SAVE UP TO 25%

when you renew your coding essentials.

Buy 1–2 items, save 15%
Buy 3–5 items, save 20%
Buy 6+ items, save 25%

ITEM #	TITLE INDICATE THE ITEMS YOU WISH TO PURCHASE	QUANTITY	PRICE PER PRODUCT	TOTAL

Subtotal	
(AK, DE, HI, MT, NH & OR are exempt) Sales Tax	
1 item $10.95 • 2–4 items $12.95 • 5+ CALL Shipping & Handling	
TOTAL AMOUNT ENCLOSED	

Save up to 25% when you renew.

Visit **www.optumcoding.com** and enter your promo code.

Call **1.800.464.3649, option 1,** and mention the promo code.

Fax this order form with purchase order to **801.982.4033.** *Optum no longer accepts credit cards by fax.*

Mail this order form with payment and/or purchase order to:
Optum, PO Box 88050, Chicago, IL 60680-9920.
Optum no longer accepts credit cards by mail.

Name

Address

Customer Number Contact Number

○ CHECK ENCLOSED (PAYABLE TO OPTUM)

○ BILL ME ○ P.O.#

( )
Telephone

( )
Fax

@
E-mail

Optum respects your right to privacy. We will not sell or rent your email address or fax number to anyone outside Optum and its business partners. If you would like to remove your name from Optum promotions, please call 1.800.464.3649, option 1.

PROMO CODE
FOBA14C

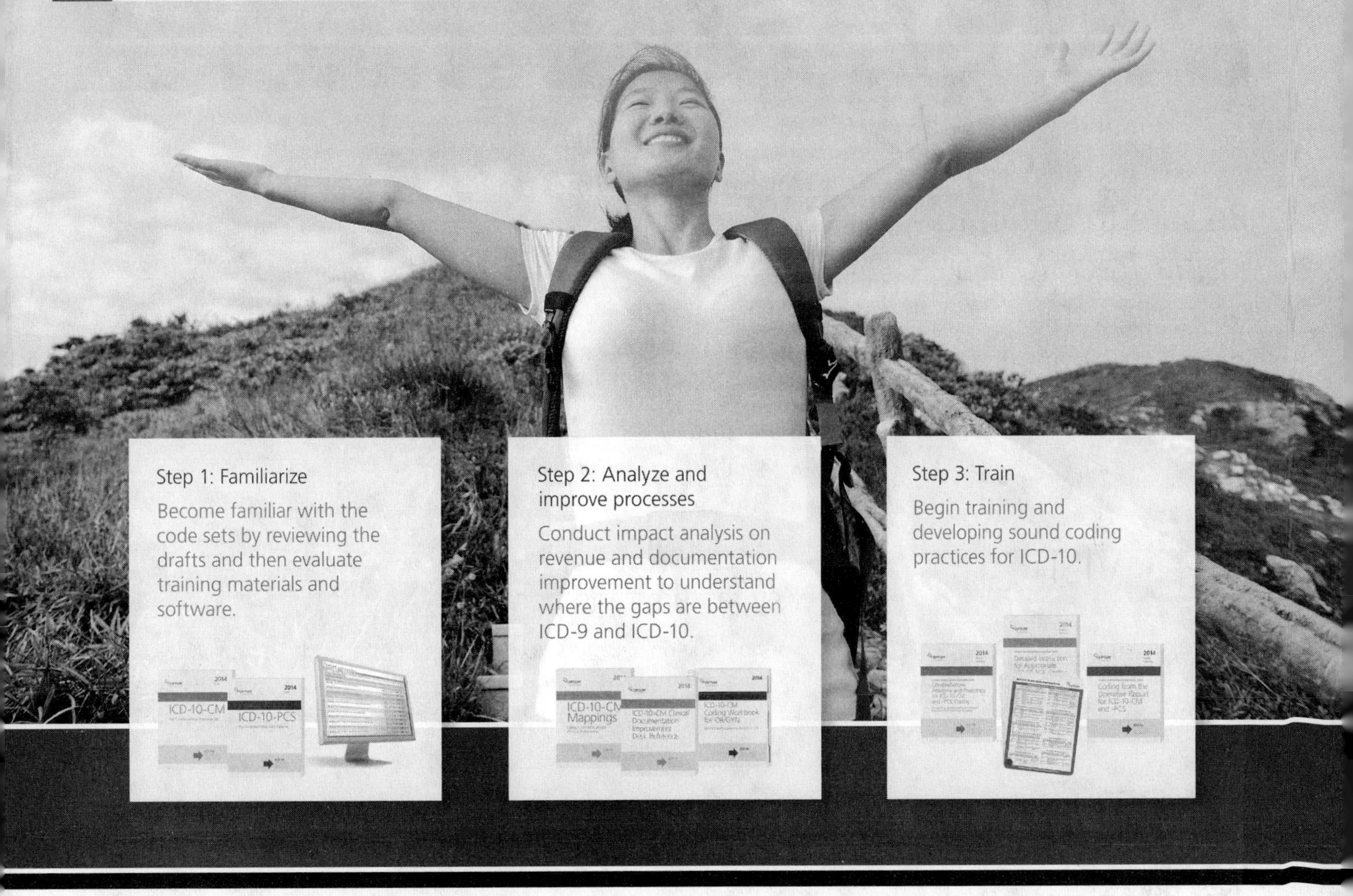

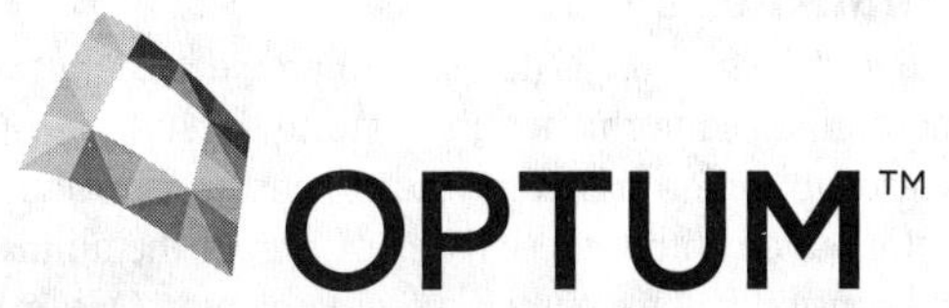

Surgical Cross Coder

Essential links from CPT® codes to ICD-9-CM and HCPCS codes

2014

Publisher's Notice

Surgical Cross Coder is designed to provide accurate and authoritative information in regard to the subject covered. Every reasonable effort has been made to ensure the accuracy of the information within these pages. However, the ultimate responsibility for accuracy lies with the user. Optum, its employees, agents, and staff, make no representation, guarantee, or warranty, express or implied, that this compilation is error-free or that the use of this publication will prevent differences of opinion or disputes with Medicare or other third-party payers, and will bear no responsibility or liability for the results or consequences of its use.

American Medical Association Notice

Fee schedules, relative value units, conversion factors and/or related components are not assigned by the AMA, are not part of CPT, and the AMA is not recommending their use. AMA does not directly or indirectly practice medicine or dispense medical services. AMA assumes no liability for data contained or not contained herein.

CPT is a registered trademark of the American Medical Association..

Our Commitment to Accuracy

Optum is committed to producing accurate and reliable materials. To report corrections, please visit www.optumcoding.com/accuracy or email accuracy@optum.com. You can also reach customer service by calling 1.800.464.3649, option 1.

Important Customer Note

The October 2013 closing of the federal government during congressional budget talks has delayed the release of the HCPCS Level II code set for 2014 and the final rules for the Medicare physician fee schedule, the hospital outpatient prospective payment system, and the ambulatory surgery center payment system. This publication went to press before the official release of these data, so the 2013 HCPCS codes and the October 2013 updates to the listed payment systems were included. To ensure excellent customer service, any significant changes to the content of this publication resulting from the 2014 updates will be communicated to customers. For updates to this product, please go to https://www.optumcoding.com/ProductUpdates/.

Copyright

Made in the USA

ISBN 978-1-60151-851-4

Acknowledgments

Kelly Armstrong, *Product Manager*
Karen Schmidt, BSN, *Technical Director*
Stacy Perry, *Manager, Desktop Publishing*
Lisa Singley, *Project Manager*
Brigid T. Caffrey, BA, BS, CCS, *Clinical/Technical Editor*
Kelly V. Canter, BA, RHIT, CCS, *Clinical/Technical Editor*
Nannette Orme, CPC, CCS-P, CPMA, CEMC, *Clinical/Technical Editor*
Tracy Betzler, *Senior Desktop Publishing Specialist*
Hope M. Dunn, *Senior Desktop Publishing Specialist*
Katie Russell, *Desktop Publishing Specialist*
Jean Parkinson, *Editor*

Technical Editors

Brigid T. Caffrey, BA, BS, CCS

Ms. Caffrey has expertise in hospital inpatient and outpatient coding and compliance and ICD-9-CM and CPT/HCPCS coding. Her experience includes teaching ICD/CPT, preparing staff for AAPC certification, conducting coding audits, providing staff education inclusive of physician education, and creating internal coding guidelines. She has a background in professional component coding, with expertise in radiology and pathology procedure coding. Most recently Ms. Caffrey was responsible for coding audits and compliance for a health information management services company. She is an active member of the American Health Information Management Association (AHIMA), the state component PHIMA and local WPHIMA.

Kelly V. Canter, BA, RHIT, CCS

Ms. Canter has expertise in hospital coding and compliance specializing in ICD-9-CM and CPT/HCPCS coding and utilization review. Her experience includes conducting coding and medical necessity audits, providing clinician and coding staff education, revenue cycle management, and hospital quality incentive programs. She has been extensively trained in ICD-10-CM and PCS. Ms. Canter has presented at multiple national conventions on a variety of coding and compliance topics. She is an active member of the American Health Information Management Association (AHIMA) and the Michigan Health Information Management Association (MHIMA).

Nannette Orme, CPC, CCS-P, CPMA, CEMC

Ms. Orme has more than 20 years of experience in the health care profession. She has extensive background in CPT/HCPCS and ICD-9-CM coding and has completed comprehensive ICD-10-CM and PCS training. Her prior experience includes physician clinics and health care consulting. Her areas of expertise include physician audits and education, compliance and HIPAA legislation, litigation support for Medicare self-disclosure cases, hospital chargemaster maintenance, workers' compensation, and emergency department coding. Ms. Orme has presented at national professional conferences and contributed articles for several professional publications. She is a member of the American Academy of Professional Coders (AAPC), American Health Information Management Association (AHIMA), and on the advisory board of a local college.

Contents

Introduction

Optum is proud to present the 2014 *Surgical Cross Coder.* The popularity of *Surgical Cross Coder* in recent years indicates that it has become the quintessential one-stop reference for medical coders. Fully comprehensive and illustrated, *Surgical Cross Coder* links more than 4,000 CPT® surgical codes to corresponding diagnosis and procedure codes. This reference is embraced by professional coders working in clinical outpatient, hospital, as well as payer settings.

Surgical Cross Coder is a single repository where every surgical CPT code instantly reveals the most appropriate diagnosis code and, the corresponding inpatient procedure codes, as well as appropriate codes for ancillary supplies and pharmaceuticals. *Surgical Cross Coder* is based on the Surgery section of *Current Procedural Terminology* (CPT®). Up-to-date CPT surgery codes link to the following related medical coding systems:

- *International Classification of Diseases, 9th Revision, Clinical Modification* (ICD-9-CM)
- *Healthcare Common Procedural Coding System* (HCPCS) *Level II*

All coding relationships in *Surgical Cross Coder* start with the surgery section of the CPT book presenting a general clinical picture of each surgery code. Pertinent surgery-related coding relationships were carefully reviewed and screened for appropriate information. For example, it is clinically unusual for a closed fracture procedure to be performed when an open fracture diagnosis code is reported. This type of unusual association is not included.

Perhaps more significantly, many acute and chronic medical conditions may eventually lead to surgical intervention. Clinical analysts point out that chronic and acute conditions are nearly always aggressively approached medically before surgery is even considered. For this reason, the number of cross-coded chronic and acute conditions are selectively culled in this reference book.

In some instances the data is abridged simply due to the enormity of the listings. For example, diagnosis codes for infections call for additional codes to identify specific organisms. The possible associations are simply too numerous and, as a result, do not appear in *Surgical Cross Coder.* In a similar vein, *Surgical Cross Coder* features codes that require accompanying etiologies or manifestations (examples include "Code first underlying disease..."). However, associated infectious and parasitic diseases are, once again, simply too numerous to list and do not appear in *Surgical Cross Coder.* For further discussion on secondary diagnosis codes, see the ICD-9-CM section later in this introduction.

Some CPT codes are omitted from the listing because consistent and reliable cross links are almost impossible to establish. Unlisted procedure codes are an obvious example. Certain types of add-on codes are also treated somewhat differently in *Surgical Cross Coder.* These codes are discussed in greater detail under the CPT Codes section later in this introduction. Add-on and unlisted codes are listed with full descriptions in appendixes A and B.

Listings for codes that are modifier 51 exempt, modifier 63 exempt, or indicate moderate (conscious) sedation can be found in *CPT 2014.*

As a coding reference, *Surgical Cross Coder* presents "most likely" scenarios as derived from clinical review. However, *Surgical Cross Coder* is not a substitute for ICD-9-CM, or any other medical coding reference, and users are urged to regularly consult all available sources. The absence of any specific code does not necessarily indicate that its association to the base procedure code is inappropriate. Assuming all rules of medical coding are followed, excepted diagnosis codes may prove appropriate to a specific code scenario.

Surgical Cross Coder does not include coding rules and guidelines. Once again, the user is urged to consult the original coding reference (e.g., current CPT, ICD-9-CM, HCPCS Level II, etc.) or one of several reputable medical coding instruction manuals. This advice may be more crucial when sorting through codes for wounds, burns, fractures, and complications.

Format

An understanding of the *Surgical Cross Coder* format allows users to easily navigate its content. Information within the main section ties back to the CPT book and codes are presented in the numeric order of the Surgery section.

Sections

Surgical Cross Coder provides linked information to the CPT code range 10021 to 69990—the surgical portion of the CPT book. The codes are divided into the same sections and subsections as the Surgery section of the CPT book. For example, the Respiratory System section is divided into anatomical subsections including nose, accessory sinuses, and larynx. Larynx is further divided into excision, introduction, endoscopy, repair, and destruction.

Codes and Code Ranges

The data within each CPT code set of *Surgical Cross Coder* is presented as follows:

- CPT code or code range
- CPT codes and descriptions
- ICD-9-CM diagnostic codes and descriptions
- ICD-9-CM procedural codes and descriptions
- HCPCS codes and descriptions

For example:

27086–27087

27086	Removal of foreign body, pelvis or hip; subcutaneous tissue
27087	Removal of foreign body, pelvis or hip; deep (subfascial or intramuscular)

ICD-9-CM Diagnostic

686.1	Pyogenic granuloma of skin and subcutaneous tissue
709.4	Foreign body granuloma of skin and subcutaneous tissue
718.15	Loose body in pelvic joint
728.82	Foreign body granuloma of muscle
729.6	Residual foreign body in soft tissue
879.7	Open wound of other and unspecified parts of trunk, complicated
890.1	Open wound of hip and thigh, complicated
890.2	Open wound of hip and thigh, with tendon involvement
919.6	Other, multiple, and unspecified sites, superficial foreign body (splinter), without major open wound and without mention of infection
919.7	Other, multiple, and unspecified sites, superficial foreign body (splinter), without major open wound, infected

ICD-9-CM Procedural

83.02	Myotomy
83.09	Other incision of soft tissue
86.05	Incision with removal of foreign body or device from skin and subcutaneous tissue

HCPCS Level II Supplies & Services

A4305	Disposable drug delivery system, flow rate of 50 ml or greater per hour

Each CPT code or code range is followed by its specific ICD-9-CM and HCPCS codes. *Surgical Cross Coder* presents full descriptions for all CPT codes and their links.

Keep in mind, though, that ICD-9-CM codes are hierarchical and their "full descriptions" are by nature incomplete. Information on a specific five-digit code is found under its three- or four-digit category. The Optum database and *Surgical Cross Coder* feature complete descriptions for ICD-9-CM codes. For example, the official ICD-9-CM description for 810.03 is a fifth-digit subclassification for use with category 810 and appears as follows:

810 Fracture of clavicle
- 0 unspecified part
  Clavicle NOS
- 1 sternal end of clavicle
- 2 shaft of clavicle
- 3 acromial end of clavicle

810.0 Closed

Surgical Cross Coder presents a closed clavicle fracture involving the acromial end as the following:

810.03 Closed fracture of the acromial end of clavicle

Complete descriptions are presented throughout this book.

Icon Key

An icon key is provided in the bottom margin on each page. These icons, or symbols, can be found next to particular ICD-9-CM diagnosis codes listed in the crosswalk, as appropriate. These icons warn of coding edits which apply to that particular code and must be followed. For instance, a procedure performed on the prostate would list diagnosis codes for prostate conditions supporting medical necessity. These codes would never be assigned to a female patient and these codes appear with the icon denoting a male only diagnosis. The following icons appear in *Surgical Cross Coder*:

♀ **Female Diagnosis.** Codes appearing with this symbol should only be used to report a diagnosis for a female patient.

♂ **Male Diagnosis.** Codes appearing with this symbol should only be used to report a diagnosis for a male patient.

Unspecified Code. Codes denoted as unspecified should only be used when the medical information to substantiate a more specific code is not available. Review the medical record documentation and/or query the physician to determine whether a more specific diagnosis is available for coding to the highest level of specificity.

Manifestation Code. A manifestation code is not allowed to be reported as the principal or first-listed diagnosis since it describes a manifestation of some other underlying disease, not the disease itself. The underlying disease is coded first and the manifestation code second. This is referred to as mandatory multiple coding of etiology and manifestation.

CPT Codes

CPT is a standardized system of five-digit codes and descriptive terms developed, maintained, and copyrighted by the American Medical Association (AMA). CPT codes are the most widely accepted procedure codes for reporting medical services performed by physicians. Federal law requires Medicare and Medicaid carriers to use CPT codes on health care claims. Commercial insurance payers often recognize only CPT codes. CPT is a trademark of the American Medical Association.

Although *Surgical Cross Coder* is organized numerically by CPT code, not all codes are presented separately. In many cases, several codes within a CPT code set have similar ICD-9-CM diagnosis or ICD-9-CM procedural codes. In these cases, a range of CPT codes is listed, followed by each individual code and its description. For example:

59840–59841

59840	Induced abortion, by dilation and curettage
59841	Induced abortion, by dilation and evacuation

Indented Procedures

Each CPT surgical procedure embraces two components: the five-digit reporting code and its precise, formal description. A simple CPT rule allows each description to stand alone while also saving space on the printed page. Codes that share a common description are grouped together. The common description is listed in its entirety in the first code. The following codes in the group are indented to indicate that they share the common descriptive portion with the preceding fully described code.

For example:

49082–49083

49082	Abdominal paracentesis (diagnostic or therapeutic); without imaging guidance
49083	with imaging guidance

The common portion of these two codes precedes the semicolon (;) in the full description of 49082. Terminology following the semicolon is unique to that code. The complete description of 49083 is:

49083 Abdominal paracentesis (diagnostic or therapeutic); with imaging guidance

Surgical Cross Coder also employs this methodology with only a minor adjustment. When the code links for indented procedures are the same as for the main code, *Surgical Cross Coder* presents the material concurrently. As in the CPT book, the description terminology following the semicolon describes the indented code.

When the cross coding links of an indented procedure vary from those of the main code, the indented code description appears in its entirety. Subsequent indented codes appear indented and are grouped if the links are the same. For example, code range 65270–65286 appears as follows in the CPT book:

65270	Repair of laceration; conjunctiva, with or without nonperforating laceration sclera, direct closure
65272	conjunctiva, by mobilization and rearrangement, without hospitalization
65273	conjunctiva, by mobilization and rearrangement, with hospitalization
65275	cornea, nonperforating, with or without removal foreign body
65280	cornea, and/or sclera, perforating, not involving uveal tissue
65285	cornea and/or sclera, perforating, with reposition or resection of uveal tissue
65286	application of tissue glue, wounds of cornea and/or sclera

Based on diagnostic links, *Surgical Cross Coder* groups these codes as follows:

65270–65273

65270*	Repair of laceration; conjunctiva, with or without nonperforating laceration sclera, direct closure
65272	conjunctiva, by mobilization and rearrangement, without hospitalization
65273	conjunctiva, by mobilization and rearrangement, with hospitalization

65275–65285

65275	Repair of laceration; cornea, nonperforating, with or without removal foreign body
65280	cornea and/or sclera, perforating, not involving uveal tissue
65285	cornea and/or sclera, perforating, with reposition or resection of uveal tissue

65286

65286	Repair of laceration; application of tissue glue, wounds of cornea and/or sclera

Not every code within a CPT surgical code set can be addressed appropriately in a cross-coding publication. Examples are found among unlisted and add-on codes.

Providers

Paragraphs 2 and 3 under Instructions for Use of the CPT Codebook on page xii of *CPT 2014,* advises coders to take note of the fact that while a particular service or procedure may be assigned to a specific section, the service or procedure itself is not limited to use only by that specialty group. Additionally, the procedures and services listed throughout the book are for use by any qualified physician or other qualified health care professional or entity; for example, hospitals, laboratories, or home health agencies).

The use of the phrase "physician or other qualified healthcare professional" was adopted to identify a health care provider other than a physician. This type of provider is further described in the CPT book as an individual "qualified by education, training, licensure/regulation (when applicable), and facility privileging (when applicable)." State licensure guidelines will determine the scope of practice and a qualified health care professional must practice within these guidelines even if more restrictive than the CPT guidelines. The qualified health care professional may report their services independently or under incident-to guidelines. The professionals within this definition are separate from "clinical staff" and are able to practice independently. CPT defines clinical staff as "a person who works under the supervision of a physician or other qualified health care professional and who is allowed, by law, regulation and facility policy to perform or assist in the performance of a specified professional service, but who does not individually report that professional service." Keep in mind that there may be other policies or guidelines that can also affect who may report a specific service.

Unlisted Procedure Codes

Unlisted codes are reported for procedures not adequately addressed by any other CPT codes. Unlisted codes are classified by general anatomy and no further description is offered. Often classified "by report," payers may require extensive documentation to accompany these manually processed claims. For obvious reasons, unlisted procedure codes cannot be reliably linked to the other medical coding systems. Consequently, *Surgical Cross Coder* does not include unlisted procedure codes from the surgery portion of the CPT book. A complete listing of these codes and their descriptions may be found in appendix B, Unlisted Codes.

Add-On Codes

Add-on codes represent procedures performed in addition to the primary procedure and as a rule are never reported separately. Three types exist: 1) those linked exclusively to one primary code; 2) those linked to a variety of primary codes; and 3) those representing procedures unrelated to the primary code, but performed concurrent to the primary procedure.

Add-on Codes Associated with Specific Primary Codes

Many add-on codes report services that are simple extensions of the primary procedure. Consider code 11732 Avulsion of nail plate, partial or complete, simple; each additional nail plate (List separately in addition to code for primary procedure). This code is an "add-on" to the preceding avulsion code and reporting 11732 without 11730 is a fundamental error.

Surgical Cross Coder usually groups this type of add-on code in a range with the primary procedure because the links to diagnosis codes are almost always identical. The preceding example is listed as the code range 11730–11732.

Add-on Codes Appropriate to Various Primary Codes

These codes report "in addition to" procedures. However, each code in this category can apply to multiple primary codes. For example, 67335 Placement of adjustable suture(s) during strabismus surgery, including postoperative adjustment(s) of suture(s) (List separately in addition to code for specific strabismus surgery), can be reported with any code in the range 67311–67334.

The primary procedure must be identified before establishing any link between the add-on code and a diagnosis. Coders should consult the instructions and references under the primary code for information also applicable to the add-on code.

Add-on Codes as Unrelated Procedures

A set of add-on codes represents procedures that are "in addition to" other surgeries, but performed for unrelated reasons.

Consider 58611 Ligation or transection of fallopian tube(s) when done at the time of cesarean section or intra-abdominal surgery (not a separate procedure) (List separately in addition to code for primary procedure). The tubal ligation is performed for a reason different from that for the primary procedure. The primary procedure (for example, cesarean) is performed for a distinct diagnosis (for example, previous cesarean scar). The cesarean is unrelated to a diagnosis linked to tubal ligation, typically performed for sterilization.

Surgical Cross Coder includes this type of unrelated add-on code as a single entry, since these codes have identifiable code-link relationships independent of the parent procedures.

A complete listing of surgical add-on codes, identified in the CPT book, is found in appendix A, Add-on Codes.

Code Links

An extensive review process by Optum links each CPT code to corresponding codes in the other major medical coding systems. But not all CPT codes link to every coding system and the listings reflect this fact.

ICD-9-CM Diagnostic Codes

ICD-9-CM, volumes 1 and 2, is a systematic listing of codes that describes the incredible variety of medical conditions known to the medical community. The system used in this country was developed and is maintained by the National Center for Health Statistics. Though designed primarily to track health statistics, ICD-9-CM diagnosis codes serve as an assurance to payers that medical services provided are warranted.

Surgical Cross Coder links each CPT surgical code with the ICD-9-CM diagnoses that would warrant such a procedure. Code associations are edited for most appropriate usage, though Optum cannot guarantee that every possible diagnosis for a given procedure is included. The diagnosis codes will generally correspond with all the CPT codes in the range; however, there may be instances where a diagnosis code will be appropriate to only some of the CPT codes listed. This crosswalk is extensive—in some instances more than 400 appropriate diagnosis codes are listed for a single procedure. In some cases the following statement appears:

The application of this code is too broad to adequately present ICD-9-CM diagnostic code links here. Refer to your ICD-9-CM book.

Third-party payers will reject claims containing invalid ICD-9-CM diagnostic codes. Invalid ICD-9-CM codes identify disease categories, yet do not give the level of detail available and necessary for processing. Valid ICD-9-CM codes can contain three, four, or five digits, which makes it difficult to recognize whether a code is at its highest level of specificity. To simplify the coder's job, *Surgical Cross Coder* includes only valid ICD-9-CM codes.

Diagnostic Coding Considerations

Surgical Cross Coder simplifies medical coding for those in physician, hospital, or payer offices. Keep in mind, though, that diagnostic coding practices in clinical settings vary from those in hospitals. The surgical facility influences coding and coders should learn the rules applicable to their medical environment.

In most sites outside the hospital, the diagnosis applicable to the procedure is generally coded first. Coexisting conditions are considered supplemental information.

Comorbidities

Comorbidities are pre-existing conditions or chronic diseases, (e.g., malignant neoplasms, diabetes, or hypertension) that occur in the background to another, significant diagnostic event. These conditions can affect the care a patient may require.

Comorbidities may affect physician reimbursement. The Centers for Medicare and Medicaid Services (CMS) advises physician coders to submit chronic disease codes only as they apply to a current patient encounter.

Hospitals are reimbursed by Diagnosis Related Groups (DRGs) for inpatient visits that are contingent on comorbidity information. For instance, the claims for two patients who undergo similar appendectomy procedures are not paid the same when one patient has underlying end stage renal disease (ESRD). Due to the extreme variability represented by comorbid diagnoses, *Surgical Cross Coder* does not link ESRD to an appendectomy code.

Coders in physician, hospital, or payer offices should reference ICD-9-CM and their own facility protocols for the role comorbidity codes should play in the patient record.

Secondary Codes

Many ICD-9-CM codes cannot be used as the primary, first listed or principal diagnosis. These codes are called manifestation diagnosis codes. ICD-9-CM notations specify to "code first" the underlying disease.

443.81 *Peripheral angiopathy in diseases classified elsewhere*
Code first underlying disease, as:
diabetes mellitus (249.7, 250.7)

The coder turns to 250.7 in ICD-9-CM to find, in addition to a fifth-digit subclassification, information required for 250.7 Diabetes with peripheral circulatory disorders.

Use additional code to identify manifestations, as:
diabetic:
gangrene (785.4)
peripheral angiopathy (443.81)

When ICD-9-CM provides specific printed code links between primary and secondary codes, those links appear in *Surgical Cross Coder* as a statement (in this case, "Code first 250.7") in parentheses following the code description. Code 443.81 appears in the crosswalk as follows:

443.81 Peripheral angiopathy in diseases classified elsewhere — (Code first 249.7, 250.7)

If 443.81 appears in a crosswalk, the primary code 249.7 or 250.7 is listed with its complete description in the numerically ordered crosswalk.

Codes appearing with parenthetical information that begins "Code first..." are manifestation codes and, consequently, not listed first on the claim form. Primary or principal diagnosis codes are identified in the parenthetical notation.

Other Related ICD-9-CM Codes

ICD-9-CM notations instruct readers to "Code also" or to "Use additional code" to give more information about the patient's condition. For example:

245.4 Iatrogenic thyroiditis
Use additional code to identify cause

Surgical Cross Coder includes specific linking data provided in ICD-9-CM. However, each of these codes may not apply to the CPT code serving as the basis for a crosswalk.

Sometimes, ICD-9-CM makes general references to other codes, such as "use additional E code to identify cause," or "use additional code to identify organism." General notes in *Surgical Cross Coder* address these situations. Consult ICD-9-CM for information about infective agents, toxic drugs or agents, E codes identifying circumstances, hypertension and neoplasm tables, or other codes broadly associated or linked to a diagnosis or procedure.

ICD-9-CM Procedural Codes

ICD-9-CM, volume 3, is a systematic listing of procedural codes for inpatient hospital coding. CMS developed and maintains these codes. *Surgical Cross Coder* cross-references each CPT procedural code to its corresponding ICD-9-CM volume 3 code or codes. Volume 3 codes are usually more general than CPT procedural codes, so in some cases numerous CPT codes link to a solitary ICD-9-CM procedural code, each remaining a one-to-one relationship.

In other cases, one CPT code may cross to several ICD-9-CM codes, each of which is a component of the CPT code.

The coder is responsible for determining from the patient record which ICD-9-CM procedure code, or codes, apply.

ICD-9-CM to ICD-10 Transition

The codes within ICD-9-CM fall short of today's medical reporting needs. ICD-9-CM was created more than 25 years ago as a modern and expandable system that was then only partially filled. Thousands of codes have been added to ICD-9-CM over the years to classify new procedures and diseases, and today the remaining space in ICD-9-CM procedure and diagnosis coding systems cannot accommodate new technologies or a new understanding of diseases.

In response to ICD-9-CM's shortcomings, new coding systems were developed and soon will be implemented in the United States. The World Health Organization (WHO) created and adopted ICD-10 in 1994 and it has been used in much of the world since then. This system is the basis for the new U.S. diagnosis coding system, International Classification of Diseases, 10th Revision, Clinical Modification (ICD-10-CM).

Concurrent to the clinical modification of ICD-10 by the National Center for Health Statistics (NCHS), the Centers for Medicare and Medicaid Services (CMS) commissioned 3M Health Information

Management to develop a new procedure coding system to replace volume 3 of ICD-9-CM, used for inpatient procedure coding. Now that the coding systems have been designed and written, they need only be implemented, but progress is slow. The government is moving cautiously toward implementation, partly because the scope of change is massive and will profoundly affect all care providers, payers, and government agencies, but also because the change is massive and costly enough to carry considerable political impact.

On January 16, 2009, the Department of Health and Human Services published a final rule in the *Federal Register,* 45 CFR part 162, "HIPAA Administrative Simplification: Modifications to Medical Data Code Set Standards to Adopt ICD-10-CM and ICD-10-PCS" (downloadable at http://edocket.access.gpo.gov/2009/pdf/E9-743.pdf). This final rule adopts modifications to standard medical data code sets for coding diagnoses and inpatient hospital procedures by adopting ICD-10-CM for diagnosis coding, including the Official ICD-10-CM Guidelines for Coding and Reporting, and ICD-10-PCS for inpatient hospital procedure coding. It is important to note that the implementation of ICD-10-CM and PCS was delayed. The final rule, published September 5, 2012, confirmed that the new implementation date is October 1, 2014.

The most current 2014 draft update release is available for public viewing, and additional updates are expected before implementation. At this time, ICD-10 codes are not valid for any purpose or use other than for reporting mortality data for death certificates. This does not mean it is not time to begin preparing, however. Now is the time to prepare, as the 2014 date is approaching rapidly, and there will be no grace period for using the new codes.

Everyone in facilities will be affected: coders, human resources staff, accountants, information systems staff, physicians—just to name a few. The proposed codes not only provide tremendous opportunities for disease and procedure tracking but also create enormous challenges. Computer hardware and software, medical documentation, and the revenue cycle are just three elements of medical reimbursement that will be shaken when implementation occurs.

Understanding the changes the World Health Organization made in moving from ICD-9 to ICD-10 is a good basis for learning about the clinical modifications to ICD-10. The first clue to the revisions is in the full title: International Statistical Classification of Diseases and Related Health Problems.

Overall, the 10th revision goes into greater clinical detail than does ICD-9-CM and addresses information about previously classified diseases, as well as those diseases discovered since the last revision. Conditions are grouped with general epidemiological purposes and the evaluation of health care in mind. New features have been added, and conditions have been reorganized, although the format and conventions of the classification remain unchanged for the most part.

Some of these revisions have included:

- Information relevant to ambulatory and managed care encounters
- Expanded injury codes
- Creation of combination diagnosis/symptom codes to reduce the number of codes needed to fully describe a condition
- The addition of sixth- and seventh-character subclassifications
- Incorporation of common fourth- and fifth-digit subclassifications
- Classifications specific to laterality
- Classification refinement for increased data granularity

This new structure also allows for further expansion than was possible with the ICD-9-CM classification system.

HCPCS Level II Codes

HCPCS is an acronym (pronounced "hick-picks") for the Healthcare Common Procedure Coding System. This coding system represents national codes to report supplies and equipment, as well as select services provided on an outpatient basis. CMS developed and maintains Level II codes for reporting different criteria than is used in CPT codes. HCPCS codes are generally used for Medicare and Medicaid reporting. Medicare may require the HCPCS Level II code instead of the CPT code. Some nongovernmental payers also use various designated HCPCS Level II codes.

In this field of *Surgical Cross Coder*, Optum provides common HCPCS supply codes linked to CPT codes, as appropriate. Confirm with your third-party payers whether they require a specific service to be reported with CPT code 99070 or a HCPCS Level II code, then report accordingly. For example:

32655–32656

32655	Thoracoscopy, surgical; with resection-plication of bullae, includes any pleural procedure when performed
32656	with parietal pleurectomy

ICD-9-CM Diagnostic

163.0	Malignant neoplasm of parietal pleura
163.8	Malignant neoplasm of other specified sites of pleura
163.9	Malignant neoplasm of pleura, unspecified site ▽
492.0	Emphysematous bleb
515	Postinflammatory pulmonary fibrosis
518.89	Other diseases of lung, not elsewhere classified

ICD-9-CM Procedural

32.21	Plication of emphysematous bleb
32.25	Thoracoscopic ablation of lung lesion or tissue
34.59	Other excision of pleura

HCPCS Level II Supplies & Services

A7042	Implanted pleural catheter, each

Site of Service

Someone other than the physician may supply many of the HCPCS supplies and services linked to codes in this crosswalk. For clarity, the crosswalk includes only those HCPCS Level II codes directly tied to the CPT code.

Sometimes, multi-specialty clinics or other free-standing facilities have in-house equipment suppliers. Always verify the patient's record before billing supplies and report only appropriate supplies issued through that facility.

While supply houses and physicians depend on HCPCS codes to report supplies and certain drugs, the same reporting system has been adapted for different reasons among hospitals and other inpatient facilities. Most often, these latter sites report supplies to Medicare with revenue codes instead of HCPCS codes. HCPCS codes are popular for inventory control, patient billing, and related purposes. *Surgical Cross Coder* provides links to appropriate HCPCS Level II codes regardless of place of service. However, HCPCS Level II codes are being required more and more by Medicare and other payers.

J Codes

The HCPCS J codes generally report drugs administered other than by an oral method. The clinical editors of *Surgical Cross Coder* have determined that consistent links to pharmaceuticals are extremely difficult to establish and only very specifically linked listings appear in this reference.

Summary

Based on the AMA's CPT code set of 10021 to 69990, *Surgical Cross Coder* links surgical procedures to appropriate ICD-9-CM diagnostic and procedural codes, and HCPCS supply codes. As a useful adjunct to these coding systems, *Surgical Cross Coder* presents a more accurate and efficient way for professional coders to link CPT surgical codes to other important medical codes. The result is a broader, comprehensive picture of a surgical event.

The Optum *Surgical Cross Coder* serves coders' needs by helping providers comply with ever emerging standards for coding, reporting, and reimbursing medical procedures. The Optum database and nationally known coding expertise combine to offer a coding book that is as accurate as possible at publication.

Optum recognizes the subjective nature of procedural coding and encourages comments or suggestions to improve the product or to illustrate regional idiosyncrasies of the reimbursement process.

As with all medical coding resources, *Surgical Cross Coder* is designed as a postprocedural reference for billing purposes only. The use of any of these listings to select surgical treatment is entirely inappropriate.

General

10021-10022

10021 Fine needle aspiration; without imaging guidance
10022 with imaging guidance

ICD-9-CM Diagnostic

032.89 Other specified diphtheria
039.8 Actinomycotic infection of other specified sites
074.8 Other specified diseases due to Coxsackievirus
075 Infectious mononucleosis
078.5 Cytomegaloviral disease — (Use additional code to identify manifestation: 484.1, 573.1)
084.9 Other pernicious complications of malaria — (Use additional code to identify complication: 573.2, 581.81)
095.8 Other specified forms of late symptomatic syphilis
116.0 Blastomycosis — (Use additional code to identify manifestation: 321.0-321.1, 380.15, 711.6)
125.0 Bancroftian filariasis
125.1 Malayan filariasis
125.2 Loiasis
125.3 Onchocerciasis
125.4 Dipetalonemiasis
125.5 Mansonella ozzardi infection
125.6 Other specified filariasis
125.7 Dracontiasis
125.9 Unspecified filariasis ▽
135 Sarcoidosis
141.0 Malignant neoplasm of base of tongue
141.1 Malignant neoplasm of dorsal surface of tongue
141.2 Malignant neoplasm of tip and lateral border of tongue
141.3 Malignant neoplasm of ventral surface of tongue
141.4 Malignant neoplasm of anterior two-thirds of tongue, part unspecified ▽
141.5 Malignant neoplasm of junctional zone of tongue
141.6 Malignant neoplasm of lingual tonsil
141.8 Malignant neoplasm of other sites of tongue
141.9 Malignant neoplasm of tongue, unspecified site ▽
142.0 Malignant neoplasm of parotid gland
142.1 Malignant neoplasm of submandibular gland
142.2 Malignant neoplasm of sublingual gland
142.8 Malignant neoplasm of other major salivary glands
142.9 Malignant neoplasm of salivary gland, unspecified ▽
143.0 Malignant neoplasm of upper gum
143.1 Malignant neoplasm of lower gum
143.8 Malignant neoplasm of other sites of gum
143.9 Malignant neoplasm of gum, unspecified site ▽
144.0 Malignant neoplasm of anterior portion of floor of mouth
144.1 Malignant neoplasm of lateral portion of floor of mouth
144.8 Malignant neoplasm of other sites of floor of mouth
144.9 Malignant neoplasm of floor of mouth, part unspecified ▽
145.0 Malignant neoplasm of cheek mucosa
145.1 Malignant neoplasm of vestibule of mouth
145.2 Malignant neoplasm of hard palate
145.3 Malignant neoplasm of soft palate
145.4 Malignant neoplasm of uvula
145.5 Malignant neoplasm of palate, unspecified ▽
145.6 Malignant neoplasm of retromolar area
145.8 Malignant neoplasm of other specified parts of mouth
145.9 Malignant neoplasm of mouth, unspecified site ▽
146.0 Malignant neoplasm of tonsil
146.1 Malignant neoplasm of tonsillar fossa
146.2 Malignant neoplasm of tonsillar pillars (anterior) (posterior)
146.3 Malignant neoplasm of vallecula
146.4 Malignant neoplasm of anterior aspect of epiglottis
146.5 Malignant neoplasm of junctional region of oropharynx
146.6 Malignant neoplasm of lateral wall of oropharynx
146.7 Malignant neoplasm of posterior wall of oropharynx
146.8 Malignant neoplasm of other specified sites of oropharynx
146.9 Malignant neoplasm of oropharynx, unspecified site ▽
147.0 Malignant neoplasm of superior wall of nasopharynx
147.1 Malignant neoplasm of posterior wall of nasopharynx
147.2 Malignant neoplasm of lateral wall of nasopharynx
147.3 Malignant neoplasm of anterior wall of nasopharynx
147.8 Malignant neoplasm of other specified sites of nasopharynx
147.9 Malignant neoplasm of nasopharynx, unspecified site ▽
148.0 Malignant neoplasm of postcricoid region of hypopharynx
148.1 Malignant neoplasm of pyriform sinus
148.2 Malignant neoplasm of aryepiglottic fold, hypopharyngeal aspect
148.3 Malignant neoplasm of posterior hypopharyngeal wall
148.8 Malignant neoplasm of other specified sites of hypopharynx
148.9 Malignant neoplasm of hypopharynx, unspecified site ▽
155.0 Malignant neoplasm of liver, primary
155.1 Malignant neoplasm of intrahepatic bile ducts
155.2 Malignant neoplasm of liver, not specified as primary or secondary ▽
157.0 Malignant neoplasm of head of pancreas
157.1 Malignant neoplasm of body of pancreas
157.2 Malignant neoplasm of tail of pancreas
157.3 Malignant neoplasm of pancreatic duct
157.4 Malignant neoplasm of islets of Langerhans — (Use additional code to identify any functional activity)
157.8 Malignant neoplasm of other specified sites of pancreas
157.9 Malignant neoplasm of pancreas, part unspecified ▽
158.0 Malignant neoplasm of retroperitoneum
158.8 Malignant neoplasm of specified parts of peritoneum
158.9 Malignant neoplasm of peritoneum, unspecified ▽
159.8 Malignant neoplasm of other sites of digestive system and intra-abdominal organs
162.2 Malignant neoplasm of main bronchus
162.3 Malignant neoplasm of upper lobe, bronchus, or lung
162.4 Malignant neoplasm of middle lobe, bronchus, or lung
162.5 Malignant neoplasm of lower lobe, bronchus, or lung
162.8 Malignant neoplasm of other parts of bronchus or lung
162.9 Malignant neoplasm of bronchus and lung, unspecified site ▽
163.0 Malignant neoplasm of parietal pleura
163.8 Malignant neoplasm of other specified sites of pleura
163.9 Malignant neoplasm of pleura, unspecified site ▽
164.2 Malignant neoplasm of anterior mediastinum
164.3 Malignant neoplasm of posterior mediastinum
164.8 Malignant neoplasm of other parts of mediastinum
164.9 Malignant neoplasm of mediastinum, part unspecified ▽
172.5 Malignant melanoma of skin of trunk, except scrotum

Code	Description
172.6	Malignant melanoma of skin of upper limb, including shoulder
172.7	Malignant melanoma of skin of lower limb, including hip
172.8	Malignant melanoma of other specified sites of skin
173.51	Basal cell carcinoma of skin of trunk, except scrotum
173.52	Squamous cell carcinoma of skin of trunk, except scrotum
173.59	Other specified malignant neoplasm of skin of trunk, except scrotum
174.0	Malignant neoplasm of nipple and areola of female breast — (Use additional code to identify estrogen receptor status: V86.0-V86.1) ♀
174.1	Malignant neoplasm of central portion of female breast — (Use additional code to identify estrogen receptor status: V86.0-V86.1) ♀
174.2	Malignant neoplasm of upper-inner quadrant of female breast — (Use additional code to identify estrogen receptor status: V86.0-V86.1) ♀
174.3	Malignant neoplasm of lower-inner quadrant of female breast — (Use additional code to identify estrogen receptor status: V86.0-V86.1) ♀
174.4	Malignant neoplasm of upper-outer quadrant of female breast — (Use additional code to identify estrogen receptor status: V86.0-V86.1) ♀
174.5	Malignant neoplasm of lower-outer quadrant of female breast — (Use additional code to identify estrogen receptor status: V86.0-V86.1) ♀
174.6	Malignant neoplasm of axillary tail of female breast — (Use additional code to identify estrogen receptor status: V86.0-V86.1) ♀
174.8	Malignant neoplasm of other specified sites of female breast — (Use additional code to identify estrogen receptor status: V86.0-V86.1) ♀
175.0	Malignant neoplasm of nipple and areola of male breast — (Use additional code to identify estrogen receptor status: V86.0-V86.1) ♂
175.9	Malignant neoplasm of other and unspecified sites of male breast — (Use additional code to identify estrogen receptor status: V86.0-V86.1) ▽ ♂
176.4	Kaposi's sarcoma of lung
180.9	Malignant neoplasm of cervix uteri, unspecified site ▽ ♀
182.0	Malignant neoplasm of corpus uteri, except isthmus ♀
183.0	Malignant neoplasm of ovary — (Use additional code to identify any functional activity) ♀
183.2	Malignant neoplasm of fallopian tube ♀
183.8	Malignant neoplasm of other specified sites of uterine adnexa ♀
185	Malignant neoplasm of prostate ♂
186.0	Malignant neoplasm of undescended testis — (Use additional code to identify any functional activity) ♂
186.9	Malignant neoplasm of other and unspecified testis — (Use additional code to identify any functional activity) ▽ ♂
187.5	Malignant neoplasm of epididymis ♂
188.9	Malignant neoplasm of bladder, part unspecified ▽
189.0	Malignant neoplasm of kidney, except pelvis
189.1	Malignant neoplasm of renal pelvis
193	Malignant neoplasm of thyroid gland — (Use additional code to identify any functional activity)
195.0	Malignant neoplasm of head, face, and neck
195.1	Malignant neoplasm of thorax
195.2	Malignant neoplasm of abdomen
195.3	Malignant neoplasm of pelvis
195.4	Malignant neoplasm of upper limb
195.5	Malignant neoplasm of lower limb
195.8	Malignant neoplasm of other specified sites
196.0	Secondary and unspecified malignant neoplasm of lymph nodes of head, face, and neck
196.1	Secondary and unspecified malignant neoplasm of intrathoracic lymph nodes
196.2	Secondary and unspecified malignant neoplasm of intra-abdominal lymph nodes
196.3	Secondary and unspecified malignant neoplasm of lymph nodes of axilla and upper limb
196.5	Secondary and unspecified malignant neoplasm of lymph nodes of inguinal region and lower limb
196.6	Secondary and unspecified malignant neoplasm of intrapelvic lymph nodes
196.8	Secondary and unspecified malignant neoplasm of lymph nodes of multiple sites
196.9	Secondary and unspecified malignant neoplasm of lymph nodes, site unspecified ▽
197.0	Secondary malignant neoplasm of lung
197.1	Secondary malignant neoplasm of mediastinum
197.2	Secondary malignant neoplasm of pleura
197.6	Secondary malignant neoplasm of retroperitoneum and peritoneum
197.7	Secondary malignant neoplasm of liver
197.8	Secondary malignant neoplasm of other digestive organs and spleen
198.0	Secondary malignant neoplasm of kidney
198.81	Secondary malignant neoplasm of breast
198.82	Secondary malignant neoplasm of genital organs
198.89	Secondary malignant neoplasm of other specified sites
199.0	Disseminated malignant neoplasm
199.1	Other malignant neoplasm of unspecified site
199.2	Malignant neoplasm associated with transplanted organ — (Code first complication of transplanted organ (996.80-996.89) Use additional code for specific malignancy)
200.00	Reticulosarcoma, unspecified site, extranodal and solid organ sites ▽
200.01	Reticulosarcoma of lymph nodes of head, face, and neck
200.04	Reticulosarcoma of lymph nodes of axilla and upper limb
200.05	Reticulosarcoma of lymph nodes of inguinal region and lower limb
200.08	Reticulosarcoma of lymph nodes of multiple sites
200.10	Lymphosarcoma, unspecified site, extranodal and solid organ sites ▽
200.14	Lymphosarcoma of lymph nodes of axilla and upper limb
200.15	Lymphosarcoma of lymph nodes of inguinal region and lower limb
200.18	Lymphosarcoma of lymph nodes of multiple sites
200.20	Burkitt's tumor or lymphoma, unspecified site, extranodal and solid organ sites ▽
200.21	Burkitt's tumor or lymphoma of lymph nodes of head, face, and neck
200.24	Burkitt's tumor or lymphoma of lymph nodes of axilla and upper limb
200.25	Burkitt's tumor or lymphoma of lymph nodes of inguinal region and lower limb
200.28	Burkitt's tumor or lymphoma of lymph nodes of multiple sites
201.00	Hodgkin's paragranuloma, unspecified site, extranodal and solid organ sites ▽
201.01	Hodgkin's paragranuloma of lymph nodes of head, face, and neck
201.04	Hodgkin's paragranuloma of lymph nodes of axilla and upper limb
201.05	Hodgkin's paragranuloma of lymph nodes of inguinal region and lower limb
201.08	Hodgkin's paragranuloma of lymph nodes of multiple sites
201.10	Hodgkin's granuloma, unspecified site, extranodal and solid organ sites ▽
201.11	Hodgkin's granuloma of lymph nodes of head, face, and neck
201.14	Hodgkin's granuloma of lymph nodes of axilla and upper limb
201.15	Hodgkin's granuloma of lymph nodes of inguinal region and lower limb
201.18	Hodgkin's granuloma of lymph nodes of multiple sites
201.20	Hodgkin's sarcoma, unspecified site, extranodal and solid organ sites ▽
201.24	Hodgkin's sarcoma of lymph nodes of axilla and upper limb
201.25	Hodgkin's sarcoma of lymph nodes of inguinal region and lower limb
201.28	Hodgkin's sarcoma of lymph nodes of multiple sites
201.40	Hodgkin's disease, lymphocytic-histiocytic predominance, unspecified site, extranodal and solid organ sites ▽
201.44	Hodgkin's disease, lymphocytic-histiocytic predominance of lymph nodes of axilla and upper limb
201.45	Hodgkin's disease, lymphocytic-histiocytic predominance of lymph nodes of inguinal region and lower limb
201.48	Hodgkin's disease, lymphocytic-histiocytic predominance of lymph nodes of multiple sites
201.51	Hodgkin's disease, nodular sclerosis, of lymph nodes of head, face, and neck
201.54	Hodgkin's disease, nodular sclerosis, of lymph nodes of axilla and upper limb
201.55	Hodgkin's disease, nodular sclerosis, of lymph nodes of inguinal region and lower limb
201.58	Hodgkin's disease, nodular sclerosis, of lymph nodes of multiple sites

201.60 Hodgkin's disease, mixed cellularity, unspecified site, extranodal and solid organ sites ▽

201.61 Hodgkin's disease, mixed cellularity, involving lymph nodes of head, face, and neck

201.65 Hodgkin's disease, mixed cellularity, of lymph nodes of inguinal region and lower limb

201.68 Hodgkin's disease, mixed cellularity, of lymph nodes of multiple sites

201.70 Hodgkin's disease, lymphocytic depletion, unspecified site, extranodal and solid organ sites ▽

201.71 Hodgkin's disease, lymphocytic depletion, of lymph nodes of head, face, and neck

201.74 Hodgkin's disease, lymphocytic depletion, of lymph nodes of axilla and upper limb

201.75 Hodgkin's disease, lymphocytic depletion, of lymph nodes of inguinal region and lower limb

201.78 Hodgkin's disease, lymphocytic depletion, of lymph nodes of multiple sites

201.90 Hodgkin's disease, unspecified type, unspecified site, extranodal and solid organ sites ▽

201.91 Hodgkin's disease, unspecified type, of lymph nodes of head, face, and neck ▽

201.94 Hodgkin's disease, unspecified type, of lymph nodes of axilla and upper limb ▽

201.95 Hodgkin's disease, unspecified type, of lymph nodes of inguinal region and lower limb ▽

201.98 Hodgkin's disease, unspecified type, of lymph nodes of multiple sites ▽

202.00 Nodular lymphoma, unspecified site, extranodal and solid organ sites ▽

202.01 Nodular lymphoma of lymph nodes of head, face, and neck

202.04 Nodular lymphoma of lymph nodes of axilla and upper limb

202.05 Nodular lymphoma of lymph nodes of inguinal region and lower limb

202.08 Nodular lymphoma of lymph nodes of multiple sites

202.10 Mycosis fungoides, unspecified site, extranodal and solid organ sites ▽

202.11 Mycosis fungoides of lymph nodes of head, face, and neck

202.14 Mycosis fungoides of lymph nodes of axilla and upper limb

202.15 Mycosis fungoides of lymph nodes of inguinal region and lower limb

202.18 Mycosis fungoides of lymph nodes of multiple sites

202.20 Sezary's disease, unspecified site, extranodal and solid organ sites ▽

202.21 Sezary's disease of lymph nodes of head, face, and neck

202.28 Sezary's disease of lymph nodes of multiple sites

202.30 Malignant histiocytosis, unspecified site, extranodal and solid organ sites ▽

202.31 Malignant histiocytosis of lymph nodes of head, face, and neck

202.34 Malignant histiocytosis of lymph nodes of axilla and upper limb

202.35 Malignant histiocytosis of lymph nodes of inguinal region and lower limb

202.38 Malignant histiocytosis of lymph nodes of multiple sites

202.40 Leukemic reticuloendotheliosis, unspecified site, extranodal and solid organ sites ▽

202.41 Leukemic reticuloendotheliosis of lymph nodes of head, face, and neck

202.44 Leukemic reticuloendotheliosis of lymph nodes of axilla and upper limb

202.45 Leukemic reticuloendotheliosis of lymph nodes of inguinal region and lower limb

202.48 Leukemic reticuloendotheliosis of lymph nodes of multiple sites

202.50 Letterer-Siwe disease, unspecified site, extranodal and solid organ sites ▽

202.51 Letterer-Siwe disease of lymph nodes of head, face, and neck

202.54 Letterer-Siwe disease of lymph nodes of axilla and upper limb

202.55 Letterer-Siwe disease of lymph nodes of inguinal region and lower limb

202.58 Letterer-Siwe disease of lymph nodes of multiple sites

202.60 Malignant mast cell tumors, unspecified site, extranodal and solid organ sites ▽

202.61 Malignant mast cell tumors of lymph nodes of head, face, and neck

202.64 Malignant mast cell tumors of lymph nodes of axilla and upper limb

202.65 Malignant mast cell tumors of lymph nodes of inguinal region and lower limb

202.68 Malignant mast cell tumors of lymph nodes of multiple sites

202.80 Other malignant lymphomas, unspecified site, extranodal and solid organ sites ▽

202.81 Other malignant lymphomas of lymph nodes of head, face, and neck

202.84 Other malignant lymphomas of lymph nodes of axilla and upper limb

202.85 Other malignant lymphomas of lymph nodes of inguinal region and lower limb

202.88 Other malignant lymphomas of lymph nodes of multiple sites

202.91 Other and unspecified malignant neoplasms of lymphoid and histiocytic tissue of lymph nodes of head, face, and neck ▽

202.94 Other and unspecified malignant neoplasms of lymphoid and histiocytic tissue of lymph nodes of axilla and upper limb ▽

202.95 Other and unspecified malignant neoplasms of lymphoid and histiocytic tissue of lymph nodes of inguinal region and lower limb ▽

202.98 Other and unspecified malignant neoplasms of lymphoid and histiocytic tissue of lymph nodes of multiple sites ▽

209.00 Malignant carcinoid tumor of the small intestine, unspecified portion — (Code first any associated multiple endocrine neoplasia syndrome: 258.01-258.03)(Use additional code to identify associated endocrine syndrome, as: carcinoid syndrome: 259.2) ▽

209.01 Malignant carcinoid tumor of the duodenum — (Code first any associated multiple endocrine neoplasia syndrome: 258.01-258.03)(Use additional code to identify associated endocrine syndrome, as: carcinoid syndrome: 259.2)

209.02 Malignant carcinoid tumor of the jejunum — (Code first any associated multiple endocrine neoplasia syndrome: 258.01-258.03)(Use additional code to identify associated endocrine syndrome, as: carcinoid syndrome: 259.2)

209.03 Malignant carcinoid tumor of the ileum — (Code first any associated multiple endocrine neoplasia syndrome: 258.01-258.03)(Use additional code to identify associated endocrine syndrome, as: carcinoid syndrome: 259.2)

209.10 Malignant carcinoid tumor of the large intestine, unspecified portion — (Code first any associated multiple endocrine neoplasia syndrome: 258.01-258.03)(Use additional code to identify associated endocrine syndrome, as: carcinoid syndrome: 259.2) ▽

209.11 Malignant carcinoid tumor of the appendix — (Code first any associated multiple endocrine neoplasia syndrome: 258.01-258.03)(Use additional code to identify associated endocrine syndrome, as: carcinoid syndrome: 259.2)

209.12 Malignant carcinoid tumor of the cecum — (Code first any associated multiple endocrine neoplasia syndrome: 258.01-258.03)(Use additional code to identify associated endocrine syndrome, as: carcinoid syndrome: 259.2)

209.13 Malignant carcinoid tumor of the ascending colon — (Code first any associated multiple endocrine neoplasia syndrome: 258.01-258.03)(Use additional code to identify associated endocrine syndrome, as: carcinoid syndrome: 259.2)

209.14 Malignant carcinoid tumor of the transverse colon — (Code first any associated multiple endocrine neoplasia syndrome: 258.01-258.03)(Use additional code to identify associated endocrine syndrome, as: carcinoid syndrome: 259.2)

209.15 Malignant carcinoid tumor of the descending colon — (Code first any associated multiple endocrine neoplasia syndrome: 258.01-258.03)(Use additional code to identify associated endocrine syndrome, as: carcinoid syndrome: 259.2)

209.16 Malignant carcinoid tumor of the sigmoid colon — (Code first any associated multiple endocrine neoplasia syndrome: 258.01-258.03)(Use additional code to identify associated endocrine syndrome, as: carcinoid syndrome: 259.2)

209.17 Malignant carcinoid tumor of the rectum — (Code first any associated multiple endocrine neoplasia syndrome: 258.01-258.03)(Use additional code to identify associated endocrine syndrome, as: carcinoid syndrome: 259.2)

209.20 Malignant carcinoid tumor of unknown primary site — (Code first any associated multiple endocrine neoplasia syndrome: 258.01-258.03)(Use additional code to identify associated endocrine syndrome, as: carcinoid syndrome: 259.2)

209.21 Malignant carcinoid tumor of the bronchus and lung — (Code first any associated multiple endocrine neoplasia syndrome: 258.01-258.03)(Use additional code to identify associated endocrine syndrome, as: carcinoid syndrome: 259.2)

209.22 Malignant carcinoid tumor of the thymus — (Code first any associated multiple endocrine neoplasia syndrome: 258.01-258.03)(Use additional code to identify associated endocrine syndrome, as: carcinoid syndrome: 259.2)

209.23 Malignant carcinoid tumor of the stomach — (Code first any associated multiple endocrine neoplasia syndrome: 258.01-258.03)(Use additional code to identify associated endocrine syndrome, as: carcinoid syndrome: 259.2)

209.24 Malignant carcinoid tumor of the kidney — (Code first any associated multiple endocrine neoplasia syndrome: 258.01-258.03; Use additional code to identify associated endocrine syndrome, as: carcinoid syndrome: 259.2)

209.25 Malignant carcinoid tumor of foregut, not otherwise specified — (Code first any associated multiple endocrine neoplasia syndrome: 258.01-258.03)(Use additional code to identify associated endocrine syndrome, as: carcinoid syndrome: 259.2)

209.26 Malignant carcinoid tumor of midgut, not otherwise specified — (Code first any associated multiple endocrine neoplasia syndrome: 258.01-258.03)(Use additional code to identify associated endocrine syndrome, as: carcinoid syndrome: 259.2)

209.27 Malignant carcinoid tumor of hindgut, not otherwise specified — (Code first any associated multiple endocrine neoplasia syndrome: 258.01-258.03)(Use additional code to identify associated endocrine syndrome, as: carcinoid syndrome: 259.2)

209.29 Malignant carcinoid tumor of other sites — (Code first any associated multiple endocrine neoplasia syndrome: 258.01-258.03)(Use additional code to identify associated endocrine syndrome, as: carcinoid syndrome: 259.2)

209.30 Malignant poorly differentiated neuroendocrine carcinoma, any site — (Code first any associated multiple endocrine neoplasia syndrome: 258.01-258.03)(Use additional code to identify associated endocrine syndrome, as: carcinoid syndrome: 259.2) ▽

209.40 Benign carcinoid tumor of the small intestine, unspecified portion — (Code first any associated multiple endocrine neoplasia syndrome: 258.01-258.03)(Use additional code to identify associated endocrine syndrome, as: carcinoid syndrome: 259.2) ▽

209.41 Benign carcinoid tumor of the duodenum — (Code first any associated multiple endocrine neoplasia syndrome: 258.01-258.03)(Use additional code to identify associated endocrine syndrome, as: carcinoid syndrome: 259.2)

209.42 Benign carcinoid tumor of the jejunum — (Code first any associated multiple endocrine neoplasia syndrome: 258.01-258.03)(Use additional code to identify associated endocrine syndrome, as: carcinoid syndrome: 259.2)

209.43 Benign carcinoid tumor of the ileum — (Code first any associated multiple endocrine neoplasia syndrome: 258.01-258.03)(Use additional code to identify associated endocrine syndrome, as: carcinoid syndrome: 259.2)

209.50 Benign carcinoid tumor of the large intestine, unspecified portion — (Code first any associated multiple endocrine neoplasia syndrome: 258.01-258.03)(Use additional code to identify associated endocrine syndrome, as: carcinoid syndrome: 259.2) ▽

209.51 Benign carcinoid tumor of the appendix — (Code first any associated multiple endocrine neoplasia syndrome: 258.01-258.03)(Use additional code to identify associated endocrine syndrome, as: carcinoid syndrome: 259.2)

209.52 Benign carcinoid tumor of the cecum — (Code first any associated multiple endocrine neoplasia syndrome: 258.01-258.03)(Use additional code to identify associated endocrine syndrome, as: carcinoid syndrome: 259.2)

209.53 Benign carcinoid tumor of the ascending colon — (Code first any associated multiple endocrine neoplasia syndrome: 258.01-258.03)(Use additional code to identify associated endocrine syndrome, as: carcinoid syndrome: 259.2)

209.54 Benign carcinoid tumor of the transverse colon — (Code first any associated multiple endocrine neoplasia syndrome: 258.01-258.03)(Use additional code to identify associated endocrine syndrome, as: carcinoid syndrome: 259.2)

209.55 Benign carcinoid tumor of the descending colon — (Code first any associated multiple endocrine neoplasia syndrome: 258.01-258.03)(Use additional code to identify associated endocrine syndrome, as: carcinoid syndrome: 259.2)

209.56 Benign carcinoid tumor of the sigmoid colon — (Code first any associated multiple endocrine neoplasia syndrome: 258.01-258.03)(Use additional code to identify associated endocrine syndrome, as: carcinoid syndrome: 259.2)

209.57 Benign carcinoid tumor of the rectum — (Code first any associated multiple endocrine neoplasia syndrome: 258.01-258.03)(Use additional code to identify associated endocrine syndrome, as: carcinoid syndrome: 259.2)

209.60 Benign carcinoid tumor of unknown primary site — (Code first any associated multiple endocrine neoplasia syndrome: 258.01-258.03)(Use additional code to identify associated endocrine syndrome, as: carcinoid syndrome: 259.2)

209.61 Benign carcinoid tumor of the bronchus and lung — (Code first any associated multiple endocrine neoplasia syndrome: 258.01-258.03)(Use additional code to identify associated endocrine syndrome, as: carcinoid syndrome: 259.2)

209.62 Benign carcinoid tumor of the thymus — (Code first any associated multiple endocrine neoplasia syndrome: 258.01-258.03)(Use additional code to identify associated endocrine syndrome, as: carcinoid syndrome: 259.2)

209.63 Benign carcinoid tumor of the stomach — (Code first any associated multiple endocrine neoplasia syndrome: 258.01-258.03)(Use additional code to identify associated endocrine syndrome, as: carcinoid syndrome: 259.2)

209.64 Benign carcinoid tumor of the kidney — (Code first any associated multiple endocrine neoplasia syndrome: 258.01-258.03; Use additional code to identify associated endocrine syndrome, as: carcinoid syndrome: 259.2)

209.65 Benign carcinoid tumor of foregut, not otherwise specified — (Code first any associated multiple endocrine neoplasia syndrome: 258.01-258.03)(Use additional code to identify associated endocrine syndrome, as: carcinoid syndrome: 259.2)

209.66 Benign carcinoid tumor of midgut, not otherwise specified — (Code first any associated multiple endocrine neoplasia syndrome: 258.01-258.03)(Use additional code to identify associated endocrine syndrome, as: carcinoid syndrome: 259.2)

209.67 Benign carcinoid tumor of hindgut, not otherwise specified — (Code first any associated multiple endocrine neoplasia syndrome: 258.01-258.03)(Use additional code to identify associated endocrine syndrome, as: carcinoid syndrome: 259.2)

209.69 Benign carcinoid tumor of other sites — (Code first any associated multiple endocrine neoplasia syndrome: 258.01-258.03)(Use additional code to identify associated endocrine syndrome, as: carcinoid syndrome: 259.2)

209.70 Secondary neuroendocrine tumor, unspecified site ▽

209.71 Secondary neuroendocrine tumor of distant lymph nodes

209.72 Secondary neuroendocrine tumor of liver

209.74 Secondary neuroendocrine tumor of peritoneum

209.79 Secondary neuroendocrine tumor of other sites

211.5 Benign neoplasm of liver and biliary passages

211.6 Benign neoplasm of pancreas, except islets of Langerhans

211.7 Benign neoplasm of islets of Langerhans — (Use additional code to identify any functional activity)

211.8 Benign neoplasm of retroperitoneum and peritoneum

211.9 Benign neoplasm of other and unspecified site of the digestive system ▽

212.3 Benign neoplasm of bronchus and lung

212.4 Benign neoplasm of pleura

212.5 Benign neoplasm of mediastinum

212.8 Benign neoplasm of other specified sites of respiratory and intrathoracic organs

214.0 Lipoma of skin and subcutaneous tissue of face

214.1 Lipoma of other skin and subcutaneous tissue

214.2 Lipoma of intrathoracic organs

214.3 Lipoma of intra-abdominal organs

214.4 Lipoma of spermatic cord ♂

214.8 Lipoma of other specified sites

214.9 Lipoma of unspecified site ▽

215.0 Other benign neoplasm of connective and other soft tissue of head, face, and neck

215.2 Other benign neoplasm of connective and other soft tissue of upper limb, including shoulder

215.3 Other benign neoplasm of connective and other soft tissue of lower limb, including hip

215.4 Other benign neoplasm of connective and other soft tissue of thorax

215.5 Other benign neoplasm of connective and other soft tissue of abdomen

215.6 Other benign neoplasm of connective and other soft tissue of pelvis

215.7 Other benign neoplasm of connective and other soft tissue of trunk, unspecified ▽

215.8 Other benign neoplasm of connective and other soft tissue of other specified sites

215.9 Other benign neoplasm of connective and other soft tissue of unspecified site ▽

217 Benign neoplasm of breast

220 Benign neoplasm of ovary — (Use additional code to identify any functional activity: 256.0-256.1) ♀

221.0 Benign neoplasm of fallopian tube and uterine ligaments ♀

222.0 Benign neoplasm of testis — (Use additional code to identify any functional activity) ♂

222.2 Benign neoplasm of prostate ♂

222.3 Benign neoplasm of epididymis ♂

223.0 Benign neoplasm of kidney, except pelvis

223.1 Benign neoplasm of renal pelvis

226 Benign neoplasm of thyroid glands — (Use additional code to identify any functional activity)

227.6 Benign neoplasm of aortic body and other paraganglia — (Use additional code to identify any functional activity)

228.04 Hemangioma of intra-abdominal structures

228.09 Hemangioma of other sites

229.0 Benign neoplasm of lymph nodes
230.1 Carcinoma in situ of esophagus
230.8 Carcinoma in situ of liver and biliary system
231.2 Carcinoma in situ of bronchus and lung
231.8 Carcinoma in situ of other specified parts of respiratory system
231.9 Carcinoma in situ of respiratory system, part unspecified ▽
233.0 Carcinoma in situ of breast
233.1 Carcinoma in situ of cervix uteri ♀
233.30 Carcinoma in situ, unspecified female genital organ ▽ ♀
233.31 Carcinoma in situ, vagina ♀
233.32 Carcinoma in situ, vulva ♀
233.39 Carcinoma in situ, other female genital organ ♀
233.4 Carcinoma in situ of prostate ♂
233.6 Carcinoma in situ of other and unspecified male genital organs ▽ ♂
233.9 Carcinoma in situ of other and unspecified urinary organs ▽
234.8 Carcinoma in situ of other specified sites
235.3 Neoplasm of uncertain behavior of liver and biliary passages
235.4 Neoplasm of uncertain behavior of retroperitoneum and peritoneum
235.5 Neoplasm of uncertain behavior of other and unspecified digestive organs ▽
235.7 Neoplasm of uncertain behavior of trachea, bronchus, and lung
235.8 Neoplasm of uncertain behavior of pleura, thymus, and mediastinum
235.9 Neoplasm of uncertain behavior of other and unspecified respiratory organs ▽
236.2 Neoplasm of uncertain behavior of ovary — (Use additional code to identify any functional activity) ♀
236.3 Neoplasm of uncertain behavior of other and unspecified female genital organs ▽ ♀
236.4 Neoplasm of uncertain behavior of testis — (Use additional code to identify any functional activity) ♂
236.5 Neoplasm of uncertain behavior of prostate ♂
236.6 Neoplasm of uncertain behavior of other and unspecified male genital organs ▽ ♂
236.91 Neoplasm of uncertain behavior of kidney and ureter
237.3 Neoplasm of uncertain behavior of paraganglia
237.4 Neoplasm of uncertain behavior of other and unspecified endocrine glands ▽
238.1 Neoplasm of uncertain behavior of connective and other soft tissue
238.3 Neoplasm of uncertain behavior of breast
238.77 Post-transplant lymphoproliferative disorder [PTLD] — (Code first complications of transplant (996.80-996.89))
238.8 Neoplasm of uncertain behavior of other specified sites
238.9 Neoplasm of uncertain behavior, site unspecified ▽
239.0 Neoplasm of unspecified nature of digestive system
239.1 Neoplasm of unspecified nature of respiratory system
239.2 Neoplasms of unspecified nature of bone, soft tissue, and skin
239.3 Neoplasm of unspecified nature of breast
239.5 Neoplasm of unspecified nature of other genitourinary organs
239.7 Neoplasm of unspecified nature of endocrine glands and other parts of nervous system
239.89 Neoplasms of unspecified nature, other specified sites
239.9 Neoplasm of unspecified nature, site unspecified ▽
240.0 Goiter, specified as simple
240.9 Goiter, unspecified ▽
241.0 Nontoxic uninodular goiter
241.1 Nontoxic multinodular goiter
241.9 Unspecified nontoxic nodular goiter ▽
242.00 Toxic diffuse goiter without mention of thyrotoxic crisis or storm
242.01 Toxic diffuse goiter with mention of thyrotoxic crisis or storm
242.10 Toxic uninodular goiter without mention of thyrotoxic crisis or storm
242.11 Toxic uninodular goiter with mention of thyrotoxic crisis or storm
242.20 Toxic multinodular goiter without mention of thyrotoxic crisis or storm
242.21 Toxic multinodular goiter with mention of thyrotoxic crisis or storm
242.30 Toxic nodular goiter, unspecified type, without mention of thyrotoxic crisis or storm ▽
242.31 Toxic nodular goiter, unspecified type, with mention of thyrotoxic crisis or storm ▽
242.40 Thyrotoxicosis from ectopic thyroid nodule without mention of thyrotoxic crisis or storm
242.41 Thyrotoxicosis from ectopic thyroid nodule with mention of thyrotoxic crisis or storm
245.0 Acute thyroiditis — (Use additional code to identify organism)
245.1 Subacute thyroiditis
245.2 Chronic lymphocytic thyroiditis
245.3 Chronic fibrous thyroiditis
245.4 Iatrogenic thyroiditis — (Use additional code to identify cause)
245.8 Other and unspecified chronic thyroiditis ▽
245.9 Unspecified thyroiditis ▽
246.2 Cyst of thyroid
246.8 Other specified disorders of thyroid
249.40 Secondary diabetes mellitus with renal manifestations, not stated as uncontrolled, or unspecified — (Use additional code to identify manifestation: 581.81, 583.81, 585.1-585.9) (Use additional code to identify any associated insulin use: V58.67)
249.41 Secondary diabetes mellitus with renal manifestations, uncontrolled — (Use additional code to identify manifestation: 581.81, 583.81, 585.1-585.9) (Use additional code to identify any associated insulin use: V58.67)
250.40 Diabetes with renal manifestations, type II or unspecified type, not stated as uncontrolled — (Use additional code to identify manifestation: 581.81, 583.81, 585.1-585.9)
250.41 Diabetes with renal manifestations, type I [juvenile type], not stated as uncontrolled — (Use additional code to identify manifestation: 581.81, 583.81, 585.1-585.9)
250.42 Diabetes with renal manifestations, type II or unspecified type, uncontrolled — (Use additional code to identify manifestation: 581.81, 583.81, 585.1-585.9)
250.43 Diabetes with renal manifestations, type I [juvenile type], uncontrolled — (Use additional code to identify manifestation: 581.81, 583.81, 585.1-585.9)
257.2 Other testicular hypofunction
277.30 Amyloidosis, unspecified — (Use additional code to identify any associated intellectual disabilities) ▽
277.31 Familial Mediterranean fever — (Use additional code to identify any associated intellectual disabilities)
277.39 Other amyloidosis — (Use additional code to identify any associated intellectual disabilities)
277.4 Disorders of bilirubin excretion — (Use additional code to identify any associated intellectual disabilities)
279.50 Graft-versus-host disease, unspecified — (Code first underlying cause: 996.80-996.89, 999.89)(Use additional code to identify any associated intellectual disabilities) (Use additional code to identify associated manifestations: 695.89, 704.09, 782.4, 787.91) ▽
279.51 Acute graft-versus-host disease — (Code first underlying cause: 996.80-996.89, 999.89)(Use additional code to identify any associated intellectual disabilities) (Use additional code to identify associated manifestations: 695.89, 704.09, 782.4, 787.91)
279.52 Chronic graft-versus-host disease — (Code first underlying cause: 996.80-996.89, 999.89)(Use additional code to identify any associated intellectual disabilities) (Use additional code to identify associated manifestations: 695.89, 704.09, 782.4, 787.91)
279.53 Acute on chronic graft-versus-host disease — (Code first underlying cause: 996.80-996.89, 999.89)(Use additional code to identify any associated intellectual disabilities) (Use additional code to identify associated manifestations: 695.89, 704.09, 782.4, 787.91)
289.1 Chronic lymphadenitis
289.3 Lymphadenitis, unspecified, except mesenteric ▽
376.00 Unspecified acute inflammation of orbit ▽
376.01 Orbital cellulitis
376.02 Orbital periostitis
376.10 Unspecified chronic inflammation of orbit ▽
376.11 Orbital granuloma
376.12 Orbital myositis

379.92 Swelling or mass of eye
403.00 Hypertensive chronic kidney disease, malignant, with chronic kidney disease stage I through stage IV, or unspecified — (Use additional code to identify the stage of chronic kidney disease: 585.1-585.4, 585.9)
403.01 Hypertensive chronic kidney disease, malignant, with chronic kidney disease stage V or end stage renal disease — (Use additional code to identify the stage of chronic kidney disease: 585.5, 585.6)
403.10 Hypertensive chronic kidney disease, benign, with chronic kidney disease stage I through stage IV, or unspecified — (Use additional code to identify the stage of chronic kidney disease: 585.1-585.4, 585.9)
403.11 Hypertensive chronic kidney disease, benign, with chronic kidney disease stage V or end stage renal disease — (Use additional code to identify the stage of chronic kidney disease: 585.5, 585.6)
403.90 Hypertensive chronic kidney disease, unspecified, with chronic kidney disease stage I through stage IV, or unspecified — (Use additional code to identify the stage of chronic kidney disease: 585.1-585.4, 585.9) ▽
403.91 Hypertensive chronic kidney disease, unspecified, with chronic kidney disease stage V or end stage renal disease — (Use additional code to identify the stage of chronic kidney disease: 585.5, 585.6) ▽
404.00 Hypertensive heart and chronic kidney disease, malignant, without heart failure and with chronic kidney disease stage I through stage IV, or unspecified — (Use additional code to identify the stage of chronic kidney disease: 585.1-585.4, 585.9)
404.01 Hypertensive heart and chronic kidney disease, malignant, with heart failure and with chronic kidney disease stage I through stage IV, or unspecified — (Use additional code to specify type of heart failure, 428.0-428.43, if known. Use additional code to identify the stage of chronic kidney disease: 585.1-585.4, 585.9)
404.02 Hypertensive heart and chronic kidney disease, malignant, without heart failure and with chronic kidney disease stage V or end stage renal disease — (Use additional code to identify the stage of chronic kidney disease: 585.5, 585.6)
404.03 Hypertensive heart and chronic kidney disease, malignant, with heart failure and with chronic kidney disease stage V or end stage renal disease — (Use additional code to specify type of heart failure, 428.0-428.43, if known. Use additional code to identify the stage of chronic kidney disease: 585.5-585.6)
404.10 Hypertensive heart and chronic kidney disease, benign, without heart failure and with chronic kidney disease stage I through stage IV, or unspecified — (Use additional code to identify the stage of chronic kidney disease: 585.1-585.4, 585.9)
404.11 Hypertensive heart and chronic kidney disease, benign, with heart failure and with chronic kidney disease stage I through stage IV, or unspecified — (Use additional code to specify type of heart failure, 428.0-428.43, if known. Use additional code to identify the stage of chronic kidney disease: 585.1-585.4, 585.9)
404.12 Hypertensive heart and chronic kidney disease, benign, without heart failure and with chronic kidney disease stage V or end stage renal disease — (Use additional code to identify the stage of chronic kidney disease: 585.5, 585.6)
404.13 Hypertensive heart and chronic kidney disease, benign, with heart failure and chronic kidney disease stage V or end stage renal disease — (Use additional code to specify type of heart failure, 428.0-428.43, if known. Use additional code to identify the stage of chronic kidney disease: 585.5-585.6)
404.90 Hypertensive heart and chronic kidney disease, unspecified, without heart failure and with chronic kidney disease stage I through stage IV, or unspecified — (Use additional code to identify the stage of chronic kidney disease: 585.1-585.4, 585.9) ▽
404.91 Hypertensive heart and chronic kidney disease, unspecified, with heart failure and with chronic kidney disease stage I through stage IV, or unspecified — (Use additional code to specify type of heart failure, 428.0-428.43, if known. Use additional code to identify the stage of chronic kidney disease: 585.1-585.4, 585.9) ▽
404.92 Hypertensive heart and chronic kidney disease, unspecified, without heart failure and with chronic kidney disease stage V or end stage renal disease — (Use additional code to identify the stage of chronic kidney disease: 585.5, 585.6) ▽
404.93 Hypertensive heart and chronic kidney disease, unspecified, with heart failure and chronic kidney disease stage V or end stage renal disease — (Use additional code to specify type of heart failure, 428.0-428.43, if known. Use additional code to identify the stage of chronic kidney disease: 585.5-585.6) ▽
457.8 Other noninfectious disorders of lymphatic channels
482.84 Legionnaires' disease
486 Pneumonia, organism unspecified ▽
511.0 Pleurisy without mention of effusion or current tuberculosis — (Use additional code to identify infectious organism)
511.81 Malignant pleural effusion — (Code first malignant neoplasm, if known)
511.89 Other specified forms of effusion, except tuberculous
518.89 Other diseases of lung, not elsewhere classified — (Use additional code to identify infectious organism)
570 Acute and subacute necrosis of liver
571.0 Alcoholic fatty liver
571.1 Acute alcoholic hepatitis
571.2 Alcoholic cirrhosis of liver
571.3 Unspecified alcoholic liver damage ▽
571.41 Chronic persistent hepatitis
571.42 Autoimmune hepatitis
571.49 Other chronic hepatitis
571.5 Cirrhosis of liver without mention of alcohol — (Code first, if applicable, viral hepatitis (acute) (chronic): 070.0-070.9)
571.6 Biliary cirrhosis
571.8 Other chronic nonalcoholic liver disease
571.9 Unspecified chronic liver disease without mention of alcohol ▽
572.0 Abscess of liver
572.1 Portal pyemia
572.2 Hepatic encephalopathy
572.4 Hepatorenal syndrome
572.8 Other sequelae of chronic liver disease
573.0 Chronic passive congestion of liver
573.1 Hepatitis in viral diseases classified elsewhere — (Code first underlying disease: 074.8, 075, 078.5) ☒
573.2 Hepatitis in other infectious diseases classified elsewhere — (Code first underlying disease: 084.9) ☒
573.3 Unspecified hepatitis — (Use additional E code to identify cause) ▽
573.4 Hepatic infarction
573.8 Other specified disorders of liver
576.8 Other specified disorders of biliary tract
577.0 Acute pancreatitis
577.1 Chronic pancreatitis
577.2 Cyst and pseudocyst of pancreas
577.8 Other specified disease of pancreas
579.4 Pancreatic steatorrhea
580.0 Acute glomerulonephritis with lesion of proliferative glomerulonephritis
580.89 Other acute glomerulonephritis with other specified pathological lesion in kidney
580.9 Acute glomerulonephritis with unspecified pathological lesion in kidney ▽
581.0 Nephrotic syndrome with lesion of proliferative glomerulonephritis
581.3 Nephrotic syndrome with lesion of minimal change glomerulonephritis
581.81 Nephrotic syndrome with other specified pathological lesion in kidney in diseases classified elsewhere — (Code first underlying disease: 084.9, 249.4, 250.4, 277.30-277.39, 446.0, 710.0) ☒
581.9 Nephrotic syndrome with unspecified pathological lesion in kidney ▽
582.0 Chronic glomerulonephritis with lesion of proliferative glomerulonephritis
582.2 Chronic glomerulonephritis with lesion of membranoproliferative glomerulonephritis
582.4 Chronic glomerulonephritis with lesion of rapidly progressive glomerulonephritis
582.81 Chronic glomerulonephritis with other specified pathological lesion in kidney in diseases classified elsewhere — (Code first underlying disease: 277.30-277.39, 710.0) ☒
582.9 Chronic glomerulonephritis with unspecified pathological lesion in kidney ▽
583.0 Nephritis and nephropathy, not specified as acute or chronic, with lesion of proliferative glomerulonephritis
583.7 Nephritis and nephropathy, not specified as acute or chronic, with lesion of renal medullary necrosis

583.81 Nephritis and nephropathy, not specified as acute or chronic, with other specified pathological lesion in kidney, in diseases classified elsewhere — (Code first underlying disease: 016.0, 098.19, 249.4, 250.4, 277.30-277.39, 446.21, 710.0) ☒

583.9 Nephritis and nephropathy, not specified as acute or chronic, with unspecified pathological lesion in kidney ▽

584.5 Acute kidney failure with lesion of tubular necrosis

584.6 Acute kidney failure with lesion of renal cortical necrosis

584.8 Acute kidney failure with other specified pathological lesion in kidney

585.1 Chronic kidney disease, Stage I — (Use additional code to identify kidney transplant status, if applicable: V42.0. Use additional code to identify manifestation: 357.4, 420.0. Code first hypertensive chronic kidney disease, if applicable: 403.00-403.91, 404.00-404.93)

585.2 Chronic kidney disease, Stage II (mild) — (Use additional code to identify kidney transplant status, if applicable: V42.0. Use additional code to identify manifestation: 357.4, 420.0. Code first hypertensive chronic kidney disease, if applicable: 403.00-403.91, 404.00-404.93)

585.3 Chronic kidney disease, Stage III (moderate) — (Use additional code to identify kidney transplant status, if applicable: V42.0. Use additional code to identify manifestation: 357.4, 420.0. Code first hypertensive chronic kidney disease, if applicable: 403.00-403.91, 404.00-404.93)

585.4 Chronic kidney disease, Stage IV (severe) — (Use additional code to identify kidney transplant status, if applicable: V42.0. Use additional code to identify manifestation: 357.4, 420.0. Code first hypertensive chronic kidney disease, if applicable: 403.00-403.91, 404.00-404.93)

585.5 Chronic kidney disease, Stage V — (Use additional code to identify kidney transplant status, if applicable: V42.0. Use additional code to identify manifestation: 357.4, 420.0. Code first hypertensive chronic kidney disease, if applicable: 403.00-403.91, 404.00-404.93)

585.6 End stage renal disease — (Use additional code to identify kidney transplant status, if applicable: V42.0. Use additional code to identify manifestation: 357.4, 420.0. Code first hypertensive chronic kidney disease, if applicable: 403.00-403.91, 404.00-404.93)

585.9 Chronic kidney disease, unspecified — (Use additional code to identify kidney transplant status, if applicable: V42.0. Use additional code to identify manifestation: 357.4, 420.0. Code first hypertensive chronic kidney disease, if applicable: 403.00-403.91, 404.00-404.93) ▽

586 Unspecified renal failure ▽

588.0 Renal osteodystrophy

593.2 Acquired cyst of kidney

593.70 Vesicoureteral reflux, unspecified or without reflex nephropathy

593.9 Unspecified disorder of kidney and ureter ▽

599.70 Hematuria, unspecified ▽

599.71 Gross hematuria

599.72 Microscopic hematuria

600.00 Hypertrophy (benign) of prostate without urinary obstruction and other lower urinary tract symptoms [LUTS] ♂

600.01 Hypertrophy (benign) of prostate with urinary obstruction and other lower urinary tract symptoms [LUTS] — (Use additional code to identify symptoms: 599.69, 788.20, 788.21, 788.30-788.39, 788.41, 788.43, 788.62, 788.63, 788.64, 788.65) ♂

600.10 Nodular prostate without urinary obstruction ♂

600.11 Nodular prostate with urinary obstruction ♂

600.20 Benign localized hyperplasia of prostate without urinary obstruction and other lower urinary tract symptoms [LUTS] ♂

600.21 Benign localized hyperplasia of prostate with urinary obstruction and other lower urinary tract symptoms [LUTS] — (Use additional code to identify symptoms: 599.69, 788.20, 788.21, 788.30-788.39, 788.41, 788.43, 788.62, 788.63, 788.64, 788.65) ♂

600.3 Cyst of prostate ♂

600.90 Hyperplasia of prostate, unspecified, without urinary obstruction and other lower urinary tract symptoms [LUTS] ▽ ♂

600.91 Hyperplasia of prostate, unspecified, with urinary obstruction and other lower urinary tract symptoms [LUTS] — (Use additional code to identify symptoms: 599.69, 788.20, 788.21, 788.30-788.39, 788.41, 788.43, 788.62, 788.63, 788.64, 788.65) ▽ ♂

601.0 Acute prostatitis — (Use additional code to identify organism: 041.0, 041.1) ♂

601.1 Chronic prostatitis — (Use additional code to identify organism: 041.0, 041.1) ♂

601.2 Abscess of prostate — (Use additional code to identify organism: 041.0, 041.1) ♂

601.3 Prostatocystitis — (Use additional code to identify organism: 041.0, 041.1) ♂

601.4 Prostatitis in diseases classified elsewhere — (Use additional code to identify organism: 041.0, 041.1. Code first underlying disease: 016.5, 039.8, 095.8, 116.0) ☒ ♂

601.8 Other specified inflammatory disease of prostate — (Use additional code to identify organism: 041.0, 041.1) ♂

602.0 Calculus of prostate ♂

602.1 Congestion or hemorrhage of prostate ♂

602.2 Atrophy of prostate ♂

602.3 Dysplasia of prostate ♂

602.8 Other specified disorder of prostate ♂

604.90 Unspecified orchitis and epididymitis — (Use additional code to identify organism: 041.00-041.09, 041.10-041.19, 041.41-041.49) ▽ ♂

604.91 Orchitis and epididymitis in disease classified elsewhere — (Use additional code to identify organism: 041.00-041.09, 041.10-041.19, 041.41-041.49. Code first underlying disease: 032.89, 095.8, 125.0-125.9) ☒ ♂

606.0 Azoospermia ♂

606.1 Oligospermia ♂

608.20 Torsion of testis, unspecified ▽ ♂

608.21 Extravaginal torsion of spermatic cord ♂

608.22 Intravaginal torsion of spermatic cord ♂

608.23 Torsion of appendix testis ♂

608.24 Torsion of appendix epididymis ♂

608.3 Atrophy of testis ♂

608.81 Specified disorder of male genital organs in diseases classified elsewhere — (Code first underlying disease: 016.5, 125.0-125.9) ☒ ♂

608.82 Hematospermia ♂

608.89 Other specified disorder of male genital organs ♂

610.0 Solitary cyst of breast

610.1 Diffuse cystic mastopathy

610.2 Fibroadenosis of breast

610.3 Fibrosclerosis of breast

610.8 Other specified benign mammary dysplasias

611.0 Inflammatory disease of breast

611.72 Lump or mass in breast

614.0 Acute salpingitis and oophoritis — (Use additional code to identify organism: 041.00-041.09, 041.10-041.19) ♀

614.1 Chronic salpingitis and oophoritis — (Use additional code to identify organism: 041.00-041.09, 041.10-041.19) ♀

614.2 Salpingitis and oophoritis not specified as acute, subacute, or chronic — (Use additional code to identify organism: 041.00-041.09, 041.10-041.19) ♀

614.3 Acute parametritis and pelvic cellulitis — (Use additional code to identify organism: 041.00-041.09, 041.10-041.19) ♀

614.4 Chronic or unspecified parametritis and pelvic cellulitis — (Use additional code to identify organism: 041.00-041.09, 041.10-041.19) ♀

614.5 Acute or unspecified pelvic peritonitis, female — (Use additional code to identify organism: 041.00-041.09, 041.10-041.19) ♀

614.6 Pelvic peritoneal adhesions, female (postoperative) (postinfection) — (Use additional code to identify organism: 041.00-041.09, 041.10-041.19) (Use additional code to identify any associated infertility: 628.2) ♀

614.7 Other chronic pelvic peritonitis, female — (Use additional code to identify organism: 041.00-041.09, 041.10-041.19) ♀

614.8 Other specified inflammatory disease of female pelvic organs and tissues — (Use additional code to identify organism: 041.00-041.09, 041.10-041.19) ♀

614.9 Unspecified inflammatory disease of female pelvic organs and tissues — (Use additional code to identify organism: 041.00-041.09, 041.10-041.19) ▽ ♀

648.10 Maternal thyroid dysfunction complicating pregnancy, childbirth, or the puerperium, unspecified as to episode of care or not applicable — (Use additional code(s) to identify the condition) ♀

648.11 Maternal thyroid dysfunction with delivery, with or without mention of antepartum condition — (Use additional code(s) to identify the condition) ♀

648.12 Maternal thyroid dysfunction with delivery, with current postpartum complication — (Use additional code(s) to identify the condition) ♀

648.13 Maternal thyroid dysfunction, antepartum condition or complication — (Use additional code(s) to identify the condition) ♀

648.14 Maternal thyroid dysfunction complicating pregnancy, childbirth, or the puerperium, postpartum condition or complication — (Use additional code(s) to identify the condition) ♀

682.0 Cellulitis and abscess of face — (Use additional code to identify organism, such as 041.1, etc.)

682.2 Cellulitis and abscess of trunk — (Use additional code to identify organism, such as 041.1, etc.)

683 Acute lymphadenitis — (Use additional code to identify organism: 041.1)

710.0 Systemic lupus erythematosus — (Use additional code to identify manifestation: 424.91, 581.81, 582.81, 583.81)

729.91 Post-traumatic seroma

729.99 Other disorders of soft tissue

751.61 Congenital biliary atresia

751.62 Congenital cystic disease of liver

753.0 Congenital renal agenesis and dysgenesis

753.10 Unspecified congenital cystic kidney disease

759.2 Congenital anomalies of other endocrine glands

780.62 Postprocedural fever

782.2 Localized superficial swelling, mass, or lump

782.4 Jaundice, unspecified, not of newborn

784.2 Swelling, mass, or lump in head and neck

785.6 Enlargement of lymph nodes

786.09 Other dyspnea and respiratory abnormalities

786.2 Cough

786.30 Hemoptysis, unspecified

786.31 Acute idiopathic pulmonary hemorrhage in infants [AIPHI]

786.39 Other hemoptysis

786.52 Painful respiration

786.6 Swelling, mass, or lump in chest

786.7 Abnormal chest sounds

786.9 Other symptoms involving respiratory system and chest

788.0 Renal colic

788.29 Other specified retention of urine — (Code, if applicable, any causal condition first, such as: 600.0-600.9, with fifth digit 1)

788.41 Urinary frequency — (Code, if applicable, any causal condition first, such as: 600.0-600.9, with fifth digit 1)

788.42 Polyuria — (Code, if applicable, any causal condition first, such as: 600.0-600.9, with fifth digit 1)

788.43 Nocturia — (Code, if applicable, any causal condition first, such as: 600.0-600.9, with fifth digit 1)

789.00 Abdominal pain, unspecified site

789.01 Abdominal pain, right upper quadrant

789.02 Abdominal pain, left upper quadrant

789.03 Abdominal pain, right lower quadrant

789.04 Abdominal pain, left lower quadrant

789.05 Abdominal pain, periumbilic

789.06 Abdominal pain, epigastric

789.07 Abdominal pain, generalized

789.09 Abdominal pain, other specified site

789.1 Hepatomegaly

789.30 Abdominal or pelvic swelling, mass or lump, unspecified site

789.31 Abdominal or pelvic swelling, mass, or lump, right upper quadrant

789.32 Abdominal or pelvic swelling, mass, or lump, left upper quadrant

789.33 Abdominal or pelvic swelling, mass, or lump, right lower quadrant

789.34 Abdominal or pelvic swelling, mass, or lump, left lower quadrant

789.35 Abdominal or pelvic swelling, mass or lump, periumbilic

789.36 Abdominal or pelvic swelling, mass, or lump, epigastric

789.37 Abdominal or pelvic swelling, mass, or lump, generalized

789.39 Abdominal or pelvic swelling, mass, or lump, other specified site

790.93 Elevated prostate specific antigen (PSA) ♂

791.0 Proteinuria

793.11 Solitary pulmonary nodule

793.19 Other nonspecific abnormal finding of lung field

793.5 Nonspecific (abnormal) findings on radiological and other examination of genitourinary organs

793.6 Nonspecific (abnormal) findings on radiological and other examination of abdominal area, including retroperitoneum

793.80 Unspecified abnormal mammogram

793.81 Mammographic microcalcification

793.89 Other (abnormal) findings on radiological examination of breast

793.91 Image test inconclusive due to excess body fat — (Use additional code to identify Body Mass Index (BMI), if known: V85.0-V85.54)

793.99 Other nonspecific (abnormal) findings on radiological and other examination of body structure

794.2 Nonspecific abnormal results of pulmonary system function study

794.5 Nonspecific abnormal results of thyroid function study

794.6 Nonspecific abnormal results of other endocrine function study

794.8 Nonspecific abnormal results of liver function study

864.01 Liver hematoma and contusion without mention of open wound into cavity

996.80 Complications of transplanted organ, unspecified site — (Use additional code to identify nature of complication: 078.5, 199.2, 238.77, 279.50-279.53)

996.81 Complications of transplanted kidney — (Use additional code to identify nature of complication: 078.5, 199.2, 238.77, 279.50-279.53)

996.82 Complications of transplanted liver — (Use additional code to identify nature of complication: 078.5, 199.2, 238.77, 279.50-279.53)

997.31 Ventilator associated pneumonia — (Use additional code to identify organism)

997.39 Other respiratory complications

ICD-9-CM Procedural

This code is too broad to adequately present ICD-9-CM procedural code links here. Refer to your ICD-9-CM Volume 3 in the appropriate anatomical site.

Integumentary System

Skin, Subcutaneous and Accessory Structures

10030

10030 Image-guided fluid collection drainage by catheter (eg, abscess, hematoma, seroma, lymphocele, cyst), soft tissue (eg, extremity, abdominal wall, neck), percutaneous

ICD-9-CM Diagnostic

457.8 Other noninfectious disorders of lymphatic channels
682.8 Cellulitis and abscess of other specified site — (Use additional code to identify organism, such as 041.1, etc.)
682.9 Cellulitis and abscess of unspecified site — (Use additional code to identify organism, such as 041.1, etc.) ▽
706.2 Sebaceous cyst
729.92 Nontraumatic hematoma of soft tissue
920 Contusion of face, scalp, and neck except eye(s)
922.2 Contusion of abdominal wall
923.03 Contusion of upper arm
923.09 Contusion of multiple sites of shoulder and upper arm
923.10 Contusion of forearm
923.9 Contusion of unspecified part of upper limb ▽
924.9 Contusion of unspecified site ▽
998.12 Hematoma complicating a procedure
998.13 Seroma complicating a procedure
998.51 Infected postoperative seroma — (Use additional code to identify organism)
998.59 Other postoperative infection — (Use additional code to identify infection)

ICD-9-CM Procedural

82.93 Aspiration of other soft tissue of hand
83.09 Other incision of soft tissue
83.95 Aspiration of other soft tissue
86.01 Aspiration of skin and subcutaneous tissue
86.04 Other incision with drainage of skin and subcutaneous tissue

10040

10040 Acne surgery (eg, marsupialization, opening or removal of multiple milia, comedones, cysts, pustules)

ICD-9-CM Diagnostic

373.13 Abscess of eyelid
374.84 Cysts of eyelids
680.0 Carbuncle and furuncle of face
680.2 Carbuncle and furuncle of trunk
686.00 Unspecified pyoderma — (Use additional code to identify any infectious organism: 041.0-041.8) ▽
686.09 Other pyoderma — (Use additional code to identify any infectious organism: 041.0-041.8)
695.3 Rosacea
704.41 Pilar cyst
704.42 Trichilemmal cyst
704.8 Other specified disease of hair and hair follicles
705.89 Other specified disorder of sweat glands
706.0 Acne varioliformis
706.1 Other acne
706.2 Sebaceous cyst
706.8 Other specified disease of sebaceous glands
709.3 Degenerative skin disorder

ICD-9-CM Procedural

08.09 Other incision of eyelid
86.04 Other incision with drainage of skin and subcutaneous tissue
86.09 Other incision of skin and subcutaneous tissue
86.3 Other local excision or destruction of lesion or tissue of skin and subcutaneous tissue

10060-10061

10060 Incision and drainage of abscess (eg, carbuncle, suppurative hidradenitis, cutaneous or subcutaneous abscess, cyst, furuncle, or paronychia); simple or single
10061 complicated or multiple

ICD-9-CM Diagnostic

110.1 Dermatophytosis of nail — (Use additional code to identify manifestation: 321.0-321.1, 380.15, 711.6)
373.13 Abscess of eyelid
528.5 Diseases of lips
680.0 Carbuncle and furuncle of face
680.1 Carbuncle and furuncle of neck
680.2 Carbuncle and furuncle of trunk
680.3 Carbuncle and furuncle of upper arm and forearm
680.4 Carbuncle and furuncle of hand
680.5 Carbuncle and furuncle of buttock
680.6 Carbuncle and furuncle of leg, except foot
680.7 Carbuncle and furuncle of foot
680.8 Carbuncle and furuncle of other specified sites
680.9 Carbuncle and furuncle of unspecified site ▽
681.00 Unspecified cellulitis and abscess of finger — (Use additional code to identify organism: 041.1) ▽
681.02 Onychia and paronychia of finger — (Use additional code to identify organism: 041.1)
681.10 Unspecified cellulitis and abscess of toe — (Use additional code to identify organism: 041.1) ▽
681.11 Onychia and paronychia of toe — (Use additional code to identify organism: 041.1)
681.9 Cellulitis and abscess of unspecified digit — (Use additional code to identify organism: 041.1) ▽
682.0 Cellulitis and abscess of face — (Use additional code to identify organism, such as 041.1, etc.)
682.1 Cellulitis and abscess of neck — (Use additional code to identify organism, such as 041.1, etc.)
682.2 Cellulitis and abscess of trunk — (Use additional code to identify organism, such as 041.1, etc.)
682.3 Cellulitis and abscess of upper arm and forearm — (Use additional code to identify organism, such as 041.1, etc.)
682.4 Cellulitis and abscess of hand, except fingers and thumb — (Use additional code to identify organism, such as 041.1, etc.)
682.5 Cellulitis and abscess of buttock — (Use additional code to identify organism, such as 041.1, etc.)
682.6 Cellulitis and abscess of leg, except foot — (Use additional code to identify organism, such as 041.1, etc.)
682.7 Cellulitis and abscess of foot, except toes — (Use additional code to identify organism, such as 041.1, etc.)
682.8 Cellulitis and abscess of other specified site — (Use additional code to identify organism, such as 041.1, etc.)
682.9 Cellulitis and abscess of unspecified site — (Use additional code to identify organism, such as 041.1, etc.) ▽

686.00 Unspecified pyoderma — (Use additional code to identify any infectious organism: 041.0-041.8) ▽

686.01 Pyoderma gangrenosum — (Use additional code to identify any infectious organism: 041.0-041.8)

686.09 Other pyoderma — (Use additional code to identify any infectious organism: 041.0-041.8)

686.1 Pyogenic granuloma of skin and subcutaneous tissue — (Use additional code to identify any infectious organism: 041.0-041.8)

686.8 Other specified local infections of skin and subcutaneous tissue — (Use additional code to identify any infectious organism: 041.0-041.8)

704.41 Pilar cyst

704.42 Trichilemmal cyst

705.83 Hidradenitis

705.89 Other specified disorder of sweat glands

706.2 Sebaceous cyst

709.8 Other specified disorder of skin

780.62 Postprocedural fever

782.2 Localized superficial swelling, mass, or lump

910.3 Face, neck, and scalp except eye, blister, infected

911.3 Trunk blister, infected

912.3 Shoulder and upper arm, blister, infected

913.3 Elbow, forearm, and wrist, blister infected

914.3 Hand(s) except finger(s) alone, blister, infected

915.3 Finger, blister, infected

916.3 Hip, thigh, leg, and ankle, blister, infected

917.3 Foot and toe(s), blister, infected

919.3 Other, multiple, and unspecified sites, blister, infected

958.3 Posttraumatic wound infection not elsewhere classified

998.51 Infected postoperative seroma — (Use additional code to identify organism)

998.59 Other postoperative infection — (Use additional code to identify infection)

ICD-9-CM Procedural

08.09 Other incision of eyelid

21.1 Incision of nose

27.0 Drainage of face and floor of mouth

86.04 Other incision with drainage of skin and subcutaneous tissue

86.09 Other incision of skin and subcutaneous tissue

10080-10081

10080 Incision and drainage of pilonidal cyst; simple

10081 complicated

ICD-9-CM Diagnostic

685.0 Pilonidal cyst with abscess

685.1 Pilonidal cyst without mention of abscess

ICD-9-CM Procedural

86.03 Incision of pilonidal sinus or cyst

10120-10121

10120 Incision and removal of foreign body, subcutaneous tissues; simple

10121 complicated

ICD-9-CM Diagnostic

709.4 Foreign body granuloma of skin and subcutaneous tissue — (Use additional code to identify foreign body (V90.01-V90.9))

729.6 Residual foreign body in soft tissue — (Use additional code to identify foreign body (V90.01-V90.9))

873.1 Open wound of scalp, complicated

873.50 Open wound of face, unspecified site, complicated ▽

873.51 Open wound of cheek, complicated

873.52 Open wound of forehead, complicated

873.54 Open wound of jaw, complicated

873.59 Open wound of face, other and multiple sites, complicated

873.9 Other and unspecified open wound of head, complicated ▽

875.1 Open wound of chest (wall), complicated

876.1 Open wound of back, complicated

877.1 Open wound of buttock, complicated

879.3 Open wound of abdominal wall, anterior, complicated

879.5 Open wound of abdominal wall, lateral, complicated

879.7 Open wound of other and unspecified parts of trunk, complicated ▽

879.9 Open wound(s) (multiple) of unspecified site(s), complicated ▽

880.12 Open wound of axillary region, complicated

881.10 Open wound of forearm, complicated

881.11 Open wound of elbow, complicated

881.12 Open wound of wrist, complicated

882.1 Open wound of hand except finger(s) alone, complicated

883.1 Open wound of finger(s), complicated

884.1 Multiple and unspecified open wound of upper limb, complicated

890.1 Open wound of hip and thigh, complicated

891.1 Open wound of knee, leg (except thigh), and ankle, complicated

894.1 Multiple and unspecified open wound of lower limb, complicated

910.6 Face, neck, and scalp, except eye, superficial foreign body (splinter), without major open wound or mention of infection

910.7 Face, neck, and scalp except eye, superficial foreign body (splinter), without major open wound, infected

911.6 Trunk, superficial foreign body (splinter), without major open wound and without mention of infection

911.7 Trunk, superficial foreign body (splinter), without major open wound, infected

913.6 Elbow, forearm, and wrist, superficial foreign body (splinter), without major open wound and without mention of infection

913.7 Elbow, forearm, and wrist, superficial foreign body (splinter), without major open wound, infected

914.6 Hand(s) except finger(s) alone, superficial foreign body (splinter), without major open wound and without mention of infection

914.7 Hand(s) except finger(s) alone, superficial foreign body (splinter) without major open wound, infected

915.6 Finger, superficial foreign body (splinter), without major open wound and without mention of infection

915.7 Finger, superficial foreign body (splinter), without major open wound, infected

916.6 Hip, thigh, leg, and ankle, superficial foreign body (splinter), without major open wound and without mention of infection

916.7 Hip, thigh, leg, and ankle, superficial foreign body (splinter), without major open wound, infected

919.6 Other, multiple, and unspecified sites, superficial foreign body (splinter), without major open wound and without mention of infection

919.7 Other, multiple, and unspecified sites, superficial foreign body (splinter), without major open wound, infected

998.4 Foreign body accidentally left during procedure, not elsewhere classified

ICD-9-CM Procedural

86.05 Incision with removal of foreign body or device from skin and subcutaneous tissue

10140

10140 Incision and drainage of hematoma, seroma or fluid collection

ICD-9-CM Diagnostic

674.30 Other complication of obstetrical surgical wounds, unspecified as to episode of care ▽ ♀

674.32 Other complication of obstetrical surgical wounds, with delivery, with mention of postpartum complication ♀

674.34 Other complications of obstetrical surgical wounds, postpartum condition or complication ♀

709.8 Other specified disorder of skin
729.91 Post-traumatic seroma
729.92 Nontraumatic hematoma of soft tissue
767.11 Birth trauma, epicranial subaponeurotic hemorrhage (massive) — (Use additional code(s) to further specify condition)
767.19 Birth trauma, other injuries to scalp — (Use additional code(s) to further specify condition)
767.8 Other specified birth trauma — (Use additional code(s) to further specify condition)
802.0 Nasal bones, closed fracture
802.1 Nasal bones, open fracture
873.1 Open wound of scalp, complicated
873.30 Open wound of nose, unspecified site, complicated ▽
873.31 Open wound of nasal septum, complicated
873.32 Open wound of nasal cavity, complicated
906.3 Late effect of contusion
920 Contusion of face, scalp, and neck except eye(s)
921.0 Black eye, not otherwise specified
921.1 Contusion of eyelids and periocular area
921.9 Unspecified contusion of eye ▽
922.1 Contusion of chest wall
922.2 Contusion of abdominal wall
922.31 Contusion of back
922.32 Contusion of buttock
922.33 Contusion of interscapular region
922.4 Contusion of genital organs
923.00 Contusion of shoulder region
923.01 Contusion of scapular region
923.03 Contusion of upper arm
923.09 Contusion of multiple sites of shoulder and upper arm
923.10 Contusion of forearm
923.11 Contusion of elbow
923.20 Contusion of hand(s)
923.21 Contusion of wrist
923.3 Contusion of finger
923.8 Contusion of multiple sites of upper limb
923.9 Contusion of unspecified part of upper limb ▽
924.00 Contusion of thigh
924.01 Contusion of hip
924.10 Contusion of lower leg
924.11 Contusion of knee
924.20 Contusion of foot
924.3 Contusion of toe
924.4 Contusion of multiple sites of lower limb
924.5 Contusion of unspecified part of lower limb ▽
924.8 Contusion of multiple sites, not elsewhere classified
924.9 Contusion of unspecified site ▽
959.01 Head injury, unspecified ▽
959.09 Injury of face and neck, other and unspecified
959.11 Other injury of chest wall
959.12 Other injury of abdomen
959.13 Fracture of corpus cavernosum penis ♂
959.14 Other injury of external genitals
959.19 Other injury of other sites of trunk
959.4 Injury, other and unspecified, hand, except finger
959.5 Injury, other and unspecified, finger
959.6 Injury, other and unspecified, hip and thigh
959.7 Injury, other and unspecified, knee, leg, ankle, and foot
959.8 Injury, other and unspecified, other specified sites, including multiple
959.9 Injury, other and unspecified, unspecified site ▽
998.11 Hemorrhage complicating a procedure
998.12 Hematoma complicating a procedure
998.13 Seroma complicating a procedure
998.51 Infected postoperative seroma — (Use additional code to identify organism)

ICD-9-CM Procedural

86.04 Other incision with drainage of skin and subcutaneous tissue

HCPCS Level II Supplies & Services

A4461 Surgical dressing holder, nonreusable, each
A4463 Surgical dressing holder, reusable, each
A4649 Surgical supply; miscellaneous

10160

10160 Puncture aspiration of abscess, hematoma, bulla, or cyst

ICD-9-CM Diagnostic

528.3 Cellulitis and abscess of oral soft tissues
528.4 Cysts of oral soft tissues
528.5 Diseases of lips
608.89 Other specified disorder of male genital organs ♂
674.30 Other complication of obstetrical surgical wounds, unspecified as to episode of care ▽ ♀
674.32 Other complication of obstetrical surgical wounds, with delivery, with mention of postpartum complication ♀
674.34 Other complications of obstetrical surgical wounds, postpartum condition or complication ♀
680.0 Carbuncle and furuncle of face
681.11 Onychia and paronychia of toe — (Use additional code to identify organism: 041.1)
682.0 Cellulitis and abscess of face — (Use additional code to identify organism, such as 041.1, etc.)
682.1 Cellulitis and abscess of neck — (Use additional code to identify organism, such as 041.1, etc.)
682.2 Cellulitis and abscess of trunk — (Use additional code to identify organism, such as 041.1, etc.)
682.3 Cellulitis and abscess of upper arm and forearm — (Use additional code to identify organism, such as 041.1, etc.)
682.4 Cellulitis and abscess of hand, except fingers and thumb — (Use additional code to identify organism, such as 041.1, etc.)
682.5 Cellulitis and abscess of buttock — (Use additional code to identify organism, such as 041.1, etc.)
682.6 Cellulitis and abscess of leg, except foot — (Use additional code to identify organism, such as 041.1, etc.)
682.7 Cellulitis and abscess of foot, except toes — (Use additional code to identify organism, such as 041.1, etc.)
704.41 Pilar cyst
704.42 Trichilemmal cyst
705.89 Other specified disorder of sweat glands
706.2 Sebaceous cyst
709.8 Other specified disorder of skin
729.92 Nontraumatic hematoma of soft tissue
767.11 Birth trauma, epicranial subaponeurotic hemorrhage (massive) — (Use additional code(s) to further specify condition)
767.19 Birth trauma, other injuries to scalp — (Use additional code(s) to further specify condition)
767.8 Other specified birth trauma — (Use additional code(s) to further specify condition)
780.62 Postprocedural fever
906.3 Late effect of contusion
920 Contusion of face, scalp, and neck except eye(s)
922.1 Contusion of chest wall
922.2 Contusion of abdominal wall
922.31 Contusion of back

922.32 Contusion of buttock
922.33 Contusion of interscapular region
922.4 Contusion of genital organs
923.00 Contusion of shoulder region
923.03 Contusion of upper arm
923.09 Contusion of multiple sites of shoulder and upper arm
923.11 Contusion of elbow
923.20 Contusion of hand(s)
923.21 Contusion of wrist
923.3 Contusion of finger
923.8 Contusion of multiple sites of upper limb
924.00 Contusion of thigh
924.01 Contusion of hip
924.10 Contusion of lower leg
924.20 Contusion of foot
924.3 Contusion of toe
924.4 Contusion of multiple sites of lower limb
959.01 Head injury, unspecified ▽
959.09 Injury of face and neck, other and unspecified
959.11 Other injury of chest wall
959.12 Other injury of abdomen
959.14 Other injury of external genitals
959.19 Other injury of other sites of trunk
959.3 Injury, other and unspecified, elbow, forearm, and wrist
959.6 Injury, other and unspecified, hip and thigh
959.7 Injury, other and unspecified, knee, leg, ankle, and foot
998.12 Hematoma complicating a procedure

ICD-9-CM Procedural

75.91 Evacuation of obstetrical incisional hematoma of perineum ♀
75.92 Evacuation of other hematoma of vulva or vagina ♀
86.01 Aspiration of skin and subcutaneous tissue

10180

10180 Incision and drainage, complex, postoperative wound infection

ICD-9-CM Diagnostic

040.42 Wound botulism
674.30 Other complication of obstetrical surgical wounds, unspecified as to episode of care ▽ ♀
674.32 Other complication of obstetrical surgical wounds, with delivery, with mention of postpartum complication ♀
674.34 Other complications of obstetrical surgical wounds, postpartum condition or complication ♀
780.62 Postprocedural fever
998.51 Infected postoperative seroma — (Use additional code to identify organism)
998.59 Other postoperative infection — (Use additional code to identify infection)

ICD-9-CM Procedural

86.04 Other incision with drainage of skin and subcutaneous tissue

11000-11001

11000 Debridement of extensive eczematous or infected skin; up to 10% of body surface
11001 each additional 10% of the body surface, or part thereof (List separately in addition to code for primary procedure)

ICD-9-CM Diagnostic

443.0 Raynaud's syndrome — (Use additional code to identify gangrene: 785.4)
681.00 Unspecified cellulitis and abscess of finger — (Use additional code to identify organism: 041.1) ▽
681.10 Unspecified cellulitis and abscess of toe — (Use additional code to identify organism: 041.1) ▽
682.0 Cellulitis and abscess of face — (Use additional code to identify organism, such as 041.1, etc.)
682.1 Cellulitis and abscess of neck — (Use additional code to identify organism, such as 041.1, etc.)
682.2 Cellulitis and abscess of trunk — (Use additional code to identify organism, such as 041.1, etc.)
682.3 Cellulitis and abscess of upper arm and forearm — (Use additional code to identify organism, such as 041.1, etc.)
682.4 Cellulitis and abscess of hand, except fingers and thumb — (Use additional code to identify organism, such as 041.1, etc.)
682.5 Cellulitis and abscess of buttock — (Use additional code to identify organism, such as 041.1, etc.)
682.6 Cellulitis and abscess of leg, except foot — (Use additional code to identify organism, such as 041.1, etc.)
682.7 Cellulitis and abscess of foot, except toes — (Use additional code to identify organism, such as 041.1, etc.)
682.8 Cellulitis and abscess of other specified site — (Use additional code to identify organism, such as 041.1, etc.)
684 Impetigo
686.00 Unspecified pyoderma — (Use additional code to identify any infectious organism: 041.0-041.8) ▽
686.01 Pyoderma gangrenosum — (Use additional code to identify any infectious organism: 041.0-041.8)
686.09 Other pyoderma — (Use additional code to identify any infectious organism: 041.0-041.8)
686.1 Pyogenic granuloma of skin and subcutaneous tissue — (Use additional code to identify any infectious organism: 041.0-041.8)
686.8 Other specified local infections of skin and subcutaneous tissue — (Use additional code to identify any infectious organism: 041.0-041.8)
686.9 Unspecified local infection of skin and subcutaneous tissue — (Use additional code to identify any infectious organism: 041.0-041.8) ▽
691.8 Other atopic dermatitis and related conditions
692.9 Contact dermatitis and other eczema, due to unspecified cause ▽
695.10 Erythema multiforme, unspecified ▽
695.11 Erythema multiforme minor
695.12 Erythema multiforme major
695.13 Stevens-Johnson syndrome
695.14 Stevens-Johnson syndrome-toxic epidermal necrolysis overlap syndrome
695.15 Toxic epidermal necrolysis
695.19 Other erythema multiforme
695.50 Exfoliation due to erythematous condition involving less than 10 percent of body surface — (Code first erythematous condition causing exfoliation: 695.13, 695.14, 695.15, 695.81)
695.51 Exfoliation due to erythematous condition involving 10-19 percent of body surface — (Code first erythematous condition causing exfoliation: 695.13, 695.14, 695.15, 695.81)
695.52 Exfoliation due to erythematous condition involving 20-29 percent of body surface — (Code first erythematous condition causing exfoliation: 695.13, 695.14, 695.15, 695.81)
695.53 Exfoliation due to erythematous condition involving 30-39 percent of body surface — (Code first erythematous condition causing exfoliation: 695.13, 695.14, 695.15, 695.81)
695.54 Exfoliation due to erythematous condition involving 40-49 percent of body surface — (Code first erythematous condition causing exfoliation: 695.13, 695.14, 695.15, 695.81)
695.55 Exfoliation due to erythematous condition involving 50-59 percent of body surface — (Code first erythematous condition causing exfoliation: 695.13, 695.14, 695.15, 695.81)

695.56 Exfoliation due to erythematous condition involving 60-69 percent of body surface — (Code first erythematous condition causing exfoliation: 695.13, 695.14, 695.15, 695.81)

695.57 Exfoliation due to erythematous condition involving 70-79 percent of body surface — (Code first erythematous condition causing exfoliation: 695.13, 695.14, 695.15, 695.81)

695.58 Exfoliation due to erythematous condition involving 80-89 percent of body surface — (Code first erythematous condition causing exfoliation: 695.13, 695.14, 695.15, 695.81)

695.59 Exfoliation due to erythematous condition involving 90 percent or more of body surface — (Code first erythematous condition causing exfoliation: 695.13, 695.14, 695.15, 695.81)

707.00 Pressure ulcer, unspecified site — (Use additional code to identify pressure ulcer stage: 707.20-707.25)

707.01 Pressure ulcer, elbow — (Use additional code to identify pressure ulcer stage: 707.20-707.25)

707.02 Pressure ulcer, upper back — (Use additional code to identify pressure ulcer stage: 707.20-707.25)

707.03 Pressure ulcer, lower back — (Use additional code to identify pressure ulcer stage: 707.20-707.25)

707.04 Pressure ulcer, hip — (Use additional code to identify pressure ulcer stage: 707.20-707.25)

707.05 Pressure ulcer, buttock — (Use additional code to identify pressure ulcer stage: 707.20-707.25)

707.06 Pressure ulcer, ankle — (Use additional code to identify pressure ulcer stage: 707.20-707.25)

707.07 Pressure ulcer, heel — (Use additional code to identify pressure ulcer stage: 707.20-707.25)

707.09 Pressure ulcer, other site — (Use additional code to identify pressure ulcer stage: 707.20-707.25)

707.10 Ulcer of lower limb, unspecified — (Code, if applicable, any causal condition first: 249.80-249.81, 250.80-250.83, 440.23, 459.11, 459.13, 459.31, 459.33)

707.11 Ulcer of thigh — (Code, if applicable, any causal condition first: 249.80-249.81, 250.80-250.83, 440.23, 459.11, 459.13, 459.31, 459.33)

707.12 Ulcer of calf — (Code, if applicable, any causal condition first: 249.80-249.81, 250.80-250.83, 440.23, 459.11, 459.13, 459.31, 459.33)

707.13 Ulcer of ankle — (Code, if applicable, any causal condition first: 249.80-249.81, 250.80-250.83, 440.23, 459.11, 459.13, 459.31, 459.33)

707.14 Ulcer of heel and midfoot — (Code, if applicable, any causal condition first: 249.80-249.81, 250.80-250.83, 440.23, 459.11, 459.13, 459.31, 459.33)

707.15 Ulcer of other part of foot — (Code, if applicable, any causal condition first: 249.80-249.81, 250.80-250.83, 440.23, 459.11, 459.13, 459.31, 459.33)

707.19 Ulcer of other part of lower limb — (Code, if applicable, any causal condition first: 249.80-249.81, 250.80-250.83, 440.23, 459.11, 459.13, 459.31, 459.33)

707.20 Pressure ulcer, unspecified stage — (Code first site of pressure ulcer: 707.00-707.09)

707.21 Pressure ulcer, stage I — (Code first site of pressure ulcer: 707.00-707.09)

707.22 Pressure ulcer stage II — (Code first site of pressure ulcer: 707.00-707.09)

707.23 Pressure ulcer stage III — (Code first site of pressure ulcer: 707.00-707.09)

707.25 Pressure ulcer, unstageable — (Code first site of pressure ulcer: 707.00-707.09)

707.8 Chronic ulcer of other specified site

785.4 Gangrene — (Code first any associated underlying condition)

910.1 Face, neck, and scalp except eye, abrasion or friction burn, infected

911.1 Trunk abrasion or friction burn, infected

912.1 Shoulder and upper arm, abrasion or friction burn, infected

913.1 Elbow, forearm, and wrist, abrasion or friction burn, infected

914.1 Hand(s) except finger(s) alone, abrasion or friction burn, infected

916.1 Hip, thigh, leg, and ankle, abrasion or friction burn, infected

ICD-9-CM Procedural

86.22 Excisional debridement of wound, infection, or burn

HCPCS Level II Supplies & Services

A4305 Disposable drug delivery system, flow rate of 50 ml or greater per hour

11004-11006

11004 Debridement of skin, subcutaneous tissue, muscle and fascia for necrotizing soft tissue infection; external genitalia and perineum

11005 abdominal wall, with or without fascial closure

11006 external genitalia, perineum and abdominal wall, with or without fascial closure

ICD-9-CM Diagnostic

035 Erysipelas

040.0 Gas gangrene

040.3 Necrobacillosis

040.42 Wound botulism

041.01 Streptococcus infection in conditions classified elsewhere and of unspecified site, group A — (Note: This code is to be used as an additional code to identify the bacterial agent in diseases classified elsewhere and bacterial infections of unspecified nature or site)

041.04 Streptococcus infection in conditions classified elsewhere and of unspecified site, group D [Enterococcus] — (Note: This code is to be used as an additional code to identify the bacterial agent in diseases classified elsewhere and bacterial infections of unspecified nature or site)

041.09 Other streptococcus infection in conditions classified elsewhere and of unspecified site — (Note: This code is to be used as an additional code to identify the bacterial agent in diseases classified elsewhere and bacterial infections of unspecified nature or site)

041.11 Methicillin susceptible Staphylococcus aureus — (Note: This code is to be used as an additional code to identify the bacterial agent in diseases classified elsewhere and bacterial infections of unspecified nature or site)

041.12 Methicillin resistant Staphylococcus aureus

041.19 Other staphylococcus infection in conditions classified elsewhere and of unspecified site — (Note: This code is to be used as an additional code to identify the bacterial agent in diseases classified elsewhere and bacterial infections of unspecified nature or site)

041.3 Klebsiella pneumoniae infection — (Note: This code is to be used as an additional code to identify the bacterial agent in diseases classified elsewhere and bacterial infections of unspecified nature or site)

041.41 Shiga toxin-producing Escherichia coli [E. coli] (STEC) O157 infection in conditions classified elsewhere and of unspecified site

041.42 Other specified Shiga toxin-producing Escherichia coli [E. coli] (STEC) infection in conditions classified elsewhere and of unspecified site

041.43 Unspecified Shiga toxin-producing Escherichia coli [E. coli] (STEC) infection in conditions classified elsewhere and of unspecified site

041.49 Other and unspecified Escherichia coli [E. coli] infection in conditions classified elsewhere and of unspecified site

041.6 Proteus (mirabilis) (morganii) infection in conditions classified elsewhere and of unspecified site — (Note: This code is to be used as an additional code to identify the bacterial agent in diseases classified elsewhere and bacterial infections of unspecified nature or site)

041.7 Pseudomonas infection in conditions classified elsewhere and of unspecified site — (Note: This code is to be used as an additional code to identify the bacterial agent in diseases classified elsewhere and bacterial infections of unspecified nature or site)

041.82 Bacterial infection in conditions classified elsewhere, Bacteroides fragilis — (Note: This code is to be used as an additional code to identify the bacterial agent in diseases classified elsewhere and bacterial infections of unspecified nature or site)

041.83 Clostridium perfringens infection in conditions classified elsewhere and of unspecified site — (Note: This code is to be used as an additional code to identify the bacterial agent in diseases classified elsewhere and bacterial infections of unspecified nature or site)

041.84 Infection due to other anaerobes in conditions classified elsewhere and of unspecified site — (Note: This code is to be used as an additional code to identify the bacterial agent in diseases classified elsewhere and bacterial infections of unspecified nature or site)

041.85 Infection due to other gram-negative organisms in conditions classified elsewhere and of unspecified site — (Note: This code is to be used as an additional code to identify the bacterial agent in diseases classified elsewhere and bacterial infections of unspecified nature or site)

249.70 Secondary diabetes mellitus with peripheral circulatory disorders, not stated as uncontrolled, or unspecified — (Use additional code to identify manifestation: 443.81, 785.4) (Use additional code to identify any associated insulin use: V58.67)

249.71 Secondary diabetes mellitus with peripheral circulatory disorders, uncontrolled — (Use additional code to identify manifestation: 443.81, 785.4) (Use additional code to identify any associated insulin use: V58.67)

249.80 Secondary diabetes mellitus with other specified manifestations, not stated as uncontrolled, or unspecified — (Use additional code to identify manifestation: 707.10-707.19, 707.8, 707.9, 731.8) (Use additional code to identify any associated insulin use: V58.67)

249.81 Secondary diabetes mellitus with other specified manifestations, uncontrolled — (Use additional code to identify manifestation: 707.10-707.19, 707.8, 707.9, 731.8) (Use additional code to identify any associated insulin use: V58.67)

249.90 Secondary diabetes mellitus with unspecified complication, not stated as uncontrolled, or unspecified — (Use additional code to identify any associated insulin use: V58.67) ▽

249.91 Secondary diabetes mellitus with unspecified complication, uncontrolled — (Use additional code to identify any associated insulin use: V58.67) ▽

250.70 Diabetes with peripheral circulatory disorders, type II or unspecified type, not stated as uncontrolled — (Use additional code to identify manifestation: 443.81, 785.4)

250.71 Diabetes with peripheral circulatory disorders, type I [juvenile type], not stated as uncontrolled — (Use additional code to identify manifestation: 443.81, 785.4)

250.72 Diabetes with peripheral circulatory disorders, type II or unspecified type, uncontrolled — (Use additional code to identify manifestation: 443.81, 785.4)

250.73 Diabetes with peripheral circulatory disorders, type I [juvenile type], uncontrolled — (Use additional code to identify manifestation: 443.81, 785.4)

443.0 Raynaud's syndrome — (Use additional code to identify gangrene: 785.4)

604.0 Orchitis, epididymitis, and epididymo-orchitis, with abscess — (Use additional code to identify organism: 041.00-041.09, 041.10-041.19, 041.41-041.49) ♂

608.83 Specified vascular disorder of male genital organs ♂

616.11 Vaginitis and vulvovaginitis in diseases classified elsewhere — (Use additional code to identify organism: 041.00-041.09, 041.10-041.19) (Code first underlying disease: 127.4) ☒ ♀

616.4 Other abscess of vulva — (Use additional code to identify organism: 041.00-041.09, 041.10-041.19) ♀

616.50 Unspecified ulceration of vulva — (Use additional code to identify organism: 041.00-041.09, 041.10-041.19) ▽ ♀

616.51 Ulceration of vulva in disease classified elsewhere — (Use additional code to identify organism: 041.00-041.09, 041.10-041.19) (Code first underlying disease: 016.7, 136.1) ☒ ♀

707.8 Chronic ulcer of other specified site

728.86 Necrotizing fasciitis — (Use additional code to identify infectious organism, 041.00-041.89, 785.4, if applicable)

785.4 Gangrene — (Code first any associated underlying condition)

996.65 Infection and inflammatory reaction due to other genitourinary device, implant, and graft — (Use additional code to identify specified infections)

998.59 Other postoperative infection — (Use additional code to identify infection)

ICD-9-CM Procedural

54.3 Excision or destruction of lesion or tissue of abdominal wall or umbilicus

61.3 Excision or destruction of lesion or tissue of scrotum ♂

71.3 Other local excision or destruction of vulva and perineum ♀

83.39 Excision of lesion of other soft tissue

83.44 Other fasciectomy

83.45 Other myectomy

86.22 Excisional debridement of wound, infection, or burn

HCPCS Level II Supplies & Services

A4461 Surgical dressing holder, nonreusable, each

A4463 Surgical dressing holder, reusable, each

A4649 Surgical supply; miscellaneous

11010-11012

11010 Debridement including removal of foreign material at the site of an open fracture and/or an open dislocation (eg, excisional debridement); skin and subcutaneous tissues

11011 skin, subcutaneous tissue, muscle fascia, and muscle

11012 skin, subcutaneous tissue, muscle fascia, muscle, and bone

ICD-9-CM Diagnostic

802.1 Nasal bones, open fracture

802.30 Open fracture of unspecified site of mandible ▽

802.31 Open fracture of condylar process of mandible

802.32 Open fracture of subcondylar process of mandible

802.33 Open fracture of coronoid process of mandible

802.34 Open fracture of unspecified part of ramus of mandible ▽

802.35 Open fracture of angle of jaw

802.36 Open fracture of symphysis of body of mandible

802.37 Open fracture of alveolar border of body of mandible

802.38 Open fracture of other and unspecified part of body of mandible ▽

802.39 Open fracture of multiple sites of mandible

802.5 Malar and maxillary bones, open fracture

802.9 Other facial bones, open fracture

804.51 Open fractures involving skull or face with other bones, without mention of intracranial injury, no loss of consciousness

804.52 Open fractures involving skull or face with other bones, without mention of intracranial injury, brief (less than one hour) loss of consciousness

804.53 Open fractures involving skull or face with other bones, without mention of intracranial injury, moderate (1-24 hours) loss of consciousness

804.54 Open fractures involving skull or face with other bones, without mention of intracranial injury, prolonged (more than 24 hours) loss of consciousness and return to pre-existing conscious level

804.55 Open fractures involving skull or face with other bones, without mention of intracranial injury, prolonged (more than 24 hours) loss of consciousness, without return to pre-existing conscious level

804.56 Open fractures involving skull or face with other bones, without mention of intracranial injury, loss of consciousness of unspecified duration ▽

804.59 Open fractures involving skull or face with other bones, without mention of intracranial injury, unspecified concussion ▽

804.60 Open fractures involving skull or face with other bones, with cerebral laceration and contusion, unspecified state of consciousness ▽

804.61 Open fractures involving skull or face with other bones, with cerebral laceration and contusion, no loss of consciousness

804.62 Open fractures involving skull or face with other bones, with cerebral laceration and contusion, brief (less than one hour) loss of consciousness

804.63 Open fractures involving skull or face with other bones, with cerebral laceration and contusion, moderate (1-24 hours) loss of consciousness

804.64 Open fractures involving skull or face with other bones, with cerebral laceration and contusion, prolonged (more than 24 hours) loss of consciousness and return to pre-existing conscious level

804.65 Open fractures involving skull or face with other bones, with cerebral laceration and contusion, prolonged (more than 24 hours) loss of consciousness, without return to pre-existing conscious level

804.66 Open fractures involving skull or face with other bones, with cerebral laceration and contusion, loss of consciousness of unspecified duration ▽

804.69 Open fractures involving skull or face with other bones, with cerebral laceration and contusion, unspecified concussion ▽

804.70 Open fractures involving skull or face with other bones with subarachnoid, subdural, and extradural hemorrhage, unspecified state of consciousness ▽

804.71 Open fractures involving skull or face with other bones with subarachnoid, subdural, and extradural hemorrhage, no loss of consciousness

804.72 Open fractures involving skull or face with other bones with subarachnoid, subdural, and extradural hemorrhage, brief (less than one hour) loss of consciousness

804.73 Open fractures involving skull or face with other bones with subarachnoid, subdural, and extradural hemorrhage, moderate (1-24 hours) loss of consciousness

804.74 Open fractures involving skull or face with other bones with subarachnoid, subdural, and extradural hemorrhage, prolonged (more than 24 hours) loss of consciousness and return to pre-existing conscious level

804.75 Open fractures involving skull or face with other bones with subarachnoid, subdural, and extradural hemorrhage, prolonged (more than 24 hours) loss of consciousness, without return to pre-existing conscious level

804.76 Open fractures involving skull or face with other bones with subarachnoid, subdural, and extradural hemorrhage, loss of consciousness of unspecified duration

804.79 Open fractures involving skull or face with other bones with subarachnoid, subdural, and extradural hemorrhage, unspecified concussion

804.80 Open fractures involving skull or face with other bones, with other and unspecified intracranial hemorrhage, unspecified state of consciousness

804.81 Open fractures involving skull or face with other bones, with other and unspecified intracranial hemorrhage, no loss of consciousness

804.82 Open fractures involving skull or face with other bones, with other and unspecified intracranial hemorrhage, brief (less than one hour) loss of consciousness

804.83 Open fractures involving skull or face with other bones, with other and unspecified intracranial hemorrhage, moderate (1-24 hours) loss of consciousness

804.84 Open fractures involving skull or face with other bones, with other and unspecified intracranial hemorrhage, prolonged (more than 24 hours) loss of consciousness and return to pre-existing conscious level

804.85 Open fractures involving skull or face with other bones, with other and unspecified intracranial hemorrhage, prolonged (more than 24 hours) loss of consciousness, without return to pre-existing conscious level

804.86 Open fractures involving skull or face with other bones, with other and unspecified intracranial hemorrhage, loss of consciousness of unspecified duration

804.89 Open fractures involving skull or face with other bones, with other and unspecified intracranial hemorrhage, unspecified concussion

804.90 Open fractures involving skull or face with other bones, with intracranial injury of other and unspecified nature, unspecified state of consciousness

804.91 Open fractures involving skull or face with other bones, with intracranial injury of other and unspecified nature, no loss of consciousness

804.92 Open fractures involving skull or face with other bones, with intracranial injury of other and unspecified nature, brief (less than one hour) loss of consciousness

804.93 Open fractures involving skull or face with other bones, with intracranial injury of other and unspecified nature, moderate (1-24 hours) loss of consciousness

804.94 Open fractures involving skull or face with other bones, with intracranial injury of other and unspecified nature, prolonged (more than 24 hours) loss of consciousness and return to pre-existing conscious level

804.95 Open fractures involving skull or face with other bones, with intracranial injury of other and unspecified nature, prolonged (more than 24 hours) loss of consciousness, without return to pre-existing level

804.96 Open fractures involving skull or face with other bones, with intracranial injury of other and unspecified nature, loss of consciousness of unspecified duration

804.99 Open fractures involving skull or face with other bones, with intracranial injury of other and unspecified nature, unspecified concussion

807.11 Open fracture of one rib

807.12 Open fracture of two ribs

807.13 Open fracture of three ribs

807.14 Open fracture of four ribs

807.15 Open fracture of five ribs

807.16 Open fracture of six ribs

807.17 Open fracture of seven ribs

807.18 Open fracture of eight or more ribs

807.6 Open fracture of larynx and trachea

808.1 Open fracture of acetabulum

808.3 Open fracture of pubis

808.51 Open fracture of ilium

808.52 Open fracture of ischium

808.53 Multiple open pelvic fractures with disruption of pelvic circle

808.59 Open fracture of other specified part of pelvis

808.9 Unspecified open fracture of pelvis

809.1 Fracture of bones of trunk, open

810.10 Unspecified part of open fracture of clavicle

810.11 Open fracture of sternal end of clavicle

810.12 Open fracture of shaft of clavicle

810.13 Open fracture of acromial end of clavicle

811.10 Open fracture of unspecified part of scapula

811.11 Open fracture of acromial process of scapula

811.12 Open fracture of coracoid process

811.13 Open fracture of glenoid cavity and neck of scapula

811.19 Open fracture of other part of scapula

812.10 Open fracture of unspecified part of upper end of humerus

812.11 Open fracture of surgical neck of humerus

812.12 Open fracture of anatomical neck of humerus

812.13 Open fracture of greater tuberosity of humerus

812.19 Other open fracture of upper end of humerus

812.30 Open fracture of unspecified part of humerus

812.31 Open fracture of shaft of humerus

812.50 Open fracture of unspecified part of lower end of humerus

812.51 Open fracture of supracondylar humerus

812.52 Open fracture of lateral condyle of humerus

812.53 Open fracture of medial condyle of humerus

812.54 Open fracture of unspecified condyle(s) of humerus

812.59 Other open fracture of lower end of humerus

813.10 Unspecified open fracture of upper end of forearm

813.11 Open fracture of olecranon process of ulna

813.12 Open fracture of coronoid process of ulna

813.13 Open Monteggia's fracture

813.14 Other and unspecified open fractures of proximal end of ulna (alone)

813.15 Open fracture of head of radius

813.17 Other and unspecified open fractures of proximal end of radius (alone)

813.18 Open fracture of radius with ulna, upper end (any part)

813.30 Unspecified open fracture of shaft of radius or ulna

813.31 Open fracture of shaft of radius (alone)

813.32 Open fracture of shaft of ulna (alone)

813.33 Open fracture of shaft of radius with ulna

813.50 Unspecified open fracture of lower end of forearm

813.51 Open Colles' fracture

813.52 Other open fractures of distal end of radius (alone)

813.53 Open fracture of distal end of ulna (alone)

813.54 Open fracture of lower end of radius with ulna

813.90 Open fracture of unspecified part of forearm

813.91 Open fracture of unspecified part of radius (alone)

813.92 Open fracture of unspecified part of ulna (alone)

813.93 Open fracture of unspecified part of radius with ulna

814.10 Unspecified open fracture of carpal bone

814.11 Open fracture of navicular (scaphoid) bone of wrist

814.12 Open fracture of lunate (semilunar) bone of wrist

814.13 Open fracture of triquetral (cuneiform) bone of wrist

814.14 Open fracture of pisiform bone of wrist

814.15 Open fracture of trapezium bone (larger multangular) of wrist

814.16 Open fracture of trapezoid bone (smaller multangular) of wrist

814.17 Open fracture of capitate bone (os magnum) of wrist
814.18 Open fracture of hamate (unciform) bone of wrist
814.19 Open fracture of other bone of wrist
815.10 Open fracture of metacarpal bone(s), site unspecified
815.11 Open fracture of base of thumb (first) metacarpal bone(s)
815.12 Open fracture of base of other metacarpal bone(s)
815.13 Open fracture of shaft of metacarpal bone(s)
815.14 Open fracture of neck of metacarpal bone(s)
815.19 Open fracture of multiple sites of metacarpus
816.10 Open fracture of phalanx or phalanges of hand, unspecified
816.11 Open fracture of middle or proximal phalanx or phalanges of hand
816.12 Open fracture of distal phalanx or phalanges of hand
816.13 Open fractures of multiple sites of phalanx or phalanges of hand
817.1 Multiple open fractures of hand bones
818.1 Ill-defined open fractures of upper limb
819.1 Multiple open fractures involving both upper limbs, and upper limb with rib(s) and sternum
820.10 Open fracture of unspecified intracapsular section of neck of femur
820.11 Open fracture of epiphysis (separation) (upper) of neck of femur
820.12 Open fracture of midcervical section of femur
820.13 Open fracture of base of neck of femur
820.19 Other open transcervical fracture of femur
820.30 Open fracture of unspecified trochanteric section of femur
820.31 Open fracture of intertrochanteric section of femur
820.32 Open fracture of subtrochanteric section of femur
820.9 Open fracture of unspecified part of neck of femur
821.10 Open fracture of unspecified part of femur
821.11 Open fracture of shaft of femur
821.30 Open fracture of unspecified part of lower end of femur
821.31 Open fracture of femoral condyle
821.32 Open fracture of lower epiphysis of femur
821.33 Open supracondylar fracture of femur
821.39 Other open fracture of lower end of femur
822.1 Open fracture of patella
823.10 Open fracture of upper end of tibia
823.11 Open fracture of upper end of fibula
823.12 Open fracture of upper end of fibula with tibia
823.30 Open fracture of shaft of tibia
823.31 Open fracture of shaft of fibula
823.32 Open fracture of shaft of fibula with tibia
823.90 Open fracture of unspecified part of tibia
823.91 Open fracture of unspecified part of fibula
823.92 Open fracture of unspecified part of fibula with tibia
824.1 Open fracture of medial malleolus
824.3 Open fracture of lateral malleolus
824.5 Open bimalleolar fracture
824.7 Open trimalleolar fracture
825.1 Open fracture of calcaneus
825.30 Open fracture of unspecified bone(s) of foot (except toes)
825.31 Open fracture of astragalus
825.32 Open fracture of navicular (scaphoid) bone of foot
825.33 Open fracture of cuboid bone
825.34 Open fracture of cuneiform bone of foot,
825.35 Open fracture of metatarsal bone(s)
825.39 Other open fractures of tarsal and metatarsal bones
826.1 Open fracture of one or more phalanges of foot
827.1 Other, multiple and ill-defined open fractures of lower limb
828.1 Multiple fractures involving both lower limbs, lower with upper limb, and lower limb(s) with rib(s) and sternum, open
829.1 Open fracture of unspecified bone
830.1 Open dislocation of jaw
831.10 Open unspecified dislocation of shoulder
831.11 Open anterior dislocation of humerus
831.12 Open posterior dislocation of humerus
831.13 Open inferior dislocation of humerus
831.14 Open dislocation of acromioclavicular (joint)
831.19 Open dislocation of other site of shoulder
832.10 Open unspecified dislocation of elbow
832.11 Open anterior dislocation of elbow
832.12 Open posterior dislocation of elbow
832.13 Open medial dislocation of elbow
832.14 Open lateral dislocation of elbow
832.19 Open dislocation of other site of elbow
833.10 Open dislocation of wrist, unspecified part
833.11 Open dislocation of distal radioulnar (joint)
833.12 Open dislocation of radiocarpal (joint)
833.13 Open dislocation of midcarpal (joint)
833.14 Open dislocation of carpometacarpal (joint)
833.15 Open dislocation of proximal end of metacarpal (bone)
833.19 Open dislocation of other part of wrist
834.10 Open dislocation of finger, unspecified part
834.11 Open dislocation of metacarpophalangeal (joint)
834.12 Open dislocation interphalangeal (joint), hand
835.10 Open dislocation of hip, unspecified site
835.11 Open posterior dislocation of hip
835.12 Open obturator dislocation of hip
835.13 Other open anterior dislocation of hip
836.4 Open dislocation of patella
836.60 Open dislocation of knee unspecified part
836.61 Open anterior dislocation of tibia, proximal end
836.62 Open posterior dislocation of tibia, proximal end
836.63 Open medial dislocation of tibia, proximal end
836.64 Open lateral dislocation of tibia, proximal end
836.69 Other open dislocation of knee
837.1 Open dislocation of ankle
838.10 Open dislocation of foot, unspecified part
838.11 Open dislocation of tarsal (bone), joint unspecified
838.12 Open dislocation of midtarsal (joint)
838.13 Open dislocation of tarsometatarsal (joint)
838.14 Open dislocation of metatarsal (bone), joint unspecified
838.15 Open dislocation of metatarsophalangeal (joint)
838.16 Open dislocation of interphalangeal (joint), foot
838.19 Open dislocation of other part of foot
839.10 Open dislocation, unspecified cervical vertebra
839.11 Open dislocation, first cervical vertebra
839.12 Open dislocation, second cervical vertebra
839.13 Open dislocation, third cervical vertebra
839.14 Open dislocation, fourth cervical vertebra
839.15 Open dislocation, fifth cervical vertebra
839.16 Open dislocation, sixth cervical vertebra
839.17 Open dislocation, seventh cervical vertebra
839.18 Open dislocation, multiple cervical vertebrae
839.30 Open dislocation, lumbar vertebra
839.31 Open dislocation, thoracic vertebra
839.50 Open dislocation, vertebra, unspecified site
839.51 Open dislocation, coccyx
839.52 Open dislocation, sacrum

839.59 Open dislocation, other vertebra
839.71 Open dislocation, sternum

ICD-9-CM Procedural

76.2 Local excision or destruction of lesion of facial bone
79.60 Debridement of open fracture, unspecified site
79.61 Debridement of open fracture of humerus
79.62 Debridement of open fracture of radius and ulna
79.63 Debridement of open fracture of carpals and metacarpals
79.64 Debridement of open fracture of phalanges of hand
79.65 Debridement of open fracture of femur
79.66 Debridement of open fracture of tibia and fibula
79.67 Debridement of open fracture of tarsals and metatarsals
79.68 Debridement of open fracture of phalanges of foot
79.69 Debridement of open fracture of other specified bone, except facial bones

HCPCS Level II Supplies & Services

A4649 Surgical supply; miscellaneous

11042-11044 [11045, 11046, 11047]

11042 Debridement, subcutaneous tissue (includes epidermis and dermis, if performed); first 20 sq cm or less
11043 Debridement, muscle and/or fascia (includes epidermis, dermis, and subcutaneous tissue, if performed); first 20 sq cm or less
11044 Debridement, bone (includes epidermis, dermis, subcutaneous tissue, muscle and/or fascia, if performed); first 20 sq cm or less
11045 each additional 20 sq cm, or part thereof (List separately in addition to code for primary procedure)
11046 each additional 20 sq cm, or part thereof (List separately in addition to code for primary procedure)
11047 each additional 20 sq cm, or part thereof (List separately in addition to code for primary procedure)

ICD-9-CM Diagnostic

249.70 Secondary diabetes mellitus with peripheral circulatory disorders, not stated as uncontrolled, or unspecified — (Use additional code to identify manifestation: 443.81, 785.4) (Use additional code to identify any associated insulin use: V58.67)
249.71 Secondary diabetes mellitus with peripheral circulatory disorders, uncontrolled — (Use additional code to identify manifestation: 443.81, 785.4) (Use additional code to identify any associated insulin use: V58.67)
249.80 Secondary diabetes mellitus with other specified manifestations, not stated as uncontrolled, or unspecified — (Use additional code to identify manifestation: 707.10-707.19, 707.8, 707.9, 731.8) (Use additional code to identify any associated insulin use: V58.67)
249.81 Secondary diabetes mellitus with other specified manifestations, uncontrolled — (Use additional code to identify manifestation: 707.10-707.19, 707.8, 707.9, 731.8) (Use additional code to identify any associated insulin use: V58.67)
249.90 Secondary diabetes mellitus with unspecified complication, not stated as uncontrolled, or unspecified — (Use additional code to identify any associated insulin use: V58.67) ▽
249.91 Secondary diabetes mellitus with unspecified complication, uncontrolled — (Use additional code to identify any associated insulin use: V58.67) ▽
250.70 Diabetes with peripheral circulatory disorders, type II or unspecified type, not stated as uncontrolled — (Use additional code to identify manifestation: 443.81, 785.4)
250.71 Diabetes with peripheral circulatory disorders, type I [juvenile type], not stated as uncontrolled — (Use additional code to identify manifestation: 443.81, 785.4)
250.72 Diabetes with peripheral circulatory disorders, type II or unspecified type, uncontrolled — (Use additional code to identify manifestation: 443.81, 785.4)
250.73 Diabetes with peripheral circulatory disorders, type I [juvenile type], uncontrolled — (Use additional code to identify manifestation: 443.81, 785.4)
440.23 Atherosclerosis of native arteries of the extremities with ulceration — (Use additional code for any associated ulceration: 707.10-707.19, 707.8, 707.9)
440.24 Atherosclerosis of native arteries of the extremities with gangrene — (Use additional code for any associated ulceration: 707.10-707.19, 707.8, 707.9)
443.0 Raynaud's syndrome — (Use additional code to identify gangrene: 785.4)
443.81 Peripheral angiopathy in diseases classified elsewhere — (Code first underlying disease: 249.7, 250.7) ☒
454.0 Varicose veins of lower extremities with ulcer
454.1 Varicose veins of lower extremities with inflammation
454.2 Varicose veins of lower extremities with ulcer and inflammation
454.8 Varicose veins of the lower extremities with other complications
459.11 Postphlebitic syndrome with ulcer
459.13 Postphlebitic syndrome with ulcer and inflammation
459.19 Postphlebitic syndrome with other complication
459.31 Chronic venous hypertension with ulcer
459.32 Chronic venous hypertension with inflammation
459.33 Chronic venous hypertension with ulcer and inflammation
459.81 Unspecified venous (peripheral) insufficiency — (Use additional code for any associated ulceration: 707.10-707.19, 707.8, 707.9) ▽
681.00 Unspecified cellulitis and abscess of finger — (Use additional code to identify organism: 041.1) ▽
681.10 Unspecified cellulitis and abscess of toe — (Use additional code to identify organism: 041.1) ▽
681.11 Onychia and paronychia of toe — (Use additional code to identify organism: 041.1)
682.0 Cellulitis and abscess of face — (Use additional code to identify organism, such as 041.1, etc.)
682.1 Cellulitis and abscess of neck — (Use additional code to identify organism, such as 041.1, etc.)
682.2 Cellulitis and abscess of trunk — (Use additional code to identify organism, such as 041.1, etc.)
682.3 Cellulitis and abscess of upper arm and forearm — (Use additional code to identify organism, such as 041.1, etc.)
682.4 Cellulitis and abscess of hand, except fingers and thumb — (Use additional code to identify organism, such as 041.1, etc.)
682.5 Cellulitis and abscess of buttock — (Use additional code to identify organism, such as 041.1, etc.)
682.6 Cellulitis and abscess of leg, except foot — (Use additional code to identify organism, such as 041.1, etc.)
682.7 Cellulitis and abscess of foot, except toes — (Use additional code to identify organism, such as 041.1, etc.)
682.8 Cellulitis and abscess of other specified site — (Use additional code to identify organism, such as 041.1, etc.)
686.09 Other pyoderma — (Use additional code to identify any infectious organism: 041.0-041.8)
686.1 Pyogenic granuloma of skin and subcutaneous tissue — (Use additional code to identify any infectious organism: 041.0-041.8)
701.5 Other abnormal granulation tissue
707.00 Pressure ulcer, unspecified site — (Use additional code to identify pressure ulcer stage: 707.20-707.25) ▽
707.01 Pressure ulcer, elbow — (Use additional code to identify pressure ulcer stage: 707.20-707.25)
707.02 Pressure ulcer, upper back — (Use additional code to identify pressure ulcer stage: 707.20-707.25)
707.03 Pressure ulcer, lower back — (Use additional code to identify pressure ulcer stage: 707.20-707.25)
707.04 Pressure ulcer, hip — (Use additional code to identify pressure ulcer stage: 707.20-707.25)
707.05 Pressure ulcer, buttock — (Use additional code to identify pressure ulcer stage: 707.20-707.25)
707.06 Pressure ulcer, ankle — (Use additional code to identify pressure ulcer stage: 707.20-707.25)
707.07 Pressure ulcer, heel — (Use additional code to identify pressure ulcer stage: 707.20-707.25)

707.09 Pressure ulcer, other site — (Use additional code to identify pressure ulcer stage: 707.20-707.25)
707.10 Ulcer of lower limb, unspecified — (Code, if applicable, any causal condition first: 249.80-249.81, 250.80-250.83, 440.23, 459.11, 459.13, 459.31, 459.33) ♥
707.11 Ulcer of thigh — (Code, if applicable, any causal condition first: 249.80-249.81, 250.80-250.83, 440.23, 459.11, 459.13, 459.31, 459.33)
707.12 Ulcer of calf — (Code, if applicable, any causal condition first: 249.80-249.81, 250.80-250.83, 440.23, 459.11, 459.13, 459.31, 459.33)
707.13 Ulcer of ankle — (Code, if applicable, any causal condition first: 249.80-249.81, 250.80-250.83, 440.23, 459.11, 459.13, 459.31, 459.33)
707.14 Ulcer of heel and midfoot — (Code, if applicable, any causal condition first: 249.80-249.81, 250.80-250.83, 440.23, 459.11, 459.13, 459.31, 459.33)
707.15 Ulcer of other part of foot — (Code, if applicable, any causal condition first: 249.80-249.81, 250.80-250.83, 440.23, 459.11, 459.13, 459.31, 459.33)
707.19 Ulcer of other part of lower limb — (Code, if applicable, any causal condition first: 249.80-249.81, 250.80-250.83, 440.23, 459.11, 459.13, 459.31, 459.33)
707.20 Pressure ulcer, unspecified stage — (Code first site of pressure ulcer: 707.00-707.09) ♥
707.23 Pressure ulcer stage III — (Code first site of pressure ulcer: 707.00-707.09)
707.24 Pressure ulcer stage IV — (Code first site of pressure ulcer: 707.00-707.09)
707.25 Pressure ulcer, unstageable — (Code first site of pressure ulcer: 707.00-707.09)
707.8 Chronic ulcer of other specified site
707.9 Chronic ulcer of unspecified site ♥
728.0 Infective myositis
728.86 Necrotizing fasciitis — (Use additional code to identify infectious organism, 041.00-041.89, 785.4, if applicable)
728.88 Rhabdomyolysis
729.4 Unspecified fasciitis ♥
785.4 Gangrene — (Code first any associated underlying condition)
872.10 Open wound of external ear, unspecified site, complicated ♥
872.11 Open wound of auricle, complicated
873.1 Open wound of scalp, complicated
873.30 Open wound of nose, unspecified site, complicated ♥
873.50 Open wound of face, unspecified site, complicated ♥
873.51 Open wound of cheek, complicated
873.52 Open wound of forehead, complicated
873.54 Open wound of jaw, complicated
873.59 Open wound of face, other and multiple sites, complicated
873.9 Other and unspecified open wound of head, complicated ♥
875.1 Open wound of chest (wall), complicated
876.1 Open wound of back, complicated
877.1 Open wound of buttock, complicated
879.1 Open wound of breast, complicated
879.3 Open wound of abdominal wall, anterior, complicated
879.5 Open wound of abdominal wall, lateral, complicated
879.7 Open wound of other and unspecified parts of trunk, complicated ♥
879.9 Open wound(s) (multiple) of unspecified site(s), complicated ♥
880.11 Open wound of scapular region, complicated
880.12 Open wound of axillary region, complicated
880.13 Open wound of upper arm, complicated
880.19 Open wound of multiple sites of shoulder and upper arm, complicated
881.10 Open wound of forearm, complicated
881.11 Open wound of elbow, complicated
881.12 Open wound of wrist, complicated
881.22 Open wound of wrist, with tendon involvement
882.1 Open wound of hand except finger(s) alone, complicated
883.1 Open wound of finger(s), complicated
884.1 Multiple and unspecified open wound of upper limb, complicated
885.1 Traumatic amputation of thumb (complete) (partial), complicated
886.1 Traumatic amputation of other finger(s) (complete) (partial), complicated
887.1 Traumatic amputation of arm and hand (complete) (partial), unilateral, below elbow, complicated
887.3 Traumatic amputation of arm and hand (complete) (partial), unilateral, at or above elbow, complicated
887.5 Traumatic amputation of arm and hand (complete) (partial), unilateral, level not specified, complicated ♥
887.7 Traumatic amputation of arm and hand (complete) (partial), bilateral (any level), complicated
890.1 Open wound of hip and thigh, complicated
891.1 Open wound of knee, leg (except thigh), and ankle, complicated
892.1 Open wound of foot except toe(s) alone, complicated
893.1 Open wound of toe(s), complicated
894.1 Multiple and unspecified open wound of lower limb, complicated
895.1 Traumatic amputation of toe(s) (complete) (partial), complicated
896.1 Traumatic amputation of foot (complete) (partial), unilateral, complicated
896.3 Traumatic amputation of foot (complete) (partial), bilateral, complicated
897.1 Traumatic amputation of leg(s) (complete) (partial), unilateral, below knee, complicated
897.3 Traumatic amputation of leg(s) (complete) (partial), unilateral, at or above knee, complicated
897.5 Traumatic amputation of leg(s) (complete) (partial), unilateral, level not specified, complicated ♥
897.7 Traumatic amputation of leg(s) (complete) (partial), bilateral (any level), complicated
925.1 Crushing injury of face and scalp — (Use additional code to identify any associated injuries, such as: 800-829, 850.0-854.1, 860.0-869.1)
925.2 Crushing injury of neck — (Use additional code to identify any associated injuries, such as: 800-829, 850.0-854.1, 860.0-869.1)
926.0 Crushing injury of external genitalia — (Use additional code to identify any associated injuries: 800-829, 850.0-854.1, 860.0-869.1)
926.11 Crushing injury of back — (Use additional code to identify any associated injuries: 800-829, 850.0-854.1, 860.0-869.1)
926.12 Crushing injury of buttock — (Use additional code to identify any associated injuries: 800-829, 850.0-854.1, 860.0-869.1)
926.19 Crushing injury of other specified sites of trunk — (Use additional code to identify any associated injuries: 800-829, 850.0-854.1, 860.0-869.1)
926.8 Crushing injury of multiple sites of trunk — (Use additional code to identify any associated injuries: 800-829, 850.0-854.1, 860.0-869.1)
926.9 Crushing injury of unspecified site of trunk — (Use additional code to identify any associated injuries: 800-829, 850.0-854.1, 860.0-869.1) ♥
927.00 Crushing injury of shoulder region — (Use additional code to identify any associated injuries: 800-829, 850.0-854.1, 860.0-869.1)
927.01 Crushing injury of scapular region — (Use additional code to identify any associated injuries: 800-829, 850.0-854.1, 860.0-869.1)
927.02 Crushing injury of axillary region — (Use additional code to identify any associated injuries: 800-829, 850.0-854.1, 860.0-869.1)
927.03 Crushing injury of upper arm — (Use additional code to identify any associated injuries: 800-829, 850.0-854.1, 860.0-869.1)
927.09 Crushing injury of multiple sites of upper arm — (Use additional code to identify any associated injuries: 800-829, 850.0-854.1, 860.0-869.1)
927.10 Crushing injury of forearm — (Use additional code to identify any associated injuries: 800-829, 850.0-854.1, 860.0-869.1)
927.11 Crushing injury of elbow — (Use additional code to identify any associated injuries: 800-829, 850.0-854.1, 860.0-869.1)
927.20 Crushing injury of hand(s) — (Use additional code to identify any associated injuries: 800-829, 850.0-854.1, 860.0-869.1)
927.21 Crushing injury of wrist — (Use additional code to identify any associated injuries: 800-829, 850.0-854.1, 860.0-869.1)
927.3 Crushing injury of finger(s) — (Use additional code to identify any associated injuries: 800-829, 850.0-854.1, 860.0-869.1)
927.8 Crushing injury of multiple sites of upper limb — (Use additional code to identify any associated injuries: 800-829, 850.0-854.1, 860.0-869.1)

928.00 Crushing injury of thigh — (Use additional code to identify any associated injuries: 800-829, 850.0-854.1, 860.0-869.1)
928.01 Crushing injury of hip — (Use additional code to identify any associated injuries: 800-829, 850.0-854.1, 860.0-869.1)
928.11 Crushing injury of knee — (Use additional code to identify any associated injuries: 800-829, 850.0-854.1, 860.0-869.1)
928.20 Crushing injury of foot — (Use additional code to identify any associated injuries: 800-829, 850.0-854.1, 860.0-869.1)
928.21 Crushing injury of ankle — (Use additional code to identify any associated injuries: 800-829, 850.0-854.1, 860.0-869.1)
928.3 Crushing injury of toe(s) — (Use additional code to identify any associated injuries: 800-829, 850.0-854.1, 860.0-869.1)
928.8 Crushing injury of multiple sites of lower limb — (Use additional code to identify any associated injuries: 800-829, 850.0-854.1, 860.0-869.1)
928.9 Crushing injury of unspecified site of lower limb — (Use additional code to identify any associated injuries: 800-829, 850.0-854.1, 860.0-869.1) ▽
929.0 Crushing injury of multiple sites, not elsewhere classified — (Use additional code to identify any associated injuries: 800-829, 850.0-854.1, 860.0-869.1)
929.9 Crushing injury of unspecified site — (Use additional code to identify any associated injuries: 800-829, 850.0-854.1, 860.0-869.1) ▽
958.3 Posttraumatic wound infection not elsewhere classified
997.62 Infection (chronic) of amputation stump — (Use additional code to identify complications)
998.2 Accidental puncture or laceration during procedure
998.30 Disruption of wound, unspecified ▽
998.33 Disruption of traumatic injury wound repair
998.59 Other postoperative infection — (Use additional code to identify infection)
998.83 Non-healing surgical wound

ICD-9-CM Procedural

77.60 Local excision of lesion or tissue of bone, unspecified site
77.61 Local excision of lesion or tissue of scapula, clavicle, and thorax (ribs and sternum)
77.62 Local excision of lesion or tissue of humerus
77.63 Local excision of lesion or tissue of radius and ulna
77.64 Local excision of lesion or tissue of carpals and metacarpals
77.65 Local excision of lesion or tissue of femur
77.66 Local excision of lesion or tissue of patella
77.67 Local excision of lesion or tissue of tibia and fibula
77.68 Local excision of lesion or tissue of tarsals and metatarsals
77.69 Local excision of lesion or tissue of other bone, except facial bones
82.36 Other myectomy of hand
83.39 Excision of lesion of other soft tissue
83.44 Other fasciectomy
83.45 Other myectomy
86.22 Excisional debridement of wound, infection, or burn

HCPCS Level II Supplies & Services

A4305 Disposable drug delivery system, flow rate of 50 ml or greater per hour
A4649 Surgical supply; miscellaneous

11055-11057

11055 Paring or cutting of benign hyperkeratotic lesion (eg, corn or callus); single lesion
11056 2 to 4 lesions
11057 more than 4 lesions

ICD-9-CM Diagnostic

700 Corns and callosities
701.1 Acquired keratoderma
702.0 Actinic keratosis
702.11 Inflamed seborrheic keratosis
702.19 Other seborrheic keratosis
702.8 Other specified dermatoses
757.39 Other specified congenital anomaly of skin

ICD-9-CM Procedural

86.3 Other local excision or destruction of lesion or tissue of skin and subcutaneous tissue

HCPCS Level II Supplies & Services

A4649 Surgical supply; miscellaneous

11100-11101

11100 Biopsy of skin, subcutaneous tissue and/or mucous membrane (including simple closure), unless otherwise listed; single lesion
11101 each separate/additional lesion (List separately in addition to code for primary procedure)

ICD-9-CM Diagnostic

140.0 Malignant neoplasm of upper lip, vermilion border
140.1 Malignant neoplasm of lower lip, vermilion border
171.0 Malignant neoplasm of connective and other soft tissue of head, face, and neck
172.0 Malignant melanoma of skin of lip
172.3 Malignant melanoma of skin of other and unspecified parts of face ▽
172.4 Malignant melanoma of skin of scalp and neck
172.5 Malignant melanoma of skin of trunk, except scrotum
172.6 Malignant melanoma of skin of upper limb, including shoulder
172.7 Malignant melanoma of skin of lower limb, including hip
172.8 Malignant melanoma of other specified sites of skin
173.00 Unspecified malignant neoplasm of skin of lip ▽
173.01 Basal cell carcinoma of skin of lip
173.02 Squamous cell carcinoma of skin of lip
173.09 Other specified malignant neoplasm of skin of lip
173.30 Unspecified malignant neoplasm of skin of other and unspecified parts of face ▽
173.31 Basal cell carcinoma of skin of other and unspecified parts of face
173.32 Squamous cell carcinoma of skin of other and unspecified parts of face
173.39 Other specified malignant neoplasm of skin of other and unspecified parts of face
173.40 Unspecified malignant neoplasm of scalp and skin of neck ▽
173.41 Basal cell carcinoma of scalp and skin of neck
173.42 Squamous cell carcinoma of scalp and skin of neck
173.49 Other specified malignant neoplasm of scalp and skin of neck
173.50 Unspecified malignant neoplasm of skin of trunk, except scrotum ▽
173.51 Basal cell carcinoma of skin of trunk, except scrotum
173.52 Squamous cell carcinoma of skin of trunk, except scrotum
173.59 Other specified malignant neoplasm of skin of trunk, except scrotum
173.60 Unspecified malignant neoplasm of skin of upper limb, including shoulder ▽
173.61 Basal cell carcinoma of skin of upper limb, including shoulder
173.62 Squamous cell carcinoma of skin of upper limb, including shoulder
173.69 Other specified malignant neoplasm of skin of upper limb, including shoulder
173.70 Unspecified malignant neoplasm of skin of lower limb, including hip ▽
173.71 Basal cell carcinoma of skin of lower limb, including hip
173.72 Squamous cell carcinoma of skin of lower limb, including hip
173.79 Other specified malignant neoplasm of skin of lower limb, including hip
173.80 Unspecified malignant neoplasm of other specified sites of skin ▽
173.81 Basal cell carcinoma of other specified sites of skin
173.82 Squamous cell carcinoma of other specified sites of skin
173.89 Other specified malignant neoplasm of other specified sites of skin
176.0 Kaposi's sarcoma of skin
195.0 Malignant neoplasm of head, face, and neck
198.2 Secondary malignant neoplasm of skin
215.0 Other benign neoplasm of connective and other soft tissue of head, face, and neck
216.3 Benign neoplasm of skin of other and unspecified parts of face ▽
216.4 Benign neoplasm of scalp and skin of neck
216.5 Benign neoplasm of skin of trunk, except scrotum
216.6 Benign neoplasm of skin of upper limb, including shoulder

216.7 Benign neoplasm of skin of lower limb, including hip
216.8 Benign neoplasm of other specified sites of skin
228.01 Hemangioma of skin and subcutaneous tissue
232.3 Carcinoma in situ of skin of other and unspecified parts of face ▽
232.4 Carcinoma in situ of scalp and skin of neck
232.5 Carcinoma in situ of skin of trunk, except scrotum
232.6 Carcinoma in situ of skin of upper limb, including shoulder
232.7 Carcinoma in situ of skin of lower limb, including hip
232.8 Carcinoma in situ of other specified sites of skin
238.2 Neoplasm of uncertain behavior of skin
239.2 Neoplasms of unspecified nature of bone, soft tissue, and skin
258.01 Multiple endocrine neoplasia [MEN] type I
258.02 Multiple endocrine neoplasia [MEN] type IIA
258.03 Multiple endocrine neoplasia [MEN] type IIB
448.1 Nevus, non-neoplastic
694.4 Pemphigus
696.1 Other psoriasis
701.5 Other abnormal granulation tissue
702.8 Other specified dermatoses
709.09 Other dyschromia
709.4 Foreign body granuloma of skin and subcutaneous tissue — (Use additional code to identify foreign body (V90.01-V90.9))
709.9 Unspecified disorder of skin and subcutaneous tissue ▽
757.32 Congenital vascular hamartomas
757.33 Congenital pigmentary anomaly of skin

ICD-9-CM Procedural

08.11 Biopsy of eyelid
21.22 Biopsy of nose
27.23 Biopsy of lip
49.22 Biopsy of perianal tissue
61.11 Biopsy of scrotum or tunica vaginalis ♂
86.11 Closed biopsy of skin and subcutaneous tissue

HCPCS Level II Supplies & Services

A4649 Surgical supply; miscellaneous

11200-11201

11200 Removal of skin tags, multiple fibrocutaneous tags, any area; up to and including 15 lesions
11201 each additional 10 lesions, or part thereof (List separately in addition to code for primary procedure)

ICD-9-CM Diagnostic

701.9 Unspecified hypertrophic and atrophic condition of skin ▽
757.39 Other specified congenital anomaly of skin

ICD-9-CM Procedural

86.3 Other local excision or destruction of lesion or tissue of skin and subcutaneous tissue

HCPCS Level II Supplies & Services

A4649 Surgical supply; miscellaneous

11300-11303

11300 Shaving of epidermal or dermal lesion, single lesion, trunk, arms or legs; lesion diameter 0.5 cm or less
11301 lesion diameter 0.6 to 1.0 cm
11302 lesion diameter 1.1 to 2.0 cm
11303 lesion diameter over 2.0 cm

ICD-9-CM Diagnostic

173.50 Unspecified malignant neoplasm of skin of trunk, except scrotum ▽
173.51 Basal cell carcinoma of skin of trunk, except scrotum
173.52 Squamous cell carcinoma of skin of trunk, except scrotum
173.59 Other specified malignant neoplasm of skin of trunk, except scrotum
173.60 Unspecified malignant neoplasm of skin of upper limb, including shoulder ▽
173.61 Basal cell carcinoma of skin of upper limb, including shoulder
173.62 Squamous cell carcinoma of skin of upper limb, including shoulder
173.69 Other specified malignant neoplasm of skin of upper limb, including shoulder
173.70 Unspecified malignant neoplasm of skin of lower limb, including hip ▽
173.71 Basal cell carcinoma of skin of lower limb, including hip
173.72 Squamous cell carcinoma of skin of lower limb, including hip
173.79 Other specified malignant neoplasm of skin of lower limb, including hip
216.5 Benign neoplasm of skin of trunk, except scrotum
216.6 Benign neoplasm of skin of upper limb, including shoulder
216.7 Benign neoplasm of skin of lower limb, including hip
228.01 Hemangioma of skin and subcutaneous tissue
232.5 Carcinoma in situ of skin of trunk, except scrotum
232.6 Carcinoma in situ of skin of upper limb, including shoulder
232.7 Carcinoma in situ of skin of lower limb, including hip
238.2 Neoplasm of uncertain behavior of skin
239.2 Neoplasms of unspecified nature of bone, soft tissue, and skin
686.1 Pyogenic granuloma of skin and subcutaneous tissue — (Use additional code to identify any infectious organism: 041.0-041.8)
701.1 Acquired keratoderma
702.0 Actinic keratosis
702.11 Inflamed seborrheic keratosis
709.00 Dyschromia, unspecified ▽
709.9 Unspecified disorder of skin and subcutaneous tissue ▽
757.39 Other specified congenital anomaly of skin

ICD-9-CM Procedural

86.3 Other local excision or destruction of lesion or tissue of skin and subcutaneous tissue

HCPCS Level II Supplies & Services

A4649 Surgical supply; miscellaneous

11305-11308

11305 Shaving of epidermal or dermal lesion, single lesion, scalp, neck, hands, feet, genitalia; lesion diameter 0.5 cm or less
11306 lesion diameter 0.6 to 1.0 cm
11307 lesion diameter 1.1 to 2.0 cm
11308 lesion diameter over 2.0 cm

ICD-9-CM Diagnostic

173.40 Unspecified malignant neoplasm of scalp and skin of neck ▽
173.41 Basal cell carcinoma of scalp and skin of neck
173.42 Squamous cell carcinoma of scalp and skin of neck
173.49 Other specified malignant neoplasm of scalp and skin of neck
173.60 Unspecified malignant neoplasm of skin of upper limb, including shoulder ▽
173.61 Basal cell carcinoma of skin of upper limb, including shoulder
173.62 Squamous cell carcinoma of skin of upper limb, including shoulder
173.69 Other specified malignant neoplasm of skin of upper limb, including shoulder
173.70 Unspecified malignant neoplasm of skin of lower limb, including hip ▽
173.71 Basal cell carcinoma of skin of lower limb, including hip
173.72 Squamous cell carcinoma of skin of lower limb, including hip
173.79 Other specified malignant neoplasm of skin of lower limb, including hip
184.1 Malignant neoplasm of labia majora ♀
184.2 Malignant neoplasm of labia minora ♀
184.4 Malignant neoplasm of vulva, unspecified site ▽ ♀
187.4 Malignant neoplasm of penis, part unspecified ▽ ♂
187.7 Malignant neoplasm of scrotum ♂
216.4 Benign neoplasm of scalp and skin of neck

216.6 Benign neoplasm of skin of upper limb, including shoulder
216.7 Benign neoplasm of skin of lower limb, including hip
221.1 Benign neoplasm of vagina ♀
221.2 Benign neoplasm of vulva ♀
221.8 Benign neoplasm of other specified sites of female genital organs ♀
221.9 Benign neoplasm of female genital organ, site unspecified ▽ ♀
222.4 Benign neoplasm of scrotum ♂
228.01 Hemangioma of skin and subcutaneous tissue
232.4 Carcinoma in situ of scalp and skin of neck
232.6 Carcinoma in situ of skin of upper limb, including shoulder
232.7 Carcinoma in situ of skin of lower limb, including hip
232.8 Carcinoma in situ of other specified sites of skin
233.30 Carcinoma in situ, unspecified female genital organ ▽ ♀
233.31 Carcinoma in situ, vagina ♀
233.32 Carcinoma in situ, vulva ♀
233.39 Carcinoma in situ, other female genital organ ♀
233.5 Carcinoma in situ of penis ♂
233.6 Carcinoma in situ of other and unspecified male genital organs ▽ ♂
236.3 Neoplasm of uncertain behavior of other and unspecified female genital organs ▽ ♀
236.6 Neoplasm of uncertain behavior of other and unspecified male genital organs ▽ ♂
238.2 Neoplasm of uncertain behavior of skin
239.2 Neoplasms of unspecified nature of bone, soft tissue, and skin
239.5 Neoplasm of unspecified nature of other genitourinary organs
686.1 Pyogenic granuloma of skin and subcutaneous tissue — (Use additional code to identify any infectious organism: 041.0-041.8)
701.1 Acquired keratoderma
701.5 Other abnormal granulation tissue
702.0 Actinic keratosis
702.11 Inflamed seborrheic keratosis
702.19 Other seborrheic keratosis
706.2 Sebaceous cyst
709.00 Dyschromia, unspecified ▽
709.9 Unspecified disorder of skin and subcutaneous tissue ▽
757.39 Other specified congenital anomaly of skin

ICD-9-CM Procedural

61.3 Excision or destruction of lesion or tissue of scrotum ♂
64.2 Local excision or destruction of lesion of penis ♂
71.09 Other incision of vulva and perineum ♀
86.3 Other local excision or destruction of lesion or tissue of skin and subcutaneous tissue

HCPCS Level II Supplies & Services

A4649 Surgical supply; miscellaneous

11310-11313

11310 Shaving of epidermal or dermal lesion, single lesion, face, ears, eyelids, nose, lips, mucous membrane; lesion diameter 0.5 cm or less
11311 lesion diameter 0.6 to 1.0 cm
11312 lesion diameter 1.1 to 2.0 cm
11313 lesion diameter over 2.0 cm

ICD-9-CM Diagnostic

173.00 Unspecified malignant neoplasm of skin of lip ▽
173.01 Basal cell carcinoma of skin of lip
173.02 Squamous cell carcinoma of skin of lip
173.09 Other specified malignant neoplasm of skin of lip
173.10 Unspecified malignant neoplasm of eyelid, including canthus ▽
173.11 Basal cell carcinoma of eyelid, including canthus
173.12 Squamous cell carcinoma of eyelid, including canthus
173.19 Other specified malignant neoplasm of eyelid, including canthus
173.20 Unspecified malignant neoplasm of skin of ear and external auditory canal ▽
173.21 Basal cell carcinoma of skin of ear and external auditory canal
173.22 Squamous cell carcinoma of skin of ear and external auditory canal
173.29 Other specified malignant neoplasm of skin of ear and external auditory canal
173.30 Unspecified malignant neoplasm of skin of other and unspecified parts of face ▽
173.31 Basal cell carcinoma of skin of other and unspecified parts of face
173.32 Squamous cell carcinoma of skin of other and unspecified parts of face
173.39 Other specified malignant neoplasm of skin of other and unspecified parts of face
198.2 Secondary malignant neoplasm of skin
198.89 Secondary malignant neoplasm of other specified sites
216.0 Benign neoplasm of skin of lip
216.1 Benign neoplasm of eyelid, including canthus
216.2 Benign neoplasm of ear and external auditory canal
216.3 Benign neoplasm of skin of other and unspecified parts of face ▽
228.01 Hemangioma of skin and subcutaneous tissue
232.0 Carcinoma in situ of skin of lip
232.1 Carcinoma in situ of eyelid, including canthus
232.2 Carcinoma in situ of skin of ear and external auditory canal
232.3 Carcinoma in situ of skin of other and unspecified parts of face ▽
238.2 Neoplasm of uncertain behavior of skin
239.2 Neoplasms of unspecified nature of bone, soft tissue, and skin
239.89 Neoplasms of unspecified nature, other specified sites
380.14 Malignant otitis externa
686.1 Pyogenic granuloma of skin and subcutaneous tissue — (Use additional code to identify any infectious organism: 041.0-041.8)
701.1 Acquired keratoderma
702.0 Actinic keratosis
702.11 Inflamed seborrheic keratosis
702.19 Other seborrheic keratosis
709.9 Unspecified disorder of skin and subcutaneous tissue ▽
757.39 Other specified congenital anomaly of skin

ICD-9-CM Procedural

08.22 Excision of other minor lesion of eyelid
18.29 Excision or destruction of other lesion of external ear
21.32 Local excision or destruction of other lesion of nose
27.43 Other excision of lesion or tissue of lip
86.3 Other local excision or destruction of lesion or tissue of skin and subcutaneous tissue

HCPCS Level II Supplies & Services

A4649 Surgical supply; miscellaneous

11400-11406

11400 Excision, benign lesion including margins, except skin tag (unless listed elsewhere), trunk, arms or legs; excised diameter 0.5 cm or less
11401 excised diameter 0.6 to 1.0 cm
11402 excised diameter 1.1 to 2.0 cm
11403 excised diameter 2.1 to 3.0 cm
11404 excised diameter 3.1 to 4.0 cm
11406 excised diameter over 4.0 cm

ICD-9-CM Diagnostic

214.1 Lipoma of other skin and subcutaneous tissue
216.5 Benign neoplasm of skin of trunk, except scrotum
216.6 Benign neoplasm of skin of upper limb, including shoulder
216.7 Benign neoplasm of skin of lower limb, including hip
228.01 Hemangioma of skin and subcutaneous tissue
238.2 Neoplasm of uncertain behavior of skin
239.2 Neoplasms of unspecified nature of bone, soft tissue, and skin
448.1 Nevus, non-neoplastic

686.1 Pyogenic granuloma of skin and subcutaneous tissue — (Use additional code to identify any infectious organism: 041.0-041.8)

701.1 Acquired keratoderma

701.3 Striae atrophicae

701.4 Keloid scar

701.5 Other abnormal granulation tissue

702.11 Inflamed seborrheic keratosis

702.19 Other seborrheic keratosis

704.41 Pilar cyst

704.42 Trichilemmal cyst

706.2 Sebaceous cyst

709.09 Other dyschromia

709.1 Vascular disorder of skin

709.2 Scar condition and fibrosis of skin

709.4 Foreign body granuloma of skin and subcutaneous tissue — (Use additional code to identify foreign body (V90.01-V90.9))

757.32 Congenital vascular hamartomas

ICD-9-CM Procedural

85.21 Local excision of lesion of breast

86.3 Other local excision or destruction of lesion or tissue of skin and subcutaneous tissue

HCPCS Level II Supplies & Services

A4305 Disposable drug delivery system, flow rate of 50 ml or greater per hour

11420-11426

11420 Excision, benign lesion including margins, except skin tag (unless listed elsewhere), scalp, neck, hands, feet, genitalia; excised diameter 0.5 cm or less

11421 excised diameter 0.6 to 1.0 cm

11422 excised diameter 1.1 to 2.0 cm

11423 excised diameter 2.1 to 3.0 cm

11424 excised diameter 3.1 to 4.0 cm

11426 excised diameter over 4.0 cm

ICD-9-CM Diagnostic

214.1 Lipoma of other skin and subcutaneous tissue

216.4 Benign neoplasm of scalp and skin of neck

216.6 Benign neoplasm of skin of upper limb, including shoulder

216.7 Benign neoplasm of skin of lower limb, including hip

216.8 Benign neoplasm of other specified sites of skin

221.2 Benign neoplasm of vulva ♀

221.8 Benign neoplasm of other specified sites of female genital organs ♀

221.9 Benign neoplasm of female genital organ, site unspecified ▽ ♀

222.1 Benign neoplasm of penis ♂

222.4 Benign neoplasm of scrotum ♂

222.9 Benign neoplasm of male genital organ, site unspecified ▽ ♂

228.01 Hemangioma of skin and subcutaneous tissue

236.3 Neoplasm of uncertain behavior of other and unspecified female genital organs ▽ ♀

236.6 Neoplasm of uncertain behavior of other and unspecified male genital organs ▽ ♂

238.2 Neoplasm of uncertain behavior of skin

239.2 Neoplasms of unspecified nature of bone, soft tissue, and skin

448.1 Nevus, non-neoplastic

624.4 Old laceration or scarring of vulva ♀

686.1 Pyogenic granuloma of skin and subcutaneous tissue — (Use additional code to identify any infectious organism: 041.0-041.8)

686.9 Unspecified local infection of skin and subcutaneous tissue — (Use additional code to identify any infectious organism: 041.0-041.8) ▽

700 Corns and callosities

701.1 Acquired keratoderma

701.4 Keloid scar

701.5 Other abnormal granulation tissue

701.8 Other specified hypertrophic and atrophic condition of skin

702.0 Actinic keratosis

702.11 Inflamed seborrheic keratosis

702.19 Other seborrheic keratosis

702.8 Other specified dermatoses

704.41 Pilar cyst

704.42 Trichilemmal cyst

706.2 Sebaceous cyst

709.00 Dyschromia, unspecified ▽

709.01 Vitiligo

709.09 Other dyschromia

709.1 Vascular disorder of skin

709.2 Scar condition and fibrosis of skin

709.4 Foreign body granuloma of skin and subcutaneous tissue — (Use additional code to identify foreign body (V90.01-V90.9))

709.9 Unspecified disorder of skin and subcutaneous tissue ▽

757.32 Congenital vascular hamartomas

757.33 Congenital pigmentary anomaly of skin

757.39 Other specified congenital anomaly of skin

782.2 Localized superficial swelling, mass, or lump

ICD-9-CM Procedural

61.3 Excision or destruction of lesion or tissue of scrotum ♂

64.2 Local excision or destruction of lesion of penis ♂

71.3 Other local excision or destruction of vulva and perineum ♀

86.3 Other local excision or destruction of lesion or tissue of skin and subcutaneous tissue

HCPCS Level II Supplies & Services

A4305 Disposable drug delivery system, flow rate of 50 ml or greater per hour

11440-11446

11440 Excision, other benign lesion including margins, except skin tag (unless listed elsewhere), face, ears, eyelids, nose, lips, mucous membrane; excised diameter 0.5 cm or less

11441 excised diameter 0.6 to 1.0 cm

11442 excised diameter 1.1 to 2.0 cm

11443 excised diameter 2.1 to 3.0 cm

11444 excised diameter 3.1 to 4.0 cm

11446 excised diameter over 4.0 cm

ICD-9-CM Diagnostic

210.0 Benign neoplasm of lip

214.0 Lipoma of skin and subcutaneous tissue of face

214.1 Lipoma of other skin and subcutaneous tissue

215.0 Other benign neoplasm of connective and other soft tissue of head, face, and neck

216.0 Benign neoplasm of skin of lip

216.1 Benign neoplasm of eyelid, including canthus

216.2 Benign neoplasm of ear and external auditory canal

216.3 Benign neoplasm of skin of other and unspecified parts of face ▽

228.01 Hemangioma of skin and subcutaneous tissue

238.1 Neoplasm of uncertain behavior of connective and other soft tissue

238.2 Neoplasm of uncertain behavior of skin

239.2 Neoplasms of unspecified nature of bone, soft tissue, and skin

448.1 Nevus, non-neoplastic

528.79 Other disturbances of oral epithelium, including tongue

686.1 Pyogenic granuloma of skin and subcutaneous tissue — (Use additional code to identify any infectious organism: 041.0-041.8)

701.1 Acquired keratoderma

701.4 Keloid scar

701.5 Other abnormal granulation tissue

701.8 Other specified hypertrophic and atrophic condition of skin

Code	Description
702.0	Actinic keratosis
702.11	Inflamed seborrheic keratosis
702.19	Other seborrheic keratosis
704.41	Pilar cyst
704.42	Trichilemmal cyst
706.2	Sebaceous cyst
709.2	Scar condition and fibrosis of skin
709.4	Foreign body granuloma of skin and subcutaneous tissue — (Use additional code to identify foreign body (V90.01-V90.9))
757.32	Congenital vascular hamartomas
757.33	Congenital pigmentary anomaly of skin
757.39	Other specified congenital anomaly of skin

ICD-9-CM Procedural

Code	Description
08.20	Removal of lesion of eyelid, not otherwise specified
08.23	Excision of major lesion of eyelid, partial-thickness
18.29	Excision or destruction of other lesion of external ear
21.30	Excision or destruction of lesion of nose, not otherwise specified
21.32	Local excision or destruction of other lesion of nose
27.43	Other excision of lesion or tissue of lip
86.3	Other local excision or destruction of lesion or tissue of skin and subcutaneous tissue

HCPCS Level II Supplies & Services

Code	Description
A4305	Disposable drug delivery system, flow rate of 50 ml or greater per hour

11450-11471

Code	Description
11450	Excision of skin and subcutaneous tissue for hidradenitis, axillary; with simple or intermediate repair
11451	with complex repair
11462	Excision of skin and subcutaneous tissue for hidradenitis, inguinal; with simple or intermediate repair
11463	with complex repair
11470	Excision of skin and subcutaneous tissue for hidradenitis, perianal, perineal, or umbilical; with simple or intermediate repair
11471	with complex repair

ICD-9-CM Diagnostic

Code	Description
705.83	Hidradenitis

ICD-9-CM Procedural

Code	Description
86.3	Other local excision or destruction of lesion or tissue of skin and subcutaneous tissue

HCPCS Level II Supplies & Services

Code	Description
A4305	Disposable drug delivery system, flow rate of 50 ml or greater per hour

11600-11606

Code	Description
11600	Excision, malignant lesion including margins, trunk, arms, or legs; excised diameter 0.5 cm or less
11601	excised diameter 0.6 to 1.0 cm
11602	excised diameter 1.1 to 2.0 cm
11603	excised diameter 2.1 to 3.0 cm
11604	excised diameter 3.1 to 4.0 cm
11606	excised diameter over 4.0 cm

ICD-9-CM Diagnostic

Code	Description
172.5	Malignant melanoma of skin of trunk, except scrotum
172.6	Malignant melanoma of skin of upper limb, including shoulder
172.7	Malignant melanoma of skin of lower limb, including hip
172.8	Malignant melanoma of other specified sites of skin
173.50	Unspecified malignant neoplasm of skin of trunk, except scrotum
173.51	Basal cell carcinoma of skin of trunk, except scrotum
173.52	Squamous cell carcinoma of skin of trunk, except scrotum
173.59	Other specified malignant neoplasm of skin of trunk, except scrotum
173.60	Unspecified malignant neoplasm of skin of upper limb, including shoulder
173.61	Basal cell carcinoma of skin of upper limb, including shoulder
173.62	Squamous cell carcinoma of skin of upper limb, including shoulder
173.69	Other specified malignant neoplasm of skin of upper limb, including shoulder
173.70	Unspecified malignant neoplasm of skin of lower limb, including hip
173.71	Basal cell carcinoma of skin of lower limb, including hip
173.72	Squamous cell carcinoma of skin of lower limb, including hip
173.79	Other specified malignant neoplasm of skin of lower limb, including hip
173.80	Unspecified malignant neoplasm of other specified sites of skin
173.81	Basal cell carcinoma of other specified sites of skin
173.82	Squamous cell carcinoma of other specified sites of skin
173.89	Other specified malignant neoplasm of other specified sites of skin
195.4	Malignant neoplasm of upper limb
198.2	Secondary malignant neoplasm of skin
209.33	Merkel cell carcinoma of the upper limb
209.34	Merkel cell carcinoma of the lower limb
209.35	Merkel cell carcinoma of the trunk
209.75	Secondary Merkel cell carcinoma
232.5	Carcinoma in situ of skin of trunk, except scrotum
232.6	Carcinoma in situ of skin of upper limb, including shoulder
232.7	Carcinoma in situ of skin of lower limb, including hip
238.2	Neoplasm of uncertain behavior of skin

ICD-9-CM Procedural

Code	Description
85.21	Local excision of lesion of breast
86.3	Other local excision or destruction of lesion or tissue of skin and subcutaneous tissue

HCPCS Level II Supplies & Services

Code	Description
A4305	Disposable drug delivery system, flow rate of 50 ml or greater per hour

11620-11626

Code	Description
11620	Excision, malignant lesion including margins, scalp, neck, hands, feet, genitalia; excised diameter 0.5 cm or less
11621	excised diameter 0.6 to 1.0 cm
11622	excised diameter 1.1 to 2.0 cm
11623	excised diameter 2.1 to 3.0 cm
11624	excised diameter 3.1 to 4.0 cm
11626	excised diameter over 4.0 cm

ICD-9-CM Diagnostic

Code	Description
171.0	Malignant neoplasm of connective and other soft tissue of head, face, and neck
171.2	Malignant neoplasm of connective and other soft tissue of upper limb, including shoulder
171.3	Malignant neoplasm of connective and other soft tissue of lower limb, including hip
171.8	Malignant neoplasm of other specified sites of connective and other soft tissue
172.4	Malignant melanoma of skin of scalp and neck
172.6	Malignant melanoma of skin of upper limb, including shoulder
172.7	Malignant melanoma of skin of lower limb, including hip
172.8	Malignant melanoma of other specified sites of skin
173.40	Unspecified malignant neoplasm of scalp and skin of neck
173.41	Basal cell carcinoma of scalp and skin of neck
173.42	Squamous cell carcinoma of scalp and skin of neck
173.49	Other specified malignant neoplasm of scalp and skin of neck
173.50	Unspecified malignant neoplasm of skin of trunk, except scrotum
173.51	Basal cell carcinoma of skin of trunk, except scrotum
173.52	Squamous cell carcinoma of skin of trunk, except scrotum
173.59	Other specified malignant neoplasm of skin of trunk, except scrotum
173.60	Unspecified malignant neoplasm of skin of upper limb, including shoulder
173.61	Basal cell carcinoma of skin of upper limb, including shoulder
173.62	Squamous cell carcinoma of skin of upper limb, including shoulder
173.69	Other specified malignant neoplasm of skin of upper limb, including shoulder
173.70	Unspecified malignant neoplasm of skin of lower limb, including hip

173.71 Basal cell carcinoma of skin of lower limb, including hip

173.72 Squamous cell carcinoma of skin of lower limb, including hip

173.79 Other specified malignant neoplasm of skin of lower limb, including hip

184.0 Malignant neoplasm of vagina ♀

184.1 Malignant neoplasm of labia majora ♀

184.2 Malignant neoplasm of labia minora ♀

184.3 Malignant neoplasm of clitoris ♀

184.4 Malignant neoplasm of vulva, unspecified site ▽ ♀

184.8 Malignant neoplasm of other specified sites of female genital organs ♀

187.1 Malignant neoplasm of prepuce ♂

187.2 Malignant neoplasm of glans penis ♂

187.3 Malignant neoplasm of body of penis ♂

187.4 Malignant neoplasm of penis, part unspecified ▽ ♂

187.7 Malignant neoplasm of scrotum ♂

187.8 Malignant neoplasm of other specified sites of male genital organs ♂

195.4 Malignant neoplasm of upper limb

195.5 Malignant neoplasm of lower limb

198.2 Secondary malignant neoplasm of skin

198.82 Secondary malignant neoplasm of genital organs

209.32 Merkel cell carcinoma of the scalp and neck

209.33 Merkel cell carcinoma of the upper limb

209.34 Merkel cell carcinoma of the lower limb

209.36 Merkel cell carcinoma of other sites

209.75 Secondary Merkel cell carcinoma

232.4 Carcinoma in situ of scalp and skin of neck

232.6 Carcinoma in situ of skin of upper limb, including shoulder

232.7 Carcinoma in situ of skin of lower limb, including hip

232.8 Carcinoma in situ of other specified sites of skin

233.30 Carcinoma in situ, unspecified female genital organ ▽ ♀

233.31 Carcinoma in situ, vagina ♀

233.32 Carcinoma in situ, vulva ♀

233.39 Carcinoma in situ, other female genital organ ♀

233.5 Carcinoma in situ of penis ♂

233.6 Carcinoma in situ of other and unspecified male genital organs ▽ ♂

236.3 Neoplasm of uncertain behavior of other and unspecified female genital organs ▽ ♀

236.6 Neoplasm of uncertain behavior of other and unspecified male genital organs ▽ ♂

ICD-9-CM Procedural

61.3 Excision or destruction of lesion or tissue of scrotum ♂

64.2 Local excision or destruction of lesion of penis ♂

71.3 Other local excision or destruction of vulva and perineum ♀

86.3 Other local excision or destruction of lesion or tissue of skin and subcutaneous tissue

HCPCS Level II Supplies & Services

A4305 Disposable drug delivery system, flow rate of 50 ml or greater per hour

11640-11646

11640 Excision, malignant lesion including margins, face, ears, eyelids, nose, lips; excised diameter 0.5 cm or less

11641 excised diameter 0.6 to 1.0 cm

11642 excised diameter 1.1 to 2.0 cm

11643 excised diameter 2.1 to 3.0 cm

11644 excised diameter 3.1 to 4.0 cm

11646 excised diameter over 4.0 cm

ICD-9-CM Diagnostic

140.0 Malignant neoplasm of upper lip, vermilion border

140.1 Malignant neoplasm of lower lip, vermilion border

140.3 Malignant neoplasm of upper lip, inner aspect

140.4 Malignant neoplasm of lower lip, inner aspect

140.8 Malignant neoplasm of other sites of lip

140.9 Malignant neoplasm of lip, vermilion border, unspecified as to upper or lower ▽

171.0 Malignant neoplasm of connective and other soft tissue of head, face, and neck

172.0 Malignant melanoma of skin of lip

172.1 Malignant melanoma of skin of eyelid, including canthus

172.2 Malignant melanoma of skin of ear and external auditory canal

172.3 Malignant melanoma of skin of other and unspecified parts of face ▽

173.00 Unspecified malignant neoplasm of skin of lip ▽

173.01 Basal cell carcinoma of skin of lip

173.02 Squamous cell carcinoma of skin of lip

173.09 Other specified malignant neoplasm of skin of lip

173.10 Unspecified malignant neoplasm of eyelid, including canthus ▽

173.11 Basal cell carcinoma of eyelid, including canthus

173.12 Squamous cell carcinoma of eyelid, including canthus

173.19 Other specified malignant neoplasm of eyelid, including canthus

173.20 Unspecified malignant neoplasm of skin of ear and external auditory canal ▽

173.21 Basal cell carcinoma of skin of ear and external auditory canal

173.22 Squamous cell carcinoma of skin of ear and external auditory canal

173.29 Other specified malignant neoplasm of skin of ear and external auditory canal

173.30 Unspecified malignant neoplasm of skin of other and unspecified parts of face ▽

173.31 Basal cell carcinoma of skin of other and unspecified parts of face

173.32 Squamous cell carcinoma of skin of other and unspecified parts of face

173.39 Other specified malignant neoplasm of skin of other and unspecified parts of face

195.0 Malignant neoplasm of head, face, and neck

198.2 Secondary malignant neoplasm of skin

198.89 Secondary malignant neoplasm of other specified sites

209.31 Merkel cell carcinoma of the face

209.36 Merkel cell carcinoma of other sites

209.75 Secondary Merkel cell carcinoma

230.0 Carcinoma in situ of lip, oral cavity, and pharynx

232.0 Carcinoma in situ of skin of lip

232.1 Carcinoma in situ of eyelid, including canthus

232.2 Carcinoma in situ of skin of ear and external auditory canal

232.3 Carcinoma in situ of skin of other and unspecified parts of face ▽

235.1 Neoplasm of uncertain behavior of lip, oral cavity, and pharynx

238.2 Neoplasm of uncertain behavior of skin

V84.09 Genetic susceptibility to other malignant neoplasm — (Use additional code, if applicable, for any associated family history of the disease: V16-V19. Code first, if applicable, any current malignant neoplasms: 140.0-195.8, 200.0-208.9, 230.0-234.9. Use additional code, if applicable, for any personal history of malignant neoplasm: V10.0-V10.9)

ICD-9-CM Procedural

08.20 Removal of lesion of eyelid, not otherwise specified

08.23 Excision of major lesion of eyelid, partial-thickness

08.24 Excision of major lesion of eyelid, full-thickness

18.29 Excision or destruction of other lesion of external ear

21.30 Excision or destruction of lesion of nose, not otherwise specified

21.32 Local excision or destruction of other lesion of nose

27.42 Wide excision of lesion of lip

27.43 Other excision of lesion or tissue of lip

86.3 Other local excision or destruction of lesion or tissue of skin and subcutaneous tissue

HCPCS Level II Supplies & Services

A4305 Disposable drug delivery system, flow rate of 50 ml or greater per hour

15760-15770

15760 Graft; composite (eg, full thickness of external ear or nasal ala), including primary closure, donor area

15770 derma-fat-fascia

ICD-9-CM Diagnostic

The application of this code is too broad to adequately present ICD-9-CM diagnostic code links here. Refer to your ICD-9-CM book.

ICD-9-CM Procedural

18.71 Construction of auricle of ear
18.79 Other plastic repair of external ear
21.89 Other repair and plastic operations on nose
83.82 Graft of muscle or fascia
86.63 Full-thickness skin graft to other sites
86.69 Other skin graft to other sites
86.71 Cutting and preparation of pedicle grafts or flaps
86.89 Other repair and reconstruction of skin and subcutaneous tissue

Nails

11719

11719 Trimming of nondystrophic nails, any number

ICD-9-CM Diagnostic

249.60 Secondary diabetes mellitus with neurological manifestations, not stated as uncontrolled, or unspecified — (Use additional code to identify manifestation: 337.1, 353.5, 354.0-355.9, 357.2, 536.3, 713.5) (Use additional code to identify any associated insulin use: V58.67)

249.61 Secondary diabetes mellitus with neurological manifestations, uncontrolled — (Use additional code to identify manifestation: 337.1, 353.5, 354.0-355.9, 357.2, 536.3, 713.5) (Use additional code to identify any associated insulin use: V58.67)

249.70 Secondary diabetes mellitus with peripheral circulatory disorders, not stated as uncontrolled, or unspecified — (Use additional code to identify manifestation: 443.81, 785.4) (Use additional code to identify any associated insulin use: V58.67)

249.71 Secondary diabetes mellitus with peripheral circulatory disorders, uncontrolled — (Use additional code to identify manifestation: 443.81, 785.4) (Use additional code to identify any associated insulin use: V58.67)

249.80 Secondary diabetes mellitus with other specified manifestations, not stated as uncontrolled, or unspecified — (Use additional code to identify manifestation: 707.10-707.19, 707.8, 707.9, 731.8) (Use additional code to identify any associated insulin use: V58.67)

249.81 Secondary diabetes mellitus with other specified manifestations, uncontrolled — (Use additional code to identify manifestation: 707.10-707.19, 707.8, 707.9, 731.8) (Use additional code to identify any associated insulin use: V58.67)

249.90 Secondary diabetes mellitus with unspecified complication, not stated as uncontrolled, or unspecified — (Use additional code to identify any associated insulin use: V58.67) ▽

249.91 Secondary diabetes mellitus with unspecified complication, uncontrolled — (Use additional code to identify any associated insulin use: V58.67) ▽

250.60 Diabetes with neurological manifestations, type II or unspecified type, not stated as uncontrolled — (Use additional code to identify manifestation: 337.1, 353.5, 354.0-355.9, 357.2, 536.3, 713.5)

250.61 Diabetes with neurological manifestations, type I [juvenile type], not stated as uncontrolled — (Use additional code to identify manifestation: 337.1, 353.5, 354.0-355.9, 357.2, 536.3, 713.5)

250.62 Diabetes with neurological manifestations, type II or unspecified type, uncontrolled — (Use additional code to identify manifestation: 337.1, 353.5, 354.0-355.9, 357.2, 536.3, 713.5)

250.63 Diabetes with neurological manifestations, type I [juvenile type], uncontrolled — (Use additional code to identify manifestation: 337.1, 353.5, 354.0-355.9, 357.2, 536.3, 713.5)

250.70 Diabetes with peripheral circulatory disorders, type II or unspecified type, not stated as uncontrolled — (Use additional code to identify manifestation: 443.81, 785.4)

250.71 Diabetes with peripheral circulatory disorders, type I [juvenile type], not stated as uncontrolled — (Use additional code to identify manifestation: 443.81, 785.4)

250.72 Diabetes with peripheral circulatory disorders, type II or unspecified type, uncontrolled — (Use additional code to identify manifestation: 443.81, 785.4)

250.73 Diabetes with peripheral circulatory disorders, type I [juvenile type], uncontrolled — (Use additional code to identify manifestation: 443.81, 785.4)

278.01 Morbid obesity — (Use additional code to identify Body Mass Index (BMI), if known: V85.0-V85.54)

342.01 Flaccid hemiplegia affecting dominant side
342.11 Spastic hemiplegia affecting dominant side
342.81 Other specified hemiplegia affecting dominant side
342.91 Unspecified hemiplegia affecting dominant side ▽
344.00 Unspecified quadriplegia ▽
344.01 Quadriplegia and quadriparesis, C1-C4, complete
344.02 Quadriplegia and quadriparesis, C1-C4, incomplete
344.03 Quadriplegia and quadriparesis, C5-C7, complete
344.04 C5-C7, incomplete
344.09 Other quadriplegia and quadriparesis
344.1 Paraplegia
344.2 Diplegia of upper limbs
344.41 Monoplegia of upper limb affecting dominant side

438.20 Hemiplegia affecting unspecified side due to cerebrovascular disease — (Use additional code to identify presence of hypertension) ▽

438.31 Monoplegia of upper limb affecting dominant side due to cerebrovascular disease — (Use additional code to identify presence of hypertension)

438.51 Other paralytic syndrome affecting dominant side due to cerebrovascular disease — (Use additional code to identify presence of hypertension. Use additional code to identify type of paralytic syndrome: 344.00-344.09, 344.81)

438.84 Ataxia as late effect of cerebrovascular disease — (Use additional code to identify presence of hypertension)

440.20 Atherosclerosis of native arteries of the extremities, unspecified ▽
440.21 Atherosclerosis of native arteries of the extremities with intermittent claudication
440.22 Atherosclerosis of native arteries of the extremities with rest pain

440.23 Atherosclerosis of native arteries of the extremities with ulceration — (Use additional code for any associated ulceration: 707.10-707.19, 707.8, 707.9)

440.24 Atherosclerosis of native arteries of the extremities with gangrene — (Use additional code for any associated ulceration: 707.10-707.19, 707.8, 707.9)

440.29 Other atherosclerosis of native arteries of the extremities
440.30 Atherosclerosis of unspecified bypass graft of extremities ▽
440.31 Atherosclerosis of autologous vein bypass graft of extremities
440.32 Atherosclerosis of nonautologous biological bypass graft of extremities
443.1 Thromboangiitis obliterans (Buerger's disease)

443.81 Peripheral angiopathy in diseases classified elsewhere — (Code first underlying disease: 249.7, 250.7) ☒

443.9 Unspecified peripheral vascular disease ▽

451.0 Phlebitis and thrombophlebitis of superficial vessels of lower extremities — (Use additional E code to identify drug, if drug-induced)

451.11 Phlebitis and thrombophlebitis of femoral vein (deep) (superficial) — (Use additional E code to identify drug, if drug-induced)

451.19 Phlebitis and thrombophlebitis of other deep vessels of lower extremities — (Use additional E code to identify drug, if drug-induced)

451.2 Phlebitis and thrombophlebitis of lower extremities, unspecified — (Use additional E code to identify drug, if drug-induced) ▽

451.81 Phlebitis and thrombophlebitis of iliac vein — (Use additional E code to identify drug, if drug-induced)

451.9 Phlebitis and thrombophlebitis of unspecified site — (Use additional E code to identify drug, if drug-induced) ▽

780.72 Functional quadriplegia

799.3 Unspecified debility ▽

ICD-9-CM Procedural

N/A

HCPCS Level II Supplies & Services

A4649 Surgical supply; miscellaneous

G0245 Initial physician evaluation and management of a diabetic patient with diabetic sensory neuropathy resulting in a loss of protective sensation (LOPS) which must include: (1) the diagnosis of LOPS, (2) a patient history, (3) a physical examination that consists of at least the following elements: (a) visual inspection of the forefoot, hindfoot, and toe web spaces, (b) evaluation of a protective sensation, (c) evaluation of foot structure and biomechanics, (d) evaluation of vascular status and skin integrity, and (e) evaluation and recommendation of footwear, and (4) patient education

G0246 Follow-up physician evaluation and management of a diabetic patient with diabetic sensory neuropathy resulting in a loss of protective sensation (LOPS) to include at least the following: (1) a patient history, (2) a physical examination that includes: (a) visual inspection of the forefoot, hindfoot, and toe web spaces, (b) evaluation of protective sensation, (c) evaluation of foot structure and biomechanics, (d) evaluation of vascular status and skin integrity, and (e) evaluation and recommendation of footwear, and (3) patient education

G0247 Routine foot care by a physician of a diabetic patient with diabetic sensory neuropathy resulting in a loss of protective sensation (LOPS) to include the local care of superficial wounds (i.e., superficial to muscle and fascia) and at least the following, if present: (1) local care of superficial wounds, (2) debridement of corns and calluses, and (3) trimming and debridement of nails

11720-11721

11720 Debridement of nail(s) by any method(s); 1 to 5

11721 6 or more

ICD-9-CM Diagnostic

110.1 Dermatophytosis of nail — (Use additional code to identify manifestation: 321.0-321.1, 380.15, 711.6)

112.3 Candidiasis of skin and nails — (Use additional code to identify manifestation: 321.0-321.1, 380.15, 711.6)

249.60 Secondary diabetes mellitus with neurological manifestations, not stated as uncontrolled, or unspecified — (Use additional code to identify manifestation: 337.1, 353.5, 354.0-355.9, 357.2, 536.3, 713.5) (Use additional code to identify any associated insulin use: V58.67)

249.61 Secondary diabetes mellitus with neurological manifestations, uncontrolled — (Use additional code to identify manifestation: 337.1, 353.5, 354.0-355.9, 357.2, 536.3, 713.5) (Use additional code to identify any associated insulin use: V58.67)

249.70 Secondary diabetes mellitus with peripheral circulatory disorders, not stated as uncontrolled, or unspecified — (Use additional code to identify manifestation: 443.81, 785.4) (Use additional code to identify any associated insulin use: V58.67)

249.71 Secondary diabetes mellitus with peripheral circulatory disorders, uncontrolled — (Use additional code to identify manifestation: 443.81, 785.4) (Use additional code to identify any associated insulin use: V58.67)

249.80 Secondary diabetes mellitus with other specified manifestations, not stated as uncontrolled, or unspecified — (Use additional code to identify manifestation: 707.10-707.19, 707.8, 707.9, 731.8) (Use additional code to identify any associated insulin use: V58.67)

249.81 Secondary diabetes mellitus with other specified manifestations, uncontrolled — (Use additional code to identify manifestation: 707.10-707.19, 707.8, 707.9, 731.8) (Use additional code to identify any associated insulin use: V58.67)

249.90 Secondary diabetes mellitus with unspecified complication, not stated as uncontrolled, or unspecified — (Use additional code to identify any associated insulin use: V58.67) ▽

249.91 Secondary diabetes mellitus with unspecified complication, uncontrolled — (Use additional code to identify any associated insulin use: V58.67) ▽

250.60 Diabetes with neurological manifestations, type II or unspecified type, not stated as uncontrolled — (Use additional code to identify manifestation: 337.1, 353.5, 354.0-355.9, 357.2, 536.3, 713.5)

250.61 Diabetes with neurological manifestations, type I [juvenile type], not stated as uncontrolled — (Use additional code to identify manifestation: 337.1, 353.5, 354.0-355.9, 357.2, 536.3, 713.5)

250.62 Diabetes with neurological manifestations, type II or unspecified type, uncontrolled — (Use additional code to identify manifestation: 337.1, 353.5, 354.0-355.9, 357.2, 536.3, 713.5)

250.63 Diabetes with neurological manifestations, type I [juvenile type], uncontrolled — (Use additional code to identify manifestation: 337.1, 353.5, 354.0-355.9, 357.2, 536.3, 713.5)

250.70 Diabetes with peripheral circulatory disorders, type II or unspecified type, not stated as uncontrolled — (Use additional code to identify manifestation: 443.81, 785.4)

250.71 Diabetes with peripheral circulatory disorders, type I [juvenile type], not stated as uncontrolled — (Use additional code to identify manifestation: 443.81, 785.4)

250.72 Diabetes with peripheral circulatory disorders, type II or unspecified type, uncontrolled — (Use additional code to identify manifestation: 443.81, 785.4)

250.73 Diabetes with peripheral circulatory disorders, type I [juvenile type], uncontrolled — (Use additional code to identify manifestation: 443.81, 785.4)

440.20 Atherosclerosis of native arteries of the extremities, unspecified ▽

440.21 Atherosclerosis of native arteries of the extremities with intermittent claudication

440.22 Atherosclerosis of native arteries of the extremities with rest pain

440.23 Atherosclerosis of native arteries of the extremities with ulceration — (Use additional code for any associated ulceration: 707.10-707.19, 707.8, 707.9)

440.24 Atherosclerosis of native arteries of the extremities with gangrene — (Use additional code for any associated ulceration: 707.10-707.19, 707.8, 707.9)

440.29 Other atherosclerosis of native arteries of the extremities

440.30 Atherosclerosis of unspecified bypass graft of extremities ▽

440.31 Atherosclerosis of autologous vein bypass graft of extremities

440.32 Atherosclerosis of nonautologous biological bypass graft of extremities

443.1 Thromboangiitis obliterans (Buerger's disease)

443.81 Peripheral angiopathy in diseases classified elsewhere — (Code first underlying disease: 249.7, 250.7) ☒

443.89 Other peripheral vascular disease

443.9 Unspecified peripheral vascular disease ▽

451.0 Phlebitis and thrombophlebitis of superficial vessels of lower extremities — (Use additional E code to identify drug, if drug-induced)

451.11 Phlebitis and thrombophlebitis of femoral vein (deep) (superficial) — (Use additional E code to identify drug, if drug-induced)

451.19 Phlebitis and thrombophlebitis of other deep vessels of lower extremities — (Use additional E code to identify drug, if drug-induced)

451.2 Phlebitis and thrombophlebitis of lower extremities, unspecified — (Use additional E code to identify drug, if drug-induced) ▽

451.81 Phlebitis and thrombophlebitis of iliac vein — (Use additional E code to identify drug, if drug-induced)

451.9 Phlebitis and thrombophlebitis of unspecified site — (Use additional E code to identify drug, if drug-induced) ▽

681.00 Unspecified cellulitis and abscess of finger — (Use additional code to identify organism: 041.1) ▽

681.02 Onychia and paronychia of finger — (Use additional code to identify organism: 041.1)

681.10 Unspecified cellulitis and abscess of toe — (Use additional code to identify organism: 041.1) ▽

681.11 Onychia and paronychia of toe — (Use additional code to identify organism: 041.1)

681.9 Cellulitis and abscess of unspecified digit — (Use additional code to identify organism: 041.1) ▽

703.0 Ingrowing nail

703.8 Other specified disease of nail

729.5 Pain in soft tissues of limb

757.5 Specified congenital anomalies of nails

924.3 Contusion of toe

928.3 Crushing injury of toe(s) — (Use additional code to identify any associated injuries: 800-829, 850.0-854.1, 860.0-869.1)

959.7 Injury, other and unspecified, knee, leg, ankle, and foot

991.1 Frostbite of hand
991.2 Frostbite of foot

ICD-9-CM Procedural

86.27 Debridement of nail, nail bed, or nail fold

HCPCS Level II Supplies & Services

A4649 Surgical supply; miscellaneous
G0247 Routine foot care by a physician of a diabetic patient with diabetic sensory neuropathy resulting in a loss of protective sensation (LOPS) to include the local care of superficial wounds (i.e., superficial to muscle and fascia) and at least the following, if present: (1) local care of superficial wounds, (2) debridement of corns and calluses, and (3) trimming and debridement of nails

11730-11732

11730 Avulsion of nail plate, partial or complete, simple; single
11732 each additional nail plate (List separately in addition to code for primary procedure)

ICD-9-CM Diagnostic

249.60 Secondary diabetes mellitus with neurological manifestations, not stated as uncontrolled, or unspecified — (Use additional code to identify manifestation: 337.1, 353.5, 354.0-355.9, 357.2, 536.3, 713.5) (Use additional code to identify any associated insulin use: V58.67)
249.61 Secondary diabetes mellitus with neurological manifestations, uncontrolled — (Use additional code to identify manifestation: 337.1, 353.5, 354.0-355.9, 357.2, 536.3, 713.5) (Use additional code to identify any associated insulin use: V58.67)
249.70 Secondary diabetes mellitus with peripheral circulatory disorders, not stated as uncontrolled, or unspecified — (Use additional code to identify manifestation: 443.81, 785.4) (Use additional code to identify any associated insulin use: V58.67)
249.71 Secondary diabetes mellitus with peripheral circulatory disorders, uncontrolled — (Use additional code to identify manifestation: 443.81, 785.4) (Use additional code to identify any associated insulin use: V58.67)
249.80 Secondary diabetes mellitus with other specified manifestations, not stated as uncontrolled, or unspecified — (Use additional code to identify manifestation: 707.10-707.19, 707.8, 707.9, 731.8) (Use additional code to identify any associated insulin use: V58.67)
249.81 Secondary diabetes mellitus with other specified manifestations, uncontrolled — (Use additional code to identify manifestation: 707.10-707.19, 707.8, 707.9, 731.8) (Use additional code to identify any associated insulin use: V58.67)
249.90 Secondary diabetes mellitus with unspecified complication, not stated as uncontrolled, or unspecified — (Use additional code to identify any associated insulin use: V58.67) ▽
249.91 Secondary diabetes mellitus with unspecified complication, uncontrolled — (Use additional code to identify any associated insulin use: V58.67) ▽
250.60 Diabetes with neurological manifestations, type II or unspecified type, not stated as uncontrolled — (Use additional code to identify manifestation: 337.1, 353.5, 354.0-355.9, 357.2, 536.3, 713.5)
250.61 Diabetes with neurological manifestations, type I [juvenile type], not stated as uncontrolled — (Use additional code to identify manifestation: 337.1, 353.5, 354.0-355.9, 357.2, 536.3, 713.5)
250.62 Diabetes with neurological manifestations, type II or unspecified type, uncontrolled — (Use additional code to identify manifestation: 337.1, 353.5, 354.0-355.9, 357.2, 536.3, 713.5)
250.63 Diabetes with neurological manifestations, type I [juvenile type], uncontrolled — (Use additional code to identify manifestation: 337.1, 353.5, 354.0-355.9, 357.2, 536.3, 713.5)
250.70 Diabetes with peripheral circulatory disorders, type II or unspecified type, not stated as uncontrolled — (Use additional code to identify manifestation: 443.81, 785.4)
250.71 Diabetes with peripheral circulatory disorders, type I [juvenile type], not stated as uncontrolled — (Use additional code to identify manifestation: 443.81, 785.4)
250.72 Diabetes with peripheral circulatory disorders, type II or unspecified type, uncontrolled — (Use additional code to identify manifestation: 443.81, 785.4)
250.73 Diabetes with peripheral circulatory disorders, type I [juvenile type], uncontrolled — (Use additional code to identify manifestation: 443.81, 785.4)
440.20 Atherosclerosis of native arteries of the extremities, unspecified ▽
440.21 Atherosclerosis of native arteries of the extremities with intermittent claudication
440.22 Atherosclerosis of native arteries of the extremities with rest pain
440.23 Atherosclerosis of native arteries of the extremities with ulceration — (Use additional code for any associated ulceration: 707.10-707.19, 707.8, 707.9)
440.24 Atherosclerosis of native arteries of the extremities with gangrene — (Use additional code for any associated ulceration: 707.10-707.19, 707.8, 707.9)
440.29 Other atherosclerosis of native arteries of the extremities
440.30 Atherosclerosis of unspecified bypass graft of extremities ▽
440.31 Atherosclerosis of autologous vein bypass graft of extremities
440.32 Atherosclerosis of nonautologous biological bypass graft of extremities
443.0 Raynaud's syndrome — (Use additional code to identify gangrene: 785.4)
443.1 Thromboangiitis obliterans (Buerger's disease)
443.81 Peripheral angiopathy in diseases classified elsewhere — (Code first underlying disease: 249.7, 250.7) ⊠
443.89 Other peripheral vascular disease
443.9 Unspecified peripheral vascular disease ▽
451.0 Phlebitis and thrombophlebitis of superficial vessels of lower extremities — (Use additional E code to identify drug, if drug-induced)
451.11 Phlebitis and thrombophlebitis of femoral vein (deep) (superficial) — (Use additional E code to identify drug, if drug-induced)
451.19 Phlebitis and thrombophlebitis of other deep vessels of lower extremities — (Use additional E code to identify drug, if drug-induced)
451.2 Phlebitis and thrombophlebitis of lower extremities, unspecified — (Use additional E code to identify drug, if drug-induced) ▽
451.81 Phlebitis and thrombophlebitis of iliac vein — (Use additional E code to identify drug, if drug-induced)
451.9 Phlebitis and thrombophlebitis of unspecified site — (Use additional E code to identify drug, if drug-induced) ▽
681.00 Unspecified cellulitis and abscess of finger — (Use additional code to identify organism: 041.1) ▽
681.02 Onychia and paronychia of finger — (Use additional code to identify organism: 041.1)
681.10 Unspecified cellulitis and abscess of toe — (Use additional code to identify organism: 041.1) ▽
681.11 Onychia and paronychia of toe — (Use additional code to identify organism: 041.1)
681.9 Cellulitis and abscess of unspecified digit — (Use additional code to identify organism: 041.1) ▽
682.8 Cellulitis and abscess of other specified site — (Use additional code to identify organism, such as 041.1, etc.)
703.0 Ingrowing nail
703.8 Other specified disease of nail
757.5 Specified congenital anomalies of nails
785.4 Gangrene — (Code first any associated underlying condition)
816.02 Closed fracture of distal phalanx or phalanges of hand
816.03 Closed fracture of multiple sites of phalanx or phalanges of hand
816.12 Open fracture of distal phalanx or phalanges of hand
816.13 Open fractures of multiple sites of phalanx or phalanges of hand
826.0 Closed fracture of one or more phalanges of foot
826.1 Open fracture of one or more phalanges of foot
883.0 Open wound of finger(s), without mention of complication
883.1 Open wound of finger(s), complicated
883.2 Open wound of finger(s), with tendon involvement
893.0 Open wound of toe(s), without mention of complication
893.1 Open wound of toe(s), complicated
893.2 Open wound of toe(s), with tendon involvement
923.3 Contusion of finger
924.3 Contusion of toe

927.3 Crushing injury of finger(s) — (Use additional code to identify any associated injuries: 800-829, 850.0-854.1, 860.0-869.1)
928.3 Crushing injury of toe(s) — (Use additional code to identify any associated injuries: 800-829, 850.0-854.1, 860.0-869.1)
991.1 Frostbite of hand
991.2 Frostbite of foot

ICD-9-CM Procedural

86.23 Removal of nail, nailbed, or nail fold

HCPCS Level II Supplies & Services

A4649 Surgical supply; miscellaneous

11740

11740 Evacuation of subungual hematoma

ICD-9-CM Diagnostic

287.8 Other specified hemorrhagic conditions
703.8 Other specified disease of nail
816.02 Closed fracture of distal phalanx or phalanges of hand
816.03 Closed fracture of multiple sites of phalanx or phalanges of hand
816.12 Open fracture of distal phalanx or phalanges of hand
816.13 Open fractures of multiple sites of phalanx or phalanges of hand
826.0 Closed fracture of one or more phalanges of foot
826.1 Open fracture of one or more phalanges of foot
883.0 Open wound of finger(s), without mention of complication
883.1 Open wound of finger(s), complicated
893.0 Open wound of toe(s), without mention of complication
893.1 Open wound of toe(s), complicated
893.2 Open wound of toe(s), with tendon involvement
923.20 Contusion of hand(s)
923.3 Contusion of finger
924.3 Contusion of toe
927.3 Crushing injury of finger(s) — (Use additional code to identify any associated injuries: 800-829, 850.0-854.1, 860.0-869.1)
928.3 Crushing injury of toe(s) — (Use additional code to identify any associated injuries: 800-829, 850.0-854.1, 860.0-869.1)
959.5 Injury, other and unspecified, finger
959.7 Injury, other and unspecified, knee, leg, ankle, and foot
998.12 Hematoma complicating a procedure

ICD-9-CM Procedural

86.04 Other incision with drainage of skin and subcutaneous tissue

HCPCS Level II Supplies & Services

A4649 Surgical supply; miscellaneous

11750-11752

11750 Excision of nail and nail matrix, partial or complete (eg, ingrown or deformed nail), for permanent removal;
11752 with amputation of tuft of distal phalanx

ICD-9-CM Diagnostic

249.60 Secondary diabetes mellitus with neurological manifestations, not stated as uncontrolled, or unspecified — (Use additional code to identify manifestation: 337.1, 353.5, 354.0-355.9, 357.2, 536.3, 713.5) (Use additional code to identify any associated insulin use: V58.67)
249.61 Secondary diabetes mellitus with neurological manifestations, uncontrolled — (Use additional code to identify manifestation: 337.1, 353.5, 354.0-355.9, 357.2, 536.3, 713.5) (Use additional code to identify any associated insulin use: V58.67)
249.70 Secondary diabetes mellitus with peripheral circulatory disorders, not stated as uncontrolled, or unspecified — (Use additional code to identify manifestation: 443.81, 785.4) (Use additional code to identify any associated insulin use: V58.67)
249.71 Secondary diabetes mellitus with peripheral circulatory disorders, uncontrolled — (Use additional code to identify manifestation: 443.81, 785.4) (Use additional code to identify any associated insulin use: V58.67)
249.80 Secondary diabetes mellitus with other specified manifestations, not stated as uncontrolled, or unspecified — (Use additional code to identify manifestation: 707.10-707.19, 707.8, 707.9, 731.8) (Use additional code to identify any associated insulin use: V58.67)
249.81 Secondary diabetes mellitus with other specified manifestations, uncontrolled — (Use additional code to identify manifestation: 707.10-707.19, 707.8, 707.9, 731.8) (Use additional code to identify any associated insulin use: V58.67)
249.90 Secondary diabetes mellitus with unspecified complication, not stated as uncontrolled, or unspecified — (Use additional code to identify any associated insulin use: V58.67) ▽
249.91 Secondary diabetes mellitus with unspecified complication, uncontrolled — (Use additional code to identify any associated insulin use: V58.67) ▽
250.60 Diabetes with neurological manifestations, type II or unspecified type, not stated as uncontrolled — (Use additional code to identify manifestation: 337.1, 353.5, 354.0-355.9, 357.2, 536.3, 713.5)
250.61 Diabetes with neurological manifestations, type I [juvenile type], not stated as uncontrolled — (Use additional code to identify manifestation: 337.1, 353.5, 354.0-355.9, 357.2, 536.3, 713.5)
250.62 Diabetes with neurological manifestations, type II or unspecified type, uncontrolled — (Use additional code to identify manifestation: 337.1, 353.5, 354.0-355.9, 357.2, 536.3, 713.5)
250.63 Diabetes with neurological manifestations, type I [juvenile type], uncontrolled — (Use additional code to identify manifestation: 337.1, 353.5, 354.0-355.9, 357.2, 536.3, 713.5)
250.70 Diabetes with peripheral circulatory disorders, type II or unspecified type, not stated as uncontrolled — (Use additional code to identify manifestation: 443.81, 785.4)
250.71 Diabetes with peripheral circulatory disorders, type I [juvenile type], not stated as uncontrolled — (Use additional code to identify manifestation: 443.81, 785.4)
250.72 Diabetes with peripheral circulatory disorders, type II or unspecified type, uncontrolled — (Use additional code to identify manifestation: 443.81, 785.4)
250.73 Diabetes with peripheral circulatory disorders, type I [juvenile type], uncontrolled — (Use additional code to identify manifestation: 443.81, 785.4)
443.0 Raynaud's syndrome — (Use additional code to identify gangrene: 785.4)
443.81 Peripheral angiopathy in diseases classified elsewhere — (Code first underlying disease: 249.7, 250.7) ☒
443.89 Other peripheral vascular disease
681.02 Onychia and paronychia of finger — (Use additional code to identify organism: 041.1)
681.10 Unspecified cellulitis and abscess of toe — (Use additional code to identify organism: 041.1) ▽
681.11 Onychia and paronychia of toe — (Use additional code to identify organism: 041.1)
681.9 Cellulitis and abscess of unspecified digit — (Use additional code to identify organism: 041.1) ▽
703.0 Ingrowing nail
703.8 Other specified disease of nail
703.9 Unspecified disease of nail ▽
757.5 Specified congenital anomalies of nails
785.4 Gangrene — (Code first any associated underlying condition)
883.0 Open wound of finger(s), without mention of complication
883.1 Open wound of finger(s), complicated
893.0 Open wound of toe(s), without mention of complication
893.1 Open wound of toe(s), complicated
927.3 Crushing injury of finger(s) — (Use additional code to identify any associated injuries: 800-829, 850.0-854.1, 860.0-869.1)
928.3 Crushing injury of toe(s) — (Use additional code to identify any associated injuries: 800-829, 850.0-854.1, 860.0-869.1)
945.31 Full-thickness skin loss due to burn (third degree NOS) of toe(s) (nail)
945.51 Deep necrosis of underlying tissues due to burn (deep third degree) of toe(s) (nail), with loss of a body part

ICD-9-CM Procedural

86.23 Removal of nail, nailbed, or nail fold

HCPCS Level II Supplies & Services

A4305 Disposable drug delivery system, flow rate of 50 ml or greater per hour

11755

11755 Biopsy of nail unit (eg, plate, bed, matrix, hyponychium, proximal and lateral nail folds) (separate procedure)

ICD-9-CM Diagnostic

110.1 Dermatophytosis of nail — (Use additional code to identify manifestation: 321.0-321.1, 380.15, 711.6)
173.60 Unspecified malignant neoplasm of skin of upper limb, including shoulder ▽
173.61 Basal cell carcinoma of skin of upper limb, including shoulder
173.62 Squamous cell carcinoma of skin of upper limb, including shoulder
173.69 Other specified malignant neoplasm of skin of upper limb, including shoulder
173.70 Unspecified malignant neoplasm of skin of lower limb, including hip ▽
173.71 Basal cell carcinoma of skin of lower limb, including hip
173.72 Squamous cell carcinoma of skin of lower limb, including hip
173.79 Other specified malignant neoplasm of skin of lower limb, including hip
198.2 Secondary malignant neoplasm of skin
216.6 Benign neoplasm of skin of upper limb, including shoulder
216.7 Benign neoplasm of skin of lower limb, including hip
216.9 Benign neoplasm of skin, site unspecified ▽
232.6 Carcinoma in situ of skin of upper limb, including shoulder
232.7 Carcinoma in situ of skin of lower limb, including hip
238.2 Neoplasm of uncertain behavior of skin
239.2 Neoplasms of unspecified nature of bone, soft tissue, and skin
697.0 Lichen planus
703.8 Other specified disease of nail

ICD-9-CM Procedural

86.11 Closed biopsy of skin and subcutaneous tissue

HCPCS Level II Supplies & Services

A4649 Surgical supply; miscellaneous

11760

11760 Repair of nail bed

ICD-9-CM Diagnostic

816.12 Open fracture of distal phalanx or phalanges of hand
816.13 Open fractures of multiple sites of phalanx or phalanges of hand
826.1 Open fracture of one or more phalanges of foot
883.0 Open wound of finger(s), without mention of complication
883.1 Open wound of finger(s), complicated
893.0 Open wound of toe(s), without mention of complication
893.1 Open wound of toe(s), complicated
893.2 Open wound of toe(s), with tendon involvement
927.3 Crushing injury of finger(s) — (Use additional code to identify any associated injuries: 800-829, 850.0-854.1, 860.0-869.1)
928.3 Crushing injury of toe(s) — (Use additional code to identify any associated injuries: 800-829, 850.0-854.1, 860.0-869.1)

ICD-9-CM Procedural

86.86 Onychoplasty

HCPCS Level II Supplies & Services

A4649 Surgical supply; miscellaneous

11762

11762 Reconstruction of nail bed with graft

ICD-9-CM Diagnostic

171.2 Malignant neoplasm of connective and other soft tissue of upper limb, including shoulder
171.3 Malignant neoplasm of connective and other soft tissue of lower limb, including hip
172.6 Malignant melanoma of skin of upper limb, including shoulder
172.7 Malignant melanoma of skin of lower limb, including hip
173.60 Unspecified malignant neoplasm of skin of upper limb, including shoulder ▽
173.61 Basal cell carcinoma of skin of upper limb, including shoulder
173.62 Squamous cell carcinoma of skin of upper limb, including shoulder
173.69 Other specified malignant neoplasm of skin of upper limb, including shoulder
173.70 Unspecified malignant neoplasm of skin of lower limb, including hip ▽
173.71 Basal cell carcinoma of skin of lower limb, including hip
173.72 Squamous cell carcinoma of skin of lower limb, including hip
173.79 Other specified malignant neoplasm of skin of lower limb, including hip
232.6 Carcinoma in situ of skin of upper limb, including shoulder
232.7 Carcinoma in situ of skin of lower limb, including hip
757.5 Specified congenital anomalies of nails
816.12 Open fracture of distal phalanx or phalanges of hand
816.13 Open fractures of multiple sites of phalanx or phalanges of hand
826.1 Open fracture of one or more phalanges of foot
883.0 Open wound of finger(s), without mention of complication
883.1 Open wound of finger(s), complicated
893.0 Open wound of toe(s), without mention of complication
893.1 Open wound of toe(s), complicated
893.2 Open wound of toe(s), with tendon involvement
906.1 Late effect of open wound of extremities without mention of tendon injury
906.7 Late effect of burn of other extremities
927.3 Crushing injury of finger(s) — (Use additional code to identify any associated injuries: 800-829, 850.0-854.1, 860.0-869.1)
928.3 Crushing injury of toe(s) — (Use additional code to identify any associated injuries: 800-829, 850.0-854.1, 860.0-869.1)
944.01 Burn of unspecified degree of single digit [finger (nail)] other than thumb ▽
944.02 Burn of unspecified degree of thumb (nail) ▽
944.03 Burn of unspecified degree of two or more digits of hand, not including thumb ▽
944.04 Burn of unspecified degree of two or more digits of hand, including thumb ▽
944.20 Blisters with epidermal loss due to burn (second degree) of unspecified site of hand ▽
944.21 Blisters with epidermal loss due to burn (second degree) of single digit [finger (nail)] other than thumb
944.23 Blisters with epidermal loss due to burn (second degree) of two or more digits of hand, not including thumb
944.24 Blisters with epidermal loss due to burn (second degree) of two or more digits of hand including thumb
944.28 Blisters with epidermal loss due to burn (second degree) of multiple sites of wrist(s) and hand(s)
944.30 Full-thickness skin loss due to burn (third degree NOS) of unspecified site of hand ▽
944.31 Full-thickness skin loss due to burn (third degree NOS) of single digit [finger (nail)] other than thumb
944.32 Full-thickness skin loss due to burn (third degree NOS) of thumb (nail)
944.33 Full-thickness skin loss due to burn (third degree NOS) of two or more digits of hand, not including thumb
944.34 Full-thickness skin loss due to burn (third degree NOS) of two or more digits of hand including thumb
944.38 Full-thickness skin loss due to burn (third degree NOS) of multiple sites of wrist(s) and hand(s)
944.41 Deep necrosis of underlying tissues due to burn (deep third degree) of single digit [finger (nail)] other than thumb, without mention of loss of a body part

▽ Unspecified code ♀ Female diagnosis ◼ Manifestation code ♂ Male diagnosis

944.42 Deep necrosis of underlying tissues due to burn (deep third degree) of thumb (nail), without mention of loss of a body part
944.43 Deep necrosis of underlying tissues due to burn (deep third degree) of two or more digits of hand, not including thumb, without mention of loss of a body part
944.44 Deep necrosis of underlying tissues due to burn (deep third degree) of two or more digits of hand including thumb, without mention of loss of a body part
944.48 Deep necrosis of underlying tissues due to burn (deep third degree) of multiple sites of wrist(s) and hand(s), without mention of loss of a body part
945.01 Burn of unspecified degree of toe(s) (nail)

ICD-9-CM Procedural
86.86 Onychoplasty

HCPCS Level II Supplies & Services
A4649 Surgical supply; miscellaneous

11765
11765 Wedge excision of skin of nail fold (eg, for ingrown toenail)

ICD-9-CM Diagnostic
681.02 Onychia and paronychia of finger — (Use additional code to identify organism: 041.1)
681.11 Onychia and paronychia of toe — (Use additional code to identify organism: 041.1)
686.1 Pyogenic granuloma of skin and subcutaneous tissue — (Use additional code to identify any infectious organism: 041.0-041.8)
703.0 Ingrowing nail
924.3 Contusion of toe
928.3 Crushing injury of toe(s) — (Use additional code to identify any associated injuries: 800-829, 850.0-854.1, 860.0-869.1)

ICD-9-CM Procedural
86.23 Removal of nail, nailbed, or nail fold

HCPCS Level II Supplies & Services
A4649 Surgical supply; miscellaneous

Pilonidal Cyst

11770-11772
11770 Excision of pilonidal cyst or sinus; simple
11771 extensive
11772 complicated

ICD-9-CM Diagnostic
685.0 Pilonidal cyst with abscess
685.1 Pilonidal cyst without mention of abscess

ICD-9-CM Procedural
86.21 Excision of pilonidal cyst or sinus

HCPCS Level II Supplies & Services
A4305 Disposable drug delivery system, flow rate of 50 ml or greater per hour

Introduction

11900-11901
11900 Injection, intralesional; up to and including 7 lesions
11901 more than 7 lesions

ICD-9-CM Diagnostic
078.10 Viral warts, unspecified
078.11 Condyloma acuminatum
078.12 Plantar wart
078.19 Other specified viral warts
215.3 Other benign neoplasm of connective and other soft tissue of lower limb, including hip
373.12 Hordeolum internum
373.2 Chalazion
695.2 Erythema nodosum
697.0 Lichen planus
698.3 Lichenification and lichen simplex chronicus
701.1 Acquired keratoderma
701.4 Keloid scar
704.01 Alopecia areata
706.1 Other acne
709.2 Scar condition and fibrosis of skin

ICD-9-CM Procedural
99.29 Injection or infusion of other therapeutic or prophylactic substance
99.77 Application or administration of adhesion barrier substance

HCPCS Level II Supplies & Services
J3301 Injection, triamcinolone acetonide, not otherwise specified, 10 mg
J3302 Injection, triamcinolone diacetate, per 5 mg
J9040 Injection, bleomycin sulfate, 15 units

11920-11922
11920 Tattooing, intradermal introduction of insoluble opaque pigments to correct color defects of skin, including micropigmentation; 6.0 sq cm or less
11921 6.1 to 20.0 sq cm
11922 each additional 20.0 sq cm, or part thereof (List separately in addition to code for primary procedure)

ICD-9-CM Diagnostic
374.53 Hypopigmentation of eyelid
709.00 Dyschromia, unspecified
709.01 Vitiligo
709.09 Other dyschromia
757.33 Congenital pigmentary anomaly of skin
757.6 Specified congenital anomalies of breast
906.0 Late effect of open wound of head, neck, and trunk
906.5 Late effect of burn of eye, face, head, and neck
906.8 Late effect of burns of other specified sites
V10.3 Personal history of malignant neoplasm of breast
V45.71 Acquired absence of breast and nipple
V50.1 Other plastic surgery for unacceptable cosmetic appearance
V51.8 Other aftercare involving the use of plastic surgery

ICD-9-CM Procedural
86.02 Injection or tattooing of skin lesion or defect

HCPCS Level II Supplies & Services
A4649 Surgical supply; miscellaneous

11950-11954
11950 Subcutaneous injection of filling material (eg, collagen); 1 cc or less
11951 1.1 to 5.0 cc
11952 5.1 to 10.0 cc
11954 over 10.0 cc

ICD-9-CM Diagnostic
374.89 Other disorders of eyelid
380.32 Acquired deformities of auricle or pinna
528.5 Diseases of lips
611.81 Ptosis of breast
611.82 Hypoplasia of breast
611.83 Capsular contracture of breast implant
611.89 Other specified disorders of breast
612.0 Deformity of reconstructed breast

612.1 Disproportion of reconstructed breast

701.8 Other specified hypertrophic and atrophic condition of skin

706.1 Other acne

709.2 Scar condition and fibrosis of skin

709.3 Degenerative skin disorder

709.8 Other specified disorder of skin

743.62 Congenital deformity of eyelid

744.3 Unspecified congenital anomaly of ear ▽

744.82 Microcheilia

757.8 Other specified congenital anomalies of the integument

757.9 Unspecified congenital anomaly of the integument ▽

906.0 Late effect of open wound of head, neck, and trunk

906.1 Late effect of open wound of extremities without mention of tendon injury

906.5 Late effect of burn of eye, face, head, and neck

906.6 Late effect of burn of wrist and hand

906.7 Late effect of burn of other extremities

906.8 Late effect of burns of other specified sites

906.9 Late effect of burn of unspecified site ▽

V50.1 Other plastic surgery for unacceptable cosmetic appearance

V51.0 Encounter for breast reconstruction following mastectomy

V51.8 Other aftercare involving the use of plastic surgery

ICD-9-CM Procedural

86.02 Injection or tattooing of skin lesion or defect

HCPCS Level II Supplies & Services

A4649 Surgical supply; miscellaneous

11960

11960 Insertion of tissue expander(s) for other than breast, including subsequent expansion

ICD-9-CM Diagnostic

709.2 Scar condition and fibrosis of skin

729.90 Disorders of soft tissue, unspecified ▽

729.99 Other disorders of soft tissue

749.11 Unilateral cleft lip, complete

749.12 Unilateral cleft lip, incomplete

752.40 Unspecified congenital anomaly of cervix, vagina, and external female genitalia ▽ ♀

752.43 Cervical agenesis ♀

752.44 Cervical duplication ♀

752.45 Vaginal agenesis ♀

752.46 Transverse vaginal septum ♀

752.47 Longitudinal vaginal septum ♀

752.49 Other congenital anomaly of cervix, vagina, and external female genitalia ♀

754.0 Congenital musculoskeletal deformities of skull, face, and jaw

872.00 Open wound of external ear, unspecified site, without mention of complication ▽

872.01 Open wound of auricle, without mention of complication

872.10 Open wound of external ear, unspecified site, complicated ▽

872.11 Open wound of auricle, complicated

873.0 Open wound of scalp, without mention of complication

873.1 Open wound of scalp, complicated

873.20 Open wound of nose, unspecified site, without mention of complication ▽

873.29 Open wound of nose, multiple sites, without mention of complication

873.30 Open wound of nose, unspecified site, complicated ▽

873.39 Open wound of nose, multiple sites, complicated

873.41 Open wound of cheek, without mention of complication

873.42 Open wound of forehead, without mention of complication

873.43 Open wound of lip, without mention of complication

873.44 Open wound of jaw, without mention of complication

873.49 Open wound of face, other and multiple sites, without mention of complication

873.51 Open wound of cheek, complicated

873.52 Open wound of forehead, complicated

873.53 Open wound of lip, complicated

873.54 Open wound of jaw, complicated

873.59 Open wound of face, other and multiple sites, complicated

874.8 Open wound of other and unspecified parts of neck, without mention of complication ▽

906.0 Late effect of open wound of head, neck, and trunk

906.5 Late effect of burn of eye, face, head, and neck

906.6 Late effect of burn of wrist and hand

906.7 Late effect of burn of other extremities

906.8 Late effect of burns of other specified sites

909.2 Late effect of radiation

909.3 Late effect of complications of surgical and medical care

941.30 Full-thickness skin loss due to burn (third degree NOS) of unspecified site of face and head ▽

941.31 Full-thickness skin loss due to burn (third degree NOS) of ear (any part)

941.32 Full-thickness skin loss due to burn (third degree NOS) of eye (with other parts of face, head, and neck)

941.33 Full-thickness skin loss due to burn (third degree NOS) of lip(s)

941.34 Full-thickness skin loss due to burn (third degree NOS) of chin

941.35 Full-thickness skin loss due to burn (third degree NOS) of nose (septum)

941.36 Full-thickness skin loss due to burn (third degree NOS) of scalp (any part)

941.38 Full-thickness skin loss due to burn (third degree NOS) of neck

941.39 Full-thickness skin loss due to burn (third degree NOS) of multiple sites (except with eye) of face, head, and neck

941.40 Deep necrosis of underlying tissues due to burn (deep third degree) of unspecified site of face and head, without mention of loss of a body part ▽

941.41 Deep necrosis of underlying tissues due to burn (deep third degree) of ear (any part), without mention of loss of a body part

941.42 Deep necrosis of underlying tissues due to burn (deep third degree) of eye (with other parts of face, head, and neck), without mention of loss of a body part

941.43 Deep necrosis of underlying tissues due to burn (deep third degree) of lip(s), without mention of loss of a body part

941.44 Deep necrosis of underlying tissues due to burn (deep third degree) of chin, without mention of loss of a body part

941.45 Deep necrosis of underlying tissues due to burn (deep third degree) of nose (septum), without mention of loss of a body part

941.46 Deep necrosis of underlying tissues due to burn (deep third degree) of scalp (any part), without mention of loss of a body part

941.47 Deep necrosis of underlying tissues due to burn (deep third degree) of forehead and cheek, without mention of loss of a body part

941.48 Deep necrosis of underlying tissues due to burn (deep third degree) of neck, without mention of loss of a body part

941.49 Deep necrosis of underlying tissues due to burn (deep third degree) of multiple sites (except with eye) of face, head, and neck, without mention of loss of a body part

941.50 Deep necrosis of underlying tissues due to burn (deep third degree) of face and head, unspecified site, with loss of a body part ▽

941.51 Deep necrosis of underlying tissues due to burn (deep third degree) of ear (any part), with loss of a body part

941.52 Deep necrosis of underlying tissues due to burn (deep third degree) of eye (with other parts of face, head, and neck), with loss of a body part

941.53 Deep necrosis of underlying tissues due to burn (deep third degree) of lip(s), with loss of a body part

941.54 Deep necrosis of underlying tissues due to burn (deep third degree) of chin, with loss of a body part

941.55 Deep necrosis of underlying tissues due to burn (deep third degree) of nose (septum), with loss of a body part

941.56 Deep necrosis of underlying tissues due to burn (deep third degree) of scalp (any part), with loss of a body part

941.57 Deep necrosis of underlying tissues due to burn (deep third degree) of forehead and cheek, with loss of a body part
941.58 Deep necrosis of underlying tissues due to burn (deep third degree) of neck, with loss of a body part
941.59 Deep necrosis of underlying tissues due to burn (deep third degree) of multiple sites (except eye) of face, head, and neck, with loss of a body part
943.30 Full-thickness skin loss due to burn (third degree NOS) of unspecified site of upper limb ♥
943.31 Full-thickness skin loss due to burn (third degree NOS) of forearm
943.32 Full-thickness skin loss due to burn (third degree NOS) of elbow
943.39 Full-thickness skin loss due to burn (third degree NOS) of multiple sites of upper limb, except wrist and hand
943.50 Deep necrosis of underlying tissues due to burn (deep third degree) of unspecified site of upper limb, with loss of a body part ♥
943.51 Deep necrosis of underlying tissues due to burn (deep third degree) of forearm, with loss of a body part
943.52 Deep necrosis of underlying tissues due to burn (deep third degree) of elbow, with loss of a body part
943.53 Deep necrosis of underlying tissues due to burn (deep third degree) of upper arm, with loss of upper a body part
943.59 Deep necrosis of underlying tissues due to burn (deep third degree) of multiple sites of upper limb, except wrist and hand, with loss of a body part
945.30 Full-thickness skin loss due to burn (third degree NOS) of unspecified site of lower limb ♥
945.34 Full-thickness skin loss due to burn (third degree NOS) of lower leg
945.35 Full-thickness skin loss due to burn (third degree NOS) of knee
945.36 Full-thickness skin loss due to burn (third degree NOS) of thigh (any part)
945.39 Full-thickness skin loss due to burn (third degree NOS) of multiple sites of lower limb(s)
945.40 Deep necrosis of underlying tissues due to burn (deep third degree) of unspecified site of lower limb (leg), without mention of loss of a body part ♥
945.44 Deep necrosis of underlying tissues due to burn (deep third degree) of lower leg, without mention of loss of a body part
945.45 Deep necrosis of underlying tissues due to burn (deep third degree) of knee, without mention of loss of a body part
945.46 Deep necrosis of underlying tissues due to burn (deep third degree) of thigh (any part), without mention of loss of a body part
945.49 Deep necrosis of underlying tissues due to burn (deep third degree) of multiple sites of lower limb(s), without mention of loss of a body part
945.50 Deep necrosis of underlying tissues due to burn (deep third degree) of unspecified site lower limb (leg), with loss of a body part ♥
945.52 Deep necrosis of underlying tissues due to burn (deep third degree) of foot, with loss of a body part
945.53 Deep necrosis of underlying tissues due to burn (deep third degree) of ankle, with loss of a body part
945.54 Deep necrosis of underlying tissues due to burn (deep third degree) of lower leg, with loss of a body part
945.55 Deep necrosis of underlying tissues due to burn (deep third degree) of knee, with loss of a body part
945.56 Deep necrosis of underlying tissues due to burn (deep third degree) of thigh (any part), with loss of a body part
945.59 Deep necrosis of underlying tissues due to burn (deep third degree) of multiple sites of lower limb(s), with loss of a body part
946.3 Full-thickness skin loss due to burn (third degree NOS) of multiple specified sites
946.4 Deep necrosis of underlying tissues due to burn (deep third degree) of multiple specified sites, without mention of loss of a body part
946.5 Deep necrosis of underlying tissues due to burn (deep third degree) of multiple specified sites, with loss of a body part
997.60 Late complications of amputation stump, unspecified — (Use additional code to identify complications) ♥
997.62 Infection (chronic) of amputation stump — (Use additional code to identify complications)
997.69 Other late amputation stump complication — (Use additional code to identify complications)
V50.1 Other plastic surgery for unacceptable cosmetic appearance
V51.8 Other aftercare involving the use of plastic surgery

ICD-9-CM Procedural

86.93 Insertion of tissue expander

HCPCS Level II Supplies & Services

A4280 Adhesive skin support attachment for use with external breast prosthesis, each
A4649 Surgical supply; miscellaneous

11970

11970 Replacement of tissue expander with permanent prosthesis

ICD-9-CM Diagnostic

709.2 Scar condition and fibrosis of skin
729.90 Disorders of soft tissue, unspecified ♥
729.99 Other disorders of soft tissue
872.00 Open wound of external ear, unspecified site, without mention of complication ♥
872.01 Open wound of auricle, without mention of complication
872.10 Open wound of external ear, unspecified site, complicated ♥
872.11 Open wound of auricle, complicated
873.0 Open wound of scalp, without mention of complication
873.1 Open wound of scalp, complicated
873.20 Open wound of nose, unspecified site, without mention of complication ♥
873.29 Open wound of nose, multiple sites, without mention of complication
873.30 Open wound of nose, unspecified site, complicated ♥
873.39 Open wound of nose, multiple sites, complicated
873.41 Open wound of cheek, without mention of complication
873.42 Open wound of forehead, without mention of complication
873.43 Open wound of lip, without mention of complication
873.44 Open wound of jaw, without mention of complication
873.49 Open wound of face, other and multiple sites, without mention of complication
873.51 Open wound of cheek, complicated
873.52 Open wound of forehead, complicated
873.53 Open wound of lip, complicated
873.54 Open wound of jaw, complicated
873.59 Open wound of face, other and multiple sites, complicated
874.8 Open wound of other and unspecified parts of neck, without mention of complication ♥
906.0 Late effect of open wound of head, neck, and trunk
906.5 Late effect of burn of eye, face, head, and neck
906.6 Late effect of burn of wrist and hand
906.7 Late effect of burn of other extremities
941.30 Full-thickness skin loss due to burn (third degree NOS) of unspecified site of face and head ♥
941.31 Full-thickness skin loss due to burn (third degree NOS) of ear (any part)
941.32 Full-thickness skin loss due to burn (third degree NOS) of eye (with other parts of face, head, and neck)
941.33 Full-thickness skin loss due to burn (third degree NOS) of lip(s)
941.34 Full-thickness skin loss due to burn (third degree NOS) of chin
941.35 Full-thickness skin loss due to burn (third degree NOS) of nose (septum)
941.36 Full-thickness skin loss due to burn (third degree NOS) of scalp (any part)
941.38 Full-thickness skin loss due to burn (third degree NOS) of neck
941.39 Full-thickness skin loss due to burn (third degree NOS) of multiple sites (except with eye) of face, head, and neck
941.40 Deep necrosis of underlying tissues due to burn (deep third degree) of unspecified site of face and head, without mention of loss of a body part ♥

941.41 Deep necrosis of underlying tissues due to burn (deep third degree) of ear (any part), without mention of loss of a body part
941.42 Deep necrosis of underlying tissues due to burn (deep third degree) of eye (with other parts of face, head, and neck), without mention of loss of a body part
941.43 Deep necrosis of underlying tissues due to burn (deep third degree) of lip(s), without mention of loss of a body part
941.44 Deep necrosis of underlying tissues due to burn (deep third degree) of chin, without mention of loss of a body part
941.45 Deep necrosis of underlying tissues due to burn (deep third degree) of nose (septum), without mention of loss of a body part
941.46 Deep necrosis of underlying tissues due to burn (deep third degree) of scalp (any part), without mention of loss of a body part
941.47 Deep necrosis of underlying tissues due to burn (deep third degree) of forehead and cheek, without mention of loss of a body part
941.48 Deep necrosis of underlying tissues due to burn (deep third degree) of neck, without mention of loss of a body part
941.49 Deep necrosis of underlying tissues due to burn (deep third degree) of multiple sites (except with eye) of face, head, and neck, without mention of loss of a body part
941.50 Deep necrosis of underlying tissues due to burn (deep third degree) of face and head, unspecified site, with loss of a body part
941.51 Deep necrosis of underlying tissues due to burn (deep third degree) of ear (any part), with loss of a body part
941.52 Deep necrosis of underlying tissues due to burn (deep third degree) of eye (with other parts of face, head, and neck), with loss of a body part
941.53 Deep necrosis of underlying tissues due to burn (deep third degree) of lip(s), with loss of a body part
941.54 Deep necrosis of underlying tissues due to burn (deep third degree) of chin, with loss of a body part
941.55 Deep necrosis of underlying tissues due to burn (deep third degree) of nose (septum), with loss of a body part
941.56 Deep necrosis of underlying tissues due to burn (deep third degree) of scalp (any part), with loss of a body part
941.57 Deep necrosis of underlying tissues due to burn (deep third degree) of forehead and cheek, with loss of a body part
941.58 Deep necrosis of underlying tissues due to burn (deep third degree) of neck, with loss of a body part
941.59 Deep necrosis of underlying tissues due to burn (deep third degree) of multiple sites (except eye) of face, head, and neck, with loss of a body part
942.30 Full-thickness skin loss due to burn (third degree NOS) of unspecified site of trunk
942.32 Full-thickness skin loss due to burn (third degree NOS) of chest wall, excluding breast and nipple
942.33 Full-thickness skin loss due to burn (third degree NOS) of abdominal wall
942.34 Full-thickness skin loss due to burn (third degree NOS) of back (any part)
942.35 Full-thickness skin loss due to burn (third degree NOS) of genitalia
942.39 Full-thickness skin loss due to burn (third degree NOS) of other and multiple sites of trunk
942.40 Deep necrosis of underlying tissues due to burn (deep third degree) of trunk, unspecified site, without mention of loss of a body part
942.42 Deep necrosis of underlying tissues due to burn (deep third degree) of chest wall, excluding breast and nipple, without mention of loss of a body part
942.43 Deep necrosis of underlying tissues due to burn (deep third degree) of abdominal wall, without mention of loss of a body part
942.44 Deep necrosis of underlying tissues due to burn (deep third degree) of back (any part), without mention of loss of a body part
942.45 Deep necrosis of underlying tissues due to burn (deep third degree) of genitalia, without mention of loss of a body part
942.49 Deep necrosis of underlying tissues due to burn (deep third degree) of other and multiple sites of trunk, without mention of loss of a body part
942.50 Deep necrosis of underlying tissues due to burn (deep third degree) of unspecified site of trunk, with loss of a body part
942.52 Deep necrosis of underlying tissues due to burn (deep third degree) of chest wall, excluding breast and nipple, with loss of a body part
942.53 Deep necrosis of underlying tissues due to burn (deep third degree) of abdominal wall with loss of a body part
942.54 Deep necrosis of underlying tissues due to burn (deep third degree) of back (any part), with loss of a body part
942.55 Deep necrosis of underlying tissues due to burn (deep third degree) of genitalia, with loss of a body part
942.59 Deep necrosis of underlying tissues due to burn (deep third degree) of other and multiple sites of trunk, with loss of a body part
943.30 Full-thickness skin loss due to burn (third degree NOS) of unspecified site of upper limb
943.31 Full-thickness skin loss due to burn (third degree NOS) of forearm
943.32 Full-thickness skin loss due to burn (third degree NOS) of elbow
943.39 Full-thickness skin loss due to burn (third degree NOS) of multiple sites of upper limb, except wrist and hand
943.50 Deep necrosis of underlying tissues due to burn (deep third degree) of unspecified site of upper limb, with loss of a body part
943.51 Deep necrosis of underlying tissues due to burn (deep third degree) of forearm, with loss of a body part
943.52 Deep necrosis of underlying tissues due to burn (deep third degree) of elbow, with loss of a body part
943.53 Deep necrosis of underlying tissues due to burn (deep third degree) of upper arm, with loss of upper a body part
943.59 Deep necrosis of underlying tissues due to burn (deep third degree) of multiple sites of upper limb, except wrist and hand, with loss of a body part
945.30 Full-thickness skin loss due to burn (third degree NOS) of unspecified site of lower limb
945.34 Full-thickness skin loss due to burn (third degree NOS) of lower leg
945.35 Full-thickness skin loss due to burn (third degree NOS) of knee
945.36 Full-thickness skin loss due to burn (third degree NOS) of thigh (any part)
945.39 Full-thickness skin loss due to burn (third degree NOS) of multiple sites of lower limb(s)
945.40 Deep necrosis of underlying tissues due to burn (deep third degree) of unspecified site of lower limb (leg), without mention of loss of a body part
945.44 Deep necrosis of underlying tissues due to burn (deep third degree) of lower leg, without mention of loss of a body part
945.45 Deep necrosis of underlying tissues due to burn (deep third degree) of knee, without mention of loss of a body part
945.46 Deep necrosis of underlying tissues due to burn (deep third degree) of thigh (any part), without mention of loss of a body part
945.49 Deep necrosis of underlying tissues due to burn (deep third degree) of multiple sites of lower limb(s), without mention of loss of a body part
945.50 Deep necrosis of underlying tissues due to burn (deep third degree) of unspecified site lower limb (leg), with loss of a body part
945.52 Deep necrosis of underlying tissues due to burn (deep third degree) of foot, with loss of a body part
945.53 Deep necrosis of underlying tissues due to burn (deep third degree) of ankle, with loss of a body part
945.54 Deep necrosis of underlying tissues due to burn (deep third degree) of lower leg, with loss of a body part
945.55 Deep necrosis of underlying tissues due to burn (deep third degree) of knee, with loss of a body part
945.56 Deep necrosis of underlying tissues due to burn (deep third degree) of thigh (any part), with loss of a body part
945.59 Deep necrosis of underlying tissues due to burn (deep third degree) of multiple sites of lower limb(s), with loss of a body part
946.3 Full-thickness skin loss due to burn (third degree NOS) of multiple specified sites
946.4 Deep necrosis of underlying tissues due to burn (deep third degree) of multiple specified sites, without mention of loss of a body part

946.5 Deep necrosis of underlying tissues due to burn (deep third degree) of multiple specified sites, with loss of a body part
997.60 Late complications of amputation stump, unspecified — (Use additional code to identify complications) ▽
997.62 Infection (chronic) of amputation stump — (Use additional code to identify complications)
997.69 Other late amputation stump complication — (Use additional code to identify complications)
V51.8 Other aftercare involving the use of plastic surgery
V52.4 Fitting and adjustment of breast prosthesis and implant ♀

ICD-9-CM Procedural

85.53 Unilateral breast implant
85.54 Bilateral breast implant
85.96 Removal of breast tissue expander (s)
86.05 Incision with removal of foreign body or device from skin and subcutaneous tissue

HCPCS Level II Supplies & Services

A4305 Disposable drug delivery system, flow rate of 50 ml or greater per hour

11971

11971 Removal of tissue expander(s) without insertion of prosthesis

ICD-9-CM Diagnostic

611.3 Fat necrosis of breast — (Code first breast necrosis due to breast graft: 996.79)
612.0 Deformity of reconstructed breast
612.1 Disproportion of reconstructed breast
704.00 Unspecified alopecia ▽
709.2 Scar condition and fibrosis of skin
996.52 Mechanical complication due to other tissue graft, not elsewhere classified
996.54 Mechanical complication due to breast prosthesis
996.69 Infection and inflammatory reaction due to other internal prosthetic device, implant, and graft — (Use additional code to identify specified infections)
996.79 Other complications due to other internal prosthetic device, implant, and graft — (Use additional code to identify complication: 338.18-338.19, 338.28-338.29)
997.60 Late complications of amputation stump, unspecified — (Use additional code to identify complications) ▽
997.62 Infection (chronic) of amputation stump — (Use additional code to identify complications)
997.69 Other late amputation stump complication — (Use additional code to identify complications)
V45.71 Acquired absence of breast and nipple
V50.1 Other plastic surgery for unacceptable cosmetic appearance
V51.8 Other aftercare involving the use of plastic surgery
V52.4 Fitting and adjustment of breast prosthesis and implant ♀

ICD-9-CM Procedural

85.96 Removal of breast tissue expander (s)
86.05 Incision with removal of foreign body or device from skin and subcutaneous tissue

HCPCS Level II Supplies & Services

A4305 Disposable drug delivery system, flow rate of 50 ml or greater per hour

11976

11976 Removal, implantable contraceptive capsules

ICD-9-CM Diagnostic

V25.43 Surveillance of previously prescribed implantable subdermal contraceptive ♀

ICD-9-CM Procedural

86.05 Incision with removal of foreign body or device from skin and subcutaneous tissue

11980

11980 Subcutaneous hormone pellet implantation (implantation of estradiol and/or testosterone pellets beneath the skin)

ICD-9-CM Diagnostic

185 Malignant neoplasm of prostate ♂
194.3 Malignant neoplasm of pituitary gland and craniopharyngeal duct
227.3 Benign neoplasm of pituitary gland and craniopharyngeal duct (pouch) — (Use additional code to identify any functional activity)
253.0 Acromegaly and gigantism
253.1 Other and unspecified anterior pituitary hyperfunction ▽
253.2 Panhypopituitarism
253.3 Pituitary dwarfism
253.4 Other anterior pituitary disorders
253.5 Diabetes insipidus
253.6 Other disorders of neurohypophysis
253.7 Iatrogenic pituitary disorders — (Use additional E code to identify cause)
253.8 Other disorders of the pituitary and other syndromes of diencephalohypophyseal origin
253.9 Unspecified disorder of the pituitary gland and its hypothalamic control ▽
256.2 Postablative ovarian failure — (Use additional code for states associated with artificial menopause: 627.4) ♀
256.31 Premature menopause — (Use additional code for states associated with natural menopause: 627.2) ♀
256.39 Other ovarian failure — (Use additional code for states associated with natural menopause: 627.2) ♀
256.8 Other ovarian dysfunction ♀
256.9 Unspecified ovarian dysfunction ▽ ♀
257.0 Testicular hyperfunction ♂
257.1 Postablative testicular hypofunction ♂
257.2 Other testicular hypofunction
257.8 Other testicular dysfunction
257.9 Unspecified testicular dysfunction ▽ ♂
259.0 Delay in sexual development and puberty, not elsewhere classified
259.1 Precocious sexual development and puberty, not elsewhere classified
259.50 Androgen insensitivity, unspecified ▽
259.51 Androgen insensitivity syndrome
259.52 Partial androgen insensitivity
346.40 Menstrual migraine, without mention of intractable migraine without mention of status migrainosus ♀
346.41 Menstrual migraine, with intractable migraine, so stated, without mention of status migrainosus ♀
346.42 Menstrual migraine, without mention of intractable migraine with status migrainosus ♀
346.43 Menstrual migraine, with intractable migraine, so stated, with status migrainosus ♀
597.80 Unspecified urethritis ▽
604.90 Unspecified orchitis and epididymitis — (Use additional code to identify organism: 041.00-041.09, 041.10-041.19, 041.41-041.49) ▽ ♂
606.1 Oligospermia ♂
608.20 Torsion of testis, unspecified ▽ ♂
608.21 Extravaginal torsion of spermatic cord ♂
608.22 Intravaginal torsion of spermatic cord ♂
608.23 Torsion of appendix testis ♂
608.24 Torsion of appendix epididymis ♂
608.3 Atrophy of testis ♂
627.0 Premenopausal menorrhagia ♀
627.1 Postmenopausal bleeding ♀
627.2 Symptomatic menopausal or female climacteric states ♀
627.3 Postmenopausal atrophic vaginitis ♀

627.4 Symptomatic states associated with artificial menopause ♀
627.8 Other specified menopausal and postmenopausal disorder ♀
627.9 Unspecified menopausal and postmenopausal disorder ▼ ♀
733.00 Unspecified osteoporosis — (Use additional code to identify major osseous defect, if applicable: 731.3) (Use additional code to identify personal history of pathologic (healed) fracture: V13.51) ▼
733.01 Senile osteoporosis — (Use additional code to identify major osseous defect, if applicable: 731.3) (Use additional code to identify personal history of pathologic (healed) fracture: V13.51)
752.51 Undescended testis ♂
752.52 Retractile testis ♂
758.7 Klinefelter's syndrome — (Use additional codes for conditions associated with the chromosomal anomalies) ♂
V10.47 Personal history of malignant neoplasm of testis ♂
V45.77 Acquired absence of organ, genital organs

ICD-9-CM Procedural

99.23 Injection of steroid

HCPCS Level II Supplies & Services

S0189 Testosterone pellet, 75 mg

11981-11983

11981 Insertion, non-biodegradable drug delivery implant
11982 Removal, non-biodegradable drug delivery implant
11983 Removal with reinsertion, non-biodegradable drug delivery implant

ICD-9-CM Diagnostic

The application of this code is too broad to adequately present ICD-9-CM diagnostic code links here. Refer to your ICD-9-CM book.

ICD-9-CM Procedural

84.56 Insertion or replacement of (cement) spacer
84.57 Removal of (cement) spacer
86.05 Incision with removal of foreign body or device from skin and subcutaneous tissue
99.21 Injection of antibiotic
99.23 Injection of steroid

HCPCS Level II Supplies & Services

J7306 Levonorgestrel (contraceptive) implant system, including implants and supplies
J7307 Etonogestrel (contraceptive) implant system, including implant and supplies

Repair (Closure)

12001-12007

12001 Simple repair of superficial wounds of scalp, neck, axillae, external genitalia, trunk and/or extremities (including hands and feet); 2.5 cm or less
12002 2.6 cm to 7.5 cm
12004 7.6 cm to 12.5 cm
12005 12.6 cm to 20.0 cm
12006 20.1 cm to 30.0 cm
12007 over 30.0 cm

ICD-9-CM Diagnostic

629.20 Female genital mutilation status, unspecified ▼ ♀
873.0 Open wound of scalp, without mention of complication
874.8 Open wound of other and unspecified parts of neck, without mention of complication ▼
878.0 Open wound of penis, without mention of complication ♂
878.2 Open wound of scrotum and testes, without mention of complication ♂
878.4 Open wound of vulva, without mention of complication ♀
878.6 Open wound of vagina, without mention of complication ♀
878.8 Open wound of other and unspecified parts of genital organs, without mention of complication ▼
879.0 Open wound of breast, without mention of complication
879.2 Open wound of abdominal wall, anterior, without mention of complication
879.4 Open wound of abdominal wall, lateral, without mention of complication
879.6 Open wound of other and unspecified parts of trunk, without mention of complication ▼
879.8 Open wound(s) (multiple) of unspecified site(s), without mention of complication ▼
880.00 Open wound of shoulder region, without mention of complication
880.01 Open wound of scapular region, without mention of complication
880.02 Open wound of axillary region, without mention of complication
880.03 Open wound of upper arm, without mention of complication
880.09 Open wound of multiple sites of shoulder and upper arm, without mention of complication
881.00 Open wound of forearm, without mention of complication
881.01 Open wound of elbow, without mention of complication
881.02 Open wound of wrist, without mention of complication
882.0 Open wound of hand except finger(s) alone, without mention of complication
883.0 Open wound of finger(s), without mention of complication
884.0 Multiple and unspecified open wound of upper limb, without mention of complication
890.0 Open wound of hip and thigh, without mention of complication
891.0 Open wound of knee, leg (except thigh), and ankle, without mention of complication
892.0 Open wound of foot except toe(s) alone, without mention of complication
893.0 Open wound of toe(s), without mention of complication
894.0 Multiple and unspecified open wound of lower limb, without mention of complication

ICD-9-CM Procedural

61.41 Suture of laceration of scrotum and tunica vaginalis ♂
64.41 Suture of laceration of penis ♂
71.71 Suture of laceration of vulva or perineum ♀
71.79 Other repair of vulva and perineum ♀
85.81 Suture of laceration of breast
86.59 Closure of skin and subcutaneous tissue of other sites

HCPCS Level II Supplies & Services

A4305 Disposable drug delivery system, flow rate of 50 ml or greater per hour

12011-12018

12011 Simple repair of superficial wounds of face, ears, eyelids, nose, lips and/or mucous membranes; 2.5 cm or less
12013 2.6 cm to 5.0 cm
12014 5.1 cm to 7.5 cm
12015 7.6 cm to 12.5 cm
12016 12.6 cm to 20.0 cm
12017 20.1 cm to 30.0 cm
12018 over 30.0 cm

ICD-9-CM Diagnostic

870.0 Laceration of skin of eyelid and periocular area
872.01 Open wound of auricle, without mention of complication
872.02 Open wound of auditory canal, without mention of complication
872.8 Open wound of ear, part unspecified, without mention of complication ▼
873.21 Open wound of nasal septum, without mention of complication
873.22 Open wound of nasal cavity, without mention of complication
873.23 Open wound of nasal sinus, without mention of complication
873.29 Open wound of nose, multiple sites, without mention of complication
873.40 Open wound of face, unspecified site, without mention of complication ▼
873.41 Open wound of cheek, without mention of complication
873.42 Open wound of forehead, without mention of complication
873.43 Open wound of lip, without mention of complication
873.44 Open wound of jaw, without mention of complication

873.49 Open wound of face, other and multiple sites, without mention of complication
873.60 Open wound of mouth, unspecified site, without mention of complication

ICD-9-CM Procedural

08.81 Linear repair of laceration of eyelid or eyebrow
18.4 Suture of laceration of external ear
21.81 Suture of laceration of nose
27.51 Suture of laceration of lip
27.52 Suture of laceration of other part of mouth
86.59 Closure of skin and subcutaneous tissue of other sites

HCPCS Level II Supplies & Services

A4305 Disposable drug delivery system, flow rate of 50 ml or greater per hour

12020-12021

12020 Treatment of superficial wound dehiscence; simple closure
12021 with packing

ICD-9-CM Diagnostic

674.10 Disruption of cesarean wound, unspecified as to episode of care ♀
674.12 Disruption of cesarean wound, with delivery, with mention of postpartum complication ♀
674.14 Disruption of cesarean wound, postpartum condition or complication ♀
674.20 Disruption of perineal wound, unspecified as to episode of care in pregnancy ♀
674.22 Disruption of perineal wound, with delivery, with mention of postpartum complication ♀
674.24 Disruption of perineal wound, postpartum condition or complication ♀
780.62 Postprocedural fever
998.30 Disruption of wound, unspecified
998.32 Disruption of external operation (surgical) wound
998.33 Disruption of traumatic injury wound repair
998.59 Other postoperative infection — (Use additional code to identify infection)
998.83 Non-healing surgical wound

ICD-9-CM Procedural

85.81 Suture of laceration of breast
86.59 Closure of skin and subcutaneous tissue of other sites
96.59 Other irrigation of wound

HCPCS Level II Supplies & Services

A4461 Surgical dressing holder, nonreusable, each
A4463 Surgical dressing holder, reusable, each

12031-12037

12031 Repair, intermediate, wounds of scalp, axillae, trunk and/or extremities (excluding hands and feet); 2.5 cm or less
12032 2.6 cm to 7.5 cm
12034 7.6 cm to 12.5 cm
12035 12.6 cm to 20.0 cm
12036 20.1 cm to 30.0 cm
12037 over 30.0 cm

ICD-9-CM Diagnostic

172.4 Malignant melanoma of skin of scalp and neck
172.5 Malignant melanoma of skin of trunk, except scrotum
172.6 Malignant melanoma of skin of upper limb, including shoulder
172.7 Malignant melanoma of skin of lower limb, including hip
172.8 Malignant melanoma of other specified sites of skin
173.40 Unspecified malignant neoplasm of scalp and skin of neck
173.41 Basal cell carcinoma of scalp and skin of neck
173.42 Squamous cell carcinoma of scalp and skin of neck
173.49 Other specified malignant neoplasm of scalp and skin of neck
173.50 Unspecified malignant neoplasm of skin of trunk, except scrotum
173.51 Basal cell carcinoma of skin of trunk, except scrotum
173.52 Squamous cell carcinoma of skin of trunk, except scrotum
173.59 Other specified malignant neoplasm of skin of trunk, except scrotum
173.60 Unspecified malignant neoplasm of skin of upper limb, including shoulder
173.61 Basal cell carcinoma of skin of upper limb, including shoulder
173.62 Squamous cell carcinoma of skin of upper limb, including shoulder
173.69 Other specified malignant neoplasm of skin of upper limb, including shoulder
173.70 Unspecified malignant neoplasm of skin of lower limb, including hip
173.71 Basal cell carcinoma of skin of lower limb, including hip
173.72 Squamous cell carcinoma of skin of lower limb, including hip
173.79 Other specified malignant neoplasm of skin of lower limb, including hip
173.80 Unspecified malignant neoplasm of other specified sites of skin
173.81 Basal cell carcinoma of other specified sites of skin
173.82 Squamous cell carcinoma of other specified sites of skin
173.89 Other specified malignant neoplasm of other specified sites of skin
209.32 Merkel cell carcinoma of the scalp and neck
209.33 Merkel cell carcinoma of the upper limb
209.34 Merkel cell carcinoma of the lower limb
209.35 Merkel cell carcinoma of the trunk
209.36 Merkel cell carcinoma of other sites
209.75 Secondary Merkel cell carcinoma
214.1 Lipoma of other skin and subcutaneous tissue
216.4 Benign neoplasm of scalp and skin of neck
216.5 Benign neoplasm of skin of trunk, except scrotum
216.6 Benign neoplasm of skin of upper limb, including shoulder
216.7 Benign neoplasm of skin of lower limb, including hip
216.8 Benign neoplasm of other specified sites of skin
232.4 Carcinoma in situ of scalp and skin of neck
232.5 Carcinoma in situ of skin of trunk, except scrotum
232.6 Carcinoma in situ of skin of upper limb, including shoulder
232.7 Carcinoma in situ of skin of lower limb, including hip
238.2 Neoplasm of uncertain behavior of skin
448.1 Nevus, non-neoplastic
686.1 Pyogenic granuloma of skin and subcutaneous tissue — (Use additional code to identify any infectious organism: 041.0-041.8)
701.1 Acquired keratoderma
701.4 Keloid scar
701.5 Other abnormal granulation tissue
701.8 Other specified hypertrophic and atrophic condition of skin
701.9 Unspecified hypertrophic and atrophic condition of skin
702.0 Actinic keratosis
702.11 Inflamed seborrheic keratosis
702.19 Other seborrheic keratosis
702.8 Other specified dermatoses
706.2 Sebaceous cyst
709.1 Vascular disorder of skin
709.2 Scar condition and fibrosis of skin
757.32 Congenital vascular hamartomas
757.33 Congenital pigmentary anomaly of skin
757.39 Other specified congenital anomaly of skin
782.2 Localized superficial swelling, mass, or lump
873.0 Open wound of scalp, without mention of complication
873.1 Open wound of scalp, complicated
874.8 Open wound of other and unspecified parts of neck, without mention of complication
875.0 Open wound of chest (wall), without mention of complication
876.0 Open wound of back, without mention of complication
877.0 Open wound of buttock, without mention of complication
879.0 Open wound of breast, without mention of complication

879.2 Open wound of abdominal wall, anterior, without mention of complication
879.4 Open wound of abdominal wall, lateral, without mention of complication
879.6 Open wound of other and unspecified parts of trunk, without mention of complication ▽
879.8 Open wound(s) (multiple) of unspecified site(s), without mention of complication ▽
880.00 Open wound of shoulder region, without mention of complication
880.03 Open wound of upper arm, without mention of complication
880.09 Open wound of multiple sites of shoulder and upper arm, without mention of complication
881.00 Open wound of forearm, without mention of complication
881.01 Open wound of elbow, without mention of complication
881.02 Open wound of wrist, without mention of complication
884.0 Multiple and unspecified open wound of upper limb, without mention of complication
890.0 Open wound of hip and thigh, without mention of complication
891.0 Open wound of knee, leg (except thigh), and ankle, without mention of complication
894.0 Multiple and unspecified open wound of lower limb, without mention of complication

ICD-9-CM Procedural

85.81 Suture of laceration of breast
86.59 Closure of skin and subcutaneous tissue of other sites

HCPCS Level II Supplies & Services

A4305 Disposable drug delivery system, flow rate of 50 ml or greater per hour

12041-12047

12041 Repair, intermediate, wounds of neck, hands, feet and/or external genitalia; 2.5 cm or less
12042 2.6 cm to 7.5 cm
12044 7.6 cm to 12.5 cm
12045 12.6 cm to 20.0 cm
12046 20.1 cm to 30.0 cm
12047 over 30.0 cm

ICD-9-CM Diagnostic

172.4 Malignant melanoma of skin of scalp and neck
172.6 Malignant melanoma of skin of upper limb, including shoulder
172.7 Malignant melanoma of skin of lower limb, including hip
172.8 Malignant melanoma of other specified sites of skin
173.40 Unspecified malignant neoplasm of scalp and skin of neck ▽
173.41 Basal cell carcinoma of scalp and skin of neck
173.42 Squamous cell carcinoma of scalp and skin of neck
173.49 Other specified malignant neoplasm of scalp and skin of neck
173.60 Unspecified malignant neoplasm of skin of upper limb, including shoulder ▽
173.61 Basal cell carcinoma of skin of upper limb, including shoulder
173.62 Squamous cell carcinoma of skin of upper limb, including shoulder
173.69 Other specified malignant neoplasm of skin of upper limb, including shoulder
173.70 Unspecified malignant neoplasm of skin of lower limb, including hip ▽
173.71 Basal cell carcinoma of skin of lower limb, including hip
173.72 Squamous cell carcinoma of skin of lower limb, including hip
173.79 Other specified malignant neoplasm of skin of lower limb, including hip
173.80 Unspecified malignant neoplasm of other specified sites of skin ▽
173.81 Basal cell carcinoma of other specified sites of skin
173.82 Squamous cell carcinoma of other specified sites of skin
173.89 Other specified malignant neoplasm of other specified sites of skin
184.1 Malignant neoplasm of labia majora ♀
184.2 Malignant neoplasm of labia minora ♀
184.4 Malignant neoplasm of vulva, unspecified site ▽ ♀
187.1 Malignant neoplasm of prepuce ♂
187.2 Malignant neoplasm of glans penis ♂
187.3 Malignant neoplasm of body of penis ♂
187.7 Malignant neoplasm of scrotum ♂
187.8 Malignant neoplasm of other specified sites of male genital organs ♂
198.2 Secondary malignant neoplasm of skin
198.82 Secondary malignant neoplasm of genital organs
209.32 Merkel cell carcinoma of the scalp and neck
209.33 Merkel cell carcinoma of the upper limb
209.34 Merkel cell carcinoma of the lower limb
209.36 Merkel cell carcinoma of other sites
209.75 Secondary Merkel cell carcinoma
214.1 Lipoma of other skin and subcutaneous tissue
216.4 Benign neoplasm of scalp and skin of neck
216.6 Benign neoplasm of skin of upper limb, including shoulder
216.7 Benign neoplasm of skin of lower limb, including hip
216.8 Benign neoplasm of other specified sites of skin
221.2 Benign neoplasm of vulva ♀
222.1 Benign neoplasm of penis ♂
222.4 Benign neoplasm of scrotum ♂
228.01 Hemangioma of skin and subcutaneous tissue
232.4 Carcinoma in situ of scalp and skin of neck
232.6 Carcinoma in situ of skin of upper limb, including shoulder
232.7 Carcinoma in situ of skin of lower limb, including hip
232.8 Carcinoma in situ of other specified sites of skin
233.30 Carcinoma in situ, unspecified female genital organ ▽ ♀
233.31 Carcinoma in situ, vagina ♀
233.32 Carcinoma in situ, vulva ♀
233.39 Carcinoma in situ, other female genital organ ♀
233.5 Carcinoma in situ of penis ♂
233.6 Carcinoma in situ of other and unspecified male genital organs ▽ ♂
238.2 Neoplasm of uncertain behavior of skin
239.89 Neoplasms of unspecified nature, other specified sites
448.1 Nevus, non-neoplastic
629.20 Female genital mutilation status, unspecified ▽ ♀
629.21 Female genital mutilation, Type I status ♀
629.22 Female genital mutilation, Type II status ♀
686.1 Pyogenic granuloma of skin and subcutaneous tissue — (Use additional code to identify any infectious organism: 041.0-041.8)
701.1 Acquired keratoderma
701.4 Keloid scar
701.5 Other abnormal granulation tissue
701.8 Other specified hypertrophic and atrophic condition of skin
701.9 Unspecified hypertrophic and atrophic condition of skin ▽
702.0 Actinic keratosis
702.11 Inflamed seborrheic keratosis
702.19 Other seborrheic keratosis
702.8 Other specified dermatoses
706.2 Sebaceous cyst
709.1 Vascular disorder of skin
709.2 Scar condition and fibrosis of skin
709.9 Unspecified disorder of skin and subcutaneous tissue ▽
757.32 Congenital vascular hamartomas
757.33 Congenital pigmentary anomaly of skin
757.39 Other specified congenital anomaly of skin
782.2 Localized superficial swelling, mass, or lump
874.8 Open wound of other and unspecified parts of neck, without mention of complication ▽
874.9 Open wound of other and unspecified parts of neck, complicated ▽
878.0 Open wound of penis, without mention of complication ♂
878.2 Open wound of scrotum and testes, without mention of complication ♂
878.3 Open wound of scrotum and testes, complicated ♂

878.4 Open wound of vulva, without mention of complication ♀
878.5 Open wound of vulva, complicated ♀
878.6 Open wound of vagina, without mention of complication ♀
878.7 Open wound of vagina, complicated ♀
878.8 Open wound of other and unspecified parts of genital organs, without mention of complication ▽
878.9 Open wound of other and unspecified parts of genital organs, complicated ▽
882.0 Open wound of hand except finger(s) alone, without mention of complication
882.1 Open wound of hand except finger(s) alone, complicated
883.0 Open wound of finger(s), without mention of complication
883.1 Open wound of finger(s), complicated
892.0 Open wound of foot except toe(s) alone, without mention of complication
892.1 Open wound of foot except toe(s) alone, complicated
893.0 Open wound of toe(s), without mention of complication
893.1 Open wound of toe(s), complicated

ICD-9-CM Procedural

61.41 Suture of laceration of scrotum and tunica vaginalis ♂
64.41 Suture of laceration of penis ♂
71.71 Suture of laceration of vulva or perineum ♀
86.59 Closure of skin and subcutaneous tissue of other sites

HCPCS Level II Supplies & Services

A4305 Disposable drug delivery system, flow rate of 50 ml or greater per hour

12051-12057

12051 Repair, intermediate, wounds of face, ears, eyelids, nose, lips and/or mucous membranes; 2.5 cm or less
12052 2.6 cm to 5.0 cm
12053 5.1 cm to 7.5 cm
12054 7.6 cm to 12.5 cm
12055 12.6 cm to 20.0 cm
12056 20.1 cm to 30.0 cm
12057 over 30.0 cm

ICD-9-CM Diagnostic

172.0 Malignant melanoma of skin of lip
172.1 Malignant melanoma of skin of eyelid, including canthus
172.2 Malignant melanoma of skin of ear and external auditory canal
172.3 Malignant melanoma of skin of other and unspecified parts of face ▽
172.8 Malignant melanoma of other specified sites of skin
173.00 Unspecified malignant neoplasm of skin of lip ▽
173.01 Basal cell carcinoma of skin of lip
173.02 Squamous cell carcinoma of skin of lip
173.09 Other specified malignant neoplasm of skin of lip
173.10 Unspecified malignant neoplasm of eyelid, including canthus ▽
173.11 Basal cell carcinoma of eyelid, including canthus
173.12 Squamous cell carcinoma of eyelid, including canthus
173.19 Other specified malignant neoplasm of eyelid, including canthus
173.20 Unspecified malignant neoplasm of skin of ear and external auditory canal ▽
173.21 Basal cell carcinoma of skin of ear and external auditory canal
173.22 Squamous cell carcinoma of skin of ear and external auditory canal
173.29 Other specified malignant neoplasm of skin of ear and external auditory canal
173.30 Unspecified malignant neoplasm of skin of other and unspecified parts of face ▽
173.31 Basal cell carcinoma of skin of other and unspecified parts of face
173.32 Squamous cell carcinoma of skin of other and unspecified parts of face
173.39 Other specified malignant neoplasm of skin of other and unspecified parts of face
173.80 Unspecified malignant neoplasm of other specified sites of skin ▽
173.81 Basal cell carcinoma of other specified sites of skin
173.82 Squamous cell carcinoma of other specified sites of skin
173.89 Other specified malignant neoplasm of other specified sites of skin
195.0 Malignant neoplasm of head, face, and neck
198.2 Secondary malignant neoplasm of skin
209.31 Merkel cell carcinoma of the face
209.36 Merkel cell carcinoma of other sites
209.75 Secondary Merkel cell carcinoma
214.0 Lipoma of skin and subcutaneous tissue of face
214.1 Lipoma of other skin and subcutaneous tissue
216.0 Benign neoplasm of skin of lip
216.1 Benign neoplasm of eyelid, including canthus
216.2 Benign neoplasm of ear and external auditory canal
216.3 Benign neoplasm of skin of other and unspecified parts of face ▽
228.01 Hemangioma of skin and subcutaneous tissue
232.0 Carcinoma in situ of skin of lip
232.1 Carcinoma in situ of eyelid, including canthus
232.2 Carcinoma in situ of skin of ear and external auditory canal
232.3 Carcinoma in situ of skin of other and unspecified parts of face ▽
235.1 Neoplasm of uncertain behavior of lip, oral cavity, and pharynx
238.2 Neoplasm of uncertain behavior of skin
239.2 Neoplasms of unspecified nature of bone, soft tissue, and skin
239.89 Neoplasms of unspecified nature, other specified sites
448.1 Nevus, non-neoplastic
686.1 Pyogenic granuloma of skin and subcutaneous tissue — (Use additional code to identify any infectious organism: 041.0-041.8)
701.1 Acquired keratoderma
701.4 Keloid scar
701.5 Other abnormal granulation tissue
701.8 Other specified hypertrophic and atrophic condition of skin
701.9 Unspecified hypertrophic and atrophic condition of skin ▽
702.0 Actinic keratosis
702.11 Inflamed seborrheic keratosis
702.19 Other seborrheic keratosis
706.2 Sebaceous cyst
709.2 Scar condition and fibrosis of skin
757.32 Congenital vascular hamartomas
757.33 Congenital pigmentary anomaly of skin
757.39 Other specified congenital anomaly of skin
870.0 Laceration of skin of eyelid and periocular area
870.1 Laceration of eyelid, full-thickness, not involving lacrimal passages
870.8 Other specified open wound of ocular adnexa
872.00 Open wound of external ear, unspecified site, without mention of complication ▽
872.01 Open wound of auricle, without mention of complication
872.02 Open wound of auditory canal, without mention of complication
872.10 Open wound of external ear, unspecified site, complicated ▽
872.11 Open wound of auricle, complicated
872.12 Open wound of auditory canal, complicated
872.69 Open wound of other and multiple sites, without mention of complication
872.79 Open wound of other and multiple sites, complicated
873.1 Open wound of scalp, complicated
873.20 Open wound of nose, unspecified site, without mention of complication ▽
873.21 Open wound of nasal septum, without mention of complication
873.22 Open wound of nasal cavity, without mention of complication
873.23 Open wound of nasal sinus, without mention of complication
873.29 Open wound of nose, multiple sites, without mention of complication
873.30 Open wound of nose, unspecified site, complicated ▽
873.31 Open wound of nasal septum, complicated
873.32 Open wound of nasal cavity, complicated
873.33 Open wound of nasal sinus, complicated
873.39 Open wound of nose, multiple sites, complicated
873.40 Open wound of face, unspecified site, without mention of complication ▽

873.41 Open wound of cheek, without mention of complication
873.42 Open wound of forehead, without mention of complication
873.43 Open wound of lip, without mention of complication
873.44 Open wound of jaw, without mention of complication
873.49 Open wound of face, other and multiple sites, without mention of complication
873.50 Open wound of face, unspecified site, complicated
873.51 Open wound of cheek, complicated
873.52 Open wound of forehead, complicated
873.53 Open wound of lip, complicated
873.54 Open wound of jaw, complicated
873.59 Open wound of face, other and multiple sites, complicated
873.60 Open wound of mouth, unspecified site, without mention of complication
873.61 Open wound of buccal mucosa, without mention of complication
873.69 Open wound of mouth, other and multiple sites, without mention of complication
873.70 Open wound of mouth, unspecified site, complicated
873.71 Open wound of buccal mucosa, complicated
873.79 Open wound of mouth, other and multiple sites, complicated
873.8 Other and unspecified open wound of head without mention of complication
873.9 Other and unspecified open wound of head, complicated
925.1 Crushing injury of face and scalp — (Use additional code to identify any associated injuries, such as: 800-829, 850.0-854.1, 860.0-869.1)
959.09 Injury of face and neck, other and unspecified

ICD-9-CM Procedural

08.81 Linear repair of laceration of eyelid or eyebrow
18.4 Suture of laceration of external ear
21.81 Suture of laceration of nose
27.51 Suture of laceration of lip
27.52 Suture of laceration of other part of mouth
86.59 Closure of skin and subcutaneous tissue of other sites

HCPCS Level II Supplies & Services

A4305 Disposable drug delivery system, flow rate of 50 ml or greater per hour

13100-13102

13100 Repair, complex, trunk; 1.1 cm to 2.5 cm
13101 2.6 cm to 7.5 cm
13102 each additional 5 cm or less (List separately in addition to code for primary procedure)

ICD-9-CM Diagnostic

172.5 Malignant melanoma of skin of trunk, except scrotum
173.50 Unspecified malignant neoplasm of skin of trunk, except scrotum
173.51 Basal cell carcinoma of skin of trunk, except scrotum
173.52 Squamous cell carcinoma of skin of trunk, except scrotum
173.59 Other specified malignant neoplasm of skin of trunk, except scrotum
198.2 Secondary malignant neoplasm of skin
209.35 Merkel cell carcinoma of the trunk
209.75 Secondary Merkel cell carcinoma
214.1 Lipoma of other skin and subcutaneous tissue
216.5 Benign neoplasm of skin of trunk, except scrotum
228.01 Hemangioma of skin and subcutaneous tissue
232.5 Carcinoma in situ of skin of trunk, except scrotum
238.2 Neoplasm of uncertain behavior of skin
448.1 Nevus, non-neoplastic
686.1 Pyogenic granuloma of skin and subcutaneous tissue — (Use additional code to identify any infectious organism: 041.0-041.8)
701.1 Acquired keratoderma
701.4 Keloid scar
701.5 Other abnormal granulation tissue
702.11 Inflamed seborrheic keratosis
702.19 Other seborrheic keratosis
706.2 Sebaceous cyst
709.1 Vascular disorder of skin
709.2 Scar condition and fibrosis of skin
709.4 Foreign body granuloma of skin and subcutaneous tissue — (Use additional code to identify foreign body (V90.01-V90.9))
757.32 Congenital vascular hamartomas
875.0 Open wound of chest (wall), without mention of complication
875.1 Open wound of chest (wall), complicated
877.0 Open wound of buttock, without mention of complication
877.1 Open wound of buttock, complicated
879.0 Open wound of breast, without mention of complication
879.1 Open wound of breast, complicated
879.2 Open wound of abdominal wall, anterior, without mention of complication
879.3 Open wound of abdominal wall, anterior, complicated
879.4 Open wound of abdominal wall, lateral, without mention of complication
879.5 Open wound of abdominal wall, lateral, complicated
879.6 Open wound of other and unspecified parts of trunk, without mention of complication
879.7 Open wound of other and unspecified parts of trunk, complicated
879.8 Open wound(s) (multiple) of unspecified site(s), without mention of complication
879.9 Open wound(s) (multiple) of unspecified site(s), complicated
880.00 Open wound of shoulder region, without mention of complication
880.01 Open wound of scapular region, without mention of complication
880.09 Open wound of multiple sites of shoulder and upper arm, without mention of complication
880.10 Open wound of shoulder region, complicated
880.11 Open wound of scapular region, complicated
880.19 Open wound of multiple sites of shoulder and upper arm, complicated
906.0 Late effect of open wound of head, neck, and trunk

ICD-9-CM Procedural

85.81 Suture of laceration of breast
86.59 Closure of skin and subcutaneous tissue of other sites
86.89 Other repair and reconstruction of skin and subcutaneous tissue

HCPCS Level II Supplies & Services

A4305 Disposable drug delivery system, flow rate of 50 ml or greater per hour

13120-13122

13120 Repair, complex, scalp, arms, and/or legs; 1.1 cm to 2.5 cm
13121 2.6 cm to 7.5 cm
13122 each additional 5 cm or less (List separately in addition to code for primary procedure)

ICD-9-CM Diagnostic

172.4 Malignant melanoma of skin of scalp and neck
172.6 Malignant melanoma of skin of upper limb, including shoulder
172.7 Malignant melanoma of skin of lower limb, including hip
172.8 Malignant melanoma of other specified sites of skin
173.40 Unspecified malignant neoplasm of scalp and skin of neck
173.41 Basal cell carcinoma of scalp and skin of neck
173.42 Squamous cell carcinoma of scalp and skin of neck
173.49 Other specified malignant neoplasm of scalp and skin of neck
173.60 Unspecified malignant neoplasm of skin of upper limb, including shoulder
173.61 Basal cell carcinoma of skin of upper limb, including shoulder
173.62 Squamous cell carcinoma of skin of upper limb, including shoulder
173.69 Other specified malignant neoplasm of skin of upper limb, including shoulder
173.70 Unspecified malignant neoplasm of skin of lower limb, including hip
173.71 Basal cell carcinoma of skin of lower limb, including hip
173.72 Squamous cell carcinoma of skin of lower limb, including hip

173.79 Other specified malignant neoplasm of skin of lower limb, including hip
195.4 Malignant neoplasm of upper limb
195.5 Malignant neoplasm of lower limb
198.2 Secondary malignant neoplasm of skin
209.32 Merkel cell carcinoma of the scalp and neck
209.33 Merkel cell carcinoma of the upper limb
209.34 Merkel cell carcinoma of the lower limb
209.75 Secondary Merkel cell carcinoma
214.1 Lipoma of other skin and subcutaneous tissue
216.4 Benign neoplasm of scalp and skin of neck
216.6 Benign neoplasm of skin of upper limb, including shoulder
216.7 Benign neoplasm of skin of lower limb, including hip
216.8 Benign neoplasm of other specified sites of skin
228.01 Hemangioma of skin and subcutaneous tissue
232.4 Carcinoma in situ of scalp and skin of neck
232.6 Carcinoma in situ of skin of upper limb, including shoulder
232.7 Carcinoma in situ of skin of lower limb, including hip
232.8 Carcinoma in situ of other specified sites of skin
238.2 Neoplasm of uncertain behavior of skin
448.1 Nevus, non-neoplastic
686.1 Pyogenic granuloma of skin and subcutaneous tissue — (Use additional code to identify any infectious organism: 041.0-041.8)
701.1 Acquired keratoderma
701.4 Keloid scar
701.5 Other abnormal granulation tissue
701.8 Other specified hypertrophic and atrophic condition of skin
701.9 Unspecified hypertrophic and atrophic condition of skin ▽
702.0 Actinic keratosis
702.11 Inflamed seborrheic keratosis
702.19 Other seborrheic keratosis
702.8 Other specified dermatoses
706.2 Sebaceous cyst
709.1 Vascular disorder of skin
709.2 Scar condition and fibrosis of skin
709.4 Foreign body granuloma of skin and subcutaneous tissue — (Use additional code to identify foreign body (V90.01-V90.9))
757.32 Congenital vascular hamartomas
757.33 Congenital pigmentary anomaly of skin
757.39 Other specified congenital anomaly of skin
782.2 Localized superficial swelling, mass, or lump
873.0 Open wound of scalp, without mention of complication
873.1 Open wound of scalp, complicated
880.03 Open wound of upper arm, without mention of complication
880.13 Open wound of upper arm, complicated
881.00 Open wound of forearm, without mention of complication
881.01 Open wound of elbow, without mention of complication
881.02 Open wound of wrist, without mention of complication
881.10 Open wound of forearm, complicated
881.11 Open wound of elbow, complicated
881.12 Open wound of wrist, complicated
884.0 Multiple and unspecified open wound of upper limb, without mention of complication
884.1 Multiple and unspecified open wound of upper limb, complicated
890.0 Open wound of hip and thigh, without mention of complication
890.1 Open wound of hip and thigh, complicated
891.0 Open wound of knee, leg (except thigh), and ankle, without mention of complication
891.1 Open wound of knee, leg (except thigh), and ankle, complicated
894.0 Multiple and unspecified open wound of lower limb, without mention of complication
894.1 Multiple and unspecified open wound of lower limb, complicated
906.0 Late effect of open wound of head, neck, and trunk

ICD-9-CM Procedural

86.51 Replantation of scalp
86.59 Closure of skin and subcutaneous tissue of other sites
86.89 Other repair and reconstruction of skin and subcutaneous tissue

HCPCS Level II Supplies & Services

A4305 Disposable drug delivery system, flow rate of 50 ml or greater per hour

13131-13133

13131 Repair, complex, forehead, cheeks, chin, mouth, neck, axillae, genitalia, hands and/or feet; 1.1 cm to 2.5 cm
13132 2.6 cm to 7.5 cm
13133 each additional 5 cm or less (List separately in addition to code for primary procedure)

ICD-9-CM Diagnostic

172.3 Malignant melanoma of skin of other and unspecified parts of face ▽
172.4 Malignant melanoma of skin of scalp and neck
172.5 Malignant melanoma of skin of trunk, except scrotum
172.6 Malignant melanoma of skin of upper limb, including shoulder
172.7 Malignant melanoma of skin of lower limb, including hip
172.8 Malignant melanoma of other specified sites of skin
173.30 Unspecified malignant neoplasm of skin of other and unspecified parts of face ▽
173.31 Basal cell carcinoma of skin of other and unspecified parts of face
173.32 Squamous cell carcinoma of skin of other and unspecified parts of face
173.39 Other specified malignant neoplasm of skin of other and unspecified parts of face
173.40 Unspecified malignant neoplasm of scalp and skin of neck ▽
173.41 Basal cell carcinoma of scalp and skin of neck
173.42 Squamous cell carcinoma of scalp and skin of neck
173.49 Other specified malignant neoplasm of scalp and skin of neck
173.60 Unspecified malignant neoplasm of skin of upper limb, including shoulder ▽
173.61 Basal cell carcinoma of skin of upper limb, including shoulder
173.62 Squamous cell carcinoma of skin of upper limb, including shoulder
173.69 Other specified malignant neoplasm of skin of upper limb, including shoulder
173.70 Unspecified malignant neoplasm of skin of lower limb, including hip ▽
173.71 Basal cell carcinoma of skin of lower limb, including hip
173.72 Squamous cell carcinoma of skin of lower limb, including hip
173.79 Other specified malignant neoplasm of skin of lower limb, including hip
173.80 Unspecified malignant neoplasm of other specified sites of skin ▽
173.81 Basal cell carcinoma of other specified sites of skin
173.82 Squamous cell carcinoma of other specified sites of skin
173.89 Other specified malignant neoplasm of other specified sites of skin
184.4 Malignant neoplasm of vulva, unspecified site ▽ ♀
187.1 Malignant neoplasm of prepuce ♂
187.2 Malignant neoplasm of glans penis ♂
187.3 Malignant neoplasm of body of penis ♂
187.4 Malignant neoplasm of penis, part unspecified ▽ ♂
187.7 Malignant neoplasm of scrotum ♂
187.8 Malignant neoplasm of other specified sites of male genital organs ♂
195.0 Malignant neoplasm of head, face, and neck
195.4 Malignant neoplasm of upper limb
195.5 Malignant neoplasm of lower limb
198.2 Secondary malignant neoplasm of skin
198.82 Secondary malignant neoplasm of genital organs
198.89 Secondary malignant neoplasm of other specified sites
209.31 Merkel cell carcinoma of the face
209.33 Merkel cell carcinoma of the upper limb
209.34 Merkel cell carcinoma of the lower limb
209.35 Merkel cell carcinoma of the trunk

209.36	Merkel cell carcinoma of other sites
209.75	Secondary Merkel cell carcinoma
214.0	Lipoma of skin and subcutaneous tissue of face
214.1	Lipoma of other skin and subcutaneous tissue
216.3	Benign neoplasm of skin of other and unspecified parts of face ▼
216.4	Benign neoplasm of scalp and skin of neck
216.6	Benign neoplasm of skin of upper limb, including shoulder
216.7	Benign neoplasm of skin of lower limb, including hip
216.8	Benign neoplasm of other specified sites of skin
221.2	Benign neoplasm of vulva ♀
222.1	Benign neoplasm of penis ♂
222.4	Benign neoplasm of scrotum ♂
228.01	Hemangioma of skin and subcutaneous tissue
230.0	Carcinoma in situ of lip, oral cavity, and pharynx
232.3	Carcinoma in situ of skin of other and unspecified parts of face ▼
232.6	Carcinoma in situ of skin of upper limb, including shoulder
232.7	Carcinoma in situ of skin of lower limb, including hip
232.8	Carcinoma in situ of other specified sites of skin
233.30	Carcinoma in situ, unspecified female genital organ ▼ ♀
233.31	Carcinoma in situ, vagina ♀
233.32	Carcinoma in situ, vulva ♀
233.39	Carcinoma in situ, other female genital organ ♀
233.5	Carcinoma in situ of penis ♂
233.6	Carcinoma in situ of other and unspecified male genital organs ▼ ♂
236.3	Neoplasm of uncertain behavior of other and unspecified female genital organs ▼ ♀
236.6	Neoplasm of uncertain behavior of other and unspecified male genital organs ▼ ♂
238.2	Neoplasm of uncertain behavior of skin
239.89	Neoplasms of unspecified nature, other specified sites
448.1	Nevus, non-neoplastic
528.79	Other disturbances of oral epithelium, including tongue
629.20	Female genital mutilation status, unspecified ▼ ♀
629.21	Female genital mutilation, Type I status ♀
629.22	Female genital mutilation, Type II status ♀
629.23	Female genital mutilation, Type III status ♀
629.29	Other female genital mutilation status ♀
629.89	Other specified disorders of female genital organs ♀
686.1	Pyogenic granuloma of skin and subcutaneous tissue — (Use additional code to identify any infectious organism: 041.0-041.8)
701.1	Acquired keratoderma
701.4	Keloid scar
701.5	Other abnormal granulation tissue
701.8	Other specified hypertrophic and atrophic condition of skin
701.9	Unspecified hypertrophic and atrophic condition of skin ▼
702.0	Actinic keratosis
702.11	Inflamed seborrheic keratosis
702.19	Other seborrheic keratosis
702.8	Other specified dermatoses
706.2	Sebaceous cyst
709.1	Vascular disorder of skin
709.2	Scar condition and fibrosis of skin
709.4	Foreign body granuloma of skin and subcutaneous tissue — (Use additional code to identify foreign body (V90.01-V90.9))
757.32	Congenital vascular hamartomas
757.33	Congenital pigmentary anomaly of skin
757.39	Other specified congenital anomaly of skin
782.2	Localized superficial swelling, mass, or lump
873.41	Open wound of cheek, without mention of complication
873.42	Open wound of forehead, without mention of complication
873.44	Open wound of jaw, without mention of complication
873.49	Open wound of face, other and multiple sites, without mention of complication
873.51	Open wound of cheek, complicated
873.52	Open wound of forehead, complicated
873.54	Open wound of jaw, complicated
873.59	Open wound of face, other and multiple sites, complicated
873.60	Open wound of mouth, unspecified site, without mention of complication ▼
873.61	Open wound of buccal mucosa, without mention of complication
873.69	Open wound of mouth, other and multiple sites, without mention of complication
873.70	Open wound of mouth, unspecified site, complicated ▼
873.71	Open wound of buccal mucosa, complicated
873.72	Open wound of gum (alveolar process), complicated
873.79	Open wound of mouth, other and multiple sites, complicated
878.0	Open wound of penis, without mention of complication ♂
878.1	Open wound of penis, complicated ♂
878.2	Open wound of scrotum and testes, without mention of complication ♂
878.3	Open wound of scrotum and testes, complicated ♂
878.4	Open wound of vulva, without mention of complication ♀
878.5	Open wound of vulva, complicated ♀
878.8	Open wound of other and unspecified parts of genital organs, without mention of complication ▼
878.9	Open wound of other and unspecified parts of genital organs, complicated ▼
880.02	Open wound of axillary region, without mention of complication
880.12	Open wound of axillary region, complicated
882.0	Open wound of hand except finger(s) alone, without mention of complication
882.1	Open wound of hand except finger(s) alone, complicated
883.0	Open wound of finger(s), without mention of complication
883.1	Open wound of finger(s), complicated
892.0	Open wound of foot except toe(s) alone, without mention of complication
892.1	Open wound of foot except toe(s) alone, complicated
893.0	Open wound of toe(s), without mention of complication
893.1	Open wound of toe(s), complicated

ICD-9-CM Procedural

27.52	Suture of laceration of other part of mouth
61.41	Suture of laceration of scrotum and tunica vaginalis ♂
64.41	Suture of laceration of penis ♂
71.71	Suture of laceration of vulva or perineum ♀
75.61	Repair of current obstetric laceration of bladder and urethra ♀
75.62	Repair of current obstetric laceration of rectum and sphincter ani ♀
75.69	Repair of other current obstetric laceration ♀
86.59	Closure of skin and subcutaneous tissue of other sites
86.89	Other repair and reconstruction of skin and subcutaneous tissue

HCPCS Level II Supplies & Services

A4305	Disposable drug delivery system, flow rate of 50 ml or greater per hour

13151-13153

13151	Repair, complex, eyelids, nose, ears and/or lips; 1.1 cm to 2.5 cm
13152	2.6 cm to 7.5 cm
13153	each additional 5 cm or less (List separately in addition to code for primary procedure)

ICD-9-CM Diagnostic

172.0	Malignant melanoma of skin of lip
172.1	Malignant melanoma of skin of eyelid, including canthus
172.2	Malignant melanoma of skin of ear and external auditory canal
172.3	Malignant melanoma of skin of other and unspecified parts of face ▼
172.8	Malignant melanoma of other specified sites of skin
173.00	Unspecified malignant neoplasm of skin of lip ▼

173.01	Basal cell carcinoma of skin of lip
173.02	Squamous cell carcinoma of skin of lip
173.09	Other specified malignant neoplasm of skin of lip
173.10	Unspecified malignant neoplasm of eyelid, including canthus ▽
173.11	Basal cell carcinoma of eyelid, including canthus
173.12	Squamous cell carcinoma of eyelid, including canthus
173.19	Other specified malignant neoplasm of eyelid, including canthus
173.20	Unspecified malignant neoplasm of skin of ear and external auditory canal ▽
173.21	Basal cell carcinoma of skin of ear and external auditory canal
173.22	Squamous cell carcinoma of skin of ear and external auditory canal
173.29	Other specified malignant neoplasm of skin of ear and external auditory canal
173.30	Unspecified malignant neoplasm of skin of other and unspecified parts of face ▽
173.31	Basal cell carcinoma of skin of other and unspecified parts of face
173.32	Squamous cell carcinoma of skin of other and unspecified parts of face
173.39	Other specified malignant neoplasm of skin of other and unspecified parts of face
173.80	Unspecified malignant neoplasm of other specified sites of skin ▽
173.81	Basal cell carcinoma of other specified sites of skin
173.82	Squamous cell carcinoma of other specified sites of skin
173.89	Other specified malignant neoplasm of other specified sites of skin
198.2	Secondary malignant neoplasm of skin
198.89	Secondary malignant neoplasm of other specified sites
209.31	Merkel cell carcinoma of the face
209.36	Merkel cell carcinoma of other sites
209.75	Secondary Merkel cell carcinoma
214.0	Lipoma of skin and subcutaneous tissue of face
214.1	Lipoma of other skin and subcutaneous tissue
216.0	Benign neoplasm of skin of lip
216.1	Benign neoplasm of eyelid, including canthus
216.2	Benign neoplasm of ear and external auditory canal
216.3	Benign neoplasm of skin of other and unspecified parts of face ▽
228.01	Hemangioma of skin and subcutaneous tissue
232.1	Carcinoma in situ of eyelid, including canthus
232.3	Carcinoma in situ of skin of other and unspecified parts of face ▽
238.2	Neoplasm of uncertain behavior of skin
239.2	Neoplasms of unspecified nature of bone, soft tissue, and skin
239.89	Neoplasms of unspecified nature, other specified sites
448.1	Nevus, non-neoplastic
686.1	Pyogenic granuloma of skin and subcutaneous tissue — (Use additional code to identify any infectious organism: 041.0-041.8)
701.1	Acquired keratoderma
701.4	Keloid scar
701.5	Other abnormal granulation tissue
701.8	Other specified hypertrophic and atrophic condition of skin
702.0	Actinic keratosis
702.11	Inflamed seborrheic keratosis
702.19	Other seborrheic keratosis
706.2	Sebaceous cyst
709.2	Scar condition and fibrosis of skin
709.4	Foreign body granuloma of skin and subcutaneous tissue — (Use additional code to identify foreign body (V90.01-V90.9))
757.32	Congenital vascular hamartomas
757.33	Congenital pigmentary anomaly of skin
757.39	Other specified congenital anomaly of skin
870.0	Laceration of skin of eyelid and periocular area
870.1	Laceration of eyelid, full-thickness, not involving lacrimal passages
870.8	Other specified open wound of ocular adnexa
872.00	Open wound of external ear, unspecified site, without mention of complication ▽
872.01	Open wound of auricle, without mention of complication
872.02	Open wound of auditory canal, without mention of complication
872.10	Open wound of external ear, unspecified site, complicated ▽
872.11	Open wound of auricle, complicated
872.12	Open wound of auditory canal, complicated
873.20	Open wound of nose, unspecified site, without mention of complication ▽
873.21	Open wound of nasal septum, without mention of complication
873.22	Open wound of nasal cavity, without mention of complication
873.29	Open wound of nose, multiple sites, without mention of complication
873.30	Open wound of nose, unspecified site, complicated ▽
873.31	Open wound of nasal septum, complicated
873.32	Open wound of nasal cavity, complicated
873.39	Open wound of nose, multiple sites, complicated
873.43	Open wound of lip, without mention of complication
873.49	Open wound of face, other and multiple sites, without mention of complication
873.53	Open wound of lip, complicated
873.59	Open wound of face, other and multiple sites, complicated
906.0	Late effect of open wound of head, neck, and trunk

ICD-9-CM Procedural

08.72	Other reconstruction of eyelid, partial-thickness
08.81	Linear repair of laceration of eyelid or eyebrow
08.83	Other repair of laceration of eyelid, partial-thickness
18.4	Suture of laceration of external ear
18.72	Reattachment of amputated ear
21.81	Suture of laceration of nose
27.51	Suture of laceration of lip
86.59	Closure of skin and subcutaneous tissue of other sites
86.89	Other repair and reconstruction of skin and subcutaneous tissue

HCPCS Level II Supplies & Services

A4305	Disposable drug delivery system, flow rate of 50 ml or greater per hour

13160

13160 Secondary closure of surgical wound or dehiscence, extensive or complicated

ICD-9-CM Diagnostic

674.10	Disruption of cesarean wound, unspecified as to episode of care ▽ ♀
674.12	Disruption of cesarean wound, with delivery, with mention of postpartum complication ♀
674.14	Disruption of cesarean wound, postpartum condition or complication ♀
674.20	Disruption of perineal wound, unspecified as to episode of care in pregnancy ▽ ♀
674.22	Disruption of perineal wound, with delivery, with mention of postpartum complication ♀
674.24	Disruption of perineal wound, postpartum condition or complication ♀
958.3	Posttraumatic wound infection not elsewhere classified
998.30	Disruption of wound, unspecified ▽
998.31	Disruption of internal operation (surgical) wound
998.32	Disruption of external operation (surgical) wound
998.83	Non-healing surgical wound
V58.41	Planned postoperative wound closure — (This code should be used in conjunction with other aftercare codes to fully identify the reason for the aftercare encounter)

ICD-9-CM Procedural

This code is too broad to adequately present ICD-9-CM procedural code links here. Refer to your ICD-9-CM Volume 3 in the appropriate anatomical site.

HCPCS Level II Supplies & Services

A4461	Surgical dressing holder, nonreusable, each
A4463	Surgical dressing holder, reusable, each

14000-14001

14000 Adjacent tissue transfer or rearrangement, trunk; defect 10 sq cm or less
14001 defect 10.1 sq cm to 30.0 sq cm

ICD-9-CM Diagnostic

172.5 Malignant melanoma of skin of trunk, except scrotum
173.50 Unspecified malignant neoplasm of skin of trunk, except scrotum ▽
173.51 Basal cell carcinoma of skin of trunk, except scrotum
173.52 Squamous cell carcinoma of skin of trunk, except scrotum
173.59 Other specified malignant neoplasm of skin of trunk, except scrotum
209.35 Merkel cell carcinoma of the trunk
209.75 Secondary Merkel cell carcinoma
216.5 Benign neoplasm of skin of trunk, except scrotum
228.01 Hemangioma of skin and subcutaneous tissue
232.5 Carcinoma in situ of skin of trunk, except scrotum
238.2 Neoplasm of uncertain behavior of skin
611.82 Hypoplasia of breast
701.4 Keloid scar
701.5 Other abnormal granulation tissue
706.2 Sebaceous cyst
707.00 Pressure ulcer, unspecified site — (Use additional code to identify pressure ulcer stage: 707.20-707.25) ▽
707.01 Pressure ulcer, elbow — (Use additional code to identify pressure ulcer stage: 707.20-707.25)
707.02 Pressure ulcer, upper back — (Use additional code to identify pressure ulcer stage: 707.20-707.25)
707.03 Pressure ulcer, lower back — (Use additional code to identify pressure ulcer stage: 707.20-707.25)
707.04 Pressure ulcer, hip — (Use additional code to identify pressure ulcer stage: 707.20-707.25)
707.05 Pressure ulcer, buttock — (Use additional code to identify pressure ulcer stage: 707.20-707.25)
707.09 Pressure ulcer, other site — (Use additional code to identify pressure ulcer stage: 707.20-707.25)
707.20 Pressure ulcer, unspecified stage — (Code first site of pressure ulcer: 707.00-707.09) ▽
707.21 Pressure ulcer, stage I — (Code first site of pressure ulcer: 707.00-707.09)
707.22 Pressure ulcer stage II — (Code first site of pressure ulcer: 707.00-707.09)
707.23 Pressure ulcer stage III — (Code first site of pressure ulcer: 707.00-707.09)
707.24 Pressure ulcer stage IV — (Code first site of pressure ulcer: 707.00-707.09)
707.25 Pressure ulcer, unstageable — (Code first site of pressure ulcer: 707.00-707.09)
707.8 Chronic ulcer of other specified site
709.2 Scar condition and fibrosis of skin
757.32 Congenital vascular hamartomas
757.6 Specified congenital anomalies of breast
757.8 Other specified congenital anomalies of the integument
757.9 Unspecified congenital anomaly of the integument ▽
875.0 Open wound of chest (wall), without mention of complication
875.1 Open wound of chest (wall), complicated
876.0 Open wound of back, without mention of complication
876.1 Open wound of back, complicated
877.0 Open wound of buttock, without mention of complication
877.1 Open wound of buttock, complicated
879.0 Open wound of breast, without mention of complication
879.1 Open wound of breast, complicated
879.2 Open wound of abdominal wall, anterior, without mention of complication
879.3 Open wound of abdominal wall, anterior, complicated
879.4 Open wound of abdominal wall, lateral, without mention of complication
879.5 Open wound of abdominal wall, lateral, complicated
879.6 Open wound of other and unspecified parts of trunk, without mention of complication ▽
879.7 Open wound of other and unspecified parts of trunk, complicated ▽
879.8 Open wound(s) (multiple) of unspecified site(s), without mention of complication ▽
879.9 Open wound(s) (multiple) of unspecified site(s), complicated ▽
906.0 Late effect of open wound of head, neck, and trunk
906.8 Late effect of burns of other specified sites
909.3 Late effect of complications of surgical and medical care
942.00 Burn of unspecified degree of trunk, unspecified site ▽
942.01 Burn of trunk, unspecified degree of breast ▽
942.02 Burn of trunk, unspecified degree of chest wall, excluding breast and nipple ▽
942.04 Burn of trunk, unspecified degree of back (any part) ▽
942.09 Burn of trunk, unspecified degree of other and multiple sites ▽
942.23 Blisters with epidermal loss due to burn (second degree) of abdominal wall
942.30 Full-thickness skin loss due to burn (third degree NOS) of unspecified site of trunk ▽
942.31 Full-thickness skin loss due to burn (third degree NOS) of breast
942.32 Full-thickness skin loss due to burn (third degree NOS) of chest wall, excluding breast and nipple
942.34 Full-thickness skin loss due to burn (third degree NOS) of back (any part)
942.39 Full-thickness skin loss due to burn (third degree NOS) of other and multiple sites of trunk
942.40 Deep necrosis of underlying tissues due to burn (deep third degree) of trunk, unspecified site, without mention of loss of a body part ▽
942.41 Deep necrosis of underlying tissues due to burn (deep third degree) of breast, without mention of loss of a body part
942.42 Deep necrosis of underlying tissues due to burn (deep third degree) of chest wall, excluding breast and nipple, without mention of loss of a body part
942.43 Deep necrosis of underlying tissues due to burn (deep third degree) of abdominal wall, without mention of loss of a body part
942.44 Deep necrosis of underlying tissues due to burn (deep third degree) of back (any part), without mention of loss of a body part
942.49 Deep necrosis of underlying tissues due to burn (deep third degree) of other and multiple sites of trunk, without mention of loss of a body part
998.30 Disruption of wound, unspecified ▽
998.32 Disruption of external operation (surgical) wound
998.33 Disruption of traumatic injury wound repair
V50.1 Other plastic surgery for unacceptable cosmetic appearance
V51.8 Other aftercare involving the use of plastic surgery

ICD-9-CM Procedural

85.89 Other mammoplasty
86.3 Other local excision or destruction of lesion or tissue of skin and subcutaneous tissue
86.70 Pedicle or flap graft, not otherwise specified
86.71 Cutting and preparation of pedicle grafts or flaps
86.72 Advancement of pedicle graft
86.74 Attachment of pedicle or flap graft to other sites
86.84 Relaxation of scar or web contracture of skin
86.89 Other repair and reconstruction of skin and subcutaneous tissue

HCPCS Level II Supplies & Services

A4461 Surgical dressing holder, nonreusable, each
A4463 Surgical dressing holder, reusable, each

14020-14021

14020 Adjacent tissue transfer or rearrangement, scalp, arms and/or legs; defect 10 sq cm or less
14021 defect 10.1 sq cm to 30.0 sq cm

ICD-9-CM Diagnostic

172.4 Malignant melanoma of skin of scalp and neck
172.6 Malignant melanoma of skin of upper limb, including shoulder

172.7 Malignant melanoma of skin of lower limb, including hip
173.40 Unspecified malignant neoplasm of scalp and skin of neck ▽
173.41 Basal cell carcinoma of scalp and skin of neck
173.42 Squamous cell carcinoma of scalp and skin of neck
173.49 Other specified malignant neoplasm of scalp and skin of neck
173.60 Unspecified malignant neoplasm of skin of upper limb, including shoulder ▽
173.61 Basal cell carcinoma of skin of upper limb, including shoulder
173.62 Squamous cell carcinoma of skin of upper limb, including shoulder
173.69 Other specified malignant neoplasm of skin of upper limb, including shoulder
173.70 Unspecified malignant neoplasm of skin of lower limb, including hip ▽
173.71 Basal cell carcinoma of skin of lower limb, including hip
173.72 Squamous cell carcinoma of skin of lower limb, including hip
173.79 Other specified malignant neoplasm of skin of lower limb, including hip
195.0 Malignant neoplasm of head, face, and neck
209.32 Merkel cell carcinoma of the scalp and neck
209.33 Merkel cell carcinoma of the upper limb
209.34 Merkel cell carcinoma of the lower limb
209.75 Secondary Merkel cell carcinoma
214.8 Lipoma of other specified sites
216.4 Benign neoplasm of scalp and skin of neck
216.6 Benign neoplasm of skin of upper limb, including shoulder
216.7 Benign neoplasm of skin of lower limb, including hip
216.8 Benign neoplasm of other specified sites of skin
232.6 Carcinoma in situ of skin of upper limb, including shoulder
238.2 Neoplasm of uncertain behavior of skin
239.2 Neoplasms of unspecified nature of bone, soft tissue, and skin
701.4 Keloid scar
701.9 Unspecified hypertrophic and atrophic condition of skin ▽
706.2 Sebaceous cyst
707.01 Pressure ulcer, elbow — (Use additional code to identify pressure ulcer stage: 707.20-707.25)
707.09 Pressure ulcer, other site — (Use additional code to identify pressure ulcer stage: 707.20-707.25)
707.10 Ulcer of lower limb, unspecified — (Code, if applicable, any causal condition first: 249.80-249.81, 250.80-250.83, 440.23, 459.11, 459.13, 459.31, 459.33) ▽
707.11 Ulcer of thigh — (Code, if applicable, any causal condition first: 249.80-249.81, 250.80-250.83, 440.23, 459.11, 459.13, 459.31, 459.33)
707.12 Ulcer of calf — (Code, if applicable, any causal condition first: 249.80-249.81, 250.80-250.83, 440.23, 459.11, 459.13, 459.31, 459.33)
707.13 Ulcer of ankle — (Code, if applicable, any causal condition first: 249.80-249.81, 250.80-250.83, 440.23, 459.11, 459.13, 459.31, 459.33)
707.19 Ulcer of other part of lower limb — (Code, if applicable, any causal condition first: 249.80-249.81, 250.80-250.83, 440.23, 459.11, 459.13, 459.31, 459.33)
707.20 Pressure ulcer, unspecified stage — (Code first site of pressure ulcer: 707.00-707.09) ▽
707.21 Pressure ulcer, stage I — (Code first site of pressure ulcer: 707.00-707.09)
707.22 Pressure ulcer stage II — (Code first site of pressure ulcer: 707.00-707.09)
707.23 Pressure ulcer stage III — (Code first site of pressure ulcer: 707.00-707.09)
707.24 Pressure ulcer stage IV — (Code first site of pressure ulcer: 707.00-707.09)
707.25 Pressure ulcer, unstageable — (Code first site of pressure ulcer: 707.00-707.09)
709.2 Scar condition and fibrosis of skin
709.4 Foreign body granuloma of skin and subcutaneous tissue — (Use additional code to identify foreign body (V90.01-V90.9))
709.9 Unspecified disorder of skin and subcutaneous tissue ▽
757.32 Congenital vascular hamartomas
757.33 Congenital pigmentary anomaly of skin
757.39 Other specified congenital anomaly of skin
757.8 Other specified congenital anomalies of the integument
785.4 Gangrene — (Code first any associated underlying condition)
873.0 Open wound of scalp, without mention of complication
873.1 Open wound of scalp, complicated
880.03 Open wound of upper arm, without mention of complication
880.09 Open wound of multiple sites of shoulder and upper arm, without mention of complication
880.13 Open wound of upper arm, complicated
880.19 Open wound of multiple sites of shoulder and upper arm, complicated
881.00 Open wound of forearm, without mention of complication
881.01 Open wound of elbow, without mention of complication
881.02 Open wound of wrist, without mention of complication
881.10 Open wound of forearm, complicated
881.11 Open wound of elbow, complicated
881.12 Open wound of wrist, complicated
884.0 Multiple and unspecified open wound of upper limb, without mention of complication
884.1 Multiple and unspecified open wound of upper limb, complicated
887.0 Traumatic amputation of arm and hand (complete) (partial), unilateral, below elbow, without mention of complication
887.1 Traumatic amputation of arm and hand (complete) (partial), unilateral, below elbow, complicated
887.2 Traumatic amputation of arm and hand (complete) (partial), unilateral, at or above elbow, without mention of complication
887.3 Traumatic amputation of arm and hand (complete) (partial), unilateral, at or above elbow, complicated
887.4 Traumatic amputation of arm and hand (complete) (partial), unilateral, level not specified, without mention of complication ▽
887.5 Traumatic amputation of arm and hand (complete) (partial), unilateral, level not specified, complicated ▽
887.6 Traumatic amputation of arm and hand (complete) (partial), bilateral (any level), without mention of complication
887.7 Traumatic amputation of arm and hand (complete) (partial), bilateral (any level), complicated
890.0 Open wound of hip and thigh, without mention of complication
890.1 Open wound of hip and thigh, complicated
891.0 Open wound of knee, leg (except thigh), and ankle, without mention of complication
891.1 Open wound of knee, leg (except thigh), and ankle, complicated
894.0 Multiple and unspecified open wound of lower limb, without mention of complication
894.1 Multiple and unspecified open wound of lower limb, complicated
897.0 Traumatic amputation of leg(s) (complete) (partial), unilateral, below knee, without mention of complication
897.1 Traumatic amputation of leg(s) (complete) (partial), unilateral, below knee, complicated
897.2 Traumatic amputation of leg(s) (complete) (partial), unilateral, at or above knee, without mention of complication
897.3 Traumatic amputation of leg(s) (complete) (partial), unilateral, at or above knee, complicated
897.4 Traumatic amputation of leg(s) (complete) (partial), unilateral, level not specified, without mention of complication ▽
897.5 Traumatic amputation of leg(s) (complete) (partial), unilateral, level not specified, complicated ▽
897.6 Traumatic amputation of leg(s) (complete) (partial), bilateral (any level), without mention of complication
897.7 Traumatic amputation of leg(s) (complete) (partial), bilateral (any level), complicated
906.0 Late effect of open wound of head, neck, and trunk
906.1 Late effect of open wound of extremities without mention of tendon injury
906.5 Late effect of burn of eye, face, head, and neck
906.6 Late effect of burn of wrist and hand
906.7 Late effect of burn of other extremities
909.3 Late effect of complications of surgical and medical care
V50.1 Other plastic surgery for unacceptable cosmetic appearance
V51.8 Other aftercare involving the use of plastic surgery

ICD-9-CM Procedural

86.3 Other local excision or destruction of lesion or tissue of skin and subcutaneous tissue

86.70 Pedicle or flap graft, not otherwise specified
86.71 Cutting and preparation of pedicle grafts or flaps
86.72 Advancement of pedicle graft
86.74 Attachment of pedicle or flap graft to other sites
86.84 Relaxation of scar or web contracture of skin
86.89 Other repair and reconstruction of skin and subcutaneous tissue

HCPCS Level II Supplies & Services

A4305 Disposable drug delivery system, flow rate of 50 ml or greater per hour

14040-14041

14040 Adjacent tissue transfer or rearrangement, forehead, cheeks, chin, mouth, neck, axillae, genitalia, hands and/or feet; defect 10 sq cm or less
14041 defect 10.1 sq cm to 30.0 sq cm

ICD-9-CM Diagnostic

171.0 Malignant neoplasm of connective and other soft tissue of head, face, and neck
171.2 Malignant neoplasm of connective and other soft tissue of upper limb, including shoulder
171.3 Malignant neoplasm of connective and other soft tissue of lower limb, including hip
171.8 Malignant neoplasm of other specified sites of connective and other soft tissue
172.0 Malignant melanoma of skin of lip
172.3 Malignant melanoma of skin of other and unspecified parts of face ▽
172.4 Malignant melanoma of skin of scalp and neck
172.5 Malignant melanoma of skin of trunk, except scrotum
172.6 Malignant melanoma of skin of upper limb, including shoulder
172.7 Malignant melanoma of skin of lower limb, including hip
173.30 Unspecified malignant neoplasm of skin of other and unspecified parts of face ▽
173.31 Basal cell carcinoma of skin of other and unspecified parts of face
173.32 Squamous cell carcinoma of skin of other and unspecified parts of face
173.39 Other specified malignant neoplasm of skin of other and unspecified parts of face
173.40 Unspecified malignant neoplasm of scalp and skin of neck ▽
173.41 Basal cell carcinoma of scalp and skin of neck
173.42 Squamous cell carcinoma of scalp and skin of neck
173.49 Other specified malignant neoplasm of scalp and skin of neck
173.50 Unspecified malignant neoplasm of skin of trunk, except scrotum ▽
173.51 Basal cell carcinoma of skin of trunk, except scrotum
173.52 Squamous cell carcinoma of skin of trunk, except scrotum
173.59 Other specified malignant neoplasm of skin of trunk, except scrotum
173.60 Unspecified malignant neoplasm of skin of upper limb, including shoulder ▽
173.61 Basal cell carcinoma of skin of upper limb, including shoulder
173.62 Squamous cell carcinoma of skin of upper limb, including shoulder
173.69 Other specified malignant neoplasm of skin of upper limb, including shoulder
173.70 Unspecified malignant neoplasm of skin of lower limb, including hip ▽
173.71 Basal cell carcinoma of skin of lower limb, including hip
173.72 Squamous cell carcinoma of skin of lower limb, including hip
173.79 Other specified malignant neoplasm of skin of lower limb, including hip
173.80 Unspecified malignant neoplasm of other specified sites of skin ▽
173.81 Basal cell carcinoma of other specified sites of skin
173.82 Squamous cell carcinoma of other specified sites of skin
173.89 Other specified malignant neoplasm of other specified sites of skin
184.0 Malignant neoplasm of vagina ♀
184.1 Malignant neoplasm of labia majora ♀
184.2 Malignant neoplasm of labia minora ♀
184.3 Malignant neoplasm of clitoris ♀
184.4 Malignant neoplasm of vulva, unspecified site ▽ ♀
184.8 Malignant neoplasm of other specified sites of female genital organs ♀
184.9 Malignant neoplasm of female genital organ, site unspecified ▽ ♀
187.1 Malignant neoplasm of prepuce ♂
187.3 Malignant neoplasm of body of penis ♂
187.4 Malignant neoplasm of penis, part unspecified ▽ ♂
187.7 Malignant neoplasm of scrotum ♂
187.8 Malignant neoplasm of other specified sites of male genital organs ♂
195.0 Malignant neoplasm of head, face, and neck
195.1 Malignant neoplasm of thorax
195.3 Malignant neoplasm of pelvis
195.4 Malignant neoplasm of upper limb
195.5 Malignant neoplasm of lower limb
195.8 Malignant neoplasm of other specified sites
198.2 Secondary malignant neoplasm of skin
198.89 Secondary malignant neoplasm of other specified sites
209.31 Merkel cell carcinoma of the face
209.33 Merkel cell carcinoma of the upper limb
209.34 Merkel cell carcinoma of the lower limb
209.35 Merkel cell carcinoma of the trunk
209.36 Merkel cell carcinoma of other sites
209.75 Secondary Merkel cell carcinoma
214.0 Lipoma of skin and subcutaneous tissue of face
214.1 Lipoma of other skin and subcutaneous tissue
215.0 Other benign neoplasm of connective and other soft tissue of head, face, and neck
215.2 Other benign neoplasm of connective and other soft tissue of upper limb, including shoulder
215.3 Other benign neoplasm of connective and other soft tissue of lower limb, including hip
215.6 Other benign neoplasm of connective and other soft tissue of pelvis
215.8 Other benign neoplasm of connective and other soft tissue of other specified sites
216.3 Benign neoplasm of skin of other and unspecified parts of face ▽
216.4 Benign neoplasm of scalp and skin of neck
216.5 Benign neoplasm of skin of trunk, except scrotum
216.8 Benign neoplasm of other specified sites of skin
228.01 Hemangioma of skin and subcutaneous tissue
229.8 Benign neoplasm of other specified sites
232.3 Carcinoma in situ of skin of other and unspecified parts of face ▽
232.4 Carcinoma in situ of scalp and skin of neck
232.5 Carcinoma in situ of skin of trunk, except scrotum
232.8 Carcinoma in situ of other specified sites of skin
234.8 Carcinoma in situ of other specified sites
238.2 Neoplasm of uncertain behavior of skin
238.8 Neoplasm of uncertain behavior of other specified sites
239.2 Neoplasms of unspecified nature of bone, soft tissue, and skin
239.89 Neoplasms of unspecified nature, other specified sites
629.20 Female genital mutilation status, unspecified ▽ ♀
629.21 Female genital mutilation, Type I status ♀
629.22 Female genital mutilation, Type II status ♀
629.23 Female genital mutilation, Type III status ♀
629.29 Other female genital mutilation status ♀
629.89 Other specified disorders of female genital organs ♀
701.4 Keloid scar
701.5 Other abnormal granulation tissue
707.8 Chronic ulcer of other specified site
709.2 Scar condition and fibrosis of skin
709.4 Foreign body granuloma of skin and subcutaneous tissue — (Use additional code to identify foreign body (V90.01-V90.9))
757.32 Congenital vascular hamartomas
757.39 Other specified congenital anomaly of skin
873.40 Open wound of face, unspecified site, without mention of complication ▽
873.41 Open wound of cheek, without mention of complication

873.42 Open wound of forehead, without mention of complication
873.43 Open wound of lip, without mention of complication
873.44 Open wound of jaw, without mention of complication
873.49 Open wound of face, other and multiple sites, without mention of complication
873.50 Open wound of face, unspecified site, complicated
873.51 Open wound of cheek, complicated
873.52 Open wound of forehead, complicated
873.53 Open wound of lip, complicated
873.54 Open wound of jaw, complicated
873.59 Open wound of face, other and multiple sites, complicated
873.70 Open wound of mouth, unspecified site, complicated
873.71 Open wound of buccal mucosa, complicated
873.74 Open wound of tongue and floor of mouth, complicated
873.79 Open wound of mouth, other and multiple sites, complicated
878.0 Open wound of penis, without mention of complication ♂
878.1 Open wound of penis, complicated ♂
878.2 Open wound of scrotum and testes, without mention of complication ♂
878.3 Open wound of scrotum and testes, complicated ♂
878.4 Open wound of vulva, without mention of complication ♀
878.5 Open wound of vulva, complicated ♀
878.6 Open wound of vagina, without mention of complication ♀
878.7 Open wound of vagina, complicated ♀
878.8 Open wound of other and unspecified parts of genital organs, without mention of complication
878.9 Open wound of other and unspecified parts of genital organs, complicated
880.02 Open wound of axillary region, without mention of complication
880.12 Open wound of axillary region, complicated
882.0 Open wound of hand except finger(s) alone, without mention of complication
882.1 Open wound of hand except finger(s) alone, complicated
883.0 Open wound of finger(s), without mention of complication
883.1 Open wound of finger(s), complicated
884.0 Multiple and unspecified open wound of upper limb, without mention of complication
884.1 Multiple and unspecified open wound of upper limb, complicated
892.0 Open wound of foot except toe(s) alone, without mention of complication
892.1 Open wound of foot except toe(s) alone, complicated
893.0 Open wound of toe(s), without mention of complication
893.1 Open wound of toe(s), complicated
894.0 Multiple and unspecified open wound of lower limb, without mention of complication
894.1 Multiple and unspecified open wound of lower limb, complicated
906.0 Late effect of open wound of head, neck, and trunk
906.1 Late effect of open wound of extremities without mention of tendon injury
906.5 Late effect of burn of eye, face, head, and neck
906.6 Late effect of burn of wrist and hand
906.7 Late effect of burn of other extremities
906.8 Late effect of burns of other specified sites
941.03 Burn of unspecified degree of lip(s)
941.07 Burn of unspecified degree of forehead and cheek
959.09 Injury of face and neck, other and unspecified
959.14 Other injury of external genitals
959.2 Injury, other and unspecified, shoulder and upper arm
959.3 Injury, other and unspecified, elbow, forearm, and wrist
959.4 Injury, other and unspecified, hand, except finger
959.7 Injury, other and unspecified, knee, leg, ankle, and foot
959.8 Injury, other and unspecified, other specified sites, including multiple
996.92 Complications of reattached hand
996.93 Complications of reattached finger(s)
996.95 Complications of reattached foot and toe(s)
997.60 Late complications of amputation stump, unspecified — (Use additional code to identify complications)
997.61 Neuroma of amputation stump — (Use additional code to identify complications)
997.62 Infection (chronic) of amputation stump — (Use additional code to identify complications)
997.69 Other late amputation stump complication — (Use additional code to identify complications)
998.30 Disruption of wound, unspecified
998.32 Disruption of external operation (surgical) wound
998.33 Disruption of traumatic injury wound repair
998.59 Other postoperative infection — (Use additional code to identify infection)
998.83 Non-healing surgical wound
V50.1 Other plastic surgery for unacceptable cosmetic appearance
V51.8 Other aftercare involving the use of plastic surgery

ICD-9-CM Procedural

27.57 Attachment of pedicle or flap graft to lip and mouth
86.3 Other local excision or destruction of lesion or tissue of skin and subcutaneous tissue
86.70 Pedicle or flap graft, not otherwise specified
86.71 Cutting and preparation of pedicle grafts or flaps
86.72 Advancement of pedicle graft
86.73 Attachment of pedicle or flap graft to hand
86.74 Attachment of pedicle or flap graft to other sites
86.84 Relaxation of scar or web contracture of skin
86.89 Other repair and reconstruction of skin and subcutaneous tissue

HCPCS Level II Supplies & Services

A4305 Disposable drug delivery system, flow rate of 50 ml or greater per hour

14060-14061

14060 Adjacent tissue transfer or rearrangement, eyelids, nose, ears and/or lips; defect 10 sq cm or less
14061 defect 10.1 sq cm to 30.0 sq cm

ICD-9-CM Diagnostic

030.0 Lepromatous leprosy (type L)
030.1 Tuberculoid leprosy (type T)
030.2 Indeterminate leprosy (group I)
030.3 Borderline leprosy (group B)
030.8 Other specified leprosy
030.9 Unspecified leprosy
102.0 Initial lesions of yaws
102.1 Multiple papillomata and wet crab yaws due to yaws
102.2 Other early skin lesions due to yaws
102.3 Hyperkeratosis due to yaws
102.4 Gummata and ulcers due to yaws
102.5 Gangosa due to yaws
102.6 Bone and joint lesions due to yaws
102.7 Other manifestations due to yaws
102.8 Latent yaws
102.9 Unspecified yaws
171.0 Malignant neoplasm of connective and other soft tissue of head, face, and neck
172.0 Malignant melanoma of skin of lip
172.1 Malignant melanoma of skin of eyelid, including canthus
172.2 Malignant melanoma of skin of ear and external auditory canal
172.3 Malignant melanoma of skin of other and unspecified parts of face
173.00 Unspecified malignant neoplasm of skin of lip
173.01 Basal cell carcinoma of skin of lip
173.02 Squamous cell carcinoma of skin of lip
173.09 Other specified malignant neoplasm of skin of lip
173.10 Unspecified malignant neoplasm of eyelid, including canthus

173.11 Basal cell carcinoma of eyelid, including canthus
173.12 Squamous cell carcinoma of eyelid, including canthus
173.19 Other specified malignant neoplasm of eyelid, including canthus
173.20 Unspecified malignant neoplasm of skin of ear and external auditory canal ▽
173.21 Basal cell carcinoma of skin of ear and external auditory canal
173.22 Squamous cell carcinoma of skin of ear and external auditory canal
173.29 Other specified malignant neoplasm of skin of ear and external auditory canal
173.30 Unspecified malignant neoplasm of skin of other and unspecified parts of face ▽
173.31 Basal cell carcinoma of skin of other and unspecified parts of face
173.32 Squamous cell carcinoma of skin of other and unspecified parts of face
173.39 Other specified malignant neoplasm of skin of other and unspecified parts of face
173.80 Unspecified malignant neoplasm of other specified sites of skin ▽
173.81 Basal cell carcinoma of other specified sites of skin
173.82 Squamous cell carcinoma of other specified sites of skin
173.89 Other specified malignant neoplasm of other specified sites of skin
195.0 Malignant neoplasm of head, face, and neck
198.2 Secondary malignant neoplasm of skin
209.31 Merkel cell carcinoma of the face
209.36 Merkel cell carcinoma of other sites
209.75 Secondary Merkel cell carcinoma
210.0 Benign neoplasm of lip
214.0 Lipoma of skin and subcutaneous tissue of face
214.1 Lipoma of other skin and subcutaneous tissue
215.0 Other benign neoplasm of connective and other soft tissue of head, face, and neck
216.0 Benign neoplasm of skin of lip
216.1 Benign neoplasm of eyelid, including canthus
216.2 Benign neoplasm of ear and external auditory canal
216.3 Benign neoplasm of skin of other and unspecified parts of face ▽
228.01 Hemangioma of skin and subcutaneous tissue
230.0 Carcinoma in situ of lip, oral cavity, and pharynx
231.8 Carcinoma in situ of other specified parts of respiratory system
232.0 Carcinoma in situ of skin of lip
232.1 Carcinoma in situ of eyelid, including canthus
232.2 Carcinoma in situ of skin of ear and external auditory canal
232.3 Carcinoma in situ of skin of other and unspecified parts of face ▽
235.1 Neoplasm of uncertain behavior of lip, oral cavity, and pharynx
238.2 Neoplasm of uncertain behavior of skin
239.2 Neoplasms of unspecified nature of bone, soft tissue, and skin
373.4 Infective dermatitis of eyelid of types resulting in deformity — (Code first underlying disease: 017.0, 030.0-030.9, 102.0-102.9) ☒
374.50 Unspecified degenerative disorder of eyelid ▽
374.84 Cysts of eyelids
374.86 Retained foreign body of eyelid — (Use additional code to identify foreign body (V90.01-V90.9))
374.89 Other disorders of eyelid
701.4 Keloid scar
701.9 Unspecified hypertrophic and atrophic condition of skin ▽
707.8 Chronic ulcer of other specified site
709.2 Scar condition and fibrosis of skin
709.4 Foreign body granuloma of skin and subcutaneous tissue — (Use additional code to identify foreign body (V90.01-V90.9))
743.62 Congenital deformity of eyelid
744.21 Congenital absence of ear lobe
744.23 Microtia
749.10 Unspecified cleft lip ▽
749.11 Unilateral cleft lip, complete
749.12 Unilateral cleft lip, incomplete
749.13 Bilateral cleft lip, complete
749.14 Bilateral cleft lip, incomplete
757.32 Congenital vascular hamartomas
757.39 Other specified congenital anomaly of skin
870.0 Laceration of skin of eyelid and periocular area
870.1 Laceration of eyelid, full-thickness, not involving lacrimal passages
870.2 Laceration of eyelid involving lacrimal passages
870.8 Other specified open wound of ocular adnexa
872.00 Open wound of external ear, unspecified site, without mention of complication ▽
872.01 Open wound of auricle, without mention of complication
872.10 Open wound of external ear, unspecified site, complicated ▽
872.11 Open wound of auricle, complicated
872.8 Open wound of ear, part unspecified, without mention of complication ▽
873.20 Open wound of nose, unspecified site, without mention of complication ▽
873.30 Open wound of nose, unspecified site, complicated ▽
873.43 Open wound of lip, without mention of complication
873.53 Open wound of lip, complicated
906.0 Late effect of open wound of head, neck, and trunk
906.2 Late effect of superficial injury
906.5 Late effect of burn of eye, face, head, and neck
941.09 Burn of unspecified degree of multiple sites (except with eye) of face, head, and neck ▽
959.09 Injury of face and neck, other and unspecified
998.30 Disruption of wound, unspecified ▽
998.32 Disruption of external operation (surgical) wound
998.33 Disruption of traumatic injury wound repair
998.59 Other postoperative infection — (Use additional code to identify infection)
998.83 Non-healing surgical wound
998.89 Other specified complications
V10.02 Personal history of malignant neoplasm of other and unspecified parts of oral cavity and pharynx ▽
V10.82 Personal history of malignant melanoma of skin
V10.83 Personal history of other malignant neoplasm of skin
V50.1 Other plastic surgery for unacceptable cosmetic appearance
V51.8 Other aftercare involving the use of plastic surgery

ICD-9-CM Procedural

08.62 Reconstruction of eyelid with mucous membrane flap or graft
08.63 Reconstruction of eyelid with hair follicle graft
08.70 Reconstruction of eyelid, not otherwise specified
18.72 Reattachment of amputated ear
18.79 Other plastic repair of external ear
27.56 Other skin graft to lip and mouth
27.57 Attachment of pedicle or flap graft to lip and mouth
86.3 Other local excision or destruction of lesion or tissue of skin and subcutaneous tissue
86.70 Pedicle or flap graft, not otherwise specified
86.71 Cutting and preparation of pedicle grafts or flaps
86.72 Advancement of pedicle graft
86.74 Attachment of pedicle or flap graft to other sites
86.84 Relaxation of scar or web contracture of skin
86.89 Other repair and reconstruction of skin and subcutaneous tissue

HCPCS Level II Supplies & Services

A4305 Disposable drug delivery system, flow rate of 50 ml or greater per hour

14301-14302

14301 Adjacent tissue transfer or rearrangement, any area; defect 30.1 sq cm to 60.0 sq cm
14302 each additional 30.0 sq cm, or part thereof (List separately in addition to code for primary procedure)

ICD-9-CM Diagnostic

140.0 Malignant neoplasm of upper lip, vermilion border
140.1 Malignant neoplasm of lower lip, vermilion border

140.3 Malignant neoplasm of upper lip, inner aspect

140.4 Malignant neoplasm of lower lip, inner aspect

140.5 Malignant neoplasm of lip, inner aspect, unspecified as to upper or lower ▽

140.6 Malignant neoplasm of commissure of lip

140.8 Malignant neoplasm of other sites of lip

140.9 Malignant neoplasm of lip, vermilion border, unspecified as to upper or lower ▽

171.0 Malignant neoplasm of connective and other soft tissue of head, face, and neck

172.0 Malignant melanoma of skin of lip

172.1 Malignant melanoma of skin of eyelid, including canthus

172.2 Malignant melanoma of skin of ear and external auditory canal

172.3 Malignant melanoma of skin of other and unspecified parts of face ▽

172.4 Malignant melanoma of skin of scalp and neck

172.5 Malignant melanoma of skin of trunk, except scrotum

172.6 Malignant melanoma of skin of upper limb, including shoulder

172.7 Malignant melanoma of skin of lower limb, including hip

172.8 Malignant melanoma of other specified sites of skin

173.00 Unspecified malignant neoplasm of skin of lip ▽

173.01 Basal cell carcinoma of skin of lip

173.02 Squamous cell carcinoma of skin of lip

173.09 Other specified malignant neoplasm of skin of lip

173.10 Unspecified malignant neoplasm of eyelid, including canthus ▽

173.11 Basal cell carcinoma of eyelid, including canthus

173.12 Squamous cell carcinoma of eyelid, including canthus

173.19 Other specified malignant neoplasm of eyelid, including canthus

173.20 Unspecified malignant neoplasm of skin of ear and external auditory canal ▽

173.21 Basal cell carcinoma of skin of ear and external auditory canal

173.22 Squamous cell carcinoma of skin of ear and external auditory canal

173.29 Other specified malignant neoplasm of skin of ear and external auditory canal

173.30 Unspecified malignant neoplasm of skin of other and unspecified parts of face ▽

173.31 Basal cell carcinoma of skin of other and unspecified parts of face

173.32 Squamous cell carcinoma of skin of other and unspecified parts of face

173.39 Other specified malignant neoplasm of skin of other and unspecified parts of face

173.40 Unspecified malignant neoplasm of scalp and skin of neck ▽

173.41 Basal cell carcinoma of scalp and skin of neck

173.42 Squamous cell carcinoma of scalp and skin of neck

173.49 Other specified malignant neoplasm of scalp and skin of neck

173.50 Unspecified malignant neoplasm of skin of trunk, except scrotum ▽

173.51 Basal cell carcinoma of skin of trunk, except scrotum

173.52 Squamous cell carcinoma of skin of trunk, except scrotum

173.59 Other specified malignant neoplasm of skin of trunk, except scrotum

173.60 Unspecified malignant neoplasm of skin of upper limb, including shoulder ▽

173.61 Basal cell carcinoma of skin of upper limb, including shoulder

173.62 Squamous cell carcinoma of skin of upper limb, including shoulder

173.69 Other specified malignant neoplasm of skin of upper limb, including shoulder

173.70 Unspecified malignant neoplasm of skin of lower limb, including hip ▽

173.71 Basal cell carcinoma of skin of lower limb, including hip

173.72 Squamous cell carcinoma of skin of lower limb, including hip

173.79 Other specified malignant neoplasm of skin of lower limb, including hip

173.80 Unspecified malignant neoplasm of other specified sites of skin ▽

173.81 Basal cell carcinoma of other specified sites of skin

173.82 Squamous cell carcinoma of other specified sites of skin

173.89 Other specified malignant neoplasm of other specified sites of skin

174.0 Malignant neoplasm of nipple and areola of female breast — (Use additional code to identify estrogen receptor status: V86.0-V86.1) ♀

174.1 Malignant neoplasm of central portion of female breast — (Use additional code to identify estrogen receptor status: V86.0-V86.1) ♀

174.2 Malignant neoplasm of upper-inner quadrant of female breast — (Use additional code to identify estrogen receptor status: V86.0-V86.1) ♀

174.3 Malignant neoplasm of lower-inner quadrant of female breast — (Use additional code to identify estrogen receptor status: V86.0-V86.1) ♀

174.4 Malignant neoplasm of upper-outer quadrant of female breast — (Use additional code to identify estrogen receptor status: V86.0-V86.1) ♀

174.5 Malignant neoplasm of lower-outer quadrant of female breast — (Use additional code to identify estrogen receptor status: V86.0-V86.1) ♀

174.6 Malignant neoplasm of axillary tail of female breast — (Use additional code to identify estrogen receptor status: V86.0-V86.1) ♀

174.8 Malignant neoplasm of other specified sites of female breast — (Use additional code to identify estrogen receptor status: V86.0-V86.1) ♀

175.0 Malignant neoplasm of nipple and areola of male breast — (Use additional code to identify estrogen receptor status: V86.0-V86.1) ♂

175.9 Malignant neoplasm of other and unspecified sites of male breast — (Use additional code to identify estrogen receptor status: V86.0-V86.1) ▽ ♂

176.0 Kaposi's sarcoma of skin

184.9 Malignant neoplasm of female genital organ, site unspecified ▽ ♀

187.8 Malignant neoplasm of other specified sites of male genital organs ♂

195.0 Malignant neoplasm of head, face, and neck

195.1 Malignant neoplasm of thorax

195.2 Malignant neoplasm of abdomen

195.3 Malignant neoplasm of pelvis

195.4 Malignant neoplasm of upper limb

195.5 Malignant neoplasm of lower limb

195.8 Malignant neoplasm of other specified sites

198.2 Secondary malignant neoplasm of skin

209.31 Merkel cell carcinoma of the face

209.32 Merkel cell carcinoma of the scalp and neck

209.33 Merkel cell carcinoma of the upper limb

209.34 Merkel cell carcinoma of the lower limb

209.35 Merkel cell carcinoma of the trunk

209.36 Merkel cell carcinoma of other sites

209.75 Secondary Merkel cell carcinoma

214.0 Lipoma of skin and subcutaneous tissue of face

214.1 Lipoma of other skin and subcutaneous tissue

215.0 Other benign neoplasm of connective and other soft tissue of head, face, and neck

215.2 Other benign neoplasm of connective and other soft tissue of upper limb, including shoulder

215.3 Other benign neoplasm of connective and other soft tissue of lower limb, including hip

215.4 Other benign neoplasm of connective and other soft tissue of thorax

215.5 Other benign neoplasm of connective and other soft tissue of abdomen

215.6 Other benign neoplasm of connective and other soft tissue of pelvis

215.7 Other benign neoplasm of connective and other soft tissue of trunk, unspecified ▽

215.8 Other benign neoplasm of connective and other soft tissue of other specified sites

216.0 Benign neoplasm of skin of lip

216.1 Benign neoplasm of eyelid, including canthus

216.2 Benign neoplasm of ear and external auditory canal

216.3 Benign neoplasm of skin of other and unspecified parts of face ▽

216.4 Benign neoplasm of scalp and skin of neck

216.5 Benign neoplasm of skin of trunk, except scrotum

216.7 Benign neoplasm of skin of lower limb, including hip

216.8 Benign neoplasm of other specified sites of skin

228.01 Hemangioma of skin and subcutaneous tissue

230.0 Carcinoma in situ of lip, oral cavity, and pharynx

232.1 Carcinoma in situ of eyelid, including canthus

232.2 Carcinoma in situ of skin of ear and external auditory canal

232.3 Carcinoma in situ of skin of other and unspecified parts of face ▽

232.4 Carcinoma in situ of scalp and skin of neck

232.5 Carcinoma in situ of skin of trunk, except scrotum

232.6 Carcinoma in situ of skin of upper limb, including shoulder
232.7 Carcinoma in situ of skin of lower limb, including hip
232.8 Carcinoma in situ of other specified sites of skin
235.1 Neoplasm of uncertain behavior of lip, oral cavity, and pharynx
238.2 Neoplasm of uncertain behavior of skin
239.2 Neoplasms of unspecified nature of bone, soft tissue, and skin
249.70 Secondary diabetes mellitus with peripheral circulatory disorders, not stated as uncontrolled, or unspecified — (Use additional code to identify manifestation: 443.81, 785.4) (Use additional code to identify any associated insulin use: V58.67)
249.71 Secondary diabetes mellitus with peripheral circulatory disorders, uncontrolled — (Use additional code to identify manifestation: 443.81, 785.4) (Use additional code to identify any associated insulin use: V58.67)
249.80 Secondary diabetes mellitus with other specified manifestations, not stated as uncontrolled, or unspecified — (Use additional code to identify manifestation: 707.10-707.19, 707.8, 707.9, 731.8) (Use additional code to identify any associated insulin use: V58.67)
249.81 Secondary diabetes mellitus with other specified manifestations, uncontrolled — (Use additional code to identify manifestation: 707.10-707.19, 707.8, 707.9, 731.8) (Use additional code to identify any associated insulin use: V58.67)
249.90 Secondary diabetes mellitus with unspecified complication, not stated as uncontrolled, or unspecified — (Use additional code to identify any associated insulin use: V58.67) ▽
249.91 Secondary diabetes mellitus with unspecified complication, uncontrolled — (Use additional code to identify any associated insulin use: V58.67) ▽
250.70 Diabetes with peripheral circulatory disorders, type II or unspecified type, not stated as uncontrolled — (Use additional code to identify manifestation: 443.81, 785.4)
250.71 Diabetes with peripheral circulatory disorders, type I [juvenile type], not stated as uncontrolled — (Use additional code to identify manifestation: 443.81, 785.4)
250.72 Diabetes with peripheral circulatory disorders, type II or unspecified type, uncontrolled — (Use additional code to identify manifestation: 443.81, 785.4)
250.73 Diabetes with peripheral circulatory disorders, type I [juvenile type], uncontrolled — (Use additional code to identify manifestation: 443.81, 785.4)
443.0 Raynaud's syndrome — (Use additional code to identify gangrene: 785.4)
612.0 Deformity of reconstructed breast
612.1 Disproportion of reconstructed breast
701.4 Keloid scar
709.2 Scar condition and fibrosis of skin
709.9 Unspecified disorder of skin and subcutaneous tissue ▽
728.86 Necrotizing fasciitis — (Use additional code to identify infectious organism, 041.00-041.89, 785.4, if applicable)
757.32 Congenital vascular hamartomas
757.39 Other specified congenital anomaly of skin
785.4 Gangrene — (Code first any associated underlying condition)
872.10 Open wound of external ear, unspecified site, complicated ▽
872.11 Open wound of auricle, complicated
873.1 Open wound of scalp, complicated
873.30 Open wound of nose, unspecified site, complicated ▽
873.50 Open wound of face, unspecified site, complicated ▽
873.51 Open wound of cheek, complicated
873.52 Open wound of forehead, complicated
873.53 Open wound of lip, complicated
873.54 Open wound of jaw, complicated
873.59 Open wound of face, other and multiple sites, complicated
873.9 Other and unspecified open wound of head, complicated ▽
874.9 Open wound of other and unspecified parts of neck, complicated ▽
875.1 Open wound of chest (wall), complicated
876.1 Open wound of back, complicated
877.1 Open wound of buttock, complicated
878.1 Open wound of penis, complicated ♂
878.3 Open wound of scrotum and testes, complicated ♂
878.5 Open wound of vulva, complicated ♀
878.9 Open wound of other and unspecified parts of genital organs, complicated ▽
879.1 Open wound of breast, complicated
879.3 Open wound of abdominal wall, anterior, complicated
879.5 Open wound of abdominal wall, lateral, complicated
879.9 Open wound(s) (multiple) of unspecified site(s), complicated ▽
880.10 Open wound of shoulder region, complicated
880.11 Open wound of scapular region, complicated
880.13 Open wound of upper arm, complicated
880.19 Open wound of multiple sites of shoulder and upper arm, complicated
882.1 Open wound of hand except finger(s) alone, complicated
883.1 Open wound of finger(s), complicated
890.1 Open wound of hip and thigh, complicated
891.1 Open wound of knee, leg (except thigh), and ankle, complicated
892.1 Open wound of foot except toe(s) alone, complicated
893.1 Open wound of toe(s), complicated
894.1 Multiple and unspecified open wound of lower limb, complicated
906.0 Late effect of open wound of head, neck, and trunk
906.1 Late effect of open wound of extremities without mention of tendon injury
906.4 Late effect of crushing
906.5 Late effect of burn of eye, face, head, and neck
906.6 Late effect of burn of wrist and hand
906.7 Late effect of burn of other extremities
906.8 Late effect of burns of other specified sites
941.19 Erythema due to burn (first degree) of multiple sites (except with eye) of face, head, and neck
941.20 Blisters, with epidermal loss due to burn (second degree) of face and head, unspecified site ▽
991.0 Frostbite of face
991.1 Frostbite of hand
991.2 Frostbite of foot
991.3 Frostbite of other and unspecified sites ▽
991.6 Effects of hypothermia
991.8 Other specified effects of reduced temperature
997.60 Late complications of amputation stump, unspecified — (Use additional code to identify complications) ▽
997.61 Neuroma of amputation stump — (Use additional code to identify complications)
997.62 Infection (chronic) of amputation stump — (Use additional code to identify complications)
997.69 Other late amputation stump complication — (Use additional code to identify complications)
998.30 Disruption of wound, unspecified ▽
998.32 Disruption of external operation (surgical) wound
998.33 Disruption of traumatic injury wound repair
998.59 Other postoperative infection — (Use additional code to identify infection)
998.83 Non-healing surgical wound
V10.02 Personal history of malignant neoplasm of other and unspecified parts of oral cavity and pharynx ▽
V10.82 Personal history of malignant melanoma of skin
V10.83 Personal history of other malignant neoplasm of skin
V51.8 Other aftercare involving the use of plastic surgery
V84.01 Genetic susceptibility to malignant neoplasm of breast — (Use additional code, if applicable, for any associated family history of the disease: V16-V19. Code first, if applicable, any current malignant neoplasms: 140.0-195.8, 200.0-208.9, 230.0-234.9. Use additional code, if applicable, for any personal history of malignant neoplasm: V10.0-V10.9)
V84.09 Genetic susceptibility to other malignant neoplasm — (Use additional code, if applicable, for any associated family history of the disease: V16-V19. Code first, if applicable, any current malignant neoplasms: 140.0-195.8, 200.0-208.9, 230.0-234.9.

Use additional code, if applicable, for any personal history of malignant neoplasm: V10.0-V10.9)

V86.0 Estrogen receptor positive status [ER+] — (Code first malignant neoplasm of breast: 174.0-174.9, 175.0-175.9)

V86.1 Estrogen receptor negative status [ER-] — (Code first malignant neoplasm of breast: 174.0-174.9, 175.0-175.9)

ICD-9-CM Procedural

21.83 Total nasal reconstruction

27.57 Attachment of pedicle or flap graft to lip and mouth

83.84 Release of clubfoot, not elsewhere classified

85.42 Bilateral simple mastectomy

85.81 Suture of laceration of breast

86.3 Other local excision or destruction of lesion or tissue of skin and subcutaneous tissue

86.70 Pedicle or flap graft, not otherwise specified

86.71 Cutting and preparation of pedicle grafts or flaps

86.72 Advancement of pedicle graft

86.73 Attachment of pedicle or flap graft to hand

86.74 Attachment of pedicle or flap graft to other sites

86.84 Relaxation of scar or web contracture of skin

86.89 Other repair and reconstruction of skin and subcutaneous tissue

HCPCS Level II Supplies & Services

A4305 Disposable drug delivery system, flow rate of 50 ml or greater per hour

14350

14350 Filleted finger or toe flap, including preparation of recipient site

ICD-9-CM Diagnostic

249.70 Secondary diabetes mellitus with peripheral circulatory disorders, not stated as uncontrolled, or unspecified — (Use additional code to identify manifestation: 443.81, 785.4) (Use additional code to identify any associated insulin use: V58.67)

249.71 Secondary diabetes mellitus with peripheral circulatory disorders, uncontrolled — (Use additional code to identify manifestation: 443.81, 785.4) (Use additional code to identify any associated insulin use: V58.67)

249.80 Secondary diabetes mellitus with other specified manifestations, not stated as uncontrolled, or unspecified — (Use additional code to identify manifestation: 707.10-707.19, 707.8, 707.9, 731.8) (Use additional code to identify any associated insulin use: V58.67)

249.81 Secondary diabetes mellitus with other specified manifestations, uncontrolled — (Use additional code to identify manifestation: 707.10-707.19, 707.8, 707.9, 731.8) (Use additional code to identify any associated insulin use: V58.67)

249.90 Secondary diabetes mellitus with unspecified complication, not stated as uncontrolled, or unspecified — (Use additional code to identify any associated insulin use: V58.67) ▽

249.91 Secondary diabetes mellitus with unspecified complication, uncontrolled — (Use additional code to identify any associated insulin use: V58.67) ▽

250.70 Diabetes with peripheral circulatory disorders, type II or unspecified type, not stated as uncontrolled — (Use additional code to identify manifestation: 443.81, 785.4)

250.71 Diabetes with peripheral circulatory disorders, type I [juvenile type], not stated as uncontrolled — (Use additional code to identify manifestation: 443.81, 785.4)

250.72 Diabetes with peripheral circulatory disorders, type II or unspecified type, uncontrolled — (Use additional code to identify manifestation: 443.81, 785.4)

250.73 Diabetes with peripheral circulatory disorders, type I [juvenile type], uncontrolled — (Use additional code to identify manifestation: 443.81, 785.4)

250.80 Diabetes with other specified manifestations, type II or unspecified type, not stated as uncontrolled — (Use additional code to identify manifestation: 707.10-707.19, 707.8, 707.9, 731.8)

250.81 Diabetes with other specified manifestations, type I [juvenile type], not stated as uncontrolled — (Use additional code to identify manifestation: 707.10-707.19, 707.8, 707.9, 731.8)

250.82 Diabetes with other specified manifestations, type II or unspecified type, uncontrolled — (Use additional code to identify manifestation: 707.10-707.19, 707.8, 707.9, 731.8)

250.83 Diabetes with other specified manifestations, type I [juvenile type], uncontrolled — (Use additional code to identify manifestation: 707.10-707.19, 707.8, 707.9, 731.8)

440.23 Atherosclerosis of native arteries of the extremities with ulceration — (Use additional code for any associated ulceration: 707.10-707.19, 707.8, 707.9)

443.0 Raynaud's syndrome — (Use additional code to identify gangrene: 785.4)

443.81 Peripheral angiopathy in diseases classified elsewhere — (Code first underlying disease: 249.7, 250.7) ☒

459.11 Postphlebitic syndrome with ulcer

459.13 Postphlebitic syndrome with ulcer and inflammation

459.31 Chronic venous hypertension with ulcer

459.33 Chronic venous hypertension with ulcer and inflammation

707.15 Ulcer of other part of foot — (Code, if applicable, any causal condition first: 249.80-249.81, 250.80-250.83, 440.23, 459.11, 459.13, 459.31, 459.33)

707.8 Chronic ulcer of other specified site

709.2 Scar condition and fibrosis of skin

785.4 Gangrene — (Code first any associated underlying condition)

816.10 Open fracture of phalanx or phalanges of hand, unspecified ▽

816.11 Open fracture of middle or proximal phalanx or phalanges of hand

816.12 Open fracture of distal phalanx or phalanges of hand

816.13 Open fractures of multiple sites of phalanx or phalanges of hand

826.1 Open fracture of one or more phalanges of foot

885.0 Traumatic amputation of thumb (complete) (partial), without mention of complication

885.1 Traumatic amputation of thumb (complete) (partial), complicated

886.0 Traumatic amputation of other finger(s) (complete) (partial), without mention of complication

886.1 Traumatic amputation of other finger(s) (complete) (partial), complicated

895.0 Traumatic amputation of toe(s) (complete) (partial), without mention of complication

895.1 Traumatic amputation of toe(s) (complete) (partial), complicated

928.3 Crushing injury of toe(s) — (Use additional code to identify any associated injuries: 800-829, 850.0-854.1, 860.0-869.1)

944.30 Full-thickness skin loss due to burn (third degree NOS) of unspecified site of hand ▽

944.31 Full-thickness skin loss due to burn (third degree NOS) of single digit [finger (nail)] other than thumb

944.32 Full-thickness skin loss due to burn (third degree NOS) of thumb (nail)

944.33 Full-thickness skin loss due to burn (third degree NOS) of two or more digits of hand, not including thumb

944.34 Full-thickness skin loss due to burn (third degree NOS) of two or more digits of hand including thumb

944.38 Full-thickness skin loss due to burn (third degree NOS) of multiple sites of wrist(s) and hand(s)

944.40 Deep necrosis of underlying tissues due to burn (deep third degree) of unspecified site of hand, without mention of loss of a body part ▽

944.41 Deep necrosis of underlying tissues due to burn (deep third degree) of single digit [finger (nail)] other than thumb, without mention of loss of a body part

944.42 Deep necrosis of underlying tissues due to burn (deep third degree) of thumb (nail), without mention of loss of a body part

944.43 Deep necrosis of underlying tissues due to burn (deep third degree) of two or more digits of hand, not including thumb, without mention of loss of a body part

944.44 Deep necrosis of underlying tissues due to burn (deep third degree) of two or more digits of hand including thumb, without mention of loss of a body part

944.48 Deep necrosis of underlying tissues due to burn (deep third degree) of multiple sites of wrist(s) and hand(s), without mention of loss of a body part

945.10 Erythema due to burn (first degree) of unspecified site of lower limb (leg) ▽

945.41 Deep necrosis of underlying tissues due to burn (deep third degree) of toe(s) (nail), without mention of loss of a body part

945.49 Deep necrosis of underlying tissues due to burn (deep third degree) of multiple sites of lower limb(s), without mention of loss of a body part

998.30 Disruption of wound, unspecified ▽

998.33 Disruption of traumatic injury wound repair
V10.82 Personal history of malignant melanoma of skin
V10.83 Personal history of other malignant neoplasm of skin
V51.8 Other aftercare involving the use of plastic surgery

ICD-9-CM Procedural

86.3 Other local excision or destruction of lesion or tissue of skin and subcutaneous tissue
86.71 Cutting and preparation of pedicle grafts or flaps
86.72 Advancement of pedicle graft
86.73 Attachment of pedicle or flap graft to hand
86.74 Attachment of pedicle or flap graft to other sites

15002-15003

15002 Surgical preparation or creation of recipient site by excision of open wounds, burn eschar, or scar (including subcutaneous tissues), or incisional release of scar contracture, trunk, arms, legs; first 100 sq cm or 1% of body area of infants and children

15003 each additional 100 sq cm, or part thereof, or each additional 1% of body area of infants and children (List separately in addition to code for primary procedure)

ICD-9-CM Diagnostic

172.5 Malignant melanoma of skin of trunk, except scrotum
172.6 Malignant melanoma of skin of upper limb, including shoulder
172.7 Malignant melanoma of skin of lower limb, including hip
172.8 Malignant melanoma of other specified sites of skin
173.50 Unspecified malignant neoplasm of skin of trunk, except scrotum ♥
173.51 Basal cell carcinoma of skin of trunk, except scrotum
173.52 Squamous cell carcinoma of skin of trunk, except scrotum
173.59 Other specified malignant neoplasm of skin of trunk, except scrotum
173.60 Unspecified malignant neoplasm of skin of upper limb, including shoulder ♥
173.61 Basal cell carcinoma of skin of upper limb, including shoulder
173.62 Squamous cell carcinoma of skin of upper limb, including shoulder
173.69 Other specified malignant neoplasm of skin of upper limb, including shoulder
173.70 Unspecified malignant neoplasm of skin of lower limb, including hip ♥
173.71 Basal cell carcinoma of skin of lower limb, including hip
173.72 Squamous cell carcinoma of skin of lower limb, including hip
173.79 Other specified malignant neoplasm of skin of lower limb, including hip
173.80 Unspecified malignant neoplasm of other specified sites of skin ♥
173.81 Basal cell carcinoma of other specified sites of skin
173.82 Squamous cell carcinoma of other specified sites of skin
173.89 Other specified malignant neoplasm of other specified sites of skin
174.0 Malignant neoplasm of nipple and areola of female breast — (Use additional code to identify estrogen receptor status: V86.0-V86.1) ♀
174.1 Malignant neoplasm of central portion of female breast — (Use additional code to identify estrogen receptor status: V86.0-V86.1) ♀
174.2 Malignant neoplasm of upper-inner quadrant of female breast — (Use additional code to identify estrogen receptor status: V86.0-V86.1) ♀
174.3 Malignant neoplasm of lower-inner quadrant of female breast — (Use additional code to identify estrogen receptor status: V86.0-V86.1) ♀
174.4 Malignant neoplasm of upper-outer quadrant of female breast — (Use additional code to identify estrogen receptor status: V86.0-V86.1) ♀
174.5 Malignant neoplasm of lower-outer quadrant of female breast — (Use additional code to identify estrogen receptor status: V86.0-V86.1) ♀
174.6 Malignant neoplasm of axillary tail of female breast — (Use additional code to identify estrogen receptor status: V86.0-V86.1) ♀
174.8 Malignant neoplasm of other specified sites of female breast — (Use additional code to identify estrogen receptor status: V86.0-V86.1) ♀
175.9 Malignant neoplasm of other and unspecified sites of male breast — (Use additional code to identify estrogen receptor status: V86.0-V86.1) ♥ ♂
176.0 Kaposi's sarcoma of skin
195.1 Malignant neoplasm of thorax
195.2 Malignant neoplasm of abdomen
195.3 Malignant neoplasm of pelvis
195.4 Malignant neoplasm of upper limb
195.5 Malignant neoplasm of lower limb
195.8 Malignant neoplasm of other specified sites
198.2 Secondary malignant neoplasm of skin
209.33 Merkel cell carcinoma of the upper limb
209.34 Merkel cell carcinoma of the lower limb
209.35 Merkel cell carcinoma of the trunk
209.75 Secondary Merkel cell carcinoma
214.1 Lipoma of other skin and subcutaneous tissue
215.2 Other benign neoplasm of connective and other soft tissue of upper limb, including shoulder
215.3 Other benign neoplasm of connective and other soft tissue of lower limb, including hip
215.4 Other benign neoplasm of connective and other soft tissue of thorax
215.5 Other benign neoplasm of connective and other soft tissue of abdomen
215.6 Other benign neoplasm of connective and other soft tissue of pelvis
215.7 Other benign neoplasm of connective and other soft tissue of trunk, unspecified ♥
215.8 Other benign neoplasm of connective and other soft tissue of other specified sites
216.5 Benign neoplasm of skin of trunk, except scrotum
216.6 Benign neoplasm of skin of upper limb, including shoulder
216.7 Benign neoplasm of skin of lower limb, including hip
216.8 Benign neoplasm of other specified sites of skin
228.01 Hemangioma of skin and subcutaneous tissue
232.5 Carcinoma in situ of skin of trunk, except scrotum
232.6 Carcinoma in situ of skin of upper limb, including shoulder
232.7 Carcinoma in situ of skin of lower limb, including hip
232.8 Carcinoma in situ of other specified sites of skin
238.2 Neoplasm of uncertain behavior of skin
239.2 Neoplasms of unspecified nature of bone, soft tissue, and skin
249.70 Secondary diabetes mellitus with peripheral circulatory disorders, not stated as uncontrolled, or unspecified — (Use additional code to identify manifestation: 443.81, 785.4) (Use additional code to identify any associated insulin use: V58.67)
249.71 Secondary diabetes mellitus with peripheral circulatory disorders, uncontrolled — (Use additional code to identify manifestation: 443.81, 785.4) (Use additional code to identify any associated insulin use: V58.67)
249.80 Secondary diabetes mellitus with other specified manifestations, not stated as uncontrolled, or unspecified — (Use additional code to identify manifestation: 707.10-707.19, 707.8, 707.9, 731.8) (Use additional code to identify any associated insulin use: V58.67)
249.81 Secondary diabetes mellitus with other specified manifestations, uncontrolled — (Use additional code to identify manifestation: 707.10-707.19, 707.8, 707.9, 731.8) (Use additional code to identify any associated insulin use: V58.67)
249.90 Secondary diabetes mellitus with unspecified complication, not stated as uncontrolled, or unspecified — (Use additional code to identify any associated insulin use: V58.67) ♥
249.91 Secondary diabetes mellitus with unspecified complication, uncontrolled — (Use additional code to identify any associated insulin use: V58.67) ♥
250.70 Diabetes with peripheral circulatory disorders, type II or unspecified type, not stated as uncontrolled — (Use additional code to identify manifestation: 443.81, 785.4)
250.71 Diabetes with peripheral circulatory disorders, type I [juvenile type], not stated as uncontrolled — (Use additional code to identify manifestation: 443.81, 785.4)
250.72 Diabetes with peripheral circulatory disorders, type II or unspecified type, uncontrolled — (Use additional code to identify manifestation: 443.81, 785.4)
250.73 Diabetes with peripheral circulatory disorders, type I [juvenile type], uncontrolled — (Use additional code to identify manifestation: 443.81, 785.4)
250.80 Diabetes with other specified manifestations, type II or unspecified type, not stated as uncontrolled — (Use additional code to identify manifestation: 707.10-707.19, 707.8, 707.9, 731.8)

250.81 Diabetes with other specified manifestations, type I [juvenile type], not stated as uncontrolled — (Use additional code to identify manifestation: 707.10-707.19, 707.8, 707.9, 731.8)
250.82 Diabetes with other specified manifestations, type II or unspecified type, uncontrolled — (Use additional code to identify manifestation: 707.10-707.19, 707.8, 707.9, 731.8)
250.83 Diabetes with other specified manifestations, type I [juvenile type], uncontrolled — (Use additional code to identify manifestation: 707.10-707.19, 707.8, 707.9, 731.8)
440.23 Atherosclerosis of native arteries of the extremities with ulceration — (Use additional code for any associated ulceration: 707.10-707.19, 707.8, 707.9)
443.0 Raynaud's syndrome — (Use additional code to identify gangrene: 785.4)
459.11 Postphlebitic syndrome with ulcer
459.13 Postphlebitic syndrome with ulcer and inflammation
459.31 Chronic venous hypertension with ulcer
459.33 Chronic venous hypertension with ulcer and inflammation
611.83 Capsular contracture of breast implant
612.0 Deformity of reconstructed breast
701.4 Keloid scar
707.00 Pressure ulcer, unspecified site — (Use additional code to identify pressure ulcer stage: 707.20-707.25)
707.01 Pressure ulcer, elbow — (Use additional code to identify pressure ulcer stage: 707.20-707.25)
707.02 Pressure ulcer, upper back — (Use additional code to identify pressure ulcer stage: 707.20-707.25)
707.03 Pressure ulcer, lower back — (Use additional code to identify pressure ulcer stage: 707.20-707.25)
707.04 Pressure ulcer, hip — (Use additional code to identify pressure ulcer stage: 707.20-707.25)
707.05 Pressure ulcer, buttock — (Use additional code to identify pressure ulcer stage: 707.20-707.25)
707.06 Pressure ulcer, ankle — (Use additional code to identify pressure ulcer stage: 707.20-707.25)
707.07 Pressure ulcer, heel — (Use additional code to identify pressure ulcer stage: 707.20-707.25)
707.10 Ulcer of lower limb, unspecified — (Code, if applicable, any causal condition first: 249.80-249.81, 250.80-250.83, 440.23, 459.11, 459.13, 459.31, 459.33)
707.11 Ulcer of thigh — (Code, if applicable, any causal condition first: 249.80-249.81, 250.80-250.83, 440.23, 459.11, 459.13, 459.31, 459.33)
707.12 Ulcer of calf — (Code, if applicable, any causal condition first: 249.80-249.81, 250.80-250.83, 440.23, 459.11, 459.13, 459.31, 459.33)
707.13 Ulcer of ankle — (Code, if applicable, any causal condition first: 249.80-249.81, 250.80-250.83, 440.23, 459.11, 459.13, 459.31, 459.33)
707.19 Ulcer of other part of lower limb — (Code, if applicable, any causal condition first: 249.80-249.81, 250.80-250.83, 440.23, 459.11, 459.13, 459.31, 459.33)
707.20 Pressure ulcer, unspecified stage — (Code first site of pressure ulcer: 707.00-707.09)
707.21 Pressure ulcer, stage I — (Code first site of pressure ulcer: 707.00-707.09)
707.22 Pressure ulcer stage II — (Code first site of pressure ulcer: 707.00-707.09)
707.23 Pressure ulcer stage III — (Code first site of pressure ulcer: 707.00-707.09)
707.24 Pressure ulcer stage IV — (Code first site of pressure ulcer: 707.00-707.09)
707.25 Pressure ulcer, unstageable — (Code first site of pressure ulcer: 707.00-707.09)
707.8 Chronic ulcer of other specified site
709.2 Scar condition and fibrosis of skin
709.4 Foreign body granuloma of skin and subcutaneous tissue — (Use additional code to identify foreign body (V90.01-V90.9))
728.86 Necrotizing fasciitis — (Use additional code to identify infectious organism, 041.00-041.89, 785.4, if applicable)
785.4 Gangrene — (Code first any associated underlying condition)
875.1 Open wound of chest (wall), complicated
876.1 Open wound of back, complicated
877.1 Open wound of buttock, complicated
879.1 Open wound of breast, complicated
879.3 Open wound of abdominal wall, anterior, complicated
879.5 Open wound of abdominal wall, lateral, complicated
879.9 Open wound(s) (multiple) of unspecified site(s), complicated
880.10 Open wound of shoulder region, complicated
880.11 Open wound of scapular region, complicated
880.12 Open wound of axillary region, complicated
880.13 Open wound of upper arm, complicated
880.19 Open wound of multiple sites of shoulder and upper arm, complicated
890.1 Open wound of hip and thigh, complicated
891.1 Open wound of knee, leg (except thigh), and ankle, complicated
894.1 Multiple and unspecified open wound of lower limb, complicated
906.0 Late effect of open wound of head, neck, and trunk
906.1 Late effect of open wound of extremities without mention of tendon injury
906.4 Late effect of crushing
906.7 Late effect of burn of other extremities
906.8 Late effect of burns of other specified sites
909.3 Late effect of complications of surgical and medical care
942.30 Full-thickness skin loss due to burn (third degree NOS) of unspecified site of trunk
942.31 Full-thickness skin loss due to burn (third degree NOS) of breast
942.33 Full-thickness skin loss due to burn (third degree NOS) of abdominal wall
942.34 Full-thickness skin loss due to burn (third degree NOS) of back (any part)
942.39 Full-thickness skin loss due to burn (third degree NOS) of other and multiple sites of trunk
942.40 Deep necrosis of underlying tissues due to burn (deep third degree) of trunk, unspecified site, without mention of loss of a body part
942.41 Deep necrosis of underlying tissues due to burn (deep third degree) of breast, without mention of loss of a body part
942.42 Deep necrosis of underlying tissues due to burn (deep third degree) of chest wall, excluding breast and nipple, without mention of loss of a body part
942.43 Deep necrosis of underlying tissues due to burn (deep third degree) of abdominal wall, without mention of loss of a body part
942.44 Deep necrosis of underlying tissues due to burn (deep third degree) of back (any part), without mention of loss of a body part
942.49 Deep necrosis of underlying tissues due to burn (deep third degree) of other and multiple sites of trunk, without mention of loss of a body part
943.30 Full-thickness skin loss due to burn (third degree NOS) of unspecified site of upper limb
943.31 Full-thickness skin loss due to burn (third degree NOS) of forearm
943.32 Full-thickness skin loss due to burn (third degree NOS) of elbow
943.33 Full-thickness skin loss due to burn (third degree NOS) of upper arm
943.34 Full-thickness skin loss due to burn (third degree NOS) of axilla
943.35 Full-thickness skin loss due to burn (third degree NOS) of shoulder
943.36 Full-thickness skin loss due to burn (third degree NOS) of scapular region
943.39 Full-thickness skin loss due to burn (third degree NOS) of multiple sites of upper limb, except wrist and hand
944.37 Full-thickness skin loss due to burn (third degree NOS) of wrist
944.38 Full-thickness skin loss due to burn (third degree NOS) of multiple sites of wrist(s) and hand(s)
944.47 Deep necrosis of underlying tissues due to burn (deep third degree) of wrist, without mention of loss of a body part
944.48 Deep necrosis of underlying tissues due to burn (deep third degree) of multiple sites of wrist(s) and hand(s), without mention of loss of a body part
945.30 Full-thickness skin loss due to burn (third degree NOS) of unspecified site of lower limb
945.34 Full-thickness skin loss due to burn (third degree NOS) of lower leg
945.35 Full-thickness skin loss due to burn (third degree NOS) of knee
945.36 Full-thickness skin loss due to burn (third degree NOS) of thigh (any part)
945.39 Full-thickness skin loss due to burn (third degree NOS) of multiple sites of lower limb(s)

Unspecified code ♀ Female diagnosis ◘ Manifestation code ♂ Male diagnosis [Resequenced code]

945.40 Deep necrosis of underlying tissues due to burn (deep third degree) of unspecified site of lower limb (leg), without mention of loss of a body part ▽

945.44 Deep necrosis of underlying tissues due to burn (deep third degree) of lower leg, without mention of loss of a body part

945.45 Deep necrosis of underlying tissues due to burn (deep third degree) of knee, without mention of loss of a body part

945.46 Deep necrosis of underlying tissues due to burn (deep third degree) of thigh (any part), without mention of loss of a body part

945.49 Deep necrosis of underlying tissues due to burn (deep third degree) of multiple sites of lower limb(s), without mention of loss of a body part

946.3 Full-thickness skin loss due to burn (third degree NOS) of multiple specified sites

946.4 Deep necrosis of underlying tissues due to burn (deep third degree) of multiple specified sites, without mention of loss of a body part

991.3 Frostbite of other and unspecified sites ▽

996.52 Mechanical complication due to other tissue graft, not elsewhere classified

997.60 Late complications of amputation stump, unspecified — (Use additional code to identify complications) ▽

998.30 Disruption of wound, unspecified ▽

998.32 Disruption of external operation (surgical) wound

998.33 Disruption of traumatic injury wound repair

998.59 Other postoperative infection — (Use additional code to identify infection)

V10.82 Personal history of malignant melanoma of skin

V10.83 Personal history of other malignant neoplasm of skin

V51.8 Other aftercare involving the use of plastic surgery

ICD-9-CM Procedural

85.21 Local excision of lesion of breast

86.3 Other local excision or destruction of lesion or tissue of skin and subcutaneous tissue

HCPCS Level II Supplies & Services

A4305 Disposable drug delivery system, flow rate of 50 ml or greater per hour

A4306 Disposable drug delivery system, flow rate of less than 50 ml per hour

15004-15005

15004 Surgical preparation or creation of recipient site by excision of open wounds, burn eschar, or scar (including subcutaneous tissues), or incisional release of scar contracture, face, scalp, eyelids, mouth, neck, ears, orbits, genitalia, hands, feet and/or multiple digits; first 100 sq cm or 1% of body area of infants and children

15005 each additional 100 sq cm, or part thereof, or each additional 1% of body area of infants and children (List separately in addition to code for primary procedure)

ICD-9-CM Diagnostic

140.0 Malignant neoplasm of upper lip, vermilion border

140.1 Malignant neoplasm of lower lip, vermilion border

140.3 Malignant neoplasm of upper lip, inner aspect

140.4 Malignant neoplasm of lower lip, inner aspect

140.5 Malignant neoplasm of lip, inner aspect, unspecified as to upper or lower ▽

140.6 Malignant neoplasm of commissure of lip

140.8 Malignant neoplasm of other sites of lip

140.9 Malignant neoplasm of lip, vermilion border, unspecified as to upper or lower ▽

172.0 Malignant melanoma of skin of lip

172.1 Malignant melanoma of skin of eyelid, including canthus

172.2 Malignant melanoma of skin of ear and external auditory canal

172.3 Malignant melanoma of skin of other and unspecified parts of face ▽

172.4 Malignant melanoma of skin of scalp and neck

172.8 Malignant melanoma of other specified sites of skin

173.00 Unspecified malignant neoplasm of skin of lip ▽

173.01 Basal cell carcinoma of skin of lip

173.02 Squamous cell carcinoma of skin of lip

173.09 Other specified malignant neoplasm of skin of lip

173.10 Unspecified malignant neoplasm of eyelid, including canthus ▽

173.11 Basal cell carcinoma of eyelid, including canthus

173.12 Squamous cell carcinoma of eyelid, including canthus

173.19 Other specified malignant neoplasm of eyelid, including canthus

173.20 Unspecified malignant neoplasm of skin of ear and external auditory canal ▽

173.21 Basal cell carcinoma of skin of ear and external auditory canal

173.22 Squamous cell carcinoma of skin of ear and external auditory canal

173.29 Other specified malignant neoplasm of skin of ear and external auditory canal

173.30 Unspecified malignant neoplasm of skin of other and unspecified parts of face ▽

173.31 Basal cell carcinoma of skin of other and unspecified parts of face

173.32 Squamous cell carcinoma of skin of other and unspecified parts of face

173.39 Other specified malignant neoplasm of skin of other and unspecified parts of face

173.40 Unspecified malignant neoplasm of scalp and skin of neck ▽

173.41 Basal cell carcinoma of scalp and skin of neck

173.42 Squamous cell carcinoma of scalp and skin of neck

173.49 Other specified malignant neoplasm of scalp and skin of neck

173.80 Unspecified malignant neoplasm of other specified sites of skin ▽

173.81 Basal cell carcinoma of other specified sites of skin

173.82 Squamous cell carcinoma of other specified sites of skin

173.89 Other specified malignant neoplasm of other specified sites of skin

176.0 Kaposi's sarcoma of skin

195.0 Malignant neoplasm of head, face, and neck

195.8 Malignant neoplasm of other specified sites

198.2 Secondary malignant neoplasm of skin

209.31 Merkel cell carcinoma of the face

209.32 Merkel cell carcinoma of the scalp and neck

209.33 Merkel cell carcinoma of the upper limb

209.34 Merkel cell carcinoma of the lower limb

209.36 Merkel cell carcinoma of other sites

209.75 Secondary Merkel cell carcinoma

214.0 Lipoma of skin and subcutaneous tissue of face

214.1 Lipoma of other skin and subcutaneous tissue

215.0 Other benign neoplasm of connective and other soft tissue of head, face, and neck

215.8 Other benign neoplasm of connective and other soft tissue of other specified sites

216.0 Benign neoplasm of skin of lip

216.1 Benign neoplasm of eyelid, including canthus

216.2 Benign neoplasm of ear and external auditory canal

216.3 Benign neoplasm of skin of other and unspecified parts of face ▽

216.4 Benign neoplasm of scalp and skin of neck

216.8 Benign neoplasm of other specified sites of skin

228.01 Hemangioma of skin and subcutaneous tissue

230.0 Carcinoma in situ of lip, oral cavity, and pharynx

232.0 Carcinoma in situ of skin of lip

232.1 Carcinoma in situ of eyelid, including canthus

232.2 Carcinoma in situ of skin of ear and external auditory canal

232.3 Carcinoma in situ of skin of other and unspecified parts of face ▽

232.4 Carcinoma in situ of scalp and skin of neck

232.8 Carcinoma in situ of other specified sites of skin

235.1 Neoplasm of uncertain behavior of lip, oral cavity, and pharynx

238.2 Neoplasm of uncertain behavior of skin

239.2 Neoplasms of unspecified nature of bone, soft tissue, and skin

249.70 Secondary diabetes mellitus with peripheral circulatory disorders, not stated as uncontrolled, or unspecified — (Use additional code to identify manifestation: 443.81, 785.4) (Use additional code to identify any associated insulin use: V58.67)

249.71 Secondary diabetes mellitus with peripheral circulatory disorders, uncontrolled — (Use additional code to identify manifestation: 443.81, 785.4) (Use additional code to identify any associated insulin use: V58.67)

249.80 Secondary diabetes mellitus with other specified manifestations, not stated as uncontrolled, or unspecified — (Use additional code to identify manifestation:

707.10-707.19, 707.8, 707.9, 731.8) (Use additional code to identify any associated insulin use: V58.67)

249.81 Secondary diabetes mellitus with other specified manifestations, uncontrolled — (Use additional code to identify manifestation: 707.10-707.19, 707.8, 707.9, 731.8) (Use additional code to identify any associated insulin use: V58.67)

249.90 Secondary diabetes mellitus with unspecified complication, not stated as uncontrolled, or unspecified — (Use additional code to identify any associated insulin use: V58.67) ▽

249.91 Secondary diabetes mellitus with unspecified complication, uncontrolled — (Use additional code to identify any associated insulin use: V58.67) ▽

250.70 Diabetes with peripheral circulatory disorders, type II or unspecified type, not stated as uncontrolled — (Use additional code to identify manifestation: 443.81, 785.4)

250.71 Diabetes with peripheral circulatory disorders, type I [juvenile type], not stated as uncontrolled — (Use additional code to identify manifestation: 443.81, 785.4)

250.72 Diabetes with peripheral circulatory disorders, type II or unspecified type, uncontrolled — (Use additional code to identify manifestation: 443.81, 785.4)

250.73 Diabetes with peripheral circulatory disorders, type I [juvenile type], uncontrolled — (Use additional code to identify manifestation: 443.81, 785.4)

250.80 Diabetes with other specified manifestations, type II or unspecified type, not stated as uncontrolled — (Use additional code to identify manifestation: 707.10-707.19, 707.8, 707.9, 731.8)

250.81 Diabetes with other specified manifestations, type I [juvenile type], not stated as uncontrolled — (Use additional code to identify manifestation: 707.10-707.19, 707.8, 707.9, 731.8)

250.82 Diabetes with other specified manifestations, type II or unspecified type, uncontrolled — (Use additional code to identify manifestation: 707.10-707.19, 707.8, 707.9, 731.8)

250.83 Diabetes with other specified manifestations, type I [juvenile type], uncontrolled — (Use additional code to identify manifestation: 707.10-707.19, 707.8, 707.9, 731.8)

443.0 Raynaud's syndrome — (Use additional code to identify gangrene: 785.4)

459.11 Postphlebitic syndrome with ulcer

459.13 Postphlebitic syndrome with ulcer and inflammation

459.31 Chronic venous hypertension with ulcer

459.33 Chronic venous hypertension with ulcer and inflammation

701.4 Keloid scar

707.14 Ulcer of heel and midfoot — (Code, if applicable, any causal condition first: 249.80-249.81, 250.80-250.83, 440.23, 459.11, 459.13, 459.31, 459.33)

707.15 Ulcer of other part of foot — (Code, if applicable, any causal condition first: 249.80-249.81, 250.80-250.83, 440.23, 459.11, 459.13, 459.31, 459.33)

707.8 Chronic ulcer of other specified site

709.2 Scar condition and fibrosis of skin

709.4 Foreign body granuloma of skin and subcutaneous tissue — (Use additional code to identify foreign body (V90.01-V90.9))

728.86 Necrotizing fasciitis — (Use additional code to identify infectious organism, 041.00-041.89, 785.4, if applicable)

785.4 Gangrene — (Code first any associated underlying condition)

872.10 Open wound of external ear, unspecified site, complicated ▽

872.11 Open wound of auricle, complicated

873.1 Open wound of scalp, complicated

873.30 Open wound of nose, unspecified site, complicated ▽

873.49 Open wound of face, other and multiple sites, without mention of complication

873.50 Open wound of face, unspecified site, complicated ▽

873.51 Open wound of cheek, complicated

873.52 Open wound of forehead, complicated

873.53 Open wound of lip, complicated

873.54 Open wound of jaw, complicated

873.59 Open wound of face, other and multiple sites, complicated

873.9 Other and unspecified open wound of head, complicated ▽

874.8 Open wound of other and unspecified parts of neck, without mention of complication ▽

874.9 Open wound of other and unspecified parts of neck, complicated ▽

878.1 Open wound of penis, complicated ♂

878.3 Open wound of scrotum and testes, complicated ♂

878.5 Open wound of vulva, complicated ♀

878.9 Open wound of other and unspecified parts of genital organs, complicated ▽

879.9 Open wound(s) (multiple) of unspecified site(s), complicated ▽

882.1 Open wound of hand except finger(s) alone, complicated

883.1 Open wound of finger(s), complicated

892.1 Open wound of foot except toe(s) alone, complicated

893.1 Open wound of toe(s), complicated

906.0 Late effect of open wound of head, neck, and trunk

906.4 Late effect of crushing

906.5 Late effect of burn of eye, face, head, and neck

909.3 Late effect of complications of surgical and medical care

941.29 Blisters, with epidermal loss due to burn (second degree) of multiple sites (except with eye) of face, head, and neck

941.30 Full-thickness skin loss due to burn (third degree NOS) of unspecified site of face and head ▽

941.31 Full-thickness skin loss due to burn (third degree NOS) of ear (any part)

941.32 Full-thickness skin loss due to burn (third degree NOS) of eye (with other parts of face, head, and neck)

941.33 Full-thickness skin loss due to burn (third degree NOS) of lip(s)

941.34 Full-thickness skin loss due to burn (third degree NOS) of chin

941.35 Full-thickness skin loss due to burn (third degree NOS) of nose (septum)

941.36 Full-thickness skin loss due to burn (third degree NOS) of scalp (any part)

941.37 Full-thickness skin loss due to burn (third degree NOS) of forehead and cheek

941.38 Full-thickness skin loss due to burn (third degree NOS) of neck

941.39 Full-thickness skin loss due to burn (third degree NOS) of multiple sites (except with eye) of face, head, and neck

941.40 Deep necrosis of underlying tissues due to burn (deep third degree) of unspecified site of face and head, without mention of loss of a body part ▽

941.41 Deep necrosis of underlying tissues due to burn (deep third degree) of ear (any part), without mention of loss of a body part

941.42 Deep necrosis of underlying tissues due to burn (deep third degree) of eye (with other parts of face, head, and neck), without mention of loss of a body part

941.43 Deep necrosis of underlying tissues due to burn (deep third degree) of lip(s), without mention of loss of a body part

941.44 Deep necrosis of underlying tissues due to burn (deep third degree) of chin, without mention of loss of a body part

941.45 Deep necrosis of underlying tissues due to burn (deep third degree) of nose (septum), without mention of loss of a body part

941.46 Deep necrosis of underlying tissues due to burn (deep third degree) of scalp (any part), without mention of loss of a body part

941.47 Deep necrosis of underlying tissues due to burn (deep third degree) of forehead and cheek, without mention of loss of a body part

941.48 Deep necrosis of underlying tissues due to burn (deep third degree) of neck, without mention of loss of a body part

941.49 Deep necrosis of underlying tissues due to burn (deep third degree) of multiple sites (except with eye) of face, head, and neck, without mention of loss of a body part

942.35 Full-thickness skin loss due to burn (third degree NOS) of genitalia

942.45 Deep necrosis of underlying tissues due to burn (deep third degree) of genitalia, without mention of loss of a body part

944.30 Full-thickness skin loss due to burn (third degree NOS) of unspecified site of hand ▽

944.31 Full-thickness skin loss due to burn (third degree NOS) of single digit [finger (nail)] other than thumb

944.32 Full-thickness skin loss due to burn (third degree NOS) of thumb (nail)

944.33 Full-thickness skin loss due to burn (third degree NOS) of two or more digits of hand, not including thumb

944.34 Full-thickness skin loss due to burn (third degree NOS) of two or more digits of hand including thumb

944.38 Full-thickness skin loss due to burn (third degree NOS) of multiple sites of wrist(s) and hand(s)
944.40 Deep necrosis of underlying tissues due to burn (deep third degree) of unspecified site of hand, without mention of loss of a body part ▽
944.41 Deep necrosis of underlying tissues due to burn (deep third degree) of single digit [finger (nail)] other than thumb, without mention of loss of a body part
944.42 Deep necrosis of underlying tissues due to burn (deep third degree) of thumb (nail), without mention of loss of a body part
944.43 Deep necrosis of underlying tissues due to burn (deep third degree) of two or more digits of hand, not including thumb, without mention of loss of a body part
944.44 Deep necrosis of underlying tissues due to burn (deep third degree) of two or more digits of hand including thumb, without mention of loss of a body part
944.45 Deep necrosis of underlying tissues due to burn (deep third degree) of palm of hand, without mention of loss of a body part
944.46 Deep necrosis of underlying tissues due to burn (deep third degree) of back of hand, without mention of loss of a body part
944.48 Deep necrosis of underlying tissues due to burn (deep third degree) of multiple sites of wrist(s) and hand(s), without mention of loss of a body part
945.31 Full-thickness skin loss due to burn (third degree NOS) of toe(s) (nail)
945.32 Full-thickness skin loss due to burn (third degree NOS) of foot
945.33 Full-thickness skin loss due to burn (third degree NOS) of ankle
945.41 Deep necrosis of underlying tissues due to burn (deep third degree) of toe(s) (nail), without mention of loss of a body part
945.42 Deep necrosis of underlying tissues due to burn (deep third degree) of foot, without mention of loss of a body part
945.43 Deep necrosis of underlying tissues due to burn (deep third degree) of ankle, without mention of loss of a body part
946.3 Full-thickness skin loss due to burn (third degree NOS) of multiple specified sites
946.4 Deep necrosis of underlying tissues due to burn (deep third degree) of multiple specified sites, without mention of loss of a body part
959.01 Head injury, unspecified ▽
959.09 Injury of face and neck, other and unspecified
991.0 Frostbite of face
991.1 Frostbite of hand
991.2 Frostbite of foot
991.3 Frostbite of other and unspecified sites ▽
996.52 Mechanical complication due to other tissue graft, not elsewhere classified
997.60 Late complications of amputation stump, unspecified — (Use additional code to identify complications) ▽
998.30 Disruption of wound, unspecified ▽
998.32 Disruption of external operation (surgical) wound
998.33 Disruption of traumatic injury wound repair
998.59 Other postoperative infection — (Use additional code to identify infection)
V10.82 Personal history of malignant melanoma of skin
V10.83 Personal history of other malignant neoplasm of skin
V51.8 Other aftercare involving the use of plastic surgery

ICD-9-CM Procedural

08.20 Removal of lesion of eyelid, not otherwise specified
08.23 Excision of major lesion of eyelid, partial-thickness
08.24 Excision of major lesion of eyelid, full-thickness
18.29 Excision or destruction of other lesion of external ear
21.32 Local excision or destruction of other lesion of nose
27.42 Wide excision of lesion of lip
27.43 Other excision of lesion or tissue of lip
49.39 Other local excision or destruction of lesion or tissue of anus
61.3 Excision or destruction of lesion or tissue of scrotum ♂
64.2 Local excision or destruction of lesion of penis ♂
86.3 Other local excision or destruction of lesion or tissue of skin and subcutaneous tissue

HCPCS Level II Supplies & Services

A4305 Disposable drug delivery system, flow rate of 50 ml or greater per hour
A4306 Disposable drug delivery system, flow rate of less than 50 ml per hour

15040

15040 Harvest of skin for tissue cultured skin autograft, 100 sq cm or less

ICD-9-CM Diagnostic

145.0 Malignant neoplasm of cheek mucosa
145.8 Malignant neoplasm of other specified parts of mouth
171.0 Malignant neoplasm of connective and other soft tissue of head, face, and neck
171.6 Malignant neoplasm of connective and other soft tissue of pelvis
171.8 Malignant neoplasm of other specified sites of connective and other soft tissue
172.0 Malignant melanoma of skin of lip
172.1 Malignant melanoma of skin of eyelid, including canthus
172.2 Malignant melanoma of skin of ear and external auditory canal
172.3 Malignant melanoma of skin of other and unspecified parts of face ▽
172.4 Malignant melanoma of skin of scalp and neck
172.5 Malignant melanoma of skin of trunk, except scrotum
172.6 Malignant melanoma of skin of upper limb, including shoulder
172.7 Malignant melanoma of skin of lower limb, including hip
172.8 Malignant melanoma of other specified sites of skin
173.00 Unspecified malignant neoplasm of skin of lip ▽
173.01 Basal cell carcinoma of skin of lip
173.02 Squamous cell carcinoma of skin of lip
173.09 Other specified malignant neoplasm of skin of lip
173.10 Unspecified malignant neoplasm of eyelid, including canthus ▽
173.11 Basal cell carcinoma of eyelid, including canthus
173.12 Squamous cell carcinoma of eyelid, including canthus
173.19 Other specified malignant neoplasm of eyelid, including canthus
173.20 Unspecified malignant neoplasm of skin of ear and external auditory canal ▽
173.21 Basal cell carcinoma of skin of ear and external auditory canal
173.22 Squamous cell carcinoma of skin of ear and external auditory canal
173.29 Other specified malignant neoplasm of skin of ear and external auditory canal
173.30 Unspecified malignant neoplasm of skin of other and unspecified parts of face ▽
173.31 Basal cell carcinoma of skin of other and unspecified parts of face
173.32 Squamous cell carcinoma of skin of other and unspecified parts of face
173.39 Other specified malignant neoplasm of skin of other and unspecified parts of face
173.40 Unspecified malignant neoplasm of scalp and skin of neck ▽
173.41 Basal cell carcinoma of scalp and skin of neck
173.42 Squamous cell carcinoma of scalp and skin of neck
173.49 Other specified malignant neoplasm of scalp and skin of neck
173.50 Unspecified malignant neoplasm of skin of trunk, except scrotum ▽
173.51 Basal cell carcinoma of skin of trunk, except scrotum
173.52 Squamous cell carcinoma of skin of trunk, except scrotum
173.59 Other specified malignant neoplasm of skin of trunk, except scrotum
173.60 Unspecified malignant neoplasm of skin of upper limb, including shoulder ▽
173.61 Basal cell carcinoma of skin of upper limb, including shoulder
173.62 Squamous cell carcinoma of skin of upper limb, including shoulder
173.69 Other specified malignant neoplasm of skin of upper limb, including shoulder
173.70 Unspecified malignant neoplasm of skin of lower limb, including hip ▽
173.71 Basal cell carcinoma of skin of lower limb, including hip
173.72 Squamous cell carcinoma of skin of lower limb, including hip
173.79 Other specified malignant neoplasm of skin of lower limb, including hip
173.80 Unspecified malignant neoplasm of other specified sites of skin ▽
173.81 Basal cell carcinoma of other specified sites of skin
173.82 Squamous cell carcinoma of other specified sites of skin
173.89 Other specified malignant neoplasm of other specified sites of skin

174.0 Malignant neoplasm of nipple and areola of female breast — (Use additional code to identify estrogen receptor status: V86.0-V86.1) ♀

174.1 Malignant neoplasm of central portion of female breast — (Use additional code to identify estrogen receptor status: V86.0-V86.1) ♀

174.2 Malignant neoplasm of upper-inner quadrant of female breast — (Use additional code to identify estrogen receptor status: V86.0-V86.1) ♀

174.3 Malignant neoplasm of lower-inner quadrant of female breast — (Use additional code to identify estrogen receptor status: V86.0-V86.1) ♀

174.4 Malignant neoplasm of upper-outer quadrant of female breast — (Use additional code to identify estrogen receptor status: V86.0-V86.1) ♀

174.5 Malignant neoplasm of lower-outer quadrant of female breast — (Use additional code to identify estrogen receptor status: V86.0-V86.1) ♀

174.6 Malignant neoplasm of axillary tail of female breast — (Use additional code to identify estrogen receptor status: V86.0-V86.1) ♀

174.8 Malignant neoplasm of other specified sites of female breast — (Use additional code to identify estrogen receptor status: V86.0-V86.1) ♀

175.0 Malignant neoplasm of nipple and areola of male breast — (Use additional code to identify estrogen receptor status: V86.0-V86.1) ♂

175.9 Malignant neoplasm of other and unspecified sites of male breast — (Use additional code to identify estrogen receptor status: V86.0-V86.1) ▽ ♂

176.0 Kaposi's sarcoma of skin

184.1 Malignant neoplasm of labia majora ♀

184.2 Malignant neoplasm of labia minora ♀

184.3 Malignant neoplasm of clitoris ♀

184.4 Malignant neoplasm of vulva, unspecified site ▽ ♀

184.8 Malignant neoplasm of other specified sites of female genital organs ♀

186.9 Malignant neoplasm of other and unspecified testis — (Use additional code to identify any functional activity) ▽ ♂

187.1 Malignant neoplasm of prepuce ♂

187.2 Malignant neoplasm of glans penis ♂

187.3 Malignant neoplasm of body of penis ♂

187.4 Malignant neoplasm of penis, part unspecified ▽ ♂

187.7 Malignant neoplasm of scrotum ♂

187.8 Malignant neoplasm of other specified sites of male genital organs ♂

195.0 Malignant neoplasm of head, face, and neck

195.1 Malignant neoplasm of thorax

195.2 Malignant neoplasm of abdomen

195.3 Malignant neoplasm of pelvis

195.4 Malignant neoplasm of upper limb

195.5 Malignant neoplasm of lower limb

195.8 Malignant neoplasm of other specified sites

198.2 Secondary malignant neoplasm of skin

198.82 Secondary malignant neoplasm of genital organs

198.89 Secondary malignant neoplasm of other specified sites

209.31 Merkel cell carcinoma of the face

209.32 Merkel cell carcinoma of the scalp and neck

209.33 Merkel cell carcinoma of the upper limb

209.34 Merkel cell carcinoma of the lower limb

209.35 Merkel cell carcinoma of the trunk

209.36 Merkel cell carcinoma of other sites

209.75 Secondary Merkel cell carcinoma

210.0 Benign neoplasm of lip

210.4 Benign neoplasm of other and unspecified parts of mouth ▽

214.0 Lipoma of skin and subcutaneous tissue of face

214.1 Lipoma of other skin and subcutaneous tissue

214.8 Lipoma of other specified sites

215.0 Other benign neoplasm of connective and other soft tissue of head, face, and neck

215.2 Other benign neoplasm of connective and other soft tissue of upper limb, including shoulder

215.3 Other benign neoplasm of connective and other soft tissue of lower limb, including hip

215.7 Other benign neoplasm of connective and other soft tissue of trunk, unspecified ▽

215.8 Other benign neoplasm of connective and other soft tissue of other specified sites

216.0 Benign neoplasm of skin of lip

216.1 Benign neoplasm of eyelid, including canthus

216.2 Benign neoplasm of ear and external auditory canal

216.3 Benign neoplasm of skin of other and unspecified parts of face ▽

216.4 Benign neoplasm of scalp and skin of neck

216.5 Benign neoplasm of skin of trunk, except scrotum

216.6 Benign neoplasm of skin of upper limb, including shoulder

216.8 Benign neoplasm of other specified sites of skin

221.2 Benign neoplasm of vulva ♀

221.8 Benign neoplasm of other specified sites of female genital organs ♀

222.1 Benign neoplasm of penis ♂

222.4 Benign neoplasm of scrotum ♂

229.8 Benign neoplasm of other specified sites

230.0 Carcinoma in situ of lip, oral cavity, and pharynx

232.0 Carcinoma in situ of skin of lip

232.1 Carcinoma in situ of eyelid, including canthus

232.2 Carcinoma in situ of skin of ear and external auditory canal

232.3 Carcinoma in situ of skin of other and unspecified parts of face ▽

232.4 Carcinoma in situ of scalp and skin of neck

232.5 Carcinoma in situ of skin of trunk, except scrotum

232.6 Carcinoma in situ of skin of upper limb, including shoulder

232.7 Carcinoma in situ of skin of lower limb, including hip

232.8 Carcinoma in situ of other specified sites of skin

233.30 Carcinoma in situ, unspecified female genital organ ▽ ♀

233.31 Carcinoma in situ, vagina ♀

233.32 Carcinoma in situ, vulva ♀

233.39 Carcinoma in situ, other female genital organ ♀

233.5 Carcinoma in situ of penis ♂

233.6 Carcinoma in situ of other and unspecified male genital organs ▽ ♂

235.1 Neoplasm of uncertain behavior of lip, oral cavity, and pharynx

236.3 Neoplasm of uncertain behavior of other and unspecified female genital organs ▽ ♀

236.6 Neoplasm of uncertain behavior of other and unspecified male genital organs ▽ ♂

238.2 Neoplasm of uncertain behavior of skin

239.2 Neoplasms of unspecified nature of bone, soft tissue, and skin

239.5 Neoplasm of unspecified nature of other genitourinary organs

249.70 Secondary diabetes mellitus with peripheral circulatory disorders, not stated as uncontrolled, or unspecified — (Use additional code to identify manifestation: 443.81, 785.4) (Use additional code to identify any associated insulin use: V58.67)

249.71 Secondary diabetes mellitus with peripheral circulatory disorders, uncontrolled — (Use additional code to identify manifestation: 443.81, 785.4) (Use additional code to identify any associated insulin use: V58.67)

249.80 Secondary diabetes mellitus with other specified manifestations, not stated as uncontrolled, or unspecified — (Use additional code to identify manifestation: 707.10-707.19, 707.8, 707.9, 731.8) (Use additional code to identify any associated insulin use: V58.67)

249.81 Secondary diabetes mellitus with other specified manifestations, uncontrolled — (Use additional code to identify manifestation: 707.10-707.19, 707.8, 707.9, 731.8) (Use additional code to identify any associated insulin use: V58.67)

249.90 Secondary diabetes mellitus with unspecified complication, not stated as uncontrolled, or unspecified — (Use additional code to identify any associated insulin use: V58.67) ▽

249.91 Secondary diabetes mellitus with unspecified complication, uncontrolled — (Use additional code to identify any associated insulin use: V58.67) ▽

250.70 Diabetes with peripheral circulatory disorders, type II or unspecified type, not stated as uncontrolled — (Use additional code to identify manifestation: 443.81, 785.4)

250.71 Diabetes with peripheral circulatory disorders, type I [juvenile type], not stated as uncontrolled — (Use additional code to identify manifestation: 443.81, 785.4)
250.72 Diabetes with peripheral circulatory disorders, type II or unspecified type, uncontrolled — (Use additional code to identify manifestation: 443.81, 785.4)
250.73 Diabetes with peripheral circulatory disorders, type I [juvenile type], uncontrolled — (Use additional code to identify manifestation: 443.81, 785.4)
250.80 Diabetes with other specified manifestations, type II or unspecified type, not stated as uncontrolled — (Use additional code to identify manifestation: 707.10-707.19, 707.8, 707.9, 731.8)
250.81 Diabetes with other specified manifestations, type I [juvenile type], not stated as uncontrolled — (Use additional code to identify manifestation: 707.10-707.19, 707.8, 707.9, 731.8)
250.82 Diabetes with other specified manifestations, type II or unspecified type, uncontrolled — (Use additional code to identify manifestation: 707.10-707.19, 707.8, 707.9, 731.8)
250.83 Diabetes with other specified manifestations, type I [juvenile type], uncontrolled — (Use additional code to identify manifestation: 707.10-707.19, 707.8, 707.9, 731.8)
374.04 Cicatricial entropion
374.50 Unspecified degenerative disorder of eyelid ▽
374.56 Other degenerative disorders of skin affecting eyelid
374.84 Cysts of eyelids
374.85 Vascular anomalies of eyelid
374.86 Retained foreign body of eyelid — (Use additional code to identify foreign body (V90.01-V90.9))
380.32 Acquired deformities of auricle or pinna
440.23 Atherosclerosis of native arteries of the extremities with ulceration — (Use additional code for any associated ulceration: 707.10-707.19, 707.8, 707.9)
443.0 Raynaud's syndrome — (Use additional code to identify gangrene: 785.4)
454.0 Varicose veins of lower extremities with ulcer
454.2 Varicose veins of lower extremities with ulcer and inflammation
459.11 Postphlebitic syndrome with ulcer
459.13 Postphlebitic syndrome with ulcer and inflammation
459.31 Chronic venous hypertension with ulcer
459.33 Chronic venous hypertension with ulcer and inflammation
629.21 Female genital mutilation, Type I status ♀
629.22 Female genital mutilation, Type II status ♀
629.23 Female genital mutilation, Type III status ♀
629.29 Other female genital mutilation status ♀
629.89 Other specified disorders of female genital organs ♀
682.2 Cellulitis and abscess of trunk — (Use additional code to identify organism, such as 041.1, etc.)
682.3 Cellulitis and abscess of upper arm and forearm — (Use additional code to identify organism, such as 041.1, etc.)
682.4 Cellulitis and abscess of hand, except fingers and thumb — (Use additional code to identify organism, such as 041.1, etc.)
682.5 Cellulitis and abscess of buttock — (Use additional code to identify organism, such as 041.1, etc.)
682.6 Cellulitis and abscess of leg, except foot — (Use additional code to identify organism, such as 041.1, etc.)
682.7 Cellulitis and abscess of foot, except toes — (Use additional code to identify organism, such as 041.1, etc.)
682.8 Cellulitis and abscess of other specified site — (Use additional code to identify organism, such as 041.1, etc.)
701.4 Keloid scar
701.5 Other abnormal granulation tissue
701.9 Unspecified hypertrophic and atrophic condition of skin ▽
707.00 Pressure ulcer, unspecified site — (Use additional code to identify pressure ulcer stage: 707.20-707.25) ▽
707.01 Pressure ulcer, elbow — (Use additional code to identify pressure ulcer stage: 707.20-707.25)
707.02 Pressure ulcer, upper back — (Use additional code to identify pressure ulcer stage: 707.20-707.25)
707.03 Pressure ulcer, lower back — (Use additional code to identify pressure ulcer stage: 707.20-707.25)
707.04 Pressure ulcer, hip — (Use additional code to identify pressure ulcer stage: 707.20-707.25)
707.05 Pressure ulcer, buttock — (Use additional code to identify pressure ulcer stage: 707.20-707.25)
707.06 Pressure ulcer, ankle — (Use additional code to identify pressure ulcer stage: 707.20-707.25)
707.07 Pressure ulcer, heel — (Use additional code to identify pressure ulcer stage: 707.20-707.25)
707.09 Pressure ulcer, other site — (Use additional code to identify pressure ulcer stage: 707.20-707.25)
707.10 Ulcer of lower limb, unspecified — (Code, if applicable, any causal condition first: 249.80-249.81, 250.80-250.83, 440.23, 459.11, 459.13, 459.31, 459.33) ▽
707.11 Ulcer of thigh — (Code, if applicable, any causal condition first: 249.80-249.81, 250.80-250.83, 440.23, 459.11, 459.13, 459.31, 459.33)
707.12 Ulcer of calf — (Code, if applicable, any causal condition first: 249.80-249.81, 250.80-250.83, 440.23, 459.11, 459.13, 459.31, 459.33)
707.13 Ulcer of ankle — (Code, if applicable, any causal condition first: 249.80-249.81, 250.80-250.83, 440.23, 459.11, 459.13, 459.31, 459.33)
707.14 Ulcer of heel and midfoot — (Code, if applicable, any causal condition first: 249.80-249.81, 250.80-250.83, 440.23, 459.11, 459.13, 459.31, 459.33)
707.15 Ulcer of other part of foot — (Code, if applicable, any causal condition first: 249.80-249.81, 250.80-250.83, 440.23, 459.11, 459.13, 459.31, 459.33)
707.19 Ulcer of other part of lower limb — (Code, if applicable, any causal condition first: 249.80-249.81, 250.80-250.83, 440.23, 459.11, 459.13, 459.31, 459.33)
707.20 Pressure ulcer, unspecified stage — (Code first site of pressure ulcer: 707.00-707.09) ▽
707.21 Pressure ulcer, stage I — (Code first site of pressure ulcer: 707.00-707.09)
707.22 Pressure ulcer stage II — (Code first site of pressure ulcer: 707.00-707.09)
707.23 Pressure ulcer stage III — (Code first site of pressure ulcer: 707.00-707.09)
707.24 Pressure ulcer stage IV — (Code first site of pressure ulcer: 707.00-707.09)
707.25 Pressure ulcer, unstageable — (Code first site of pressure ulcer: 707.00-707.09)
707.8 Chronic ulcer of other specified site
709.2 Scar condition and fibrosis of skin
709.3 Degenerative skin disorder
709.4 Foreign body granuloma of skin and subcutaneous tissue — (Use additional code to identify foreign body (V90.01-V90.9))
709.8 Other specified disorder of skin
709.9 Unspecified disorder of skin and subcutaneous tissue ▽
744.29 Other congenital anomaly of ear
752.40 Unspecified congenital anomaly of cervix, vagina, and external female genitalia ▽ ♀
752.43 Cervical agenesis ♀
752.44 Cervical duplication ♀
752.45 Vaginal agenesis ♀
752.46 Transverse vaginal septum ♀
752.47 Longitudinal vaginal septum ♀
752.49 Other congenital anomaly of cervix, vagina, and external female genitalia ♀
757.39 Other specified congenital anomaly of skin
785.4 Gangrene — (Code first any associated underlying condition)
870.0 Laceration of skin of eyelid and periocular area
870.1 Laceration of eyelid, full-thickness, not involving lacrimal passages
870.2 Laceration of eyelid involving lacrimal passages
872.00 Open wound of external ear, unspecified site, without mention of complication ▽
872.01 Open wound of auricle, without mention of complication
872.10 Open wound of external ear, unspecified site, complicated ▽
872.11 Open wound of auricle, complicated
872.8 Open wound of ear, part unspecified, without mention of complication ▽

- 873.0 Open wound of scalp, without mention of complication
- 873.1 Open wound of scalp, complicated
- 873.21 Open wound of nasal septum, without mention of complication
- 873.31 Open wound of nasal septum, complicated
- 873.40 Open wound of face, unspecified site, without mention of complication ▽
- 873.41 Open wound of cheek, without mention of complication
- 873.42 Open wound of forehead, without mention of complication
- 873.43 Open wound of lip, without mention of complication
- 873.44 Open wound of jaw, without mention of complication
- 873.49 Open wound of face, other and multiple sites, without mention of complication
- 873.50 Open wound of face, unspecified site, complicated ▽
- 873.51 Open wound of cheek, complicated
- 873.52 Open wound of forehead, complicated
- 873.53 Open wound of lip, complicated
- 873.54 Open wound of jaw, complicated
- 873.59 Open wound of face, other and multiple sites, complicated
- 873.9 Other and unspecified open wound of head, complicated ▽
- 874.8 Open wound of other and unspecified parts of neck, without mention of complication ▽
- 875.0 Open wound of chest (wall), without mention of complication
- 875.1 Open wound of chest (wall), complicated
- 876.0 Open wound of back, without mention of complication
- 876.1 Open wound of back, complicated
- 877.0 Open wound of buttock, without mention of complication
- 877.1 Open wound of buttock, complicated
- 878.1 Open wound of penis, complicated ♂
- 878.2 Open wound of scrotum and testes, without mention of complication ♂
- 878.3 Open wound of scrotum and testes, complicated ♂
- 878.4 Open wound of vulva, without mention of complication ♀
- 878.5 Open wound of vulva, complicated ♀
- 878.8 Open wound of other and unspecified parts of genital organs, without mention of complication ▽
- 878.9 Open wound of other and unspecified parts of genital organs, complicated ▽
- 879.0 Open wound of breast, without mention of complication
- 879.1 Open wound of breast, complicated
- 879.2 Open wound of abdominal wall, anterior, without mention of complication
- 879.3 Open wound of abdominal wall, anterior, complicated
- 879.4 Open wound of abdominal wall, lateral, without mention of complication
- 879.5 Open wound of abdominal wall, lateral, complicated
- 879.6 Open wound of other and unspecified parts of trunk, without mention of complication ▽
- 879.7 Open wound of other and unspecified parts of trunk, complicated ▽
- 879.8 Open wound(s) (multiple) of unspecified site(s), without mention of complication ▽
- 879.9 Open wound(s) (multiple) of unspecified site(s), complicated ▽
- 880.00 Open wound of shoulder region, without mention of complication
- 880.01 Open wound of scapular region, without mention of complication
- 880.02 Open wound of axillary region, without mention of complication
- 880.03 Open wound of upper arm, without mention of complication
- 880.09 Open wound of multiple sites of shoulder and upper arm, without mention of complication
- 880.10 Open wound of shoulder region, complicated
- 880.11 Open wound of scapular region, complicated
- 880.12 Open wound of axillary region, complicated
- 880.13 Open wound of upper arm, complicated
- 880.19 Open wound of multiple sites of shoulder and upper arm, complicated
- 880.20 Open wound of shoulder region, with tendon involvement
- 880.21 Open wound of scapular region, with tendon involvement
- 880.22 Open wound of axillary region, with tendon involvement
- 880.23 Open wound of upper arm, with tendon involvement
- 880.29 Open wound of multiple sites of shoulder and upper arm, with tendon involvement
- 881.00 Open wound of forearm, without mention of complication
- 881.01 Open wound of elbow, without mention of complication
- 881.02 Open wound of wrist, without mention of complication
- 881.10 Open wound of forearm, complicated
- 881.11 Open wound of elbow, complicated
- 881.12 Open wound of wrist, complicated
- 881.20 Open wound of forearm, with tendon involvement
- 881.21 Open wound of elbow, with tendon involvement
- 881.22 Open wound of wrist, with tendon involvement
- 882.0 Open wound of hand except finger(s) alone, without mention of complication
- 882.1 Open wound of hand except finger(s) alone, complicated
- 882.2 Open wound of hand except finger(s) alone, with tendon involvement
- 883.0 Open wound of finger(s), without mention of complication
- 883.1 Open wound of finger(s), complicated
- 883.2 Open wound of finger(s), with tendon involvement
- 884.0 Multiple and unspecified open wound of upper limb, without mention of complication
- 884.1 Multiple and unspecified open wound of upper limb, complicated
- 884.2 Multiple and unspecified open wound of upper limb, with tendon involvement
- 885.0 Traumatic amputation of thumb (complete) (partial), without mention of complication
- 885.1 Traumatic amputation of thumb (complete) (partial), complicated
- 886.0 Traumatic amputation of other finger(s) (complete) (partial), without mention of complication
- 886.1 Traumatic amputation of other finger(s) (complete) (partial), complicated
- 887.0 Traumatic amputation of arm and hand (complete) (partial), unilateral, below elbow, without mention of complication
- 887.1 Traumatic amputation of arm and hand (complete) (partial), unilateral, below elbow, complicated
- 887.2 Traumatic amputation of arm and hand (complete) (partial), unilateral, at or above elbow, without mention of complication
- 887.3 Traumatic amputation of arm and hand (complete) (partial), unilateral, at or above elbow, complicated
- 887.4 Traumatic amputation of arm and hand (complete) (partial), unilateral, level not specified, without mention of complication ▽
- 887.5 Traumatic amputation of arm and hand (complete) (partial), unilateral, level not specified, complicated ▽
- 887.6 Traumatic amputation of arm and hand (complete) (partial), bilateral (any level), without mention of complication
- 887.7 Traumatic amputation of arm and hand (complete) (partial), bilateral (any level), complicated
- 890.0 Open wound of hip and thigh, without mention of complication
- 890.1 Open wound of hip and thigh, complicated
- 890.2 Open wound of hip and thigh, with tendon involvement
- 891.0 Open wound of knee, leg (except thigh), and ankle, without mention of complication
- 891.1 Open wound of knee, leg (except thigh), and ankle, complicated
- 891.2 Open wound of knee, leg (except thigh), and ankle, with tendon involvement
- 892.0 Open wound of foot except toe(s) alone, without mention of complication
- 892.1 Open wound of foot except toe(s) alone, complicated
- 892.2 Open wound of foot except toe(s) alone, with tendon involvement
- 893.0 Open wound of toe(s), without mention of complication
- 893.1 Open wound of toe(s), complicated
- 893.2 Open wound of toe(s), with tendon involvement
- 894.1 Multiple and unspecified open wound of lower limb, complicated
- 894.2 Multiple and unspecified open wound of lower limb, with tendon involvement
- 895.0 Traumatic amputation of toe(s) (complete) (partial), without mention of complication
- 895.1 Traumatic amputation of toe(s) (complete) (partial), complicated
- 896.0 Traumatic amputation of foot (complete) (partial), unilateral, without mention of complication
- 896.1 Traumatic amputation of foot (complete) (partial), unilateral, complicated

▽ Unspecified code ☒ Manifestation code [Resequenced code]
♀ Female diagnosis ♂ Male diagnosis

896.2 Traumatic amputation of foot (complete) (partial), bilateral, without mention of complication
896.3 Traumatic amputation of foot (complete) (partial), bilateral, complicated
897.0 Traumatic amputation of leg(s) (complete) (partial), unilateral, below knee, without mention of complication
897.1 Traumatic amputation of leg(s) (complete) (partial), unilateral, below knee, complicated
897.2 Traumatic amputation of leg(s) (complete) (partial), unilateral, at or above knee, without mention of complication
897.3 Traumatic amputation of leg(s) (complete) (partial), unilateral, at or above knee, complicated
897.4 Traumatic amputation of leg(s) (complete) (partial), unilateral, level not specified, without mention of complication ▽
897.5 Traumatic amputation of leg(s) (complete) (partial), unilateral, level not specified, complicated ▽
897.6 Traumatic amputation of leg(s) (complete) (partial), bilateral (any level), without mention of complication
897.7 Traumatic amputation of leg(s) (complete) (partial), bilateral (any level), complicated
906.0 Late effect of open wound of head, neck, and trunk
906.1 Late effect of open wound of extremities without mention of tendon injury
906.4 Late effect of crushing
906.5 Late effect of burn of eye, face, head, and neck
906.6 Late effect of burn of wrist and hand
906.7 Late effect of burn of other extremities
906.8 Late effect of burns of other specified sites
908.6 Late effect of certain complications of trauma
909.2 Late effect of radiation
909.3 Late effect of complications of surgical and medical care
909.4 Late effect of certain other external causes
925.1 Crushing injury of face and scalp — (Use additional code to identify any associated injuries, such as: 800-829, 850.0-854.1, 860.0-869.1)
925.2 Crushing injury of neck — (Use additional code to identify any associated injuries, such as: 800-829, 850.0-854.1, 860.0-869.1)
926.0 Crushing injury of external genitalia — (Use additional code to identify any associated injuries: 800-829, 850.0-854.1, 860.0-869.1)
926.11 Crushing injury of back — (Use additional code to identify any associated injuries: 800-829, 850.0-854.1, 860.0-869.1)
926.12 Crushing injury of buttock — (Use additional code to identify any associated injuries: 800-829, 850.0-854.1, 860.0-869.1)
926.19 Crushing injury of other specified sites of trunk — (Use additional code to identify any associated injuries: 800-829, 850.0-854.1, 860.0-869.1)
926.8 Crushing injury of multiple sites of trunk — (Use additional code to identify any associated injuries: 800-829, 850.0-854.1, 860.0-869.1)
926.9 Crushing injury of unspecified site of trunk — (Use additional code to identify any associated injuries: 800-829, 850.0-854.1, 860.0-869.1) ▽
927.00 Crushing injury of shoulder region — (Use additional code to identify any associated injuries: 800-829, 850.0-854.1, 860.0-869.1)
927.01 Crushing injury of scapular region — (Use additional code to identify any associated injuries: 800-829, 850.0-854.1, 860.0-869.1)
927.02 Crushing injury of axillary region — (Use additional code to identify any associated injuries: 800-829, 850.0-854.1, 860.0-869.1)
927.03 Crushing injury of upper arm — (Use additional code to identify any associated injuries: 800-829, 850.0-854.1, 860.0-869.1)
927.09 Crushing injury of multiple sites of upper arm — (Use additional code to identify any associated injuries: 800-829, 850.0-854.1, 860.0-869.1)
927.10 Crushing injury of forearm — (Use additional code to identify any associated injuries: 800-829, 850.0-854.1, 860.0-869.1)
927.11 Crushing injury of elbow — (Use additional code to identify any associated injuries: 800-829, 850.0-854.1, 860.0-869.1)
927.20 Crushing injury of hand(s) — (Use additional code to identify any associated injuries: 800-829, 850.0-854.1, 860.0-869.1)
927.21 Crushing injury of wrist — (Use additional code to identify any associated injuries: 800-829, 850.0-854.1, 860.0-869.1)
927.3 Crushing injury of finger(s) — (Use additional code to identify any associated injuries: 800-829, 850.0-854.1, 860.0-869.1)
927.8 Crushing injury of multiple sites of upper limb — (Use additional code to identify any associated injuries: 800-829, 850.0-854.1, 860.0-869.1)
927.9 Crushing injury of unspecified site of upper limb — (Use additional code to identify any associated injuries: 800-829, 850.0-854.1, 860.0-869.1) ▽
928.00 Crushing injury of thigh — (Use additional code to identify any associated injuries: 800-829, 850.0-854.1, 860.0-869.1)
928.01 Crushing injury of hip — (Use additional code to identify any associated injuries: 800-829, 850.0-854.1, 860.0-869.1)
928.10 Crushing injury of lower leg — (Use additional code to identify any associated injuries: 800-829, 850.0-854.1, 860.0-869.1)
928.11 Crushing injury of knee — (Use additional code to identify any associated injuries: 800-829, 850.0-854.1, 860.0-869.1)
928.20 Crushing injury of foot — (Use additional code to identify any associated injuries: 800-829, 850.0-854.1, 860.0-869.1)
928.21 Crushing injury of ankle — (Use additional code to identify any associated injuries: 800-829, 850.0-854.1, 860.0-869.1)
928.3 Crushing injury of toe(s) — (Use additional code to identify any associated injuries: 800-829, 850.0-854.1, 860.0-869.1)
928.8 Crushing injury of multiple sites of lower limb — (Use additional code to identify any associated injuries: 800-829, 850.0-854.1, 860.0-869.1)
928.9 Crushing injury of unspecified site of lower limb — (Use additional code to identify any associated injuries: 800-829, 850.0-854.1, 860.0-869.1) ▽
929.0 Crushing injury of multiple sites, not elsewhere classified — (Use additional code to identify any associated injuries: 800-829, 850.0-854.1, 860.0-869.1)
940.0 Chemical burn of eyelids and periocular area
940.1 Other burns of eyelids and periocular area
941.30 Full-thickness skin loss due to burn (third degree NOS) of unspecified site of face and head ▽
941.31 Full-thickness skin loss due to burn (third degree NOS) of ear (any part)
941.32 Full-thickness skin loss due to burn (third degree NOS) of eye (with other parts of face, head, and neck)
941.33 Full-thickness skin loss due to burn (third degree NOS) of lip(s)
941.34 Full-thickness skin loss due to burn (third degree NOS) of chin
941.35 Full-thickness skin loss due to burn (third degree NOS) of nose (septum)
941.36 Full-thickness skin loss due to burn (third degree NOS) of scalp (any part)
941.37 Full-thickness skin loss due to burn (third degree NOS) of forehead and cheek
941.38 Full-thickness skin loss due to burn (third degree NOS) of neck
941.39 Full-thickness skin loss due to burn (third degree NOS) of multiple sites (except with eye) of face, head, and neck
941.40 Deep necrosis of underlying tissues due to burn (deep third degree) of unspecified site of face and head, without mention of loss of a body part ▽
941.41 Deep necrosis of underlying tissues due to burn (deep third degree) of ear (any part), without mention of loss of a body part
941.42 Deep necrosis of underlying tissues due to burn (deep third degree) of eye (with other parts of face, head, and neck), without mention of loss of a body part
941.43 Deep necrosis of underlying tissues due to burn (deep third degree) of lip(s), without mention of loss of a body part
941.44 Deep necrosis of underlying tissues due to burn (deep third degree) of chin, without mention of loss of a body part
941.45 Deep necrosis of underlying tissues due to burn (deep third degree) of nose (septum), without mention of loss of a body part
941.46 Deep necrosis of underlying tissues due to burn (deep third degree) of scalp (any part), without mention of loss of a body part
941.47 Deep necrosis of underlying tissues due to burn (deep third degree) of forehead and cheek, without mention of loss of a body part
941.48 Deep necrosis of underlying tissues due to burn (deep third degree) of neck, without mention of loss of a body part

941.49 Deep necrosis of underlying tissues due to burn (deep third degree) of multiple sites (except with eye) of face, head, and neck, without mention of loss of a body part

941.50 Deep necrosis of underlying tissues due to burn (deep third degree) of face and head, unspecified site, with loss of a body part ▽

941.51 Deep necrosis of underlying tissues due to burn (deep third degree) of ear (any part), with loss of a body part

941.52 Deep necrosis of underlying tissues due to burn (deep third degree) of eye (with other parts of face, head, and neck), with loss of a body part

941.53 Deep necrosis of underlying tissues due to burn (deep third degree) of lip(s), with loss of a body part

941.54 Deep necrosis of underlying tissues due to burn (deep third degree) of chin, with loss of a body part

941.55 Deep necrosis of underlying tissues due to burn (deep third degree) of nose (septum), with loss of a body part

941.56 Deep necrosis of underlying tissues due to burn (deep third degree) of scalp (any part), with loss of a body part

941.57 Deep necrosis of underlying tissues due to burn (deep third degree) of forehead and cheek, with loss of a body part

941.58 Deep necrosis of underlying tissues due to burn (deep third degree) of neck, with loss of a body part

941.59 Deep necrosis of underlying tissues due to burn (deep third degree) of multiple sites (except eye) of face, head, and neck, with loss of a body part

942.30 Full-thickness skin loss due to burn (third degree NOS) of unspecified site of trunk ▽

942.31 Full-thickness skin loss due to burn (third degree NOS) of breast

942.32 Full-thickness skin loss due to burn (third degree NOS) of chest wall, excluding breast and nipple

942.33 Full-thickness skin loss due to burn (third degree NOS) of abdominal wall

942.34 Full-thickness skin loss due to burn (third degree NOS) of back (any part)

942.35 Full-thickness skin loss due to burn (third degree NOS) of genitalia

942.39 Full-thickness skin loss due to burn (third degree NOS) of other and multiple sites of trunk

942.40 Deep necrosis of underlying tissues due to burn (deep third degree) of trunk, unspecified site, without mention of loss of a body part ▽

942.41 Deep necrosis of underlying tissues due to burn (deep third degree) of breast, without mention of loss of a body part

942.42 Deep necrosis of underlying tissues due to burn (deep third degree) of chest wall, excluding breast and nipple, without mention of loss of a body part

942.43 Deep necrosis of underlying tissues due to burn (deep third degree) of abdominal wall, without mention of loss of a body part

942.44 Deep necrosis of underlying tissues due to burn (deep third degree) of back (any part), without mention of loss of a body part

942.45 Deep necrosis of underlying tissues due to burn (deep third degree) of genitalia, without mention of loss of a body part

942.49 Deep necrosis of underlying tissues due to burn (deep third degree) of other and multiple sites of trunk, without mention of loss of a body part

942.50 Deep necrosis of underlying tissues due to burn (deep third degree) of unspecified site of trunk, with loss of a body part ▽

942.51 Deep necrosis of underlying tissues due to burn (deep third degree) of breast, with loss of a body part

942.52 Deep necrosis of underlying tissues due to burn (deep third degree) of chest wall, excluding breast and nipple, with loss of a body part

942.53 Deep necrosis of underlying tissues due to burn (deep third degree) of abdominal wall with loss of a body part

942.54 Deep necrosis of underlying tissues due to burn (deep third degree) of back (any part), with loss of a body part

942.55 Deep necrosis of underlying tissues due to burn (deep third degree) of genitalia, with loss of a body part

942.59 Deep necrosis of underlying tissues due to burn (deep third degree) of other and multiple sites of trunk, with loss of a body part

943.30 Full-thickness skin loss due to burn (third degree NOS) of unspecified site of upper limb ▽

943.31 Full-thickness skin loss due to burn (third degree NOS) of forearm

943.32 Full-thickness skin loss due to burn (third degree NOS) of elbow

943.33 Full-thickness skin loss due to burn (third degree NOS) of upper arm

943.34 Full-thickness skin loss due to burn (third degree NOS) of axilla

943.35 Full-thickness skin loss due to burn (third degree NOS) of shoulder

943.36 Full-thickness skin loss due to burn (third degree NOS) of scapular region

943.39 Full-thickness skin loss due to burn (third degree NOS) of multiple sites of upper limb, except wrist and hand

943.40 Deep necrosis of underlying tissues due to burn (deep third degree) of unspecified site of upper limb, without mention of loss of a body part ▽

943.41 Deep necrosis of underlying tissues due to burn (deep third degree) of forearm, without mention of loss of a body part

943.42 Deep necrosis of underlying tissues due to burn (deep third degree) of elbow, without mention of loss of a body part

943.43 Deep necrosis of underlying tissues due to burn (deep third degree) of upper arm, without mention of loss of a body part

943.44 Deep necrosis of underlying tissues due to burn (deep third degree) of axilla, without mention of loss of a body part

943.45 Deep necrosis of underlying tissues due to burn (deep third degree) of shoulder, without mention of loss of a body part

943.46 Deep necrosis of underlying tissues due to burn (deep third degree) of scapular region, without mention of loss of a body part

943.49 Deep necrosis of underlying tissues due to burn (deep third degree) of multiple sites of upper limb, except wrist and hand, without mention of loss of a body part

943.50 Deep necrosis of underlying tissues due to burn (deep third degree) of unspecified site of upper limb, with loss of a body part ▽

943.51 Deep necrosis of underlying tissues due to burn (deep third degree) of forearm, with loss of a body part

943.52 Deep necrosis of underlying tissues due to burn (deep third degree) of elbow, with loss of a body part

943.53 Deep necrosis of underlying tissues due to burn (deep third degree) of upper arm, with loss of upper a body part

943.54 Deep necrosis of underlying tissues due to burn (deep third degree) of axilla, with loss of a body part

943.55 Deep necrosis of underlying tissues due to burn (deep third degree) of shoulder, with loss of a body part

943.56 Deep necrosis of underlying tissues due to burn (deep third degree) of scapular region, with loss of a body part

943.59 Deep necrosis of underlying tissues due to burn (deep third degree) of multiple sites of upper limb, except wrist and hand, with loss of a body part

944.30 Full-thickness skin loss due to burn (third degree NOS) of unspecified site of hand ▽

944.31 Full-thickness skin loss due to burn (third degree NOS) of single digit [finger (nail)] other than thumb

944.32 Full-thickness skin loss due to burn (third degree NOS) of thumb (nail)

944.33 Full-thickness skin loss due to burn (third degree NOS) of two or more digits of hand, not including thumb

944.34 Full-thickness skin loss due to burn (third degree NOS) of two or more digits of hand including thumb

944.35 Full-thickness skin loss due to burn (third degree NOS) of palm of hand

944.36 Full-thickness skin loss due to burn (third degree NOS) of back of hand

944.37 Full-thickness skin loss due to burn (third degree NOS) of wrist

944.38 Full-thickness skin loss due to burn (third degree NOS) of multiple sites of wrist(s) and hand(s)

944.40 Deep necrosis of underlying tissues due to burn (deep third degree) of unspecified site of hand, without mention of loss of a body part ▽

944.41 Deep necrosis of underlying tissues due to burn (deep third degree) of single digit [finger (nail)] other than thumb, without mention of loss of a body part

944.42 Deep necrosis of underlying tissues due to burn (deep third degree) of thumb (nail), without mention of loss of a body part

944.43 Deep necrosis of underlying tissues due to burn (deep third degree) of two or more digits of hand, not including thumb, without mention of loss of a body part

944.44 Deep necrosis of underlying tissues due to burn (deep third degree) of two or more digits of hand including thumb, without mention of loss of a body part
944.45 Deep necrosis of underlying tissues due to burn (deep third degree) of palm of hand, without mention of loss of a body part
944.46 Deep necrosis of underlying tissues due to burn (deep third degree) of back of hand, without mention of loss of a body part
944.47 Deep necrosis of underlying tissues due to burn (deep third degree) of wrist, without mention of loss of a body part
944.48 Deep necrosis of underlying tissues due to burn (deep third degree) of multiple sites of wrist(s) and hand(s), without mention of loss of a body part
944.50 Deep necrosis of underlying tissues due to burn (deep third degree) of unspecified site of hand, with loss of a body part ▽
944.51 Deep necrosis of underlying tissues due to burn (deep third degree) of single digit (finger (nail)) other than thumb, with loss of a body part
944.52 Deep necrosis of underlying tissues due to burn (deep third degree) of thumb (nail), with loss of a body part
944.53 Deep necrosis of underlying tissues due to burn (deep third degree) of two or more digits of hand, not including thumb, with loss of a body part
944.54 Deep necrosis of underlying tissues due to burn (deep third degree) of two or more digits of hand including thumb, with loss of a body part
944.55 Deep necrosis of underlying tissues due to burn (deep third degree) of palm of hand, with loss of a body part
944.56 Deep necrosis of underlying tissues due to burn (deep third degree) of back of hand, with loss of a body part
944.57 Deep necrosis of underlying tissues due to burn (deep third degree) of wrist, with loss of a body part
944.58 Deep necrosis of underlying tissues due to burn (deep third degree) of multiple sites of wrist(s) and hand(s), with loss of a body part
945.30 Full-thickness skin loss due to burn (third degree NOS) of unspecified site of lower limb ▽
945.31 Full-thickness skin loss due to burn (third degree NOS) of toe(s) (nail)
945.32 Full-thickness skin loss due to burn (third degree NOS) of foot
945.33 Full-thickness skin loss due to burn (third degree NOS) of ankle
945.34 Full-thickness skin loss due to burn (third degree NOS) of lower leg
945.35 Full-thickness skin loss due to burn (third degree NOS) of knee
945.36 Full-thickness skin loss due to burn (third degree NOS) of thigh (any part)
945.39 Full-thickness skin loss due to burn (third degree NOS) of multiple sites of lower limb(s)
945.40 Deep necrosis of underlying tissues due to burn (deep third degree) of unspecified site of lower limb (leg), without mention of loss of a body part ▽
945.42 Deep necrosis of underlying tissues due to burn (deep third degree) of foot, without mention of loss of a body part
945.43 Deep necrosis of underlying tissues due to burn (deep third degree) of ankle, without mention of loss of a body part
945.44 Deep necrosis of underlying tissues due to burn (deep third degree) of lower leg, without mention of loss of a body part
945.45 Deep necrosis of underlying tissues due to burn (deep third degree) of knee, without mention of loss of a body part
945.46 Deep necrosis of underlying tissues due to burn (deep third degree) of thigh (any part), without mention of loss of a body part
945.49 Deep necrosis of underlying tissues due to burn (deep third degree) of multiple sites of lower limb(s), without mention of loss of a body part
945.50 Deep necrosis of underlying tissues due to burn (deep third degree) of unspecified site lower limb (leg), with loss of a body part ▽
945.51 Deep necrosis of underlying tissues due to burn (deep third degree) of toe(s) (nail), with loss of a body part
945.52 Deep necrosis of underlying tissues due to burn (deep third degree) of foot, with loss of a body part
945.53 Deep necrosis of underlying tissues due to burn (deep third degree) of ankle, with loss of a body part
945.54 Deep necrosis of underlying tissues due to burn (deep third degree) of lower leg, with loss of a body part
945.55 Deep necrosis of underlying tissues due to burn (deep third degree) of knee, with loss of a body part
945.56 Deep necrosis of underlying tissues due to burn (deep third degree) of thigh (any part), with loss of a body part
945.59 Deep necrosis of underlying tissues due to burn (deep third degree) of multiple sites of lower limb(s), with loss of a body part
946.3 Full-thickness skin loss due to burn (third degree NOS) of multiple specified sites
946.4 Deep necrosis of underlying tissues due to burn (deep third degree) of multiple specified sites, without mention of loss of a body part
946.5 Deep necrosis of underlying tissues due to burn (deep third degree) of multiple specified sites, with loss of a body part
948.00 Burn (any degree) involving less than 10% of body surface with third degree burn of less than 10% or unspecified amount
948.10 Burn (any degree) involving 10-19% of body surface with third degree burn of less than 10% or unspecified amount
948.11 Burn (any degree) involving 10-19% of body surface with third degree burn of 10-19%
948.20 Burn (any degree) involving 20-29% of body surface with third degree burn of less than 10% or unspecified amount
948.21 Burn (any degree) involving 20-29% of body surface with third degree burn of 10-19%
948.22 Burn (any degree) involving 20-29% of body surface with third degree burn of 20-29%
948.30 Burn (any degree) involving 30-39% of body surface with third degree burn of less than 10% or unspecified amount
948.31 Burn (any degree) involving 30-39% of body surface with third degree burn of 10-19%
948.32 Burn (any degree) involving 30-39% of body surface with third degree burn of 20-29%
948.33 Burn (any degree) involving 30-39% of body surface with third degree burn of 30-39%
948.40 Burn (any degree) involving 40-49% of body surface with third degree burn of less than 10% or unspecified amount
948.41 Burn (any degree) involving 40-49% of body surface with third degree burn of 10-19%
948.42 Burn (any degree) involving 40-49% of body surface with third degree burn of 20-29%
948.43 Burn (any degree) involving 40-49% of body surface with third degree burn of 30-39%
948.44 Burn (any degree) involving 40-49% of body surface with third degree burn of 40-49%
948.50 Burn (any degree) involving 50-59% of body surface with third degree burn of less than 10% or unspecified amount
948.51 Burn (any degree) involving 50-59% of body surface with third degree burn of 10-19%
948.52 Burn (any degree) involving 50-59% of body surface with third degree burn of 20-29%
948.53 Burn (any degree) involving 50-59% of body surface with third degree burn of 30-39%
948.54 Burn (any degree) involving 50-59% of body surface with third degree burn of 40-49%
948.55 Burn (any degree) involving 50-59% of body surface with third degree burn of 50-59%
948.60 Burn (any degree) involving 60-69% of body surface with third degree burn of less than 10% or unspecified amount
948.61 Burn (any degree) involving 60-69% of body surface with third degree burn of 10-19%
948.62 Burn (any degree) involving 60-69% of body surface with third degree burn of 20-29%
948.63 Burn (any degree) involving 60-69% of body surface with third degree burn of 30-39%
948.64 Burn (any degree) involving 60-69% of body surface with third degree burn of 40-49%
948.65 Burn (any degree) involving 60-69% of body surface with third degree burn of 50-59%
948.66 Burn (any degree) involving 60-69% of body surface with third degree burn of 60-69%
948.70 Burn (any degree) involving 70-79% of body surface with third degree burn of less than 10% or unspecified amount
948.71 Burn (any degree) involving 70-79% of body surface with third degree burn of 10-19%
948.72 Burn (any degree) involving 70-79% of body surface with third degree burn of 20-29%
948.73 Burn (any degree) involving 70-79% of body surface with third degree burn of 30-39%
948.74 Burn (any degree) involving 70-79% of body surface with third degree burn of 40-49%
948.75 Burn (any degree) involving 70-79% of body surface with third degree burn of 50-59%
948.76 Burn (any degree) involving 70-79% of body surface with third degree burn of 60-69%
948.77 Burn (any degree) involving 70-79% of body surface with third degree burn of 70-79%
948.80 Burn (any degree) involving 80-89% of body surface with third degree burn of less than 10% or unspecified amount
948.81 Burn (any degree) involving 80-89% of body surface with third degree burn of 10-19%

948.82 Burn (any degree) involving 80-89% of body surface with third degree burn of 20-29%

948.83 Burn (any degree) involving 80-89% of body surface with third degree burn of 30-39%

948.84 Burn (any degree) involving 80-89% of body surface with third degree burn of 40-49%

948.85 Burn (any degree) involving 80-89% of body surface with third degree burn of 50-59%

948.86 Burn (any degree) involving 80-89% of body surface with third degree burn of 60-69%

948.87 Burn (any degree) involving 80-89% of body surface with third degree burn of 70-79%

948.88 Burn (any degree) involving 80-89% of body surface with third degree burn of 80-89%

948.90 Burn (any degree) involving 90% or more of body surface with third degree burn of less than 10% or unspecified amount

948.91 Burn (any degree) involving 90% or more of body surface with third degree burn of 10-19%

948.92 Burn (any degree) involving 90% or more of body surface with third degree burn of 20-29%

948.93 Burn (any degree) involving 90% or more of body surface with third degree burn of 30-39%

948.94 Burn (any degree) involving 90% or more of body surface with third degree burn of 40-49%

948.95 Burn (any degree) involving 90% or more of body surface with third degree burn of 50-59%

948.96 Burn (any degree) involving 90% or more of body surface with third degree burn of 60-69%

948.97 Burn (any degree) involving 90% or more of body surface with third degree burn of 70-79%

948.98 Burn (any degree) involving 90% or more of body surface with third degree burn of 80-89%

948.99 Burn (any degree) involving 90% or more of body surface with third degree burn of 90% or more of body surface

949.3 Full-thickness skin loss due to burn (third degree NOS), unspecified site ▽

949.4 Deep necrosis of underlying tissue due to burn (deep third degree), unspecified site without mention of loss of body part ▽

949.5 Deep necrosis of underlying tissues due to burn (deep third degree, unspecified site with loss of body part ▽

959.01 Head injury, unspecified ▽

959.09 Injury of face and neck, other and unspecified

959.14 Other injury of external genitals

959.4 Injury, other and unspecified, hand, except finger

959.5 Injury, other and unspecified, finger

959.7 Injury, other and unspecified, knee, leg, ankle, and foot

959.8 Injury, other and unspecified, other specified sites, including multiple

991.0 Frostbite of face

991.1 Frostbite of hand

991.2 Frostbite of foot

991.3 Frostbite of other and unspecified sites ▽

996.52 Mechanical complication due to other tissue graft, not elsewhere classified

996.91 Complications of reattached forearm

996.92 Complications of reattached hand

996.93 Complications of reattached finger(s)

996.94 Complications of reattached upper extremity, other and unspecified ▽

996.95 Complications of reattached foot and toe(s)

996.96 Complications of reattached lower extremity, other and unspecified ▽

997.61 Neuroma of amputation stump — (Use additional code to identify complications)

997.62 Infection (chronic) of amputation stump — (Use additional code to identify complications)

997.69 Other late amputation stump complication — (Use additional code to identify complications)

998.30 Disruption of wound, unspecified ▽

998.32 Disruption of external operation (surgical) wound

998.33 Disruption of traumatic injury wound repair

998.59 Other postoperative infection — (Use additional code to identify infection)

998.83 Non-healing surgical wound

V51.0 Encounter for breast reconstruction following mastectomy

V51.8 Other aftercare involving the use of plastic surgery

ICD-9-CM Procedural

86.91 Excision of skin for graft

15050

15050 Pinch graft, single or multiple, to cover small ulcer, tip of digit, or other minimal open area (except on face), up to defect size 2 cm diameter

ICD-9-CM Diagnostic

171.2 Malignant neoplasm of connective and other soft tissue of upper limb, including shoulder

172.6 Malignant melanoma of skin of upper limb, including shoulder

172.7 Malignant melanoma of skin of lower limb, including hip

173.60 Unspecified malignant neoplasm of skin of upper limb, including shoulder ▽

173.61 Basal cell carcinoma of skin of upper limb, including shoulder

173.62 Squamous cell carcinoma of skin of upper limb, including shoulder

173.69 Other specified malignant neoplasm of skin of upper limb, including shoulder

173.70 Unspecified malignant neoplasm of skin of lower limb, including hip ▽

173.71 Basal cell carcinoma of skin of lower limb, including hip

173.72 Squamous cell carcinoma of skin of lower limb, including hip

173.79 Other specified malignant neoplasm of skin of lower limb, including hip

209.33 Merkel cell carcinoma of the upper limb

209.34 Merkel cell carcinoma of the lower limb

209.36 Merkel cell carcinoma of other sites

209.75 Secondary Merkel cell carcinoma

232.8 Carcinoma in situ of other specified sites of skin

238.2 Neoplasm of uncertain behavior of skin

249.70 Secondary diabetes mellitus with peripheral circulatory disorders, not stated as uncontrolled, or unspecified — (Use additional code to identify manifestation: 443.81, 785.4) (Use additional code to identify any associated insulin use: V58.67)

249.71 Secondary diabetes mellitus with peripheral circulatory disorders, uncontrolled — (Use additional code to identify manifestation: 443.81, 785.4) (Use additional code to identify any associated insulin use: V58.67)

249.80 Secondary diabetes mellitus with other specified manifestations, not stated as uncontrolled, or unspecified — (Use additional code to identify manifestation: 707.10-707.19, 707.8, 707.9, 731.8) (Use additional code to identify any associated insulin use: V58.67)

249.81 Secondary diabetes mellitus with other specified manifestations, uncontrolled — (Use additional code to identify manifestation: 707.10-707.19, 707.8, 707.9, 731.8) (Use additional code to identify any associated insulin use: V58.67)

249.90 Secondary diabetes mellitus with unspecified complication, not stated as uncontrolled, or unspecified — (Use additional code to identify any associated insulin use: V58.67) ▽

249.91 Secondary diabetes mellitus with unspecified complication, uncontrolled — (Use additional code to identify any associated insulin use: V58.67) ▽

250.70 Diabetes with peripheral circulatory disorders, type II or unspecified type, not stated as uncontrolled — (Use additional code to identify manifestation: 443.81, 785.4)

250.71 Diabetes with peripheral circulatory disorders, type I [juvenile type], not stated as uncontrolled — (Use additional code to identify manifestation: 443.81, 785.4)

250.72 Diabetes with peripheral circulatory disorders, type II or unspecified type, uncontrolled — (Use additional code to identify manifestation: 443.81, 785.4)

250.73 Diabetes with peripheral circulatory disorders, type I [juvenile type], uncontrolled — (Use additional code to identify manifestation: 443.81, 785.4)

250.80 Diabetes with other specified manifestations, type II or unspecified type, not stated as uncontrolled — (Use additional code to identify manifestation: 707.10-707.19, 707.8, 707.9, 731.8)

250.81 Diabetes with other specified manifestations, type I [juvenile type], not stated as uncontrolled — (Use additional code to identify manifestation: 707.10-707.19, 707.8, 707.9, 731.8)

250.82 Diabetes with other specified manifestations, type II or unspecified type, uncontrolled — (Use additional code to identify manifestation: 707.10-707.19, 707.8, 707.9, 731.8)

250.83 Diabetes with other specified manifestations, type I [juvenile type], uncontrolled — (Use additional code to identify manifestation: 707.10-707.19, 707.8, 707.9, 731.8)

440.23 Atherosclerosis of native arteries of the extremities with ulceration — (Use additional code for any associated ulceration: 707.10-707.19, 707.8, 707.9)

443.81 Peripheral angiopathy in diseases classified elsewhere — (Code first underlying disease: 249.7, 250.7) ☒

459.11 Postphlebitic syndrome with ulcer

459.13 Postphlebitic syndrome with ulcer and inflammation

459.31 Chronic venous hypertension with ulcer

459.33 Chronic venous hypertension with ulcer and inflammation

681.01 Felon — (Use additional code to identify organism: 041.1)

707.00 Pressure ulcer, unspecified site — (Use additional code to identify pressure ulcer stage: 707.20-707.25) ▽

707.01 Pressure ulcer, elbow — (Use additional code to identify pressure ulcer stage: 707.20-707.25)

707.02 Pressure ulcer, upper back — (Use additional code to identify pressure ulcer stage: 707.20-707.25)

707.03 Pressure ulcer, lower back — (Use additional code to identify pressure ulcer stage: 707.20-707.25)

707.04 Pressure ulcer, hip — (Use additional code to identify pressure ulcer stage: 707.20-707.25)

707.05 Pressure ulcer, buttock — (Use additional code to identify pressure ulcer stage: 707.20-707.25)

707.06 Pressure ulcer, ankle — (Use additional code to identify pressure ulcer stage: 707.20-707.25)

707.07 Pressure ulcer, heel — (Use additional code to identify pressure ulcer stage: 707.20-707.25)

707.09 Pressure ulcer, other site — (Use additional code to identify pressure ulcer stage: 707.20-707.25)

707.10 Ulcer of lower limb, unspecified — (Code, if applicable, any causal condition first: 249.80-249.81, 250.80-250.83, 440.23, 459.11, 459.13, 459.31, 459.33) ▽

707.11 Ulcer of thigh — (Code, if applicable, any causal condition first: 249.80-249.81, 250.80-250.83, 440.23, 459.11, 459.13, 459.31, 459.33)

707.12 Ulcer of calf — (Code, if applicable, any causal condition first: 249.80-249.81, 250.80-250.83, 440.23, 459.11, 459.13, 459.31, 459.33)

707.13 Ulcer of ankle — (Code, if applicable, any causal condition first: 249.80-249.81, 250.80-250.83, 440.23, 459.11, 459.13, 459.31, 459.33)

707.14 Ulcer of heel and midfoot — (Code, if applicable, any causal condition first: 249.80-249.81, 250.80-250.83, 440.23, 459.11, 459.13, 459.31, 459.33)

707.15 Ulcer of other part of foot — (Code, if applicable, any causal condition first: 249.80-249.81, 250.80-250.83, 440.23, 459.11, 459.13, 459.31, 459.33)

707.19 Ulcer of other part of lower limb — (Code, if applicable, any causal condition first: 249.80-249.81, 250.80-250.83, 440.23, 459.11, 459.13, 459.31, 459.33)

707.20 Pressure ulcer, unspecified stage — (Code first site of pressure ulcer: 707.00-707.09) ▽

707.21 Pressure ulcer, stage I — (Code first site of pressure ulcer: 707.00-707.09)

707.22 Pressure ulcer stage II — (Code first site of pressure ulcer: 707.00-707.09)

707.23 Pressure ulcer stage III — (Code first site of pressure ulcer: 707.00-707.09)

707.24 Pressure ulcer stage IV — (Code first site of pressure ulcer: 707.00-707.09)

707.25 Pressure ulcer, unstageable — (Code first site of pressure ulcer: 707.00-707.09)

707.8 Chronic ulcer of other specified site

707.9 Chronic ulcer of unspecified site ▽

785.4 Gangrene — (Code first any associated underlying condition)

816.12 Open fracture of distal phalanx or phalanges of hand

882.0 Open wound of hand except finger(s) alone, without mention of complication

882.1 Open wound of hand except finger(s) alone, complicated

882.2 Open wound of hand except finger(s) alone, with tendon involvement

883.0 Open wound of finger(s), without mention of complication

883.1 Open wound of finger(s), complicated

883.2 Open wound of finger(s), with tendon involvement

885.0 Traumatic amputation of thumb (complete) (partial), without mention of complication

885.1 Traumatic amputation of thumb (complete) (partial), complicated

886.0 Traumatic amputation of other finger(s) (complete) (partial), without mention of complication

886.1 Traumatic amputation of other finger(s) (complete) (partial), complicated

893.0 Open wound of toe(s), without mention of complication

893.1 Open wound of toe(s), complicated

893.2 Open wound of toe(s), with tendon involvement

895.0 Traumatic amputation of toe(s) (complete) (partial), without mention of complication

895.1 Traumatic amputation of toe(s) (complete) (partial), complicated

906.4 Late effect of crushing

906.6 Late effect of burn of wrist and hand

906.7 Late effect of burn of other extremities

906.8 Late effect of burns of other specified sites

908.6 Late effect of certain complications of trauma

908.9 Late effect of unspecified injury ▽

909.3 Late effect of complications of surgical and medical care

927.3 Crushing injury of finger(s) — (Use additional code to identify any associated injuries: 800-829, 850.0-854.1, 860.0-869.1)

928.3 Crushing injury of toe(s) — (Use additional code to identify any associated injuries: 800-829, 850.0-854.1, 860.0-869.1)

V51.8 Other aftercare involving the use of plastic surgery

ICD-9-CM Procedural

86.60 Free skin graft, not otherwise specified

86.62 Other skin graft to hand

15100-15101

15100 Split-thickness autograft, trunk, arms, legs; first 100 sq cm or less, or 1% of body area of infants and children (except 15050)

15101 each additional 100 sq cm, or each additional 1% of body area of infants and children, or part thereof (List separately in addition to code for primary procedure)

ICD-9-CM Diagnostic

172.5 Malignant melanoma of skin of trunk, except scrotum

172.6 Malignant melanoma of skin of upper limb, including shoulder

172.7 Malignant melanoma of skin of lower limb, including hip

172.8 Malignant melanoma of other specified sites of skin

173.50 Unspecified malignant neoplasm of skin of trunk, except scrotum ▽

173.51 Basal cell carcinoma of skin of trunk, except scrotum

173.52 Squamous cell carcinoma of skin of trunk, except scrotum

173.59 Other specified malignant neoplasm of skin of trunk, except scrotum

173.60 Unspecified malignant neoplasm of skin of upper limb, including shoulder ▽

173.61 Basal cell carcinoma of skin of upper limb, including shoulder

173.62 Squamous cell carcinoma of skin of upper limb, including shoulder

173.69 Other specified malignant neoplasm of skin of upper limb, including shoulder

173.70 Unspecified malignant neoplasm of skin of lower limb, including hip ▽

173.71 Basal cell carcinoma of skin of lower limb, including hip

173.72 Squamous cell carcinoma of skin of lower limb, including hip

173.79 Other specified malignant neoplasm of skin of lower limb, including hip

173.80 Unspecified malignant neoplasm of other specified sites of skin ▽

173.81 Basal cell carcinoma of other specified sites of skin

173.82 Squamous cell carcinoma of other specified sites of skin

173.89 Other specified malignant neoplasm of other specified sites of skin

174.0 Malignant neoplasm of nipple and areola of female breast — (Use additional code to identify estrogen receptor status: V86.0-V86.1) ♀

174.1 Malignant neoplasm of central portion of female breast — (Use additional code to identify estrogen receptor status: V86.0-V86.1) ♀

174.2 Malignant neoplasm of upper-inner quadrant of female breast — (Use additional code to identify estrogen receptor status: V86.0-V86.1) ♀
174.3 Malignant neoplasm of lower-inner quadrant of female breast — (Use additional code to identify estrogen receptor status: V86.0-V86.1) ♀
174.4 Malignant neoplasm of upper-outer quadrant of female breast — (Use additional code to identify estrogen receptor status: V86.0-V86.1) ♀
174.5 Malignant neoplasm of lower-outer quadrant of female breast — (Use additional code to identify estrogen receptor status: V86.0-V86.1) ♀
174.6 Malignant neoplasm of axillary tail of female breast — (Use additional code to identify estrogen receptor status: V86.0-V86.1) ♀
174.8 Malignant neoplasm of other specified sites of female breast — (Use additional code to identify estrogen receptor status: V86.0-V86.1) ♀
175.0 Malignant neoplasm of nipple and areola of male breast — (Use additional code to identify estrogen receptor status: V86.0-V86.1) ♂
175.9 Malignant neoplasm of other and unspecified sites of male breast — (Use additional code to identify estrogen receptor status: V86.0-V86.1) ▽ ♂
195.1 Malignant neoplasm of thorax
195.2 Malignant neoplasm of abdomen
195.3 Malignant neoplasm of pelvis
195.4 Malignant neoplasm of upper limb
195.5 Malignant neoplasm of lower limb
195.8 Malignant neoplasm of other specified sites
198.2 Secondary malignant neoplasm of skin
209.33 Merkel cell carcinoma of the upper limb
209.34 Merkel cell carcinoma of the lower limb
209.35 Merkel cell carcinoma of the trunk
209.75 Secondary Merkel cell carcinoma
232.5 Carcinoma in situ of skin of trunk, except scrotum
232.6 Carcinoma in situ of skin of upper limb, including shoulder
232.7 Carcinoma in situ of skin of lower limb, including hip
232.8 Carcinoma in situ of other specified sites of skin
238.2 Neoplasm of uncertain behavior of skin
239.2 Neoplasms of unspecified nature of bone, soft tissue, and skin
249.70 Secondary diabetes mellitus with peripheral circulatory disorders, not stated as uncontrolled, or unspecified — (Use additional code to identify manifestation: 443.81, 785.4) (Use additional code to identify any associated insulin use: V58.67)
249.71 Secondary diabetes mellitus with peripheral circulatory disorders, uncontrolled — (Use additional code to identify manifestation: 443.81, 785.4) (Use additional code to identify any associated insulin use: V58.67)
249.80 Secondary diabetes mellitus with other specified manifestations, not stated as uncontrolled, or unspecified — (Use additional code to identify manifestation: 707.10-707.19, 707.8, 707.9, 731.8) (Use additional code to identify any associated insulin use: V58.67)
249.81 Secondary diabetes mellitus with other specified manifestations, uncontrolled — (Use additional code to identify manifestation: 707.10-707.19, 707.8, 707.9, 731.8) (Use additional code to identify any associated insulin use: V58.67)
249.90 Secondary diabetes mellitus with unspecified complication, not stated as uncontrolled, or unspecified — (Use additional code to identify any associated insulin use: V58.67) ▽
249.91 Secondary diabetes mellitus with unspecified complication, uncontrolled — (Use additional code to identify any associated insulin use: V58.67) ▽
250.70 Diabetes with peripheral circulatory disorders, type II or unspecified type, not stated as uncontrolled — (Use additional code to identify manifestation: 443.81, 785.4)
250.71 Diabetes with peripheral circulatory disorders, type I [juvenile type], not stated as uncontrolled — (Use additional code to identify manifestation: 443.81, 785.4)
250.72 Diabetes with peripheral circulatory disorders, type II or unspecified type, uncontrolled — (Use additional code to identify manifestation: 443.81, 785.4)
250.73 Diabetes with peripheral circulatory disorders, type I [juvenile type], uncontrolled — (Use additional code to identify manifestation: 443.81, 785.4)
250.80 Diabetes with other specified manifestations, type II or unspecified type, not stated as uncontrolled — (Use additional code to identify manifestation: 707.10-707.19, 707.8, 707.9, 731.8)
250.81 Diabetes with other specified manifestations, type I [juvenile type], not stated as uncontrolled — (Use additional code to identify manifestation: 707.10-707.19, 707.8, 707.9, 731.8)
250.82 Diabetes with other specified manifestations, type II or unspecified type, uncontrolled — (Use additional code to identify manifestation: 707.10-707.19, 707.8, 707.9, 731.8)
250.83 Diabetes with other specified manifestations, type I [juvenile type], uncontrolled — (Use additional code to identify manifestation: 707.10-707.19, 707.8, 707.9, 731.8)
440.23 Atherosclerosis of native arteries of the extremities with ulceration — (Use additional code for any associated ulceration: 707.10-707.19, 707.8, 707.9)
443.0 Raynaud's syndrome — (Use additional code to identify gangrene: 785.4)
443.81 Peripheral angiopathy in diseases classified elsewhere — (Code first underlying disease: 249.7, 250.7) ☒
454.0 Varicose veins of lower extremities with ulcer
454.2 Varicose veins of lower extremities with ulcer and inflammation
454.8 Varicose veins of the lower extremities with other complications
459.11 Postphlebitic syndrome with ulcer
459.13 Postphlebitic syndrome with ulcer and inflammation
459.19 Postphlebitic syndrome with other complication
459.31 Chronic venous hypertension with ulcer
459.33 Chronic venous hypertension with ulcer and inflammation
459.39 Chronic venous hypertension with other complication
459.81 Unspecified venous (peripheral) insufficiency — (Use additional code for any associated ulceration: 707.10-707.19, 707.8, 707.9) ▽
682.2 Cellulitis and abscess of trunk — (Use additional code to identify organism, such as 041.1, etc.)
682.3 Cellulitis and abscess of upper arm and forearm — (Use additional code to identify organism, such as 041.1, etc.)
682.5 Cellulitis and abscess of buttock — (Use additional code to identify organism, such as 041.1, etc.)
682.6 Cellulitis and abscess of leg, except foot — (Use additional code to identify organism, such as 041.1, etc.)
682.8 Cellulitis and abscess of other specified site — (Use additional code to identify organism, such as 041.1, etc.)
701.4 Keloid scar
701.5 Other abnormal granulation tissue
701.9 Unspecified hypertrophic and atrophic condition of skin ▽
707.00 Pressure ulcer, unspecified site — (Use additional code to identify pressure ulcer stage: 707.20-707.25) ▽
707.01 Pressure ulcer, elbow — (Use additional code to identify pressure ulcer stage: 707.20-707.25)
707.02 Pressure ulcer, upper back — (Use additional code to identify pressure ulcer stage: 707.20-707.25)
707.03 Pressure ulcer, lower back — (Use additional code to identify pressure ulcer stage: 707.20-707.25)
707.04 Pressure ulcer, hip — (Use additional code to identify pressure ulcer stage: 707.20-707.25)
707.05 Pressure ulcer, buttock — (Use additional code to identify pressure ulcer stage: 707.20-707.25)
707.06 Pressure ulcer, ankle — (Use additional code to identify pressure ulcer stage: 707.20-707.25)
707.07 Pressure ulcer, heel — (Use additional code to identify pressure ulcer stage: 707.20-707.25)
707.09 Pressure ulcer, other site — (Use additional code to identify pressure ulcer stage: 707.20-707.25)
707.10 Ulcer of lower limb, unspecified — (Code, if applicable, any causal condition first: 249.80-249.81, 250.80-250.83, 440.23, 459.11, 459.13, 459.31, 459.33) ▽

707.11 Ulcer of thigh — (Code, if applicable, any causal condition first: 249.80-249.81, 250.80-250.83, 440.23, 459.11, 459.13, 459.31, 459.33)

707.12 Ulcer of calf — (Code, if applicable, any causal condition first: 249.80-249.81, 250.80-250.83, 440.23, 459.11, 459.13, 459.31, 459.33)

707.13 Ulcer of ankle — (Code, if applicable, any causal condition first: 249.80-249.81, 250.80-250.83, 440.23, 459.11, 459.13, 459.31, 459.33)

707.20 Pressure ulcer, unspecified stage — (Code first site of pressure ulcer: 707.00-707.09) ▽

707.21 Pressure ulcer, stage I — (Code first site of pressure ulcer: 707.00-707.09)

707.22 Pressure ulcer stage II — (Code first site of pressure ulcer: 707.00-707.09)

707.23 Pressure ulcer stage III — (Code first site of pressure ulcer: 707.00-707.09)

707.24 Pressure ulcer stage IV — (Code first site of pressure ulcer: 707.00-707.09)

707.25 Pressure ulcer, unstageable — (Code first site of pressure ulcer: 707.00-707.09)

707.8 Chronic ulcer of other specified site

709.2 Scar condition and fibrosis of skin

709.4 Foreign body granuloma of skin and subcutaneous tissue — (Use additional code to identify foreign body (V90.01-V90.9))

709.9 Unspecified disorder of skin and subcutaneous tissue ▽

785.4 Gangrene — (Code first any associated underlying condition)

875.0 Open wound of chest (wall), without mention of complication

875.1 Open wound of chest (wall), complicated

876.0 Open wound of back, without mention of complication

876.1 Open wound of back, complicated

877.0 Open wound of buttock, without mention of complication

877.1 Open wound of buttock, complicated

879.0 Open wound of breast, without mention of complication

879.1 Open wound of breast, complicated

879.2 Open wound of abdominal wall, anterior, without mention of complication

879.3 Open wound of abdominal wall, anterior, complicated

879.4 Open wound of abdominal wall, lateral, without mention of complication

879.5 Open wound of abdominal wall, lateral, complicated

879.6 Open wound of other and unspecified parts of trunk, without mention of complication ▽

879.7 Open wound of other and unspecified parts of trunk, complicated ▽

879.8 Open wound(s) (multiple) of unspecified site(s), without mention of complication ▽

879.9 Open wound(s) (multiple) of unspecified site(s), complicated ▽

880.00 Open wound of shoulder region, without mention of complication

880.01 Open wound of scapular region, without mention of complication

880.02 Open wound of axillary region, without mention of complication

880.03 Open wound of upper arm, without mention of complication

880.09 Open wound of multiple sites of shoulder and upper arm, without mention of complication

881.00 Open wound of forearm, without mention of complication

881.01 Open wound of elbow, without mention of complication

881.02 Open wound of wrist, without mention of complication

881.10 Open wound of forearm, complicated

881.11 Open wound of elbow, complicated

881.12 Open wound of wrist, complicated

881.20 Open wound of forearm, with tendon involvement

881.21 Open wound of elbow, with tendon involvement

881.22 Open wound of wrist, with tendon involvement

884.0 Multiple and unspecified open wound of upper limb, without mention of complication

884.1 Multiple and unspecified open wound of upper limb, complicated

884.2 Multiple and unspecified open wound of upper limb, with tendon involvement

887.0 Traumatic amputation of arm and hand (complete) (partial), unilateral, below elbow, without mention of complication

887.1 Traumatic amputation of arm and hand (complete) (partial), unilateral, below elbow, complicated

887.2 Traumatic amputation of arm and hand (complete) (partial), unilateral, at or above elbow, without mention of complication

887.3 Traumatic amputation of arm and hand (complete) (partial), unilateral, at or above elbow, complicated

887.4 Traumatic amputation of arm and hand (complete) (partial), unilateral, level not specified, without mention of complication ▽

887.5 Traumatic amputation of arm and hand (complete) (partial), unilateral, level not specified, complicated ▽

887.6 Traumatic amputation of arm and hand (complete) (partial), bilateral (any level), without mention of complication

887.7 Traumatic amputation of arm and hand (complete) (partial), bilateral (any level), complicated

890.0 Open wound of hip and thigh, without mention of complication

890.1 Open wound of hip and thigh, complicated

890.2 Open wound of hip and thigh, with tendon involvement

891.0 Open wound of knee, leg (except thigh), and ankle, without mention of complication

891.1 Open wound of knee, leg (except thigh), and ankle, complicated

891.2 Open wound of knee, leg (except thigh), and ankle, with tendon involvement

894.0 Multiple and unspecified open wound of lower limb, without mention of complication

894.1 Multiple and unspecified open wound of lower limb, complicated

894.2 Multiple and unspecified open wound of lower limb, with tendon involvement

897.0 Traumatic amputation of leg(s) (complete) (partial), unilateral, below knee, without mention of complication

897.1 Traumatic amputation of leg(s) (complete) (partial), unilateral, below knee, complicated

897.2 Traumatic amputation of leg(s) (complete) (partial), unilateral, at or above knee, without mention of complication

897.3 Traumatic amputation of leg(s) (complete) (partial), unilateral, at or above knee, complicated

897.4 Traumatic amputation of leg(s) (complete) (partial), unilateral, level not specified, without mention of complication ▽

897.5 Traumatic amputation of leg(s) (complete) (partial), unilateral, level not specified, complicated ▽

897.6 Traumatic amputation of leg(s) (complete) (partial), bilateral (any level), without mention of complication

897.7 Traumatic amputation of leg(s) (complete) (partial), bilateral (any level), complicated

906.0 Late effect of open wound of head, neck, and trunk

906.1 Late effect of open wound of extremities without mention of tendon injury

906.4 Late effect of crushing

906.6 Late effect of burn of wrist and hand

906.7 Late effect of burn of other extremities

906.8 Late effect of burns of other specified sites

908.0 Late effect of internal injury to chest

908.1 Late effect of internal injury to intra-abdominal organs

908.2 Late effect of internal injury to other internal organs

908.3 Late effect of injury to blood vessel of head, neck, and extremities

908.4 Late effect of injury to blood vessel of thorax, abdomen, and pelvis

908.6 Late effect of certain complications of trauma

909.2 Late effect of radiation

948.00 Burn (any degree) involving less than 10% of body surface with third degree burn of less than 10% or unspecified amount

948.10 Burn (any degree) involving 10-19% of body surface with third degree burn of less than 10% or unspecified amount

948.11 Burn (any degree) involving 10-19% of body surface with third degree burn of 10-19%

948.20 Burn (any degree) involving 20-29% of body surface with third degree burn of less than 10% or unspecified amount

948.21 Burn (any degree) involving 20-29% of body surface with third degree burn of 10-19%

948.22 Burn (any degree) involving 20-29% of body surface with third degree burn of 20-29%

948.30 Burn (any degree) involving 30-39% of body surface with third degree burn of less than 10% or unspecified amount

948.31 Burn (any degree) involving 30-39% of body surface with third degree burn of 10-19%

948.32 Burn (any degree) involving 30-39% of body surface with third degree burn of 20-29%

948.33 Burn (any degree) involving 30-39% of body surface with third degree burn of 30-39%

948.40 Burn (any degree) involving 40-49% of body surface with third degree burn of less than 10% or unspecified amount
948.41 Burn (any degree) involving 40-49% of body surface with third degree burn of 10-19%
948.42 Burn (any degree) involving 40-49% of body surface with third degree burn of 20-29%
948.43 Burn (any degree) involving 40-49% of body surface with third degree burn of 30-39%
948.44 Burn (any degree) involving 40-49% of body surface with third degree burn of 40-49%
948.50 Burn (any degree) involving 50-59% of body surface with third degree burn of less than 10% or unspecified amount
948.51 Burn (any degree) involving 50-59% of body surface with third degree burn of 10-19%
948.52 Burn (any degree) involving 50-59% of body surface with third degree burn of 20-29%
948.53 Burn (any degree) involving 50-59% of body surface with third degree burn of 30-39%
948.54 Burn (any degree) involving 50-59% of body surface with third degree burn of 40-49%
948.55 Burn (any degree) involving 50-59% of body surface with third degree burn of 50-59%
948.60 Burn (any degree) involving 60-69% of body surface with third degree burn of less than 10% or unspecified amount
948.61 Burn (any degree) involving 60-69% of body surface with third degree burn of 10-19%
948.62 Burn (any degree) involving 60-69% of body surface with third degree burn of 20-29%
948.63 Burn (any degree) involving 60-69% of body surface with third degree burn of 30-39%
948.64 Burn (any degree) involving 60-69% of body surface with third degree burn of 40-49%
948.65 Burn (any degree) involving 60-69% of body surface with third degree burn of 50-59%
948.66 Burn (any degree) involving 60-69% of body surface with third degree burn of 60-69%
948.70 Burn (any degree) involving 70-79% of body surface with third degree burn of less than 10% or unspecified amount
948.71 Burn (any degree) involving 70-79% of body surface with third degree burn of 10-19%
948.72 Burn (any degree) involving 70-79% of body surface with third degree burn of 20-29%
948.73 Burn (any degree) involving 70-79% of body surface with third degree burn of 30-39%
948.74 Burn (any degree) involving 70-79% of body surface with third degree burn of 40-49%
948.75 Burn (any degree) involving 70-79% of body surface with third degree burn of 50-59%
948.76 Burn (any degree) involving 70-79% of body surface with third degree burn of 60-69%
948.77 Burn (any degree) involving 70-79% of body surface with third degree burn of 70-79%
948.80 Burn (any degree) involving 80-89% of body surface with third degree burn of less than 10% or unspecified amount
948.81 Burn (any degree) involving 80-89% of body surface with third degree burn of 10-19%
948.82 Burn (any degree) involving 80-89% of body surface with third degree burn of 20-29%
948.83 Burn (any degree) involving 80-89% of body surface with third degree burn of 30-39%
948.84 Burn (any degree) involving 80-89% of body surface with third degree burn of 40-49%
948.85 Burn (any degree) involving 80-89% of body surface with third degree burn of 50-59%
948.86 Burn (any degree) involving 80-89% of body surface with third degree burn of 60-69%
948.87 Burn (any degree) involving 80-89% of body surface with third degree burn of 70-79%
948.88 Burn (any degree) involving 80-89% of body surface with third degree burn of 80-89%
958.3 Posttraumatic wound infection not elsewhere classified
991.3 Frostbite of other and unspecified sites ♥
996.52 Mechanical complication due to other tissue graft, not elsewhere classified
996.91 Complications of reattached forearm
996.94 Complications of reattached upper extremity, other and unspecified ♥
996.96 Complications of reattached lower extremity, other and unspecified ♥
997.61 Neuroma of amputation stump — (Use additional code to identify complications)
997.62 Infection (chronic) of amputation stump — (Use additional code to identify complications)
997.69 Other late amputation stump complication — (Use additional code to identify complications)
998.30 Disruption of wound, unspecified ♥
998.32 Disruption of external operation (surgical) wound
998.33 Disruption of traumatic injury wound repair
998.59 Other postoperative infection — (Use additional code to identify infection)
998.83 Non-healing surgical wound
V51.8 Other aftercare involving the use of plastic surgery

ICD-9-CM Procedural

85.82 Split-thickness graft to breast
86.60 Free skin graft, not otherwise specified
86.69 Other skin graft to other sites

15110-15111

15110 Epidermal autograft, trunk, arms, legs; first 100 sq cm or less, or 1% of body area of infants and children
15111 each additional 100 sq cm, or each additional 1% of body area of infants and children, or part thereof (List separately in addition to code for primary procedure)

ICD-9-CM Diagnostic

172.5 Malignant melanoma of skin of trunk, except scrotum
172.6 Malignant melanoma of skin of upper limb, including shoulder
172.7 Malignant melanoma of skin of lower limb, including hip
172.8 Malignant melanoma of other specified sites of skin
173.50 Unspecified malignant neoplasm of skin of trunk, except scrotum ♥
173.51 Basal cell carcinoma of skin of trunk, except scrotum
173.52 Squamous cell carcinoma of skin of trunk, except scrotum
173.59 Other specified malignant neoplasm of skin of trunk, except scrotum
173.60 Unspecified malignant neoplasm of skin of upper limb, including shoulder ♥
173.61 Basal cell carcinoma of skin of upper limb, including shoulder
173.62 Squamous cell carcinoma of skin of upper limb, including shoulder
173.69 Other specified malignant neoplasm of skin of upper limb, including shoulder
173.70 Unspecified malignant neoplasm of skin of lower limb, including hip ♥
173.71 Basal cell carcinoma of skin of lower limb, including hip
173.72 Squamous cell carcinoma of skin of lower limb, including hip
173.79 Other specified malignant neoplasm of skin of lower limb, including hip
173.80 Unspecified malignant neoplasm of other specified sites of skin ♥
173.81 Basal cell carcinoma of other specified sites of skin
173.82 Squamous cell carcinoma of other specified sites of skin
173.89 Other specified malignant neoplasm of other specified sites of skin
174.0 Malignant neoplasm of nipple and areola of female breast — (Use additional code to identify estrogen receptor status: V86.0-V86.1) ♀
174.1 Malignant neoplasm of central portion of female breast — (Use additional code to identify estrogen receptor status: V86.0-V86.1) ♀
174.2 Malignant neoplasm of upper-inner quadrant of female breast — (Use additional code to identify estrogen receptor status: V86.0-V86.1) ♀
174.3 Malignant neoplasm of lower-inner quadrant of female breast — (Use additional code to identify estrogen receptor status: V86.0-V86.1) ♀
174.4 Malignant neoplasm of upper-outer quadrant of female breast — (Use additional code to identify estrogen receptor status: V86.0-V86.1) ♀
174.5 Malignant neoplasm of lower-outer quadrant of female breast — (Use additional code to identify estrogen receptor status: V86.0-V86.1) ♀
174.6 Malignant neoplasm of axillary tail of female breast — (Use additional code to identify estrogen receptor status: V86.0-V86.1) ♀
174.8 Malignant neoplasm of other specified sites of female breast — (Use additional code to identify estrogen receptor status: V86.0-V86.1) ♀
175.0 Malignant neoplasm of nipple and areola of male breast — (Use additional code to identify estrogen receptor status: V86.0-V86.1) ♂
175.9 Malignant neoplasm of other and unspecified sites of male breast — (Use additional code to identify estrogen receptor status: V86.0-V86.1) ♥ ♂
176.0 Kaposi's sarcoma of skin
195.1 Malignant neoplasm of thorax
195.2 Malignant neoplasm of abdomen
195.3 Malignant neoplasm of pelvis
195.4 Malignant neoplasm of upper limb
195.5 Malignant neoplasm of lower limb
195.8 Malignant neoplasm of other specified sites
198.2 Secondary malignant neoplasm of skin
209.33 Merkel cell carcinoma of the upper limb
209.34 Merkel cell carcinoma of the lower limb

209.35 Merkel cell carcinoma of the trunk
209.75 Secondary Merkel cell carcinoma
214.1 Lipoma of other skin and subcutaneous tissue
215.7 Other benign neoplasm of connective and other soft tissue of trunk, unspecified
216.5 Benign neoplasm of skin of trunk, except scrotum
216.6 Benign neoplasm of skin of upper limb, including shoulder
232.5 Carcinoma in situ of skin of trunk, except scrotum
232.6 Carcinoma in situ of skin of upper limb, including shoulder
232.7 Carcinoma in situ of skin of lower limb, including hip
232.8 Carcinoma in situ of other specified sites of skin
238.2 Neoplasm of uncertain behavior of skin
239.2 Neoplasms of unspecified nature of bone, soft tissue, and skin
249.70 Secondary diabetes mellitus with peripheral circulatory disorders, not stated as uncontrolled, or unspecified — (Use additional code to identify manifestation: 443.81, 785.4) (Use additional code to identify any associated insulin use: V58.67)
249.71 Secondary diabetes mellitus with peripheral circulatory disorders, uncontrolled — (Use additional code to identify manifestation: 443.81, 785.4) (Use additional code to identify any associated insulin use: V58.67)
249.80 Secondary diabetes mellitus with other specified manifestations, not stated as uncontrolled, or unspecified — (Use additional code to identify manifestation: 707.10-707.19, 707.8, 707.9, 731.8) (Use additional code to identify any associated insulin use: V58.67)
249.81 Secondary diabetes mellitus with other specified manifestations, uncontrolled — (Use additional code to identify manifestation: 707.10-707.19, 707.8, 707.9, 731.8) (Use additional code to identify any associated insulin use: V58.67)
249.90 Secondary diabetes mellitus with unspecified complication, not stated as uncontrolled, or unspecified — (Use additional code to identify any associated insulin use: V58.67)
249.91 Secondary diabetes mellitus with unspecified complication, uncontrolled — (Use additional code to identify any associated insulin use: V58.67)
250.70 Diabetes with peripheral circulatory disorders, type II or unspecified type, not stated as uncontrolled — (Use additional code to identify manifestation: 443.81, 785.4)
250.71 Diabetes with peripheral circulatory disorders, type I [juvenile type], not stated as uncontrolled — (Use additional code to identify manifestation: 443.81, 785.4)
250.72 Diabetes with peripheral circulatory disorders, type II or unspecified type, uncontrolled — (Use additional code to identify manifestation: 443.81, 785.4)
250.73 Diabetes with peripheral circulatory disorders, type I [juvenile type], uncontrolled — (Use additional code to identify manifestation: 443.81, 785.4)
250.80 Diabetes with other specified manifestations, type II or unspecified type, not stated as uncontrolled — (Use additional code to identify manifestation: 707.10-707.19, 707.8, 707.9, 731.8)
250.81 Diabetes with other specified manifestations, type I [juvenile type], not stated as uncontrolled — (Use additional code to identify manifestation: 707.10-707.19, 707.8, 707.9, 731.8)
250.82 Diabetes with other specified manifestations, type II or unspecified type, uncontrolled — (Use additional code to identify manifestation: 707.10-707.19, 707.8, 707.9, 731.8)
250.83 Diabetes with other specified manifestations, type I [juvenile type], uncontrolled — (Use additional code to identify manifestation: 707.10-707.19, 707.8, 707.9, 731.8)
440.23 Atherosclerosis of native arteries of the extremities with ulceration — (Use additional code for any associated ulceration: 707.10-707.19, 707.8, 707.9)
454.0 Varicose veins of lower extremities with ulcer
454.2 Varicose veins of lower extremities with ulcer and inflammation
459.11 Postphlebitic syndrome with ulcer
459.13 Postphlebitic syndrome with ulcer and inflammation
459.31 Chronic venous hypertension with ulcer
459.33 Chronic venous hypertension with ulcer and inflammation
459.81 Unspecified venous (peripheral) insufficiency — (Use additional code for any associated ulceration: 707.10-707.19, 707.8, 707.9)
682.2 Cellulitis and abscess of trunk — (Use additional code to identify organism, such as 041.1, etc.)
682.3 Cellulitis and abscess of upper arm and forearm — (Use additional code to identify organism, such as 041.1, etc.)
682.5 Cellulitis and abscess of buttock — (Use additional code to identify organism, such as 041.1, etc.)
682.6 Cellulitis and abscess of leg, except foot — (Use additional code to identify organism, such as 041.1, etc.)
682.8 Cellulitis and abscess of other specified site — (Use additional code to identify organism, such as 041.1, etc.)
701.4 Keloid scar
701.5 Other abnormal granulation tissue
701.9 Unspecified hypertrophic and atrophic condition of skin
707.00 Pressure ulcer, unspecified site — (Use additional code to identify pressure ulcer stage: 707.20-707.25)
707.01 Pressure ulcer, elbow — (Use additional code to identify pressure ulcer stage: 707.20-707.25)
707.02 Pressure ulcer, upper back — (Use additional code to identify pressure ulcer stage: 707.20-707.25)
707.03 Pressure ulcer, lower back — (Use additional code to identify pressure ulcer stage: 707.20-707.25)
707.04 Pressure ulcer, hip — (Use additional code to identify pressure ulcer stage: 707.20-707.25)
707.05 Pressure ulcer, buttock — (Use additional code to identify pressure ulcer stage: 707.20-707.25)
707.06 Pressure ulcer, ankle — (Use additional code to identify pressure ulcer stage: 707.20-707.25)
707.09 Pressure ulcer, other site — (Use additional code to identify pressure ulcer stage: 707.20-707.25)
707.10 Ulcer of lower limb, unspecified — (Code, if applicable, any causal condition first: 249.80-249.81, 250.80-250.83, 440.23, 459.11, 459.13, 459.31, 459.33)
707.11 Ulcer of thigh — (Code, if applicable, any causal condition first: 249.80-249.81, 250.80-250.83, 440.23, 459.11, 459.13, 459.31, 459.33)
707.12 Ulcer of calf — (Code, if applicable, any causal condition first: 249.80-249.81, 250.80-250.83, 440.23, 459.11, 459.13, 459.31, 459.33)
707.13 Ulcer of ankle — (Code, if applicable, any causal condition first: 249.80-249.81, 250.80-250.83, 440.23, 459.11, 459.13, 459.31, 459.33)
707.20 Pressure ulcer, unspecified stage — (Code first site of pressure ulcer: 707.00-707.09)
707.21 Pressure ulcer, stage I — (Code first site of pressure ulcer: 707.00-707.09)
707.22 Pressure ulcer stage II — (Code first site of pressure ulcer: 707.00-707.09)
707.23 Pressure ulcer stage III — (Code first site of pressure ulcer: 707.00-707.09)
707.24 Pressure ulcer stage IV — (Code first site of pressure ulcer: 707.00-707.09)
707.25 Pressure ulcer, unstageable — (Code first site of pressure ulcer: 707.00-707.09)
707.8 Chronic ulcer of other specified site
709.2 Scar condition and fibrosis of skin
709.3 Degenerative skin disorder
709.4 Foreign body granuloma of skin and subcutaneous tissue — (Use additional code to identify foreign body (V90.01-V90.9))
709.8 Other specified disorder of skin
709.9 Unspecified disorder of skin and subcutaneous tissue
785.4 Gangrene — (Code first any associated underlying condition)
875.0 Open wound of chest (wall), without mention of complication
875.1 Open wound of chest (wall), complicated
876.0 Open wound of back, without mention of complication
876.1 Open wound of back, complicated
877.0 Open wound of buttock, without mention of complication
877.1 Open wound of buttock, complicated
879.0 Open wound of breast, without mention of complication
879.1 Open wound of breast, complicated
879.2 Open wound of abdominal wall, anterior, without mention of complication
879.3 Open wound of abdominal wall, anterior, complicated

Code	Description
879.4	Open wound of abdominal wall, lateral, without mention of complication
879.5	Open wound of abdominal wall, lateral, complicated
879.6	Open wound of other and unspecified parts of trunk, without mention of complication
879.7	Open wound of other and unspecified parts of trunk, complicated
879.8	Open wound(s) (multiple) of unspecified site(s), without mention of complication
879.9	Open wound(s) (multiple) of unspecified site(s), complicated
880.00	Open wound of shoulder region, without mention of complication
880.01	Open wound of scapular region, without mention of complication
880.02	Open wound of axillary region, without mention of complication
880.03	Open wound of upper arm, without mention of complication
880.09	Open wound of multiple sites of shoulder and upper arm, without mention of complication
880.10	Open wound of shoulder region, complicated
880.11	Open wound of scapular region, complicated
880.12	Open wound of axillary region, complicated
880.13	Open wound of upper arm, complicated
880.19	Open wound of multiple sites of shoulder and upper arm, complicated
880.20	Open wound of shoulder region, with tendon involvement
880.21	Open wound of scapular region, with tendon involvement
880.22	Open wound of axillary region, with tendon involvement
880.23	Open wound of upper arm, with tendon involvement
880.29	Open wound of multiple sites of shoulder and upper arm, with tendon involvement
881.00	Open wound of forearm, without mention of complication
881.01	Open wound of elbow, without mention of complication
881.02	Open wound of wrist, without mention of complication
881.10	Open wound of forearm, complicated
881.11	Open wound of elbow, complicated
881.12	Open wound of wrist, complicated
881.20	Open wound of forearm, with tendon involvement
881.21	Open wound of elbow, with tendon involvement
881.22	Open wound of wrist, with tendon involvement
884.0	Multiple and unspecified open wound of upper limb, without mention of complication
884.1	Multiple and unspecified open wound of upper limb, complicated
884.2	Multiple and unspecified open wound of upper limb, with tendon involvement
887.0	Traumatic amputation of arm and hand (complete) (partial), unilateral, below elbow, without mention of complication
887.1	Traumatic amputation of arm and hand (complete) (partial), unilateral, below elbow, complicated
887.2	Traumatic amputation of arm and hand (complete) (partial), unilateral, at or above elbow, without mention of complication
887.3	Traumatic amputation of arm and hand (complete) (partial), unilateral, at or above elbow, complicated
887.4	Traumatic amputation of arm and hand (complete) (partial), unilateral, level not specified, without mention of complication
887.5	Traumatic amputation of arm and hand (complete) (partial), unilateral, level not specified, complicated
887.6	Traumatic amputation of arm and hand (complete) (partial), bilateral (any level), without mention of complication
887.7	Traumatic amputation of arm and hand (complete) (partial), bilateral (any level), complicated
890.0	Open wound of hip and thigh, without mention of complication
890.1	Open wound of hip and thigh, complicated
890.2	Open wound of hip and thigh, with tendon involvement
891.0	Open wound of knee, leg (except thigh), and ankle, without mention of complication
891.1	Open wound of knee, leg (except thigh), and ankle, complicated
891.2	Open wound of knee, leg (except thigh), and ankle, with tendon involvement
894.0	Multiple and unspecified open wound of lower limb, without mention of complication
894.1	Multiple and unspecified open wound of lower limb, complicated
894.2	Multiple and unspecified open wound of lower limb, with tendon involvement
897.0	Traumatic amputation of leg(s) (complete) (partial), unilateral, below knee, without mention of complication
897.1	Traumatic amputation of leg(s) (complete) (partial), unilateral, below knee, complicated
897.2	Traumatic amputation of leg(s) (complete) (partial), unilateral, at or above knee, without mention of complication
897.3	Traumatic amputation of leg(s) (complete) (partial), unilateral, at or above knee, complicated
897.4	Traumatic amputation of leg(s) (complete) (partial), unilateral, level not specified, without mention of complication
897.5	Traumatic amputation of leg(s) (complete) (partial), unilateral, level not specified, complicated
897.6	Traumatic amputation of leg(s) (complete) (partial), bilateral (any level), without mention of complication
897.7	Traumatic amputation of leg(s) (complete) (partial), bilateral (any level), complicated
906.0	Late effect of open wound of head, neck, and trunk
906.1	Late effect of open wound of extremities without mention of tendon injury
906.4	Late effect of crushing
906.6	Late effect of burn of wrist and hand
906.7	Late effect of burn of other extremities
906.8	Late effect of burns of other specified sites
908.6	Late effect of certain complications of trauma
909.2	Late effect of radiation
909.3	Late effect of complications of surgical and medical care
909.4	Late effect of certain other external causes
926.11	Crushing injury of back — (Use additional code to identify any associated injuries: 800-829, 850.0-854.1, 860.0-869.1)
926.12	Crushing injury of buttock — (Use additional code to identify any associated injuries: 800-829, 850.0-854.1, 860.0-869.1)
926.19	Crushing injury of other specified sites of trunk — (Use additional code to identify any associated injuries: 800-829, 850.0-854.1, 860.0-869.1)
926.8	Crushing injury of multiple sites of trunk — (Use additional code to identify any associated injuries: 800-829, 850.0-854.1, 860.0-869.1)
926.9	Crushing injury of unspecified site of trunk — (Use additional code to identify any associated injuries: 800-829, 850.0-854.1, 860.0-869.1)
927.00	Crushing injury of shoulder region — (Use additional code to identify any associated injuries: 800-829, 850.0-854.1, 860.0-869.1)
927.01	Crushing injury of scapular region — (Use additional code to identify any associated injuries: 800-829, 850.0-854.1, 860.0-869.1)
927.02	Crushing injury of axillary region — (Use additional code to identify any associated injuries: 800-829, 850.0-854.1, 860.0-869.1)
927.03	Crushing injury of upper arm — (Use additional code to identify any associated injuries: 800-829, 850.0-854.1, 860.0-869.1)
927.09	Crushing injury of multiple sites of upper arm — (Use additional code to identify any associated injuries: 800-829, 850.0-854.1, 860.0-869.1)
927.10	Crushing injury of forearm — (Use additional code to identify any associated injuries: 800-829, 850.0-854.1, 860.0-869.1)
927.11	Crushing injury of elbow — (Use additional code to identify any associated injuries: 800-829, 850.0-854.1, 860.0-869.1)
927.21	Crushing injury of wrist — (Use additional code to identify any associated injuries: 800-829, 850.0-854.1, 860.0-869.1)
927.8	Crushing injury of multiple sites of upper limb — (Use additional code to identify any associated injuries: 800-829, 850.0-854.1, 860.0-869.1)
927.9	Crushing injury of unspecified site of upper limb — (Use additional code to identify any associated injuries: 800-829, 850.0-854.1, 860.0-869.1)
928.00	Crushing injury of thigh — (Use additional code to identify any associated injuries: 800-829, 850.0-854.1, 860.0-869.1)
928.01	Crushing injury of hip — (Use additional code to identify any associated injuries: 800-829, 850.0-854.1, 860.0-869.1)
928.10	Crushing injury of lower leg — (Use additional code to identify any associated injuries: 800-829, 850.0-854.1, 860.0-869.1)

Unspecified code ♀ Female diagnosis ■ Manifestation code ♂ Male diagnosis [Resequenced code]

928.11 Crushing injury of knee — (Use additional code to identify any associated injuries: 800-829, 850.0-854.1, 860.0-869.1)

928.21 Crushing injury of ankle — (Use additional code to identify any associated injuries: 800-829, 850.0-854.1, 860.0-869.1)

928.8 Crushing injury of multiple sites of lower limb — (Use additional code to identify any associated injuries: 800-829, 850.0-854.1, 860.0-869.1)

928.9 Crushing injury of unspecified site of lower limb — (Use additional code to identify any associated injuries: 800-829, 850.0-854.1, 860.0-869.1) ▽

929.0 Crushing injury of multiple sites, not elsewhere classified — (Use additional code to identify any associated injuries: 800-829, 850.0-854.1, 860.0-869.1)

942.20 Blisters with epidermal loss due to burn (second degree) of unspecified site of trunk ▽

942.21 Blisters with epidermal loss due to burn (second degree) of breast

942.22 Blisters with epidermal loss due to burn (second degree) of chest wall, excluding breast and nipple

942.23 Blisters with epidermal loss due to burn (second degree) of abdominal wall

942.24 Blisters with epidermal loss due to burn (second degree) of back (any part)

942.29 Blisters with epidermal loss due to burn (second degree) of other and multiple sites of trunk

942.30 Full-thickness skin loss due to burn (third degree NOS) of unspecified site of trunk ▽

942.31 Full-thickness skin loss due to burn (third degree NOS) of breast

942.32 Full-thickness skin loss due to burn (third degree NOS) of chest wall, excluding breast and nipple

942.33 Full-thickness skin loss due to burn (third degree NOS) of abdominal wall

942.34 Full-thickness skin loss due to burn (third degree NOS) of back (any part)

942.39 Full-thickness skin loss due to burn (third degree NOS) of other and multiple sites of trunk

942.40 Deep necrosis of underlying tissues due to burn (deep third degree) of trunk, unspecified site, without mention of loss of a body part ▽

942.41 Deep necrosis of underlying tissues due to burn (deep third degree) of breast, without mention of loss of a body part

942.42 Deep necrosis of underlying tissues due to burn (deep third degree) of chest wall, excluding breast and nipple, without mention of loss of a body part

942.43 Deep necrosis of underlying tissues due to burn (deep third degree) of abdominal wall, without mention of loss of a body part

942.44 Deep necrosis of underlying tissues due to burn (deep third degree) of back (any part), without mention of loss of a body part

942.49 Deep necrosis of underlying tissues due to burn (deep third degree) of other and multiple sites of trunk, without mention of loss of a body part

942.50 Deep necrosis of underlying tissues due to burn (deep third degree) of unspecified site of trunk, with loss of a body part ▽

942.51 Deep necrosis of underlying tissues due to burn (deep third degree) of breast, with loss of a body part

942.52 Deep necrosis of underlying tissues due to burn (deep third degree) of chest wall, excluding breast and nipple, with loss of a body part

942.53 Deep necrosis of underlying tissues due to burn (deep third degree) of abdominal wall with loss of a body part

942.54 Deep necrosis of underlying tissues due to burn (deep third degree) of back (any part), with loss of a body part

942.59 Deep necrosis of underlying tissues due to burn (deep third degree) of other and multiple sites of trunk, with loss of a body part

943.30 Full-thickness skin loss due to burn (third degree NOS) of unspecified site of upper limb ▽

943.31 Full-thickness skin loss due to burn (third degree NOS) of forearm

943.32 Full-thickness skin loss due to burn (third degree NOS) of elbow

943.33 Full-thickness skin loss due to burn (third degree NOS) of upper arm

943.34 Full-thickness skin loss due to burn (third degree NOS) of axilla

943.35 Full-thickness skin loss due to burn (third degree NOS) of shoulder

943.36 Full-thickness skin loss due to burn (third degree NOS) of scapular region

943.39 Full-thickness skin loss due to burn (third degree NOS) of multiple sites of upper limb, except wrist and hand

943.40 Deep necrosis of underlying tissues due to burn (deep third degree) of unspecified site of upper limb, without mention of loss of a body part ▽

943.41 Deep necrosis of underlying tissues due to burn (deep third degree) of forearm, without mention of loss of a body part

943.42 Deep necrosis of underlying tissues due to burn (deep third degree) of elbow, without mention of loss of a body part

943.43 Deep necrosis of underlying tissues due to burn (deep third degree) of upper arm, without mention of loss of a body part

943.44 Deep necrosis of underlying tissues due to burn (deep third degree) of axilla, without mention of loss of a body part

943.45 Deep necrosis of underlying tissues due to burn (deep third degree) of shoulder, without mention of loss of a body part

943.46 Deep necrosis of underlying tissues due to burn (deep third degree) of scapular region, without mention of loss of a body part

943.49 Deep necrosis of underlying tissues due to burn (deep third degree) of multiple sites of upper limb, except wrist and hand, without mention of loss of a body part

943.50 Deep necrosis of underlying tissues due to burn (deep third degree) of unspecified site of upper limb, with loss of a body part ▽

943.51 Deep necrosis of underlying tissues due to burn (deep third degree) of forearm, with loss of a body part

943.52 Deep necrosis of underlying tissues due to burn (deep third degree) of elbow, with loss of a body part

943.53 Deep necrosis of underlying tissues due to burn (deep third degree) of upper arm, with loss of upper a body part

943.54 Deep necrosis of underlying tissues due to burn (deep third degree) of axilla, with loss of a body part

943.55 Deep necrosis of underlying tissues due to burn (deep third degree) of shoulder, with loss of a body part

943.56 Deep necrosis of underlying tissues due to burn (deep third degree) of scapular region, with loss of a body part

943.59 Deep necrosis of underlying tissues due to burn (deep third degree) of multiple sites of upper limb, except wrist and hand, with loss of a body part

945.30 Full-thickness skin loss due to burn (third degree NOS) of unspecified site of lower limb ▽

945.33 Full-thickness skin loss due to burn (third degree NOS) of ankle

945.34 Full-thickness skin loss due to burn (third degree NOS) of lower leg

945.35 Full-thickness skin loss due to burn (third degree NOS) of knee

945.36 Full-thickness skin loss due to burn (third degree NOS) of thigh (any part)

945.39 Full-thickness skin loss due to burn (third degree NOS) of multiple sites of lower limb(s)

945.40 Deep necrosis of underlying tissues due to burn (deep third degree) of unspecified site of lower limb (leg), without mention of loss of a body part ▽

945.43 Deep necrosis of underlying tissues due to burn (deep third degree) of ankle, without mention of loss of a body part

945.44 Deep necrosis of underlying tissues due to burn (deep third degree) of lower leg, without mention of loss of a body part

945.45 Deep necrosis of underlying tissues due to burn (deep third degree) of knee, without mention of loss of a body part

945.46 Deep necrosis of underlying tissues due to burn (deep third degree) of thigh (any part), without mention of loss of a body part

945.49 Deep necrosis of underlying tissues due to burn (deep third degree) of multiple sites of lower limb(s), without mention of loss of a body part

945.50 Deep necrosis of underlying tissues due to burn (deep third degree) of unspecified site lower limb (leg), with loss of a body part ▽

945.53 Deep necrosis of underlying tissues due to burn (deep third degree) of ankle, with loss of a body part

945.54 Deep necrosis of underlying tissues due to burn (deep third degree) of lower leg, with loss of a body part

945.55 Deep necrosis of underlying tissues due to burn (deep third degree) of knee, with loss of a body part

945.56 Deep necrosis of underlying tissues due to burn (deep third degree) of thigh (any part), with loss of a body part
945.59 Deep necrosis of underlying tissues due to burn (deep third degree) of multiple sites of lower limb(s), with loss of a body part
946.3 Full-thickness skin loss due to burn (third degree NOS) of multiple specified sites
946.4 Deep necrosis of underlying tissues due to burn (deep third degree) of multiple specified sites, without mention of loss of a body part
946.5 Deep necrosis of underlying tissues due to burn (deep third degree) of multiple specified sites, with loss of a body part
948.00 Burn (any degree) involving less than 10% of body surface with third degree burn of less than 10% or unspecified amount
948.10 Burn (any degree) involving 10-19% of body surface with third degree burn of less than 10% or unspecified amount
948.11 Burn (any degree) involving 10-19% of body surface with third degree burn of 10-19%
948.20 Burn (any degree) involving 20-29% of body surface with third degree burn of less than 10% or unspecified amount
948.21 Burn (any degree) involving 20-29% of body surface with third degree burn of 10-19%
948.22 Burn (any degree) involving 20-29% of body surface with third degree burn of 20-29%
948.30 Burn (any degree) involving 30-39% of body surface with third degree burn of less than 10% or unspecified amount
948.31 Burn (any degree) involving 30-39% of body surface with third degree burn of 10-19%
948.32 Burn (any degree) involving 30-39% of body surface with third degree burn of 20-29%
948.33 Burn (any degree) involving 30-39% of body surface with third degree burn of 30-39%
948.40 Burn (any degree) involving 40-49% of body surface with third degree burn of less than 10% or unspecified amount
948.41 Burn (any degree) involving 40-49% of body surface with third degree burn of 10-19%
948.42 Burn (any degree) involving 40-49% of body surface with third degree burn of 20-29%
948.43 Burn (any degree) involving 40-49% of body surface with third degree burn of 30-39%
948.44 Burn (any degree) involving 40-49% of body surface with third degree burn of 40-49%
948.50 Burn (any degree) involving 50-59% of body surface with third degree burn of less than 10% or unspecified amount
948.51 Burn (any degree) involving 50-59% of body surface with third degree burn of 10-19%
948.52 Burn (any degree) involving 50-59% of body surface with third degree burn of 20-29%
948.53 Burn (any degree) involving 50-59% of body surface with third degree burn of 30-39%
948.54 Burn (any degree) involving 50-59% of body surface with third degree burn of 40-49%
948.55 Burn (any degree) involving 50-59% of body surface with third degree burn of 50-59%
948.60 Burn (any degree) involving 60-69% of body surface with third degree burn of less than 10% or unspecified amount
948.61 Burn (any degree) involving 60-69% of body surface with third degree burn of 10-19%
948.62 Burn (any degree) involving 60-69% of body surface with third degree burn of 20-29%
948.63 Burn (any degree) involving 60-69% of body surface with third degree burn of 30-39%
948.64 Burn (any degree) involving 60-69% of body surface with third degree burn of 40-49%
948.65 Burn (any degree) involving 60-69% of body surface with third degree burn of 50-59%
948.66 Burn (any degree) involving 60-69% of body surface with third degree burn of 60-69%
948.70 Burn (any degree) involving 70-79% of body surface with third degree burn of less than 10% or unspecified amount
948.71 Burn (any degree) involving 70-79% of body surface with third degree burn of 10-19%
948.72 Burn (any degree) involving 70-79% of body surface with third degree burn of 20-29%
948.73 Burn (any degree) involving 70-79% of body surface with third degree burn of 30-39%
948.74 Burn (any degree) involving 70-79% of body surface with third degree burn of 40-49%
948.75 Burn (any degree) involving 70-79% of body surface with third degree burn of 50-59%
948.76 Burn (any degree) involving 70-79% of body surface with third degree burn of 60-69%
948.77 Burn (any degree) involving 70-79% of body surface with third degree burn of 70-79%
948.80 Burn (any degree) involving 80-89% of body surface with third degree burn of less than 10% or unspecified amount
948.81 Burn (any degree) involving 80-89% of body surface with third degree burn of 10-19%
948.82 Burn (any degree) involving 80-89% of body surface with third degree burn of 20-29%
948.83 Burn (any degree) involving 80-89% of body surface with third degree burn of 30-39%
948.84 Burn (any degree) involving 80-89% of body surface with third degree burn of 40-49%
948.85 Burn (any degree) involving 80-89% of body surface with third degree burn of 50-59%
948.86 Burn (any degree) involving 80-89% of body surface with third degree burn of 60-69%
948.87 Burn (any degree) involving 80-89% of body surface with third degree burn of 70-79%
948.88 Burn (any degree) involving 80-89% of body surface with third degree burn of 80-89%
948.90 Burn (any degree) involving 90% or more of body surface with third degree burn of less than 10% or unspecified amount
948.91 Burn (any degree) involving 90% or more of body surface with third degree burn of 10-19%
948.92 Burn (any degree) involving 90% or more of body surface with third degree burn of 20-29%
948.93 Burn (any degree) involving 90% or more of body surface with third degree burn of 30-39%
948.94 Burn (any degree) involving 90% or more of body surface with third degree burn of 40-49%
948.95 Burn (any degree) involving 90% or more of body surface with third degree burn of 50-59%
948.96 Burn (any degree) involving 90% or more of body surface with third degree burn of 60-69%
948.97 Burn (any degree) involving 90% or more of body surface with third degree burn of 70-79%
948.98 Burn (any degree) involving 90% or more of body surface with third degree burn of 80-89%
948.99 Burn (any degree) involving 90% or more of body surface with third degree burn of 90% or more of body surface
949.3 Full-thickness skin loss due to burn (third degree NOS), unspecified site ▽
949.4 Deep necrosis of underlying tissue due to burn (deep third degree), unspecified site without mention of loss of body part ▽
949.5 Deep necrosis of underlying tissues due to burn (deep third degree, unspecified site with loss of body part ▽
958.3 Posttraumatic wound infection not elsewhere classified
991.3 Frostbite of other and unspecified sites ▽
996.52 Mechanical complication due to other tissue graft, not elsewhere classified
996.91 Complications of reattached forearm
996.94 Complications of reattached upper extremity, other and unspecified ▽
996.96 Complications of reattached lower extremity, other and unspecified ▽
997.61 Neuroma of amputation stump — (Use additional code to identify complications)
997.62 Infection (chronic) of amputation stump — (Use additional code to identify complications)
997.69 Other late amputation stump complication — (Use additional code to identify complications)
998.30 Disruption of wound, unspecified ▽
998.32 Disruption of external operation (surgical) wound
998.33 Disruption of traumatic injury wound repair
998.59 Other postoperative infection — (Use additional code to identify infection)
998.83 Non-healing surgical wound
V51.8 Other aftercare involving the use of plastic surgery

ICD-9-CM Procedural

86.60 Free skin graft, not otherwise specified
86.69 Other skin graft to other sites

15115-15116

15115 Epidermal autograft, face, scalp, eyelids, mouth, neck, ears, orbits, genitalia, hands, feet, and/or multiple digits; first 100 sq cm or less, or 1% of body area of infants and children
15116 each additional 100 sq cm, or each additional 1% of body area of infants and children, or part thereof (List separately in addition to code for primary procedure)

ICD-9-CM Diagnostic

145.0 Malignant neoplasm of cheek mucosa
145.8 Malignant neoplasm of other specified parts of mouth
171.0 Malignant neoplasm of connective and other soft tissue of head, face, and neck

Code	Description
171.6	Malignant neoplasm of connective and other soft tissue of pelvis
171.8	Malignant neoplasm of other specified sites of connective and other soft tissue
172.0	Malignant melanoma of skin of lip
172.1	Malignant melanoma of skin of eyelid, including canthus
172.2	Malignant melanoma of skin of ear and external auditory canal
172.3	Malignant melanoma of skin of other and unspecified parts of face ▽
172.4	Malignant melanoma of skin of scalp and neck
172.6	Malignant melanoma of skin of upper limb, including shoulder
172.7	Malignant melanoma of skin of lower limb, including hip
172.8	Malignant melanoma of other specified sites of skin
173.00	Unspecified malignant neoplasm of skin of lip ▽
173.01	Basal cell carcinoma of skin of lip
173.02	Squamous cell carcinoma of skin of lip
173.09	Other specified malignant neoplasm of skin of lip
173.10	Unspecified malignant neoplasm of eyelid, including canthus ▽
173.11	Basal cell carcinoma of eyelid, including canthus
173.12	Squamous cell carcinoma of eyelid, including canthus
173.19	Other specified malignant neoplasm of eyelid, including canthus
173.20	Unspecified malignant neoplasm of skin of ear and external auditory canal ▽
173.21	Basal cell carcinoma of skin of ear and external auditory canal
173.22	Squamous cell carcinoma of skin of ear and external auditory canal
173.29	Other specified malignant neoplasm of skin of ear and external auditory canal
173.30	Unspecified malignant neoplasm of skin of other and unspecified parts of face ▽
173.31	Basal cell carcinoma of skin of other and unspecified parts of face
173.32	Squamous cell carcinoma of skin of other and unspecified parts of face
173.39	Other specified malignant neoplasm of skin of other and unspecified parts of face
173.40	Unspecified malignant neoplasm of scalp and skin of neck ▽
173.41	Basal cell carcinoma of scalp and skin of neck
173.42	Squamous cell carcinoma of scalp and skin of neck
173.49	Other specified malignant neoplasm of scalp and skin of neck
173.60	Unspecified malignant neoplasm of skin of upper limb, including shoulder ▽
173.61	Basal cell carcinoma of skin of upper limb, including shoulder
173.62	Squamous cell carcinoma of skin of upper limb, including shoulder
173.69	Other specified malignant neoplasm of skin of upper limb, including shoulder
173.70	Unspecified malignant neoplasm of skin of lower limb, including hip ▽
173.71	Basal cell carcinoma of skin of lower limb, including hip
173.72	Squamous cell carcinoma of skin of lower limb, including hip
173.79	Other specified malignant neoplasm of skin of lower limb, including hip
173.80	Unspecified malignant neoplasm of other specified sites of skin ▽
173.81	Basal cell carcinoma of other specified sites of skin
173.82	Squamous cell carcinoma of other specified sites of skin
173.89	Other specified malignant neoplasm of other specified sites of skin
176.0	Kaposi's sarcoma of skin
184.1	Malignant neoplasm of labia majora ♀
184.2	Malignant neoplasm of labia minora ♀
184.3	Malignant neoplasm of clitoris ♀
184.4	Malignant neoplasm of vulva, unspecified site ▽ ♀
184.8	Malignant neoplasm of other specified sites of female genital organs ♀
186.9	Malignant neoplasm of other and unspecified testis — (Use additional code to identify any functional activity) ▽ ♂
187.1	Malignant neoplasm of prepuce ♂
187.2	Malignant neoplasm of glans penis ♂
187.3	Malignant neoplasm of body of penis ♂
187.4	Malignant neoplasm of penis, part unspecified ▽ ♂
187.7	Malignant neoplasm of scrotum ♂
187.8	Malignant neoplasm of other specified sites of male genital organs ♂
195.0	Malignant neoplasm of head, face, and neck
195.4	Malignant neoplasm of upper limb
195.5	Malignant neoplasm of lower limb
195.8	Malignant neoplasm of other specified sites
198.2	Secondary malignant neoplasm of skin
198.82	Secondary malignant neoplasm of genital organs
198.89	Secondary malignant neoplasm of other specified sites
209.31	Merkel cell carcinoma of the face
209.32	Merkel cell carcinoma of the scalp and neck
209.33	Merkel cell carcinoma of the upper limb
209.34	Merkel cell carcinoma of the lower limb
209.36	Merkel cell carcinoma of other sites
209.75	Secondary Merkel cell carcinoma
210.0	Benign neoplasm of lip
210.4	Benign neoplasm of other and unspecified parts of mouth ▽
214.0	Lipoma of skin and subcutaneous tissue of face
214.1	Lipoma of other skin and subcutaneous tissue
214.8	Lipoma of other specified sites
215.0	Other benign neoplasm of connective and other soft tissue of head, face, and neck
215.2	Other benign neoplasm of connective and other soft tissue of upper limb, including shoulder
215.3	Other benign neoplasm of connective and other soft tissue of lower limb, including hip
215.8	Other benign neoplasm of connective and other soft tissue of other specified sites
216.0	Benign neoplasm of skin of lip
216.1	Benign neoplasm of eyelid, including canthus
216.2	Benign neoplasm of ear and external auditory canal
216.3	Benign neoplasm of skin of other and unspecified parts of face ▽
216.4	Benign neoplasm of scalp and skin of neck
216.6	Benign neoplasm of skin of upper limb, including shoulder
216.7	Benign neoplasm of skin of lower limb, including hip
216.8	Benign neoplasm of other specified sites of skin
221.2	Benign neoplasm of vulva ♀
221.8	Benign neoplasm of other specified sites of female genital organs ♀
222.1	Benign neoplasm of penis ♂
222.4	Benign neoplasm of scrotum ♂
229.8	Benign neoplasm of other specified sites
230.0	Carcinoma in situ of lip, oral cavity, and pharynx
232.0	Carcinoma in situ of skin of lip
232.1	Carcinoma in situ of eyelid, including canthus
232.2	Carcinoma in situ of skin of ear and external auditory canal
232.3	Carcinoma in situ of skin of other and unspecified parts of face ▽
232.4	Carcinoma in situ of scalp and skin of neck
232.6	Carcinoma in situ of skin of upper limb, including shoulder
232.7	Carcinoma in situ of skin of lower limb, including hip
232.8	Carcinoma in situ of other specified sites of skin
233.30	Carcinoma in situ, unspecified female genital organ ▽ ♀
233.31	Carcinoma in situ, vagina ♀
233.32	Carcinoma in situ, vulva ♀
233.39	Carcinoma in situ, other female genital organ ♀
233.5	Carcinoma in situ of penis ♂
233.6	Carcinoma in situ of other and unspecified male genital organs ▽ ♂
235.1	Neoplasm of uncertain behavior of lip, oral cavity, and pharynx
236.3	Neoplasm of uncertain behavior of other and unspecified female genital organs ▽ ♀
236.6	Neoplasm of uncertain behavior of other and unspecified male genital organs ▽ ♂
238.2	Neoplasm of uncertain behavior of skin
239.2	Neoplasms of unspecified nature of bone, soft tissue, and skin
239.5	Neoplasm of unspecified nature of other genitourinary organs

249.70 Secondary diabetes mellitus with peripheral circulatory disorders, not stated as uncontrolled, or unspecified — (Use additional code to identify manifestation: 443.81, 785.4) (Use additional code to identify any associated insulin use: V58.67)

249.71 Secondary diabetes mellitus with peripheral circulatory disorders, uncontrolled — (Use additional code to identify manifestation: 443.81, 785.4) (Use additional code to identify any associated insulin use: V58.67)

249.80 Secondary diabetes mellitus with other specified manifestations, not stated as uncontrolled, or unspecified — (Use additional code to identify manifestation: 707.10-707.19, 707.8, 707.9, 731.8) (Use additional code to identify any associated insulin use: V58.67)

249.81 Secondary diabetes mellitus with other specified manifestations, uncontrolled — (Use additional code to identify manifestation: 707.10-707.19, 707.8, 707.9, 731.8) (Use additional code to identify any associated insulin use: V58.67)

249.90 Secondary diabetes mellitus with unspecified complication, not stated as uncontrolled, or unspecified — (Use additional code to identify any associated insulin use: V58.67) ▼

249.91 Secondary diabetes mellitus with unspecified complication, uncontrolled — (Use additional code to identify any associated insulin use: V58.67) ▼

250.70 Diabetes with peripheral circulatory disorders, type II or unspecified type, not stated as uncontrolled — (Use additional code to identify manifestation: 443.81, 785.4)

250.71 Diabetes with peripheral circulatory disorders, type I [juvenile type], not stated as uncontrolled — (Use additional code to identify manifestation: 443.81, 785.4)

250.72 Diabetes with peripheral circulatory disorders, type II or unspecified type, uncontrolled — (Use additional code to identify manifestation: 443.81, 785.4)

250.73 Diabetes with peripheral circulatory disorders, type I [juvenile type], uncontrolled — (Use additional code to identify manifestation: 443.81, 785.4)

250.80 Diabetes with other specified manifestations, type II or unspecified type, not stated as uncontrolled — (Use additional code to identify manifestation: 707.10-707.19, 707.8, 707.9, 731.8)

250.81 Diabetes with other specified manifestations, type I [juvenile type], not stated as uncontrolled — (Use additional code to identify manifestation: 707.10-707.19, 707.8, 707.9, 731.8)

250.82 Diabetes with other specified manifestations, type II or unspecified type, uncontrolled — (Use additional code to identify manifestation: 707.10-707.19, 707.8, 707.9, 731.8)

250.83 Diabetes with other specified manifestations, type I [juvenile type], uncontrolled — (Use additional code to identify manifestation: 707.10-707.19, 707.8, 707.9, 731.8)

374.04 Cicatricial entropion

374.50 Unspecified degenerative disorder of eyelid ▼

374.56 Other degenerative disorders of skin affecting eyelid

374.84 Cysts of eyelids

374.85 Vascular anomalies of eyelid

374.86 Retained foreign body of eyelid — (Use additional code to identify foreign body (V90.01-V90.9))

380.32 Acquired deformities of auricle or pinna

440.23 Atherosclerosis of native arteries of the extremities with ulceration — (Use additional code for any associated ulceration: 707.10-707.19, 707.8, 707.9)

459.11 Postphlebitic syndrome with ulcer

459.13 Postphlebitic syndrome with ulcer and inflammation

459.31 Chronic venous hypertension with ulcer

459.33 Chronic venous hypertension with ulcer and inflammation

629.20 Female genital mutilation status, unspecified ▼ ♀

629.21 Female genital mutilation, Type I status ♀

629.22 Female genital mutilation, Type II status ♀

629.23 Female genital mutilation, Type III status ♀

629.29 Other female genital mutilation status ♀

629.89 Other specified disorders of female genital organs ♀

682.4 Cellulitis and abscess of hand, except fingers and thumb — (Use additional code to identify organism, such as 041.1, etc.)

682.7 Cellulitis and abscess of foot, except toes — (Use additional code to identify organism, such as 041.1, etc.)

701.4 Keloid scar

701.5 Other abnormal granulation tissue

701.9 Unspecified hypertrophic and atrophic condition of skin ▼

707.00 Pressure ulcer, unspecified site — (Use additional code to identify pressure ulcer stage: 707.20-707.25) ▼

707.07 Pressure ulcer, heel — (Use additional code to identify pressure ulcer stage: 707.20-707.25)

707.09 Pressure ulcer, other site — (Use additional code to identify pressure ulcer stage: 707.20-707.25)

707.14 Ulcer of heel and midfoot — (Code, if applicable, any causal condition first: 249.80-249.81, 250.80-250.83, 440.23, 459.11, 459.13, 459.31, 459.33)

707.15 Ulcer of other part of foot — (Code, if applicable, any causal condition first: 249.80-249.81, 250.80-250.83, 440.23, 459.11, 459.13, 459.31, 459.33)

707.20 Pressure ulcer, unspecified stage — (Code first site of pressure ulcer: 707.00-707.09) ▼

707.21 Pressure ulcer, stage I — (Code first site of pressure ulcer: 707.00-707.09)

707.22 Pressure ulcer stage II — (Code first site of pressure ulcer: 707.00-707.09)

707.23 Pressure ulcer stage III — (Code first site of pressure ulcer: 707.00-707.09)

707.24 Pressure ulcer stage IV — (Code first site of pressure ulcer: 707.00-707.09)

707.25 Pressure ulcer, unstageable — (Code first site of pressure ulcer: 707.00-707.09)

707.8 Chronic ulcer of other specified site

709.2 Scar condition and fibrosis of skin

709.3 Degenerative skin disorder

709.4 Foreign body granuloma of skin and subcutaneous tissue — (Use additional code to identify foreign body (V90.01-V90.9))

744.29 Other congenital anomaly of ear

752.40 Unspecified congenital anomaly of cervix, vagina, and external female genitalia ▼ ♀

752.43 Cervical agenesis ♀

752.44 Cervical duplication ♀

752.45 Vaginal agenesis ♀

752.46 Transverse vaginal septum ♀

752.47 Longitudinal vaginal septum ♀

752.49 Other congenital anomaly of cervix, vagina, and external female genitalia ♀

757.39 Other specified congenital anomaly of skin

785.4 Gangrene — (Code first any associated underlying condition)

870.0 Laceration of skin of eyelid and periocular area

870.1 Laceration of eyelid, full-thickness, not involving lacrimal passages

870.2 Laceration of eyelid involving lacrimal passages

872.00 Open wound of external ear, unspecified site, without mention of complication ▼

872.01 Open wound of auricle, without mention of complication

872.10 Open wound of external ear, unspecified site, complicated ▼

872.11 Open wound of auricle, complicated

872.8 Open wound of ear, part unspecified, without mention of complication ▼

873.0 Open wound of scalp, without mention of complication

873.1 Open wound of scalp, complicated

873.21 Open wound of nasal septum, without mention of complication

873.31 Open wound of nasal septum, complicated

873.40 Open wound of face, unspecified site, without mention of complication ▼

873.41 Open wound of cheek, without mention of complication

873.42 Open wound of forehead, without mention of complication

873.43 Open wound of lip, without mention of complication

873.44 Open wound of jaw, without mention of complication

873.49 Open wound of face, other and multiple sites, without mention of complication

873.50 Open wound of face, unspecified site, complicated ▼

873.51 Open wound of cheek, complicated

873.52 Open wound of forehead, complicated

873.53 Open wound of lip, complicated

873.54 Open wound of jaw, complicated

873.59 Open wound of face, other and multiple sites, complicated

873.9 Other and unspecified open wound of head, complicated ♥
874.8 Open wound of other and unspecified parts of neck, without mention of complication ♥
878.0 Open wound of penis, without mention of complication ♂
878.1 Open wound of penis, complicated ♂
878.2 Open wound of scrotum and testes, without mention of complication ♂
878.3 Open wound of scrotum and testes, complicated ♂
878.4 Open wound of vulva, without mention of complication ♀
878.5 Open wound of vulva, complicated ♀
878.8 Open wound of other and unspecified parts of genital organs, without mention of complication ♥
878.9 Open wound of other and unspecified parts of genital organs, complicated ♥
882.0 Open wound of hand except finger(s) alone, without mention of complication
882.1 Open wound of hand except finger(s) alone, complicated
882.2 Open wound of hand except finger(s) alone, with tendon involvement
883.0 Open wound of finger(s), without mention of complication
883.1 Open wound of finger(s), complicated
883.2 Open wound of finger(s), with tendon involvement
885.0 Traumatic amputation of thumb (complete) (partial), without mention of complication
885.1 Traumatic amputation of thumb (complete) (partial), complicated
886.0 Traumatic amputation of other finger(s) (complete) (partial), without mention of complication
886.1 Traumatic amputation of other finger(s) (complete) (partial), complicated
892.0 Open wound of foot except toe(s) alone, without mention of complication
892.1 Open wound of foot except toe(s) alone, complicated
892.2 Open wound of foot except toe(s) alone, with tendon involvement
893.0 Open wound of toe(s), without mention of complication
893.1 Open wound of toe(s), complicated
893.2 Open wound of toe(s), with tendon involvement
895.0 Traumatic amputation of toe(s) (complete) (partial), without mention of complication
895.1 Traumatic amputation of toe(s) (complete) (partial), complicated
896.0 Traumatic amputation of foot (complete) (partial), unilateral, without mention of complication
896.1 Traumatic amputation of foot (complete) (partial), unilateral, complicated
896.2 Traumatic amputation of foot (complete) (partial), bilateral, without mention of complication
896.3 Traumatic amputation of foot (complete) (partial), bilateral, complicated
906.0 Late effect of open wound of head, neck, and trunk
906.1 Late effect of open wound of extremities without mention of tendon injury
906.4 Late effect of crushing
906.5 Late effect of burn of eye, face, head, and neck
906.6 Late effect of burn of wrist and hand
906.7 Late effect of burn of other extremities
906.8 Late effect of burns of other specified sites
909.2 Late effect of radiation
909.3 Late effect of complications of surgical and medical care
909.4 Late effect of certain other external causes
925.1 Crushing injury of face and scalp — (Use additional code to identify any associated injuries, such as: 800-829, 850.0-854.1, 860.0-869.1)
925.2 Crushing injury of neck — (Use additional code to identify any associated injuries, such as: 800-829, 850.0-854.1, 860.0-869.1)
926.0 Crushing injury of external genitalia — (Use additional code to identify any associated injuries: 800-829, 850.0-854.1, 860.0-869.1)
927.20 Crushing injury of hand(s) — (Use additional code to identify any associated injuries: 800-829, 850.0-854.1, 860.0-869.1)
927.3 Crushing injury of finger(s) — (Use additional code to identify any associated injuries: 800-829, 850.0-854.1, 860.0-869.1)
927.8 Crushing injury of multiple sites of upper limb — (Use additional code to identify any associated injuries: 800-829, 850.0-854.1, 860.0-869.1)
928.20 Crushing injury of foot — (Use additional code to identify any associated injuries: 800-829, 850.0-854.1, 860.0-869.1)
928.3 Crushing injury of toe(s) — (Use additional code to identify any associated injuries: 800-829, 850.0-854.1, 860.0-869.1)
928.8 Crushing injury of multiple sites of lower limb — (Use additional code to identify any associated injuries: 800-829, 850.0-854.1, 860.0-869.1)
929.0 Crushing injury of multiple sites, not elsewhere classified — (Use additional code to identify any associated injuries: 800-829, 850.0-854.1, 860.0-869.1)
940.0 Chemical burn of eyelids and periocular area
940.1 Other burns of eyelids and periocular area
941.30 Full-thickness skin loss due to burn (third degree NOS) of unspecified site of face and head ♥
941.31 Full-thickness skin loss due to burn (third degree NOS) of ear (any part)
941.32 Full-thickness skin loss due to burn (third degree NOS) of eye (with other parts of face, head, and neck)
941.33 Full-thickness skin loss due to burn (third degree NOS) of lip(s)
941.34 Full-thickness skin loss due to burn (third degree NOS) of chin
941.35 Full-thickness skin loss due to burn (third degree NOS) of nose (septum)
941.36 Full-thickness skin loss due to burn (third degree NOS) of scalp (any part)
941.37 Full-thickness skin loss due to burn (third degree NOS) of forehead and cheek
941.38 Full-thickness skin loss due to burn (third degree NOS) of neck
941.39 Full-thickness skin loss due to burn (third degree NOS) of multiple sites (except with eye) of face, head, and neck
941.40 Deep necrosis of underlying tissues due to burn (deep third degree) of unspecified site of face and head, without mention of loss of a body part ♥
941.41 Deep necrosis of underlying tissues due to burn (deep third degree) of ear (any part), without mention of loss of a body part
941.42 Deep necrosis of underlying tissues due to burn (deep third degree) of eye (with other parts of face, head, and neck), without mention of loss of a body part
941.43 Deep necrosis of underlying tissues due to burn (deep third degree) of lip(s), without mention of loss of a body part
941.44 Deep necrosis of underlying tissues due to burn (deep third degree) of chin, without mention of loss of a body part
941.45 Deep necrosis of underlying tissues due to burn (deep third degree) of nose (septum), without mention of loss of a body part
941.46 Deep necrosis of underlying tissues due to burn (deep third degree) of scalp (any part), without mention of loss of a body part
941.47 Deep necrosis of underlying tissues due to burn (deep third degree) of forehead and cheek, without mention of loss of a body part
941.48 Deep necrosis of underlying tissues due to burn (deep third degree) of neck, without mention of loss of a body part
941.49 Deep necrosis of underlying tissues due to burn (deep third degree) of multiple sites (except with eye) of face, head, and neck, without mention of loss of a body part
941.50 Deep necrosis of underlying tissues due to burn (deep third degree) of face and head, unspecified site, with loss of a body part ♥
941.51 Deep necrosis of underlying tissues due to burn (deep third degree) of ear (any part), with loss of a body part
941.52 Deep necrosis of underlying tissues due to burn (deep third degree) of eye (with other parts of face, head, and neck), with loss of a body part
941.53 Deep necrosis of underlying tissues due to burn (deep third degree) of lip(s), with loss of a body part
941.54 Deep necrosis of underlying tissues due to burn (deep third degree) of chin, with loss of a body part
941.55 Deep necrosis of underlying tissues due to burn (deep third degree) of nose (septum), with loss of a body part
941.56 Deep necrosis of underlying tissues due to burn (deep third degree) of scalp (any part), with loss of a body part
941.57 Deep necrosis of underlying tissues due to burn (deep third degree) of forehead and cheek, with loss of a body part
941.58 Deep necrosis of underlying tissues due to burn (deep third degree) of neck, with loss of a body part

941.59 Deep necrosis of underlying tissues due to burn (deep third degree) of multiple sites (except eye) of face, head, and neck, with loss of a body part
942.35 Full-thickness skin loss due to burn (third degree NOS) of genitalia
942.45 Deep necrosis of underlying tissues due to burn (deep third degree) of genitalia, without mention of loss of a body part
942.55 Deep necrosis of underlying tissues due to burn (deep third degree) of genitalia, with loss of a body part
944.30 Full-thickness skin loss due to burn (third degree NOS) of unspecified site of hand
944.31 Full-thickness skin loss due to burn (third degree NOS) of single digit [finger (nail)] other than thumb
944.32 Full-thickness skin loss due to burn (third degree NOS) of thumb (nail)
944.33 Full-thickness skin loss due to burn (third degree NOS) of two or more digits of hand, not including thumb
944.34 Full-thickness skin loss due to burn (third degree NOS) of two or more digits of hand including thumb
944.35 Full-thickness skin loss due to burn (third degree NOS) of palm of hand
944.36 Full-thickness skin loss due to burn (third degree NOS) of back of hand
944.38 Full-thickness skin loss due to burn (third degree NOS) of multiple sites of wrist(s) and hand(s)
944.40 Deep necrosis of underlying tissues due to burn (deep third degree) of unspecified site of hand, without mention of loss of a body part
944.41 Deep necrosis of underlying tissues due to burn (deep third degree) of single digit [finger (nail)] other than thumb, without mention of loss of a body part
944.42 Deep necrosis of underlying tissues due to burn (deep third degree) of thumb (nail), without mention of loss of a body part
944.43 Deep necrosis of underlying tissues due to burn (deep third degree) of two or more digits of hand, not including thumb, without mention of loss of a body part
944.44 Deep necrosis of underlying tissues due to burn (deep third degree) of two or more digits of hand including thumb, without mention of loss of a body part
944.45 Deep necrosis of underlying tissues due to burn (deep third degree) of palm of hand, without mention of loss of a body part
944.46 Deep necrosis of underlying tissues due to burn (deep third degree) of back of hand, without mention of loss of a body part
944.48 Deep necrosis of underlying tissues due to burn (deep third degree) of multiple sites of wrist(s) and hand(s), without mention of loss of a body part
944.50 Deep necrosis of underlying tissues due to burn (deep third degree) of unspecified site of hand, with loss of a body part
944.51 Deep necrosis of underlying tissues due to burn (deep third degree) of single digit (finger (nail)) other than thumb, with loss of a body part
944.52 Deep necrosis of underlying tissues due to burn (deep third degree) of thumb (nail), with loss of a body part
944.53 Deep necrosis of underlying tissues due to burn (deep third degree) of two or more digits of hand, not including thumb, with loss of a body part
944.54 Deep necrosis of underlying tissues due to burn (deep third degree) of two or more digits of hand including thumb, with loss of a body part
944.55 Deep necrosis of underlying tissues due to burn (deep third degree) of palm of hand, with loss of a body part
944.56 Deep necrosis of underlying tissues due to burn (deep third degree) of back of hand, with loss of a body part
944.58 Deep necrosis of underlying tissues due to burn (deep third degree) of multiple sites of wrist(s) and hand(s), with loss of a body part
945.31 Full-thickness skin loss due to burn (third degree NOS) of toe(s) (nail)
945.32 Full-thickness skin loss due to burn (third degree NOS) of foot
945.39 Full-thickness skin loss due to burn (third degree NOS) of multiple sites of lower limb(s)
945.41 Deep necrosis of underlying tissues due to burn (deep third degree) of toe(s) (nail), without mention of loss of a body part
945.42 Deep necrosis of underlying tissues due to burn (deep third degree) of foot, without mention of loss of a body part
945.49 Deep necrosis of underlying tissues due to burn (deep third degree) of multiple sites of lower limb(s), without mention of loss of a body part
945.51 Deep necrosis of underlying tissues due to burn (deep third degree) of toe(s) (nail), with loss of a body part
945.52 Deep necrosis of underlying tissues due to burn (deep third degree) of foot, with loss of a body part
945.59 Deep necrosis of underlying tissues due to burn (deep third degree) of multiple sites of lower limb(s), with loss of a body part
946.3 Full-thickness skin loss due to burn (third degree NOS) of multiple specified sites
946.4 Deep necrosis of underlying tissues due to burn (deep third degree) of multiple specified sites, without mention of loss of a body part
946.5 Deep necrosis of underlying tissues due to burn (deep third degree) of multiple specified sites, with loss of a body part
947.0 Burn of mouth and pharynx
948.00 Burn (any degree) involving less than 10% of body surface with third degree burn of less than 10% or unspecified amount
948.10 Burn (any degree) involving 10-19% of body surface with third degree burn of less than 10% or unspecified amount
948.11 Burn (any degree) involving 10-19% of body surface with third degree burn of 10-19%
948.20 Burn (any degree) involving 20-29% of body surface with third degree burn of less than 10% or unspecified amount
948.21 Burn (any degree) involving 20-29% of body surface with third degree burn of 10-19%
948.22 Burn (any degree) involving 20-29% of body surface with third degree burn of 20-29%
948.30 Burn (any degree) involving 30-39% of body surface with third degree burn of less than 10% or unspecified amount
948.31 Burn (any degree) involving 30-39% of body surface with third degree burn of 10-19%
948.32 Burn (any degree) involving 30-39% of body surface with third degree burn of 20-29%
948.33 Burn (any degree) involving 30-39% of body surface with third degree burn of 30-39%
948.40 Burn (any degree) involving 40-49% of body surface with third degree burn of less than 10% or unspecified amount
948.41 Burn (any degree) involving 40-49% of body surface with third degree burn of 10-19%
948.42 Burn (any degree) involving 40-49% of body surface with third degree burn of 20-29%
948.43 Burn (any degree) involving 40-49% of body surface with third degree burn of 30-39%
948.44 Burn (any degree) involving 40-49% of body surface with third degree burn of 40-49%
948.50 Burn (any degree) involving 50-59% of body surface with third degree burn of less than 10% or unspecified amount
948.51 Burn (any degree) involving 50-59% of body surface with third degree burn of 10-19%
948.52 Burn (any degree) involving 50-59% of body surface with third degree burn of 20-29%
948.53 Burn (any degree) involving 50-59% of body surface with third degree burn of 30-39%
948.54 Burn (any degree) involving 50-59% of body surface with third degree burn of 40-49%
948.55 Burn (any degree) involving 50-59% of body surface with third degree burn of 50-59%
948.60 Burn (any degree) involving 60-69% of body surface with third degree burn of less than 10% or unspecified amount
948.61 Burn (any degree) involving 60-69% of body surface with third degree burn of 10-19%
948.62 Burn (any degree) involving 60-69% of body surface with third degree burn of 20-29%
948.63 Burn (any degree) involving 60-69% of body surface with third degree burn of 30-39%
948.64 Burn (any degree) involving 60-69% of body surface with third degree burn of 40-49%
948.65 Burn (any degree) involving 60-69% of body surface with third degree burn of 50-59%
948.66 Burn (any degree) involving 60-69% of body surface with third degree burn of 60-69%
948.70 Burn (any degree) involving 70-79% of body surface with third degree burn of less than 10% or unspecified amount
948.71 Burn (any degree) involving 70-79% of body surface with third degree burn of 10-19%
948.72 Burn (any degree) involving 70-79% of body surface with third degree burn of 20-29%
948.73 Burn (any degree) involving 70-79% of body surface with third degree burn of 30-39%
948.74 Burn (any degree) involving 70-79% of body surface with third degree burn of 40-49%
948.75 Burn (any degree) involving 70-79% of body surface with third degree burn of 50-59%
948.76 Burn (any degree) involving 70-79% of body surface with third degree burn of 60-69%
948.77 Burn (any degree) involving 70-79% of body surface with third degree burn of 70-79%
948.80 Burn (any degree) involving 80-89% of body surface with third degree burn of less than 10% or unspecified amount
948.81 Burn (any degree) involving 80-89% of body surface with third degree burn of 10-19%
948.82 Burn (any degree) involving 80-89% of body surface with third degree burn of 20-29%

948.83 Burn (any degree) involving 80-89% of body surface with third degree burn of 30-39%
948.84 Burn (any degree) involving 80-89% of body surface with third degree burn of 40-49%
948.85 Burn (any degree) involving 80-89% of body surface with third degree burn of 50-59%
948.86 Burn (any degree) involving 80-89% of body surface with third degree burn of 60-69%
948.87 Burn (any degree) involving 80-89% of body surface with third degree burn of 70-79%
948.88 Burn (any degree) involving 80-89% of body surface with third degree burn of 80-89%
948.90 Burn (any degree) involving 90% or more of body surface with third degree burn of less than 10% or unspecified amount
948.91 Burn (any degree) involving 90% or more of body surface with third degree burn of 10-19%
948.92 Burn (any degree) involving 90% or more of body surface with third degree burn of 20-29%
948.93 Burn (any degree) involving 90% or more of body surface with third degree burn of 30-39%
948.94 Burn (any degree) involving 90% or more of body surface with third degree burn of 40-49%
948.95 Burn (any degree) involving 90% or more of body surface with third degree burn of 50-59%
948.96 Burn (any degree) involving 90% or more of body surface with third degree burn of 60-69%
948.97 Burn (any degree) involving 90% or more of body surface with third degree burn of 70-79%
948.98 Burn (any degree) involving 90% or more of body surface with third degree burn of 80-89%
948.99 Burn (any degree) involving 90% or more of body surface with third degree burn of 90% or more of body surface
949.2 Blisters with epidermal loss due to burn (second degree), unspecified site ▽
949.3 Full-thickness skin loss due to burn (third degree NOS), unspecified site ▽
949.4 Deep necrosis of underlying tissue due to burn (deep third degree), unspecified site without mention of loss of body part ▽
949.5 Deep necrosis of underlying tissues due to burn (deep third degree, unspecified site with loss of body part ▽
959.01 Head injury, unspecified ▽
959.09 Injury of face and neck, other and unspecified
959.14 Other injury of external genitals
959.4 Injury, other and unspecified, hand, except finger
959.5 Injury, other and unspecified, finger
959.7 Injury, other and unspecified, knee, leg, ankle, and foot
959.8 Injury, other and unspecified, other specified sites, including multiple
991.0 Frostbite of face
991.1 Frostbite of hand
991.2 Frostbite of foot
996.52 Mechanical complication due to other tissue graft, not elsewhere classified
996.92 Complications of reattached hand
996.93 Complications of reattached finger(s)
996.95 Complications of reattached foot and toe(s)
997.62 Infection (chronic) of amputation stump — (Use additional code to identify complications)
997.69 Other late amputation stump complication — (Use additional code to identify complications)
998.30 Disruption of wound, unspecified ▽
998.32 Disruption of external operation (surgical) wound
998.33 Disruption of traumatic injury wound repair
998.83 Non-healing surgical wound
V51.8 Other aftercare involving the use of plastic surgery

ICD-9-CM Procedural

08.61 Reconstruction of eyelid with skin flap or graft
16.65 Secondary graft to exenteration cavity
18.6 Reconstruction of external auditory canal
18.79 Other plastic repair of external ear
27.56 Other skin graft to lip and mouth
86.62 Other skin graft to hand
86.69 Other skin graft to other sites

15120-15121

15120 Split-thickness autograft, face, scalp, eyelids, mouth, neck, ears, orbits, genitalia, hands, feet, and/or multiple digits; first 100 sq cm or less, or 1% of body area of infants and children (except 15050)
15121 each additional 100 sq cm, or each additional 1% of body area of infants and children, or part thereof (List separately in addition to code for primary procedure)

ICD-9-CM Diagnostic

145.0 Malignant neoplasm of cheek mucosa
171.0 Malignant neoplasm of connective and other soft tissue of head, face, and neck
171.6 Malignant neoplasm of connective and other soft tissue of pelvis
172.0 Malignant melanoma of skin of lip
172.1 Malignant melanoma of skin of eyelid, including canthus
172.2 Malignant melanoma of skin of ear and external auditory canal
172.4 Malignant melanoma of skin of scalp and neck
172.6 Malignant melanoma of skin of upper limb, including shoulder
172.7 Malignant melanoma of skin of lower limb, including hip
173.00 Unspecified malignant neoplasm of skin of lip ▽
173.01 Basal cell carcinoma of skin of lip
173.02 Squamous cell carcinoma of skin of lip
173.09 Other specified malignant neoplasm of skin of lip
173.10 Unspecified malignant neoplasm of eyelid, including canthus ▽
173.11 Basal cell carcinoma of eyelid, including canthus
173.12 Squamous cell carcinoma of eyelid, including canthus
173.19 Other specified malignant neoplasm of eyelid, including canthus
173.20 Unspecified malignant neoplasm of skin of ear and external auditory canal ▽
173.21 Basal cell carcinoma of skin of ear and external auditory canal
173.22 Squamous cell carcinoma of skin of ear and external auditory canal
173.29 Other specified malignant neoplasm of skin of ear and external auditory canal
173.30 Unspecified malignant neoplasm of skin of other and unspecified parts of face ▽
173.31 Basal cell carcinoma of skin of other and unspecified parts of face
173.32 Squamous cell carcinoma of skin of other and unspecified parts of face
173.39 Other specified malignant neoplasm of skin of other and unspecified parts of face
173.40 Unspecified malignant neoplasm of scalp and skin of neck ▽
173.41 Basal cell carcinoma of scalp and skin of neck
173.42 Squamous cell carcinoma of scalp and skin of neck
173.49 Other specified malignant neoplasm of scalp and skin of neck
173.60 Unspecified malignant neoplasm of skin of upper limb, including shoulder ▽
173.61 Basal cell carcinoma of skin of upper limb, including shoulder
173.62 Squamous cell carcinoma of skin of upper limb, including shoulder
173.69 Other specified malignant neoplasm of skin of upper limb, including shoulder
173.70 Unspecified malignant neoplasm of skin of lower limb, including hip ▽
173.71 Basal cell carcinoma of skin of lower limb, including hip
173.72 Squamous cell carcinoma of skin of lower limb, including hip
173.79 Other specified malignant neoplasm of skin of lower limb, including hip
184.0 Malignant neoplasm of vagina ♀
184.2 Malignant neoplasm of labia minora ♀
184.3 Malignant neoplasm of clitoris ♀
184.4 Malignant neoplasm of vulva, unspecified site ▽ ♀
184.8 Malignant neoplasm of other specified sites of female genital organs ♀
187.1 Malignant neoplasm of prepuce ♂
187.2 Malignant neoplasm of glans penis ♂
187.3 Malignant neoplasm of body of penis ♂
187.4 Malignant neoplasm of penis, part unspecified ▽ ♂
187.7 Malignant neoplasm of scrotum ♂

187.8	Malignant neoplasm of other specified sites of male genital organs ♂
195.0	Malignant neoplasm of head, face, and neck
195.4	Malignant neoplasm of upper limb
195.5	Malignant neoplasm of lower limb
198.82	Secondary malignant neoplasm of genital organs
209.31	Merkel cell carcinoma of the face
209.32	Merkel cell carcinoma of the scalp and neck
209.33	Merkel cell carcinoma of the upper limb
209.34	Merkel cell carcinoma of the lower limb
209.36	Merkel cell carcinoma of other sites
209.75	Secondary Merkel cell carcinoma
210.4	Benign neoplasm of other and unspecified parts of mouth ▽
216.0	Benign neoplasm of skin of lip
216.1	Benign neoplasm of eyelid, including canthus
216.2	Benign neoplasm of ear and external auditory canal
216.3	Benign neoplasm of skin of other and unspecified parts of face ▽
216.4	Benign neoplasm of scalp and skin of neck
221.2	Benign neoplasm of vulva ♀
221.8	Benign neoplasm of other specified sites of female genital organs ♀
222.1	Benign neoplasm of penis ♂
222.4	Benign neoplasm of scrotum ♂
230.0	Carcinoma in situ of lip, oral cavity, and pharynx
232.0	Carcinoma in situ of skin of lip
232.1	Carcinoma in situ of eyelid, including canthus
232.2	Carcinoma in situ of skin of ear and external auditory canal
232.3	Carcinoma in situ of skin of other and unspecified parts of face ▽
232.4	Carcinoma in situ of scalp and skin of neck
233.30	Carcinoma in situ, unspecified female genital organ ▽ ♀
233.31	Carcinoma in situ, vagina ♀
233.32	Carcinoma in situ, vulva ♀
233.39	Carcinoma in situ, other female genital organ ♀
233.5	Carcinoma in situ of penis ♂
233.6	Carcinoma in situ of other and unspecified male genital organs ▽ ♂
235.1	Neoplasm of uncertain behavior of lip, oral cavity, and pharynx
236.3	Neoplasm of uncertain behavior of other and unspecified female genital organs ▽ ♀
236.6	Neoplasm of uncertain behavior of other and unspecified male genital organs ▽ ♂
239.5	Neoplasm of unspecified nature of other genitourinary organs
374.04	Cicatricial entropion
374.50	Unspecified degenerative disorder of eyelid ▽
374.56	Other degenerative disorders of skin affecting eyelid
374.84	Cysts of eyelids
374.85	Vascular anomalies of eyelid
374.86	Retained foreign body of eyelid — (Use additional code to identify foreign body (V90.01-V90.9))
380.32	Acquired deformities of auricle or pinna
380.50	Acquired stenosis of external ear canal unspecified as to cause ▽
459.11	Postphlebitic syndrome with ulcer
459.13	Postphlebitic syndrome with ulcer and inflammation
459.31	Chronic venous hypertension with ulcer
459.33	Chronic venous hypertension with ulcer and inflammation
525.20	Unspecified atrophy of edentulous alveolar ridge ▽
525.21	Minimal atrophy of the mandible
525.22	Moderate atrophy of the mandible
525.23	Severe atrophy of the mandible
525.24	Minimal atrophy of the maxilla
525.25	Moderate atrophy of the maxilla
525.26	Severe atrophy of the maxilla
629.20	Female genital mutilation status, unspecified ▽ ♀
629.21	Female genital mutilation, Type I status ♀
629.22	Female genital mutilation, Type II status ♀
629.23	Female genital mutilation, Type III status ♀
629.29	Other female genital mutilation status ♀
629.89	Other specified disorders of female genital organs ♀
682.4	Cellulitis and abscess of hand, except fingers and thumb — (Use additional code to identify organism, such as 041.1, etc.)
682.7	Cellulitis and abscess of foot, except toes — (Use additional code to identify organism, such as 041.1, etc.)
701.4	Keloid scar
701.5	Other abnormal granulation tissue
701.9	Unspecified hypertrophic and atrophic condition of skin ▽
707.00	Pressure ulcer, unspecified site — (Use additional code to identify pressure ulcer stage: 707.20-707.25) ▽
707.07	Pressure ulcer, heel — (Use additional code to identify pressure ulcer stage: 707.20-707.25)
707.09	Pressure ulcer, other site — (Use additional code to identify pressure ulcer stage: 707.20-707.25)
707.14	Ulcer of heel and midfoot — (Code, if applicable, any causal condition first: 249.80-249.81, 250.80-250.83, 440.23, 459.11, 459.13, 459.31, 459.33)
707.15	Ulcer of other part of foot — (Code, if applicable, any causal condition first: 249.80-249.81, 250.80-250.83, 440.23, 459.11, 459.13, 459.31, 459.33)
707.20	Pressure ulcer, unspecified stage — (Code first site of pressure ulcer: 707.00-707.09) ▽
707.21	Pressure ulcer, stage I — (Code first site of pressure ulcer: 707.00-707.09)
707.22	Pressure ulcer stage II — (Code first site of pressure ulcer: 707.00-707.09)
707.23	Pressure ulcer stage III — (Code first site of pressure ulcer: 707.00-707.09)
707.24	Pressure ulcer stage IV — (Code first site of pressure ulcer: 707.00-707.09)
707.25	Pressure ulcer, unstageable — (Code first site of pressure ulcer: 707.00-707.09)
707.8	Chronic ulcer of other specified site
709.2	Scar condition and fibrosis of skin
709.3	Degenerative skin disorder
709.4	Foreign body granuloma of skin and subcutaneous tissue — (Use additional code to identify foreign body (V90.01-V90.9))
744.23	Microtia
744.29	Other congenital anomaly of ear
752.40	Unspecified congenital anomaly of cervix, vagina, and external female genitalia ▽ ♀
752.43	Cervical agenesis ♀
752.44	Cervical duplication ♀
752.45	Vaginal agenesis ♀
752.46	Transverse vaginal septum ♀
752.47	Longitudinal vaginal septum ♀
752.49	Other congenital anomaly of cervix, vagina, and external female genitalia ♀
785.4	Gangrene — (Code first any associated underlying condition)
870.0	Laceration of skin of eyelid and periocular area
870.1	Laceration of eyelid, full-thickness, not involving lacrimal passages
870.2	Laceration of eyelid involving lacrimal passages
872.00	Open wound of external ear, unspecified site, without mention of complication ▽
872.01	Open wound of auricle, without mention of complication
872.10	Open wound of external ear, unspecified site, complicated ▽
872.11	Open wound of auricle, complicated
872.8	Open wound of ear, part unspecified, without mention of complication ▽
873.0	Open wound of scalp, without mention of complication
873.1	Open wound of scalp, complicated
873.40	Open wound of face, unspecified site, without mention of complication ▽
873.41	Open wound of cheek, without mention of complication
873.42	Open wound of forehead, without mention of complication
873.43	Open wound of lip, without mention of complication
873.44	Open wound of jaw, without mention of complication

873.49 Open wound of face, other and multiple sites, without mention of complication
873.50 Open wound of face, unspecified site, complicated ▽
873.51 Open wound of cheek, complicated
873.52 Open wound of forehead, complicated
873.53 Open wound of lip, complicated
873.54 Open wound of jaw, complicated
873.59 Open wound of face, other and multiple sites, complicated
873.70 Open wound of mouth, unspecified site, complicated ▽
873.71 Open wound of buccal mucosa, complicated
873.74 Open wound of tongue and floor of mouth, complicated
874.8 Open wound of other and unspecified parts of neck, without mention of complication ▽
878.0 Open wound of penis, without mention of complication ♂
878.1 Open wound of penis, complicated ♂
878.2 Open wound of scrotum and testes, without mention of complication ♂
878.3 Open wound of scrotum and testes, complicated ♂
878.4 Open wound of vulva, without mention of complication ♀
878.5 Open wound of vulva, complicated ♀
878.6 Open wound of vagina, without mention of complication ♀
878.7 Open wound of vagina, complicated ♀
878.8 Open wound of other and unspecified parts of genital organs, without mention of complication ▽
878.9 Open wound of other and unspecified parts of genital organs, complicated ▽
882.0 Open wound of hand except finger(s) alone, without mention of complication
882.1 Open wound of hand except finger(s) alone, complicated
882.2 Open wound of hand except finger(s) alone, with tendon involvement
883.0 Open wound of finger(s), without mention of complication
883.1 Open wound of finger(s), complicated
883.2 Open wound of finger(s), with tendon involvement
885.0 Traumatic amputation of thumb (complete) (partial), without mention of complication
885.1 Traumatic amputation of thumb (complete) (partial), complicated
886.0 Traumatic amputation of other finger(s) (complete) (partial), without mention of complication
886.1 Traumatic amputation of other finger(s) (complete) (partial), complicated
892.0 Open wound of foot except toe(s) alone, without mention of complication
892.1 Open wound of foot except toe(s) alone, complicated
892.2 Open wound of foot except toe(s) alone, with tendon involvement
893.0 Open wound of toe(s), without mention of complication
893.1 Open wound of toe(s), complicated
893.2 Open wound of toe(s), with tendon involvement
895.0 Traumatic amputation of toe(s) (complete) (partial), without mention of complication
895.1 Traumatic amputation of toe(s) (complete) (partial), complicated
896.0 Traumatic amputation of foot (complete) (partial), unilateral, without mention of complication
896.1 Traumatic amputation of foot (complete) (partial), unilateral, complicated
896.2 Traumatic amputation of foot (complete) (partial), bilateral, without mention of complication
896.3 Traumatic amputation of foot (complete) (partial), bilateral, complicated
906.0 Late effect of open wound of head, neck, and trunk
906.5 Late effect of burn of eye, face, head, and neck
906.6 Late effect of burn of wrist and hand
906.7 Late effect of burn of other extremities
908.3 Late effect of injury to blood vessel of head, neck, and extremities
926.0 Crushing injury of external genitalia — (Use additional code to identify any associated injuries: 800-829, 850.0-854.1, 860.0-869.1)
940.0 Chemical burn of eyelids and periocular area
940.1 Other burns of eyelids and periocular area
941.01 Burn of unspecified degree of ear (any part) ▽
941.31 Full-thickness skin loss due to burn (third degree NOS) of ear (any part)
941.32 Full-thickness skin loss due to burn (third degree NOS) of eye (with other parts of face, head, and neck)
941.33 Full-thickness skin loss due to burn (third degree NOS) of lip(s)
941.34 Full-thickness skin loss due to burn (third degree NOS) of chin
941.35 Full-thickness skin loss due to burn (third degree NOS) of nose (septum)
941.36 Full-thickness skin loss due to burn (third degree NOS) of scalp (any part)
941.37 Full-thickness skin loss due to burn (third degree NOS) of forehead and cheek
941.38 Full-thickness skin loss due to burn (third degree NOS) of neck
941.39 Full-thickness skin loss due to burn (third degree NOS) of multiple sites (except with eye) of face, head, and neck
941.40 Deep necrosis of underlying tissues due to burn (deep third degree) of unspecified site of face and head, without mention of loss of a body part ▽
941.46 Deep necrosis of underlying tissues due to burn (deep third degree) of scalp (any part), without mention of loss of a body part
941.48 Deep necrosis of underlying tissues due to burn (deep third degree) of neck, without mention of loss of a body part
941.49 Deep necrosis of underlying tissues due to burn (deep third degree) of multiple sites (except with eye) of face, head, and neck, without mention of loss of a body part
947.0 Burn of mouth and pharynx
948.00 Burn (any degree) involving less than 10% of body surface with third degree burn of less than 10% or unspecified amount
948.10 Burn (any degree) involving 10-19% of body surface with third degree burn of less than 10% or unspecified amount
948.11 Burn (any degree) involving 10-19% of body surface with third degree burn of 10-19%
948.20 Burn (any degree) involving 20-29% of body surface with third degree burn of less than 10% or unspecified amount
948.21 Burn (any degree) involving 20-29% of body surface with third degree burn of 10-19%
948.22 Burn (any degree) involving 20-29% of body surface with third degree burn of 20-29%
948.30 Burn (any degree) involving 30-39% of body surface with third degree burn of less than 10% or unspecified amount
948.31 Burn (any degree) involving 30-39% of body surface with third degree burn of 10-19%
948.32 Burn (any degree) involving 30-39% of body surface with third degree burn of 20-29%
948.33 Burn (any degree) involving 30-39% of body surface with third degree burn of 30-39%
948.40 Burn (any degree) involving 40-49% of body surface with third degree burn of less than 10% or unspecified amount
948.41 Burn (any degree) involving 40-49% of body surface with third degree burn of 10-19%
948.42 Burn (any degree) involving 40-49% of body surface with third degree burn of 20-29%
948.43 Burn (any degree) involving 40-49% of body surface with third degree burn of 30-39%
948.44 Burn (any degree) involving 40-49% of body surface with third degree burn of 40-49%
948.50 Burn (any degree) involving 50-59% of body surface with third degree burn of less than 10% or unspecified amount
948.51 Burn (any degree) involving 50-59% of body surface with third degree burn of 10-19%
948.52 Burn (any degree) involving 50-59% of body surface with third degree burn of 20-29%
948.53 Burn (any degree) involving 50-59% of body surface with third degree burn of 30-39%
948.54 Burn (any degree) involving 50-59% of body surface with third degree burn of 40-49%
948.55 Burn (any degree) involving 50-59% of body surface with third degree burn of 50-59%
948.60 Burn (any degree) involving 60-69% of body surface with third degree burn of less than 10% or unspecified amount
948.61 Burn (any degree) involving 60-69% of body surface with third degree burn of 10-19%
948.62 Burn (any degree) involving 60-69% of body surface with third degree burn of 20-29%
948.63 Burn (any degree) involving 60-69% of body surface with third degree burn of 30-39%
948.64 Burn (any degree) involving 60-69% of body surface with third degree burn of 40-49%
948.65 Burn (any degree) involving 60-69% of body surface with third degree burn of 50-59%
948.66 Burn (any degree) involving 60-69% of body surface with third degree burn of 60-69%
948.70 Burn (any degree) involving 70-79% of body surface with third degree burn of less than 10% or unspecified amount
948.71 Burn (any degree) involving 70-79% of body surface with third degree burn of 10-19%
948.72 Burn (any degree) involving 70-79% of body surface with third degree burn of 20-29%
948.73 Burn (any degree) involving 70-79% of body surface with third degree burn of 30-39%
948.74 Burn (any degree) involving 70-79% of body surface with third degree burn of 40-49%

948.75 Burn (any degree) involving 70-79% of body surface with third degree burn of 50-59%
948.76 Burn (any degree) involving 70-79% of body surface with third degree burn of 60-69%
948.77 Burn (any degree) involving 70-79% of body surface with third degree burn of 70-79%
948.80 Burn (any degree) involving 80-89% of body surface with third degree burn of less than 10% or unspecified amount
948.81 Burn (any degree) involving 80-89% of body surface with third degree burn of 10-19%
948.82 Burn (any degree) involving 80-89% of body surface with third degree burn of 20-29%
948.83 Burn (any degree) involving 80-89% of body surface with third degree burn of 30-39%
948.84 Burn (any degree) involving 80-89% of body surface with third degree burn of 40-49%
948.85 Burn (any degree) involving 80-89% of body surface with third degree burn of 50-59%
948.86 Burn (any degree) involving 80-89% of body surface with third degree burn of 60-69%
948.87 Burn (any degree) involving 80-89% of body surface with third degree burn of 70-79%
948.88 Burn (any degree) involving 80-89% of body surface with third degree burn of 80-89%
949.2 Blisters with epidermal loss due to burn (second degree), unspecified site ▽
959.01 Head injury, unspecified ▽
959.09 Injury of face and neck, other and unspecified
959.14 Other injury of external genitals
959.5 Injury, other and unspecified, finger
959.7 Injury, other and unspecified, knee, leg, ankle, and foot
959.8 Injury, other and unspecified, other specified sites, including multiple
991.0 Frostbite of face
991.1 Frostbite of hand
991.2 Frostbite of foot
996.52 Mechanical complication due to other tissue graft, not elsewhere classified
997.62 Infection (chronic) of amputation stump — (Use additional code to identify complications)
997.69 Other late amputation stump complication — (Use additional code to identify complications)
998.30 Disruption of wound, unspecified ▽
998.32 Disruption of external operation (surgical) wound
998.33 Disruption of traumatic injury wound repair
998.83 Non-healing surgical wound
V51.8 Other aftercare involving the use of plastic surgery

ICD-9-CM Procedural

08.61 Reconstruction of eyelid with skin flap or graft
16.65 Secondary graft to exenteration cavity
18.6 Reconstruction of external auditory canal
18.79 Other plastic repair of external ear
27.56 Other skin graft to lip and mouth
61.49 Other repair of scrotum and tunica vaginalis ♂
64.49 Other repair of penis ♂
70.79 Other repair of vagina ♀
71.79 Other repair of vulva and perineum ♀
86.62 Other skin graft to hand
86.69 Other skin graft to other sites

15130-15131

15130 Dermal autograft, trunk, arms, legs; first 100 sq cm or less, or 1% of body area of infants and children

15131 each additional 100 sq cm, or each additional 1% of body area of infants and children, or part thereof (List separately in addition to code for primary procedure)

ICD-9-CM Diagnostic

172.5 Malignant melanoma of skin of trunk, except scrotum
172.6 Malignant melanoma of skin of upper limb, including shoulder
172.7 Malignant melanoma of skin of lower limb, including hip
172.8 Malignant melanoma of other specified sites of skin
173.50 Unspecified malignant neoplasm of skin of trunk, except scrotum ▽
173.51 Basal cell carcinoma of skin of trunk, except scrotum
173.52 Squamous cell carcinoma of skin of trunk, except scrotum
173.59 Other specified malignant neoplasm of skin of trunk, except scrotum
173.60 Unspecified malignant neoplasm of skin of upper limb, including shoulder ▽
173.61 Basal cell carcinoma of skin of upper limb, including shoulder
173.62 Squamous cell carcinoma of skin of upper limb, including shoulder
173.69 Other specified malignant neoplasm of skin of upper limb, including shoulder
173.70 Unspecified malignant neoplasm of skin of lower limb, including hip ▽
173.71 Basal cell carcinoma of skin of lower limb, including hip
173.72 Squamous cell carcinoma of skin of lower limb, including hip
173.79 Other specified malignant neoplasm of skin of lower limb, including hip
173.80 Unspecified malignant neoplasm of other specified sites of skin ▽
173.81 Basal cell carcinoma of other specified sites of skin
173.82 Squamous cell carcinoma of other specified sites of skin
173.89 Other specified malignant neoplasm of other specified sites of skin
174.0 Malignant neoplasm of nipple and areola of female breast — (Use additional code to identify estrogen receptor status: V86.0-V86.1) ♀
174.1 Malignant neoplasm of central portion of female breast — (Use additional code to identify estrogen receptor status: V86.0-V86.1) ♀
174.2 Malignant neoplasm of upper-inner quadrant of female breast — (Use additional code to identify estrogen receptor status: V86.0-V86.1) ♀
174.3 Malignant neoplasm of lower-inner quadrant of female breast — (Use additional code to identify estrogen receptor status: V86.0-V86.1) ♀
174.4 Malignant neoplasm of upper-outer quadrant of female breast — (Use additional code to identify estrogen receptor status: V86.0-V86.1) ♀
174.5 Malignant neoplasm of lower-outer quadrant of female breast — (Use additional code to identify estrogen receptor status: V86.0-V86.1) ♀
174.6 Malignant neoplasm of axillary tail of female breast — (Use additional code to identify estrogen receptor status: V86.0-V86.1) ♀
174.8 Malignant neoplasm of other specified sites of female breast — (Use additional code to identify estrogen receptor status: V86.0-V86.1) ♀
175.0 Malignant neoplasm of nipple and areola of male breast — (Use additional code to identify estrogen receptor status: V86.0-V86.1) ♂
175.9 Malignant neoplasm of other and unspecified sites of male breast — (Use additional code to identify estrogen receptor status: V86.0-V86.1) ▽ ♂
176.0 Kaposi's sarcoma of skin
195.1 Malignant neoplasm of thorax
195.2 Malignant neoplasm of abdomen
195.3 Malignant neoplasm of pelvis
195.4 Malignant neoplasm of upper limb
195.5 Malignant neoplasm of lower limb
195.8 Malignant neoplasm of other specified sites
198.2 Secondary malignant neoplasm of skin
209.33 Merkel cell carcinoma of the upper limb
209.34 Merkel cell carcinoma of the lower limb
209.35 Merkel cell carcinoma of the trunk
209.75 Secondary Merkel cell carcinoma
214.1 Lipoma of other skin and subcutaneous tissue
215.7 Other benign neoplasm of connective and other soft tissue of trunk, unspecified ▽
216.5 Benign neoplasm of skin of trunk, except scrotum
216.6 Benign neoplasm of skin of upper limb, including shoulder
232.5 Carcinoma in situ of skin of trunk, except scrotum
232.6 Carcinoma in situ of skin of upper limb, including shoulder
232.7 Carcinoma in situ of skin of lower limb, including hip
232.8 Carcinoma in situ of other specified sites of skin
238.2 Neoplasm of uncertain behavior of skin
239.2 Neoplasms of unspecified nature of bone, soft tissue, and skin
249.70 Secondary diabetes mellitus with peripheral circulatory disorders, not stated as uncontrolled, or unspecified — (Use additional code to identify manifestation: 443.81, 785.4) (Use additional code to identify any associated insulin use: V58.67)

249.71 Secondary diabetes mellitus with peripheral circulatory disorders, uncontrolled — (Use additional code to identify manifestation: 443.81, 785.4) (Use additional code to identify any associated insulin use: V58.67)

249.80 Secondary diabetes mellitus with other specified manifestations, not stated as uncontrolled, or unspecified — (Use additional code to identify manifestation: 707.10-707.19, 707.8, 707.9, 731.8) (Use additional code to identify any associated insulin use: V58.67)

249.81 Secondary diabetes mellitus with other specified manifestations, uncontrolled — (Use additional code to identify manifestation: 707.10-707.19, 707.8, 707.9, 731.8) (Use additional code to identify any associated insulin use: V58.67)

249.90 Secondary diabetes mellitus with unspecified complication, not stated as uncontrolled, or unspecified — (Use additional code to identify any associated insulin use: V58.67) ▽

249.91 Secondary diabetes mellitus with unspecified complication, uncontrolled — (Use additional code to identify any associated insulin use: V58.67) ▽

250.70 Diabetes with peripheral circulatory disorders, type II or unspecified type, not stated as uncontrolled — (Use additional code to identify manifestation: 443.81, 785.4)

250.71 Diabetes with peripheral circulatory disorders, type I [juvenile type], not stated as uncontrolled — (Use additional code to identify manifestation: 443.81, 785.4)

250.72 Diabetes with peripheral circulatory disorders, type II or unspecified type, uncontrolled — (Use additional code to identify manifestation: 443.81, 785.4)

250.73 Diabetes with peripheral circulatory disorders, type I [juvenile type], uncontrolled — (Use additional code to identify manifestation: 443.81, 785.4)

250.80 Diabetes with other specified manifestations, type II or unspecified type, not stated as uncontrolled — (Use additional code to identify manifestation: 707.10-707.19, 707.8, 707.9, 731.8)

250.81 Diabetes with other specified manifestations, type I [juvenile type], not stated as uncontrolled — (Use additional code to identify manifestation: 707.10-707.19, 707.8, 707.9, 731.8)

250.82 Diabetes with other specified manifestations, type II or unspecified type, uncontrolled — (Use additional code to identify manifestation: 707.10-707.19, 707.8, 707.9, 731.8)

250.83 Diabetes with other specified manifestations, type I [juvenile type], uncontrolled — (Use additional code to identify manifestation: 707.10-707.19, 707.8, 707.9, 731.8)

440.23 Atherosclerosis of native arteries of the extremities with ulceration — (Use additional code for any associated ulceration: 707.10-707.19, 707.8, 707.9)

454.0 Varicose veins of lower extremities with ulcer

454.2 Varicose veins of lower extremities with ulcer and inflammation

459.11 Postphlebitic syndrome with ulcer

459.13 Postphlebitic syndrome with ulcer and inflammation

459.31 Chronic venous hypertension with ulcer

459.33 Chronic venous hypertension with ulcer and inflammation

459.81 Unspecified venous (peripheral) insufficiency — (Use additional code for any associated ulceration: 707.10-707.19, 707.8, 707.9) ▽

682.2 Cellulitis and abscess of trunk — (Use additional code to identify organism, such as 041.1, etc.)

682.3 Cellulitis and abscess of upper arm and forearm — (Use additional code to identify organism, such as 041.1, etc.)

682.5 Cellulitis and abscess of buttock — (Use additional code to identify organism, such as 041.1, etc.)

682.6 Cellulitis and abscess of leg, except foot — (Use additional code to identify organism, such as 041.1, etc.)

682.8 Cellulitis and abscess of other specified site — (Use additional code to identify organism, such as 041.1, etc.)

701.4 Keloid scar

701.5 Other abnormal granulation tissue

701.9 Unspecified hypertrophic and atrophic condition of skin ▽

707.00 Pressure ulcer, unspecified site — (Use additional code to identify pressure ulcer stage: 707.20-707.25) ▽

707.01 Pressure ulcer, elbow — (Use additional code to identify pressure ulcer stage: 707.20-707.25)

707.02 Pressure ulcer, upper back — (Use additional code to identify pressure ulcer stage: 707.20-707.25)

707.03 Pressure ulcer, lower back — (Use additional code to identify pressure ulcer stage: 707.20-707.25)

707.04 Pressure ulcer, hip — (Use additional code to identify pressure ulcer stage: 707.20-707.25)

707.05 Pressure ulcer, buttock — (Use additional code to identify pressure ulcer stage: 707.20-707.25)

707.06 Pressure ulcer, ankle — (Use additional code to identify pressure ulcer stage: 707.20-707.25)

707.09 Pressure ulcer, other site — (Use additional code to identify pressure ulcer stage: 707.20-707.25)

707.10 Ulcer of lower limb, unspecified — (Code, if applicable, any causal condition first: 249.80-249.81, 250.80-250.83, 440.23, 459.11, 459.13, 459.31, 459.33) ▽

707.11 Ulcer of thigh — (Code, if applicable, any causal condition first: 249.80-249.81, 250.80-250.83, 440.23, 459.11, 459.13, 459.31, 459.33)

707.12 Ulcer of calf — (Code, if applicable, any causal condition first: 249.80-249.81, 250.80-250.83, 440.23, 459.11, 459.13, 459.31, 459.33)

707.13 Ulcer of ankle — (Code, if applicable, any causal condition first: 249.80-249.81, 250.80-250.83, 440.23, 459.11, 459.13, 459.31, 459.33)

707.19 Ulcer of other part of lower limb — (Code, if applicable, any causal condition first: 249.80-249.81, 250.80-250.83, 440.23, 459.11, 459.13, 459.31, 459.33)

707.20 Pressure ulcer, unspecified stage — (Code first site of pressure ulcer: 707.00-707.09) ▽

707.21 Pressure ulcer, stage I — (Code first site of pressure ulcer: 707.00-707.09)

707.22 Pressure ulcer stage II — (Code first site of pressure ulcer: 707.00-707.09)

707.23 Pressure ulcer stage III — (Code first site of pressure ulcer: 707.00-707.09)

707.24 Pressure ulcer stage IV — (Code first site of pressure ulcer: 707.00-707.09)

707.25 Pressure ulcer, unstageable — (Code first site of pressure ulcer: 707.00-707.09)

707.8 Chronic ulcer of other specified site

709.2 Scar condition and fibrosis of skin

709.3 Degenerative skin disorder

709.4 Foreign body granuloma of skin and subcutaneous tissue — (Use additional code to identify foreign body (V90.01-V90.9))

709.8 Other specified disorder of skin

709.9 Unspecified disorder of skin and subcutaneous tissue ▽

785.4 Gangrene — (Code first any associated underlying condition)

875.0 Open wound of chest (wall), without mention of complication

875.1 Open wound of chest (wall), complicated

876.0 Open wound of back, without mention of complication

876.1 Open wound of back, complicated

877.0 Open wound of buttock, without mention of complication

877.1 Open wound of buttock, complicated

879.0 Open wound of breast, without mention of complication

879.1 Open wound of breast, complicated

879.2 Open wound of abdominal wall, anterior, without mention of complication

879.3 Open wound of abdominal wall, anterior, complicated

879.4 Open wound of abdominal wall, lateral, without mention of complication

879.5 Open wound of abdominal wall, lateral, complicated

879.6 Open wound of other and unspecified parts of trunk, without mention of complication ▽

879.7 Open wound of other and unspecified parts of trunk, complicated ▽

879.8 Open wound(s) (multiple) of unspecified site(s), without mention of complication ▽

879.9 Open wound(s) (multiple) of unspecified site(s), complicated ▽

880.00 Open wound of shoulder region, without mention of complication

880.01 Open wound of scapular region, without mention of complication

880.02 Open wound of axillary region, without mention of complication

880.03 Open wound of upper arm, without mention of complication

880.09 Open wound of multiple sites of shoulder and upper arm, without mention of complication

880.10 Open wound of shoulder region, complicated
880.11 Open wound of scapular region, complicated
880.12 Open wound of axillary region, complicated
880.13 Open wound of upper arm, complicated
880.19 Open wound of multiple sites of shoulder and upper arm, complicated
880.20 Open wound of shoulder region, with tendon involvement
880.21 Open wound of scapular region, with tendon involvement
880.22 Open wound of axillary region, with tendon involvement
880.23 Open wound of upper arm, with tendon involvement
880.29 Open wound of multiple sites of shoulder and upper arm, with tendon involvement
881.00 Open wound of forearm, without mention of complication
881.01 Open wound of elbow, without mention of complication
881.02 Open wound of wrist, without mention of complication
881.10 Open wound of forearm, complicated
881.11 Open wound of elbow, complicated
881.12 Open wound of wrist, complicated
881.20 Open wound of forearm, with tendon involvement
881.21 Open wound of elbow, with tendon involvement
881.22 Open wound of wrist, with tendon involvement
884.0 Multiple and unspecified open wound of upper limb, without mention of complication
884.1 Multiple and unspecified open wound of upper limb, complicated
884.2 Multiple and unspecified open wound of upper limb, with tendon involvement
887.0 Traumatic amputation of arm and hand (complete) (partial), unilateral, below elbow, without mention of complication
887.1 Traumatic amputation of arm and hand (complete) (partial), unilateral, below elbow, complicated
887.2 Traumatic amputation of arm and hand (complete) (partial), unilateral, at or above elbow, without mention of complication
887.3 Traumatic amputation of arm and hand (complete) (partial), unilateral, at or above elbow, complicated
887.4 Traumatic amputation of arm and hand (complete) (partial), unilateral, level not specified, without mention of complication ▽
887.5 Traumatic amputation of arm and hand (complete) (partial), unilateral, level not specified, complicated ▽
887.6 Traumatic amputation of arm and hand (complete) (partial), bilateral (any level), without mention of complication
887.7 Traumatic amputation of arm and hand (complete) (partial), bilateral (any level), complicated
890.0 Open wound of hip and thigh, without mention of complication
890.1 Open wound of hip and thigh, complicated
890.2 Open wound of hip and thigh, with tendon involvement
891.0 Open wound of knee, leg (except thigh), and ankle, without mention of complication
891.1 Open wound of knee, leg (except thigh), and ankle, complicated
891.2 Open wound of knee, leg (except thigh), and ankle, with tendon involvement
894.0 Multiple and unspecified open wound of lower limb, without mention of complication
894.1 Multiple and unspecified open wound of lower limb, complicated
894.2 Multiple and unspecified open wound of lower limb, with tendon involvement
897.0 Traumatic amputation of leg(s) (complete) (partial), unilateral, below knee, without mention of complication
897.1 Traumatic amputation of leg(s) (complete) (partial), unilateral, below knee, complicated
897.2 Traumatic amputation of leg(s) (complete) (partial), unilateral, at or above knee, without mention of complication
897.3 Traumatic amputation of leg(s) (complete) (partial), unilateral, at or above knee, complicated
897.4 Traumatic amputation of leg(s) (complete) (partial), unilateral, level not specified, without mention of complication ▽
897.5 Traumatic amputation of leg(s) (complete) (partial), unilateral, level not specified, complicated ▽
897.6 Traumatic amputation of leg(s) (complete) (partial), bilateral (any level), without mention of complication
897.7 Traumatic amputation of leg(s) (complete) (partial), bilateral (any level), complicated
906.0 Late effect of open wound of head, neck, and trunk
906.1 Late effect of open wound of extremities without mention of tendon injury
906.4 Late effect of crushing
906.6 Late effect of burn of wrist and hand
906.7 Late effect of burn of other extremities
906.8 Late effect of burns of other specified sites
908.6 Late effect of certain complications of trauma
909.2 Late effect of radiation
909.3 Late effect of complications of surgical and medical care
909.4 Late effect of certain other external causes
926.11 Crushing injury of back — (Use additional code to identify any associated injuries: 800-829, 850.0-854.1, 860.0-869.1)
926.12 Crushing injury of buttock — (Use additional code to identify any associated injuries: 800-829, 850.0-854.1, 860.0-869.1)
926.19 Crushing injury of other specified sites of trunk — (Use additional code to identify any associated injuries: 800-829, 850.0-854.1, 860.0-869.1)
926.8 Crushing injury of multiple sites of trunk — (Use additional code to identify any associated injuries: 800-829, 850.0-854.1, 860.0-869.1)
926.9 Crushing injury of unspecified site of trunk — (Use additional code to identify any associated injuries: 800-829, 850.0-854.1, 860.0-869.1) ▽
927.00 Crushing injury of shoulder region — (Use additional code to identify any associated injuries: 800-829, 850.0-854.1, 860.0-869.1)
927.01 Crushing injury of scapular region — (Use additional code to identify any associated injuries: 800-829, 850.0-854.1, 860.0-869.1)
927.02 Crushing injury of axillary region — (Use additional code to identify any associated injuries: 800-829, 850.0-854.1, 860.0-869.1)
927.03 Crushing injury of upper arm — (Use additional code to identify any associated injuries: 800-829, 850.0-854.1, 860.0-869.1)
927.09 Crushing injury of multiple sites of upper arm — (Use additional code to identify any associated injuries: 800-829, 850.0-854.1, 860.0-869.1)
927.10 Crushing injury of forearm — (Use additional code to identify any associated injuries: 800-829, 850.0-854.1, 860.0-869.1)
927.11 Crushing injury of elbow — (Use additional code to identify any associated injuries: 800-829, 850.0-854.1, 860.0-869.1)
927.21 Crushing injury of wrist — (Use additional code to identify any associated injuries: 800-829, 850.0-854.1, 860.0-869.1)
927.8 Crushing injury of multiple sites of upper limb — (Use additional code to identify any associated injuries: 800-829, 850.0-854.1, 860.0-869.1)
927.9 Crushing injury of unspecified site of upper limb — (Use additional code to identify any associated injuries: 800-829, 850.0-854.1, 860.0-869.1) ▽
928.00 Crushing injury of thigh — (Use additional code to identify any associated injuries: 800-829, 850.0-854.1, 860.0-869.1)
928.01 Crushing injury of hip — (Use additional code to identify any associated injuries: 800-829, 850.0-854.1, 860.0-869.1)
928.10 Crushing injury of lower leg — (Use additional code to identify any associated injuries: 800-829, 850.0-854.1, 860.0-869.1)
928.11 Crushing injury of knee — (Use additional code to identify any associated injuries: 800-829, 850.0-854.1, 860.0-869.1)
928.21 Crushing injury of ankle — (Use additional code to identify any associated injuries: 800-829, 850.0-854.1, 860.0-869.1)
928.8 Crushing injury of multiple sites of lower limb — (Use additional code to identify any associated injuries: 800-829, 850.0-854.1, 860.0-869.1)
928.9 Crushing injury of unspecified site of lower limb — (Use additional code to identify any associated injuries: 800-829, 850.0-854.1, 860.0-869.1) ▽
929.0 Crushing injury of multiple sites, not elsewhere classified — (Use additional code to identify any associated injuries: 800-829, 850.0-854.1, 860.0-869.1)
942.20 Blisters with epidermal loss due to burn (second degree) of unspecified site of trunk ▽
942.21 Blisters with epidermal loss due to burn (second degree) of breast
942.22 Blisters with epidermal loss due to burn (second degree) of chest wall, excluding breast and nipple

942.23 Blisters with epidermal loss due to burn (second degree) of abdominal wall
942.24 Blisters with epidermal loss due to burn (second degree) of back (any part)
942.29 Blisters with epidermal loss due to burn (second degree) of other and multiple sites of trunk
942.30 Full-thickness skin loss due to burn (third degree NOS) of unspecified site of trunk
942.31 Full-thickness skin loss due to burn (third degree NOS) of breast
942.32 Full-thickness skin loss due to burn (third degree NOS) of chest wall, excluding breast and nipple
942.33 Full-thickness skin loss due to burn (third degree NOS) of abdominal wall
942.34 Full-thickness skin loss due to burn (third degree NOS) of back (any part)
942.39 Full-thickness skin loss due to burn (third degree NOS) of other and multiple sites of trunk
942.40 Deep necrosis of underlying tissues due to burn (deep third degree) of trunk, unspecified site, without mention of loss of a body part
942.41 Deep necrosis of underlying tissues due to burn (deep third degree) of breast, without mention of loss of a body part
942.42 Deep necrosis of underlying tissues due to burn (deep third degree) of chest wall, excluding breast and nipple, without mention of loss of a body part
942.43 Deep necrosis of underlying tissues due to burn (deep third degree) of abdominal wall, without mention of loss of a body part
942.44 Deep necrosis of underlying tissues due to burn (deep third degree) of back (any part), without mention of loss of a body part
942.49 Deep necrosis of underlying tissues due to burn (deep third degree) of other and multiple sites of trunk, without mention of loss of a body part
942.50 Deep necrosis of underlying tissues due to burn (deep third degree) of unspecified site of trunk, with loss of a body part
942.51 Deep necrosis of underlying tissues due to burn (deep third degree) of breast, with loss of a body part
942.52 Deep necrosis of underlying tissues due to burn (deep third degree) of chest wall, excluding breast and nipple, with loss of a body part
942.53 Deep necrosis of underlying tissues due to burn (deep third degree) of abdominal wall with loss of a body part
942.54 Deep necrosis of underlying tissues due to burn (deep third degree) of back (any part), with loss of a body part
942.59 Deep necrosis of underlying tissues due to burn (deep third degree) of other and multiple sites of trunk, with loss of a body part
943.30 Full-thickness skin loss due to burn (third degree NOS) of unspecified site of upper limb
943.31 Full-thickness skin loss due to burn (third degree NOS) of forearm
943.32 Full-thickness skin loss due to burn (third degree NOS) of elbow
943.33 Full-thickness skin loss due to burn (third degree NOS) of upper arm
943.34 Full-thickness skin loss due to burn (third degree NOS) of axilla
943.35 Full-thickness skin loss due to burn (third degree NOS) of shoulder
943.36 Full-thickness skin loss due to burn (third degree NOS) of scapular region
943.39 Full-thickness skin loss due to burn (third degree NOS) of multiple sites of upper limb, except wrist and hand
943.40 Deep necrosis of underlying tissues due to burn (deep third degree) of unspecified site of upper limb, without mention of loss of a body part
943.41 Deep necrosis of underlying tissues due to burn (deep third degree) of forearm, without mention of loss of a body part
943.42 Deep necrosis of underlying tissues due to burn (deep third degree) of elbow, without mention of loss of a body part
943.43 Deep necrosis of underlying tissues due to burn (deep third degree) of upper arm, without mention of loss of a body part
943.44 Deep necrosis of underlying tissues due to burn (deep third degree) of axilla, without mention of loss of a body part
943.45 Deep necrosis of underlying tissues due to burn (deep third degree) of shoulder, without mention of loss of a body part
943.46 Deep necrosis of underlying tissues due to burn (deep third degree) of scapular region, without mention of loss of a body part
943.49 Deep necrosis of underlying tissues due to burn (deep third degree) of multiple sites of upper limb, except wrist and hand, without mention of loss of a body part
943.50 Deep necrosis of underlying tissues due to burn (deep third degree) of unspecified site of upper limb, with loss of a body part
943.51 Deep necrosis of underlying tissues due to burn (deep third degree) of forearm, with loss of a body part
943.52 Deep necrosis of underlying tissues due to burn (deep third degree) of elbow, with loss of a body part
943.53 Deep necrosis of underlying tissues due to burn (deep third degree) of upper arm, with loss of upper a body part
943.54 Deep necrosis of underlying tissues due to burn (deep third degree) of axilla, with loss of a body part
943.55 Deep necrosis of underlying tissues due to burn (deep third degree) of shoulder, with loss of a body part
943.56 Deep necrosis of underlying tissues due to burn (deep third degree) of scapular region, with loss of a body part
943.59 Deep necrosis of underlying tissues due to burn (deep third degree) of multiple sites of upper limb, except wrist and hand, with loss of a body part
945.30 Full-thickness skin loss due to burn (third degree NOS) of unspecified site of lower limb
945.33 Full-thickness skin loss due to burn (third degree NOS) of ankle
945.34 Full-thickness skin loss due to burn (third degree NOS) of lower leg
945.35 Full-thickness skin loss due to burn (third degree NOS) of knee
945.36 Full-thickness skin loss due to burn (third degree NOS) of thigh (any part)
945.39 Full-thickness skin loss due to burn (third degree NOS) of multiple sites of lower limb(s)
945.40 Deep necrosis of underlying tissues due to burn (deep third degree) of unspecified site of lower limb (leg), without mention of loss of a body part
945.43 Deep necrosis of underlying tissues due to burn (deep third degree) of ankle, without mention of loss of a body part
945.44 Deep necrosis of underlying tissues due to burn (deep third degree) of lower leg, without mention of loss of a body part
945.45 Deep necrosis of underlying tissues due to burn (deep third degree) of knee, without mention of loss of a body part
945.46 Deep necrosis of underlying tissues due to burn (deep third degree) of thigh (any part), without mention of loss of a body part
945.49 Deep necrosis of underlying tissues due to burn (deep third degree) of multiple sites of lower limb(s), without mention of loss of a body part
945.50 Deep necrosis of underlying tissues due to burn (deep third degree) of unspecified site lower limb (leg), with loss of a body part
945.53 Deep necrosis of underlying tissues due to burn (deep third degree) of ankle, with loss of a body part
945.54 Deep necrosis of underlying tissues due to burn (deep third degree) of lower leg, with loss of a body part
945.55 Deep necrosis of underlying tissues due to burn (deep third degree) of knee, with loss of a body part
945.56 Deep necrosis of underlying tissues due to burn (deep third degree) of thigh (any part), with loss of a body part
945.59 Deep necrosis of underlying tissues due to burn (deep third degree) of multiple sites of lower limb(s), with loss of a body part
946.3 Full-thickness skin loss due to burn (third degree NOS) of multiple specified sites
946.4 Deep necrosis of underlying tissues due to burn (deep third degree) of multiple specified sites, without mention of loss of a body part
946.5 Deep necrosis of underlying tissues due to burn (deep third degree) of multiple specified sites, with loss of a body part
948.00 Burn (any degree) involving less than 10% of body surface with third degree burn of less than 10% or unspecified amount
948.10 Burn (any degree) involving 10-19% of body surface with third degree burn of less than 10% or unspecified amount
948.11 Burn (any degree) involving 10-19% of body surface with third degree burn of 10-19%

948.20 Burn (any degree) involving 20-29% of body surface with third degree burn of less than 10% or unspecified amount
948.21 Burn (any degree) involving 20-29% of body surface with third degree burn of 10-19%
948.22 Burn (any degree) involving 20-29% of body surface with third degree burn of 20-29%
948.30 Burn (any degree) involving 30-39% of body surface with third degree burn of less than 10% or unspecified amount
948.31 Burn (any degree) involving 30-39% of body surface with third degree burn of 10-19%
948.32 Burn (any degree) involving 30-39% of body surface with third degree burn of 20-29%
948.33 Burn (any degree) involving 30-39% of body surface with third degree burn of 30-39%
948.40 Burn (any degree) involving 40-49% of body surface with third degree burn of less than 10% or unspecified amount
948.41 Burn (any degree) involving 40-49% of body surface with third degree burn of 10-19%
948.42 Burn (any degree) involving 40-49% of body surface with third degree burn of 20-29%
948.43 Burn (any degree) involving 40-49% of body surface with third degree burn of 30-39%
948.44 Burn (any degree) involving 40-49% of body surface with third degree burn of 40-49%
948.50 Burn (any degree) involving 50-59% of body surface with third degree burn of less than 10% or unspecified amount
948.51 Burn (any degree) involving 50-59% of body surface with third degree burn of 10-19%
948.52 Burn (any degree) involving 50-59% of body surface with third degree burn of 20-29%
948.53 Burn (any degree) involving 50-59% of body surface with third degree burn of 30-39%
948.54 Burn (any degree) involving 50-59% of body surface with third degree burn of 40-49%
948.55 Burn (any degree) involving 50-59% of body surface with third degree burn of 50-59%
948.60 Burn (any degree) involving 60-69% of body surface with third degree burn of less than 10% or unspecified amount
948.61 Burn (any degree) involving 60-69% of body surface with third degree burn of 10-19%
948.62 Burn (any degree) involving 60-69% of body surface with third degree burn of 20-29%
948.63 Burn (any degree) involving 60-69% of body surface with third degree burn of 30-39%
948.64 Burn (any degree) involving 60-69% of body surface with third degree burn of 40-49%
948.65 Burn (any degree) involving 60-69% of body surface with third degree burn of 50-59%
948.66 Burn (any degree) involving 60-69% of body surface with third degree burn of 60-69%
948.70 Burn (any degree) involving 70-79% of body surface with third degree burn of less than 10% or unspecified amount
948.71 Burn (any degree) involving 70-79% of body surface with third degree burn of 10-19%
948.72 Burn (any degree) involving 70-79% of body surface with third degree burn of 20-29%
948.73 Burn (any degree) involving 70-79% of body surface with third degree burn of 30-39%
948.74 Burn (any degree) involving 70-79% of body surface with third degree burn of 40-49%
948.75 Burn (any degree) involving 70-79% of body surface with third degree burn of 50-59%
948.76 Burn (any degree) involving 70-79% of body surface with third degree burn of 60-69%
948.77 Burn (any degree) involving 70-79% of body surface with third degree burn of 70-79%
948.80 Burn (any degree) involving 80-89% of body surface with third degree burn of less than 10% or unspecified amount
948.81 Burn (any degree) involving 80-89% of body surface with third degree burn of 10-19%
948.82 Burn (any degree) involving 80-89% of body surface with third degree burn of 20-29%
948.83 Burn (any degree) involving 80-89% of body surface with third degree burn of 30-39%
948.84 Burn (any degree) involving 80-89% of body surface with third degree burn of 40-49%
948.85 Burn (any degree) involving 80-89% of body surface with third degree burn of 50-59%
948.86 Burn (any degree) involving 80-89% of body surface with third degree burn of 60-69%
948.87 Burn (any degree) involving 80-89% of body surface with third degree burn of 70-79%
948.88 Burn (any degree) involving 80-89% of body surface with third degree burn of 80-89%
948.90 Burn (any degree) involving 90% or more of body surface with third degree burn of less than 10% or unspecified amount
948.91 Burn (any degree) involving 90% or more of body surface with third degree burn of 10-19%
948.92 Burn (any degree) involving 90% or more of body surface with third degree burn of 20-29%
948.93 Burn (any degree) involving 90% or more of body surface with third degree burn of 30-39%
948.94 Burn (any degree) involving 90% or more of body surface with third degree burn of 40-49%
948.95 Burn (any degree) involving 90% or more of body surface with third degree burn of 50-59%
948.96 Burn (any degree) involving 90% or more of body surface with third degree burn of 60-69%
948.97 Burn (any degree) involving 90% or more of body surface with third degree burn of 70-79%
948.98 Burn (any degree) involving 90% or more of body surface with third degree burn of 80-89%
948.99 Burn (any degree) involving 90% or more of body surface with third degree burn of 90% or more of body surface
949.3 Full-thickness skin loss due to burn (third degree NOS), unspecified site ▽
949.4 Deep necrosis of underlying tissue due to burn (deep third degree), unspecified site without mention of loss of body part ▽
949.5 Deep necrosis of underlying tissues due to burn (deep third degree, unspecified site with loss of body part ▽
958.3 Posttraumatic wound infection not elsewhere classified
991.3 Frostbite of other and unspecified sites ▽
996.52 Mechanical complication due to other tissue graft, not elsewhere classified
996.91 Complications of reattached forearm
996.94 Complications of reattached upper extremity, other and unspecified ▽
996.96 Complications of reattached lower extremity, other and unspecified ▽
997.61 Neuroma of amputation stump — (Use additional code to identify complications)
997.62 Infection (chronic) of amputation stump — (Use additional code to identify complications)
997.69 Other late amputation stump complication — (Use additional code to identify complications)
998.30 Disruption of wound, unspecified ▽
998.32 Disruption of external operation (surgical) wound
998.33 Disruption of traumatic injury wound repair
998.59 Other postoperative infection — (Use additional code to identify infection)
998.83 Non-healing surgical wound
V51.8 Other aftercare involving the use of plastic surgery

ICD-9-CM Procedural

86.69 Other skin graft to other sites

15135-15136

15135 Dermal autograft, face, scalp, eyelids, mouth, neck, ears, orbits, genitalia, hands, feet, and/or multiple digits; first 100 sq cm or less, or 1% of body area of infants and children

15136 each additional 100 sq cm, or each additional 1% of body area of infants and children, or part thereof (List separately in addition to code for primary procedure)

ICD-9-CM Diagnostic

145.0 Malignant neoplasm of cheek mucosa
145.8 Malignant neoplasm of other specified parts of mouth
171.0 Malignant neoplasm of connective and other soft tissue of head, face, and neck
171.6 Malignant neoplasm of connective and other soft tissue of pelvis
171.8 Malignant neoplasm of other specified sites of connective and other soft tissue
172.0 Malignant melanoma of skin of lip
172.1 Malignant melanoma of skin of eyelid, including canthus
172.2 Malignant melanoma of skin of ear and external auditory canal
172.3 Malignant melanoma of skin of other and unspecified parts of face ▽
172.4 Malignant melanoma of skin of scalp and neck
172.6 Malignant melanoma of skin of upper limb, including shoulder
172.7 Malignant melanoma of skin of lower limb, including hip
172.8 Malignant melanoma of other specified sites of skin
173.00 Unspecified malignant neoplasm of skin of lip ▽
173.01 Basal cell carcinoma of skin of lip
173.02 Squamous cell carcinoma of skin of lip
173.09 Other specified malignant neoplasm of skin of lip

173.10 Unspecified malignant neoplasm of eyelid, including canthus ▼
173.11 Basal cell carcinoma of eyelid, including canthus
173.12 Squamous cell carcinoma of eyelid, including canthus
173.19 Other specified malignant neoplasm of eyelid, including canthus
173.20 Unspecified malignant neoplasm of skin of ear and external auditory canal ▼
173.21 Basal cell carcinoma of skin of ear and external auditory canal
173.22 Squamous cell carcinoma of skin of ear and external auditory canal
173.29 Other specified malignant neoplasm of skin of ear and external auditory canal
173.30 Unspecified malignant neoplasm of skin of other and unspecified parts of face ▼
173.31 Basal cell carcinoma of skin of other and unspecified parts of face
173.32 Squamous cell carcinoma of skin of other and unspecified parts of face
173.39 Other specified malignant neoplasm of skin of other and unspecified parts of face
173.40 Unspecified malignant neoplasm of scalp and skin of neck ▼
173.41 Basal cell carcinoma of scalp and skin of neck
173.42 Squamous cell carcinoma of scalp and skin of neck
173.49 Other specified malignant neoplasm of scalp and skin of neck
173.60 Unspecified malignant neoplasm of skin of upper limb, including shoulder ▼
173.61 Basal cell carcinoma of skin of upper limb, including shoulder
173.62 Squamous cell carcinoma of skin of upper limb, including shoulder
173.69 Other specified malignant neoplasm of skin of upper limb, including shoulder
173.70 Unspecified malignant neoplasm of skin of lower limb, including hip ▼
173.71 Basal cell carcinoma of skin of lower limb, including hip
173.72 Squamous cell carcinoma of skin of lower limb, including hip
173.79 Other specified malignant neoplasm of skin of lower limb, including hip
173.80 Unspecified malignant neoplasm of other specified sites of skin ▼
173.81 Basal cell carcinoma of other specified sites of skin
173.82 Squamous cell carcinoma of other specified sites of skin
173.89 Other specified malignant neoplasm of other specified sites of skin
176.0 Kaposi's sarcoma of skin
184.1 Malignant neoplasm of labia majora ♀
184.2 Malignant neoplasm of labia minora ♀
184.3 Malignant neoplasm of clitoris ♀
184.4 Malignant neoplasm of vulva, unspecified site ▼ ♀
184.8 Malignant neoplasm of other specified sites of female genital organs ♀
186.9 Malignant neoplasm of other and unspecified testis — (Use additional code to identify any functional activity) ▼ ♂
187.1 Malignant neoplasm of prepuce ♂
187.2 Malignant neoplasm of glans penis ♂
187.3 Malignant neoplasm of body of penis ♂
187.4 Malignant neoplasm of penis, part unspecified ▼ ♂
187.7 Malignant neoplasm of scrotum ♂
187.8 Malignant neoplasm of other specified sites of male genital organs ♂
195.0 Malignant neoplasm of head, face, and neck
195.4 Malignant neoplasm of upper limb
195.5 Malignant neoplasm of lower limb
195.8 Malignant neoplasm of other specified sites
198.2 Secondary malignant neoplasm of skin
198.82 Secondary malignant neoplasm of genital organs
198.89 Secondary malignant neoplasm of other specified sites
209.31 Merkel cell carcinoma of the face
209.32 Merkel cell carcinoma of the scalp and neck
209.33 Merkel cell carcinoma of the upper limb
209.34 Merkel cell carcinoma of the lower limb
209.36 Merkel cell carcinoma of other sites
209.75 Secondary Merkel cell carcinoma
210.0 Benign neoplasm of lip
210.4 Benign neoplasm of other and unspecified parts of mouth ▼
214.0 Lipoma of skin and subcutaneous tissue of face
214.1 Lipoma of other skin and subcutaneous tissue
214.8 Lipoma of other specified sites
215.0 Other benign neoplasm of connective and other soft tissue of head, face, and neck
215.2 Other benign neoplasm of connective and other soft tissue of upper limb, including shoulder
215.3 Other benign neoplasm of connective and other soft tissue of lower limb, including hip
215.8 Other benign neoplasm of connective and other soft tissue of other specified sites
216.0 Benign neoplasm of skin of lip
216.1 Benign neoplasm of eyelid, including canthus
216.2 Benign neoplasm of ear and external auditory canal
216.3 Benign neoplasm of skin of other and unspecified parts of face ▼
216.4 Benign neoplasm of scalp and skin of neck
216.6 Benign neoplasm of skin of upper limb, including shoulder
216.7 Benign neoplasm of skin of lower limb, including hip
216.8 Benign neoplasm of other specified sites of skin
221.2 Benign neoplasm of vulva ♀
221.8 Benign neoplasm of other specified sites of female genital organs ♀
222.1 Benign neoplasm of penis ♂
222.4 Benign neoplasm of scrotum ♂
229.8 Benign neoplasm of other specified sites
230.0 Carcinoma in situ of lip, oral cavity, and pharynx
232.0 Carcinoma in situ of skin of lip
232.1 Carcinoma in situ of eyelid, including canthus
232.2 Carcinoma in situ of skin of ear and external auditory canal
232.3 Carcinoma in situ of skin of other and unspecified parts of face ▼
232.4 Carcinoma in situ of scalp and skin of neck
232.6 Carcinoma in situ of skin of upper limb, including shoulder
232.7 Carcinoma in situ of skin of lower limb, including hip
232.8 Carcinoma in situ of other specified sites of skin
233.30 Carcinoma in situ, unspecified female genital organ ▼ ♀
233.31 Carcinoma in situ, vagina ♀
233.32 Carcinoma in situ, vulva ♀
233.39 Carcinoma in situ, other female genital organ ♀
233.5 Carcinoma in situ of penis ♂
233.6 Carcinoma in situ of other and unspecified male genital organs ▼ ♂
235.1 Neoplasm of uncertain behavior of lip, oral cavity, and pharynx
236.3 Neoplasm of uncertain behavior of other and unspecified female genital organs ▼ ♀
236.6 Neoplasm of uncertain behavior of other and unspecified male genital organs ▼ ♂
238.2 Neoplasm of uncertain behavior of skin
239.2 Neoplasms of unspecified nature of bone, soft tissue, and skin
239.5 Neoplasm of unspecified nature of other genitourinary organs
249.70 Secondary diabetes mellitus with peripheral circulatory disorders, not stated as uncontrolled, or unspecified — (Use additional code to identify manifestation: 443.81, 785.4) (Use additional code to identify any associated insulin use: V58.67)
249.71 Secondary diabetes mellitus with peripheral circulatory disorders, uncontrolled — (Use additional code to identify manifestation: 443.81, 785.4) (Use additional code to identify any associated insulin use: V58.67)
249.80 Secondary diabetes mellitus with other specified manifestations, not stated as uncontrolled, or unspecified — (Use additional code to identify manifestation: 707.10-707.19, 707.8, 707.9, 731.8) (Use additional code to identify any associated insulin use: V58.67)
249.81 Secondary diabetes mellitus with other specified manifestations, uncontrolled — (Use additional code to identify manifestation: 707.10-707.19, 707.8, 707.9, 731.8) (Use additional code to identify any associated insulin use: V58.67)
249.90 Secondary diabetes mellitus with unspecified complication, not stated as uncontrolled, or unspecified — (Use additional code to identify any associated insulin use: V58.67) ▼

249.91 Secondary diabetes mellitus with unspecified complication, uncontrolled — (Use additional code to identify any associated insulin use: V58.67) ▽

250.70 Diabetes with peripheral circulatory disorders, type II or unspecified type, not stated as uncontrolled — (Use additional code to identify manifestation: 443.81, 785.4)

250.71 Diabetes with peripheral circulatory disorders, type I [juvenile type], not stated as uncontrolled — (Use additional code to identify manifestation: 443.81, 785.4)

250.72 Diabetes with peripheral circulatory disorders, type II or unspecified type, uncontrolled — (Use additional code to identify manifestation: 443.81, 785.4)

250.73 Diabetes with peripheral circulatory disorders, type I [juvenile type], uncontrolled — (Use additional code to identify manifestation: 443.81, 785.4)

250.80 Diabetes with other specified manifestations, type II or unspecified type, not stated as uncontrolled — (Use additional code to identify manifestation: 707.10-707.19, 707.8, 707.9, 731.8)

250.81 Diabetes with other specified manifestations, type I [juvenile type], not stated as uncontrolled — (Use additional code to identify manifestation: 707.10-707.19, 707.8, 707.9, 731.8)

250.82 Diabetes with other specified manifestations, type II or unspecified type, uncontrolled — (Use additional code to identify manifestation: 707.10-707.19, 707.8, 707.9, 731.8)

250.83 Diabetes with other specified manifestations, type I [juvenile type], uncontrolled — (Use additional code to identify manifestation: 707.10-707.19, 707.8, 707.9, 731.8)

374.04 Cicatricial entropion

374.50 Unspecified degenerative disorder of eyelid ▽

374.56 Other degenerative disorders of skin affecting eyelid

374.84 Cysts of eyelids

374.85 Vascular anomalies of eyelid

374.86 Retained foreign body of eyelid — (Use additional code to identify foreign body (V90.01-V90.9))

380.32 Acquired deformities of auricle or pinna

440.23 Atherosclerosis of native arteries of the extremities with ulceration — (Use additional code for any associated ulceration: 707.10-707.19, 707.8, 707.9)

459.11 Postphlebitic syndrome with ulcer

459.13 Postphlebitic syndrome with ulcer and inflammation

459.31 Chronic venous hypertension with ulcer

459.33 Chronic venous hypertension with ulcer and inflammation

629.20 Female genital mutilation status, unspecified ▽ ♀

629.21 Female genital mutilation, Type I status ♀

629.22 Female genital mutilation, Type II status ♀

629.23 Female genital mutilation, Type III status ♀

629.29 Other female genital mutilation status ♀

629.89 Other specified disorders of female genital organs ♀

682.4 Cellulitis and abscess of hand, except fingers and thumb — (Use additional code to identify organism, such as 041.1, etc.)

682.7 Cellulitis and abscess of foot, except toes — (Use additional code to identify organism, such as 041.1, etc.)

701.4 Keloid scar

701.5 Other abnormal granulation tissue

701.9 Unspecified hypertrophic and atrophic condition of skin ▽

707.00 Pressure ulcer, unspecified site — (Use additional code to identify pressure ulcer stage: 707.20-707.25) ▽

707.07 Pressure ulcer, heel — (Use additional code to identify pressure ulcer stage: 707.20-707.25)

707.09 Pressure ulcer, other site — (Use additional code to identify pressure ulcer stage: 707.20-707.25)

707.14 Ulcer of heel and midfoot — (Code, if applicable, any causal condition first: 249.80-249.81, 250.80-250.83, 440.23, 459.11, 459.13, 459.31, 459.33)

707.15 Ulcer of other part of foot — (Code, if applicable, any causal condition first: 249.80-249.81, 250.80-250.83, 440.23, 459.11, 459.13, 459.31, 459.33)

707.20 Pressure ulcer, unspecified stage — (Code first site of pressure ulcer: 707.00-707.09) ▽

707.21 Pressure ulcer, stage I — (Code first site of pressure ulcer: 707.00-707.09)

707.22 Pressure ulcer stage II — (Code first site of pressure ulcer: 707.00-707.09)

707.23 Pressure ulcer stage III — (Code first site of pressure ulcer: 707.00-707.09)

707.24 Pressure ulcer stage IV — (Code first site of pressure ulcer: 707.00-707.09)

707.25 Pressure ulcer, unstageable — (Code first site of pressure ulcer: 707.00-707.09)

707.8 Chronic ulcer of other specified site

709.2 Scar condition and fibrosis of skin

709.3 Degenerative skin disorder

709.4 Foreign body granuloma of skin and subcutaneous tissue — (Use additional code to identify foreign body (V90.01-V90.9))

744.29 Other congenital anomaly of ear

752.40 Unspecified congenital anomaly of cervix, vagina, and external female genitalia ▽ ♀

752.43 Cervical agenesis ♀

752.44 Cervical duplication ♀

752.45 Vaginal agenesis ♀

752.46 Transverse vaginal septum ♀

752.47 Longitudinal vaginal septum ♀

752.49 Other congenital anomaly of cervix, vagina, and external female genitalia ♀

757.39 Other specified congenital anomaly of skin

785.4 Gangrene — (Code first any associated underlying condition)

870.0 Laceration of skin of eyelid and periocular area

870.1 Laceration of eyelid, full-thickness, not involving lacrimal passages

870.2 Laceration of eyelid involving lacrimal passages

872.00 Open wound of external ear, unspecified site, without mention of complication ▽

872.01 Open wound of auricle, without mention of complication

872.10 Open wound of external ear, unspecified site, complicated ▽

872.11 Open wound of auricle, complicated

872.8 Open wound of ear, part unspecified, without mention of complication ▽

873.0 Open wound of scalp, without mention of complication

873.1 Open wound of scalp, complicated

873.21 Open wound of nasal septum, without mention of complication

873.31 Open wound of nasal septum, complicated

873.40 Open wound of face, unspecified site, without mention of complication ▽

873.41 Open wound of cheek, without mention of complication

873.42 Open wound of forehead, without mention of complication

873.43 Open wound of lip, without mention of complication

873.44 Open wound of jaw, without mention of complication

873.49 Open wound of face, other and multiple sites, without mention of complication

873.50 Open wound of face, unspecified site, complicated ▽

873.51 Open wound of cheek, complicated

873.52 Open wound of forehead, complicated

873.53 Open wound of lip, complicated

873.54 Open wound of jaw, complicated

873.59 Open wound of face, other and multiple sites, complicated

873.9 Other and unspecified open wound of head, complicated ▽

874.8 Open wound of other and unspecified parts of neck, without mention of complication ▽

878.0 Open wound of penis, without mention of complication ♂

878.1 Open wound of penis, complicated ♂

878.2 Open wound of scrotum and testes, without mention of complication ♂

878.3 Open wound of scrotum and testes, complicated ♂

878.4 Open wound of vulva, without mention of complication ♀

878.5 Open wound of vulva, complicated ♀

878.8 Open wound of other and unspecified parts of genital organs, without mention of complication ▽

878.9 Open wound of other and unspecified parts of genital organs, complicated ▽

882.0 Open wound of hand except finger(s) alone, without mention of complication

882.1 Open wound of hand except finger(s) alone, complicated

882.2 Open wound of hand except finger(s) alone, with tendon involvement

883.0 Open wound of finger(s), without mention of complication
883.1 Open wound of finger(s), complicated
883.2 Open wound of finger(s), with tendon involvement
885.0 Traumatic amputation of thumb (complete) (partial), without mention of complication
885.1 Traumatic amputation of thumb (complete) (partial), complicated
886.0 Traumatic amputation of other finger(s) (complete) (partial), without mention of complication
886.1 Traumatic amputation of other finger(s) (complete) (partial), complicated
892.0 Open wound of foot except toe(s) alone, without mention of complication
892.1 Open wound of foot except toe(s) alone, complicated
892.2 Open wound of foot except toe(s) alone, with tendon involvement
893.0 Open wound of toe(s), without mention of complication
893.1 Open wound of toe(s), complicated
893.2 Open wound of toe(s), with tendon involvement
895.0 Traumatic amputation of toe(s) (complete) (partial), without mention of complication
895.1 Traumatic amputation of toe(s) (complete) (partial), complicated
896.0 Traumatic amputation of foot (complete) (partial), unilateral, without mention of complication
896.1 Traumatic amputation of foot (complete) (partial), unilateral, complicated
896.2 Traumatic amputation of foot (complete) (partial), bilateral, without mention of complication
896.3 Traumatic amputation of foot (complete) (partial), bilateral, complicated
906.0 Late effect of open wound of head, neck, and trunk
906.1 Late effect of open wound of extremities without mention of tendon injury
906.4 Late effect of crushing
906.5 Late effect of burn of eye, face, head, and neck
906.6 Late effect of burn of wrist and hand
906.7 Late effect of burn of other extremities
906.8 Late effect of burns of other specified sites
909.2 Late effect of radiation
909.3 Late effect of complications of surgical and medical care
909.4 Late effect of certain other external causes
925.1 Crushing injury of face and scalp — (Use additional code to identify any associated injuries, such as: 800-829, 850.0-854.1, 860.0-869.1)
925.2 Crushing injury of neck — (Use additional code to identify any associated injuries, such as: 800-829, 850.0-854.1, 860.0-869.1)
926.0 Crushing injury of external genitalia — (Use additional code to identify any associated injuries: 800-829, 850.0-854.1, 860.0-869.1)
927.20 Crushing injury of hand(s) — (Use additional code to identify any associated injuries: 800-829, 850.0-854.1, 860.0-869.1)
927.3 Crushing injury of finger(s) — (Use additional code to identify any associated injuries: 800-829, 850.0-854.1, 860.0-869.1)
927.8 Crushing injury of multiple sites of upper limb — (Use additional code to identify any associated injuries: 800-829, 850.0-854.1, 860.0-869.1)
928.20 Crushing injury of foot — (Use additional code to identify any associated injuries: 800-829, 850.0-854.1, 860.0-869.1)
928.3 Crushing injury of toe(s) — (Use additional code to identify any associated injuries: 800-829, 850.0-854.1, 860.0-869.1)
928.8 Crushing injury of multiple sites of lower limb — (Use additional code to identify any associated injuries: 800-829, 850.0-854.1, 860.0-869.1)
929.0 Crushing injury of multiple sites, not elsewhere classified — (Use additional code to identify any associated injuries: 800-829, 850.0-854.1, 860.0-869.1)
940.0 Chemical burn of eyelids and periocular area
940.1 Other burns of eyelids and periocular area
941.30 Full-thickness skin loss due to burn (third degree NOS) of unspecified site of face and head ▽
941.31 Full-thickness skin loss due to burn (third degree NOS) of ear (any part)
941.32 Full-thickness skin loss due to burn (third degree NOS) of eye (with other parts of face, head, and neck)
941.33 Full-thickness skin loss due to burn (third degree NOS) of lip(s)
941.34 Full-thickness skin loss due to burn (third degree NOS) of chin
941.35 Full-thickness skin loss due to burn (third degree NOS) of nose (septum)
941.36 Full-thickness skin loss due to burn (third degree NOS) of scalp (any part)
941.37 Full-thickness skin loss due to burn (third degree NOS) of forehead and cheek
941.38 Full-thickness skin loss due to burn (third degree NOS) of neck
941.39 Full-thickness skin loss due to burn (third degree NOS) of multiple sites (except with eye) of face, head, and neck
941.40 Deep necrosis of underlying tissues due to burn (deep third degree) of unspecified site of face and head, without mention of loss of a body part ▽
941.41 Deep necrosis of underlying tissues due to burn (deep third degree) of ear (any part), without mention of loss of a body part
941.42 Deep necrosis of underlying tissues due to burn (deep third degree) of eye (with other parts of face, head, and neck), without mention of loss of a body part
941.43 Deep necrosis of underlying tissues due to burn (deep third degree) of lip(s), without mention of loss of a body part
941.44 Deep necrosis of underlying tissues due to burn (deep third degree) of chin, without mention of loss of a body part
941.45 Deep necrosis of underlying tissues due to burn (deep third degree) of nose (septum), without mention of loss of a body part
941.46 Deep necrosis of underlying tissues due to burn (deep third degree) of scalp (any part), without mention of loss of a body part
941.47 Deep necrosis of underlying tissues due to burn (deep third degree) of forehead and cheek, without mention of loss of a body part
941.48 Deep necrosis of underlying tissues due to burn (deep third degree) of neck, without mention of loss of a body part
941.49 Deep necrosis of underlying tissues due to burn (deep third degree) of multiple sites (except with eye) of face, head, and neck, without mention of loss of a body part
941.50 Deep necrosis of underlying tissues due to burn (deep third degree) of face and head, unspecified site, with loss of a body part ▽
941.51 Deep necrosis of underlying tissues due to burn (deep third degree) of ear (any part), with loss of a body part
941.52 Deep necrosis of underlying tissues due to burn (deep third degree) of eye (with other parts of face, head, and neck), with loss of a body part
941.53 Deep necrosis of underlying tissues due to burn (deep third degree) of lip(s), with loss of a body part
941.54 Deep necrosis of underlying tissues due to burn (deep third degree) of chin, with loss of a body part
941.55 Deep necrosis of underlying tissues due to burn (deep third degree) of nose (septum), with loss of a body part
941.56 Deep necrosis of underlying tissues due to burn (deep third degree) of scalp (any part), with loss of a body part
941.57 Deep necrosis of underlying tissues due to burn (deep third degree) of forehead and cheek, with loss of a body part
941.58 Deep necrosis of underlying tissues due to burn (deep third degree) of neck, with loss of a body part
941.59 Deep necrosis of underlying tissues due to burn (deep third degree) of multiple sites (except eye) of face, head, and neck, with loss of a body part
942.35 Full-thickness skin loss due to burn (third degree NOS) of genitalia
942.45 Deep necrosis of underlying tissues due to burn (deep third degree) of genitalia, without mention of loss of a body part
942.55 Deep necrosis of underlying tissues due to burn (deep third degree) of genitalia, with loss of a body part
944.30 Full-thickness skin loss due to burn (third degree NOS) of unspecified site of hand ▽
944.31 Full-thickness skin loss due to burn (third degree NOS) of single digit [finger (nail)] other than thumb
944.32 Full-thickness skin loss due to burn (third degree NOS) of thumb (nail)
944.33 Full-thickness skin loss due to burn (third degree NOS) of two or more digits of hand, not including thumb
944.34 Full-thickness skin loss due to burn (third degree NOS) of two or more digits of hand including thumb
944.35 Full-thickness skin loss due to burn (third degree NOS) of palm of hand

944.36 Full-thickness skin loss due to burn (third degree NOS) of back of hand
944.38 Full-thickness skin loss due to burn (third degree NOS) of multiple sites of wrist(s) and hand(s)
944.40 Deep necrosis of underlying tissues due to burn (deep third degree) of unspecified site of hand, without mention of loss of a body part
944.41 Deep necrosis of underlying tissues due to burn (deep third degree) of single digit [finger (nail)] other than thumb, without mention of loss of a body part
944.42 Deep necrosis of underlying tissues due to burn (deep third degree) of thumb (nail), without mention of loss of a body part
944.43 Deep necrosis of underlying tissues due to burn (deep third degree) of two or more digits of hand, not including thumb, without mention of loss of a body part
944.44 Deep necrosis of underlying tissues due to burn (deep third degree) of two or more digits of hand including thumb, without mention of loss of a body part
944.45 Deep necrosis of underlying tissues due to burn (deep third degree) of palm of hand, without mention of loss of a body part
944.46 Deep necrosis of underlying tissues due to burn (deep third degree) of back of hand, without mention of loss of a body part
944.48 Deep necrosis of underlying tissues due to burn (deep third degree) of multiple sites of wrist(s) and hand(s), without mention of loss of a body part
944.50 Deep necrosis of underlying tissues due to burn (deep third degree) of unspecified site of hand, with loss of a body part
944.51 Deep necrosis of underlying tissues due to burn (deep third degree) of single digit (finger (nail)) other than thumb, with loss of a body part
944.52 Deep necrosis of underlying tissues due to burn (deep third degree) of thumb (nail), with loss of a body part
944.53 Deep necrosis of underlying tissues due to burn (deep third degree) of two or more digits of hand, not including thumb, with loss of a body part
944.54 Deep necrosis of underlying tissues due to burn (deep third degree) of two or more digits of hand including thumb, with loss of a body part
944.55 Deep necrosis of underlying tissues due to burn (deep third degree) of palm of hand, with loss of a body part
944.56 Deep necrosis of underlying tissues due to burn (deep third degree) of back of hand, with loss of a body part
944.58 Deep necrosis of underlying tissues due to burn (deep third degree) of multiple sites of wrist(s) and hand(s), with loss of a body part
945.31 Full-thickness skin loss due to burn (third degree NOS) of toe(s) (nail)
945.32 Full-thickness skin loss due to burn (third degree NOS) of foot
945.39 Full-thickness skin loss due to burn (third degree NOS) of multiple sites of lower limb(s)
945.41 Deep necrosis of underlying tissues due to burn (deep third degree) of toe(s) (nail), without mention of loss of a body part
945.42 Deep necrosis of underlying tissues due to burn (deep third degree) of foot, without mention of loss of a body part
945.49 Deep necrosis of underlying tissues due to burn (deep third degree) of multiple sites of lower limb(s), without mention of loss of a body part
945.51 Deep necrosis of underlying tissues due to burn (deep third degree) of toe(s) (nail), with loss of a body part
945.52 Deep necrosis of underlying tissues due to burn (deep third degree) of foot, with loss of a body part
945.59 Deep necrosis of underlying tissues due to burn (deep third degree) of multiple sites of lower limb(s), with loss of a body part
946.3 Full-thickness skin loss due to burn (third degree NOS) of multiple specified sites
946.4 Deep necrosis of underlying tissues due to burn (deep third degree) of multiple specified sites, without mention of loss of a body part
946.5 Deep necrosis of underlying tissues due to burn (deep third degree) of multiple specified sites, with loss of a body part
947.0 Burn of mouth and pharynx
948.00 Burn (any degree) involving less than 10% of body surface with third degree burn of less than 10% or unspecified amount
948.10 Burn (any degree) involving 10-19% of body surface with third degree burn of less than 10% or unspecified amount
948.11 Burn (any degree) involving 10-19% of body surface with third degree burn of 10-19%
948.20 Burn (any degree) involving 20-29% of body surface with third degree burn of less than 10% or unspecified amount
948.21 Burn (any degree) involving 20-29% of body surface with third degree burn of 10-19%
948.22 Burn (any degree) involving 20-29% of body surface with third degree burn of 20-29%
948.30 Burn (any degree) involving 30-39% of body surface with third degree burn of less than 10% or unspecified amount
948.31 Burn (any degree) involving 30-39% of body surface with third degree burn of 10-19%
948.32 Burn (any degree) involving 30-39% of body surface with third degree burn of 20-29%
948.33 Burn (any degree) involving 30-39% of body surface with third degree burn of 30-39%
948.40 Burn (any degree) involving 40-49% of body surface with third degree burn of less than 10% or unspecified amount
948.41 Burn (any degree) involving 40-49% of body surface with third degree burn of 10-19%
948.42 Burn (any degree) involving 40-49% of body surface with third degree burn of 20-29%
948.43 Burn (any degree) involving 40-49% of body surface with third degree burn of 30-39%
948.44 Burn (any degree) involving 40-49% of body surface with third degree burn of 40-49%
948.50 Burn (any degree) involving 50-59% of body surface with third degree burn of less than 10% or unspecified amount
948.51 Burn (any degree) involving 50-59% of body surface with third degree burn of 10-19%
948.52 Burn (any degree) involving 50-59% of body surface with third degree burn of 20-29%
948.53 Burn (any degree) involving 50-59% of body surface with third degree burn of 30-39%
948.54 Burn (any degree) involving 50-59% of body surface with third degree burn of 40-49%
948.55 Burn (any degree) involving 50-59% of body surface with third degree burn of 50-59%
948.60 Burn (any degree) involving 60-69% of body surface with third degree burn of less than 10% or unspecified amount
948.61 Burn (any degree) involving 60-69% of body surface with third degree burn of 10-19%
948.62 Burn (any degree) involving 60-69% of body surface with third degree burn of 20-29%
948.63 Burn (any degree) involving 60-69% of body surface with third degree burn of 30-39%
948.64 Burn (any degree) involving 60-69% of body surface with third degree burn of 40-49%
948.65 Burn (any degree) involving 60-69% of body surface with third degree burn of 50-59%
948.66 Burn (any degree) involving 60-69% of body surface with third degree burn of 60-69%
948.70 Burn (any degree) involving 70-79% of body surface with third degree burn of less than 10% or unspecified amount
948.71 Burn (any degree) involving 70-79% of body surface with third degree burn of 10-19%
948.72 Burn (any degree) involving 70-79% of body surface with third degree burn of 20-29%
948.73 Burn (any degree) involving 70-79% of body surface with third degree burn of 30-39%
948.74 Burn (any degree) involving 70-79% of body surface with third degree burn of 40-49%
948.75 Burn (any degree) involving 70-79% of body surface with third degree burn of 50-59%
948.76 Burn (any degree) involving 70-79% of body surface with third degree burn of 60-69%
948.77 Burn (any degree) involving 70-79% of body surface with third degree burn of 70-79%
948.80 Burn (any degree) involving 80-89% of body surface with third degree burn of less than 10% or unspecified amount
948.81 Burn (any degree) involving 80-89% of body surface with third degree burn of 10-19%
948.82 Burn (any degree) involving 80-89% of body surface with third degree burn of 20-29%
948.83 Burn (any degree) involving 80-89% of body surface with third degree burn of 30-39%
948.84 Burn (any degree) involving 80-89% of body surface with third degree burn of 40-49%
948.85 Burn (any degree) involving 80-89% of body surface with third degree burn of 50-59%
948.86 Burn (any degree) involving 80-89% of body surface with third degree burn of 60-69%
948.87 Burn (any degree) involving 80-89% of body surface with third degree burn of 70-79%
948.88 Burn (any degree) involving 80-89% of body surface with third degree burn of 80-89%
948.90 Burn (any degree) involving 90% or more of body surface with third degree burn of less than 10% or unspecified amount
948.91 Burn (any degree) involving 90% or more of body surface with third degree burn of 10-19%
948.92 Burn (any degree) involving 90% or more of body surface with third degree burn of 20-29%
948.93 Burn (any degree) involving 90% or more of body surface with third degree burn of 30-39%
948.94 Burn (any degree) involving 90% or more of body surface with third degree burn of 40-49%

948.95 Burn (any degree) involving 90% or more of body surface with third degree burn of 50-59%
948.96 Burn (any degree) involving 90% or more of body surface with third degree burn of 60-69%
948.97 Burn (any degree) involving 90% or more of body surface with third degree burn of 70-79%
948.98 Burn (any degree) involving 90% or more of body surface with third degree burn of 80-89%
948.99 Burn (any degree) involving 90% or more of body surface with third degree burn of 90% or more of body surface
949.3 Full-thickness skin loss due to burn (third degree NOS), unspecified site ▽
949.4 Deep necrosis of underlying tissue due to burn (deep third degree), unspecified site without mention of loss of body part ▽
949.5 Deep necrosis of underlying tissues due to burn (deep third degree, unspecified site with loss of body part ▽
959.01 Head injury, unspecified ▽
959.09 Injury of face and neck, other and unspecified
959.14 Other injury of external genitals
959.4 Injury, other and unspecified, hand, except finger
959.5 Injury, other and unspecified, finger
959.7 Injury, other and unspecified, knee, leg, ankle, and foot
959.8 Injury, other and unspecified, other specified sites, including multiple
991.0 Frostbite of face
991.1 Frostbite of hand
991.2 Frostbite of foot
996.52 Mechanical complication due to other tissue graft, not elsewhere classified
996.92 Complications of reattached hand
996.93 Complications of reattached finger(s)
996.95 Complications of reattached foot and toe(s)
997.62 Infection (chronic) of amputation stump — (Use additional code to identify complications)
997.69 Other late amputation stump complication — (Use additional code to identify complications)
998.30 Disruption of wound, unspecified ▽
998.32 Disruption of external operation (surgical) wound
998.33 Disruption of traumatic injury wound repair
998.83 Non-healing surgical wound
V51.8 Other aftercare involving the use of plastic surgery

ICD-9-CM Procedural

08.61 Reconstruction of eyelid with skin flap or graft
16.65 Secondary graft to exenteration cavity
18.6 Reconstruction of external auditory canal
18.79 Other plastic repair of external ear
27.56 Other skin graft to lip and mouth
61.49 Other repair of scrotum and tunica vaginalis ♂
64.49 Other repair of penis ♂
70.79 Other repair of vagina ♀
71.79 Other repair of vulva and perineum ♀
86.62 Other skin graft to hand
86.69 Other skin graft to other sites

15150-15152

15150 Tissue cultured skin autograft, trunk, arms, legs; first 25 sq cm or less
15151 additional 1 sq cm to 75 sq cm (List separately in addition to code for primary procedure)
15152 each additional 100 sq cm, or each additional 1% of body area of infants and children, or part thereof (List separately in addition to code for primary procedure)

ICD-9-CM Diagnostic

172.5 Malignant melanoma of skin of trunk, except scrotum
172.6 Malignant melanoma of skin of upper limb, including shoulder
172.7 Malignant melanoma of skin of lower limb, including hip
172.8 Malignant melanoma of other specified sites of skin
173.50 Unspecified malignant neoplasm of skin of trunk, except scrotum ▽
173.51 Basal cell carcinoma of skin of trunk, except scrotum
173.52 Squamous cell carcinoma of skin of trunk, except scrotum
173.59 Other specified malignant neoplasm of skin of trunk, except scrotum
173.60 Unspecified malignant neoplasm of skin of upper limb, including shoulder ▽
173.61 Basal cell carcinoma of skin of upper limb, including shoulder
173.62 Squamous cell carcinoma of skin of upper limb, including shoulder
173.69 Other specified malignant neoplasm of skin of upper limb, including shoulder
173.70 Unspecified malignant neoplasm of skin of lower limb, including hip ▽
173.71 Basal cell carcinoma of skin of lower limb, including hip
173.72 Squamous cell carcinoma of skin of lower limb, including hip
173.79 Other specified malignant neoplasm of skin of lower limb, including hip
173.80 Unspecified malignant neoplasm of other specified sites of skin ▽
173.81 Basal cell carcinoma of other specified sites of skin
173.82 Squamous cell carcinoma of other specified sites of skin
173.89 Other specified malignant neoplasm of other specified sites of skin
174.0 Malignant neoplasm of nipple and areola of female breast — (Use additional code to identify estrogen receptor status: V86.0-V86.1) ♀
174.1 Malignant neoplasm of central portion of female breast — (Use additional code to identify estrogen receptor status: V86.0-V86.1) ♀
174.2 Malignant neoplasm of upper-inner quadrant of female breast — (Use additional code to identify estrogen receptor status: V86.0-V86.1) ♀
174.3 Malignant neoplasm of lower-inner quadrant of female breast — (Use additional code to identify estrogen receptor status: V86.0-V86.1) ♀
174.4 Malignant neoplasm of upper-outer quadrant of female breast — (Use additional code to identify estrogen receptor status: V86.0-V86.1) ♀
174.5 Malignant neoplasm of lower-outer quadrant of female breast — (Use additional code to identify estrogen receptor status: V86.0-V86.1) ♀
174.6 Malignant neoplasm of axillary tail of female breast — (Use additional code to identify estrogen receptor status: V86.0-V86.1) ♀
174.8 Malignant neoplasm of other specified sites of female breast — (Use additional code to identify estrogen receptor status: V86.0-V86.1) ♀
175.0 Malignant neoplasm of nipple and areola of male breast — (Use additional code to identify estrogen receptor status: V86.0-V86.1) ♂
175.9 Malignant neoplasm of other and unspecified sites of male breast — (Use additional code to identify estrogen receptor status: V86.0-V86.1) ▽ ♂
176.0 Kaposi's sarcoma of skin
195.1 Malignant neoplasm of thorax
195.2 Malignant neoplasm of abdomen
195.3 Malignant neoplasm of pelvis
195.4 Malignant neoplasm of upper limb
195.5 Malignant neoplasm of lower limb
195.8 Malignant neoplasm of other specified sites
198.2 Secondary malignant neoplasm of skin
209.33 Merkel cell carcinoma of the upper limb
209.34 Merkel cell carcinoma of the lower limb
209.35 Merkel cell carcinoma of the trunk
209.75 Secondary Merkel cell carcinoma
214.1 Lipoma of other skin and subcutaneous tissue
215.7 Other benign neoplasm of connective and other soft tissue of trunk, unspecified ▽
216.5 Benign neoplasm of skin of trunk, except scrotum
216.6 Benign neoplasm of skin of upper limb, including shoulder
232.5 Carcinoma in situ of skin of trunk, except scrotum
232.6 Carcinoma in situ of skin of upper limb, including shoulder
232.7 Carcinoma in situ of skin of lower limb, including hip
232.8 Carcinoma in situ of other specified sites of skin

238.2 Neoplasm of uncertain behavior of skin
239.2 Neoplasms of unspecified nature of bone, soft tissue, and skin
249.70 Secondary diabetes mellitus with peripheral circulatory disorders, not stated as uncontrolled, or unspecified — (Use additional code to identify manifestation: 443.81, 785.4) (Use additional code to identify any associated insulin use: V58.67)
249.71 Secondary diabetes mellitus with peripheral circulatory disorders, uncontrolled — (Use additional code to identify manifestation: 443.81, 785.4) (Use additional code to identify any associated insulin use: V58.67)
249.80 Secondary diabetes mellitus with other specified manifestations, not stated as uncontrolled, or unspecified — (Use additional code to identify manifestation: 707.10-707.19, 707.8, 707.9, 731.8) (Use additional code to identify any associated insulin use: V58.67)
249.81 Secondary diabetes mellitus with other specified manifestations, uncontrolled — (Use additional code to identify manifestation: 707.10-707.19, 707.8, 707.9, 731.8) (Use additional code to identify any associated insulin use: V58.67)
249.90 Secondary diabetes mellitus with unspecified complication, not stated as uncontrolled, or unspecified — (Use additional code to identify any associated insulin use: V58.67) ▽
249.91 Secondary diabetes mellitus with unspecified complication, uncontrolled — (Use additional code to identify any associated insulin use: V58.67) ▽
250.70 Diabetes with peripheral circulatory disorders, type II or unspecified type, not stated as uncontrolled — (Use additional code to identify manifestation: 443.81, 785.4)
250.71 Diabetes with peripheral circulatory disorders, type I [juvenile type], not stated as uncontrolled — (Use additional code to identify manifestation: 443.81, 785.4)
250.72 Diabetes with peripheral circulatory disorders, type II or unspecified type, uncontrolled — (Use additional code to identify manifestation: 443.81, 785.4)
250.73 Diabetes with peripheral circulatory disorders, type I [juvenile type], uncontrolled — (Use additional code to identify manifestation: 443.81, 785.4)
250.80 Diabetes with other specified manifestations, type II or unspecified type, not stated as uncontrolled — (Use additional code to identify manifestation: 707.10-707.19, 707.8, 707.9, 731.8)
250.81 Diabetes with other specified manifestations, type I [juvenile type], not stated as uncontrolled — (Use additional code to identify manifestation: 707.10-707.19, 707.8, 707.9, 731.8)
250.82 Diabetes with other specified manifestations, type II or unspecified type, uncontrolled — (Use additional code to identify manifestation: 707.10-707.19, 707.8, 707.9, 731.8)
250.83 Diabetes with other specified manifestations, type I [juvenile type], uncontrolled — (Use additional code to identify manifestation: 707.10-707.19, 707.8, 707.9, 731.8)
440.23 Atherosclerosis of native arteries of the extremities with ulceration — (Use additional code for any associated ulceration: 707.10-707.19, 707.8, 707.9)
454.0 Varicose veins of lower extremities with ulcer
454.2 Varicose veins of lower extremities with ulcer and inflammation
459.11 Postphlebitic syndrome with ulcer
459.13 Postphlebitic syndrome with ulcer and inflammation
459.31 Chronic venous hypertension with ulcer
459.33 Chronic venous hypertension with ulcer and inflammation
682.2 Cellulitis and abscess of trunk — (Use additional code to identify organism, such as 041.1, etc.)
682.3 Cellulitis and abscess of upper arm and forearm — (Use additional code to identify organism, such as 041.1, etc.)
682.5 Cellulitis and abscess of buttock — (Use additional code to identify organism, such as 041.1, etc.)
682.6 Cellulitis and abscess of leg, except foot — (Use additional code to identify organism, such as 041.1, etc.)
682.8 Cellulitis and abscess of other specified site — (Use additional code to identify organism, such as 041.1, etc.)
701.4 Keloid scar
701.5 Other abnormal granulation tissue
701.9 Unspecified hypertrophic and atrophic condition of skin ▽
707.00 Pressure ulcer, unspecified site — (Use additional code to identify pressure ulcer stage: 707.20-707.25) ▽
707.01 Pressure ulcer, elbow — (Use additional code to identify pressure ulcer stage: 707.20-707.25)
707.02 Pressure ulcer, upper back — (Use additional code to identify pressure ulcer stage: 707.20-707.25)
707.03 Pressure ulcer, lower back — (Use additional code to identify pressure ulcer stage: 707.20-707.25)
707.04 Pressure ulcer, hip — (Use additional code to identify pressure ulcer stage: 707.20-707.25)
707.05 Pressure ulcer, buttock — (Use additional code to identify pressure ulcer stage: 707.20-707.25)
707.06 Pressure ulcer, ankle — (Use additional code to identify pressure ulcer stage: 707.20-707.25)
707.09 Pressure ulcer, other site — (Use additional code to identify pressure ulcer stage: 707.20-707.25)
707.10 Ulcer of lower limb, unspecified — (Code, if applicable, any causal condition first: 249.80-249.81, 250.80-250.83, 440.23, 459.11, 459.13, 459.31, 459.33) ▽
707.11 Ulcer of thigh — (Code, if applicable, any causal condition first: 249.80-249.81, 250.80-250.83, 440.23, 459.11, 459.13, 459.31, 459.33)
707.12 Ulcer of calf — (Code, if applicable, any causal condition first: 249.80-249.81, 250.80-250.83, 440.23, 459.11, 459.13, 459.31, 459.33)
707.13 Ulcer of ankle — (Code, if applicable, any causal condition first: 249.80-249.81, 250.80-250.83, 440.23, 459.11, 459.13, 459.31, 459.33)
707.19 Ulcer of other part of lower limb — (Code, if applicable, any causal condition first: 249.80-249.81, 250.80-250.83, 440.23, 459.11, 459.13, 459.31, 459.33)
707.20 Pressure ulcer, unspecified stage — (Code first site of pressure ulcer: 707.00-707.09) ▽
707.21 Pressure ulcer, stage I — (Code first site of pressure ulcer: 707.00-707.09)
707.22 Pressure ulcer stage II — (Code first site of pressure ulcer: 707.00-707.09)
707.23 Pressure ulcer stage III — (Code first site of pressure ulcer: 707.00-707.09)
707.24 Pressure ulcer stage IV — (Code first site of pressure ulcer: 707.00-707.09)
707.25 Pressure ulcer, unstageable — (Code first site of pressure ulcer: 707.00-707.09)
707.8 Chronic ulcer of other specified site
709.2 Scar condition and fibrosis of skin
709.3 Degenerative skin disorder
709.4 Foreign body granuloma of skin and subcutaneous tissue — (Use additional code to identify foreign body (V90.01-V90.9))
709.8 Other specified disorder of skin
709.9 Unspecified disorder of skin and subcutaneous tissue ▽
785.4 Gangrene — (Code first any associated underlying condition)
875.0 Open wound of chest (wall), without mention of complication
875.1 Open wound of chest (wall), complicated
876.0 Open wound of back, without mention of complication
876.1 Open wound of back, complicated
877.0 Open wound of buttock, without mention of complication
877.1 Open wound of buttock, complicated
879.0 Open wound of breast, without mention of complication
879.1 Open wound of breast, complicated
879.2 Open wound of abdominal wall, anterior, without mention of complication
879.3 Open wound of abdominal wall, anterior, complicated
879.4 Open wound of abdominal wall, lateral, without mention of complication
879.5 Open wound of abdominal wall, lateral, complicated
879.6 Open wound of other and unspecified parts of trunk, without mention of complication ▽
879.7 Open wound of other and unspecified parts of trunk, complicated ▽
879.8 Open wound(s) (multiple) of unspecified site(s), without mention of complication ▽
879.9 Open wound(s) (multiple) of unspecified site(s), complicated ▽
880.00 Open wound of shoulder region, without mention of complication
880.01 Open wound of scapular region, without mention of complication
880.02 Open wound of axillary region, without mention of complication
880.03 Open wound of upper arm, without mention of complication

880.09 Open wound of multiple sites of shoulder and upper arm, without mention of complication

880.10 Open wound of shoulder region, complicated

880.11 Open wound of scapular region, complicated

880.12 Open wound of axillary region, complicated

880.13 Open wound of upper arm, complicated

880.19 Open wound of multiple sites of shoulder and upper arm, complicated

880.20 Open wound of shoulder region, with tendon involvement

880.21 Open wound of scapular region, with tendon involvement

880.22 Open wound of axillary region, with tendon involvement

880.23 Open wound of upper arm, with tendon involvement

880.29 Open wound of multiple sites of shoulder and upper arm, with tendon involvement

881.00 Open wound of forearm, without mention of complication

881.01 Open wound of elbow, without mention of complication

881.02 Open wound of wrist, without mention of complication

881.10 Open wound of forearm, complicated

881.11 Open wound of elbow, complicated

881.12 Open wound of wrist, complicated

881.20 Open wound of forearm, with tendon involvement

881.21 Open wound of elbow, with tendon involvement

881.22 Open wound of wrist, with tendon involvement

884.0 Multiple and unspecified open wound of upper limb, without mention of complication

884.1 Multiple and unspecified open wound of upper limb, complicated

884.2 Multiple and unspecified open wound of upper limb, with tendon involvement

887.0 Traumatic amputation of arm and hand (complete) (partial), unilateral, below elbow, without mention of complication

887.1 Traumatic amputation of arm and hand (complete) (partial), unilateral, below elbow, complicated

887.2 Traumatic amputation of arm and hand (complete) (partial), unilateral, at or above elbow, without mention of complication

887.3 Traumatic amputation of arm and hand (complete) (partial), unilateral, at or above elbow, complicated

887.4 Traumatic amputation of arm and hand (complete) (partial), unilateral, level not specified, without mention of complication

887.5 Traumatic amputation of arm and hand (complete) (partial), unilateral, level not specified, complicated

887.6 Traumatic amputation of arm and hand (complete) (partial), bilateral (any level), without mention of complication

887.7 Traumatic amputation of arm and hand (complete) (partial), bilateral (any level), complicated

890.0 Open wound of hip and thigh, without mention of complication

890.1 Open wound of hip and thigh, complicated

890.2 Open wound of hip and thigh, with tendon involvement

891.0 Open wound of knee, leg (except thigh), and ankle, without mention of complication

891.1 Open wound of knee, leg (except thigh), and ankle, complicated

891.2 Open wound of knee, leg (except thigh), and ankle, with tendon involvement

894.0 Multiple and unspecified open wound of lower limb, without mention of complication

894.1 Multiple and unspecified open wound of lower limb, complicated

894.2 Multiple and unspecified open wound of lower limb, with tendon involvement

897.0 Traumatic amputation of leg(s) (complete) (partial), unilateral, below knee, without mention of complication

897.1 Traumatic amputation of leg(s) (complete) (partial), unilateral, below knee, complicated

897.2 Traumatic amputation of leg(s) (complete) (partial), unilateral, at or above knee, without mention of complication

897.3 Traumatic amputation of leg(s) (complete) (partial), unilateral, at or above knee, complicated

897.4 Traumatic amputation of leg(s) (complete) (partial), unilateral, level not specified, without mention of complication

897.5 Traumatic amputation of leg(s) (complete) (partial), unilateral, level not specified, complicated

897.6 Traumatic amputation of leg(s) (complete) (partial), bilateral (any level), without mention of complication

897.7 Traumatic amputation of leg(s) (complete) (partial), bilateral (any level), complicated

906.0 Late effect of open wound of head, neck, and trunk

906.1 Late effect of open wound of extremities without mention of tendon injury

906.4 Late effect of crushing

906.6 Late effect of burn of wrist and hand

906.7 Late effect of burn of other extremities

906.8 Late effect of burns of other specified sites

908.6 Late effect of certain complications of trauma

909.2 Late effect of radiation

909.3 Late effect of complications of surgical and medical care

909.4 Late effect of certain other external causes

926.11 Crushing injury of back — (Use additional code to identify any associated injuries: 800-829, 850.0-854.1, 860.0-869.1)

926.12 Crushing injury of buttock — (Use additional code to identify any associated injuries: 800-829, 850.0-854.1, 860.0-869.1)

926.19 Crushing injury of other specified sites of trunk — (Use additional code to identify any associated injuries: 800-829, 850.0-854.1, 860.0-869.1)

926.8 Crushing injury of multiple sites of trunk — (Use additional code to identify any associated injuries: 800-829, 850.0-854.1, 860.0-869.1)

926.9 Crushing injury of unspecified site of trunk — (Use additional code to identify any associated injuries: 800-829, 850.0-854.1, 860.0-869.1)

927.00 Crushing injury of shoulder region — (Use additional code to identify any associated injuries: 800-829, 850.0-854.1, 860.0-869.1)

927.01 Crushing injury of scapular region — (Use additional code to identify any associated injuries: 800-829, 850.0-854.1, 860.0-869.1)

927.02 Crushing injury of axillary region — (Use additional code to identify any associated injuries: 800-829, 850.0-854.1, 860.0-869.1)

927.03 Crushing injury of upper arm — (Use additional code to identify any associated injuries: 800-829, 850.0-854.1, 860.0-869.1)

927.09 Crushing injury of multiple sites of upper arm — (Use additional code to identify any associated injuries: 800-829, 850.0-854.1, 860.0-869.1)

927.10 Crushing injury of forearm — (Use additional code to identify any associated injuries: 800-829, 850.0-854.1, 860.0-869.1)

927.11 Crushing injury of elbow — (Use additional code to identify any associated injuries: 800-829, 850.0-854.1, 860.0-869.1)

927.21 Crushing injury of wrist — (Use additional code to identify any associated injuries: 800-829, 850.0-854.1, 860.0-869.1)

927.8 Crushing injury of multiple sites of upper limb — (Use additional code to identify any associated injuries: 800-829, 850.0-854.1, 860.0-869.1)

927.9 Crushing injury of unspecified site of upper limb — (Use additional code to identify any associated injuries: 800-829, 850.0-854.1, 860.0-869.1)

928.00 Crushing injury of thigh — (Use additional code to identify any associated injuries: 800-829, 850.0-854.1, 860.0-869.1)

928.01 Crushing injury of hip — (Use additional code to identify any associated injuries: 800-829, 850.0-854.1, 860.0-869.1)

928.10 Crushing injury of lower leg — (Use additional code to identify any associated injuries: 800-829, 850.0-854.1, 860.0-869.1)

928.11 Crushing injury of knee — (Use additional code to identify any associated injuries: 800-829, 850.0-854.1, 860.0-869.1)

928.21 Crushing injury of ankle — (Use additional code to identify any associated injuries: 800-829, 850.0-854.1, 860.0-869.1)

928.8 Crushing injury of multiple sites of lower limb — (Use additional code to identify any associated injuries: 800-829, 850.0-854.1, 860.0-869.1)

928.9 Crushing injury of unspecified site of lower limb — (Use additional code to identify any associated injuries: 800-829, 850.0-854.1, 860.0-869.1)

929.0 Crushing injury of multiple sites, not elsewhere classified — (Use additional code to identify any associated injuries: 800-829, 850.0-854.1, 860.0-869.1)

942.20 Blisters with epidermal loss due to burn (second degree) of unspecified site of trunk

942.21 Blisters with epidermal loss due to burn (second degree) of breast

942.22 Blisters with epidermal loss due to burn (second degree) of chest wall, excluding breast and nipple
942.23 Blisters with epidermal loss due to burn (second degree) of abdominal wall
942.24 Blisters with epidermal loss due to burn (second degree) of back (any part)
942.29 Blisters with epidermal loss due to burn (second degree) of other and multiple sites of trunk
942.30 Full-thickness skin loss due to burn (third degree NOS) of unspecified site of trunk ▽
942.31 Full-thickness skin loss due to burn (third degree NOS) of breast
942.32 Full-thickness skin loss due to burn (third degree NOS) of chest wall, excluding breast and nipple
942.33 Full-thickness skin loss due to burn (third degree NOS) of abdominal wall
942.34 Full-thickness skin loss due to burn (third degree NOS) of back (any part)
942.39 Full-thickness skin loss due to burn (third degree NOS) of other and multiple sites of trunk
942.40 Deep necrosis of underlying tissues due to burn (deep third degree) of trunk, unspecified site, without mention of loss of a body part ▽
942.41 Deep necrosis of underlying tissues due to burn (deep third degree) of breast, without mention of loss of a body part
942.42 Deep necrosis of underlying tissues due to burn (deep third degree) of chest wall, excluding breast and nipple, without mention of loss of a body part
942.43 Deep necrosis of underlying tissues due to burn (deep third degree) of abdominal wall, without mention of loss of a body part
942.44 Deep necrosis of underlying tissues due to burn (deep third degree) of back (any part), without mention of loss of a body part
942.49 Deep necrosis of underlying tissues due to burn (deep third degree) of other and multiple sites of trunk, without mention of loss of a body part
942.50 Deep necrosis of underlying tissues due to burn (deep third degree) of unspecified site of trunk, with loss of a body part ▽
942.51 Deep necrosis of underlying tissues due to burn (deep third degree) of breast, with loss of a body part
942.52 Deep necrosis of underlying tissues due to burn (deep third degree) of chest wall, excluding breast and nipple, with loss of a body part
942.53 Deep necrosis of underlying tissues due to burn (deep third degree) of abdominal wall with loss of a body part
942.54 Deep necrosis of underlying tissues due to burn (deep third degree) of back (any part), with loss of a body part
942.59 Deep necrosis of underlying tissues due to burn (deep third degree) of other and multiple sites of trunk, with loss of a body part
943.30 Full-thickness skin loss due to burn (third degree NOS) of unspecified site of upper limb ▽
943.31 Full-thickness skin loss due to burn (third degree NOS) of forearm
943.32 Full-thickness skin loss due to burn (third degree NOS) of elbow
943.33 Full-thickness skin loss due to burn (third degree NOS) of upper arm
943.34 Full-thickness skin loss due to burn (third degree NOS) of axilla
943.35 Full-thickness skin loss due to burn (third degree NOS) of shoulder
943.36 Full-thickness skin loss due to burn (third degree NOS) of scapular region
943.39 Full-thickness skin loss due to burn (third degree NOS) of multiple sites of upper limb, except wrist and hand
943.40 Deep necrosis of underlying tissues due to burn (deep third degree) of unspecified site of upper limb, without mention of loss of a body part ▽
943.41 Deep necrosis of underlying tissues due to burn (deep third degree) of forearm, without mention of loss of a body part
943.42 Deep necrosis of underlying tissues due to burn (deep third degree) of elbow, without mention of loss of a body part
943.43 Deep necrosis of underlying tissues due to burn (deep third degree) of upper arm, without mention of loss of a body part
943.44 Deep necrosis of underlying tissues due to burn (deep third degree) of axilla, without mention of loss of a body part
943.45 Deep necrosis of underlying tissues due to burn (deep third degree) of shoulder, without mention of loss of a body part
943.46 Deep necrosis of underlying tissues due to burn (deep third degree) of scapular region, without mention of loss of a body part
943.49 Deep necrosis of underlying tissues due to burn (deep third degree) of multiple sites of upper limb, except wrist and hand, without mention of loss of a body part
943.50 Deep necrosis of underlying tissues due to burn (deep third degree) of unspecified site of upper limb, with loss of a body part ▽
943.51 Deep necrosis of underlying tissues due to burn (deep third degree) of forearm, with loss of a body part
943.52 Deep necrosis of underlying tissues due to burn (deep third degree) of elbow, with loss of a body part
943.53 Deep necrosis of underlying tissues due to burn (deep third degree) of upper arm, with loss of upper a body part
943.54 Deep necrosis of underlying tissues due to burn (deep third degree) of axilla, with loss of a body part
943.55 Deep necrosis of underlying tissues due to burn (deep third degree) of shoulder, with loss of a body part
943.56 Deep necrosis of underlying tissues due to burn (deep third degree) of scapular region, with loss of a body part
943.59 Deep necrosis of underlying tissues due to burn (deep third degree) of multiple sites of upper limb, except wrist and hand, with loss of a body part
945.30 Full-thickness skin loss due to burn (third degree NOS) of unspecified site of lower limb ▽
945.33 Full-thickness skin loss due to burn (third degree NOS) of ankle
945.34 Full-thickness skin loss due to burn (third degree NOS) of lower leg
945.35 Full-thickness skin loss due to burn (third degree NOS) of knee
945.36 Full-thickness skin loss due to burn (third degree NOS) of thigh (any part)
945.39 Full-thickness skin loss due to burn (third degree NOS) of multiple sites of lower limb(s)
945.40 Deep necrosis of underlying tissues due to burn (deep third degree) of unspecified site of lower limb (leg), without mention of loss of a body part ▽
945.43 Deep necrosis of underlying tissues due to burn (deep third degree) of ankle, without mention of loss of a body part
945.44 Deep necrosis of underlying tissues due to burn (deep third degree) of lower leg, without mention of loss of a body part
945.45 Deep necrosis of underlying tissues due to burn (deep third degree) of knee, without mention of loss of a body part
945.46 Deep necrosis of underlying tissues due to burn (deep third degree) of thigh (any part), without mention of loss of a body part
945.49 Deep necrosis of underlying tissues due to burn (deep third degree) of multiple sites of lower limb(s), without mention of loss of a body part
945.50 Deep necrosis of underlying tissues due to burn (deep third degree) of unspecified site lower limb (leg), with loss of a body part ▽
945.53 Deep necrosis of underlying tissues due to burn (deep third degree) of ankle, with loss of a body part
945.54 Deep necrosis of underlying tissues due to burn (deep third degree) of lower leg, with loss of a body part
945.55 Deep necrosis of underlying tissues due to burn (deep third degree) of knee, with loss of a body part
945.56 Deep necrosis of underlying tissues due to burn (deep third degree) of thigh (any part), with loss of a body part
945.59 Deep necrosis of underlying tissues due to burn (deep third degree) of multiple sites of lower limb(s), with loss of a body part
946.3 Full-thickness skin loss due to burn (third degree NOS) of multiple specified sites
946.4 Deep necrosis of underlying tissues due to burn (deep third degree) of multiple specified sites, without mention of loss of a body part
946.5 Deep necrosis of underlying tissues due to burn (deep third degree) of multiple specified sites, with loss of a body part
948.00 Burn (any degree) involving less than 10% of body surface with third degree burn of less than 10% or unspecified amount
948.10 Burn (any degree) involving 10-19% of body surface with third degree burn of less than 10% or unspecified amount

948.11 Burn (any degree) involving 10-19% of body surface with third degree burn of 10-19%
948.20 Burn (any degree) involving 20-29% of body surface with third degree burn of less than 10% or unspecified amount
948.21 Burn (any degree) involving 20-29% of body surface with third degree burn of 10-19%
948.22 Burn (any degree) involving 20-29% of body surface with third degree burn of 20-29%
948.30 Burn (any degree) involving 30-39% of body surface with third degree burn of less than 10% or unspecified amount
948.31 Burn (any degree) involving 30-39% of body surface with third degree burn of 10-19%
948.32 Burn (any degree) involving 30-39% of body surface with third degree burn of 20-29%
948.33 Burn (any degree) involving 30-39% of body surface with third degree burn of 30-39%
948.40 Burn (any degree) involving 40-49% of body surface with third degree burn of less than 10% or unspecified amount
948.41 Burn (any degree) involving 40-49% of body surface with third degree burn of 10-19%
948.42 Burn (any degree) involving 40-49% of body surface with third degree burn of 20-29%
948.43 Burn (any degree) involving 40-49% of body surface with third degree burn of 30-39%
948.44 Burn (any degree) involving 40-49% of body surface with third degree burn of 40-49%
948.50 Burn (any degree) involving 50-59% of body surface with third degree burn of less than 10% or unspecified amount
948.51 Burn (any degree) involving 50-59% of body surface with third degree burn of 10-19%
948.52 Burn (any degree) involving 50-59% of body surface with third degree burn of 20-29%
948.53 Burn (any degree) involving 50-59% of body surface with third degree burn of 30-39%
948.54 Burn (any degree) involving 50-59% of body surface with third degree burn of 40-49%
948.55 Burn (any degree) involving 50-59% of body surface with third degree burn of 50-59%
948.60 Burn (any degree) involving 60-69% of body surface with third degree burn of less than 10% or unspecified amount
948.61 Burn (any degree) involving 60-69% of body surface with third degree burn of 10-19%
948.62 Burn (any degree) involving 60-69% of body surface with third degree burn of 20-29%
948.63 Burn (any degree) involving 60-69% of body surface with third degree burn of 30-39%
948.64 Burn (any degree) involving 60-69% of body surface with third degree burn of 40-49%
948.65 Burn (any degree) involving 60-69% of body surface with third degree burn of 50-59%
948.66 Burn (any degree) involving 60-69% of body surface with third degree burn of 60-69%
948.70 Burn (any degree) involving 70-79% of body surface with third degree burn of less than 10% or unspecified amount
948.71 Burn (any degree) involving 70-79% of body surface with third degree burn of 10-19%
948.72 Burn (any degree) involving 70-79% of body surface with third degree burn of 20-29%
948.73 Burn (any degree) involving 70-79% of body surface with third degree burn of 30-39%
948.74 Burn (any degree) involving 70-79% of body surface with third degree burn of 40-49%
948.75 Burn (any degree) involving 70-79% of body surface with third degree burn of 50-59%
948.76 Burn (any degree) involving 70-79% of body surface with third degree burn of 60-69%
948.77 Burn (any degree) involving 70-79% of body surface with third degree burn of 70-79%
948.80 Burn (any degree) involving 80-89% of body surface with third degree burn of less than 10% or unspecified amount
948.81 Burn (any degree) involving 80-89% of body surface with third degree burn of 10-19%
948.82 Burn (any degree) involving 80-89% of body surface with third degree burn of 20-29%
948.83 Burn (any degree) involving 80-89% of body surface with third degree burn of 30-39%
948.84 Burn (any degree) involving 80-89% of body surface with third degree burn of 40-49%
948.85 Burn (any degree) involving 80-89% of body surface with third degree burn of 50-59%
948.86 Burn (any degree) involving 80-89% of body surface with third degree burn of 60-69%
948.87 Burn (any degree) involving 80-89% of body surface with third degree burn of 70-79%
948.88 Burn (any degree) involving 80-89% of body surface with third degree burn of 80-89%
948.90 Burn (any degree) involving 90% or more of body surface with third degree burn of less than 10% or unspecified amount
948.91 Burn (any degree) involving 90% or more of body surface with third degree burn of 10-19%
948.92 Burn (any degree) involving 90% or more of body surface with third degree burn of 20-29%
948.93 Burn (any degree) involving 90% or more of body surface with third degree burn of 30-39%
948.94 Burn (any degree) involving 90% or more of body surface with third degree burn of 40-49%
948.95 Burn (any degree) involving 90% or more of body surface with third degree burn of 50-59%
948.96 Burn (any degree) involving 90% or more of body surface with third degree burn of 60-69%
948.97 Burn (any degree) involving 90% or more of body surface with third degree burn of 70-79%
948.98 Burn (any degree) involving 90% or more of body surface with third degree burn of 80-89%
948.99 Burn (any degree) involving 90% or more of body surface with third degree burn of 90% or more of body surface
949.3 Full-thickness skin loss due to burn (third degree NOS), unspecified site ▽
949.4 Deep necrosis of underlying tissue due to burn (deep third degree), unspecified site without mention of loss of body part ▽
949.5 Deep necrosis of underlying tissues due to burn (deep third degree, unspecified site with loss of body part ▽
958.3 Posttraumatic wound infection not elsewhere classified
991.3 Frostbite of other and unspecified sites ▽
996.52 Mechanical complication due to other tissue graft, not elsewhere classified
996.91 Complications of reattached forearm
996.94 Complications of reattached upper extremity, other and unspecified ▽
996.96 Complications of reattached lower extremity, other and unspecified ▽
997.61 Neuroma of amputation stump — (Use additional code to identify complications)
997.62 Infection (chronic) of amputation stump — (Use additional code to identify complications)
997.69 Other late amputation stump complication — (Use additional code to identify complications)
998.30 Disruption of wound, unspecified ▽
998.32 Disruption of external operation (surgical) wound
998.33 Disruption of traumatic injury wound repair
998.59 Other postoperative infection — (Use additional code to identify infection)
998.83 Non-healing surgical wound
V51.8 Other aftercare involving the use of plastic surgery

ICD-9-CM Procedural

86.60 Free skin graft, not otherwise specified
86.67 Dermal regenerative graft
86.69 Other skin graft to other sites

15155-15157

15155 Tissue cultured skin autograft, face, scalp, eyelids, mouth, neck, ears, orbits, genitalia, hands, feet, and/or multiple digits; first 25 sq cm or less
15156 additional 1 sq cm to 75 sq cm (List separately in addition to code for primary procedure)
15157 each additional 100 sq cm, or each additional 1% of body area of infants and children, or part thereof (List separately in addition to code for primary procedure)

ICD-9-CM Diagnostic

145.0 Malignant neoplasm of cheek mucosa
145.8 Malignant neoplasm of other specified parts of mouth
171.0 Malignant neoplasm of connective and other soft tissue of head, face, and neck
171.6 Malignant neoplasm of connective and other soft tissue of pelvis
172.0 Malignant melanoma of skin of lip
172.1 Malignant melanoma of skin of eyelid, including canthus
172.2 Malignant melanoma of skin of ear and external auditory canal
172.3 Malignant melanoma of skin of other and unspecified parts of face ▽
172.4 Malignant melanoma of skin of scalp and neck
172.6 Malignant melanoma of skin of upper limb, including shoulder
172.7 Malignant melanoma of skin of lower limb, including hip
173.00 Unspecified malignant neoplasm of skin of lip ▽
173.01 Basal cell carcinoma of skin of lip
173.02 Squamous cell carcinoma of skin of lip

173.09 Other specified malignant neoplasm of skin of lip
173.10 Unspecified malignant neoplasm of eyelid, including canthus ▽
173.11 Basal cell carcinoma of eyelid, including canthus
173.12 Squamous cell carcinoma of eyelid, including canthus
173.19 Other specified malignant neoplasm of eyelid, including canthus
173.20 Unspecified malignant neoplasm of skin of ear and external auditory canal ▽
173.21 Basal cell carcinoma of skin of ear and external auditory canal
173.22 Squamous cell carcinoma of skin of ear and external auditory canal
173.29 Other specified malignant neoplasm of skin of ear and external auditory canal
173.30 Unspecified malignant neoplasm of skin of other and unspecified parts of face ▽
173.31 Basal cell carcinoma of skin of other and unspecified parts of face
173.32 Squamous cell carcinoma of skin of other and unspecified parts of face
173.39 Other specified malignant neoplasm of skin of other and unspecified parts of face
173.40 Unspecified malignant neoplasm of scalp and skin of neck ▽
173.41 Basal cell carcinoma of scalp and skin of neck
173.42 Squamous cell carcinoma of scalp and skin of neck
173.49 Other specified malignant neoplasm of scalp and skin of neck
173.60 Unspecified malignant neoplasm of skin of upper limb, including shoulder ▽
173.61 Basal cell carcinoma of skin of upper limb, including shoulder
173.62 Squamous cell carcinoma of skin of upper limb, including shoulder
173.69 Other specified malignant neoplasm of skin of upper limb, including shoulder
173.70 Unspecified malignant neoplasm of skin of lower limb, including hip ▽
173.71 Basal cell carcinoma of skin of lower limb, including hip
173.72 Squamous cell carcinoma of skin of lower limb, including hip
173.79 Other specified malignant neoplasm of skin of lower limb, including hip
176.0 Kaposi's sarcoma of skin
184.1 Malignant neoplasm of labia majora ♀
184.2 Malignant neoplasm of labia minora ♀
184.3 Malignant neoplasm of clitoris ♀
184.4 Malignant neoplasm of vulva, unspecified site ▽ ♀
184.8 Malignant neoplasm of other specified sites of female genital organs ♀
186.9 Malignant neoplasm of other and unspecified testis — (Use additional code to identify any functional activity) ▽ ♂
187.1 Malignant neoplasm of prepuce ♂
187.2 Malignant neoplasm of glans penis ♂
187.3 Malignant neoplasm of body of penis ♂
187.4 Malignant neoplasm of penis, part unspecified ▽ ♂
187.7 Malignant neoplasm of scrotum ♂
187.8 Malignant neoplasm of other specified sites of male genital organs ♂
195.0 Malignant neoplasm of head, face, and neck
195.4 Malignant neoplasm of upper limb
195.5 Malignant neoplasm of lower limb
195.8 Malignant neoplasm of other specified sites
198.2 Secondary malignant neoplasm of skin
198.82 Secondary malignant neoplasm of genital organs
198.89 Secondary malignant neoplasm of other specified sites
209.31 Merkel cell carcinoma of the face
209.32 Merkel cell carcinoma of the scalp and neck
209.33 Merkel cell carcinoma of the upper limb
209.34 Merkel cell carcinoma of the lower limb
209.36 Merkel cell carcinoma of other sites
209.75 Secondary Merkel cell carcinoma
210.0 Benign neoplasm of lip
210.4 Benign neoplasm of other and unspecified parts of mouth ▽
214.0 Lipoma of skin and subcutaneous tissue of face
214.1 Lipoma of other skin and subcutaneous tissue
214.8 Lipoma of other specified sites
215.0 Other benign neoplasm of connective and other soft tissue of head, face, and neck
215.2 Other benign neoplasm of connective and other soft tissue of upper limb, including shoulder
215.3 Other benign neoplasm of connective and other soft tissue of lower limb, including hip
215.8 Other benign neoplasm of connective and other soft tissue of other specified sites
216.0 Benign neoplasm of skin of lip
216.1 Benign neoplasm of eyelid, including canthus
216.2 Benign neoplasm of ear and external auditory canal
216.3 Benign neoplasm of skin of other and unspecified parts of face ▽
216.4 Benign neoplasm of scalp and skin of neck
216.6 Benign neoplasm of skin of upper limb, including shoulder
216.7 Benign neoplasm of skin of lower limb, including hip
216.8 Benign neoplasm of other specified sites of skin
221.2 Benign neoplasm of vulva ♀
221.8 Benign neoplasm of other specified sites of female genital organs ♀
222.1 Benign neoplasm of penis ♂
222.4 Benign neoplasm of scrotum ♂
229.8 Benign neoplasm of other specified sites
230.0 Carcinoma in situ of lip, oral cavity, and pharynx
232.0 Carcinoma in situ of skin of lip
232.1 Carcinoma in situ of eyelid, including canthus
232.2 Carcinoma in situ of skin of ear and external auditory canal
232.3 Carcinoma in situ of skin of other and unspecified parts of face ▽
232.4 Carcinoma in situ of scalp and skin of neck
232.6 Carcinoma in situ of skin of upper limb, including shoulder
232.7 Carcinoma in situ of skin of lower limb, including hip
232.8 Carcinoma in situ of other specified sites of skin
233.30 Carcinoma in situ, unspecified female genital organ ▽ ♀
233.31 Carcinoma in situ, vagina ♀
233.32 Carcinoma in situ, vulva ♀
233.39 Carcinoma in situ, other female genital organ ♀
233.5 Carcinoma in situ of penis ♂
233.6 Carcinoma in situ of other and unspecified male genital organs ▽ ♂
235.1 Neoplasm of uncertain behavior of lip, oral cavity, and pharynx
236.3 Neoplasm of uncertain behavior of other and unspecified female genital organs ▽ ♀
236.6 Neoplasm of uncertain behavior of other and unspecified male genital organs ▽ ♂
238.2 Neoplasm of uncertain behavior of skin
239.2 Neoplasms of unspecified nature of bone, soft tissue, and skin
239.5 Neoplasm of unspecified nature of other genitourinary organs
249.70 Secondary diabetes mellitus with peripheral circulatory disorders, not stated as uncontrolled, or unspecified — (Use additional code to identify manifestation: 443.81, 785.4) (Use additional code to identify any associated insulin use: V58.67)
249.71 Secondary diabetes mellitus with peripheral circulatory disorders, uncontrolled — (Use additional code to identify manifestation: 443.81, 785.4) (Use additional code to identify any associated insulin use: V58.67)
249.80 Secondary diabetes mellitus with other specified manifestations, not stated as uncontrolled, or unspecified — (Use additional code to identify manifestation: 707.10-707.19, 707.8, 707.9, 731.8) (Use additional code to identify any associated insulin use: V58.67)
249.81 Secondary diabetes mellitus with other specified manifestations, uncontrolled — (Use additional code to identify manifestation: 707.10-707.19, 707.8, 707.9, 731.8) (Use additional code to identify any associated insulin use: V58.67)
249.90 Secondary diabetes mellitus with unspecified complication, not stated as uncontrolled, or unspecified — (Use additional code to identify any associated insulin use: V58.67) ▽
249.91 Secondary diabetes mellitus with unspecified complication, uncontrolled — (Use additional code to identify any associated insulin use: V58.67) ▽
250.70 Diabetes with peripheral circulatory disorders, type II or unspecified type, not stated as uncontrolled — (Use additional code to identify manifestation: 443.81, 785.4)

250.71 Diabetes with peripheral circulatory disorders, type I [juvenile type], not stated as uncontrolled — (Use additional code to identify manifestation: 443.81, 785.4)
250.72 Diabetes with peripheral circulatory disorders, type II or unspecified type, uncontrolled — (Use additional code to identify manifestation: 443.81, 785.4)
250.73 Diabetes with peripheral circulatory disorders, type I [juvenile type], uncontrolled — (Use additional code to identify manifestation: 443.81, 785.4)
250.80 Diabetes with other specified manifestations, type II or unspecified type, not stated as uncontrolled — (Use additional code to identify manifestation: 707.10-707.19, 707.8, 707.9, 731.8)
250.81 Diabetes with other specified manifestations, type I [juvenile type], not stated as uncontrolled — (Use additional code to identify manifestation: 707.10-707.19, 707.8, 707.9, 731.8)
250.82 Diabetes with other specified manifestations, type II or unspecified type, uncontrolled — (Use additional code to identify manifestation: 707.10-707.19, 707.8, 707.9, 731.8)
250.83 Diabetes with other specified manifestations, type I [juvenile type], uncontrolled — (Use additional code to identify manifestation: 707.10-707.19, 707.8, 707.9, 731.8)
374.04 Cicatricial entropion
374.50 Unspecified degenerative disorder of eyelid ▽
374.56 Other degenerative disorders of skin affecting eyelid
374.84 Cysts of eyelids
374.85 Vascular anomalies of eyelid
374.86 Retained foreign body of eyelid — (Use additional code to identify foreign body (V90.01-V90.9))
380.32 Acquired deformities of auricle or pinna
440.23 Atherosclerosis of native arteries of the extremities with ulceration — (Use additional code for any associated ulceration: 707.10-707.19, 707.8, 707.9)
459.11 Postphlebitic syndrome with ulcer
459.13 Postphlebitic syndrome with ulcer and inflammation
459.31 Chronic venous hypertension with ulcer
459.33 Chronic venous hypertension with ulcer and inflammation
629.20 Female genital mutilation status, unspecified ▽ ♀
629.21 Female genital mutilation, Type I status ♀
629.22 Female genital mutilation, Type II status ♀
629.23 Female genital mutilation, Type III status ♀
629.29 Other female genital mutilation status ♀
629.89 Other specified disorders of female genital organs ♀
682.4 Cellulitis and abscess of hand, except fingers and thumb — (Use additional code to identify organism, such as 041.1, etc.)
682.7 Cellulitis and abscess of foot, except toes — (Use additional code to identify organism, such as 041.1, etc.)
701.4 Keloid scar
701.5 Other abnormal granulation tissue
701.9 Unspecified hypertrophic and atrophic condition of skin ▽
707.00 Pressure ulcer, unspecified site — (Use additional code to identify pressure ulcer stage: 707.20-707.25) ▽
707.07 Pressure ulcer, heel — (Use additional code to identify pressure ulcer stage: 707.20-707.25)
707.09 Pressure ulcer, other site — (Use additional code to identify pressure ulcer stage: 707.20-707.25)
707.14 Ulcer of heel and midfoot — (Code, if applicable, any causal condition first: 249.80-249.81, 250.80-250.83, 440.23, 459.11, 459.13, 459.31, 459.33)
707.15 Ulcer of other part of foot — (Code, if applicable, any causal condition first: 249.80-249.81, 250.80-250.83, 440.23, 459.11, 459.13, 459.31, 459.33)
707.20 Pressure ulcer, unspecified stage — (Code first site of pressure ulcer: 707.00-707.09) ▽
707.21 Pressure ulcer, stage I — (Code first site of pressure ulcer: 707.00-707.09)
707.22 Pressure ulcer stage II — (Code first site of pressure ulcer: 707.00-707.09)
707.23 Pressure ulcer stage III — (Code first site of pressure ulcer: 707.00-707.09)
707.24 Pressure ulcer stage IV — (Code first site of pressure ulcer: 707.00-707.09)
707.25 Pressure ulcer, unstageable — (Code first site of pressure ulcer: 707.00-707.09)
707.8 Chronic ulcer of other specified site
709.2 Scar condition and fibrosis of skin
709.3 Degenerative skin disorder
709.4 Foreign body granuloma of skin and subcutaneous tissue — (Use additional code to identify foreign body (V90.01-V90.9))
744.29 Other congenital anomaly of ear
752.40 Unspecified congenital anomaly of cervix, vagina, and external female genitalia ▽ ♀
752.43 Cervical agenesis ♀
752.44 Cervical duplication ♀
752.45 Vaginal agenesis ♀
752.46 Transverse vaginal septum ♀
752.47 Longitudinal vaginal septum ♀
752.49 Other congenital anomaly of cervix, vagina, and external female genitalia ♀
757.39 Other specified congenital anomaly of skin
785.4 Gangrene — (Code first any associated underlying condition)
870.0 Laceration of skin of eyelid and periocular area
870.1 Laceration of eyelid, full-thickness, not involving lacrimal passages
870.2 Laceration of eyelid involving lacrimal passages
872.00 Open wound of external ear, unspecified site, without mention of complication ▽
872.01 Open wound of auricle, without mention of complication
872.10 Open wound of external ear, unspecified site, complicated ▽
872.11 Open wound of auricle, complicated
872.8 Open wound of ear, part unspecified, without mention of complication ▽
873.0 Open wound of scalp, without mention of complication
873.1 Open wound of scalp, complicated
873.21 Open wound of nasal septum, without mention of complication
873.31 Open wound of nasal septum, complicated
873.40 Open wound of face, unspecified site, without mention of complication ▽
873.41 Open wound of cheek, without mention of complication
873.42 Open wound of forehead, without mention of complication
873.43 Open wound of lip, without mention of complication
873.44 Open wound of jaw, without mention of complication
873.49 Open wound of face, other and multiple sites, without mention of complication
873.50 Open wound of face, unspecified site, complicated ▽
873.51 Open wound of cheek, complicated
873.52 Open wound of forehead, complicated
873.53 Open wound of lip, complicated
873.54 Open wound of jaw, complicated
873.59 Open wound of face, other and multiple sites, complicated
873.9 Other and unspecified open wound of head, complicated ▽
874.8 Open wound of other and unspecified parts of neck, without mention of complication ▽
878.0 Open wound of penis, without mention of complication ♂
878.1 Open wound of penis, complicated ♂
878.2 Open wound of scrotum and testes, without mention of complication ♂
878.3 Open wound of scrotum and testes, complicated ♂
878.4 Open wound of vulva, without mention of complication ♀
878.5 Open wound of vulva, complicated ♀
878.8 Open wound of other and unspecified parts of genital organs, without mention of complication ▽
878.9 Open wound of other and unspecified parts of genital organs, complicated ▽
882.0 Open wound of hand except finger(s) alone, without mention of complication
882.1 Open wound of hand except finger(s) alone, complicated
882.2 Open wound of hand except finger(s) alone, with tendon involvement
883.0 Open wound of finger(s), without mention of complication
883.1 Open wound of finger(s), complicated
883.2 Open wound of finger(s), with tendon involvement

885.0 Traumatic amputation of thumb (complete) (partial), without mention of complication
885.1 Traumatic amputation of thumb (complete) (partial), complicated
886.0 Traumatic amputation of other finger(s) (complete) (partial), without mention of complication
886.1 Traumatic amputation of other finger(s) (complete) (partial), complicated
892.0 Open wound of foot except toe(s) alone, without mention of complication
892.1 Open wound of foot except toe(s) alone, complicated
892.2 Open wound of foot except toe(s) alone, with tendon involvement
893.0 Open wound of toe(s), without mention of complication
893.1 Open wound of toe(s), complicated
893.2 Open wound of toe(s), with tendon involvement
895.0 Traumatic amputation of toe(s) (complete) (partial), without mention of complication
895.1 Traumatic amputation of toe(s) (complete) (partial), complicated
896.0 Traumatic amputation of foot (complete) (partial), unilateral, without mention of complication
896.1 Traumatic amputation of foot (complete) (partial), unilateral, complicated
896.2 Traumatic amputation of foot (complete) (partial), bilateral, without mention of complication
896.3 Traumatic amputation of foot (complete) (partial), bilateral, complicated
906.0 Late effect of open wound of head, neck, and trunk
906.1 Late effect of open wound of extremities without mention of tendon injury
906.4 Late effect of crushing
906.5 Late effect of burn of eye, face, head, and neck
906.6 Late effect of burn of wrist and hand
906.7 Late effect of burn of other extremities
906.8 Late effect of burns of other specified sites
909.2 Late effect of radiation
909.3 Late effect of complications of surgical and medical care
909.4 Late effect of certain other external causes
925.1 Crushing injury of face and scalp — (Use additional code to identify any associated injuries, such as: 800-829, 850.0-854.1, 860.0-869.1)
925.2 Crushing injury of neck — (Use additional code to identify any associated injuries, such as: 800-829, 850.0-854.1, 860.0-869.1)
926.0 Crushing injury of external genitalia — (Use additional code to identify any associated injuries: 800-829, 850.0-854.1, 860.0-869.1)
927.20 Crushing injury of hand(s) — (Use additional code to identify any associated injuries: 800-829, 850.0-854.1, 860.0-869.1)
927.3 Crushing injury of finger(s) — (Use additional code to identify any associated injuries: 800-829, 850.0-854.1, 860.0-869.1)
927.8 Crushing injury of multiple sites of upper limb — (Use additional code to identify any associated injuries: 800-829, 850.0-854.1, 860.0-869.1)
928.20 Crushing injury of foot — (Use additional code to identify any associated injuries: 800-829, 850.0-854.1, 860.0-869.1)
928.3 Crushing injury of toe(s) — (Use additional code to identify any associated injuries: 800-829, 850.0-854.1, 860.0-869.1)
928.8 Crushing injury of multiple sites of lower limb — (Use additional code to identify any associated injuries: 800-829, 850.0-854.1, 860.0-869.1)
929.0 Crushing injury of multiple sites, not elsewhere classified — (Use additional code to identify any associated injuries: 800-829, 850.0-854.1, 860.0-869.1)
940.0 Chemical burn of eyelids and periocular area
940.1 Other burns of eyelids and periocular area
941.30 Full-thickness skin loss due to burn (third degree NOS) of unspecified site of face and head ▽
941.31 Full-thickness skin loss due to burn (third degree NOS) of ear (any part)
941.32 Full-thickness skin loss due to burn (third degree NOS) of eye (with other parts of face, head, and neck)
941.33 Full-thickness skin loss due to burn (third degree NOS) of lip(s)
941.34 Full-thickness skin loss due to burn (third degree NOS) of chin
941.35 Full-thickness skin loss due to burn (third degree NOS) of nose (septum)
941.36 Full-thickness skin loss due to burn (third degree NOS) of scalp (any part)
941.37 Full-thickness skin loss due to burn (third degree NOS) of forehead and cheek
941.38 Full-thickness skin loss due to burn (third degree NOS) of neck
941.39 Full-thickness skin loss due to burn (third degree NOS) of multiple sites (except with eye) of face, head, and neck
941.40 Deep necrosis of underlying tissues due to burn (deep third degree) of unspecified site of face and head, without mention of loss of a body part ▽
941.41 Deep necrosis of underlying tissues due to burn (deep third degree) of ear (any part), without mention of loss of a body part
941.42 Deep necrosis of underlying tissues due to burn (deep third degree) of eye (with other parts of face, head, and neck), without mention of loss of a body part
941.43 Deep necrosis of underlying tissues due to burn (deep third degree) of lip(s), without mention of loss of a body part
941.44 Deep necrosis of underlying tissues due to burn (deep third degree) of chin, without mention of loss of a body part
941.45 Deep necrosis of underlying tissues due to burn (deep third degree) of nose (septum), without mention of loss of a body part
941.46 Deep necrosis of underlying tissues due to burn (deep third degree) of scalp (any part), without mention of loss of a body part
941.47 Deep necrosis of underlying tissues due to burn (deep third degree) of forehead and cheek, without mention of loss of a body part
941.48 Deep necrosis of underlying tissues due to burn (deep third degree) of neck, without mention of loss of a body part
941.49 Deep necrosis of underlying tissues due to burn (deep third degree) of multiple sites (except with eye) of face, head, and neck, without mention of loss of a body part
941.50 Deep necrosis of underlying tissues due to burn (deep third degree) of face and head, unspecified site, with loss of a body part ▽
941.51 Deep necrosis of underlying tissues due to burn (deep third degree) of ear (any part), with loss of a body part
941.52 Deep necrosis of underlying tissues due to burn (deep third degree) of eye (with other parts of face, head, and neck), with loss of a body part
941.53 Deep necrosis of underlying tissues due to burn (deep third degree) of lip(s), with loss of a body part
941.54 Deep necrosis of underlying tissues due to burn (deep third degree) of chin, with loss of a body part
941.55 Deep necrosis of underlying tissues due to burn (deep third degree) of nose (septum), with loss of a body part
941.56 Deep necrosis of underlying tissues due to burn (deep third degree) of scalp (any part), with loss of a body part
941.57 Deep necrosis of underlying tissues due to burn (deep third degree) of forehead and cheek, with loss of a body part
941.58 Deep necrosis of underlying tissues due to burn (deep third degree) of neck, with loss of a body part
941.59 Deep necrosis of underlying tissues due to burn (deep third degree) of multiple sites (except eye) of face, head, and neck, with loss of a body part
942.35 Full-thickness skin loss due to burn (third degree NOS) of genitalia
942.45 Deep necrosis of underlying tissues due to burn (deep third degree) of genitalia, without mention of loss of a body part
942.55 Deep necrosis of underlying tissues due to burn (deep third degree) of genitalia, with loss of a body part
944.30 Full-thickness skin loss due to burn (third degree NOS) of unspecified site of hand ▽
944.31 Full-thickness skin loss due to burn (third degree NOS) of single digit [finger (nail)] other than thumb
944.32 Full-thickness skin loss due to burn (third degree NOS) of thumb (nail)
944.33 Full-thickness skin loss due to burn (third degree NOS) of two or more digits of hand, not including thumb
944.34 Full-thickness skin loss due to burn (third degree NOS) of two or more digits of hand including thumb
944.35 Full-thickness skin loss due to burn (third degree NOS) of palm of hand
944.36 Full-thickness skin loss due to burn (third degree NOS) of back of hand
944.38 Full-thickness skin loss due to burn (third degree NOS) of multiple sites of wrist(s) and hand(s)

944.40 Deep necrosis of underlying tissues due to burn (deep third degree) of unspecified site of hand, without mention of loss of a body part
944.41 Deep necrosis of underlying tissues due to burn (deep third degree) of single digit [finger (nail)] other than thumb, without mention of loss of a body part
944.42 Deep necrosis of underlying tissues due to burn (deep third degree) of thumb (nail), without mention of loss of a body part
944.43 Deep necrosis of underlying tissues due to burn (deep third degree) of two or more digits of hand, not including thumb, without mention of loss of a body part
944.44 Deep necrosis of underlying tissues due to burn (deep third degree) of two or more digits of hand including thumb, without mention of loss of a body part
944.45 Deep necrosis of underlying tissues due to burn (deep third degree) of palm of hand, without mention of loss of a body part
944.46 Deep necrosis of underlying tissues due to burn (deep third degree) of back of hand, without mention of loss of a body part
944.48 Deep necrosis of underlying tissues due to burn (deep third degree) of multiple sites of wrist(s) and hand(s), without mention of loss of a body part
944.50 Deep necrosis of underlying tissues due to burn (deep third degree) of unspecified site of hand, with loss of a body part
944.51 Deep necrosis of underlying tissues due to burn (deep third degree) of single digit (finger (nail)) other than thumb, with loss of a body part
944.52 Deep necrosis of underlying tissues due to burn (deep third degree) of thumb (nail), with loss of a body part
944.53 Deep necrosis of underlying tissues due to burn (deep third degree) of two or more digits of hand, not including thumb, with loss of a body part
944.54 Deep necrosis of underlying tissues due to burn (deep third degree) of two or more digits of hand including thumb, with loss of a body part
944.55 Deep necrosis of underlying tissues due to burn (deep third degree) of palm of hand, with loss of a body part
944.56 Deep necrosis of underlying tissues due to burn (deep third degree) of back of hand, with loss of a body part
944.58 Deep necrosis of underlying tissues due to burn (deep third degree) of multiple sites of wrist(s) and hand(s), with loss of a body part
945.31 Full-thickness skin loss due to burn (third degree NOS) of toe(s) (nail)
945.32 Full-thickness skin loss due to burn (third degree NOS) of foot
945.39 Full-thickness skin loss due to burn (third degree NOS) of multiple sites of lower limb(s)
945.41 Deep necrosis of underlying tissues due to burn (deep third degree) of toe(s) (nail), without mention of loss of a body part
945.42 Deep necrosis of underlying tissues due to burn (deep third degree) of foot, without mention of loss of a body part
945.49 Deep necrosis of underlying tissues due to burn (deep third degree) of multiple sites of lower limb(s), without mention of loss of a body part
945.51 Deep necrosis of underlying tissues due to burn (deep third degree) of toe(s) (nail), with loss of a body part
945.52 Deep necrosis of underlying tissues due to burn (deep third degree) of foot, with loss of a body part
945.59 Deep necrosis of underlying tissues due to burn (deep third degree) of multiple sites of lower limb(s), with loss of a body part
946.3 Full-thickness skin loss due to burn (third degree NOS) of multiple specified sites
946.4 Deep necrosis of underlying tissues due to burn (deep third degree) of multiple specified sites, without mention of loss of a body part
946.5 Deep necrosis of underlying tissues due to burn (deep third degree) of multiple specified sites, with loss of a body part
947.0 Burn of mouth and pharynx
948.00 Burn (any degree) involving less than 10% of body surface with third degree burn of less than 10% or unspecified amount
948.10 Burn (any degree) involving 10-19% of body surface with third degree burn of less than 10% or unspecified amount
948.11 Burn (any degree) involving 10-19% of body surface with third degree burn of 10-19%
948.20 Burn (any degree) involving 20-29% of body surface with third degree burn of less than 10% or unspecified amount
948.21 Burn (any degree) involving 20-29% of body surface with third degree burn of 10-19%
948.22 Burn (any degree) involving 20-29% of body surface with third degree burn of 20-29%
948.30 Burn (any degree) involving 30-39% of body surface with third degree burn of less than 10% or unspecified amount
948.31 Burn (any degree) involving 30-39% of body surface with third degree burn of 10-19%
948.32 Burn (any degree) involving 30-39% of body surface with third degree burn of 20-29%
948.33 Burn (any degree) involving 30-39% of body surface with third degree burn of 30-39%
948.40 Burn (any degree) involving 40-49% of body surface with third degree burn of less than 10% or unspecified amount
948.41 Burn (any degree) involving 40-49% of body surface with third degree burn of 10-19%
948.42 Burn (any degree) involving 40-49% of body surface with third degree burn of 20-29%
948.43 Burn (any degree) involving 40-49% of body surface with third degree burn of 30-39%
948.44 Burn (any degree) involving 40-49% of body surface with third degree burn of 40-49%
948.50 Burn (any degree) involving 50-59% of body surface with third degree burn of less than 10% or unspecified amount
948.51 Burn (any degree) involving 50-59% of body surface with third degree burn of 10-19%
948.52 Burn (any degree) involving 50-59% of body surface with third degree burn of 20-29%
948.53 Burn (any degree) involving 50-59% of body surface with third degree burn of 30-39%
948.54 Burn (any degree) involving 50-59% of body surface with third degree burn of 40-49%
948.55 Burn (any degree) involving 50-59% of body surface with third degree burn of 50-59%
948.60 Burn (any degree) involving 60-69% of body surface with third degree burn of less than 10% or unspecified amount
948.61 Burn (any degree) involving 60-69% of body surface with third degree burn of 10-19%
948.62 Burn (any degree) involving 60-69% of body surface with third degree burn of 20-29%
948.63 Burn (any degree) involving 60-69% of body surface with third degree burn of 30-39%
948.64 Burn (any degree) involving 60-69% of body surface with third degree burn of 40-49%
948.65 Burn (any degree) involving 60-69% of body surface with third degree burn of 50-59%
948.66 Burn (any degree) involving 60-69% of body surface with third degree burn of 60-69%
948.70 Burn (any degree) involving 70-79% of body surface with third degree burn of less than 10% or unspecified amount
948.71 Burn (any degree) involving 70-79% of body surface with third degree burn of 10-19%
948.72 Burn (any degree) involving 70-79% of body surface with third degree burn of 20-29%
948.73 Burn (any degree) involving 70-79% of body surface with third degree burn of 30-39%
948.74 Burn (any degree) involving 70-79% of body surface with third degree burn of 40-49%
948.75 Burn (any degree) involving 70-79% of body surface with third degree burn of 50-59%
948.76 Burn (any degree) involving 70-79% of body surface with third degree burn of 60-69%
948.77 Burn (any degree) involving 70-79% of body surface with third degree burn of 70-79%
948.80 Burn (any degree) involving 80-89% of body surface with third degree burn of less than 10% or unspecified amount
948.81 Burn (any degree) involving 80-89% of body surface with third degree burn of 10-19%
948.82 Burn (any degree) involving 80-89% of body surface with third degree burn of 20-29%
948.83 Burn (any degree) involving 80-89% of body surface with third degree burn of 30-39%
948.84 Burn (any degree) involving 80-89% of body surface with third degree burn of 40-49%
948.85 Burn (any degree) involving 80-89% of body surface with third degree burn of 50-59%
948.86 Burn (any degree) involving 80-89% of body surface with third degree burn of 60-69%
948.87 Burn (any degree) involving 80-89% of body surface with third degree burn of 70-79%
948.88 Burn (any degree) involving 80-89% of body surface with third degree burn of 80-89%
948.90 Burn (any degree) involving 90% or more of body surface with third degree burn of less than 10% or unspecified amount
948.91 Burn (any degree) involving 90% or more of body surface with third degree burn of 10-19%
948.92 Burn (any degree) involving 90% or more of body surface with third degree burn of 20-29%
948.93 Burn (any degree) involving 90% or more of body surface with third degree burn of 30-39%
948.94 Burn (any degree) involving 90% or more of body surface with third degree burn of 40-49%
948.95 Burn (any degree) involving 90% or more of body surface with third degree burn of 50-59%

948.96 Burn (any degree) involving 90% or more of body surface with third degree burn of 60-69%
948.97 Burn (any degree) involving 90% or more of body surface with third degree burn of 70-79%
948.98 Burn (any degree) involving 90% or more of body surface with third degree burn of 80-89%
948.99 Burn (any degree) involving 90% or more of body surface with third degree burn of 90% or more of body surface
949.3 Full-thickness skin loss due to burn (third degree NOS), unspecified site ▽
949.4 Deep necrosis of underlying tissue due to burn (deep third degree), unspecified site without mention of loss of body part ▽
949.5 Deep necrosis of underlying tissues due to burn (deep third degree, unspecified site with loss of body part ▽
959.01 Head injury, unspecified ▽
959.09 Injury of face and neck, other and unspecified
959.14 Other injury of external genitals
959.4 Injury, other and unspecified, hand, except finger
959.5 Injury, other and unspecified, finger
959.7 Injury, other and unspecified, knee, leg, ankle, and foot
959.8 Injury, other and unspecified, other specified sites, including multiple
991.0 Frostbite of face
991.1 Frostbite of hand
991.2 Frostbite of foot
996.52 Mechanical complication due to other tissue graft, not elsewhere classified
996.92 Complications of reattached hand
996.93 Complications of reattached finger(s)
996.95 Complications of reattached foot and toe(s)
997.62 Infection (chronic) of amputation stump — (Use additional code to identify complications)
997.69 Other late amputation stump complication — (Use additional code to identify complications)
998.30 Disruption of wound, unspecified ▽
998.32 Disruption of external operation (surgical) wound
998.33 Disruption of traumatic injury wound repair
998.59 Other postoperative infection — (Use additional code to identify infection)
998.83 Non-healing surgical wound
V51.8 Other aftercare involving the use of plastic surgery

ICD-9-CM Procedural

08.61 Reconstruction of eyelid with skin flap or graft
16.65 Secondary graft to exenteration cavity
18.6 Reconstruction of external auditory canal
18.79 Other plastic repair of external ear
27.56 Other skin graft to lip and mouth
86.62 Other skin graft to hand
86.67 Dermal regenerative graft
86.69 Other skin graft to other sites

15200-15201

15200 Full thickness graft, free, including direct closure of donor site, trunk; 20 sq cm or less
15201 each additional 20 sq cm, or part thereof (List separately in addition to code for primary procedure)

ICD-9-CM Diagnostic

171.4 Malignant neoplasm of connective and other soft tissue of thorax
171.5 Malignant neoplasm of connective and other soft tissue of abdomen
171.6 Malignant neoplasm of connective and other soft tissue of pelvis
172.5 Malignant melanoma of skin of trunk, except scrotum
173.50 Unspecified malignant neoplasm of skin of trunk, except scrotum ▽
173.51 Basal cell carcinoma of skin of trunk, except scrotum
173.52 Squamous cell carcinoma of skin of trunk, except scrotum
173.59 Other specified malignant neoplasm of skin of trunk, except scrotum
174.0 Malignant neoplasm of nipple and areola of female breast — (Use additional code to identify estrogen receptor status: V86.0-V86.1) ♀
174.1 Malignant neoplasm of central portion of female breast — (Use additional code to identify estrogen receptor status: V86.0-V86.1) ♀
174.2 Malignant neoplasm of upper-inner quadrant of female breast — (Use additional code to identify estrogen receptor status: V86.0-V86.1) ♀
174.3 Malignant neoplasm of lower-inner quadrant of female breast — (Use additional code to identify estrogen receptor status: V86.0-V86.1) ♀
174.4 Malignant neoplasm of upper-outer quadrant of female breast — (Use additional code to identify estrogen receptor status: V86.0-V86.1) ♀
174.5 Malignant neoplasm of lower-outer quadrant of female breast — (Use additional code to identify estrogen receptor status: V86.0-V86.1) ♀
174.6 Malignant neoplasm of axillary tail of female breast — (Use additional code to identify estrogen receptor status: V86.0-V86.1) ♀
174.8 Malignant neoplasm of other specified sites of female breast — (Use additional code to identify estrogen receptor status: V86.0-V86.1) ♀
174.9 Malignant neoplasm of breast (female), unspecified site — (Use additional code to identify estrogen receptor status: V86.0-V86.1) ▽ ♀
175.0 Malignant neoplasm of nipple and areola of male breast — (Use additional code to identify estrogen receptor status: V86.0-V86.1) ♂
175.9 Malignant neoplasm of other and unspecified sites of male breast — (Use additional code to identify estrogen receptor status: V86.0-V86.1) ▽ ♂
209.35 Merkel cell carcinoma of the trunk
209.75 Secondary Merkel cell carcinoma
215.4 Other benign neoplasm of connective and other soft tissue of thorax
215.5 Other benign neoplasm of connective and other soft tissue of abdomen
215.6 Other benign neoplasm of connective and other soft tissue of pelvis
215.7 Other benign neoplasm of connective and other soft tissue of trunk, unspecified ▽
232.5 Carcinoma in situ of skin of trunk, except scrotum
238.2 Neoplasm of uncertain behavior of skin
239.2 Neoplasms of unspecified nature of bone, soft tissue, and skin
249.70 Secondary diabetes mellitus with peripheral circulatory disorders, not stated as uncontrolled, or unspecified — (Use additional code to identify manifestation: 443.81, 785.4) (Use additional code to identify any associated insulin use: V58.67)
249.71 Secondary diabetes mellitus with peripheral circulatory disorders, uncontrolled — (Use additional code to identify manifestation: 443.81, 785.4) (Use additional code to identify any associated insulin use: V58.67)
249.80 Secondary diabetes mellitus with other specified manifestations, not stated as uncontrolled, or unspecified — (Use additional code to identify manifestation: 707.10-707.19, 707.8, 707.9, 731.8) (Use additional code to identify any associated insulin use: V58.67)
249.81 Secondary diabetes mellitus with other specified manifestations, uncontrolled — (Use additional code to identify manifestation: 707.10-707.19, 707.8, 707.9, 731.8) (Use additional code to identify any associated insulin use: V58.67)
249.90 Secondary diabetes mellitus with unspecified complication, not stated as uncontrolled, or unspecified — (Use additional code to identify any associated insulin use: V58.67) ▽
249.91 Secondary diabetes mellitus with unspecified complication, uncontrolled — (Use additional code to identify any associated insulin use: V58.67) ▽
250.70 Diabetes with peripheral circulatory disorders, type II or unspecified type, not stated as uncontrolled — (Use additional code to identify manifestation: 443.81, 785.4)
250.71 Diabetes with peripheral circulatory disorders, type I [juvenile type], not stated as uncontrolled — (Use additional code to identify manifestation: 443.81, 785.4)
250.72 Diabetes with peripheral circulatory disorders, type II or unspecified type, uncontrolled — (Use additional code to identify manifestation: 443.81, 785.4)
250.73 Diabetes with peripheral circulatory disorders, type I [juvenile type], uncontrolled — (Use additional code to identify manifestation: 443.81, 785.4)
443.0 Raynaud's syndrome — (Use additional code to identify gangrene: 785.4)

▽ Unspecified code ■ Manifestation code [Resequenced code]
♀ Female diagnosis ♂ Male diagnosis

707.00 Pressure ulcer, unspecified site — (Use additional code to identify pressure ulcer stage: 707.20-707.25) ▼
707.02 Pressure ulcer, upper back — (Use additional code to identify pressure ulcer stage: 707.20-707.25)
707.03 Pressure ulcer, lower back — (Use additional code to identify pressure ulcer stage: 707.20-707.25)
707.04 Pressure ulcer, hip — (Use additional code to identify pressure ulcer stage: 707.20-707.25)
707.05 Pressure ulcer, buttock — (Use additional code to identify pressure ulcer stage: 707.20-707.25)
707.09 Pressure ulcer, other site — (Use additional code to identify pressure ulcer stage: 707.20-707.25)
707.20 Pressure ulcer, unspecified stage — (Code first site of pressure ulcer: 707.00-707.09) ▼
707.21 Pressure ulcer, stage I — (Code first site of pressure ulcer: 707.00-707.09)
707.22 Pressure ulcer stage II — (Code first site of pressure ulcer: 707.00-707.09)
707.23 Pressure ulcer stage III — (Code first site of pressure ulcer: 707.00-707.09)
707.24 Pressure ulcer stage IV — (Code first site of pressure ulcer: 707.00-707.09)
707.25 Pressure ulcer, unstageable — (Code first site of pressure ulcer: 707.00-707.09)
707.8 Chronic ulcer of other specified site
728.86 Necrotizing fasciitis — (Use additional code to identify infectious organism, 041.00-041.89, 785.4, if applicable)
785.4 Gangrene — (Code first any associated underlying condition)
875.0 Open wound of chest (wall), without mention of complication
875.1 Open wound of chest (wall), complicated
876.0 Open wound of back, without mention of complication
876.1 Open wound of back, complicated
877.0 Open wound of buttock, without mention of complication
877.1 Open wound of buttock, complicated
879.0 Open wound of breast, without mention of complication
879.1 Open wound of breast, complicated
879.2 Open wound of abdominal wall, anterior, without mention of complication
879.3 Open wound of abdominal wall, anterior, complicated
879.4 Open wound of abdominal wall, lateral, without mention of complication
879.5 Open wound of abdominal wall, lateral, complicated
879.6 Open wound of other and unspecified parts of trunk, without mention of complication ▼
879.7 Open wound of other and unspecified parts of trunk, complicated ▼
879.8 Open wound(s) (multiple) of unspecified site(s), without mention of complication ▼
879.9 Open wound(s) (multiple) of unspecified site(s), complicated ▼
906.8 Late effect of burns of other specified sites
908.0 Late effect of internal injury to chest
908.1 Late effect of internal injury to intra-abdominal organs
908.2 Late effect of internal injury to other internal organs
909.2 Late effect of radiation
909.3 Late effect of complications of surgical and medical care
942.30 Full-thickness skin loss due to burn (third degree NOS) of unspecified site of trunk ▼
942.31 Full-thickness skin loss due to burn (third degree NOS) of breast
942.32 Full-thickness skin loss due to burn (third degree NOS) of chest wall, excluding breast and nipple
942.33 Full-thickness skin loss due to burn (third degree NOS) of abdominal wall
942.34 Full-thickness skin loss due to burn (third degree NOS) of back (any part)
942.35 Full-thickness skin loss due to burn (third degree NOS) of genitalia
942.40 Deep necrosis of underlying tissues due to burn (deep third degree) of trunk, unspecified site, without mention of loss of a body part ▼
942.41 Deep necrosis of underlying tissues due to burn (deep third degree) of breast, without mention of loss of a body part
942.42 Deep necrosis of underlying tissues due to burn (deep third degree) of chest wall, excluding breast and nipple, without mention of loss of a body part
942.43 Deep necrosis of underlying tissues due to burn (deep third degree) of abdominal wall, without mention of loss of a body part
942.44 Deep necrosis of underlying tissues due to burn (deep third degree) of back (any part), without mention of loss of a body part
942.45 Deep necrosis of underlying tissues due to burn (deep third degree) of genitalia, without mention of loss of a body part
943.34 Full-thickness skin loss due to burn (third degree NOS) of axilla
943.35 Full-thickness skin loss due to burn (third degree NOS) of shoulder
943.36 Full-thickness skin loss due to burn (third degree NOS) of scapular region
943.44 Deep necrosis of underlying tissues due to burn (deep third degree) of axilla, without mention of loss of a body part
943.45 Deep necrosis of underlying tissues due to burn (deep third degree) of shoulder, without mention of loss of a body part
943.46 Deep necrosis of underlying tissues due to burn (deep third degree) of scapular region, without mention of loss of a body part
943.54 Deep necrosis of underlying tissues due to burn (deep third degree) of axilla, with loss of a body part
943.56 Deep necrosis of underlying tissues due to burn (deep third degree) of scapular region, with loss of a body part
948.00 Burn (any degree) involving less than 10% of body surface with third degree burn of less than 10% or unspecified amount
948.10 Burn (any degree) involving 10-19% of body surface with third degree burn of less than 10% or unspecified amount
948.11 Burn (any degree) involving 10-19% of body surface with third degree burn of 10-19%
948.20 Burn (any degree) involving 20-29% of body surface with third degree burn of less than 10% or unspecified amount
948.21 Burn (any degree) involving 20-29% of body surface with third degree burn of 10-19%
948.22 Burn (any degree) involving 20-29% of body surface with third degree burn of 20-29%
948.30 Burn (any degree) involving 30-39% of body surface with third degree burn of less than 10% or unspecified amount
948.31 Burn (any degree) involving 30-39% of body surface with third degree burn of 10-19%
948.32 Burn (any degree) involving 30-39% of body surface with third degree burn of 20-29%
948.33 Burn (any degree) involving 30-39% of body surface with third degree burn of 30-39%
948.40 Burn (any degree) involving 40-49% of body surface with third degree burn of less than 10% or unspecified amount
948.41 Burn (any degree) involving 40-49% of body surface with third degree burn of 10-19%
948.42 Burn (any degree) involving 40-49% of body surface with third degree burn of 20-29%
948.43 Burn (any degree) involving 40-49% of body surface with third degree burn of 30-39%
948.44 Burn (any degree) involving 40-49% of body surface with third degree burn of 40-49%
948.50 Burn (any degree) involving 50-59% of body surface with third degree burn of less than 10% or unspecified amount
948.51 Burn (any degree) involving 50-59% of body surface with third degree burn of 10-19%
948.52 Burn (any degree) involving 50-59% of body surface with third degree burn of 20-29%
948.53 Burn (any degree) involving 50-59% of body surface with third degree burn of 30-39%
948.54 Burn (any degree) involving 50-59% of body surface with third degree burn of 40-49%
948.55 Burn (any degree) involving 50-59% of body surface with third degree burn of 50-59%
948.60 Burn (any degree) involving 60-69% of body surface with third degree burn of less than 10% or unspecified amount
948.61 Burn (any degree) involving 60-69% of body surface with third degree burn of 10-19%
948.62 Burn (any degree) involving 60-69% of body surface with third degree burn of 20-29%
948.63 Burn (any degree) involving 60-69% of body surface with third degree burn of 30-39%
948.64 Burn (any degree) involving 60-69% of body surface with third degree burn of 40-49%
948.65 Burn (any degree) involving 60-69% of body surface with third degree burn of 50-59%
948.66 Burn (any degree) involving 60-69% of body surface with third degree burn of 60-69%
948.70 Burn (any degree) involving 70-79% of body surface with third degree burn of less than 10% or unspecified amount
948.71 Burn (any degree) involving 70-79% of body surface with third degree burn of 10-19%
948.72 Burn (any degree) involving 70-79% of body surface with third degree burn of 20-29%
948.73 Burn (any degree) involving 70-79% of body surface with third degree burn of 30-39%
948.74 Burn (any degree) involving 70-79% of body surface with third degree burn of 40-49%

948.75 Burn (any degree) involving 70-79% of body surface with third degree burn of 50-59%
948.76 Burn (any degree) involving 70-79% of body surface with third degree burn of 60-69%
948.77 Burn (any degree) involving 70-79% of body surface with third degree burn of 70-79%
948.80 Burn (any degree) involving 80-89% of body surface with third degree burn of less than 10% or unspecified amount
948.81 Burn (any degree) involving 80-89% of body surface with third degree burn of 10-19%
948.82 Burn (any degree) involving 80-89% of body surface with third degree burn of 20-29%
948.83 Burn (any degree) involving 80-89% of body surface with third degree burn of 30-39%
948.84 Burn (any degree) involving 80-89% of body surface with third degree burn of 40-49%
948.85 Burn (any degree) involving 80-89% of body surface with third degree burn of 50-59%
948.86 Burn (any degree) involving 80-89% of body surface with third degree burn of 60-69%
948.87 Burn (any degree) involving 80-89% of body surface with third degree burn of 70-79%
948.88 Burn (any degree) involving 80-89% of body surface with third degree burn of 80-89%
958.3 Posttraumatic wound infection not elsewhere classified
959.11 Other injury of chest wall
959.12 Other injury of abdomen
959.19 Other injury of other sites of trunk
983.0 Toxic effect of corrosive aromatics — (Use additional code to specify the nature of the toxic effect)
983.1 Toxic effect of acids — (Use additional code to specify the nature of the toxic effect)
983.2 Toxic effect of caustic alkalis — (Use additional code to specify the nature of the toxic effect)
991.3 Frostbite of other and unspecified sites ▽
998.30 Disruption of wound, unspecified ▽
998.32 Disruption of external operation (surgical) wound
998.33 Disruption of traumatic injury wound repair
998.59 Other postoperative infection — (Use additional code to identify infection)
998.83 Non-healing surgical wound
V10.3 Personal history of malignant neoplasm of breast
V10.40 Personal history of malignant neoplasm of unspecified female genital organ ▽ ♀
V10.49 Personal history of malignant neoplasm of other male genital organs ♂
V10.84 Personal history of malignant neoplasm of eye
V51.8 Other aftercare involving the use of plastic surgery

ICD-9-CM Procedural

85.83 Full-thickness graft to breast
86.63 Full-thickness skin graft to other sites

15220-15221

15220 Full thickness graft, free, including direct closure of donor site, scalp, arms, and/or legs; 20 sq cm or less
15221 each additional 20 sq cm, or part thereof (List separately in addition to code for primary procedure)

ICD-9-CM Diagnostic

172.4 Malignant melanoma of skin of scalp and neck
172.6 Malignant melanoma of skin of upper limb, including shoulder
172.7 Malignant melanoma of skin of lower limb, including hip
172.8 Malignant melanoma of other specified sites of skin
173.40 Unspecified malignant neoplasm of scalp and skin of neck ▽
173.41 Basal cell carcinoma of scalp and skin of neck
173.42 Squamous cell carcinoma of scalp and skin of neck
173.49 Other specified malignant neoplasm of scalp and skin of neck
173.60 Unspecified malignant neoplasm of skin of upper limb, including shoulder ▽
173.61 Basal cell carcinoma of skin of upper limb, including shoulder
173.62 Squamous cell carcinoma of skin of upper limb, including shoulder
173.69 Other specified malignant neoplasm of skin of upper limb, including shoulder
173.70 Unspecified malignant neoplasm of skin of lower limb, including hip ▽
173.71 Basal cell carcinoma of skin of lower limb, including hip
173.72 Squamous cell carcinoma of skin of lower limb, including hip
173.79 Other specified malignant neoplasm of skin of lower limb, including hip
173.80 Unspecified malignant neoplasm of other specified sites of skin ▽
173.81 Basal cell carcinoma of other specified sites of skin
173.82 Squamous cell carcinoma of other specified sites of skin
173.89 Other specified malignant neoplasm of other specified sites of skin
195.0 Malignant neoplasm of head, face, and neck
195.4 Malignant neoplasm of upper limb
195.5 Malignant neoplasm of lower limb
209.32 Merkel cell carcinoma of the scalp and neck
209.33 Merkel cell carcinoma of the upper limb
209.34 Merkel cell carcinoma of the lower limb
209.75 Secondary Merkel cell carcinoma
216.4 Benign neoplasm of scalp and skin of neck
216.6 Benign neoplasm of skin of upper limb, including shoulder
216.7 Benign neoplasm of skin of lower limb, including hip
232.4 Carcinoma in situ of scalp and skin of neck
232.6 Carcinoma in situ of skin of upper limb, including shoulder
232.7 Carcinoma in situ of skin of lower limb, including hip
238.2 Neoplasm of uncertain behavior of skin
239.2 Neoplasms of unspecified nature of bone, soft tissue, and skin
249.70 Secondary diabetes mellitus with peripheral circulatory disorders, not stated as uncontrolled, or unspecified — (Use additional code to identify manifestation: 443.81, 785.4) (Use additional code to identify any associated insulin use: V58.67)
249.71 Secondary diabetes mellitus with peripheral circulatory disorders, uncontrolled — (Use additional code to identify manifestation: 443.81, 785.4) (Use additional code to identify any associated insulin use: V58.67)
249.80 Secondary diabetes mellitus with other specified manifestations, not stated as uncontrolled, or unspecified — (Use additional code to identify manifestation: 707.10-707.19, 707.8, 707.9, 731.8) (Use additional code to identify any associated insulin use: V58.67)
249.81 Secondary diabetes mellitus with other specified manifestations, uncontrolled — (Use additional code to identify manifestation: 707.10-707.19, 707.8, 707.9, 731.8) (Use additional code to identify any associated insulin use: V58.67)
249.90 Secondary diabetes mellitus with unspecified complication, not stated as uncontrolled, or unspecified — (Use additional code to identify any associated insulin use: V58.67) ▽
249.91 Secondary diabetes mellitus with unspecified complication, uncontrolled — (Use additional code to identify any associated insulin use: V58.67) ▽
250.70 Diabetes with peripheral circulatory disorders, type II or unspecified type, not stated as uncontrolled — (Use additional code to identify manifestation: 443.81, 785.4)
250.71 Diabetes with peripheral circulatory disorders, type I [juvenile type], not stated as uncontrolled — (Use additional code to identify manifestation: 443.81, 785.4)
250.72 Diabetes with peripheral circulatory disorders, type II or unspecified type, uncontrolled — (Use additional code to identify manifestation: 443.81, 785.4)
250.73 Diabetes with peripheral circulatory disorders, type I [juvenile type], uncontrolled — (Use additional code to identify manifestation: 443.81, 785.4)
250.80 Diabetes with other specified manifestations, type II or unspecified type, not stated as uncontrolled — (Use additional code to identify manifestation: 707.10-707.19, 707.8, 707.9, 731.8)
250.81 Diabetes with other specified manifestations, type I [juvenile type], not stated as uncontrolled — (Use additional code to identify manifestation: 707.10-707.19, 707.8, 707.9, 731.8)
250.82 Diabetes with other specified manifestations, type II or unspecified type, uncontrolled — (Use additional code to identify manifestation: 707.10-707.19, 707.8, 707.9, 731.8)
250.83 Diabetes with other specified manifestations, type I [juvenile type], uncontrolled — (Use additional code to identify manifestation: 707.10-707.19, 707.8, 707.9, 731.8)
440.23 Atherosclerosis of native arteries of the extremities with ulceration — (Use additional code for any associated ulceration: 707.10-707.19, 707.8, 707.9)
443.0 Raynaud's syndrome — (Use additional code to identify gangrene: 785.4)
454.0 Varicose veins of lower extremities with ulcer

454.2 Varicose veins of lower extremities with ulcer and inflammation

454.8 Varicose veins of the lower extremities with other complications

459.11 Postphlebitic syndrome with ulcer

459.13 Postphlebitic syndrome with ulcer and inflammation

459.19 Postphlebitic syndrome with other complication

459.31 Chronic venous hypertension with ulcer

459.33 Chronic venous hypertension with ulcer and inflammation

459.39 Chronic venous hypertension with other complication

701.4 Keloid scar

707.00 Pressure ulcer, unspecified site — (Use additional code to identify pressure ulcer stage: 707.20-707.25) ▽

707.06 Pressure ulcer, ankle — (Use additional code to identify pressure ulcer stage: 707.20-707.25)

707.09 Pressure ulcer, other site — (Use additional code to identify pressure ulcer stage: 707.20-707.25)

707.10 Ulcer of lower limb, unspecified — (Code, if applicable, any causal condition first: 249.80-249.81, 250.80-250.83, 440.23, 459.11, 459.13, 459.31, 459.33) ▽

707.11 Ulcer of thigh — (Code, if applicable, any causal condition first: 249.80-249.81, 250.80-250.83, 440.23, 459.11, 459.13, 459.31, 459.33)

707.12 Ulcer of calf — (Code, if applicable, any causal condition first: 249.80-249.81, 250.80-250.83, 440.23, 459.11, 459.13, 459.31, 459.33)

707.13 Ulcer of ankle — (Code, if applicable, any causal condition first: 249.80-249.81, 250.80-250.83, 440.23, 459.11, 459.13, 459.31, 459.33)

707.19 Ulcer of other part of lower limb — (Code, if applicable, any causal condition first: 249.80-249.81, 250.80-250.83, 440.23, 459.11, 459.13, 459.31, 459.33)

707.20 Pressure ulcer, unspecified stage — (Code first site of pressure ulcer: 707.00-707.09) ▽

707.21 Pressure ulcer, stage I — (Code first site of pressure ulcer: 707.00-707.09)

707.22 Pressure ulcer stage II — (Code first site of pressure ulcer: 707.00-707.09)

707.23 Pressure ulcer stage III — (Code first site of pressure ulcer: 707.00-707.09)

707.24 Pressure ulcer stage IV — (Code first site of pressure ulcer: 707.00-707.09)

707.25 Pressure ulcer, unstageable — (Code first site of pressure ulcer: 707.00-707.09)

707.8 Chronic ulcer of other specified site

709.2 Scar condition and fibrosis of skin

728.86 Necrotizing fasciitis — (Use additional code to identify infectious organism, 041.00-041.89, 785.4, if applicable)

785.4 Gangrene — (Code first any associated underlying condition)

873.0 Open wound of scalp, without mention of complication

873.1 Open wound of scalp, complicated

880.01 Open wound of scapular region, without mention of complication

880.02 Open wound of axillary region, without mention of complication

880.03 Open wound of upper arm, without mention of complication

880.09 Open wound of multiple sites of shoulder and upper arm, without mention of complication

880.13 Open wound of upper arm, complicated

880.19 Open wound of multiple sites of shoulder and upper arm, complicated

881.00 Open wound of forearm, without mention of complication

881.01 Open wound of elbow, without mention of complication

881.02 Open wound of wrist, without mention of complication

881.10 Open wound of forearm, complicated

881.11 Open wound of elbow, complicated

881.12 Open wound of wrist, complicated

881.21 Open wound of elbow, with tendon involvement

884.0 Multiple and unspecified open wound of upper limb, without mention of complication

884.1 Multiple and unspecified open wound of upper limb, complicated

884.2 Multiple and unspecified open wound of upper limb, with tendon involvement

887.0 Traumatic amputation of arm and hand (complete) (partial), unilateral, below elbow, without mention of complication

887.1 Traumatic amputation of arm and hand (complete) (partial), unilateral, below elbow, complicated

887.2 Traumatic amputation of arm and hand (complete) (partial), unilateral, at or above elbow, without mention of complication

887.3 Traumatic amputation of arm and hand (complete) (partial), unilateral, at or above elbow, complicated

887.4 Traumatic amputation of arm and hand (complete) (partial), unilateral, level not specified, without mention of complication ▽

887.5 Traumatic amputation of arm and hand (complete) (partial), unilateral, level not specified, complicated ▽

887.6 Traumatic amputation of arm and hand (complete) (partial), bilateral (any level), without mention of complication

887.7 Traumatic amputation of arm and hand (complete) (partial), bilateral (any level), complicated

890.0 Open wound of hip and thigh, without mention of complication

890.1 Open wound of hip and thigh, complicated

890.2 Open wound of hip and thigh, with tendon involvement

891.0 Open wound of knee, leg (except thigh), and ankle, without mention of complication

891.2 Open wound of knee, leg (except thigh), and ankle, with tendon involvement

892.1 Open wound of foot except toe(s) alone, complicated

894.0 Multiple and unspecified open wound of lower limb, without mention of complication

894.1 Multiple and unspecified open wound of lower limb, complicated

894.2 Multiple and unspecified open wound of lower limb, with tendon involvement

897.0 Traumatic amputation of leg(s) (complete) (partial), unilateral, below knee, without mention of complication

897.1 Traumatic amputation of leg(s) (complete) (partial), unilateral, below knee, complicated

897.3 Traumatic amputation of leg(s) (complete) (partial), unilateral, at or above knee, complicated

897.4 Traumatic amputation of leg(s) (complete) (partial), unilateral, level not specified, without mention of complication ▽

897.5 Traumatic amputation of leg(s) (complete) (partial), unilateral, level not specified, complicated ▽

897.6 Traumatic amputation of leg(s) (complete) (partial), bilateral (any level), without mention of complication

897.7 Traumatic amputation of leg(s) (complete) (partial), bilateral (any level), complicated

906.0 Late effect of open wound of head, neck, and trunk

906.1 Late effect of open wound of extremities without mention of tendon injury

906.4 Late effect of crushing

906.5 Late effect of burn of eye, face, head, and neck

906.7 Late effect of burn of other extremities

908.6 Late effect of certain complications of trauma

909.2 Late effect of radiation

941.36 Full-thickness skin loss due to burn (third degree NOS) of scalp (any part)

941.46 Deep necrosis of underlying tissues due to burn (deep third degree) of scalp (any part), without mention of loss of a body part

943.30 Full-thickness skin loss due to burn (third degree NOS) of unspecified site of upper limb ▽

943.31 Full-thickness skin loss due to burn (third degree NOS) of forearm

943.32 Full-thickness skin loss due to burn (third degree NOS) of elbow

943.33 Full-thickness skin loss due to burn (third degree NOS) of upper arm

943.34 Full-thickness skin loss due to burn (third degree NOS) of axilla

943.35 Full-thickness skin loss due to burn (third degree NOS) of shoulder

943.36 Full-thickness skin loss due to burn (third degree NOS) of scapular region

943.39 Full-thickness skin loss due to burn (third degree NOS) of multiple sites of upper limb, except wrist and hand

943.40 Deep necrosis of underlying tissues due to burn (deep third degree) of unspecified site of upper limb, without mention of loss of a body part ▽

943.41 Deep necrosis of underlying tissues due to burn (deep third degree) of forearm, without mention of loss of a body part

943.42 Deep necrosis of underlying tissues due to burn (deep third degree) of elbow, without mention of loss of a body part

943.43 Deep necrosis of underlying tissues due to burn (deep third degree) of upper arm, without mention of loss of a body part
943.49 Deep necrosis of underlying tissues due to burn (deep third degree) of multiple sites of upper limb, except wrist and hand, without mention of loss of a body part
943.50 Deep necrosis of underlying tissues due to burn (deep third degree) of unspecified site of upper limb, with loss of a body part
943.51 Deep necrosis of underlying tissues due to burn (deep third degree) of forearm, with loss of a body part
943.52 Deep necrosis of underlying tissues due to burn (deep third degree) of elbow, with loss of a body part
943.53 Deep necrosis of underlying tissues due to burn (deep third degree) of upper arm, with loss of upper a body part
943.59 Deep necrosis of underlying tissues due to burn (deep third degree) of multiple sites of upper limb, except wrist and hand, with loss of a body part
945.33 Full-thickness skin loss due to burn (third degree NOS) of ankle
945.34 Full-thickness skin loss due to burn (third degree NOS) of lower leg
945.35 Full-thickness skin loss due to burn (third degree NOS) of knee
945.36 Full-thickness skin loss due to burn (third degree NOS) of thigh (any part)
945.39 Full-thickness skin loss due to burn (third degree NOS) of multiple sites of lower limb(s)
945.40 Deep necrosis of underlying tissues due to burn (deep third degree) of unspecified site of lower limb (leg), without mention of loss of a body part
945.43 Deep necrosis of underlying tissues due to burn (deep third degree) of ankle, without mention of loss of a body part
945.44 Deep necrosis of underlying tissues due to burn (deep third degree) of lower leg, without mention of loss of a body part
945.45 Deep necrosis of underlying tissues due to burn (deep third degree) of knee, without mention of loss of a body part
945.46 Deep necrosis of underlying tissues due to burn (deep third degree) of thigh (any part), without mention of loss of a body part
945.49 Deep necrosis of underlying tissues due to burn (deep third degree) of multiple sites of lower limb(s), without mention of loss of a body part
945.50 Deep necrosis of underlying tissues due to burn (deep third degree) of unspecified site lower limb (leg), with loss of a body part
945.53 Deep necrosis of underlying tissues due to burn (deep third degree) of ankle, with loss of a body part
945.54 Deep necrosis of underlying tissues due to burn (deep third degree) of lower leg, with loss of a body part
945.55 Deep necrosis of underlying tissues due to burn (deep third degree) of knee, with loss of a body part
945.56 Deep necrosis of underlying tissues due to burn (deep third degree) of thigh (any part), with loss of a body part
945.59 Deep necrosis of underlying tissues due to burn (deep third degree) of multiple sites of lower limb(s), with loss of a body part
946.3 Full-thickness skin loss due to burn (third degree NOS) of multiple specified sites
946.4 Deep necrosis of underlying tissues due to burn (deep third degree) of multiple specified sites, without mention of loss of a body part
946.5 Deep necrosis of underlying tissues due to burn (deep third degree) of multiple specified sites, with loss of a body part
948.00 Burn (any degree) involving less than 10% of body surface with third degree burn of less than 10% or unspecified amount
948.10 Burn (any degree) involving 10-19% of body surface with third degree burn of less than 10% or unspecified amount
948.11 Burn (any degree) involving 10-19% of body surface with third degree burn of 10-19%
948.20 Burn (any degree) involving 20-29% of body surface with third degree burn of less than 10% or unspecified amount
948.21 Burn (any degree) involving 20-29% of body surface with third degree burn of 10-19%
948.22 Burn (any degree) involving 20-29% of body surface with third degree burn of 20-29%
948.30 Burn (any degree) involving 30-39% of body surface with third degree burn of less than 10% or unspecified amount
948.31 Burn (any degree) involving 30-39% of body surface with third degree burn of 10-19%
948.32 Burn (any degree) involving 30-39% of body surface with third degree burn of 20-29%
948.33 Burn (any degree) involving 30-39% of body surface with third degree burn of 30-39%
948.40 Burn (any degree) involving 40-49% of body surface with third degree burn of less than 10% or unspecified amount
948.41 Burn (any degree) involving 40-49% of body surface with third degree burn of 10-19%
948.42 Burn (any degree) involving 40-49% of body surface with third degree burn of 20-29%
948.43 Burn (any degree) involving 40-49% of body surface with third degree burn of 30-39%
948.44 Burn (any degree) involving 40-49% of body surface with third degree burn of 40-49%
948.50 Burn (any degree) involving 50-59% of body surface with third degree burn of less than 10% or unspecified amount
948.51 Burn (any degree) involving 50-59% of body surface with third degree burn of 10-19%
948.52 Burn (any degree) involving 50-59% of body surface with third degree burn of 20-29%
948.53 Burn (any degree) involving 50-59% of body surface with third degree burn of 30-39%
948.54 Burn (any degree) involving 50-59% of body surface with third degree burn of 40-49%
948.55 Burn (any degree) involving 50-59% of body surface with third degree burn of 50-59%
948.60 Burn (any degree) involving 60-69% of body surface with third degree burn of less than 10% or unspecified amount
948.61 Burn (any degree) involving 60-69% of body surface with third degree burn of 10-19%
948.62 Burn (any degree) involving 60-69% of body surface with third degree burn of 20-29%
948.63 Burn (any degree) involving 60-69% of body surface with third degree burn of 30-39%
948.64 Burn (any degree) involving 60-69% of body surface with third degree burn of 40-49%
948.65 Burn (any degree) involving 60-69% of body surface with third degree burn of 50-59%
948.66 Burn (any degree) involving 60-69% of body surface with third degree burn of 60-69%
948.70 Burn (any degree) involving 70-79% of body surface with third degree burn of less than 10% or unspecified amount
948.71 Burn (any degree) involving 70-79% of body surface with third degree burn of 10-19%
948.72 Burn (any degree) involving 70-79% of body surface with third degree burn of 20-29%
948.73 Burn (any degree) involving 70-79% of body surface with third degree burn of 30-39%
948.74 Burn (any degree) involving 70-79% of body surface with third degree burn of 40-49%
948.75 Burn (any degree) involving 70-79% of body surface with third degree burn of 50-59%
948.76 Burn (any degree) involving 70-79% of body surface with third degree burn of 60-69%
948.77 Burn (any degree) involving 70-79% of body surface with third degree burn of 70-79%
948.80 Burn (any degree) involving 80-89% of body surface with third degree burn of less than 10% or unspecified amount
948.81 Burn (any degree) involving 80-89% of body surface with third degree burn of 10-19%
948.82 Burn (any degree) involving 80-89% of body surface with third degree burn of 20-29%
998.30 Disruption of wound, unspecified
998.32 Disruption of external operation (surgical) wound
998.33 Disruption of traumatic injury wound repair
998.59 Other postoperative infection — (Use additional code to identify infection)
998.83 Non-healing surgical wound
V51.8 Other aftercare involving the use of plastic surgery

ICD-9-CM Procedural

86.63 Full-thickness skin graft to other sites
86.64 Hair transplant

15240-15241

15240 Full thickness graft, free, including direct closure of donor site, forehead, cheeks, chin, mouth, neck, axillae, genitalia, hands, and/or feet; 20 sq cm or less
15241 each additional 20 sq cm, or part thereof (List separately in addition to code for primary procedure)

ICD-9-CM Diagnostic

140.3 Malignant neoplasm of upper lip, inner aspect
140.4 Malignant neoplasm of lower lip, inner aspect
140.5 Malignant neoplasm of lip, inner aspect, unspecified as to upper or lower
145.0 Malignant neoplasm of cheek mucosa
149.8 Malignant neoplasm of other sites within the lip and oral cavity
149.9 Malignant neoplasm of ill-defined sites of lip and oral cavity
171.6 Malignant neoplasm of connective and other soft tissue of pelvis

172.3	Malignant melanoma of skin of other and unspecified parts of face ▽
172.4	Malignant melanoma of skin of scalp and neck
172.5	Malignant melanoma of skin of trunk, except scrotum
172.6	Malignant melanoma of skin of upper limb, including shoulder
172.7	Malignant melanoma of skin of lower limb, including hip
172.8	Malignant melanoma of other specified sites of skin
173.30	Unspecified malignant neoplasm of skin of other and unspecified parts of face ▽
173.31	Basal cell carcinoma of skin of other and unspecified parts of face
173.32	Squamous cell carcinoma of skin of other and unspecified parts of face
173.39	Other specified malignant neoplasm of skin of other and unspecified parts of face
173.40	Unspecified malignant neoplasm of scalp and skin of neck ▽
173.41	Basal cell carcinoma of scalp and skin of neck
173.42	Squamous cell carcinoma of scalp and skin of neck
173.49	Other specified malignant neoplasm of scalp and skin of neck
184.0	Malignant neoplasm of vagina ♀
184.1	Malignant neoplasm of labia majora ♀
184.2	Malignant neoplasm of labia minora ♀
184.3	Malignant neoplasm of clitoris ♀
184.4	Malignant neoplasm of vulva, unspecified site ▽ ♀
184.8	Malignant neoplasm of other specified sites of female genital organs ♀
184.9	Malignant neoplasm of female genital organ, site unspecified ▽ ♀
187.1	Malignant neoplasm of prepuce ♂
187.2	Malignant neoplasm of glans penis ♂
187.3	Malignant neoplasm of body of penis ♂
187.4	Malignant neoplasm of penis, part unspecified ▽ ♂
187.7	Malignant neoplasm of scrotum ♂
187.9	Malignant neoplasm of male genital organ, site unspecified ▽ ♂
198.82	Secondary malignant neoplasm of genital organs
198.89	Secondary malignant neoplasm of other specified sites
209.31	Merkel cell carcinoma of the face
209.32	Merkel cell carcinoma of the scalp and neck
209.33	Merkel cell carcinoma of the upper limb
209.34	Merkel cell carcinoma of the lower limb
209.35	Merkel cell carcinoma of the trunk
209.36	Merkel cell carcinoma of other sites
209.75	Secondary Merkel cell carcinoma
210.4	Benign neoplasm of other and unspecified parts of mouth ▽
216.3	Benign neoplasm of skin of other and unspecified parts of face ▽
216.4	Benign neoplasm of scalp and skin of neck
216.6	Benign neoplasm of skin of upper limb, including shoulder
216.7	Benign neoplasm of skin of lower limb, including hip
216.8	Benign neoplasm of other specified sites of skin
222.4	Benign neoplasm of scrotum ♂
230.0	Carcinoma in situ of lip, oral cavity, and pharynx
232.3	Carcinoma in situ of skin of other and unspecified parts of face ▽
232.4	Carcinoma in situ of scalp and skin of neck
232.6	Carcinoma in situ of skin of upper limb, including shoulder
232.7	Carcinoma in situ of skin of lower limb, including hip
232.8	Carcinoma in situ of other specified sites of skin
233.30	Carcinoma in situ, unspecified female genital organ ▽ ♀
233.31	Carcinoma in situ, vagina ♀
233.32	Carcinoma in situ, vulva ♀
233.39	Carcinoma in situ, other female genital organ ♀
233.5	Carcinoma in situ of penis ♂
233.6	Carcinoma in situ of other and unspecified male genital organs ▽ ♂
235.1	Neoplasm of uncertain behavior of lip, oral cavity, and pharynx
236.3	Neoplasm of uncertain behavior of other and unspecified female genital organs ▽ ♀
236.6	Neoplasm of uncertain behavior of other and unspecified male genital organs ▽ ♂
238.2	Neoplasm of uncertain behavior of skin
239.5	Neoplasm of unspecified nature of other genitourinary organs
249.70	Secondary diabetes mellitus with peripheral circulatory disorders, not stated as uncontrolled, or unspecified — (Use additional code to identify manifestation: 443.81, 785.4) (Use additional code to identify any associated insulin use: V58.67)
249.71	Secondary diabetes mellitus with peripheral circulatory disorders, uncontrolled — (Use additional code to identify manifestation: 443.81, 785.4) (Use additional code to identify any associated insulin use: V58.67)
249.80	Secondary diabetes mellitus with other specified manifestations, not stated as uncontrolled, or unspecified — (Use additional code to identify manifestation: 707.10-707.19, 707.8, 707.9, 731.8) (Use additional code to identify any associated insulin use: V58.67)
249.81	Secondary diabetes mellitus with other specified manifestations, uncontrolled — (Use additional code to identify manifestation: 707.10-707.19, 707.8, 707.9, 731.8) (Use additional code to identify any associated insulin use: V58.67)
249.90	Secondary diabetes mellitus with unspecified complication, not stated as uncontrolled, or unspecified — (Use additional code to identify any associated insulin use: V58.67) ▽
249.91	Secondary diabetes mellitus with unspecified complication, uncontrolled — (Use additional code to identify any associated insulin use: V58.67) ▽
250.70	Diabetes with peripheral circulatory disorders, type II or unspecified type, not stated as uncontrolled — (Use additional code to identify manifestation: 443.81, 785.4)
250.71	Diabetes with peripheral circulatory disorders, type I [juvenile type], not stated as uncontrolled — (Use additional code to identify manifestation: 443.81, 785.4)
250.72	Diabetes with peripheral circulatory disorders, type II or unspecified type, uncontrolled — (Use additional code to identify manifestation: 443.81, 785.4)
250.73	Diabetes with peripheral circulatory disorders, type I [juvenile type], uncontrolled — (Use additional code to identify manifestation: 443.81, 785.4)
250.80	Diabetes with other specified manifestations, type II or unspecified type, not stated as uncontrolled — (Use additional code to identify manifestation: 707.10-707.19, 707.8, 707.9, 731.8)
250.81	Diabetes with other specified manifestations, type I [juvenile type], not stated as uncontrolled — (Use additional code to identify manifestation: 707.10-707.19, 707.8, 707.9, 731.8)
250.82	Diabetes with other specified manifestations, type II or unspecified type, uncontrolled — (Use additional code to identify manifestation: 707.10-707.19, 707.8, 707.9, 731.8)
250.83	Diabetes with other specified manifestations, type I [juvenile type], uncontrolled — (Use additional code to identify manifestation: 707.10-707.19, 707.8, 707.9, 731.8)
440.23	Atherosclerosis of native arteries of the extremities with ulceration — (Use additional code for any associated ulceration: 707.10-707.19, 707.8, 707.9)
459.11	Postphlebitic syndrome with ulcer
459.13	Postphlebitic syndrome with ulcer and inflammation
459.31	Chronic venous hypertension with ulcer
459.33	Chronic venous hypertension with ulcer and inflammation
607.2	Other inflammatory disorders of penis — (Use additional code to identify organism) ♂
629.20	Female genital mutilation status, unspecified ▽ ♀
629.21	Female genital mutilation, Type I status ♀
629.22	Female genital mutilation, Type II status ♀
629.23	Female genital mutilation, Type III status ♀
629.29	Other female genital mutilation status ♀
629.89	Other specified disorders of female genital organs ♀
707.00	Pressure ulcer, unspecified site — (Use additional code to identify pressure ulcer stage: 707.20-707.25) ▽
707.07	Pressure ulcer, heel — (Use additional code to identify pressure ulcer stage: 707.20-707.25)
707.09	Pressure ulcer, other site — (Use additional code to identify pressure ulcer stage: 707.20-707.25)
707.14	Ulcer of heel and midfoot — (Code, if applicable, any causal condition first: 249.80-249.81, 250.80-250.83, 440.23, 459.11, 459.13, 459.31, 459.33)

707.15 Ulcer of other part of foot — (Code, if applicable, any causal condition first: 249.80-249.81, 250.80-250.83, 440.23, 459.11, 459.13, 459.31, 459.33)
707.20 Pressure ulcer, unspecified stage — (Code first site of pressure ulcer: 707.00-707.09) ▽
707.21 Pressure ulcer, stage I — (Code first site of pressure ulcer: 707.00-707.09)
707.22 Pressure ulcer stage II — (Code first site of pressure ulcer: 707.00-707.09)
707.23 Pressure ulcer stage III — (Code first site of pressure ulcer: 707.00-707.09)
707.24 Pressure ulcer stage IV — (Code first site of pressure ulcer: 707.00-707.09)
707.25 Pressure ulcer, unstageable — (Code first site of pressure ulcer: 707.00-707.09)
709.2 Scar condition and fibrosis of skin
709.9 Unspecified disorder of skin and subcutaneous tissue ▽
728.86 Necrotizing fasciitis — (Use additional code to identify infectious organism, 041.00-041.89, 785.4, if applicable)
752.40 Unspecified congenital anomaly of cervix, vagina, and external female genitalia ▽ ♀
752.43 Cervical agenesis ♀
752.44 Cervical duplication ♀
752.45 Vaginal agenesis ♀
752.46 Transverse vaginal septum ♀
752.47 Longitudinal vaginal septum ♀
752.49 Other congenital anomaly of cervix, vagina, and external female genitalia ♀
752.64 Micropenis ♂
752.69 Other penile anomalies ♂
752.7 Indeterminate sex and pseudohermaphroditism
752.81 Scrotal transposition ♂
752.89 Other specified anomalies of genital organs
752.9 Unspecified congenital anomaly of genital organs ▽
757.33 Congenital pigmentary anomaly of skin
785.4 Gangrene — (Code first any associated underlying condition)
873.50 Open wound of face, unspecified site, complicated ▽
873.51 Open wound of cheek, complicated
873.52 Open wound of forehead, complicated
873.54 Open wound of jaw, complicated
873.59 Open wound of face, other and multiple sites, complicated
873.70 Open wound of mouth, unspecified site, complicated ▽
873.71 Open wound of buccal mucosa, complicated
873.74 Open wound of tongue and floor of mouth, complicated
878.1 Open wound of penis, complicated ♂
878.3 Open wound of scrotum and testes, complicated ♂
878.5 Open wound of vulva, complicated ♀
878.7 Open wound of vagina, complicated ♀
878.9 Open wound of other and unspecified parts of genital organs, complicated ▽
880.12 Open wound of axillary region, complicated
882.1 Open wound of hand except finger(s) alone, complicated
882.2 Open wound of hand except finger(s) alone, with tendon involvement
883.1 Open wound of finger(s), complicated
883.2 Open wound of finger(s), with tendon involvement
884.1 Multiple and unspecified open wound of upper limb, complicated
884.2 Multiple and unspecified open wound of upper limb, with tendon involvement
885.0 Traumatic amputation of thumb (complete) (partial), without mention of complication
885.1 Traumatic amputation of thumb (complete) (partial), complicated
886.0 Traumatic amputation of other finger(s) (complete) (partial), without mention of complication
886.1 Traumatic amputation of other finger(s) (complete) (partial), complicated
887.0 Traumatic amputation of arm and hand (complete) (partial), unilateral, below elbow, without mention of complication
887.1 Traumatic amputation of arm and hand (complete) (partial), unilateral, below elbow, complicated
887.6 Traumatic amputation of arm and hand (complete) (partial), bilateral (any level), without mention of complication
887.7 Traumatic amputation of arm and hand (complete) (partial), bilateral (any level), complicated
892.1 Open wound of foot except toe(s) alone, complicated
892.2 Open wound of foot except toe(s) alone, with tendon involvement
893.1 Open wound of toe(s), complicated
893.2 Open wound of toe(s), with tendon involvement
894.1 Multiple and unspecified open wound of lower limb, complicated
894.2 Multiple and unspecified open wound of lower limb, with tendon involvement
895.0 Traumatic amputation of toe(s) (complete) (partial), without mention of complication
895.1 Traumatic amputation of toe(s) (complete) (partial), complicated
896.0 Traumatic amputation of foot (complete) (partial), unilateral, without mention of complication
896.1 Traumatic amputation of foot (complete) (partial), unilateral, complicated
896.2 Traumatic amputation of foot (complete) (partial), bilateral, without mention of complication
896.3 Traumatic amputation of foot (complete) (partial), bilateral, complicated
906.0 Late effect of open wound of head, neck, and trunk
906.5 Late effect of burn of eye, face, head, and neck
906.6 Late effect of burn of wrist and hand
906.8 Late effect of burns of other specified sites
926.0 Crushing injury of external genitalia — (Use additional code to identify any associated injuries: 800-829, 850.0-854.1, 860.0-869.1)
941.30 Full-thickness skin loss due to burn (third degree NOS) of unspecified site of face and head ▽
941.33 Full-thickness skin loss due to burn (third degree NOS) of lip(s)
941.34 Full-thickness skin loss due to burn (third degree NOS) of chin
941.37 Full-thickness skin loss due to burn (third degree NOS) of forehead and cheek
941.38 Full-thickness skin loss due to burn (third degree NOS) of neck
941.39 Full-thickness skin loss due to burn (third degree NOS) of multiple sites (except with eye) of face, head, and neck
941.40 Deep necrosis of underlying tissues due to burn (deep third degree) of unspecified site of face and head, without mention of loss of a body part ▽
941.44 Deep necrosis of underlying tissues due to burn (deep third degree) of chin, without mention of loss of a body part
941.47 Deep necrosis of underlying tissues due to burn (deep third degree) of forehead and cheek, without mention of loss of a body part
941.48 Deep necrosis of underlying tissues due to burn (deep third degree) of neck, without mention of loss of a body part
941.49 Deep necrosis of underlying tissues due to burn (deep third degree) of multiple sites (except with eye) of face, head, and neck, without mention of loss of a body part
941.50 Deep necrosis of underlying tissues due to burn (deep third degree) of face and head, unspecified site, with loss of a body part ▽
941.57 Deep necrosis of underlying tissues due to burn (deep third degree) of forehead and cheek, with loss of a body part
941.58 Deep necrosis of underlying tissues due to burn (deep third degree) of neck, with loss of a body part
941.59 Deep necrosis of underlying tissues due to burn (deep third degree) of multiple sites (except eye) of face, head, and neck, with loss of a body part
942.05 Burn of trunk, unspecified degree of genitalia ▽
943.34 Full-thickness skin loss due to burn (third degree NOS) of axilla
943.44 Deep necrosis of underlying tissues due to burn (deep third degree) of axilla, without mention of loss of a body part
943.54 Deep necrosis of underlying tissues due to burn (deep third degree) of axilla, with loss of a body part
944.30 Full-thickness skin loss due to burn (third degree NOS) of unspecified site of hand ▽
944.31 Full-thickness skin loss due to burn (third degree NOS) of single digit [finger (nail)] other than thumb
944.32 Full-thickness skin loss due to burn (third degree NOS) of thumb (nail)
944.33 Full-thickness skin loss due to burn (third degree NOS) of two or more digits of hand, not including thumb

944.34 Full-thickness skin loss due to burn (third degree NOS) of two or more digits of hand including thumb
944.35 Full-thickness skin loss due to burn (third degree NOS) of palm of hand
944.36 Full-thickness skin loss due to burn (third degree NOS) of back of hand
944.37 Full-thickness skin loss due to burn (third degree NOS) of wrist
944.38 Full-thickness skin loss due to burn (third degree NOS) of multiple sites of wrist(s) and hand(s)
944.40 Deep necrosis of underlying tissues due to burn (deep third degree) of unspecified site of hand, without mention of loss of a body part ▽
944.41 Deep necrosis of underlying tissues due to burn (deep third degree) of single digit [finger (nail)] other than thumb, without mention of loss of a body part
944.42 Deep necrosis of underlying tissues due to burn (deep third degree) of thumb (nail), without mention of loss of a body part
944.43 Deep necrosis of underlying tissues due to burn (deep third degree) of two or more digits of hand, not including thumb, without mention of loss of a body part
944.44 Deep necrosis of underlying tissues due to burn (deep third degree) of two or more digits of hand including thumb, without mention of loss of a body part
944.45 Deep necrosis of underlying tissues due to burn (deep third degree) of palm of hand, without mention of loss of a body part
944.46 Deep necrosis of underlying tissues due to burn (deep third degree) of back of hand, without mention of loss of a body part
944.47 Deep necrosis of underlying tissues due to burn (deep third degree) of wrist, without mention of loss of a body part
944.48 Deep necrosis of underlying tissues due to burn (deep third degree) of multiple sites of wrist(s) and hand(s), without mention of loss of a body part
944.50 Deep necrosis of underlying tissues due to burn (deep third degree) of unspecified site of hand, with loss of a body part ▽
944.51 Deep necrosis of underlying tissues due to burn (deep third degree) of single digit (finger (nail)) other than thumb, with loss of a body part
944.52 Deep necrosis of underlying tissues due to burn (deep third degree) of thumb (nail), with loss of a body part
944.53 Deep necrosis of underlying tissues due to burn (deep third degree) of two or more digits of hand, not including thumb, with loss of a body part
944.54 Deep necrosis of underlying tissues due to burn (deep third degree) of two or more digits of hand including thumb, with loss of a body part
944.55 Deep necrosis of underlying tissues due to burn (deep third degree) of palm of hand, with loss of a body part
944.56 Deep necrosis of underlying tissues due to burn (deep third degree) of back of hand, with loss of a body part
944.57 Deep necrosis of underlying tissues due to burn (deep third degree) of wrist, with loss of a body part
944.58 Deep necrosis of underlying tissues due to burn (deep third degree) of multiple sites of wrist(s) and hand(s), with loss of a body part
945.32 Full-thickness skin loss due to burn (third degree NOS) of foot
945.42 Deep necrosis of underlying tissues due to burn (deep third degree) of foot, without mention of loss of a body part
945.52 Deep necrosis of underlying tissues due to burn (deep third degree) of foot, with loss of a body part
946.3 Full-thickness skin loss due to burn (third degree NOS) of multiple specified sites
946.4 Deep necrosis of underlying tissues due to burn (deep third degree) of multiple specified sites, without mention of loss of a body part
946.5 Deep necrosis of underlying tissues due to burn (deep third degree) of multiple specified sites, with loss of a body part
947.0 Burn of mouth and pharynx
959.09 Injury of face and neck, other and unspecified
959.14 Other injury of external genitals
959.4 Injury, other and unspecified, hand, except finger
959.5 Injury, other and unspecified, finger
959.7 Injury, other and unspecified, knee, leg, ankle, and foot
959.8 Injury, other and unspecified, other specified sites, including multiple
991.0 Frostbite of face
991.1 Frostbite of hand
991.2 Frostbite of foot
996.52 Mechanical complication due to other tissue graft, not elsewhere classified
996.64 Infection and inflammatory reaction due to indwelling urinary catheter — (Use additional code to identify specified infections: 038.0-038.9, 595.0-595.9)
997.60 Late complications of amputation stump, unspecified — (Use additional code to identify complications) ▽
997.62 Infection (chronic) of amputation stump — (Use additional code to identify complications)
997.69 Other late amputation stump complication — (Use additional code to identify complications)
998.30 Disruption of wound, unspecified ▽
998.32 Disruption of external operation (surgical) wound
998.33 Disruption of traumatic injury wound repair
998.83 Non-healing surgical wound
V51.8 Other aftercare involving the use of plastic surgery

ICD-9-CM Procedural

27.55 Full-thickness skin graft to lip and mouth
61.49 Other repair of scrotum and tunica vaginalis ♂
64.49 Other repair of penis ♂
70.79 Other repair of vagina ♀
71.79 Other repair of vulva and perineum ♀
86.61 Full-thickness skin graft to hand
86.63 Full-thickness skin graft to other sites

15260-15261

15260 Full thickness graft, free, including direct closure of donor site, nose, ears, eyelids, and/or lips; 20 sq cm or less
15261 each additional 20 sq cm, or part thereof (List separately in addition to code for primary procedure)

ICD-9-CM Diagnostic

140.0 Malignant neoplasm of upper lip, vermilion border
140.1 Malignant neoplasm of lower lip, vermilion border
140.3 Malignant neoplasm of upper lip, inner aspect
140.4 Malignant neoplasm of lower lip, inner aspect
140.5 Malignant neoplasm of lip, inner aspect, unspecified as to upper or lower ▽
140.6 Malignant neoplasm of commissure of lip
140.8 Malignant neoplasm of other sites of lip
140.9 Malignant neoplasm of lip, vermilion border, unspecified as to upper or lower ▽
172.0 Malignant melanoma of skin of lip
172.1 Malignant melanoma of skin of eyelid, including canthus
172.2 Malignant melanoma of skin of ear and external auditory canal
172.3 Malignant melanoma of skin of other and unspecified parts of face ▽
172.8 Malignant melanoma of other specified sites of skin
173.00 Unspecified malignant neoplasm of skin of lip ▽
173.01 Basal cell carcinoma of skin of lip
173.02 Squamous cell carcinoma of skin of lip
173.09 Other specified malignant neoplasm of skin of lip
173.10 Unspecified malignant neoplasm of eyelid, including canthus ▽
173.11 Basal cell carcinoma of eyelid, including canthus
173.12 Squamous cell carcinoma of eyelid, including canthus
173.19 Other specified malignant neoplasm of eyelid, including canthus
173.20 Unspecified malignant neoplasm of skin of ear and external auditory canal ▽
173.21 Basal cell carcinoma of skin of ear and external auditory canal
173.22 Squamous cell carcinoma of skin of ear and external auditory canal
173.29 Other specified malignant neoplasm of skin of ear and external auditory canal
173.30 Unspecified malignant neoplasm of skin of other and unspecified parts of face ▽
173.31 Basal cell carcinoma of skin of other and unspecified parts of face

173.32 Squamous cell carcinoma of skin of other and unspecified parts of face
173.39 Other specified malignant neoplasm of skin of other and unspecified parts of face
173.80 Unspecified malignant neoplasm of other specified sites of skin ♥
173.81 Basal cell carcinoma of other specified sites of skin
173.82 Squamous cell carcinoma of other specified sites of skin
173.89 Other specified malignant neoplasm of other specified sites of skin
195.0 Malignant neoplasm of head, face, and neck
198.2 Secondary malignant neoplasm of skin
209.31 Merkel cell carcinoma of the face
209.75 Secondary Merkel cell carcinoma
210.0 Benign neoplasm of lip
210.4 Benign neoplasm of other and unspecified parts of mouth ♥
216.0 Benign neoplasm of skin of lip
216.1 Benign neoplasm of eyelid, including canthus
216.2 Benign neoplasm of ear and external auditory canal
216.3 Benign neoplasm of skin of other and unspecified parts of face ♥
230.0 Carcinoma in situ of lip, oral cavity, and pharynx
232.1 Carcinoma in situ of eyelid, including canthus
232.2 Carcinoma in situ of skin of ear and external auditory canal
232.3 Carcinoma in situ of skin of other and unspecified parts of face ♥
238.2 Neoplasm of uncertain behavior of skin
239.0 Neoplasm of unspecified nature of digestive system
239.2 Neoplasms of unspecified nature of bone, soft tissue, and skin
374.04 Cicatricial entropion
374.14 Cicatricial ectropion
374.41 Eyelid retraction or lag
380.32 Acquired deformities of auricle or pinna
682.0 Cellulitis and abscess of face — (Use additional code to identify organism, such as 041.1, etc.)
709.2 Scar condition and fibrosis of skin
743.62 Congenital deformity of eyelid
744.01 Congenital absence of external ear causing impairment of hearing
744.09 Other congenital anomalies of ear causing impairment of hearing
744.23 Microtia
744.3 Unspecified congenital anomaly of ear ♥
744.5 Congenital webbing of neck
744.82 Microcheilia
748.1 Other congenital anomaly of nose
749.00 Unspecified cleft palate ♥
749.10 Unspecified cleft lip ♥
749.11 Unilateral cleft lip, complete
749.12 Unilateral cleft lip, incomplete
749.13 Bilateral cleft lip, complete
749.14 Bilateral cleft lip, incomplete
749.20 Unspecified cleft palate with cleft lip ♥
749.21 Unilateral cleft palate with cleft lip, complete
749.22 Unilateral cleft palate with cleft lip, incomplete
749.23 Bilateral cleft palate with cleft lip, complete
749.24 Bilateral cleft palate with cleft lip, incomplete
785.4 Gangrene — (Code first any associated underlying condition)
870.0 Laceration of skin of eyelid and periocular area
870.1 Laceration of eyelid, full-thickness, not involving lacrimal passages
870.2 Laceration of eyelid involving lacrimal passages
872.00 Open wound of external ear, unspecified site, without mention of complication ♥
872.01 Open wound of auricle, without mention of complication
872.02 Open wound of auditory canal, without mention of complication
872.10 Open wound of external ear, unspecified site, complicated ♥
872.11 Open wound of auricle, complicated
872.12 Open wound of auditory canal, complicated
872.8 Open wound of ear, part unspecified, without mention of complication ♥
872.9 Open wound of ear, part unspecified, complicated ♥
873.20 Open wound of nose, unspecified site, without mention of complication ♥
873.23 Open wound of nasal sinus, without mention of complication
873.30 Open wound of nose, unspecified site, complicated ♥
873.31 Open wound of nasal septum, complicated
873.32 Open wound of nasal cavity, complicated
873.33 Open wound of nasal sinus, complicated
873.39 Open wound of nose, multiple sites, complicated
873.43 Open wound of lip, without mention of complication
873.53 Open wound of lip, complicated
906.0 Late effect of open wound of head, neck, and trunk
906.5 Late effect of burn of eye, face, head, and neck
941.01 Burn of unspecified degree of ear (any part) ♥
941.02 Burn of unspecified degree of eye (with other parts of face, head, and neck) ♥
941.03 Burn of unspecified degree of lip(s) ♥
941.05 Burn of unspecified degree of nose (septum) ♥
941.09 Burn of unspecified degree of multiple sites (except with eye) of face, head, and neck ♥
941.31 Full-thickness skin loss due to burn (third degree NOS) of ear (any part)
941.32 Full-thickness skin loss due to burn (third degree NOS) of eye (with other parts of face, head, and neck)
941.33 Full-thickness skin loss due to burn (third degree NOS) of lip(s)
941.35 Full-thickness skin loss due to burn (third degree NOS) of nose (septum)
941.39 Full-thickness skin loss due to burn (third degree NOS) of multiple sites (except with eye) of face, head, and neck
941.49 Deep necrosis of underlying tissues due to burn (deep third degree) of multiple sites (except with eye) of face, head, and neck, without mention of loss of a body part
941.51 Deep necrosis of underlying tissues due to burn (deep third degree) of ear (any part), with loss of a body part
941.52 Deep necrosis of underlying tissues due to burn (deep third degree) of eye (with other parts of face, head, and neck), with loss of a body part
941.53 Deep necrosis of underlying tissues due to burn (deep third degree) of lip(s), with loss of a body part
941.55 Deep necrosis of underlying tissues due to burn (deep third degree) of nose (septum), with loss of a body part
941.59 Deep necrosis of underlying tissues due to burn (deep third degree) of multiple sites (except eye) of face, head, and neck, with loss of a body part
946.3 Full-thickness skin loss due to burn (third degree NOS) of multiple specified sites
946.4 Deep necrosis of underlying tissues due to burn (deep third degree) of multiple specified sites, without mention of loss of a body part
946.5 Deep necrosis of underlying tissues due to burn (deep third degree) of multiple specified sites, with loss of a body part
948.00 Burn (any degree) involving less than 10% of body surface with third degree burn of less than 10% or unspecified amount
948.10 Burn (any degree) involving 10-19% of body surface with third degree burn of less than 10% or unspecified amount
948.11 Burn (any degree) involving 10-19% of body surface with third degree burn of 10-19%
948.20 Burn (any degree) involving 20-29% of body surface with third degree burn of less than 10% or unspecified amount
948.21 Burn (any degree) involving 20-29% of body surface with third degree burn of 10-19%
948.22 Burn (any degree) involving 20-29% of body surface with third degree burn of 20-29%
948.30 Burn (any degree) involving 30-39% of body surface with third degree burn of less than 10% or unspecified amount
948.31 Burn (any degree) involving 30-39% of body surface with third degree burn of 10-19%
948.32 Burn (any degree) involving 30-39% of body surface with third degree burn of 20-29%
948.33 Burn (any degree) involving 30-39% of body surface with third degree burn of 30-39%
948.40 Burn (any degree) involving 40-49% of body surface with third degree burn of less than 10% or unspecified amount
948.41 Burn (any degree) involving 40-49% of body surface with third degree burn of 10-19%

948.42 Burn (any degree) involving 40-49% of body surface with third degree burn of 20-29%
948.43 Burn (any degree) involving 40-49% of body surface with third degree burn of 30-39%
948.44 Burn (any degree) involving 40-49% of body surface with third degree burn of 40-49%
948.50 Burn (any degree) involving 50-59% of body surface with third degree burn of less than 10% or unspecified amount
948.51 Burn (any degree) involving 50-59% of body surface with third degree burn of 10-19%
948.52 Burn (any degree) involving 50-59% of body surface with third degree burn of 20-29%
948.53 Burn (any degree) involving 50-59% of body surface with third degree burn of 30-39%
948.54 Burn (any degree) involving 50-59% of body surface with third degree burn of 40-49%
948.55 Burn (any degree) involving 50-59% of body surface with third degree burn of 50-59%
948.60 Burn (any degree) involving 60-69% of body surface with third degree burn of less than 10% or unspecified amount
948.61 Burn (any degree) involving 60-69% of body surface with third degree burn of 10-19%
948.62 Burn (any degree) involving 60-69% of body surface with third degree burn of 20-29%
948.63 Burn (any degree) involving 60-69% of body surface with third degree burn of 30-39%
948.64 Burn (any degree) involving 60-69% of body surface with third degree burn of 40-49%
948.65 Burn (any degree) involving 60-69% of body surface with third degree burn of 50-59%
948.66 Burn (any degree) involving 60-69% of body surface with third degree burn of 60-69%
948.70 Burn (any degree) involving 70-79% of body surface with third degree burn of less than 10% or unspecified amount
948.71 Burn (any degree) involving 70-79% of body surface with third degree burn of 10-19%
948.72 Burn (any degree) involving 70-79% of body surface with third degree burn of 20-29%
948.73 Burn (any degree) involving 70-79% of body surface with third degree burn of 30-39%
948.74 Burn (any degree) involving 70-79% of body surface with third degree burn of 40-49%
948.75 Burn (any degree) involving 70-79% of body surface with third degree burn of 50-59%
948.76 Burn (any degree) involving 70-79% of body surface with third degree burn of 60-69%
948.77 Burn (any degree) involving 70-79% of body surface with third degree burn of 70-79%
948.80 Burn (any degree) involving 80-89% of body surface with third degree burn of less than 10% or unspecified amount
948.81 Burn (any degree) involving 80-89% of body surface with third degree burn of 10-19%
948.82 Burn (any degree) involving 80-89% of body surface with third degree burn of 20-29%
948.83 Burn (any degree) involving 80-89% of body surface with third degree burn of 30-39%
948.84 Burn (any degree) involving 80-89% of body surface with third degree burn of 40-49%
948.85 Burn (any degree) involving 80-89% of body surface with third degree burn of 50-59%
948.86 Burn (any degree) involving 80-89% of body surface with third degree burn of 60-69%
948.87 Burn (any degree) involving 80-89% of body surface with third degree burn of 70-79%
948.88 Burn (any degree) involving 80-89% of body surface with third degree burn of 80-89%
959.01 Head injury, unspecified
959.09 Injury of face and neck, other and unspecified
996.52 Mechanical complication due to other tissue graft, not elsewhere classified
998.30 Disruption of wound, unspecified
998.32 Disruption of external operation (surgical) wound
998.33 Disruption of traumatic injury wound repair
998.59 Other postoperative infection — (Use additional code to identify infection)
998.83 Non-healing surgical wound
V10.02 Personal history of malignant neoplasm of other and unspecified parts of oral cavity and pharynx
V51.8 Other aftercare involving the use of plastic surgery

ICD-9-CM Procedural

08.61 Reconstruction of eyelid with skin flap or graft
16.63 Revision of enucleation socket with graft
21.89 Other repair and plastic operations on nose
27.55 Full-thickness skin graft to lip and mouth
86.63 Full-thickness skin graft to other sites

15271-15274

15271 Application of skin substitute graft to trunk, arms, legs, total wound surface area up to 100 sq cm; first 25 sq cm or less wound surface area
15272 each additional 25 sq cm wound surface area, or part thereof (List separately in addition to code for primary procedure)
15273 Application of skin substitute graft to trunk, arms, legs, total wound surface area greater than or equal to 100 sq cm; first 100 sq cm wound surface area, or 1% of body area of infants and children
15274 each additional 100 sq cm wound surface area, or part thereof, or each additional 1% of body area of infants and children, or part thereof (List separately in addition to code for primary procedure)

ICD-9-CM Diagnostic

The application of this code is too broad to adequately present ICD-9-CM diagnostic code links here. Refer to your ICD-9-CM book.

ICD-9-CM Procedural

86.60 Free skin graft, not otherwise specified
86.65 Heterograft to skin
86.67 Dermal regenerative graft
86.69 Other skin graft to other sites

HCPCS Level II Supplies & Services

A4305 Disposable drug delivery system, flow rate of 50 ml or greater per hour
A4306 Disposable drug delivery system, flow rate of less than 50 ml per hour
C9358 Dermal substitute, native, nondenatured collagen, fetal bovine origin (SurgiMend Collagen Matrix), per 0.5 sq cm
C9360 Dermal substitute, native, nondenatured collagen, neonatal bovine origin (SurgiMend Collagen Matrix), per 0.5 sq cm
C9363 Skin substitute (Integra Meshed Bilayer Wound Matrix), per square cm
C9364 Porcine implant, Permacol, per sq cm
Q4100 Skin substitute, not otherwise specified
Q4101 Apligraf, per sq cm
Q4102 Oasis wound matrix, per sq cm
Q4104 Integra bilayer matrix wound dressing (BMWD), per sq cm
Q4105 Integra dermal regeneration template (DRT), per sq cm
Q4106 Dermagraft, per sq cm
Q4107 GRAFTJACKET, per sq cm
Q4108 Integra matrix, per sq cm
Q4110 PriMatrix, per sq cm
Q4111 GammaGraft, per sq cm
Q4115 AlloSkin, per sq cm
Q4116 AlloDerm, per sq cm
Q4117 HYALOMATRIX, per sq cm
Q4118 MatriStem micromatrix, 1 mg
Q4119 MatriStem Wound Matrix, PSMX, RS, or PSM, per sq cm
Q4120 MatriStem burn matrix, per sq cm
Q4121 TheraSkin, per sq cm
Q4122 DermACELL, per sq cm
Q4123 AlloSkin RT, per sq cm
Q4124 OASIS ultra tri-layer wound matrix, per sq cm
Q4125 Arthroflex, per sq cm
Q4126 MemoDerm, DermaSpan, TranZgraft or InteguPly, per sq cm
Q4127 Talymed, per sq cm
Q4128 FlexHD, AllopatchHD, or Matrix HD, per sq cm
Q4129 Unite biomatrix, per sq cm
Q4130 Strattice TM, per sq cm
Q4131 EpiFix, per sq cm
Q4132 Grafix core, per sq cm
Q4133 Grafix prime, per sq cm
Q4134 hMatrix, per sq cm
Q4135 Mediskin, per sq cm

Q4136 E-Z Derm, per sq cm

15275-15278

15275 Application of skin substitute graft to face, scalp, eyelids, mouth, neck, ears, orbits, genitalia, hands, feet, and/or multiple digits, total wound surface area up to 100 sq cm; first 25 sq cm or less wound surface area

15276 each additional 25 sq cm wound surface area, or part thereof (List separately in addition to code for primary procedure)

15277 Application of skin substitute graft to face, scalp, eyelids, mouth, neck, ears, orbits, genitalia, hands, feet, and/or multiple digits, total wound surface area greater than or equal to 100 sq cm; first 100 sq cm wound surface area, or 1% of body area of infants and children

15278 each additional 100 sq cm wound surface area, or part thereof, or each additional 1% of body area of infants and children, or part thereof (List separately in addition to code for primary procedure)

ICD-9-CM Diagnostic

The application of this code is too broad to adequately present ICD-9-CM diagnostic code links here. Refer to your ICD-9-CM book.

ICD-9-CM Procedural

08.61 Reconstruction of eyelid with skin flap or graft
16.63 Revision of enucleation socket with graft
16.65 Secondary graft to exenteration cavity
18.6 Reconstruction of external auditory canal
18.79 Other plastic repair of external ear
21.86 Limited rhinoplasty
21.89 Other repair and plastic operations on nose
27.56 Other skin graft to lip and mouth
61.49 Other repair of scrotum and tunica vaginalis ♂
64.44 Reconstruction of penis ♂
64.49 Other repair of penis ♂
70.79 Other repair of vagina ♀
71.79 Other repair of vulva and perineum ♀
86.67 Dermal regenerative graft

HCPCS Level II Supplies & Services

A4305 Disposable drug delivery system, flow rate of 50 ml or greater per hour
A4306 Disposable drug delivery system, flow rate of less than 50 ml per hour
C9358 Dermal substitute, native, nondenatured collagen, fetal bovine origin (SurgiMend Collagen Matrix), per 0.5 sq cm
C9360 Dermal substitute, native, nondenatured collagen, neonatal bovine origin (SurgiMend Collagen Matrix), per 0.5 sq cm
C9363 Skin substitute (Integra Meshed Bilayer Wound Matrix), per square cm
C9364 Porcine implant, Permacol, per sq cm
Q4100 Skin substitute, not otherwise specified
Q4101 Apligraf, per sq cm
Q4102 Oasis wound matrix, per sq cm
Q4104 Integra bilayer matrix wound dressing (BMWD), per sq cm
Q4105 Integra dermal regeneration template (DRT), per sq cm
Q4106 Dermagraft, per sq cm
Q4107 GRAFTJACKET, per sq cm
Q4108 Integra matrix, per sq cm
Q4110 PriMatrix, per sq cm
Q4111 GammaGraft, per sq cm
Q4115 AlloSkin, per sq cm
Q4116 AlloDerm, per sq cm
Q4117 HYALOMATRIX, per sq cm
Q4118 MatriStem micromatrix, 1 mg
Q4119 MatriStem Wound Matrix, PSMX, RS, or PSM, per sq cm
Q4120 MatriStem burn matrix, per sq cm
Q4121 TheraSkin, per sq cm
Q4122 DermACELL, per sq cm
Q4123 AlloSkin RT, per sq cm
Q4124 OASIS ultra tri-layer wound matrix, per sq cm
Q4125 Arthroflex, per sq cm
Q4126 MemoDerm, DermaSpan, TranZgraft or InteguPly, per sq cm
Q4127 Talymed, per sq cm
Q4128 FlexHD, AllopatchHD, or Matrix HD, per sq cm
Q4129 Unite biomatrix, per sq cm
Q4131 EpiFix, per sq cm
Q4132 Grafix core, per sq cm
Q4133 Grafix prime, per sq cm
Q4134 hMatrix, per sq cm
Q4135 Mediskin, per sq cm
Q4136 E-Z Derm, per sq cm

15570

15570 Formation of direct or tubed pedicle, with or without transfer; trunk

ICD-9-CM Diagnostic

171.4 Malignant neoplasm of connective and other soft tissue of thorax
171.6 Malignant neoplasm of connective and other soft tissue of pelvis
171.7 Malignant neoplasm of connective and other soft tissue of trunk, unspecified site ▽
171.8 Malignant neoplasm of other specified sites of connective and other soft tissue
172.5 Malignant melanoma of skin of trunk, except scrotum
173.50 Unspecified malignant neoplasm of skin of trunk, except scrotum ▽
173.51 Basal cell carcinoma of skin of trunk, except scrotum
173.52 Squamous cell carcinoma of skin of trunk, except scrotum
173.59 Other specified malignant neoplasm of skin of trunk, except scrotum
174.0 Malignant neoplasm of nipple and areola of female breast — (Use additional code to identify estrogen receptor status: V86.0-V86.1) ♀
174.1 Malignant neoplasm of central portion of female breast — (Use additional code to identify estrogen receptor status: V86.0-V86.1) ♀
174.2 Malignant neoplasm of upper-inner quadrant of female breast — (Use additional code to identify estrogen receptor status: V86.0-V86.1) ♀
174.3 Malignant neoplasm of lower-inner quadrant of female breast — (Use additional code to identify estrogen receptor status: V86.0-V86.1) ♀
174.4 Malignant neoplasm of upper-outer quadrant of female breast — (Use additional code to identify estrogen receptor status: V86.0-V86.1) ♀
174.5 Malignant neoplasm of lower-outer quadrant of female breast — (Use additional code to identify estrogen receptor status: V86.0-V86.1) ♀
174.6 Malignant neoplasm of axillary tail of female breast — (Use additional code to identify estrogen receptor status: V86.0-V86.1) ♀
174.8 Malignant neoplasm of other specified sites of female breast — (Use additional code to identify estrogen receptor status: V86.0-V86.1) ♀
175.9 Malignant neoplasm of other and unspecified sites of male breast — (Use additional code to identify estrogen receptor status: V86.0-V86.1) ▽ ♂
198.81 Secondary malignant neoplasm of breast
209.35 Merkel cell carcinoma of the trunk
209.75 Secondary Merkel cell carcinoma
233.0 Carcinoma in situ of breast
238.3 Neoplasm of uncertain behavior of breast
239.2 Neoplasms of unspecified nature of bone, soft tissue, and skin
239.3 Neoplasm of unspecified nature of breast
519.2 Mediastinitis — (Use additional code to identify infectious organism)
682.2 Cellulitis and abscess of trunk — (Use additional code to identify organism, such as 041.1, etc.)
682.5 Cellulitis and abscess of buttock — (Use additional code to identify organism, such as 041.1, etc.)
707.00 Pressure ulcer, unspecified site — (Use additional code to identify pressure ulcer stage: 707.20-707.25) ▽

707.02	Pressure ulcer, upper back — (Use additional code to identify pressure ulcer stage: 707.20-707.25)
707.03	Pressure ulcer, lower back — (Use additional code to identify pressure ulcer stage: 707.20-707.25)
707.04	Pressure ulcer, hip — (Use additional code to identify pressure ulcer stage: 707.20-707.25)
707.05	Pressure ulcer, buttock — (Use additional code to identify pressure ulcer stage: 707.20-707.25)
707.09	Pressure ulcer, other site — (Use additional code to identify pressure ulcer stage: 707.20-707.25)
707.20	Pressure ulcer, unspecified stage — (Code first site of pressure ulcer: 707.00-707.09)
707.21	Pressure ulcer, stage I — (Code first site of pressure ulcer: 707.00-707.09)
707.22	Pressure ulcer stage II — (Code first site of pressure ulcer: 707.00-707.09)
707.23	Pressure ulcer stage III — (Code first site of pressure ulcer: 707.00-707.09)
707.24	Pressure ulcer stage IV — (Code first site of pressure ulcer: 707.00-707.09)
707.25	Pressure ulcer, unstageable — (Code first site of pressure ulcer: 707.00-707.09)
707.8	Chronic ulcer of other specified site
709.2	Scar condition and fibrosis of skin
738.3	Acquired deformity of chest and rib
741.00	Spina bifida with hydrocephalus, unspecified region
754.81	Pectus excavatum
875.0	Open wound of chest (wall), without mention of complication
875.1	Open wound of chest (wall), complicated
876.0	Open wound of back, without mention of complication
876.1	Open wound of back, complicated
877.0	Open wound of buttock, without mention of complication
877.1	Open wound of buttock, complicated
879.0	Open wound of breast, without mention of complication
879.1	Open wound of breast, complicated
879.2	Open wound of abdominal wall, anterior, without mention of complication
879.3	Open wound of abdominal wall, anterior, complicated
879.4	Open wound of abdominal wall, lateral, without mention of complication
879.5	Open wound of abdominal wall, lateral, complicated
879.6	Open wound of other and unspecified parts of trunk, without mention of complication
879.7	Open wound of other and unspecified parts of trunk, complicated
942.30	Full-thickness skin loss due to burn (third degree NOS) of unspecified site of trunk
942.31	Full-thickness skin loss due to burn (third degree NOS) of breast
942.33	Full-thickness skin loss due to burn (third degree NOS) of abdominal wall
942.34	Full-thickness skin loss due to burn (third degree NOS) of back (any part)
942.39	Full-thickness skin loss due to burn (third degree NOS) of other and multiple sites of trunk
942.40	Deep necrosis of underlying tissues due to burn (deep third degree) of trunk, unspecified site, without mention of loss of a body part
942.41	Deep necrosis of underlying tissues due to burn (deep third degree) of breast, without mention of loss of a body part
942.42	Deep necrosis of underlying tissues due to burn (deep third degree) of chest wall, excluding breast and nipple, without mention of loss of a body part
942.43	Deep necrosis of underlying tissues due to burn (deep third degree) of abdominal wall, without mention of loss of a body part
942.44	Deep necrosis of underlying tissues due to burn (deep third degree) of back (any part), without mention of loss of a body part
942.49	Deep necrosis of underlying tissues due to burn (deep third degree) of other and multiple sites of trunk, without mention of loss of a body part
942.50	Deep necrosis of underlying tissues due to burn (deep third degree) of unspecified site of trunk, with loss of a body part
942.51	Deep necrosis of underlying tissues due to burn (deep third degree) of breast, with loss of a body part
942.52	Deep necrosis of underlying tissues due to burn (deep third degree) of chest wall, excluding breast and nipple, with loss of a body part
942.53	Deep necrosis of underlying tissues due to burn (deep third degree) of abdominal wall with loss of a body part
942.54	Deep necrosis of underlying tissues due to burn (deep third degree) of back (any part), with loss of a body part
942.59	Deep necrosis of underlying tissues due to burn (deep third degree) of other and multiple sites of trunk, with loss of a body part
V51.8	Other aftercare involving the use of plastic surgery

ICD-9-CM Procedural

86.71	Cutting and preparation of pedicle grafts or flaps
86.74	Attachment of pedicle or flap graft to other sites

15572

15572 Formation of direct or tubed pedicle, with or without transfer; scalp, arms, or legs

ICD-9-CM Diagnostic

171.0	Malignant neoplasm of connective and other soft tissue of head, face, and neck
171.2	Malignant neoplasm of connective and other soft tissue of upper limb, including shoulder
171.3	Malignant neoplasm of connective and other soft tissue of lower limb, including hip
172.4	Malignant melanoma of skin of scalp and neck
173.40	Unspecified malignant neoplasm of scalp and skin of neck
173.41	Basal cell carcinoma of scalp and skin of neck
173.42	Squamous cell carcinoma of scalp and skin of neck
173.49	Other specified malignant neoplasm of scalp and skin of neck
173.60	Unspecified malignant neoplasm of skin of upper limb, including shoulder
173.61	Basal cell carcinoma of skin of upper limb, including shoulder
173.62	Squamous cell carcinoma of skin of upper limb, including shoulder
173.69	Other specified malignant neoplasm of skin of upper limb, including shoulder
173.70	Unspecified malignant neoplasm of skin of lower limb, including hip
173.71	Basal cell carcinoma of skin of lower limb, including hip
173.72	Squamous cell carcinoma of skin of lower limb, including hip
173.79	Other specified malignant neoplasm of skin of lower limb, including hip
209.32	Merkel cell carcinoma of the scalp and neck
209.33	Merkel cell carcinoma of the upper limb
209.34	Merkel cell carcinoma of the lower limb
209.75	Secondary Merkel cell carcinoma
216.4	Benign neoplasm of scalp and skin of neck
232.4	Carcinoma in situ of scalp and skin of neck
238.1	Neoplasm of uncertain behavior of connective and other soft tissue
238.2	Neoplasm of uncertain behavior of skin
239.2	Neoplasms of unspecified nature of bone, soft tissue, and skin
682.3	Cellulitis and abscess of upper arm and forearm — (Use additional code to identify organism, such as 041.1, etc.)
682.6	Cellulitis and abscess of leg, except foot — (Use additional code to identify organism, such as 041.1, etc.)
682.8	Cellulitis and abscess of other specified site — (Use additional code to identify organism, such as 041.1, etc.)
701.4	Keloid scar
707.00	Pressure ulcer, unspecified site — (Use additional code to identify pressure ulcer stage: 707.20-707.25)
707.01	Pressure ulcer, elbow — (Use additional code to identify pressure ulcer stage: 707.20-707.25)
707.06	Pressure ulcer, ankle — (Use additional code to identify pressure ulcer stage: 707.20-707.25)
707.07	Pressure ulcer, heel — (Use additional code to identify pressure ulcer stage: 707.20-707.25)
707.09	Pressure ulcer, other site — (Use additional code to identify pressure ulcer stage: 707.20-707.25)

707.10 Ulcer of lower limb, unspecified — (Code, if applicable, any causal condition first: 249.80-249.81, 250.80-250.83, 440.23, 459.11, 459.13, 459.31, 459.33) ▽
707.11 Ulcer of thigh — (Code, if applicable, any causal condition first: 249.80-249.81, 250.80-250.83, 440.23, 459.11, 459.13, 459.31, 459.33)
707.12 Ulcer of calf — (Code, if applicable, any causal condition first: 249.80-249.81, 250.80-250.83, 440.23, 459.11, 459.13, 459.31, 459.33)
707.13 Ulcer of ankle — (Code, if applicable, any causal condition first: 249.80-249.81, 250.80-250.83, 440.23, 459.11, 459.13, 459.31, 459.33)
707.19 Ulcer of other part of lower limb — (Code, if applicable, any causal condition first: 249.80-249.81, 250.80-250.83, 440.23, 459.11, 459.13, 459.31, 459.33)
707.20 Pressure ulcer, unspecified stage — (Code first site of pressure ulcer: 707.00-707.09) ▽
707.21 Pressure ulcer, stage I — (Code first site of pressure ulcer: 707.00-707.09)
707.22 Pressure ulcer stage II — (Code first site of pressure ulcer: 707.00-707.09)
707.23 Pressure ulcer stage III — (Code first site of pressure ulcer: 707.00-707.09)
707.24 Pressure ulcer stage IV — (Code first site of pressure ulcer: 707.00-707.09)
707.25 Pressure ulcer, unstageable — (Code first site of pressure ulcer: 707.00-707.09)
707.8 Chronic ulcer of other specified site
709.2 Scar condition and fibrosis of skin
754.0 Congenital musculoskeletal deformities of skull, face, and jaw
873.0 Open wound of scalp, without mention of complication
873.1 Open wound of scalp, complicated
880.12 Open wound of axillary region, complicated
880.13 Open wound of upper arm, complicated
880.19 Open wound of multiple sites of shoulder and upper arm, complicated
880.20 Open wound of shoulder region, with tendon involvement
880.21 Open wound of scapular region, with tendon involvement
880.22 Open wound of axillary region, with tendon involvement
880.23 Open wound of upper arm, with tendon involvement
880.29 Open wound of multiple sites of shoulder and upper arm, with tendon involvement
881.11 Open wound of elbow, complicated
881.12 Open wound of wrist, complicated
881.20 Open wound of forearm, with tendon involvement
881.21 Open wound of elbow, with tendon involvement
881.22 Open wound of wrist, with tendon involvement
884.1 Multiple and unspecified open wound of upper limb, complicated
884.2 Multiple and unspecified open wound of upper limb, with tendon involvement
890.1 Open wound of hip and thigh, complicated
890.2 Open wound of hip and thigh, with tendon involvement
891.1 Open wound of knee, leg (except thigh), and ankle, complicated
891.2 Open wound of knee, leg (except thigh), and ankle, with tendon involvement
894.1 Multiple and unspecified open wound of lower limb, complicated
894.2 Multiple and unspecified open wound of lower limb, with tendon involvement
906.0 Late effect of open wound of head, neck, and trunk
906.5 Late effect of burn of eye, face, head, and neck
941.36 Full-thickness skin loss due to burn (third degree NOS) of scalp (any part)
941.46 Deep necrosis of underlying tissues due to burn (deep third degree) of scalp (any part), without mention of loss of a body part
941.56 Deep necrosis of underlying tissues due to burn (deep third degree) of scalp (any part), with loss of a body part
943.30 Full-thickness skin loss due to burn (third degree NOS) of unspecified site of upper limb ▽
943.31 Full-thickness skin loss due to burn (third degree NOS) of forearm
943.32 Full-thickness skin loss due to burn (third degree NOS) of elbow
943.33 Full-thickness skin loss due to burn (third degree NOS) of upper arm
943.39 Full-thickness skin loss due to burn (third degree NOS) of multiple sites of upper limb, except wrist and hand
944.40 Deep necrosis of underlying tissues due to burn (deep third degree) of unspecified site of hand, without mention of loss of a body part ▽
944.41 Deep necrosis of underlying tissues due to burn (deep third degree) of single digit [finger (nail)] other than thumb, without mention of loss of a body part
944.42 Deep necrosis of underlying tissues due to burn (deep third degree) of thumb (nail), without mention of loss of a body part
944.43 Deep necrosis of underlying tissues due to burn (deep third degree) of two or more digits of hand, not including thumb, without mention of loss of a body part
945.30 Full-thickness skin loss due to burn (third degree NOS) of unspecified site of lower limb ▽
945.33 Full-thickness skin loss due to burn (third degree NOS) of ankle
945.34 Full-thickness skin loss due to burn (third degree NOS) of lower leg
945.35 Full-thickness skin loss due to burn (third degree NOS) of knee
945.36 Full-thickness skin loss due to burn (third degree NOS) of thigh (any part)
945.39 Full-thickness skin loss due to burn (third degree NOS) of multiple sites of lower limb(s)
945.40 Deep necrosis of underlying tissues due to burn (deep third degree) of unspecified site of lower limb (leg), without mention of loss of a body part ▽
945.43 Deep necrosis of underlying tissues due to burn (deep third degree) of ankle, without mention of loss of a body part
945.44 Deep necrosis of underlying tissues due to burn (deep third degree) of lower leg, without mention of loss of a body part
945.45 Deep necrosis of underlying tissues due to burn (deep third degree) of knee, without mention of loss of a body part
945.46 Deep necrosis of underlying tissues due to burn (deep third degree) of thigh (any part), without mention of loss of a body part
945.49 Deep necrosis of underlying tissues due to burn (deep third degree) of multiple sites of lower limb(s), without mention of loss of a body part
V51.8 Other aftercare involving the use of plastic surgery

ICD-9-CM Procedural

86.71 Cutting and preparation of pedicle grafts or flaps
86.74 Attachment of pedicle or flap graft to other sites

15574

15574 Formation of direct or tubed pedicle, with or without transfer; forehead, cheeks, chin, mouth, neck, axillae, genitalia, hands or feet

ICD-9-CM Diagnostic

145.0 Malignant neoplasm of cheek mucosa
171.0 Malignant neoplasm of connective and other soft tissue of head, face, and neck
171.2 Malignant neoplasm of connective and other soft tissue of upper limb, including shoulder
171.3 Malignant neoplasm of connective and other soft tissue of lower limb, including hip
171.4 Malignant neoplasm of connective and other soft tissue of thorax
172.3 Malignant melanoma of skin of other and unspecified parts of face ▽
172.4 Malignant melanoma of skin of scalp and neck
173.30 Unspecified malignant neoplasm of skin of other and unspecified parts of face ▽
173.31 Basal cell carcinoma of skin of other and unspecified parts of face
173.32 Squamous cell carcinoma of skin of other and unspecified parts of face
173.39 Other specified malignant neoplasm of skin of other and unspecified parts of face
173.40 Unspecified malignant neoplasm of scalp and skin of neck ▽
173.41 Basal cell carcinoma of scalp and skin of neck
173.42 Squamous cell carcinoma of scalp and skin of neck
173.49 Other specified malignant neoplasm of scalp and skin of neck
173.50 Unspecified malignant neoplasm of skin of trunk, except scrotum ▽
173.51 Basal cell carcinoma of skin of trunk, except scrotum
173.52 Squamous cell carcinoma of skin of trunk, except scrotum
173.59 Other specified malignant neoplasm of skin of trunk, except scrotum
173.60 Unspecified malignant neoplasm of skin of upper limb, including shoulder ▽
173.61 Basal cell carcinoma of skin of upper limb, including shoulder
173.62 Squamous cell carcinoma of skin of upper limb, including shoulder
173.69 Other specified malignant neoplasm of skin of upper limb, including shoulder

173.70 Unspecified malignant neoplasm of skin of lower limb, including hip ▽
173.71 Basal cell carcinoma of skin of lower limb, including hip
173.72 Squamous cell carcinoma of skin of lower limb, including hip
173.79 Other specified malignant neoplasm of skin of lower limb, including hip
195.0 Malignant neoplasm of head, face, and neck
195.3 Malignant neoplasm of pelvis
195.4 Malignant neoplasm of upper limb
198.89 Secondary malignant neoplasm of other specified sites
209.31 Merkel cell carcinoma of the face
209.32 Merkel cell carcinoma of the scalp and neck
209.33 Merkel cell carcinoma of the upper limb
209.34 Merkel cell carcinoma of the lower limb
209.35 Merkel cell carcinoma of the trunk
209.36 Merkel cell carcinoma of other sites
209.75 Secondary Merkel cell carcinoma
210.3 Benign neoplasm of floor of mouth
210.4 Benign neoplasm of other and unspecified parts of mouth ▽
216.8 Benign neoplasm of other specified sites of skin
221.2 Benign neoplasm of vulva ♀
222.1 Benign neoplasm of penis ♂
222.4 Benign neoplasm of scrotum ♂
230.0 Carcinoma in situ of lip, oral cavity, and pharynx
233.30 Carcinoma in situ, unspecified female genital organ ▽ ♀
233.31 Carcinoma in situ, vagina ♀
233.32 Carcinoma in situ, vulva ♀
233.39 Carcinoma in situ, other female genital organ ♀
233.5 Carcinoma in situ of penis ♂
233.6 Carcinoma in situ of other and unspecified male genital organs ▽ ♂
235.1 Neoplasm of uncertain behavior of lip, oral cavity, and pharynx
236.3 Neoplasm of uncertain behavior of other and unspecified female genital organs ▽ ♀
236.6 Neoplasm of uncertain behavior of other and unspecified male genital organs ▽ ♂
239.0 Neoplasm of unspecified nature of digestive system
239.2 Neoplasms of unspecified nature of bone, soft tissue, and skin
249.70 Secondary diabetes mellitus with peripheral circulatory disorders, not stated as uncontrolled, or unspecified — (Use additional code to identify manifestation: 443.81, 785.4) (Use additional code to identify any associated insulin use: V58.67)
249.71 Secondary diabetes mellitus with peripheral circulatory disorders, uncontrolled — (Use additional code to identify manifestation: 443.81, 785.4) (Use additional code to identify any associated insulin use: V58.67)
249.80 Secondary diabetes mellitus with other specified manifestations, not stated as uncontrolled, or unspecified — (Use additional code to identify manifestation: 707.10-707.19, 707.8, 707.9, 731.8) (Use additional code to identify any associated insulin use: V58.67)
249.81 Secondary diabetes mellitus with other specified manifestations, uncontrolled — (Use additional code to identify manifestation: 707.10-707.19, 707.8, 707.9, 731.8) (Use additional code to identify any associated insulin use: V58.67)
249.90 Secondary diabetes mellitus with unspecified complication, not stated as uncontrolled, or unspecified — (Use additional code to identify any associated insulin use: V58.67) ▽
249.91 Secondary diabetes mellitus with unspecified complication, uncontrolled — (Use additional code to identify any associated insulin use: V58.67) ▽
250.80 Diabetes with other specified manifestations, type II or unspecified type, not stated as uncontrolled — (Use additional code to identify manifestation: 707.10-707.19, 707.8, 707.9, 731.8)
250.81 Diabetes with other specified manifestations, type I [juvenile type], not stated as uncontrolled — (Use additional code to identify manifestation: 707.10-707.19, 707.8, 707.9, 731.8)
250.82 Diabetes with other specified manifestations, type II or unspecified type, uncontrolled — (Use additional code to identify manifestation: 707.10-707.19, 707.8, 707.9, 731.8)
250.83 Diabetes with other specified manifestations, type I [juvenile type], uncontrolled — (Use additional code to identify manifestation: 707.10-707.19, 707.8, 707.9, 731.8)
440.23 Atherosclerosis of native arteries of the extremities with ulceration — (Use additional code for any associated ulceration: 707.10-707.19, 707.8, 707.9)
459.11 Postphlebitic syndrome with ulcer
459.13 Postphlebitic syndrome with ulcer and inflammation
459.31 Chronic venous hypertension with ulcer
459.33 Chronic venous hypertension with ulcer and inflammation
629.20 Female genital mutilation status, unspecified ▽ ♀
629.21 Female genital mutilation, Type I status ♀
629.22 Female genital mutilation, Type II status ♀
629.23 Female genital mutilation, Type III status ♀
629.29 Other female genital mutilation status ♀
629.89 Other specified disorders of female genital organs ♀
682.0 Cellulitis and abscess of face — (Use additional code to identify organism, such as 041.1, etc.)
682.1 Cellulitis and abscess of neck — (Use additional code to identify organism, such as 041.1, etc.)
682.4 Cellulitis and abscess of hand, except fingers and thumb — (Use additional code to identify organism, such as 041.1, etc.)
682.7 Cellulitis and abscess of foot, except toes — (Use additional code to identify organism, such as 041.1, etc.)
707.00 Pressure ulcer, unspecified site — (Use additional code to identify pressure ulcer stage: 707.20-707.25) ▽
707.07 Pressure ulcer, heel — (Use additional code to identify pressure ulcer stage: 707.20-707.25)
707.09 Pressure ulcer, other site — (Use additional code to identify pressure ulcer stage: 707.20-707.25)
707.14 Ulcer of heel and midfoot — (Code, if applicable, any causal condition first: 249.80-249.81, 250.80-250.83, 440.23, 459.11, 459.13, 459.31, 459.33)
707.15 Ulcer of other part of foot — (Code, if applicable, any causal condition first: 249.80-249.81, 250.80-250.83, 440.23, 459.11, 459.13, 459.31, 459.33)
707.20 Pressure ulcer, unspecified stage — (Code first site of pressure ulcer: 707.00-707.09) ▽
707.21 Pressure ulcer, stage I — (Code first site of pressure ulcer: 707.00-707.09)
707.22 Pressure ulcer stage II — (Code first site of pressure ulcer: 707.00-707.09)
707.23 Pressure ulcer stage III — (Code first site of pressure ulcer: 707.00-707.09)
707.24 Pressure ulcer stage IV — (Code first site of pressure ulcer: 707.00-707.09)
707.25 Pressure ulcer, unstageable — (Code first site of pressure ulcer: 707.00-707.09)
709.2 Scar condition and fibrosis of skin
741.01 Spina bifida with hydrocephalus, cervical region
741.91 Spina bifida without mention of hydrocephalus, cervical region
754.0 Congenital musculoskeletal deformities of skull, face, and jaw
754.1 Congenital musculoskeletal deformity of sternocleidomastoid muscle
873.20 Open wound of nose, unspecified site, without mention of complication ▽
873.30 Open wound of nose, unspecified site, complicated ▽
873.41 Open wound of cheek, without mention of complication
873.42 Open wound of forehead, without mention of complication
873.43 Open wound of lip, without mention of complication
873.44 Open wound of jaw, without mention of complication
873.49 Open wound of face, other and multiple sites, without mention of complication
873.51 Open wound of cheek, complicated
873.52 Open wound of forehead, complicated
873.53 Open wound of lip, complicated
873.54 Open wound of jaw, complicated
873.59 Open wound of face, other and multiple sites, complicated
873.70 Open wound of mouth, unspecified site, complicated ▽
873.71 Open wound of buccal mucosa, complicated
873.79 Open wound of mouth, other and multiple sites, complicated

874.8 Open wound of other and unspecified parts of neck, without mention of complication 🅤

874.9 Open wound of other and unspecified parts of neck, complicated 🅤

878.0 Open wound of penis, without mention of complication ♂

878.1 Open wound of penis, complicated ♂

878.2 Open wound of scrotum and testes, without mention of complication ♂

878.3 Open wound of scrotum and testes, complicated ♂

878.4 Open wound of vulva, without mention of complication ♀

878.5 Open wound of vulva, complicated ♀

878.7 Open wound of vagina, complicated ♀

878.8 Open wound of other and unspecified parts of genital organs, without mention of complication 🅤

878.9 Open wound of other and unspecified parts of genital organs, complicated 🅤

882.0 Open wound of hand except finger(s) alone, without mention of complication

882.1 Open wound of hand except finger(s) alone, complicated

882.2 Open wound of hand except finger(s) alone, with tendon involvement

883.0 Open wound of finger(s), without mention of complication

883.1 Open wound of finger(s), complicated

883.2 Open wound of finger(s), with tendon involvement

885.0 Traumatic amputation of thumb (complete) (partial), without mention of complication

885.1 Traumatic amputation of thumb (complete) (partial), complicated

886.0 Traumatic amputation of other finger(s) (complete) (partial), without mention of complication

886.1 Traumatic amputation of other finger(s) (complete) (partial), complicated

887.0 Traumatic amputation of arm and hand (complete) (partial), unilateral, below elbow, without mention of complication

887.1 Traumatic amputation of arm and hand (complete) (partial), unilateral, below elbow, complicated

887.4 Traumatic amputation of arm and hand (complete) (partial), unilateral, level not specified, without mention of complication 🅤

887.5 Traumatic amputation of arm and hand (complete) (partial), unilateral, level not specified, complicated 🅤

887.6 Traumatic amputation of arm and hand (complete) (partial), bilateral (any level), without mention of complication

887.7 Traumatic amputation of arm and hand (complete) (partial), bilateral (any level), complicated

892.0 Open wound of foot except toe(s) alone, without mention of complication

892.1 Open wound of foot except toe(s) alone, complicated

892.2 Open wound of foot except toe(s) alone, with tendon involvement

893.0 Open wound of toe(s), without mention of complication

893.1 Open wound of toe(s), complicated

893.2 Open wound of toe(s), with tendon involvement

895.0 Traumatic amputation of toe(s) (complete) (partial), without mention of complication

895.1 Traumatic amputation of toe(s) (complete) (partial), complicated

896.0 Traumatic amputation of foot (complete) (partial), unilateral, without mention of complication

896.1 Traumatic amputation of foot (complete) (partial), unilateral, complicated

896.2 Traumatic amputation of foot (complete) (partial), bilateral, without mention of complication

906.0 Late effect of open wound of head, neck, and trunk

906.1 Late effect of open wound of extremities without mention of tendon injury

906.4 Late effect of crushing

906.5 Late effect of burn of eye, face, head, and neck

906.6 Late effect of burn of wrist and hand

906.7 Late effect of burn of other extremities

906.8 Late effect of burns of other specified sites

925.1 Crushing injury of face and scalp — (Use additional code to identify any associated injuries, such as: 800-829, 850.0-854.1, 860.0-869.1)

925.2 Crushing injury of neck — (Use additional code to identify any associated injuries, such as: 800-829, 850.0-854.1, 860.0-869.1)

926.0 Crushing injury of external genitalia — (Use additional code to identify any associated injuries: 800-829, 850.0-854.1, 860.0-869.1)

927.20 Crushing injury of hand(s) — (Use additional code to identify any associated injuries: 800-829, 850.0-854.1, 860.0-869.1)

927.21 Crushing injury of wrist — (Use additional code to identify any associated injuries: 800-829, 850.0-854.1, 860.0-869.1)

928.20 Crushing injury of foot — (Use additional code to identify any associated injuries: 800-829, 850.0-854.1, 860.0-869.1)

928.3 Crushing injury of toe(s) — (Use additional code to identify any associated injuries: 800-829, 850.0-854.1, 860.0-869.1)

928.8 Crushing injury of multiple sites of lower limb — (Use additional code to identify any associated injuries: 800-829, 850.0-854.1, 860.0-869.1)

941.30 Full-thickness skin loss due to burn (third degree NOS) of unspecified site of face and head 🅤

941.33 Full-thickness skin loss due to burn (third degree NOS) of lip(s)

941.35 Full-thickness skin loss due to burn (third degree NOS) of nose (septum)

941.37 Full-thickness skin loss due to burn (third degree NOS) of forehead and cheek

941.38 Full-thickness skin loss due to burn (third degree NOS) of neck

941.39 Full-thickness skin loss due to burn (third degree NOS) of multiple sites (except with eye) of face, head, and neck

941.40 Deep necrosis of underlying tissues due to burn (deep third degree) of unspecified site of face and head, without mention of loss of a body part 🅤

941.43 Deep necrosis of underlying tissues due to burn (deep third degree) of lip(s), without mention of loss of a body part

941.44 Deep necrosis of underlying tissues due to burn (deep third degree) of chin, without mention of loss of a body part

941.45 Deep necrosis of underlying tissues due to burn (deep third degree) of nose (septum), without mention of loss of a body part

941.47 Deep necrosis of underlying tissues due to burn (deep third degree) of forehead and cheek, without mention of loss of a body part

941.48 Deep necrosis of underlying tissues due to burn (deep third degree) of neck, without mention of loss of a body part

941.49 Deep necrosis of underlying tissues due to burn (deep third degree) of multiple sites (except with eye) of face, head, and neck, without mention of loss of a body part

941.50 Deep necrosis of underlying tissues due to burn (deep third degree) of face and head, unspecified site, with loss of a body part 🅤

941.53 Deep necrosis of underlying tissues due to burn (deep third degree) of lip(s), with loss of a body part

941.54 Deep necrosis of underlying tissues due to burn (deep third degree) of chin, with loss of a body part

941.55 Deep necrosis of underlying tissues due to burn (deep third degree) of nose (septum), with loss of a body part

941.57 Deep necrosis of underlying tissues due to burn (deep third degree) of forehead and cheek, with loss of a body part

941.58 Deep necrosis of underlying tissues due to burn (deep third degree) of neck, with loss of a body part

941.59 Deep necrosis of underlying tissues due to burn (deep third degree) of multiple sites (except eye) of face, head, and neck, with loss of a body part

942.35 Full-thickness skin loss due to burn (third degree NOS) of genitalia

942.45 Deep necrosis of underlying tissues due to burn (deep third degree) of genitalia, without mention of loss of a body part

942.52 Deep necrosis of underlying tissues due to burn (deep third degree) of chest wall, excluding breast and nipple, with loss of a body part

942.55 Deep necrosis of underlying tissues due to burn (deep third degree) of genitalia, with loss of a body part

944.30 Full-thickness skin loss due to burn (third degree NOS) of unspecified site of hand 🅤

944.31 Full-thickness skin loss due to burn (third degree NOS) of single digit [finger (nail)] other than thumb

944.32 Full-thickness skin loss due to burn (third degree NOS) of thumb (nail)

944.33 Full-thickness skin loss due to burn (third degree NOS) of two or more digits of hand, not including thumb
944.34 Full-thickness skin loss due to burn (third degree NOS) of two or more digits of hand including thumb
944.35 Full-thickness skin loss due to burn (third degree NOS) of palm of hand
944.36 Full-thickness skin loss due to burn (third degree NOS) of back of hand
944.37 Full-thickness skin loss due to burn (third degree NOS) of wrist
944.38 Full-thickness skin loss due to burn (third degree NOS) of multiple sites of wrist(s) and hand(s)
944.40 Deep necrosis of underlying tissues due to burn (deep third degree) of unspecified site of hand, without mention of loss of a body part
944.41 Deep necrosis of underlying tissues due to burn (deep third degree) of single digit [finger (nail)] other than thumb, without mention of loss of a body part
944.42 Deep necrosis of underlying tissues due to burn (deep third degree) of thumb (nail), without mention of loss of a body part
944.43 Deep necrosis of underlying tissues due to burn (deep third degree) of two or more digits of hand, not including thumb, without mention of loss of a body part
944.44 Deep necrosis of underlying tissues due to burn (deep third degree) of two or more digits of hand including thumb, without mention of loss of a body part
944.45 Deep necrosis of underlying tissues due to burn (deep third degree) of palm of hand, without mention of loss of a body part
944.46 Deep necrosis of underlying tissues due to burn (deep third degree) of back of hand, without mention of loss of a body part
944.47 Deep necrosis of underlying tissues due to burn (deep third degree) of wrist, without mention of loss of a body part
944.48 Deep necrosis of underlying tissues due to burn (deep third degree) of multiple sites of wrist(s) and hand(s), without mention of loss of a body part
944.50 Deep necrosis of underlying tissues due to burn (deep third degree) of unspecified site of hand, with loss of a body part
944.51 Deep necrosis of underlying tissues due to burn (deep third degree) of single digit (finger (nail)) other than thumb, with loss of a body part
944.52 Deep necrosis of underlying tissues due to burn (deep third degree) of thumb (nail), with loss of a body part
945.32 Full-thickness skin loss due to burn (third degree NOS) of foot
945.42 Deep necrosis of underlying tissues due to burn (deep third degree) of foot, without mention of loss of a body part
947.0 Burn of mouth and pharynx
959.09 Injury of face and neck, other and unspecified
959.14 Other injury of external genitals
997.62 Infection (chronic) of amputation stump — (Use additional code to identify complications)
997.69 Other late amputation stump complication — (Use additional code to identify complications)
998.30 Disruption of wound, unspecified
998.32 Disruption of external operation (surgical) wound
998.33 Disruption of traumatic injury wound repair
998.83 Non-healing surgical wound
V10.02 Personal history of malignant neoplasm of other and unspecified parts of oral cavity and pharynx
V10.21 Personal history of malignant neoplasm of larynx
V51.8 Other aftercare involving the use of plastic surgery

ICD-9-CM Procedural

27.57 Attachment of pedicle or flap graft to lip and mouth
71.9 Other operations on female genital organs ♀
86.71 Cutting and preparation of pedicle grafts or flaps
86.73 Attachment of pedicle or flap graft to hand
86.74 Attachment of pedicle or flap graft to other sites

15576

15576 Formation of direct or tubed pedicle, with or without transfer; eyelids, nose, ears, lips, or intraoral

ICD-9-CM Diagnostic

140.0 Malignant neoplasm of upper lip, vermilion border
140.1 Malignant neoplasm of lower lip, vermilion border
140.3 Malignant neoplasm of upper lip, inner aspect
140.4 Malignant neoplasm of lower lip, inner aspect
140.5 Malignant neoplasm of lip, inner aspect, unspecified as to upper or lower
140.6 Malignant neoplasm of commissure of lip
140.8 Malignant neoplasm of other sites of lip
140.9 Malignant neoplasm of lip, vermilion border, unspecified as to upper or lower
144.0 Malignant neoplasm of anterior portion of floor of mouth
144.1 Malignant neoplasm of lateral portion of floor of mouth
144.8 Malignant neoplasm of other sites of floor of mouth
144.9 Malignant neoplasm of floor of mouth, part unspecified
145.0 Malignant neoplasm of cheek mucosa
145.1 Malignant neoplasm of vestibule of mouth
145.2 Malignant neoplasm of hard palate
145.3 Malignant neoplasm of soft palate
145.8 Malignant neoplasm of other specified parts of mouth
145.9 Malignant neoplasm of mouth, unspecified site
172.0 Malignant melanoma of skin of lip
172.1 Malignant melanoma of skin of eyelid, including canthus
172.2 Malignant melanoma of skin of ear and external auditory canal
172.3 Malignant melanoma of skin of other and unspecified parts of face
172.8 Malignant melanoma of other specified sites of skin
173.00 Unspecified malignant neoplasm of skin of lip
173.01 Basal cell carcinoma of skin of lip
173.02 Squamous cell carcinoma of skin of lip
173.09 Other specified malignant neoplasm of skin of lip
173.10 Unspecified malignant neoplasm of eyelid, including canthus
173.11 Basal cell carcinoma of eyelid, including canthus
173.12 Squamous cell carcinoma of eyelid, including canthus
173.19 Other specified malignant neoplasm of eyelid, including canthus
173.20 Unspecified malignant neoplasm of skin of ear and external auditory canal
173.21 Basal cell carcinoma of skin of ear and external auditory canal
173.22 Squamous cell carcinoma of skin of ear and external auditory canal
173.29 Other specified malignant neoplasm of skin of ear and external auditory canal
173.30 Unspecified malignant neoplasm of skin of other and unspecified parts of face
173.31 Basal cell carcinoma of skin of other and unspecified parts of face
173.32 Squamous cell carcinoma of skin of other and unspecified parts of face
173.39 Other specified malignant neoplasm of skin of other and unspecified parts of face
173.80 Unspecified malignant neoplasm of other specified sites of skin
173.81 Basal cell carcinoma of other specified sites of skin
173.82 Squamous cell carcinoma of other specified sites of skin
173.89 Other specified malignant neoplasm of other specified sites of skin
195.0 Malignant neoplasm of head, face, and neck
198.2 Secondary malignant neoplasm of skin
209.31 Merkel cell carcinoma of the face
209.75 Secondary Merkel cell carcinoma
210.0 Benign neoplasm of lip
210.4 Benign neoplasm of other and unspecified parts of mouth
216.0 Benign neoplasm of skin of lip
216.1 Benign neoplasm of eyelid, including canthus
216.2 Benign neoplasm of ear and external auditory canal
216.3 Benign neoplasm of skin of other and unspecified parts of face
230.0 Carcinoma in situ of lip, oral cavity, and pharynx

232.1 Carcinoma in situ of eyelid, including canthus
232.2 Carcinoma in situ of skin of ear and external auditory canal
232.3 Carcinoma in situ of skin of other and unspecified parts of face ♥
235.1 Neoplasm of uncertain behavior of lip, oral cavity, and pharynx
238.1 Neoplasm of uncertain behavior of connective and other soft tissue
238.2 Neoplasm of uncertain behavior of skin
239.0 Neoplasm of unspecified nature of digestive system
239.2 Neoplasms of unspecified nature of bone, soft tissue, and skin
380.32 Acquired deformities of auricle or pinna
682.0 Cellulitis and abscess of face — (Use additional code to identify organism, such as 041.1, etc.)
709.2 Scar condition and fibrosis of skin
709.9 Unspecified disorder of skin and subcutaneous tissue ♥
743.62 Congenital deformity of eyelid
744.01 Congenital absence of external ear causing impairment of hearing
744.02 Other congenital anomaly of external ear causing impairment of hearing
744.09 Other congenital anomalies of ear causing impairment of hearing
744.23 Microtia
744.3 Unspecified congenital anomaly of ear ♥
744.5 Congenital webbing of neck
744.82 Microcheilia
748.1 Other congenital anomaly of nose
749.01 Unilateral cleft palate, complete
749.02 Unilateral cleft palate, incomplete
749.03 Bilateral cleft palate, complete
749.04 Bilateral cleft palate, incomplete
749.10 Unspecified cleft lip ♥
749.11 Unilateral cleft lip, complete
749.12 Unilateral cleft lip, incomplete
749.13 Bilateral cleft lip, complete
749.14 Bilateral cleft lip, incomplete
749.20 Unspecified cleft palate with cleft lip ♥
749.21 Unilateral cleft palate with cleft lip, complete
749.22 Unilateral cleft palate with cleft lip, incomplete
749.23 Bilateral cleft palate with cleft lip, complete
749.24 Bilateral cleft palate with cleft lip, incomplete
785.4 Gangrene — (Code first any associated underlying condition)
870.0 Laceration of skin of eyelid and periocular area
870.1 Laceration of eyelid, full-thickness, not involving lacrimal passages
870.2 Laceration of eyelid involving lacrimal passages
872.00 Open wound of external ear, unspecified site, without mention of complication ♥
872.01 Open wound of auricle, without mention of complication
872.02 Open wound of auditory canal, without mention of complication
872.10 Open wound of external ear, unspecified site, complicated ♥
872.11 Open wound of auricle, complicated
872.12 Open wound of auditory canal, complicated
872.8 Open wound of ear, part unspecified, without mention of complication ♥
872.9 Open wound of ear, part unspecified, complicated ♥
873.20 Open wound of nose, unspecified site, without mention of complication ♥
873.30 Open wound of nose, unspecified site, complicated ♥
873.31 Open wound of nasal septum, complicated
873.32 Open wound of nasal cavity, complicated
873.33 Open wound of nasal sinus, complicated
873.39 Open wound of nose, multiple sites, complicated
873.43 Open wound of lip, without mention of complication
873.53 Open wound of lip, complicated
906.0 Late effect of open wound of head, neck, and trunk
906.5 Late effect of burn of eye, face, head, and neck
941.01 Burn of unspecified degree of ear (any part) ♥
941.02 Burn of unspecified degree of eye (with other parts of face, head, and neck) ♥
941.03 Burn of unspecified degree of lip(s) ♥
941.05 Burn of unspecified degree of nose (septum) ♥
941.09 Burn of unspecified degree of multiple sites (except with eye) of face, head, and neck ♥
941.31 Full-thickness skin loss due to burn (third degree NOS) of ear (any part)
941.32 Full-thickness skin loss due to burn (third degree NOS) of eye (with other parts of face, head, and neck)
941.33 Full-thickness skin loss due to burn (third degree NOS) of lip(s)
941.35 Full-thickness skin loss due to burn (third degree NOS) of nose (septum)
941.39 Full-thickness skin loss due to burn (third degree NOS) of multiple sites (except with eye) of face, head, and neck
941.41 Deep necrosis of underlying tissues due to burn (deep third degree) of ear (any part), without mention of loss of a body part
941.45 Deep necrosis of underlying tissues due to burn (deep third degree) of nose (septum), without mention of loss of a body part
941.49 Deep necrosis of underlying tissues due to burn (deep third degree) of multiple sites (except with eye) of face, head, and neck, without mention of loss of a body part
941.51 Deep necrosis of underlying tissues due to burn (deep third degree) of ear (any part), with loss of a body part
941.52 Deep necrosis of underlying tissues due to burn (deep third degree) of eye (with other parts of face, head, and neck), with loss of a body part
941.53 Deep necrosis of underlying tissues due to burn (deep third degree) of lip(s), with loss of a body part
941.55 Deep necrosis of underlying tissues due to burn (deep third degree) of nose (septum), with loss of a body part
941.59 Deep necrosis of underlying tissues due to burn (deep third degree) of multiple sites (except eye) of face, head, and neck, with loss of a body part
946.3 Full-thickness skin loss due to burn (third degree NOS) of multiple specified sites
946.4 Deep necrosis of underlying tissues due to burn (deep third degree) of multiple specified sites, without mention of loss of a body part
946.5 Deep necrosis of underlying tissues due to burn (deep third degree) of multiple specified sites, with loss of a body part
947.0 Burn of mouth and pharynx
948.00 Burn (any degree) involving less than 10% of body surface with third degree burn of less than 10% or unspecified amount
948.10 Burn (any degree) involving 10-19% of body surface with third degree burn of less than 10% or unspecified amount
948.11 Burn (any degree) involving 10-19% of body surface with third degree burn of 10-19%
948.20 Burn (any degree) involving 20-29% of body surface with third degree burn of less than 10% or unspecified amount
948.21 Burn (any degree) involving 20-29% of body surface with third degree burn of 10-19%
948.22 Burn (any degree) involving 20-29% of body surface with third degree burn of 20-29%
948.30 Burn (any degree) involving 30-39% of body surface with third degree burn of less than 10% or unspecified amount
948.31 Burn (any degree) involving 30-39% of body surface with third degree burn of 10-19%
948.32 Burn (any degree) involving 30-39% of body surface with third degree burn of 20-29%
948.33 Burn (any degree) involving 30-39% of body surface with third degree burn of 30-39%
948.40 Burn (any degree) involving 40-49% of body surface with third degree burn of less than 10% or unspecified amount
948.41 Burn (any degree) involving 40-49% of body surface with third degree burn of 10-19%
948.42 Burn (any degree) involving 40-49% of body surface with third degree burn of 20-29%
948.43 Burn (any degree) involving 40-49% of body surface with third degree burn of 30-39%
948.44 Burn (any degree) involving 40-49% of body surface with third degree burn of 40-49%
948.50 Burn (any degree) involving 50-59% of body surface with third degree burn of less than 10% or unspecified amount
948.51 Burn (any degree) involving 50-59% of body surface with third degree burn of 10-19%
948.52 Burn (any degree) involving 50-59% of body surface with third degree burn of 20-29%
948.53 Burn (any degree) involving 50-59% of body surface with third degree burn of 30-39%
948.54 Burn (any degree) involving 50-59% of body surface with third degree burn of 40-49%
948.55 Burn (any degree) involving 50-59% of body surface with third degree burn of 50-59%

948.60 Burn (any degree) involving 60-69% of body surface with third degree burn of less than 10% or unspecified amount
948.61 Burn (any degree) involving 60-69% of body surface with third degree burn of 10-19%
948.62 Burn (any degree) involving 60-69% of body surface with third degree burn of 20-29%
948.63 Burn (any degree) involving 60-69% of body surface with third degree burn of 30-39%
948.64 Burn (any degree) involving 60-69% of body surface with third degree burn of 40-49%
948.65 Burn (any degree) involving 60-69% of body surface with third degree burn of 50-59%
948.66 Burn (any degree) involving 60-69% of body surface with third degree burn of 60-69%
948.70 Burn (any degree) involving 70-79% of body surface with third degree burn of less than 10% or unspecified amount
948.71 Burn (any degree) involving 70-79% of body surface with third degree burn of 10-19%
948.72 Burn (any degree) involving 70-79% of body surface with third degree burn of 20-29%
948.73 Burn (any degree) involving 70-79% of body surface with third degree burn of 30-39%
948.74 Burn (any degree) involving 70-79% of body surface with third degree burn of 40-49%
948.75 Burn (any degree) involving 70-79% of body surface with third degree burn of 50-59%
948.76 Burn (any degree) involving 70-79% of body surface with third degree burn of 60-69%
948.77 Burn (any degree) involving 70-79% of body surface with third degree burn of 70-79%
948.80 Burn (any degree) involving 80-89% of body surface with third degree burn of less than 10% or unspecified amount
948.81 Burn (any degree) involving 80-89% of body surface with third degree burn of 10-19%
948.82 Burn (any degree) involving 80-89% of body surface with third degree burn of 20-29%
948.83 Burn (any degree) involving 80-89% of body surface with third degree burn of 30-39%
948.84 Burn (any degree) involving 80-89% of body surface with third degree burn of 40-49%
948.85 Burn (any degree) involving 80-89% of body surface with third degree burn of 50-59%
948.86 Burn (any degree) involving 80-89% of body surface with third degree burn of 60-69%
948.87 Burn (any degree) involving 80-89% of body surface with third degree burn of 70-79%
948.88 Burn (any degree) involving 80-89% of body surface with third degree burn of 80-89%
959.09 Injury of face and neck, other and unspecified
996.52 Mechanical complication due to other tissue graft, not elsewhere classified
998.30 Disruption of wound, unspecified ▽
998.32 Disruption of external operation (surgical) wound
998.33 Disruption of traumatic injury wound repair
998.59 Other postoperative infection — (Use additional code to identify infection)
998.83 Non-healing surgical wound
V10.02 Personal history of malignant neoplasm of other and unspecified parts of oral cavity and pharynx ▽
V51.8 Other aftercare involving the use of plastic surgery

ICD-9-CM Procedural

18.71 Construction of auricle of ear
18.79 Other plastic repair of external ear
27.56 Other skin graft to lip and mouth
27.57 Attachment of pedicle or flap graft to lip and mouth
86.71 Cutting and preparation of pedicle grafts or flaps
86.74 Attachment of pedicle or flap graft to other sites

15600

15600 Delay of flap or sectioning of flap (division and inset); at trunk

ICD-9-CM Diagnostic

171.4 Malignant neoplasm of connective and other soft tissue of thorax
171.6 Malignant neoplasm of connective and other soft tissue of pelvis
171.7 Malignant neoplasm of connective and other soft tissue of trunk, unspecified site ▽
171.8 Malignant neoplasm of other specified sites of connective and other soft tissue
172.5 Malignant melanoma of skin of trunk, except scrotum
173.50 Unspecified malignant neoplasm of skin of trunk, except scrotum ▽
173.51 Basal cell carcinoma of skin of trunk, except scrotum
173.52 Squamous cell carcinoma of skin of trunk, except scrotum
173.59 Other specified malignant neoplasm of skin of trunk, except scrotum
174.0 Malignant neoplasm of nipple and areola of female breast — (Use additional code to identify estrogen receptor status: V86.0-V86.1) ♀
174.1 Malignant neoplasm of central portion of female breast — (Use additional code to identify estrogen receptor status: V86.0-V86.1) ♀
174.2 Malignant neoplasm of upper-inner quadrant of female breast — (Use additional code to identify estrogen receptor status: V86.0-V86.1) ♀
174.3 Malignant neoplasm of lower-inner quadrant of female breast — (Use additional code to identify estrogen receptor status: V86.0-V86.1) ♀
174.4 Malignant neoplasm of upper-outer quadrant of female breast — (Use additional code to identify estrogen receptor status: V86.0-V86.1) ♀
174.5 Malignant neoplasm of lower-outer quadrant of female breast — (Use additional code to identify estrogen receptor status: V86.0-V86.1) ♀
174.6 Malignant neoplasm of axillary tail of female breast — (Use additional code to identify estrogen receptor status: V86.0-V86.1) ♀
174.8 Malignant neoplasm of other specified sites of female breast — (Use additional code to identify estrogen receptor status: V86.0-V86.1) ♀
175.9 Malignant neoplasm of other and unspecified sites of male breast — (Use additional code to identify estrogen receptor status: V86.0-V86.1) ▽ ♂
198.81 Secondary malignant neoplasm of breast
209.35 Merkel cell carcinoma of the trunk
209.75 Secondary Merkel cell carcinoma
233.0 Carcinoma in situ of breast
238.2 Neoplasm of uncertain behavior of skin
238.3 Neoplasm of uncertain behavior of breast
239.2 Neoplasms of unspecified nature of bone, soft tissue, and skin
239.3 Neoplasm of unspecified nature of breast
519.2 Mediastinitis — (Use additional code to identify infectious organism)
682.2 Cellulitis and abscess of trunk — (Use additional code to identify organism, such as 041.1, etc.)
682.5 Cellulitis and abscess of buttock — (Use additional code to identify organism, such as 041.1, etc.)
707.00 Pressure ulcer, unspecified site — (Use additional code to identify pressure ulcer stage: 707.20-707.25) ▽
707.02 Pressure ulcer, upper back — (Use additional code to identify pressure ulcer stage: 707.20-707.25)
707.03 Pressure ulcer, lower back — (Use additional code to identify pressure ulcer stage: 707.20-707.25)
707.04 Pressure ulcer, hip — (Use additional code to identify pressure ulcer stage: 707.20-707.25)
707.05 Pressure ulcer, buttock — (Use additional code to identify pressure ulcer stage: 707.20-707.25)
707.09 Pressure ulcer, other site — (Use additional code to identify pressure ulcer stage: 707.20-707.25)
707.20 Pressure ulcer, unspecified stage — (Code first site of pressure ulcer: 707.00-707.09) ▽
707.21 Pressure ulcer, stage I — (Code first site of pressure ulcer: 707.00-707.09)
707.22 Pressure ulcer stage II — (Code first site of pressure ulcer: 707.00-707.09)
707.23 Pressure ulcer stage III — (Code first site of pressure ulcer: 707.00-707.09)
707.24 Pressure ulcer stage IV — (Code first site of pressure ulcer: 707.00-707.09)
707.25 Pressure ulcer, unstageable — (Code first site of pressure ulcer: 707.00-707.09)
707.8 Chronic ulcer of other specified site
709.2 Scar condition and fibrosis of skin
738.3 Acquired deformity of chest and rib
741.00 Spina bifida with hydrocephalus, unspecified region ▽
754.81 Pectus excavatum
875.0 Open wound of chest (wall), without mention of complication
875.1 Open wound of chest (wall), complicated
876.0 Open wound of back, without mention of complication
876.1 Open wound of back, complicated
877.0 Open wound of buttock, without mention of complication

877.1 Open wound of buttock, complicated
879.0 Open wound of breast, without mention of complication
879.1 Open wound of breast, complicated
879.2 Open wound of abdominal wall, anterior, without mention of complication
879.3 Open wound of abdominal wall, anterior, complicated
879.4 Open wound of abdominal wall, lateral, without mention of complication
879.5 Open wound of abdominal wall, lateral, complicated
879.6 Open wound of other and unspecified parts of trunk, without mention of complication
879.7 Open wound of other and unspecified parts of trunk, complicated
942.30 Full-thickness skin loss due to burn (third degree NOS) of unspecified site of trunk
942.31 Full-thickness skin loss due to burn (third degree NOS) of breast
942.33 Full-thickness skin loss due to burn (third degree NOS) of abdominal wall
942.34 Full-thickness skin loss due to burn (third degree NOS) of back (any part)
942.39 Full-thickness skin loss due to burn (third degree NOS) of other and multiple sites of trunk
942.40 Deep necrosis of underlying tissues due to burn (deep third degree) of trunk, unspecified site, without mention of loss of a body part
942.41 Deep necrosis of underlying tissues due to burn (deep third degree) of breast, without mention of loss of a body part
942.42 Deep necrosis of underlying tissues due to burn (deep third degree) of chest wall, excluding breast and nipple, without mention of loss of a body part
942.43 Deep necrosis of underlying tissues due to burn (deep third degree) of abdominal wall, without mention of loss of a body part
942.44 Deep necrosis of underlying tissues due to burn (deep third degree) of back (any part), without mention of loss of a body part
942.49 Deep necrosis of underlying tissues due to burn (deep third degree) of other and multiple sites of trunk, without mention of loss of a body part
942.50 Deep necrosis of underlying tissues due to burn (deep third degree) of unspecified site of trunk, with loss of a body part
942.51 Deep necrosis of underlying tissues due to burn (deep third degree) of breast, with loss of a body part
942.52 Deep necrosis of underlying tissues due to burn (deep third degree) of chest wall, excluding breast and nipple, with loss of a body part
942.53 Deep necrosis of underlying tissues due to burn (deep third degree) of abdominal wall with loss of a body part
942.54 Deep necrosis of underlying tissues due to burn (deep third degree) of back (any part), with loss of a body part
942.59 Deep necrosis of underlying tissues due to burn (deep third degree) of other and multiple sites of trunk, with loss of a body part
V51.8 Other aftercare involving the use of plastic surgery

ICD-9-CM Procedural

86.71 Cutting and preparation of pedicle grafts or flaps

15610

15610 Delay of flap or sectioning of flap (division and inset); at scalp, arms, or legs

ICD-9-CM Diagnostic

171.0 Malignant neoplasm of connective and other soft tissue of head, face, and neck
171.2 Malignant neoplasm of connective and other soft tissue of upper limb, including shoulder
171.3 Malignant neoplasm of connective and other soft tissue of lower limb, including hip
172.4 Malignant melanoma of skin of scalp and neck
173.40 Unspecified malignant neoplasm of scalp and skin of neck
173.41 Basal cell carcinoma of scalp and skin of neck
173.42 Squamous cell carcinoma of scalp and skin of neck
173.49 Other specified malignant neoplasm of scalp and skin of neck
173.60 Unspecified malignant neoplasm of skin of upper limb, including shoulder
173.61 Basal cell carcinoma of skin of upper limb, including shoulder
173.62 Squamous cell carcinoma of skin of upper limb, including shoulder
173.69 Other specified malignant neoplasm of skin of upper limb, including shoulder
173.70 Unspecified malignant neoplasm of skin of lower limb, including hip
173.71 Basal cell carcinoma of skin of lower limb, including hip
173.72 Squamous cell carcinoma of skin of lower limb, including hip
173.79 Other specified malignant neoplasm of skin of lower limb, including hip
209.32 Merkel cell carcinoma of the scalp and neck
209.33 Merkel cell carcinoma of the upper limb
209.34 Merkel cell carcinoma of the lower limb
209.75 Secondary Merkel cell carcinoma
216.4 Benign neoplasm of scalp and skin of neck
232.4 Carcinoma in situ of scalp and skin of neck
238.1 Neoplasm of uncertain behavior of connective and other soft tissue
238.2 Neoplasm of uncertain behavior of skin
239.2 Neoplasms of unspecified nature of bone, soft tissue, and skin
682.3 Cellulitis and abscess of upper arm and forearm — (Use additional code to identify organism, such as 041.1, etc.)
682.6 Cellulitis and abscess of leg, except foot — (Use additional code to identify organism, such as 041.1, etc.)
682.8 Cellulitis and abscess of other specified site — (Use additional code to identify organism, such as 041.1, etc.)
701.4 Keloid scar
707.00 Pressure ulcer, unspecified site — (Use additional code to identify pressure ulcer stage: 707.20-707.25)
707.01 Pressure ulcer, elbow — (Use additional code to identify pressure ulcer stage: 707.20-707.25)
707.06 Pressure ulcer, ankle — (Use additional code to identify pressure ulcer stage: 707.20-707.25)
707.09 Pressure ulcer, other site — (Use additional code to identify pressure ulcer stage: 707.20-707.25)
707.10 Ulcer of lower limb, unspecified — (Code, if applicable, any causal condition first: 249.80-249.81, 250.80-250.83, 440.23, 459.11, 459.13, 459.31, 459.33)
707.11 Ulcer of thigh — (Code, if applicable, any causal condition first: 249.80-249.81, 250.80-250.83, 440.23, 459.11, 459.13, 459.31, 459.33)
707.12 Ulcer of calf — (Code, if applicable, any causal condition first: 249.80-249.81, 250.80-250.83, 440.23, 459.11, 459.13, 459.31, 459.33)
707.13 Ulcer of ankle — (Code, if applicable, any causal condition first: 249.80-249.81, 250.80-250.83, 440.23, 459.11, 459.13, 459.31, 459.33)
707.19 Ulcer of other part of lower limb — (Code, if applicable, any causal condition first: 249.80-249.81, 250.80-250.83, 440.23, 459.11, 459.13, 459.31, 459.33)
707.20 Pressure ulcer, unspecified stage — (Code first site of pressure ulcer: 707.00-707.09)
707.21 Pressure ulcer, stage I — (Code first site of pressure ulcer: 707.00-707.09)
707.22 Pressure ulcer stage II — (Code first site of pressure ulcer: 707.00-707.09)
707.23 Pressure ulcer stage III — (Code first site of pressure ulcer: 707.00-707.09)
707.24 Pressure ulcer stage IV — (Code first site of pressure ulcer: 707.00-707.09)
707.25 Pressure ulcer, unstageable — (Code first site of pressure ulcer: 707.00-707.09)
707.8 Chronic ulcer of other specified site
709.2 Scar condition and fibrosis of skin
754.0 Congenital musculoskeletal deformities of skull, face, and jaw
873.0 Open wound of scalp, without mention of complication
873.1 Open wound of scalp, complicated
880.12 Open wound of axillary region, complicated
880.13 Open wound of upper arm, complicated
880.19 Open wound of multiple sites of shoulder and upper arm, complicated
880.20 Open wound of shoulder region, with tendon involvement
880.21 Open wound of scapular region, with tendon involvement
880.22 Open wound of axillary region, with tendon involvement
880.23 Open wound of upper arm, with tendon involvement
880.29 Open wound of multiple sites of shoulder and upper arm, with tendon involvement
881.11 Open wound of elbow, complicated

881.12 Open wound of wrist, complicated
881.20 Open wound of forearm, with tendon involvement
881.21 Open wound of elbow, with tendon involvement
881.22 Open wound of wrist, with tendon involvement
884.1 Multiple and unspecified open wound of upper limb, complicated
884.2 Multiple and unspecified open wound of upper limb, with tendon involvement
890.1 Open wound of hip and thigh, complicated
890.2 Open wound of hip and thigh, with tendon involvement
891.1 Open wound of knee, leg (except thigh), and ankle, complicated
891.2 Open wound of knee, leg (except thigh), and ankle, with tendon involvement
894.1 Multiple and unspecified open wound of lower limb, complicated
894.2 Multiple and unspecified open wound of lower limb, with tendon involvement
906.0 Late effect of open wound of head, neck, and trunk
906.5 Late effect of burn of eye, face, head, and neck
941.36 Full-thickness skin loss due to burn (third degree NOS) of scalp (any part)
941.46 Deep necrosis of underlying tissues due to burn (deep third degree) of scalp (any part), without mention of loss of a body part
941.56 Deep necrosis of underlying tissues due to burn (deep third degree) of scalp (any part), with loss of a body part
943.30 Full-thickness skin loss due to burn (third degree NOS) of unspecified site of upper limb ▽
943.31 Full-thickness skin loss due to burn (third degree NOS) of forearm
943.32 Full-thickness skin loss due to burn (third degree NOS) of elbow
943.33 Full-thickness skin loss due to burn (third degree NOS) of upper arm
943.39 Full-thickness skin loss due to burn (third degree NOS) of multiple sites of upper limb, except wrist and hand
945.30 Full-thickness skin loss due to burn (third degree NOS) of unspecified site of lower limb ▽
945.33 Full-thickness skin loss due to burn (third degree NOS) of ankle
945.34 Full-thickness skin loss due to burn (third degree NOS) of lower leg
945.35 Full-thickness skin loss due to burn (third degree NOS) of knee
945.36 Full-thickness skin loss due to burn (third degree NOS) of thigh (any part)
945.39 Full-thickness skin loss due to burn (third degree NOS) of multiple sites of lower limb(s)
945.40 Deep necrosis of underlying tissues due to burn (deep third degree) of unspecified site of lower limb (leg), without mention of loss of a body part ▽
945.43 Deep necrosis of underlying tissues due to burn (deep third degree) of ankle, without mention of loss of a body part
945.44 Deep necrosis of underlying tissues due to burn (deep third degree) of lower leg, without mention of loss of a body part
945.45 Deep necrosis of underlying tissues due to burn (deep third degree) of knee, without mention of loss of a body part
945.46 Deep necrosis of underlying tissues due to burn (deep third degree) of thigh (any part), without mention of loss of a body part
945.49 Deep necrosis of underlying tissues due to burn (deep third degree) of multiple sites of lower limb(s), without mention of loss of a body part
948.00 Burn (any degree) involving less than 10% of body surface with third degree burn of less than 10% or unspecified amount
V51.8 Other aftercare involving the use of plastic surgery

ICD-9-CM Procedural

86.71 Cutting and preparation of pedicle grafts or flaps
86.74 Attachment of pedicle or flap graft to other sites

15620

15620 Delay of flap or sectioning of flap (division and inset); at forehead, cheeks, chin, neck, axillae, genitalia, hands, or feet

ICD-9-CM Diagnostic

171.0 Malignant neoplasm of connective and other soft tissue of head, face, and neck
171.2 Malignant neoplasm of connective and other soft tissue of upper limb, including shoulder
171.3 Malignant neoplasm of connective and other soft tissue of lower limb, including hip
171.4 Malignant neoplasm of connective and other soft tissue of thorax
172.3 Malignant melanoma of skin of other and unspecified parts of face ▽
172.4 Malignant melanoma of skin of scalp and neck
173.30 Unspecified malignant neoplasm of skin of other and unspecified parts of face ▽
173.31 Basal cell carcinoma of skin of other and unspecified parts of face
173.32 Squamous cell carcinoma of skin of other and unspecified parts of face
173.39 Other specified malignant neoplasm of skin of other and unspecified parts of face
173.40 Unspecified malignant neoplasm of scalp and skin of neck ▽
173.41 Basal cell carcinoma of scalp and skin of neck
173.42 Squamous cell carcinoma of scalp and skin of neck
173.49 Other specified malignant neoplasm of scalp and skin of neck
173.50 Unspecified malignant neoplasm of skin of trunk, except scrotum ▽
173.51 Basal cell carcinoma of skin of trunk, except scrotum
173.52 Squamous cell carcinoma of skin of trunk, except scrotum
173.59 Other specified malignant neoplasm of skin of trunk, except scrotum
173.60 Unspecified malignant neoplasm of skin of upper limb, including shoulder ▽
173.61 Basal cell carcinoma of skin of upper limb, including shoulder
173.62 Squamous cell carcinoma of skin of upper limb, including shoulder
173.69 Other specified malignant neoplasm of skin of upper limb, including shoulder
173.70 Unspecified malignant neoplasm of skin of lower limb, including hip ▽
173.71 Basal cell carcinoma of skin of lower limb, including hip
173.72 Squamous cell carcinoma of skin of lower limb, including hip
173.79 Other specified malignant neoplasm of skin of lower limb, including hip
184.0 Malignant neoplasm of vagina ♀
184.1 Malignant neoplasm of labia majora ♀
184.2 Malignant neoplasm of labia minora ♀
184.3 Malignant neoplasm of clitoris ♀
184.4 Malignant neoplasm of vulva, unspecified site ▽ ♀
184.8 Malignant neoplasm of other specified sites of female genital organs ♀
184.9 Malignant neoplasm of female genital organ, site unspecified ▽ ♀
186.9 Malignant neoplasm of other and unspecified testis — (Use additional code to identify any functional activity) ▽ ♂
187.3 Malignant neoplasm of body of penis ♂
187.4 Malignant neoplasm of penis, part unspecified ▽ ♂
187.7 Malignant neoplasm of scrotum ♂
187.8 Malignant neoplasm of other specified sites of male genital organs ♂
187.9 Malignant neoplasm of male genital organ, site unspecified ▽ ♂
195.0 Malignant neoplasm of head, face, and neck
195.3 Malignant neoplasm of pelvis
195.4 Malignant neoplasm of upper limb
198.2 Secondary malignant neoplasm of skin
209.31 Merkel cell carcinoma of the face
209.32 Merkel cell carcinoma of the scalp and neck
209.33 Merkel cell carcinoma of the upper limb
209.34 Merkel cell carcinoma of the lower limb
209.35 Merkel cell carcinoma of the trunk
209.36 Merkel cell carcinoma of other sites
209.75 Secondary Merkel cell carcinoma
210.0 Benign neoplasm of lip
210.3 Benign neoplasm of floor of mouth
210.4 Benign neoplasm of other and unspecified parts of mouth ▽
216.5 Benign neoplasm of skin of trunk, except scrotum
216.8 Benign neoplasm of other specified sites of skin
221.2 Benign neoplasm of vulva ♀
222.1 Benign neoplasm of penis ♂

222.4 Benign neoplasm of scrotum ♂
230.0 Carcinoma in situ of lip, oral cavity, and pharynx
232.0 Carcinoma in situ of skin of lip
232.5 Carcinoma in situ of skin of trunk, except scrotum
233.30 Carcinoma in situ, unspecified female genital organ ▼ ♀
233.31 Carcinoma in situ, vagina ♀
233.32 Carcinoma in situ, vulva ♀
233.39 Carcinoma in situ, other female genital organ ♀
233.5 Carcinoma in situ of penis ♂
233.6 Carcinoma in situ of other and unspecified male genital organs ▼ ♂
235.1 Neoplasm of uncertain behavior of lip, oral cavity, and pharynx
236.3 Neoplasm of uncertain behavior of other and unspecified female genital organs ▼ ♀
236.6 Neoplasm of uncertain behavior of other and unspecified male genital organs ▼ ♂
238.1 Neoplasm of uncertain behavior of connective and other soft tissue
239.2 Neoplasms of unspecified nature of bone, soft tissue, and skin
619.2 Genital tract-skin fistula, female ♀
619.8 Other specified fistula involving female genital tract ♀
629.20 Female genital mutilation status, unspecified ▼ ♀
629.21 Female genital mutilation, Type I status ♀
629.22 Female genital mutilation, Type II status ♀
629.23 Female genital mutilation, Type III status ♀
629.29 Other female genital mutilation status ♀
629.89 Other specified disorders of female genital organs ♀
681.00 Unspecified cellulitis and abscess of finger — (Use additional code to identify organism: 041.1) ▼
681.10 Unspecified cellulitis and abscess of toe — (Use additional code to identify organism: 041.1) ▼
682.0 Cellulitis and abscess of face — (Use additional code to identify organism, such as 041.1, etc.)
682.1 Cellulitis and abscess of neck — (Use additional code to identify organism, such as 041.1, etc.)
682.4 Cellulitis and abscess of hand, except fingers and thumb — (Use additional code to identify organism, such as 041.1, etc.)
682.7 Cellulitis and abscess of foot, except toes — (Use additional code to identify organism, such as 041.1, etc.)
707.00 Pressure ulcer, unspecified site — (Use additional code to identify pressure ulcer stage: 707.20-707.25) ▼
707.07 Pressure ulcer, heel — (Use additional code to identify pressure ulcer stage: 707.20-707.25)
707.09 Pressure ulcer, other site — (Use additional code to identify pressure ulcer stage: 707.20-707.25)
707.14 Ulcer of heel and midfoot — (Code, if applicable, any causal condition first: 249.80-249.81, 250.80-250.83, 440.23, 459.11, 459.13, 459.31, 459.33)
707.15 Ulcer of other part of foot — (Code, if applicable, any causal condition first: 249.80-249.81, 250.80-250.83, 440.23, 459.11, 459.13, 459.31, 459.33)
707.20 Pressure ulcer, unspecified stage — (Code first site of pressure ulcer: 707.00-707.09) ▼
707.21 Pressure ulcer, stage I — (Code first site of pressure ulcer: 707.00-707.09)
707.22 Pressure ulcer stage II — (Code first site of pressure ulcer: 707.00-707.09)
707.23 Pressure ulcer stage III — (Code first site of pressure ulcer: 707.00-707.09)
707.24 Pressure ulcer stage IV — (Code first site of pressure ulcer: 707.00-707.09)
707.25 Pressure ulcer, unstageable — (Code first site of pressure ulcer: 707.00-707.09)
709.2 Scar condition and fibrosis of skin
752.40 Unspecified congenital anomaly of cervix, vagina, and external female genitalia ▼ ♀
752.43 Cervical agenesis ♀
752.44 Cervical duplication ♀
752.45 Vaginal agenesis ♀
752.46 Transverse vaginal septum ♀
752.47 Longitudinal vaginal septum ♀
752.49 Other congenital anomaly of cervix, vagina, and external female genitalia ♀
752.69 Other penile anomalies ♂
752.81 Scrotal transposition ♂
752.89 Other specified anomalies of genital organs
754.0 Congenital musculoskeletal deformities of skull, face, and jaw
754.1 Congenital musculoskeletal deformity of sternocleidomastoid muscle
755.10 Syndactyly of multiple and unspecified sites
755.11 Syndactyly of fingers without fusion of bone
755.12 Syndactyly of fingers with fusion of bone
873.41 Open wound of cheek, without mention of complication
873.42 Open wound of forehead, without mention of complication
873.43 Open wound of lip, without mention of complication
873.44 Open wound of jaw, without mention of complication
873.49 Open wound of face, other and multiple sites, without mention of complication
873.51 Open wound of cheek, complicated
873.52 Open wound of forehead, complicated
873.53 Open wound of lip, complicated
873.54 Open wound of jaw, complicated
873.59 Open wound of face, other and multiple sites, complicated
874.8 Open wound of other and unspecified parts of neck, without mention of complication ▼
874.9 Open wound of other and unspecified parts of neck, complicated ▼
878.0 Open wound of penis, without mention of complication ♂
878.1 Open wound of penis, complicated ♂
878.2 Open wound of scrotum and testes, without mention of complication ♂
878.3 Open wound of scrotum and testes, complicated ♂
878.4 Open wound of vulva, without mention of complication ♀
878.5 Open wound of vulva, complicated ♀
878.7 Open wound of vagina, complicated ♀
878.8 Open wound of other and unspecified parts of genital organs, without mention of complication ▼
878.9 Open wound of other and unspecified parts of genital organs, complicated ▼
882.0 Open wound of hand except finger(s) alone, without mention of complication
882.1 Open wound of hand except finger(s) alone, complicated
882.2 Open wound of hand except finger(s) alone, with tendon involvement
883.0 Open wound of finger(s), without mention of complication
883.1 Open wound of finger(s), complicated
883.2 Open wound of finger(s), with tendon involvement
885.0 Traumatic amputation of thumb (complete) (partial), without mention of complication
885.1 Traumatic amputation of thumb (complete) (partial), complicated
886.0 Traumatic amputation of other finger(s) (complete) (partial), without mention of complication
886.1 Traumatic amputation of other finger(s) (complete) (partial), complicated
887.0 Traumatic amputation of arm and hand (complete) (partial), unilateral, below elbow, without mention of complication
887.1 Traumatic amputation of arm and hand (complete) (partial), unilateral, below elbow, complicated
887.4 Traumatic amputation of arm and hand (complete) (partial), unilateral, level not specified, without mention of complication ▼
887.5 Traumatic amputation of arm and hand (complete) (partial), unilateral, level not specified, complicated ▼
887.6 Traumatic amputation of arm and hand (complete) (partial), bilateral (any level), without mention of complication
887.7 Traumatic amputation of arm and hand (complete) (partial), bilateral (any level), complicated
892.0 Open wound of foot except toe(s) alone, without mention of complication
892.1 Open wound of foot except toe(s) alone, complicated
892.2 Open wound of foot except toe(s) alone, with tendon involvement
893.0 Open wound of toe(s), without mention of complication

893.1 Open wound of toe(s), complicated
893.2 Open wound of toe(s), with tendon involvement
895.0 Traumatic amputation of toe(s) (complete) (partial), without mention of complication
895.1 Traumatic amputation of toe(s) (complete) (partial), complicated
896.0 Traumatic amputation of foot (complete) (partial), unilateral, without mention of complication
896.1 Traumatic amputation of foot (complete) (partial), unilateral, complicated
896.2 Traumatic amputation of foot (complete) (partial), bilateral, without mention of complication
906.0 Late effect of open wound of head, neck, and trunk
906.1 Late effect of open wound of extremities without mention of tendon injury
906.4 Late effect of crushing
906.5 Late effect of burn of eye, face, head, and neck
906.6 Late effect of burn of wrist and hand
906.7 Late effect of burn of other extremities
906.8 Late effect of burns of other specified sites
909.3 Late effect of complications of surgical and medical care
925.2 Crushing injury of neck — (Use additional code to identify any associated injuries, such as: 800-829, 850.0-854.1, 860.0-869.1)
926.0 Crushing injury of external genitalia — (Use additional code to identify any associated injuries: 800-829, 850.0-854.1, 860.0-869.1)
927.20 Crushing injury of hand(s) — (Use additional code to identify any associated injuries: 800-829, 850.0-854.1, 860.0-869.1)
927.21 Crushing injury of wrist — (Use additional code to identify any associated injuries: 800-829, 850.0-854.1, 860.0-869.1)
928.20 Crushing injury of foot — (Use additional code to identify any associated injuries: 800-829, 850.0-854.1, 860.0-869.1)
928.3 Crushing injury of toe(s) — (Use additional code to identify any associated injuries: 800-829, 850.0-854.1, 860.0-869.1)
928.8 Crushing injury of multiple sites of lower limb — (Use additional code to identify any associated injuries: 800-829, 850.0-854.1, 860.0-869.1)
941.30 Full-thickness skin loss due to burn (third degree NOS) of unspecified site of face and head ▽
941.33 Full-thickness skin loss due to burn (third degree NOS) of lip(s)
941.35 Full-thickness skin loss due to burn (third degree NOS) of nose (septum)
941.37 Full-thickness skin loss due to burn (third degree NOS) of forehead and cheek
941.38 Full-thickness skin loss due to burn (third degree NOS) of neck
941.39 Full-thickness skin loss due to burn (third degree NOS) of multiple sites (except with eye) of face, head, and neck
941.40 Deep necrosis of underlying tissues due to burn (deep third degree) of unspecified site of face and head, without mention of loss of a body part ▽
941.43 Deep necrosis of underlying tissues due to burn (deep third degree) of lip(s), without mention of loss of a body part
941.44 Deep necrosis of underlying tissues due to burn (deep third degree) of chin, without mention of loss of a body part
941.45 Deep necrosis of underlying tissues due to burn (deep third degree) of nose (septum), without mention of loss of a body part
941.47 Deep necrosis of underlying tissues due to burn (deep third degree) of forehead and cheek, without mention of loss of a body part
941.48 Deep necrosis of underlying tissues due to burn (deep third degree) of neck, without mention of loss of a body part
941.49 Deep necrosis of underlying tissues due to burn (deep third degree) of multiple sites (except with eye) of face, head, and neck, without mention of loss of a body part
941.50 Deep necrosis of underlying tissues due to burn (deep third degree) of face and head, unspecified site, with loss of a body part ▽
941.53 Deep necrosis of underlying tissues due to burn (deep third degree) of lip(s), with loss of a body part
941.54 Deep necrosis of underlying tissues due to burn (deep third degree) of chin, with loss of a body part
941.55 Deep necrosis of underlying tissues due to burn (deep third degree) of nose (septum), with loss of a body part
941.57 Deep necrosis of underlying tissues due to burn (deep third degree) of forehead and cheek, with loss of a body part
941.58 Deep necrosis of underlying tissues due to burn (deep third degree) of neck, with loss of a body part
941.59 Deep necrosis of underlying tissues due to burn (deep third degree) of multiple sites (except eye) of face, head, and neck, with loss of a body part
942.35 Full-thickness skin loss due to burn (third degree NOS) of genitalia
942.45 Deep necrosis of underlying tissues due to burn (deep third degree) of genitalia, without mention of loss of a body part
942.52 Deep necrosis of underlying tissues due to burn (deep third degree) of chest wall, excluding breast and nipple, with loss of a body part
942.55 Deep necrosis of underlying tissues due to burn (deep third degree) of genitalia, with loss of a body part
944.30 Full-thickness skin loss due to burn (third degree NOS) of unspecified site of hand ▽
944.31 Full-thickness skin loss due to burn (third degree NOS) of single digit [finger (nail)] other than thumb
944.32 Full-thickness skin loss due to burn (third degree NOS) of thumb (nail)
944.33 Full-thickness skin loss due to burn (third degree NOS) of two or more digits of hand, not including thumb
944.34 Full-thickness skin loss due to burn (third degree NOS) of two or more digits of hand including thumb
944.35 Full-thickness skin loss due to burn (third degree NOS) of palm of hand
944.36 Full-thickness skin loss due to burn (third degree NOS) of back of hand
944.37 Full-thickness skin loss due to burn (third degree NOS) of wrist
944.38 Full-thickness skin loss due to burn (third degree NOS) of multiple sites of wrist(s) and hand(s)
944.40 Deep necrosis of underlying tissues due to burn (deep third degree) of unspecified site of hand, without mention of loss of a body part ▽
944.41 Deep necrosis of underlying tissues due to burn (deep third degree) of single digit [finger (nail)] other than thumb, without mention of loss of a body part
944.42 Deep necrosis of underlying tissues due to burn (deep third degree) of thumb (nail), without mention of loss of a body part
944.43 Deep necrosis of underlying tissues due to burn (deep third degree) of two or more digits of hand, not including thumb, without mention of loss of a body part
944.44 Deep necrosis of underlying tissues due to burn (deep third degree) of two or more digits of hand including thumb, without mention of loss of a body part
944.45 Deep necrosis of underlying tissues due to burn (deep third degree) of palm of hand, without mention of loss of a body part
944.46 Deep necrosis of underlying tissues due to burn (deep third degree) of back of hand, without mention of loss of a body part
944.47 Deep necrosis of underlying tissues due to burn (deep third degree) of wrist, without mention of loss of a body part
944.48 Deep necrosis of underlying tissues due to burn (deep third degree) of multiple sites of wrist(s) and hand(s), without mention of loss of a body part
944.50 Deep necrosis of underlying tissues due to burn (deep third degree) of unspecified site of hand, with loss of a body part ▽
944.51 Deep necrosis of underlying tissues due to burn (deep third degree) of single digit (finger (nail)) other than thumb, with loss of a body part
944.52 Deep necrosis of underlying tissues due to burn (deep third degree) of thumb (nail), with loss of a body part
945.32 Full-thickness skin loss due to burn (third degree NOS) of foot
945.42 Deep necrosis of underlying tissues due to burn (deep third degree) of foot, without mention of loss of a body part
959.09 Injury of face and neck, other and unspecified
959.14 Other injury of external genitals
991.1 Frostbite of hand
996.52 Mechanical complication due to other tissue graft, not elsewhere classified
997.62 Infection (chronic) of amputation stump — (Use additional code to identify complications)
997.69 Other late amputation stump complication — (Use additional code to identify complications)

998.30 Disruption of wound, unspecified ▽
998.32 Disruption of external operation (surgical) wound
998.33 Disruption of traumatic injury wound repair
998.59 Other postoperative infection — (Use additional code to identify infection)
998.83 Non-healing surgical wound
V51.8 Other aftercare involving the use of plastic surgery

ICD-9-CM Procedural

86.71 Cutting and preparation of pedicle grafts or flaps
86.74 Attachment of pedicle or flap graft to other sites

15630

15630 Delay of flap or sectioning of flap (division and inset); at eyelids, nose, ears, or lips

ICD-9-CM Diagnostic

140.0 Malignant neoplasm of upper lip, vermilion border
140.1 Malignant neoplasm of lower lip, vermilion border
140.3 Malignant neoplasm of upper lip, inner aspect
140.4 Malignant neoplasm of lower lip, inner aspect
140.5 Malignant neoplasm of lip, inner aspect, unspecified as to upper or lower ▽
140.6 Malignant neoplasm of commissure of lip
140.8 Malignant neoplasm of other sites of lip
140.9 Malignant neoplasm of lip, vermilion border, unspecified as to upper or lower ▽
172.0 Malignant melanoma of skin of lip
172.1 Malignant melanoma of skin of eyelid, including canthus
172.2 Malignant melanoma of skin of ear and external auditory canal
172.8 Malignant melanoma of other specified sites of skin
173.00 Unspecified malignant neoplasm of skin of lip ▽
173.01 Basal cell carcinoma of skin of lip
173.02 Squamous cell carcinoma of skin of lip
173.09 Other specified malignant neoplasm of skin of lip
173.10 Unspecified malignant neoplasm of eyelid, including canthus ▽
173.11 Basal cell carcinoma of eyelid, including canthus
173.12 Squamous cell carcinoma of eyelid, including canthus
173.19 Other specified malignant neoplasm of eyelid, including canthus
173.20 Unspecified malignant neoplasm of skin of ear and external auditory canal ▽
173.21 Basal cell carcinoma of skin of ear and external auditory canal
173.22 Squamous cell carcinoma of skin of ear and external auditory canal
173.29 Other specified malignant neoplasm of skin of ear and external auditory canal
173.30 Unspecified malignant neoplasm of skin of other and unspecified parts of face ▽
173.31 Basal cell carcinoma of skin of other and unspecified parts of face
173.32 Squamous cell carcinoma of skin of other and unspecified parts of face
173.39 Other specified malignant neoplasm of skin of other and unspecified parts of face
173.80 Unspecified malignant neoplasm of other specified sites of skin ▽
173.81 Basal cell carcinoma of other specified sites of skin
173.82 Squamous cell carcinoma of other specified sites of skin
173.89 Other specified malignant neoplasm of other specified sites of skin
195.0 Malignant neoplasm of head, face, and neck
209.31 Merkel cell carcinoma of the face
209.75 Secondary Merkel cell carcinoma
210.0 Benign neoplasm of lip
210.4 Benign neoplasm of other and unspecified parts of mouth ▽
216.0 Benign neoplasm of skin of lip
216.1 Benign neoplasm of eyelid, including canthus
216.2 Benign neoplasm of ear and external auditory canal
216.3 Benign neoplasm of skin of other and unspecified parts of face ▽
230.0 Carcinoma in situ of lip, oral cavity, and pharynx
232.1 Carcinoma in situ of eyelid, including canthus
232.2 Carcinoma in situ of skin of ear and external auditory canal
232.3 Carcinoma in situ of skin of other and unspecified parts of face ▽
238.2 Neoplasm of uncertain behavior of skin
239.0 Neoplasm of unspecified nature of digestive system
239.2 Neoplasms of unspecified nature of bone, soft tissue, and skin
380.32 Acquired deformities of auricle or pinna
682.0 Cellulitis and abscess of face — (Use additional code to identify organism, such as 041.1, etc.)
709.2 Scar condition and fibrosis of skin
709.9 Unspecified disorder of skin and subcutaneous tissue ▽
744.01 Congenital absence of external ear causing impairment of hearing
744.09 Other congenital anomalies of ear causing impairment of hearing
744.23 Microtia
744.3 Unspecified congenital anomaly of ear ▽
744.5 Congenital webbing of neck
744.82 Microcheilia
748.1 Other congenital anomaly of nose
749.01 Unilateral cleft palate, complete
749.02 Unilateral cleft palate, incomplete
749.03 Bilateral cleft palate, complete
749.04 Bilateral cleft palate, incomplete
749.10 Unspecified cleft lip ▽
749.11 Unilateral cleft lip, complete
749.12 Unilateral cleft lip, incomplete
749.13 Bilateral cleft lip, complete
749.14 Bilateral cleft lip, incomplete
749.20 Unspecified cleft palate with cleft lip ▽
749.21 Unilateral cleft palate with cleft lip, complete
749.22 Unilateral cleft palate with cleft lip, incomplete
749.23 Bilateral cleft palate with cleft lip, complete
749.24 Bilateral cleft palate with cleft lip, incomplete
785.4 Gangrene — (Code first any associated underlying condition)
870.0 Laceration of skin of eyelid and periocular area
870.1 Laceration of eyelid, full-thickness, not involving lacrimal passages
870.2 Laceration of eyelid involving lacrimal passages
872.00 Open wound of external ear, unspecified site, without mention of complication ▽
872.01 Open wound of auricle, without mention of complication
872.02 Open wound of auditory canal, without mention of complication
872.10 Open wound of external ear, unspecified site, complicated ▽
872.11 Open wound of auricle, complicated
872.12 Open wound of auditory canal, complicated
872.8 Open wound of ear, part unspecified, without mention of complication ▽
872.9 Open wound of ear, part unspecified, complicated ▽
873.20 Open wound of nose, unspecified site, without mention of complication ▽
873.30 Open wound of nose, unspecified site, complicated ▽
873.31 Open wound of nasal septum, complicated
873.32 Open wound of nasal cavity, complicated
873.33 Open wound of nasal sinus, complicated
873.39 Open wound of nose, multiple sites, complicated
873.41 Open wound of cheek, without mention of complication
873.42 Open wound of forehead, without mention of complication
873.43 Open wound of lip, without mention of complication
873.44 Open wound of jaw, without mention of complication
873.51 Open wound of cheek, complicated
873.52 Open wound of forehead, complicated
873.53 Open wound of lip, complicated
873.54 Open wound of jaw, complicated
874.8 Open wound of other and unspecified parts of neck, without mention of complication ▽
906.0 Late effect of open wound of head, neck, and trunk
906.5 Late effect of burn of eye, face, head, and neck

941.01 Burn of unspecified degree of ear (any part)

941.02 Burn of unspecified degree of eye (with other parts of face, head, and neck)

941.03 Burn of unspecified degree of lip(s)

941.05 Burn of unspecified degree of nose (septum)

941.09 Burn of unspecified degree of multiple sites (except with eye) of face, head, and neck

941.31 Full-thickness skin loss due to burn (third degree NOS) of ear (any part)

941.32 Full-thickness skin loss due to burn (third degree NOS) of eye (with other parts of face, head, and neck)

941.33 Full-thickness skin loss due to burn (third degree NOS) of lip(s)

941.35 Full-thickness skin loss due to burn (third degree NOS) of nose (septum)

941.39 Full-thickness skin loss due to burn (third degree NOS) of multiple sites (except with eye) of face, head, and neck

941.49 Deep necrosis of underlying tissues due to burn (deep third degree) of multiple sites (except with eye) of face, head, and neck, without mention of loss of a body part

941.51 Deep necrosis of underlying tissues due to burn (deep third degree) of ear (any part), with loss of a body part

941.52 Deep necrosis of underlying tissues due to burn (deep third degree) of eye (with other parts of face, head, and neck), with loss of a body part

941.53 Deep necrosis of underlying tissues due to burn (deep third degree) of lip(s), with loss of a body part

941.55 Deep necrosis of underlying tissues due to burn (deep third degree) of nose (septum), with loss of a body part

941.59 Deep necrosis of underlying tissues due to burn (deep third degree) of multiple sites (except eye) of face, head, and neck, with loss of a body part

946.3 Full-thickness skin loss due to burn (third degree NOS) of multiple specified sites

946.4 Deep necrosis of underlying tissues due to burn (deep third degree) of multiple specified sites, without mention of loss of a body part

946.5 Deep necrosis of underlying tissues due to burn (deep third degree) of multiple specified sites, with loss of a body part

948.00 Burn (any degree) involving less than 10% of body surface with third degree burn of less than 10% or unspecified amount

948.10 Burn (any degree) involving 10-19% of body surface with third degree burn of less than 10% or unspecified amount

948.11 Burn (any degree) involving 10-19% of body surface with third degree burn of 10-19%

948.20 Burn (any degree) involving 20-29% of body surface with third degree burn of less than 10% or unspecified amount

948.21 Burn (any degree) involving 20-29% of body surface with third degree burn of 10-19%

948.22 Burn (any degree) involving 20-29% of body surface with third degree burn of 20-29%

948.30 Burn (any degree) involving 30-39% of body surface with third degree burn of less than 10% or unspecified amount

948.31 Burn (any degree) involving 30-39% of body surface with third degree burn of 10-19%

948.32 Burn (any degree) involving 30-39% of body surface with third degree burn of 20-29%

948.33 Burn (any degree) involving 30-39% of body surface with third degree burn of 30-39%

948.40 Burn (any degree) involving 40-49% of body surface with third degree burn of less than 10% or unspecified amount

948.41 Burn (any degree) involving 40-49% of body surface with third degree burn of 10-19%

948.42 Burn (any degree) involving 40-49% of body surface with third degree burn of 20-29%

948.43 Burn (any degree) involving 40-49% of body surface with third degree burn of 30-39%

948.44 Burn (any degree) involving 40-49% of body surface with third degree burn of 40-49%

948.50 Burn (any degree) involving 50-59% of body surface with third degree burn of less than 10% or unspecified amount

948.51 Burn (any degree) involving 50-59% of body surface with third degree burn of 10-19%

948.52 Burn (any degree) involving 50-59% of body surface with third degree burn of 20-29%

948.53 Burn (any degree) involving 50-59% of body surface with third degree burn of 30-39%

948.54 Burn (any degree) involving 50-59% of body surface with third degree burn of 40-49%

948.55 Burn (any degree) involving 50-59% of body surface with third degree burn of 50-59%

948.60 Burn (any degree) involving 60-69% of body surface with third degree burn of less than 10% or unspecified amount

948.61 Burn (any degree) involving 60-69% of body surface with third degree burn of 10-19%

948.62 Burn (any degree) involving 60-69% of body surface with third degree burn of 20-29%

948.63 Burn (any degree) involving 60-69% of body surface with third degree burn of 30-39%

948.64 Burn (any degree) involving 60-69% of body surface with third degree burn of 40-49%

948.65 Burn (any degree) involving 60-69% of body surface with third degree burn of 50-59%

948.66 Burn (any degree) involving 60-69% of body surface with third degree burn of 60-69%

948.70 Burn (any degree) involving 70-79% of body surface with third degree burn of less than 10% or unspecified amount

948.71 Burn (any degree) involving 70-79% of body surface with third degree burn of 10-19%

948.72 Burn (any degree) involving 70-79% of body surface with third degree burn of 20-29%

948.73 Burn (any degree) involving 70-79% of body surface with third degree burn of 30-39%

948.74 Burn (any degree) involving 70-79% of body surface with third degree burn of 40-49%

948.75 Burn (any degree) involving 70-79% of body surface with third degree burn of 50-59%

948.76 Burn (any degree) involving 70-79% of body surface with third degree burn of 60-69%

948.77 Burn (any degree) involving 70-79% of body surface with third degree burn of 70-79%

948.80 Burn (any degree) involving 80-89% of body surface with third degree burn of less than 10% or unspecified amount

948.81 Burn (any degree) involving 80-89% of body surface with third degree burn of 10-19%

948.82 Burn (any degree) involving 80-89% of body surface with third degree burn of 20-29%

948.83 Burn (any degree) involving 80-89% of body surface with third degree burn of 30-39%

948.84 Burn (any degree) involving 80-89% of body surface with third degree burn of 40-49%

948.85 Burn (any degree) involving 80-89% of body surface with third degree burn of 50-59%

948.86 Burn (any degree) involving 80-89% of body surface with third degree burn of 60-69%

948.87 Burn (any degree) involving 80-89% of body surface with third degree burn of 70-79%

948.88 Burn (any degree) involving 80-89% of body surface with third degree burn of 80-89%

959.09 Injury of face and neck, other and unspecified

996.52 Mechanical complication due to other tissue graft, not elsewhere classified

998.30 Disruption of wound, unspecified

998.32 Disruption of external operation (surgical) wound

998.33 Disruption of traumatic injury wound repair

998.59 Other postoperative infection — (Use additional code to identify infection)

998.83 Non-healing surgical wound

V10.02 Personal history of malignant neoplasm of other and unspecified parts of oral cavity and pharynx

V51.8 Other aftercare involving the use of plastic surgery

ICD-9-CM Procedural

18.79 Other plastic repair of external ear

27.57 Attachment of pedicle or flap graft to lip and mouth

86.71 Cutting and preparation of pedicle grafts or flaps

15650

15650 Transfer, intermediate, of any pedicle flap (eg, abdomen to wrist, Walking tube), any location

ICD-9-CM Diagnostic

172.0 Malignant melanoma of skin of lip

172.1 Malignant melanoma of skin of eyelid, including canthus

172.2 Malignant melanoma of skin of ear and external auditory canal

172.3 Malignant melanoma of skin of other and unspecified parts of face

172.4 Malignant melanoma of skin of scalp and neck

172.5 Malignant melanoma of skin of trunk, except scrotum

172.6 Malignant melanoma of skin of upper limb, including shoulder

172.7 Malignant melanoma of skin of lower limb, including hip

172.8 Malignant melanoma of other specified sites of skin

173.00 Unspecified malignant neoplasm of skin of lip

173.01 Basal cell carcinoma of skin of lip

173.02 Squamous cell carcinoma of skin of lip

173.09 Other specified malignant neoplasm of skin of lip

173.10 Unspecified malignant neoplasm of eyelid, including canthus

173.11 Basal cell carcinoma of eyelid, including canthus

173.12 Squamous cell carcinoma of eyelid, including canthus
173.19 Other specified malignant neoplasm of eyelid, including canthus
173.20 Unspecified malignant neoplasm of skin of ear and external auditory canal ▽
173.21 Basal cell carcinoma of skin of ear and external auditory canal
173.22 Squamous cell carcinoma of skin of ear and external auditory canal
173.29 Other specified malignant neoplasm of skin of ear and external auditory canal
173.30 Unspecified malignant neoplasm of skin of other and unspecified parts of face ▽
173.31 Basal cell carcinoma of skin of other and unspecified parts of face
173.32 Squamous cell carcinoma of skin of other and unspecified parts of face
173.39 Other specified malignant neoplasm of skin of other and unspecified parts of face
173.40 Unspecified malignant neoplasm of scalp and skin of neck ▽
173.41 Basal cell carcinoma of scalp and skin of neck
173.42 Squamous cell carcinoma of scalp and skin of neck
173.49 Other specified malignant neoplasm of scalp and skin of neck
173.50 Unspecified malignant neoplasm of skin of trunk, except scrotum ▽
173.51 Basal cell carcinoma of skin of trunk, except scrotum
173.52 Squamous cell carcinoma of skin of trunk, except scrotum
173.59 Other specified malignant neoplasm of skin of trunk, except scrotum
173.60 Unspecified malignant neoplasm of skin of upper limb, including shoulder ▽
173.61 Basal cell carcinoma of skin of upper limb, including shoulder
173.62 Squamous cell carcinoma of skin of upper limb, including shoulder
173.69 Other specified malignant neoplasm of skin of upper limb, including shoulder
173.70 Unspecified malignant neoplasm of skin of lower limb, including hip ▽
173.71 Basal cell carcinoma of skin of lower limb, including hip
173.72 Squamous cell carcinoma of skin of lower limb, including hip
173.79 Other specified malignant neoplasm of skin of lower limb, including hip
173.80 Unspecified malignant neoplasm of other specified sites of skin ▽
173.81 Basal cell carcinoma of other specified sites of skin
173.82 Squamous cell carcinoma of other specified sites of skin
173.89 Other specified malignant neoplasm of other specified sites of skin
174.0 Malignant neoplasm of nipple and areola of female breast — (Use additional code to identify estrogen receptor status: V86.0-V86.1) ♀
175.0 Malignant neoplasm of nipple and areola of male breast — (Use additional code to identify estrogen receptor status: V86.0-V86.1) ♂
198.2 Secondary malignant neoplasm of skin
209.31 Merkel cell carcinoma of the face
209.32 Merkel cell carcinoma of the scalp and neck
209.33 Merkel cell carcinoma of the upper limb
209.34 Merkel cell carcinoma of the lower limb
209.35 Merkel cell carcinoma of the trunk
209.36 Merkel cell carcinoma of other sites
209.75 Secondary Merkel cell carcinoma
210.0 Benign neoplasm of lip
232.0 Carcinoma in situ of skin of lip
232.1 Carcinoma in situ of eyelid, including canthus
232.2 Carcinoma in situ of skin of ear and external auditory canal
232.3 Carcinoma in situ of skin of other and unspecified parts of face ▽
232.4 Carcinoma in situ of scalp and skin of neck
232.5 Carcinoma in situ of skin of trunk, except scrotum
232.6 Carcinoma in situ of skin of upper limb, including shoulder
232.7 Carcinoma in situ of skin of lower limb, including hip
232.8 Carcinoma in situ of other specified sites of skin
235.1 Neoplasm of uncertain behavior of lip, oral cavity, and pharynx
238.2 Neoplasm of uncertain behavior of skin
239.0 Neoplasm of unspecified nature of digestive system
239.2 Neoplasms of unspecified nature of bone, soft tissue, and skin
249.70 Secondary diabetes mellitus with peripheral circulatory disorders, not stated as uncontrolled, or unspecified — (Use additional code to identify manifestation: 443.81, 785.4) (Use additional code to identify any associated insulin use: V58.67)
249.71 Secondary diabetes mellitus with peripheral circulatory disorders, uncontrolled — (Use additional code to identify manifestation: 443.81, 785.4) (Use additional code to identify any associated insulin use: V58.67)
249.80 Secondary diabetes mellitus with other specified manifestations, not stated as uncontrolled, or unspecified — (Use additional code to identify manifestation: 707.10-707.19, 707.8, 707.9, 731.8) (Use additional code to identify any associated insulin use: V58.67)
249.81 Secondary diabetes mellitus with other specified manifestations, uncontrolled — (Use additional code to identify manifestation: 707.10-707.19, 707.8, 707.9, 731.8) (Use additional code to identify any associated insulin use: V58.67)
249.90 Secondary diabetes mellitus with unspecified complication, not stated as uncontrolled, or unspecified — (Use additional code to identify any associated insulin use: V58.67) ▽
249.91 Secondary diabetes mellitus with unspecified complication, uncontrolled — (Use additional code to identify any associated insulin use: V58.67) ▽
250.70 Diabetes with peripheral circulatory disorders, type II or unspecified type, not stated as uncontrolled — (Use additional code to identify manifestation: 443.81, 785.4)
250.71 Diabetes with peripheral circulatory disorders, type I [juvenile type], not stated as uncontrolled — (Use additional code to identify manifestation: 443.81, 785.4)
250.72 Diabetes with peripheral circulatory disorders, type II or unspecified type, uncontrolled — (Use additional code to identify manifestation: 443.81, 785.4)
250.73 Diabetes with peripheral circulatory disorders, type I [juvenile type], uncontrolled — (Use additional code to identify manifestation: 443.81, 785.4)
440.23 Atherosclerosis of native arteries of the extremities with ulceration — (Use additional code for any associated ulceration: 707.10-707.19, 707.8, 707.9)
443.81 Peripheral angiopathy in diseases classified elsewhere — (Code first underlying disease: 249.7, 250.7) ☒
454.0 Varicose veins of lower extremities with ulcer
454.2 Varicose veins of lower extremities with ulcer and inflammation
454.8 Varicose veins of the lower extremities with other complications
459.11 Postphlebitic syndrome with ulcer
459.13 Postphlebitic syndrome with ulcer and inflammation
459.19 Postphlebitic syndrome with other complication
459.31 Chronic venous hypertension with ulcer
459.33 Chronic venous hypertension with ulcer and inflammation
459.39 Chronic venous hypertension with other complication
681.00 Unspecified cellulitis and abscess of finger — (Use additional code to identify organism: 041.1) ▽
681.01 Felon — (Use additional code to identify organism: 041.1)
681.02 Onychia and paronychia of finger — (Use additional code to identify organism: 041.1)
681.10 Unspecified cellulitis and abscess of toe — (Use additional code to identify organism: 041.1) ▽
681.11 Onychia and paronychia of toe — (Use additional code to identify organism: 041.1)
682.0 Cellulitis and abscess of face — (Use additional code to identify organism, such as 041.1, etc.)
682.1 Cellulitis and abscess of neck — (Use additional code to identify organism, such as 041.1, etc.)
682.2 Cellulitis and abscess of trunk — (Use additional code to identify organism, such as 041.1, etc.)
682.3 Cellulitis and abscess of upper arm and forearm — (Use additional code to identify organism, such as 041.1, etc.)
682.4 Cellulitis and abscess of hand, except fingers and thumb — (Use additional code to identify organism, such as 041.1, etc.)
682.5 Cellulitis and abscess of buttock — (Use additional code to identify organism, such as 041.1, etc.)
682.6 Cellulitis and abscess of leg, except foot — (Use additional code to identify organism, such as 041.1, etc.)
682.7 Cellulitis and abscess of foot, except toes — (Use additional code to identify organism, such as 041.1, etc.)
682.8 Cellulitis and abscess of other specified site — (Use additional code to identify organism, such as 041.1, etc.)

707.00 Pressure ulcer, unspecified site — (Use additional code to identify pressure ulcer stage: 707.20-707.25)

707.01 Pressure ulcer, elbow — (Use additional code to identify pressure ulcer stage: 707.20-707.25)

707.02 Pressure ulcer, upper back — (Use additional code to identify pressure ulcer stage: 707.20-707.25)

707.03 Pressure ulcer, lower back — (Use additional code to identify pressure ulcer stage: 707.20-707.25)

707.04 Pressure ulcer, hip — (Use additional code to identify pressure ulcer stage: 707.20-707.25)

707.05 Pressure ulcer, buttock — (Use additional code to identify pressure ulcer stage: 707.20-707.25)

707.06 Pressure ulcer, ankle — (Use additional code to identify pressure ulcer stage: 707.20-707.25)

707.07 Pressure ulcer, heel — (Use additional code to identify pressure ulcer stage: 707.20-707.25)

707.09 Pressure ulcer, other site — (Use additional code to identify pressure ulcer stage: 707.20-707.25)

707.10 Ulcer of lower limb, unspecified — (Code, if applicable, any causal condition first: 249.80-249.81, 250.80-250.83, 440.23, 459.11, 459.13, 459.31, 459.33)

707.11 Ulcer of thigh — (Code, if applicable, any causal condition first: 249.80-249.81, 250.80-250.83, 440.23, 459.11, 459.13, 459.31, 459.33)

707.12 Ulcer of calf — (Code, if applicable, any causal condition first: 249.80-249.81, 250.80-250.83, 440.23, 459.11, 459.13, 459.31, 459.33)

707.13 Ulcer of ankle — (Code, if applicable, any causal condition first: 249.80-249.81, 250.80-250.83, 440.23, 459.11, 459.13, 459.31, 459.33)

707.14 Ulcer of heel and midfoot — (Code, if applicable, any causal condition first: 249.80-249.81, 250.80-250.83, 440.23, 459.11, 459.13, 459.31, 459.33)

707.15 Ulcer of other part of foot — (Code, if applicable, any causal condition first: 249.80-249.81, 250.80-250.83, 440.23, 459.11, 459.13, 459.31, 459.33)

707.19 Ulcer of other part of lower limb — (Code, if applicable, any causal condition first: 249.80-249.81, 250.80-250.83, 440.23, 459.11, 459.13, 459.31, 459.33)

707.20 Pressure ulcer, unspecified stage — (Code first site of pressure ulcer: 707.00-707.09)

707.21 Pressure ulcer, stage I — (Code first site of pressure ulcer: 707.00-707.09)

707.22 Pressure ulcer stage II — (Code first site of pressure ulcer: 707.00-707.09)

707.23 Pressure ulcer stage III — (Code first site of pressure ulcer: 707.00-707.09)

707.24 Pressure ulcer stage IV — (Code first site of pressure ulcer: 707.00-707.09)

707.25 Pressure ulcer, unstageable — (Code first site of pressure ulcer: 707.00-707.09)

707.8 Chronic ulcer of other specified site

707.9 Chronic ulcer of unspecified site

709.2 Scar condition and fibrosis of skin

709.9 Unspecified disorder of skin and subcutaneous tissue

728.86 Necrotizing fasciitis — (Use additional code to identify infectious organism, 041.00-041.89, 785.4, if applicable)

754.0 Congenital musculoskeletal deformities of skull, face, and jaw

756.70 Unspecified congenital anomaly of abdominal wall

756.71 Prune belly syndrome

756.79 Other congenital anomalies of abdominal wall

785.4 Gangrene — (Code first any associated underlying condition)

880.00 Open wound of shoulder region, without mention of complication

880.01 Open wound of scapular region, without mention of complication

880.02 Open wound of axillary region, without mention of complication

880.03 Open wound of upper arm, without mention of complication

880.09 Open wound of multiple sites of shoulder and upper arm, without mention of complication

880.10 Open wound of shoulder region, complicated

880.11 Open wound of scapular region, complicated

880.12 Open wound of axillary region, complicated

880.13 Open wound of upper arm, complicated

880.19 Open wound of multiple sites of shoulder and upper arm, complicated

880.20 Open wound of shoulder region, with tendon involvement

880.21 Open wound of scapular region, with tendon involvement

880.22 Open wound of axillary region, with tendon involvement

880.23 Open wound of upper arm, with tendon involvement

880.29 Open wound of multiple sites of shoulder and upper arm, with tendon involvement

881.00 Open wound of forearm, without mention of complication

881.01 Open wound of elbow, without mention of complication

881.02 Open wound of wrist, without mention of complication

881.10 Open wound of forearm, complicated

881.11 Open wound of elbow, complicated

881.12 Open wound of wrist, complicated

881.20 Open wound of forearm, with tendon involvement

881.21 Open wound of elbow, with tendon involvement

881.22 Open wound of wrist, with tendon involvement

882.0 Open wound of hand except finger(s) alone, without mention of complication

882.1 Open wound of hand except finger(s) alone, complicated

882.2 Open wound of hand except finger(s) alone, with tendon involvement

883.0 Open wound of finger(s), without mention of complication

883.1 Open wound of finger(s), complicated

883.2 Open wound of finger(s), with tendon involvement

884.0 Multiple and unspecified open wound of upper limb, without mention of complication

884.1 Multiple and unspecified open wound of upper limb, complicated

884.2 Multiple and unspecified open wound of upper limb, with tendon involvement

885.0 Traumatic amputation of thumb (complete) (partial), without mention of complication

885.1 Traumatic amputation of thumb (complete) (partial), complicated

886.0 Traumatic amputation of other finger(s) (complete) (partial), without mention of complication

886.1 Traumatic amputation of other finger(s) (complete) (partial), complicated

887.2 Traumatic amputation of arm and hand (complete) (partial), unilateral, at or above elbow, without mention of complication

887.3 Traumatic amputation of arm and hand (complete) (partial), unilateral, at or above elbow, complicated

887.4 Traumatic amputation of arm and hand (complete) (partial), unilateral, level not specified, without mention of complication

887.5 Traumatic amputation of arm and hand (complete) (partial), unilateral, level not specified, complicated

887.6 Traumatic amputation of arm and hand (complete) (partial), bilateral (any level), without mention of complication

887.7 Traumatic amputation of arm and hand (complete) (partial), bilateral (any level), complicated

890.0 Open wound of hip and thigh, without mention of complication

890.1 Open wound of hip and thigh, complicated

890.2 Open wound of hip and thigh, with tendon involvement

891.0 Open wound of knee, leg (except thigh), and ankle, without mention of complication

891.1 Open wound of knee, leg (except thigh), and ankle, complicated

891.2 Open wound of knee, leg (except thigh), and ankle, with tendon involvement

892.0 Open wound of foot except toe(s) alone, without mention of complication

892.1 Open wound of foot except toe(s) alone, complicated

892.2 Open wound of foot except toe(s) alone, with tendon involvement

893.0 Open wound of toe(s), without mention of complication

893.1 Open wound of toe(s), complicated

893.2 Open wound of toe(s), with tendon involvement

894.0 Multiple and unspecified open wound of lower limb, without mention of complication

894.1 Multiple and unspecified open wound of lower limb, complicated

894.2 Multiple and unspecified open wound of lower limb, with tendon involvement

895.0 Traumatic amputation of toe(s) (complete) (partial), without mention of complication

895.1 Traumatic amputation of toe(s) (complete) (partial), complicated

896.0 Traumatic amputation of foot (complete) (partial), unilateral, without mention of complication

896.1 Traumatic amputation of foot (complete) (partial), unilateral, complicated
896.2 Traumatic amputation of foot (complete) (partial), bilateral, without mention of complication
896.3 Traumatic amputation of foot (complete) (partial), bilateral, complicated
897.0 Traumatic amputation of leg(s) (complete) (partial), unilateral, below knee, without mention of complication
897.1 Traumatic amputation of leg(s) (complete) (partial), unilateral, below knee, complicated
897.2 Traumatic amputation of leg(s) (complete) (partial), unilateral, at or above knee, without mention of complication
897.3 Traumatic amputation of leg(s) (complete) (partial), unilateral, at or above knee, complicated
897.4 Traumatic amputation of leg(s) (complete) (partial), unilateral, level not specified, without mention of complication ▽
897.5 Traumatic amputation of leg(s) (complete) (partial), unilateral, level not specified, complicated ▽
897.6 Traumatic amputation of leg(s) (complete) (partial), bilateral (any level), without mention of complication
897.7 Traumatic amputation of leg(s) (complete) (partial), bilateral (any level), complicated
906.0 Late effect of open wound of head, neck, and trunk
906.1 Late effect of open wound of extremities without mention of tendon injury
906.5 Late effect of burn of eye, face, head, and neck
906.6 Late effect of burn of wrist and hand
906.7 Late effect of burn of other extremities
906.8 Late effect of burns of other specified sites
906.9 Late effect of burn of unspecified site ▽
941.30 Full-thickness skin loss due to burn (third degree NOS) of unspecified site of face and head ▽
941.31 Full-thickness skin loss due to burn (third degree NOS) of ear (any part)
941.32 Full-thickness skin loss due to burn (third degree NOS) of eye (with other parts of face, head, and neck)
941.33 Full-thickness skin loss due to burn (third degree NOS) of lip(s)
941.34 Full-thickness skin loss due to burn (third degree NOS) of chin
941.35 Full-thickness skin loss due to burn (third degree NOS) of nose (septum)
941.36 Full-thickness skin loss due to burn (third degree NOS) of scalp (any part)
941.37 Full-thickness skin loss due to burn (third degree NOS) of forehead and cheek
941.38 Full-thickness skin loss due to burn (third degree NOS) of neck
941.39 Full-thickness skin loss due to burn (third degree NOS) of multiple sites (except with eye) of face, head, and neck
941.40 Deep necrosis of underlying tissues due to burn (deep third degree) of unspecified site of face and head, without mention of loss of a body part ▽
941.41 Deep necrosis of underlying tissues due to burn (deep third degree) of ear (any part), without mention of loss of a body part
941.42 Deep necrosis of underlying tissues due to burn (deep third degree) of eye (with other parts of face, head, and neck), without mention of loss of a body part
941.43 Deep necrosis of underlying tissues due to burn (deep third degree) of lip(s), without mention of loss of a body part
941.44 Deep necrosis of underlying tissues due to burn (deep third degree) of chin, without mention of loss of a body part
941.45 Deep necrosis of underlying tissues due to burn (deep third degree) of nose (septum), without mention of loss of a body part
941.46 Deep necrosis of underlying tissues due to burn (deep third degree) of scalp (any part), without mention of loss of a body part
941.47 Deep necrosis of underlying tissues due to burn (deep third degree) of forehead and cheek, without mention of loss of a body part
941.48 Deep necrosis of underlying tissues due to burn (deep third degree) of neck, without mention of loss of a body part
941.49 Deep necrosis of underlying tissues due to burn (deep third degree) of multiple sites (except with eye) of face, head, and neck, without mention of loss of a body part
941.50 Deep necrosis of underlying tissues due to burn (deep third degree) of face and head, unspecified site, with loss of a body part ▽
941.51 Deep necrosis of underlying tissues due to burn (deep third degree) of ear (any part), with loss of a body part
941.52 Deep necrosis of underlying tissues due to burn (deep third degree) of eye (with other parts of face, head, and neck), with loss of a body part
941.53 Deep necrosis of underlying tissues due to burn (deep third degree) of lip(s), with loss of a body part
941.54 Deep necrosis of underlying tissues due to burn (deep third degree) of chin, with loss of a body part
941.55 Deep necrosis of underlying tissues due to burn (deep third degree) of nose (septum), with loss of a body part
941.56 Deep necrosis of underlying tissues due to burn (deep third degree) of scalp (any part), with loss of a body part
941.57 Deep necrosis of underlying tissues due to burn (deep third degree) of forehead and cheek, with loss of a body part
941.58 Deep necrosis of underlying tissues due to burn (deep third degree) of neck, with loss of a body part
941.59 Deep necrosis of underlying tissues due to burn (deep third degree) of multiple sites (except eye) of face, head, and neck, with loss of a body part
942.30 Full-thickness skin loss due to burn (third degree NOS) of unspecified site of trunk ▽
942.31 Full-thickness skin loss due to burn (third degree NOS) of breast
942.32 Full-thickness skin loss due to burn (third degree NOS) of chest wall, excluding breast and nipple
942.33 Full-thickness skin loss due to burn (third degree NOS) of abdominal wall
942.34 Full-thickness skin loss due to burn (third degree NOS) of back (any part)
942.35 Full-thickness skin loss due to burn (third degree NOS) of genitalia
942.39 Full-thickness skin loss due to burn (third degree NOS) of other and multiple sites of trunk
942.40 Deep necrosis of underlying tissues due to burn (deep third degree) of trunk, unspecified site, without mention of loss of a body part ▽
942.41 Deep necrosis of underlying tissues due to burn (deep third degree) of breast, without mention of loss of a body part
942.42 Deep necrosis of underlying tissues due to burn (deep third degree) of chest wall, excluding breast and nipple, without mention of loss of a body part
942.43 Deep necrosis of underlying tissues due to burn (deep third degree) of abdominal wall, without mention of loss of a body part
942.44 Deep necrosis of underlying tissues due to burn (deep third degree) of back (any part), without mention of loss of a body part
942.45 Deep necrosis of underlying tissues due to burn (deep third degree) of genitalia, without mention of loss of a body part
942.49 Deep necrosis of underlying tissues due to burn (deep third degree) of other and multiple sites of trunk, without mention of loss of a body part
942.50 Deep necrosis of underlying tissues due to burn (deep third degree) of unspecified site of trunk, with loss of a body part ▽
942.51 Deep necrosis of underlying tissues due to burn (deep third degree) of breast, with loss of a body part
942.52 Deep necrosis of underlying tissues due to burn (deep third degree) of chest wall, excluding breast and nipple, with loss of a body part
942.53 Deep necrosis of underlying tissues due to burn (deep third degree) of abdominal wall with loss of a body part
942.54 Deep necrosis of underlying tissues due to burn (deep third degree) of back (any part), with loss of a body part
942.55 Deep necrosis of underlying tissues due to burn (deep third degree) of genitalia, with loss of a body part
942.59 Deep necrosis of underlying tissues due to burn (deep third degree) of other and multiple sites of trunk, with loss of a body part
943.30 Full-thickness skin loss due to burn (third degree NOS) of unspecified site of upper limb ▽
943.31 Full-thickness skin loss due to burn (third degree NOS) of forearm
943.32 Full-thickness skin loss due to burn (third degree NOS) of elbow
943.33 Full-thickness skin loss due to burn (third degree NOS) of upper arm
943.34 Full-thickness skin loss due to burn (third degree NOS) of axilla

943.35 Full-thickness skin loss due to burn (third degree NOS) of shoulder

943.36 Full-thickness skin loss due to burn (third degree NOS) of scapular region

943.39 Full-thickness skin loss due to burn (third degree NOS) of multiple sites of upper limb, except wrist and hand

943.40 Deep necrosis of underlying tissues due to burn (deep third degree) of unspecified site of upper limb, without mention of loss of a body part ▽

943.41 Deep necrosis of underlying tissues due to burn (deep third degree) of forearm, without mention of loss of a body part

943.42 Deep necrosis of underlying tissues due to burn (deep third degree) of elbow, without mention of loss of a body part

943.43 Deep necrosis of underlying tissues due to burn (deep third degree) of upper arm, without mention of loss of a body part

943.44 Deep necrosis of underlying tissues due to burn (deep third degree) of axilla, without mention of loss of a body part

943.45 Deep necrosis of underlying tissues due to burn (deep third degree) of shoulder, without mention of loss of a body part

943.46 Deep necrosis of underlying tissues due to burn (deep third degree) of scapular region, without mention of loss of a body part

943.49 Deep necrosis of underlying tissues due to burn (deep third degree) of multiple sites of upper limb, except wrist and hand, without mention of loss of a body part

943.50 Deep necrosis of underlying tissues due to burn (deep third degree) of unspecified site of upper limb, with loss of a body part ▽

943.51 Deep necrosis of underlying tissues due to burn (deep third degree) of forearm, with loss of a body part

943.52 Deep necrosis of underlying tissues due to burn (deep third degree) of elbow, with loss of a body part

943.53 Deep necrosis of underlying tissues due to burn (deep third degree) of upper arm, with loss of upper a body part

943.54 Deep necrosis of underlying tissues due to burn (deep third degree) of axilla, with loss of a body part

943.55 Deep necrosis of underlying tissues due to burn (deep third degree) of shoulder, with loss of a body part

943.56 Deep necrosis of underlying tissues due to burn (deep third degree) of scapular region, with loss of a body part

943.59 Deep necrosis of underlying tissues due to burn (deep third degree) of multiple sites of upper limb, except wrist and hand, with loss of a body part

944.30 Full-thickness skin loss due to burn (third degree NOS) of unspecified site of hand ▽

944.31 Full-thickness skin loss due to burn (third degree NOS) of single digit [finger (nail)] other than thumb

944.32 Full-thickness skin loss due to burn (third degree NOS) of thumb (nail)

944.33 Full-thickness skin loss due to burn (third degree NOS) of two or more digits of hand, not including thumb

944.34 Full-thickness skin loss due to burn (third degree NOS) of two or more digits of hand including thumb

944.35 Full-thickness skin loss due to burn (third degree NOS) of palm of hand

944.36 Full-thickness skin loss due to burn (third degree NOS) of back of hand

944.37 Full-thickness skin loss due to burn (third degree NOS) of wrist

944.38 Full-thickness skin loss due to burn (third degree NOS) of multiple sites of wrist(s) and hand(s)

944.40 Deep necrosis of underlying tissues due to burn (deep third degree) of unspecified site of hand, without mention of loss of a body part ▽

944.41 Deep necrosis of underlying tissues due to burn (deep third degree) of single digit [finger (nail)] other than thumb, without mention of loss of a body part

944.42 Deep necrosis of underlying tissues due to burn (deep third degree) of thumb (nail), without mention of loss of a body part

944.43 Deep necrosis of underlying tissues due to burn (deep third degree) of two or more digits of hand, not including thumb, without mention of loss of a body part

944.44 Deep necrosis of underlying tissues due to burn (deep third degree) of two or more digits of hand including thumb, without mention of loss of a body part

944.45 Deep necrosis of underlying tissues due to burn (deep third degree) of palm of hand, without mention of loss of a body part

944.46 Deep necrosis of underlying tissues due to burn (deep third degree) of back of hand, without mention of loss of a body part

944.47 Deep necrosis of underlying tissues due to burn (deep third degree) of wrist, without mention of loss of a body part

944.48 Deep necrosis of underlying tissues due to burn (deep third degree) of multiple sites of wrist(s) and hand(s), without mention of loss of a body part

944.50 Deep necrosis of underlying tissues due to burn (deep third degree) of unspecified site of hand, with loss of a body part ▽

944.51 Deep necrosis of underlying tissues due to burn (deep third degree) of single digit (finger (nail)) other than thumb, with loss of a body part

944.52 Deep necrosis of underlying tissues due to burn (deep third degree) of thumb (nail), with loss of a body part

944.53 Deep necrosis of underlying tissues due to burn (deep third degree) of two or more digits of hand, not including thumb, with loss of a body part

944.54 Deep necrosis of underlying tissues due to burn (deep third degree) of two or more digits of hand including thumb, with loss of a body part

944.55 Deep necrosis of underlying tissues due to burn (deep third degree) of palm of hand, with loss of a body part

944.56 Deep necrosis of underlying tissues due to burn (deep third degree) of back of hand, with loss of a body part

944.57 Deep necrosis of underlying tissues due to burn (deep third degree) of wrist, with loss of a body part

944.58 Deep necrosis of underlying tissues due to burn (deep third degree) of multiple sites of wrist(s) and hand(s), with loss of a body part

945.30 Full-thickness skin loss due to burn (third degree NOS) of unspecified site of lower limb ▽

945.31 Full-thickness skin loss due to burn (third degree NOS) of toe(s) (nail)

945.32 Full-thickness skin loss due to burn (third degree NOS) of foot

945.33 Full-thickness skin loss due to burn (third degree NOS) of ankle

945.34 Full-thickness skin loss due to burn (third degree NOS) of lower leg

945.35 Full-thickness skin loss due to burn (third degree NOS) of knee

945.36 Full-thickness skin loss due to burn (third degree NOS) of thigh (any part)

945.39 Full-thickness skin loss due to burn (third degree NOS) of multiple sites of lower limb(s)

945.40 Deep necrosis of underlying tissues due to burn (deep third degree) of unspecified site of lower limb (leg), without mention of loss of a body part ▽

945.41 Deep necrosis of underlying tissues due to burn (deep third degree) of toe(s) (nail), without mention of loss of a body part

945.42 Deep necrosis of underlying tissues due to burn (deep third degree) of foot, without mention of loss of a body part

945.43 Deep necrosis of underlying tissues due to burn (deep third degree) of ankle, without mention of loss of a body part

945.44 Deep necrosis of underlying tissues due to burn (deep third degree) of lower leg, without mention of loss of a body part

945.45 Deep necrosis of underlying tissues due to burn (deep third degree) of knee, without mention of loss of a body part

945.46 Deep necrosis of underlying tissues due to burn (deep third degree) of thigh (any part), without mention of loss of a body part

945.49 Deep necrosis of underlying tissues due to burn (deep third degree) of multiple sites of lower limb(s), without mention of loss of a body part

945.50 Deep necrosis of underlying tissues due to burn (deep third degree) of unspecified site lower limb (leg), with loss of a body part ▽

945.51 Deep necrosis of underlying tissues due to burn (deep third degree) of toe(s) (nail), with loss of a body part

945.52 Deep necrosis of underlying tissues due to burn (deep third degree) of foot, with loss of a body part

945.53 Deep necrosis of underlying tissues due to burn (deep third degree) of ankle, with loss of a body part

945.54 Deep necrosis of underlying tissues due to burn (deep third degree) of lower leg, with loss of a body part

945.55 Deep necrosis of underlying tissues due to burn (deep third degree) of knee, with loss of a body part
945.56 Deep necrosis of underlying tissues due to burn (deep third degree) of thigh (any part), with loss of a body part
945.59 Deep necrosis of underlying tissues due to burn (deep third degree) of multiple sites of lower limb(s), with loss of a body part
946.3 Full-thickness skin loss due to burn (third degree NOS) of multiple specified sites
946.4 Deep necrosis of underlying tissues due to burn (deep third degree) of multiple specified sites, without mention of loss of a body part
946.5 Deep necrosis of underlying tissues due to burn (deep third degree) of multiple specified sites, with loss of a body part
948.00 Burn (any degree) involving less than 10% of body surface with third degree burn of less than 10% or unspecified amount
948.10 Burn (any degree) involving 10-19% of body surface with third degree burn of less than 10% or unspecified amount
948.11 Burn (any degree) involving 10-19% of body surface with third degree burn of 10-19%
948.20 Burn (any degree) involving 20-29% of body surface with third degree burn of less than 10% or unspecified amount
948.21 Burn (any degree) involving 20-29% of body surface with third degree burn of 10-19%
948.22 Burn (any degree) involving 20-29% of body surface with third degree burn of 20-29%
948.30 Burn (any degree) involving 30-39% of body surface with third degree burn of less than 10% or unspecified amount
948.31 Burn (any degree) involving 30-39% of body surface with third degree burn of 10-19%
948.32 Burn (any degree) involving 30-39% of body surface with third degree burn of 20-29%
948.33 Burn (any degree) involving 30-39% of body surface with third degree burn of 30-39%
948.40 Burn (any degree) involving 40-49% of body surface with third degree burn of less than 10% or unspecified amount
948.41 Burn (any degree) involving 40-49% of body surface with third degree burn of 10-19%
948.42 Burn (any degree) involving 40-49% of body surface with third degree burn of 20-29%
948.43 Burn (any degree) involving 40-49% of body surface with third degree burn of 30-39%
948.44 Burn (any degree) involving 40-49% of body surface with third degree burn of 40-49%
948.50 Burn (any degree) involving 50-59% of body surface with third degree burn of less than 10% or unspecified amount
948.51 Burn (any degree) involving 50-59% of body surface with third degree burn of 10-19%
948.52 Burn (any degree) involving 50-59% of body surface with third degree burn of 20-29%
948.53 Burn (any degree) involving 50-59% of body surface with third degree burn of 30-39%
948.54 Burn (any degree) involving 50-59% of body surface with third degree burn of 40-49%
948.55 Burn (any degree) involving 50-59% of body surface with third degree burn of 50-59%
948.60 Burn (any degree) involving 60-69% of body surface with third degree burn of less than 10% or unspecified amount
948.61 Burn (any degree) involving 60-69% of body surface with third degree burn of 10-19%
948.62 Burn (any degree) involving 60-69% of body surface with third degree burn of 20-29%
948.63 Burn (any degree) involving 60-69% of body surface with third degree burn of 30-39%
948.64 Burn (any degree) involving 60-69% of body surface with third degree burn of 40-49%
948.65 Burn (any degree) involving 60-69% of body surface with third degree burn of 50-59%
948.66 Burn (any degree) involving 60-69% of body surface with third degree burn of 60-69%
948.70 Burn (any degree) involving 70-79% of body surface with third degree burn of less than 10% or unspecified amount
948.71 Burn (any degree) involving 70-79% of body surface with third degree burn of 10-19%
948.72 Burn (any degree) involving 70-79% of body surface with third degree burn of 20-29%
948.73 Burn (any degree) involving 70-79% of body surface with third degree burn of 30-39%
948.74 Burn (any degree) involving 70-79% of body surface with third degree burn of 40-49%
948.75 Burn (any degree) involving 70-79% of body surface with third degree burn of 50-59%
948.76 Burn (any degree) involving 70-79% of body surface with third degree burn of 60-69%
948.77 Burn (any degree) involving 70-79% of body surface with third degree burn of 70-79%
948.80 Burn (any degree) involving 80-89% of body surface with third degree burn of less than 10% or unspecified amount
948.81 Burn (any degree) involving 80-89% of body surface with third degree burn of 10-19%
948.82 Burn (any degree) involving 80-89% of body surface with third degree burn of 20-29%
948.83 Burn (any degree) involving 80-89% of body surface with third degree burn of 30-39%
948.84 Burn (any degree) involving 80-89% of body surface with third degree burn of 40-49%
948.85 Burn (any degree) involving 80-89% of body surface with third degree burn of 50-59%
948.86 Burn (any degree) involving 80-89% of body surface with third degree burn of 60-69%
948.87 Burn (any degree) involving 80-89% of body surface with third degree burn of 70-79%
948.88 Burn (any degree) involving 80-89% of body surface with third degree burn of 80-89%
948.90 Burn (any degree) involving 90% or more of body surface with third degree burn of less than 10% or unspecified amount
948.91 Burn (any degree) involving 90% or more of body surface with third degree burn of 10-19%
948.92 Burn (any degree) involving 90% or more of body surface with third degree burn of 20-29%
948.93 Burn (any degree) involving 90% or more of body surface with third degree burn of 30-39%
948.94 Burn (any degree) involving 90% or more of body surface with third degree burn of 40-49%
948.95 Burn (any degree) involving 90% or more of body surface with third degree burn of 50-59%
948.96 Burn (any degree) involving 90% or more of body surface with third degree burn of 60-69%
948.97 Burn (any degree) involving 90% or more of body surface with third degree burn of 70-79%
948.98 Burn (any degree) involving 90% or more of body surface with third degree burn of 80-89%
948.99 Burn (any degree) involving 90% or more of body surface with third degree burn of 90% or more of body surface
991.0 Frostbite of face
991.1 Frostbite of hand
991.2 Frostbite of foot
991.3 Frostbite of other and unspecified sites ▽
996.52 Mechanical complication due to other tissue graft, not elsewhere classified
998.30 Disruption of wound, unspecified ▽
998.32 Disruption of external operation (surgical) wound
998.33 Disruption of traumatic injury wound repair
998.59 Other postoperative infection — (Use additional code to identify infection)
998.83 Non-healing surgical wound
V51.8 Other aftercare involving the use of plastic surgery

ICD-9-CM Procedural

86.72 Advancement of pedicle graft
86.73 Attachment of pedicle or flap graft to hand
86.74 Attachment of pedicle or flap graft to other sites

15731

15731 Forehead flap with preservation of vascular pedicle (eg, axial pattern flap, paramedian forehead flap)

ICD-9-CM Diagnostic

170.0 Malignant neoplasm of bones of skull and face, except mandible
171.0 Malignant neoplasm of connective and other soft tissue of head, face, and neck
172.3 Malignant melanoma of skin of other and unspecified parts of face ▽
172.4 Malignant melanoma of skin of scalp and neck
173.30 Unspecified malignant neoplasm of skin of other and unspecified parts of face ▽
173.31 Basal cell carcinoma of skin of other and unspecified parts of face
173.32 Squamous cell carcinoma of skin of other and unspecified parts of face
173.39 Other specified malignant neoplasm of skin of other and unspecified parts of face
173.40 Unspecified malignant neoplasm of scalp and skin of neck ▽
173.41 Basal cell carcinoma of scalp and skin of neck
173.42 Squamous cell carcinoma of scalp and skin of neck
173.49 Other specified malignant neoplasm of scalp and skin of neck
195.0 Malignant neoplasm of head, face, and neck

196.0	Secondary and unspecified malignant neoplasm of lymph nodes of head, face, and neck
209.31	Merkel cell carcinoma of the face
209.32	Merkel cell carcinoma of the scalp and neck
209.75	Secondary Merkel cell carcinoma
215.0	Other benign neoplasm of connective and other soft tissue of head, face, and neck
234.8	Carcinoma in situ of other specified sites
238.1	Neoplasm of uncertain behavior of connective and other soft tissue
238.2	Neoplasm of uncertain behavior of skin
239.2	Neoplasms of unspecified nature of bone, soft tissue, and skin
873.0	Open wound of scalp, without mention of complication
873.1	Open wound of scalp, complicated
873.40	Open wound of face, unspecified site, without mention of complication ▽
873.42	Open wound of forehead, without mention of complication
873.49	Open wound of face, other and multiple sites, without mention of complication
873.50	Open wound of face, unspecified site, complicated ▽
873.52	Open wound of forehead, complicated
873.59	Open wound of face, other and multiple sites, complicated
906.5	Late effect of burn of eye, face, head, and neck
909.2	Late effect of radiation
909.3	Late effect of complications of surgical and medical care
925.1	Crushing injury of face and scalp — (Use additional code to identify any associated injuries, such as: 800-829, 850.0-854.1, 860.0-869.1)
941.30	Full-thickness skin loss due to burn (third degree NOS) of unspecified site of face and head ▽
941.36	Full-thickness skin loss due to burn (third degree NOS) of scalp (any part)
941.37	Full-thickness skin loss due to burn (third degree NOS) of forehead and cheek
941.39	Full-thickness skin loss due to burn (third degree NOS) of multiple sites (except with eye) of face, head, and neck
941.40	Deep necrosis of underlying tissues due to burn (deep third degree) of unspecified site of face and head, without mention of loss of a body part ▽
941.46	Deep necrosis of underlying tissues due to burn (deep third degree) of scalp (any part), without mention of loss of a body part
941.47	Deep necrosis of underlying tissues due to burn (deep third degree) of forehead and cheek, without mention of loss of a body part
941.49	Deep necrosis of underlying tissues due to burn (deep third degree) of multiple sites (except with eye) of face, head, and neck, without mention of loss of a body part
941.50	Deep necrosis of underlying tissues due to burn (deep third degree) of face and head, unspecified site, with loss of a body part ▽
941.56	Deep necrosis of underlying tissues due to burn (deep third degree) of scalp (any part), with loss of a body part
959.01	Head injury, unspecified ▽
959.09	Injury of face and neck, other and unspecified
V51.8	Other aftercare involving the use of plastic surgery

ICD-9-CM Procedural

86.70	Pedicle or flap graft, not otherwise specified
86.71	Cutting and preparation of pedicle grafts or flaps
86.72	Advancement of pedicle graft
86.74	Attachment of pedicle or flap graft to other sites
86.75	Revision of pedicle or flap graft

15732

15732 Muscle, myocutaneous, or fasciocutaneous flap; head and neck (eg, temporalis, masseter muscle, sternocleidomastoid, levator scapulae)

ICD-9-CM Diagnostic

142.0	Malignant neoplasm of parotid gland
142.1	Malignant neoplasm of submandibular gland
142.2	Malignant neoplasm of sublingual gland
143.0	Malignant neoplasm of upper gum
143.1	Malignant neoplasm of lower gum
143.8	Malignant neoplasm of other sites of gum
144.8	Malignant neoplasm of other sites of floor of mouth
145.0	Malignant neoplasm of cheek mucosa
145.1	Malignant neoplasm of vestibule of mouth
145.5	Malignant neoplasm of palate, unspecified ▽
145.8	Malignant neoplasm of other specified parts of mouth
147.0	Malignant neoplasm of superior wall of nasopharynx
147.1	Malignant neoplasm of posterior wall of nasopharynx
147.2	Malignant neoplasm of lateral wall of nasopharynx
147.3	Malignant neoplasm of anterior wall of nasopharynx
148.0	Malignant neoplasm of postcricoid region of hypopharynx
148.1	Malignant neoplasm of pyriform sinus
148.2	Malignant neoplasm of aryepiglottic fold, hypopharyngeal aspect
148.3	Malignant neoplasm of posterior hypopharyngeal wall
148.8	Malignant neoplasm of other specified sites of hypopharynx
149.0	Malignant neoplasm of pharynx, unspecified ▽
149.8	Malignant neoplasm of other sites within the lip and oral cavity
160.0	Malignant neoplasm of nasal cavities
160.1	Malignant neoplasm of auditory tube, middle ear, and mastoid air cells
160.2	Malignant neoplasm of maxillary sinus
160.3	Malignant neoplasm of ethmoidal sinus
160.4	Malignant neoplasm of frontal sinus
160.5	Malignant neoplasm of sphenoidal sinus
160.8	Malignant neoplasm of other sites of nasal cavities, middle ear, and accessory sinuses
161.8	Malignant neoplasm of other specified sites of larynx
170.0	Malignant neoplasm of bones of skull and face, except mandible
170.1	Malignant neoplasm of mandible
171.0	Malignant neoplasm of connective and other soft tissue of head, face, and neck
172.2	Malignant melanoma of skin of ear and external auditory canal
172.3	Malignant melanoma of skin of other and unspecified parts of face ▽
172.4	Malignant melanoma of skin of scalp and neck
173.40	Unspecified malignant neoplasm of scalp and skin of neck ▽
173.41	Basal cell carcinoma of scalp and skin of neck
173.42	Squamous cell carcinoma of scalp and skin of neck
173.49	Other specified malignant neoplasm of scalp and skin of neck
195.0	Malignant neoplasm of head, face, and neck
196.0	Secondary and unspecified malignant neoplasm of lymph nodes of head, face, and neck
209.31	Merkel cell carcinoma of the face
209.32	Merkel cell carcinoma of the scalp and neck
209.75	Secondary Merkel cell carcinoma
215.0	Other benign neoplasm of connective and other soft tissue of head, face, and neck
230.0	Carcinoma in situ of lip, oral cavity, and pharynx
232.1	Carcinoma in situ of eyelid, including canthus
232.2	Carcinoma in situ of skin of ear and external auditory canal
234.8	Carcinoma in situ of other specified sites
235.0	Neoplasm of uncertain behavior of major salivary glands
235.1	Neoplasm of uncertain behavior of lip, oral cavity, and pharynx
235.9	Neoplasm of uncertain behavior of other and unspecified respiratory organs ▽
238.0	Neoplasm of uncertain behavior of bone and articular cartilage
238.1	Neoplasm of uncertain behavior of connective and other soft tissue
238.2	Neoplasm of uncertain behavior of skin
239.0	Neoplasm of unspecified nature of digestive system
239.1	Neoplasm of unspecified nature of respiratory system
239.2	Neoplasms of unspecified nature of bone, soft tissue, and skin
873.0	Open wound of scalp, without mention of complication
873.1	Open wound of scalp, complicated
873.40	Open wound of face, unspecified site, without mention of complication ▽

873.41 Open wound of cheek, without mention of complication
873.42 Open wound of forehead, without mention of complication
873.44 Open wound of jaw, without mention of complication
873.49 Open wound of face, other and multiple sites, without mention of complication
873.50 Open wound of face, unspecified site, complicated ▽
873.51 Open wound of cheek, complicated
873.52 Open wound of forehead, complicated
873.54 Open wound of jaw, complicated
873.59 Open wound of face, other and multiple sites, complicated
874.8 Open wound of other and unspecified parts of neck, without mention of complication ▽
874.9 Open wound of other and unspecified parts of neck, complicated ▽
905.0 Late effect of fracture of skull and face bones
906.5 Late effect of burn of eye, face, head, and neck
909.2 Late effect of radiation
909.3 Late effect of complications of surgical and medical care
925.1 Crushing injury of face and scalp — (Use additional code to identify any associated injuries, such as: 800-829, 850.0-854.1, 860.0-869.1)
925.2 Crushing injury of neck — (Use additional code to identify any associated injuries, such as: 800-829, 850.0-854.1, 860.0-869.1)
941.30 Full-thickness skin loss due to burn (third degree NOS) of unspecified site of face and head ▽
941.34 Full-thickness skin loss due to burn (third degree NOS) of chin
941.36 Full-thickness skin loss due to burn (third degree NOS) of scalp (any part)
941.37 Full-thickness skin loss due to burn (third degree NOS) of forehead and cheek
941.38 Full-thickness skin loss due to burn (third degree NOS) of neck
941.39 Full-thickness skin loss due to burn (third degree NOS) of multiple sites (except with eye) of face, head, and neck
941.40 Deep necrosis of underlying tissues due to burn (deep third degree) of unspecified site of face and head, without mention of loss of a body part ▽
941.44 Deep necrosis of underlying tissues due to burn (deep third degree) of chin, without mention of loss of a body part
941.46 Deep necrosis of underlying tissues due to burn (deep third degree) of scalp (any part), without mention of loss of a body part
941.47 Deep necrosis of underlying tissues due to burn (deep third degree) of forehead and cheek, without mention of loss of a body part
941.48 Deep necrosis of underlying tissues due to burn (deep third degree) of neck, without mention of loss of a body part
941.49 Deep necrosis of underlying tissues due to burn (deep third degree) of multiple sites (except with eye) of face, head, and neck, without mention of loss of a body part
941.50 Deep necrosis of underlying tissues due to burn (deep third degree) of face and head, unspecified site, with loss of a body part ▽
941.54 Deep necrosis of underlying tissues due to burn (deep third degree) of chin, with loss of a body part
941.56 Deep necrosis of underlying tissues due to burn (deep third degree) of scalp (any part), with loss of a body part
941.58 Deep necrosis of underlying tissues due to burn (deep third degree) of neck, with loss of a body part
959.01 Head injury, unspecified ▽
959.09 Injury of face and neck, other and unspecified
V10.02 Personal history of malignant neoplasm of other and unspecified parts of oral cavity and pharynx ▽
V51.8 Other aftercare involving the use of plastic surgery

ICD-9-CM Procedural

18.71 Construction of auricle of ear
18.79 Other plastic repair of external ear
27.57 Attachment of pedicle or flap graft to lip and mouth
83.82 Graft of muscle or fascia
86.71 Cutting and preparation of pedicle grafts or flaps
86.74 Attachment of pedicle or flap graft to other sites

15734

15734 Muscle, myocutaneous, or fasciocutaneous flap; trunk

ICD-9-CM Diagnostic

171.4 Malignant neoplasm of connective and other soft tissue of thorax
171.6 Malignant neoplasm of connective and other soft tissue of pelvis
171.7 Malignant neoplasm of connective and other soft tissue of trunk, unspecified site ▽
171.8 Malignant neoplasm of other specified sites of connective and other soft tissue
172.5 Malignant melanoma of skin of trunk, except scrotum
173.50 Unspecified malignant neoplasm of skin of trunk, except scrotum ▽
173.51 Basal cell carcinoma of skin of trunk, except scrotum
173.52 Squamous cell carcinoma of skin of trunk, except scrotum
173.59 Other specified malignant neoplasm of skin of trunk, except scrotum
174.0 Malignant neoplasm of nipple and areola of female breast — (Use additional code to identify estrogen receptor status: V86.0-V86.1) ♀
174.1 Malignant neoplasm of central portion of female breast — (Use additional code to identify estrogen receptor status: V86.0-V86.1) ♀
174.2 Malignant neoplasm of upper-inner quadrant of female breast — (Use additional code to identify estrogen receptor status: V86.0-V86.1) ♀
174.3 Malignant neoplasm of lower-inner quadrant of female breast — (Use additional code to identify estrogen receptor status: V86.0-V86.1) ♀
174.4 Malignant neoplasm of upper-outer quadrant of female breast — (Use additional code to identify estrogen receptor status: V86.0-V86.1) ♀
174.5 Malignant neoplasm of lower-outer quadrant of female breast — (Use additional code to identify estrogen receptor status: V86.0-V86.1) ♀
174.6 Malignant neoplasm of axillary tail of female breast — (Use additional code to identify estrogen receptor status: V86.0-V86.1) ♀
174.8 Malignant neoplasm of other specified sites of female breast — (Use additional code to identify estrogen receptor status: V86.0-V86.1) ♀
175.9 Malignant neoplasm of other and unspecified sites of male breast — (Use additional code to identify estrogen receptor status: V86.0-V86.1) ▽ ♂
197.0 Secondary malignant neoplasm of lung
197.1 Secondary malignant neoplasm of mediastinum
197.3 Secondary malignant neoplasm of other respiratory organs
197.8 Secondary malignant neoplasm of other digestive organs and spleen
198.2 Secondary malignant neoplasm of skin
198.81 Secondary malignant neoplasm of breast
209.35 Merkel cell carcinoma of the trunk
209.75 Secondary Merkel cell carcinoma
232.5 Carcinoma in situ of skin of trunk, except scrotum
233.0 Carcinoma in situ of breast
235.7 Neoplasm of uncertain behavior of trachea, bronchus, and lung
235.8 Neoplasm of uncertain behavior of pleura, thymus, and mediastinum
238.2 Neoplasm of uncertain behavior of skin
238.3 Neoplasm of uncertain behavior of breast
239.2 Neoplasms of unspecified nature of bone, soft tissue, and skin
239.3 Neoplasm of unspecified nature of breast
519.2 Mediastinitis — (Use additional code to identify infectious organism)
682.2 Cellulitis and abscess of trunk — (Use additional code to identify organism, such as 041.1, etc.)
682.5 Cellulitis and abscess of buttock — (Use additional code to identify organism, such as 041.1, etc.)
707.00 Pressure ulcer, unspecified site — (Use additional code to identify pressure ulcer stage: 707.20-707.25) ▽
707.02 Pressure ulcer, upper back — (Use additional code to identify pressure ulcer stage: 707.20-707.25)
707.03 Pressure ulcer, lower back — (Use additional code to identify pressure ulcer stage: 707.20-707.25)
707.04 Pressure ulcer, hip — (Use additional code to identify pressure ulcer stage: 707.20-707.25)

707.05 Pressure ulcer, buttock — (Use additional code to identify pressure ulcer stage: 707.20-707.25)

707.09 Pressure ulcer, other site — (Use additional code to identify pressure ulcer stage: 707.20-707.25)

707.20 Pressure ulcer, unspecified stage — (Code first site of pressure ulcer: 707.00-707.09) ▽

707.21 Pressure ulcer, stage I — (Code first site of pressure ulcer: 707.00-707.09)

707.22 Pressure ulcer stage II — (Code first site of pressure ulcer: 707.00-707.09)

707.23 Pressure ulcer stage III — (Code first site of pressure ulcer: 707.00-707.09)

707.24 Pressure ulcer stage IV — (Code first site of pressure ulcer: 707.00-707.09)

707.25 Pressure ulcer, unstageable — (Code first site of pressure ulcer: 707.00-707.09)

707.8 Chronic ulcer of other specified site

709.2 Scar condition and fibrosis of skin

728.82 Foreign body granuloma of muscle — (Use additional code to identify foreign body (V90.01-V90.9))

728.86 Necrotizing fasciitis — (Use additional code to identify infectious organism, 041.00-041.89, 785.4, if applicable)

728.88 Rhabdomyolysis

729.4 Unspecified fasciitis ▽

730.15 Chronic osteomyelitis, pelvic region and thigh — (Use additional code to identify organism: 041.1. Use additional code to identify major osseous defect, if applicable: 731.3)

730.18 Chronic osteomyelitis, other specified sites — (Use additional code to identify organism: 041.1. Use additional code to identify major osseous defect, if applicable: 731.3)

738.3 Acquired deformity of chest and rib

741.00 Spina bifida with hydrocephalus, unspecified region ▽

754.81 Pectus excavatum

810.11 Open fracture of sternal end of clavicle

810.12 Open fracture of shaft of clavicle

810.13 Open fracture of acromial end of clavicle

811.10 Open fracture of unspecified part of scapula ▽

811.11 Open fracture of acromial process of scapula

811.12 Open fracture of coracoid process

811.13 Open fracture of glenoid cavity and neck of scapula

811.19 Open fracture of other part of scapula

860.1 Traumatic pneumothorax with open wound into thorax

860.3 Traumatic hemothorax with open wound into thorax

860.5 Traumatic pneumohemothorax with open wound into thorax

861.30 Unspecified lung injury with open wound into thorax ▽

861.31 Lung contusion with open wound into thorax

861.32 Lung laceration with open wound into thorax

862.1 Diaphragm injury with open wound into cavity

862.31 Bronchus injury with open wound into cavity

862.32 Esophagus injury with open wound into cavity

862.39 Injury to other specified intrathoracic organs with open wound into cavity

863.30 Small intestine injury, unspecified site, with open wound into cavity ▽

863.31 Duodenum injury with open wound into cavity

863.39 Other injury to small intestine with open wound into cavity

863.50 Colon injury, unspecified site, with open wound into cavity ▽

863.51 Ascending (right) colon injury with open wound into cavity

863.52 Transverse colon injury with open wound into cavity

863.53 Descending (left) colon injury with open wound into cavity

863.54 Sigmoid colon injury with open wound into cavity

863.55 Rectum injury with open wound into cavity

863.56 Injury to multiple sites in colon and rectum with open wound into cavity

863.59 Other injury to colon and rectum with open wound into cavity

863.90 Gastrointestinal tract injury, unspecified site, with open wound into cavity ▽

863.91 Pancreas head injury with open wound into cavity

863.92 Pancreas body injury with open wound into cavity

863.93 Pancreas tail injury with open wound into cavity

863.94 Pancreas injury, multiple and unspecified sites, with open wound into cavity

863.95 Appendix injury with open wound into cavity

863.99 Injury to other and unspecified gastrointestinal sites with open wound into cavity

864.10 Unspecified liver injury with open wound into cavity ▽

864.11 Liver hematoma and contusion with open wound into cavity

864.12 Liver laceration, minor, with open wound into cavity

864.13 Liver laceration, moderate, with open wound into cavity

864.14 Liver laceration, major, with open wound into cavity

864.15 Liver injury with open wound into cavity, unspecified laceration ▽

864.19 Other liver injury with open wound into cavity

865.10 Unspecified spleen injury with open wound into cavity ▽

865.11 Spleen hematoma, without rupture of capsule, with open wound into cavity

865.12 Capsular tears to spleen, without major disruption of parenchyma, with open wound into cavity

865.13 Spleen laceration extending into parenchyma, with open wound into cavity

865.14 Massive parenchyma disruption of spleen with open wound into cavity

865.19 Other spleen injury with open wound into cavity

866.10 Unspecified kidney injury with open wound into cavity ▽

866.11 Kidney hematoma, without rupture of capsule, with open wound into cavity

866.12 Kidney laceration with open wound into cavity

866.13 Complete disruption of kidney parenchyma, with open wound into cavity

867.1 Bladder and urethra injury with open wound into cavity

867.3 Ureter injury with open wound into cavity

867.5 Uterus injury with open wound into cavity ♀

867.7 Injury to other specified pelvic organs with open wound into cavity

868.10 Injury to unspecified intra-abdominal organ, with open wound into cavity ▽

868.11 Adrenal gland injury, with open wound into cavity

868.12 Bile duct and gallbladder injury, with open wound into cavity

868.13 Peritoneum injury with open wound into cavity

868.14 Retroperitoneum injury with open wound into cavity

868.19 Injury to other and multiple intra-abdominal organs, with open wound into cavity

869.1 Internal injury to unspecified or ill-defined organs with open wound into cavity ▽

875.1 Open wound of chest (wall), complicated

876.0 Open wound of back, without mention of complication

876.1 Open wound of back, complicated

877.1 Open wound of buttock, complicated

879.5 Open wound of abdominal wall, lateral, complicated

879.8 Open wound(s) (multiple) of unspecified site(s), without mention of complication ▽

879.9 Open wound(s) (multiple) of unspecified site(s), complicated ▽

906.0 Late effect of open wound of head, neck, and trunk

906.4 Late effect of crushing

906.8 Late effect of burns of other specified sites

908.0 Late effect of internal injury to chest

908.1 Late effect of internal injury to intra-abdominal organs

908.2 Late effect of internal injury to other internal organs

908.4 Late effect of injury to blood vessel of thorax, abdomen, and pelvis

908.6 Late effect of certain complications of trauma

926.0 Crushing injury of external genitalia — (Use additional code to identify any associated injuries: 800-829, 850.0-854.1, 860.0-869.1)

926.11 Crushing injury of back — (Use additional code to identify any associated injuries: 800-829, 850.0-854.1, 860.0-869.1)

926.12 Crushing injury of buttock — (Use additional code to identify any associated injuries: 800-829, 850.0-854.1, 860.0-869.1)

926.19 Crushing injury of other specified sites of trunk — (Use additional code to identify any associated injuries: 800-829, 850.0-854.1, 860.0-869.1)

942.30 Full-thickness skin loss due to burn (third degree NOS) of unspecified site of trunk ▽

942.31 Full-thickness skin loss due to burn (third degree NOS) of breast

942.33 Full-thickness skin loss due to burn (third degree NOS) of abdominal wall

942.34 Full-thickness skin loss due to burn (third degree NOS) of back (any part)

942.35 Full-thickness skin loss due to burn (third degree NOS) of genitalia

942.39 Full-thickness skin loss due to burn (third degree NOS) of other and multiple sites of trunk

942.40 Deep necrosis of underlying tissues due to burn (deep third degree) of trunk, unspecified site, without mention of loss of a body part ▽

942.41 Deep necrosis of underlying tissues due to burn (deep third degree) of breast, without mention of loss of a body part

942.42 Deep necrosis of underlying tissues due to burn (deep third degree) of chest wall, excluding breast and nipple, without mention of loss of a body part

942.43 Deep necrosis of underlying tissues due to burn (deep third degree) of abdominal wall, without mention of loss of a body part

942.44 Deep necrosis of underlying tissues due to burn (deep third degree) of back (any part), without mention of loss of a body part

942.45 Deep necrosis of underlying tissues due to burn (deep third degree) of genitalia, without mention of loss of a body part

942.49 Deep necrosis of underlying tissues due to burn (deep third degree) of other and multiple sites of trunk, without mention of loss of a body part

942.50 Deep necrosis of underlying tissues due to burn (deep third degree) of unspecified site of trunk, with loss of a body part ▽

942.51 Deep necrosis of underlying tissues due to burn (deep third degree) of breast, with loss of a body part

942.52 Deep necrosis of underlying tissues due to burn (deep third degree) of chest wall, excluding breast and nipple, with loss of a body part

942.53 Deep necrosis of underlying tissues due to burn (deep third degree) of abdominal wall with loss of a body part

942.54 Deep necrosis of underlying tissues due to burn (deep third degree) of back (any part), with loss of a body part

942.55 Deep necrosis of underlying tissues due to burn (deep third degree) of genitalia, with loss of a body part

942.59 Deep necrosis of underlying tissues due to burn (deep third degree) of other and multiple sites of trunk, with loss of a body part

996.52 Mechanical complication due to other tissue graft, not elsewhere classified

998.30 Disruption of wound, unspecified ▽

998.31 Disruption of internal operation (surgical) wound

998.32 Disruption of external operation (surgical) wound

998.33 Disruption of traumatic injury wound repair

998.59 Other postoperative infection — (Use additional code to identify infection)

998.83 Non-healing surgical wound

V51.8 Other aftercare involving the use of plastic surgery

ICD-9-CM Procedural

83.82 Graft of muscle or fascia

86.71 Cutting and preparation of pedicle grafts or flaps

86.74 Attachment of pedicle or flap graft to other sites

15736

15736 Muscle, myocutaneous, or fasciocutaneous flap; upper extremity

ICD-9-CM Diagnostic

171.2 Malignant neoplasm of connective and other soft tissue of upper limb, including shoulder

172.6 Malignant melanoma of skin of upper limb, including shoulder

173.60 Unspecified malignant neoplasm of skin of upper limb, including shoulder ▽

173.61 Basal cell carcinoma of skin of upper limb, including shoulder

173.62 Squamous cell carcinoma of skin of upper limb, including shoulder

173.69 Other specified malignant neoplasm of skin of upper limb, including shoulder

198.2 Secondary malignant neoplasm of skin

209.33 Merkel cell carcinoma of the upper limb

209.75 Secondary Merkel cell carcinoma

232.6 Carcinoma in situ of skin of upper limb, including shoulder

232.8 Carcinoma in situ of other specified sites of skin

682.3 Cellulitis and abscess of upper arm and forearm — (Use additional code to identify organism, such as 041.1, etc.)

682.4 Cellulitis and abscess of hand, except fingers and thumb — (Use additional code to identify organism, such as 041.1, etc.)

701.5 Other abnormal granulation tissue

709.2 Scar condition and fibrosis of skin

728.82 Foreign body granuloma of muscle — (Use additional code to identify foreign body (V90.01-V90.9))

728.86 Necrotizing fasciitis — (Use additional code to identify infectious organism, 041.00-041.89, 785.4, if applicable)

728.88 Rhabdomyolysis

812.10 Open fracture of unspecified part of upper end of humerus ▽

812.12 Open fracture of anatomical neck of humerus

812.13 Open fracture of greater tuberosity of humerus

812.19 Other open fracture of upper end of humerus

812.30 Open fracture of unspecified part of humerus ▽

812.31 Open fracture of shaft of humerus

812.50 Open fracture of unspecified part of lower end of humerus ▽

812.51 Open fracture of supracondylar humerus

812.52 Open fracture of lateral condyle of humerus

812.53 Open fracture of medial condyle of humerus

812.54 Open fracture of unspecified condyle(s) of humerus ▽

812.59 Other open fracture of lower end of humerus

813.10 Unspecified open fracture of upper end of forearm ▽

813.11 Open fracture of olecranon process of ulna

813.12 Open fracture of coronoid process of ulna

813.13 Open Monteggia's fracture

813.14 Other and unspecified open fractures of proximal end of ulna (alone) ▽

813.15 Open fracture of head of radius

813.16 Open fracture of neck of radius

813.17 Other and unspecified open fractures of proximal end of radius (alone) ▽

813.18 Open fracture of radius with ulna, upper end (any part)

813.30 Unspecified open fracture of shaft of radius or ulna ▽

813.31 Open fracture of shaft of radius (alone)

813.32 Open fracture of shaft of ulna (alone)

813.33 Open fracture of shaft of radius with ulna

813.50 Unspecified open fracture of lower end of forearm ▽

813.51 Open Colles' fracture

813.52 Other open fractures of distal end of radius (alone)

813.53 Open fracture of distal end of ulna (alone)

813.54 Open fracture of lower end of radius with ulna

813.90 Open fracture of unspecified part of forearm ▽

813.91 Open fracture of unspecified part of radius (alone) ▽

813.92 Open fracture of unspecified part of ulna (alone) ▽

813.93 Open fracture of unspecified part of radius with ulna ▽

819.1 Multiple open fractures involving both upper limbs, and upper limb with rib(s) and sternum

880.03 Open wound of upper arm, without mention of complication

880.09 Open wound of multiple sites of shoulder and upper arm, without mention of complication

880.13 Open wound of upper arm, complicated

880.19 Open wound of multiple sites of shoulder and upper arm, complicated

880.23 Open wound of upper arm, with tendon involvement

880.29 Open wound of multiple sites of shoulder and upper arm, with tendon involvement

881.00 Open wound of forearm, without mention of complication

881.01 Open wound of elbow, without mention of complication

881.02 Open wound of wrist, without mention of complication

881.10 Open wound of forearm, complicated

881.11 Open wound of elbow, complicated

881.12 Open wound of wrist, complicated

881.20 Open wound of forearm, with tendon involvement

881.21 Open wound of elbow, with tendon involvement

881.22 Open wound of wrist, with tendon involvement

882.0 Open wound of hand except finger(s) alone, without mention of complication

882.1 Open wound of hand except finger(s) alone, complicated

882.2 Open wound of hand except finger(s) alone, with tendon involvement

883.0 Open wound of finger(s), without mention of complication

883.1 Open wound of finger(s), complicated

883.2 Open wound of finger(s), with tendon involvement

884.0 Multiple and unspecified open wound of upper limb, without mention of complication

884.1 Multiple and unspecified open wound of upper limb, complicated

884.2 Multiple and unspecified open wound of upper limb, with tendon involvement

885.0 Traumatic amputation of thumb (complete) (partial), without mention of complication

885.1 Traumatic amputation of thumb (complete) (partial), complicated

886.0 Traumatic amputation of other finger(s) (complete) (partial), without mention of complication

886.1 Traumatic amputation of other finger(s) (complete) (partial), complicated

887.0 Traumatic amputation of arm and hand (complete) (partial), unilateral, below elbow, without mention of complication

887.1 Traumatic amputation of arm and hand (complete) (partial), unilateral, below elbow, complicated

887.2 Traumatic amputation of arm and hand (complete) (partial), unilateral, at or above elbow, without mention of complication

887.3 Traumatic amputation of arm and hand (complete) (partial), unilateral, at or above elbow, complicated

887.4 Traumatic amputation of arm and hand (complete) (partial), unilateral, level not specified, without mention of complication ▼

887.5 Traumatic amputation of arm and hand (complete) (partial), unilateral, level not specified, complicated ▼

887.6 Traumatic amputation of arm and hand (complete) (partial), bilateral (any level), without mention of complication

887.7 Traumatic amputation of arm and hand (complete) (partial), bilateral (any level), complicated

906.1 Late effect of open wound of extremities without mention of tendon injury

906.6 Late effect of burn of wrist and hand

906.7 Late effect of burn of other extremities

908.6 Late effect of certain complications of trauma

909.3 Late effect of complications of surgical and medical care

927.03 Crushing injury of upper arm — (Use additional code to identify any associated injuries: 800-829, 850.0-854.1, 860.0-869.1)

927.09 Crushing injury of multiple sites of upper arm — (Use additional code to identify any associated injuries: 800-829, 850.0-854.1, 860.0-869.1)

927.10 Crushing injury of forearm — (Use additional code to identify any associated injuries: 800-829, 850.0-854.1, 860.0-869.1)

927.11 Crushing injury of elbow — (Use additional code to identify any associated injuries: 800-829, 850.0-854.1, 860.0-869.1)

927.20 Crushing injury of hand(s) — (Use additional code to identify any associated injuries: 800-829, 850.0-854.1, 860.0-869.1)

927.21 Crushing injury of wrist — (Use additional code to identify any associated injuries: 800-829, 850.0-854.1, 860.0-869.1)

927.3 Crushing injury of finger(s) — (Use additional code to identify any associated injuries: 800-829, 850.0-854.1, 860.0-869.1)

927.8 Crushing injury of multiple sites of upper limb — (Use additional code to identify any associated injuries: 800-829, 850.0-854.1, 860.0-869.1)

943.30 Full-thickness skin loss due to burn (third degree NOS) of unspecified site of upper limb ▼

943.31 Full-thickness skin loss due to burn (third degree NOS) of forearm

943.32 Full-thickness skin loss due to burn (third degree NOS) of elbow

943.33 Full-thickness skin loss due to burn (third degree NOS) of upper arm

943.39 Full-thickness skin loss due to burn (third degree NOS) of multiple sites of upper limb, except wrist and hand

943.40 Deep necrosis of underlying tissues due to burn (deep third degree) of unspecified site of upper limb, without mention of loss of a body part ▼

943.41 Deep necrosis of underlying tissues due to burn (deep third degree) of forearm, without mention of loss of a body part

943.42 Deep necrosis of underlying tissues due to burn (deep third degree) of elbow, without mention of loss of a body part

943.44 Deep necrosis of underlying tissues due to burn (deep third degree) of axilla, without mention of loss of a body part

943.49 Deep necrosis of underlying tissues due to burn (deep third degree) of multiple sites of upper limb, except wrist and hand, without mention of loss of a body part

943.50 Deep necrosis of underlying tissues due to burn (deep third degree) of unspecified site of upper limb, with loss of a body part ▼

943.51 Deep necrosis of underlying tissues due to burn (deep third degree) of forearm, with loss of a body part

943.52 Deep necrosis of underlying tissues due to burn (deep third degree) of elbow, with loss of a body part

943.53 Deep necrosis of underlying tissues due to burn (deep third degree) of upper arm, with loss of upper a body part

943.59 Deep necrosis of underlying tissues due to burn (deep third degree) of multiple sites of upper limb, except wrist and hand, with loss of a body part

944.30 Full-thickness skin loss due to burn (third degree NOS) of unspecified site of hand ▼

944.31 Full-thickness skin loss due to burn (third degree NOS) of single digit [finger (nail)] other than thumb

944.32 Full-thickness skin loss due to burn (third degree NOS) of thumb (nail)

944.33 Full-thickness skin loss due to burn (third degree NOS) of two or more digits of hand, not including thumb

944.34 Full-thickness skin loss due to burn (third degree NOS) of two or more digits of hand including thumb

944.35 Full-thickness skin loss due to burn (third degree NOS) of palm of hand

944.36 Full-thickness skin loss due to burn (third degree NOS) of back of hand

944.37 Full-thickness skin loss due to burn (third degree NOS) of wrist

944.38 Full-thickness skin loss due to burn (third degree NOS) of multiple sites of wrist(s) and hand(s)

944.40 Deep necrosis of underlying tissues due to burn (deep third degree) of unspecified site of hand, without mention of loss of a body part ▼

944.41 Deep necrosis of underlying tissues due to burn (deep third degree) of single digit [finger (nail)] other than thumb, without mention of loss of a body part

944.42 Deep necrosis of underlying tissues due to burn (deep third degree) of thumb (nail), without mention of loss of a body part

944.43 Deep necrosis of underlying tissues due to burn (deep third degree) of two or more digits of hand, not including thumb, without mention of loss of a body part

944.44 Deep necrosis of underlying tissues due to burn (deep third degree) of two or more digits of hand including thumb, without mention of loss of a body part

944.46 Deep necrosis of underlying tissues due to burn (deep third degree) of back of hand, without mention of loss of a body part

944.47 Deep necrosis of underlying tissues due to burn (deep third degree) of wrist, without mention of loss of a body part

944.48 Deep necrosis of underlying tissues due to burn (deep third degree) of multiple sites of wrist(s) and hand(s), without mention of loss of a body part

944.50 Deep necrosis of underlying tissues due to burn (deep third degree) of unspecified site of hand, with loss of a body part ▼

944.51 Deep necrosis of underlying tissues due to burn (deep third degree) of single digit (finger (nail)) other than thumb, with loss of a body part

944.52 Deep necrosis of underlying tissues due to burn (deep third degree) of thumb (nail), with loss of a body part

944.53 Deep necrosis of underlying tissues due to burn (deep third degree) of two or more digits of hand, not including thumb, with loss of a body part

944.54 Deep necrosis of underlying tissues due to burn (deep third degree) of two or more digits of hand including thumb, with loss of a body part
944.55 Deep necrosis of underlying tissues due to burn (deep third degree) of palm of hand, with loss of a body part
944.56 Deep necrosis of underlying tissues due to burn (deep third degree) of back of hand, with loss of a body part
944.57 Deep necrosis of underlying tissues due to burn (deep third degree) of wrist, with loss of a body part
944.58 Deep necrosis of underlying tissues due to burn (deep third degree) of multiple sites of wrist(s) and hand(s), with loss of a body part
995.4 Shock due to anesthesia not elsewhere classified
997.60 Late complications of amputation stump, unspecified — (Use additional code to identify complications) ▽
997.62 Infection (chronic) of amputation stump — (Use additional code to identify complications)
997.69 Other late amputation stump complication — (Use additional code to identify complications)
998.30 Disruption of wound, unspecified ▽
998.32 Disruption of external operation (surgical) wound
998.33 Disruption of traumatic injury wound repair
998.59 Other postoperative infection — (Use additional code to identify infection)
998.83 Non-healing surgical wound
V10.82 Personal history of malignant melanoma of skin
V51.8 Other aftercare involving the use of plastic surgery

ICD-9-CM Procedural

83.82 Graft of muscle or fascia
86.71 Cutting and preparation of pedicle grafts or flaps
86.74 Attachment of pedicle or flap graft to other sites

15738

15738 Muscle, myocutaneous, or fasciocutaneous flap; lower extremity

ICD-9-CM Diagnostic

171.3 Malignant neoplasm of connective and other soft tissue of lower limb, including hip
172.7 Malignant melanoma of skin of lower limb, including hip
173.70 Unspecified malignant neoplasm of skin of lower limb, including hip ▽
173.71 Basal cell carcinoma of skin of lower limb, including hip
173.72 Squamous cell carcinoma of skin of lower limb, including hip
173.79 Other specified malignant neoplasm of skin of lower limb, including hip
195.5 Malignant neoplasm of lower limb
209.34 Merkel cell carcinoma of the lower limb
209.75 Secondary Merkel cell carcinoma
440.23 Atherosclerosis of native arteries of the extremities with ulceration — (Use additional code for any associated ulceration: 707.10-707.19, 707.8, 707.9)
459.11 Postphlebitic syndrome with ulcer
459.13 Postphlebitic syndrome with ulcer and inflammation
459.31 Chronic venous hypertension with ulcer
459.33 Chronic venous hypertension with ulcer and inflammation
707.00 Pressure ulcer, unspecified site — (Use additional code to identify pressure ulcer stage: 707.20-707.25) ▽
707.06 Pressure ulcer, ankle — (Use additional code to identify pressure ulcer stage: 707.20-707.25)
707.07 Pressure ulcer, heel — (Use additional code to identify pressure ulcer stage: 707.20-707.25)
707.09 Pressure ulcer, other site — (Use additional code to identify pressure ulcer stage: 707.20-707.25)
707.10 Ulcer of lower limb, unspecified — (Code, if applicable, any causal condition first: 249.80-249.81, 250.80-250.83, 440.23, 459.11, 459.13, 459.31, 459.33) ▽
707.11 Ulcer of thigh — (Code, if applicable, any causal condition first: 249.80-249.81, 250.80-250.83, 440.23, 459.11, 459.13, 459.31, 459.33)
707.12 Ulcer of calf — (Code, if applicable, any causal condition first: 249.80-249.81, 250.80-250.83, 440.23, 459.11, 459.13, 459.31, 459.33)
707.13 Ulcer of ankle — (Code, if applicable, any causal condition first: 249.80-249.81, 250.80-250.83, 440.23, 459.11, 459.13, 459.31, 459.33)
707.14 Ulcer of heel and midfoot — (Code, if applicable, any causal condition first: 249.80-249.81, 250.80-250.83, 440.23, 459.11, 459.13, 459.31, 459.33)
707.15 Ulcer of other part of foot — (Code, if applicable, any causal condition first: 249.80-249.81, 250.80-250.83, 440.23, 459.11, 459.13, 459.31, 459.33)
707.19 Ulcer of other part of lower limb — (Code, if applicable, any causal condition first: 249.80-249.81, 250.80-250.83, 440.23, 459.11, 459.13, 459.31, 459.33)
707.20 Pressure ulcer, unspecified stage — (Code first site of pressure ulcer: 707.00-707.09) ▽
707.21 Pressure ulcer, stage I — (Code first site of pressure ulcer: 707.00-707.09)
707.22 Pressure ulcer stage II — (Code first site of pressure ulcer: 707.00-707.09)
707.23 Pressure ulcer stage III — (Code first site of pressure ulcer: 707.00-707.09)
707.24 Pressure ulcer stage IV — (Code first site of pressure ulcer: 707.00-707.09)
707.25 Pressure ulcer, unstageable — (Code first site of pressure ulcer: 707.00-707.09)
730.16 Chronic osteomyelitis, lower leg — (Use additional code to identify organism: 041.1. Use additional code to identify major osseous defect, if applicable: 731.3)
730.17 Chronic osteomyelitis, ankle and foot — (Use additional code to identify organism: 041.1. Use additional code to identify major osseous defect, if applicable: 731.3)
730.26 Unspecified osteomyelitis, lower leg — (Use additional code to identify organism: 041.1. Use additional code to identify major osseous defect, if applicable: 731.3) ▽
821.10 Open fracture of unspecified part of femur ▽
823.92 Open fracture of unspecified part of fibula with tibia ▽
825.1 Open fracture of calcaneus
825.30 Open fracture of unspecified bone(s) of foot (except toes) ▽
826.1 Open fracture of one or more phalanges of foot
827.1 Other, multiple and ill-defined open fractures of lower limb
828.1 Multiple fractures involving both lower limbs, lower with upper limb, and lower limb(s) with rib(s) and sternum, open
829.1 Open fracture of unspecified bone ▽
890.1 Open wound of hip and thigh, complicated
891.0 Open wound of knee, leg (except thigh), and ankle, without mention of complication
891.1 Open wound of knee, leg (except thigh), and ankle, complicated
892.1 Open wound of foot except toe(s) alone, complicated
896.1 Traumatic amputation of foot (complete) (partial), unilateral, complicated
V51.8 Other aftercare involving the use of plastic surgery

ICD-9-CM Procedural

83.82 Graft of muscle or fascia
86.71 Cutting and preparation of pedicle grafts or flaps
86.74 Attachment of pedicle or flap graft to other sites

15740

15740 Flap; island pedicle requiring identification and dissection of an anatomically named axial vessel

ICD-9-CM Diagnostic

140.9 Malignant neoplasm of lip, vermilion border, unspecified as to upper or lower ▽
149.8 Malignant neoplasm of other sites within the lip and oral cavity
149.9 Malignant neoplasm of ill-defined sites of lip and oral cavity
172.1 Malignant melanoma of skin of eyelid, including canthus
172.2 Malignant melanoma of skin of ear and external auditory canal
172.4 Malignant melanoma of skin of scalp and neck
172.6 Malignant melanoma of skin of upper limb, including shoulder
172.7 Malignant melanoma of skin of lower limb, including hip
173.00 Unspecified malignant neoplasm of skin of lip ▽
173.01 Basal cell carcinoma of skin of lip
173.02 Squamous cell carcinoma of skin of lip
173.09 Other specified malignant neoplasm of skin of lip

173.10 Unspecified malignant neoplasm of eyelid, including canthus
173.11 Basal cell carcinoma of eyelid, including canthus
173.12 Squamous cell carcinoma of eyelid, including canthus
173.19 Other specified malignant neoplasm of eyelid, including canthus
173.20 Unspecified malignant neoplasm of skin of ear and external auditory canal
173.21 Basal cell carcinoma of skin of ear and external auditory canal
173.22 Squamous cell carcinoma of skin of ear and external auditory canal
173.29 Other specified malignant neoplasm of skin of ear and external auditory canal
173.40 Unspecified malignant neoplasm of scalp and skin of neck
173.41 Basal cell carcinoma of scalp and skin of neck
173.42 Squamous cell carcinoma of scalp and skin of neck
173.49 Other specified malignant neoplasm of scalp and skin of neck
173.60 Unspecified malignant neoplasm of skin of upper limb, including shoulder
173.61 Basal cell carcinoma of skin of upper limb, including shoulder
173.62 Squamous cell carcinoma of skin of upper limb, including shoulder
173.69 Other specified malignant neoplasm of skin of upper limb, including shoulder
173.70 Unspecified malignant neoplasm of skin of lower limb, including hip
173.71 Basal cell carcinoma of skin of lower limb, including hip
173.72 Squamous cell carcinoma of skin of lower limb, including hip
173.79 Other specified malignant neoplasm of skin of lower limb, including hip
173.80 Unspecified malignant neoplasm of other specified sites of skin
173.81 Basal cell carcinoma of other specified sites of skin
173.82 Squamous cell carcinoma of other specified sites of skin
173.89 Other specified malignant neoplasm of other specified sites of skin
184.0 Malignant neoplasm of vagina ♀
184.1 Malignant neoplasm of labia majora ♀
184.2 Malignant neoplasm of labia minora ♀
184.3 Malignant neoplasm of clitoris ♀
184.4 Malignant neoplasm of vulva, unspecified site ♀
184.8 Malignant neoplasm of other specified sites of female genital organs ♀
187.1 Malignant neoplasm of prepuce ♂
187.2 Malignant neoplasm of glans penis ♂
187.3 Malignant neoplasm of body of penis ♂
187.4 Malignant neoplasm of penis, part unspecified ♂
187.7 Malignant neoplasm of scrotum ♂
187.9 Malignant neoplasm of male genital organ, site unspecified ♂
195.0 Malignant neoplasm of head, face, and neck
198.2 Secondary malignant neoplasm of skin
209.31 Merkel cell carcinoma of the face
209.32 Merkel cell carcinoma of the scalp and neck
209.33 Merkel cell carcinoma of the upper limb
209.34 Merkel cell carcinoma of the lower limb
209.35 Merkel cell carcinoma of the trunk
209.36 Merkel cell carcinoma of other sites
209.75 Secondary Merkel cell carcinoma
210.0 Benign neoplasm of lip
210.4 Benign neoplasm of other and unspecified parts of mouth
216.1 Benign neoplasm of eyelid, including canthus
216.2 Benign neoplasm of ear and external auditory canal
216.4 Benign neoplasm of scalp and skin of neck
216.6 Benign neoplasm of skin of upper limb, including shoulder
216.7 Benign neoplasm of skin of lower limb, including hip
216.8 Benign neoplasm of other specified sites of skin
232.0 Carcinoma in situ of skin of lip
232.1 Carcinoma in situ of eyelid, including canthus
232.2 Carcinoma in situ of skin of ear and external auditory canal
232.4 Carcinoma in situ of scalp and skin of neck
232.6 Carcinoma in situ of skin of upper limb, including shoulder
232.7 Carcinoma in situ of skin of lower limb, including hip
232.8 Carcinoma in situ of other specified sites of skin
238.1 Neoplasm of uncertain behavior of connective and other soft tissue
239.0 Neoplasm of unspecified nature of digestive system
239.2 Neoplasms of unspecified nature of bone, soft tissue, and skin
380.32 Acquired deformities of auricle or pinna
607.2 Other inflammatory disorders of penis — (Use additional code to identify organism) ♂
629.20 Female genital mutilation status, unspecified ♀
629.21 Female genital mutilation, Type I status ♀
629.22 Female genital mutilation, Type II status ♀
629.23 Female genital mutilation, Type III status ♀
629.29 Other female genital mutilation status ♀
629.89 Other specified disorders of female genital organs ♀
682.0 Cellulitis and abscess of face — (Use additional code to identify organism, such as 041.1, etc.)
707.00 Pressure ulcer, unspecified site — (Use additional code to identify pressure ulcer stage: 707.20-707.25)
707.01 Pressure ulcer, elbow — (Use additional code to identify pressure ulcer stage: 707.20-707.25)
707.02 Pressure ulcer, upper back — (Use additional code to identify pressure ulcer stage: 707.20-707.25)
707.03 Pressure ulcer, lower back — (Use additional code to identify pressure ulcer stage: 707.20-707.25)
707.04 Pressure ulcer, hip — (Use additional code to identify pressure ulcer stage: 707.20-707.25)
707.05 Pressure ulcer, buttock — (Use additional code to identify pressure ulcer stage: 707.20-707.25)
707.06 Pressure ulcer, ankle — (Use additional code to identify pressure ulcer stage: 707.20-707.25)
707.07 Pressure ulcer, heel — (Use additional code to identify pressure ulcer stage: 707.20-707.25)
707.09 Pressure ulcer, other site — (Use additional code to identify pressure ulcer stage: 707.20-707.25)
707.10 Ulcer of lower limb, unspecified — (Code, if applicable, any causal condition first: 249.80-249.81, 250.80-250.83, 440.23, 459.11, 459.13, 459.31, 459.33)
707.11 Ulcer of thigh — (Code, if applicable, any causal condition first: 249.80-249.81, 250.80-250.83, 440.23, 459.11, 459.13, 459.31, 459.33)
707.12 Ulcer of calf — (Code, if applicable, any causal condition first: 249.80-249.81, 250.80-250.83, 440.23, 459.11, 459.13, 459.31, 459.33)
707.13 Ulcer of ankle — (Code, if applicable, any causal condition first: 249.80-249.81, 250.80-250.83, 440.23, 459.11, 459.13, 459.31, 459.33)
707.14 Ulcer of heel and midfoot — (Code, if applicable, any causal condition first: 249.80-249.81, 250.80-250.83, 440.23, 459.11, 459.13, 459.31, 459.33)
707.15 Ulcer of other part of foot — (Code, if applicable, any causal condition first: 249.80-249.81, 250.80-250.83, 440.23, 459.11, 459.13, 459.31, 459.33)
707.19 Ulcer of other part of lower limb — (Code, if applicable, any causal condition first: 249.80-249.81, 250.80-250.83, 440.23, 459.11, 459.13, 459.31, 459.33)
707.20 Pressure ulcer, unspecified stage — (Code first site of pressure ulcer: 707.00-707.09)
707.21 Pressure ulcer, stage I — (Code first site of pressure ulcer: 707.00-707.09)
707.22 Pressure ulcer stage II — (Code first site of pressure ulcer: 707.00-707.09)
707.23 Pressure ulcer stage III — (Code first site of pressure ulcer: 707.00-707.09)
707.24 Pressure ulcer stage IV — (Code first site of pressure ulcer: 707.00-707.09)
707.25 Pressure ulcer, unstageable — (Code first site of pressure ulcer: 707.00-707.09)
707.8 Chronic ulcer of other specified site
728.86 Necrotizing fasciitis — (Use additional code to identify infectious organism, 041.00-041.89, 785.4, if applicable)
743.62 Congenital deformity of eyelid
744.01 Congenital absence of external ear causing impairment of hearing
744.09 Other congenital anomalies of ear causing impairment of hearing

Code	Description
744.23	Microtia
744.3	Unspecified congenital anomaly of ear ▽
744.5	Congenital webbing of neck
744.82	Microcheilia
748.1	Other congenital anomaly of nose
749.10	Unspecified cleft lip ▽
749.11	Unilateral cleft lip, complete
749.12	Unilateral cleft lip, incomplete
749.13	Bilateral cleft lip, complete
749.14	Bilateral cleft lip, incomplete
749.20	Unspecified cleft palate with cleft lip ▽
749.21	Unilateral cleft palate with cleft lip, complete
749.22	Unilateral cleft palate with cleft lip, incomplete
749.23	Bilateral cleft palate with cleft lip, complete
749.24	Bilateral cleft palate with cleft lip, incomplete
752.40	Unspecified congenital anomaly of cervix, vagina, and external female genitalia ▽ ♀
752.43	Cervical agenesis ♀
752.44	Cervical duplication ♀
752.45	Vaginal agenesis ♀
752.46	Transverse vaginal septum ♀
752.47	Longitudinal vaginal septum ♀
752.49	Other congenital anomaly of cervix, vagina, and external female genitalia ♀
752.64	Micropenis ♂
752.69	Other penile anomalies ♂
752.7	Indeterminate sex and pseudohermaphroditism
752.81	Scrotal transposition ♂
752.89	Other specified anomalies of genital organs
752.9	Unspecified congenital anomaly of genital organs ▽
757.33	Congenital pigmentary anomaly of skin
785.4	Gangrene — (Code first any associated underlying condition)
870.0	Laceration of skin of eyelid and periocular area
870.1	Laceration of eyelid, full-thickness, not involving lacrimal passages
870.2	Laceration of eyelid involving lacrimal passages
872.00	Open wound of external ear, unspecified site, without mention of complication ▽
872.01	Open wound of auricle, without mention of complication
872.02	Open wound of auditory canal, without mention of complication
872.10	Open wound of external ear, unspecified site, complicated ▽
872.11	Open wound of auricle, complicated
872.8	Open wound of ear, part unspecified, without mention of complication ▽
872.9	Open wound of ear, part unspecified, complicated ▽
873.30	Open wound of nose, unspecified site, complicated ▽
873.31	Open wound of nasal septum, complicated
873.32	Open wound of nasal cavity, complicated
873.33	Open wound of nasal sinus, complicated
873.39	Open wound of nose, multiple sites, complicated
873.43	Open wound of lip, without mention of complication
873.50	Open wound of face, unspecified site, complicated ▽
873.52	Open wound of forehead, complicated
873.54	Open wound of jaw, complicated
873.59	Open wound of face, other and multiple sites, complicated
874.8	Open wound of other and unspecified parts of neck, without mention of complication ▽
874.9	Open wound of other and unspecified parts of neck, complicated ▽
876.0	Open wound of back, without mention of complication
876.1	Open wound of back, complicated
878.1	Open wound of penis, complicated ♂
878.3	Open wound of scrotum and testes, complicated ♂
878.5	Open wound of vulva, complicated ♀
878.7	Open wound of vagina, complicated ♀
878.9	Open wound of other and unspecified parts of genital organs, complicated ▽
880.12	Open wound of axillary region, complicated
882.1	Open wound of hand except finger(s) alone, complicated
882.2	Open wound of hand except finger(s) alone, with tendon involvement
883.1	Open wound of finger(s), complicated
883.2	Open wound of finger(s), with tendon involvement
884.1	Multiple and unspecified open wound of upper limb, complicated
884.2	Multiple and unspecified open wound of upper limb, with tendon involvement
885.0	Traumatic amputation of thumb (complete) (partial), without mention of complication
885.1	Traumatic amputation of thumb (complete) (partial), complicated
886.0	Traumatic amputation of other finger(s) (complete) (partial), without mention of complication
886.1	Traumatic amputation of other finger(s) (complete) (partial), complicated
887.0	Traumatic amputation of arm and hand (complete) (partial), unilateral, below elbow, without mention of complication
887.1	Traumatic amputation of arm and hand (complete) (partial), unilateral, below elbow, complicated
887.6	Traumatic amputation of arm and hand (complete) (partial), bilateral (any level), without mention of complication
887.7	Traumatic amputation of arm and hand (complete) (partial), bilateral (any level), complicated
892.1	Open wound of foot except toe(s) alone, complicated
892.2	Open wound of foot except toe(s) alone, with tendon involvement
893.1	Open wound of toe(s), complicated
893.2	Open wound of toe(s), with tendon involvement
894.1	Multiple and unspecified open wound of lower limb, complicated
894.2	Multiple and unspecified open wound of lower limb, with tendon involvement
895.0	Traumatic amputation of toe(s) (complete) (partial), without mention of complication
895.1	Traumatic amputation of toe(s) (complete) (partial), complicated
896.0	Traumatic amputation of foot (complete) (partial), unilateral, without mention of complication
896.1	Traumatic amputation of foot (complete) (partial), unilateral, complicated
896.2	Traumatic amputation of foot (complete) (partial), bilateral, without mention of complication
896.3	Traumatic amputation of foot (complete) (partial), bilateral, complicated
906.0	Late effect of open wound of head, neck, and trunk
906.6	Late effect of burn of wrist and hand
941.01	Burn of unspecified degree of ear (any part) ▽
941.02	Burn of unspecified degree of eye (with other parts of face, head, and neck) ▽
941.03	Burn of unspecified degree of lip(s) ▽
941.05	Burn of unspecified degree of nose (septum) ▽
941.09	Burn of unspecified degree of multiple sites (except with eye) of face, head, and neck ▽
941.30	Full-thickness skin loss due to burn (third degree NOS) of unspecified site of face and head ▽
941.31	Full-thickness skin loss due to burn (third degree NOS) of ear (any part)
941.32	Full-thickness skin loss due to burn (third degree NOS) of eye (with other parts of face, head, and neck)
941.34	Full-thickness skin loss due to burn (third degree NOS) of chin
941.35	Full-thickness skin loss due to burn (third degree NOS) of nose (septum)
941.37	Full-thickness skin loss due to burn (third degree NOS) of forehead and cheek
941.38	Full-thickness skin loss due to burn (third degree NOS) of neck
941.40	Deep necrosis of underlying tissues due to burn (deep third degree) of unspecified site of face and head, without mention of loss of a body part ▽
941.43	Deep necrosis of underlying tissues due to burn (deep third degree) of lip(s), without mention of loss of a body part
941.44	Deep necrosis of underlying tissues due to burn (deep third degree) of chin, without mention of loss of a body part

941.47 Deep necrosis of underlying tissues due to burn (deep third degree) of forehead and cheek, without mention of loss of a body part
941.48 Deep necrosis of underlying tissues due to burn (deep third degree) of neck, without mention of loss of a body part
941.49 Deep necrosis of underlying tissues due to burn (deep third degree) of multiple sites (except with eye) of face, head, and neck, without mention of loss of a body part
941.50 Deep necrosis of underlying tissues due to burn (deep third degree) of face and head, unspecified site, with loss of a body part ▽
941.51 Deep necrosis of underlying tissues due to burn (deep third degree) of ear (any part), with loss of a body part
941.52 Deep necrosis of underlying tissues due to burn (deep third degree) of eye (with other parts of face, head, and neck), with loss of a body part
941.55 Deep necrosis of underlying tissues due to burn (deep third degree) of nose (septum), with loss of a body part
941.57 Deep necrosis of underlying tissues due to burn (deep third degree) of forehead and cheek, with loss of a body part
941.58 Deep necrosis of underlying tissues due to burn (deep third degree) of neck, with loss of a body part
943.34 Full-thickness skin loss due to burn (third degree NOS) of axilla
943.44 Deep necrosis of underlying tissues due to burn (deep third degree) of axilla, without mention of loss of a body part
943.54 Deep necrosis of underlying tissues due to burn (deep third degree) of axilla, with loss of a body part
944.30 Full-thickness skin loss due to burn (third degree NOS) of unspecified site of hand ▽
944.31 Full-thickness skin loss due to burn (third degree NOS) of single digit [finger (nail)] other than thumb
944.32 Full-thickness skin loss due to burn (third degree NOS) of thumb (nail)
944.33 Full-thickness skin loss due to burn (third degree NOS) of two or more digits of hand, not including thumb
944.34 Full-thickness skin loss due to burn (third degree NOS) of two or more digits of hand including thumb
944.35 Full-thickness skin loss due to burn (third degree NOS) of palm of hand
944.36 Full-thickness skin loss due to burn (third degree NOS) of back of hand
944.37 Full-thickness skin loss due to burn (third degree NOS) of wrist
944.38 Full-thickness skin loss due to burn (third degree NOS) of multiple sites of wrist(s) and hand(s)
944.40 Deep necrosis of underlying tissues due to burn (deep third degree) of unspecified site of hand, without mention of loss of a body part ▽
944.41 Deep necrosis of underlying tissues due to burn (deep third degree) of single digit [finger (nail)] other than thumb, without mention of loss of a body part
944.42 Deep necrosis of underlying tissues due to burn (deep third degree) of thumb (nail), without mention of loss of a body part
944.43 Deep necrosis of underlying tissues due to burn (deep third degree) of two or more digits of hand, not including thumb, without mention of loss of a body part
944.44 Deep necrosis of underlying tissues due to burn (deep third degree) of two or more digits of hand including thumb, without mention of loss of a body part
944.45 Deep necrosis of underlying tissues due to burn (deep third degree) of palm of hand, without mention of loss of a body part
944.46 Deep necrosis of underlying tissues due to burn (deep third degree) of back of hand, without mention of loss of a body part
944.47 Deep necrosis of underlying tissues due to burn (deep third degree) of wrist, without mention of loss of a body part
944.48 Deep necrosis of underlying tissues due to burn (deep third degree) of multiple sites of wrist(s) and hand(s), without mention of loss of a body part
944.50 Deep necrosis of underlying tissues due to burn (deep third degree) of unspecified site of hand, with loss of a body part ▽
944.51 Deep necrosis of underlying tissues due to burn (deep third degree) of single digit (finger (nail)) other than thumb, with loss of a body part
944.52 Deep necrosis of underlying tissues due to burn (deep third degree) of thumb (nail), with loss of a body part
944.53 Deep necrosis of underlying tissues due to burn (deep third degree) of two or more digits of hand, not including thumb, with loss of a body part
944.54 Deep necrosis of underlying tissues due to burn (deep third degree) of two or more digits of hand including thumb, with loss of a body part
944.55 Deep necrosis of underlying tissues due to burn (deep third degree) of palm of hand, with loss of a body part
944.56 Deep necrosis of underlying tissues due to burn (deep third degree) of back of hand, with loss of a body part
944.57 Deep necrosis of underlying tissues due to burn (deep third degree) of wrist, with loss of a body part
944.58 Deep necrosis of underlying tissues due to burn (deep third degree) of multiple sites of wrist(s) and hand(s), with loss of a body part
945.32 Full-thickness skin loss due to burn (third degree NOS) of foot
945.42 Deep necrosis of underlying tissues due to burn (deep third degree) of foot, without mention of loss of a body part
945.52 Deep necrosis of underlying tissues due to burn (deep third degree) of foot, with loss of a body part
948.00 Burn (any degree) involving less than 10% of body surface with third degree burn of less than 10% or unspecified amount
948.10 Burn (any degree) involving 10-19% of body surface with third degree burn of less than 10% or unspecified amount
948.11 Burn (any degree) involving 10-19% of body surface with third degree burn of 10-19%
948.20 Burn (any degree) involving 20-29% of body surface with third degree burn of less than 10% or unspecified amount
948.21 Burn (any degree) involving 20-29% of body surface with third degree burn of 10-19%
948.22 Burn (any degree) involving 20-29% of body surface with third degree burn of 20-29%
948.30 Burn (any degree) involving 30-39% of body surface with third degree burn of less than 10% or unspecified amount
948.31 Burn (any degree) involving 30-39% of body surface with third degree burn of 10-19%
948.32 Burn (any degree) involving 30-39% of body surface with third degree burn of 20-29%
948.33 Burn (any degree) involving 30-39% of body surface with third degree burn of 30-39%
948.40 Burn (any degree) involving 40-49% of body surface with third degree burn of less than 10% or unspecified amount
948.41 Burn (any degree) involving 40-49% of body surface with third degree burn of 10-19%
948.42 Burn (any degree) involving 40-49% of body surface with third degree burn of 20-29%
948.43 Burn (any degree) involving 40-49% of body surface with third degree burn of 30-39%
948.44 Burn (any degree) involving 40-49% of body surface with third degree burn of 40-49%
948.50 Burn (any degree) involving 50-59% of body surface with third degree burn of less than 10% or unspecified amount
948.51 Burn (any degree) involving 50-59% of body surface with third degree burn of 10-19%
948.52 Burn (any degree) involving 50-59% of body surface with third degree burn of 20-29%
948.53 Burn (any degree) involving 50-59% of body surface with third degree burn of 30-39%
948.54 Burn (any degree) involving 50-59% of body surface with third degree burn of 40-49%
948.55 Burn (any degree) involving 50-59% of body surface with third degree burn of 50-59%
948.60 Burn (any degree) involving 60-69% of body surface with third degree burn of less than 10% or unspecified amount
948.61 Burn (any degree) involving 60-69% of body surface with third degree burn of 10-19%
948.62 Burn (any degree) involving 60-69% of body surface with third degree burn of 20-29%
948.63 Burn (any degree) involving 60-69% of body surface with third degree burn of 30-39%
948.64 Burn (any degree) involving 60-69% of body surface with third degree burn of 40-49%
948.65 Burn (any degree) involving 60-69% of body surface with third degree burn of 50-59%
948.66 Burn (any degree) involving 60-69% of body surface with third degree burn of 60-69%
948.70 Burn (any degree) involving 70-79% of body surface with third degree burn of less than 10% or unspecified amount
948.71 Burn (any degree) involving 70-79% of body surface with third degree burn of 10-19%
948.72 Burn (any degree) involving 70-79% of body surface with third degree burn of 20-29%
948.73 Burn (any degree) involving 70-79% of body surface with third degree burn of 30-39%
948.74 Burn (any degree) involving 70-79% of body surface with third degree burn of 40-49%
948.75 Burn (any degree) involving 70-79% of body surface with third degree burn of 50-59%
948.76 Burn (any degree) involving 70-79% of body surface with third degree burn of 60-69%

948.77 Burn (any degree) involving 70-79% of body surface with third degree burn of 70-79%
948.80 Burn (any degree) involving 80-89% of body surface with third degree burn of less than 10% or unspecified amount
948.81 Burn (any degree) involving 80-89% of body surface with third degree burn of 10-19%
948.82 Burn (any degree) involving 80-89% of body surface with third degree burn of 20-29%
948.83 Burn (any degree) involving 80-89% of body surface with third degree burn of 30-39%
948.84 Burn (any degree) involving 80-89% of body surface with third degree burn of 40-49%
948.85 Burn (any degree) involving 80-89% of body surface with third degree burn of 50-59%
948.86 Burn (any degree) involving 80-89% of body surface with third degree burn of 60-69%
948.87 Burn (any degree) involving 80-89% of body surface with third degree burn of 70-79%
948.88 Burn (any degree) involving 80-89% of body surface with third degree burn of 80-89%
959.11 Other injury of chest wall
959.12 Other injury of abdomen
959.14 Other injury of external genitals
959.19 Other injury of other sites of trunk
959.4 Injury, other and unspecified, hand, except finger
959.5 Injury, other and unspecified, finger
959.7 Injury, other and unspecified, knee, leg, ankle, and foot
959.8 Injury, other and unspecified, other specified sites, including multiple
991.0 Frostbite of face
991.1 Frostbite of hand
991.2 Frostbite of foot
997.60 Late complications of amputation stump, unspecified — (Use additional code to identify complications) ▽
997.62 Infection (chronic) of amputation stump — (Use additional code to identify complications)
997.69 Other late amputation stump complication — (Use additional code to identify complications)
998.59 Other postoperative infection — (Use additional code to identify infection)
V51.8 Other aftercare involving the use of plastic surgery

ICD-9-CM Procedural

08.61 Reconstruction of eyelid with skin flap or graft
08.69 Other reconstruction of eyelid with flaps or grafts
18.79 Other plastic repair of external ear
21.89 Other repair and plastic operations on nose
27.99 Other operations on oral cavity
61.49 Other repair of scrotum and tunica vaginalis ♂
64.99 Other operations on male genital organs ♂
71.79 Other repair of vulva and perineum ♀
86.70 Pedicle or flap graft, not otherwise specified

15750

15750 Flap; neurovascular pedicle

ICD-9-CM Diagnostic

142.0 Malignant neoplasm of parotid gland
142.1 Malignant neoplasm of submandibular gland
142.2 Malignant neoplasm of sublingual gland
143.0 Malignant neoplasm of upper gum
143.1 Malignant neoplasm of lower gum
143.8 Malignant neoplasm of other sites of gum
144.8 Malignant neoplasm of other sites of floor of mouth
145.0 Malignant neoplasm of cheek mucosa
145.1 Malignant neoplasm of vestibule of mouth
145.8 Malignant neoplasm of other specified parts of mouth
145.9 Malignant neoplasm of mouth, unspecified site ▽
146.9 Malignant neoplasm of oropharynx, unspecified site ▽
147.0 Malignant neoplasm of superior wall of nasopharynx
147.1 Malignant neoplasm of posterior wall of nasopharynx
147.2 Malignant neoplasm of lateral wall of nasopharynx
147.3 Malignant neoplasm of anterior wall of nasopharynx
149.8 Malignant neoplasm of other sites within the lip and oral cavity
160.0 Malignant neoplasm of nasal cavities
160.1 Malignant neoplasm of auditory tube, middle ear, and mastoid air cells
160.2 Malignant neoplasm of maxillary sinus
160.3 Malignant neoplasm of ethmoidal sinus
160.4 Malignant neoplasm of frontal sinus
160.5 Malignant neoplasm of sphenoidal sinus
160.8 Malignant neoplasm of other sites of nasal cavities, middle ear, and accessory sinuses
161.8 Malignant neoplasm of other specified sites of larynx
161.9 Malignant neoplasm of larynx, unspecified site ▽
170.0 Malignant neoplasm of bones of skull and face, except mandible
170.1 Malignant neoplasm of mandible
171.0 Malignant neoplasm of connective and other soft tissue of head, face, and neck
171.2 Malignant neoplasm of connective and other soft tissue of upper limb, including shoulder
171.4 Malignant neoplasm of connective and other soft tissue of thorax
171.6 Malignant neoplasm of connective and other soft tissue of pelvis
171.7 Malignant neoplasm of connective and other soft tissue of trunk, unspecified site ▽
171.8 Malignant neoplasm of other specified sites of connective and other soft tissue
172.2 Malignant melanoma of skin of ear and external auditory canal
172.3 Malignant melanoma of skin of other and unspecified parts of face ▽
172.5 Malignant melanoma of skin of trunk, except scrotum
172.6 Malignant melanoma of skin of upper limb, including shoulder
173.50 Unspecified malignant neoplasm of skin of trunk, except scrotum ▽
173.51 Basal cell carcinoma of skin of trunk, except scrotum
173.52 Squamous cell carcinoma of skin of trunk, except scrotum
173.59 Other specified malignant neoplasm of skin of trunk, except scrotum
173.60 Unspecified malignant neoplasm of skin of upper limb, including shoulder ▽
173.61 Basal cell carcinoma of skin of upper limb, including shoulder
173.62 Squamous cell carcinoma of skin of upper limb, including shoulder
173.69 Other specified malignant neoplasm of skin of upper limb, including shoulder
173.70 Unspecified malignant neoplasm of skin of lower limb, including hip ▽
173.71 Basal cell carcinoma of skin of lower limb, including hip
173.72 Squamous cell carcinoma of skin of lower limb, including hip
173.79 Other specified malignant neoplasm of skin of lower limb, including hip
174.0 Malignant neoplasm of nipple and areola of female breast — (Use additional code to identify estrogen receptor status: V86.0-V86.1) ♀
174.1 Malignant neoplasm of central portion of female breast — (Use additional code to identify estrogen receptor status: V86.0-V86.1) ♀
174.2 Malignant neoplasm of upper-inner quadrant of female breast — (Use additional code to identify estrogen receptor status: V86.0-V86.1) ♀
174.3 Malignant neoplasm of lower-inner quadrant of female breast — (Use additional code to identify estrogen receptor status: V86.0-V86.1) ♀
174.4 Malignant neoplasm of upper-outer quadrant of female breast — (Use additional code to identify estrogen receptor status: V86.0-V86.1) ♀
174.5 Malignant neoplasm of lower-outer quadrant of female breast — (Use additional code to identify estrogen receptor status: V86.0-V86.1) ♀
174.6 Malignant neoplasm of axillary tail of female breast — (Use additional code to identify estrogen receptor status: V86.0-V86.1) ♀
174.8 Malignant neoplasm of other specified sites of female breast — (Use additional code to identify estrogen receptor status: V86.0-V86.1) ♀
175.9 Malignant neoplasm of other and unspecified sites of male breast — (Use additional code to identify estrogen receptor status: V86.0-V86.1) ▽ ♂
195.0 Malignant neoplasm of head, face, and neck
195.5 Malignant neoplasm of lower limb
196.0 Secondary and unspecified malignant neoplasm of lymph nodes of head, face, and neck

197.1 Secondary malignant neoplasm of mediastinum
197.8 Secondary malignant neoplasm of other digestive organs and spleen
198.2 Secondary malignant neoplasm of skin
198.81 Secondary malignant neoplasm of breast
209.31 Merkel cell carcinoma of the face
209.32 Merkel cell carcinoma of the scalp and neck
209.33 Merkel cell carcinoma of the upper limb
209.34 Merkel cell carcinoma of the lower limb
209.35 Merkel cell carcinoma of the trunk
209.36 Merkel cell carcinoma of other sites
209.75 Secondary Merkel cell carcinoma
215.0 Other benign neoplasm of connective and other soft tissue of head, face, and neck
230.0 Carcinoma in situ of lip, oral cavity, and pharynx
232.1 Carcinoma in situ of eyelid, including canthus
232.2 Carcinoma in situ of skin of ear and external auditory canal
232.5 Carcinoma in situ of skin of trunk, except scrotum
232.6 Carcinoma in situ of skin of upper limb, including shoulder
232.8 Carcinoma in situ of other specified sites of skin
233.0 Carcinoma in situ of breast
234.8 Carcinoma in situ of other specified sites
235.0 Neoplasm of uncertain behavior of major salivary glands
235.1 Neoplasm of uncertain behavior of lip, oral cavity, and pharynx
235.9 Neoplasm of uncertain behavior of other and unspecified respiratory organs ▽
238.0 Neoplasm of uncertain behavior of bone and articular cartilage
238.1 Neoplasm of uncertain behavior of connective and other soft tissue
238.2 Neoplasm of uncertain behavior of skin
238.3 Neoplasm of uncertain behavior of breast
239.0 Neoplasm of unspecified nature of digestive system
239.1 Neoplasm of unspecified nature of respiratory system
239.2 Neoplasms of unspecified nature of bone, soft tissue, and skin
239.3 Neoplasm of unspecified nature of breast
519.2 Mediastinitis — (Use additional code to identify infectious organism)
682.2 Cellulitis and abscess of trunk — (Use additional code to identify organism, such as 041.1, etc.)
682.3 Cellulitis and abscess of upper arm and forearm — (Use additional code to identify organism, such as 041.1, etc.)
682.4 Cellulitis and abscess of hand, except fingers and thumb — (Use additional code to identify organism, such as 041.1, etc.)
682.5 Cellulitis and abscess of buttock — (Use additional code to identify organism, such as 041.1, etc.)
701.5 Other abnormal granulation tissue
707.00 Pressure ulcer, unspecified site — (Use additional code to identify pressure ulcer stage: 707.20-707.25) ▽
707.01 Pressure ulcer, elbow — (Use additional code to identify pressure ulcer stage: 707.20-707.25)
707.02 Pressure ulcer, upper back — (Use additional code to identify pressure ulcer stage: 707.20-707.25)
707.03 Pressure ulcer, lower back — (Use additional code to identify pressure ulcer stage: 707.20-707.25)
707.04 Pressure ulcer, hip — (Use additional code to identify pressure ulcer stage: 707.20-707.25)
707.05 Pressure ulcer, buttock — (Use additional code to identify pressure ulcer stage: 707.20-707.25)
707.06 Pressure ulcer, ankle — (Use additional code to identify pressure ulcer stage: 707.20-707.25)
707.07 Pressure ulcer, heel — (Use additional code to identify pressure ulcer stage: 707.20-707.25)
707.09 Pressure ulcer, other site — (Use additional code to identify pressure ulcer stage: 707.20-707.25)
707.10 Ulcer of lower limb, unspecified — (Code, if applicable, any causal condition first: 249.80-249.81, 250.80-250.83, 440.23, 459.11, 459.13, 459.31, 459.33) ▽
707.11 Ulcer of thigh — (Code, if applicable, any causal condition first: 249.80-249.81, 250.80-250.83, 440.23, 459.11, 459.13, 459.31, 459.33)
707.12 Ulcer of calf — (Code, if applicable, any causal condition first: 249.80-249.81, 250.80-250.83, 440.23, 459.11, 459.13, 459.31, 459.33)
707.13 Ulcer of ankle — (Code, if applicable, any causal condition first: 249.80-249.81, 250.80-250.83, 440.23, 459.11, 459.13, 459.31, 459.33)
707.14 Ulcer of heel and midfoot — (Code, if applicable, any causal condition first: 249.80-249.81, 250.80-250.83, 440.23, 459.11, 459.13, 459.31, 459.33)
707.15 Ulcer of other part of foot — (Code, if applicable, any causal condition first: 249.80-249.81, 250.80-250.83, 440.23, 459.11, 459.13, 459.31, 459.33)
707.19 Ulcer of other part of lower limb — (Code, if applicable, any causal condition first: 249.80-249.81, 250.80-250.83, 440.23, 459.11, 459.13, 459.31, 459.33)
707.20 Pressure ulcer, unspecified stage — (Code first site of pressure ulcer: 707.00-707.09) ▽
707.21 Pressure ulcer, stage I — (Code first site of pressure ulcer: 707.00-707.09)
707.22 Pressure ulcer stage II — (Code first site of pressure ulcer: 707.00-707.09)
707.23 Pressure ulcer stage III — (Code first site of pressure ulcer: 707.00-707.09)
707.24 Pressure ulcer stage IV — (Code first site of pressure ulcer: 707.00-707.09)
707.25 Pressure ulcer, unstageable — (Code first site of pressure ulcer: 707.00-707.09)
707.8 Chronic ulcer of other specified site
709.2 Scar condition and fibrosis of skin
728.82 Foreign body granuloma of muscle — (Use additional code to identify foreign body (V90.01-V90.9))
728.86 Necrotizing fasciitis — (Use additional code to identify infectious organism, 041.00-041.89, 785.4, if applicable)
729.4 Unspecified fasciitis ▽
730.16 Chronic osteomyelitis, lower leg — (Use additional code to identify organism: 041.1. Use additional code to identify major osseous defect, if applicable: 731.3)
730.17 Chronic osteomyelitis, ankle and foot — (Use additional code to identify organism: 041.1. Use additional code to identify major osseous defect, if applicable: 731.3)
730.26 Unspecified osteomyelitis, lower leg — (Use additional code to identify organism: 041.1. Use additional code to identify major osseous defect, if applicable: 731.3) ▽
738.3 Acquired deformity of chest and rib
741.00 Spina bifida with hydrocephalus, unspecified region ▽
754.81 Pectus excavatum
810.10 Unspecified part of open fracture of clavicle ▽
810.11 Open fracture of sternal end of clavicle
810.12 Open fracture of shaft of clavicle
810.13 Open fracture of acromial end of clavicle
811.10 Open fracture of unspecified part of scapula ▽
811.11 Open fracture of acromial process of scapula
811.12 Open fracture of coracoid process
811.13 Open fracture of glenoid cavity and neck of scapula
811.19 Open fracture of other part of scapula
812.10 Open fracture of unspecified part of upper end of humerus ▽
812.12 Open fracture of anatomical neck of humerus
812.13 Open fracture of greater tuberosity of humerus
812.19 Other open fracture of upper end of humerus
812.30 Open fracture of unspecified part of humerus ▽
812.31 Open fracture of shaft of humerus
812.50 Open fracture of unspecified part of lower end of humerus ▽
812.51 Open fracture of supracondylar humerus
812.52 Open fracture of lateral condyle of humerus
812.53 Open fracture of medial condyle of humerus
812.54 Open fracture of unspecified condyle(s) of humerus ▽
812.59 Other open fracture of lower end of humerus
813.10 Unspecified open fracture of upper end of forearm ▽
813.11 Open fracture of olecranon process of ulna

Code	Description
813.12	Open fracture of coronoid process of ulna
813.13	Open Monteggia's fracture
813.14	Other and unspecified open fractures of proximal end of ulna (alone)
813.15	Open fracture of head of radius
813.16	Open fracture of neck of radius
813.17	Other and unspecified open fractures of proximal end of radius (alone)
813.18	Open fracture of radius with ulna, upper end (any part)
813.30	Unspecified open fracture of shaft of radius or ulna
813.31	Open fracture of shaft of radius (alone)
813.32	Open fracture of shaft of ulna (alone)
813.33	Open fracture of shaft of radius with ulna
813.50	Unspecified open fracture of lower end of forearm
813.51	Open Colles' fracture
813.52	Other open fractures of distal end of radius (alone)
813.53	Open fracture of distal end of ulna (alone)
813.54	Open fracture of lower end of radius with ulna
813.90	Open fracture of unspecified part of forearm
813.91	Open fracture of unspecified part of radius (alone)
813.92	Open fracture of unspecified part of ulna (alone)
813.93	Open fracture of unspecified part of radius with ulna
819.1	Multiple open fractures involving both upper limbs, and upper limb with rib(s) and sternum
823.92	Open fracture of unspecified part of fibula with tibia
860.1	Traumatic pneumothorax with open wound into thorax
860.3	Traumatic hemothorax with open wound into thorax
860.5	Traumatic pneumohemothorax with open wound into thorax
861.30	Unspecified lung injury with open wound into thorax
861.31	Lung contusion with open wound into thorax
861.32	Lung laceration with open wound into thorax
862.1	Diaphragm injury with open wound into cavity
862.31	Bronchus injury with open wound into cavity
862.32	Esophagus injury with open wound into cavity
862.39	Injury to other specified intrathoracic organs with open wound into cavity
863.30	Small intestine injury, unspecified site, with open wound into cavity
863.31	Duodenum injury with open wound into cavity
863.39	Other injury to small intestine with open wound into cavity
863.50	Colon injury, unspecified site, with open wound into cavity
863.51	Ascending (right) colon injury with open wound into cavity
863.52	Transverse colon injury with open wound into cavity
863.53	Descending (left) colon injury with open wound into cavity
863.54	Sigmoid colon injury with open wound into cavity
863.55	Rectum injury with open wound into cavity
863.56	Injury to multiple sites in colon and rectum with open wound into cavity
863.59	Other injury to colon and rectum with open wound into cavity
863.91	Pancreas head injury with open wound into cavity
863.92	Pancreas body injury with open wound into cavity
863.93	Pancreas tail injury with open wound into cavity
863.94	Pancreas injury, multiple and unspecified sites, with open wound into cavity
863.95	Appendix injury with open wound into cavity
863.99	Injury to other and unspecified gastrointestinal sites with open wound into cavity
864.10	Unspecified liver injury with open wound into cavity
864.11	Liver hematoma and contusion with open wound into cavity
864.12	Liver laceration, minor, with open wound into cavity
864.13	Liver laceration, moderate, with open wound into cavity
864.14	Liver laceration, major, with open wound into cavity
864.15	Liver injury with open wound into cavity, unspecified laceration
864.19	Other liver injury with open wound into cavity
865.10	Unspecified spleen injury with open wound into cavity
865.11	Spleen hematoma, without rupture of capsule, with open wound into cavity
865.12	Capsular tears to spleen, without major disruption of parenchyma, with open wound into cavity
865.13	Spleen laceration extending into parenchyma, with open wound into cavity
865.14	Massive parenchyma disruption of spleen with open wound into cavity
865.19	Other spleen injury with open wound into cavity
866.11	Kidney hematoma, without rupture of capsule, with open wound into cavity
866.12	Kidney laceration with open wound into cavity
866.13	Complete disruption of kidney parenchyma, with open wound into cavity
867.1	Bladder and urethra injury with open wound into cavity
867.3	Ureter injury with open wound into cavity
867.5	Uterus injury with open wound into cavity ♀
867.7	Injury to other specified pelvic organs with open wound into cavity
868.10	Injury to unspecified intra-abdominal organ, with open wound into cavity
868.11	Adrenal gland injury, with open wound into cavity
868.12	Bile duct and gallbladder injury, with open wound into cavity
868.13	Peritoneum injury with open wound into cavity
868.14	Retroperitoneum injury with open wound into cavity
868.19	Injury to other and multiple intra-abdominal organs, with open wound into cavity
869.1	Internal injury to unspecified or ill-defined organs with open wound into cavity
873.0	Open wound of scalp, without mention of complication
873.1	Open wound of scalp, complicated
873.40	Open wound of face, unspecified site, without mention of complication
873.41	Open wound of cheek, without mention of complication
873.42	Open wound of forehead, without mention of complication
873.49	Open wound of face, other and multiple sites, without mention of complication
873.50	Open wound of face, unspecified site, complicated
873.51	Open wound of cheek, complicated
873.52	Open wound of forehead, complicated
873.54	Open wound of jaw, complicated
873.59	Open wound of face, other and multiple sites, complicated
874.8	Open wound of other and unspecified parts of neck, without mention of complication
875.1	Open wound of chest (wall), complicated
876.0	Open wound of back, without mention of complication
876.1	Open wound of back, complicated
877.1	Open wound of buttock, complicated
879.5	Open wound of abdominal wall, lateral, complicated
879.8	Open wound(s) (multiple) of unspecified site(s), without mention of complication
879.9	Open wound(s) (multiple) of unspecified site(s), complicated
880.03	Open wound of upper arm, without mention of complication
880.09	Open wound of multiple sites of shoulder and upper arm, without mention of complication
880.13	Open wound of upper arm, complicated
880.19	Open wound of multiple sites of shoulder and upper arm, complicated
880.23	Open wound of upper arm, with tendon involvement
880.29	Open wound of multiple sites of shoulder and upper arm, with tendon involvement
881.00	Open wound of forearm, without mention of complication
881.01	Open wound of elbow, without mention of complication
881.02	Open wound of wrist, without mention of complication
881.10	Open wound of forearm, complicated
881.11	Open wound of elbow, complicated
881.12	Open wound of wrist, complicated
881.20	Open wound of forearm, with tendon involvement
881.21	Open wound of elbow, with tendon involvement
881.22	Open wound of wrist, with tendon involvement
882.0	Open wound of hand except finger(s) alone, without mention of complication
882.1	Open wound of hand except finger(s) alone, complicated
882.2	Open wound of hand except finger(s) alone, with tendon involvement

Unspecified code ♀ Female diagnosis ■ Manifestation code ♂ Male diagnosis [Resequenced code]

883.0 Open wound of finger(s), without mention of complication
883.1 Open wound of finger(s), complicated
883.2 Open wound of finger(s), with tendon involvement
884.0 Multiple and unspecified open wound of upper limb, without mention of complication
884.1 Multiple and unspecified open wound of upper limb, complicated
884.2 Multiple and unspecified open wound of upper limb, with tendon involvement
885.0 Traumatic amputation of thumb (complete) (partial), without mention of complication
885.1 Traumatic amputation of thumb (complete) (partial), complicated
886.0 Traumatic amputation of other finger(s) (complete) (partial), without mention of complication
886.1 Traumatic amputation of other finger(s) (complete) (partial), complicated
887.0 Traumatic amputation of arm and hand (complete) (partial), unilateral, below elbow, without mention of complication
887.1 Traumatic amputation of arm and hand (complete) (partial), unilateral, below elbow, complicated
887.2 Traumatic amputation of arm and hand (complete) (partial), unilateral, at or above elbow, without mention of complication
887.3 Traumatic amputation of arm and hand (complete) (partial), unilateral, at or above elbow, complicated
887.4 Traumatic amputation of arm and hand (complete) (partial), unilateral, level not specified, without mention of complication ▽
887.5 Traumatic amputation of arm and hand (complete) (partial), unilateral, level not specified, complicated ▽
887.6 Traumatic amputation of arm and hand (complete) (partial), bilateral (any level), without mention of complication
887.7 Traumatic amputation of arm and hand (complete) (partial), bilateral (any level), complicated
890.1 Open wound of hip and thigh, complicated
891.0 Open wound of knee, leg (except thigh), and ankle, without mention of complication
891.1 Open wound of knee, leg (except thigh), and ankle, complicated
892.1 Open wound of foot except toe(s) alone, complicated
896.1 Traumatic amputation of foot (complete) (partial), unilateral, complicated
905.0 Late effect of fracture of skull and face bones
906.0 Late effect of open wound of head, neck, and trunk
906.1 Late effect of open wound of extremities without mention of tendon injury
906.4 Late effect of crushing
906.6 Late effect of burn of wrist and hand
906.7 Late effect of burn of other extremities
906.8 Late effect of burns of other specified sites
908.0 Late effect of internal injury to chest
908.1 Late effect of internal injury to intra-abdominal organs
908.2 Late effect of internal injury to other internal organs
908.4 Late effect of injury to blood vessel of thorax, abdomen, and pelvis
908.6 Late effect of certain complications of trauma
909.2 Late effect of radiation
909.3 Late effect of complications of surgical and medical care
925.1 Crushing injury of face and scalp — (Use additional code to identify any associated injuries, such as: 800-829, 850.0-854.1, 860.0-869.1)
925.2 Crushing injury of neck — (Use additional code to identify any associated injuries, such as: 800-829, 850.0-854.1, 860.0-869.1)
926.0 Crushing injury of external genitalia — (Use additional code to identify any associated injuries: 800-829, 850.0-854.1, 860.0-869.1)
926.11 Crushing injury of back — (Use additional code to identify any associated injuries: 800-829, 850.0-854.1, 860.0-869.1)
926.12 Crushing injury of buttock — (Use additional code to identify any associated injuries: 800-829, 850.0-854.1, 860.0-869.1)
926.19 Crushing injury of other specified sites of trunk — (Use additional code to identify any associated injuries: 800-829, 850.0-854.1, 860.0-869.1)
927.03 Crushing injury of upper arm — (Use additional code to identify any associated injuries: 800-829, 850.0-854.1, 860.0-869.1)
927.09 Crushing injury of multiple sites of upper arm — (Use additional code to identify any associated injuries: 800-829, 850.0-854.1, 860.0-869.1)
927.10 Crushing injury of forearm — (Use additional code to identify any associated injuries: 800-829, 850.0-854.1, 860.0-869.1)
927.11 Crushing injury of elbow — (Use additional code to identify any associated injuries: 800-829, 850.0-854.1, 860.0-869.1)
927.20 Crushing injury of hand(s) — (Use additional code to identify any associated injuries: 800-829, 850.0-854.1, 860.0-869.1)
927.21 Crushing injury of wrist — (Use additional code to identify any associated injuries: 800-829, 850.0-854.1, 860.0-869.1)
927.3 Crushing injury of finger(s) — (Use additional code to identify any associated injuries: 800-829, 850.0-854.1, 860.0-869.1)
927.8 Crushing injury of multiple sites of upper limb — (Use additional code to identify any associated injuries: 800-829, 850.0-854.1, 860.0-869.1)
941.30 Full-thickness skin loss due to burn (third degree NOS) of unspecified site of face and head ▽
941.36 Full-thickness skin loss due to burn (third degree NOS) of scalp (any part)
941.37 Full-thickness skin loss due to burn (third degree NOS) of forehead and cheek
941.38 Full-thickness skin loss due to burn (third degree NOS) of neck
941.39 Full-thickness skin loss due to burn (third degree NOS) of multiple sites (except with eye) of face, head, and neck
941.40 Deep necrosis of underlying tissues due to burn (deep third degree) of unspecified site of face and head, without mention of loss of a body part ▽
941.44 Deep necrosis of underlying tissues due to burn (deep third degree) of chin, without mention of loss of a body part
941.46 Deep necrosis of underlying tissues due to burn (deep third degree) of scalp (any part), without mention of loss of a body part
941.47 Deep necrosis of underlying tissues due to burn (deep third degree) of forehead and cheek, without mention of loss of a body part
941.48 Deep necrosis of underlying tissues due to burn (deep third degree) of neck, without mention of loss of a body part
941.49 Deep necrosis of underlying tissues due to burn (deep third degree) of multiple sites (except with eye) of face, head, and neck, without mention of loss of a body part
941.50 Deep necrosis of underlying tissues due to burn (deep third degree) of face and head, unspecified site, with loss of a body part ▽
941.54 Deep necrosis of underlying tissues due to burn (deep third degree) of chin, with loss of a body part
941.56 Deep necrosis of underlying tissues due to burn (deep third degree) of scalp (any part), with loss of a body part
941.58 Deep necrosis of underlying tissues due to burn (deep third degree) of neck, with loss of a body part
942.30 Full-thickness skin loss due to burn (third degree NOS) of unspecified site of trunk ▽
942.31 Full-thickness skin loss due to burn (third degree NOS) of breast
942.33 Full-thickness skin loss due to burn (third degree NOS) of abdominal wall
942.34 Full-thickness skin loss due to burn (third degree NOS) of back (any part)
942.35 Full-thickness skin loss due to burn (third degree NOS) of genitalia
942.39 Full-thickness skin loss due to burn (third degree NOS) of other and multiple sites of trunk
942.40 Deep necrosis of underlying tissues due to burn (deep third degree) of trunk, unspecified site, without mention of loss of a body part ▽
942.41 Deep necrosis of underlying tissues due to burn (deep third degree) of breast, without mention of loss of a body part
942.42 Deep necrosis of underlying tissues due to burn (deep third degree) of chest wall, excluding breast and nipple, without mention of loss of a body part
942.43 Deep necrosis of underlying tissues due to burn (deep third degree) of abdominal wall, without mention of loss of a body part
942.44 Deep necrosis of underlying tissues due to burn (deep third degree) of back (any part), without mention of loss of a body part
942.45 Deep necrosis of underlying tissues due to burn (deep third degree) of genitalia, without mention of loss of a body part

942.49 Deep necrosis of underlying tissues due to burn (deep third degree) of other and multiple sites of trunk, without mention of loss of a body part
942.50 Deep necrosis of underlying tissues due to burn (deep third degree) of unspecified site of trunk, with loss of a body part
942.51 Deep necrosis of underlying tissues due to burn (deep third degree) of breast, with loss of a body part
942.52 Deep necrosis of underlying tissues due to burn (deep third degree) of chest wall, excluding breast and nipple, with loss of a body part
942.53 Deep necrosis of underlying tissues due to burn (deep third degree) of abdominal wall with loss of a body part
942.54 Deep necrosis of underlying tissues due to burn (deep third degree) of back (any part), with loss of a body part
942.55 Deep necrosis of underlying tissues due to burn (deep third degree) of genitalia, with loss of a body part
942.59 Deep necrosis of underlying tissues due to burn (deep third degree) of other and multiple sites of trunk, with loss of a body part
943.30 Full-thickness skin loss due to burn (third degree NOS) of unspecified site of upper limb
943.31 Full-thickness skin loss due to burn (third degree NOS) of forearm
943.32 Full-thickness skin loss due to burn (third degree NOS) of elbow
943.33 Full-thickness skin loss due to burn (third degree NOS) of upper arm
943.39 Full-thickness skin loss due to burn (third degree NOS) of multiple sites of upper limb, except wrist and hand
943.40 Deep necrosis of underlying tissues due to burn (deep third degree) of unspecified site of upper limb, without mention of loss of a body part
943.41 Deep necrosis of underlying tissues due to burn (deep third degree) of forearm, without mention of loss of a body part
943.42 Deep necrosis of underlying tissues due to burn (deep third degree) of elbow, without mention of loss of a body part
943.44 Deep necrosis of underlying tissues due to burn (deep third degree) of axilla, without mention of loss of a body part
943.49 Deep necrosis of underlying tissues due to burn (deep third degree) of multiple sites of upper limb, except wrist and hand, without mention of loss of a body part
943.50 Deep necrosis of underlying tissues due to burn (deep third degree) of unspecified site of upper limb, with loss of a body part
943.51 Deep necrosis of underlying tissues due to burn (deep third degree) of forearm, with loss of a body part
943.52 Deep necrosis of underlying tissues due to burn (deep third degree) of elbow, with loss of a body part
943.53 Deep necrosis of underlying tissues due to burn (deep third degree) of upper arm, with loss of upper a body part
943.59 Deep necrosis of underlying tissues due to burn (deep third degree) of multiple sites of upper limb, except wrist and hand, with loss of a body part
944.30 Full-thickness skin loss due to burn (third degree NOS) of unspecified site of hand
944.31 Full-thickness skin loss due to burn (third degree NOS) of single digit [finger (nail)] other than thumb
944.32 Full-thickness skin loss due to burn (third degree NOS) of thumb (nail)
944.33 Full-thickness skin loss due to burn (third degree NOS) of two or more digits of hand, not including thumb
944.34 Full-thickness skin loss due to burn (third degree NOS) of two or more digits of hand including thumb
944.35 Full-thickness skin loss due to burn (third degree NOS) of palm of hand
944.36 Full-thickness skin loss due to burn (third degree NOS) of back of hand
944.37 Full-thickness skin loss due to burn (third degree NOS) of wrist
944.38 Full-thickness skin loss due to burn (third degree NOS) of multiple sites of wrist(s) and hand(s)
944.40 Deep necrosis of underlying tissues due to burn (deep third degree) of unspecified site of hand, without mention of loss of a body part
944.41 Deep necrosis of underlying tissues due to burn (deep third degree) of single digit [finger (nail)] other than thumb, without mention of loss of a body part
944.42 Deep necrosis of underlying tissues due to burn (deep third degree) of thumb (nail), without mention of loss of a body part
944.43 Deep necrosis of underlying tissues due to burn (deep third degree) of two or more digits of hand, not including thumb, without mention of loss of a body part
944.44 Deep necrosis of underlying tissues due to burn (deep third degree) of two or more digits of hand including thumb, without mention of loss of a body part
944.46 Deep necrosis of underlying tissues due to burn (deep third degree) of back of hand, without mention of loss of a body part
944.47 Deep necrosis of underlying tissues due to burn (deep third degree) of wrist, without mention of loss of a body part
944.48 Deep necrosis of underlying tissues due to burn (deep third degree) of multiple sites of wrist(s) and hand(s), without mention of loss of a body part
944.50 Deep necrosis of underlying tissues due to burn (deep third degree) of unspecified site of hand, with loss of a body part
944.51 Deep necrosis of underlying tissues due to burn (deep third degree) of single digit (finger (nail)) other than thumb, with loss of a body part
944.52 Deep necrosis of underlying tissues due to burn (deep third degree) of thumb (nail), with loss of a body part
944.53 Deep necrosis of underlying tissues due to burn (deep third degree) of two or more digits of hand, not including thumb, with loss of a body part
944.54 Deep necrosis of underlying tissues due to burn (deep third degree) of two or more digits of hand including thumb, with loss of a body part
944.55 Deep necrosis of underlying tissues due to burn (deep third degree) of palm of hand, with loss of a body part
944.56 Deep necrosis of underlying tissues due to burn (deep third degree) of back of hand, with loss of a body part
944.57 Deep necrosis of underlying tissues due to burn (deep third degree) of wrist, with loss of a body part
944.58 Deep necrosis of underlying tissues due to burn (deep third degree) of multiple sites of wrist(s) and hand(s), with loss of a body part
996.52 Mechanical complication due to other tissue graft, not elsewhere classified
997.60 Late complications of amputation stump, unspecified — (Use additional code to identify complications)
997.62 Infection (chronic) of amputation stump — (Use additional code to identify complications)
997.69 Other late amputation stump complication — (Use additional code to identify complications)
998.30 Disruption of wound, unspecified
998.31 Disruption of internal operation (surgical) wound
998.32 Disruption of external operation (surgical) wound
998.33 Disruption of traumatic injury wound repair
998.59 Other postoperative infection — (Use additional code to identify infection)
998.83 Non-healing surgical wound
V10.02 Personal history of malignant neoplasm of other and unspecified parts of oral cavity and pharynx
V10.82 Personal history of malignant melanoma of skin
V51.8 Other aftercare involving the use of plastic surgery

ICD-9-CM Procedural

04.5 Cranial or peripheral nerve graft
86.70 Pedicle or flap graft, not otherwise specified

15756

15756 Free muscle or myocutaneous flap with microvascular anastomosis

ICD-9-CM Diagnostic

140.3 Malignant neoplasm of upper lip, inner aspect
140.5 Malignant neoplasm of lip, inner aspect, unspecified as to upper or lower
140.8 Malignant neoplasm of other sites of lip
141.0 Malignant neoplasm of base of tongue
142.0 Malignant neoplasm of parotid gland
142.1 Malignant neoplasm of submandibular gland

142.2 Malignant neoplasm of sublingual gland
142.8 Malignant neoplasm of other major salivary glands
143.0 Malignant neoplasm of upper gum
143.1 Malignant neoplasm of lower gum
143.8 Malignant neoplasm of other sites of gum
143.9 Malignant neoplasm of gum, unspecified site ▽
144.0 Malignant neoplasm of anterior portion of floor of mouth
144.1 Malignant neoplasm of lateral portion of floor of mouth
144.8 Malignant neoplasm of other sites of floor of mouth
145.0 Malignant neoplasm of cheek mucosa
145.1 Malignant neoplasm of vestibule of mouth
145.8 Malignant neoplasm of other specified parts of mouth
146.3 Malignant neoplasm of vallecula
146.4 Malignant neoplasm of anterior aspect of epiglottis
146.5 Malignant neoplasm of junctional region of oropharynx
146.6 Malignant neoplasm of lateral wall of oropharynx
146.7 Malignant neoplasm of posterior wall of oropharynx
146.8 Malignant neoplasm of other specified sites of oropharynx
147.0 Malignant neoplasm of superior wall of nasopharynx
147.1 Malignant neoplasm of posterior wall of nasopharynx
147.2 Malignant neoplasm of lateral wall of nasopharynx
147.3 Malignant neoplasm of anterior wall of nasopharynx
149.8 Malignant neoplasm of other sites within the lip and oral cavity
149.9 Malignant neoplasm of ill-defined sites of lip and oral cavity
150.0 Malignant neoplasm of cervical esophagus
150.1 Malignant neoplasm of thoracic esophagus
160.0 Malignant neoplasm of nasal cavities
160.1 Malignant neoplasm of auditory tube, middle ear, and mastoid air cells
160.2 Malignant neoplasm of maxillary sinus
160.3 Malignant neoplasm of ethmoidal sinus
160.4 Malignant neoplasm of frontal sinus
160.5 Malignant neoplasm of sphenoidal sinus
160.8 Malignant neoplasm of other sites of nasal cavities, middle ear, and accessory sinuses
171.0 Malignant neoplasm of connective and other soft tissue of head, face, and neck
171.2 Malignant neoplasm of connective and other soft tissue of upper limb, including shoulder
171.3 Malignant neoplasm of connective and other soft tissue of lower limb, including hip
171.4 Malignant neoplasm of connective and other soft tissue of thorax
171.7 Malignant neoplasm of connective and other soft tissue of trunk, unspecified site ▽
171.8 Malignant neoplasm of other specified sites of connective and other soft tissue
172.0 Malignant melanoma of skin of lip
172.1 Malignant melanoma of skin of eyelid, including canthus
172.2 Malignant melanoma of skin of ear and external auditory canal
172.4 Malignant melanoma of skin of scalp and neck
172.5 Malignant melanoma of skin of trunk, except scrotum
172.6 Malignant melanoma of skin of upper limb, including shoulder
172.7 Malignant melanoma of skin of lower limb, including hip
172.8 Malignant melanoma of other specified sites of skin
193 Malignant neoplasm of thyroid gland — (Use additional code to identify any functional activity)
195.0 Malignant neoplasm of head, face, and neck
195.1 Malignant neoplasm of thorax
196.0 Secondary and unspecified malignant neoplasm of lymph nodes of head, face, and neck
196.1 Secondary and unspecified malignant neoplasm of intrathoracic lymph nodes
209.31 Merkel cell carcinoma of the face
209.32 Merkel cell carcinoma of the scalp and neck
209.33 Merkel cell carcinoma of the upper limb
209.34 Merkel cell carcinoma of the lower limb
209.35 Merkel cell carcinoma of the trunk
209.36 Merkel cell carcinoma of other sites
209.75 Secondary Merkel cell carcinoma
235.0 Neoplasm of uncertain behavior of major salivary glands
235.1 Neoplasm of uncertain behavior of lip, oral cavity, and pharynx
238.1 Neoplasm of uncertain behavior of connective and other soft tissue
239.2 Neoplasms of unspecified nature of bone, soft tissue, and skin
682.2 Cellulitis and abscess of trunk — (Use additional code to identify organism, such as 041.1, etc.)
707.00 Pressure ulcer, unspecified site — (Use additional code to identify pressure ulcer stage: 707.20-707.25) ▽
707.01 Pressure ulcer, elbow — (Use additional code to identify pressure ulcer stage: 707.20-707.25)
707.02 Pressure ulcer, upper back — (Use additional code to identify pressure ulcer stage: 707.20-707.25)
707.03 Pressure ulcer, lower back — (Use additional code to identify pressure ulcer stage: 707.20-707.25)
707.04 Pressure ulcer, hip — (Use additional code to identify pressure ulcer stage: 707.20-707.25)
707.05 Pressure ulcer, buttock — (Use additional code to identify pressure ulcer stage: 707.20-707.25)
707.06 Pressure ulcer, ankle — (Use additional code to identify pressure ulcer stage: 707.20-707.25)
707.07 Pressure ulcer, heel — (Use additional code to identify pressure ulcer stage: 707.20-707.25)
707.09 Pressure ulcer, other site — (Use additional code to identify pressure ulcer stage: 707.20-707.25)
707.20 Pressure ulcer, unspecified stage — (Code first site of pressure ulcer: 707.00-707.09) ▽
707.21 Pressure ulcer, stage I — (Code first site of pressure ulcer: 707.00-707.09)
707.22 Pressure ulcer stage II — (Code first site of pressure ulcer: 707.00-707.09)
707.23 Pressure ulcer stage III — (Code first site of pressure ulcer: 707.00-707.09)
707.24 Pressure ulcer stage IV — (Code first site of pressure ulcer: 707.00-707.09)
707.25 Pressure ulcer, unstageable — (Code first site of pressure ulcer: 707.00-707.09)
810.10 Unspecified part of open fracture of clavicle ▽
810.11 Open fracture of sternal end of clavicle
810.12 Open fracture of shaft of clavicle
810.13 Open fracture of acromial end of clavicle
813.10 Unspecified open fracture of upper end of forearm ▽
813.11 Open fracture of olecranon process of ulna
813.12 Open fracture of coronoid process of ulna
813.13 Open Monteggia's fracture
813.14 Other and unspecified open fractures of proximal end of ulna (alone) ▽
813.15 Open fracture of head of radius
813.16 Open fracture of neck of radius
813.17 Other and unspecified open fractures of proximal end of radius (alone) ▽
813.18 Open fracture of radius with ulna, upper end (any part)
813.30 Unspecified open fracture of shaft of radius or ulna ▽
813.31 Open fracture of shaft of radius (alone)
813.32 Open fracture of shaft of ulna (alone)
813.33 Open fracture of shaft of radius with ulna
813.50 Unspecified open fracture of lower end of forearm ▽
813.51 Open Colles' fracture
813.52 Other open fractures of distal end of radius (alone)
813.53 Open fracture of distal end of ulna (alone)
813.54 Open fracture of lower end of radius with ulna
813.90 Open fracture of unspecified part of forearm ▽
813.91 Open fracture of unspecified part of radius (alone) ▽
813.92 Open fracture of unspecified part of ulna (alone) ▽

813.93 Open fracture of unspecified part of radius with ulna ▽
823.10 Open fracture of upper end of tibia
823.11 Open fracture of upper end of fibula
823.12 Open fracture of upper end of fibula with tibia
823.30 Open fracture of shaft of tibia
823.31 Open fracture of shaft of fibula
823.32 Open fracture of shaft of fibula with tibia
823.90 Open fracture of unspecified part of tibia ▽
823.91 Open fracture of unspecified part of fibula ▽
823.92 Open fracture of unspecified part of fibula with tibia ▽
873.50 Open wound of face, unspecified site, complicated ▽
873.51 Open wound of cheek, complicated
873.52 Open wound of forehead, complicated
873.53 Open wound of lip, complicated
873.54 Open wound of jaw, complicated
873.9 Other and unspecified open wound of head, complicated ▽
874.10 Open wound of larynx with trachea, complicated
874.11 Open wound of larynx, complicated
874.12 Open wound of trachea, complicated
874.3 Open wound of thyroid gland, complicated
874.5 Open wound of pharynx, complicated
874.9 Open wound of other and unspecified parts of neck, complicated ▽
875.1 Open wound of chest (wall), complicated
876.1 Open wound of back, complicated
880.10 Open wound of shoulder region, complicated
880.11 Open wound of scapular region, complicated
880.12 Open wound of axillary region, complicated
880.13 Open wound of upper arm, complicated
880.19 Open wound of multiple sites of shoulder and upper arm, complicated
881.10 Open wound of forearm, complicated
881.11 Open wound of elbow, complicated
881.12 Open wound of wrist, complicated
882.1 Open wound of hand except finger(s) alone, complicated
884.1 Multiple and unspecified open wound of upper limb, complicated
891.1 Open wound of knee, leg (except thigh), and ankle, complicated
959.01 Head injury, unspecified ▽
959.09 Injury of face and neck, other and unspecified
959.11 Other injury of chest wall
959.12 Other injury of abdomen
959.19 Other injury of other sites of trunk
998.30 Disruption of wound, unspecified ▽
998.32 Disruption of external operation (surgical) wound
998.33 Disruption of traumatic injury wound repair
998.83 Non-healing surgical wound
V51.8 Other aftercare involving the use of plastic surgery

ICD-9-CM Procedural

39.31 Suture of artery
39.32 Suture of vein
82.72 Plastic operation on hand with graft of muscle or fascia
83.77 Muscle transfer or transplantation
86.61 Full-thickness skin graft to hand
86.63 Full-thickness skin graft to other sites

15757

15757 Free skin flap with microvascular anastomosis

ICD-9-CM Diagnostic

140.9 Malignant neoplasm of lip, vermilion border, unspecified as to upper or lower ▽
149.8 Malignant neoplasm of other sites within the lip and oral cavity
149.9 Malignant neoplasm of ill-defined sites of lip and oral cavity
172.1 Malignant melanoma of skin of eyelid, including canthus
172.2 Malignant melanoma of skin of ear and external auditory canal
172.4 Malignant melanoma of skin of scalp and neck
172.5 Malignant melanoma of skin of trunk, except scrotum
172.6 Malignant melanoma of skin of upper limb, including shoulder
172.7 Malignant melanoma of skin of lower limb, including hip
173.00 Unspecified malignant neoplasm of skin of lip ▽
173.01 Basal cell carcinoma of skin of lip
173.02 Squamous cell carcinoma of skin of lip
173.09 Other specified malignant neoplasm of skin of lip
173.10 Unspecified malignant neoplasm of eyelid, including canthus ▽
173.11 Basal cell carcinoma of eyelid, including canthus
173.12 Squamous cell carcinoma of eyelid, including canthus
173.19 Other specified malignant neoplasm of eyelid, including canthus
173.20 Unspecified malignant neoplasm of skin of ear and external auditory canal ▽
173.21 Basal cell carcinoma of skin of ear and external auditory canal
173.22 Squamous cell carcinoma of skin of ear and external auditory canal
173.29 Other specified malignant neoplasm of skin of ear and external auditory canal
173.40 Unspecified malignant neoplasm of scalp and skin of neck ▽
173.41 Basal cell carcinoma of scalp and skin of neck
173.42 Squamous cell carcinoma of scalp and skin of neck
173.49 Other specified malignant neoplasm of scalp and skin of neck
173.50 Unspecified malignant neoplasm of skin of trunk, except scrotum ▽
173.51 Basal cell carcinoma of skin of trunk, except scrotum
173.52 Squamous cell carcinoma of skin of trunk, except scrotum
173.59 Other specified malignant neoplasm of skin of trunk, except scrotum
173.60 Unspecified malignant neoplasm of skin of upper limb, including shoulder ▽
173.61 Basal cell carcinoma of skin of upper limb, including shoulder
173.62 Squamous cell carcinoma of skin of upper limb, including shoulder
173.69 Other specified malignant neoplasm of skin of upper limb, including shoulder
173.70 Unspecified malignant neoplasm of skin of lower limb, including hip ▽
173.71 Basal cell carcinoma of skin of lower limb, including hip
173.72 Squamous cell carcinoma of skin of lower limb, including hip
173.79 Other specified malignant neoplasm of skin of lower limb, including hip
173.80 Unspecified malignant neoplasm of other specified sites of skin ▽
173.81 Basal cell carcinoma of other specified sites of skin
173.82 Squamous cell carcinoma of other specified sites of skin
173.89 Other specified malignant neoplasm of other specified sites of skin
184.0 Malignant neoplasm of vagina ♀
184.1 Malignant neoplasm of labia majora ♀
184.2 Malignant neoplasm of labia minora ♀
184.3 Malignant neoplasm of clitoris ♀
184.4 Malignant neoplasm of vulva, unspecified site ▽ ♀
184.8 Malignant neoplasm of other specified sites of female genital organs ♀
187.1 Malignant neoplasm of prepuce ♂
187.2 Malignant neoplasm of glans penis ♂
187.3 Malignant neoplasm of body of penis ♂
187.4 Malignant neoplasm of penis, part unspecified ▽ ♂
187.7 Malignant neoplasm of scrotum ♂
187.9 Malignant neoplasm of male genital organ, site unspecified ▽ ♂
195.0 Malignant neoplasm of head, face, and neck
198.2 Secondary malignant neoplasm of skin
209.31 Merkel cell carcinoma of the face
209.32 Merkel cell carcinoma of the scalp and neck
209.33 Merkel cell carcinoma of the upper limb
209.34 Merkel cell carcinoma of the lower limb
209.35 Merkel cell carcinoma of the trunk

209.36 Merkel cell carcinoma of other sites
209.75 Secondary Merkel cell carcinoma
210.0 Benign neoplasm of lip
210.4 Benign neoplasm of other and unspecified parts of mouth ▽
216.1 Benign neoplasm of eyelid, including canthus
216.2 Benign neoplasm of ear and external auditory canal
216.4 Benign neoplasm of scalp and skin of neck
216.6 Benign neoplasm of skin of upper limb, including shoulder
216.7 Benign neoplasm of skin of lower limb, including hip
216.8 Benign neoplasm of other specified sites of skin
232.0 Carcinoma in situ of skin of lip
232.1 Carcinoma in situ of eyelid, including canthus
232.2 Carcinoma in situ of skin of ear and external auditory canal
232.4 Carcinoma in situ of scalp and skin of neck
232.6 Carcinoma in situ of skin of upper limb, including shoulder
232.7 Carcinoma in situ of skin of lower limb, including hip
232.8 Carcinoma in situ of other specified sites of skin
239.0 Neoplasm of unspecified nature of digestive system
239.2 Neoplasms of unspecified nature of bone, soft tissue, and skin
380.32 Acquired deformities of auricle or pinna
440.23 Atherosclerosis of native arteries of the extremities with ulceration — (Use additional code for any associated ulceration: 707.10-707.19, 707.8, 707.9)
443.0 Raynaud's syndrome — (Use additional code to identify gangrene: 785.4)
459.11 Postphlebitic syndrome with ulcer
459.13 Postphlebitic syndrome with ulcer and inflammation
459.31 Chronic venous hypertension with ulcer
459.33 Chronic venous hypertension with ulcer and inflammation
607.2 Other inflammatory disorders of penis — (Use additional code to identify organism) ♂
682.0 Cellulitis and abscess of face — (Use additional code to identify organism, such as 041.1, etc.)
682.2 Cellulitis and abscess of trunk — (Use additional code to identify organism, such as 041.1, etc.)
707.00 Pressure ulcer, unspecified site — (Use additional code to identify pressure ulcer stage: 707.20-707.25) ▽
707.01 Pressure ulcer, elbow — (Use additional code to identify pressure ulcer stage: 707.20-707.25)
707.02 Pressure ulcer, upper back — (Use additional code to identify pressure ulcer stage: 707.20-707.25)
707.03 Pressure ulcer, lower back — (Use additional code to identify pressure ulcer stage: 707.20-707.25)
707.04 Pressure ulcer, hip — (Use additional code to identify pressure ulcer stage: 707.20-707.25)
707.05 Pressure ulcer, buttock — (Use additional code to identify pressure ulcer stage: 707.20-707.25)
707.06 Pressure ulcer, ankle — (Use additional code to identify pressure ulcer stage: 707.20-707.25)
707.07 Pressure ulcer, heel — (Use additional code to identify pressure ulcer stage: 707.20-707.25)
707.09 Pressure ulcer, other site — (Use additional code to identify pressure ulcer stage: 707.20-707.25)
707.10 Ulcer of lower limb, unspecified — (Code, if applicable, any causal condition first: 249.80-249.81, 250.80-250.83, 440.23, 459.11, 459.13, 459.31, 459.33) ▽
707.11 Ulcer of thigh — (Code, if applicable, any causal condition first: 249.80-249.81, 250.80-250.83, 440.23, 459.11, 459.13, 459.31, 459.33)
707.12 Ulcer of calf — (Code, if applicable, any causal condition first: 249.80-249.81, 250.80-250.83, 440.23, 459.11, 459.13, 459.31, 459.33)
707.13 Ulcer of ankle — (Code, if applicable, any causal condition first: 249.80-249.81, 250.80-250.83, 440.23, 459.11, 459.13, 459.31, 459.33)
707.14 Ulcer of heel and midfoot — (Code, if applicable, any causal condition first: 249.80-249.81, 250.80-250.83, 440.23, 459.11, 459.13, 459.31, 459.33)
707.15 Ulcer of other part of foot — (Code, if applicable, any causal condition first: 249.80-249.81, 250.80-250.83, 440.23, 459.11, 459.13, 459.31, 459.33)
707.19 Ulcer of other part of lower limb — (Code, if applicable, any causal condition first: 249.80-249.81, 250.80-250.83, 440.23, 459.11, 459.13, 459.31, 459.33)
707.20 Pressure ulcer, unspecified stage — (Code first site of pressure ulcer: 707.00-707.09) ▽
707.21 Pressure ulcer, stage I — (Code first site of pressure ulcer: 707.00-707.09)
707.22 Pressure ulcer stage II — (Code first site of pressure ulcer: 707.00-707.09)
707.23 Pressure ulcer stage III — (Code first site of pressure ulcer: 707.00-707.09)
707.24 Pressure ulcer stage IV — (Code first site of pressure ulcer: 707.00-707.09)
707.25 Pressure ulcer, unstageable — (Code first site of pressure ulcer: 707.00-707.09)
707.8 Chronic ulcer of other specified site
728.86 Necrotizing fasciitis — (Use additional code to identify infectious organism, 041.00-041.89, 785.4, if applicable)
743.62 Congenital deformity of eyelid
744.01 Congenital absence of external ear causing impairment of hearing
744.09 Other congenital anomalies of ear causing impairment of hearing
744.23 Microtia
744.3 Unspecified congenital anomaly of ear ▽
744.5 Congenital webbing of neck
744.82 Microcheilia
748.1 Other congenital anomaly of nose
749.11 Unilateral cleft lip, complete
749.12 Unilateral cleft lip, incomplete
749.13 Bilateral cleft lip, complete
749.14 Bilateral cleft lip, incomplete
749.20 Unspecified cleft palate with cleft lip ▽
749.21 Unilateral cleft palate with cleft lip, complete
749.22 Unilateral cleft palate with cleft lip, incomplete
749.23 Bilateral cleft palate with cleft lip, complete
749.24 Bilateral cleft palate with cleft lip, incomplete
752.40 Unspecified congenital anomaly of cervix, vagina, and external female genitalia ▽ ♀
752.43 Cervical agenesis ♀
752.44 Cervical duplication ♀
752.45 Vaginal agenesis ♀
752.46 Transverse vaginal septum ♀
752.47 Longitudinal vaginal septum ♀
752.49 Other congenital anomaly of cervix, vagina, and external female genitalia ♀
752.64 Micropenis ♂
752.69 Other penile anomalies ♂
752.7 Indeterminate sex and pseudohermaphroditism
752.81 Scrotal transposition ♂
752.89 Other specified anomalies of genital organs
752.9 Unspecified congenital anomaly of genital organs ▽
757.33 Congenital pigmentary anomaly of skin
785.4 Gangrene — (Code first any associated underlying condition)
870.0 Laceration of skin of eyelid and periocular area
870.1 Laceration of eyelid, full-thickness, not involving lacrimal passages
870.2 Laceration of eyelid involving lacrimal passages
872.00 Open wound of external ear, unspecified site, without mention of complication ▽
872.01 Open wound of auricle, without mention of complication
872.02 Open wound of auditory canal, without mention of complication
872.10 Open wound of external ear, unspecified site, complicated ▽
872.11 Open wound of auricle, complicated
872.12 Open wound of auditory canal, complicated
872.8 Open wound of ear, part unspecified, without mention of complication ▽
872.9 Open wound of ear, part unspecified, complicated ▽
873.30 Open wound of nose, unspecified site, complicated ▽

873.31 Open wound of nasal septum, complicated
873.32 Open wound of nasal cavity, complicated
873.33 Open wound of nasal sinus, complicated
873.39 Open wound of nose, multiple sites, complicated
873.43 Open wound of lip, without mention of complication
873.50 Open wound of face, unspecified site, complicated
873.52 Open wound of forehead, complicated
873.54 Open wound of jaw, complicated
873.59 Open wound of face, other and multiple sites, complicated
874.8 Open wound of other and unspecified parts of neck, without mention of complication
874.9 Open wound of other and unspecified parts of neck, complicated
876.0 Open wound of back, without mention of complication
876.1 Open wound of back, complicated
878.1 Open wound of penis, complicated ♂
878.3 Open wound of scrotum and testes, complicated ♂
878.5 Open wound of vulva, complicated ♀
878.7 Open wound of vagina, complicated ♀
878.9 Open wound of other and unspecified parts of genital organs, complicated
880.12 Open wound of axillary region, complicated
882.1 Open wound of hand except finger(s) alone, complicated
882.2 Open wound of hand except finger(s) alone, with tendon involvement
883.1 Open wound of finger(s), complicated
883.2 Open wound of finger(s), with tendon involvement
884.1 Multiple and unspecified open wound of upper limb, complicated
884.2 Multiple and unspecified open wound of upper limb, with tendon involvement
885.0 Traumatic amputation of thumb (complete) (partial), without mention of complication
885.1 Traumatic amputation of thumb (complete) (partial), complicated
886.0 Traumatic amputation of other finger(s) (complete) (partial), without mention of complication
886.1 Traumatic amputation of other finger(s) (complete) (partial), complicated
887.0 Traumatic amputation of arm and hand (complete) (partial), unilateral, below elbow, without mention of complication
887.1 Traumatic amputation of arm and hand (complete) (partial), unilateral, below elbow, complicated
887.6 Traumatic amputation of arm and hand (complete) (partial), bilateral (any level), without mention of complication
887.7 Traumatic amputation of arm and hand (complete) (partial), bilateral (any level), complicated
892.1 Open wound of foot except toe(s) alone, complicated
892.2 Open wound of foot except toe(s) alone, with tendon involvement
893.1 Open wound of toe(s), complicated
893.2 Open wound of toe(s), with tendon involvement
894.1 Multiple and unspecified open wound of lower limb, complicated
894.2 Multiple and unspecified open wound of lower limb, with tendon involvement
895.0 Traumatic amputation of toe(s) (complete) (partial), without mention of complication
895.1 Traumatic amputation of toe(s) (complete) (partial), complicated
896.0 Traumatic amputation of foot (complete) (partial), unilateral, without mention of complication
896.1 Traumatic amputation of foot (complete) (partial), unilateral, complicated
896.2 Traumatic amputation of foot (complete) (partial), bilateral, without mention of complication
896.3 Traumatic amputation of foot (complete) (partial), bilateral, complicated
906.0 Late effect of open wound of head, neck, and trunk
906.6 Late effect of burn of wrist and hand
941.01 Burn of unspecified degree of ear (any part)
941.02 Burn of unspecified degree of eye (with other parts of face, head, and neck)
941.03 Burn of unspecified degree of lip(s)
941.05 Burn of unspecified degree of nose (septum)
941.09 Burn of unspecified degree of multiple sites (except with eye) of face, head, and neck
941.30 Full-thickness skin loss due to burn (third degree NOS) of unspecified site of face and head
941.31 Full-thickness skin loss due to burn (third degree NOS) of ear (any part)
941.32 Full-thickness skin loss due to burn (third degree NOS) of eye (with other parts of face, head, and neck)
941.34 Full-thickness skin loss due to burn (third degree NOS) of chin
941.35 Full-thickness skin loss due to burn (third degree NOS) of nose (septum)
941.37 Full-thickness skin loss due to burn (third degree NOS) of forehead and cheek
941.38 Full-thickness skin loss due to burn (third degree NOS) of neck
941.40 Deep necrosis of underlying tissues due to burn (deep third degree) of unspecified site of face and head, without mention of loss of a body part
941.43 Deep necrosis of underlying tissues due to burn (deep third degree) of lip(s), without mention of loss of a body part
941.44 Deep necrosis of underlying tissues due to burn (deep third degree) of chin, without mention of loss of a body part
941.47 Deep necrosis of underlying tissues due to burn (deep third degree) of forehead and cheek, without mention of loss of a body part
941.48 Deep necrosis of underlying tissues due to burn (deep third degree) of neck, without mention of loss of a body part
941.49 Deep necrosis of underlying tissues due to burn (deep third degree) of multiple sites (except with eye) of face, head, and neck, without mention of loss of a body part
941.50 Deep necrosis of underlying tissues due to burn (deep third degree) of face and head, unspecified site, with loss of a body part
941.51 Deep necrosis of underlying tissues due to burn (deep third degree) of ear (any part), with loss of a body part
941.52 Deep necrosis of underlying tissues due to burn (deep third degree) of eye (with other parts of face, head, and neck), with loss of a body part
941.55 Deep necrosis of underlying tissues due to burn (deep third degree) of nose (septum), with loss of a body part
941.57 Deep necrosis of underlying tissues due to burn (deep third degree) of forehead and cheek, with loss of a body part
941.58 Deep necrosis of underlying tissues due to burn (deep third degree) of neck, with loss of a body part
943.34 Full-thickness skin loss due to burn (third degree NOS) of axilla
943.44 Deep necrosis of underlying tissues due to burn (deep third degree) of axilla, without mention of loss of a body part
943.54 Deep necrosis of underlying tissues due to burn (deep third degree) of axilla, with loss of a body part
944.30 Full-thickness skin loss due to burn (third degree NOS) of unspecified site of hand
944.31 Full-thickness skin loss due to burn (third degree NOS) of single digit [finger (nail)] other than thumb
944.32 Full-thickness skin loss due to burn (third degree NOS) of thumb (nail)
944.33 Full-thickness skin loss due to burn (third degree NOS) of two or more digits of hand, not including thumb
944.34 Full-thickness skin loss due to burn (third degree NOS) of two or more digits of hand including thumb
944.35 Full-thickness skin loss due to burn (third degree NOS) of palm of hand
944.36 Full-thickness skin loss due to burn (third degree NOS) of back of hand
944.37 Full-thickness skin loss due to burn (third degree NOS) of wrist
944.38 Full-thickness skin loss due to burn (third degree NOS) of multiple sites of wrist(s) and hand(s)
944.40 Deep necrosis of underlying tissues due to burn (deep third degree) of unspecified site of hand, without mention of loss of a body part
944.41 Deep necrosis of underlying tissues due to burn (deep third degree) of single digit [finger (nail)] other than thumb, without mention of loss of a body part
944.42 Deep necrosis of underlying tissues due to burn (deep third degree) of thumb (nail), without mention of loss of a body part
944.43 Deep necrosis of underlying tissues due to burn (deep third degree) of two or more digits of hand, not including thumb, without mention of loss of a body part

944.44 Deep necrosis of underlying tissues due to burn (deep third degree) of two or more digits of hand including thumb, without mention of loss of a body part

944.45 Deep necrosis of underlying tissues due to burn (deep third degree) of palm of hand, without mention of loss of a body part

944.46 Deep necrosis of underlying tissues due to burn (deep third degree) of back of hand, without mention of loss of a body part

944.47 Deep necrosis of underlying tissues due to burn (deep third degree) of wrist, without mention of loss of a body part

944.48 Deep necrosis of underlying tissues due to burn (deep third degree) of multiple sites of wrist(s) and hand(s), without mention of loss of a body part

944.50 Deep necrosis of underlying tissues due to burn (deep third degree) of unspecified site of hand, with loss of a body part

944.51 Deep necrosis of underlying tissues due to burn (deep third degree) of single digit (finger (nail)) other than thumb, with loss of a body part

944.52 Deep necrosis of underlying tissues due to burn (deep third degree) of thumb (nail), with loss of a body part

944.53 Deep necrosis of underlying tissues due to burn (deep third degree) of two or more digits of hand, not including thumb, with loss of a body part

944.54 Deep necrosis of underlying tissues due to burn (deep third degree) of two or more digits of hand including thumb, with loss of a body part

944.55 Deep necrosis of underlying tissues due to burn (deep third degree) of palm of hand, with loss of a body part

944.56 Deep necrosis of underlying tissues due to burn (deep third degree) of back of hand, with loss of a body part

944.57 Deep necrosis of underlying tissues due to burn (deep third degree) of wrist, with loss of a body part

944.58 Deep necrosis of underlying tissues due to burn (deep third degree) of multiple sites of wrist(s) and hand(s), with loss of a body part

945.32 Full-thickness skin loss due to burn (third degree NOS) of foot

945.42 Deep necrosis of underlying tissues due to burn (deep third degree) of foot, without mention of loss of a body part

945.52 Deep necrosis of underlying tissues due to burn (deep third degree) of foot, with loss of a body part

948.00 Burn (any degree) involving less than 10% of body surface with third degree burn of less than 10% or unspecified amount

948.10 Burn (any degree) involving 10-19% of body surface with third degree burn of less than 10% or unspecified amount

948.11 Burn (any degree) involving 10-19% of body surface with third degree burn of 10-19%

948.20 Burn (any degree) involving 20-29% of body surface with third degree burn of less than 10% or unspecified amount

948.21 Burn (any degree) involving 20-29% of body surface with third degree burn of 10-19%

948.22 Burn (any degree) involving 20-29% of body surface with third degree burn of 20-29%

948.30 Burn (any degree) involving 30-39% of body surface with third degree burn of less than 10% or unspecified amount

948.31 Burn (any degree) involving 30-39% of body surface with third degree burn of 10-19%

948.32 Burn (any degree) involving 30-39% of body surface with third degree burn of 20-29%

948.33 Burn (any degree) involving 30-39% of body surface with third degree burn of 30-39%

948.40 Burn (any degree) involving 40-49% of body surface with third degree burn of less than 10% or unspecified amount

948.41 Burn (any degree) involving 40-49% of body surface with third degree burn of 10-19%

948.42 Burn (any degree) involving 40-49% of body surface with third degree burn of 20-29%

948.43 Burn (any degree) involving 40-49% of body surface with third degree burn of 30-39%

948.44 Burn (any degree) involving 40-49% of body surface with third degree burn of 40-49%

948.50 Burn (any degree) involving 50-59% of body surface with third degree burn of less than 10% or unspecified amount

948.51 Burn (any degree) involving 50-59% of body surface with third degree burn of 10-19%

948.52 Burn (any degree) involving 50-59% of body surface with third degree burn of 20-29%

948.53 Burn (any degree) involving 50-59% of body surface with third degree burn of 30-39%

948.54 Burn (any degree) involving 50-59% of body surface with third degree burn of 40-49%

948.55 Burn (any degree) involving 50-59% of body surface with third degree burn of 50-59%

948.60 Burn (any degree) involving 60-69% of body surface with third degree burn of less than 10% or unspecified amount

948.61 Burn (any degree) involving 60-69% of body surface with third degree burn of 10-19%

948.62 Burn (any degree) involving 60-69% of body surface with third degree burn of 20-29%

948.63 Burn (any degree) involving 60-69% of body surface with third degree burn of 30-39%

948.64 Burn (any degree) involving 60-69% of body surface with third degree burn of 40-49%

948.65 Burn (any degree) involving 60-69% of body surface with third degree burn of 50-59%

948.66 Burn (any degree) involving 60-69% of body surface with third degree burn of 60-69%

948.70 Burn (any degree) involving 70-79% of body surface with third degree burn of less than 10% or unspecified amount

948.71 Burn (any degree) involving 70-79% of body surface with third degree burn of 10-19%

948.72 Burn (any degree) involving 70-79% of body surface with third degree burn of 20-29%

948.73 Burn (any degree) involving 70-79% of body surface with third degree burn of 30-39%

948.74 Burn (any degree) involving 70-79% of body surface with third degree burn of 40-49%

948.75 Burn (any degree) involving 70-79% of body surface with third degree burn of 50-59%

948.76 Burn (any degree) involving 70-79% of body surface with third degree burn of 60-69%

948.77 Burn (any degree) involving 70-79% of body surface with third degree burn of 70-79%

948.80 Burn (any degree) involving 80-89% of body surface with third degree burn of less than 10% or unspecified amount

948.81 Burn (any degree) involving 80-89% of body surface with third degree burn of 10-19%

948.82 Burn (any degree) involving 80-89% of body surface with third degree burn of 20-29%

948.83 Burn (any degree) involving 80-89% of body surface with third degree burn of 30-39%

948.84 Burn (any degree) involving 80-89% of body surface with third degree burn of 40-49%

948.85 Burn (any degree) involving 80-89% of body surface with third degree burn of 50-59%

948.86 Burn (any degree) involving 80-89% of body surface with third degree burn of 60-69%

948.87 Burn (any degree) involving 80-89% of body surface with third degree burn of 70-79%

948.88 Burn (any degree) involving 80-89% of body surface with third degree burn of 80-89%

959.01 Head injury, unspecified

959.09 Injury of face and neck, other and unspecified

959.11 Other injury of chest wall

959.12 Other injury of abdomen

959.14 Other injury of external genitals

959.19 Other injury of other sites of trunk

959.4 Injury, other and unspecified, hand, except finger

959.5 Injury, other and unspecified, finger

959.7 Injury, other and unspecified, knee, leg, ankle, and foot

959.8 Injury, other and unspecified, other specified sites, including multiple

991.0 Frostbite of face

991.1 Frostbite of hand

991.2 Frostbite of foot

996.64 Infection and inflammatory reaction due to indwelling urinary catheter — (Use additional code to identify specified infections: 038.0-038.9, 595.0-595.9)

997.60 Late complications of amputation stump, unspecified — (Use additional code to identify complications)

997.61 Neuroma of amputation stump — (Use additional code to identify complications)

997.62 Infection (chronic) of amputation stump — (Use additional code to identify complications)

997.69 Other late amputation stump complication — (Use additional code to identify complications)

998.30 Disruption of wound, unspecified

998.32 Disruption of external operation (surgical) wound

998.33 Disruption of traumatic injury wound repair

998.59 Other postoperative infection — (Use additional code to identify infection)

998.83 Non-healing surgical wound

V51.8 Other aftercare involving the use of plastic surgery

ICD-9-CM Procedural

39.31 Suture of artery

39.32 Suture of vein

86.70 Pedicle or flap graft, not otherwise specified

86.71 Cutting and preparation of pedicle grafts or flaps
86.73 Attachment of pedicle or flap graft to hand
86.74 Attachment of pedicle or flap graft to other sites
86.75 Revision of pedicle or flap graft

15758

15758 Free fascial flap with microvascular anastomosis

ICD-9-CM Diagnostic

135 Sarcoidosis
142.0 Malignant neoplasm of parotid gland
142.1 Malignant neoplasm of submandibular gland
142.2 Malignant neoplasm of sublingual gland
142.8 Malignant neoplasm of other major salivary glands
142.9 Malignant neoplasm of salivary gland, unspecified ▽
143.0 Malignant neoplasm of upper gum
143.1 Malignant neoplasm of lower gum
143.8 Malignant neoplasm of other sites of gum
143.9 Malignant neoplasm of gum, unspecified site ▽
145.1 Malignant neoplasm of vestibule of mouth
145.9 Malignant neoplasm of mouth, unspecified site ▽
161.0 Malignant neoplasm of glottis
161.1 Malignant neoplasm of supraglottis
161.2 Malignant neoplasm of subglottis
161.3 Malignant neoplasm of laryngeal cartilages
161.8 Malignant neoplasm of other specified sites of larynx
161.9 Malignant neoplasm of larynx, unspecified site ▽
170.0 Malignant neoplasm of bones of skull and face, except mandible
170.1 Malignant neoplasm of mandible
171.0 Malignant neoplasm of connective and other soft tissue of head, face, and neck
193 Malignant neoplasm of thyroid gland — (Use additional code to identify any functional activity)
194.5 Malignant neoplasm of carotid body
194.6 Malignant neoplasm of aortic body and other paraganglia
195.0 Malignant neoplasm of head, face, and neck
202.31 Malignant histiocytosis of lymph nodes of head, face, and neck
209.29 Malignant carcinoid tumor of other sites — (Code first any associated multiple endocrine neoplasia syndrome: 258.01-258.03)(Use additional code to identify associated endocrine syndrome, as: carcinoid syndrome: 259.2)
209.69 Benign carcinoid tumor of other sites — (Code first any associated multiple endocrine neoplasia syndrome: 258.01-258.03)(Use additional code to identify associated endocrine syndrome, as: carcinoid syndrome: 259.2)
209.79 Secondary neuroendocrine tumor of other sites
210.2 Benign neoplasm of major salivary glands
212.1 Benign neoplasm of larynx
215.0 Other benign neoplasm of connective and other soft tissue of head, face, and neck
227.5 Benign neoplasm of carotid body — (Use additional code to identify any functional activity)
227.6 Benign neoplasm of aortic body and other paraganglia — (Use additional code to identify any functional activity)
235.0 Neoplasm of uncertain behavior of major salivary glands
235.1 Neoplasm of uncertain behavior of lip, oral cavity, and pharynx
237.3 Neoplasm of uncertain behavior of paraganglia
237.4 Neoplasm of uncertain behavior of other and unspecified endocrine glands ▽
237.71 Neurofibromatosis, Type 1 (von Recklinghausen's disease)
237.72 Neurofibromatosis, Type 2 (acoustic neurofibromatosis)
237.79 Other neurofibromatosis
277.30 Amyloidosis, unspecified — (Use additional code to identify any associated intellectual disabilities) ▽
277.39 Other amyloidosis — (Use additional code to identify any associated intellectual disabilities)
351.0 Bell's palsy
478.5 Other diseases of vocal cords — (Use additional code to identify infectious organism)
523.8 Other specified periodontal diseases
526.0 Developmental odontogenic cysts
526.4 Inflammatory conditions of jaw
526.5 Alveolitis of jaw
526.89 Other specified disease of the jaws
709.2 Scar condition and fibrosis of skin
710.2 Sicca syndrome
728.89 Other disorder of muscle, ligament, and fascia — (Use additional E code to identify drug, if drug-induced)
729.99 Other disorders of soft tissue
767.5 Facial nerve injury, birth trauma — (Use additional code(s) to further specify condition)
802.39 Open fracture of multiple sites of mandible
802.5 Malar and maxillary bones, open fracture
802.9 Other facial bones, open fracture
873.49 Open wound of face, other and multiple sites, without mention of complication
873.59 Open wound of face, other and multiple sites, complicated
874.8 Open wound of other and unspecified parts of neck, without mention of complication ▽
874.9 Open wound of other and unspecified parts of neck, complicated ▽
881.10 Open wound of forearm, complicated
881.11 Open wound of elbow, complicated
881.12 Open wound of wrist, complicated
881.20 Open wound of forearm, with tendon involvement
881.21 Open wound of elbow, with tendon involvement
881.22 Open wound of wrist, with tendon involvement
882.1 Open wound of hand except finger(s) alone, complicated
882.2 Open wound of hand except finger(s) alone, with tendon involvement
883.1 Open wound of finger(s), complicated
883.2 Open wound of finger(s), with tendon involvement
892.1 Open wound of foot except toe(s) alone, complicated
892.2 Open wound of foot except toe(s) alone, with tendon involvement
893.1 Open wound of toe(s), complicated
893.2 Open wound of toe(s), with tendon involvement
905.0 Late effect of fracture of skull and face bones
906.0 Late effect of open wound of head, neck, and trunk
906.1 Late effect of open wound of extremities without mention of tendon injury
906.4 Late effect of crushing
906.5 Late effect of burn of eye, face, head, and neck
906.6 Late effect of burn of wrist and hand
906.7 Late effect of burn of other extremities
909.3 Late effect of complications of surgical and medical care
925.1 Crushing injury of face and scalp — (Use additional code to identify any associated injuries, such as: 800-829, 850.0-854.1, 860.0-869.1)
925.2 Crushing injury of neck — (Use additional code to identify any associated injuries, such as: 800-829, 850.0-854.1, 860.0-869.1)
927.10 Crushing injury of forearm — (Use additional code to identify any associated injuries: 800-829, 850.0-854.1, 860.0-869.1)
927.11 Crushing injury of elbow — (Use additional code to identify any associated injuries: 800-829, 850.0-854.1, 860.0-869.1)
927.20 Crushing injury of hand(s) — (Use additional code to identify any associated injuries: 800-829, 850.0-854.1, 860.0-869.1)
927.21 Crushing injury of wrist — (Use additional code to identify any associated injuries: 800-829, 850.0-854.1, 860.0-869.1)
927.3 Crushing injury of finger(s) — (Use additional code to identify any associated injuries: 800-829, 850.0-854.1, 860.0-869.1)

927.8 Crushing injury of multiple sites of upper limb — (Use additional code to identify any associated injuries: 800-829, 850.0-854.1, 860.0-869.1)

928.10 Crushing injury of lower leg — (Use additional code to identify any associated injuries: 800-829, 850.0-854.1, 860.0-869.1)

928.11 Crushing injury of knee — (Use additional code to identify any associated injuries: 800-829, 850.0-854.1, 860.0-869.1)

928.20 Crushing injury of foot — (Use additional code to identify any associated injuries: 800-829, 850.0-854.1, 860.0-869.1)

928.21 Crushing injury of ankle — (Use additional code to identify any associated injuries: 800-829, 850.0-854.1, 860.0-869.1)

928.3 Crushing injury of toe(s) — (Use additional code to identify any associated injuries: 800-829, 850.0-854.1, 860.0-869.1)

928.8 Crushing injury of multiple sites of lower limb — (Use additional code to identify any associated injuries: 800-829, 850.0-854.1, 860.0-869.1)

928.9 Crushing injury of unspecified site of lower limb — (Use additional code to identify any associated injuries: 800-829, 850.0-854.1, 860.0-869.1) ▽

941.50 Deep necrosis of underlying tissues due to burn (deep third degree) of face and head, unspecified site, with loss of a body part ▽

941.59 Deep necrosis of underlying tissues due to burn (deep third degree) of multiple sites (except eye) of face, head, and neck, with loss of a body part

943.31 Full-thickness skin loss due to burn (third degree NOS) of forearm

943.39 Full-thickness skin loss due to burn (third degree NOS) of multiple sites of upper limb, except wrist and hand

943.41 Deep necrosis of underlying tissues due to burn (deep third degree) of forearm, without mention of loss of a body part

943.49 Deep necrosis of underlying tissues due to burn (deep third degree) of multiple sites of upper limb, except wrist and hand, without mention of loss of a body part

944.30 Full-thickness skin loss due to burn (third degree NOS) of unspecified site of hand ▽

944.31 Full-thickness skin loss due to burn (third degree NOS) of single digit [finger (nail)] other than thumb

944.32 Full-thickness skin loss due to burn (third degree NOS) of thumb (nail)

944.33 Full-thickness skin loss due to burn (third degree NOS) of two or more digits of hand, not including thumb

944.34 Full-thickness skin loss due to burn (third degree NOS) of two or more digits of hand including thumb

944.35 Full-thickness skin loss due to burn (third degree NOS) of palm of hand

944.36 Full-thickness skin loss due to burn (third degree NOS) of back of hand

944.37 Full-thickness skin loss due to burn (third degree NOS) of wrist

944.38 Full-thickness skin loss due to burn (third degree NOS) of multiple sites of wrist(s) and hand(s)

944.41 Deep necrosis of underlying tissues due to burn (deep third degree) of single digit [finger (nail)] other than thumb, without mention of loss of a body part

944.42 Deep necrosis of underlying tissues due to burn (deep third degree) of thumb (nail), without mention of loss of a body part

944.43 Deep necrosis of underlying tissues due to burn (deep third degree) of two or more digits of hand, not including thumb, without mention of loss of a body part

944.44 Deep necrosis of underlying tissues due to burn (deep third degree) of two or more digits of hand including thumb, without mention of loss of a body part

944.45 Deep necrosis of underlying tissues due to burn (deep third degree) of palm of hand, without mention of loss of a body part

944.46 Deep necrosis of underlying tissues due to burn (deep third degree) of back of hand, without mention of loss of a body part

944.47 Deep necrosis of underlying tissues due to burn (deep third degree) of wrist, without mention of loss of a body part

944.48 Deep necrosis of underlying tissues due to burn (deep third degree) of multiple sites of wrist(s) and hand(s), without mention of loss of a body part

959.3 Injury, other and unspecified, elbow, forearm, and wrist

959.4 Injury, other and unspecified, hand, except finger

959.5 Injury, other and unspecified, finger

959.7 Injury, other and unspecified, knee, leg, ankle, and foot

997.09 Other nervous system complications — (Use additional code to identify complications)

ICD-9-CM Procedural

39.31 Suture of artery

39.32 Suture of vein

82.72 Plastic operation on hand with graft of muscle or fascia

83.82 Graft of muscle or fascia

15775-15776

15775 Punch graft for hair transplant; 1 to 15 punch grafts

15776 more than 15 punch grafts

ICD-9-CM Diagnostic

374.55 Hypotrichosis of eyelid

704.00 Unspecified alopecia ▽

704.01 Alopecia areata

704.02 Telogen effluvium

757.4 Specified congenital anomalies of hair

873.0 Open wound of scalp, without mention of complication

873.1 Open wound of scalp, complicated

941.27 Blisters, with epidermal loss due to burn (second degree) of forehead and cheek

941.32 Full-thickness skin loss due to burn (third degree NOS) of eye (with other parts of face, head, and neck)

941.36 Full-thickness skin loss due to burn (third degree NOS) of scalp (any part)

941.37 Full-thickness skin loss due to burn (third degree NOS) of forehead and cheek

941.42 Deep necrosis of underlying tissues due to burn (deep third degree) of eye (with other parts of face, head, and neck), without mention of loss of a body part

941.46 Deep necrosis of underlying tissues due to burn (deep third degree) of scalp (any part), without mention of loss of a body part

941.49 Deep necrosis of underlying tissues due to burn (deep third degree) of multiple sites (except with eye) of face, head, and neck, without mention of loss of a body part

V50.0 Elective hair transplant for purposes other than remedying health states

ICD-9-CM Procedural

86.64 Hair transplant

15777

15777 Implantation of biologic implant (eg, acellular dermal matrix) for soft tissue reinforcement (ie, breast, trunk) (List separately in addition to code for primary procedure)

ICD-9-CM Diagnostic

The ICD-9-CM diagnostic code(s) would be the same as the actual procedure performed because these are in-addition-to codes.

ICD-9-CM Procedural

86.67 Dermal regenerative graft

HCPCS Level II Supplies & Services

C9360 Dermal substitute, native, nondenatured collagen, neonatal bovine origin (SurgiMend Collagen Matrix), per 0.5 sq cm

C9364 Porcine implant, Permacol, per sq cm

Q4130 Strattice TM, per sq cm

15780-15781

15780 Dermabrasion; total face (eg, for acne scarring, fine wrinkling, rhytids, general keratosis)

15781 segmental, face

ICD-9-CM Diagnostic

701.5 Other abnormal granulation tissue

701.8 Other specified hypertrophic and atrophic condition of skin

701.9 Unspecified hypertrophic and atrophic condition of skin ▽

702.0 Actinic keratosis

702.11 Inflamed seborrheic keratosis

709.2 Scar condition and fibrosis of skin
906.0 Late effect of open wound of head, neck, and trunk
908.6 Late effect of certain complications of trauma
909.3 Late effect of complications of surgical and medical care
V50.1 Other plastic surgery for unacceptable cosmetic appearance

ICD-9-CM Procedural

86.25 Dermabrasion

HCPCS Level II Supplies & Services

A4305 Disposable drug delivery system, flow rate of 50 ml or greater per hour

15782

15782 Dermabrasion; regional, other than face

ICD-9-CM Diagnostic

701.1 Acquired keratoderma
701.4 Keloid scar
701.5 Other abnormal granulation tissue
701.8 Other specified hypertrophic and atrophic condition of skin
701.9 Unspecified hypertrophic and atrophic condition of skin ▽
702.0 Actinic keratosis
702.11 Inflamed seborrheic keratosis
702.19 Other seborrheic keratosis
709.09 Other dyschromia
709.2 Scar condition and fibrosis of skin
906.8 Late effect of burns of other specified sites
909.3 Late effect of complications of surgical and medical care

ICD-9-CM Procedural

86.25 Dermabrasion

HCPCS Level II Supplies & Services

A4305 Disposable drug delivery system, flow rate of 50 ml or greater per hour

15783

15783 Dermabrasion; superficial, any site (eg, tattoo removal)

ICD-9-CM Diagnostic

701.1 Acquired keratoderma
702.0 Actinic keratosis
702.11 Inflamed seborrheic keratosis
702.19 Other seborrheic keratosis
709.09 Other dyschromia
709.2 Scar condition and fibrosis of skin
906.0 Late effect of open wound of head, neck, and trunk
908.6 Late effect of certain complications of trauma
V50.1 Other plastic surgery for unacceptable cosmetic appearance

ICD-9-CM Procedural

86.25 Dermabrasion

HCPCS Level II Supplies & Services

A4305 Disposable drug delivery system, flow rate of 50 ml or greater per hour

15786-15787

15786 Abrasion; single lesion (eg, keratosis, scar)
15787 each additional 4 lesions or less (List separately in addition to code for primary procedure)

ICD-9-CM Diagnostic

701.1 Acquired keratoderma
701.4 Keloid scar
702.0 Actinic keratosis
702.11 Inflamed seborrheic keratosis
702.19 Other seborrheic keratosis
709.09 Other dyschromia
709.2 Scar condition and fibrosis of skin
757.32 Congenital vascular hamartomas
757.39 Other specified congenital anomaly of skin
906.0 Late effect of open wound of head, neck, and trunk
906.8 Late effect of burns of other specified sites

ICD-9-CM Procedural

86.25 Dermabrasion

HCPCS Level II Supplies & Services

A4305 Disposable drug delivery system, flow rate of 50 ml or greater per hour

15788-15789

15788 Chemical peel, facial; epidermal
15789 dermal

ICD-9-CM Diagnostic

701.4 Keloid scar
701.5 Other abnormal granulation tissue
701.8 Other specified hypertrophic and atrophic condition of skin
701.9 Unspecified hypertrophic and atrophic condition of skin ▽
706.0 Acne varioliformis
706.1 Other acne
709.09 Other dyschromia
709.2 Scar condition and fibrosis of skin
757.32 Congenital vascular hamartomas
757.33 Congenital pigmentary anomaly of skin
757.39 Other specified congenital anomaly of skin
V50.1 Other plastic surgery for unacceptable cosmetic appearance

ICD-9-CM Procedural

86.24 Chemosurgery of skin

HCPCS Level II Supplies & Services

A4305 Disposable drug delivery system, flow rate of 50 ml or greater per hour

15792-15793

15792 Chemical peel, nonfacial; epidermal
15793 dermal

ICD-9-CM Diagnostic

701.1 Acquired keratoderma
701.4 Keloid scar
701.5 Other abnormal granulation tissue
701.8 Other specified hypertrophic and atrophic condition of skin
702.0 Actinic keratosis
702.11 Inflamed seborrheic keratosis
702.19 Other seborrheic keratosis
706.0 Acne varioliformis
706.1 Other acne
709.09 Other dyschromia
709.2 Scar condition and fibrosis of skin
757.32 Congenital vascular hamartomas
757.33 Congenital pigmentary anomaly of skin
757.39 Other specified congenital anomaly of skin
V50.1 Other plastic surgery for unacceptable cosmetic appearance

ICD-9-CM Procedural

86.24 Chemosurgery of skin

HCPCS Level II Supplies & Services

A4305 Disposable drug delivery system, flow rate of 50 ml or greater per hour

15819

15819 Cervicoplasty

ICD-9-CM Diagnostic

214.1 Lipoma of other skin and subcutaneous tissue
701.8 Other specified hypertrophic and atrophic condition of skin
709.2 Scar condition and fibrosis of skin
906.0 Late effect of open wound of head, neck, and trunk
V10.83 Personal history of other malignant neoplasm of skin
V10.89 Personal history of malignant neoplasm of other site
V50.1 Other plastic surgery for unacceptable cosmetic appearance

ICD-9-CM Procedural

86.83 Size reduction plastic operation
86.89 Other repair and reconstruction of skin and subcutaneous tissue

15820-15823

15820 Blepharoplasty, lower eyelid;
15821 with extensive herniated fat pad
15822 Blepharoplasty, upper eyelid;
15823 with excessive skin weighting down lid

ICD-9-CM Diagnostic

351.8 Other facial nerve disorders
368.40 Unspecified visual field defect ▽
368.44 Other localized visual field defect
368.45 Generalized contraction or constriction in visual field
368.46 Homonymous bilateral field defects in visual field
368.47 Heteronymous bilateral field defects in visual field
374.01 Senile entropion
374.03 Spastic entropion
374.11 Senile ectropion
374.30 Unspecified ptosis of eyelid ▽
374.31 Paralytic ptosis
374.32 Myogenic ptosis
374.34 Blepharochalasis
374.87 Dermatochalasis
374.89 Other disorders of eyelid
376.52 Enophthalmos due to trauma or surgery
701.8 Other specified hypertrophic and atrophic condition of skin
701.9 Unspecified hypertrophic and atrophic condition of skin ▽
709.2 Scar condition and fibrosis of skin
743.62 Congenital deformity of eyelid
743.63 Other specified congenital anomaly of eyelid
V50.1 Other plastic surgery for unacceptable cosmetic appearance
V51.8 Other aftercare involving the use of plastic surgery
V52.2 Fitting and adjustment of artificial eye

ICD-9-CM Procedural

08.70 Reconstruction of eyelid, not otherwise specified
08.86 Lower eyelid rhytidectomy
08.87 Upper eyelid rhytidectomy

15824

15824 Rhytidectomy; forehead

ICD-9-CM Diagnostic

374.34 Blepharochalasis
692.79 Other dermatitis due to solar radiation
701.8 Other specified hypertrophic and atrophic condition of skin
709.2 Scar condition and fibrosis of skin
709.3 Degenerative skin disorder
906.0 Late effect of open wound of head, neck, and trunk
V50.1 Other plastic surgery for unacceptable cosmetic appearance

ICD-9-CM Procedural

86.82 Facial rhytidectomy

15825

15825 Rhytidectomy; neck with platysmal tightening (platysmal flap, P-flap)

ICD-9-CM Diagnostic

701.8 Other specified hypertrophic and atrophic condition of skin
701.9 Unspecified hypertrophic and atrophic condition of skin ▽
V50.1 Other plastic surgery for unacceptable cosmetic appearance
V51.8 Other aftercare involving the use of plastic surgery

ICD-9-CM Procedural

86.82 Facial rhytidectomy
86.89 Other repair and reconstruction of skin and subcutaneous tissue

15826

15826 Rhytidectomy; glabellar frown lines

ICD-9-CM Diagnostic

692.79 Other dermatitis due to solar radiation
701.8 Other specified hypertrophic and atrophic condition of skin
709.3 Degenerative skin disorder
V50.1 Other plastic surgery for unacceptable cosmetic appearance

ICD-9-CM Procedural

86.82 Facial rhytidectomy
86.89 Other repair and reconstruction of skin and subcutaneous tissue

15828-15829

15828 Rhytidectomy; cheek, chin, and neck
15829 superficial musculoaponeurotic system (SMAS) flap

ICD-9-CM Diagnostic

692.79 Other dermatitis due to solar radiation
701.8 Other specified hypertrophic and atrophic condition of skin
701.9 Unspecified hypertrophic and atrophic condition of skin ▽
V50.1 Other plastic surgery for unacceptable cosmetic appearance

ICD-9-CM Procedural

86.82 Facial rhytidectomy

15830-15839

15830 Excision, excessive skin and subcutaneous tissue (includes lipectomy); abdomen, infraumbilical panniculectomy
15832 thigh
15833 leg
15834 hip
15835 buttock
15836 arm
15837 forearm or hand
15838 submental fat pad
15839 other area

ICD-9-CM Diagnostic

278.00 Obesity, unspecified — (Use additional code to identify Body Mass Index (BMI), if known: V85.0-V85.54) (Use additional code to identify any associated intellectual disabilities) ▽

278.01	Morbid obesity — (Use additional code to identify Body Mass Index (BMI), if known: V85.0-V85.54)
278.02	Overweight — (Use additional code to identify Body Mass Index (BMI), if known: V85.0-V85.54) (Use additional code to identify any associated intellectual disabilities)
278.1	Localized adiposity — (Use additional code to identify any associated intellectual disabilities.)
701.9	Unspecified hypertrophic and atrophic condition of skin ♥
729.39	Panniculitis of other sites

ICD-9-CM Procedural

86.83 Size reduction plastic operation

HCPCS Level II Supplies & Services

A4461 Surgical dressing holder, nonreusable, each
A4463 Surgical dressing holder, reusable, each

15840-15845

15840 Graft for facial nerve paralysis; free fascia graft (including obtaining fascia)
15841 free muscle graft (including obtaining graft)
15842 free muscle flap by microsurgical technique
15845 regional muscle transfer

ICD-9-CM Diagnostic

350.1 Trigeminal neuralgia
350.8 Other specified trigeminal nerve disorders
351.0 Bell's palsy
351.1 Geniculate ganglionitis
351.8 Other facial nerve disorders
742.8 Other specified congenital anomalies of nervous system
767.5 Facial nerve injury, birth trauma — (Use additional code(s) to further specify condition)
906.0 Late effect of open wound of head, neck, and trunk
906.5 Late effect of burn of eye, face, head, and neck
909.3 Late effect of complications of surgical and medical care
951.4 Injury to facial nerve

ICD-9-CM Procedural

83.82 Graft of muscle or fascia
86.81 Repair for facial weakness

HCPCS Level II Supplies & Services

C1762 Connective tissue, human (includes fascia lata)

15847

15847 Excision, excessive skin and subcutaneous tissue (includes lipectomy), abdomen (eg, abdominoplasty) (includes umbilical transposition and fascial plication) (List separately in addition to code for primary procedure)

ICD-9-CM Diagnostic

278.00 Obesity, unspecified — (Use additional code to identify Body Mass Index (BMI), if known: V85.0-V85.54) (Use additional code to identify any associated intellectual disabilities) ♥
278.01 Morbid obesity — (Use additional code to identify Body Mass Index (BMI), if known: V85.0-V85.54)
278.02 Overweight — (Use additional code to identify Body Mass Index (BMI), if known: V85.0-V85.54) (Use additional code to identify any associated intellectual disabilities)
278.1 Localized adiposity — (Use additional code to identify any associated intellectual disabilities.)
701.9 Unspecified hypertrophic and atrophic condition of skin ♥
729.39 Panniculitis of other sites

ICD-9-CM Procedural

86.83 Size reduction plastic operation

15850-15851

15850 Removal of sutures under anesthesia (other than local), same surgeon
15851 Removal of sutures under anesthesia (other than local), other surgeon

ICD-9-CM Diagnostic

729.90 Disorders of soft tissue, unspecified ♥
729.91 Post-traumatic seroma
998.30 Disruption of wound, unspecified ♥
998.31 Disruption of internal operation (surgical) wound
998.32 Disruption of external operation (surgical) wound
998.33 Disruption of traumatic injury wound repair
998.51 Infected postoperative seroma — (Use additional code to identify organism)
998.59 Other postoperative infection — (Use additional code to identify infection)
V58.32 Encounter for removal of sutures

ICD-9-CM Procedural

97.38 Removal of sutures from head and neck
97.43 Removal of sutures from thorax
97.83 Removal of abdominal wall sutures
97.84 Removal of sutures from trunk, not elsewhere classified
97.89 Removal of other therapeutic device

HCPCS Level II Supplies & Services

A4649 Surgical supply; miscellaneous

15852

15852 Dressing change (for other than burns) under anesthesia (other than local)

ICD-9-CM Diagnostic

440.23 Atherosclerosis of native arteries of the extremities with ulceration — (Use additional code for any associated ulceration: 707.10-707.19, 707.8, 707.9)
440.24 Atherosclerosis of native arteries of the extremities with gangrene — (Use additional code for any associated ulceration: 707.10-707.19, 707.8, 707.9)
459.11 Postphlebitic syndrome with ulcer
459.13 Postphlebitic syndrome with ulcer and inflammation
459.31 Chronic venous hypertension with ulcer
459.33 Chronic venous hypertension with ulcer and inflammation
707.00 Pressure ulcer, unspecified site — (Use additional code to identify pressure ulcer stage: 707.20-707.25) ♥
707.01 Pressure ulcer, elbow — (Use additional code to identify pressure ulcer stage: 707.20-707.25)
707.02 Pressure ulcer, upper back — (Use additional code to identify pressure ulcer stage: 707.20-707.25)
707.03 Pressure ulcer, lower back — (Use additional code to identify pressure ulcer stage: 707.20-707.25)
707.04 Pressure ulcer, hip — (Use additional code to identify pressure ulcer stage: 707.20-707.25)
707.05 Pressure ulcer, buttock — (Use additional code to identify pressure ulcer stage: 707.20-707.25)
707.06 Pressure ulcer, ankle — (Use additional code to identify pressure ulcer stage: 707.20-707.25)
707.07 Pressure ulcer, heel — (Use additional code to identify pressure ulcer stage: 707.20-707.25)
707.09 Pressure ulcer, other site — (Use additional code to identify pressure ulcer stage: 707.20-707.25)
707.10 Ulcer of lower limb, unspecified — (Code, if applicable, any causal condition first: 249.80-249.81, 250.80-250.83, 440.23, 459.11, 459.13, 459.31, 459.33) ♥
707.11 Ulcer of thigh — (Code, if applicable, any causal condition first: 249.80-249.81, 250.80-250.83, 440.23, 459.11, 459.13, 459.31, 459.33)
707.12 Ulcer of calf — (Code, if applicable, any causal condition first: 249.80-249.81, 250.80-250.83, 440.23, 459.11, 459.13, 459.31, 459.33)

707.13 Ulcer of ankle — (Code, if applicable, any causal condition first: 249.80-249.81, 250.80-250.83, 440.23, 459.11, 459.13, 459.31, 459.33)

707.14 Ulcer of heel and midfoot — (Code, if applicable, any causal condition first: 249.80-249.81, 250.80-250.83, 440.23, 459.11, 459.13, 459.31, 459.33)

707.15 Ulcer of other part of foot — (Code, if applicable, any causal condition first: 249.80-249.81, 250.80-250.83, 440.23, 459.11, 459.13, 459.31, 459.33)

707.19 Ulcer of other part of lower limb — (Code, if applicable, any causal condition first: 249.80-249.81, 250.80-250.83, 440.23, 459.11, 459.13, 459.31, 459.33)

707.20 Pressure ulcer, unspecified stage — (Code first site of pressure ulcer: 707.00-707.09) ▽

707.21 Pressure ulcer, stage I — (Code first site of pressure ulcer: 707.00-707.09)

707.22 Pressure ulcer stage II — (Code first site of pressure ulcer: 707.00-707.09)

707.23 Pressure ulcer stage III — (Code first site of pressure ulcer: 707.00-707.09)

707.24 Pressure ulcer stage IV — (Code first site of pressure ulcer: 707.00-707.09)

707.25 Pressure ulcer, unstageable — (Code first site of pressure ulcer: 707.00-707.09)

707.9 Chronic ulcer of unspecified site ▽

709.8 Other specified disorder of skin

729.91 Post-traumatic seroma

729.92 Nontraumatic hematoma of soft tissue

785.4 Gangrene — (Code first any associated underlying condition)

872.01 Open wound of auricle, without mention of complication

872.10 Open wound of external ear, unspecified site, complicated ▽

872.11 Open wound of auricle, complicated

872.12 Open wound of auditory canal, complicated

872.9 Open wound of ear, part unspecified, complicated ▽

873.30 Open wound of nose, unspecified site, complicated ▽

873.31 Open wound of nasal septum, complicated

873.32 Open wound of nasal cavity, complicated

873.33 Open wound of nasal sinus, complicated

873.39 Open wound of nose, multiple sites, complicated

873.43 Open wound of lip, without mention of complication

873.50 Open wound of face, unspecified site, complicated ▽

873.52 Open wound of forehead, complicated

873.54 Open wound of jaw, complicated

873.59 Open wound of face, other and multiple sites, complicated

878.1 Open wound of penis, complicated ♂

878.3 Open wound of scrotum and testes, complicated ♂

878.5 Open wound of vulva, complicated ♀

878.7 Open wound of vagina, complicated ♀

878.9 Open wound of other and unspecified parts of genital organs, complicated ▽

880.12 Open wound of axillary region, complicated

882.1 Open wound of hand except finger(s) alone, complicated

882.2 Open wound of hand except finger(s) alone, with tendon involvement

883.1 Open wound of finger(s), complicated

883.2 Open wound of finger(s), with tendon involvement

884.1 Multiple and unspecified open wound of upper limb, complicated

884.2 Multiple and unspecified open wound of upper limb, with tendon involvement

892.1 Open wound of foot except toe(s) alone, complicated

892.2 Open wound of foot except toe(s) alone, with tendon involvement

893.2 Open wound of toe(s), with tendon involvement

894.1 Multiple and unspecified open wound of lower limb, complicated

894.2 Multiple and unspecified open wound of lower limb, with tendon involvement

925.1 Crushing injury of face and scalp — (Use additional code to identify any associated injuries, such as: 800-829, 850.0-854.1, 860.0-869.1)

925.2 Crushing injury of neck — (Use additional code to identify any associated injuries, such as: 800-829, 850.0-854.1, 860.0-869.1)

926.0 Crushing injury of external genitalia — (Use additional code to identify any associated injuries: 800-829, 850.0-854.1, 860.0-869.1)

926.11 Crushing injury of back — (Use additional code to identify any associated injuries: 800-829, 850.0-854.1, 860.0-869.1)

926.12 Crushing injury of buttock — (Use additional code to identify any associated injuries: 800-829, 850.0-854.1, 860.0-869.1)

926.19 Crushing injury of other specified sites of trunk — (Use additional code to identify any associated injuries: 800-829, 850.0-854.1, 860.0-869.1)

926.8 Crushing injury of multiple sites of trunk — (Use additional code to identify any associated injuries: 800-829, 850.0-854.1, 860.0-869.1)

926.9 Crushing injury of unspecified site of trunk — (Use additional code to identify any associated injuries: 800-829, 850.0-854.1, 860.0-869.1) ▽

927.00 Crushing injury of shoulder region — (Use additional code to identify any associated injuries: 800-829, 850.0-854.1, 860.0-869.1)

927.01 Crushing injury of scapular region — (Use additional code to identify any associated injuries: 800-829, 850.0-854.1, 860.0-869.1)

927.02 Crushing injury of axillary region — (Use additional code to identify any associated injuries: 800-829, 850.0-854.1, 860.0-869.1)

927.03 Crushing injury of upper arm — (Use additional code to identify any associated injuries: 800-829, 850.0-854.1, 860.0-869.1)

927.09 Crushing injury of multiple sites of upper arm — (Use additional code to identify any associated injuries: 800-829, 850.0-854.1, 860.0-869.1)

927.10 Crushing injury of forearm — (Use additional code to identify any associated injuries: 800-829, 850.0-854.1, 860.0-869.1)

927.11 Crushing injury of elbow — (Use additional code to identify any associated injuries: 800-829, 850.0-854.1, 860.0-869.1)

927.20 Crushing injury of hand(s) — (Use additional code to identify any associated injuries: 800-829, 850.0-854.1, 860.0-869.1)

927.21 Crushing injury of wrist — (Use additional code to identify any associated injuries: 800-829, 850.0-854.1, 860.0-869.1)

927.3 Crushing injury of finger(s) — (Use additional code to identify any associated injuries: 800-829, 850.0-854.1, 860.0-869.1)

927.8 Crushing injury of multiple sites of upper limb — (Use additional code to identify any associated injuries: 800-829, 850.0-854.1, 860.0-869.1)

927.9 Crushing injury of unspecified site of upper limb — (Use additional code to identify any associated injuries: 800-829, 850.0-854.1, 860.0-869.1) ▽

928.00 Crushing injury of thigh — (Use additional code to identify any associated injuries: 800-829, 850.0-854.1, 860.0-869.1)

928.01 Crushing injury of hip — (Use additional code to identify any associated injuries: 800-829, 850.0-854.1, 860.0-869.1)

928.11 Crushing injury of knee — (Use additional code to identify any associated injuries: 800-829, 850.0-854.1, 860.0-869.1)

928.20 Crushing injury of foot — (Use additional code to identify any associated injuries: 800-829, 850.0-854.1, 860.0-869.1)

928.21 Crushing injury of ankle — (Use additional code to identify any associated injuries: 800-829, 850.0-854.1, 860.0-869.1)

928.3 Crushing injury of toe(s) — (Use additional code to identify any associated injuries: 800-829, 850.0-854.1, 860.0-869.1)

928.8 Crushing injury of multiple sites of lower limb — (Use additional code to identify any associated injuries: 800-829, 850.0-854.1, 860.0-869.1)

928.9 Crushing injury of unspecified site of lower limb — (Use additional code to identify any associated injuries: 800-829, 850.0-854.1, 860.0-869.1) ▽

929.0 Crushing injury of multiple sites, not elsewhere classified — (Use additional code to identify any associated injuries: 800-829, 850.0-854.1, 860.0-869.1)

983.1 Toxic effect of acids — (Use additional code to specify the nature of the toxic effect)

998.30 Disruption of wound, unspecified ▽

998.32 Disruption of external operation (surgical) wound

998.33 Disruption of traumatic injury wound repair

998.51 Infected postoperative seroma — (Use additional code to identify organism)

998.59 Other postoperative infection — (Use additional code to identify infection)

998.6 Persistent postoperative fistula, not elsewhere classified

V58.30 Encounter for change or removal of nonsurgical wound dressing

V58.31 Encounter for change or removal of surgical wound dressing

V58.49 Other specified aftercare following surgery — (This code should be used in conjunction with other aftercare codes to fully identify the reason for the aftercare encounter)

ICD-9-CM Procedural

93.57 Application of other wound dressing

HCPCS Level II Supplies & Services

A4461 Surgical dressing holder, nonreusable, each
A4463 Surgical dressing holder, reusable, each
Q4102 Oasis wound matrix, per sq cm
Q4124 OASIS ultra tri-layer wound matrix, per sq cm

15860

15860 Intravenous injection of agent (eg, fluorescein) to test vascular flow in flap or graft

ICD-9-CM Diagnostic

The application of this code is too broad to adequately present ICD-9-CM diagnostic code links here. Refer to your ICD-9-CM book.

ICD-9-CM Procedural

88.90 Diagnostic imaging, not elsewhere classified
99.99 Other miscellaneous procedures

15876

15876 Suction assisted lipectomy; head and neck

ICD-9-CM Diagnostic

214.0 Lipoma of skin and subcutaneous tissue of face
214.1 Lipoma of other skin and subcutaneous tissue
272.6 Lipodystrophy — (Use additional code to identify any associated intellectual disabilities) (Use additional E code to identify cause, if iatrogenic)
272.8 Other disorders of lipoid metabolism — (Use additional code to identify any associated intellectual disabilities)
278.1 Localized adiposity — (Use additional code to identify any associated intellectual disabilities.)
V50.1 Other plastic surgery for unacceptable cosmetic appearance

ICD-9-CM Procedural

86.83 Size reduction plastic operation

HCPCS Level II Supplies & Services

A4305 Disposable drug delivery system, flow rate of 50 ml or greater per hour

15877-15879

15877 Suction assisted lipectomy; trunk
15878 upper extremity
15879 lower extremity

ICD-9-CM Diagnostic

214.1 Lipoma of other skin and subcutaneous tissue
272.6 Lipodystrophy — (Use additional code to identify any associated intellectual disabilities) (Use additional E code to identify cause, if iatrogenic)
272.8 Other disorders of lipoid metabolism — (Use additional code to identify any associated intellectual disabilities)
278.1 Localized adiposity — (Use additional code to identify any associated intellectual disabilities.)
V50.1 Other plastic surgery for unacceptable cosmetic appearance

ICD-9-CM Procedural

86.83 Size reduction plastic operation

HCPCS Level II Supplies & Services

A4305 Disposable drug delivery system, flow rate of 50 ml or greater per hour
A4461 Surgical dressing holder, nonreusable, each
A4463 Surgical dressing holder, reusable, each

15920-15922

15920 Excision, coccygeal pressure ulcer, with coccygectomy; with primary suture
15922 with flap closure

ICD-9-CM Diagnostic

707.00 Pressure ulcer, unspecified site — (Use additional code to identify pressure ulcer stage: 707.20-707.25)
707.05 Pressure ulcer, buttock — (Use additional code to identify pressure ulcer stage: 707.20-707.25)
707.09 Pressure ulcer, other site — (Use additional code to identify pressure ulcer stage: 707.20-707.25)
707.20 Pressure ulcer, unspecified stage — (Code first site of pressure ulcer: 707.00-707.09)
707.21 Pressure ulcer, stage I — (Code first site of pressure ulcer: 707.00-707.09)
707.22 Pressure ulcer stage II — (Code first site of pressure ulcer: 707.00-707.09)
707.23 Pressure ulcer stage III — (Code first site of pressure ulcer: 707.00-707.09)
707.24 Pressure ulcer stage IV — (Code first site of pressure ulcer: 707.00-707.09)
707.25 Pressure ulcer, unstageable — (Code first site of pressure ulcer: 707.00-707.09)
730.18 Chronic osteomyelitis, other specified sites — (Use additional code to identify organism: 041.1. Use additional code to identify major osseous defect, if applicable: 731.3)
785.4 Gangrene — (Code first any associated underlying condition)

ICD-9-CM Procedural

77.99 Total ostectomy of other bone, except facial bones
86.3 Other local excision or destruction of lesion or tissue of skin and subcutaneous tissue
86.4 Radical excision of skin lesion
86.74 Attachment of pedicle or flap graft to other sites

15931-15933

15931 Excision, sacral pressure ulcer, with primary suture;
15933 with ostectomy

ICD-9-CM Diagnostic

707.03 Pressure ulcer, lower back — (Use additional code to identify pressure ulcer stage: 707.20-707.25)
707.20 Pressure ulcer, unspecified stage — (Code first site of pressure ulcer: 707.00-707.09)
707.21 Pressure ulcer, stage I — (Code first site of pressure ulcer: 707.00-707.09)
707.22 Pressure ulcer stage II — (Code first site of pressure ulcer: 707.00-707.09)
707.23 Pressure ulcer stage III — (Code first site of pressure ulcer: 707.00-707.09)
707.24 Pressure ulcer stage IV — (Code first site of pressure ulcer: 707.00-707.09)
707.25 Pressure ulcer, unstageable — (Code first site of pressure ulcer: 707.00-707.09)
730.18 Chronic osteomyelitis, other specified sites — (Use additional code to identify organism: 041.1. Use additional code to identify major osseous defect, if applicable: 731.3)
785.4 Gangrene — (Code first any associated underlying condition)

ICD-9-CM Procedural

77.89 Other partial ostectomy of other bone, except facial bones
86.3 Other local excision or destruction of lesion or tissue of skin and subcutaneous tissue
86.4 Radical excision of skin lesion

15934-15935

15934 Excision, sacral pressure ulcer, with skin flap closure;
15935 with ostectomy

ICD-9-CM Diagnostic

707.03 Pressure ulcer, lower back — (Use additional code to identify pressure ulcer stage: 707.20-707.25)
707.20 Pressure ulcer, unspecified stage — (Code first site of pressure ulcer: 707.00-707.09)
707.21 Pressure ulcer, stage I — (Code first site of pressure ulcer: 707.00-707.09)

707.22 Pressure ulcer stage II — (Code first site of pressure ulcer: 707.00-707.09)
707.23 Pressure ulcer stage III — (Code first site of pressure ulcer: 707.00-707.09)
707.24 Pressure ulcer stage IV — (Code first site of pressure ulcer: 707.00-707.09)
707.25 Pressure ulcer, unstageable — (Code first site of pressure ulcer: 707.00-707.09)
730.18 Chronic osteomyelitis, other specified sites — (Use additional code to identify organism: 041.1. Use additional code to identify major osseous defect, if applicable: 731.3)
785.4 Gangrene — (Code first any associated underlying condition)

ICD-9-CM Procedural

77.89 Other partial ostectomy of other bone, except facial bones
86.3 Other local excision or destruction of lesion or tissue of skin and subcutaneous tissue
86.4 Radical excision of skin lesion
86.74 Attachment of pedicle or flap graft to other sites

15936-15937

15936 Excision, sacral pressure ulcer, in preparation for muscle or myocutaneous flap or skin graft closure;
15937 with ostectomy

ICD-9-CM Diagnostic

707.03 Pressure ulcer, lower back — (Use additional code to identify pressure ulcer stage: 707.20-707.25)
707.20 Pressure ulcer, unspecified stage — (Code first site of pressure ulcer: 707.00-707.09) ▽
707.21 Pressure ulcer, stage I — (Code first site of pressure ulcer: 707.00-707.09)
707.22 Pressure ulcer stage II — (Code first site of pressure ulcer: 707.00-707.09)
707.23 Pressure ulcer stage III — (Code first site of pressure ulcer: 707.00-707.09)
707.24 Pressure ulcer stage IV — (Code first site of pressure ulcer: 707.00-707.09)
707.25 Pressure ulcer, unstageable — (Code first site of pressure ulcer: 707.00-707.09)
730.18 Chronic osteomyelitis, other specified sites — (Use additional code to identify organism: 041.1. Use additional code to identify major osseous defect, if applicable: 731.3)
785.4 Gangrene — (Code first any associated underlying condition)

ICD-9-CM Procedural

77.89 Other partial ostectomy of other bone, except facial bones
83.82 Graft of muscle or fascia
86.3 Other local excision or destruction of lesion or tissue of skin and subcutaneous tissue
86.4 Radical excision of skin lesion
86.74 Attachment of pedicle or flap graft to other sites

15940-15941

15940 Excision, ischial pressure ulcer, with primary suture;
15941 with ostectomy (ischiectomy)

ICD-9-CM Diagnostic

707.00 Pressure ulcer, unspecified site — (Use additional code to identify pressure ulcer stage: 707.20-707.25) ▽
707.04 Pressure ulcer, hip — (Use additional code to identify pressure ulcer stage: 707.20-707.25)
707.09 Pressure ulcer, other site — (Use additional code to identify pressure ulcer stage: 707.20-707.25)
707.20 Pressure ulcer, unspecified stage — (Code first site of pressure ulcer: 707.00-707.09) ▽
707.21 Pressure ulcer, stage I — (Code first site of pressure ulcer: 707.00-707.09)
707.22 Pressure ulcer stage II — (Code first site of pressure ulcer: 707.00-707.09)
707.23 Pressure ulcer stage III — (Code first site of pressure ulcer: 707.00-707.09)
707.24 Pressure ulcer stage IV — (Code first site of pressure ulcer: 707.00-707.09)
707.25 Pressure ulcer, unstageable — (Code first site of pressure ulcer: 707.00-707.09)
730.15 Chronic osteomyelitis, pelvic region and thigh — (Use additional code to identify organism: 041.1. Use additional code to identify major osseous defect, if applicable: 731.3)
785.4 Gangrene — (Code first any associated underlying condition)

ICD-9-CM Procedural

77.89 Other partial ostectomy of other bone, except facial bones
77.99 Total ostectomy of other bone, except facial bones
86.3 Other local excision or destruction of lesion or tissue of skin and subcutaneous tissue
86.4 Radical excision of skin lesion

15944-15945

15944 Excision, ischial pressure ulcer, with skin flap closure;
15945 with ostectomy

ICD-9-CM Diagnostic

707.00 Pressure ulcer, unspecified site — (Use additional code to identify pressure ulcer stage: 707.20-707.25) ▽
707.04 Pressure ulcer, hip — (Use additional code to identify pressure ulcer stage: 707.20-707.25)
707.09 Pressure ulcer, other site — (Use additional code to identify pressure ulcer stage: 707.20-707.25)
707.20 Pressure ulcer, unspecified stage — (Code first site of pressure ulcer: 707.00-707.09) ▽
707.21 Pressure ulcer, stage I — (Code first site of pressure ulcer: 707.00-707.09)
707.22 Pressure ulcer stage II — (Code first site of pressure ulcer: 707.00-707.09)
707.23 Pressure ulcer stage III — (Code first site of pressure ulcer: 707.00-707.09)
707.24 Pressure ulcer stage IV — (Code first site of pressure ulcer: 707.00-707.09)
707.25 Pressure ulcer, unstageable — (Code first site of pressure ulcer: 707.00-707.09)
730.15 Chronic osteomyelitis, pelvic region and thigh — (Use additional code to identify organism: 041.1. Use additional code to identify major osseous defect, if applicable: 731.3)
785.4 Gangrene — (Code first any associated underlying condition)

ICD-9-CM Procedural

77.89 Other partial ostectomy of other bone, except facial bones
77.99 Total ostectomy of other bone, except facial bones
86.3 Other local excision or destruction of lesion or tissue of skin and subcutaneous tissue
86.4 Radical excision of skin lesion
86.74 Attachment of pedicle or flap graft to other sites

15946

15946 Excision, ischial pressure ulcer, with ostectomy, in preparation for muscle or myocutaneous flap or skin graft closure

ICD-9-CM Diagnostic

707.00 Pressure ulcer, unspecified site — (Use additional code to identify pressure ulcer stage: 707.20-707.25) ▽
707.04 Pressure ulcer, hip — (Use additional code to identify pressure ulcer stage: 707.20-707.25)
707.09 Pressure ulcer, other site — (Use additional code to identify pressure ulcer stage: 707.20-707.25)
707.20 Pressure ulcer, unspecified stage — (Code first site of pressure ulcer: 707.00-707.09) ▽
707.21 Pressure ulcer, stage I — (Code first site of pressure ulcer: 707.00-707.09)
707.22 Pressure ulcer stage II — (Code first site of pressure ulcer: 707.00-707.09)
707.23 Pressure ulcer stage III — (Code first site of pressure ulcer: 707.00-707.09)
707.24 Pressure ulcer stage IV — (Code first site of pressure ulcer: 707.00-707.09)
707.25 Pressure ulcer, unstageable — (Code first site of pressure ulcer: 707.00-707.09)
730.15 Chronic osteomyelitis, pelvic region and thigh — (Use additional code to identify organism: 041.1. Use additional code to identify major osseous defect, if applicable: 731.3)

785.4 Gangrene — (Code first any associated underlying condition)

ICD-9-CM Procedural

77.89 Other partial ostectomy of other bone, except facial bones
77.99 Total ostectomy of other bone, except facial bones
83.82 Graft of muscle or fascia
86.3 Other local excision or destruction of lesion or tissue of skin and subcutaneous tissue
86.4 Radical excision of skin lesion
86.74 Attachment of pedicle or flap graft to other sites

15950-15951

15950 Excision, trochanteric pressure ulcer, with primary suture;
15951 with ostectomy

ICD-9-CM Diagnostic

707.00 Pressure ulcer, unspecified site — (Use additional code to identify pressure ulcer stage: 707.20-707.25) ▽
707.04 Pressure ulcer, hip — (Use additional code to identify pressure ulcer stage: 707.20-707.25)
707.09 Pressure ulcer, other site — (Use additional code to identify pressure ulcer stage: 707.20-707.25)
707.20 Pressure ulcer, unspecified stage — (Code first site of pressure ulcer: 707.00-707.09) ▽
707.21 Pressure ulcer, stage I — (Code first site of pressure ulcer: 707.00-707.09)
707.22 Pressure ulcer stage II — (Code first site of pressure ulcer: 707.00-707.09)
707.23 Pressure ulcer stage III — (Code first site of pressure ulcer: 707.00-707.09)
707.24 Pressure ulcer stage IV — (Code first site of pressure ulcer: 707.00-707.09)
707.25 Pressure ulcer, unstageable — (Code first site of pressure ulcer: 707.00-707.09)
730.15 Chronic osteomyelitis, pelvic region and thigh — (Use additional code to identify organism: 041.1. Use additional code to identify major osseous defect, if applicable: 731.3)
785.4 Gangrene — (Code first any associated underlying condition)

ICD-9-CM Procedural

77.85 Other partial ostectomy of femur
86.3 Other local excision or destruction of lesion or tissue of skin and subcutaneous tissue
86.4 Radical excision of skin lesion

15952-15953

15952 Excision, trochanteric pressure ulcer, with skin flap closure;
15953 with ostectomy

ICD-9-CM Diagnostic

707.00 Pressure ulcer, unspecified site — (Use additional code to identify pressure ulcer stage: 707.20-707.25) ▽
707.04 Pressure ulcer, hip — (Use additional code to identify pressure ulcer stage: 707.20-707.25)
707.09 Pressure ulcer, other site — (Use additional code to identify pressure ulcer stage: 707.20-707.25)
707.20 Pressure ulcer, unspecified stage — (Code first site of pressure ulcer: 707.00-707.09) ▽
707.21 Pressure ulcer, stage I — (Code first site of pressure ulcer: 707.00-707.09)
707.22 Pressure ulcer stage II — (Code first site of pressure ulcer: 707.00-707.09)
707.23 Pressure ulcer stage III — (Code first site of pressure ulcer: 707.00-707.09)
707.24 Pressure ulcer stage IV — (Code first site of pressure ulcer: 707.00-707.09)
707.25 Pressure ulcer, unstageable — (Code first site of pressure ulcer: 707.00-707.09)
730.15 Chronic osteomyelitis, pelvic region and thigh — (Use additional code to identify organism: 041.1. Use additional code to identify major osseous defect, if applicable: 731.3)
785.4 Gangrene — (Code first any associated underlying condition)

ICD-9-CM Procedural

77.85 Other partial ostectomy of femur
86.3 Other local excision or destruction of lesion or tissue of skin and subcutaneous tissue
86.4 Radical excision of skin lesion
86.74 Attachment of pedicle or flap graft to other sites

15956-15958

15956 Excision, trochanteric pressure ulcer, in preparation for muscle or myocutaneous flap or skin graft closure;
15958 with ostectomy

ICD-9-CM Diagnostic

707.00 Pressure ulcer, unspecified site — (Use additional code to identify pressure ulcer stage: 707.20-707.25) ▽
707.04 Pressure ulcer, hip — (Use additional code to identify pressure ulcer stage: 707.20-707.25)
707.09 Pressure ulcer, other site — (Use additional code to identify pressure ulcer stage: 707.20-707.25)
707.20 Pressure ulcer, unspecified stage — (Code first site of pressure ulcer: 707.00-707.09) ▽
707.21 Pressure ulcer, stage I — (Code first site of pressure ulcer: 707.00-707.09)
707.22 Pressure ulcer stage II — (Code first site of pressure ulcer: 707.00-707.09)
707.23 Pressure ulcer stage III — (Code first site of pressure ulcer: 707.00-707.09)
707.24 Pressure ulcer stage IV — (Code first site of pressure ulcer: 707.00-707.09)
707.25 Pressure ulcer, unstageable — (Code first site of pressure ulcer: 707.00-707.09)
730.15 Chronic osteomyelitis, pelvic region and thigh — (Use additional code to identify organism: 041.1. Use additional code to identify major osseous defect, if applicable: 731.3)
785.4 Gangrene — (Code first any associated underlying condition)

ICD-9-CM Procedural

77.85 Other partial ostectomy of femur
83.82 Graft of muscle or fascia
86.3 Other local excision or destruction of lesion or tissue of skin and subcutaneous tissue
86.4 Radical excision of skin lesion
86.74 Attachment of pedicle or flap graft to other sites

16000

16000 Initial treatment, first degree burn, when no more than local treatment is required

ICD-9-CM Diagnostic

941.10 Erythema due to burn (first degree) of unspecified site of face and head ▽
941.11 Erythema due to burn (first degree) of ear (any part)
941.12 Erythema due to burn (first degree) of eye (with other parts face, head, and neck)
941.13 Erythema due to burn (first degree) of lip(s)
941.14 Erythema due to burn (first degree) of chin
941.15 Erythema due to burn (first degree) of nose (septum)
941.16 Erythema due to burn (first degree) of scalp (any part)
941.17 Erythema due to burn (first degree) of forehead and cheek
941.18 Erythema due to burn (first degree) of neck
941.19 Erythema due to burn (first degree) of multiple sites (except with eye) of face, head, and neck
942.10 Erythema due to burn (first degree) of unspecified site of trunk ▽
942.11 Erythema due to burn (first degree) of breast
942.12 Erythema due to burn (first degree) of chest wall, excluding breast and nipple
942.13 Erythema due to burn (first degree) of abdominal wall
942.14 Erythema due to burn (first degree) of back (any part)
942.15 Erythema due to burn (first degree) of genitalia
942.19 Erythema due to burn (first degree) of other and multiple sites of trunk
943.10 Erythema due to burn (first degree) of unspecified site of upper limb ▽
943.11 Erythema due to burn (first degree) of forearm
943.12 Erythema due to burn (first degree) of elbow
943.13 Erythema due to burn (first degree) of upper arm

943.14 Erythema due to burn (first degree) of axilla
943.15 Erythema due to burn (first degree) of shoulder
943.16 Erythema due to burn (first degree) of scapular region
943.19 Erythema due to burn (first degree) of multiple sites of upper limb, except wrist and hand
944.10 Erythema due to burn (first degree) of unspecified site of hand
944.11 Erythema due to burn (first degree) of single digit [finger (nail)] other than thumb
944.12 Erythema due to burn (first degree) of thumb (nail)
944.13 Erythema due to burn (first degree) of two or more digits of hand, not including thumb
944.14 Erythema due to burn (first degree) of two or more digits of hand including thumb
944.15 Erythema due to burn (first degree) of palm of hand
944.16 Erythema due to burn (first degree) of back of hand
944.17 Erythema due to burn (first degree) of wrist
944.18 Erythema due to burn (first degree) of multiple sites of wrist(s) and hand(s)
945.10 Erythema due to burn (first degree) of unspecified site of lower limb (leg)
945.11 Erythema due to burn (first degree) of toe(s) (nail)
945.12 Erythema due to burn (first degree) of foot
945.13 Erythema due to burn (first degree) of ankle
945.14 Erythema due to burn (first degree) of lower leg
945.15 Erythema due to burn (first degree) of knee
945.16 Erythema due to burn (first degree) of thigh (any part)
945.19 Erythema due to burn (first degree) of multiple sites of lower limb(s)
946.1 Erythema due to burn (first degree) of multiple specified sites
947.0 Burn of mouth and pharynx
948.00 Burn (any degree) involving less than 10% of body surface with third degree burn of less than 10% or unspecified amount

ICD-9-CM Procedural

93.57 Application of other wound dressing

HCPCS Level II Supplies & Services

A4649 Surgical supply; miscellaneous

16020-16030

16020 Dressings and/or debridement of partial-thickness burns, initial or subsequent; small (less than 5% total body surface area)
16025 medium (eg, whole face or whole extremity, or 5% to 10% total body surface area)
16030 large (eg, more than 1 extremity, or greater than 10% total body surface area)

ICD-9-CM Diagnostic

941.20 Blisters, with epidermal loss due to burn (second degree) of face and head, unspecified site
941.21 Blisters, with epidermal loss due to burn (second degree) of ear (any part)
941.22 Blisters, with epidermal loss due to burn (second degree) of eye (with other parts of face, head, and neck)
941.23 Blisters, with epidermal loss due to burn (second degree) of lip(s)
941.24 Blisters, with epidermal loss due to burn (second degree) of chin
941.25 Blisters, with epidermal loss due to burn (second degree) of nose (septum)
941.26 Blisters, with epidermal loss due to burn (second degree) of scalp (any part)
941.27 Blisters, with epidermal loss due to burn (second degree) of forehead and cheek
941.28 Blisters, with epidermal loss due to burn (second degree) of neck
941.29 Blisters, with epidermal loss due to burn (second degree) of multiple sites (except with eye) of face, head, and neck
941.30 Full-thickness skin loss due to burn (third degree NOS) of unspecified site of face and head
941.31 Full-thickness skin loss due to burn (third degree NOS) of ear (any part)
941.32 Full-thickness skin loss due to burn (third degree NOS) of eye (with other parts of face, head, and neck)
941.33 Full-thickness skin loss due to burn (third degree NOS) of lip(s)
941.34 Full-thickness skin loss due to burn (third degree NOS) of chin
941.35 Full-thickness skin loss due to burn (third degree NOS) of nose (septum)
941.36 Full-thickness skin loss due to burn (third degree NOS) of scalp (any part)
941.37 Full-thickness skin loss due to burn (third degree NOS) of forehead and cheek
941.38 Full-thickness skin loss due to burn (third degree NOS) of neck
941.39 Full-thickness skin loss due to burn (third degree NOS) of multiple sites (except with eye) of face, head, and neck
941.40 Deep necrosis of underlying tissues due to burn (deep third degree) of unspecified site of face and head, without mention of loss of a body part
941.41 Deep necrosis of underlying tissues due to burn (deep third degree) of ear (any part), without mention of loss of a body part
941.42 Deep necrosis of underlying tissues due to burn (deep third degree) of eye (with other parts of face, head, and neck), without mention of loss of a body part
941.43 Deep necrosis of underlying tissues due to burn (deep third degree) of lip(s), without mention of loss of a body part
941.44 Deep necrosis of underlying tissues due to burn (deep third degree) of chin, without mention of loss of a body part
941.45 Deep necrosis of underlying tissues due to burn (deep third degree) of nose (septum), without mention of loss of a body part
941.46 Deep necrosis of underlying tissues due to burn (deep third degree) of scalp (any part), without mention of loss of a body part
941.47 Deep necrosis of underlying tissues due to burn (deep third degree) of forehead and cheek, without mention of loss of a body part
941.48 Deep necrosis of underlying tissues due to burn (deep third degree) of neck, without mention of loss of a body part
941.49 Deep necrosis of underlying tissues due to burn (deep third degree) of multiple sites (except with eye) of face, head, and neck, without mention of loss of a body part
942.20 Blisters with epidermal loss due to burn (second degree) of unspecified site of trunk
942.21 Blisters with epidermal loss due to burn (second degree) of breast
942.22 Blisters with epidermal loss due to burn (second degree) of chest wall, excluding breast and nipple
942.23 Blisters with epidermal loss due to burn (second degree) of abdominal wall
942.24 Blisters with epidermal loss due to burn (second degree) of back (any part)
942.25 Blisters with epidermal loss due to burn (second degree) of genitalia
942.30 Full-thickness skin loss due to burn (third degree NOS) of unspecified site of trunk
942.31 Full-thickness skin loss due to burn (third degree NOS) of breast
942.32 Full-thickness skin loss due to burn (third degree NOS) of chest wall, excluding breast and nipple
942.33 Full-thickness skin loss due to burn (third degree NOS) of abdominal wall
942.34 Full-thickness skin loss due to burn (third degree NOS) of back (any part)
942.35 Full-thickness skin loss due to burn (third degree NOS) of genitalia
942.40 Deep necrosis of underlying tissues due to burn (deep third degree) of trunk, unspecified site, without mention of loss of a body part
942.41 Deep necrosis of underlying tissues due to burn (deep third degree) of breast, without mention of loss of a body part
942.42 Deep necrosis of underlying tissues due to burn (deep third degree) of chest wall, excluding breast and nipple, without mention of loss of a body part
942.43 Deep necrosis of underlying tissues due to burn (deep third degree) of abdominal wall, without mention of loss of a body part
942.44 Deep necrosis of underlying tissues due to burn (deep third degree) of back (any part), without mention of loss of a body part
942.45 Deep necrosis of underlying tissues due to burn (deep third degree) of genitalia, without mention of loss of a body part
942.50 Deep necrosis of underlying tissues due to burn (deep third degree) of unspecified site of trunk, with loss of a body part
942.51 Deep necrosis of underlying tissues due to burn (deep third degree) of breast, with loss of a body part
942.52 Deep necrosis of underlying tissues due to burn (deep third degree) of chest wall, excluding breast and nipple, with loss of a body part
942.53 Deep necrosis of underlying tissues due to burn (deep third degree) of abdominal wall with loss of a body part

942.54 Deep necrosis of underlying tissues due to burn (deep third degree) of back (any part), with loss of a body part
942.55 Deep necrosis of underlying tissues due to burn (deep third degree) of genitalia, with loss of a body part
943.20 Blisters with epidermal loss due to burn (second degree) of unspecified site of upper limb ▽
943.21 Blisters with epidermal loss due to burn (second degree) of forearm
943.22 Blisters with epidermal loss due to burn (second degree) of elbow
943.23 Blisters with epidermal loss due to burn (second degree) of upper arm
943.24 Blisters with epidermal loss due to burn (second degree) of axilla
943.25 Blisters with epidermal loss due to burn (second degree) of shoulder
943.26 Blisters with epidermal loss due to burn (second degree) of scapular region
943.29 Blisters with epidermal loss due to burn (second degree) of multiple sites of upper limb, except wrist and hand
943.30 Full-thickness skin loss due to burn (third degree NOS) of unspecified site of upper limb ▽
943.31 Full-thickness skin loss due to burn (third degree NOS) of forearm
943.32 Full-thickness skin loss due to burn (third degree NOS) of elbow
943.33 Full-thickness skin loss due to burn (third degree NOS) of upper arm
943.34 Full-thickness skin loss due to burn (third degree NOS) of axilla
943.35 Full-thickness skin loss due to burn (third degree NOS) of shoulder
943.36 Full-thickness skin loss due to burn (third degree NOS) of scapular region
943.39 Full-thickness skin loss due to burn (third degree NOS) of multiple sites of upper limb, except wrist and hand
943.40 Deep necrosis of underlying tissues due to burn (deep third degree) of unspecified site of upper limb, without mention of loss of a body part ▽
943.41 Deep necrosis of underlying tissues due to burn (deep third degree) of forearm, without mention of loss of a body part
943.42 Deep necrosis of underlying tissues due to burn (deep third degree) of elbow, without mention of loss of a body part
943.43 Deep necrosis of underlying tissues due to burn (deep third degree) of upper arm, without mention of loss of a body part
943.44 Deep necrosis of underlying tissues due to burn (deep third degree) of axilla, without mention of loss of a body part
943.45 Deep necrosis of underlying tissues due to burn (deep third degree) of shoulder, without mention of loss of a body part
943.46 Deep necrosis of underlying tissues due to burn (deep third degree) of scapular region, without mention of loss of a body part
943.49 Deep necrosis of underlying tissues due to burn (deep third degree) of multiple sites of upper limb, except wrist and hand, without mention of loss of a body part
943.50 Deep necrosis of underlying tissues due to burn (deep third degree) of unspecified site of upper limb, with loss of a body part ▽
943.51 Deep necrosis of underlying tissues due to burn (deep third degree) of forearm, with loss of a body part
943.52 Deep necrosis of underlying tissues due to burn (deep third degree) of elbow, with loss of a body part
943.53 Deep necrosis of underlying tissues due to burn (deep third degree) of upper arm, with loss of upper a body part
943.54 Deep necrosis of underlying tissues due to burn (deep third degree) of axilla, with loss of a body part
943.55 Deep necrosis of underlying tissues due to burn (deep third degree) of shoulder, with loss of a body part
943.56 Deep necrosis of underlying tissues due to burn (deep third degree) of scapular region, with loss of a body part
943.59 Deep necrosis of underlying tissues due to burn (deep third degree) of multiple sites of upper limb, except wrist and hand, with loss of a body part
944.20 Blisters with epidermal loss due to burn (second degree) of unspecified site of hand ▽
944.21 Blisters with epidermal loss due to burn (second degree) of single digit [finger (nail)] other than thumb
944.22 Blisters with epidermal loss due to burn of (second degree) of thumb (nail)
944.23 Blisters with epidermal loss due to burn (second degree) of two or more digits of hand, not including thumb
944.24 Blisters with epidermal loss due to burn (second degree) of two or more digits of hand including thumb
944.25 Blisters with epidermal loss due to burn (second degree) of palm of hand
944.26 Blisters with epidermal loss due to burn (second degree) of back of hand
944.27 Blisters with epidermal loss due to burn (second degree) of wrist
944.28 Blisters with epidermal loss due to burn (second degree) of multiple sites of wrist(s) and hand(s)
944.30 Full-thickness skin loss due to burn (third degree NOS) of unspecified site of hand ▽
944.31 Full-thickness skin loss due to burn (third degree NOS) of single digit [finger (nail)] other than thumb
944.32 Full-thickness skin loss due to burn (third degree NOS) of thumb (nail)
944.33 Full-thickness skin loss due to burn (third degree NOS) of two or more digits of hand, not including thumb
944.34 Full-thickness skin loss due to burn (third degree NOS) of two or more digits of hand including thumb
944.35 Full-thickness skin loss due to burn (third degree NOS) of palm of hand
944.36 Full-thickness skin loss due to burn (third degree NOS) of back of hand
944.37 Full-thickness skin loss due to burn (third degree NOS) of wrist
944.38 Full-thickness skin loss due to burn (third degree NOS) of multiple sites of wrist(s) and hand(s)
944.40 Deep necrosis of underlying tissues due to burn (deep third degree) of unspecified site of hand, without mention of loss of a body part ▽
944.41 Deep necrosis of underlying tissues due to burn (deep third degree) of single digit [finger (nail)] other than thumb, without mention of loss of a body part
944.42 Deep necrosis of underlying tissues due to burn (deep third degree) of thumb (nail), without mention of loss of a body part
944.43 Deep necrosis of underlying tissues due to burn (deep third degree) of two or more digits of hand, not including thumb, without mention of loss of a body part
944.44 Deep necrosis of underlying tissues due to burn (deep third degree) of two or more digits of hand including thumb, without mention of loss of a body part
944.45 Deep necrosis of underlying tissues due to burn (deep third degree) of palm of hand, without mention of loss of a body part
944.46 Deep necrosis of underlying tissues due to burn (deep third degree) of back of hand, without mention of loss of a body part
944.47 Deep necrosis of underlying tissues due to burn (deep third degree) of wrist, without mention of loss of a body part
944.48 Deep necrosis of underlying tissues due to burn (deep third degree) of multiple sites of wrist(s) and hand(s), without mention of loss of a body part
944.50 Deep necrosis of underlying tissues due to burn (deep third degree) of unspecified site of hand, with loss of a body part ▽
944.51 Deep necrosis of underlying tissues due to burn (deep third degree) of single digit (finger (nail)) other than thumb, with loss of a body part
944.52 Deep necrosis of underlying tissues due to burn (deep third degree) of thumb (nail), with loss of a body part
944.53 Deep necrosis of underlying tissues due to burn (deep third degree) of two or more digits of hand, not including thumb, with loss of a body part
944.54 Deep necrosis of underlying tissues due to burn (deep third degree) of two or more digits of hand including thumb, with loss of a body part
944.55 Deep necrosis of underlying tissues due to burn (deep third degree) of palm of hand, with loss of a body part
944.56 Deep necrosis of underlying tissues due to burn (deep third degree) of back of hand, with loss of a body part
944.57 Deep necrosis of underlying tissues due to burn (deep third degree) of wrist, with loss of a body part
944.58 Deep necrosis of underlying tissues due to burn (deep third degree) of multiple sites of wrist(s) and hand(s), with loss of a body part
945.20 Blisters with epidermal loss due to burn (second degree) of unspecified site of lower limb (leg) ▽
945.21 Blisters with epidermal loss due to burn (second degree) of toe(s) (nail)

945.22 Blisters with epidermal loss due to burn (second degree) of foot
945.23 Blisters with epidermal loss due to burn (second degree) of ankle
945.24 Blisters with epidermal loss due to burn (second degree) of lower leg
945.25 Blisters with epidermal loss due to burn (second degree) of knee
945.26 Blisters with epidermal loss due to burn (second degree) of thigh (any part)
945.29 Blisters with epidermal loss due to burn (second degree) of multiple sites of lower limb(s)
945.30 Full-thickness skin loss due to burn (third degree NOS) of unspecified site of lower limb
945.31 Full-thickness skin loss due to burn (third degree NOS) of toe(s) (nail)
945.32 Full-thickness skin loss due to burn (third degree NOS) of foot
945.33 Full-thickness skin loss due to burn (third degree NOS) of ankle
945.34 Full-thickness skin loss due to burn (third degree NOS) of lower leg
945.35 Full-thickness skin loss due to burn (third degree NOS) of knee
945.36 Full-thickness skin loss due to burn (third degree NOS) of thigh (any part)
945.39 Full-thickness skin loss due to burn (third degree NOS) of multiple sites of lower limb(s)
945.40 Deep necrosis of underlying tissues due to burn (deep third degree) of unspecified site of lower limb (leg), without mention of loss of a body part
945.41 Deep necrosis of underlying tissues due to burn (deep third degree) of toe(s) (nail), without mention of loss of a body part
945.42 Deep necrosis of underlying tissues due to burn (deep third degree) of foot, without mention of loss of a body part
945.49 Deep necrosis of underlying tissues due to burn (deep third degree) of multiple sites of lower limb(s), without mention of loss of a body part
945.50 Deep necrosis of underlying tissues due to burn (deep third degree) of unspecified site lower limb (leg), with loss of a body part
945.51 Deep necrosis of underlying tissues due to burn (deep third degree) of toe(s) (nail), with loss of a body part
945.52 Deep necrosis of underlying tissues due to burn (deep third degree) of foot, with loss of a body part
945.53 Deep necrosis of underlying tissues due to burn (deep third degree) of ankle, with loss of a body part
945.54 Deep necrosis of underlying tissues due to burn (deep third degree) of lower leg, with loss of a body part
945.55 Deep necrosis of underlying tissues due to burn (deep third degree) of knee, with loss of a body part
945.56 Deep necrosis of underlying tissues due to burn (deep third degree) of thigh (any part), with loss of a body part
945.59 Deep necrosis of underlying tissues due to burn (deep third degree) of multiple sites of lower limb(s), with loss of a body part
947.0 Burn of mouth and pharynx
948.00 Burn (any degree) involving less than 10% of body surface with third degree burn of less than 10% or unspecified amount
948.11 Burn (any degree) involving 10-19% of body surface with third degree burn of 10-19%
948.20 Burn (any degree) involving 20-29% of body surface with third degree burn of less than 10% or unspecified amount
948.21 Burn (any degree) involving 20-29% of body surface with third degree burn of 10-19%
948.22 Burn (any degree) involving 20-29% of body surface with third degree burn of 20-29%

ICD-9-CM Procedural

86.22 Excisional debridement of wound, infection, or burn
86.28 Nonexcisional debridement of wound, infection, or burn
93.56 Application of pressure dressing
93.57 Application of other wound dressing

HCPCS Level II Supplies & Services

A4305 Disposable drug delivery system, flow rate of 50 ml or greater per hour
Q4103 Oasis burn matrix, per sq cm

16035-16036

16035 Escharotomy; initial incision
16036 each additional incision (List separately in addition to code for primary procedure)

ICD-9-CM Diagnostic

709.2 Scar condition and fibrosis of skin
906.5 Late effect of burn of eye, face, head, and neck
906.6 Late effect of burn of wrist and hand
906.7 Late effect of burn of other extremities
906.8 Late effect of burns of other specified sites
940.0 Chemical burn of eyelids and periocular area
940.1 Other burns of eyelids and periocular area
941.20 Blisters, with epidermal loss due to burn (second degree) of face and head, unspecified site
941.21 Blisters, with epidermal loss due to burn (second degree) of ear (any part)
941.22 Blisters, with epidermal loss due to burn (second degree) of eye (with other parts of face, head, and neck)
941.23 Blisters, with epidermal loss due to burn (second degree) of lip(s)
941.24 Blisters, with epidermal loss due to burn (second degree) of chin
941.25 Blisters, with epidermal loss due to burn (second degree) of nose (septum)
941.26 Blisters, with epidermal loss due to burn (second degree) of scalp (any part)
941.27 Blisters, with epidermal loss due to burn (second degree) of forehead and cheek
941.28 Blisters, with epidermal loss due to burn (second degree) of neck
941.29 Blisters, with epidermal loss due to burn (second degree) of multiple sites (except with eye) of face, head, and neck
941.30 Full-thickness skin loss due to burn (third degree NOS) of unspecified site of face and head
941.31 Full-thickness skin loss due to burn (third degree NOS) of ear (any part)
941.32 Full-thickness skin loss due to burn (third degree NOS) of eye (with other parts of face, head, and neck)
941.33 Full-thickness skin loss due to burn (third degree NOS) of lip(s)
941.34 Full-thickness skin loss due to burn (third degree NOS) of chin
941.35 Full-thickness skin loss due to burn (third degree NOS) of nose (septum)
941.36 Full-thickness skin loss due to burn (third degree NOS) of scalp (any part)
941.37 Full-thickness skin loss due to burn (third degree NOS) of forehead and cheek
941.38 Full-thickness skin loss due to burn (third degree NOS) of neck
941.39 Full-thickness skin loss due to burn (third degree NOS) of multiple sites (except with eye) of face, head, and neck
941.40 Deep necrosis of underlying tissues due to burn (deep third degree) of unspecified site of face and head, without mention of loss of a body part
941.41 Deep necrosis of underlying tissues due to burn (deep third degree) of ear (any part), without mention of loss of a body part
941.42 Deep necrosis of underlying tissues due to burn (deep third degree) of eye (with other parts of face, head, and neck), without mention of loss of a body part
941.43 Deep necrosis of underlying tissues due to burn (deep third degree) of lip(s), without mention of loss of a body part
941.44 Deep necrosis of underlying tissues due to burn (deep third degree) of chin, without mention of loss of a body part
941.45 Deep necrosis of underlying tissues due to burn (deep third degree) of nose (septum), without mention of loss of a body part
941.46 Deep necrosis of underlying tissues due to burn (deep third degree) of scalp (any part), without mention of loss of a body part
941.47 Deep necrosis of underlying tissues due to burn (deep third degree) of forehead and cheek, without mention of loss of a body part
941.48 Deep necrosis of underlying tissues due to burn (deep third degree) of neck, without mention of loss of a body part
941.49 Deep necrosis of underlying tissues due to burn (deep third degree) of multiple sites (except with eye) of face, head, and neck, without mention of loss of a body part
941.50 Deep necrosis of underlying tissues due to burn (deep third degree) of face and head, unspecified site, with loss of a body part

941.51 Deep necrosis of underlying tissues due to burn (deep third degree) of ear (any part), with loss of a body part
941.52 Deep necrosis of underlying tissues due to burn (deep third degree) of eye (with other parts of face, head, and neck), with loss of a body part
941.53 Deep necrosis of underlying tissues due to burn (deep third degree) of lip(s), with loss of a body part
941.54 Deep necrosis of underlying tissues due to burn (deep third degree) of chin, with loss of a body part
941.55 Deep necrosis of underlying tissues due to burn (deep third degree) of nose (septum), with loss of a body part
941.56 Deep necrosis of underlying tissues due to burn (deep third degree) of scalp (any part), with loss of a body part
941.57 Deep necrosis of underlying tissues due to burn (deep third degree) of forehead and cheek, with loss of a body part
941.58 Deep necrosis of underlying tissues due to burn (deep third degree) of neck, with loss of a body part
941.59 Deep necrosis of underlying tissues due to burn (deep third degree) of multiple sites (except eye) of face, head, and neck, with loss of a body part
942.20 Blisters with epidermal loss due to burn (second degree) of unspecified site of trunk ▽
942.21 Blisters with epidermal loss due to burn (second degree) of breast
942.22 Blisters with epidermal loss due to burn (second degree) of chest wall, excluding breast and nipple
942.23 Blisters with epidermal loss due to burn (second degree) of abdominal wall
942.24 Blisters with epidermal loss due to burn (second degree) of back (any part)
942.25 Blisters with epidermal loss due to burn (second degree) of genitalia
942.29 Blisters with epidermal loss due to burn (second degree) of other and multiple sites of trunk
942.30 Full-thickness skin loss due to burn (third degree NOS) of unspecified site of trunk ▽
942.31 Full-thickness skin loss due to burn (third degree NOS) of breast
942.32 Full-thickness skin loss due to burn (third degree NOS) of chest wall, excluding breast and nipple
942.33 Full-thickness skin loss due to burn (third degree NOS) of abdominal wall
942.34 Full-thickness skin loss due to burn (third degree NOS) of back (any part)
942.35 Full-thickness skin loss due to burn (third degree NOS) of genitalia
942.39 Full-thickness skin loss due to burn (third degree NOS) of other and multiple sites of trunk
942.40 Deep necrosis of underlying tissues due to burn (deep third degree) of trunk, unspecified site, without mention of loss of a body part ▽
942.41 Deep necrosis of underlying tissues due to burn (deep third degree) of breast, without mention of loss of a body part
942.42 Deep necrosis of underlying tissues due to burn (deep third degree) of chest wall, excluding breast and nipple, without mention of loss of a body part
942.43 Deep necrosis of underlying tissues due to burn (deep third degree) of abdominal wall, without mention of loss of a body part
942.44 Deep necrosis of underlying tissues due to burn (deep third degree) of back (any part), without mention of loss of a body part
942.45 Deep necrosis of underlying tissues due to burn (deep third degree) of genitalia, without mention of loss of a body part
942.49 Deep necrosis of underlying tissues due to burn (deep third degree) of other and multiple sites of trunk, without mention of loss of a body part
943.20 Blisters with epidermal loss due to burn (second degree) of unspecified site of upper limb ▽
943.21 Blisters with epidermal loss due to burn (second degree) of forearm
943.22 Blisters with epidermal loss due to burn (second degree) of elbow
943.23 Blisters with epidermal loss due to burn (second degree) of upper arm
943.24 Blisters with epidermal loss due to burn (second degree) of axilla
943.25 Blisters with epidermal loss due to burn (second degree) of shoulder
943.26 Blisters with epidermal loss due to burn (second degree) of scapular region
943.29 Blisters with epidermal loss due to burn (second degree) of multiple sites of upper limb, except wrist and hand
943.30 Full-thickness skin loss due to burn (third degree NOS) of unspecified site of upper limb ▽
943.31 Full-thickness skin loss due to burn (third degree NOS) of forearm
943.32 Full-thickness skin loss due to burn (third degree NOS) of elbow
943.33 Full-thickness skin loss due to burn (third degree NOS) of upper arm
943.34 Full-thickness skin loss due to burn (third degree NOS) of axilla
943.35 Full-thickness skin loss due to burn (third degree NOS) of shoulder
943.36 Full-thickness skin loss due to burn (third degree NOS) of scapular region
943.39 Full-thickness skin loss due to burn (third degree NOS) of multiple sites of upper limb, except wrist and hand
943.40 Deep necrosis of underlying tissues due to burn (deep third degree) of unspecified site of upper limb, without mention of loss of a body part ▽
943.41 Deep necrosis of underlying tissues due to burn (deep third degree) of forearm, without mention of loss of a body part
943.42 Deep necrosis of underlying tissues due to burn (deep third degree) of elbow, without mention of loss of a body part
943.43 Deep necrosis of underlying tissues due to burn (deep third degree) of upper arm, without mention of loss of a body part
943.44 Deep necrosis of underlying tissues due to burn (deep third degree) of axilla, without mention of loss of a body part
943.45 Deep necrosis of underlying tissues due to burn (deep third degree) of shoulder, without mention of loss of a body part
943.46 Deep necrosis of underlying tissues due to burn (deep third degree) of scapular region, without mention of loss of a body part
943.49 Deep necrosis of underlying tissues due to burn (deep third degree) of multiple sites of upper limb, except wrist and hand, without mention of loss of a body part
943.50 Deep necrosis of underlying tissues due to burn (deep third degree) of unspecified site of upper limb, with loss of a body part ▽
943.51 Deep necrosis of underlying tissues due to burn (deep third degree) of forearm, with loss of a body part
943.52 Deep necrosis of underlying tissues due to burn (deep third degree) of elbow, with loss of a body part
943.53 Deep necrosis of underlying tissues due to burn (deep third degree) of upper arm, with loss of upper a body part
943.54 Deep necrosis of underlying tissues due to burn (deep third degree) of axilla, with loss of a body part
943.55 Deep necrosis of underlying tissues due to burn (deep third degree) of shoulder, with loss of a body part
943.56 Deep necrosis of underlying tissues due to burn (deep third degree) of scapular region, with loss of a body part
943.59 Deep necrosis of underlying tissues due to burn (deep third degree) of multiple sites of upper limb, except wrist and hand, with loss of a body part
944.20 Blisters with epidermal loss due to burn (second degree) of unspecified site of hand ▽
944.21 Blisters with epidermal loss due to burn (second degree) of single digit [finger (nail)] other than thumb
944.22 Blisters with epidermal loss due to burn of (second degree) of thumb (nail)
944.23 Blisters with epidermal loss due to burn (second degree) of two or more digits of hand, not including thumb
944.24 Blisters with epidermal loss due to burn (second degree) of two or more digits of hand including thumb
944.25 Blisters with epidermal loss due to burn (second degree) of palm of hand
944.26 Blisters with epidermal loss due to burn (second degree) of back of hand
944.27 Blisters with epidermal loss due to burn (second degree) of wrist
944.28 Blisters with epidermal loss due to burn (second degree) of multiple sites of wrist(s) and hand(s)
944.30 Full-thickness skin loss due to burn (third degree NOS) of unspecified site of hand ▽
944.31 Full-thickness skin loss due to burn (third degree NOS) of single digit [finger (nail)] other than thumb
944.32 Full-thickness skin loss due to burn (third degree NOS) of thumb (nail)
944.33 Full-thickness skin loss due to burn (third degree NOS) of two or more digits of hand, not including thumb

944.34 Full-thickness skin loss due to burn (third degree NOS) of two or more digits of hand including thumb
944.35 Full-thickness skin loss due to burn (third degree NOS) of palm of hand
944.36 Full-thickness skin loss due to burn (third degree NOS) of back of hand
944.37 Full-thickness skin loss due to burn (third degree NOS) of wrist
944.38 Full-thickness skin loss due to burn (third degree NOS) of multiple sites of wrist(s) and hand(s)
944.40 Deep necrosis of underlying tissues due to burn (deep third degree) of unspecified site of hand, without mention of loss of a body part
944.41 Deep necrosis of underlying tissues due to burn (deep third degree) of single digit [finger (nail)] other than thumb, without mention of loss of a body part
944.42 Deep necrosis of underlying tissues due to burn (deep third degree) of thumb (nail), without mention of loss of a body part
944.43 Deep necrosis of underlying tissues due to burn (deep third degree) of two or more digits of hand, not including thumb, without mention of loss of a body part
944.44 Deep necrosis of underlying tissues due to burn (deep third degree) of two or more digits of hand including thumb, without mention of loss of a body part
944.45 Deep necrosis of underlying tissues due to burn (deep third degree) of palm of hand, without mention of loss of a body part
944.46 Deep necrosis of underlying tissues due to burn (deep third degree) of back of hand, without mention of loss of a body part
944.47 Deep necrosis of underlying tissues due to burn (deep third degree) of wrist, without mention of loss of a body part
944.48 Deep necrosis of underlying tissues due to burn (deep third degree) of multiple sites of wrist(s) and hand(s), without mention of loss of a body part
944.50 Deep necrosis of underlying tissues due to burn (deep third degree) of unspecified site of hand, with loss of a body part
944.51 Deep necrosis of underlying tissues due to burn (deep third degree) of single digit (finger (nail)) other than thumb, with loss of a body part
944.52 Deep necrosis of underlying tissues due to burn (deep third degree) of thumb (nail), with loss of a body part
944.53 Deep necrosis of underlying tissues due to burn (deep third degree) of two or more digits of hand, not including thumb, with loss of a body part
944.54 Deep necrosis of underlying tissues due to burn (deep third degree) of two or more digits of hand including thumb, with loss of a body part
944.55 Deep necrosis of underlying tissues due to burn (deep third degree) of palm of hand, with loss of a body part
944.56 Deep necrosis of underlying tissues due to burn (deep third degree) of back of hand, with loss of a body part
944.57 Deep necrosis of underlying tissues due to burn (deep third degree) of wrist, with loss of a body part
944.58 Deep necrosis of underlying tissues due to burn (deep third degree) of multiple sites of wrist(s) and hand(s), with loss of a body part
945.20 Blisters with epidermal loss due to burn (second degree) of unspecified site of lower limb (leg)
945.21 Blisters with epidermal loss due to burn (second degree) of toe(s) (nail)
945.22 Blisters with epidermal loss due to burn (second degree) of foot
945.23 Blisters with epidermal loss due to burn (second degree) of ankle
945.24 Blisters with epidermal loss due to burn (second degree) of lower leg
945.25 Blisters with epidermal loss due to burn (second degree) of knee
945.26 Blisters with epidermal loss due to burn (second degree) of thigh (any part)
945.29 Blisters with epidermal loss due to burn (second degree) of multiple sites of lower limb(s)
945.30 Full-thickness skin loss due to burn (third degree NOS) of unspecified site of lower limb
945.31 Full-thickness skin loss due to burn (third degree NOS) of toe(s) (nail)
945.32 Full-thickness skin loss due to burn (third degree NOS) of foot
945.33 Full-thickness skin loss due to burn (third degree NOS) of ankle
945.34 Full-thickness skin loss due to burn (third degree NOS) of lower leg
945.35 Full-thickness skin loss due to burn (third degree NOS) of knee
945.36 Full-thickness skin loss due to burn (third degree NOS) of thigh (any part)
945.39 Full-thickness skin loss due to burn (third degree NOS) of multiple sites of lower limb(s)
945.40 Deep necrosis of underlying tissues due to burn (deep third degree) of unspecified site of lower limb (leg), without mention of loss of a body part
945.41 Deep necrosis of underlying tissues due to burn (deep third degree) of toe(s) (nail), without mention of loss of a body part
945.42 Deep necrosis of underlying tissues due to burn (deep third degree) of foot, without mention of loss of a body part
945.43 Deep necrosis of underlying tissues due to burn (deep third degree) of ankle, without mention of loss of a body part
945.44 Deep necrosis of underlying tissues due to burn (deep third degree) of lower leg, without mention of loss of a body part
945.45 Deep necrosis of underlying tissues due to burn (deep third degree) of knee, without mention of loss of a body part
945.46 Deep necrosis of underlying tissues due to burn (deep third degree) of thigh (any part), without mention of loss of a body part
945.49 Deep necrosis of underlying tissues due to burn (deep third degree) of multiple sites of lower limb(s), without mention of loss of a body part
945.50 Deep necrosis of underlying tissues due to burn (deep third degree) of unspecified site lower limb (leg), with loss of a body part
945.51 Deep necrosis of underlying tissues due to burn (deep third degree) of toe(s) (nail), with loss of a body part
945.52 Deep necrosis of underlying tissues due to burn (deep third degree) of foot, with loss of a body part
945.53 Deep necrosis of underlying tissues due to burn (deep third degree) of ankle, with loss of a body part
945.54 Deep necrosis of underlying tissues due to burn (deep third degree) of lower leg, with loss of a body part
945.55 Deep necrosis of underlying tissues due to burn (deep third degree) of knee, with loss of a body part
945.56 Deep necrosis of underlying tissues due to burn (deep third degree) of thigh (any part), with loss of a body part
945.59 Deep necrosis of underlying tissues due to burn (deep third degree) of multiple sites of lower limb(s), with loss of a body part
946.2 Blisters with epidermal loss due to burn (second degree) of multiple specified sites
946.3 Full-thickness skin loss due to burn (third degree NOS) of multiple specified sites
946.4 Deep necrosis of underlying tissues due to burn (deep third degree) of multiple specified sites, without mention of loss of a body part
946.5 Deep necrosis of underlying tissues due to burn (deep third degree) of multiple specified sites, with loss of a body part
948.00 Burn (any degree) involving less than 10% of body surface with third degree burn of less than 10% or unspecified amount
948.10 Burn (any degree) involving 10-19% of body surface with third degree burn of less than 10% or unspecified amount
948.11 Burn (any degree) involving 10-19% of body surface with third degree burn of 10-19%
948.20 Burn (any degree) involving 20-29% of body surface with third degree burn of less than 10% or unspecified amount
948.21 Burn (any degree) involving 20-29% of body surface with third degree burn of 10-19%
948.22 Burn (any degree) involving 20-29% of body surface with third degree burn of 20-29%
948.30 Burn (any degree) involving 30-39% of body surface with third degree burn of less than 10% or unspecified amount
948.31 Burn (any degree) involving 30-39% of body surface with third degree burn of 10-19%
948.32 Burn (any degree) involving 30-39% of body surface with third degree burn of 20-29%
948.33 Burn (any degree) involving 30-39% of body surface with third degree burn of 30-39%
948.40 Burn (any degree) involving 40-49% of body surface with third degree burn of less than 10% or unspecified amount
948.41 Burn (any degree) involving 40-49% of body surface with third degree burn of 10-19%
948.42 Burn (any degree) involving 40-49% of body surface with third degree burn of 20-29%
948.43 Burn (any degree) involving 40-49% of body surface with third degree burn of 30-39%
948.44 Burn (any degree) involving 40-49% of body surface with third degree burn of 40-49%

948.50 Burn (any degree) involving 50-59% of body surface with third degree burn of less than 10% or unspecified amount
948.51 Burn (any degree) involving 50-59% of body surface with third degree burn of 10-19%
948.52 Burn (any degree) involving 50-59% of body surface with third degree burn of 20-29%
948.53 Burn (any degree) involving 50-59% of body surface with third degree burn of 30-39%
948.54 Burn (any degree) involving 50-59% of body surface with third degree burn of 40-49%
948.55 Burn (any degree) involving 50-59% of body surface with third degree burn of 50-59%
948.60 Burn (any degree) involving 60-69% of body surface with third degree burn of less than 10% or unspecified amount
948.61 Burn (any degree) involving 60-69% of body surface with third degree burn of 10-19%
948.62 Burn (any degree) involving 60-69% of body surface with third degree burn of 20-29%
948.63 Burn (any degree) involving 60-69% of body surface with third degree burn of 30-39%
948.64 Burn (any degree) involving 60-69% of body surface with third degree burn of 40-49%
948.65 Burn (any degree) involving 60-69% of body surface with third degree burn of 50-59%
948.66 Burn (any degree) involving 60-69% of body surface with third degree burn of 60-69%
948.70 Burn (any degree) involving 70-79% of body surface with third degree burn of less than 10% or unspecified amount
948.71 Burn (any degree) involving 70-79% of body surface with third degree burn of 10-19%
948.72 Burn (any degree) involving 70-79% of body surface with third degree burn of 20-29%
948.73 Burn (any degree) involving 70-79% of body surface with third degree burn of 30-39%
948.74 Burn (any degree) involving 70-79% of body surface with third degree burn of 40-49%
948.75 Burn (any degree) involving 70-79% of body surface with third degree burn of 50-59%
948.76 Burn (any degree) involving 70-79% of body surface with third degree burn of 60-69%
948.77 Burn (any degree) involving 70-79% of body surface with third degree burn of 70-79%
948.80 Burn (any degree) involving 80-89% of body surface with third degree burn of less than 10% or unspecified amount
948.81 Burn (any degree) involving 80-89% of body surface with third degree burn of 10-19%
948.82 Burn (any degree) involving 80-89% of body surface with third degree burn of 20-29%
948.83 Burn (any degree) involving 80-89% of body surface with third degree burn of 30-39%
948.84 Burn (any degree) involving 80-89% of body surface with third degree burn of 40-49%
948.85 Burn (any degree) involving 80-89% of body surface with third degree burn of 50-59%
948.86 Burn (any degree) involving 80-89% of body surface with third degree burn of 60-69%
948.87 Burn (any degree) involving 80-89% of body surface with third degree burn of 70-79%
948.88 Burn (any degree) involving 80-89% of body surface with third degree burn of 80-89%
948.90 Burn (any degree) involving 90% or more of body surface with third degree burn of less than 10% or unspecified amount
948.91 Burn (any degree) involving 90% or more of body surface with third degree burn of 10-19%
948.92 Burn (any degree) involving 90% or more of body surface with third degree burn of 20-29%
948.93 Burn (any degree) involving 90% or more of body surface with third degree burn of 30-39%
948.94 Burn (any degree) involving 90% or more of body surface with third degree burn of 40-49%
948.95 Burn (any degree) involving 90% or more of body surface with third degree burn of 50-59%
948.96 Burn (any degree) involving 90% or more of body surface with third degree burn of 60-69%
948.97 Burn (any degree) involving 90% or more of body surface with third degree burn of 70-79%
948.98 Burn (any degree) involving 90% or more of body surface with third degree burn of 80-89%
948.99 Burn (any degree) involving 90% or more of body surface with third degree burn of 90% or more of body surface

ICD-9-CM Procedural

86.09 Other incision of skin and subcutaneous tissue

Destruction

17000-17004

17000 Destruction (eg, laser surgery, electrosurgery, cryosurgery, chemosurgery, surgical curettement), premalignant lesions (eg, actinic keratoses); first lesion
17003 second through 14 lesions, each (List separately in addition to code for first lesion)
17004 Destruction (eg, laser surgery, electrosurgery, cryosurgery, chemosurgery, surgical curettement), premalignant lesions (eg, actinic keratoses), 15 or more lesions

ICD-9-CM Diagnostic

095.8 Other specified forms of late symptomatic syphilis
232.0 Carcinoma in situ of skin of lip
232.1 Carcinoma in situ of eyelid, including canthus
232.2 Carcinoma in situ of skin of ear and external auditory canal
232.3 Carcinoma in situ of skin of other and unspecified parts of face ▽
232.4 Carcinoma in situ of scalp and skin of neck
232.5 Carcinoma in situ of skin of trunk, except scrotum
232.6 Carcinoma in situ of skin of upper limb, including shoulder
232.7 Carcinoma in situ of skin of lower limb, including hip
232.8 Carcinoma in situ of other specified sites of skin
232.9 Carcinoma in situ of skin, site unspecified ▽
233.5 Carcinoma in situ of penis ♂
233.6 Carcinoma in situ of other and unspecified male genital organs ▽ ♂
569.49 Other specified disorder of rectum and anus — (Use additional code for any associated fecal incontinence (787.60-787.63))
702.0 Actinic keratosis
702.8 Other specified dermatoses
V50.1 Other plastic surgery for unacceptable cosmetic appearance

ICD-9-CM Procedural

08.25 Destruction of lesion of eyelid
18.29 Excision or destruction of other lesion of external ear
21.32 Local excision or destruction of other lesion of nose
86.24 Chemosurgery of skin
86.3 Other local excision or destruction of lesion or tissue of skin and subcutaneous tissue

HCPCS Level II Supplies & Services

A4257 Replacement lens shield cartridge for use with laser skin piercing device, each

17106-17108

17106 Destruction of cutaneous vascular proliferative lesions (eg, laser technique); less than 10 sq cm
17107 10.0 to 50.0 sq cm
17108 over 50.0 sq cm

ICD-9-CM Diagnostic

216.1 Benign neoplasm of eyelid, including canthus
216.2 Benign neoplasm of ear and external auditory canal
216.3 Benign neoplasm of skin of other and unspecified parts of face ▽
216.4 Benign neoplasm of scalp and skin of neck
216.5 Benign neoplasm of skin of trunk, except scrotum
216.6 Benign neoplasm of skin of upper limb, including shoulder
216.7 Benign neoplasm of skin of lower limb, including hip
216.8 Benign neoplasm of other specified sites of skin
228.01 Hemangioma of skin and subcutaneous tissue
228.09 Hemangioma of other sites
228.1 Lymphangioma, any site
448.1 Nevus, non-neoplastic
448.9 Other and unspecified capillary diseases ▽
709.1 Vascular disorder of skin

747.60 Congenital anomaly of the peripheral vascular system, unspecified site ▽
757.32 Congenital vascular hamartomas
759.6 Other congenital hamartoses, not elsewhere classified

ICD-9-CM Procedural

08.25 Destruction of lesion of eyelid
18.29 Excision or destruction of other lesion of external ear
21.32 Local excision or destruction of other lesion of nose
86.3 Other local excision or destruction of lesion or tissue of skin and subcutaneous tissue

HCPCS Level II Supplies & Services

A4257 Replacement lens shield cartridge for use with laser skin piercing device, each

17110-17111

17110 Destruction (eg, laser surgery, electrosurgery, cryosurgery, chemosurgery, surgical curettement), of benign lesions other than skin tags or cutaneous vascular proliferative lesions; up to 14 lesions
17111 15 or more lesions

ICD-9-CM Diagnostic

078.0 Molluscum contagiosum
078.10 Viral warts, unspecified ▽
078.11 Condyloma acuminatum
078.12 Plantar wart
078.19 Other specified viral warts
216.0 Benign neoplasm of skin of lip
216.1 Benign neoplasm of eyelid, including canthus
216.2 Benign neoplasm of ear and external auditory canal
216.3 Benign neoplasm of skin of other and unspecified parts of face ▽
216.4 Benign neoplasm of scalp and skin of neck
216.5 Benign neoplasm of skin of trunk, except scrotum
216.6 Benign neoplasm of skin of upper limb, including shoulder
216.7 Benign neoplasm of skin of lower limb, including hip
216.8 Benign neoplasm of other specified sites of skin
692.75 Disseminated superficial actinic porokeratosis (DSAP)
695.3 Rosacea
702.11 Inflamed seborrheic keratosis
706.2 Sebaceous cyst
709.00 Dyschromia, unspecified ▽
709.3 Degenerative skin disorder

ICD-9-CM Procedural

08.25 Destruction of lesion of eyelid
18.29 Excision or destruction of other lesion of external ear
21.32 Local excision or destruction of other lesion of nose
49.39 Other local excision or destruction of lesion or tissue of anus
86.24 Chemosurgery of skin
86.3 Other local excision or destruction of lesion or tissue of skin and subcutaneous tissue

HCPCS Level II Supplies & Services

A4257 Replacement lens shield cartridge for use with laser skin piercing device, each

17250

17250 Chemical cauterization of granulation tissue (proud flesh, sinus or fistula)

ICD-9-CM Diagnostic

701.5 Other abnormal granulation tissue
909.3 Late effect of complications of surgical and medical care
998.30 Disruption of wound, unspecified ▽
998.33 Disruption of traumatic injury wound repair
998.59 Other postoperative infection — (Use additional code to identify infection)
998.6 Persistent postoperative fistula, not elsewhere classified
998.83 Non-healing surgical wound

ICD-9-CM Procedural

18.29 Excision or destruction of other lesion of external ear
86.24 Chemosurgery of skin
86.3 Other local excision or destruction of lesion or tissue of skin and subcutaneous tissue

17260-17266

17260 Destruction, malignant lesion (eg, laser surgery, electrosurgery, cryosurgery, chemosurgery, surgical curettement), trunk, arms or legs; lesion diameter 0.5 cm or less
17261 lesion diameter 0.6 to 1.0 cm
17262 lesion diameter 1.1 to 2.0 cm
17263 lesion diameter 2.1 to 3.0 cm
17264 lesion diameter 3.1 to 4.0 cm
17266 lesion diameter over 4.0 cm

ICD-9-CM Diagnostic

173.50 Unspecified malignant neoplasm of skin of trunk, except scrotum ▽
173.51 Basal cell carcinoma of skin of trunk, except scrotum
173.52 Squamous cell carcinoma of skin of trunk, except scrotum
173.59 Other specified malignant neoplasm of skin of trunk, except scrotum
173.60 Unspecified malignant neoplasm of skin of upper limb, including shoulder ▽
173.61 Basal cell carcinoma of skin of upper limb, including shoulder
173.62 Squamous cell carcinoma of skin of upper limb, including shoulder
173.69 Other specified malignant neoplasm of skin of upper limb, including shoulder
173.70 Unspecified malignant neoplasm of skin of lower limb, including hip ▽
173.71 Basal cell carcinoma of skin of lower limb, including hip
173.72 Squamous cell carcinoma of skin of lower limb, including hip
173.79 Other specified malignant neoplasm of skin of lower limb, including hip
209.33 Merkel cell carcinoma of the upper limb
209.34 Merkel cell carcinoma of the lower limb
209.35 Merkel cell carcinoma of the trunk
209.75 Secondary Merkel cell carcinoma
232.5 Carcinoma in situ of skin of trunk, except scrotum
232.6 Carcinoma in situ of skin of upper limb, including shoulder
232.7 Carcinoma in situ of skin of lower limb, including hip
238.2 Neoplasm of uncertain behavior of skin

ICD-9-CM Procedural

86.3 Other local excision or destruction of lesion or tissue of skin and subcutaneous tissue

HCPCS Level II Supplies & Services

A4305 Disposable drug delivery system, flow rate of 50 ml or greater per hour

17270-17276

17270 Destruction, malignant lesion (eg, laser surgery, electrosurgery, cryosurgery, chemosurgery, surgical curettement), scalp, neck, hands, feet, genitalia; lesion diameter 0.5 cm or less
17271 lesion diameter 0.6 to 1.0 cm
17272 lesion diameter 1.1 to 2.0 cm
17273 lesion diameter 2.1 to 3.0 cm
17274 lesion diameter 3.1 to 4.0 cm
17276 lesion diameter over 4.0 cm

ICD-9-CM Diagnostic

173.40 Unspecified malignant neoplasm of scalp and skin of neck ▽
173.41 Basal cell carcinoma of scalp and skin of neck
173.42 Squamous cell carcinoma of scalp and skin of neck
173.49 Other specified malignant neoplasm of scalp and skin of neck
173.60 Unspecified malignant neoplasm of skin of upper limb, including shoulder ▽
173.61 Basal cell carcinoma of skin of upper limb, including shoulder
173.62 Squamous cell carcinoma of skin of upper limb, including shoulder

[Resequenced code]
▽ Unspecified code
♀ Female diagnosis
☒ Manifestation code
♂ Male diagnosis

173.69 Other specified malignant neoplasm of skin of upper limb, including shoulder
173.70 Unspecified malignant neoplasm of skin of lower limb, including hip ▽
173.71 Basal cell carcinoma of skin of lower limb, including hip
173.72 Squamous cell carcinoma of skin of lower limb, including hip
173.79 Other specified malignant neoplasm of skin of lower limb, including hip
184.0 Malignant neoplasm of vagina ♀
184.1 Malignant neoplasm of labia majora ♀
184.2 Malignant neoplasm of labia minora ♀
184.3 Malignant neoplasm of clitoris ♀
184.4 Malignant neoplasm of vulva, unspecified site ▽ ♀
184.8 Malignant neoplasm of other specified sites of female genital organs ♀
187.1 Malignant neoplasm of prepuce ♂
187.2 Malignant neoplasm of glans penis ♂
187.3 Malignant neoplasm of body of penis ♂
187.4 Malignant neoplasm of penis, part unspecified ▽ ♂
187.7 Malignant neoplasm of scrotum ♂
187.8 Malignant neoplasm of other specified sites of male genital organs ♂
209.32 Merkel cell carcinoma of the scalp and neck
209.33 Merkel cell carcinoma of the upper limb
209.34 Merkel cell carcinoma of the lower limb
209.36 Merkel cell carcinoma of other sites
209.75 Secondary Merkel cell carcinoma
232.4 Carcinoma in situ of scalp and skin of neck
232.6 Carcinoma in situ of skin of upper limb, including shoulder
232.7 Carcinoma in situ of skin of lower limb, including hip
232.8 Carcinoma in situ of other specified sites of skin
233.30 Carcinoma in situ, unspecified female genital organ ▽ ♀
233.31 Carcinoma in situ, vagina ♀
233.32 Carcinoma in situ, vulva ♀
233.39 Carcinoma in situ, other female genital organ ♀
233.5 Carcinoma in situ of penis ♂
233.6 Carcinoma in situ of other and unspecified male genital organs ▽ ♂
236.3 Neoplasm of uncertain behavior of other and unspecified female genital organs ▽ ♀
236.6 Neoplasm of uncertain behavior of other and unspecified male genital organs ▽ ♂
238.2 Neoplasm of uncertain behavior of skin

ICD-9-CM Procedural

61.3 Excision or destruction of lesion or tissue of scrotum ♂
64.2 Local excision or destruction of lesion of penis ♂
71.3 Other local excision or destruction of vulva and perineum ♀
86.3 Other local excision or destruction of lesion or tissue of skin and subcutaneous tissue

HCPCS Level II Supplies & Services

A4305 Disposable drug delivery system, flow rate of 50 ml or greater per hour

17280-17286

17280 Destruction, malignant lesion (eg, laser surgery, electrosurgery, cryosurgery, chemosurgery, surgical curettement), face, ears, eyelids, nose, lips, mucous membrane; lesion diameter 0.5 cm or less
17281 lesion diameter 0.6 to 1.0 cm
17282 lesion diameter 1.1 to 2.0 cm
17283 lesion diameter 2.1 to 3.0 cm
17284 lesion diameter 3.1 to 4.0 cm
17286 lesion diameter over 4.0 cm

ICD-9-CM Diagnostic

140.0 Malignant neoplasm of upper lip, vermilion border
140.1 Malignant neoplasm of lower lip, vermilion border
140.3 Malignant neoplasm of upper lip, inner aspect
140.4 Malignant neoplasm of lower lip, inner aspect
140.5 Malignant neoplasm of lip, inner aspect, unspecified as to upper or lower ▽
140.6 Malignant neoplasm of commissure of lip
140.8 Malignant neoplasm of other sites of lip
143.0 Malignant neoplasm of upper gum
143.1 Malignant neoplasm of lower gum
143.8 Malignant neoplasm of other sites of gum
143.9 Malignant neoplasm of gum, unspecified site ▽
144.0 Malignant neoplasm of anterior portion of floor of mouth
144.1 Malignant neoplasm of lateral portion of floor of mouth
144.8 Malignant neoplasm of other sites of floor of mouth
145.0 Malignant neoplasm of cheek mucosa
145.1 Malignant neoplasm of vestibule of mouth
145.2 Malignant neoplasm of hard palate
145.3 Malignant neoplasm of soft palate
145.4 Malignant neoplasm of uvula
145.5 Malignant neoplasm of palate, unspecified ▽
145.6 Malignant neoplasm of retromolar area
145.8 Malignant neoplasm of other specified parts of mouth
145.9 Malignant neoplasm of mouth, unspecified site ▽
171.0 Malignant neoplasm of connective and other soft tissue of head, face, and neck
172.0 Malignant melanoma of skin of lip
172.1 Malignant melanoma of skin of eyelid, including canthus
172.2 Malignant melanoma of skin of ear and external auditory canal
172.3 Malignant melanoma of skin of other and unspecified parts of face ▽
173.00 Unspecified malignant neoplasm of skin of lip ▽
173.01 Basal cell carcinoma of skin of lip
173.02 Squamous cell carcinoma of skin of lip
173.09 Other specified malignant neoplasm of skin of lip
173.10 Unspecified malignant neoplasm of eyelid, including canthus ▽
173.11 Basal cell carcinoma of eyelid, including canthus
173.12 Squamous cell carcinoma of eyelid, including canthus
173.19 Other specified malignant neoplasm of eyelid, including canthus
173.20 Unspecified malignant neoplasm of skin of ear and external auditory canal ▽
173.21 Basal cell carcinoma of skin of ear and external auditory canal
173.22 Squamous cell carcinoma of skin of ear and external auditory canal
173.29 Other specified malignant neoplasm of skin of ear and external auditory canal
173.30 Unspecified malignant neoplasm of skin of other and unspecified parts of face ▽
173.31 Basal cell carcinoma of skin of other and unspecified parts of face
173.32 Squamous cell carcinoma of skin of other and unspecified parts of face
173.39 Other specified malignant neoplasm of skin of other and unspecified parts of face
198.2 Secondary malignant neoplasm of skin
198.89 Secondary malignant neoplasm of other specified sites
209.31 Merkel cell carcinoma of the face
209.75 Secondary Merkel cell carcinoma
232.0 Carcinoma in situ of skin of lip
232.1 Carcinoma in situ of eyelid, including canthus
232.2 Carcinoma in situ of skin of ear and external auditory canal
232.3 Carcinoma in situ of skin of other and unspecified parts of face ▽
235.1 Neoplasm of uncertain behavior of lip, oral cavity, and pharynx
238.2 Neoplasm of uncertain behavior of skin

ICD-9-CM Procedural

08.25 Destruction of lesion of eyelid
18.29 Excision or destruction of other lesion of external ear
21.32 Local excision or destruction of other lesion of nose
86.24 Chemosurgery of skin
86.3 Other local excision or destruction of lesion or tissue of skin and subcutaneous tissue

HCPCS Level II Supplies & Services

A4305	Disposable drug delivery system, flow rate of 50 ml or greater per hour

17311-17315

17311 Mohs micrographic technique, including removal of all gross tumor, surgical excision of tissue specimens, mapping, color coding of specimens, microscopic examination of specimens by the surgeon, and histopathologic preparation including routine stain(s) (eg, hematoxylin and eosin, toluidine blue), head, neck, hands, feet, genitalia, or any location with surgery directly involving muscle, cartilage, bone, tendon, major nerves, or vessels; first stage, up to 5 tissue blocks

17312 each additional stage after the first stage, up to 5 tissue blocks (List separately in addition to code for primary procedure)

17313 Mohs micrographic technique, including removal of all gross tumor, surgical excision of tissue specimens, mapping, color coding of specimens, microscopic examination of specimens by the surgeon, and histopathologic preparation including routine stain(s) (eg, hematoxylin and eosin, toluidine blue), of the trunk, arms, or legs; first stage, up to 5 tissue blocks

17314 each additional stage after the first stage, up to 5 tissue blocks (List separately in addition to code for primary procedure)

17315 Mohs micrographic technique, including removal of all gross tumor, surgical excision of tissue specimens, mapping, color coding of specimens, microscopic examination of specimens by the surgeon, and histopathologic preparation including routine stain(s) (eg, hematoxylin and eosin, toluidine blue), each additional block after the first 5 tissue blocks, any stage (List separately in addition to code for primary procedure)

ICD-9-CM Diagnostic

140.0	Malignant neoplasm of upper lip, vermilion border
140.1	Malignant neoplasm of lower lip, vermilion border
140.3	Malignant neoplasm of upper lip, inner aspect
140.4	Malignant neoplasm of lower lip, inner aspect
140.5	Malignant neoplasm of lip, inner aspect, unspecified as to upper or lower ▽
140.6	Malignant neoplasm of commissure of lip
140.8	Malignant neoplasm of other sites of lip
143.0	Malignant neoplasm of upper gum
143.1	Malignant neoplasm of lower gum
143.8	Malignant neoplasm of other sites of gum
144.0	Malignant neoplasm of anterior portion of floor of mouth
144.1	Malignant neoplasm of lateral portion of floor of mouth
144.8	Malignant neoplasm of other sites of floor of mouth
145.0	Malignant neoplasm of cheek mucosa
145.1	Malignant neoplasm of vestibule of mouth
145.2	Malignant neoplasm of hard palate
145.3	Malignant neoplasm of soft palate
145.4	Malignant neoplasm of uvula
145.5	Malignant neoplasm of palate, unspecified ▽
145.6	Malignant neoplasm of retromolar area
145.8	Malignant neoplasm of other specified parts of mouth
145.9	Malignant neoplasm of mouth, unspecified site ▽
171.0	Malignant neoplasm of connective and other soft tissue of head, face, and neck
172.0	Malignant melanoma of skin of lip
172.1	Malignant melanoma of skin of eyelid, including canthus
172.2	Malignant melanoma of skin of ear and external auditory canal
172.3	Malignant melanoma of skin of other and unspecified parts of face ▽
172.4	Malignant melanoma of skin of scalp and neck
172.5	Malignant melanoma of skin of trunk, except scrotum
172.6	Malignant melanoma of skin of upper limb, including shoulder
172.7	Malignant melanoma of skin of lower limb, including hip
172.8	Malignant melanoma of other specified sites of skin
172.9	Melanoma of skin, site unspecified ▽
173.00	Unspecified malignant neoplasm of skin of lip ▽
173.01	Basal cell carcinoma of skin of lip
173.02	Squamous cell carcinoma of skin of lip
173.09	Other specified malignant neoplasm of skin of lip
173.10	Unspecified malignant neoplasm of eyelid, including canthus ▽
173.11	Basal cell carcinoma of eyelid, including canthus
173.12	Squamous cell carcinoma of eyelid, including canthus
173.19	Other specified malignant neoplasm of eyelid, including canthus
173.20	Unspecified malignant neoplasm of skin of ear and external auditory canal ▽
173.21	Basal cell carcinoma of skin of ear and external auditory canal
173.22	Squamous cell carcinoma of skin of ear and external auditory canal
173.29	Other specified malignant neoplasm of skin of ear and external auditory canal
173.30	Unspecified malignant neoplasm of skin of other and unspecified parts of face ▽
173.31	Basal cell carcinoma of skin of other and unspecified parts of face
173.32	Squamous cell carcinoma of skin of other and unspecified parts of face
173.39	Other specified malignant neoplasm of skin of other and unspecified parts of face
173.40	Unspecified malignant neoplasm of scalp and skin of neck ▽
173.41	Basal cell carcinoma of scalp and skin of neck
173.42	Squamous cell carcinoma of scalp and skin of neck
173.49	Other specified malignant neoplasm of scalp and skin of neck
173.50	Unspecified malignant neoplasm of skin of trunk, except scrotum ▽
173.51	Basal cell carcinoma of skin of trunk, except scrotum
173.52	Squamous cell carcinoma of skin of trunk, except scrotum
173.59	Other specified malignant neoplasm of skin of trunk, except scrotum
173.60	Unspecified malignant neoplasm of skin of upper limb, including shoulder ▽
173.61	Basal cell carcinoma of skin of upper limb, including shoulder
173.62	Squamous cell carcinoma of skin of upper limb, including shoulder
173.69	Other specified malignant neoplasm of skin of upper limb, including shoulder
173.70	Unspecified malignant neoplasm of skin of lower limb, including hip ▽
173.71	Basal cell carcinoma of skin of lower limb, including hip
173.72	Squamous cell carcinoma of skin of lower limb, including hip
173.79	Other specified malignant neoplasm of skin of lower limb, including hip
173.80	Unspecified malignant neoplasm of other specified sites of skin ▽
173.81	Basal cell carcinoma of other specified sites of skin
173.82	Squamous cell carcinoma of other specified sites of skin
173.89	Other specified malignant neoplasm of other specified sites of skin
173.90	Unspecified malignant neoplasm of skin, site unspecified ▽
173.91	Basal cell carcinoma of skin, site unspecified
173.92	Squamous cell carcinoma of skin, site unspecified
173.99	Other specified malignant neoplasm of skin, site unspecified
184.0	Malignant neoplasm of vagina ♀
184.1	Malignant neoplasm of labia majora ♀
184.2	Malignant neoplasm of labia minora ♀
184.3	Malignant neoplasm of clitoris ♀
184.8	Malignant neoplasm of other specified sites of female genital organs ♀
184.9	Malignant neoplasm of female genital organ, site unspecified ▽ ♀
187.1	Malignant neoplasm of prepuce ♂
187.2	Malignant neoplasm of glans penis ♂
187.3	Malignant neoplasm of body of penis ♂
187.7	Malignant neoplasm of scrotum ♂
187.8	Malignant neoplasm of other specified sites of male genital organs ♂
195.0	Malignant neoplasm of head, face, and neck
195.1	Malignant neoplasm of thorax
195.2	Malignant neoplasm of abdomen
195.3	Malignant neoplasm of pelvis
195.4	Malignant neoplasm of upper limb
195.8	Malignant neoplasm of other specified sites
209.31	Merkel cell carcinoma of the face
209.32	Merkel cell carcinoma of the scalp and neck

209.33 Merkel cell carcinoma of the upper limb
209.34 Merkel cell carcinoma of the lower limb
209.35 Merkel cell carcinoma of the trunk
209.36 Merkel cell carcinoma of other sites
209.75 Secondary Merkel cell carcinoma
232.0 Carcinoma in situ of skin of lip
232.1 Carcinoma in situ of eyelid, including canthus
232.2 Carcinoma in situ of skin of ear and external auditory canal
232.4 Carcinoma in situ of scalp and skin of neck
232.5 Carcinoma in situ of skin of trunk, except scrotum
232.8 Carcinoma in situ of other specified sites of skin
233.30 Carcinoma in situ, unspecified female genital organ ▽ ♀
233.31 Carcinoma in situ, vagina ♀
233.32 Carcinoma in situ, vulva ♀
233.39 Carcinoma in situ, other female genital organ ♀
233.5 Carcinoma in situ of penis ♂
233.6 Carcinoma in situ of other and unspecified male genital organs ▽ ♂

ICD-9-CM Procedural

86.24 Chemosurgery of skin

HCPCS Level II Supplies & Services

A4305 Disposable drug delivery system, flow rate of 50 ml or greater per hour

17340-17360

17340 Cryotherapy (CO2 slush, liquid N2) for acne
17360 Chemical exfoliation for acne (eg, acne paste, acid)

ICD-9-CM Diagnostic

695.3 Rosacea
706.0 Acne varioliformis
706.1 Other acne

ICD-9-CM Procedural

86.24 Chemosurgery of skin
86.3 Other local excision or destruction of lesion or tissue of skin and subcutaneous tissue

17380

17380 Electrolysis epilation, each 30 minutes

ICD-9-CM Diagnostic

704.1 Hirsutism
757.4 Specified congenital anomalies of hair
V50.1 Other plastic surgery for unacceptable cosmetic appearance

ICD-9-CM Procedural

86.92 Electrolysis and other epilation of skin

Breast

19000-19001

19000 Puncture aspiration of cyst of breast;
19001 each additional cyst (List separately in addition to code for primary procedure)

ICD-9-CM Diagnostic

610.0 Solitary cyst of breast
610.1 Diffuse cystic mastopathy
610.8 Other specified benign mammary dysplasias
611.5 Galactocele
611.72 Lump or mass in breast
611.89 Other specified disorders of breast
793.80 Unspecified abnormal mammogram ▽
793.89 Other (abnormal) findings on radiological examination of breast

ICD-9-CM Procedural

85.91 Aspiration of breast

19020

19020 Mastotomy with exploration or drainage of abscess, deep

ICD-9-CM Diagnostic

611.0 Inflammatory disease of breast
675.10 Abscess of breast associated with childbirth, unspecified as to episode of care ▽ ♀
675.11 Abscess of breast associated with childbirth, delivered, with or without mention of antepartum condition ♀
675.12 Abscess of breast associated with childbirth, delivered, with mention of postpartum complication ♀
675.13 Abscess of breast, antepartum ♀
675.14 Abscess of breast, postpartum condition or complication ♀
996.69 Infection and inflammatory reaction due to other internal prosthetic device, implant, and graft — (Use additional code to identify specified infections)
998.51 Infected postoperative seroma — (Use additional code to identify organism)
998.59 Other postoperative infection — (Use additional code to identify infection)

ICD-9-CM Procedural

85.0 Mastotomy

19030

19030 Injection procedure only for mammary ductogram or galactogram

ICD-9-CM Diagnostic

217 Benign neoplasm of breast
610.0 Solitary cyst of breast
610.1 Diffuse cystic mastopathy
610.4 Mammary duct ectasia
610.8 Other specified benign mammary dysplasias
611.0 Inflammatory disease of breast
611.1 Hypertrophy of breast
611.5 Galactocele
611.6 Galactorrhea not associated with childbirth
611.71 Mastodynia
611.72 Lump or mass in breast
611.79 Other sign and symptom in breast
611.89 Other specified disorders of breast

ICD-9-CM Procedural

87.35 Contrast radiogram of mammary ducts

19081-19086

19081 Biopsy, breast, with placement of breast localization device(s) (eg, clip, metallic pellet), when performed, and imaging of the biopsy specimen, when performed, percutaneous; first lesion, including stereotactic guidance
19082 each additional lesion, including stereotactic guidance (List separately in addition to code for primary procedure)
19083 Biopsy, breast, with placement of breast localization device(s) (eg, clip, metallic pellet), when performed, and imaging of the biopsy specimen, when performed, percutaneous; first lesion, including ultrasound guidance
19084 each additional lesion, including ultrasound guidance (List separately in addition to code for primary procedure)
19085 Biopsy, breast, with placement of breast localization device(s) (eg, clip, metallic pellet), when performed, and imaging of the biopsy specimen, when performed, percutaneous; first lesion, including magnetic resonance guidance
19086 each additional lesion, including magnetic resonance guidance (List separately in addition to code for primary procedure)

ICD-9-CM Diagnostic

172.5 Malignant melanoma of skin of trunk, except scrotum

173.50 Unspecified malignant neoplasm of skin of trunk, except scrotum ▽

173.51 Basal cell carcinoma of skin of trunk, except scrotum

173.52 Squamous cell carcinoma of skin of trunk, except scrotum

173.59 Other specified malignant neoplasm of skin of trunk, except scrotum

174.0 Malignant neoplasm of nipple and areola of female breast — (Use additional code to identify estrogen receptor status: V86.0-V86.1) ♀

174.1 Malignant neoplasm of central portion of female breast — (Use additional code to identify estrogen receptor status: V86.0-V86.1) ♀

174.2 Malignant neoplasm of upper-inner quadrant of female breast — (Use additional code to identify estrogen receptor status: V86.0-V86.1) ♀

174.3 Malignant neoplasm of lower-inner quadrant of female breast — (Use additional code to identify estrogen receptor status: V86.0-V86.1) ♀

174.4 Malignant neoplasm of upper-outer quadrant of female breast — (Use additional code to identify estrogen receptor status: V86.0-V86.1) ♀

174.5 Malignant neoplasm of lower-outer quadrant of female breast — (Use additional code to identify estrogen receptor status: V86.0-V86.1) ♀

174.6 Malignant neoplasm of axillary tail of female breast — (Use additional code to identify estrogen receptor status: V86.0-V86.1) ♀

174.8 Malignant neoplasm of other specified sites of female breast — (Use additional code to identify estrogen receptor status: V86.0-V86.1) ♀

174.9 Malignant neoplasm of breast (female), unspecified site — (Use additional code to identify estrogen receptor status: V86.0-V86.1) ▽ ♀

175.0 Malignant neoplasm of nipple and areola of male breast — (Use additional code to identify estrogen receptor status: V86.0-V86.1) ♂

175.9 Malignant neoplasm of other and unspecified sites of male breast — (Use additional code to identify estrogen receptor status: V86.0-V86.1) ▽ ♂

198.2 Secondary malignant neoplasm of skin

198.81 Secondary malignant neoplasm of breast

232.5 Carcinoma in situ of skin of trunk, except scrotum

238.2 Neoplasm of uncertain behavior of skin

238.3 Neoplasm of uncertain behavior of breast

239.2 Neoplasms of unspecified nature of bone, soft tissue, and skin

239.3 Neoplasm of unspecified nature of breast

610.0 Solitary cyst of breast

610.1 Diffuse cystic mastopathy

610.2 Fibroadenosis of breast

610.3 Fibrosclerosis of breast

610.4 Mammary duct ectasia

610.8 Other specified benign mammary dysplasias

610.9 Unspecified benign mammary dysplasia ▽

611.0 Inflammatory disease of breast

611.2 Fissure of nipple

611.3 Fat necrosis of breast — (Code first breast necrosis due to breast graft: 996.79)

611.5 Galactocele

611.72 Lump or mass in breast

611.79 Other sign and symptom in breast

611.89 Other specified disorders of breast

611.9 Unspecified breast disorder ▽

ICD-9-CM Procedural

85.11 Closed (percutaneous) (needle) biopsy of breast

19100-19101

19100 Biopsy of breast; percutaneous, needle core, not using imaging guidance (separate procedure)

19101 open, incisional

ICD-9-CM Diagnostic

174.0 Malignant neoplasm of nipple and areola of female breast — (Use additional code to identify estrogen receptor status: V86.0-V86.1) ♀

174.1 Malignant neoplasm of central portion of female breast — (Use additional code to identify estrogen receptor status: V86.0-V86.1) ♀

174.2 Malignant neoplasm of upper-inner quadrant of female breast — (Use additional code to identify estrogen receptor status: V86.0-V86.1) ♀

174.3 Malignant neoplasm of lower-inner quadrant of female breast — (Use additional code to identify estrogen receptor status: V86.0-V86.1) ♀

174.4 Malignant neoplasm of upper-outer quadrant of female breast — (Use additional code to identify estrogen receptor status: V86.0-V86.1) ♀

174.5 Malignant neoplasm of lower-outer quadrant of female breast — (Use additional code to identify estrogen receptor status: V86.0-V86.1) ♀

174.6 Malignant neoplasm of axillary tail of female breast — (Use additional code to identify estrogen receptor status: V86.0-V86.1) ♀

174.8 Malignant neoplasm of other specified sites of female breast — (Use additional code to identify estrogen receptor status: V86.0-V86.1) ♀

175.0 Malignant neoplasm of nipple and areola of male breast — (Use additional code to identify estrogen receptor status: V86.0-V86.1) ♂

175.9 Malignant neoplasm of other and unspecified sites of male breast — (Use additional code to identify estrogen receptor status: V86.0-V86.1) ▽ ♂

198.81 Secondary malignant neoplasm of breast

217 Benign neoplasm of breast

233.0 Carcinoma in situ of breast

238.3 Neoplasm of uncertain behavior of breast

239.3 Neoplasm of unspecified nature of breast

610.0 Solitary cyst of breast

610.1 Diffuse cystic mastopathy

610.2 Fibroadenosis of breast

610.3 Fibrosclerosis of breast

610.8 Other specified benign mammary dysplasias

611.0 Inflammatory disease of breast

611.72 Lump or mass in breast

611.89 Other specified disorders of breast

793.80 Unspecified abnormal mammogram ▽

793.81 Mammographic microcalcification

793.89 Other (abnormal) findings on radiological examination of breast

ICD-9-CM Procedural

85.11 Closed (percutaneous) (needle) biopsy of breast

85.12 Open biopsy of breast

87.37 Other mammography

19105

19105 Ablation, cryosurgical, of fibroadenoma, including ultrasound guidance, each fibroadenoma

ICD-9-CM Diagnostic

217 Benign neoplasm of breast

ICD-9-CM Procedural

85.20 Excision or destruction of breast tissue, not otherwise specified

85.21 Local excision of lesion of breast

19110

19110 Nipple exploration, with or without excision of a solitary lactiferous duct or a papilloma lactiferous duct

ICD-9-CM Diagnostic

174.0 Malignant neoplasm of nipple and areola of female breast — (Use additional code to identify estrogen receptor status: V86.0-V86.1) ♀

174.8 Malignant neoplasm of other specified sites of female breast — (Use additional code to identify estrogen receptor status: V86.0-V86.1) ♀

217 Benign neoplasm of breast

233.0 Carcinoma in situ of breast

238.3 Neoplasm of uncertain behavior of breast
239.3 Neoplasm of unspecified nature of breast
610.0 Solitary cyst of breast
610.4 Mammary duct ectasia
611.0 Inflammatory disease of breast
611.5 Galactocele
611.72 Lump or mass in breast
611.79 Other sign and symptom in breast
611.89 Other specified disorders of breast
757.6 Specified congenital anomalies of breast

ICD-9-CM Procedural

85.0 Mastotomy
85.20 Excision or destruction of breast tissue, not otherwise specified
85.25 Excision of nipple

19112

19112 Excision of lactiferous duct fistula

ICD-9-CM Diagnostic

611.0 Inflammatory disease of breast
675.10 Abscess of breast associated with childbirth, unspecified as to episode of care ▼ ♀
675.11 Abscess of breast associated with childbirth, delivered, with or without mention of antepartum condition ♀
675.12 Abscess of breast associated with childbirth, delivered, with mention of postpartum complication ♀
675.13 Abscess of breast, antepartum ♀
675.14 Abscess of breast, postpartum condition or complication ♀

ICD-9-CM Procedural

85.20 Excision or destruction of breast tissue, not otherwise specified

19120

19120 Excision of cyst, fibroadenoma, or other benign or malignant tumor, aberrant breast tissue, duct lesion, nipple or areolar lesion (except 19300), open, male or female, 1 or more lesions

ICD-9-CM Diagnostic

174.0 Malignant neoplasm of nipple and areola of female breast — (Use additional code to identify estrogen receptor status: V86.0-V86.1) ♀
174.1 Malignant neoplasm of central portion of female breast — (Use additional code to identify estrogen receptor status: V86.0-V86.1) ♀
174.2 Malignant neoplasm of upper-inner quadrant of female breast — (Use additional code to identify estrogen receptor status: V86.0-V86.1) ♀
174.3 Malignant neoplasm of lower-inner quadrant of female breast — (Use additional code to identify estrogen receptor status: V86.0-V86.1) ♀
174.4 Malignant neoplasm of upper-outer quadrant of female breast — (Use additional code to identify estrogen receptor status: V86.0-V86.1) ♀
174.5 Malignant neoplasm of lower-outer quadrant of female breast — (Use additional code to identify estrogen receptor status: V86.0-V86.1) ♀
174.6 Malignant neoplasm of axillary tail of female breast — (Use additional code to identify estrogen receptor status: V86.0-V86.1) ♀
174.8 Malignant neoplasm of other specified sites of female breast — (Use additional code to identify estrogen receptor status: V86.0-V86.1) ♀
175.0 Malignant neoplasm of nipple and areola of male breast — (Use additional code to identify estrogen receptor status: V86.0-V86.1) ♂
175.9 Malignant neoplasm of other and unspecified sites of male breast — (Use additional code to identify estrogen receptor status: V86.0-V86.1) ▼ ♂
198.81 Secondary malignant neoplasm of breast
217 Benign neoplasm of breast
233.0 Carcinoma in situ of breast
238.3 Neoplasm of uncertain behavior of breast
239.3 Neoplasm of unspecified nature of breast
610.0 Solitary cyst of breast
610.1 Diffuse cystic mastopathy
610.2 Fibroadenosis of breast
610.3 Fibrosclerosis of breast
610.4 Mammary duct ectasia
610.8 Other specified benign mammary dysplasias
611.0 Inflammatory disease of breast
611.72 Lump or mass in breast
611.79 Other sign and symptom in breast
611.89 Other specified disorders of breast

ICD-9-CM Procedural

85.20 Excision or destruction of breast tissue, not otherwise specified
85.21 Local excision of lesion of breast
85.24 Excision of ectopic breast tissue
85.25 Excision of nipple

HCPCS Level II Supplies & Services

A4280 Adhesive skin support attachment for use with external breast prosthesis, each

19125-19126

19125 Excision of breast lesion identified by preoperative placement of radiological marker, open; single lesion
19126 each additional lesion separately identified by a preoperative radiological marker (List separately in addition to code for primary procedure)

ICD-9-CM Diagnostic

174.0 Malignant neoplasm of nipple and areola of female breast — (Use additional code to identify estrogen receptor status: V86.0-V86.1) ♀
174.1 Malignant neoplasm of central portion of female breast — (Use additional code to identify estrogen receptor status: V86.0-V86.1) ♀
174.2 Malignant neoplasm of upper-inner quadrant of female breast — (Use additional code to identify estrogen receptor status: V86.0-V86.1) ♀
174.3 Malignant neoplasm of lower-inner quadrant of female breast — (Use additional code to identify estrogen receptor status: V86.0-V86.1) ♀
174.4 Malignant neoplasm of upper-outer quadrant of female breast — (Use additional code to identify estrogen receptor status: V86.0-V86.1) ♀
174.5 Malignant neoplasm of lower-outer quadrant of female breast — (Use additional code to identify estrogen receptor status: V86.0-V86.1) ♀
174.6 Malignant neoplasm of axillary tail of female breast — (Use additional code to identify estrogen receptor status: V86.0-V86.1) ♀
174.8 Malignant neoplasm of other specified sites of female breast — (Use additional code to identify estrogen receptor status: V86.0-V86.1) ♀
175.0 Malignant neoplasm of nipple and areola of male breast — (Use additional code to identify estrogen receptor status: V86.0-V86.1) ♂
175.9 Malignant neoplasm of other and unspecified sites of male breast — (Use additional code to identify estrogen receptor status: V86.0-V86.1) ▼ ♂
198.81 Secondary malignant neoplasm of breast
217 Benign neoplasm of breast
233.0 Carcinoma in situ of breast
238.3 Neoplasm of uncertain behavior of breast
239.3 Neoplasm of unspecified nature of breast
610.0 Solitary cyst of breast
610.1 Diffuse cystic mastopathy
610.3 Fibrosclerosis of breast
611.0 Inflammatory disease of breast
611.72 Lump or mass in breast
611.79 Other sign and symptom in breast
611.89 Other specified disorders of breast
793.81 Mammographic microcalcification

793.89 Other (abnormal) findings on radiological examination of breast

ICD-9-CM Procedural

85.21 Local excision of lesion of breast

HCPCS Level II Supplies & Services

A4305 Disposable drug delivery system, flow rate of 50 ml or greater per hour

19260-19272

19260 Excision of chest wall tumor including ribs
19271 Excision of chest wall tumor involving ribs, with plastic reconstruction; without mediastinal lymphadenectomy
19272 with mediastinal lymphadenectomy

ICD-9-CM Diagnostic

170.3 Malignant neoplasm of ribs, sternum, and clavicle
171.4 Malignant neoplasm of connective and other soft tissue of thorax
195.1 Malignant neoplasm of thorax
196.1 Secondary and unspecified malignant neoplasm of intrathoracic lymph nodes
198.2 Secondary malignant neoplasm of skin
198.5 Secondary malignant neoplasm of bone and bone marrow
198.81 Secondary malignant neoplasm of breast
198.89 Secondary malignant neoplasm of other specified sites
209.73 Secondary neuroendocrine tumor of bone
213.3 Benign neoplasm of ribs, sternum, and clavicle
214.8 Lipoma of other specified sites
229.8 Benign neoplasm of other specified sites
234.8 Carcinoma in situ of other specified sites
238.0 Neoplasm of uncertain behavior of bone and articular cartilage
238.1 Neoplasm of uncertain behavior of connective and other soft tissue
239.2 Neoplasms of unspecified nature of bone, soft tissue, and skin

ICD-9-CM Procedural

34.4 Excision or destruction of lesion of chest wall
40.3 Regional lymph node excision
40.59 Radical excision of other lymph nodes
77.61 Local excision of lesion or tissue of scapula, clavicle, and thorax (ribs and sternum)

19281-19288

19281 Placement of breast localization device(s) (eg, clip, metallic pellet, wire/needle, radioactive seeds), percutaneous; first lesion, including mammographic guidance
19282 each additional lesion, including mammographic guidance (List separately in addition to code for primary procedure)
19283 Placement of breast localization device(s) (eg, clip, metallic pellet, wire/needle, radioactive seeds), percutaneous; first lesion, including stereotactic guidance
19284 each additional lesion, including stereotactic guidance (List separately in addition to code for primary procedure)
19285 Placement of breast localization device(s) (eg, clip, metallic pellet, wire/needle, radioactive seeds), percutaneous; first lesion, including ultrasound guidance
19286 each additional lesion, including ultrasound guidance (List separately in addition to code for primary procedure)
19287 Placement of breast localization device(s) (eg clip, metallic pellet, wire/needle, radioactive seeds), percutaneous; first lesion, including magnetic resonance guidance
19288 each additional lesion, including magnetic resonance guidance (List separately in addition to code for primary procedure)

ICD-9-CM Diagnostic

172.5 Malignant melanoma of skin of trunk, except scrotum
173.50 Unspecified malignant neoplasm of skin of trunk, except scrotum ▽
173.51 Basal cell carcinoma of skin of trunk, except scrotum
173.52 Squamous cell carcinoma of skin of trunk, except scrotum
173.59 Other specified malignant neoplasm of skin of trunk, except scrotum
174.0 Malignant neoplasm of nipple and areola of female breast — (Use additional code to identify estrogen receptor status: V86.0-V86.1) ♀
174.1 Malignant neoplasm of central portion of female breast — (Use additional code to identify estrogen receptor status: V86.0-V86.1) ♀
174.2 Malignant neoplasm of upper-inner quadrant of female breast — (Use additional code to identify estrogen receptor status: V86.0-V86.1) ♀
174.3 Malignant neoplasm of lower-inner quadrant of female breast — (Use additional code to identify estrogen receptor status: V86.0-V86.1) ♀
174.4 Malignant neoplasm of upper-outer quadrant of female breast — (Use additional code to identify estrogen receptor status: V86.0-V86.1) ♀
174.5 Malignant neoplasm of lower-outer quadrant of female breast — (Use additional code to identify estrogen receptor status: V86.0-V86.1) ♀
174.6 Malignant neoplasm of axillary tail of female breast — (Use additional code to identify estrogen receptor status: V86.0-V86.1) ♀
174.8 Malignant neoplasm of other specified sites of female breast — (Use additional code to identify estrogen receptor status: V86.0-V86.1) ♀
174.9 Malignant neoplasm of breast (female), unspecified site — (Use additional code to identify estrogen receptor status: V86.0-V86.1) ▽ ♀
175.0 Malignant neoplasm of nipple and areola of male breast — (Use additional code to identify estrogen receptor status: V86.0-V86.1) ♂
175.9 Malignant neoplasm of other and unspecified sites of male breast — (Use additional code to identify estrogen receptor status: V86.0-V86.1) ▽ ♂
198.2 Secondary malignant neoplasm of skin
198.81 Secondary malignant neoplasm of breast
232.5 Carcinoma in situ of skin of trunk, except scrotum
238.2 Neoplasm of uncertain behavior of skin
238.3 Neoplasm of uncertain behavior of breast
239.2 Neoplasms of unspecified nature of bone, soft tissue, and skin
239.3 Neoplasm of unspecified nature of breast
610.0 Solitary cyst of breast
610.1 Diffuse cystic mastopathy
610.2 Fibroadenosis of breast
610.3 Fibrosclerosis of breast
610.4 Mammary duct ectasia
610.8 Other specified benign mammary dysplasias
610.9 Unspecified benign mammary dysplasia ▽
611.0 Inflammatory disease of breast
611.2 Fissure of nipple
611.3 Fat necrosis of breast — (Code first breast necrosis due to breast graft: 996.79)
611.5 Galactocele
611.72 Lump or mass in breast
611.79 Other sign and symptom in breast
611.89 Other specified disorders of breast
611.9 Unspecified breast disorder ▽

ICD-9-CM Procedural

85.99 Other operations on the breast

19296-19297

19296 Placement of radiotherapy afterloading expandable catheter (single or multichannel) into the breast for interstitial radioelement application following partial mastectomy, includes imaging guidance; on date separate from partial mastectomy
19297 concurrent with partial mastectomy (List separately in addition to code for primary procedure)

ICD-9-CM Diagnostic

174.0 Malignant neoplasm of nipple and areola of female breast — (Use additional code to identify estrogen receptor status: V86.0-V86.1) ♀
174.1 Malignant neoplasm of central portion of female breast — (Use additional code to identify estrogen receptor status: V86.0-V86.1) ♀

174.2 Malignant neoplasm of upper-inner quadrant of female breast — (Use additional code to identify estrogen receptor status: V86.0-V86.1) ♀
174.3 Malignant neoplasm of lower-inner quadrant of female breast — (Use additional code to identify estrogen receptor status: V86.0-V86.1) ♀
174.4 Malignant neoplasm of upper-outer quadrant of female breast — (Use additional code to identify estrogen receptor status: V86.0-V86.1) ♀
174.5 Malignant neoplasm of lower-outer quadrant of female breast — (Use additional code to identify estrogen receptor status: V86.0-V86.1) ♀
174.6 Malignant neoplasm of axillary tail of female breast — (Use additional code to identify estrogen receptor status: V86.0-V86.1) ♀
174.8 Malignant neoplasm of other specified sites of female breast — (Use additional code to identify estrogen receptor status: V86.0-V86.1) ♀
175.0 Malignant neoplasm of nipple and areola of male breast — (Use additional code to identify estrogen receptor status: V86.0-V86.1) ♂
175.9 Malignant neoplasm of other and unspecified sites of male breast — (Use additional code to identify estrogen receptor status: V86.0-V86.1) ▽ ♂
196.3 Secondary and unspecified malignant neoplasm of lymph nodes of axilla and upper limb
198.81 Secondary malignant neoplasm of breast
233.0 Carcinoma in situ of breast
238.3 Neoplasm of uncertain behavior of breast
239.3 Neoplasm of unspecified nature of breast

ICD-9-CM Procedural

85.0 Mastotomy
92.27 Implantation or insertion of radioactive elements

19298

19298 Placement of radiotherapy afterloading brachytherapy catheters (multiple tube and button type) into the breast for interstitial radioelement application following (at the time of or subsequent to) partial mastectomy, includes imaging guidance

ICD-9-CM Diagnostic

174.0 Malignant neoplasm of nipple and areola of female breast — (Use additional code to identify estrogen receptor status: V86.0-V86.1) ♀
174.1 Malignant neoplasm of central portion of female breast — (Use additional code to identify estrogen receptor status: V86.0-V86.1) ♀
174.2 Malignant neoplasm of upper-inner quadrant of female breast — (Use additional code to identify estrogen receptor status: V86.0-V86.1) ♀
174.3 Malignant neoplasm of lower-inner quadrant of female breast — (Use additional code to identify estrogen receptor status: V86.0-V86.1) ♀
174.4 Malignant neoplasm of upper-outer quadrant of female breast — (Use additional code to identify estrogen receptor status: V86.0-V86.1) ♀
174.5 Malignant neoplasm of lower-outer quadrant of female breast — (Use additional code to identify estrogen receptor status: V86.0-V86.1) ♀
174.6 Malignant neoplasm of axillary tail of female breast — (Use additional code to identify estrogen receptor status: V86.0-V86.1) ♀
174.8 Malignant neoplasm of other specified sites of female breast — (Use additional code to identify estrogen receptor status: V86.0-V86.1) ♀
175.0 Malignant neoplasm of nipple and areola of male breast — (Use additional code to identify estrogen receptor status: V86.0-V86.1) ♂
175.9 Malignant neoplasm of other and unspecified sites of male breast — (Use additional code to identify estrogen receptor status: V86.0-V86.1) ▽ ♂
196.3 Secondary and unspecified malignant neoplasm of lymph nodes of axilla and upper limb
198.81 Secondary malignant neoplasm of breast
238.3 Neoplasm of uncertain behavior of breast
239.3 Neoplasm of unspecified nature of breast

ICD-9-CM Procedural

85.0 Mastotomy
92.27 Implantation or insertion of radioactive elements

19300

19300 Mastectomy for gynecomastia

ICD-9-CM Diagnostic

611.1 Hypertrophy of breast

ICD-9-CM Procedural

85.31 Unilateral reduction mammoplasty
85.32 Bilateral reduction mammoplasty
85.34 Other unilateral subcutaneous mammectomy
85.36 Other bilateral subcutaneous mammectomy

19301-19302

19301 Mastectomy, partial (eg, lumpectomy, tylectomy, quadrantectomy, segmentectomy);
19302 with axillary lymphadenectomy

ICD-9-CM Diagnostic

174.0 Malignant neoplasm of nipple and areola of female breast — (Use additional code to identify estrogen receptor status: V86.0-V86.1) ♀
174.1 Malignant neoplasm of central portion of female breast — (Use additional code to identify estrogen receptor status: V86.0-V86.1) ♀
174.2 Malignant neoplasm of upper-inner quadrant of female breast — (Use additional code to identify estrogen receptor status: V86.0-V86.1) ♀
174.3 Malignant neoplasm of lower-inner quadrant of female breast — (Use additional code to identify estrogen receptor status: V86.0-V86.1) ♀
174.4 Malignant neoplasm of upper-outer quadrant of female breast — (Use additional code to identify estrogen receptor status: V86.0-V86.1) ♀
174.5 Malignant neoplasm of lower-outer quadrant of female breast — (Use additional code to identify estrogen receptor status: V86.0-V86.1) ♀
174.6 Malignant neoplasm of axillary tail of female breast — (Use additional code to identify estrogen receptor status: V86.0-V86.1) ♀
174.8 Malignant neoplasm of other specified sites of female breast — (Use additional code to identify estrogen receptor status: V86.0-V86.1) ♀
175.0 Malignant neoplasm of nipple and areola of male breast — (Use additional code to identify estrogen receptor status: V86.0-V86.1) ♂
175.9 Malignant neoplasm of other and unspecified sites of male breast — (Use additional code to identify estrogen receptor status: V86.0-V86.1) ▽ ♂
196.3 Secondary and unspecified malignant neoplasm of lymph nodes of axilla and upper limb
198.81 Secondary malignant neoplasm of breast
238.3 Neoplasm of uncertain behavior of breast
239.3 Neoplasm of unspecified nature of breast

ICD-9-CM Procedural

40.23 Excision of axillary lymph node
40.3 Regional lymph node excision
85.22 Resection of quadrant of breast
85.23 Subtotal mastectomy

19303

19303 Mastectomy, simple, complete

ICD-9-CM Diagnostic

174.0 Malignant neoplasm of nipple and areola of female breast — (Use additional code to identify estrogen receptor status: V86.0-V86.1) ♀
174.1 Malignant neoplasm of central portion of female breast — (Use additional code to identify estrogen receptor status: V86.0-V86.1) ♀
174.2 Malignant neoplasm of upper-inner quadrant of female breast — (Use additional code to identify estrogen receptor status: V86.0-V86.1) ♀
174.3 Malignant neoplasm of lower-inner quadrant of female breast — (Use additional code to identify estrogen receptor status: V86.0-V86.1) ♀

174.4 Malignant neoplasm of upper-outer quadrant of female breast — (Use additional code to identify estrogen receptor status: V86.0-V86.1) ♀
174.5 Malignant neoplasm of lower-outer quadrant of female breast — (Use additional code to identify estrogen receptor status: V86.0-V86.1) ♀
174.6 Malignant neoplasm of axillary tail of female breast — (Use additional code to identify estrogen receptor status: V86.0-V86.1) ♀
174.8 Malignant neoplasm of other specified sites of female breast — (Use additional code to identify estrogen receptor status: V86.0-V86.1) ♀
175.0 Malignant neoplasm of nipple and areola of male breast — (Use additional code to identify estrogen receptor status: V86.0-V86.1) ♂
175.9 Malignant neoplasm of other and unspecified sites of male breast — (Use additional code to identify estrogen receptor status: V86.0-V86.1) ▽ ♂
198.81 Secondary malignant neoplasm of breast
233.0 Carcinoma in situ of breast
238.3 Neoplasm of uncertain behavior of breast
239.3 Neoplasm of unspecified nature of breast
610.1 Diffuse cystic mastopathy
611.1 Hypertrophy of breast
611.72 Lump or mass in breast
V50.41 Prophylactic breast removal

ICD-9-CM Procedural

85.41 Unilateral simple mastectomy
85.42 Bilateral simple mastectomy

19304

19304 Mastectomy, subcutaneous

ICD-9-CM Diagnostic

173.50 Unspecified malignant neoplasm of skin of trunk, except scrotum ▽
173.51 Basal cell carcinoma of skin of trunk, except scrotum
173.52 Squamous cell carcinoma of skin of trunk, except scrotum
173.59 Other specified malignant neoplasm of skin of trunk, except scrotum
174.0 Malignant neoplasm of nipple and areola of female breast — (Use additional code to identify estrogen receptor status: V86.0-V86.1) ♀
174.1 Malignant neoplasm of central portion of female breast — (Use additional code to identify estrogen receptor status: V86.0-V86.1) ♀
174.2 Malignant neoplasm of upper-inner quadrant of female breast — (Use additional code to identify estrogen receptor status: V86.0-V86.1) ♀
174.3 Malignant neoplasm of lower-inner quadrant of female breast — (Use additional code to identify estrogen receptor status: V86.0-V86.1) ♀
174.4 Malignant neoplasm of upper-outer quadrant of female breast — (Use additional code to identify estrogen receptor status: V86.0-V86.1) ♀
174.5 Malignant neoplasm of lower-outer quadrant of female breast — (Use additional code to identify estrogen receptor status: V86.0-V86.1) ♀
174.6 Malignant neoplasm of axillary tail of female breast — (Use additional code to identify estrogen receptor status: V86.0-V86.1) ♀
174.8 Malignant neoplasm of other specified sites of female breast — (Use additional code to identify estrogen receptor status: V86.0-V86.1) ♀
175.0 Malignant neoplasm of nipple and areola of male breast — (Use additional code to identify estrogen receptor status: V86.0-V86.1) ♂
175.9 Malignant neoplasm of other and unspecified sites of male breast — (Use additional code to identify estrogen receptor status: V86.0-V86.1) ▽ ♂
198.81 Secondary malignant neoplasm of breast
233.0 Carcinoma in situ of breast
238.3 Neoplasm of uncertain behavior of breast
239.2 Neoplasms of unspecified nature of bone, soft tissue, and skin
239.3 Neoplasm of unspecified nature of breast
757.6 Specified congenital anomalies of breast
V50.41 Prophylactic breast removal

ICD-9-CM Procedural

85.33 Unilateral subcutaneous mammectomy with synchronous implant
85.34 Other unilateral subcutaneous mammectomy
85.35 Bilateral subcutaneous mammectomy with synchronous implant
85.36 Other bilateral subcutaneous mammectomy

19305-19306

19305 Mastectomy, radical, including pectoral muscles, axillary lymph nodes
19306 Mastectomy, radical, including pectoral muscles, axillary and internal mammary lymph nodes (Urban type operation)

ICD-9-CM Diagnostic

174.0 Malignant neoplasm of nipple and areola of female breast — (Use additional code to identify estrogen receptor status: V86.0-V86.1) ♀
174.1 Malignant neoplasm of central portion of female breast — (Use additional code to identify estrogen receptor status: V86.0-V86.1) ♀
174.2 Malignant neoplasm of upper-inner quadrant of female breast — (Use additional code to identify estrogen receptor status: V86.0-V86.1) ♀
174.3 Malignant neoplasm of lower-inner quadrant of female breast — (Use additional code to identify estrogen receptor status: V86.0-V86.1) ♀
174.4 Malignant neoplasm of upper-outer quadrant of female breast — (Use additional code to identify estrogen receptor status: V86.0-V86.1) ♀
174.5 Malignant neoplasm of lower-outer quadrant of female breast — (Use additional code to identify estrogen receptor status: V86.0-V86.1) ♀
174.6 Malignant neoplasm of axillary tail of female breast — (Use additional code to identify estrogen receptor status: V86.0-V86.1) ♀
174.8 Malignant neoplasm of other specified sites of female breast — (Use additional code to identify estrogen receptor status: V86.0-V86.1) ♀
175.0 Malignant neoplasm of nipple and areola of male breast — (Use additional code to identify estrogen receptor status: V86.0-V86.1) ♂
175.9 Malignant neoplasm of other and unspecified sites of male breast — (Use additional code to identify estrogen receptor status: V86.0-V86.1) ▽ ♂
196.3 Secondary and unspecified malignant neoplasm of lymph nodes of axilla and upper limb
198.81 Secondary malignant neoplasm of breast
233.0 Carcinoma in situ of breast
238.3 Neoplasm of uncertain behavior of breast
239.3 Neoplasm of unspecified nature of breast
V50.41 Prophylactic breast removal

ICD-9-CM Procedural

85.45 Unilateral radical mastectomy
85.46 Bilateral radical mastectomy
85.47 Unilateral extended radical mastectomy
85.48 Bilateral extended radical mastectomy

19307

19307 Mastectomy, modified radical, including axillary lymph nodes, with or without pectoralis minor muscle, but excluding pectoralis major muscle

ICD-9-CM Diagnostic

174.0 Malignant neoplasm of nipple and areola of female breast — (Use additional code to identify estrogen receptor status: V86.0-V86.1) ♀
174.1 Malignant neoplasm of central portion of female breast — (Use additional code to identify estrogen receptor status: V86.0-V86.1) ♀
174.2 Malignant neoplasm of upper-inner quadrant of female breast — (Use additional code to identify estrogen receptor status: V86.0-V86.1) ♀
174.3 Malignant neoplasm of lower-inner quadrant of female breast — (Use additional code to identify estrogen receptor status: V86.0-V86.1) ♀
174.4 Malignant neoplasm of upper-outer quadrant of female breast — (Use additional code to identify estrogen receptor status: V86.0-V86.1) ♀

174.5 Malignant neoplasm of lower-outer quadrant of female breast — (Use additional code to identify estrogen receptor status: V86.0-V86.1) ♀

174.6 Malignant neoplasm of axillary tail of female breast — (Use additional code to identify estrogen receptor status: V86.0-V86.1) ♀

174.8 Malignant neoplasm of other specified sites of female breast — (Use additional code to identify estrogen receptor status: V86.0-V86.1) ♀

175.0 Malignant neoplasm of nipple and areola of male breast — (Use additional code to identify estrogen receptor status: V86.0-V86.1) ♂

175.9 Malignant neoplasm of other and unspecified sites of male breast — (Use additional code to identify estrogen receptor status: V86.0-V86.1) ▽ ♂

196.3 Secondary and unspecified malignant neoplasm of lymph nodes of axilla and upper limb

198.81 Secondary malignant neoplasm of breast

233.0 Carcinoma in situ of breast

238.3 Neoplasm of uncertain behavior of breast

239.3 Neoplasm of unspecified nature of breast

V50.41 Prophylactic breast removal

ICD-9-CM Procedural

85.43 Unilateral extended simple mastectomy

85.44 Bilateral extended simple mastectomy

19316

19316 Mastopexy

ICD-9-CM Diagnostic

611.1 Hypertrophy of breast

611.4 Atrophy of breast

611.81 Ptosis of breast

611.82 Hypoplasia of breast

611.83 Capsular contracture of breast implant

611.89 Other specified disorders of breast

612.0 Deformity of reconstructed breast

612.1 Disproportion of reconstructed breast

V50.1 Other plastic surgery for unacceptable cosmetic appearance

V51.0 Encounter for breast reconstruction following mastectomy

V51.8 Other aftercare involving the use of plastic surgery

ICD-9-CM Procedural

85.6 Mastopexy

19318

19318 Reduction mammaplasty

ICD-9-CM Diagnostic

611.1 Hypertrophy of breast

611.4 Atrophy of breast

611.71 Mastodynia

611.81 Ptosis of breast

611.89 Other specified disorders of breast

612.0 Deformity of reconstructed breast

612.1 Disproportion of reconstructed breast

V50.1 Other plastic surgery for unacceptable cosmetic appearance

ICD-9-CM Procedural

85.31 Unilateral reduction mammoplasty

85.32 Bilateral reduction mammoplasty

19324-19325

19324 Mammaplasty, augmentation; without prosthetic implant

19325 with prosthetic implant

ICD-9-CM Diagnostic

611.4 Atrophy of breast

611.82 Hypoplasia of breast

611.89 Other specified disorders of breast

612.0 Deformity of reconstructed breast

612.1 Disproportion of reconstructed breast

757.6 Specified congenital anomalies of breast

757.8 Other specified congenital anomalies of the integument

V50.1 Other plastic surgery for unacceptable cosmetic appearance

V51.8 Other aftercare involving the use of plastic surgery

ICD-9-CM Procedural

85.50 Augmentation mammoplasty, not otherwise specified

85.53 Unilateral breast implant

85.54 Bilateral breast implant

HCPCS Level II Supplies & Services

C1789 Prosthesis, breast (implantable)

L8031 Breast prosthesis, silicone or equal, with integral adhesive

L8032 Nipple prosthesis, reusable, any type, each

L8600 Implantable breast prosthesis, silicone or equal

19328-19330

19328 Removal of intact mammary implant

19330 Removal of mammary implant material

ICD-9-CM Diagnostic

611.71 Mastodynia

611.89 Other specified disorders of breast

686.1 Pyogenic granuloma of skin and subcutaneous tissue — (Use additional code to identify any infectious organism: 041.0-041.8)

909.3 Late effect of complications of surgical and medical care

996.54 Mechanical complication due to breast prosthesis

996.69 Infection and inflammatory reaction due to other internal prosthetic device, implant, and graft — (Use additional code to identify specified infections)

996.79 Other complications due to other internal prosthetic device, implant, and graft — (Use additional code to identify complication: 338.18-338.19, 338.28-338.29)

998.51 Infected postoperative seroma — (Use additional code to identify organism)

998.59 Other postoperative infection — (Use additional code to identify infection)

998.83 Non-healing surgical wound

V50.1 Other plastic surgery for unacceptable cosmetic appearance

V51.8 Other aftercare involving the use of plastic surgery

V52.4 Fitting and adjustment of breast prosthesis and implant ♀

V65.8 Other reasons for seeking consultation

ICD-9-CM Procedural

85.94 Removal of implant of breast

19340

19340 Immediate insertion of breast prosthesis following mastopexy, mastectomy or in reconstruction

ICD-9-CM Diagnostic

174.0 Malignant neoplasm of nipple and areola of female breast — (Use additional code to identify estrogen receptor status: V86.0-V86.1) ♀

174.1 Malignant neoplasm of central portion of female breast — (Use additional code to identify estrogen receptor status: V86.0-V86.1) ♀

174.2 Malignant neoplasm of upper-inner quadrant of female breast — (Use additional code to identify estrogen receptor status: V86.0-V86.1) ♀

174.3 Malignant neoplasm of lower-inner quadrant of female breast — (Use additional code to identify estrogen receptor status: V86.0-V86.1) ♀
174.4 Malignant neoplasm of upper-outer quadrant of female breast — (Use additional code to identify estrogen receptor status: V86.0-V86.1) ♀
174.5 Malignant neoplasm of lower-outer quadrant of female breast — (Use additional code to identify estrogen receptor status: V86.0-V86.1) ♀
174.6 Malignant neoplasm of axillary tail of female breast — (Use additional code to identify estrogen receptor status: V86.0-V86.1) ♀
174.8 Malignant neoplasm of other specified sites of female breast — (Use additional code to identify estrogen receptor status: V86.0-V86.1) ♀
174.9 Malignant neoplasm of breast (female), unspecified site — (Use additional code to identify estrogen receptor status: V86.0-V86.1) ▽ ♀
233.0 Carcinoma in situ of breast
610.1 Diffuse cystic mastopathy
611.1 Hypertrophy of breast
611.4 Atrophy of breast
611.81 Ptosis of breast
611.82 Hypoplasia of breast
611.83 Capsular contracture of breast implant
611.89 Other specified disorders of breast
612.0 Deformity of reconstructed breast
612.1 Disproportion of reconstructed breast
757.6 Specified congenital anomalies of breast
V45.71 Acquired absence of breast and nipple
V50.1 Other plastic surgery for unacceptable cosmetic appearance
V50.41 Prophylactic breast removal
V51.0 Encounter for breast reconstruction following mastectomy
V51.8 Other aftercare involving the use of plastic surgery

ICD-9-CM Procedural

85.53 Unilateral breast implant
85.54 Bilateral breast implant

HCPCS Level II Supplies & Services

A4461 Surgical dressing holder, nonreusable, each
A4463 Surgical dressing holder, reusable, each
C1789 Prosthesis, breast (implantable)
L8031 Breast prosthesis, silicone or equal, with integral adhesive
L8032 Nipple prosthesis, reusable, any type, each
L8600 Implantable breast prosthesis, silicone or equal

19342

19342 Delayed insertion of breast prosthesis following mastopexy, mastectomy or in reconstruction

ICD-9-CM Diagnostic

611.81 Ptosis of breast
611.82 Hypoplasia of breast
611.83 Capsular contracture of breast implant
611.89 Other specified disorders of breast
612.0 Deformity of reconstructed breast
612.1 Disproportion of reconstructed breast
757.6 Specified congenital anomalies of breast
V45.71 Acquired absence of breast and nipple
V50.1 Other plastic surgery for unacceptable cosmetic appearance
V50.41 Prophylactic breast removal
V51.0 Encounter for breast reconstruction following mastectomy
V51.8 Other aftercare involving the use of plastic surgery

ICD-9-CM Procedural

85.53 Unilateral breast implant
85.54 Bilateral breast implant

HCPCS Level II Supplies & Services

A4461 Surgical dressing holder, nonreusable, each
A4463 Surgical dressing holder, reusable, each
C1789 Prosthesis, breast (implantable)
L8031 Breast prosthesis, silicone or equal, with integral adhesive
L8032 Nipple prosthesis, reusable, any type, each
L8600 Implantable breast prosthesis, silicone or equal

19350

19350 Nipple/areola reconstruction

ICD-9-CM Diagnostic

611.2 Fissure of nipple
611.83 Capsular contracture of breast implant
611.89 Other specified disorders of breast
612.0 Deformity of reconstructed breast
612.1 Disproportion of reconstructed breast
757.6 Specified congenital anomalies of breast
V10.3 Personal history of malignant neoplasm of breast
V16.3 Family history of malignant neoplasm of breast
V45.71 Acquired absence of breast and nipple
V50.1 Other plastic surgery for unacceptable cosmetic appearance
V51.0 Encounter for breast reconstruction following mastectomy
V51.8 Other aftercare involving the use of plastic surgery
V84.01 Genetic susceptibility to malignant neoplasm of breast — (Use additional code, if applicable, for any associated family history of the disease: V16-V19. Code first, if applicable, any current malignant neoplasms: 140.0-195.8, 200.0-208.9, 230.0-234.9. Use additional code, if applicable, for any personal history of malignant neoplasm: V10.0-V10.9)

ICD-9-CM Procedural

85.87 Other repair or reconstruction of nipple

HCPCS Level II Supplies & Services

L8032 Nipple prosthesis, reusable, any type, each

19355

19355 Correction of inverted nipples

ICD-9-CM Diagnostic

611.79 Other sign and symptom in breast
611.82 Hypoplasia of breast
611.89 Other specified disorders of breast
676.31 Other and unspecified disorder of breast associated with childbirth, delivered, with or without mention of antepartum condition ▽ ♀
676.32 Other and unspecified disorder of breast associated with childbirth, delivered, with mention of postpartum complication ▽ ♀
676.34 Other and unspecified disorder of breast associated with childbirth, postpartum condition or complication ▽ ♀
757.6 Specified congenital anomalies of breast

ICD-9-CM Procedural

85.87 Other repair or reconstruction of nipple

HCPCS Level II Supplies & Services

L8032 Nipple prosthesis, reusable, any type, each

19357

19357 Breast reconstruction, immediate or delayed, with tissue expander, including subsequent expansion

ICD-9-CM Diagnostic

174.0 Malignant neoplasm of nipple and areola of female breast — (Use additional code to identify estrogen receptor status: V86.0-V86.1) ♀

174.1 Malignant neoplasm of central portion of female breast — (Use additional code to identify estrogen receptor status: V86.0-V86.1) ♀

174.2 Malignant neoplasm of upper-inner quadrant of female breast — (Use additional code to identify estrogen receptor status: V86.0-V86.1) ♀

174.3 Malignant neoplasm of lower-inner quadrant of female breast — (Use additional code to identify estrogen receptor status: V86.0-V86.1) ♀

174.4 Malignant neoplasm of upper-outer quadrant of female breast — (Use additional code to identify estrogen receptor status: V86.0-V86.1) ♀

174.5 Malignant neoplasm of lower-outer quadrant of female breast — (Use additional code to identify estrogen receptor status: V86.0-V86.1) ♀

174.6 Malignant neoplasm of axillary tail of female breast — (Use additional code to identify estrogen receptor status: V86.0-V86.1) ♀

174.8 Malignant neoplasm of other specified sites of female breast — (Use additional code to identify estrogen receptor status: V86.0-V86.1) ♀

198.81 Secondary malignant neoplasm of breast

233.0 Carcinoma in situ of breast

610.1 Diffuse cystic mastopathy

610.3 Fibrosclerosis of breast

611.0 Inflammatory disease of breast

611.72 Lump or mass in breast

611.81 Ptosis of breast

611.82 Hypoplasia of breast

611.83 Capsular contracture of breast implant

611.89 Other specified disorders of breast

612.0 Deformity of reconstructed breast

612.1 Disproportion of reconstructed breast

V45.71 Acquired absence of breast and nipple

V50.1 Other plastic surgery for unacceptable cosmetic appearance

V50.41 Prophylactic breast removal

V51.0 Encounter for breast reconstruction following mastectomy

V51.8 Other aftercare involving the use of plastic surgery

ICD-9-CM Procedural

85.95 Insertion of breast tissue expander

HCPCS Level II Supplies & Services

A4461 Surgical dressing holder, nonreusable, each

A4463 Surgical dressing holder, reusable, each

19361

19361 Breast reconstruction with latissimus dorsi flap, without prosthetic implant

ICD-9-CM Diagnostic

174.0 Malignant neoplasm of nipple and areola of female breast — (Use additional code to identify estrogen receptor status: V86.0-V86.1) ♀

174.1 Malignant neoplasm of central portion of female breast — (Use additional code to identify estrogen receptor status: V86.0-V86.1) ♀

174.2 Malignant neoplasm of upper-inner quadrant of female breast — (Use additional code to identify estrogen receptor status: V86.0-V86.1) ♀

174.3 Malignant neoplasm of lower-inner quadrant of female breast — (Use additional code to identify estrogen receptor status: V86.0-V86.1) ♀

174.4 Malignant neoplasm of upper-outer quadrant of female breast — (Use additional code to identify estrogen receptor status: V86.0-V86.1) ♀

174.5 Malignant neoplasm of lower-outer quadrant of female breast — (Use additional code to identify estrogen receptor status: V86.0-V86.1) ♀

174.6 Malignant neoplasm of axillary tail of female breast — (Use additional code to identify estrogen receptor status: V86.0-V86.1) ♀

174.8 Malignant neoplasm of other specified sites of female breast — (Use additional code to identify estrogen receptor status: V86.0-V86.1) ♀

198.81 Secondary malignant neoplasm of breast

233.0 Carcinoma in situ of breast

610.1 Diffuse cystic mastopathy

610.3 Fibrosclerosis of breast

611.0 Inflammatory disease of breast

611.72 Lump or mass in breast

611.81 Ptosis of breast

611.82 Hypoplasia of breast

611.83 Capsular contracture of breast implant

611.89 Other specified disorders of breast

612.0 Deformity of reconstructed breast

612.1 Disproportion of reconstructed breast

V10.3 Personal history of malignant neoplasm of breast

V16.3 Family history of malignant neoplasm of breast

V45.71 Acquired absence of breast and nipple

V50.1 Other plastic surgery for unacceptable cosmetic appearance

V51.0 Encounter for breast reconstruction following mastectomy

V51.8 Other aftercare involving the use of plastic surgery

V84.01 Genetic susceptibility to malignant neoplasm of breast — (Use additional code, if applicable, for any associated family history of the disease: V16-V19. Code first, if applicable, any current malignant neoplasms: 140.0-195.8, 200.0-208.9, 230.0-234.9. Use additional code, if applicable, for any personal history of malignant neoplasm: V10.0-V10.9)

ICD-9-CM Procedural

85.42 Bilateral simple mastectomy

85.71 Latissimus dorsi myocutaneous flap

HCPCS Level II Supplies & Services

A4461 Surgical dressing holder, nonreusable, each

A4463 Surgical dressing holder, reusable, each

19364

19364 Breast reconstruction with free flap

ICD-9-CM Diagnostic

174.0 Malignant neoplasm of nipple and areola of female breast — (Use additional code to identify estrogen receptor status: V86.0-V86.1) ♀

174.1 Malignant neoplasm of central portion of female breast — (Use additional code to identify estrogen receptor status: V86.0-V86.1) ♀

174.2 Malignant neoplasm of upper-inner quadrant of female breast — (Use additional code to identify estrogen receptor status: V86.0-V86.1) ♀

174.3 Malignant neoplasm of lower-inner quadrant of female breast — (Use additional code to identify estrogen receptor status: V86.0-V86.1) ♀

174.4 Malignant neoplasm of upper-outer quadrant of female breast — (Use additional code to identify estrogen receptor status: V86.0-V86.1) ♀

174.5 Malignant neoplasm of lower-outer quadrant of female breast — (Use additional code to identify estrogen receptor status: V86.0-V86.1) ♀

174.6 Malignant neoplasm of axillary tail of female breast — (Use additional code to identify estrogen receptor status: V86.0-V86.1) ♀

174.8 Malignant neoplasm of other specified sites of female breast — (Use additional code to identify estrogen receptor status: V86.0-V86.1) ♀

198.81 Secondary malignant neoplasm of breast

233.0 Carcinoma in situ of breast

610.1 Diffuse cystic mastopathy

610.3 Fibrosclerosis of breast

611.0 Inflammatory disease of breast

611.72 Lump or mass in breast

611.81 Ptosis of breast
611.82 Hypoplasia of breast
611.83 Capsular contracture of breast implant
611.89 Other specified disorders of breast
612.0 Deformity of reconstructed breast
612.1 Disproportion of reconstructed breast
V45.71 Acquired absence of breast and nipple
V50.41 Prophylactic breast removal
V51.0 Encounter for breast reconstruction following mastectomy
V51.8 Other aftercare involving the use of plastic surgery

ICD-9-CM Procedural

85.73 Transverse rectus abdominis myocutaneous (TRAM) flap, free
85.74 Deep inferior epigastric artery perforator (DIEP) flap, free
85.75 Superficial inferior epigastric artery (SIEA) flap, free
85.76 Gluteal artery perforator (GAP) flap, free

HCPCS Level II Supplies & Services

A4461 Surgical dressing holder, nonreusable, each
A4463 Surgical dressing holder, reusable, each

19366

19366 Breast reconstruction with other technique

ICD-9-CM Diagnostic

174.0 Malignant neoplasm of nipple and areola of female breast — (Use additional code to identify estrogen receptor status: V86.0-V86.1) ♀
174.1 Malignant neoplasm of central portion of female breast — (Use additional code to identify estrogen receptor status: V86.0-V86.1) ♀
174.2 Malignant neoplasm of upper-inner quadrant of female breast — (Use additional code to identify estrogen receptor status: V86.0-V86.1) ♀
174.3 Malignant neoplasm of lower-inner quadrant of female breast — (Use additional code to identify estrogen receptor status: V86.0-V86.1) ♀
174.4 Malignant neoplasm of upper-outer quadrant of female breast — (Use additional code to identify estrogen receptor status: V86.0-V86.1) ♀
174.5 Malignant neoplasm of lower-outer quadrant of female breast — (Use additional code to identify estrogen receptor status: V86.0-V86.1) ♀
174.6 Malignant neoplasm of axillary tail of female breast — (Use additional code to identify estrogen receptor status: V86.0-V86.1) ♀
174.8 Malignant neoplasm of other specified sites of female breast — (Use additional code to identify estrogen receptor status: V86.0-V86.1) ♀
198.81 Secondary malignant neoplasm of breast
233.0 Carcinoma in situ of breast
610.1 Diffuse cystic mastopathy
610.3 Fibrosclerosis of breast
611.0 Inflammatory disease of breast
611.72 Lump or mass in breast
611.81 Ptosis of breast
611.82 Hypoplasia of breast
611.83 Capsular contracture of breast implant
611.89 Other specified disorders of breast
612.0 Deformity of reconstructed breast
612.1 Disproportion of reconstructed breast
V45.71 Acquired absence of breast and nipple
V50.41 Prophylactic breast removal
V51.0 Encounter for breast reconstruction following mastectomy
V51.8 Other aftercare involving the use of plastic surgery

ICD-9-CM Procedural

85.55 Fat graft to breast
85.70 Total reconstruction of breast, not otherwise specified
85.79 Other total reconstruction of breast
85.85 Muscle flap graft to breast

HCPCS Level II Supplies & Services

A4461 Surgical dressing holder, nonreusable, each
A4463 Surgical dressing holder, reusable, each

19367-19369

19367 Breast reconstruction with transverse rectus abdominis myocutaneous flap (TRAM), single pedicle, including closure of donor site;
19368 with microvascular anastomosis (supercharging)
19369 Breast reconstruction with transverse rectus abdominis myocutaneous flap (TRAM), double pedicle, including closure of donor site

ICD-9-CM Diagnostic

174.0 Malignant neoplasm of nipple and areola of female breast — (Use additional code to identify estrogen receptor status: V86.0-V86.1) ♀
174.1 Malignant neoplasm of central portion of female breast — (Use additional code to identify estrogen receptor status: V86.0-V86.1) ♀
174.2 Malignant neoplasm of upper-inner quadrant of female breast — (Use additional code to identify estrogen receptor status: V86.0-V86.1) ♀
174.3 Malignant neoplasm of lower-inner quadrant of female breast — (Use additional code to identify estrogen receptor status: V86.0-V86.1) ♀
174.4 Malignant neoplasm of upper-outer quadrant of female breast — (Use additional code to identify estrogen receptor status: V86.0-V86.1) ♀
174.5 Malignant neoplasm of lower-outer quadrant of female breast — (Use additional code to identify estrogen receptor status: V86.0-V86.1) ♀
174.6 Malignant neoplasm of axillary tail of female breast — (Use additional code to identify estrogen receptor status: V86.0-V86.1) ♀
174.8 Malignant neoplasm of other specified sites of female breast — (Use additional code to identify estrogen receptor status: V86.0-V86.1) ♀
198.81 Secondary malignant neoplasm of breast
233.0 Carcinoma in situ of breast
610.1 Diffuse cystic mastopathy
610.3 Fibrosclerosis of breast
611.0 Inflammatory disease of breast
611.72 Lump or mass in breast
611.81 Ptosis of breast
611.82 Hypoplasia of breast
611.83 Capsular contracture of breast implant
611.89 Other specified disorders of breast
612.0 Deformity of reconstructed breast
612.1 Disproportion of reconstructed breast
V45.71 Acquired absence of breast and nipple
V50.1 Other plastic surgery for unacceptable cosmetic appearance
V50.41 Prophylactic breast removal
V51.0 Encounter for breast reconstruction following mastectomy
V51.8 Other aftercare involving the use of plastic surgery

ICD-9-CM Procedural

85.72 Transverse rectus abdominis myocutaneous (TRAM) flap, pedicled

HCPCS Level II Supplies & Services

A4461 Surgical dressing holder, nonreusable, each
A4463 Surgical dressing holder, reusable, each

19370-19371

19370 Open periprosthetic capsulotomy, breast
19371 Periprosthetic capsulectomy, breast

ICD-9-CM Diagnostic

611.71 Mastodynia
611.83 Capsular contracture of breast implant
611.89 Other specified disorders of breast

686.1 Pyogenic granuloma of skin and subcutaneous tissue — (Use additional code to identify any infectious organism: 041.0-041.8)
909.3 Late effect of complications of surgical and medical care
996.54 Mechanical complication due to breast prosthesis
996.69 Infection and inflammatory reaction due to other internal prosthetic device, implant, and graft — (Use additional code to identify specified infections)
996.79 Other complications due to other internal prosthetic device, implant, and graft — (Use additional code to identify complication: 338.18-338.19, 338.28-338.29)
998.51 Infected postoperative seroma — (Use additional code to identify organism)
998.59 Other postoperative infection — (Use additional code to identify infection)
998.83 Non-healing surgical wound
V45.71 Acquired absence of breast and nipple
V50.1 Other plastic surgery for unacceptable cosmetic appearance
V51.8 Other aftercare involving the use of plastic surgery

ICD-9-CM Procedural

85.0 Mastotomy
85.21 Local excision of lesion of breast

HCPCS Level II Supplies & Services

A4461 Surgical dressing holder, nonreusable, each
A4463 Surgical dressing holder, reusable, each

19380

19380 Revision of reconstructed breast

ICD-9-CM Diagnostic

611.83 Capsular contracture of breast implant
611.89 Other specified disorders of breast
612.0 Deformity of reconstructed breast
612.1 Disproportion of reconstructed breast
709.2 Scar condition and fibrosis of skin
909.3 Late effect of complications of surgical and medical care
996.54 Mechanical complication due to breast prosthesis
996.79 Other complications due to other internal prosthetic device, implant, and graft — (Use additional code to identify complication: 338.18-338.19, 338.28-338.29)
V45.71 Acquired absence of breast and nipple
V50.1 Other plastic surgery for unacceptable cosmetic appearance
V51.0 Encounter for breast reconstruction following mastectomy
V51.8 Other aftercare involving the use of plastic surgery

ICD-9-CM Procedural

85.93 Revision of implant of breast

HCPCS Level II Supplies & Services

A4461 Surgical dressing holder, nonreusable, each
A4463 Surgical dressing holder, reusable, each

Musculoskeletal System

General

20005

20005 Incision and drainage of soft tissue abscess, subfascial (ie, involves the soft tissue below the deep fascia)

ICD-9-CM Diagnostic

567.31 Psoas muscle abscess

728.89 Other disorder of muscle, ligament, and fascia — (Use additional E code to identify drug, if drug-induced)

996.66 Infection and inflammatory reaction due to internal joint prosthesis — (Use additional code to identify specified infections. Use additional code to identify infected prosthetic joint: V43.60-V43.69)

996.67 Infection and inflammatory reaction due to other internal orthopedic device, implant, and graft — (Use additional code to identify specified infections)

998.59 Other postoperative infection — (Use additional code to identify infection)

ICD-9-CM Procedural

82.02 Myotomy of hand

82.09 Other incision of soft tissue of hand

83.02 Myotomy

83.09 Other incision of soft tissue

20100

20100 Exploration of penetrating wound (separate procedure); neck

ICD-9-CM Diagnostic

874.00 Open wound of larynx with trachea, without mention of complication

874.01 Open wound of larynx, without mention of complication

874.02 Open wound of trachea, without mention of complication

874.10 Open wound of larynx with trachea, complicated

874.11 Open wound of larynx, complicated

874.12 Open wound of trachea, complicated

874.2 Open wound of thyroid gland, without mention of complication

874.3 Open wound of thyroid gland, complicated

874.4 Open wound of pharynx, without mention of complication

874.5 Open wound of pharynx, complicated

874.8 Open wound of other and unspecified parts of neck, without mention of complication ▽

874.9 Open wound of other and unspecified parts of neck, complicated ▽

959.09 Injury of face and neck, other and unspecified

959.8 Injury, other and unspecified, other specified sites, including multiple

ICD-9-CM Procedural

06.09 Other incision of thyroid field

83.02 Myotomy

83.09 Other incision of soft tissue

83.65 Other suture of muscle or fascia

84.99 Other operations on musculoskeletal system

86.05 Incision with removal of foreign body or device from skin and subcutaneous tissue

86.09 Other incision of skin and subcutaneous tissue

86.22 Excisional debridement of wound, infection, or burn

86.28 Nonexcisional debridement of wound, infection, or burn

HCPCS Level II Supplies & Services

A4305 Disposable drug delivery system, flow rate of 50 ml or greater per hour

20101

20101 Exploration of penetrating wound (separate procedure); chest

ICD-9-CM Diagnostic

875.0 Open wound of chest (wall), without mention of complication

875.1 Open wound of chest (wall), complicated

879.0 Open wound of breast, without mention of complication

879.1 Open wound of breast, complicated

879.8 Open wound(s) (multiple) of unspecified site(s), without mention of complication ▽

879.9 Open wound(s) (multiple) of unspecified site(s), complicated ▽

959.11 Other injury of chest wall

959.8 Injury, other and unspecified, other specified sites, including multiple

ICD-9-CM Procedural

34.71 Suture of laceration of chest wall

34.79 Other repair of chest wall

83.02 Myotomy

83.09 Other incision of soft tissue

83.14 Fasciotomy

83.65 Other suture of muscle or fascia

84.99 Other operations on musculoskeletal system

85.0 Mastotomy

86.05 Incision with removal of foreign body or device from skin and subcutaneous tissue

86.09 Other incision of skin and subcutaneous tissue

86.22 Excisional debridement of wound, infection, or burn

86.28 Nonexcisional debridement of wound, infection, or burn

HCPCS Level II Supplies & Services

A4305 Disposable drug delivery system, flow rate of 50 ml or greater per hour

20102

20102 Exploration of penetrating wound (separate procedure); abdomen/flank/back

ICD-9-CM Diagnostic

876.0 Open wound of back, without mention of complication

876.1 Open wound of back, complicated

877.0 Open wound of buttock, without mention of complication

877.1 Open wound of buttock, complicated

879.2 Open wound of abdominal wall, anterior, without mention of complication

879.3 Open wound of abdominal wall, anterior, complicated

879.4 Open wound of abdominal wall, lateral, without mention of complication

879.5 Open wound of abdominal wall, lateral, complicated

879.6 Open wound of other and unspecified parts of trunk, without mention of complication ▽

879.7 Open wound of other and unspecified parts of trunk, complicated ▽

879.8 Open wound(s) (multiple) of unspecified site(s), without mention of complication ▽

879.9 Open wound(s) (multiple) of unspecified site(s), complicated ▽

959.12 Other injury of abdomen

959.19 Other injury of other sites of trunk

959.8 Injury, other and unspecified, other specified sites, including multiple

ICD-9-CM Procedural

54.0 Incision of abdominal wall

54.63 Other suture of abdominal wall

54.72 Other repair of abdominal wall

83.02 Myotomy

83.09	Other incision of soft tissue
83.65	Other suture of muscle or fascia
84.99	Other operations on musculoskeletal system
86.05	Incision with removal of foreign body or device from skin and subcutaneous tissue
86.09	Other incision of skin and subcutaneous tissue
86.22	Excisional debridement of wound, infection, or burn
86.28	Nonexcisional debridement of wound, infection, or burn

HCPCS Level II Supplies & Services

A4305	Disposable drug delivery system, flow rate of 50 ml or greater per hour

20103

20103 Exploration of penetrating wound (separate procedure); extremity

ICD-9-CM Diagnostic

880.00	Open wound of shoulder region, without mention of complication
880.01	Open wound of scapular region, without mention of complication
880.02	Open wound of axillary region, without mention of complication
880.03	Open wound of upper arm, without mention of complication
880.09	Open wound of multiple sites of shoulder and upper arm, without mention of complication
880.10	Open wound of shoulder region, complicated
880.11	Open wound of scapular region, complicated
880.12	Open wound of axillary region, complicated
880.13	Open wound of upper arm, complicated
880.19	Open wound of multiple sites of shoulder and upper arm, complicated
881.00	Open wound of forearm, without mention of complication
881.01	Open wound of elbow, without mention of complication
881.02	Open wound of wrist, without mention of complication
881.10	Open wound of forearm, complicated
881.11	Open wound of elbow, complicated
881.12	Open wound of wrist, complicated
882.0	Open wound of hand except finger(s) alone, without mention of complication
882.1	Open wound of hand except finger(s) alone, complicated
883.0	Open wound of finger(s), without mention of complication
883.1	Open wound of finger(s), complicated
884.0	Multiple and unspecified open wound of upper limb, without mention of complication
884.1	Multiple and unspecified open wound of upper limb, complicated
890.0	Open wound of hip and thigh, without mention of complication
890.1	Open wound of hip and thigh, complicated
891.0	Open wound of knee, leg (except thigh), and ankle, without mention of complication
891.1	Open wound of knee, leg (except thigh), and ankle, complicated
892.0	Open wound of foot except toe(s) alone, without mention of complication
892.1	Open wound of foot except toe(s) alone, complicated
893.0	Open wound of toe(s), without mention of complication
893.1	Open wound of toe(s), complicated
894.0	Multiple and unspecified open wound of lower limb, without mention of complication
894.1	Multiple and unspecified open wound of lower limb, complicated
959.2	Injury, other and unspecified, shoulder and upper arm
959.3	Injury, other and unspecified, elbow, forearm, and wrist
959.4	Injury, other and unspecified, hand, except finger
959.5	Injury, other and unspecified, finger
959.6	Injury, other and unspecified, hip and thigh
959.7	Injury, other and unspecified, knee, leg, ankle, and foot
959.8	Injury, other and unspecified, other specified sites, including multiple

ICD-9-CM Procedural

82.01	Exploration of tendon sheath of hand
82.02	Myotomy of hand
83.01	Exploration of tendon sheath
83.02	Myotomy

83.09	Other incision of soft tissue
83.65	Other suture of muscle or fascia
84.99	Other operations on musculoskeletal system
86.05	Incision with removal of foreign body or device from skin and subcutaneous tissue
86.09	Other incision of skin and subcutaneous tissue
86.22	Excisional debridement of wound, infection, or burn
86.28	Nonexcisional debridement of wound, infection, or burn

HCPCS Level II Supplies & Services

A4305	Disposable drug delivery system, flow rate of 50 ml or greater per hour

20150

20150 Excision of epiphyseal bar, with or without autogenous soft tissue graft obtained through same fascial incision

ICD-9-CM Diagnostic

733.91	Arrest of bone development or growth
736.00	Unspecified deformity of forearm, excluding fingers ▼
736.30	Unspecified acquired deformity of hip ▼
736.39	Other acquired deformities of hip
736.6	Other acquired deformities of knee
736.70	Unspecified deformity of ankle and foot, acquired ▼
736.79	Other acquired deformity of ankle and foot
736.81	Unequal leg length (acquired)
736.89	Other acquired deformity of other parts of limb
905.2	Late effect of fracture of upper extremities
905.3	Late effect of fracture of neck of femur
905.4	Late effect of fracture of lower extremities
906.4	Late effect of crushing

ICD-9-CM Procedural

78.20	Limb shortening procedures, unspecified site
78.22	Limb shortening procedures, humerus
78.23	Limb shortening procedures, radius and ulna
78.24	Limb shortening procedures, carpals and metacarpals
78.25	Limb shortening procedures, femur
78.27	Limb shortening procedures, tibia and fibula
78.28	Limb shortening procedures, tarsals and metatarsals
78.29	Limb shortening procedures, other
78.42	Other repair or plastic operation on humerus
78.43	Other repair or plastic operations on radius and ulna
78.45	Other repair or plastic operations on femur
78.47	Other repair or plastic operations on tibia and fibula
78.49	Other repair or plastic operations on other bone, except facial bones

20200-20206

20200 Biopsy, muscle; superficial
20205 deep
20206 Biopsy, muscle, percutaneous needle

ICD-9-CM Diagnostic

135	Sarcoidosis
171.0	Malignant neoplasm of connective and other soft tissue of head, face, and neck
171.2	Malignant neoplasm of connective and other soft tissue of upper limb, including shoulder
171.3	Malignant neoplasm of connective and other soft tissue of lower limb, including hip
171.4	Malignant neoplasm of connective and other soft tissue of thorax
171.5	Malignant neoplasm of connective and other soft tissue of abdomen
171.6	Malignant neoplasm of connective and other soft tissue of pelvis
171.7	Malignant neoplasm of connective and other soft tissue of trunk, unspecified site ▼
171.8	Malignant neoplasm of other specified sites of connective and other soft tissue

198.89 Secondary malignant neoplasm of other specified sites
209.29 Malignant carcinoid tumor of other sites — (Code first any associated multiple endocrine neoplasia syndrome: 258.01-258.03)(Use additional code to identify associated endocrine syndrome, as: carcinoid syndrome: 259.2)
209.69 Benign carcinoid tumor of other sites — (Code first any associated multiple endocrine neoplasia syndrome: 258.01-258.03)(Use additional code to identify associated endocrine syndrome, as: carcinoid syndrome: 259.2)
215.0 Other benign neoplasm of connective and other soft tissue of head, face, and neck
215.2 Other benign neoplasm of connective and other soft tissue of upper limb, including shoulder
215.3 Other benign neoplasm of connective and other soft tissue of lower limb, including hip
215.4 Other benign neoplasm of connective and other soft tissue of thorax
215.5 Other benign neoplasm of connective and other soft tissue of abdomen
215.6 Other benign neoplasm of connective and other soft tissue of pelvis
215.7 Other benign neoplasm of connective and other soft tissue of trunk, unspecified ▽
215.8 Other benign neoplasm of connective and other soft tissue of other specified sites
229.8 Benign neoplasm of other specified sites
238.1 Neoplasm of uncertain behavior of connective and other soft tissue
239.2 Neoplasms of unspecified nature of bone, soft tissue, and skin
277.30 Amyloidosis, unspecified — (Use additional code to identify any associated intellectual disabilities) ▽
277.31 Familial Mediterranean fever — (Use additional code to identify any associated intellectual disabilities)
277.39 Other amyloidosis — (Use additional code to identify any associated intellectual disabilities)
277.81 Primary carnitine deficiency — (Use additional code to identify any associated intellectual disabilities)
277.82 Carnitine deficiency due to inborn errors of metabolism — (Use additional code to identify any associated intellectual disabilities)
277.83 Iatrogenic carnitine deficiency — (Use additional code to identify any associated intellectual disabilities)
277.84 Other secondary carnitine deficiency — (Use additional code to identify any associated intellectual disabilities)
277.89 Other specified disorders of metabolism — (Use additional code to identify any associated intellectual disabilities)
359.0 Congenital hereditary muscular dystrophy
359.1 Hereditary progressive muscular dystrophy
359.6 Symptomatic inflammatory myopathy in diseases classified elsewhere — (Code first underlying disease: 135, 140.0-208.9, 277.30-277.39, 446.0, 710.0, 710.1, 710.2, 714.0) ☒
359.81 Critical illness myopathy
359.89 Other myopathies
728.0 Infective myositis
728.19 Other muscular calcification and ossification
728.79 Other fibromatoses of muscle, ligament, and fascia
728.81 Interstitial myositis
728.88 Rhabdomyolysis
729.1 Unspecified myalgia and myositis ▽

ICD-9-CM Procedural

82.93 Aspiration of other soft tissue of hand
83.21 Open biopsy of soft tissue
83.95 Aspiration of other soft tissue

20220-20225

20220 Biopsy, bone, trocar, or needle; superficial (eg, ilium, sternum, spinous process, ribs)
20225 deep (eg, vertebral body, femur)

ICD-9-CM Diagnostic

002.0 Typhoid fever
015.10 Tuberculosis of hip, confirmation unspecified — (Use additional code to identify manifestation: 711.4, 727.01, 730.8) ▽
015.20 Tuberculosis of knee, confirmation unspecified — (Use additional code to identify manifestation: 711.4, 727.01, 730.8) ▽
015.50 Tuberculosis of limb bones, confirmation unspecified — (Use additional code to identify manifestation: 711.4, 727.01, 730.8) ▽
015.60 Tuberculosis of mastoid, confirmation unspecified — (Use additional code to identify manifestation: 711.4, 727.01, 730.8) ▽
015.70 Tuberculosis of other specified bone, unspecified — (Use additional code to identify manifestation: 711.4, 727.01, 730.8) ▽
015.80 Tuberculosis of other specified joint, confirmation unspecified — (Use additional code to identify manifestation: 711.4, 727.01, 730.8) ▽
015.90 Tuberculosis of unspecified bones and joints, confirmation unspecified — (Use additional code to identify manifestation: 711.4, 727.01, 730.8) ▽
170.0 Malignant neoplasm of bones of skull and face, except mandible
170.1 Malignant neoplasm of mandible
170.2 Malignant neoplasm of vertebral column, excluding sacrum and coccyx
170.3 Malignant neoplasm of ribs, sternum, and clavicle
170.4 Malignant neoplasm of scapula and long bones of upper limb
170.5 Malignant neoplasm of short bones of upper limb
170.6 Malignant neoplasm of pelvic bones, sacrum, and coccyx
170.7 Malignant neoplasm of long bones of lower limb
170.8 Malignant neoplasm of short bones of lower limb
170.9 Malignant neoplasm of bone and articular cartilage, site unspecified ▽
198.5 Secondary malignant neoplasm of bone and bone marrow
209.73 Secondary neuroendocrine tumor of bone
213.0 Benign neoplasm of bones of skull and face
213.1 Benign neoplasm of lower jaw bone
213.2 Benign neoplasm of vertebral column, excluding sacrum and coccyx
213.3 Benign neoplasm of ribs, sternum, and clavicle
213.4 Benign neoplasm of scapula and long bones of upper limb
213.5 Benign neoplasm of short bones of upper limb
213.6 Benign neoplasm of pelvic bones, sacrum, and coccyx
213.7 Benign neoplasm of long bones of lower limb
213.8 Benign neoplasm of short bones of lower limb
238.0 Neoplasm of uncertain behavior of bone and articular cartilage
239.2 Neoplasms of unspecified nature of bone, soft tissue, and skin
273.1 Monoclonal paraproteinemia — (Use additional code to identify any associated intellectual disabilities)
284.81 Red cell aplasia (acquired) (adult) (with thymoma)
284.89 Other specified aplastic anemias
285.9 Unspecified anemia ▽
730.10 Chronic osteomyelitis, site unspecified — (Use additional code to identify organism: 041.1. Use additional code to identify major osseous defect, if applicable: 731.3) ▽
730.11 Chronic osteomyelitis, shoulder region — (Use additional code to identify organism: 041.1. Use additional code to identify major osseous defect, if applicable: 731.3)
730.12 Chronic osteomyelitis, upper arm — (Use additional code to identify organism: 041.1. Use additional code to identify major osseous defect, if applicable: 731.3)
730.13 Chronic osteomyelitis, forearm — (Use additional code to identify organism: 041.1. Use additional code to identify major osseous defect, if applicable: 731.3)
730.14 Chronic osteomyelitis, hand — (Use additional code to identify organism: 041.1. Use additional code to identify major osseous defect, if applicable: 731.3)
730.15 Chronic osteomyelitis, pelvic region and thigh — (Use additional code to identify organism: 041.1. Use additional code to identify major osseous defect, if applicable: 731.3)
730.16 Chronic osteomyelitis, lower leg — (Use additional code to identify organism: 041.1. Use additional code to identify major osseous defect, if applicable: 731.3)
730.17 Chronic osteomyelitis, ankle and foot — (Use additional code to identify organism: 041.1. Use additional code to identify major osseous defect, if applicable: 731.3)

730.18 Chronic osteomyelitis, other specified sites — (Use additional code to identify organism: 041.1. Use additional code to identify major osseous defect, if applicable: 731.3)

730.19 Chronic osteomyelitis, multiple sites — (Use additional code to identify organism: 041.1. Use additional code to identify major osseous defect, if applicable: 731.3)

730.20 Unspecified osteomyelitis, site unspecified — (Use additional code to identify organism: 041.1. Use additional code to identify major osseous defect, if applicable: 731.3) ▽

730.21 Unspecified osteomyelitis, shoulder region — (Use additional code to identify organism: 041.1. Use additional code to identify major osseous defect, if applicable: 731.3) ▽

730.22 Unspecified osteomyelitis, upper arm — (Use additional code to identify organism: 041.1. Use additional code to identify major osseous defect, if applicable: 731.3) ▽

730.23 Unspecified osteomyelitis, forearm — (Use additional code to identify organism: 041.1. Use additional code to identify major osseous defect, if applicable: 731.3) ▽

730.24 Unspecified osteomyelitis, hand — (Use additional code to identify organism: 041.1. Use additional code to identify major osseous defect, if applicable: 731.3) ▽

730.25 Unspecified osteomyelitis, pelvic region and thigh — (Use additional code to identify organism: 041.1. Use additional code to identify major osseous defect, if applicable: 731.3) ▽

730.26 Unspecified osteomyelitis, lower leg — (Use additional code to identify organism: 041.1. Use additional code to identify major osseous defect, if applicable: 731.3) ▽

730.27 Unspecified osteomyelitis, ankle and foot — (Use additional code to identify organism: 041.1. Use additional code to identify major osseous defect, if applicable: 731.3) ▽

730.28 Unspecified osteomyelitis, other specified sites — (Use additional code to identify organism: 041.1. Use additional code to identify major osseous defect, if applicable: 731.3) ▽

730.29 Unspecified osteomyelitis, multiple sites — (Use additional code to identify organism: 041.1. Use additional code to identify major osseous defect, if applicable: 731.3) ▽

730.80 Other infections involving bone in diseases classified elsewhere, site unspecified — (Use additional code to identify organism: 041.1. Code first underlying disease: 002.0, 015.0-015.9) ▽ ☒

730.81 Other infections involving bone diseases classified elsewhere, shoulder region — (Use additional code to identify organism: 041.1. Code first underlying disease: 002.0, 015.0-015.9) ☒

730.82 Other infections involving bone diseases classified elsewhere, upper arm — (Use additional code to identify organism: 041.1. Code first underlying disease: 002.0, 015.0-015.9) ☒

730.83 Other infections involving bone in diseases classified elsewhere, forearm — (Use additional code to identify organism: 041.1. Code first underlying disease: 002.0, 015.0-015.9) ☒

730.84 Other infections involving diseases classified elsewhere, hand bone — (Use additional code to identify organism: 041.1. Code first underlying disease: 002.0, 015.0-015.9) ☒

730.85 Other infections involving bone diseases classified elsewhere, pelvic region and thigh — (Use additional code to identify organism: 041.1. Code first underlying disease: 002.0, 015.0-015.9) ☒

730.86 Other infections involving bone diseases classified elsewhere, lower leg — (Use additional code to identify organism: 041.1. Code first underlying disease: 002.0, 015.0-015.9) ☒

730.87 Other infections involving bone diseases classified elsewhere, ankle and foot — (Use additional code to identify organism: 041.1. Code first underlying disease: 002.0, 015.0-015.9) ☒

730.88 Other infections involving bone diseases classified elsewhere, other specified sites — (Use additional code to identify organism: 041.1. Code first underlying disease: 002.0, 015.0-015.9) ☒

730.89 Other infections involving bone diseases classified elsewhere, multiple sites — (Use additional code to identify organism: 041.1. Code first underlying disease: 002.0, 015.0-015.9) ☒

731.3 Major osseous defects — (Code first underlying disease: 170.0-170.9, 730.00-730.29, 733.00-733.09, 733.40-733.49, 996.45)

V10.00 Personal history of malignant neoplasm of unspecified site in gastrointestinal tract ▽

V10.01 Personal history of malignant neoplasm of tongue

V10.02 Personal history of malignant neoplasm of other and unspecified parts of oral cavity and pharynx ▽

V10.03 Personal history of malignant neoplasm of esophagus

V10.04 Personal history of malignant neoplasm of stomach

V10.05 Personal history of malignant neoplasm of large intestine

V10.06 Personal history of malignant neoplasm of rectum, rectosigmoid junction, and anus

V10.07 Personal history of malignant neoplasm of liver

V10.09 Personal history of malignant neoplasm of other site in gastrointestinal tract

V10.11 Personal history of malignant neoplasm of bronchus and lung

V10.12 Personal history of malignant neoplasm of trachea

V10.3 Personal history of malignant neoplasm of breast

V10.40 Personal history of malignant neoplasm of unspecified female genital organ ▽ ♀

V10.41 Personal history of malignant neoplasm of cervix uteri ♀

V10.42 Personal history of malignant neoplasm of other parts of uterus ♀

V10.43 Personal history of malignant neoplasm of ovary ♀

V10.44 Personal history of malignant neoplasm of other female genital organs ♀

V10.45 Personal history of malignant neoplasm of unspecified male genital organ ▽ ♂

V10.46 Personal history of malignant neoplasm of prostate ♂

V10.47 Personal history of malignant neoplasm of testis ♂

V10.49 Personal history of malignant neoplasm of other male genital organs ♂

V10.50 Personal history of malignant neoplasm of unspecified urinary organ ▽

V10.51 Personal history of malignant neoplasm of bladder

V10.52 Personal history of malignant neoplasm of kidney

V10.53 Personal history of malignant neoplasm, renal pelvis

V10.59 Personal history of malignant neoplasm of other urinary organ

V10.81 Personal history of malignant neoplasm of bone

V10.90 Personal history of unspecified malignant neoplasm ▽

V10.91 Personal history of malignant neuroendocrine tumor — (Code first any continuing functional activity, such as: carcinoid syndrome (259.2))

ICD-9-CM Procedural

01.15 Biopsy of skull

76.11 Biopsy of facial bone

77.40 Biopsy of bone, unspecified site

77.41 Biopsy of scapula, clavicle, and thorax (ribs and sternum)

77.42 Biopsy of humerus

77.43 Biopsy of radius and ulna

77.44 Biopsy of carpals and metacarpals

77.45 Biopsy of femur

77.46 Biopsy of patella

77.47 Biopsy of tibia and fibula

77.48 Biopsy of tarsals and metatarsals

77.49 Biopsy of other bone, except facial bones

20240-20245

20240 Biopsy, bone, open; superficial (eg, ilium, sternum, spinous process, ribs, trochanter of femur)

20245 deep (eg, humerus, ischium, femur)

ICD-9-CM Diagnostic

002.0 Typhoid fever

170.0 Malignant neoplasm of bones of skull and face, except mandible

170.1 Malignant neoplasm of mandible

170.2 Malignant neoplasm of vertebral column, excluding sacrum and coccyx

170.3 Malignant neoplasm of ribs, sternum, and clavicle

170.4 Malignant neoplasm of scapula and long bones of upper limb

170.5 Malignant neoplasm of short bones of upper limb

170.6 Malignant neoplasm of pelvic bones, sacrum, and coccyx

170.7 Malignant neoplasm of long bones of lower limb

170.8 Malignant neoplasm of short bones of lower limb

170.9 Malignant neoplasm of bone and articular cartilage, site unspecified ▼

198.5 Secondary malignant neoplasm of bone and bone marrow

209.73 Secondary neuroendocrine tumor of bone

213.0 Benign neoplasm of bones of skull and face

213.1 Benign neoplasm of lower jaw bone

213.2 Benign neoplasm of vertebral column, excluding sacrum and coccyx

213.3 Benign neoplasm of ribs, sternum, and clavicle

213.4 Benign neoplasm of scapula and long bones of upper limb

213.5 Benign neoplasm of short bones of upper limb

213.6 Benign neoplasm of pelvic bones, sacrum, and coccyx

213.7 Benign neoplasm of long bones of lower limb

213.8 Benign neoplasm of short bones of lower limb

238.0 Neoplasm of uncertain behavior of bone and articular cartilage

239.2 Neoplasms of unspecified nature of bone, soft tissue, and skin

249.80 Secondary diabetes mellitus with other specified manifestations, not stated as uncontrolled, or unspecified — (Use additional code to identify manifestation: 707.10-707.19, 707.8, 707.9, 731.8) (Use additional code to identify any associated insulin use: V58.67)

249.81 Secondary diabetes mellitus with other specified manifestations, uncontrolled — (Use additional code to identify manifestation: 707.10-707.19, 707.8, 707.9, 731.8) (Use additional code to identify any associated insulin use: V58.67)

250.80 Diabetes with other specified manifestations, type II or unspecified type, not stated as uncontrolled — (Use additional code to identify manifestation: 707.10-707.19, 707.8, 707.9, 731.8)

250.81 Diabetes with other specified manifestations, type I [juvenile type], not stated as uncontrolled — (Use additional code to identify manifestation: 707.10-707.19, 707.8, 707.9, 731.8)

250.82 Diabetes with other specified manifestations, type II or unspecified type, uncontrolled — (Use additional code to identify manifestation: 707.10-707.19, 707.8, 707.9, 731.8)

250.83 Diabetes with other specified manifestations, type I [juvenile type], uncontrolled — (Use additional code to identify manifestation: 707.10-707.19, 707.8, 707.9, 731.8)

730.10 Chronic osteomyelitis, site unspecified — (Use additional code to identify organism: 041.1. Use additional code to identify major osseous defect, if applicable: 731.3) ▼

730.11 Chronic osteomyelitis, shoulder region — (Use additional code to identify organism: 041.1. Use additional code to identify major osseous defect, if applicable: 731.3)

730.12 Chronic osteomyelitis, upper arm — (Use additional code to identify organism: 041.1. Use additional code to identify major osseous defect, if applicable: 731.3)

730.13 Chronic osteomyelitis, forearm — (Use additional code to identify organism: 041.1. Use additional code to identify major osseous defect, if applicable: 731.3)

730.14 Chronic osteomyelitis, hand — (Use additional code to identify organism: 041.1. Use additional code to identify major osseous defect, if applicable: 731.3)

730.15 Chronic osteomyelitis, pelvic region and thigh — (Use additional code to identify organism: 041.1. Use additional code to identify major osseous defect, if applicable: 731.3)

730.16 Chronic osteomyelitis, lower leg — (Use additional code to identify organism: 041.1. Use additional code to identify major osseous defect, if applicable: 731.3)

730.17 Chronic osteomyelitis, ankle and foot — (Use additional code to identify organism: 041.1. Use additional code to identify major osseous defect, if applicable: 731.3)

730.18 Chronic osteomyelitis, other specified sites — (Use additional code to identify organism: 041.1. Use additional code to identify major osseous defect, if applicable: 731.3)

730.19 Chronic osteomyelitis, multiple sites — (Use additional code to identify organism: 041.1. Use additional code to identify major osseous defect, if applicable: 731.3)

730.20 Unspecified osteomyelitis, site unspecified — (Use additional code to identify organism: 041.1. Use additional code to identify major osseous defect, if applicable: 731.3) ▼

730.21 Unspecified osteomyelitis, shoulder region — (Use additional code to identify organism: 041.1. Use additional code to identify major osseous defect, if applicable: 731.3) ▼

730.22 Unspecified osteomyelitis, upper arm — (Use additional code to identify organism: 041.1. Use additional code to identify major osseous defect, if applicable: 731.3) ▼

730.23 Unspecified osteomyelitis, forearm — (Use additional code to identify organism: 041.1. Use additional code to identify major osseous defect, if applicable: 731.3) ▼

730.24 Unspecified osteomyelitis, hand — (Use additional code to identify organism: 041.1. Use additional code to identify major osseous defect, if applicable: 731.3) ▼

730.25 Unspecified osteomyelitis, pelvic region and thigh — (Use additional code to identify organism: 041.1. Use additional code to identify major osseous defect, if applicable: 731.3) ▼

730.26 Unspecified osteomyelitis, lower leg — (Use additional code to identify organism: 041.1. Use additional code to identify major osseous defect, if applicable: 731.3) ▼

730.27 Unspecified osteomyelitis, ankle and foot — (Use additional code to identify organism: 041.1. Use additional code to identify major osseous defect, if applicable: 731.3) ▼

730.28 Unspecified osteomyelitis, other specified sites — (Use additional code to identify organism: 041.1. Use additional code to identify major osseous defect, if applicable: 731.3) ▼

730.29 Unspecified osteomyelitis, multiple sites — (Use additional code to identify organism: 041.1. Use additional code to identify major osseous defect, if applicable: 731.3) ▼

730.80 Other infections involving bone in diseases classified elsewhere, site unspecified — (Use additional code to identify organism: 041.1. Code first underlying disease: 002.0, 015.0-015.9) ▼ ☒

730.81 Other infections involving bone diseases classified elsewhere, shoulder region — (Use additional code to identify organism: 041.1. Code first underlying disease: 002.0, 015.0-015.9) ☒

730.82 Other infections involving bone diseases classified elsewhere, upper arm — (Use additional code to identify organism: 041.1. Code first underlying disease: 002.0, 015.0-015.9) ☒

730.83 Other infections involving bone in diseases classified elsewhere, forearm — (Use additional code to identify organism: 041.1. Code first underlying disease: 002.0, 015.0-015.9) ☒

730.84 Other infections involving diseases classified elsewhere, hand bone — (Use additional code to identify organism: 041.1. Code first underlying disease: 002.0, 015.0-015.9) ☒

730.85 Other infections involving bone diseases classified elsewhere, pelvic region and thigh — (Use additional code to identify organism: 041.1. Code first underlying disease: 002.0, 015.0-015.9) ☒

730.86 Other infections involving bone diseases classified elsewhere, lower leg — (Use additional code to identify organism: 041.1. Code first underlying disease: 002.0, 015.0-015.9) ☒

730.87 Other infections involving bone diseases classified elsewhere, ankle and foot — (Use additional code to identify organism: 041.1. Code first underlying disease: 002.0, 015.0-015.9) ☒

730.88 Other infections involving bone diseases classified elsewhere, other specified sites — (Use additional code to identify organism: 041.1. Code first underlying disease: 002.0, 015.0-015.9) ☒

730.89 Other infections involving bone diseases classified elsewhere, multiple sites — (Use additional code to identify organism: 041.1. Code first underlying disease: 002.0, 015.0-015.9) ☒

731.0 Osteitis deformans without mention of bone tumor

731.1 Osteitis deformans in diseases classified elsewhere — (Code first underlying disease: 170.0-170.9) ☒

731.2 Hypertrophic pulmonary osteoarthropathy

731.3 Major osseous defects — (Code first underlying disease: 170.0-170.9, 730.00-730.29, 733.00-733.09, 733.40-733.49, 996.45)

731.8 Other bone involvement in diseases classified elsewhere — (Code first underlying disease: 249.8, 250.8. Use additional code to specify bone condition: 730.00-730.09) ☒

V10.00 Personal history of malignant neoplasm of unspecified site in gastrointestinal tract ▼

V10.03 Personal history of malignant neoplasm of esophagus

V10.04 Personal history of malignant neoplasm of stomach

V10.05 Personal history of malignant neoplasm of large intestine

V10.06 Personal history of malignant neoplasm of rectum, rectosigmoid junction, and anus

V10.07 Personal history of malignant neoplasm of liver

V10.09 Personal history of malignant neoplasm of other site in gastrointestinal tract
V10.11 Personal history of malignant neoplasm of bronchus and lung
V10.12 Personal history of malignant neoplasm of trachea
V10.20 Personal history of malignant neoplasm of unspecified respiratory organ ▽
V10.3 Personal history of malignant neoplasm of breast
V10.40 Personal history of malignant neoplasm of unspecified female genital organ ▽ ♀
V10.41 Personal history of malignant neoplasm of cervix uteri ♀
V10.42 Personal history of malignant neoplasm of other parts of uterus ♀
V10.43 Personal history of malignant neoplasm of ovary ♀
V10.44 Personal history of malignant neoplasm of other female genital organs ♀
V10.45 Personal history of malignant neoplasm of unspecified male genital organ ▽ ♂
V10.46 Personal history of malignant neoplasm of prostate ♂
V10.47 Personal history of malignant neoplasm of testis ♂
V10.49 Personal history of malignant neoplasm of other male genital organs ♂
V10.50 Personal history of malignant neoplasm of unspecified urinary organ ▽
V10.51 Personal history of malignant neoplasm of bladder
V10.52 Personal history of malignant neoplasm of kidney
V10.53 Personal history of malignant neoplasm, renal pelvis
V10.59 Personal history of malignant neoplasm of other urinary organ
V10.81 Personal history of malignant neoplasm of bone
V10.90 Personal history of unspecified malignant neoplasm ▽
V10.91 Personal history of malignant neuroendocrine tumor — (Code first any continuing functional activity, such as: carcinoid syndrome (259.2))

ICD-9-CM Procedural

01.15 Biopsy of skull
76.11 Biopsy of facial bone
77.40 Biopsy of bone, unspecified site
77.41 Biopsy of scapula, clavicle, and thorax (ribs and sternum)
77.42 Biopsy of humerus
77.43 Biopsy of radius and ulna
77.44 Biopsy of carpals and metacarpals
77.45 Biopsy of femur
77.46 Biopsy of patella
77.47 Biopsy of tibia and fibula
77.48 Biopsy of tarsals and metatarsals
77.49 Biopsy of other bone, except facial bones

20250-20251

20250 Biopsy, vertebral body, open; thoracic
20251 lumbar or cervical

ICD-9-CM Diagnostic

170.2 Malignant neoplasm of vertebral column, excluding sacrum and coccyx
198.5 Secondary malignant neoplasm of bone and bone marrow
198.89 Secondary malignant neoplasm of other specified sites
209.73 Secondary neuroendocrine tumor of bone
213.2 Benign neoplasm of vertebral column, excluding sacrum and coccyx
237.70 Neurofibromatosis, unspecified ▽
237.71 Neurofibromatosis, Type 1 (von Recklinghausen's disease)
237.72 Neurofibromatosis, Type 2 (acoustic neurofibromatosis)
237.73 Schwannomatosis
237.79 Other neurofibromatosis
238.0 Neoplasm of uncertain behavior of bone and articular cartilage
239.2 Neoplasms of unspecified nature of bone, soft tissue, and skin
252.00 Hyperparathyroidism, unspecified ▽
252.01 Primary hyperparathyroidism
252.02 Secondary hyperparathyroidism, non-renal
252.08 Other hyperparathyroidism
277.5 Mucopolysaccharidosis — (Use additional code to identify any associated intellectual disabilities)
336.9 Unspecified disease of spinal cord ▽
356.1 Peroneal muscular atrophy
720.81 Inflammatory spondylopathies in diseases classified elsewhere — (Code first underlying disease: 015.0) ☒
720.89 Other inflammatory spondylopathies
723.4 Brachial neuritis or radiculitis NOS ▽
724.4 Thoracic or lumbosacral neuritis or radiculitis, unspecified ▽
724.5 Unspecified backache ▽
724.9 Other unspecified back disorder
729.2 Unspecified neuralgia, neuritis, and radiculitis ▽
730.18 Chronic osteomyelitis, other specified sites — (Use additional code to identify organism: 041.1. Use additional code to identify major osseous defect, if applicable: 731.3)
730.28 Unspecified osteomyelitis, other specified sites — (Use additional code to identify organism: 041.1. Use additional code to identify major osseous defect, if applicable: 731.3) ▽
730.80 Other infections involving bone in diseases classified elsewhere, site unspecified — (Use additional code to identify organism: 041.1. Code first underlying disease: 002.0, 015.0-015.9) ▽ ☒
730.88 Other infections involving bone diseases classified elsewhere, other specified sites — (Use additional code to identify organism: 041.1. Code first underlying disease: 002.0, 015.0-015.9) ☒
730.89 Other infections involving bone diseases classified elsewhere, multiple sites — (Use additional code to identify organism: 041.1. Code first underlying disease: 002.0, 015.0-015.9) ☒
730.98 Unspecified infection of bone of other specified site — (Use additional code to identify organism: 041.1) ▽
731.0 Osteitis deformans without mention of bone tumor
731.3 Major osseous defects — (Code first underlying disease: 170.0-170.9, 730.00-730.29, 733.00-733.09, 733.40-733.49, 996.45)
733.00 Unspecified osteoporosis — (Use additional code to identify major osseous defect, if applicable: 731.3) (Use additional code to identify personal history of pathologic (healed) fracture: V13.51) ▽
733.01 Senile osteoporosis — (Use additional code to identify major osseous defect, if applicable: 731.3) (Use additional code to identify personal history of pathologic (healed) fracture: V13.51)
733.02 Idiopathic osteoporosis — (Use additional code to identify major osseous defect, if applicable: 731.3) (Use additional code to identify personal history of pathologic (healed) fracture: V13.51)
733.03 Disuse osteoporosis — (Use additional code to identify major osseous defect, if applicable: 731.3) (Use additional code to identify personal history of pathologic (healed) fracture: V13.51)
733.09 Other osteoporosis — (Use additional code to identify major osseous defect, if applicable: 731.3) (Use additional code to identify personal history of pathologic (healed) fracture: V13.51) (Use additional E code to identify drug)
737.40 Unspecified curvature of spine associated with other condition — (Code first associated condition: 015.0, 138, 237.7, 252.01, 277.5, 356.1, 731.0, 733.00-733.09) ☒
737.41 Kyphosis associated with other condition — (Code first associated condition: 015.0, 138, 237.7, 252.01, 277.5, 356.1, 731.0, 733.00-733.09) ☒
737.42 Lordosis associated with other condition — (Code first associated condition: 015.0, 138, 237.7, 252.01, 277.5, 356.1, 731.0, 733.00-733.09) ☒
737.43 Scoliosis associated with other condition — (Code first associated condition: 015.0, 138, 237.7, 252.01, 277.5, 356.1, 731.0, 733.00-733.09) ☒
V10.90 Personal history of unspecified malignant neoplasm ▽
V10.91 Personal history of malignant neuroendocrine tumor — (Code first any continuing functional activity, such as: carcinoid syndrome (259.2))

ICD-9-CM Procedural

77.49 Biopsy of other bone, except facial bones

20500

20500 Injection of sinus tract; therapeutic (separate procedure)

ICD-9-CM Diagnostic

510.0 Empyema with fistula — (Use additional code to identify infectious organism: 041.00-041.9)
522.7 Periapical abscess with sinus
527.4 Fistula of salivary gland
528.3 Cellulitis and abscess of oral soft tissues
567.22 Peritoneal abscess
567.23 Spontaneous bacterial peritonitis
567.29 Other suppurative peritonitis
567.31 Psoas muscle abscess
567.38 Other retroperitoneal abscess
567.39 Other retroperitoneal infections
685.0 Pilonidal cyst with abscess
685.1 Pilonidal cyst without mention of abscess
686.9 Unspecified local infection of skin and subcutaneous tissue — (Use additional code to identify any infectious organism: 041.0-041.8) ▽
719.80 Other specified disorders of joint, site unspecified ▽
719.81 Other specified disorders of shoulder joint
719.82 Other specified disorders of upper arm joint
719.83 Other specified disorders of forearm joint
719.84 Other specified disorders of hand joint
719.85 Other specified disorders of pelvic joint
719.86 Other specified disorders of lower leg joint
719.87 Other specified disorders of ankle and foot joint
719.88 Other specified disorders of joint of other specified site
719.89 Other specified disorders of joints of multiple sites
733.99 Other disorders of bone and cartilage
998.6 Persistent postoperative fistula, not elsewhere classified

ICD-9-CM Procedural

82.96 Other injection of locally-acting therapeutic substance into soft tissue of hand
83.98 Injection of locally acting therapeutic substance into other soft tissue
99.21 Injection of antibiotic
99.23 Injection of steroid
99.29 Injection or infusion of other therapeutic or prophylactic substance

20501

20501 Injection of sinus tract; diagnostic (sinogram)

ICD-9-CM Diagnostic

349.81 Cerebrospinal fluid rhinorrhea
360.32 Ocular fistula causing hypotony
375.61 Lacrimal fistula
380.89 Other disorder of external ear
383.81 Postauricular fistula
386.40 Unspecified labyrinthine fistula ▽
386.41 Round window fistula
386.42 Oval window fistula
386.43 Semicircular canal fistula
386.48 Labyrinthine fistula of combined sites
478.79 Other diseases of larynx — (Use additional code to identify infectious organism)
510.0 Empyema with fistula — (Use additional code to identify infectious organism: 041.00-041.9)
526.89 Other specified disease of the jaws
528.5 Diseases of lips
530.84 Tracheoesophageal fistula
530.89 Other specified disorder of the esophagus
537.4 Fistula of stomach or duodenum
543.9 Other and unspecified diseases of appendix ▽
569.69 Other complication of colostomy or enterostomy
569.81 Fistula of intestine, excluding rectum and anus
575.5 Fistula of gallbladder
576.4 Fistula of bile duct
577.8 Other specified disease of pancreas
593.81 Vascular disorders of kidney
593.82 Ureteral fistula
596.1 Intestinovesical fistula — (Use additional code to identify urinary incontinence: 625.6, 788.30-788.39)
596.2 Vesical fistula, not elsewhere classified — (Use additional code to identify urinary incontinence: 625.6, 788.30-788.39)
608.89 Other specified disorder of male genital organs ♂
611.0 Inflammatory disease of breast
619.0 Urinary-genital tract fistula, female ♀
619.1 Digestive-genital tract fistula, female ♀
619.2 Genital tract-skin fistula, female ♀
619.8 Other specified fistula involving female genital tract ♀
686.9 Unspecified local infection of skin and subcutaneous tissue — (Use additional code to identify any infectious organism: 041.0-041.8) ▽
719.80 Other specified disorders of joint, site unspecified ▽
719.81 Other specified disorders of shoulder joint
719.82 Other specified disorders of upper arm joint
719.83 Other specified disorders of forearm joint
719.84 Other specified disorders of hand joint
719.85 Other specified disorders of pelvic joint
719.86 Other specified disorders of lower leg joint
719.87 Other specified disorders of ankle and foot joint
719.88 Other specified disorders of joint of other specified site
719.89 Other specified disorders of joints of multiple sites
733.99 Other disorders of bone and cartilage
744.41 Congenital branchial cleft sinus or fistula
744.46 Congenital preauricular sinus or fistula
744.49 Other congenital branchial cleft cyst or fistula; preauricular sinus
748.3 Other congenital anomaly of larynx, trachea, and bronchus
750.25 Congenital fistula of lip
998.6 Persistent postoperative fistula, not elsewhere classified

ICD-9-CM Procedural

87.38 Sinogram of chest wall
88.03 Sinogram of abdominal wall
88.14 Retroperitoneal fistulogram

20520-20525

20520 Removal of foreign body in muscle or tendon sheath; simple
20525 deep or complicated

ICD-9-CM Diagnostic

709.4 Foreign body granuloma of skin and subcutaneous tissue — (Use additional code to identify foreign body (V90.01-V90.9))
728.82 Foreign body granuloma of muscle — (Use additional code to identify foreign body (V90.01-V90.9))
729.6 Residual foreign body in soft tissue — (Use additional code to identify foreign body (V90.01-V90.9))
870.4 Penetrating wound of orbit with foreign body
873.50 Open wound of face, unspecified site, complicated ▽
873.51 Open wound of cheek, complicated
873.52 Open wound of forehead, complicated
873.53 Open wound of lip, complicated

873.54 Open wound of jaw, complicated
873.59 Open wound of face, other and multiple sites, complicated
874.9 Open wound of other and unspecified parts of neck, complicated
875.1 Open wound of chest (wall), complicated
876.1 Open wound of back, complicated
879.3 Open wound of abdominal wall, anterior, complicated
879.5 Open wound of abdominal wall, lateral, complicated
879.9 Open wound(s) (multiple) of unspecified site(s), complicated
880.10 Open wound of shoulder region, complicated
880.11 Open wound of scapular region, complicated
880.12 Open wound of axillary region, complicated
880.13 Open wound of upper arm, complicated
880.19 Open wound of multiple sites of shoulder and upper arm, complicated
880.20 Open wound of shoulder region, with tendon involvement
880.21 Open wound of scapular region, with tendon involvement
880.22 Open wound of axillary region, with tendon involvement
880.23 Open wound of upper arm, with tendon involvement
880.29 Open wound of multiple sites of shoulder and upper arm, with tendon involvement
881.10 Open wound of forearm, complicated
881.11 Open wound of elbow, complicated
881.12 Open wound of wrist, complicated
881.20 Open wound of forearm, with tendon involvement
881.21 Open wound of elbow, with tendon involvement
881.22 Open wound of wrist, with tendon involvement
882.1 Open wound of hand except finger(s) alone, complicated
882.2 Open wound of hand except finger(s) alone, with tendon involvement
883.1 Open wound of finger(s), complicated
883.2 Open wound of finger(s), with tendon involvement
890.1 Open wound of hip and thigh, complicated
890.2 Open wound of hip and thigh, with tendon involvement
891.1 Open wound of knee, leg (except thigh), and ankle, complicated
891.2 Open wound of knee, leg (except thigh), and ankle, with tendon involvement
892.1 Open wound of foot except toe(s) alone, complicated
893.1 Open wound of toe(s), complicated
893.2 Open wound of toe(s), with tendon involvement
894.1 Multiple and unspecified open wound of lower limb, complicated
894.2 Multiple and unspecified open wound of lower limb, with tendon involvement
930.8 Foreign body in other and combined sites on external eye

ICD-9-CM Procedural

82.01 Exploration of tendon sheath of hand
82.02 Myotomy of hand
83.01 Exploration of tendon sheath
83.02 Myotomy

HCPCS Level II Supplies & Services

A4305 Disposable drug delivery system, flow rate of 50 ml or greater per hour

20526

20526 Injection, therapeutic (eg, local anesthetic, corticosteroid), carpal tunnel

ICD-9-CM Diagnostic

354.0 Carpal tunnel syndrome

ICD-9-CM Procedural

99.23 Injection of steroid
99.29 Injection or infusion of other therapeutic or prophylactic substance

HCPCS Level II Supplies & Services

J0702 Injection, betamethasone acetate 3 mg and betamethasone sodium phosphate 3 mg
J1020 Injection, methylprednisolone acetate, 20 mg
J1030 Injection, methylprednisolone acetate, 40 mg
J1040 Injection, methylprednisolone acetate, 80 mg
J1094 Injection, dexamethasone acetate, 1 mg
J1100 Injection, dexamethasone sodium phosphate, 1 mg
J1700 Injection, hydrocortisone acetate, up to 25 mg
J1710 Injection, hydrocortisone sodium phosphate, up to 50 mg
J1720 Injection, hydrocortisone sodium succinate, up to 100 mg
J2920 Injection, methylprednisolone sodium succinate, up to 40 mg
J2930 Injection, methylprednisolone sodium succinate, up to 125 mg
J3301 Injection, triamcinolone acetonide, not otherwise specified, 10 mg
J3302 Injection, triamcinolone diacetate, per 5 mg
J3303 Injection, triamcinolone hexacetonide, per 5 mg
S0020 Injection, bupivicaine HCl, 30 ml

20550

20550 Injection(s); single tendon sheath, or ligament, aponeurosis (eg, plantar "fascia")

ICD-9-CM Diagnostic

135 Sarcoidosis
277.30 Amyloidosis, unspecified — (Use additional code to identify any associated intellectual disabilities)
277.31 Familial Mediterranean fever — (Use additional code to identify any associated intellectual disabilities)
277.39 Other amyloidosis — (Use additional code to identify any associated intellectual disabilities)
338.0 Central pain syndrome — (Use additional code to identify pain associated with psychological factors: 307.89)
338.11 Acute pain due to trauma — (Use additional code to identify pain associated with psychological factors: 307.89)
338.12 Acute post-thoracotomy pain — (Use additional code to identify pain associated with psychological factors: 307.89)
338.18 Other acute postoperative pain — (Use additional code to identify pain associated with psychological factors: 307.89)
338.19 Other acute pain — (Use additional code to identify pain associated with psychological factors: 307.89)
338.21 Chronic pain due to trauma — (Use additional code to identify pain associated with psychological factors: 307.89)
338.22 Chronic post-thoracotomy pain — (Use additional code to identify pain associated with psychological factors: 307.89)
338.28 Other chronic postoperative pain — (Use additional code to identify pain associated with psychological factors: 307.89)
338.29 Other chronic pain — (Use additional code to identify pain associated with psychological factors: 307.89)
338.4 Chronic pain syndrome — (Use additional code to identify pain associated with psychological factors: 307.89)
351.1 Geniculate ganglionitis
353.0 Brachial plexus lesions
353.1 Lumbosacral plexus lesions
353.2 Cervical root lesions, not elsewhere classified
353.3 Thoracic root lesions, not elsewhere classified
353.4 Lumbosacral root lesions, not elsewhere classified
353.8 Other nerve root and plexus disorders
354.0 Carpal tunnel syndrome
354.1 Other lesion of median nerve
354.2 Lesion of ulnar nerve
354.3 Lesion of radial nerve
354.5 Mononeuritis multiplex
354.8 Other mononeuritis of upper limb
355.6 Lesion of plantar nerve
357.1 Polyneuropathy in collagen vascular disease — (Code first underlying disease: 446.0, 710.0, 714.0)

357.4 Polyneuropathy in other diseases classified elsewhere — (Code first underlying disease, as: 032.0-032.9,135, 251.2, 265.0, 265.2, 266.0-266.9, 277.1, 277.30-277.39, 585.9, 586) ☒
359.6 Symptomatic inflammatory myopathy in diseases classified elsewhere — (Code first underlying disease: 135, 140.0-208.9, 277.30-277.39, 446.0, 710.0, 710.1, 710.2, 714.0) ☒
446.0 Polyarteritis nodosa
710.0 Systemic lupus erythematosus — (Use additional code to identify manifestation: 424.91, 581.81, 582.81, 583.81)
710.1 Systemic sclerosis — (Use additional code to identify manifestation: 359.6, 517.2)
710.2 Sicca syndrome
714.0 Rheumatoid arthritis — (Use additional code to identify manifestation: 357.1, 359.6)
715.00 Generalized osteoarthrosis, unspecified site ▽
715.04 Generalized osteoarthrosis, involving hand
715.09 Generalized osteoarthrosis, involving multiple sites
716.50 Unspecified polyarthropathy or polyarthritis, site unspecified ▽
716.51 Unspecified polyarthropathy or polyarthritis, shoulder region ▽
716.52 Unspecified polyarthropathy or polyarthritis, upper arm ▽
716.53 Unspecified polyarthropathy or polyarthritis, forearm ▽
716.54 Unspecified polyarthropathy or polyarthritis, hand ▽
716.55 Unspecified polyarthropathy or polyarthritis, pelvic region and thigh ▽
716.56 Unspecified polyarthropathy or polyarthritis, lower leg ▽
716.57 Unspecified polyarthropathy or polyarthritis, ankle and foot ▽
716.58 Unspecified polyarthropathy or polyarthritis, other specified sites ▽
716.59 Unspecified polyarthropathy or polyarthritis, multiple sites ▽
716.60 Unspecified monoarthritis, site unspecified ▽
716.61 Unspecified monoarthritis, shoulder region ▽
716.62 Unspecified monoarthritis, upper arm ▽
716.63 Unspecified monoarthritis, forearm ▽
716.64 Unspecified monoarthritis, hand ▽
716.65 Unspecified monoarthritis, pelvic region and thigh ▽
716.66 Unspecified monoarthritis, lower leg ▽
716.67 Unspecified monoarthritis, ankle and foot ▽
716.68 Unspecified monoarthritis, other specified sites ▽
716.90 Unspecified arthropathy, site unspecified ▽
716.91 Unspecified arthropathy, shoulder region ▽
716.92 Unspecified arthropathy, upper arm ▽
716.93 Unspecified arthropathy, forearm ▽
716.94 Unspecified arthropathy, hand ▽
716.95 Unspecified arthropathy, pelvic region and thigh ▽
716.96 Unspecified arthropathy, lower leg ▽
716.97 Unspecified arthropathy, ankle and foot ▽
716.99 Unspecified arthropathy, multiple sites ▽
719.40 Pain in joint, site unspecified ▽
719.41 Pain in joint, shoulder region
719.42 Pain in joint, upper arm
719.43 Pain in joint, forearm
719.44 Pain in joint, hand
719.45 Pain in joint, pelvic region and thigh
719.46 Pain in joint, lower leg
719.47 Pain in joint, ankle and foot
719.48 Pain in joint, other specified sites
719.49 Pain in joint, multiple sites
720.0 Ankylosing spondylitis
726.0 Adhesive capsulitis of shoulder
726.10 Unspecified disorders of bursae and tendons in shoulder region ▽
726.11 Calcifying tendinitis of shoulder
726.12 Bicipital tenosynovitis
726.19 Other specified disorders of rotator cuff syndrome of shoulder and allied disorders
726.2 Other affections of shoulder region, not elsewhere classified
726.32 Lateral epicondylitis of elbow
727.00 Unspecified synovitis and tenosynovitis ▽
727.02 Giant cell tumor of tendon sheath
727.03 Trigger finger (acquired)
727.04 Radial styloid tenosynovitis
727.05 Other tenosynovitis of hand and wrist
727.06 Tenosynovitis of foot and ankle
727.09 Other synovitis and tenosynovitis
727.2 Specific bursitides often of occupational origin
727.3 Other bursitis disorders
728.71 Plantar fascial fibromatosis
729.4 Unspecified fasciitis ▽
729.5 Pain in soft tissues of limb
729.91 Post-traumatic seroma
729.92 Nontraumatic hematoma of soft tissue
729.99 Other disorders of soft tissue

ICD-9-CM Procedural

81.92 Injection of therapeutic substance into joint or ligament
82.96 Other injection of locally-acting therapeutic substance into soft tissue of hand
83.97 Injection of therapeutic substance into tendon
83.98 Injection of locally acting therapeutic substance into other soft tissue

HCPCS Level II Supplies & Services

J0702 Injection, betamethasone acetate 3 mg and betamethasone sodium phosphate 3 mg
J1020 Injection, methylprednisolone acetate, 20 mg
J1030 Injection, methylprednisolone acetate, 40 mg
J1040 Injection, methylprednisolone acetate, 80 mg
J1094 Injection, dexamethasone acetate, 1 mg
J1100 Injection, dexamethasone sodium phosphate, 1 mg
J1700 Injection, hydrocortisone acetate, up to 25 mg
J1710 Injection, hydrocortisone sodium phosphate, up to 50 mg
J1720 Injection, hydrocortisone sodium succinate, up to 100 mg
J2920 Injection, methylprednisolone sodium succinate, up to 40 mg
J2930 Injection, methylprednisolone sodium succinate, up to 125 mg
S0020 Injection, bupivicaine HCl, 30 ml

20551

20551 Injection(s); single tendon origin/insertion

ICD-9-CM Diagnostic

135 Sarcoidosis
277.30 Amyloidosis, unspecified — (Use additional code to identify any associated intellectual disabilities) ▽
277.31 Familial Mediterranean fever — (Use additional code to identify any associated intellectual disabilities)
277.39 Other amyloidosis — (Use additional code to identify any associated intellectual disabilities)
338.0 Central pain syndrome — (Use additional code to identify pain associated with psychological factors: 307.89)
338.11 Acute pain due to trauma — (Use additional code to identify pain associated with psychological factors: 307.89)
338.12 Acute post-thoracotomy pain — (Use additional code to identify pain associated with psychological factors: 307.89)
338.18 Other acute postoperative pain — (Use additional code to identify pain associated with psychological factors: 307.89)
338.19 Other acute pain — (Use additional code to identify pain associated with psychological factors: 307.89)

338.21 Chronic pain due to trauma — (Use additional code to identify pain associated with psychological factors: 307.89)
338.22 Chronic post-thoracotomy pain — (Use additional code to identify pain associated with psychological factors: 307.89)
338.28 Other chronic postoperative pain — (Use additional code to identify pain associated with psychological factors: 307.89)
338.29 Other chronic pain — (Use additional code to identify pain associated with psychological factors: 307.89)
338.4 Chronic pain syndrome — (Use additional code to identify pain associated with psychological factors: 307.89)
353.0 Brachial plexus lesions
353.1 Lumbosacral plexus lesions
353.2 Cervical root lesions, not elsewhere classified
353.3 Thoracic root lesions, not elsewhere classified
353.4 Lumbosacral root lesions, not elsewhere classified
353.8 Other nerve root and plexus disorders
354.0 Carpal tunnel syndrome
354.1 Other lesion of median nerve
354.2 Lesion of ulnar nerve
354.3 Lesion of radial nerve
354.5 Mononeuritis multiplex
354.8 Other mononeuritis of upper limb
355.2 Other lesion of femoral nerve
355.3 Lesion of lateral popliteal nerve
355.4 Lesion of medial popliteal nerve
355.5 Tarsal tunnel syndrome
355.6 Lesion of plantar nerve
355.71 Causalgia of lower limb
355.79 Other mononeuritis of lower limb
355.8 Unspecified mononeuritis of lower limb
355.9 Mononeuritis of unspecified site
357.1 Polyneuropathy in collagen vascular disease — (Code first underlying disease: 446.0, 710.0, 714.0)
357.4 Polyneuropathy in other diseases classified elsewhere — (Code first underlying disease, as: 032.0-032.9,135, 251.2, 265.0, 265.2, 266.0-266.9, 277.1, 277.30-277.39, 585.9, 586)
359.6 Symptomatic inflammatory myopathy in diseases classified elsewhere — (Code first underlying disease: 135, 140.0-208.9, 277.30-277.39, 446.0, 710.0, 710.1, 710.2, 714.0)
446.0 Polyarteritis nodosa
710.0 Systemic lupus erythematosus — (Use additional code to identify manifestation: 424.91, 581.81, 582.81, 583.81)
710.1 Systemic sclerosis — (Use additional code to identify manifestation: 359.6, 517.2)
710.2 Sicca syndrome
714.0 Rheumatoid arthritis — (Use additional code to identify manifestation: 357.1, 359.6)
715.00 Generalized osteoarthrosis, unspecified site
715.04 Generalized osteoarthrosis, involving hand
715.09 Generalized osteoarthrosis, involving multiple sites
715.16 Primary localized osteoarthrosis, lower leg
715.17 Primary localized osteoarthrosis, ankle and foot
715.18 Primary localized osteoarthrosis, other specified sites
715.35 Localized osteoarthrosis not specified whether primary or secondary, pelvic region and thigh
715.36 Localized osteoarthrosis not specified whether primary or secondary, lower leg
715.37 Localized osteoarthrosis not specified whether primary or secondary, ankle and foot
715.38 Localized osteoarthrosis not specified whether primary or secondary, other specified sites
716.50 Unspecified polyarthropathy or polyarthritis, site unspecified
716.51 Unspecified polyarthropathy or polyarthritis, shoulder region
716.52 Unspecified polyarthropathy or polyarthritis, upper arm
716.53 Unspecified polyarthropathy or polyarthritis, forearm
716.54 Unspecified polyarthropathy or polyarthritis, hand
716.55 Unspecified polyarthropathy or polyarthritis, pelvic region and thigh
716.56 Unspecified polyarthropathy or polyarthritis, lower leg
716.57 Unspecified polyarthropathy or polyarthritis, ankle and foot
716.58 Unspecified polyarthropathy or polyarthritis, other specified sites
716.59 Unspecified polyarthropathy or polyarthritis, multiple sites
716.60 Unspecified monoarthritis, site unspecified
716.61 Unspecified monoarthritis, shoulder region
716.62 Unspecified monoarthritis, upper arm
716.63 Unspecified monoarthritis, forearm
716.64 Unspecified monoarthritis, hand
716.65 Unspecified monoarthritis, pelvic region and thigh
716.66 Unspecified monoarthritis, lower leg
716.67 Unspecified monoarthritis, ankle and foot
716.68 Unspecified monoarthritis, other specified sites
716.90 Unspecified arthropathy, site unspecified
716.91 Unspecified arthropathy, shoulder region
716.92 Unspecified arthropathy, upper arm
716.93 Unspecified arthropathy, forearm
716.94 Unspecified arthropathy, hand
716.95 Unspecified arthropathy, pelvic region and thigh
716.96 Unspecified arthropathy, lower leg
716.97 Unspecified arthropathy, ankle and foot
716.99 Unspecified arthropathy, multiple sites
719.40 Pain in joint, site unspecified
719.41 Pain in joint, shoulder region
719.42 Pain in joint, upper arm
719.43 Pain in joint, forearm
719.44 Pain in joint, hand
719.45 Pain in joint, pelvic region and thigh
719.46 Pain in joint, lower leg
719.47 Pain in joint, ankle and foot
719.48 Pain in joint, other specified sites
719.49 Pain in joint, multiple sites
720.0 Ankylosing spondylitis
726.10 Unspecified disorders of bursae and tendons in shoulder region
726.32 Lateral epicondylitis of elbow
727.00 Unspecified synovitis and tenosynovitis
727.02 Giant cell tumor of tendon sheath
727.03 Trigger finger (acquired)
727.04 Radial styloid tenosynovitis
727.05 Other tenosynovitis of hand and wrist
727.06 Tenosynovitis of foot and ankle
727.09 Other synovitis and tenosynovitis
727.2 Specific bursitides often of occupational origin
727.3 Other bursitis disorders
728.71 Plantar fascial fibromatosis
729.4 Unspecified fasciitis
729.5 Pain in soft tissues of limb
729.91 Post-traumatic seroma
729.92 Nontraumatic hematoma of soft tissue
729.99 Other disorders of soft tissue

ICD-9-CM Procedural

81.92 Injection of therapeutic substance into joint or ligament
82.95 Injection of therapeutic substance into tendon of hand
83.97 Injection of therapeutic substance into tendon

Unspecified code · Female diagnosis · Manifestation code · Male diagnosis · [Resequenced code]

HCPCS Level II Supplies & Services

J0702 Injection, betamethasone acetate 3 mg and betamethasone sodium phosphate 3 mg
J1020 Injection, methylprednisolone acetate, 20 mg
J1030 Injection, methylprednisolone acetate, 40 mg
J1040 Injection, methylprednisolone acetate, 80 mg
J1094 Injection, dexamethasone acetate, 1 mg
J1100 Injection, dexamethasone sodium phosphate, 1 mg
J1700 Injection, hydrocortisone acetate, up to 25 mg
J1710 Injection, hydrocortisone sodium phosphate, up to 50 mg
J1720 Injection, hydrocortisone sodium succinate, up to 100 mg
J2920 Injection, methylprednisolone sodium succinate, up to 40 mg
S0020 Injection, bupivicaine HCl, 30 ml

20552-20553

20552 Injection(s); single or multiple trigger point(s), 1 or 2 muscle(s)
20553 single or multiple trigger point(s), 3 or more muscle(s)

ICD-9-CM Diagnostic

135 Sarcoidosis
277.30 Amyloidosis, unspecified — (Use additional code to identify any associated intellectual disabilities) ▽
277.31 Familial Mediterranean fever — (Use additional code to identify any associated intellectual disabilities)
277.39 Other amyloidosis — (Use additional code to identify any associated intellectual disabilities)
338.0 Central pain syndrome — (Use additional code to identify pain associated with psychological factors: 307.89)
338.11 Acute pain due to trauma — (Use additional code to identify pain associated with psychological factors: 307.89)
338.12 Acute post-thoracotomy pain — (Use additional code to identify pain associated with psychological factors: 307.89)
338.18 Other acute postoperative pain — (Use additional code to identify pain associated with psychological factors: 307.89)
338.19 Other acute pain — (Use additional code to identify pain associated with psychological factors: 307.89)
338.21 Chronic pain due to trauma — (Use additional code to identify pain associated with psychological factors: 307.89)
338.22 Chronic post-thoracotomy pain — (Use additional code to identify pain associated with psychological factors: 307.89)
338.28 Other chronic postoperative pain — (Use additional code to identify pain associated with psychological factors: 307.89)
338.29 Other chronic pain — (Use additional code to identify pain associated with psychological factors: 307.89)
338.4 Chronic pain syndrome — (Use additional code to identify pain associated with psychological factors: 307.89)
359.6 Symptomatic inflammatory myopathy in diseases classified elsewhere — (Code first underlying disease: 135, 140.0-208.9, 277.30-277.39, 446.0, 710.0, 710.1, 710.2, 714.0) ☒
710.0 Systemic lupus erythematosus — (Use additional code to identify manifestation: 424.91, 581.81, 582.81, 583.81)
710.1 Systemic sclerosis — (Use additional code to identify manifestation: 359.6, 517.2)
710.2 Sicca syndrome
720.1 Spinal enthesopathy
720.2 Sacroiliitis, not elsewhere classified
723.1 Cervicalgia
723.9 Unspecified musculoskeletal disorders and symptoms referable to neck ▽
724.1 Pain in thoracic spine
724.2 Lumbago
724.4 Thoracic or lumbosacral neuritis or radiculitis, unspecified ▽
724.5 Unspecified backache ▽
724.8 Other symptoms referable to back
726.0 Adhesive capsulitis of shoulder
726.10 Unspecified disorders of bursae and tendons in shoulder region ▽
726.11 Calcifying tendinitis of shoulder
726.12 Bicipital tenosynovitis
726.19 Other specified disorders of rotator cuff syndrome of shoulder and allied disorders
726.30 Unspecified enthesopathy of elbow ▽
726.31 Medial epicondylitis of elbow
726.32 Lateral epicondylitis of elbow
726.33 Olecranon bursitis
726.39 Other enthesopathy of elbow region
726.4 Enthesopathy of wrist and carpus
726.5 Enthesopathy of hip region
727.00 Unspecified synovitis and tenosynovitis ▽
727.01 Synovitis and tenosynovitis in diseases classified elsewhere — (Code first underlying disease: 015.0-015.9) ☒
727.02 Giant cell tumor of tendon sheath
727.03 Trigger finger (acquired)
727.04 Radial styloid tenosynovitis
727.05 Other tenosynovitis of hand and wrist
727.06 Tenosynovitis of foot and ankle
727.09 Other synovitis and tenosynovitis
727.40 Unspecified synovial cyst ▽
728.71 Plantar fascial fibromatosis
728.79 Other fibromatoses of muscle, ligament, and fascia
728.81 Interstitial myositis
728.85 Spasm of muscle
729.1 Unspecified myalgia and myositis ▽
729.4 Unspecified fasciitis ▽
729.5 Pain in soft tissues of limb

ICD-9-CM Procedural

81.92 Injection of therapeutic substance into joint or ligament
82.96 Other injection of locally-acting therapeutic substance into soft tissue of hand
83.98 Injection of locally acting therapeutic substance into other soft tissue
99.23 Injection of steroid
99.29 Injection or infusion of other therapeutic or prophylactic substance

HCPCS Level II Supplies & Services

J0702 Injection, betamethasone acetate 3 mg and betamethasone sodium phosphate 3 mg
J1020 Injection, methylprednisolone acetate, 20 mg
J1030 Injection, methylprednisolone acetate, 40 mg
J1040 Injection, methylprednisolone acetate, 80 mg
J1094 Injection, dexamethasone acetate, 1 mg
J1100 Injection, dexamethasone sodium phosphate, 1 mg
J1700 Injection, hydrocortisone acetate, up to 25 mg
J1710 Injection, hydrocortisone sodium phosphate, up to 50 mg
J1720 Injection, hydrocortisone sodium succinate, up to 100 mg
J2920 Injection, methylprednisolone sodium succinate, up to 40 mg
J2930 Injection, methylprednisolone sodium succinate, up to 125 mg
S0020 Injection, bupivicaine HCl, 30 ml

20555

20555 Placement of needles or catheters into muscle and/or soft tissue for subsequent interstitial radioelement application (at the time of or subsequent to the procedure)

ICD-9-CM Diagnostic

171.2 Malignant neoplasm of connective and other soft tissue of upper limb, including shoulder
171.3 Malignant neoplasm of connective and other soft tissue of lower limb, including hip
171.4 Malignant neoplasm of connective and other soft tissue of thorax
171.7 Malignant neoplasm of connective and other soft tissue of trunk, unspecified site ▽

171.8	Malignant neoplasm of other specified sites of connective and other soft tissue
171.9	Malignant neoplasm of connective and other soft tissue, site unspecified ▽
172.6	Malignant melanoma of skin of upper limb, including shoulder
195.4	Malignant neoplasm of upper limb
198.89	Secondary malignant neoplasm of other specified sites
238.1	Neoplasm of uncertain behavior of connective and other soft tissue
238.8	Neoplasm of uncertain behavior of other specified sites

ICD-9-CM Procedural

92.27	Implantation or insertion of radioactive elements

20600

20600	Arthrocentesis, aspiration and/or injection; small joint or bursa (eg, fingers, toes)

ICD-9-CM Diagnostic

275.40	Unspecified disorder of calcium metabolism — (Use additional code to identify any associated intellectual disabilities) ▽
275.41	Hypocalcemia — (Use additional code to identify any associated intellectual disabilities)
275.42	Hypercalcemia — (Use additional code to identify any associated intellectual disabilities)
275.49	Other disorders of calcium metabolism — (Use additional code to identify any associated intellectual disabilities)
275.5	Hungry bone syndrome — (Use additional code to identify any associated intellectual disabilities)
277.30	Amyloidosis, unspecified — (Use additional code to identify any associated intellectual disabilities) ▽
277.31	Familial Mediterranean fever — (Use additional code to identify any associated intellectual disabilities)
277.39	Other amyloidosis — (Use additional code to identify any associated intellectual disabilities)
278.4	Hypervitaminosis D — (Use additional code to identify any associated intellectual disabilities)
338.0	Central pain syndrome — (Use additional code to identify pain associated with psychological factors: 307.89)
338.11	Acute pain due to trauma — (Use additional code to identify pain associated with psychological factors: 307.89)
338.12	Acute post-thoracotomy pain — (Use additional code to identify pain associated with psychological factors: 307.89)
338.18	Other acute postoperative pain — (Use additional code to identify pain associated with psychological factors: 307.89)
338.19	Other acute pain — (Use additional code to identify pain associated with psychological factors: 307.89)
338.21	Chronic pain due to trauma — (Use additional code to identify pain associated with psychological factors: 307.89)
338.22	Chronic post-thoracotomy pain — (Use additional code to identify pain associated with psychological factors: 307.89)
338.28	Other chronic postoperative pain — (Use additional code to identify pain associated with psychological factors: 307.89)
338.29	Other chronic pain — (Use additional code to identify pain associated with psychological factors: 307.89)
338.4	Chronic pain syndrome — (Use additional code to identify pain associated with psychological factors: 307.89)
353.5	Neuralgic amyotrophy — (Code first any associated underlying disease as: 249.6, 250.6)
354.0	Carpal tunnel syndrome
354.1	Other lesion of median nerve
354.2	Lesion of ulnar nerve
354.3	Lesion of radial nerve
354.5	Mononeuritis multiplex
354.8	Other mononeuritis of upper limb
354.9	Unspecified mononeuritis of upper limb ▽
355.6	Lesion of plantar nerve
357.1	Polyneuropathy in collagen vascular disease — (Code first underlying disease: 446.0, 710.0, 714.0) ⊠
359.6	Symptomatic inflammatory myopathy in diseases classified elsewhere — (Code first underlying disease: 135, 140.0-208.9, 277.30-277.39, 446.0, 710.0, 710.1, 710.2, 714.0) ⊠
712.17	Chondrocalcinosis due to dicalcium phosphate crystals, ankle and foot — (Code first underlying disease: 275.4) ⊠
712.24	Chondrocalcinosis due to pyrophosphate crystals, hand — (Code first underlying disease: 275.4) ⊠
712.34	Chondrocalcinosis, cause unspecified, involving hand — (Code first underlying disease: 275.4) ⊠
712.37	Chondrocalcinosis, cause unspecified, involving ankle and foot — (Code first underlying disease: 275.4) ⊠
712.84	Other specified crystal arthropathies, hand
712.87	Other specified crystal arthropathies, ankle and foot
712.94	Unspecified crystal arthropathy, hand ▽
712.97	Unspecified crystal arthropathy, ankle and foot ▽
714.0	Rheumatoid arthritis — (Use additional code to identify manifestation: 357.1, 359.6)
715.00	Generalized osteoarthrosis, unspecified site ▽
715.04	Generalized osteoarthrosis, involving hand
715.09	Generalized osteoarthrosis, involving multiple sites
716.14	Traumatic arthropathy, hand
716.17	Traumatic arthropathy, ankle and foot
716.18	Traumatic arthropathy, other specified sites
716.19	Traumatic arthropathy, multiple sites
716.27	Allergic arthritis, ankle and foot
716.64	Unspecified monoarthritis, hand ▽
716.68	Unspecified monoarthritis, other specified sites ▽
716.84	Other specified arthropathy, hand
716.87	Other specified arthropathy, ankle and foot
716.88	Other specified arthropathy, other specified sites
716.89	Other specified arthropathy, multiple sites
716.94	Unspecified arthropathy, hand ▽
716.97	Unspecified arthropathy, ankle and foot ▽
716.98	Unspecified arthropathy, other specified sites ▽
716.99	Unspecified arthropathy, multiple sites ▽
719.00	Effusion of joint, site unspecified ▽
719.04	Effusion of hand joint
719.07	Effusion of ankle and foot joint
719.09	Effusion of joint, multiple sites
719.40	Pain in joint, site unspecified ▽
719.44	Pain in joint, hand
719.47	Pain in joint, ankle and foot
719.49	Pain in joint, multiple sites
727.00	Unspecified synovitis and tenosynovitis ▽
727.03	Trigger finger (acquired)
727.05	Other tenosynovitis of hand and wrist
727.06	Tenosynovitis of foot and ankle
727.09	Other synovitis and tenosynovitis
727.2	Specific bursitides often of occupational origin
727.40	Unspecified synovial cyst ▽
727.49	Other ganglion and cyst of synovium, tendon, and bursa

ICD-9-CM Procedural

81.91	Arthrocentesis
81.92	Injection of therapeutic substance into joint or ligament
82.92	Aspiration of bursa of hand
82.94	Injection of therapeutic substance into bursa of hand
82.95	Injection of therapeutic substance into tendon of hand

83.94 Aspiration of bursa
83.96 Injection of therapeutic substance into bursa

HCPCS Level II Supplies & Services

J0702 Injection, betamethasone acetate 3 mg and betamethasone sodium phosphate 3 mg
J1020 Injection, methylprednisolone acetate, 20 mg
J1030 Injection, methylprednisolone acetate, 40 mg
J1040 Injection, methylprednisolone acetate, 80 mg
J1094 Injection, dexamethasone acetate, 1 mg
J1700 Injection, hydrocortisone acetate, up to 25 mg
J1710 Injection, hydrocortisone sodium phosphate, up to 50 mg
J1720 Injection, hydrocortisone sodium succinate, up to 100 mg
J2920 Injection, methylprednisolone sodium succinate, up to 40 mg
J2930 Injection, methylprednisolone sodium succinate, up to 125 mg
J3301 Injection, triamcinolone acetonide, not otherwise specified, 10 mg
J3302 Injection, triamcinolone diacetate, per 5 mg
J3303 Injection, triamcinolone hexacetonide, per 5 mg
S0020 Injection, bupivicaine HCl, 30 ml

20605

20605 Arthrocentesis, aspiration and/or injection; intermediate joint or bursa (eg, temporomandibular, acromioclavicular, wrist, elbow or ankle, olecranon bursa)

ICD-9-CM Diagnostic

274.00 Gouty arthropathy, unspecified — (Use additional code to identify any associated intellectual disabilities) ▽
274.01 Acute gouty arthropathy — (Use additional code to identify any associated intellectual disabilities)
274.02 Chronic gouty arthropathy without mention of tophus (tophi) — (Use additional code to identify any associated intellectual disabilities)
274.03 Chronic gouty arthropathy with tophus (tophi) — (Use additional code to identify any associated intellectual disabilities)
275.40 Unspecified disorder of calcium metabolism — (Use additional code to identify any associated intellectual disabilities) ▽
275.42 Hypercalcemia — (Use additional code to identify any associated intellectual disabilities)
275.49 Other disorders of calcium metabolism — (Use additional code to identify any associated intellectual disabilities)
275.5 Hungry bone syndrome — (Use additional code to identify any associated intellectual disabilities)
277.1 Disorders of porphyrin metabolism — (Use additional code to identify any associated intellectual disabilities)
277.30 Amyloidosis, unspecified — (Use additional code to identify any associated intellectual disabilities) ▽
277.31 Familial Mediterranean fever — (Use additional code to identify any associated intellectual disabilities)
277.39 Other amyloidosis — (Use additional code to identify any associated intellectual disabilities)
338.0 Central pain syndrome — (Use additional code to identify pain associated with psychological factors: 307.89)
338.11 Acute pain due to trauma — (Use additional code to identify pain associated with psychological factors: 307.89)
338.12 Acute post-thoracotomy pain — (Use additional code to identify pain associated with psychological factors: 307.89)
338.18 Other acute postoperative pain — (Use additional code to identify pain associated with psychological factors: 307.89)
338.19 Other acute pain — (Use additional code to identify pain associated with psychological factors: 307.89)
338.21 Chronic pain due to trauma — (Use additional code to identify pain associated with psychological factors: 307.89)
338.22 Chronic post-thoracotomy pain — (Use additional code to identify pain associated with psychological factors: 307.89)
338.28 Other chronic postoperative pain — (Use additional code to identify pain associated with psychological factors: 307.89)
338.29 Other chronic pain — (Use additional code to identify pain associated with psychological factors: 307.89)
338.4 Chronic pain syndrome — (Use additional code to identify pain associated with psychological factors: 307.89)
357.1 Polyneuropathy in collagen vascular disease — (Code first underlying disease: 446.0, 710.0, 714.0) ☒
359.6 Symptomatic inflammatory myopathy in diseases classified elsewhere — (Code first underlying disease: 135, 140.0-208.9, 277.30-277.39, 446.0, 710.0, 710.1, 710.2, 714.0) ☒
524.60 Unspecified temporomandibular joint disorders ▽
524.61 Adhesions and ankylosis (bony or fibrous) of temporomandibular joint
524.62 Arthralgia of temporomandibular joint
524.69 Other specified temporomandibular joint disorders
526.1 Fissural cysts of jaw
526.2 Other cysts of jaws
526.4 Inflammatory conditions of jaw
526.9 Unspecified disease of the jaws ▽
712.12 Chondrocalcinosis due to dicalcium phosphate crystals, upper arm — (Code first underlying disease: 275.4) ☒
712.13 Chondrocalcinosis due to dicalcium phosphate crystals, forearm — (Code first underlying disease: 275.4) ☒
712.17 Chondrocalcinosis due to dicalcium phosphate crystals, ankle and foot — (Code first underlying disease: 275.4) ☒
712.18 Chondrocalcinosis due to dicalcium phosphate crystals, other specified sites — (Code first underlying disease: 275.4) ☒
712.82 Other specified crystal arthropathies, upper arm
712.83 Other specified crystal arthropathies, forearm
712.87 Other specified crystal arthropathies, ankle and foot
712.88 Other specified crystal arthropathies, other specified sites
712.92 Unspecified crystal arthropathy, upper arm ▽
712.93 Unspecified crystal arthropathy, forearm ▽
712.97 Unspecified crystal arthropathy, ankle and foot ▽
712.98 Unspecified crystal arthropathy, other specified sites ▽
714.0 Rheumatoid arthritis — (Use additional code to identify manifestation: 357.1, 359.6)
715.00 Generalized osteoarthrosis, unspecified site ▽
715.04 Generalized osteoarthrosis, involving hand
715.12 Primary localized osteoarthrosis, upper arm
715.13 Primary localized osteoarthrosis, forearm
715.14 Primary localized osteoarthrosis, hand
715.17 Primary localized osteoarthrosis, ankle and foot
715.20 Secondary localized osteoarthrosis, unspecified site ▽
715.22 Secondary localized osteoarthrosis, upper arm
715.23 Secondary localized osteoarthrosis, forearm
715.24 Secondary localized osteoarthrosis, involving hand
715.27 Secondary localized osteoarthrosis, ankle and foot
715.30 Localized osteoarthrosis not specified whether primary or secondary, unspecified site ▽
715.32 Localized osteoarthrosis not specified whether primary or secondary, upper arm
715.33 Localized osteoarthrosis not specified whether primary or secondary, forearm
715.34 Localized osteoarthrosis not specified whether primary or secondary, hand
715.37 Localized osteoarthrosis not specified whether primary or secondary, ankle and foot
715.38 Localized osteoarthrosis not specified whether primary or secondary, other specified sites
715.89 Osteoarthrosis involving multiple sites, but not specified as generalized
715.92 Osteoarthrosis, unspecified whether generalized or localized, upper arm ▽
715.93 Osteoarthrosis, unspecified whether generalized or localized, forearm ▽
715.94 Osteoarthrosis, unspecified whether generalized or localized, hand ▽

715.97 Osteoarthrosis, unspecified whether generalized or localized, ankle and foot ▽
716.10 Traumatic arthropathy, site unspecified ▽
716.12 Traumatic arthropathy, upper arm
716.13 Traumatic arthropathy, forearm
716.14 Traumatic arthropathy, hand
716.17 Traumatic arthropathy, ankle and foot
716.92 Unspecified arthropathy, upper arm ▽
716.93 Unspecified arthropathy, forearm ▽
716.94 Unspecified arthropathy, hand ▽
716.97 Unspecified arthropathy, ankle and foot ▽
719.00 Effusion of joint, site unspecified ▽
719.02 Effusion of upper arm joint
719.03 Effusion of forearm joint
719.04 Effusion of hand joint
719.07 Effusion of ankle and foot joint
719.10 Hemarthrosis, site unspecified ▽
719.12 Hemarthrosis, upper arm
719.13 Hemarthrosis, forearm
719.14 Hemarthrosis, hand
719.17 Hemarthrosis, ankle and foot
719.40 Pain in joint, site unspecified ▽
719.42 Pain in joint, upper arm
719.43 Pain in joint, forearm
719.44 Pain in joint, hand
719.47 Pain in joint, ankle and foot
726.30 Unspecified enthesopathy of elbow ▽
726.31 Medial epicondylitis of elbow
726.32 Lateral epicondylitis of elbow
726.33 Olecranon bursitis
726.39 Other enthesopathy of elbow region
726.4 Enthesopathy of wrist and carpus
726.70 Unspecified enthesopathy of ankle and tarsus ▽
726.71 Achilles bursitis or tendinitis
726.79 Other enthesopathy of ankle and tarsus
727.00 Unspecified synovitis and tenosynovitis ▽
727.04 Radial styloid tenosynovitis
727.05 Other tenosynovitis of hand and wrist
727.06 Tenosynovitis of foot and ankle
727.09 Other synovitis and tenosynovitis
784.92 Jaw pain
830.0 Closed dislocation of jaw
848.1 Sprain and strain of jaw
905.0 Late effect of fracture of skull and face bones

ICD-9-CM Procedural

76.96 Injection of therapeutic substance into temporomandibular joint
81.91 Arthrocentesis
81.92 Injection of therapeutic substance into joint or ligament
83.94 Aspiration of bursa
83.96 Injection of therapeutic substance into bursa

HCPCS Level II Supplies & Services

J0702 Injection, betamethasone acetate 3 mg and betamethasone sodium phosphate 3 mg
J1020 Injection, methylprednisolone acetate, 20 mg
J1030 Injection, methylprednisolone acetate, 40 mg
J1040 Injection, methylprednisolone acetate, 80 mg
J1094 Injection, dexamethasone acetate, 1 mg
J1100 Injection, dexamethasone sodium phosphate, 1 mg
J1700 Injection, hydrocortisone acetate, up to 25 mg
J1710 Injection, hydrocortisone sodium phosphate, up to 50 mg
J1720 Injection, hydrocortisone sodium succinate, up to 100 mg
J2920 Injection, methylprednisolone sodium succinate, up to 40 mg
J2930 Injection, methylprednisolone sodium succinate, up to 125 mg
J3301 Injection, triamcinolone acetonide, not otherwise specified, 10 mg
J3302 Injection, triamcinolone diacetate, per 5 mg
J3303 Injection, triamcinolone hexacetonide, per 5 mg
S0020 Injection, bupivicaine HCl, 30 ml

20610

20610 Arthrocentesis, aspiration and/or injection; major joint or bursa (eg, shoulder, hip, knee joint, subacromial bursa)

ICD-9-CM Diagnostic

274.00 Gouty arthropathy, unspecified — (Use additional code to identify any associated intellectual disabilities) ▽
274.01 Acute gouty arthropathy — (Use additional code to identify any associated intellectual disabilities)
274.02 Chronic gouty arthropathy without mention of tophus (tophi) — (Use additional code to identify any associated intellectual disabilities)
274.03 Chronic gouty arthropathy with tophus (tophi) — (Use additional code to identify any associated intellectual disabilities)
275.40 Unspecified disorder of calcium metabolism — (Use additional code to identify any associated intellectual disabilities) ▽
275.42 Hypercalcemia — (Use additional code to identify any associated intellectual disabilities)
275.49 Other disorders of calcium metabolism — (Use additional code to identify any associated intellectual disabilities)
275.5 Hungry bone syndrome — (Use additional code to identify any associated intellectual disabilities)
338.0 Central pain syndrome — (Use additional code to identify pain associated with psychological factors: 307.89)
338.11 Acute pain due to trauma — (Use additional code to identify pain associated with psychological factors: 307.89)
338.12 Acute post-thoracotomy pain — (Use additional code to identify pain associated with psychological factors: 307.89)
338.18 Other acute postoperative pain — (Use additional code to identify pain associated with psychological factors: 307.89)
338.19 Other acute pain — (Use additional code to identify pain associated with psychological factors: 307.89)
338.21 Chronic pain due to trauma — (Use additional code to identify pain associated with psychological factors: 307.89)
338.22 Chronic post-thoracotomy pain — (Use additional code to identify pain associated with psychological factors: 307.89)
338.28 Other chronic postoperative pain — (Use additional code to identify pain associated with psychological factors: 307.89)
338.29 Other chronic pain — (Use additional code to identify pain associated with psychological factors: 307.89)
338.4 Chronic pain syndrome — (Use additional code to identify pain associated with psychological factors: 307.89)
357.1 Polyneuropathy in collagen vascular disease — (Code first underlying disease: 446.0, 710.0, 714.0) ☒
359.6 Symptomatic inflammatory myopathy in diseases classified elsewhere — (Code first underlying disease: 135, 140.0-208.9, 277.30-277.39, 446.0, 710.0, 710.1, 710.2, 714.0) ☒
712.11 Chondrocalcinosis due to dicalcium phosphate crystals, shoulder region — (Code first underlying disease: 275.4) ☒
712.15 Chondrocalcinosis due to dicalcium phosphate crystals, pelvic region and thigh — (Code first underlying disease: 275.4) ☒
712.16 Chondrocalcinosis due to dicalcium phosphate crystals, lower leg — (Code first underlying disease: 275.4) ☒
712.18 Chondrocalcinosis due to dicalcium phosphate crystals, other specified sites — (Code first underlying disease: 275.4) ☒

712.19 Chondrocalcinosis due to dicalcium phosphate crystals, multiple sites — (Code first underlying disease: 275.4) ☒
712.21 Chondrocalcinosis due to pyrophosphate crystals, shoulder region — (Code first underlying disease: 275.4) ☒
712.25 Chondrocalcinosis due to pyrophosphate crystals, pelvic region and thigh — (Code first underlying disease: 275.4) ☒
712.26 Chondrocalcinosis due to pyrophosphate crystals, lower leg — (Code first underlying disease: 275.4) ☒
712.28 Chondrocalcinosis due to pyrophosphate crystals, other specified sites — (Code first underlying disease: 275.4) ☒
712.29 Chondrocalcinosis due to pyrophosphate crystals, multiple sites — (Code first underlying disease: 275.4) ☒
712.31 Chondrocalcinosis, cause unspecified, involving shoulder region — (Code first underlying disease: 275.4) ☒
712.39 Chondrocalcinosis, cause unspecified, involving multiple sites — (Code first underlying disease: 275.4) ☒
714.0 Rheumatoid arthritis — (Use additional code to identify manifestation: 357.1, 359.6)
715.00 Generalized osteoarthrosis, unspecified site ▽
715.09 Generalized osteoarthrosis, involving multiple sites
715.11 Primary localized osteoarthrosis, shoulder region
715.15 Primary localized osteoarthrosis, pelvic region and thigh
715.16 Primary localized osteoarthrosis, lower leg
715.18 Primary localized osteoarthrosis, other specified sites
715.91 Osteoarthrosis, unspecified whether generalized or localized, shoulder region ▽
715.95 Osteoarthrosis, unspecified whether generalized or localized, pelvic region and thigh ▽
715.96 Osteoarthrosis, unspecified whether generalized or localized, lower leg ▽
715.98 Osteoarthrosis, unspecified whether generalized or localized, other specified sites ▽
716.90 Unspecified arthropathy, site unspecified ▽
716.91 Unspecified arthropathy, shoulder region ▽
716.95 Unspecified arthropathy, pelvic region and thigh ▽
716.96 Unspecified arthropathy, lower leg ▽
716.98 Unspecified arthropathy, other specified sites ▽
716.99 Unspecified arthropathy, multiple sites ▽
717.9 Unspecified internal derangement of knee ▽
719.01 Effusion of shoulder joint
719.05 Effusion of pelvic joint
719.06 Effusion of lower leg joint
719.09 Effusion of joint, multiple sites
719.10 Hemarthrosis, site unspecified ▽
719.11 Hemarthrosis, shoulder region
719.15 Hemarthrosis, pelvic region and thigh
719.16 Hemarthrosis, lower leg
719.19 Hemarthrosis, multiple sites
719.20 Villonodular synovitis, site unspecified ▽
719.21 Villonodular synovitis, shoulder region
719.25 Villonodular synovitis, pelvic region and thigh
719.26 Villonodular synovitis, lower leg
719.28 Villonodular synovitis, other specified sites
719.29 Villonodular synovitis, multiple sites
719.41 Pain in joint, shoulder region
719.45 Pain in joint, pelvic region and thigh
719.46 Pain in joint, lower leg
719.49 Pain in joint, multiple sites
726.5 Enthesopathy of hip region
726.60 Unspecified enthesopathy of knee ▽
726.61 Pes anserinus tendinitis or bursitis
726.62 Tibial collateral ligament bursitis
726.63 Fibular collateral ligament bursitis
726.64 Patellar tendinitis
726.65 Prepatellar bursitis
726.69 Other enthesopathy of knee
727.3 Other bursitis disorders

ICD-9-CM Procedural

81.91 Arthrocentesis
81.92 Injection of therapeutic substance into joint or ligament
83.94 Aspiration of bursa
83.96 Injection of therapeutic substance into bursa

HCPCS Level II Supplies & Services

J0702 Injection, betamethasone acetate 3 mg and betamethasone sodium phosphate 3 mg
J1020 Injection, methylprednisolone acetate, 20 mg
J1030 Injection, methylprednisolone acetate, 40 mg
J1040 Injection, methylprednisolone acetate, 80 mg
J1094 Injection, dexamethasone acetate, 1 mg
J1100 Injection, dexamethasone sodium phosphate, 1 mg
J1700 Injection, hydrocortisone acetate, up to 25 mg
J1710 Injection, hydrocortisone sodium phosphate, up to 50 mg
J1720 Injection, hydrocortisone sodium succinate, up to 100 mg
J2920 Injection, methylprednisolone sodium succinate, up to 40 mg
J2930 Injection, methylprednisolone sodium succinate, up to 125 mg
J3301 Injection, triamcinolone acetonide, not otherwise specified, 10 mg
J3302 Injection, triamcinolone diacetate, per 5 mg
J3303 Injection, triamcinolone hexacetonide, per 5 mg
S0020 Injection, bupivicaine HCl, 30 ml

20612

20612 Aspiration and/or injection of ganglion cyst(s) any location

ICD-9-CM Diagnostic

727.40 Unspecified synovial cyst ▽
727.41 Ganglion of joint
727.42 Ganglion of tendon sheath
727.43 Unspecified ganglion ▽
727.49 Other ganglion and cyst of synovium, tendon, and bursa

ICD-9-CM Procedural

05.39 Other injection into sympathetic nerve or ganglion
82.93 Aspiration of other soft tissue of hand
83.95 Aspiration of other soft tissue

HCPCS Level II Supplies & Services

J0702 Injection, betamethasone acetate 3 mg and betamethasone sodium phosphate 3 mg
J1020 Injection, methylprednisolone acetate, 20 mg
J1030 Injection, methylprednisolone acetate, 40 mg
J1040 Injection, methylprednisolone acetate, 80 mg
S0020 Injection, bupivicaine HCl, 30 ml

20615

20615 Aspiration and injection for treatment of bone cyst

ICD-9-CM Diagnostic

526.0 Developmental odontogenic cysts
526.1 Fissural cysts of jaw
526.2 Other cysts of jaws
526.89 Other specified disease of the jaws
733.20 Unspecified cyst of bone (localized) ▽
733.21 Solitary bone cyst
733.22 Aneurysmal bone cyst
733.29 Other cyst of bone

ICD-9-CM Procedural

78.40 Other repair or plastic operations on bone, unspecified site
78.41 Other repair or plastic operations on scapula, clavicle, and thorax (ribs and sternum)
78.43 Other repair or plastic operations on radius and ulna
78.44 Other repair or plastic operations on carpals and metacarpals
78.45 Other repair or plastic operations on femur
78.46 Other repair or plastic operations on patella
78.47 Other repair or plastic operations on tibia and fibula
78.48 Other repair or plastic operations on tarsals and metatarsals
78.49 Other repair or plastic operations on other bone, except facial bones

20650

20650 Insertion of wire or pin with application of skeletal traction, including removal (separate procedure)

ICD-9-CM Diagnostic

733.93 Stress fracture of tibia or fibula — (Use additional external cause code(s) to identify the cause of the stress fracture)
733.95 Stress fracture of other bone — (Use additional external cause code(s) to identify the cause of the stress fracture)
733.96 Stress fracture of femoral neck — (Use additional external cause code(s) to identify the cause of the stress fracture)
733.97 Stress fracture of shaft of femur — (Use additional external cause code(s) to identify the cause of the stress fracture)
733.98 Stress fracture of pelvis — (Use additional external cause code(s) to identify the cause of the stress fracture)
808.0 Closed fracture of acetabulum
808.1 Open fracture of acetabulum
808.53 Multiple open pelvic fractures with disruption of pelvic circle
812.00 Closed fracture of unspecified part of upper end of humerus ▽
812.01 Closed fracture of surgical neck of humerus
812.02 Closed fracture of anatomical neck of humerus
812.03 Closed fracture of greater tuberosity of humerus
812.09 Other closed fractures of upper end of humerus
812.10 Open fracture of unspecified part of upper end of humerus ▽
812.11 Open fracture of surgical neck of humerus
812.12 Open fracture of anatomical neck of humerus
812.13 Open fracture of greater tuberosity of humerus
812.20 Closed fracture of unspecified part of humerus ▽
812.21 Closed fracture of shaft of humerus
812.30 Open fracture of unspecified part of humerus ▽
812.31 Open fracture of shaft of humerus
812.40 Closed fracture of unspecified part of lower end of humerus ▽
812.41 Closed fracture of supracondylar humerus
812.42 Closed fracture of lateral condyle of humerus
812.43 Closed fracture of medial condyle of humerus
812.44 Closed fracture of unspecified condyle(s) of humerus ▽
812.49 Other closed fracture of lower end of humerus
812.50 Open fracture of unspecified part of lower end of humerus ▽
812.51 Open fracture of supracondylar humerus
812.52 Open fracture of lateral condyle of humerus
812.53 Open fracture of medial condyle of humerus
812.54 Open fracture of unspecified condyle(s) of humerus ▽
812.59 Other open fracture of lower end of humerus
813.07 Other and unspecified closed fractures of proximal end of radius (alone) ▽
813.17 Other and unspecified open fractures of proximal end of radius (alone) ▽
820.00 Closed fracture of unspecified intracapsular section of neck of femur ▽
820.01 Closed fracture of epiphysis (separation) (upper) of neck of femur
820.02 Closed fracture of midcervical section of femur
820.09 Other closed transcervical fracture of femur
820.10 Open fracture of unspecified intracapsular section of neck of femur ▽
820.11 Open fracture of epiphysis (separation) (upper) of neck of femur
820.12 Open fracture of midcervical section of femur
820.13 Open fracture of base of neck of femur
820.19 Other open transcervical fracture of femur
820.20 Closed fracture of unspecified trochanteric section of femur ▽
820.21 Closed fracture of intertrochanteric section of femur
820.22 Closed fracture of subtrochanteric section of femur
820.30 Open fracture of unspecified trochanteric section of femur ▽
820.31 Open fracture of intertrochanteric section of femur
820.8 Closed fracture of unspecified part of neck of femur ▽
820.9 Open fracture of unspecified part of neck of femur ▽
821.00 Closed fracture of unspecified part of femur ▽
821.01 Closed fracture of shaft of femur
821.10 Open fracture of unspecified part of femur ▽
821.11 Open fracture of shaft of femur
821.20 Closed fracture of unspecified part of lower end of femur ▽
821.21 Closed fracture of femoral condyle
821.22 Closed fracture of lower epiphysis of femur
821.23 Closed supracondylar fracture of femur
821.30 Open fracture of unspecified part of lower end of femur ▽
821.31 Open fracture of femoral condyle
821.32 Open fracture of lower epiphysis of femur
821.33 Open supracondylar fracture of femur
821.39 Other open fracture of lower end of femur
823.00 Closed fracture of upper end of tibia
823.01 Closed fracture of upper end of fibula
823.02 Closed fracture of upper end of fibula with tibia
823.10 Open fracture of upper end of tibia
823.11 Open fracture of upper end of fibula
823.12 Open fracture of upper end of fibula with tibia
823.20 Closed fracture of shaft of tibia
823.21 Closed fracture of shaft of fibula
823.22 Closed fracture of shaft of fibula with tibia
823.30 Open fracture of shaft of tibia
823.31 Open fracture of shaft of fibula
823.32 Open fracture of shaft of fibula with tibia
823.80 Closed fracture of unspecified part of tibia ▽
823.81 Closed fracture of unspecified part of fibula ▽
823.82 Closed fracture of unspecified part of fibula with tibia ▽
823.90 Open fracture of unspecified part of tibia ▽
823.91 Open fracture of unspecified part of fibula ▽
823.92 Open fracture of unspecified part of fibula with tibia ▽
996.40 Unspecified mechanical complication of internal orthopedic device, implant, and graft — (Use additional code to identify prosthetic joint with mechanical complication, V43.60-V43.69) ▽
996.49 Other mechanical complication of other internal orthopedic device, implant, and graft — (Use additional code to identify prosthetic joint with mechanical complication, V43.60-V43.69)
996.67 Infection and inflammatory reaction due to other internal orthopedic device, implant, and graft — (Use additional code to identify specified infections)
996.78 Other complications due to other internal orthopedic device, implant, and graft — (Use additional code to identify complication: 338.18-338.19, 338.28-338.29)

ICD-9-CM Procedural

93.44 Other skeletal traction

HCPCS Level II Supplies & Services

A4305 Disposable drug delivery system, flow rate of 50 ml or greater per hour

20660

20660 Application of cranial tongs, caliper, or stereotactic frame, including removal (separate procedure)

ICD-9-CM Diagnostic

805.00 Closed fracture of cervical vertebra, unspecified level without mention of spinal cord injury ▽
805.01 Closed fracture of first cervical vertebra without mention of spinal cord injury
805.02 Closed fracture of second cervical vertebra without mention of spinal cord injury
805.03 Closed fracture of third cervical vertebra without mention of spinal cord injury
805.04 Closed fracture of fourth cervical vertebra without mention of spinal cord injury
805.05 Closed fracture of fifth cervical vertebra without mention of spinal cord injury
805.06 Closed fracture of sixth cervical vertebra without mention of spinal cord injury
805.07 Closed fracture of seventh cervical vertebra without mention of spinal cord injury
805.08 Closed fracture of multiple cervical vertebrae without mention of spinal cord injury
805.10 Open fracture of cervical vertebra, unspecified level without mention of spinal cord injury ▽
805.11 Open fracture of first cervical vertebra without mention of spinal cord injury
805.12 Open fracture of second cervical vertebra without mention of spinal cord injury
805.13 Open fracture of third cervical vertebra without mention of spinal cord injury
805.14 Open fracture of fourth cervical vertebra without mention of spinal cord injury
805.15 Open fracture of fifth cervical vertebra without mention of spinal cord injury
805.16 Open fracture of sixth cervical vertebra without mention of spinal cord injury
805.17 Open fracture of seventh cervical vertebra without mention of spinal cord injury
805.18 Open fracture of multiple cervical vertebrae without mention of spinal cord injury
806.00 Closed fracture of C1-C4 level with unspecified spinal cord injury ▽
806.01 Closed fracture of C1-C4 level with complete lesion of cord
806.02 Closed fracture of C1-C4 level with anterior cord syndrome
806.03 Closed fracture of C1-C4 level with central cord syndrome
806.04 Closed fracture of C1-C4 level with other specified spinal cord injury
806.05 Closed fracture of C5-C7 level with unspecified spinal cord injury ▽
806.06 Closed fracture of C5-C7 level with complete lesion of cord
806.07 Closed fracture of C5-C7 level with anterior cord syndrome
806.08 Closed fracture of C5-C7 level with central cord syndrome
806.09 Closed fracture of C5-C7 level with other specified spinal cord injury
806.10 Open fracture of C1-C4 level with unspecified spinal cord injury ▽
806.11 Open fracture of C1-C4 level with complete lesion of cord
806.12 Open fracture of C1-C4 level with anterior cord syndrome
806.13 Open fracture of C1-C4 level with central cord syndrome
806.14 Open fracture of C1-C4 level with other specified spinal cord injury
806.15 Open fracture of C5-C7 level with unspecified spinal cord injury ▽
806.16 Open fracture of C5-C7 level with complete lesion of cord
806.17 Open fracture of C5-C7 level with anterior cord syndrome
806.18 Open fracture of C5-C7 level with central cord syndrome
806.19 Open fracture of C5-C7 level with other specified spinal cord injury
996.40 Unspecified mechanical complication of internal orthopedic device, implant, and graft — (Use additional code to identify prosthetic joint with mechanical complication, V43.60-V43.69) ▽
996.49 Other mechanical complication of other internal orthopedic device, implant, and graft — (Use additional code to identify prosthetic joint with mechanical complication, V43.60-V43.69)
996.67 Infection and inflammatory reaction due to other internal orthopedic device, implant, and graft — (Use additional code to identify specified infections)
996.78 Other complications due to other internal orthopedic device, implant, and graft — (Use additional code to identify complication: 338.18-338.19, 338.28-338.29)

ICD-9-CM Procedural

02.94 Insertion or replacement of skull tongs or halo traction device
02.95 Removal of skull tongs or halo traction device
93.41 Spinal traction using skull device

20661

20661 Application of halo, including removal; cranial

ICD-9-CM Diagnostic

805.00 Closed fracture of cervical vertebra, unspecified level without mention of spinal cord injury ▽
805.01 Closed fracture of first cervical vertebra without mention of spinal cord injury
805.02 Closed fracture of second cervical vertebra without mention of spinal cord injury
805.03 Closed fracture of third cervical vertebra without mention of spinal cord injury
805.04 Closed fracture of fourth cervical vertebra without mention of spinal cord injury
805.05 Closed fracture of fifth cervical vertebra without mention of spinal cord injury
805.06 Closed fracture of sixth cervical vertebra without mention of spinal cord injury
805.07 Closed fracture of seventh cervical vertebra without mention of spinal cord injury
805.08 Closed fracture of multiple cervical vertebrae without mention of spinal cord injury
805.10 Open fracture of cervical vertebra, unspecified level without mention of spinal cord injury ▽
805.11 Open fracture of first cervical vertebra without mention of spinal cord injury
805.12 Open fracture of second cervical vertebra without mention of spinal cord injury
805.13 Open fracture of third cervical vertebra without mention of spinal cord injury
805.14 Open fracture of fourth cervical vertebra without mention of spinal cord injury
805.15 Open fracture of fifth cervical vertebra without mention of spinal cord injury
805.16 Open fracture of sixth cervical vertebra without mention of spinal cord injury
805.17 Open fracture of seventh cervical vertebra without mention of spinal cord injury
805.18 Open fracture of multiple cervical vertebrae without mention of spinal cord injury
806.00 Closed fracture of C1-C4 level with unspecified spinal cord injury ▽
806.01 Closed fracture of C1-C4 level with complete lesion of cord
806.02 Closed fracture of C1-C4 level with anterior cord syndrome
806.03 Closed fracture of C1-C4 level with central cord syndrome
806.04 Closed fracture of C1-C4 level with other specified spinal cord injury
806.05 Closed fracture of C5-C7 level with unspecified spinal cord injury ▽
806.06 Closed fracture of C5-C7 level with complete lesion of cord
806.07 Closed fracture of C5-C7 level with anterior cord syndrome
806.08 Closed fracture of C5-C7 level with central cord syndrome
806.09 Closed fracture of C5-C7 level with other specified spinal cord injury
806.10 Open fracture of C1-C4 level with unspecified spinal cord injury ▽
806.11 Open fracture of C1-C4 level with complete lesion of cord
806.12 Open fracture of C1-C4 level with anterior cord syndrome
806.13 Open fracture of C1-C4 level with central cord syndrome
806.14 Open fracture of C1-C4 level with other specified spinal cord injury
806.15 Open fracture of C5-C7 level with unspecified spinal cord injury ▽
806.16 Open fracture of C5-C7 level with complete lesion of cord
806.17 Open fracture of C5-C7 level with anterior cord syndrome
806.18 Open fracture of C5-C7 level with central cord syndrome
806.19 Open fracture of C5-C7 level with other specified spinal cord injury
996.40 Unspecified mechanical complication of internal orthopedic device, implant, and graft — (Use additional code to identify prosthetic joint with mechanical complication, V43.60-V43.69) ▽
996.49 Other mechanical complication of other internal orthopedic device, implant, and graft — (Use additional code to identify prosthetic joint with mechanical complication, V43.60-V43.69)
996.67 Infection and inflammatory reaction due to other internal orthopedic device, implant, and graft — (Use additional code to identify specified infections)
996.78 Other complications due to other internal orthopedic device, implant, and graft — (Use additional code to identify complication: 338.18-338.19, 338.28-338.29)

ICD-9-CM Procedural

02.94 Insertion or replacement of skull tongs or halo traction device
02.95 Removal of skull tongs or halo traction device
93.41 Spinal traction using skull device

HCPCS Level II Supplies & Services

L0810 Halo procedure, cervical halo incorporated into jacket vest

20662

20662 Application of halo, including removal; pelvic

ICD-9-CM Diagnostic

808.0 Closed fracture of acetabulum
808.1 Open fracture of acetabulum
808.2 Closed fracture of pubis
808.3 Open fracture of pubis
808.41 Closed fracture of ilium
808.42 Closed fracture of ischium
808.43 Multiple closed pelvic fractures with disruption of pelvic circle
808.49 Closed fracture of other specified part of pelvis
808.51 Open fracture of ilium
808.52 Open fracture of ischium
808.53 Multiple open pelvic fractures with disruption of pelvic circle
808.59 Open fracture of other specified part of pelvis
996.40 Unspecified mechanical complication of internal orthopedic device, implant, and graft — (Use additional code to identify prosthetic joint with mechanical complication, V43.60-V43.69) ▼
996.49 Other mechanical complication of other internal orthopedic device, implant, and graft — (Use additional code to identify prosthetic joint with mechanical complication, V43.60-V43.69)
996.67 Infection and inflammatory reaction due to other internal orthopedic device, implant, and graft — (Use additional code to identify specified infections)
996.78 Other complications due to other internal orthopedic device, implant, and graft — (Use additional code to identify complication: 338.18-338.19, 338.28-338.29)

ICD-9-CM Procedural

02.94 Insertion or replacement of skull tongs or halo traction device
02.95 Removal of skull tongs or halo traction device
93.41 Spinal traction using skull device

HCPCS Level II Supplies & Services

L0830 Halo procedure, cervical halo incorporated into Milwaukee type orthotic

20663

20663 Application of halo, including removal; femoral

ICD-9-CM Diagnostic

820.00 Closed fracture of unspecified intracapsular section of neck of femur ▼
820.01 Closed fracture of epiphysis (separation) (upper) of neck of femur
820.02 Closed fracture of midcervical section of femur
820.03 Closed fracture of base of neck of femur
820.09 Other closed transcervical fracture of femur
820.10 Open fracture of unspecified intracapsular section of neck of femur ▼
820.11 Open fracture of epiphysis (separation) (upper) of neck of femur
820.12 Open fracture of midcervical section of femur
820.13 Open fracture of base of neck of femur
820.19 Other open transcervical fracture of femur
820.20 Closed fracture of unspecified trochanteric section of femur ▼
820.21 Closed fracture of intertrochanteric section of femur
820.22 Closed fracture of subtrochanteric section of femur
820.30 Open fracture of unspecified trochanteric section of femur ▼
820.31 Open fracture of intertrochanteric section of femur
820.32 Open fracture of subtrochanteric section of femur
820.8 Closed fracture of unspecified part of neck of femur ▼
821.01 Closed fracture of shaft of femur
821.11 Open fracture of shaft of femur
821.21 Closed fracture of femoral condyle
821.22 Closed fracture of lower epiphysis of femur
821.23 Closed supracondylar fracture of femur
821.29 Other closed fracture of lower end of femur
821.31 Open fracture of femoral condyle
821.32 Open fracture of lower epiphysis of femur
821.33 Open supracondylar fracture of femur
821.39 Other open fracture of lower end of femur
996.40 Unspecified mechanical complication of internal orthopedic device, implant, and graft — (Use additional code to identify prosthetic joint with mechanical complication, V43.60-V43.69) ▼
996.49 Other mechanical complication of other internal orthopedic device, implant, and graft — (Use additional code to identify prosthetic joint with mechanical complication, V43.60-V43.69)
996.67 Infection and inflammatory reaction due to other internal orthopedic device, implant, and graft — (Use additional code to identify specified infections)
996.78 Other complications due to other internal orthopedic device, implant, and graft — (Use additional code to identify complication: 338.18-338.19, 338.28-338.29)

ICD-9-CM Procedural

02.94 Insertion or replacement of skull tongs or halo traction device
02.95 Removal of skull tongs or halo traction device
93.41 Spinal traction using skull device

HCPCS Level II Supplies & Services

L0830 Halo procedure, cervical halo incorporated into Milwaukee type orthotic

20664

20664 Application of halo, including removal, cranial, 6 or more pins placed, for thin skull osteology (eg, pediatric patients, hydrocephalus, osteogenesis imperfecta)

ICD-9-CM Diagnostic

733.90 Disorder of bone and cartilage, unspecified ▼
741.00 Spina bifida with hydrocephalus, unspecified region ▼
741.01 Spina bifida with hydrocephalus, cervical region
741.02 Spina bifida with hydrocephalus, dorsal (thoracic) region
741.03 Spina bifida with hydrocephalus, lumbar region
742.3 Congenital hydrocephalus
756.0 Congenital anomalies of skull and face bones
756.51 Osteogenesis imperfecta
805.01 Closed fracture of first cervical vertebra without mention of spinal cord injury
805.02 Closed fracture of second cervical vertebra without mention of spinal cord injury
805.03 Closed fracture of third cervical vertebra without mention of spinal cord injury
805.04 Closed fracture of fourth cervical vertebra without mention of spinal cord injury
805.05 Closed fracture of fifth cervical vertebra without mention of spinal cord injury
805.06 Closed fracture of sixth cervical vertebra without mention of spinal cord injury
805.07 Closed fracture of seventh cervical vertebra without mention of spinal cord injury
805.08 Closed fracture of multiple cervical vertebrae without mention of spinal cord injury
805.11 Open fracture of first cervical vertebra without mention of spinal cord injury
805.12 Open fracture of second cervical vertebra without mention of spinal cord injury
805.13 Open fracture of third cervical vertebra without mention of spinal cord injury
805.14 Open fracture of fourth cervical vertebra without mention of spinal cord injury
805.15 Open fracture of fifth cervical vertebra without mention of spinal cord injury
805.16 Open fracture of sixth cervical vertebra without mention of spinal cord injury
805.17 Open fracture of seventh cervical vertebra without mention of spinal cord injury
805.18 Open fracture of multiple cervical vertebrae without mention of spinal cord injury
806.00 Closed fracture of C1-C4 level with unspecified spinal cord injury ▼
806.01 Closed fracture of C1-C4 level with complete lesion of cord
806.02 Closed fracture of C1-C4 level with anterior cord syndrome
806.03 Closed fracture of C1-C4 level with central cord syndrome
806.04 Closed fracture of C1-C4 level with other specified spinal cord injury

806.05 Closed fracture of C5-C7 level with unspecified spinal cord injury
806.06 Closed fracture of C5-C7 level with complete lesion of cord
806.07 Closed fracture of C5-C7 level with anterior cord syndrome
806.08 Closed fracture of C5-C7 level with central cord syndrome
806.09 Closed fracture of C5-C7 level with other specified spinal cord injury
806.10 Open fracture of C1-C4 level with unspecified spinal cord injury
806.11 Open fracture of C1-C4 level with complete lesion of cord
806.12 Open fracture of C1-C4 level with anterior cord syndrome
806.13 Open fracture of C1-C4 level with central cord syndrome
806.14 Open fracture of C1-C4 level with other specified spinal cord injury
806.15 Open fracture of C5-C7 level with unspecified spinal cord injury
806.16 Open fracture of C5-C7 level with complete lesion of cord
806.17 Open fracture of C5-C7 level with anterior cord syndrome
806.18 Open fracture of C5-C7 level with central cord syndrome
806.19 Open fracture of C5-C7 level with other specified spinal cord injury
996.40 Unspecified mechanical complication of internal orthopedic device, implant, and graft — (Use additional code to identify prosthetic joint with mechanical complication, V43.60-V43.69)
996.49 Other mechanical complication of other internal orthopedic device, implant, and graft — (Use additional code to identify prosthetic joint with mechanical complication, V43.60-V43.69)
996.67 Infection and inflammatory reaction due to other internal orthopedic device, implant, and graft — (Use additional code to identify specified infections)
996.78 Other complications due to other internal orthopedic device, implant, and graft — (Use additional code to identify complication: 338.18-338.19, 338.28-338.29)

ICD-9-CM Procedural

02.94 Insertion or replacement of skull tongs or halo traction device
02.95 Removal of skull tongs or halo traction device
93.41 Spinal traction using skull device

HCPCS Level II Supplies & Services

L0810 Halo procedure, cervical halo incorporated into jacket vest

20665

20665 Removal of tongs or halo applied by another individual

ICD-9-CM Diagnostic

805.01 Closed fracture of first cervical vertebra without mention of spinal cord injury
805.02 Closed fracture of second cervical vertebra without mention of spinal cord injury
805.03 Closed fracture of third cervical vertebra without mention of spinal cord injury
805.04 Closed fracture of fourth cervical vertebra without mention of spinal cord injury
805.05 Closed fracture of fifth cervical vertebra without mention of spinal cord injury
805.06 Closed fracture of sixth cervical vertebra without mention of spinal cord injury
805.07 Closed fracture of seventh cervical vertebra without mention of spinal cord injury
805.08 Closed fracture of multiple cervical vertebrae without mention of spinal cord injury
805.10 Open fracture of cervical vertebra, unspecified level without mention of spinal cord injury
805.11 Open fracture of first cervical vertebra without mention of spinal cord injury
805.12 Open fracture of second cervical vertebra without mention of spinal cord injury
805.13 Open fracture of third cervical vertebra without mention of spinal cord injury
805.14 Open fracture of fourth cervical vertebra without mention of spinal cord injury
805.15 Open fracture of fifth cervical vertebra without mention of spinal cord injury
805.16 Open fracture of sixth cervical vertebra without mention of spinal cord injury
805.17 Open fracture of seventh cervical vertebra without mention of spinal cord injury
805.18 Open fracture of multiple cervical vertebrae without mention of spinal cord injury
806.01 Closed fracture of C1-C4 level with complete lesion of cord
806.02 Closed fracture of C1-C4 level with anterior cord syndrome
806.03 Closed fracture of C1-C4 level with central cord syndrome
806.04 Closed fracture of C1-C4 level with other specified spinal cord injury
806.05 Closed fracture of C5-C7 level with unspecified spinal cord injury
806.06 Closed fracture of C5-C7 level with complete lesion of cord
806.07 Closed fracture of C5-C7 level with anterior cord syndrome
806.08 Closed fracture of C5-C7 level with central cord syndrome
806.09 Closed fracture of C5-C7 level with other specified spinal cord injury
806.10 Open fracture of C1-C4 level with unspecified spinal cord injury
806.11 Open fracture of C1-C4 level with complete lesion of cord
806.12 Open fracture of C1-C4 level with anterior cord syndrome
806.13 Open fracture of C1-C4 level with central cord syndrome
806.14 Open fracture of C1-C4 level with other specified spinal cord injury
806.15 Open fracture of C5-C7 level with unspecified spinal cord injury
806.16 Open fracture of C5-C7 level with complete lesion of cord
806.17 Open fracture of C5-C7 level with anterior cord syndrome
806.18 Open fracture of C5-C7 level with central cord syndrome
806.19 Open fracture of C5-C7 level with other specified spinal cord injury
808.2 Closed fracture of pubis
808.3 Open fracture of pubis
808.41 Closed fracture of ilium
808.42 Closed fracture of ischium
808.43 Multiple closed pelvic fractures with disruption of pelvic circle
808.51 Open fracture of ilium
808.52 Open fracture of ischium
808.53 Multiple open pelvic fractures with disruption of pelvic circle
821.01 Closed fracture of shaft of femur
821.11 Open fracture of shaft of femur
821.20 Closed fracture of unspecified part of lower end of femur
821.29 Other closed fracture of lower end of femur
821.30 Open fracture of unspecified part of lower end of femur
821.39 Other open fracture of lower end of femur
996.40 Unspecified mechanical complication of internal orthopedic device, implant, and graft — (Use additional code to identify prosthetic joint with mechanical complication, V43.60-V43.69)
996.49 Other mechanical complication of other internal orthopedic device, implant, and graft — (Use additional code to identify prosthetic joint with mechanical complication, V43.60-V43.69)
996.67 Infection and inflammatory reaction due to other internal orthopedic device, implant, and graft — (Use additional code to identify specified infections)
996.78 Other complications due to other internal orthopedic device, implant, and graft — (Use additional code to identify complication: 338.18-338.19, 338.28-338.29)
V54.01 Encounter for removal of internal fixation device
V54.17 Aftercare for healing traumatic fracture of vertebrae
V54.89 Other orthopedic aftercare
V67.4 Treatment of healed fracture follow-up examination

ICD-9-CM Procedural

02.95 Removal of skull tongs or halo traction device

20670-20680

20670 Removal of implant; superficial (eg, buried wire, pin or rod) (separate procedure)
20680 deep (eg, buried wire, pin, screw, metal band, nail, rod or plate)

ICD-9-CM Diagnostic

996.40 Unspecified mechanical complication of internal orthopedic device, implant, and graft — (Use additional code to identify prosthetic joint with mechanical complication, V43.60-V43.69)
996.49 Other mechanical complication of other internal orthopedic device, implant, and graft — (Use additional code to identify prosthetic joint with mechanical complication, V43.60-V43.69)
996.67 Infection and inflammatory reaction due to other internal orthopedic device, implant, and graft — (Use additional code to identify specified infections)
996.78 Other complications due to other internal orthopedic device, implant, and graft — (Use additional code to identify complication: 338.18-338.19, 338.28-338.29)

V54.01 Encounter for removal of internal fixation device
V54.10 Aftercare for healing traumatic fracture of arm, unspecified
V54.11 Aftercare for healing traumatic fracture of upper arm
V54.12 Aftercare for healing traumatic fracture of lower arm
V54.13 Aftercare for healing traumatic fracture of hip
V54.14 Aftercare for healing traumatic fracture of leg, unspecified
V54.15 Aftercare for healing traumatic fracture of upper leg
V54.16 Aftercare for healing traumatic fracture of lower leg
V54.19 Aftercare for healing traumatic fracture of other bone
V54.20 Aftercare for healing pathologic fracture of arm, unspecified
V54.21 Aftercare for healing pathologic fracture of upper arm
V54.22 Aftercare for healing pathologic fracture of lower arm
V54.23 Aftercare for healing pathologic fracture of hip
V54.24 Aftercare for healing pathologic fracture of leg, unspecified
V54.25 Aftercare for healing pathologic fracture of upper leg
V54.26 Aftercare for healing pathologic fracture of lower leg
V54.29 Aftercare for healing pathologic fracture of other bone
V54.81 Aftercare following joint replacement — (Use additional code to identify joint replacement site: V43.60-V43.69)
V54.89 Other orthopedic aftercare

ICD-9-CM Procedural

76.97 Removal of internal fixation device from facial bone
78.60 Removal of implanted device, unspecified site
78.61 Removal of implanted device from scapula, clavicle, and thorax (ribs and sternum)
78.62 Removal of implanted device from humerus
78.63 Removal of implanted device from radius and ulna
78.64 Removal of implanted device from carpals and metacarpals
78.65 Removal of implanted device from femur
78.66 Removal of implanted device from patella
78.67 Removal of implanted device from tibia and fibula
78.68 Removal of implanted device from tarsal and metatarsals
78.69 Removal of implanted device from other bone
80.02 Arthrotomy for removal of prosthesis without replacement, elbow
84.57 Removal of (cement) spacer
97.35 Removal of dental prosthesis
97.36 Removal of other external mandibular fixation device

HCPCS Level II Supplies & Services

A4305 Disposable drug delivery system, flow rate of 50 ml or greater per hour

20690-20692

20690 Application of a uniplane (pins or wires in 1 plane), unilateral, external fixation system
20692 Application of a multiplane (pins or wires in more than 1 plane), unilateral, external fixation system (eg, Ilizarov, Monticelli type)

ICD-9-CM Diagnostic

This is designated as an add-on code by Optum only. Refer to the corresponding primary procedure code for ICD-9-CM diagnosis code links.

ICD-9-CM Procedural

78.10 Application of external fixator device, unspecified site
78.11 Application of external fixator device, scapula, clavicle, and thorax [ribs and sternum]
78.12 Application of external fixator device, humerus
78.13 Application of external fixator device, radius and ulna
78.14 Application of external fixator device, carpals and metacarpals
78.15 Application of external fixator device, femur
78.16 Application of external fixator device, patella
78.17 Application of external fixator device, tibia and fibula
78.18 Application of external fixator device, tarsals and metatarsals
78.19 Application of external fixator device, other

HCPCS Level II Supplies & Services

A4305 Disposable drug delivery system, flow rate of 50 ml or greater per hour

20693

20693 Adjustment or revision of external fixation system requiring anesthesia (eg, new pin[s] or wire[s] and/or new ring[s] or bar[s])

ICD-9-CM Diagnostic

733.93 Stress fracture of tibia or fibula — (Use additional external cause code(s) to identify the cause of the stress fracture)
733.95 Stress fracture of other bone — (Use additional external cause code(s) to identify the cause of the stress fracture)
733.96 Stress fracture of femoral neck — (Use additional external cause code(s) to identify the cause of the stress fracture)
733.97 Stress fracture of shaft of femur — (Use additional external cause code(s) to identify the cause of the stress fracture)
733.98 Stress fracture of pelvis — (Use additional external cause code(s) to identify the cause of the stress fracture)
808.0 Closed fracture of acetabulum
808.1 Open fracture of acetabulum
808.2 Closed fracture of pubis
808.3 Open fracture of pubis
808.41 Closed fracture of ilium
808.42 Closed fracture of ischium
808.43 Multiple closed pelvic fractures with disruption of pelvic circle
808.49 Closed fracture of other specified part of pelvis
808.51 Open fracture of ilium
808.52 Open fracture of ischium
808.53 Multiple open pelvic fractures with disruption of pelvic circle
808.59 Open fracture of other specified part of pelvis
812.01 Closed fracture of surgical neck of humerus
812.02 Closed fracture of anatomical neck of humerus
812.09 Other closed fractures of upper end of humerus
812.11 Open fracture of surgical neck of humerus
812.12 Open fracture of anatomical neck of humerus
812.13 Open fracture of greater tuberosity of humerus
812.19 Other open fracture of upper end of humerus
812.21 Closed fracture of shaft of humerus
812.31 Open fracture of shaft of humerus
812.41 Closed fracture of supracondylar humerus
812.42 Closed fracture of lateral condyle of humerus
812.43 Closed fracture of medial condyle of humerus
812.44 Closed fracture of unspecified condyle(s) of humerus
812.49 Other closed fracture of lower end of humerus
812.51 Open fracture of supracondylar humerus
812.52 Open fracture of lateral condyle of humerus
812.53 Open fracture of medial condyle of humerus
812.54 Open fracture of unspecified condyle(s) of humerus
812.59 Other open fracture of lower end of humerus
813.01 Closed fracture of olecranon process of ulna
813.02 Closed fracture of coronoid process of ulna
813.03 Closed Monteggia's fracture
813.04 Other and unspecified closed fractures of proximal end of ulna (alone)
813.05 Closed fracture of head of radius
813.06 Closed fracture of neck of radius
813.07 Other and unspecified closed fractures of proximal end of radius (alone)
813.08 Closed fracture of radius with ulna, upper end (any part)
813.11 Open fracture of olecranon process of ulna
813.12 Open fracture of coronoid process of ulna
813.13 Open Monteggia's fracture

813.14	Other and unspecified open fractures of proximal end of ulna (alone) ▽
813.15	Open fracture of head of radius
813.16	Open fracture of neck of radius
813.17	Other and unspecified open fractures of proximal end of radius (alone) ▽
813.18	Open fracture of radius with ulna, upper end (any part)
813.21	Closed fracture of shaft of radius (alone)
813.22	Closed fracture of shaft of ulna (alone)
813.23	Closed fracture of shaft of radius with ulna
813.31	Open fracture of shaft of radius (alone)
813.32	Open fracture of shaft of ulna (alone)
813.33	Open fracture of shaft of radius with ulna
813.41	Closed Colles' fracture
813.42	Other closed fractures of distal end of radius (alone)
813.43	Closed fracture of distal end of ulna (alone)
813.44	Closed fracture of lower end of radius with ulna
813.45	Torus fracture of radius (alone)
813.46	Torus fracture of ulna (alone)
813.47	Torus fracture of radius and ulna
813.51	Open Colles' fracture
813.52	Other open fractures of distal end of radius (alone)
813.53	Open fracture of distal end of ulna (alone)
813.54	Open fracture of lower end of radius with ulna
813.81	Closed fracture of unspecified part of radius (alone) ▽
813.82	Closed fracture of unspecified part of ulna (alone) ▽
813.83	Closed fracture of unspecified part of radius with ulna ▽
813.91	Open fracture of unspecified part of radius (alone) ▽
813.92	Open fracture of unspecified part of ulna (alone) ▽
813.93	Open fracture of unspecified part of radius with ulna ▽
814.00	Unspecified closed fracture of carpal bone ▽
814.10	Unspecified open fracture of carpal bone ▽
815.00	Closed fracture of metacarpal bone(s), site unspecified ▽
815.09	Closed fracture of multiple sites of metacarpus
815.10	Open fracture of metacarpal bone(s), site unspecified ▽
815.19	Open fracture of multiple sites of metacarpus
816.03	Closed fracture of multiple sites of phalanx or phalanges of hand
816.13	Open fractures of multiple sites of phalanx or phalanges of hand
819.0	Multiple closed fractures involving both upper limbs, and upper limb with rib(s) and sternum
819.1	Multiple open fractures involving both upper limbs, and upper limb with rib(s) and sternum
820.00	Closed fracture of unspecified intracapsular section of neck of femur ▽
820.10	Open fracture of unspecified intracapsular section of neck of femur ▽
820.19	Other open transcervical fracture of femur
820.20	Closed fracture of unspecified trochanteric section of femur ▽
820.30	Open fracture of unspecified trochanteric section of femur ▽
821.01	Closed fracture of shaft of femur
821.11	Open fracture of shaft of femur
821.20	Closed fracture of unspecified part of lower end of femur ▽
821.21	Closed fracture of femoral condyle
821.22	Closed fracture of lower epiphysis of femur
821.23	Closed supracondylar fracture of femur
821.29	Other closed fracture of lower end of femur
821.30	Open fracture of unspecified part of lower end of femur ▽
821.31	Open fracture of femoral condyle
821.32	Open fracture of lower epiphysis of femur
821.33	Open supracondylar fracture of femur
821.39	Other open fracture of lower end of femur
823.00	Closed fracture of upper end of tibia
823.01	Closed fracture of upper end of fibula
823.02	Closed fracture of upper end of fibula with tibia
823.10	Open fracture of upper end of tibia
823.11	Open fracture of upper end of fibula
823.12	Open fracture of upper end of fibula with tibia
823.20	Closed fracture of shaft of tibia
823.21	Closed fracture of shaft of fibula
823.22	Closed fracture of shaft of fibula with tibia
823.30	Open fracture of shaft of tibia
823.31	Open fracture of shaft of fibula
823.32	Open fracture of shaft of fibula with tibia
824.0	Closed fracture of medial malleolus
824.1	Open fracture of medial malleolus
824.2	Closed fracture of lateral malleolus
824.3	Open fracture of lateral malleolus
824.4	Closed bimalleolar fracture
824.5	Open bimalleolar fracture
824.6	Closed trimalleolar fracture
824.7	Open trimalleolar fracture
824.8	Unspecified closed fracture of ankle ▽
824.9	Unspecified open fracture of ankle ▽
827.0	Other, multiple and ill-defined closed fractures of lower limb
827.1	Other, multiple and ill-defined open fractures of lower limb
828.0	Multiple closed fractures involving both lower limbs, lower with upper limb, and lower limb(s) with rib(s) and sternum
828.1	Multiple fractures involving both lower limbs, lower with upper limb, and lower limb(s) with rib(s) and sternum, open
996.40	Unspecified mechanical complication of internal orthopedic device, implant, and graft — (Use additional code to identify prosthetic joint with mechanical complication, V43.60-V43.69) ▽
996.49	Other mechanical complication of other internal orthopedic device, implant, and graft — (Use additional code to identify prosthetic joint with mechanical complication, V43.60-V43.69)
996.67	Infection and inflammatory reaction due to other internal orthopedic device, implant, and graft — (Use additional code to identify specified infections)
996.78	Other complications due to other internal orthopedic device, implant, and graft — (Use additional code to identify complication: 338.18-338.19, 338.28-338.29)
V53.7	Fitting and adjustment of orthopedic device
V54.89	Other orthopedic aftercare

ICD-9-CM Procedural

93.44	Other skeletal traction

20694

20694 Removal, under anesthesia, of external fixation system

ICD-9-CM Diagnostic

733.93	Stress fracture of tibia or fibula — (Use additional external cause code(s) to identify the cause of the stress fracture)
733.95	Stress fracture of other bone — (Use additional external cause code(s) to identify the cause of the stress fracture)
733.96	Stress fracture of femoral neck — (Use additional external cause code(s) to identify the cause of the stress fracture)
733.97	Stress fracture of shaft of femur — (Use additional external cause code(s) to identify the cause of the stress fracture)
733.98	Stress fracture of pelvis — (Use additional external cause code(s) to identify the cause of the stress fracture)
808.0	Closed fracture of acetabulum
808.1	Open fracture of acetabulum
808.2	Closed fracture of pubis
808.3	Open fracture of pubis

808.41 Closed fracture of ilium
808.42 Closed fracture of ischium
808.43 Multiple closed pelvic fractures with disruption of pelvic circle
808.49 Closed fracture of other specified part of pelvis
808.51 Open fracture of ilium
808.52 Open fracture of ischium
808.53 Multiple open pelvic fractures with disruption of pelvic circle
808.59 Open fracture of other specified part of pelvis
812.01 Closed fracture of surgical neck of humerus
812.02 Closed fracture of anatomical neck of humerus
812.09 Other closed fractures of upper end of humerus
812.11 Open fracture of surgical neck of humerus
812.12 Open fracture of anatomical neck of humerus
812.13 Open fracture of greater tuberosity of humerus
812.19 Other open fracture of upper end of humerus
812.21 Closed fracture of shaft of humerus
812.31 Open fracture of shaft of humerus
812.41 Closed fracture of supracondylar humerus
812.42 Closed fracture of lateral condyle of humerus
812.43 Closed fracture of medial condyle of humerus
812.44 Closed fracture of unspecified condyle(s) of humerus ▽
812.49 Other closed fracture of lower end of humerus
812.51 Open fracture of supracondylar humerus
812.52 Open fracture of lateral condyle of humerus
812.53 Open fracture of medial condyle of humerus
812.54 Open fracture of unspecified condyle(s) of humerus ▽
812.59 Other open fracture of lower end of humerus
813.01 Closed fracture of olecranon process of ulna
813.02 Closed fracture of coronoid process of ulna
813.03 Closed Monteggia's fracture
813.04 Other and unspecified closed fractures of proximal end of ulna (alone) ▽
813.05 Closed fracture of head of radius
813.06 Closed fracture of neck of radius
813.07 Other and unspecified closed fractures of proximal end of radius (alone) ▽
813.08 Closed fracture of radius with ulna, upper end (any part)
813.11 Open fracture of olecranon process of ulna
813.12 Open fracture of coronoid process of ulna
813.13 Open Monteggia's fracture
813.14 Other and unspecified open fractures of proximal end of ulna (alone) ▽
813.15 Open fracture of head of radius
813.16 Open fracture of neck of radius
813.17 Other and unspecified open fractures of proximal end of radius (alone) ▽
813.18 Open fracture of radius with ulna, upper end (any part)
813.21 Closed fracture of shaft of radius (alone)
813.22 Closed fracture of shaft of ulna (alone)
813.23 Closed fracture of shaft of radius with ulna
813.31 Open fracture of shaft of radius (alone)
813.32 Open fracture of shaft of ulna (alone)
813.33 Open fracture of shaft of radius with ulna
813.41 Closed Colles' fracture
813.42 Other closed fractures of distal end of radius (alone)
813.43 Closed fracture of distal end of ulna (alone)
813.44 Closed fracture of lower end of radius with ulna
813.45 Torus fracture of radius (alone)
813.46 Torus fracture of ulna (alone)
813.47 Torus fracture of radius and ulna
813.51 Open Colles' fracture
813.52 Other open fractures of distal end of radius (alone)
813.53 Open fracture of distal end of ulna (alone)
813.54 Open fracture of lower end of radius with ulna
813.81 Closed fracture of unspecified part of radius (alone) ▽
813.82 Closed fracture of unspecified part of ulna (alone) ▽
813.83 Closed fracture of unspecified part of radius with ulna ▽
813.91 Open fracture of unspecified part of radius (alone) ▽
813.92 Open fracture of unspecified part of ulna (alone) ▽
813.93 Open fracture of unspecified part of radius with ulna ▽
814.00 Unspecified closed fracture of carpal bone ▽
814.10 Unspecified open fracture of carpal bone ▽
815.00 Closed fracture of metacarpal bone(s), site unspecified ▽
815.09 Closed fracture of multiple sites of metacarpus
815.10 Open fracture of metacarpal bone(s), site unspecified ▽
815.19 Open fracture of multiple sites of metacarpus
816.03 Closed fracture of multiple sites of phalanx or phalanges of hand
816.13 Open fractures of multiple sites of phalanx or phalanges of hand
819.0 Multiple closed fractures involving both upper limbs, and upper limb with rib(s) and sternum
819.1 Multiple open fractures involving both upper limbs, and upper limb with rib(s) and sternum
820.00 Closed fracture of unspecified intracapsular section of neck of femur ▽
820.10 Open fracture of unspecified intracapsular section of neck of femur ▽
820.19 Other open transcervical fracture of femur
820.20 Closed fracture of unspecified trochanteric section of femur ▽
820.30 Open fracture of unspecified trochanteric section of femur ▽
821.01 Closed fracture of shaft of femur
821.11 Open fracture of shaft of femur
821.20 Closed fracture of unspecified part of lower end of femur ▽
821.21 Closed fracture of femoral condyle
821.22 Closed fracture of lower epiphysis of femur
821.23 Closed supracondylar fracture of femur
821.29 Other closed fracture of lower end of femur
821.30 Open fracture of unspecified part of lower end of femur ▽
821.31 Open fracture of femoral condyle
821.32 Open fracture of lower epiphysis of femur
821.33 Open supracondylar fracture of femur
821.39 Other open fracture of lower end of femur
823.00 Closed fracture of upper end of tibia
823.01 Closed fracture of upper end of fibula
823.02 Closed fracture of upper end of fibula with tibia
823.10 Open fracture of upper end of tibia
823.11 Open fracture of upper end of fibula
823.12 Open fracture of upper end of fibula with tibia
823.20 Closed fracture of shaft of tibia
823.21 Closed fracture of shaft of fibula
823.22 Closed fracture of shaft of fibula with tibia
823.30 Open fracture of shaft of tibia
823.31 Open fracture of shaft of fibula
823.32 Open fracture of shaft of fibula with tibia
824.0 Closed fracture of medial malleolus
824.1 Open fracture of medial malleolus
824.2 Closed fracture of lateral malleolus
824.3 Open fracture of lateral malleolus
824.4 Closed bimalleolar fracture
824.5 Open bimalleolar fracture
824.6 Closed trimalleolar fracture
824.7 Open trimalleolar fracture
824.8 Unspecified closed fracture of ankle ▽
824.9 Unspecified open fracture of ankle ▽

827.0 Other, multiple and ill-defined closed fractures of lower limb
827.1 Other, multiple and ill-defined open fractures of lower limb
828.0 Multiple closed fractures involving both lower limbs, lower with upper limb, and lower limb(s) with rib(s) and sternum
828.1 Multiple fractures involving both lower limbs, lower with upper limb, and lower limb(s) with rib(s) and sternum, open
996.40 Unspecified mechanical complication of internal orthopedic device, implant, and graft — (Use additional code to identify prosthetic joint with mechanical complication, V43.60-V43.69) ▼
996.49 Other mechanical complication of other internal orthopedic device, implant, and graft — (Use additional code to identify prosthetic joint with mechanical complication, V43.60-V43.69)
996.67 Infection and inflammatory reaction due to other internal orthopedic device, implant, and graft — (Use additional code to identify specified infections)
996.78 Other complications due to other internal orthopedic device, implant, and graft — (Use additional code to identify complication: 338.18-338.19, 338.28-338.29)
V54.10 Aftercare for healing traumatic fracture of arm, unspecified ▼
V54.11 Aftercare for healing traumatic fracture of upper arm
V54.12 Aftercare for healing traumatic fracture of lower arm
V54.14 Aftercare for healing traumatic fracture of leg, unspecified ▼
V54.16 Aftercare for healing traumatic fracture of lower leg
V54.19 Aftercare for healing traumatic fracture of other bone
V54.20 Aftercare for healing pathologic fracture of arm, unspecified ▼
V54.21 Aftercare for healing pathologic fracture of upper arm
V54.22 Aftercare for healing pathologic fracture of lower arm
V54.24 Aftercare for healing pathologic fracture of leg, unspecified ▼
V54.25 Aftercare for healing pathologic fracture of upper leg
V54.26 Aftercare for healing pathologic fracture of lower leg
V54.29 Aftercare for healing pathologic fracture of other bone
V54.89 Other orthopedic aftercare

ICD-9-CM Procedural

78.60 Removal of implanted device, unspecified site
78.61 Removal of implanted device from scapula, clavicle, and thorax (ribs and sternum)
78.62 Removal of implanted device from humerus
78.63 Removal of implanted device from radius and ulna
78.64 Removal of implanted device from carpals and metacarpals
78.65 Removal of implanted device from femur
78.66 Removal of implanted device from patella
78.67 Removal of implanted device from tibia and fibula
78.68 Removal of implanted device from tarsal and metatarsals
78.69 Removal of implanted device from other bone

20696-20697

20696 Application of multiplane (pins or wires in more than 1 plane), unilateral, external fixation with stereotactic computer-assisted adjustment (eg, spatial frame), including imaging; initial and subsequent alignment(s), assessment(s), and computation(s) of adjustment schedule(s)
20697 exchange (ie, removal and replacement) of strut, each

ICD-9-CM Diagnostic

The application of this code is too broad to adequately present ICD-9-CM diagnostic code links here. Refer to your ICD-9-CM book.

ICD-9-CM Procedural

00.39 Other computer assisted surgery
78.10 Application of external fixator device, unspecified site
78.11 Application of external fixator device, scapula, clavicle, and thorax [ribs and sternum]
78.12 Application of external fixator device, humerus
78.13 Application of external fixator device, radius and ulna
78.14 Application of external fixator device, carpals and metacarpals
78.15 Application of external fixator device, femur
78.16 Application of external fixator device, patella
78.17 Application of external fixator device, tibia and fibula
78.18 Application of external fixator device, tarsals and metatarsals
78.19 Application of external fixator device, other

20802

20802 Replantation, arm (includes surgical neck of humerus through elbow joint), complete amputation

ICD-9-CM Diagnostic

887.2 Traumatic amputation of arm and hand (complete) (partial), unilateral, at or above elbow, without mention of complication
887.3 Traumatic amputation of arm and hand (complete) (partial), unilateral, at or above elbow, complicated
887.6 Traumatic amputation of arm and hand (complete) (partial), bilateral (any level), without mention of complication
887.7 Traumatic amputation of arm and hand (complete) (partial), bilateral (any level), complicated

ICD-9-CM Procedural

84.24 Upper arm reattachment

20805

20805 Replantation, forearm (includes radius and ulna to radial carpal joint), complete amputation

ICD-9-CM Diagnostic

887.0 Traumatic amputation of arm and hand (complete) (partial), unilateral, below elbow, without mention of complication
887.1 Traumatic amputation of arm and hand (complete) (partial), unilateral, below elbow, complicated
887.6 Traumatic amputation of arm and hand (complete) (partial), bilateral (any level), without mention of complication
887.7 Traumatic amputation of arm and hand (complete) (partial), bilateral (any level), complicated

ICD-9-CM Procedural

84.23 Forearm, wrist, or hand reattachment

20808

20808 Replantation, hand (includes hand through metacarpophalangeal joints), complete amputation

ICD-9-CM Diagnostic

887.0 Traumatic amputation of arm and hand (complete) (partial), unilateral, below elbow, without mention of complication
887.1 Traumatic amputation of arm and hand (complete) (partial), unilateral, below elbow, complicated
887.4 Traumatic amputation of arm and hand (complete) (partial), unilateral, level not specified, without mention of complication ▼
887.5 Traumatic amputation of arm and hand (complete) (partial), unilateral, level not specified, complicated ▼
887.6 Traumatic amputation of arm and hand (complete) (partial), bilateral (any level), without mention of complication
887.7 Traumatic amputation of arm and hand (complete) (partial), bilateral (any level), complicated

ICD-9-CM Procedural

84.23 Forearm, wrist, or hand reattachment

20816-20822

20816 Replantation, digit, excluding thumb (includes metacarpophalangeal joint to insertion of flexor sublimis tendon), complete amputation
20822 Replantation, digit, excluding thumb (includes distal tip to sublimis tendon insertion), complete amputation

ICD-9-CM Diagnostic

886.0 Traumatic amputation of other finger(s) (complete) (partial), without mention of complication
886.1 Traumatic amputation of other finger(s) (complete) (partial), complicated
895.0 Traumatic amputation of toe(s) (complete) (partial), without mention of complication
895.1 Traumatic amputation of toe(s) (complete) (partial), complicated

ICD-9-CM Procedural

84.22 Finger reattachment
84.25 Toe reattachment

20824-20827

20824 Replantation, thumb (includes carpometacarpal joint to MP joint), complete amputation
20827 Replantation, thumb (includes distal tip to MP joint), complete amputation

ICD-9-CM Diagnostic

885.0 Traumatic amputation of thumb (complete) (partial), without mention of complication
885.1 Traumatic amputation of thumb (complete) (partial), complicated

ICD-9-CM Procedural

84.21 Thumb reattachment

20838

20838 Replantation, foot, complete amputation

ICD-9-CM Diagnostic

896.0 Traumatic amputation of foot (complete) (partial), unilateral, without mention of complication
896.1 Traumatic amputation of foot (complete) (partial), unilateral, complicated
896.2 Traumatic amputation of foot (complete) (partial), bilateral, without mention of complication
896.3 Traumatic amputation of foot (complete) (partial), bilateral, complicated

ICD-9-CM Procedural

84.26 Foot reattachment

20900-20902

20900 Bone graft, any donor area; minor or small (eg, dowel or button)
20902 major or large

ICD-9-CM Diagnostic

The application of this code is too broad to adequately present ICD-9-CM diagnostic code links here. Refer to your ICD-9-CM book.

ICD-9-CM Procedural

77.70 Excision of bone for graft, unspecified site
77.71 Excision of scapula, clavicle, and thorax (ribs and sternum) for graft
77.72 Excision of humerus for graft
77.73 Excision of radius and ulna for graft
77.74 Excision of carpals and metacarpals for graft
77.75 Excision of femur for graft
77.76 Excision of patella for graft
77.77 Excision of tibia and fibula for graft
77.78 Excision of tarsals and metatarsals for graft
77.79 Excision of other bone for graft, except facial bones

HCPCS Level II Supplies & Services

A4305 Disposable drug delivery system, flow rate of 50 ml or greater per hour

20910

20910 Cartilage graft; costochondral

ICD-9-CM Diagnostic

The application of this code is too broad to adequately present ICD-9-CM diagnostic code links here. Refer to your ICD-9-CM book.

ICD-9-CM Procedural

80.49 Division of joint capsule, ligament, or cartilage of other specified site
81.99 Other operations on joint structures

20912

20912 Cartilage graft; nasal septum

ICD-9-CM Diagnostic

The application of this code is too broad to adequately present ICD-9-CM diagnostic code links here. Refer to your ICD-9-CM book.

ICD-9-CM Procedural

21.88 Other septoplasty
21.99 Other operations on nose
76.99 Other operations on facial bones and joints

20920-20922

20920 Fascia lata graft; by stripper
20922 by incision and area exposure, complex or sheet

ICD-9-CM Diagnostic

The application of this code is too broad to adequately present ICD-9-CM diagnostic code links here. Refer to your ICD-9-CM book.

ICD-9-CM Procedural

83.43 Excision of muscle or fascia for graft

20924

20924 Tendon graft, from a distance (eg, palmaris, toe extensor, plantaris)

ICD-9-CM Diagnostic

The application of this code is too broad to adequately present ICD-9-CM diagnostic code links here. Refer to your ICD-9-CM book.

ICD-9-CM Procedural

82.32 Excision of tendon of hand for graft
82.53 Reattachment of tendon of hand
82.99 Other operations on muscle, tendon, and fascia of hand
83.41 Excision of tendon for graft
83.73 Reattachment of tendon
83.75 Tendon transfer or transplantation

20926

20926 Tissue grafts, other (eg, paratenon, fat, dermis)

ICD-9-CM Diagnostic

The application of this code is too broad to adequately present ICD-9-CM diagnostic code links here. Refer to your ICD-9-CM book.

ICD-9-CM Procedural

86.69 Other skin graft to other sites
86.87 Fat graft of skin and subcutaneous tissue

20930-20931

20930 Allograft, morselized, or placement of osteopromotive material, for spine surgery only (List separately in addition to code for primary procedure)

20931 Allograft, structural, for spine surgery only (List separately in addition to code for primary procedure)

ICD-9-CM Diagnostic

This is an add-on code. Refer to the corresponding primary procedure code for ICD-9-CM diagnosis code links.

ICD-9-CM Procedural

84.52 Insertion of recombinant bone morphogenetic protein

20936-20938

20936 Autograft for spine surgery only (includes harvesting the graft); local (eg, ribs, spinous process, or laminar fragments) obtained from same incision (List separately in addition to code for primary procedure)

20937 morselized (through separate skin or fascial incision) (List separately in addition to code for primary procedure)

20938 structural, bicortical or tricortical (through separate skin or fascial incision) (List separately in addition to code for primary procedure)

ICD-9-CM Diagnostic

This is an add-on code. Refer to the corresponding primary procedure code for ICD-9-CM diagnosis code links.

ICD-9-CM Procedural

77.70 Excision of bone for graft, unspecified site

77.79 Excision of other bone for graft, except facial bones

20950

20950 Monitoring of interstitial fluid pressure (includes insertion of device, eg, wick catheter technique, needle manometer technique) in detection of muscle compartment syndrome

ICD-9-CM Diagnostic

249.70 Secondary diabetes mellitus with peripheral circulatory disorders, not stated as uncontrolled, or unspecified — (Use additional code to identify manifestation: 443.81, 785.4) (Use additional code to identify any associated insulin use: V58.67)

249.71 Secondary diabetes mellitus with peripheral circulatory disorders, uncontrolled — (Use additional code to identify manifestation: 443.81, 785.4) (Use additional code to identify any associated insulin use: V58.67)

250.70 Diabetes with peripheral circulatory disorders, type II or unspecified type, not stated as uncontrolled — (Use additional code to identify manifestation: 443.81, 785.4)

250.71 Diabetes with peripheral circulatory disorders, type I [juvenile type], not stated as uncontrolled — (Use additional code to identify manifestation: 443.81, 785.4)

250.72 Diabetes with peripheral circulatory disorders, type II or unspecified type, uncontrolled — (Use additional code to identify manifestation: 443.81, 785.4)

250.73 Diabetes with peripheral circulatory disorders, type I [juvenile type], uncontrolled — (Use additional code to identify manifestation: 443.81, 785.4)

286.6 Defibrination syndrome

443.0 Raynaud's syndrome — (Use additional code to identify gangrene: 785.4)

728.86 Necrotizing fasciitis — (Use additional code to identify infectious organism, 041.00-041.89, 785.4, if applicable)

729.71 Nontraumatic compartment syndrome of upper extremity — (Code first, if applicable, postprocedural complication: 998.89)

729.72 Nontraumatic compartment syndrome of lower extremity — (Code first, if applicable, postprocedural complication: 998.89)

729.73 Nontraumatic compartment syndrome of abdomen — (Code first, if applicable, postprocedural complication: 998.89)

729.79 Nontraumatic compartment syndrome of other sites — (Code first, if applicable, postprocedural complication: 998.89)

785.4 Gangrene — (Code first any associated underlying condition)

925.1 Crushing injury of face and scalp — (Use additional code to identify any associated injuries, such as: 800-829, 850.0-854.1, 860.0-869.1)

925.2 Crushing injury of neck — (Use additional code to identify any associated injuries, such as: 800-829, 850.0-854.1, 860.0-869.1)

926.0 Crushing injury of external genitalia — (Use additional code to identify any associated injuries: 800-829, 850.0-854.1, 860.0-869.1)

926.11 Crushing injury of back — (Use additional code to identify any associated injuries: 800-829, 850.0-854.1, 860.0-869.1)

926.12 Crushing injury of buttock — (Use additional code to identify any associated injuries: 800-829, 850.0-854.1, 860.0-869.1)

926.19 Crushing injury of other specified sites of trunk — (Use additional code to identify any associated injuries: 800-829, 850.0-854.1, 860.0-869.1)

926.8 Crushing injury of multiple sites of trunk — (Use additional code to identify any associated injuries: 800-829, 850.0-854.1, 860.0-869.1)

927.00 Crushing injury of shoulder region — (Use additional code to identify any associated injuries: 800-829, 850.0-854.1, 860.0-869.1)

927.01 Crushing injury of scapular region — (Use additional code to identify any associated injuries: 800-829, 850.0-854.1, 860.0-869.1)

927.02 Crushing injury of axillary region — (Use additional code to identify any associated injuries: 800-829, 850.0-854.1, 860.0-869.1)

927.03 Crushing injury of upper arm — (Use additional code to identify any associated injuries: 800-829, 850.0-854.1, 860.0-869.1)

927.09 Crushing injury of multiple sites of upper arm — (Use additional code to identify any associated injuries: 800-829, 850.0-854.1, 860.0-869.1)

927.10 Crushing injury of forearm — (Use additional code to identify any associated injuries: 800-829, 850.0-854.1, 860.0-869.1)

927.11 Crushing injury of elbow — (Use additional code to identify any associated injuries: 800-829, 850.0-854.1, 860.0-869.1)

927.3 Crushing injury of finger(s) — (Use additional code to identify any associated injuries: 800-829, 850.0-854.1, 860.0-869.1)

927.8 Crushing injury of multiple sites of upper limb — (Use additional code to identify any associated injuries: 800-829, 850.0-854.1, 860.0-869.1)

928.00 Crushing injury of thigh — (Use additional code to identify any associated injuries: 800-829, 850.0-854.1, 860.0-869.1)

928.01 Crushing injury of hip — (Use additional code to identify any associated injuries: 800-829, 850.0-854.1, 860.0-869.1)

928.10 Crushing injury of lower leg — (Use additional code to identify any associated injuries: 800-829, 850.0-854.1, 860.0-869.1)

928.11 Crushing injury of knee — (Use additional code to identify any associated injuries: 800-829, 850.0-854.1, 860.0-869.1)

928.20 Crushing injury of foot — (Use additional code to identify any associated injuries: 800-829, 850.0-854.1, 860.0-869.1)

928.21 Crushing injury of ankle — (Use additional code to identify any associated injuries: 800-829, 850.0-854.1, 860.0-869.1)

928.3 Crushing injury of toe(s) — (Use additional code to identify any associated injuries: 800-829, 850.0-854.1, 860.0-869.1)

928.8 Crushing injury of multiple sites of lower limb — (Use additional code to identify any associated injuries: 800-829, 850.0-854.1, 860.0-869.1)

958.90 Compartment syndrome, unspecified ▽

958.91 Traumatic compartment syndrome of upper extremity

958.92 Traumatic compartment syndrome of lower extremity

958.93 Traumatic compartment syndrome of abdomen

958.99 Traumatic compartment syndrome of other sites

ICD-9-CM Procedural

83.29 Other diagnostic procedures on muscle, tendon, fascia, and bursa, including that of hand

20955

20955 Bone graft with microvascular anastomosis; fibula

ICD-9-CM Diagnostic

170.1 Malignant neoplasm of mandible
198.5 Secondary malignant neoplasm of bone and bone marrow
213.0 Benign neoplasm of bones of skull and face
213.1 Benign neoplasm of lower jaw bone
239.2 Neoplasms of unspecified nature of bone, soft tissue, and skin
524.00 Unspecified major anomaly of jaw size ♥
524.03 Maxillary hypoplasia
524.04 Mandibular hypoplasia
524.06 Microgenia
524.07 Excessive tuberosity of jaw
524.09 Other specified major anomaly of jaw size
524.11 Maxillary asymmetry
524.12 Other jaw asymmetry
524.19 Other specified anomaly of relationship of jaw to cranial base
524.69 Other specified temporomandibular joint disorders
524.74 Alveolar mandibular hypoplasia
526.89 Other specified disease of the jaws
730.16 Chronic osteomyelitis, lower leg — (Use additional code to identify organism: 041.1. Use additional code to identify major osseous defect, if applicable: 731.3)
730.18 Chronic osteomyelitis, other specified sites — (Use additional code to identify organism: 041.1. Use additional code to identify major osseous defect, if applicable: 731.3)
731.3 Major osseous defects — (Code first underlying disease: 170.0-170.9, 730.00-730.29, 733.00-733.09, 733.40-733.49, 996.45)
733.49 Aseptic necrosis of other bone site — (Use additional code to identify major osseous defect, if applicable: 731.3)
733.81 Malunion of fracture
733.82 Nonunion of fracture
905.0 Late effect of fracture of skull and face bones
925.1 Crushing injury of face and scalp — (Use additional code to identify any associated injuries, such as: 800-829, 850.0-854.1, 860.0-869.1)

ICD-9-CM Procedural

76.41 Total mandibulectomy with synchronous reconstruction
76.44 Total ostectomy of other facial bone with synchronous reconstruction
76.91 Bone graft to facial bone
77.77 Excision of tibia and fibula for graft
78.07 Bone graft of tibia and fibula

20956

20956 Bone graft with microvascular anastomosis; iliac crest

ICD-9-CM Diagnostic

170.0 Malignant neoplasm of bones of skull and face, except mandible
170.1 Malignant neoplasm of mandible
170.2 Malignant neoplasm of vertebral column, excluding sacrum and coccyx
170.3 Malignant neoplasm of ribs, sternum, and clavicle
170.4 Malignant neoplasm of scapula and long bones of upper limb
170.5 Malignant neoplasm of short bones of upper limb
170.6 Malignant neoplasm of pelvic bones, sacrum, and coccyx
170.7 Malignant neoplasm of long bones of lower limb
170.8 Malignant neoplasm of short bones of lower limb
198.5 Secondary malignant neoplasm of bone and bone marrow
209.73 Secondary neuroendocrine tumor of bone
213.0 Benign neoplasm of bones of skull and face
213.1 Benign neoplasm of lower jaw bone
213.2 Benign neoplasm of vertebral column, excluding sacrum and coccyx
213.3 Benign neoplasm of ribs, sternum, and clavicle
213.4 Benign neoplasm of scapula and long bones of upper limb
213.5 Benign neoplasm of short bones of upper limb
213.6 Benign neoplasm of pelvic bones, sacrum, and coccyx
213.7 Benign neoplasm of long bones of lower limb
213.8 Benign neoplasm of short bones of lower limb
238.0 Neoplasm of uncertain behavior of bone and articular cartilage
239.2 Neoplasms of unspecified nature of bone, soft tissue, and skin
524.00 Unspecified major anomaly of jaw size ♥
524.03 Maxillary hypoplasia
524.04 Mandibular hypoplasia
524.06 Microgenia
524.07 Excessive tuberosity of jaw
524.09 Other specified major anomaly of jaw size
524.11 Maxillary asymmetry
524.12 Other jaw asymmetry
524.19 Other specified anomaly of relationship of jaw to cranial base
524.69 Other specified temporomandibular joint disorders
526.2 Other cysts of jaws
526.4 Inflammatory conditions of jaw
526.89 Other specified disease of the jaws
730.11 Chronic osteomyelitis, shoulder region — (Use additional code to identify organism: 041.1. Use additional code to identify major osseous defect, if applicable: 731.3)
730.12 Chronic osteomyelitis, upper arm — (Use additional code to identify organism: 041.1. Use additional code to identify major osseous defect, if applicable: 731.3)
730.13 Chronic osteomyelitis, forearm — (Use additional code to identify organism: 041.1. Use additional code to identify major osseous defect, if applicable: 731.3)
730.14 Chronic osteomyelitis, hand — (Use additional code to identify organism: 041.1. Use additional code to identify major osseous defect, if applicable: 731.3)
730.15 Chronic osteomyelitis, pelvic region and thigh — (Use additional code to identify organism: 041.1. Use additional code to identify major osseous defect, if applicable: 731.3)
730.16 Chronic osteomyelitis, lower leg — (Use additional code to identify organism: 041.1. Use additional code to identify major osseous defect, if applicable: 731.3)
730.17 Chronic osteomyelitis, ankle and foot — (Use additional code to identify organism: 041.1. Use additional code to identify major osseous defect, if applicable: 731.3)
730.18 Chronic osteomyelitis, other specified sites — (Use additional code to identify organism: 041.1. Use additional code to identify major osseous defect, if applicable: 731.3)
731.3 Major osseous defects — (Code first underlying disease: 170.0-170.9, 730.00-730.29, 733.00-733.09, 733.40-733.49, 996.45)
733.82 Nonunion of fracture
756.9 Other and unspecified congenital anomaly of musculoskeletal system ♥
873.54 Open wound of jaw, complicated
V10.90 Personal history of unspecified malignant neoplasm ♥
V10.91 Personal history of malignant neuroendocrine tumor — (Code first any continuing functional activity, such as: carcinoid syndrome (259.2))

ICD-9-CM Procedural

76.91 Bone graft to facial bone
77.79 Excision of other bone for graft, except facial bones
78.09 Bone graft of other bone, except facial bones

20957

20957 Bone graft with microvascular anastomosis; metatarsal

ICD-9-CM Diagnostic

170.1 Malignant neoplasm of mandible
170.5 Malignant neoplasm of short bones of upper limb
170.8 Malignant neoplasm of short bones of lower limb
198.5 Secondary malignant neoplasm of bone and bone marrow

213.0 Benign neoplasm of bones of skull and face
213.1 Benign neoplasm of lower jaw bone
213.5 Benign neoplasm of short bones of upper limb
213.8 Benign neoplasm of short bones of lower limb
238.0 Neoplasm of uncertain behavior of bone and articular cartilage
239.2 Neoplasms of unspecified nature of bone, soft tissue, and skin
524.00 Unspecified major anomaly of jaw size
524.03 Maxillary hypoplasia
524.04 Mandibular hypoplasia
524.06 Microgenia
524.07 Excessive tuberosity of jaw
524.09 Other specified major anomaly of jaw size
524.11 Maxillary asymmetry
524.12 Other jaw asymmetry
524.19 Other specified anomaly of relationship of jaw to cranial base
524.69 Other specified temporomandibular joint disorders
730.14 Chronic osteomyelitis, hand — (Use additional code to identify organism: 041.1. Use additional code to identify major osseous defect, if applicable: 731.3)
730.17 Chronic osteomyelitis, ankle and foot — (Use additional code to identify organism: 041.1. Use additional code to identify major osseous defect, if applicable: 731.3)
730.18 Chronic osteomyelitis, other specified sites — (Use additional code to identify organism: 041.1. Use additional code to identify major osseous defect, if applicable: 731.3)
731.3 Major osseous defects — (Code first underlying disease: 170.0-170.9, 730.00-730.29, 733.00-733.09, 733.40-733.49, 996.45)
733.19 Pathologic fracture of other specified site
733.81 Malunion of fracture
733.82 Nonunion of fracture
756.9 Other and unspecified congenital anomaly of musculoskeletal system
892.1 Open wound of foot except toe(s) alone, complicated
893.1 Open wound of toe(s), complicated
927.20 Crushing injury of hand(s) — (Use additional code to identify any associated injuries: 800-829, 850.0-854.1, 860.0-869.1)
927.3 Crushing injury of finger(s) — (Use additional code to identify any associated injuries: 800-829, 850.0-854.1, 860.0-869.1)
928.20 Crushing injury of foot — (Use additional code to identify any associated injuries: 800-829, 850.0-854.1, 860.0-869.1)

ICD-9-CM Procedural

76.91 Bone graft to facial bone
77.78 Excision of tarsals and metatarsals for graft
78.08 Bone graft of tarsals and metatarsals

20962

20962 Bone graft with microvascular anastomosis; other than fibula, iliac crest, or metatarsal

ICD-9-CM Diagnostic

170.1 Malignant neoplasm of mandible
170.2 Malignant neoplasm of vertebral column, excluding sacrum and coccyx
170.3 Malignant neoplasm of ribs, sternum, and clavicle
170.4 Malignant neoplasm of scapula and long bones of upper limb
170.5 Malignant neoplasm of short bones of upper limb
170.6 Malignant neoplasm of pelvic bones, sacrum, and coccyx
170.7 Malignant neoplasm of long bones of lower limb
170.8 Malignant neoplasm of short bones of lower limb
198.5 Secondary malignant neoplasm of bone and bone marrow
209.73 Secondary neuroendocrine tumor of bone
213.0 Benign neoplasm of bones of skull and face
213.1 Benign neoplasm of lower jaw bone
213.2 Benign neoplasm of vertebral column, excluding sacrum and coccyx
213.3 Benign neoplasm of ribs, sternum, and clavicle
213.4 Benign neoplasm of scapula and long bones of upper limb
213.5 Benign neoplasm of short bones of upper limb
213.6 Benign neoplasm of pelvic bones, sacrum, and coccyx
213.7 Benign neoplasm of long bones of lower limb
213.8 Benign neoplasm of short bones of lower limb
238.0 Neoplasm of uncertain behavior of bone and articular cartilage
239.2 Neoplasms of unspecified nature of bone, soft tissue, and skin
524.00 Unspecified major anomaly of jaw size
524.03 Maxillary hypoplasia
524.04 Mandibular hypoplasia
524.06 Microgenia
524.07 Excessive tuberosity of jaw
524.09 Other specified major anomaly of jaw size
524.11 Maxillary asymmetry
524.12 Other jaw asymmetry
524.19 Other specified anomaly of relationship of jaw to cranial base
524.69 Other specified temporomandibular joint disorders
730.11 Chronic osteomyelitis, shoulder region — (Use additional code to identify organism: 041.1. Use additional code to identify major osseous defect, if applicable: 731.3)
730.12 Chronic osteomyelitis, upper arm — (Use additional code to identify organism: 041.1. Use additional code to identify major osseous defect, if applicable: 731.3)
730.13 Chronic osteomyelitis, forearm — (Use additional code to identify organism: 041.1. Use additional code to identify major osseous defect, if applicable: 731.3)
730.14 Chronic osteomyelitis, hand — (Use additional code to identify organism: 041.1. Use additional code to identify major osseous defect, if applicable: 731.3)
730.15 Chronic osteomyelitis, pelvic region and thigh — (Use additional code to identify organism: 041.1. Use additional code to identify major osseous defect, if applicable: 731.3)
730.16 Chronic osteomyelitis, lower leg — (Use additional code to identify organism: 041.1. Use additional code to identify major osseous defect, if applicable: 731.3)
730.17 Chronic osteomyelitis, ankle and foot — (Use additional code to identify organism: 041.1. Use additional code to identify major osseous defect, if applicable: 731.3)
730.18 Chronic osteomyelitis, other specified sites — (Use additional code to identify organism: 041.1. Use additional code to identify major osseous defect, if applicable: 731.3)
731.3 Major osseous defects — (Code first underlying disease: 170.0-170.9, 730.00-730.29, 733.00-733.09, 733.40-733.49, 996.45)
733.11 Pathologic fracture of humerus
733.12 Pathologic fracture of distal radius and ulna
733.13 Pathologic fracture of vertebrae
733.14 Pathologic fracture of neck of femur
733.15 Pathologic fracture of other specified part of femur
733.16 Pathologic fracture of tibia and fibula
733.19 Pathologic fracture of other specified site
733.40 Aseptic necrosis of bone, site unspecified — (Use additional code to identify major osseous defect, if applicable: 731.3)
733.42 Aseptic necrosis of head and neck of femur — (Use additional code to identify major osseous defect, if applicable: 731.3)
733.43 Aseptic necrosis of medial femoral condyle — (Use additional code to identify major osseous defect, if applicable: 731.3)
733.44 Aseptic necrosis of talus — (Use additional code to identify major osseous defect, if applicable: 731.3)
733.45 Aseptic necrosis of bone, jaw
733.49 Aseptic necrosis of other bone site — (Use additional code to identify major osseous defect, if applicable: 731.3)
733.81 Malunion of fracture
733.82 Nonunion of fracture
733.93 Stress fracture of tibia or fibula — (Use additional external cause code(s) to identify the cause of the stress fracture)
733.95 Stress fracture of other bone — (Use additional external cause code(s) to identify the cause of the stress fracture)

733.96 Stress fracture of femoral neck — (Use additional external cause code(s) to identify the cause of the stress fracture)
733.97 Stress fracture of shaft of femur — (Use additional external cause code(s) to identify the cause of the stress fracture)
733.98 Stress fracture of pelvis — (Use additional external cause code(s) to identify the cause of the stress fracture)
927.03 Crushing injury of upper arm — (Use additional code to identify any associated injuries: 800-829, 850.0-854.1, 860.0-869.1)
927.10 Crushing injury of forearm — (Use additional code to identify any associated injuries: 800-829, 850.0-854.1, 860.0-869.1)
927.20 Crushing injury of hand(s) — (Use additional code to identify any associated injuries: 800-829, 850.0-854.1, 860.0-869.1)
927.21 Crushing injury of wrist — (Use additional code to identify any associated injuries: 800-829, 850.0-854.1, 860.0-869.1)
928.00 Crushing injury of thigh — (Use additional code to identify any associated injuries: 800-829, 850.0-854.1, 860.0-869.1)
928.10 Crushing injury of lower leg — (Use additional code to identify any associated injuries: 800-829, 850.0-854.1, 860.0-869.1)
928.11 Crushing injury of knee — (Use additional code to identify any associated injuries: 800-829, 850.0-854.1, 860.0-869.1)
928.20 Crushing injury of foot — (Use additional code to identify any associated injuries: 800-829, 850.0-854.1, 860.0-869.1)
928.21 Crushing injury of ankle — (Use additional code to identify any associated injuries: 800-829, 850.0-854.1, 860.0-869.1)
V10.90 Personal history of unspecified malignant neoplasm ▽
V10.91 Personal history of malignant neuroendocrine tumor — (Code first any continuing functional activity, such as: carcinoid syndrome (259.2))

ICD-9-CM Procedural

76.91 Bone graft to facial bone
77.70 Excision of bone for graft, unspecified site
77.71 Excision of scapula, clavicle, and thorax (ribs and sternum) for graft
77.72 Excision of humerus for graft
77.73 Excision of radius and ulna for graft
77.74 Excision of carpals and metacarpals for graft
77.76 Excision of patella for graft
77.78 Excision of tarsals and metatarsals for graft
77.79 Excision of other bone for graft, except facial bones
78.00 Bone graft, unspecified site
78.01 Bone graft of scapula, clavicle, and thorax (ribs and sternum)

20969

20969 Free osteocutaneous flap with microvascular anastomosis; other than iliac crest, metatarsal, or great toe

ICD-9-CM Diagnostic

170.1 Malignant neoplasm of mandible
170.2 Malignant neoplasm of vertebral column, excluding sacrum and coccyx
170.3 Malignant neoplasm of ribs, sternum, and clavicle
170.4 Malignant neoplasm of scapula and long bones of upper limb
170.5 Malignant neoplasm of short bones of upper limb
170.6 Malignant neoplasm of pelvic bones, sacrum, and coccyx
170.7 Malignant neoplasm of long bones of lower limb
170.8 Malignant neoplasm of short bones of lower limb
198.5 Secondary malignant neoplasm of bone and bone marrow
209.73 Secondary neuroendocrine tumor of bone
213.0 Benign neoplasm of bones of skull and face
213.1 Benign neoplasm of lower jaw bone
213.2 Benign neoplasm of vertebral column, excluding sacrum and coccyx
213.3 Benign neoplasm of ribs, sternum, and clavicle
213.4 Benign neoplasm of scapula and long bones of upper limb
213.5 Benign neoplasm of short bones of upper limb
213.6 Benign neoplasm of pelvic bones, sacrum, and coccyx
213.7 Benign neoplasm of long bones of lower limb
213.8 Benign neoplasm of short bones of lower limb
238.0 Neoplasm of uncertain behavior of bone and articular cartilage
239.2 Neoplasms of unspecified nature of bone, soft tissue, and skin
730.11 Chronic osteomyelitis, shoulder region — (Use additional code to identify organism: 041.1. Use additional code to identify major osseous defect, if applicable: 731.3)
730.12 Chronic osteomyelitis, upper arm — (Use additional code to identify organism: 041.1. Use additional code to identify major osseous defect, if applicable: 731.3)
730.13 Chronic osteomyelitis, forearm — (Use additional code to identify organism: 041.1. Use additional code to identify major osseous defect, if applicable: 731.3)
730.14 Chronic osteomyelitis, hand — (Use additional code to identify organism: 041.1. Use additional code to identify major osseous defect, if applicable: 731.3)
730.15 Chronic osteomyelitis, pelvic region and thigh — (Use additional code to identify organism: 041.1. Use additional code to identify major osseous defect, if applicable: 731.3)
730.16 Chronic osteomyelitis, lower leg — (Use additional code to identify organism: 041.1. Use additional code to identify major osseous defect, if applicable: 731.3)
730.17 Chronic osteomyelitis, ankle and foot — (Use additional code to identify organism: 041.1. Use additional code to identify major osseous defect, if applicable: 731.3)
730.18 Chronic osteomyelitis, other specified sites — (Use additional code to identify organism: 041.1. Use additional code to identify major osseous defect, if applicable: 731.3)
731.3 Major osseous defects — (Code first underlying disease: 170.0-170.9, 730.00-730.29, 733.00-733.09, 733.40-733.49, 996.45)
733.11 Pathologic fracture of humerus
733.12 Pathologic fracture of distal radius and ulna
733.13 Pathologic fracture of vertebrae
733.14 Pathologic fracture of neck of femur
733.15 Pathologic fracture of other specified part of femur
733.16 Pathologic fracture of tibia and fibula
733.19 Pathologic fracture of other specified site
733.81 Malunion of fracture
733.82 Nonunion of fracture
733.93 Stress fracture of tibia or fibula — (Use additional external cause code(s) to identify the cause of the stress fracture)
733.95 Stress fracture of other bone — (Use additional external cause code(s) to identify the cause of the stress fracture)
733.96 Stress fracture of femoral neck — (Use additional external cause code(s) to identify the cause of the stress fracture)
733.97 Stress fracture of shaft of femur — (Use additional external cause code(s) to identify the cause of the stress fracture)
733.98 Stress fracture of pelvis — (Use additional external cause code(s) to identify the cause of the stress fracture)
927.03 Crushing injury of upper arm — (Use additional code to identify any associated injuries: 800-829, 850.0-854.1, 860.0-869.1)
927.10 Crushing injury of forearm — (Use additional code to identify any associated injuries: 800-829, 850.0-854.1, 860.0-869.1)
927.20 Crushing injury of hand(s) — (Use additional code to identify any associated injuries: 800-829, 850.0-854.1, 860.0-869.1)
927.21 Crushing injury of wrist — (Use additional code to identify any associated injuries: 800-829, 850.0-854.1, 860.0-869.1)
928.00 Crushing injury of thigh — (Use additional code to identify any associated injuries: 800-829, 850.0-854.1, 860.0-869.1)
928.10 Crushing injury of lower leg — (Use additional code to identify any associated injuries: 800-829, 850.0-854.1, 860.0-869.1)
928.11 Crushing injury of knee — (Use additional code to identify any associated injuries: 800-829, 850.0-854.1, 860.0-869.1)
928.20 Crushing injury of foot — (Use additional code to identify any associated injuries: 800-829, 850.0-854.1, 860.0-869.1)

928.21 Crushing injury of ankle — (Use additional code to identify any associated injuries: 800-829, 850.0-854.1, 860.0-869.1)

ICD-9-CM Procedural

77.70 Excision of bone for graft, unspecified site
77.71 Excision of scapula, clavicle, and thorax (ribs and sternum) for graft
77.72 Excision of humerus for graft
77.73 Excision of radius and ulna for graft
77.74 Excision of carpals and metacarpals for graft
77.75 Excision of femur for graft
77.76 Excision of patella for graft
77.77 Excision of tibia and fibula for graft
77.78 Excision of tarsals and metatarsals for graft
77.79 Excision of other bone for graft, except facial bones
86.09 Other incision of skin and subcutaneous tissue

20970

20970 Free osteocutaneous flap with microvascular anastomosis; iliac crest

ICD-9-CM Diagnostic

170.0 Malignant neoplasm of bones of skull and face, except mandible
170.1 Malignant neoplasm of mandible
170.2 Malignant neoplasm of vertebral column, excluding sacrum and coccyx
170.3 Malignant neoplasm of ribs, sternum, and clavicle
170.4 Malignant neoplasm of scapula and long bones of upper limb
170.5 Malignant neoplasm of short bones of upper limb
170.6 Malignant neoplasm of pelvic bones, sacrum, and coccyx
170.7 Malignant neoplasm of long bones of lower limb
170.8 Malignant neoplasm of short bones of lower limb
198.5 Secondary malignant neoplasm of bone and bone marrow
209.73 Secondary neuroendocrine tumor of bone
213.0 Benign neoplasm of bones of skull and face
213.1 Benign neoplasm of lower jaw bone
213.2 Benign neoplasm of vertebral column, excluding sacrum and coccyx
213.3 Benign neoplasm of ribs, sternum, and clavicle
213.4 Benign neoplasm of scapula and long bones of upper limb
213.5 Benign neoplasm of short bones of upper limb
213.6 Benign neoplasm of pelvic bones, sacrum, and coccyx
213.7 Benign neoplasm of long bones of lower limb
213.8 Benign neoplasm of short bones of lower limb
238.0 Neoplasm of uncertain behavior of bone and articular cartilage
239.2 Neoplasms of unspecified nature of bone, soft tissue, and skin
524.03 Maxillary hypoplasia
524.04 Mandibular hypoplasia
524.07 Excessive tuberosity of jaw
524.09 Other specified major anomaly of jaw size
524.11 Maxillary asymmetry
524.12 Other jaw asymmetry
524.69 Other specified temporomandibular joint disorders
526.2 Other cysts of jaws
526.4 Inflammatory conditions of jaw
526.89 Other specified disease of the jaws
730.11 Chronic osteomyelitis, shoulder region — (Use additional code to identify organism: 041.1. Use additional code to identify major osseous defect, if applicable: 731.3)
730.12 Chronic osteomyelitis, upper arm — (Use additional code to identify organism: 041.1. Use additional code to identify major osseous defect, if applicable: 731.3)
730.13 Chronic osteomyelitis, forearm — (Use additional code to identify organism: 041.1. Use additional code to identify major osseous defect, if applicable: 731.3)
730.14 Chronic osteomyelitis, hand — (Use additional code to identify organism: 041.1. Use additional code to identify major osseous defect, if applicable: 731.3)
730.15 Chronic osteomyelitis, pelvic region and thigh — (Use additional code to identify organism: 041.1. Use additional code to identify major osseous defect, if applicable: 731.3)
730.16 Chronic osteomyelitis, lower leg — (Use additional code to identify organism: 041.1. Use additional code to identify major osseous defect, if applicable: 731.3)
730.17 Chronic osteomyelitis, ankle and foot — (Use additional code to identify organism: 041.1. Use additional code to identify major osseous defect, if applicable: 731.3)
730.18 Chronic osteomyelitis, other specified sites — (Use additional code to identify organism: 041.1. Use additional code to identify major osseous defect, if applicable: 731.3)
731.3 Major osseous defects — (Code first underlying disease: 170.0-170.9, 730.00-730.29, 733.00-733.09, 733.40-733.49, 996.45)
733.82 Nonunion of fracture
756.9 Other and unspecified congenital anomaly of musculoskeletal system ▽
873.54 Open wound of jaw, complicated
V10.90 Personal history of unspecified malignant neoplasm ▽
V10.91 Personal history of malignant neuroendocrine tumor — (Code first any continuing functional activity, such as: carcinoid syndrome (259.2))

ICD-9-CM Procedural

77.79 Excision of other bone for graft, except facial bones
86.09 Other incision of skin and subcutaneous tissue

20972

20972 Free osteocutaneous flap with microvascular anastomosis; metatarsal

ICD-9-CM Diagnostic

170.1 Malignant neoplasm of mandible
170.5 Malignant neoplasm of short bones of upper limb
170.8 Malignant neoplasm of short bones of lower limb
198.5 Secondary malignant neoplasm of bone and bone marrow
213.5 Benign neoplasm of short bones of upper limb
213.8 Benign neoplasm of short bones of lower limb
238.0 Neoplasm of uncertain behavior of bone and articular cartilage
239.2 Neoplasms of unspecified nature of bone, soft tissue, and skin
730.14 Chronic osteomyelitis, hand — (Use additional code to identify organism: 041.1. Use additional code to identify major osseous defect, if applicable: 731.3)
730.17 Chronic osteomyelitis, ankle and foot — (Use additional code to identify organism: 041.1. Use additional code to identify major osseous defect, if applicable: 731.3)
730.18 Chronic osteomyelitis, other specified sites — (Use additional code to identify organism: 041.1. Use additional code to identify major osseous defect, if applicable: 731.3)
731.3 Major osseous defects — (Code first underlying disease: 170.0-170.9, 730.00-730.29, 733.00-733.09, 733.40-733.49, 996.45)
733.19 Pathologic fracture of other specified site
733.81 Malunion of fracture
733.82 Nonunion of fracture
756.9 Other and unspecified congenital anomaly of musculoskeletal system ▽
892.1 Open wound of foot except toe(s) alone, complicated
893.1 Open wound of toe(s), complicated
927.20 Crushing injury of hand(s) — (Use additional code to identify any associated injuries: 800-829, 850.0-854.1, 860.0-869.1)
927.3 Crushing injury of finger(s) — (Use additional code to identify any associated injuries: 800-829, 850.0-854.1, 860.0-869.1)
928.20 Crushing injury of foot — (Use additional code to identify any associated injuries: 800-829, 850.0-854.1, 860.0-869.1)

ICD-9-CM Procedural

77.78 Excision of tarsals and metatarsals for graft
86.09 Other incision of skin and subcutaneous tissue

20973

20973 Free osteocutaneous flap with microvascular anastomosis; great toe with web space

ICD-9-CM Diagnostic

755.29 Congenital longitudinal deficiency, phalanges, complete or partial
885.0 Traumatic amputation of thumb (complete) (partial), without mention of complication
885.1 Traumatic amputation of thumb (complete) (partial), complicated
886.0 Traumatic amputation of other finger(s) (complete) (partial), without mention of complication
886.1 Traumatic amputation of other finger(s) (complete) (partial), complicated
927.3 Crushing injury of finger(s) — (Use additional code to identify any associated injuries: 800-829, 850.0-854.1, 860.0-869.1)

ICD-9-CM Procedural

77.79 Excision of other bone for graft, except facial bones
86.09 Other incision of skin and subcutaneous tissue

20974-20975

20974 Electrical stimulation to aid bone healing; noninvasive (nonoperative)
20975 invasive (operative)

ICD-9-CM Diagnostic

721.0 Cervical spondylosis without myelopathy
721.1 Cervical spondylosis with myelopathy
721.2 Thoracic spondylosis without myelopathy
721.3 Lumbosacral spondylosis without myelopathy
721.5 Kissing spine
721.6 Ankylosing vertebral hyperostosis
721.7 Traumatic spondylopathy
721.8 Other allied disorders of spine
721.90 Spondylosis of unspecified site without mention of myelopathy ▼
721.91 Spondylosis of unspecified site with myelopathy ▼
723.0 Spinal stenosis in cervical region
723.9 Unspecified musculoskeletal disorders and symptoms referable to neck ▼
724.00 Spinal stenosis, unspecified region other than cervical ▼
724.01 Spinal stenosis of thoracic region
724.02 Spinal stenosis of lumbar region, without neurogenic claudication
724.03 Spinal stenosis of lumbar region, with neurogenic claudication
724.09 Spinal stenosis, other region other than cervical
724.9 Other unspecified back disorder
733.11 Pathologic fracture of humerus
733.12 Pathologic fracture of distal radius and ulna
733.13 Pathologic fracture of vertebrae
733.14 Pathologic fracture of neck of femur
733.15 Pathologic fracture of other specified part of femur
733.16 Pathologic fracture of tibia and fibula
733.19 Pathologic fracture of other specified site
733.81 Malunion of fracture
733.82 Nonunion of fracture
733.93 Stress fracture of tibia or fibula — (Use additional external cause code(s) to identify the cause of the stress fracture)
733.95 Stress fracture of other bone — (Use additional external cause code(s) to identify the cause of the stress fracture)
733.96 Stress fracture of femoral neck — (Use additional external cause code(s) to identify the cause of the stress fracture)
733.97 Stress fracture of shaft of femur — (Use additional external cause code(s) to identify the cause of the stress fracture)
733.98 Stress fracture of pelvis — (Use additional external cause code(s) to identify the cause of the stress fracture)
738.4 Acquired spondylolisthesis
754.40 Congenital genu recurvatum
754.41 Congenital dislocation of knee (with genu recurvatum)
754.42 Congenital bowing of femur
754.43 Congenital bowing of tibia and fibula
754.44 Congenital bowing of unspecified long bones of leg ▼
755.50 Unspecified congenital anomaly of upper limb ▼
755.51 Congenital deformity of clavicle
755.52 Congenital elevation of scapula
755.53 Radioulnar synostosis
755.54 Madelung's deformity
755.55 Acrocephalosyndactyly
755.56 Accessory carpal bones
755.57 Macrodactylia (fingers)
755.58 Congenital cleft hand
755.59 Other congenital anomaly of upper limb, including shoulder girdle
755.60 Unspecified congenital anomaly of lower limb ▼
755.61 Congenital coxa valga
755.62 Congenital coxa vara
755.63 Other congenital deformity of hip (joint)
755.64 Congenital deformity of knee (joint)
755.65 Macrodactylia of toes
755.66 Other congenital anomaly of toes
755.67 Congenital anomalies of foot, not elsewhere classified
755.69 Other congenital anomaly of lower limb, including pelvic girdle
756.12 Congenital spondylolisthesis
805.01 Closed fracture of first cervical vertebra without mention of spinal cord injury
805.02 Closed fracture of second cervical vertebra without mention of spinal cord injury
805.03 Closed fracture of third cervical vertebra without mention of spinal cord injury
805.04 Closed fracture of fourth cervical vertebra without mention of spinal cord injury
805.05 Closed fracture of fifth cervical vertebra without mention of spinal cord injury
805.06 Closed fracture of sixth cervical vertebra without mention of spinal cord injury
805.07 Closed fracture of seventh cervical vertebra without mention of spinal cord injury
805.08 Closed fracture of multiple cervical vertebrae without mention of spinal cord injury
805.11 Open fracture of first cervical vertebra without mention of spinal cord injury
805.12 Open fracture of second cervical vertebra without mention of spinal cord injury
805.13 Open fracture of third cervical vertebra without mention of spinal cord injury
805.14 Open fracture of fourth cervical vertebra without mention of spinal cord injury
805.15 Open fracture of fifth cervical vertebra without mention of spinal cord injury
805.16 Open fracture of sixth cervical vertebra without mention of spinal cord injury
805.17 Open fracture of seventh cervical vertebra without mention of spinal cord injury
805.18 Open fracture of multiple cervical vertebrae without mention of spinal cord injury
805.2 Closed fracture of dorsal (thoracic) vertebra without mention of spinal cord injury
805.3 Open fracture of dorsal (thoracic) vertebra without mention of spinal cord injury
805.4 Closed fracture of lumbar vertebra without mention of spinal cord injury
805.5 Open fracture of lumbar vertebra without mention of spinal cord injury
805.6 Closed fracture of sacrum and coccyx without mention of spinal cord injury
805.7 Open fracture of sacrum and coccyx without mention of spinal cord injury
808.0 Closed fracture of acetabulum
808.1 Open fracture of acetabulum
808.2 Closed fracture of pubis
808.3 Open fracture of pubis
808.41 Closed fracture of ilium
808.42 Closed fracture of ischium
810.01 Closed fracture of sternal end of clavicle
810.02 Closed fracture of shaft of clavicle
810.03 Closed fracture of acromial end of clavicle
810.11 Open fracture of sternal end of clavicle
810.12 Open fracture of shaft of clavicle
810.13 Open fracture of acromial end of clavicle
811.01 Closed fracture of acromial process of scapula

811.02 Closed fracture of coracoid process of scapula
811.03 Closed fracture of glenoid cavity and neck of scapula
811.11 Open fracture of acromial process of scapula
811.12 Open fracture of coracoid process
811.13 Open fracture of glenoid cavity and neck of scapula
812.00 Closed fracture of unspecified part of upper end of humerus ▽
812.01 Closed fracture of surgical neck of humerus
812.02 Closed fracture of anatomical neck of humerus
812.03 Closed fracture of greater tuberosity of humerus
812.09 Other closed fractures of upper end of humerus
812.10 Open fracture of unspecified part of upper end of humerus ▽
812.11 Open fracture of surgical neck of humerus
812.12 Open fracture of anatomical neck of humerus
812.13 Open fracture of greater tuberosity of humerus
812.19 Other open fracture of upper end of humerus
812.20 Closed fracture of unspecified part of humerus ▽
812.21 Closed fracture of shaft of humerus
812.30 Open fracture of unspecified part of humerus ▽
812.31 Open fracture of shaft of humerus
812.40 Closed fracture of unspecified part of lower end of humerus ▽
812.41 Closed fracture of supracondylar humerus
812.42 Closed fracture of lateral condyle of humerus
812.43 Closed fracture of medial condyle of humerus
812.44 Closed fracture of unspecified condyle(s) of humerus ▽
812.49 Other closed fracture of lower end of humerus
812.50 Open fracture of unspecified part of lower end of humerus ▽
812.51 Open fracture of supracondylar humerus
812.52 Open fracture of lateral condyle of humerus
812.53 Open fracture of medial condyle of humerus
812.54 Open fracture of unspecified condyle(s) of humerus ▽
812.59 Other open fracture of lower end of humerus
813.00 Unspecified fracture of radius and ulna, upper end of forearm, closed ▽
813.01 Closed fracture of olecranon process of ulna
813.02 Closed fracture of coronoid process of ulna
813.03 Closed Monteggia's fracture
813.04 Other and unspecified closed fractures of proximal end of ulna (alone) ▽
813.05 Closed fracture of head of radius
813.06 Closed fracture of neck of radius
813.07 Other and unspecified closed fractures of proximal end of radius (alone) ▽
813.08 Closed fracture of radius with ulna, upper end (any part)
813.10 Unspecified open fracture of upper end of forearm ▽
813.11 Open fracture of olecranon process of ulna
813.12 Open fracture of coronoid process of ulna
813.13 Open Monteggia's fracture
813.14 Other and unspecified open fractures of proximal end of ulna (alone) ▽
813.15 Open fracture of head of radius
813.16 Open fracture of neck of radius
813.17 Other and unspecified open fractures of proximal end of radius (alone) ▽
813.18 Open fracture of radius with ulna, upper end (any part)
813.20 Unspecified closed fracture of shaft of radius or ulna ▽
813.21 Closed fracture of shaft of radius (alone)
813.22 Closed fracture of shaft of ulna (alone)
813.23 Closed fracture of shaft of radius with ulna
813.30 Unspecified open fracture of shaft of radius or ulna ▽
813.31 Open fracture of shaft of radius (alone)
813.32 Open fracture of shaft of ulna (alone)
813.33 Open fracture of shaft of radius with ulna
813.40 Unspecified closed fracture of lower end of forearm ▽
813.41 Closed Colles' fracture
813.42 Other closed fractures of distal end of radius (alone)
813.43 Closed fracture of distal end of ulna (alone)
813.44 Closed fracture of lower end of radius with ulna
813.45 Torus fracture of radius (alone)
813.46 Torus fracture of ulna (alone)
813.47 Torus fracture of radius and ulna
813.50 Unspecified open fracture of lower end of forearm ▽
813.51 Open Colles' fracture
813.52 Other open fractures of distal end of radius (alone)
813.53 Open fracture of distal end of ulna (alone)
813.54 Open fracture of lower end of radius with ulna
813.80 Closed fracture of unspecified part of forearm ▽
813.81 Closed fracture of unspecified part of radius (alone) ▽
813.82 Closed fracture of unspecified part of ulna (alone) ▽
813.83 Closed fracture of unspecified part of radius with ulna ▽
813.90 Open fracture of unspecified part of forearm ▽
813.91 Open fracture of unspecified part of radius (alone) ▽
813.92 Open fracture of unspecified part of ulna (alone) ▽
813.93 Open fracture of unspecified part of radius with ulna ▽
817.0 Multiple closed fractures of hand bones
817.1 Multiple open fractures of hand bones
820.00 Closed fracture of unspecified intracapsular section of neck of femur ▽
820.01 Closed fracture of epiphysis (separation) (upper) of neck of femur
820.02 Closed fracture of midcervical section of femur
820.03 Closed fracture of base of neck of femur
820.09 Other closed transcervical fracture of femur
820.10 Open fracture of unspecified intracapsular section of neck of femur ▽
820.11 Open fracture of epiphysis (separation) (upper) of neck of femur
820.12 Open fracture of midcervical section of femur
820.13 Open fracture of base of neck of femur
820.19 Other open transcervical fracture of femur
820.20 Closed fracture of unspecified trochanteric section of femur ▽
820.21 Closed fracture of intertrochanteric section of femur
820.22 Closed fracture of subtrochanteric section of femur
820.30 Open fracture of unspecified trochanteric section of femur ▽
820.31 Open fracture of intertrochanteric section of femur
820.32 Open fracture of subtrochanteric section of femur
820.8 Closed fracture of unspecified part of neck of femur ▽
820.9 Open fracture of unspecified part of neck of femur ▽
821.00 Closed fracture of unspecified part of femur ▽
821.01 Closed fracture of shaft of femur
821.10 Open fracture of unspecified part of femur ▽
821.11 Open fracture of shaft of femur
821.20 Closed fracture of unspecified part of lower end of femur ▽
821.21 Closed fracture of femoral condyle
821.22 Closed fracture of lower epiphysis of femur
821.23 Closed supracondylar fracture of femur
821.29 Other closed fracture of lower end of femur
821.30 Open fracture of unspecified part of lower end of femur ▽
821.31 Open fracture of femoral condyle
821.32 Open fracture of lower epiphysis of femur
821.33 Open supracondylar fracture of femur
821.39 Other open fracture of lower end of femur
823.00 Closed fracture of upper end of tibia
823.01 Closed fracture of upper end of fibula
823.02 Closed fracture of upper end of fibula with tibia
823.10 Open fracture of upper end of tibia

823.11 Open fracture of upper end of fibula
823.12 Open fracture of upper end of fibula with tibia
823.20 Closed fracture of shaft of tibia
823.21 Closed fracture of shaft of fibula
823.22 Closed fracture of shaft of fibula with tibia
823.30 Open fracture of shaft of tibia
823.31 Open fracture of shaft of fibula
823.32 Open fracture of shaft of fibula with tibia
823.80 Closed fracture of unspecified part of tibia ▽
823.81 Closed fracture of unspecified part of fibula ▽
823.82 Closed fracture of unspecified part of fibula with tibia ▽
823.90 Open fracture of unspecified part of tibia ▽
823.91 Open fracture of unspecified part of fibula ▽
823.92 Open fracture of unspecified part of fibula with tibia ▽
824.0 Closed fracture of medial malleolus
824.1 Open fracture of medial malleolus
824.2 Closed fracture of lateral malleolus
824.3 Open fracture of lateral malleolus
824.4 Closed bimalleolar fracture
824.5 Open bimalleolar fracture
824.6 Closed trimalleolar fracture
824.7 Open trimalleolar fracture
825.0 Closed fracture of calcaneus
825.1 Open fracture of calcaneus
825.25 Closed fracture of metatarsal bone(s)
825.35 Open fracture of metatarsal bone(s)
905.0 Late effect of fracture of skull and face bones
905.1 Late effect of fracture of spine and trunk without mention of spinal cord lesion
905.2 Late effect of fracture of upper extremities
905.3 Late effect of fracture of neck of femur
905.4 Late effect of fracture of lower extremities
905.5 Late effect of fracture of multiple and unspecified bones
909.3 Late effect of complications of surgical and medical care
996.40 Unspecified mechanical complication of internal orthopedic device, implant, and graft — (Use additional code to identify prosthetic joint with mechanical complication, V43.60-V43.69) ▽
996.41 Mechanical loosening of prosthetic joint — (Use additional code to identify prosthetic joint with mechanical complication, V43.60-V43.69)
996.42 Dislocation of prosthetic joint — (Use additional code to identify prosthetic joint with mechanical complication, V43.60-V43.69)
996.43 Broken prosthetic joint implant — (Use additional code to identify prosthetic joint with mechanical complication, V43.60-V43.69)
996.44 Peri-prosthetic fracture around prosthetic joint — (Use additional code to identify prosthetic joint with mechanical complication, V43.60-V43.69.
996.45 Peri-prosthetic osteolysis — (Use additional code to identify prosthetic joint with mechanical complication, V43.60-V43.69. Use additional code to identify major osseous defect, if applicable: 731.3)
996.46 Articular bearing surface wear of prosthetic joint — (Use additional code to identify prosthetic joint with mechanical complication, V43.60-V43.69)
996.47 Other mechanical complication of prosthetic joint implant — (Use additional code to identify prosthetic joint with mechanical complication, V43.60-V43.69)
996.49 Other mechanical complication of other internal orthopedic device, implant, and graft — (Use additional code to identify prosthetic joint with mechanical complication, V43.60-V43.69)

ICD-9-CM Procedural

78.90 Insertion of bone growth stimulator, unspecified site
78.91 Insertion of bone growth stimulator into scapula, clavicle and thorax (ribs and sternum)
78.92 Insertion of bone growth stimulator into humerus
78.93 Insertion of bone growth stimulator into radius and ulna
78.94 Insertion of bone growth stimulator into carpals and metacarpals
78.95 Insertion of bone growth stimulator into femur
78.96 Insertion of bone growth stimulator into patella
78.97 Insertion of bone growth stimulator into tibia and fibula
78.98 Insertion of bone growth stimulator into tarsals and metatarsals
78.99 Insertion of bone growth stimulator into other bone
99.86 Non-invasive placement of bone growth stimulator

HCPCS Level II Supplies & Services

E0747 Osteogenesis stimulator, electrical, noninvasive, other than spinal applications
E0748 Osteogenesis stimulator, electrical, noninvasive, spinal applications
E0749 Osteogenesis stimulator, electrical, surgically implanted

20979

20979 Low intensity ultrasound stimulation to aid bone healing, noninvasive (nonoperative)

ICD-9-CM Diagnostic

733.11 Pathologic fracture of humerus
733.12 Pathologic fracture of distal radius and ulna
733.13 Pathologic fracture of vertebrae
733.14 Pathologic fracture of neck of femur
733.15 Pathologic fracture of other specified part of femur
733.16 Pathologic fracture of tibia and fibula
733.19 Pathologic fracture of other specified site
733.82 Nonunion of fracture
733.93 Stress fracture of tibia or fibula — (Use additional external cause code(s) to identify the cause of the stress fracture)
733.95 Stress fracture of other bone — (Use additional external cause code(s) to identify the cause of the stress fracture)
733.96 Stress fracture of femoral neck — (Use additional external cause code(s) to identify the cause of the stress fracture)
733.97 Stress fracture of shaft of femur — (Use additional external cause code(s) to identify the cause of the stress fracture)
733.98 Stress fracture of pelvis — (Use additional external cause code(s) to identify the cause of the stress fracture)
805.01 Closed fracture of first cervical vertebra without mention of spinal cord injury
805.02 Closed fracture of second cervical vertebra without mention of spinal cord injury
805.03 Closed fracture of third cervical vertebra without mention of spinal cord injury
805.04 Closed fracture of fourth cervical vertebra without mention of spinal cord injury
805.05 Closed fracture of fifth cervical vertebra without mention of spinal cord injury
805.06 Closed fracture of sixth cervical vertebra without mention of spinal cord injury
805.07 Closed fracture of seventh cervical vertebra without mention of spinal cord injury
805.08 Closed fracture of multiple cervical vertebrae without mention of spinal cord injury
805.11 Open fracture of first cervical vertebra without mention of spinal cord injury
805.12 Open fracture of second cervical vertebra without mention of spinal cord injury
805.13 Open fracture of third cervical vertebra without mention of spinal cord injury
805.14 Open fracture of fourth cervical vertebra without mention of spinal cord injury
805.15 Open fracture of fifth cervical vertebra without mention of spinal cord injury
805.16 Open fracture of sixth cervical vertebra without mention of spinal cord injury
805.17 Open fracture of seventh cervical vertebra without mention of spinal cord injury
805.18 Open fracture of multiple cervical vertebrae without mention of spinal cord injury
805.2 Closed fracture of dorsal (thoracic) vertebra without mention of spinal cord injury
805.3 Open fracture of dorsal (thoracic) vertebra without mention of spinal cord injury
805.4 Closed fracture of lumbar vertebra without mention of spinal cord injury
805.5 Open fracture of lumbar vertebra without mention of spinal cord injury
805.6 Closed fracture of sacrum and coccyx without mention of spinal cord injury
805.7 Open fracture of sacrum and coccyx without mention of spinal cord injury
808.0 Closed fracture of acetabulum
808.1 Open fracture of acetabulum
808.2 Closed fracture of pubis
808.3 Open fracture of pubis

808.41 Closed fracture of ilium
808.42 Closed fracture of ischium
810.01 Closed fracture of sternal end of clavicle
810.02 Closed fracture of shaft of clavicle
810.03 Closed fracture of acromial end of clavicle
810.11 Open fracture of sternal end of clavicle
810.12 Open fracture of shaft of clavicle
810.13 Open fracture of acromial end of clavicle
811.01 Closed fracture of acromial process of scapula
811.02 Closed fracture of coracoid process of scapula
811.03 Closed fracture of glenoid cavity and neck of scapula
811.11 Open fracture of acromial process of scapula
811.12 Open fracture of coracoid process
811.13 Open fracture of glenoid cavity and neck of scapula
812.01 Closed fracture of surgical neck of humerus
812.02 Closed fracture of anatomical neck of humerus
812.03 Closed fracture of greater tuberosity of humerus
812.09 Other closed fractures of upper end of humerus
812.11 Open fracture of surgical neck of humerus
812.12 Open fracture of anatomical neck of humerus
812.13 Open fracture of greater tuberosity of humerus
812.19 Other open fracture of upper end of humerus
812.20 Closed fracture of unspecified part of humerus ▽
812.21 Closed fracture of shaft of humerus
812.30 Open fracture of unspecified part of humerus ▽
812.31 Open fracture of shaft of humerus
812.40 Closed fracture of unspecified part of lower end of humerus ▽
812.41 Closed fracture of supracondylar humerus
812.42 Closed fracture of lateral condyle of humerus
812.43 Closed fracture of medial condyle of humerus
812.44 Closed fracture of unspecified condyle(s) of humerus ▽
812.49 Other closed fracture of lower end of humerus
812.51 Open fracture of supracondylar humerus
812.52 Open fracture of lateral condyle of humerus
812.53 Open fracture of medial condyle of humerus
812.54 Open fracture of unspecified condyle(s) of humerus ▽
812.59 Other open fracture of lower end of humerus
817.0 Multiple closed fractures of hand bones
817.1 Multiple open fractures of hand bones
821.00 Closed fracture of unspecified part of femur ▽
821.01 Closed fracture of shaft of femur
821.20 Closed fracture of unspecified part of lower end of femur ▽
821.21 Closed fracture of femoral condyle
821.22 Closed fracture of lower epiphysis of femur
821.23 Closed supracondylar fracture of femur
821.29 Other closed fracture of lower end of femur
821.30 Open fracture of unspecified part of lower end of femur ▽
821.31 Open fracture of femoral condyle
821.32 Open fracture of lower epiphysis of femur
821.33 Open supracondylar fracture of femur
821.39 Other open fracture of lower end of femur
823.00 Closed fracture of upper end of tibia
823.01 Closed fracture of upper end of fibula
823.02 Closed fracture of upper end of fibula with tibia
823.10 Open fracture of upper end of tibia
823.11 Open fracture of upper end of fibula
823.12 Open fracture of upper end of fibula with tibia
823.20 Closed fracture of shaft of tibia
823.21 Closed fracture of shaft of fibula
823.22 Closed fracture of shaft of fibula with tibia
823.30 Open fracture of shaft of tibia
823.31 Open fracture of shaft of fibula
823.32 Open fracture of shaft of fibula with tibia
823.80 Closed fracture of unspecified part of tibia ▽
823.81 Closed fracture of unspecified part of fibula ▽
823.82 Closed fracture of unspecified part of fibula with tibia ▽
824.0 Closed fracture of medial malleolus
824.1 Open fracture of medial malleolus
824.2 Closed fracture of lateral malleolus
824.3 Open fracture of lateral malleolus
824.4 Closed bimalleolar fracture
824.5 Open bimalleolar fracture
824.6 Closed trimalleolar fracture
824.7 Open trimalleolar fracture
825.0 Closed fracture of calcaneus
825.1 Open fracture of calcaneus
905.0 Late effect of fracture of skull and face bones
905.1 Late effect of fracture of spine and trunk without mention of spinal cord lesion
905.2 Late effect of fracture of upper extremities
905.3 Late effect of fracture of neck of femur
905.4 Late effect of fracture of lower extremities
905.5 Late effect of fracture of multiple and unspecified bones
909.3 Late effect of complications of surgical and medical care
996.40 Unspecified mechanical complication of internal orthopedic device, implant, and graft — (Use additional code to identify prosthetic joint with mechanical complication, V43.60-V43.69) ▽
996.44 Peri-prosthetic fracture around prosthetic joint — (Use additional code to identify prosthetic joint with mechanical complication, V43.60-V43.69.
996.45 Peri-prosthetic osteolysis — (Use additional code to identify prosthetic joint with mechanical complication, V43.60-V43.69. Use additional code to identify major osseous defect, if applicable: 731.3)
996.47 Other mechanical complication of prosthetic joint implant — (Use additional code to identify prosthetic joint with mechanical complication, V43.60-V43.69)
996.49 Other mechanical complication of other internal orthopedic device, implant, and graft — (Use additional code to identify prosthetic joint with mechanical complication, V43.60-V43.69)
V54.89 Other orthopedic aftercare

ICD-9-CM Procedural

93.35 Other heat therapy

HCPCS Level II Supplies & Services

E0760 Osteogenesis stimulator, low intensity ultrasound, noninvasive
E1399 Durable medical equipment, miscellaneous

20982

20982 Ablation, bone tumor(s) (eg, osteoid osteoma, metastasis) radiofrequency, percutaneous, including computed tomographic guidance

ICD-9-CM Diagnostic

170.0 Malignant neoplasm of bones of skull and face, except mandible
170.1 Malignant neoplasm of mandible
170.2 Malignant neoplasm of vertebral column, excluding sacrum and coccyx
170.3 Malignant neoplasm of ribs, sternum, and clavicle
170.4 Malignant neoplasm of scapula and long bones of upper limb
170.5 Malignant neoplasm of short bones of upper limb
170.6 Malignant neoplasm of pelvic bones, sacrum, and coccyx
170.7 Malignant neoplasm of long bones of lower limb
170.8 Malignant neoplasm of short bones of lower limb
170.9 Malignant neoplasm of bone and articular cartilage, site unspecified ▽

198.5 Secondary malignant neoplasm of bone and bone marrow
209.73 Secondary neuroendocrine tumor of bone
213.0 Benign neoplasm of bones of skull and face
213.1 Benign neoplasm of lower jaw bone
213.2 Benign neoplasm of vertebral column, excluding sacrum and coccyx
213.3 Benign neoplasm of ribs, sternum, and clavicle
213.4 Benign neoplasm of scapula and long bones of upper limb
213.5 Benign neoplasm of short bones of upper limb
213.6 Benign neoplasm of pelvic bones, sacrum, and coccyx
213.7 Benign neoplasm of long bones of lower limb
213.8 Benign neoplasm of short bones of lower limb
213.9 Benign neoplasm of bone and articular cartilage, site unspecified ▽
238.0 Neoplasm of uncertain behavior of bone and articular cartilage
239.2 Neoplasms of unspecified nature of bone, soft tissue, and skin

ICD-9-CM Procedural

01.6 Excision of lesion of skull
76.2 Local excision or destruction of lesion of facial bone
77.60 Local excision of lesion or tissue of bone, unspecified site
77.61 Local excision of lesion or tissue of scapula, clavicle, and thorax (ribs and sternum)
77.62 Local excision of lesion or tissue of humerus
77.63 Local excision of lesion or tissue of radius and ulna
77.64 Local excision of lesion or tissue of carpals and metacarpals
77.65 Local excision of lesion or tissue of femur
77.66 Local excision of lesion or tissue of patella
77.67 Local excision of lesion or tissue of tibia and fibula
77.68 Local excision of lesion or tissue of tarsals and metatarsals
77.69 Local excision of lesion or tissue of other bone, except facial bones

20985

20985 Computer-assisted surgical navigational procedure for musculoskeletal procedures, image-less (List separately in addition to code for primary procedure)

ICD-9-CM Diagnostic

The application of this code is too broad to adequately present ICD-9-CM diagnostic code links here. Refer to your ICD-9-CM book.

ICD-9-CM Procedural

00.34 Imageless computer assisted surgery

Head

21010

21010 Arthrotomy, temporomandibular joint

ICD-9-CM Diagnostic

524.60 Unspecified temporomandibular joint disorders ▽
524.61 Adhesions and ankylosis (bony or fibrous) of temporomandibular joint
524.62 Arthralgia of temporomandibular joint
524.69 Other specified temporomandibular joint disorders
526.4 Inflammatory conditions of jaw
715.18 Primary localized osteoarthrosis, other specified sites
715.28 Secondary localized osteoarthrosis, other specified site
718.58 Ankylosis of joint of other specified site
830.0 Closed dislocation of jaw
905.0 Late effect of fracture of skull and face bones
959.09 Injury of face and neck, other and unspecified

ICD-9-CM Procedural

76.99 Other operations on facial bones and joints

21011-21016

21011 Excision, tumor, soft tissue of face or scalp, subcutaneous; less than 2 cm
21012 2 cm or greater
21013 Excision, tumor, soft tissue of face and scalp, subfascial (eg, subgaleal, intramuscular); less than 2 cm
21014 2 cm or greater
21015 Radical resection of tumor (eg, sarcoma), soft tissue of face or scalp; less than 2 cm
21016 2 cm or greater

ICD-9-CM Diagnostic

171.0 Malignant neoplasm of connective and other soft tissue of head, face, and neck
171.8 Malignant neoplasm of other specified sites of connective and other soft tissue
172.3 Malignant melanoma of skin of other and unspecified parts of face ▽
172.4 Malignant melanoma of skin of scalp and neck
172.8 Malignant melanoma of other specified sites of skin
173.30 Unspecified malignant neoplasm of skin of other and unspecified parts of face ▽
173.31 Basal cell carcinoma of skin of other and unspecified parts of face
173.32 Squamous cell carcinoma of skin of other and unspecified parts of face
173.39 Other specified malignant neoplasm of skin of other and unspecified parts of face
173.40 Unspecified malignant neoplasm of scalp and skin of neck ▽
173.41 Basal cell carcinoma of scalp and skin of neck
173.42 Squamous cell carcinoma of scalp and skin of neck
173.49 Other specified malignant neoplasm of scalp and skin of neck
173.80 Unspecified malignant neoplasm of other specified sites of skin ▽
173.81 Basal cell carcinoma of other specified sites of skin
173.82 Squamous cell carcinoma of other specified sites of skin
173.89 Other specified malignant neoplasm of other specified sites of skin
209.31 Merkel cell carcinoma of the face
209.32 Merkel cell carcinoma of the scalp and neck
209.75 Secondary Merkel cell carcinoma
214.0 Lipoma of skin and subcutaneous tissue of face
238.1 Neoplasm of uncertain behavior of connective and other soft tissue
238.2 Neoplasm of uncertain behavior of skin
239.2 Neoplasms of unspecified nature of bone, soft tissue, and skin

ICD-9-CM Procedural

83.39 Excision of lesion of other soft tissue
83.49 Other excision of soft tissue
86.3 Other local excision or destruction of lesion or tissue of skin and subcutaneous tissue
86.4 Radical excision of skin lesion

21025-21026

21025 Excision of bone (eg, for osteomyelitis or bone abscess); mandible
21026 facial bone(s)

ICD-9-CM Diagnostic

015.60 Tuberculosis of mastoid, confirmation unspecified — (Use additional code to identify manifestation: 711.4, 727.01, 730.8) ▽
015.61 Tuberculosis of mastoid, bacteriological or histological examination not done — (Use additional code to identify manifestation: 711.4, 727.01, 730.8)
015.62 Tuberculosis of mastoid, bacteriological or histological examination unknown (at present) — (Use additional code to identify manifestation: 711.4, 727.01, 730.8)
015.63 Tuberculosis of mastoid, tubercle bacilli found (in sputum) by microscopy — (Use additional code to identify manifestation: 711.4, 727.01, 730.8)
015.65 Tuberculosis of mastoid, tubercle bacilli not found by bacteriological examination, but tuberculosis confirmed histologically — (Use additional code to identify manifestation: 711.4, 727.01, 730.8)
015.66 Tuberculosis of mastoid, tubercle bacilli not found by bacteriological or histological examination but tuberculosis confirmed by other methods [inoculation of animals] — (Use additional code to identify manifestation: 711.4, 727.01, 730.8)
383.01 Subperiosteal abscess of mastoid
383.02 Acute mastoiditis with other complications

383.1 Chronic mastoiditis
383.20 Unspecified petrositis ♥
383.21 Acute petrositis
383.22 Chronic petrositis
383.9 Unspecified mastoiditis ♥
473.0 Chronic maxillary sinusitis — (Use additional code to identify infectious organism)
473.1 Chronic frontal sinusitis — (Use additional code to identify infectious organism)
473.2 Chronic ethmoidal sinusitis — (Use additional code to identify infectious organism)
473.3 Chronic sphenoidal sinusitis — (Use additional code to identify infectious organism)
473.9 Unspecified sinusitis (chronic) — (Use additional code to identify infectious organism) ♥
526.2 Other cysts of jaws
526.4 Inflammatory conditions of jaw
526.89 Other specified disease of the jaws
730.08 Acute osteomyelitis, other specified site — (Use additional code to identify organism: 041.1. Use additional code to identify major osseous defect, if applicable: 731.3)
730.09 Acute osteomyelitis, multiple sites — (Use additional code to identify organism: 041.1. Use additional code to identify major osseous defect, if applicable: 731.3)
730.18 Chronic osteomyelitis, other specified sites — (Use additional code to identify organism: 041.1. Use additional code to identify major osseous defect, if applicable: 731.3)
730.19 Chronic osteomyelitis, multiple sites — (Use additional code to identify organism: 041.1. Use additional code to identify major osseous defect, if applicable: 731.3)
730.28 Unspecified osteomyelitis, other specified sites — (Use additional code to identify organism: 041.1. Use additional code to identify major osseous defect, if applicable: 731.3) ♥
730.29 Unspecified osteomyelitis, multiple sites — (Use additional code to identify organism: 041.1. Use additional code to identify major osseous defect, if applicable: 731.3) ♥
730.88 Other infections involving bone diseases classified elsewhere, other specified sites — (Use additional code to identify organism: 041.1. Code first underlying disease: 002.0, 015.0-015.9) ☒
730.89 Other infections involving bone diseases classified elsewhere, multiple sites — (Use additional code to identify organism: 041.1. Code first underlying disease: 002.0, 015.0-015.9) ☒
733.45 Aseptic necrosis of bone, jaw
905.0 Late effect of fracture of skull and face bones
906.0 Late effect of open wound of head, neck, and trunk
906.4 Late effect of crushing
906.5 Late effect of burn of eye, face, head, and neck
908.9 Late effect of unspecified injury ♥
909.2 Late effect of radiation
909.3 Late effect of complications of surgical and medical care
996.66 Infection and inflammatory reaction due to internal joint prosthesis — (Use additional code to identify specified infections. Use additional code to identify infected prosthetic joint: V43.60-V43.69)
998.59 Other postoperative infection — (Use additional code to identify infection)

ICD-9-CM Procedural

76.2 Local excision or destruction of lesion of facial bone
76.31 Partial mandibulectomy
76.39 Partial ostectomy of other facial bone
76.41 Total mandibulectomy with synchronous reconstruction
76.42 Other total mandibulectomy
76.44 Total ostectomy of other facial bone with synchronous reconstruction
76.45 Other total ostectomy of other facial bone

21029

21029 Removal by contouring of benign tumor of facial bone (eg, fibrous dysplasia)

ICD-9-CM Diagnostic

213.0 Benign neoplasm of bones of skull and face
213.1 Benign neoplasm of lower jaw bone
526.0 Developmental odontogenic cysts
526.1 Fissural cysts of jaw
526.2 Other cysts of jaws
526.3 Central giant cell (reparative) granuloma
526.89 Other specified disease of the jaws
733.21 Solitary bone cyst
733.22 Aneurysmal bone cyst
733.29 Other cyst of bone
738.11 Zygomatic hyperplasia
756.54 Polyostotic fibrous dysplasia of bone

ICD-9-CM Procedural

76.2 Local excision or destruction of lesion of facial bone
76.69 Other facial bone repair

21030

21030 Excision of benign tumor or cyst of maxilla or zygoma by enucleation and curettage

ICD-9-CM Diagnostic

213.0 Benign neoplasm of bones of skull and face
521.6 Ankylosis of teeth
526.0 Developmental odontogenic cysts
526.1 Fissural cysts of jaw
526.2 Other cysts of jaws
526.3 Central giant cell (reparative) granuloma
526.81 Exostosis of jaw
526.89 Other specified disease of the jaws
528.1 Cancrum oris
733.20 Unspecified cyst of bone (localized) ♥
733.21 Solitary bone cyst
733.22 Aneurysmal bone cyst
733.29 Other cyst of bone
738.11 Zygomatic hyperplasia

ICD-9-CM Procedural

76.2 Local excision or destruction of lesion of facial bone

HCPCS Level II Supplies & Services

A4305 Disposable drug delivery system, flow rate of 50 ml or greater per hour

21031

21031 Excision of torus mandibularis

ICD-9-CM Diagnostic

526.81 Exostosis of jaw

ICD-9-CM Procedural

76.2 Local excision or destruction of lesion of facial bone

HCPCS Level II Supplies & Services

A4305 Disposable drug delivery system, flow rate of 50 ml or greater per hour

21032

21032 Excision of maxillary torus palatinus

ICD-9-CM Diagnostic

526.81 Exostosis of jaw

ICD-9-CM Procedural

76.2 Local excision or destruction of lesion of facial bone

21034

21034 Excision of malignant tumor of maxilla or zygoma

ICD-9-CM Diagnostic

170.0 Malignant neoplasm of bones of skull and face, except mandible
198.5 Secondary malignant neoplasm of bone and bone marrow

ICD-9-CM Procedural

76.2 Local excision or destruction of lesion of facial bone

21040

21040 Excision of benign tumor or cyst of mandible, by enucleation and/or curettage

ICD-9-CM Diagnostic

213.1 Benign neoplasm of lower jaw bone
521.6 Ankylosis of teeth
526.0 Developmental odontogenic cysts
526.1 Fissural cysts of jaw
526.2 Other cysts of jaws
526.3 Central giant cell (reparative) granuloma
526.81 Exostosis of jaw
526.89 Other specified disease of the jaws
528.1 Cancrum oris
733.20 Unspecified cyst of bone (localized) ▽
733.21 Solitary bone cyst
733.22 Aneurysmal bone cyst
733.29 Other cyst of bone
733.99 Other disorders of bone and cartilage

ICD-9-CM Procedural

24.4 Excision of dental lesion of jaw
76.31 Partial mandibulectomy

HCPCS Level II Supplies & Services

A4305 Disposable drug delivery system, flow rate of 50 ml or greater per hour

21044-21045

21044 Excision of malignant tumor of mandible;
21045 radical resection

ICD-9-CM Diagnostic

170.1 Malignant neoplasm of mandible
195.0 Malignant neoplasm of head, face, and neck
198.5 Secondary malignant neoplasm of bone and bone marrow
199.0 Disseminated malignant neoplasm
209.30 Malignant poorly differentiated neuroendocrine carcinoma, any site — (Code first any associated multiple endocrine neoplasia syndrome: 258.01-258.03)(Use additional code to identify associated endocrine syndrome, as: carcinoid syndrome: 259.2) ▽

ICD-9-CM Procedural

24.4 Excision of dental lesion of jaw
76.2 Local excision or destruction of lesion of facial bone
76.31 Partial mandibulectomy
76.41 Total mandibulectomy with synchronous reconstruction
76.42 Other total mandibulectomy

21046-21047

21046 Excision of benign tumor or cyst of mandible; requiring intra-oral osteotomy (eg, locally aggressive or destructive lesion[s])
21047 requiring extra-oral osteotomy and partial mandibulectomy (eg, locally aggressive or destructive lesion[s])

ICD-9-CM Diagnostic

213.1 Benign neoplasm of lower jaw bone
521.6 Ankylosis of teeth
526.0 Developmental odontogenic cysts
526.1 Fissural cysts of jaw
526.2 Other cysts of jaws
526.3 Central giant cell (reparative) granuloma
526.81 Exostosis of jaw
526.89 Other specified disease of the jaws
528.1 Cancrum oris
733.20 Unspecified cyst of bone (localized) ▽
733.21 Solitary bone cyst
733.22 Aneurysmal bone cyst
733.29 Other cyst of bone

ICD-9-CM Procedural

76.2 Local excision or destruction of lesion of facial bone
76.31 Partial mandibulectomy
76.61 Closed osteoplasty (osteotomy) of mandibular ramus
76.62 Open osteoplasty (osteotomy) of mandibular ramus
76.63 Osteoplasty (osteotomy) of body of mandible

21048-21049

21048 Excision of benign tumor or cyst of maxilla; requiring intra-oral osteotomy (eg, locally aggressive or destructive lesion[s])
21049 requiring extra-oral osteotomy and partial maxillectomy (eg, locally aggressive or destructive lesion[s])

ICD-9-CM Diagnostic

213.0 Benign neoplasm of bones of skull and face
521.6 Ankylosis of teeth
526.0 Developmental odontogenic cysts
526.1 Fissural cysts of jaw
526.2 Other cysts of jaws
526.3 Central giant cell (reparative) granuloma
526.81 Exostosis of jaw
526.89 Other specified disease of the jaws
528.1 Cancrum oris
733.20 Unspecified cyst of bone (localized) ▽
733.21 Solitary bone cyst
733.22 Aneurysmal bone cyst
733.29 Other cyst of bone

ICD-9-CM Procedural

76.2 Local excision or destruction of lesion of facial bone
76.39 Partial ostectomy of other facial bone
76.65 Segmental osteoplasty (osteotomy) of maxilla
76.66 Total osteoplasty (osteotomy) of maxilla

21050

21050 Condylectomy, temporomandibular joint (separate procedure)

ICD-9-CM Diagnostic

170.1 Malignant neoplasm of mandible
357.1 Polyneuropathy in collagen vascular disease — (Code first underlying disease: 446.0, 710.0, 714.0) ☒
359.6 Symptomatic inflammatory myopathy in diseases classified elsewhere — (Code first underlying disease: 135, 140.0-208.9, 277.30-277.39, 446.0, 710.0, 710.1, 710.2, 714.0) ☒
524.61 Adhesions and ankylosis (bony or fibrous) of temporomandibular joint
524.62 Arthralgia of temporomandibular joint
524.63 Articular disc disorder (reducing or non-reducing) of temporomandibular joint
524.69 Other specified temporomandibular joint disorders
526.89 Other specified disease of the jaws

714.0 Rheumatoid arthritis — (Use additional code to identify manifestation: 357.1, 359.6)
802.21 Closed fracture of condylar process of mandible
802.31 Open fracture of condylar process of mandible
905.0 Late effect of fracture of skull and face bones

ICD-9-CM Procedural

76.5 Temporomandibular arthroplasty

21060

21060 Meniscectomy, partial or complete, temporomandibular joint (separate procedure)

ICD-9-CM Diagnostic

524.50 Dentofacial functional abnormality, unspecified ♥
524.51 Abnormal jaw closure
524.52 Limited mandibular range of motion
524.53 Deviation in opening and closing of the mandible
524.59 Other dentofacial functional abnormalities
524.60 Unspecified temporomandibular joint disorders ♥
524.61 Adhesions and ankylosis (bony or fibrous) of temporomandibular joint
524.63 Articular disc disorder (reducing or non-reducing) of temporomandibular joint
524.64 Temporomandibular joint sounds on opening and/or closing the jaw
524.69 Other specified temporomandibular joint disorders
715.18 Primary localized osteoarthrosis, other specified sites
715.38 Localized osteoarthrosis not specified whether primary or secondary, other specified sites
830.0 Closed dislocation of jaw
830.1 Open dislocation of jaw
905.0 Late effect of fracture of skull and face bones
906.0 Late effect of open wound of head, neck, and trunk

ICD-9-CM Procedural

76.5 Temporomandibular arthroplasty

21070

21070 Coronoidectomy (separate procedure)

ICD-9-CM Diagnostic

524.02 Mandibular hyperplasia
524.07 Excessive tuberosity of jaw
524.09 Other specified major anomaly of jaw size
524.12 Other jaw asymmetry
524.19 Other specified anomaly of relationship of jaw to cranial base
524.21 Malocclusion, Angle's class I
524.22 Malocclusion, Angle's class II
524.23 Malocclusion, Angle's class III
524.29 Other anomalies of dental arch relationship
524.52 Limited mandibular range of motion
524.53 Deviation in opening and closing of the mandible
524.59 Other dentofacial functional abnormalities
524.89 Other specified dentofacial anomalies
526.89 Other specified disease of the jaws
802.23 Closed fracture of coronoid process of mandible
802.33 Open fracture of coronoid process of mandible
905.0 Late effect of fracture of skull and face bones

ICD-9-CM Procedural

76.31 Partial mandibulectomy

21073

21073 Manipulation of temporomandibular joint(s) (TMJ), therapeutic, requiring an anesthesia service (ie, general or monitored anesthesia care)

ICD-9-CM Diagnostic

524.60 Unspecified temporomandibular joint disorders ♥
524.61 Adhesions and ankylosis (bony or fibrous) of temporomandibular joint
524.63 Articular disc disorder (reducing or non-reducing) of temporomandibular joint
524.69 Other specified temporomandibular joint disorders
830.0 Closed dislocation of jaw
830.1 Open dislocation of jaw
925.1 Crushing injury of face and scalp — (Use additional code to identify any associated injuries, such as: 800-829, 850.0-854.1, 860.0-869.1)

ICD-9-CM Procedural

76.93 Closed reduction of temporomandibular dislocation
76.95 Other manipulation of temporomandibular joint

HCPCS Level II Supplies & Services

A4305 Disposable drug delivery system, flow rate of 50 ml or greater per hour

21076

21076 Impression and custom preparation; surgical obturator prosthesis

ICD-9-CM Diagnostic

145.2 Malignant neoplasm of hard palate
145.3 Malignant neoplasm of soft palate
525.8 Other specified disorders of the teeth and supporting structures
749.00 Unspecified cleft palate ♥
749.01 Unilateral cleft palate, complete
749.02 Unilateral cleft palate, incomplete
749.03 Bilateral cleft palate, complete
749.04 Bilateral cleft palate, incomplete
749.20 Unspecified cleft palate with cleft lip ♥
749.21 Unilateral cleft palate with cleft lip, complete
749.22 Unilateral cleft palate with cleft lip, incomplete
749.23 Bilateral cleft palate with cleft lip, complete
749.24 Bilateral cleft palate with cleft lip, incomplete
749.25 Other combinations of cleft palate with cleft lip
756.0 Congenital anomalies of skull and face bones
873.65 Open wound of palate, without mention of complication
873.75 Open wound of palate, complicated
905.0 Late effect of fracture of skull and face bones
V51.8 Other aftercare involving the use of plastic surgery
V52.8 Fitting and adjustment of other specified prosthetic device
V58.42 Aftercare following surgery for neoplasm — (This code should be used in conjunction with other aftercare codes to fully identify the reason for the aftercare encounter)

ICD-9-CM Procedural

23.6 Prosthetic dental implant

21077

21077 Impression and custom preparation; orbital prosthesis

ICD-9-CM Diagnostic

170.0 Malignant neoplasm of bones of skull and face, except mandible
730.18 Chronic osteomyelitis, other specified sites — (Use additional code to identify organism: 041.1. Use additional code to identify major osseous defect, if applicable: 731.3)
733.45 Aseptic necrosis of bone, jaw
733.49 Aseptic necrosis of other bone site — (Use additional code to identify major osseous defect, if applicable: 731.3)

802.6 Orbital floor (blow-out), closed fracture
802.7 Orbital floor (blow-out), open fracture
802.8 Other facial bones, closed fracture
802.9 Other facial bones, open fracture
870.3 Penetrating wound of orbit, without mention of foreign body
870.4 Penetrating wound of orbit with foreign body
905.0 Late effect of fracture of skull and face bones
906.0 Late effect of open wound of head, neck, and trunk
906.4 Late effect of crushing
925.1 Crushing injury of face and scalp — (Use additional code to identify any associated injuries, such as: 800-829, 850.0-854.1, 860.0-869.1)
V58.42 Aftercare following surgery for neoplasm — (This code should be used in conjunction with other aftercare codes to fully identify the reason for the aftercare encounter)

ICD-9-CM Procedural

95.34 Ocular prosthetics

HCPCS Level II Supplies & Services

L8042 Orbital prosthesis, provided by a nonphysician

21079-21080

21079 Impression and custom preparation; interim obturator prosthesis
21080 definitive obturator prosthesis

ICD-9-CM Diagnostic

145.2 Malignant neoplasm of hard palate
145.3 Malignant neoplasm of soft palate
170.0 Malignant neoplasm of bones of skull and face, except mandible
749.00 Unspecified cleft palate ▽
749.01 Unilateral cleft palate, complete
749.02 Unilateral cleft palate, incomplete
749.03 Bilateral cleft palate, complete
749.04 Bilateral cleft palate, incomplete
749.20 Unspecified cleft palate with cleft lip ▽
749.21 Unilateral cleft palate with cleft lip, complete
749.22 Unilateral cleft palate with cleft lip, incomplete
749.23 Bilateral cleft palate with cleft lip, complete
749.24 Bilateral cleft palate with cleft lip, incomplete
749.25 Other combinations of cleft palate with cleft lip
756.0 Congenital anomalies of skull and face bones
873.65 Open wound of palate, without mention of complication
873.75 Open wound of palate, complicated
905.0 Late effect of fracture of skull and face bones
V52.8 Fitting and adjustment of other specified prosthetic device
V58.42 Aftercare following surgery for neoplasm — (This code should be used in conjunction with other aftercare codes to fully identify the reason for the aftercare encounter)

ICD-9-CM Procedural

23.6 Prosthetic dental implant

21081

21081 Impression and custom preparation; mandibular resection prosthesis

ICD-9-CM Diagnostic

170.1 Malignant neoplasm of mandible
213.1 Benign neoplasm of lower jaw bone
524.04 Mandibular hypoplasia
524.12 Other jaw asymmetry
524.74 Alveolar mandibular hypoplasia
526.89 Other specified disease of the jaws
733.91 Arrest of bone development or growth
873.54 Open wound of jaw, complicated
905.0 Late effect of fracture of skull and face bones
V52.8 Fitting and adjustment of other specified prosthetic device
V58.42 Aftercare following surgery for neoplasm — (This code should be used in conjunction with other aftercare codes to fully identify the reason for the aftercare encounter)

ICD-9-CM Procedural

23.6 Prosthetic dental implant

21082-21083

21082 Impression and custom preparation; palatal augmentation prosthesis
21083 palatal lift prosthesis

ICD-9-CM Diagnostic

749.00 Unspecified cleft palate ▽
749.01 Unilateral cleft palate, complete
749.02 Unilateral cleft palate, incomplete
749.03 Bilateral cleft palate, complete
749.04 Bilateral cleft palate, incomplete
749.20 Unspecified cleft palate with cleft lip ▽
749.21 Unilateral cleft palate with cleft lip, complete
749.22 Unilateral cleft palate with cleft lip, incomplete
749.23 Bilateral cleft palate with cleft lip, complete
749.24 Bilateral cleft palate with cleft lip, incomplete
749.25 Other combinations of cleft palate with cleft lip
784.51 Dysarthria
784.59 Other speech disturbance
787.20 Dysphagia, unspecified ▽
787.21 Dysphagia, oral phase
787.22 Dysphagia, oropharyngeal phase
787.23 Dysphagia, pharyngeal phase
787.24 Dysphagia, pharyngoesophageal phase
787.29 Other dysphagia
V52.8 Fitting and adjustment of other specified prosthetic device
V58.42 Aftercare following surgery for neoplasm — (This code should be used in conjunction with other aftercare codes to fully identify the reason for the aftercare encounter)

ICD-9-CM Procedural

23.6 Prosthetic dental implant

21084

21084 Impression and custom preparation; speech aid prosthesis

ICD-9-CM Diagnostic

446.4 Wegener's granulomatosis
528.9 Other and unspecified diseases of the oral soft tissues ▽
749.00 Unspecified cleft palate ▽
749.01 Unilateral cleft palate, complete
749.02 Unilateral cleft palate, incomplete
749.03 Bilateral cleft palate, complete
749.04 Bilateral cleft palate, incomplete
749.20 Unspecified cleft palate with cleft lip ▽
749.21 Unilateral cleft palate with cleft lip, complete
749.22 Unilateral cleft palate with cleft lip, incomplete
749.23 Bilateral cleft palate with cleft lip, complete
749.24 Bilateral cleft palate with cleft lip, incomplete
749.25 Other combinations of cleft palate with cleft lip
750.29 Other specified congenital anomaly of pharynx
784.51 Dysarthria
784.52 Fluency disorder in conditions classified elsewhere — (Code first underlying disease or condition, such as: Parkinson's disease (332.0)) ☒
784.59 Other speech disturbance

787.20 Dysphagia, unspecified
787.21 Dysphagia, oral phase
787.22 Dysphagia, oropharyngeal phase
787.23 Dysphagia, pharyngeal phase
787.24 Dysphagia, pharyngoesophageal phase
787.29 Other dysphagia
V52.8 Fitting and adjustment of other specified prosthetic device
V58.42 Aftercare following surgery for neoplasm — (This code should be used in conjunction with other aftercare codes to fully identify the reason for the aftercare encounter)

ICD-9-CM Procedural

27.69 Other plastic repair of palate

21085

21085 Impression and custom preparation; oral surgical splint

ICD-9-CM Diagnostic

170.0 Malignant neoplasm of bones of skull and face, except mandible
170.1 Malignant neoplasm of mandible
327.20 Organic sleep apnea, unspecified
327.21 Primary central sleep apnea
327.22 High altitude periodic breathing
327.23 Obstructive sleep apnea (adult) (pediatric)
327.24 Idiopathic sleep related nonobstructive alveolar hypoventilation
327.25 Congenital central alveolar hypoventilation syndrome
327.26 Sleep related hypoventilation/hypoxemia in conditions classifiable elsewhere — (Code first underlying condition)
327.27 Central sleep apnea in conditions classified elsewhere — (Code first underlying condition)
327.29 Other organic sleep apnea
523.40 Chronic periodontitis, unspecified
523.41 Chronic periodontitis, localized
523.42 Chronic periodontitis, generalized
524.01 Maxillary hyperplasia
524.02 Mandibular hyperplasia
524.03 Maxillary hypoplasia
524.04 Mandibular hypoplasia
524.12 Other jaw asymmetry
524.28 Anomaly of dental arch relationship, anomalies of interarch distance
524.29 Other anomalies of dental arch relationship
524.51 Abnormal jaw closure
524.59 Other dentofacial functional abnormalities
524.72 Alveolar mandibular hyperplasia
524.74 Alveolar mandibular hypoplasia
526.89 Other specified disease of the jaws
780.53 Hypersomnia with sleep apnea, unspecified
780.57 Unspecified sleep apnea
V51.8 Other aftercare involving the use of plastic surgery
V58.42 Aftercare following surgery for neoplasm — (This code should be used in conjunction with other aftercare codes to fully identify the reason for the aftercare encounter)

ICD-9-CM Procedural

23.6 Prosthetic dental implant

21086

21086 Impression and custom preparation; auricular prosthesis

ICD-9-CM Diagnostic

171.0 Malignant neoplasm of connective and other soft tissue of head, face, and neck
172.2 Malignant melanoma of skin of ear and external auditory canal
173.20 Unspecified malignant neoplasm of skin of ear and external auditory canal
173.21 Basal cell carcinoma of skin of ear and external auditory canal
173.22 Squamous cell carcinoma of skin of ear and external auditory canal
173.29 Other specified malignant neoplasm of skin of ear and external auditory canal
380.32 Acquired deformities of auricle or pinna
388.8 Other disorders of ear
744.01 Congenital absence of external ear causing impairment of hearing
744.02 Other congenital anomaly of external ear causing impairment of hearing
744.09 Other congenital anomalies of ear causing impairment of hearing
744.23 Microtia
872.11 Open wound of auricle, complicated
906.5 Late effect of burn of eye, face, head, and neck
925.1 Crushing injury of face and scalp — (Use additional code to identify any associated injuries, such as: 800-829, 850.0-854.1, 860.0-869.1)
941.31 Full-thickness skin loss due to burn (third degree NOS) of ear (any part)
941.51 Deep necrosis of underlying tissues due to burn (deep third degree) of ear (any part), with loss of a body part
V51.8 Other aftercare involving the use of plastic surgery
V58.42 Aftercare following surgery for neoplasm — (This code should be used in conjunction with other aftercare codes to fully identify the reason for the aftercare encounter)

ICD-9-CM Procedural

18.71 Construction of auricle of ear

HCPCS Level II Supplies & Services

L8045 Auricular prosthesis, provided by a nonphysician

21087

21087 Impression and custom preparation; nasal prosthesis

ICD-9-CM Diagnostic

738.0 Acquired deformity of nose
748.1 Other congenital anomaly of nose
756.0 Congenital anomalies of skull and face bones
802.0 Nasal bones, closed fracture
802.1 Nasal bones, open fracture
873.30 Open wound of nose, unspecified site, complicated
873.31 Open wound of nasal septum, complicated
873.32 Open wound of nasal cavity, complicated
873.33 Open wound of nasal sinus, complicated
873.39 Open wound of nose, multiple sites, complicated
906.5 Late effect of burn of eye, face, head, and neck
V58.42 Aftercare following surgery for neoplasm — (This code should be used in conjunction with other aftercare codes to fully identify the reason for the aftercare encounter)

ICD-9-CM Procedural

99.99 Other miscellaneous procedures

HCPCS Level II Supplies & Services

L8040 Nasal prosthesis, provided by a nonphysician

21088

21088 Impression and custom preparation; facial prosthesis

ICD-9-CM Diagnostic

733.45 Aseptic necrosis of bone, jaw
744.89 Other specified congenital anomaly of face and neck
756.0 Congenital anomalies of skull and face bones
906.5 Late effect of burn of eye, face, head, and neck
V58.42 Aftercare following surgery for neoplasm — (This code should be used in conjunction with other aftercare codes to fully identify the reason for the aftercare encounter)

ICD-9-CM Procedural

99.99 Other miscellaneous procedures

HCPCS Level II Supplies & Services

L8041 Midfacial prosthesis, provided by a nonphysician

21100

21100 Application of halo type appliance for maxillofacial fixation, includes removal (separate procedure)

ICD-9-CM Diagnostic

170.0 Malignant neoplasm of bones of skull and face, except mandible
170.1 Malignant neoplasm of mandible
524.01 Maxillary hyperplasia
524.02 Mandibular hyperplasia
524.06 Microgenia
524.07 Excessive tuberosity of jaw
524.09 Other specified major anomaly of jaw size
524.10 Unspecified anomaly of relationship of jaw to cranial base ▽
524.11 Maxillary asymmetry
524.12 Other jaw asymmetry
524.19 Other specified anomaly of relationship of jaw to cranial base
524.69 Other specified temporomandibular joint disorders
754.0 Congenital musculoskeletal deformities of skull, face, and jaw
756.0 Congenital anomalies of skull and face bones
802.22 Closed fracture of subcondylar process of mandible
802.25 Closed fracture of angle of jaw
802.26 Closed fracture of symphysis of body of mandible
802.28 Closed fracture of other and unspecified part of body of mandible ▽
802.29 Closed fracture of multiple sites of mandible
802.32 Open fracture of subcondylar process of mandible
802.35 Open fracture of angle of jaw
802.36 Open fracture of symphysis of body of mandible
802.38 Open fracture of other and unspecified part of body of mandible ▽
802.39 Open fracture of multiple sites of mandible
802.4 Malar and maxillary bones, closed fracture
802.5 Malar and maxillary bones, open fracture
830.0 Closed dislocation of jaw
830.1 Open dislocation of jaw
996.40 Unspecified mechanical complication of internal orthopedic device, implant, and graft — (Use additional code to identify prosthetic joint with mechanical complication, V43.60-V43.69) ▽
996.49 Other mechanical complication of other internal orthopedic device, implant, and graft — (Use additional code to identify prosthetic joint with mechanical complication, V43.60-V43.69)
996.67 Infection and inflammatory reaction due to other internal orthopedic device, implant, and graft — (Use additional code to identify specified infections)
996.78 Other complications due to other internal orthopedic device, implant, and graft — (Use additional code to identify complication: 338.18-338.19, 338.28-338.29)

ICD-9-CM Procedural

78.19 Application of external fixator device, other
97.36 Removal of other external mandibular fixation device

HCPCS Level II Supplies & Services

A4305 Disposable drug delivery system, flow rate of 50 ml or greater per hour

21110

21110 Application of interdental fixation device for conditions other than fracture or dislocation, includes removal

ICD-9-CM Diagnostic

143.0 Malignant neoplasm of upper gum
143.1 Malignant neoplasm of lower gum
143.8 Malignant neoplasm of other sites of gum
143.9 Malignant neoplasm of gum, unspecified site ▽
145.2 Malignant neoplasm of hard palate
145.3 Malignant neoplasm of soft palate
145.5 Malignant neoplasm of palate, unspecified ▽
145.6 Malignant neoplasm of retromolar area
170.0 Malignant neoplasm of bones of skull and face, except mandible
170.1 Malignant neoplasm of mandible
278.00 Obesity, unspecified — (Use additional code to identify Body Mass Index (BMI), if known: V85.0-V85.54) (Use additional code to identify any associated intellectual disabilities) ▽
278.01 Morbid obesity — (Use additional code to identify Body Mass Index (BMI), if known: V85.0-V85.54)
524.01 Maxillary hyperplasia
524.02 Mandibular hyperplasia
524.06 Microgenia
524.07 Excessive tuberosity of jaw
524.09 Other specified major anomaly of jaw size
524.10 Unspecified anomaly of relationship of jaw to cranial base ▽
524.11 Maxillary asymmetry
524.12 Other jaw asymmetry
524.19 Other specified anomaly of relationship of jaw to cranial base
524.28 Anomaly of dental arch relationship, anomalies of interarch distance
524.29 Other anomalies of dental arch relationship
524.51 Abnormal jaw closure
524.52 Limited mandibular range of motion
524.53 Deviation in opening and closing of the mandible
524.56 Dentofacial functional abnormality, non-working side interference
524.59 Other dentofacial functional abnormalities
524.60 Unspecified temporomandibular joint disorders ▽
524.61 Adhesions and ankylosis (bony or fibrous) of temporomandibular joint
524.62 Arthralgia of temporomandibular joint
524.63 Articular disc disorder (reducing or non-reducing) of temporomandibular joint
524.64 Temporomandibular joint sounds on opening and/or closing the jaw
524.69 Other specified temporomandibular joint disorders
525.0 Exfoliation of teeth due to systemic causes
525.10 Unspecified acquired absence of teeth — (Code first class of edentulism: 525.40-525.44, 525.50-525.54) ▽ ☒
525.11 Loss of teeth due to trauma — (Code first class of edentulism: 525.40-525.44, 525.50-525.54) ☒
525.12 Loss of teeth due to periodontal disease — (Code first class of edentulism: 525.40-525.44, 525.50-525.54) ☒
525.13 Loss of teeth due to caries — (Code first class of edentulism: 525.40-525.44, 525.50-525.54) ☒
525.19 Other loss of teeth — (Code first class of edentulism: 525.40-525.44, 525.50-525.54) ☒
525.20 Unspecified atrophy of edentulous alveolar ridge ▽
525.21 Minimal atrophy of the mandible
525.22 Moderate atrophy of the mandible
525.23 Severe atrophy of the mandible
525.24 Minimal atrophy of the maxilla
525.25 Moderate atrophy of the maxilla
525.26 Severe atrophy of the maxilla
525.50 Partial edentulism, unspecified — (Use additional code to identify cause of edentulism: 525.10-525.19) ▽
525.51 Partial edentulism, class I — (Use additional code to identify cause of edentulism: 525.10-525.19)
525.52 Partial edentulism, class II — (Use additional code to identify cause of edentulism: 525.10-525.19)

525.53 Partial edentulism, class III — (Use additional code to identify cause of edentulism: 525.10-525.19)
525.54 Partial edentulism, class IV — (Use additional code to identify cause of edentulism: 525.10-525.19)
525.8 Other specified disorders of the teeth and supporting structures
525.9 Unspecified disorder of the teeth and supporting structures ♥
526.4 Inflammatory conditions of jaw
714.0 Rheumatoid arthritis — (Use additional code to identify manifestation: 357.1, 359.6)
715.80 Osteoarthrosis involving more than one site, but not specified as generalized, unspecified site ♥
715.89 Osteoarthrosis involving multiple sites, but not specified as generalized
715.98 Osteoarthrosis, unspecified whether generalized or localized, other specified sites ♥
716.90 Unspecified arthropathy, site unspecified ♥
716.98 Unspecified arthropathy, other specified sites ♥
716.99 Unspecified arthropathy, multiple sites ♥
754.0 Congenital musculoskeletal deformities of skull, face, and jaw
756.0 Congenital anomalies of skull and face bones
905.0 Late effect of fracture of skull and face bones

ICD-9-CM Procedural

24.7 Application of orthodontic appliance
78.59 Internal fixation of other bone, except facial bones, without fracture reduction

HCPCS Level II Supplies & Services

A4305 Disposable drug delivery system, flow rate of 50 ml or greater per hour

21116

21116 Injection procedure for temporomandibular joint arthrography

ICD-9-CM Diagnostic

170.1 Malignant neoplasm of mandible
524.60 Unspecified temporomandibular joint disorders ♥
524.61 Adhesions and ankylosis (bony or fibrous) of temporomandibular joint
524.62 Arthralgia of temporomandibular joint
524.63 Articular disc disorder (reducing or non-reducing) of temporomandibular joint
524.64 Temporomandibular joint sounds on opening and/or closing the jaw
524.69 Other specified temporomandibular joint disorders
719.08 Effusion of joint, other specified site
719.48 Pain in joint, other specified sites
802.21 Closed fracture of condylar process of mandible
802.31 Open fracture of condylar process of mandible
830.0 Closed dislocation of jaw
830.1 Open dislocation of jaw
905.0 Late effect of fracture of skull and face bones
925.1 Crushing injury of face and scalp — (Use additional code to identify any associated injuries, such as: 800-829, 850.0-854.1, 860.0-869.1)

ICD-9-CM Procedural

76.99 Other operations on facial bones and joints
87.13 Temporomandibular contrast arthrogram

21120

21120 Genioplasty; augmentation (autograft, allograft, prosthetic material)

ICD-9-CM Diagnostic

170.1 Malignant neoplasm of mandible
524.04 Mandibular hypoplasia
524.06 Microgenia
524.89 Other specified dentofacial anomalies
733.45 Aseptic necrosis of bone, jaw
754.0 Congenital musculoskeletal deformities of skull, face, and jaw
787.20 Dysphagia, unspecified ♥
787.21 Dysphagia, oral phase
787.22 Dysphagia, oropharyngeal phase
787.23 Dysphagia, pharyngeal phase
787.24 Dysphagia, pharyngoesophageal phase
787.29 Other dysphagia
V41.6 Problems with swallowing and mastication
V50.1 Other plastic surgery for unacceptable cosmetic appearance
V51.8 Other aftercare involving the use of plastic surgery
V58.42 Aftercare following surgery for neoplasm — (This code should be used in conjunction with other aftercare codes to fully identify the reason for the aftercare encounter)

ICD-9-CM Procedural

76.68 Augmentation genioplasty

21121-21123

21121 Genioplasty; sliding osteotomy, single piece
21122 sliding osteotomies, 2 or more osteotomies (eg, wedge excision or bone wedge reversal for asymmetrical chin)
21123 sliding, augmentation with interpositional bone grafts (includes obtaining autografts)

ICD-9-CM Diagnostic

170.1 Malignant neoplasm of mandible
524.02 Mandibular hyperplasia
524.04 Mandibular hypoplasia
524.05 Macrogenia
524.06 Microgenia
524.07 Excessive tuberosity of jaw
524.09 Other specified major anomaly of jaw size
524.29 Other anomalies of dental arch relationship
524.30 Anomaly of tooth position, unspecified ♥
524.39 Other anomalies of tooth position
524.89 Other specified dentofacial anomalies
526.89 Other specified disease of the jaws
733.45 Aseptic necrosis of bone, jaw
754.0 Congenital musculoskeletal deformities of skull, face, and jaw
V51.8 Other aftercare involving the use of plastic surgery
V58.42 Aftercare following surgery for neoplasm — (This code should be used in conjunction with other aftercare codes to fully identify the reason for the aftercare encounter)

ICD-9-CM Procedural

76.62 Open osteoplasty (osteotomy) of mandibular ramus
76.68 Augmentation genioplasty
76.91 Bone graft to facial bone

21125-21127

21125 Augmentation, mandibular body or angle; prosthetic material
21127 with bone graft, onlay or interpositional (includes obtaining autograft)

ICD-9-CM Diagnostic

170.1 Malignant neoplasm of mandible
524.04 Mandibular hypoplasia
524.07 Excessive tuberosity of jaw
524.09 Other specified major anomaly of jaw size
524.19 Other specified anomaly of relationship of jaw to cranial base
524.20 Unspecified anomaly of dental arch relationship ♥
524.21 Malocclusion, Angle's class I
524.22 Malocclusion, Angle's class II
524.23 Malocclusion, Angle's class III
524.24 Anomaly of dental arch relationship, open anterior occlusal relationship
524.25 Anomaly of dental arch relationship, open posterior occlusal relationship
524.26 Anomaly of dental arch relationship, excessive horizontal overlap

524.27 Anomaly of dental arch relationship, reverse articulation
524.28 Anomaly of dental arch relationship, anomalies of interarch distance
524.52 Limited mandibular range of motion
524.53 Deviation in opening and closing of the mandible
524.56 Dentofacial functional abnormality, non-working side interference
524.59 Other dentofacial functional abnormalities
524.89 Other specified dentofacial anomalies
526.89 Other specified disease of the jaws
733.45 Aseptic necrosis of bone, jaw
787.20 Dysphagia, unspecified ▽
787.21 Dysphagia, oral phase
787.22 Dysphagia, oropharyngeal phase
787.23 Dysphagia, pharyngeal phase
787.24 Dysphagia, pharyngoesophageal phase
787.29 Other dysphagia
V50.1 Other plastic surgery for unacceptable cosmetic appearance
V51.8 Other aftercare involving the use of plastic surgery

ICD-9-CM Procedural

76.43 Other reconstruction of mandible
76.68 Augmentation genioplasty
76.91 Bone graft to facial bone
76.92 Insertion of synthetic implant in facial bone

21137

21137 Reduction forehead; contouring only

ICD-9-CM Diagnostic

733.3 Hyperostosis of skull
738.19 Other specified acquired deformity of head
754.0 Congenital musculoskeletal deformities of skull, face, and jaw
756.0 Congenital anomalies of skull and face bones
905.0 Late effect of fracture of skull and face bones
906.3 Late effect of contusion
906.4 Late effect of crushing

ICD-9-CM Procedural

76.99 Other operations on facial bones and joints

21138-21139

21138 Reduction forehead; contouring and application of prosthetic material or bone graft (includes obtaining autograft)
21139 contouring and setback of anterior frontal sinus wall

ICD-9-CM Diagnostic

160.4 Malignant neoplasm of frontal sinus
170.0 Malignant neoplasm of bones of skull and face, except mandible
733.3 Hyperostosis of skull
738.19 Other specified acquired deformity of head
754.0 Congenital musculoskeletal deformities of skull, face, and jaw
756.0 Congenital anomalies of skull and face bones
905.0 Late effect of fracture of skull and face bones
906.4 Late effect of crushing

ICD-9-CM Procedural

76.91 Bone graft to facial bone
76.92 Insertion of synthetic implant in facial bone
76.99 Other operations on facial bones and joints

21141-21143

21141 Reconstruction midface, LeFort I; single piece, segment movement in any direction (eg, for Long Face Syndrome), without bone graft
21142 2 pieces, segment movement in any direction, without bone graft
21143 3 or more pieces, segment movement in any direction, without bone graft

ICD-9-CM Diagnostic

327.20 Organic sleep apnea, unspecified ▽
327.21 Primary central sleep apnea
327.22 High altitude periodic breathing
327.23 Obstructive sleep apnea (adult) (pediatric)
327.24 Idiopathic sleep related nonobstructive alveolar hypoventilation
327.25 Congenital central alveolar hypoventilation syndrome
327.26 Sleep related hypoventilation/hypoxemia in conditions classifiable elsewhere — (Code first underlying condition) ☒
327.27 Central sleep apnea in conditions classified elsewhere — (Code first underlying condition) ☒
327.29 Other organic sleep apnea
524.01 Maxillary hyperplasia
524.03 Maxillary hypoplasia
524.09 Other specified major anomaly of jaw size
524.11 Maxillary asymmetry
524.12 Other jaw asymmetry
524.19 Other specified anomaly of relationship of jaw to cranial base
524.29 Other anomalies of dental arch relationship
524.9 Unspecified dentofacial anomalies ▽
733.45 Aseptic necrosis of bone, jaw
733.91 Arrest of bone development or growth
744.9 Unspecified congenital anomaly of face and neck ▽
756.0 Congenital anomalies of skull and face bones
780.53 Hypersomnia with sleep apnea, unspecified ▽
780.57 Unspecified sleep apnea ▽

ICD-9-CM Procedural

76.46 Other reconstruction of other facial bone

21145-21147

21145 Reconstruction midface, LeFort I; single piece, segment movement in any direction, requiring bone grafts (includes obtaining autografts)
21146 2 pieces, segment movement in any direction, requiring bone grafts (includes obtaining autografts) (eg, ungrafted unilateral alveolar cleft)
21147 3 or more pieces, segment movement in any direction, requiring bone grafts (includes obtaining autografts) (eg, ungrafted bilateral alveolar cleft or multiple osteotomies)

ICD-9-CM Diagnostic

327.20 Organic sleep apnea, unspecified ▽
327.21 Primary central sleep apnea
327.22 High altitude periodic breathing
327.23 Obstructive sleep apnea (adult) (pediatric)
327.24 Idiopathic sleep related nonobstructive alveolar hypoventilation
327.25 Congenital central alveolar hypoventilation syndrome
327.26 Sleep related hypoventilation/hypoxemia in conditions classifiable elsewhere — (Code first underlying condition) ☒
327.27 Central sleep apnea in conditions classified elsewhere — (Code first underlying condition) ☒
327.29 Other organic sleep apnea
524.01 Maxillary hyperplasia
524.03 Maxillary hypoplasia
524.09 Other specified major anomaly of jaw size
524.11 Maxillary asymmetry

524.12 Other jaw asymmetry
524.19 Other specified anomaly of relationship of jaw to cranial base
524.29 Other anomalies of dental arch relationship
524.72 Alveolar mandibular hyperplasia
524.9 Unspecified dentofacial anomalies
733.45 Aseptic necrosis of bone, jaw
733.91 Arrest of bone development or growth
744.9 Unspecified congenital anomaly of face and neck
756.0 Congenital anomalies of skull and face bones
780.53 Hypersomnia with sleep apnea, unspecified
780.57 Unspecified sleep apnea

ICD-9-CM Procedural

76.46 Other reconstruction of other facial bone
76.91 Bone graft to facial bone

21150-21151

21150 Reconstruction midface, LeFort II; anterior intrusion (eg, Treacher-Collins Syndrome)
21151 any direction, requiring bone grafts (includes obtaining autografts)

ICD-9-CM Diagnostic

524.01 Maxillary hyperplasia
524.03 Maxillary hypoplasia
524.09 Other specified major anomaly of jaw size
524.10 Unspecified anomaly of relationship of jaw to cranial base
524.11 Maxillary asymmetry
524.12 Other jaw asymmetry
524.19 Other specified anomaly of relationship of jaw to cranial base
524.29 Other anomalies of dental arch relationship
524.59 Other dentofacial functional abnormalities
524.72 Alveolar mandibular hyperplasia
524.89 Other specified dentofacial anomalies
524.9 Unspecified dentofacial anomalies
733.45 Aseptic necrosis of bone, jaw
733.81 Malunion of fracture
733.91 Arrest of bone development or growth
738.10 Unspecified acquired deformity of head
738.11 Zygomatic hyperplasia
738.12 Zygomatic hypoplasia
738.19 Other specified acquired deformity of head
744.9 Unspecified congenital anomaly of face and neck
754.0 Congenital musculoskeletal deformities of skull, face, and jaw
756.0 Congenital anomalies of skull and face bones
905.0 Late effect of fracture of skull and face bones

ICD-9-CM Procedural

76.46 Other reconstruction of other facial bone
76.91 Bone graft to facial bone

21154-21155

21154 Reconstruction midface, LeFort III (extracranial), any type, requiring bone grafts (includes obtaining autografts); without LeFort I
21155 with LeFort I

ICD-9-CM Diagnostic

376.40 Unspecified deformity of orbit
376.43 Local deformities of orbit due to bone disease
376.44 Orbital deformities associated with craniofacial deformities
524.01 Maxillary hyperplasia
524.03 Maxillary hypoplasia
524.09 Other specified major anomaly of jaw size
524.11 Maxillary asymmetry
524.12 Other jaw asymmetry
524.19 Other specified anomaly of relationship of jaw to cranial base
524.59 Other dentofacial functional abnormalities
524.72 Alveolar mandibular hyperplasia
524.89 Other specified dentofacial anomalies
524.9 Unspecified dentofacial anomalies
733.45 Aseptic necrosis of bone, jaw
738.19 Other specified acquired deformity of head
743.66 Specified congenital anomaly of orbit
744.9 Unspecified congenital anomaly of face and neck
755.55 Acrocephalosyndactyly
756.0 Congenital anomalies of skull and face bones

ICD-9-CM Procedural

76.46 Other reconstruction of other facial bone
76.91 Bone graft to facial bone

21159-21160

21159 Reconstruction midface, LeFort III (extra and intracranial) with forehead advancement (eg, mono bloc), requiring bone grafts (includes obtaining autografts); without LeFort I
21160 with LeFort I

ICD-9-CM Diagnostic

376.40 Unspecified deformity of orbit
376.43 Local deformities of orbit due to bone disease
376.44 Orbital deformities associated with craniofacial deformities
376.47 Deformity of orbit due to trauma or surgery
524.01 Maxillary hyperplasia
524.03 Maxillary hypoplasia
524.09 Other specified major anomaly of jaw size
524.11 Maxillary asymmetry
524.12 Other jaw asymmetry
524.19 Other specified anomaly of relationship of jaw to cranial base
524.29 Other anomalies of dental arch relationship
524.70 Unspecified alveolar anomaly
524.71 Alveolar maxillary hyperplasia
524.72 Alveolar mandibular hyperplasia
524.73 Alveolar maxillary hypoplasia
524.79 Other specified alveolar anomaly
524.89 Other specified dentofacial anomalies
524.9 Unspecified dentofacial anomalies
733.45 Aseptic necrosis of bone, jaw
738.10 Unspecified acquired deformity of head
738.11 Zygomatic hyperplasia
738.12 Zygomatic hypoplasia
738.19 Other specified acquired deformity of head
743.66 Specified congenital anomaly of orbit
744.9 Unspecified congenital anomaly of face and neck
756.0 Congenital anomalies of skull and face bones
905.0 Late effect of fracture of skull and face bones

ICD-9-CM Procedural

76.46 Other reconstruction of other facial bone
76.91 Bone graft to facial bone

21172

21172 Reconstruction superior-lateral orbital rim and lower forehead, advancement or alteration, with or without grafts (includes obtaining autografts)

ICD-9-CM Diagnostic

170.0 Malignant neoplasm of bones of skull and face, except mandible
238.0 Neoplasm of uncertain behavior of bone and articular cartilage
239.2 Neoplasms of unspecified nature of bone, soft tissue, and skin
376.40 Unspecified deformity of orbit ▽
376.43 Local deformities of orbit due to bone disease
376.44 Orbital deformities associated with craniofacial deformities
376.45 Atrophy of orbit
376.46 Enlargement of orbit
376.47 Deformity of orbit due to trauma or surgery
738.19 Other specified acquired deformity of head
744.9 Unspecified congenital anomaly of face and neck ▽
756.0 Congenital anomalies of skull and face bones
905.0 Late effect of fracture of skull and face bones

ICD-9-CM Procedural

16.98 Other operations on orbit
76.46 Other reconstruction of other facial bone
76.91 Bone graft to facial bone

21175

21175 Reconstruction, bifrontal, superior-lateral orbital rims and lower forehead, advancement or alteration (eg, plagiocephaly, trigonocephaly, brachycephaly), with or without grafts (includes obtaining autografts)

ICD-9-CM Diagnostic

170.0 Malignant neoplasm of bones of skull and face, except mandible
238.0 Neoplasm of uncertain behavior of bone and articular cartilage
239.2 Neoplasms of unspecified nature of bone, soft tissue, and skin
376.40 Unspecified deformity of orbit ▽
376.43 Local deformities of orbit due to bone disease
376.44 Orbital deformities associated with craniofacial deformities
376.45 Atrophy of orbit
376.46 Enlargement of orbit
376.47 Deformity of orbit due to trauma or surgery
738.10 Unspecified acquired deformity of head ▽
738.19 Other specified acquired deformity of head
744.9 Unspecified congenital anomaly of face and neck ▽
756.0 Congenital anomalies of skull and face bones
905.0 Late effect of fracture of skull and face bones

ICD-9-CM Procedural

16.98 Other operations on orbit
76.46 Other reconstruction of other facial bone
76.91 Bone graft to facial bone

21179-21180

21179 Reconstruction, entire or majority of forehead and/or supraorbital rims; with grafts (allograft or prosthetic material)
21180 with autograft (includes obtaining grafts)

ICD-9-CM Diagnostic

170.0 Malignant neoplasm of bones of skull and face, except mandible
238.0 Neoplasm of uncertain behavior of bone and articular cartilage
239.2 Neoplasms of unspecified nature of bone, soft tissue, and skin
376.40 Unspecified deformity of orbit ▽
376.43 Local deformities of orbit due to bone disease
376.44 Orbital deformities associated with craniofacial deformities
376.45 Atrophy of orbit
376.46 Enlargement of orbit
376.47 Deformity of orbit due to trauma or surgery
738.10 Unspecified acquired deformity of head ▽
738.19 Other specified acquired deformity of head
744.9 Unspecified congenital anomaly of face and neck ▽
756.0 Congenital anomalies of skull and face bones
905.0 Late effect of fracture of skull and face bones

ICD-9-CM Procedural

16.98 Other operations on orbit
76.46 Other reconstruction of other facial bone
76.91 Bone graft to facial bone
76.92 Insertion of synthetic implant in facial bone

21181

21181 Reconstruction by contouring of benign tumor of cranial bones (eg, fibrous dysplasia), extracranial

ICD-9-CM Diagnostic

213.0 Benign neoplasm of bones of skull and face
238.0 Neoplasm of uncertain behavior of bone and articular cartilage
239.2 Neoplasms of unspecified nature of bone, soft tissue, and skin
252.00 Hyperparathyroidism, unspecified ▽
252.01 Primary hyperparathyroidism
252.02 Secondary hyperparathyroidism, non-renal
252.08 Other hyperparathyroidism
733.20 Unspecified cyst of bone (localized) ▽
733.21 Solitary bone cyst
733.22 Aneurysmal bone cyst
733.29 Other cyst of bone
738.11 Zygomatic hyperplasia
756.50 Unspecified congenital osteodystrophy ▽
756.54 Polyostotic fibrous dysplasia of bone
756.59 Other congenital osteodystrophy

ICD-9-CM Procedural

02.99 Other operations on skull, brain, and cerebral meninges
76.91 Bone graft to facial bone

21182-21184

21182 Reconstruction of orbital walls, rims, forehead, nasoethmoid complex following intra- and extracranial excision of benign tumor of cranial bone (eg, fibrous dysplasia), with multiple autografts (includes obtaining grafts); total area of bone grafting less than 40 sq cm
21183 total area of bone grafting greater than 40 sq cm but less than 80 sq cm
21184 total area of bone grafting greater than 80 sq cm

ICD-9-CM Diagnostic

213.0 Benign neoplasm of bones of skull and face
238.0 Neoplasm of uncertain behavior of bone and articular cartilage
239.2 Neoplasms of unspecified nature of bone, soft tissue, and skin
252.00 Hyperparathyroidism, unspecified ▽
252.01 Primary hyperparathyroidism
252.02 Secondary hyperparathyroidism, non-renal
252.08 Other hyperparathyroidism
376.40 Unspecified deformity of orbit ▽
376.42 Exostosis of orbit
376.43 Local deformities of orbit due to bone disease
376.44 Orbital deformities associated with craniofacial deformities
376.47 Deformity of orbit due to trauma or surgery

733.29 Other cyst of bone
738.11 Zygomatic hyperplasia
738.19 Other specified acquired deformity of head
756.0 Congenital anomalies of skull and face bones
756.54 Polyostotic fibrous dysplasia of bone
756.59 Other congenital osteodystrophy

ICD-9-CM Procedural

16.98 Other operations on orbit
76.46 Other reconstruction of other facial bone
76.91 Bone graft to facial bone

21188

21188 Reconstruction midface, osteotomies (other than LeFort type) and bone grafts (includes obtaining autografts)

ICD-9-CM Diagnostic

143.0 Malignant neoplasm of upper gum
170.0 Malignant neoplasm of bones of skull and face, except mandible
198.5 Secondary malignant neoplasm of bone and bone marrow
238.0 Neoplasm of uncertain behavior of bone and articular cartilage
239.2 Neoplasms of unspecified nature of bone, soft tissue, and skin
524.00 Unspecified major anomaly of jaw size ▽
524.03 Maxillary hypoplasia
524.09 Other specified major anomaly of jaw size
524.11 Maxillary asymmetry
524.12 Other jaw asymmetry
524.19 Other specified anomaly of relationship of jaw to cranial base
733.45 Aseptic necrosis of bone, jaw
738.19 Other specified acquired deformity of head
754.0 Congenital musculoskeletal deformities of skull, face, and jaw
756.0 Congenital anomalies of skull and face bones
802.4 Malar and maxillary bones, closed fracture
802.5 Malar and maxillary bones, open fracture
905.0 Late effect of fracture of skull and face bones
V10.22 Personal history of malignant neoplasm of nasal cavities, middle ear, and accessory sinuses

ICD-9-CM Procedural

76.46 Other reconstruction of other facial bone
76.91 Bone graft to facial bone

21193-21194

21193 Reconstruction of mandibular rami, horizontal, vertical, C, or L osteotomy; without bone graft
21194 with bone graft (includes obtaining graft)

ICD-9-CM Diagnostic

170.1 Malignant neoplasm of mandible
198.5 Secondary malignant neoplasm of bone and bone marrow
238.0 Neoplasm of uncertain behavior of bone and articular cartilage
239.2 Neoplasms of unspecified nature of bone, soft tissue, and skin
524.02 Mandibular hyperplasia
524.04 Mandibular hypoplasia
524.09 Other specified major anomaly of jaw size
524.19 Other specified anomaly of relationship of jaw to cranial base
524.52 Limited mandibular range of motion
524.53 Deviation in opening and closing of the mandible
524.59 Other dentofacial functional abnormalities
524.69 Other specified temporomandibular joint disorders
524.89 Other specified dentofacial anomalies
526.89 Other specified disease of the jaws
733.45 Aseptic necrosis of bone, jaw
733.81 Malunion of fracture
733.82 Nonunion of fracture
754.0 Congenital musculoskeletal deformities of skull, face, and jaw
787.20 Dysphagia, unspecified ▽
787.21 Dysphagia, oral phase
787.22 Dysphagia, oropharyngeal phase
787.23 Dysphagia, pharyngeal phase
787.24 Dysphagia, pharyngoesophageal phase
787.29 Other dysphagia
905.0 Late effect of fracture of skull and face bones
V50.1 Other plastic surgery for unacceptable cosmetic appearance

ICD-9-CM Procedural

76.43 Other reconstruction of mandible
76.91 Bone graft to facial bone

21195-21196

21195 Reconstruction of mandibular rami and/or body, sagittal split; without internal rigid fixation
21196 with internal rigid fixation

ICD-9-CM Diagnostic

170.1 Malignant neoplasm of mandible
198.5 Secondary malignant neoplasm of bone and bone marrow
238.0 Neoplasm of uncertain behavior of bone and articular cartilage
239.2 Neoplasms of unspecified nature of bone, soft tissue, and skin
524.00 Unspecified major anomaly of jaw size ▽
524.02 Mandibular hyperplasia
524.04 Mandibular hypoplasia
524.09 Other specified major anomaly of jaw size
524.19 Other specified anomaly of relationship of jaw to cranial base
524.29 Other anomalies of dental arch relationship
524.69 Other specified temporomandibular joint disorders
524.89 Other specified dentofacial anomalies
526.89 Other specified disease of the jaws
733.45 Aseptic necrosis of bone, jaw
754.0 Congenital musculoskeletal deformities of skull, face, and jaw
787.20 Dysphagia, unspecified ▽
787.21 Dysphagia, oral phase
787.22 Dysphagia, oropharyngeal phase
787.23 Dysphagia, pharyngeal phase
787.24 Dysphagia, pharyngoesophageal phase
787.29 Other dysphagia
905.0 Late effect of fracture of skull and face bones
V50.1 Other plastic surgery for unacceptable cosmetic appearance

ICD-9-CM Procedural

76.43 Other reconstruction of mandible
76.61 Closed osteoplasty (osteotomy) of mandibular ramus
76.63 Osteoplasty (osteotomy) of body of mandible

21198-21199

21198 Osteotomy, mandible, segmental;
21199 with genioglossus advancement

ICD-9-CM Diagnostic

524.02 Mandibular hyperplasia
524.04 Mandibular hypoplasia
524.12 Other jaw asymmetry

524.72 Alveolar mandibular hyperplasia
524.74 Alveolar mandibular hypoplasia
524.79 Other specified alveolar anomaly
524.89 Other specified dentofacial anomalies
524.9 Unspecified dentofacial anomalies ▽
526.89 Other specified disease of the jaws
733.45 Aseptic necrosis of bone, jaw
754.0 Congenital musculoskeletal deformities of skull, face, and jaw
V50.1 Other plastic surgery for unacceptable cosmetic appearance

ICD-9-CM Procedural

76.63 Osteoplasty (osteotomy) of body of mandible
76.64 Other orthognathic surgery on mandible

21206

21206 Osteotomy, maxilla, segmental (eg, Wassmund or Schuchard)

ICD-9-CM Diagnostic

143.0 Malignant neoplasm of upper gum
170.0 Malignant neoplasm of bones of skull and face, except mandible
198.5 Secondary malignant neoplasm of bone and bone marrow
524.01 Maxillary hyperplasia
524.11 Maxillary asymmetry
524.21 Malocclusion, Angle's class I
524.22 Malocclusion, Angle's class II
524.23 Malocclusion, Angle's class III
524.28 Anomaly of dental arch relationship, anomalies of interarch distance
524.29 Other anomalies of dental arch relationship
524.59 Other dentofacial functional abnormalities
524.9 Unspecified dentofacial anomalies ▽
733.45 Aseptic necrosis of bone, jaw
738.19 Other specified acquired deformity of head
754.0 Congenital musculoskeletal deformities of skull, face, and jaw
756.0 Congenital anomalies of skull and face bones

ICD-9-CM Procedural

76.65 Segmental osteoplasty (osteotomy) of maxilla

21208

21208 Osteoplasty, facial bones; augmentation (autograft, allograft, or prosthetic implant)

ICD-9-CM Diagnostic

524.03 Maxillary hypoplasia
524.04 Mandibular hypoplasia
524.06 Microgenia
524.07 Excessive tuberosity of jaw
524.09 Other specified major anomaly of jaw size
524.11 Maxillary asymmetry
524.12 Other jaw asymmetry
524.19 Other specified anomaly of relationship of jaw to cranial base
524.73 Alveolar maxillary hypoplasia
524.74 Alveolar mandibular hypoplasia
524.79 Other specified alveolar anomaly
524.89 Other specified dentofacial anomalies
526.89 Other specified disease of the jaws
733.45 Aseptic necrosis of bone, jaw
738.12 Zygomatic hypoplasia
738.19 Other specified acquired deformity of head
905.0 Late effect of fracture of skull and face bones
V50.1 Other plastic surgery for unacceptable cosmetic appearance

ICD-9-CM Procedural

76.63 Osteoplasty (osteotomy) of body of mandible
76.66 Total osteoplasty (osteotomy) of maxilla
76.69 Other facial bone repair
76.91 Bone graft to facial bone
76.92 Insertion of synthetic implant in facial bone

21209

21209 Osteoplasty, facial bones; reduction

ICD-9-CM Diagnostic

524.01 Maxillary hyperplasia
524.02 Mandibular hyperplasia
524.05 Macrogenia
524.07 Excessive tuberosity of jaw
524.09 Other specified major anomaly of jaw size
524.10 Unspecified anomaly of relationship of jaw to cranial base ▽
524.11 Maxillary asymmetry
524.12 Other jaw asymmetry
524.19 Other specified anomaly of relationship of jaw to cranial base
524.61 Adhesions and ankylosis (bony or fibrous) of temporomandibular joint
524.69 Other specified temporomandibular joint disorders
524.89 Other specified dentofacial anomalies
526.89 Other specified disease of the jaws
733.45 Aseptic necrosis of bone, jaw
738.11 Zygomatic hyperplasia
738.12 Zygomatic hypoplasia
738.19 Other specified acquired deformity of head
V50.1 Other plastic surgery for unacceptable cosmetic appearance

ICD-9-CM Procedural

76.31 Partial mandibulectomy
76.63 Osteoplasty (osteotomy) of body of mandible
76.66 Total osteoplasty (osteotomy) of maxilla
76.67 Reduction genioplasty
76.69 Other facial bone repair

21210

21210 Graft, bone; nasal, maxillary or malar areas (includes obtaining graft)

ICD-9-CM Diagnostic

160.2 Malignant neoplasm of maxillary sinus
160.8 Malignant neoplasm of other sites of nasal cavities, middle ear, and accessory sinuses
170.0 Malignant neoplasm of bones of skull and face, except mandible
213.0 Benign neoplasm of bones of skull and face
376.50 Enophthalmos, unspecified as to cause ▽
376.51 Enophthalmos due to atrophy of orbital tissue
376.52 Enophthalmos due to trauma or surgery
473.0 Chronic maxillary sinusitis — (Use additional code to identify infectious organism)
522.8 Radicular cyst of dental pulp
523.40 Chronic periodontitis, unspecified ▽
523.41 Chronic periodontitis, localized
523.42 Chronic periodontitis, generalized
524.03 Maxillary hypoplasia
524.09 Other specified major anomaly of jaw size
524.11 Maxillary asymmetry
524.12 Other jaw asymmetry
524.19 Other specified anomaly of relationship of jaw to cranial base
733.45 Aseptic necrosis of bone, jaw
733.81 Malunion of fracture

738.0 Acquired deformity of nose
748.1 Other congenital anomaly of nose
749.01 Unilateral cleft palate, complete
749.02 Unilateral cleft palate, incomplete
749.03 Bilateral cleft palate, complete
749.04 Bilateral cleft palate, incomplete
749.20 Unspecified cleft palate with cleft lip ▽
749.21 Unilateral cleft palate with cleft lip, complete
749.22 Unilateral cleft palate with cleft lip, incomplete
749.23 Bilateral cleft palate with cleft lip, complete
754.0 Congenital musculoskeletal deformities of skull, face, and jaw
756.0 Congenital anomalies of skull and face bones
802.0 Nasal bones, closed fracture
802.1 Nasal bones, open fracture
802.4 Malar and maxillary bones, closed fracture
802.5 Malar and maxillary bones, open fracture
802.6 Orbital floor (blow-out), closed fracture
802.7 Orbital floor (blow-out), open fracture
802.8 Other facial bones, closed fracture
905.0 Late effect of fracture of skull and face bones
906.5 Late effect of burn of eye, face, head, and neck
V50.1 Other plastic surgery for unacceptable cosmetic appearance
V51.8 Other aftercare involving the use of plastic surgery

ICD-9-CM Procedural

21.89 Other repair and plastic operations on nose
76.91 Bone graft to facial bone

21215

21215 Graft, bone; mandible (includes obtaining graft)

ICD-9-CM Diagnostic

170.1 Malignant neoplasm of mandible
213.1 Benign neoplasm of lower jaw bone
238.0 Neoplasm of uncertain behavior of bone and articular cartilage
239.2 Neoplasms of unspecified nature of bone, soft tissue, and skin
522.8 Radicular cyst of dental pulp
523.40 Chronic periodontitis, unspecified ▽
523.41 Chronic periodontitis, localized
523.42 Chronic periodontitis, generalized
524.04 Mandibular hypoplasia
524.06 Microgenia
524.09 Other specified major anomaly of jaw size
524.10 Unspecified anomaly of relationship of jaw to cranial base ▽
524.12 Other jaw asymmetry
524.19 Other specified anomaly of relationship of jaw to cranial base
524.74 Alveolar mandibular hypoplasia
524.79 Other specified alveolar anomaly
524.89 Other specified dentofacial anomalies
525.20 Unspecified atrophy of edentulous alveolar ridge ▽
525.21 Minimal atrophy of the mandible
525.22 Moderate atrophy of the mandible
525.23 Severe atrophy of the mandible
525.8 Other specified disorders of the teeth and supporting structures
526.89 Other specified disease of the jaws
733.45 Aseptic necrosis of bone, jaw
733.81 Malunion of fracture
733.82 Nonunion of fracture
738.19 Other specified acquired deformity of head
802.20 Closed fracture of unspecified site of mandible ▽
802.22 Closed fracture of subcondylar process of mandible
802.25 Closed fracture of angle of jaw
802.26 Closed fracture of symphysis of body of mandible
802.28 Closed fracture of other and unspecified part of body of mandible ▽
802.30 Open fracture of unspecified site of mandible ▽
802.32 Open fracture of subcondylar process of mandible
802.35 Open fracture of angle of jaw
802.36 Open fracture of symphysis of body of mandible
802.38 Open fracture of other and unspecified part of body of mandible ▽
905.0 Late effect of fracture of skull and face bones
V50.1 Other plastic surgery for unacceptable cosmetic appearance
V51.8 Other aftercare involving the use of plastic surgery

ICD-9-CM Procedural

76.91 Bone graft to facial bone

21230-21235

21230 Graft; rib cartilage, autogenous, to face, chin, nose or ear (includes obtaining graft)
21235 ear cartilage, autogenous, to nose or ear (includes obtaining graft)

ICD-9-CM Diagnostic

160.0 Malignant neoplasm of nasal cavities
171.0 Malignant neoplasm of connective and other soft tissue of head, face, and neck
172.2 Malignant melanoma of skin of ear and external auditory canal
173.20 Unspecified malignant neoplasm of skin of ear and external auditory canal ▽
173.21 Basal cell carcinoma of skin of ear and external auditory canal
173.22 Squamous cell carcinoma of skin of ear and external auditory canal
173.29 Other specified malignant neoplasm of skin of ear and external auditory canal
173.30 Unspecified malignant neoplasm of skin of other and unspecified parts of face ▽
173.31 Basal cell carcinoma of skin of other and unspecified parts of face
173.32 Squamous cell carcinoma of skin of other and unspecified parts of face
173.39 Other specified malignant neoplasm of skin of other and unspecified parts of face
198.89 Secondary malignant neoplasm of other specified sites
235.9 Neoplasm of uncertain behavior of other and unspecified respiratory organs ▽
238.1 Neoplasm of uncertain behavior of connective and other soft tissue
239.1 Neoplasm of unspecified nature of respiratory system
239.2 Neoplasms of unspecified nature of bone, soft tissue, and skin
380.32 Acquired deformities of auricle or pinna
524.00 Unspecified major anomaly of jaw size ▽
524.04 Mandibular hypoplasia
524.06 Microgenia
524.09 Other specified major anomaly of jaw size
524.10 Unspecified anomaly of relationship of jaw to cranial base ▽
524.19 Other specified anomaly of relationship of jaw to cranial base
524.89 Other specified dentofacial anomalies
524.9 Unspecified dentofacial anomalies ▽
738.0 Acquired deformity of nose
738.19 Other specified acquired deformity of head
738.7 Cauliflower ear
744.01 Congenital absence of external ear causing impairment of hearing
744.02 Other congenital anomaly of external ear causing impairment of hearing
744.09 Other congenital anomalies of ear causing impairment of hearing
744.23 Microtia
744.3 Unspecified congenital anomaly of ear ▽
748.0 Congenital choanal atresia
748.1 Other congenital anomaly of nose
754.0 Congenital musculoskeletal deformities of skull, face, and jaw
756.0 Congenital anomalies of skull and face bones
872.11 Open wound of auricle, complicated
905.0 Late effect of fracture of skull and face bones

906.0 Late effect of open wound of head, neck, and trunk
906.5 Late effect of burn of eye, face, head, and neck
925.1 Crushing injury of face and scalp — (Use additional code to identify any associated injuries, such as: 800-829, 850.0-854.1, 860.0-869.1)
V50.1 Other plastic surgery for unacceptable cosmetic appearance
V51.8 Other aftercare involving the use of plastic surgery

ICD-9-CM Procedural

18.79 Other plastic repair of external ear
76.91 Bone graft to facial bone
76.99 Other operations on facial bones and joints

21240-21242

21240 Arthroplasty, temporomandibular joint, with or without autograft (includes obtaining graft)
21242 Arthroplasty, temporomandibular joint, with allograft

ICD-9-CM Diagnostic

170.1 Malignant neoplasm of mandible
357.1 Polyneuropathy in collagen vascular disease — (Code first underlying disease: 446.0, 710.0, 714.0) ☒
359.6 Symptomatic inflammatory myopathy in diseases classified elsewhere — (Code first underlying disease: 135, 140.0-208.9, 277.30-277.39, 446.0, 710.0, 710.1, 710.2, 714.0) ☒
524.60 Unspecified temporomandibular joint disorders ▽
524.61 Adhesions and ankylosis (bony or fibrous) of temporomandibular joint
524.62 Arthralgia of temporomandibular joint
524.63 Articular disc disorder (reducing or non-reducing) of temporomandibular joint
524.64 Temporomandibular joint sounds on opening and/or closing the jaw
524.69 Other specified temporomandibular joint disorders
714.0 Rheumatoid arthritis — (Use additional code to identify manifestation: 357.1, 359.6)
830.0 Closed dislocation of jaw
830.1 Open dislocation of jaw
905.0 Late effect of fracture of skull and face bones
905.6 Late effect of dislocation

ICD-9-CM Procedural

76.5 Temporomandibular arthroplasty
76.91 Bone graft to facial bone

21243

21243 Arthroplasty, temporomandibular joint, with prosthetic joint replacement

ICD-9-CM Diagnostic

170.1 Malignant neoplasm of mandible
357.1 Polyneuropathy in collagen vascular disease — (Code first underlying disease: 446.0, 710.0, 714.0) ☒
359.6 Symptomatic inflammatory myopathy in diseases classified elsewhere — (Code first underlying disease: 135, 140.0-208.9, 277.30-277.39, 446.0, 710.0, 710.1, 710.2, 714.0) ☒
524.60 Unspecified temporomandibular joint disorders ▽
524.61 Adhesions and ankylosis (bony or fibrous) of temporomandibular joint
524.62 Arthralgia of temporomandibular joint
524.63 Articular disc disorder (reducing or non-reducing) of temporomandibular joint
524.64 Temporomandibular joint sounds on opening and/or closing the jaw
524.69 Other specified temporomandibular joint disorders
714.0 Rheumatoid arthritis — (Use additional code to identify manifestation: 357.1, 359.6)
718.08 Articular cartilage disorder, other specified site
830.0 Closed dislocation of jaw
830.1 Open dislocation of jaw
905.0 Late effect of fracture of skull and face bones
905.6 Late effect of dislocation

ICD-9-CM Procedural

76.5 Temporomandibular arthroplasty
76.92 Insertion of synthetic implant in facial bone

21244

21244 Reconstruction of mandible, extraoral, with transosteal bone plate (eg, mandibular staple bone plate)

ICD-9-CM Diagnostic

170.1 Malignant neoplasm of mandible
198.5 Secondary malignant neoplasm of bone and bone marrow
524.04 Mandibular hypoplasia
524.06 Microgenia
524.09 Other specified major anomaly of jaw size
524.12 Other jaw asymmetry
524.19 Other specified anomaly of relationship of jaw to cranial base
524.29 Other anomalies of dental arch relationship
524.52 Limited mandibular range of motion
524.53 Deviation in opening and closing of the mandible
524.59 Other dentofacial functional abnormalities
524.74 Alveolar mandibular hypoplasia
524.79 Other specified alveolar anomaly
525.20 Unspecified atrophy of edentulous alveolar ridge ▽
525.21 Minimal atrophy of the mandible
525.22 Moderate atrophy of the mandible
525.23 Severe atrophy of the mandible
526.4 Inflammatory conditions of jaw
733.45 Aseptic necrosis of bone, jaw
733.81 Malunion of fracture
733.82 Nonunion of fracture
738.19 Other specified acquired deformity of head
905.0 Late effect of fracture of skull and face bones

ICD-9-CM Procedural

76.43 Other reconstruction of mandible

21245-21246

21245 Reconstruction of mandible or maxilla, subperiosteal implant; partial
21246 complete

ICD-9-CM Diagnostic

170.0 Malignant neoplasm of bones of skull and face, except mandible
170.1 Malignant neoplasm of mandible
198.5 Secondary malignant neoplasm of bone and bone marrow
520.0 Anodontia
520.6 Disturbances in tooth eruption
521.40 Diseases of hard tissues of teeth, pathological resorption, unspecified ▽
521.41 Diseases of hard tissues of teeth, pathological resorption, internal
521.42 Diseases of hard tissues of teeth, pathological resorption, external
523.40 Chronic periodontitis, unspecified ▽
523.41 Chronic periodontitis, localized
523.42 Chronic periodontitis, generalized
524.12 Other jaw asymmetry
524.39 Other anomalies of tooth position
524.73 Alveolar maxillary hypoplasia
524.74 Alveolar mandibular hypoplasia
524.79 Other specified alveolar anomaly
524.89 Other specified dentofacial anomalies
525.0 Exfoliation of teeth due to systemic causes

525.10 Unspecified acquired absence of teeth — (Code first class of edentulism: 525.40-525.44, 525.50-525.54) ▽ ☒
525.11 Loss of teeth due to trauma — (Code first class of edentulism: 525.40-525.44, 525.50-525.54) ☒
525.12 Loss of teeth due to periodontal disease — (Code first class of edentulism: 525.40-525.44, 525.50-525.54) ☒
525.13 Loss of teeth due to caries — (Code first class of edentulism: 525.40-525.44, 525.50-525.54) ☒
525.19 Other loss of teeth — (Code first class of edentulism: 525.40-525.44, 525.50-525.54) ☒
525.20 Unspecified atrophy of edentulous alveolar ridge ▽
525.21 Minimal atrophy of the mandible
525.22 Moderate atrophy of the mandible
525.23 Severe atrophy of the mandible
525.24 Minimal atrophy of the maxilla
525.25 Moderate atrophy of the maxilla
525.26 Severe atrophy of the maxilla
525.43 Complete edentulism, class III — (Use additional code to identify cause of edentulism: 525.10-525.19)
525.44 Complete edentulism, class IV — (Use additional code to identify cause of edentulism: 525.10-525.19)
525.53 Partial edentulism, class III — (Use additional code to identify cause of edentulism: 525.10-525.19)
525.54 Partial edentulism, class IV — (Use additional code to identify cause of edentulism: 525.10-525.19)
525.8 Other specified disorders of the teeth and supporting structures
526.4 Inflammatory conditions of jaw
733.45 Aseptic necrosis of bone, jaw
738.19 Other specified acquired deformity of head
905.0 Late effect of fracture of skull and face bones
909.3 Late effect of complications of surgical and medical care
V41.6 Problems with swallowing and mastication
V51.8 Other aftercare involving the use of plastic surgery

ICD-9-CM Procedural

76.41 Total mandibulectomy with synchronous reconstruction
76.43 Other reconstruction of mandible
76.91 Bone graft to facial bone
76.92 Insertion of synthetic implant in facial bone

21247

21247 Reconstruction of mandibular condyle with bone and cartilage autografts (includes obtaining grafts) (eg, for hemifacial microsomia)

ICD-9-CM Diagnostic

170.1 Malignant neoplasm of mandible
198.5 Secondary malignant neoplasm of bone and bone marrow
524.04 Mandibular hypoplasia
524.09 Other specified major anomaly of jaw size
524.12 Other jaw asymmetry
524.19 Other specified anomaly of relationship of jaw to cranial base
524.52 Limited mandibular range of motion
524.53 Deviation in opening and closing of the mandible
524.59 Other dentofacial functional abnormalities
524.62 Arthralgia of temporomandibular joint
524.63 Articular disc disorder (reducing or non-reducing) of temporomandibular joint
524.89 Other specified dentofacial anomalies
526.89 Other specified disease of the jaws
733.45 Aseptic necrosis of bone, jaw
733.81 Malunion of fracture
733.82 Nonunion of fracture
738.19 Other specified acquired deformity of head
754.0 Congenital musculoskeletal deformities of skull, face, and jaw
905.0 Late effect of fracture of skull and face bones

ICD-9-CM Procedural

76.46 Other reconstruction of other facial bone
76.91 Bone graft to facial bone

21248-21249

21248 Reconstruction of mandible or maxilla, endosteal implant (eg, blade, cylinder); partial
21249 complete

ICD-9-CM Diagnostic

170.0 Malignant neoplasm of bones of skull and face, except mandible
170.1 Malignant neoplasm of mandible
352.1 Glossopharyngeal neuralgia
520.0 Anodontia
520.6 Disturbances in tooth eruption
521.40 Diseases of hard tissues of teeth, pathological resorption, unspecified ▽
521.41 Diseases of hard tissues of teeth, pathological resorption, internal
521.42 Diseases of hard tissues of teeth, pathological resorption, external
521.49 Diseases of hard tissues of teeth, other pathological resorption
523.40 Chronic periodontitis, unspecified ▽
523.41 Chronic periodontitis, localized
523.42 Chronic periodontitis, generalized
524.30 Anomaly of tooth position, unspecified ▽
524.39 Other anomalies of tooth position
524.73 Alveolar maxillary hypoplasia
524.74 Alveolar mandibular hypoplasia
524.79 Other specified alveolar anomaly
524.89 Other specified dentofacial anomalies
525.0 Exfoliation of teeth due to systemic causes
525.10 Unspecified acquired absence of teeth — (Code first class of edentulism: 525.40-525.44, 525.50-525.54) ▽ ☒
525.11 Loss of teeth due to trauma — (Code first class of edentulism: 525.40-525.44, 525.50-525.54) ☒
525.12 Loss of teeth due to periodontal disease — (Code first class of edentulism: 525.40-525.44, 525.50-525.54) ☒
525.13 Loss of teeth due to caries — (Code first class of edentulism: 525.40-525.44, 525.50-525.54) ☒
525.19 Other loss of teeth — (Code first class of edentulism: 525.40-525.44, 525.50-525.54) ☒
525.20 Unspecified atrophy of edentulous alveolar ridge ▽
525.21 Minimal atrophy of the mandible
525.22 Moderate atrophy of the mandible
525.23 Severe atrophy of the mandible
525.24 Minimal atrophy of the maxilla
525.25 Moderate atrophy of the maxilla
525.26 Severe atrophy of the maxilla
525.43 Complete edentulism, class III — (Use additional code to identify cause of edentulism: 525.10-525.19)
525.44 Complete edentulism, class IV — (Use additional code to identify cause of edentulism: 525.10-525.19)
525.53 Partial edentulism, class III — (Use additional code to identify cause of edentulism: 525.10-525.19)
525.54 Partial edentulism, class IV — (Use additional code to identify cause of edentulism: 525.10-525.19)
525.8 Other specified disorders of the teeth and supporting structures
525.9 Unspecified disorder of the teeth and supporting structures ▽
526.4 Inflammatory conditions of jaw
733.45 Aseptic necrosis of bone, jaw

733.99 Other disorders of bone and cartilage
905.0 Late effect of fracture of skull and face bones
V41.6 Problems with swallowing and mastication
V51.8 Other aftercare involving the use of plastic surgery

ICD-9-CM Procedural

76.41 Total mandibulectomy with synchronous reconstruction
76.43 Other reconstruction of mandible
76.46 Other reconstruction of other facial bone

21255

21255 Reconstruction of zygomatic arch and glenoid fossa with bone and cartilage (includes obtaining autografts)

ICD-9-CM Diagnostic

170.0 Malignant neoplasm of bones of skull and face, except mandible
198.5 Secondary malignant neoplasm of bone and bone marrow
213.0 Benign neoplasm of bones of skull and face
238.0 Neoplasm of uncertain behavior of bone and articular cartilage
239.2 Neoplasms of unspecified nature of bone, soft tissue, and skin
733.45 Aseptic necrosis of bone, jaw
733.81 Malunion of fracture
733.82 Nonunion of fracture
738.11 Zygomatic hyperplasia
738.12 Zygomatic hypoplasia
738.19 Other specified acquired deformity of head
905.0 Late effect of fracture of skull and face bones
925.1 Crushing injury of face and scalp — (Use additional code to identify any associated injuries, such as: 800-829, 850.0-854.1, 860.0-869.1)
V10.02 Personal history of malignant neoplasm of other and unspecified parts of oral cavity and pharynx ▽
V51.8 Other aftercare involving the use of plastic surgery

ICD-9-CM Procedural

76.46 Other reconstruction of other facial bone
76.91 Bone graft to facial bone

21256

21256 Reconstruction of orbit with osteotomies (extracranial) and with bone grafts (includes obtaining autografts) (eg, micro-ophthalmia)

ICD-9-CM Diagnostic

170.0 Malignant neoplasm of bones of skull and face, except mandible
198.5 Secondary malignant neoplasm of bone and bone marrow
213.0 Benign neoplasm of bones of skull and face
238.0 Neoplasm of uncertain behavior of bone and articular cartilage
239.2 Neoplasms of unspecified nature of bone, soft tissue, and skin
376.40 Unspecified deformity of orbit ▽
376.42 Exostosis of orbit
376.43 Local deformities of orbit due to bone disease
376.44 Orbital deformities associated with craniofacial deformities
376.45 Atrophy of orbit
376.47 Deformity of orbit due to trauma or surgery
376.50 Enophthalmos, unspecified as to cause ▽
376.51 Enophthalmos due to atrophy of orbital tissue
376.52 Enophthalmos due to trauma or surgery
733.21 Solitary bone cyst
733.81 Malunion of fracture
733.82 Nonunion of fracture
738.19 Other specified acquired deformity of head
743.10 Unspecified microphthalmos ▽
743.11 Simple microphthalmos
743.12 Microphthalmos associated with other anomalies of eye and adnexa
756.0 Congenital anomalies of skull and face bones
759.89 Other specified multiple congenital anomalies, so described
905.0 Late effect of fracture of skull and face bones
925.1 Crushing injury of face and scalp — (Use additional code to identify any associated injuries, such as: 800-829, 850.0-854.1, 860.0-869.1)

ICD-9-CM Procedural

76.69 Other facial bone repair
76.91 Bone graft to facial bone

21260-21263

21260 Periorbital osteotomies for orbital hypertelorism, with bone grafts; extracranial approach
21261 combined intra- and extracranial approach
21263 with forehead advancement

ICD-9-CM Diagnostic

376.41 Hypertelorism of orbit
376.44 Orbital deformities associated with craniofacial deformities
754.0 Congenital musculoskeletal deformities of skull, face, and jaw
756.0 Congenital anomalies of skull and face bones

ICD-9-CM Procedural

76.69 Other facial bone repair
76.91 Bone graft to facial bone

21267-21268

21267 Orbital repositioning, periorbital osteotomies, unilateral, with bone grafts; extracranial approach
21268 combined intra- and extracranial approach

ICD-9-CM Diagnostic

376.40 Unspecified deformity of orbit ▽
376.43 Local deformities of orbit due to bone disease
376.44 Orbital deformities associated with craniofacial deformities
376.45 Atrophy of orbit
376.47 Deformity of orbit due to trauma or surgery
376.52 Enophthalmos due to trauma or surgery
733.81 Malunion of fracture
738.10 Unspecified acquired deformity of head ▽
738.11 Zygomatic hyperplasia
738.12 Zygomatic hypoplasia
738.19 Other specified acquired deformity of head
743.10 Unspecified microphthalmos ▽
743.11 Simple microphthalmos
743.12 Microphthalmos associated with other anomalies of eye and adnexa
754.0 Congenital musculoskeletal deformities of skull, face, and jaw
756.0 Congenital anomalies of skull and face bones
756.9 Other and unspecified congenital anomaly of musculoskeletal system ▽
905.0 Late effect of fracture of skull and face bones
925.1 Crushing injury of face and scalp — (Use additional code to identify any associated injuries, such as: 800-829, 850.0-854.1, 860.0-869.1)

ICD-9-CM Procedural

76.69 Other facial bone repair
76.91 Bone graft to facial bone

21270

21270 Malar augmentation, prosthetic material

ICD-9-CM Diagnostic

524.03 Maxillary hypoplasia
524.06 Microgenia
524.07 Excessive tuberosity of jaw
524.09 Other specified major anomaly of jaw size
524.11 Maxillary asymmetry
524.12 Other jaw asymmetry
524.19 Other specified anomaly of relationship of jaw to cranial base
524.73 Alveolar maxillary hypoplasia
524.89 Other specified dentofacial anomalies
526.89 Other specified disease of the jaws
738.12 Zygomatic hypoplasia
754.0 Congenital musculoskeletal deformities of skull, face, and jaw
756.0 Congenital anomalies of skull and face bones
905.0 Late effect of fracture of skull and face bones
925.1 Crushing injury of face and scalp — (Use additional code to identify any associated injuries, such as: 800-829, 850.0-854.1, 860.0-869.1)
V50.1 Other plastic surgery for unacceptable cosmetic appearance

ICD-9-CM Procedural

76.69 Other facial bone repair
76.92 Insertion of synthetic implant in facial bone

21275

21275 Secondary revision of orbitocraniofacial reconstruction

ICD-9-CM Diagnostic

170.0 Malignant neoplasm of bones of skull and face, except mandible
198.5 Secondary malignant neoplasm of bone and bone marrow
376.41 Hypertelorism of orbit
376.42 Exostosis of orbit
376.43 Local deformities of orbit due to bone disease
376.44 Orbital deformities associated with craniofacial deformities
376.45 Atrophy of orbit
376.46 Enlargement of orbit
376.47 Deformity of orbit due to trauma or surgery
376.52 Enophthalmos due to trauma or surgery
738.12 Zygomatic hypoplasia
738.19 Other specified acquired deformity of head
743.10 Unspecified microphthalmos ▽
743.11 Simple microphthalmos
756.0 Congenital anomalies of skull and face bones
756.51 Osteogenesis imperfecta

ICD-9-CM Procedural

76.69 Other facial bone repair

21280

21280 Medial canthopexy (separate procedure)

ICD-9-CM Diagnostic

376.41 Hypertelorism of orbit
376.47 Deformity of orbit due to trauma or surgery
743.11 Simple microphthalmos
743.63 Other specified congenital anomaly of eyelid
756.0 Congenital anomalies of skull and face bones
802.8 Other facial bones, closed fracture
802.9 Other facial bones, open fracture
870.8 Other specified open wound of ocular adnexa
906.0 Late effect of open wound of head, neck, and trunk
918.0 Superficial injury of eyelids and periocular area
921.1 Contusion of eyelids and periocular area

ICD-9-CM Procedural

08.59 Other adjustment of lid position

21282

21282 Lateral canthopexy

ICD-9-CM Diagnostic

376.47 Deformity of orbit due to trauma or surgery
743.10 Unspecified microphthalmos ▽
743.11 Simple microphthalmos
743.63 Other specified congenital anomaly of eyelid
756.0 Congenital anomalies of skull and face bones
802.4 Malar and maxillary bones, closed fracture
802.5 Malar and maxillary bones, open fracture
802.8 Other facial bones, closed fracture
802.9 Other facial bones, open fracture
870.8 Other specified open wound of ocular adnexa
906.0 Late effect of open wound of head, neck, and trunk
V50.1 Other plastic surgery for unacceptable cosmetic appearance

ICD-9-CM Procedural

08.59 Other adjustment of lid position

21295-21296

21295 Reduction of masseter muscle and bone (eg, for treatment of benign masseteric hypertrophy); extraoral approach
21296 intraoral approach

ICD-9-CM Diagnostic

728.9 Unspecified disorder of muscle, ligament, and fascia ▽

ICD-9-CM Procedural

76.64 Other orthognathic surgery on mandible
83.49 Other excision of soft tissue

21310-21320

21310 Closed treatment of nasal bone fracture without manipulation
21315 Closed treatment of nasal bone fracture; without stabilization
21320 with stabilization

ICD-9-CM Diagnostic

802.0 Nasal bones, closed fracture

ICD-9-CM Procedural

21.71 Closed reduction of nasal fracture
21.99 Other operations on nose
93.54 Application of splint

HCPCS Level II Supplies & Services

A4305 Disposable drug delivery system, flow rate of 50 ml or greater per hour

21325

21325 Open treatment of nasal fracture; uncomplicated

ICD-9-CM Diagnostic

733.81 Malunion of fracture
733.82 Nonunion of fracture
802.0 Nasal bones, closed fracture
802.1 Nasal bones, open fracture

ICD-9-CM Procedural

21.72 Open reduction of nasal fracture

HCPCS Level II Supplies & Services

A4570 Splint

21330

21330 Open treatment of nasal fracture; complicated, with internal and/or external skeletal fixation

ICD-9-CM Diagnostic

733.81 Malunion of fracture

733.82 Nonunion of fracture

802.0 Nasal bones, closed fracture

802.1 Nasal bones, open fracture

ICD-9-CM Procedural

21.72 Open reduction of nasal fracture

21335

21335 Open treatment of nasal fracture; with concomitant open treatment of fractured septum

ICD-9-CM Diagnostic

733.81 Malunion of fracture

733.82 Nonunion of fracture

802.0 Nasal bones, closed fracture

802.1 Nasal bones, open fracture

ICD-9-CM Procedural

21.5 Submucous resection of nasal septum

21.72 Open reduction of nasal fracture

21.88 Other septoplasty

21336

21336 Open treatment of nasal septal fracture, with or without stabilization

ICD-9-CM Diagnostic

470 Deviated nasal septum

802.0 Nasal bones, closed fracture

802.1 Nasal bones, open fracture

ICD-9-CM Procedural

21.5 Submucous resection of nasal septum

21.72 Open reduction of nasal fracture

21.88 Other septoplasty

21337

21337 Closed treatment of nasal septal fracture, with or without stabilization

ICD-9-CM Diagnostic

470 Deviated nasal septum

802.0 Nasal bones, closed fracture

ICD-9-CM Procedural

21.71 Closed reduction of nasal fracture

21338-21339

21338 Open treatment of nasoethmoid fracture; without external fixation

21339 with external fixation

ICD-9-CM Diagnostic

801.00 Closed fracture of base of skull without mention of intracranial injury, unspecified state of consciousness

801.01 Closed fracture of base of skull without mention of intracranial injury, no loss of consciousness

801.02 Closed fracture of base of skull without mention of intracranial injury, brief (less than one hour) loss of consciousness

801.03 Closed fracture of base of skull without mention of intracranial injury, moderate (1-24 hours) loss of consciousness

801.04 Closed fracture of base of skull without mention of intracranial injury, prolonged (more than 24 hours) loss of consciousness and return to pre-existing conscious level

801.05 Closed fracture of base of skull without mention of intracranial injury, prolonged (more than 24 hours) loss of consciousness, without return to pre-existing conscious level

801.06 Closed fracture of base of skull without mention of intracranial injury, loss of consciousness of unspecified duration

801.09 Closed fracture of base of skull without mention of intracranial injury, unspecified concussion

801.10 Closed fracture of base of skull with cerebral laceration and contusion, unspecified state of consciousness

801.11 Closed fracture of base of skull with cerebral laceration and contusion, no loss of consciousness

801.12 Closed fracture of base of skull with cerebral laceration and contusion, brief (less than one hour) loss of consciousness

801.13 Closed fracture of base of skull with cerebral laceration and contusion, moderate (1-24 hours) loss of consciousness

801.14 Closed fracture of base of skull with cerebral laceration and contusion, prolonged (more than 24 hours) loss of consciousness and return to pre-existing conscious level

801.15 Closed fracture of base of skull with cerebral laceration and contusion, prolonged (more than 24 hours) loss of consciousness, without return to pre-existing conscious level

801.16 Closed fracture of base of skull with cerebral laceration and contusion, loss of consciousness of unspecified duration

801.19 Closed fracture of base of skull with cerebral laceration and contusion, unspecified concussion

801.20 Closed fracture of base of skull with subarachnoid, subdural, and extradural hemorrhage, unspecified state of consciousness

801.21 Closed fracture of base of skull with subarachnoid, subdural, and extradural hemorrhage, no loss of consciousness

801.22 Closed fracture of base of skull with subarachnoid, subdural, and extradural hemorrhage, brief (less than one hour) loss of consciousness

801.23 Closed fracture of base of skull with subarachnoid, subdural, and extradural hemorrhage, moderate (1-24 hours) loss of consciousness

801.24 Closed fracture of base of skull with subarachnoid, subdural, and extradural hemorrhage, prolonged (more than 24 hours) loss of consciousness and return to pre-existing conscious level

801.25 Closed fracture of base of skull with subarachnoid, subdural, and extradural hemorrhage, prolonged (more than 24 hours) loss of consciousness, without return to pre-existing conscious level

801.26 Closed fracture of base of skull with subarachnoid, subdural, and extradural hemorrhage, loss of consciousness of unspecified duration

801.29 Closed fracture of base of skull with subarachnoid, subdural, and extradural hemorrhage, unspecified concussion

801.30 Closed fracture of base of skull with other and unspecified intracranial hemorrhage, unspecified state of consciousness

801.31 Closed fracture of base of skull with other and unspecified intracranial hemorrhage, no loss of consciousness

801.32 Closed fracture of base of skull with other and unspecified intracranial hemorrhage, brief (less than one hour) loss of consciousness

801.33 Closed fracture of base of skull with other and unspecified intracranial hemorrhage, moderate (1-24 hours) loss of consciousness

801.34 Closed fracture of base of skull with other and unspecified intracranial hemorrhage, prolonged (more than 24 hours) loss of consciousness and return to pre-existing conscious level

801.35 Closed fracture of base of skull with other and unspecified intracranial hemorrhage, prolonged (more than 24 hours) loss of consciousness, without return to pre-existing conscious level

801.36 Closed fracture of base of skull with other and unspecified intracranial hemorrhage, loss of consciousness of unspecified duration

801.39 Closed fracture of base of skull with other and unspecified intracranial hemorrhage, unspecified concussion

801.40 Closed fracture of base of skull with intracranial injury of other and unspecified nature, unspecified state of consciousness

801.41 Closed fracture of base of skull with intracranial injury of other and unspecified nature, no loss of consciousness

801.42 Closed fracture of base of skull with intracranial injury of other and unspecified nature, brief (less than one hour) loss of consciousness

801.43 Closed fracture of base of skull with intracranial injury of other and unspecified nature, moderate (1-24 hours) loss of consciousness

801.44 Closed fracture of base of skull with intracranial injury of other and unspecified nature, prolonged (more than 24 hours) loss of consciousness and return to pre-existing conscious level

801.45 Closed fracture of base of skull with intracranial injury of other and unspecified nature, prolonged (more than 24 hours) loss of consciousness, without return to pre-existing conscious level

801.46 Closed fracture of base of skull with intracranial injury of other and unspecified nature, loss of consciousness of unspecified duration

801.49 Closed fracture of base of skull with intracranial injury of other and unspecified nature, unspecified concussion

801.50 Open fracture of base of skull without mention of intracranial injury, unspecified state of consciousness

801.51 Open fracture of base of skull without mention of intracranial injury, no loss of consciousness

801.52 Open fracture of base of skull without mention of intracranial injury, brief (less than one hour) loss of consciousness

801.53 Open fracture of base of skull without mention of intracranial injury, moderate (1-24 hours) loss of consciousness

801.54 Open fracture of base of skull without mention of intracranial injury, prolonged (more than 24 hours) loss of consciousness and return to pre-existing conscious level

801.55 Open fracture of base of skull without mention of intracranial injury, prolonged (more than 24 hours) loss of consciousness, without return to pre-existing conscious level

801.56 Open fracture of base of skull without mention of intracranial injury, loss of consciousness of unspecified duration

801.59 Open fracture of base of skull without mention of intracranial injury, unspecified concussion

801.60 Open fracture of base of skull with cerebral laceration and contusion, unspecified state of consciousness

801.61 Open fracture of base of skull with cerebral laceration and contusion, no loss of consciousness

801.62 Open fracture of base of skull with cerebral laceration and contusion, brief (less than one hour) loss of consciousness

801.63 Open fracture of base of skull with cerebral laceration and contusion, moderate (1-24 hours) loss of consciousness

801.64 Open fracture of base of skull with cerebral laceration and contusion, prolonged (more than 24 hours) loss of consciousness and return to pre-existing conscious level

801.65 Open fracture of base of skull with cerebral laceration and contusion, prolonged (more than 24 hours) loss of consciousness, without return to pre-existing conscious level

801.66 Open fracture of base of skull with cerebral laceration and contusion, loss of consciousness of unspecified duration

801.69 Open fracture of base of skull with cerebral laceration and contusion, unspecified concussion

801.70 Open fracture of base of skull with subarachnoid, subdural, and extradural hemorrhage, unspecified state of consciousness

801.71 Open fracture of base of skull with subarachnoid, subdural, and extradural hemorrhage, no loss of consciousness

801.72 Open fracture of base of skull with subarachnoid, subdural, and extradural hemorrhage, brief (less than one hour) loss of consciousness

801.73 Open fracture of base of skull with subarachnoid, subdural, and extradural hemorrhage, moderate (1-24 hours) loss of consciousness

801.74 Open fracture of base of skull with subarachnoid, subdural, and extradural hemorrhage, prolonged (more than 24 hours) loss of consciousness and return to pre-existing conscious level

801.75 Open fracture of base of skull with subarachnoid, subdural, and extradural hemorrhage, prolonged (more than 24 hours) loss of consciousness, without return to pre-existing conscious level

801.76 Open fracture of base of skull with subarachnoid, subdural, and extradural hemorrhage, loss of consciousness of unspecified duration

801.79 Open fracture of base of skull with subarachnoid, subdural, and extradural hemorrhage, unspecified concussion

801.80 Open fracture of base of skull with other and unspecified intracranial hemorrhage, unspecified state of consciousness

801.81 Open fracture of base of skull with other and unspecified intracranial hemorrhage, no loss of consciousness

801.82 Open fracture of base of skull with other and unspecified intracranial hemorrhage, brief (less than one hour) loss of consciousness

801.83 Open fracture of base of skull with other and unspecified intracranial hemorrhage, moderate (1-24 hours) loss of consciousness

801.84 Open fracture of base of skull with other and unspecified intracranial hemorrhage, prolonged (more than 24 hours) loss of consciousness and return to pre-existing conscious level

801.85 Open fracture of base of skull with other and unspecified intracranial hemorrhage, prolonged (more than 24 hours) loss of consciousness, without return to pre-existing conscious level

801.86 Open fracture of base of skull with other and unspecified intracranial hemorrhage, loss of consciousness of unspecified duration

801.89 Open fracture of base of skull with other and unspecified intracranial hemorrhage, unspecified concussion

801.90 Open fracture of base of skull with intracranial injury of other and unspecified nature, unspecified state of consciousness

801.91 Open fracture of base of skull with intracranial injury of other and unspecified nature, no loss of consciousness

801.92 Open fracture of base of skull with intracranial injury of other and unspecified nature, brief (less than one hour) loss of consciousness

801.93 Open fracture of base of skull with intracranial injury of other and unspecified nature, moderate (1-24 hours) loss of consciousness

801.94 Open fracture of base of skull with intracranial injury of other and unspecified nature, prolonged (more than 24 hours) loss of consciousness and return to pre-existing conscious level

801.95 Open fracture of base of skull with intracranial injury of other and unspecified nature, prolonged (more than 24 hours) loss of consciousness, without return to pre-existing conscious level

801.96 Open fracture of base of skull with intracranial injury of other and unspecified nature, loss of consciousness of unspecified duration

801.99 Open fracture of base of skull with intracranial injury of other and unspecified nature, unspecified concussion

802.0 Nasal bones, closed fracture

802.1 Nasal bones, open fracture

ICD-9-CM Procedural

21.72 Open reduction of nasal fracture

21.99 Other operations on nose

22.79 Other repair of nasal sinus

76.70 Reduction of facial fracture, not otherwise specified

21340

21340 Percutaneous treatment of nasoethmoid complex fracture, with splint, wire or headcap fixation, including repair of canthal ligaments and/or the nasolacrimal apparatus

ICD-9-CM Diagnostic

733.82 Nonunion of fracture

801.00 Closed fracture of base of skull without mention of intracranial injury, unspecified state of consciousness ▽

801.01 Closed fracture of base of skull without mention of intracranial injury, no loss of consciousness

801.02 Closed fracture of base of skull without mention of intracranial injury, brief (less than one hour) loss of consciousness

801.03 Closed fracture of base of skull without mention of intracranial injury, moderate (1-24 hours) loss of consciousness

801.04 Closed fracture of base of skull without mention of intracranial injury, prolonged (more than 24 hours) loss of consciousness and return to pre-existing conscious level

801.05 Closed fracture of base of skull without mention of intracranial injury, prolonged (more than 24 hours) loss of consciousness, without return to pre-existing conscious level

801.06 Closed fracture of base of skull without mention of intracranial injury, loss of consciousness of unspecified duration ▽

801.09 Closed fracture of base of skull without mention of intracranial injury, unspecified concussion ▽

801.10 Closed fracture of base of skull with cerebral laceration and contusion, unspecified state of consciousness ▽

801.11 Closed fracture of base of skull with cerebral laceration and contusion, no loss of consciousness

801.12 Closed fracture of base of skull with cerebral laceration and contusion, brief (less than one hour) loss of consciousness

801.13 Closed fracture of base of skull with cerebral laceration and contusion, moderate (1-24 hours) loss of consciousness

801.14 Closed fracture of base of skull with cerebral laceration and contusion, prolonged (more than 24 hours) loss of consciousness and return to pre-existing conscious level

801.15 Closed fracture of base of skull with cerebral laceration and contusion, prolonged (more than 24 hours) loss of consciousness, without return to pre-existing conscious level

801.16 Closed fracture of base of skull with cerebral laceration and contusion, loss of consciousness of unspecified duration ▽

801.19 Closed fracture of base of skull with cerebral laceration and contusion, unspecified concussion ▽

801.20 Closed fracture of base of skull with subarachnoid, subdural, and extradural hemorrhage, unspecified state of consciousness ▽

801.21 Closed fracture of base of skull with subarachnoid, subdural, and extradural hemorrhage, no loss of consciousness

801.22 Closed fracture of base of skull with subarachnoid, subdural, and extradural hemorrhage, brief (less than one hour) loss of consciousness

801.23 Closed fracture of base of skull with subarachnoid, subdural, and extradural hemorrhage, moderate (1-24 hours) loss of consciousness

801.24 Closed fracture of base of skull with subarachnoid, subdural, and extradural hemorrhage, prolonged (more than 24 hours) loss of consciousness and return to pre-existing conscious level

801.25 Closed fracture of base of skull with subarachnoid, subdural, and extradural hemorrhage, prolonged (more than 24 hours) loss of consciousness, without return to pre-existing conscious level

801.26 Closed fracture of base of skull with subarachnoid, subdural, and extradural hemorrhage, loss of consciousness of unspecified duration ▽

801.29 Closed fracture of base of skull with subarachnoid, subdural, and extradural hemorrhage, unspecified concussion ▽

801.30 Closed fracture of base of skull with other and unspecified intracranial hemorrhage, unspecified state of consciousness ▽

801.31 Closed fracture of base of skull with other and unspecified intracranial hemorrhage, no loss of consciousness ▽

801.32 Closed fracture of base of skull with other and unspecified intracranial hemorrhage, brief (less than one hour) loss of consciousness ▽

801.33 Closed fracture of base of skull with other and unspecified intracranial hemorrhage, moderate (1-24 hours) loss of consciousness ▽

801.34 Closed fracture of base of skull with other and unspecified intracranial hemorrhage, prolonged (more than 24 hours) loss of consciousness and return to pre-existing conscious level ▽

801.35 Closed fracture of base of skull with other and unspecified intracranial hemorrhage, prolonged (more than 24 hours) loss of consciousness, without return to pre-existing conscious level ▽

801.36 Closed fracture of base of skull with other and unspecified intracranial hemorrhage, loss of consciousness of unspecified duration ▽

801.39 Closed fracture of base of skull with other and unspecified intracranial hemorrhage, unspecified concussion ▽

801.40 Closed fracture of base of skull with intracranial injury of other and unspecified nature, unspecified state of consciousness ▽

801.41 Closed fracture of base of skull with intracranial injury of other and unspecified nature, no loss of consciousness ▽

801.42 Closed fracture of base of skull with intracranial injury of other and unspecified nature, brief (less than one hour) loss of consciousness ▽

801.43 Closed fracture of base of skull with intracranial injury of other and unspecified nature, moderate (1-24 hours) loss of consciousness ▽

801.44 Closed fracture of base of skull with intracranial injury of other and unspecified nature, prolonged (more than 24 hours) loss of consciousness and return to pre-existing conscious level ▽

801.45 Closed fracture of base of skull with intracranial injury of other and unspecified nature, prolonged (more than 24 hours) loss of consciousness, without return to pre-existing conscious level ▽

801.46 Closed fracture of base of skull with intracranial injury of other and unspecified nature, loss of consciousness of unspecified duration ▽

801.49 Closed fracture of base of skull with intracranial injury of other and unspecified nature, unspecified concussion ▽

801.50 Open fracture of base of skull without mention of intracranial injury, unspecified state of consciousness ▽

801.51 Open fracture of base of skull without mention of intracranial injury, no loss of consciousness

801.52 Open fracture of base of skull without mention of intracranial injury, brief (less than one hour) loss of consciousness

801.53 Open fracture of base of skull without mention of intracranial injury, moderate (1-24 hours) loss of consciousness

801.54 Open fracture of base of skull without mention of intracranial injury, prolonged (more than 24 hours) loss of consciousness and return to pre-existing conscious level

801.55 Open fracture of base of skull without mention of intracranial injury, prolonged (more than 24 hours) loss of consciousness, without return to pre-existing conscious level

801.56 Open fracture of base of skull without mention of intracranial injury, loss of consciousness of unspecified duration ▽

801.59 Open fracture of base of skull without mention of intracranial injury, unspecified concussion ▽

801.60 Open fracture of base of skull with cerebral laceration and contusion, unspecified state of consciousness ▽

801.61 Open fracture of base of skull with cerebral laceration and contusion, no loss of consciousness

801.62 Open fracture of base of skull with cerebral laceration and contusion, brief (less than one hour) loss of consciousness

801.63 Open fracture of base of skull with cerebral laceration and contusion, moderate (1-24 hours) loss of consciousness

801.64 Open fracture of base of skull with cerebral laceration and contusion, prolonged (more than 24 hours) loss of consciousness and return to pre-existing conscious level

801.65 Open fracture of base of skull with cerebral laceration and contusion, prolonged (more than 24 hours) loss of consciousness, without return to pre-existing conscious level

801.66 Open fracture of base of skull with cerebral laceration and contusion, loss of consciousness of unspecified duration ▽
801.69 Open fracture of base of skull with cerebral laceration and contusion, unspecified concussion ▽
801.70 Open fracture of base of skull with subarachnoid, subdural, and extradural hemorrhage, unspecified state of consciousness ▽
801.71 Open fracture of base of skull with subarachnoid, subdural, and extradural hemorrhage, no loss of consciousness
801.72 Open fracture of base of skull with subarachnoid, subdural, and extradural hemorrhage, brief (less than one hour) loss of consciousness
801.73 Open fracture of base of skull with subarachnoid, subdural, and extradural hemorrhage, moderate (1-24 hours) loss of consciousness
801.74 Open fracture of base of skull with subarachnoid, subdural, and extradural hemorrhage, prolonged (more than 24 hours) loss of consciousness and return to pre-existing conscious level
801.75 Open fracture of base of skull with subarachnoid, subdural, and extradural hemorrhage, prolonged (more than 24 hours) loss of consciousness, without return to pre-existing conscious level
801.76 Open fracture of base of skull with subarachnoid, subdural, and extradural hemorrhage, loss of consciousness of unspecified duration ▽
801.79 Open fracture of base of skull with subarachnoid, subdural, and extradural hemorrhage, unspecified concussion ▽
801.80 Open fracture of base of skull with other and unspecified intracranial hemorrhage, unspecified state of consciousness ▽
801.81 Open fracture of base of skull with other and unspecified intracranial hemorrhage, no loss of consciousness ▽
801.82 Open fracture of base of skull with other and unspecified intracranial hemorrhage, brief (less than one hour) loss of consciousness ▽
801.83 Open fracture of base of skull with other and unspecified intracranial hemorrhage, moderate (1-24 hours) loss of consciousness ▽
801.84 Open fracture of base of skull with other and unspecified intracranial hemorrhage, prolonged (more than 24 hours) loss of consciousness and return to pre-existing conscious level ▽
801.85 Open fracture of base of skull with other and unspecified intracranial hemorrhage, prolonged (more than 24 hours) loss of consciousness, without return to pre-existing conscious level ▽
801.86 Open fracture of base of skull with other and unspecified intracranial hemorrhage, loss of consciousness of unspecified duration ▽
801.89 Open fracture of base of skull with other and unspecified intracranial hemorrhage, unspecified concussion ▽
801.90 Open fracture of base of skull with intracranial injury of other and unspecified nature, unspecified state of consciousness ▽
801.91 Open fracture of base of skull with intracranial injury of other and unspecified nature, no loss of consciousness ▽
801.92 Open fracture of base of skull with intracranial injury of other and unspecified nature, brief (less than one hour) loss of consciousness ▽
801.93 Open fracture of base of skull with intracranial injury of other and unspecified nature, moderate (1-24 hours) loss of consciousness ▽
801.94 Open fracture of base of skull with intracranial injury of other and unspecified nature, prolonged (more than 24 hours) loss of consciousness and return to pre-existing conscious level ▽
801.95 Open fracture of base of skull with intracranial injury of other and unspecified nature, prolonged (more than 24 hours) loss of consciousness, without return to pre-existing conscious level ▽
801.96 Open fracture of base of skull with intracranial injury of other and unspecified nature, loss of consciousness of unspecified duration ▽
801.99 Open fracture of base of skull with intracranial injury of other and unspecified nature, unspecified concussion ▽
802.0 Nasal bones, closed fracture
802.1 Nasal bones, open fracture
802.8 Other facial bones, closed fracture
802.9 Other facial bones, open fracture
870.2 Laceration of eyelid involving lacrimal passages
870.8 Other specified open wound of ocular adnexa

ICD-9-CM Procedural

21.71 Closed reduction of nasal fracture
76.78 Other closed reduction of facial fracture

21343

21343 Open treatment of depressed frontal sinus fracture

ICD-9-CM Diagnostic

801.00 Closed fracture of base of skull without mention of intracranial injury, unspecified state of consciousness ▽
801.01 Closed fracture of base of skull without mention of intracranial injury, no loss of consciousness
801.02 Closed fracture of base of skull without mention of intracranial injury, brief (less than one hour) loss of consciousness
801.03 Closed fracture of base of skull without mention of intracranial injury, moderate (1-24 hours) loss of consciousness
801.04 Closed fracture of base of skull without mention of intracranial injury, prolonged (more than 24 hours) loss of consciousness and return to pre-existing conscious level
801.05 Closed fracture of base of skull without mention of intracranial injury, prolonged (more than 24 hours) loss of consciousness, without return to pre-existing conscious level
801.06 Closed fracture of base of skull without mention of intracranial injury, loss of consciousness of unspecified duration ▽
801.09 Closed fracture of base of skull without mention of intracranial injury, unspecified concussion ▽
801.10 Closed fracture of base of skull with cerebral laceration and contusion, unspecified state of consciousness ▽
801.11 Closed fracture of base of skull with cerebral laceration and contusion, no loss of consciousness
801.12 Closed fracture of base of skull with cerebral laceration and contusion, brief (less than one hour) loss of consciousness
801.13 Closed fracture of base of skull with cerebral laceration and contusion, moderate (1-24 hours) loss of consciousness
801.14 Closed fracture of base of skull with cerebral laceration and contusion, prolonged (more than 24 hours) loss of consciousness and return to pre-existing conscious level
801.15 Closed fracture of base of skull with cerebral laceration and contusion, prolonged (more than 24 hours) loss of consciousness, without return to pre-existing conscious level
801.16 Closed fracture of base of skull with cerebral laceration and contusion, loss of consciousness of unspecified duration ▽
801.19 Closed fracture of base of skull with cerebral laceration and contusion, unspecified concussion ▽
801.20 Closed fracture of base of skull with subarachnoid, subdural, and extradural hemorrhage, unspecified state of consciousness ▽
801.21 Closed fracture of base of skull with subarachnoid, subdural, and extradural hemorrhage, no loss of consciousness
801.22 Closed fracture of base of skull with subarachnoid, subdural, and extradural hemorrhage, brief (less than one hour) loss of consciousness
801.23 Closed fracture of base of skull with subarachnoid, subdural, and extradural hemorrhage, moderate (1-24 hours) loss of consciousness
801.24 Closed fracture of base of skull with subarachnoid, subdural, and extradural hemorrhage, prolonged (more than 24 hours) loss of consciousness and return to pre-existing conscious level
801.25 Closed fracture of base of skull with subarachnoid, subdural, and extradural hemorrhage, prolonged (more than 24 hours) loss of consciousness, without return to pre-existing conscious level
801.26 Closed fracture of base of skull with subarachnoid, subdural, and extradural hemorrhage, loss of consciousness of unspecified duration ▽

801.29 Closed fracture of base of skull with subarachnoid, subdural, and extradural hemorrhage, unspecified concussion
801.30 Closed fracture of base of skull with other and unspecified intracranial hemorrhage, unspecified state of consciousness
801.31 Closed fracture of base of skull with other and unspecified intracranial hemorrhage, no loss of consciousness
801.32 Closed fracture of base of skull with other and unspecified intracranial hemorrhage, brief (less than one hour) loss of consciousness
801.33 Closed fracture of base of skull with other and unspecified intracranial hemorrhage, moderate (1-24 hours) loss of consciousness
801.34 Closed fracture of base of skull with other and unspecified intracranial hemorrhage, prolonged (more than 24 hours) loss of consciousness and return to pre-existing conscious level
801.35 Closed fracture of base of skull with other and unspecified intracranial hemorrhage, prolonged (more than 24 hours) loss of consciousness, without return to pre-existing conscious level
801.36 Closed fracture of base of skull with other and unspecified intracranial hemorrhage, loss of consciousness of unspecified duration
801.39 Closed fracture of base of skull with other and unspecified intracranial hemorrhage, unspecified concussion
801.40 Closed fracture of base of skull with intracranial injury of other and unspecified nature, unspecified state of consciousness
801.41 Closed fracture of base of skull with intracranial injury of other and unspecified nature, no loss of consciousness
801.42 Closed fracture of base of skull with intracranial injury of other and unspecified nature, brief (less than one hour) loss of consciousness
801.43 Closed fracture of base of skull with intracranial injury of other and unspecified nature, moderate (1-24 hours) loss of consciousness
801.44 Closed fracture of base of skull with intracranial injury of other and unspecified nature, prolonged (more than 24 hours) loss of consciousness and return to pre-existing conscious level
801.45 Closed fracture of base of skull with intracranial injury of other and unspecified nature, prolonged (more than 24 hours) loss of consciousness, without return to pre-existing conscious level
801.46 Closed fracture of base of skull with intracranial injury of other and unspecified nature, loss of consciousness of unspecified duration
801.49 Closed fracture of base of skull with intracranial injury of other and unspecified nature, unspecified concussion
801.50 Open fracture of base of skull without mention of intracranial injury, unspecified state of consciousness
801.51 Open fracture of base of skull without mention of intracranial injury, no loss of consciousness
801.52 Open fracture of base of skull without mention of intracranial injury, brief (less than one hour) loss of consciousness
801.53 Open fracture of base of skull without mention of intracranial injury, moderate (1-24 hours) loss of consciousness
801.54 Open fracture of base of skull without mention of intracranial injury, prolonged (more than 24 hours) loss of consciousness and return to pre-existing conscious level
801.55 Open fracture of base of skull without mention of intracranial injury, prolonged (more than 24 hours) loss of consciousness, without return to pre-existing conscious level
801.56 Open fracture of base of skull without mention of intracranial injury, loss of consciousness of unspecified duration
801.59 Open fracture of base of skull without mention of intracranial injury, unspecified concussion
801.60 Open fracture of base of skull with cerebral laceration and contusion, unspecified state of consciousness
801.61 Open fracture of base of skull with cerebral laceration and contusion, no loss of consciousness
801.62 Open fracture of base of skull with cerebral laceration and contusion, brief (less than one hour) loss of consciousness
801.63 Open fracture of base of skull with cerebral laceration and contusion, moderate (1-24 hours) loss of consciousness
801.64 Open fracture of base of skull with cerebral laceration and contusion, prolonged (more than 24 hours) loss of consciousness and return to pre-existing conscious level
801.65 Open fracture of base of skull with cerebral laceration and contusion, prolonged (more than 24 hours) loss of consciousness, without return to pre-existing conscious level
801.66 Open fracture of base of skull with cerebral laceration and contusion, loss of consciousness of unspecified duration
801.69 Open fracture of base of skull with cerebral laceration and contusion, unspecified concussion
801.70 Open fracture of base of skull with subarachnoid, subdural, and extradural hemorrhage, unspecified state of consciousness
801.71 Open fracture of base of skull with subarachnoid, subdural, and extradural hemorrhage, no loss of consciousness
801.72 Open fracture of base of skull with subarachnoid, subdural, and extradural hemorrhage, brief (less than one hour) loss of consciousness
801.73 Open fracture of base of skull with subarachnoid, subdural, and extradural hemorrhage, moderate (1-24 hours) loss of consciousness
801.74 Open fracture of base of skull with subarachnoid, subdural, and extradural hemorrhage, prolonged (more than 24 hours) loss of consciousness and return to pre-existing conscious level
801.75 Open fracture of base of skull with subarachnoid, subdural, and extradural hemorrhage, prolonged (more than 24 hours) loss of consciousness, without return to pre-existing conscious level
801.76 Open fracture of base of skull with subarachnoid, subdural, and extradural hemorrhage, loss of consciousness of unspecified duration
801.79 Open fracture of base of skull with subarachnoid, subdural, and extradural hemorrhage, unspecified concussion
801.80 Open fracture of base of skull with other and unspecified intracranial hemorrhage, unspecified state of consciousness
801.81 Open fracture of base of skull with other and unspecified intracranial hemorrhage, no loss of consciousness
801.82 Open fracture of base of skull with other and unspecified intracranial hemorrhage, brief (less than one hour) loss of consciousness
801.83 Open fracture of base of skull with other and unspecified intracranial hemorrhage, moderate (1-24 hours) loss of consciousness
801.84 Open fracture of base of skull with other and unspecified intracranial hemorrhage, prolonged (more than 24 hours) loss of consciousness and return to pre-existing conscious level
801.85 Open fracture of base of skull with other and unspecified intracranial hemorrhage, prolonged (more than 24 hours) loss of consciousness, without return to pre-existing conscious level
801.86 Open fracture of base of skull with other and unspecified intracranial hemorrhage, loss of consciousness of unspecified duration
801.89 Open fracture of base of skull with other and unspecified intracranial hemorrhage, unspecified concussion
801.90 Open fracture of base of skull with intracranial injury of other and unspecified nature, unspecified state of consciousness
801.91 Open fracture of base of skull with intracranial injury of other and unspecified nature, no loss of consciousness
801.92 Open fracture of base of skull with intracranial injury of other and unspecified nature, brief (less than one hour) loss of consciousness
801.93 Open fracture of base of skull with intracranial injury of other and unspecified nature, moderate (1-24 hours) loss of consciousness
801.94 Open fracture of base of skull with intracranial injury of other and unspecified nature, prolonged (more than 24 hours) loss of consciousness and return to pre-existing conscious level
801.95 Open fracture of base of skull with intracranial injury of other and unspecified nature, prolonged (more than 24 hours) loss of consciousness, without return to pre-existing conscious level

801.96 Open fracture of base of skull with intracranial injury of other and unspecified nature, loss of consciousness of unspecified duration

801.99 Open fracture of base of skull with intracranial injury of other and unspecified nature, unspecified concussion

ICD-9-CM Procedural

22.41 Frontal sinusotomy

22.79 Other repair of nasal sinus

76.70 Reduction of facial fracture, not otherwise specified

21344

21344 Open treatment of complicated (eg, comminuted or involving posterior wall) frontal sinus fracture, via coronal or multiple approaches

ICD-9-CM Diagnostic

801.00 Closed fracture of base of skull without mention of intracranial injury, unspecified state of consciousness

801.01 Closed fracture of base of skull without mention of intracranial injury, no loss of consciousness

801.02 Closed fracture of base of skull without mention of intracranial injury, brief (less than one hour) loss of consciousness

801.03 Closed fracture of base of skull without mention of intracranial injury, moderate (1-24 hours) loss of consciousness

801.04 Closed fracture of base of skull without mention of intracranial injury, prolonged (more than 24 hours) loss of consciousness and return to pre-existing conscious level

801.05 Closed fracture of base of skull without mention of intracranial injury, prolonged (more than 24 hours) loss of consciousness, without return to pre-existing conscious level

801.06 Closed fracture of base of skull without mention of intracranial injury, loss of consciousness of unspecified duration

801.09 Closed fracture of base of skull without mention of intracranial injury, unspecified concussion

801.10 Closed fracture of base of skull with cerebral laceration and contusion, unspecified state of consciousness

801.11 Closed fracture of base of skull with cerebral laceration and contusion, no loss of consciousness

801.12 Closed fracture of base of skull with cerebral laceration and contusion, brief (less than one hour) loss of consciousness

801.13 Closed fracture of base of skull with cerebral laceration and contusion, moderate (1-24 hours) loss of consciousness

801.14 Closed fracture of base of skull with cerebral laceration and contusion, prolonged (more than 24 hours) loss of consciousness and return to pre-existing conscious level

801.15 Closed fracture of base of skull with cerebral laceration and contusion, prolonged (more than 24 hours) loss of consciousness, without return to pre-existing conscious level

801.16 Closed fracture of base of skull with cerebral laceration and contusion, loss of consciousness of unspecified duration

801.19 Closed fracture of base of skull with cerebral laceration and contusion, unspecified concussion

801.20 Closed fracture of base of skull with subarachnoid, subdural, and extradural hemorrhage, unspecified state of consciousness

801.21 Closed fracture of base of skull with subarachnoid, subdural, and extradural hemorrhage, no loss of consciousness

801.22 Closed fracture of base of skull with subarachnoid, subdural, and extradural hemorrhage, brief (less than one hour) loss of consciousness

801.23 Closed fracture of base of skull with subarachnoid, subdural, and extradural hemorrhage, moderate (1-24 hours) loss of consciousness

801.24 Closed fracture of base of skull with subarachnoid, subdural, and extradural hemorrhage, prolonged (more than 24 hours) loss of consciousness and return to pre-existing conscious level

801.25 Closed fracture of base of skull with subarachnoid, subdural, and extradural hemorrhage, prolonged (more than 24 hours) loss of consciousness, without return to pre-existing conscious level

801.26 Closed fracture of base of skull with subarachnoid, subdural, and extradural hemorrhage, loss of consciousness of unspecified duration

801.29 Closed fracture of base of skull with subarachnoid, subdural, and extradural hemorrhage, unspecified concussion

801.30 Closed fracture of base of skull with other and unspecified intracranial hemorrhage, unspecified state of consciousness

801.31 Closed fracture of base of skull with other and unspecified intracranial hemorrhage, no loss of consciousness

801.32 Closed fracture of base of skull with other and unspecified intracranial hemorrhage, brief (less than one hour) loss of consciousness

801.33 Closed fracture of base of skull with other and unspecified intracranial hemorrhage, moderate (1-24 hours) loss of consciousness

801.34 Closed fracture of base of skull with other and unspecified intracranial hemorrhage, prolonged (more than 24 hours) loss of consciousness and return to pre-existing conscious level

801.35 Closed fracture of base of skull with other and unspecified intracranial hemorrhage, prolonged (more than 24 hours) loss of consciousness, without return to pre-existing conscious level

801.36 Closed fracture of base of skull with other and unspecified intracranial hemorrhage, loss of consciousness of unspecified duration

801.39 Closed fracture of base of skull with other and unspecified intracranial hemorrhage, unspecified concussion

801.40 Closed fracture of base of skull with intracranial injury of other and unspecified nature, unspecified state of consciousness

801.41 Closed fracture of base of skull with intracranial injury of other and unspecified nature, no loss of consciousness

801.42 Closed fracture of base of skull with intracranial injury of other and unspecified nature, brief (less than one hour) loss of consciousness

801.43 Closed fracture of base of skull with intracranial injury of other and unspecified nature, moderate (1-24 hours) loss of consciousness

801.44 Closed fracture of base of skull with intracranial injury of other and unspecified nature, prolonged (more than 24 hours) loss of consciousness and return to pre-existing conscious level

801.45 Closed fracture of base of skull with intracranial injury of other and unspecified nature, prolonged (more than 24 hours) loss of consciousness, without return to pre-existing conscious level

801.46 Closed fracture of base of skull with intracranial injury of other and unspecified nature, loss of consciousness of unspecified duration

801.49 Closed fracture of base of skull with intracranial injury of other and unspecified nature, unspecified concussion

801.50 Open fracture of base of skull without mention of intracranial injury, unspecified state of consciousness

801.51 Open fracture of base of skull without mention of intracranial injury, no loss of consciousness

801.52 Open fracture of base of skull without mention of intracranial injury, brief (less than one hour) loss of consciousness

801.53 Open fracture of base of skull without mention of intracranial injury, moderate (1-24 hours) loss of consciousness

801.54 Open fracture of base of skull without mention of intracranial injury, prolonged (more than 24 hours) loss of consciousness and return to pre-existing conscious level

801.55 Open fracture of base of skull without mention of intracranial injury, prolonged (more than 24 hours) loss of consciousness, without return to pre-existing conscious level

801.56 Open fracture of base of skull without mention of intracranial injury, loss of consciousness of unspecified duration

801.59 Open fracture of base of skull without mention of intracranial injury, unspecified concussion

801.60 Open fracture of base of skull with cerebral laceration and contusion, unspecified state of consciousness

801.61 Open fracture of base of skull with cerebral laceration and contusion, no loss of consciousness
801.62 Open fracture of base of skull with cerebral laceration and contusion, brief (less than one hour) loss of consciousness
801.63 Open fracture of base of skull with cerebral laceration and contusion, moderate (1-24 hours) loss of consciousness
801.64 Open fracture of base of skull with cerebral laceration and contusion, prolonged (more than 24 hours) loss of consciousness and return to pre-existing conscious level
801.65 Open fracture of base of skull with cerebral laceration and contusion, prolonged (more than 24 hours) loss of consciousness, without return to pre-existing conscious level
801.66 Open fracture of base of skull with cerebral laceration and contusion, loss of consciousness of unspecified duration
801.69 Open fracture of base of skull with cerebral laceration and contusion, unspecified concussion
801.70 Open fracture of base of skull with subarachnoid, subdural, and extradural hemorrhage, unspecified state of consciousness
801.71 Open fracture of base of skull with subarachnoid, subdural, and extradural hemorrhage, no loss of consciousness
801.72 Open fracture of base of skull with subarachnoid, subdural, and extradural hemorrhage, brief (less than one hour) loss of consciousness
801.73 Open fracture of base of skull with subarachnoid, subdural, and extradural hemorrhage, moderate (1-24 hours) loss of consciousness
801.74 Open fracture of base of skull with subarachnoid, subdural, and extradural hemorrhage, prolonged (more than 24 hours) loss of consciousness and return to pre-existing conscious level
801.75 Open fracture of base of skull with subarachnoid, subdural, and extradural hemorrhage, prolonged (more than 24 hours) loss of consciousness, without return to pre-existing conscious level
801.76 Open fracture of base of skull with subarachnoid, subdural, and extradural hemorrhage, loss of consciousness of unspecified duration
801.79 Open fracture of base of skull with subarachnoid, subdural, and extradural hemorrhage, unspecified concussion
801.80 Open fracture of base of skull with other and unspecified intracranial hemorrhage, unspecified state of consciousness
801.81 Open fracture of base of skull with other and unspecified intracranial hemorrhage, no loss of consciousness
801.82 Open fracture of base of skull with other and unspecified intracranial hemorrhage, brief (less than one hour) loss of consciousness
801.83 Open fracture of base of skull with other and unspecified intracranial hemorrhage, moderate (1-24 hours) loss of consciousness
801.84 Open fracture of base of skull with other and unspecified intracranial hemorrhage, prolonged (more than 24 hours) loss of consciousness and return to pre-existing conscious level
801.85 Open fracture of base of skull with other and unspecified intracranial hemorrhage, prolonged (more than 24 hours) loss of consciousness, without return to pre-existing conscious level
801.86 Open fracture of base of skull with other and unspecified intracranial hemorrhage, loss of consciousness of unspecified duration
801.89 Open fracture of base of skull with other and unspecified intracranial hemorrhage, unspecified concussion
801.90 Open fracture of base of skull with intracranial injury of other and unspecified nature, unspecified state of consciousness
801.91 Open fracture of base of skull with intracranial injury of other and unspecified nature, no loss of consciousness
801.92 Open fracture of base of skull with intracranial injury of other and unspecified nature, brief (less than one hour) loss of consciousness
801.93 Open fracture of base of skull with intracranial injury of other and unspecified nature, moderate (1-24 hours) loss of consciousness
801.94 Open fracture of base of skull with intracranial injury of other and unspecified nature, prolonged (more than 24 hours) loss of consciousness and return to pre-existing conscious level
801.95 Open fracture of base of skull with intracranial injury of other and unspecified nature, prolonged (more than 24 hours) loss of consciousness, without return to pre-existing conscious level
801.96 Open fracture of base of skull with intracranial injury of other and unspecified nature, loss of consciousness of unspecified duration
801.99 Open fracture of base of skull with intracranial injury of other and unspecified nature, unspecified concussion
925.1 Crushing injury of face and scalp — (Use additional code to identify any associated injuries, such as: 800-829, 850.0-854.1, 860.0-869.1)

ICD-9-CM Procedural

22.41 Frontal sinusotomy
22.79 Other repair of nasal sinus
76.70 Reduction of facial fracture, not otherwise specified

21345

21345 Closed treatment of nasomaxillary complex fracture (LeFort II type), with interdental wire fixation or fixation of denture or splint

ICD-9-CM Diagnostic

802.0 Nasal bones, closed fracture
802.4 Malar and maxillary bones, closed fracture

ICD-9-CM Procedural

21.71 Closed reduction of nasal fracture
76.73 Closed reduction of maxillary fracture
76.78 Other closed reduction of facial fracture

21346-21348

21346 Open treatment of nasomaxillary complex fracture (LeFort II type); with wiring and/or local fixation
21347 requiring multiple open approaches
21348 with bone grafting (includes obtaining graft)

ICD-9-CM Diagnostic

733.82 Nonunion of fracture
802.0 Nasal bones, closed fracture
802.1 Nasal bones, open fracture
802.4 Malar and maxillary bones, closed fracture
802.5 Malar and maxillary bones, open fracture

ICD-9-CM Procedural

76.79 Other open reduction of facial fracture
76.91 Bone graft to facial bone

21355

21355 Percutaneous treatment of fracture of malar area, including zygomatic arch and malar tripod, with manipulation

ICD-9-CM Diagnostic

733.82 Nonunion of fracture
802.4 Malar and maxillary bones, closed fracture
802.5 Malar and maxillary bones, open fracture

ICD-9-CM Procedural

76.71 Closed reduction of malar and zygomatic fracture

HCPCS Level II Supplies & Services

A4305 Disposable drug delivery system, flow rate of 50 ml or greater per hour

21356

21356 Open treatment of depressed zygomatic arch fracture (eg, Gillies approach)

ICD-9-CM Diagnostic

733.82 Nonunion of fracture

802.4 Malar and maxillary bones, closed fracture
802.5 Malar and maxillary bones, open fracture

ICD-9-CM Procedural

76.72 Open reduction of malar and zygomatic fracture

21360

21360 Open treatment of depressed malar fracture, including zygomatic arch and malar tripod

ICD-9-CM Diagnostic

733.82 Nonunion of fracture
802.4 Malar and maxillary bones, closed fracture
802.5 Malar and maxillary bones, open fracture

ICD-9-CM Procedural

76.72 Open reduction of malar and zygomatic fracture

21365-21366

21365 Open treatment of complicated (eg, comminuted or involving cranial nerve foramina) fracture(s) of malar area, including zygomatic arch and malar tripod; with internal fixation and multiple surgical approaches
21366 with bone grafting (includes obtaining graft)

ICD-9-CM Diagnostic

802.4 Malar and maxillary bones, closed fracture
802.5 Malar and maxillary bones, open fracture
951.4 Injury to facial nerve
951.9 Injury to unspecified cranial nerve ▽

ICD-9-CM Procedural

76.71 Closed reduction of malar and zygomatic fracture
76.72 Open reduction of malar and zygomatic fracture
76.91 Bone graft to facial bone

21385-21387

21385 Open treatment of orbital floor blowout fracture; transantral approach (Caldwell-Luc type operation)
21386 periorbital approach
21387 combined approach

ICD-9-CM Diagnostic

802.6 Orbital floor (blow-out), closed fracture
802.7 Orbital floor (blow-out), open fracture

ICD-9-CM Procedural

76.79 Other open reduction of facial fracture

21390-21395

21390 Open treatment of orbital floor blowout fracture; periorbital approach, with alloplastic or other implant
21395 periorbital approach with bone graft (includes obtaining graft)

ICD-9-CM Diagnostic

802.6 Orbital floor (blow-out), closed fracture
802.7 Orbital floor (blow-out), open fracture

ICD-9-CM Procedural

76.79 Other open reduction of facial fracture
76.91 Bone graft to facial bone
76.92 Insertion of synthetic implant in facial bone

21400-21401

21400 Closed treatment of fracture of orbit, except blowout; without manipulation
21401 with manipulation

ICD-9-CM Diagnostic

801.00 Closed fracture of base of skull without mention of intracranial injury, unspecified state of consciousness ▽
801.01 Closed fracture of base of skull without mention of intracranial injury, no loss of consciousness
801.02 Closed fracture of base of skull without mention of intracranial injury, brief (less than one hour) loss of consciousness
801.03 Closed fracture of base of skull without mention of intracranial injury, moderate (1-24 hours) loss of consciousness
801.04 Closed fracture of base of skull without mention of intracranial injury, prolonged (more than 24 hours) loss of consciousness and return to pre-existing conscious level
801.05 Closed fracture of base of skull without mention of intracranial injury, prolonged (more than 24 hours) loss of consciousness, without return to pre-existing conscious level
801.06 Closed fracture of base of skull without mention of intracranial injury, loss of consciousness of unspecified duration ▽
801.09 Closed fracture of base of skull without mention of intracranial injury, unspecified concussion ▽
801.10 Closed fracture of base of skull with cerebral laceration and contusion, unspecified state of consciousness ▽
801.12 Closed fracture of base of skull with cerebral laceration and contusion, brief (less than one hour) loss of consciousness
801.13 Closed fracture of base of skull with cerebral laceration and contusion, moderate (1-24 hours) loss of consciousness
801.14 Closed fracture of base of skull with cerebral laceration and contusion, prolonged (more than 24 hours) loss of consciousness and return to pre-existing conscious level
801.15 Closed fracture of base of skull with cerebral laceration and contusion, prolonged (more than 24 hours) loss of consciousness, without return to pre-existing conscious level
801.16 Closed fracture of base of skull with cerebral laceration and contusion, loss of consciousness of unspecified duration ▽
801.19 Closed fracture of base of skull with cerebral laceration and contusion, unspecified concussion ▽
801.20 Closed fracture of base of skull with subarachnoid, subdural, and extradural hemorrhage, unspecified state of consciousness ▽
801.21 Closed fracture of base of skull with subarachnoid, subdural, and extradural hemorrhage, no loss of consciousness
801.22 Closed fracture of base of skull with subarachnoid, subdural, and extradural hemorrhage, brief (less than one hour) loss of consciousness
801.23 Closed fracture of base of skull with subarachnoid, subdural, and extradural hemorrhage, moderate (1-24 hours) loss of consciousness
801.24 Closed fracture of base of skull with subarachnoid, subdural, and extradural hemorrhage, prolonged (more than 24 hours) loss of consciousness and return to pre-existing conscious level
801.25 Closed fracture of base of skull with subarachnoid, subdural, and extradural hemorrhage, prolonged (more than 24 hours) loss of consciousness, without return to pre-existing conscious level
801.26 Closed fracture of base of skull with subarachnoid, subdural, and extradural hemorrhage, loss of consciousness of unspecified duration ▽
801.29 Closed fracture of base of skull with subarachnoid, subdural, and extradural hemorrhage, unspecified concussion ▽
801.30 Closed fracture of base of skull with other and unspecified intracranial hemorrhage, unspecified state of consciousness ▽
801.31 Closed fracture of base of skull with other and unspecified intracranial hemorrhage, no loss of consciousness ▽
801.32 Closed fracture of base of skull with other and unspecified intracranial hemorrhage, brief (less than one hour) loss of consciousness ▽

801.33 Closed fracture of base of skull with other and unspecified intracranial hemorrhage, moderate (1-24 hours) loss of consciousness
801.34 Closed fracture of base of skull with other and unspecified intracranial hemorrhage, prolonged (more than 24 hours) loss of consciousness and return to pre-existing conscious level
801.35 Closed fracture of base of skull with other and unspecified intracranial hemorrhage, prolonged (more than 24 hours) loss of consciousness, without return to pre-existing conscious level
801.36 Closed fracture of base of skull with other and unspecified intracranial hemorrhage, loss of consciousness of unspecified duration
801.39 Closed fracture of base of skull with other and unspecified intracranial hemorrhage, unspecified concussion
801.40 Closed fracture of base of skull with intracranial injury of other and unspecified nature, unspecified state of consciousness
801.41 Closed fracture of base of skull with intracranial injury of other and unspecified nature, no loss of consciousness
801.42 Closed fracture of base of skull with intracranial injury of other and unspecified nature, brief (less than one hour) loss of consciousness
801.43 Closed fracture of base of skull with intracranial injury of other and unspecified nature, moderate (1-24 hours) loss of consciousness
801.44 Closed fracture of base of skull with intracranial injury of other and unspecified nature, prolonged (more than 24 hours) loss of consciousness and return to pre-existing conscious level
801.45 Closed fracture of base of skull with intracranial injury of other and unspecified nature, prolonged (more than 24 hours) loss of consciousness, without return to pre-existing conscious level
801.46 Closed fracture of base of skull with intracranial injury of other and unspecified nature, loss of consciousness of unspecified duration
801.49 Closed fracture of base of skull with intracranial injury of other and unspecified nature, unspecified concussion
802.4 Malar and maxillary bones, closed fracture
802.8 Other facial bones, closed fracture

ICD-9-CM Procedural

76.78 Other closed reduction of facial fracture
93.59 Other immobilization, pressure, and attention to wound

HCPCS Level II Supplies & Services

A4305 Disposable drug delivery system, flow rate of 50 ml or greater per hour

21406-21408

21406 Open treatment of fracture of orbit, except blowout; without implant
21407 with implant
21408 with bone grafting (includes obtaining graft)

ICD-9-CM Diagnostic

801.00 Closed fracture of base of skull without mention of intracranial injury, unspecified state of consciousness
801.01 Closed fracture of base of skull without mention of intracranial injury, no loss of consciousness
801.02 Closed fracture of base of skull without mention of intracranial injury, brief (less than one hour) loss of consciousness
801.03 Closed fracture of base of skull without mention of intracranial injury, moderate (1-24 hours) loss of consciousness
801.04 Closed fracture of base of skull without mention of intracranial injury, prolonged (more than 24 hours) loss of consciousness and return to pre-existing conscious level
801.05 Closed fracture of base of skull without mention of intracranial injury, prolonged (more than 24 hours) loss of consciousness, without return to pre-existing conscious level
801.06 Closed fracture of base of skull without mention of intracranial injury, loss of consciousness of unspecified duration
801.09 Closed fracture of base of skull without mention of intracranial injury, unspecified concussion
801.10 Closed fracture of base of skull with cerebral laceration and contusion, unspecified state of consciousness
801.11 Closed fracture of base of skull with cerebral laceration and contusion, no loss of consciousness
801.12 Closed fracture of base of skull with cerebral laceration and contusion, brief (less than one hour) loss of consciousness
801.13 Closed fracture of base of skull with cerebral laceration and contusion, moderate (1-24 hours) loss of consciousness
801.14 Closed fracture of base of skull with cerebral laceration and contusion, prolonged (more than 24 hours) loss of consciousness and return to pre-existing conscious level
801.15 Closed fracture of base of skull with cerebral laceration and contusion, prolonged (more than 24 hours) loss of consciousness, without return to pre-existing conscious level
801.16 Closed fracture of base of skull with cerebral laceration and contusion, loss of consciousness of unspecified duration
801.19 Closed fracture of base of skull with cerebral laceration and contusion, unspecified concussion
801.20 Closed fracture of base of skull with subarachnoid, subdural, and extradural hemorrhage, unspecified state of consciousness
801.21 Closed fracture of base of skull with subarachnoid, subdural, and extradural hemorrhage, no loss of consciousness
801.22 Closed fracture of base of skull with subarachnoid, subdural, and extradural hemorrhage, brief (less than one hour) loss of consciousness
801.23 Closed fracture of base of skull with subarachnoid, subdural, and extradural hemorrhage, moderate (1-24 hours) loss of consciousness
801.24 Closed fracture of base of skull with subarachnoid, subdural, and extradural hemorrhage, prolonged (more than 24 hours) loss of consciousness and return to pre-existing conscious level
801.25 Closed fracture of base of skull with subarachnoid, subdural, and extradural hemorrhage, prolonged (more than 24 hours) loss of consciousness, without return to pre-existing conscious level
801.26 Closed fracture of base of skull with subarachnoid, subdural, and extradural hemorrhage, loss of consciousness of unspecified duration
801.29 Closed fracture of base of skull with subarachnoid, subdural, and extradural hemorrhage, unspecified concussion
801.30 Closed fracture of base of skull with other and unspecified intracranial hemorrhage, unspecified state of consciousness
801.31 Closed fracture of base of skull with other and unspecified intracranial hemorrhage, no loss of consciousness
801.32 Closed fracture of base of skull with other and unspecified intracranial hemorrhage, brief (less than one hour) loss of consciousness
801.33 Closed fracture of base of skull with other and unspecified intracranial hemorrhage, moderate (1-24 hours) loss of consciousness
801.34 Closed fracture of base of skull with other and unspecified intracranial hemorrhage, prolonged (more than 24 hours) loss of consciousness and return to pre-existing conscious level
801.35 Closed fracture of base of skull with other and unspecified intracranial hemorrhage, prolonged (more than 24 hours) loss of consciousness, without return to pre-existing conscious level
801.36 Closed fracture of base of skull with other and unspecified intracranial hemorrhage, loss of consciousness of unspecified duration
801.39 Closed fracture of base of skull with other and unspecified intracranial hemorrhage, unspecified concussion
801.40 Closed fracture of base of skull with intracranial injury of other and unspecified nature, unspecified state of consciousness
801.41 Closed fracture of base of skull with intracranial injury of other and unspecified nature, no loss of consciousness
801.42 Closed fracture of base of skull with intracranial injury of other and unspecified nature, brief (less than one hour) loss of consciousness
801.43 Closed fracture of base of skull with intracranial injury of other and unspecified nature, moderate (1-24 hours) loss of consciousness

801.44 Closed fracture of base of skull with intracranial injury of other and unspecified nature, prolonged (more than 24 hours) loss of consciousness and return to pre-existing conscious level ▽
801.45 Closed fracture of base of skull with intracranial injury of other and unspecified nature, prolonged (more than 24 hours) loss of consciousness, without return to pre-existing conscious level ▽
801.46 Closed fracture of base of skull with intracranial injury of other and unspecified nature, loss of consciousness of unspecified duration ▽
801.49 Closed fracture of base of skull with intracranial injury of other and unspecified nature, unspecified concussion ▽
801.50 Open fracture of base of skull without mention of intracranial injury, unspecified state of consciousness ▽
801.51 Open fracture of base of skull without mention of intracranial injury, no loss of consciousness
801.52 Open fracture of base of skull without mention of intracranial injury, brief (less than one hour) loss of consciousness
801.53 Open fracture of base of skull without mention of intracranial injury, moderate (1-24 hours) loss of consciousness
801.54 Open fracture of base of skull without mention of intracranial injury, prolonged (more than 24 hours) loss of consciousness and return to pre-existing conscious level
801.56 Open fracture of base of skull without mention of intracranial injury, loss of consciousness of unspecified duration ▽
801.59 Open fracture of base of skull without mention of intracranial injury, unspecified concussion ▽
801.60 Open fracture of base of skull with cerebral laceration and contusion, unspecified state of consciousness ▽
801.61 Open fracture of base of skull with cerebral laceration and contusion, no loss of consciousness
801.62 Open fracture of base of skull with cerebral laceration and contusion, brief (less than one hour) loss of consciousness
801.63 Open fracture of base of skull with cerebral laceration and contusion, moderate (1-24 hours) loss of consciousness
801.64 Open fracture of base of skull with cerebral laceration and contusion, prolonged (more than 24 hours) loss of consciousness and return to pre-existing conscious level
801.65 Open fracture of base of skull with cerebral laceration and contusion, prolonged (more than 24 hours) loss of consciousness, without return to pre-existing conscious level
801.66 Open fracture of base of skull with cerebral laceration and contusion, loss of consciousness of unspecified duration ▽
801.69 Open fracture of base of skull with cerebral laceration and contusion, unspecified concussion ▽
801.70 Open fracture of base of skull with subarachnoid, subdural, and extradural hemorrhage, unspecified state of consciousness ▽
801.71 Open fracture of base of skull with subarachnoid, subdural, and extradural hemorrhage, no loss of consciousness
801.72 Open fracture of base of skull with subarachnoid, subdural, and extradural hemorrhage, brief (less than one hour) loss of consciousness
801.73 Open fracture of base of skull with subarachnoid, subdural, and extradural hemorrhage, moderate (1-24 hours) loss of consciousness
801.74 Open fracture of base of skull with subarachnoid, subdural, and extradural hemorrhage, prolonged (more than 24 hours) loss of consciousness and return to pre-existing conscious level
801.75 Open fracture of base of skull with subarachnoid, subdural, and extradural hemorrhage, prolonged (more than 24 hours) loss of consciousness, without return to pre-existing conscious level
801.76 Open fracture of base of skull with subarachnoid, subdural, and extradural hemorrhage, loss of consciousness of unspecified duration ▽
801.79 Open fracture of base of skull with subarachnoid, subdural, and extradural hemorrhage, unspecified concussion ▽
801.80 Open fracture of base of skull with other and unspecified intracranial hemorrhage, unspecified state of consciousness ▽
801.81 Open fracture of base of skull with other and unspecified intracranial hemorrhage, no loss of consciousness ▽
801.82 Open fracture of base of skull with other and unspecified intracranial hemorrhage, brief (less than one hour) loss of consciousness ▽
801.83 Open fracture of base of skull with other and unspecified intracranial hemorrhage, moderate (1-24 hours) loss of consciousness ▽
801.84 Open fracture of base of skull with other and unspecified intracranial hemorrhage, prolonged (more than 24 hours) loss of consciousness and return to pre-existing conscious level ▽
801.85 Open fracture of base of skull with other and unspecified intracranial hemorrhage, prolonged (more than 24 hours) loss of consciousness, without return to pre-existing conscious level ▽
801.86 Open fracture of base of skull with other and unspecified intracranial hemorrhage, loss of consciousness of unspecified duration ▽
801.89 Open fracture of base of skull with other and unspecified intracranial hemorrhage, unspecified concussion ▽
801.90 Open fracture of base of skull with intracranial injury of other and unspecified nature, unspecified state of consciousness ▽
801.91 Open fracture of base of skull with intracranial injury of other and unspecified nature, no loss of consciousness ▽
801.92 Open fracture of base of skull with intracranial injury of other and unspecified nature, brief (less than one hour) loss of consciousness ▽
801.93 Open fracture of base of skull with intracranial injury of other and unspecified nature, moderate (1-24 hours) loss of consciousness ▽
801.94 Open fracture of base of skull with intracranial injury of other and unspecified nature, prolonged (more than 24 hours) loss of consciousness and return to pre-existing conscious level ▽
801.95 Open fracture of base of skull with intracranial injury of other and unspecified nature, prolonged (more than 24 hours) loss of consciousness, without return to pre-existing conscious level ▽
801.96 Open fracture of base of skull with intracranial injury of other and unspecified nature, loss of consciousness of unspecified duration ▽
801.99 Open fracture of base of skull with intracranial injury of other and unspecified nature, unspecified concussion ▽
802.4 Malar and maxillary bones, closed fracture
802.5 Malar and maxillary bones, open fracture
802.8 Other facial bones, closed fracture
802.9 Other facial bones, open fracture

ICD-9-CM Procedural

76.79 Other open reduction of facial fracture
76.91 Bone graft to facial bone
76.92 Insertion of synthetic implant in facial bone

21421

21421 Closed treatment of palatal or maxillary fracture (LeFort I type), with interdental wire fixation or fixation of denture or splint

ICD-9-CM Diagnostic

802.4 Malar and maxillary bones, closed fracture
802.8 Other facial bones, closed fracture

ICD-9-CM Procedural

76.73 Closed reduction of maxillary fracture
76.78 Other closed reduction of facial fracture

21422

21422 Open treatment of palatal or maxillary fracture (LeFort I type);

ICD-9-CM Diagnostic

802.4 Malar and maxillary bones, closed fracture
802.5 Malar and maxillary bones, open fracture

802.8 Other facial bones, closed fracture
802.9 Other facial bones, open fracture

ICD-9-CM Procedural

76.74 Open reduction of maxillary fracture
76.79 Other open reduction of facial fracture

21423

21423 Open treatment of palatal or maxillary fracture (LeFort I type); complicated (comminuted or involving cranial nerve foramina), multiple approaches

ICD-9-CM Diagnostic

802.4 Malar and maxillary bones, closed fracture
802.5 Malar and maxillary bones, open fracture
802.8 Other facial bones, closed fracture
802.9 Other facial bones, open fracture

ICD-9-CM Procedural

76.74 Open reduction of maxillary fracture
76.78 Other closed reduction of facial fracture

21431

21431 Closed treatment of craniofacial separation (LeFort III type) using interdental wire fixation of denture or splint

ICD-9-CM Diagnostic

800.00 Closed fracture of vault of skull without mention of intracranial injury, unspecified state of consciousness ▽
800.01 Closed fracture of vault of skull without mention of intracranial injury, no loss of consciousness
800.02 Closed fracture of vault of skull without mention of intracranial injury, brief (less than one hour) loss of consciousness
800.03 Closed fracture of vault of skull without mention of intracranial injury, moderate (1-24 hours) loss of consciousness
800.04 Closed fracture of vault of skull without mention of intracranial injury, prolonged (more than 24 hours) loss of consciousness and return to pre-existing conscious level
800.05 Closed fracture of vault of skull without mention of intracranial injury, prolonged (more than 24 hours) loss of consciousness, without return to pre-existing conscious level
800.06 Closed fracture of vault of skull without mention of intracranial injury, loss of consciousness of unspecified duration ▽
800.09 Closed fracture of vault of skull without mention of intracranial injury, unspecified concussion ▽
800.10 Closed fracture of vault of skull with cerebral laceration and contusion, unspecified state of consciousness ▽
800.11 Closed fracture of vault of skull with cerebral laceration and contusion, no loss of consciousness
800.12 Closed fracture of vault of skull with cerebral laceration and contusion, brief (less than one hour) loss of consciousness
800.13 Closed fracture of vault of skull with cerebral laceration and contusion, moderate (1-24 hours) loss of consciousness
800.14 Closed fracture of vault of skull with cerebral laceration and contusion, prolonged (more than 24 hours) loss of consciousness and return to pre-existing conscious level
800.15 Closed fracture of vault of skull with cerebral laceration and contusion, prolonged (more than 24 hours) loss of consciousness, without return to pre-existing conscious level
800.16 Closed fracture of vault of skull with cerebral laceration and contusion, loss of consciousness of unspecified duration ▽
800.19 Closed fracture of vault of skull with cerebral laceration and contusion, unspecified concussion ▽
800.20 Closed fracture of vault of skull with subarachnoid, subdural, and extradural hemorrhage, unspecified state of consciousness ▽
800.21 Closed fracture of vault of skull with subarachnoid, subdural, and extradural hemorrhage, no loss of consciousness
800.22 Closed fracture of vault of skull with subarachnoid, subdural, and extradural hemorrhage, brief (less than one hour) loss of consciousness
800.23 Closed fracture of vault of skull with subarachnoid, subdural, and extradural hemorrhage, moderate (1-24 hours) loss of consciousness
800.24 Closed fracture of vault of skull with subarachnoid, subdural, and extradural hemorrhage, prolonged (more than 24 hours) loss of consciousness and return to pre-existing conscious level
800.25 Closed fracture of vault of skull with subarachnoid, subdural, and extradural hemorrhage, prolonged (more than 24 hours) loss of consciousness, without return to pre-existing conscious level
800.26 Closed fracture of vault of skull with subarachnoid, subdural, and extradural hemorrhage, loss of consciousness of unspecified duration ▽
800.30 Closed fracture of vault of skull with other and unspecified intracranial hemorrhage, unspecified state of consciousness ▽
800.31 Closed fracture of vault of skull with other and unspecified intracranial hemorrhage, no loss of consciousness ▽
800.32 Closed fracture of vault of skull with other and unspecified intracranial hemorrhage, brief (less than one hour) loss of consciousness ▽
800.33 Closed fracture of vault of skull with other and unspecified intracranial hemorrhage, moderate (1-24 hours) loss of consciousness ▽
800.34 Closed fracture of vault of skull with other and unspecified intracranial hemorrhage, prolonged (more than 24 hours) loss of consciousness and return to pre-existing conscious level ▽
800.35 Closed fracture of vault of skull with other and unspecified intracranial hemorrhage, prolonged (more than 24 hours) loss of consciousness, without return to pre-existing conscious level ▽
800.36 Closed fracture of vault of skull with other and unspecified intracranial hemorrhage, loss of consciousness of unspecified duration ▽
800.39 Closed fracture of vault of skull with other and unspecified intracranial hemorrhage, unspecified concussion ▽
800.40 Closed fracture of vault of skull with intracranial injury of other and unspecified nature, unspecified state of consciousness ▽
800.41 Closed fracture of vault of skull with intracranial injury of other and unspecified nature, no loss of consciousness ▽
800.42 Closed fracture of vault of skull with intracranial injury of other and unspecified nature, brief (less than one hour) loss of consciousness ▽
800.43 Closed fracture of vault of skull with intracranial injury of other and unspecified nature, moderate (1-24 hours) loss of consciousness ▽
800.44 Closed fracture of vault of skull with intracranial injury of other and unspecified nature, prolonged (more than 24 hours) loss of consciousness and return to pre-existing conscious level ▽
800.45 Closed fracture of vault of skull with intracranial injury of other and unspecified nature, prolonged (more than 24 hours) loss of consciousness, without return to pre-existing conscious level ▽
800.46 Closed fracture of vault of skull with intracranial injury of other and unspecified nature, loss of consciousness of unspecified duration ▽
800.49 Closed fracture of vault of skull with intracranial injury of other and unspecified nature, unspecified concussion ▽
801.00 Closed fracture of base of skull without mention of intracranial injury, unspecified state of consciousness ▽
801.01 Closed fracture of base of skull without mention of intracranial injury, no loss of consciousness
801.02 Closed fracture of base of skull without mention of intracranial injury, brief (less than one hour) loss of consciousness
801.03 Closed fracture of base of skull without mention of intracranial injury, moderate (1-24 hours) loss of consciousness
801.04 Closed fracture of base of skull without mention of intracranial injury, prolonged (more than 24 hours) loss of consciousness and return to pre-existing conscious level

801.05 Closed fracture of base of skull without mention of intracranial injury, prolonged (more than 24 hours) loss of consciousness, without return to pre-existing conscious level

801.06 Closed fracture of base of skull without mention of intracranial injury, loss of consciousness of unspecified duration ▽

801.09 Closed fracture of base of skull without mention of intracranial injury, unspecified concussion ▽

801.10 Closed fracture of base of skull with cerebral laceration and contusion, unspecified state of consciousness ▽

801.11 Closed fracture of base of skull with cerebral laceration and contusion, no loss of consciousness

801.12 Closed fracture of base of skull with cerebral laceration and contusion, brief (less than one hour) loss of consciousness

801.13 Closed fracture of base of skull with cerebral laceration and contusion, moderate (1-24 hours) loss of consciousness

801.14 Closed fracture of base of skull with cerebral laceration and contusion, prolonged (more than 24 hours) loss of consciousness and return to pre-existing conscious level

801.15 Closed fracture of base of skull with cerebral laceration and contusion, prolonged (more than 24 hours) loss of consciousness, without return to pre-existing conscious level

801.16 Closed fracture of base of skull with cerebral laceration and contusion, loss of consciousness of unspecified duration ▽

801.19 Closed fracture of base of skull with cerebral laceration and contusion, unspecified concussion ▽

801.20 Closed fracture of base of skull with subarachnoid, subdural, and extradural hemorrhage, unspecified state of consciousness ▽

801.21 Closed fracture of base of skull with subarachnoid, subdural, and extradural hemorrhage, no loss of consciousness

801.22 Closed fracture of base of skull with subarachnoid, subdural, and extradural hemorrhage, brief (less than one hour) loss of consciousness

801.23 Closed fracture of base of skull with subarachnoid, subdural, and extradural hemorrhage, moderate (1-24 hours) loss of consciousness

801.24 Closed fracture of base of skull with subarachnoid, subdural, and extradural hemorrhage, prolonged (more than 24 hours) loss of consciousness and return to pre-existing conscious level

801.25 Closed fracture of base of skull with subarachnoid, subdural, and extradural hemorrhage, prolonged (more than 24 hours) loss of consciousness, without return to pre-existing conscious level

801.26 Closed fracture of base of skull with subarachnoid, subdural, and extradural hemorrhage, loss of consciousness of unspecified duration ▽

801.30 Closed fracture of base of skull with other and unspecified intracranial hemorrhage, unspecified state of consciousness ▽

801.31 Closed fracture of base of skull with other and unspecified intracranial hemorrhage, no loss of consciousness ▽

801.32 Closed fracture of base of skull with other and unspecified intracranial hemorrhage, brief (less than one hour) loss of consciousness ▽

801.33 Closed fracture of base of skull with other and unspecified intracranial hemorrhage, moderate (1-24 hours) loss of consciousness ▽

801.34 Closed fracture of base of skull with other and unspecified intracranial hemorrhage, prolonged (more than 24 hours) loss of consciousness and return to pre-existing conscious level ▽

801.35 Closed fracture of base of skull with other and unspecified intracranial hemorrhage, prolonged (more than 24 hours) loss of consciousness, without return to pre-existing conscious level ▽

801.36 Closed fracture of base of skull with other and unspecified intracranial hemorrhage, loss of consciousness of unspecified duration ▽

801.39 Closed fracture of base of skull with other and unspecified intracranial hemorrhage, unspecified concussion ▽

801.40 Closed fracture of base of skull with intracranial injury of other and unspecified nature, unspecified state of consciousness ▽

801.41 Closed fracture of base of skull with intracranial injury of other and unspecified nature, no loss of consciousness ▽

801.42 Closed fracture of base of skull with intracranial injury of other and unspecified nature, brief (less than one hour) loss of consciousness ▽

801.43 Closed fracture of base of skull with intracranial injury of other and unspecified nature, moderate (1-24 hours) loss of consciousness ▽

801.44 Closed fracture of base of skull with intracranial injury of other and unspecified nature, prolonged (more than 24 hours) loss of consciousness and return to pre-existing conscious level ▽

801.45 Closed fracture of base of skull with intracranial injury of other and unspecified nature, prolonged (more than 24 hours) loss of consciousness, without return to pre-existing conscious level ▽

801.46 Closed fracture of base of skull with intracranial injury of other and unspecified nature, loss of consciousness of unspecified duration ▽

801.49 Closed fracture of base of skull with intracranial injury of other and unspecified nature, unspecified concussion ▽

802.4 Malar and maxillary bones, closed fracture

802.5 Malar and maxillary bones, open fracture

802.8 Other facial bones, closed fracture

802.9 Other facial bones, open fracture

804.00 Closed fractures involving skull or face with other bones, without mention of intracranial injury, unspecified state of consciousness ▽

804.01 Closed fractures involving skull or face with other bones, without mention of intracranial injury, no loss of consciousness

804.02 Closed fractures involving skull or face with other bones, without mention of intracranial injury, brief (less than one hour) loss of consciousness

804.03 Closed fractures involving skull or face with other bones, without mention of intracranial injury, moderate (1-24 hours) loss of consciousness

804.04 Closed fractures involving skull or face with other bones, without mention or intracranial injury, prolonged (more than 24 hours) loss of consciousness and return to pre-existing conscious level

804.05 Closed fractures involving skull of face with other bones, without mention of intracranial injury, prolonged (more than 24 hours) loss of consciousness, without return to pre-existing conscious level

804.06 Closed fractures involving skull of face with other bones, without mention of intracranial injury, loss of consciousness of unspecified duration ▽

804.09 Closed fractures involving skull of face with other bones, without mention of intracranial injury, unspecified concussion ▽

804.10 Closed fractures involving skull or face with other bones, with cerebral laceration and contusion, unspecified state of consciousness ▽

804.11 Closed fractures involving skull or face with other bones, with cerebral laceration and contusion, no loss of consciousness

804.12 Closed fractures involving skull or face with other bones, with cerebral laceration and contusion, brief (less than one hour) loss of consciousness

804.13 Closed fractures involving skull or face with other bones, with cerebral laceration and contusion, moderate (1-24 hours) loss of consciousness

804.14 Closed fractures involving skull or face with other bones, with cerebral laceration and contusion, prolonged (more than 24 hours) loss of consciousness and return to pre-existing conscious level

804.15 Closed fractures involving skull or face with other bones, with cerebral laceration and contusion, prolonged (more than 24 hours) loss of consciousness, without return to pre-existing conscious level

804.16 Closed fractures involving skull or face with other bones, with cerebral laceration and contusion, loss of consciousness of unspecified duration ▽

804.19 Closed fractures involving skull or face with other bones, with cerebral laceration and contusion, unspecified concussion ▽

804.20 Closed fractures involving skull or face with other bones with subarachnoid, subdural, and extradural hemorrhage, unspecified state of consciousness ▽

804.21 Closed fractures involving skull or face with other bones with subarachnoid, subdural, and extradural hemorrhage, no loss of consciousness

▽ Unspecified code ☒ Manifestation code
♀ Female diagnosis ♂ Male diagnosis

804.22 Closed fractures involving skull or face with other bones with subarachnoid, subdural, and extradural hemorrhage, brief (less than one hour) loss of consciousness

804.23 Closed fractures involving skull or face with other bones with subarachnoid, subdural, and extradural hemorrhage, moderate (1-24 hours) loss of consciousness

804.24 Closed fractures involving skull or face with other bones with subarachnoid, subdural, and extradural hemorrhage, prolonged (more than 24 hours) loss of consciousness and return to pre-existing conscious level

804.25 Closed fractures involving skull or face with other bones with subarachnoid, subdural, and extradural hemorrhage, prolonged (more than 24 hours) loss of consciousness, without return to pre-existing conscious level

804.26 Closed fractures involving skull or face with other bones with subarachnoid, subdural, and extradural hemorrhage, loss of consciousness of unspecified duration ▽

804.29 Closed fractures involving skull or face with other bones with subarachnoid, subdural, and extradural hemorrhage, unspecified concussion ▽

804.30 Closed fractures involving skull or face with other bones, with other and unspecified intracranial hemorrhage, unspecified state of consciousness ▽

804.31 Closed fractures involving skull or face with other bones, with other and unspecified intracranial hemorrhage, no loss of consciousness ▽

804.32 Closed fractures involving skull or face with other bones, with other and unspecified intracranial hemorrhage, brief (less than one hour) loss of consciousness ▽

804.33 Closed fractures involving skull or face with other bones, with other and unspecified intracranial hemorrhage, moderate (1-24 hours) loss of consciousness ▽

804.34 Closed fractures involving skull or face with other bones, with other and unspecified intracranial hemorrhage, prolonged (more than 24 hours) loss of consciousness and return to preexisting conscious level ▽

804.35 Closed fractures involving skull or face with other bones, with other and unspecified intracranial hemorrhage, prolonged (more than 24 hours) loss of consciousness, without return to pre-existing conscious level ▽

804.36 Closed fractures involving skull or face with other bones, with other and unspecified intracranial hemorrhage, loss of consciousness of unspecified duration ▽

804.39 Closed fractures involving skull or face with other bones, with other and unspecified intracranial hemorrhage, unspecified concussion ▽

804.40 Closed fractures involving skull or face with other bones, with intracranial injury of other and unspecified nature, unspecified state of consciousness ▽

804.41 Closed fractures involving skull or face with other bones, with intracranial injury of other and unspecified nature, no loss of consciousness ▽

804.42 Closed fractures involving skull or face with other bones, with intracranial injury of other and unspecified nature, brief (less than one hour) loss of consciousness ▽

804.43 Closed fractures involving skull or face with other bones, with intracranial injury of other and unspecified nature, moderate (1-24 hours) loss of consciousness ▽

804.44 Closed fractures involving skull or face with other bones, with intracranial injury of other and unspecified nature, prolonged (more than 24 hours) loss of consciousness and return to pre-existing conscious level ▽

804.45 Closed fractures involving skull or face with other bones, with intracranial injury of other and unspecified nature, prolonged (more than 24 hours) loss of consciousness, without return to pre-existing conscious level ▽

804.46 Closed fractures involving skull or face with other bones, with intracranial injury of other and unspecified nature, loss of consciousness of unspecified duration ▽

804.49 Closed fractures involving skull or face with other bones, with intracranial injury of other and unspecified nature, unspecified concussion ▽

ICD-9-CM Procedural

76.78 Other closed reduction of facial fracture

21432-21436

21432 Open treatment of craniofacial separation (LeFort III type); with wiring and/or internal fixation

21433 complicated (eg, comminuted or involving cranial nerve foramina), multiple surgical approaches

21435 complicated, utilizing internal and/or external fixation techniques (eg, head cap, halo device, and/or intermaxillary fixation)

21436 complicated, multiple surgical approaches, internal fixation, with bone grafting (includes obtaining graft)

ICD-9-CM Diagnostic

733.82 Nonunion of fracture

800.00 Closed fracture of vault of skull without mention of intracranial injury, unspecified state of consciousness ▽

800.01 Closed fracture of vault of skull without mention of intracranial injury, no loss of consciousness

800.02 Closed fracture of vault of skull without mention of intracranial injury, brief (less than one hour) loss of consciousness

800.03 Closed fracture of vault of skull without mention of intracranial injury, moderate (1-24 hours) loss of consciousness

800.04 Closed fracture of vault of skull without mention of intracranial injury, prolonged (more than 24 hours) loss of consciousness and return to pre-existing conscious level

800.05 Closed fracture of vault of skull without mention of intracranial injury, prolonged (more than 24 hours) loss of consciousness, without return to pre-existing conscious level

800.06 Closed fracture of vault of skull without mention of intracranial injury, loss of consciousness of unspecified duration ▽

800.09 Closed fracture of vault of skull without mention of intracranial injury, unspecified concussion ▽

800.10 Closed fracture of vault of skull with cerebral laceration and contusion, unspecified state of consciousness ▽

800.11 Closed fracture of vault of skull with cerebral laceration and contusion, no loss of consciousness

800.12 Closed fracture of vault of skull with cerebral laceration and contusion, brief (less than one hour) loss of consciousness

800.13 Closed fracture of vault of skull with cerebral laceration and contusion, moderate (1-24 hours) loss of consciousness

800.14 Closed fracture of vault of skull with cerebral laceration and contusion, prolonged (more than 24 hours) loss of consciousness and return to pre-existing conscious level

800.15 Closed fracture of vault of skull with cerebral laceration and contusion, prolonged (more than 24 hours) loss of consciousness, without return to pre-existing conscious level

800.16 Closed fracture of vault of skull with cerebral laceration and contusion, loss of consciousness of unspecified duration ▽

800.19 Closed fracture of vault of skull with cerebral laceration and contusion, unspecified concussion ▽

800.20 Closed fracture of vault of skull with subarachnoid, subdural, and extradural hemorrhage, unspecified state of consciousness ▽

800.21 Closed fracture of vault of skull with subarachnoid, subdural, and extradural hemorrhage, no loss of consciousness

800.22 Closed fracture of vault of skull with subarachnoid, subdural, and extradural hemorrhage, brief (less than one hour) loss of consciousness

800.23 Closed fracture of vault of skull with subarachnoid, subdural, and extradural hemorrhage, moderate (1-24 hours) loss of consciousness

800.24 Closed fracture of vault of skull with subarachnoid, subdural, and extradural hemorrhage, prolonged (more than 24 hours) loss of consciousness and return to pre-existing conscious level

800.25 Closed fracture of vault of skull with subarachnoid, subdural, and extradural hemorrhage, prolonged (more than 24 hours) loss of consciousness, without return to pre-existing conscious level

800.26 Closed fracture of vault of skull with subarachnoid, subdural, and extradural hemorrhage, loss of consciousness of unspecified duration ▽

800.30 Closed fracture of vault of skull with other and unspecified intracranial hemorrhage, unspecified state of consciousness

800.31 Closed fracture of vault of skull with other and unspecified intracranial hemorrhage, no loss of consciousness

800.32 Closed fracture of vault of skull with other and unspecified intracranial hemorrhage, brief (less than one hour) loss of consciousness

800.33 Closed fracture of vault of skull with other and unspecified intracranial hemorrhage, moderate (1-24 hours) loss of consciousness

800.34 Closed fracture of vault of skull with other and unspecified intracranial hemorrhage, prolonged (more than 24 hours) loss of consciousness and return to pre-existing conscious level

800.35 Closed fracture of vault of skull with other and unspecified intracranial hemorrhage, prolonged (more than 24 hours) loss of consciousness, without return to pre-existing conscious level

800.36 Closed fracture of vault of skull with other and unspecified intracranial hemorrhage, loss of consciousness of unspecified duration

800.39 Closed fracture of vault of skull with other and unspecified intracranial hemorrhage, unspecified concussion

800.40 Closed fracture of vault of skull with intracranial injury of other and unspecified nature, unspecified state of consciousness

800.41 Closed fracture of vault of skull with intracranial injury of other and unspecified nature, no loss of consciousness

800.42 Closed fracture of vault of skull with intracranial injury of other and unspecified nature, brief (less than one hour) loss of consciousness

800.43 Closed fracture of vault of skull with intracranial injury of other and unspecified nature, moderate (1-24 hours) loss of consciousness

800.44 Closed fracture of vault of skull with intracranial injury of other and unspecified nature, prolonged (more than 24 hours) loss of consciousness and return to pre-existing conscious level

800.45 Closed fracture of vault of skull with intracranial injury of other and unspecified nature, prolonged (more than 24 hours) loss of consciousness, without return to pre-existing conscious level

800.46 Closed fracture of vault of skull with intracranial injury of other and unspecified nature, loss of consciousness of unspecified duration

800.49 Closed fracture of vault of skull with intracranial injury of other and unspecified nature, unspecified concussion

800.50 Open fracture of vault of skull without mention of intracranial injury, unspecified state of consciousness

800.51 Open fracture of vault of skull without mention of intracranial injury, no loss of consciousness

800.52 Open fracture of vault of skull without mention of intracranial injury, brief (less than one hour) loss of consciousness

800.53 Open fracture of vault of skull without mention of intracranial injury, moderate (1-24 hours) loss of consciousness

800.54 Open fracture of vault of skull without mention of intracranial injury, prolonged (more than 24 hours) loss of consciousness and return to pre-existing conscious level

800.55 Open fracture of vault of skull without mention of intracranial injury, prolonged (more than 24 hours) loss of consciousness, without return to pre-existing conscious level

800.56 Open fracture of vault of skull without mention of intracranial injury, loss of consciousness of unspecified duration

800.59 Open fracture of vault of skull without mention of intracranial injury, unspecified concussion

800.60 Open fracture of vault of skull with cerebral laceration and contusion, unspecified state of consciousness

800.61 Open fracture of vault of skull with cerebral laceration and contusion, no loss of consciousness

800.62 Open fracture of vault of skull with cerebral laceration and contusion, brief (less than one hour) loss of consciousness

800.63 Open fracture of vault of skull with cerebral laceration and contusion, moderate (1-24 hours) loss of consciousness

800.64 Open fracture of vault of skull with cerebral laceration and contusion, prolonged (more than 24 hours) loss of consciousness and return to pre-existing conscious level

800.65 Open fracture of vault of skull with cerebral laceration and contusion, prolonged (more than 24 hours) loss of consciousness, without return to pre-existing conscious level

800.66 Open fracture of vault of skull with cerebral laceration and contusion, loss of consciousness of unspecified duration

800.69 Open fracture of vault of skull with cerebral laceration and contusion, unspecified concussion

800.70 Open fracture of vault of skull with subarachnoid, subdural, and extradural hemorrhage, unspecified state of consciousness

800.71 Open fracture of vault of skull with subarachnoid, subdural, and extradural hemorrhage, no loss of consciousness

800.72 Open fracture of vault of skull with subarachnoid, subdural, and extradural hemorrhage, brief (less than one hour) loss of consciousness

800.73 Open fracture of vault of skull with subarachnoid, subdural, and extradural hemorrhage, moderate (1-24 hours) loss of consciousness

800.74 Open fracture of vault of skull with subarachnoid, subdural, and extradural hemorrhage, prolonged (more than 24 hours) loss of consciousness and return to pre-existing conscious level

800.75 Open fracture of vault of skull with subarachnoid, subdural, and extradural hemorrhage, prolonged (more than 24 hours) loss of consciousness, without return to pre-existing conscious level

800.79 Open fracture of vault of skull with subarachnoid, subdural, and extradural hemorrhage, unspecified concussion

800.80 Open fracture of vault of skull with other and unspecified intracranial hemorrhage, unspecified state of consciousness

800.90 Open fracture of vault of skull with intracranial injury of other and unspecified nature, unspecified state of consciousness

800.91 Open fracture of vault of skull with intracranial injury of other and unspecified nature, no loss of consciousness

800.92 Open fracture of vault of skull with intracranial injury of other and unspecified nature, brief (less than one hour) loss of consciousness

800.93 Open fracture of vault of skull with intracranial injury of other and unspecified nature, moderate (1-24 hours) loss of consciousness

800.94 Open fracture of vault of skull with intracranial injury of other and unspecified nature, prolonged (more than 24 hours) loss of consciousness and return to pre-existing conscious level

800.95 Open fracture of vault of skull with intracranial injury of other and unspecified nature, prolonged (more than 24 hours) loss of consciousness, without return to pre-existing conscious level

800.96 Open fracture of vault of skull with intracranial injury of other and unspecified nature, loss of consciousness of unspecified duration

800.99 Open fracture of vault of skull with intracranial injury of other and unspecified nature, unspecified concussion

801.00 Closed fracture of base of skull without mention of intracranial injury, unspecified state of consciousness

801.01 Closed fracture of base of skull without mention of intracranial injury, no loss of consciousness

801.02 Closed fracture of base of skull without mention of intracranial injury, brief (less than one hour) loss of consciousness

801.03 Closed fracture of base of skull without mention of intracranial injury, moderate (1-24 hours) loss of consciousness

801.04 Closed fracture of base of skull without mention of intracranial injury, prolonged (more than 24 hours) loss of consciousness and return to pre-existing conscious level

801.05 Closed fracture of base of skull without mention of intracranial injury, prolonged (more than 24 hours) loss of consciousness, without return to pre-existing conscious level

801.06 Closed fracture of base of skull without mention of intracranial injury, loss of consciousness of unspecified duration

801.09 Closed fracture of base of skull without mention of intracranial injury, unspecified concussion ▽

801.10 Closed fracture of base of skull with cerebral laceration and contusion, unspecified state of consciousness ▽

801.11 Closed fracture of base of skull with cerebral laceration and contusion, no loss of consciousness

801.12 Closed fracture of base of skull with cerebral laceration and contusion, brief (less than one hour) loss of consciousness

801.13 Closed fracture of base of skull with cerebral laceration and contusion, moderate (1-24 hours) loss of consciousness

801.14 Closed fracture of base of skull with cerebral laceration and contusion, prolonged (more than 24 hours) loss of consciousness and return to pre-existing conscious level

801.15 Closed fracture of base of skull with cerebral laceration and contusion, prolonged (more than 24 hours) loss of consciousness, without return to pre-existing conscious level

801.16 Closed fracture of base of skull with cerebral laceration and contusion, loss of consciousness of unspecified duration ▽

801.19 Closed fracture of base of skull with cerebral laceration and contusion, unspecified concussion ▽

801.20 Closed fracture of base of skull with subarachnoid, subdural, and extradural hemorrhage, unspecified state of consciousness ▽

801.21 Closed fracture of base of skull with subarachnoid, subdural, and extradural hemorrhage, no loss of consciousness

801.22 Closed fracture of base of skull with subarachnoid, subdural, and extradural hemorrhage, brief (less than one hour) loss of consciousness

801.23 Closed fracture of base of skull with subarachnoid, subdural, and extradural hemorrhage, moderate (1-24 hours) loss of consciousness

801.24 Closed fracture of base of skull with subarachnoid, subdural, and extradural hemorrhage, prolonged (more than 24 hours) loss of consciousness and return to pre-existing conscious level

801.25 Closed fracture of base of skull with subarachnoid, subdural, and extradural hemorrhage, prolonged (more than 24 hours) loss of consciousness, without return to pre-existing conscious level

801.26 Closed fracture of base of skull with subarachnoid, subdural, and extradural hemorrhage, loss of consciousness of unspecified duration ▽

801.30 Closed fracture of base of skull with other and unspecified intracranial hemorrhage, unspecified state of consciousness ▽

801.31 Closed fracture of base of skull with other and unspecified intracranial hemorrhage, no loss of consciousness ▽

801.32 Closed fracture of base of skull with other and unspecified intracranial hemorrhage, brief (less than one hour) loss of consciousness ▽

801.33 Closed fracture of base of skull with other and unspecified intracranial hemorrhage, moderate (1-24 hours) loss of consciousness ▽

801.34 Closed fracture of base of skull with other and unspecified intracranial hemorrhage, prolonged (more than 24 hours) loss of consciousness and return to pre-existing conscious level ▽

801.35 Closed fracture of base of skull with other and unspecified intracranial hemorrhage, prolonged (more than 24 hours) loss of consciousness, without return to pre-existing conscious level ▽

801.36 Closed fracture of base of skull with other and unspecified intracranial hemorrhage, loss of consciousness of unspecified duration ▽

801.39 Closed fracture of base of skull with other and unspecified intracranial hemorrhage, unspecified concussion ▽

801.41 Closed fracture of base of skull with intracranial injury of other and unspecified nature, no loss of consciousness ▽

801.42 Closed fracture of base of skull with intracranial injury of other and unspecified nature, brief (less than one hour) loss of consciousness ▽

801.43 Closed fracture of base of skull with intracranial injury of other and unspecified nature, moderate (1-24 hours) loss of consciousness ▽

801.44 Closed fracture of base of skull with intracranial injury of other and unspecified nature, prolonged (more than 24 hours) loss of consciousness and return to pre-existing conscious level ▽

801.45 Closed fracture of base of skull with intracranial injury of other and unspecified nature, prolonged (more than 24 hours) loss of consciousness, without return to pre-existing conscious level ▽

801.46 Closed fracture of base of skull with intracranial injury of other and unspecified nature, loss of consciousness of unspecified duration ▽

801.49 Closed fracture of base of skull with intracranial injury of other and unspecified nature, unspecified concussion ▽

802.4 Malar and maxillary bones, closed fracture

802.5 Malar and maxillary bones, open fracture

802.8 Other facial bones, closed fracture

802.9 Other facial bones, open fracture

804.00 Closed fractures involving skull or face with other bones, without mention of intracranial injury, unspecified state of consciousness ▽

804.01 Closed fractures involving skull or face with other bones, without mention of intracranial injury, no loss of consciousness

804.02 Closed fractures involving skull or face with other bones, without mention of intracranial injury, brief (less than one hour) loss of consciousness

804.03 Closed fractures involving skull or face with other bones, without mention of intracranial injury, moderate (1-24 hours) loss of consciousness

804.04 Closed fractures involving skull or face with other bones, without mention or intracranial injury, prolonged (more than 24 hours) loss of consciousness and return to pre-existing conscious level

804.05 Closed fractures involving skull of face with other bones, without mention of intracranial injury, prolonged (more than 24 hours) loss of consciousness, without return to pre-existing conscious level

804.06 Closed fractures involving skull of face with other bones, without mention of intracranial injury, loss of consciousness of unspecified duration ▽

804.09 Closed fractures involving skull of face with other bones, without mention of intracranial injury, unspecified concussion ▽

804.10 Closed fractures involving skull or face with other bones, with cerebral laceration and contusion, unspecified state of consciousness ▽

804.11 Closed fractures involving skull or face with other bones, with cerebral laceration and contusion, no loss of consciousness

804.12 Closed fractures involving skull or face with other bones, with cerebral laceration and contusion, brief (less than one hour) loss of consciousness

804.13 Closed fractures involving skull or face with other bones, with cerebral laceration and contusion, moderate (1-24 hours) loss of consciousness

804.14 Closed fractures involving skull or face with other bones, with cerebral laceration and contusion, prolonged (more than 24 hours) loss of consciousness and return to pre-existing conscious level

804.15 Closed fractures involving skull or face with other bones, with cerebral laceration and contusion, prolonged (more than 24 hours) loss of consciousness, without return to pre-existing conscious level

804.16 Closed fractures involving skull or face with other bones, with cerebral laceration and contusion, loss of consciousness of unspecified duration ▽

804.19 Closed fractures involving skull or face with other bones, with cerebral laceration and contusion, unspecified concussion ▽

804.20 Closed fractures involving skull or face with other bones with subarachnoid, subdural, and extradural hemorrhage, unspecified state of consciousness ▽

804.21 Closed fractures involving skull or face with other bones with subarachnoid, subdural, and extradural hemorrhage, no loss of consciousness

804.22 Closed fractures involving skull or face with other bones with subarachnoid, subdural, and extradural hemorrhage, brief (less than one hour) loss of consciousness

804.23 Closed fractures involving skull or face with other bones with subarachnoid, subdural, and extradural hemorrhage, moderate (1-24 hours) loss of consciousness

804.24 Closed fractures involving skull or face with other bones with subarachnoid, subdural, and extradural hemorrhage, prolonged (more than 24 hours) loss of consciousness and return to pre-existing conscious level

▽ Unspecified code ♀ Female diagnosis ☒ Manifestation code ♂ Male diagnosis [Resequenced code]

804.25 Closed fractures involving skull or face with other bones with subarachnoid, subdural, and extradural hemorrhage, prolonged (more than 24 hours) loss of consciousness, without return to pre-existing conscious level

804.26 Closed fractures involving skull or face with other bones with subarachnoid, subdural, and extradural hemorrhage, loss of consciousness of unspecified duration ▽

804.29 Closed fractures involving skull or face with other bones with subarachnoid, subdural, and extradural hemorrhage, unspecified concussion ▽

804.30 Closed fractures involving skull or face with other bones, with other and unspecified intracranial hemorrhage, unspecified state of consciousness ▽

804.31 Closed fractures involving skull or face with other bones, with other and unspecified intracranial hemorrhage, no loss of consciousness ▽

804.32 Closed fractures involving skull or face with other bones, with other and unspecified intracranial hemorrhage, brief (less than one hour) loss of consciousness ▽

804.33 Closed fractures involving skull or face with other bones, with other and unspecified intracranial hemorrhage, moderate (1-24 hours) loss of consciousness ▽

804.34 Closed fractures involving skull or face with other bones, with other and unspecified intracranial hemorrhage, prolonged (more than 24 hours) loss of consciousness and return to preexisting conscious level ▽

804.35 Closed fractures involving skull or face with other bones, with other and unspecified intracranial hemorrhage, prolonged (more than 24 hours) loss of consciousness, without return to pre-existing conscious level ▽

804.36 Closed fractures involving skull or face with other bones, with other and unspecified intracranial hemorrhage, loss of consciousness of unspecified duration ▽

804.39 Closed fractures involving skull or face with other bones, with other and unspecified intracranial hemorrhage, unspecified concussion ▽

804.40 Closed fractures involving skull or face with other bones, with intracranial injury of other and unspecified nature, unspecified state of consciousness ▽

804.41 Closed fractures involving skull or face with other bones, with intracranial injury of other and unspecified nature, no loss of consciousness ▽

804.42 Closed fractures involving skull or face with other bones, with intracranial injury of other and unspecified nature, brief (less than one hour) loss of consciousness ▽

804.43 Closed fractures involving skull or face with other bones, with intracranial injury of other and unspecified nature, moderate (1-24 hours) loss of consciousness ▽

804.44 Closed fractures involving skull or face with other bones, with intracranial injury of other and unspecified nature, prolonged (more than 24 hours) loss of consciousness and return to pre-existing conscious level ▽

804.45 Closed fractures involving skull or face with other bones, with intracranial injury of other and unspecified nature, prolonged (more than 24 hours) loss of consciousness, without return to pre-existing conscious level ▽

804.46 Closed fractures involving skull or face with other bones, with intracranial injury of other and unspecified nature, loss of consciousness of unspecified duration ▽

804.49 Closed fractures involving skull or face with other bones, with intracranial injury of other and unspecified nature, unspecified concussion ▽

804.50 Open fractures involving skull or face with other bones, without mention of intracranial injury, unspecified state of consciousness ▽

804.51 Open fractures involving skull or face with other bones, without mention of intracranial injury, no loss of consciousness

804.52 Open fractures involving skull or face with other bones, without mention of intracranial injury, brief (less than one hour) loss of consciousness

804.53 Open fractures involving skull or face with other bones, without mention of intracranial injury, moderate (1-24 hours) loss of consciousness

804.54 Open fractures involving skull or face with other bones, without mention of intracranial injury, prolonged (more than 24 hours) loss of consciousness and return to pre-existing conscious level

804.55 Open fractures involving skull or face with other bones, without mention of intracranial injury, prolonged (more than 24 hours) loss of consciousness, without return to pre-existing conscious level

804.56 Open fractures involving skull or face with other bones, without mention of intracranial injury, loss of consciousness of unspecified duration ▽

804.59 Open fractures involving skull or face with other bones, without mention of intracranial injury, unspecified concussion ▽

804.60 Open fractures involving skull or face with other bones, with cerebral laceration and contusion, unspecified state of consciousness ▽

804.61 Open fractures involving skull or face with other bones, with cerebral laceration and contusion, no loss of consciousness

804.62 Open fractures involving skull or face with other bones, with cerebral laceration and contusion, brief (less than one hour) loss of consciousness

804.63 Open fractures involving skull or face with other bones, with cerebral laceration and contusion, moderate (1-24 hours) loss of consciousness

804.64 Open fractures involving skull or face with other bones, with cerebral laceration and contusion, prolonged (more than 24 hours) loss of consciousness and return to pre-existing conscious level

804.65 Open fractures involving skull or face with other bones, with cerebral laceration and contusion, prolonged (more than 24 hours) loss of consciousness, without return to pre-existing conscious level

804.66 Open fractures involving skull or face with other bones, with cerebral laceration and contusion, loss of consciousness of unspecified duration ▽

804.69 Open fractures involving skull or face with other bones, with cerebral laceration and contusion, unspecified concussion ▽

804.70 Open fractures involving skull or face with other bones with subarachnoid, subdural, and extradural hemorrhage, unspecified state of consciousness ▽

804.71 Open fractures involving skull or face with other bones with subarachnoid, subdural, and extradural hemorrhage, no loss of consciousness

804.72 Open fractures involving skull or face with other bones with subarachnoid, subdural, and extradural hemorrhage, brief (less than one hour) loss of consciousness

804.73 Open fractures involving skull or face with other bones with subarachnoid, subdural, and extradural hemorrhage, moderate (1-24 hours) loss of consciousness

804.74 Open fractures involving skull or face with other bones with subarachnoid, subdural, and extradural hemorrhage, prolonged (more than 24 hours) loss of consciousness and return to pre-existing conscious level

804.75 Open fractures involving skull or face with other bones with subarachnoid, subdural, and extradural hemorrhage, prolonged (more than 24 hours) loss of consciousness, without return to pre-existing conscious level

804.76 Open fractures involving skull or face with other bones with subarachnoid, subdural, and extradural hemorrhage, loss of consciousness of unspecified duration ▽

804.79 Open fractures involving skull or face with other bones with subarachnoid, subdural, and extradural hemorrhage, unspecified concussion ▽

804.80 Open fractures involving skull or face with other bones, with other and unspecified intracranial hemorrhage, unspecified state of consciousness ▽

804.81 Open fractures involving skull or face with other bones, with other and unspecified intracranial hemorrhage, no loss of consciousness ▽

804.82 Open fractures involving skull or face with other bones, with other and unspecified intracranial hemorrhage, brief (less than one hour) loss of consciousness ▽

804.83 Open fractures involving skull or face with other bones, with other and unspecified intracranial hemorrhage, moderate (1-24 hours) loss of consciousness ▽

804.84 Open fractures involving skull or face with other bones, with other and unspecified intracranial hemorrhage, prolonged (more than 24 hours) loss of consciousness and return to pre-existing conscious level ▽

804.85 Open fractures involving skull or face with other bones, with other and unspecified intracranial hemorrhage, prolonged (more than 24 hours) loss of consciousness, without return to pre-existing conscious level ▽

804.86 Open fractures involving skull or face with other bones, with other and unspecified intracranial hemorrhage, loss of consciousness of unspecified duration ▽

804.89 Open fractures involving skull or face with other bones, with other and unspecified intracranial hemorrhage, unspecified concussion ▽

804.90 Open fractures involving skull or face with other bones, with intracranial injury of other and unspecified nature, unspecified state of consciousness ▽

804.91 Open fractures involving skull or face with other bones, with intracranial injury of other and unspecified nature, no loss of consciousness ▽

804.92 Open fractures involving skull or face with other bones, with intracranial injury of other and unspecified nature, brief (less than one hour) loss of consciousness ▽

804.93 Open fractures involving skull or face with other bones, with intracranial injury of other and unspecified nature, moderate (1-24 hours) loss of consciousness ▽
804.94 Open fractures involving skull or face with other bones, with intracranial injury of other and unspecified nature, prolonged (more than 24 hours) loss of consciousness and return to pre-existing conscious level ▽
804.95 Open fractures involving skull or face with other bones, with intracranial injury of other and unspecified nature, prolonged (more than 24 hours) loss of consciousness, without return to pre-existing level ▽
804.96 Open fractures involving skull or face with other bones, with intracranial injury of other and unspecified nature, loss of consciousness of unspecified duration ▽
804.99 Open fractures involving skull or face with other bones, with intracranial injury of other and unspecified nature, unspecified concussion ▽

ICD-9-CM Procedural
76.79 Other open reduction of facial fracture
76.91 Bone graft to facial bone

21440
21440 Closed treatment of mandibular or maxillary alveolar ridge fracture (separate procedure)

ICD-9-CM Diagnostic
802.27 Closed fracture of alveolar border of body of mandible
802.29 Closed fracture of multiple sites of mandible
802.4 Malar and maxillary bones, closed fracture
802.8 Other facial bones, closed fracture

ICD-9-CM Procedural
76.73 Closed reduction of maxillary fracture
76.75 Closed reduction of mandibular fracture

HCPCS Level II Supplies & Services
A4570 Splint

21445
21445 Open treatment of mandibular or maxillary alveolar ridge fracture (separate procedure)

ICD-9-CM Diagnostic
802.27 Closed fracture of alveolar border of body of mandible
802.29 Closed fracture of multiple sites of mandible
802.37 Open fracture of alveolar border of body of mandible
802.39 Open fracture of multiple sites of mandible
802.4 Malar and maxillary bones, closed fracture
802.5 Malar and maxillary bones, open fracture

ICD-9-CM Procedural
76.77 Open reduction of alveolar fracture

21450-21451
21450 Closed treatment of mandibular fracture; without manipulation
21451 with manipulation

ICD-9-CM Diagnostic
802.20 Closed fracture of unspecified site of mandible ▽
802.21 Closed fracture of condylar process of mandible
802.22 Closed fracture of subcondylar process of mandible
802.23 Closed fracture of coronoid process of mandible
802.24 Closed fracture of unspecified part of ramus of mandible ▽
802.25 Closed fracture of angle of jaw
802.26 Closed fracture of symphysis of body of mandible
802.29 Closed fracture of multiple sites of mandible

ICD-9-CM Procedural
76.75 Closed reduction of mandibular fracture
93.59 Other immobilization, pressure, and attention to wound

HCPCS Level II Supplies & Services
A4305 Disposable drug delivery system, flow rate of 50 ml or greater per hour

21452
21452 Percutaneous treatment of mandibular fracture, with external fixation

ICD-9-CM Diagnostic
733.82 Nonunion of fracture
802.20 Closed fracture of unspecified site of mandible ▽
802.21 Closed fracture of condylar process of mandible
802.22 Closed fracture of subcondylar process of mandible
802.23 Closed fracture of coronoid process of mandible
802.24 Closed fracture of unspecified part of ramus of mandible ▽
802.25 Closed fracture of angle of jaw
802.26 Closed fracture of symphysis of body of mandible
802.27 Closed fracture of alveolar border of body of mandible
802.28 Closed fracture of other and unspecified part of body of mandible ▽
802.29 Closed fracture of multiple sites of mandible

ICD-9-CM Procedural
76.75 Closed reduction of mandibular fracture
78.19 Application of external fixator device, other

HCPCS Level II Supplies & Services
A4305 Disposable drug delivery system, flow rate of 50 ml or greater per hour

21453
21453 Closed treatment of mandibular fracture with interdental fixation

ICD-9-CM Diagnostic
733.82 Nonunion of fracture
802.20 Closed fracture of unspecified site of mandible ▽
802.21 Closed fracture of condylar process of mandible
802.22 Closed fracture of subcondylar process of mandible
802.23 Closed fracture of coronoid process of mandible
802.24 Closed fracture of unspecified part of ramus of mandible ▽
802.25 Closed fracture of angle of jaw
802.26 Closed fracture of symphysis of body of mandible
802.27 Closed fracture of alveolar border of body of mandible
802.28 Closed fracture of other and unspecified part of body of mandible ▽
802.29 Closed fracture of multiple sites of mandible

ICD-9-CM Procedural
76.75 Closed reduction of mandibular fracture

21454
21454 Open treatment of mandibular fracture with external fixation

ICD-9-CM Diagnostic
733.82 Nonunion of fracture
802.21 Closed fracture of condylar process of mandible
802.22 Closed fracture of subcondylar process of mandible
802.23 Closed fracture of coronoid process of mandible
802.24 Closed fracture of unspecified part of ramus of mandible ▽
802.25 Closed fracture of angle of jaw
802.26 Closed fracture of symphysis of body of mandible
802.27 Closed fracture of alveolar border of body of mandible
802.28 Closed fracture of other and unspecified part of body of mandible ▽
802.29 Closed fracture of multiple sites of mandible
802.31 Open fracture of condylar process of mandible

802.32 Open fracture of subcondylar process of mandible
802.34 Open fracture of unspecified part of ramus of mandible ▽
802.35 Open fracture of angle of jaw
802.36 Open fracture of symphysis of body of mandible
802.37 Open fracture of alveolar border of body of mandible
802.38 Open fracture of other and unspecified part of body of mandible ▽
802.39 Open fracture of multiple sites of mandible

ICD-9-CM Procedural

76.76 Open reduction of mandibular fracture
78.19 Application of external fixator device, other

21461-21462

21461 Open treatment of mandibular fracture; without interdental fixation
21462 with interdental fixation

ICD-9-CM Diagnostic

733.82 Nonunion of fracture
802.21 Closed fracture of condylar process of mandible
802.22 Closed fracture of subcondylar process of mandible
802.23 Closed fracture of coronoid process of mandible
802.24 Closed fracture of unspecified part of ramus of mandible ▽
802.25 Closed fracture of angle of jaw
802.26 Closed fracture of symphysis of body of mandible
802.27 Closed fracture of alveolar border of body of mandible
802.28 Closed fracture of other and unspecified part of body of mandible ▽
802.29 Closed fracture of multiple sites of mandible
802.30 Open fracture of unspecified site of mandible ▽
802.31 Open fracture of condylar process of mandible
802.32 Open fracture of subcondylar process of mandible
802.33 Open fracture of coronoid process of mandible
802.34 Open fracture of unspecified part of ramus of mandible ▽
802.35 Open fracture of angle of jaw
802.36 Open fracture of symphysis of body of mandible
802.37 Open fracture of alveolar border of body of mandible
802.38 Open fracture of other and unspecified part of body of mandible ▽
802.39 Open fracture of multiple sites of mandible

ICD-9-CM Procedural

76.76 Open reduction of mandibular fracture

21465

21465 Open treatment of mandibular condylar fracture

ICD-9-CM Diagnostic

733.82 Nonunion of fracture
802.21 Closed fracture of condylar process of mandible
802.22 Closed fracture of subcondylar process of mandible
802.29 Closed fracture of multiple sites of mandible
802.30 Open fracture of unspecified site of mandible ▽
802.31 Open fracture of condylar process of mandible
802.32 Open fracture of subcondylar process of mandible
802.33 Open fracture of coronoid process of mandible
802.39 Open fracture of multiple sites of mandible

ICD-9-CM Procedural

76.76 Open reduction of mandibular fracture

21470

21470 Open treatment of complicated mandibular fracture by multiple surgical approaches including internal fixation, interdental fixation, and/or wiring of dentures or splints

ICD-9-CM Diagnostic

733.82 Nonunion of fracture
802.21 Closed fracture of condylar process of mandible
802.22 Closed fracture of subcondylar process of mandible
802.23 Closed fracture of coronoid process of mandible
802.24 Closed fracture of unspecified part of ramus of mandible ▽
802.25 Closed fracture of angle of jaw
802.26 Closed fracture of symphysis of body of mandible
802.27 Closed fracture of alveolar border of body of mandible
802.28 Closed fracture of other and unspecified part of body of mandible ▽
802.29 Closed fracture of multiple sites of mandible
802.30 Open fracture of unspecified site of mandible ▽
802.31 Open fracture of condylar process of mandible
802.32 Open fracture of subcondylar process of mandible
802.33 Open fracture of coronoid process of mandible
802.34 Open fracture of unspecified part of ramus of mandible ▽
802.35 Open fracture of angle of jaw
802.36 Open fracture of symphysis of body of mandible
802.37 Open fracture of alveolar border of body of mandible
802.38 Open fracture of other and unspecified part of body of mandible ▽
802.39 Open fracture of multiple sites of mandible

ICD-9-CM Procedural

76.76 Open reduction of mandibular fracture
78.19 Application of external fixator device, other

21480-21485

21480 Closed treatment of temporomandibular dislocation; initial or subsequent
21485 complicated (eg, recurrent requiring intermaxillary fixation or splinting), initial or subsequent

ICD-9-CM Diagnostic

524.63 Articular disc disorder (reducing or non-reducing) of temporomandibular joint
524.64 Temporomandibular joint sounds on opening and/or closing the jaw
524.69 Other specified temporomandibular joint disorders
830.0 Closed dislocation of jaw
925.1 Crushing injury of face and scalp — (Use additional code to identify any associated injuries, such as: 800-829, 850.0-854.1, 860.0-869.1)

ICD-9-CM Procedural

76.93 Closed reduction of temporomandibular dislocation
76.95 Other manipulation of temporomandibular joint

HCPCS Level II Supplies & Services

A4305 Disposable drug delivery system, flow rate of 50 ml or greater per hour

21490

21490 Open treatment of temporomandibular dislocation

ICD-9-CM Diagnostic

524.63 Articular disc disorder (reducing or non-reducing) of temporomandibular joint
524.64 Temporomandibular joint sounds on opening and/or closing the jaw
524.69 Other specified temporomandibular joint disorders
830.0 Closed dislocation of jaw
830.1 Open dislocation of jaw

ICD-9-CM Procedural

76.94 Open reduction of temporomandibular dislocation

21495

21495 Open treatment of hyoid fracture

ICD-9-CM Diagnostic

807.5 Closed fracture of larynx and trachea
807.6 Open fracture of larynx and trachea
925.2 Crushing injury of neck — (Use additional code to identify any associated injuries, such as: 800-829, 850.0-854.1, 860.0-869.1)

ICD-9-CM Procedural

31.64 Repair of laryngeal fracture

21497

21497 Interdental wiring, for condition other than fracture

ICD-9-CM Diagnostic

170.0 Malignant neoplasm of bones of skull and face, except mandible
170.1 Malignant neoplasm of mandible
213.0 Benign neoplasm of bones of skull and face
213.1 Benign neoplasm of lower jaw bone
278.00 Obesity, unspecified — (Use additional code to identify Body Mass Index (BMI), if known: V85.0-V85.54) (Use additional code to identify any associated intellectual disabilities) ▽
278.01 Morbid obesity — (Use additional code to identify Body Mass Index (BMI), if known: V85.0-V85.54)
524.01 Maxillary hyperplasia
524.02 Mandibular hyperplasia
524.04 Mandibular hypoplasia
524.69 Other specified temporomandibular joint disorders
526.89 Other specified disease of the jaws
830.0 Closed dislocation of jaw
830.1 Open dislocation of jaw
839.8 Closed dislocation, multiple and ill-defined sites
941.09 Burn of unspecified degree of multiple sites (except with eye) of face, head, and neck ▽

ICD-9-CM Procedural

24.7 Application of orthodontic appliance
93.55 Dental wiring

HCPCS Level II Supplies & Services

A4305 Disposable drug delivery system, flow rate of 50 ml or greater per hour

Neck (Soft Tissues) and Thorax

21501-21502

21501 Incision and drainage, deep abscess or hematoma, soft tissues of neck or thorax;
21502 with partial rib ostectomy

ICD-9-CM Diagnostic

682.1 Cellulitis and abscess of neck — (Use additional code to identify organism, such as 041.1, etc.)
682.2 Cellulitis and abscess of trunk — (Use additional code to identify organism, such as 041.1, etc.)
729.92 Nontraumatic hematoma of soft tissue
784.2 Swelling, mass, or lump in head and neck
920 Contusion of face, scalp, and neck except eye(s)
922.1 Contusion of chest wall
998.59 Other postoperative infection — (Use additional code to identify infection)

ICD-9-CM Procedural

77.81 Other partial ostectomy of scapula, clavicle, and thorax (ribs and sternum)
83.02 Myotomy
83.09 Other incision of soft tissue

HCPCS Level II Supplies & Services

A4305 Disposable drug delivery system, flow rate of 50 ml or greater per hour

21510

21510 Incision, deep, with opening of bone cortex (eg, for osteomyelitis or bone abscess), thorax

ICD-9-CM Diagnostic

682.2 Cellulitis and abscess of trunk — (Use additional code to identify organism, such as 041.1, etc.)
730.18 Chronic osteomyelitis, other specified sites — (Use additional code to identify organism: 041.1. Use additional code to identify major osseous defect, if applicable: 731.3)
730.19 Chronic osteomyelitis, multiple sites — (Use additional code to identify organism: 041.1. Use additional code to identify major osseous defect, if applicable: 731.3)
730.28 Unspecified osteomyelitis, other specified sites — (Use additional code to identify organism: 041.1. Use additional code to identify major osseous defect, if applicable: 731.3) ▽
730.29 Unspecified osteomyelitis, multiple sites — (Use additional code to identify organism: 041.1. Use additional code to identify major osseous defect, if applicable: 731.3) ▽
731.3 Major osseous defects — (Code first underlying disease: 170.0-170.9, 730.00-730.29, 733.00-733.09, 733.40-733.49, 996.45)
786.6 Swelling, mass, or lump in chest
998.51 Infected postoperative seroma — (Use additional code to identify organism)
998.59 Other postoperative infection — (Use additional code to identify infection)

ICD-9-CM Procedural

34.01 Incision of chest wall
77.01 Sequestrectomy of scapula, clavicle, and thorax (ribs and sternum)

21550

21550 Biopsy, soft tissue of neck or thorax

ICD-9-CM Diagnostic

171.0 Malignant neoplasm of connective and other soft tissue of head, face, and neck
171.4 Malignant neoplasm of connective and other soft tissue of thorax
195.0 Malignant neoplasm of head, face, and neck
195.1 Malignant neoplasm of thorax
198.89 Secondary malignant neoplasm of other specified sites
215.0 Other benign neoplasm of connective and other soft tissue of head, face, and neck
215.4 Other benign neoplasm of connective and other soft tissue of thorax
229.8 Benign neoplasm of other specified sites
234.8 Carcinoma in situ of other specified sites
238.1 Neoplasm of uncertain behavior of connective and other soft tissue
239.89 Neoplasms of unspecified nature, other specified sites
709.9 Unspecified disorder of skin and subcutaneous tissue ▽
782.2 Localized superficial swelling, mass, or lump
784.2 Swelling, mass, or lump in head and neck

ICD-9-CM Procedural

34.23 Biopsy of chest wall
83.21 Open biopsy of soft tissue

21555-21558 [21552, 21554]

21552 Excision, tumor, soft tissue of neck or anterior thorax, subcutaneous; 3 cm or greater
21554 Excision, tumor, soft tissue of neck or anterior thorax, subfascial (eg, intramuscular); 5 cm or greater
21555 Excision, tumor, soft tissue of neck or anterior thorax, subcutaneous; less than 3 cm
21556 Excision, tumor, soft tissue of neck or anterior thorax, subfascial (eg, intramuscular); less than 5 cm
21557 Radical resection of tumor (eg, sarcoma), soft tissue of neck or anterior thorax; less than 5 cm
21558 5 cm or greater

ICD-9-CM Diagnostic

171.0 Malignant neoplasm of connective and other soft tissue of head, face, and neck
171.4 Malignant neoplasm of connective and other soft tissue of thorax
171.8 Malignant neoplasm of other specified sites of connective and other soft tissue
195.0 Malignant neoplasm of head, face, and neck
195.1 Malignant neoplasm of thorax
198.89 Secondary malignant neoplasm of other specified sites
199.0 Disseminated malignant neoplasm
199.1 Other malignant neoplasm of unspecified site
209.32 Merkel cell carcinoma of the scalp and neck
209.35 Merkel cell carcinoma of the trunk
209.75 Secondary Merkel cell carcinoma
214.1 Lipoma of other skin and subcutaneous tissue
214.8 Lipoma of other specified sites
215.0 Other benign neoplasm of connective and other soft tissue of head, face, and neck
215.4 Other benign neoplasm of connective and other soft tissue of thorax
229.8 Benign neoplasm of other specified sites
234.8 Carcinoma in situ of other specified sites
238.1 Neoplasm of uncertain behavior of connective and other soft tissue
239.2 Neoplasms of unspecified nature of bone, soft tissue, and skin
782.2 Localized superficial swelling, mass, or lump
784.2 Swelling, mass, or lump in head and neck
786.6 Swelling, mass, or lump in chest

ICD-9-CM Procedural

83.32 Excision of lesion of muscle
83.39 Excision of lesion of other soft tissue
83.49 Other excision of soft tissue
86.3 Other local excision or destruction of lesion or tissue of skin and subcutaneous tissue
86.4 Radical excision of skin lesion

21600

21600 Excision of rib, partial

ICD-9-CM Diagnostic

170.3 Malignant neoplasm of ribs, sternum, and clavicle
198.5 Secondary malignant neoplasm of bone and bone marrow
209.73 Secondary neuroendocrine tumor of bone
213.3 Benign neoplasm of ribs, sternum, and clavicle
229.8 Benign neoplasm of other specified sites
238.0 Neoplasm of uncertain behavior of bone and articular cartilage
239.2 Neoplasms of unspecified nature of bone, soft tissue, and skin
730.18 Chronic osteomyelitis, other specified sites — (Use additional code to identify organism: 041.1. Use additional code to identify major osseous defect, if applicable: 731.3)
730.88 Other infections involving bone diseases classified elsewhere, other specified sites — (Use additional code to identify organism: 041.1. Code first underlying disease: 002.0, 015.0-015.9) ☒
731.3 Major osseous defects — (Code first underlying disease: 170.0-170.9, 730.00-730.29, 733.00-733.09, 733.40-733.49, 996.45)
756.2 Cervical rib
756.3 Other congenital anomaly of ribs and sternum
V10.90 Personal history of unspecified malignant neoplasm ▽
V10.91 Personal history of malignant neuroendocrine tumor — (Code first any continuing functional activity, such as: carcinoid syndrome (259.2))

ICD-9-CM Procedural

77.81 Other partial ostectomy of scapula, clavicle, and thorax (ribs and sternum)

21610

21610 Costotransversectomy (separate procedure)

ICD-9-CM Diagnostic

170.2 Malignant neoplasm of vertebral column, excluding sacrum and coccyx
170.3 Malignant neoplasm of ribs, sternum, and clavicle
198.5 Secondary malignant neoplasm of bone and bone marrow
209.73 Secondary neuroendocrine tumor of bone
213.2 Benign neoplasm of vertebral column, excluding sacrum and coccyx
213.3 Benign neoplasm of ribs, sternum, and clavicle
229.8 Benign neoplasm of other specified sites
238.0 Neoplasm of uncertain behavior of bone and articular cartilage
239.2 Neoplasms of unspecified nature of bone, soft tissue, and skin
715.09 Generalized osteoarthrosis, involving multiple sites
715.18 Primary localized osteoarthrosis, other specified sites
715.98 Osteoarthrosis, unspecified whether generalized or localized, other specified sites ▽
730.18 Chronic osteomyelitis, other specified sites — (Use additional code to identify organism: 041.1. Use additional code to identify major osseous defect, if applicable: 731.3)
730.88 Other infections involving bone diseases classified elsewhere, other specified sites — (Use additional code to identify organism: 041.1. Code first underlying disease: 002.0, 015.0-015.9) ☒
731.3 Major osseous defects — (Code first underlying disease: 170.0-170.9, 730.00-730.29, 733.00-733.09, 733.40-733.49, 996.45)
756.3 Other congenital anomaly of ribs and sternum
V10.90 Personal history of unspecified malignant neoplasm ▽
V10.91 Personal history of malignant neuroendocrine tumor — (Code first any continuing functional activity, such as: carcinoid syndrome (259.2))

ICD-9-CM Procedural

77.91 Total ostectomy of scapula, clavicle, and thorax (ribs and sternum)

21615-21616

21615 Excision first and/or cervical rib;
21616 with sympathectomy

ICD-9-CM Diagnostic

353.0 Brachial plexus lesions
443.0 Raynaud's syndrome — (Use additional code to identify gangrene: 785.4)
444.21 Embolism and thrombosis of arteries of upper extremity
723.1 Cervicalgia
723.4 Brachial neuritis or radiculitis NOS ▽
756.2 Cervical rib
786.52 Painful respiration
786.6 Swelling, mass, or lump in chest

ICD-9-CM Procedural

05.22 Cervical sympathectomy
77.91 Total ostectomy of scapula, clavicle, and thorax (ribs and sternum)

21620

21620 Ostectomy of sternum, partial

ICD-9-CM Diagnostic

170.3 Malignant neoplasm of ribs, sternum, and clavicle
198.5 Secondary malignant neoplasm of bone and bone marrow
209.73 Secondary neuroendocrine tumor of bone
213.3 Benign neoplasm of ribs, sternum, and clavicle
238.0 Neoplasm of uncertain behavior of bone and articular cartilage
239.2 Neoplasms of unspecified nature of bone, soft tissue, and skin
519.2 Mediastinitis — (Use additional code to identify infectious organism)
730.18 Chronic osteomyelitis, other specified sites — (Use additional code to identify organism: 041.1. Use additional code to identify major osseous defect, if applicable: 731.3)
730.28 Unspecified osteomyelitis, other specified sites — (Use additional code to identify organism: 041.1. Use additional code to identify major osseous defect, if applicable: 731.3) ▽
730.88 Other infections involving bone diseases classified elsewhere, other specified sites — (Use additional code to identify organism: 041.1. Code first underlying disease: 002.0, 015.0-015.9) ☒
731.3 Major osseous defects — (Code first underlying disease: 170.0-170.9, 730.00-730.29, 733.00-733.09, 733.40-733.49, 996.45)
733.49 Aseptic necrosis of other bone site — (Use additional code to identify major osseous defect, if applicable: 731.3)
733.99 Other disorders of bone and cartilage
V10.90 Personal history of unspecified malignant neoplasm ▽
V10.91 Personal history of malignant neuroendocrine tumor — (Code first any continuing functional activity, such as: carcinoid syndrome (259.2))

ICD-9-CM Procedural

77.81 Other partial ostectomy of scapula, clavicle, and thorax (ribs and sternum)

21627

21627 Sternal debridement

ICD-9-CM Diagnostic

170.3 Malignant neoplasm of ribs, sternum, and clavicle
198.5 Secondary malignant neoplasm of bone and bone marrow
209.73 Secondary neuroendocrine tumor of bone
213.3 Benign neoplasm of ribs, sternum, and clavicle
238.0 Neoplasm of uncertain behavior of bone and articular cartilage
239.2 Neoplasms of unspecified nature of bone, soft tissue, and skin
519.2 Mediastinitis — (Use additional code to identify infectious organism)
730.18 Chronic osteomyelitis, other specified sites — (Use additional code to identify organism: 041.1. Use additional code to identify major osseous defect, if applicable: 731.3)
730.28 Unspecified osteomyelitis, other specified sites — (Use additional code to identify organism: 041.1. Use additional code to identify major osseous defect, if applicable: 731.3) ▽
730.88 Other infections involving bone diseases classified elsewhere, other specified sites — (Use additional code to identify organism: 041.1. Code first underlying disease: 002.0, 015.0-015.9) ☒
731.3 Major osseous defects — (Code first underlying disease: 170.0-170.9, 730.00-730.29, 733.00-733.09, 733.40-733.49, 996.45)
733.49 Aseptic necrosis of other bone site — (Use additional code to identify major osseous defect, if applicable: 731.3)
875.1 Open wound of chest (wall), complicated
998.51 Infected postoperative seroma — (Use additional code to identify organism)
998.59 Other postoperative infection — (Use additional code to identify infection)
998.83 Non-healing surgical wound

ICD-9-CM Procedural

77.61 Local excision of lesion or tissue of scapula, clavicle, and thorax (ribs and sternum)

21630-21632

21630 Radical resection of sternum;
21632 with mediastinal lymphadenectomy

ICD-9-CM Diagnostic

170.3 Malignant neoplasm of ribs, sternum, and clavicle
196.1 Secondary and unspecified malignant neoplasm of intrathoracic lymph nodes
197.1 Secondary malignant neoplasm of mediastinum
198.5 Secondary malignant neoplasm of bone and bone marrow
209.73 Secondary neuroendocrine tumor of bone
213.3 Benign neoplasm of ribs, sternum, and clavicle
238.0 Neoplasm of uncertain behavior of bone and articular cartilage
730.18 Chronic osteomyelitis, other specified sites — (Use additional code to identify organism: 041.1. Use additional code to identify major osseous defect, if applicable: 731.3)
730.28 Unspecified osteomyelitis, other specified sites — (Use additional code to identify organism: 041.1. Use additional code to identify major osseous defect, if applicable: 731.3) ▽
730.88 Other infections involving bone diseases classified elsewhere, other specified sites — (Use additional code to identify organism: 041.1. Code first underlying disease: 002.0, 015.0-015.9) ☒
731.3 Major osseous defects — (Code first underlying disease: 170.0-170.9, 730.00-730.29, 733.00-733.09, 733.40-733.49, 996.45)
733.49 Aseptic necrosis of other bone site — (Use additional code to identify major osseous defect, if applicable: 731.3)
875.1 Open wound of chest (wall), complicated
998.59 Other postoperative infection — (Use additional code to identify infection)
V10.90 Personal history of unspecified malignant neoplasm ▽
V10.91 Personal history of malignant neuroendocrine tumor — (Code first any continuing functional activity, such as: carcinoid syndrome (259.2))

ICD-9-CM Procedural

40.22 Excision of internal mammary lymph node
40.3 Regional lymph node excision
40.59 Radical excision of other lymph nodes
77.81 Other partial ostectomy of scapula, clavicle, and thorax (ribs and sternum)
77.91 Total ostectomy of scapula, clavicle, and thorax (ribs and sternum)

21685

21685 Hyoid myotomy and suspension

ICD-9-CM Diagnostic

327.20 Organic sleep apnea, unspecified ▽
327.23 Obstructive sleep apnea (adult) (pediatric)
327.29 Other organic sleep apnea
780.50 Unspecified sleep disturbance
780.51 Insomnia with sleep apnea, unspecified ▽
780.53 Hypersomnia with sleep apnea, unspecified ▽
780.57 Unspecified sleep apnea ▽

ICD-9-CM Procedural

83.02 Myotomy

21700-21705

21700 Division of scalenus anticus; without resection of cervical rib
21705 with resection of cervical rib

ICD-9-CM Diagnostic

353.0 Brachial plexus lesions

728.85 Spasm of muscle
756.2 Cervical rib

ICD-9-CM Procedural

77.81 Other partial ostectomy of scapula, clavicle, and thorax (ribs and sternum)
83.19 Other division of soft tissue

21720-21725

21720 Division of sternocleidomastoid for torticollis, open operation; without cast application
21725 with cast application

ICD-9-CM Diagnostic

333.83 Spasmodic torticollis — (Use additional E code to identify drug, if drug-induced)
723.5 Torticollis, unspecified ▽
754.1 Congenital musculoskeletal deformity of sternocleidomastoid muscle
781.93 Ocular torticollis

ICD-9-CM Procedural

83.19 Other division of soft tissue
93.52 Application of neck support
93.53 Application of other cast

21740-21743

21740 Reconstructive repair of pectus excavatum or carinatum; open
21742 minimally invasive approach (Nuss procedure), without thoracoscopy
21743 minimally invasive approach (Nuss procedure), with thoracoscopy

ICD-9-CM Diagnostic

277.5 Mucopolysaccharidosis — (Use additional code to identify any associated intellectual disabilities)
754.81 Pectus excavatum
754.82 Pectus carinatum
756.51 Osteogenesis imperfecta
758.6 Gonadal dysgenesis — (Use additional codes for conditions associated with the chromosomal anomalies)
759.82 Marfan's syndrome

ICD-9-CM Procedural

34.21 Transpleural thoracoscopy
34.74 Repair of pectus deformity

21750

21750 Closure of median sternotomy separation with or without debridement (separate procedure)

ICD-9-CM Diagnostic

733.81 Malunion of fracture
733.82 Nonunion of fracture
998.31 Disruption of internal operation (surgical) wound
998.59 Other postoperative infection — (Use additional code to identify infection)
998.83 Non-healing surgical wound

ICD-9-CM Procedural

77.61 Local excision of lesion or tissue of scapula, clavicle, and thorax (ribs and sternum)
78.49 Other repair or plastic operations on other bone, except facial bones
84.94 Insertion of sternal fixation device with rigid plates

21800

21800 Closed treatment of rib fracture, uncomplicated, each

ICD-9-CM Diagnostic

786.52 Painful respiration
807.00 Closed fracture of rib(s), unspecified ▽
807.01 Closed fracture of one rib
807.02 Closed fracture of two ribs
807.03 Closed fracture of three ribs
807.04 Closed fracture of four ribs
807.05 Closed fracture of five ribs
807.06 Closed fracture of six ribs
807.07 Closed fracture of seven ribs
807.08 Closed fracture of eight or more ribs
807.09 Closed fracture of multiple ribs, unspecified ▽

ICD-9-CM Procedural

79.09 Closed reduction of fracture of other specified bone, except facial bones, without internal fixation

21805

21805 Open treatment of rib fracture without fixation, each

ICD-9-CM Diagnostic

807.01 Closed fracture of one rib
807.02 Closed fracture of two ribs
807.03 Closed fracture of three ribs
807.04 Closed fracture of four ribs
807.05 Closed fracture of five ribs
807.06 Closed fracture of six ribs
807.07 Closed fracture of seven ribs
807.08 Closed fracture of eight or more ribs
807.11 Open fracture of one rib
807.12 Open fracture of two ribs
807.13 Open fracture of three ribs
807.14 Open fracture of four ribs
807.15 Open fracture of five ribs
807.16 Open fracture of six ribs
807.17 Open fracture of seven ribs
807.18 Open fracture of eight or more ribs

ICD-9-CM Procedural

79.29 Open reduction of fracture of other specified bone, except facial bones, without internal fixation

21810

21810 Treatment of rib fracture requiring external fixation (flail chest)

ICD-9-CM Diagnostic

807.4 Flail chest

ICD-9-CM Procedural

78.11 Application of external fixator device, scapula, clavicle, and thorax [ribs and sternum]
79.09 Closed reduction of fracture of other specified bone, except facial bones, without internal fixation

21820

21820 Closed treatment of sternum fracture

ICD-9-CM Diagnostic

807.2 Closed fracture of sternum

ICD-9-CM Procedural

79.09 Closed reduction of fracture of other specified bone, except facial bones, without internal fixation

HCPCS Level II Supplies & Services

A4649 Surgical supply; miscellaneous

21825

21825 Open treatment of sternum fracture with or without skeletal fixation

ICD-9-CM Diagnostic

733.81 Malunion of fracture
733.82 Nonunion of fracture
807.2 Closed fracture of sternum
807.3 Open fracture of sternum

ICD-9-CM Procedural

79.29 Open reduction of fracture of other specified bone, except facial bones, without internal fixation
79.39 Open reduction of fracture of other specified bone, except facial bones, with internal fixation
84.94 Insertion of sternal fixation device with rigid plates

Back and Flank

21920-21925

21920 Biopsy, soft tissue of back or flank; superficial
21925 deep

ICD-9-CM Diagnostic

171.7 Malignant neoplasm of connective and other soft tissue of trunk, unspecified site ▽
195.8 Malignant neoplasm of other specified sites
198.89 Secondary malignant neoplasm of other specified sites
214.1 Lipoma of other skin and subcutaneous tissue
215.7 Other benign neoplasm of connective and other soft tissue of trunk, unspecified ▽
229.8 Benign neoplasm of other specified sites
238.1 Neoplasm of uncertain behavior of connective and other soft tissue
238.8 Neoplasm of uncertain behavior of other specified sites
239.2 Neoplasms of unspecified nature of bone, soft tissue, and skin
239.89 Neoplasms of unspecified nature, other specified sites
782.2 Localized superficial swelling, mass, or lump

ICD-9-CM Procedural

83.21 Open biopsy of soft tissue

21930-21936

21930 Excision, tumor, soft tissue of back or flank, subcutaneous; less than 3 cm
21931 3 cm or greater
21932 Excision, tumor, soft tissue of back or flank, subfascial (eg, intramuscular); less than 5 cm
21933 5 cm or greater
21935 Radical resection of tumor (eg, sarcoma), soft tissue of back or flank; less than 5 cm
21936 5 cm or greater

ICD-9-CM Diagnostic

171.7 Malignant neoplasm of connective and other soft tissue of trunk, unspecified site ▽
172.5 Malignant melanoma of skin of trunk, except scrotum
195.8 Malignant neoplasm of other specified sites
198.89 Secondary malignant neoplasm of other specified sites
209.35 Merkel cell carcinoma of the trunk
209.75 Secondary Merkel cell carcinoma
214.1 Lipoma of other skin and subcutaneous tissue
215.7 Other benign neoplasm of connective and other soft tissue of trunk, unspecified ▽
228.01 Hemangioma of skin and subcutaneous tissue
238.1 Neoplasm of uncertain behavior of connective and other soft tissue
239.2 Neoplasms of unspecified nature of bone, soft tissue, and skin
782.2 Localized superficial swelling, mass, or lump

ICD-9-CM Procedural

83.32 Excision of lesion of muscle
83.39 Excision of lesion of other soft tissue
83.49 Other excision of soft tissue
86.3 Other local excision or destruction of lesion or tissue of skin and subcutaneous tissue
86.4 Radical excision of skin lesion

HCPCS Level II Supplies & Services

A4305 Disposable drug delivery system, flow rate of 50 ml or greater per hour

Spine (Vertebral Column)

22010-22015

22010 Incision and drainage, open, of deep abscess (subfascial), posterior spine; cervical, thoracic, or cervicothoracic
22015 lumbar, sacral, or lumbosacral

ICD-9-CM Diagnostic

324.9 Intracranial and intraspinal abscess of unspecified site ▽
682.1 Cellulitis and abscess of neck — (Use additional code to identify organism, such as 041.1, etc.)
682.2 Cellulitis and abscess of trunk — (Use additional code to identify organism, such as 041.1, etc.)
682.8 Cellulitis and abscess of other specified site — (Use additional code to identify organism, such as 041.1, etc.)
728.86 Necrotizing fasciitis — (Use additional code to identify infectious organism, 041.00-041.89, 785.4, if applicable)
728.89 Other disorder of muscle, ligament, and fascia — (Use additional E code to identify drug, if drug-induced)
730.08 Acute osteomyelitis, other specified site — (Use additional code to identify organism: 041.1. Use additional code to identify major osseous defect, if applicable: 731.3)
731.3 Major osseous defects — (Code first underlying disease: 170.0-170.9, 730.00-730.29, 733.00-733.09, 733.40-733.49, 996.45)
996.63 Infection and inflammatory reaction due to nervous system device, implant, and graft — (Use additional code to identify specified infections)
996.67 Infection and inflammatory reaction due to other internal orthopedic device, implant, and graft — (Use additional code to identify specified infections)
996.78 Other complications due to other internal orthopedic device, implant, and graft — (Use additional code to identify complication: 338.18-338.19, 338.28-338.29)
998.59 Other postoperative infection — (Use additional code to identify infection)

ICD-9-CM Procedural

83.09 Other incision of soft tissue

22100-22103

22100 Partial excision of posterior vertebral component (eg, spinous process, lamina or facet) for intrinsic bony lesion, single vertebral segment; cervical
22101 thoracic
22102 lumbar
22103 each additional segment (List separately in addition to code for primary procedure)

ICD-9-CM Diagnostic

170.2 Malignant neoplasm of vertebral column, excluding sacrum and coccyx
198.5 Secondary malignant neoplasm of bone and bone marrow
209.73 Secondary neuroendocrine tumor of bone
213.2 Benign neoplasm of vertebral column, excluding sacrum and coccyx
238.0 Neoplasm of uncertain behavior of bone and articular cartilage
239.2 Neoplasms of unspecified nature of bone, soft tissue, and skin
720.0 Ankylosing spondylitis
720.1 Spinal enthesopathy
720.81 Inflammatory spondylopathies in diseases classified elsewhere — (Code first underlying disease: 015.0) ☒
720.89 Other inflammatory spondylopathies
720.9 Unspecified inflammatory spondylopathy ▽
721.0 Cervical spondylosis without myelopathy

721.1	Cervical spondylosis with myelopathy
721.2	Thoracic spondylosis without myelopathy
721.3	Lumbosacral spondylosis without myelopathy
721.41	Spondylosis with myelopathy, thoracic region
721.42	Spondylosis with myelopathy, lumbar region
721.5	Kissing spine
721.8	Other allied disorders of spine
723.0	Spinal stenosis in cervical region
730.18	Chronic osteomyelitis, other specified sites — (Use additional code to identify organism: 041.1. Use additional code to identify major osseous defect, if applicable: 731.3)
730.28	Unspecified osteomyelitis, other specified sites — (Use additional code to identify organism: 041.1. Use additional code to identify major osseous defect, if applicable: 731.3) ▽
731.3	Major osseous defects — (Code first underlying disease: 170.0-170.9, 730.00-730.29, 733.00-733.09, 733.40-733.49, 996.45)
733.13	Pathologic fracture of vertebrae
733.20	Unspecified cyst of bone (localized) ▽
733.21	Solitary bone cyst
733.22	Aneurysmal bone cyst
733.29	Other cyst of bone
733.95	Stress fracture of other bone — (Use additional external cause code(s) to identify the cause of the stress fracture)
738.5	Other acquired deformity of back or spine
756.15	Congenital fusion of spine (vertebra)

ICD-9-CM Procedural

77.89	Other partial ostectomy of other bone, except facial bones

22110-22116

22110	Partial excision of vertebral body, for intrinsic bony lesion, without decompression of spinal cord or nerve root(s), single vertebral segment; cervical
22112	thoracic
22114	lumbar
22116	each additional vertebral segment (List separately in addition to code for primary procedure)

ICD-9-CM Diagnostic

094.0	Tabes dorsalis — (Use additional code to identify any associated mental disorder. Use additional code to identify manifestation: 713.5)
098.53	Gonococcal spondylitis
170.2	Malignant neoplasm of vertebral column, excluding sacrum and coccyx
198.5	Secondary malignant neoplasm of bone and bone marrow
209.73	Secondary neuroendocrine tumor of bone
213.2	Benign neoplasm of vertebral column, excluding sacrum and coccyx
238.0	Neoplasm of uncertain behavior of bone and articular cartilage
239.2	Neoplasms of unspecified nature of bone, soft tissue, and skin
721.5	Kissing spine
722.31	Schmorl's nodes, thoracic region
722.32	Schmorl's nodes, lumbar region
722.39	Schmorl's nodes, other spinal region
723.0	Spinal stenosis in cervical region
724.01	Spinal stenosis of thoracic region
724.02	Spinal stenosis of lumbar region, without neurogenic claudication
724.03	Spinal stenosis of lumbar region, with neurogenic claudication
730.18	Chronic osteomyelitis, other specified sites — (Use additional code to identify organism: 041.1. Use additional code to identify major osseous defect, if applicable: 731.3)
730.28	Unspecified osteomyelitis, other specified sites — (Use additional code to identify organism: 041.1. Use additional code to identify major osseous defect, if applicable: 731.3) ▽
730.88	Other infections involving bone diseases classified elsewhere, other specified sites — (Use additional code to identify organism: 041.1. Code first underlying disease: 002.0, 015.0-015.9) ☒
731.3	Major osseous defects — (Code first underlying disease: 170.0-170.9, 730.00-730.29, 733.00-733.09, 733.40-733.49, 996.45)
733.21	Solitary bone cyst
733.22	Aneurysmal bone cyst
733.29	Other cyst of bone

ICD-9-CM Procedural

77.89	Other partial ostectomy of other bone, except facial bones

22206

22206	Osteotomy of spine, posterior or posterolateral approach, 3 columns, 1 vertebral segment (eg, pedicle/vertebral body subtraction); thoracic

ICD-9-CM Diagnostic

138	Late effects of acute poliomyelitis — (Note: This category is to be used to indicate conditions classifiable to 045 as the cause of late effects, which are themselves classified elsewhere. The "late effects" include those specified as such, as sequelae, or as due to old or inactive poliomyelitis, without evidence of active disease.)
237.70	Neurofibromatosis, unspecified ▽
237.71	Neurofibromatosis, Type 1 (von Recklinghausen's disease)
237.72	Neurofibromatosis, Type 2 (acoustic neurofibromatosis)
237.73	Schwannomatosis
237.79	Other neurofibromatosis
268.1	Rickets, late effect — (Use additional code to identify the nature of late effect)
720.0	Ankylosing spondylitis
721.7	Traumatic spondylopathy
731.0	Osteitis deformans without mention of bone tumor
732.0	Juvenile osteochondrosis of spine
733.13	Pathologic fracture of vertebrae
733.90	Disorder of bone and cartilage, unspecified ▽
733.95	Stress fracture of other bone — (Use additional external cause code(s) to identify the cause of the stress fracture)
737.10	Kyphosis (acquired) (postural)
737.11	Kyphosis due to radiation
737.12	Kyphosis, postlaminectomy
737.19	Other kyphosis (acquired)
737.20	Lordosis (acquired) (postural)
737.30	Scoliosis (and kyphoscoliosis), idiopathic
737.41	Kyphosis associated with other condition — (Code first associated condition: 015.0, 138, 237.7, 252.01, 277.5, 356.1, 731.0, 733.00-733.09) ☒
738.5	Other acquired deformity of back or spine
754.2	Congenital musculoskeletal deformity of spine
756.12	Congenital spondylolisthesis
756.15	Congenital fusion of spine (vertebra)
756.19	Other congenital anomaly of spine
805.00	Closed fracture of cervical vertebra, unspecified level without mention of spinal cord injury ▽
805.10	Open fracture of cervical vertebra, unspecified level without mention of spinal cord injury ▽
805.2	Closed fracture of dorsal (thoracic) vertebra without mention of spinal cord injury
805.3	Open fracture of dorsal (thoracic) vertebra without mention of spinal cord injury
805.4	Closed fracture of lumbar vertebra without mention of spinal cord injury
805.5	Open fracture of lumbar vertebra without mention of spinal cord injury
905.1	Late effect of fracture of spine and trunk without mention of spinal cord lesion

ICD-9-CM Procedural

77.29	Wedge osteotomy of other bone, except facial bones
77.39	Other division of other bone, except facial bones

22207

22207 Osteotomy of spine, posterior or posterolateral approach, 3 columns, 1 vertebral segment (eg, pedicle/vertebral body subtraction); lumbar

ICD-9-CM Diagnostic

138 Late effects of acute poliomyelitis — (Note: This category is to be used to indicate conditions classifiable to 045 as the cause of late effects, which are themselves classified elsewhere. The "late effects" include those specified as such, as sequelae, or as due to old or inactive poliomyelitis, without evidence of active disease.)
237.70 Neurofibromatosis, unspecified ▽
237.71 Neurofibromatosis, Type 1 (von Recklinghausen's disease)
237.72 Neurofibromatosis, Type 2 (acoustic neurofibromatosis)
237.73 Schwannomatosis
237.79 Other neurofibromatosis
268.1 Rickets, late effect — (Use additional code to identify the nature of late effect)
720.0 Ankylosing spondylitis
721.7 Traumatic spondylopathy
731.0 Osteitis deformans without mention of bone tumor
732.0 Juvenile osteochondrosis of spine
733.13 Pathologic fracture of vertebrae
733.90 Disorder of bone and cartilage, unspecified ▽
733.95 Stress fracture of other bone — (Use additional external cause code(s) to identify the cause of the stress fracture)
737.10 Kyphosis (acquired) (postural)
737.11 Kyphosis due to radiation
737.12 Kyphosis, postlaminectomy
737.19 Other kyphosis (acquired)
737.20 Lordosis (acquired) (postural)
737.30 Scoliosis (and kyphoscoliosis), idiopathic
737.41 Kyphosis associated with other condition — (Code first associated condition: 015.0, 138, 237.7, 252.01, 277.5, 356.1, 731.0, 733.00-733.09) ☒
738.5 Other acquired deformity of back or spine
754.2 Congenital musculoskeletal deformity of spine
756.12 Congenital spondylolisthesis
756.15 Congenital fusion of spine (vertebra)
756.19 Other congenital anomaly of spine
805.00 Closed fracture of cervical vertebra, unspecified level without mention of spinal cord injury ▽
805.10 Open fracture of cervical vertebra, unspecified level without mention of spinal cord injury ▽
805.2 Closed fracture of dorsal (thoracic) vertebra without mention of spinal cord injury
805.3 Open fracture of dorsal (thoracic) vertebra without mention of spinal cord injury
805.4 Closed fracture of lumbar vertebra without mention of spinal cord injury
805.5 Open fracture of lumbar vertebra without mention of spinal cord injury
905.1 Late effect of fracture of spine and trunk without mention of spinal cord lesion

ICD-9-CM Procedural

77.29 Wedge osteotomy of other bone, except facial bones
77.39 Other division of other bone, except facial bones

22208

22208 Osteotomy of spine, posterior or posterolateral approach, 3 columns, 1 vertebral segment (eg, pedicle/vertebral body subtraction); each additional vertebral segment (List separately in addition to code for primary procedure)

ICD-9-CM Diagnostic

237.70 Neurofibromatosis, unspecified ▽
237.71 Neurofibromatosis, Type 1 (von Recklinghausen's disease)
237.72 Neurofibromatosis, Type 2 (acoustic neurofibromatosis)
237.73 Schwannomatosis
237.79 Other neurofibromatosis
720.0 Ankylosing spondylitis
721.7 Traumatic spondylopathy
722.0 Displacement of cervical intervertebral disc without myelopathy
722.10 Displacement of lumbar intervertebral disc without myelopathy
722.11 Displacement of thoracic intervertebral disc without myelopathy
722.4 Degeneration of cervical intervertebral disc
722.51 Degeneration of thoracic or thoracolumbar intervertebral disc
722.52 Degeneration of lumbar or lumbosacral intervertebral disc
722.71 Intervertebral cervical disc disorder with myelopathy, cervical region
722.72 Intervertebral thoracic disc disorder with myelopathy, thoracic region
722.73 Intervertebral lumbar disc disorder with myelopathy, lumbar region
731.0 Osteitis deformans without mention of bone tumor
732.0 Juvenile osteochondrosis of spine
733.13 Pathologic fracture of vertebrae
733.95 Stress fracture of other bone — (Use additional external cause code(s) to identify the cause of the stress fracture)
737.10 Kyphosis (acquired) (postural)
737.11 Kyphosis due to radiation
737.12 Kyphosis, postlaminectomy
737.19 Other kyphosis (acquired)
737.20 Lordosis (acquired) (postural)
737.30 Scoliosis (and kyphoscoliosis), idiopathic
737.41 Kyphosis associated with other condition — (Code first associated condition: 015.0, 138, 237.7, 252.01, 277.5, 356.1, 731.0, 733.00-733.09) ☒
738.5 Other acquired deformity of back or spine
756.12 Congenital spondylolisthesis
756.15 Congenital fusion of spine (vertebra)
756.19 Other congenital anomaly of spine
905.1 Late effect of fracture of spine and trunk without mention of spinal cord lesion
907.2 Late effect of spinal cord injury

ICD-9-CM Procedural

77.29 Wedge osteotomy of other bone, except facial bones
77.39 Other division of other bone, except facial bones

22210-22216

22210 Osteotomy of spine, posterior or posterolateral approach, 1 vertebral segment; cervical
22212 thoracic
22214 lumbar
22216 each additional vertebral segment (List separately in addition to primary procedure)

ICD-9-CM Diagnostic

138 Late effects of acute poliomyelitis — (Note: This category is to be used to indicate conditions classifiable to 045 as the cause of late effects, which are themselves classified elsewhere. The "late effects" include those specified as such, as sequelae, or as due to old or inactive poliomyelitis, without evidence of active disease.)
237.70 Neurofibromatosis, unspecified ▽
237.71 Neurofibromatosis, Type 1 (von Recklinghausen's disease)
237.72 Neurofibromatosis, Type 2 (acoustic neurofibromatosis)
237.73 Schwannomatosis
237.79 Other neurofibromatosis
268.1 Rickets, late effect — (Use additional code to identify the nature of late effect)
720.0 Ankylosing spondylitis
721.7 Traumatic spondylopathy
731.0 Osteitis deformans without mention of bone tumor
732.0 Juvenile osteochondrosis of spine
733.13 Pathologic fracture of vertebrae
733.90 Disorder of bone and cartilage, unspecified ▽
733.95 Stress fracture of other bone — (Use additional external cause code(s) to identify the cause of the stress fracture)
737.10 Kyphosis (acquired) (postural)

737.11 Kyphosis due to radiation
737.12 Kyphosis, postlaminectomy
737.19 Other kyphosis (acquired)
737.20 Lordosis (acquired) (postural)
737.30 Scoliosis (and kyphoscoliosis), idiopathic
737.41 Kyphosis associated with other condition — (Code first associated condition: 015.0, 138, 237.7, 252.01, 277.5, 356.1, 731.0, 733.00-733.09) ☒
738.5 Other acquired deformity of back or spine
756.12 Congenital spondylolisthesis
756.15 Congenital fusion of spine (vertebra)
756.19 Other congenital anomaly of spine
805.00 Closed fracture of cervical vertebra, unspecified level without mention of spinal cord injury ▽
805.10 Open fracture of cervical vertebra, unspecified level without mention of spinal cord injury ▽
805.2 Closed fracture of dorsal (thoracic) vertebra without mention of spinal cord injury
805.3 Open fracture of dorsal (thoracic) vertebra without mention of spinal cord injury
805.4 Closed fracture of lumbar vertebra without mention of spinal cord injury
805.5 Open fracture of lumbar vertebra without mention of spinal cord injury
905.1 Late effect of fracture of spine and trunk without mention of spinal cord lesion

ICD-9-CM Procedural

77.29 Wedge osteotomy of other bone, except facial bones
77.39 Other division of other bone, except facial bones

22220-22226

22220 Osteotomy of spine, including discectomy, anterior approach, single vertebral segment; cervical
22222 thoracic
22224 lumbar
22226 each additional vertebral segment (List separately in addition to code for primary procedure)

ICD-9-CM Diagnostic

138 Late effects of acute poliomyelitis — (Note: This category is to be used to indicate conditions classifiable to 045 as the cause of late effects, which are themselves classified elsewhere. The "late effects" include those specified as such, as sequelae, or as due to old or inactive poliomyelitis, without evidence of active disease.)
237.70 Neurofibromatosis, unspecified ▽
237.71 Neurofibromatosis, Type 1 (von Recklinghausen's disease)
237.72 Neurofibromatosis, Type 2 (acoustic neurofibromatosis)
237.73 Schwannomatosis
237.79 Other neurofibromatosis
268.1 Rickets, late effect — (Use additional code to identify the nature of late effect)
720.0 Ankylosing spondylitis
721.7 Traumatic spondylopathy
722.0 Displacement of cervical intervertebral disc without myelopathy
722.10 Displacement of lumbar intervertebral disc without myelopathy
722.11 Displacement of thoracic intervertebral disc without myelopathy
722.4 Degeneration of cervical intervertebral disc
722.51 Degeneration of thoracic or thoracolumbar intervertebral disc
722.52 Degeneration of lumbar or lumbosacral intervertebral disc
722.71 Intervertebral cervical disc disorder with myelopathy, cervical region
722.72 Intervertebral thoracic disc disorder with myelopathy, thoracic region
722.73 Intervertebral lumbar disc disorder with myelopathy, lumbar region
731.0 Osteitis deformans without mention of bone tumor
732.0 Juvenile osteochondrosis of spine
733.13 Pathologic fracture of vertebrae
733.90 Disorder of bone and cartilage, unspecified ▽
733.95 Stress fracture of other bone — (Use additional external cause code(s) to identify the cause of the stress fracture)
737.10 Kyphosis (acquired) (postural)
737.11 Kyphosis due to radiation
737.12 Kyphosis, postlaminectomy
737.19 Other kyphosis (acquired)
737.20 Lordosis (acquired) (postural)
737.30 Scoliosis (and kyphoscoliosis), idiopathic
737.41 Kyphosis associated with other condition — (Code first associated condition: 015.0, 138, 237.7, 252.01, 277.5, 356.1, 731.0, 733.00-733.09) ☒
738.5 Other acquired deformity of back or spine
756.12 Congenital spondylolisthesis
756.15 Congenital fusion of spine (vertebra)
756.19 Other congenital anomaly of spine
905.1 Late effect of fracture of spine and trunk without mention of spinal cord lesion
907.2 Late effect of spinal cord injury

ICD-9-CM Procedural

77.29 Wedge osteotomy of other bone, except facial bones
77.39 Other division of other bone, except facial bones
80.51 Excision of intervertebral disc

22305-22310

22305 Closed treatment of vertebral process fracture(s)
22310 Closed treatment of vertebral body fracture(s), without manipulation, requiring and including casting or bracing

ICD-9-CM Diagnostic

336.9 Unspecified disease of spinal cord ▽
731.3 Major osseous defects — (Code first underlying disease: 170.0-170.9, 730.00-730.29, 733.00-733.09, 733.40-733.49, 996.45)
733.00 Unspecified osteoporosis — (Use additional code to identify major osseous defect, if applicable: 731.3) (Use additional code to identify personal history of pathologic (healed) fracture: V13.51) ▽
733.01 Senile osteoporosis — (Use additional code to identify major osseous defect, if applicable: 731.3) (Use additional code to identify personal history of pathologic (healed) fracture: V13.51)
733.02 Idiopathic osteoporosis — (Use additional code to identify major osseous defect, if applicable: 731.3) (Use additional code to identify personal history of pathologic (healed) fracture: V13.51)
733.13 Pathologic fracture of vertebrae
733.95 Stress fracture of other bone — (Use additional external cause code(s) to identify the cause of the stress fracture)
805.01 Closed fracture of first cervical vertebra without mention of spinal cord injury
805.02 Closed fracture of second cervical vertebra without mention of spinal cord injury
805.03 Closed fracture of third cervical vertebra without mention of spinal cord injury
805.04 Closed fracture of fourth cervical vertebra without mention of spinal cord injury
805.05 Closed fracture of fifth cervical vertebra without mention of spinal cord injury
805.06 Closed fracture of sixth cervical vertebra without mention of spinal cord injury
805.07 Closed fracture of seventh cervical vertebra without mention of spinal cord injury
805.08 Closed fracture of multiple cervical vertebrae without mention of spinal cord injury
805.2 Closed fracture of dorsal (thoracic) vertebra without mention of spinal cord injury
805.4 Closed fracture of lumbar vertebra without mention of spinal cord injury
805.6 Closed fracture of sacrum and coccyx without mention of spinal cord injury
806.00 Closed fracture of C1-C4 level with unspecified spinal cord injury ▽
806.01 Closed fracture of C1-C4 level with complete lesion of cord
806.02 Closed fracture of C1-C4 level with anterior cord syndrome
806.03 Closed fracture of C1-C4 level with central cord syndrome
806.04 Closed fracture of C1-C4 level with other specified spinal cord injury
806.05 Closed fracture of C5-C7 level with unspecified spinal cord injury ▽
806.06 Closed fracture of C5-C7 level with complete lesion of cord
806.07 Closed fracture of C5-C7 level with anterior cord syndrome
806.08 Closed fracture of C5-C7 level with central cord syndrome

806.09 Closed fracture of C5-C7 level with other specified spinal cord injury
806.20 Closed fracture of T1-T6 level with unspecified spinal cord injury ♥
806.21 Closed fracture of T1-T6 level with complete lesion of cord
806.22 Closed fracture of T1-T6 level with anterior cord syndrome
806.23 Closed fracture of T1-T6 level with central cord syndrome
806.24 Closed fracture of T1-T6 level with other specified spinal cord injury
806.25 Closed fracture of T7-T12 level with unspecified spinal cord injury ♥
806.26 Closed fracture of T7-T12 level with complete lesion of cord
806.27 Closed fracture of T7-T12 level with anterior cord syndrome
806.28 Closed fracture of T7-T12 level with central cord syndrome
806.29 Closed fracture of T7-T12 level with other specified spinal cord injury
806.4 Closed fracture of lumbar spine with spinal cord injury

ICD-9-CM Procedural

03.53 Repair of vertebral fracture

HCPCS Level II Supplies & Services

A4580 Cast supplies (e.g., plaster)

22315

22315 Closed treatment of vertebral fracture(s) and/or dislocation(s) requiring casting or bracing, with and including casting and/or bracing by manipulation or traction

ICD-9-CM Diagnostic

336.9 Unspecified disease of spinal cord ♥
731.3 Major osseous defects — (Code first underlying disease: 170.0-170.9, 730.00-730.29, 733.00-733.09, 733.40-733.49, 996.45)
733.00 Unspecified osteoporosis — (Use additional code to identify major osseous defect, if applicable: 731.3) (Use additional code to identify personal history of pathologic (healed) fracture: V13.51) ♥
733.01 Senile osteoporosis — (Use additional code to identify major osseous defect, if applicable: 731.3) (Use additional code to identify personal history of pathologic (healed) fracture: V13.51)
733.02 Idiopathic osteoporosis — (Use additional code to identify major osseous defect, if applicable: 731.3) (Use additional code to identify personal history of pathologic (healed) fracture: V13.51)
733.13 Pathologic fracture of vertebrae
733.95 Stress fracture of other bone — (Use additional external cause code(s) to identify the cause of the stress fracture)
805.00 Closed fracture of cervical vertebra, unspecified level without mention of spinal cord injury ♥
805.01 Closed fracture of first cervical vertebra without mention of spinal cord injury
805.02 Closed fracture of second cervical vertebra without mention of spinal cord injury
805.03 Closed fracture of third cervical vertebra without mention of spinal cord injury
805.04 Closed fracture of fourth cervical vertebra without mention of spinal cord injury
805.05 Closed fracture of fifth cervical vertebra without mention of spinal cord injury
805.06 Closed fracture of sixth cervical vertebra without mention of spinal cord injury
805.07 Closed fracture of seventh cervical vertebra without mention of spinal cord injury
805.08 Closed fracture of multiple cervical vertebrae without mention of spinal cord injury
805.2 Closed fracture of dorsal (thoracic) vertebra without mention of spinal cord injury
805.4 Closed fracture of lumbar vertebra without mention of spinal cord injury
805.6 Closed fracture of sacrum and coccyx without mention of spinal cord injury
806.00 Closed fracture of C1-C4 level with unspecified spinal cord injury ♥
806.01 Closed fracture of C1-C4 level with complete lesion of cord
806.02 Closed fracture of C1-C4 level with anterior cord syndrome
806.03 Closed fracture of C1-C4 level with central cord syndrome
806.04 Closed fracture of C1-C4 level with other specified spinal cord injury
806.05 Closed fracture of C5-C7 level with unspecified spinal cord injury ♥
806.06 Closed fracture of C5-C7 level with complete lesion of cord
806.07 Closed fracture of C5-C7 level with anterior cord syndrome
806.08 Closed fracture of C5-C7 level with central cord syndrome
806.09 Closed fracture of C5-C7 level with other specified spinal cord injury
806.20 Closed fracture of T1-T6 level with unspecified spinal cord injury ♥
806.21 Closed fracture of T1-T6 level with complete lesion of cord
806.22 Closed fracture of T1-T6 level with anterior cord syndrome
806.23 Closed fracture of T1-T6 level with central cord syndrome
806.24 Closed fracture of T1-T6 level with other specified spinal cord injury
806.25 Closed fracture of T7-T12 level with unspecified spinal cord injury ♥
806.26 Closed fracture of T7-T12 level with complete lesion of cord
806.27 Closed fracture of T7-T12 level with anterior cord syndrome
806.28 Closed fracture of T7-T12 level with central cord syndrome
806.29 Closed fracture of T7-T12 level with other specified spinal cord injury
806.4 Closed fracture of lumbar spine with spinal cord injury
806.60 Closed fracture of sacrum and coccyx with unspecified spinal cord injury ♥
839.01 Closed dislocation, first cervical vertebra
839.02 Closed dislocation, second cervical vertebra
839.03 Closed dislocation, third cervical vertebra
839.04 Closed dislocation, fourth cervical vertebra
839.05 Closed dislocation, fifth cervical vertebra
839.06 Closed dislocation, sixth cervical vertebra
839.07 Closed dislocation, seventh cervical vertebra
839.08 Closed dislocation, multiple cervical vertebrae
839.20 Closed dislocation, lumbar vertebra
839.21 Closed dislocation, thoracic vertebra
839.41 Closed dislocation, coccyx
839.42 Closed dislocation, sacrum
839.49 Closed dislocation, other vertebra

ICD-9-CM Procedural

02.94 Insertion or replacement of skull tongs or halo traction device
03.53 Repair of vertebral fracture
93.41 Spinal traction using skull device
93.42 Other spinal traction

HCPCS Level II Supplies & Services

A4580 Cast supplies (e.g., plaster)

22318-22319

22318 Open treatment and/or reduction of odontoid fracture(s) and or dislocation(s) (including os odontoideum), anterior approach, including placement of internal fixation; without grafting
22319 with grafting

ICD-9-CM Diagnostic

756.10 Congenital anomaly of spine, unspecified ♥
805.02 Closed fracture of second cervical vertebra without mention of spinal cord injury
805.12 Open fracture of second cervical vertebra without mention of spinal cord injury
806.00 Closed fracture of C1-C4 level with unspecified spinal cord injury ♥
806.01 Closed fracture of C1-C4 level with complete lesion of cord
806.02 Closed fracture of C1-C4 level with anterior cord syndrome
806.03 Closed fracture of C1-C4 level with central cord syndrome
806.04 Closed fracture of C1-C4 level with other specified spinal cord injury
806.10 Open fracture of C1-C4 level with unspecified spinal cord injury ♥
806.11 Open fracture of C1-C4 level with complete lesion of cord
806.12 Open fracture of C1-C4 level with anterior cord syndrome
806.13 Open fracture of C1-C4 level with central cord syndrome
806.14 Open fracture of C1-C4 level with other specified spinal cord injury
839.02 Closed dislocation, second cervical vertebra
839.12 Open dislocation, second cervical vertebra

ICD-9-CM Procedural

03.53 Repair of vertebral fracture

78.09 Bone graft of other bone, except facial bones
78.59 Internal fixation of other bone, except facial bones, without fracture reduction
79.39 Open reduction of fracture of other specified bone, except facial bones, with internal fixation
79.89 Open reduction of dislocation of other specified site, except temporomandibular

22325-22328

22325 Open treatment and/or reduction of vertebral fracture(s) and/or dislocation(s), posterior approach, 1 fractured vertebra or dislocated segment; lumbar
22326 cervical
22327 thoracic
22328 each additional fractured vertebra or dislocated segment (List separately in addition to code for primary procedure)

ICD-9-CM Diagnostic

733.13 Pathologic fracture of vertebrae
733.81 Malunion of fracture
733.82 Nonunion of fracture
733.95 Stress fracture of other bone — (Use additional external cause code(s) to identify the cause of the stress fracture)
805.00 Closed fracture of cervical vertebra, unspecified level without mention of spinal cord injury ▽
805.01 Closed fracture of first cervical vertebra without mention of spinal cord injury
805.02 Closed fracture of second cervical vertebra without mention of spinal cord injury
805.03 Closed fracture of third cervical vertebra without mention of spinal cord injury
805.04 Closed fracture of fourth cervical vertebra without mention of spinal cord injury
805.05 Closed fracture of fifth cervical vertebra without mention of spinal cord injury
805.06 Closed fracture of sixth cervical vertebra without mention of spinal cord injury
805.07 Closed fracture of seventh cervical vertebra without mention of spinal cord injury
805.08 Closed fracture of multiple cervical vertebrae without mention of spinal cord injury
805.10 Open fracture of cervical vertebra, unspecified level without mention of spinal cord injury ▽
805.11 Open fracture of first cervical vertebra without mention of spinal cord injury
805.12 Open fracture of second cervical vertebra without mention of spinal cord injury
805.13 Open fracture of third cervical vertebra without mention of spinal cord injury
805.14 Open fracture of fourth cervical vertebra without mention of spinal cord injury
805.15 Open fracture of fifth cervical vertebra without mention of spinal cord injury
805.16 Open fracture of sixth cervical vertebra without mention of spinal cord injury
805.17 Open fracture of seventh cervical vertebra without mention of spinal cord injury
805.18 Open fracture of multiple cervical vertebrae without mention of spinal cord injury
805.2 Closed fracture of dorsal (thoracic) vertebra without mention of spinal cord injury
805.3 Open fracture of dorsal (thoracic) vertebra without mention of spinal cord injury
805.4 Closed fracture of lumbar vertebra without mention of spinal cord injury
805.5 Open fracture of lumbar vertebra without mention of spinal cord injury
806.10 Open fracture of C1-C4 level with unspecified spinal cord injury ▽
806.11 Open fracture of C1-C4 level with complete lesion of cord
806.12 Open fracture of C1-C4 level with anterior cord syndrome
806.13 Open fracture of C1-C4 level with central cord syndrome
806.14 Open fracture of C1-C4 level with other specified spinal cord injury
806.15 Open fracture of C5-C7 level with unspecified spinal cord injury ▽
806.16 Open fracture of C5-C7 level with complete lesion of cord
806.17 Open fracture of C5-C7 level with anterior cord syndrome
806.18 Open fracture of C5-C7 level with central cord syndrome
806.19 Open fracture of C5-C7 level with other specified spinal cord injury
806.20 Closed fracture of T1-T6 level with unspecified spinal cord injury ▽
806.21 Closed fracture of T1-T6 level with complete lesion of cord
806.22 Closed fracture of T1-T6 level with anterior cord syndrome
806.23 Closed fracture of T1-T6 level with central cord syndrome
806.24 Closed fracture of T1-T6 level with other specified spinal cord injury
806.25 Closed fracture of T7-T12 level with unspecified spinal cord injury ▽
806.26 Closed fracture of T7-T12 level with complete lesion of cord
806.27 Closed fracture of T7-T12 level with anterior cord syndrome
806.28 Closed fracture of T7-T12 level with central cord syndrome
806.29 Closed fracture of T7-T12 level with other specified spinal cord injury
806.30 Open fracture of T1-T6 level with unspecified spinal cord injury ▽
806.31 Open fracture of T1-T6 level with complete lesion of cord
806.32 Open fracture of T1-T6 level with anterior cord syndrome
806.33 Open fracture of T1-T6 level with central cord syndrome
806.34 Open fracture of T1-T6 level with other specified spinal cord injury
806.35 Open fracture of T7-T12 level with unspecified spinal cord injury ▽
806.36 Open fracture of T7-T12 level with complete lesion of cord
806.37 Open fracture of T7-T12 level with anterior cord syndrome
806.38 Open fracture of T7-T12 level with central cord syndrome
806.39 Open fracture of T7-T12 level with other specified spinal cord injury
806.4 Closed fracture of lumbar spine with spinal cord injury
806.5 Open fracture of lumbar spine with spinal cord injury
839.00 Closed dislocation, unspecified cervical vertebra ▽
839.01 Closed dislocation, first cervical vertebra
839.02 Closed dislocation, second cervical vertebra
839.03 Closed dislocation, third cervical vertebra
839.04 Closed dislocation, fourth cervical vertebra
839.05 Closed dislocation, fifth cervical vertebra
839.06 Closed dislocation, sixth cervical vertebra
839.07 Closed dislocation, seventh cervical vertebra
839.08 Closed dislocation, multiple cervical vertebrae
839.10 Open dislocation, unspecified cervical vertebra ▽
839.11 Open dislocation, first cervical vertebra
839.12 Open dislocation, second cervical vertebra
839.13 Open dislocation, third cervical vertebra
839.14 Open dislocation, fourth cervical vertebra
839.15 Open dislocation, fifth cervical vertebra
839.16 Open dislocation, sixth cervical vertebra
839.17 Open dislocation, seventh cervical vertebra
839.18 Open dislocation, multiple cervical vertebrae
839.20 Closed dislocation, lumbar vertebra
839.21 Closed dislocation, thoracic vertebra
839.30 Open dislocation, lumbar vertebra
839.31 Open dislocation, thoracic vertebra

ICD-9-CM Procedural

03.53 Repair of vertebral fracture

22505

22505 Manipulation of spine requiring anesthesia, any region

ICD-9-CM Diagnostic

720.2 Sacroiliitis, not elsewhere classified
722.0 Displacement of cervical intervertebral disc without myelopathy
722.10 Displacement of lumbar intervertebral disc without myelopathy
722.11 Displacement of thoracic intervertebral disc without myelopathy
722.2 Displacement of intervertebral disc, site unspecified, without myelopathy ▽
722.4 Degeneration of cervical intervertebral disc
722.51 Degeneration of thoracic or thoracolumbar intervertebral disc
722.52 Degeneration of lumbar or lumbosacral intervertebral disc
722.90 Other and unspecified disc disorder of unspecified region ▽
722.92 Other and unspecified disc disorder of thoracic region ▽
722.93 Other and unspecified disc disorder of lumbar region ▽
723.5 Torticollis, unspecified ▽
724.00 Spinal stenosis, unspecified region other than cervical ▽
724.01 Spinal stenosis of thoracic region

724.02 Spinal stenosis of lumbar region, without neurogenic claudication
724.03 Spinal stenosis of lumbar region, with neurogenic claudication
724.2 Lumbago
724.3 Sciatica
728.85 Spasm of muscle
729.2 Unspecified neuralgia, neuritis, and radiculitis
739.2 Nonallopathic lesion of thoracic region, not elsewhere classified
739.3 Nonallopathic lesion of lumbar region, not elsewhere classified
739.4 Nonallopathic lesion of sacral region, not elsewhere classified
781.93 Ocular torticollis
839.00 Closed dislocation, unspecified cervical vertebra
839.01 Closed dislocation, first cervical vertebra
839.02 Closed dislocation, second cervical vertebra
839.03 Closed dislocation, third cervical vertebra
839.04 Closed dislocation, fourth cervical vertebra
839.05 Closed dislocation, fifth cervical vertebra
839.06 Closed dislocation, sixth cervical vertebra
839.07 Closed dislocation, seventh cervical vertebra
839.08 Closed dislocation, multiple cervical vertebrae
839.20 Closed dislocation, lumbar vertebra
839.21 Closed dislocation, thoracic vertebra
839.40 Closed dislocation, vertebra, unspecified site
839.41 Closed dislocation, coccyx
839.42 Closed dislocation, sacrum
839.49 Closed dislocation, other vertebra
847.0 Neck sprain and strain
953.0 Injury to cervical nerve root
956.0 Injury to sciatic nerve

ICD-9-CM Procedural

93.29 Other forcible correction of musculoskeletal deformity

22520-22522

22520 Percutaneous vertebroplasty (bone biopsy included when performed), 1 vertebral body, unilateral or bilateral injection; thoracic
22521 lumbar
22522 each additional thoracic or lumbar vertebral body (List separately in addition to code for primary procedure)

ICD-9-CM Diagnostic

170.2 Malignant neoplasm of vertebral column, excluding sacrum and coccyx
198.5 Secondary malignant neoplasm of bone and bone marrow
203.00 Multiple myeloma, without mention of having achieved remission
203.01 Multiple myeloma in remission
203.02 Multiple myeloma, in relapse
209.73 Secondary neuroendocrine tumor of bone
213.2 Benign neoplasm of vertebral column, excluding sacrum and coccyx
213.6 Benign neoplasm of pelvic bones, sacrum, and coccyx
238.0 Neoplasm of uncertain behavior of bone and articular cartilage
238.6 Neoplasm of uncertain behavior of plasma cells
239.2 Neoplasms of unspecified nature of bone, soft tissue, and skin
731.0 Osteitis deformans without mention of bone tumor
731.3 Major osseous defects — (Code first underlying disease: 170.0-170.9, 730.00-730.29, 733.00-733.09, 733.40-733.49, 996.45)
733.00 Unspecified osteoporosis — (Use additional code to identify major osseous defect, if applicable: 731.3) (Use additional code to identify personal history of pathologic (healed) fracture: V13.51)
733.01 Senile osteoporosis — (Use additional code to identify major osseous defect, if applicable: 731.3) (Use additional code to identify personal history of pathologic (healed) fracture: V13.51)
733.02 Idiopathic osteoporosis — (Use additional code to identify major osseous defect, if applicable: 731.3) (Use additional code to identify personal history of pathologic (healed) fracture: V13.51)
733.03 Disuse osteoporosis — (Use additional code to identify major osseous defect, if applicable: 731.3) (Use additional code to identify personal history of pathologic (healed) fracture: V13.51)
733.09 Other osteoporosis — (Use additional code to identify major osseous defect, if applicable: 731.3) (Use additional code to identify personal history of pathologic (healed) fracture: V13.51) (Use additional E code to identify drug)
733.13 Pathologic fracture of vertebrae
733.22 Aneurysmal bone cyst
733.7 Algoneurodystrophy
733.95 Stress fracture of other bone — (Use additional external cause code(s) to identify the cause of the stress fracture)
805.2 Closed fracture of dorsal (thoracic) vertebra without mention of spinal cord injury
805.4 Closed fracture of lumbar vertebra without mention of spinal cord injury

ICD-9-CM Procedural

81.65 Percutaneous vertebroplasty

22523-22525

22523 Percutaneous vertebral augmentation, including cavity creation (fracture reduction and bone biopsy included when performed) using mechanical device, 1 vertebral body, unilateral or bilateral cannulation (eg, kyphoplasty); thoracic
22524 lumbar
22525 each additional thoracic or lumbar vertebral body (List separately in addition to code for primary procedure)

ICD-9-CM Diagnostic

170.2 Malignant neoplasm of vertebral column, excluding sacrum and coccyx
198.5 Secondary malignant neoplasm of bone and bone marrow
203.00 Multiple myeloma, without mention of having achieved remission
203.01 Multiple myeloma in remission
203.02 Multiple myeloma, in relapse
209.73 Secondary neuroendocrine tumor of bone
213.2 Benign neoplasm of vertebral column, excluding sacrum and coccyx
237.5 Neoplasm of uncertain behavior of brain and spinal cord
238.0 Neoplasm of uncertain behavior of bone and articular cartilage
239.2 Neoplasms of unspecified nature of bone, soft tissue, and skin
731.0 Osteitis deformans without mention of bone tumor
733.00 Unspecified osteoporosis — (Use additional code to identify major osseous defect, if applicable: 731.3) (Use additional code to identify personal history of pathologic (healed) fracture: V13.51)
733.01 Senile osteoporosis — (Use additional code to identify major osseous defect, if applicable: 731.3) (Use additional code to identify personal history of pathologic (healed) fracture: V13.51)
733.02 Idiopathic osteoporosis — (Use additional code to identify major osseous defect, if applicable: 731.3) (Use additional code to identify personal history of pathologic (healed) fracture: V13.51)
733.03 Disuse osteoporosis — (Use additional code to identify major osseous defect, if applicable: 731.3) (Use additional code to identify personal history of pathologic (healed) fracture: V13.51)
733.09 Other osteoporosis — (Use additional code to identify major osseous defect, if applicable: 731.3) (Use additional code to identify personal history of pathologic (healed) fracture: V13.51) (Use additional E code to identify drug)
733.13 Pathologic fracture of vertebrae
733.95 Stress fracture of other bone — (Use additional external cause code(s) to identify the cause of the stress fracture)
733.96 Stress fracture of femoral neck — (Use additional external cause code(s) to identify the cause of the stress fracture)
733.97 Stress fracture of shaft of femur — (Use additional external cause code(s) to identify the cause of the stress fracture)

Unspecified code ♀ Female diagnosis ☒ Manifestation code ♂ Male diagnosis [Resequenced code]

733.98 Stress fracture of pelvis — (Use additional external cause code(s) to identify the cause of the stress fracture)
805.2 Closed fracture of dorsal (thoracic) vertebra without mention of spinal cord injury
805.4 Closed fracture of lumbar vertebra without mention of spinal cord injury

ICD-9-CM Procedural

81.66 Percutaneous vertebral augmentation

22526-22527

22526 Percutaneous intradiscal electrothermal annuloplasty, unilateral or bilateral including fluoroscopic guidance; single level
22527 1 or more additional levels (List separately in addition to code for primary procedure)

ICD-9-CM Diagnostic

721.0 Cervical spondylosis without myelopathy
721.1 Cervical spondylosis with myelopathy
721.2 Thoracic spondylosis without myelopathy
721.3 Lumbosacral spondylosis without myelopathy
721.41 Spondylosis with myelopathy, thoracic region
721.42 Spondylosis with myelopathy, lumbar region
721.8 Other allied disorders of spine
721.90 Spondylosis of unspecified site without mention of myelopathy ▽
721.91 Spondylosis of unspecified site with myelopathy ▽
722.0 Displacement of cervical intervertebral disc without myelopathy
722.10 Displacement of lumbar intervertebral disc without myelopathy
722.11 Displacement of thoracic intervertebral disc without myelopathy
722.2 Displacement of intervertebral disc, site unspecified, without myelopathy ▽
722.30 Schmorl's nodes, unspecified region ▽
722.31 Schmorl's nodes, thoracic region
722.32 Schmorl's nodes, lumbar region
722.39 Schmorl's nodes, other spinal region
722.4 Degeneration of cervical intervertebral disc
722.51 Degeneration of thoracic or thoracolumbar intervertebral disc
722.52 Degeneration of lumbar or lumbosacral intervertebral disc
722.6 Degeneration of intervertebral disc, site unspecified ▽
722.70 Intervertebral disc disorder with myelopathy, unspecified region ▽
722.71 Intervertebral cervical disc disorder with myelopathy, cervical region
722.72 Intervertebral thoracic disc disorder with myelopathy, thoracic region
722.73 Intervertebral lumbar disc disorder with myelopathy, lumbar region
724.4 Thoracic or lumbosacral neuritis or radiculitis, unspecified ▽

ICD-9-CM Procedural

80.59 Other destruction of intervertebral disc

22532-22534

22532 Arthrodesis, lateral extracavitary technique, including minimal discectomy to prepare interspace (other than for decompression); thoracic
22533 lumbar
22534 thoracic or lumbar, each additional vertebral segment (List separately in addition to code for primary procedure)

ICD-9-CM Diagnostic

170.2 Malignant neoplasm of vertebral column, excluding sacrum and coccyx
198.5 Secondary malignant neoplasm of bone and bone marrow
209.73 Secondary neuroendocrine tumor of bone
213.2 Benign neoplasm of vertebral column, excluding sacrum and coccyx
238.0 Neoplasm of uncertain behavior of bone and articular cartilage
336.9 Unspecified disease of spinal cord ▽
721.0 Cervical spondylosis without myelopathy
721.1 Cervical spondylosis with myelopathy
721.2 Thoracic spondylosis without myelopathy
721.3 Lumbosacral spondylosis without myelopathy
721.41 Spondylosis with myelopathy, thoracic region
721.42 Spondylosis with myelopathy, lumbar region
721.8 Other allied disorders of spine
722.0 Displacement of cervical intervertebral disc without myelopathy
722.10 Displacement of lumbar intervertebral disc without myelopathy
722.11 Displacement of thoracic intervertebral disc without myelopathy
722.31 Schmorl's nodes, thoracic region
722.4 Degeneration of cervical intervertebral disc
722.51 Degeneration of thoracic or thoracolumbar intervertebral disc
722.52 Degeneration of lumbar or lumbosacral intervertebral disc
722.71 Intervertebral cervical disc disorder with myelopathy, cervical region
722.72 Intervertebral thoracic disc disorder with myelopathy, thoracic region
722.73 Intervertebral lumbar disc disorder with myelopathy, lumbar region
722.81 Postlaminectomy syndrome, cervical region
722.82 Postlaminectomy syndrome, thoracic region
722.83 Postlaminectomy syndrome, lumbar region
722.91 Other and unspecified disc disorder of cervical region ▽
722.92 Other and unspecified disc disorder of thoracic region ▽
722.93 Other and unspecified disc disorder of lumbar region ▽
723.0 Spinal stenosis in cervical region
724.01 Spinal stenosis of thoracic region
724.02 Spinal stenosis of lumbar region, without neurogenic claudication
724.03 Spinal stenosis of lumbar region, with neurogenic claudication
724.2 Lumbago
724.3 Sciatica
724.4 Thoracic or lumbosacral neuritis or radiculitis, unspecified ▽
724.5 Unspecified backache ▽
724.9 Other unspecified back disorder
731.0 Osteitis deformans without mention of bone tumor
733.13 Pathologic fracture of vertebrae
733.82 Nonunion of fracture
733.95 Stress fracture of other bone — (Use additional external cause code(s) to identify the cause of the stress fracture)
738.2 Acquired deformity of neck
738.5 Other acquired deformity of back or spine
756.11 Congenital spondylolysis, lumbosacral region
756.12 Congenital spondylolisthesis
756.19 Other congenital anomaly of spine
805.00 Closed fracture of cervical vertebra, unspecified level without mention of spinal cord injury ▽
805.03 Closed fracture of third cervical vertebra without mention of spinal cord injury
805.04 Closed fracture of fourth cervical vertebra without mention of spinal cord injury
805.05 Closed fracture of fifth cervical vertebra without mention of spinal cord injury
805.06 Closed fracture of sixth cervical vertebra without mention of spinal cord injury
805.07 Closed fracture of seventh cervical vertebra without mention of spinal cord injury
805.08 Closed fracture of multiple cervical vertebrae without mention of spinal cord injury
805.10 Open fracture of cervical vertebra, unspecified level without mention of spinal cord injury ▽
805.13 Open fracture of third cervical vertebra without mention of spinal cord injury
805.14 Open fracture of fourth cervical vertebra without mention of spinal cord injury
805.15 Open fracture of fifth cervical vertebra without mention of spinal cord injury
805.16 Open fracture of sixth cervical vertebra without mention of spinal cord injury
805.17 Open fracture of seventh cervical vertebra without mention of spinal cord injury
805.18 Open fracture of multiple cervical vertebrae without mention of spinal cord injury
805.2 Closed fracture of dorsal (thoracic) vertebra without mention of spinal cord injury
805.3 Open fracture of dorsal (thoracic) vertebra without mention of spinal cord injury
805.4 Closed fracture of lumbar vertebra without mention of spinal cord injury
805.5 Open fracture of lumbar vertebra without mention of spinal cord injury

806.00 Closed fracture of C1-C4 level with unspecified spinal cord injury
806.01 Closed fracture of C1-C4 level with complete lesion of cord
806.02 Closed fracture of C1-C4 level with anterior cord syndrome
806.03 Closed fracture of C1-C4 level with central cord syndrome
806.04 Closed fracture of C1-C4 level with other specified spinal cord injury
806.05 Closed fracture of C5-C7 level with unspecified spinal cord injury
806.06 Closed fracture of C5-C7 level with complete lesion of cord
806.07 Closed fracture of C5-C7 level with anterior cord syndrome
806.08 Closed fracture of C5-C7 level with central cord syndrome
806.09 Closed fracture of C5-C7 level with other specified spinal cord injury
806.10 Open fracture of C1-C4 level with unspecified spinal cord injury
806.11 Open fracture of C1-C4 level with complete lesion of cord
806.12 Open fracture of C1-C4 level with anterior cord syndrome
806.13 Open fracture of C1-C4 level with central cord syndrome
806.14 Open fracture of C1-C4 level with other specified spinal cord injury
806.15 Open fracture of C5-C7 level with unspecified spinal cord injury
806.16 Open fracture of C5-C7 level with complete lesion of cord
806.17 Open fracture of C5-C7 level with anterior cord syndrome
806.18 Open fracture of C5-C7 level with central cord syndrome
806.19 Open fracture of C5-C7 level with other specified spinal cord injury
806.20 Closed fracture of T1-T6 level with unspecified spinal cord injury
806.21 Closed fracture of T1-T6 level with complete lesion of cord
806.22 Closed fracture of T1-T6 level with anterior cord syndrome
806.23 Closed fracture of T1-T6 level with central cord syndrome
806.24 Closed fracture of T1-T6 level with other specified spinal cord injury
806.25 Closed fracture of T7-T12 level with unspecified spinal cord injury
806.26 Closed fracture of T7-T12 level with complete lesion of cord
806.27 Closed fracture of T7-T12 level with anterior cord syndrome
806.28 Closed fracture of T7-T12 level with central cord syndrome
806.29 Closed fracture of T7-T12 level with other specified spinal cord injury
806.30 Open fracture of T1-T6 level with unspecified spinal cord injury
806.31 Open fracture of T1-T6 level with complete lesion of cord
806.32 Open fracture of T1-T6 level with anterior cord syndrome
806.33 Open fracture of T1-T6 level with central cord syndrome
806.34 Open fracture of T1-T6 level with other specified spinal cord injury
806.35 Open fracture of T7-T12 level with unspecified spinal cord injury
806.36 Open fracture of T7-T12 level with complete lesion of cord
806.37 Open fracture of T7-T12 level with anterior cord syndrome
806.38 Open fracture of T7-T12 level with central cord syndrome
806.39 Open fracture of T7-T12 level with other specified spinal cord injury
806.4 Closed fracture of lumbar spine with spinal cord injury
806.5 Open fracture of lumbar spine with spinal cord injury
839.03 Closed dislocation, third cervical vertebra
839.04 Closed dislocation, fourth cervical vertebra
839.05 Closed dislocation, fifth cervical vertebra
839.06 Closed dislocation, sixth cervical vertebra
839.07 Closed dislocation, seventh cervical vertebra
839.08 Closed dislocation, multiple cervical vertebrae
839.13 Open dislocation, third cervical vertebra
839.14 Open dislocation, fourth cervical vertebra
839.15 Open dislocation, fifth cervical vertebra
839.16 Open dislocation, sixth cervical vertebra
839.17 Open dislocation, seventh cervical vertebra
839.18 Open dislocation, multiple cervical vertebrae
839.20 Closed dislocation, lumbar vertebra
839.21 Closed dislocation, thoracic vertebra
839.30 Open dislocation, lumbar vertebra
839.31 Open dislocation, thoracic vertebra

ICD-9-CM Procedural

81.00 Spinal fusion, not otherwise specified

22548

22548 Arthrodesis, anterior transoral or extraoral technique, clivus-C1-C2 (atlas-axis), with or without excision of odontoid process

ICD-9-CM Diagnostic

170.2 Malignant neoplasm of vertebral column, excluding sacrum and coccyx
198.5 Secondary malignant neoplasm of bone and bone marrow
209.73 Secondary neuroendocrine tumor of bone
213.2 Benign neoplasm of vertebral column, excluding sacrum and coccyx
238.0 Neoplasm of uncertain behavior of bone and articular cartilage
721.1 Cervical spondylosis with myelopathy
721.8 Other allied disorders of spine
723.2 Cervicocranial syndrome
723.3 Cervicobrachial syndrome (diffuse)
738.5 Other acquired deformity of back or spine
805.01 Closed fracture of first cervical vertebra without mention of spinal cord injury
805.02 Closed fracture of second cervical vertebra without mention of spinal cord injury
805.08 Closed fracture of multiple cervical vertebrae without mention of spinal cord injury
805.11 Open fracture of first cervical vertebra without mention of spinal cord injury
805.12 Open fracture of second cervical vertebra without mention of spinal cord injury
806.00 Closed fracture of C1-C4 level with unspecified spinal cord injury
806.01 Closed fracture of C1-C4 level with complete lesion of cord
806.02 Closed fracture of C1-C4 level with anterior cord syndrome
806.03 Closed fracture of C1-C4 level with central cord syndrome
806.04 Closed fracture of C1-C4 level with other specified spinal cord injury
806.10 Open fracture of C1-C4 level with unspecified spinal cord injury
806.11 Open fracture of C1-C4 level with complete lesion of cord
806.12 Open fracture of C1-C4 level with anterior cord syndrome
806.13 Open fracture of C1-C4 level with central cord syndrome
806.14 Open fracture of C1-C4 level with other specified spinal cord injury

ICD-9-CM Procedural

81.01 Atlas-axis spinal fusion
81.31 Refusion of Atlas-axis spine
81.62 Fusion or refusion of 2-3 vertebrae

22551-22585

22551 Arthrodesis, anterior interbody, including disc space preparation, discectomy, osteophytectomy and decompression of spinal cord and/or nerve roots; cervical below C2
22552 cervical below C2, each additional interspace (List separately in addition to code for separate procedure)
22554 Arthrodesis, anterior interbody technique, including minimal discectomy to prepare interspace (other than for decompression); cervical below C2
22556 thoracic
22558 lumbar
22585 each additional interspace (List separately in addition to code for primary procedure)

ICD-9-CM Diagnostic

170.2 Malignant neoplasm of vertebral column, excluding sacrum and coccyx
198.5 Secondary malignant neoplasm of bone and bone marrow
209.73 Secondary neuroendocrine tumor of bone
213.2 Benign neoplasm of vertebral column, excluding sacrum and coccyx
238.0 Neoplasm of uncertain behavior of bone and articular cartilage
336.9 Unspecified disease of spinal cord
721.0 Cervical spondylosis without myelopathy
721.1 Cervical spondylosis with myelopathy

Code	Description
721.2	Thoracic spondylosis without myelopathy
721.3	Lumbosacral spondylosis without myelopathy
721.41	Spondylosis with myelopathy, thoracic region
721.42	Spondylosis with myelopathy, lumbar region
721.8	Other allied disorders of spine
722.0	Displacement of cervical intervertebral disc without myelopathy
722.10	Displacement of lumbar intervertebral disc without myelopathy
722.11	Displacement of thoracic intervertebral disc without myelopathy
722.31	Schmorl's nodes, thoracic region
722.4	Degeneration of cervical intervertebral disc
722.51	Degeneration of thoracic or thoracolumbar intervertebral disc
722.52	Degeneration of lumbar or lumbosacral intervertebral disc
722.71	Intervertebral cervical disc disorder with myelopathy, cervical region
722.72	Intervertebral thoracic disc disorder with myelopathy, thoracic region
722.73	Intervertebral lumbar disc disorder with myelopathy, lumbar region
722.81	Postlaminectomy syndrome, cervical region
722.82	Postlaminectomy syndrome, thoracic region
722.83	Postlaminectomy syndrome, lumbar region
722.91	Other and unspecified disc disorder of cervical region ▽
722.92	Other and unspecified disc disorder of thoracic region ▽
722.93	Other and unspecified disc disorder of lumbar region ▽
723.0	Spinal stenosis in cervical region
724.01	Spinal stenosis of thoracic region
724.02	Spinal stenosis of lumbar region, without neurogenic claudication
724.03	Spinal stenosis of lumbar region, with neurogenic claudication
724.2	Lumbago
724.3	Sciatica
724.4	Thoracic or lumbosacral neuritis or radiculitis, unspecified ▽
724.5	Unspecified backache ▽
724.9	Other unspecified back disorder
731.0	Osteitis deformans without mention of bone tumor
733.13	Pathologic fracture of vertebrae
733.82	Nonunion of fracture
733.95	Stress fracture of other bone — (Use additional external cause code(s) to identify the cause of the stress fracture)
738.2	Acquired deformity of neck
738.5	Other acquired deformity of back or spine
756.11	Congenital spondylolysis, lumbosacral region
756.12	Congenital spondylolisthesis
756.19	Other congenital anomaly of spine
805.00	Closed fracture of cervical vertebra, unspecified level without mention of spinal cord injury ▽
805.03	Closed fracture of third cervical vertebra without mention of spinal cord injury
805.04	Closed fracture of fourth cervical vertebra without mention of spinal cord injury
805.05	Closed fracture of fifth cervical vertebra without mention of spinal cord injury
805.06	Closed fracture of sixth cervical vertebra without mention of spinal cord injury
805.07	Closed fracture of seventh cervical vertebra without mention of spinal cord injury
805.08	Closed fracture of multiple cervical vertebrae without mention of spinal cord injury
805.10	Open fracture of cervical vertebra, unspecified level without mention of spinal cord injury ▽
805.13	Open fracture of third cervical vertebra without mention of spinal cord injury
805.14	Open fracture of fourth cervical vertebra without mention of spinal cord injury
805.15	Open fracture of fifth cervical vertebra without mention of spinal cord injury
805.16	Open fracture of sixth cervical vertebra without mention of spinal cord injury
805.17	Open fracture of seventh cervical vertebra without mention of spinal cord injury
805.18	Open fracture of multiple cervical vertebrae without mention of spinal cord injury
805.2	Closed fracture of dorsal (thoracic) vertebra without mention of spinal cord injury
805.3	Open fracture of dorsal (thoracic) vertebra without mention of spinal cord injury
805.4	Closed fracture of lumbar vertebra without mention of spinal cord injury
805.5	Open fracture of lumbar vertebra without mention of spinal cord injury
806.00	Closed fracture of C1-C4 level with unspecified spinal cord injury ▽
806.01	Closed fracture of C1-C4 level with complete lesion of cord
806.02	Closed fracture of C1-C4 level with anterior cord syndrome
806.03	Closed fracture of C1-C4 level with central cord syndrome
806.04	Closed fracture of C1-C4 level with other specified spinal cord injury
806.05	Closed fracture of C5-C7 level with unspecified spinal cord injury ▽
806.06	Closed fracture of C5-C7 level with complete lesion of cord
806.07	Closed fracture of C5-C7 level with anterior cord syndrome
806.08	Closed fracture of C5-C7 level with central cord syndrome
806.09	Closed fracture of C5-C7 level with other specified spinal cord injury
806.10	Open fracture of C1-C4 level with unspecified spinal cord injury ▽
806.11	Open fracture of C1-C4 level with complete lesion of cord
806.12	Open fracture of C1-C4 level with anterior cord syndrome
806.13	Open fracture of C1-C4 level with central cord syndrome
806.14	Open fracture of C1-C4 level with other specified spinal cord injury
806.15	Open fracture of C5-C7 level with unspecified spinal cord injury ▽
806.16	Open fracture of C5-C7 level with complete lesion of cord
806.17	Open fracture of C5-C7 level with anterior cord syndrome
806.18	Open fracture of C5-C7 level with central cord syndrome
806.19	Open fracture of C5-C7 level with other specified spinal cord injury
806.20	Closed fracture of T1-T6 level with unspecified spinal cord injury ▽
806.21	Closed fracture of T1-T6 level with complete lesion of cord
806.22	Closed fracture of T1-T6 level with anterior cord syndrome
806.23	Closed fracture of T1-T6 level with central cord syndrome
806.24	Closed fracture of T1-T6 level with other specified spinal cord injury
806.25	Closed fracture of T7-T12 level with unspecified spinal cord injury ▽
806.26	Closed fracture of T7-T12 level with complete lesion of cord
806.27	Closed fracture of T7-T12 level with anterior cord syndrome
806.28	Closed fracture of T7-T12 level with central cord syndrome
806.29	Closed fracture of T7-T12 level with other specified spinal cord injury
806.30	Open fracture of T1-T6 level with unspecified spinal cord injury ▽
806.31	Open fracture of T1-T6 level with complete lesion of cord
806.32	Open fracture of T1-T6 level with anterior cord syndrome
806.33	Open fracture of T1-T6 level with central cord syndrome
806.34	Open fracture of T1-T6 level with other specified spinal cord injury
806.35	Open fracture of T7-T12 level with unspecified spinal cord injury ▽
806.36	Open fracture of T7-T12 level with complete lesion of cord
806.37	Open fracture of T7-T12 level with anterior cord syndrome
806.38	Open fracture of T7-T12 level with central cord syndrome
806.39	Open fracture of T7-T12 level with other specified spinal cord injury
806.4	Closed fracture of lumbar spine with spinal cord injury
806.5	Open fracture of lumbar spine with spinal cord injury
839.03	Closed dislocation, third cervical vertebra
839.04	Closed dislocation, fourth cervical vertebra
839.05	Closed dislocation, fifth cervical vertebra
839.06	Closed dislocation, sixth cervical vertebra
839.07	Closed dislocation, seventh cervical vertebra
839.08	Closed dislocation, multiple cervical vertebrae
839.13	Open dislocation, third cervical vertebra
839.14	Open dislocation, fourth cervical vertebra
839.15	Open dislocation, fifth cervical vertebra
839.16	Open dislocation, sixth cervical vertebra
839.17	Open dislocation, seventh cervical vertebra
839.18	Open dislocation, multiple cervical vertebrae
839.20	Closed dislocation, lumbar vertebra
839.21	Closed dislocation, thoracic vertebra
839.30	Open dislocation, lumbar vertebra
839.31	Open dislocation, thoracic vertebra

ICD-9-CM Procedural

81.00 Spinal fusion, not otherwise specified
81.02 Other cervical fusion of the anterior column, anterior technique
81.04 Dorsal and dorsolumbar fusion of the anterior column, anterior technique
81.06 Lumbar and lumbosacral fusion of the anterior column, anterior technique
81.32 Refusion of other cervical spine, anterior column, anterior technique
81.34 Refusion of dorsal and dorsolumbar spine, anterior column, anterior technique
81.36 Refusion of lumbar and lumbosacral spine, anterior column, anterior technique
81.62 Fusion or refusion of 2-3 vertebrae
81.63 Fusion or refusion of 4-8 vertebrae
81.64 Fusion or refusion of 9 or more vertebrae

22586

22586 Arthrodesis, pre-sacral interbody technique, including disc space preparation, discectomy, with posterior instrumentation, with image guidance, includes bone graft when performed, L5-S1 interspace

ICD-9-CM Diagnostic

170.2 Malignant neoplasm of vertebral column, excluding sacrum and coccyx
198.5 Secondary malignant neoplasm of bone and bone marrow
209.73 Secondary neuroendocrine tumor of bone
213.2 Benign neoplasm of vertebral column, excluding sacrum and coccyx
238.0 Neoplasm of uncertain behavior of bone and articular cartilage
239.2 Neoplasms of unspecified nature of bone, soft tissue, and skin
721.3 Lumbosacral spondylosis without myelopathy
721.42 Spondylosis with myelopathy, lumbar region
722.10 Displacement of lumbar intervertebral disc without myelopathy
722.32 Schmorl's nodes, lumbar region
722.52 Degeneration of lumbar or lumbosacral intervertebral disc
722.73 Intervertebral lumbar disc disorder with myelopathy, lumbar region
722.83 Postlaminectomy syndrome, lumbar region
722.93 Other and unspecified disc disorder of lumbar region ▽
724.02 Spinal stenosis of lumbar region, without neurogenic claudication
724.03 Spinal stenosis of lumbar region, with neurogenic claudication
724.2 Lumbago
724.3 Sciatica
733.13 Pathologic fracture of vertebrae
733.95 Stress fracture of other bone — (Use additional external cause code(s) to identify the cause of the stress fracture)
738.4 Acquired spondylolisthesis
756.11 Congenital spondylolysis, lumbosacral region
756.12 Congenital spondylolisthesis
805.4 Closed fracture of lumbar vertebra without mention of spinal cord injury
805.5 Open fracture of lumbar vertebra without mention of spinal cord injury
806.4 Closed fracture of lumbar spine with spinal cord injury
806.5 Open fracture of lumbar spine with spinal cord injury
839.20 Closed dislocation, lumbar vertebra
839.30 Open dislocation, lumbar vertebra
996.40 Unspecified mechanical complication of internal orthopedic device, implant, and graft — (Use additional code to identify prosthetic joint with mechanical complication, V43.60-V43.69) ▽
996.49 Other mechanical complication of other internal orthopedic device, implant, and graft — (Use additional code to identify prosthetic joint with mechanical complication, V43.60-V43.69)
996.67 Infection and inflammatory reaction due to other internal orthopedic device, implant, and graft — (Use additional code to identify specified infections)
996.78 Other complications due to other internal orthopedic device, implant, and graft — (Use additional code to identify complication: 338.18-338.19, 338.28-338.29)
998.89 Other specified complications

ICD-9-CM Procedural

80.51 Excision of intervertebral disc
81.06 Lumbar and lumbosacral fusion of the anterior column, anterior technique
81.08 Lumbar and lumbosacral fusion of the anterior column, posterior technique
81.36 Refusion of lumbar and lumbosacral spine, anterior column, anterior technique
81.62 Fusion or refusion of 2-3 vertebrae
84.51 Insertion of interbody spinal fusion device

22590

22590 Arthrodesis, posterior technique, craniocervical (occiput-C2)

ICD-9-CM Diagnostic

170.2 Malignant neoplasm of vertebral column, excluding sacrum and coccyx
198.5 Secondary malignant neoplasm of bone and bone marrow
209.73 Secondary neuroendocrine tumor of bone
213.2 Benign neoplasm of vertebral column, excluding sacrum and coccyx
238.0 Neoplasm of uncertain behavior of bone and articular cartilage
721.1 Cervical spondylosis with myelopathy
721.8 Other allied disorders of spine
723.2 Cervicocranial syndrome
723.3 Cervicobrachial syndrome (diffuse)
733.81 Malunion of fracture
733.82 Nonunion of fracture
738.5 Other acquired deformity of back or spine
756.12 Congenital spondylolisthesis
805.01 Closed fracture of first cervical vertebra without mention of spinal cord injury
805.02 Closed fracture of second cervical vertebra without mention of spinal cord injury
805.11 Open fracture of first cervical vertebra without mention of spinal cord injury
805.12 Open fracture of second cervical vertebra without mention of spinal cord injury
806.00 Closed fracture of C1-C4 level with unspecified spinal cord injury ▽
806.01 Closed fracture of C1-C4 level with complete lesion of cord
806.02 Closed fracture of C1-C4 level with anterior cord syndrome
806.03 Closed fracture of C1-C4 level with central cord syndrome
806.04 Closed fracture of C1-C4 level with other specified spinal cord injury
806.10 Open fracture of C1-C4 level with unspecified spinal cord injury ▽
806.11 Open fracture of C1-C4 level with complete lesion of cord
806.12 Open fracture of C1-C4 level with anterior cord syndrome
806.13 Open fracture of C1-C4 level with central cord syndrome
806.14 Open fracture of C1-C4 level with other specified spinal cord injury
839.01 Closed dislocation, first cervical vertebra
839.02 Closed dislocation, second cervical vertebra
839.11 Open dislocation, first cervical vertebra
839.12 Open dislocation, second cervical vertebra

ICD-9-CM Procedural

81.01 Atlas-axis spinal fusion
81.03 Other cervical fusion of the posterior column, posterior technique
81.31 Refusion of Atlas-axis spine
81.33 Refusion of other cervical spine, posterior column, posterior technique
81.62 Fusion or refusion of 2-3 vertebrae

22595

22595 Arthrodesis, posterior technique, atlas-axis (C1-C2)

ICD-9-CM Diagnostic

170.2 Malignant neoplasm of vertebral column, excluding sacrum and coccyx
198.5 Secondary malignant neoplasm of bone and bone marrow
209.73 Secondary neuroendocrine tumor of bone
213.2 Benign neoplasm of vertebral column, excluding sacrum and coccyx
238.0 Neoplasm of uncertain behavior of bone and articular cartilage

721.0 Cervical spondylosis without myelopathy
721.1 Cervical spondylosis with myelopathy
721.8 Other allied disorders of spine
723.0 Spinal stenosis in cervical region
723.1 Cervicalgia
723.2 Cervicocranial syndrome
723.4 Brachial neuritis or radiculitis NOS ▽
733.13 Pathologic fracture of vertebrae
733.81 Malunion of fracture
733.82 Nonunion of fracture
733.95 Stress fracture of other bone — (Use additional external cause code(s) to identify the cause of the stress fracture)
756.12 Congenital spondylolisthesis
756.19 Other congenital anomaly of spine
805.01 Closed fracture of first cervical vertebra without mention of spinal cord injury
805.02 Closed fracture of second cervical vertebra without mention of spinal cord injury
805.11 Open fracture of first cervical vertebra without mention of spinal cord injury
805.12 Open fracture of second cervical vertebra without mention of spinal cord injury
806.00 Closed fracture of C1-C4 level with unspecified spinal cord injury ▽
806.01 Closed fracture of C1-C4 level with complete lesion of cord
806.02 Closed fracture of C1-C4 level with anterior cord syndrome
806.03 Closed fracture of C1-C4 level with central cord syndrome
806.04 Closed fracture of C1-C4 level with other specified spinal cord injury
806.10 Open fracture of C1-C4 level with unspecified spinal cord injury ▽
806.11 Open fracture of C1-C4 level with complete lesion of cord
806.12 Open fracture of C1-C4 level with anterior cord syndrome
806.13 Open fracture of C1-C4 level with central cord syndrome
806.14 Open fracture of C1-C4 level with other specified spinal cord injury
839.01 Closed dislocation, first cervical vertebra
839.02 Closed dislocation, second cervical vertebra
839.11 Open dislocation, first cervical vertebra
839.12 Open dislocation, second cervical vertebra

ICD-9-CM Procedural

81.01 Atlas-axis spinal fusion
81.31 Refusion of Atlas-axis spine
81.62 Fusion or refusion of 2-3 vertebrae

22600-22614

22600 Arthrodesis, posterior or posterolateral technique, single level; cervical below C2 segment
22610 thoracic (with lateral transverse technique, when performed)
22612 lumbar (with lateral transverse technique, when performed)
22614 each additional vertebral segment (List separately in addition to code for primary procedure)

ICD-9-CM Diagnostic

170.2 Malignant neoplasm of vertebral column, excluding sacrum and coccyx
198.5 Secondary malignant neoplasm of bone and bone marrow
209.73 Secondary neuroendocrine tumor of bone
213.2 Benign neoplasm of vertebral column, excluding sacrum and coccyx
238.0 Neoplasm of uncertain behavior of bone and articular cartilage
336.9 Unspecified disease of spinal cord ▽
721.0 Cervical spondylosis without myelopathy
721.1 Cervical spondylosis with myelopathy
721.2 Thoracic spondylosis without myelopathy
721.3 Lumbosacral spondylosis without myelopathy
721.41 Spondylosis with myelopathy, thoracic region
721.42 Spondylosis with myelopathy, lumbar region
721.8 Other allied disorders of spine
722.0 Displacement of cervical intervertebral disc without myelopathy
722.10 Displacement of lumbar intervertebral disc without myelopathy
722.11 Displacement of thoracic intervertebral disc without myelopathy
722.31 Schmorl's nodes, thoracic region
722.4 Degeneration of cervical intervertebral disc
722.51 Degeneration of thoracic or thoracolumbar intervertebral disc
722.52 Degeneration of lumbar or lumbosacral intervertebral disc
722.71 Intervertebral cervical disc disorder with myelopathy, cervical region
722.72 Intervertebral thoracic disc disorder with myelopathy, thoracic region
722.73 Intervertebral lumbar disc disorder with myelopathy, lumbar region
722.81 Postlaminectomy syndrome, cervical region
722.82 Postlaminectomy syndrome, thoracic region
722.83 Postlaminectomy syndrome, lumbar region
722.91 Other and unspecified disc disorder of cervical region ▽
722.92 Other and unspecified disc disorder of thoracic region ▽
722.93 Other and unspecified disc disorder of lumbar region ▽
723.0 Spinal stenosis in cervical region
724.01 Spinal stenosis of thoracic region
724.02 Spinal stenosis of lumbar region, without neurogenic claudication
724.03 Spinal stenosis of lumbar region, with neurogenic claudication
724.2 Lumbago
724.3 Sciatica
724.4 Thoracic or lumbosacral neuritis or radiculitis, unspecified ▽
724.9 Other unspecified back disorder
731.0 Osteitis deformans without mention of bone tumor
733.13 Pathologic fracture of vertebrae
733.82 Nonunion of fracture
733.95 Stress fracture of other bone — (Use additional external cause code(s) to identify the cause of the stress fracture)
738.2 Acquired deformity of neck
738.5 Other acquired deformity of back or spine
756.11 Congenital spondylolysis, lumbosacral region
756.12 Congenital spondylolisthesis
756.19 Other congenital anomaly of spine
805.00 Closed fracture of cervical vertebra, unspecified level without mention of spinal cord injury ▽
805.03 Closed fracture of third cervical vertebra without mention of spinal cord injury
805.04 Closed fracture of fourth cervical vertebra without mention of spinal cord injury
805.05 Closed fracture of fifth cervical vertebra without mention of spinal cord injury
805.06 Closed fracture of sixth cervical vertebra without mention of spinal cord injury
805.07 Closed fracture of seventh cervical vertebra without mention of spinal cord injury
805.08 Closed fracture of multiple cervical vertebrae without mention of spinal cord injury
805.10 Open fracture of cervical vertebra, unspecified level without mention of spinal cord injury ▽
805.13 Open fracture of third cervical vertebra without mention of spinal cord injury
805.14 Open fracture of fourth cervical vertebra without mention of spinal cord injury
805.15 Open fracture of fifth cervical vertebra without mention of spinal cord injury
805.16 Open fracture of sixth cervical vertebra without mention of spinal cord injury
805.17 Open fracture of seventh cervical vertebra without mention of spinal cord injury
805.18 Open fracture of multiple cervical vertebrae without mention of spinal cord injury
805.2 Closed fracture of dorsal (thoracic) vertebra without mention of spinal cord injury
805.3 Open fracture of dorsal (thoracic) vertebra without mention of spinal cord injury
805.4 Closed fracture of lumbar vertebra without mention of spinal cord injury
805.5 Open fracture of lumbar vertebra without mention of spinal cord injury
806.00 Closed fracture of C1-C4 level with unspecified spinal cord injury ▽
806.01 Closed fracture of C1-C4 level with complete lesion of cord
806.02 Closed fracture of C1-C4 level with anterior cord syndrome
806.03 Closed fracture of C1-C4 level with central cord syndrome
806.04 Closed fracture of C1-C4 level with other specified spinal cord injury

806.05 Closed fracture of C5-C7 level with unspecified spinal cord injury

806.06 Closed fracture of C5-C7 level with complete lesion of cord

806.07 Closed fracture of C5-C7 level with anterior cord syndrome

806.08 Closed fracture of C5-C7 level with central cord syndrome

806.09 Closed fracture of C5-C7 level with other specified spinal cord injury

806.10 Open fracture of C1-C4 level with unspecified spinal cord injury

806.11 Open fracture of C1-C4 level with complete lesion of cord

806.12 Open fracture of C1-C4 level with anterior cord syndrome

806.13 Open fracture of C1-C4 level with central cord syndrome

806.14 Open fracture of C1-C4 level with other specified spinal cord injury

806.15 Open fracture of C5-C7 level with unspecified spinal cord injury

806.16 Open fracture of C5-C7 level with complete lesion of cord

806.17 Open fracture of C5-C7 level with anterior cord syndrome

806.18 Open fracture of C5-C7 level with central cord syndrome

806.19 Open fracture of C5-C7 level with other specified spinal cord injury

806.20 Closed fracture of T1-T6 level with unspecified spinal cord injury

806.21 Closed fracture of T1-T6 level with complete lesion of cord

806.22 Closed fracture of T1-T6 level with anterior cord syndrome

806.23 Closed fracture of T1-T6 level with central cord syndrome

806.24 Closed fracture of T1-T6 level with other specified spinal cord injury

806.25 Closed fracture of T7-T12 level with unspecified spinal cord injury

806.26 Closed fracture of T7-T12 level with complete lesion of cord

806.27 Closed fracture of T7-T12 level with anterior cord syndrome

806.28 Closed fracture of T7-T12 level with central cord syndrome

806.29 Closed fracture of T7-T12 level with other specified spinal cord injury

806.30 Open fracture of T1-T6 level with unspecified spinal cord injury

806.31 Open fracture of T1-T6 level with complete lesion of cord

806.32 Open fracture of T1-T6 level with anterior cord syndrome

806.33 Open fracture of T1-T6 level with central cord syndrome

806.34 Open fracture of T1-T6 level with other specified spinal cord injury

806.35 Open fracture of T7-T12 level with unspecified spinal cord injury

806.36 Open fracture of T7-T12 level with complete lesion of cord

806.37 Open fracture of T7-T12 level with anterior cord syndrome

806.38 Open fracture of T7-T12 level with central cord syndrome

806.39 Open fracture of T7-T12 level with other specified spinal cord injury

806.4 Closed fracture of lumbar spine with spinal cord injury

806.5 Open fracture of lumbar spine with spinal cord injury

839.03 Closed dislocation, third cervical vertebra

839.04 Closed dislocation, fourth cervical vertebra

839.05 Closed dislocation, fifth cervical vertebra

839.06 Closed dislocation, sixth cervical vertebra

839.07 Closed dislocation, seventh cervical vertebra

839.08 Closed dislocation, multiple cervical vertebrae

839.13 Open dislocation, third cervical vertebra

839.14 Open dislocation, fourth cervical vertebra

839.15 Open dislocation, fifth cervical vertebra

839.16 Open dislocation, sixth cervical vertebra

839.17 Open dislocation, seventh cervical vertebra

839.18 Open dislocation, multiple cervical vertebrae

839.20 Closed dislocation, lumbar vertebra

839.21 Closed dislocation, thoracic vertebra

839.30 Open dislocation, lumbar vertebra

839.31 Open dislocation, thoracic vertebra

ICD-9-CM Procedural

81.00 Spinal fusion, not otherwise specified

81.01 Atlas-axis spinal fusion

81.03 Other cervical fusion of the posterior column, posterior technique

81.05 Dorsal and dorsolumbar fusion of the posterior column, posterior technique

81.07 Lumbar and lumbosacral fusion of the posterior column, posterior technique

81.08 Lumbar and lumbosacral fusion of the anterior column, posterior technique

81.31 Refusion of Atlas-axis spine

81.33 Refusion of other cervical spine, posterior column, posterior technique

81.35 Refusion of dorsal and dorsolumbar spine, posterior column, posterior technique

81.37 Refusion of lumbar and lumbosacral spine, posterior column, posterior technique

81.38 Refusion of lumbar and lumbosacral spine, anterior column, posterior technique

81.62 Fusion or refusion of 2-3 vertebrae

81.63 Fusion or refusion of 4-8 vertebrae

81.64 Fusion or refusion of 9 or more vertebrae

22630-22632

22630 Arthrodesis, posterior interbody technique, including laminectomy and/or discectomy to prepare interspace (other than for decompression), single interspace; lumbar

22632 each additional interspace (List separately in addition to code for primary procedure)

ICD-9-CM Diagnostic

170.2 Malignant neoplasm of vertebral column, excluding sacrum and coccyx

198.5 Secondary malignant neoplasm of bone and bone marrow

209.73 Secondary neuroendocrine tumor of bone

213.2 Benign neoplasm of vertebral column, excluding sacrum and coccyx

238.0 Neoplasm of uncertain behavior of bone and articular cartilage

239.2 Neoplasms of unspecified nature of bone, soft tissue, and skin

336.9 Unspecified disease of spinal cord

721.3 Lumbosacral spondylosis without myelopathy

721.42 Spondylosis with myelopathy, lumbar region

722.10 Displacement of lumbar intervertebral disc without myelopathy

722.52 Degeneration of lumbar or lumbosacral intervertebral disc

722.73 Intervertebral lumbar disc disorder with myelopathy, lumbar region

722.83 Postlaminectomy syndrome, lumbar region

722.93 Other and unspecified disc disorder of lumbar region

724.02 Spinal stenosis of lumbar region, without neurogenic claudication

724.03 Spinal stenosis of lumbar region, with neurogenic claudication

724.2 Lumbago

724.3 Sciatica

724.4 Thoracic or lumbosacral neuritis or radiculitis, unspecified

731.0 Osteitis deformans without mention of bone tumor

733.13 Pathologic fracture of vertebrae

733.95 Stress fracture of other bone — (Use additional external cause code(s) to identify the cause of the stress fracture)

756.11 Congenital spondylolysis, lumbosacral region

756.12 Congenital spondylolisthesis

805.4 Closed fracture of lumbar vertebra without mention of spinal cord injury

805.5 Open fracture of lumbar vertebra without mention of spinal cord injury

806.4 Closed fracture of lumbar spine with spinal cord injury

806.5 Open fracture of lumbar spine with spinal cord injury

839.20 Closed dislocation, lumbar vertebra

839.30 Open dislocation, lumbar vertebra

ICD-9-CM Procedural

81.07 Lumbar and lumbosacral fusion of the posterior column, posterior technique

81.08 Lumbar and lumbosacral fusion of the anterior column, posterior technique

81.37 Refusion of lumbar and lumbosacral spine, posterior column, posterior technique

81.38 Refusion of lumbar and lumbosacral spine, anterior column, posterior technique

81.62 Fusion or refusion of 2-3 vertebrae

81.63 Fusion or refusion of 4-8 vertebrae

81.64 Fusion or refusion of 9 or more vertebrae

22633-22634

22633 Arthrodesis, combined posterior or posterolateral technique with posterior interbody technique including laminectomy and/or discectomy sufficient to prepare interspace (other than for decompression), single interspace and segment; lumbar

22634 each additional interspace and segment (List separately in addition to code for primary procedure)

ICD-9-CM Diagnostic

170.2 Malignant neoplasm of vertebral column, excluding sacrum and coccyx
198.5 Secondary malignant neoplasm of bone and bone marrow
209.73 Secondary neuroendocrine tumor of bone
213.2 Benign neoplasm of vertebral column, excluding sacrum and coccyx
238.0 Neoplasm of uncertain behavior of bone and articular cartilage
239.2 Neoplasms of unspecified nature of bone, soft tissue, and skin
336.9 Unspecified disease of spinal cord ▽
721.3 Lumbosacral spondylosis without myelopathy
721.42 Spondylosis with myelopathy, lumbar region
722.10 Displacement of lumbar intervertebral disc without myelopathy
722.52 Degeneration of lumbar or lumbosacral intervertebral disc
722.73 Intervertebral lumbar disc disorder with myelopathy, lumbar region
722.83 Postlaminectomy syndrome, lumbar region
722.93 Other and unspecified disc disorder of lumbar region ▽
724.02 Spinal stenosis of lumbar region, without neurogenic claudication
724.03 Spinal stenosis of lumbar region, with neurogenic claudication
724.2 Lumbago
724.3 Sciatica
724.4 Thoracic or lumbosacral neuritis or radiculitis, unspecified ▽
731.0 Osteitis deformans without mention of bone tumor
733.13 Pathologic fracture of vertebrae
733.95 Stress fracture of other bone — (Use additional external cause code(s) to identify the cause of the stress fracture)
756.11 Congenital spondylolysis, lumbosacral region
756.12 Congenital spondylolisthesis
805.4 Closed fracture of lumbar vertebra without mention of spinal cord injury
805.5 Open fracture of lumbar vertebra without mention of spinal cord injury
806.4 Closed fracture of lumbar spine with spinal cord injury
806.5 Open fracture of lumbar spine with spinal cord injury
839.20 Closed dislocation, lumbar vertebra
839.30 Open dislocation, lumbar vertebra

ICD-9-CM Procedural

80.51 Excision of intervertebral disc
81.07 Lumbar and lumbosacral fusion of the posterior column, posterior technique
81.08 Lumbar and lumbosacral fusion of the anterior column, posterior technique
81.37 Refusion of lumbar and lumbosacral spine, posterior column, posterior technique
81.38 Refusion of lumbar and lumbosacral spine, anterior column, posterior technique
81.62 Fusion or refusion of 2-3 vertebrae
81.63 Fusion or refusion of 4-8 vertebrae
81.64 Fusion or refusion of 9 or more vertebrae

22800-22804

22800 Arthrodesis, posterior, for spinal deformity, with or without cast; up to 6 vertebral segments

22802 7 to 12 vertebral segments

22804 13 or more vertebral segments

ICD-9-CM Diagnostic

138 Late effects of acute poliomyelitis — (Note: This category is to be used to indicate conditions classifiable to 045 as the cause of late effects, which are themselves classified elsewhere. The "late effects" include those specified as such, as sequelae, or as due to old or inactive poliomyelitis, without evidence of active disease.)
237.70 Neurofibromatosis, unspecified ▽
237.71 Neurofibromatosis, Type 1 (von Recklinghausen's disease)
237.72 Neurofibromatosis, Type 2 (acoustic neurofibromatosis)
237.73 Schwannomatosis
237.79 Other neurofibromatosis
252.00 Hyperparathyroidism, unspecified ▽
252.01 Primary hyperparathyroidism
252.02 Secondary hyperparathyroidism, non-renal
252.08 Other hyperparathyroidism
277.5 Mucopolysaccharidosis — (Use additional code to identify any associated intellectual disabilities)
356.1 Peroneal muscular atrophy
731.0 Osteitis deformans without mention of bone tumor
731.3 Major osseous defects — (Code first underlying disease: 170.0-170.9, 730.00-730.29, 733.00-733.09, 733.40-733.49, 996.45)
732.0 Juvenile osteochondrosis of spine
732.8 Other specified forms of osteochondropathy
733.00 Unspecified osteoporosis — (Use additional code to identify major osseous defect, if applicable: 731.3) (Use additional code to identify personal history of pathologic (healed) fracture: V13.51) ▽
733.01 Senile osteoporosis — (Use additional code to identify major osseous defect, if applicable: 731.3) (Use additional code to identify personal history of pathologic (healed) fracture: V13.51)
733.02 Idiopathic osteoporosis — (Use additional code to identify major osseous defect, if applicable: 731.3) (Use additional code to identify personal history of pathologic (healed) fracture: V13.51)
733.03 Disuse osteoporosis — (Use additional code to identify major osseous defect, if applicable: 731.3) (Use additional code to identify personal history of pathologic (healed) fracture: V13.51)
733.09 Other osteoporosis — (Use additional code to identify major osseous defect, if applicable: 731.3) (Use additional code to identify personal history of pathologic (healed) fracture: V13.51) (Use additional E code to identify drug)
737.0 Adolescent postural kyphosis
737.10 Kyphosis (acquired) (postural)
737.20 Lordosis (acquired) (postural)
737.30 Scoliosis (and kyphoscoliosis), idiopathic
737.32 Progressive infantile idiopathic scoliosis
737.33 Scoliosis due to radiation
737.34 Thoracogenic scoliosis
737.40 Unspecified curvature of spine associated with other condition — (Code first associated condition: 015.0, 138, 237.7, 252.01, 277.5, 356.1, 731.0, 733.00-733.09) ☒
737.41 Kyphosis associated with other condition — (Code first associated condition: 015.0, 138, 237.7, 252.01, 277.5, 356.1, 731.0, 733.00-733.09) ☒
737.42 Lordosis associated with other condition — (Code first associated condition: 015.0, 138, 237.7, 252.01, 277.5, 356.1, 731.0, 733.00-733.09) ☒
737.43 Scoliosis associated with other condition — (Code first associated condition: 015.0, 138, 237.7, 252.01, 277.5, 356.1, 731.0, 733.00-733.09) ☒
737.8 Other curvatures of spine associated with other conditions
737.9 Unspecified curvature of spine associated with other condition ▽
738.5 Other acquired deformity of back or spine
754.2 Congenital musculoskeletal deformity of spine
756.10 Congenital anomaly of spine, unspecified ▽
756.12 Congenital spondylolisthesis

ICD-9-CM Procedural

81.00 Spinal fusion, not otherwise specified
81.01 Atlas-axis spinal fusion
81.03 Other cervical fusion of the posterior column, posterior technique
81.05 Dorsal and dorsolumbar fusion of the posterior column, posterior technique
81.07 Lumbar and lumbosacral fusion of the posterior column, posterior technique
81.08 Lumbar and lumbosacral fusion of the anterior column, posterior technique

81.31 Refusion of Atlas-axis spine
81.33 Refusion of other cervical spine, posterior column, posterior technique
81.35 Refusion of dorsal and dorsolumbar spine, posterior column, posterior technique
81.37 Refusion of lumbar and lumbosacral spine, posterior column, posterior technique
81.38 Refusion of lumbar and lumbosacral spine, anterior column, posterior technique
81.62 Fusion or refusion of 2-3 vertebrae
81.63 Fusion or refusion of 4-8 vertebrae
81.64 Fusion or refusion of 9 or more vertebrae

22808-22812

22808 Arthrodesis, anterior, for spinal deformity, with or without cast; 2 to 3 vertebral segments
22810 4 to 7 vertebral segments
22812 8 or more vertebral segments

ICD-9-CM Diagnostic

138 Late effects of acute poliomyelitis — (Note: This category is to be used to indicate conditions classifiable to 045 as the cause of late effects, which are themselves classified elsewhere. The "late effects" include those specified as such, as sequelae, or as due to old or inactive poliomyelitis, without evidence of active disease.)
237.70 Neurofibromatosis, unspecified ▽
237.71 Neurofibromatosis, Type 1 (von Recklinghausen's disease)
237.72 Neurofibromatosis, Type 2 (acoustic neurofibromatosis)
237.73 Schwannomatosis
237.79 Other neurofibromatosis
252.00 Hyperparathyroidism, unspecified ▽
252.01 Primary hyperparathyroidism
252.02 Secondary hyperparathyroidism, non-renal
252.08 Other hyperparathyroidism
277.5 Mucopolysaccharidosis — (Use additional code to identify any associated intellectual disabilities)
356.1 Peroneal muscular atrophy
731.0 Osteitis deformans without mention of bone tumor
731.3 Major osseous defects — (Code first underlying disease: 170.0-170.9, 730.00-730.29, 733.00-733.09, 733.40-733.49, 996.45)
732.0 Juvenile osteochondrosis of spine
732.8 Other specified forms of osteochondropathy
733.00 Unspecified osteoporosis — (Use additional code to identify major osseous defect, if applicable: 731.3) (Use additional code to identify personal history of pathologic (healed) fracture: V13.51) ▽
733.01 Senile osteoporosis — (Use additional code to identify major osseous defect, if applicable: 731.3) (Use additional code to identify personal history of pathologic (healed) fracture: V13.51)
733.02 Idiopathic osteoporosis — (Use additional code to identify major osseous defect, if applicable: 731.3) (Use additional code to identify personal history of pathologic (healed) fracture: V13.51)
733.03 Disuse osteoporosis — (Use additional code to identify major osseous defect, if applicable: 731.3) (Use additional code to identify personal history of pathologic (healed) fracture: V13.51)
733.09 Other osteoporosis — (Use additional code to identify major osseous defect, if applicable: 731.3) (Use additional code to identify personal history of pathologic (healed) fracture: V13.51) (Use additional E code to identify drug)
737.0 Adolescent postural kyphosis
737.10 Kyphosis (acquired) (postural)
737.20 Lordosis (acquired) (postural)
737.30 Scoliosis (and kyphoscoliosis), idiopathic
737.32 Progressive infantile idiopathic scoliosis
737.33 Scoliosis due to radiation
737.34 Thoracogenic scoliosis
737.40 Unspecified curvature of spine associated with other condition — (Code first associated condition: 015.0, 138, 237.7, 252.01, 277.5, 356.1, 731.0, 733.00-733.09) ☒
737.41 Kyphosis associated with other condition — (Code first associated condition: 015.0, 138, 237.7, 252.01, 277.5, 356.1, 731.0, 733.00-733.09) ☒
737.42 Lordosis associated with other condition — (Code first associated condition: 015.0, 138, 237.7, 252.01, 277.5, 356.1, 731.0, 733.00-733.09) ☒
737.43 Scoliosis associated with other condition — (Code first associated condition: 015.0, 138, 237.7, 252.01, 277.5, 356.1, 731.0, 733.00-733.09) ☒
737.8 Other curvatures of spine associated with other conditions
737.9 Unspecified curvature of spine associated with other condition ▽
738.5 Other acquired deformity of back or spine
754.2 Congenital musculoskeletal deformity of spine
756.10 Congenital anomaly of spine, unspecified ▽
756.12 Congenital spondylolisthesis

ICD-9-CM Procedural

81.00 Spinal fusion, not otherwise specified
81.01 Atlas-axis spinal fusion
81.02 Other cervical fusion of the anterior column, anterior technique
81.04 Dorsal and dorsolumbar fusion of the anterior column, anterior technique
81.06 Lumbar and lumbosacral fusion of the anterior column, anterior technique
81.31 Refusion of Atlas-axis spine
81.32 Refusion of other cervical spine, anterior column, anterior technique
81.34 Refusion of dorsal and dorsolumbar spine, anterior column, anterior technique
81.36 Refusion of lumbar and lumbosacral spine, anterior column, anterior technique
81.62 Fusion or refusion of 2-3 vertebrae
81.63 Fusion or refusion of 4-8 vertebrae
81.64 Fusion or refusion of 9 or more vertebrae

22818-22819

22818 Kyphectomy, circumferential exposure of spine and resection of vertebral segment(s) (including body and posterior elements); single or 2 segments
22819 3 or more segments

ICD-9-CM Diagnostic

737.10 Kyphosis (acquired) (postural)
737.30 Scoliosis (and kyphoscoliosis), idiopathic
737.32 Progressive infantile idiopathic scoliosis
737.41 Kyphosis associated with other condition — (Code first associated condition: 015.0, 138, 237.7, 252.01, 277.5, 356.1, 731.0, 733.00-733.09) ☒
737.43 Scoliosis associated with other condition — (Code first associated condition: 015.0, 138, 237.7, 252.01, 277.5, 356.1, 731.0, 733.00-733.09) ☒
738.5 Other acquired deformity of back or spine
741.00 Spina bifida with hydrocephalus, unspecified region ▽
741.02 Spina bifida with hydrocephalus, dorsal (thoracic) region
741.03 Spina bifida with hydrocephalus, lumbar region
741.90 Spina bifida without mention of hydrocephalus, unspecified region ▽
741.92 Spina bifida without mention of hydrocephalus, dorsal (thoracic) region
741.93 Spina bifida without mention of hydrocephalus, lumbar region
742.59 Other specified congenital anomaly of spinal cord
754.2 Congenital musculoskeletal deformity of spine
756.19 Other congenital anomaly of spine

ICD-9-CM Procedural

77.99 Total ostectomy of other bone, except facial bones

22830

22830 Exploration of spinal fusion

ICD-9-CM Diagnostic

324.1 Intraspinal abscess
722.81 Postlaminectomy syndrome, cervical region
722.82 Postlaminectomy syndrome, thoracic region

722.83 Postlaminectomy syndrome, lumbar region
724.4 Thoracic or lumbosacral neuritis or radiculitis, unspecified ▽
733.13 Pathologic fracture of vertebrae
733.81 Malunion of fracture
733.82 Nonunion of fracture
733.95 Stress fracture of other bone — (Use additional external cause code(s) to identify the cause of the stress fracture)
996.40 Unspecified mechanical complication of internal orthopedic device, implant, and graft — (Use additional code to identify prosthetic joint with mechanical complication, V43.60-V43.69) ▽
996.49 Other mechanical complication of other internal orthopedic device, implant, and graft — (Use additional code to identify prosthetic joint with mechanical complication, V43.60-V43.69)
996.67 Infection and inflammatory reaction due to other internal orthopedic device, implant, and graft — (Use additional code to identify specified infections)
996.78 Other complications due to other internal orthopedic device, implant, and graft — (Use additional code to identify complication: 338.18-338.19, 338.28-338.29)
V45.4 Arthrodesis status

ICD-9-CM Procedural

03.09 Other exploration and decompression of spinal canal

22840

22840 Posterior non-segmental instrumentation (eg, Harrington rod technique, pedicle fixation across 1 interspace, atlantoaxial transarticular screw fixation, sublaminar wiring at C1, facet screw fixation) (List separately in addition to code for primary procedure)

ICD-9-CM Diagnostic

The ICD-9-CM diagnostic code(s) would be the same as the actual procedure performed because these are in-addition-to codes.

ICD-9-CM Procedural

78.59 Internal fixation of other bone, except facial bones, without fracture reduction
81.00 Spinal fusion, not otherwise specified
81.01 Atlas-axis spinal fusion
81.03 Other cervical fusion of the posterior column, posterior technique
81.05 Dorsal and dorsolumbar fusion of the posterior column, posterior technique
81.07 Lumbar and lumbosacral fusion of the posterior column, posterior technique
81.08 Lumbar and lumbosacral fusion of the anterior column, posterior technique

22841

22841 Internal spinal fixation by wiring of spinous processes (List separately in addition to code for primary procedure)

ICD-9-CM Diagnostic

The ICD-9-CM diagnostic code(s) would be the same as the actual procedure performed because these are in-addition-to codes.

ICD-9-CM Procedural

78.59 Internal fixation of other bone, except facial bones, without fracture reduction
81.01 Atlas-axis spinal fusion
81.02 Other cervical fusion of the anterior column, anterior technique
81.03 Other cervical fusion of the posterior column, posterior technique
81.04 Dorsal and dorsolumbar fusion of the anterior column, anterior technique
81.05 Dorsal and dorsolumbar fusion of the posterior column, posterior technique
81.06 Lumbar and lumbosacral fusion of the anterior column, anterior technique
81.07 Lumbar and lumbosacral fusion of the posterior column, posterior technique
81.08 Lumbar and lumbosacral fusion of the anterior column, posterior technique

22842-22844

22842 Posterior segmental instrumentation (eg, pedicle fixation, dual rods with multiple hooks and sublaminar wires); 3 to 6 vertebral segments (List separately in addition to code for primary procedure)
22843 7 to 12 vertebral segments (List separately in addition to code for primary procedure)
22844 13 or more vertebral segments (List separately in addition to code for primary procedure)

ICD-9-CM Diagnostic

The ICD-9-CM diagnostic code(s) would be the same as the actual procedure performed because these are in-addition-to codes.

ICD-9-CM Procedural

78.59 Internal fixation of other bone, except facial bones, without fracture reduction
81.01 Atlas-axis spinal fusion
81.03 Other cervical fusion of the posterior column, posterior technique
81.05 Dorsal and dorsolumbar fusion of the posterior column, posterior technique
81.07 Lumbar and lumbosacral fusion of the posterior column, posterior technique

22845-22847

22845 Anterior instrumentation; 2 to 3 vertebral segments (List separately in addition to code for primary procedure)
22846 4 to 7 vertebral segments (List separately in addition to code for primary procedure)
22847 8 or more vertebral segments (List separately in addition to code for primary procedure)

ICD-9-CM Diagnostic

The ICD-9-CM diagnostic code(s) would be the same as the actual procedure performed because these are in-addition-to codes.

ICD-9-CM Procedural

78.59 Internal fixation of other bone, except facial bones, without fracture reduction
81.01 Atlas-axis spinal fusion
81.02 Other cervical fusion of the anterior column, anterior technique
81.04 Dorsal and dorsolumbar fusion of the anterior column, anterior technique
81.06 Lumbar and lumbosacral fusion of the anterior column, anterior technique
81.08 Lumbar and lumbosacral fusion of the anterior column, posterior technique

22848

22848 Pelvic fixation (attachment of caudal end of instrumentation to pelvic bony structures) other than sacrum (List separately in addition to code for primary procedure)

ICD-9-CM Diagnostic

The ICD-9-CM diagnostic code(s) would be the same as the actual procedure performed because these are in-addition-to codes.

ICD-9-CM Procedural

78.59 Internal fixation of other bone, except facial bones, without fracture reduction

22849

22849 Reinsertion of spinal fixation device

ICD-9-CM Diagnostic

996.40 Unspecified mechanical complication of internal orthopedic device, implant, and graft — (Use additional code to identify prosthetic joint with mechanical complication, V43.60-V43.69) ▽
996.49 Other mechanical complication of other internal orthopedic device, implant, and graft — (Use additional code to identify prosthetic joint with mechanical complication, V43.60-V43.69)
996.67 Infection and inflammatory reaction due to other internal orthopedic device, implant, and graft — (Use additional code to identify specified infections)
996.78 Other complications due to other internal orthopedic device, implant, and graft — (Use additional code to identify complication: 338.18-338.19, 338.28-338.29)

V45.4 Arthrodesis status

ICD-9-CM Procedural

78.59 Internal fixation of other bone, except facial bones, without fracture reduction
84.51 Insertion of interbody spinal fusion device
84.59 Insertion of other spinal devices

22850

22850 Removal of posterior nonsegmental instrumentation (eg, Harrington rod)

ICD-9-CM Diagnostic

996.40 Unspecified mechanical complication of internal orthopedic device, implant, and graft — (Use additional code to identify prosthetic joint with mechanical complication, V43.60-V43.69) ▽
996.49 Other mechanical complication of other internal orthopedic device, implant, and graft — (Use additional code to identify prosthetic joint with mechanical complication, V43.60-V43.69)
996.67 Infection and inflammatory reaction due to other internal orthopedic device, implant, and graft — (Use additional code to identify specified infections)
996.78 Other complications due to other internal orthopedic device, implant, and graft — (Use additional code to identify complication: 338.18-338.19, 338.28-338.29)
V54.01 Encounter for removal of internal fixation device

ICD-9-CM Procedural

78.69 Removal of implanted device from other bone

22851

22851 Application of intervertebral biomechanical device(s) (eg, synthetic cage(s), methylmethacrylate) to vertebral defect or interspace (List separately in addition to code for primary procedure)

ICD-9-CM Diagnostic

The ICD-9-CM diagnostic code(s) would be the same as the actual procedure performed because these are in-addition-to codes.

ICD-9-CM Procedural

84.51 Insertion of interbody spinal fusion device
84.56 Insertion or replacement of (cement) spacer
84.59 Insertion of other spinal devices

22852

22852 Removal of posterior segmental instrumentation

ICD-9-CM Diagnostic

996.40 Unspecified mechanical complication of internal orthopedic device, implant, and graft — (Use additional code to identify prosthetic joint with mechanical complication, V43.60-V43.69) ▽
996.49 Other mechanical complication of other internal orthopedic device, implant, and graft — (Use additional code to identify prosthetic joint with mechanical complication, V43.60-V43.69)
996.67 Infection and inflammatory reaction due to other internal orthopedic device, implant, and graft — (Use additional code to identify specified infections)
996.78 Other complications due to other internal orthopedic device, implant, and graft — (Use additional code to identify complication: 338.18-338.19, 338.28-338.29)
V54.01 Encounter for removal of internal fixation device

ICD-9-CM Procedural

78.69 Removal of implanted device from other bone

22855

22855 Removal of anterior instrumentation

ICD-9-CM Diagnostic

996.40 Unspecified mechanical complication of internal orthopedic device, implant, and graft — (Use additional code to identify prosthetic joint with mechanical complication, V43.60-V43.69) ▽
996.49 Other mechanical complication of other internal orthopedic device, implant, and graft — (Use additional code to identify prosthetic joint with mechanical complication, V43.60-V43.69)
996.67 Infection and inflammatory reaction due to other internal orthopedic device, implant, and graft — (Use additional code to identify specified infections)
996.78 Other complications due to other internal orthopedic device, implant, and graft — (Use additional code to identify complication: 338.18-338.19, 338.28-338.29)
V45.4 Arthrodesis status
V54.01 Encounter for removal of internal fixation device

ICD-9-CM Procedural

78.69 Removal of implanted device from other bone

22856-22865

22856 Total disc arthroplasty (artificial disc), anterior approach, including discectomy with end plate preparation (includes osteophytectomy for nerve root or spinal cord decompression and microdissection), single interspace, cervical
22857 Total disc arthroplasty (artificial disc), anterior approach, including discectomy to prepare interspace (other than for decompression), single interspace, lumbar
22861 Revision including replacement of total disc arthroplasty (artificial disc), anterior approach, single interspace; cervical
22862 lumbar
22864 Removal of total disc arthroplasty (artificial disc), anterior approach, single interspace; cervical
22865 lumbar

ICD-9-CM Diagnostic

170.2 Malignant neoplasm of vertebral column, excluding sacrum and coccyx
198.5 Secondary malignant neoplasm of bone and bone marrow
213.2 Benign neoplasm of vertebral column, excluding sacrum and coccyx
238.0 Neoplasm of uncertain behavior of bone and articular cartilage
239.2 Neoplasms of unspecified nature of bone, soft tissue, and skin
336.9 Unspecified disease of spinal cord ▽
721.0 Cervical spondylosis without myelopathy
721.1 Cervical spondylosis with myelopathy
721.3 Lumbosacral spondylosis without myelopathy
721.42 Spondylosis with myelopathy, lumbar region
721.8 Other allied disorders of spine
722.0 Displacement of cervical intervertebral disc without myelopathy
722.10 Displacement of lumbar intervertebral disc without myelopathy
722.4 Degeneration of cervical intervertebral disc
722.51 Degeneration of thoracic or thoracolumbar intervertebral disc
722.52 Degeneration of lumbar or lumbosacral intervertebral disc
722.71 Intervertebral cervical disc disorder with myelopathy, cervical region
722.73 Intervertebral lumbar disc disorder with myelopathy, lumbar region
722.81 Postlaminectomy syndrome, cervical region
722.83 Postlaminectomy syndrome, lumbar region
722.91 Other and unspecified disc disorder of cervical region ▽
722.93 Other and unspecified disc disorder of lumbar region ▽
723.0 Spinal stenosis in cervical region
723.8 Other syndromes affecting cervical region
724.02 Spinal stenosis of lumbar region, without neurogenic claudication
724.03 Spinal stenosis of lumbar region, with neurogenic claudication
724.4 Thoracic or lumbosacral neuritis or radiculitis, unspecified ▽
731.0 Osteitis deformans without mention of bone tumor

733.13 Pathologic fracture of vertebrae
738.5 Other acquired deformity of back or spine
756.11 Congenital spondylolysis, lumbosacral region
756.12 Congenital spondylolisthesis
756.19 Other congenital anomaly of spine
805.00 Closed fracture of cervical vertebra, unspecified level without mention of spinal cord injury ▽
805.01 Closed fracture of first cervical vertebra without mention of spinal cord injury
805.02 Closed fracture of second cervical vertebra without mention of spinal cord injury
805.03 Closed fracture of third cervical vertebra without mention of spinal cord injury
805.04 Closed fracture of fourth cervical vertebra without mention of spinal cord injury
805.05 Closed fracture of fifth cervical vertebra without mention of spinal cord injury
805.06 Closed fracture of sixth cervical vertebra without mention of spinal cord injury
805.07 Closed fracture of seventh cervical vertebra without mention of spinal cord injury
805.08 Closed fracture of multiple cervical vertebrae without mention of spinal cord injury
805.10 Open fracture of cervical vertebra, unspecified level without mention of spinal cord injury ▽
805.11 Open fracture of first cervical vertebra without mention of spinal cord injury
805.12 Open fracture of second cervical vertebra without mention of spinal cord injury
805.13 Open fracture of third cervical vertebra without mention of spinal cord injury
805.14 Open fracture of fourth cervical vertebra without mention of spinal cord injury
805.15 Open fracture of fifth cervical vertebra without mention of spinal cord injury
805.16 Open fracture of sixth cervical vertebra without mention of spinal cord injury
805.17 Open fracture of seventh cervical vertebra without mention of spinal cord injury
805.18 Open fracture of multiple cervical vertebrae without mention of spinal cord injury
805.4 Closed fracture of lumbar vertebra without mention of spinal cord injury
805.5 Open fracture of lumbar vertebra without mention of spinal cord injury
806.00 Closed fracture of C1-C4 level with unspecified spinal cord injury ▽
806.01 Closed fracture of C1-C4 level with complete lesion of cord
806.02 Closed fracture of C1-C4 level with anterior cord syndrome
806.03 Closed fracture of C1-C4 level with central cord syndrome
806.04 Closed fracture of C1-C4 level with other specified spinal cord injury
806.05 Closed fracture of C5-C7 level with unspecified spinal cord injury ▽
806.06 Closed fracture of C5-C7 level with complete lesion of cord
806.07 Closed fracture of C5-C7 level with anterior cord syndrome
806.08 Closed fracture of C5-C7 level with central cord syndrome
806.09 Closed fracture of C5-C7 level with other specified spinal cord injury
806.10 Open fracture of C1-C4 level with unspecified spinal cord injury ▽
806.11 Open fracture of C1-C4 level with complete lesion of cord
806.12 Open fracture of C1-C4 level with anterior cord syndrome
806.13 Open fracture of C1-C4 level with central cord syndrome
806.14 Open fracture of C1-C4 level with other specified spinal cord injury
806.15 Open fracture of C5-C7 level with unspecified spinal cord injury ▽
806.16 Open fracture of C5-C7 level with complete lesion of cord
806.17 Open fracture of C5-C7 level with anterior cord syndrome
806.18 Open fracture of C5-C7 level with central cord syndrome
806.19 Open fracture of C5-C7 level with other specified spinal cord injury
806.4 Closed fracture of lumbar spine with spinal cord injury
806.5 Open fracture of lumbar spine with spinal cord injury
839.00 Closed dislocation, unspecified cervical vertebra ▽
839.01 Closed dislocation, first cervical vertebra
839.02 Closed dislocation, second cervical vertebra
839.03 Closed dislocation, third cervical vertebra
839.04 Closed dislocation, fourth cervical vertebra
839.05 Closed dislocation, fifth cervical vertebra
839.06 Closed dislocation, sixth cervical vertebra
839.07 Closed dislocation, seventh cervical vertebra
839.08 Closed dislocation, multiple cervical vertebrae
839.10 Open dislocation, unspecified cervical vertebra ▽
839.11 Open dislocation, first cervical vertebra
839.12 Open dislocation, second cervical vertebra
839.13 Open dislocation, third cervical vertebra
839.14 Open dislocation, fourth cervical vertebra
839.15 Open dislocation, fifth cervical vertebra
839.16 Open dislocation, sixth cervical vertebra
839.17 Open dislocation, seventh cervical vertebra
839.18 Open dislocation, multiple cervical vertebrae
839.20 Closed dislocation, lumbar vertebra
839.30 Open dislocation, lumbar vertebra
996.40 Unspecified mechanical complication of internal orthopedic device, implant, and graft — (Use additional code to identify prosthetic joint with mechanical complication, V43.60-V43.69) ▽
996.49 Other mechanical complication of other internal orthopedic device, implant, and graft — (Use additional code to identify prosthetic joint with mechanical complication, V43.60-V43.69)
996.67 Infection and inflammatory reaction due to other internal orthopedic device, implant, and graft — (Use additional code to identify specified infections)
996.78 Other complications due to other internal orthopedic device, implant, and graft — (Use additional code to identify complication: 338.18-338.19, 338.28-338.29)

ICD-9-CM Procedural

80.09 Arthrotomy for removal of prosthesis without replacement, other specified site
84.62 Insertion of total spinal disc prosthesis, cervical
84.65 Insertion of total spinal disc prosthesis, lumbosacral
84.66 Revision or replacement of artificial spinal disc prosthesis, cervical
84.68 Revision or replacement of artificial spinal disc prosthesis, lumbosacral
84.69 Revision or replacement of artificial spinal disc prosthesis, not otherwise specified

Abdomen

22900-22905

22900 Excision, tumor, soft tissue of abdominal wall, subfascial (eg, intramuscular); less than 5 cm
22901 5 cm or greater
22902 Excision, tumor, soft tissue of abdominal wall, subcutaneous; less than 3 cm
22903 3 cm or greater
22904 Radical resection of tumor (eg, sarcoma), soft tissue of abdominal wall; less than 5 cm
22905 5 cm or greater

ICD-9-CM Diagnostic

171.5 Malignant neoplasm of connective and other soft tissue of abdomen
198.89 Secondary malignant neoplasm of other specified sites
209.35 Merkel cell carcinoma of the trunk
209.75 Secondary Merkel cell carcinoma
214.1 Lipoma of other skin and subcutaneous tissue
215.5 Other benign neoplasm of connective and other soft tissue of abdomen
238.1 Neoplasm of uncertain behavior of connective and other soft tissue
239.2 Neoplasms of unspecified nature of bone, soft tissue, and skin

ICD-9-CM Procedural

54.3 Excision or destruction of lesion or tissue of abdominal wall or umbilicus
83.39 Excision of lesion of other soft tissue
83.49 Other excision of soft tissue
86.3 Other local excision or destruction of lesion or tissue of skin and subcutaneous tissue
86.4 Radical excision of skin lesion

HCPCS Level II Supplies & Services

A4305 Disposable drug delivery system, flow rate of 50 ml or greater per hour

Shoulder

23000

23000 Removal of subdeltoid calcareous deposits, open

ICD-9-CM Diagnostic

712.11 Chondrocalcinosis due to dicalcium phosphate crystals, shoulder region — (Code first underlying disease: 275.4) ☒
712.21 Chondrocalcinosis due to pyrophosphate crystals, shoulder region — (Code first underlying disease: 275.4) ☒
712.31 Chondrocalcinosis, cause unspecified, involving shoulder region — (Code first underlying disease: 275.4) ☒
712.81 Other specified crystal arthropathies, shoulder region
726.11 Calcifying tendinitis of shoulder
726.19 Other specified disorders of rotator cuff syndrome of shoulder and allied disorders
726.2 Other affections of shoulder region, not elsewhere classified
727.82 Calcium deposits in tendon and bursa
727.89 Other disorders of synovium, tendon, and bursa
728.11 Progressive myositis ossificans
728.12 Traumatic myositis ossificans
728.13 Postoperative heterotopic calcification
728.19 Other muscular calcification and ossification

ICD-9-CM Procedural

83.39 Excision of lesion of other soft tissue

23020

23020 Capsular contracture release (eg, Sever type procedure)

ICD-9-CM Diagnostic

718.41 Contracture of shoulder joint

ICD-9-CM Procedural

80.41 Division of joint capsule, ligament, or cartilage of shoulder
83.19 Other division of soft tissue

23030

23030 Incision and drainage, shoulder area; deep abscess or hematoma

ICD-9-CM Diagnostic

682.3 Cellulitis and abscess of upper arm and forearm — (Use additional code to identify organism, such as 041.1, etc.)
711.41 Arthropathy associated with other bacterial diseases, shoulder region — (Code first underlying disease, such as diseases classifiable to 010-040 (except 036.82), 090-099 (except 098.50)) ☒
719.11 Hemarthrosis, shoulder region
727.89 Other disorders of synovium, tendon, and bursa
729.92 Nontraumatic hematoma of soft tissue
730.11 Chronic osteomyelitis, shoulder region — (Use additional code to identify organism: 041.1. Use additional code to identify major osseous defect, if applicable: 731.3)
730.21 Unspecified osteomyelitis, shoulder region — (Use additional code to identify organism: 041.1. Use additional code to identify major osseous defect, if applicable: 731.3) ▽
730.31 Periostitis, without mention of osteomyelitis, shoulder region — (Use additional code to identify organism: 041.1)
731.3 Major osseous defects — (Code first underlying disease: 170.0-170.9, 730.00-730.29, 733.00-733.09, 733.40-733.49, 996.45)
780.62 Postprocedural fever
923.00 Contusion of shoulder region
998.12 Hematoma complicating a procedure
998.51 Infected postoperative seroma — (Use additional code to identify organism)
998.59 Other postoperative infection — (Use additional code to identify infection)

ICD-9-CM Procedural

83.02 Myotomy

HCPCS Level II Supplies & Services

A4305 Disposable drug delivery system, flow rate of 50 ml or greater per hour

23031

23031 Incision and drainage, shoulder area; infected bursa

ICD-9-CM Diagnostic

726.10 Unspecified disorders of bursae and tendons in shoulder region ▽
727.3 Other bursitis disorders
727.89 Other disorders of synovium, tendon, and bursa
730.01 Acute osteomyelitis, shoulder region — (Use additional code to identify organism: 041.1. Use additional code to identify major osseous defect, if applicable: 731.3)
730.11 Chronic osteomyelitis, shoulder region — (Use additional code to identify organism: 041.1. Use additional code to identify major osseous defect, if applicable: 731.3)
730.21 Unspecified osteomyelitis, shoulder region — (Use additional code to identify organism: 041.1. Use additional code to identify major osseous defect, if applicable: 731.3) ▽
731.3 Major osseous defects — (Code first underlying disease: 170.0-170.9, 730.00-730.29, 733.00-733.09, 733.40-733.49, 996.45)
998.51 Infected postoperative seroma — (Use additional code to identify organism)
998.59 Other postoperative infection — (Use additional code to identify infection)

ICD-9-CM Procedural

83.03 Bursotomy

HCPCS Level II Supplies & Services

A4305 Disposable drug delivery system, flow rate of 50 ml or greater per hour

23035

23035 Incision, bone cortex (eg, osteomyelitis or bone abscess), shoulder area

ICD-9-CM Diagnostic

682.3 Cellulitis and abscess of upper arm and forearm — (Use additional code to identify organism, such as 041.1, etc.)
730.11 Chronic osteomyelitis, shoulder region — (Use additional code to identify organism: 041.1. Use additional code to identify major osseous defect, if applicable: 731.3)
730.21 Unspecified osteomyelitis, shoulder region — (Use additional code to identify organism: 041.1. Use additional code to identify major osseous defect, if applicable: 731.3) ▽
730.81 Other infections involving bone diseases classified elsewhere, shoulder region — (Use additional code to identify organism: 041.1. Code first underlying disease: 002.0, 015.0-015.9) ☒
731.3 Major osseous defects — (Code first underlying disease: 170.0-170.9, 730.00-730.29, 733.00-733.09, 733.40-733.49, 996.45)
998.51 Infected postoperative seroma — (Use additional code to identify organism)
998.59 Other postoperative infection — (Use additional code to identify infection)

ICD-9-CM Procedural

77.11 Other incision of scapula, clavicle, and thorax (ribs and sternum) without division
77.12 Other incision of humerus without division

23040-23044

23040 Arthrotomy, glenohumeral joint, including exploration, drainage, or removal of foreign body
23044 Arthrotomy, acromioclavicular, sternoclavicular joint, including exploration, drainage, or removal of foreign body

ICD-9-CM Diagnostic

711.01 Pyogenic arthritis, shoulder region — (Use additional code to identify infectious organism: 041.0-041.8)

711.81 Arthropathy associated with other infectious and parasitic diseases, shoulder region — (Code first underlying disease: 080-088, 100-104, 130-136) ☒
711.91 Unspecified infective arthritis, shoulder region ▽
715.00 Generalized osteoarthrosis, unspecified site ▽
715.09 Generalized osteoarthrosis, involving multiple sites
715.11 Primary localized osteoarthrosis, shoulder region
716.11 Traumatic arthropathy, shoulder region
718.01 Articular cartilage disorder, shoulder region
718.11 Loose body in shoulder joint
718.21 Pathological dislocation of shoulder joint
718.41 Contracture of shoulder joint
718.51 Ankylosis of joint of shoulder region
718.71 Developmental dislocation of joint, shoulder region
719.01 Effusion of shoulder joint
719.11 Hemarthrosis, shoulder region
719.41 Pain in joint, shoulder region
719.81 Other specified disorders of shoulder joint
729.6 Residual foreign body in soft tissue — (Use additional code to identify foreign body (V90.01-V90.9))
998.51 Infected postoperative seroma — (Use additional code to identify organism)
998.59 Other postoperative infection — (Use additional code to identify infection)

ICD-9-CM Procedural

80.11 Other arthrotomy of shoulder
80.19 Other arthrotomy of other specified site

23065-23066

23065 Biopsy, soft tissue of shoulder area; superficial
23066 deep

ICD-9-CM Diagnostic

171.2 Malignant neoplasm of connective and other soft tissue of upper limb, including shoulder
195.4 Malignant neoplasm of upper limb
198.89 Secondary malignant neoplasm of other specified sites
214.1 Lipoma of other skin and subcutaneous tissue
215.2 Other benign neoplasm of connective and other soft tissue of upper limb, including shoulder
238.1 Neoplasm of uncertain behavior of connective and other soft tissue
239.2 Neoplasms of unspecified nature of bone, soft tissue, and skin
728.82 Foreign body granuloma of muscle — (Use additional code to identify foreign body (V90.01-V90.9))
782.2 Localized superficial swelling, mass, or lump

ICD-9-CM Procedural

83.21 Open biopsy of soft tissue

23075-23078 [23071, 23073]

23071 Excision, tumor, soft tissue of shoulder area, subcutaneous; 3 cm or greater
23073 Excision, tumor, soft tissue of shoulder area, subfascial (eg, intramuscular); 5 cm or greater
23075 Excision, tumor, soft tissue of shoulder area, subcutaneous; less than 3 cm
23076 Excision, tumor, soft tissue of shoulder area, subfascial (eg, intramuscular); less than 5 cm
23077 Radical resection of tumor (eg, sarcoma), soft tissue of shoulder area; less than 5 cm
23078 5 cm or greater

ICD-9-CM Diagnostic

171.2 Malignant neoplasm of connective and other soft tissue of upper limb, including shoulder
172.6 Malignant melanoma of skin of upper limb, including shoulder
173.60 Unspecified malignant neoplasm of skin of upper limb, including shoulder ▽
173.61 Basal cell carcinoma of skin of upper limb, including shoulder
173.62 Squamous cell carcinoma of skin of upper limb, including shoulder
173.69 Other specified malignant neoplasm of skin of upper limb, including shoulder
195.4 Malignant neoplasm of upper limb
198.89 Secondary malignant neoplasm of other specified sites
209.33 Merkel cell carcinoma of the upper limb
209.35 Merkel cell carcinoma of the trunk
209.75 Secondary Merkel cell carcinoma
214.1 Lipoma of other skin and subcutaneous tissue
215.2 Other benign neoplasm of connective and other soft tissue of upper limb, including shoulder
228.01 Hemangioma of skin and subcutaneous tissue
238.1 Neoplasm of uncertain behavior of connective and other soft tissue
239.2 Neoplasms of unspecified nature of bone, soft tissue, and skin
728.82 Foreign body granuloma of muscle — (Use additional code to identify foreign body (V90.01-V90.9))
782.2 Localized superficial swelling, mass, or lump

ICD-9-CM Procedural

83.32 Excision of lesion of muscle
83.39 Excision of lesion of other soft tissue
83.49 Other excision of soft tissue
86.3 Other local excision or destruction of lesion or tissue of skin and subcutaneous tissue
86.4 Radical excision of skin lesion

HCPCS Level II Supplies & Services

A4305 Disposable drug delivery system, flow rate of 50 ml or greater per hour

23100

23100 Arthrotomy, glenohumeral joint, including biopsy

ICD-9-CM Diagnostic

170.4 Malignant neoplasm of scapula and long bones of upper limb
171.2 Malignant neoplasm of connective and other soft tissue of upper limb, including shoulder
198.5 Secondary malignant neoplasm of bone and bone marrow
198.89 Secondary malignant neoplasm of other specified sites
213.4 Benign neoplasm of scapula and long bones of upper limb
215.2 Other benign neoplasm of connective and other soft tissue of upper limb, including shoulder
238.0 Neoplasm of uncertain behavior of bone and articular cartilage
238.1 Neoplasm of uncertain behavior of connective and other soft tissue
239.2 Neoplasms of unspecified nature of bone, soft tissue, and skin
275.40 Unspecified disorder of calcium metabolism — (Use additional code to identify any associated intellectual disabilities) ▽
275.42 Hypercalcemia — (Use additional code to identify any associated intellectual disabilities)
275.49 Other disorders of calcium metabolism — (Use additional code to identify any associated intellectual disabilities)
275.5 Hungry bone syndrome — (Use additional code to identify any associated intellectual disabilities)
357.1 Polyneuropathy in collagen vascular disease — (Code first underlying disease: 446.0, 710.0, 714.0) ☒
359.6 Symptomatic inflammatory myopathy in diseases classified elsewhere — (Code first underlying disease: 135, 140.0-208.9, 277.30-277.39, 446.0, 710.0, 710.1, 710.2, 714.0) ☒
446.0 Polyarteritis nodosa
710.0 Systemic lupus erythematosus — (Use additional code to identify manifestation: 424.91, 581.81, 582.81, 583.81)
714.0 Rheumatoid arthritis — (Use additional code to identify manifestation: 357.1, 359.6)
998.51 Infected postoperative seroma — (Use additional code to identify organism)
998.59 Other postoperative infection — (Use additional code to identify infection)

▽ Unspecified code ☒ Manifestation code
♀ Female diagnosis ♂ Male diagnosis

V64.43 Arthroscopic surgical procedure converted to open procedure

ICD-9-CM Procedural

80.11 Other arthrotomy of shoulder

80.31 Biopsy of joint structure of shoulder

23101

23101 Arthrotomy, acromioclavicular joint or sternoclavicular joint, including biopsy and/or excision of torn cartilage

ICD-9-CM Diagnostic

170.4 Malignant neoplasm of scapula and long bones of upper limb

171.2 Malignant neoplasm of connective and other soft tissue of upper limb, including shoulder

195.4 Malignant neoplasm of upper limb

198.89 Secondary malignant neoplasm of other specified sites

213.4 Benign neoplasm of scapula and long bones of upper limb

215.2 Other benign neoplasm of connective and other soft tissue of upper limb, including shoulder

239.2 Neoplasms of unspecified nature of bone, soft tissue, and skin

275.40 Unspecified disorder of calcium metabolism — (Use additional code to identify any associated intellectual disabilities) ▽

275.42 Hypercalcemia — (Use additional code to identify any associated intellectual disabilities)

275.49 Other disorders of calcium metabolism — (Use additional code to identify any associated intellectual disabilities)

275.5 Hungry bone syndrome — (Use additional code to identify any associated intellectual disabilities)

357.1 Polyneuropathy in collagen vascular disease — (Code first underlying disease: 446.0, 710.0, 714.0) ☒

359.6 Symptomatic inflammatory myopathy in diseases classified elsewhere — (Code first underlying disease: 135, 140.0-208.9, 277.30-277.39, 446.0, 710.0, 710.1, 710.2, 714.0) ☒

446.0 Polyarteritis nodosa

710.0 Systemic lupus erythematosus — (Use additional code to identify manifestation: 424.91, 581.81, 582.81, 583.81)

714.0 Rheumatoid arthritis — (Use additional code to identify manifestation: 357.1, 359.6)

718.01 Articular cartilage disorder, shoulder region

719.41 Pain in joint, shoulder region

V64.43 Arthroscopic surgical procedure converted to open procedure

ICD-9-CM Procedural

80.31 Biopsy of joint structure of shoulder

80.91 Other excision of shoulder joint

23075

23105 Arthrotomy; glenohumeral joint, with synovectomy, with or without biopsy

23106 sternoclavicular joint, with synovectomy, with or without biopsy

ICD-9-CM Diagnostic

357.1 Polyneuropathy in collagen vascular disease — (Code first underlying disease: 446.0, 710.0, 714.0) ☒

359.6 Symptomatic inflammatory myopathy in diseases classified elsewhere — (Code first underlying disease: 135, 140.0-208.9, 277.30-277.39, 446.0, 710.0, 710.1, 710.2, 714.0) ☒

446.0 Polyarteritis nodosa

710.0 Systemic lupus erythematosus — (Use additional code to identify manifestation: 424.91, 581.81, 582.81, 583.81)

714.0 Rheumatoid arthritis — (Use additional code to identify manifestation: 357.1, 359.6)

715.91 Osteoarthrosis, unspecified whether generalized or localized, shoulder region ▽

716.61 Unspecified monoarthritis, shoulder region ▽

719.21 Villonodular synovitis, shoulder region

719.41 Pain in joint, shoulder region

727.00 Unspecified synovitis and tenosynovitis ▽

727.01 Synovitis and tenosynovitis in diseases classified elsewhere — (Code first underlying disease: 015.0-015.9) ☒

727.02 Giant cell tumor of tendon sheath

V64.43 Arthroscopic surgical procedure converted to open procedure

ICD-9-CM Procedural

80.11 Other arthrotomy of shoulder

80.19 Other arthrotomy of other specified site

80.31 Biopsy of joint structure of shoulder

80.71 Synovectomy of shoulder

23107

23107 Arthrotomy, glenohumeral joint, with joint exploration, with or without removal of loose or foreign body

ICD-9-CM Diagnostic

275.40 Unspecified disorder of calcium metabolism — (Use additional code to identify any associated intellectual disabilities) ▽

275.41 Hypocalcemia — (Use additional code to identify any associated intellectual disabilities)

275.42 Hypercalcemia — (Use additional code to identify any associated intellectual disabilities)

275.49 Other disorders of calcium metabolism — (Use additional code to identify any associated intellectual disabilities)

275.5 Hungry bone syndrome — (Use additional code to identify any associated intellectual disabilities)

357.1 Polyneuropathy in collagen vascular disease — (Code first underlying disease: 446.0, 710.0, 714.0) ☒

359.6 Symptomatic inflammatory myopathy in diseases classified elsewhere — (Code first underlying disease: 135, 140.0-208.9, 277.30-277.39, 446.0, 710.0, 710.1, 710.2, 714.0) ☒

446.0 Polyarteritis nodosa

710.0 Systemic lupus erythematosus — (Use additional code to identify manifestation: 424.91, 581.81, 582.81, 583.81)

712.11 Chondrocalcinosis due to dicalcium phosphate crystals, shoulder region — (Code first underlying disease: 275.4) ☒

712.21 Chondrocalcinosis due to pyrophosphate crystals, shoulder region — (Code first underlying disease: 275.4) ☒

714.0 Rheumatoid arthritis — (Use additional code to identify manifestation: 357.1, 359.6)

715.91 Osteoarthrosis, unspecified whether generalized or localized, shoulder region ▽

716.61 Unspecified monoarthritis, shoulder region ▽

718.11 Loose body in shoulder joint

719.41 Pain in joint, shoulder region

727.02 Giant cell tumor of tendon sheath

V64.43 Arthroscopic surgical procedure converted to open procedure

ICD-9-CM Procedural

80.11 Other arthrotomy of shoulder

23120-23125

23120 Claviculectomy; partial

23125 total

ICD-9-CM Diagnostic

170.3 Malignant neoplasm of ribs, sternum, and clavicle

196.3 Secondary and unspecified malignant neoplasm of lymph nodes of axilla and upper limb

198.5 Secondary malignant neoplasm of bone and bone marrow

198.89 Secondary malignant neoplasm of other specified sites

209.73 Secondary neuroendocrine tumor of bone

213.3 Benign neoplasm of ribs, sternum, and clavicle

238.0 Neoplasm of uncertain behavior of bone and articular cartilage
239.2 Neoplasms of unspecified nature of bone, soft tissue, and skin
715.11 Primary localized osteoarthrosis, shoulder region
715.21 Secondary localized osteoarthrosis, shoulder region
716.11 Traumatic arthropathy, shoulder region
716.61 Unspecified monoarthritis, shoulder region ▽
718.01 Articular cartilage disorder, shoulder region
718.31 Recurrent dislocation of shoulder joint
728.86 Necrotizing fasciitis — (Use additional code to identify infectious organism, 041.00-041.89, 785.4, if applicable)
730.11 Chronic osteomyelitis, shoulder region — (Use additional code to identify organism: 041.1. Use additional code to identify major osseous defect, if applicable: 731.3)
731.3 Major osseous defects — (Code first underlying disease: 170.0-170.9, 730.00-730.29, 733.00-733.09, 733.40-733.49, 996.45)
733.49 Aseptic necrosis of other bone site — (Use additional code to identify major osseous defect, if applicable: 731.3)
733.90 Disorder of bone and cartilage, unspecified ▽
738.8 Acquired musculoskeletal deformity of other specified site
785.4 Gangrene — (Code first any associated underlying condition)
831.04 Closed dislocation of acromioclavicular (joint)

ICD-9-CM Procedural

77.81 Other partial ostectomy of scapula, clavicle, and thorax (ribs and sternum)
77.91 Total ostectomy of scapula, clavicle, and thorax (ribs and sternum)

23130

23130 Acromioplasty or acromionectomy, partial, with or without coracoacromial ligament release

ICD-9-CM Diagnostic

715.11 Primary localized osteoarthrosis, shoulder region
715.21 Secondary localized osteoarthrosis, shoulder region
716.11 Traumatic arthropathy, shoulder region
716.61 Unspecified monoarthritis, shoulder region ▽
716.91 Unspecified arthropathy, shoulder region ▽
718.01 Articular cartilage disorder, shoulder region
719.41 Pain in joint, shoulder region
726.10 Unspecified disorders of bursae and tendons in shoulder region ▽
726.13 Partial tear of rotator cuff
726.2 Other affections of shoulder region, not elsewhere classified
727.61 Complete rupture of rotator cuff
811.01 Closed fracture of acromial process of scapula
811.11 Open fracture of acromial process of scapula
831.14 Open dislocation of acromioclavicular (joint)

ICD-9-CM Procedural

77.81 Other partial ostectomy of scapula, clavicle, and thorax (ribs and sternum)
81.81 Partial shoulder replacement
81.82 Repair of recurrent dislocation of shoulder
81.83 Other repair of shoulder

23140-23146

23140 Excision or curettage of bone cyst or benign tumor of clavicle or scapula;
23145 with autograft (includes obtaining graft)
23146 with allograft

ICD-9-CM Diagnostic

213.3 Benign neoplasm of ribs, sternum, and clavicle
213.4 Benign neoplasm of scapula and long bones of upper limb
238.0 Neoplasm of uncertain behavior of bone and articular cartilage
239.2 Neoplasms of unspecified nature of bone, soft tissue, and skin
733.21 Solitary bone cyst
733.22 Aneurysmal bone cyst
733.29 Other cyst of bone

ICD-9-CM Procedural

77.61 Local excision of lesion or tissue of scapula, clavicle, and thorax (ribs and sternum)
77.77 Excision of tibia and fibula for graft
77.79 Excision of other bone for graft, except facial bones
78.01 Bone graft of scapula, clavicle, and thorax (ribs and sternum)

23150-23156

23150 Excision or curettage of bone cyst or benign tumor of proximal humerus;
23155 with autograft (includes obtaining graft)
23156 with allograft

ICD-9-CM Diagnostic

213.4 Benign neoplasm of scapula and long bones of upper limb
238.0 Neoplasm of uncertain behavior of bone and articular cartilage
239.2 Neoplasms of unspecified nature of bone, soft tissue, and skin
733.21 Solitary bone cyst
733.22 Aneurysmal bone cyst
733.29 Other cyst of bone

ICD-9-CM Procedural

77.62 Local excision of lesion or tissue of humerus
77.77 Excision of tibia and fibula for graft
77.79 Excision of other bone for graft, except facial bones
78.02 Bone graft of humerus

23170-23172

23170 Sequestrectomy (eg, for osteomyelitis or bone abscess), clavicle
23172 Sequestrectomy (eg, for osteomyelitis or bone abscess), scapula

ICD-9-CM Diagnostic

730.01 Acute osteomyelitis, shoulder region — (Use additional code to identify organism: 041.1. Use additional code to identify major osseous defect, if applicable: 731.3)
730.11 Chronic osteomyelitis, shoulder region — (Use additional code to identify organism: 041.1. Use additional code to identify major osseous defect, if applicable: 731.3)
730.21 Unspecified osteomyelitis, shoulder region — (Use additional code to identify organism: 041.1. Use additional code to identify major osseous defect, if applicable: 731.3) ▽
730.31 Periostitis, without mention of osteomyelitis, shoulder region — (Use additional code to identify organism: 041.1)
730.88 Other infections involving bone diseases classified elsewhere, other specified sites — (Use additional code to identify organism: 041.1. Code first underlying disease: 002.0, 015.0-015.9) ☒
731.3 Major osseous defects — (Code first underlying disease: 170.0-170.9, 730.00-730.29, 733.00-733.09, 733.40-733.49, 996.45)
733.49 Aseptic necrosis of other bone site — (Use additional code to identify major osseous defect, if applicable: 731.3)

ICD-9-CM Procedural

77.01 Sequestrectomy of scapula, clavicle, and thorax (ribs and sternum)

23174

23174 Sequestrectomy (eg, for osteomyelitis or bone abscess), humeral head to surgical neck

ICD-9-CM Diagnostic

730.02 Acute osteomyelitis, upper arm — (Use additional code to identify organism: 041.1. Use additional code to identify major osseous defect, if applicable: 731.3)
730.12 Chronic osteomyelitis, upper arm — (Use additional code to identify organism: 041.1. Use additional code to identify major osseous defect, if applicable: 731.3)
730.22 Unspecified osteomyelitis, upper arm — (Use additional code to identify organism: 041.1. Use additional code to identify major osseous defect, if applicable: 731.3) ▽

730.32 Periostitis, without mention of osteomyelitis, upper arm — (Use additional code to identify organism: 041.1)
730.82 Other infections involving bone diseases classified elsewhere, upper arm — (Use additional code to identify organism: 041.1. Code first underlying disease: 002.0, 015.0-015.9) ☒
731.3 Major osseous defects — (Code first underlying disease: 170.0-170.9, 730.00-730.29, 733.00-733.09, 733.40-733.49, 996.45)
733.41 Aseptic necrosis of head of humerus — (Use additional code to identify major osseous defect, if applicable: 731.3)

ICD-9-CM Procedural

77.02 Sequestrectomy of humerus

23180-23182

23180 Partial excision (craterization, saucerization, or diaphysectomy) bone (eg, osteomyelitis), clavicle
23182 Partial excision (craterization, saucerization, or diaphysectomy) bone (eg, osteomyelitis), scapula

ICD-9-CM Diagnostic

730.11 Chronic osteomyelitis, shoulder region — (Use additional code to identify organism: 041.1. Use additional code to identify major osseous defect, if applicable: 731.3)
730.21 Unspecified osteomyelitis, shoulder region — (Use additional code to identify organism: 041.1. Use additional code to identify major osseous defect, if applicable: 731.3) ▽
730.31 Periostitis, without mention of osteomyelitis, shoulder region — (Use additional code to identify organism: 041.1)
730.81 Other infections involving bone diseases classified elsewhere, shoulder region — (Use additional code to identify organism: 041.1. Code first underlying disease: 002.0, 015.0-015.9) ☒
731.3 Major osseous defects — (Code first underlying disease: 170.0-170.9, 730.00-730.29, 733.00-733.09, 733.40-733.49, 996.45)
733.49 Aseptic necrosis of other bone site — (Use additional code to identify major osseous defect, if applicable: 731.3)

ICD-9-CM Procedural

77.81 Other partial ostectomy of scapula, clavicle, and thorax (ribs and sternum)

23184

23184 Partial excision (craterization, saucerization, or diaphysectomy) bone (eg, osteomyelitis), proximal humerus

ICD-9-CM Diagnostic

730.12 Chronic osteomyelitis, upper arm — (Use additional code to identify organism: 041.1. Use additional code to identify major osseous defect, if applicable: 731.3)
730.22 Unspecified osteomyelitis, upper arm — (Use additional code to identify organism: 041.1. Use additional code to identify major osseous defect, if applicable: 731.3) ▽
730.32 Periostitis, without mention of osteomyelitis, upper arm — (Use additional code to identify organism: 041.1)
730.82 Other infections involving bone diseases classified elsewhere, upper arm — (Use additional code to identify organism: 041.1. Code first underlying disease: 002.0, 015.0-015.9) ☒
731.3 Major osseous defects — (Code first underlying disease: 170.0-170.9, 730.00-730.29, 733.00-733.09, 733.40-733.49, 996.45)
733.41 Aseptic necrosis of head of humerus — (Use additional code to identify major osseous defect, if applicable: 731.3)

ICD-9-CM Procedural

77.82 Other partial ostectomy of humerus

23190

23190 Ostectomy of scapula, partial (eg, superior medial angle)

ICD-9-CM Diagnostic

170.4 Malignant neoplasm of scapula and long bones of upper limb
171.4 Malignant neoplasm of connective and other soft tissue of thorax
195.1 Malignant neoplasm of thorax
198.5 Secondary malignant neoplasm of bone and bone marrow
213.4 Benign neoplasm of scapula and long bones of upper limb
238.0 Neoplasm of uncertain behavior of bone and articular cartilage
239.2 Neoplasms of unspecified nature of bone, soft tissue, and skin
731.3 Major osseous defects — (Code first underlying disease: 170.0-170.9, 730.00-730.29, 733.00-733.09, 733.40-733.49, 996.45)
733.90 Disorder of bone and cartilage, unspecified ▽
736.89 Other acquired deformity of other parts of limb

ICD-9-CM Procedural

77.81 Other partial ostectomy of scapula, clavicle, and thorax (ribs and sternum)

23195

23195 Resection, humeral head

ICD-9-CM Diagnostic

170.4 Malignant neoplasm of scapula and long bones of upper limb
195.4 Malignant neoplasm of upper limb
213.4 Benign neoplasm of scapula and long bones of upper limb
357.1 Polyneuropathy in collagen vascular disease — (Code first underlying disease: 446.0, 710.0, 714.0) ☒
359.6 Symptomatic inflammatory myopathy in diseases classified elsewhere — (Code first underlying disease: 135, 140.0-208.9, 277.30-277.39, 446.0, 710.0, 710.1, 710.2, 714.0) ☒
446.0 Polyarteritis nodosa
710.0 Systemic lupus erythematosus — (Use additional code to identify manifestation: 424.91, 581.81, 582.81, 583.81)
714.0 Rheumatoid arthritis — (Use additional code to identify manifestation: 357.1, 359.6)
715.11 Primary localized osteoarthrosis, shoulder region
715.12 Primary localized osteoarthrosis, upper arm
715.31 Localized osteoarthrosis not specified whether primary or secondary, shoulder region
715.32 Localized osteoarthrosis not specified whether primary or secondary, upper arm
716.11 Traumatic arthropathy, shoulder region
716.12 Traumatic arthropathy, upper arm
716.61 Unspecified monoarthritis, shoulder region ▽
716.62 Unspecified monoarthritis, upper arm ▽
718.81 Other joint derangement, not elsewhere classified, shoulder region
718.82 Other joint derangement, not elsewhere classified, upper arm
731.3 Major osseous defects — (Code first underlying disease: 170.0-170.9, 730.00-730.29, 733.00-733.09, 733.40-733.49, 996.45)
733.41 Aseptic necrosis of head of humerus — (Use additional code to identify major osseous defect, if applicable: 731.3)
733.82 Nonunion of fracture
812.03 Closed fracture of greater tuberosity of humerus
812.09 Other closed fractures of upper end of humerus

ICD-9-CM Procedural

77.82 Other partial ostectomy of humerus

23200-23210

23200 Radical resection of tumor; clavicle
23210 scapula

ICD-9-CM Diagnostic

170.3 Malignant neoplasm of ribs, sternum, and clavicle

170.4 Malignant neoplasm of scapula and long bones of upper limb
171.0 Malignant neoplasm of connective and other soft tissue of head, face, and neck
171.4 Malignant neoplasm of connective and other soft tissue of thorax
171.7 Malignant neoplasm of connective and other soft tissue of trunk, unspecified site
198.5 Secondary malignant neoplasm of bone and bone marrow
199.0 Disseminated malignant neoplasm
209.73 Secondary neuroendocrine tumor of bone
213.3 Benign neoplasm of ribs, sternum, and clavicle
213.4 Benign neoplasm of scapula and long bones of upper limb
238.0 Neoplasm of uncertain behavior of bone and articular cartilage
239.2 Neoplasms of unspecified nature of bone, soft tissue, and skin
731.3 Major osseous defects — (Code first underlying disease: 170.0-170.9, 730.00-730.29, 733.00-733.09, 733.40-733.49, 996.45)

ICD-9-CM Procedural

77.81 Other partial ostectomy of scapula, clavicle, and thorax (ribs and sternum)

23220

23220 Radical resection of tumor, proximal humerus

ICD-9-CM Diagnostic

170.4 Malignant neoplasm of scapula and long bones of upper limb
171.2 Malignant neoplasm of connective and other soft tissue of upper limb, including shoulder
198.5 Secondary malignant neoplasm of bone and bone marrow
199.0 Disseminated malignant neoplasm
209.73 Secondary neuroendocrine tumor of bone
213.4 Benign neoplasm of scapula and long bones of upper limb
238.0 Neoplasm of uncertain behavior of bone and articular cartilage
239.2 Neoplasms of unspecified nature of bone, soft tissue, and skin
731.3 Major osseous defects — (Code first underlying disease: 170.0-170.9, 730.00-730.29, 733.00-733.09, 733.40-733.49, 996.45)

ICD-9-CM Procedural

77.82 Other partial ostectomy of humerus

23330-23333

23330 Removal of foreign body, shoulder; subcutaneous
23333 deep (subfascial or intramuscular)

ICD-9-CM Diagnostic

709.4 Foreign body granuloma of skin and subcutaneous tissue — (Use additional code to identify foreign body (V90.01-V90.9))
728.82 Foreign body granuloma of muscle — (Use additional code to identify foreign body (V90.01-V90.9))
729.6 Residual foreign body in soft tissue — (Use additional code to identify foreign body (V90.01-V90.9))
880.10 Open wound of shoulder region, complicated
912.6 Shoulder and upper arm, superficial foreign body (splinter), without major open wound and without mention of infection
912.7 Shoulder and upper arm, superficial foreign body (splinter), without major open wound, infected
998.4 Foreign body accidentally left during procedure, not elsewhere classified

ICD-9-CM Procedural

83.02 Myotomy
83.09 Other incision of soft tissue
86.05 Incision with removal of foreign body or device from skin and subcutaneous tissue
98.27 Removal of foreign body without incision from upper limb, except hand

HCPCS Level II Supplies & Services

A4305 Disposable drug delivery system, flow rate of 50 ml or greater per hour

23334-23335

23334 Removal of prosthesis, includes debridement and synovectomy when performed; humeral or glenoid component
23335 humeral and glenoid components (eg, total shoulder)

ICD-9-CM Diagnostic

996.41 Mechanical loosening of prosthetic joint — (Use additional code to identify prosthetic joint with mechanical complication, V43.60-V43.69)
996.42 Dislocation of prosthetic joint — (Use additional code to identify prosthetic joint with mechanical complication, V43.60-V43.69)
996.43 Broken prosthetic joint implant — (Use additional code to identify prosthetic joint with mechanical complication, V43.60-V43.69)
996.45 Peri-prosthetic osteolysis — (Use additional code to identify prosthetic joint with mechanical complication, V43.60-V43.69. Use additional code to identify major osseous defect, if applicable: 731.3)
996.46 Articular bearing surface wear of prosthetic joint — (Use additional code to identify prosthetic joint with mechanical complication, V43.60-V43.69)
996.47 Other mechanical complication of prosthetic joint implant — (Use additional code to identify prosthetic joint with mechanical complication, V43.60-V43.69)
996.66 Infection and inflammatory reaction due to internal joint prosthesis — (Use additional code to identify specified infections. Use additional code to identify infected prosthetic joint: V43.60-V43.69)
996.77 Other complications due to internal joint prosthesis — (Use additional code to identify complication: 338.18-338.19, 338.28-338.29)

ICD-9-CM Procedural

80.01 Arthrotomy for removal of prosthesis without replacement, shoulder

23350

23350 Injection procedure for shoulder arthrography or enhanced CT/MRI shoulder arthrography

ICD-9-CM Diagnostic

275.40 Unspecified disorder of calcium metabolism — (Use additional code to identify any associated intellectual disabilities)
275.42 Hypercalcemia — (Use additional code to identify any associated intellectual disabilities)
275.49 Other disorders of calcium metabolism — (Use additional code to identify any associated intellectual disabilities)
275.5 Hungry bone syndrome — (Use additional code to identify any associated intellectual disabilities)
715.11 Primary localized osteoarthrosis, shoulder region
715.21 Secondary localized osteoarthrosis, shoulder region
715.31 Localized osteoarthrosis not specified whether primary or secondary, shoulder region
715.91 Osteoarthrosis, unspecified whether generalized or localized, shoulder region
716.11 Traumatic arthropathy, shoulder region
716.41 Transient arthropathy, shoulder region
716.61 Unspecified monoarthritis, shoulder region
716.81 Other specified arthropathy, shoulder region
716.91 Unspecified arthropathy, shoulder region
718.01 Articular cartilage disorder, shoulder region
718.11 Loose body in shoulder joint
718.21 Pathological dislocation of shoulder joint
718.31 Recurrent dislocation of shoulder joint
718.41 Contracture of shoulder joint
718.71 Developmental dislocation of joint, shoulder region
719.01 Effusion of shoulder joint
719.41 Pain in joint, shoulder region
719.42 Pain in joint, upper arm
726.13 Partial tear of rotator cuff
726.90 Enthesopathy of unspecified site
727.61 Complete rupture of rotator cuff

831.00 Closed dislocation of shoulder, unspecified site ▽
831.01 Closed anterior dislocation of humerus
831.02 Closed posterior dislocation of humerus
831.03 Closed inferior dislocation of humerus
831.04 Closed dislocation of acromioclavicular (joint)
831.09 Closed dislocation of other site of shoulder
831.10 Open unspecified dislocation of shoulder ▽
831.11 Open anterior dislocation of humerus
831.12 Open posterior dislocation of humerus
831.13 Open inferior dislocation of humerus
831.14 Open dislocation of acromioclavicular (joint)
831.19 Open dislocation of other site of shoulder
840.0 Acromioclavicular (joint) (ligament) sprain and strain
840.1 Coracoclavicular (ligament) sprain and strain
840.2 Coracohumeral (ligament) sprain and strain
840.3 Infraspinatus (muscle) (tendon) sprain and strain
840.4 Rotator cuff (capsule) sprain and strain
923.00 Contusion of shoulder region

ICD-9-CM Procedural

81.92 Injection of therapeutic substance into joint or ligament
88.32 Contrast arthrogram

23395-23397

23395 Muscle transfer, any type, shoulder or upper arm; single
23397 multiple

ICD-9-CM Diagnostic

880.10 Open wound of shoulder region, complicated
880.11 Open wound of scapular region, complicated
880.12 Open wound of axillary region, complicated
880.13 Open wound of upper arm, complicated
880.19 Open wound of multiple sites of shoulder and upper arm, complicated
880.20 Open wound of shoulder region, with tendon involvement
880.21 Open wound of scapular region, with tendon involvement
880.22 Open wound of axillary region, with tendon involvement
880.23 Open wound of upper arm, with tendon involvement
880.29 Open wound of multiple sites of shoulder and upper arm, with tendon involvement
906.1 Late effect of open wound of extremities without mention of tendon injury
906.7 Late effect of burn of other extremities
927.00 Crushing injury of shoulder region — (Use additional code to identify any associated injuries: 800-829, 850.0-854.1, 860.0-869.1)
927.01 Crushing injury of scapular region — (Use additional code to identify any associated injuries: 800-829, 850.0-854.1, 860.0-869.1)
927.02 Crushing injury of axillary region — (Use additional code to identify any associated injuries: 800-829, 850.0-854.1, 860.0-869.1)
927.03 Crushing injury of upper arm — (Use additional code to identify any associated injuries: 800-829, 850.0-854.1, 860.0-869.1)
927.09 Crushing injury of multiple sites of upper arm — (Use additional code to identify any associated injuries: 800-829, 850.0-854.1, 860.0-869.1)
953.4 Injury to brachial plexus
V10.89 Personal history of malignant neoplasm of other site

ICD-9-CM Procedural

83.77 Muscle transfer or transplantation

23400

23400 Scapulopexy (eg, Sprengels deformity or for paralysis)

ICD-9-CM Diagnostic

342.10 Spastic hemiplegia affecting unspecified side ▽
342.11 Spastic hemiplegia affecting dominant side
342.12 Spastic hemiplegia affecting nondominant side
353.0 Brachial plexus lesions
718.41 Contracture of shoulder joint
755.52 Congenital elevation of scapula

ICD-9-CM Procedural

78.41 Other repair or plastic operations on scapula, clavicle, and thorax (ribs and sternum)

23405-23406

23405 Tenotomy, shoulder area; single tendon
23406 multiple tendons through same incision

ICD-9-CM Diagnostic

342.10 Spastic hemiplegia affecting unspecified side ▽
342.11 Spastic hemiplegia affecting dominant side
342.12 Spastic hemiplegia affecting nondominant side
718.41 Contracture of shoulder joint
727.02 Giant cell tumor of tendon sheath
755.52 Congenital elevation of scapula
756.89 Other specified congenital anomaly of muscle, tendon, fascia, and connective tissue

ICD-9-CM Procedural

83.13 Other tenotomy

23410-23412

23410 Repair of ruptured musculotendinous cuff (eg, rotator cuff) open; acute
23412 chronic

ICD-9-CM Diagnostic

715.10 Primary localized osteoarthrosis, unspecified site ▽
715.11 Primary localized osteoarthrosis, shoulder region
715.21 Secondary localized osteoarthrosis, shoulder region
715.31 Localized osteoarthrosis not specified whether primary or secondary, shoulder region
716.11 Traumatic arthropathy, shoulder region
716.61 Unspecified monoarthritis, shoulder region ▽
719.41 Pain in joint, shoulder region
726.10 Unspecified disorders of bursae and tendons in shoulder region ▽
726.13 Partial tear of rotator cuff
727.61 Complete rupture of rotator cuff
831.00 Closed dislocation of shoulder, unspecified site ▽
831.01 Closed anterior dislocation of humerus
831.02 Closed posterior dislocation of humerus
831.03 Closed inferior dislocation of humerus
831.10 Open unspecified dislocation of shoulder ▽
831.11 Open anterior dislocation of humerus
831.12 Open posterior dislocation of humerus
831.13 Open inferior dislocation of humerus
840.4 Rotator cuff (capsule) sprain and strain
880.20 Open wound of shoulder region, with tendon involvement
927.00 Crushing injury of shoulder region — (Use additional code to identify any associated injuries: 800-829, 850.0-854.1, 860.0-869.1)
959.2 Injury, other and unspecified, shoulder and upper arm

ICD-9-CM Procedural

83.63 Rotator cuff repair

23415

23415 Coracoacromial ligament release, with or without acromioplasty

ICD-9-CM Diagnostic

715.11 Primary localized osteoarthrosis, shoulder region
715.31 Localized osteoarthrosis not specified whether primary or secondary, shoulder region

716.11 Traumatic arthropathy, shoulder region
716.91 Unspecified arthropathy, shoulder region ▽
719.41 Pain in joint, shoulder region
726.10 Unspecified disorders of bursae and tendons in shoulder region ▽
726.11 Calcifying tendinitis of shoulder
726.13 Partial tear of rotator cuff
726.2 Other affections of shoulder region, not elsewhere classified
727.61 Complete rupture of rotator cuff
840.4 Rotator cuff (capsule) sprain and strain

ICD-9-CM Procedural

80.41 Division of joint capsule, ligament, or cartilage of shoulder
81.83 Other repair of shoulder

23420

23420 Reconstruction of complete shoulder (rotator) cuff avulsion, chronic (includes acromioplasty)

ICD-9-CM Diagnostic

715.11 Primary localized osteoarthrosis, shoulder region
715.21 Secondary localized osteoarthrosis, shoulder region
715.31 Localized osteoarthrosis not specified whether primary or secondary, shoulder region
716.61 Unspecified monoarthritis, shoulder region ▽
719.41 Pain in joint, shoulder region
726.10 Unspecified disorders of bursae and tendons in shoulder region ▽
727.61 Complete rupture of rotator cuff
840.4 Rotator cuff (capsule) sprain and strain
V64.43 Arthroscopic surgical procedure converted to open procedure

ICD-9-CM Procedural

81.82 Repair of recurrent dislocation of shoulder
83.63 Rotator cuff repair

23430

23430 Tenodesis of long tendon of biceps

ICD-9-CM Diagnostic

718.91 Unspecified derangement, shoulder region ▽
719.42 Pain in joint, upper arm
719.61 Other symptoms referable to shoulder joint
726.12 Bicipital tenosynovitis
727.62 Nontraumatic rupture of tendons of biceps (long head)
840.8 Sprain and strain of other specified sites of shoulder and upper arm
880.20 Open wound of shoulder region, with tendon involvement
927.03 Crushing injury of upper arm — (Use additional code to identify any associated injuries: 800-829, 850.0-854.1, 860.0-869.1)

ICD-9-CM Procedural

83.88 Other plastic operations on tendon

23440

23440 Resection or transplantation of long tendon of biceps

ICD-9-CM Diagnostic

726.12 Bicipital tenosynovitis
727.62 Nontraumatic rupture of tendons of biceps (long head)
880.20 Open wound of shoulder region, with tendon involvement
880.23 Open wound of upper arm, with tendon involvement
927.03 Crushing injury of upper arm — (Use additional code to identify any associated injuries: 800-829, 850.0-854.1, 860.0-869.1)

ICD-9-CM Procedural

83.42 Other tenonectomy
83.75 Tendon transfer or transplantation

23450-23455

23450 Capsulorrhaphy, anterior; Putti-Platt procedure or Magnuson type operation
23455 with labral repair (eg, Bankart procedure)

ICD-9-CM Diagnostic

718.21 Pathological dislocation of shoulder joint
718.31 Recurrent dislocation of shoulder joint
831.01 Closed anterior dislocation of humerus
831.11 Open anterior dislocation of humerus
840.5 Subscapularis (muscle) sprain and strain
840.7 Superior glenoid labrum lesions (SLAP)
V64.43 Arthroscopic surgical procedure converted to open procedure

ICD-9-CM Procedural

81.82 Repair of recurrent dislocation of shoulder
81.83 Other repair of shoulder
81.93 Suture of capsule or ligament of upper extremity

23460-23462

23460 Capsulorrhaphy, anterior, any type; with bone block
23462 with coracoid process transfer

ICD-9-CM Diagnostic

718.21 Pathological dislocation of shoulder joint
718.31 Recurrent dislocation of shoulder joint
831.01 Closed anterior dislocation of humerus
831.11 Open anterior dislocation of humerus
840.2 Coracohumeral (ligament) sprain and strain
840.5 Subscapularis (muscle) sprain and strain
840.7 Superior glenoid labrum lesions (SLAP)
V64.43 Arthroscopic surgical procedure converted to open procedure

ICD-9-CM Procedural

81.82 Repair of recurrent dislocation of shoulder
81.83 Other repair of shoulder
81.93 Suture of capsule or ligament of upper extremity

23465

23465 Capsulorrhaphy, glenohumeral joint, posterior, with or without bone block

ICD-9-CM Diagnostic

718.21 Pathological dislocation of shoulder joint
718.31 Recurrent dislocation of shoulder joint
718.51 Ankylosis of joint of shoulder region
831.00 Closed dislocation of shoulder, unspecified site ▽
831.02 Closed posterior dislocation of humerus
831.10 Open unspecified dislocation of shoulder ▽
831.12 Open posterior dislocation of humerus
840.4 Rotator cuff (capsule) sprain and strain
V64.43 Arthroscopic surgical procedure converted to open procedure

ICD-9-CM Procedural

81.82 Repair of recurrent dislocation of shoulder
81.83 Other repair of shoulder
81.93 Suture of capsule or ligament of upper extremity

23466

23466 Capsulorrhaphy, glenohumeral joint, any type multi-directional instability

ICD-9-CM Diagnostic

718.21 Pathological dislocation of shoulder joint

718.31 Recurrent dislocation of shoulder joint
831.00 Closed dislocation of shoulder, unspecified site ▽
831.01 Closed anterior dislocation of humerus
831.02 Closed posterior dislocation of humerus
831.03 Closed inferior dislocation of humerus
831.10 Open unspecified dislocation of shoulder ▽
831.11 Open anterior dislocation of humerus
831.12 Open posterior dislocation of humerus
831.13 Open inferior dislocation of humerus
840.4 Rotator cuff (capsule) sprain and strain
V64.43 Arthroscopic surgical procedure converted to open procedure

ICD-9-CM Procedural

81.82 Repair of recurrent dislocation of shoulder
81.83 Other repair of shoulder
81.93 Suture of capsule or ligament of upper extremity

23470

23470 Arthroplasty, glenohumeral joint; hemiarthroplasty

ICD-9-CM Diagnostic

170.4 Malignant neoplasm of scapula and long bones of upper limb
171.2 Malignant neoplasm of connective and other soft tissue of upper limb, including shoulder
198.5 Secondary malignant neoplasm of bone and bone marrow
238.0 Neoplasm of uncertain behavior of bone and articular cartilage
239.2 Neoplasms of unspecified nature of bone, soft tissue, and skin
357.1 Polyneuropathy in collagen vascular disease — (Code first underlying disease: 446.0, 710.0, 714.0) ☒
359.6 Symptomatic inflammatory myopathy in diseases classified elsewhere — (Code first underlying disease: 135, 140.0-208.9, 277.30-277.39, 446.0, 710.0, 710.1, 710.2, 714.0) ☒
446.0 Polyarteritis nodosa
710.0 Systemic lupus erythematosus — (Use additional code to identify manifestation: 424.91, 581.81, 582.81, 583.81)
714.0 Rheumatoid arthritis — (Use additional code to identify manifestation: 357.1, 359.6)
715.11 Primary localized osteoarthrosis, shoulder region
715.21 Secondary localized osteoarthrosis, shoulder region
715.31 Localized osteoarthrosis not specified whether primary or secondary, shoulder region
715.91 Osteoarthrosis, unspecified whether generalized or localized, shoulder region ▽
716.11 Traumatic arthropathy, shoulder region
716.61 Unspecified monoarthritis, shoulder region ▽
716.81 Other specified arthropathy, shoulder region
718.01 Articular cartilage disorder, shoulder region
726.10 Unspecified disorders of bursae and tendons in shoulder region ▽
726.19 Other specified disorders of rotator cuff syndrome of shoulder and allied disorders
727.61 Complete rupture of rotator cuff
730.11 Chronic osteomyelitis, shoulder region — (Use additional code to identify organism: 041.1. Use additional code to identify major osseous defect, if applicable: 731.3)
730.12 Chronic osteomyelitis, upper arm — (Use additional code to identify organism: 041.1. Use additional code to identify major osseous defect, if applicable: 731.3)
730.81 Other infections involving bone diseases classified elsewhere, shoulder region — (Use additional code to identify organism: 041.1. Code first underlying disease: 002.0, 015.0-015.9) ☒
731.3 Major osseous defects — (Code first underlying disease: 170.0-170.9, 730.00-730.29, 733.00-733.09, 733.40-733.49, 996.45)
733.41 Aseptic necrosis of head of humerus — (Use additional code to identify major osseous defect, if applicable: 731.3)
812.00 Closed fracture of unspecified part of upper end of humerus ▽
812.10 Open fracture of unspecified part of upper end of humerus ▽
927.00 Crushing injury of shoulder region — (Use additional code to identify any associated injuries: 800-829, 850.0-854.1, 860.0-869.1)
V88.29 Acquired absence of other joint

ICD-9-CM Procedural

81.81 Partial shoulder replacement
81.97 Revision of joint replacement of upper extremity

23472

23472 Arthroplasty, glenohumeral joint; total shoulder (glenoid and proximal humeral replacement (eg, total shoulder))

ICD-9-CM Diagnostic

170.4 Malignant neoplasm of scapula and long bones of upper limb
171.2 Malignant neoplasm of connective and other soft tissue of upper limb, including shoulder
198.5 Secondary malignant neoplasm of bone and bone marrow
238.0 Neoplasm of uncertain behavior of bone and articular cartilage
239.2 Neoplasms of unspecified nature of bone, soft tissue, and skin
357.1 Polyneuropathy in collagen vascular disease — (Code first underlying disease: 446.0, 710.0, 714.0) ☒
359.6 Symptomatic inflammatory myopathy in diseases classified elsewhere — (Code first underlying disease: 135, 140.0-208.9, 277.30-277.39, 446.0, 710.0, 710.1, 710.2, 714.0) ☒
446.0 Polyarteritis nodosa
710.0 Systemic lupus erythematosus — (Use additional code to identify manifestation: 424.91, 581.81, 582.81, 583.81)
710.1 Systemic sclerosis — (Use additional code to identify manifestation: 359.6, 517.2)
710.2 Sicca syndrome
714.0 Rheumatoid arthritis — (Use additional code to identify manifestation: 357.1, 359.6)
715.11 Primary localized osteoarthrosis, shoulder region
715.21 Secondary localized osteoarthrosis, shoulder region
715.31 Localized osteoarthrosis not specified whether primary or secondary, shoulder region
715.91 Osteoarthrosis, unspecified whether generalized or localized, shoulder region ▽
716.11 Traumatic arthropathy, shoulder region
716.61 Unspecified monoarthritis, shoulder region ▽
716.81 Other specified arthropathy, shoulder region
718.01 Articular cartilage disorder, shoulder region
730.11 Chronic osteomyelitis, shoulder region — (Use additional code to identify organism: 041.1. Use additional code to identify major osseous defect, if applicable: 731.3)
730.12 Chronic osteomyelitis, upper arm — (Use additional code to identify organism: 041.1. Use additional code to identify major osseous defect, if applicable: 731.3)
730.81 Other infections involving bone diseases classified elsewhere, shoulder region — (Use additional code to identify organism: 041.1. Code first underlying disease: 002.0, 015.0-015.9) ☒
731.3 Major osseous defects — (Code first underlying disease: 170.0-170.9, 730.00-730.29, 733.00-733.09, 733.40-733.49, 996.45)
733.41 Aseptic necrosis of head of humerus — (Use additional code to identify major osseous defect, if applicable: 731.3)
733.81 Malunion of fracture
733.82 Nonunion of fracture
812.03 Closed fracture of greater tuberosity of humerus
927.00 Crushing injury of shoulder region — (Use additional code to identify any associated injuries: 800-829, 850.0-854.1, 860.0-869.1)
V88.29 Acquired absence of other joint

ICD-9-CM Procedural

81.80 Other total shoulder replacement
81.88 Reverse total shoulder replacement
81.97 Revision of joint replacement of upper extremity

23473-23474

23473 Revision of total shoulder arthroplasty, including allograft when performed; humeral or glenoid component
23474 humeral and glenoid component

ICD-9-CM Diagnostic

733.11 Pathologic fracture of humerus
733.95 Stress fracture of other bone — (Use additional external cause code(s) to identify the cause of the stress fracture)
996.41 Mechanical loosening of prosthetic joint — (Use additional code to identify prosthetic joint with mechanical complication, V43.60-V43.69)
996.42 Dislocation of prosthetic joint — (Use additional code to identify prosthetic joint with mechanical complication, V43.60-V43.69)
996.43 Broken prosthetic joint implant — (Use additional code to identify prosthetic joint with mechanical complication, V43.60-V43.69)
996.44 Peri-prosthetic fracture around prosthetic joint — (Use additional code to identify prosthetic joint with mechanical complication, V43.60-V43.69.
996.45 Peri-prosthetic osteolysis — (Use additional code to identify prosthetic joint with mechanical complication, V43.60-V43.69. Use additional code to identify major osseous defect, if applicable: 731.3)
996.46 Articular bearing surface wear of prosthetic joint — (Use additional code to identify prosthetic joint with mechanical complication, V43.60-V43.69)
996.47 Other mechanical complication of prosthetic joint implant — (Use additional code to identify prosthetic joint with mechanical complication, V43.60-V43.69)
996.66 Infection and inflammatory reaction due to internal joint prosthesis — (Use additional code to identify specified infections. Use additional code to identify infected prosthetic joint: V43.60-V43.69)
996.77 Other complications due to internal joint prosthesis — (Use additional code to identify complication: 338.18-338.19, 338.28-338.29)
V54.82 Aftercare following explantation of joint prosthesis

ICD-9-CM Procedural

81.97 Revision of joint replacement of upper extremity

23480-23485

23480 Osteotomy, clavicle, with or without internal fixation;
23485 with bone graft for nonunion or malunion (includes obtaining graft and/or necessary fixation)

ICD-9-CM Diagnostic

170.3 Malignant neoplasm of ribs, sternum, and clavicle
213.3 Benign neoplasm of ribs, sternum, and clavicle
730.11 Chronic osteomyelitis, shoulder region — (Use additional code to identify organism: 041.1. Use additional code to identify major osseous defect, if applicable: 731.3)
731.3 Major osseous defects — (Code first underlying disease: 170.0-170.9, 730.00-730.29, 733.00-733.09, 733.40-733.49, 996.45)
733.81 Malunion of fracture
733.82 Nonunion of fracture
738.8 Acquired musculoskeletal deformity of other specified site
755.51 Congenital deformity of clavicle
905.1 Late effect of fracture of spine and trunk without mention of spinal cord lesion

ICD-9-CM Procedural

77.21 Wedge osteotomy of scapula, clavicle, and thorax (ribs and sternum)
77.31 Other division of scapula, clavicle, and thorax (ribs and sternum)
77.71 Excision of scapula, clavicle, and thorax (ribs and sternum) for graft
77.77 Excision of tibia and fibula for graft
77.79 Excision of other bone for graft, except facial bones
78.01 Bone graft of scapula, clavicle, and thorax (ribs and sternum)
78.41 Other repair or plastic operations on scapula, clavicle, and thorax (ribs and sternum)

23490-23491

23490 Prophylactic treatment (nailing, pinning, plating or wiring) with or without methylmethacrylate; clavicle
23491 proximal humerus

ICD-9-CM Diagnostic

170.4 Malignant neoplasm of scapula and long bones of upper limb
198.5 Secondary malignant neoplasm of bone and bone marrow
238.0 Neoplasm of uncertain behavior of bone and articular cartilage
239.2 Neoplasms of unspecified nature of bone, soft tissue, and skin
731.3 Major osseous defects — (Code first underlying disease: 170.0-170.9, 730.00-730.29, 733.00-733.09, 733.40-733.49, 996.45)
733.00 Unspecified osteoporosis — (Use additional code to identify major osseous defect, if applicable: 731.3) (Use additional code to identify personal history of pathologic (healed) fracture: V13.51) ▽
733.01 Senile osteoporosis — (Use additional code to identify major osseous defect, if applicable: 731.3) (Use additional code to identify personal history of pathologic (healed) fracture: V13.51)
733.02 Idiopathic osteoporosis — (Use additional code to identify major osseous defect, if applicable: 731.3) (Use additional code to identify personal history of pathologic (healed) fracture: V13.51)
733.7 Algoneurodystrophy
831.00 Closed dislocation of shoulder, unspecified site ▽
831.01 Closed anterior dislocation of humerus
831.02 Closed posterior dislocation of humerus
831.03 Closed inferior dislocation of humerus
831.04 Closed dislocation of acromioclavicular (joint)
831.10 Open unspecified dislocation of shoulder ▽
831.11 Open anterior dislocation of humerus
831.12 Open posterior dislocation of humerus
831.13 Open inferior dislocation of humerus
831.14 Open dislocation of acromioclavicular (joint)
831.14 Open dislocation of acromioclavicular (joint)

ICD-9-CM Procedural

78.51 Internal fixation of scapula, clavicle, and thorax (ribs and sternum) without fracture reduction
78.52 Internal fixation of humerus without fracture reduction
84.55 Insertion of bone void filler

23500-23505

23500 Closed treatment of clavicular fracture; without manipulation
23505 with manipulation

ICD-9-CM Diagnostic

733.19 Pathologic fracture of other specified site
810.00 Unspecified part of closed fracture of clavicle ▽
810.01 Closed fracture of sternal end of clavicle
810.02 Closed fracture of shaft of clavicle
810.03 Closed fracture of acromial end of clavicle

ICD-9-CM Procedural

79.09 Closed reduction of fracture of other specified bone, except facial bones, without internal fixation
93.54 Application of splint

HCPCS Level II Supplies & Services

A4565 Slings

23515

23515 Open treatment of clavicular fracture, includes internal fixation, when performed

ICD-9-CM Diagnostic

733.19 Pathologic fracture of other specified site
733.81 Malunion of fracture
733.82 Nonunion of fracture
810.00 Unspecified part of closed fracture of clavicle 🆄
810.02 Closed fracture of shaft of clavicle
810.03 Closed fracture of acromial end of clavicle
810.10 Unspecified part of open fracture of clavicle 🆄
810.11 Open fracture of sternal end of clavicle
810.12 Open fracture of shaft of clavicle
810.13 Open fracture of acromial end of clavicle

ICD-9-CM Procedural

79.29 Open reduction of fracture of other specified bone, except facial bones, without internal fixation
79.39 Open reduction of fracture of other specified bone, except facial bones, with internal fixation

23520-23525

23520 Closed treatment of sternoclavicular dislocation; without manipulation
23525 with manipulation

ICD-9-CM Diagnostic

718.21 Pathological dislocation of shoulder joint
718.71 Developmental dislocation of joint, shoulder region
839.61 Closed dislocation, sternum

ICD-9-CM Procedural

79.79 Closed reduction of dislocation of other specified site, except temporomandibular
93.54 Application of splint
93.59 Other immobilization, pressure, and attention to wound

HCPCS Level II Supplies & Services

A4565 Slings

23530-23532

23530 Open treatment of sternoclavicular dislocation, acute or chronic;
23532 with fascial graft (includes obtaining graft)

ICD-9-CM Diagnostic

718.21 Pathological dislocation of shoulder joint
718.31 Recurrent dislocation of shoulder joint
718.71 Developmental dislocation of joint, shoulder region
718.78 Developmental dislocation of joint, other specified sites
839.61 Closed dislocation, sternum
839.71 Open dislocation, sternum

ICD-9-CM Procedural

79.89 Open reduction of dislocation of other specified site, except temporomandibular
83.82 Graft of muscle or fascia

23540-23545

23540 Closed treatment of acromioclavicular dislocation; without manipulation
23545 with manipulation

ICD-9-CM Diagnostic

718.21 Pathological dislocation of shoulder joint
718.31 Recurrent dislocation of shoulder joint
718.71 Developmental dislocation of joint, shoulder region
831.04 Closed dislocation of acromioclavicular (joint)
840.0 Acromioclavicular (joint) (ligament) sprain and strain

ICD-9-CM Procedural

79.79 Closed reduction of dislocation of other specified site, except temporomandibular
93.59 Other immobilization, pressure, and attention to wound

HCPCS Level II Supplies & Services

A4565 Slings

23550-23552

23550 Open treatment of acromioclavicular dislocation, acute or chronic;
23552 with fascial graft (includes obtaining graft)

ICD-9-CM Diagnostic

718.21 Pathological dislocation of shoulder joint
718.31 Recurrent dislocation of shoulder joint
718.71 Developmental dislocation of joint, shoulder region
831.04 Closed dislocation of acromioclavicular (joint)
831.14 Open dislocation of acromioclavicular (joint)
840.0 Acromioclavicular (joint) (ligament) sprain and strain

ICD-9-CM Procedural

79.89 Open reduction of dislocation of other specified site, except temporomandibular
83.82 Graft of muscle or fascia

HCPCS Level II Supplies & Services

A4565 Slings

23570-23575

23570 Closed treatment of scapular fracture; without manipulation
23575 with manipulation, with or without skeletal traction (with or without shoulder joint involvement)

ICD-9-CM Diagnostic

733.19 Pathologic fracture of other specified site
811.01 Closed fracture of acromial process of scapula
811.02 Closed fracture of coracoid process of scapula
811.03 Closed fracture of glenoid cavity and neck of scapula
811.09 Closed fracture of other part of scapula

ICD-9-CM Procedural

79.09 Closed reduction of fracture of other specified bone, except facial bones, without internal fixation
79.19 Closed reduction of fracture of other specified bone, except facial bones, with internal fixation
93.44 Other skeletal traction
93.54 Application of splint
93.59 Other immobilization, pressure, and attention to wound

HCPCS Level II Supplies & Services

A4565 Slings

23585

23585 Open treatment of scapular fracture (body, glenoid or acromion) includes internal fixation, when performed

ICD-9-CM Diagnostic

733.19 Pathologic fracture of other specified site
733.81 Malunion of fracture
733.82 Nonunion of fracture
811.01 Closed fracture of acromial process of scapula
811.03 Closed fracture of glenoid cavity and neck of scapula
811.09 Closed fracture of other part of scapula
811.11 Open fracture of acromial process of scapula
811.13 Open fracture of glenoid cavity and neck of scapula

811.19 Open fracture of other part of scapula

ICD-9-CM Procedural

79.29 Open reduction of fracture of other specified bone, except facial bones, without internal fixation

79.39 Open reduction of fracture of other specified bone, except facial bones, with internal fixation

23600-23605

23600 Closed treatment of proximal humeral (surgical or anatomical neck) fracture; without manipulation

23605 with manipulation, with or without skeletal traction

ICD-9-CM Diagnostic

733.11 Pathologic fracture of humerus

812.01 Closed fracture of surgical neck of humerus

812.02 Closed fracture of anatomical neck of humerus

ICD-9-CM Procedural

79.01 Closed reduction of fracture of humerus without internal fixation

79.11 Closed reduction of fracture of humerus with internal fixation

93.54 Application of splint

HCPCS Level II Supplies & Services

A4565 Slings

23615-23616

23615 Open treatment of proximal humeral (surgical or anatomical neck) fracture, includes internal fixation, when performed, includes repair of tuberosity(s), when performed;

23616 with proximal humeral prosthetic replacement

ICD-9-CM Diagnostic

733.11 Pathologic fracture of humerus

733.81 Malunion of fracture

733.82 Nonunion of fracture

812.01 Closed fracture of surgical neck of humerus

812.02 Closed fracture of anatomical neck of humerus

812.03 Closed fracture of greater tuberosity of humerus

812.09 Other closed fractures of upper end of humerus

812.11 Open fracture of surgical neck of humerus

812.12 Open fracture of anatomical neck of humerus

812.13 Open fracture of greater tuberosity of humerus

812.19 Other open fracture of upper end of humerus

ICD-9-CM Procedural

79.21 Open reduction of fracture of humerus without internal fixation

79.31 Open reduction of fracture of humerus with internal fixation

81.81 Partial shoulder replacement

23620-23625

23620 Closed treatment of greater humeral tuberosity fracture; without manipulation

23625 with manipulation

ICD-9-CM Diagnostic

733.11 Pathologic fracture of humerus

812.03 Closed fracture of greater tuberosity of humerus

ICD-9-CM Procedural

79.01 Closed reduction of fracture of humerus without internal fixation

93.54 Application of splint

HCPCS Level II Supplies & Services

A4565 Slings

23630

23630 Open treatment of greater humeral tuberosity fracture, includes internal fixation, when performed

ICD-9-CM Diagnostic

733.19 Pathologic fracture of other specified site

733.81 Malunion of fracture

733.82 Nonunion of fracture

812.03 Closed fracture of greater tuberosity of humerus

812.13 Open fracture of greater tuberosity of humerus

ICD-9-CM Procedural

79.21 Open reduction of fracture of humerus without internal fixation

79.31 Open reduction of fracture of humerus with internal fixation

23650-23655

23650 Closed treatment of shoulder dislocation, with manipulation; without anesthesia

23655 requiring anesthesia

ICD-9-CM Diagnostic

718.21 Pathological dislocation of shoulder joint

718.31 Recurrent dislocation of shoulder joint

718.71 Developmental dislocation of joint, shoulder region

831.00 Closed dislocation of shoulder, unspecified site ▽

831.01 Closed anterior dislocation of humerus

831.02 Closed posterior dislocation of humerus

831.03 Closed inferior dislocation of humerus

831.09 Closed dislocation of other site of shoulder

ICD-9-CM Procedural

79.71 Closed reduction of dislocation of shoulder

HCPCS Level II Supplies & Services

A4565 Slings

23660

23660 Open treatment of acute shoulder dislocation

ICD-9-CM Diagnostic

718.21 Pathological dislocation of shoulder joint

718.71 Developmental dislocation of joint, shoulder region

831.00 Closed dislocation of shoulder, unspecified site ▽

831.01 Closed anterior dislocation of humerus

831.02 Closed posterior dislocation of humerus

831.03 Closed inferior dislocation of humerus

831.04 Closed dislocation of acromioclavicular (joint)

831.09 Closed dislocation of other site of shoulder

831.10 Open unspecified dislocation of shoulder ▽

831.11 Open anterior dislocation of humerus

831.12 Open posterior dislocation of humerus

831.13 Open inferior dislocation of humerus

831.14 Open dislocation of acromioclavicular (joint)

831.19 Open dislocation of other site of shoulder

ICD-9-CM Procedural

79.81 Open reduction of dislocation of shoulder

23665

23665 Closed treatment of shoulder dislocation, with fracture of greater humeral tuberosity, with manipulation

ICD-9-CM Diagnostic

733.11 Pathologic fracture of humerus

812.03 Closed fracture of greater tuberosity of humerus
831.00 Closed dislocation of shoulder, unspecified site

ICD-9-CM Procedural

79.01 Closed reduction of fracture of humerus without internal fixation
79.71 Closed reduction of dislocation of shoulder

23670

23670 Open treatment of shoulder dislocation, with fracture of greater humeral tuberosity, includes internal fixation, when performed

ICD-9-CM Diagnostic

733.11 Pathologic fracture of humerus
812.03 Closed fracture of greater tuberosity of humerus
812.13 Open fracture of greater tuberosity of humerus
831.00 Closed dislocation of shoulder, unspecified site
831.10 Open unspecified dislocation of shoulder
831.19 Open dislocation of other site of shoulder

ICD-9-CM Procedural

79.21 Open reduction of fracture of humerus without internal fixation
79.31 Open reduction of fracture of humerus with internal fixation
79.81 Open reduction of dislocation of shoulder

23675

23675 Closed treatment of shoulder dislocation, with surgical or anatomical neck fracture, with manipulation

ICD-9-CM Diagnostic

733.11 Pathologic fracture of humerus
812.01 Closed fracture of surgical neck of humerus
812.02 Closed fracture of anatomical neck of humerus
831.00 Closed dislocation of shoulder, unspecified site

ICD-9-CM Procedural

79.01 Closed reduction of fracture of humerus without internal fixation
79.71 Closed reduction of dislocation of shoulder

23680

23680 Open treatment of shoulder dislocation, with surgical or anatomical neck fracture, includes internal fixation, when performed

ICD-9-CM Diagnostic

733.11 Pathologic fracture of humerus
812.01 Closed fracture of surgical neck of humerus
812.02 Closed fracture of anatomical neck of humerus
812.11 Open fracture of surgical neck of humerus
812.12 Open fracture of anatomical neck of humerus
831.00 Closed dislocation of shoulder, unspecified site
831.10 Open unspecified dislocation of shoulder
831.19 Open dislocation of other site of shoulder

ICD-9-CM Procedural

79.21 Open reduction of fracture of humerus without internal fixation
79.31 Open reduction of fracture of humerus with internal fixation
79.81 Open reduction of dislocation of shoulder

23700

23700 Manipulation under anesthesia, shoulder joint, including application of fixation apparatus (dislocation excluded)

ICD-9-CM Diagnostic

354.4 Causalgia of upper limb
719.41 Pain in joint, shoulder region
723.4 Brachial neuritis or radiculitis NOS
726.0 Adhesive capsulitis of shoulder
726.10 Unspecified disorders of bursae and tendons in shoulder region
726.11 Calcifying tendinitis of shoulder
726.2 Other affections of shoulder region, not elsewhere classified
727.82 Calcium deposits in tendon and bursa
728.85 Spasm of muscle
729.1 Unspecified myalgia and myositis
729.2 Unspecified neuralgia, neuritis, and radiculitis
739.7 Nonallopathic lesion of upper extremities, not elsewhere classified

ICD-9-CM Procedural

78.11 Application of external fixator device, scapula, clavicle, and thorax [ribs and sternum]
78.12 Application of external fixator device, humerus
78.19 Application of external fixator device, other
84.71 Application of external fixator device, monoplanar system
84.72 Application of external fixator device, ring system
84.73 Application of hybrid external fixator device
93.25 Forced extension of limb
93.26 Manual rupture of joint adhesions

23800-23802

23800 Arthrodesis, glenohumeral joint;
23802 with autogenous graft (includes obtaining graft)

ICD-9-CM Diagnostic

171.2 Malignant neoplasm of connective and other soft tissue of upper limb, including shoulder
198.5 Secondary malignant neoplasm of bone and bone marrow
238.0 Neoplasm of uncertain behavior of bone and articular cartilage
239.2 Neoplasms of unspecified nature of bone, soft tissue, and skin
357.1 Polyneuropathy in collagen vascular disease — (Code first underlying disease: 446.0, 710.0, 714.0)
359.6 Symptomatic inflammatory myopathy in diseases classified elsewhere — (Code first underlying disease: 135, 140.0-208.9, 277.30-277.39, 446.0, 710.0, 710.1, 710.2, 714.0)
711.01 Pyogenic arthritis, shoulder region — (Use additional code to identify infectious organism: 041.0-041.8)
714.0 Rheumatoid arthritis — (Use additional code to identify manifestation: 357.1, 359.6)
715.11 Primary localized osteoarthrosis, shoulder region
715.21 Secondary localized osteoarthrosis, shoulder region
715.31 Localized osteoarthrosis not specified whether primary or secondary, shoulder region
715.91 Osteoarthrosis, unspecified whether generalized or localized, shoulder region
716.11 Traumatic arthropathy, shoulder region
718.01 Articular cartilage disorder, shoulder region
718.31 Recurrent dislocation of shoulder joint
730.11 Chronic osteomyelitis, shoulder region — (Use additional code to identify organism: 041.1. Use additional code to identify major osseous defect, if applicable: 731.3)
731.3 Major osseous defects — (Code first underlying disease: 170.0-170.9, 730.00-730.29, 733.00-733.09, 733.40-733.49, 996.45)
V88.29 Acquired absence of other joint

ICD-9-CM Procedural

77.71 Excision of scapula, clavicle, and thorax (ribs and sternum) for graft
77.77 Excision of tibia and fibula for graft
77.79 Excision of other bone for graft, except facial bones
78.02 Bone graft of humerus
81.23 Arthrodesis of shoulder

23900

23900 Interthoracoscapular amputation (forequarter)

ICD-9-CM Diagnostic

170.4 Malignant neoplasm of scapula and long bones of upper limb
171.2 Malignant neoplasm of connective and other soft tissue of upper limb, including shoulder
199.0 Disseminated malignant neoplasm
238.0 Neoplasm of uncertain behavior of bone and articular cartilage
728.86 Necrotizing fasciitis — (Use additional code to identify infectious organism, 041.00-041.89, 785.4, if applicable)
785.4 Gangrene — (Code first any associated underlying condition)
880.10 Open wound of shoulder region, complicated
880.11 Open wound of scapular region, complicated
880.12 Open wound of axillary region, complicated
880.13 Open wound of upper arm, complicated
880.20 Open wound of shoulder region, with tendon involvement
880.21 Open wound of scapular region, with tendon involvement
880.22 Open wound of axillary region, with tendon involvement
880.23 Open wound of upper arm, with tendon involvement
887.2 Traumatic amputation of arm and hand (complete) (partial), unilateral, at or above elbow, without mention of complication
887.3 Traumatic amputation of arm and hand (complete) (partial), unilateral, at or above elbow, complicated
906.7 Late effect of burn of other extremities
927.00 Crushing injury of shoulder region — (Use additional code to identify any associated injuries: 800-829, 850.0-854.1, 860.0-869.1)
927.01 Crushing injury of scapular region — (Use additional code to identify any associated injuries: 800-829, 850.0-854.1, 860.0-869.1)
927.02 Crushing injury of axillary region — (Use additional code to identify any associated injuries: 800-829, 850.0-854.1, 860.0-869.1)

ICD-9-CM Procedural

84.09 Interthoracoscapular amputation

23920

23920 Disarticulation of shoulder;

ICD-9-CM Diagnostic

170.4 Malignant neoplasm of scapula and long bones of upper limb
171.2 Malignant neoplasm of connective and other soft tissue of upper limb, including shoulder
199.0 Disseminated malignant neoplasm
238.0 Neoplasm of uncertain behavior of bone and articular cartilage
728.86 Necrotizing fasciitis — (Use additional code to identify infectious organism, 041.00-041.89, 785.4, if applicable)
785.4 Gangrene — (Code first any associated underlying condition)
880.10 Open wound of shoulder region, complicated
880.12 Open wound of axillary region, complicated
880.13 Open wound of upper arm, complicated
880.19 Open wound of multiple sites of shoulder and upper arm, complicated
880.20 Open wound of shoulder region, with tendon involvement
880.22 Open wound of axillary region, with tendon involvement
880.23 Open wound of upper arm, with tendon involvement
880.29 Open wound of multiple sites of shoulder and upper arm, with tendon involvement
887.2 Traumatic amputation of arm and hand (complete) (partial), unilateral, at or above elbow, without mention of complication
887.3 Traumatic amputation of arm and hand (complete) (partial), unilateral, at or above elbow, complicated
906.7 Late effect of burn of other extremities
908.6 Late effect of certain complications of trauma
927.00 Crushing injury of shoulder region — (Use additional code to identify any associated injuries: 800-829, 850.0-854.1, 860.0-869.1)
927.01 Crushing injury of scapular region — (Use additional code to identify any associated injuries: 800-829, 850.0-854.1, 860.0-869.1)
927.02 Crushing injury of axillary region — (Use additional code to identify any associated injuries: 800-829, 850.0-854.1, 860.0-869.1)
927.03 Crushing injury of upper arm — (Use additional code to identify any associated injuries: 800-829, 850.0-854.1, 860.0-869.1)
927.09 Crushing injury of multiple sites of upper arm — (Use additional code to identify any associated injuries: 800-829, 850.0-854.1, 860.0-869.1)

ICD-9-CM Procedural

84.08 Disarticulation of shoulder

23921

23921 Disarticulation of shoulder; secondary closure or scar revision

ICD-9-CM Diagnostic

997.60 Late complications of amputation stump, unspecified — (Use additional code to identify complications) ♥
997.61 Neuroma of amputation stump — (Use additional code to identify complications)
997.62 Infection (chronic) of amputation stump — (Use additional code to identify complications)
997.69 Other late amputation stump complication — (Use additional code to identify complications)
V49.67 Upper limb amputation, shoulder
V51.8 Other aftercare involving the use of plastic surgery

ICD-9-CM Procedural

84.3 Revision of amputation stump

Humerus (Upper Arm) and Elbow

23930

23930 Incision and drainage, upper arm or elbow area; deep abscess or hematoma

ICD-9-CM Diagnostic

682.3 Cellulitis and abscess of upper arm and forearm — (Use additional code to identify organism, such as 041.1, etc.)
719.12 Hemarthrosis, upper arm
719.82 Other specified disorders of upper arm joint
727.89 Other disorders of synovium, tendon, and bursa
729.4 Unspecified fasciitis ♥
730.12 Chronic osteomyelitis, upper arm — (Use additional code to identify organism: 041.1. Use additional code to identify major osseous defect, if applicable: 731.3)
780.62 Postprocedural fever
903.1 Brachial blood vessels injury
923.03 Contusion of upper arm
923.11 Contusion of elbow
958.8 Other early complications of trauma
996.1 Mechanical complication of other vascular device, implant, and graft
998.59 Other postoperative infection — (Use additional code to identify infection)

ICD-9-CM Procedural

83.09 Other incision of soft tissue

23931

23931 Incision and drainage, upper arm or elbow area; bursa

ICD-9-CM Diagnostic

711.02 Pyogenic arthritis, upper arm — (Use additional code to identify infectious organism: 041.0-041.8)
719.02 Effusion of upper arm joint

726.33 Olecranon bursitis
728.0 Infective myositis
729.5 Pain in soft tissues of limb
730.02 Acute osteomyelitis, upper arm — (Use additional code to identify organism: 041.1. Use additional code to identify major osseous defect, if applicable: 731.3)
730.12 Chronic osteomyelitis, upper arm — (Use additional code to identify organism: 041.1. Use additional code to identify major osseous defect, if applicable: 731.3)
780.62 Postprocedural fever

ICD-9-CM Procedural

83.03 Bursotomy

23935

23935 Incision, deep, with opening of bone cortex (eg, for osteomyelitis or bone abscess), humerus or elbow

ICD-9-CM Diagnostic

682.3 Cellulitis and abscess of upper arm and forearm — (Use additional code to identify organism, such as 041.1, etc.)
730.12 Chronic osteomyelitis, upper arm — (Use additional code to identify organism: 041.1. Use additional code to identify major osseous defect, if applicable: 731.3)
730.22 Unspecified osteomyelitis, upper arm — (Use additional code to identify organism: 041.1. Use additional code to identify major osseous defect, if applicable: 731.3) ▽
730.28 Unspecified osteomyelitis, other specified sites — (Use additional code to identify organism: 041.1. Use additional code to identify major osseous defect, if applicable: 731.3) ▽
730.29 Unspecified osteomyelitis, multiple sites — (Use additional code to identify organism: 041.1. Use additional code to identify major osseous defect, if applicable: 731.3) ▽
730.30 Periostitis, without mention of osteomyelitis, unspecified site — (Use additional code to identify organism: 041.1) ▽
730.32 Periostitis, without mention of osteomyelitis, upper arm — (Use additional code to identify organism: 041.1)
730.80 Other infections involving bone in diseases classified elsewhere, site unspecified — (Use additional code to identify organism: 041.1. Code first underlying disease: 002.0, 015.0-015.9) ▽ ⊠
730.82 Other infections involving bone diseases classified elsewhere, upper arm — (Use additional code to identify organism: 041.1. Code first underlying disease: 002.0, 015.0-015.9) ⊠
730.88 Other infections involving bone diseases classified elsewhere, other specified sites — (Use additional code to identify organism: 041.1. Code first underlying disease: 002.0, 015.0-015.9) ⊠
730.92 Unspecified infection of bone, upper arm — (Use additional code to identify organism: 041.1) ▽
731.3 Major osseous defects — (Code first underlying disease: 170.0-170.9, 730.00-730.29, 733.00-733.09, 733.40-733.49, 996.45)

ICD-9-CM Procedural

77.12 Other incision of humerus without division
77.19 Other incision of other bone, except facial bones, without division

24000

24000 Arthrotomy, elbow, including exploration, drainage, or removal of foreign body

ICD-9-CM Diagnostic

711.02 Pyogenic arthritis, upper arm — (Use additional code to identify infectious organism: 041.0-041.8)
711.92 Unspecified infective arthritis, upper arm ▽
711.98 Unspecified infective arthritis, other specified sites ▽
715.92 Osteoarthrosis, unspecified whether generalized or localized, upper arm ▽
718.12 Loose body in upper arm joint
719.02 Effusion of upper arm joint
719.12 Hemarthrosis, upper arm
726.33 Olecranon bursitis
729.6 Residual foreign body in soft tissue — (Use additional code to identify foreign body (V90.01-V90.9))
881.01 Open wound of elbow, without mention of complication
881.11 Open wound of elbow, complicated
998.51 Infected postoperative seroma — (Use additional code to identify organism)
998.59 Other postoperative infection — (Use additional code to identify infection)
V64.43 Arthroscopic surgical procedure converted to open procedure

ICD-9-CM Procedural

80.12 Other arthrotomy of elbow

24006

24006 Arthrotomy of the elbow, with capsular excision for capsular release (separate procedure)

ICD-9-CM Diagnostic

711.02 Pyogenic arthritis, upper arm — (Use additional code to identify infectious organism: 041.0-041.8)
711.92 Unspecified infective arthritis, upper arm ▽
715.12 Primary localized osteoarthrosis, upper arm
715.92 Osteoarthrosis, unspecified whether generalized or localized, upper arm ▽
716.12 Traumatic arthropathy, upper arm
718.42 Contracture of upper arm joint
718.52 Ankylosis of upper arm joint
726.30 Unspecified enthesopathy of elbow ▽
726.31 Medial epicondylitis of elbow
726.32 Lateral epicondylitis of elbow
726.33 Olecranon bursitis
726.39 Other enthesopathy of elbow region
V64.43 Arthroscopic surgical procedure converted to open procedure

ICD-9-CM Procedural

80.92 Other excision of elbow joint

24065-24066

24065 Biopsy, soft tissue of upper arm or elbow area; superficial
24066 deep (subfascial or intramuscular)

ICD-9-CM Diagnostic

171.2 Malignant neoplasm of connective and other soft tissue of upper limb, including shoulder
195.4 Malignant neoplasm of upper limb
198.89 Secondary malignant neoplasm of other specified sites
214.1 Lipoma of other skin and subcutaneous tissue
215.2 Other benign neoplasm of connective and other soft tissue of upper limb, including shoulder
238.1 Neoplasm of uncertain behavior of connective and other soft tissue
239.2 Neoplasms of unspecified nature of bone, soft tissue, and skin
682.3 Cellulitis and abscess of upper arm and forearm — (Use additional code to identify organism, such as 041.1, etc.)
686.8 Other specified local infections of skin and subcutaneous tissue — (Use additional code to identify any infectious organism: 041.0-041.8)
709.9 Unspecified disorder of skin and subcutaneous tissue ▽
728.82 Foreign body granuloma of muscle — (Use additional code to identify foreign body (V90.01-V90.9))

ICD-9-CM Procedural

83.21 Open biopsy of soft tissue

HCPCS Level II Supplies & Services

A4570 Splint

24075-24079 [24071, 24073]

24071 Excision, tumor, soft tissue of upper arm or elbow area, subcutaneous; 3 cm or greater

24073 Excision, tumor, soft tissue of upper arm or elbow area, subfascial (eg, intramuscular); 5 cm or greater

24075 Excision, tumor, soft tissue of upper arm or elbow area, subcutaneous; less than 3 cm

24076 Excision, tumor, soft tissue of upper arm or elbow area, subfascial (eg, intramuscular); less than 5 cm

24077 Radical resection of tumor (eg, sarcoma), soft tissue of upper arm or elbow area; less than 5 cm

24079 5 cm or greater

ICD-9-CM Diagnostic

171.2 Malignant neoplasm of connective and other soft tissue of upper limb, including shoulder

172.6 Malignant melanoma of skin of upper limb, including shoulder

173.60 Unspecified malignant neoplasm of skin of upper limb, including shoulder ▽

173.61 Basal cell carcinoma of skin of upper limb, including shoulder

173.62 Squamous cell carcinoma of skin of upper limb, including shoulder

173.69 Other specified malignant neoplasm of skin of upper limb, including shoulder

195.4 Malignant neoplasm of upper limb

209.33 Merkel cell carcinoma of the upper limb

209.75 Secondary Merkel cell carcinoma

214.1 Lipoma of other skin and subcutaneous tissue

214.8 Lipoma of other specified sites

215.2 Other benign neoplasm of connective and other soft tissue of upper limb, including shoulder

238.1 Neoplasm of uncertain behavior of connective and other soft tissue

239.2 Neoplasms of unspecified nature of bone, soft tissue, and skin

782.2 Localized superficial swelling, mass, or lump

ICD-9-CM Procedural

83.32 Excision of lesion of muscle

83.39 Excision of lesion of other soft tissue

83.49 Other excision of soft tissue

86.3 Other local excision or destruction of lesion or tissue of skin and subcutaneous tissue

86.4 Radical excision of skin lesion

HCPCS Level II Supplies & Services

A4570 Splint

24100-24102

24100 Arthrotomy, elbow; with synovial biopsy only

24101 with joint exploration, with or without biopsy, with or without removal of loose or foreign body

24102 with synovectomy

ICD-9-CM Diagnostic

171.2 Malignant neoplasm of connective and other soft tissue of upper limb, including shoulder

198.89 Secondary malignant neoplasm of other specified sites

215.2 Other benign neoplasm of connective and other soft tissue of upper limb, including shoulder

238.1 Neoplasm of uncertain behavior of connective and other soft tissue

239.2 Neoplasms of unspecified nature of bone, soft tissue, and skin

357.1 Polyneuropathy in collagen vascular disease — (Code first underlying disease: 446.0, 710.0, 714.0) ☒

359.6 Symptomatic inflammatory myopathy in diseases classified elsewhere — (Code first underlying disease: 135, 140.0-208.9, 277.30-277.39, 446.0, 710.0, 710.1, 710.2, 714.0) ☒

446.0 Polyarteritis nodosa

710.0 Systemic lupus erythematosus — (Use additional code to identify manifestation: 424.91, 581.81, 582.81, 583.81)

710.1 Systemic sclerosis — (Use additional code to identify manifestation: 359.6, 517.2)

710.2 Sicca syndrome

711.02 Pyogenic arthritis, upper arm — (Use additional code to identify infectious organism: 041.0-041.8)

711.32 Postdysenteric arthropathy, upper arm — (Code first underlying disease: 002.0-002.9, 008.0-009.3) ☒

711.42 Arthropathy associated with other bacterial diseases, upper arm — (Code first underlying disease, such as diseases classifiable to 010-040 (except 036.82), 090-099 (except 098.50)) ☒

711.52 Arthropathy associated with other viral diseases, upper arm — (Code first underlying disease: 045-049, 050-079, 480, 487) ☒

711.62 Arthropathy associated with mycoses, upper arm — (Code first underlying disease: 110.0-118) ☒

711.82 Arthropathy associated with other infectious and parasitic diseases, upper arm — (Code first underlying disease: 080-088, 100-104, 130-136) ☒

711.92 Unspecified infective arthritis, upper arm ▽

714.0 Rheumatoid arthritis — (Use additional code to identify manifestation: 357.1, 359.6)

714.1 Felty's syndrome

714.30 Polyarticular juvenile rheumatoid arthritis, chronic or unspecified

714.31 Polyarticular juvenile rheumatoid arthritis, acute

714.32 Pauciarticular juvenile rheumatoid arthritis

714.33 Monoarticular juvenile rheumatoid arthritis

714.4 Chronic postrheumatic arthropathy

714.89 Other specified inflammatory polyarthropathies

715.12 Primary localized osteoarthrosis, upper arm

715.22 Secondary localized osteoarthrosis, upper arm

715.32 Localized osteoarthrosis not specified whether primary or secondary, upper arm

716.62 Unspecified monoarthritis, upper arm ▽

716.92 Unspecified arthropathy, upper arm ▽

718.12 Loose body in upper arm joint

719.02 Effusion of upper arm joint

719.22 Villonodular synovitis, upper arm

719.42 Pain in joint, upper arm

719.62 Other symptoms referable to upper arm joint

727.00 Unspecified synovitis and tenosynovitis ▽

727.09 Other synovitis and tenosynovitis

727.9 Unspecified disorder of synovium, tendon, and bursa ▽

732.7 Osteochondritis dissecans

V64.43 Arthroscopic surgical procedure converted to open procedure

ICD-9-CM Procedural

80.32 Biopsy of joint structure of elbow

80.72 Synovectomy of elbow

80.92 Other excision of elbow joint

24105

24105 Excision, olecranon bursa

ICD-9-CM Diagnostic

357.1 Polyneuropathy in collagen vascular disease — (Code first underlying disease: 446.0, 710.0, 714.0) ☒

359.6 Symptomatic inflammatory myopathy in diseases classified elsewhere — (Code first underlying disease: 135, 140.0-208.9, 277.30-277.39, 446.0, 710.0, 710.1, 710.2, 714.0) ☒

446.0 Polyarteritis nodosa

710.0 Systemic lupus erythematosus — (Use additional code to identify manifestation: 424.91, 581.81, 582.81, 583.81)

710.1 Systemic sclerosis — (Use additional code to identify manifestation: 359.6, 517.2)

710.2 Sicca syndrome

714.0 Rheumatoid arthritis — (Use additional code to identify manifestation: 357.1, 359.6)

719.42 Pain in joint, upper arm

719.43 Pain in joint, forearm
719.62 Other symptoms referable to upper arm joint
726.33 Olecranon bursitis
727.2 Specific bursitides often of occupational origin
727.3 Other bursitis disorders
727.49 Other ganglion and cyst of synovium, tendon, and bursa

ICD-9-CM Procedural

83.5 Bursectomy

24110-24116

24110 Excision or curettage of bone cyst or benign tumor, humerus;
24115 with autograft (includes obtaining graft)
24116 with allograft

ICD-9-CM Diagnostic

213.4 Benign neoplasm of scapula and long bones of upper limb
238.0 Neoplasm of uncertain behavior of bone and articular cartilage
239.2 Neoplasms of unspecified nature of bone, soft tissue, and skin
726.91 Exostosis of unspecified site ▽
733.21 Solitary bone cyst
733.22 Aneurysmal bone cyst
733.29 Other cyst of bone

ICD-9-CM Procedural

77.62 Local excision of lesion or tissue of humerus
77.77 Excision of tibia and fibula for graft
77.79 Excision of other bone for graft, except facial bones
78.02 Bone graft of humerus

24120-24126

24120 Excision or curettage of bone cyst or benign tumor of head or neck of radius or olecranon process;
24125 with autograft (includes obtaining graft)
24126 with allograft

ICD-9-CM Diagnostic

213.4 Benign neoplasm of scapula and long bones of upper limb
229.8 Benign neoplasm of other specified sites
238.0 Neoplasm of uncertain behavior of bone and articular cartilage
239.2 Neoplasms of unspecified nature of bone, soft tissue, and skin
726.91 Exostosis of unspecified site ▽
733.21 Solitary bone cyst
733.22 Aneurysmal bone cyst
733.29 Other cyst of bone

ICD-9-CM Procedural

77.63 Local excision of lesion or tissue of radius and ulna
77.77 Excision of tibia and fibula for graft
77.79 Excision of other bone for graft, except facial bones
78.03 Bone graft of radius and ulna

24130

24130 Excision, radial head

ICD-9-CM Diagnostic

170.4 Malignant neoplasm of scapula and long bones of upper limb
171.2 Malignant neoplasm of connective and other soft tissue of upper limb, including shoulder
195.4 Malignant neoplasm of upper limb
213.4 Benign neoplasm of scapula and long bones of upper limb
238.0 Neoplasm of uncertain behavior of bone and articular cartilage
239.2 Neoplasms of unspecified nature of bone, soft tissue, and skin
277.30 Amyloidosis, unspecified — (Use additional code to identify any associated intellectual disabilities) ▽
277.31 Familial Mediterranean fever — (Use additional code to identify any associated intellectual disabilities)
277.39 Other amyloidosis — (Use additional code to identify any associated intellectual disabilities)
357.1 Polyneuropathy in collagen vascular disease — (Code first underlying disease: 446.0, 710.0, 714.0) ☒
359.6 Symptomatic inflammatory myopathy in diseases classified elsewhere — (Code first underlying disease: 135, 140.0-208.9, 277.30-277.39, 446.0, 710.0, 710.1, 710.2, 714.0) ☒
446.0 Polyarteritis nodosa
710.0 Systemic lupus erythematosus — (Use additional code to identify manifestation: 424.91, 581.81, 582.81, 583.81)
710.1 Systemic sclerosis — (Use additional code to identify manifestation: 359.6, 517.2)
710.2 Sicca syndrome
714.0 Rheumatoid arthritis — (Use additional code to identify manifestation: 357.1, 359.6)
715.13 Primary localized osteoarthrosis, forearm
718.93 Unspecified derangement, forearm joint ▽
719.43 Pain in joint, forearm
733.81 Malunion of fracture
754.89 Other specified nonteratogenic anomalies

ICD-9-CM Procedural

77.83 Other partial ostectomy of radius and ulna

24134

24134 Sequestrectomy (eg, for osteomyelitis or bone abscess), shaft or distal humerus

ICD-9-CM Diagnostic

715.12 Primary localized osteoarthrosis, upper arm
715.32 Localized osteoarthrosis not specified whether primary or secondary, upper arm
715.92 Osteoarthrosis, unspecified whether generalized or localized, upper arm ▽
716.62 Unspecified monoarthritis, upper arm ▽
730.12 Chronic osteomyelitis, upper arm — (Use additional code to identify organism: 041.1. Use additional code to identify major osseous defect, if applicable: 731.3)
730.22 Unspecified osteomyelitis, upper arm — (Use additional code to identify organism: 041.1. Use additional code to identify major osseous defect, if applicable: 731.3) ▽
730.32 Periostitis, without mention of osteomyelitis, upper arm — (Use additional code to identify organism: 041.1)
730.72 Osteopathy resulting from poliomyelitis, upper arm — (Use additional code to identify organism: 041.1. Code first underlying disease: 045.0-045.9) ☒
730.82 Other infections involving bone diseases classified elsewhere, upper arm — (Use additional code to identify organism: 041.1. Code first underlying disease: 002.0, 015.0-015.9) ☒
731.3 Major osseous defects — (Code first underlying disease: 170.0-170.9, 730.00-730.29, 733.00-733.09, 733.40-733.49, 996.45)
733.49 Aseptic necrosis of other bone site — (Use additional code to identify major osseous defect, if applicable: 731.3)
905.2 Late effect of fracture of upper extremities

ICD-9-CM Procedural

77.02 Sequestrectomy of humerus

24136-24138

24136 Sequestrectomy (eg, for osteomyelitis or bone abscess), radial head or neck
24138 Sequestrectomy (eg, for osteomyelitis or bone abscess), olecranon process

ICD-9-CM Diagnostic

715.12 Primary localized osteoarthrosis, upper arm
715.32 Localized osteoarthrosis not specified whether primary or secondary, upper arm
715.92 Osteoarthrosis, unspecified whether generalized or localized, upper arm ▽

716.62 Unspecified monoarthritis, upper arm ▽

730.12 Chronic osteomyelitis, upper arm — (Use additional code to identify organism: 041.1. Use additional code to identify major osseous defect, if applicable: 731.3)

730.22 Unspecified osteomyelitis, upper arm — (Use additional code to identify organism: 041.1. Use additional code to identify major osseous defect, if applicable: 731.3) ▽

730.32 Periostitis, without mention of osteomyelitis, upper arm — (Use additional code to identify organism: 041.1)

730.72 Osteopathy resulting from poliomyelitis, upper arm — (Use additional code to identify organism: 041.1. Code first underlying disease: 045.0-045.9) ☒

730.82 Other infections involving bone diseases classified elsewhere, upper arm — (Use additional code to identify organism: 041.1. Code first underlying disease: 002.0, 015.0-015.9) ☒

730.92 Unspecified infection of bone, upper arm — (Use additional code to identify organism: 041.1) ▽

731.3 Major osseous defects — (Code first underlying disease: 170.0-170.9, 730.00-730.29, 733.00-733.09, 733.40-733.49, 996.45)

733.49 Aseptic necrosis of other bone site — (Use additional code to identify major osseous defect, if applicable: 731.3)

905.2 Late effect of fracture of upper extremities

ICD-9-CM Procedural

77.03 Sequestrectomy of radius and ulna

77.09 Sequestrectomy of other bone, except facial bones

24140

24140 Partial excision (craterization, saucerization, or diaphysectomy) bone (eg, osteomyelitis), humerus

ICD-9-CM Diagnostic

729.5 Pain in soft tissues of limb

730.12 Chronic osteomyelitis, upper arm — (Use additional code to identify organism: 041.1. Use additional code to identify major osseous defect, if applicable: 731.3)

730.22 Unspecified osteomyelitis, upper arm — (Use additional code to identify organism: 041.1. Use additional code to identify major osseous defect, if applicable: 731.3) ▽

730.32 Periostitis, without mention of osteomyelitis, upper arm — (Use additional code to identify organism: 041.1)

730.72 Osteopathy resulting from poliomyelitis, upper arm — (Use additional code to identify organism: 041.1. Code first underlying disease: 045.0-045.9) ☒

730.82 Other infections involving bone diseases classified elsewhere, upper arm — (Use additional code to identify organism: 041.1. Code first underlying disease: 002.0, 015.0-015.9) ☒

730.92 Unspecified infection of bone, upper arm — (Use additional code to identify organism: 041.1) ▽

731.3 Major osseous defects — (Code first underlying disease: 170.0-170.9, 730.00-730.29, 733.00-733.09, 733.40-733.49, 996.45)

733.49 Aseptic necrosis of other bone site — (Use additional code to identify major osseous defect, if applicable: 731.3)

ICD-9-CM Procedural

77.82 Other partial ostectomy of humerus

24145-24147

24145 Partial excision (craterization, saucerization, or diaphysectomy) bone (eg, osteomyelitis), radial head or neck

24147 Partial excision (craterization, saucerization, or diaphysectomy) bone (eg, osteomyelitis), olecranon process

ICD-9-CM Diagnostic

729.5 Pain in soft tissues of limb

730.12 Chronic osteomyelitis, upper arm — (Use additional code to identify organism: 041.1. Use additional code to identify major osseous defect, if applicable: 731.3)

730.13 Chronic osteomyelitis, forearm — (Use additional code to identify organism: 041.1. Use additional code to identify major osseous defect, if applicable: 731.3)

730.22 Unspecified osteomyelitis, upper arm — (Use additional code to identify organism: 041.1. Use additional code to identify major osseous defect, if applicable: 731.3) ▽

730.23 Unspecified osteomyelitis, forearm — (Use additional code to identify organism: 041.1. Use additional code to identify major osseous defect, if applicable: 731.3) ▽

730.32 Periostitis, without mention of osteomyelitis, upper arm — (Use additional code to identify organism: 041.1)

730.33 Periostitis, without mention of osteomyelitis, forearm — (Use additional code to identify organism: 041.1)

730.73 Osteopathy resulting from poliomyelitis, forearm — (Use additional code to identify organism: 041.1. Code first underlying disease: 045.0-045.9) ☒

730.82 Other infections involving bone diseases classified elsewhere, upper arm — (Use additional code to identify organism: 041.1. Code first underlying disease: 002.0, 015.0-015.9) ☒

730.83 Other infections involving bone in diseases classified elsewhere, forearm — (Use additional code to identify organism: 041.1. Code first underlying disease: 002.0, 015.0-015.9) ☒

730.92 Unspecified infection of bone, upper arm — (Use additional code to identify organism: 041.1) ▽

730.93 Unspecified infection of bone, forearm — (Use additional code to identify organism: 041.1) ▽

731.3 Major osseous defects — (Code first underlying disease: 170.0-170.9, 730.00-730.29, 733.00-733.09, 733.40-733.49, 996.45)

733.49 Aseptic necrosis of other bone site — (Use additional code to identify major osseous defect, if applicable: 731.3)

ICD-9-CM Procedural

77.83 Other partial ostectomy of radius and ulna

77.89 Other partial ostectomy of other bone, except facial bones

24149

24149 Radical resection of capsule, soft tissue, and heterotopic bone, elbow, with contracture release (separate procedure)

ICD-9-CM Diagnostic

357.1 Polyneuropathy in collagen vascular disease — (Code first underlying disease: 446.0, 710.0, 714.0) ☒

359.6 Symptomatic inflammatory myopathy in diseases classified elsewhere — (Code first underlying disease: 135, 140.0-208.9, 277.30-277.39, 446.0, 710.0, 710.1, 710.2, 714.0) ☒

446.0 Polyarteritis nodosa

710.0 Systemic lupus erythematosus — (Use additional code to identify manifestation: 424.91, 581.81, 582.81, 583.81)

710.1 Systemic sclerosis — (Use additional code to identify manifestation: 359.6, 517.2)

710.2 Sicca syndrome

711.02 Pyogenic arthritis, upper arm — (Use additional code to identify infectious organism: 041.0-041.8)

711.92 Unspecified infective arthritis, upper arm ▽

714.0 Rheumatoid arthritis — (Use additional code to identify manifestation: 357.1, 359.6)

718.52 Ankylosis of upper arm joint

719.22 Villonodular synovitis, upper arm

719.42 Pain in joint, upper arm

730.12 Chronic osteomyelitis, upper arm — (Use additional code to identify organism: 041.1. Use additional code to identify major osseous defect, if applicable: 731.3)

730.22 Unspecified osteomyelitis, upper arm — (Use additional code to identify organism: 041.1. Use additional code to identify major osseous defect, if applicable: 731.3) ▽

730.92 Unspecified infection of bone, upper arm — (Use additional code to identify organism: 041.1) ▽

731.3 Major osseous defects — (Code first underlying disease: 170.0-170.9, 730.00-730.29, 733.00-733.09, 733.40-733.49, 996.45)

733.49 Aseptic necrosis of other bone site — (Use additional code to identify major osseous defect, if applicable: 731.3)

905.2 Late effect of fracture of upper extremities

905.6 Late effect of dislocation
906.4 Late effect of crushing
927.11 Crushing injury of elbow — (Use additional code to identify any associated injuries: 800-829, 850.0-854.1, 860.0-869.1)

ICD-9-CM Procedural

77.62 Local excision of lesion or tissue of humerus
80.42 Division of joint capsule, ligament, or cartilage of elbow
83.49 Other excision of soft tissue

24150

24150 Radical resection of tumor, shaft or distal humerus

ICD-9-CM Diagnostic

170.4 Malignant neoplasm of scapula and long bones of upper limb
198.5 Secondary malignant neoplasm of bone and bone marrow
209.73 Secondary neuroendocrine tumor of bone
238.0 Neoplasm of uncertain behavior of bone and articular cartilage
239.2 Neoplasms of unspecified nature of bone, soft tissue, and skin

ICD-9-CM Procedural

77.82 Other partial ostectomy of humerus

24152

24152 Radical resection of tumor, radial head or neck

ICD-9-CM Diagnostic

170.4 Malignant neoplasm of scapula and long bones of upper limb
198.5 Secondary malignant neoplasm of bone and bone marrow
209.73 Secondary neuroendocrine tumor of bone
238.0 Neoplasm of uncertain behavior of bone and articular cartilage
239.2 Neoplasms of unspecified nature of bone, soft tissue, and skin

ICD-9-CM Procedural

77.83 Other partial ostectomy of radius and ulna

24155

24155 Resection of elbow joint (arthrectomy)

ICD-9-CM Diagnostic

170.4 Malignant neoplasm of scapula and long bones of upper limb
195.4 Malignant neoplasm of upper limb
238.0 Neoplasm of uncertain behavior of bone and articular cartilage
239.2 Neoplasms of unspecified nature of bone, soft tissue, and skin
239.89 Neoplasms of unspecified nature, other specified sites
357.1 Polyneuropathy in collagen vascular disease — (Code first underlying disease: 446.0, 710.0, 714.0) ☒
359.6 Symptomatic inflammatory myopathy in diseases classified elsewhere — (Code first underlying disease: 135, 140.0-208.9, 277.30-277.39, 446.0, 710.0, 710.1, 710.2, 714.0) ☒
446.0 Polyarteritis nodosa
710.0 Systemic lupus erythematosus — (Use additional code to identify manifestation: 424.91, 581.81, 582.81, 583.81)
710.1 Systemic sclerosis — (Use additional code to identify manifestation: 359.6, 517.2)
710.2 Sicca syndrome
711.02 Pyogenic arthritis, upper arm — (Use additional code to identify infectious organism: 041.0-041.8)
711.92 Unspecified infective arthritis, upper arm ♥
714.0 Rheumatoid arthritis — (Use additional code to identify manifestation: 357.1, 359.6)
718.52 Ankylosis of upper arm joint
718.72 Developmental dislocation of joint, upper arm
719.22 Villonodular synovitis, upper arm
719.42 Pain in joint, upper arm
730.12 Chronic osteomyelitis, upper arm — (Use additional code to identify organism: 041.1. Use additional code to identify major osseous defect, if applicable: 731.3)
730.22 Unspecified osteomyelitis, upper arm — (Use additional code to identify organism: 041.1. Use additional code to identify major osseous defect, if applicable: 731.3) ♥
730.92 Unspecified infection of bone, upper arm — (Use additional code to identify organism: 041.1) ♥
731.3 Major osseous defects — (Code first underlying disease: 170.0-170.9, 730.00-730.29, 733.00-733.09, 733.40-733.49, 996.45)
733.49 Aseptic necrosis of other bone site — (Use additional code to identify major osseous defect, if applicable: 731.3)
812.41 Closed fracture of supracondylar humerus
812.42 Closed fracture of lateral condyle of humerus
812.43 Closed fracture of medial condyle of humerus
812.44 Closed fracture of unspecified condyle(s) of humerus ♥
812.49 Other closed fracture of lower end of humerus
812.51 Open fracture of supracondylar humerus
812.52 Open fracture of lateral condyle of humerus
812.53 Open fracture of medial condyle of humerus
812.54 Open fracture of unspecified condyle(s) of humerus ♥
812.59 Other open fracture of lower end of humerus
813.01 Closed fracture of olecranon process of ulna
813.02 Closed fracture of coronoid process of ulna
813.04 Other and unspecified closed fractures of proximal end of ulna (alone) ♥
813.05 Closed fracture of head of radius
813.06 Closed fracture of neck of radius
813.07 Other and unspecified closed fractures of proximal end of radius (alone) ♥
813.08 Closed fracture of radius with ulna, upper end (any part)
813.11 Open fracture of olecranon process of ulna
813.12 Open fracture of coronoid process of ulna
813.15 Open fracture of head of radius
813.16 Open fracture of neck of radius
813.17 Other and unspecified open fractures of proximal end of radius (alone) ♥
813.18 Open fracture of radius with ulna, upper end (any part)
832.00 Closed unspecified dislocation of elbow
832.01 Closed anterior dislocation of elbow
832.02 Closed posterior dislocation of elbow
832.10 Open unspecified dislocation of elbow ♥
832.11 Open anterior dislocation of elbow
832.12 Open posterior dislocation of elbow
832.13 Open medial dislocation of elbow
832.14 Open lateral dislocation of elbow
832.19 Open dislocation of other site of elbow
927.11 Crushing injury of elbow — (Use additional code to identify any associated injuries: 800-829, 850.0-854.1, 860.0-869.1)

ICD-9-CM Procedural

80.92 Other excision of elbow joint

24160-24164

24160 Removal of prosthesis, includes debridement and synovectomy when performed; humeral and ulnar components
24164 radial head

ICD-9-CM Diagnostic

731.3 Major osseous defects — (Code first underlying disease: 170.0-170.9, 730.00-730.29, 733.00-733.09, 733.40-733.49, 996.45)
996.40 Unspecified mechanical complication of internal orthopedic device, implant, and graft — (Use additional code to identify prosthetic joint with mechanical complication, V43.60-V43.69) ♥
996.41 Mechanical loosening of prosthetic joint — (Use additional code to identify prosthetic joint with mechanical complication, V43.60-V43.69)

996.42 Dislocation of prosthetic joint — (Use additional code to identify prosthetic joint with mechanical complication, V43.60-V43.69)
996.43 Broken prosthetic joint implant — (Use additional code to identify prosthetic joint with mechanical complication, V43.60-V43.69)
996.44 Peri-prosthetic fracture around prosthetic joint — (Use additional code to identify prosthetic joint with mechanical complication, V43.60-V43.69.
996.45 Peri-prosthetic osteolysis — (Use additional code to identify prosthetic joint with mechanical complication, V43.60-V43.69. Use additional code to identify major osseous defect, if applicable: 731.3)
996.47 Other mechanical complication of prosthetic joint implant — (Use additional code to identify prosthetic joint with mechanical complication, V43.60-V43.69)
996.49 Other mechanical complication of other internal orthopedic device, implant, and graft — (Use additional code to identify prosthetic joint with mechanical complication, V43.60-V43.69)
996.66 Infection and inflammatory reaction due to internal joint prosthesis — (Use additional code to identify specified infections. Use additional code to identify infected prosthetic joint: V43.60-V43.69)
996.67 Infection and inflammatory reaction due to other internal orthopedic device, implant, and graft — (Use additional code to identify specified infections)
996.77 Other complications due to internal joint prosthesis — (Use additional code to identify complication: 338.18-338.19, 338.28-338.29)
996.78 Other complications due to other internal orthopedic device, implant, and graft — (Use additional code to identify complication: 338.18-338.19, 338.28-338.29)
996.79 Other complications due to other internal prosthetic device, implant, and graft — (Use additional code to identify complication: 338.18-338.19, 338.28-338.29)
998.59 Other postoperative infection — (Use additional code to identify infection)
V43.62 Elbow joint replacement by other means

ICD-9-CM Procedural

78.63 Removal of implanted device from radius and ulna
78.69 Removal of implanted device from other bone

24200-24201

24200 Removal of foreign body, upper arm or elbow area; subcutaneous
24201 deep (subfascial or intramuscular)

ICD-9-CM Diagnostic

709.4 Foreign body granuloma of skin and subcutaneous tissue — (Use additional code to identify foreign body (V90.01-V90.9))
728.82 Foreign body granuloma of muscle — (Use additional code to identify foreign body (V90.01-V90.9))
729.6 Residual foreign body in soft tissue — (Use additional code to identify foreign body (V90.01-V90.9))
733.99 Other disorders of bone and cartilage
880.13 Open wound of upper arm, complicated
881.11 Open wound of elbow, complicated
906.1 Late effect of open wound of extremities without mention of tendon injury
913.6 Elbow, forearm, and wrist, superficial foreign body (splinter), without major open wound and without mention of infection
913.7 Elbow, forearm, and wrist, superficial foreign body (splinter), without major open wound, infected
998.4 Foreign body accidentally left during procedure, not elsewhere classified

ICD-9-CM Procedural

83.02 Myotomy
83.09 Other incision of soft tissue
86.05 Incision with removal of foreign body or device from skin and subcutaneous tissue

HCPCS Level II Supplies & Services

A4570 Splint

24220

24220 Injection procedure for elbow arthrography

ICD-9-CM Diagnostic

229.8 Benign neoplasm of other specified sites
275.40 Unspecified disorder of calcium metabolism — (Use additional code to identify any associated intellectual disabilities) ▽
275.42 Hypercalcemia — (Use additional code to identify any associated intellectual disabilities)
275.49 Other disorders of calcium metabolism — (Use additional code to identify any associated intellectual disabilities)
275.5 Hungry bone syndrome — (Use additional code to identify any associated intellectual disabilities)
357.1 Polyneuropathy in collagen vascular disease — (Code first underlying disease: 446.0, 710.0, 714.0) ☒
359.6 Symptomatic inflammatory myopathy in diseases classified elsewhere — (Code first underlying disease: 135, 140.0-208.9, 277.30-277.39, 446.0, 710.0, 710.1, 710.2, 714.0) ☒
446.0 Polyarteritis nodosa
710.0 Systemic lupus erythematosus — (Use additional code to identify manifestation: 424.91, 581.81, 582.81, 583.81)
710.1 Systemic sclerosis — (Use additional code to identify manifestation: 359.6, 517.2)
710.2 Sicca syndrome
714.0 Rheumatoid arthritis — (Use additional code to identify manifestation: 357.1, 359.6)
715.12 Primary localized osteoarthrosis, upper arm
715.92 Osteoarthrosis, unspecified whether generalized or localized, upper arm ▽
716.12 Traumatic arthropathy, upper arm
718.12 Loose body in upper arm joint
718.72 Developmental dislocation of joint, upper arm
718.82 Other joint derangement, not elsewhere classified, upper arm
719.42 Pain in joint, upper arm
719.52 Stiffness of joint, not elsewhere classified, upper arm
719.82 Other specified disorders of upper arm joint
812.40 Closed fracture of unspecified part of lower end of humerus ▽
812.41 Closed fracture of supracondylar humerus
812.42 Closed fracture of lateral condyle of humerus
812.43 Closed fracture of medial condyle of humerus
812.44 Closed fracture of unspecified condyle(s) of humerus ▽
812.49 Other closed fracture of lower end of humerus
813.01 Closed fracture of olecranon process of ulna
813.02 Closed fracture of coronoid process of ulna
813.04 Other and unspecified closed fractures of proximal end of ulna (alone) ▽
813.05 Closed fracture of head of radius
813.07 Other and unspecified closed fractures of proximal end of radius (alone) ▽
832.00 Closed unspecified dislocation of elbow
832.01 Closed anterior dislocation of elbow
832.02 Closed posterior dislocation of elbow
832.03 Closed medial dislocation of elbow
832.04 Closed lateral dislocation of elbow
832.09 Closed dislocation of other site of elbow
832.2 Nursemaid's elbow

ICD-9-CM Procedural

81.99 Other operations on joint structures
88.32 Contrast arthrogram

24300

24300 Manipulation, elbow, under anesthesia

ICD-9-CM Diagnostic

357.1 Polyneuropathy in collagen vascular disease — (Code first underlying disease: 446.0, 710.0, 714.0) ☒
359.6 Symptomatic inflammatory myopathy in diseases classified elsewhere — (Code first underlying disease: 135, 140.0-208.9, 277.30-277.39, 446.0, 710.0, 710.1, 710.2, 714.0) ☒
446.0 Polyarteritis nodosa
710.0 Systemic lupus erythematosus — (Use additional code to identify manifestation: 424.91, 581.81, 582.81, 583.81)
710.1 Systemic sclerosis — (Use additional code to identify manifestation: 359.6, 517.2)
710.2 Sicca syndrome
714.0 Rheumatoid arthritis — (Use additional code to identify manifestation: 357.1, 359.6)
715.12 Primary localized osteoarthrosis, upper arm
715.92 Osteoarthrosis, unspecified whether generalized or localized, upper arm ♥
718.42 Contracture of upper arm joint
718.52 Ankylosis of upper arm joint
719.22 Villonodular synovitis, upper arm
719.52 Stiffness of joint, not elsewhere classified, upper arm
726.30 Unspecified enthesopathy of elbow ♥
726.31 Medial epicondylitis of elbow
726.32 Lateral epicondylitis of elbow
726.33 Olecranon bursitis
726.39 Other enthesopathy of elbow region

ICD-9-CM Procedural

93.25 Forced extension of limb
93.26 Manual rupture of joint adhesions
93.29 Other forcible correction of musculoskeletal deformity

24301

24301 Muscle or tendon transfer, any type, upper arm or elbow, single (excluding 24320-24331)

ICD-9-CM Diagnostic

342.10 Spastic hemiplegia affecting unspecified side ♥
342.11 Spastic hemiplegia affecting dominant side
342.12 Spastic hemiplegia affecting nondominant side
343.0 Diplegic infantile cerebral palsy
343.1 Hemiplegic infantile cerebral palsy
343.2 Quadriplegic infantile cerebral palsy
343.3 Monoplegic infantile cerebral palsy
718.32 Recurrent dislocation of upper arm joint
726.30 Unspecified enthesopathy of elbow ♥
726.39 Other enthesopathy of elbow region
727.62 Nontraumatic rupture of tendons of biceps (long head)
727.63 Nontraumatic rupture of extensor tendons of hand and wrist
727.64 Nontraumatic rupture of flexor tendons of hand and wrist
728.4 Laxity of ligament
728.5 Hypermobility syndrome
841.0 Radial collateral ligament sprain and strain
841.1 Ulnar collateral ligament sprain and strain
841.2 Radiohumeral (joint) sprain and strain
841.3 Ulnohumeral (joint) sprain and strain
841.8 Sprain and strain of other specified sites of elbow and forearm
841.9 Sprain and strain of unspecified site of elbow and forearm ♥
881.11 Open wound of elbow, complicated
881.21 Open wound of elbow, with tendon involvement
884.1 Multiple and unspecified open wound of upper limb, complicated
884.2 Multiple and unspecified open wound of upper limb, with tendon involvement

ICD-9-CM Procedural

83.75 Tendon transfer or transplantation
83.77 Muscle transfer or transplantation

24305

24305 Tendon lengthening, upper arm or elbow, each tendon

ICD-9-CM Diagnostic

343.0 Diplegic infantile cerebral palsy
715.31 Localized osteoarthrosis not specified whether primary or secondary, shoulder region
718.41 Contracture of shoulder joint
718.42 Contracture of upper arm joint
728.3 Other specific muscle disorders
840.8 Sprain and strain of other specified sites of shoulder and upper arm
840.9 Sprain and strain of unspecified site of shoulder and upper arm ♥
841.0 Radial collateral ligament sprain and strain
841.1 Ulnar collateral ligament sprain and strain
841.2 Radiohumeral (joint) sprain and strain
841.3 Ulnohumeral (joint) sprain and strain
841.8 Sprain and strain of other specified sites of elbow and forearm
841.9 Sprain and strain of unspecified site of elbow and forearm ♥

ICD-9-CM Procedural

83.85 Other change in muscle or tendon length

24310

24310 Tenotomy, open, elbow to shoulder, each tendon

ICD-9-CM Diagnostic

716.51 Unspecified polyarthropathy or polyarthritis, shoulder region ♥
716.52 Unspecified polyarthropathy or polyarthritis, upper arm ♥
718.41 Contracture of shoulder joint
718.42 Contracture of upper arm joint
718.51 Ankylosis of joint of shoulder region
718.52 Ankylosis of upper arm joint
718.81 Other joint derangement, not elsewhere classified, shoulder region
718.82 Other joint derangement, not elsewhere classified, upper arm
718.91 Unspecified derangement, shoulder region ♥
718.92 Unspecified derangement, upper arm joint ♥
728.3 Other specific muscle disorders
840.8 Sprain and strain of other specified sites of shoulder and upper arm

ICD-9-CM Procedural

83.13 Other tenotomy

24320

24320 Tenoplasty, with muscle transfer, with or without free graft, elbow to shoulder, single (Seddon-Brookes type procedure)

ICD-9-CM Diagnostic

343.0 Diplegic infantile cerebral palsy
718.41 Contracture of shoulder joint
718.42 Contracture of upper arm joint
718.81 Other joint derangement, not elsewhere classified, shoulder region
718.82 Other joint derangement, not elsewhere classified, upper arm
718.91 Unspecified derangement, shoulder region ♥
718.92 Unspecified derangement, upper arm joint ♥
718.98 Unspecified derangement of joint, other specified sites ♥
727.62 Nontraumatic rupture of tendons of biceps (long head)
880.23 Open wound of upper arm, with tendon involvement

881.21 Open wound of elbow, with tendon involvement

ICD-9-CM Procedural

83.77 Muscle transfer or transplantation
83.81 Tendon graft
83.88 Other plastic operations on tendon

24330-24331

24330 Flexor-plasty, elbow (eg, Steindler type advancement);
24331 with extensor advancement

ICD-9-CM Diagnostic

343.0 Diplegic infantile cerebral palsy
344.2 Diplegia of upper limbs
344.40 Monoplegia of upper limb affecting unspecified side ▽
344.41 Monoplegia of upper limb affecting dominant side
344.42 Monoplegia of upper limb affecting nondominant side
718.32 Recurrent dislocation of upper arm joint
718.42 Contracture of upper arm joint
718.82 Other joint derangement, not elsewhere classified, upper arm
718.92 Unspecified derangement, upper arm joint ▽
719.42 Pain in joint, upper arm
767.6 Injury to brachial plexus, birth trauma — (Use additional code(s) to further specify condition)
953.4 Injury to brachial plexus

ICD-9-CM Procedural

83.71 Advancement of tendon
83.77 Muscle transfer or transplantation
83.81 Tendon graft

24332

24332 Tenolysis, triceps

ICD-9-CM Diagnostic

357.1 Polyneuropathy in collagen vascular disease — (Code first underlying disease: 446.0, 710.0, 714.0) ☒
359.6 Symptomatic inflammatory myopathy in diseases classified elsewhere — (Code first underlying disease: 135, 140.0-208.9, 277.30-277.39, 446.0, 710.0, 710.1, 710.2, 714.0) ☒
446.0 Polyarteritis nodosa
710.0 Systemic lupus erythematosus — (Use additional code to identify manifestation: 424.91, 581.81, 582.81, 583.81)
710.1 Systemic sclerosis — (Use additional code to identify manifestation: 359.6, 517.2)
710.2 Sicca syndrome
714.0 Rheumatoid arthritis — (Use additional code to identify manifestation: 357.1, 359.6)
718.52 Ankylosis of upper arm joint
719.52 Stiffness of joint, not elsewhere classified, upper arm
727.00 Unspecified synovitis and tenosynovitis ▽
727.01 Synovitis and tenosynovitis in diseases classified elsewhere — (Code first underlying disease: 015.0-015.9) ☒
727.09 Other synovitis and tenosynovitis
727.81 Contracture of tendon (sheath)
727.82 Calcium deposits in tendon and bursa
727.89 Other disorders of synovium, tendon, and bursa
727.9 Unspecified disorder of synovium, tendon, and bursa ▽

ICD-9-CM Procedural

83.91 Lysis of adhesions of muscle, tendon, fascia, and bursa

24340

24340 Tenodesis of biceps tendon at elbow (separate procedure)

ICD-9-CM Diagnostic

727.62 Nontraumatic rupture of tendons of biceps (long head)
728.83 Rupture of muscle, nontraumatic
841.8 Sprain and strain of other specified sites of elbow and forearm

ICD-9-CM Procedural

83.88 Other plastic operations on tendon

24341

24341 Repair, tendon or muscle, upper arm or elbow, each tendon or muscle, primary or secondary (excludes rotator cuff)

ICD-9-CM Diagnostic

727.62 Nontraumatic rupture of tendons of biceps (long head)
727.69 Nontraumatic rupture of other tendon
831.00 Closed dislocation of shoulder, unspecified site ▽
831.02 Closed posterior dislocation of humerus
831.03 Closed inferior dislocation of humerus
831.04 Closed dislocation of acromioclavicular (joint)
831.09 Closed dislocation of other site of shoulder
831.10 Open unspecified dislocation of shoulder ▽
831.11 Open anterior dislocation of humerus
831.12 Open posterior dislocation of humerus
831.13 Open inferior dislocation of humerus
831.14 Open dislocation of acromioclavicular (joint)
831.19 Open dislocation of other site of shoulder
832.00 Closed unspecified dislocation of elbow
832.01 Closed anterior dislocation of elbow
832.02 Closed posterior dislocation of elbow
832.03 Closed medial dislocation of elbow
832.04 Closed lateral dislocation of elbow
832.09 Closed dislocation of other site of elbow
832.10 Open unspecified dislocation of elbow ▽
832.11 Open anterior dislocation of elbow
832.12 Open posterior dislocation of elbow
832.13 Open medial dislocation of elbow
832.14 Open lateral dislocation of elbow
832.19 Open dislocation of other site of elbow
840.8 Sprain and strain of other specified sites of shoulder and upper arm
840.9 Sprain and strain of unspecified site of shoulder and upper arm ▽
841.8 Sprain and strain of other specified sites of elbow and forearm
841.9 Sprain and strain of unspecified site of elbow and forearm ▽
880.03 Open wound of upper arm, without mention of complication
880.09 Open wound of multiple sites of shoulder and upper arm, without mention of complication
880.10 Open wound of shoulder region, complicated
880.19 Open wound of multiple sites of shoulder and upper arm, complicated
880.20 Open wound of shoulder region, with tendon involvement
880.23 Open wound of upper arm, with tendon involvement
880.29 Open wound of multiple sites of shoulder and upper arm, with tendon involvement
884.1 Multiple and unspecified open wound of upper limb, complicated
884.2 Multiple and unspecified open wound of upper limb, with tendon involvement
927.00 Crushing injury of shoulder region — (Use additional code to identify any associated injuries: 800-829, 850.0-854.1, 860.0-869.1)
927.01 Crushing injury of scapular region — (Use additional code to identify any associated injuries: 800-829, 850.0-854.1, 860.0-869.1)
927.02 Crushing injury of axillary region — (Use additional code to identify any associated injuries: 800-829, 850.0-854.1, 860.0-869.1)

927.03 Crushing injury of upper arm — (Use additional code to identify any associated injuries: 800-829, 850.0-854.1, 860.0-869.1)
927.09 Crushing injury of multiple sites of upper arm — (Use additional code to identify any associated injuries: 800-829, 850.0-854.1, 860.0-869.1)
927.11 Crushing injury of elbow — (Use additional code to identify any associated injuries: 800-829, 850.0-854.1, 860.0-869.1)
998.2 Accidental puncture or laceration during procedure

ICD-9-CM Procedural

83.64 Other suture of tendon
83.65 Other suture of muscle or fascia
83.87 Other plastic operations on muscle
83.88 Other plastic operations on tendon

24342

24342 Reinsertion of ruptured biceps or triceps tendon, distal, with or without tendon graft

ICD-9-CM Diagnostic

727.62 Nontraumatic rupture of tendons of biceps (long head)
841.8 Sprain and strain of other specified sites of elbow and forearm
880.23 Open wound of upper arm, with tendon involvement

ICD-9-CM Procedural

83.75 Tendon transfer or transplantation
83.82 Graft of muscle or fascia

24343-24346

24343 Repair lateral collateral ligament, elbow, with local tissue
24344 Reconstruction lateral collateral ligament, elbow, with tendon graft (includes harvesting of graft)
24345 Repair medial collateral ligament, elbow, with local tissue
24346 Reconstruction medial collateral ligament, elbow, with tendon graft (includes harvesting of graft)

ICD-9-CM Diagnostic

716.12 Traumatic arthropathy, upper arm
718.02 Articular cartilage disorder, upper arm
718.32 Recurrent dislocation of upper arm joint
718.82 Other joint derangement, not elsewhere classified, upper arm
728.89 Other disorder of muscle, ligament, and fascia — (Use additional E code to identify drug, if drug-induced)
728.9 Unspecified disorder of muscle, ligament, and fascia ▽
812.40 Closed fracture of unspecified part of lower end of humerus ▽
812.41 Closed fracture of supracondylar humerus
812.42 Closed fracture of lateral condyle of humerus
812.43 Closed fracture of medial condyle of humerus
812.44 Closed fracture of unspecified condyle(s) of humerus ▽
812.49 Other closed fracture of lower end of humerus
812.50 Open fracture of unspecified part of lower end of humerus ▽
812.51 Open fracture of supracondylar humerus
812.52 Open fracture of lateral condyle of humerus
812.53 Open fracture of medial condyle of humerus
812.54 Open fracture of unspecified condyle(s) of humerus ▽
812.59 Other open fracture of lower end of humerus
813.00 Unspecified fracture of radius and ulna, upper end of forearm, closed ▽
813.01 Closed fracture of olecranon process of ulna
813.02 Closed fracture of coronoid process of ulna
813.03 Closed Monteggia's fracture
813.04 Other and unspecified closed fractures of proximal end of ulna (alone) ▽
813.05 Closed fracture of head of radius
813.06 Closed fracture of neck of radius
813.07 Other and unspecified closed fractures of proximal end of radius (alone) ▽
813.08 Closed fracture of radius with ulna, upper end (any part)
813.10 Unspecified open fracture of upper end of forearm ▽
813.11 Open fracture of olecranon process of ulna
813.12 Open fracture of coronoid process of ulna
813.13 Open Monteggia's fracture
813.14 Other and unspecified open fractures of proximal end of ulna (alone) ▽
813.15 Open fracture of head of radius
813.16 Open fracture of neck of radius
813.17 Other and unspecified open fractures of proximal end of radius (alone) ▽
813.18 Open fracture of radius with ulna, upper end (any part)
832.00 Closed unspecified dislocation of elbow
832.01 Closed anterior dislocation of elbow
832.02 Closed posterior dislocation of elbow
832.03 Closed medial dislocation of elbow
832.04 Closed lateral dislocation of elbow
832.09 Closed dislocation of other site of elbow
832.10 Open unspecified dislocation of elbow ▽
832.11 Open anterior dislocation of elbow
832.12 Open posterior dislocation of elbow
832.13 Open medial dislocation of elbow
832.14 Open lateral dislocation of elbow
832.19 Open dislocation of other site of elbow
841.0 Radial collateral ligament sprain and strain
841.1 Ulnar collateral ligament sprain and strain
841.2 Radiohumeral (joint) sprain and strain
841.3 Ulnohumeral (joint) sprain and strain
841.8 Sprain and strain of other specified sites of elbow and forearm
841.9 Sprain and strain of unspecified site of elbow and forearm ▽
880.23 Open wound of upper arm, with tendon involvement
881.21 Open wound of elbow, with tendon involvement
884.2 Multiple and unspecified open wound of upper limb, with tendon involvement
927.11 Crushing injury of elbow — (Use additional code to identify any associated injuries: 800-829, 850.0-854.1, 860.0-869.1)

ICD-9-CM Procedural

81.96 Other repair of joint
83.81 Tendon graft

24357

24357 Tenotomy, elbow, lateral or medial (eg, epicondylitis, tennis elbow, golfer's elbow); percutaneous

ICD-9-CM Diagnostic

719.42 Pain in joint, upper arm
726.31 Medial epicondylitis of elbow
726.32 Lateral epicondylitis of elbow
726.39 Other enthesopathy of elbow region
726.90 Enthesopathy of unspecified site ▽
727.09 Other synovitis and tenosynovitis
729.71 Nontraumatic compartment syndrome of upper extremity — (Code first, if applicable, postprocedural complication: 998.89)
958.91 Traumatic compartment syndrome of upper extremity

ICD-9-CM Procedural

77.89 Other partial ostectomy of other bone, except facial bones
80.99 Other excision of joint of other specified site
83.14 Fasciotomy
83.82 Graft of muscle or fascia

24358

24358 Tenotomy, elbow, lateral or medial (eg, epicondylitis, tennis elbow, golfer's elbow); debridement, soft tissue and/or bone, open

ICD-9-CM Diagnostic

719.42 Pain in joint, upper arm
726.31 Medial epicondylitis of elbow
726.32 Lateral epicondylitis of elbow
726.39 Other enthesopathy of elbow region
726.90 Enthesopathy of unspecified site ▽
727.09 Other synovitis and tenosynovitis
729.71 Nontraumatic compartment syndrome of upper extremity — (Code first, if applicable, postprocedural complication: 998.89)
958.91 Traumatic compartment syndrome of upper extremity

ICD-9-CM Procedural

77.89 Other partial ostectomy of other bone, except facial bones
80.99 Other excision of joint of other specified site
83.14 Fasciotomy
83.82 Graft of muscle or fascia

24359

24359 Tenotomy, elbow, lateral or medial (eg, epicondylitis, tennis elbow, golfer's elbow); debridement, soft tissue and/or bone, open with tendon repair or reattachment

ICD-9-CM Diagnostic

719.42 Pain in joint, upper arm
726.31 Medial epicondylitis of elbow
726.32 Lateral epicondylitis of elbow
726.39 Other enthesopathy of elbow region
726.90 Enthesopathy of unspecified site ▽
727.09 Other synovitis and tenosynovitis
729.71 Nontraumatic compartment syndrome of upper extremity — (Code first, if applicable, postprocedural complication: 998.89)
958.91 Traumatic compartment syndrome of upper extremity

ICD-9-CM Procedural

77.89 Other partial ostectomy of other bone, except facial bones
80.99 Other excision of joint of other specified site
83.14 Fasciotomy
83.82 Graft of muscle or fascia

24360

24360 Arthroplasty, elbow; with membrane (eg, fascial)

ICD-9-CM Diagnostic

357.1 Polyneuropathy in collagen vascular disease — (Code first underlying disease: 446.0, 710.0, 714.0) ☒
359.6 Symptomatic inflammatory myopathy in diseases classified elsewhere — (Code first underlying disease: 135, 140.0-208.9, 277.30-277.39, 446.0, 710.0, 710.1, 710.2, 714.0) ☒
446.0 Polyarteritis nodosa
710.0 Systemic lupus erythematosus — (Use additional code to identify manifestation: 424.91, 581.81, 582.81, 583.81)
710.1 Systemic sclerosis — (Use additional code to identify manifestation: 359.6, 517.2)
710.2 Sicca syndrome
711.02 Pyogenic arthritis, upper arm — (Use additional code to identify infectious organism: 041.0-041.8)
711.92 Unspecified infective arthritis, upper arm ▽
714.0 Rheumatoid arthritis — (Use additional code to identify manifestation: 357.1, 359.6)
715.12 Primary localized osteoarthrosis, upper arm
715.32 Localized osteoarthrosis not specified whether primary or secondary, upper arm
716.12 Traumatic arthropathy, upper arm
716.22 Allergic arthritis, upper arm
716.62 Unspecified monoarthritis, upper arm ▽
719.42 Pain in joint, upper arm
730.12 Chronic osteomyelitis, upper arm — (Use additional code to identify organism: 041.1. Use additional code to identify major osseous defect, if applicable: 731.3)
730.22 Unspecified osteomyelitis, upper arm — (Use additional code to identify organism: 041.1. Use additional code to identify major osseous defect, if applicable: 731.3) ▽
730.32 Periostitis, without mention of osteomyelitis, upper arm — (Use additional code to identify organism: 041.1)
730.82 Other infections involving bone diseases classified elsewhere, upper arm — (Use additional code to identify organism: 041.1. Code first underlying disease: 002.0, 015.0-015.9) ☒
731.0 Osteitis deformans without mention of bone tumor
731.3 Major osseous defects — (Code first underlying disease: 170.0-170.9, 730.00-730.29, 733.00-733.09, 733.40-733.49, 996.45)
733.49 Aseptic necrosis of other bone site — (Use additional code to identify major osseous defect, if applicable: 731.3)
733.82 Nonunion of fracture
736.00 Unspecified deformity of forearm, excluding fingers ▽
754.89 Other specified nonteratogenic anomalies
756.51 Osteogenesis imperfecta
812.40 Closed fracture of unspecified part of lower end of humerus ▽
812.41 Closed fracture of supracondylar humerus
812.42 Closed fracture of lateral condyle of humerus
812.43 Closed fracture of medial condyle of humerus
812.44 Closed fracture of unspecified condyle(s) of humerus ▽
812.49 Other closed fracture of lower end of humerus
812.50 Open fracture of unspecified part of lower end of humerus ▽
812.51 Open fracture of supracondylar humerus
812.52 Open fracture of lateral condyle of humerus
812.53 Open fracture of medial condyle of humerus
812.54 Open fracture of unspecified condyle(s) of humerus ▽
812.59 Other open fracture of lower end of humerus
813.00 Unspecified fracture of radius and ulna, upper end of forearm, closed ▽
813.02 Closed fracture of coronoid process of ulna
813.03 Closed Monteggia's fracture
813.04 Other and unspecified closed fractures of proximal end of ulna (alone) ▽
813.05 Closed fracture of head of radius
813.06 Closed fracture of neck of radius
813.07 Other and unspecified closed fractures of proximal end of radius (alone) ▽
813.08 Closed fracture of radius with ulna, upper end (any part)
813.10 Unspecified open fracture of upper end of forearm ▽
813.11 Open fracture of olecranon process of ulna
813.12 Open fracture of coronoid process of ulna
813.13 Open Monteggia's fracture
813.14 Other and unspecified open fractures of proximal end of ulna (alone) ▽
813.15 Open fracture of head of radius
813.16 Open fracture of neck of radius
813.17 Other and unspecified open fractures of proximal end of radius (alone) ▽
813.18 Open fracture of radius with ulna, upper end (any part)

ICD-9-CM Procedural

81.85 Other repair of elbow

24361-24362

24361 Arthroplasty, elbow; with distal humeral prosthetic replacement
24362 with implant and fascia lata ligament reconstruction

ICD-9-CM Diagnostic

357.1 Polyneuropathy in collagen vascular disease — (Code first underlying disease: 446.0, 710.0, 714.0) ⊠
359.6 Symptomatic inflammatory myopathy in diseases classified elsewhere — (Code first underlying disease: 135, 140.0-208.9, 277.30-277.39, 446.0, 710.0, 710.1, 710.2, 714.0) ⊠
446.0 Polyarteritis nodosa
710.0 Systemic lupus erythematosus — (Use additional code to identify manifestation: 424.91, 581.81, 582.81, 583.81)
710.1 Systemic sclerosis — (Use additional code to identify manifestation: 359.6, 517.2)
710.2 Sicca syndrome
711.02 Pyogenic arthritis, upper arm — (Use additional code to identify infectious organism: 041.0-041.8)
711.92 Unspecified infective arthritis, upper arm ▽
714.0 Rheumatoid arthritis — (Use additional code to identify manifestation: 357.1, 359.6)
715.12 Primary localized osteoarthrosis, upper arm
715.32 Localized osteoarthrosis not specified whether primary or secondary, upper arm
716.12 Traumatic arthropathy, upper arm
716.22 Allergic arthritis, upper arm
716.62 Unspecified monoarthritis, upper arm ▽
719.22 Villonodular synovitis, upper arm
719.42 Pain in joint, upper arm
730.12 Chronic osteomyelitis, upper arm — (Use additional code to identify organism: 041.1. Use additional code to identify major osseous defect, if applicable: 731.3)
730.22 Unspecified osteomyelitis, upper arm — (Use additional code to identify organism: 041.1. Use additional code to identify major osseous defect, if applicable: 731.3) ▽
730.32 Periostitis, without mention of osteomyelitis, upper arm — (Use additional code to identify organism: 041.1)
730.82 Other infections involving bone diseases classified elsewhere, upper arm — (Use additional code to identify organism: 041.1. Code first underlying disease: 002.0, 015.0-015.9) ⊠
731.0 Osteitis deformans without mention of bone tumor
731.3 Major osseous defects — (Code first underlying disease: 170.0-170.9, 730.00-730.29, 733.00-733.09, 733.40-733.49, 996.45)
733.49 Aseptic necrosis of other bone site — (Use additional code to identify major osseous defect, if applicable: 731.3)
733.82 Nonunion of fracture
736.00 Unspecified deformity of forearm, excluding fingers ▽
754.89 Other specified nonteratogenic anomalies
755.50 Unspecified congenital anomaly of upper limb ▽
756.51 Osteogenesis imperfecta
V88.29 Acquired absence of other joint

ICD-9-CM Procedural

81.85 Other repair of elbow

24363

24363 Arthroplasty, elbow; with distal humerus and proximal ulnar prosthetic replacement (eg, total elbow)

ICD-9-CM Diagnostic

357.1 Polyneuropathy in collagen vascular disease — (Code first underlying disease: 446.0, 710.0, 714.0) ⊠
359.6 Symptomatic inflammatory myopathy in diseases classified elsewhere — (Code first underlying disease: 135, 140.0-208.9, 277.30-277.39, 446.0, 710.0, 710.1, 710.2, 714.0) ⊠
446.0 Polyarteritis nodosa
710.0 Systemic lupus erythematosus — (Use additional code to identify manifestation: 424.91, 581.81, 582.81, 583.81)
710.1 Systemic sclerosis — (Use additional code to identify manifestation: 359.6, 517.2)
710.2 Sicca syndrome
711.02 Pyogenic arthritis, upper arm — (Use additional code to identify infectious organism: 041.0-041.8)
711.92 Unspecified infective arthritis, upper arm ▽
714.0 Rheumatoid arthritis — (Use additional code to identify manifestation: 357.1, 359.6)
715.12 Primary localized osteoarthrosis, upper arm
715.32 Localized osteoarthrosis not specified whether primary or secondary, upper arm
716.12 Traumatic arthropathy, upper arm
716.22 Allergic arthritis, upper arm
716.62 Unspecified monoarthritis, upper arm ▽
719.22 Villonodular synovitis, upper arm
719.42 Pain in joint, upper arm
730.12 Chronic osteomyelitis, upper arm — (Use additional code to identify organism: 041.1. Use additional code to identify major osseous defect, if applicable: 731.3)
730.22 Unspecified osteomyelitis, upper arm — (Use additional code to identify organism: 041.1. Use additional code to identify major osseous defect, if applicable: 731.3) ▽
730.32 Periostitis, without mention of osteomyelitis, upper arm — (Use additional code to identify organism: 041.1)
730.82 Other infections involving bone diseases classified elsewhere, upper arm — (Use additional code to identify organism: 041.1. Code first underlying disease: 002.0, 015.0-015.9) ⊠
731.0 Osteitis deformans without mention of bone tumor
731.3 Major osseous defects — (Code first underlying disease: 170.0-170.9, 730.00-730.29, 733.00-733.09, 733.40-733.49, 996.45)
733.49 Aseptic necrosis of other bone site — (Use additional code to identify major osseous defect, if applicable: 731.3)
733.82 Nonunion of fracture
736.00 Unspecified deformity of forearm, excluding fingers ▽
754.89 Other specified nonteratogenic anomalies
755.50 Unspecified congenital anomaly of upper limb ▽
756.51 Osteogenesis imperfecta
812.40 Closed fracture of unspecified part of lower end of humerus ▽
812.41 Closed fracture of supracondylar humerus
812.49 Other closed fracture of lower end of humerus
812.50 Open fracture of unspecified part of lower end of humerus ▽
812.51 Open fracture of supracondylar humerus
812.59 Other open fracture of lower end of humerus
813.01 Closed fracture of olecranon process of ulna
813.02 Closed fracture of coronoid process of ulna
813.03 Closed Monteggia's fracture
813.04 Other and unspecified closed fractures of proximal end of ulna (alone) ▽
813.11 Open fracture of olecranon process of ulna
813.12 Open fracture of coronoid process of ulna
813.13 Open Monteggia's fracture
813.14 Other and unspecified open fractures of proximal end of ulna (alone) ▽
V88.29 Acquired absence of other joint

ICD-9-CM Procedural

81.84 Total elbow replacement

24365-24366

24365 Arthroplasty, radial head;
24366 with implant

ICD-9-CM Diagnostic

357.1 Polyneuropathy in collagen vascular disease — (Code first underlying disease: 446.0, 710.0, 714.0) ⊠

▽ Unspecified code ⊠ Manifestation code [Resequenced code]
♀ Female diagnosis ♂ Male diagnosis

359.6 Symptomatic inflammatory myopathy in diseases classified elsewhere — (Code first underlying disease: 135, 140.0-208.9, 277.30-277.39, 446.0, 710.0, 710.1, 710.2, 714.0) ☒
446.0 Polyarteritis nodosa
710.0 Systemic lupus erythematosus — (Use additional code to identify manifestation: 424.91, 581.81, 582.81, 583.81)
710.1 Systemic sclerosis — (Use additional code to identify manifestation: 359.6, 517.2)
710.2 Sicca syndrome
711.02 Pyogenic arthritis, upper arm — (Use additional code to identify infectious organism: 041.0-041.8)
711.92 Unspecified infective arthritis, upper arm ▽
714.0 Rheumatoid arthritis — (Use additional code to identify manifestation: 357.1, 359.6)
715.00 Generalized osteoarthrosis, unspecified site ▽
715.12 Primary localized osteoarthrosis, upper arm
715.32 Localized osteoarthrosis not specified whether primary or secondary, upper arm
716.12 Traumatic arthropathy, upper arm
716.22 Allergic arthritis, upper arm
716.62 Unspecified monoarthritis, upper arm ▽
718.82 Other joint derangement, not elsewhere classified, upper arm
719.22 Villonodular synovitis, upper arm
719.42 Pain in joint, upper arm
719.52 Stiffness of joint, not elsewhere classified, upper arm
730.12 Chronic osteomyelitis, upper arm — (Use additional code to identify organism: 041.1. Use additional code to identify major osseous defect, if applicable: 731.3)
730.22 Unspecified osteomyelitis, upper arm — (Use additional code to identify organism: 041.1. Use additional code to identify major osseous defect, if applicable: 731.3) ▽
730.32 Periostitis, without mention of osteomyelitis, upper arm — (Use additional code to identify organism: 041.1)
730.82 Other infections involving bone diseases classified elsewhere, upper arm — (Use additional code to identify organism: 041.1. Code first underlying disease: 002.0, 015.0-015.9) ☒
731.0 Osteitis deformans without mention of bone tumor
731.3 Major osseous defects — (Code first underlying disease: 170.0-170.9, 730.00-730.29, 733.00-733.09, 733.40-733.49, 996.45)
733.49 Aseptic necrosis of other bone site — (Use additional code to identify major osseous defect, if applicable: 731.3)
733.82 Nonunion of fracture
736.00 Unspecified deformity of forearm, excluding fingers ▽
756.51 Osteogenesis imperfecta

ICD-9-CM Procedural

81.85 Other repair of elbow

24370-24371

24370 Revision of total elbow arthroplasty, including allograft when performed; humeral or ulnar component
24371 humeral and ulnar component

ICD-9-CM Diagnostic

733.11 Pathologic fracture of humerus
733.19 Pathologic fracture of other specified site
733.95 Stress fracture of other bone — (Use additional external cause code(s) to identify the cause of the stress fracture)
996.41 Mechanical loosening of prosthetic joint — (Use additional code to identify prosthetic joint with mechanical complication, V43.60-V43.69)
996.42 Dislocation of prosthetic joint — (Use additional code to identify prosthetic joint with mechanical complication, V43.60-V43.69)
996.43 Broken prosthetic joint implant — (Use additional code to identify prosthetic joint with mechanical complication, V43.60-V43.69)
996.44 Peri-prosthetic fracture around prosthetic joint — (Use additional code to identify prosthetic joint with mechanical complication, V43.60-V43.69.
996.45 Peri-prosthetic osteolysis — (Use additional code to identify prosthetic joint with mechanical complication, V43.60-V43.69. Use additional code to identify major osseous defect, if applicable: 731.3)
996.46 Articular bearing surface wear of prosthetic joint — (Use additional code to identify prosthetic joint with mechanical complication, V43.60-V43.69)
996.47 Other mechanical complication of prosthetic joint implant — (Use additional code to identify prosthetic joint with mechanical complication, V43.60-V43.69)
996.66 Infection and inflammatory reaction due to internal joint prosthesis — (Use additional code to identify specified infections. Use additional code to identify infected prosthetic joint: V43.60-V43.69)
996.77 Other complications due to internal joint prosthesis — (Use additional code to identify complication: 338.18-338.19, 338.28-338.29)
998.89 Other specified complications
V54.82 Aftercare following explantation of joint prosthesis

ICD-9-CM Procedural

81.97 Revision of joint replacement of upper extremity

24400

24400 Osteotomy, humerus, with or without internal fixation

ICD-9-CM Diagnostic

170.4 Malignant neoplasm of scapula and long bones of upper limb
213.4 Benign neoplasm of scapula and long bones of upper limb
715.10 Primary localized osteoarthrosis, unspecified site ▽
715.22 Secondary localized osteoarthrosis, upper arm
715.32 Localized osteoarthrosis not specified whether primary or secondary, upper arm
730.12 Chronic osteomyelitis, upper arm — (Use additional code to identify organism: 041.1. Use additional code to identify major osseous defect, if applicable: 731.3)
731.3 Major osseous defects — (Code first underlying disease: 170.0-170.9, 730.00-730.29, 733.00-733.09, 733.40-733.49, 996.45)
733.11 Pathologic fracture of humerus
733.41 Aseptic necrosis of head of humerus — (Use additional code to identify major osseous defect, if applicable: 731.3)
733.81 Malunion of fracture
733.82 Nonunion of fracture
736.89 Other acquired deformity of other parts of limb
756.4 Chondrodystrophy
756.51 Osteogenesis imperfecta
812.21 Closed fracture of shaft of humerus
812.31 Open fracture of shaft of humerus
812.49 Other closed fracture of lower end of humerus

ICD-9-CM Procedural

77.22 Wedge osteotomy of humerus
77.32 Other division of humerus

24410

24410 Multiple osteotomies with realignment on intramedullary rod, humeral shaft (Sofield type procedure)

ICD-9-CM Diagnostic

170.4 Malignant neoplasm of scapula and long bones of upper limb
213.4 Benign neoplasm of scapula and long bones of upper limb
715.12 Primary localized osteoarthrosis, upper arm
715.22 Secondary localized osteoarthrosis, upper arm
715.32 Localized osteoarthrosis not specified whether primary or secondary, upper arm
730.12 Chronic osteomyelitis, upper arm — (Use additional code to identify organism: 041.1. Use additional code to identify major osseous defect, if applicable: 731.3)
731.3 Major osseous defects — (Code first underlying disease: 170.0-170.9, 730.00-730.29, 733.00-733.09, 733.40-733.49, 996.45)
733.11 Pathologic fracture of humerus

▽ Unspecified code ☒ Manifestation code
♀ Female diagnosis ♂ Male diagnosis

733.41 Aseptic necrosis of head of humerus — (Use additional code to identify major osseous defect, if applicable: 731.3)
733.81 Malunion of fracture
733.82 Nonunion of fracture
736.89 Other acquired deformity of other parts of limb
756.4 Chondrodystrophy
756.51 Osteogenesis imperfecta
V54.02 Encounter for lengthening/adjustment of growth rod

ICD-9-CM Procedural

77.32 Other division of humerus

24420

24420 Osteoplasty, humerus (eg, shortening or lengthening) (excluding 64876)

ICD-9-CM Diagnostic

170.4 Malignant neoplasm of scapula and long bones of upper limb
198.5 Secondary malignant neoplasm of bone and bone marrow
213.4 Benign neoplasm of scapula and long bones of upper limb
715.10 Primary localized osteoarthrosis, unspecified site ▽
715.22 Secondary localized osteoarthrosis, upper arm
715.31 Localized osteoarthrosis not specified whether primary or secondary, shoulder region
715.32 Localized osteoarthrosis not specified whether primary or secondary, upper arm
730.12 Chronic osteomyelitis, upper arm — (Use additional code to identify organism: 041.1. Use additional code to identify major osseous defect, if applicable: 731.3)
731.3 Major osseous defects — (Code first underlying disease: 170.0-170.9, 730.00-730.29, 733.00-733.09, 733.40-733.49, 996.45)
733.41 Aseptic necrosis of head of humerus — (Use additional code to identify major osseous defect, if applicable: 731.3)
733.81 Malunion of fracture
733.82 Nonunion of fracture
733.91 Arrest of bone development or growth
736.89 Other acquired deformity of other parts of limb
756.4 Chondrodystrophy
756.51 Osteogenesis imperfecta

ICD-9-CM Procedural

77.32 Other division of humerus
78.12 Application of external fixator device, humerus
78.22 Limb shortening procedures, humerus
78.32 Limb lengthening procedures, humerus
84.53 Implantation of internal limb lengthening device with kinetic distraction
84.54 Implantation of other internal limb lengthening device
84.71 Application of external fixator device, monoplanar system
84.72 Application of external fixator device, ring system
84.73 Application of hybrid external fixator device

24430-24435

24430 Repair of nonunion or malunion, humerus; without graft (eg, compression technique)
24435 with iliac or other autograft (includes obtaining graft)

ICD-9-CM Diagnostic

733.81 Malunion of fracture
733.82 Nonunion of fracture

ICD-9-CM Procedural

77.79 Excision of other bone for graft, except facial bones
78.02 Bone graft of humerus
78.42 Other repair or plastic operation on humerus

24470

24470 Hemiepiphyseal arrest (eg, cubitus varus or valgus, distal humerus)

ICD-9-CM Diagnostic

268.1 Rickets, late effect — (Use additional code to identify the nature of late effect)
736.01 Cubitus valgus (acquired)
736.02 Cubitus varus (acquired)
755.59 Other congenital anomaly of upper limb, including shoulder girdle

ICD-9-CM Procedural

78.22 Limb shortening procedures, humerus

24495

24495 Decompression fasciotomy, forearm, with brachial artery exploration

ICD-9-CM Diagnostic

682.3 Cellulitis and abscess of upper arm and forearm — (Use additional code to identify organism, such as 041.1, etc.)
728.88 Rhabdomyolysis
729.71 Nontraumatic compartment syndrome of upper extremity — (Code first, if applicable, postprocedural complication: 998.89)
813.21 Closed fracture of shaft of radius (alone)
813.22 Closed fracture of shaft of ulna (alone)
813.23 Closed fracture of shaft of radius with ulna
813.31 Open fracture of shaft of radius (alone)
813.32 Open fracture of shaft of ulna (alone)
813.33 Open fracture of shaft of radius with ulna
813.80 Closed fracture of unspecified part of forearm ▽
813.90 Open fracture of unspecified part of forearm ▽
832.00 Closed unspecified dislocation of elbow
832.10 Open unspecified dislocation of elbow ▽
881.01 Open wound of elbow, without mention of complication
881.10 Open wound of forearm, complicated
881.11 Open wound of elbow, complicated
881.20 Open wound of forearm, with tendon involvement
903.1 Brachial blood vessels injury
923.10 Contusion of forearm
923.11 Contusion of elbow
927.10 Crushing injury of forearm — (Use additional code to identify any associated injuries: 800-829, 850.0-854.1, 860.0-869.1)
927.11 Crushing injury of elbow — (Use additional code to identify any associated injuries: 800-829, 850.0-854.1, 860.0-869.1)
958.8 Other early complications of trauma
958.91 Traumatic compartment syndrome of upper extremity

ICD-9-CM Procedural

83.14 Fasciotomy

24498

24498 Prophylactic treatment (nailing, pinning, plating or wiring), with or without methylmethacrylate, humeral shaft

ICD-9-CM Diagnostic

170.4 Malignant neoplasm of scapula and long bones of upper limb
198.5 Secondary malignant neoplasm of bone and bone marrow
213.4 Benign neoplasm of scapula and long bones of upper limb
238.0 Neoplasm of uncertain behavior of bone and articular cartilage
239.2 Neoplasms of unspecified nature of bone, soft tissue, and skin
732.3 Juvenile osteochondrosis of upper extremity
733.11 Pathologic fracture of humerus
756.4 Chondrodystrophy
756.51 Osteogenesis imperfecta

ICD-9-CM Procedural

78.52 Internal fixation of humerus without fracture reduction
84.55 Insertion of bone void filler

24500-24505

24500 Closed treatment of humeral shaft fracture; without manipulation
24505 with manipulation, with or without skeletal traction

ICD-9-CM Diagnostic

733.11 Pathologic fracture of humerus
812.21 Closed fracture of shaft of humerus

ICD-9-CM Procedural

79.01 Closed reduction of fracture of humerus without internal fixation
93.43 Intermittent skeletal traction
93.44 Other skeletal traction
93.53 Application of other cast
93.54 Application of splint

HCPCS Level II Supplies & Services

A4565 Slings

24515-24516

24515 Open treatment of humeral shaft fracture with plate/screws, with or without cerclage
24516 Treatment of humeral shaft fracture, with insertion of intramedullary implant, with or without cerclage and/or locking screws

ICD-9-CM Diagnostic

733.11 Pathologic fracture of humerus
812.21 Closed fracture of shaft of humerus
812.31 Open fracture of shaft of humerus

ICD-9-CM Procedural

79.21 Open reduction of fracture of humerus without internal fixation
79.31 Open reduction of fracture of humerus with internal fixation

24530-24535

24530 Closed treatment of supracondylar or transcondylar humeral fracture, with or without intercondylar extension; without manipulation
24535 with manipulation, with or without skin or skeletal traction

ICD-9-CM Diagnostic

733.11 Pathologic fracture of humerus
812.40 Closed fracture of unspecified part of lower end of humerus ▽
812.41 Closed fracture of supracondylar humerus
812.42 Closed fracture of lateral condyle of humerus
812.43 Closed fracture of medial condyle of humerus
812.44 Closed fracture of unspecified condyle(s) of humerus ▽
812.49 Other closed fracture of lower end of humerus

ICD-9-CM Procedural

79.01 Closed reduction of fracture of humerus without internal fixation
79.11 Closed reduction of fracture of humerus with internal fixation
93.43 Intermittent skeletal traction
93.44 Other skeletal traction
93.46 Other skin traction of limbs
93.53 Application of other cast
93.54 Application of splint

HCPCS Level II Supplies & Services

A4570 Splint

24538

24538 Percutaneous skeletal fixation of supracondylar or transcondylar humeral fracture, with or without intercondylar extension

ICD-9-CM Diagnostic

733.11 Pathologic fracture of humerus
812.20 Closed fracture of unspecified part of humerus ▽
812.40 Closed fracture of unspecified part of lower end of humerus ▽
812.41 Closed fracture of supracondylar humerus
812.42 Closed fracture of lateral condyle of humerus
812.43 Closed fracture of medial condyle of humerus
812.49 Other closed fracture of lower end of humerus

ICD-9-CM Procedural

78.52 Internal fixation of humerus without fracture reduction
79.11 Closed reduction of fracture of humerus with internal fixation

HCPCS Level II Supplies & Services

A4565 Slings

24545-24546

24545 Open treatment of humeral supracondylar or transcondylar fracture, includes internal fixation, when performed; without intercondylar extension
24546 with intercondylar extension

ICD-9-CM Diagnostic

733.11 Pathologic fracture of humerus
812.40 Closed fracture of unspecified part of lower end of humerus ▽
812.41 Closed fracture of supracondylar humerus
812.42 Closed fracture of lateral condyle of humerus
812.43 Closed fracture of medial condyle of humerus
812.49 Other closed fracture of lower end of humerus
812.50 Open fracture of unspecified part of lower end of humerus ▽
812.51 Open fracture of supracondylar humerus
812.52 Open fracture of lateral condyle of humerus
812.53 Open fracture of medial condyle of humerus
812.54 Open fracture of unspecified condyle(s) of humerus ▽
812.59 Other open fracture of lower end of humerus

ICD-9-CM Procedural

79.21 Open reduction of fracture of humerus without internal fixation
79.31 Open reduction of fracture of humerus with internal fixation

24560-24565

24560 Closed treatment of humeral epicondylar fracture, medial or lateral; without manipulation
24565 with manipulation

ICD-9-CM Diagnostic

733.11 Pathologic fracture of humerus
812.40 Closed fracture of unspecified part of lower end of humerus ▽
812.42 Closed fracture of lateral condyle of humerus
812.43 Closed fracture of medial condyle of humerus
812.44 Closed fracture of unspecified condyle(s) of humerus ▽
812.49 Other closed fracture of lower end of humerus

ICD-9-CM Procedural

79.01 Closed reduction of fracture of humerus without internal fixation
93.54 Application of splint

HCPCS Level II Supplies & Services

A4570 Splint

24566

24566 Percutaneous skeletal fixation of humeral epicondylar fracture, medial or lateral, with manipulation

ICD-9-CM Diagnostic

733.11 Pathologic fracture of humerus
812.40 Closed fracture of unspecified part of lower end of humerus ▽
812.42 Closed fracture of lateral condyle of humerus
812.43 Closed fracture of medial condyle of humerus
812.44 Closed fracture of unspecified condyle(s) of humerus ▽
812.49 Other closed fracture of lower end of humerus

ICD-9-CM Procedural

79.11 Closed reduction of fracture of humerus with internal fixation

HCPCS Level II Supplies & Services

A4305 Disposable drug delivery system, flow rate of 50 ml or greater per hour

24575

24575 Open treatment of humeral epicondylar fracture, medial or lateral, includes internal fixation, when performed

ICD-9-CM Diagnostic

733.11 Pathologic fracture of humerus
812.40 Closed fracture of unspecified part of lower end of humerus ▽
812.42 Closed fracture of lateral condyle of humerus
812.43 Closed fracture of medial condyle of humerus
812.49 Other closed fracture of lower end of humerus
812.50 Open fracture of unspecified part of lower end of humerus ▽
812.52 Open fracture of lateral condyle of humerus
812.53 Open fracture of medial condyle of humerus
812.54 Open fracture of unspecified condyle(s) of humerus ▽
812.59 Other open fracture of lower end of humerus

ICD-9-CM Procedural

79.21 Open reduction of fracture of humerus without internal fixation
79.31 Open reduction of fracture of humerus with internal fixation

24576-24577

24576 Closed treatment of humeral condylar fracture, medial or lateral; without manipulation
24577 with manipulation

ICD-9-CM Diagnostic

733.11 Pathologic fracture of humerus
812.40 Closed fracture of unspecified part of lower end of humerus ▽
812.41 Closed fracture of supracondylar humerus
812.42 Closed fracture of lateral condyle of humerus
812.43 Closed fracture of medial condyle of humerus
812.44 Closed fracture of unspecified condyle(s) of humerus ▽
812.49 Other closed fracture of lower end of humerus

ICD-9-CM Procedural

79.01 Closed reduction of fracture of humerus without internal fixation
93.54 Application of splint

HCPCS Level II Supplies & Services

A4570 Splint

24579

24579 Open treatment of humeral condylar fracture, medial or lateral, includes internal fixation, when performed

ICD-9-CM Diagnostic

733.11 Pathologic fracture of humerus
812.40 Closed fracture of unspecified part of lower end of humerus ▽
812.42 Closed fracture of lateral condyle of humerus
812.43 Closed fracture of medial condyle of humerus
812.44 Closed fracture of unspecified condyle(s) of humerus ▽
812.49 Other closed fracture of lower end of humerus
812.50 Open fracture of unspecified part of lower end of humerus ▽
812.52 Open fracture of lateral condyle of humerus
812.53 Open fracture of medial condyle of humerus
812.54 Open fracture of unspecified condyle(s) of humerus ▽
812.59 Other open fracture of lower end of humerus

ICD-9-CM Procedural

79.21 Open reduction of fracture of humerus without internal fixation
79.31 Open reduction of fracture of humerus with internal fixation

24582

24582 Percutaneous skeletal fixation of humeral condylar fracture, medial or lateral, with manipulation

ICD-9-CM Diagnostic

733.11 Pathologic fracture of humerus
812.40 Closed fracture of unspecified part of lower end of humerus ▽
812.42 Closed fracture of lateral condyle of humerus
812.43 Closed fracture of medial condyle of humerus
812.44 Closed fracture of unspecified condyle(s) of humerus ▽
812.49 Other closed fracture of lower end of humerus

ICD-9-CM Procedural

79.11 Closed reduction of fracture of humerus with internal fixation

HCPCS Level II Supplies & Services

A4570 Splint

24586-24587

24586 Open treatment of periarticular fracture and/or dislocation of the elbow (fracture distal humerus and proximal ulna and/or proximal radius);
24587 with implant arthroplasty

ICD-9-CM Diagnostic

718.72 Developmental dislocation of joint, upper arm
733.11 Pathologic fracture of humerus
733.19 Pathologic fracture of other specified site
812.40 Closed fracture of unspecified part of lower end of humerus ▽
812.41 Closed fracture of supracondylar humerus
812.42 Closed fracture of lateral condyle of humerus
812.43 Closed fracture of medial condyle of humerus
812.44 Closed fracture of unspecified condyle(s) of humerus ▽
812.49 Other closed fracture of lower end of humerus
812.50 Open fracture of unspecified part of lower end of humerus ▽
812.51 Open fracture of supracondylar humerus
812.52 Open fracture of lateral condyle of humerus
812.53 Open fracture of medial condyle of humerus
812.54 Open fracture of unspecified condyle(s) of humerus ▽
812.59 Other open fracture of lower end of humerus
813.00 Unspecified fracture of radius and ulna, upper end of forearm, closed ▽
813.01 Closed fracture of olecranon process of ulna
813.02 Closed fracture of coronoid process of ulna
813.04 Other and unspecified closed fractures of proximal end of ulna (alone) ▽
813.05 Closed fracture of head of radius
813.06 Closed fracture of neck of radius
813.07 Other and unspecified closed fractures of proximal end of radius (alone) ▽

813.08 Closed fracture of radius with ulna, upper end (any part)
813.10 Unspecified open fracture of upper end of forearm ▽
813.11 Open fracture of olecranon process of ulna
813.12 Open fracture of coronoid process of ulna
813.14 Other and unspecified open fractures of proximal end of ulna (alone) ▽
813.15 Open fracture of head of radius
813.17 Other and unspecified open fractures of proximal end of radius (alone) ▽
813.18 Open fracture of radius with ulna, upper end (any part)
832.01 Closed anterior dislocation of elbow
832.02 Closed posterior dislocation of elbow
832.03 Closed medial dislocation of elbow
832.04 Closed lateral dislocation of elbow
832.09 Closed dislocation of other site of elbow
832.10 Open unspecified dislocation of elbow ▽
832.11 Open anterior dislocation of elbow
832.12 Open posterior dislocation of elbow
832.13 Open medial dislocation of elbow
832.14 Open lateral dislocation of elbow
832.19 Open dislocation of other site of elbow

ICD-9-CM Procedural

79.21 Open reduction of fracture of humerus without internal fixation
79.32 Open reduction of fracture of radius and ulna with internal fixation
79.82 Open reduction of dislocation of elbow
81.84 Total elbow replacement

24600-24605

24600 Treatment of closed elbow dislocation; without anesthesia
24605 requiring anesthesia

ICD-9-CM Diagnostic

718.72 Developmental dislocation of joint, upper arm
832.00 Closed unspecified dislocation of elbow
832.01 Closed anterior dislocation of elbow
832.02 Closed posterior dislocation of elbow
832.03 Closed medial dislocation of elbow
832.04 Closed lateral dislocation of elbow
832.09 Closed dislocation of other site of elbow
832.2 Nursemaid's elbow

ICD-9-CM Procedural

79.72 Closed reduction of dislocation of elbow

HCPCS Level II Supplies & Services

A4570 Splint

24615

24615 Open treatment of acute or chronic elbow dislocation

ICD-9-CM Diagnostic

718.32 Recurrent dislocation of upper arm joint
718.72 Developmental dislocation of joint, upper arm
754.89 Other specified nonteratogenic anomalies
832.01 Closed anterior dislocation of elbow
832.02 Closed posterior dislocation of elbow
832.03 Closed medial dislocation of elbow
832.04 Closed lateral dislocation of elbow
832.09 Closed dislocation of other site of elbow
832.10 Open unspecified dislocation of elbow ▽
832.11 Open anterior dislocation of elbow
832.12 Open posterior dislocation of elbow
832.13 Open medial dislocation of elbow
832.14 Open lateral dislocation of elbow
832.19 Open dislocation of other site of elbow

ICD-9-CM Procedural

79.82 Open reduction of dislocation of elbow

24620

24620 Closed treatment of Monteggia type of fracture dislocation at elbow (fracture proximal end of ulna with dislocation of radial head), with manipulation

ICD-9-CM Diagnostic

733.19 Pathologic fracture of other specified site
813.03 Closed Monteggia's fracture
813.13 Open Monteggia's fracture

ICD-9-CM Procedural

79.02 Closed reduction of fracture of radius and ulna without internal fixation
79.72 Closed reduction of dislocation of elbow

HCPCS Level II Supplies & Services

A4570 Splint

24635

24635 Open treatment of Monteggia type of fracture dislocation at elbow (fracture proximal end of ulna with dislocation of radial head), includes internal fixation, when performed

ICD-9-CM Diagnostic

813.03 Closed Monteggia's fracture
813.13 Open Monteggia's fracture

ICD-9-CM Procedural

79.22 Open reduction of fracture of radius and ulna without internal fixation
79.32 Open reduction of fracture of radius and ulna with internal fixation
79.82 Open reduction of dislocation of elbow
81.85 Other repair of elbow

24640

24640 Closed treatment of radial head subluxation in child, nursemaid elbow, with manipulation

ICD-9-CM Diagnostic

832.2 Nursemaid's elbow

ICD-9-CM Procedural

79.72 Closed reduction of dislocation of elbow

HCPCS Level II Supplies & Services

A4570 Splint

24650-24655

24650 Closed treatment of radial head or neck fracture; without manipulation
24655 with manipulation

ICD-9-CM Diagnostic

733.19 Pathologic fracture of other specified site
813.05 Closed fracture of head of radius
813.06 Closed fracture of neck of radius
813.07 Other and unspecified closed fractures of proximal end of radius (alone) ▽

ICD-9-CM Procedural

79.02 Closed reduction of fracture of radius and ulna without internal fixation
93.54 Application of splint

HCPCS Level II Supplies & Services

A4570 Splint

24665-24666

24665 Open treatment of radial head or neck fracture, includes internal fixation or radial head excision, when performed;
24666 with radial head prosthetic replacement

ICD-9-CM Diagnostic

733.19 Pathologic fracture of other specified site
733.81 Malunion of fracture
813.05 Closed fracture of head of radius
813.06 Closed fracture of neck of radius
813.07 Other and unspecified closed fractures of proximal end of radius (alone) ▽
813.15 Open fracture of head of radius
813.16 Open fracture of neck of radius
813.17 Other and unspecified open fractures of proximal end of radius (alone) ▽

ICD-9-CM Procedural

77.83 Other partial ostectomy of radius and ulna
79.22 Open reduction of fracture of radius and ulna without internal fixation
79.32 Open reduction of fracture of radius and ulna with internal fixation
81.85 Other repair of elbow

24670-24675

24670 Closed treatment of ulnar fracture, proximal end (eg, olecranon or coronoid process[es]); without manipulation
24675 with manipulation

ICD-9-CM Diagnostic

733.19 Pathologic fracture of other specified site
813.01 Closed fracture of olecranon process of ulna
813.02 Closed fracture of coronoid process of ulna
813.04 Other and unspecified closed fractures of proximal end of ulna (alone) ▽

ICD-9-CM Procedural

79.02 Closed reduction of fracture of radius and ulna without internal fixation
93.54 Application of splint

HCPCS Level II Supplies & Services

A4570 Splint

24685

24685 Open treatment of ulnar fracture, proximal end (eg, olecranon or coronoid process[es]), includes internal fixation, when performed

ICD-9-CM Diagnostic

733.19 Pathologic fracture of other specified site
733.82 Nonunion of fracture
813.01 Closed fracture of olecranon process of ulna
813.02 Closed fracture of coronoid process of ulna
813.04 Other and unspecified closed fractures of proximal end of ulna (alone) ▽
813.11 Open fracture of olecranon process of ulna
813.12 Open fracture of coronoid process of ulna
813.14 Other and unspecified open fractures of proximal end of ulna (alone) ▽

ICD-9-CM Procedural

79.22 Open reduction of fracture of radius and ulna without internal fixation
79.32 Open reduction of fracture of radius and ulna with internal fixation

24800-24802

24800 Arthrodesis, elbow joint; local
24802 with autogenous graft (includes obtaining graft)

ICD-9-CM Diagnostic

171.2 Malignant neoplasm of connective and other soft tissue of upper limb, including shoulder
198.5 Secondary malignant neoplasm of bone and bone marrow
238.0 Neoplasm of uncertain behavior of bone and articular cartilage
239.2 Neoplasms of unspecified nature of bone, soft tissue, and skin
357.1 Polyneuropathy in collagen vascular disease — (Code first underlying disease: 446.0, 710.0, 714.0) ☒
359.6 Symptomatic inflammatory myopathy in diseases classified elsewhere — (Code first underlying disease: 135, 140.0-208.9, 277.30-277.39, 446.0, 710.0, 710.1, 710.2, 714.0) ☒
446.0 Polyarteritis nodosa
710.0 Systemic lupus erythematosus — (Use additional code to identify manifestation: 424.91, 581.81, 582.81, 583.81)
710.1 Systemic sclerosis — (Use additional code to identify manifestation: 359.6, 517.2)
710.2 Sicca syndrome
711.02 Pyogenic arthritis, upper arm — (Use additional code to identify infectious organism: 041.0-041.8)
714.0 Rheumatoid arthritis — (Use additional code to identify manifestation: 357.1, 359.6)
714.1 Felty's syndrome
714.2 Other rheumatoid arthritis with visceral or systemic involvement
714.4 Chronic postrheumatic arthropathy
714.9 Unspecified inflammatory polyarthropathy ▽
715.12 Primary localized osteoarthrosis, upper arm
715.32 Localized osteoarthrosis not specified whether primary or secondary, upper arm
716.12 Traumatic arthropathy, upper arm
716.82 Other specified arthropathy, upper arm
716.92 Unspecified arthropathy, upper arm ▽
719.42 Pain in joint, upper arm
728.0 Infective myositis
728.10 Unspecified calcification and ossification ▽
728.11 Progressive myositis ossificans
728.12 Traumatic myositis ossificans
728.13 Postoperative heterotopic calcification
728.19 Other muscular calcification and ossification
728.3 Other specific muscle disorders
728.81 Interstitial myositis
730.12 Chronic osteomyelitis, upper arm — (Use additional code to identify organism: 041.1. Use additional code to identify major osseous defect, if applicable: 731.3)
731.3 Major osseous defects — (Code first underlying disease: 170.0-170.9, 730.00-730.29, 733.00-733.09, 733.40-733.49, 996.45)
V88.29 Acquired absence of other joint

ICD-9-CM Procedural

81.24 Arthrodesis of elbow

24900-24920

24900 Amputation, arm through humerus; with primary closure
24920 open, circular (guillotine)

ICD-9-CM Diagnostic

170.4 Malignant neoplasm of scapula and long bones of upper limb
171.2 Malignant neoplasm of connective and other soft tissue of upper limb, including shoulder
198.5 Secondary malignant neoplasm of bone and bone marrow
249.70 Secondary diabetes mellitus with peripheral circulatory disorders, not stated as uncontrolled, or unspecified — (Use additional code to identify manifestation: 443.81, 785.4) (Use additional code to identify any associated insulin use: V58.67)
249.71 Secondary diabetes mellitus with peripheral circulatory disorders, uncontrolled — (Use additional code to identify manifestation: 443.81, 785.4) (Use additional code to identify any associated insulin use: V58.67)
250.70 Diabetes with peripheral circulatory disorders, type II or unspecified type, not stated as uncontrolled — (Use additional code to identify manifestation: 443.81, 785.4)

250.71 Diabetes with peripheral circulatory disorders, type I [juvenile type], not stated as uncontrolled — (Use additional code to identify manifestation: 443.81, 785.4)
250.72 Diabetes with peripheral circulatory disorders, type II or unspecified type, uncontrolled — (Use additional code to identify manifestation: 443.81, 785.4)
250.73 Diabetes with peripheral circulatory disorders, type I [juvenile type], uncontrolled — (Use additional code to identify manifestation: 443.81, 785.4)
250.80 Diabetes with other specified manifestations, type II or unspecified type, not stated as uncontrolled — (Use additional code to identify manifestation: 707.10-707.19, 707.8, 707.9, 731.8)
250.81 Diabetes with other specified manifestations, type I [juvenile type], not stated as uncontrolled — (Use additional code to identify manifestation: 707.10-707.19, 707.8, 707.9, 731.8)
250.82 Diabetes with other specified manifestations, type II or unspecified type, uncontrolled — (Use additional code to identify manifestation: 707.10-707.19, 707.8, 707.9, 731.8)
250.83 Diabetes with other specified manifestations, type I [juvenile type], uncontrolled — (Use additional code to identify manifestation: 707.10-707.19, 707.8, 707.9, 731.8)
440.24 Atherosclerosis of native arteries of the extremities with gangrene — (Use additional code for any associated ulceration: 707.10-707.19, 707.8, 707.9)
443.81 Peripheral angiopathy in diseases classified elsewhere — (Code first underlying disease: 249.7, 250.7) ☒
443.9 Unspecified peripheral vascular disease ▽
444.21 Embolism and thrombosis of arteries of upper extremity
445.01 Atheroembolism of upper extremity
446.0 Polyarteritis nodosa
728.86 Necrotizing fasciitis — (Use additional code to identify infectious organism, 041.00-041.89, 785.4, if applicable)
730.12 Chronic osteomyelitis, upper arm — (Use additional code to identify organism: 041.1. Use additional code to identify major osseous defect, if applicable: 731.3)
731.1 Osteitis deformans in diseases classified elsewhere — (Code first underlying disease: 170.0-170.9) ☒
731.3 Major osseous defects — (Code first underlying disease: 170.0-170.9, 730.00-730.29, 733.00-733.09, 733.40-733.49, 996.45)
731.8 Other bone involvement in diseases classified elsewhere — (Code first underlying disease: 249.8, 250.8. Use additional code to specify bone condition: 730.00-730.09) ☒
785.4 Gangrene — (Code first any associated underlying condition)
812.49 Other closed fracture of lower end of humerus
812.59 Other open fracture of lower end of humerus
880.13 Open wound of upper arm, complicated
880.23 Open wound of upper arm, with tendon involvement
887.2 Traumatic amputation of arm and hand (complete) (partial), unilateral, at or above elbow, without mention of complication
887.3 Traumatic amputation of arm and hand (complete) (partial), unilateral, at or above elbow, complicated
887.6 Traumatic amputation of arm and hand (complete) (partial), bilateral (any level), without mention of complication
887.7 Traumatic amputation of arm and hand (complete) (partial), bilateral (any level), complicated
927.03 Crushing injury of upper arm — (Use additional code to identify any associated injuries: 800-829, 850.0-854.1, 860.0-869.1)
943.52 Deep necrosis of underlying tissues due to burn (deep third degree) of elbow, with loss of a body part
943.53 Deep necrosis of underlying tissues due to burn (deep third degree) of upper arm, with loss of upper a body part
996.94 Complications of reattached upper extremity, other and unspecified ▽

ICD-9-CM Procedural

84.07 Amputation through humerus

24925

24925 Amputation, arm through humerus; secondary closure or scar revision

ICD-9-CM Diagnostic

249.70 Secondary diabetes mellitus with peripheral circulatory disorders, not stated as uncontrolled, or unspecified — (Use additional code to identify manifestation: 443.81, 785.4) (Use additional code to identify any associated insulin use: V58.67)
249.71 Secondary diabetes mellitus with peripheral circulatory disorders, uncontrolled — (Use additional code to identify manifestation: 443.81, 785.4) (Use additional code to identify any associated insulin use: V58.67)
250.70 Diabetes with peripheral circulatory disorders, type II or unspecified type, not stated as uncontrolled — (Use additional code to identify manifestation: 443.81, 785.4)
250.71 Diabetes with peripheral circulatory disorders, type I [juvenile type], not stated as uncontrolled — (Use additional code to identify manifestation: 443.81, 785.4)
250.72 Diabetes with peripheral circulatory disorders, type II or unspecified type, uncontrolled — (Use additional code to identify manifestation: 443.81, 785.4)
250.73 Diabetes with peripheral circulatory disorders, type I [juvenile type], uncontrolled — (Use additional code to identify manifestation: 443.81, 785.4)
440.24 Atherosclerosis of native arteries of the extremities with gangrene — (Use additional code for any associated ulceration: 707.10-707.19, 707.8, 707.9)
443.81 Peripheral angiopathy in diseases classified elsewhere — (Code first underlying disease: 249.7, 250.7) ☒
443.9 Unspecified peripheral vascular disease ▽
446.0 Polyarteritis nodosa
682.3 Cellulitis and abscess of upper arm and forearm — (Use additional code to identify organism, such as 041.1, etc.)
707.00 Pressure ulcer, unspecified site — (Use additional code to identify pressure ulcer stage: 707.20-707.25) ▽
707.01 Pressure ulcer, elbow — (Use additional code to identify pressure ulcer stage: 707.20-707.25)
707.09 Pressure ulcer, other site — (Use additional code to identify pressure ulcer stage: 707.20-707.25)
707.20 Pressure ulcer, unspecified stage — (Code first site of pressure ulcer: 707.00-707.09) ▽
707.21 Pressure ulcer, stage I — (Code first site of pressure ulcer: 707.00-707.09)
707.22 Pressure ulcer stage II — (Code first site of pressure ulcer: 707.00-707.09)
707.23 Pressure ulcer stage III — (Code first site of pressure ulcer: 707.00-707.09)
707.24 Pressure ulcer stage IV — (Code first site of pressure ulcer: 707.00-707.09)
707.25 Pressure ulcer, unstageable — (Code first site of pressure ulcer: 707.00-707.09)
707.8 Chronic ulcer of other specified site
728.86 Necrotizing fasciitis — (Use additional code to identify infectious organism, 041.00-041.89, 785.4, if applicable)
730.12 Chronic osteomyelitis, upper arm — (Use additional code to identify organism: 041.1. Use additional code to identify major osseous defect, if applicable: 731.3)
731.3 Major osseous defects — (Code first underlying disease: 170.0-170.9, 730.00-730.29, 733.00-733.09, 733.40-733.49, 996.45)
785.4 Gangrene — (Code first any associated underlying condition)
880.13 Open wound of upper arm, complicated
880.23 Open wound of upper arm, with tendon involvement
997.60 Late complications of amputation stump, unspecified — (Use additional code to identify complications) ▽
997.61 Neuroma of amputation stump — (Use additional code to identify complications)
997.62 Infection (chronic) of amputation stump — (Use additional code to identify complications)
997.69 Other late amputation stump complication — (Use additional code to identify complications)
V51.8 Other aftercare involving the use of plastic surgery
V58.41 Planned postoperative wound closure — (This code should be used in conjunction with other aftercare codes to fully identify the reason for the aftercare encounter)

ICD-9-CM Procedural

84.3 Revision of amputation stump

24930

24930 Amputation, arm through humerus; re-amputation

ICD-9-CM Diagnostic

170.4 Malignant neoplasm of scapula and long bones of upper limb
171.2 Malignant neoplasm of connective and other soft tissue of upper limb, including shoulder
198.5 Secondary malignant neoplasm of bone and bone marrow
249.70 Secondary diabetes mellitus with peripheral circulatory disorders, not stated as uncontrolled, or unspecified — (Use additional code to identify manifestation: 443.81, 785.4) (Use additional code to identify any associated insulin use: V58.67)
249.71 Secondary diabetes mellitus with peripheral circulatory disorders, uncontrolled — (Use additional code to identify manifestation: 443.81, 785.4) (Use additional code to identify any associated insulin use: V58.67)
249.80 Secondary diabetes mellitus with other specified manifestations, not stated as uncontrolled, or unspecified — (Use additional code to identify manifestation: 707.10-707.19, 707.8, 707.9, 731.8) (Use additional code to identify any associated insulin use: V58.67)
249.81 Secondary diabetes mellitus with other specified manifestations, uncontrolled — (Use additional code to identify manifestation: 707.10-707.19, 707.8, 707.9, 731.8) (Use additional code to identify any associated insulin use: V58.67)
250.70 Diabetes with peripheral circulatory disorders, type II or unspecified type, not stated as uncontrolled — (Use additional code to identify manifestation: 443.81, 785.4)
250.71 Diabetes with peripheral circulatory disorders, type I [juvenile type], not stated as uncontrolled — (Use additional code to identify manifestation: 443.81, 785.4)
250.72 Diabetes with peripheral circulatory disorders, type II or unspecified type, uncontrolled — (Use additional code to identify manifestation: 443.81, 785.4)
250.73 Diabetes with peripheral circulatory disorders, type I [juvenile type], uncontrolled — (Use additional code to identify manifestation: 443.81, 785.4)
250.80 Diabetes with other specified manifestations, type II or unspecified type, not stated as uncontrolled — (Use additional code to identify manifestation: 707.10-707.19, 707.8, 707.9, 731.8)
250.81 Diabetes with other specified manifestations, type I [juvenile type], not stated as uncontrolled — (Use additional code to identify manifestation: 707.10-707.19, 707.8, 707.9, 731.8)
250.82 Diabetes with other specified manifestations, type II or unspecified type, uncontrolled — (Use additional code to identify manifestation: 707.10-707.19, 707.8, 707.9, 731.8)
250.83 Diabetes with other specified manifestations, type I [juvenile type], uncontrolled — (Use additional code to identify manifestation: 707.10-707.19, 707.8, 707.9, 731.8)
730.12 Chronic osteomyelitis, upper arm — (Use additional code to identify organism: 041.1. Use additional code to identify major osseous defect, if applicable: 731.3)
731.8 Other bone involvement in diseases classified elsewhere — (Code first underlying disease: 249.8, 250.8. Use additional code to specify bone condition: 730.00-730.09) ☒
785.4 Gangrene — (Code first any associated underlying condition)
997.60 Late complications of amputation stump, unspecified — (Use additional code to identify complications) ▽
997.61 Neuroma of amputation stump — (Use additional code to identify complications)
997.62 Infection (chronic) of amputation stump — (Use additional code to identify complications)
997.69 Other late amputation stump complication — (Use additional code to identify complications)
V49.66 Upper limb amputation, above elbow

ICD-9-CM Procedural

84.07 Amputation through humerus
84.3 Revision of amputation stump

24931

24931 Amputation, arm through humerus; with implant

ICD-9-CM Diagnostic

170.4 Malignant neoplasm of scapula and long bones of upper limb
171.2 Malignant neoplasm of connective and other soft tissue of upper limb, including shoulder
198.5 Secondary malignant neoplasm of bone and bone marrow
228.1 Lymphangioma, any site
249.70 Secondary diabetes mellitus with peripheral circulatory disorders, not stated as uncontrolled, or unspecified — (Use additional code to identify manifestation: 443.81, 785.4) (Use additional code to identify any associated insulin use: V58.67)
249.71 Secondary diabetes mellitus with peripheral circulatory disorders, uncontrolled — (Use additional code to identify manifestation: 443.81, 785.4) (Use additional code to identify any associated insulin use: V58.67)
249.80 Secondary diabetes mellitus with other specified manifestations, not stated as uncontrolled, or unspecified — (Use additional code to identify manifestation: 707.10-707.19, 707.8, 707.9, 731.8) (Use additional code to identify any associated insulin use: V58.67)
249.81 Secondary diabetes mellitus with other specified manifestations, uncontrolled — (Use additional code to identify manifestation: 707.10-707.19, 707.8, 707.9, 731.8) (Use additional code to identify any associated insulin use: V58.67)
250.70 Diabetes with peripheral circulatory disorders, type II or unspecified type, not stated as uncontrolled — (Use additional code to identify manifestation: 443.81, 785.4)
250.71 Diabetes with peripheral circulatory disorders, type I [juvenile type], not stated as uncontrolled — (Use additional code to identify manifestation: 443.81, 785.4)
250.72 Diabetes with peripheral circulatory disorders, type II or unspecified type, uncontrolled — (Use additional code to identify manifestation: 443.81, 785.4)
250.73 Diabetes with peripheral circulatory disorders, type I [juvenile type], uncontrolled — (Use additional code to identify manifestation: 443.81, 785.4)
250.80 Diabetes with other specified manifestations, type II or unspecified type, not stated as uncontrolled — (Use additional code to identify manifestation: 707.10-707.19, 707.8, 707.9, 731.8)
250.81 Diabetes with other specified manifestations, type I [juvenile type], not stated as uncontrolled — (Use additional code to identify manifestation: 707.10-707.19, 707.8, 707.9, 731.8)
250.82 Diabetes with other specified manifestations, type II or unspecified type, uncontrolled — (Use additional code to identify manifestation: 707.10-707.19, 707.8, 707.9, 731.8)
250.83 Diabetes with other specified manifestations, type I [juvenile type], uncontrolled — (Use additional code to identify manifestation: 707.10-707.19, 707.8, 707.9, 731.8)
440.24 Atherosclerosis of native arteries of the extremities with gangrene — (Use additional code for any associated ulceration: 707.10-707.19, 707.8, 707.9)
443.9 Unspecified peripheral vascular disease ▽
444.21 Embolism and thrombosis of arteries of upper extremity
445.01 Atheroembolism of upper extremity
446.0 Polyarteritis nodosa
728.86 Necrotizing fasciitis — (Use additional code to identify infectious organism, 041.00-041.89, 785.4, if applicable)
730.12 Chronic osteomyelitis, upper arm — (Use additional code to identify organism: 041.1. Use additional code to identify major osseous defect, if applicable: 731.3)
731.1 Osteitis deformans in diseases classified elsewhere — (Code first underlying disease: 170.0-170.9) ☒
731.3 Major osseous defects — (Code first underlying disease: 170.0-170.9, 730.00-730.29, 733.00-733.09, 733.40-733.49, 996.45)
731.8 Other bone involvement in diseases classified elsewhere — (Code first underlying disease: 249.8, 250.8. Use additional code to specify bone condition: 730.00-730.09) ☒
785.4 Gangrene — (Code first any associated underlying condition)
812.21 Closed fracture of shaft of humerus
812.41 Closed fracture of supracondylar humerus
812.49 Other closed fracture of lower end of humerus

812.51 Open fracture of supracondylar humerus
812.54 Open fracture of unspecified condyle(s) of humerus ♈
812.59 Other open fracture of lower end of humerus
813.31 Open fracture of shaft of radius (alone)
880.13 Open wound of upper arm, complicated
880.23 Open wound of upper arm, with tendon involvement
887.2 Traumatic amputation of arm and hand (complete) (partial), unilateral, at or above elbow, without mention of complication
887.3 Traumatic amputation of arm and hand (complete) (partial), unilateral, at or above elbow, complicated
887.6 Traumatic amputation of arm and hand (complete) (partial), bilateral (any level), without mention of complication
887.7 Traumatic amputation of arm and hand (complete) (partial), bilateral (any level), complicated
927.03 Crushing injury of upper arm — (Use additional code to identify any associated injuries: 800-829, 850.0-854.1, 860.0-869.1)
943.52 Deep necrosis of underlying tissues due to burn (deep third degree) of elbow, with loss of a body part
943.53 Deep necrosis of underlying tissues due to burn (deep third degree) of upper arm, with loss of upper a body part
996.94 Complications of reattached upper extremity, other and unspecified ♈

ICD-9-CM Procedural

81.96 Other repair of joint
84.07 Amputation through humerus
84.44 Implantation of prosthetic device of arm

24935

24935 Stump elongation, upper extremity

ICD-9-CM Diagnostic

V51.8 Other aftercare involving the use of plastic surgery
V58.49 Other specified aftercare following surgery — (This code should be used in conjunction with other aftercare codes to fully identify the reason for the aftercare encounter)

ICD-9-CM Procedural

77.77 Excision of tibia and fibula for graft
77.79 Excision of other bone for graft, except facial bones
78.02 Bone graft of humerus
78.03 Bone graft of radius and ulna
78.32 Limb lengthening procedures, humerus
78.33 Limb lengthening procedures, radius and ulna

24940

24940 Cineplasty, upper extremity, complete procedure

ICD-9-CM Diagnostic

170.4 Malignant neoplasm of scapula and long bones of upper limb
170.5 Malignant neoplasm of short bones of upper limb
171.2 Malignant neoplasm of connective and other soft tissue of upper limb, including shoulder
198.5 Secondary malignant neoplasm of bone and bone marrow
249.70 Secondary diabetes mellitus with peripheral circulatory disorders, not stated as uncontrolled, or unspecified — (Use additional code to identify manifestation: 443.81, 785.4) (Use additional code to identify any associated insulin use: V58.67)
249.71 Secondary diabetes mellitus with peripheral circulatory disorders, uncontrolled — (Use additional code to identify manifestation: 443.81, 785.4) (Use additional code to identify any associated insulin use: V58.67)
250.70 Diabetes with peripheral circulatory disorders, type II or unspecified type, not stated as uncontrolled — (Use additional code to identify manifestation: 443.81, 785.4)
250.71 Diabetes with peripheral circulatory disorders, type I [juvenile type], not stated as uncontrolled — (Use additional code to identify manifestation: 443.81, 785.4)
250.72 Diabetes with peripheral circulatory disorders, type II or unspecified type, uncontrolled — (Use additional code to identify manifestation: 443.81, 785.4)
250.73 Diabetes with peripheral circulatory disorders, type I [juvenile type], uncontrolled — (Use additional code to identify manifestation: 443.81, 785.4)
440.24 Atherosclerosis of native arteries of the extremities with gangrene — (Use additional code for any associated ulceration: 707.10-707.19, 707.8, 707.9)
443.81 Peripheral angiopathy in diseases classified elsewhere — (Code first underlying disease: 249.7, 250.7) ☒
443.9 Unspecified peripheral vascular disease ♈
444.21 Embolism and thrombosis of arteries of upper extremity
445.01 Atheroembolism of upper extremity
446.0 Polyarteritis nodosa
728.86 Necrotizing fasciitis — (Use additional code to identify infectious organism, 041.00-041.89, 785.4, if applicable)
730.12 Chronic osteomyelitis, upper arm — (Use additional code to identify organism: 041.1. Use additional code to identify major osseous defect, if applicable: 731.3)
731.1 Osteitis deformans in diseases classified elsewhere — (Code first underlying disease: 170.0-170.9) ☒
731.3 Major osseous defects — (Code first underlying disease: 170.0-170.9, 730.00-730.29, 733.00-733.09, 733.40-733.49, 996.45)
785.4 Gangrene — (Code first any associated underlying condition)
812.49 Other closed fracture of lower end of humerus
812.59 Other open fracture of lower end of humerus
880.13 Open wound of upper arm, complicated
880.23 Open wound of upper arm, with tendon involvement
887.2 Traumatic amputation of arm and hand (complete) (partial), unilateral, at or above elbow, without mention of complication
887.3 Traumatic amputation of arm and hand (complete) (partial), unilateral, at or above elbow, complicated
887.6 Traumatic amputation of arm and hand (complete) (partial), bilateral (any level), without mention of complication
887.7 Traumatic amputation of arm and hand (complete) (partial), bilateral (any level), complicated
927.03 Crushing injury of upper arm — (Use additional code to identify any associated injuries: 800-829, 850.0-854.1, 860.0-869.1)
943.52 Deep necrosis of underlying tissues due to burn (deep third degree) of elbow, with loss of a body part
943.53 Deep necrosis of underlying tissues due to burn (deep third degree) of upper arm, with loss of upper a body part
996.94 Complications of reattached upper extremity, other and unspecified ♈
V49.66 Upper limb amputation, above elbow
V51.8 Other aftercare involving the use of plastic surgery
V58.41 Planned postoperative wound closure — (This code should be used in conjunction with other aftercare codes to fully identify the reason for the aftercare encounter)
V58.49 Other specified aftercare following surgery — (This code should be used in conjunction with other aftercare codes to fully identify the reason for the aftercare encounter)

ICD-9-CM Procedural

84.07 Amputation through humerus
84.44 Implantation of prosthetic device of arm

Forearm and Wrist

25000-25001

25000 Incision, extensor tendon sheath, wrist (eg, deQuervains disease)
25001 Incision, flexor tendon sheath, wrist (eg, flexor carpi radialis)

ICD-9-CM Diagnostic

719.23 Villonodular synovitis, forearm
726.4 Enthesopathy of wrist and carpus
727.00 Unspecified synovitis and tenosynovitis ♈
727.04 Radial styloid tenosynovitis

727.05 Other tenosynovitis of hand and wrist
727.2 Specific bursitides often of occupational origin

ICD-9-CM Procedural

83.01 Exploration of tendon sheath

25020-25023

25020 Decompression fasciotomy, forearm and/or wrist, flexor OR extensor compartment; without debridement of nonviable muscle and/or nerve
25023 with debridement of nonviable muscle and/or nerve

ICD-9-CM Diagnostic

682.3 Cellulitis and abscess of upper arm and forearm — (Use additional code to identify organism, such as 041.1, etc.)
682.4 Cellulitis and abscess of hand, except fingers and thumb — (Use additional code to identify organism, such as 041.1, etc.)
728.86 Necrotizing fasciitis — (Use additional code to identify infectious organism, 041.00-041.89, 785.4, if applicable)
728.88 Rhabdomyolysis
729.4 Unspecified fasciitis
729.71 Nontraumatic compartment syndrome of upper extremity — (Code first, if applicable, postprocedural complication: 998.89)
785.4 Gangrene — (Code first any associated underlying condition)
813.21 Closed fracture of shaft of radius (alone)
813.22 Closed fracture of shaft of ulna (alone)
813.23 Closed fracture of shaft of radius with ulna
813.31 Open fracture of shaft of radius (alone)
813.32 Open fracture of shaft of ulna (alone)
813.33 Open fracture of shaft of radius with ulna
813.80 Closed fracture of unspecified part of forearm
813.90 Open fracture of unspecified part of forearm
832.00 Closed unspecified dislocation of elbow
832.10 Open unspecified dislocation of elbow
881.01 Open wound of elbow, without mention of complication
881.10 Open wound of forearm, complicated
881.11 Open wound of elbow, complicated
881.12 Open wound of wrist, complicated
881.20 Open wound of forearm, with tendon involvement
881.22 Open wound of wrist, with tendon involvement
923.10 Contusion of forearm
923.11 Contusion of elbow
927.10 Crushing injury of forearm — (Use additional code to identify any associated injuries: 800-829, 850.0-854.1, 860.0-869.1)
927.11 Crushing injury of elbow — (Use additional code to identify any associated injuries: 800-829, 850.0-854.1, 860.0-869.1)
927.21 Crushing injury of wrist — (Use additional code to identify any associated injuries: 800-829, 850.0-854.1, 860.0-869.1)
943.01 Burn of unspecified degree of forearm
943.21 Blisters with epidermal loss due to burn (second degree) of forearm
943.31 Full-thickness skin loss due to burn (third degree NOS) of forearm
943.41 Deep necrosis of underlying tissues due to burn (deep third degree) of forearm, without mention of loss of a body part
948.00 Burn (any degree) involving less than 10% of body surface with third degree burn of less than 10% or unspecified amount
958.8 Other early complications of trauma
958.91 Traumatic compartment syndrome of upper extremity

ICD-9-CM Procedural

04.07 Other excision or avulsion of cranial and peripheral nerves
83.14 Fasciotomy
83.45 Other myectomy

HCPCS Level II Supplies & Services

A4305 Disposable drug delivery system, flow rate of 50 ml or greater per hour

25024-25025

25024 Decompression fasciotomy, forearm and/or wrist, flexor AND extensor compartment; without debridement of nonviable muscle and/or nerve
25025 with debridement of nonviable muscle and/or nerve

ICD-9-CM Diagnostic

682.3 Cellulitis and abscess of upper arm and forearm — (Use additional code to identify organism, such as 041.1, etc.)
682.4 Cellulitis and abscess of hand, except fingers and thumb — (Use additional code to identify organism, such as 041.1, etc.)
728.86 Necrotizing fasciitis — (Use additional code to identify infectious organism, 041.00-041.89, 785.4, if applicable)
728.88 Rhabdomyolysis
729.4 Unspecified fasciitis
729.71 Nontraumatic compartment syndrome of upper extremity — (Code first, if applicable, postprocedural complication: 998.89)
785.4 Gangrene — (Code first any associated underlying condition)
813.21 Closed fracture of shaft of radius (alone)
813.22 Closed fracture of shaft of ulna (alone)
813.23 Closed fracture of shaft of radius with ulna
813.31 Open fracture of shaft of radius (alone)
813.32 Open fracture of shaft of ulna (alone)
813.33 Open fracture of shaft of radius with ulna
813.80 Closed fracture of unspecified part of forearm
813.90 Open fracture of unspecified part of forearm
832.00 Closed unspecified dislocation of elbow
832.10 Open unspecified dislocation of elbow
881.01 Open wound of elbow, without mention of complication
881.10 Open wound of forearm, complicated
881.11 Open wound of elbow, complicated
881.12 Open wound of wrist, complicated
881.20 Open wound of forearm, with tendon involvement
881.22 Open wound of wrist, with tendon involvement
923.10 Contusion of forearm
923.11 Contusion of elbow
927.10 Crushing injury of forearm — (Use additional code to identify any associated injuries: 800-829, 850.0-854.1, 860.0-869.1)
927.11 Crushing injury of elbow — (Use additional code to identify any associated injuries: 800-829, 850.0-854.1, 860.0-869.1)
927.21 Crushing injury of wrist — (Use additional code to identify any associated injuries: 800-829, 850.0-854.1, 860.0-869.1)
943.01 Burn of unspecified degree of forearm
943.21 Blisters with epidermal loss due to burn (second degree) of forearm
943.31 Full-thickness skin loss due to burn (third degree NOS) of forearm
943.41 Deep necrosis of underlying tissues due to burn (deep third degree) of forearm, without mention of loss of a body part
948.00 Burn (any degree) involving less than 10% of body surface with third degree burn of less than 10% or unspecified amount
958.8 Other early complications of trauma
958.91 Traumatic compartment syndrome of upper extremity

ICD-9-CM Procedural

04.07 Other excision or avulsion of cranial and peripheral nerves
83.14 Fasciotomy
83.45 Other myectomy

25028

25028 Incision and drainage, forearm and/or wrist; deep abscess or hematoma

ICD-9-CM Diagnostic

682.3 Cellulitis and abscess of upper arm and forearm — (Use additional code to identify organism, such as 041.1, etc.)
682.4 Cellulitis and abscess of hand, except fingers and thumb — (Use additional code to identify organism, such as 041.1, etc.)
727.89 Other disorders of synovium, tendon, and bursa
730.33 Periostitis, without mention of osteomyelitis, forearm — (Use additional code to identify organism: 041.1)
780.62 Postprocedural fever
881.10 Open wound of forearm, complicated
881.12 Open wound of wrist, complicated
923.10 Contusion of forearm
923.21 Contusion of wrist
927.10 Crushing injury of forearm — (Use additional code to identify any associated injuries: 800-829, 850.0-854.1, 860.0-869.1)
927.21 Crushing injury of wrist — (Use additional code to identify any associated injuries: 800-829, 850.0-854.1, 860.0-869.1)
927.8 Crushing injury of multiple sites of upper limb — (Use additional code to identify any associated injuries: 800-829, 850.0-854.1, 860.0-869.1)
998.59 Other postoperative infection — (Use additional code to identify infection)

ICD-9-CM Procedural

83.02 Myotomy
83.09 Other incision of soft tissue

HCPCS Level II Supplies & Services

A4305 Disposable drug delivery system, flow rate of 50 ml or greater per hour

25031

25031 Incision and drainage, forearm and/or wrist; bursa

ICD-9-CM Diagnostic

711.03 Pyogenic arthritis, forearm — (Use additional code to identify infectious organism: 041.0-041.8)
711.93 Unspecified infective arthritis, forearm ▽
716.93 Unspecified arthropathy, forearm ▽
726.4 Enthesopathy of wrist and carpus
727.2 Specific bursitides often of occupational origin
727.3 Other bursitis disorders
727.89 Other disorders of synovium, tendon, and bursa
906.3 Late effect of contusion
906.4 Late effect of crushing
998.51 Infected postoperative seroma — (Use additional code to identify organism)
998.59 Other postoperative infection — (Use additional code to identify infection)

ICD-9-CM Procedural

83.03 Bursotomy

HCPCS Level II Supplies & Services

A4305 Disposable drug delivery system, flow rate of 50 ml or greater per hour

25035

25035 Incision, deep, bone cortex, forearm and/or wrist (eg, osteomyelitis or bone abscess)

ICD-9-CM Diagnostic

730.13 Chronic osteomyelitis, forearm — (Use additional code to identify organism: 041.1. Use additional code to identify major osseous defect, if applicable: 731.3)
730.23 Unspecified osteomyelitis, forearm — (Use additional code to identify organism: 041.1. Use additional code to identify major osseous defect, if applicable: 731.3) ▽
730.83 Other infections involving bone in diseases classified elsewhere, forearm — (Use additional code to identify organism: 041.1. Code first underlying disease: 002.0, 015.0-015.9) ☒
730.88 Other infections involving bone diseases classified elsewhere, other specified sites — (Use additional code to identify organism: 041.1. Code first underlying disease: 002.0, 015.0-015.9) ☒
731.3 Major osseous defects — (Code first underlying disease: 170.0-170.9, 730.00-730.29, 733.00-733.09, 733.40-733.49, 996.45)
998.59 Other postoperative infection — (Use additional code to identify infection)

ICD-9-CM Procedural

77.13 Other incision of radius and ulna without division
77.14 Other incision of carpals and metacarpals without division

25040

25040 Arthrotomy, radiocarpal or midcarpal joint, with exploration, drainage, or removal of foreign body

ICD-9-CM Diagnostic

357.1 Polyneuropathy in collagen vascular disease — (Code first underlying disease: 446.0, 710.0, 714.0) ☒
359.6 Symptomatic inflammatory myopathy in diseases classified elsewhere — (Code first underlying disease: 135, 140.0-208.9, 277.30-277.39, 446.0, 710.0, 710.1, 710.2, 714.0) ☒
446.0 Polyarteritis nodosa
710.0 Systemic lupus erythematosus — (Use additional code to identify manifestation: 424.91, 581.81, 582.81, 583.81)
710.1 Systemic sclerosis — (Use additional code to identify manifestation: 359.6, 517.2)
710.2 Sicca syndrome
711.03 Pyogenic arthritis, forearm — (Use additional code to identify infectious organism: 041.0-041.8)
714.0 Rheumatoid arthritis — (Use additional code to identify manifestation: 357.1, 359.6)
715.13 Primary localized osteoarthrosis, forearm
715.33 Localized osteoarthrosis not specified whether primary or secondary, forearm
716.13 Traumatic arthropathy, forearm
716.63 Unspecified monoarthritis, forearm ▽
718.13 Loose body in forearm joint
719.03 Effusion of forearm joint
719.23 Villonodular synovitis, forearm
730.03 Acute osteomyelitis, forearm — (Use additional code to identify organism: 041.1. Use additional code to identify major osseous defect, if applicable: 731.3)
730.13 Chronic osteomyelitis, forearm — (Use additional code to identify organism: 041.1. Use additional code to identify major osseous defect, if applicable: 731.3)
731.3 Major osseous defects — (Code first underlying disease: 170.0-170.9, 730.00-730.29, 733.00-733.09, 733.40-733.49, 996.45)
881.12 Open wound of wrist, complicated

ICD-9-CM Procedural

80.13 Other arthrotomy of wrist

25065-25066

25065 Biopsy, soft tissue of forearm and/or wrist; superficial
25066 deep (subfascial or intramuscular)

ICD-9-CM Diagnostic

171.2 Malignant neoplasm of connective and other soft tissue of upper limb, including shoulder
195.4 Malignant neoplasm of upper limb
198.89 Secondary malignant neoplasm of other specified sites
215.2 Other benign neoplasm of connective and other soft tissue of upper limb, including shoulder
238.1 Neoplasm of uncertain behavior of connective and other soft tissue

239.2 Neoplasms of unspecified nature of bone, soft tissue, and skin

ICD-9-CM Procedural

83.21 Open biopsy of soft tissue

25075-25078 [25071, 25073]

25071 Excision, tumor, soft tissue of forearm and/or wrist area, subcutaneous; 3 cm or greater
25073 Excision, tumor, soft tissue of forearm and/or wrist area, subfascial (eg, intramuscular); 3 cm or greater
25075 Excision, tumor, soft tissue of forearm and/or wrist area, subcutaneous; less than 3 cm
25076 Excision, tumor, soft tissue of forearm and/or wrist area, subfascial (eg, intramuscular); less than 3 cm
25077 Radical resection of tumor (eg, sarcoma), soft tissue of forearm and/or wrist area; less than 3 cm
25078 3 cm or greater

ICD-9-CM Diagnostic

171.2 Malignant neoplasm of connective and other soft tissue of upper limb, including shoulder
172.6 Malignant melanoma of skin of upper limb, including shoulder
173.60 Unspecified malignant neoplasm of skin of upper limb, including shoulder ▽
173.61 Basal cell carcinoma of skin of upper limb, including shoulder
173.62 Squamous cell carcinoma of skin of upper limb, including shoulder
173.69 Other specified malignant neoplasm of skin of upper limb, including shoulder
195.4 Malignant neoplasm of upper limb
198.89 Secondary malignant neoplasm of other specified sites
209.33 Merkel cell carcinoma of the upper limb
209.75 Secondary Merkel cell carcinoma
214.1 Lipoma of other skin and subcutaneous tissue
215.2 Other benign neoplasm of connective and other soft tissue of upper limb, including shoulder
232.6 Carcinoma in situ of skin of upper limb, including shoulder
238.1 Neoplasm of uncertain behavior of connective and other soft tissue
239.2 Neoplasms of unspecified nature of bone, soft tissue, and skin
782.2 Localized superficial swelling, mass, or lump

ICD-9-CM Procedural

83.31 Excision of lesion of tendon sheath
83.32 Excision of lesion of muscle
83.39 Excision of lesion of other soft tissue
83.49 Other excision of soft tissue
86.3 Other local excision or destruction of lesion or tissue of skin and subcutaneous tissue
86.4 Radical excision of skin lesion

HCPCS Level II Supplies & Services

A4305 Disposable drug delivery system, flow rate of 50 ml or greater per hour

25085

25085 Capsulotomy, wrist (eg, contracture)

ICD-9-CM Diagnostic

718.43 Contracture of forearm joint
728.10 Unspecified calcification and ossification ▽

ICD-9-CM Procedural

80.43 Division of joint capsule, ligament, or cartilage of wrist

25100

25100 Arthrotomy, wrist joint; with biopsy

ICD-9-CM Diagnostic

170.5 Malignant neoplasm of short bones of upper limb
171.2 Malignant neoplasm of connective and other soft tissue of upper limb, including shoulder
195.4 Malignant neoplasm of upper limb
198.5 Secondary malignant neoplasm of bone and bone marrow
198.89 Secondary malignant neoplasm of other specified sites
213.5 Benign neoplasm of short bones of upper limb
229.8 Benign neoplasm of other specified sites
238.0 Neoplasm of uncertain behavior of bone and articular cartilage
238.8 Neoplasm of uncertain behavior of other specified sites
239.2 Neoplasms of unspecified nature of bone, soft tissue, and skin
275.40 Unspecified disorder of calcium metabolism — (Use additional code to identify any associated intellectual disabilities) ▽
275.42 Hypercalcemia — (Use additional code to identify any associated intellectual disabilities)
275.49 Other disorders of calcium metabolism — (Use additional code to identify any associated intellectual disabilities)
275.5 Hungry bone syndrome — (Use additional code to identify any associated intellectual disabilities)
357.1 Polyneuropathy in collagen vascular disease — (Code first underlying disease: 446.0, 710.0, 714.0) ☒
359.6 Symptomatic inflammatory myopathy in diseases classified elsewhere — (Code first underlying disease: 135, 140.0-208.9, 277.30-277.39, 446.0, 710.0, 710.1, 710.2, 714.0) ☒
446.0 Polyarteritis nodosa
710.0 Systemic lupus erythematosus — (Use additional code to identify manifestation: 424.91, 581.81, 582.81, 583.81)
710.1 Systemic sclerosis — (Use additional code to identify manifestation: 359.6, 517.2)
710.2 Sicca syndrome
711.03 Pyogenic arthritis, forearm — (Use additional code to identify infectious organism: 041.0-041.8)
711.93 Unspecified infective arthritis, forearm ▽
714.0 Rheumatoid arthritis — (Use additional code to identify manifestation: 357.1, 359.6)
715.13 Primary localized osteoarthrosis, forearm
715.33 Localized osteoarthrosis not specified whether primary or secondary, forearm
716.63 Unspecified monoarthritis, forearm ▽
719.23 Villonodular synovitis, forearm
V64.43 Arthroscopic surgical procedure converted to open procedure

ICD-9-CM Procedural

80.33 Biopsy of joint structure of wrist

HCPCS Level II Supplies & Services

A4305 Disposable drug delivery system, flow rate of 50 ml or greater per hour

25101-25105

25101 Arthrotomy, wrist joint; with joint exploration, with or without biopsy, with or without removal of loose or foreign body
25105 with synovectomy

ICD-9-CM Diagnostic

170.5 Malignant neoplasm of short bones of upper limb
171.2 Malignant neoplasm of connective and other soft tissue of upper limb, including shoulder
195.4 Malignant neoplasm of upper limb
198.5 Secondary malignant neoplasm of bone and bone marrow
198.89 Secondary malignant neoplasm of other specified sites
213.5 Benign neoplasm of short bones of upper limb
215.2 Other benign neoplasm of connective and other soft tissue of upper limb, including shoulder
229.8 Benign neoplasm of other specified sites
238.0 Neoplasm of uncertain behavior of bone and articular cartilage
239.2 Neoplasms of unspecified nature of bone, soft tissue, and skin

357.1 Polyneuropathy in collagen vascular disease — (Code first underlying disease: 446.0, 710.0, 714.0) ☒
359.6 Symptomatic inflammatory myopathy in diseases classified elsewhere — (Code first underlying disease: 135, 140.0-208.9, 277.30-277.39, 446.0, 710.0, 710.1, 710.2, 714.0) ☒
446.0 Polyarteritis nodosa
710.0 Systemic lupus erythematosus — (Use additional code to identify manifestation: 424.91, 581.81, 582.81, 583.81)
710.1 Systemic sclerosis — (Use additional code to identify manifestation: 359.6, 517.2)
710.2 Sicca syndrome
711.03 Pyogenic arthritis, forearm — (Use additional code to identify infectious organism: 041.0-041.8)
711.93 Unspecified infective arthritis, forearm ▽
714.0 Rheumatoid arthritis — (Use additional code to identify manifestation: 357.1, 359.6)
715.13 Primary localized osteoarthrosis, forearm
715.33 Localized osteoarthrosis not specified whether primary or secondary, forearm
716.63 Unspecified monoarthritis, forearm ▽
718.13 Loose body in forearm joint
718.93 Unspecified derangement, forearm joint ▽
719.23 Villonodular synovitis, forearm
727.05 Other tenosynovitis of hand and wrist
729.6 Residual foreign body in soft tissue — (Use additional code to identify foreign body (V90.01-V90.9))
906.3 Late effect of contusion
906.4 Late effect of crushing
V64.43 Arthroscopic surgical procedure converted to open procedure

ICD-9-CM Procedural

80.13 Other arthrotomy of wrist
80.33 Biopsy of joint structure of wrist
80.73 Synovectomy of wrist

HCPCS Level II Supplies & Services

A4305 Disposable drug delivery system, flow rate of 50 ml or greater per hour

25107

25107 Arthrotomy, distal radioulnar joint including repair of triangular cartilage, complex

ICD-9-CM Diagnostic

718.03 Articular cartilage disorder, forearm
718.73 Developmental dislocation of joint, forearm
718.83 Other joint derangement, not elsewhere classified, forearm
718.93 Unspecified derangement, forearm joint ▽
813.40 Unspecified closed fracture of lower end of forearm ▽
813.41 Closed Colles' fracture
813.42 Other closed fractures of distal end of radius (alone)
813.43 Closed fracture of distal end of ulna (alone)
813.44 Closed fracture of lower end of radius with ulna
813.45 Torus fracture of radius (alone)
813.46 Torus fracture of ulna (alone)
813.47 Torus fracture of radius and ulna
813.50 Unspecified open fracture of lower end of forearm ▽
813.51 Open Colles' fracture
813.52 Other open fractures of distal end of radius (alone)
813.53 Open fracture of distal end of ulna (alone)
813.54 Open fracture of lower end of radius with ulna
833.01 Closed dislocation of distal radioulnar (joint)
833.11 Open dislocation of distal radioulnar (joint)
842.09 Other wrist sprain and strain
881.12 Open wound of wrist, complicated
881.22 Open wound of wrist, with tendon involvement

ICD-9-CM Procedural

81.96 Other repair of joint

25109

25109 Excision of tendon, forearm and/or wrist, flexor or extensor, each

ICD-9-CM Diagnostic

171.2 Malignant neoplasm of connective and other soft tissue of upper limb, including shoulder
215.2 Other benign neoplasm of connective and other soft tissue of upper limb, including shoulder
238.1 Neoplasm of uncertain behavior of connective and other soft tissue
239.2 Neoplasms of unspecified nature of bone, soft tissue, and skin
719.93 Unspecified disorder of forearm joint ▽
727.00 Unspecified synovitis and tenosynovitis ▽
727.01 Synovitis and tenosynovitis in diseases classified elsewhere — (Code first underlying disease: 015.0-015.9) ☒
727.02 Giant cell tumor of tendon sheath
727.04 Radial styloid tenosynovitis
727.05 Other tenosynovitis of hand and wrist
782.2 Localized superficial swelling, mass, or lump

ICD-9-CM Procedural

83.41 Excision of tendon for graft
83.42 Other tenonectomy

25110

25110 Excision, lesion of tendon sheath, forearm and/or wrist

ICD-9-CM Diagnostic

171.2 Malignant neoplasm of connective and other soft tissue of upper limb, including shoulder
215.2 Other benign neoplasm of connective and other soft tissue of upper limb, including shoulder
216.6 Benign neoplasm of skin of upper limb, including shoulder
238.1 Neoplasm of uncertain behavior of connective and other soft tissue
239.2 Neoplasms of unspecified nature of bone, soft tissue, and skin
719.93 Unspecified disorder of forearm joint ▽
727.02 Giant cell tumor of tendon sheath
727.05 Other tenosynovitis of hand and wrist
782.2 Localized superficial swelling, mass, or lump

ICD-9-CM Procedural

83.31 Excision of lesion of tendon sheath

HCPCS Level II Supplies & Services

A4305 Disposable drug delivery system, flow rate of 50 ml or greater per hour

25111-25112

25111 Excision of ganglion, wrist (dorsal or volar); primary
25112 recurrent

ICD-9-CM Diagnostic

727.41 Ganglion of joint
727.42 Ganglion of tendon sheath

ICD-9-CM Procedural

82.21 Excision of lesion of tendon sheath of hand

HCPCS Level II Supplies & Services

A4305 Disposable drug delivery system, flow rate of 50 ml or greater per hour

25115-25116

25115 Radical excision of bursa, synovia of wrist, or forearm tendon sheaths (eg, tenosynovitis, fungus, Tbc, or other granulomas, rheumatoid arthritis); flexors
25116 extensors, with or without transposition of dorsal retinaculum

ICD-9-CM Diagnostic

357.1 Polyneuropathy in collagen vascular disease — (Code first underlying disease: 446.0, 710.0, 714.0) ☒
359.6 Symptomatic inflammatory myopathy in diseases classified elsewhere — (Code first underlying disease: 135, 140.0-208.9, 277.30-277.39, 446.0, 710.0, 710.1, 710.2, 714.0) ☒
446.0 Polyarteritis nodosa
517.8 Lung involvement in other diseases classified elsewhere — (Use additional code to identify infectious organism. Code first underlying disease: 135, 277.30-277.39, 710.0, 710.2, 710.4) ☒
710.0 Systemic lupus erythematosus — (Use additional code to identify manifestation: 424.91, 581.81, 582.81, 583.81)
710.1 Systemic sclerosis — (Use additional code to identify manifestation: 359.6, 517.2)
710.2 Sicca syndrome
710.9 Unspecified diffuse connective tissue disease ▽
711.03 Pyogenic arthritis, forearm — (Use additional code to identify infectious organism: 041.0-041.8)
711.13 Arthropathy associated with Reiter's disease and nonspecific urethritis, forearm — (Code first underlying disease: 099.3, 099.4) ☒
711.93 Unspecified infective arthritis, forearm ▽
714.0 Rheumatoid arthritis — (Use additional code to identify manifestation: 357.1, 359.6)
719.23 Villonodular synovitis, forearm
727.00 Unspecified synovitis and tenosynovitis ▽
727.01 Synovitis and tenosynovitis in diseases classified elsewhere — (Code first underlying disease: 015.0-015.9) ☒
727.02 Giant cell tumor of tendon sheath
727.05 Other tenosynovitis of hand and wrist
727.42 Ganglion of tendon sheath
727.49 Other ganglion and cyst of synovium, tendon, and bursa

ICD-9-CM Procedural

83.31 Excision of lesion of tendon sheath
83.39 Excision of lesion of other soft tissue
83.5 Bursectomy

25118-25119

25118 Synovectomy, extensor tendon sheath, wrist, single compartment;
25119 with resection of distal ulna

ICD-9-CM Diagnostic

171.2 Malignant neoplasm of connective and other soft tissue of upper limb, including shoulder
198.89 Secondary malignant neoplasm of other specified sites
215.2 Other benign neoplasm of connective and other soft tissue of upper limb, including shoulder
238.1 Neoplasm of uncertain behavior of connective and other soft tissue
239.2 Neoplasms of unspecified nature of bone, soft tissue, and skin
354.5 Mononeuritis multiplex
357.1 Polyneuropathy in collagen vascular disease — (Code first underlying disease: 446.0, 710.0, 714.0) ☒
359.6 Symptomatic inflammatory myopathy in diseases classified elsewhere — (Code first underlying disease: 135, 140.0-208.9, 277.30-277.39, 446.0, 710.0, 710.1, 710.2, 714.0) ☒
446.0 Polyarteritis nodosa
710.0 Systemic lupus erythematosus — (Use additional code to identify manifestation: 424.91, 581.81, 582.81, 583.81)
710.1 Systemic sclerosis — (Use additional code to identify manifestation: 359.6, 517.2)
710.2 Sicca syndrome
714.0 Rheumatoid arthritis — (Use additional code to identify manifestation: 357.1, 359.6)
715.13 Primary localized osteoarthrosis, forearm
716.13 Traumatic arthropathy, forearm
719.23 Villonodular synovitis, forearm
727.00 Unspecified synovitis and tenosynovitis ▽
727.01 Synovitis and tenosynovitis in diseases classified elsewhere — (Code first underlying disease: 015.0-015.9) ☒
727.04 Radial styloid tenosynovitis
727.05 Other tenosynovitis of hand and wrist
727.40 Unspecified synovial cyst ▽
727.49 Other ganglion and cyst of synovium, tendon, and bursa
881.22 Open wound of wrist, with tendon involvement
V64.43 Arthroscopic surgical procedure converted to open procedure

ICD-9-CM Procedural

77.83 Other partial ostectomy of radius and ulna
80.73 Synovectomy of wrist
83.42 Other tenonectomy

HCPCS Level II Supplies & Services

A4305 Disposable drug delivery system, flow rate of 50 ml or greater per hour

25120-25126

25120 Excision or curettage of bone cyst or benign tumor of radius or ulna (excluding head or neck of radius and olecranon process);
25125 with autograft (includes obtaining graft)
25126 with allograft

ICD-9-CM Diagnostic

213.4 Benign neoplasm of scapula and long bones of upper limb
238.0 Neoplasm of uncertain behavior of bone and articular cartilage
239.2 Neoplasms of unspecified nature of bone, soft tissue, and skin
726.91 Exostosis of unspecified site ▽
733.21 Solitary bone cyst
733.22 Aneurysmal bone cyst
733.29 Other cyst of bone

ICD-9-CM Procedural

77.79 Excision of other bone for graft, except facial bones
78.03 Bone graft of radius and ulna
80.83 Other local excision or destruction of lesion of wrist joint

25130-25136

25130 Excision or curettage of bone cyst or benign tumor of carpal bones;
25135 with autograft (includes obtaining graft)
25136 with allograft

ICD-9-CM Diagnostic

213.5 Benign neoplasm of short bones of upper limb
238.0 Neoplasm of uncertain behavior of bone and articular cartilage
239.2 Neoplasms of unspecified nature of bone, soft tissue, and skin
726.91 Exostosis of unspecified site ▽
733.21 Solitary bone cyst
733.22 Aneurysmal bone cyst
733.29 Other cyst of bone

ICD-9-CM Procedural

77.77 Excision of tibia and fibula for graft
77.79 Excision of other bone for graft, except facial bones
78.04 Bone graft of carpals and metacarpals
80.83 Other local excision or destruction of lesion of wrist joint

25145

25145 Sequestrectomy (eg, for osteomyelitis or bone abscess), forearm and/or wrist

ICD-9-CM Diagnostic

715.13 Primary localized osteoarthrosis, forearm
715.33 Localized osteoarthrosis not specified whether primary or secondary, forearm
716.63 Unspecified monoarthritis, forearm ▽
730.13 Chronic osteomyelitis, forearm — (Use additional code to identify organism: 041.1. Use additional code to identify major osseous defect, if applicable: 731.3)
730.23 Unspecified osteomyelitis, forearm — (Use additional code to identify organism: 041.1. Use additional code to identify major osseous defect, if applicable: 731.3) ▽
730.33 Periostitis, without mention of osteomyelitis, forearm — (Use additional code to identify organism: 041.1)
730.83 Other infections involving bone in diseases classified elsewhere, forearm — (Use additional code to identify organism: 041.1. Code first underlying disease: 002.0, 015.0-015.9) ☒
731.3 Major osseous defects — (Code first underlying disease: 170.0-170.9, 730.00-730.29, 733.00-733.09, 733.40-733.49, 996.45)
905.2 Late effect of fracture of upper extremities

ICD-9-CM Procedural

77.03 Sequestrectomy of radius and ulna
77.04 Sequestrectomy of carpals and metacarpals
77.09 Sequestrectomy of other bone, except facial bones

25150-25151

25150 Partial excision (craterization, saucerization, or diaphysectomy) of bone (eg, for osteomyelitis); ulna
25151 radius

ICD-9-CM Diagnostic

715.13 Primary localized osteoarthrosis, forearm
715.33 Localized osteoarthrosis not specified whether primary or secondary, forearm
716.63 Unspecified monoarthritis, forearm ▽
730.13 Chronic osteomyelitis, forearm — (Use additional code to identify organism: 041.1. Use additional code to identify major osseous defect, if applicable: 731.3)
730.23 Unspecified osteomyelitis, forearm — (Use additional code to identify organism: 041.1. Use additional code to identify major osseous defect, if applicable: 731.3) ▽
730.33 Periostitis, without mention of osteomyelitis, forearm — (Use additional code to identify organism: 041.1)
730.83 Other infections involving bone in diseases classified elsewhere, forearm — (Use additional code to identify organism: 041.1. Code first underlying disease: 002.0, 015.0-015.9) ☒
731.3 Major osseous defects — (Code first underlying disease: 170.0-170.9, 730.00-730.29, 733.00-733.09, 733.40-733.49, 996.45)
905.2 Late effect of fracture of upper extremities

ICD-9-CM Procedural

77.83 Other partial ostectomy of radius and ulna

25170

25170 Radical resection of tumor, radius or ulna

ICD-9-CM Diagnostic

170.4 Malignant neoplasm of scapula and long bones of upper limb
198.5 Secondary malignant neoplasm of bone and bone marrow
209.73 Secondary neuroendocrine tumor of bone
238.0 Neoplasm of uncertain behavior of bone and articular cartilage
239.2 Neoplasms of unspecified nature of bone, soft tissue, and skin

ICD-9-CM Procedural

77.63 Local excision of lesion or tissue of radius and ulna

25210-25215

25210 Carpectomy; 1 bone
25215 all bones of proximal row

ICD-9-CM Diagnostic

357.1 Polyneuropathy in collagen vascular disease — (Code first underlying disease: 446.0, 710.0, 714.0) ☒
359.6 Symptomatic inflammatory myopathy in diseases classified elsewhere — (Code first underlying disease: 135, 140.0-208.9, 277.30-277.39, 446.0, 710.0, 710.1, 710.2, 714.0) ☒
446.0 Polyarteritis nodosa
710.0 Systemic lupus erythematosus — (Use additional code to identify manifestation: 424.91, 581.81, 582.81, 583.81)
710.1 Systemic sclerosis — (Use additional code to identify manifestation: 359.6, 517.2)
710.2 Sicca syndrome
714.0 Rheumatoid arthritis — (Use additional code to identify manifestation: 357.1, 359.6)
715.04 Generalized osteoarthrosis, involving hand
715.14 Primary localized osteoarthrosis, hand
715.34 Localized osteoarthrosis not specified whether primary or secondary, hand
715.94 Osteoarthrosis, unspecified whether generalized or localized, hand ▽
716.14 Traumatic arthropathy, hand
716.64 Unspecified monoarthritis, hand ▽
716.94 Unspecified arthropathy, hand ▽
718.83 Other joint derangement, not elsewhere classified, forearm
726.91 Exostosis of unspecified site ▽
727.05 Other tenosynovitis of hand and wrist
730.14 Chronic osteomyelitis, hand — (Use additional code to identify organism: 041.1. Use additional code to identify major osseous defect, if applicable: 731.3)
730.24 Unspecified osteomyelitis, hand — (Use additional code to identify organism: 041.1. Use additional code to identify major osseous defect, if applicable: 731.3) ▽
730.84 Other infections involving diseases classified elsewhere, hand bone — (Use additional code to identify organism: 041.1. Code first underlying disease: 002.0, 015.0-015.9) ☒
730.94 Unspecified infection of bone, hand — (Use additional code to identify organism: 041.1) ▽
731.3 Major osseous defects — (Code first underlying disease: 170.0-170.9, 730.00-730.29, 733.00-733.09, 733.40-733.49, 996.45)
733.49 Aseptic necrosis of other bone site — (Use additional code to identify major osseous defect, if applicable: 731.3)
733.82 Nonunion of fracture
814.00 Unspecified closed fracture of carpal bone ▽
814.01 Closed fracture of navicular (scaphoid) bone of wrist
814.02 Closed fracture of lunate (semilunar) bone of wrist
814.03 Closed fracture of triquetral (cuneiform) bone of wrist
814.04 Closed fracture of pisiform bone of wrist
814.05 Closed fracture of trapezium bone (larger multangular) of wrist
814.06 Closed fracture of trapezoid bone (smaller multangular) of wrist
814.07 Closed fracture of capitate bone (os magnum) of wrist
814.08 Closed fracture of hamate (unciform) bone of wrist
814.09 Closed fracture of other bone of wrist
814.10 Unspecified open fracture of carpal bone ▽
814.11 Open fracture of navicular (scaphoid) bone of wrist
814.12 Open fracture of lunate (semilunar) bone of wrist
814.13 Open fracture of triquetral (cuneiform) bone of wrist
814.14 Open fracture of pisiform bone of wrist
814.15 Open fracture of trapezium bone (larger multangular) of wrist
814.16 Open fracture of trapezoid bone (smaller multangular) of wrist
814.17 Open fracture of capitate bone (os magnum) of wrist
814.18 Open fracture of hamate (unciform) bone of wrist
814.19 Open fracture of other bone of wrist

906.4 Late effect of crushing

927.21 Crushing injury of wrist — (Use additional code to identify any associated injuries: 800-829, 850.0-854.1, 860.0-869.1)

ICD-9-CM Procedural

77.84 Other partial ostectomy of carpals and metacarpals

77.94 Total ostectomy of carpals and metacarpals

25230

25230 Radial styloidectomy (separate procedure)

ICD-9-CM Diagnostic

170.5 Malignant neoplasm of short bones of upper limb

198.5 Secondary malignant neoplasm of bone and bone marrow

213.5 Benign neoplasm of short bones of upper limb

238.0 Neoplasm of uncertain behavior of bone and articular cartilage

239.2 Neoplasms of unspecified nature of bone, soft tissue, and skin

357.1 Polyneuropathy in collagen vascular disease — (Code first underlying disease: 446.0, 710.0, 714.0) ☒

359.6 Symptomatic inflammatory myopathy in diseases classified elsewhere — (Code first underlying disease: 135, 140.0-208.9, 277.30-277.39, 446.0, 710.0, 710.1, 710.2, 714.0) ☒

446.0 Polyarteritis nodosa

710.0 Systemic lupus erythematosus — (Use additional code to identify manifestation: 424.91, 581.81, 582.81, 583.81)

710.1 Systemic sclerosis — (Use additional code to identify manifestation: 359.6, 517.2)

710.2 Sicca syndrome

714.0 Rheumatoid arthritis — (Use additional code to identify manifestation: 357.1, 359.6)

715.13 Primary localized osteoarthrosis, forearm

715.93 Osteoarthrosis, unspecified whether generalized or localized, forearm ▽

716.13 Traumatic arthropathy, forearm

716.93 Unspecified arthropathy, forearm ▽

718.83 Other joint derangement, not elsewhere classified, forearm

727.00 Unspecified synovitis and tenosynovitis ▽

727.04 Radial styloid tenosynovitis

727.05 Other tenosynovitis of hand and wrist

729.5 Pain in soft tissues of limb

730.13 Chronic osteomyelitis, forearm — (Use additional code to identify organism: 041.1. Use additional code to identify major osseous defect, if applicable: 731.3)

730.23 Unspecified osteomyelitis, forearm — (Use additional code to identify organism: 041.1. Use additional code to identify major osseous defect, if applicable: 731.3) ▽

730.83 Other infections involving bone in diseases classified elsewhere, forearm — (Use additional code to identify organism: 041.1. Code first underlying disease: 002.0, 015.0-015.9) ☒

731.3 Major osseous defects — (Code first underlying disease: 170.0-170.9, 730.00-730.29, 733.00-733.09, 733.40-733.49, 996.45)

732.3 Juvenile osteochondrosis of upper extremity

733.81 Malunion of fracture

733.82 Nonunion of fracture

ICD-9-CM Procedural

77.83 Other partial ostectomy of radius and ulna

25240

25240 Excision distal ulna partial or complete (eg, Darrach type or matched resection)

ICD-9-CM Diagnostic

238.0 Neoplasm of uncertain behavior of bone and articular cartilage

239.2 Neoplasms of unspecified nature of bone, soft tissue, and skin

357.1 Polyneuropathy in collagen vascular disease — (Code first underlying disease: 446.0, 710.0, 714.0) ☒

359.6 Symptomatic inflammatory myopathy in diseases classified elsewhere — (Code first underlying disease: 135, 140.0-208.9, 277.30-277.39, 446.0, 710.0, 710.1, 710.2, 714.0) ☒

446.0 Polyarteritis nodosa

710.0 Systemic lupus erythematosus — (Use additional code to identify manifestation: 424.91, 581.81, 582.81, 583.81)

710.1 Systemic sclerosis — (Use additional code to identify manifestation: 359.6, 517.2)

710.2 Sicca syndrome

714.0 Rheumatoid arthritis — (Use additional code to identify manifestation: 357.1, 359.6)

715.13 Primary localized osteoarthrosis, forearm

715.93 Osteoarthrosis, unspecified whether generalized or localized, forearm ▽

716.13 Traumatic arthropathy, forearm

716.93 Unspecified arthropathy, forearm ▽

718.83 Other joint derangement, not elsewhere classified, forearm

727.00 Unspecified synovitis and tenosynovitis ▽

727.05 Other tenosynovitis of hand and wrist

730.13 Chronic osteomyelitis, forearm — (Use additional code to identify organism: 041.1. Use additional code to identify major osseous defect, if applicable: 731.3)

730.23 Unspecified osteomyelitis, forearm — (Use additional code to identify organism: 041.1. Use additional code to identify major osseous defect, if applicable: 731.3) ▽

730.83 Other infections involving bone in diseases classified elsewhere, forearm — (Use additional code to identify organism: 041.1. Code first underlying disease: 002.0, 015.0-015.9) ☒

731.3 Major osseous defects — (Code first underlying disease: 170.0-170.9, 730.00-730.29, 733.00-733.09, 733.40-733.49, 996.45)

732.3 Juvenile osteochondrosis of upper extremity

733.81 Malunion of fracture

733.82 Nonunion of fracture

736.09 Other acquired deformities of forearm, excluding fingers

ICD-9-CM Procedural

77.83 Other partial ostectomy of radius and ulna

25246

25246 Injection procedure for wrist arthrography

ICD-9-CM Diagnostic

275.40 Unspecified disorder of calcium metabolism — (Use additional code to identify any associated intellectual disabilities) ▽

275.42 Hypercalcemia — (Use additional code to identify any associated intellectual disabilities)

275.49 Other disorders of calcium metabolism — (Use additional code to identify any associated intellectual disabilities)

275.5 Hungry bone syndrome — (Use additional code to identify any associated intellectual disabilities)

718.03 Articular cartilage disorder, forearm

718.13 Loose body in forearm joint

718.73 Developmental dislocation of joint, forearm

718.93 Unspecified derangement, forearm joint ▽

814.00 Unspecified closed fracture of carpal bone ▽

814.01 Closed fracture of navicular (scaphoid) bone of wrist

814.02 Closed fracture of lunate (semilunar) bone of wrist

814.03 Closed fracture of triquetral (cuneiform) bone of wrist

814.04 Closed fracture of pisiform bone of wrist

814.05 Closed fracture of trapezium bone (larger multangular) of wrist

814.06 Closed fracture of trapezoid bone (smaller multangular) of wrist

814.07 Closed fracture of capitate bone (os magnum) of wrist

814.08 Closed fracture of hamate (unciform) bone of wrist

814.09 Closed fracture of other bone of wrist

814.10 Unspecified open fracture of carpal bone ▽

814.11 Open fracture of navicular (scaphoid) bone of wrist

814.12 Open fracture of lunate (semilunar) bone of wrist
814.13 Open fracture of triquetral (cuneiform) bone of wrist
814.14 Open fracture of pisiform bone of wrist
814.15 Open fracture of trapezium bone (larger multangular) of wrist
814.16 Open fracture of trapezoid bone (smaller multangular) of wrist
814.17 Open fracture of capitate bone (os magnum) of wrist
814.18 Open fracture of hamate (unciform) bone of wrist
814.19 Open fracture of other bone of wrist
833.00 Closed dislocation of wrist, unspecified part ▽
833.01 Closed dislocation of distal radioulnar (joint)
833.02 Closed dislocation of radiocarpal (joint)
833.03 Closed dislocation of midcarpal (joint)
833.04 Closed dislocation of carpometacarpal (joint)
833.05 Closed dislocation of proximal end of metacarpal (bone)
833.09 Closed dislocation of other part of wrist
833.10 Open dislocation of wrist, unspecified part ▽
833.11 Open dislocation of distal radioulnar (joint)
833.12 Open dislocation of radiocarpal (joint)
833.13 Open dislocation of midcarpal (joint)
833.14 Open dislocation of carpometacarpal (joint)
833.15 Open dislocation of proximal end of metacarpal (bone)
833.19 Open dislocation of other part of wrist
842.00 Sprain and strain of unspecified site of wrist ▽
842.01 Sprain and strain of carpal (joint) of wrist
842.02 Sprain and strain of radiocarpal (joint) (ligament) of wrist
842.09 Other wrist sprain and strain
881.12 Open wound of wrist, complicated
881.22 Open wound of wrist, with tendon involvement
927.21 Crushing injury of wrist — (Use additional code to identify any associated injuries: 800-829, 850.0-854.1, 860.0-869.1)
959.3 Injury, other and unspecified, elbow, forearm, and wrist

ICD-9-CM Procedural

81.92 Injection of therapeutic substance into joint or ligament
88.32 Contrast arthrogram

25248

25248 Exploration with removal of deep foreign body, forearm or wrist

ICD-9-CM Diagnostic

728.82 Foreign body granuloma of muscle — (Use additional code to identify foreign body (V90.01-V90.9))
729.6 Residual foreign body in soft tissue — (Use additional code to identify foreign body (V90.01-V90.9))
881.10 Open wound of forearm, complicated
881.12 Open wound of wrist, complicated
959.3 Injury, other and unspecified, elbow, forearm, and wrist

ICD-9-CM Procedural

81.91 Arthrocentesis
83.02 Myotomy
83.09 Other incision of soft tissue
98.27 Removal of foreign body without incision from upper limb, except hand

25250-25251

25250 Removal of wrist prosthesis; (separate procedure)
25251 complicated, including total wrist

ICD-9-CM Diagnostic

731.3 Major osseous defects — (Code first underlying disease: 170.0-170.9, 730.00-730.29, 733.00-733.09, 733.40-733.49, 996.45)
996.40 Unspecified mechanical complication of internal orthopedic device, implant, and graft — (Use additional code to identify prosthetic joint with mechanical complication, V43.60-V43.69) ▽
996.41 Mechanical loosening of prosthetic joint — (Use additional code to identify prosthetic joint with mechanical complication, V43.60-V43.69)
996.42 Dislocation of prosthetic joint — (Use additional code to identify prosthetic joint with mechanical complication, V43.60-V43.69)
996.43 Broken prosthetic joint implant — (Use additional code to identify prosthetic joint with mechanical complication, V43.60-V43.69)
996.44 Peri-prosthetic fracture around prosthetic joint — (Use additional code to identify prosthetic joint with mechanical complication, V43.60-V43.69.
996.45 Peri-prosthetic osteolysis — (Use additional code to identify prosthetic joint with mechanical complication, V43.60-V43.69. Use additional code to identify major osseous defect, if applicable: 731.3)
996.47 Other mechanical complication of prosthetic joint implant — (Use additional code to identify prosthetic joint with mechanical complication, V43.60-V43.69)
996.49 Other mechanical complication of other internal orthopedic device, implant, and graft — (Use additional code to identify prosthetic joint with mechanical complication, V43.60-V43.69)
996.66 Infection and inflammatory reaction due to internal joint prosthesis — (Use additional code to identify specified infections. Use additional code to identify infected prosthetic joint: V43.60-V43.69)
996.67 Infection and inflammatory reaction due to other internal orthopedic device, implant, and graft — (Use additional code to identify specified infections)
996.77 Other complications due to internal joint prosthesis — (Use additional code to identify complication: 338.18-338.19, 338.28-338.29)
996.78 Other complications due to other internal orthopedic device, implant, and graft — (Use additional code to identify complication: 338.18-338.19, 338.28-338.29)
998.6 Persistent postoperative fistula, not elsewhere classified
998.83 Non-healing surgical wound
V43.63 Wrist joint replacement by other means
V88.29 Acquired absence of other joint

ICD-9-CM Procedural

80.03 Arthrotomy for removal of prosthesis without replacement, wrist
84.57 Removal of (cement) spacer

25259

25259 Manipulation, wrist, under anesthesia

ICD-9-CM Diagnostic

357.1 Polyneuropathy in collagen vascular disease — (Code first underlying disease: 446.0, 710.0, 714.0) ☒
359.6 Symptomatic inflammatory myopathy in diseases classified elsewhere — (Code first underlying disease: 135, 140.0-208.9, 277.30-277.39, 446.0, 710.0, 710.1, 710.2, 714.0) ☒
446.0 Polyarteritis nodosa
710.0 Systemic lupus erythematosus — (Use additional code to identify manifestation: 424.91, 581.81, 582.81, 583.81)
710.1 Systemic sclerosis — (Use additional code to identify manifestation: 359.6, 517.2)
710.2 Sicca syndrome
714.0 Rheumatoid arthritis — (Use additional code to identify manifestation: 357.1, 359.6)
715.13 Primary localized osteoarthrosis, forearm
715.93 Osteoarthrosis, unspecified whether generalized or localized, forearm ▽
718.43 Contracture of forearm joint
718.53 Ankylosis of forearm joint
719.23 Villonodular synovitis, forearm
719.53 Stiffness of joint, not elsewhere classified, forearm
726.4 Enthesopathy of wrist and carpus

ICD-9-CM Procedural

93.25 Forced extension of limb

93.26 Manual rupture of joint adhesions
93.29 Other forcible correction of musculoskeletal deformity

25260-25265

25260 Repair, tendon or muscle, flexor, forearm and/or wrist; primary, single, each tendon or muscle
25263 secondary, single, each tendon or muscle
25265 secondary, with free graft (includes obtaining graft), each tendon or muscle

ICD-9-CM Diagnostic

727.64 Nontraumatic rupture of flexor tendons of hand and wrist
727.69 Nontraumatic rupture of other tendon
727.9 Unspecified disorder of synovium, tendon, and bursa ▽
841.8 Sprain and strain of other specified sites of elbow and forearm
842.00 Sprain and strain of unspecified site of wrist ▽
842.01 Sprain and strain of carpal (joint) of wrist
842.02 Sprain and strain of radiocarpal (joint) (ligament) of wrist
842.09 Other wrist sprain and strain
881.20 Open wound of forearm, with tendon involvement
881.22 Open wound of wrist, with tendon involvement
884.2 Multiple and unspecified open wound of upper limb, with tendon involvement
905.8 Late effect of tendon injury
959.3 Injury, other and unspecified, elbow, forearm, and wrist

ICD-9-CM Procedural

83.64 Other suture of tendon
83.65 Other suture of muscle or fascia
83.81 Tendon graft
83.82 Graft of muscle or fascia
83.88 Other plastic operations on tendon
83.99 Other operations on muscle, tendon, fascia, and bursa

25270-25274

25270 Repair, tendon or muscle, extensor, forearm and/or wrist; primary, single, each tendon or muscle
25272 secondary, single, each tendon or muscle
25274 secondary, with free graft (includes obtaining graft), each tendon or muscle

ICD-9-CM Diagnostic

727.63 Nontraumatic rupture of extensor tendons of hand and wrist
727.69 Nontraumatic rupture of other tendon
727.9 Unspecified disorder of synovium, tendon, and bursa ▽
841.8 Sprain and strain of other specified sites of elbow and forearm
842.00 Sprain and strain of unspecified site of wrist ▽
842.01 Sprain and strain of carpal (joint) of wrist
842.02 Sprain and strain of radiocarpal (joint) (ligament) of wrist
842.09 Other wrist sprain and strain
881.20 Open wound of forearm, with tendon involvement
881.22 Open wound of wrist, with tendon involvement
884.2 Multiple and unspecified open wound of upper limb, with tendon involvement
905.7 Late effect of sprain and strain without mention of tendon injury
905.8 Late effect of tendon injury
959.3 Injury, other and unspecified, elbow, forearm, and wrist

ICD-9-CM Procedural

83.64 Other suture of tendon
83.65 Other suture of muscle or fascia
83.81 Tendon graft
83.88 Other plastic operations on tendon
83.99 Other operations on muscle, tendon, fascia, and bursa

HCPCS Level II Supplies & Services

A4570 Splint

25275

25275 Repair, tendon sheath, extensor, forearm and/or wrist, with free graft (includes obtaining graft) (eg, for extensor carpi ulnaris subluxation)

ICD-9-CM Diagnostic

727.63 Nontraumatic rupture of extensor tendons of hand and wrist
727.69 Nontraumatic rupture of other tendon
727.9 Unspecified disorder of synovium, tendon, and bursa ▽
841.8 Sprain and strain of other specified sites of elbow and forearm
842.00 Sprain and strain of unspecified site of wrist ▽
842.01 Sprain and strain of carpal (joint) of wrist
842.02 Sprain and strain of radiocarpal (joint) (ligament) of wrist
842.09 Other wrist sprain and strain
881.20 Open wound of forearm, with tendon involvement
881.22 Open wound of wrist, with tendon involvement
884.2 Multiple and unspecified open wound of upper limb, with tendon involvement
905.7 Late effect of sprain and strain without mention of tendon injury
905.8 Late effect of tendon injury
959.3 Injury, other and unspecified, elbow, forearm, and wrist

ICD-9-CM Procedural

83.61 Suture of tendon sheath
83.81 Tendon graft

25280

25280 Lengthening or shortening of flexor or extensor tendon, forearm and/or wrist, single, each tendon

ICD-9-CM Diagnostic

342.10 Spastic hemiplegia affecting unspecified side ▽
342.11 Spastic hemiplegia affecting dominant side
342.12 Spastic hemiplegia affecting nondominant side
342.80 Other specified hemiplegia affecting unspecified side ▽
342.81 Other specified hemiplegia affecting dominant side
342.82 Other specified hemiplegia affecting nondominant side
343.9 Unspecified infantile cerebral palsy ▽
344.89 Other specified paralytic syndrome
718.33 Recurrent dislocation of forearm joint
718.43 Contracture of forearm joint
727.81 Contracture of tendon (sheath)

ICD-9-CM Procedural

83.85 Other change in muscle or tendon length

25290

25290 Tenotomy, open, flexor or extensor tendon, forearm and/or wrist, single, each tendon

ICD-9-CM Diagnostic

718.43 Contracture of forearm joint
726.4 Enthesopathy of wrist and carpus
727.00 Unspecified synovitis and tenosynovitis ▽
727.01 Synovitis and tenosynovitis in diseases classified elsewhere — (Code first underlying disease: 015.0-015.9) ☒
727.02 Giant cell tumor of tendon sheath
727.03 Trigger finger (acquired)
727.04 Radial styloid tenosynovitis
727.05 Other tenosynovitis of hand and wrist
727.81 Contracture of tendon (sheath)

ICD-9-CM Procedural

83.13 Other tenotomy

25295

25295 Tenolysis, flexor or extensor tendon, forearm and/or wrist, single, each tendon

ICD-9-CM Diagnostic

342.10 Spastic hemiplegia affecting unspecified side ▽
342.11 Spastic hemiplegia affecting dominant side
342.12 Spastic hemiplegia affecting nondominant side
343.9 Unspecified infantile cerebral palsy ▽
344.81 Locked-in state
357.1 Polyneuropathy in collagen vascular disease — (Code first underlying disease: 446.0, 710.0, 714.0) ☒
359.6 Symptomatic inflammatory myopathy in diseases classified elsewhere — (Code first underlying disease: 135, 140.0-208.9, 277.30-277.39, 446.0, 710.0, 710.1, 710.2, 714.0) ☒
446.0 Polyarteritis nodosa
710.0 Systemic lupus erythematosus — (Use additional code to identify manifestation: 424.91, 581.81, 582.81, 583.81)
710.1 Systemic sclerosis — (Use additional code to identify manifestation: 359.6, 517.2)
710.2 Sicca syndrome
714.0 Rheumatoid arthritis — (Use additional code to identify manifestation: 357.1, 359.6)
727.05 Other tenosynovitis of hand and wrist
727.42 Ganglion of tendon sheath
727.81 Contracture of tendon (sheath)
727.82 Calcium deposits in tendon and bursa
727.89 Other disorders of synovium, tendon, and bursa
727.9 Unspecified disorder of synovium, tendon, and bursa ▽
905.8 Late effect of tendon injury

ICD-9-CM Procedural

83.91 Lysis of adhesions of muscle, tendon, fascia, and bursa

25300-25301

25300 Tenodesis at wrist; flexors of fingers
25301 extensors of fingers

ICD-9-CM Diagnostic

138 Late effects of acute poliomyelitis — (Note: This category is to be used to indicate conditions classifiable to 045 as the cause of late effects, which are themselves classified elsewhere. The "late effects" include those specified as such, as sequelae, or as due to old or inactive poliomyelitis, without evidence of active disease.)
343.8 Other specified infantile cerebral palsy
718.73 Developmental dislocation of joint, forearm
718.74 Developmental dislocation of joint, hand
726.4 Enthesopathy of wrist and carpus
727.63 Nontraumatic rupture of extensor tendons of hand and wrist
727.64 Nontraumatic rupture of flexor tendons of hand and wrist
727.9 Unspecified disorder of synovium, tendon, and bursa ▽
833.00 Closed dislocation of wrist, unspecified part ▽
833.01 Closed dislocation of distal radioulnar (joint)
833.02 Closed dislocation of radiocarpal (joint)
833.03 Closed dislocation of midcarpal (joint)
833.04 Closed dislocation of carpometacarpal (joint)
833.05 Closed dislocation of proximal end of metacarpal (bone)
833.09 Closed dislocation of other part of wrist
834.00 Closed dislocation of finger, unspecified part ▽
834.01 Closed dislocation of metacarpophalangeal (joint)
834.02 Closed dislocation of interphalangeal (joint), hand
834.10 Open dislocation of finger, unspecified part ▽
834.11 Open dislocation of metacarpophalangeal (joint)
834.12 Open dislocation interphalangeal (joint), hand
881.22 Open wound of wrist, with tendon involvement
883.2 Open wound of finger(s), with tendon involvement
884.2 Multiple and unspecified open wound of upper limb, with tendon involvement
905.8 Late effect of tendon injury

ICD-9-CM Procedural

82.85 Other tenodesis of hand
83.88 Other plastic operations on tendon

25310-25312

25310 Tendon transplantation or transfer, flexor or extensor, forearm and/or wrist, single; each tendon
25312 with tendon graft(s) (includes obtaining graft), each tendon

ICD-9-CM Diagnostic

138 Late effects of acute poliomyelitis — (Note: This category is to be used to indicate conditions classifiable to 045 as the cause of late effects, which are themselves classified elsewhere. The "late effects" include those specified as such, as sequelae, or as due to old or inactive poliomyelitis, without evidence of active disease.)
343.8 Other specified infantile cerebral palsy
357.1 Polyneuropathy in collagen vascular disease — (Code first underlying disease: 446.0, 710.0, 714.0) ☒
359.6 Symptomatic inflammatory myopathy in diseases classified elsewhere — (Code first underlying disease: 135, 140.0-208.9, 277.30-277.39, 446.0, 710.0, 710.1, 710.2, 714.0) ☒
446.0 Polyarteritis nodosa
710.0 Systemic lupus erythematosus — (Use additional code to identify manifestation: 424.91, 581.81, 582.81, 583.81)
710.1 Systemic sclerosis — (Use additional code to identify manifestation: 359.6, 517.2)
710.2 Sicca syndrome
714.0 Rheumatoid arthritis — (Use additional code to identify manifestation: 357.1, 359.6)
715.13 Primary localized osteoarthrosis, forearm
715.33 Localized osteoarthrosis not specified whether primary or secondary, forearm
715.93 Osteoarthrosis, unspecified whether generalized or localized, forearm ▽
726.4 Enthesopathy of wrist and carpus
727.63 Nontraumatic rupture of extensor tendons of hand and wrist
727.64 Nontraumatic rupture of flexor tendons of hand and wrist
881.20 Open wound of forearm, with tendon involvement
881.22 Open wound of wrist, with tendon involvement
905.8 Late effect of tendon injury

ICD-9-CM Procedural

83.75 Tendon transfer or transplantation
83.81 Tendon graft

25315-25316

25315 Flexor origin slide (eg, for cerebral palsy, Volkmann contracture), forearm and/or wrist;
25316 with tendon(s) transfer

ICD-9-CM Diagnostic

138 Late effects of acute poliomyelitis — (Note: This category is to be used to indicate conditions classifiable to 045 as the cause of late effects, which are themselves classified elsewhere. The "late effects" include those specified as such, as sequelae, or as due to old or inactive poliomyelitis, without evidence of active disease.)
343.0 Diplegic infantile cerebral palsy
343.1 Hemiplegic infantile cerebral palsy
343.2 Quadriplegic infantile cerebral palsy
343.3 Monoplegic infantile cerebral palsy
343.4 Infantile hemiplegia

343.8	Other specified infantile cerebral palsy
343.9	Unspecified infantile cerebral palsy ▽
726.4	Enthesopathy of wrist and carpus
728.88	Rhabdomyolysis
755.26	Congenital longitudinal deficiency, radial, complete or partial (with or without distal deficiencies, incomplete)
881.20	Open wound of forearm, with tendon involvement
881.22	Open wound of wrist, with tendon involvement
905.8	Late effect of tendon injury
958.6	Volkmann's ischemic contracture

ICD-9-CM Procedural

82.85	Other tenodesis of hand
83.75	Tendon transfer or transplantation
83.88	Other plastic operations on tendon

25320

25320 Capsulorrhaphy or reconstruction, wrist, open (eg, capsulodesis, ligament repair, tendon transfer or graft) (includes synovectomy, capsulotomy and open reduction) for carpal instability

ICD-9-CM Diagnostic

170.5	Malignant neoplasm of short bones of upper limb
357.1	Polyneuropathy in collagen vascular disease — (Code first underlying disease: 446.0, 710.0, 714.0) ☒
359.6	Symptomatic inflammatory myopathy in diseases classified elsewhere — (Code first underlying disease: 135, 140.0-208.9, 277.30-277.39, 446.0, 710.0, 710.1, 710.2, 714.0) ☒
446.0	Polyarteritis nodosa
710.0	Systemic lupus erythematosus — (Use additional code to identify manifestation: 424.91, 581.81, 582.81, 583.81)
710.1	Systemic sclerosis — (Use additional code to identify manifestation: 359.6, 517.2)
710.2	Sicca syndrome
710.3	Dermatomyositis
710.4	Polymyositis
710.5	Eosinophilia myalgia syndrome — (Use additional E code to identify drug, if drug-induced)
710.8	Other specified diffuse disease of connective tissue
710.9	Unspecified diffuse connective tissue disease ▽
714.0	Rheumatoid arthritis — (Use additional code to identify manifestation: 357.1, 359.6)
714.9	Unspecified inflammatory polyarthropathy ▽
715.13	Primary localized osteoarthrosis, forearm
715.93	Osteoarthrosis, unspecified whether generalized or localized, forearm ▽
718.03	Articular cartilage disorder, forearm
718.73	Developmental dislocation of joint, forearm
718.83	Other joint derangement, not elsewhere classified, forearm
727.63	Nontraumatic rupture of extensor tendons of hand and wrist
727.64	Nontraumatic rupture of flexor tendons of hand and wrist
727.9	Unspecified disorder of synovium, tendon, and bursa ▽
731.1	Osteitis deformans in diseases classified elsewhere — (Code first underlying disease: 170.0-170.9) ☒
833.00	Closed dislocation of wrist, unspecified part ▽
833.10	Open dislocation of wrist, unspecified part ▽
881.12	Open wound of wrist, complicated
881.22	Open wound of wrist, with tendon involvement
884.1	Multiple and unspecified open wound of upper limb, complicated

ICD-9-CM Procedural

81.75	Arthroplasty of carpocarpal or carpometacarpal joint without implant
81.93	Suture of capsule or ligament of upper extremity
83.73	Reattachment of tendon
83.75	Tendon transfer or transplantation

25332

25332 Arthroplasty, wrist, with or without interposition, with or without external or internal fixation

ICD-9-CM Diagnostic

357.1	Polyneuropathy in collagen vascular disease — (Code first underlying disease: 446.0, 710.0, 714.0) ☒
359.6	Symptomatic inflammatory myopathy in diseases classified elsewhere — (Code first underlying disease: 135, 140.0-208.9, 277.30-277.39, 446.0, 710.0, 710.1, 710.2, 714.0) ☒
446.0	Polyarteritis nodosa
710.0	Systemic lupus erythematosus — (Use additional code to identify manifestation: 424.91, 581.81, 582.81, 583.81)
710.1	Systemic sclerosis — (Use additional code to identify manifestation: 359.6, 517.2)
710.2	Sicca syndrome
714.0	Rheumatoid arthritis — (Use additional code to identify manifestation: 357.1, 359.6)
714.9	Unspecified inflammatory polyarthropathy ▽
715.13	Primary localized osteoarthrosis, forearm
715.93	Osteoarthrosis, unspecified whether generalized or localized, forearm ▽
716.93	Unspecified arthropathy, forearm ▽
719.13	Hemarthrosis, forearm
733.81	Malunion of fracture
733.82	Nonunion of fracture
905.2	Late effect of fracture of upper extremities

ICD-9-CM Procedural

81.74	Arthroplasty of carpocarpal or carpometacarpal joint with implant

25335

25335 Centralization of wrist on ulna (eg, radial club hand)

ICD-9-CM Diagnostic

357.1	Polyneuropathy in collagen vascular disease — (Code first underlying disease: 446.0, 710.0, 714.0) ☒
359.6	Symptomatic inflammatory myopathy in diseases classified elsewhere — (Code first underlying disease: 135, 140.0-208.9, 277.30-277.39, 446.0, 710.0, 710.1, 710.2, 714.0) ☒
446.0	Polyarteritis nodosa
710.0	Systemic lupus erythematosus — (Use additional code to identify manifestation: 424.91, 581.81, 582.81, 583.81)
710.1	Systemic sclerosis — (Use additional code to identify manifestation: 359.6, 517.2)
710.2	Sicca syndrome
714.0	Rheumatoid arthritis — (Use additional code to identify manifestation: 357.1, 359.6)
736.00	Unspecified deformity of forearm, excluding fingers ▽
736.07	Club hand, acquired
736.09	Other acquired deformities of forearm, excluding fingers
754.89	Other specified nonteratogenic anomalies
755.50	Unspecified congenital anomaly of upper limb ▽

ICD-9-CM Procedural

78.54	Internal fixation of carpals and metacarpals without fracture reduction
80.43	Division of joint capsule, ligament, or cartilage of wrist
81.75	Arthroplasty of carpocarpal or carpometacarpal joint without implant

25337

25337 Reconstruction for stabilization of unstable distal ulna or distal radioulnar joint, secondary by soft tissue stabilization (eg, tendon transfer, tendon graft or weave, or tenodesis) with or without open reduction of distal radioulnar joint

ICD-9-CM Diagnostic

716.13 Traumatic arthropathy, forearm
718.73 Developmental dislocation of joint, forearm
718.83 Other joint derangement, not elsewhere classified, forearm
726.90 Enthesopathy of unspecified site ▽
727.05 Other tenosynovitis of hand and wrist
727.63 Nontraumatic rupture of extensor tendons of hand and wrist
727.64 Nontraumatic rupture of flexor tendons of hand and wrist
728.4 Laxity of ligament
728.5 Hypermobility syndrome
813.43 Closed fracture of distal end of ulna (alone)
813.53 Open fracture of distal end of ulna (alone)
813.92 Open fracture of unspecified part of ulna (alone) ▽
833.01 Closed dislocation of distal radioulnar (joint)
833.09 Closed dislocation of other part of wrist
833.11 Open dislocation of distal radioulnar (joint)
833.19 Open dislocation of other part of wrist
881.20 Open wound of forearm, with tendon involvement
927.10 Crushing injury of forearm — (Use additional code to identify any associated injuries: 800-829, 850.0-854.1, 860.0-869.1)

ICD-9-CM Procedural

78.43 Other repair or plastic operations on radius and ulna
79.22 Open reduction of fracture of radius and ulna without internal fixation
83.75 Tendon transfer or transplantation
83.81 Tendon graft

25350-25355

25350 Osteotomy, radius; distal third
25355 middle or proximal third

ICD-9-CM Diagnostic

170.4 Malignant neoplasm of scapula and long bones of upper limb
198.5 Secondary malignant neoplasm of bone and bone marrow
213.4 Benign neoplasm of scapula and long bones of upper limb
715.13 Primary localized osteoarthrosis, forearm
715.23 Secondary localized osteoarthrosis, forearm
718.83 Other joint derangement, not elsewhere classified, forearm
731.1 Osteitis deformans in diseases classified elsewhere — (Code first underlying disease: 170.0-170.9) ☒
731.3 Major osseous defects — (Code first underlying disease: 170.0-170.9, 730.00-730.29, 733.00-733.09, 733.40-733.49, 996.45)
733.12 Pathologic fracture of distal radius and ulna
733.49 Aseptic necrosis of other bone site — (Use additional code to identify major osseous defect, if applicable: 731.3)
733.81 Malunion of fracture
733.82 Nonunion of fracture
736.89 Other acquired deformity of other parts of limb
755.53 Radioulnar synostosis
756.51 Osteogenesis imperfecta
813.41 Closed Colles' fracture
813.42 Other closed fractures of distal end of radius (alone)
813.45 Torus fracture of radius (alone)
813.51 Open Colles' fracture
813.52 Other open fractures of distal end of radius (alone)
905.2 Late effect of fracture of upper extremities

ICD-9-CM Procedural

77.23 Wedge osteotomy of radius and ulna
77.33 Other division of radius and ulna

25360-25365

25360 Osteotomy; ulna
25365 radius AND ulna

ICD-9-CM Diagnostic

170.4 Malignant neoplasm of scapula and long bones of upper limb
198.5 Secondary malignant neoplasm of bone and bone marrow
213.4 Benign neoplasm of scapula and long bones of upper limb
715.13 Primary localized osteoarthrosis, forearm
715.23 Secondary localized osteoarthrosis, forearm
731.1 Osteitis deformans in diseases classified elsewhere — (Code first underlying disease: 170.0-170.9) ☒
731.3 Major osseous defects — (Code first underlying disease: 170.0-170.9, 730.00-730.29, 733.00-733.09, 733.40-733.49, 996.45)
733.49 Aseptic necrosis of other bone site — (Use additional code to identify major osseous defect, if applicable: 731.3)
733.81 Malunion of fracture
733.82 Nonunion of fracture
736.89 Other acquired deformity of other parts of limb
755.53 Radioulnar synostosis
756.51 Osteogenesis imperfecta
905.2 Late effect of fracture of upper extremities

ICD-9-CM Procedural

77.23 Wedge osteotomy of radius and ulna
77.33 Other division of radius and ulna

25370-25375

25370 Multiple osteotomies, with realignment on intramedullary rod (Sofield type procedure); radius OR ulna
25375 radius AND ulna

ICD-9-CM Diagnostic

170.4 Malignant neoplasm of scapula and long bones of upper limb
198.5 Secondary malignant neoplasm of bone and bone marrow
209.73 Secondary neuroendocrine tumor of bone
213.4 Benign neoplasm of scapula and long bones of upper limb
715.13 Primary localized osteoarthrosis, forearm
716.13 Traumatic arthropathy, forearm
716.53 Unspecified polyarthropathy or polyarthritis, forearm ▽
716.93 Unspecified arthropathy, forearm ▽
731.1 Osteitis deformans in diseases classified elsewhere — (Code first underlying disease: 170.0-170.9) ☒
731.3 Major osseous defects — (Code first underlying disease: 170.0-170.9, 730.00-730.29, 733.00-733.09, 733.40-733.49, 996.45)
733.81 Malunion of fracture
733.82 Nonunion of fracture
736.89 Other acquired deformity of other parts of limb
755.50 Unspecified congenital anomaly of upper limb ▽
755.59 Other congenital anomaly of upper limb, including shoulder girdle
756.51 Osteogenesis imperfecta
756.53 Osteopoikilosis
V54.02 Encounter for lengthening/adjustment of growth rod

ICD-9-CM Procedural

77.23 Wedge osteotomy of radius and ulna
77.33 Other division of radius and ulna

78.43 Other repair or plastic operations on radius and ulna

25390

25390 Osteoplasty, radius OR ulna; shortening

ICD-9-CM Diagnostic

718.83 Other joint derangement, not elsewhere classified, forearm
732.3 Juvenile osteochondrosis of upper extremity
733.99 Other disorders of bone and cartilage
736.00 Unspecified deformity of forearm, excluding fingers ▽
736.09 Other acquired deformities of forearm, excluding fingers
755.50 Unspecified congenital anomaly of upper limb ▽
755.54 Madelung's deformity
755.59 Other congenital anomaly of upper limb, including shoulder girdle

ICD-9-CM Procedural

78.23 Limb shortening procedures, radius and ulna

25391

25391 Osteoplasty, radius OR ulna; lengthening with autograft

ICD-9-CM Diagnostic

718.83 Other joint derangement, not elsewhere classified, forearm
733.81 Malunion of fracture
733.82 Nonunion of fracture
733.99 Other disorders of bone and cartilage
736.00 Unspecified deformity of forearm, excluding fingers ▽
736.09 Other acquired deformities of forearm, excluding fingers
755.20 Congenital unspecified reduction deformity of upper limb ▽
755.26 Congenital longitudinal deficiency, radial, complete or partial (with or without distal deficiencies, incomplete)
755.27 Congenital longitudinal deficiency, ulnar, complete or partial (with or without distal deficiencies, incomplete)
755.50 Unspecified congenital anomaly of upper limb ▽

ICD-9-CM Procedural

77.79 Excision of other bone for graft, except facial bones
78.03 Bone graft of radius and ulna
78.13 Application of external fixator device, radius and ulna
78.33 Limb lengthening procedures, radius and ulna
84.53 Implantation of internal limb lengthening device with kinetic distraction
84.54 Implantation of other internal limb lengthening device
84.71 Application of external fixator device, monoplanar system
84.72 Application of external fixator device, ring system
84.73 Application of hybrid external fixator device

25392

25392 Osteoplasty, radius AND ulna; shortening (excluding 64876)

ICD-9-CM Diagnostic

718.83 Other joint derangement, not elsewhere classified, forearm
732.3 Juvenile osteochondrosis of upper extremity
733.99 Other disorders of bone and cartilage
736.00 Unspecified deformity of forearm, excluding fingers ▽
736.09 Other acquired deformities of forearm, excluding fingers
755.50 Unspecified congenital anomaly of upper limb ▽
755.59 Other congenital anomaly of upper limb, including shoulder girdle

ICD-9-CM Procedural

78.23 Limb shortening procedures, radius and ulna

25393

25393 Osteoplasty, radius AND ulna; lengthening with autograft

ICD-9-CM Diagnostic

718.83 Other joint derangement, not elsewhere classified, forearm
733.81 Malunion of fracture
733.82 Nonunion of fracture
733.99 Other disorders of bone and cartilage
736.00 Unspecified deformity of forearm, excluding fingers ▽
736.09 Other acquired deformities of forearm, excluding fingers
755.20 Congenital unspecified reduction deformity of upper limb ▽
755.26 Congenital longitudinal deficiency, radial, complete or partial (with or without distal deficiencies, incomplete)
755.27 Congenital longitudinal deficiency, ulnar, complete or partial (with or without distal deficiencies, incomplete)
755.50 Unspecified congenital anomaly of upper limb ▽

ICD-9-CM Procedural

77.79 Excision of other bone for graft, except facial bones
78.03 Bone graft of radius and ulna
78.13 Application of external fixator device, radius and ulna
78.33 Limb lengthening procedures, radius and ulna
84.53 Implantation of internal limb lengthening device with kinetic distraction
84.54 Implantation of other internal limb lengthening device
84.71 Application of external fixator device, monoplanar system
84.72 Application of external fixator device, ring system
84.73 Application of hybrid external fixator device

25394

25394 Osteoplasty, carpal bone, shortening

ICD-9-CM Diagnostic

718.83 Other joint derangement, not elsewhere classified, forearm
732.3 Juvenile osteochondrosis of upper extremity
733.99 Other disorders of bone and cartilage
736.00 Unspecified deformity of forearm, excluding fingers ▽
736.09 Other acquired deformities of forearm, excluding fingers
755.50 Unspecified congenital anomaly of upper limb ▽
755.59 Other congenital anomaly of upper limb, including shoulder girdle

ICD-9-CM Procedural

78.24 Limb shortening procedures, carpals and metacarpals

25400-25405

25400 Repair of nonunion or malunion, radius OR ulna; without graft (eg, compression technique)
25405 with autograft (includes obtaining graft)

ICD-9-CM Diagnostic

733.81 Malunion of fracture
733.82 Nonunion of fracture
905.2 Late effect of fracture of upper extremities

ICD-9-CM Procedural

77.77 Excision of tibia and fibula for graft
77.79 Excision of other bone for graft, except facial bones
78.03 Bone graft of radius and ulna
78.43 Other repair or plastic operations on radius and ulna

25415-25420

25415 Repair of nonunion or malunion, radius AND ulna; without graft (eg, compression technique)

25420 with autograft (includes obtaining graft)

ICD-9-CM Diagnostic

733.81 Malunion of fracture

733.82 Nonunion of fracture

905.2 Late effect of fracture of upper extremities

ICD-9-CM Procedural

77.77 Excision of tibia and fibula for graft

77.79 Excision of other bone for graft, except facial bones

78.03 Bone graft of radius and ulna

78.43 Other repair or plastic operations on radius and ulna

25425-25426

25425 Repair of defect with autograft; radius OR ulna

25426 radius AND ulna

ICD-9-CM Diagnostic

730.13 Chronic osteomyelitis, forearm — (Use additional code to identify organism: 041.1. Use additional code to identify major osseous defect, if applicable: 731.3)

730.83 Other infections involving bone in diseases classified elsewhere, forearm — (Use additional code to identify organism: 041.1. Code first underlying disease: 002.0, 015.0-015.9) ☒

731.3 Major osseous defects — (Code first underlying disease: 170.0-170.9, 730.00-730.29, 733.00-733.09, 733.40-733.49, 996.45)

732.3 Juvenile osteochondrosis of upper extremity

733.12 Pathologic fracture of distal radius and ulna

733.49 Aseptic necrosis of other bone site — (Use additional code to identify major osseous defect, if applicable: 731.3)

733.81 Malunion of fracture

733.82 Nonunion of fracture

736.00 Unspecified deformity of forearm, excluding fingers ▽

736.05 Wrist drop (acquired)

736.09 Other acquired deformities of forearm, excluding fingers

755.26 Congenital longitudinal deficiency, radial, complete or partial (with or without distal deficiencies, incomplete)

755.27 Congenital longitudinal deficiency, ulnar, complete or partial (with or without distal deficiencies, incomplete)

905.2 Late effect of fracture of upper extremities

996.40 Unspecified mechanical complication of internal orthopedic device, implant, and graft — (Use additional code to identify prosthetic joint with mechanical complication, V43.60-V43.69) ▽

996.49 Other mechanical complication of other internal orthopedic device, implant, and graft — (Use additional code to identify prosthetic joint with mechanical complication, V43.60-V43.69)

ICD-9-CM Procedural

77.77 Excision of tibia and fibula for graft

77.79 Excision of other bone for graft, except facial bones

78.03 Bone graft of radius and ulna

78.43 Other repair or plastic operations on radius and ulna

25430

25430 Insertion of vascular pedicle into carpal bone (eg, Hori procedure)

ICD-9-CM Diagnostic

170.5 Malignant neoplasm of short bones of upper limb

198.5 Secondary malignant neoplasm of bone and bone marrow

213.5 Benign neoplasm of short bones of upper limb

238.0 Neoplasm of uncertain behavior of bone and articular cartilage

239.2 Neoplasms of unspecified nature of bone, soft tissue, and skin

730.13 Chronic osteomyelitis, forearm — (Use additional code to identify organism: 041.1. Use additional code to identify major osseous defect, if applicable: 731.3)

730.14 Chronic osteomyelitis, hand — (Use additional code to identify organism: 041.1. Use additional code to identify major osseous defect, if applicable: 731.3)

730.23 Unspecified osteomyelitis, forearm — (Use additional code to identify organism: 041.1. Use additional code to identify major osseous defect, if applicable: 731.3) ▽

730.24 Unspecified osteomyelitis, hand — (Use additional code to identify organism: 041.1. Use additional code to identify major osseous defect, if applicable: 731.3) ▽

731.3 Major osseous defects — (Code first underlying disease: 170.0-170.9, 730.00-730.29, 733.00-733.09, 733.40-733.49, 996.45)

733.19 Pathologic fracture of other specified site

733.49 Aseptic necrosis of other bone site — (Use additional code to identify major osseous defect, if applicable: 731.3)

733.82 Nonunion of fracture

733.90 Disorder of bone and cartilage, unspecified ▽

733.99 Other disorders of bone and cartilage

814.00 Unspecified closed fracture of carpal bone ▽

814.01 Closed fracture of navicular (scaphoid) bone of wrist

814.02 Closed fracture of lunate (semilunar) bone of wrist

814.03 Closed fracture of triquetral (cuneiform) bone of wrist

814.04 Closed fracture of pisiform bone of wrist

814.05 Closed fracture of trapezium bone (larger multangular) of wrist

814.06 Closed fracture of trapezoid bone (smaller multangular) of wrist

814.07 Closed fracture of capitate bone (os magnum) of wrist

814.08 Closed fracture of hamate (unciform) bone of wrist

814.09 Closed fracture of other bone of wrist

814.10 Unspecified open fracture of carpal bone ▽

814.11 Open fracture of navicular (scaphoid) bone of wrist

814.12 Open fracture of lunate (semilunar) bone of wrist

814.13 Open fracture of triquetral (cuneiform) bone of wrist

814.14 Open fracture of pisiform bone of wrist

814.15 Open fracture of trapezium bone (larger multangular) of wrist

814.16 Open fracture of trapezoid bone (smaller multangular) of wrist

814.17 Open fracture of capitate bone (os magnum) of wrist

814.18 Open fracture of hamate (unciform) bone of wrist

814.19 Open fracture of other bone of wrist

905.2 Late effect of fracture of upper extremities

927.20 Crushing injury of hand(s) — (Use additional code to identify any associated injuries: 800-829, 850.0-854.1, 860.0-869.1)

927.21 Crushing injury of wrist — (Use additional code to identify any associated injuries: 800-829, 850.0-854.1, 860.0-869.1)

ICD-9-CM Procedural

86.73 Attachment of pedicle or flap graft to hand

86.74 Attachment of pedicle or flap graft to other sites

25431

25431 Repair of nonunion of carpal bone (excluding carpal scaphoid (navicular)) (includes obtaining graft and necessary fixation), each bone

ICD-9-CM Diagnostic

733.82 Nonunion of fracture

905.2 Late effect of fracture of upper extremities

ICD-9-CM Procedural

77.77 Excision of tibia and fibula for graft

78.04 Bone graft of carpals and metacarpals

78.79 Osteoclasis of other bone, except facial bones

25440

25440 Repair of nonunion, scaphoid carpal (navicular) bone, with or without radial styloidectomy (includes obtaining graft and necessary fixation)

ICD-9-CM Diagnostic

733.82 Nonunion of fracture

905.2 Late effect of fracture of upper extremities

ICD-9-CM Procedural

77.77 Excision of tibia and fibula for graft

77.79 Excision of other bone for graft, except facial bones

78.04 Bone graft of carpals and metacarpals

25441

25441 Arthroplasty with prosthetic replacement; distal radius

ICD-9-CM Diagnostic

357.1 Polyneuropathy in collagen vascular disease — (Code first underlying disease: 446.0, 710.0, 714.0) ☒

359.6 Symptomatic inflammatory myopathy in diseases classified elsewhere — (Code first underlying disease: 135, 140.0-208.9, 277.30-277.39, 446.0, 710.0, 710.1, 710.2, 714.0) ☒

446.0 Polyarteritis nodosa

710.0 Systemic lupus erythematosus — (Use additional code to identify manifestation: 424.91, 581.81, 582.81, 583.81)

710.1 Systemic sclerosis — (Use additional code to identify manifestation: 359.6, 517.2)

710.2 Sicca syndrome

711.03 Pyogenic arthritis, forearm — (Use additional code to identify infectious organism: 041.0-041.8)

711.93 Unspecified infective arthritis, forearm ▽

714.0 Rheumatoid arthritis — (Use additional code to identify manifestation: 357.1, 359.6)

715.13 Primary localized osteoarthrosis, forearm

715.23 Secondary localized osteoarthrosis, forearm

715.33 Localized osteoarthrosis not specified whether primary or secondary, forearm

716.13 Traumatic arthropathy, forearm

716.23 Allergic arthritis, forearm

716.63 Unspecified monoarthritis, forearm ▽

716.93 Unspecified arthropathy, forearm ▽

718.83 Other joint derangement, not elsewhere classified, forearm

719.23 Villonodular synovitis, forearm

719.63 Other symptoms referable to forearm joint

730.13 Chronic osteomyelitis, forearm — (Use additional code to identify organism: 041.1. Use additional code to identify major osseous defect, if applicable: 731.3)

730.23 Unspecified osteomyelitis, forearm — (Use additional code to identify organism: 041.1. Use additional code to identify major osseous defect, if applicable: 731.3) ▽

730.33 Periostitis, without mention of osteomyelitis, forearm — (Use additional code to identify organism: 041.1)

731.3 Major osseous defects — (Code first underlying disease: 170.0-170.9, 730.00-730.29, 733.00-733.09, 733.40-733.49, 996.45)

905.2 Late effect of fracture of upper extremities

ICD-9-CM Procedural

81.74 Arthroplasty of carpocarpal or carpometacarpal joint with implant

25442

25442 Arthroplasty with prosthetic replacement; distal ulna

ICD-9-CM Diagnostic

357.1 Polyneuropathy in collagen vascular disease — (Code first underlying disease: 446.0, 710.0, 714.0) ☒

359.6 Symptomatic inflammatory myopathy in diseases classified elsewhere — (Code first underlying disease: 135, 140.0-208.9, 277.30-277.39, 446.0, 710.0, 710.1, 710.2, 714.0) ☒

446.0 Polyarteritis nodosa

710.0 Systemic lupus erythematosus — (Use additional code to identify manifestation: 424.91, 581.81, 582.81, 583.81)

710.1 Systemic sclerosis — (Use additional code to identify manifestation: 359.6, 517.2)

710.2 Sicca syndrome

711.03 Pyogenic arthritis, forearm — (Use additional code to identify infectious organism: 041.0-041.8)

711.93 Unspecified infective arthritis, forearm ▽

714.0 Rheumatoid arthritis — (Use additional code to identify manifestation: 357.1, 359.6)

715.13 Primary localized osteoarthrosis, forearm

715.23 Secondary localized osteoarthrosis, forearm

715.33 Localized osteoarthrosis not specified whether primary or secondary, forearm

716.13 Traumatic arthropathy, forearm

716.63 Unspecified monoarthritis, forearm ▽

716.93 Unspecified arthropathy, forearm ▽

718.83 Other joint derangement, not elsewhere classified, forearm

719.23 Villonodular synovitis, forearm

719.63 Other symptoms referable to forearm joint

730.13 Chronic osteomyelitis, forearm — (Use additional code to identify organism: 041.1. Use additional code to identify major osseous defect, if applicable: 731.3)

730.23 Unspecified osteomyelitis, forearm — (Use additional code to identify organism: 041.1. Use additional code to identify major osseous defect, if applicable: 731.3) ▽

730.33 Periostitis, without mention of osteomyelitis, forearm — (Use additional code to identify organism: 041.1)

731.0 Osteitis deformans without mention of bone tumor

731.3 Major osseous defects — (Code first underlying disease: 170.0-170.9, 730.00-730.29, 733.00-733.09, 733.40-733.49, 996.45)

733.49 Aseptic necrosis of other bone site — (Use additional code to identify major osseous defect, if applicable: 731.3)

733.82 Nonunion of fracture

736.00 Unspecified deformity of forearm, excluding fingers ▽

756.51 Osteogenesis imperfecta

905.2 Late effect of fracture of upper extremities

ICD-9-CM Procedural

81.74 Arthroplasty of carpocarpal or carpometacarpal joint with implant

25443

25443 Arthroplasty with prosthetic replacement; scaphoid carpal (navicular)

ICD-9-CM Diagnostic

357.1 Polyneuropathy in collagen vascular disease — (Code first underlying disease: 446.0, 710.0, 714.0) ☒

359.6 Symptomatic inflammatory myopathy in diseases classified elsewhere — (Code first underlying disease: 135, 140.0-208.9, 277.30-277.39, 446.0, 710.0, 710.1, 710.2, 714.0) ☒

446.0 Polyarteritis nodosa

710.0 Systemic lupus erythematosus — (Use additional code to identify manifestation: 424.91, 581.81, 582.81, 583.81)

710.1 Systemic sclerosis — (Use additional code to identify manifestation: 359.6, 517.2)

710.2 Sicca syndrome

711.03 Pyogenic arthritis, forearm — (Use additional code to identify infectious organism: 041.0-041.8)

711.04 Pyogenic arthritis, hand — (Use additional code to identify infectious organism: 041.0-041.8)

711.93 Unspecified infective arthritis, forearm ▽

711.94 Unspecified infective arthritis, hand ▽

714.0 Rheumatoid arthritis — (Use additional code to identify manifestation: 357.1, 359.6)

715.13 Primary localized osteoarthrosis, forearm
715.14 Primary localized osteoarthrosis, hand
715.23 Secondary localized osteoarthrosis, forearm
715.24 Secondary localized osteoarthrosis, involving hand
715.33 Localized osteoarthrosis not specified whether primary or secondary, forearm
715.34 Localized osteoarthrosis not specified whether primary or secondary, hand
716.13 Traumatic arthropathy, forearm
716.14 Traumatic arthropathy, hand
716.63 Unspecified monoarthritis, forearm
716.64 Unspecified monoarthritis, hand
716.93 Unspecified arthropathy, forearm
716.94 Unspecified arthropathy, hand
718.83 Other joint derangement, not elsewhere classified, forearm
718.84 Other joint derangement, not elsewhere classified, hand
719.23 Villonodular synovitis, forearm
719.24 Villonodular synovitis, hand
719.63 Other symptoms referable to forearm joint
719.64 Other symptoms referable to hand joint
730.13 Chronic osteomyelitis, forearm — (Use additional code to identify organism: 041.1. Use additional code to identify major osseous defect, if applicable: 731.3)
730.14 Chronic osteomyelitis, hand — (Use additional code to identify organism: 041.1. Use additional code to identify major osseous defect, if applicable: 731.3)
730.23 Unspecified osteomyelitis, forearm — (Use additional code to identify organism: 041.1. Use additional code to identify major osseous defect, if applicable: 731.3)
730.24 Unspecified osteomyelitis, hand — (Use additional code to identify organism: 041.1. Use additional code to identify major osseous defect, if applicable: 731.3)
730.33 Periostitis, without mention of osteomyelitis, forearm — (Use additional code to identify organism: 041.1)
730.34 Periostitis, without mention of osteomyelitis, hand — (Use additional code to identify organism: 041.1)
731.0 Osteitis deformans without mention of bone tumor
731.3 Major osseous defects — (Code first underlying disease: 170.0-170.9, 730.00-730.29, 733.00-733.09, 733.40-733.49, 996.45)
733.49 Aseptic necrosis of other bone site — (Use additional code to identify major osseous defect, if applicable: 731.3)
733.82 Nonunion of fracture
736.00 Unspecified deformity of forearm, excluding fingers
756.51 Osteogenesis imperfecta
905.2 Late effect of fracture of upper extremities

ICD-9-CM Procedural

81.74 Arthroplasty of carpocarpal or carpometacarpal joint with implant

25444

25444 Arthroplasty with prosthetic replacement; lunate

ICD-9-CM Diagnostic

357.1 Polyneuropathy in collagen vascular disease — (Code first underlying disease: 446.0, 710.0, 714.0)
359.6 Symptomatic inflammatory myopathy in diseases classified elsewhere — (Code first underlying disease: 135, 140.0-208.9, 277.30-277.39, 446.0, 710.0, 710.1, 710.2, 714.0)
446.0 Polyarteritis nodosa
710.0 Systemic lupus erythematosus — (Use additional code to identify manifestation: 424.91, 581.81, 582.81, 583.81)
710.1 Systemic sclerosis — (Use additional code to identify manifestation: 359.6, 517.2)
710.2 Sicca syndrome
711.03 Pyogenic arthritis, forearm — (Use additional code to identify infectious organism: 041.0-041.8)
711.04 Pyogenic arthritis, hand — (Use additional code to identify infectious organism: 041.0-041.8)
711.93 Unspecified infective arthritis, forearm
711.94 Unspecified infective arthritis, hand
714.0 Rheumatoid arthritis — (Use additional code to identify manifestation: 357.1, 359.6)
715.13 Primary localized osteoarthrosis, forearm
715.14 Primary localized osteoarthrosis, hand
715.23 Secondary localized osteoarthrosis, forearm
715.24 Secondary localized osteoarthrosis, involving hand
715.33 Localized osteoarthrosis not specified whether primary or secondary, forearm
715.34 Localized osteoarthrosis not specified whether primary or secondary, hand
716.13 Traumatic arthropathy, forearm
716.14 Traumatic arthropathy, hand
716.63 Unspecified monoarthritis, forearm
716.64 Unspecified monoarthritis, hand
716.93 Unspecified arthropathy, forearm
716.94 Unspecified arthropathy, hand
718.83 Other joint derangement, not elsewhere classified, forearm
718.84 Other joint derangement, not elsewhere classified, hand
719.23 Villonodular synovitis, forearm
719.24 Villonodular synovitis, hand
719.63 Other symptoms referable to forearm joint
719.64 Other symptoms referable to hand joint
730.13 Chronic osteomyelitis, forearm — (Use additional code to identify organism: 041.1. Use additional code to identify major osseous defect, if applicable: 731.3)
730.14 Chronic osteomyelitis, hand — (Use additional code to identify organism: 041.1. Use additional code to identify major osseous defect, if applicable: 731.3)
730.23 Unspecified osteomyelitis, forearm — (Use additional code to identify organism: 041.1. Use additional code to identify major osseous defect, if applicable: 731.3)
730.24 Unspecified osteomyelitis, hand — (Use additional code to identify organism: 041.1. Use additional code to identify major osseous defect, if applicable: 731.3)
730.33 Periostitis, without mention of osteomyelitis, forearm — (Use additional code to identify organism: 041.1)
730.34 Periostitis, without mention of osteomyelitis, hand — (Use additional code to identify organism: 041.1)
731.0 Osteitis deformans without mention of bone tumor
731.3 Major osseous defects — (Code first underlying disease: 170.0-170.9, 730.00-730.29, 733.00-733.09, 733.40-733.49, 996.45)
733.49 Aseptic necrosis of other bone site — (Use additional code to identify major osseous defect, if applicable: 731.3)
733.82 Nonunion of fracture
736.00 Unspecified deformity of forearm, excluding fingers
756.51 Osteogenesis imperfecta
905.2 Late effect of fracture of upper extremities

ICD-9-CM Procedural

81.74 Arthroplasty of carpocarpal or carpometacarpal joint with implant

25445

25445 Arthroplasty with prosthetic replacement; trapezium

ICD-9-CM Diagnostic

357.1 Polyneuropathy in collagen vascular disease — (Code first underlying disease: 446.0, 710.0, 714.0)
359.6 Symptomatic inflammatory myopathy in diseases classified elsewhere — (Code first underlying disease: 135, 140.0-208.9, 277.30-277.39, 446.0, 710.0, 710.1, 710.2, 714.0)
446.0 Polyarteritis nodosa
710.0 Systemic lupus erythematosus — (Use additional code to identify manifestation: 424.91, 581.81, 582.81, 583.81)
710.1 Systemic sclerosis — (Use additional code to identify manifestation: 359.6, 517.2)
710.2 Sicca syndrome

711.03 Pyogenic arthritis, forearm — (Use additional code to identify infectious organism: 041.0-041.8)
711.04 Pyogenic arthritis, hand — (Use additional code to identify infectious organism: 041.0-041.8)
711.93 Unspecified infective arthritis, forearm
711.94 Unspecified infective arthritis, hand
714.0 Rheumatoid arthritis — (Use additional code to identify manifestation: 357.1, 359.6)
715.13 Primary localized osteoarthrosis, forearm
715.14 Primary localized osteoarthrosis, hand
715.23 Secondary localized osteoarthrosis, forearm
715.24 Secondary localized osteoarthrosis, involving hand
715.33 Localized osteoarthrosis not specified whether primary or secondary, forearm
715.34 Localized osteoarthrosis not specified whether primary or secondary, hand
716.13 Traumatic arthropathy, forearm
716.14 Traumatic arthropathy, hand
716.63 Unspecified monoarthritis, forearm
716.64 Unspecified monoarthritis, hand
716.93 Unspecified arthropathy, forearm
716.94 Unspecified arthropathy, hand
718.04 Articular cartilage disorder, hand
718.83 Other joint derangement, not elsewhere classified, forearm
718.84 Other joint derangement, not elsewhere classified, hand
719.23 Villonodular synovitis, forearm
719.24 Villonodular synovitis, hand
719.63 Other symptoms referable to forearm joint
719.64 Other symptoms referable to hand joint
730.13 Chronic osteomyelitis, forearm — (Use additional code to identify organism: 041.1. Use additional code to identify major osseous defect, if applicable: 731.3)
730.14 Chronic osteomyelitis, hand — (Use additional code to identify organism: 041.1. Use additional code to identify major osseous defect, if applicable: 731.3)
730.23 Unspecified osteomyelitis, forearm — (Use additional code to identify organism: 041.1. Use additional code to identify major osseous defect, if applicable: 731.3)
730.24 Unspecified osteomyelitis, hand — (Use additional code to identify organism: 041.1. Use additional code to identify major osseous defect, if applicable: 731.3)
730.33 Periostitis, without mention of osteomyelitis, forearm — (Use additional code to identify organism: 041.1)
730.34 Periostitis, without mention of osteomyelitis, hand — (Use additional code to identify organism: 041.1)
731.0 Osteitis deformans without mention of bone tumor
731.3 Major osseous defects — (Code first underlying disease: 170.0-170.9, 730.00-730.29, 733.00-733.09, 733.40-733.49, 996.45)
733.49 Aseptic necrosis of other bone site — (Use additional code to identify major osseous defect, if applicable: 731.3)
733.82 Nonunion of fracture
736.00 Unspecified deformity of forearm, excluding fingers
756.51 Osteogenesis imperfecta
905.2 Late effect of fracture of upper extremities

ICD-9-CM Procedural

81.79 Other repair of hand, fingers, and wrist

25446

25446 Arthroplasty with prosthetic replacement; distal radius and partial or entire carpus (total wrist)

ICD-9-CM Diagnostic

357.1 Polyneuropathy in collagen vascular disease — (Code first underlying disease: 446.0, 710.0, 714.0)
359.6 Symptomatic inflammatory myopathy in diseases classified elsewhere — (Code first underlying disease: 135, 140.0-208.9, 277.30-277.39, 446.0, 710.0, 710.1, 710.2, 714.0)
446.0 Polyarteritis nodosa
710.0 Systemic lupus erythematosus — (Use additional code to identify manifestation: 424.91, 581.81, 582.81, 583.81)
710.1 Systemic sclerosis — (Use additional code to identify manifestation: 359.6, 517.2)
710.2 Sicca syndrome
711.03 Pyogenic arthritis, forearm — (Use additional code to identify infectious organism: 041.0-041.8)
711.04 Pyogenic arthritis, hand — (Use additional code to identify infectious organism: 041.0-041.8)
711.93 Unspecified infective arthritis, forearm
711.94 Unspecified infective arthritis, hand
714.0 Rheumatoid arthritis — (Use additional code to identify manifestation: 357.1, 359.6)
715.04 Generalized osteoarthrosis, involving hand
715.13 Primary localized osteoarthrosis, forearm
715.14 Primary localized osteoarthrosis, hand
715.23 Secondary localized osteoarthrosis, forearm
715.24 Secondary localized osteoarthrosis, involving hand
715.33 Localized osteoarthrosis not specified whether primary or secondary, forearm
715.34 Localized osteoarthrosis not specified whether primary or secondary, hand
716.13 Traumatic arthropathy, forearm
716.14 Traumatic arthropathy, hand
716.63 Unspecified monoarthritis, forearm
716.64 Unspecified monoarthritis, hand
716.93 Unspecified arthropathy, forearm
716.94 Unspecified arthropathy, hand
718.83 Other joint derangement, not elsewhere classified, forearm
718.84 Other joint derangement, not elsewhere classified, hand
719.23 Villonodular synovitis, forearm
719.24 Villonodular synovitis, hand
719.63 Other symptoms referable to forearm joint
719.64 Other symptoms referable to hand joint
730.13 Chronic osteomyelitis, forearm — (Use additional code to identify organism: 041.1. Use additional code to identify major osseous defect, if applicable: 731.3)
730.14 Chronic osteomyelitis, hand — (Use additional code to identify organism: 041.1. Use additional code to identify major osseous defect, if applicable: 731.3)
730.23 Unspecified osteomyelitis, forearm — (Use additional code to identify organism: 041.1. Use additional code to identify major osseous defect, if applicable: 731.3)
730.24 Unspecified osteomyelitis, hand — (Use additional code to identify organism: 041.1. Use additional code to identify major osseous defect, if applicable: 731.3)
730.33 Periostitis, without mention of osteomyelitis, forearm — (Use additional code to identify organism: 041.1)
730.34 Periostitis, without mention of osteomyelitis, hand — (Use additional code to identify organism: 041.1)
731.0 Osteitis deformans without mention of bone tumor
731.3 Major osseous defects — (Code first underlying disease: 170.0-170.9, 730.00-730.29, 733.00-733.09, 733.40-733.49, 996.45)
733.49 Aseptic necrosis of other bone site — (Use additional code to identify major osseous defect, if applicable: 731.3)
733.82 Nonunion of fracture
736.00 Unspecified deformity of forearm, excluding fingers
756.51 Osteogenesis imperfecta
905.2 Late effect of fracture of upper extremities

ICD-9-CM Procedural

81.73 Total wrist replacement

25447

25447 Arthroplasty, interposition, intercarpal or carpometacarpal joints

ICD-9-CM Diagnostic

357.1 Polyneuropathy in collagen vascular disease — (Code first underlying disease: 446.0, 710.0, 714.0) ☒

359.6 Symptomatic inflammatory myopathy in diseases classified elsewhere — (Code first underlying disease: 135, 140.0-208.9, 277.30-277.39, 446.0, 710.0, 710.1, 710.2, 714.0) ☒

446.0 Polyarteritis nodosa

710.0 Systemic lupus erythematosus — (Use additional code to identify manifestation: 424.91, 581.81, 582.81, 583.81)

710.1 Systemic sclerosis — (Use additional code to identify manifestation: 359.6, 517.2)

710.2 Sicca syndrome

714.0 Rheumatoid arthritis — (Use additional code to identify manifestation: 357.1, 359.6)

715.04 Generalized osteoarthrosis, involving hand

715.14 Primary localized osteoarthrosis, hand

715.94 Osteoarthrosis, unspecified whether generalized or localized, hand ▽

716.14 Traumatic arthropathy, hand

716.94 Unspecified arthropathy, hand ▽

814.00 Unspecified closed fracture of carpal bone ▽

905.2 Late effect of fracture of upper extremities

ICD-9-CM Procedural

81.74 Arthroplasty of carpocarpal or carpometacarpal joint with implant

25449

25449 Revision of arthroplasty, including removal of implant, wrist joint

ICD-9-CM Diagnostic

711.03 Pyogenic arthritis, forearm — (Use additional code to identify infectious organism: 041.0-041.8)

711.04 Pyogenic arthritis, hand — (Use additional code to identify infectious organism: 041.0-041.8)

711.83 Arthropathy associated with other infectious and parasitic diseases, forearm — (Code first underlying disease: 080-088, 100-104, 130-136) ☒

711.84 Arthropathy associated with other infectious and parasitic diseases, hand — (Code first underlying disease: 080-088, 100-104, 130-136) ☒

711.93 Unspecified infective arthritis, forearm ▽

711.94 Unspecified infective arthritis, hand ▽

730.13 Chronic osteomyelitis, forearm — (Use additional code to identify organism: 041.1. Use additional code to identify major osseous defect, if applicable: 731.3)

730.14 Chronic osteomyelitis, hand — (Use additional code to identify organism: 041.1. Use additional code to identify major osseous defect, if applicable: 731.3)

731.3 Major osseous defects — (Code first underlying disease: 170.0-170.9, 730.00-730.29, 733.00-733.09, 733.40-733.49, 996.45)

996.40 Unspecified mechanical complication of internal orthopedic device, implant, and graft — (Use additional code to identify prosthetic joint with mechanical complication, V43.60-V43.69) ▽

996.41 Mechanical loosening of prosthetic joint — (Use additional code to identify prosthetic joint with mechanical complication, V43.60-V43.69)

996.42 Dislocation of prosthetic joint — (Use additional code to identify prosthetic joint with mechanical complication, V43.60-V43.69)

996.43 Broken prosthetic joint implant — (Use additional code to identify prosthetic joint with mechanical complication, V43.60-V43.69)

996.44 Peri-prosthetic fracture around prosthetic joint — (Use additional code to identify prosthetic joint with mechanical complication, V43.60-V43.69.

996.45 Peri-prosthetic osteolysis — (Use additional code to identify prosthetic joint with mechanical complication, V43.60-V43.69. Use additional code to identify major osseous defect, if applicable: 731.3)

996.47 Other mechanical complication of prosthetic joint implant — (Use additional code to identify prosthetic joint with mechanical complication, V43.60-V43.69)

996.66 Infection and inflammatory reaction due to internal joint prosthesis — (Use additional code to identify specified infections. Use additional code to identify infected prosthetic joint: V43.60-V43.69)

996.77 Other complications due to internal joint prosthesis — (Use additional code to identify complication: 338.18-338.19, 338.28-338.29)

998.59 Other postoperative infection — (Use additional code to identify infection)

998.6 Persistent postoperative fistula, not elsewhere classified

V43.63 Wrist joint replacement by other means

ICD-9-CM Procedural

78.64 Removal of implanted device from carpals and metacarpals

81.75 Arthroplasty of carpocarpal or carpometacarpal joint without implant

25450-25455

25450 Epiphyseal arrest by epiphysiodesis or stapling; distal radius OR ulna

25455 distal radius AND ulna

ICD-9-CM Diagnostic

732.3 Juvenile osteochondrosis of upper extremity

ICD-9-CM Procedural

78.23 Limb shortening procedures, radius and ulna

25490-25492

25490 Prophylactic treatment (nailing, pinning, plating or wiring) with or without methylmethacrylate; radius

25491 ulna

25492 radius AND ulna

ICD-9-CM Diagnostic

170.4 Malignant neoplasm of scapula and long bones of upper limb

198.5 Secondary malignant neoplasm of bone and bone marrow

213.4 Benign neoplasm of scapula and long bones of upper limb

238.0 Neoplasm of uncertain behavior of bone and articular cartilage

239.2 Neoplasms of unspecified nature of bone, soft tissue, and skin

731.3 Major osseous defects — (Code first underlying disease: 170.0-170.9, 730.00-730.29, 733.00-733.09, 733.40-733.49, 996.45)

733.49 Aseptic necrosis of other bone site — (Use additional code to identify major osseous defect, if applicable: 731.3)

ICD-9-CM Procedural

78.53 Internal fixation of radius and ulna without fracture reduction

84.55 Insertion of bone void filler

25500-25505

25500 Closed treatment of radial shaft fracture; without manipulation

25505 with manipulation

ICD-9-CM Diagnostic

733.19 Pathologic fracture of other specified site

813.21 Closed fracture of shaft of radius (alone)

ICD-9-CM Procedural

79.02 Closed reduction of fracture of radius and ulna without internal fixation

93.53 Application of other cast

HCPCS Level II Supplies & Services

A4580 Cast supplies (e.g., plaster)

25515

25515 Open treatment of radial shaft fracture, includes internal fixation, when performed

ICD-9-CM Diagnostic

733.19 Pathologic fracture of other specified site

733.81 Malunion of fracture

733.82 Nonunion of fracture
813.21 Closed fracture of shaft of radius (alone)
813.31 Open fracture of shaft of radius (alone)

ICD-9-CM Procedural

79.22 Open reduction of fracture of radius and ulna without internal fixation
79.32 Open reduction of fracture of radius and ulna with internal fixation

25520

25520 Closed treatment of radial shaft fracture and closed treatment of dislocation of distal radioulnar joint (Galeazzi fracture/dislocation)

ICD-9-CM Diagnostic

733.19 Pathologic fracture of other specified site
813.00 Unspecified fracture of radius and ulna, upper end of forearm, closed ▼
813.20 Unspecified closed fracture of shaft of radius or ulna ▼
813.21 Closed fracture of shaft of radius (alone)
833.01 Closed dislocation of distal radioulnar (joint)

ICD-9-CM Procedural

79.02 Closed reduction of fracture of radius and ulna without internal fixation
79.79 Closed reduction of dislocation of other specified site, except temporomandibular

HCPCS Level II Supplies & Services

A4580 Cast supplies (e.g., plaster)

25525

25525 Open treatment of radial shaft fracture, includes internal fixation, when performed, and closed treatment of distal radioulnar joint dislocation (Galeazzi fracture/dislocation), includes percutaneous skeletal fixation, when performed

ICD-9-CM Diagnostic

733.19 Pathologic fracture of other specified site
733.81 Malunion of fracture
733.82 Nonunion of fracture
813.21 Closed fracture of shaft of radius (alone)
813.31 Open fracture of shaft of radius (alone)
833.01 Closed dislocation of distal radioulnar (joint)
833.11 Open dislocation of distal radioulnar (joint)

ICD-9-CM Procedural

79.22 Open reduction of fracture of radius and ulna without internal fixation
79.32 Open reduction of fracture of radius and ulna with internal fixation
79.73 Closed reduction of dislocation of wrist
84.71 Application of external fixator device, monoplanar system
84.72 Application of external fixator device, ring system
84.73 Application of hybrid external fixator device

25526

25526 Open treatment of radial shaft fracture, includes internal fixation, when performed, and open treatment of distal radioulnar joint dislocation (Galeazzi fracture/dislocation), includes internal fixation, when performed, includes repair of triangular fibrocartilage complex

ICD-9-CM Diagnostic

733.19 Pathologic fracture of other specified site
733.81 Malunion of fracture
733.82 Nonunion of fracture
813.21 Closed fracture of shaft of radius (alone)
813.31 Open fracture of shaft of radius (alone)
833.01 Closed dislocation of distal radioulnar (joint)
833.11 Open dislocation of distal radioulnar (joint)

ICD-9-CM Procedural

79.22 Open reduction of fracture of radius and ulna without internal fixation
79.32 Open reduction of fracture of radius and ulna with internal fixation
79.83 Open reduction of dislocation of wrist

25530-25535

25530 Closed treatment of ulnar shaft fracture; without manipulation
25535 with manipulation

ICD-9-CM Diagnostic

733.19 Pathologic fracture of other specified site
813.22 Closed fracture of shaft of ulna (alone)

ICD-9-CM Procedural

79.02 Closed reduction of fracture of radius and ulna without internal fixation
93.53 Application of other cast

HCPCS Level II Supplies & Services

A4580 Cast supplies (e.g., plaster)

25545

25545 Open treatment of ulnar shaft fracture, includes internal fixation, when performed

ICD-9-CM Diagnostic

733.19 Pathologic fracture of other specified site
733.81 Malunion of fracture
733.82 Nonunion of fracture
813.22 Closed fracture of shaft of ulna (alone)
813.32 Open fracture of shaft of ulna (alone)

ICD-9-CM Procedural

79.22 Open reduction of fracture of radius and ulna without internal fixation
79.32 Open reduction of fracture of radius and ulna with internal fixation

25560-25565

25560 Closed treatment of radial and ulnar shaft fractures; without manipulation
25565 with manipulation

ICD-9-CM Diagnostic

733.19 Pathologic fracture of other specified site
813.23 Closed fracture of shaft of radius with ulna

ICD-9-CM Procedural

79.02 Closed reduction of fracture of radius and ulna without internal fixation
93.53 Application of other cast

HCPCS Level II Supplies & Services

A4580 Cast supplies (e.g., plaster)

25574-25575

25574 Open treatment of radial AND ulnar shaft fractures, with internal fixation, when performed; of radius OR ulna
25575 of radius AND ulna

ICD-9-CM Diagnostic

733.19 Pathologic fracture of other specified site
813.23 Closed fracture of shaft of radius with ulna
813.33 Open fracture of shaft of radius with ulna
927.10 Crushing injury of forearm — (Use additional code to identify any associated injuries: 800-829, 850.0-854.1, 860.0-869.1)

ICD-9-CM Procedural

79.32 Open reduction of fracture of radius and ulna with internal fixation

25600-25605

25600 Closed treatment of distal radial fracture (eg, Colles or Smith type) or epiphyseal separation, includes closed treatment of fracture of ulnar styloid, when performed; without manipulation

25605 with manipulation

ICD-9-CM Diagnostic

732.9 Unspecified osteochondropathy ▽
733.12 Pathologic fracture of distal radius and ulna
813.40 Unspecified closed fracture of lower end of forearm ▽
813.41 Closed Colles' fracture
813.42 Other closed fractures of distal end of radius (alone)
813.44 Closed fracture of lower end of radius with ulna
813.45 Torus fracture of radius (alone)
813.47 Torus fracture of radius and ulna

ICD-9-CM Procedural

79.02 Closed reduction of fracture of radius and ulna without internal fixation
79.42 Closed reduction of separated epiphysis of radius and ulna
93.53 Application of other cast
93.54 Application of splint

HCPCS Level II Supplies & Services

A4580 Cast supplies (e.g., plaster)

25606

25606 Percutaneous skeletal fixation of distal radial fracture or epiphyseal separation

ICD-9-CM Diagnostic

732.9 Unspecified osteochondropathy ▽
733.12 Pathologic fracture of distal radius and ulna
813.40 Unspecified closed fracture of lower end of forearm ▽
813.41 Closed Colles' fracture
813.42 Other closed fractures of distal end of radius (alone)
813.44 Closed fracture of lower end of radius with ulna
813.45 Torus fracture of radius (alone)
813.47 Torus fracture of radius and ulna

ICD-9-CM Procedural

79.12 Closed reduction of fracture of radius and ulna with internal fixation
79.42 Closed reduction of separated epiphysis of radius and ulna

25607-25609

25607 Open treatment of distal radial extra-articular fracture or epiphyseal separation, with internal fixation

25608 Open treatment of distal radial intra-articular fracture or epiphyseal separation; with internal fixation of 2 fragments

25609 with internal fixation of 3 or more fragments

ICD-9-CM Diagnostic

732.9 Unspecified osteochondropathy ▽
733.12 Pathologic fracture of distal radius and ulna
733.82 Nonunion of fracture
813.40 Unspecified closed fracture of lower end of forearm ▽
813.41 Closed Colles' fracture
813.42 Other closed fractures of distal end of radius (alone)
813.44 Closed fracture of lower end of radius with ulna
813.45 Torus fracture of radius (alone)
813.47 Torus fracture of radius and ulna
813.50 Unspecified open fracture of lower end of forearm ▽
813.51 Open Colles' fracture
813.52 Other open fractures of distal end of radius (alone)
813.54 Open fracture of lower end of radius with ulna

ICD-9-CM Procedural

79.32 Open reduction of fracture of radius and ulna with internal fixation
79.52 Open reduction of separated epiphysis of radius and ulna

25622-25624

25622 Closed treatment of carpal scaphoid (navicular) fracture; without manipulation

25624 with manipulation

ICD-9-CM Diagnostic

733.19 Pathologic fracture of other specified site
814.01 Closed fracture of navicular (scaphoid) bone of wrist

ICD-9-CM Procedural

79.03 Closed reduction of fracture of carpals and metacarpals without internal fixation
93.53 Application of other cast

HCPCS Level II Supplies & Services

A4580 Cast supplies (e.g., plaster)

25628

25628 Open treatment of carpal scaphoid (navicular) fracture, includes internal fixation, when performed

ICD-9-CM Diagnostic

733.19 Pathologic fracture of other specified site
814.01 Closed fracture of navicular (scaphoid) bone of wrist
814.11 Open fracture of navicular (scaphoid) bone of wrist

ICD-9-CM Procedural

78.14 Application of external fixator device, carpals and metacarpals
79.23 Open reduction of fracture of carpals and metacarpals without internal fixation
79.33 Open reduction of fracture of carpals and metacarpals with internal fixation

HCPCS Level II Supplies & Services

A4305 Disposable drug delivery system, flow rate of 50 ml or greater per hour

25630-25635

25630 Closed treatment of carpal bone fracture (excluding carpal scaphoid [navicular]); without manipulation, each bone

25635 with manipulation, each bone

ICD-9-CM Diagnostic

733.19 Pathologic fracture of other specified site
814.02 Closed fracture of lunate (semilunar) bone of wrist
814.03 Closed fracture of triquetral (cuneiform) bone of wrist
814.04 Closed fracture of pisiform bone of wrist
814.05 Closed fracture of trapezium bone (larger multangular) of wrist
814.06 Closed fracture of trapezoid bone (smaller multangular) of wrist
814.07 Closed fracture of capitate bone (os magnum) of wrist
814.08 Closed fracture of hamate (unciform) bone of wrist
814.09 Closed fracture of other bone of wrist

ICD-9-CM Procedural

79.03 Closed reduction of fracture of carpals and metacarpals without internal fixation
93.53 Application of other cast
93.54 Application of splint

HCPCS Level II Supplies & Services

A4580 Cast supplies (e.g., plaster)

25645

25645 Open treatment of carpal bone fracture (other than carpal scaphoid [navicular]), each bone

ICD-9-CM Diagnostic

733.19 Pathologic fracture of other specified site
814.02 Closed fracture of lunate (semilunar) bone of wrist
814.03 Closed fracture of triquetral (cuneiform) bone of wrist
814.04 Closed fracture of pisiform bone of wrist
814.05 Closed fracture of trapezium bone (larger multangular) of wrist
814.06 Closed fracture of trapezoid bone (smaller multangular) of wrist
814.07 Closed fracture of capitate bone (os magnum) of wrist
814.08 Closed fracture of hamate (unciform) bone of wrist
814.09 Closed fracture of other bone of wrist
814.12 Open fracture of lunate (semilunar) bone of wrist
814.13 Open fracture of triquetral (cuneiform) bone of wrist
814.14 Open fracture of pisiform bone of wrist
814.15 Open fracture of trapezium bone (larger multangular) of wrist
814.16 Open fracture of trapezoid bone (smaller multangular) of wrist
814.17 Open fracture of capitate bone (os magnum) of wrist
814.18 Open fracture of hamate (unciform) bone of wrist
814.19 Open fracture of other bone of wrist

ICD-9-CM Procedural

79.23 Open reduction of fracture of carpals and metacarpals without internal fixation
79.33 Open reduction of fracture of carpals and metacarpals with internal fixation

25650

25650 Closed treatment of ulnar styloid fracture

ICD-9-CM Diagnostic

733.12 Pathologic fracture of distal radius and ulna
813.43 Closed fracture of distal end of ulna (alone)

ICD-9-CM Procedural

93.53 Application of other cast
93.54 Application of splint

HCPCS Level II Supplies & Services

A4580 Cast supplies (e.g., plaster)

25651

25651 Percutaneous skeletal fixation of ulnar styloid fracture

ICD-9-CM Diagnostic

733.12 Pathologic fracture of distal radius and ulna
813.43 Closed fracture of distal end of ulna (alone)

ICD-9-CM Procedural

78.13 Application of external fixator device, radius and ulna
79.12 Closed reduction of fracture of radius and ulna with internal fixation
84.71 Application of external fixator device, monoplanar system
84.72 Application of external fixator device, ring system
84.73 Application of hybrid external fixator device

25652

25652 Open treatment of ulnar styloid fracture

ICD-9-CM Diagnostic

733.12 Pathologic fracture of distal radius and ulna
733.81 Malunion of fracture
733.82 Nonunion of fracture
813.43 Closed fracture of distal end of ulna (alone)
813.53 Open fracture of distal end of ulna (alone)

ICD-9-CM Procedural

79.22 Open reduction of fracture of radius and ulna without internal fixation

25660

25660 Closed treatment of radiocarpal or intercarpal dislocation, 1 or more bones, with manipulation

ICD-9-CM Diagnostic

718.23 Pathological dislocation of forearm joint
718.24 Pathological dislocation of hand joint
718.33 Recurrent dislocation of forearm joint
718.34 Recurrent dislocation of hand joint
718.73 Developmental dislocation of joint, forearm
833.02 Closed dislocation of radiocarpal (joint)
833.03 Closed dislocation of midcarpal (joint)

ICD-9-CM Procedural

79.73 Closed reduction of dislocation of wrist

HCPCS Level II Supplies & Services

A4580 Cast supplies (e.g., plaster)

25670

25670 Open treatment of radiocarpal or intercarpal dislocation, 1 or more bones

ICD-9-CM Diagnostic

718.23 Pathological dislocation of forearm joint
718.24 Pathological dislocation of hand joint
718.33 Recurrent dislocation of forearm joint
718.34 Recurrent dislocation of hand joint
718.73 Developmental dislocation of joint, forearm
833.02 Closed dislocation of radiocarpal (joint)
833.03 Closed dislocation of midcarpal (joint)
833.12 Open dislocation of radiocarpal (joint)
833.13 Open dislocation of midcarpal (joint)

ICD-9-CM Procedural

79.83 Open reduction of dislocation of wrist

25671

25671 Percutaneous skeletal fixation of distal radioulnar dislocation

ICD-9-CM Diagnostic

718.23 Pathological dislocation of forearm joint
718.33 Recurrent dislocation of forearm joint
718.73 Developmental dislocation of joint, forearm
833.01 Closed dislocation of distal radioulnar (joint)

ICD-9-CM Procedural

79.73 Closed reduction of dislocation of wrist

25675

25675 Closed treatment of distal radioulnar dislocation with manipulation

ICD-9-CM Diagnostic

718.23 Pathological dislocation of forearm joint
718.33 Recurrent dislocation of forearm joint
718.73 Developmental dislocation of joint, forearm
833.01 Closed dislocation of distal radioulnar (joint)

ICD-9-CM Procedural

79.73 Closed reduction of dislocation of wrist

HCPCS Level II Supplies & Services

A4580 Cast supplies (e.g., plaster)

25676

25676 Open treatment of distal radioulnar dislocation, acute or chronic

ICD-9-CM Diagnostic

718.23 Pathological dislocation of forearm joint
718.33 Recurrent dislocation of forearm joint
718.73 Developmental dislocation of joint, forearm
833.01 Closed dislocation of distal radioulnar (joint)
833.11 Open dislocation of distal radioulnar (joint)

ICD-9-CM Procedural

79.83 Open reduction of dislocation of wrist

25680

25680 Closed treatment of trans-scaphoperilunar type of fracture dislocation, with manipulation

ICD-9-CM Diagnostic

733.19 Pathologic fracture of other specified site
814.01 Closed fracture of navicular (scaphoid) bone of wrist
833.03 Closed dislocation of midcarpal (joint)

ICD-9-CM Procedural

79.03 Closed reduction of fracture of carpals and metacarpals without internal fixation
79.73 Closed reduction of dislocation of wrist

HCPCS Level II Supplies & Services

A4570 Splint

25685

25685 Open treatment of trans-scaphoperilunar type of fracture dislocation

ICD-9-CM Diagnostic

733.19 Pathologic fracture of other specified site
814.01 Closed fracture of navicular (scaphoid) bone of wrist
814.11 Open fracture of navicular (scaphoid) bone of wrist
833.03 Closed dislocation of midcarpal (joint)
833.13 Open dislocation of midcarpal (joint)

ICD-9-CM Procedural

79.83 Open reduction of dislocation of wrist

25690

25690 Closed treatment of lunate dislocation, with manipulation

ICD-9-CM Diagnostic

718.24 Pathological dislocation of hand joint
718.34 Recurrent dislocation of hand joint
718.73 Developmental dislocation of joint, forearm
833.03 Closed dislocation of midcarpal (joint)

ICD-9-CM Procedural

79.73 Closed reduction of dislocation of wrist

HCPCS Level II Supplies & Services

A4580 Cast supplies (e.g., plaster)

25695

25695 Open treatment of lunate dislocation

ICD-9-CM Diagnostic

718.23 Pathological dislocation of forearm joint
718.24 Pathological dislocation of hand joint
718.33 Recurrent dislocation of forearm joint
718.34 Recurrent dislocation of hand joint
718.73 Developmental dislocation of joint, forearm
833.03 Closed dislocation of midcarpal (joint)
833.13 Open dislocation of midcarpal (joint)

ICD-9-CM Procedural

79.83 Open reduction of dislocation of wrist

25800-25810

25800 Arthrodesis, wrist; complete, without bone graft (includes radiocarpal and/or intercarpal and/or carpometacarpal joints)
25805 with sliding graft
25810 with iliac or other autograft (includes obtaining graft)

ICD-9-CM Diagnostic

170.4 Malignant neoplasm of scapula and long bones of upper limb
170.5 Malignant neoplasm of short bones of upper limb
171.2 Malignant neoplasm of connective and other soft tissue of upper limb, including shoulder
198.5 Secondary malignant neoplasm of bone and bone marrow
238.0 Neoplasm of uncertain behavior of bone and articular cartilage
239.2 Neoplasms of unspecified nature of bone, soft tissue, and skin
357.1 Polyneuropathy in collagen vascular disease — (Code first underlying disease: 446.0, 710.0, 714.0) ☒
359.6 Symptomatic inflammatory myopathy in diseases classified elsewhere — (Code first underlying disease: 135, 140.0-208.9, 277.30-277.39, 446.0, 710.0, 710.1, 710.2, 714.0) ☒
446.0 Polyarteritis nodosa
710.0 Systemic lupus erythematosus — (Use additional code to identify manifestation: 424.91, 581.81, 582.81, 583.81)
710.1 Systemic sclerosis — (Use additional code to identify manifestation: 359.6, 517.2)
710.2 Sicca syndrome
711.03 Pyogenic arthritis, forearm — (Use additional code to identify infectious organism: 041.0-041.8)
711.04 Pyogenic arthritis, hand — (Use additional code to identify infectious organism: 041.0-041.8)
714.0 Rheumatoid arthritis — (Use additional code to identify manifestation: 357.1, 359.6)
714.30 Polyarticular juvenile rheumatoid arthritis, chronic or unspecified
715.13 Primary localized osteoarthrosis, forearm
715.14 Primary localized osteoarthrosis, hand
715.23 Secondary localized osteoarthrosis, forearm
715.24 Secondary localized osteoarthrosis, involving hand
716.03 Kaschin-Beck disease, forearm
716.04 Kaschin-Beck disease, hand
716.13 Traumatic arthropathy, forearm
716.14 Traumatic arthropathy, hand
716.93 Unspecified arthropathy, forearm ▽
716.94 Unspecified arthropathy, hand ▽
718.03 Articular cartilage disorder, forearm
718.04 Articular cartilage disorder, hand
718.33 Recurrent dislocation of forearm joint
718.34 Recurrent dislocation of hand joint
718.83 Other joint derangement, not elsewhere classified, forearm
718.84 Other joint derangement, not elsewhere classified, hand
719.03 Effusion of forearm joint
719.04 Effusion of hand joint
719.23 Villonodular synovitis, forearm
719.24 Villonodular synovitis, hand

731.3 Major osseous defects — (Code first underlying disease: 170.0-170.9, 730.00-730.29, 733.00-733.09, 733.40-733.49, 996.45)
733.81 Malunion of fracture
959.3 Injury, other and unspecified, elbow, forearm, and wrist

ICD-9-CM Procedural

81.25 Carporadial fusion
81.26 Metacarpocarpal fusion
81.29 Arthrodesis of other specified joint

25820-25825

25820 Arthrodesis, wrist; limited, without bone graft (eg, intercarpal or radiocarpal)
25825 with autograft (includes obtaining graft)

ICD-9-CM Diagnostic

357.1 Polyneuropathy in collagen vascular disease — (Code first underlying disease: 446.0, 710.0, 714.0) ☒
359.6 Symptomatic inflammatory myopathy in diseases classified elsewhere — (Code first underlying disease: 135, 140.0-208.9, 277.30-277.39, 446.0, 710.0, 710.1, 710.2, 714.0) ☒
446.0 Polyarteritis nodosa
710.0 Systemic lupus erythematosus — (Use additional code to identify manifestation: 424.91, 581.81, 582.81, 583.81)
710.1 Systemic sclerosis — (Use additional code to identify manifestation: 359.6, 517.2)
710.2 Sicca syndrome
714.0 Rheumatoid arthritis — (Use additional code to identify manifestation: 357.1, 359.6)
714.31 Polyarticular juvenile rheumatoid arthritis, acute
715.04 Generalized osteoarthrosis, involving hand
715.14 Primary localized osteoarthrosis, hand
715.24 Secondary localized osteoarthrosis, involving hand
715.34 Localized osteoarthrosis not specified whether primary or secondary, hand
715.93 Osteoarthrosis, unspecified whether generalized or localized, forearm ▽
715.94 Osteoarthrosis, unspecified whether generalized or localized, hand ▽
716.03 Kaschin-Beck disease, forearm
716.04 Kaschin-Beck disease, hand
716.14 Traumatic arthropathy, hand
718.03 Articular cartilage disorder, forearm
718.04 Articular cartilage disorder, hand
718.84 Other joint derangement, not elsewhere classified, hand
731.3 Major osseous defects — (Code first underlying disease: 170.0-170.9, 730.00-730.29, 733.00-733.09, 733.40-733.49, 996.45)
733.49 Aseptic necrosis of other bone site — (Use additional code to identify major osseous defect, if applicable: 731.3)
733.81 Malunion of fracture

ICD-9-CM Procedural

81.25 Carporadial fusion
81.29 Arthrodesis of other specified joint

25830

25830 Arthrodesis, distal radioulnar joint with segmental resection of ulna, with or without bone graft (eg, Sauve-Kapandji procedure)

ICD-9-CM Diagnostic

170.5 Malignant neoplasm of short bones of upper limb
198.5 Secondary malignant neoplasm of bone and bone marrow
238.0 Neoplasm of uncertain behavior of bone and articular cartilage
239.2 Neoplasms of unspecified nature of bone, soft tissue, and skin
715.33 Localized osteoarthrosis not specified whether primary or secondary, forearm
715.93 Osteoarthrosis, unspecified whether generalized or localized, forearm ▽
716.13 Traumatic arthropathy, forearm
718.33 Recurrent dislocation of forearm joint
731.3 Major osseous defects — (Code first underlying disease: 170.0-170.9, 730.00-730.29, 733.00-733.09, 733.40-733.49, 996.45)
733.49 Aseptic necrosis of other bone site — (Use additional code to identify major osseous defect, if applicable: 731.3)
733.81 Malunion of fracture

ICD-9-CM Procedural

81.29 Arthrodesis of other specified joint

25900-25905

25900 Amputation, forearm, through radius and ulna;
25905 open, circular (guillotine)

ICD-9-CM Diagnostic

170.5 Malignant neoplasm of short bones of upper limb
170.9 Malignant neoplasm of bone and articular cartilage, site unspecified ▽
198.5 Secondary malignant neoplasm of bone and bone marrow
249.70 Secondary diabetes mellitus with peripheral circulatory disorders, not stated as uncontrolled, or unspecified — (Use additional code to identify manifestation: 443.81, 785.4) (Use additional code to identify any associated insulin use: V58.67)
249.71 Secondary diabetes mellitus with peripheral circulatory disorders, uncontrolled — (Use additional code to identify manifestation: 443.81, 785.4) (Use additional code to identify any associated insulin use: V58.67)
249.80 Secondary diabetes mellitus with other specified manifestations, not stated as uncontrolled, or unspecified — (Use additional code to identify manifestation: 707.10-707.19, 707.8, 707.9, 731.8) (Use additional code to identify any associated insulin use: V58.67)
249.81 Secondary diabetes mellitus with other specified manifestations, uncontrolled — (Use additional code to identify manifestation: 707.10-707.19, 707.8, 707.9, 731.8) (Use additional code to identify any associated insulin use: V58.67)
250.70 Diabetes with peripheral circulatory disorders, type II or unspecified type, not stated as uncontrolled — (Use additional code to identify manifestation: 443.81, 785.4)
250.71 Diabetes with peripheral circulatory disorders, type I [juvenile type], not stated as uncontrolled — (Use additional code to identify manifestation: 443.81, 785.4)
250.72 Diabetes with peripheral circulatory disorders, type II or unspecified type, uncontrolled — (Use additional code to identify manifestation: 443.81, 785.4)
250.73 Diabetes with peripheral circulatory disorders, type I [juvenile type], uncontrolled — (Use additional code to identify manifestation: 443.81, 785.4)
250.80 Diabetes with other specified manifestations, type II or unspecified type, not stated as uncontrolled — (Use additional code to identify manifestation: 707.10-707.19, 707.8, 707.9, 731.8)
250.81 Diabetes with other specified manifestations, type I [juvenile type], not stated as uncontrolled — (Use additional code to identify manifestation: 707.10-707.19, 707.8, 707.9, 731.8)
250.82 Diabetes with other specified manifestations, type II or unspecified type, uncontrolled — (Use additional code to identify manifestation: 707.10-707.19, 707.8, 707.9, 731.8)
250.83 Diabetes with other specified manifestations, type I [juvenile type], uncontrolled — (Use additional code to identify manifestation: 707.10-707.19, 707.8, 707.9, 731.8)
440.24 Atherosclerosis of native arteries of the extremities with gangrene — (Use additional code for any associated ulceration: 707.10-707.19, 707.8, 707.9)
443.81 Peripheral angiopathy in diseases classified elsewhere — (Code first underlying disease: 249.7, 250.7) ☒
446.0 Polyarteritis nodosa
682.3 Cellulitis and abscess of upper arm and forearm — (Use additional code to identify organism, such as 041.1, etc.)
728.86 Necrotizing fasciitis — (Use additional code to identify infectious organism, 041.00-041.89, 785.4, if applicable)
730.13 Chronic osteomyelitis, forearm — (Use additional code to identify organism: 041.1. Use additional code to identify major osseous defect, if applicable: 731.3)
731.1 Osteitis deformans in diseases classified elsewhere — (Code first underlying disease: 170.0-170.9) ☒

731.3 Major osseous defects — (Code first underlying disease: 170.0-170.9, 730.00-730.29, 733.00-733.09, 733.40-733.49, 996.45)

731.8 Other bone involvement in diseases classified elsewhere — (Code first underlying disease: 249.8, 250.8. Use additional code to specify bone condition: 730.00-730.09) ☒

785.4 Gangrene — (Code first any associated underlying condition)

887.0 Traumatic amputation of arm and hand (complete) (partial), unilateral, below elbow, without mention of complication

887.1 Traumatic amputation of arm and hand (complete) (partial), unilateral, below elbow, complicated

887.6 Traumatic amputation of arm and hand (complete) (partial), bilateral (any level), without mention of complication

887.7 Traumatic amputation of arm and hand (complete) (partial), bilateral (any level), complicated

927.10 Crushing injury of forearm — (Use additional code to identify any associated injuries: 800-829, 850.0-854.1, 860.0-869.1)

927.21 Crushing injury of wrist — (Use additional code to identify any associated injuries: 800-829, 850.0-854.1, 860.0-869.1)

943.51 Deep necrosis of underlying tissues due to burn (deep third degree) of forearm, with loss of a body part

958.3 Posttraumatic wound infection not elsewhere classified

ICD-9-CM Procedural

84.05 Amputation through forearm

25907

25907 Amputation, forearm, through radius and ulna; secondary closure or scar revision

ICD-9-CM Diagnostic

170.5 Malignant neoplasm of short bones of upper limb

170.9 Malignant neoplasm of bone and articular cartilage, site unspecified ▽

198.5 Secondary malignant neoplasm of bone and bone marrow

249.70 Secondary diabetes mellitus with peripheral circulatory disorders, not stated as uncontrolled, or unspecified — (Use additional code to identify manifestation: 443.81, 785.4) (Use additional code to identify any associated insulin use: V58.67)

249.71 Secondary diabetes mellitus with peripheral circulatory disorders, uncontrolled — (Use additional code to identify manifestation: 443.81, 785.4) (Use additional code to identify any associated insulin use: V58.67)

249.80 Secondary diabetes mellitus with other specified manifestations, not stated as uncontrolled, or unspecified — (Use additional code to identify manifestation: 707.10-707.19, 707.8, 707.9, 731.8) (Use additional code to identify any associated insulin use: V58.67)

249.81 Secondary diabetes mellitus with other specified manifestations, uncontrolled — (Use additional code to identify manifestation: 707.10-707.19, 707.8, 707.9, 731.8) (Use additional code to identify any associated insulin use: V58.67)

250.70 Diabetes with peripheral circulatory disorders, type II or unspecified type, not stated as uncontrolled — (Use additional code to identify manifestation: 443.81, 785.4)

250.71 Diabetes with peripheral circulatory disorders, type I [juvenile type], not stated as uncontrolled — (Use additional code to identify manifestation: 443.81, 785.4)

250.72 Diabetes with peripheral circulatory disorders, type II or unspecified type, uncontrolled — (Use additional code to identify manifestation: 443.81, 785.4)

250.73 Diabetes with peripheral circulatory disorders, type I [juvenile type], uncontrolled — (Use additional code to identify manifestation: 443.81, 785.4)

250.80 Diabetes with other specified manifestations, type II or unspecified type, not stated as uncontrolled — (Use additional code to identify manifestation: 707.10-707.19, 707.8, 707.9, 731.8)

250.81 Diabetes with other specified manifestations, type I [juvenile type], not stated as uncontrolled — (Use additional code to identify manifestation: 707.10-707.19, 707.8, 707.9, 731.8)

250.82 Diabetes with other specified manifestations, type II or unspecified type, uncontrolled — (Use additional code to identify manifestation: 707.10-707.19, 707.8, 707.9, 731.8)

250.83 Diabetes with other specified manifestations, type I [juvenile type], uncontrolled — (Use additional code to identify manifestation: 707.10-707.19, 707.8, 707.9, 731.8)

440.24 Atherosclerosis of native arteries of the extremities with gangrene — (Use additional code for any associated ulceration: 707.10-707.19, 707.8, 707.9)

443.81 Peripheral angiopathy in diseases classified elsewhere — (Code first underlying disease: 249.7, 250.7) ☒

443.9 Unspecified peripheral vascular disease ▽

446.0 Polyarteritis nodosa

682.3 Cellulitis and abscess of upper arm and forearm — (Use additional code to identify organism, such as 041.1, etc.)

707.00 Pressure ulcer, unspecified site — (Use additional code to identify pressure ulcer stage: 707.20-707.25) ▽

707.01 Pressure ulcer, elbow — (Use additional code to identify pressure ulcer stage: 707.20-707.25)

707.09 Pressure ulcer, other site — (Use additional code to identify pressure ulcer stage: 707.20-707.25)

707.8 Chronic ulcer of other specified site

728.86 Necrotizing fasciitis — (Use additional code to identify infectious organism, 041.00-041.89, 785.4, if applicable)

730.12 Chronic osteomyelitis, upper arm — (Use additional code to identify organism: 041.1. Use additional code to identify major osseous defect, if applicable: 731.3)

730.13 Chronic osteomyelitis, forearm — (Use additional code to identify organism: 041.1. Use additional code to identify major osseous defect, if applicable: 731.3)

731.3 Major osseous defects — (Code first underlying disease: 170.0-170.9, 730.00-730.29, 733.00-733.09, 733.40-733.49, 996.45)

731.8 Other bone involvement in diseases classified elsewhere — (Code first underlying disease: 249.8, 250.8. Use additional code to specify bone condition: 730.00-730.09) ☒

785.4 Gangrene — (Code first any associated underlying condition)

944.58 Deep necrosis of underlying tissues due to burn (deep third degree) of multiple sites of wrist(s) and hand(s), with loss of a body part

997.60 Late complications of amputation stump, unspecified — (Use additional code to identify complications) ▽

997.61 Neuroma of amputation stump — (Use additional code to identify complications)

997.62 Infection (chronic) of amputation stump — (Use additional code to identify complications)

997.69 Other late amputation stump complication — (Use additional code to identify complications)

V51.8 Other aftercare involving the use of plastic surgery

V58.41 Planned postoperative wound closure — (This code should be used in conjunction with other aftercare codes to fully identify the reason for the aftercare encounter)

ICD-9-CM Procedural

84.3 Revision of amputation stump

HCPCS Level II Supplies & Services

A4305 Disposable drug delivery system, flow rate of 50 ml or greater per hour

25909

25909 Amputation, forearm, through radius and ulna; re-amputation

ICD-9-CM Diagnostic

249.70 Secondary diabetes mellitus with peripheral circulatory disorders, not stated as uncontrolled, or unspecified — (Use additional code to identify manifestation: 443.81, 785.4) (Use additional code to identify any associated insulin use: V58.67)

249.71 Secondary diabetes mellitus with peripheral circulatory disorders, uncontrolled — (Use additional code to identify manifestation: 443.81, 785.4) (Use additional code to identify any associated insulin use: V58.67)

249.80 Secondary diabetes mellitus with other specified manifestations, not stated as uncontrolled, or unspecified — (Use additional code to identify manifestation: 707.10-707.19, 707.8, 707.9, 731.8) (Use additional code to identify any associated insulin use: V58.67)

249.81 Secondary diabetes mellitus with other specified manifestations, uncontrolled — (Use additional code to identify manifestation: 707.10-707.19, 707.8, 707.9, 731.8) (Use additional code to identify any associated insulin use: V58.67)
250.70 Diabetes with peripheral circulatory disorders, type II or unspecified type, not stated as uncontrolled — (Use additional code to identify manifestation: 443.81, 785.4)
250.71 Diabetes with peripheral circulatory disorders, type I [juvenile type], not stated as uncontrolled — (Use additional code to identify manifestation: 443.81, 785.4)
250.72 Diabetes with peripheral circulatory disorders, type II or unspecified type, uncontrolled — (Use additional code to identify manifestation: 443.81, 785.4)
250.73 Diabetes with peripheral circulatory disorders, type I [juvenile type], uncontrolled — (Use additional code to identify manifestation: 443.81, 785.4)
250.80 Diabetes with other specified manifestations, type II or unspecified type, not stated as uncontrolled — (Use additional code to identify manifestation: 707.10-707.19, 707.8, 707.9, 731.8)
250.81 Diabetes with other specified manifestations, type I [juvenile type], not stated as uncontrolled — (Use additional code to identify manifestation: 707.10-707.19, 707.8, 707.9, 731.8)
250.82 Diabetes with other specified manifestations, type II or unspecified type, uncontrolled — (Use additional code to identify manifestation: 707.10-707.19, 707.8, 707.9, 731.8)
250.83 Diabetes with other specified manifestations, type I [juvenile type], uncontrolled — (Use additional code to identify manifestation: 707.10-707.19, 707.8, 707.9, 731.8)
730.13 Chronic osteomyelitis, forearm — (Use additional code to identify organism: 041.1. Use additional code to identify major osseous defect, if applicable: 731.3)
731.3 Major osseous defects — (Code first underlying disease: 170.0-170.9, 730.00-730.29, 733.00-733.09, 733.40-733.49, 996.45)
731.8 Other bone involvement in diseases classified elsewhere — (Code first underlying disease: 249.8, 250.8. Use additional code to specify bone condition: 730.00-730.09) ☒
785.4 Gangrene — (Code first any associated underlying condition)
997.60 Late complications of amputation stump, unspecified — (Use additional code to identify complications) ▽
997.61 Neuroma of amputation stump — (Use additional code to identify complications)
997.62 Infection (chronic) of amputation stump — (Use additional code to identify complications)
997.69 Other late amputation stump complication — (Use additional code to identify complications)
V49.66 Upper limb amputation, above elbow
V51.8 Other aftercare involving the use of plastic surgery

ICD-9-CM Procedural

84.05 Amputation through forearm
84.3 Revision of amputation stump

25915

25915 Krukenberg procedure

ICD-9-CM Diagnostic

170.5 Malignant neoplasm of short bones of upper limb
198.5 Secondary malignant neoplasm of bone and bone marrow
249.70 Secondary diabetes mellitus with peripheral circulatory disorders, not stated as uncontrolled, or unspecified — (Use additional code to identify manifestation: 443.81, 785.4) (Use additional code to identify any associated insulin use: V58.67)
249.71 Secondary diabetes mellitus with peripheral circulatory disorders, uncontrolled — (Use additional code to identify manifestation: 443.81, 785.4) (Use additional code to identify any associated insulin use: V58.67)
250.70 Diabetes with peripheral circulatory disorders, type II or unspecified type, not stated as uncontrolled — (Use additional code to identify manifestation: 443.81, 785.4)
250.71 Diabetes with peripheral circulatory disorders, type I [juvenile type], not stated as uncontrolled — (Use additional code to identify manifestation: 443.81, 785.4)
250.72 Diabetes with peripheral circulatory disorders, type II or unspecified type, uncontrolled — (Use additional code to identify manifestation: 443.81, 785.4)
250.73 Diabetes with peripheral circulatory disorders, type I [juvenile type], uncontrolled — (Use additional code to identify manifestation: 443.81, 785.4)
440.24 Atherosclerosis of native arteries of the extremities with gangrene — (Use additional code for any associated ulceration: 707.10-707.19, 707.8, 707.9)
443.81 Peripheral angiopathy in diseases classified elsewhere — (Code first underlying disease: 249.7, 250.7) ☒
682.3 Cellulitis and abscess of upper arm and forearm — (Use additional code to identify organism, such as 041.1, etc.)
728.86 Necrotizing fasciitis — (Use additional code to identify infectious organism, 041.00-041.89, 785.4, if applicable)
736.00 Unspecified deformity of forearm, excluding fingers ▽
755.50 Unspecified congenital anomaly of upper limb ▽
785.4 Gangrene — (Code first any associated underlying condition)
997.60 Late complications of amputation stump, unspecified — (Use additional code to identify complications) ▽
997.61 Neuroma of amputation stump — (Use additional code to identify complications)

ICD-9-CM Procedural

82.89 Other plastic operations on hand

25920-25924

25920 Disarticulation through wrist;
25922 secondary closure or scar revision
25924 re-amputation

ICD-9-CM Diagnostic

170.5 Malignant neoplasm of short bones of upper limb
171.2 Malignant neoplasm of connective and other soft tissue of upper limb, including shoulder
195.5 Malignant neoplasm of lower limb
249.70 Secondary diabetes mellitus with peripheral circulatory disorders, not stated as uncontrolled, or unspecified — (Use additional code to identify manifestation: 443.81, 785.4) (Use additional code to identify any associated insulin use: V58.67)
249.71 Secondary diabetes mellitus with peripheral circulatory disorders, uncontrolled — (Use additional code to identify manifestation: 443.81, 785.4) (Use additional code to identify any associated insulin use: V58.67)
249.80 Secondary diabetes mellitus with other specified manifestations, not stated as uncontrolled, or unspecified — (Use additional code to identify manifestation: 707.10-707.19, 707.8, 707.9, 731.8) (Use additional code to identify any associated insulin use: V58.67)
249.81 Secondary diabetes mellitus with other specified manifestations, uncontrolled — (Use additional code to identify manifestation: 707.10-707.19, 707.8, 707.9, 731.8) (Use additional code to identify any associated insulin use: V58.67)
250.70 Diabetes with peripheral circulatory disorders, type II or unspecified type, not stated as uncontrolled — (Use additional code to identify manifestation: 443.81, 785.4)
250.71 Diabetes with peripheral circulatory disorders, type I [juvenile type], not stated as uncontrolled — (Use additional code to identify manifestation: 443.81, 785.4)
250.72 Diabetes with peripheral circulatory disorders, type II or unspecified type, uncontrolled — (Use additional code to identify manifestation: 443.81, 785.4)
250.73 Diabetes with peripheral circulatory disorders, type I [juvenile type], uncontrolled — (Use additional code to identify manifestation: 443.81, 785.4)
250.80 Diabetes with other specified manifestations, type II or unspecified type, not stated as uncontrolled — (Use additional code to identify manifestation: 707.10-707.19, 707.8, 707.9, 731.8)
250.81 Diabetes with other specified manifestations, type I [juvenile type], not stated as uncontrolled — (Use additional code to identify manifestation: 707.10-707.19, 707.8, 707.9, 731.8)
250.82 Diabetes with other specified manifestations, type II or unspecified type, uncontrolled — (Use additional code to identify manifestation: 707.10-707.19, 707.8, 707.9, 731.8)
250.83 Diabetes with other specified manifestations, type I [juvenile type], uncontrolled — (Use additional code to identify manifestation: 707.10-707.19, 707.8, 707.9, 731.8)

440.24 Atherosclerosis of native arteries of the extremities with gangrene — (Use additional code for any associated ulceration: 707.10-707.19, 707.8, 707.9)
443.81 Peripheral angiopathy in diseases classified elsewhere — (Code first underlying disease: 249.7, 250.7) ☒
446.0 Polyarteritis nodosa
682.3 Cellulitis and abscess of upper arm and forearm — (Use additional code to identify organism, such as 041.1, etc.)
707.09 Pressure ulcer, other site — (Use additional code to identify pressure ulcer stage: 707.20-707.25)
707.8 Chronic ulcer of other specified site
709.2 Scar condition and fibrosis of skin
728.86 Necrotizing fasciitis — (Use additional code to identify infectious organism, 041.00-041.89, 785.4, if applicable)
731.8 Other bone involvement in diseases classified elsewhere — (Code first underlying disease: 249.8, 250.8. Use additional code to specify bone condition: 730.00-730.09) ☒
785.4 Gangrene — (Code first any associated underlying condition)
817.1 Multiple open fractures of hand bones
887.0 Traumatic amputation of arm and hand (complete) (partial), unilateral, below elbow, without mention of complication
887.1 Traumatic amputation of arm and hand (complete) (partial), unilateral, below elbow, complicated
887.6 Traumatic amputation of arm and hand (complete) (partial), bilateral (any level), without mention of complication
887.7 Traumatic amputation of arm and hand (complete) (partial), bilateral (any level), complicated
927.21 Crushing injury of wrist — (Use additional code to identify any associated injuries: 800-829, 850.0-854.1, 860.0-869.1)
997.60 Late complications of amputation stump, unspecified — (Use additional code to identify complications) ▽
997.61 Neuroma of amputation stump — (Use additional code to identify complications)
997.62 Infection (chronic) of amputation stump — (Use additional code to identify complications)
997.69 Other late amputation stump complication — (Use additional code to identify complications)
998.59 Other postoperative infection — (Use additional code to identify infection)
998.6 Persistent postoperative fistula, not elsewhere classified
998.83 Non-healing surgical wound
V51.8 Other aftercare involving the use of plastic surgery
V58.41 Planned postoperative wound closure — (This code should be used in conjunction with other aftercare codes to fully identify the reason for the aftercare encounter)

ICD-9-CM Procedural

84.04 Disarticulation of wrist
84.3 Revision of amputation stump

HCPCS Level II Supplies & Services

A4305 Disposable drug delivery system, flow rate of 50 ml or greater per hour

25927-25931

25927 Transmetacarpal amputation;
25929 secondary closure or scar revision
25931 re-amputation

ICD-9-CM Diagnostic

170.5 Malignant neoplasm of short bones of upper limb
171.2 Malignant neoplasm of connective and other soft tissue of upper limb, including shoulder
198.5 Secondary malignant neoplasm of bone and bone marrow
249.70 Secondary diabetes mellitus with peripheral circulatory disorders, not stated as uncontrolled, or unspecified — (Use additional code to identify manifestation: 443.81, 785.4) (Use additional code to identify any associated insulin use: V58.67)
249.71 Secondary diabetes mellitus with peripheral circulatory disorders, uncontrolled — (Use additional code to identify manifestation: 443.81, 785.4) (Use additional code to identify any associated insulin use: V58.67)
249.80 Secondary diabetes mellitus with other specified manifestations, not stated as uncontrolled, or unspecified — (Use additional code to identify manifestation: 707.10-707.19, 707.8, 707.9, 731.8) (Use additional code to identify any associated insulin use: V58.67)
249.81 Secondary diabetes mellitus with other specified manifestations, uncontrolled — (Use additional code to identify manifestation: 707.10-707.19, 707.8, 707.9, 731.8) (Use additional code to identify any associated insulin use: V58.67)
250.70 Diabetes with peripheral circulatory disorders, type II or unspecified type, not stated as uncontrolled — (Use additional code to identify manifestation: 443.81, 785.4)
250.71 Diabetes with peripheral circulatory disorders, type I [juvenile type], not stated as uncontrolled — (Use additional code to identify manifestation: 443.81, 785.4)
250.72 Diabetes with peripheral circulatory disorders, type II or unspecified type, uncontrolled — (Use additional code to identify manifestation: 443.81, 785.4)
250.73 Diabetes with peripheral circulatory disorders, type I [juvenile type], uncontrolled — (Use additional code to identify manifestation: 443.81, 785.4)
250.80 Diabetes with other specified manifestations, type II or unspecified type, not stated as uncontrolled — (Use additional code to identify manifestation: 707.10-707.19, 707.8, 707.9, 731.8)
250.81 Diabetes with other specified manifestations, type I [juvenile type], not stated as uncontrolled — (Use additional code to identify manifestation: 707.10-707.19, 707.8, 707.9, 731.8)
250.82 Diabetes with other specified manifestations, type II or unspecified type, uncontrolled — (Use additional code to identify manifestation: 707.10-707.19, 707.8, 707.9, 731.8)
250.83 Diabetes with other specified manifestations, type I [juvenile type], uncontrolled — (Use additional code to identify manifestation: 707.10-707.19, 707.8, 707.9, 731.8)
440.24 Atherosclerosis of native arteries of the extremities with gangrene — (Use additional code for any associated ulceration: 707.10-707.19, 707.8, 707.9)
443.81 Peripheral angiopathy in diseases classified elsewhere — (Code first underlying disease: 249.7, 250.7) ☒
681.00 Unspecified cellulitis and abscess of finger — (Use additional code to identify organism: 041.1) ▽
682.3 Cellulitis and abscess of upper arm and forearm — (Use additional code to identify organism, such as 041.1, etc.)
707.00 Pressure ulcer, unspecified site — (Use additional code to identify pressure ulcer stage: 707.20-707.25) ▽
707.09 Pressure ulcer, other site — (Use additional code to identify pressure ulcer stage: 707.20-707.25)
707.8 Chronic ulcer of other specified site
709.2 Scar condition and fibrosis of skin
728.86 Necrotizing fasciitis — (Use additional code to identify infectious organism, 041.00-041.89, 785.4, if applicable)
731.8 Other bone involvement in diseases classified elsewhere — (Code first underlying disease: 249.8, 250.8. Use additional code to specify bone condition: 730.00-730.09) ☒
785.4 Gangrene — (Code first any associated underlying condition)
883.1 Open wound of finger(s), complicated
886.0 Traumatic amputation of other finger(s) (complete) (partial), without mention of complication
886.1 Traumatic amputation of other finger(s) (complete) (partial), complicated
887.0 Traumatic amputation of arm and hand (complete) (partial), unilateral, below elbow, without mention of complication
887.1 Traumatic amputation of arm and hand (complete) (partial), unilateral, below elbow, complicated
927.20 Crushing injury of hand(s) — (Use additional code to identify any associated injuries: 800-829, 850.0-854.1, 860.0-869.1)
944.58 Deep necrosis of underlying tissues due to burn (deep third degree) of multiple sites of wrist(s) and hand(s), with loss of a body part
959.4 Injury, other and unspecified, hand, except finger

959.5 Injury, other and unspecified, finger
997.60 Late complications of amputation stump, unspecified — (Use additional code to identify complications) ▽
997.61 Neuroma of amputation stump — (Use additional code to identify complications)
997.62 Infection (chronic) of amputation stump — (Use additional code to identify complications)
997.69 Other late amputation stump complication — (Use additional code to identify complications)
998.59 Other postoperative infection — (Use additional code to identify infection)
998.6 Persistent postoperative fistula, not elsewhere classified
998.83 Non-healing surgical wound
V51.8 Other aftercare involving the use of plastic surgery
V58.41 Planned postoperative wound closure — (This code should be used in conjunction with other aftercare codes to fully identify the reason for the aftercare encounter)

ICD-9-CM Procedural

84.03 Amputation through hand
84.3 Revision of amputation stump

HCPCS Level II Supplies & Services

A4305 Disposable drug delivery system, flow rate of 50 ml or greater per hour

Hand and Fingers

20527

20527 Injection, enzyme (eg, collagenase), palmar fascial cord (ie, Dupuytren's contracture)

ICD-9-CM Diagnostic

728.6 Contracture of palmar fascia

ICD-9-CM Procedural

82.96 Other injection of locally-acting therapeutic substance into soft tissue of hand

26010-26011

26010 Drainage of finger abscess; simple
26011 complicated (eg, felon)

ICD-9-CM Diagnostic

681.00 Unspecified cellulitis and abscess of finger — (Use additional code to identify organism: 041.1) ▽
681.01 Felon — (Use additional code to identify organism: 041.1)
681.02 Onychia and paronychia of finger — (Use additional code to identify organism: 041.1)
780.62 Postprocedural fever
883.1 Open wound of finger(s), complicated

ICD-9-CM Procedural

86.04 Other incision with drainage of skin and subcutaneous tissue

26020

26020 Drainage of tendon sheath, digit and/or palm, each

ICD-9-CM Diagnostic

727.05 Other tenosynovitis of hand and wrist
727.89 Other disorders of synovium, tendon, and bursa
780.62 Postprocedural fever
882.1 Open wound of hand except finger(s) alone, complicated
882.2 Open wound of hand except finger(s) alone, with tendon involvement
883.1 Open wound of finger(s), complicated
883.2 Open wound of finger(s), with tendon involvement

ICD-9-CM Procedural

82.01 Exploration of tendon sheath of hand
82.04 Incision and drainage of palmar or thenar space
83.01 Exploration of tendon sheath

HCPCS Level II Supplies & Services

A4305 Disposable drug delivery system, flow rate of 50 ml or greater per hour

26025-26030

26025 Drainage of palmar bursa; single, bursa
26030 multiple bursa

ICD-9-CM Diagnostic

682.4 Cellulitis and abscess of hand, except fingers and thumb — (Use additional code to identify organism, such as 041.1, etc.)
727.05 Other tenosynovitis of hand and wrist
727.3 Other bursitis disorders
727.89 Other disorders of synovium, tendon, and bursa
882.1 Open wound of hand except finger(s) alone, complicated
882.2 Open wound of hand except finger(s) alone, with tendon involvement
958.8 Other early complications of trauma

ICD-9-CM Procedural

82.03 Bursotomy of hand

HCPCS Level II Supplies & Services

A4305 Disposable drug delivery system, flow rate of 50 ml or greater per hour

26034

26034 Incision, bone cortex, hand or finger (eg, osteomyelitis or bone abscess)

ICD-9-CM Diagnostic

681.00 Unspecified cellulitis and abscess of finger — (Use additional code to identify organism: 041.1) ▽
681.02 Onychia and paronychia of finger — (Use additional code to identify organism: 041.1)
682.4 Cellulitis and abscess of hand, except fingers and thumb — (Use additional code to identify organism, such as 041.1, etc.)
730.04 Acute osteomyelitis, hand — (Use additional code to identify organism: 041.1. Use additional code to identify major osseous defect, if applicable: 731.3)
730.14 Chronic osteomyelitis, hand — (Use additional code to identify organism: 041.1. Use additional code to identify major osseous defect, if applicable: 731.3)
730.24 Unspecified osteomyelitis, hand — (Use additional code to identify organism: 041.1. Use additional code to identify major osseous defect, if applicable: 731.3) ▽
730.34 Periostitis, without mention of osteomyelitis, hand — (Use additional code to identify organism: 041.1)
730.84 Other infections involving diseases classified elsewhere, hand bone — (Use additional code to identify organism: 041.1. Code first underlying disease: 002.0, 015.0-015.9) ☒
730.94 Unspecified infection of bone, hand — (Use additional code to identify organism: 041.1) ▽
731.3 Major osseous defects — (Code first underlying disease: 170.0-170.9, 730.00-730.29, 733.00-733.09, 733.40-733.49, 996.45)
883.1 Open wound of finger(s), complicated

ICD-9-CM Procedural

77.14 Other incision of carpals and metacarpals without division
77.19 Other incision of other bone, except facial bones, without division

HCPCS Level II Supplies & Services

A4305 Disposable drug delivery system, flow rate of 50 ml or greater per hour

26035

26035 Decompression fingers and/or hand, injection injury (eg, grease gun)

ICD-9-CM Diagnostic

882.1 Open wound of hand except finger(s) alone, complicated
882.2 Open wound of hand except finger(s) alone, with tendon involvement
883.1 Open wound of finger(s), complicated
883.2 Open wound of finger(s), with tendon involvement

ICD-9-CM Procedural

77.14 Other incision of carpals and metacarpals without division
82.02 Myotomy of hand
82.09 Other incision of soft tissue of hand
82.12 Fasciotomy of hand
82.19 Other division of soft tissue of hand
82.96 Other injection of locally-acting therapeutic substance into soft tissue of hand

HCPCS Level II Supplies & Services

A4305 Disposable drug delivery system, flow rate of 50 ml or greater per hour

26037

26037 Decompressive fasciotomy, hand (excludes 26035)

ICD-9-CM Diagnostic

682.4 Cellulitis and abscess of hand, except fingers and thumb — (Use additional code to identify organism, such as 041.1, etc.)
728.0 Infective myositis
728.86 Necrotizing fasciitis — (Use additional code to identify infectious organism, 041.00-041.89, 785.4, if applicable)
728.88 Rhabdomyolysis
728.89 Other disorder of muscle, ligament, and fascia — (Use additional E code to identify drug, if drug-induced)
729.4 Unspecified fasciitis ▽
729.71 Nontraumatic compartment syndrome of upper extremity — (Code first, if applicable, postprocedural complication: 998.89)
882.1 Open wound of hand except finger(s) alone, complicated
927.20 Crushing injury of hand(s) — (Use additional code to identify any associated injuries: 800-829, 850.0-854.1, 860.0-869.1)
958.8 Other early complications of trauma
958.91 Traumatic compartment syndrome of upper extremity

ICD-9-CM Procedural

82.12 Fasciotomy of hand

HCPCS Level II Supplies & Services

A4305 Disposable drug delivery system, flow rate of 50 ml or greater per hour

26040-26045

26040 Fasciotomy, palmar (eg, Dupuytren's contracture); percutaneous
26045 open, partial

ICD-9-CM Diagnostic

728.6 Contracture of palmar fascia

ICD-9-CM Procedural

82.12 Fasciotomy of hand

HCPCS Level II Supplies & Services

A4305 Disposable drug delivery system, flow rate of 50 ml or greater per hour

26055

26055 Tendon sheath incision (eg, for trigger finger)

ICD-9-CM Diagnostic

357.1 Polyneuropathy in collagen vascular disease — (Code first underlying disease: 446.0, 710.0, 714.0) ☒
359.6 Symptomatic inflammatory myopathy in diseases classified elsewhere — (Code first underlying disease: 135, 140.0-208.9, 277.30-277.39, 446.0, 710.0, 710.1, 710.2, 714.0) ☒
446.0 Polyarteritis nodosa
710.0 Systemic lupus erythematosus — (Use additional code to identify manifestation: 424.91, 581.81, 582.81, 583.81)
710.1 Systemic sclerosis — (Use additional code to identify manifestation: 359.6, 517.2)
710.2 Sicca syndrome
711.04 Pyogenic arthritis, hand — (Use additional code to identify infectious organism: 041.0-041.8)
711.84 Arthropathy associated with other infectious and parasitic diseases, hand — (Code first underlying disease: 080-088, 100-104, 130-136) ☒
711.94 Unspecified infective arthritis, hand ▽
714.0 Rheumatoid arthritis — (Use additional code to identify manifestation: 357.1, 359.6)
716.04 Kaschin-Beck disease, hand
716.14 Traumatic arthropathy, hand
716.54 Unspecified polyarthropathy or polyarthritis, hand ▽
716.64 Unspecified monoarthritis, hand ▽
716.84 Other specified arthropathy, hand
716.94 Unspecified arthropathy, hand ▽
718.44 Contracture of hand joint
718.94 Unspecified derangement of hand joint ▽
727.00 Unspecified synovitis and tenosynovitis ▽
727.01 Synovitis and tenosynovitis in diseases classified elsewhere — (Code first underlying disease: 015.0-015.9) ☒
727.03 Trigger finger (acquired)
727.04 Radial styloid tenosynovitis
727.05 Other tenosynovitis of hand and wrist
727.89 Other disorders of synovium, tendon, and bursa
736.20 Unspecified deformity of finger ▽
736.29 Other acquired deformity of finger
756.89 Other specified congenital anomaly of muscle, tendon, fascia, and connective tissue
905.8 Late effect of tendon injury

ICD-9-CM Procedural

82.01 Exploration of tendon sheath of hand

26060

26060 Tenotomy, percutaneous, single, each digit

ICD-9-CM Diagnostic

727.00 Unspecified synovitis and tenosynovitis ▽
727.01 Synovitis and tenosynovitis in diseases classified elsewhere — (Code first underlying disease: 015.0-015.9) ☒
727.02 Giant cell tumor of tendon sheath
727.03 Trigger finger (acquired)
727.04 Radial styloid tenosynovitis
727.05 Other tenosynovitis of hand and wrist
727.09 Other synovitis and tenosynovitis
727.81 Contracture of tendon (sheath)
727.82 Calcium deposits in tendon and bursa
727.89 Other disorders of synovium, tendon, and bursa

ICD-9-CM Procedural

82.11 Tenotomy of hand

26070-26080

26070 Arthrotomy, with exploration, drainage, or removal of loose or foreign body; carpometacarpal joint
26075 metacarpophalangeal joint, each
26080 interphalangeal joint, each

ICD-9-CM Diagnostic

682.4 Cellulitis and abscess of hand, except fingers and thumb — (Use additional code to identify organism, such as 041.1, etc.)
709.4 Foreign body granuloma of skin and subcutaneous tissue — (Use additional code to identify foreign body (V90.01-V90.9))
711.04 Pyogenic arthritis, hand — (Use additional code to identify infectious organism: 041.0-041.8)

716.14 Traumatic arthropathy, hand
728.0 Infective myositis
728.82 Foreign body granuloma of muscle — (Use additional code to identify foreign body (V90.01-V90.9))
728.89 Other disorder of muscle, ligament, and fascia — (Use additional E code to identify drug, if drug-induced)
729.4 Unspecified fasciitis
729.6 Residual foreign body in soft tissue — (Use additional code to identify foreign body (V90.01-V90.9))
730.04 Acute osteomyelitis, hand — (Use additional code to identify organism: 041.1. Use additional code to identify major osseous defect, if applicable: 731.3)
730.14 Chronic osteomyelitis, hand — (Use additional code to identify organism: 041.1. Use additional code to identify major osseous defect, if applicable: 731.3)
730.24 Unspecified osteomyelitis, hand — (Use additional code to identify organism: 041.1. Use additional code to identify major osseous defect, if applicable: 731.3)
730.34 Periostitis, without mention of osteomyelitis, hand — (Use additional code to identify organism: 041.1)
730.84 Other infections involving diseases classified elsewhere, hand bone — (Use additional code to identify organism: 041.1. Code first underlying disease: 002.0, 015.0-015.9)
731.3 Major osseous defects — (Code first underlying disease: 170.0-170.9, 730.00-730.29, 733.00-733.09, 733.40-733.49, 996.45)
882.1 Open wound of hand except finger(s) alone, complicated
883.1 Open wound of finger(s), complicated
V64.43 Arthroscopic surgical procedure converted to open procedure

ICD-9-CM Procedural

80.14 Other arthrotomy of hand and finger

HCPCS Level II Supplies & Services

A4305 Disposable drug delivery system, flow rate of 50 ml or greater per hour

26100-26110

26100 Arthrotomy with biopsy; carpometacarpal joint, each
26105 metacarpophalangeal joint, each
26110 interphalangeal joint, each

ICD-9-CM Diagnostic

357.1 Polyneuropathy in collagen vascular disease — (Code first underlying disease: 446.0, 710.0, 714.0)
359.6 Symptomatic inflammatory myopathy in diseases classified elsewhere — (Code first underlying disease: 135, 140.0-208.9, 277.30-277.39, 446.0, 710.0, 710.1, 710.2, 714.0)
446.0 Polyarteritis nodosa
710.0 Systemic lupus erythematosus — (Use additional code to identify manifestation: 424.91, 581.81, 582.81, 583.81)
710.1 Systemic sclerosis — (Use additional code to identify manifestation: 359.6, 517.2)
710.2 Sicca syndrome
711.04 Pyogenic arthritis, hand — (Use additional code to identify infectious organism: 041.0-041.8)
711.44 Arthropathy, associated with other bacterial diseases, hand — (Code first underlying disease, such as diseases classifiable to 010-040 (except 036.82), 090-099 (except 098.50))
711.54 Arthropathy associated with other viral diseases, hand — (Code first underlying disease: 045-049, 050-079, 480, 487)
711.64 Arthropathy associated with mycoses, hand — (Code first underlying disease: 110.0-118)
713.8 Arthropathy associated with other conditions classifiable elsewhere — (Code first underlying disease as conditions classifiable elsewhere except as in: 711.1-711.8, 712, 713.0-713.7)
714.0 Rheumatoid arthritis — (Use additional code to identify manifestation: 357.1, 359.6)
714.30 Polyarticular juvenile rheumatoid arthritis, chronic or unspecified
714.9 Unspecified inflammatory polyarthropathy
716.04 Kaschin-Beck disease, hand
716.64 Unspecified monoarthritis, hand
719.24 Villonodular synovitis, hand
726.4 Enthesopathy of wrist and carpus
727.00 Unspecified synovitis and tenosynovitis
727.01 Synovitis and tenosynovitis in diseases classified elsewhere — (Code first underlying disease: 015.0-015.9)
727.05 Other tenosynovitis of hand and wrist
V64.43 Arthroscopic surgical procedure converted to open procedure

ICD-9-CM Procedural

80.34 Biopsy of joint structure of hand and finger

HCPCS Level II Supplies & Services

A4305 Disposable drug delivery system, flow rate of 50 ml or greater per hour

26115-26118 [26111, 26113]

26111 Excision, tumor or vascular malformation, soft tissue of hand or finger, subcutaneous; 1.5 cm or greater
26113 Excision, tumor, soft tissue, or vascular malformation, of hand or finger, subfascial (eg, intramuscular); 1.5 cm or greater
26115 Excision, tumor or vascular malformation, soft tissue of hand or finger, subcutaneous; less than 1.5 cm
26116 Excision, tumor, soft tissue, or vascular malformation, of hand or finger, subfascial (eg, intramuscular); less than 1.5 cm
26117 Radical resection of tumor (eg, sarcoma), soft tissue of hand or finger; less than 3 cm
26118 3 cm or greater

ICD-9-CM Diagnostic

171.2 Malignant neoplasm of connective and other soft tissue of upper limb, including shoulder
195.4 Malignant neoplasm of upper limb
198.89 Secondary malignant neoplasm of other specified sites
209.33 Merkel cell carcinoma of the upper limb
209.75 Secondary Merkel cell carcinoma
214.1 Lipoma of other skin and subcutaneous tissue
215.2 Other benign neoplasm of connective and other soft tissue of upper limb, including shoulder
228.01 Hemangioma of skin and subcutaneous tissue
238.1 Neoplasm of uncertain behavior of connective and other soft tissue
239.2 Neoplasms of unspecified nature of bone, soft tissue, and skin
686.1 Pyogenic granuloma of skin and subcutaneous tissue — (Use additional code to identify any infectious organism: 041.0-041.8)
727.02 Giant cell tumor of tendon sheath
728.79 Other fibromatoses of muscle, ligament, and fascia
747.63 Congenital upper limb vessel anomaly
747.69 Congenital anomaly of other specified site of peripheral vascular system
782.2 Localized superficial swelling, mass, or lump

ICD-9-CM Procedural

82.21 Excision of lesion of tendon sheath of hand
82.22 Excision of lesion of muscle of hand
82.29 Excision of other lesion of soft tissue of hand
83.49 Other excision of soft tissue
86.3 Other local excision or destruction of lesion or tissue of skin and subcutaneous tissue
86.4 Radical excision of skin lesion

HCPCS Level II Supplies & Services

A4305 Disposable drug delivery system, flow rate of 50 ml or greater per hour

26121-26125

26121 Fasciectomy, palm only, with or without Z-plasty, other local tissue rearrangement, or skin grafting (includes obtaining graft)

26123 Fasciectomy, partial palmar with release of single digit including proximal interphalangeal joint, with or without Z-plasty, other local tissue rearrangement, or skin grafting (includes obtaining graft);

26125 each additional digit (List separately in addition to code for primary procedure)

ICD-9-CM Diagnostic

239.2 Neoplasms of unspecified nature of bone, soft tissue, and skin

682.4 Cellulitis and abscess of hand, except fingers and thumb — (Use additional code to identify organism, such as 041.1, etc.)

718.44 Contracture of hand joint

727.03 Trigger finger (acquired)

727.81 Contracture of tendon (sheath)

728.0 Infective myositis

728.6 Contracture of palmar fascia

729.4 Unspecified fasciitis ▽

736.29 Other acquired deformity of finger

882.1 Open wound of hand except finger(s) alone, complicated

ICD-9-CM Procedural

82.35 Other fasciectomy of hand

86.61 Full-thickness skin graft to hand

86.84 Relaxation of scar or web contracture of skin

26130

26130 Synovectomy, carpometacarpal joint

ICD-9-CM Diagnostic

275.40 Unspecified disorder of calcium metabolism — (Use additional code to identify any associated intellectual disabilities) ▽

275.42 Hypercalcemia — (Use additional code to identify any associated intellectual disabilities)

275.49 Other disorders of calcium metabolism — (Use additional code to identify any associated intellectual disabilities)

357.1 Polyneuropathy in collagen vascular disease — (Code first underlying disease: 446.0, 710.0, 714.0) ☒

359.6 Symptomatic inflammatory myopathy in diseases classified elsewhere — (Code first underlying disease: 135, 140.0-208.9, 277.30-277.39, 446.0, 710.0, 710.1, 710.2, 714.0) ☒

446.0 Polyarteritis nodosa

710.0 Systemic lupus erythematosus — (Use additional code to identify manifestation: 424.91, 581.81, 582.81, 583.81)

710.1 Systemic sclerosis — (Use additional code to identify manifestation: 359.6, 517.2)

710.2 Sicca syndrome

711.04 Pyogenic arthritis, hand — (Use additional code to identify infectious organism: 041.0-041.8)

711.44 Arthropathy, associated with other bacterial diseases, hand — (Code first underlying disease, such as diseases classifiable to 010-040 (except 036.82), 090-099 (except 098.50)) ☒

711.54 Arthropathy associated with other viral diseases, hand — (Code first underlying disease: 045-049, 050-079, 480, 487) ☒

711.64 Arthropathy associated with mycoses, hand — (Code first underlying disease: 110.0-118) ☒

711.94 Unspecified infective arthritis, hand ▽

712.84 Other specified crystal arthropathies, hand

713.8 Arthropathy associated with other conditions classifiable elsewhere — (Code first underlying disease as conditions classifiable elsewhere except as in: 711.1-711.8, 712, 713.0-713.7) ☒

714.0 Rheumatoid arthritis — (Use additional code to identify manifestation: 357.1, 359.6)

714.30 Polyarticular juvenile rheumatoid arthritis, chronic or unspecified

714.31 Polyarticular juvenile rheumatoid arthritis, acute

714.32 Pauciarticular juvenile rheumatoid arthritis

714.33 Monoarticular juvenile rheumatoid arthritis

714.9 Unspecified inflammatory polyarthropathy ▽

716.04 Kaschin-Beck disease, hand

716.14 Traumatic arthropathy, hand

716.64 Unspecified monoarthritis, hand ▽

719.24 Villonodular synovitis, hand

726.4 Enthesopathy of wrist and carpus

727.00 Unspecified synovitis and tenosynovitis ▽

727.50 Unspecified rupture of synovium ▽

ICD-9-CM Procedural

80.79 Synovectomy of other specified site

HCPCS Level II Supplies & Services

A4305 Disposable drug delivery system, flow rate of 50 ml or greater per hour

26135

26135 Synovectomy, metacarpophalangeal joint including intrinsic release and extensor hood reconstruction, each digit

ICD-9-CM Diagnostic

275.40 Unspecified disorder of calcium metabolism — (Use additional code to identify any associated intellectual disabilities) ▽

275.42 Hypercalcemia — (Use additional code to identify any associated intellectual disabilities)

275.49 Other disorders of calcium metabolism — (Use additional code to identify any associated intellectual disabilities)

275.5 Hungry bone syndrome — (Use additional code to identify any associated intellectual disabilities)

357.1 Polyneuropathy in collagen vascular disease — (Code first underlying disease: 446.0, 710.0, 714.0) ☒

359.6 Symptomatic inflammatory myopathy in diseases classified elsewhere — (Code first underlying disease: 135, 140.0-208.9, 277.30-277.39, 446.0, 710.0, 710.1, 710.2, 714.0) ☒

446.0 Polyarteritis nodosa

710.0 Systemic lupus erythematosus — (Use additional code to identify manifestation: 424.91, 581.81, 582.81, 583.81)

710.1 Systemic sclerosis — (Use additional code to identify manifestation: 359.6, 517.2)

710.2 Sicca syndrome

711.04 Pyogenic arthritis, hand — (Use additional code to identify infectious organism: 041.0-041.8)

711.44 Arthropathy, associated with other bacterial diseases, hand — (Code first underlying disease, such as diseases classifiable to 010-040 (except 036.82), 090-099 (except 098.50)) ☒

711.54 Arthropathy associated with other viral diseases, hand — (Code first underlying disease: 045-049, 050-079, 480, 487) ☒

711.64 Arthropathy associated with mycoses, hand — (Code first underlying disease: 110.0-118) ☒

711.94 Unspecified infective arthritis, hand ▽

712.84 Other specified crystal arthropathies, hand

713.8 Arthropathy associated with other conditions classifiable elsewhere — (Code first underlying disease as conditions classifiable elsewhere except as in: 711.1-711.8, 712, 713.0-713.7) ☒

714.0 Rheumatoid arthritis — (Use additional code to identify manifestation: 357.1, 359.6)

714.31 Polyarticular juvenile rheumatoid arthritis, acute

716.14 Traumatic arthropathy, hand

718.44 Contracture of hand joint

719.24 Villonodular synovitis, hand

727.00 Unspecified synovitis and tenosynovitis ▽

727.01 Synovitis and tenosynovitis in diseases classified elsewhere — (Code first underlying disease: 015.0-015.9) ☒
727.05 Other tenosynovitis of hand and wrist

ICD-9-CM Procedural

80.74 Synovectomy of hand and finger

HCPCS Level II Supplies & Services

A4305 Disposable drug delivery system, flow rate of 50 ml or greater per hour

26140

26140 Synovectomy, proximal interphalangeal joint, including extensor reconstruction, each interphalangeal joint

ICD-9-CM Diagnostic

275.40 Unspecified disorder of calcium metabolism — (Use additional code to identify any associated intellectual disabilities) ▽
275.42 Hypercalcemia — (Use additional code to identify any associated intellectual disabilities)
275.49 Other disorders of calcium metabolism — (Use additional code to identify any associated intellectual disabilities)
277.30 Amyloidosis, unspecified — (Use additional code to identify any associated intellectual disabilities) ▽
277.31 Familial Mediterranean fever — (Use additional code to identify any associated intellectual disabilities)
277.39 Other amyloidosis — (Use additional code to identify any associated intellectual disabilities)
357.1 Polyneuropathy in collagen vascular disease — (Code first underlying disease: 446.0, 710.0, 714.0) ☒
359.6 Symptomatic inflammatory myopathy in diseases classified elsewhere — (Code first underlying disease: 135, 140.0-208.9, 277.30-277.39, 446.0, 710.0, 710.1, 710.2, 714.0) ☒
446.0 Polyarteritis nodosa
710.0 Systemic lupus erythematosus — (Use additional code to identify manifestation: 424.91, 581.81, 582.81, 583.81)
710.1 Systemic sclerosis — (Use additional code to identify manifestation: 359.6, 517.2)
710.2 Sicca syndrome
711.04 Pyogenic arthritis, hand — (Use additional code to identify infectious organism: 041.0-041.8)
711.44 Arthropathy, associated with other bacterial diseases, hand — (Code first underlying disease, such as diseases classifiable to 010-040 (except 036.82), 090-099 (except 098.50)) ☒
711.54 Arthropathy associated with other viral diseases, hand — (Code first underlying disease: 045-049, 050-079, 480, 487) ☒
711.64 Arthropathy associated with mycoses, hand — (Code first underlying disease: 110.0-118) ☒
711.94 Unspecified infective arthritis, hand ▽
712.84 Other specified crystal arthropathies, hand
713.8 Arthropathy associated with other conditions classifiable elsewhere — (Code first underlying disease as conditions classifiable elsewhere except as in: 711.1-711.8, 712, 713.0-713.7) ☒
714.0 Rheumatoid arthritis — (Use additional code to identify manifestation: 357.1, 359.6)
714.1 Felty's syndrome
718.44 Contracture of hand joint
727.00 Unspecified synovitis and tenosynovitis ▽
727.01 Synovitis and tenosynovitis in diseases classified elsewhere — (Code first underlying disease: 015.0-015.9) ☒
727.05 Other tenosynovitis of hand and wrist
736.21 Boutonniere deformity

ICD-9-CM Procedural

80.74 Synovectomy of hand and finger

HCPCS Level II Supplies & Services

A4305 Disposable drug delivery system, flow rate of 50 ml or greater per hour

26145

26145 Synovectomy, tendon sheath, radical (tenosynovectomy), flexor tendon, palm and/or finger, each tendon

ICD-9-CM Diagnostic

171.2 Malignant neoplasm of connective and other soft tissue of upper limb, including shoulder
238.1 Neoplasm of uncertain behavior of connective and other soft tissue
239.2 Neoplasms of unspecified nature of bone, soft tissue, and skin
357.1 Polyneuropathy in collagen vascular disease — (Code first underlying disease: 446.0, 710.0, 714.0) ☒
359.6 Symptomatic inflammatory myopathy in diseases classified elsewhere — (Code first underlying disease: 135, 140.0-208.9, 277.30-277.39, 446.0, 710.0, 710.1, 710.2, 714.0) ☒
446.0 Polyarteritis nodosa
710.0 Systemic lupus erythematosus — (Use additional code to identify manifestation: 424.91, 581.81, 582.81, 583.81)
710.1 Systemic sclerosis — (Use additional code to identify manifestation: 359.6, 517.2)
710.2 Sicca syndrome
714.0 Rheumatoid arthritis — (Use additional code to identify manifestation: 357.1, 359.6)
714.1 Felty's syndrome

ICD-9-CM Procedural

80.74 Synovectomy of hand and finger

26160

26160 Excision of lesion of tendon sheath or joint capsule (eg, cyst, mucous cyst, or ganglion), hand or finger

ICD-9-CM Diagnostic

215.2 Other benign neoplasm of connective and other soft tissue of upper limb, including shoulder
229.8 Benign neoplasm of other specified sites
238.8 Neoplasm of uncertain behavior of other specified sites
239.2 Neoplasms of unspecified nature of bone, soft tissue, and skin
727.00 Unspecified synovitis and tenosynovitis ▽
727.02 Giant cell tumor of tendon sheath
727.04 Radial styloid tenosynovitis
727.41 Ganglion of joint
727.42 Ganglion of tendon sheath
727.9 Unspecified disorder of synovium, tendon, and bursa ▽
782.2 Localized superficial swelling, mass, or lump

ICD-9-CM Procedural

82.21 Excision of lesion of tendon sheath of hand

HCPCS Level II Supplies & Services

A4305 Disposable drug delivery system, flow rate of 50 ml or greater per hour

26115

26170 Excision of tendon, palm, flexor or extensor, single, each tendon
26180 Excision of tendon, finger, flexor or extensor, each tendon

ICD-9-CM Diagnostic

357.1 Polyneuropathy in collagen vascular disease — (Code first underlying disease: 446.0, 710.0, 714.0) ☒
359.6 Symptomatic inflammatory myopathy in diseases classified elsewhere — (Code first underlying disease: 135, 140.0-208.9, 277.30-277.39, 446.0, 710.0, 710.1, 710.2, 714.0) ☒
446.0 Polyarteritis nodosa

682.4 Cellulitis and abscess of hand, except fingers and thumb — (Use additional code to identify organism, such as 041.1, etc.)
710.0 Systemic lupus erythematosus — (Use additional code to identify manifestation: 424.91, 581.81, 582.81, 583.81)
710.1 Systemic sclerosis — (Use additional code to identify manifestation: 359.6, 517.2)
710.2 Sicca syndrome
714.0 Rheumatoid arthritis — (Use additional code to identify manifestation: 357.1, 359.6)
716.14 Traumatic arthropathy, hand
727.81 Contracture of tendon (sheath)
727.89 Other disorders of synovium, tendon, and bursa
728.6 Contracture of palmar fascia
882.2 Open wound of hand except finger(s) alone, with tendon involvement
905.8 Late effect of tendon injury

ICD-9-CM Procedural
82.33 Other tenonectomy of hand

HCPCS Level II Supplies & Services
A4305 Disposable drug delivery system, flow rate of 50 ml or greater per hour

26185
26185 Sesamoidectomy, thumb or finger (separate procedure)

ICD-9-CM Diagnostic
170.5 Malignant neoplasm of short bones of upper limb
213.5 Benign neoplasm of short bones of upper limb
357.1 Polyneuropathy in collagen vascular disease — (Code first underlying disease: 446.0, 710.0, 714.0) ☒
359.6 Symptomatic inflammatory myopathy in diseases classified elsewhere — (Code first underlying disease: 135, 140.0-208.9, 277.30-277.39, 446.0, 710.0, 710.1, 710.2, 714.0) ☒
446.0 Polyarteritis nodosa
710.0 Systemic lupus erythematosus — (Use additional code to identify manifestation: 424.91, 581.81, 582.81, 583.81)
710.1 Systemic sclerosis — (Use additional code to identify manifestation: 359.6, 517.2)
710.2 Sicca syndrome
714.0 Rheumatoid arthritis — (Use additional code to identify manifestation: 357.1, 359.6)
715.09 Generalized osteoarthrosis, involving multiple sites
715.14 Primary localized osteoarthrosis, hand
726.4 Enthesopathy of wrist and carpus
726.90 Enthesopathy of unspecified site ▽
732.9 Unspecified osteochondropathy ▽
733.99 Other disorders of bone and cartilage

ICD-9-CM Procedural
77.99 Total ostectomy of other bone, except facial bones

HCPCS Level II Supplies & Services
A4305 Disposable drug delivery system, flow rate of 50 ml or greater per hour

26200-26205
26200 Excision or curettage of bone cyst or benign tumor of metacarpal;
26205 with autograft (includes obtaining graft)

ICD-9-CM Diagnostic
213.5 Benign neoplasm of short bones of upper limb
238.0 Neoplasm of uncertain behavior of bone and articular cartilage
239.2 Neoplasms of unspecified nature of bone, soft tissue, and skin
726.91 Exostosis of unspecified site ▽
733.21 Solitary bone cyst
733.22 Aneurysmal bone cyst
733.29 Other cyst of bone

ICD-9-CM Procedural
77.64 Local excision of lesion or tissue of carpals and metacarpals

HCPCS Level II Supplies & Services
A4305 Disposable drug delivery system, flow rate of 50 ml or greater per hour

26210-26215
26210 Excision or curettage of bone cyst or benign tumor of proximal, middle, or distal phalanx of finger;
26215 with autograft (includes obtaining graft)

ICD-9-CM Diagnostic
213.5 Benign neoplasm of short bones of upper limb
238.0 Neoplasm of uncertain behavior of bone and articular cartilage
239.2 Neoplasms of unspecified nature of bone, soft tissue, and skin
726.91 Exostosis of unspecified site ▽
733.21 Solitary bone cyst
733.22 Aneurysmal bone cyst
733.29 Other cyst of bone

ICD-9-CM Procedural
77.64 Local excision of lesion or tissue of carpals and metacarpals

HCPCS Level II Supplies & Services
A4305 Disposable drug delivery system, flow rate of 50 ml or greater per hour

26230-26236
26230 Partial excision (craterization, saucerization, or diaphysectomy) bone (eg, osteomyelitis); metacarpal
26235 proximal or middle phalanx of finger
26236 distal phalanx of finger

ICD-9-CM Diagnostic
730.14 Chronic osteomyelitis, hand — (Use additional code to identify organism: 041.1. Use additional code to identify major osseous defect, if applicable: 731.3)
730.18 Chronic osteomyelitis, other specified sites — (Use additional code to identify organism: 041.1. Use additional code to identify major osseous defect, if applicable: 731.3)
730.24 Unspecified osteomyelitis, hand — (Use additional code to identify organism: 041.1. Use additional code to identify major osseous defect, if applicable: 731.3) ▽
730.84 Other infections involving diseases classified elsewhere, hand bone — (Use additional code to identify organism: 041.1. Code first underlying disease: 002.0, 015.0-015.9) ☒
731.3 Major osseous defects — (Code first underlying disease: 170.0-170.9, 730.00-730.29, 733.00-733.09, 733.40-733.49, 996.45)
733.49 Aseptic necrosis of other bone site — (Use additional code to identify major osseous defect, if applicable: 731.3)

ICD-9-CM Procedural
77.89 Other partial ostectomy of other bone, except facial bones

HCPCS Level II Supplies & Services
A4305 Disposable drug delivery system, flow rate of 50 ml or greater per hour

26250-26262
26250 Radical resection of tumor, metacarpal
26260 Radical resection of tumor, proximal or middle phalanx of finger
26262 Radical resection of tumor, distal phalanx of finger

ICD-9-CM Diagnostic
170.5 Malignant neoplasm of short bones of upper limb
195.4 Malignant neoplasm of upper limb
198.5 Secondary malignant neoplasm of bone and bone marrow
198.89 Secondary malignant neoplasm of other specified sites

209.73 Secondary neuroendocrine tumor of bone
238.0 Neoplasm of uncertain behavior of bone and articular cartilage
238.1 Neoplasm of uncertain behavior of connective and other soft tissue
239.2 Neoplasms of unspecified nature of bone, soft tissue, and skin

ICD-9-CM Procedural

77.64 Local excision of lesion or tissue of carpals and metacarpals

HCPCS Level II Supplies & Services

A4305 Disposable drug delivery system, flow rate of 50 ml or greater per hour

26320

26320 Removal of implant from finger or hand

ICD-9-CM Diagnostic

357.1 Polyneuropathy in collagen vascular disease — (Code first underlying disease: 446.0, 710.0, 714.0) ☒
359.6 Symptomatic inflammatory myopathy in diseases classified elsewhere — (Code first underlying disease: 135, 140.0-208.9, 277.30-277.39, 446.0, 710.0, 710.1, 710.2, 714.0) ☒
446.0 Polyarteritis nodosa
710.0 Systemic lupus erythematosus — (Use additional code to identify manifestation: 424.91, 581.81, 582.81, 583.81)
710.1 Systemic sclerosis — (Use additional code to identify manifestation: 359.6, 517.2)
710.2 Sicca syndrome
714.0 Rheumatoid arthritis — (Use additional code to identify manifestation: 357.1, 359.6)
731.3 Major osseous defects — (Code first underlying disease: 170.0-170.9, 730.00-730.29, 733.00-733.09, 733.40-733.49, 996.45)
905.2 Late effect of fracture of upper extremities
996.40 Unspecified mechanical complication of internal orthopedic device, implant, and graft — (Use additional code to identify prosthetic joint with mechanical complication, V43.60-V43.69) ▽
996.41 Mechanical loosening of prosthetic joint — (Use additional code to identify prosthetic joint with mechanical complication, V43.60-V43.69)
996.42 Dislocation of prosthetic joint — (Use additional code to identify prosthetic joint with mechanical complication, V43.60-V43.69)
996.43 Broken prosthetic joint implant — (Use additional code to identify prosthetic joint with mechanical complication, V43.60-V43.69)
996.44 Peri-prosthetic fracture around prosthetic joint — (Use additional code to identify prosthetic joint with mechanical complication, V43.60-V43.69.
996.45 Peri-prosthetic osteolysis — (Use additional code to identify prosthetic joint with mechanical complication, V43.60-V43.69. Use additional code to identify major osseous defect, if applicable: 731.3)
996.47 Other mechanical complication of prosthetic joint implant — (Use additional code to identify prosthetic joint with mechanical complication, V43.60-V43.69)
996.49 Other mechanical complication of other internal orthopedic device, implant, and graft — (Use additional code to identify prosthetic joint with mechanical complication, V43.60-V43.69)
996.66 Infection and inflammatory reaction due to internal joint prosthesis — (Use additional code to identify specified infections. Use additional code to identify infected prosthetic joint: V43.60-V43.69)
996.67 Infection and inflammatory reaction due to other internal orthopedic device, implant, and graft — (Use additional code to identify specified infections)
996.77 Other complications due to internal joint prosthesis — (Use additional code to identify complication: 338.18-338.19, 338.28-338.29)
996.78 Other complications due to other internal orthopedic device, implant, and graft — (Use additional code to identify complication: 338.18-338.19, 338.28-338.29)
998.51 Infected postoperative seroma — (Use additional code to identify organism)
998.59 Other postoperative infection — (Use additional code to identify infection)
V43.69 Other joint replacement by other means

ICD-9-CM Procedural

78.64 Removal of implanted device from carpals and metacarpals
80.04 Arthrotomy for removal of prosthesis without replacement, hand and finger
84.57 Removal of (cement) spacer

HCPCS Level II Supplies & Services

A4305 Disposable drug delivery system, flow rate of 50 ml or greater per hour

26340

26340 Manipulation, finger joint, under anesthesia, each joint

ICD-9-CM Diagnostic

357.1 Polyneuropathy in collagen vascular disease — (Code first underlying disease: 446.0, 710.0, 714.0) ☒
359.6 Symptomatic inflammatory myopathy in diseases classified elsewhere — (Code first underlying disease: 135, 140.0-208.9, 277.30-277.39, 446.0, 710.0, 710.1, 710.2, 714.0) ☒
446.0 Polyarteritis nodosa
710.0 Systemic lupus erythematosus — (Use additional code to identify manifestation: 424.91, 581.81, 582.81, 583.81)
710.1 Systemic sclerosis — (Use additional code to identify manifestation: 359.6, 517.2)
710.2 Sicca syndrome
714.0 Rheumatoid arthritis — (Use additional code to identify manifestation: 357.1, 359.6)
715.14 Primary localized osteoarthrosis, hand
715.94 Osteoarthrosis, unspecified whether generalized or localized, hand ▽
718.44 Contracture of hand joint
718.54 Ankylosis of hand joint
719.24 Villonodular synovitis, hand
719.54 Stiffness of joint, not elsewhere classified, hand
726.8 Other peripheral enthesopathies

ICD-9-CM Procedural

93.25 Forced extension of limb
93.26 Manual rupture of joint adhesions
93.29 Other forcible correction of musculoskeletal deformity

26341

26341 Manipulation, palmar fascial cord (ie, Dupuytren's cord), post enzyme injection (eg, collagenase), single cord

ICD-9-CM Diagnostic

728.6 Contracture of palmar fascia

ICD-9-CM Procedural

93.28 Stretching of fascia

26350-26352

26350 Repair or advancement, flexor tendon, not in zone 2 digital flexor tendon sheath (eg, no man's land); primary or secondary without free graft, each tendon
26352 secondary with free graft (includes obtaining graft), each tendon

ICD-9-CM Diagnostic

357.1 Polyneuropathy in collagen vascular disease — (Code first underlying disease: 446.0, 710.0, 714.0) ☒
359.6 Symptomatic inflammatory myopathy in diseases classified elsewhere — (Code first underlying disease: 135, 140.0-208.9, 277.30-277.39, 446.0, 710.0, 710.1, 710.2, 714.0) ☒
446.0 Polyarteritis nodosa
710.0 Systemic lupus erythematosus — (Use additional code to identify manifestation: 424.91, 581.81, 582.81, 583.81)
710.1 Systemic sclerosis — (Use additional code to identify manifestation: 359.6, 517.2)
710.2 Sicca syndrome
714.0 Rheumatoid arthritis — (Use additional code to identify manifestation: 357.1, 359.6)
727.64 Nontraumatic rupture of flexor tendons of hand and wrist
881.22 Open wound of wrist, with tendon involvement

882.2 Open wound of hand except finger(s) alone, with tendon involvement
883.2 Open wound of finger(s), with tendon involvement
884.2 Multiple and unspecified open wound of upper limb, with tendon involvement
886.1 Traumatic amputation of other finger(s) (complete) (partial), complicated
959.4 Injury, other and unspecified, hand, except finger
998.2 Accidental puncture or laceration during procedure

ICD-9-CM Procedural

82.42 Delayed suture of flexor tendon of hand
82.44 Other suture of flexor tendon of hand
82.51 Advancement of tendon of hand
83.71 Advancement of tendon
83.88 Other plastic operations on tendon

26356-26358

26356 Repair or advancement, flexor tendon, in zone 2 digital flexor tendon sheath (eg, no man's land); primary, without free graft, each tendon
26357 secondary, without free graft, each tendon
26358 secondary, with free graft (includes obtaining graft), each tendon

ICD-9-CM Diagnostic

357.1 Polyneuropathy in collagen vascular disease — (Code first underlying disease: 446.0, 710.0, 714.0) ☒
359.6 Symptomatic inflammatory myopathy in diseases classified elsewhere — (Code first underlying disease: 135, 140.0-208.9, 277.30-277.39, 446.0, 710.0, 710.1, 710.2, 714.0) ☒
446.0 Polyarteritis nodosa
710.0 Systemic lupus erythematosus — (Use additional code to identify manifestation: 424.91, 581.81, 582.81, 583.81)
710.1 Systemic sclerosis — (Use additional code to identify manifestation: 359.6, 517.2)
710.2 Sicca syndrome
714.0 Rheumatoid arthritis — (Use additional code to identify manifestation: 357.1, 359.6)
727.64 Nontraumatic rupture of flexor tendons of hand and wrist
881.22 Open wound of wrist, with tendon involvement
882.2 Open wound of hand except finger(s) alone, with tendon involvement
883.2 Open wound of finger(s), with tendon involvement
884.2 Multiple and unspecified open wound of upper limb, with tendon involvement
886.1 Traumatic amputation of other finger(s) (complete) (partial), complicated
959.4 Injury, other and unspecified, hand, except finger
998.2 Accidental puncture or laceration during procedure

ICD-9-CM Procedural

82.42 Delayed suture of flexor tendon of hand
82.44 Other suture of flexor tendon of hand
82.51 Advancement of tendon of hand
83.71 Advancement of tendon
83.88 Other plastic operations on tendon

26370-26373

26370 Repair or advancement of profundus tendon, with intact superficialis tendon; primary, each tendon
26372 secondary with free graft (includes obtaining graft), each tendon
26373 secondary without free graft, each tendon

ICD-9-CM Diagnostic

357.1 Polyneuropathy in collagen vascular disease — (Code first underlying disease: 446.0, 710.0, 714.0) ☒
359.6 Symptomatic inflammatory myopathy in diseases classified elsewhere — (Code first underlying disease: 135, 140.0-208.9, 277.30-277.39, 446.0, 710.0, 710.1, 710.2, 714.0) ☒
446.0 Polyarteritis nodosa
710.0 Systemic lupus erythematosus — (Use additional code to identify manifestation: 424.91, 581.81, 582.81, 583.81)
710.1 Systemic sclerosis — (Use additional code to identify manifestation: 359.6, 517.2)
710.2 Sicca syndrome
714.0 Rheumatoid arthritis — (Use additional code to identify manifestation: 357.1, 359.6)
727.64 Nontraumatic rupture of flexor tendons of hand and wrist
881.22 Open wound of wrist, with tendon involvement
882.2 Open wound of hand except finger(s) alone, with tendon involvement
883.2 Open wound of finger(s), with tendon involvement
884.2 Multiple and unspecified open wound of upper limb, with tendon involvement
886.1 Traumatic amputation of other finger(s) (complete) (partial), complicated
959.4 Injury, other and unspecified, hand, except finger
998.2 Accidental puncture or laceration during procedure

ICD-9-CM Procedural

82.42 Delayed suture of flexor tendon of hand
82.44 Other suture of flexor tendon of hand
82.51 Advancement of tendon of hand
83.71 Advancement of tendon
83.88 Other plastic operations on tendon

26390-26392

26390 Excision flexor tendon, with implantation of synthetic rod for delayed tendon graft, hand or finger, each rod
26392 Removal of synthetic rod and insertion of flexor tendon graft, hand or finger (includes obtaining graft), each rod

ICD-9-CM Diagnostic

727.64 Nontraumatic rupture of flexor tendons of hand and wrist
727.69 Nontraumatic rupture of other tendon
881.22 Open wound of wrist, with tendon involvement
882.2 Open wound of hand except finger(s) alone, with tendon involvement
883.2 Open wound of finger(s), with tendon involvement
884.2 Multiple and unspecified open wound of upper limb, with tendon involvement
906.1 Late effect of open wound of extremities without mention of tendon injury
998.2 Accidental puncture or laceration during procedure
V51.8 Other aftercare involving the use of plastic surgery
V54.01 Encounter for removal of internal fixation device
V54.02 Encounter for lengthening/adjustment of growth rod
V54.09 Other aftercare involving internal fixation device

ICD-9-CM Procedural

78.64 Removal of implanted device from carpals and metacarpals
82.33 Other tenonectomy of hand
82.79 Plastic operation on hand with other graft or implant
83.81 Tendon graft

26410-26412

26410 Repair, extensor tendon, hand, primary or secondary; without free graft, each tendon
26412 with free graft (includes obtaining graft), each tendon

ICD-9-CM Diagnostic

727.63 Nontraumatic rupture of extensor tendons of hand and wrist
881.22 Open wound of wrist, with tendon involvement
882.2 Open wound of hand except finger(s) alone, with tendon involvement
884.2 Multiple and unspecified open wound of upper limb, with tendon involvement
927.20 Crushing injury of hand(s) — (Use additional code to identify any associated injuries: 800-829, 850.0-854.1, 860.0-869.1)
959.4 Injury, other and unspecified, hand, except finger
998.2 Accidental puncture or laceration during procedure

ICD-9-CM Procedural

82.43 Delayed suture of other tendon of hand
82.45 Other suture of other tendon of hand
83.81 Tendon graft
83.88 Other plastic operations on tendon

26415-26416

26415 Excision of extensor tendon, with implantation of synthetic rod for delayed tendon graft, hand or finger, each rod
26416 Removal of synthetic rod and insertion of extensor tendon graft (includes obtaining graft), hand or finger, each rod

ICD-9-CM Diagnostic

727.63 Nontraumatic rupture of extensor tendons of hand and wrist
881.22 Open wound of wrist, with tendon involvement
882.2 Open wound of hand except finger(s) alone, with tendon involvement
883.2 Open wound of finger(s), with tendon involvement
884.2 Multiple and unspecified open wound of upper limb, with tendon involvement
887.1 Traumatic amputation of arm and hand (complete) (partial), unilateral, below elbow, complicated
998.2 Accidental puncture or laceration during procedure
V51.8 Other aftercare involving the use of plastic surgery
V54.01 Encounter for removal of internal fixation device
V54.02 Encounter for lengthening/adjustment of growth rod
V54.09 Other aftercare involving internal fixation device

ICD-9-CM Procedural

78.64 Removal of implanted device from carpals and metacarpals
82.33 Other tenonectomy of hand
82.79 Plastic operation on hand with other graft or implant

26418-26420

26418 Repair, extensor tendon, finger, primary or secondary; without free graft, each tendon
26420 with free graft (includes obtaining graft) each tendon

ICD-9-CM Diagnostic

357.1 Polyneuropathy in collagen vascular disease — (Code first underlying disease: 446.0, 710.0, 714.0) ☒
359.6 Symptomatic inflammatory myopathy in diseases classified elsewhere — (Code first underlying disease: 135, 140.0-208.9, 277.30-277.39, 446.0, 710.0, 710.1, 710.2, 714.0) ☒
446.0 Polyarteritis nodosa
710.0 Systemic lupus erythematosus — (Use additional code to identify manifestation: 424.91, 581.81, 582.81, 583.81)
710.1 Systemic sclerosis — (Use additional code to identify manifestation: 359.6, 517.2)
710.2 Sicca syndrome
714.0 Rheumatoid arthritis — (Use additional code to identify manifestation: 357.1, 359.6)
727.63 Nontraumatic rupture of extensor tendons of hand and wrist
727.9 Unspecified disorder of synovium, tendon, and bursa ♥
883.2 Open wound of finger(s), with tendon involvement

ICD-9-CM Procedural

82.43 Delayed suture of other tendon of hand
82.45 Other suture of other tendon of hand
82.51 Advancement of tendon of hand

26426-26428

26426 Repair of extensor tendon, central slip, secondary (eg, boutonniere deformity); using local tissue(s), including lateral band(s), each finger
26428 with free graft (includes obtaining graft), each finger

ICD-9-CM Diagnostic

357.1 Polyneuropathy in collagen vascular disease — (Code first underlying disease: 446.0, 710.0, 714.0) ☒
359.6 Symptomatic inflammatory myopathy in diseases classified elsewhere — (Code first underlying disease: 135, 140.0-208.9, 277.30-277.39, 446.0, 710.0, 710.1, 710.2, 714.0) ☒
446.0 Polyarteritis nodosa
710.0 Systemic lupus erythematosus — (Use additional code to identify manifestation: 424.91, 581.81, 582.81, 583.81)
710.1 Systemic sclerosis — (Use additional code to identify manifestation: 359.6, 517.2)
710.2 Sicca syndrome
714.0 Rheumatoid arthritis — (Use additional code to identify manifestation: 357.1, 359.6)
714.1 Felty's syndrome
736.21 Boutonniere deformity
883.2 Open wound of finger(s), with tendon involvement
905.2 Late effect of fracture of upper extremities

ICD-9-CM Procedural

83.88 Other plastic operations on tendon

26432

26432 Closed treatment of distal extensor tendon insertion, with or without percutaneous pinning (eg, mallet finger)

ICD-9-CM Diagnostic

736.1 Mallet finger

ICD-9-CM Procedural

82.84 Repair of mallet finger
83.88 Other plastic operations on tendon

26433-26434

26433 Repair of extensor tendon, distal insertion, primary or secondary; without graft (eg, mallet finger)
26434 with free graft (includes obtaining graft)

ICD-9-CM Diagnostic

736.1 Mallet finger

ICD-9-CM Procedural

82.84 Repair of mallet finger
83.88 Other plastic operations on tendon

26437

26437 Realignment of extensor tendon, hand, each tendon

ICD-9-CM Diagnostic

357.1 Polyneuropathy in collagen vascular disease — (Code first underlying disease: 446.0, 710.0, 714.0) ☒
359.6 Symptomatic inflammatory myopathy in diseases classified elsewhere — (Code first underlying disease: 135, 140.0-208.9, 277.30-277.39, 446.0, 710.0, 710.1, 710.2, 714.0) ☒
446.0 Polyarteritis nodosa
710.0 Systemic lupus erythematosus — (Use additional code to identify manifestation: 424.91, 581.81, 582.81, 583.81)
710.1 Systemic sclerosis — (Use additional code to identify manifestation: 359.6, 517.2)
710.2 Sicca syndrome
714.0 Rheumatoid arthritis — (Use additional code to identify manifestation: 357.1, 359.6)
882.2 Open wound of hand except finger(s) alone, with tendon involvement

ICD-9-CM Procedural

83.88 Other plastic operations on tendon

26440-26442

26440 Tenolysis, flexor tendon; palm OR finger, each tendon
26442 palm AND finger, each tendon

ICD-9-CM Diagnostic

357.1 Polyneuropathy in collagen vascular disease — (Code first underlying disease: 446.0, 710.0, 714.0) ☒
359.6 Symptomatic inflammatory myopathy in diseases classified elsewhere — (Code first underlying disease: 135, 140.0-208.9, 277.30-277.39, 446.0, 710.0, 710.1, 710.2, 714.0) ☒
446.0 Polyarteritis nodosa
710.0 Systemic lupus erythematosus — (Use additional code to identify manifestation: 424.91, 581.81, 582.81, 583.81)
710.1 Systemic sclerosis — (Use additional code to identify manifestation: 359.6, 517.2)
710.2 Sicca syndrome
714.0 Rheumatoid arthritis — (Use additional code to identify manifestation: 357.1, 359.6)
727.00 Unspecified synovitis and tenosynovitis ▼
727.05 Other tenosynovitis of hand and wrist
727.81 Contracture of tendon (sheath)
727.89 Other disorders of synovium, tendon, and bursa
736.29 Other acquired deformity of finger
883.2 Open wound of finger(s), with tendon involvement
905.8 Late effect of tendon injury

ICD-9-CM Procedural

82.91 Lysis of adhesions of hand
83.91 Lysis of adhesions of muscle, tendon, fascia, and bursa

26445-26449

26445 Tenolysis, extensor tendon, hand OR finger, each tendon
26449 Tenolysis, complex, extensor tendon, finger, including forearm, each tendon

ICD-9-CM Diagnostic

357.1 Polyneuropathy in collagen vascular disease — (Code first underlying disease: 446.0, 710.0, 714.0) ☒
359.6 Symptomatic inflammatory myopathy in diseases classified elsewhere — (Code first underlying disease: 135, 140.0-208.9, 277.30-277.39, 446.0, 710.0, 710.1, 710.2, 714.0) ☒
446.0 Polyarteritis nodosa
710.0 Systemic lupus erythematosus — (Use additional code to identify manifestation: 424.91, 581.81, 582.81, 583.81)
710.1 Systemic sclerosis — (Use additional code to identify manifestation: 359.6, 517.2)
710.2 Sicca syndrome
714.0 Rheumatoid arthritis — (Use additional code to identify manifestation: 357.1, 359.6)
727.00 Unspecified synovitis and tenosynovitis ▼
727.04 Radial styloid tenosynovitis
727.05 Other tenosynovitis of hand and wrist
727.89 Other disorders of synovium, tendon, and bursa
736.29 Other acquired deformity of finger
882.2 Open wound of hand except finger(s) alone, with tendon involvement
883.2 Open wound of finger(s), with tendon involvement
905.8 Late effect of tendon injury

ICD-9-CM Procedural

82.91 Lysis of adhesions of hand
83.91 Lysis of adhesions of muscle, tendon, fascia, and bursa

26450-26460

26450 Tenotomy, flexor, palm, open, each tendon
26455 Tenotomy, flexor, finger, open, each tendon
26460 Tenotomy, extensor, hand or finger, open, each tendon

ICD-9-CM Diagnostic

718.44 Contracture of hand joint
727.00 Unspecified synovitis and tenosynovitis ▼
727.05 Other tenosynovitis of hand and wrist
727.81 Contracture of tendon (sheath)
728.6 Contracture of palmar fascia
736.29 Other acquired deformity of finger
755.50 Unspecified congenital anomaly of upper limb ▼
883.2 Open wound of finger(s), with tendon involvement
905.8 Late effect of tendon injury

ICD-9-CM Procedural

82.11 Tenotomy of hand

HCPCS Level II Supplies & Services

A4305 Disposable drug delivery system, flow rate of 50 ml or greater per hour

26471-26474

26471 Tenodesis; of proximal interphalangeal joint, each joint
26474 of distal joint, each joint

ICD-9-CM Diagnostic

714.1 Felty's syndrome
715.14 Primary localized osteoarthrosis, hand
718.44 Contracture of hand joint
718.84 Other joint derangement, not elsewhere classified, hand
727.64 Nontraumatic rupture of flexor tendons of hand and wrist
816.11 Open fracture of middle or proximal phalanx or phalanges of hand
816.12 Open fracture of distal phalanx or phalanges of hand
833.15 Open dislocation of proximal end of metacarpal (bone)
834.11 Open dislocation of metacarpophalangeal (joint)
883.2 Open wound of finger(s), with tendon involvement
886.1 Traumatic amputation of other finger(s) (complete) (partial), complicated
927.3 Crushing injury of finger(s) — (Use additional code to identify any associated injuries: 800-829, 850.0-854.1, 860.0-869.1)

ICD-9-CM Procedural

82.85 Other tenodesis of hand

26476

26476 Lengthening of tendon, extensor, hand or finger, each tendon

ICD-9-CM Diagnostic

715.14 Primary localized osteoarthrosis, hand
718.44 Contracture of hand joint
755.50 Unspecified congenital anomaly of upper limb ▼
816.00 Closed fracture of unspecified phalanx or phalanges of hand ▼
816.01 Closed fracture of middle or proximal phalanx or phalanges of hand
816.10 Open fracture of phalanx or phalanges of hand, unspecified ▼
816.11 Open fracture of middle or proximal phalanx or phalanges of hand
834.01 Closed dislocation of metacarpophalangeal (joint)
883.2 Open wound of finger(s), with tendon involvement
886.1 Traumatic amputation of other finger(s) (complete) (partial), complicated
905.2 Late effect of fracture of upper extremities
906.4 Late effect of crushing
927.3 Crushing injury of finger(s) — (Use additional code to identify any associated injuries: 800-829, 850.0-854.1, 860.0-869.1)

ICD-9-CM Procedural

82.55 Other change in muscle or tendon length of hand

26477

26477 Shortening of tendon, extensor, hand or finger, each tendon

ICD-9-CM Diagnostic

715.14 Primary localized osteoarthrosis, hand
755.50 Unspecified congenital anomaly of upper limb ▽
816.00 Closed fracture of unspecified phalanx or phalanges of hand ▽
816.01 Closed fracture of middle or proximal phalanx or phalanges of hand
816.10 Open fracture of phalanx or phalanges of hand, unspecified ▽
816.11 Open fracture of middle or proximal phalanx or phalanges of hand
833.15 Open dislocation of proximal end of metacarpal (bone)
834.01 Closed dislocation of metacarpophalangeal (joint)
834.11 Open dislocation of metacarpophalangeal (joint)
842.12 Sprain and strain of metacarpophalangeal (joint) of hand
883.2 Open wound of finger(s), with tendon involvement
886.1 Traumatic amputation of other finger(s) (complete) (partial), complicated
905.2 Late effect of fracture of upper extremities
906.4 Late effect of crushing
927.3 Crushing injury of finger(s) — (Use additional code to identify any associated injuries: 800-829, 850.0-854.1, 860.0-869.1)

ICD-9-CM Procedural

82.55 Other change in muscle or tendon length of hand

26478

26478 Lengthening of tendon, flexor, hand or finger, each tendon

ICD-9-CM Diagnostic

718.44 Contracture of hand joint
727.64 Nontraumatic rupture of flexor tendons of hand and wrist
728.6 Contracture of palmar fascia
755.50 Unspecified congenital anomaly of upper limb ▽
816.11 Open fracture of middle or proximal phalanx or phalanges of hand
833.15 Open dislocation of proximal end of metacarpal (bone)
834.11 Open dislocation of metacarpophalangeal (joint)
842.12 Sprain and strain of metacarpophalangeal (joint) of hand
882.2 Open wound of hand except finger(s) alone, with tendon involvement
883.2 Open wound of finger(s), with tendon involvement
886.1 Traumatic amputation of other finger(s) (complete) (partial), complicated
905.2 Late effect of fracture of upper extremities
906.4 Late effect of crushing

ICD-9-CM Procedural

82.55 Other change in muscle or tendon length of hand

26479

26479 Shortening of tendon, flexor, hand or finger, each tendon

ICD-9-CM Diagnostic

727.64 Nontraumatic rupture of flexor tendons of hand and wrist
728.6 Contracture of palmar fascia
755.50 Unspecified congenital anomaly of upper limb ▽
816.11 Open fracture of middle or proximal phalanx or phalanges of hand
833.15 Open dislocation of proximal end of metacarpal (bone)
834.11 Open dislocation of metacarpophalangeal (joint)
842.12 Sprain and strain of metacarpophalangeal (joint) of hand
882.2 Open wound of hand except finger(s) alone, with tendon involvement
883.2 Open wound of finger(s), with tendon involvement
886.1 Traumatic amputation of other finger(s) (complete) (partial), complicated
905.2 Late effect of fracture of upper extremities
906.4 Late effect of crushing

ICD-9-CM Procedural

82.55 Other change in muscle or tendon length of hand

26480-26483

26480 Transfer or transplant of tendon, carpometacarpal area or dorsum of hand; without free graft, each tendon
26483 with free tendon graft (includes obtaining graft), each tendon

ICD-9-CM Diagnostic

138 Late effects of acute poliomyelitis — (Note: This category is to be used to indicate conditions classifiable to 045 as the cause of late effects, which are themselves classified elsewhere. The "late effects" include those specified as such, as sequelae, or as due to old or inactive poliomyelitis, without evidence of active disease.)
343.0 Diplegic infantile cerebral palsy
714.4 Chronic postrheumatic arthropathy
716.14 Traumatic arthropathy, hand
718.54 Ankylosis of hand joint
718.84 Other joint derangement, not elsewhere classified, hand
719.14 Hemarthrosis, hand
727.63 Nontraumatic rupture of extensor tendons of hand and wrist
755.50 Unspecified congenital anomaly of upper limb ▽
842.12 Sprain and strain of metacarpophalangeal (joint) of hand
882.2 Open wound of hand except finger(s) alone, with tendon involvement
883.2 Open wound of finger(s), with tendon involvement
886.1 Traumatic amputation of other finger(s) (complete) (partial), complicated
905.2 Late effect of fracture of upper extremities
906.4 Late effect of crushing

ICD-9-CM Procedural

82.56 Other hand tendon transfer or transplantation

26485-26489

26485 Transfer or transplant of tendon, palmar; without free tendon graft, each tendon
26489 with free tendon graft (includes obtaining graft), each tendon

ICD-9-CM Diagnostic

138 Late effects of acute poliomyelitis — (Note: This category is to be used to indicate conditions classifiable to 045 as the cause of late effects, which are themselves classified elsewhere. The "late effects" include those specified as such, as sequelae, or as due to old or inactive poliomyelitis, without evidence of active disease.)
343.0 Diplegic infantile cerebral palsy
714.4 Chronic postrheumatic arthropathy
716.14 Traumatic arthropathy, hand
718.54 Ankylosis of hand joint
718.84 Other joint derangement, not elsewhere classified, hand
719.14 Hemarthrosis, hand
727.63 Nontraumatic rupture of extensor tendons of hand and wrist
755.50 Unspecified congenital anomaly of upper limb ▽
842.12 Sprain and strain of metacarpophalangeal (joint) of hand
882.2 Open wound of hand except finger(s) alone, with tendon involvement
883.2 Open wound of finger(s), with tendon involvement
886.1 Traumatic amputation of other finger(s) (complete) (partial), complicated
905.2 Late effect of fracture of upper extremities
906.4 Late effect of crushing

ICD-9-CM Procedural

82.56 Other hand tendon transfer or transplantation
82.79 Plastic operation on hand with other graft or implant

26490-26496

26490 Opponensplasty; superficialis tendon transfer type, each tendon
26492 tendon transfer with graft (includes obtaining graft), each tendon
26494 hypothenar muscle transfer
26496 other methods

ICD-9-CM Diagnostic

138 Late effects of acute poliomyelitis — (Note: This category is to be used to indicate conditions classifiable to 045 as the cause of late effects, which are themselves classified elsewhere. The "late effects" include those specified as such, as sequelae, or as due to old or inactive poliomyelitis, without evidence of active disease.)
718.44 Contracture of hand joint
718.84 Other joint derangement, not elsewhere classified, hand
727.63 Nontraumatic rupture of extensor tendons of hand and wrist
728.6 Contracture of palmar fascia
736.29 Other acquired deformity of finger
755.21 Congenital transverse deficiency of upper limb
755.50 Unspecified congenital anomaly of upper limb ▽
816.00 Closed fracture of unspecified phalanx or phalanges of hand ▽
816.01 Closed fracture of middle or proximal phalanx or phalanges of hand
816.03 Closed fracture of multiple sites of phalanx or phalanges of hand
816.10 Open fracture of phalanx or phalanges of hand, unspecified ▽
816.11 Open fracture of middle or proximal phalanx or phalanges of hand
816.12 Open fracture of distal phalanx or phalanges of hand
816.13 Open fractures of multiple sites of phalanx or phalanges of hand
842.01 Sprain and strain of carpal (joint) of wrist
883.2 Open wound of finger(s), with tendon involvement
886.1 Traumatic amputation of other finger(s) (complete) (partial), complicated
905.2 Late effect of fracture of upper extremities
905.9 Late effect of traumatic amputation
906.4 Late effect of crushing
927.3 Crushing injury of finger(s) — (Use additional code to identify any associated injuries: 800-829, 850.0-854.1, 860.0-869.1)

ICD-9-CM Procedural

82.56 Other hand tendon transfer or transplantation

26497-26498

26497 Transfer of tendon to restore intrinsic function; ring and small finger
26498 all 4 fingers

ICD-9-CM Diagnostic

138 Late effects of acute poliomyelitis — (Note: This category is to be used to indicate conditions classifiable to 045 as the cause of late effects, which are themselves classified elsewhere. The "late effects" include those specified as such, as sequelae, or as due to old or inactive poliomyelitis, without evidence of active disease.)
343.0 Diplegic infantile cerebral palsy
718.44 Contracture of hand joint
718.84 Other joint derangement, not elsewhere classified, hand
727.63 Nontraumatic rupture of extensor tendons of hand and wrist
736.29 Other acquired deformity of finger
755.21 Congenital transverse deficiency of upper limb
816.00 Closed fracture of unspecified phalanx or phalanges of hand ▽
816.01 Closed fracture of middle or proximal phalanx or phalanges of hand
816.03 Closed fracture of multiple sites of phalanx or phalanges of hand
816.10 Open fracture of phalanx or phalanges of hand, unspecified ▽
816.11 Open fracture of middle or proximal phalanx or phalanges of hand
816.12 Open fracture of distal phalanx or phalanges of hand
816.13 Open fractures of multiple sites of phalanx or phalanges of hand
883.2 Open wound of finger(s), with tendon involvement
886.1 Traumatic amputation of other finger(s) (complete) (partial), complicated
905.2 Late effect of fracture of upper extremities
905.9 Late effect of traumatic amputation
906.4 Late effect of crushing
927.3 Crushing injury of finger(s) — (Use additional code to identify any associated injuries: 800-829, 850.0-854.1, 860.0-869.1)

ICD-9-CM Procedural

82.56 Other hand tendon transfer or transplantation

26499

26499 Correction claw finger, other methods

ICD-9-CM Diagnostic

736.06 Claw hand (acquired)

ICD-9-CM Procedural

80.44 Division of joint capsule, ligament, or cartilage of hand and finger
81.28 Interphalangeal fusion
82.55 Other change in muscle or tendon length of hand

26500-26502

26500 Reconstruction of tendon pulley, each tendon; with local tissues (separate procedure)
26502 with tendon or fascial graft (includes obtaining graft) (separate procedure)

ICD-9-CM Diagnostic

138 Late effects of acute poliomyelitis — (Note: This category is to be used to indicate conditions classifiable to 045 as the cause of late effects, which are themselves classified elsewhere. The "late effects" include those specified as such, as sequelae, or as due to old or inactive poliomyelitis, without evidence of active disease.)
344.89 Other specified paralytic syndrome
715.14 Primary localized osteoarthrosis, hand
718.44 Contracture of hand joint
718.84 Other joint derangement, not elsewhere classified, hand
727.64 Nontraumatic rupture of flexor tendons of hand and wrist
727.89 Other disorders of synovium, tendon, and bursa
816.00 Closed fracture of unspecified phalanx or phalanges of hand ▽
816.01 Closed fracture of middle or proximal phalanx or phalanges of hand
816.02 Closed fracture of distal phalanx or phalanges of hand
816.03 Closed fracture of multiple sites of phalanx or phalanges of hand
816.10 Open fracture of phalanx or phalanges of hand, unspecified ▽
816.11 Open fracture of middle or proximal phalanx or phalanges of hand
816.12 Open fracture of distal phalanx or phalanges of hand
816.13 Open fractures of multiple sites of phalanx or phalanges of hand
842.13 Sprain and strain of interphalangeal (joint) of hand
883.2 Open wound of finger(s), with tendon involvement
886.1 Traumatic amputation of other finger(s) (complete) (partial), complicated
905.2 Late effect of fracture of upper extremities
905.8 Late effect of tendon injury
905.9 Late effect of traumatic amputation
927.3 Crushing injury of finger(s) — (Use additional code to identify any associated injuries: 800-829, 850.0-854.1, 860.0-869.1)

ICD-9-CM Procedural

82.71 Tendon pulley reconstruction on hand
82.79 Plastic operation on hand with other graft or implant
83.83 Tendon pulley reconstruction on muscle, tendon, and fascia

26508

26508 Release of thenar muscle(s) (eg, thumb contracture)

ICD-9-CM Diagnostic

344.89 Other specified paralytic syndrome

357.1	Polyneuropathy in collagen vascular disease — (Code first underlying disease: 446.0, 710.0, 714.0) ☒
359.6	Symptomatic inflammatory myopathy in diseases classified elsewhere — (Code first underlying disease: 135, 140.0-208.9, 277.30-277.39, 446.0, 710.0, 710.1, 710.2, 714.0) ☒
446.0	Polyarteritis nodosa
710.0	Systemic lupus erythematosus — (Use additional code to identify manifestation: 424.91, 581.81, 582.81, 583.81)
710.1	Systemic sclerosis — (Use additional code to identify manifestation: 359.6, 517.2)
710.2	Sicca syndrome
714.0	Rheumatoid arthritis — (Use additional code to identify manifestation: 357.1, 359.6)
715.14	Primary localized osteoarthrosis, hand
718.44	Contracture of hand joint
728.2	Muscular wasting and disuse atrophy, not elsewhere classified
728.88	Rhabdomyolysis
728.89	Other disorder of muscle, ligament, and fascia — (Use additional E code to identify drug, if drug-induced)
736.29	Other acquired deformity of finger
905.8	Late effect of tendon injury
906.4	Late effect of crushing
906.6	Late effect of burn of wrist and hand
909.3	Late effect of complications of surgical and medical care
958.6	Volkmann's ischemic contracture

ICD-9-CM Procedural

82.19	Other division of soft tissue of hand

26510

26510	Cross intrinsic transfer, each tendon

ICD-9-CM Diagnostic

344.89	Other specified paralytic syndrome
357.1	Polyneuropathy in collagen vascular disease — (Code first underlying disease: 446.0, 710.0, 714.0) ☒
359.6	Symptomatic inflammatory myopathy in diseases classified elsewhere — (Code first underlying disease: 135, 140.0-208.9, 277.30-277.39, 446.0, 710.0, 710.1, 710.2, 714.0) ☒
446.0	Polyarteritis nodosa
710.0	Systemic lupus erythematosus — (Use additional code to identify manifestation: 424.91, 581.81, 582.81, 583.81)
710.1	Systemic sclerosis — (Use additional code to identify manifestation: 359.6, 517.2)
710.2	Sicca syndrome
714.0	Rheumatoid arthritis — (Use additional code to identify manifestation: 357.1, 359.6)
715.14	Primary localized osteoarthrosis, hand
718.44	Contracture of hand joint
727.63	Nontraumatic rupture of extensor tendons of hand and wrist
727.64	Nontraumatic rupture of flexor tendons of hand and wrist
728.2	Muscular wasting and disuse atrophy, not elsewhere classified
728.88	Rhabdomyolysis
728.89	Other disorder of muscle, ligament, and fascia — (Use additional E code to identify drug, if drug-induced)
842.12	Sprain and strain of metacarpophalangeal (joint) of hand
883.2	Open wound of finger(s), with tendon involvement
886.1	Traumatic amputation of other finger(s) (complete) (partial), complicated
905.8	Late effect of tendon injury
905.9	Late effect of traumatic amputation
906.4	Late effect of crushing
906.6	Late effect of burn of wrist and hand
927.3	Crushing injury of finger(s) — (Use additional code to identify any associated injuries: 800-829, 850.0-854.1, 860.0-869.1)
958.6	Volkmann's ischemic contracture

ICD-9-CM Procedural

83.75	Tendon transfer or transplantation

26516-26518

26516	Capsulodesis, metacarpophalangeal joint; single digit
26517	2 digits
26518	3 or 4 digits

ICD-9-CM Diagnostic

343.0	Diplegic infantile cerebral palsy
343.1	Hemiplegic infantile cerebral palsy
343.2	Quadriplegic infantile cerebral palsy
343.3	Monoplegic infantile cerebral palsy
343.4	Infantile hemiplegia
343.8	Other specified infantile cerebral palsy
343.9	Unspecified infantile cerebral palsy ▽
344.81	Locked-in state
344.89	Other specified paralytic syndrome
357.1	Polyneuropathy in collagen vascular disease — (Code first underlying disease: 446.0, 710.0, 714.0) ☒
359.6	Symptomatic inflammatory myopathy in diseases classified elsewhere — (Code first underlying disease: 135, 140.0-208.9, 277.30-277.39, 446.0, 710.0, 710.1, 710.2, 714.0) ☒
446.0	Polyarteritis nodosa
710.0	Systemic lupus erythematosus — (Use additional code to identify manifestation: 424.91, 581.81, 582.81, 583.81)
710.1	Systemic sclerosis — (Use additional code to identify manifestation: 359.6, 517.2)
710.2	Sicca syndrome
714.0	Rheumatoid arthritis — (Use additional code to identify manifestation: 357.1, 359.6)
715.14	Primary localized osteoarthrosis, hand
718.44	Contracture of hand joint
718.74	Developmental dislocation of joint, hand
718.84	Other joint derangement, not elsewhere classified, hand
719.94	Unspecified disorder of hand joint ▽
728.2	Muscular wasting and disuse atrophy, not elsewhere classified
728.88	Rhabdomyolysis
728.89	Other disorder of muscle, ligament, and fascia — (Use additional E code to identify drug, if drug-induced)
736.06	Claw hand (acquired)
834.11	Open dislocation of metacarpophalangeal (joint)
882.1	Open wound of hand except finger(s) alone, complicated
882.2	Open wound of hand except finger(s) alone, with tendon involvement
883.1	Open wound of finger(s), complicated
883.2	Open wound of finger(s), with tendon involvement
886.1	Traumatic amputation of other finger(s) (complete) (partial), complicated
906.1	Late effect of open wound of extremities without mention of tendon injury
906.4	Late effect of crushing
906.6	Late effect of burn of wrist and hand
927.20	Crushing injury of hand(s) — (Use additional code to identify any associated injuries: 800-829, 850.0-854.1, 860.0-869.1)
927.3	Crushing injury of finger(s) — (Use additional code to identify any associated injuries: 800-829, 850.0-854.1, 860.0-869.1)
944.04	Burn of unspecified degree of two or more digits of hand, including thumb ▽
944.08	Burn of unspecified degree of multiple sites of wrist(s) and hand(s) ▽
944.42	Deep necrosis of underlying tissues due to burn (deep third degree) of thumb (nail), without mention of loss of a body part
955.4	Injury to musculocutaneous nerve
958.6	Volkmann's ischemic contracture

ICD-9-CM Procedural

81.27	Metacarpophalangeal fusion

26520-26525

26520 Capsulectomy or capsulotomy; metacarpophalangeal joint, each joint
26525 interphalangeal joint, each joint

ICD-9-CM Diagnostic

357.1 Polyneuropathy in collagen vascular disease — (Code first underlying disease: 446.0, 710.0, 714.0) ☒
359.6 Symptomatic inflammatory myopathy in diseases classified elsewhere — (Code first underlying disease: 135, 140.0-208.9, 277.30-277.39, 446.0, 710.0, 710.1, 710.2, 714.0) ☒
446.0 Polyarteritis nodosa
710.0 Systemic lupus erythematosus — (Use additional code to identify manifestation: 424.91, 581.81, 582.81, 583.81)
710.1 Systemic sclerosis — (Use additional code to identify manifestation: 359.6, 517.2)
710.2 Sicca syndrome
714.0 Rheumatoid arthritis — (Use additional code to identify manifestation: 357.1, 359.6)
714.4 Chronic postrheumatic arthropathy
715.14 Primary localized osteoarthrosis, hand
716.14 Traumatic arthropathy, hand
718.44 Contracture of hand joint
719.54 Stiffness of joint, not elsewhere classified, hand
728.89 Other disorder of muscle, ligament, and fascia — (Use additional E code to identify drug, if drug-induced)
736.20 Unspecified deformity of finger ▽
736.29 Other acquired deformity of finger
756.89 Other specified congenital anomaly of muscle, tendon, fascia, and connective tissue
906.4 Late effect of crushing
959.5 Injury, other and unspecified, finger
996.92 Complications of reattached hand
996.93 Complications of reattached finger(s)
998.59 Other postoperative infection — (Use additional code to identify infection)

ICD-9-CM Procedural

80.44 Division of joint capsule, ligament, or cartilage of hand and finger
80.94 Other excision of joint of hand and finger

26530-26531

26530 Arthroplasty, metacarpophalangeal joint; each joint
26531 with prosthetic implant, each joint

ICD-9-CM Diagnostic

357.1 Polyneuropathy in collagen vascular disease — (Code first underlying disease: 446.0, 710.0, 714.0) ☒
359.6 Symptomatic inflammatory myopathy in diseases classified elsewhere — (Code first underlying disease: 135, 140.0-208.9, 277.30-277.39, 446.0, 710.0, 710.1, 710.2, 714.0) ☒
446.0 Polyarteritis nodosa
710.0 Systemic lupus erythematosus — (Use additional code to identify manifestation: 424.91, 581.81, 582.81, 583.81)
710.1 Systemic sclerosis — (Use additional code to identify manifestation: 359.6, 517.2)
710.2 Sicca syndrome
714.0 Rheumatoid arthritis — (Use additional code to identify manifestation: 357.1, 359.6)
714.4 Chronic postrheumatic arthropathy
715.14 Primary localized osteoarthrosis, hand
715.94 Osteoarthrosis, unspecified whether generalized or localized, hand ▽
716.14 Traumatic arthropathy, hand
718.04 Articular cartilage disorder, hand
718.74 Developmental dislocation of joint, hand
730.14 Chronic osteomyelitis, hand — (Use additional code to identify organism: 041.1. Use additional code to identify major osseous defect, if applicable: 731.3)
731.3 Major osseous defects — (Code first underlying disease: 170.0-170.9, 730.00-730.29, 733.00-733.09, 733.40-733.49, 996.45)
733.82 Nonunion of fracture
815.02 Closed fracture of base of other metacarpal bone(s)
815.12 Open fracture of base of other metacarpal bone(s)
834.01 Closed dislocation of metacarpophalangeal (joint)
834.11 Open dislocation of metacarpophalangeal (joint)
882.1 Open wound of hand except finger(s) alone, complicated
882.2 Open wound of hand except finger(s) alone, with tendon involvement
905.2 Late effect of fracture of upper extremities
927.20 Crushing injury of hand(s) — (Use additional code to identify any associated injuries: 800-829, 850.0-854.1, 860.0-869.1)
927.3 Crushing injury of finger(s) — (Use additional code to identify any associated injuries: 800-829, 850.0-854.1, 860.0-869.1)

ICD-9-CM Procedural

81.71 Arthroplasty of metacarpophalangeal and interphalangeal joint with implant
81.72 Arthroplasty of metacarpophalangeal and interphalangeal joint without implant

26535-26536

26535 Arthroplasty, interphalangeal joint; each joint
26536 with prosthetic implant, each joint

ICD-9-CM Diagnostic

357.1 Polyneuropathy in collagen vascular disease — (Code first underlying disease: 446.0, 710.0, 714.0) ☒
359.6 Symptomatic inflammatory myopathy in diseases classified elsewhere — (Code first underlying disease: 135, 140.0-208.9, 277.30-277.39, 446.0, 710.0, 710.1, 710.2, 714.0) ☒
446.0 Polyarteritis nodosa
710.0 Systemic lupus erythematosus — (Use additional code to identify manifestation: 424.91, 581.81, 582.81, 583.81)
710.1 Systemic sclerosis — (Use additional code to identify manifestation: 359.6, 517.2)
710.2 Sicca syndrome
714.0 Rheumatoid arthritis — (Use additional code to identify manifestation: 357.1, 359.6)
714.4 Chronic postrheumatic arthropathy
715.14 Primary localized osteoarthrosis, hand
715.94 Osteoarthrosis, unspecified whether generalized or localized, hand ▽
716.14 Traumatic arthropathy, hand
718.44 Contracture of hand joint
718.74 Developmental dislocation of joint, hand
730.14 Chronic osteomyelitis, hand — (Use additional code to identify organism: 041.1. Use additional code to identify major osseous defect, if applicable: 731.3)
731.3 Major osseous defects — (Code first underlying disease: 170.0-170.9, 730.00-730.29, 733.00-733.09, 733.40-733.49, 996.45)
736.29 Other acquired deformity of finger
816.01 Closed fracture of middle or proximal phalanx or phalanges of hand
816.02 Closed fracture of distal phalanx or phalanges of hand
816.03 Closed fracture of multiple sites of phalanx or phalanges of hand
816.11 Open fracture of middle or proximal phalanx or phalanges of hand
816.12 Open fracture of distal phalanx or phalanges of hand
816.13 Open fractures of multiple sites of phalanx or phalanges of hand
817.0 Multiple closed fractures of hand bones
817.1 Multiple open fractures of hand bones
834.02 Closed dislocation of interphalangeal (joint), hand
834.12 Open dislocation interphalangeal (joint), hand
883.1 Open wound of finger(s), complicated
883.2 Open wound of finger(s), with tendon involvement
905.2 Late effect of fracture of upper extremities
905.9 Late effect of traumatic amputation
906.4 Late effect of crushing

927.3 Crushing injury of finger(s) — (Use additional code to identify any associated injuries: 800-829, 850.0-854.1, 860.0-869.1)

ICD-9-CM Procedural

81.71 Arthroplasty of metacarpophalangeal and interphalangeal joint with implant
81.72 Arthroplasty of metacarpophalangeal and interphalangeal joint without implant

26540

26540 Repair of collateral ligament, metacarpophalangeal or interphalangeal joint

ICD-9-CM Diagnostic

716.14 Traumatic arthropathy, hand
718.34 Recurrent dislocation of hand joint
718.74 Developmental dislocation of joint, hand
718.84 Other joint derangement, not elsewhere classified, hand
728.89 Other disorder of muscle, ligament, and fascia — (Use additional E code to identify drug, if drug-induced)
816.01 Closed fracture of middle or proximal phalanx or phalanges of hand
816.02 Closed fracture of distal phalanx or phalanges of hand
816.03 Closed fracture of multiple sites of phalanx or phalanges of hand
816.11 Open fracture of middle or proximal phalanx or phalanges of hand
816.12 Open fracture of distal phalanx or phalanges of hand
816.13 Open fractures of multiple sites of phalanx or phalanges of hand
834.01 Closed dislocation of metacarpophalangeal (joint)
834.02 Closed dislocation of interphalangeal (joint), hand
834.11 Open dislocation of metacarpophalangeal (joint)
834.12 Open dislocation interphalangeal (joint), hand
842.12 Sprain and strain of metacarpophalangeal (joint) of hand
842.13 Sprain and strain of interphalangeal (joint) of hand
882.1 Open wound of hand except finger(s) alone, complicated
882.2 Open wound of hand except finger(s) alone, with tendon involvement
883.1 Open wound of finger(s), complicated
883.2 Open wound of finger(s), with tendon involvement
927.3 Crushing injury of finger(s) — (Use additional code to identify any associated injuries: 800-829, 850.0-854.1, 860.0-869.1)

ICD-9-CM Procedural

81.93 Suture of capsule or ligament of upper extremity

26541-26545

26541 Reconstruction, collateral ligament, metacarpophalangeal joint, single; with tendon or fascial graft (includes obtaining graft)
26542 with local tissue (eg, adductor advancement)
26545 Reconstruction, collateral ligament, interphalangeal joint, single, including graft, each joint

ICD-9-CM Diagnostic

716.14 Traumatic arthropathy, hand
718.34 Recurrent dislocation of hand joint
718.74 Developmental dislocation of joint, hand
718.84 Other joint derangement, not elsewhere classified, hand
728.89 Other disorder of muscle, ligament, and fascia — (Use additional E code to identify drug, if drug-induced)
816.01 Closed fracture of middle or proximal phalanx or phalanges of hand
816.02 Closed fracture of distal phalanx or phalanges of hand
816.03 Closed fracture of multiple sites of phalanx or phalanges of hand
816.11 Open fracture of middle or proximal phalanx or phalanges of hand
816.12 Open fracture of distal phalanx or phalanges of hand
816.13 Open fractures of multiple sites of phalanx or phalanges of hand
834.01 Closed dislocation of metacarpophalangeal (joint)
834.02 Closed dislocation of interphalangeal (joint), hand
834.11 Open dislocation of metacarpophalangeal (joint)
834.12 Open dislocation interphalangeal (joint), hand
842.12 Sprain and strain of metacarpophalangeal (joint) of hand
842.13 Sprain and strain of interphalangeal (joint) of hand
882.1 Open wound of hand except finger(s) alone, complicated
882.2 Open wound of hand except finger(s) alone, with tendon involvement
883.1 Open wound of finger(s), complicated
883.2 Open wound of finger(s), with tendon involvement
927.3 Crushing injury of finger(s) — (Use additional code to identify any associated injuries: 800-829, 850.0-854.1, 860.0-869.1)

ICD-9-CM Procedural

81.93 Suture of capsule or ligament of upper extremity
82.72 Plastic operation on hand with graft of muscle or fascia
83.41 Excision of tendon for graft
83.81 Tendon graft

26546

26546 Repair non-union, metacarpal or phalanx (includes obtaining bone graft with or without external or internal fixation)

ICD-9-CM Diagnostic

733.82 Nonunion of fracture
905.2 Late effect of fracture of upper extremities

ICD-9-CM Procedural

77.77 Excision of tibia and fibula for graft
77.78 Excision of tarsals and metatarsals for graft
77.99 Total ostectomy of other bone, except facial bones
78.09 Bone graft of other bone, except facial bones
78.44 Other repair or plastic operations on carpals and metacarpals
78.49 Other repair or plastic operations on other bone, except facial bones

26548

26548 Repair and reconstruction, finger, volar plate, interphalangeal joint

ICD-9-CM Diagnostic

716.14 Traumatic arthropathy, hand
718.04 Articular cartilage disorder, hand
718.24 Pathological dislocation of hand joint
718.34 Recurrent dislocation of hand joint
718.74 Developmental dislocation of joint, hand
718.84 Other joint derangement, not elsewhere classified, hand
816.01 Closed fracture of middle or proximal phalanx or phalanges of hand
816.02 Closed fracture of distal phalanx or phalanges of hand
816.03 Closed fracture of multiple sites of phalanx or phalanges of hand
816.11 Open fracture of middle or proximal phalanx or phalanges of hand
816.12 Open fracture of distal phalanx or phalanges of hand
816.13 Open fractures of multiple sites of phalanx or phalanges of hand
834.02 Closed dislocation of interphalangeal (joint), hand
834.12 Open dislocation interphalangeal (joint), hand
842.13 Sprain and strain of interphalangeal (joint) of hand
883.2 Open wound of finger(s), with tendon involvement
905.9 Late effect of traumatic amputation
927.3 Crushing injury of finger(s) — (Use additional code to identify any associated injuries: 800-829, 850.0-854.1, 860.0-869.1)

ICD-9-CM Procedural

81.96 Other repair of joint

26550

26550 Pollicization of a digit

ICD-9-CM Diagnostic

755.29 Congenital longitudinal deficiency, phalanges, complete or partial
906.4 Late effect of crushing
906.6 Late effect of burn of wrist and hand
V10.81 Personal history of malignant neoplasm of bone
V49.61 Upper limb amputation, thumb
V49.62 Upper limb amputation, other finger(s)
V51.8 Other aftercare involving the use of plastic surgery

ICD-9-CM Procedural

82.61 Pollicization operation carrying over nerves and blood supply

26551

26551 Transfer, toe-to-hand with microvascular anastomosis; great toe wrap-around with bone graft

ICD-9-CM Diagnostic

755.29 Congenital longitudinal deficiency, phalanges, complete or partial
906.4 Late effect of crushing
906.6 Late effect of burn of wrist and hand
V10.81 Personal history of malignant neoplasm of bone
V49.61 Upper limb amputation, thumb
V51.8 Other aftercare involving the use of plastic surgery

ICD-9-CM Procedural

82.69 Other reconstruction of thumb
84.11 Amputation of toe

26553-26554

26553 Transfer, toe-to-hand with microvascular anastomosis; other than great toe, single
26554 other than great toe, double

ICD-9-CM Diagnostic

755.29 Congenital longitudinal deficiency, phalanges, complete or partial
906.1 Late effect of open wound of extremities without mention of tendon injury
906.4 Late effect of crushing
906.6 Late effect of burn of wrist and hand
V10.81 Personal history of malignant neoplasm of bone
V49.62 Upper limb amputation, other finger(s)
V51.8 Other aftercare involving the use of plastic surgery

ICD-9-CM Procedural

82.81 Transfer of finger, except thumb
82.89 Other plastic operations on hand

26555

26555 Transfer, finger to another position without microvascular anastomosis

ICD-9-CM Diagnostic

755.29 Congenital longitudinal deficiency, phalanges, complete or partial
906.1 Late effect of open wound of extremities without mention of tendon injury
906.4 Late effect of crushing
906.6 Late effect of burn of wrist and hand
V10.81 Personal history of malignant neoplasm of bone
V49.62 Upper limb amputation, other finger(s)
V51.8 Other aftercare involving the use of plastic surgery

ICD-9-CM Procedural

82.81 Transfer of finger, except thumb
82.89 Other plastic operations on hand

26556

26556 Transfer, free toe joint, with microvascular anastomosis

ICD-9-CM Diagnostic

755.29 Congenital longitudinal deficiency, phalanges, complete or partial
755.50 Unspecified congenital anomaly of upper limb ▽
755.8 Other specified congenital anomalies of unspecified limb
906.4 Late effect of crushing
906.6 Late effect of burn of wrist and hand
V10.81 Personal history of malignant neoplasm of bone
V49.61 Upper limb amputation, thumb
V49.62 Upper limb amputation, other finger(s)
V51.8 Other aftercare involving the use of plastic surgery

ICD-9-CM Procedural

80.98 Other excision of joint of foot and toe
81.72 Arthroplasty of metacarpophalangeal and interphalangeal joint without implant

26560-26562

26560 Repair of syndactyly (web finger) each web space; with skin flaps
26561 with skin flaps and grafts
26562 complex (eg, involving bone, nails)

ICD-9-CM Diagnostic

755.10 Syndactyly of multiple and unspecified sites
755.11 Syndactyly of fingers without fusion of bone
755.12 Syndactyly of fingers with fusion of bone

ICD-9-CM Procedural

86.85 Correction of syndactyly

26565-26567

26565 Osteotomy; metacarpal, each
26567 phalanx of finger, each

ICD-9-CM Diagnostic

357.1 Polyneuropathy in collagen vascular disease — (Code first underlying disease: 446.0, 710.0, 714.0) ☒
359.6 Symptomatic inflammatory myopathy in diseases classified elsewhere — (Code first underlying disease: 135, 140.0-208.9, 277.30-277.39, 446.0, 710.0, 710.1, 710.2, 714.0) ☒
446.0 Polyarteritis nodosa
710.0 Systemic lupus erythematosus — (Use additional code to identify manifestation: 424.91, 581.81, 582.81, 583.81)
710.1 Systemic sclerosis — (Use additional code to identify manifestation: 359.6, 517.2)
710.2 Sicca syndrome
714.0 Rheumatoid arthritis — (Use additional code to identify manifestation: 357.1, 359.6)
714.4 Chronic postrheumatic arthropathy
715.14 Primary localized osteoarthrosis, hand
716.14 Traumatic arthropathy, hand
736.00 Unspecified deformity of forearm, excluding fingers ▽
736.07 Club hand, acquired
736.09 Other acquired deformities of forearm, excluding fingers
736.20 Unspecified deformity of finger ▽
736.29 Other acquired deformity of finger
738.9 Acquired musculoskeletal deformity of unspecified site ▽
754.89 Other specified nonteratogenic anomalies
755.28 Congenital longitudinal deficiency, carpals or metacarpals, complete or partial (with or without incomplete phalangeal deficiency)
756.9 Other and unspecified congenital anomaly of musculoskeletal system ▽
905.2 Late effect of fracture of upper extremities
909.3 Late effect of complications of surgical and medical care

998.59 Other postoperative infection — (Use additional code to identify infection)

ICD-9-CM Procedural

77.24 Wedge osteotomy of carpals and metacarpals
77.34 Other division of carpals and metacarpals
77.39 Other division of other bone, except facial bones

26568

26568 Osteoplasty, lengthening, metacarpal or phalanx

ICD-9-CM Diagnostic

714.4 Chronic postrheumatic arthropathy
715.14 Primary localized osteoarthrosis, hand
716.14 Traumatic arthropathy, hand
733.81 Malunion of fracture
736.06 Claw hand (acquired)
736.20 Unspecified deformity of finger ▽
736.29 Other acquired deformity of finger
738.9 Acquired musculoskeletal deformity of unspecified site ▽
755.28 Congenital longitudinal deficiency, carpals or metacarpals, complete or partial (with or without incomplete phalangeal deficiency)
756.9 Other and unspecified congenital anomaly of musculoskeletal system ▽
905.2 Late effect of fracture of upper extremities

ICD-9-CM Procedural

78.14 Application of external fixator device, carpals and metacarpals
78.19 Application of external fixator device, other
78.34 Limb lengthening procedures, carpals and metacarpals
78.39 Other limb lengthening procedures
84.53 Implantation of internal limb lengthening device with kinetic distraction
84.54 Implantation of other internal limb lengthening device
84.71 Application of external fixator device, monoplanar system
84.72 Application of external fixator device, ring system
84.73 Application of hybrid external fixator device

26580

26580 Repair cleft hand

ICD-9-CM Diagnostic

755.58 Congenital cleft hand

ICD-9-CM Procedural

82.82 Repair of cleft hand

26587

26587 Reconstruction of polydactylous digit, soft tissue and bone

ICD-9-CM Diagnostic

755.01 Polydactyly of fingers

ICD-9-CM Procedural

82.89 Other plastic operations on hand

26590

26590 Repair macrodactylia, each digit

ICD-9-CM Diagnostic

755.57 Macrodactylia (fingers)

ICD-9-CM Procedural

82.83 Repair of macrodactyly

26591

26591 Repair, intrinsic muscles of hand, each muscle

ICD-9-CM Diagnostic

727.64 Nontraumatic rupture of flexor tendons of hand and wrist
728.2 Muscular wasting and disuse atrophy, not elsewhere classified
728.83 Rupture of muscle, nontraumatic
842.12 Sprain and strain of metacarpophalangeal (joint) of hand
882.1 Open wound of hand except finger(s) alone, complicated
882.2 Open wound of hand except finger(s) alone, with tendon involvement
927.20 Crushing injury of hand(s) — (Use additional code to identify any associated injuries: 800-829, 850.0-854.1, 860.0-869.1)

ICD-9-CM Procedural

82.46 Suture of muscle or fascia of hand
82.72 Plastic operation on hand with graft of muscle or fascia
82.89 Other plastic operations on hand

26593

26593 Release, intrinsic muscles of hand, each muscle

ICD-9-CM Diagnostic

343.0 Diplegic infantile cerebral palsy
343.3 Monoplegic infantile cerebral palsy
344.89 Other specified paralytic syndrome
714.4 Chronic postrheumatic arthropathy
728.6 Contracture of palmar fascia
728.88 Rhabdomyolysis
728.89 Other disorder of muscle, ligament, and fascia — (Use additional E code to identify drug, if drug-induced)
736.06 Claw hand (acquired)
756.89 Other specified congenital anomaly of muscle, tendon, fascia, and connective tissue
905.2 Late effect of fracture of upper extremities
905.7 Late effect of sprain and strain without mention of tendon injury
905.8 Late effect of tendon injury
905.9 Late effect of traumatic amputation
906.1 Late effect of open wound of extremities without mention of tendon injury
906.6 Late effect of burn of wrist and hand
907.4 Late effect of injury to peripheral nerve of shoulder girdle and upper limb
927.20 Crushing injury of hand(s) — (Use additional code to identify any associated injuries: 800-829, 850.0-854.1, 860.0-869.1)
958.6 Volkmann's ischemic contracture

ICD-9-CM Procedural

82.19 Other division of soft tissue of hand

26596

26596 Excision of constricting ring of finger, with multiple Z-plasties

ICD-9-CM Diagnostic

709.2 Scar condition and fibrosis of skin
718.44 Contracture of hand joint
727.81 Contracture of tendon (sheath)
728.6 Contracture of palmar fascia
905.8 Late effect of tendon injury
905.9 Late effect of traumatic amputation
906.1 Late effect of open wound of extremities without mention of tendon injury
906.4 Late effect of crushing
906.6 Late effect of burn of wrist and hand

ICD-9-CM Procedural

86.84 Relaxation of scar or web contracture of skin

26600-26607

26600 Closed treatment of metacarpal fracture, single; without manipulation, each bone
26605 with manipulation, each bone
26607 Closed treatment of metacarpal fracture, with manipulation, with external fixation, each bone

ICD-9-CM Diagnostic

733.19 Pathologic fracture of other specified site
815.00 Closed fracture of metacarpal bone(s), site unspecified
815.02 Closed fracture of base of other metacarpal bone(s)
815.03 Closed fracture of shaft of metacarpal bone(s)
815.04 Closed fracture of neck of metacarpal bone(s)
815.09 Closed fracture of multiple sites of metacarpus
817.0 Multiple closed fractures of hand bones

ICD-9-CM Procedural

79.03 Closed reduction of fracture of carpals and metacarpals without internal fixation
79.13 Closed reduction of fracture of carpals and metacarpals with internal fixation
79.14 Closed reduction of fracture of phalanges of hand with internal fixation
93.54 Application of splint

HCPCS Level II Supplies & Services

A4580 Cast supplies (e.g., plaster)

26608

26608 Percutaneous skeletal fixation of metacarpal fracture, each bone

ICD-9-CM Diagnostic

733.19 Pathologic fracture of other specified site
815.00 Closed fracture of metacarpal bone(s), site unspecified
815.02 Closed fracture of base of other metacarpal bone(s)
815.03 Closed fracture of shaft of metacarpal bone(s)
815.04 Closed fracture of neck of metacarpal bone(s)
815.09 Closed fracture of multiple sites of metacarpus
817.0 Multiple closed fractures of hand bones

ICD-9-CM Procedural

78.54 Internal fixation of carpals and metacarpals without fracture reduction
79.13 Closed reduction of fracture of carpals and metacarpals with internal fixation

HCPCS Level II Supplies & Services

A4570 Splint

26615

26615 Open treatment of metacarpal fracture, single, includes internal fixation, when performed, each bone

ICD-9-CM Diagnostic

733.19 Pathologic fracture of other specified site
733.81 Malunion of fracture
733.82 Nonunion of fracture
815.00 Closed fracture of metacarpal bone(s), site unspecified
815.02 Closed fracture of base of other metacarpal bone(s)
815.03 Closed fracture of shaft of metacarpal bone(s)
815.04 Closed fracture of neck of metacarpal bone(s)
815.09 Closed fracture of multiple sites of metacarpus
815.10 Open fracture of metacarpal bone(s), site unspecified
815.12 Open fracture of base of other metacarpal bone(s)
815.13 Open fracture of shaft of metacarpal bone(s)
815.14 Open fracture of neck of metacarpal bone(s)
815.19 Open fracture of multiple sites of metacarpus
817.0 Multiple closed fractures of hand bones
817.1 Multiple open fractures of hand bones

ICD-9-CM Procedural

79.23 Open reduction of fracture of carpals and metacarpals without internal fixation
79.33 Open reduction of fracture of carpals and metacarpals with internal fixation

HCPCS Level II Supplies & Services

A4570 Splint

26641-26645

26641 Closed treatment of carpometacarpal dislocation, thumb, with manipulation
26645 Closed treatment of carpometacarpal fracture dislocation, thumb (Bennett fracture), with manipulation

ICD-9-CM Diagnostic

718.24 Pathological dislocation of hand joint
718.30 Recurrent dislocation of joint, site unspecified
718.34 Recurrent dislocation of hand joint
718.74 Developmental dislocation of joint, hand
733.19 Pathologic fracture of other specified site
815.01 Closed fracture of base of thumb (first) metacarpal bone(s)
833.04 Closed dislocation of carpometacarpal (joint)

ICD-9-CM Procedural

79.03 Closed reduction of fracture of carpals and metacarpals without internal fixation
79.13 Closed reduction of fracture of carpals and metacarpals with internal fixation
79.74 Closed reduction of dislocation of hand and finger

HCPCS Level II Supplies & Services

A4570 Splint

26650

26650 Percutaneous skeletal fixation of carpometacarpal fracture dislocation, thumb (Bennett fracture), with manipulation

ICD-9-CM Diagnostic

733.19 Pathologic fracture of other specified site
815.01 Closed fracture of base of thumb (first) metacarpal bone(s)
815.11 Open fracture of base of thumb (first) metacarpal bone(s)

ICD-9-CM Procedural

78.14 Application of external fixator device, carpals and metacarpals
79.03 Closed reduction of fracture of carpals and metacarpals without internal fixation

HCPCS Level II Supplies & Services

A4570 Splint

26665

26665 Open treatment of carpometacarpal fracture dislocation, thumb (Bennett fracture), includes internal fixation, when performed

ICD-9-CM Diagnostic

733.19 Pathologic fracture of other specified site
733.81 Malunion of fracture
733.82 Nonunion of fracture
815.01 Closed fracture of base of thumb (first) metacarpal bone(s)
815.11 Open fracture of base of thumb (first) metacarpal bone(s)

ICD-9-CM Procedural

79.23 Open reduction of fracture of carpals and metacarpals without internal fixation
79.33 Open reduction of fracture of carpals and metacarpals with internal fixation
79.84 Open reduction of dislocation of hand and finger

HCPCS Level II Supplies & Services

A4570 Splint

26670-26675

26670 Closed treatment of carpometacarpal dislocation, other than thumb, with manipulation, each joint; without anesthesia
26675 requiring anesthesia

ICD-9-CM Diagnostic

718.24 Pathological dislocation of hand joint
718.30 Recurrent dislocation of joint, site unspecified ♥
718.34 Recurrent dislocation of hand joint
718.74 Developmental dislocation of joint, hand
833.04 Closed dislocation of carpometacarpal (joint)

ICD-9-CM Procedural

79.74 Closed reduction of dislocation of hand and finger

HCPCS Level II Supplies & Services

A4570 Splint

26676

26676 Percutaneous skeletal fixation of carpometacarpal dislocation, other than thumb, with manipulation, each joint

ICD-9-CM Diagnostic

718.24 Pathological dislocation of hand joint
718.34 Recurrent dislocation of hand joint
718.74 Developmental dislocation of joint, hand
833.04 Closed dislocation of carpometacarpal (joint)
833.14 Open dislocation of carpometacarpal (joint)

ICD-9-CM Procedural

78.54 Internal fixation of carpals and metacarpals without fracture reduction
79.74 Closed reduction of dislocation of hand and finger

HCPCS Level II Supplies & Services

A4570 Splint

26685-26686

26685 Open treatment of carpometacarpal dislocation, other than thumb; includes internal fixation, when performed, each joint
26686 complex, multiple, or delayed reduction

ICD-9-CM Diagnostic

718.24 Pathological dislocation of hand joint
718.34 Recurrent dislocation of hand joint
718.74 Developmental dislocation of joint, hand
833.04 Closed dislocation of carpometacarpal (joint)
833.14 Open dislocation of carpometacarpal (joint)

ICD-9-CM Procedural

78.54 Internal fixation of carpals and metacarpals without fracture reduction
79.84 Open reduction of dislocation of hand and finger

HCPCS Level II Supplies & Services

A4570 Splint

26700-26705

26700 Closed treatment of metacarpophalangeal dislocation, single, with manipulation; without anesthesia
26705 requiring anesthesia

ICD-9-CM Diagnostic

718.24 Pathological dislocation of hand joint
718.34 Recurrent dislocation of hand joint
718.74 Developmental dislocation of joint, hand
834.01 Closed dislocation of metacarpophalangeal (joint)

ICD-9-CM Procedural

79.74 Closed reduction of dislocation of hand and finger

HCPCS Level II Supplies & Services

A4570 Splint

26706

26706 Percutaneous skeletal fixation of metacarpophalangeal dislocation, single, with manipulation

ICD-9-CM Diagnostic

718.24 Pathological dislocation of hand joint
718.34 Recurrent dislocation of hand joint
718.74 Developmental dislocation of joint, hand
834.01 Closed dislocation of metacarpophalangeal (joint)

ICD-9-CM Procedural

78.54 Internal fixation of carpals and metacarpals without fracture reduction
79.74 Closed reduction of dislocation of hand and finger

HCPCS Level II Supplies & Services

A4570 Splint

26715

26715 Open treatment of metacarpophalangeal dislocation, single, includes internal fixation, when performed

ICD-9-CM Diagnostic

718.24 Pathological dislocation of hand joint
718.74 Developmental dislocation of joint, hand
834.01 Closed dislocation of metacarpophalangeal (joint)
834.11 Open dislocation of metacarpophalangeal (joint)

ICD-9-CM Procedural

79.84 Open reduction of dislocation of hand and finger

HCPCS Level II Supplies & Services

A4570 Splint

26720-26725

26720 Closed treatment of phalangeal shaft fracture, proximal or middle phalanx, finger or thumb; without manipulation, each
26725 with manipulation, with or without skin or skeletal traction, each

ICD-9-CM Diagnostic

733.19 Pathologic fracture of other specified site
816.01 Closed fracture of middle or proximal phalanx or phalanges of hand
816.03 Closed fracture of multiple sites of phalanx or phalanges of hand
817.0 Multiple closed fractures of hand bones
927.3 Crushing injury of finger(s) — (Use additional code to identify any associated injuries: 800-829, 850.0-854.1, 860.0-869.1)

ICD-9-CM Procedural

79.04 Closed reduction of fracture of phalanges of hand without internal fixation
93.54 Application of splint

HCPCS Level II Supplies & Services

A4570 Splint

26727

26727 Percutaneous skeletal fixation of unstable phalangeal shaft fracture, proximal or middle phalanx, finger or thumb, with manipulation, each

ICD-9-CM Diagnostic

733.19 Pathologic fracture of other specified site

816.01 Closed fracture of middle or proximal phalanx or phalanges of hand
816.03 Closed fracture of multiple sites of phalanx or phalanges of hand
817.0 Multiple closed fractures of hand bones
927.3 Crushing injury of finger(s) — (Use additional code to identify any associated injuries: 800-829, 850.0-854.1, 860.0-869.1)

ICD-9-CM Procedural

79.14 Closed reduction of fracture of phalanges of hand with internal fixation

HCPCS Level II Supplies & Services

A4570 Splint

26735

26735 Open treatment of phalangeal shaft fracture, proximal or middle phalanx, finger or thumb, includes internal fixation, when performed, each

ICD-9-CM Diagnostic

733.19 Pathologic fracture of other specified site
733.81 Malunion of fracture
816.01 Closed fracture of middle or proximal phalanx or phalanges of hand
816.03 Closed fracture of multiple sites of phalanx or phalanges of hand
816.11 Open fracture of middle or proximal phalanx or phalanges of hand
816.13 Open fractures of multiple sites of phalanx or phalanges of hand
817.0 Multiple closed fractures of hand bones
817.1 Multiple open fractures of hand bones
927.3 Crushing injury of finger(s) — (Use additional code to identify any associated injuries: 800-829, 850.0-854.1, 860.0-869.1)

ICD-9-CM Procedural

79.24 Open reduction of fracture of phalanges of hand without internal fixation
79.34 Open reduction of fracture of phalanges of hand with internal fixation
79.80 Open reduction of dislocation of unspecified site

HCPCS Level II Supplies & Services

A4570 Splint

26740-26742

26740 Closed treatment of articular fracture, involving metacarpophalangeal or interphalangeal joint; without manipulation, each
26742 with manipulation, each

ICD-9-CM Diagnostic

733.19 Pathologic fracture of other specified site
815.01 Closed fracture of base of thumb (first) metacarpal bone(s)
815.02 Closed fracture of base of other metacarpal bone(s)
815.04 Closed fracture of neck of metacarpal bone(s)
815.09 Closed fracture of multiple sites of metacarpus
816.01 Closed fracture of middle or proximal phalanx or phalanges of hand
816.03 Closed fracture of multiple sites of phalanx or phalanges of hand
817.0 Multiple closed fractures of hand bones
927.20 Crushing injury of hand(s) — (Use additional code to identify any associated injuries: 800-829, 850.0-854.1, 860.0-869.1)
927.3 Crushing injury of finger(s) — (Use additional code to identify any associated injuries: 800-829, 850.0-854.1, 860.0-869.1)

ICD-9-CM Procedural

79.04 Closed reduction of fracture of phalanges of hand without internal fixation
93.54 Application of splint

HCPCS Level II Supplies & Services

A4570 Splint

26746

26746 Open treatment of articular fracture, involving metacarpophalangeal or interphalangeal joint, includes internal fixation, when performed, each

ICD-9-CM Diagnostic

733.19 Pathologic fracture of other specified site
733.82 Nonunion of fracture
815.01 Closed fracture of base of thumb (first) metacarpal bone(s)
815.02 Closed fracture of base of other metacarpal bone(s)
815.04 Closed fracture of neck of metacarpal bone(s)
815.09 Closed fracture of multiple sites of metacarpus
815.11 Open fracture of base of thumb (first) metacarpal bone(s)
815.12 Open fracture of base of other metacarpal bone(s)
815.14 Open fracture of neck of metacarpal bone(s)
815.19 Open fracture of multiple sites of metacarpus
816.01 Closed fracture of middle or proximal phalanx or phalanges of hand
816.03 Closed fracture of multiple sites of phalanx or phalanges of hand
817.0 Multiple closed fractures of hand bones
817.1 Multiple open fractures of hand bones

ICD-9-CM Procedural

79.24 Open reduction of fracture of phalanges of hand without internal fixation
79.34 Open reduction of fracture of phalanges of hand with internal fixation

HCPCS Level II Supplies & Services

A4570 Splint

26750-26755

26750 Closed treatment of distal phalangeal fracture, finger or thumb; without manipulation, each
26755 with manipulation, each

ICD-9-CM Diagnostic

733.19 Pathologic fracture of other specified site
816.02 Closed fracture of distal phalanx or phalanges of hand
816.03 Closed fracture of multiple sites of phalanx or phalanges of hand
817.0 Multiple closed fractures of hand bones

ICD-9-CM Procedural

79.04 Closed reduction of fracture of phalanges of hand without internal fixation
93.54 Application of splint

HCPCS Level II Supplies & Services

A4570 Splint

26756

26756 Percutaneous skeletal fixation of distal phalangeal fracture, finger or thumb, each

ICD-9-CM Diagnostic

733.19 Pathologic fracture of other specified site
816.02 Closed fracture of distal phalanx or phalanges of hand
816.03 Closed fracture of multiple sites of phalanx or phalanges of hand
816.12 Open fracture of distal phalanx or phalanges of hand
816.13 Open fractures of multiple sites of phalanx or phalanges of hand
817.0 Multiple closed fractures of hand bones

ICD-9-CM Procedural

78.59 Internal fixation of other bone, except facial bones, without fracture reduction

HCPCS Level II Supplies & Services

A4570 Splint

26765

26765 Open treatment of distal phalangeal fracture, finger or thumb, includes internal fixation, when performed, each

ICD-9-CM Diagnostic

733.19 Pathologic fracture of other specified site
816.02 Closed fracture of distal phalanx or phalanges of hand
816.03 Closed fracture of multiple sites of phalanx or phalanges of hand
816.12 Open fracture of distal phalanx or phalanges of hand
816.13 Open fractures of multiple sites of phalanx or phalanges of hand
817.0 Multiple closed fractures of hand bones
817.1 Multiple open fractures of hand bones

ICD-9-CM Procedural

79.24 Open reduction of fracture of phalanges of hand without internal fixation
79.34 Open reduction of fracture of phalanges of hand with internal fixation

HCPCS Level II Supplies & Services

A4570 Splint

26770-26775

26770 Closed treatment of interphalangeal joint dislocation, single, with manipulation; without anesthesia
26775 requiring anesthesia

ICD-9-CM Diagnostic

718.24 Pathological dislocation of hand joint
718.34 Recurrent dislocation of hand joint
718.74 Developmental dislocation of joint, hand
834.02 Closed dislocation of interphalangeal (joint), hand

ICD-9-CM Procedural

79.70 Closed reduction of dislocation of unspecified site

HCPCS Level II Supplies & Services

A4570 Splint

26776

26776 Percutaneous skeletal fixation of interphalangeal joint dislocation, single, with manipulation

ICD-9-CM Diagnostic

718.24 Pathological dislocation of hand joint
718.34 Recurrent dislocation of hand joint
718.74 Developmental dislocation of joint, hand
834.02 Closed dislocation of interphalangeal (joint), hand

ICD-9-CM Procedural

78.59 Internal fixation of other bone, except facial bones, without fracture reduction
79.74 Closed reduction of dislocation of hand and finger

HCPCS Level II Supplies & Services

A4570 Splint

26785

26785 Open treatment of interphalangeal joint dislocation, includes internal fixation, when performed, single

ICD-9-CM Diagnostic

718.24 Pathological dislocation of hand joint
718.34 Recurrent dislocation of hand joint
718.74 Developmental dislocation of joint, hand
834.02 Closed dislocation of interphalangeal (joint), hand
834.12 Open dislocation interphalangeal (joint), hand

ICD-9-CM Procedural

79.80 Open reduction of dislocation of unspecified site

HCPCS Level II Supplies & Services

A4570 Splint

26820

26820 Fusion in opposition, thumb, with autogenous graft (includes obtaining graft)

ICD-9-CM Diagnostic

357.1 Polyneuropathy in collagen vascular disease — (Code first underlying disease: 446.0, 710.0, 714.0) ☒
359.6 Symptomatic inflammatory myopathy in diseases classified elsewhere — (Code first underlying disease: 135, 140.0-208.9, 277.30-277.39, 446.0, 710.0, 710.1, 710.2, 714.0) ☒
446.0 Polyarteritis nodosa
710.0 Systemic lupus erythematosus — (Use additional code to identify manifestation: 424.91, 581.81, 582.81, 583.81)
710.1 Systemic sclerosis — (Use additional code to identify manifestation: 359.6, 517.2)
710.2 Sicca syndrome
714.0 Rheumatoid arthritis — (Use additional code to identify manifestation: 357.1, 359.6)
715.34 Localized osteoarthrosis not specified whether primary or secondary, hand
716.14 Traumatic arthropathy, hand
718.24 Pathological dislocation of hand joint
718.34 Recurrent dislocation of hand joint
726.4 Enthesopathy of wrist and carpus
733.81 Malunion of fracture
905.2 Late effect of fracture of upper extremities
905.6 Late effect of dislocation
906.4 Late effect of crushing

ICD-9-CM Procedural

81.29 Arthrodesis of other specified joint

26841-26842

26841 Arthrodesis, carpometacarpal joint, thumb, with or without internal fixation;
26842 with autograft (includes obtaining graft)

ICD-9-CM Diagnostic

357.1 Polyneuropathy in collagen vascular disease — (Code first underlying disease: 446.0, 710.0, 714.0) ☒
359.6 Symptomatic inflammatory myopathy in diseases classified elsewhere — (Code first underlying disease: 135, 140.0-208.9, 277.30-277.39, 446.0, 710.0, 710.1, 710.2, 714.0) ☒
446.0 Polyarteritis nodosa
710.0 Systemic lupus erythematosus — (Use additional code to identify manifestation: 424.91, 581.81, 582.81, 583.81)
710.1 Systemic sclerosis — (Use additional code to identify manifestation: 359.6, 517.2)
710.2 Sicca syndrome
714.0 Rheumatoid arthritis — (Use additional code to identify manifestation: 357.1, 359.6)
715.34 Localized osteoarthrosis not specified whether primary or secondary, hand
716.14 Traumatic arthropathy, hand
718.24 Pathological dislocation of hand joint
718.34 Recurrent dislocation of hand joint
726.4 Enthesopathy of wrist and carpus
727.00 Unspecified synovitis and tenosynovitis ▽
733.81 Malunion of fracture
755.56 Accessory carpal bones
905.2 Late effect of fracture of upper extremities
905.6 Late effect of dislocation
906.4 Late effect of crushing

ICD-9-CM Procedural

81.29 Arthrodesis of other specified joint

26843-26844

26843 Arthrodesis, carpometacarpal joint, digit, other than thumb, each;
26844 with autograft (includes obtaining graft)

ICD-9-CM Diagnostic

357.1 Polyneuropathy in collagen vascular disease — (Code first underlying disease: 446.0, 710.0, 714.0) ☒
359.6 Symptomatic inflammatory myopathy in diseases classified elsewhere — (Code first underlying disease: 135, 140.0-208.9, 277.30-277.39, 446.0, 710.0, 710.1, 710.2, 714.0) ☒
446.0 Polyarteritis nodosa
710.0 Systemic lupus erythematosus — (Use additional code to identify manifestation: 424.91, 581.81, 582.81, 583.81)
710.1 Systemic sclerosis — (Use additional code to identify manifestation: 359.6, 517.2)
710.2 Sicca syndrome
714.0 Rheumatoid arthritis — (Use additional code to identify manifestation: 357.1, 359.6)
715.34 Localized osteoarthrosis not specified whether primary or secondary, hand
716.14 Traumatic arthropathy, hand
718.24 Pathological dislocation of hand joint
718.34 Recurrent dislocation of hand joint
726.4 Enthesopathy of wrist and carpus
727.00 Unspecified synovitis and tenosynovitis ▽
733.81 Malunion of fracture
755.56 Accessory carpal bones
905.2 Late effect of fracture of upper extremities
905.6 Late effect of dislocation
906.4 Late effect of crushing

ICD-9-CM Procedural

81.29 Arthrodesis of other specified joint

26850-26852

26850 Arthrodesis, metacarpophalangeal joint, with or without internal fixation;
26852 with autograft (includes obtaining graft)

ICD-9-CM Diagnostic

357.1 Polyneuropathy in collagen vascular disease — (Code first underlying disease: 446.0, 710.0, 714.0) ☒
359.6 Symptomatic inflammatory myopathy in diseases classified elsewhere — (Code first underlying disease: 135, 140.0-208.9, 277.30-277.39, 446.0, 710.0, 710.1, 710.2, 714.0) ☒
446.0 Polyarteritis nodosa
710.0 Systemic lupus erythematosus — (Use additional code to identify manifestation: 424.91, 581.81, 582.81, 583.81)
710.1 Systemic sclerosis — (Use additional code to identify manifestation: 359.6, 517.2)
710.2 Sicca syndrome
714.0 Rheumatoid arthritis — (Use additional code to identify manifestation: 357.1, 359.6)
715.34 Localized osteoarthrosis not specified whether primary or secondary, hand
716.14 Traumatic arthropathy, hand
718.24 Pathological dislocation of hand joint
718.34 Recurrent dislocation of hand joint
726.91 Exostosis of unspecified site ▽
727.00 Unspecified synovitis and tenosynovitis ▽
733.81 Malunion of fracture
905.2 Late effect of fracture of upper extremities
905.6 Late effect of dislocation
906.4 Late effect of crushing

ICD-9-CM Procedural

81.27 Metacarpophalangeal fusion

26860-26863

26860 Arthrodesis, interphalangeal joint, with or without internal fixation;
26861 each additional interphalangeal joint (List separately in addition to code for primary procedure)
26862 with autograft (includes obtaining graft)
26863 with autograft (includes obtaining graft), each additional joint (List separately in addition to code for primary procedure)

ICD-9-CM Diagnostic

357.1 Polyneuropathy in collagen vascular disease — (Code first underlying disease: 446.0, 710.0, 714.0) ☒
359.6 Symptomatic inflammatory myopathy in diseases classified elsewhere — (Code first underlying disease: 135, 140.0-208.9, 277.30-277.39, 446.0, 710.0, 710.1, 710.2, 714.0) ☒
446.0 Polyarteritis nodosa
710.0 Systemic lupus erythematosus — (Use additional code to identify manifestation: 424.91, 581.81, 582.81, 583.81)
710.1 Systemic sclerosis — (Use additional code to identify manifestation: 359.6, 517.2)
710.2 Sicca syndrome
714.0 Rheumatoid arthritis — (Use additional code to identify manifestation: 357.1, 359.6)
715.14 Primary localized osteoarthrosis, hand
715.34 Localized osteoarthrosis not specified whether primary or secondary, hand
716.14 Traumatic arthropathy, hand
718.24 Pathological dislocation of hand joint
718.34 Recurrent dislocation of hand joint
718.94 Unspecified derangement of hand joint ▽
733.81 Malunion of fracture
736.1 Mallet finger
736.20 Unspecified deformity of finger ▽
736.29 Other acquired deformity of finger
905.2 Late effect of fracture of upper extremities
905.6 Late effect of dislocation
906.4 Late effect of crushing
927.3 Crushing injury of finger(s) — (Use additional code to identify any associated injuries: 800-829, 850.0-854.1, 860.0-869.1)
959.5 Injury, other and unspecified, finger

ICD-9-CM Procedural

81.28 Interphalangeal fusion

26910

26910 Amputation, metacarpal, with finger or thumb (ray amputation), single, with or without interosseous transfer

ICD-9-CM Diagnostic

170.5 Malignant neoplasm of short bones of upper limb
198.5 Secondary malignant neoplasm of bone and bone marrow
238.0 Neoplasm of uncertain behavior of bone and articular cartilage
239.2 Neoplasms of unspecified nature of bone, soft tissue, and skin
249.70 Secondary diabetes mellitus with peripheral circulatory disorders, not stated as uncontrolled, or unspecified — (Use additional code to identify manifestation: 443.81, 785.4) (Use additional code to identify any associated insulin use: V58.67)
249.71 Secondary diabetes mellitus with peripheral circulatory disorders, uncontrolled — (Use additional code to identify manifestation: 443.81, 785.4) (Use additional code to identify any associated insulin use: V58.67)
250.70 Diabetes with peripheral circulatory disorders, type II or unspecified type, not stated as uncontrolled — (Use additional code to identify manifestation: 443.81, 785.4)
250.71 Diabetes with peripheral circulatory disorders, type I [juvenile type], not stated as uncontrolled — (Use additional code to identify manifestation: 443.81, 785.4)

250.72 Diabetes with peripheral circulatory disorders, type II or unspecified type, uncontrolled — (Use additional code to identify manifestation: 443.81, 785.4)
250.73 Diabetes with peripheral circulatory disorders, type I [juvenile type], uncontrolled — (Use additional code to identify manifestation: 443.81, 785.4)
443.81 Peripheral angiopathy in diseases classified elsewhere — (Code first underlying disease: 249.7, 250.7) ☒
443.9 Unspecified peripheral vascular disease ▽
730.14 Chronic osteomyelitis, hand — (Use additional code to identify organism: 041.1. Use additional code to identify major osseous defect, if applicable: 731.3)
731.3 Major osseous defects — (Code first underlying disease: 170.0-170.9, 730.00-730.29, 733.00-733.09, 733.40-733.49, 996.45)
755.01 Polydactyly of fingers
785.4 Gangrene — (Code first any associated underlying condition)
882.1 Open wound of hand except finger(s) alone, complicated
883.1 Open wound of finger(s), complicated
885.0 Traumatic amputation of thumb (complete) (partial), without mention of complication
886.0 Traumatic amputation of other finger(s) (complete) (partial), without mention of complication
906.4 Late effect of crushing
906.6 Late effect of burn of wrist and hand
927.20 Crushing injury of hand(s) — (Use additional code to identify any associated injuries: 800-829, 850.0-854.1, 860.0-869.1)
927.3 Crushing injury of finger(s) — (Use additional code to identify any associated injuries: 800-829, 850.0-854.1, 860.0-869.1)
944.40 Deep necrosis of underlying tissues due to burn (deep third degree) of unspecified site of hand, without mention of loss of a body part ▽
944.41 Deep necrosis of underlying tissues due to burn (deep third degree) of single digit [finger (nail)] other than thumb, without mention of loss of a body part
944.42 Deep necrosis of underlying tissues due to burn (deep third degree) of thumb (nail), without mention of loss of a body part
944.43 Deep necrosis of underlying tissues due to burn (deep third degree) of two or more digits of hand, not including thumb, without mention of loss of a body part
944.44 Deep necrosis of underlying tissues due to burn (deep third degree) of two or more digits of hand including thumb, without mention of loss of a body part
944.45 Deep necrosis of underlying tissues due to burn (deep third degree) of palm of hand, without mention of loss of a body part
944.46 Deep necrosis of underlying tissues due to burn (deep third degree) of back of hand, without mention of loss of a body part
948.00 Burn (any degree) involving less than 10% of body surface with third degree burn of less than 10% or unspecified amount
948.10 Burn (any degree) involving 10-19% of body surface with third degree burn of less than 10% or unspecified amount
948.11 Burn (any degree) involving 10-19% of body surface with third degree burn of 10-19%
991.1 Frostbite of hand
998.59 Other postoperative infection — (Use additional code to identify infection)

ICD-9-CM Procedural

84.01 Amputation and disarticulation of finger
84.03 Amputation through hand
84.91 Amputation, not otherwise specified

26951-26952

26951 Amputation, finger or thumb, primary or secondary, any joint or phalanx, single, including neurectomies; with direct closure
26952 with local advancement flaps (V-Y, hood)

ICD-9-CM Diagnostic

170.5 Malignant neoplasm of short bones of upper limb
198.5 Secondary malignant neoplasm of bone and bone marrow
238.0 Neoplasm of uncertain behavior of bone and articular cartilage
239.2 Neoplasms of unspecified nature of bone, soft tissue, and skin
249.70 Secondary diabetes mellitus with peripheral circulatory disorders, not stated as uncontrolled, or unspecified — (Use additional code to identify manifestation: 443.81, 785.4) (Use additional code to identify any associated insulin use: V58.67)
249.71 Secondary diabetes mellitus with peripheral circulatory disorders, uncontrolled — (Use additional code to identify manifestation: 443.81, 785.4) (Use additional code to identify any associated insulin use: V58.67)
250.70 Diabetes with peripheral circulatory disorders, type II or unspecified type, not stated as uncontrolled — (Use additional code to identify manifestation: 443.81, 785.4)
250.71 Diabetes with peripheral circulatory disorders, type I [juvenile type], not stated as uncontrolled — (Use additional code to identify manifestation: 443.81, 785.4)
250.72 Diabetes with peripheral circulatory disorders, type II or unspecified type, uncontrolled — (Use additional code to identify manifestation: 443.81, 785.4)
250.73 Diabetes with peripheral circulatory disorders, type I [juvenile type], uncontrolled — (Use additional code to identify manifestation: 443.81, 785.4)
443.81 Peripheral angiopathy in diseases classified elsewhere — (Code first underlying disease: 249.7, 250.7) ☒
443.9 Unspecified peripheral vascular disease ▽
730.14 Chronic osteomyelitis, hand — (Use additional code to identify organism: 041.1. Use additional code to identify major osseous defect, if applicable: 731.3)
730.24 Unspecified osteomyelitis, hand — (Use additional code to identify organism: 041.1. Use additional code to identify major osseous defect, if applicable: 731.3) ▽
731.3 Major osseous defects — (Code first underlying disease: 170.0-170.9, 730.00-730.29, 733.00-733.09, 733.40-733.49, 996.45)
733.49 Aseptic necrosis of other bone site — (Use additional code to identify major osseous defect, if applicable: 731.3)
736.20 Unspecified deformity of finger ▽
755.01 Polydactyly of fingers
785.4 Gangrene — (Code first any associated underlying condition)
883.0 Open wound of finger(s), without mention of complication
883.1 Open wound of finger(s), complicated
883.2 Open wound of finger(s), with tendon involvement
885.0 Traumatic amputation of thumb (complete) (partial), without mention of complication
886.0 Traumatic amputation of other finger(s) (complete) (partial), without mention of complication
906.1 Late effect of open wound of extremities without mention of tendon injury
906.4 Late effect of crushing
906.6 Late effect of burn of wrist and hand
927.3 Crushing injury of finger(s) — (Use additional code to identify any associated injuries: 800-829, 850.0-854.1, 860.0-869.1)
944.40 Deep necrosis of underlying tissues due to burn (deep third degree) of unspecified site of hand, without mention of loss of a body part ▽
944.41 Deep necrosis of underlying tissues due to burn (deep third degree) of single digit [finger (nail)] other than thumb, without mention of loss of a body part
944.42 Deep necrosis of underlying tissues due to burn (deep third degree) of thumb (nail), without mention of loss of a body part
944.43 Deep necrosis of underlying tissues due to burn (deep third degree) of two or more digits of hand, not including thumb, without mention of loss of a body part
944.44 Deep necrosis of underlying tissues due to burn (deep third degree) of two or more digits of hand including thumb, without mention of loss of a body part
944.54 Deep necrosis of underlying tissues due to burn (deep third degree) of two or more digits of hand including thumb, with loss of a body part
948.00 Burn (any degree) involving less than 10% of body surface with third degree burn of less than 10% or unspecified amount
948.10 Burn (any degree) involving 10-19% of body surface with third degree burn of less than 10% or unspecified amount
948.11 Burn (any degree) involving 10-19% of body surface with third degree burn of 10-19%
991.1 Frostbite of hand
998.59 Other postoperative infection — (Use additional code to identify infection)

ICD-9-CM Procedural

84.01 Amputation and disarticulation of finger
84.02 Amputation and disarticulation of thumb

84.91 Amputation, not otherwise specified

Pelvis and Hip Joint

26990

26990 Incision and drainage, pelvis or hip joint area; deep abscess or hematoma

ICD-9-CM Diagnostic

682.6 Cellulitis and abscess of leg, except foot — (Use additional code to identify organism, such as 041.1, etc.)
711.05 Pyogenic arthritis, pelvic region and thigh — (Use additional code to identify infectious organism: 041.0-041.8)
728.89 Other disorder of muscle, ligament, and fascia — (Use additional E code to identify drug, if drug-induced)
730.15 Chronic osteomyelitis, pelvic region and thigh — (Use additional code to identify organism: 041.1. Use additional code to identify major osseous defect, if applicable: 731.3)
782.2 Localized superficial swelling, mass, or lump
924.01 Contusion of hip
998.59 Other postoperative infection — (Use additional code to identify infection)

ICD-9-CM Procedural

77.19 Other incision of other bone, except facial bones, without division
83.01 Exploration of tendon sheath
83.02 Myotomy
83.09 Other incision of soft tissue

HCPCS Level II Supplies & Services

A4305 Disposable drug delivery system, flow rate of 50 ml or greater per hour

26991

26991 Incision and drainage, pelvis or hip joint area; infected bursa

ICD-9-CM Diagnostic

726.5 Enthesopathy of hip region

ICD-9-CM Procedural

83.03 Bursotomy

HCPCS Level II Supplies & Services

A4305 Disposable drug delivery system, flow rate of 50 ml or greater per hour

26992

26992 Incision, bone cortex, pelvis and/or hip joint (eg, osteomyelitis or bone abscess)

ICD-9-CM Diagnostic

730.05 Acute osteomyelitis, pelvic region and thigh — (Use additional code to identify organism: 041.1. Use additional code to identify major osseous defect, if applicable: 731.3)
730.15 Chronic osteomyelitis, pelvic region and thigh — (Use additional code to identify organism: 041.1. Use additional code to identify major osseous defect, if applicable: 731.3)
730.35 Periostitis, without mention of osteomyelitis, pelvic region and thigh — (Use additional code to identify organism: 041.1)
730.85 Other infections involving bone diseases classified elsewhere, pelvic region and thigh — (Use additional code to identify organism: 041.1. Code first underlying disease: 002.0, 015.0-015.9) ☒
731.3 Major osseous defects — (Code first underlying disease: 170.0-170.9, 730.00-730.29, 733.00-733.09, 733.40-733.49, 996.45)

ICD-9-CM Procedural

77.19 Other incision of other bone, except facial bones, without division

27000

27000 Tenotomy, adductor of hip, percutaneous (separate procedure)

ICD-9-CM Diagnostic

343.9 Unspecified infantile cerebral palsy ▽
357.1 Polyneuropathy in collagen vascular disease — (Code first underlying disease: 446.0, 710.0, 714.0) ☒
359.6 Symptomatic inflammatory myopathy in diseases classified elsewhere — (Code first underlying disease: 135, 140.0-208.9, 277.30-277.39, 446.0, 710.0, 710.1, 710.2, 714.0) ☒
714.0 Rheumatoid arthritis — (Use additional code to identify manifestation: 357.1, 359.6)
715.95 Osteoarthrosis, unspecified whether generalized or localized, pelvic region and thigh ▽
718.45 Contracture of pelvic joint
726.5 Enthesopathy of hip region
727.09 Other synovitis and tenosynovitis
727.81 Contracture of tendon (sheath)
732.1 Juvenile osteochondrosis of hip and pelvis
754.30 Congenital dislocation of hip, unilateral

ICD-9-CM Procedural

83.12 Adductor tenotomy of hip

27001-27003

27001 Tenotomy, adductor of hip, open
27003 Tenotomy, adductor, subcutaneous, open, with obturator neurectomy

ICD-9-CM Diagnostic

343.9 Unspecified infantile cerebral palsy ▽
715.95 Osteoarthrosis, unspecified whether generalized or localized, pelvic region and thigh ▽
718.45 Contracture of pelvic joint
727.09 Other synovitis and tenosynovitis
727.81 Contracture of tendon (sheath)
732.1 Juvenile osteochondrosis of hip and pelvis
737.32 Progressive infantile idiopathic scoliosis
754.30 Congenital dislocation of hip, unilateral
754.32 Congenital subluxation of hip, unilateral

ICD-9-CM Procedural

04.07 Other excision or avulsion of cranial and peripheral nerves
83.12 Adductor tenotomy of hip

27005

27005 Tenotomy, hip flexor(s), open (separate procedure)

ICD-9-CM Diagnostic

343.9 Unspecified infantile cerebral palsy ▽
718.35 Recurrent dislocation of pelvic region and thigh joint
718.45 Contracture of pelvic joint
726.5 Enthesopathy of hip region
727.81 Contracture of tendon (sheath)
754.30 Congenital dislocation of hip, unilateral
754.32 Congenital subluxation of hip, unilateral

ICD-9-CM Procedural

83.12 Adductor tenotomy of hip
83.13 Other tenotomy

27006

27006 Tenotomy, abductors and/or extensor(s) of hip, open (separate procedure)

ICD-9-CM Diagnostic

343.9 Unspecified infantile cerebral palsy ▽
718.45 Contracture of pelvic joint
727.81 Contracture of tendon (sheath)
737.32 Progressive infantile idiopathic scoliosis

ICD-9-CM Procedural

83.13 Other tenotomy

27025-27027

27025 Fasciotomy, hip or thigh, any type
27027 Decompression fasciotomy(ies), pelvic (buttock) compartment(s) (eg, gluteus medius-minimus, gluteus maximus, iliopsoas, and/or tensor fascia lata muscle), unilateral

ICD-9-CM Diagnostic

343.9 Unspecified infantile cerebral palsy ▽
718.35 Recurrent dislocation of pelvic region and thigh joint
718.45 Contracture of pelvic joint
726.5 Enthesopathy of hip region
727.81 Contracture of tendon (sheath)
728.89 Other disorder of muscle, ligament, and fascia — (Use additional E code to identify drug, if drug-induced)
729.72 Nontraumatic compartment syndrome of lower extremity — (Code first, if applicable, postprocedural complication: 998.89)
737.32 Progressive infantile idiopathic scoliosis
754.30 Congenital dislocation of hip, unilateral
754.32 Congenital subluxation of hip, unilateral
958.92 Traumatic compartment syndrome of lower extremity

ICD-9-CM Procedural

83.14 Fasciotomy
83.44 Other fasciectomy

27030

27030 Arthrotomy, hip, with drainage (eg, infection)

ICD-9-CM Diagnostic

711.05 Pyogenic arthritis, pelvic region and thigh — (Use additional code to identify infectious organism: 041.0-041.8)
719.85 Other specified disorders of pelvic joint
996.66 Infection and inflammatory reaction due to internal joint prosthesis — (Use additional code to identify specified infections. Use additional code to identify infected prosthetic joint: V43.60-V43.69)
996.67 Infection and inflammatory reaction due to other internal orthopedic device, implant, and graft — (Use additional code to identify specified infections)
998.51 Infected postoperative seroma — (Use additional code to identify organism)
998.59 Other postoperative infection — (Use additional code to identify infection)

ICD-9-CM Procedural

80.15 Other arthrotomy of hip

27033

27033 Arthrotomy, hip, including exploration or removal of loose or foreign body

ICD-9-CM Diagnostic

718.15 Loose body in pelvic joint
719.85 Other specified disorders of pelvic joint
728.12 Traumatic myositis ossificans
754.32 Congenital subluxation of hip, unilateral
890.1 Open wound of hip and thigh, complicated
996.40 Unspecified mechanical complication of internal orthopedic device, implant, and graft — (Use additional code to identify prosthetic joint with mechanical complication, V43.60-V43.69) ▽
996.49 Other mechanical complication of other internal orthopedic device, implant, and graft — (Use additional code to identify prosthetic joint with mechanical complication, V43.60-V43.69)
996.67 Infection and inflammatory reaction due to other internal orthopedic device, implant, and graft — (Use additional code to identify specified infections)
996.78 Other complications due to other internal orthopedic device, implant, and graft — (Use additional code to identify complication: 338.18-338.19, 338.28-338.29)
V64.43 Arthroscopic surgical procedure converted to open procedure

ICD-9-CM Procedural

80.15 Other arthrotomy of hip

27035

27035 Denervation, hip joint, intrapelvic or extrapelvic intra-articular branches of sciatic, femoral, or obturator nerves

ICD-9-CM Diagnostic

343.9 Unspecified infantile cerebral palsy ▽
355.0 Lesion of sciatic nerve
355.79 Other mononeuritis of lower limb
718.45 Contracture of pelvic joint
737.32 Progressive infantile idiopathic scoliosis

ICD-9-CM Procedural

04.03 Division or crushing of other cranial and peripheral nerves
04.04 Other incision of cranial and peripheral nerves

27036

27036 Capsulectomy or capsulotomy, hip, with or without excision of heterotopic bone, with release of hip flexor muscles (ie, gluteus medius, gluteus minimus, tensor fascia latae, rectus femoris, sartorius, iliopsoas)

ICD-9-CM Diagnostic

719.85 Other specified disorders of pelvic joint
733.90 Disorder of bone and cartilage, unspecified ▽
733.99 Other disorders of bone and cartilage
754.30 Congenital dislocation of hip, unilateral
755.69 Other congenital anomaly of lower limb, including pelvic girdle

ICD-9-CM Procedural

80.45 Division of joint capsule, ligament, or cartilage of hip
80.85 Other local excision or destruction of lesion of hip joint
80.95 Other excision of hip joint
83.19 Other division of soft tissue

27040-27041

27040 Biopsy, soft tissue of pelvis and hip area; superficial
27041 deep, subfascial or intramuscular

ICD-9-CM Diagnostic

171.3 Malignant neoplasm of connective and other soft tissue of lower limb, including hip
171.6 Malignant neoplasm of connective and other soft tissue of pelvis
172.7 Malignant melanoma of skin of lower limb, including hip
198.89 Secondary malignant neoplasm of other specified sites
214.1 Lipoma of other skin and subcutaneous tissue
215.3 Other benign neoplasm of connective and other soft tissue of lower limb, including hip
215.6 Other benign neoplasm of connective and other soft tissue of pelvis
238.1 Neoplasm of uncertain behavior of connective and other soft tissue

239.2 Neoplasms of unspecified nature of bone, soft tissue, and skin
682.6 Cellulitis and abscess of leg, except foot — (Use additional code to identify organism, such as 041.1, etc.)
728.82 Foreign body granuloma of muscle — (Use additional code to identify foreign body (V90.01-V90.9))
728.89 Other disorder of muscle, ligament, and fascia — (Use additional E code to identify drug, if drug-induced)
729.89 Other musculoskeletal symptoms referable to limbs

ICD-9-CM Procedural

83.21 Open biopsy of soft tissue

HCPCS Level II Supplies & Services

A4305 Disposable drug delivery system, flow rate of 50 ml or greater per hour

27047-27049 [27043, 27045, 27059]

27043 Excision, tumor, soft tissue of pelvis and hip area, subcutaneous; 3 cm or greater
27045 Excision, tumor, soft tissue of pelvis and hip area, subfascial (eg, intramuscular); 5 cm or greater
27047 Excision, tumor, soft tissue of pelvis and hip area, subcutaneous; less than 3 cm
27048 Excision, tumor, soft tissue of pelvis and hip area, subfascial (eg, intramuscular); less than 5 cm
27049 Radical resection of tumor (eg, sarcoma), soft tissue of pelvis and hip area; less than 5 cm
27059 5 cm or greater

ICD-9-CM Diagnostic

170.6 Malignant neoplasm of pelvic bones, sacrum, and coccyx
170.7 Malignant neoplasm of long bones of lower limb
171.3 Malignant neoplasm of connective and other soft tissue of lower limb, including hip
171.6 Malignant neoplasm of connective and other soft tissue of pelvis
195.3 Malignant neoplasm of pelvis
195.5 Malignant neoplasm of lower limb
198.89 Secondary malignant neoplasm of other specified sites
209.35 Merkel cell carcinoma of the trunk
209.75 Secondary Merkel cell carcinoma
214.1 Lipoma of other skin and subcutaneous tissue
215.3 Other benign neoplasm of connective and other soft tissue of lower limb, including hip
215.6 Other benign neoplasm of connective and other soft tissue of pelvis
238.1 Neoplasm of uncertain behavior of connective and other soft tissue
239.2 Neoplasms of unspecified nature of bone, soft tissue, and skin
709.4 Foreign body granuloma of skin and subcutaneous tissue — (Use additional code to identify foreign body (V90.01-V90.9))

ICD-9-CM Procedural

83.31 Excision of lesion of tendon sheath
83.32 Excision of lesion of muscle
83.39 Excision of lesion of other soft tissue
83.49 Other excision of soft tissue
86.3 Other local excision or destruction of lesion or tissue of skin and subcutaneous tissue
86.4 Radical excision of skin lesion

HCPCS Level II Supplies & Services

A4305 Disposable drug delivery system, flow rate of 50 ml or greater per hour

27050

27050 Arthrotomy, with biopsy; sacroiliac joint

ICD-9-CM Diagnostic

170.6 Malignant neoplasm of pelvic bones, sacrum, and coccyx
198.5 Secondary malignant neoplasm of bone and bone marrow
209.73 Secondary neuroendocrine tumor of bone
215.6 Other benign neoplasm of connective and other soft tissue of pelvis
238.0 Neoplasm of uncertain behavior of bone and articular cartilage
239.2 Neoplasms of unspecified nature of bone, soft tissue, and skin
275.40 Unspecified disorder of calcium metabolism — (Use additional code to identify any associated intellectual disabilities) ▽
275.42 Hypercalcemia — (Use additional code to identify any associated intellectual disabilities)
275.49 Other disorders of calcium metabolism — (Use additional code to identify any associated intellectual disabilities)
275.5 Hungry bone syndrome — (Use additional code to identify any associated intellectual disabilities)
720.2 Sacroiliitis, not elsewhere classified

ICD-9-CM Procedural

80.39 Biopsy of joint structure of other specified site

27052

27052 Arthrotomy, with biopsy; hip joint

ICD-9-CM Diagnostic

170.3 Malignant neoplasm of ribs, sternum, and clavicle
170.6 Malignant neoplasm of pelvic bones, sacrum, and coccyx
170.7 Malignant neoplasm of long bones of lower limb
198.5 Secondary malignant neoplasm of bone and bone marrow
209.73 Secondary neuroendocrine tumor of bone
213.6 Benign neoplasm of pelvic bones, sacrum, and coccyx
213.7 Benign neoplasm of long bones of lower limb
215.3 Other benign neoplasm of connective and other soft tissue of lower limb, including hip
238.0 Neoplasm of uncertain behavior of bone and articular cartilage
239.2 Neoplasms of unspecified nature of bone, soft tissue, and skin
275.40 Unspecified disorder of calcium metabolism — (Use additional code to identify any associated intellectual disabilities) ▽
275.42 Hypercalcemia — (Use additional code to identify any associated intellectual disabilities)
275.49 Other disorders of calcium metabolism — (Use additional code to identify any associated intellectual disabilities)
275.5 Hungry bone syndrome — (Use additional code to identify any associated intellectual disabilities)
711.05 Pyogenic arthritis, pelvic region and thigh — (Use additional code to identify infectious organism: 041.0-041.8)
727.02 Giant cell tumor of tendon sheath
727.41 Ganglion of joint
727.82 Calcium deposits in tendon and bursa
730.15 Chronic osteomyelitis, pelvic region and thigh — (Use additional code to identify organism: 041.1. Use additional code to identify major osseous defect, if applicable: 731.3)
731.3 Major osseous defects — (Code first underlying disease: 170.0-170.9, 730.00-730.29, 733.00-733.09, 733.40-733.49, 996.45)
733.20 Unspecified cyst of bone (localized) ▽
733.42 Aseptic necrosis of head and neck of femur — (Use additional code to identify major osseous defect, if applicable: 731.3)

ICD-9-CM Procedural

80.35 Biopsy of joint structure of hip

27054

27054 Arthrotomy with synovectomy, hip joint

ICD-9-CM Diagnostic

275.40 Unspecified disorder of calcium metabolism — (Use additional code to identify any associated intellectual disabilities) ▽

275.42 Hypercalcemia — (Use additional code to identify any associated intellectual disabilities)
275.49 Other disorders of calcium metabolism — (Use additional code to identify any associated intellectual disabilities)
275.5 Hungry bone syndrome — (Use additional code to identify any associated intellectual disabilities)
719.25 Villonodular synovitis, pelvic region and thigh
726.5 Enthesopathy of hip region
727.09 Other synovitis and tenosynovitis
727.40 Unspecified synovial cyst ▽
V64.43 Arthroscopic surgical procedure converted to open procedure

ICD-9-CM Procedural

80.75 Synovectomy of hip

27057

27057 Decompression fasciotomy(ies), pelvic (buttock) compartment(s) (eg, gluteus medius-minimus, gluteus maximus, iliopsoas, and/or tensor fascia lata muscle) with debridement of nonviable muscle, unilateral

ICD-9-CM Diagnostic

343.9 Unspecified infantile cerebral palsy ▽
718.35 Recurrent dislocation of pelvic region and thigh joint
718.45 Contracture of pelvic joint
726.5 Enthesopathy of hip region
727.81 Contracture of tendon (sheath)
728.89 Other disorder of muscle, ligament, and fascia — (Use additional E code to identify drug, if drug-induced)
729.72 Nontraumatic compartment syndrome of lower extremity — (Code first, if applicable, postprocedural complication: 998.89)
737.32 Progressive infantile idiopathic scoliosis
754.30 Congenital dislocation of hip, unilateral
754.32 Congenital subluxation of hip, unilateral
958.92 Traumatic compartment syndrome of lower extremity

ICD-9-CM Procedural

83.14 Fasciotomy
83.45 Other myectomy

27060-27062

27060 Excision; ischial bursa
27062 trochanteric bursa or calcification

ICD-9-CM Diagnostic

215.6 Other benign neoplasm of connective and other soft tissue of pelvis
726.5 Enthesopathy of hip region
727.3 Other bursitis disorders
727.49 Other ganglion and cyst of synovium, tendon, and bursa
727.82 Calcium deposits in tendon and bursa
727.9 Unspecified disorder of synovium, tendon, and bursa ▽

ICD-9-CM Procedural

83.5 Bursectomy

27065-27067

27065 Excision of bone cyst or benign tumor, wing of ilium, symphysis pubis, or greater trochanter of femur; superficial, includes autograft, when performed
27066 deep (subfascial), includes autograft, when performed
27067 with autograft requiring separate incision

ICD-9-CM Diagnostic

213.6 Benign neoplasm of pelvic bones, sacrum, and coccyx
213.7 Benign neoplasm of long bones of lower limb
238.0 Neoplasm of uncertain behavior of bone and articular cartilage
239.2 Neoplasms of unspecified nature of bone, soft tissue, and skin
732.1 Juvenile osteochondrosis of hip and pelvis
732.4 Juvenile osteochondrosis of lower extremity, excluding foot
732.9 Unspecified osteochondropathy ▽
733.21 Solitary bone cyst
733.22 Aneurysmal bone cyst
733.29 Other cyst of bone

ICD-9-CM Procedural

77.65 Local excision of lesion or tissue of femur
77.69 Local excision of lesion or tissue of other bone, except facial bones
77.75 Excision of femur for graft
77.79 Excision of other bone for graft, except facial bones
78.05 Bone graft of femur
78.09 Bone graft of other bone, except facial bones

27070-27071

27070 Partial excision, wing of ilium, symphysis pubis, or greater trochanter of femur, (craterization, saucerization) (eg, osteomyelitis or bone abscess); superficial
27071 deep (subfascial or intramuscular)

ICD-9-CM Diagnostic

715.15 Primary localized osteoarthrosis, pelvic region and thigh
728.13 Postoperative heterotopic calcification
730.05 Acute osteomyelitis, pelvic region and thigh — (Use additional code to identify organism: 041.1. Use additional code to identify major osseous defect, if applicable: 731.3)
730.15 Chronic osteomyelitis, pelvic region and thigh — (Use additional code to identify organism: 041.1. Use additional code to identify major osseous defect, if applicable: 731.3)
730.25 Unspecified osteomyelitis, pelvic region and thigh — (Use additional code to identify organism: 041.1. Use additional code to identify major osseous defect, if applicable: 731.3) ▽
730.85 Other infections involving bone diseases classified elsewhere, pelvic region and thigh — (Use additional code to identify organism: 041.1. Code first underlying disease: 002.0, 015.0-015.9) ☒
731.3 Major osseous defects — (Code first underlying disease: 170.0-170.9, 730.00-730.29, 733.00-733.09, 733.40-733.49, 996.45)
733.99 Other disorders of bone and cartilage
996.66 Infection and inflammatory reaction due to internal joint prosthesis — (Use additional code to identify specified infections. Use additional code to identify infected prosthetic joint: V43.60-V43.69)
996.67 Infection and inflammatory reaction due to other internal orthopedic device, implant, and graft — (Use additional code to identify specified infections)

ICD-9-CM Procedural

77.65 Local excision of lesion or tissue of femur
77.69 Local excision of lesion or tissue of other bone, except facial bones
77.85 Other partial ostectomy of femur
77.89 Other partial ostectomy of other bone, except facial bones

27075

27075 Radical resection of tumor; wing of ilium, 1 pubic or ischial ramus or symphysis pubis

ICD-9-CM Diagnostic

170.6 Malignant neoplasm of pelvic bones, sacrum, and coccyx
170.7 Malignant neoplasm of long bones of lower limb
198.5 Secondary malignant neoplasm of bone and bone marrow
209.73 Secondary neuroendocrine tumor of bone
213.6 Benign neoplasm of pelvic bones, sacrum, and coccyx
213.7 Benign neoplasm of long bones of lower limb

238.0 Neoplasm of uncertain behavior of bone and articular cartilage
239.2 Neoplasms of unspecified nature of bone, soft tissue, and skin
731.3 Major osseous defects — (Code first underlying disease: 170.0-170.9, 730.00-730.29, 733.00-733.09, 733.40-733.49, 996.45)

ICD-9-CM Procedural

77.89 Other partial ostectomy of other bone, except facial bones
77.99 Total ostectomy of other bone, except facial bones

27076

27076 Radical resection of tumor; ilium, including acetabulum, both pubic rami, or ischium and acetabulum

ICD-9-CM Diagnostic

170.6 Malignant neoplasm of pelvic bones, sacrum, and coccyx
170.7 Malignant neoplasm of long bones of lower limb
198.5 Secondary malignant neoplasm of bone and bone marrow
209.73 Secondary neuroendocrine tumor of bone
213.6 Benign neoplasm of pelvic bones, sacrum, and coccyx
213.7 Benign neoplasm of long bones of lower limb
238.0 Neoplasm of uncertain behavior of bone and articular cartilage
239.2 Neoplasms of unspecified nature of bone, soft tissue, and skin
731.3 Major osseous defects — (Code first underlying disease: 170.0-170.9, 730.00-730.29, 733.00-733.09, 733.40-733.49, 996.45)

ICD-9-CM Procedural

77.89 Other partial ostectomy of other bone, except facial bones
77.99 Total ostectomy of other bone, except facial bones

27077

27077 Radical resection of tumor; innominate bone, total

ICD-9-CM Diagnostic

170.6 Malignant neoplasm of pelvic bones, sacrum, and coccyx
170.7 Malignant neoplasm of long bones of lower limb
198.5 Secondary malignant neoplasm of bone and bone marrow
209.73 Secondary neuroendocrine tumor of bone
213.6 Benign neoplasm of pelvic bones, sacrum, and coccyx
213.7 Benign neoplasm of long bones of lower limb
238.0 Neoplasm of uncertain behavior of bone and articular cartilage
239.2 Neoplasms of unspecified nature of bone, soft tissue, and skin
731.3 Major osseous defects — (Code first underlying disease: 170.0-170.9, 730.00-730.29, 733.00-733.09, 733.40-733.49, 996.45)

ICD-9-CM Procedural

77.89 Other partial ostectomy of other bone, except facial bones
77.99 Total ostectomy of other bone, except facial bones

27078

27078 Radical resection of tumor; ischial tuberosity and greater trochanter of femur

ICD-9-CM Diagnostic

170.6 Malignant neoplasm of pelvic bones, sacrum, and coccyx
170.7 Malignant neoplasm of long bones of lower limb
198.5 Secondary malignant neoplasm of bone and bone marrow
209.73 Secondary neuroendocrine tumor of bone
213.6 Benign neoplasm of pelvic bones, sacrum, and coccyx
213.7 Benign neoplasm of long bones of lower limb
238.0 Neoplasm of uncertain behavior of bone and articular cartilage
239.2 Neoplasms of unspecified nature of bone, soft tissue, and skin
731.3 Major osseous defects — (Code first underlying disease: 170.0-170.9, 730.00-730.29, 733.00-733.09, 733.40-733.49, 996.45)

ICD-9-CM Procedural

77.85 Other partial ostectomy of femur
77.89 Other partial ostectomy of other bone, except facial bones
77.95 Total ostectomy of femur
77.99 Total ostectomy of other bone, except facial bones

27080

27080 Coccygectomy, primary

ICD-9-CM Diagnostic

170.6 Malignant neoplasm of pelvic bones, sacrum, and coccyx
198.5 Secondary malignant neoplasm of bone and bone marrow
209.73 Secondary neuroendocrine tumor of bone
213.6 Benign neoplasm of pelvic bones, sacrum, and coccyx
238.0 Neoplasm of uncertain behavior of bone and articular cartilage
239.2 Neoplasms of unspecified nature of bone, soft tissue, and skin
707.05 Pressure ulcer, buttock — (Use additional code to identify pressure ulcer stage: 707.20-707.25)
707.09 Pressure ulcer, other site — (Use additional code to identify pressure ulcer stage: 707.20-707.25)
724.70 Unspecified disorder of coccyx ▽
730.15 Chronic osteomyelitis, pelvic region and thigh — (Use additional code to identify organism: 041.1. Use additional code to identify major osseous defect, if applicable: 731.3)
730.35 Periostitis, without mention of osteomyelitis, pelvic region and thigh — (Use additional code to identify organism: 041.1)
731.3 Major osseous defects — (Code first underlying disease: 170.0-170.9, 730.00-730.29, 733.00-733.09, 733.40-733.49, 996.45)

ICD-9-CM Procedural

77.99 Total ostectomy of other bone, except facial bones

27086-27087

27086 Removal of foreign body, pelvis or hip; subcutaneous tissue
27087 deep (subfascial or intramuscular)

ICD-9-CM Diagnostic

686.1 Pyogenic granuloma of skin and subcutaneous tissue — (Use additional code to identify any infectious organism: 041.0-041.8)
709.4 Foreign body granuloma of skin and subcutaneous tissue — (Use additional code to identify foreign body (V90.01-V90.9))
718.15 Loose body in pelvic joint
728.82 Foreign body granuloma of muscle — (Use additional code to identify foreign body (V90.01-V90.9))
729.6 Residual foreign body in soft tissue — (Use additional code to identify foreign body (V90.01-V90.9))
879.7 Open wound of other and unspecified parts of trunk, complicated ▽
890.1 Open wound of hip and thigh, complicated
890.2 Open wound of hip and thigh, with tendon involvement
919.6 Other, multiple, and unspecified sites, superficial foreign body (splinter), without major open wound and without mention of infection
919.7 Other, multiple, and unspecified sites, superficial foreign body (splinter), without major open wound, infected

ICD-9-CM Procedural

83.02 Myotomy
83.09 Other incision of soft tissue
86.05 Incision with removal of foreign body or device from skin and subcutaneous tissue

HCPCS Level II Supplies & Services

A4305 Disposable drug delivery system, flow rate of 50 ml or greater per hour

27090-27091

27090 Removal of hip prosthesis; (separate procedure)
27091 complicated, including total hip prosthesis, methylmethacrylate with or without insertion of spacer

ICD-9-CM Diagnostic

731.3 Major osseous defects — (Code first underlying disease: 170.0-170.9, 730.00-730.29, 733.00-733.09, 733.40-733.49, 996.45)
996.40 Unspecified mechanical complication of internal orthopedic device, implant, and graft — (Use additional code to identify prosthetic joint with mechanical complication, V43.60-V43.69) ▼
996.41 Mechanical loosening of prosthetic joint — (Use additional code to identify prosthetic joint with mechanical complication, V43.60-V43.69)
996.42 Dislocation of prosthetic joint — (Use additional code to identify prosthetic joint with mechanical complication, V43.60-V43.69)
996.43 Broken prosthetic joint implant — (Use additional code to identify prosthetic joint with mechanical complication, V43.60-V43.69)
996.44 Peri-prosthetic fracture around prosthetic joint — (Use additional code to identify prosthetic joint with mechanical complication, V43.60-V43.69.
996.45 Peri-prosthetic osteolysis — (Use additional code to identify prosthetic joint with mechanical complication, V43.60-V43.69. Use additional code to identify major osseous defect, if applicable: 731.3)
996.46 Articular bearing surface wear of prosthetic joint — (Use additional code to identify prosthetic joint with mechanical complication, V43.60-V43.69)
996.47 Other mechanical complication of prosthetic joint implant — (Use additional code to identify prosthetic joint with mechanical complication, V43.60-V43.69)
996.66 Infection and inflammatory reaction due to internal joint prosthesis — (Use additional code to identify specified infections. Use additional code to identify infected prosthetic joint: V43.60-V43.69)
996.77 Other complications due to internal joint prosthesis — (Use additional code to identify complication: 338.18-338.19, 338.28-338.29)
998.51 Infected postoperative seroma — (Use additional code to identify organism)
998.59 Other postoperative infection — (Use additional code to identify infection)
998.7 Acute reaction to foreign substance accidentally left during procedure, not elsewhere classified
V43.64 Hip joint replacement by other means

ICD-9-CM Procedural

80.05 Arthrotomy for removal of prosthesis without replacement, hip
84.56 Insertion or replacement of (cement) spacer
84.57 Removal of (cement) spacer

27093-27095

27093 Injection procedure for hip arthrography; without anesthesia
27095 with anesthesia

ICD-9-CM Diagnostic

213.6 Benign neoplasm of pelvic bones, sacrum, and coccyx
357.1 Polyneuropathy in collagen vascular disease — (Code first underlying disease: 446.0, 710.0, 714.0) ☒
359.6 Symptomatic inflammatory myopathy in diseases classified elsewhere — (Code first underlying disease: 135, 140.0-208.9, 277.30-277.39, 446.0, 710.0, 710.1, 710.2, 714.0) ☒
446.0 Polyarteritis nodosa
696.0 Psoriatic arthropathy
710.0 Systemic lupus erythematosus — (Use additional code to identify manifestation: 424.91, 581.81, 582.81, 583.81)
710.1 Systemic sclerosis — (Use additional code to identify manifestation: 359.6, 517.2)
710.2 Sicca syndrome
711.05 Pyogenic arthritis, pelvic region and thigh — (Use additional code to identify infectious organism: 041.0-041.8)
711.95 Unspecified infective arthritis, pelvic region and thigh ▼
714.0 Rheumatoid arthritis — (Use additional code to identify manifestation: 357.1, 359.6)
714.9 Unspecified inflammatory polyarthropathy ▼
715.09 Generalized osteoarthrosis, involving multiple sites
715.15 Primary localized osteoarthrosis, pelvic region and thigh
715.35 Localized osteoarthrosis not specified whether primary or secondary, pelvic region and thigh
715.90 Osteoarthrosis, unspecified whether generalized or localized, unspecified site ▼
715.95 Osteoarthrosis, unspecified whether generalized or localized, pelvic region and thigh ▼
716.15 Traumatic arthropathy, pelvic region and thigh
716.95 Unspecified arthropathy, pelvic region and thigh ▼
716.99 Unspecified arthropathy, multiple sites ▼
718.15 Loose body in pelvic joint
718.35 Recurrent dislocation of pelvic region and thigh joint
718.65 Unspecified intrapelvic protrusion acetabulum, pelvic region and thigh ▼
718.75 Developmental dislocation of joint, pelvic region and thigh
718.85 Other joint derangement, not elsewhere classified, pelvic region and thigh
719.05 Effusion of pelvic joint
719.45 Pain in joint, pelvic region and thigh
726.5 Enthesopathy of hip region
727.00 Unspecified synovitis and tenosynovitis ▼
727.09 Other synovitis and tenosynovitis
731.3 Major osseous defects — (Code first underlying disease: 170.0-170.9, 730.00-730.29, 733.00-733.09, 733.40-733.49, 996.45)
732.1 Juvenile osteochondrosis of hip and pelvis
733.40 Aseptic necrosis of bone, site unspecified — (Use additional code to identify major osseous defect, if applicable: 731.3) ▼
733.42 Aseptic necrosis of head and neck of femur — (Use additional code to identify major osseous defect, if applicable: 731.3)
733.90 Disorder of bone and cartilage, unspecified ▼
754.30 Congenital dislocation of hip, unilateral
754.31 Congenital dislocation of hip, bilateral
754.32 Congenital subluxation of hip, unilateral
755.62 Congenital coxa vara
755.63 Other congenital deformity of hip (joint)
820.8 Closed fracture of unspecified part of neck of femur ▼
835.00 Closed dislocation of hip, unspecified site ▼
959.6 Injury, other and unspecified, hip and thigh
996.40 Unspecified mechanical complication of internal orthopedic device, implant, and graft — (Use additional code to identify prosthetic joint with mechanical complication, V43.60-V43.69) ▼
996.41 Mechanical loosening of prosthetic joint — (Use additional code to identify prosthetic joint with mechanical complication, V43.60-V43.69)
996.42 Dislocation of prosthetic joint — (Use additional code to identify prosthetic joint with mechanical complication, V43.60-V43.69)
996.43 Broken prosthetic joint implant — (Use additional code to identify prosthetic joint with mechanical complication, V43.60-V43.69)
996.44 Peri-prosthetic fracture around prosthetic joint — (Use additional code to identify prosthetic joint with mechanical complication, V43.60-V43.69.
996.45 Peri-prosthetic osteolysis — (Use additional code to identify prosthetic joint with mechanical complication, V43.60-V43.69. Use additional code to identify major osseous defect, if applicable: 731.3)
996.46 Articular bearing surface wear of prosthetic joint — (Use additional code to identify prosthetic joint with mechanical complication, V43.60-V43.69)
996.47 Other mechanical complication of prosthetic joint implant — (Use additional code to identify prosthetic joint with mechanical complication, V43.60-V43.69)
996.66 Infection and inflammatory reaction due to internal joint prosthesis — (Use additional code to identify specified infections. Use additional code to identify infected prosthetic joint: V43.60-V43.69)

996.67 Infection and inflammatory reaction due to other internal orthopedic device, implant, and graft — (Use additional code to identify specified infections)
996.77 Other complications due to internal joint prosthesis — (Use additional code to identify complication: 338.18-338.19, 338.28-338.29)
996.78 Other complications due to other internal orthopedic device, implant, and graft — (Use additional code to identify complication: 338.18-338.19, 338.28-338.29)

ICD-9-CM Procedural

81.99 Other operations on joint structures
88.32 Contrast arthrogram

27096

27096 Injection procedure for sacroiliac joint, anesthetic/steroid, with image guidance (fluoroscopy or CT) including arthrography when performed

ICD-9-CM Diagnostic

338.21 Chronic pain due to trauma — (Use additional code to identify pain associated with psychological factors: 307.89)
338.29 Other chronic pain — (Use additional code to identify pain associated with psychological factors: 307.89)
359.6 Symptomatic inflammatory myopathy in diseases classified elsewhere — (Code first underlying disease: 135, 140.0-208.9, 277.30-277.39, 446.0, 710.0, 710.1, 710.2, 714.0) ☒
710.0 Systemic lupus erythematosus — (Use additional code to identify manifestation: 424.91, 581.81, 582.81, 583.81)
710.1 Systemic sclerosis — (Use additional code to identify manifestation: 359.6, 517.2)
710.2 Sicca syndrome
711.05 Pyogenic arthritis, pelvic region and thigh — (Use additional code to identify infectious organism: 041.0-041.8)
711.95 Unspecified infective arthritis, pelvic region and thigh ▽
714.0 Rheumatoid arthritis — (Use additional code to identify manifestation: 357.1, 359.6)
715.09 Generalized osteoarthrosis, involving multiple sites
715.15 Primary localized osteoarthrosis, pelvic region and thigh
715.25 Secondary localized osteoarthrosis, pelvic region and thigh
715.35 Localized osteoarthrosis not specified whether primary or secondary, pelvic region and thigh
715.89 Osteoarthrosis involving multiple sites, but not specified as generalized
715.95 Osteoarthrosis, unspecified whether generalized or localized, pelvic region and thigh ▽
716.15 Traumatic arthropathy, pelvic region and thigh
716.95 Unspecified arthropathy, pelvic region and thigh ▽
718.25 Pathological dislocation of pelvic region and thigh joint
718.35 Recurrent dislocation of pelvic region and thigh joint
718.55 Ankylosis of pelvic region and thigh joint
719.45 Pain in joint, pelvic region and thigh
719.85 Other specified disorders of pelvic joint
719.95 Unspecified disorder of joint of pelvic region and thigh ▽
720.2 Sacroiliitis, not elsewhere classified
724.6 Disorders of sacrum
755.69 Other congenital anomaly of lower limb, including pelvic girdle
805.6 Closed fracture of sacrum and coccyx without mention of spinal cord injury
805.7 Open fracture of sacrum and coccyx without mention of spinal cord injury
808.41 Closed fracture of ilium
808.43 Multiple closed pelvic fractures with disruption of pelvic circle
808.51 Open fracture of ilium
808.53 Multiple open pelvic fractures with disruption of pelvic circle
839.42 Closed dislocation, sacrum
839.52 Open dislocation, sacrum

ICD-9-CM Procedural

81.92 Injection of therapeutic substance into joint or ligament
88.32 Contrast arthrogram
99.23 Injection of steroid
99.29 Injection or infusion of other therapeutic or prophylactic substance

HCPCS Level II Supplies & Services

G0260 Injection procedure for sacroiliac joint; provision of anesthetic, steroid and/or other therapeutic agent, with or without arthrography

27097

27097 Release or recession, hamstring, proximal

ICD-9-CM Diagnostic

343.9 Unspecified infantile cerebral palsy ▽
716.15 Traumatic arthropathy, pelvic region and thigh
718.25 Pathological dislocation of pelvic region and thigh joint
718.45 Contracture of pelvic joint
726.5 Enthesopathy of hip region
741.93 Spina bifida without mention of hydrocephalus, lumbar region
890.1 Open wound of hip and thigh, complicated
890.2 Open wound of hip and thigh, with tendon involvement

ICD-9-CM Procedural

83.14 Fasciotomy
83.72 Recession of tendon

27098

27098 Transfer, adductor to ischium

ICD-9-CM Diagnostic

343.9 Unspecified infantile cerebral palsy ▽
718.25 Pathological dislocation of pelvic region and thigh joint
718.45 Contracture of pelvic joint
741.93 Spina bifida without mention of hydrocephalus, lumbar region
890.2 Open wound of hip and thigh, with tendon involvement

ICD-9-CM Procedural

83.75 Tendon transfer or transplantation

27100

27100 Transfer external oblique muscle to greater trochanter including fascial or tendon extension (graft)

ICD-9-CM Diagnostic

138 Late effects of acute poliomyelitis — (Note: This category is to be used to indicate conditions classifiable to 045 as the cause of late effects, which are themselves classified elsewhere. The "late effects" include those specified as such, as sequelae, or as due to old or inactive poliomyelitis, without evidence of active disease.)
343.9 Unspecified infantile cerebral palsy ▽
718.45 Contracture of pelvic joint
741.93 Spina bifida without mention of hydrocephalus, lumbar region

ICD-9-CM Procedural

83.77 Muscle transfer or transplantation
83.82 Graft of muscle or fascia

27105

27105 Transfer paraspinal muscle to hip (includes fascial or tendon extension graft)

ICD-9-CM Diagnostic

343.9 Unspecified infantile cerebral palsy ▽
718.25 Pathological dislocation of pelvic region and thigh joint
718.45 Contracture of pelvic joint
741.93 Spina bifida without mention of hydrocephalus, lumbar region
835.00 Closed dislocation of hip, unspecified site ▽

ICD-9-CM Procedural

83.77 Muscle transfer or transplantation
83.82 Graft of muscle or fascia
83.83 Tendon pulley reconstruction on muscle, tendon, and fascia

27110

27110 Transfer iliopsoas; to greater trochanter of femur

ICD-9-CM Diagnostic

343.9 Unspecified infantile cerebral palsy ▽
718.25 Pathological dislocation of pelvic region and thigh joint
718.45 Contracture of pelvic joint
741.93 Spina bifida without mention of hydrocephalus, lumbar region
835.00 Closed dislocation of hip, unspecified site ▽

ICD-9-CM Procedural

83.77 Muscle transfer or transplantation

27111

27111 Transfer iliopsoas; to femoral neck

ICD-9-CM Diagnostic

343.9 Unspecified infantile cerebral palsy ▽
718.25 Pathological dislocation of pelvic region and thigh joint
718.45 Contracture of pelvic joint
718.75 Developmental dislocation of joint, pelvic region and thigh
741.93 Spina bifida without mention of hydrocephalus, lumbar region
835.01 Closed posterior dislocation of hip

ICD-9-CM Procedural

83.77 Muscle transfer or transplantation

27120

27120 Acetabuloplasty; (eg, Whitman, Colonna, Haygroves, or cup type)

ICD-9-CM Diagnostic

715.15 Primary localized osteoarthrosis, pelvic region and thigh
732.1 Juvenile osteochondrosis of hip and pelvis
733.21 Solitary bone cyst
754.30 Congenital dislocation of hip, unilateral
808.0 Closed fracture of acetabulum
808.1 Open fracture of acetabulum
835.00 Closed dislocation of hip, unspecified site ▽
835.10 Open dislocation of hip, unspecified site ▽

ICD-9-CM Procedural

81.40 Repair of hip, not elsewhere classified

27122

27122 Acetabuloplasty; resection, femoral head (eg, Girdlestone procedure)

ICD-9-CM Diagnostic

718.45 Contracture of pelvic joint
730.15 Chronic osteomyelitis, pelvic region and thigh — (Use additional code to identify organism: 041.1. Use additional code to identify major osseous defect, if applicable: 731.3)
733.42 Aseptic necrosis of head and neck of femur — (Use additional code to identify major osseous defect, if applicable: 731.3)
835.12 Open obturator dislocation of hip

ICD-9-CM Procedural

77.85 Other partial ostectomy of femur

27125

27125 Hemiarthroplasty, hip, partial (eg, femoral stem prosthesis, bipolar arthroplasty)

ICD-9-CM Diagnostic

170.1 Malignant neoplasm of mandible
170.7 Malignant neoplasm of long bones of lower limb
198.5 Secondary malignant neoplasm of bone and bone marrow
213.7 Benign neoplasm of long bones of lower limb
238.0 Neoplasm of uncertain behavior of bone and articular cartilage
239.2 Neoplasms of unspecified nature of bone, soft tissue, and skin
357.1 Polyneuropathy in collagen vascular disease — (Code first underlying disease: 446.0, 710.0, 714.0) ☒
359.6 Symptomatic inflammatory myopathy in diseases classified elsewhere — (Code first underlying disease: 135, 140.0-208.9, 277.30-277.39, 446.0, 710.0, 710.1, 710.2, 714.0) ☒
446.0 Polyarteritis nodosa
710.0 Systemic lupus erythematosus — (Use additional code to identify manifestation: 424.91, 581.81, 582.81, 583.81)
710.1 Systemic sclerosis — (Use additional code to identify manifestation: 359.6, 517.2)
710.2 Sicca syndrome
714.0 Rheumatoid arthritis — (Use additional code to identify manifestation: 357.1, 359.6)
715.15 Primary localized osteoarthrosis, pelvic region and thigh
715.35 Localized osteoarthrosis not specified whether primary or secondary, pelvic region and thigh
715.95 Osteoarthrosis, unspecified whether generalized or localized, pelvic region and thigh ▽
716.15 Traumatic arthropathy, pelvic region and thigh
716.95 Unspecified arthropathy, pelvic region and thigh ▽
718.05 Articular cartilage disorder, pelvic region and thigh
718.15 Loose body in pelvic joint
718.95 Unspecified pelvic joint derangement ▽
731.3 Major osseous defects — (Code first underlying disease: 170.0-170.9, 730.00-730.29, 733.00-733.09, 733.40-733.49, 996.45)
732.1 Juvenile osteochondrosis of hip and pelvis
733.42 Aseptic necrosis of head and neck of femur — (Use additional code to identify major osseous defect, if applicable: 731.3)
733.81 Malunion of fracture
733.82 Nonunion of fracture
733.99 Other disorders of bone and cartilage
820.01 Closed fracture of epiphysis (separation) (upper) of neck of femur
820.02 Closed fracture of midcervical section of femur
820.11 Open fracture of epiphysis (separation) (upper) of neck of femur
820.12 Open fracture of midcervical section of femur
820.21 Closed fracture of intertrochanteric section of femur
820.22 Closed fracture of subtrochanteric section of femur
820.31 Open fracture of intertrochanteric section of femur
820.32 Open fracture of subtrochanteric section of femur
905.3 Late effect of fracture of neck of femur
905.4 Late effect of fracture of lower extremities

ICD-9-CM Procedural

00.74 Hip bearing surface, metal-on-polyethylene
00.75 Hip bearing surface, metal-on-metal
00.76 Hip bearing surface, ceramic-on-ceramic
00.77 Hip bearing surface, ceramic-on-polyethylene
81.52 Partial hip replacement

27130

27130 Arthroplasty, acetabular and proximal femoral prosthetic replacement (total hip arthroplasty), with or without autograft or allograft

ICD-9-CM Diagnostic

357.1 Polyneuropathy in collagen vascular disease — (Code first underlying disease: 446.0, 710.0, 714.0) ☒

359.6 Symptomatic inflammatory myopathy in diseases classified elsewhere — (Code first underlying disease: 135, 140.0-208.9, 277.30-277.39, 446.0, 710.0, 710.1, 710.2, 714.0) ☒

446.0 Polyarteritis nodosa

710.0 Systemic lupus erythematosus — (Use additional code to identify manifestation: 424.91, 581.81, 582.81, 583.81)

710.1 Systemic sclerosis — (Use additional code to identify manifestation: 359.6, 517.2)

710.2 Sicca syndrome

714.0 Rheumatoid arthritis — (Use additional code to identify manifestation: 357.1, 359.6)

715.09 Generalized osteoarthrosis, involving multiple sites

715.15 Primary localized osteoarthrosis, pelvic region and thigh

715.25 Secondary localized osteoarthrosis, pelvic region and thigh

715.35 Localized osteoarthrosis not specified whether primary or secondary, pelvic region and thigh

715.95 Osteoarthrosis, unspecified whether generalized or localized, pelvic region and thigh ▽

716.05 Kaschin-Beck disease pelvic, region and thigh

716.15 Traumatic arthropathy, pelvic region and thigh

716.95 Unspecified arthropathy, pelvic region and thigh ▽

718.65 Unspecified intrapelvic protrusion acetabulum, pelvic region and thigh ▽

719.35 Palindromic rheumatism, pelvic region and thigh

731.3 Major osseous defects — (Code first underlying disease: 170.0-170.9, 730.00-730.29, 733.00-733.09, 733.40-733.49, 996.45)

733.14 Pathologic fracture of neck of femur

733.42 Aseptic necrosis of head and neck of femur — (Use additional code to identify major osseous defect, if applicable: 731.3)

733.82 Nonunion of fracture

754.30 Congenital dislocation of hip, unilateral

755.63 Other congenital deformity of hip (joint)

905.4 Late effect of fracture of lower extremities

ICD-9-CM Procedural

00.74 Hip bearing surface, metal-on-polyethylene

00.75 Hip bearing surface, metal-on-metal

00.76 Hip bearing surface, ceramic-on-ceramic

00.77 Hip bearing surface, ceramic-on-polyethylene

81.51 Total hip replacement

27132

27132 Conversion of previous hip surgery to total hip arthroplasty, with or without autograft or allograft

ICD-9-CM Diagnostic

357.1 Polyneuropathy in collagen vascular disease — (Code first underlying disease: 446.0, 710.0, 714.0) ☒

359.6 Symptomatic inflammatory myopathy in diseases classified elsewhere — (Code first underlying disease: 135, 140.0-208.9, 277.30-277.39, 446.0, 710.0, 710.1, 710.2, 714.0) ☒

446.0 Polyarteritis nodosa

710.0 Systemic lupus erythematosus — (Use additional code to identify manifestation: 424.91, 581.81, 582.81, 583.81)

710.1 Systemic sclerosis — (Use additional code to identify manifestation: 359.6, 517.2)

710.2 Sicca syndrome

714.0 Rheumatoid arthritis — (Use additional code to identify manifestation: 357.1, 359.6)

715.09 Generalized osteoarthrosis, involving multiple sites

715.15 Primary localized osteoarthrosis, pelvic region and thigh

715.25 Secondary localized osteoarthrosis, pelvic region and thigh

715.35 Localized osteoarthrosis not specified whether primary or secondary, pelvic region and thigh

715.95 Osteoarthrosis, unspecified whether generalized or localized, pelvic region and thigh ▽

716.05 Kaschin-Beck disease pelvic, region and thigh

716.15 Traumatic arthropathy, pelvic region and thigh

716.95 Unspecified arthropathy, pelvic region and thigh ▽

718.05 Articular cartilage disorder, pelvic region and thigh

718.25 Pathological dislocation of pelvic region and thigh joint

718.35 Recurrent dislocation of pelvic region and thigh joint

718.85 Other joint derangement, not elsewhere classified, pelvic region and thigh

719.35 Palindromic rheumatism, pelvic region and thigh

719.95 Unspecified disorder of joint of pelvic region and thigh ▽

731.3 Major osseous defects — (Code first underlying disease: 170.0-170.9, 730.00-730.29, 733.00-733.09, 733.40-733.49, 996.45)

733.14 Pathologic fracture of neck of femur

733.42 Aseptic necrosis of head and neck of femur — (Use additional code to identify major osseous defect, if applicable: 731.3)

733.82 Nonunion of fracture

754.30 Congenital dislocation of hip, unilateral

755.63 Other congenital deformity of hip (joint)

905.4 Late effect of fracture of lower extremities

996.40 Unspecified mechanical complication of internal orthopedic device, implant, and graft — (Use additional code to identify prosthetic joint with mechanical complication, V43.60-V43.69) ▽

996.49 Other mechanical complication of other internal orthopedic device, implant, and graft — (Use additional code to identify prosthetic joint with mechanical complication, V43.60-V43.69)

996.67 Infection and inflammatory reaction due to other internal orthopedic device, implant, and graft — (Use additional code to identify specified infections)

996.78 Other complications due to other internal orthopedic device, implant, and graft — (Use additional code to identify complication: 338.18-338.19, 338.28-338.29)

ICD-9-CM Procedural

00.74 Hip bearing surface, metal-on-polyethylene

00.75 Hip bearing surface, metal-on-metal

00.76 Hip bearing surface, ceramic-on-ceramic

00.77 Hip bearing surface, ceramic-on-polyethylene

81.51 Total hip replacement

81.53 Revision of hip replacement, not otherwise specified

27134

27134 Revision of total hip arthroplasty; both components, with or without autograft or allograft

ICD-9-CM Diagnostic

357.1 Polyneuropathy in collagen vascular disease — (Code first underlying disease: 446.0, 710.0, 714.0) ☒

359.6 Symptomatic inflammatory myopathy in diseases classified elsewhere — (Code first underlying disease: 135, 140.0-208.9, 277.30-277.39, 446.0, 710.0, 710.1, 710.2, 714.0) ☒

446.0 Polyarteritis nodosa

710.0 Systemic lupus erythematosus — (Use additional code to identify manifestation: 424.91, 581.81, 582.81, 583.81)

710.1 Systemic sclerosis — (Use additional code to identify manifestation: 359.6, 517.2)

710.2 Sicca syndrome

714.0 Rheumatoid arthritis — (Use additional code to identify manifestation: 357.1, 359.6)

715.09 Generalized osteoarthrosis, involving multiple sites

715.15 Primary localized osteoarthrosis, pelvic region and thigh
715.25 Secondary localized osteoarthrosis, pelvic region and thigh
715.35 Localized osteoarthrosis not specified whether primary or secondary, pelvic region and thigh
715.95 Osteoarthrosis, unspecified whether generalized or localized, pelvic region and thigh
716.05 Kaschin-Beck disease pelvic, region and thigh
716.15 Traumatic arthropathy, pelvic region and thigh
718.05 Articular cartilage disorder, pelvic region and thigh
718.25 Pathological dislocation of pelvic region and thigh joint
718.35 Recurrent dislocation of pelvic region and thigh joint
718.85 Other joint derangement, not elsewhere classified, pelvic region and thigh
719.95 Unspecified disorder of joint of pelvic region and thigh
731.3 Major osseous defects — (Code first underlying disease: 170.0-170.9, 730.00-730.29, 733.00-733.09, 733.40-733.49, 996.45)
733.14 Pathologic fracture of neck of femur
996.40 Unspecified mechanical complication of internal orthopedic device, implant, and graft — (Use additional code to identify prosthetic joint with mechanical complication, V43.60-V43.69)
996.41 Mechanical loosening of prosthetic joint — (Use additional code to identify prosthetic joint with mechanical complication, V43.60-V43.69)
996.42 Dislocation of prosthetic joint — (Use additional code to identify prosthetic joint with mechanical complication, V43.60-V43.69)
996.43 Broken prosthetic joint implant — (Use additional code to identify prosthetic joint with mechanical complication, V43.60-V43.69)
996.44 Peri-prosthetic fracture around prosthetic joint — (Use additional code to identify prosthetic joint with mechanical complication, V43.60-V43.69.
996.45 Peri-prosthetic osteolysis — (Use additional code to identify prosthetic joint with mechanical complication, V43.60-V43.69. Use additional code to identify major osseous defect, if applicable: 731.3)
996.46 Articular bearing surface wear of prosthetic joint — (Use additional code to identify prosthetic joint with mechanical complication, V43.60-V43.69)
996.47 Other mechanical complication of prosthetic joint implant — (Use additional code to identify prosthetic joint with mechanical complication, V43.60-V43.69)
996.66 Infection and inflammatory reaction due to internal joint prosthesis — (Use additional code to identify specified infections. Use additional code to identify infected prosthetic joint: V43.60-V43.69)
996.77 Other complications due to internal joint prosthesis — (Use additional code to identify complication: 338.18-338.19, 338.28-338.29)
998.59 Other postoperative infection — (Use additional code to identify infection)
V43.64 Hip joint replacement by other means

ICD-9-CM Procedural

00.70 Revision of hip replacement, both acetabular and femoral components
00.74 Hip bearing surface, metal-on-polyethylene
00.75 Hip bearing surface, metal-on-metal
00.76 Hip bearing surface, ceramic-on-ceramic
00.77 Hip bearing surface, ceramic-on-polyethylene

27137

27137 Revision of total hip arthroplasty; acetabular component only, with or without autograft or allograft

ICD-9-CM Diagnostic

357.1 Polyneuropathy in collagen vascular disease — (Code first underlying disease: 446.0, 710.0, 714.0)
359.6 Symptomatic inflammatory myopathy in diseases classified elsewhere — (Code first underlying disease: 135, 140.0-208.9, 277.30-277.39, 446.0, 710.0, 710.1, 710.2, 714.0)
446.0 Polyarteritis nodosa
710.0 Systemic lupus erythematosus — (Use additional code to identify manifestation: 424.91, 581.81, 582.81, 583.81)
710.1 Systemic sclerosis — (Use additional code to identify manifestation: 359.6, 517.2)
710.2 Sicca syndrome
714.0 Rheumatoid arthritis — (Use additional code to identify manifestation: 357.1, 359.6)
714.33 Monoarticular juvenile rheumatoid arthritis
715.09 Generalized osteoarthrosis, involving multiple sites
715.15 Primary localized osteoarthrosis, pelvic region and thigh
715.25 Secondary localized osteoarthrosis, pelvic region and thigh
715.35 Localized osteoarthrosis not specified whether primary or secondary, pelvic region and thigh
715.95 Osteoarthrosis, unspecified whether generalized or localized, pelvic region and thigh
716.05 Kaschin-Beck disease pelvic, region and thigh
716.15 Traumatic arthropathy, pelvic region and thigh
718.05 Articular cartilage disorder, pelvic region and thigh
718.15 Loose body in pelvic joint
718.25 Pathological dislocation of pelvic region and thigh joint
718.35 Recurrent dislocation of pelvic region and thigh joint
718.85 Other joint derangement, not elsewhere classified, pelvic region and thigh
719.95 Unspecified disorder of joint of pelvic region and thigh
731.3 Major osseous defects — (Code first underlying disease: 170.0-170.9, 730.00-730.29, 733.00-733.09, 733.40-733.49, 996.45)
733.14 Pathologic fracture of neck of femur
996.40 Unspecified mechanical complication of internal orthopedic device, implant, and graft — (Use additional code to identify prosthetic joint with mechanical complication, V43.60-V43.69)
996.41 Mechanical loosening of prosthetic joint — (Use additional code to identify prosthetic joint with mechanical complication, V43.60-V43.69)
996.42 Dislocation of prosthetic joint — (Use additional code to identify prosthetic joint with mechanical complication, V43.60-V43.69)
996.43 Broken prosthetic joint implant — (Use additional code to identify prosthetic joint with mechanical complication, V43.60-V43.69)
996.44 Peri-prosthetic fracture around prosthetic joint — (Use additional code to identify prosthetic joint with mechanical complication, V43.60-V43.69.
996.45 Peri-prosthetic osteolysis — (Use additional code to identify prosthetic joint with mechanical complication, V43.60-V43.69. Use additional code to identify major osseous defect, if applicable: 731.3)
996.46 Articular bearing surface wear of prosthetic joint — (Use additional code to identify prosthetic joint with mechanical complication, V43.60-V43.69)
996.47 Other mechanical complication of prosthetic joint implant — (Use additional code to identify prosthetic joint with mechanical complication, V43.60-V43.69)
996.66 Infection and inflammatory reaction due to internal joint prosthesis — (Use additional code to identify specified infections. Use additional code to identify infected prosthetic joint: V43.60-V43.69)
996.77 Other complications due to internal joint prosthesis — (Use additional code to identify complication: 338.18-338.19, 338.28-338.29)
998.59 Other postoperative infection — (Use additional code to identify infection)
V43.64 Hip joint replacement by other means

ICD-9-CM Procedural

00.71 Revision of hip replacement, acetabular component
00.73 Revision of hip replacement, acetabular liner and/or femoral head only
00.74 Hip bearing surface, metal-on-polyethylene
00.75 Hip bearing surface, metal-on-metal
00.76 Hip bearing surface, ceramic-on-ceramic
00.77 Hip bearing surface, ceramic-on-polyethylene

27138

27138 Revision of total hip arthroplasty; femoral component only, with or without allograft

ICD-9-CM Diagnostic

357.1 Polyneuropathy in collagen vascular disease — (Code first underlying disease: 446.0, 710.0, 714.0) ✖
359.6 Symptomatic inflammatory myopathy in diseases classified elsewhere — (Code first underlying disease: 135, 140.0-208.9, 277.30-277.39, 446.0, 710.0, 710.1, 710.2, 714.0) ✖
446.0 Polyarteritis nodosa
710.0 Systemic lupus erythematosus — (Use additional code to identify manifestation: 424.91, 581.81, 582.81, 583.81)
710.1 Systemic sclerosis — (Use additional code to identify manifestation: 359.6, 517.2)
710.2 Sicca syndrome
714.0 Rheumatoid arthritis — (Use additional code to identify manifestation: 357.1, 359.6)
715.09 Generalized osteoarthrosis, involving multiple sites
715.15 Primary localized osteoarthrosis, pelvic region and thigh
715.25 Secondary localized osteoarthrosis, pelvic region and thigh
715.35 Localized osteoarthrosis not specified whether primary or secondary, pelvic region and thigh
715.95 Osteoarthrosis, unspecified whether generalized or localized, pelvic region and thigh ▽
716.05 Kaschin-Beck disease pelvic, region and thigh
718.25 Pathological dislocation of pelvic region and thigh joint
718.35 Recurrent dislocation of pelvic region and thigh joint
718.85 Other joint derangement, not elsewhere classified, pelvic region and thigh
731.3 Major osseous defects — (Code first underlying disease: 170.0-170.9, 730.00-730.29, 733.00-733.09, 733.40-733.49, 996.45)
733.14 Pathologic fracture of neck of femur
996.40 Unspecified mechanical complication of internal orthopedic device, implant, and graft — (Use additional code to identify prosthetic joint with mechanical complication, V43.60-V43.69) ▽
996.41 Mechanical loosening of prosthetic joint — (Use additional code to identify prosthetic joint with mechanical complication, V43.60-V43.69)
996.42 Dislocation of prosthetic joint — (Use additional code to identify prosthetic joint with mechanical complication, V43.60-V43.69)
996.43 Broken prosthetic joint implant — (Use additional code to identify prosthetic joint with mechanical complication, V43.60-V43.69)
996.44 Peri-prosthetic fracture around prosthetic joint — (Use additional code to identify prosthetic joint with mechanical complication, V43.60-V43.69.
996.45 Peri-prosthetic osteolysis — (Use additional code to identify prosthetic joint with mechanical complication, V43.60-V43.69. Use additional code to identify major osseous defect, if applicable: 731.3)
996.46 Articular bearing surface wear of prosthetic joint — (Use additional code to identify prosthetic joint with mechanical complication, V43.60-V43.69)
996.47 Other mechanical complication of prosthetic joint implant — (Use additional code to identify prosthetic joint with mechanical complication, V43.60-V43.69)
996.66 Infection and inflammatory reaction due to internal joint prosthesis — (Use additional code to identify specified infections. Use additional code to identify infected prosthetic joint: V43.60-V43.69)
996.77 Other complications due to internal joint prosthesis — (Use additional code to identify complication: 338.18-338.19, 338.28-338.29)
998.59 Other postoperative infection — (Use additional code to identify infection)
V43.64 Hip joint replacement by other means

ICD-9-CM Procedural

00.72 Revision of hip replacement, femoral component
00.73 Revision of hip replacement, acetabular liner and/or femoral head only
00.74 Hip bearing surface, metal-on-polyethylene
00.75 Hip bearing surface, metal-on-metal
00.76 Hip bearing surface, ceramic-on-ceramic
00.77 Hip bearing surface, ceramic-on-polyethylene

27140

27140 Osteotomy and transfer of greater trochanter of femur (separate procedure)

ICD-9-CM Diagnostic

718.25 Pathological dislocation of pelvic region and thigh joint
718.35 Recurrent dislocation of pelvic region and thigh joint
733.15 Pathologic fracture of other specified part of femur
733.81 Malunion of fracture
736.39 Other acquired deformities of hip
996.40 Unspecified mechanical complication of internal orthopedic device, implant, and graft — (Use additional code to identify prosthetic joint with mechanical complication, V43.60-V43.69) ▽
996.49 Other mechanical complication of other internal orthopedic device, implant, and graft — (Use additional code to identify prosthetic joint with mechanical complication, V43.60-V43.69)
996.67 Infection and inflammatory reaction due to other internal orthopedic device, implant, and graft — (Use additional code to identify specified infections)
996.78 Other complications due to other internal orthopedic device, implant, and graft — (Use additional code to identify complication: 338.18-338.19, 338.28-338.29)

ICD-9-CM Procedural

77.35 Other division of femur

27146-27147

27146 Osteotomy, iliac, acetabular or innominate bone;
27147 with open reduction of hip

ICD-9-CM Diagnostic

343.9 Unspecified infantile cerebral palsy ▽
718.35 Recurrent dislocation of pelvic region and thigh joint
718.85 Other joint derangement, not elsewhere classified, pelvic region and thigh
754.30 Congenital dislocation of hip, unilateral
754.31 Congenital dislocation of hip, bilateral
754.32 Congenital subluxation of hip, unilateral
754.33 Congenital subluxation of hip, bilateral
755.61 Congenital coxa valga
755.63 Other congenital deformity of hip (joint)

ICD-9-CM Procedural

77.39 Other division of other bone, except facial bones
77.85 Other partial ostectomy of femur
79.85 Open reduction of dislocation of hip

27151-27156

27151 Osteotomy, iliac, acetabular or innominate bone; with femoral osteotomy
27156 with femoral osteotomy and with open reduction of hip

ICD-9-CM Diagnostic

343.9 Unspecified infantile cerebral palsy ▽
718.35 Recurrent dislocation of pelvic region and thigh joint
718.85 Other joint derangement, not elsewhere classified, pelvic region and thigh
754.30 Congenital dislocation of hip, unilateral
754.31 Congenital dislocation of hip, bilateral
754.32 Congenital subluxation of hip, unilateral
754.33 Congenital subluxation of hip, bilateral
755.61 Congenital coxa valga
755.63 Other congenital deformity of hip (joint)

ICD-9-CM Procedural

77.35 Other division of femur
77.39 Other division of other bone, except facial bones
79.85 Open reduction of dislocation of hip

27158

27158 Osteotomy, pelvis, bilateral (eg, congenital malformation)

ICD-9-CM Diagnostic

755.63 Other congenital deformity of hip (joint)

ICD-9-CM Procedural

77.39 Other division of other bone, except facial bones

27161

27161 Osteotomy, femoral neck (separate procedure)

ICD-9-CM Diagnostic

343.9 Unspecified infantile cerebral palsy ▽
733.14 Pathologic fracture of neck of femur
733.81 Malunion of fracture
736.30 Unspecified acquired deformity of hip ▽
754.32 Congenital subluxation of hip, unilateral

ICD-9-CM Procedural

77.35 Other division of femur

27165

27165 Osteotomy, intertrochanteric or subtrochanteric including internal or external fixation and/or cast

ICD-9-CM Diagnostic

343.9 Unspecified infantile cerebral palsy ▽
715.15 Primary localized osteoarthrosis, pelvic region and thigh
718.25 Pathological dislocation of pelvic region and thigh joint
731.3 Major osseous defects — (Code first underlying disease: 170.0-170.9, 730.00-730.29, 733.00-733.09, 733.40-733.49, 996.45)
733.14 Pathologic fracture of neck of femur
733.42 Aseptic necrosis of head and neck of femur — (Use additional code to identify major osseous defect, if applicable: 731.3)
733.82 Nonunion of fracture
754.30 Congenital dislocation of hip, unilateral
754.31 Congenital dislocation of hip, bilateral
754.32 Congenital subluxation of hip, unilateral
754.33 Congenital subluxation of hip, bilateral
755.61 Congenital coxa valga
755.62 Congenital coxa vara

ICD-9-CM Procedural

77.35 Other division of femur
78.15 Application of external fixator device, femur
84.71 Application of external fixator device, monoplanar system
84.72 Application of external fixator device, ring system
84.73 Application of hybrid external fixator device

27170

27170 Bone graft, femoral head, neck, intertrochanteric or subtrochanteric area (includes obtaining bone graft)

ICD-9-CM Diagnostic

239.2 Neoplasms of unspecified nature of bone, soft tissue, and skin
733.14 Pathologic fracture of neck of femur
733.20 Unspecified cyst of bone (localized) ▽
733.21 Solitary bone cyst
733.42 Aseptic necrosis of head and neck of femur — (Use additional code to identify major osseous defect, if applicable: 731.3)
733.82 Nonunion of fracture
820.01 Closed fracture of epiphysis (separation) (upper) of neck of femur
820.11 Open fracture of epiphysis (separation) (upper) of neck of femur
820.13 Open fracture of base of neck of femur
820.20 Closed fracture of unspecified trochanteric section of femur ▽
820.21 Closed fracture of intertrochanteric section of femur
820.22 Closed fracture of subtrochanteric section of femur

ICD-9-CM Procedural

77.77 Excision of tibia and fibula for graft
77.79 Excision of other bone for graft, except facial bones
78.05 Bone graft of femur

27175-27176

27175 Treatment of slipped femoral epiphysis; by traction, without reduction
27176 by single or multiple pinning, in situ

ICD-9-CM Diagnostic

732.2 Nontraumatic slipped upper femoral epiphysis
732.9 Unspecified osteochondropathy ▽
820.01 Closed fracture of epiphysis (separation) (upper) of neck of femur

ICD-9-CM Procedural

78.55 Internal fixation of femur without fracture reduction
93.44 Other skeletal traction
93.45 Thomas' splint traction

27177

27177 Open treatment of slipped femoral epiphysis; single or multiple pinning or bone graft (includes obtaining graft)

ICD-9-CM Diagnostic

732.2 Nontraumatic slipped upper femoral epiphysis
732.9 Unspecified osteochondropathy ▽
820.01 Closed fracture of epiphysis (separation) (upper) of neck of femur

ICD-9-CM Procedural

77.79 Excision of other bone for graft, except facial bones
78.05 Bone graft of femur
78.55 Internal fixation of femur without fracture reduction
79.55 Open reduction of separated epiphysis of femur

27178

27178 Open treatment of slipped femoral epiphysis; closed manipulation with single or multiple pinning

ICD-9-CM Diagnostic

732.2 Nontraumatic slipped upper femoral epiphysis
732.9 Unspecified osteochondropathy ▽
820.01 Closed fracture of epiphysis (separation) (upper) of neck of femur

ICD-9-CM Procedural

78.55 Internal fixation of femur without fracture reduction
79.55 Open reduction of separated epiphysis of femur

27179

27179 Open treatment of slipped femoral epiphysis; osteoplasty of femoral neck (Heyman type procedure)

ICD-9-CM Diagnostic

732.2 Nontraumatic slipped upper femoral epiphysis
732.9 Unspecified osteochondropathy ▽
820.01 Closed fracture of epiphysis (separation) (upper) of neck of femur

ICD-9-CM Procedural

78.45 Other repair or plastic operations on femur

79.55 Open reduction of separated epiphysis of femur

27181

27181 Open treatment of slipped femoral epiphysis; osteotomy and internal fixation

ICD-9-CM Diagnostic

732.2 Nontraumatic slipped upper femoral epiphysis
732.9 Unspecified osteochondropathy ▽
820.01 Closed fracture of epiphysis (separation) (upper) of neck of femur

ICD-9-CM Procedural

77.25 Wedge osteotomy of femur
78.55 Internal fixation of femur without fracture reduction
79.55 Open reduction of separated epiphysis of femur

27185

27185 Epiphyseal arrest by epiphysiodesis or stapling, greater trochanter of femur

ICD-9-CM Diagnostic

733.91 Arrest of bone development or growth
736.32 Coxa vara (acquired)
755.30 Congenital unspecified reduction deformity of lower limb ▽
755.31 Congenital transverse deficiency of lower limb

ICD-9-CM Procedural

78.25 Limb shortening procedures, femur

27187

27187 Prophylactic treatment (nailing, pinning, plating or wiring) with or without methylmethacrylate, femoral neck and proximal femur

ICD-9-CM Diagnostic

170.7 Malignant neoplasm of long bones of lower limb
198.5 Secondary malignant neoplasm of bone and bone marrow
213.7 Benign neoplasm of long bones of lower limb
238.0 Neoplasm of uncertain behavior of bone and articular cartilage
239.2 Neoplasms of unspecified nature of bone, soft tissue, and skin
731.3 Major osseous defects — (Code first underlying disease: 170.0-170.9, 730.00-730.29, 733.00-733.09, 733.40-733.49, 996.45)
733.00 Unspecified osteoporosis — (Use additional code to identify major osseous defect, if applicable: 731.3) (Use additional code to identify personal history of pathologic (healed) fracture: V13.51) ▽
733.09 Other osteoporosis — (Use additional code to identify major osseous defect, if applicable: 731.3) (Use additional code to identify personal history of pathologic (healed) fracture: V13.51) (Use additional E code to identify drug)

ICD-9-CM Procedural

78.55 Internal fixation of femur without fracture reduction
84.55 Insertion of bone void filler

27193-27194

27193 Closed treatment of pelvic ring fracture, dislocation, diastasis or subluxation; without manipulation
27194 with manipulation, requiring more than local anesthesia

ICD-9-CM Diagnostic

724.6 Disorders of sacrum
733.19 Pathologic fracture of other specified site
805.6 Closed fracture of sacrum and coccyx without mention of spinal cord injury
806.61 Closed fracture of sacrum and coccyx with complete cauda equina lesion
806.62 Closed fracture of sacrum and coccyx with other cauda equina injury
806.79 Open fracture of sacrum and coccyx with other spinal cord injury
808.0 Closed fracture of acetabulum
808.2 Closed fracture of pubis
808.41 Closed fracture of ilium
808.42 Closed fracture of ischium
808.43 Multiple closed pelvic fractures with disruption of pelvic circle
808.49 Closed fracture of other specified part of pelvis
839.41 Closed dislocation, coccyx
839.42 Closed dislocation, sacrum
839.69 Closed dislocation, other location

ICD-9-CM Procedural

79.09 Closed reduction of fracture of other specified bone, except facial bones, without internal fixation
79.79 Closed reduction of dislocation of other specified site, except temporomandibular
93.59 Other immobilization, pressure, and attention to wound

27200

27200 Closed treatment of coccygeal fracture

ICD-9-CM Diagnostic

733.19 Pathologic fracture of other specified site
805.6 Closed fracture of sacrum and coccyx without mention of spinal cord injury
806.60 Closed fracture of sacrum and coccyx with unspecified spinal cord injury ▽
806.61 Closed fracture of sacrum and coccyx with complete cauda equina lesion
806.62 Closed fracture of sacrum and coccyx with other cauda equina injury
806.69 Closed fracture of sacrum and coccyx with other spinal cord injury
808.44 Multiple closed pelvic fractures without disruption of pelvic circle
808.54 Multiple open pelvic fractures without disruption of pelvic circle

ICD-9-CM Procedural

03.53 Repair of vertebral fracture

27202

27202 Open treatment of coccygeal fracture

ICD-9-CM Diagnostic

733.19 Pathologic fracture of other specified site
805.6 Closed fracture of sacrum and coccyx without mention of spinal cord injury
805.7 Open fracture of sacrum and coccyx without mention of spinal cord injury
805.8 Closed fracture of unspecified part of vertebral column without mention of spinal cord injury ▽
806.60 Closed fracture of sacrum and coccyx with unspecified spinal cord injury ▽
806.61 Closed fracture of sacrum and coccyx with complete cauda equina lesion
806.69 Closed fracture of sacrum and coccyx with other spinal cord injury
808.44 Multiple closed pelvic fractures without disruption of pelvic circle
808.54 Multiple open pelvic fractures without disruption of pelvic circle

ICD-9-CM Procedural

03.53 Repair of vertebral fracture

27215

27215 Open treatment of iliac spine(s), tuberosity avulsion, or iliac wing fracture(s), unilateral, for pelvic bone fracture patterns that do not disrupt the pelvic ring, includes internal fixation, when performed

ICD-9-CM Diagnostic

733.19 Pathologic fracture of other specified site
733.98 Stress fracture of pelvis — (Use additional external cause code(s) to identify the cause of the stress fracture)
808.41 Closed fracture of ilium
808.44 Multiple closed pelvic fractures without disruption of pelvic circle
808.51 Open fracture of ilium
808.54 Multiple open pelvic fractures without disruption of pelvic circle

ICD-9-CM Procedural

79.29 Open reduction of fracture of other specified bone, except facial bones, without internal fixation

79.39 Open reduction of fracture of other specified bone, except facial bones, with internal fixation

27216

27216 Percutaneous skeletal fixation of posterior pelvic bone fracture and/or dislocation, for fracture patterns that disrupt the pelvic ring, unilateral (includes ipsilateral ilium, sacroiliac joint and/or sacrum)

ICD-9-CM Diagnostic

724.6 Disorders of sacrum

733.19 Pathologic fracture of other specified site

733.98 Stress fracture of pelvis — (Use additional external cause code(s) to identify the cause of the stress fracture)

805.6 Closed fracture of sacrum and coccyx without mention of spinal cord injury

808.41 Closed fracture of ilium

808.43 Multiple closed pelvic fractures with disruption of pelvic circle

808.49 Closed fracture of other specified part of pelvis

808.51 Open fracture of ilium

808.53 Multiple open pelvic fractures with disruption of pelvic circle

839.42 Closed dislocation, sacrum

839.52 Open dislocation, sacrum

ICD-9-CM Procedural

78.59 Internal fixation of other bone, except facial bones, without fracture reduction

79.19 Closed reduction of fracture of other specified bone, except facial bones, with internal fixation

79.79 Closed reduction of dislocation of other specified site, except temporomandibular

27217

27217 Open treatment of anterior pelvic bone fracture and/or dislocation for fracture patterns that disrupt the pelvic ring, unilateral, includes internal fixation, when performed (includes pubic symphysis and/or ipsilateral superior/inferior rami)

ICD-9-CM Diagnostic

733.19 Pathologic fracture of other specified site

733.98 Stress fracture of pelvis — (Use additional external cause code(s) to identify the cause of the stress fracture)

808.2 Closed fracture of pubis

808.3 Open fracture of pubis

808.43 Multiple closed pelvic fractures with disruption of pelvic circle

808.53 Multiple open pelvic fractures with disruption of pelvic circle

839.69 Closed dislocation, other location

839.79 Open dislocation, other location

ICD-9-CM Procedural

79.29 Open reduction of fracture of other specified bone, except facial bones, without internal fixation

79.39 Open reduction of fracture of other specified bone, except facial bones, with internal fixation

79.89 Open reduction of dislocation of other specified site, except temporomandibular

27218

27218 Open treatment of posterior pelvic bone fracture and/or dislocation, for fracture patterns that disrupt the pelvic ring, unilateral, includes internal fixation, when performed (includes ipsilateral ilium, sacroiliac joint and/or sacrum)

ICD-9-CM Diagnostic

733.19 Pathologic fracture of other specified site

733.98 Stress fracture of pelvis — (Use additional external cause code(s) to identify the cause of the stress fracture)

805.6 Closed fracture of sacrum and coccyx without mention of spinal cord injury

806.61 Closed fracture of sacrum and coccyx with complete cauda equina lesion

806.62 Closed fracture of sacrum and coccyx with other cauda equina injury

806.79 Open fracture of sacrum and coccyx with other spinal cord injury

808.41 Closed fracture of ilium

808.43 Multiple closed pelvic fractures with disruption of pelvic circle

808.51 Open fracture of ilium

808.53 Multiple open pelvic fractures with disruption of pelvic circle

839.42 Closed dislocation, sacrum

839.52 Open dislocation, sacrum

839.79 Open dislocation, other location

ICD-9-CM Procedural

79.29 Open reduction of fracture of other specified bone, except facial bones, without internal fixation

79.39 Open reduction of fracture of other specified bone, except facial bones, with internal fixation

79.89 Open reduction of dislocation of other specified site, except temporomandibular

27220-27222

27220 Closed treatment of acetabulum (hip socket) fracture(s); without manipulation

27222 with manipulation, with or without skeletal traction

ICD-9-CM Diagnostic

733.19 Pathologic fracture of other specified site

808.0 Closed fracture of acetabulum

ICD-9-CM Procedural

79.09 Closed reduction of fracture of other specified bone, except facial bones, without internal fixation

93.44 Other skeletal traction

93.46 Other skin traction of limbs

93.59 Other immobilization, pressure, and attention to wound

27226

27226 Open treatment of posterior or anterior acetabular wall fracture, with internal fixation

ICD-9-CM Diagnostic

733.19 Pathologic fracture of other specified site

808.0 Closed fracture of acetabulum

808.1 Open fracture of acetabulum

808.43 Multiple closed pelvic fractures with disruption of pelvic circle

808.53 Multiple open pelvic fractures with disruption of pelvic circle

ICD-9-CM Procedural

79.39 Open reduction of fracture of other specified bone, except facial bones, with internal fixation

27227

27227 Open treatment of acetabular fracture(s) involving anterior or posterior (1) column, or a fracture running transversely across the acetabulum, with internal fixation

ICD-9-CM Diagnostic

733.19 Pathologic fracture of other specified site

808.0 Closed fracture of acetabulum

808.1 Open fracture of acetabulum

808.43 Multiple closed pelvic fractures with disruption of pelvic circle

808.53 Multiple open pelvic fractures with disruption of pelvic circle

ICD-9-CM Procedural

79.39 Open reduction of fracture of other specified bone, except facial bones, with internal fixation

27228

27228 Open treatment of acetabular fracture(s) involving anterior and posterior (2) columns, includes T-fracture and both column fracture with complete articular detachment, or single column or transverse fracture with associated acetabular wall fracture, with internal fixation

ICD-9-CM Diagnostic

733.19 Pathologic fracture of other specified site
808.0 Closed fracture of acetabulum
808.1 Open fracture of acetabulum
808.43 Multiple closed pelvic fractures with disruption of pelvic circle
808.53 Multiple open pelvic fractures with disruption of pelvic circle
808.59 Open fracture of other specified part of pelvis

ICD-9-CM Procedural

79.39 Open reduction of fracture of other specified bone, except facial bones, with internal fixation

27230-27232

27230 Closed treatment of femoral fracture, proximal end, neck; without manipulation
27232 with manipulation, with or without skeletal traction

ICD-9-CM Diagnostic

733.14 Pathologic fracture of neck of femur
733.81 Malunion of fracture
820.00 Closed fracture of unspecified intracapsular section of neck of femur ▽
820.01 Closed fracture of epiphysis (separation) (upper) of neck of femur
820.02 Closed fracture of midcervical section of femur
820.03 Closed fracture of base of neck of femur
820.09 Other closed transcervical fracture of femur
820.8 Closed fracture of unspecified part of neck of femur ▽

ICD-9-CM Procedural

79.05 Closed reduction of fracture of femur without internal fixation
93.44 Other skeletal traction
93.46 Other skin traction of limbs
93.53 Application of other cast

27235

27235 Percutaneous skeletal fixation of femoral fracture, proximal end, neck

ICD-9-CM Diagnostic

733.14 Pathologic fracture of neck of femur
820.00 Closed fracture of unspecified intracapsular section of neck of femur ▽
820.01 Closed fracture of epiphysis (separation) (upper) of neck of femur
820.02 Closed fracture of midcervical section of femur
820.03 Closed fracture of base of neck of femur
820.09 Other closed transcervical fracture of femur
820.8 Closed fracture of unspecified part of neck of femur ▽

ICD-9-CM Procedural

78.55 Internal fixation of femur without fracture reduction
79.15 Closed reduction of fracture of femur with internal fixation

27236

27236 Open treatment of femoral fracture, proximal end, neck, internal fixation or prosthetic replacement

ICD-9-CM Diagnostic

733.14 Pathologic fracture of neck of femur
733.81 Malunion of fracture
820.01 Closed fracture of epiphysis (separation) (upper) of neck of femur
820.02 Closed fracture of midcervical section of femur
820.03 Closed fracture of base of neck of femur
820.09 Other closed transcervical fracture of femur
820.10 Open fracture of unspecified intracapsular section of neck of femur ▽
820.11 Open fracture of epiphysis (separation) (upper) of neck of femur
820.12 Open fracture of midcervical section of femur
820.13 Open fracture of base of neck of femur
820.19 Other open transcervical fracture of femur
820.8 Closed fracture of unspecified part of neck of femur ▽
820.9 Open fracture of unspecified part of neck of femur ▽
827.0 Other, multiple and ill-defined closed fractures of lower limb
827.1 Other, multiple and ill-defined open fractures of lower limb
828.0 Multiple closed fractures involving both lower limbs, lower with upper limb, and lower limb(s) with rib(s) and sternum
828.1 Multiple fractures involving both lower limbs, lower with upper limb, and lower limb(s) with rib(s) and sternum, open

ICD-9-CM Procedural

00.74 Hip bearing surface, metal-on-polyethylene
00.75 Hip bearing surface, metal-on-metal
00.76 Hip bearing surface, ceramic-on-ceramic
79.35 Open reduction of fracture of femur with internal fixation
81.52 Partial hip replacement

27238-27240

27238 Closed treatment of intertrochanteric, peritrochanteric, or subtrochanteric femoral fracture; without manipulation
27240 with manipulation, with or without skin or skeletal traction

ICD-9-CM Diagnostic

733.15 Pathologic fracture of other specified part of femur
820.20 Closed fracture of unspecified trochanteric section of femur ▽
820.21 Closed fracture of intertrochanteric section of femur
820.22 Closed fracture of subtrochanteric section of femur
820.8 Closed fracture of unspecified part of neck of femur ▽

ICD-9-CM Procedural

79.05 Closed reduction of fracture of femur without internal fixation
93.44 Other skeletal traction
93.46 Other skin traction of limbs
93.53 Application of other cast

27244-27245

27244 Treatment of intertrochanteric, peritrochanteric, or subtrochanteric femoral fracture; with plate/screw type implant, with or without cerclage
27245 with intramedullary implant, with or without interlocking screws and/or cerclage

ICD-9-CM Diagnostic

733.15 Pathologic fracture of other specified part of femur
733.81 Malunion of fracture
820.20 Closed fracture of unspecified trochanteric section of femur ▽
820.21 Closed fracture of intertrochanteric section of femur
820.22 Closed fracture of subtrochanteric section of femur
820.30 Open fracture of unspecified trochanteric section of femur ▽
820.31 Open fracture of intertrochanteric section of femur
820.32 Open fracture of subtrochanteric section of femur
827.0 Other, multiple and ill-defined closed fractures of lower limb
827.1 Other, multiple and ill-defined open fractures of lower limb
828.0 Multiple closed fractures involving both lower limbs, lower with upper limb, and lower limb(s) with rib(s) and sternum
828.1 Multiple fractures involving both lower limbs, lower with upper limb, and lower limb(s) with rib(s) and sternum, open
829.0 Closed fracture of unspecified bone ▽

ICD-9-CM Procedural
79.35 Open reduction of fracture of femur with internal fixation

27246-27248
27246 Closed treatment of greater trochanteric fracture, without manipulation
27248 Open treatment of greater trochanteric fracture, includes internal fixation, when performed

ICD-9-CM Diagnostic
733.15 Pathologic fracture of other specified part of femur
820.20 Closed fracture of unspecified trochanteric section of femur ▽
820.21 Closed fracture of intertrochanteric section of femur
820.22 Closed fracture of subtrochanteric section of femur
820.30 Open fracture of unspecified trochanteric section of femur ▽
820.31 Open fracture of intertrochanteric section of femur
820.32 Open fracture of subtrochanteric section of femur

ICD-9-CM Procedural
79.35 Open reduction of fracture of femur with internal fixation
93.53 Application of other cast

27250-27252
27250 Closed treatment of hip dislocation, traumatic; without anesthesia
27252 requiring anesthesia

ICD-9-CM Diagnostic
835.00 Closed dislocation of hip, unspecified site ▽
835.01 Closed posterior dislocation of hip
835.02 Closed obturator dislocation of hip
835.03 Other closed anterior dislocation of hip

ICD-9-CM Procedural
79.75 Closed reduction of dislocation of hip

HCPCS Level II Supplies & Services
A4570 Splint

27253
27253 Open treatment of hip dislocation, traumatic, without internal fixation

ICD-9-CM Diagnostic
835.01 Closed posterior dislocation of hip
835.02 Closed obturator dislocation of hip
835.03 Other closed anterior dislocation of hip
835.11 Open posterior dislocation of hip
835.12 Open obturator dislocation of hip
835.13 Other open anterior dislocation of hip

ICD-9-CM Procedural
79.85 Open reduction of dislocation of hip

27254
27254 Open treatment of hip dislocation, traumatic, with acetabular wall and femoral head fracture, with or without internal or external fixation

ICD-9-CM Diagnostic
733.15 Pathologic fracture of other specified part of femur
808.0 Closed fracture of acetabulum
808.1 Open fracture of acetabulum
808.43 Multiple closed pelvic fractures with disruption of pelvic circle
808.53 Multiple open pelvic fractures with disruption of pelvic circle
808.59 Open fracture of other specified part of pelvis
820.01 Closed fracture of epiphysis (separation) (upper) of neck of femur
820.02 Closed fracture of midcervical section of femur
820.09 Other closed transcervical fracture of femur
820.11 Open fracture of epiphysis (separation) (upper) of neck of femur
820.12 Open fracture of midcervical section of femur
820.19 Other open transcervical fracture of femur
820.8 Closed fracture of unspecified part of neck of femur ▽
820.9 Open fracture of unspecified part of neck of femur ▽
835.01 Closed posterior dislocation of hip
835.02 Closed obturator dislocation of hip
835.03 Other closed anterior dislocation of hip
835.11 Open posterior dislocation of hip
835.12 Open obturator dislocation of hip
835.13 Other open anterior dislocation of hip

ICD-9-CM Procedural
78.15 Application of external fixator device, femur
79.25 Open reduction of fracture of femur without internal fixation
79.35 Open reduction of fracture of femur with internal fixation
79.85 Open reduction of dislocation of hip
84.71 Application of external fixator device, monoplanar system
84.72 Application of external fixator device, ring system
84.73 Application of hybrid external fixator device

27256-27257
27256 Treatment of spontaneous hip dislocation (developmental, including congenital or pathological), by abduction, splint or traction; without anesthesia, without manipulation
27257 with manipulation, requiring anesthesia

ICD-9-CM Diagnostic
718.25 Pathological dislocation of pelvic region and thigh joint
718.35 Recurrent dislocation of pelvic region and thigh joint
736.31 Coxa valga (acquired)
754.30 Congenital dislocation of hip, unilateral
754.31 Congenital dislocation of hip, bilateral

ICD-9-CM Procedural
79.70 Closed reduction of dislocation of unspecified site
79.75 Closed reduction of dislocation of hip
79.79 Closed reduction of dislocation of other specified site, except temporomandibular
93.44 Other skeletal traction
93.46 Other skin traction of limbs
93.53 Application of other cast

HCPCS Level II Supplies & Services
A4305 Disposable drug delivery system, flow rate of 50 ml or greater per hour

27258-27259
27258 Open treatment of spontaneous hip dislocation (developmental, including congenital or pathological), replacement of femoral head in acetabulum (including tenotomy, etc);
27259 with femoral shaft shortening

ICD-9-CM Diagnostic
718.25 Pathological dislocation of pelvic region and thigh joint
718.35 Recurrent dislocation of pelvic region and thigh joint
718.75 Developmental dislocation of joint, pelvic region and thigh
736.31 Coxa valga (acquired)
754.30 Congenital dislocation of hip, unilateral
754.31 Congenital dislocation of hip, bilateral

ICD-9-CM Procedural
78.25 Limb shortening procedures, femur

79.85 Open reduction of dislocation of hip

27265-27266

27265 Closed treatment of post hip arthroplasty dislocation; without anesthesia
27266 requiring regional or general anesthesia

ICD-9-CM Diagnostic

718.35 Recurrent dislocation of pelvic region and thigh joint
835.00 Closed dislocation of hip, unspecified site
835.01 Closed posterior dislocation of hip
835.02 Closed obturator dislocation of hip
835.03 Other closed anterior dislocation of hip
996.42 Dislocation of prosthetic joint — (Use additional code to identify prosthetic joint with mechanical complication, V43.60-V43.69)
996.66 Infection and inflammatory reaction due to internal joint prosthesis — (Use additional code to identify specified infections. Use additional code to identify infected prosthetic joint: V43.60-V43.69)
996.77 Other complications due to internal joint prosthesis — (Use additional code to identify complication: 338.18-338.19, 338.28-338.29)

ICD-9-CM Procedural

79.75 Closed reduction of dislocation of hip

HCPCS Level II Supplies & Services

A4305 Disposable drug delivery system, flow rate of 50 ml or greater per hour

27267-27268

27267 Closed treatment of femoral fracture, proximal end, head; without manipulation
27268 with manipulation

ICD-9-CM Diagnostic

733.14 Pathologic fracture of neck of femur
733.15 Pathologic fracture of other specified part of femur
820.00 Closed fracture of unspecified intracapsular section of neck of femur
820.01 Closed fracture of epiphysis (separation) (upper) of neck of femur
820.02 Closed fracture of midcervical section of femur
820.03 Closed fracture of base of neck of femur
820.09 Other closed transcervical fracture of femur
820.10 Open fracture of unspecified intracapsular section of neck of femur
820.11 Open fracture of epiphysis (separation) (upper) of neck of femur
820.12 Open fracture of midcervical section of femur
820.13 Open fracture of base of neck of femur
820.19 Other open transcervical fracture of femur
820.20 Closed fracture of unspecified trochanteric section of femur
820.21 Closed fracture of intertrochanteric section of femur
820.22 Closed fracture of subtrochanteric section of femur
820.8 Closed fracture of unspecified part of neck of femur
820.9 Open fracture of unspecified part of neck of femur
821.00 Closed fracture of unspecified part of femur
827.0 Other, multiple and ill-defined closed fractures of lower limb
828.0 Multiple closed fractures involving both lower limbs, lower with upper limb, and lower limb(s) with rib(s) and sternum
905.3 Late effect of fracture of neck of femur

ICD-9-CM Procedural

79.05 Closed reduction of fracture of femur without internal fixation
79.15 Closed reduction of fracture of femur with internal fixation

27269

27269 Open treatment of femoral fracture, proximal end, head, includes internal fixation, when performed

ICD-9-CM Diagnostic

733.14 Pathologic fracture of neck of femur
733.15 Pathologic fracture of other specified part of femur
820.00 Closed fracture of unspecified intracapsular section of neck of femur
820.01 Closed fracture of epiphysis (separation) (upper) of neck of femur
820.02 Closed fracture of midcervical section of femur
820.03 Closed fracture of base of neck of femur
820.09 Other closed transcervical fracture of femur
820.10 Open fracture of unspecified intracapsular section of neck of femur
820.11 Open fracture of epiphysis (separation) (upper) of neck of femur
820.12 Open fracture of midcervical section of femur
820.13 Open fracture of base of neck of femur
820.19 Other open transcervical fracture of femur
820.20 Closed fracture of unspecified trochanteric section of femur
820.21 Closed fracture of intertrochanteric section of femur
820.22 Closed fracture of subtrochanteric section of femur
820.30 Open fracture of unspecified trochanteric section of femur
820.31 Open fracture of intertrochanteric section of femur
820.32 Open fracture of subtrochanteric section of femur
820.8 Closed fracture of unspecified part of neck of femur
820.9 Open fracture of unspecified part of neck of femur
821.10 Open fracture of unspecified part of femur
821.11 Open fracture of shaft of femur
827.0 Other, multiple and ill-defined closed fractures of lower limb
827.1 Other, multiple and ill-defined open fractures of lower limb
828.0 Multiple closed fractures involving both lower limbs, lower with upper limb, and lower limb(s) with rib(s) and sternum
828.1 Multiple fractures involving both lower limbs, lower with upper limb, and lower limb(s) with rib(s) and sternum, open
905.3 Late effect of fracture of neck of femur

ICD-9-CM Procedural

78.55 Internal fixation of femur without fracture reduction
79.25 Open reduction of fracture of femur without internal fixation
79.35 Open reduction of fracture of femur with internal fixation
79.65 Debridement of open fracture of femur

27275

27275 Manipulation, hip joint, requiring general anesthesia

ICD-9-CM Diagnostic

718.55 Ankylosis of pelvic region and thigh joint
718.56 Ankylosis of lower leg joint
996.40 Unspecified mechanical complication of internal orthopedic device, implant, and graft — (Use additional code to identify prosthetic joint with mechanical complication, V43.60-V43.69)
996.47 Other mechanical complication of prosthetic joint implant — (Use additional code to identify prosthetic joint with mechanical complication, V43.60-V43.69)
996.49 Other mechanical complication of other internal orthopedic device, implant, and graft — (Use additional code to identify prosthetic joint with mechanical complication, V43.60-V43.69)
996.77 Other complications due to internal joint prosthesis — (Use additional code to identify complication: 338.18-338.19, 338.28-338.29)
996.78 Other complications due to other internal orthopedic device, implant, and graft — (Use additional code to identify complication: 338.18-338.19, 338.28-338.29)

ICD-9-CM Procedural

93.26 Manual rupture of joint adhesions

93.29 Other forcible correction of musculoskeletal deformity

27280

27280 Arthrodesis, sacroiliac joint (including obtaining graft)

ICD-9-CM Diagnostic

357.1 Polyneuropathy in collagen vascular disease — (Code first underlying disease: 446.0, 710.0, 714.0) ⊠
359.6 Symptomatic inflammatory myopathy in diseases classified elsewhere — (Code first underlying disease: 135, 140.0-208.9, 277.30-277.39, 446.0, 710.0, 710.1, 710.2, 714.0) ⊠
446.0 Polyarteritis nodosa
710.0 Systemic lupus erythematosus — (Use additional code to identify manifestation: 424.91, 581.81, 582.81, 583.81)
710.1 Systemic sclerosis — (Use additional code to identify manifestation: 359.6, 517.2)
710.2 Sicca syndrome
714.0 Rheumatoid arthritis — (Use additional code to identify manifestation: 357.1, 359.6)
730.15 Chronic osteomyelitis, pelvic region and thigh — (Use additional code to identify organism: 041.1. Use additional code to identify major osseous defect, if applicable: 731.3)
731.3 Major osseous defects — (Code first underlying disease: 170.0-170.9, 730.00-730.29, 733.00-733.09, 733.40-733.49, 996.45)
808.43 Multiple closed pelvic fractures with disruption of pelvic circle
808.53 Multiple open pelvic fractures with disruption of pelvic circle
839.42 Closed dislocation, sacrum
839.52 Open dislocation, sacrum

ICD-9-CM Procedural

81.29 Arthrodesis of other specified joint

27282

27282 Arthrodesis, symphysis pubis (including obtaining graft)

ICD-9-CM Diagnostic

357.1 Polyneuropathy in collagen vascular disease — (Code first underlying disease: 446.0, 710.0, 714.0) ⊠
359.6 Symptomatic inflammatory myopathy in diseases classified elsewhere — (Code first underlying disease: 135, 140.0-208.9, 277.30-277.39, 446.0, 710.0, 710.1, 710.2, 714.0) ⊠
446.0 Polyarteritis nodosa
710.0 Systemic lupus erythematosus — (Use additional code to identify manifestation: 424.91, 581.81, 582.81, 583.81)
710.1 Systemic sclerosis — (Use additional code to identify manifestation: 359.6, 517.2)
710.2 Sicca syndrome
714.0 Rheumatoid arthritis — (Use additional code to identify manifestation: 357.1, 359.6)
730.15 Chronic osteomyelitis, pelvic region and thigh — (Use additional code to identify organism: 041.1. Use additional code to identify major osseous defect, if applicable: 731.3)
731.3 Major osseous defects — (Code first underlying disease: 170.0-170.9, 730.00-730.29, 733.00-733.09, 733.40-733.49, 996.45)
808.2 Closed fracture of pubis
808.3 Open fracture of pubis
808.43 Multiple closed pelvic fractures with disruption of pelvic circle
808.53 Multiple open pelvic fractures with disruption of pelvic circle
839.69 Closed dislocation, other location
839.79 Open dislocation, other location

ICD-9-CM Procedural

81.29 Arthrodesis of other specified joint

27284-27286

27284 Arthrodesis, hip joint (including obtaining graft);
27286 with subtrochanteric osteotomy

ICD-9-CM Diagnostic

715.35 Localized osteoarthrosis not specified whether primary or secondary, pelvic region and thigh
726.5 Enthesopathy of hip region
730.15 Chronic osteomyelitis, pelvic region and thigh — (Use additional code to identify organism: 041.1. Use additional code to identify major osseous defect, if applicable: 731.3)
731.3 Major osseous defects — (Code first underlying disease: 170.0-170.9, 730.00-730.29, 733.00-733.09, 733.40-733.49, 996.45)
733.42 Aseptic necrosis of head and neck of femur — (Use additional code to identify major osseous defect, if applicable: 731.3)
733.81 Malunion of fracture
733.82 Nonunion of fracture
808.0 Closed fracture of acetabulum
808.1 Open fracture of acetabulum
V88.21 Acquired absence of hip joint

ICD-9-CM Procedural

77.39 Other division of other bone, except facial bones
81.21 Arthrodesis of hip

27290

27290 Interpelviabdominal amputation (hindquarter amputation)

ICD-9-CM Diagnostic

158.8 Malignant neoplasm of specified parts of peritoneum
170.6 Malignant neoplasm of pelvic bones, sacrum, and coccyx
171.6 Malignant neoplasm of connective and other soft tissue of pelvis
195.3 Malignant neoplasm of pelvis
197.6 Secondary malignant neoplasm of retroperitoneum and peritoneum
198.5 Secondary malignant neoplasm of bone and bone marrow
200.06 Reticulosarcoma of intrapelvic lymph nodes
200.16 Lymphosarcoma of intrapelvic lymph nodes
209.73 Secondary neuroendocrine tumor of bone
730.15 Chronic osteomyelitis, pelvic region and thigh — (Use additional code to identify organism: 041.1. Use additional code to identify major osseous defect, if applicable: 731.3)
731.3 Major osseous defects — (Code first underlying disease: 170.0-170.9, 730.00-730.29, 733.00-733.09, 733.40-733.49, 996.45)
926.12 Crushing injury of buttock — (Use additional code to identify any associated injuries: 800-829, 850.0-854.1, 860.0-869.1)

ICD-9-CM Procedural

84.19 Abdominopelvic amputation

27295

27295 Disarticulation of hip

ICD-9-CM Diagnostic

170.7 Malignant neoplasm of long bones of lower limb
198.5 Secondary malignant neoplasm of bone and bone marrow
249.70 Secondary diabetes mellitus with peripheral circulatory disorders, not stated as uncontrolled, or unspecified — (Use additional code to identify manifestation: 443.81, 785.4) (Use additional code to identify any associated insulin use: V58.67)
249.71 Secondary diabetes mellitus with peripheral circulatory disorders, uncontrolled — (Use additional code to identify manifestation: 443.81, 785.4) (Use additional code to identify any associated insulin use: V58.67)
249.80 Secondary diabetes mellitus with other specified manifestations, not stated as uncontrolled, or unspecified — (Use additional code to identify manifestation:

707.10-707.19, 707.8, 707.9, 731.8) (Use additional code to identify any associated insulin use: V58.67)

249.81 Secondary diabetes mellitus with other specified manifestations, uncontrolled — (Use additional code to identify manifestation: 707.10-707.19, 707.8, 707.9, 731.8) (Use additional code to identify any associated insulin use: V58.67)

250.70 Diabetes with peripheral circulatory disorders, type II or unspecified type, not stated as uncontrolled — (Use additional code to identify manifestation: 443.81, 785.4)

250.71 Diabetes with peripheral circulatory disorders, type I [juvenile type], not stated as uncontrolled — (Use additional code to identify manifestation: 443.81, 785.4)

250.72 Diabetes with peripheral circulatory disorders, type II or unspecified type, uncontrolled — (Use additional code to identify manifestation: 443.81, 785.4)

250.73 Diabetes with peripheral circulatory disorders, type I [juvenile type], uncontrolled — (Use additional code to identify manifestation: 443.81, 785.4)

250.80 Diabetes with other specified manifestations, type II or unspecified type, not stated as uncontrolled — (Use additional code to identify manifestation: 707.10-707.19, 707.8, 707.9, 731.8)

250.81 Diabetes with other specified manifestations, type I [juvenile type], not stated as uncontrolled — (Use additional code to identify manifestation: 707.10-707.19, 707.8, 707.9, 731.8)

250.82 Diabetes with other specified manifestations, type II or unspecified type, uncontrolled — (Use additional code to identify manifestation: 707.10-707.19, 707.8, 707.9, 731.8)

250.83 Diabetes with other specified manifestations, type I [juvenile type], uncontrolled — (Use additional code to identify manifestation: 707.10-707.19, 707.8, 707.9, 731.8)

730.15 Chronic osteomyelitis, pelvic region and thigh — (Use additional code to identify organism: 041.1. Use additional code to identify major osseous defect, if applicable: 731.3)

731.3 Major osseous defects — (Code first underlying disease: 170.0-170.9, 730.00-730.29, 733.00-733.09, 733.40-733.49, 996.45)

731.8 Other bone involvement in diseases classified elsewhere — (Code first underlying disease: 249.8, 250.8. Use additional code to specify bone condition: 730.00-730.09) ☒

890.1 Open wound of hip and thigh, complicated

897.3 Traumatic amputation of leg(s) (complete) (partial), unilateral, at or above knee, complicated

897.5 Traumatic amputation of leg(s) (complete) (partial), unilateral, level not specified, complicated ▽

905.4 Late effect of fracture of lower extremities

928.01 Crushing injury of hip — (Use additional code to identify any associated injuries: 800-829, 850.0-854.1, 860.0-869.1)

ICD-9-CM Procedural

84.18 Disarticulation of hip

Femur (Thigh Region) and Knee Joint

27301

27301 Incision and drainage, deep abscess, bursa, or hematoma, thigh or knee region

ICD-9-CM Diagnostic

680.6 Carbuncle and furuncle of leg, except foot

682.6 Cellulitis and abscess of leg, except foot — (Use additional code to identify organism, such as 041.1, etc.)

686.9 Unspecified local infection of skin and subcutaneous tissue — (Use additional code to identify any infectious organism: 041.0-041.8) ▽

696.0 Psoriatic arthropathy

711.06 Pyogenic arthritis, lower leg — (Use additional code to identify infectious organism: 041.0-041.8)

726.60 Unspecified enthesopathy of knee ▽

726.65 Prepatellar bursitis

780.62 Postprocedural fever

890.0 Open wound of hip and thigh, without mention of complication

890.1 Open wound of hip and thigh, complicated

891.0 Open wound of knee, leg (except thigh), and ankle, without mention of complication

891.1 Open wound of knee, leg (except thigh), and ankle, complicated

904.8 Injury to unspecified blood vessel of lower extremity ▽

924.00 Contusion of thigh

924.11 Contusion of knee

928.11 Crushing injury of knee — (Use additional code to identify any associated injuries: 800-829, 850.0-854.1, 860.0-869.1)

958.3 Posttraumatic wound infection not elsewhere classified

996.66 Infection and inflammatory reaction due to internal joint prosthesis — (Use additional code to identify specified infections. Use additional code to identify infected prosthetic joint: V43.60-V43.69)

998.11 Hemorrhage complicating a procedure

998.31 Disruption of internal operation (surgical) wound

998.32 Disruption of external operation (surgical) wound

998.59 Other postoperative infection — (Use additional code to identify infection)

ICD-9-CM Procedural

83.02 Myotomy

83.03 Bursotomy

83.09 Other incision of soft tissue

HCPCS Level II Supplies & Services

A4305 Disposable drug delivery system, flow rate of 50 ml or greater per hour

27303

27303 Incision, deep, with opening of bone cortex, femur or knee (eg, osteomyelitis or bone abscess)

ICD-9-CM Diagnostic

198.5 Secondary malignant neoplasm of bone and bone marrow

213.7 Benign neoplasm of long bones of lower limb

711.05 Pyogenic arthritis, pelvic region and thigh — (Use additional code to identify infectious organism: 041.0-041.8)

711.06 Pyogenic arthritis, lower leg — (Use additional code to identify infectious organism: 041.0-041.8)

730.05 Acute osteomyelitis, pelvic region and thigh — (Use additional code to identify organism: 041.1. Use additional code to identify major osseous defect, if applicable: 731.3)

730.06 Acute osteomyelitis, lower leg — (Use additional code to identify organism: 041.1. Use additional code to identify major osseous defect, if applicable: 731.3)

730.15 Chronic osteomyelitis, pelvic region and thigh — (Use additional code to identify organism: 041.1. Use additional code to identify major osseous defect, if applicable: 731.3)

730.16 Chronic osteomyelitis, lower leg — (Use additional code to identify organism: 041.1. Use additional code to identify major osseous defect, if applicable: 731.3)

730.25 Unspecified osteomyelitis, pelvic region and thigh — (Use additional code to identify organism: 041.1. Use additional code to identify major osseous defect, if applicable: 731.3) ▽

730.26 Unspecified osteomyelitis, lower leg — (Use additional code to identify organism: 041.1. Use additional code to identify major osseous defect, if applicable: 731.3) ▽

730.95 Unspecified infection of bone, pelvic region and thigh — (Use additional code to identify organism: 041.1) ▽

730.96 Unspecified infection of bone, lower leg — (Use additional code to identify organism: 041.1) ▽

731.3 Major osseous defects — (Code first underlying disease: 170.0-170.9, 730.00-730.29, 733.00-733.09, 733.40-733.49, 996.45)

733.20 Unspecified cyst of bone (localized) ▽

733.22 Aneurysmal bone cyst

733.49 Aseptic necrosis of other bone site — (Use additional code to identify major osseous defect, if applicable: 731.3)

996.66 Infection and inflammatory reaction due to internal joint prosthesis — (Use additional code to identify specified infections. Use additional code to identify infected prosthetic joint: V43.60-V43.69)
996.67 Infection and inflammatory reaction due to other internal orthopedic device, implant, and graft — (Use additional code to identify specified infections)
998.59 Other postoperative infection — (Use additional code to identify infection)

ICD-9-CM Procedural

77.15 Other incision of femur without division
77.16 Other incision of patella without division
77.17 Other incision of tibia and fibula without division

27305

27305 Fasciotomy, iliotibial (tenotomy), open

ICD-9-CM Diagnostic

716.16 Traumatic arthropathy, lower leg
726.69 Other enthesopathy of knee
726.72 Tibialis tendinitis
727.09 Other synovitis and tenosynovitis
727.81 Contracture of tendon (sheath)
728.88 Rhabdomyolysis
729.72 Nontraumatic compartment syndrome of lower extremity — (Code first, if applicable, postprocedural complication: 998.89)
736.41 Genu valgum (acquired)
836.51 Closed anterior dislocation of tibia, proximal end
836.52 Closed posterior dislocation of tibia, proximal end
836.61 Open anterior dislocation of tibia, proximal end
836.62 Open posterior dislocation of tibia, proximal end
844.8 Sprain and strain of other specified sites of knee and leg
844.9 Sprain and strain of unspecified site of knee and leg ▽
891.2 Open wound of knee, leg (except thigh), and ankle, with tendon involvement
958.8 Other early complications of trauma
958.92 Traumatic compartment syndrome of lower extremity

ICD-9-CM Procedural

83.14 Fasciotomy

27306-27307

27306 Tenotomy, percutaneous, adductor or hamstring; single tendon (separate procedure)
27307 multiple tendons

ICD-9-CM Diagnostic

359.6 Symptomatic inflammatory myopathy in diseases classified elsewhere — (Code first underlying disease: 135, 140.0-208.9, 277.30-277.39, 446.0, 710.0, 710.1, 710.2, 714.0) ☒
446.0 Polyarteritis nodosa
710.0 Systemic lupus erythematosus — (Use additional code to identify manifestation: 424.91, 581.81, 582.81, 583.81)
710.1 Systemic sclerosis — (Use additional code to identify manifestation: 359.6, 517.2)
711.05 Pyogenic arthritis, pelvic region and thigh — (Use additional code to identify infectious organism: 041.0-041.8)
714.0 Rheumatoid arthritis — (Use additional code to identify manifestation: 357.1, 359.6)
726.69 Other enthesopathy of knee
727.89 Other disorders of synovium, tendon, and bursa
755.60 Unspecified congenital anomaly of lower limb ▽
755.61 Congenital coxa valga
755.62 Congenital coxa vara
890.2 Open wound of hip and thigh, with tendon involvement
905.8 Late effect of tendon injury
928.01 Crushing injury of hip — (Use additional code to identify any associated injuries: 800-829, 850.0-854.1, 860.0-869.1)
928.11 Crushing injury of knee — (Use additional code to identify any associated injuries: 800-829, 850.0-854.1, 860.0-869.1)
996.67 Infection and inflammatory reaction due to other internal orthopedic device, implant, and graft — (Use additional code to identify specified infections)

ICD-9-CM Procedural

83.12 Adductor tenotomy of hip
83.13 Other tenotomy

27310

27310 Arthrotomy, knee, with exploration, drainage, or removal of foreign body (eg, infection)

ICD-9-CM Diagnostic

711.06 Pyogenic arthritis, lower leg — (Use additional code to identify infectious organism: 041.0-041.8)
719.46 Pain in joint, lower leg
726.60 Unspecified enthesopathy of knee ▽
891.0 Open wound of knee, leg (except thigh), and ankle, without mention of complication
891.1 Open wound of knee, leg (except thigh), and ankle, complicated
996.66 Infection and inflammatory reaction due to internal joint prosthesis — (Use additional code to identify specified infections. Use additional code to identify infected prosthetic joint: V43.60-V43.69)
996.67 Infection and inflammatory reaction due to other internal orthopedic device, implant, and graft — (Use additional code to identify specified infections)
998.4 Foreign body accidentally left during procedure, not elsewhere classified
998.59 Other postoperative infection — (Use additional code to identify infection)

ICD-9-CM Procedural

80.16 Other arthrotomy of knee

27323-27324

27323 Biopsy, soft tissue of thigh or knee area; superficial
27324 deep (subfascial or intramuscular)

ICD-9-CM Diagnostic

171.3 Malignant neoplasm of connective and other soft tissue of lower limb, including hip
172.7 Malignant melanoma of skin of lower limb, including hip
195.5 Malignant neoplasm of lower limb
198.89 Secondary malignant neoplasm of other specified sites
214.1 Lipoma of other skin and subcutaneous tissue
215.3 Other benign neoplasm of connective and other soft tissue of lower limb, including hip
238.1 Neoplasm of uncertain behavior of connective and other soft tissue
239.2 Neoplasms of unspecified nature of bone, soft tissue, and skin
355.2 Other lesion of femoral nerve
359.6 Symptomatic inflammatory myopathy in diseases classified elsewhere — (Code first underlying disease: 135, 140.0-208.9, 277.30-277.39, 446.0, 710.0, 710.1, 710.2, 714.0) ☒
446.0 Polyarteritis nodosa
682.6 Cellulitis and abscess of leg, except foot — (Use additional code to identify organism, such as 041.1, etc.)
696.1 Other psoriasis
709.4 Foreign body granuloma of skin and subcutaneous tissue — (Use additional code to identify foreign body (V90.01-V90.9))
710.0 Systemic lupus erythematosus — (Use additional code to identify manifestation: 424.91, 581.81, 582.81, 583.81)
710.1 Systemic sclerosis — (Use additional code to identify manifestation: 359.6, 517.2)
710.2 Sicca syndrome
710.4 Polymyositis
710.9 Unspecified diffuse connective tissue disease ▽
714.0 Rheumatoid arthritis — (Use additional code to identify manifestation: 357.1, 359.6)
727.51 Synovial cyst of popliteal space

728.82 Foreign body granuloma of muscle — (Use additional code to identify foreign body (V90.01-V90.9))
728.89 Other disorder of muscle, ligament, and fascia — (Use additional E code to identify drug, if drug-induced)
730.26 Unspecified osteomyelitis, lower leg — (Use additional code to identify organism: 041.1. Use additional code to identify major osseous defect, if applicable: 731.3) ▽
731.3 Major osseous defects — (Code first underlying disease: 170.0-170.9, 730.00-730.29, 733.00-733.09, 733.40-733.49, 996.45)
733.90 Disorder of bone and cartilage, unspecified ▽
782.2 Localized superficial swelling, mass, or lump

ICD-9-CM Procedural

83.21 Open biopsy of soft tissue

27325

27325 Neurectomy, hamstring muscle

ICD-9-CM Diagnostic

249.60 Secondary diabetes mellitus with neurological manifestations, not stated as uncontrolled, or unspecified — (Use additional code to identify manifestation: 337.1, 353.5, 354.0-355.9, 357.2, 536.3, 713.5) (Use additional code to identify any associated insulin use: V58.67)
249.61 Secondary diabetes mellitus with neurological manifestations, uncontrolled — (Use additional code to identify manifestation: 337.1, 353.5, 354.0-355.9, 357.2, 536.3, 713.5) (Use additional code to identify any associated insulin use: V58.67)
250.60 Diabetes with neurological manifestations, type II or unspecified type, not stated as uncontrolled — (Use additional code to identify manifestation: 337.1, 353.5, 354.0-355.9, 357.2, 536.3, 713.5)
250.61 Diabetes with neurological manifestations, type I [juvenile type], not stated as uncontrolled — (Use additional code to identify manifestation: 337.1, 353.5, 354.0-355.9, 357.2, 536.3, 713.5)
250.62 Diabetes with neurological manifestations, type II or unspecified type, uncontrolled — (Use additional code to identify manifestation: 337.1, 353.5, 354.0-355.9, 357.2, 536.3, 713.5)
250.63 Diabetes with neurological manifestations, type I [juvenile type], uncontrolled — (Use additional code to identify manifestation: 337.1, 353.5, 354.0-355.9, 357.2, 536.3, 713.5)
336.0 Syringomyelia and syringobulbia
337.1 Peripheral autonomic neuropathy in disorders classified elsewhere — (Code first underlying disease: 249.6, 250.6, 277.30-277.39) ☒
355.1 Meralgia paresthetica
355.2 Other lesion of femoral nerve
355.71 Causalgia of lower limb
355.79 Other mononeuritis of lower limb
357.2 Polyneuropathy in diabetes — (Code first underlying disease: 249.6, 250.6) ☒
713.5 Arthropathy associated with neurological disorders — (Code first underlying disease: 094.0, 249.6, 250.6, 336.0) ☒
727.42 Ganglion of tendon sheath
729.2 Unspecified neuralgia, neuritis, and radiculitis ▽

ICD-9-CM Procedural

04.07 Other excision or avulsion of cranial and peripheral nerves

27326

27326 Neurectomy, popliteal (gastrocnemius)

ICD-9-CM Diagnostic

249.60 Secondary diabetes mellitus with neurological manifestations, not stated as uncontrolled, or unspecified — (Use additional code to identify manifestation: 337.1, 353.5, 354.0-355.9, 357.2, 536.3, 713.5) (Use additional code to identify any associated insulin use: V58.67)
249.61 Secondary diabetes mellitus with neurological manifestations, uncontrolled — (Use additional code to identify manifestation: 337.1, 353.5, 354.0-355.9, 357.2, 536.3, 713.5) (Use additional code to identify any associated insulin use: V58.67)
250.60 Diabetes with neurological manifestations, type II or unspecified type, not stated as uncontrolled — (Use additional code to identify manifestation: 337.1, 353.5, 354.0-355.9, 357.2, 536.3, 713.5)
250.61 Diabetes with neurological manifestations, type I [juvenile type], not stated as uncontrolled — (Use additional code to identify manifestation: 337.1, 353.5, 354.0-355.9, 357.2, 536.3, 713.5)
250.62 Diabetes with neurological manifestations, type II or unspecified type, uncontrolled — (Use additional code to identify manifestation: 337.1, 353.5, 354.0-355.9, 357.2, 536.3, 713.5)
250.63 Diabetes with neurological manifestations, type I [juvenile type], uncontrolled — (Use additional code to identify manifestation: 337.1, 353.5, 354.0-355.9, 357.2, 536.3, 713.5)
336.0 Syringomyelia and syringobulbia
355.1 Meralgia paresthetica
355.2 Other lesion of femoral nerve
355.3 Lesion of lateral popliteal nerve
355.4 Lesion of medial popliteal nerve
355.71 Causalgia of lower limb
355.79 Other mononeuritis of lower limb
713.5 Arthropathy associated with neurological disorders — (Code first underlying disease: 094.0, 249.6, 250.6, 336.0) ☒
727.42 Ganglion of tendon sheath
729.2 Unspecified neuralgia, neuritis, and radiculitis ▽

ICD-9-CM Procedural

04.07 Other excision or avulsion of cranial and peripheral nerves

27327-27364 [27329, 27337, 27339]

27327 Excision, tumor, soft tissue of thigh or knee area, subcutaneous; less than 3 cm
27328 Excision, tumor, soft tissue of thigh or knee area, subfascial (eg, intramuscular); less than 5 cm
27329 Radical resection of tumor (eg, sarcoma), soft tissue of thigh or knee area; less than 5 cm
27337 3 cm or greater
27339 5 cm or greater
27364 5 cm or greater

ICD-9-CM Diagnostic

171.3 Malignant neoplasm of connective and other soft tissue of lower limb, including hip
173.70 Unspecified malignant neoplasm of skin of lower limb, including hip ▽
173.71 Basal cell carcinoma of skin of lower limb, including hip
173.72 Squamous cell carcinoma of skin of lower limb, including hip
173.79 Other specified malignant neoplasm of skin of lower limb, including hip
195.5 Malignant neoplasm of lower limb
198.89 Secondary malignant neoplasm of other specified sites
209.34 Merkel cell carcinoma of the lower limb
209.75 Secondary Merkel cell carcinoma
214.1 Lipoma of other skin and subcutaneous tissue
214.8 Lipoma of other specified sites
215.3 Other benign neoplasm of connective and other soft tissue of lower limb, including hip
228.1 Lymphangioma, any site
238.1 Neoplasm of uncertain behavior of connective and other soft tissue
239.2 Neoplasms of unspecified nature of bone, soft tissue, and skin
782.2 Localized superficial swelling, mass, or lump

ICD-9-CM Procedural

83.31 Excision of lesion of tendon sheath
83.32 Excision of lesion of muscle

83.39 Excision of lesion of other soft tissue
83.49 Other excision of soft tissue
86.3 Other local excision or destruction of lesion or tissue of skin and subcutaneous tissue
86.4 Radical excision of skin lesion

HCPCS Level II Supplies & Services

A4305 Disposable drug delivery system, flow rate of 50 ml or greater per hour

27330-27331

27330 Arthrotomy, knee; with synovial biopsy only
27331 including joint exploration, biopsy, or removal of loose or foreign bodies

ICD-9-CM Diagnostic

171.3 Malignant neoplasm of connective and other soft tissue of lower limb, including hip
198.89 Secondary malignant neoplasm of other specified sites
215.3 Other benign neoplasm of connective and other soft tissue of lower limb, including hip
238.1 Neoplasm of uncertain behavior of connective and other soft tissue
239.2 Neoplasms of unspecified nature of bone, soft tissue, and skin
275.40 Unspecified disorder of calcium metabolism — (Use additional code to identify any associated intellectual disabilities) ▽
275.42 Hypercalcemia — (Use additional code to identify any associated intellectual disabilities)
275.49 Other disorders of calcium metabolism — (Use additional code to identify any associated intellectual disabilities)
275.5 Hungry bone syndrome — (Use additional code to identify any associated intellectual disabilities)
711.06 Pyogenic arthritis, lower leg — (Use additional code to identify infectious organism: 041.0-041.8)
712.96 Unspecified crystal arthropathy, lower leg ▽
714.9 Unspecified inflammatory polyarthropathy ▽
715.96 Osteoarthrosis, unspecified whether generalized or localized, lower leg ▽
717.5 Derangement of meniscus, not elsewhere classified
717.6 Loose body in knee
717.9 Unspecified internal derangement of knee ▽
718.46 Contracture of lower leg joint
718.76 Developmental dislocation of joint, lower leg
719.26 Villonodular synovitis, lower leg
719.46 Pain in joint, lower leg
719.66 Other symptoms referable to lower leg joint
727.50 Unspecified rupture of synovium ▽
727.51 Synovial cyst of popliteal space
727.83 Plica syndrome
727.89 Other disorders of synovium, tendon, and bursa
732.7 Osteochondritis dissecans
836.2 Other tear of cartilage or meniscus of knee, current
891.1 Open wound of knee, leg (except thigh), and ankle, complicated
996.40 Unspecified mechanical complication of internal orthopedic device, implant, and graft — (Use additional code to identify prosthetic joint with mechanical complication, V43.60-V43.69) ▽
996.47 Other mechanical complication of prosthetic joint implant — (Use additional code to identify prosthetic joint with mechanical complication, V43.60-V43.69)
996.49 Other mechanical complication of other internal orthopedic device, implant, and graft — (Use additional code to identify prosthetic joint with mechanical complication, V43.60-V43.69)
996.66 Infection and inflammatory reaction due to internal joint prosthesis — (Use additional code to identify specified infections. Use additional code to identify infected prosthetic joint: V43.60-V43.69)
996.67 Infection and inflammatory reaction due to other internal orthopedic device, implant, and graft — (Use additional code to identify specified infections)
996.77 Other complications due to internal joint prosthesis — (Use additional code to identify complication: 338.18-338.19, 338.28-338.29)
996.78 Other complications due to other internal orthopedic device, implant, and graft — (Use additional code to identify complication: 338.18-338.19, 338.28-338.29)
V64.43 Arthroscopic surgical procedure converted to open procedure

ICD-9-CM Procedural

80.16 Other arthrotomy of knee
80.36 Biopsy of joint structure of knee

27332-27333

27332 Arthrotomy, with excision of semilunar cartilage (meniscectomy) knee; medial OR lateral
27333 medial AND lateral

ICD-9-CM Diagnostic

717.0 Old bucket handle tear of medial meniscus
717.1 Derangement of anterior horn of medial meniscus
717.2 Derangement of posterior horn of medial meniscus
717.3 Other and unspecified derangement of medial meniscus ▽
717.40 Unspecified derangement of lateral meniscus ▽
717.41 Bucket handle tear of lateral meniscus
717.42 Derangement of anterior horn of lateral meniscus
717.43 Derangement of posterior horn of lateral meniscus
717.49 Other derangement of lateral meniscus
717.5 Derangement of meniscus, not elsewhere classified
717.9 Unspecified internal derangement of knee ▽
718.76 Developmental dislocation of joint, lower leg
719.66 Other symptoms referable to lower leg joint
719.86 Other specified disorders of lower leg joint
719.96 Unspecified disorder of lower leg joint ▽
836.0 Tear of medial cartilage or meniscus of knee, current
836.1 Tear of lateral cartilage or meniscus of knee, current
836.2 Other tear of cartilage or meniscus of knee, current
836.50 Closed dislocation of knee, unspecified part ▽
836.51 Closed anterior dislocation of tibia, proximal end
836.52 Closed posterior dislocation of tibia, proximal end
836.53 Closed medial dislocation of tibia, proximal end
836.54 Closed lateral dislocation of tibia, proximal end
836.59 Other closed dislocation of knee
959.7 Injury, other and unspecified, knee, leg, ankle, and foot
V64.43 Arthroscopic surgical procedure converted to open procedure

ICD-9-CM Procedural

80.6 Excision of semilunar cartilage of knee
81.42 Five-in-one repair of knee
81.43 Triad knee repair

27334-27335

27334 Arthrotomy, with synovectomy, knee; anterior OR posterior
27335 anterior AND posterior including popliteal area

ICD-9-CM Diagnostic

711.06 Pyogenic arthritis, lower leg — (Use additional code to identify infectious organism: 041.0-041.8)
714.9 Unspecified inflammatory polyarthropathy ▽
715.96 Osteoarthrosis, unspecified whether generalized or localized, lower leg ▽
719.26 Villonodular synovitis, lower leg
719.46 Pain in joint, lower leg
726.60 Unspecified enthesopathy of knee ▽
726.65 Prepatellar bursitis

727.41 Ganglion of joint
727.42 Ganglion of tendon sheath
727.83 Plica syndrome
727.89 Other disorders of synovium, tendon, and bursa
727.9 Unspecified disorder of synovium, tendon, and bursa ▽
V64.43 Arthroscopic surgical procedure converted to open procedure

ICD-9-CM Procedural

80.76 Synovectomy of knee

27340

27340 Excision, prepatellar bursa

ICD-9-CM Diagnostic

726.60 Unspecified enthesopathy of knee ▽
726.65 Prepatellar bursitis
727.3 Other bursitis disorders
727.83 Plica syndrome
727.89 Other disorders of synovium, tendon, and bursa
782.2 Localized superficial swelling, mass, or lump

ICD-9-CM Procedural

83.5 Bursectomy

27345

27345 Excision of synovial cyst of popliteal space (eg, Baker's cyst)

ICD-9-CM Diagnostic

727.51 Synovial cyst of popliteal space

ICD-9-CM Procedural

83.39 Excision of lesion of other soft tissue

27347

27347 Excision of lesion of meniscus or capsule (eg, cyst, ganglion), knee

ICD-9-CM Diagnostic

717.0 Old bucket handle tear of medial meniscus
717.1 Derangement of anterior horn of medial meniscus
717.2 Derangement of posterior horn of medial meniscus
717.3 Other and unspecified derangement of medial meniscus ▽
717.40 Unspecified derangement of lateral meniscus ▽
717.41 Bucket handle tear of lateral meniscus
717.42 Derangement of anterior horn of lateral meniscus
717.43 Derangement of posterior horn of lateral meniscus
717.49 Other derangement of lateral meniscus
717.5 Derangement of meniscus, not elsewhere classified
727.40 Unspecified synovial cyst ▽
727.41 Ganglion of joint

ICD-9-CM Procedural

80.6 Excision of semilunar cartilage of knee
80.96 Other excision of knee joint

27350

27350 Patellectomy or hemipatellectomy

ICD-9-CM Diagnostic

713.8 Arthropathy associated with other conditions classifiable elsewhere — (Code first underlying disease as conditions classifiable elsewhere except as in: 711.1-711.8, 712, 713.0-713.7) ☒
715.16 Primary localized osteoarthrosis, lower leg
715.36 Localized osteoarthrosis not specified whether primary or secondary, lower leg
715.96 Osteoarthrosis, unspecified whether generalized or localized, lower leg ▽
717.7 Chondromalacia of patella
717.81 Old disruption of lateral collateral ligament
718.76 Developmental dislocation of joint, lower leg
727.65 Nontraumatic rupture of quadriceps tendon
730.16 Chronic osteomyelitis, lower leg — (Use additional code to identify organism: 041.1. Use additional code to identify major osseous defect, if applicable: 731.3)
731.3 Major osseous defects — (Code first underlying disease: 170.0-170.9, 730.00-730.29, 733.00-733.09, 733.40-733.49, 996.45)
755.64 Congenital deformity of knee (joint)
822.0 Closed fracture of patella
822.1 Open fracture of patella
836.3 Closed dislocation of patella
836.4 Open dislocation of patella
996.40 Unspecified mechanical complication of internal orthopedic device, implant, and graft — (Use additional code to identify prosthetic joint with mechanical complication, V43.60-V43.69) ▽
996.47 Other mechanical complication of prosthetic joint implant — (Use additional code to identify prosthetic joint with mechanical complication, V43.60-V43.69)
996.49 Other mechanical complication of other internal orthopedic device, implant, and graft — (Use additional code to identify prosthetic joint with mechanical complication, V43.60-V43.69)
996.66 Infection and inflammatory reaction due to internal joint prosthesis — (Use additional code to identify specified infections. Use additional code to identify infected prosthetic joint: V43.60-V43.69)
996.67 Infection and inflammatory reaction due to other internal orthopedic device, implant, and graft — (Use additional code to identify specified infections)
996.77 Other complications due to internal joint prosthesis — (Use additional code to identify complication: 338.18-338.19, 338.28-338.29)
996.78 Other complications due to other internal orthopedic device, implant, and graft — (Use additional code to identify complication: 338.18-338.19, 338.28-338.29)

ICD-9-CM Procedural

77.86 Other partial ostectomy of patella
77.96 Total ostectomy of patella

27355-27358

27355 Excision or curettage of bone cyst or benign tumor of femur;
27356 with allograft
27357 with autograft (includes obtaining graft)
27358 with internal fixation (List in addition to code for primary procedure)

ICD-9-CM Diagnostic

213.7 Benign neoplasm of long bones of lower limb
238.0 Neoplasm of uncertain behavior of bone and articular cartilage
239.2 Neoplasms of unspecified nature of bone, soft tissue, and skin
733.21 Solitary bone cyst
733.29 Other cyst of bone
733.90 Disorder of bone and cartilage, unspecified ▽
756.4 Chondrodystrophy

ICD-9-CM Procedural

77.65 Local excision of lesion or tissue of femur
77.79 Excision of other bone for graft, except facial bones
78.05 Bone graft of femur
78.55 Internal fixation of femur without fracture reduction

27360

27360 Partial excision (craterization, saucerization, or diaphysectomy) bone, femur, proximal tibia and/or fibula (eg, osteomyelitis or bone abscess)

ICD-9-CM Diagnostic

730.06 Acute osteomyelitis, lower leg — (Use additional code to identify organism: 041.1. Use additional code to identify major osseous defect, if applicable: 731.3)

730.16 Chronic osteomyelitis, lower leg — (Use additional code to identify organism: 041.1. Use additional code to identify major osseous defect, if applicable: 731.3)

730.25 Unspecified osteomyelitis, pelvic region and thigh — (Use additional code to identify organism: 041.1. Use additional code to identify major osseous defect, if applicable: 731.3) ▽

730.26 Unspecified osteomyelitis, lower leg — (Use additional code to identify organism: 041.1. Use additional code to identify major osseous defect, if applicable: 731.3) ▽

730.35 Periostitis, without mention of osteomyelitis, pelvic region and thigh — (Use additional code to identify organism: 041.1)

730.36 Periostitis, without mention of osteomyelitis, lower leg — (Use additional code to identify organism: 041.1)

730.95 Unspecified infection of bone, pelvic region and thigh — (Use additional code to identify organism: 041.1) ▽

730.96 Unspecified infection of bone, lower leg — (Use additional code to identify organism: 041.1) ▽

731.3 Major osseous defects — (Code first underlying disease: 170.0-170.9, 730.00-730.29, 733.00-733.09, 733.40-733.49, 996.45)

732.4 Juvenile osteochondrosis of lower extremity, excluding foot

732.6 Other juvenile osteochondrosis

732.9 Unspecified osteochondropathy ▽

733.40 Aseptic necrosis of bone, site unspecified — (Use additional code to identify major osseous defect, if applicable: 731.3) ▽

733.92 Chondromalacia

ICD-9-CM Procedural

77.85 Other partial ostectomy of femur

77.87 Other partial ostectomy of tibia and fibula

27365

27365 Radical resection of tumor, femur or knee

ICD-9-CM Diagnostic

170.7 Malignant neoplasm of long bones of lower limb

170.8 Malignant neoplasm of short bones of lower limb

195.5 Malignant neoplasm of lower limb

198.5 Secondary malignant neoplasm of bone and bone marrow

209.73 Secondary neuroendocrine tumor of bone

213.7 Benign neoplasm of long bones of lower limb

213.8 Benign neoplasm of short bones of lower limb

229.8 Benign neoplasm of other specified sites

238.0 Neoplasm of uncertain behavior of bone and articular cartilage

238.8 Neoplasm of uncertain behavior of other specified sites

239.2 Neoplasms of unspecified nature of bone, soft tissue, and skin

ICD-9-CM Procedural

77.65 Local excision of lesion or tissue of femur

77.66 Local excision of lesion or tissue of patella

77.67 Local excision of lesion or tissue of tibia and fibula

77.85 Other partial ostectomy of femur

77.86 Other partial ostectomy of patella

77.95 Total ostectomy of femur

77.96 Total ostectomy of patella

27370

27370 Injection procedure for knee arthrography

ICD-9-CM Diagnostic

275.40 Unspecified disorder of calcium metabolism — (Use additional code to identify any associated intellectual disabilities) ▽

275.42 Hypercalcemia — (Use additional code to identify any associated intellectual disabilities)

275.49 Other disorders of calcium metabolism — (Use additional code to identify any associated intellectual disabilities)

275.5 Hungry bone syndrome — (Use additional code to identify any associated intellectual disabilities)

357.1 Polyneuropathy in collagen vascular disease — (Code first underlying disease: 446.0, 710.0, 714.0) ☒

359.6 Symptomatic inflammatory myopathy in diseases classified elsewhere — (Code first underlying disease: 135, 140.0-208.9, 277.30-277.39, 446.0, 710.0, 710.1, 710.2, 714.0) ☒

446.0 Polyarteritis nodosa

710.0 Systemic lupus erythematosus — (Use additional code to identify manifestation: 424.91, 581.81, 582.81, 583.81)

710.1 Systemic sclerosis — (Use additional code to identify manifestation: 359.6, 517.2)

710.2 Sicca syndrome

714.0 Rheumatoid arthritis — (Use additional code to identify manifestation: 357.1, 359.6)

715.16 Primary localized osteoarthrosis, lower leg

715.96 Osteoarthrosis, unspecified whether generalized or localized, lower leg ▽

716.96 Unspecified arthropathy, lower leg ▽

717.1 Derangement of anterior horn of medial meniscus

717.42 Derangement of anterior horn of lateral meniscus

717.6 Loose body in knee

718.76 Developmental dislocation of joint, lower leg

719.06 Effusion of lower leg joint

719.16 Hemarthrosis, lower leg

719.26 Villonodular synovitis, lower leg

719.36 Palindromic rheumatism, lower leg

719.46 Pain in joint, lower leg

719.56 Stiffness of joint, not elsewhere classified, lower leg

719.86 Other specified disorders of lower leg joint

719.96 Unspecified disorder of lower leg joint ▽

725 Polymyalgia rheumatica

836.2 Other tear of cartilage or meniscus of knee, current

836.50 Closed dislocation of knee, unspecified part ▽

836.60 Open dislocation of knee unspecified part ▽

ICD-9-CM Procedural

81.99 Other operations on joint structures

88.32 Contrast arthrogram

27372

27372 Removal of foreign body, deep, thigh region or knee area

ICD-9-CM Diagnostic

709.4 Foreign body granuloma of skin and subcutaneous tissue — (Use additional code to identify foreign body (V90.01-V90.9))

717.6 Loose body in knee

728.82 Foreign body granuloma of muscle — (Use additional code to identify foreign body (V90.01-V90.9))

729.6 Residual foreign body in soft tissue — (Use additional code to identify foreign body (V90.01-V90.9))

890.1 Open wound of hip and thigh, complicated

891.1 Open wound of knee, leg (except thigh), and ankle, complicated

916.6 Hip, thigh, leg, and ankle, superficial foreign body (splinter), without major open wound and without mention of infection
998.4 Foreign body accidentally left during procedure, not elsewhere classified

ICD-9-CM Procedural

83.02 Myotomy
83.09 Other incision of soft tissue
98.29 Removal of foreign body without incision from lower limb, except foot

27380-27381

27380 Suture of infrapatellar tendon; primary
27381 secondary reconstruction, including fascial or tendon graft

ICD-9-CM Diagnostic

717.89 Other internal derangement of knee
718.36 Recurrent dislocation of lower leg joint
727.66 Nontraumatic rupture of patellar tendon
822.0 Closed fracture of patella
822.1 Open fracture of patella
844.8 Sprain and strain of other specified sites of knee and leg
891.2 Open wound of knee, leg (except thigh), and ankle, with tendon involvement

ICD-9-CM Procedural

83.62 Delayed suture of tendon
83.64 Other suture of tendon
83.81 Tendon graft
83.82 Graft of muscle or fascia

27385-27386

27385 Suture of quadriceps or hamstring muscle rupture; primary
27386 secondary reconstruction, including fascial or tendon graft

ICD-9-CM Diagnostic

727.65 Nontraumatic rupture of quadriceps tendon
821.01 Closed fracture of shaft of femur
822.0 Closed fracture of patella
843.8 Sprain and strain of other specified sites of hip and thigh
844.8 Sprain and strain of other specified sites of knee and leg
890.1 Open wound of hip and thigh, complicated
890.2 Open wound of hip and thigh, with tendon involvement
905.7 Late effect of sprain and strain without mention of tendon injury
905.8 Late effect of tendon injury
906.1 Late effect of open wound of extremities without mention of tendon injury
906.3 Late effect of contusion
906.4 Late effect of crushing

ICD-9-CM Procedural

83.65 Other suture of muscle or fascia
83.81 Tendon graft
83.82 Graft of muscle or fascia
83.87 Other plastic operations on muscle

27390-27392

27390 Tenotomy, open, hamstring, knee to hip; single tendon
27391 multiple tendons, 1 leg
27392 multiple tendons, bilateral

ICD-9-CM Diagnostic

718.45 Contracture of pelvic joint
727.09 Other synovitis and tenosynovitis
727.81 Contracture of tendon (sheath)
727.82 Calcium deposits in tendon and bursa
727.89 Other disorders of synovium, tendon, and bursa
727.9 Unspecified disorder of synovium, tendon, and bursa ▽
728.0 Infective myositis
728.13 Postoperative heterotopic calcification
728.85 Spasm of muscle
728.9 Unspecified disorder of muscle, ligament, and fascia ▽
736.89 Other acquired deformity of other parts of limb
785.4 Gangrene — (Code first any associated underlying condition)
924.00 Contusion of thigh

ICD-9-CM Procedural

83.13 Other tenotomy

27393-27395

27393 Lengthening of hamstring tendon; single tendon
27394 multiple tendons, 1 leg
27395 multiple tendons, bilateral

ICD-9-CM Diagnostic

343.9 Unspecified infantile cerebral palsy ▽
718.45 Contracture of pelvic joint
727.81 Contracture of tendon (sheath)
728.85 Spasm of muscle
728.89 Other disorder of muscle, ligament, and fascia — (Use additional E code to identify drug, if drug-induced)
754.30 Congenital dislocation of hip, unilateral

ICD-9-CM Procedural

83.85 Other change in muscle or tendon length

27396-27397

27396 Transplant or transfer (with muscle redirection or rerouting), thigh (eg, extensor to flexor); single tendon
27397 multiple tendons

ICD-9-CM Diagnostic

333.71 Athetoid cerebral palsy
333.72 Acute dystonia due to drugs — (Use additional E code to identify drug)
333.79 Other acquired torsion dystonia
343.2 Quadriplegic infantile cerebral palsy
343.9 Unspecified infantile cerebral palsy ▽
355.8 Unspecified mononeuritis of lower limb ▽
718.46 Contracture of lower leg joint
729.99 Other disorders of soft tissue
754.89 Other specified nonteratogenic anomalies
785.4 Gangrene — (Code first any associated underlying condition)
843.8 Sprain and strain of other specified sites of hip and thigh
843.9 Sprain and strain of unspecified site of hip and thigh ▽
890.1 Open wound of hip and thigh, complicated
890.2 Open wound of hip and thigh, with tendon involvement
928.00 Crushing injury of thigh — (Use additional code to identify any associated injuries: 800-829, 850.0-854.1, 860.0-869.1)
928.10 Crushing injury of lower leg — (Use additional code to identify any associated injuries: 800-829, 850.0-854.1, 860.0-869.1)
928.11 Crushing injury of knee — (Use additional code to identify any associated injuries: 800-829, 850.0-854.1, 860.0-869.1)

ICD-9-CM Procedural

83.75 Tendon transfer or transplantation

27400

27400 Transfer, tendon or muscle, hamstrings to femur (eg, Egger's type procedure)

ICD-9-CM Diagnostic

718.46 Contracture of lower leg joint
726.5 Enthesopathy of hip region
736.41 Genu valgum (acquired)
754.41 Congenital dislocation of knee (with genu recurvatum)
754.42 Congenital bowing of femur
755.35 Congenital longitudinal deficiency, tibiofibular, complete or partial (with or without distal deficiencies, incomplete)
755.61 Congenital coxa valga
781.2 Abnormality of gait

ICD-9-CM Procedural

83.75 Tendon transfer or transplantation
83.79 Other muscle transposition

27403

27403 Arthrotomy with meniscus repair, knee

ICD-9-CM Diagnostic

717.0 Old bucket handle tear of medial meniscus
717.1 Derangement of anterior horn of medial meniscus
717.2 Derangement of posterior horn of medial meniscus
717.3 Other and unspecified derangement of medial meniscus ▽
717.40 Unspecified derangement of lateral meniscus ▽
717.41 Bucket handle tear of lateral meniscus
717.42 Derangement of anterior horn of lateral meniscus
717.43 Derangement of posterior horn of lateral meniscus
717.5 Derangement of meniscus, not elsewhere classified
717.6 Loose body in knee
836.0 Tear of medial cartilage or meniscus of knee, current
836.1 Tear of lateral cartilage or meniscus of knee, current
836.2 Other tear of cartilage or meniscus of knee, current
V64.43 Arthroscopic surgical procedure converted to open procedure

ICD-9-CM Procedural

81.47 Other repair of knee

27405-27409

27405 Repair, primary, torn ligament and/or capsule, knee; collateral
27407 cruciate
27409 collateral and cruciate ligaments

ICD-9-CM Diagnostic

716.16 Traumatic arthropathy, lower leg
717.81 Old disruption of lateral collateral ligament
717.82 Old disruption of medial collateral ligament
717.83 Old disruption of anterior cruciate ligament
717.84 Old disruption of posterior cruciate ligament
717.85 Old disruption of other ligament of knee
717.89 Other internal derangement of knee
836.0 Tear of medial cartilage or meniscus of knee, current
836.1 Tear of lateral cartilage or meniscus of knee, current
844.0 Sprain and strain of lateral collateral ligament of knee
844.1 Sprain and strain of medial collateral ligament of knee
844.2 Sprain and strain of cruciate ligament of knee
844.8 Sprain and strain of other specified sites of knee and leg
844.9 Sprain and strain of unspecified site of knee and leg ▽
891.1 Open wound of knee, leg (except thigh), and ankle, complicated

ICD-9-CM Procedural

81.42 Five-in-one repair of knee
81.43 Triad knee repair
81.45 Other repair of the cruciate ligaments
81.46 Other repair of the collateral ligaments
81.95 Suture of capsule or ligament of other lower extremity

27412

27412 Autologous chondrocyte implantation, knee

ICD-9-CM Diagnostic

714.30 Polyarticular juvenile rheumatoid arthritis, chronic or unspecified
715.16 Primary localized osteoarthrosis, lower leg
715.26 Secondary localized osteoarthrosis, lower leg
715.36 Localized osteoarthrosis not specified whether primary or secondary, lower leg
715.96 Osteoarthrosis, unspecified whether generalized or localized, lower leg ▽
717.0 Old bucket handle tear of medial meniscus
717.1 Derangement of anterior horn of medial meniscus
717.2 Derangement of posterior horn of medial meniscus
717.3 Other and unspecified derangement of medial meniscus ▽
717.7 Chondromalacia of patella
717.83 Old disruption of anterior cruciate ligament
719.96 Unspecified disorder of lower leg joint ▽
732.4 Juvenile osteochondrosis of lower extremity, excluding foot
732.7 Osteochondritis dissecans
732.9 Unspecified osteochondropathy ▽
733.90 Disorder of bone and cartilage, unspecified ▽
844.2 Sprain and strain of cruciate ligament of knee

ICD-9-CM Procedural

81.47 Other repair of knee

HCPCS Level II Supplies & Services

J7330 Autologous cultured chondrocytes, implant

27415

27415 Osteochondral allograft, knee, open

ICD-9-CM Diagnostic

714.30 Polyarticular juvenile rheumatoid arthritis, chronic or unspecified
715.16 Primary localized osteoarthrosis, lower leg
715.26 Secondary localized osteoarthrosis, lower leg
715.36 Localized osteoarthrosis not specified whether primary or secondary, lower leg
715.96 Osteoarthrosis, unspecified whether generalized or localized, lower leg ▽
717.0 Old bucket handle tear of medial meniscus
717.1 Derangement of anterior horn of medial meniscus
717.2 Derangement of posterior horn of medial meniscus
717.3 Other and unspecified derangement of medial meniscus ▽
717.7 Chondromalacia of patella
717.83 Old disruption of anterior cruciate ligament
719.96 Unspecified disorder of lower leg joint ▽
732.4 Juvenile osteochondrosis of lower extremity, excluding foot
732.7 Osteochondritis dissecans
732.9 Unspecified osteochondropathy ▽
844.2 Sprain and strain of cruciate ligament of knee

ICD-9-CM Procedural

81.47 Other repair of knee

HCPCS Level II Supplies & Services

J7330 Autologous cultured chondrocytes, implant
S2112 Arthroscopy, knee, surgical for harvesting of cartilage (chondrocyte cells)

27416

27416 Osteochondral autograft(s), knee, open (eg, mosaicplasty) (includes harvesting of autograft[s])

ICD-9-CM Diagnostic

714.30 Polyarticular juvenile rheumatoid arthritis, chronic or unspecified
715.16 Primary localized osteoarthrosis, lower leg
715.26 Secondary localized osteoarthrosis, lower leg
715.36 Localized osteoarthrosis not specified whether primary or secondary, lower leg
715.96 Osteoarthrosis, unspecified whether generalized or localized, lower leg ▽
717.0 Old bucket handle tear of medial meniscus
717.1 Derangement of anterior horn of medial meniscus
717.2 Derangement of posterior horn of medial meniscus
717.3 Other and unspecified derangement of medial meniscus ▽
717.7 Chondromalacia of patella
717.83 Old disruption of anterior cruciate ligament
719.96 Unspecified disorder of lower leg joint ▽
732.4 Juvenile osteochondrosis of lower extremity, excluding foot
732.7 Osteochondritis dissecans
732.9 Unspecified osteochondropathy ▽
844.2 Sprain and strain of cruciate ligament of knee

ICD-9-CM Procedural

81.47 Other repair of knee

27418

27418 Anterior tibial tubercleplasty (eg, Maquet type procedure)

ICD-9-CM Diagnostic

713.8 Arthropathy associated with other conditions classifiable elsewhere — (Code first underlying disease as conditions classifiable elsewhere except as in: 711.1-711.8, 712, 713.0-713.7) ☒
717.7 Chondromalacia of patella
717.81 Old disruption of lateral collateral ligament
717.82 Old disruption of medial collateral ligament
717.83 Old disruption of anterior cruciate ligament
717.84 Old disruption of posterior cruciate ligament
717.85 Old disruption of other ligament of knee
717.89 Other internal derangement of knee
755.30 Congenital unspecified reduction deformity of lower limb ▽
755.64 Congenital deformity of knee (joint)
755.69 Other congenital anomaly of lower limb, including pelvic girdle
836.3 Closed dislocation of patella
836.4 Open dislocation of patella

ICD-9-CM Procedural

77.87 Other partial ostectomy of tibia and fibula

27420

27420 Reconstruction of dislocating patella; (eg, Hauser type procedure)

ICD-9-CM Diagnostic

713.8 Arthropathy associated with other conditions classifiable elsewhere — (Code first underlying disease as conditions classifiable elsewhere except as in: 711.1-711.8, 712, 713.0-713.7) ☒
717.7 Chondromalacia of patella
718.36 Recurrent dislocation of lower leg joint
718.86 Other joint derangement, not elsewhere classified, lower leg
719.46 Pain in joint, lower leg
736.41 Genu valgum (acquired)
736.5 Genu recurvatum (acquired)
754.40 Congenital genu recurvatum
754.41 Congenital dislocation of knee (with genu recurvatum)
755.35 Congenital longitudinal deficiency, tibiofibular, complete or partial (with or without distal deficiencies, incomplete)
755.61 Congenital coxa valga
755.64 Congenital deformity of knee (joint)
755.69 Other congenital anomaly of lower limb, including pelvic girdle
836.3 Closed dislocation of patella
836.4 Open dislocation of patella

ICD-9-CM Procedural

81.44 Patellar stabilization

27422

27422 Reconstruction of dislocating patella; with extensor realignment and/or muscle advancement or release (eg, Campbell, Goldwaite type procedure)

ICD-9-CM Diagnostic

713.8 Arthropathy associated with other conditions classifiable elsewhere — (Code first underlying disease as conditions classifiable elsewhere except as in: 711.1-711.8, 712, 713.0-713.7) ☒
717.7 Chondromalacia of patella
718.36 Recurrent dislocation of lower leg joint
718.86 Other joint derangement, not elsewhere classified, lower leg
719.46 Pain in joint, lower leg
736.41 Genu valgum (acquired)
736.5 Genu recurvatum (acquired)
754.40 Congenital genu recurvatum
754.41 Congenital dislocation of knee (with genu recurvatum)
755.35 Congenital longitudinal deficiency, tibiofibular, complete or partial (with or without distal deficiencies, incomplete)
755.61 Congenital coxa valga
755.64 Congenital deformity of knee (joint)
755.69 Other congenital anomaly of lower limb, including pelvic girdle
836.3 Closed dislocation of patella
836.4 Open dislocation of patella

ICD-9-CM Procedural

81.44 Patellar stabilization

27424

27424 Reconstruction of dislocating patella; with patellectomy

ICD-9-CM Diagnostic

713.8 Arthropathy associated with other conditions classifiable elsewhere — (Code first underlying disease as conditions classifiable elsewhere except as in: 711.1-711.8, 712, 713.0-713.7) ☒
717.7 Chondromalacia of patella
718.36 Recurrent dislocation of lower leg joint
718.86 Other joint derangement, not elsewhere classified, lower leg
719.46 Pain in joint, lower leg
736.41 Genu valgum (acquired)
736.5 Genu recurvatum (acquired)
754.40 Congenital genu recurvatum
754.41 Congenital dislocation of knee (with genu recurvatum)
755.35 Congenital longitudinal deficiency, tibiofibular, complete or partial (with or without distal deficiencies, incomplete)
755.61 Congenital coxa valga
755.64 Congenital deformity of knee (joint)
755.69 Other congenital anomaly of lower limb, including pelvic girdle
836.3 Closed dislocation of patella
836.4 Open dislocation of patella

ICD-9-CM Procedural

77.96 Total ostectomy of patella
81.44 Patellar stabilization

27425

27425 Lateral retinacular release, open

ICD-9-CM Diagnostic

715.16 Primary localized osteoarthrosis, lower leg
715.96 Osteoarthrosis, unspecified whether generalized or localized, lower leg ▽
717.6 Loose body in knee
717.7 Chondromalacia of patella
717.9 Unspecified internal derangement of knee ▽
718.36 Recurrent dislocation of lower leg joint
718.46 Contracture of lower leg joint
718.56 Ankylosis of lower leg joint
718.86 Other joint derangement, not elsewhere classified, lower leg
719.26 Villonodular synovitis, lower leg
719.86 Other specified disorders of lower leg joint
733.92 Chondromalacia
755.64 Congenital deformity of knee (joint)
822.1 Open fracture of patella
836.3 Closed dislocation of patella
836.50 Closed dislocation of knee, unspecified part ▽
836.54 Closed lateral dislocation of tibia, proximal end
844.2 Sprain and strain of cruciate ligament of knee
V64.43 Arthroscopic surgical procedure converted to open procedure

ICD-9-CM Procedural

80.46 Division of joint capsule, ligament, or cartilage of knee

27427-27429

27427 Ligamentous reconstruction (augmentation), knee; extra-articular
27428 intra-articular (open)
27429 intra-articular (open) and extra-articular

ICD-9-CM Diagnostic

717.81 Old disruption of lateral collateral ligament
717.82 Old disruption of medial collateral ligament
717.83 Old disruption of anterior cruciate ligament
717.84 Old disruption of posterior cruciate ligament
717.89 Other internal derangement of knee
717.9 Unspecified internal derangement of knee ▽
718.56 Ankylosis of lower leg joint
718.86 Other joint derangement, not elsewhere classified, lower leg
728.89 Other disorder of muscle, ligament, and fascia — (Use additional E code to identify drug, if drug-induced)
728.9 Unspecified disorder of muscle, ligament, and fascia ▽
836.2 Other tear of cartilage or meniscus of knee, current
844.0 Sprain and strain of lateral collateral ligament of knee
844.1 Sprain and strain of medial collateral ligament of knee
844.2 Sprain and strain of cruciate ligament of knee
844.8 Sprain and strain of other specified sites of knee and leg
844.9 Sprain and strain of unspecified site of knee and leg ▽
891.2 Open wound of knee, leg (except thigh), and ankle, with tendon involvement

ICD-9-CM Procedural

81.45 Other repair of the cruciate ligaments
81.46 Other repair of the collateral ligaments
81.47 Other repair of knee

27430

27430 Quadricepsplasty (eg, Bennett or Thompson type)

ICD-9-CM Diagnostic

713.8 Arthropathy associated with other conditions classifiable elsewhere — (Code first underlying disease as conditions classifiable elsewhere except as in: 711.1-711.8, 712, 713.0-713.7) ☒
718.46 Contracture of lower leg joint
890.1 Open wound of hip and thigh, complicated

ICD-9-CM Procedural

83.86 Quadricepsplasty

27435

27435 Capsulotomy, posterior capsular release, knee

ICD-9-CM Diagnostic

715.96 Osteoarthrosis, unspecified whether generalized or localized, lower leg ▽
716.16 Traumatic arthropathy, lower leg
717.41 Bucket handle tear of lateral meniscus
717.7 Chondromalacia of patella
717.81 Old disruption of lateral collateral ligament
719.26 Villonodular synovitis, lower leg
726.60 Unspecified enthesopathy of knee ▽
726.61 Pes anserinus tendinitis or bursitis
727.00 Unspecified synovitis and tenosynovitis ▽
727.60 Nontraumatic rupture of unspecified tendon ▽
727.65 Nontraumatic rupture of quadriceps tendon
727.66 Nontraumatic rupture of patellar tendon
727.9 Unspecified disorder of synovium, tendon, and bursa ▽
844.0 Sprain and strain of lateral collateral ligament of knee
844.1 Sprain and strain of medial collateral ligament of knee
844.2 Sprain and strain of cruciate ligament of knee
844.8 Sprain and strain of other specified sites of knee and leg

ICD-9-CM Procedural

80.46 Division of joint capsule, ligament, or cartilage of knee

27437-27438

27437 Arthroplasty, patella; without prosthesis
27438 with prosthesis

ICD-9-CM Diagnostic

715.09 Generalized osteoarthrosis, involving multiple sites
715.16 Primary localized osteoarthrosis, lower leg
715.89 Osteoarthrosis involving multiple sites, but not specified as generalized
715.96 Osteoarthrosis, unspecified whether generalized or localized, lower leg ▽
717.7 Chondromalacia of patella
718.26 Pathological dislocation of lower leg joint
718.36 Recurrent dislocation of lower leg joint
718.86 Other joint derangement, not elsewhere classified, lower leg
726.64 Patellar tendinitis
730.16 Chronic osteomyelitis, lower leg — (Use additional code to identify organism: 041.1. Use additional code to identify major osseous defect, if applicable: 731.3)
731.3 Major osseous defects — (Code first underlying disease: 170.0-170.9, 730.00-730.29, 733.00-733.09, 733.40-733.49, 996.45)
732.4 Juvenile osteochondrosis of lower extremity, excluding foot
822.0 Closed fracture of patella
822.1 Open fracture of patella
836.3 Closed dislocation of patella
836.4 Open dislocation of patella
V88.22 Acquired absence of knee joint

ICD-9-CM Procedural

81.47 Other repair of knee
81.54 Total knee replacement

27440-27441

27440 Arthroplasty, knee, tibial plateau;
27441 with debridement and partial synovectomy

ICD-9-CM Diagnostic

715.16 Primary localized osteoarthrosis, lower leg
715.96 Osteoarthrosis, unspecified whether generalized or localized, lower leg
716.96 Unspecified arthropathy, lower leg
718.56 Ankylosis of lower leg joint
719.26 Villonodular synovitis, lower leg
719.66 Other symptoms referable to lower leg joint
726.60 Unspecified enthesopathy of knee
726.91 Exostosis of unspecified site
727.00 Unspecified synovitis and tenosynovitis
727.09 Other synovitis and tenosynovitis
730.16 Chronic osteomyelitis, lower leg — (Use additional code to identify organism: 041.1. Use additional code to identify major osseous defect, if applicable: 731.3)
730.36 Periostitis, without mention of osteomyelitis, lower leg — (Use additional code to identify organism: 041.1)
731.3 Major osseous defects — (Code first underlying disease: 170.0-170.9, 730.00-730.29, 733.00-733.09, 733.40-733.49, 996.45)
733.81 Malunion of fracture
733.82 Nonunion of fracture
733.92 Chondromalacia
823.00 Closed fracture of upper end of tibia
V88.22 Acquired absence of knee joint

ICD-9-CM Procedural

80.76 Synovectomy of knee
81.47 Other repair of knee

27442-27443

27442 Arthroplasty, femoral condyles or tibial plateau(s), knee;
27443 with debridement and partial synovectomy

ICD-9-CM Diagnostic

357.1 Polyneuropathy in collagen vascular disease — (Code first underlying disease: 446.0, 710.0, 714.0) ☒
359.6 Symptomatic inflammatory myopathy in diseases classified elsewhere — (Code first underlying disease: 135, 140.0-208.9, 277.30-277.39, 446.0, 710.0, 710.1, 710.2, 714.0) ☒
446.0 Polyarteritis nodosa
710.0 Systemic lupus erythematosus — (Use additional code to identify manifestation: 424.91, 581.81, 582.81, 583.81)
710.1 Systemic sclerosis — (Use additional code to identify manifestation: 359.6, 517.2)
710.2 Sicca syndrome
714.0 Rheumatoid arthritis — (Use additional code to identify manifestation: 357.1, 359.6)
715.16 Primary localized osteoarthrosis, lower leg
715.96 Osteoarthrosis, unspecified whether generalized or localized, lower leg
716.16 Traumatic arthropathy, lower leg
716.96 Unspecified arthropathy, lower leg
717.41 Bucket handle tear of lateral meniscus
717.42 Derangement of anterior horn of lateral meniscus
717.5 Derangement of meniscus, not elsewhere classified
717.83 Old disruption of anterior cruciate ligament
717.84 Old disruption of posterior cruciate ligament
719.26 Villonodular synovitis, lower leg
726.60 Unspecified enthesopathy of knee
726.91 Exostosis of unspecified site
727.00 Unspecified synovitis and tenosynovitis
727.09 Other synovitis and tenosynovitis
V88.22 Acquired absence of knee joint

ICD-9-CM Procedural

80.76 Synovectomy of knee
81.47 Other repair of knee

27445

27445 Arthroplasty, knee, hinge prosthesis (eg, Walldius type)

ICD-9-CM Diagnostic

714.4 Chronic postrheumatic arthropathy
715.16 Primary localized osteoarthrosis, lower leg
715.36 Localized osteoarthrosis not specified whether primary or secondary, lower leg
715.96 Osteoarthrosis, unspecified whether generalized or localized, lower leg
716.16 Traumatic arthropathy, lower leg
716.96 Unspecified arthropathy, lower leg
719.46 Pain in joint, lower leg
V88.22 Acquired absence of knee joint

ICD-9-CM Procedural

81.54 Total knee replacement

27446-27447

27446 Arthroplasty, knee, condyle and plateau; medial OR lateral compartment
27447 medial AND lateral compartments with or without patella resurfacing (total knee arthroplasty)

ICD-9-CM Diagnostic

357.1 Polyneuropathy in collagen vascular disease — (Code first underlying disease: 446.0, 710.0, 714.0) ☒
359.6 Symptomatic inflammatory myopathy in diseases classified elsewhere — (Code first underlying disease: 135, 140.0-208.9, 277.30-277.39, 446.0, 710.0, 710.1, 710.2, 714.0) ☒
446.0 Polyarteritis nodosa
710.0 Systemic lupus erythematosus — (Use additional code to identify manifestation: 424.91, 581.81, 582.81, 583.81)
710.1 Systemic sclerosis — (Use additional code to identify manifestation: 359.6, 517.2)
710.2 Sicca syndrome
714.0 Rheumatoid arthritis — (Use additional code to identify manifestation: 357.1, 359.6)
714.30 Polyarticular juvenile rheumatoid arthritis, chronic or unspecified
714.31 Polyarticular juvenile rheumatoid arthritis, acute
714.4 Chronic postrheumatic arthropathy
715.09 Generalized osteoarthrosis, involving multiple sites
715.16 Primary localized osteoarthrosis, lower leg
715.26 Secondary localized osteoarthrosis, lower leg
715.36 Localized osteoarthrosis not specified whether primary or secondary, lower leg
715.96 Osteoarthrosis, unspecified whether generalized or localized, lower leg
716.06 Kaschin-Beck disease, lower leg
716.16 Traumatic arthropathy, lower leg
716.96 Unspecified arthropathy, lower leg
719.46 Pain in joint, lower leg
731.3 Major osseous defects — (Code first underlying disease: 170.0-170.9, 730.00-730.29, 733.00-733.09, 733.40-733.49, 996.45)
733.49 Aseptic necrosis of other bone site — (Use additional code to identify major osseous defect, if applicable: 731.3)
755.64 Congenital deformity of knee (joint)
V88.22 Acquired absence of knee joint

ICD-9-CM Procedural

81.47 Other repair of knee
81.54 Total knee replacement

HCPCS Level II Supplies & Services

C1776 Joint device (implantable)

27448-27450

27448 Osteotomy, femur, shaft or supracondylar; without fixation
27450 with fixation

ICD-9-CM Diagnostic

715.96 Osteoarthrosis, unspecified whether generalized or localized, lower leg ▽
733.81 Malunion of fracture
733.82 Nonunion of fracture
733.91 Arrest of bone development or growth
736.81 Unequal leg length (acquired)
736.89 Other acquired deformity of other parts of limb
755.60 Unspecified congenital anomaly of lower limb ▽
755.61 Congenital coxa valga
755.62 Congenital coxa vara
755.63 Other congenital deformity of hip (joint)

ICD-9-CM Procedural

77.25 Wedge osteotomy of femur
77.35 Other division of femur
78.55 Internal fixation of femur without fracture reduction

27454

27454 Osteotomy, multiple, with realignment on intramedullary rod, femoral shaft (eg, Sofield type procedure)

ICD-9-CM Diagnostic

170.7 Malignant neoplasm of long bones of lower limb
730.05 Acute osteomyelitis, pelvic region and thigh — (Use additional code to identify organism: 041.1. Use additional code to identify major osseous defect, if applicable: 731.3)
731.3 Major osseous defects — (Code first underlying disease: 170.0-170.9, 730.00-730.29, 733.00-733.09, 733.40-733.49, 996.45)
732.9 Unspecified osteochondropathy ▽
733.81 Malunion of fracture
733.82 Nonunion of fracture
733.91 Arrest of bone development or growth
736.81 Unequal leg length (acquired)
736.89 Other acquired deformity of other parts of limb
755.60 Unspecified congenital anomaly of lower limb ▽
755.61 Congenital coxa valga
755.62 Congenital coxa vara
755.63 Other congenital deformity of hip (joint)
V54.02 Encounter for lengthening/adjustment of growth rod

ICD-9-CM Procedural

77.35 Other division of femur
78.55 Internal fixation of femur without fracture reduction

27455-27457

27455 Osteotomy, proximal tibia, including fibular excision or osteotomy (includes correction of genu varus [bowleg] or genu valgus [knock-knee]); before epiphyseal closure
27457 after epiphyseal closure

ICD-9-CM Diagnostic

268.1 Rickets, late effect — (Use additional code to identify the nature of late effect)
343.9 Unspecified infantile cerebral palsy ▽
715.16 Primary localized osteoarthrosis, lower leg
715.96 Osteoarthrosis, unspecified whether generalized or localized, lower leg ▽
716.96 Unspecified arthropathy, lower leg ▽
718.36 Recurrent dislocation of lower leg joint
719.66 Other symptoms referable to lower leg joint
732.4 Juvenile osteochondrosis of lower extremity, excluding foot
732.7 Osteochondritis dissecans
733.81 Malunion of fracture
733.82 Nonunion of fracture
736.41 Genu valgum (acquired)
736.42 Genu varum (acquired)
736.81 Unequal leg length (acquired)
736.89 Other acquired deformity of other parts of limb
754.43 Congenital bowing of tibia and fibula
755.64 Congenital deformity of knee (joint)

ICD-9-CM Procedural

77.37 Other division of tibia and fibula
77.87 Other partial ostectomy of tibia and fibula

27465-27468

27465 Osteoplasty, femur; shortening (excluding 64876)
27466 lengthening
27468 combined, lengthening and shortening with femoral segment transfer

ICD-9-CM Diagnostic

732.2 Nontraumatic slipped upper femoral epiphysis
732.4 Juvenile osteochondrosis of lower extremity, excluding foot
733.15 Pathologic fracture of other specified part of femur
733.81 Malunion of fracture
733.82 Nonunion of fracture
733.99 Other disorders of bone and cartilage
736.81 Unequal leg length (acquired)
754.89 Other specified nonteratogenic anomalies
755.30 Congenital unspecified reduction deformity of lower limb ▽
755.33 Congenital longitudinal deficiency, combined, involving femur, tibia, and fibula (complete or incomplete)

ICD-9-CM Procedural

78.15 Application of external fixator device, femur
78.25 Limb shortening procedures, femur
78.35 Limb lengthening procedures, femur
84.53 Implantation of internal limb lengthening device with kinetic distraction
84.54 Implantation of other internal limb lengthening device
84.71 Application of external fixator device, monoplanar system
84.72 Application of external fixator device, ring system
84.73 Application of hybrid external fixator device

27470-27472

27470 Repair, nonunion or malunion, femur, distal to head and neck; without graft (eg, compression technique)
27472 with iliac or other autogenous bone graft (includes obtaining graft)

ICD-9-CM Diagnostic

733.81 Malunion of fracture
733.82 Nonunion of fracture
996.77 Other complications due to internal joint prosthesis — (Use additional code to identify complication: 338.18-338.19, 338.28-338.29)
996.78 Other complications due to other internal orthopedic device, implant, and graft — (Use additional code to identify complication: 338.18-338.19, 338.28-338.29)

ICD-9-CM Procedural

77.79 Excision of other bone for graft, except facial bones
78.05 Bone graft of femur
78.45 Other repair or plastic operations on femur
78.75 Osteoclasis of femur

27475-27479

27475 Arrest, epiphyseal, any method (eg, epiphysiodesis); distal femur
27477 tibia and fibula, proximal
27479 combined distal femur, proximal tibia and fibula

ICD-9-CM Diagnostic

715.96 Osteoarthrosis, unspecified whether generalized or localized, lower leg
716.16 Traumatic arthropathy, lower leg
716.96 Unspecified arthropathy, lower leg
718.56 Ankylosis of lower leg joint
730.16 Chronic osteomyelitis, lower leg — (Use additional code to identify organism: 041.1. Use additional code to identify major osseous defect, if applicable: 731.3)
731.3 Major osseous defects — (Code first underlying disease: 170.0-170.9, 730.00-730.29, 733.00-733.09, 733.40-733.49, 996.45)
736.41 Genu valgum (acquired)
736.42 Genu varum (acquired)
736.81 Unequal leg length (acquired)
755.30 Congenital unspecified reduction deformity of lower limb

ICD-9-CM Procedural

78.25 Limb shortening procedures, femur
78.27 Limb shortening procedures, tibia and fibula

27485

27485 Arrest, hemiepiphyseal, distal femur or proximal tibia or fibula (eg, genu varus or valgus)

ICD-9-CM Diagnostic

718.56 Ankylosis of lower leg joint
736.41 Genu valgum (acquired)
736.42 Genu varum (acquired)
736.81 Unequal leg length (acquired)
755.30 Congenital unspecified reduction deformity of lower limb
755.64 Congenital deformity of knee (joint)

ICD-9-CM Procedural

78.25 Limb shortening procedures, femur
78.27 Limb shortening procedures, tibia and fibula
78.45 Other repair or plastic operations on femur

27486-27487

27486 Revision of total knee arthroplasty, with or without allograft; 1 component
27487 femoral and entire tibial component

ICD-9-CM Diagnostic

357.1 Polyneuropathy in collagen vascular disease — (Code first underlying disease: 446.0, 710.0, 714.0)
359.6 Symptomatic inflammatory myopathy in diseases classified elsewhere — (Code first underlying disease: 135, 140.0-208.9, 277.30-277.39, 446.0, 710.0, 710.1, 710.2, 714.0)
446.0 Polyarteritis nodosa
710.0 Systemic lupus erythematosus — (Use additional code to identify manifestation: 424.91, 581.81, 582.81, 583.81)
710.1 Systemic sclerosis — (Use additional code to identify manifestation: 359.6, 517.2)
710.2 Sicca syndrome
714.0 Rheumatoid arthritis — (Use additional code to identify manifestation: 357.1, 359.6)
715.16 Primary localized osteoarthrosis, lower leg
715.96 Osteoarthrosis, unspecified whether generalized or localized, lower leg
716.16 Traumatic arthropathy, lower leg
716.96 Unspecified arthropathy, lower leg
717.6 Loose body in knee
718.36 Recurrent dislocation of lower leg joint
718.46 Contracture of lower leg joint
718.56 Ankylosis of lower leg joint
718.86 Other joint derangement, not elsewhere classified, lower leg
731.3 Major osseous defects — (Code first underlying disease: 170.0-170.9, 730.00-730.29, 733.00-733.09, 733.40-733.49, 996.45)
736.41 Genu valgum (acquired)
996.40 Unspecified mechanical complication of internal orthopedic device, implant, and graft — (Use additional code to identify prosthetic joint with mechanical complication, V43.60-V43.69)
996.41 Mechanical loosening of prosthetic joint — (Use additional code to identify prosthetic joint with mechanical complication, V43.60-V43.69)
996.42 Dislocation of prosthetic joint — (Use additional code to identify prosthetic joint with mechanical complication, V43.60-V43.69)
996.43 Broken prosthetic joint implant — (Use additional code to identify prosthetic joint with mechanical complication, V43.60-V43.69)
996.44 Peri-prosthetic fracture around prosthetic joint — (Use additional code to identify prosthetic joint with mechanical complication, V43.60-V43.69.
996.45 Peri-prosthetic osteolysis — (Use additional code to identify prosthetic joint with mechanical complication, V43.60-V43.69. Use additional code to identify major osseous defect, if applicable: 731.3)
996.46 Articular bearing surface wear of prosthetic joint — (Use additional code to identify prosthetic joint with mechanical complication, V43.60-V43.69)
996.47 Other mechanical complication of prosthetic joint implant — (Use additional code to identify prosthetic joint with mechanical complication, V43.60-V43.69)
996.66 Infection and inflammatory reaction due to internal joint prosthesis — (Use additional code to identify specified infections. Use additional code to identify infected prosthetic joint: V43.60-V43.69)
996.77 Other complications due to internal joint prosthesis — (Use additional code to identify complication: 338.18-338.19, 338.28-338.29)
V43.65 Knee joint replacement by other means

ICD-9-CM Procedural

00.80 Revision of knee replacement, total (all components)
00.81 Revision of knee replacement, tibial component
00.82 Revision of knee replacement, femoral component
00.83 Revision of knee replacement, patellar component
00.84 Revision of total knee replacement, tibial insert (liner)

27488

27488 Removal of prosthesis, including total knee prosthesis, methylmethacrylate with or without insertion of spacer, knee

ICD-9-CM Diagnostic

711.06 Pyogenic arthritis, lower leg — (Use additional code to identify infectious organism: 041.0-041.8)
711.96 Unspecified infective arthritis, lower leg
715.16 Primary localized osteoarthrosis, lower leg
715.96 Osteoarthrosis, unspecified whether generalized or localized, lower leg
716.86 Other specified arthropathy, lower leg
717.6 Loose body in knee
719.26 Villonodular synovitis, lower leg
730.06 Acute osteomyelitis, lower leg — (Use additional code to identify organism: 041.1. Use additional code to identify major osseous defect, if applicable: 731.3)
730.16 Chronic osteomyelitis, lower leg — (Use additional code to identify organism: 041.1. Use additional code to identify major osseous defect, if applicable: 731.3)

731.3 Major osseous defects — (Code first underlying disease: 170.0-170.9, 730.00-730.29, 733.00-733.09, 733.40-733.49, 996.45)
736.6 Other acquired deformities of knee
996.40 Unspecified mechanical complication of internal orthopedic device, implant, and graft — (Use additional code to identify prosthetic joint with mechanical complication, V43.60-V43.69) ▽
996.41 Mechanical loosening of prosthetic joint — (Use additional code to identify prosthetic joint with mechanical complication, V43.60-V43.69)
996.42 Dislocation of prosthetic joint — (Use additional code to identify prosthetic joint with mechanical complication, V43.60-V43.69)
996.43 Broken prosthetic joint implant — (Use additional code to identify prosthetic joint with mechanical complication, V43.60-V43.69)
996.44 Peri-prosthetic fracture around prosthetic joint — (Use additional code to identify prosthetic joint with mechanical complication, V43.60-V43.69.
996.45 Peri-prosthetic osteolysis — (Use additional code to identify prosthetic joint with mechanical complication, V43.60-V43.69. Use additional code to identify major osseous defect, if applicable: 731.3)
996.46 Articular bearing surface wear of prosthetic joint — (Use additional code to identify prosthetic joint with mechanical complication, V43.60-V43.69)
996.47 Other mechanical complication of prosthetic joint implant — (Use additional code to identify prosthetic joint with mechanical complication, V43.60-V43.69)
996.66 Infection and inflammatory reaction due to internal joint prosthesis — (Use additional code to identify specified infections. Use additional code to identify infected prosthetic joint: V43.60-V43.69)
996.77 Other complications due to internal joint prosthesis — (Use additional code to identify complication: 338.18-338.19, 338.28-338.29)
V43.65 Knee joint replacement by other means

ICD-9-CM Procedural

80.06 Arthrotomy for removal of prosthesis without replacement, knee
84.56 Insertion or replacement of (cement) spacer

27495

27495 Prophylactic treatment (nailing, pinning, plating, or wiring) with or without methylmethacrylate, femur

ICD-9-CM Diagnostic

170.7 Malignant neoplasm of long bones of lower limb
198.5 Secondary malignant neoplasm of bone and bone marrow
213.7 Benign neoplasm of long bones of lower limb
238.0 Neoplasm of uncertain behavior of bone and articular cartilage
239.2 Neoplasms of unspecified nature of bone, soft tissue, and skin
268.1 Rickets, late effect — (Use additional code to identify the nature of late effect)
275.40 Unspecified disorder of calcium metabolism — (Use additional code to identify any associated intellectual disabilities) ▽
275.41 Hypocalcemia — (Use additional code to identify any associated intellectual disabilities)
275.42 Hypercalcemia — (Use additional code to identify any associated intellectual disabilities)
275.49 Other disorders of calcium metabolism — (Use additional code to identify any associated intellectual disabilities)
275.5 Hungry bone syndrome — (Use additional code to identify any associated intellectual disabilities)
731.3 Major osseous defects — (Code first underlying disease: 170.0-170.9, 730.00-730.29, 733.00-733.09, 733.40-733.49, 996.45)
733.00 Unspecified osteoporosis — (Use additional code to identify major osseous defect, if applicable: 731.3) (Use additional code to identify personal history of pathologic (healed) fracture: V13.51) ▽
733.02 Idiopathic osteoporosis — (Use additional code to identify major osseous defect, if applicable: 731.3) (Use additional code to identify personal history of pathologic (healed) fracture: V13.51)
733.09 Other osteoporosis — (Use additional code to identify major osseous defect, if applicable: 731.3) (Use additional code to identify personal history of pathologic (healed) fracture: V13.51) (Use additional E code to identify drug)
756.51 Osteogenesis imperfecta
756.52 Osteopetrosis
821.01 Closed fracture of shaft of femur

ICD-9-CM Procedural

78.55 Internal fixation of femur without fracture reduction
84.55 Insertion of bone void filler

27496-27497

27496 Decompression fasciotomy, thigh and/or knee, 1 compartment (flexor or extensor or adductor);
27497 with debridement of nonviable muscle and/or nerve

ICD-9-CM Diagnostic

287.8 Other specified hemorrhagic conditions
682.6 Cellulitis and abscess of leg, except foot — (Use additional code to identify organism, such as 041.1, etc.)
728.0 Infective myositis
728.81 Interstitial myositis
728.88 Rhabdomyolysis
729.72 Nontraumatic compartment syndrome of lower extremity — (Code first, if applicable, postprocedural complication: 998.89)
906.4 Late effect of crushing
906.7 Late effect of burn of other extremities
928.00 Crushing injury of thigh — (Use additional code to identify any associated injuries: 800-829, 850.0-854.1, 860.0-869.1)
928.01 Crushing injury of hip — (Use additional code to identify any associated injuries: 800-829, 850.0-854.1, 860.0-869.1)
928.10 Crushing injury of lower leg — (Use additional code to identify any associated injuries: 800-829, 850.0-854.1, 860.0-869.1)
928.11 Crushing injury of knee — (Use additional code to identify any associated injuries: 800-829, 850.0-854.1, 860.0-869.1)
945.44 Deep necrosis of underlying tissues due to burn (deep third degree) of lower leg, without mention of loss of a body part
945.45 Deep necrosis of underlying tissues due to burn (deep third degree) of knee, without mention of loss of a body part
945.46 Deep necrosis of underlying tissues due to burn (deep third degree) of thigh (any part), without mention of loss of a body part
958.8 Other early complications of trauma
958.92 Traumatic compartment syndrome of lower extremity
959.6 Injury, other and unspecified, hip and thigh
998.59 Other postoperative infection — (Use additional code to identify infection)

ICD-9-CM Procedural

83.14 Fasciotomy
83.45 Other myectomy

27498-27499

27498 Decompression fasciotomy, thigh and/or knee, multiple compartments;
27499 with debridement of nonviable muscle and/or nerve

ICD-9-CM Diagnostic

287.8 Other specified hemorrhagic conditions
682.6 Cellulitis and abscess of leg, except foot — (Use additional code to identify organism, such as 041.1, etc.)
728.0 Infective myositis
728.81 Interstitial myositis
728.88 Rhabdomyolysis
906.4 Late effect of crushing
906.7 Late effect of burn of other extremities

928.00 Crushing injury of thigh — (Use additional code to identify any associated injuries: 800-829, 850.0-854.1, 860.0-869.1)
928.01 Crushing injury of hip — (Use additional code to identify any associated injuries: 800-829, 850.0-854.1, 860.0-869.1)
928.10 Crushing injury of lower leg — (Use additional code to identify any associated injuries: 800-829, 850.0-854.1, 860.0-869.1)
928.11 Crushing injury of knee — (Use additional code to identify any associated injuries: 800-829, 850.0-854.1, 860.0-869.1)
945.44 Deep necrosis of underlying tissues due to burn (deep third degree) of lower leg, without mention of loss of a body part
945.45 Deep necrosis of underlying tissues due to burn (deep third degree) of knee, without mention of loss of a body part
945.46 Deep necrosis of underlying tissues due to burn (deep third degree) of thigh (any part), without mention of loss of a body part
945.49 Deep necrosis of underlying tissues due to burn (deep third degree) of multiple sites of lower limb(s), without mention of loss of a body part
958.8 Other early complications of trauma
959.6 Injury, other and unspecified, hip and thigh

ICD-9-CM Procedural

83.14 Fasciotomy
83.45 Other myectomy

27500

27500 Closed treatment of femoral shaft fracture, without manipulation

ICD-9-CM Diagnostic

733.15 Pathologic fracture of other specified part of femur
756.51 Osteogenesis imperfecta
821.01 Closed fracture of shaft of femur
827.0 Other, multiple and ill-defined closed fractures of lower limb
828.0 Multiple closed fractures involving both lower limbs, lower with upper limb, and lower limb(s) with rib(s) and sternum
928.00 Crushing injury of thigh — (Use additional code to identify any associated injuries: 800-829, 850.0-854.1, 860.0-869.1)

ICD-9-CM Procedural

93.53 Application of other cast

27501

27501 Closed treatment of supracondylar or transcondylar femoral fracture with or without intercondylar extension, without manipulation

ICD-9-CM Diagnostic

731.3 Major osseous defects — (Code first underlying disease: 170.0-170.9, 730.00-730.29, 733.00-733.09, 733.40-733.49, 996.45)
733.15 Pathologic fracture of other specified part of femur
733.43 Aseptic necrosis of medial femoral condyle — (Use additional code to identify major osseous defect, if applicable: 731.3)
756.51 Osteogenesis imperfecta
821.20 Closed fracture of unspecified part of lower end of femur ▼
821.21 Closed fracture of femoral condyle
821.22 Closed fracture of lower epiphysis of femur
821.23 Closed supracondylar fracture of femur
821.29 Other closed fracture of lower end of femur
828.0 Multiple closed fractures involving both lower limbs, lower with upper limb, and lower limb(s) with rib(s) and sternum

ICD-9-CM Procedural

93.53 Application of other cast

27502

27502 Closed treatment of femoral shaft fracture, with manipulation, with or without skin or skeletal traction

ICD-9-CM Diagnostic

733.15 Pathologic fracture of other specified part of femur
756.51 Osteogenesis imperfecta
821.01 Closed fracture of shaft of femur
827.0 Other, multiple and ill-defined closed fractures of lower limb
828.0 Multiple closed fractures involving both lower limbs, lower with upper limb, and lower limb(s) with rib(s) and sternum

ICD-9-CM Procedural

79.05 Closed reduction of fracture of femur without internal fixation
93.44 Other skeletal traction
93.46 Other skin traction of limbs

27503

27503 Closed treatment of supracondylar or transcondylar femoral fracture with or without intercondylar extension, with manipulation, with or without skin or skeletal traction

ICD-9-CM Diagnostic

731.3 Major osseous defects — (Code first underlying disease: 170.0-170.9, 730.00-730.29, 733.00-733.09, 733.40-733.49, 996.45)
733.15 Pathologic fracture of other specified part of femur
733.43 Aseptic necrosis of medial femoral condyle — (Use additional code to identify major osseous defect, if applicable: 731.3)
756.51 Osteogenesis imperfecta
821.20 Closed fracture of unspecified part of lower end of femur ▼
821.21 Closed fracture of femoral condyle
821.22 Closed fracture of lower epiphysis of femur
821.23 Closed supracondylar fracture of femur
821.29 Other closed fracture of lower end of femur
828.0 Multiple closed fractures involving both lower limbs, lower with upper limb, and lower limb(s) with rib(s) and sternum

ICD-9-CM Procedural

79.05 Closed reduction of fracture of femur without internal fixation
93.44 Other skeletal traction
93.46 Other skin traction of limbs

27506

27506 Open treatment of femoral shaft fracture, with or without external fixation, with insertion of intramedullary implant, with or without cerclage and/or locking screws

ICD-9-CM Diagnostic

731.3 Major osseous defects — (Code first underlying disease: 170.0-170.9, 730.00-730.29, 733.00-733.09, 733.40-733.49, 996.45)
733.15 Pathologic fracture of other specified part of femur
733.81 Malunion of fracture
733.82 Nonunion of fracture
756.51 Osteogenesis imperfecta
821.01 Closed fracture of shaft of femur
821.10 Open fracture of unspecified part of femur ▼
821.11 Open fracture of shaft of femur
827.0 Other, multiple and ill-defined closed fractures of lower limb
827.1 Other, multiple and ill-defined open fractures of lower limb
828.0 Multiple closed fractures involving both lower limbs, lower with upper limb, and lower limb(s) with rib(s) and sternum
928.00 Crushing injury of thigh — (Use additional code to identify any associated injuries: 800-829, 850.0-854.1, 860.0-869.1)

ICD-9-CM Procedural

78.15 Application of external fixator device, femur
79.35 Open reduction of fracture of femur with internal fixation
84.71 Application of external fixator device, monoplanar system
84.72 Application of external fixator device, ring system
84.73 Application of hybrid external fixator device

27507

27507 Open treatment of femoral shaft fracture with plate/screws, with or without cerclage

ICD-9-CM Diagnostic

733.15 Pathologic fracture of other specified part of femur
733.81 Malunion of fracture
733.82 Nonunion of fracture
821.01 Closed fracture of shaft of femur
821.11 Open fracture of shaft of femur
827.0 Other, multiple and ill-defined closed fractures of lower limb
827.1 Other, multiple and ill-defined open fractures of lower limb
828.0 Multiple closed fractures involving both lower limbs, lower with upper limb, and lower limb(s) with rib(s) and sternum
928.00 Crushing injury of thigh — (Use additional code to identify any associated injuries: 800-829, 850.0-854.1, 860.0-869.1)

ICD-9-CM Procedural

79.35 Open reduction of fracture of femur with internal fixation

27508

27508 Closed treatment of femoral fracture, distal end, medial or lateral condyle, without manipulation

ICD-9-CM Diagnostic

731.3 Major osseous defects — (Code first underlying disease: 170.0-170.9, 730.00-730.29, 733.00-733.09, 733.40-733.49, 996.45)
733.01 Senile osteoporosis — (Use additional code to identify major osseous defect, if applicable: 731.3) (Use additional code to identify personal history of pathologic (healed) fracture: V13.51)
733.15 Pathologic fracture of other specified part of femur
733.43 Aseptic necrosis of medial femoral condyle — (Use additional code to identify major osseous defect, if applicable: 731.3)
756.51 Osteogenesis imperfecta
821.20 Closed fracture of unspecified part of lower end of femur ▽
821.21 Closed fracture of femoral condyle
821.22 Closed fracture of lower epiphysis of femur
821.23 Closed supracondylar fracture of femur
821.29 Other closed fracture of lower end of femur
827.0 Other, multiple and ill-defined closed fractures of lower limb
828.0 Multiple closed fractures involving both lower limbs, lower with upper limb, and lower limb(s) with rib(s) and sternum

ICD-9-CM Procedural

93.53 Application of other cast

27509

27509 Percutaneous skeletal fixation of femoral fracture, distal end, medial or lateral condyle, or supracondylar or transcondylar, with or without intercondylar extension, or distal femoral epiphyseal separation

ICD-9-CM Diagnostic

731.3 Major osseous defects — (Code first underlying disease: 170.0-170.9, 730.00-730.29, 733.00-733.09, 733.40-733.49, 996.45)
733.15 Pathologic fracture of other specified part of femur
733.43 Aseptic necrosis of medial femoral condyle — (Use additional code to identify major osseous defect, if applicable: 731.3)
756.51 Osteogenesis imperfecta
821.20 Closed fracture of unspecified part of lower end of femur ▽
821.21 Closed fracture of femoral condyle
821.22 Closed fracture of lower epiphysis of femur
821.23 Closed supracondylar fracture of femur
821.29 Other closed fracture of lower end of femur
827.0 Other, multiple and ill-defined closed fractures of lower limb
828.0 Multiple closed fractures involving both lower limbs, lower with upper limb, and lower limb(s) with rib(s) and sternum

ICD-9-CM Procedural

78.55 Internal fixation of femur without fracture reduction

27510

27510 Closed treatment of femoral fracture, distal end, medial or lateral condyle, with manipulation

ICD-9-CM Diagnostic

731.3 Major osseous defects — (Code first underlying disease: 170.0-170.9, 730.00-730.29, 733.00-733.09, 733.40-733.49, 996.45)
733.15 Pathologic fracture of other specified part of femur
733.43 Aseptic necrosis of medial femoral condyle — (Use additional code to identify major osseous defect, if applicable: 731.3)
756.51 Osteogenesis imperfecta
821.20 Closed fracture of unspecified part of lower end of femur ▽
821.21 Closed fracture of femoral condyle
821.22 Closed fracture of lower epiphysis of femur
821.23 Closed supracondylar fracture of femur
821.29 Other closed fracture of lower end of femur
821.30 Open fracture of unspecified part of lower end of femur ▽
821.31 Open fracture of femoral condyle
821.32 Open fracture of lower epiphysis of femur
821.33 Open supracondylar fracture of femur
821.39 Other open fracture of lower end of femur
827.0 Other, multiple and ill-defined closed fractures of lower limb
827.1 Other, multiple and ill-defined open fractures of lower limb
828.0 Multiple closed fractures involving both lower limbs, lower with upper limb, and lower limb(s) with rib(s) and sternum
828.1 Multiple fractures involving both lower limbs, lower with upper limb, and lower limb(s) with rib(s) and sternum, open

ICD-9-CM Procedural

79.05 Closed reduction of fracture of femur without internal fixation

27511-27513

27511 Open treatment of femoral supracondylar or transcondylar fracture without intercondylar extension, includes internal fixation, when performed
27513 Open treatment of femoral supracondylar or transcondylar fracture with intercondylar extension, includes internal fixation, when performed

ICD-9-CM Diagnostic

731.3 Major osseous defects — (Code first underlying disease: 170.0-170.9, 730.00-730.29, 733.00-733.09, 733.40-733.49, 996.45)
732.7 Osteochondritis dissecans
733.15 Pathologic fracture of other specified part of femur
733.43 Aseptic necrosis of medial femoral condyle — (Use additional code to identify major osseous defect, if applicable: 731.3)
733.81 Malunion of fracture
733.82 Nonunion of fracture
756.51 Osteogenesis imperfecta

821.20 Closed fracture of unspecified part of lower end of femur ▽
821.21 Closed fracture of femoral condyle
821.22 Closed fracture of lower epiphysis of femur
821.23 Closed supracondylar fracture of femur
821.29 Other closed fracture of lower end of femur
821.30 Open fracture of unspecified part of lower end of femur ▽
821.31 Open fracture of femoral condyle
821.32 Open fracture of lower epiphysis of femur
821.33 Open supracondylar fracture of femur
821.39 Other open fracture of lower end of femur
827.0 Other, multiple and ill-defined closed fractures of lower limb
827.1 Other, multiple and ill-defined open fractures of lower limb
828.0 Multiple closed fractures involving both lower limbs, lower with upper limb, and lower limb(s) with rib(s) and sternum
828.1 Multiple fractures involving both lower limbs, lower with upper limb, and lower limb(s) with rib(s) and sternum, open

ICD-9-CM Procedural

79.25 Open reduction of fracture of femur without internal fixation
79.35 Open reduction of fracture of femur with internal fixation

27514

27514 Open treatment of femoral fracture, distal end, medial or lateral condyle, includes internal fixation, when performed

ICD-9-CM Diagnostic

732.7 Osteochondritis dissecans
733.15 Pathologic fracture of other specified part of femur
733.81 Malunion of fracture
733.82 Nonunion of fracture
756.51 Osteogenesis imperfecta
821.20 Closed fracture of unspecified part of lower end of femur ▽
821.21 Closed fracture of femoral condyle
821.22 Closed fracture of lower epiphysis of femur
821.23 Closed supracondylar fracture of femur
821.29 Other closed fracture of lower end of femur
821.30 Open fracture of unspecified part of lower end of femur ▽
821.31 Open fracture of femoral condyle
821.32 Open fracture of lower epiphysis of femur
821.33 Open supracondylar fracture of femur
821.39 Other open fracture of lower end of femur
827.0 Other, multiple and ill-defined closed fractures of lower limb
827.1 Other, multiple and ill-defined open fractures of lower limb
828.0 Multiple closed fractures involving both lower limbs, lower with upper limb, and lower limb(s) with rib(s) and sternum
828.1 Multiple fractures involving both lower limbs, lower with upper limb, and lower limb(s) with rib(s) and sternum, open

ICD-9-CM Procedural

79.25 Open reduction of fracture of femur without internal fixation
79.35 Open reduction of fracture of femur with internal fixation

27516-27517

27516 Closed treatment of distal femoral epiphyseal separation; without manipulation
27517 with manipulation, with or without skin or skeletal traction

ICD-9-CM Diagnostic

732.2 Nontraumatic slipped upper femoral epiphysis
732.6 Other juvenile osteochondrosis
732.9 Unspecified osteochondropathy ▽
733.15 Pathologic fracture of other specified part of femur
821.22 Closed fracture of lower epiphysis of femur

ICD-9-CM Procedural

79.45 Closed reduction of separated epiphysis of femur
93.44 Other skeletal traction
93.46 Other skin traction of limbs
93.53 Application of other cast

27519

27519 Open treatment of distal femoral epiphyseal separation, includes internal fixation, when performed

ICD-9-CM Diagnostic

732.6 Other juvenile osteochondrosis
732.7 Osteochondritis dissecans
732.9 Unspecified osteochondropathy ▽
733.15 Pathologic fracture of other specified part of femur
821.22 Closed fracture of lower epiphysis of femur
821.32 Open fracture of lower epiphysis of femur

ICD-9-CM Procedural

79.55 Open reduction of separated epiphysis of femur

27520

27520 Closed treatment of patellar fracture, without manipulation

ICD-9-CM Diagnostic

715.96 Osteoarthrosis, unspecified whether generalized or localized, lower leg ▽
719.46 Pain in joint, lower leg
732.7 Osteochondritis dissecans
733.19 Pathologic fracture of other specified site
756.51 Osteogenesis imperfecta
822.0 Closed fracture of patella

ICD-9-CM Procedural

93.53 Application of other cast
93.54 Application of splint

27524

27524 Open treatment of patellar fracture, with internal fixation and/or partial or complete patellectomy and soft tissue repair

ICD-9-CM Diagnostic

715.96 Osteoarthrosis, unspecified whether generalized or localized, lower leg ▽
732.7 Osteochondritis dissecans
733.19 Pathologic fracture of other specified site
756.51 Osteogenesis imperfecta
822.0 Closed fracture of patella
822.1 Open fracture of patella

ICD-9-CM Procedural

77.86 Other partial ostectomy of patella
77.96 Total ostectomy of patella
79.36 Open reduction of fracture of tibia and fibula with internal fixation
79.39 Open reduction of fracture of other specified bone, except facial bones, with internal fixation
83.09 Other incision of soft tissue

27530-27532

27530 Closed treatment of tibial fracture, proximal (plateau); without manipulation
27532 with or without manipulation, with skeletal traction

ICD-9-CM Diagnostic

733.16 Pathologic fracture of tibia and fibula

733.93 Stress fracture of tibia or fibula — (Use additional external cause code(s) to identify the cause of the stress fracture)
756.51 Osteogenesis imperfecta
823.00 Closed fracture of upper end of tibia
823.02 Closed fracture of upper end of fibula with tibia
823.40 Torus fracture of tibia alone
827.0 Other, multiple and ill-defined closed fractures of lower limb
828.0 Multiple closed fractures involving both lower limbs, lower with upper limb, and lower limb(s) with rib(s) and sternum

ICD-9-CM Procedural

79.06 Closed reduction of fracture of tibia and fibula without internal fixation
93.44 Other skeletal traction
93.53 Application of other cast

27535-27536

27535 Open treatment of tibial fracture, proximal (plateau); unicondylar, includes internal fixation, when performed
27536 bicondylar, with or without internal fixation

ICD-9-CM Diagnostic

733.16 Pathologic fracture of tibia and fibula
733.81 Malunion of fracture
733.82 Nonunion of fracture
733.93 Stress fracture of tibia or fibula — (Use additional external cause code(s) to identify the cause of the stress fracture)
756.51 Osteogenesis imperfecta
823.00 Closed fracture of upper end of tibia
823.02 Closed fracture of upper end of fibula with tibia
823.10 Open fracture of upper end of tibia
823.12 Open fracture of upper end of fibula with tibia
827.0 Other, multiple and ill-defined closed fractures of lower limb
827.1 Other, multiple and ill-defined open fractures of lower limb
828.0 Multiple closed fractures involving both lower limbs, lower with upper limb, and lower limb(s) with rib(s) and sternum
828.1 Multiple fractures involving both lower limbs, lower with upper limb, and lower limb(s) with rib(s) and sternum, open

ICD-9-CM Procedural

79.26 Open reduction of fracture of tibia and fibula without internal fixation
79.36 Open reduction of fracture of tibia and fibula with internal fixation

27538

27538 Closed treatment of intercondylar spine(s) and/or tuberosity fracture(s) of knee, with or without manipulation

ICD-9-CM Diagnostic

733.16 Pathologic fracture of tibia and fibula
733.93 Stress fracture of tibia or fibula — (Use additional external cause code(s) to identify the cause of the stress fracture)
756.51 Osteogenesis imperfecta
823.00 Closed fracture of upper end of tibia
823.02 Closed fracture of upper end of fibula with tibia
827.0 Other, multiple and ill-defined closed fractures of lower limb

ICD-9-CM Procedural

79.06 Closed reduction of fracture of tibia and fibula without internal fixation
93.53 Application of other cast
93.54 Application of splint

27540

27540 Open treatment of intercondylar spine(s) and/or tuberosity fracture(s) of the knee, includes internal fixation, when performed

ICD-9-CM Diagnostic

733.16 Pathologic fracture of tibia and fibula
733.81 Malunion of fracture
733.82 Nonunion of fracture
733.93 Stress fracture of tibia or fibula — (Use additional external cause code(s) to identify the cause of the stress fracture)
756.51 Osteogenesis imperfecta
823.00 Closed fracture of upper end of tibia
823.10 Open fracture of upper end of tibia
827.0 Other, multiple and ill-defined closed fractures of lower limb
827.1 Other, multiple and ill-defined open fractures of lower limb

ICD-9-CM Procedural

79.26 Open reduction of fracture of tibia and fibula without internal fixation
79.36 Open reduction of fracture of tibia and fibula with internal fixation

27550-27552

27550 Closed treatment of knee dislocation; without anesthesia
27552 requiring anesthesia

ICD-9-CM Diagnostic

717.85 Old disruption of other ligament of knee
718.26 Pathological dislocation of lower leg joint
718.36 Recurrent dislocation of lower leg joint
718.76 Developmental dislocation of joint, lower leg
754.41 Congenital dislocation of knee (with genu recurvatum)
836.0 Tear of medial cartilage or meniscus of knee, current
836.1 Tear of lateral cartilage or meniscus of knee, current
836.2 Other tear of cartilage or meniscus of knee, current
836.3 Closed dislocation of patella
836.50 Closed dislocation of knee, unspecified part ▽
836.51 Closed anterior dislocation of tibia, proximal end
836.52 Closed posterior dislocation of tibia, proximal end
836.53 Closed medial dislocation of tibia, proximal end
836.54 Closed lateral dislocation of tibia, proximal end

ICD-9-CM Procedural

79.76 Closed reduction of dislocation of knee

27556-27557

27556 Open treatment of knee dislocation, includes internal fixation, when performed; without primary ligamentous repair or augmentation/reconstruction
27557 with primary ligamentous repair

ICD-9-CM Diagnostic

717.81 Old disruption of lateral collateral ligament
717.82 Old disruption of medial collateral ligament
717.83 Old disruption of anterior cruciate ligament
717.84 Old disruption of posterior cruciate ligament
718.26 Pathological dislocation of lower leg joint
718.36 Recurrent dislocation of lower leg joint
718.76 Developmental dislocation of joint, lower leg
754.41 Congenital dislocation of knee (with genu recurvatum)
836.3 Closed dislocation of patella
836.4 Open dislocation of patella
836.50 Closed dislocation of knee, unspecified part ▽
836.51 Closed anterior dislocation of tibia, proximal end
836.52 Closed posterior dislocation of tibia, proximal end

836.53 Closed medial dislocation of tibia, proximal end
836.54 Closed lateral dislocation of tibia, proximal end
836.60 Open dislocation of knee unspecified part ▽
836.61 Open anterior dislocation of tibia, proximal end
836.62 Open posterior dislocation of tibia, proximal end
836.63 Open medial dislocation of tibia, proximal end
836.64 Open lateral dislocation of tibia, proximal end

ICD-9-CM Procedural

79.86 Open reduction of dislocation of knee
81.47 Other repair of knee
81.96 Other repair of joint

27558

27558 Open treatment of knee dislocation, includes internal fixation, when performed; with primary ligamentous repair, with augmentation/reconstruction

ICD-9-CM Diagnostic

717.81 Old disruption of lateral collateral ligament
717.82 Old disruption of medial collateral ligament
717.83 Old disruption of anterior cruciate ligament
717.84 Old disruption of posterior cruciate ligament
718.26 Pathological dislocation of lower leg joint
718.36 Recurrent dislocation of lower leg joint
718.76 Developmental dislocation of joint, lower leg
754.41 Congenital dislocation of knee (with genu recurvatum)
836.3 Closed dislocation of patella
836.4 Open dislocation of patella
836.50 Closed dislocation of knee, unspecified part ▽
836.51 Closed anterior dislocation of tibia, proximal end
836.52 Closed posterior dislocation of tibia, proximal end
836.53 Closed medial dislocation of tibia, proximal end
836.54 Closed lateral dislocation of tibia, proximal end
836.60 Open dislocation of knee unspecified part ▽
836.61 Open anterior dislocation of tibia, proximal end
836.62 Open posterior dislocation of tibia, proximal end
836.63 Open medial dislocation of tibia, proximal end
836.64 Open lateral dislocation of tibia, proximal end

ICD-9-CM Procedural

79.86 Open reduction of dislocation of knee
81.47 Other repair of knee
81.96 Other repair of joint

27560-27562

27560 Closed treatment of patellar dislocation; without anesthesia
27562 requiring anesthesia

ICD-9-CM Diagnostic

718.36 Recurrent dislocation of lower leg joint
718.76 Developmental dislocation of joint, lower leg
836.3 Closed dislocation of patella
905.7 Late effect of sprain and strain without mention of tendon injury
905.8 Late effect of tendon injury

ICD-9-CM Procedural

79.79 Closed reduction of dislocation of other specified site, except temporomandibular

27566

27566 Open treatment of patellar dislocation, with or without partial or total patellectomy

ICD-9-CM Diagnostic

718.36 Recurrent dislocation of lower leg joint
718.76 Developmental dislocation of joint, lower leg
836.3 Closed dislocation of patella
836.4 Open dislocation of patella

ICD-9-CM Procedural

77.86 Other partial ostectomy of patella
77.96 Total ostectomy of patella
79.89 Open reduction of dislocation of other specified site, except temporomandibular

27570

27570 Manipulation of knee joint under general anesthesia (includes application of traction or other fixation devices)

ICD-9-CM Diagnostic

357.1 Polyneuropathy in collagen vascular disease — (Code first underlying disease: 446.0, 710.0, 714.0) ☒
359.6 Symptomatic inflammatory myopathy in diseases classified elsewhere — (Code first underlying disease: 135, 140.0-208.9, 277.30-277.39, 446.0, 710.0, 710.1, 710.2, 714.0) ☒
446.0 Polyarteritis nodosa
710.0 Systemic lupus erythematosus — (Use additional code to identify manifestation: 424.91, 581.81, 582.81, 583.81)
710.1 Systemic sclerosis — (Use additional code to identify manifestation: 359.6, 517.2)
710.2 Sicca syndrome
714.0 Rheumatoid arthritis — (Use additional code to identify manifestation: 357.1, 359.6)
715.16 Primary localized osteoarthrosis, lower leg
715.96 Osteoarthrosis, unspecified whether generalized or localized, lower leg ▽
717.7 Chondromalacia of patella
717.83 Old disruption of anterior cruciate ligament
717.84 Old disruption of posterior cruciate ligament
718.26 Pathological dislocation of lower leg joint
718.46 Contracture of lower leg joint
718.56 Ankylosis of lower leg joint
718.76 Developmental dislocation of joint, lower leg
719.26 Villonodular synovitis, lower leg
719.56 Stiffness of joint, not elsewhere classified, lower leg
726.60 Unspecified enthesopathy of knee ▽
V43.65 Knee joint replacement by other means

ICD-9-CM Procedural

78.15 Application of external fixator device, femur
78.17 Application of external fixator device, tibia and fibula
84.71 Application of external fixator device, monoplanar system
84.72 Application of external fixator device, ring system
84.73 Application of hybrid external fixator device
93.25 Forced extension of limb
93.26 Manual rupture of joint adhesions
93.44 Other skeletal traction

27580

27580 Arthrodesis, knee, any technique

ICD-9-CM Diagnostic

136.1 Behcet's syndrome
711.16 Arthropathy associated with Reiter's disease and nonspecific urethritis, lower leg — (Code first underlying disease: 099.3, 099.4) ☒

711.26 Arthropathy in Behcet's syndrome, lower leg — (Code first underlying disease: 136.1) ☒
718.26 Pathological dislocation of lower leg joint
718.36 Recurrent dislocation of lower leg joint
718.46 Contracture of lower leg joint
718.56 Ankylosis of lower leg joint
718.86 Other joint derangement, not elsewhere classified, lower leg
726.60 Unspecified enthesopathy of knee ▽
733.15 Pathologic fracture of other specified part of femur
733.81 Malunion of fracture
733.82 Nonunion of fracture
733.92 Chondromalacia
756.51 Osteogenesis imperfecta

ICD-9-CM Procedural

81.22 Arthrodesis of knee

27590-27592

27590 Amputation, thigh, through femur, any level;
27591 immediate fitting technique including first cast
27592 open, circular (guillotine)

ICD-9-CM Diagnostic

170.7 Malignant neoplasm of long bones of lower limb
195.5 Malignant neoplasm of lower limb
198.5 Secondary malignant neoplasm of bone and bone marrow
249.70 Secondary diabetes mellitus with peripheral circulatory disorders, not stated as uncontrolled, or unspecified — (Use additional code to identify manifestation: 443.81, 785.4) (Use additional code to identify any associated insulin use: V58.67)
249.71 Secondary diabetes mellitus with peripheral circulatory disorders, uncontrolled — (Use additional code to identify manifestation: 443.81, 785.4) (Use additional code to identify any associated insulin use: V58.67)
249.80 Secondary diabetes mellitus with other specified manifestations, not stated as uncontrolled, or unspecified — (Use additional code to identify manifestation: 707.10-707.19, 707.8, 707.9, 731.8) (Use additional code to identify any associated insulin use: V58.67)
249.80 Secondary diabetes mellitus with other specified manifestations, not stated as uncontrolled, or unspecified — (Use additional code to identify manifestation: 707.10-707.19, 707.8, 707.9, 731.8) (Use additional code to identify any associated insulin use: V58.67)
249.81 Secondary diabetes mellitus with other specified manifestations, uncontrolled — (Use additional code to identify manifestation: 707.10-707.19, 707.8, 707.9, 731.8) (Use additional code to identify any associated insulin use: V58.67)
249.81 Secondary diabetes mellitus with other specified manifestations, uncontrolled — (Use additional code to identify manifestation: 707.10-707.19, 707.8, 707.9, 731.8) (Use additional code to identify any associated insulin use: V58.67)
250.70 Diabetes with peripheral circulatory disorders, type II or unspecified type, not stated as uncontrolled — (Use additional code to identify manifestation: 443.81, 785.4)
250.71 Diabetes with peripheral circulatory disorders, type I [juvenile type], not stated as uncontrolled — (Use additional code to identify manifestation: 443.81, 785.4)
250.72 Diabetes with peripheral circulatory disorders, type II or unspecified type, uncontrolled — (Use additional code to identify manifestation: 443.81, 785.4)
250.73 Diabetes with peripheral circulatory disorders, type I [juvenile type], uncontrolled — (Use additional code to identify manifestation: 443.81, 785.4)
250.80 Diabetes with other specified manifestations, type II or unspecified type, not stated as uncontrolled — (Use additional code to identify manifestation: 707.10-707.19, 707.8, 707.9, 731.8)
250.81 Diabetes with other specified manifestations, type I [juvenile type], not stated as uncontrolled — (Use additional code to identify manifestation: 707.10-707.19, 707.8, 707.9, 731.8)
250.82 Diabetes with other specified manifestations, type II or unspecified type, uncontrolled — (Use additional code to identify manifestation: 707.10-707.19, 707.8, 707.9, 731.8)
250.83 Diabetes with other specified manifestations, type I [juvenile type], uncontrolled — (Use additional code to identify manifestation: 707.10-707.19, 707.8, 707.9, 731.8)
440.20 Atherosclerosis of native arteries of the extremities, unspecified ▽
440.21 Atherosclerosis of native arteries of the extremities with intermittent claudication
440.22 Atherosclerosis of native arteries of the extremities with rest pain
440.23 Atherosclerosis of native arteries of the extremities with ulceration — (Use additional code for any associated ulceration: 707.10-707.19, 707.8, 707.9)
440.24 Atherosclerosis of native arteries of the extremities with gangrene — (Use additional code for any associated ulceration: 707.10-707.19, 707.8, 707.9)
443.1 Thromboangiitis obliterans (Buerger's disease)
443.81 Peripheral angiopathy in diseases classified elsewhere — (Code first underlying disease: 249.7, 250.7) ☒
443.9 Unspecified peripheral vascular disease ▽
444.22 Embolism and thrombosis of arteries of lower extremity
445.02 Atheroembolism of lower extremity
446.0 Polyarteritis nodosa
446.6 Thrombotic microangiopathy
447.5 Necrosis of artery
682.6 Cellulitis and abscess of leg, except foot — (Use additional code to identify organism, such as 041.1, etc.)
707.10 Ulcer of lower limb, unspecified — (Code, if applicable, any causal condition first: 249.80-249.81, 250.80-250.83, 440.23, 459.11, 459.13, 459.31, 459.33) ▽
707.11 Ulcer of thigh — (Code, if applicable, any causal condition first: 249.80-249.81, 250.80-250.83, 440.23, 459.11, 459.13, 459.31, 459.33)
728.89 Other disorder of muscle, ligament, and fascia — (Use additional E code to identify drug, if drug-induced)
730.15 Chronic osteomyelitis, pelvic region and thigh — (Use additional code to identify organism: 041.1. Use additional code to identify major osseous defect, if applicable: 731.3)
730.16 Chronic osteomyelitis, lower leg — (Use additional code to identify organism: 041.1. Use additional code to identify major osseous defect, if applicable: 731.3)
731.1 Osteitis deformans in diseases classified elsewhere — (Code first underlying disease: 170.0-170.9) ☒
731.3 Major osseous defects — (Code first underlying disease: 170.0-170.9, 730.00-730.29, 733.00-733.09, 733.40-733.49, 996.45)
731.8 Other bone involvement in diseases classified elsewhere — (Code first underlying disease: 249.8, 250.8. Use additional code to specify bone condition: 730.00-730.09) ☒
733.43 Aseptic necrosis of medial femoral condyle — (Use additional code to identify major osseous defect, if applicable: 731.3)
785.4 Gangrene — (Code first any associated underlying condition)
890.1 Open wound of hip and thigh, complicated
897.7 Traumatic amputation of leg(s) (complete) (partial), bilateral (any level), complicated
928.00 Crushing injury of thigh — (Use additional code to identify any associated injuries: 800-829, 850.0-854.1, 860.0-869.1)

ICD-9-CM Procedural

84.17 Amputation above knee
84.45 Fitting of prosthesis above knee

27594

27594 Amputation, thigh, through femur, any level; secondary closure or scar revision

ICD-9-CM Diagnostic

170.7 Malignant neoplasm of long bones of lower limb
195.5 Malignant neoplasm of lower limb
198.5 Secondary malignant neoplasm of bone and bone marrow

249.70 Secondary diabetes mellitus with peripheral circulatory disorders, not stated as uncontrolled, or unspecified — (Use additional code to identify manifestation: 443.81, 785.4) (Use additional code to identify any associated insulin use: V58.67)

249.71 Secondary diabetes mellitus with peripheral circulatory disorders, uncontrolled — (Use additional code to identify manifestation: 443.81, 785.4) (Use additional code to identify any associated insulin use: V58.67)

249.80 Secondary diabetes mellitus with other specified manifestations, not stated as uncontrolled, or unspecified — (Use additional code to identify manifestation: 707.10-707.19, 707.8, 707.9, 731.8) (Use additional code to identify any associated insulin use: V58.67)

249.81 Secondary diabetes mellitus with other specified manifestations, uncontrolled — (Use additional code to identify manifestation: 707.10-707.19, 707.8, 707.9, 731.8) (Use additional code to identify any associated insulin use: V58.67)

250.70 Diabetes with peripheral circulatory disorders, type II or unspecified type, not stated as uncontrolled — (Use additional code to identify manifestation: 443.81, 785.4)

250.71 Diabetes with peripheral circulatory disorders, type I [juvenile type], not stated as uncontrolled — (Use additional code to identify manifestation: 443.81, 785.4)

250.72 Diabetes with peripheral circulatory disorders, type II or unspecified type, uncontrolled — (Use additional code to identify manifestation: 443.81, 785.4)

250.73 Diabetes with peripheral circulatory disorders, type I [juvenile type], uncontrolled — (Use additional code to identify manifestation: 443.81, 785.4)

440.24 Atherosclerosis of native arteries of the extremities with gangrene — (Use additional code for any associated ulceration: 707.10-707.19, 707.8, 707.9)

682.6 Cellulitis and abscess of leg, except foot — (Use additional code to identify organism, such as 041.1, etc.)

707.10 Ulcer of lower limb, unspecified — (Code, if applicable, any causal condition first: 249.80-249.81, 250.80-250.83, 440.23, 459.11, 459.13, 459.31, 459.33) ▽

707.11 Ulcer of thigh — (Code, if applicable, any causal condition first: 249.80-249.81, 250.80-250.83, 440.23, 459.11, 459.13, 459.31, 459.33)

709.2 Scar condition and fibrosis of skin

730.15 Chronic osteomyelitis, pelvic region and thigh — (Use additional code to identify organism: 041.1. Use additional code to identify major osseous defect, if applicable: 731.3)

731.3 Major osseous defects — (Code first underlying disease: 170.0-170.9, 730.00-730.29, 733.00-733.09, 733.40-733.49, 996.45)

785.4 Gangrene — (Code first any associated underlying condition)

897.3 Traumatic amputation of leg(s) (complete) (partial), unilateral, at or above knee, complicated

897.7 Traumatic amputation of leg(s) (complete) (partial), bilateral (any level), complicated

928.00 Crushing injury of thigh — (Use additional code to identify any associated injuries: 800-829, 850.0-854.1, 860.0-869.1)

997.60 Late complications of amputation stump, unspecified — (Use additional code to identify complications) ▽

997.61 Neuroma of amputation stump — (Use additional code to identify complications)

997.62 Infection (chronic) of amputation stump — (Use additional code to identify complications)

997.69 Other late amputation stump complication — (Use additional code to identify complications)

ICD-9-CM Procedural

84.3 Revision of amputation stump

27596

27596 Amputation, thigh, through femur, any level; re-amputation

ICD-9-CM Diagnostic

249.70 Secondary diabetes mellitus with peripheral circulatory disorders, not stated as uncontrolled, or unspecified — (Use additional code to identify manifestation: 443.81, 785.4) (Use additional code to identify any associated insulin use: V58.67)

249.71 Secondary diabetes mellitus with peripheral circulatory disorders, uncontrolled — (Use additional code to identify manifestation: 443.81, 785.4) (Use additional code to identify any associated insulin use: V58.67)

249.80 Secondary diabetes mellitus with other specified manifestations, not stated as uncontrolled, or unspecified — (Use additional code to identify manifestation: 707.10-707.19, 707.8, 707.9, 731.8) (Use additional code to identify any associated insulin use: V58.67)

249.81 Secondary diabetes mellitus with other specified manifestations, uncontrolled — (Use additional code to identify manifestation: 707.10-707.19, 707.8, 707.9, 731.8) (Use additional code to identify any associated insulin use: V58.67)

250.70 Diabetes with peripheral circulatory disorders, type II or unspecified type, not stated as uncontrolled — (Use additional code to identify manifestation: 443.81, 785.4)

250.71 Diabetes with peripheral circulatory disorders, type I [juvenile type], not stated as uncontrolled — (Use additional code to identify manifestation: 443.81, 785.4)

250.72 Diabetes with peripheral circulatory disorders, type II or unspecified type, uncontrolled — (Use additional code to identify manifestation: 443.81, 785.4)

250.73 Diabetes with peripheral circulatory disorders, type I [juvenile type], uncontrolled — (Use additional code to identify manifestation: 443.81, 785.4)

250.80 Diabetes with other specified manifestations, type II or unspecified type, not stated as uncontrolled — (Use additional code to identify manifestation: 707.10-707.19, 707.8, 707.9, 731.8)

250.81 Diabetes with other specified manifestations, type I [juvenile type], not stated as uncontrolled — (Use additional code to identify manifestation: 707.10-707.19, 707.8, 707.9, 731.8)

250.82 Diabetes with other specified manifestations, type II or unspecified type, uncontrolled — (Use additional code to identify manifestation: 707.10-707.19, 707.8, 707.9, 731.8)

250.83 Diabetes with other specified manifestations, type I [juvenile type], uncontrolled — (Use additional code to identify manifestation: 707.10-707.19, 707.8, 707.9, 731.8)

440.24 Atherosclerosis of native arteries of the extremities with gangrene — (Use additional code for any associated ulceration: 707.10-707.19, 707.8, 707.9)

682.6 Cellulitis and abscess of leg, except foot — (Use additional code to identify organism, such as 041.1, etc.)

707.10 Ulcer of lower limb, unspecified — (Code, if applicable, any causal condition first: 249.80-249.81, 250.80-250.83, 440.23, 459.11, 459.13, 459.31, 459.33) ▽

707.11 Ulcer of thigh — (Code, if applicable, any causal condition first: 249.80-249.81, 250.80-250.83, 440.23, 459.11, 459.13, 459.31, 459.33)

728.86 Necrotizing fasciitis — (Use additional code to identify infectious organism, 041.00-041.89, 785.4, if applicable)

730.15 Chronic osteomyelitis, pelvic region and thigh — (Use additional code to identify organism: 041.1. Use additional code to identify major osseous defect, if applicable: 731.3)

730.16 Chronic osteomyelitis, lower leg — (Use additional code to identify organism: 041.1. Use additional code to identify major osseous defect, if applicable: 731.3)

731.8 Other bone involvement in diseases classified elsewhere — (Code first underlying disease: 249.8, 250.8. Use additional code to specify bone condition: 730.00-730.09) ■

733.15 Pathologic fracture of other specified part of femur

785.4 Gangrene — (Code first any associated underlying condition)

897.2 Traumatic amputation of leg(s) (complete) (partial), unilateral, at or above knee, without mention of complication

928.00 Crushing injury of thigh — (Use additional code to identify any associated injuries: 800-829, 850.0-854.1, 860.0-869.1)

997.60 Late complications of amputation stump, unspecified — (Use additional code to identify complications) ▽

997.61 Neuroma of amputation stump — (Use additional code to identify complications)

997.62 Infection (chronic) of amputation stump — (Use additional code to identify complications)

997.69 Other late amputation stump complication — (Use additional code to identify complications)

ICD-9-CM Procedural

84.3 Revision of amputation stump

27598

27598 Disarticulation at knee

ICD-9-CM Diagnostic

170.7 Malignant neoplasm of long bones of lower limb
195.5 Malignant neoplasm of lower limb
198.5 Secondary malignant neoplasm of bone and bone marrow
249.70 Secondary diabetes mellitus with peripheral circulatory disorders, not stated as uncontrolled, or unspecified — (Use additional code to identify manifestation: 443.81, 785.4) (Use additional code to identify any associated insulin use: V58.67)
249.71 Secondary diabetes mellitus with peripheral circulatory disorders, uncontrolled — (Use additional code to identify manifestation: 443.81, 785.4) (Use additional code to identify any associated insulin use: V58.67)
249.80 Secondary diabetes mellitus with other specified manifestations, not stated as uncontrolled, or unspecified — (Use additional code to identify manifestation: 707.10-707.19, 707.8, 707.9, 731.8) (Use additional code to identify any associated insulin use: V58.67)
249.81 Secondary diabetes mellitus with other specified manifestations, uncontrolled — (Use additional code to identify manifestation: 707.10-707.19, 707.8, 707.9, 731.8) (Use additional code to identify any associated insulin use: V58.67)
250.70 Diabetes with peripheral circulatory disorders, type II or unspecified type, not stated as uncontrolled — (Use additional code to identify manifestation: 443.81, 785.4)
250.71 Diabetes with peripheral circulatory disorders, type I [juvenile type], not stated as uncontrolled — (Use additional code to identify manifestation: 443.81, 785.4)
250.72 Diabetes with peripheral circulatory disorders, type II or unspecified type, uncontrolled — (Use additional code to identify manifestation: 443.81, 785.4)
250.73 Diabetes with peripheral circulatory disorders, type I [juvenile type], uncontrolled — (Use additional code to identify manifestation: 443.81, 785.4)
250.80 Diabetes with other specified manifestations, type II or unspecified type, not stated as uncontrolled — (Use additional code to identify manifestation: 707.10-707.19, 707.8, 707.9, 731.8)
250.81 Diabetes with other specified manifestations, type I [juvenile type], not stated as uncontrolled — (Use additional code to identify manifestation: 707.10-707.19, 707.8, 707.9, 731.8)
250.82 Diabetes with other specified manifestations, type II or unspecified type, uncontrolled — (Use additional code to identify manifestation: 707.10-707.19, 707.8, 707.9, 731.8)
250.83 Diabetes with other specified manifestations, type I [juvenile type], uncontrolled — (Use additional code to identify manifestation: 707.10-707.19, 707.8, 707.9, 731.8)
440.20 Atherosclerosis of native arteries of the extremities, unspecified ▽
440.21 Atherosclerosis of native arteries of the extremities with intermittent claudication
440.22 Atherosclerosis of native arteries of the extremities with rest pain
440.23 Atherosclerosis of native arteries of the extremities with ulceration — (Use additional code for any associated ulceration: 707.10-707.19, 707.8, 707.9)
440.24 Atherosclerosis of native arteries of the extremities with gangrene — (Use additional code for any associated ulceration: 707.10-707.19, 707.8, 707.9)
443.1 Thromboangiitis obliterans (Buerger's disease)
443.81 Peripheral angiopathy in diseases classified elsewhere — (Code first underlying disease: 249.7, 250.7) ☒
682.6 Cellulitis and abscess of leg, except foot — (Use additional code to identify organism, such as 041.1, etc.)
730.16 Chronic osteomyelitis, lower leg — (Use additional code to identify organism: 041.1. Use additional code to identify major osseous defect, if applicable: 731.3)
731.1 Osteitis deformans in diseases classified elsewhere — (Code first underlying disease: 170.0-170.9) ☒
731.3 Major osseous defects — (Code first underlying disease: 170.0-170.9, 730.00-730.29, 733.00-733.09, 733.40-733.49, 996.45)
731.8 Other bone involvement in diseases classified elsewhere — (Code first underlying disease: 249.8, 250.8. Use additional code to specify bone condition: 730.00-730.09) ☒
733.43 Aseptic necrosis of medial femoral condyle — (Use additional code to identify major osseous defect, if applicable: 731.3)
785.4 Gangrene — (Code first any associated underlying condition)
891.1 Open wound of knee, leg (except thigh), and ankle, complicated
897.3 Traumatic amputation of leg(s) (complete) (partial), unilateral, at or above knee, complicated
928.10 Crushing injury of lower leg — (Use additional code to identify any associated injuries: 800-829, 850.0-854.1, 860.0-869.1)
928.11 Crushing injury of knee — (Use additional code to identify any associated injuries: 800-829, 850.0-854.1, 860.0-869.1)

ICD-9-CM Procedural

84.16 Disarticulation of knee

Leg (Tibia and Fibula) and Ankle Joint

27600-27602

27600 Decompression fasciotomy, leg; anterior and/or lateral compartments only
27601 posterior compartment(s) only
27602 anterior and/or lateral, and posterior compartment(s)

ICD-9-CM Diagnostic

728.0 Infective myositis
728.81 Interstitial myositis
728.88 Rhabdomyolysis
729.72 Nontraumatic compartment syndrome of lower extremity — (Code first, if applicable, postprocedural complication: 998.89)
906.4 Late effect of crushing
906.7 Late effect of burn of other extremities
928.10 Crushing injury of lower leg — (Use additional code to identify any associated injuries: 800-829, 850.0-854.1, 860.0-869.1)
928.11 Crushing injury of knee — (Use additional code to identify any associated injuries: 800-829, 850.0-854.1, 860.0-869.1)
945.44 Deep necrosis of underlying tissues due to burn (deep third degree) of lower leg, without mention of loss of a body part
945.45 Deep necrosis of underlying tissues due to burn (deep third degree) of knee, without mention of loss of a body part
945.49 Deep necrosis of underlying tissues due to burn (deep third degree) of multiple sites of lower limb(s), without mention of loss of a body part
958.8 Other early complications of trauma
958.92 Traumatic compartment syndrome of lower extremity

ICD-9-CM Procedural

83.14 Fasciotomy

27603

27603 Incision and drainage, leg or ankle; deep abscess or hematoma

ICD-9-CM Diagnostic

682.6 Cellulitis and abscess of leg, except foot — (Use additional code to identify organism, such as 041.1, etc.)
707.10 Ulcer of lower limb, unspecified — (Code, if applicable, any causal condition first: 249.80-249.81, 250.80-250.83, 440.23, 459.11, 459.13, 459.31, 459.33) ▽
707.11 Ulcer of thigh — (Code, if applicable, any causal condition first: 249.80-249.81, 250.80-250.83, 440.23, 459.11, 459.13, 459.31, 459.33)
707.12 Ulcer of calf — (Code, if applicable, any causal condition first: 249.80-249.81, 250.80-250.83, 440.23, 459.11, 459.13, 459.31, 459.33)
707.13 Ulcer of ankle — (Code, if applicable, any causal condition first: 249.80-249.81, 250.80-250.83, 440.23, 459.11, 459.13, 459.31, 459.33)
719.17 Hemarthrosis, ankle and foot
719.47 Pain in joint, ankle and foot
730.26 Unspecified osteomyelitis, lower leg — (Use additional code to identify organism: 041.1. Use additional code to identify major osseous defect, if applicable: 731.3) ▽
731.3 Major osseous defects — (Code first underlying disease: 170.0-170.9, 730.00-730.29, 733.00-733.09, 733.40-733.49, 996.45)

780.62 Postprocedural fever
891.1 Open wound of knee, leg (except thigh), and ankle, complicated
924.10 Contusion of lower leg
924.21 Contusion of ankle
998.11 Hemorrhage complicating a procedure
998.12 Hematoma complicating a procedure
998.13 Seroma complicating a procedure

ICD-9-CM Procedural

83.02 Myotomy
83.09 Other incision of soft tissue

HCPCS Level II Supplies & Services

A4305 Disposable drug delivery system, flow rate of 50 ml or greater per hour

27604

27604 Incision and drainage, leg or ankle; infected bursa

ICD-9-CM Diagnostic

726.70 Unspecified enthesopathy of ankle and tarsus ▽
726.71 Achilles bursitis or tendinitis
726.79 Other enthesopathy of ankle and tarsus

ICD-9-CM Procedural

83.03 Bursotomy

HCPCS Level II Supplies & Services

A4305 Disposable drug delivery system, flow rate of 50 ml or greater per hour

27605-27606

27605 Tenotomy, percutaneous, Achilles tendon (separate procedure); local anesthesia
27606 general anesthesia

ICD-9-CM Diagnostic

726.71 Achilles bursitis or tendinitis
727.06 Tenosynovitis of foot and ankle
727.81 Contracture of tendon (sheath)

ICD-9-CM Procedural

83.11 Achillotenotomy

HCPCS Level II Supplies & Services

A4580 Cast supplies (e.g., plaster)

27607

27607 Incision (eg, osteomyelitis or bone abscess), leg or ankle

ICD-9-CM Diagnostic

682.6 Cellulitis and abscess of leg, except foot — (Use additional code to identify organism, such as 041.1, etc.)
711.06 Pyogenic arthritis, lower leg — (Use additional code to identify infectious organism: 041.0-041.8)
711.07 Pyogenic arthritis, ankle and foot — (Use additional code to identify infectious organism: 041.0-041.8)
730.16 Chronic osteomyelitis, lower leg — (Use additional code to identify organism: 041.1. Use additional code to identify major osseous defect, if applicable: 731.3)
730.17 Chronic osteomyelitis, ankle and foot — (Use additional code to identify organism: 041.1. Use additional code to identify major osseous defect, if applicable: 731.3)
730.26 Unspecified osteomyelitis, lower leg — (Use additional code to identify organism: 041.1. Use additional code to identify major osseous defect, if applicable: 731.3) ▽
730.27 Unspecified osteomyelitis, ankle and foot — (Use additional code to identify organism: 041.1. Use additional code to identify major osseous defect, if applicable: 731.3) ▽
730.97 Unspecified infection of bone, ankle and foot — (Use additional code to identify organism: 041.1) ▽
731.3 Major osseous defects — (Code first underlying disease: 170.0-170.9, 730.00-730.29, 733.00-733.09, 733.40-733.49, 996.45)
891.1 Open wound of knee, leg (except thigh), and ankle, complicated
996.66 Infection and inflammatory reaction due to internal joint prosthesis — (Use additional code to identify specified infections. Use additional code to identify infected prosthetic joint: V43.60-V43.69)
996.67 Infection and inflammatory reaction due to other internal orthopedic device, implant, and graft — (Use additional code to identify specified infections)
998.59 Other postoperative infection — (Use additional code to identify infection)

ICD-9-CM Procedural

77.17 Other incision of tibia and fibula without division
77.18 Other incision of tarsals and metatarsals without division

27610

27610 Arthrotomy, ankle, including exploration, drainage, or removal of foreign body

ICD-9-CM Diagnostic

711.07 Pyogenic arthritis, ankle and foot — (Use additional code to identify infectious organism: 041.0-041.8)
715.37 Localized osteoarthrosis not specified whether primary or secondary, ankle and foot
718.17 Loose body in ankle and foot joint
719.07 Effusion of ankle and foot joint
730.17 Chronic osteomyelitis, ankle and foot — (Use additional code to identify organism: 041.1. Use additional code to identify major osseous defect, if applicable: 731.3)
730.27 Unspecified osteomyelitis, ankle and foot — (Use additional code to identify organism: 041.1. Use additional code to identify major osseous defect, if applicable: 731.3) ▽
730.97 Unspecified infection of bone, ankle and foot — (Use additional code to identify organism: 041.1) ▽
731.3 Major osseous defects — (Code first underlying disease: 170.0-170.9, 730.00-730.29, 733.00-733.09, 733.40-733.49, 996.45)
996.66 Infection and inflammatory reaction due to internal joint prosthesis — (Use additional code to identify specified infections. Use additional code to identify infected prosthetic joint: V43.60-V43.69)
996.67 Infection and inflammatory reaction due to other internal orthopedic device, implant, and graft — (Use additional code to identify specified infections)
V64.43 Arthroscopic surgical procedure converted to open procedure

ICD-9-CM Procedural

80.17 Other arthrotomy of ankle

27612

27612 Arthrotomy, posterior capsular release, ankle, with or without Achilles tendon lengthening

ICD-9-CM Diagnostic

718.47 Contracture of ankle and foot joint
727.81 Contracture of tendon (sheath)
736.71 Acquired equinovarus deformity
736.72 Equinus deformity of foot, acquired
754.50 Congenital talipes varus
754.51 Congenital talipes equinovarus
754.69 Other congenital valgus deformity of feet

ICD-9-CM Procedural

80.47 Division of joint capsule, ligament, or cartilage of ankle
83.85 Other change in muscle or tendon length

27613-27614

27613 Biopsy, soft tissue of leg or ankle area; superficial
27614 deep (subfascial or intramuscular)

ICD-9-CM Diagnostic

171.3 Malignant neoplasm of connective and other soft tissue of lower limb, including hip
172.7 Malignant melanoma of skin of lower limb, including hip
215.3 Other benign neoplasm of connective and other soft tissue of lower limb, including hip
238.1 Neoplasm of uncertain behavior of connective and other soft tissue
239.2 Neoplasms of unspecified nature of bone, soft tissue, and skin
682.6 Cellulitis and abscess of leg, except foot — (Use additional code to identify organism, such as 041.1, etc.)
782.2 Localized superficial swelling, mass, or lump

ICD-9-CM Procedural

83.21 Open biopsy of soft tissue

HCPCS Level II Supplies & Services

A4305 Disposable drug delivery system, flow rate of 50 ml or greater per hour

27615-27619 [27632, 27634]

27615 Radical resection of tumor (eg, sarcoma), soft tissue of leg or ankle area; less than 5 cm
27616 5 cm or greater
27618 Excision, tumor, soft tissue of leg or ankle area, subcutaneous; less than 3 cm
27619 Excision, tumor, soft tissue of leg or ankle area, subfascial (eg, intramuscular); less than 5 cm
27632 3 cm or greater
27634 5 cm or greater

ICD-9-CM Diagnostic

171.3 Malignant neoplasm of connective and other soft tissue of lower limb, including hip
172.7 Malignant melanoma of skin of lower limb, including hip
173.70 Unspecified malignant neoplasm of skin of lower limb, including hip ▽
173.71 Basal cell carcinoma of skin of lower limb, including hip
173.72 Squamous cell carcinoma of skin of lower limb, including hip
173.79 Other specified malignant neoplasm of skin of lower limb, including hip
195.5 Malignant neoplasm of lower limb
209.34 Merkel cell carcinoma of the lower limb
209.75 Secondary Merkel cell carcinoma
214.1 Lipoma of other skin and subcutaneous tissue
215.3 Other benign neoplasm of connective and other soft tissue of lower limb, including hip
238.1 Neoplasm of uncertain behavior of connective and other soft tissue
239.2 Neoplasms of unspecified nature of bone, soft tissue, and skin

ICD-9-CM Procedural

83.31 Excision of lesion of tendon sheath
83.32 Excision of lesion of muscle
83.39 Excision of lesion of other soft tissue
83.49 Other excision of soft tissue
86.3 Other local excision or destruction of lesion or tissue of skin and subcutaneous tissue
86.4 Radical excision of skin lesion

HCPCS Level II Supplies & Services

A4305 Disposable drug delivery system, flow rate of 50 ml or greater per hour

27620

27620 Arthrotomy, ankle, with joint exploration, with or without biopsy, with or without removal of loose or foreign body

ICD-9-CM Diagnostic

275.40 Unspecified disorder of calcium metabolism — (Use additional code to identify any associated intellectual disabilities) ▽
275.42 Hypercalcemia — (Use additional code to identify any associated intellectual disabilities)
275.49 Other disorders of calcium metabolism — (Use additional code to identify any associated intellectual disabilities)
275.5 Hungry bone syndrome — (Use additional code to identify any associated intellectual disabilities)
715.17 Primary localized osteoarthrosis, ankle and foot
715.27 Secondary localized osteoarthrosis, ankle and foot
715.97 Osteoarthrosis, unspecified whether generalized or localized, ankle and foot ▽
716.17 Traumatic arthropathy, ankle and foot
716.97 Unspecified arthropathy, ankle and foot ▽
718.17 Loose body in ankle and foot joint
718.87 Other joint derangement, not elsewhere classified, ankle and foot
719.47 Pain in joint, ankle and foot
726.91 Exostosis of unspecified site ▽
732.7 Osteochondritis dissecans
733.82 Nonunion of fracture
733.90 Disorder of bone and cartilage, unspecified ▽
996.40 Unspecified mechanical complication of internal orthopedic device, implant, and graft — (Use additional code to identify prosthetic joint with mechanical complication, V43.60-V43.69) ▽
996.49 Other mechanical complication of other internal orthopedic device, implant, and graft — (Use additional code to identify prosthetic joint with mechanical complication, V43.60-V43.69)
996.67 Infection and inflammatory reaction due to other internal orthopedic device, implant, and graft — (Use additional code to identify specified infections)
996.78 Other complications due to other internal orthopedic device, implant, and graft — (Use additional code to identify complication: 338.18-338.19, 338.28-338.29)
V64.43 Arthroscopic surgical procedure converted to open procedure

ICD-9-CM Procedural

80.17 Other arthrotomy of ankle
80.37 Biopsy of joint structure of ankle

27625-27626

27625 Arthrotomy, with synovectomy, ankle;
27626 including tenosynovectomy

ICD-9-CM Diagnostic

357.1 Polyneuropathy in collagen vascular disease — (Code first underlying disease: 446.0, 710.0, 714.0) ☒
359.6 Symptomatic inflammatory myopathy in diseases classified elsewhere — (Code first underlying disease: 135, 140.0-208.9, 277.30-277.39, 446.0, 710.0, 710.1, 710.2, 714.0) ☒
446.0 Polyarteritis nodosa
710.0 Systemic lupus erythematosus — (Use additional code to identify manifestation: 424.91, 581.81, 582.81, 583.81)
710.1 Systemic sclerosis — (Use additional code to identify manifestation: 359.6, 517.2)
710.2 Sicca syndrome
714.0 Rheumatoid arthritis — (Use additional code to identify manifestation: 357.1, 359.6)
719.27 Villonodular synovitis, ankle and foot
V64.43 Arthroscopic surgical procedure converted to open procedure

ICD-9-CM Procedural

80.77 Synovectomy of ankle

83.42 Other tenonectomy

27630

27630 Excision of lesion of tendon sheath or capsule (eg, cyst or ganglion), leg and/or ankle

ICD-9-CM Diagnostic

215.3 Other benign neoplasm of connective and other soft tissue of lower limb, including hip
719.27 Villonodular synovitis, ankle and foot
727.42 Ganglion of tendon sheath

ICD-9-CM Procedural

83.31 Excision of lesion of tendon sheath

HCPCS Level II Supplies & Services

A4305 Disposable drug delivery system, flow rate of 50 ml or greater per hour

27635-27638

27635 Excision or curettage of bone cyst or benign tumor, tibia or fibula;
27637 with autograft (includes obtaining graft)
27638 with allograft

ICD-9-CM Diagnostic

213.7 Benign neoplasm of long bones of lower limb
238.0 Neoplasm of uncertain behavior of bone and articular cartilage
239.2 Neoplasms of unspecified nature of bone, soft tissue, and skin
726.91 Exostosis of unspecified site
730.26 Unspecified osteomyelitis, lower leg — (Use additional code to identify organism: 041.1. Use additional code to identify major osseous defect, if applicable: 731.3)
731.3 Major osseous defects — (Code first underlying disease: 170.0-170.9, 730.00-730.29, 733.00-733.09, 733.40-733.49, 996.45)
733.21 Solitary bone cyst
733.99 Other disorders of bone and cartilage
756.4 Chondrodystrophy

ICD-9-CM Procedural

77.67 Local excision of lesion or tissue of tibia and fibula
77.77 Excision of tibia and fibula for graft
78.07 Bone graft of tibia and fibula

HCPCS Level II Supplies & Services

A4305 Disposable drug delivery system, flow rate of 50 ml or greater per hour

27640-27641

27640 Partial excision (craterization, saucerization, or diaphysectomy), bone (eg, osteomyelitis); tibia
27641 fibula

ICD-9-CM Diagnostic

730.06 Acute osteomyelitis, lower leg — (Use additional code to identify organism: 041.1. Use additional code to identify major osseous defect, if applicable: 731.3)
730.16 Chronic osteomyelitis, lower leg — (Use additional code to identify organism: 041.1. Use additional code to identify major osseous defect, if applicable: 731.3)
730.26 Unspecified osteomyelitis, lower leg — (Use additional code to identify organism: 041.1. Use additional code to identify major osseous defect, if applicable: 731.3)
730.36 Periostitis, without mention of osteomyelitis, lower leg — (Use additional code to identify organism: 041.1)
731.3 Major osseous defects — (Code first underlying disease: 170.0-170.9, 730.00-730.29, 733.00-733.09, 733.40-733.49, 996.45)

ICD-9-CM Procedural

77.87 Other partial ostectomy of tibia and fibula

27645-27647

27645 Radical resection of tumor; tibia
27646 fibula
27647 talus or calcaneus

ICD-9-CM Diagnostic

170.7 Malignant neoplasm of long bones of lower limb
170.8 Malignant neoplasm of short bones of lower limb
198.5 Secondary malignant neoplasm of bone and bone marrow
209.73 Secondary neuroendocrine tumor of bone
238.0 Neoplasm of uncertain behavior of bone and articular cartilage
239.2 Neoplasms of unspecified nature of bone, soft tissue, and skin

ICD-9-CM Procedural

77.97 Total ostectomy of tibia and fibula
77.99 Total ostectomy of other bone, except facial bones

27648

27648 Injection procedure for ankle arthrography

ICD-9-CM Diagnostic

275.40 Unspecified disorder of calcium metabolism — (Use additional code to identify any associated intellectual disabilities)
275.42 Hypercalcemia — (Use additional code to identify any associated intellectual disabilities)
275.49 Other disorders of calcium metabolism — (Use additional code to identify any associated intellectual disabilities)
275.5 Hungry bone syndrome — (Use additional code to identify any associated intellectual disabilities)
357.1 Polyneuropathy in collagen vascular disease — (Code first underlying disease: 446.0, 710.0, 714.0) ☒
359.6 Symptomatic inflammatory myopathy in diseases classified elsewhere — (Code first underlying disease: 135, 140.0-208.9, 277.30-277.39, 446.0, 710.0, 710.1, 710.2, 714.0) ☒
446.0 Polyarteritis nodosa
710.0 Systemic lupus erythematosus — (Use additional code to identify manifestation: 424.91, 581.81, 582.81, 583.81)
710.1 Systemic sclerosis — (Use additional code to identify manifestation: 359.6, 517.2)
710.2 Sicca syndrome
714.0 Rheumatoid arthritis — (Use additional code to identify manifestation: 357.1, 359.6)
715.97 Osteoarthrosis, unspecified whether generalized or localized, ankle and foot
718.17 Loose body in ankle and foot joint
719.07 Effusion of ankle and foot joint
732.7 Osteochondritis dissecans
905.4 Late effect of fracture of lower extremities

ICD-9-CM Procedural

81.99 Other operations on joint structures
88.32 Contrast arthrogram

27650-27652

27650 Repair, primary, open or percutaneous, ruptured Achilles tendon;
27652 with graft (includes obtaining graft)

ICD-9-CM Diagnostic

727.67 Nontraumatic rupture of Achilles tendon
845.09 Other ankle sprain and strain
891.2 Open wound of knee, leg (except thigh), and ankle, with tendon involvement
928.20 Crushing injury of foot — (Use additional code to identify any associated injuries: 800-829, 850.0-854.1, 860.0-869.1)

ICD-9-CM Procedural

83.64 Other suture of tendon

27654

27654 Repair, secondary, Achilles tendon, with or without graft

ICD-9-CM Diagnostic

727.67 Nontraumatic rupture of Achilles tendon
845.09 Other ankle sprain and strain
892.1 Open wound of foot except toe(s) alone, complicated
928.20 Crushing injury of foot — (Use additional code to identify any associated injuries: 800-829, 850.0-854.1, 860.0-869.1)

ICD-9-CM Procedural

83.41 Excision of tendon for graft
83.62 Delayed suture of tendon
83.81 Tendon graft

27656

27656 Repair, fascial defect of leg

ICD-9-CM Diagnostic

728.89 Other disorder of muscle, ligament, and fascia — (Use additional E code to identify drug, if drug-induced)
729.4 Unspecified fasciitis ▽

ICD-9-CM Procedural

83.89 Other plastic operations on fascia

27658-27659

27658 Repair, flexor tendon, leg; primary, without graft, each tendon
27659 secondary, with or without graft, each tendon

ICD-9-CM Diagnostic

727.68 Nontraumatic rupture of other tendons of foot and ankle
727.69 Nontraumatic rupture of other tendon
891.2 Open wound of knee, leg (except thigh), and ankle, with tendon involvement
894.1 Multiple and unspecified open wound of lower limb, complicated
894.2 Multiple and unspecified open wound of lower limb, with tendon involvement
905.8 Late effect of tendon injury
906.4 Late effect of crushing

ICD-9-CM Procedural

83.41 Excision of tendon for graft
83.62 Delayed suture of tendon
83.64 Other suture of tendon
83.81 Tendon graft

27664-27665

27664 Repair, extensor tendon, leg; primary, without graft, each tendon
27665 secondary, with or without graft, each tendon

ICD-9-CM Diagnostic

727.68 Nontraumatic rupture of other tendons of foot and ankle
727.69 Nontraumatic rupture of other tendon
891.2 Open wound of knee, leg (except thigh), and ankle, with tendon involvement
894.2 Multiple and unspecified open wound of lower limb, with tendon involvement
905.8 Late effect of tendon injury
906.4 Late effect of crushing
959.7 Injury, other and unspecified, knee, leg, ankle, and foot

ICD-9-CM Procedural

83.41 Excision of tendon for graft
83.62 Delayed suture of tendon
83.64 Other suture of tendon
83.81 Tendon graft

27675-27676

27675 Repair, dislocating peroneal tendons; without fibular osteotomy
27676 with fibular osteotomy

ICD-9-CM Diagnostic

718.37 Recurrent dislocation of ankle and foot joint
718.77 Developmental dislocation of joint, ankle and foot
718.87 Other joint derangement, not elsewhere classified, ankle and foot
726.79 Other enthesopathy of ankle and tarsus
727.00 Unspecified synovitis and tenosynovitis ▽
837.0 Closed dislocation of ankle
845.00 Unspecified site of ankle sprain and strain ▽
891.2 Open wound of knee, leg (except thigh), and ankle, with tendon involvement

ICD-9-CM Procedural

77.17 Other incision of tibia and fibula without division
83.64 Other suture of tendon
83.76 Other tendon transposition
83.88 Other plastic operations on tendon

27680-27681

27680 Tenolysis, flexor or extensor tendon, leg and/or ankle; single, each tendon
27681 multiple tendons (through separate incision[s])

ICD-9-CM Diagnostic

718.57 Ankylosis of ankle and foot joint
719.57 Stiffness of joint, not elsewhere classified, ankle and foot
727.81 Contracture of tendon (sheath)
959.7 Injury, other and unspecified, knee, leg, ankle, and foot

ICD-9-CM Procedural

83.91 Lysis of adhesions of muscle, tendon, fascia, and bursa

27685-27686

27685 Lengthening or shortening of tendon, leg or ankle; single tendon (separate procedure)
27686 multiple tendons (through same incision), each

ICD-9-CM Diagnostic

718.46 Contracture of lower leg joint
718.47 Contracture of ankle and foot joint
727.81 Contracture of tendon (sheath)
736.70 Unspecified deformity of ankle and foot, acquired ▽
736.72 Equinus deformity of foot, acquired
736.79 Other acquired deformity of ankle and foot
754.51 Congenital talipes equinovarus
754.69 Other congenital valgus deformity of feet
754.79 Other congenital deformity of feet

ICD-9-CM Procedural

83.85 Other change in muscle or tendon length

27687

27687 Gastrocnemius recession (eg, Strayer procedure)

ICD-9-CM Diagnostic

343.9 Unspecified infantile cerebral palsy ▽
727.81 Contracture of tendon (sheath)

ICD-9-CM Procedural

83.72 Recession of tendon

27690-27692

27690 Transfer or transplant of single tendon (with muscle redirection or rerouting); superficial (eg, anterior tibial extensors into midfoot)

27691 deep (eg, anterior tibial or posterior tibial through interosseous space, flexor digitorum longus, flexor hallucis longus, or peroneal tendon to midfoot or hindfoot)

27692 each additional tendon (List separately in addition to code for primary procedure)

ICD-9-CM Diagnostic

718.47 Contracture of ankle and foot joint
726.72 Tibialis tendinitis
726.90 Enthesopathy of unspecified site ▽
727.06 Tenosynovitis of foot and ankle
727.68 Nontraumatic rupture of other tendons of foot and ankle
727.81 Contracture of tendon (sheath)
736.72 Equinus deformity of foot, acquired
754.51 Congenital talipes equinovarus

ICD-9-CM Procedural

83.75 Tendon transfer or transplantation
83.79 Other muscle transposition

27695-27696

27695 Repair, primary, disrupted ligament, ankle; collateral
27696 both collateral ligaments

ICD-9-CM Diagnostic

837.1 Open dislocation of ankle
845.00 Unspecified site of ankle sprain and strain ▽
845.01 Sprain and strain of deltoid (ligament) of ankle
845.02 Sprain and strain of calcaneofibular (ligament)
845.03 Sprain and strain of tibiofibular (ligament)
845.09 Other ankle sprain and strain
891.1 Open wound of knee, leg (except thigh), and ankle, complicated
959.7 Injury, other and unspecified, knee, leg, ankle, and foot

ICD-9-CM Procedural

81.94 Suture of capsule or ligament of ankle and foot

27698

27698 Repair, secondary, disrupted ligament, ankle, collateral (eg, Watson-Jones procedure)

ICD-9-CM Diagnostic

718.37 Recurrent dislocation of ankle and foot joint
726.79 Other enthesopathy of ankle and tarsus
845.01 Sprain and strain of deltoid (ligament) of ankle
845.02 Sprain and strain of calcaneofibular (ligament)
845.03 Sprain and strain of tibiofibular (ligament)
845.09 Other ankle sprain and strain
959.7 Injury, other and unspecified, knee, leg, ankle, and foot

ICD-9-CM Procedural

81.49 Other repair of ankle
81.94 Suture of capsule or ligament of ankle and foot

27700

27700 Arthroplasty, ankle;

ICD-9-CM Diagnostic

357.1 Polyneuropathy in collagen vascular disease — (Code first underlying disease: 446.0, 710.0, 714.0) ☒
359.6 Symptomatic inflammatory myopathy in diseases classified elsewhere — (Code first underlying disease: 135, 140.0-208.9, 277.30-277.39, 446.0, 710.0, 710.1, 710.2, 714.0) ☒
446.0 Polyarteritis nodosa
710.0 Systemic lupus erythematosus — (Use additional code to identify manifestation: 424.91, 581.81, 582.81, 583.81)
710.1 Systemic sclerosis — (Use additional code to identify manifestation: 359.6, 517.2)
710.2 Sicca syndrome
714.0 Rheumatoid arthritis — (Use additional code to identify manifestation: 357.1, 359.6)
715.17 Primary localized osteoarthrosis, ankle and foot
715.97 Osteoarthrosis, unspecified whether generalized or localized, ankle and foot ▽
718.57 Ankylosis of ankle and foot joint
718.87 Other joint derangement, not elsewhere classified, ankle and foot
V88.29 Acquired absence of other joint

ICD-9-CM Procedural

81.49 Other repair of ankle

27702

27702 Arthroplasty, ankle; with implant (total ankle)

ICD-9-CM Diagnostic

357.1 Polyneuropathy in collagen vascular disease — (Code first underlying disease: 446.0, 710.0, 714.0) ☒
359.6 Symptomatic inflammatory myopathy in diseases classified elsewhere — (Code first underlying disease: 135, 140.0-208.9, 277.30-277.39, 446.0, 710.0, 710.1, 710.2, 714.0) ☒
446.0 Polyarteritis nodosa
710.0 Systemic lupus erythematosus — (Use additional code to identify manifestation: 424.91, 581.81, 582.81, 583.81)
710.1 Systemic sclerosis — (Use additional code to identify manifestation: 359.6, 517.2)
710.2 Sicca syndrome
714.0 Rheumatoid arthritis — (Use additional code to identify manifestation: 357.1, 359.6)
715.17 Primary localized osteoarthrosis, ankle and foot
715.97 Osteoarthrosis, unspecified whether generalized or localized, ankle and foot ▽
718.57 Ankylosis of ankle and foot joint
718.87 Other joint derangement, not elsewhere classified, ankle and foot
730.27 Unspecified osteomyelitis, ankle and foot — (Use additional code to identify organism: 041.1. Use additional code to identify major osseous defect, if applicable: 731.3) ▽
731.3 Major osseous defects — (Code first underlying disease: 170.0-170.9, 730.00-730.29, 733.00-733.09, 733.40-733.49, 996.45)
824.9 Unspecified open fracture of ankle ▽
V88.29 Acquired absence of other joint

ICD-9-CM Procedural

81.56 Total ankle replacement

27703

27703 Arthroplasty, ankle; revision, total ankle

ICD-9-CM Diagnostic

357.1 Polyneuropathy in collagen vascular disease — (Code first underlying disease: 446.0, 710.0, 714.0) ☒
359.6 Symptomatic inflammatory myopathy in diseases classified elsewhere — (Code first underlying disease: 135, 140.0-208.9, 277.30-277.39, 446.0, 710.0, 710.1, 710.2, 714.0) ☒
446.0 Polyarteritis nodosa
710.0 Systemic lupus erythematosus — (Use additional code to identify manifestation: 424.91, 581.81, 582.81, 583.81)
710.1 Systemic sclerosis — (Use additional code to identify manifestation: 359.6, 517.2)
710.2 Sicca syndrome
714.0 Rheumatoid arthritis — (Use additional code to identify manifestation: 357.1, 359.6)

715.17 Primary localized osteoarthrosis, ankle and foot
715.27 Secondary localized osteoarthrosis, ankle and foot
715.97 Osteoarthrosis, unspecified whether generalized or localized, ankle and foot
718.57 Ankylosis of ankle and foot joint
718.87 Other joint derangement, not elsewhere classified, ankle and foot
731.3 Major osseous defects — (Code first underlying disease: 170.0-170.9, 730.00-730.29, 733.00-733.09, 733.40-733.49, 996.45)
733.16 Pathologic fracture of tibia and fibula
996.40 Unspecified mechanical complication of internal orthopedic device, implant, and graft — (Use additional code to identify prosthetic joint with mechanical complication, V43.60-V43.69)
996.41 Mechanical loosening of prosthetic joint — (Use additional code to identify prosthetic joint with mechanical complication, V43.60-V43.69)
996.42 Dislocation of prosthetic joint — (Use additional code to identify prosthetic joint with mechanical complication, V43.60-V43.69)
996.43 Broken prosthetic joint implant — (Use additional code to identify prosthetic joint with mechanical complication, V43.60-V43.69)
996.44 Peri-prosthetic fracture around prosthetic joint — (Use additional code to identify prosthetic joint with mechanical complication, V43.60-V43.69.
996.45 Peri-prosthetic osteolysis — (Use additional code to identify prosthetic joint with mechanical complication, V43.60-V43.69. Use additional code to identify major osseous defect, if applicable: 731.3)
996.46 Articular bearing surface wear of prosthetic joint — (Use additional code to identify prosthetic joint with mechanical complication, V43.60-V43.69)
996.47 Other mechanical complication of prosthetic joint implant — (Use additional code to identify prosthetic joint with mechanical complication, V43.60-V43.69)
996.66 Infection and inflammatory reaction due to internal joint prosthesis — (Use additional code to identify specified infections. Use additional code to identify infected prosthetic joint: V43.60-V43.69)
996.77 Other complications due to internal joint prosthesis — (Use additional code to identify complication: 338.18-338.19, 338.28-338.29)
V43.66 Ankle joint replacement by other means

ICD-9-CM Procedural

81.59 Revision of joint replacement of lower extremity, not elsewhere classified

27704

27704 Removal of ankle implant

ICD-9-CM Diagnostic

731.3 Major osseous defects — (Code first underlying disease: 170.0-170.9, 730.00-730.29, 733.00-733.09, 733.40-733.49, 996.45)
996.40 Unspecified mechanical complication of internal orthopedic device, implant, and graft — (Use additional code to identify prosthetic joint with mechanical complication, V43.60-V43.69)
996.41 Mechanical loosening of prosthetic joint — (Use additional code to identify prosthetic joint with mechanical complication, V43.60-V43.69)
996.42 Dislocation of prosthetic joint — (Use additional code to identify prosthetic joint with mechanical complication, V43.60-V43.69)
996.43 Broken prosthetic joint implant — (Use additional code to identify prosthetic joint with mechanical complication, V43.60-V43.69)
996.44 Peri-prosthetic fracture around prosthetic joint — (Use additional code to identify prosthetic joint with mechanical complication, V43.60-V43.69.
996.45 Peri-prosthetic osteolysis — (Use additional code to identify prosthetic joint with mechanical complication, V43.60-V43.69. Use additional code to identify major osseous defect, if applicable: 731.3)
996.46 Articular bearing surface wear of prosthetic joint — (Use additional code to identify prosthetic joint with mechanical complication, V43.60-V43.69)
996.47 Other mechanical complication of prosthetic joint implant — (Use additional code to identify prosthetic joint with mechanical complication, V43.60-V43.69)
996.49 Other mechanical complication of other internal orthopedic device, implant, and graft — (Use additional code to identify prosthetic joint with mechanical complication, V43.60-V43.69)
996.66 Infection and inflammatory reaction due to internal joint prosthesis — (Use additional code to identify specified infections. Use additional code to identify infected prosthetic joint: V43.60-V43.69)
996.67 Infection and inflammatory reaction due to other internal orthopedic device, implant, and graft — (Use additional code to identify specified infections)
996.77 Other complications due to internal joint prosthesis — (Use additional code to identify complication: 338.18-338.19, 338.28-338.29)
996.78 Other complications due to other internal orthopedic device, implant, and graft — (Use additional code to identify complication: 338.18-338.19, 338.28-338.29)
998.59 Other postoperative infection — (Use additional code to identify infection)
V43.66 Ankle joint replacement by other means
V54.01 Encounter for removal of internal fixation device

ICD-9-CM Procedural

80.07 Arthrotomy for removal of prosthesis without replacement, ankle
84.57 Removal of (cement) spacer

27705-27709

27705 Osteotomy; tibia
27707 fibula
27709 tibia and fibula

ICD-9-CM Diagnostic

715.96 Osteoarthrosis, unspecified whether generalized or localized, lower leg
733.5 Osteitis condensans
733.81 Malunion of fracture
733.82 Nonunion of fracture
733.90 Disorder of bone and cartilage, unspecified
736.41 Genu valgum (acquired)
736.42 Genu varum (acquired)
736.81 Unequal leg length (acquired)
756.51 Osteogenesis imperfecta

ICD-9-CM Procedural

77.27 Wedge osteotomy of tibia and fibula
77.37 Other division of tibia and fibula

27712

27712 Osteotomy; multiple, with realignment on intramedullary rod (eg, Sofield type procedure)

ICD-9-CM Diagnostic

733.81 Malunion of fracture
733.82 Nonunion of fracture
736.41 Genu valgum (acquired)
736.42 Genu varum (acquired)
756.51 Osteogenesis imperfecta
V54.02 Encounter for lengthening/adjustment of growth rod

ICD-9-CM Procedural

77.39 Other division of other bone, except facial bones

27715

27715 Osteoplasty, tibia and fibula, lengthening or shortening

ICD-9-CM Diagnostic

733.81 Malunion of fracture
733.82 Nonunion of fracture
736.81 Unequal leg length (acquired)
755.30 Congenital unspecified reduction deformity of lower limb

755.32 Congenital longitudinal deficiency of lower limb, not elsewhere classified

ICD-9-CM Procedural

78.17 Application of external fixator device, tibia and fibula
78.27 Limb shortening procedures, tibia and fibula
78.37 Limb lengthening procedures, tibia and fibula
84.53 Implantation of internal limb lengthening device with kinetic distraction
84.54 Implantation of other internal limb lengthening device
84.71 Application of external fixator device, monoplanar system
84.72 Application of external fixator device, ring system
84.73 Application of hybrid external fixator device

27720-27725

27720 Repair of nonunion or malunion, tibia; without graft, (eg, compression technique)
27722 with sliding graft
27724 with iliac or other autograft (includes obtaining graft)
27725 by synostosis, with fibula, any method

ICD-9-CM Diagnostic

733.81 Malunion of fracture
733.82 Nonunion of fracture

ICD-9-CM Procedural

77.77 Excision of tibia and fibula for graft
78.07 Bone graft of tibia and fibula
78.47 Other repair or plastic operations on tibia and fibula

27726

27726 Repair of fibula nonunion and/or malunion with internal fixation

ICD-9-CM Diagnostic

733.81 Malunion of fracture
733.82 Nonunion of fracture
905.4 Late effect of fracture of lower extremities
905.5 Late effect of fracture of multiple and unspecified bones

ICD-9-CM Procedural

77.77 Excision of tibia and fibula for graft
78.07 Bone graft of tibia and fibula
78.47 Other repair or plastic operations on tibia and fibula
78.57 Internal fixation of tibia and fibula without fracture reduction

27727

27727 Repair of congenital pseudarthrosis, tibia

ICD-9-CM Diagnostic

755.69 Other congenital anomaly of lower limb, including pelvic girdle

ICD-9-CM Procedural

78.47 Other repair or plastic operations on tibia and fibula

27730-27734

27730 Arrest, epiphyseal (epiphysiodesis), open; distal tibia
27732 distal fibula
27734 distal tibia and fibula

ICD-9-CM Diagnostic

733.91 Arrest of bone development or growth
736.81 Unequal leg length (acquired)
755.30 Congenital unspecified reduction deformity of lower limb ▽
755.32 Congenital longitudinal deficiency of lower limb, not elsewhere classified

ICD-9-CM Procedural

78.27 Limb shortening procedures, tibia and fibula

27740-27742

27740 Arrest, epiphyseal (epiphysiodesis), any method, combined, proximal and distal tibia and fibula;
27742 and distal femur

ICD-9-CM Diagnostic

733.91 Arrest of bone development or growth
736.81 Unequal leg length (acquired)
736.89 Other acquired deformity of other parts of limb
755.30 Congenital unspecified reduction deformity of lower limb ▽
755.32 Congenital longitudinal deficiency of lower limb, not elsewhere classified
755.60 Unspecified congenital anomaly of lower limb ▽

ICD-9-CM Procedural

78.25 Limb shortening procedures, femur
78.27 Limb shortening procedures, tibia and fibula

27745

27745 Prophylactic treatment (nailing, pinning, plating or wiring) with or without methylmethacrylate, tibia

ICD-9-CM Diagnostic

170.7 Malignant neoplasm of long bones of lower limb
198.5 Secondary malignant neoplasm of bone and bone marrow
213.7 Benign neoplasm of long bones of lower limb
238.0 Neoplasm of uncertain behavior of bone and articular cartilage
239.2 Neoplasms of unspecified nature of bone, soft tissue, and skin
731.3 Major osseous defects — (Code first underlying disease: 170.0-170.9, 730.00-730.29, 733.00-733.09, 733.40-733.49, 996.45)
733.00 Unspecified osteoporosis — (Use additional code to identify major osseous defect, if applicable: 731.3) (Use additional code to identify personal history of pathologic (healed) fracture: V13.51) ▽
733.02 Idiopathic osteoporosis — (Use additional code to identify major osseous defect, if applicable: 731.3) (Use additional code to identify personal history of pathologic (healed) fracture: V13.51)
733.09 Other osteoporosis — (Use additional code to identify major osseous defect, if applicable: 731.3) (Use additional code to identify personal history of pathologic (healed) fracture: V13.51) (Use additional E code to identify drug)
733.90 Disorder of bone and cartilage, unspecified ▽

ICD-9-CM Procedural

78.57 Internal fixation of tibia and fibula without fracture reduction
84.55 Insertion of bone void filler

27750-27752

27750 Closed treatment of tibial shaft fracture (with or without fibular fracture); without manipulation
27752 with manipulation, with or without skeletal traction

ICD-9-CM Diagnostic

733.16 Pathologic fracture of tibia and fibula
733.93 Stress fracture of tibia or fibula — (Use additional external cause code(s) to identify the cause of the stress fracture)
823.20 Closed fracture of shaft of tibia
823.22 Closed fracture of shaft of fibula with tibia
823.40 Torus fracture of tibia alone
823.42 Torus fracture of fibula with tibia

ICD-9-CM Procedural

79.06 Closed reduction of fracture of tibia and fibula without internal fixation
93.44 Other skeletal traction
93.53 Application of other cast
93.54 Application of splint

HCPCS Level II Supplies & Services

A4570 Splint

27756

27756 Percutaneous skeletal fixation of tibial shaft fracture (with or without fibular fracture) (eg, pins or screws)

ICD-9-CM Diagnostic

733.16 Pathologic fracture of tibia and fibula

733.93 Stress fracture of tibia or fibula — (Use additional external cause code(s) to identify the cause of the stress fracture)

823.21 Closed fracture of shaft of fibula

823.22 Closed fracture of shaft of fibula with tibia

ICD-9-CM Procedural

78.57 Internal fixation of tibia and fibula without fracture reduction

27758-27759

27758 Open treatment of tibial shaft fracture (with or without fibular fracture), with plate/screws, with or without cerclage

27759 Treatment of tibial shaft fracture (with or without fibular fracture) by intramedullary implant, with or without interlocking screws and/or cerclage

ICD-9-CM Diagnostic

733.16 Pathologic fracture of tibia and fibula

733.93 Stress fracture of tibia or fibula — (Use additional external cause code(s) to identify the cause of the stress fracture)

823.20 Closed fracture of shaft of tibia

823.22 Closed fracture of shaft of fibula with tibia

823.30 Open fracture of shaft of tibia

823.32 Open fracture of shaft of fibula with tibia

ICD-9-CM Procedural

79.36 Open reduction of fracture of tibia and fibula with internal fixation

27760-27762

27760 Closed treatment of medial malleolus fracture; without manipulation

27762 with manipulation, with or without skin or skeletal traction

ICD-9-CM Diagnostic

733.16 Pathologic fracture of tibia and fibula

733.93 Stress fracture of tibia or fibula — (Use additional external cause code(s) to identify the cause of the stress fracture)

824.0 Closed fracture of medial malleolus

ICD-9-CM Procedural

79.09 Closed reduction of fracture of other specified bone, except facial bones, without internal fixation

93.44 Other skeletal traction

93.46 Other skin traction of limbs

93.53 Application of other cast

HCPCS Level II Supplies & Services

A4580 Cast supplies (e.g., plaster)

27766

27766 Open treatment of medial malleolus fracture, includes internal fixation, when performed

ICD-9-CM Diagnostic

733.16 Pathologic fracture of tibia and fibula

733.93 Stress fracture of tibia or fibula — (Use additional external cause code(s) to identify the cause of the stress fracture)

824.0 Closed fracture of medial malleolus

824.1 Open fracture of medial malleolus

ICD-9-CM Procedural

79.29 Open reduction of fracture of other specified bone, except facial bones, without internal fixation

79.39 Open reduction of fracture of other specified bone, except facial bones, with internal fixation

27767-27768

27767 Closed treatment of posterior malleolus fracture; without manipulation

27768 with manipulation

ICD-9-CM Diagnostic

733.16 Pathologic fracture of tibia and fibula

733.93 Stress fracture of tibia or fibula — (Use additional external cause code(s) to identify the cause of the stress fracture)

824.8 Unspecified closed fracture of ankle ▽

824.9 Unspecified open fracture of ankle ▽

ICD-9-CM Procedural

79.09 Closed reduction of fracture of other specified bone, except facial bones, without internal fixation

93.44 Other skeletal traction

93.46 Other skin traction of limbs

93.53 Application of other cast

HCPCS Level II Supplies & Services

A4580 Cast supplies (e.g., plaster)

27769

27769 Open treatment of posterior malleolus fracture, includes internal fixation, when performed

ICD-9-CM Diagnostic

733.16 Pathologic fracture of tibia and fibula

733.93 Stress fracture of tibia or fibula — (Use additional external cause code(s) to identify the cause of the stress fracture)

824.8 Unspecified closed fracture of ankle ▽

824.9 Unspecified open fracture of ankle ▽

ICD-9-CM Procedural

79.29 Open reduction of fracture of other specified bone, except facial bones, without internal fixation

79.39 Open reduction of fracture of other specified bone, except facial bones, with internal fixation

93.44 Other skeletal traction

93.46 Other skin traction of limbs

93.53 Application of other cast

HCPCS Level II Supplies & Services

A4580 Cast supplies (e.g., plaster)

27780-27781

27780 Closed treatment of proximal fibula or shaft fracture; without manipulation

27781 with manipulation

ICD-9-CM Diagnostic

733.16 Pathologic fracture of tibia and fibula

733.93 Stress fracture of tibia or fibula — (Use additional external cause code(s) to identify the cause of the stress fracture)

823.01 Closed fracture of upper end of fibula

823.21 Closed fracture of shaft of fibula

823.41 Torus fracture of fibula alone

ICD-9-CM Procedural

79.06 Closed reduction of fracture of tibia and fibula without internal fixation

93.53 Application of other cast

HCPCS Level II Supplies & Services

A4580 Cast supplies (e.g., plaster)

27784

27784 Open treatment of proximal fibula or shaft fracture, includes internal fixation, when performed

ICD-9-CM Diagnostic

733.16 Pathologic fracture of tibia and fibula

733.93 Stress fracture of tibia or fibula — (Use additional external cause code(s) to identify the cause of the stress fracture)

823.01 Closed fracture of upper end of fibula

823.11 Open fracture of upper end of fibula

823.21 Closed fracture of shaft of fibula

823.31 Open fracture of shaft of fibula

ICD-9-CM Procedural

79.26 Open reduction of fracture of tibia and fibula without internal fixation

79.36 Open reduction of fracture of tibia and fibula with internal fixation

27786-27788

27786 Closed treatment of distal fibular fracture (lateral malleolus); without manipulation

27788 with manipulation

ICD-9-CM Diagnostic

733.16 Pathologic fracture of tibia and fibula

733.93 Stress fracture of tibia or fibula — (Use additional external cause code(s) to identify the cause of the stress fracture)

824.2 Closed fracture of lateral malleolus

ICD-9-CM Procedural

79.06 Closed reduction of fracture of tibia and fibula without internal fixation

93.53 Application of other cast

HCPCS Level II Supplies & Services

A4570 Splint

27792

27792 Open treatment of distal fibular fracture (lateral malleolus), includes internal fixation, when performed

ICD-9-CM Diagnostic

733.16 Pathologic fracture of tibia and fibula

733.93 Stress fracture of tibia or fibula — (Use additional external cause code(s) to identify the cause of the stress fracture)

824.2 Closed fracture of lateral malleolus

824.3 Open fracture of lateral malleolus

ICD-9-CM Procedural

79.26 Open reduction of fracture of tibia and fibula without internal fixation

79.36 Open reduction of fracture of tibia and fibula with internal fixation

27808-27810

27808 Closed treatment of bimalleolar ankle fracture (eg, lateral and medial malleoli, or lateral and posterior malleoli or medial and posterior malleoli); without manipulation

27810 with manipulation

ICD-9-CM Diagnostic

733.16 Pathologic fracture of tibia and fibula

733.93 Stress fracture of tibia or fibula — (Use additional external cause code(s) to identify the cause of the stress fracture)

824.2 Closed fracture of lateral malleolus

824.4 Closed bimalleolar fracture

ICD-9-CM Procedural

79.09 Closed reduction of fracture of other specified bone, except facial bones, without internal fixation

93.53 Application of other cast

HCPCS Level II Supplies & Services

A4570 Splint

27814

27814 Open treatment of bimalleolar ankle fracture (eg, lateral and medial malleoli, or lateral and posterior malleoli, or medial and posterior malleoli), includes internal fixation, when performed

ICD-9-CM Diagnostic

733.16 Pathologic fracture of tibia and fibula

733.93 Stress fracture of tibia or fibula — (Use additional external cause code(s) to identify the cause of the stress fracture)

824.4 Closed bimalleolar fracture

824.5 Open bimalleolar fracture

ICD-9-CM Procedural

79.29 Open reduction of fracture of other specified bone, except facial bones, without internal fixation

79.39 Open reduction of fracture of other specified bone, except facial bones, with internal fixation

27816-27818

27816 Closed treatment of trimalleolar ankle fracture; without manipulation

27818 with manipulation

ICD-9-CM Diagnostic

733.16 Pathologic fracture of tibia and fibula

733.93 Stress fracture of tibia or fibula — (Use additional external cause code(s) to identify the cause of the stress fracture)

824.6 Closed trimalleolar fracture

ICD-9-CM Procedural

79.09 Closed reduction of fracture of other specified bone, except facial bones, without internal fixation

93.53 Application of other cast

HCPCS Level II Supplies & Services

A4570 Splint

27822-27823

27822 Open treatment of trimalleolar ankle fracture, includes internal fixation, when performed, medial and/or lateral malleolus; without fixation of posterior lip

27823 with fixation of posterior lip

ICD-9-CM Diagnostic

733.16 Pathologic fracture of tibia and fibula

733.93 Stress fracture of tibia or fibula — (Use additional external cause code(s) to identify the cause of the stress fracture)

824.6 Closed trimalleolar fracture

824.7 Open trimalleolar fracture

ICD-9-CM Procedural

79.29 Open reduction of fracture of other specified bone, except facial bones, without internal fixation

79.36 Open reduction of fracture of tibia and fibula with internal fixation

79.39 Open reduction of fracture of other specified bone, except facial bones, with internal fixation

27824-27825

27824 Closed treatment of fracture of weight bearing articular portion of distal tibia (eg, pilon or tibial plafond), with or without anesthesia; without manipulation
27825 with skeletal traction and/or requiring manipulation

ICD-9-CM Diagnostic

733.16 Pathologic fracture of tibia and fibula
733.93 Stress fracture of tibia or fibula — (Use additional external cause code(s) to identify the cause of the stress fracture)
733.95 Stress fracture of other bone — (Use additional external cause code(s) to identify the cause of the stress fracture)
824.8 Unspecified closed fracture of ankle ▽

ICD-9-CM Procedural

79.06 Closed reduction of fracture of tibia and fibula without internal fixation
93.44 Other skeletal traction
93.53 Application of other cast

27826-27828

27826 Open treatment of fracture of weight bearing articular surface/portion of distal tibia (eg, pilon or tibial plafond), with internal fixation, when performed; of fibula only
27827 of tibia only
27828 of both tibia and fibula

ICD-9-CM Diagnostic

733.16 Pathologic fracture of tibia and fibula
733.93 Stress fracture of tibia or fibula — (Use additional external cause code(s) to identify the cause of the stress fracture)
733.95 Stress fracture of other bone — (Use additional external cause code(s) to identify the cause of the stress fracture)
823.82 Closed fracture of unspecified part of fibula with tibia ▽
823.92 Open fracture of unspecified part of fibula with tibia ▽
824.8 Unspecified closed fracture of ankle ▽
824.9 Unspecified open fracture of ankle ▽

ICD-9-CM Procedural

79.26 Open reduction of fracture of tibia and fibula without internal fixation
79.36 Open reduction of fracture of tibia and fibula with internal fixation

27829

27829 Open treatment of distal tibiofibular joint (syndesmosis) disruption, includes internal fixation, when performed

ICD-9-CM Diagnostic

718.77 Developmental dislocation of joint, ankle and foot
837.0 Closed dislocation of ankle
837.1 Open dislocation of ankle

ICD-9-CM Procedural

79.26 Open reduction of fracture of tibia and fibula without internal fixation
79.36 Open reduction of fracture of tibia and fibula with internal fixation

27830-27831

27830 Closed treatment of proximal tibiofibular joint dislocation; without anesthesia
27831 requiring anesthesia

ICD-9-CM Diagnostic

718.76 Developmental dislocation of joint, lower leg
836.59 Other closed dislocation of knee

ICD-9-CM Procedural

79.79 Closed reduction of dislocation of other specified site, except temporomandibular

HCPCS Level II Supplies & Services

A4570 Splint

27832

27832 Open treatment of proximal tibiofibular joint dislocation, includes internal fixation, when performed, or with excision of proximal fibula

ICD-9-CM Diagnostic

718.76 Developmental dislocation of joint, lower leg
836.59 Other closed dislocation of knee
836.69 Other open dislocation of knee

ICD-9-CM Procedural

79.89 Open reduction of dislocation of other specified site, except temporomandibular

27840-27842

27840 Closed treatment of ankle dislocation; without anesthesia
27842 requiring anesthesia, with or without percutaneous skeletal fixation

ICD-9-CM Diagnostic

718.77 Developmental dislocation of joint, ankle and foot
837.0 Closed dislocation of ankle

ICD-9-CM Procedural

79.09 Closed reduction of fracture of other specified bone, except facial bones, without internal fixation
79.77 Closed reduction of dislocation of ankle

HCPCS Level II Supplies & Services

A4570 Splint

27846-27848

27846 Open treatment of ankle dislocation, with or without percutaneous skeletal fixation; without repair or internal fixation
27848 with repair or internal or external fixation

ICD-9-CM Diagnostic

718.77 Developmental dislocation of joint, ankle and foot
837.0 Closed dislocation of ankle
837.1 Open dislocation of ankle

ICD-9-CM Procedural

79.87 Open reduction of dislocation of ankle
81.49 Other repair of ankle

27860

27860 Manipulation of ankle under general anesthesia (includes application of traction or other fixation apparatus)

ICD-9-CM Diagnostic

718.57 Ankylosis of ankle and foot joint
719.47 Pain in joint, ankle and foot
726.71 Achilles bursitis or tendinitis
728.71 Plantar fascial fibromatosis
996.40 Unspecified mechanical complication of internal orthopedic device, implant, and graft — (Use additional code to identify prosthetic joint with mechanical complication, V43.60-V43.69) ▽
996.47 Other mechanical complication of prosthetic joint implant — (Use additional code to identify prosthetic joint with mechanical complication, V43.60-V43.69)
996.49 Other mechanical complication of other internal orthopedic device, implant, and graft — (Use additional code to identify prosthetic joint with mechanical complication, V43.60-V43.69)
996.77 Other complications due to internal joint prosthesis — (Use additional code to identify complication: 338.18-338.19, 338.28-338.29)
996.78 Other complications due to other internal orthopedic device, implant, and graft — (Use additional code to identify complication: 338.18-338.19, 338.28-338.29)

ICD-9-CM Procedural

79.77 Closed reduction of dislocation of ankle
93.26 Manual rupture of joint adhesions
93.29 Other forcible correction of musculoskeletal deformity

HCPCS Level II Supplies & Services

A4305 Disposable drug delivery system, flow rate of 50 ml or greater per hour

27870

27870 Arthrodesis, ankle, open

ICD-9-CM Diagnostic

711.07 Pyogenic arthritis, ankle and foot — (Use additional code to identify infectious organism: 041.0-041.8)
711.67 Arthropathy associated with mycoses, ankle and foot — (Code first underlying disease: 110.0-118) ☒
712.17 Chondrocalcinosis due to dicalcium phosphate crystals, ankle and foot — (Code first underlying disease: 275.4) ☒
712.27 Chondrocalcinosis due to pyrophosphate crystals, ankle and foot — (Code first underlying disease: 275.4) ☒
713.5 Arthropathy associated with neurological disorders — (Code first underlying disease: 094.0, 249.6, 250.6, 336.0) ☒
714.0 Rheumatoid arthritis — (Use additional code to identify manifestation: 357.1, 359.6)
714.4 Chronic postrheumatic arthropathy
715.17 Primary localized osteoarthrosis, ankle and foot
715.27 Secondary localized osteoarthrosis, ankle and foot
715.97 Osteoarthrosis, unspecified whether generalized or localized, ankle and foot ▽
716.17 Traumatic arthropathy, ankle and foot
718.87 Other joint derangement, not elsewhere classified, ankle and foot
730.17 Chronic osteomyelitis, ankle and foot — (Use additional code to identify organism: 041.1. Use additional code to identify major osseous defect, if applicable: 731.3)
731.3 Major osseous defects — (Code first underlying disease: 170.0-170.9, 730.00-730.29, 733.00-733.09, 733.40-733.49, 996.45)
733.81 Malunion of fracture
736.70 Unspecified deformity of ankle and foot, acquired ▽
754.51 Congenital talipes equinovarus
905.4 Late effect of fracture of lower extremities
906.4 Late effect of crushing
996.77 Other complications due to internal joint prosthesis — (Use additional code to identify complication: 338.18-338.19, 338.28-338.29)
V64.43 Arthroscopic surgical procedure converted to open procedure
V88.29 Acquired absence of other joint

ICD-9-CM Procedural

81.11 Ankle fusion

27871

27871 Arthrodesis, tibiofibular joint, proximal or distal

ICD-9-CM Diagnostic

718.36 Recurrent dislocation of lower leg joint
718.77 Developmental dislocation of joint, ankle and foot
718.86 Other joint derangement, not elsewhere classified, lower leg
718.87 Other joint derangement, not elsewhere classified, ankle and foot
718.97 Unspecified ankle and foot joint derangement ▽

ICD-9-CM Procedural

81.29 Arthrodesis of other specified joint

27880-27882

27880 Amputation, leg, through tibia and fibula;
27881 with immediate fitting technique including application of first cast
27882 open, circular (guillotine)

ICD-9-CM Diagnostic

170.7 Malignant neoplasm of long bones of lower limb
170.8 Malignant neoplasm of short bones of lower limb
171.3 Malignant neoplasm of connective and other soft tissue of lower limb, including hip
195.5 Malignant neoplasm of lower limb
198.5 Secondary malignant neoplasm of bone and bone marrow
238.0 Neoplasm of uncertain behavior of bone and articular cartilage
249.70 Secondary diabetes mellitus with peripheral circulatory disorders, not stated as uncontrolled, or unspecified — (Use additional code to identify manifestation: 443.81, 785.4) (Use additional code to identify any associated insulin use: V58.67)
249.71 Secondary diabetes mellitus with peripheral circulatory disorders, uncontrolled — (Use additional code to identify manifestation: 443.81, 785.4) (Use additional code to identify any associated insulin use: V58.67)
249.80 Secondary diabetes mellitus with other specified manifestations, not stated as uncontrolled, or unspecified — (Use additional code to identify manifestation: 707.10-707.19, 707.8, 707.9, 731.8) (Use additional code to identify any associated insulin use: V58.67)
249.81 Secondary diabetes mellitus with other specified manifestations, uncontrolled — (Use additional code to identify manifestation: 707.10-707.19, 707.8, 707.9, 731.8) (Use additional code to identify any associated insulin use: V58.67)
250.70 Diabetes with peripheral circulatory disorders, type II or unspecified type, not stated as uncontrolled — (Use additional code to identify manifestation: 443.81, 785.4)
250.71 Diabetes with peripheral circulatory disorders, type I [juvenile type], not stated as uncontrolled — (Use additional code to identify manifestation: 443.81, 785.4)
250.72 Diabetes with peripheral circulatory disorders, type II or unspecified type, uncontrolled — (Use additional code to identify manifestation: 443.81, 785.4)
250.73 Diabetes with peripheral circulatory disorders, type I [juvenile type], uncontrolled — (Use additional code to identify manifestation: 443.81, 785.4)
250.80 Diabetes with other specified manifestations, type II or unspecified type, not stated as uncontrolled — (Use additional code to identify manifestation: 707.10-707.19, 707.8, 707.9, 731.8)
250.81 Diabetes with other specified manifestations, type I [juvenile type], not stated as uncontrolled — (Use additional code to identify manifestation: 707.10-707.19, 707.8, 707.9, 731.8)
250.82 Diabetes with other specified manifestations, type II or unspecified type, uncontrolled — (Use additional code to identify manifestation: 707.10-707.19, 707.8, 707.9, 731.8)
250.83 Diabetes with other specified manifestations, type I [juvenile type], uncontrolled — (Use additional code to identify manifestation: 707.10-707.19, 707.8, 707.9, 731.8)
440.20 Atherosclerosis of native arteries of the extremities, unspecified ▽
440.21 Atherosclerosis of native arteries of the extremities with intermittent claudication
440.22 Atherosclerosis of native arteries of the extremities with rest pain
440.23 Atherosclerosis of native arteries of the extremities with ulceration — (Use additional code for any associated ulceration: 707.10-707.19, 707.8, 707.9)
440.24 Atherosclerosis of native arteries of the extremities with gangrene — (Use additional code for any associated ulceration: 707.10-707.19, 707.8, 707.9)
443.81 Peripheral angiopathy in diseases classified elsewhere — (Code first underlying disease: 249.7, 250.7) ☒
682.6 Cellulitis and abscess of leg, except foot — (Use additional code to identify organism, such as 041.1, etc.)
682.7 Cellulitis and abscess of foot, except toes — (Use additional code to identify organism, such as 041.1, etc.)
707.10 Ulcer of lower limb, unspecified — (Code, if applicable, any causal condition first: 249.80-249.81, 250.80-250.83, 440.23, 459.11, 459.13, 459.31, 459.33) ▽
707.12 Ulcer of calf — (Code, if applicable, any causal condition first: 249.80-249.81, 250.80-250.83, 440.23, 459.11, 459.13, 459.31, 459.33)

707.13 Ulcer of ankle — (Code, if applicable, any causal condition first: 249.80-249.81, 250.80-250.83, 440.23, 459.11, 459.13, 459.31, 459.33)
730.16 Chronic osteomyelitis, lower leg — (Use additional code to identify organism: 041.1. Use additional code to identify major osseous defect, if applicable: 731.3)
730.17 Chronic osteomyelitis, ankle and foot — (Use additional code to identify organism: 041.1. Use additional code to identify major osseous defect, if applicable: 731.3)
731.3 Major osseous defects — (Code first underlying disease: 170.0-170.9, 730.00-730.29, 733.00-733.09, 733.40-733.49, 996.45)
731.8 Other bone involvement in diseases classified elsewhere — (Code first underlying disease: 249.8, 250.8. Use additional code to specify bone condition: 730.00-730.09) ☒
733.49 Aseptic necrosis of other bone site — (Use additional code to identify major osseous defect, if applicable: 731.3)
785.4 Gangrene — (Code first any associated underlying condition)
897.0 Traumatic amputation of leg(s) (complete) (partial), unilateral, below knee, without mention of complication
897.1 Traumatic amputation of leg(s) (complete) (partial), unilateral, below knee, complicated

ICD-9-CM Procedural

84.15 Other amputation below knee
84.46 Fitting of prosthesis below knee

27884

27884 Amputation, leg, through tibia and fibula; secondary closure or scar revision

ICD-9-CM Diagnostic

249.70 Secondary diabetes mellitus with peripheral circulatory disorders, not stated as uncontrolled, or unspecified — (Use additional code to identify manifestation: 443.81, 785.4) (Use additional code to identify any associated insulin use: V58.67)
249.71 Secondary diabetes mellitus with peripheral circulatory disorders, uncontrolled — (Use additional code to identify manifestation: 443.81, 785.4) (Use additional code to identify any associated insulin use: V58.67)
249.80 Secondary diabetes mellitus with other specified manifestations, not stated as uncontrolled, or unspecified — (Use additional code to identify manifestation: 707.10-707.19, 707.8, 707.9, 731.8) (Use additional code to identify any associated insulin use: V58.67)
249.81 Secondary diabetes mellitus with other specified manifestations, uncontrolled — (Use additional code to identify manifestation: 707.10-707.19, 707.8, 707.9, 731.8) (Use additional code to identify any associated insulin use: V58.67)
250.70 Diabetes with peripheral circulatory disorders, type II or unspecified type, not stated as uncontrolled — (Use additional code to identify manifestation: 443.81, 785.4)
250.71 Diabetes with peripheral circulatory disorders, type I [juvenile type], not stated as uncontrolled — (Use additional code to identify manifestation: 443.81, 785.4)
250.72 Diabetes with peripheral circulatory disorders, type II or unspecified type, uncontrolled — (Use additional code to identify manifestation: 443.81, 785.4)
250.73 Diabetes with peripheral circulatory disorders, type I [juvenile type], uncontrolled — (Use additional code to identify manifestation: 443.81, 785.4)
250.80 Diabetes with other specified manifestations, type II or unspecified type, not stated as uncontrolled — (Use additional code to identify manifestation: 707.10-707.19, 707.8, 707.9, 731.8)
250.81 Diabetes with other specified manifestations, type I [juvenile type], not stated as uncontrolled — (Use additional code to identify manifestation: 707.10-707.19, 707.8, 707.9, 731.8)
250.82 Diabetes with other specified manifestations, type II or unspecified type, uncontrolled — (Use additional code to identify manifestation: 707.10-707.19, 707.8, 707.9, 731.8)
250.83 Diabetes with other specified manifestations, type I [juvenile type], uncontrolled — (Use additional code to identify manifestation: 707.10-707.19, 707.8, 707.9, 731.8)
443.81 Peripheral angiopathy in diseases classified elsewhere — (Code first underlying disease: 249.7, 250.7) ☒
459.89 Other specified circulatory system disorders
682.6 Cellulitis and abscess of leg, except foot — (Use additional code to identify organism, such as 041.1, etc.)
707.10 Ulcer of lower limb, unspecified — (Code, if applicable, any causal condition first: 249.80-249.81, 250.80-250.83, 440.23, 459.11, 459.13, 459.31, 459.33) ▽
707.12 Ulcer of calf — (Code, if applicable, any causal condition first: 249.80-249.81, 250.80-250.83, 440.23, 459.11, 459.13, 459.31, 459.33)
709.2 Scar condition and fibrosis of skin
731.8 Other bone involvement in diseases classified elsewhere — (Code first underlying disease: 249.8, 250.8. Use additional code to specify bone condition: 730.00-730.09) ☒
785.4 Gangrene — (Code first any associated underlying condition)
997.60 Late complications of amputation stump, unspecified — (Use additional code to identify complications) ▽
997.61 Neuroma of amputation stump — (Use additional code to identify complications)
997.62 Infection (chronic) of amputation stump — (Use additional code to identify complications)
997.69 Other late amputation stump complication — (Use additional code to identify complications)

ICD-9-CM Procedural

84.15 Other amputation below knee
84.3 Revision of amputation stump

HCPCS Level II Supplies & Services

A4580 Cast supplies (e.g., plaster)
L8470 Prosthetic sock, single ply, fitting, below knee, each

27886

27886 Amputation, leg, through tibia and fibula; re-amputation

ICD-9-CM Diagnostic

249.70 Secondary diabetes mellitus with peripheral circulatory disorders, not stated as uncontrolled, or unspecified — (Use additional code to identify manifestation: 443.81, 785.4) (Use additional code to identify any associated insulin use: V58.67)
249.71 Secondary diabetes mellitus with peripheral circulatory disorders, uncontrolled — (Use additional code to identify manifestation: 443.81, 785.4) (Use additional code to identify any associated insulin use: V58.67)
250.70 Diabetes with peripheral circulatory disorders, type II or unspecified type, not stated as uncontrolled — (Use additional code to identify manifestation: 443.81, 785.4)
250.71 Diabetes with peripheral circulatory disorders, type I [juvenile type], not stated as uncontrolled — (Use additional code to identify manifestation: 443.81, 785.4)
250.72 Diabetes with peripheral circulatory disorders, type II or unspecified type, uncontrolled — (Use additional code to identify manifestation: 443.81, 785.4)
250.73 Diabetes with peripheral circulatory disorders, type I [juvenile type], uncontrolled — (Use additional code to identify manifestation: 443.81, 785.4)
250.80 Diabetes with other specified manifestations, type II or unspecified type, not stated as uncontrolled — (Use additional code to identify manifestation: 707.10-707.19, 707.8, 707.9, 731.8)
250.81 Diabetes with other specified manifestations, type I [juvenile type], not stated as uncontrolled — (Use additional code to identify manifestation: 707.10-707.19, 707.8, 707.9, 731.8)
250.82 Diabetes with other specified manifestations, type II or unspecified type, uncontrolled — (Use additional code to identify manifestation: 707.10-707.19, 707.8, 707.9, 731.8)
250.83 Diabetes with other specified manifestations, type I [juvenile type], uncontrolled — (Use additional code to identify manifestation: 707.10-707.19, 707.8, 707.9, 731.8)
443.81 Peripheral angiopathy in diseases classified elsewhere — (Code first underlying disease: 249.7, 250.7) ☒
443.9 Unspecified peripheral vascular disease ▽
682.6 Cellulitis and abscess of leg, except foot — (Use additional code to identify organism, such as 041.1, etc.)
707.10 Ulcer of lower limb, unspecified — (Code, if applicable, any causal condition first: 249.80-249.81, 250.80-250.83, 440.23, 459.11, 459.13, 459.31, 459.33) ▽
707.12 Ulcer of calf — (Code, if applicable, any causal condition first: 249.80-249.81, 250.80-250.83, 440.23, 459.11, 459.13, 459.31, 459.33)

709.2 Scar condition and fibrosis of skin
730.16 Chronic osteomyelitis, lower leg — (Use additional code to identify organism: 041.1. Use additional code to identify major osseous defect, if applicable: 731.3)
785.4 Gangrene — (Code first any associated underlying condition)
997.60 Late complications of amputation stump, unspecified — (Use additional code to identify complications) ▽
997.61 Neuroma of amputation stump — (Use additional code to identify complications)
997.62 Infection (chronic) of amputation stump — (Use additional code to identify complications)
997.69 Other late amputation stump complication — (Use additional code to identify complications)

ICD-9-CM Procedural

84.15 Other amputation below knee
84.3 Revision of amputation stump

27888

27888 Amputation, ankle, through malleoli of tibia and fibula (eg, Syme, Pirogoff type procedures), with plastic closure and resection of nerves

ICD-9-CM Diagnostic

170.8 Malignant neoplasm of short bones of lower limb
195.5 Malignant neoplasm of lower limb
198.5 Secondary malignant neoplasm of bone and bone marrow
198.89 Secondary malignant neoplasm of other specified sites
238.0 Neoplasm of uncertain behavior of bone and articular cartilage
249.70 Secondary diabetes mellitus with peripheral circulatory disorders, not stated as uncontrolled, or unspecified — (Use additional code to identify manifestation: 443.81, 785.4) (Use additional code to identify any associated insulin use: V58.67)
249.71 Secondary diabetes mellitus with peripheral circulatory disorders, uncontrolled — (Use additional code to identify manifestation: 443.81, 785.4) (Use additional code to identify any associated insulin use: V58.67)
249.80 Secondary diabetes mellitus with other specified manifestations, not stated as uncontrolled, or unspecified — (Use additional code to identify manifestation: 707.10-707.19, 707.8, 707.9, 731.8) (Use additional code to identify any associated insulin use: V58.67)
249.81 Secondary diabetes mellitus with other specified manifestations, uncontrolled — (Use additional code to identify manifestation: 707.10-707.19, 707.8, 707.9, 731.8) (Use additional code to identify any associated insulin use: V58.67)
250.70 Diabetes with peripheral circulatory disorders, type II or unspecified type, not stated as uncontrolled — (Use additional code to identify manifestation: 443.81, 785.4)
250.71 Diabetes with peripheral circulatory disorders, type I [juvenile type], not stated as uncontrolled — (Use additional code to identify manifestation: 443.81, 785.4)
250.72 Diabetes with peripheral circulatory disorders, type II or unspecified type, uncontrolled — (Use additional code to identify manifestation: 443.81, 785.4)
250.73 Diabetes with peripheral circulatory disorders, type I [juvenile type], uncontrolled — (Use additional code to identify manifestation: 443.81, 785.4)
250.80 Diabetes with other specified manifestations, type II or unspecified type, not stated as uncontrolled — (Use additional code to identify manifestation: 707.10-707.19, 707.8, 707.9, 731.8)
250.81 Diabetes with other specified manifestations, type I [juvenile type], not stated as uncontrolled — (Use additional code to identify manifestation: 707.10-707.19, 707.8, 707.9, 731.8)
250.82 Diabetes with other specified manifestations, type II or unspecified type, uncontrolled — (Use additional code to identify manifestation: 707.10-707.19, 707.8, 707.9, 731.8)
250.83 Diabetes with other specified manifestations, type I [juvenile type], uncontrolled — (Use additional code to identify manifestation: 707.10-707.19, 707.8, 707.9, 731.8)
355.79 Other mononeuritis of lower limb
355.8 Unspecified mononeuritis of lower limb ▽
440.20 Atherosclerosis of native arteries of the extremities, unspecified ▽
440.21 Atherosclerosis of native arteries of the extremities with intermittent claudication
440.22 Atherosclerosis of native arteries of the extremities with rest pain
440.23 Atherosclerosis of native arteries of the extremities with ulceration — (Use additional code for any associated ulceration: 707.10-707.19, 707.8, 707.9)
440.24 Atherosclerosis of native arteries of the extremities with gangrene — (Use additional code for any associated ulceration: 707.10-707.19, 707.8, 707.9)
443.81 Peripheral angiopathy in diseases classified elsewhere — (Code first underlying disease: 249.7, 250.7) ☒
446.0 Polyarteritis nodosa
707.10 Ulcer of lower limb, unspecified — (Code, if applicable, any causal condition first: 249.80-249.81, 250.80-250.83, 440.23, 459.11, 459.13, 459.31, 459.33) ▽
707.13 Ulcer of ankle — (Code, if applicable, any causal condition first: 249.80-249.81, 250.80-250.83, 440.23, 459.11, 459.13, 459.31, 459.33)
707.14 Ulcer of heel and midfoot — (Code, if applicable, any causal condition first: 249.80-249.81, 250.80-250.83, 440.23, 459.11, 459.13, 459.31, 459.33)
707.15 Ulcer of other part of foot — (Code, if applicable, any causal condition first: 249.80-249.81, 250.80-250.83, 440.23, 459.11, 459.13, 459.31, 459.33)
728.86 Necrotizing fasciitis — (Use additional code to identify infectious organism, 041.00-041.89, 785.4, if applicable)
730.17 Chronic osteomyelitis, ankle and foot — (Use additional code to identify organism: 041.1. Use additional code to identify major osseous defect, if applicable: 731.3)
731.1 Osteitis deformans in diseases classified elsewhere — (Code first underlying disease: 170.0-170.9) ☒
731.3 Major osseous defects — (Code first underlying disease: 170.0-170.9, 730.00-730.29, 733.00-733.09, 733.40-733.49, 996.45)
731.8 Other bone involvement in diseases classified elsewhere — (Code first underlying disease: 249.8, 250.8. Use additional code to specify bone condition: 730.00-730.09) ☒
785.4 Gangrene — (Code first any associated underlying condition)
896.0 Traumatic amputation of foot (complete) (partial), unilateral, without mention of complication
896.1 Traumatic amputation of foot (complete) (partial), unilateral, complicated
928.20 Crushing injury of foot — (Use additional code to identify any associated injuries: 800-829, 850.0-854.1, 860.0-869.1)
945.34 Full-thickness skin loss due to burn (third degree NOS) of lower leg
945.44 Deep necrosis of underlying tissues due to burn (deep third degree) of lower leg, without mention of loss of a body part

ICD-9-CM Procedural

84.14 Amputation of ankle through malleoli of tibia and fibula

27889

27889 Ankle disarticulation

ICD-9-CM Diagnostic

170.8 Malignant neoplasm of short bones of lower limb
195.5 Malignant neoplasm of lower limb
198.5 Secondary malignant neoplasm of bone and bone marrow
238.0 Neoplasm of uncertain behavior of bone and articular cartilage
249.70 Secondary diabetes mellitus with peripheral circulatory disorders, not stated as uncontrolled, or unspecified — (Use additional code to identify manifestation: 443.81, 785.4) (Use additional code to identify any associated insulin use: V58.67)
249.71 Secondary diabetes mellitus with peripheral circulatory disorders, uncontrolled — (Use additional code to identify manifestation: 443.81, 785.4) (Use additional code to identify any associated insulin use: V58.67)
249.80 Secondary diabetes mellitus with other specified manifestations, not stated as uncontrolled, or unspecified — (Use additional code to identify manifestation: 707.10-707.19, 707.8, 707.9, 731.8) (Use additional code to identify any associated insulin use: V58.67)
249.81 Secondary diabetes mellitus with other specified manifestations, uncontrolled — (Use additional code to identify manifestation: 707.10-707.19, 707.8, 707.9, 731.8) (Use additional code to identify any associated insulin use: V58.67)

250.70 Diabetes with peripheral circulatory disorders, type II or unspecified type, not stated as uncontrolled — (Use additional code to identify manifestation: 443.81, 785.4)
250.71 Diabetes with peripheral circulatory disorders, type I [juvenile type], not stated as uncontrolled — (Use additional code to identify manifestation: 443.81, 785.4)
250.72 Diabetes with peripheral circulatory disorders, type II or unspecified type, uncontrolled — (Use additional code to identify manifestation: 443.81, 785.4)
250.73 Diabetes with peripheral circulatory disorders, type I [juvenile type], uncontrolled — (Use additional code to identify manifestation: 443.81, 785.4)
250.80 Diabetes with other specified manifestations, type II or unspecified type, not stated as uncontrolled — (Use additional code to identify manifestation: 707.10-707.19, 707.8, 707.9, 731.8)
250.81 Diabetes with other specified manifestations, type I [juvenile type], not stated as uncontrolled — (Use additional code to identify manifestation: 707.10-707.19, 707.8, 707.9, 731.8)
250.82 Diabetes with other specified manifestations, type II or unspecified type, uncontrolled — (Use additional code to identify manifestation: 707.10-707.19, 707.8, 707.9, 731.8)
250.83 Diabetes with other specified manifestations, type I [juvenile type], uncontrolled — (Use additional code to identify manifestation: 707.10-707.19, 707.8, 707.9, 731.8)
355.79 Other mononeuritis of lower limb
355.8 Unspecified mononeuritis of lower limb ▽
440.20 Atherosclerosis of native arteries of the extremities, unspecified ▽
440.21 Atherosclerosis of native arteries of the extremities with intermittent claudication
440.22 Atherosclerosis of native arteries of the extremities with rest pain
440.23 Atherosclerosis of native arteries of the extremities with ulceration — (Use additional code for any associated ulceration: 707.10-707.19, 707.8, 707.9)
440.24 Atherosclerosis of native arteries of the extremities with gangrene — (Use additional code for any associated ulceration: 707.10-707.19, 707.8, 707.9)
443.81 Peripheral angiopathy in diseases classified elsewhere — (Code first underlying disease: 249.7, 250.7) ☒
446.0 Polyarteritis nodosa
707.10 Ulcer of lower limb, unspecified — (Code, if applicable, any causal condition first: 249.80-249.81, 250.80-250.83, 440.23, 459.11, 459.13, 459.31, 459.33) ▽
707.13 Ulcer of ankle — (Code, if applicable, any causal condition first: 249.80-249.81, 250.80-250.83, 440.23, 459.11, 459.13, 459.31, 459.33)
707.14 Ulcer of heel and midfoot — (Code, if applicable, any causal condition first: 249.80-249.81, 250.80-250.83, 440.23, 459.11, 459.13, 459.31, 459.33)
707.15 Ulcer of other part of foot — (Code, if applicable, any causal condition first: 249.80-249.81, 250.80-250.83, 440.23, 459.11, 459.13, 459.31, 459.33)
728.86 Necrotizing fasciitis — (Use additional code to identify infectious organism, 041.00-041.89, 785.4, if applicable)
730.17 Chronic osteomyelitis, ankle and foot — (Use additional code to identify organism: 041.1. Use additional code to identify major osseous defect, if applicable: 731.3)
731.1 Osteitis deformans in diseases classified elsewhere — (Code first underlying disease: 170.0-170.9) ☒
731.3 Major osseous defects — (Code first underlying disease: 170.0-170.9, 730.00-730.29, 733.00-733.09, 733.40-733.49, 996.45)
731.8 Other bone involvement in diseases classified elsewhere — (Code first underlying disease: 249.8, 250.8. Use additional code to specify bone condition: 730.00-730.09) ☒
785.4 Gangrene — (Code first any associated underlying condition)
896.0 Traumatic amputation of foot (complete) (partial), unilateral, without mention of complication
896.1 Traumatic amputation of foot (complete) (partial), unilateral, complicated
928.20 Crushing injury of foot — (Use additional code to identify any associated injuries: 800-829, 850.0-854.1, 860.0-869.1)
945.34 Full-thickness skin loss due to burn (third degree NOS) of lower leg
945.44 Deep necrosis of underlying tissues due to burn (deep third degree) of lower leg, without mention of loss of a body part

ICD-9-CM Procedural

84.13 Disarticulation of ankle

27892-27894

27892 Decompression fasciotomy, leg; anterior and/or lateral compartments only, with debridement of nonviable muscle and/or nerve
27893 posterior compartment(s) only, with debridement of nonviable muscle and/or nerve
27894 anterior and/or lateral, and posterior compartment(s), with debridement of nonviable muscle and/or nerve

ICD-9-CM Diagnostic

444.22 Embolism and thrombosis of arteries of lower extremity
445.02 Atheroembolism of lower extremity
682.6 Cellulitis and abscess of leg, except foot — (Use additional code to identify organism, such as 041.1, etc.)
728.86 Necrotizing fasciitis — (Use additional code to identify infectious organism, 041.00-041.89, 785.4, if applicable)
728.88 Rhabdomyolysis
729.4 Unspecified fasciitis ▽
729.72 Nontraumatic compartment syndrome of lower extremity — (Code first, if applicable, postprocedural complication: 998.89)
785.4 Gangrene — (Code first any associated underlying condition)
823.22 Closed fracture of shaft of fibula with tibia
823.30 Open fracture of shaft of tibia
823.32 Open fracture of shaft of fibula with tibia
928.10 Crushing injury of lower leg — (Use additional code to identify any associated injuries: 800-829, 850.0-854.1, 860.0-869.1)
945.34 Full-thickness skin loss due to burn (third degree NOS) of lower leg
945.44 Deep necrosis of underlying tissues due to burn (deep third degree) of lower leg, without mention of loss of a body part
958.6 Volkmann's ischemic contracture
958.8 Other early complications of trauma
958.92 Traumatic compartment syndrome of lower extremity
996.74 Other complications due to other vascular device, implant, and graft — (Use additional code to identify complication: 338.18-338.19, 338.28-338.29)

ICD-9-CM Procedural

83.14 Fasciotomy

Foot and Toes

28001

28001 Incision and drainage, bursa, foot

ICD-9-CM Diagnostic

249.70 Secondary diabetes mellitus with peripheral circulatory disorders, not stated as uncontrolled, or unspecified — (Use additional code to identify manifestation: 443.81, 785.4) (Use additional code to identify any associated insulin use: V58.67)
249.71 Secondary diabetes mellitus with peripheral circulatory disorders, uncontrolled — (Use additional code to identify manifestation: 443.81, 785.4) (Use additional code to identify any associated insulin use: V58.67)
250.70 Diabetes with peripheral circulatory disorders, type II or unspecified type, not stated as uncontrolled — (Use additional code to identify manifestation: 443.81, 785.4)
250.71 Diabetes with peripheral circulatory disorders, type I [juvenile type], not stated as uncontrolled — (Use additional code to identify manifestation: 443.81, 785.4)
250.72 Diabetes with peripheral circulatory disorders, type II or unspecified type, uncontrolled — (Use additional code to identify manifestation: 443.81, 785.4)
250.73 Diabetes with peripheral circulatory disorders, type I [juvenile type], uncontrolled — (Use additional code to identify manifestation: 443.81, 785.4)
443.81 Peripheral angiopathy in diseases classified elsewhere — (Code first underlying disease: 249.7, 250.7) ☒
681.9 Cellulitis and abscess of unspecified digit — (Use additional code to identify organism: 041.1) ▽

682.7 Cellulitis and abscess of foot, except toes — (Use additional code to identify organism, such as 041.1, etc.)
686.1 Pyogenic granuloma of skin and subcutaneous tissue — (Use additional code to identify any infectious organism: 041.0-041.8)
726.70 Unspecified enthesopathy of ankle and tarsus ♥
726.79 Other enthesopathy of ankle and tarsus
727.3 Other bursitis disorders
727.89 Other disorders of synovium, tendon, and bursa

ICD-9-CM Procedural

83.03 Bursotomy

HCPCS Level II Supplies & Services

A4305 Disposable drug delivery system, flow rate of 50 ml or greater per hour

28002-28003

28002 Incision and drainage below fascia, with or without tendon sheath involvement, foot; single bursal space
28003 multiple areas

ICD-9-CM Diagnostic

249.70 Secondary diabetes mellitus with peripheral circulatory disorders, not stated as uncontrolled, or unspecified — (Use additional code to identify manifestation: 443.81, 785.4) (Use additional code to identify any associated insulin use: V58.67)
249.71 Secondary diabetes mellitus with peripheral circulatory disorders, uncontrolled — (Use additional code to identify manifestation: 443.81, 785.4) (Use additional code to identify any associated insulin use: V58.67)
249.80 Secondary diabetes mellitus with other specified manifestations, not stated as uncontrolled, or unspecified — (Use additional code to identify manifestation: 707.10-707.19, 707.8, 707.9, 731.8) (Use additional code to identify any associated insulin use: V58.67)
249.81 Secondary diabetes mellitus with other specified manifestations, uncontrolled — (Use additional code to identify manifestation: 707.10-707.19, 707.8, 707.9, 731.8) (Use additional code to identify any associated insulin use: V58.67)
250.70 Diabetes with peripheral circulatory disorders, type II or unspecified type, not stated as uncontrolled — (Use additional code to identify manifestation: 443.81, 785.4)
250.71 Diabetes with peripheral circulatory disorders, type I [juvenile type], not stated as uncontrolled — (Use additional code to identify manifestation: 443.81, 785.4)
250.72 Diabetes with peripheral circulatory disorders, type II or unspecified type, uncontrolled — (Use additional code to identify manifestation: 443.81, 785.4)
250.73 Diabetes with peripheral circulatory disorders, type I [juvenile type], uncontrolled — (Use additional code to identify manifestation: 443.81, 785.4)
250.80 Diabetes with other specified manifestations, type II or unspecified type, not stated as uncontrolled — (Use additional code to identify manifestation: 707.10-707.19, 707.8, 707.9, 731.8)
250.81 Diabetes with other specified manifestations, type I [juvenile type], not stated as uncontrolled — (Use additional code to identify manifestation: 707.10-707.19, 707.8, 707.9, 731.8)
250.82 Diabetes with other specified manifestations, type II or unspecified type, uncontrolled — (Use additional code to identify manifestation: 707.10-707.19, 707.8, 707.9, 731.8)
250.83 Diabetes with other specified manifestations, type I [juvenile type], uncontrolled — (Use additional code to identify manifestation: 707.10-707.19, 707.8, 707.9, 731.8)
443.81 Peripheral angiopathy in diseases classified elsewhere — (Code first underlying disease: 249.7, 250.7) ☒
682.7 Cellulitis and abscess of foot, except toes — (Use additional code to identify organism, such as 041.1, etc.)
707.10 Ulcer of lower limb, unspecified — (Code, if applicable, any causal condition first: 249.80-249.81, 250.80-250.83, 440.23, 459.11, 459.13, 459.31, 459.33) ♥
707.14 Ulcer of heel and midfoot — (Code, if applicable, any causal condition first: 249.80-249.81, 250.80-250.83, 440.23, 459.11, 459.13, 459.31, 459.33)
707.15 Ulcer of other part of foot — (Code, if applicable, any causal condition first: 249.80-249.81, 250.80-250.83, 440.23, 459.11, 459.13, 459.31, 459.33)
711.07 Pyogenic arthritis, ankle and foot — (Use additional code to identify infectious organism: 041.0-041.8)
726.70 Unspecified enthesopathy of ankle and tarsus ♥
785.4 Gangrene — (Code first any associated underlying condition)
892.1 Open wound of foot except toe(s) alone, complicated
998.51 Infected postoperative seroma — (Use additional code to identify organism)
998.59 Other postoperative infection — (Use additional code to identify infection)

ICD-9-CM Procedural

83.01 Exploration of tendon sheath
83.03 Bursotomy

HCPCS Level II Supplies & Services

A4305 Disposable drug delivery system, flow rate of 50 ml or greater per hour

28005

28005 Incision, bone cortex (eg, osteomyelitis or bone abscess), foot

ICD-9-CM Diagnostic

249.70 Secondary diabetes mellitus with peripheral circulatory disorders, not stated as uncontrolled, or unspecified — (Use additional code to identify manifestation: 443.81, 785.4) (Use additional code to identify any associated insulin use: V58.67)
249.71 Secondary diabetes mellitus with peripheral circulatory disorders, uncontrolled — (Use additional code to identify manifestation: 443.81, 785.4) (Use additional code to identify any associated insulin use: V58.67)
249.80 Secondary diabetes mellitus with other specified manifestations, not stated as uncontrolled, or unspecified — (Use additional code to identify manifestation: 707.10-707.19, 707.8, 707.9, 731.8) (Use additional code to identify any associated insulin use: V58.67)
249.81 Secondary diabetes mellitus with other specified manifestations, uncontrolled — (Use additional code to identify manifestation: 707.10-707.19, 707.8, 707.9, 731.8) (Use additional code to identify any associated insulin use: V58.67)
250.70 Diabetes with peripheral circulatory disorders, type II or unspecified type, not stated as uncontrolled — (Use additional code to identify manifestation: 443.81, 785.4)
250.71 Diabetes with peripheral circulatory disorders, type I [juvenile type], not stated as uncontrolled — (Use additional code to identify manifestation: 443.81, 785.4)
250.72 Diabetes with peripheral circulatory disorders, type II or unspecified type, uncontrolled — (Use additional code to identify manifestation: 443.81, 785.4)
250.73 Diabetes with peripheral circulatory disorders, type I [juvenile type], uncontrolled — (Use additional code to identify manifestation: 443.81, 785.4)
250.80 Diabetes with other specified manifestations, type II or unspecified type, not stated as uncontrolled — (Use additional code to identify manifestation: 707.10-707.19, 707.8, 707.9, 731.8)
250.81 Diabetes with other specified manifestations, type I [juvenile type], not stated as uncontrolled — (Use additional code to identify manifestation: 707.10-707.19, 707.8, 707.9, 731.8)
250.82 Diabetes with other specified manifestations, type II or unspecified type, uncontrolled — (Use additional code to identify manifestation: 707.10-707.19, 707.8, 707.9, 731.8)
250.83 Diabetes with other specified manifestations, type I [juvenile type], uncontrolled — (Use additional code to identify manifestation: 707.10-707.19, 707.8, 707.9, 731.8)
355.79 Other mononeuritis of lower limb
355.8 Unspecified mononeuritis of lower limb ♥
440.20 Atherosclerosis of native arteries of the extremities, unspecified ♥
440.24 Atherosclerosis of native arteries of the extremities with gangrene — (Use additional code for any associated ulceration: 707.10-707.19, 707.8, 707.9)
443.81 Peripheral angiopathy in diseases classified elsewhere — (Code first underlying disease: 249.7, 250.7) ☒
446.0 Polyarteritis nodosa
707.10 Ulcer of lower limb, unspecified — (Code, if applicable, any causal condition first: 249.80-249.81, 250.80-250.83, 440.23, 459.11, 459.13, 459.31, 459.33) ♥
707.14 Ulcer of heel and midfoot — (Code, if applicable, any causal condition first: 249.80-249.81, 250.80-250.83, 440.23, 459.11, 459.13, 459.31, 459.33)

707.15 Ulcer of other part of foot — (Code, if applicable, any causal condition first: 249.80-249.81, 250.80-250.83, 440.23, 459.11, 459.13, 459.31, 459.33)
728.86 Necrotizing fasciitis — (Use additional code to identify infectious organism, 041.00-041.89, 785.4, if applicable)
730.17 Chronic osteomyelitis, ankle and foot — (Use additional code to identify organism: 041.1. Use additional code to identify major osseous defect, if applicable: 731.3)
731.1 Osteitis deformans in diseases classified elsewhere — (Code first underlying disease: 170.0-170.9) ☒
731.3 Major osseous defects — (Code first underlying disease: 170.0-170.9, 730.00-730.29, 733.00-733.09, 733.40-733.49, 996.45)
731.8 Other bone involvement in diseases classified elsewhere — (Code first underlying disease: 249.8, 250.8. Use additional code to specify bone condition: 730.00-730.09) ☒
785.4 Gangrene — (Code first any associated underlying condition)
896.0 Traumatic amputation of foot (complete) (partial), unilateral, without mention of complication
896.1 Traumatic amputation of foot (complete) (partial), unilateral, complicated
928.20 Crushing injury of foot — (Use additional code to identify any associated injuries: 800-829, 850.0-854.1, 860.0-869.1)
945.34 Full-thickness skin loss due to burn (third degree NOS) of lower leg
945.44 Deep necrosis of underlying tissues due to burn (deep third degree) of lower leg, without mention of loss of a body part

ICD-9-CM Procedural

77.18 Other incision of tarsals and metatarsals without division

28008

28008 Fasciotomy, foot and/or toe

ICD-9-CM Diagnostic

249.70 Secondary diabetes mellitus with peripheral circulatory disorders, not stated as uncontrolled, or unspecified — (Use additional code to identify manifestation: 443.81, 785.4) (Use additional code to identify any associated insulin use: V58.67)
249.71 Secondary diabetes mellitus with peripheral circulatory disorders, uncontrolled — (Use additional code to identify manifestation: 443.81, 785.4) (Use additional code to identify any associated insulin use: V58.67)
250.70 Diabetes with peripheral circulatory disorders, type II or unspecified type, not stated as uncontrolled — (Use additional code to identify manifestation: 443.81, 785.4)
250.71 Diabetes with peripheral circulatory disorders, type I [juvenile type], not stated as uncontrolled — (Use additional code to identify manifestation: 443.81, 785.4)
250.72 Diabetes with peripheral circulatory disorders, type II or unspecified type, uncontrolled — (Use additional code to identify manifestation: 443.81, 785.4)
250.73 Diabetes with peripheral circulatory disorders, type I [juvenile type], uncontrolled — (Use additional code to identify manifestation: 443.81, 785.4)
443.81 Peripheral angiopathy in diseases classified elsewhere — (Code first underlying disease: 249.7, 250.7) ☒
682.6 Cellulitis and abscess of leg, except foot — (Use additional code to identify organism, such as 041.1, etc.)
726.73 Calcaneal spur
726.91 Exostosis of unspecified site ▽
728.71 Plantar fascial fibromatosis
728.86 Necrotizing fasciitis — (Use additional code to identify infectious organism, 041.00-041.89, 785.4, if applicable)
728.88 Rhabdomyolysis
729.4 Unspecified fasciitis ▽
729.72 Nontraumatic compartment syndrome of lower extremity — (Code first, if applicable, postprocedural complication: 998.89)
735.8 Other acquired deformity of toe
785.4 Gangrene — (Code first any associated underlying condition)
945.34 Full-thickness skin loss due to burn (third degree NOS) of lower leg
945.44 Deep necrosis of underlying tissues due to burn (deep third degree) of lower leg, without mention of loss of a body part
958.6 Volkmann's ischemic contracture
958.8 Other early complications of trauma
958.92 Traumatic compartment syndrome of lower extremity

ICD-9-CM Procedural

83.14 Fasciotomy

HCPCS Level II Supplies & Services

A4580 Cast supplies (e.g., plaster)

28010-28011

28010 Tenotomy, percutaneous, toe; single tendon
28011 multiple tendons

ICD-9-CM Diagnostic

735.0 Hallux valgus (acquired)
735.1 Hallux varus (acquired)
735.2 Hallux rigidus
735.3 Hallux malleus
735.4 Other hammer toe (acquired)
735.5 Claw toe (acquired)
735.8 Other acquired deformity of toe
755.66 Other congenital anomaly of toes

ICD-9-CM Procedural

83.13 Other tenotomy

HCPCS Level II Supplies & Services

A4305 Disposable drug delivery system, flow rate of 50 ml or greater per hour

28020-28024

28020 Arthrotomy, including exploration, drainage, or removal of loose or foreign body; intertarsal or tarsometatarsal joint
28022 metatarsophalangeal joint
28024 interphalangeal joint

ICD-9-CM Diagnostic

355.5 Tarsal tunnel syndrome
682.7 Cellulitis and abscess of foot, except toes — (Use additional code to identify organism, such as 041.1, etc.)
711.07 Pyogenic arthritis, ankle and foot — (Use additional code to identify infectious organism: 041.0-041.8)
718.17 Loose body in ankle and foot joint
726.70 Unspecified enthesopathy of ankle and tarsus ▽
729.6 Residual foreign body in soft tissue — (Use additional code to identify foreign body (V90.01-V90.9))
730.17 Chronic osteomyelitis, ankle and foot — (Use additional code to identify organism: 041.1. Use additional code to identify major osseous defect, if applicable: 731.3)
731.3 Major osseous defects — (Code first underlying disease: 170.0-170.9, 730.00-730.29, 733.00-733.09, 733.40-733.49, 996.45)
892.1 Open wound of foot except toe(s) alone, complicated
893.0 Open wound of toe(s), without mention of complication
893.1 Open wound of toe(s), complicated
996.40 Unspecified mechanical complication of internal orthopedic device, implant, and graft — (Use additional code to identify prosthetic joint with mechanical complication, V43.60-V43.69) ▽
996.47 Other mechanical complication of prosthetic joint implant — (Use additional code to identify prosthetic joint with mechanical complication, V43.60-V43.69)
996.49 Other mechanical complication of other internal orthopedic device, implant, and graft — (Use additional code to identify prosthetic joint with mechanical complication, V43.60-V43.69)
996.66 Infection and inflammatory reaction due to internal joint prosthesis — (Use additional code to identify specified infections. Use additional code to identify infected prosthetic joint: V43.60-V43.69)

996.67 Infection and inflammatory reaction due to other internal orthopedic device, implant, and graft — (Use additional code to identify specified infections)

996.77 Other complications due to internal joint prosthesis — (Use additional code to identify complication: 338.18-338.19, 338.28-338.29)

996.78 Other complications due to other internal orthopedic device, implant, and graft — (Use additional code to identify complication: 338.18-338.19, 338.28-338.29)

ICD-9-CM Procedural

80.18 Other arthrotomy of foot and toe

HCPCS Level II Supplies & Services

A4305 Disposable drug delivery system, flow rate of 50 ml or greater per hour

28035

28035 Release, tarsal tunnel (posterior tibial nerve decompression)

ICD-9-CM Diagnostic

355.5 Tarsal tunnel syndrome

ICD-9-CM Procedural

04.44 Release of tarsal tunnel

28043-28047 [28039, 28041]

28039 Excision, tumor, soft tissue of foot or toe, subcutaneous; 1.5 cm or greater

28041 Excision, tumor, soft tissue of foot or toe, subfascial (eg, intramuscular); 1.5 cm or greater

28043 Excision, tumor, soft tissue of foot or toe, subcutaneous; less than 1.5 cm

28045 Excision, tumor, soft tissue of foot or toe, subfascial (eg, intramuscular); less than 1.5 cm

28046 Radical resection of tumor (eg, sarcoma), soft tissue of foot or toe; less than 3 cm

28047 3 cm or greater

ICD-9-CM Diagnostic

171.3 Malignant neoplasm of connective and other soft tissue of lower limb, including hip

172.7 Malignant melanoma of skin of lower limb, including hip

195.5 Malignant neoplasm of lower limb

198.89 Secondary malignant neoplasm of other specified sites

209.34 Merkel cell carcinoma of the lower limb

209.75 Secondary Merkel cell carcinoma

214.1 Lipoma of other skin and subcutaneous tissue

215.3 Other benign neoplasm of connective and other soft tissue of lower limb, including hip

238.1 Neoplasm of uncertain behavior of connective and other soft tissue

239.2 Neoplasms of unspecified nature of bone, soft tissue, and skin

ICD-9-CM Procedural

83.31 Excision of lesion of tendon sheath

83.32 Excision of lesion of muscle

83.49 Other excision of soft tissue

86.3 Other local excision or destruction of lesion or tissue of skin and subcutaneous tissue

86.4 Radical excision of skin lesion

HCPCS Level II Supplies & Services

A4305 Disposable drug delivery system, flow rate of 50 ml or greater per hour

28050-28054

28050 Arthrotomy with biopsy; intertarsal or tarsometatarsal joint

28052 metatarsophalangeal joint

28054 interphalangeal joint

ICD-9-CM Diagnostic

170.8 Malignant neoplasm of short bones of lower limb

171.3 Malignant neoplasm of connective and other soft tissue of lower limb, including hip

213.8 Benign neoplasm of short bones of lower limb

215.3 Other benign neoplasm of connective and other soft tissue of lower limb, including hip

238.0 Neoplasm of uncertain behavior of bone and articular cartilage

238.1 Neoplasm of uncertain behavior of connective and other soft tissue

239.2 Neoplasms of unspecified nature of bone, soft tissue, and skin

357.1 Polyneuropathy in collagen vascular disease — (Code first underlying disease: 446.0, 710.0, 714.0) ☒

359.6 Symptomatic inflammatory myopathy in diseases classified elsewhere — (Code first underlying disease: 135, 140.0-208.9, 277.30-277.39, 446.0, 710.0, 710.1, 710.2, 714.0) ☒

446.0 Polyarteritis nodosa

710.0 Systemic lupus erythematosus — (Use additional code to identify manifestation: 424.91, 581.81, 582.81, 583.81)

710.1 Systemic sclerosis — (Use additional code to identify manifestation: 359.6, 517.2)

710.2 Sicca syndrome

714.0 Rheumatoid arthritis — (Use additional code to identify manifestation: 357.1, 359.6)

714.1 Felty's syndrome

714.2 Other rheumatoid arthritis with visceral or systemic involvement

714.30 Polyarticular juvenile rheumatoid arthritis, chronic or unspecified

714.31 Polyarticular juvenile rheumatoid arthritis, acute

714.32 Pauciarticular juvenile rheumatoid arthritis

714.33 Monoarticular juvenile rheumatoid arthritis

714.4 Chronic postrheumatic arthropathy

714.89 Other specified inflammatory polyarthropathies

716.07 Kaschin-Beck disease, ankle and foot

719.17 Hemarthrosis, ankle and foot

719.27 Villonodular synovitis, ankle and foot

727.00 Unspecified synovitis and tenosynovitis ▽

732.5 Juvenile osteochondrosis of foot

ICD-9-CM Procedural

80.38 Biopsy of joint structure of foot and toe

HCPCS Level II Supplies & Services

A4305 Disposable drug delivery system, flow rate of 50 ml or greater per hour

28055

28055 Neurectomy, intrinsic musculature of foot

ICD-9-CM Diagnostic

215.3 Other benign neoplasm of connective and other soft tissue of lower limb, including hip

355.6 Lesion of plantar nerve

355.8 Unspecified mononeuritis of lower limb ▽

729.2 Unspecified neuralgia, neuritis, and radiculitis ▽

ICD-9-CM Procedural

04.07 Other excision or avulsion of cranial and peripheral nerves

28060-28062

28060 Fasciectomy, plantar fascia; partial (separate procedure)

28062 radical (separate procedure)

ICD-9-CM Diagnostic

237.70 Neurofibromatosis, unspecified ▽

237.71 Neurofibromatosis, Type 1 (von Recklinghausen's disease)

237.72 Neurofibromatosis, Type 2 (acoustic neurofibromatosis)

237.73 Schwannomatosis

237.79 Other neurofibromatosis

355.6 Lesion of plantar nerve

728.6 Contracture of palmar fascia

728.71 Plantar fascial fibromatosis

ICD-9-CM Procedural

83.44 Other fasciectomy

HCPCS Level II Supplies & Services

A4305 Disposable drug delivery system, flow rate of 50 ml or greater per hour

28070-28072

28070 Synovectomy; intertarsal or tarsometatarsal joint, each
28072 metatarsophalangeal joint, each

ICD-9-CM Diagnostic

357.1 Polyneuropathy in collagen vascular disease — (Code first underlying disease: 446.0, 710.0, 714.0) ☒
359.6 Symptomatic inflammatory myopathy in diseases classified elsewhere — (Code first underlying disease: 135, 140.0-208.9, 277.30-277.39, 446.0, 710.0, 710.1, 710.2, 714.0) ☒
446.0 Polyarteritis nodosa
710.0 Systemic lupus erythematosus — (Use additional code to identify manifestation: 424.91, 581.81, 582.81, 583.81)
710.1 Systemic sclerosis — (Use additional code to identify manifestation: 359.6, 517.2)
710.2 Sicca syndrome
714.0 Rheumatoid arthritis — (Use additional code to identify manifestation: 357.1, 359.6)
719.27 Villonodular synovitis, ankle and foot
727.00 Unspecified synovitis and tenosynovitis ▽

ICD-9-CM Procedural

80.78 Synovectomy of foot and toe

28080

28080 Excision, interdigital (Morton) neuroma, single, each

ICD-9-CM Diagnostic

355.6 Lesion of plantar nerve

ICD-9-CM Procedural

04.07 Other excision or avulsion of cranial and peripheral nerves

HCPCS Level II Supplies & Services

A4305 Disposable drug delivery system, flow rate of 50 ml or greater per hour

28086-28088

28086 Synovectomy, tendon sheath, foot; flexor
28088 extensor

ICD-9-CM Diagnostic

357.1 Polyneuropathy in collagen vascular disease — (Code first underlying disease: 446.0, 710.0, 714.0) ☒
359.6 Symptomatic inflammatory myopathy in diseases classified elsewhere — (Code first underlying disease: 135, 140.0-208.9, 277.30-277.39, 446.0, 710.0, 710.1, 710.2, 714.0) ☒
446.0 Polyarteritis nodosa
710.0 Systemic lupus erythematosus — (Use additional code to identify manifestation: 424.91, 581.81, 582.81, 583.81)
710.1 Systemic sclerosis — (Use additional code to identify manifestation: 359.6, 517.2)
710.2 Sicca syndrome
714.0 Rheumatoid arthritis — (Use additional code to identify manifestation: 357.1, 359.6)
726.70 Unspecified enthesopathy of ankle and tarsus ▽
726.71 Achilles bursitis or tendinitis
726.72 Tibialis tendinitis
726.73 Calcaneal spur
726.79 Other enthesopathy of ankle and tarsus
727.42 Ganglion of tendon sheath
727.49 Other ganglion and cyst of synovium, tendon, and bursa

ICD-9-CM Procedural

80.78 Synovectomy of foot and toe
83.42 Other tenonectomy

28090-28092

28090 Excision of lesion, tendon, tendon sheath, or capsule (including synovectomy) (eg, cyst or ganglion); foot
28092 toe(s), each

ICD-9-CM Diagnostic

357.1 Polyneuropathy in collagen vascular disease — (Code first underlying disease: 446.0, 710.0, 714.0) ☒
359.6 Symptomatic inflammatory myopathy in diseases classified elsewhere — (Code first underlying disease: 135, 140.0-208.9, 277.30-277.39, 446.0, 710.0, 710.1, 710.2, 714.0) ☒
446.0 Polyarteritis nodosa
701.5 Other abnormal granulation tissue
710.0 Systemic lupus erythematosus — (Use additional code to identify manifestation: 424.91, 581.81, 582.81, 583.81)
710.1 Systemic sclerosis — (Use additional code to identify manifestation: 359.6, 517.2)
710.2 Sicca syndrome
714.0 Rheumatoid arthritis — (Use additional code to identify manifestation: 357.1, 359.6)
716.67 Unspecified monoarthritis, ankle and foot ▽
726.71 Achilles bursitis or tendinitis
727.41 Ganglion of joint
727.42 Ganglion of tendon sheath
727.49 Other ganglion and cyst of synovium, tendon, and bursa
727.82 Calcium deposits in tendon and bursa
728.71 Plantar fascial fibromatosis

ICD-9-CM Procedural

80.78 Synovectomy of foot and toe
80.88 Other local excision or destruction of lesion of joint of foot and toe
83.31 Excision of lesion of tendon sheath
83.39 Excision of lesion of other soft tissue

HCPCS Level II Supplies & Services

A4305 Disposable drug delivery system, flow rate of 50 ml or greater per hour

28100-28103

28100 Excision or curettage of bone cyst or benign tumor, talus or calcaneus;
28102 with iliac or other autograft (includes obtaining graft)
28103 with allograft

ICD-9-CM Diagnostic

213.8 Benign neoplasm of short bones of lower limb
732.5 Juvenile osteochondrosis of foot
733.21 Solitary bone cyst
733.22 Aneurysmal bone cyst
733.29 Other cyst of bone
733.5 Osteitis condensans

ICD-9-CM Procedural

77.68 Local excision of lesion or tissue of tarsals and metatarsals
77.78 Excision of tarsals and metatarsals for graft
78.08 Bone graft of tarsals and metatarsals

HCPCS Level II Supplies & Services

E0112 Crutches, underarm, wood, adjustable or fixed, pair, with pads, tips, and handgrips

28104-28108

28104 Excision or curettage of bone cyst or benign tumor, tarsal or metatarsal, except talus or calcaneus;
28106 with iliac or other autograft (includes obtaining graft)
28107 with allograft
28108 Excision or curettage of bone cyst or benign tumor, phalanges of foot

ICD-9-CM Diagnostic

213.8 Benign neoplasm of short bones of lower limb
733.21 Solitary bone cyst
733.22 Aneurysmal bone cyst
733.29 Other cyst of bone
733.5 Osteitis condensans

ICD-9-CM Procedural

77.68 Local excision of lesion or tissue of tarsals and metatarsals
77.69 Local excision of lesion or tissue of other bone, except facial bones
77.78 Excision of tarsals and metatarsals for graft
78.08 Bone graft of tarsals and metatarsals

HCPCS Level II Supplies & Services

E0112 Crutches, underarm, wood, adjustable or fixed, pair, with pads, tips, and handgrips

28110

28110 Ostectomy, partial excision, fifth metatarsal head (bunionette) (separate procedure)

ICD-9-CM Diagnostic

726.91 Exostosis of unspecified site ▽
727.1 Bunion
733.99 Other disorders of bone and cartilage
735.4 Other hammer toe (acquired)
736.74 Claw foot, acquired
736.79 Other acquired deformity of ankle and foot
754.52 Congenital metatarsus primus varus

ICD-9-CM Procedural

77.54 Excision or correction of bunionette
77.88 Other partial ostectomy of tarsals and metatarsals

28111-28114

28111 Ostectomy, complete excision; first metatarsal head
28112 other metatarsal head (second, third or fourth)
28113 fifth metatarsal head
28114 all metatarsal heads, with partial proximal phalangectomy, excluding first metatarsal (eg, Clayton type procedure)

ICD-9-CM Diagnostic

213.8 Benign neoplasm of short bones of lower limb
357.1 Polyneuropathy in collagen vascular disease — (Code first underlying disease: 446.0, 710.0, 714.0) ☒
359.6 Symptomatic inflammatory myopathy in diseases classified elsewhere — (Code first underlying disease: 135, 140.0-208.9, 277.30-277.39, 446.0, 710.0, 710.1, 710.2, 714.0) ☒
446.0 Polyarteritis nodosa
710.0 Systemic lupus erythematosus — (Use additional code to identify manifestation: 424.91, 581.81, 582.81, 583.81)
710.1 Systemic sclerosis — (Use additional code to identify manifestation: 359.6, 517.2)
710.2 Sicca syndrome
714.0 Rheumatoid arthritis — (Use additional code to identify manifestation: 357.1, 359.6)
714.1 Felty's syndrome
714.2 Other rheumatoid arthritis with visceral or systemic involvement
714.30 Polyarticular juvenile rheumatoid arthritis, chronic or unspecified
714.31 Polyarticular juvenile rheumatoid arthritis, acute
714.32 Pauciarticular juvenile rheumatoid arthritis
714.33 Monoarticular juvenile rheumatoid arthritis
714.4 Chronic postrheumatic arthropathy
715.17 Primary localized osteoarthrosis, ankle and foot
715.27 Secondary localized osteoarthrosis, ankle and foot
727.1 Bunion
730.17 Chronic osteomyelitis, ankle and foot — (Use additional code to identify organism: 041.1. Use additional code to identify major osseous defect, if applicable: 731.3)
731.3 Major osseous defects — (Code first underlying disease: 170.0-170.9, 730.00-730.29, 733.00-733.09, 733.40-733.49, 996.45)
733.49 Aseptic necrosis of other bone site — (Use additional code to identify major osseous defect, if applicable: 731.3)
733.81 Malunion of fracture
733.82 Nonunion of fracture
733.94 Stress fracture of the metatarsals — (Use additional external cause code(s) to identify the cause of the stress fracture)
733.99 Other disorders of bone and cartilage
735.0 Hallux valgus (acquired)
735.4 Other hammer toe (acquired)
735.8 Other acquired deformity of toe
785.4 Gangrene — (Code first any associated underlying condition)
825.25 Closed fracture of metatarsal bone(s)
825.35 Open fracture of metatarsal bone(s)
905.4 Late effect of fracture of lower extremities
928.20 Crushing injury of foot — (Use additional code to identify any associated injuries: 800-829, 850.0-854.1, 860.0-869.1)

ICD-9-CM Procedural

77.88 Other partial ostectomy of tarsals and metatarsals

28116

28116 Ostectomy, excision of tarsal coalition

ICD-9-CM Diagnostic

755.56 Accessory carpal bones
755.67 Congenital anomalies of foot, not elsewhere classified

ICD-9-CM Procedural

77.98 Total ostectomy of tarsals and metatarsals

28118

28118 Ostectomy, calcaneus;

ICD-9-CM Diagnostic

213.8 Benign neoplasm of short bones of lower limb
726.73 Calcaneal spur
726.91 Exostosis of unspecified site ▽
732.5 Juvenile osteochondrosis of foot
733.90 Disorder of bone and cartilage, unspecified ▽
736.76 Other acquired calcaneus deformity
755.67 Congenital anomalies of foot, not elsewhere classified

ICD-9-CM Procedural

77.88 Other partial ostectomy of tarsals and metatarsals
77.98 Total ostectomy of tarsals and metatarsals

28119

28119 Ostectomy, calcaneus; for spur, with or without plantar fascial release

ICD-9-CM Diagnostic

355.6 Lesion of plantar nerve
726.73 Calcaneal spur
726.79 Other enthesopathy of ankle and tarsus

726.91 Exostosis of unspecified site ▽
729.4 Unspecified fasciitis ▽
729.5 Pain in soft tissues of limb
732.5 Juvenile osteochondrosis of foot
732.6 Other juvenile osteochondrosis
733.99 Other disorders of bone and cartilage
736.76 Other acquired calcaneus deformity

ICD-9-CM Procedural

77.88 Other partial ostectomy of tarsals and metatarsals
83.09 Other incision of soft tissue

28120-28124

28120 Partial excision (craterization, saucerization, sequestrectomy, or diaphysectomy) bone (eg, osteomyelitis or bossing); talus or calcaneus
28122 tarsal or metatarsal bone, except talus or calcaneus
28124 phalanx of toe

ICD-9-CM Diagnostic

213.8 Benign neoplasm of short bones of lower limb
239.2 Neoplasms of unspecified nature of bone, soft tissue, and skin
357.1 Polyneuropathy in collagen vascular disease — (Code first underlying disease: 446.0, 710.0, 714.0) ☒
359.6 Symptomatic inflammatory myopathy in diseases classified elsewhere — (Code first underlying disease: 135, 140.0-208.9, 277.30-277.39, 446.0, 710.0, 710.1, 710.2, 714.0) ☒
446.0 Polyarteritis nodosa
681.11 Onychia and paronychia of toe — (Use additional code to identify organism: 041.1)
703.8 Other specified disease of nail
707.10 Ulcer of lower limb, unspecified — (Code, if applicable, any causal condition first: 249.80-249.81, 250.80-250.83, 440.23, 459.11, 459.13, 459.31, 459.33) ▽
707.13 Ulcer of ankle — (Code, if applicable, any causal condition first: 249.80-249.81, 250.80-250.83, 440.23, 459.11, 459.13, 459.31, 459.33)
707.14 Ulcer of heel and midfoot — (Code, if applicable, any causal condition first: 249.80-249.81, 250.80-250.83, 440.23, 459.11, 459.13, 459.31, 459.33)
707.15 Ulcer of other part of foot — (Code, if applicable, any causal condition first: 249.80-249.81, 250.80-250.83, 440.23, 459.11, 459.13, 459.31, 459.33)
710.0 Systemic lupus erythematosus — (Use additional code to identify manifestation: 424.91, 581.81, 582.81, 583.81)
710.1 Systemic sclerosis — (Use additional code to identify manifestation: 359.6, 517.2)
710.2 Sicca syndrome
714.0 Rheumatoid arthritis — (Use additional code to identify manifestation: 357.1, 359.6)
715.17 Primary localized osteoarthrosis, ankle and foot
719.40 Pain in joint, site unspecified ▽
719.47 Pain in joint, ankle and foot
726.73 Calcaneal spur
726.79 Other enthesopathy of ankle and tarsus
726.8 Other peripheral enthesopathies
726.90 Enthesopathy of unspecified site ▽
726.91 Exostosis of unspecified site ▽
727.1 Bunion
730.17 Chronic osteomyelitis, ankle and foot — (Use additional code to identify organism: 041.1. Use additional code to identify major osseous defect, if applicable: 731.3)
730.87 Other infections involving bone diseases classified elsewhere, ankle and foot — (Use additional code to identify organism: 041.1. Code first underlying disease: 002.0, 015.0-015.9) ☒
731.3 Major osseous defects — (Code first underlying disease: 170.0-170.9, 730.00-730.29, 733.00-733.09, 733.40-733.49, 996.45)
732.5 Juvenile osteochondrosis of foot
733.49 Aseptic necrosis of other bone site — (Use additional code to identify major osseous defect, if applicable: 731.3)
733.99 Other disorders of bone and cartilage
735.0 Hallux valgus (acquired)
735.1 Hallux varus (acquired)
735.2 Hallux rigidus
735.3 Hallux malleus
735.4 Other hammer toe (acquired)
735.5 Claw toe (acquired)
735.8 Other acquired deformity of toe
735.9 Unspecified acquired deformity of toe ▽
736.76 Other acquired calcaneus deformity
755.67 Congenital anomalies of foot, not elsewhere classified
785.4 Gangrene — (Code first any associated underlying condition)
826.1 Open fracture of one or more phalanges of foot
905.4 Late effect of fracture of lower extremities
996.66 Infection and inflammatory reaction due to internal joint prosthesis — (Use additional code to identify specified infections. Use additional code to identify infected prosthetic joint: V43.60-V43.69)
996.67 Infection and inflammatory reaction due to other internal orthopedic device, implant, and graft — (Use additional code to identify specified infections)

ICD-9-CM Procedural

77.88 Other partial ostectomy of tarsals and metatarsals
77.89 Other partial ostectomy of other bone, except facial bones

HCPCS Level II Supplies & Services

A4580 Cast supplies (e.g., plaster)

28126

28126 Resection, partial or complete, phalangeal base, each toe

ICD-9-CM Diagnostic

213.8 Benign neoplasm of short bones of lower limb
726.91 Exostosis of unspecified site ▽
727.1 Bunion
733.99 Other disorders of bone and cartilage
735.0 Hallux valgus (acquired)
735.4 Other hammer toe (acquired)
735.8 Other acquired deformity of toe
755.66 Other congenital anomaly of toes

ICD-9-CM Procedural

77.89 Other partial ostectomy of other bone, except facial bones

28130

28130 Talectomy (astragalectomy)

ICD-9-CM Diagnostic

726.70 Unspecified enthesopathy of ankle and tarsus ▽
728.0 Infective myositis
730.17 Chronic osteomyelitis, ankle and foot — (Use additional code to identify organism: 041.1. Use additional code to identify major osseous defect, if applicable: 731.3)
730.87 Other infections involving bone diseases classified elsewhere, ankle and foot — (Use additional code to identify organism: 041.1. Code first underlying disease: 002.0, 015.0-015.9) ☒
731.3 Major osseous defects — (Code first underlying disease: 170.0-170.9, 730.00-730.29, 733.00-733.09, 733.40-733.49, 996.45)
733.44 Aseptic necrosis of talus — (Use additional code to identify major osseous defect, if applicable: 731.3)
733.81 Malunion of fracture

ICD-9-CM Procedural

77.98 Total ostectomy of tarsals and metatarsals

28140

28140 Metatarsectomy

ICD-9-CM Diagnostic

170.8 Malignant neoplasm of short bones of lower limb
198.5 Secondary malignant neoplasm of bone and bone marrow
238.0 Neoplasm of uncertain behavior of bone and articular cartilage
707.14 Ulcer of heel and midfoot — (Code, if applicable, any causal condition first: 249.80-249.81, 250.80-250.83, 440.23, 459.11, 459.13, 459.31, 459.33)
726.91 Exostosis of unspecified site ▽
728.0 Infective myositis
730.17 Chronic osteomyelitis, ankle and foot — (Use additional code to identify organism: 041.1. Use additional code to identify major osseous defect, if applicable: 731.3)
730.87 Other infections involving bone diseases classified elsewhere, ankle and foot — (Use additional code to identify organism: 041.1. Code first underlying disease: 002.0, 015.0-015.9) ☒
731.3 Major osseous defects — (Code first underlying disease: 170.0-170.9, 730.00-730.29, 733.00-733.09, 733.40-733.49, 996.45)
732.5 Juvenile osteochondrosis of foot
733.49 Aseptic necrosis of other bone site — (Use additional code to identify major osseous defect, if applicable: 731.3)
733.81 Malunion of fracture
733.82 Nonunion of fracture
733.99 Other disorders of bone and cartilage
735.9 Unspecified acquired deformity of toe ▽
736.70 Unspecified deformity of ankle and foot, acquired ▽
755.67 Congenital anomalies of foot, not elsewhere classified
785.4 Gangrene — (Code first any associated underlying condition)
825.35 Open fracture of metatarsal bone(s)
905.4 Late effect of fracture of lower extremities
928.20 Crushing injury of foot — (Use additional code to identify any associated injuries: 800-829, 850.0-854.1, 860.0-869.1)
996.66 Infection and inflammatory reaction due to internal joint prosthesis — (Use additional code to identify specified infections. Use additional code to identify infected prosthetic joint: V43.60-V43.69)
996.67 Infection and inflammatory reaction due to other internal orthopedic device, implant, and graft — (Use additional code to identify specified infections)

ICD-9-CM Procedural

77.98 Total ostectomy of tarsals and metatarsals

28150

28150 Phalangectomy, toe, each toe

ICD-9-CM Diagnostic

357.1 Polyneuropathy in collagen vascular disease — (Code first underlying disease: 446.0, 710.0, 714.0) ☒
359.6 Symptomatic inflammatory myopathy in diseases classified elsewhere — (Code first underlying disease: 135, 140.0-208.9, 277.30-277.39, 446.0, 710.0, 710.1, 710.2, 714.0) ☒
446.0 Polyarteritis nodosa
707.10 Ulcer of lower limb, unspecified — (Code, if applicable, any causal condition first: 249.80-249.81, 250.80-250.83, 440.23, 459.11, 459.13, 459.31, 459.33) ▽
707.15 Ulcer of other part of foot — (Code, if applicable, any causal condition first: 249.80-249.81, 250.80-250.83, 440.23, 459.11, 459.13, 459.31, 459.33)
710.0 Systemic lupus erythematosus — (Use additional code to identify manifestation: 424.91, 581.81, 582.81, 583.81)
710.1 Systemic sclerosis — (Use additional code to identify manifestation: 359.6, 517.2)
710.2 Sicca syndrome
714.0 Rheumatoid arthritis — (Use additional code to identify manifestation: 357.1, 359.6)
726.91 Exostosis of unspecified site ▽
728.0 Infective myositis
728.12 Traumatic myositis ossificans
730.17 Chronic osteomyelitis, ankle and foot — (Use additional code to identify organism: 041.1. Use additional code to identify major osseous defect, if applicable: 731.3)
731.3 Major osseous defects — (Code first underlying disease: 170.0-170.9, 730.00-730.29, 733.00-733.09, 733.40-733.49, 996.45)
735.0 Hallux valgus (acquired)
735.1 Hallux varus (acquired)
735.2 Hallux rigidus
735.3 Hallux malleus
735.4 Other hammer toe (acquired)
735.5 Claw toe (acquired)
735.8 Other acquired deformity of toe
755.66 Other congenital anomaly of toes
785.4 Gangrene — (Code first any associated underlying condition)
879.8 Open wound(s) (multiple) of unspecified site(s), without mention of complication ▽

ICD-9-CM Procedural

77.89 Other partial ostectomy of other bone, except facial bones
77.99 Total ostectomy of other bone, except facial bones

28153

28153 Resection, condyle(s), distal end of phalanx, each toe

ICD-9-CM Diagnostic

213.8 Benign neoplasm of short bones of lower limb
700 Corns and callosities
726.90 Enthesopathy of unspecified site ▽
726.91 Exostosis of unspecified site ▽
727.1 Bunion
728.0 Infective myositis
730.17 Chronic osteomyelitis, ankle and foot — (Use additional code to identify organism: 041.1. Use additional code to identify major osseous defect, if applicable: 731.3)
732.5 Juvenile osteochondrosis of foot
733.90 Disorder of bone and cartilage, unspecified ▽
733.99 Other disorders of bone and cartilage
735.0 Hallux valgus (acquired)
735.1 Hallux varus (acquired)
735.2 Hallux rigidus
735.3 Hallux malleus
735.4 Other hammer toe (acquired)
735.5 Claw toe (acquired)
735.8 Other acquired deformity of toe
755.66 Other congenital anomaly of toes
785.4 Gangrene — (Code first any associated underlying condition)

ICD-9-CM Procedural

77.89 Other partial ostectomy of other bone, except facial bones

28160

28160 Hemiphalangectomy or interphalangeal joint excision, toe, proximal end of phalanx, each

ICD-9-CM Diagnostic

357.1 Polyneuropathy in collagen vascular disease — (Code first underlying disease: 446.0, 710.0, 714.0) ☒
359.6 Symptomatic inflammatory myopathy in diseases classified elsewhere — (Code first underlying disease: 135, 140.0-208.9, 277.30-277.39, 446.0, 710.0, 710.1, 710.2, 714.0) ☒
446.0 Polyarteritis nodosa
710.0 Systemic lupus erythematosus — (Use additional code to identify manifestation: 424.91, 581.81, 582.81, 583.81)

710.1 Systemic sclerosis — (Use additional code to identify manifestation: 359.6, 517.2)
710.2 Sicca syndrome
714.0 Rheumatoid arthritis — (Use additional code to identify manifestation: 357.1, 359.6)
726.91 Exostosis of unspecified site ♥
733.99 Other disorders of bone and cartilage
735.0 Hallux valgus (acquired)
735.1 Hallux varus (acquired)
735.2 Hallux rigidus
735.3 Hallux malleus
735.4 Other hammer toe (acquired)
735.5 Claw toe (acquired)
735.8 Other acquired deformity of toe
755.66 Other congenital anomaly of toes

ICD-9-CM Procedural

77.89 Other partial ostectomy of other bone, except facial bones

28171-28175

28171 Radical resection of tumor; tarsal (except talus or calcaneus)
28173 metatarsal
28175 phalanx of toe

ICD-9-CM Diagnostic

170.8 Malignant neoplasm of short bones of lower limb
171.3 Malignant neoplasm of connective and other soft tissue of lower limb, including hip
172.7 Malignant melanoma of skin of lower limb, including hip
173.70 Unspecified malignant neoplasm of skin of lower limb, including hip ♥
173.71 Basal cell carcinoma of skin of lower limb, including hip
173.72 Squamous cell carcinoma of skin of lower limb, including hip
173.79 Other specified malignant neoplasm of skin of lower limb, including hip
198.5 Secondary malignant neoplasm of bone and bone marrow
209.73 Secondary neuroendocrine tumor of bone
213.8 Benign neoplasm of short bones of lower limb
238.0 Neoplasm of uncertain behavior of bone and articular cartilage
239.2 Neoplasms of unspecified nature of bone, soft tissue, and skin

ICD-9-CM Procedural

77.88 Other partial ostectomy of tarsals and metatarsals
77.89 Other partial ostectomy of other bone, except facial bones
77.98 Total ostectomy of tarsals and metatarsals
77.99 Total ostectomy of other bone, except facial bones

28190-28193

28190 Removal of foreign body, foot; subcutaneous
28192 deep
28193 complicated

ICD-9-CM Diagnostic

709.4 Foreign body granuloma of skin and subcutaneous tissue — (Use additional code to identify foreign body (V90.01-V90.9))
728.82 Foreign body granuloma of muscle — (Use additional code to identify foreign body (V90.01-V90.9))
729.6 Residual foreign body in soft tissue — (Use additional code to identify foreign body (V90.01-V90.9))
892.1 Open wound of foot except toe(s) alone, complicated
893.1 Open wound of toe(s), complicated
917.6 Foot and toe(s), superficial foreign body (splinter), without major open wound and without mention of infection
917.7 Foot and toe(s), superficial foreign body (splinter), without major open wound, infected
917.9 Other and unspecified superficial injury of foot and toes, infected ♥

ICD-9-CM Procedural

83.02 Myotomy
83.09 Other incision of soft tissue
86.05 Incision with removal of foreign body or device from skin and subcutaneous tissue

HCPCS Level II Supplies & Services

A4305 Disposable drug delivery system, flow rate of 50 ml or greater per hour

28200-28202

28200 Repair, tendon, flexor, foot; primary or secondary, without free graft, each tendon
28202 secondary with free graft, each tendon (includes obtaining graft)

ICD-9-CM Diagnostic

727.68 Nontraumatic rupture of other tendons of foot and ankle
845.10 Sprain and strain of unspecified site of foot ♥
845.11 Sprain and strain of tarsometatarsal (joint) (ligament)
845.12 Sprain and strain of metatarsophalangeal (joint)
845.13 Sprain and strain of interphalangeal (joint), of toe
845.19 Other foot sprain and strain
892.2 Open wound of foot except toe(s) alone, with tendon involvement
893.2 Open wound of toe(s), with tendon involvement
905.8 Late effect of tendon injury
928.3 Crushing injury of toe(s) — (Use additional code to identify any associated injuries: 800-829, 850.0-854.1, 860.0-869.1)
998.31 Disruption of internal operation (surgical) wound

ICD-9-CM Procedural

83.61 Suture of tendon sheath
83.62 Delayed suture of tendon

HCPCS Level II Supplies & Services

A4305 Disposable drug delivery system, flow rate of 50 ml or greater per hour

28208-28210

28208 Repair, tendon, extensor, foot; primary or secondary, each tendon
28210 secondary with free graft, each tendon (includes obtaining graft)

ICD-9-CM Diagnostic

727.68 Nontraumatic rupture of other tendons of foot and ankle
727.69 Nontraumatic rupture of other tendon
845.10 Sprain and strain of unspecified site of foot ♥
845.11 Sprain and strain of tarsometatarsal (joint) (ligament)
845.12 Sprain and strain of metatarsophalangeal (joint)
845.13 Sprain and strain of interphalangeal (joint), of toe
845.19 Other foot sprain and strain
892.2 Open wound of foot except toe(s) alone, with tendon involvement
893.2 Open wound of toe(s), with tendon involvement
905.8 Late effect of tendon injury
928.3 Crushing injury of toe(s) — (Use additional code to identify any associated injuries: 800-829, 850.0-854.1, 860.0-869.1)

ICD-9-CM Procedural

83.61 Suture of tendon sheath
83.62 Delayed suture of tendon

HCPCS Level II Supplies & Services

A4580 Cast supplies (e.g., plaster)

28220-28222

28220 Tenolysis, flexor, foot; single tendon
28222 multiple tendons

ICD-9-CM Diagnostic

727.01 Synovitis and tenosynovitis in diseases classified elsewhere — (Code first underlying disease: 015.0-015.9) ☒
727.06 Tenosynovitis of foot and ankle
727.82 Calcium deposits in tendon and bursa
727.89 Other disorders of synovium, tendon, and bursa
735.8 Other acquired deformity of toe

ICD-9-CM Procedural

83.91 Lysis of adhesions of muscle, tendon, fascia, and bursa

HCPCS Level II Supplies & Services

A4305 Disposable drug delivery system, flow rate of 50 ml or greater per hour

28225-28226

28225 Tenolysis, extensor, foot; single tendon
28226 multiple tendons

ICD-9-CM Diagnostic

727.01 Synovitis and tenosynovitis in diseases classified elsewhere — (Code first underlying disease: 015.0-015.9) ☒
727.06 Tenosynovitis of foot and ankle
727.82 Calcium deposits in tendon and bursa
727.89 Other disorders of synovium, tendon, and bursa
735.8 Other acquired deformity of toe

ICD-9-CM Procedural

83.91 Lysis of adhesions of muscle, tendon, fascia, and bursa

HCPCS Level II Supplies & Services

A4305 Disposable drug delivery system, flow rate of 50 ml or greater per hour

28230-28232

28230 Tenotomy, open, tendon flexor; foot, single or multiple tendon(s) (separate procedure)
28232 toe, single tendon (separate procedure)

ICD-9-CM Diagnostic

357.1 Polyneuropathy in collagen vascular disease — (Code first underlying disease: 446.0, 710.0, 714.0) ☒
359.6 Symptomatic inflammatory myopathy in diseases classified elsewhere — (Code first underlying disease: 135, 140.0-208.9, 277.30-277.39, 446.0, 710.0, 710.1, 710.2, 714.0) ☒
446.0 Polyarteritis nodosa
710.0 Systemic lupus erythematosus — (Use additional code to identify manifestation: 424.91, 581.81, 582.81, 583.81)
710.1 Systemic sclerosis — (Use additional code to identify manifestation: 359.6, 517.2)
710.2 Sicca syndrome
714.0 Rheumatoid arthritis — (Use additional code to identify manifestation: 357.1, 359.6)
718.47 Contracture of ankle and foot joint
727.81 Contracture of tendon (sheath)
735.0 Hallux valgus (acquired)
735.1 Hallux varus (acquired)
735.2 Hallux rigidus
735.3 Hallux malleus
735.4 Other hammer toe (acquired)
735.5 Claw toe (acquired)
735.8 Other acquired deformity of toe
736.71 Acquired equinovarus deformity
736.72 Equinus deformity of foot, acquired
736.73 Cavus deformity of foot, acquired
736.74 Claw foot, acquired
736.75 Cavovarus deformity of foot, acquired
736.79 Other acquired deformity of ankle and foot

ICD-9-CM Procedural

83.13 Other tenotomy

HCPCS Level II Supplies & Services

A4305 Disposable drug delivery system, flow rate of 50 ml or greater per hour

28234

28234 Tenotomy, open, extensor, foot or toe, each tendon

ICD-9-CM Diagnostic

357.1 Polyneuropathy in collagen vascular disease — (Code first underlying disease: 446.0, 710.0, 714.0) ☒
359.6 Symptomatic inflammatory myopathy in diseases classified elsewhere — (Code first underlying disease: 135, 140.0-208.9, 277.30-277.39, 446.0, 710.0, 710.1, 710.2, 714.0) ☒
446.0 Polyarteritis nodosa
710.0 Systemic lupus erythematosus — (Use additional code to identify manifestation: 424.91, 581.81, 582.81, 583.81)
710.1 Systemic sclerosis — (Use additional code to identify manifestation: 359.6, 517.2)
710.2 Sicca syndrome
714.0 Rheumatoid arthritis — (Use additional code to identify manifestation: 357.1, 359.6)
718.47 Contracture of ankle and foot joint
727.81 Contracture of tendon (sheath)
735.0 Hallux valgus (acquired)
735.1 Hallux varus (acquired)
735.2 Hallux rigidus
735.3 Hallux malleus
735.4 Other hammer toe (acquired)
735.5 Claw toe (acquired)
735.8 Other acquired deformity of toe
736.71 Acquired equinovarus deformity
736.72 Equinus deformity of foot, acquired
736.73 Cavus deformity of foot, acquired
736.74 Claw foot, acquired
736.75 Cavovarus deformity of foot, acquired
736.79 Other acquired deformity of ankle and foot
906.4 Late effect of crushing

ICD-9-CM Procedural

83.13 Other tenotomy

HCPCS Level II Supplies & Services

A4305 Disposable drug delivery system, flow rate of 50 ml or greater per hour

28238

28238 Reconstruction (advancement), posterior tibial tendon with excision of accessory tarsal navicular bone (eg, Kidner type procedure)

ICD-9-CM Diagnostic

138 Late effects of acute poliomyelitis — (Note: This category is to be used to indicate conditions classifiable to 045 as the cause of late effects, which are themselves classified elsewhere. The "late effects" include those specified as such, as sequelae, or as due to old or inactive poliomyelitis, without evidence of active disease.)
726.72 Tibialis tendinitis
727.68 Nontraumatic rupture of other tendons of foot and ankle
727.81 Contracture of tendon (sheath)
727.89 Other disorders of synovium, tendon, and bursa
754.50 Congenital talipes varus

754.51 Congenital talipes equinovarus
754.52 Congenital metatarsus primus varus
754.53 Congenital metatarsus varus
754.59 Other congenital varus deformity of feet

ICD-9-CM Procedural

77.68 Local excision of lesion or tissue of tarsals and metatarsals
83.71 Advancement of tendon

28240

28240 Tenotomy, lengthening, or release, abductor hallucis muscle

ICD-9-CM Diagnostic

727.1 Bunion
727.81 Contracture of tendon (sheath)
735.1 Hallux varus (acquired)
735.2 Hallux rigidus
736.71 Acquired equinovarus deformity
736.72 Equinus deformity of foot, acquired
736.73 Cavus deformity of foot, acquired
736.74 Claw foot, acquired
736.75 Cavovarus deformity of foot, acquired
736.76 Other acquired calcaneus deformity
736.79 Other acquired deformity of ankle and foot

ICD-9-CM Procedural

83.19 Other division of soft tissue
83.85 Other change in muscle or tendon length

28250

28250 Division of plantar fascia and muscle (eg, Steindler stripping) (separate procedure)

ICD-9-CM Diagnostic

726.73 Calcaneal spur
728.71 Plantar fascial fibromatosis
734 Flat foot
736.73 Cavus deformity of foot, acquired
736.75 Cavovarus deformity of foot, acquired
754.50 Congenital talipes varus
754.51 Congenital talipes equinovarus
754.52 Congenital metatarsus primus varus
754.53 Congenital metatarsus varus
754.59 Other congenital varus deformity of feet
754.60 Congenital talipes valgus
754.61 Congenital pes planus
754.62 Talipes calcaneovalgus
754.69 Other congenital valgus deformity of feet
754.71 Talipes cavus
754.79 Other congenital deformity of feet

ICD-9-CM Procedural

83.14 Fasciotomy

28260-28262

28260 Capsulotomy, midfoot; medial release only (separate procedure)
28261 with tendon lengthening
28262 extensive, including posterior talotibial capsulotomy and tendon(s) lengthening (eg, resistant clubfoot deformity)

ICD-9-CM Diagnostic

357.1 Polyneuropathy in collagen vascular disease — (Code first underlying disease: 446.0, 710.0, 714.0) ☒
359.6 Symptomatic inflammatory myopathy in diseases classified elsewhere — (Code first underlying disease: 135, 140.0-208.9, 277.30-277.39, 446.0, 710.0, 710.1, 710.2, 714.0) ☒
446.0 Polyarteritis nodosa
710.0 Systemic lupus erythematosus — (Use additional code to identify manifestation: 424.91, 581.81, 582.81, 583.81)
710.1 Systemic sclerosis — (Use additional code to identify manifestation: 359.6, 517.2)
710.2 Sicca syndrome
714.0 Rheumatoid arthritis — (Use additional code to identify manifestation: 357.1, 359.6)
727.1 Bunion
727.81 Contracture of tendon (sheath)
735.4 Other hammer toe (acquired)
754.50 Congenital talipes varus
754.60 Congenital talipes valgus
754.70 Unspecified talipes ▽
754.71 Talipes cavus
754.79 Other congenital deformity of feet
755.66 Other congenital anomaly of toes
893.2 Open wound of toe(s), with tendon involvement

ICD-9-CM Procedural

80.48 Division of joint capsule, ligament, or cartilage of foot and toe
83.84 Release of clubfoot, not elsewhere classified

HCPCS Level II Supplies & Services

A4580 Cast supplies (e.g., plaster)

28264

28264 Capsulotomy, midtarsal (eg, Heyman type procedure)

ICD-9-CM Diagnostic

727.1 Bunion
735.4 Other hammer toe (acquired)
736.73 Cavus deformity of foot, acquired
754.50 Congenital talipes varus
754.60 Congenital talipes valgus

ICD-9-CM Procedural

80.48 Division of joint capsule, ligament, or cartilage of foot and toe

HCPCS Level II Supplies & Services

A4580 Cast supplies (e.g., plaster)

28270-28272

28270 Capsulotomy; metatarsophalangeal joint, with or without tenorrhaphy, each joint (separate procedure)
28272 interphalangeal joint, each joint (separate procedure)

ICD-9-CM Diagnostic

357.1 Polyneuropathy in collagen vascular disease — (Code first underlying disease: 446.0, 710.0, 714.0) ☒
359.6 Symptomatic inflammatory myopathy in diseases classified elsewhere — (Code first underlying disease: 135, 140.0-208.9, 277.30-277.39, 446.0, 710.0, 710.1, 710.2, 714.0) ☒
446.0 Polyarteritis nodosa
710.0 Systemic lupus erythematosus — (Use additional code to identify manifestation: 424.91, 581.81, 582.81, 583.81)
710.1 Systemic sclerosis — (Use additional code to identify manifestation: 359.6, 517.2)
710.2 Sicca syndrome
714.0 Rheumatoid arthritis — (Use additional code to identify manifestation: 357.1, 359.6)
718.40 Contracture of joint, site unspecified ▽
718.47 Contracture of ankle and foot joint
727.81 Contracture of tendon (sheath)

733.99 Other disorders of bone and cartilage
735.4 Other hammer toe (acquired)
735.5 Claw toe (acquired)
735.8 Other acquired deformity of toe
754.71 Talipes cavus
755.66 Other congenital anomaly of toes
893.2 Open wound of toe(s), with tendon involvement

ICD-9-CM Procedural

80.48 Division of joint capsule, ligament, or cartilage of foot and toe
83.64 Other suture of tendon

28280

28280 Syndactylization, toes (eg, webbing or Kelikian type procedure)

ICD-9-CM Diagnostic

735.8 Other acquired deformity of toe
755.39 Congenital longitudinal deficiency, phalanges, complete or partial

ICD-9-CM Procedural

86.89 Other repair and reconstruction of skin and subcutaneous tissue

28285

28285 Correction, hammertoe (eg, interphalangeal fusion, partial or total phalangectomy)

ICD-9-CM Diagnostic

735.3 Hallux malleus
735.4 Other hammer toe (acquired)
735.8 Other acquired deformity of toe
755.66 Other congenital anomaly of toes

ICD-9-CM Procedural

77.56 Repair of hammer toe

28286

28286 Correction, cock-up fifth toe, with plastic skin closure (eg, Ruiz-Mora type procedure)

ICD-9-CM Diagnostic

735.2 Hallux rigidus
735.4 Other hammer toe (acquired)
735.8 Other acquired deformity of toe
755.66 Other congenital anomaly of toes

ICD-9-CM Procedural

77.58 Other excision, fusion, and repair of toes

28288

28288 Ostectomy, partial, exostectomy or condylectomy, metatarsal head, each metatarsal head

ICD-9-CM Diagnostic

213.8 Benign neoplasm of short bones of lower limb
357.1 Polyneuropathy in collagen vascular disease — (Code first underlying disease: 446.0, 710.0, 714.0) ☒
359.6 Symptomatic inflammatory myopathy in diseases classified elsewhere — (Code first underlying disease: 135, 140.0-208.9, 277.30-277.39, 446.0, 710.0, 710.1, 710.2, 714.0) ☒
446.0 Polyarteritis nodosa
700 Corns and callosities
710.0 Systemic lupus erythematosus — (Use additional code to identify manifestation: 424.91, 581.81, 582.81, 583.81)
710.1 Systemic sclerosis — (Use additional code to identify manifestation: 359.6, 517.2)
710.2 Sicca syndrome
714.0 Rheumatoid arthritis — (Use additional code to identify manifestation: 357.1, 359.6)
727.1 Bunion
733.99 Other disorders of bone and cartilage
735.0 Hallux valgus (acquired)
735.1 Hallux varus (acquired)
735.2 Hallux rigidus
735.3 Hallux malleus
735.4 Other hammer toe (acquired)
735.5 Claw toe (acquired)
735.8 Other acquired deformity of toe
755.66 Other congenital anomaly of toes
755.67 Congenital anomalies of foot, not elsewhere classified
825.25 Closed fracture of metatarsal bone(s)
825.35 Open fracture of metatarsal bone(s)

ICD-9-CM Procedural

77.51 Bunionectomy with soft tissue correction and osteotomy of the first metatarsal
77.88 Other partial ostectomy of tarsals and metatarsals

28289

28289 Hallux rigidus correction with cheilectomy, debridement and capsular release of the first metatarsophalangeal joint

ICD-9-CM Diagnostic

735.2 Hallux rigidus

ICD-9-CM Procedural

77.58 Other excision, fusion, and repair of toes
77.68 Local excision of lesion or tissue of tarsals and metatarsals
77.88 Other partial ostectomy of tarsals and metatarsals

28290

28290 Correction, hallux valgus (bunion), with or without sesamoidectomy; simple exostectomy (eg, Silver type procedure)

ICD-9-CM Diagnostic

727.1 Bunion
735.0 Hallux valgus (acquired)
735.2 Hallux rigidus
735.8 Other acquired deformity of toe
755.66 Other congenital anomaly of toes

ICD-9-CM Procedural

77.59 Other bunionectomy

28292

28292 Correction, hallux valgus (bunion), with or without sesamoidectomy; Keller, McBride, or Mayo type procedure

ICD-9-CM Diagnostic

727.1 Bunion
728.13 Postoperative heterotopic calcification
733.99 Other disorders of bone and cartilage
735.0 Hallux valgus (acquired)
735.1 Hallux varus (acquired)
735.2 Hallux rigidus
735.3 Hallux malleus
754.52 Congenital metatarsus primus varus
755.66 Other congenital anomaly of toes

ICD-9-CM Procedural

77.53 Other bunionectomy with soft tissue correction
77.59 Other bunionectomy

28293

28293 Correction, hallux valgus (bunion), with or without sesamoidectomy; resection of joint with implant

ICD-9-CM Diagnostic

357.1 Polyneuropathy in collagen vascular disease — (Code first underlying disease: 446.0, 710.0, 714.0) ☒

359.6 Symptomatic inflammatory myopathy in diseases classified elsewhere — (Code first underlying disease: 135, 140.0-208.9, 277.30-277.39, 446.0, 710.0, 710.1, 710.2, 714.0) ☒

446.0 Polyarteritis nodosa

710.0 Systemic lupus erythematosus — (Use additional code to identify manifestation: 424.91, 581.81, 582.81, 583.81)

710.1 Systemic sclerosis — (Use additional code to identify manifestation: 359.6, 517.2)

710.2 Sicca syndrome

714.0 Rheumatoid arthritis — (Use additional code to identify manifestation: 357.1, 359.6)

714.89 Other specified inflammatory polyarthropathies

715.09 Generalized osteoarthrosis, involving multiple sites

715.17 Primary localized osteoarthrosis, ankle and foot

715.37 Localized osteoarthrosis not specified whether primary or secondary, ankle and foot

715.97 Osteoarthrosis, unspecified whether generalized or localized, ankle and foot ▽

718.47 Contracture of ankle and foot joint

719.57 Stiffness of joint, not elsewhere classified, ankle and foot

726.73 Calcaneal spur

726.91 Exostosis of unspecified site ▽

727.1 Bunion

735.0 Hallux valgus (acquired)

735.1 Hallux varus (acquired)

735.2 Hallux rigidus

735.3 Hallux malleus

735.8 Other acquired deformity of toe

755.66 Other congenital anomaly of toes

ICD-9-CM Procedural

77.59 Other bunionectomy

28294

28294 Correction, hallux valgus (bunion), with or without sesamoidectomy; with tendon transplants (eg, Joplin type procedure)

ICD-9-CM Diagnostic

727.06 Tenosynovitis of foot and ankle

727.1 Bunion

733.99 Other disorders of bone and cartilage

735.0 Hallux valgus (acquired)

735.1 Hallux varus (acquired)

735.2 Hallux rigidus

735.3 Hallux malleus

735.4 Other hammer toe (acquired)

755.66 Other congenital anomaly of toes

ICD-9-CM Procedural

77.53 Other bunionectomy with soft tissue correction

28296

28296 Correction, hallux valgus (bunion), with or without sesamoidectomy; with metatarsal osteotomy (eg, Mitchell, Chevron, or concentric type procedures)

ICD-9-CM Diagnostic

727.1 Bunion

733.99 Other disorders of bone and cartilage

735.0 Hallux valgus (acquired)

735.1 Hallux varus (acquired)

735.2 Hallux rigidus

735.3 Hallux malleus

735.8 Other acquired deformity of toe

754.52 Congenital metatarsus primus varus

755.66 Other congenital anomaly of toes

ICD-9-CM Procedural

77.51 Bunionectomy with soft tissue correction and osteotomy of the first metatarsal

77.59 Other bunionectomy

28297

28297 Correction, hallux valgus (bunion), with or without sesamoidectomy; Lapidus-type procedure

ICD-9-CM Diagnostic

727.1 Bunion

733.99 Other disorders of bone and cartilage

735.0 Hallux valgus (acquired)

735.1 Hallux varus (acquired)

735.2 Hallux rigidus

735.3 Hallux malleus

755.66 Other congenital anomaly of toes

ICD-9-CM Procedural

77.51 Bunionectomy with soft tissue correction and osteotomy of the first metatarsal

28298

28298 Correction, hallux valgus (bunion), with or without sesamoidectomy; by phalanx osteotomy

ICD-9-CM Diagnostic

727.1 Bunion

733.99 Other disorders of bone and cartilage

735.0 Hallux valgus (acquired)

735.1 Hallux varus (acquired)

735.2 Hallux rigidus

735.3 Hallux malleus

735.8 Other acquired deformity of toe

755.66 Other congenital anomaly of toes

ICD-9-CM Procedural

77.59 Other bunionectomy

28299

28299 Correction, hallux valgus (bunion), with or without sesamoidectomy; by double osteotomy

ICD-9-CM Diagnostic

727.1 Bunion

733.99 Other disorders of bone and cartilage

735.0 Hallux valgus (acquired)

735.1 Hallux varus (acquired)

735.2 Hallux rigidus

735.3 Hallux malleus

754.52 Congenital metatarsus primus varus

755.66 Other congenital anomaly of toes

ICD-9-CM Procedural

77.59 Other bunionectomy

28300-28302

28300 Osteotomy; calcaneus (eg, Dwyer or Chambers type procedure), with or without internal fixation

28302 talus

ICD-9-CM Diagnostic

239.2 Neoplasms of unspecified nature of bone, soft tissue, and skin
732.5 Juvenile osteochondrosis of foot
736.70 Unspecified deformity of ankle and foot, acquired
736.72 Equinus deformity of foot, acquired
736.73 Cavus deformity of foot, acquired
736.76 Other acquired calcaneus deformity
736.79 Other acquired deformity of ankle and foot
738.9 Acquired musculoskeletal deformity of unspecified site
754.50 Congenital talipes varus
754.59 Other congenital varus deformity of feet
754.60 Congenital talipes valgus
754.62 Talipes calcaneovalgus
754.69 Other congenital valgus deformity of feet

ICD-9-CM Procedural

77.28 Wedge osteotomy of tarsals and metatarsals
77.38 Other division of tarsals and metatarsals
78.58 Internal fixation of tarsals and metatarsals without fracture reduction

28304-28305

28304 Osteotomy, tarsal bones, other than calcaneus or talus;

28305 with autograft (includes obtaining graft) (eg, Fowler type)

ICD-9-CM Diagnostic

732.5 Juvenile osteochondrosis of foot
736.70 Unspecified deformity of ankle and foot, acquired
736.71 Acquired equinovarus deformity
736.73 Cavus deformity of foot, acquired
754.51 Congenital talipes equinovarus
754.53 Congenital metatarsus varus
754.70 Unspecified talipes
754.71 Talipes cavus
754.79 Other congenital deformity of feet
756.89 Other specified congenital anomaly of muscle, tendon, fascia, and connective tissue

ICD-9-CM Procedural

77.28 Wedge osteotomy of tarsals and metatarsals
77.38 Other division of tarsals and metatarsals
77.77 Excision of tibia and fibula for graft
77.79 Excision of other bone for graft, except facial bones
78.08 Bone graft of tarsals and metatarsals

28306-28308

28306 Osteotomy, with or without lengthening, shortening or angular correction, metatarsal; first metatarsal

28307 first metatarsal with autograft (other than first toe)

28308 other than first metatarsal, each

ICD-9-CM Diagnostic

357.1 Polyneuropathy in collagen vascular disease — (Code first underlying disease: 446.0, 710.0, 714.0) ☒
359.6 Symptomatic inflammatory myopathy in diseases classified elsewhere — (Code first underlying disease: 135, 140.0-208.9, 277.30-277.39, 446.0, 710.0, 710.1, 710.2, 714.0) ☒
446.0 Polyarteritis nodosa
710.0 Systemic lupus erythematosus — (Use additional code to identify manifestation: 424.91, 581.81, 582.81, 583.81)
710.1 Systemic sclerosis — (Use additional code to identify manifestation: 359.6, 517.2)
710.2 Sicca syndrome
714.0 Rheumatoid arthritis — (Use additional code to identify manifestation: 357.1, 359.6)
715.17 Primary localized osteoarthrosis, ankle and foot
715.97 Osteoarthrosis, unspecified whether generalized or localized, ankle and foot
718.47 Contracture of ankle and foot joint
719.47 Pain in joint, ankle and foot
726.91 Exostosis of unspecified site
727.1 Bunion
733.91 Arrest of bone development or growth
733.99 Other disorders of bone and cartilage
735.0 Hallux valgus (acquired)
735.1 Hallux varus (acquired)
735.2 Hallux rigidus
735.3 Hallux malleus
735.4 Other hammer toe (acquired)
735.5 Claw toe (acquired)
735.8 Other acquired deformity of toe
736.79 Other acquired deformity of ankle and foot
754.50 Congenital talipes varus
754.52 Congenital metatarsus primus varus
754.53 Congenital metatarsus varus
754.59 Other congenital varus deformity of feet
754.60 Congenital talipes valgus
754.71 Talipes cavus
755.38 Congenital longitudinal deficiency, tarsals or metatarsals, complete or partial (with or without incomplete phalangeal deficiency)
755.67 Congenital anomalies of foot, not elsewhere classified

ICD-9-CM Procedural

77.28 Wedge osteotomy of tarsals and metatarsals
77.38 Other division of tarsals and metatarsals
77.79 Excision of other bone for graft, except facial bones
78.08 Bone graft of tarsals and metatarsals
78.18 Application of external fixator device, tarsals and metatarsals
78.28 Limb shortening procedures, tarsals and metatarsals
78.38 Limb lengthening procedures, tarsals and metatarsals
84.53 Implantation of internal limb lengthening device with kinetic distraction
84.54 Implantation of other internal limb lengthening device

28309

28309 Osteotomy, with or without lengthening, shortening or angular correction, metatarsal; multiple (eg, Swanson type cavus foot procedure)

ICD-9-CM Diagnostic

735.8 Other acquired deformity of toe
736.73 Cavus deformity of foot, acquired
736.75 Cavovarus deformity of foot, acquired
754.71 Talipes cavus
755.67 Congenital anomalies of foot, not elsewhere classified

ICD-9-CM Procedural

77.29 Wedge osteotomy of other bone, except facial bones
77.38 Other division of tarsals and metatarsals
78.18 Application of external fixator device, tarsals and metatarsals
78.28 Limb shortening procedures, tarsals and metatarsals
78.38 Limb lengthening procedures, tarsals and metatarsals
84.53 Implantation of internal limb lengthening device with kinetic distraction
84.54 Implantation of other internal limb lengthening device

28310-28312

28310 Osteotomy, shortening, angular or rotational correction; proximal phalanx, first toe (separate procedure)
28312 other phalanges, any toe

ICD-9-CM Diagnostic

357.1 Polyneuropathy in collagen vascular disease — (Code first underlying disease: 446.0, 710.0, 714.0) ☒
359.6 Symptomatic inflammatory myopathy in diseases classified elsewhere — (Code first underlying disease: 135, 140.0-208.9, 277.30-277.39, 446.0, 710.0, 710.1, 710.2, 714.0) ☒
446.0 Polyarteritis nodosa
700 Corns and callosities
710.0 Systemic lupus erythematosus — (Use additional code to identify manifestation: 424.91, 581.81, 582.81, 583.81)
710.1 Systemic sclerosis — (Use additional code to identify manifestation: 359.6, 517.2)
710.2 Sicca syndrome
714.0 Rheumatoid arthritis — (Use additional code to identify manifestation: 357.1, 359.6)
718.47 Contracture of ankle and foot joint
727.1 Bunion
733.91 Arrest of bone development or growth
733.99 Other disorders of bone and cartilage
735.0 Hallux valgus (acquired)
735.1 Hallux varus (acquired)
735.2 Hallux rigidus
735.3 Hallux malleus
735.4 Other hammer toe (acquired)
735.5 Claw toe (acquired)
735.8 Other acquired deformity of toe
736.74 Claw foot, acquired
736.79 Other acquired deformity of ankle and foot
754.52 Congenital metatarsus primus varus
754.53 Congenital metatarsus varus
754.69 Other congenital valgus deformity of feet
755.66 Other congenital anomaly of toes
755.67 Congenital anomalies of foot, not elsewhere classified

ICD-9-CM Procedural

77.29 Wedge osteotomy of other bone, except facial bones
78.29 Limb shortening procedures, other

28313

28313 Reconstruction, angular deformity of toe, soft tissue procedures only (eg, overlapping second toe, fifth toe, curly toes)

ICD-9-CM Diagnostic

718.47 Contracture of ankle and foot joint
733.90 Disorder of bone and cartilage, unspecified ▽
735.4 Other hammer toe (acquired)
735.5 Claw toe (acquired)
735.8 Other acquired deformity of toe
755.66 Other congenital anomaly of toes

ICD-9-CM Procedural

83.09 Other incision of soft tissue
83.75 Tendon transfer or transplantation

28315

28315 Sesamoidectomy, first toe (separate procedure)

ICD-9-CM Diagnostic

357.1 Polyneuropathy in collagen vascular disease — (Code first underlying disease: 446.0, 710.0, 714.0) ☒
359.6 Symptomatic inflammatory myopathy in diseases classified elsewhere — (Code first underlying disease: 135, 140.0-208.9, 277.30-277.39, 446.0, 710.0, 710.1, 710.2, 714.0) ☒
446.0 Polyarteritis nodosa
710.0 Systemic lupus erythematosus — (Use additional code to identify manifestation: 424.91, 581.81, 582.81, 583.81)
710.1 Systemic sclerosis — (Use additional code to identify manifestation: 359.6, 517.2)
710.2 Sicca syndrome
714.0 Rheumatoid arthritis — (Use additional code to identify manifestation: 357.1, 359.6)
733.99 Other disorders of bone and cartilage
735.0 Hallux valgus (acquired)
735.1 Hallux varus (acquired)
754.52 Congenital metatarsus primus varus
755.67 Congenital anomalies of foot, not elsewhere classified

ICD-9-CM Procedural

77.98 Total ostectomy of tarsals and metatarsals

28320-28322

28320 Repair, nonunion or malunion; tarsal bones
28322 metatarsal, with or without bone graft (includes obtaining graft)

ICD-9-CM Diagnostic

733.81 Malunion of fracture
733.82 Nonunion of fracture
905.4 Late effect of fracture of lower extremities

ICD-9-CM Procedural

77.78 Excision of tarsals and metatarsals for graft
78.08 Bone graft of tarsals and metatarsals
78.48 Other repair or plastic operations on tarsals and metatarsals

28340-28341

28340 Reconstruction, toe, macrodactyly; soft tissue resection
28341 requiring bone resection

ICD-9-CM Diagnostic

755.65 Macrodactylia of toes

ICD-9-CM Procedural

77.39 Other division of other bone, except facial bones
78.48 Other repair or plastic operations on tarsals and metatarsals
83.49 Other excision of soft tissue

28344

28344 Reconstruction, toe(s); polydactyly

ICD-9-CM Diagnostic

755.02 Polydactyly of toes

ICD-9-CM Procedural

77.69 Local excision of lesion or tissue of other bone, except facial bones
78.49 Other repair or plastic operations on other bone, except facial bones

28345

28345 Reconstruction, toe(s); syndactyly, with or without skin graft(s), each web

ICD-9-CM Diagnostic

755.13 Syndactyly of toes without fusion of bone
755.14 Syndactyly of toes with fusion of bone

ICD-9-CM Procedural

77.69 Local excision of lesion or tissue of other bone, except facial bones
78.49 Other repair or plastic operations on other bone, except facial bones

28360

28360 Reconstruction, cleft foot

ICD-9-CM Diagnostic

755.66 Other congenital anomaly of toes
755.67 Congenital anomalies of foot, not elsewhere classified

ICD-9-CM Procedural

83.85 Other change in muscle or tendon length

28400-28405

28400 Closed treatment of calcaneal fracture; without manipulation
28405 with manipulation

ICD-9-CM Diagnostic

733.19 Pathologic fracture of other specified site
733.95 Stress fracture of other bone — (Use additional external cause code(s) to identify the cause of the stress fracture)
825.0 Closed fracture of calcaneus
928.20 Crushing injury of foot — (Use additional code to identify any associated injuries: 800-829, 850.0-854.1, 860.0-869.1)

ICD-9-CM Procedural

79.07 Closed reduction of fracture of tarsals and metatarsals without internal fixation
93.53 Application of other cast
93.54 Application of splint

HCPCS Level II Supplies & Services

A4570 Splint

28406

28406 Percutaneous skeletal fixation of calcaneal fracture, with manipulation

ICD-9-CM Diagnostic

733.19 Pathologic fracture of other specified site
733.95 Stress fracture of other bone — (Use additional external cause code(s) to identify the cause of the stress fracture)
825.0 Closed fracture of calcaneus
928.20 Crushing injury of foot — (Use additional code to identify any associated injuries: 800-829, 850.0-854.1, 860.0-869.1)

ICD-9-CM Procedural

79.17 Closed reduction of fracture of tarsals and metatarsals with internal fixation

28415

28415 Open treatment of calcaneal fracture, includes internal fixation, when performed;

ICD-9-CM Diagnostic

733.19 Pathologic fracture of other specified site
733.81 Malunion of fracture
733.82 Nonunion of fracture
733.95 Stress fracture of other bone — (Use additional external cause code(s) to identify the cause of the stress fracture)
825.0 Closed fracture of calcaneus
825.1 Open fracture of calcaneus
928.20 Crushing injury of foot — (Use additional code to identify any associated injuries: 800-829, 850.0-854.1, 860.0-869.1)

ICD-9-CM Procedural

79.27 Open reduction of fracture of tarsals and metatarsals without internal fixation
79.37 Open reduction of fracture of tarsals and metatarsals with internal fixation

HCPCS Level II Supplies & Services

A4305 Disposable drug delivery system, flow rate of 50 ml or greater per hour

28420

28420 Open treatment of calcaneal fracture, includes internal fixation, when performed; with primary iliac or other autogenous bone graft (includes obtaining graft)

ICD-9-CM Diagnostic

733.19 Pathologic fracture of other specified site
733.81 Malunion of fracture
733.82 Nonunion of fracture
733.95 Stress fracture of other bone — (Use additional external cause code(s) to identify the cause of the stress fracture)
825.0 Closed fracture of calcaneus
825.1 Open fracture of calcaneus
928.20 Crushing injury of foot — (Use additional code to identify any associated injuries: 800-829, 850.0-854.1, 860.0-869.1)

ICD-9-CM Procedural

77.77 Excision of tibia and fibula for graft
77.79 Excision of other bone for graft, except facial bones
78.08 Bone graft of tarsals and metatarsals
79.27 Open reduction of fracture of tarsals and metatarsals without internal fixation
79.37 Open reduction of fracture of tarsals and metatarsals with internal fixation

28430-28435

28430 Closed treatment of talus fracture; without manipulation
28435 with manipulation

ICD-9-CM Diagnostic

733.19 Pathologic fracture of other specified site
733.95 Stress fracture of other bone — (Use additional external cause code(s) to identify the cause of the stress fracture)
825.21 Closed fracture of astragalus
825.29 Other closed fracture of tarsal and metatarsal bones
928.20 Crushing injury of foot — (Use additional code to identify any associated injuries: 800-829, 850.0-854.1, 860.0-869.1)
928.21 Crushing injury of ankle — (Use additional code to identify any associated injuries: 800-829, 850.0-854.1, 860.0-869.1)

ICD-9-CM Procedural

79.07 Closed reduction of fracture of tarsals and metatarsals without internal fixation
93.53 Application of other cast
93.54 Application of splint

HCPCS Level II Supplies & Services

A4570 Splint

28436

28436 Percutaneous skeletal fixation of talus fracture, with manipulation

ICD-9-CM Diagnostic

733.19 Pathologic fracture of other specified site
733.95 Stress fracture of other bone — (Use additional external cause code(s) to identify the cause of the stress fracture)
825.21 Closed fracture of astragalus

825.29 Other closed fracture of tarsal and metatarsal bones
928.20 Crushing injury of foot — (Use additional code to identify any associated injuries: 800-829, 850.0-854.1, 860.0-869.1)
928.21 Crushing injury of ankle — (Use additional code to identify any associated injuries: 800-829, 850.0-854.1, 860.0-869.1)

ICD-9-CM Procedural

79.17 Closed reduction of fracture of tarsals and metatarsals with internal fixation

HCPCS Level II Supplies & Services

A4570 Splint

28445

28445 Open treatment of talus fracture, includes internal fixation, when performed

ICD-9-CM Diagnostic

733.19 Pathologic fracture of other specified site
733.81 Malunion of fracture
733.82 Nonunion of fracture
733.95 Stress fracture of other bone — (Use additional external cause code(s) to identify the cause of the stress fracture)
825.21 Closed fracture of astragalus
825.29 Other closed fracture of tarsal and metatarsal bones
825.31 Open fracture of astragalus
825.39 Other open fractures of tarsal and metatarsal bones
905.4 Late effect of fracture of lower extremities
928.20 Crushing injury of foot — (Use additional code to identify any associated injuries: 800-829, 850.0-854.1, 860.0-869.1)
928.21 Crushing injury of ankle — (Use additional code to identify any associated injuries: 800-829, 850.0-854.1, 860.0-869.1)

ICD-9-CM Procedural

79.27 Open reduction of fracture of tarsals and metatarsals without internal fixation
79.37 Open reduction of fracture of tarsals and metatarsals with internal fixation

HCPCS Level II Supplies & Services

A4570 Splint

28446

28446 Open osteochondral autograft, talus (includes obtaining graft[s])

ICD-9-CM Diagnostic

732.7 Osteochondritis dissecans
823.80 Closed fracture of unspecified part of tibia ▽
824.0 Closed fracture of medial malleolus
825.21 Closed fracture of astragalus
825.31 Open fracture of astragalus

ICD-9-CM Procedural

77.79 Excision of other bone for graft, except facial bones
78.57 Internal fixation of tibia and fibula without fracture reduction
78.58 Internal fixation of tarsals and metatarsals without fracture reduction
79.26 Open reduction of fracture of tibia and fibula without internal fixation
79.27 Open reduction of fracture of tarsals and metatarsals without internal fixation
79.36 Open reduction of fracture of tibia and fibula with internal fixation
79.37 Open reduction of fracture of tarsals and metatarsals with internal fixation
80.87 Other local excision or destruction of lesion of ankle joint
80.90 Other excision of joint, unspecified site

28450-28455

28450 Treatment of tarsal bone fracture (except talus and calcaneus); without manipulation, each
28455 with manipulation, each

ICD-9-CM Diagnostic

733.19 Pathologic fracture of other specified site
733.95 Stress fracture of other bone — (Use additional external cause code(s) to identify the cause of the stress fracture)
825.22 Closed fracture of navicular (scaphoid) bone of foot
825.23 Closed fracture of cuboid bone
825.24 Closed fracture of cuneiform bone of foot
825.29 Other closed fracture of tarsal and metatarsal bones

ICD-9-CM Procedural

79.07 Closed reduction of fracture of tarsals and metatarsals without internal fixation
79.97 Unspecified operation on bone injury of tarsals and metatarsals
93.53 Application of other cast
93.54 Application of splint

HCPCS Level II Supplies & Services

A4570 Splint

28456

28456 Percutaneous skeletal fixation of tarsal bone fracture (except talus and calcaneus), with manipulation, each

ICD-9-CM Diagnostic

733.19 Pathologic fracture of other specified site
733.95 Stress fracture of other bone — (Use additional external cause code(s) to identify the cause of the stress fracture)
825.22 Closed fracture of navicular (scaphoid) bone of foot
825.23 Closed fracture of cuboid bone
825.24 Closed fracture of cuneiform bone of foot
825.29 Other closed fracture of tarsal and metatarsal bones

ICD-9-CM Procedural

79.17 Closed reduction of fracture of tarsals and metatarsals with internal fixation

HCPCS Level II Supplies & Services

A4570 Splint

28465

28465 Open treatment of tarsal bone fracture (except talus and calcaneus), includes internal fixation, when performed, each

ICD-9-CM Diagnostic

733.19 Pathologic fracture of other specified site
733.81 Malunion of fracture
733.82 Nonunion of fracture
733.95 Stress fracture of other bone — (Use additional external cause code(s) to identify the cause of the stress fracture)
825.22 Closed fracture of navicular (scaphoid) bone of foot
825.23 Closed fracture of cuboid bone
825.24 Closed fracture of cuneiform bone of foot
825.29 Other closed fracture of tarsal and metatarsal bones
825.32 Open fracture of navicular (scaphoid) bone of foot
825.33 Open fracture of cuboid bone
825.34 Open fracture of cuneiform bone of foot,
825.39 Other open fractures of tarsal and metatarsal bones
905.4 Late effect of fracture of lower extremities

ICD-9-CM Procedural

79.27 Open reduction of fracture of tarsals and metatarsals without internal fixation

79.37 Open reduction of fracture of tarsals and metatarsals with internal fixation

28470-28475

28470 Closed treatment of metatarsal fracture; without manipulation, each
28475 with manipulation, each

ICD-9-CM Diagnostic

733.19 Pathologic fracture of other specified site
733.94 Stress fracture of the metatarsals — (Use additional external cause code(s) to identify the cause of the stress fracture)
825.25 Closed fracture of metatarsal bone(s)
825.29 Other closed fracture of tarsal and metatarsal bones
928.20 Crushing injury of foot — (Use additional code to identify any associated injuries: 800-829, 850.0-854.1, 860.0-869.1)

ICD-9-CM Procedural

79.07 Closed reduction of fracture of tarsals and metatarsals without internal fixation
93.53 Application of other cast
93.54 Application of splint

HCPCS Level II Supplies & Services

A4570 Splint

28476

28476 Percutaneous skeletal fixation of metatarsal fracture, with manipulation, each

ICD-9-CM Diagnostic

733.19 Pathologic fracture of other specified site
733.94 Stress fracture of the metatarsals — (Use additional external cause code(s) to identify the cause of the stress fracture)
825.25 Closed fracture of metatarsal bone(s)
825.29 Other closed fracture of tarsal and metatarsal bones
928.20 Crushing injury of foot — (Use additional code to identify any associated injuries: 800-829, 850.0-854.1, 860.0-869.1)

ICD-9-CM Procedural

79.17 Closed reduction of fracture of tarsals and metatarsals with internal fixation

HCPCS Level II Supplies & Services

A4570 Splint

28485

28485 Open treatment of metatarsal fracture, includes internal fixation, when performed, each

ICD-9-CM Diagnostic

733.19 Pathologic fracture of other specified site
733.81 Malunion of fracture
733.82 Nonunion of fracture
733.94 Stress fracture of the metatarsals — (Use additional external cause code(s) to identify the cause of the stress fracture)
825.25 Closed fracture of metatarsal bone(s)
825.29 Other closed fracture of tarsal and metatarsal bones
825.35 Open fracture of metatarsal bone(s)
825.39 Other open fractures of tarsal and metatarsal bones

ICD-9-CM Procedural

79.27 Open reduction of fracture of tarsals and metatarsals without internal fixation
79.37 Open reduction of fracture of tarsals and metatarsals with internal fixation

HCPCS Level II Supplies & Services

A4570 Splint

28490-28495

28490 Closed treatment of fracture great toe, phalanx or phalanges; without manipulation
28495 with manipulation

ICD-9-CM Diagnostic

733.19 Pathologic fracture of other specified site
733.95 Stress fracture of other bone — (Use additional external cause code(s) to identify the cause of the stress fracture)
826.0 Closed fracture of one or more phalanges of foot

ICD-9-CM Procedural

79.08 Closed reduction of fracture of phalanges of foot without internal fixation
93.53 Application of other cast
93.54 Application of splint

HCPCS Level II Supplies & Services

A4570 Splint

28496

28496 Percutaneous skeletal fixation of fracture great toe, phalanx or phalanges, with manipulation

ICD-9-CM Diagnostic

733.19 Pathologic fracture of other specified site
733.95 Stress fracture of other bone — (Use additional external cause code(s) to identify the cause of the stress fracture)
826.0 Closed fracture of one or more phalanges of foot

ICD-9-CM Procedural

79.18 Closed reduction of fracture of phalanges of foot with internal fixation

HCPCS Level II Supplies & Services

A4570 Splint

28505

28505 Open treatment of fracture, great toe, phalanx or phalanges, includes internal fixation, when performed

ICD-9-CM Diagnostic

733.19 Pathologic fracture of other specified site
733.81 Malunion of fracture
733.82 Nonunion of fracture
733.95 Stress fracture of other bone — (Use additional external cause code(s) to identify the cause of the stress fracture)
826.0 Closed fracture of one or more phalanges of foot
826.1 Open fracture of one or more phalanges of foot
905.4 Late effect of fracture of lower extremities

ICD-9-CM Procedural

79.28 Open reduction of fracture of phalanges of foot without internal fixation
79.38 Open reduction of fracture of phalanges of foot with internal fixation

HCPCS Level II Supplies & Services

A4570 Splint

28510-28515

28510 Closed treatment of fracture, phalanx or phalanges, other than great toe; without manipulation, each
28515 with manipulation, each

ICD-9-CM Diagnostic

733.19 Pathologic fracture of other specified site
733.95 Stress fracture of other bone — (Use additional external cause code(s) to identify the cause of the stress fracture)
826.0 Closed fracture of one or more phalanges of foot

ICD-9-CM Procedural

79.08 Closed reduction of fracture of phalanges of foot without internal fixation
93.53 Application of other cast
93.54 Application of splint

HCPCS Level II Supplies & Services

A4570 Splint

28525

28525 Open treatment of fracture, phalanx or phalanges, other than great toe, includes internal fixation, when performed, each

ICD-9-CM Diagnostic

733.19 Pathologic fracture of other specified site
733.81 Malunion of fracture
733.95 Stress fracture of other bone — (Use additional external cause code(s) to identify the cause of the stress fracture)
826.0 Closed fracture of one or more phalanges of foot
826.1 Open fracture of one or more phalanges of foot
905.4 Late effect of fracture of lower extremities

ICD-9-CM Procedural

79.28 Open reduction of fracture of phalanges of foot without internal fixation
79.38 Open reduction of fracture of phalanges of foot with internal fixation

HCPCS Level II Supplies & Services

A4305 Disposable drug delivery system, flow rate of 50 ml or greater per hour

28530

28530 Closed treatment of sesamoid fracture

ICD-9-CM Diagnostic

733.19 Pathologic fracture of other specified site
733.95 Stress fracture of other bone — (Use additional external cause code(s) to identify the cause of the stress fracture)
825.29 Other closed fracture of tarsal and metatarsal bones

ICD-9-CM Procedural

79.09 Closed reduction of fracture of other specified bone, except facial bones, without internal fixation
79.19 Closed reduction of fracture of other specified bone, except facial bones, with internal fixation

HCPCS Level II Supplies & Services

A4570 Splint

28531

28531 Open treatment of sesamoid fracture, with or without internal fixation

ICD-9-CM Diagnostic

733.19 Pathologic fracture of other specified site
733.81 Malunion of fracture
733.82 Nonunion of fracture
733.95 Stress fracture of other bone — (Use additional external cause code(s) to identify the cause of the stress fracture)
825.29 Other closed fracture of tarsal and metatarsal bones
825.39 Other open fractures of tarsal and metatarsal bones
893.1 Open wound of toe(s), complicated

ICD-9-CM Procedural

79.29 Open reduction of fracture of other specified bone, except facial bones, without internal fixation
79.39 Open reduction of fracture of other specified bone, except facial bones, with internal fixation

HCPCS Level II Supplies & Services

A4305 Disposable drug delivery system, flow rate of 50 ml or greater per hour

28540-28545

28540 Closed treatment of tarsal bone dislocation, other than talotarsal; without anesthesia
28545 requiring anesthesia

ICD-9-CM Diagnostic

718.77 Developmental dislocation of joint, ankle and foot
837.0 Closed dislocation of ankle
838.01 Closed dislocation of tarsal (bone), joint unspecified ▽
838.02 Closed dislocation of midtarsal (joint)

ICD-9-CM Procedural

79.78 Closed reduction of dislocation of foot and toe

HCPCS Level II Supplies & Services

A4570 Splint

28546

28546 Percutaneous skeletal fixation of tarsal bone dislocation, other than talotarsal, with manipulation

ICD-9-CM Diagnostic

718.77 Developmental dislocation of joint, ankle and foot
838.02 Closed dislocation of midtarsal (joint)
838.03 Closed dislocation of tarsometatarsal (joint)

ICD-9-CM Procedural

78.58 Internal fixation of tarsals and metatarsals without fracture reduction
79.78 Closed reduction of dislocation of foot and toe

HCPCS Level II Supplies & Services

A4570 Splint

28555

28555 Open treatment of tarsal bone dislocation, includes internal fixation, when performed

ICD-9-CM Diagnostic

718.77 Developmental dislocation of joint, ankle and foot
837.0 Closed dislocation of ankle
837.1 Open dislocation of ankle
838.01 Closed dislocation of tarsal (bone), joint unspecified ▽
838.02 Closed dislocation of midtarsal (joint)
838.03 Closed dislocation of tarsometatarsal (joint)
838.11 Open dislocation of tarsal (bone), joint unspecified ▽
838.12 Open dislocation of midtarsal (joint)
838.13 Open dislocation of tarsometatarsal (joint)

ICD-9-CM Procedural

79.88 Open reduction of dislocation of foot and toe

HCPCS Level II Supplies & Services

A4580 Cast supplies (e.g., plaster)

28570-28575

28570 Closed treatment of talotarsal joint dislocation; without anesthesia
28575 requiring anesthesia

ICD-9-CM Diagnostic

718.77 Developmental dislocation of joint, ankle and foot
837.0 Closed dislocation of ankle
838.02 Closed dislocation of midtarsal (joint)

ICD-9-CM Procedural

79.78 Closed reduction of dislocation of foot and toe

HCPCS Level II Supplies & Services

A4580 Cast supplies (e.g., plaster)

28576

28576 Percutaneous skeletal fixation of talotarsal joint dislocation, with manipulation

ICD-9-CM Diagnostic

718.77 Developmental dislocation of joint, ankle and foot
837.0 Closed dislocation of ankle
838.02 Closed dislocation of midtarsal (joint)

ICD-9-CM Procedural

78.58 Internal fixation of tarsals and metatarsals without fracture reduction
79.77 Closed reduction of dislocation of ankle

HCPCS Level II Supplies & Services

A4580 Cast supplies (e.g., plaster)

28585

28585 Open treatment of talotarsal joint dislocation, includes internal fixation, when performed

ICD-9-CM Diagnostic

718.77 Developmental dislocation of joint, ankle and foot
838.02 Closed dislocation of midtarsal (joint)
838.12 Open dislocation of midtarsal (joint)

ICD-9-CM Procedural

78.58 Internal fixation of tarsals and metatarsals without fracture reduction
79.88 Open reduction of dislocation of foot and toe

HCPCS Level II Supplies & Services

A4580 Cast supplies (e.g., plaster)

28600-28605

28600 Closed treatment of tarsometatarsal joint dislocation; without anesthesia
28605 requiring anesthesia

ICD-9-CM Diagnostic

718.77 Developmental dislocation of joint, ankle and foot
838.02 Closed dislocation of midtarsal (joint)
838.03 Closed dislocation of tarsometatarsal (joint)

ICD-9-CM Procedural

79.78 Closed reduction of dislocation of foot and toe

HCPCS Level II Supplies & Services

A4580 Cast supplies (e.g., plaster)

28606

28606 Percutaneous skeletal fixation of tarsometatarsal joint dislocation, with manipulation

ICD-9-CM Diagnostic

718.77 Developmental dislocation of joint, ankle and foot
838.02 Closed dislocation of midtarsal (joint)
838.03 Closed dislocation of tarsometatarsal (joint)

ICD-9-CM Procedural

78.58 Internal fixation of tarsals and metatarsals without fracture reduction
79.78 Closed reduction of dislocation of foot and toe

HCPCS Level II Supplies & Services

A4580 Cast supplies (e.g., plaster)

28615

28615 Open treatment of tarsometatarsal joint dislocation, includes internal fixation, when performed

ICD-9-CM Diagnostic

718.77 Developmental dislocation of joint, ankle and foot
838.02 Closed dislocation of midtarsal (joint)
838.03 Closed dislocation of tarsometatarsal (joint)
838.11 Open dislocation of tarsal (bone), joint unspecified ▽
838.12 Open dislocation of midtarsal (joint)

ICD-9-CM Procedural

79.88 Open reduction of dislocation of foot and toe

HCPCS Level II Supplies & Services

A4580 Cast supplies (e.g., plaster)

28630-28635

28630 Closed treatment of metatarsophalangeal joint dislocation; without anesthesia
28635 requiring anesthesia

ICD-9-CM Diagnostic

718.77 Developmental dislocation of joint, ankle and foot
838.05 Closed dislocation of metatarsophalangeal (joint)

ICD-9-CM Procedural

79.78 Closed reduction of dislocation of foot and toe

HCPCS Level II Supplies & Services

A4580 Cast supplies (e.g., plaster)

28636

28636 Percutaneous skeletal fixation of metatarsophalangeal joint dislocation, with manipulation

ICD-9-CM Diagnostic

718.77 Developmental dislocation of joint, ankle and foot
838.05 Closed dislocation of metatarsophalangeal (joint)

ICD-9-CM Procedural

78.58 Internal fixation of tarsals and metatarsals without fracture reduction
79.78 Closed reduction of dislocation of foot and toe

HCPCS Level II Supplies & Services

A4580 Cast supplies (e.g., plaster)

28645

28645 Open treatment of metatarsophalangeal joint dislocation, includes internal fixation, when performed

ICD-9-CM Diagnostic

718.77 Developmental dislocation of joint, ankle and foot
838.05 Closed dislocation of metatarsophalangeal (joint)
838.15 Open dislocation of metatarsophalangeal (joint)

ICD-9-CM Procedural

79.88 Open reduction of dislocation of foot and toe

HCPCS Level II Supplies & Services

A4580 Cast supplies (e.g., plaster)

28660-28665

28660 Closed treatment of interphalangeal joint dislocation; without anesthesia
28665 requiring anesthesia

ICD-9-CM Diagnostic

718.77 Developmental dislocation of joint, ankle and foot
838.06 Closed dislocation of interphalangeal (joint), foot

ICD-9-CM Procedural

79.78 Closed reduction of dislocation of foot and toe

HCPCS Level II Supplies & Services

A4570 Splint

28666

28666 Percutaneous skeletal fixation of interphalangeal joint dislocation, with manipulation

ICD-9-CM Diagnostic

718.77 Developmental dislocation of joint, ankle and foot
838.06 Closed dislocation of interphalangeal (joint), foot

ICD-9-CM Procedural

78.59 Internal fixation of other bone, except facial bones, without fracture reduction
79.78 Closed reduction of dislocation of foot and toe

HCPCS Level II Supplies & Services

A4570 Splint

28675

28675 Open treatment of interphalangeal joint dislocation, includes internal fixation, when performed

ICD-9-CM Diagnostic

718.77 Developmental dislocation of joint, ankle and foot
838.06 Closed dislocation of interphalangeal (joint), foot
838.16 Open dislocation of interphalangeal (joint), foot

ICD-9-CM Procedural

79.88 Open reduction of dislocation of foot and toe

HCPCS Level II Supplies & Services

A4570 Splint

28705

28705 Arthrodesis; pantalar

ICD-9-CM Diagnostic

357.1 Polyneuropathy in collagen vascular disease — (Code first underlying disease: 446.0, 710.0, 714.0) ☒
359.6 Symptomatic inflammatory myopathy in diseases classified elsewhere — (Code first underlying disease: 135, 140.0-208.9, 277.30-277.39, 446.0, 710.0, 710.1, 710.2, 714.0) ☒
446.0 Polyarteritis nodosa
710.0 Systemic lupus erythematosus — (Use additional code to identify manifestation: 424.91, 581.81, 582.81, 583.81)
710.1 Systemic sclerosis — (Use additional code to identify manifestation: 359.6, 517.2)
710.2 Sicca syndrome
714.0 Rheumatoid arthritis — (Use additional code to identify manifestation: 357.1, 359.6)
715.17 Primary localized osteoarthrosis, ankle and foot
715.27 Secondary localized osteoarthrosis, ankle and foot
715.37 Localized osteoarthrosis not specified whether primary or secondary, ankle and foot
715.89 Osteoarthrosis involving multiple sites, but not specified as generalized
715.97 Osteoarthrosis, unspecified whether generalized or localized, ankle and foot ▽
716.17 Traumatic arthropathy, ankle and foot
718.87 Other joint derangement, not elsewhere classified, ankle and foot
731.3 Major osseous defects — (Code first underlying disease: 170.0-170.9, 730.00-730.29, 733.00-733.09, 733.40-733.49, 996.45)
733.44 Aseptic necrosis of talus — (Use additional code to identify major osseous defect, if applicable: 731.3)
733.81 Malunion of fracture
733.82 Nonunion of fracture

ICD-9-CM Procedural

81.11 Ankle fusion

28715

28715 Arthrodesis; triple

ICD-9-CM Diagnostic

138 Late effects of acute poliomyelitis — (Note: This category is to be used to indicate conditions classifiable to 045 as the cause of late effects, which are themselves classified elsewhere. The "late effects" include those specified as such, as sequelae, or as due to old or inactive poliomyelitis, without evidence of active disease.)
356.1 Peroneal muscular atrophy
357.1 Polyneuropathy in collagen vascular disease — (Code first underlying disease: 446.0, 710.0, 714.0) ☒
359.6 Symptomatic inflammatory myopathy in diseases classified elsewhere — (Code first underlying disease: 135, 140.0-208.9, 277.30-277.39, 446.0, 710.0, 710.1, 710.2, 714.0) ☒
446.0 Polyarteritis nodosa
710.0 Systemic lupus erythematosus — (Use additional code to identify manifestation: 424.91, 581.81, 582.81, 583.81)
710.1 Systemic sclerosis — (Use additional code to identify manifestation: 359.6, 517.2)
710.2 Sicca syndrome
714.0 Rheumatoid arthritis — (Use additional code to identify manifestation: 357.1, 359.6)
714.1 Felty's syndrome
715.17 Primary localized osteoarthrosis, ankle and foot
715.27 Secondary localized osteoarthrosis, ankle and foot
715.37 Localized osteoarthrosis not specified whether primary or secondary, ankle and foot
715.97 Osteoarthrosis, unspecified whether generalized or localized, ankle and foot ▽
716.17 Traumatic arthropathy, ankle and foot
718.87 Other joint derangement, not elsewhere classified, ankle and foot
719.47 Pain in joint, ankle and foot
733.81 Malunion of fracture
736.71 Acquired equinovarus deformity
736.72 Equinus deformity of foot, acquired
736.73 Cavus deformity of foot, acquired
736.74 Claw foot, acquired
736.75 Cavovarus deformity of foot, acquired
736.76 Other acquired calcaneus deformity
736.79 Other acquired deformity of ankle and foot
754.61 Congenital pes planus
754.62 Talipes calcaneovalgus
754.69 Other congenital valgus deformity of feet
755.67 Congenital anomalies of foot, not elsewhere classified
825.22 Closed fracture of navicular (scaphoid) bone of foot
928.20 Crushing injury of foot — (Use additional code to identify any associated injuries: 800-829, 850.0-854.1, 860.0-869.1)
928.21 Crushing injury of ankle — (Use additional code to identify any associated injuries: 800-829, 850.0-854.1, 860.0-869.1)

ICD-9-CM Procedural

81.12 Triple arthrodesis

28725

28725 Arthrodesis; subtalar

ICD-9-CM Diagnostic

357.1 Polyneuropathy in collagen vascular disease — (Code first underlying disease: 446.0, 710.0, 714.0) ☒
359.6 Symptomatic inflammatory myopathy in diseases classified elsewhere — (Code first underlying disease: 135, 140.0-208.9, 277.30-277.39, 446.0, 710.0, 710.1, 710.2, 714.0) ☒
446.0 Polyarteritis nodosa
710.0 Systemic lupus erythematosus — (Use additional code to identify manifestation: 424.91, 581.81, 582.81, 583.81)
710.1 Systemic sclerosis — (Use additional code to identify manifestation: 359.6, 517.2)
710.2 Sicca syndrome
714.0 Rheumatoid arthritis — (Use additional code to identify manifestation: 357.1, 359.6)
716.17 Traumatic arthropathy, ankle and foot
731.3 Major osseous defects — (Code first underlying disease: 170.0-170.9, 730.00-730.29, 733.00-733.09, 733.40-733.49, 996.45)
733.44 Aseptic necrosis of talus — (Use additional code to identify major osseous defect, if applicable: 731.3)
733.81 Malunion of fracture
736.76 Other acquired calcaneus deformity
736.79 Other acquired deformity of ankle and foot
754.61 Congenital pes planus
754.62 Talipes calcaneovalgus
754.69 Other congenital valgus deformity of feet
755.67 Congenital anomalies of foot, not elsewhere classified
825.0 Closed fracture of calcaneus
825.1 Open fracture of calcaneus
825.20 Closed fracture of unspecified bone(s) of foot (except toes) ▽
928.20 Crushing injury of foot — (Use additional code to identify any associated injuries: 800-829, 850.0-854.1, 860.0-869.1)
928.21 Crushing injury of ankle — (Use additional code to identify any associated injuries: 800-829, 850.0-854.1, 860.0-869.1)

ICD-9-CM Procedural

81.13 Subtalar fusion

28730-28735

28730 Arthrodesis, midtarsal or tarsometatarsal, multiple or transverse;
28735 with osteotomy (eg, flatfoot correction)

ICD-9-CM Diagnostic

357.1 Polyneuropathy in collagen vascular disease — (Code first underlying disease: 446.0, 710.0, 714.0) ☒
359.6 Symptomatic inflammatory myopathy in diseases classified elsewhere — (Code first underlying disease: 135, 140.0-208.9, 277.30-277.39, 446.0, 710.0, 710.1, 710.2, 714.0) ☒
446.0 Polyarteritis nodosa
710.0 Systemic lupus erythematosus — (Use additional code to identify manifestation: 424.91, 581.81, 582.81, 583.81)
710.1 Systemic sclerosis — (Use additional code to identify manifestation: 359.6, 517.2)
710.2 Sicca syndrome
714.0 Rheumatoid arthritis — (Use additional code to identify manifestation: 357.1, 359.6)
715.17 Primary localized osteoarthrosis, ankle and foot
715.37 Localized osteoarthrosis not specified whether primary or secondary, ankle and foot
715.97 Osteoarthrosis, unspecified whether generalized or localized, ankle and foot ▽
716.17 Traumatic arthropathy, ankle and foot
718.87 Other joint derangement, not elsewhere classified, ankle and foot
731.3 Major osseous defects — (Code first underlying disease: 170.0-170.9, 730.00-730.29, 733.00-733.09, 733.40-733.49, 996.45)
733.49 Aseptic necrosis of other bone site — (Use additional code to identify major osseous defect, if applicable: 731.3)
733.81 Malunion of fracture
733.82 Nonunion of fracture
734 Flat foot
736.71 Acquired equinovarus deformity
736.72 Equinus deformity of foot, acquired
736.73 Cavus deformity of foot, acquired
754.70 Unspecified talipes ▽
825.20 Closed fracture of unspecified bone(s) of foot (except toes) ▽
825.22 Closed fracture of navicular (scaphoid) bone of foot
825.29 Other closed fracture of tarsal and metatarsal bones

ICD-9-CM Procedural

77.38 Other division of tarsals and metatarsals
81.15 Tarsometatarsal fusion
81.18 Subtalar joint arthroereisis

28737

28737 Arthrodesis, with tendon lengthening and advancement, midtarsal, tarsal navicular-cuneiform (eg, Miller type procedure)

ICD-9-CM Diagnostic

715.17 Primary localized osteoarthrosis, ankle and foot
715.97 Osteoarthrosis, unspecified whether generalized or localized, ankle and foot ▽
716.17 Traumatic arthropathy, ankle and foot
754.50 Congenital talipes varus
754.51 Congenital talipes equinovarus
754.52 Congenital metatarsus primus varus
754.53 Congenital metatarsus varus
754.59 Other congenital varus deformity of feet
754.60 Congenital talipes valgus
754.61 Congenital pes planus
754.62 Talipes calcaneovalgus
754.69 Other congenital valgus deformity of feet
754.70 Unspecified talipes ▽
754.71 Talipes cavus

ICD-9-CM Procedural

81.14 Midtarsal fusion
83.71 Advancement of tendon
83.75 Tendon transfer or transplantation

28740

28740 Arthrodesis, midtarsal or tarsometatarsal, single joint

ICD-9-CM Diagnostic

355.5 Tarsal tunnel syndrome
357.1 Polyneuropathy in collagen vascular disease — (Code first underlying disease: 446.0, 710.0, 714.0) ☒
359.6 Symptomatic inflammatory myopathy in diseases classified elsewhere — (Code first underlying disease: 135, 140.0-208.9, 277.30-277.39, 446.0, 710.0, 710.1, 710.2, 714.0) ☒
446.0 Polyarteritis nodosa
710.0 Systemic lupus erythematosus — (Use additional code to identify manifestation: 424.91, 581.81, 582.81, 583.81)
710.1 Systemic sclerosis — (Use additional code to identify manifestation: 359.6, 517.2)
710.2 Sicca syndrome
714.0 Rheumatoid arthritis — (Use additional code to identify manifestation: 357.1, 359.6)
715.17 Primary localized osteoarthrosis, ankle and foot
715.37 Localized osteoarthrosis not specified whether primary or secondary, ankle and foot

715.97 Osteoarthrosis, unspecified whether generalized or localized, ankle and foot ▽
716.17 Traumatic arthropathy, ankle and foot
718.47 Contracture of ankle and foot joint
718.77 Developmental dislocation of joint, ankle and foot
719.67 Other symptoms referable to ankle and foot joint
719.87 Other specified disorders of ankle and foot joint
733.81 Malunion of fracture
733.82 Nonunion of fracture
736.74 Claw foot, acquired
754.50 Congenital talipes varus
754.51 Congenital talipes equinovarus
754.59 Other congenital varus deformity of feet
754.60 Congenital talipes valgus
754.70 Unspecified talipes ▽
754.89 Other specified nonteratogenic anomalies
825.25 Closed fracture of metatarsal bone(s)
838.02 Closed dislocation of midtarsal (joint)
905.4 Late effect of fracture of lower extremities

ICD-9-CM Procedural

81.14 Midtarsal fusion

28750

28750 Arthrodesis, great toe; metatarsophalangeal joint

ICD-9-CM Diagnostic

356.1 Peroneal muscular atrophy
357.1 Polyneuropathy in collagen vascular disease — (Code first underlying disease: 446.0, 710.0, 714.0) ☒
359.6 Symptomatic inflammatory myopathy in diseases classified elsewhere — (Code first underlying disease: 135, 140.0-208.9, 277.30-277.39, 446.0, 710.0, 710.1, 710.2, 714.0) ☒
446.0 Polyarteritis nodosa
710.0 Systemic lupus erythematosus — (Use additional code to identify manifestation: 424.91, 581.81, 582.81, 583.81)
710.1 Systemic sclerosis — (Use additional code to identify manifestation: 359.6, 517.2)
710.2 Sicca syndrome
714.0 Rheumatoid arthritis — (Use additional code to identify manifestation: 357.1, 359.6)
714.30 Polyarticular juvenile rheumatoid arthritis, chronic or unspecified
714.32 Pauciarticular juvenile rheumatoid arthritis
715.17 Primary localized osteoarthrosis, ankle and foot
715.27 Secondary localized osteoarthrosis, ankle and foot
715.37 Localized osteoarthrosis not specified whether primary or secondary, ankle and foot
715.97 Osteoarthrosis, unspecified whether generalized or localized, ankle and foot ▽
716.17 Traumatic arthropathy, ankle and foot
718.47 Contracture of ankle and foot joint
727.1 Bunion
733.81 Malunion of fracture
733.82 Nonunion of fracture
735.0 Hallux valgus (acquired)
735.1 Hallux varus (acquired)
735.2 Hallux rigidus
735.3 Hallux malleus
735.4 Other hammer toe (acquired)
735.5 Claw toe (acquired)
735.8 Other acquired deformity of toe
735.9 Unspecified acquired deformity of toe ▽
736.70 Unspecified deformity of ankle and foot, acquired ▽
736.71 Acquired equinovarus deformity
736.72 Equinus deformity of foot, acquired
736.73 Cavus deformity of foot, acquired
755.39 Congenital longitudinal deficiency, phalanges, complete or partial
755.67 Congenital anomalies of foot, not elsewhere classified
838.05 Closed dislocation of metatarsophalangeal (joint)
928.3 Crushing injury of toe(s) — (Use additional code to identify any associated injuries: 800-829, 850.0-854.1, 860.0-869.1)

ICD-9-CM Procedural

81.16 Metatarsophalangeal fusion

HCPCS Level II Supplies & Services

A4305 Disposable drug delivery system, flow rate of 50 ml or greater per hour

28755

28755 Arthrodesis, great toe; interphalangeal joint

ICD-9-CM Diagnostic

357.1 Polyneuropathy in collagen vascular disease — (Code first underlying disease: 446.0, 710.0, 714.0) ☒
359.6 Symptomatic inflammatory myopathy in diseases classified elsewhere — (Code first underlying disease: 135, 140.0-208.9, 277.30-277.39, 446.0, 710.0, 710.1, 710.2, 714.0) ☒
446.0 Polyarteritis nodosa
710.0 Systemic lupus erythematosus — (Use additional code to identify manifestation: 424.91, 581.81, 582.81, 583.81)
710.1 Systemic sclerosis — (Use additional code to identify manifestation: 359.6, 517.2)
710.2 Sicca syndrome
714.0 Rheumatoid arthritis — (Use additional code to identify manifestation: 357.1, 359.6)
715.97 Osteoarthrosis, unspecified whether generalized or localized, ankle and foot ▽
716.17 Traumatic arthropathy, ankle and foot
718.87 Other joint derangement, not elsewhere classified, ankle and foot
719.57 Stiffness of joint, not elsewhere classified, ankle and foot
735.1 Hallux varus (acquired)
735.2 Hallux rigidus
735.8 Other acquired deformity of toe
755.66 Other congenital anomaly of toes
928.3 Crushing injury of toe(s) — (Use additional code to identify any associated injuries: 800-829, 850.0-854.1, 860.0-869.1)

ICD-9-CM Procedural

77.58 Other excision, fusion, and repair of toes

HCPCS Level II Supplies & Services

A4305 Disposable drug delivery system, flow rate of 50 ml or greater per hour

28760

28760 Arthrodesis, with extensor hallucis longus transfer to first metatarsal neck, great toe, interphalangeal joint (eg, Jones type procedure)

ICD-9-CM Diagnostic

138 Late effects of acute poliomyelitis — (Note: This category is to be used to indicate conditions classifiable to 045 as the cause of late effects, which are themselves classified elsewhere. The "late effects" include those specified as such, as sequelae, or as due to old or inactive poliomyelitis, without evidence of active disease.)
715.27 Secondary localized osteoarthrosis, ankle and foot
715.37 Localized osteoarthrosis not specified whether primary or secondary, ankle and foot
715.97 Osteoarthrosis, unspecified whether generalized or localized, ankle and foot ▽
716.17 Traumatic arthropathy, ankle and foot
719.57 Stiffness of joint, not elsewhere classified, ankle and foot
735.1 Hallux varus (acquired)
735.3 Hallux malleus
735.4 Other hammer toe (acquired)
735.5 Claw toe (acquired)

755.66 Other congenital anomaly of toes
826.0 Closed fracture of one or more phalanges of foot
826.1 Open fracture of one or more phalanges of foot
928.3 Crushing injury of toe(s) — (Use additional code to identify any associated injuries: 800-829, 850.0-854.1, 860.0-869.1)

ICD-9-CM Procedural

77.57 Repair of claw toe

HCPCS Level II Supplies & Services

A4305 Disposable drug delivery system, flow rate of 50 ml or greater per hour

28800

28800 Amputation, foot; midtarsal (eg, Chopart type procedure)

ICD-9-CM Diagnostic

249.70 Secondary diabetes mellitus with peripheral circulatory disorders, not stated as uncontrolled, or unspecified — (Use additional code to identify manifestation: 443.81, 785.4) (Use additional code to identify any associated insulin use: V58.67)
249.71 Secondary diabetes mellitus with peripheral circulatory disorders, uncontrolled — (Use additional code to identify manifestation: 443.81, 785.4) (Use additional code to identify any associated insulin use: V58.67)
250.70 Diabetes with peripheral circulatory disorders, type II or unspecified type, not stated as uncontrolled — (Use additional code to identify manifestation: 443.81, 785.4)
250.71 Diabetes with peripheral circulatory disorders, type I [juvenile type], not stated as uncontrolled — (Use additional code to identify manifestation: 443.81, 785.4)
250.72 Diabetes with peripheral circulatory disorders, type II or unspecified type, uncontrolled — (Use additional code to identify manifestation: 443.81, 785.4)
250.73 Diabetes with peripheral circulatory disorders, type I [juvenile type], uncontrolled — (Use additional code to identify manifestation: 443.81, 785.4)
440.23 Atherosclerosis of native arteries of the extremities with ulceration — (Use additional code for any associated ulceration: 707.10-707.19, 707.8, 707.9)
443.81 Peripheral angiopathy in diseases classified elsewhere — (Code first underlying disease: 249.7, 250.7) ☒
444.22 Embolism and thrombosis of arteries of lower extremity
445.02 Atheroembolism of lower extremity
447.1 Stricture of artery
707.10 Ulcer of lower limb, unspecified — (Code, if applicable, any causal condition first: 249.80-249.81, 250.80-250.83, 440.23, 459.11, 459.13, 459.31, 459.33) ▽
707.14 Ulcer of heel and midfoot — (Code, if applicable, any causal condition first: 249.80-249.81, 250.80-250.83, 440.23, 459.11, 459.13, 459.31, 459.33)
707.15 Ulcer of other part of foot — (Code, if applicable, any causal condition first: 249.80-249.81, 250.80-250.83, 440.23, 459.11, 459.13, 459.31, 459.33)
730.17 Chronic osteomyelitis, ankle and foot — (Use additional code to identify organism: 041.1. Use additional code to identify major osseous defect, if applicable: 731.3)
730.37 Periostitis, without mention of osteomyelitis, ankle and foot — (Use additional code to identify organism: 041.1)
731.3 Major osseous defects — (Code first underlying disease: 170.0-170.9, 730.00-730.29, 733.00-733.09, 733.40-733.49, 996.45)
733.49 Aseptic necrosis of other bone site — (Use additional code to identify major osseous defect, if applicable: 731.3)
785.4 Gangrene — (Code first any associated underlying condition)
892.1 Open wound of foot except toe(s) alone, complicated
895.0 Traumatic amputation of toe(s) (complete) (partial), without mention of complication
896.0 Traumatic amputation of foot (complete) (partial), unilateral, without mention of complication
928.20 Crushing injury of foot — (Use additional code to identify any associated injuries: 800-829, 850.0-854.1, 860.0-869.1)

ICD-9-CM Procedural

84.12 Amputation through foot

28805

28805 Amputation, foot; transmetatarsal

ICD-9-CM Diagnostic

249.70 Secondary diabetes mellitus with peripheral circulatory disorders, not stated as uncontrolled, or unspecified — (Use additional code to identify manifestation: 443.81, 785.4) (Use additional code to identify any associated insulin use: V58.67)
249.71 Secondary diabetes mellitus with peripheral circulatory disorders, uncontrolled — (Use additional code to identify manifestation: 443.81, 785.4) (Use additional code to identify any associated insulin use: V58.67)
250.70 Diabetes with peripheral circulatory disorders, type II or unspecified type, not stated as uncontrolled — (Use additional code to identify manifestation: 443.81, 785.4)
250.71 Diabetes with peripheral circulatory disorders, type I [juvenile type], not stated as uncontrolled — (Use additional code to identify manifestation: 443.81, 785.4)
250.72 Diabetes with peripheral circulatory disorders, type II or unspecified type, uncontrolled — (Use additional code to identify manifestation: 443.81, 785.4)
250.73 Diabetes with peripheral circulatory disorders, type I [juvenile type], uncontrolled — (Use additional code to identify manifestation: 443.81, 785.4)
440.23 Atherosclerosis of native arteries of the extremities with ulceration — (Use additional code for any associated ulceration: 707.10-707.19, 707.8, 707.9)
443.81 Peripheral angiopathy in diseases classified elsewhere — (Code first underlying disease: 249.7, 250.7) ☒
444.22 Embolism and thrombosis of arteries of lower extremity
445.02 Atheroembolism of lower extremity
447.1 Stricture of artery
707.10 Ulcer of lower limb, unspecified — (Code, if applicable, any causal condition first: 249.80-249.81, 250.80-250.83, 440.23, 459.11, 459.13, 459.31, 459.33) ▽
707.14 Ulcer of heel and midfoot — (Code, if applicable, any causal condition first: 249.80-249.81, 250.80-250.83, 440.23, 459.11, 459.13, 459.31, 459.33)
707.15 Ulcer of other part of foot — (Code, if applicable, any causal condition first: 249.80-249.81, 250.80-250.83, 440.23, 459.11, 459.13, 459.31, 459.33)
730.17 Chronic osteomyelitis, ankle and foot — (Use additional code to identify organism: 041.1. Use additional code to identify major osseous defect, if applicable: 731.3)
730.37 Periostitis, without mention of osteomyelitis, ankle and foot — (Use additional code to identify organism: 041.1)
731.3 Major osseous defects — (Code first underlying disease: 170.0-170.9, 730.00-730.29, 733.00-733.09, 733.40-733.49, 996.45)
733.49 Aseptic necrosis of other bone site — (Use additional code to identify major osseous defect, if applicable: 731.3)
785.4 Gangrene — (Code first any associated underlying condition)
892.1 Open wound of foot except toe(s) alone, complicated
895.0 Traumatic amputation of toe(s) (complete) (partial), without mention of complication
896.0 Traumatic amputation of foot (complete) (partial), unilateral, without mention of complication
928.20 Crushing injury of foot — (Use additional code to identify any associated injuries: 800-829, 850.0-854.1, 860.0-869.1)

ICD-9-CM Procedural

84.12 Amputation through foot

28810

28810 Amputation, metatarsal, with toe, single

ICD-9-CM Diagnostic

249.70 Secondary diabetes mellitus with peripheral circulatory disorders, not stated as uncontrolled, or unspecified — (Use additional code to identify manifestation: 443.81, 785.4) (Use additional code to identify any associated insulin use: V58.67)
249.71 Secondary diabetes mellitus with peripheral circulatory disorders, uncontrolled — (Use additional code to identify manifestation: 443.81, 785.4) (Use additional code to identify any associated insulin use: V58.67)
249.80 Secondary diabetes mellitus with other specified manifestations, not stated as uncontrolled, or unspecified — (Use additional code to identify manifestation:

707.10-707.19, 707.8, 707.9, 731.8) (Use additional code to identify any associated insulin use: V58.67)

249.81 Secondary diabetes mellitus with other specified manifestations, uncontrolled — (Use additional code to identify manifestation: 707.10-707.19, 707.8, 707.9, 731.8) (Use additional code to identify any associated insulin use: V58.67)

250.70 Diabetes with peripheral circulatory disorders, type II or unspecified type, not stated as uncontrolled — (Use additional code to identify manifestation: 443.81, 785.4)

250.71 Diabetes with peripheral circulatory disorders, type I [juvenile type], not stated as uncontrolled — (Use additional code to identify manifestation: 443.81, 785.4)

250.72 Diabetes with peripheral circulatory disorders, type II or unspecified type, uncontrolled — (Use additional code to identify manifestation: 443.81, 785.4)

250.73 Diabetes with peripheral circulatory disorders, type I [juvenile type], uncontrolled — (Use additional code to identify manifestation: 443.81, 785.4)

250.80 Diabetes with other specified manifestations, type II or unspecified type, not stated as uncontrolled — (Use additional code to identify manifestation: 707.10-707.19, 707.8, 707.9, 731.8)

250.81 Diabetes with other specified manifestations, type I [juvenile type], not stated as uncontrolled — (Use additional code to identify manifestation: 707.10-707.19, 707.8, 707.9, 731.8)

250.82 Diabetes with other specified manifestations, type II or unspecified type, uncontrolled — (Use additional code to identify manifestation: 707.10-707.19, 707.8, 707.9, 731.8)

250.83 Diabetes with other specified manifestations, type I [juvenile type], uncontrolled — (Use additional code to identify manifestation: 707.10-707.19, 707.8, 707.9, 731.8)

250.90 Diabetes with unspecified complication, type II or unspecified type, not stated as uncontrolled ♥

250.91 Diabetes with unspecified complication, type I [juvenile type], not stated as uncontrolled ♥

250.92 Diabetes with unspecified complication, type II or unspecified type, uncontrolled ♥

250.93 Diabetes with unspecified complication, type I [juvenile type], uncontrolled ♥

440.24 Atherosclerosis of native arteries of the extremities with gangrene — (Use additional code for any associated ulceration: 707.10-707.19, 707.8, 707.9)

443.81 Peripheral angiopathy in diseases classified elsewhere — (Code first underlying disease: 249.7, 250.7) ☒

444.22 Embolism and thrombosis of arteries of lower extremity

445.02 Atheroembolism of lower extremity

682.7 Cellulitis and abscess of foot, except toes — (Use additional code to identify organism, such as 041.1, etc.)

707.10 Ulcer of lower limb, unspecified — (Code, if applicable, any causal condition first: 249.80-249.81, 250.80-250.83, 440.23, 459.11, 459.13, 459.31, 459.33) ♥

707.14 Ulcer of heel and midfoot — (Code, if applicable, any causal condition first: 249.80-249.81, 250.80-250.83, 440.23, 459.11, 459.13, 459.31, 459.33)

707.15 Ulcer of other part of foot — (Code, if applicable, any causal condition first: 249.80-249.81, 250.80-250.83, 440.23, 459.11, 459.13, 459.31, 459.33)

730.07 Acute osteomyelitis, ankle and foot — (Use additional code to identify organism: 041.1. Use additional code to identify major osseous defect, if applicable: 731.3)

730.17 Chronic osteomyelitis, ankle and foot — (Use additional code to identify organism: 041.1. Use additional code to identify major osseous defect, if applicable: 731.3)

730.37 Periostitis, without mention of osteomyelitis, ankle and foot — (Use additional code to identify organism: 041.1)

730.87 Other infections involving bone diseases classified elsewhere, ankle and foot — (Use additional code to identify organism: 041.1. Code first underlying disease: 002.0, 015.0-015.9) ☒

731.3 Major osseous defects — (Code first underlying disease: 170.0-170.9, 730.00-730.29, 733.00-733.09, 733.40-733.49, 996.45)

731.8 Other bone involvement in diseases classified elsewhere — (Code first underlying disease: 249.8, 250.8. Use additional code to specify bone condition: 730.00-730.09) ☒

785.4 Gangrene — (Code first any associated underlying condition)

892.1 Open wound of foot except toe(s) alone, complicated

895.0 Traumatic amputation of toe(s) (complete) (partial), without mention of complication

896.0 Traumatic amputation of foot (complete) (partial), unilateral, without mention of complication

928.3 Crushing injury of toe(s) — (Use additional code to identify any associated injuries: 800-829, 850.0-854.1, 860.0-869.1)

ICD-9-CM Procedural

84.12 Amputation through foot

28820

28820 Amputation, toe; metatarsophalangeal joint

ICD-9-CM Diagnostic

213.8 Benign neoplasm of short bones of lower limb

249.70 Secondary diabetes mellitus with peripheral circulatory disorders, not stated as uncontrolled, or unspecified — (Use additional code to identify manifestation: 443.81, 785.4) (Use additional code to identify any associated insulin use: V58.67)

249.71 Secondary diabetes mellitus with peripheral circulatory disorders, uncontrolled — (Use additional code to identify manifestation: 443.81, 785.4) (Use additional code to identify any associated insulin use: V58.67)

249.80 Secondary diabetes mellitus with other specified manifestations, not stated as uncontrolled, or unspecified — (Use additional code to identify manifestation: 707.10-707.19, 707.8, 707.9, 731.8) (Use additional code to identify any associated insulin use: V58.67)

249.81 Secondary diabetes mellitus with other specified manifestations, uncontrolled — (Use additional code to identify manifestation: 707.10-707.19, 707.8, 707.9, 731.8) (Use additional code to identify any associated insulin use: V58.67)

250.70 Diabetes with peripheral circulatory disorders, type II or unspecified type, not stated as uncontrolled — (Use additional code to identify manifestation: 443.81, 785.4)

250.71 Diabetes with peripheral circulatory disorders, type I [juvenile type], not stated as uncontrolled — (Use additional code to identify manifestation: 443.81, 785.4)

250.72 Diabetes with peripheral circulatory disorders, type II or unspecified type, uncontrolled — (Use additional code to identify manifestation: 443.81, 785.4)

250.73 Diabetes with peripheral circulatory disorders, type I [juvenile type], uncontrolled — (Use additional code to identify manifestation: 443.81, 785.4)

250.80 Diabetes with other specified manifestations, type II or unspecified type, not stated as uncontrolled — (Use additional code to identify manifestation: 707.10-707.19, 707.8, 707.9, 731.8)

250.81 Diabetes with other specified manifestations, type I [juvenile type], not stated as uncontrolled — (Use additional code to identify manifestation: 707.10-707.19, 707.8, 707.9, 731.8)

250.82 Diabetes with other specified manifestations, type II or unspecified type, uncontrolled — (Use additional code to identify manifestation: 707.10-707.19, 707.8, 707.9, 731.8)

250.83 Diabetes with other specified manifestations, type I [juvenile type], uncontrolled — (Use additional code to identify manifestation: 707.10-707.19, 707.8, 707.9, 731.8)

250.90 Diabetes with unspecified complication, type II or unspecified type, not stated as uncontrolled ♥

250.91 Diabetes with unspecified complication, type I [juvenile type], not stated as uncontrolled ♥

250.92 Diabetes with unspecified complication, type II or unspecified type, uncontrolled ♥

250.93 Diabetes with unspecified complication, type I [juvenile type], uncontrolled ♥

357.1 Polyneuropathy in collagen vascular disease — (Code first underlying disease: 446.0, 710.0, 714.0) ☒

359.6 Symptomatic inflammatory myopathy in diseases classified elsewhere — (Code first underlying disease: 135, 140.0-208.9, 277.30-277.39, 446.0, 710.0, 710.1, 710.2, 714.0) ☒

440.21 Atherosclerosis of native arteries of the extremities with intermittent claudication

443.81 Peripheral angiopathy in diseases classified elsewhere — (Code first underlying disease: 249.7, 250.7) ☒

443.9 Unspecified peripheral vascular disease ♥

444.22 Embolism and thrombosis of arteries of lower extremity

445.02 Atheroembolism of lower extremity

459.9 Unspecified circulatory system disorder ▽
707.10 Ulcer of lower limb, unspecified — (Code, if applicable, any causal condition first: 249.80-249.81, 250.80-250.83, 440.23, 459.11, 459.13, 459.31, 459.33) ▽
707.14 Ulcer of heel and midfoot — (Code, if applicable, any causal condition first: 249.80-249.81, 250.80-250.83, 440.23, 459.11, 459.13, 459.31, 459.33)
707.15 Ulcer of other part of foot — (Code, if applicable, any causal condition first: 249.80-249.81, 250.80-250.83, 440.23, 459.11, 459.13, 459.31, 459.33)
714.0 Rheumatoid arthritis — (Use additional code to identify manifestation: 357.1, 359.6)
730.07 Acute osteomyelitis, ankle and foot — (Use additional code to identify organism: 041.1. Use additional code to identify major osseous defect, if applicable: 731.3)
730.17 Chronic osteomyelitis, ankle and foot — (Use additional code to identify organism: 041.1. Use additional code to identify major osseous defect, if applicable: 731.3)
731.3 Major osseous defects — (Code first underlying disease: 170.0-170.9, 730.00-730.29, 733.00-733.09, 733.40-733.49, 996.45)
731.8 Other bone involvement in diseases classified elsewhere — (Code first underlying disease: 249.8, 250.8. Use additional code to specify bone condition: 730.00-730.09) ☒
733.40 Aseptic necrosis of bone, site unspecified — (Use additional code to identify major osseous defect, if applicable: 731.3) ▽
735.0 Hallux valgus (acquired)
735.1 Hallux varus (acquired)
735.2 Hallux rigidus
735.3 Hallux malleus
735.4 Other hammer toe (acquired)
735.5 Claw toe (acquired)
735.8 Other acquired deformity of toe
785.4 Gangrene — (Code first any associated underlying condition)
893.0 Open wound of toe(s), without mention of complication
895.0 Traumatic amputation of toe(s) (complete) (partial), without mention of complication
895.1 Traumatic amputation of toe(s) (complete) (partial), complicated
896.0 Traumatic amputation of foot (complete) (partial), unilateral, without mention of complication
928.3 Crushing injury of toe(s) — (Use additional code to identify any associated injuries: 800-829, 850.0-854.1, 860.0-869.1)

ICD-9-CM Procedural

84.11 Amputation of toe

28825

28825 Amputation, toe; interphalangeal joint

ICD-9-CM Diagnostic

239.2 Neoplasms of unspecified nature of bone, soft tissue, and skin
249.60 Secondary diabetes mellitus with neurological manifestations, not stated as uncontrolled, or unspecified — (Use additional code to identify manifestation: 337.1, 353.5, 354.0-355.9, 357.2, 536.3, 713.5) (Use additional code to identify any associated insulin use: V58.67)
249.61 Secondary diabetes mellitus with neurological manifestations, uncontrolled — (Use additional code to identify manifestation: 337.1, 353.5, 354.0-355.9, 357.2, 536.3, 713.5) (Use additional code to identify any associated insulin use: V58.67)
249.70 Secondary diabetes mellitus with peripheral circulatory disorders, not stated as uncontrolled, or unspecified — (Use additional code to identify manifestation: 443.81, 785.4) (Use additional code to identify any associated insulin use: V58.67)
249.71 Secondary diabetes mellitus with peripheral circulatory disorders, uncontrolled — (Use additional code to identify manifestation: 443.81, 785.4) (Use additional code to identify any associated insulin use: V58.67)
249.80 Secondary diabetes mellitus with other specified manifestations, not stated as uncontrolled, or unspecified — (Use additional code to identify manifestation: 707.10-707.19, 707.8, 707.9, 731.8) (Use additional code to identify any associated insulin use: V58.67)
249.81 Secondary diabetes mellitus with other specified manifestations, uncontrolled — (Use additional code to identify manifestation: 707.10-707.19, 707.8, 707.9, 731.8) (Use additional code to identify any associated insulin use: V58.67)
250.60 Diabetes with neurological manifestations, type II or unspecified type, not stated as uncontrolled — (Use additional code to identify manifestation: 337.1, 353.5, 354.0-355.9, 357.2, 536.3, 713.5)
250.61 Diabetes with neurological manifestations, type I [juvenile type], not stated as uncontrolled — (Use additional code to identify manifestation: 337.1, 353.5, 354.0-355.9, 357.2, 536.3, 713.5)
250.62 Diabetes with neurological manifestations, type II or unspecified type, uncontrolled — (Use additional code to identify manifestation: 337.1, 353.5, 354.0-355.9, 357.2, 536.3, 713.5)
250.63 Diabetes with neurological manifestations, type I [juvenile type], uncontrolled — (Use additional code to identify manifestation: 337.1, 353.5, 354.0-355.9, 357.2, 536.3, 713.5)
250.70 Diabetes with peripheral circulatory disorders, type II or unspecified type, not stated as uncontrolled — (Use additional code to identify manifestation: 443.81, 785.4)
250.71 Diabetes with peripheral circulatory disorders, type I [juvenile type], not stated as uncontrolled — (Use additional code to identify manifestation: 443.81, 785.4)
250.72 Diabetes with peripheral circulatory disorders, type II or unspecified type, uncontrolled — (Use additional code to identify manifestation: 443.81, 785.4)
250.73 Diabetes with peripheral circulatory disorders, type I [juvenile type], uncontrolled — (Use additional code to identify manifestation: 443.81, 785.4)
250.80 Diabetes with other specified manifestations, type II or unspecified type, not stated as uncontrolled — (Use additional code to identify manifestation: 707.10-707.19, 707.8, 707.9, 731.8)
250.81 Diabetes with other specified manifestations, type I [juvenile type], not stated as uncontrolled — (Use additional code to identify manifestation: 707.10-707.19, 707.8, 707.9, 731.8)
250.82 Diabetes with other specified manifestations, type II or unspecified type, uncontrolled — (Use additional code to identify manifestation: 707.10-707.19, 707.8, 707.9, 731.8)
250.83 Diabetes with other specified manifestations, type I [juvenile type], uncontrolled — (Use additional code to identify manifestation: 707.10-707.19, 707.8, 707.9, 731.8)
337.1 Peripheral autonomic neuropathy in disorders classified elsewhere — (Code first underlying disease: 249.6, 250.6, 277.30-277.39) ☒
355.0 Lesion of sciatic nerve
355.1 Meralgia paresthetica
355.2 Other lesion of femoral nerve
355.3 Lesion of lateral popliteal nerve
355.4 Lesion of medial popliteal nerve
355.5 Tarsal tunnel syndrome
355.6 Lesion of plantar nerve
355.71 Causalgia of lower limb
355.79 Other mononeuritis of lower limb
355.8 Unspecified mononeuritis of lower limb ▽
355.9 Mononeuritis of unspecified site ▽
357.2 Polyneuropathy in diabetes — (Code first underlying disease: 249.6, 250.6) ☒
359.6 Symptomatic inflammatory myopathy in diseases classified elsewhere — (Code first underlying disease: 135, 140.0-208.9, 277.30-277.39, 446.0, 710.0, 710.1, 710.2, 714.0) ☒
440.21 Atherosclerosis of native arteries of the extremities with intermittent claudication
443.81 Peripheral angiopathy in diseases classified elsewhere — (Code first underlying disease: 249.7, 250.7) ☒
444.22 Embolism and thrombosis of arteries of lower extremity
445.02 Atheroembolism of lower extremity
703.8 Other specified disease of nail
707.10 Ulcer of lower limb, unspecified — (Code, if applicable, any causal condition first: 249.80-249.81, 250.80-250.83, 440.23, 459.11, 459.13, 459.31, 459.33) ▽
707.14 Ulcer of heel and midfoot — (Code, if applicable, any causal condition first: 249.80-249.81, 250.80-250.83, 440.23, 459.11, 459.13, 459.31, 459.33)

707.15 Ulcer of other part of foot — (Code, if applicable, any causal condition first: 249.80-249.81, 250.80-250.83, 440.23, 459.11, 459.13, 459.31, 459.33)
713.5 Arthropathy associated with neurological disorders — (Code first underlying disease: 094.0, 249.6, 250.6, 336.0) ☒
714.0 Rheumatoid arthritis — (Use additional code to identify manifestation: 357.1, 359.6)
730.17 Chronic osteomyelitis, ankle and foot — (Use additional code to identify organism: 041.1. Use additional code to identify major osseous defect, if applicable: 731.3)
730.37 Periostitis, without mention of osteomyelitis, ankle and foot — (Use additional code to identify organism: 041.1)
730.77 Osteopathy resulting from poliomyelitis, ankle and foot — (Use additional code to identify organism: 041.1. Code first underlying disease: 045.0-045.9) ☒
731.3 Major osseous defects — (Code first underlying disease: 170.0-170.9, 730.00-730.29, 733.00-733.09, 733.40-733.49, 996.45)
731.8 Other bone involvement in diseases classified elsewhere — (Code first underlying disease: 249.8, 250.8. Use additional code to specify bone condition: 730.00-730.09) ☒
735.8 Other acquired deformity of toe
785.4 Gangrene — (Code first any associated underlying condition)
893.1 Open wound of toe(s), complicated
895.0 Traumatic amputation of toe(s) (complete) (partial), without mention of complication
928.3 Crushing injury of toe(s) — (Use additional code to identify any associated injuries: 800-829, 850.0-854.1, 860.0-869.1)

ICD-9-CM Procedural

84.11 Amputation of toe

HCPCS Level II Supplies & Services

A4305 Disposable drug delivery system, flow rate of 50 ml or greater per hour

28890

28890 Extracorporeal shock wave, high energy, performed by a physician or other qualified health care professional, requiring anesthesia other than local, including ultrasound guidance, involving the plantar fascia

ICD-9-CM Diagnostic

728.71 Plantar fascial fibromatosis

ICD-9-CM Procedural

00.09 Other therapeutic ultrasound

Application of Casts and Strapping

29000

29000 Application of halo type body cast (see 20661-20663 for insertion)

ICD-9-CM Diagnostic

805.00 Closed fracture of cervical vertebra, unspecified level without mention of spinal cord injury ▽
805.01 Closed fracture of first cervical vertebra without mention of spinal cord injury
805.02 Closed fracture of second cervical vertebra without mention of spinal cord injury
805.03 Closed fracture of third cervical vertebra without mention of spinal cord injury
805.04 Closed fracture of fourth cervical vertebra without mention of spinal cord injury
805.05 Closed fracture of fifth cervical vertebra without mention of spinal cord injury
805.06 Closed fracture of sixth cervical vertebra without mention of spinal cord injury
805.07 Closed fracture of seventh cervical vertebra without mention of spinal cord injury
805.08 Closed fracture of multiple cervical vertebrae without mention of spinal cord injury
805.10 Open fracture of cervical vertebra, unspecified level without mention of spinal cord injury ▽
805.11 Open fracture of first cervical vertebra without mention of spinal cord injury
805.12 Open fracture of second cervical vertebra without mention of spinal cord injury
805.13 Open fracture of third cervical vertebra without mention of spinal cord injury
805.14 Open fracture of fourth cervical vertebra without mention of spinal cord injury
805.15 Open fracture of fifth cervical vertebra without mention of spinal cord injury
805.16 Open fracture of sixth cervical vertebra without mention of spinal cord injury
805.17 Open fracture of seventh cervical vertebra without mention of spinal cord injury
805.18 Open fracture of multiple cervical vertebrae without mention of spinal cord injury
806.00 Closed fracture of C1-C4 level with unspecified spinal cord injury ▽
806.01 Closed fracture of C1-C4 level with complete lesion of cord
806.02 Closed fracture of C1-C4 level with anterior cord syndrome
806.03 Closed fracture of C1-C4 level with central cord syndrome
806.04 Closed fracture of C1-C4 level with other specified spinal cord injury
806.05 Closed fracture of C5-C7 level with unspecified spinal cord injury ▽
806.06 Closed fracture of C5-C7 level with complete lesion of cord
806.07 Closed fracture of C5-C7 level with anterior cord syndrome
806.08 Closed fracture of C5-C7 level with central cord syndrome
806.09 Closed fracture of C5-C7 level with other specified spinal cord injury
806.10 Open fracture of C1-C4 level with unspecified spinal cord injury ▽
806.11 Open fracture of C1-C4 level with complete lesion of cord
806.12 Open fracture of C1-C4 level with anterior cord syndrome
806.13 Open fracture of C1-C4 level with central cord syndrome
806.14 Open fracture of C1-C4 level with other specified spinal cord injury
806.15 Open fracture of C5-C7 level with unspecified spinal cord injury ▽
806.16 Open fracture of C5-C7 level with complete lesion of cord
806.17 Open fracture of C5-C7 level with anterior cord syndrome
806.18 Open fracture of C5-C7 level with central cord syndrome
806.19 Open fracture of C5-C7 level with other specified spinal cord injury
V54.17 Aftercare for healing traumatic fracture of vertebrae
V54.19 Aftercare for healing traumatic fracture of other bone
V54.27 Aftercare for healing pathologic fracture of vertebrae
V54.29 Aftercare for healing pathologic fracture of other bone

ICD-9-CM Procedural

93.51 Application of plaster jacket
93.52 Application of neck support
97.13 Replacement of other cast

HCPCS Level II Supplies & Services

A6441 Padding bandage, nonelastic, nonwoven/nonknitted, width greater than or equal to 3 in and less than 5 in, per yd
Q4001 Casting supplies, body cast adult, with or without head, plaster
Q4002 Cast supplies, body cast adult, with or without head, fiberglass

29010-29015

29010 Application of Risser jacket, localizer, body; only
29015 including head

ICD-9-CM Diagnostic

268.1 Rickets, late effect — (Use additional code to identify the nature of late effect)
737.0 Adolescent postural kyphosis
737.10 Kyphosis (acquired) (postural)
737.11 Kyphosis due to radiation
737.12 Kyphosis, postlaminectomy
737.19 Other kyphosis (acquired)
737.20 Lordosis (acquired) (postural)
737.21 Lordosis, postlaminectomy
737.22 Other postsurgical lordosis
737.29 Other lordosis (acquired)
737.30 Scoliosis (and kyphoscoliosis), idiopathic
737.34 Thoracogenic scoliosis
737.39 Other kyphoscoliosis and scoliosis
738.5 Other acquired deformity of back or spine
756.19 Other congenital anomaly of spine
V54.17 Aftercare for healing traumatic fracture of vertebrae
V54.19 Aftercare for healing traumatic fracture of other bone

V54.27 Aftercare for healing pathologic fracture of vertebrae
V54.29 Aftercare for healing pathologic fracture of other bone

ICD-9-CM Procedural

93.51 Application of plaster jacket
93.52 Application of neck support
97.13 Replacement of other cast

HCPCS Level II Supplies & Services

A6441 Padding bandage, nonelastic, nonwoven/nonknitted, width greater than or equal to 3 in and less than 5 in, per yd
Q4001 Casting supplies, body cast adult, with or without head, plaster
Q4002 Cast supplies, body cast adult, with or without head, fiberglass

29020-29025

29020 Application of turnbuckle jacket, body; only
29025 including head

ICD-9-CM Diagnostic

268.1 Rickets, late effect — (Use additional code to identify the nature of late effect)
737.0 Adolescent postural kyphosis
737.10 Kyphosis (acquired) (postural)
737.11 Kyphosis due to radiation
737.12 Kyphosis, postlaminectomy
737.19 Other kyphosis (acquired)
737.20 Lordosis (acquired) (postural)
737.21 Lordosis, postlaminectomy
737.22 Other postsurgical lordosis
737.29 Other lordosis (acquired)
737.30 Scoliosis (and kyphoscoliosis), idiopathic
737.32 Progressive infantile idiopathic scoliosis
737.34 Thoracogenic scoliosis
737.39 Other kyphoscoliosis and scoliosis
738.5 Other acquired deformity of back or spine
756.19 Other congenital anomaly of spine
V54.17 Aftercare for healing traumatic fracture of vertebrae
V54.19 Aftercare for healing traumatic fracture of other bone
V54.27 Aftercare for healing pathologic fracture of vertebrae
V54.29 Aftercare for healing pathologic fracture of other bone

ICD-9-CM Procedural

93.51 Application of plaster jacket
93.52 Application of neck support
97.13 Replacement of other cast

HCPCS Level II Supplies & Services

A4580 Cast supplies (e.g., plaster)
Q4001 Casting supplies, body cast adult, with or without head, plaster
Q4002 Cast supplies, body cast adult, with or without head, fiberglass

29035-29046

29035 Application of body cast, shoulder to hips;
29040 including head, Minerva type
29044 including 1 thigh
29046 including both thighs

ICD-9-CM Diagnostic

805.00 Closed fracture of cervical vertebra, unspecified level without mention of spinal cord injury ▽
805.01 Closed fracture of first cervical vertebra without mention of spinal cord injury
805.02 Closed fracture of second cervical vertebra without mention of spinal cord injury
805.03 Closed fracture of third cervical vertebra without mention of spinal cord injury
805.04 Closed fracture of fourth cervical vertebra without mention of spinal cord injury
805.05 Closed fracture of fifth cervical vertebra without mention of spinal cord injury
805.06 Closed fracture of sixth cervical vertebra without mention of spinal cord injury
805.07 Closed fracture of seventh cervical vertebra without mention of spinal cord injury
805.08 Closed fracture of multiple cervical vertebrae without mention of spinal cord injury
805.10 Open fracture of cervical vertebra, unspecified level without mention of spinal cord injury ▽
805.11 Open fracture of first cervical vertebra without mention of spinal cord injury
805.12 Open fracture of second cervical vertebra without mention of spinal cord injury
805.13 Open fracture of third cervical vertebra without mention of spinal cord injury
805.14 Open fracture of fourth cervical vertebra without mention of spinal cord injury
805.16 Open fracture of sixth cervical vertebra without mention of spinal cord injury
805.17 Open fracture of seventh cervical vertebra without mention of spinal cord injury
805.18 Open fracture of multiple cervical vertebrae without mention of spinal cord injury
805.2 Closed fracture of dorsal (thoracic) vertebra without mention of spinal cord injury
805.3 Open fracture of dorsal (thoracic) vertebra without mention of spinal cord injury
805.4 Closed fracture of lumbar vertebra without mention of spinal cord injury
805.5 Open fracture of lumbar vertebra without mention of spinal cord injury
805.6 Closed fracture of sacrum and coccyx without mention of spinal cord injury
805.7 Open fracture of sacrum and coccyx without mention of spinal cord injury
805.8 Closed fracture of unspecified part of vertebral column without mention of spinal cord injury ▽
805.9 Open fracture of unspecified part of vertebral column without mention of spinal cord injury ▽
806.00 Closed fracture of C1-C4 level with unspecified spinal cord injury ▽
806.01 Closed fracture of C1-C4 level with complete lesion of cord
806.02 Closed fracture of C1-C4 level with anterior cord syndrome
806.03 Closed fracture of C1-C4 level with central cord syndrome
806.04 Closed fracture of C1-C4 level with other specified spinal cord injury
806.05 Closed fracture of C5-C7 level with unspecified spinal cord injury ▽
806.06 Closed fracture of C5-C7 level with complete lesion of cord
806.07 Closed fracture of C5-C7 level with anterior cord syndrome
806.08 Closed fracture of C5-C7 level with central cord syndrome
806.09 Closed fracture of C5-C7 level with other specified spinal cord injury
806.10 Open fracture of C1-C4 level with unspecified spinal cord injury ▽
806.11 Open fracture of C1-C4 level with complete lesion of cord
806.12 Open fracture of C1-C4 level with anterior cord syndrome
806.13 Open fracture of C1-C4 level with central cord syndrome
806.14 Open fracture of C1-C4 level with other specified spinal cord injury
806.15 Open fracture of C5-C7 level with unspecified spinal cord injury ▽
806.16 Open fracture of C5-C7 level with complete lesion of cord
806.17 Open fracture of C5-C7 level with anterior cord syndrome
806.18 Open fracture of C5-C7 level with central cord syndrome
806.19 Open fracture of C5-C7 level with other specified spinal cord injury
806.20 Closed fracture of T1-T6 level with unspecified spinal cord injury ▽
806.21 Closed fracture of T1-T6 level with complete lesion of cord
806.22 Closed fracture of T1-T6 level with anterior cord syndrome
806.23 Closed fracture of T1-T6 level with central cord syndrome
806.24 Closed fracture of T1-T6 level with other specified spinal cord injury
806.25 Closed fracture of T7-T12 level with unspecified spinal cord injury ▽
806.26 Closed fracture of T7-T12 level with complete lesion of cord
806.27 Closed fracture of T7-T12 level with anterior cord syndrome
806.28 Closed fracture of T7-T12 level with central cord syndrome
806.29 Closed fracture of T7-T12 level with other specified spinal cord injury
806.30 Open fracture of T1-T6 level with unspecified spinal cord injury ▽
806.31 Open fracture of T1-T6 level with complete lesion of cord
806.32 Open fracture of T1-T6 level with anterior cord syndrome
806.33 Open fracture of T1-T6 level with central cord syndrome
806.34 Open fracture of T1-T6 level with other specified spinal cord injury
806.35 Open fracture of T7-T12 level with unspecified spinal cord injury ▽

806.36 Open fracture of T7-T12 level with complete lesion of cord
806.37 Open fracture of T7-T12 level with anterior cord syndrome
806.38 Open fracture of T7-T12 level with central cord syndrome
806.39 Open fracture of T7-T12 level with other specified spinal cord injury
806.4 Closed fracture of lumbar spine with spinal cord injury
806.5 Open fracture of lumbar spine with spinal cord injury
806.60 Closed fracture of sacrum and coccyx with unspecified spinal cord injury ▽
806.61 Closed fracture of sacrum and coccyx with complete cauda equina lesion
806.62 Closed fracture of sacrum and coccyx with other cauda equina injury
806.69 Closed fracture of sacrum and coccyx with other spinal cord injury
806.70 Open fracture of sacrum and coccyx with unspecified spinal cord injury ▽
806.71 Open fracture of sacrum and coccyx with complete cauda equina lesion
806.72 Open fracture of sacrum and coccyx with other cauda equina injury
806.79 Open fracture of sacrum and coccyx with other spinal cord injury
808.0 Closed fracture of acetabulum
808.1 Open fracture of acetabulum
808.2 Closed fracture of pubis
808.3 Open fracture of pubis
808.41 Closed fracture of ilium
808.42 Closed fracture of ischium
808.43 Multiple closed pelvic fractures with disruption of pelvic circle
808.49 Closed fracture of other specified part of pelvis
808.51 Open fracture of ilium
808.52 Open fracture of ischium
808.53 Multiple open pelvic fractures with disruption of pelvic circle
808.59 Open fracture of other specified part of pelvis
V54.13 Aftercare for healing traumatic fracture of hip
V54.17 Aftercare for healing traumatic fracture of vertebrae
V54.19 Aftercare for healing traumatic fracture of other bone
V54.23 Aftercare for healing pathologic fracture of hip
V54.27 Aftercare for healing pathologic fracture of vertebrae
V54.29 Aftercare for healing pathologic fracture of other bone

ICD-9-CM Procedural

93.52 Application of neck support
93.53 Application of other cast
97.13 Replacement of other cast

HCPCS Level II Supplies & Services

A6441 Padding bandage, nonelastic, nonwoven/nonknitted, width greater than or equal to 3 in and less than 5 in, per yd
Q4001 Casting supplies, body cast adult, with or without head, plaster
Q4002 Cast supplies, body cast adult, with or without head, fiberglass

29049-29058

29049 Application, cast; figure-of-eight
29055 shoulder spica
29058 plaster Velpeau

ICD-9-CM Diagnostic

718.71 Developmental dislocation of joint, shoulder region
810.01 Closed fracture of sternal end of clavicle
810.02 Closed fracture of shaft of clavicle
810.03 Closed fracture of acromial end of clavicle
811.00 Closed fracture of unspecified part of scapula ▽
811.01 Closed fracture of acromial process of scapula
811.02 Closed fracture of coracoid process of scapula
811.03 Closed fracture of glenoid cavity and neck of scapula
811.09 Closed fracture of other part of scapula
811.10 Open fracture of unspecified part of scapula ▽
811.11 Open fracture of acromial process of scapula
811.12 Open fracture of coracoid process
811.13 Open fracture of glenoid cavity and neck of scapula
811.19 Open fracture of other part of scapula
812.00 Closed fracture of unspecified part of upper end of humerus ▽
812.01 Closed fracture of surgical neck of humerus
812.02 Closed fracture of anatomical neck of humerus
812.03 Closed fracture of greater tuberosity of humerus
812.09 Other closed fractures of upper end of humerus
831.01 Closed anterior dislocation of humerus
831.02 Closed posterior dislocation of humerus
831.03 Closed inferior dislocation of humerus
831.04 Closed dislocation of acromioclavicular (joint)
831.09 Closed dislocation of other site of shoulder
840.0 Acromioclavicular (joint) (ligament) sprain and strain
840.1 Coracoclavicular (ligament) sprain and strain
840.2 Coracohumeral (ligament) sprain and strain
840.3 Infraspinatus (muscle) (tendon) sprain and strain
840.4 Rotator cuff (capsule) sprain and strain
840.5 Subscapularis (muscle) sprain and strain
840.6 Supraspinatus (muscle) (tendon) sprain and strain
840.8 Sprain and strain of other specified sites of shoulder and upper arm
V54.11 Aftercare for healing traumatic fracture of upper arm
V54.19 Aftercare for healing traumatic fracture of other bone
V54.21 Aftercare for healing pathologic fracture of upper arm
V54.29 Aftercare for healing pathologic fracture of other bone

ICD-9-CM Procedural

93.53 Application of other cast
97.11 Replacement of cast on upper limb

HCPCS Level II Supplies & Services

A4580 Cast supplies (e.g., plaster)
Q4003 Cast supplies, shoulder cast, adult (11 years +), plaster
Q4004 Cast supplies, shoulder cast, adult (11 years +), fiberglass
Q4050 Cast supplies, for unlisted types and materials of casts

29065

29065 Application, cast; shoulder to hand (long arm)

ICD-9-CM Diagnostic

733.81 Malunion of fracture
733.82 Nonunion of fracture
812.00 Closed fracture of unspecified part of upper end of humerus ▽
812.01 Closed fracture of surgical neck of humerus
812.03 Closed fracture of greater tuberosity of humerus
812.09 Other closed fractures of upper end of humerus
812.20 Closed fracture of unspecified part of humerus ▽
812.21 Closed fracture of shaft of humerus
812.40 Closed fracture of unspecified part of lower end of humerus ▽
812.41 Closed fracture of supracondylar humerus
812.42 Closed fracture of lateral condyle of humerus
812.43 Closed fracture of medial condyle of humerus
812.44 Closed fracture of unspecified condyle(s) of humerus ▽
812.49 Other closed fracture of lower end of humerus
813.00 Unspecified fracture of radius and ulna, upper end of forearm, closed ▽
813.01 Closed fracture of olecranon process of ulna
813.02 Closed fracture of coronoid process of ulna
813.03 Closed Monteggia's fracture
813.04 Other and unspecified closed fractures of proximal end of ulna (alone) ▽
813.05 Closed fracture of head of radius

813.06 Closed fracture of neck of radius
813.07 Other and unspecified closed fractures of proximal end of radius (alone) ▽
813.08 Closed fracture of radius with ulna, upper end (any part)
813.46 Torus fracture of ulna (alone)
813.47 Torus fracture of radius and ulna
V54.10 Aftercare for healing traumatic fracture of arm, unspecified ▽
V54.11 Aftercare for healing traumatic fracture of upper arm
V54.12 Aftercare for healing traumatic fracture of lower arm
V54.20 Aftercare for healing pathologic fracture of arm, unspecified ▽
V54.21 Aftercare for healing pathologic fracture of upper arm
V54.22 Aftercare for healing pathologic fracture of lower arm

ICD-9-CM Procedural

93.53 Application of other cast
97.11 Replacement of cast on upper limb

HCPCS Level II Supplies & Services

A4580 Cast supplies (e.g., plaster)

29075

29075 Application, cast; elbow to finger (short arm)

ICD-9-CM Diagnostic

718.23 Pathological dislocation of forearm joint
718.24 Pathological dislocation of hand joint
718.33 Recurrent dislocation of forearm joint
718.34 Recurrent dislocation of hand joint
718.73 Developmental dislocation of joint, forearm
718.74 Developmental dislocation of joint, hand
727.02 Giant cell tumor of tendon sheath
727.03 Trigger finger (acquired)
727.04 Radial styloid tenosynovitis
727.05 Other tenosynovitis of hand and wrist
727.09 Other synovitis and tenosynovitis
727.2 Specific bursitides often of occupational origin
727.59 Other rupture of synovium
727.63 Nontraumatic rupture of extensor tendons of hand and wrist
727.64 Nontraumatic rupture of flexor tendons of hand and wrist
727.69 Nontraumatic rupture of other tendon
727.81 Contracture of tendon (sheath)
727.82 Calcium deposits in tendon and bursa
727.89 Other disorders of synovium, tendon, and bursa
728.4 Laxity of ligament
728.5 Hypermobility syndrome
728.6 Contracture of palmar fascia
733.12 Pathologic fracture of distal radius and ulna
733.19 Pathologic fracture of other specified site
733.21 Solitary bone cyst
733.22 Aneurysmal bone cyst
733.29 Other cyst of bone
733.40 Aseptic necrosis of bone, site unspecified — (Use additional code to identify major osseous defect, if applicable: 731.3) ▽
733.81 Malunion of fracture
733.82 Nonunion of fracture
736.00 Unspecified deformity of forearm, excluding fingers ▽
736.01 Cubitus valgus (acquired)
736.02 Cubitus varus (acquired)
736.03 Valgus deformity of wrist (acquired)
736.04 Varus deformity of wrist (acquired)
736.05 Wrist drop (acquired)
736.06 Claw hand (acquired)
736.07 Club hand, acquired
736.09 Other acquired deformities of forearm, excluding fingers
736.21 Boutonniere deformity
736.22 Swan-neck deformity
736.29 Other acquired deformity of finger
755.53 Radioulnar synostosis
755.56 Accessory carpal bones
755.57 Macrodactylia (fingers)
755.58 Congenital cleft hand
755.59 Other congenital anomaly of upper limb, including shoulder girdle
813.01 Closed fracture of olecranon process of ulna
813.02 Closed fracture of coronoid process of ulna
813.03 Closed Monteggia's fracture
813.05 Closed fracture of head of radius
813.06 Closed fracture of neck of radius
813.08 Closed fracture of radius with ulna, upper end (any part)
813.10 Unspecified open fracture of upper end of forearm ▽
813.11 Open fracture of olecranon process of ulna
813.12 Open fracture of coronoid process of ulna
813.15 Open fracture of head of radius
813.16 Open fracture of neck of radius
813.18 Open fracture of radius with ulna, upper end (any part)
813.21 Closed fracture of shaft of radius (alone)
813.22 Closed fracture of shaft of ulna (alone)
813.23 Closed fracture of shaft of radius with ulna
813.31 Open fracture of shaft of radius (alone)
813.32 Open fracture of shaft of ulna (alone)
813.33 Open fracture of shaft of radius with ulna
813.40 Unspecified closed fracture of lower end of forearm ▽
813.41 Closed Colles' fracture
813.42 Other closed fractures of distal end of radius (alone)
813.43 Closed fracture of distal end of ulna (alone)
813.44 Closed fracture of lower end of radius with ulna
813.45 Torus fracture of radius (alone)
813.46 Torus fracture of ulna (alone)
813.47 Torus fracture of radius and ulna
813.50 Unspecified open fracture of lower end of forearm ▽
813.51 Open Colles' fracture
813.52 Other open fractures of distal end of radius (alone)
813.53 Open fracture of distal end of ulna (alone)
813.54 Open fracture of lower end of radius with ulna
813.80 Closed fracture of unspecified part of forearm ▽
813.81 Closed fracture of unspecified part of radius (alone) ▽
813.82 Closed fracture of unspecified part of ulna (alone) ▽
813.83 Closed fracture of unspecified part of radius with ulna ▽
813.91 Open fracture of unspecified part of radius (alone) ▽
813.92 Open fracture of unspecified part of ulna (alone) ▽
814.01 Closed fracture of navicular (scaphoid) bone of wrist
814.02 Closed fracture of lunate (semilunar) bone of wrist
814.03 Closed fracture of triquetral (cuneiform) bone of wrist
814.04 Closed fracture of pisiform bone of wrist
814.05 Closed fracture of trapezium bone (larger multangular) of wrist
814.06 Closed fracture of trapezoid bone (smaller multangular) of wrist
814.07 Closed fracture of capitate bone (os magnum) of wrist
814.08 Closed fracture of hamate (unciform) bone of wrist
814.09 Closed fracture of other bone of wrist
814.11 Open fracture of navicular (scaphoid) bone of wrist
814.12 Open fracture of lunate (semilunar) bone of wrist
814.13 Open fracture of triquetral (cuneiform) bone of wrist

814.14 Open fracture of pisiform bone of wrist
814.15 Open fracture of trapezium bone (larger multangular) of wrist
814.16 Open fracture of trapezoid bone (smaller multangular) of wrist
814.17 Open fracture of capitate bone (os magnum) of wrist
814.18 Open fracture of hamate (unciform) bone of wrist
814.19 Open fracture of other bone of wrist
815.01 Closed fracture of base of thumb (first) metacarpal bone(s)
815.02 Closed fracture of base of other metacarpal bone(s)
815.03 Closed fracture of shaft of metacarpal bone(s)
815.04 Closed fracture of neck of metacarpal bone(s)
815.09 Closed fracture of multiple sites of metacarpus
815.10 Open fracture of metacarpal bone(s), site unspecified
815.11 Open fracture of base of thumb (first) metacarpal bone(s)
815.12 Open fracture of base of other metacarpal bone(s)
815.13 Open fracture of shaft of metacarpal bone(s)
815.14 Open fracture of neck of metacarpal bone(s)
815.19 Open fracture of multiple sites of metacarpus
816.00 Closed fracture of unspecified phalanx or phalanges of hand
816.01 Closed fracture of middle or proximal phalanx or phalanges of hand
816.02 Closed fracture of distal phalanx or phalanges of hand
816.03 Closed fracture of multiple sites of phalanx or phalanges of hand
816.10 Open fracture of phalanx or phalanges of hand, unspecified
816.11 Open fracture of middle or proximal phalanx or phalanges of hand
816.12 Open fracture of distal phalanx or phalanges of hand
816.13 Open fractures of multiple sites of phalanx or phalanges of hand
817.0 Multiple closed fractures of hand bones
817.1 Multiple open fractures of hand bones
818.0 Ill-defined closed fractures of upper limb
818.1 Ill-defined open fractures of upper limb
833.01 Closed dislocation of distal radioulnar (joint)
833.02 Closed dislocation of radiocarpal (joint)
833.03 Closed dislocation of midcarpal (joint)
833.04 Closed dislocation of carpometacarpal (joint)
833.05 Closed dislocation of proximal end of metacarpal (bone)
833.09 Closed dislocation of other part of wrist
833.10 Open dislocation of wrist, unspecified part
833.11 Open dislocation of distal radioulnar (joint)
833.12 Open dislocation of radiocarpal (joint)
833.13 Open dislocation of midcarpal (joint)
833.14 Open dislocation of carpometacarpal (joint)
833.15 Open dislocation of proximal end of metacarpal (bone)
833.19 Open dislocation of other part of wrist
834.00 Closed dislocation of finger, unspecified part
834.01 Closed dislocation of metacarpophalangeal (joint)
834.02 Closed dislocation of interphalangeal (joint), hand
834.11 Open dislocation of metacarpophalangeal (joint)
834.12 Open dislocation interphalangeal (joint), hand
842.01 Sprain and strain of carpal (joint) of wrist
842.02 Sprain and strain of radiocarpal (joint) (ligament) of wrist
842.09 Other wrist sprain and strain
842.11 Sprain and strain of carpometacarpal (joint) of hand
842.12 Sprain and strain of metacarpophalangeal (joint) of hand
842.13 Sprain and strain of interphalangeal (joint) of hand
842.19 Other hand sprain and strain
881.00 Open wound of forearm, without mention of complication
881.02 Open wound of wrist, without mention of complication
881.10 Open wound of forearm, complicated
881.12 Open wound of wrist, complicated
881.20 Open wound of forearm, with tendon involvement
881.22 Open wound of wrist, with tendon involvement
883.0 Open wound of finger(s), without mention of complication
883.1 Open wound of finger(s), complicated
883.2 Open wound of finger(s), with tendon involvement
884.0 Multiple and unspecified open wound of upper limb, without mention of complication
884.1 Multiple and unspecified open wound of upper limb, complicated
884.2 Multiple and unspecified open wound of upper limb, with tendon involvement
905.2 Late effect of fracture of upper extremities
959.3 Injury, other and unspecified, elbow, forearm, and wrist
V54.12 Aftercare for healing traumatic fracture of lower arm
V54.19 Aftercare for healing traumatic fracture of other bone
V54.22 Aftercare for healing pathologic fracture of lower arm
V54.29 Aftercare for healing pathologic fracture of other bone
V54.89 Other orthopedic aftercare
V67.00 Follow-up examination, following unspecified surgery
V67.09 Follow-up examination, following other surgery

ICD-9-CM Procedural

93.53 Application of other cast
97.11 Replacement of cast on upper limb

HCPCS Level II Supplies & Services

A4580 Cast supplies (e.g., plaster)

29085

29085 Application, cast; hand and lower forearm (gauntlet)

ICD-9-CM Diagnostic

716.13 Traumatic arthropathy, forearm
718.83 Other joint derangement, not elsewhere classified, forearm
718.84 Other joint derangement, not elsewhere classified, hand
733.82 Nonunion of fracture
813.05 Closed fracture of head of radius
813.06 Closed fracture of neck of radius
813.21 Closed fracture of shaft of radius (alone)
813.22 Closed fracture of shaft of ulna (alone)
813.40 Unspecified closed fracture of lower end of forearm
813.41 Closed Colles' fracture
813.42 Other closed fractures of distal end of radius (alone)
813.43 Closed fracture of distal end of ulna (alone)
813.44 Closed fracture of lower end of radius with ulna
813.45 Torus fracture of radius (alone)
813.46 Torus fracture of ulna (alone)
813.47 Torus fracture of radius and ulna
813.50 Unspecified open fracture of lower end of forearm
813.51 Open Colles' fracture
813.52 Other open fractures of distal end of radius (alone)
813.53 Open fracture of distal end of ulna (alone)
813.54 Open fracture of lower end of radius with ulna
813.91 Open fracture of unspecified part of radius (alone)
813.92 Open fracture of unspecified part of ulna (alone)
814.01 Closed fracture of navicular (scaphoid) bone of wrist
814.02 Closed fracture of lunate (semilunar) bone of wrist
814.03 Closed fracture of triquetral (cuneiform) bone of wrist
814.04 Closed fracture of pisiform bone of wrist
814.05 Closed fracture of trapezium bone (larger multangular) of wrist
814.06 Closed fracture of trapezoid bone (smaller multangular) of wrist
814.07 Closed fracture of capitate bone (os magnum) of wrist
814.08 Closed fracture of hamate (unciform) bone of wrist
814.09 Closed fracture of other bone of wrist

814.11	Open fracture of navicular (scaphoid) bone of wrist
814.12	Open fracture of lunate (semilunar) bone of wrist
814.13	Open fracture of triquetral (cuneiform) bone of wrist
814.14	Open fracture of pisiform bone of wrist
814.15	Open fracture of trapezium bone (larger multangular) of wrist
814.16	Open fracture of trapezoid bone (smaller multangular) of wrist
814.17	Open fracture of capitate bone (os magnum) of wrist
814.18	Open fracture of hamate (unciform) bone of wrist
814.19	Open fracture of other bone of wrist
815.00	Closed fracture of metacarpal bone(s), site unspecified ▽
815.01	Closed fracture of base of thumb (first) metacarpal bone(s)
815.02	Closed fracture of base of other metacarpal bone(s)
815.03	Closed fracture of shaft of metacarpal bone(s)
815.04	Closed fracture of neck of metacarpal bone(s)
815.09	Closed fracture of multiple sites of metacarpus
815.10	Open fracture of metacarpal bone(s), site unspecified ▽
815.11	Open fracture of base of thumb (first) metacarpal bone(s)
815.12	Open fracture of base of other metacarpal bone(s)
815.13	Open fracture of shaft of metacarpal bone(s)
815.14	Open fracture of neck of metacarpal bone(s)
815.19	Open fracture of multiple sites of metacarpus
816.00	Closed fracture of unspecified phalanx or phalanges of hand ▽
816.01	Closed fracture of middle or proximal phalanx or phalanges of hand
816.02	Closed fracture of distal phalanx or phalanges of hand
816.03	Closed fracture of multiple sites of phalanx or phalanges of hand
816.10	Open fracture of phalanx or phalanges of hand, unspecified ▽
816.11	Open fracture of middle or proximal phalanx or phalanges of hand
816.12	Open fracture of distal phalanx or phalanges of hand
816.13	Open fractures of multiple sites of phalanx or phalanges of hand
817.0	Multiple closed fractures of hand bones
817.1	Multiple open fractures of hand bones
959.4	Injury, other and unspecified, hand, except finger
959.5	Injury, other and unspecified, finger
V54.12	Aftercare for healing traumatic fracture of lower arm
V54.19	Aftercare for healing traumatic fracture of other bone
V54.22	Aftercare for healing pathologic fracture of lower arm
V54.29	Aftercare for healing pathologic fracture of other bone

ICD-9-CM Procedural

93.53	Application of other cast
97.11	Replacement of cast on upper limb

HCPCS Level II Supplies & Services

A4580	Cast supplies (e.g., plaster)

29086

29086 Application, cast; finger (eg, contracture)

ICD-9-CM Diagnostic

718.74	Developmental dislocation of joint, hand
727.03	Trigger finger (acquired)
727.05	Other tenosynovitis of hand and wrist
728.6	Contracture of palmar fascia
736.1	Mallet finger
736.20	Unspecified deformity of finger ▽
736.21	Boutonniere deformity
736.22	Swan-neck deformity
736.29	Other acquired deformity of finger
816.00	Closed fracture of unspecified phalanx or phalanges of hand ▽
816.01	Closed fracture of middle or proximal phalanx or phalanges of hand
816.02	Closed fracture of distal phalanx or phalanges of hand
816.03	Closed fracture of multiple sites of phalanx or phalanges of hand
834.00	Closed dislocation of finger, unspecified part ▽
834.01	Closed dislocation of metacarpophalangeal (joint)
834.02	Closed dislocation of interphalangeal (joint), hand
842.12	Sprain and strain of metacarpophalangeal (joint) of hand
842.13	Sprain and strain of interphalangeal (joint) of hand
883.0	Open wound of finger(s), without mention of complication
883.1	Open wound of finger(s), complicated
883.2	Open wound of finger(s), with tendon involvement
927.3	Crushing injury of finger(s) — (Use additional code to identify any associated injuries: 800-829, 850.0-854.1, 860.0-869.1)
959.5	Injury, other and unspecified, finger
V54.19	Aftercare for healing traumatic fracture of other bone
V54.29	Aftercare for healing pathologic fracture of other bone

ICD-9-CM Procedural

93.53	Application of other cast

HCPCS Level II Supplies & Services

A4580	Cast supplies (e.g., plaster)

29105

29105 Application of long arm splint (shoulder to hand)

ICD-9-CM Diagnostic

357.1	Polyneuropathy in collagen vascular disease — (Code first underlying disease: 446.0, 710.0, 714.0) ☒
359.6	Symptomatic inflammatory myopathy in diseases classified elsewhere — (Code first underlying disease: 135, 140.0-208.9, 277.30-277.39, 446.0, 710.0, 710.1, 710.2, 714.0) ☒
446.0	Polyarteritis nodosa
710.0	Systemic lupus erythematosus — (Use additional code to identify manifestation: 424.91, 581.81, 582.81, 583.81)
710.1	Systemic sclerosis — (Use additional code to identify manifestation: 359.6, 517.2)
710.2	Sicca syndrome
714.0	Rheumatoid arthritis — (Use additional code to identify manifestation: 357.1, 359.6)
718.82	Other joint derangement, not elsewhere classified, upper arm
718.83	Other joint derangement, not elsewhere classified, forearm
726.30	Unspecified enthesopathy of elbow ▽
726.31	Medial epicondylitis of elbow
726.32	Lateral epicondylitis of elbow
726.33	Olecranon bursitis
726.39	Other enthesopathy of elbow region
726.90	Enthesopathy of unspecified site ▽
727.00	Unspecified synovitis and tenosynovitis ▽
727.05	Other tenosynovitis of hand and wrist
810.00	Unspecified part of closed fracture of clavicle ▽
812.00	Closed fracture of unspecified part of upper end of humerus ▽
812.01	Closed fracture of surgical neck of humerus
812.03	Closed fracture of greater tuberosity of humerus
812.09	Other closed fractures of upper end of humerus
812.20	Closed fracture of unspecified part of humerus ▽
812.21	Closed fracture of shaft of humerus
812.40	Closed fracture of unspecified part of lower end of humerus ▽
812.41	Closed fracture of supracondylar humerus
812.42	Closed fracture of lateral condyle of humerus
812.43	Closed fracture of medial condyle of humerus
812.44	Closed fracture of unspecified condyle(s) of humerus ▽
812.49	Other closed fracture of lower end of humerus
813.00	Unspecified fracture of radius and ulna, upper end of forearm, closed ▽

813.01 Closed fracture of olecranon process of ulna
813.02 Closed fracture of coronoid process of ulna
813.03 Closed Monteggia's fracture
813.04 Other and unspecified closed fractures of proximal end of ulna (alone) ▽
813.05 Closed fracture of head of radius
813.06 Closed fracture of neck of radius
813.07 Other and unspecified closed fractures of proximal end of radius (alone) ▽
813.08 Closed fracture of radius with ulna, upper end (any part)
813.21 Closed fracture of shaft of radius (alone)
813.22 Closed fracture of shaft of ulna (alone)
813.23 Closed fracture of shaft of radius with ulna
813.40 Unspecified closed fracture of lower end of forearm ▽
813.41 Closed Colles' fracture
813.42 Other closed fractures of distal end of radius (alone)
813.43 Closed fracture of distal end of ulna (alone)
813.44 Closed fracture of lower end of radius with ulna
813.45 Torus fracture of radius (alone)
813.46 Torus fracture of ulna (alone)
813.47 Torus fracture of radius and ulna
813.80 Closed fracture of unspecified part of forearm ▽
813.81 Closed fracture of unspecified part of radius (alone) ▽
813.82 Closed fracture of unspecified part of ulna (alone) ▽
813.83 Closed fracture of unspecified part of radius with ulna ▽
814.01 Closed fracture of navicular (scaphoid) bone of wrist
814.02 Closed fracture of lunate (semilunar) bone of wrist
814.03 Closed fracture of triquetral (cuneiform) bone of wrist
814.04 Closed fracture of pisiform bone of wrist
814.05 Closed fracture of trapezium bone (larger multangular) of wrist
814.06 Closed fracture of trapezoid bone (smaller multangular) of wrist
814.07 Closed fracture of capitate bone (os magnum) of wrist
814.08 Closed fracture of hamate (unciform) bone of wrist
815.00 Closed fracture of metacarpal bone(s), site unspecified ▽
815.01 Closed fracture of base of thumb (first) metacarpal bone(s)
815.02 Closed fracture of base of other metacarpal bone(s)
815.03 Closed fracture of shaft of metacarpal bone(s)
815.04 Closed fracture of neck of metacarpal bone(s)
815.09 Closed fracture of multiple sites of metacarpus
816.00 Closed fracture of unspecified phalanx or phalanges of hand ▽
816.01 Closed fracture of middle or proximal phalanx or phalanges of hand
816.02 Closed fracture of distal phalanx or phalanges of hand
817.0 Multiple closed fractures of hand bones
832.2 Nursemaid's elbow
842.11 Sprain and strain of carpometacarpal (joint) of hand
842.12 Sprain and strain of metacarpophalangeal (joint) of hand
842.13 Sprain and strain of interphalangeal (joint) of hand
923.10 Contusion of forearm
923.20 Contusion of hand(s)
923.21 Contusion of wrist
V54.10 Aftercare for healing traumatic fracture of arm, unspecified ▽
V54.11 Aftercare for healing traumatic fracture of upper arm
V54.12 Aftercare for healing traumatic fracture of lower arm
V54.20 Aftercare for healing pathologic fracture of arm, unspecified ▽
V54.21 Aftercare for healing pathologic fracture of upper arm
V54.22 Aftercare for healing pathologic fracture of lower arm

ICD-9-CM Procedural

93.54 Application of splint
97.14 Replacement of other device for musculoskeletal immobilization

HCPCS Level II Supplies & Services

A4570 Splint

29125-29126

29125 Application of short arm splint (forearm to hand); static
29126 dynamic

ICD-9-CM Diagnostic

354.0 Carpal tunnel syndrome
357.1 Polyneuropathy in collagen vascular disease — (Code first underlying disease: 446.0, 710.0, 714.0) ☒
359.6 Symptomatic inflammatory myopathy in diseases classified elsewhere — (Code first underlying disease: 135, 140.0-208.9, 277.30-277.39, 446.0, 710.0, 710.1, 710.2, 714.0) ☒
446.0 Polyarteritis nodosa
710.0 Systemic lupus erythematosus — (Use additional code to identify manifestation: 424.91, 581.81, 582.81, 583.81)
710.1 Systemic sclerosis — (Use additional code to identify manifestation: 359.6, 517.2)
710.2 Sicca syndrome
714.0 Rheumatoid arthritis — (Use additional code to identify manifestation: 357.1, 359.6)
715.14 Primary localized osteoarthrosis, hand
715.93 Osteoarthrosis, unspecified whether generalized or localized, forearm ▽
715.94 Osteoarthrosis, unspecified whether generalized or localized, hand ▽
718.83 Other joint derangement, not elsewhere classified, forearm
718.84 Other joint derangement, not elsewhere classified, hand
726.90 Enthesopathy of unspecified site ▽
727.05 Other tenosynovitis of hand and wrist
729.81 Swelling of limb
813.21 Closed fracture of shaft of radius (alone)
813.22 Closed fracture of shaft of ulna (alone)
813.23 Closed fracture of shaft of radius with ulna
813.40 Unspecified closed fracture of lower end of forearm ▽
813.41 Closed Colles' fracture
813.42 Other closed fractures of distal end of radius (alone)
813.43 Closed fracture of distal end of ulna (alone)
813.44 Closed fracture of lower end of radius with ulna
813.45 Torus fracture of radius (alone)
813.46 Torus fracture of ulna (alone)
813.47 Torus fracture of radius and ulna
813.80 Closed fracture of unspecified part of forearm ▽
813.81 Closed fracture of unspecified part of radius (alone) ▽
813.82 Closed fracture of unspecified part of ulna (alone) ▽
813.83 Closed fracture of unspecified part of radius with ulna ▽
814.01 Closed fracture of navicular (scaphoid) bone of wrist
814.02 Closed fracture of lunate (semilunar) bone of wrist
814.03 Closed fracture of triquetral (cuneiform) bone of wrist
814.04 Closed fracture of pisiform bone of wrist
814.05 Closed fracture of trapezium bone (larger multangular) of wrist
814.06 Closed fracture of trapezoid bone (smaller multangular) of wrist
814.07 Closed fracture of capitate bone (os magnum) of wrist
814.08 Closed fracture of hamate (unciform) bone of wrist
815.00 Closed fracture of metacarpal bone(s), site unspecified ▽
815.01 Closed fracture of base of thumb (first) metacarpal bone(s)
815.02 Closed fracture of base of other metacarpal bone(s)
815.03 Closed fracture of shaft of metacarpal bone(s)
815.04 Closed fracture of neck of metacarpal bone(s)
815.09 Closed fracture of multiple sites of metacarpus
816.00 Closed fracture of unspecified phalanx or phalanges of hand ▽
816.01 Closed fracture of middle or proximal phalanx or phalanges of hand

816.02 Closed fracture of distal phalanx or phalanges of hand
816.03 Closed fracture of multiple sites of phalanx or phalanges of hand
817.0 Multiple closed fractures of hand bones
818.0 Ill-defined closed fractures of upper limb
841.9 Sprain and strain of unspecified site of elbow and forearm ▽
842.00 Sprain and strain of unspecified site of wrist ▽
842.10 Sprain and strain of unspecified site of hand ▽
842.11 Sprain and strain of carpometacarpal (joint) of hand
842.12 Sprain and strain of metacarpophalangeal (joint) of hand
842.13 Sprain and strain of interphalangeal (joint) of hand
842.19 Other hand sprain and strain
923.10 Contusion of forearm
923.20 Contusion of hand(s)
923.21 Contusion of wrist
959.3 Injury, other and unspecified, elbow, forearm, and wrist
959.4 Injury, other and unspecified, hand, except finger
959.5 Injury, other and unspecified, finger
V54.10 Aftercare for healing traumatic fracture of arm, unspecified ▽
V54.12 Aftercare for healing traumatic fracture of lower arm
V54.20 Aftercare for healing pathologic fracture of arm, unspecified ▽
V54.22 Aftercare for healing pathologic fracture of lower arm
V67.4 Treatment of healed fracture follow-up examination

ICD-9-CM Procedural

93.54 Application of splint
97.14 Replacement of other device for musculoskeletal immobilization

HCPCS Level II Supplies & Services

A4570 Splint

29130-29131

29130 Application of finger splint; static
29131 dynamic

ICD-9-CM Diagnostic

718.74 Developmental dislocation of joint, hand
727.03 Trigger finger (acquired)
727.05 Other tenosynovitis of hand and wrist
728.6 Contracture of palmar fascia
736.1 Mallet finger
736.20 Unspecified deformity of finger ▽
736.21 Boutonniere deformity
736.22 Swan-neck deformity
736.29 Other acquired deformity of finger
816.00 Closed fracture of unspecified phalanx or phalanges of hand ▽
816.01 Closed fracture of middle or proximal phalanx or phalanges of hand
816.02 Closed fracture of distal phalanx or phalanges of hand
816.03 Closed fracture of multiple sites of phalanx or phalanges of hand
834.00 Closed dislocation of finger, unspecified part ▽
834.01 Closed dislocation of metacarpophalangeal (joint)
834.02 Closed dislocation of interphalangeal (joint), hand
842.12 Sprain and strain of metacarpophalangeal (joint) of hand
842.13 Sprain and strain of interphalangeal (joint) of hand
883.0 Open wound of finger(s), without mention of complication
883.1 Open wound of finger(s), complicated
883.2 Open wound of finger(s), with tendon involvement
927.3 Crushing injury of finger(s) — (Use additional code to identify any associated injuries: 800-829, 850.0-854.1, 860.0-869.1)
959.5 Injury, other and unspecified, finger
V54.19 Aftercare for healing traumatic fracture of other bone
V54.29 Aftercare for healing pathologic fracture of other bone

ICD-9-CM Procedural

93.54 Application of splint
97.14 Replacement of other device for musculoskeletal immobilization

HCPCS Level II Supplies & Services

A4570 Splint

29200

29200 Strapping; thorax

ICD-9-CM Diagnostic

807.01 Closed fracture of one rib
807.02 Closed fracture of two ribs
807.03 Closed fracture of three ribs
807.04 Closed fracture of four ribs
807.05 Closed fracture of five ribs
807.06 Closed fracture of six ribs
807.07 Closed fracture of seven ribs
807.08 Closed fracture of eight or more ribs
807.09 Closed fracture of multiple ribs, unspecified ▽
807.2 Closed fracture of sternum
839.21 Closed dislocation, thoracic vertebra
839.69 Closed dislocation, other location
848.8 Other specified sites of sprains and strains
V54.17 Aftercare for healing traumatic fracture of vertebrae
V54.19 Aftercare for healing traumatic fracture of other bone
V54.27 Aftercare for healing pathologic fracture of vertebrae
V54.29 Aftercare for healing pathologic fracture of other bone

ICD-9-CM Procedural

93.59 Other immobilization, pressure, and attention to wound
97.14 Replacement of other device for musculoskeletal immobilization

HCPCS Level II Supplies & Services

A4450 Tape, nonwaterproof, per 18 sq in

29240

29240 Strapping; shoulder (eg, Velpeau)

ICD-9-CM Diagnostic

718.31 Recurrent dislocation of shoulder joint
719.41 Pain in joint, shoulder region
719.81 Other specified disorders of shoulder joint
726.10 Unspecified disorders of bursae and tendons in shoulder region ▽
726.11 Calcifying tendinitis of shoulder
726.12 Bicipital tenosynovitis
726.19 Other specified disorders of rotator cuff syndrome of shoulder and allied disorders
726.2 Other affections of shoulder region, not elsewhere classified
810.03 Closed fracture of acromial end of clavicle
811.01 Closed fracture of acromial process of scapula
811.03 Closed fracture of glenoid cavity and neck of scapula
812.00 Closed fracture of unspecified part of upper end of humerus ▽
812.01 Closed fracture of surgical neck of humerus
812.02 Closed fracture of anatomical neck of humerus
812.03 Closed fracture of greater tuberosity of humerus
812.09 Other closed fractures of upper end of humerus
812.20 Closed fracture of unspecified part of humerus ▽
812.21 Closed fracture of shaft of humerus
812.40 Closed fracture of unspecified part of lower end of humerus ▽
812.41 Closed fracture of supracondylar humerus
840.0 Acromioclavicular (joint) (ligament) sprain and strain

840.1 Coracoclavicular (ligament) sprain and strain
840.2 Coracohumeral (ligament) sprain and strain
840.3 Infraspinatus (muscle) (tendon) sprain and strain
840.4 Rotator cuff (capsule) sprain and strain
840.5 Subscapularis (muscle) sprain and strain
840.6 Supraspinatus (muscle) (tendon) sprain and strain
840.7 Superior glenoid labrum lesions (SLAP)
840.8 Sprain and strain of other specified sites of shoulder and upper arm
840.9 Sprain and strain of unspecified site of shoulder and upper arm ♡
V54.11 Aftercare for healing traumatic fracture of upper arm
V54.19 Aftercare for healing traumatic fracture of other bone

ICD-9-CM Procedural

93.59 Other immobilization, pressure, and attention to wound
97.14 Replacement of other device for musculoskeletal immobilization

HCPCS Level II Supplies & Services

A4450 Tape, nonwaterproof, per 18 sq in

29260-29280

29260 Strapping; elbow or wrist
29280 hand or finger

ICD-9-CM Diagnostic

354.0 Carpal tunnel syndrome
715.94 Osteoarthrosis, unspecified whether generalized or localized, hand ♡
718.72 Developmental dislocation of joint, upper arm
718.73 Developmental dislocation of joint, forearm
718.74 Developmental dislocation of joint, hand
727.05 Other tenosynovitis of hand and wrist
814.01 Closed fracture of navicular (scaphoid) bone of wrist
815.00 Closed fracture of metacarpal bone(s), site unspecified ♡
815.01 Closed fracture of base of thumb (first) metacarpal bone(s)
815.02 Closed fracture of base of other metacarpal bone(s)
815.03 Closed fracture of shaft of metacarpal bone(s)
815.04 Closed fracture of neck of metacarpal bone(s)
815.09 Closed fracture of multiple sites of metacarpus
816.00 Closed fracture of unspecified phalanx or phalanges of hand ♡
816.01 Closed fracture of middle or proximal phalanx or phalanges of hand
816.02 Closed fracture of distal phalanx or phalanges of hand
816.03 Closed fracture of multiple sites of phalanx or phalanges of hand
817.0 Multiple closed fractures of hand bones
833.05 Closed dislocation of proximal end of metacarpal (bone)
834.00 Closed dislocation of finger, unspecified part ♡
834.01 Closed dislocation of metacarpophalangeal (joint)
834.02 Closed dislocation of interphalangeal (joint), hand
834.11 Open dislocation of metacarpophalangeal (joint)
841.0 Radial collateral ligament sprain and strain
841.1 Ulnar collateral ligament sprain and strain
841.2 Radiohumeral (joint) sprain and strain
841.3 Ulnohumeral (joint) sprain and strain
841.8 Sprain and strain of other specified sites of elbow and forearm
841.9 Sprain and strain of unspecified site of elbow and forearm ♡
842.00 Sprain and strain of unspecified site of wrist ♡
842.01 Sprain and strain of carpal (joint) of wrist
842.02 Sprain and strain of radiocarpal (joint) (ligament) of wrist
842.09 Other wrist sprain and strain
842.10 Sprain and strain of unspecified site of hand ♡
842.11 Sprain and strain of carpometacarpal (joint) of hand
842.12 Sprain and strain of metacarpophalangeal (joint) of hand
842.13 Sprain and strain of interphalangeal (joint) of hand
842.19 Other hand sprain and strain
927.20 Crushing injury of hand(s) — (Use additional code to identify any associated injuries: 800-829, 850.0-854.1, 860.0-869.1)
927.3 Crushing injury of finger(s) — (Use additional code to identify any associated injuries: 800-829, 850.0-854.1, 860.0-869.1)
959.4 Injury, other and unspecified, hand, except finger
959.5 Injury, other and unspecified, finger
V54.12 Aftercare for healing traumatic fracture of lower arm
V54.19 Aftercare for healing traumatic fracture of other bone

ICD-9-CM Procedural

93.59 Other immobilization, pressure, and attention to wound
97.14 Replacement of other device for musculoskeletal immobilization

HCPCS Level II Supplies & Services

A4450 Tape, nonwaterproof, per 18 sq in

29305-29325

29305 Application of hip spica cast; 1 leg
29325 1 and 1/2 spica or both legs

ICD-9-CM Diagnostic

718.45 Contracture of pelvic joint
718.46 Contracture of lower leg joint
736.89 Other acquired deformity of other parts of limb
754.30 Congenital dislocation of hip, unilateral
754.31 Congenital dislocation of hip, bilateral
754.32 Congenital subluxation of hip, unilateral
756.11 Congenital spondylolysis, lumbosacral region
820.8 Closed fracture of unspecified part of neck of femur ♡
821.00 Closed fracture of unspecified part of femur ♡
821.01 Closed fracture of shaft of femur
821.20 Closed fracture of unspecified part of lower end of femur ♡
827.0 Other, multiple and ill-defined closed fractures of lower limb
V54.13 Aftercare for healing traumatic fracture of hip
V54.14 Aftercare for healing traumatic fracture of leg, unspecified ♡
V54.15 Aftercare for healing traumatic fracture of upper leg
V54.19 Aftercare for healing traumatic fracture of other bone
V54.23 Aftercare for healing pathologic fracture of hip
V54.24 Aftercare for healing pathologic fracture of leg, unspecified ♡
V54.25 Aftercare for healing pathologic fracture of upper leg
V54.29 Aftercare for healing pathologic fracture of other bone

ICD-9-CM Procedural

93.53 Application of other cast
97.12 Replacement of cast on lower limb

HCPCS Level II Supplies & Services

A4580 Cast supplies (e.g., plaster)

29345-29355

29345 Application of long leg cast (thigh to toes);
29355 walker or ambulatory type

ICD-9-CM Diagnostic

718.46 Contracture of lower leg joint
718.76 Developmental dislocation of joint, lower leg
718.86 Other joint derangement, not elsewhere classified, lower leg
727.65 Nontraumatic rupture of quadriceps tendon
727.66 Nontraumatic rupture of patellar tendon
727.67 Nontraumatic rupture of Achilles tendon
727.68 Nontraumatic rupture of other tendons of foot and ankle

732.4 Juvenile osteochondrosis of lower extremity, excluding foot

733.81 Malunion of fracture

733.82 Nonunion of fracture

733.93 Stress fracture of tibia or fibula — (Use additional external cause code(s) to identify the cause of the stress fracture)

733.95 Stress fracture of other bone — (Use additional external cause code(s) to identify the cause of the stress fracture)

733.97 Stress fracture of shaft of femur — (Use additional external cause code(s) to identify the cause of the stress fracture)

821.01 Closed fracture of shaft of femur

821.20 Closed fracture of unspecified part of lower end of femur

821.21 Closed fracture of femoral condyle

821.22 Closed fracture of lower epiphysis of femur

821.23 Closed supracondylar fracture of femur

821.32 Open fracture of lower epiphysis of femur

821.33 Open supracondylar fracture of femur

822.0 Closed fracture of patella

823.00 Closed fracture of upper end of tibia

823.01 Closed fracture of upper end of fibula

823.02 Closed fracture of upper end of fibula with tibia

823.10 Open fracture of upper end of tibia

823.20 Closed fracture of shaft of tibia

823.21 Closed fracture of shaft of fibula

823.22 Closed fracture of shaft of fibula with tibia

823.30 Open fracture of shaft of tibia

823.32 Open fracture of shaft of fibula with tibia

823.40 Torus fracture of tibia alone

823.41 Torus fracture of fibula alone

823.42 Torus fracture of fibula with tibia

823.80 Closed fracture of unspecified part of tibia

823.81 Closed fracture of unspecified part of fibula

823.82 Closed fracture of unspecified part of fibula with tibia

823.90 Open fracture of unspecified part of tibia

823.91 Open fracture of unspecified part of fibula

823.92 Open fracture of unspecified part of fibula with tibia

836.0 Tear of medial cartilage or meniscus of knee, current

836.1 Tear of lateral cartilage or meniscus of knee, current

836.2 Other tear of cartilage or meniscus of knee, current

836.3 Closed dislocation of patella

836.50 Closed dislocation of knee, unspecified part

928.10 Crushing injury of lower leg — (Use additional code to identify any associated injuries: 800-829, 850.0-854.1, 860.0-869.1)

928.11 Crushing injury of knee — (Use additional code to identify any associated injuries: 800-829, 850.0-854.1, 860.0-869.1)

928.21 Crushing injury of ankle — (Use additional code to identify any associated injuries: 800-829, 850.0-854.1, 860.0-869.1)

V54.14 Aftercare for healing traumatic fracture of leg, unspecified

V54.15 Aftercare for healing traumatic fracture of upper leg

V54.16 Aftercare for healing traumatic fracture of lower leg

V54.19 Aftercare for healing traumatic fracture of other bone

V54.24 Aftercare for healing pathologic fracture of leg, unspecified

V54.25 Aftercare for healing pathologic fracture of upper leg

V54.26 Aftercare for healing pathologic fracture of lower leg

V54.29 Aftercare for healing pathologic fracture of other bone

V67.00 Follow-up examination, following unspecified surgery

V67.09 Follow-up examination, following other surgery

ICD-9-CM Procedural

93.53 Application of other cast

97.12 Replacement of cast on lower limb

HCPCS Level II Supplies & Services

A4580 Cast supplies (e.g., plaster)

29358

29358 Application of long leg cast brace

ICD-9-CM Diagnostic

718.76 Developmental dislocation of joint, lower leg

733.93 Stress fracture of tibia or fibula — (Use additional external cause code(s) to identify the cause of the stress fracture)

733.95 Stress fracture of other bone — (Use additional external cause code(s) to identify the cause of the stress fracture)

733.97 Stress fracture of shaft of femur — (Use additional external cause code(s) to identify the cause of the stress fracture)

821.01 Closed fracture of shaft of femur

821.20 Closed fracture of unspecified part of lower end of femur

821.21 Closed fracture of femoral condyle

821.22 Closed fracture of lower epiphysis of femur

821.23 Closed supracondylar fracture of femur

822.0 Closed fracture of patella

823.00 Closed fracture of upper end of tibia

823.01 Closed fracture of upper end of fibula

823.02 Closed fracture of upper end of fibula with tibia

823.20 Closed fracture of shaft of tibia

823.21 Closed fracture of shaft of fibula

823.22 Closed fracture of shaft of fibula with tibia

823.30 Open fracture of shaft of tibia

823.40 Torus fracture of tibia alone

823.41 Torus fracture of fibula alone

823.42 Torus fracture of fibula with tibia

823.80 Closed fracture of unspecified part of tibia

823.81 Closed fracture of unspecified part of fibula

823.82 Closed fracture of unspecified part of fibula with tibia

823.90 Open fracture of unspecified part of tibia

823.91 Open fracture of unspecified part of fibula

823.92 Open fracture of unspecified part of fibula with tibia

836.0 Tear of medial cartilage or meniscus of knee, current

836.1 Tear of lateral cartilage or meniscus of knee, current

836.2 Other tear of cartilage or meniscus of knee, current

836.3 Closed dislocation of patella

836.50 Closed dislocation of knee, unspecified part

V54.14 Aftercare for healing traumatic fracture of leg, unspecified

V54.15 Aftercare for healing traumatic fracture of upper leg

V54.16 Aftercare for healing traumatic fracture of lower leg

V54.19 Aftercare for healing traumatic fracture of other bone

V54.24 Aftercare for healing pathologic fracture of leg, unspecified

V54.25 Aftercare for healing pathologic fracture of upper leg

V54.26 Aftercare for healing pathologic fracture of lower leg

V54.29 Aftercare for healing pathologic fracture of other bone

V67.00 Follow-up examination, following unspecified surgery

V67.09 Follow-up examination, following other surgery

ICD-9-CM Procedural

93.53 Application of other cast

97.12 Replacement of cast on lower limb

HCPCS Level II Supplies & Services

A4580 Cast supplies (e.g., plaster)

29365

29365 Application of cylinder cast (thigh to ankle)

ICD-9-CM Diagnostic

- 715.16 Primary localized osteoarthrosis, lower leg
- 717.3 Other and unspecified derangement of medial meniscus ▼
- 717.7 Chondromalacia of patella
- 717.81 Old disruption of lateral collateral ligament
- 717.82 Old disruption of medial collateral ligament
- 717.83 Old disruption of anterior cruciate ligament
- 717.84 Old disruption of posterior cruciate ligament
- 717.85 Old disruption of other ligament of knee
- 717.89 Other internal derangement of knee
- 718.36 Recurrent dislocation of lower leg joint
- 718.76 Developmental dislocation of joint, lower leg
- 727.65 Nontraumatic rupture of quadriceps tendon
- 727.66 Nontraumatic rupture of patellar tendon
- 732.4 Juvenile osteochondrosis of lower extremity, excluding foot
- 733.93 Stress fracture of tibia or fibula — (Use additional external cause code(s) to identify the cause of the stress fracture)
- 733.95 Stress fracture of other bone — (Use additional external cause code(s) to identify the cause of the stress fracture)
- 733.97 Stress fracture of shaft of femur — (Use additional external cause code(s) to identify the cause of the stress fracture)
- 821.01 Closed fracture of shaft of femur
- 821.20 Closed fracture of unspecified part of lower end of femur ▼
- 821.21 Closed fracture of femoral condyle
- 821.22 Closed fracture of lower epiphysis of femur
- 821.23 Closed supracondylar fracture of femur
- 821.29 Other closed fracture of lower end of femur
- 821.30 Open fracture of unspecified part of lower end of femur ▼
- 821.31 Open fracture of femoral condyle
- 821.32 Open fracture of lower epiphysis of femur
- 821.33 Open supracondylar fracture of femur
- 821.39 Other open fracture of lower end of femur
- 822.0 Closed fracture of patella
- 823.00 Closed fracture of upper end of tibia
- 823.01 Closed fracture of upper end of fibula
- 823.02 Closed fracture of upper end of fibula with tibia
- 823.10 Open fracture of upper end of tibia
- 823.11 Open fracture of upper end of fibula
- 823.12 Open fracture of upper end of fibula with tibia
- 823.20 Closed fracture of shaft of tibia
- 823.21 Closed fracture of shaft of fibula
- 823.40 Torus fracture of tibia alone
- 823.41 Torus fracture of fibula alone
- 823.42 Torus fracture of fibula with tibia
- 823.80 Closed fracture of unspecified part of tibia ▼
- 823.81 Closed fracture of unspecified part of fibula ▼
- 823.82 Closed fracture of unspecified part of fibula with tibia ▼
- 823.90 Open fracture of unspecified part of tibia ▼
- 823.91 Open fracture of unspecified part of fibula ▼
- 823.92 Open fracture of unspecified part of fibula with tibia ▼
- 836.0 Tear of medial cartilage or meniscus of knee, current
- 836.2 Other tear of cartilage or meniscus of knee, current
- 836.3 Closed dislocation of patella
- 844.1 Sprain and strain of medial collateral ligament of knee
- 844.2 Sprain and strain of cruciate ligament of knee
- 928.10 Crushing injury of lower leg — (Use additional code to identify any associated injuries: 800-829, 850.0-854.1, 860.0-869.1)
- 928.11 Crushing injury of knee — (Use additional code to identify any associated injuries: 800-829, 850.0-854.1, 860.0-869.1)
- V54.14 Aftercare for healing traumatic fracture of leg, unspecified ▼
- V54.15 Aftercare for healing traumatic fracture of upper leg
- V54.16 Aftercare for healing traumatic fracture of lower leg
- V54.19 Aftercare for healing traumatic fracture of other bone
- V54.24 Aftercare for healing pathologic fracture of leg, unspecified ▼
- V54.25 Aftercare for healing pathologic fracture of upper leg
- V54.26 Aftercare for healing pathologic fracture of lower leg
- V54.29 Aftercare for healing pathologic fracture of other bone
- V67.00 Follow-up examination, following unspecified surgery ▼
- V67.09 Follow-up examination, following other surgery
- V67.4 Treatment of healed fracture follow-up examination

ICD-9-CM Procedural

- 93.53 Application of other cast
- 97.12 Replacement of cast on lower limb

HCPCS Level II Supplies & Services

- A4580 Cast supplies (e.g., plaster)

29405-29425

29405 Application of short leg cast (below knee to toes);
29425 walking or ambulatory type

ICD-9-CM Diagnostic

- 355.3 Lesion of lateral popliteal nerve
- 355.4 Lesion of medial popliteal nerve
- 355.5 Tarsal tunnel syndrome
- 355.6 Lesion of plantar nerve
- 718.07 Articular cartilage disorder, ankle and foot
- 718.17 Loose body in ankle and foot joint
- 718.27 Pathological dislocation of ankle and foot joint
- 718.37 Recurrent dislocation of ankle and foot joint
- 718.40 Contracture of joint, site unspecified ▼
- 718.47 Contracture of ankle and foot joint
- 718.57 Ankylosis of ankle and foot joint
- 718.77 Developmental dislocation of joint, ankle and foot
- 718.87 Other joint derangement, not elsewhere classified, ankle and foot
- 719.87 Other specified disorders of ankle and foot joint
- 726.71 Achilles bursitis or tendinitis
- 726.72 Tibialis tendinitis
- 726.73 Calcaneal spur
- 726.79 Other enthesopathy of ankle and tarsus
- 726.8 Other peripheral enthesopathies
- 726.90 Enthesopathy of unspecified site ▼
- 726.91 Exostosis of unspecified site ▼
- 727.00 Unspecified synovitis and tenosynovitis ▼
- 727.01 Synovitis and tenosynovitis in diseases classified elsewhere — (Code first underlying disease: 015.0-015.9) ☒
- 727.02 Giant cell tumor of tendon sheath
- 727.06 Tenosynovitis of foot and ankle
- 727.09 Other synovitis and tenosynovitis
- 727.1 Bunion
- 727.3 Other bursitis disorders
- 727.67 Nontraumatic rupture of Achilles tendon
- 727.68 Nontraumatic rupture of other tendons of foot and ankle
- 727.81 Contracture of tendon (sheath)
- 728.71 Plantar fascial fibromatosis

732.5	Juvenile osteochondrosis of foot
733.16	Pathologic fracture of tibia and fibula
733.19	Pathologic fracture of other specified site
733.21	Solitary bone cyst
733.22	Aneurysmal bone cyst
733.29	Other cyst of bone
733.44	Aseptic necrosis of talus — (Use additional code to identify major osseous defect, if applicable: 731.3)
733.49	Aseptic necrosis of other bone site — (Use additional code to identify major osseous defect, if applicable: 731.3)
733.81	Malunion of fracture
733.82	Nonunion of fracture
733.93	Stress fracture of tibia or fibula — (Use additional external cause code(s) to identify the cause of the stress fracture)
733.94	Stress fracture of the metatarsals — (Use additional external cause code(s) to identify the cause of the stress fracture)
733.95	Stress fracture of other bone — (Use additional external cause code(s) to identify the cause of the stress fracture)
733.99	Other disorders of bone and cartilage
735.0	Hallux valgus (acquired)
735.1	Hallux varus (acquired)
735.2	Hallux rigidus
735.3	Hallux malleus
735.4	Other hammer toe (acquired)
735.5	Claw toe (acquired)
735.8	Other acquired deformity of toe
736.71	Acquired equinovarus deformity
736.72	Equinus deformity of foot, acquired
736.73	Cavus deformity of foot, acquired
736.74	Claw foot, acquired
736.75	Cavovarus deformity of foot, acquired
736.76	Other acquired calcaneus deformity
736.79	Other acquired deformity of ankle and foot
736.81	Unequal leg length (acquired)
736.89	Other acquired deformity of other parts of limb
736.9	Acquired deformity of limb, site unspecified ▽
754.50	Congenital talipes varus
754.51	Congenital talipes equinovarus
754.52	Congenital metatarsus primus varus
754.53	Congenital metatarsus varus
754.59	Other congenital varus deformity of feet
754.60	Congenital talipes valgus
754.61	Congenital pes planus
754.62	Talipes calcaneovalgus
754.69	Other congenital valgus deformity of feet
754.70	Unspecified talipes ▽
754.71	Talipes cavus
754.79	Other congenital deformity of feet
755.66	Other congenital anomaly of toes
755.67	Congenital anomalies of foot, not elsewhere classified
755.69	Other congenital anomaly of lower limb, including pelvic girdle
755.8	Other specified congenital anomalies of unspecified limb
823.20	Closed fracture of shaft of tibia
823.21	Closed fracture of shaft of fibula
823.22	Closed fracture of shaft of fibula with tibia
823.30	Open fracture of shaft of tibia
823.31	Open fracture of shaft of fibula
823.32	Open fracture of shaft of fibula with tibia
823.40	Torus fracture of tibia alone
823.41	Torus fracture of fibula alone
823.42	Torus fracture of fibula with tibia
824.0	Closed fracture of medial malleolus
824.1	Open fracture of medial malleolus
824.2	Closed fracture of lateral malleolus
824.3	Open fracture of lateral malleolus
824.4	Closed bimalleolar fracture
824.5	Open bimalleolar fracture
824.6	Closed trimalleolar fracture
824.7	Open trimalleolar fracture
825.0	Closed fracture of calcaneus
825.1	Open fracture of calcaneus
825.21	Closed fracture of astragalus
825.22	Closed fracture of navicular (scaphoid) bone of foot
825.23	Closed fracture of cuboid bone
825.24	Closed fracture of cuneiform bone of foot
825.25	Closed fracture of metatarsal bone(s)
825.29	Other closed fracture of tarsal and metatarsal bones
825.31	Open fracture of astragalus
825.33	Open fracture of cuboid bone
825.34	Open fracture of cuneiform bone of foot,
825.35	Open fracture of metatarsal bone(s)
825.39	Other open fractures of tarsal and metatarsal bones
826.0	Closed fracture of one or more phalanges of foot
826.1	Open fracture of one or more phalanges of foot
827.0	Other, multiple and ill-defined closed fractures of lower limb
827.1	Other, multiple and ill-defined open fractures of lower limb
837.0	Closed dislocation of ankle
837.1	Open dislocation of ankle
838.01	Closed dislocation of tarsal (bone), joint unspecified ▽
838.02	Closed dislocation of midtarsal (joint)
838.03	Closed dislocation of tarsometatarsal (joint)
838.04	Closed dislocation of metatarsal (bone), joint unspecified ▽
838.05	Closed dislocation of metatarsophalangeal (joint)
838.06	Closed dislocation of interphalangeal (joint), foot
838.09	Closed dislocation of other part of foot
838.10	Open dislocation of foot, unspecified part ▽
838.11	Open dislocation of tarsal (bone), joint unspecified ▽
838.12	Open dislocation of midtarsal (joint)
838.13	Open dislocation of tarsometatarsal (joint)
838.14	Open dislocation of metatarsal (bone), joint unspecified ▽
838.15	Open dislocation of metatarsophalangeal (joint)
838.16	Open dislocation of interphalangeal (joint), foot
838.19	Open dislocation of other part of foot
845.01	Sprain and strain of deltoid (ligament) of ankle
845.02	Sprain and strain of calcaneofibular (ligament)
845.03	Sprain and strain of tibiofibular (ligament)
845.09	Other ankle sprain and strain
845.10	Sprain and strain of unspecified site of foot ▽
845.11	Sprain and strain of tarsometatarsal (joint) (ligament)
845.12	Sprain and strain of metatarsophalangeal (joint)
845.13	Sprain and strain of interphalangeal (joint), of toe
845.19	Other foot sprain and strain
891.0	Open wound of knee, leg (except thigh), and ankle, without mention of complication
891.1	Open wound of knee, leg (except thigh), and ankle, complicated
891.2	Open wound of knee, leg (except thigh), and ankle, with tendon involvement
892.0	Open wound of foot except toe(s) alone, without mention of complication
892.1	Open wound of foot except toe(s) alone, complicated
892.2	Open wound of foot except toe(s) alone, with tendon involvement

- 893.0 Open wound of toe(s), without mention of complication
- 893.1 Open wound of toe(s), complicated
- 893.2 Open wound of toe(s), with tendon involvement
- 894.0 Multiple and unspecified open wound of lower limb, without mention of complication
- 894.1 Multiple and unspecified open wound of lower limb, complicated
- 894.2 Multiple and unspecified open wound of lower limb, with tendon involvement
- 905.4 Late effect of fracture of lower extremities
- 928.10 Crushing injury of lower leg — (Use additional code to identify any associated injuries: 800-829, 850.0-854.1, 860.0-869.1)
- 928.20 Crushing injury of foot — (Use additional code to identify any associated injuries: 800-829, 850.0-854.1, 860.0-869.1)
- 928.21 Crushing injury of ankle — (Use additional code to identify any associated injuries: 800-829, 850.0-854.1, 860.0-869.1)
- 959.7 Injury, other and unspecified, knee, leg, ankle, and foot
- V54.16 Aftercare for healing traumatic fracture of lower leg
- V54.19 Aftercare for healing traumatic fracture of other bone
- V54.26 Aftercare for healing pathologic fracture of lower leg
- V54.29 Aftercare for healing pathologic fracture of other bone
- V54.89 Other orthopedic aftercare
- V67.00 Follow-up examination, following unspecified surgery
- V67.09 Follow-up examination, following other surgery

ICD-9-CM Procedural

- 93.53 Application of other cast
- 97.12 Replacement of cast on lower limb

HCPCS Level II Supplies & Services

- A4580 Cast supplies (e.g., plaster)

29435

29435 Application of patellar tendon bearing (PTB) cast

ICD-9-CM Diagnostic

- 717.83 Old disruption of anterior cruciate ligament
- 732.4 Juvenile osteochondrosis of lower extremity, excluding foot
- 733.93 Stress fracture of tibia or fibula — (Use additional external cause code(s) to identify the cause of the stress fracture)
- 823.20 Closed fracture of shaft of tibia
- 823.21 Closed fracture of shaft of fibula
- 823.22 Closed fracture of shaft of fibula with tibia
- 823.40 Torus fracture of tibia alone
- 823.41 Torus fracture of fibula alone
- 823.42 Torus fracture of fibula with tibia
- 823.80 Closed fracture of unspecified part of tibia
- 823.81 Closed fracture of unspecified part of fibula
- 823.82 Closed fracture of unspecified part of fibula with tibia
- 836.0 Tear of medial cartilage or meniscus of knee, current
- V54.16 Aftercare for healing traumatic fracture of lower leg
- V54.26 Aftercare for healing pathologic fracture of lower leg
- V54.89 Other orthopedic aftercare

ICD-9-CM Procedural

- 93.53 Application of other cast
- 97.12 Replacement of cast on lower limb

HCPCS Level II Supplies & Services

- A4580 Cast supplies (e.g., plaster)

29440

29440 Adding walker to previously applied cast

ICD-9-CM Diagnostic

- 733.93 Stress fracture of tibia or fibula — (Use additional external cause code(s) to identify the cause of the stress fracture)
- 733.94 Stress fracture of the metatarsals — (Use additional external cause code(s) to identify the cause of the stress fracture)
- 733.95 Stress fracture of other bone — (Use additional external cause code(s) to identify the cause of the stress fracture)
- 733.97 Stress fracture of shaft of femur — (Use additional external cause code(s) to identify the cause of the stress fracture)
- 733.99 Other disorders of bone and cartilage
- 822.0 Closed fracture of patella
- 822.1 Open fracture of patella
- 823.00 Closed fracture of upper end of tibia
- 823.01 Closed fracture of upper end of fibula
- 823.02 Closed fracture of upper end of fibula with tibia
- 823.10 Open fracture of upper end of tibia
- 823.11 Open fracture of upper end of fibula
- 823.12 Open fracture of upper end of fibula with tibia
- 823.20 Closed fracture of shaft of tibia
- 823.21 Closed fracture of shaft of fibula
- 823.22 Closed fracture of shaft of fibula with tibia
- 823.30 Open fracture of shaft of tibia
- 823.31 Open fracture of shaft of fibula
- 823.32 Open fracture of shaft of fibula with tibia
- 823.40 Torus fracture of tibia alone
- 823.41 Torus fracture of fibula alone
- 823.42 Torus fracture of fibula with tibia
- 823.80 Closed fracture of unspecified part of tibia
- 823.81 Closed fracture of unspecified part of fibula
- 823.82 Closed fracture of unspecified part of fibula with tibia
- 823.90 Open fracture of unspecified part of tibia
- 823.91 Open fracture of unspecified part of fibula
- 823.92 Open fracture of unspecified part of fibula with tibia
- 824.0 Closed fracture of medial malleolus
- 824.1 Open fracture of medial malleolus
- 824.2 Closed fracture of lateral malleolus
- 824.3 Open fracture of lateral malleolus
- 824.4 Closed bimalleolar fracture
- 824.5 Open bimalleolar fracture
- 824.6 Closed trimalleolar fracture
- 824.7 Open trimalleolar fracture
- 824.9 Unspecified open fracture of ankle
- V54.16 Aftercare for healing traumatic fracture of lower leg
- V54.19 Aftercare for healing traumatic fracture of other bone
- V54.26 Aftercare for healing pathologic fracture of lower leg
- V54.29 Aftercare for healing pathologic fracture of other bone
- V54.89 Other orthopedic aftercare

ICD-9-CM Procedural

- 93.59 Other immobilization, pressure, and attention to wound

HCPCS Level II Supplies & Services

- A4580 Cast supplies (e.g., plaster)

29445

29445 Application of rigid total contact leg cast

ICD-9-CM Diagnostic

454.0 Varicose veins of lower extremities with ulcer
454.1 Varicose veins of lower extremities with inflammation
454.2 Varicose veins of lower extremities with ulcer and inflammation
454.8 Varicose veins of the lower extremities with other complications
454.9 Asymptomatic varicose veins
459.10 Postphlebitic syndrome without complications
459.11 Postphlebitic syndrome with ulcer
459.12 Postphlebitic syndrome with inflammation
459.13 Postphlebitic syndrome with ulcer and inflammation
459.19 Postphlebitic syndrome with other complication
459.30 Chronic venous hypertension without complications
459.31 Chronic venous hypertension with ulcer
459.32 Chronic venous hypertension with inflammation
459.33 Chronic venous hypertension with ulcer and inflammation
459.39 Chronic venous hypertension with other complication
459.81 Unspecified venous (peripheral) insufficiency — (Use additional code for any associated ulceration: 707.10-707.19, 707.8, 707.9) ▽
707.06 Pressure ulcer, ankle — (Use additional code to identify pressure ulcer stage: 707.20-707.25)
707.09 Pressure ulcer, other site — (Use additional code to identify pressure ulcer stage: 707.20-707.25)
707.11 Ulcer of thigh — (Code, if applicable, any causal condition first: 249.80-249.81, 250.80-250.83, 440.23, 459.11, 459.13, 459.31, 459.33)

ICD-9-CM Procedural

93.53 Application of other cast
97.12 Replacement of cast on lower limb

HCPCS Level II Supplies & Services

A4580 Cast supplies (e.g., plaster)

29450

29450 Application of clubfoot cast with molding or manipulation, long or short leg

ICD-9-CM Diagnostic

736.71 Acquired equinovarus deformity
736.76 Other acquired calcaneus deformity
736.89 Other acquired deformity of other parts of limb
754.50 Congenital talipes varus
754.51 Congenital talipes equinovarus
754.52 Congenital metatarsus primus varus
754.53 Congenital metatarsus varus
754.59 Other congenital varus deformity of feet
754.60 Congenital talipes valgus
754.61 Congenital pes planus
754.62 Talipes calcaneovalgus
754.70 Unspecified talipes ▽
754.79 Other congenital deformity of feet
755.67 Congenital anomalies of foot, not elsewhere classified
V54.89 Other orthopedic aftercare

ICD-9-CM Procedural

93.53 Application of other cast
97.12 Replacement of cast on lower limb

HCPCS Level II Supplies & Services

A4580 Cast supplies (e.g., plaster)

29505

29505 Application of long leg splint (thigh to ankle or toes)

ICD-9-CM Diagnostic

717.7 Chondromalacia of patella
717.83 Old disruption of anterior cruciate ligament
718.36 Recurrent dislocation of lower leg joint
719.06 Effusion of lower leg joint
726.60 Unspecified enthesopathy of knee ▽
726.64 Patellar tendinitis
727.65 Nontraumatic rupture of quadriceps tendon
727.66 Nontraumatic rupture of patellar tendon
727.67 Nontraumatic rupture of Achilles tendon
732.4 Juvenile osteochondrosis of lower extremity, excluding foot
733.93 Stress fracture of tibia or fibula — (Use additional external cause code(s) to identify the cause of the stress fracture)
733.95 Stress fracture of other bone — (Use additional external cause code(s) to identify the cause of the stress fracture)
733.97 Stress fracture of shaft of femur — (Use additional external cause code(s) to identify the cause of the stress fracture)
754.42 Congenital bowing of femur
821.01 Closed fracture of shaft of femur
821.22 Closed fracture of lower epiphysis of femur
821.23 Closed supracondylar fracture of femur
822.0 Closed fracture of patella
822.1 Open fracture of patella
823.02 Closed fracture of upper end of fibula with tibia
823.10 Open fracture of upper end of tibia
823.32 Open fracture of shaft of fibula with tibia
836.0 Tear of medial cartilage or meniscus of knee, current
836.2 Other tear of cartilage or meniscus of knee, current
836.3 Closed dislocation of patella
836.60 Open dislocation of knee unspecified part ▽
844.0 Sprain and strain of lateral collateral ligament of knee
844.1 Sprain and strain of medial collateral ligament of knee
844.2 Sprain and strain of cruciate ligament of knee
844.3 Sprain and strain of tibiofibular (joint) (ligament) superior, of knee
844.8 Sprain and strain of other specified sites of knee and leg
844.9 Sprain and strain of unspecified site of knee and leg ▽
924.11 Contusion of knee
928.10 Crushing injury of lower leg — (Use additional code to identify any associated injuries: 800-829, 850.0-854.1, 860.0-869.1)
928.11 Crushing injury of knee — (Use additional code to identify any associated injuries: 800-829, 850.0-854.1, 860.0-869.1)
928.21 Crushing injury of ankle — (Use additional code to identify any associated injuries: 800-829, 850.0-854.1, 860.0-869.1)
V54.14 Aftercare for healing traumatic fracture of leg, unspecified ▽
V54.15 Aftercare for healing traumatic fracture of upper leg
V54.16 Aftercare for healing traumatic fracture of lower leg
V54.19 Aftercare for healing traumatic fracture of other bone
V54.24 Aftercare for healing pathologic fracture of leg, unspecified ▽
V54.25 Aftercare for healing pathologic fracture of upper leg
V54.26 Aftercare for healing pathologic fracture of lower leg
V54.29 Aftercare for healing pathologic fracture of other bone

ICD-9-CM Procedural

93.45 Thomas' splint traction
93.54 Application of splint
97.14 Replacement of other device for musculoskeletal immobilization

HCPCS Level II Supplies & Services

A4570 Splint

29515

29515 Application of short leg splint (calf to foot)

ICD-9-CM Diagnostic

718.87 Other joint derangement, not elsewhere classified, ankle and foot
727.67 Nontraumatic rupture of Achilles tendon
845.00 Unspecified site of ankle sprain and strain ▽
845.01 Sprain and strain of deltoid (ligament) of ankle
845.02 Sprain and strain of calcaneofibular (ligament)
845.03 Sprain and strain of tibiofibular (ligament)
845.09 Other ankle sprain and strain
928.21 Crushing injury of ankle — (Use additional code to identify any associated injuries: 800-829, 850.0-854.1, 860.0-869.1)
V54.16 Aftercare for healing traumatic fracture of lower leg
V54.19 Aftercare for healing traumatic fracture of other bone
V54.26 Aftercare for healing pathologic fracture of lower leg
V54.29 Aftercare for healing pathologic fracture of other bone

ICD-9-CM Procedural

93.54 Application of splint
97.14 Replacement of other device for musculoskeletal immobilization

HCPCS Level II Supplies & Services

A4570 Splint

29520

29520 Strapping; hip

ICD-9-CM Diagnostic

718.75 Developmental dislocation of joint, pelvic region and thigh
835.00 Closed dislocation of hip, unspecified site ▽
835.01 Closed posterior dislocation of hip
835.02 Closed obturator dislocation of hip
835.03 Other closed anterior dislocation of hip
843.0 Iliofemoral (ligament) sprain and strain
843.1 Ischiocapsular (ligament) sprain and strain
843.8 Sprain and strain of other specified sites of hip and thigh
843.9 Sprain and strain of unspecified site of hip and thigh ▽
V54.89 Other orthopedic aftercare

ICD-9-CM Procedural

93.59 Other immobilization, pressure, and attention to wound
97.14 Replacement of other device for musculoskeletal immobilization

HCPCS Level II Supplies & Services

A4450 Tape, nonwaterproof, per 18 sq in

29530

29530 Strapping; knee

ICD-9-CM Diagnostic

717.7 Chondromalacia of patella
717.81 Old disruption of lateral collateral ligament
717.82 Old disruption of medial collateral ligament
717.83 Old disruption of anterior cruciate ligament
718.36 Recurrent dislocation of lower leg joint
719.06 Effusion of lower leg joint
726.60 Unspecified enthesopathy of knee ▽
726.64 Patellar tendinitis
726.65 Prepatellar bursitis
729.4 Unspecified fasciitis ▽
729.81 Swelling of limb
836.0 Tear of medial cartilage or meniscus of knee, current
836.1 Tear of lateral cartilage or meniscus of knee, current
836.2 Other tear of cartilage or meniscus of knee, current
836.3 Closed dislocation of patella
844.0 Sprain and strain of lateral collateral ligament of knee
844.1 Sprain and strain of medial collateral ligament of knee
844.2 Sprain and strain of cruciate ligament of knee
844.3 Sprain and strain of tibiofibular (joint) (ligament) superior, of knee
844.8 Sprain and strain of other specified sites of knee and leg
844.9 Sprain and strain of unspecified site of knee and leg ▽
891.0 Open wound of knee, leg (except thigh), and ankle, without mention of complication
924.11 Contusion of knee
V54.89 Other orthopedic aftercare

ICD-9-CM Procedural

93.59 Other immobilization, pressure, and attention to wound
97.14 Replacement of other device for musculoskeletal immobilization

HCPCS Level II Supplies & Services

A4450 Tape, nonwaterproof, per 18 sq in

29540

29540 Strapping; ankle and/or foot

ICD-9-CM Diagnostic

718.37 Recurrent dislocation of ankle and foot joint
718.87 Other joint derangement, not elsewhere classified, ankle and foot
719.27 Villonodular synovitis, ankle and foot
726.70 Unspecified enthesopathy of ankle and tarsus ▽
726.73 Calcaneal spur
726.79 Other enthesopathy of ankle and tarsus
727.06 Tenosynovitis of foot and ankle
727.67 Nontraumatic rupture of Achilles tendon
727.68 Nontraumatic rupture of other tendons of foot and ankle
728.71 Plantar fascial fibromatosis
736.79 Other acquired deformity of ankle and foot
845.01 Sprain and strain of deltoid (ligament) of ankle
924.21 Contusion of ankle
959.7 Injury, other and unspecified, knee, leg, ankle, and foot
V54.89 Other orthopedic aftercare

ICD-9-CM Procedural

93.59 Other immobilization, pressure, and attention to wound
97.14 Replacement of other device for musculoskeletal immobilization

HCPCS Level II Supplies & Services

A4450 Tape, nonwaterproof, per 18 sq in

29550

29550 Strapping; toes

ICD-9-CM Diagnostic

681.11 Onychia and paronychia of toe — (Use additional code to identify organism: 041.1)
735.0 Hallux valgus (acquired)
735.1 Hallux varus (acquired)
735.2 Hallux rigidus
735.3 Hallux malleus
735.4 Other hammer toe (acquired)
735.5 Claw toe (acquired)
735.8 Other acquired deformity of toe

826.0 Closed fracture of one or more phalanges of foot
826.1 Open fracture of one or more phalanges of foot
845.10 Sprain and strain of unspecified site of foot
924.3 Contusion of toe
V54.19 Aftercare for healing traumatic fracture of other bone
V54.29 Aftercare for healing pathologic fracture of other bone
V54.89 Other orthopedic aftercare

ICD-9-CM Procedural

93.59 Other immobilization, pressure, and attention to wound
97.14 Replacement of other device for musculoskeletal immobilization

HCPCS Level II Supplies & Services

A4450 Tape, nonwaterproof, per 18 sq in

29580

29580 Strapping; Unna boot

ICD-9-CM Diagnostic

249.70 Secondary diabetes mellitus with peripheral circulatory disorders, not stated as uncontrolled, or unspecified — (Use additional code to identify manifestation: 443.81, 785.4) (Use additional code to identify any associated insulin use: V58.67)
249.71 Secondary diabetes mellitus with peripheral circulatory disorders, uncontrolled — (Use additional code to identify manifestation: 443.81, 785.4) (Use additional code to identify any associated insulin use: V58.67)
249.80 Secondary diabetes mellitus with other specified manifestations, not stated as uncontrolled, or unspecified — (Use additional code to identify manifestation: 707.10-707.19, 707.8, 707.9, 731.8) (Use additional code to identify any associated insulin use: V58.67)
249.81 Secondary diabetes mellitus with other specified manifestations, uncontrolled — (Use additional code to identify manifestation: 707.10-707.19, 707.8, 707.9, 731.8) (Use additional code to identify any associated insulin use: V58.67)
250.70 Diabetes with peripheral circulatory disorders, type II or unspecified type, not stated as uncontrolled — (Use additional code to identify manifestation: 443.81, 785.4)
250.71 Diabetes with peripheral circulatory disorders, type I [juvenile type], not stated as uncontrolled — (Use additional code to identify manifestation: 443.81, 785.4)
250.72 Diabetes with peripheral circulatory disorders, type II or unspecified type, uncontrolled — (Use additional code to identify manifestation: 443.81, 785.4)
250.73 Diabetes with peripheral circulatory disorders, type I [juvenile type], uncontrolled — (Use additional code to identify manifestation: 443.81, 785.4)
250.80 Diabetes with other specified manifestations, type II or unspecified type, not stated as uncontrolled — (Use additional code to identify manifestation: 707.10-707.19, 707.8, 707.9, 731.8)
250.81 Diabetes with other specified manifestations, type I [juvenile type], not stated as uncontrolled — (Use additional code to identify manifestation: 707.10-707.19, 707.8, 707.9, 731.8)
250.82 Diabetes with other specified manifestations, type II or unspecified type, uncontrolled — (Use additional code to identify manifestation: 707.10-707.19, 707.8, 707.9, 731.8)
250.83 Diabetes with other specified manifestations, type I [juvenile type], uncontrolled — (Use additional code to identify manifestation: 707.10-707.19, 707.8, 707.9, 731.8)
443.81 Peripheral angiopathy in diseases classified elsewhere — (Code first underlying disease: 249.7, 250.7)
443.9 Unspecified peripheral vascular disease
451.9 Phlebitis and thrombophlebitis of unspecified site — (Use additional E code to identify drug, if drug-induced)
454.0 Varicose veins of lower extremities with ulcer
454.1 Varicose veins of lower extremities with inflammation
454.2 Varicose veins of lower extremities with ulcer and inflammation
454.8 Varicose veins of the lower extremities with other complications
457.1 Other noninfectious lymphedema
459.10 Postphlebitic syndrome without complications
459.11 Postphlebitic syndrome with ulcer
459.12 Postphlebitic syndrome with inflammation
459.13 Postphlebitic syndrome with ulcer and inflammation
459.19 Postphlebitic syndrome with other complication
459.30 Chronic venous hypertension without complications
459.31 Chronic venous hypertension with ulcer
459.32 Chronic venous hypertension with inflammation
459.33 Chronic venous hypertension with ulcer and inflammation
459.39 Chronic venous hypertension with other complication
459.81 Unspecified venous (peripheral) insufficiency — (Use additional code for any associated ulceration: 707.10-707.19, 707.8, 707.9)
682.7 Cellulitis and abscess of foot, except toes — (Use additional code to identify organism, such as 041.1, etc.)
707.10 Ulcer of lower limb, unspecified — (Code, if applicable, any causal condition first: 249.80-249.81, 250.80-250.83, 440.23, 459.11, 459.13, 459.31, 459.33)
707.13 Ulcer of ankle — (Code, if applicable, any causal condition first: 249.80-249.81, 250.80-250.83, 440.23, 459.11, 459.13, 459.31, 459.33)
707.14 Ulcer of heel and midfoot — (Code, if applicable, any causal condition first: 249.80-249.81, 250.80-250.83, 440.23, 459.11, 459.13, 459.31, 459.33)
707.15 Ulcer of other part of foot — (Code, if applicable, any causal condition first: 249.80-249.81, 250.80-250.83, 440.23, 459.11, 459.13, 459.31, 459.33)
707.8 Chronic ulcer of other specified site
707.9 Chronic ulcer of unspecified site
728.71 Plantar fascial fibromatosis
731.8 Other bone involvement in diseases classified elsewhere — (Code first underlying disease: 249.8, 250.8. Use additional code to specify bone condition: 730.00-730.09)
782.3 Edema
785.4 Gangrene — (Code first any associated underlying condition)
891.0 Open wound of knee, leg (except thigh), and ankle, without mention of complication
891.1 Open wound of knee, leg (except thigh), and ankle, complicated
892.1 Open wound of foot except toe(s) alone, complicated
V54.89 Other orthopedic aftercare

ICD-9-CM Procedural

93.59 Other immobilization, pressure, and attention to wound
97.14 Replacement of other device for musculoskeletal immobilization

HCPCS Level II Supplies & Services

L3260 Surgical boot/shoe, each

29581-29584

29581 Application of multi-layer compression system; leg (below knee), including ankle and foot
29582 thigh and leg, including ankle and foot, when performed
29583 upper arm and forearm
29584 upper arm, forearm, hand, and fingers

ICD-9-CM Diagnostic

440.23 Atherosclerosis of native arteries of the extremities with ulceration — (Use additional code for any associated ulceration: 707.10-707.19, 707.8, 707.9)
454.0 Varicose veins of lower extremities with ulcer
454.2 Varicose veins of lower extremities with ulcer and inflammation
456.8 Varices of other sites
457.0 Postmastectomy lymphedema syndrome
457.1 Other noninfectious lymphedema
459.11 Postphlebitic syndrome with ulcer
459.13 Postphlebitic syndrome with ulcer and inflammation
459.31 Chronic venous hypertension with ulcer
459.33 Chronic venous hypertension with ulcer and inflammation
707.10 Ulcer of lower limb, unspecified — (Code, if applicable, any causal condition first: 249.80-249.81, 250.80-250.83, 440.23, 459.11, 459.13, 459.31, 459.33)

707.12 Ulcer of calf — (Code, if applicable, any causal condition first: 249.80-249.81, 250.80-250.83, 440.23, 459.11, 459.13, 459.31, 459.33)
707.13 Ulcer of ankle — (Code, if applicable, any causal condition first: 249.80-249.81, 250.80-250.83, 440.23, 459.11, 459.13, 459.31, 459.33)
707.14 Ulcer of heel and midfoot — (Code, if applicable, any causal condition first: 249.80-249.81, 250.80-250.83, 440.23, 459.11, 459.13, 459.31, 459.33)
707.15 Ulcer of other part of foot — (Code, if applicable, any causal condition first: 249.80-249.81, 250.80-250.83, 440.23, 459.11, 459.13, 459.31, 459.33)
707.19 Ulcer of other part of lower limb — (Code, if applicable, any causal condition first: 249.80-249.81, 250.80-250.83, 440.23, 459.11, 459.13, 459.31, 459.33)
707.8 Chronic ulcer of other specified site
729.81 Swelling of limb

ICD-9-CM Procedural

93.56 Application of pressure dressing
93.57 Application of other wound dressing
93.59 Other immobilization, pressure, and attention to wound
97.14 Replacement of other device for musculoskeletal immobilization

HCPCS Level II Supplies & Services

A6448 Light compression bandage, elastic, knitted/woven, width less than 3 in, per yd
A6449 Light compression bandage, elastic, knitted/woven, width greater than or equal to 3 in and less than 5 in, per yd
A6450 Light compression bandage, elastic, knitted/woven, width greater than or equal to 5 in, per yd
A6451 Moderate compression bandage, elastic, knitted/woven, load resistance of 1.25 to 1.34 ft lbs at 50% maximum stretch, width greater than or equal to 3 in and less than 5 in, per yd
A6452 High compression bandage, elastic, knitted/woven, load resistance greater than or equal to 1.35 ft lbs at 50% maximum stretch, width greater than or equal to 3 in and less than 5 in, per yd
A6453 Self-adherent bandage, elastic, nonknitted/nonwoven, width less than 3 in, per yd
A6454 Self-adherent bandage, elastic, nonknitted/nonwoven, width greater than or equal to 3 in and less than 5 in, per yd
A6455 Self-adherent bandage, elastic, nonknitted/nonwoven, width greater than or equal to 5 in, per yd
A6456 Zinc paste impregnated bandage, nonelastic, knitted/woven, width greater than or equal to 3 in and less than 5 in, per yd
A6545 Gradient compression wrap, nonelastic, below knee, 30-50 mm Hg, each

29700-29715

29700 Removal or bivalving; gauntlet, boot or body cast
29705 full arm or full leg cast
29710 shoulder or hip spica, Minerva, or Risser jacket, etc.
29715 turnbuckle jacket

ICD-9-CM Diagnostic

V54.10 Aftercare for healing traumatic fracture of arm, unspecified ▽
V54.11 Aftercare for healing traumatic fracture of upper arm
V54.12 Aftercare for healing traumatic fracture of lower arm
V54.13 Aftercare for healing traumatic fracture of hip
V54.14 Aftercare for healing traumatic fracture of leg, unspecified ▽
V54.15 Aftercare for healing traumatic fracture of upper leg
V54.16 Aftercare for healing traumatic fracture of lower leg
V54.19 Aftercare for healing traumatic fracture of other bone
V54.20 Aftercare for healing pathologic fracture of arm, unspecified ▽
V54.21 Aftercare for healing pathologic fracture of upper arm
V54.22 Aftercare for healing pathologic fracture of lower arm
V54.23 Aftercare for healing pathologic fracture of hip
V54.24 Aftercare for healing pathologic fracture of leg, unspecified ▽
V54.25 Aftercare for healing pathologic fracture of upper leg
V54.26 Aftercare for healing pathologic fracture of lower leg
V54.29 Aftercare for healing pathologic fracture of other bone
V54.89 Other orthopedic aftercare

ICD-9-CM Procedural

97.88 Removal of external immobilization device

HCPCS Level II Supplies & Services

A4649 Surgical supply; miscellaneous

29720

29720 Repair of spica, body cast or jacket

ICD-9-CM Diagnostic

V54.13 Aftercare for healing traumatic fracture of hip
V54.14 Aftercare for healing traumatic fracture of leg, unspecified ▽
V54.15 Aftercare for healing traumatic fracture of upper leg
V54.16 Aftercare for healing traumatic fracture of lower leg
V54.19 Aftercare for healing traumatic fracture of other bone
V54.23 Aftercare for healing pathologic fracture of hip
V54.24 Aftercare for healing pathologic fracture of leg, unspecified ▽
V54.25 Aftercare for healing pathologic fracture of upper leg
V54.26 Aftercare for healing pathologic fracture of lower leg
V54.29 Aftercare for healing pathologic fracture of other bone
V54.89 Other orthopedic aftercare

ICD-9-CM Procedural

93.59 Other immobilization, pressure, and attention to wound

HCPCS Level II Supplies & Services

A4580 Cast supplies (e.g., plaster)

29730-29750

29730 Windowing of cast
29740 Wedging of cast (except clubfoot casts)
29750 Wedging of clubfoot cast

ICD-9-CM Diagnostic

V54.10 Aftercare for healing traumatic fracture of arm, unspecified ▽
V54.11 Aftercare for healing traumatic fracture of upper arm
V54.12 Aftercare for healing traumatic fracture of lower arm
V54.13 Aftercare for healing traumatic fracture of hip
V54.14 Aftercare for healing traumatic fracture of leg, unspecified ▽
V54.15 Aftercare for healing traumatic fracture of upper leg
V54.16 Aftercare for healing traumatic fracture of lower leg
V54.19 Aftercare for healing traumatic fracture of other bone
V54.20 Aftercare for healing pathologic fracture of arm, unspecified ▽
V54.21 Aftercare for healing pathologic fracture of upper arm
V54.22 Aftercare for healing pathologic fracture of lower arm
V54.23 Aftercare for healing pathologic fracture of hip
V54.24 Aftercare for healing pathologic fracture of leg, unspecified ▽
V54.25 Aftercare for healing pathologic fracture of upper leg
V54.26 Aftercare for healing pathologic fracture of lower leg
V54.29 Aftercare for healing pathologic fracture of other bone
V54.89 Other orthopedic aftercare

ICD-9-CM Procedural

93.59 Other immobilization, pressure, and attention to wound

HCPCS Level II Supplies & Services

A4580 Cast supplies (e.g., plaster)

Endoscopy/Arthroscopy

29800

29800 Arthroscopy, temporomandibular joint, diagnostic, with or without synovial biopsy (separate procedure)

ICD-9-CM Diagnostic

170.0 Malignant neoplasm of bones of skull and face, except mandible
524.29 Other anomalies of dental arch relationship
524.60 Unspecified temporomandibular joint disorders ▽
524.61 Adhesions and ankylosis (bony or fibrous) of temporomandibular joint
524.62 Arthralgia of temporomandibular joint
524.63 Articular disc disorder (reducing or non-reducing) of temporomandibular joint
524.64 Temporomandibular joint sounds on opening and/or closing the jaw
524.69 Other specified temporomandibular joint disorders
525.8 Other specified disorders of the teeth and supporting structures
526.1 Fissural cysts of jaw
714.0 Rheumatoid arthritis — (Use additional code to identify manifestation: 357.1, 359.6)
830.0 Closed dislocation of jaw

ICD-9-CM Procedural

76.19 Other diagnostic procedures on facial bones and joints
76.99 Other operations on facial bones and joints

HCPCS Level II Supplies & Services

A4305 Disposable drug delivery system, flow rate of 50 ml or greater per hour

29804

29804 Arthroscopy, temporomandibular joint, surgical

ICD-9-CM Diagnostic

524.02 Mandibular hyperplasia
524.04 Mandibular hypoplasia
524.11 Maxillary asymmetry
524.59 Other dentofacial functional abnormalities
524.61 Adhesions and ankylosis (bony or fibrous) of temporomandibular joint
524.62 Arthralgia of temporomandibular joint
524.63 Articular disc disorder (reducing or non-reducing) of temporomandibular joint
524.64 Temporomandibular joint sounds on opening and/or closing the jaw
524.69 Other specified temporomandibular joint disorders
714.0 Rheumatoid arthritis — (Use additional code to identify manifestation: 357.1, 359.6)
830.0 Closed dislocation of jaw
830.1 Open dislocation of jaw

ICD-9-CM Procedural

76.99 Other operations on facial bones and joints

HCPCS Level II Supplies & Services

A4305 Disposable drug delivery system, flow rate of 50 ml or greater per hour

29805

29805 Arthroscopy, shoulder, diagnostic, with or without synovial biopsy (separate procedure)

ICD-9-CM Diagnostic

171.2 Malignant neoplasm of connective and other soft tissue of upper limb, including shoulder
195.4 Malignant neoplasm of upper limb
198.89 Secondary malignant neoplasm of other specified sites
215.2 Other benign neoplasm of connective and other soft tissue of upper limb, including shoulder
238.0 Neoplasm of uncertain behavior of bone and articular cartilage
238.1 Neoplasm of uncertain behavior of connective and other soft tissue
275.40 Unspecified disorder of calcium metabolism — (Use additional code to identify any associated intellectual disabilities) ▽
275.41 Hypocalcemia — (Use additional code to identify any associated intellectual disabilities)
275.42 Hypercalcemia — (Use additional code to identify any associated intellectual disabilities)
275.49 Other disorders of calcium metabolism — (Use additional code to identify any associated intellectual disabilities)
275.5 Hungry bone syndrome — (Use additional code to identify any associated intellectual disabilities)
357.1 Polyneuropathy in collagen vascular disease — (Code first underlying disease: 446.0, 710.0, 714.0) ☒
359.6 Symptomatic inflammatory myopathy in diseases classified elsewhere — (Code first underlying disease: 135, 140.0-208.9, 277.30-277.39, 446.0, 710.0, 710.1, 710.2, 714.0) ☒
446.0 Polyarteritis nodosa
710.0 Systemic lupus erythematosus — (Use additional code to identify manifestation: 424.91, 581.81, 582.81, 583.81)
710.1 Systemic sclerosis — (Use additional code to identify manifestation: 359.6, 517.2)
710.2 Sicca syndrome
711.01 Pyogenic arthritis, shoulder region — (Use additional code to identify infectious organism: 041.0-041.8)
712.11 Chondrocalcinosis due to dicalcium phosphate crystals, shoulder region — (Code first underlying disease: 275.4) ☒
712.21 Chondrocalcinosis due to pyrophosphate crystals, shoulder region — (Code first underlying disease: 275.4) ☒
714.0 Rheumatoid arthritis — (Use additional code to identify manifestation: 357.1, 359.6)
715.11 Primary localized osteoarthrosis, shoulder region
715.21 Secondary localized osteoarthrosis, shoulder region
715.91 Osteoarthrosis, unspecified whether generalized or localized, shoulder region ▽
716.11 Traumatic arthropathy, shoulder region
716.91 Unspecified arthropathy, shoulder region ▽
718.01 Articular cartilage disorder, shoulder region
718.21 Pathological dislocation of shoulder joint
718.31 Recurrent dislocation of shoulder joint
718.41 Contracture of shoulder joint
718.71 Developmental dislocation of joint, shoulder region
718.81 Other joint derangement, not elsewhere classified, shoulder region
719.01 Effusion of shoulder joint
719.11 Hemarthrosis, shoulder region
719.21 Villonodular synovitis, shoulder region
719.31 Palindromic rheumatism, shoulder region
719.41 Pain in joint, shoulder region
719.51 Stiffness of joint, not elsewhere classified, shoulder region
719.81 Other specified disorders of shoulder joint
726.0 Adhesive capsulitis of shoulder
726.11 Calcifying tendinitis of shoulder
726.12 Bicipital tenosynovitis
726.13 Partial tear of rotator cuff
726.19 Other specified disorders of rotator cuff syndrome of shoulder and allied disorders
726.2 Other affections of shoulder region, not elsewhere classified
727.61 Complete rupture of rotator cuff
755.59 Other congenital anomaly of upper limb, including shoulder girdle
831.00 Closed dislocation of shoulder, unspecified site ▽
831.01 Closed anterior dislocation of humerus
831.03 Closed inferior dislocation of humerus
840.0 Acromioclavicular (joint) (ligament) sprain and strain
840.1 Coracoclavicular (ligament) sprain and strain
840.2 Coracohumeral (ligament) sprain and strain
840.3 Infraspinatus (muscle) (tendon) sprain and strain

840.4 Rotator cuff (capsule) sprain and strain
840.5 Subscapularis (muscle) sprain and strain
840.6 Supraspinatus (muscle) (tendon) sprain and strain
840.9 Sprain and strain of unspecified site of shoulder and upper arm ▽
905.2 Late effect of fracture of upper extremities
905.6 Late effect of dislocation

ICD-9-CM Procedural

80.21 Arthroscopy of shoulder
80.31 Biopsy of joint structure of shoulder

29806

29806 Arthroscopy, shoulder, surgical; capsulorrhaphy

ICD-9-CM Diagnostic

718.21 Pathological dislocation of shoulder joint
718.31 Recurrent dislocation of shoulder joint
831.00 Closed dislocation of shoulder, unspecified site ▽
831.01 Closed anterior dislocation of humerus
831.02 Closed posterior dislocation of humerus
831.03 Closed inferior dislocation of humerus
831.10 Open unspecified dislocation of shoulder ▽
831.11 Open anterior dislocation of humerus
831.12 Open posterior dislocation of humerus
831.13 Open inferior dislocation of humerus
840.2 Coracohumeral (ligament) sprain and strain
840.4 Rotator cuff (capsule) sprain and strain
840.5 Subscapularis (muscle) sprain and strain

ICD-9-CM Procedural

81.93 Suture of capsule or ligament of upper extremity

29807

29807 Arthroscopy, shoulder, surgical; repair of SLAP lesion

ICD-9-CM Diagnostic

718.31 Recurrent dislocation of shoulder joint
840.7 Superior glenoid labrum lesions (SLAP)

ICD-9-CM Procedural

81.96 Other repair of joint

29819

29819 Arthroscopy, shoulder, surgical; with removal of loose body or foreign body

ICD-9-CM Diagnostic

275.40 Unspecified disorder of calcium metabolism — (Use additional code to identify any associated intellectual disabilities) ▽
275.42 Hypercalcemia — (Use additional code to identify any associated intellectual disabilities)
275.49 Other disorders of calcium metabolism — (Use additional code to identify any associated intellectual disabilities)
718.01 Articular cartilage disorder, shoulder region
718.11 Loose body in shoulder joint
729.6 Residual foreign body in soft tissue — (Use additional code to identify foreign body (V90.01-V90.9))

ICD-9-CM Procedural

80.21 Arthroscopy of shoulder

29820-29821

29820 Arthroscopy, shoulder, surgical; synovectomy, partial
29821 synovectomy, complete

ICD-9-CM Diagnostic

170.4 Malignant neoplasm of scapula and long bones of upper limb
171.2 Malignant neoplasm of connective and other soft tissue of upper limb, including shoulder
195.4 Malignant neoplasm of upper limb
213.4 Benign neoplasm of scapula and long bones of upper limb
215.2 Other benign neoplasm of connective and other soft tissue of upper limb, including shoulder
238.0 Neoplasm of uncertain behavior of bone and articular cartilage
239.2 Neoplasms of unspecified nature of bone, soft tissue, and skin
275.41 Hypocalcemia — (Use additional code to identify any associated intellectual disabilities)
275.42 Hypercalcemia — (Use additional code to identify any associated intellectual disabilities)
275.5 Hungry bone syndrome — (Use additional code to identify any associated intellectual disabilities)
357.1 Polyneuropathy in collagen vascular disease — (Code first underlying disease: 446.0, 710.0, 714.0) ☒
359.6 Symptomatic inflammatory myopathy in diseases classified elsewhere — (Code first underlying disease: 135, 140.0-208.9, 277.30-277.39, 446.0, 710.0, 710.1, 710.2, 714.0) ☒
446.0 Polyarteritis nodosa
710.0 Systemic lupus erythematosus — (Use additional code to identify manifestation: 424.91, 581.81, 582.81, 583.81)
710.1 Systemic sclerosis — (Use additional code to identify manifestation: 359.6, 517.2)
710.2 Sicca syndrome
712.11 Chondrocalcinosis due to dicalcium phosphate crystals, shoulder region — (Code first underlying disease: 275.4) ☒
712.12 Chondrocalcinosis due to dicalcium phosphate crystals, upper arm — (Code first underlying disease: 275.4) ☒
714.0 Rheumatoid arthritis — (Use additional code to identify manifestation: 357.1, 359.6)
715.11 Primary localized osteoarthrosis, shoulder region
719.21 Villonodular synovitis, shoulder region
726.0 Adhesive capsulitis of shoulder
726.11 Calcifying tendinitis of shoulder
726.12 Bicipital tenosynovitis
727.00 Unspecified synovitis and tenosynovitis ▽

ICD-9-CM Procedural

80.71 Synovectomy of shoulder

29822-29823

29822 Arthroscopy, shoulder, surgical; debridement, limited
29823 debridement, extensive

ICD-9-CM Diagnostic

357.1 Polyneuropathy in collagen vascular disease — (Code first underlying disease: 446.0, 710.0, 714.0) ☒
359.6 Symptomatic inflammatory myopathy in diseases classified elsewhere — (Code first underlying disease: 135, 140.0-208.9, 277.30-277.39, 446.0, 710.0, 710.1, 710.2, 714.0) ☒
446.0 Polyarteritis nodosa
710.0 Systemic lupus erythematosus — (Use additional code to identify manifestation: 424.91, 581.81, 582.81, 583.81)
710.1 Systemic sclerosis — (Use additional code to identify manifestation: 359.6, 517.2)
710.2 Sicca syndrome
714.0 Rheumatoid arthritis — (Use additional code to identify manifestation: 357.1, 359.6)
715.11 Primary localized osteoarthrosis, shoulder region
715.31 Localized osteoarthrosis not specified whether primary or secondary, shoulder region

715.91 Osteoarthrosis, unspecified whether generalized or localized, shoulder region ▽
716.01 Kaschin-Beck disease, shoulder region
716.11 Traumatic arthropathy, shoulder region
718.01 Articular cartilage disorder, shoulder region
718.31 Recurrent dislocation of shoulder joint
718.81 Other joint derangement, not elsewhere classified, shoulder region
719.01 Effusion of shoulder joint
719.21 Villonodular synovitis, shoulder region
719.41 Pain in joint, shoulder region
726.0 Adhesive capsulitis of shoulder
726.10 Unspecified disorders of bursae and tendons in shoulder region ▽
726.11 Calcifying tendinitis of shoulder
726.12 Bicipital tenosynovitis
726.19 Other specified disorders of rotator cuff syndrome of shoulder and allied disorders
726.2 Other affections of shoulder region, not elsewhere classified
727.00 Unspecified synovitis and tenosynovitis ▽
733.90 Disorder of bone and cartilage, unspecified ▽
840.0 Acromioclavicular (joint) (ligament) sprain and strain
840.4 Rotator cuff (capsule) sprain and strain
840.6 Supraspinatus (muscle) (tendon) sprain and strain
840.8 Sprain and strain of other specified sites of shoulder and upper arm

ICD-9-CM Procedural

80.81 Other local excision or destruction of lesion of shoulder joint

29824

29824 Arthroscopy, shoulder, surgical; distal claviculectomy including distal articular surface (Mumford procedure)

ICD-9-CM Diagnostic

170.3 Malignant neoplasm of ribs, sternum, and clavicle
196.3 Secondary and unspecified malignant neoplasm of lymph nodes of axilla and upper limb
198.5 Secondary malignant neoplasm of bone and bone marrow
198.89 Secondary malignant neoplasm of other specified sites
213.3 Benign neoplasm of ribs, sternum, and clavicle
238.0 Neoplasm of uncertain behavior of bone and articular cartilage
239.2 Neoplasms of unspecified nature of bone, soft tissue, and skin
715.11 Primary localized osteoarthrosis, shoulder region
715.21 Secondary localized osteoarthrosis, shoulder region
716.11 Traumatic arthropathy, shoulder region
716.61 Unspecified monoarthritis, shoulder region ▽
718.01 Articular cartilage disorder, shoulder region
718.31 Recurrent dislocation of shoulder joint
728.86 Necrotizing fasciitis — (Use additional code to identify infectious organism, 041.00-041.89, 785.4, if applicable)
730.11 Chronic osteomyelitis, shoulder region — (Use additional code to identify organism: 041.1. Use additional code to identify major osseous defect, if applicable: 731.3)
731.3 Major osseous defects — (Code first underlying disease: 170.0-170.9, 730.00-730.29, 733.00-733.09, 733.40-733.49, 996.45)
733.49 Aseptic necrosis of other bone site — (Use additional code to identify major osseous defect, if applicable: 731.3)
733.90 Disorder of bone and cartilage, unspecified ▽
738.8 Acquired musculoskeletal deformity of other specified site
785.4 Gangrene — (Code first any associated underlying condition)
831.04 Closed dislocation of acromioclavicular (joint)

ICD-9-CM Procedural

77.81 Other partial ostectomy of scapula, clavicle, and thorax (ribs and sternum)

29825

29825 Arthroscopy, shoulder, surgical; with lysis and resection of adhesions, with or without manipulation

ICD-9-CM Diagnostic

357.1 Polyneuropathy in collagen vascular disease — (Code first underlying disease: 446.0, 710.0, 714.0) ☒
359.6 Symptomatic inflammatory myopathy in diseases classified elsewhere — (Code first underlying disease: 135, 140.0-208.9, 277.30-277.39, 446.0, 710.0, 710.1, 710.2, 714.0) ☒
446.0 Polyarteritis nodosa
710.0 Systemic lupus erythematosus — (Use additional code to identify manifestation: 424.91, 581.81, 582.81, 583.81)
710.1 Systemic sclerosis — (Use additional code to identify manifestation: 359.6, 517.2)
710.2 Sicca syndrome
714.0 Rheumatoid arthritis — (Use additional code to identify manifestation: 357.1, 359.6)
715.11 Primary localized osteoarthrosis, shoulder region
715.31 Localized osteoarthrosis not specified whether primary or secondary, shoulder region
715.91 Osteoarthrosis, unspecified whether generalized or localized, shoulder region ▽
716.11 Traumatic arthropathy, shoulder region
718.31 Recurrent dislocation of shoulder joint
718.41 Contracture of shoulder joint
718.51 Ankylosis of joint of shoulder region
726.0 Adhesive capsulitis of shoulder
726.10 Unspecified disorders of bursae and tendons in shoulder region ▽
726.11 Calcifying tendinitis of shoulder
726.12 Bicipital tenosynovitis
726.19 Other specified disorders of rotator cuff syndrome of shoulder and allied disorders
726.2 Other affections of shoulder region, not elsewhere classified
840.0 Acromioclavicular (joint) (ligament) sprain and strain
840.4 Rotator cuff (capsule) sprain and strain
840.6 Supraspinatus (muscle) (tendon) sprain and strain
840.9 Sprain and strain of unspecified site of shoulder and upper arm ▽

ICD-9-CM Procedural

80.41 Division of joint capsule, ligament, or cartilage of shoulder

29826

29826 Arthroscopy, shoulder, surgical; decompression of subacromial space with partial acromioplasty, with coracoacromial ligament (ie, arch) release, when performed (List separately in addition to code for primary procedure)

ICD-9-CM Diagnostic

353.0 Brachial plexus lesions
715.11 Primary localized osteoarthrosis, shoulder region
715.21 Secondary localized osteoarthrosis, shoulder region
715.31 Localized osteoarthrosis not specified whether primary or secondary, shoulder region
715.91 Osteoarthrosis, unspecified whether generalized or localized, shoulder region ▽
716.11 Traumatic arthropathy, shoulder region
718.01 Articular cartilage disorder, shoulder region
718.31 Recurrent dislocation of shoulder joint
718.51 Ankylosis of joint of shoulder region
718.81 Other joint derangement, not elsewhere classified, shoulder region
726.0 Adhesive capsulitis of shoulder
726.10 Unspecified disorders of bursae and tendons in shoulder region ▽
726.11 Calcifying tendinitis of shoulder
726.12 Bicipital tenosynovitis
726.13 Partial tear of rotator cuff
726.19 Other specified disorders of rotator cuff syndrome of shoulder and allied disorders
726.2 Other affections of shoulder region, not elsewhere classified
727.61 Complete rupture of rotator cuff

840.0 Acromioclavicular (joint) (ligament) sprain and strain
840.4 Rotator cuff (capsule) sprain and strain
840.8 Sprain and strain of other specified sites of shoulder and upper arm

ICD-9-CM Procedural

81.82 Repair of recurrent dislocation of shoulder
81.83 Other repair of shoulder

29827

29827 Arthroscopy, shoulder, surgical; with rotator cuff repair

ICD-9-CM Diagnostic

715.10 Primary localized osteoarthrosis, unspecified site ▽
715.11 Primary localized osteoarthrosis, shoulder region
715.21 Secondary localized osteoarthrosis, shoulder region
715.31 Localized osteoarthrosis not specified whether primary or secondary, shoulder region
716.11 Traumatic arthropathy, shoulder region
716.61 Unspecified monoarthritis, shoulder region ▽
719.41 Pain in joint, shoulder region
726.10 Unspecified disorders of bursae and tendons in shoulder region ▽
726.13 Partial tear of rotator cuff
727.61 Complete rupture of rotator cuff
831.00 Closed dislocation of shoulder, unspecified site ▽
831.01 Closed anterior dislocation of humerus
831.02 Closed posterior dislocation of humerus
831.03 Closed inferior dislocation of humerus
840.4 Rotator cuff (capsule) sprain and strain
927.00 Crushing injury of shoulder region — (Use additional code to identify any associated injuries: 800-829, 850.0-854.1, 860.0-869.1)
959.2 Injury, other and unspecified, shoulder and upper arm

ICD-9-CM Procedural

83.63 Rotator cuff repair

HCPCS Level II Supplies & Services

Q4113 GRAFTJACKET XPRESS, injectable, 1cc

29828

29828 Arthroscopy, shoulder, surgical; biceps tenodesis

ICD-9-CM Diagnostic

170.4 Malignant neoplasm of scapula and long bones of upper limb
195.4 Malignant neoplasm of upper limb
213.4 Benign neoplasm of scapula and long bones of upper limb
215.2 Other benign neoplasm of connective and other soft tissue of upper limb, including shoulder
238.0 Neoplasm of uncertain behavior of bone and articular cartilage
239.2 Neoplasms of unspecified nature of bone, soft tissue, and skin
275.40 Unspecified disorder of calcium metabolism — (Use additional code to identify any associated intellectual disabilities) ▽
275.41 Hypocalcemia — (Use additional code to identify any associated intellectual disabilities)
275.42 Hypercalcemia — (Use additional code to identify any associated intellectual disabilities)
275.49 Other disorders of calcium metabolism — (Use additional code to identify any associated intellectual disabilities)
275.5 Hungry bone syndrome — (Use additional code to identify any associated intellectual disabilities)
357.1 Polyneuropathy in collagen vascular disease — (Code first underlying disease: 446.0, 710.0, 714.0) ☒
359.6 Symptomatic inflammatory myopathy in diseases classified elsewhere — (Code first underlying disease: 135, 140.0-208.9, 277.30-277.39, 446.0, 710.0, 710.1, 710.2, 714.0) ☒
446.0 Polyarteritis nodosa
710.0 Systemic lupus erythematosus — (Use additional code to identify manifestation: 424.91, 581.81, 582.81, 583.81)
710.1 Systemic sclerosis — (Use additional code to identify manifestation: 359.6, 517.2)
710.2 Sicca syndrome
711.01 Pyogenic arthritis, shoulder region — (Use additional code to identify infectious organism: 041.0-041.8)
712.11 Chondrocalcinosis due to dicalcium phosphate crystals, shoulder region — (Code first underlying disease: 275.4) ☒
712.21 Chondrocalcinosis due to pyrophosphate crystals, shoulder region — (Code first underlying disease: 275.4) ☒
714.0 Rheumatoid arthritis — (Use additional code to identify manifestation: 357.1, 359.6)
715.10 Primary localized osteoarthrosis, unspecified site ▽
715.11 Primary localized osteoarthrosis, shoulder region
715.21 Secondary localized osteoarthrosis, shoulder region
715.31 Localized osteoarthrosis not specified whether primary or secondary, shoulder region
715.91 Osteoarthrosis, unspecified whether generalized or localized, shoulder region ▽
716.11 Traumatic arthropathy, shoulder region
716.61 Unspecified monoarthritis, shoulder region ▽
716.91 Unspecified arthropathy, shoulder region ▽
718.01 Articular cartilage disorder, shoulder region
718.21 Pathological dislocation of shoulder joint
718.31 Recurrent dislocation of shoulder joint
718.41 Contracture of shoulder joint
718.71 Developmental dislocation of joint, shoulder region
718.81 Other joint derangement, not elsewhere classified, shoulder region
718.91 Unspecified derangement, shoulder region ▽
719.01 Effusion of shoulder joint
719.11 Hemarthrosis, shoulder region
719.21 Villonodular synovitis, shoulder region
719.31 Palindromic rheumatism, shoulder region
719.41 Pain in joint, shoulder region
719.51 Stiffness of joint, not elsewhere classified, shoulder region
719.61 Other symptoms referable to shoulder joint
719.81 Other specified disorders of shoulder joint
726.0 Adhesive capsulitis of shoulder
726.10 Unspecified disorders of bursae and tendons in shoulder region ▽
726.11 Calcifying tendinitis of shoulder
726.12 Bicipital tenosynovitis
726.13 Partial tear of rotator cuff
726.19 Other specified disorders of rotator cuff syndrome of shoulder and allied disorders
726.2 Other affections of shoulder region, not elsewhere classified
727.61 Complete rupture of rotator cuff
727.62 Nontraumatic rupture of tendons of biceps (long head)
755.59 Other congenital anomaly of upper limb, including shoulder girdle
831.00 Closed dislocation of shoulder, unspecified site ▽
831.01 Closed anterior dislocation of humerus
831.02 Closed posterior dislocation of humerus
831.03 Closed inferior dislocation of humerus
840.0 Acromioclavicular (joint) (ligament) sprain and strain
840.1 Coracoclavicular (ligament) sprain and strain
840.2 Coracohumeral (ligament) sprain and strain
840.3 Infraspinatus (muscle) (tendon) sprain and strain
840.4 Rotator cuff (capsule) sprain and strain
840.5 Subscapularis (muscle) sprain and strain
840.6 Supraspinatus (muscle) (tendon) sprain and strain
840.8 Sprain and strain of other specified sites of shoulder and upper arm
840.9 Sprain and strain of unspecified site of shoulder and upper arm ▽
880.20 Open wound of shoulder region, with tendon involvement

905.2 Late effect of fracture of upper extremities
905.6 Late effect of dislocation
927.00 Crushing injury of shoulder region — (Use additional code to identify any associated injuries: 800-829, 850.0-854.1, 860.0-869.1)
927.03 Crushing injury of upper arm — (Use additional code to identify any associated injuries: 800-829, 850.0-854.1, 860.0-869.1)
959.2 Injury, other and unspecified, shoulder and upper arm

ICD-9-CM Procedural

81.96 Other repair of joint
83.01 Exploration of tendon sheath
83.13 Other tenotomy
83.42 Other tenonectomy
83.61 Suture of tendon sheath
83.62 Delayed suture of tendon
83.64 Other suture of tendon
83.71 Advancement of tendon
83.72 Recession of tendon
83.73 Reattachment of tendon
83.75 Tendon transfer or transplantation
83.76 Other tendon transposition
83.88 Other plastic operations on tendon

29830

29830 Arthroscopy, elbow, diagnostic, with or without synovial biopsy (separate procedure)

ICD-9-CM Diagnostic

170.4 Malignant neoplasm of scapula and long bones of upper limb
171.2 Malignant neoplasm of connective and other soft tissue of upper limb, including shoulder
195.4 Malignant neoplasm of upper limb
213.4 Benign neoplasm of scapula and long bones of upper limb
215.2 Other benign neoplasm of connective and other soft tissue of upper limb, including shoulder
229.8 Benign neoplasm of other specified sites
232.6 Carcinoma in situ of skin of upper limb, including shoulder
238.0 Neoplasm of uncertain behavior of bone and articular cartilage
238.1 Neoplasm of uncertain behavior of connective and other soft tissue
239.2 Neoplasms of unspecified nature of bone, soft tissue, and skin
275.40 Unspecified disorder of calcium metabolism — (Use additional code to identify any associated intellectual disabilities) ▽
275.41 Hypocalcemia — (Use additional code to identify any associated intellectual disabilities)
275.42 Hypercalcemia — (Use additional code to identify any associated intellectual disabilities)
275.49 Other disorders of calcium metabolism — (Use additional code to identify any associated intellectual disabilities)
275.5 Hungry bone syndrome — (Use additional code to identify any associated intellectual disabilities)
357.1 Polyneuropathy in collagen vascular disease — (Code first underlying disease: 446.0, 710.0, 714.0) ☒
359.6 Symptomatic inflammatory myopathy in diseases classified elsewhere — (Code first underlying disease: 135, 140.0-208.9, 277.30-277.39, 446.0, 710.0, 710.1, 710.2, 714.0) ☒
446.0 Polyarteritis nodosa
710.0 Systemic lupus erythematosus — (Use additional code to identify manifestation: 424.91, 581.81, 582.81, 583.81)
710.1 Systemic sclerosis — (Use additional code to identify manifestation: 359.6, 517.2)
710.2 Sicca syndrome
714.0 Rheumatoid arthritis — (Use additional code to identify manifestation: 357.1, 359.6)
715.12 Primary localized osteoarthrosis, upper arm
715.22 Secondary localized osteoarthrosis, upper arm
716.12 Traumatic arthropathy, upper arm
718.02 Articular cartilage disorder, upper arm
718.22 Pathological dislocation of upper arm joint
718.32 Recurrent dislocation of upper arm joint
718.42 Contracture of upper arm joint
719.22 Villonodular synovitis, upper arm
727.00 Unspecified synovitis and tenosynovitis ▽

ICD-9-CM Procedural

80.22 Arthroscopy of elbow
80.32 Biopsy of joint structure of elbow

HCPCS Level II Supplies & Services

A4305 Disposable drug delivery system, flow rate of 50 ml or greater per hour

29834

29834 Arthroscopy, elbow, surgical; with removal of loose body or foreign body

ICD-9-CM Diagnostic

718.02 Articular cartilage disorder, upper arm
718.12 Loose body in upper arm joint
729.6 Residual foreign body in soft tissue — (Use additional code to identify foreign body (V90.01-V90.9))
733.99 Other disorders of bone and cartilage

ICD-9-CM Procedural

80.22 Arthroscopy of elbow

HCPCS Level II Supplies & Services

A4305 Disposable drug delivery system, flow rate of 50 ml or greater per hour

29835-29836

29835 Arthroscopy, elbow, surgical; synovectomy, partial
29836 synovectomy, complete

ICD-9-CM Diagnostic

275.40 Unspecified disorder of calcium metabolism — (Use additional code to identify any associated intellectual disabilities) ▽
275.41 Hypocalcemia — (Use additional code to identify any associated intellectual disabilities)
275.49 Other disorders of calcium metabolism — (Use additional code to identify any associated intellectual disabilities)
275.5 Hungry bone syndrome — (Use additional code to identify any associated intellectual disabilities)
357.1 Polyneuropathy in collagen vascular disease — (Code first underlying disease: 446.0, 710.0, 714.0) ☒
359.6 Symptomatic inflammatory myopathy in diseases classified elsewhere — (Code first underlying disease: 135, 140.0-208.9, 277.30-277.39, 446.0, 710.0, 710.1, 710.2, 714.0) ☒
446.0 Polyarteritis nodosa
710.0 Systemic lupus erythematosus — (Use additional code to identify manifestation: 424.91, 581.81, 582.81, 583.81)
710.1 Systemic sclerosis — (Use additional code to identify manifestation: 359.6, 517.2)
710.2 Sicca syndrome
712.12 Chondrocalcinosis due to dicalcium phosphate crystals, upper arm — (Code first underlying disease: 275.4) ☒
712.22 Chondrocalcinosis due to pyrophosphate crystals, upper arm — (Code first underlying disease: 275.4) ☒
714.0 Rheumatoid arthritis — (Use additional code to identify manifestation: 357.1, 359.6)
715.12 Primary localized osteoarthrosis, upper arm
718.32 Recurrent dislocation of upper arm joint
718.82 Other joint derangement, not elsewhere classified, upper arm
719.12 Hemarthrosis, upper arm
719.22 Villonodular synovitis, upper arm

727.00 Unspecified synovitis and tenosynovitis ▽

ICD-9-CM Procedural

80.72 Synovectomy of elbow

HCPCS Level II Supplies & Services

A4305 Disposable drug delivery system, flow rate of 50 ml or greater per hour

29837-29838

29837 Arthroscopy, elbow, surgical; debridement, limited
29838 debridement, extensive

ICD-9-CM Diagnostic

275.41 Hypocalcemia — (Use additional code to identify any associated intellectual disabilities)
275.42 Hypercalcemia — (Use additional code to identify any associated intellectual disabilities)
275.5 Hungry bone syndrome — (Use additional code to identify any associated intellectual disabilities)
357.1 Polyneuropathy in collagen vascular disease — (Code first underlying disease: 446.0, 710.0, 714.0) ☒
359.6 Symptomatic inflammatory myopathy in diseases classified elsewhere — (Code first underlying disease: 135, 140.0-208.9, 277.30-277.39, 446.0, 710.0, 710.1, 710.2, 714.0) ☒
446.0 Polyarteritis nodosa
710.0 Systemic lupus erythematosus — (Use additional code to identify manifestation: 424.91, 581.81, 582.81, 583.81)
710.1 Systemic sclerosis — (Use additional code to identify manifestation: 359.6, 517.2)
710.2 Sicca syndrome
712.12 Chondrocalcinosis due to dicalcium phosphate crystals, upper arm — (Code first underlying disease: 275.4) ☒
712.22 Chondrocalcinosis due to pyrophosphate crystals, upper arm — (Code first underlying disease: 275.4) ☒
714.0 Rheumatoid arthritis — (Use additional code to identify manifestation: 357.1, 359.6)
715.12 Primary localized osteoarthrosis, upper arm
718.22 Pathological dislocation of upper arm joint
718.32 Recurrent dislocation of upper arm joint
718.82 Other joint derangement, not elsewhere classified, upper arm
719.22 Villonodular synovitis, upper arm
727.00 Unspecified synovitis and tenosynovitis ▽

ICD-9-CM Procedural

80.82 Other local excision or destruction of lesion of elbow joint

HCPCS Level II Supplies & Services

A4305 Disposable drug delivery system, flow rate of 50 ml or greater per hour

29840

29840 Arthroscopy, wrist, diagnostic, with or without synovial biopsy (separate procedure)

ICD-9-CM Diagnostic

170.5 Malignant neoplasm of short bones of upper limb
171.2 Malignant neoplasm of connective and other soft tissue of upper limb, including shoulder
198.5 Secondary malignant neoplasm of bone and bone marrow
198.89 Secondary malignant neoplasm of other specified sites
213.5 Benign neoplasm of short bones of upper limb
215.2 Other benign neoplasm of connective and other soft tissue of upper limb, including shoulder
238.0 Neoplasm of uncertain behavior of bone and articular cartilage
238.1 Neoplasm of uncertain behavior of connective and other soft tissue
239.2 Neoplasms of unspecified nature of bone, soft tissue, and skin
275.40 Unspecified disorder of calcium metabolism — (Use additional code to identify any associated intellectual disabilities) ▽
275.42 Hypercalcemia — (Use additional code to identify any associated intellectual disabilities)
275.49 Other disorders of calcium metabolism — (Use additional code to identify any associated intellectual disabilities)
357.1 Polyneuropathy in collagen vascular disease — (Code first underlying disease: 446.0, 710.0, 714.0) ☒
359.6 Symptomatic inflammatory myopathy in diseases classified elsewhere — (Code first underlying disease: 135, 140.0-208.9, 277.30-277.39, 446.0, 710.0, 710.1, 710.2, 714.0) ☒
446.0 Polyarteritis nodosa
710.0 Systemic lupus erythematosus — (Use additional code to identify manifestation: 424.91, 581.81, 582.81, 583.81)
710.1 Systemic sclerosis — (Use additional code to identify manifestation: 359.6, 517.2)
710.2 Sicca syndrome
714.0 Rheumatoid arthritis — (Use additional code to identify manifestation: 357.1, 359.6)
715.23 Secondary localized osteoarthrosis, forearm
716.13 Traumatic arthropathy, forearm
718.03 Articular cartilage disorder, forearm
718.23 Pathological dislocation of forearm joint
718.33 Recurrent dislocation of forearm joint
718.43 Contracture of forearm joint
718.73 Developmental dislocation of joint, forearm
719.23 Villonodular synovitis, forearm
727.09 Other synovitis and tenosynovitis

ICD-9-CM Procedural

80.23 Arthroscopy of wrist
80.33 Biopsy of joint structure of wrist

HCPCS Level II Supplies & Services

A4305 Disposable drug delivery system, flow rate of 50 ml or greater per hour

29843

29843 Arthroscopy, wrist, surgical; for infection, lavage and drainage

ICD-9-CM Diagnostic

711.03 Pyogenic arthritis, forearm — (Use additional code to identify infectious organism: 041.0-041.8)
711.43 Arthropathy associated with other bacterial diseases, forearm — (Code first underlying disease, such as diseases classifiable to 010-040 (except 036.82), 090-099 (except 098.50)) ☒
711.53 Arthropathy associated with other viral diseases, forearm — (Code first underlying disease: 045-049, 050-079, 480, 487) ☒
711.63 Arthropathy associated with mycoses, forearm — (Code first underlying disease: 110.0-118) ☒
711.83 Arthropathy associated with other infectious and parasitic diseases, forearm — (Code first underlying disease: 080-088, 100-104, 130-136) ☒
711.93 Unspecified infective arthritis, forearm ▽
996.67 Infection and inflammatory reaction due to other internal orthopedic device, implant, and graft — (Use additional code to identify specified infections)
996.69 Infection and inflammatory reaction due to other internal prosthetic device, implant, and graft — (Use additional code to identify specified infections)
998.51 Infected postoperative seroma — (Use additional code to identify organism)
998.59 Other postoperative infection — (Use additional code to identify infection)

ICD-9-CM Procedural

80.23 Arthroscopy of wrist

HCPCS Level II Supplies & Services

A4305 Disposable drug delivery system, flow rate of 50 ml or greater per hour

29844-29845

29844 Arthroscopy, wrist, surgical; synovectomy, partial
29845 synovectomy, complete

ICD-9-CM Diagnostic

171.2 Malignant neoplasm of connective and other soft tissue of upper limb, including shoulder
198.89 Secondary malignant neoplasm of other specified sites
215.2 Other benign neoplasm of connective and other soft tissue of upper limb, including shoulder
238.1 Neoplasm of uncertain behavior of connective and other soft tissue
239.2 Neoplasms of unspecified nature of bone, soft tissue, and skin
275.40 Unspecified disorder of calcium metabolism — (Use additional code to identify any associated intellectual disabilities) ▼
275.41 Hypocalcemia — (Use additional code to identify any associated intellectual disabilities)
275.49 Other disorders of calcium metabolism — (Use additional code to identify any associated intellectual disabilities)
275.5 Hungry bone syndrome — (Use additional code to identify any associated intellectual disabilities)
357.1 Polyneuropathy in collagen vascular disease — (Code first underlying disease: 446.0, 710.0, 714.0) ☒
359.6 Symptomatic inflammatory myopathy in diseases classified elsewhere — (Code first underlying disease: 135, 140.0-208.9, 277.30-277.39, 446.0, 710.0, 710.1, 710.2, 714.0) ☒
446.0 Polyarteritis nodosa
710.0 Systemic lupus erythematosus — (Use additional code to identify manifestation: 424.91, 581.81, 582.81, 583.81)
710.1 Systemic sclerosis — (Use additional code to identify manifestation: 359.6, 517.2)
710.2 Sicca syndrome
712.12 Chondrocalcinosis due to dicalcium phosphate crystals, upper arm — (Code first underlying disease: 275.4) ☒
712.23 Chondrocalcinosis due to pyrophosphate crystals, forearm — (Code first underlying disease: 275.4) ☒
714.0 Rheumatoid arthritis — (Use additional code to identify manifestation: 357.1, 359.6)
715.13 Primary localized osteoarthrosis, forearm
719.23 Villonodular synovitis, forearm
727.00 Unspecified synovitis and tenosynovitis ▼

ICD-9-CM Procedural

80.73 Synovectomy of wrist

HCPCS Level II Supplies & Services

A4305 Disposable drug delivery system, flow rate of 50 ml or greater per hour

29846

29846 Arthroscopy, wrist, surgical; excision and/or repair of triangular fibrocartilage and/or joint debridement

ICD-9-CM Diagnostic

718.03 Articular cartilage disorder, forearm
718.83 Other joint derangement, not elsewhere classified, forearm

ICD-9-CM Procedural

80.83 Other local excision or destruction of lesion of wrist joint
81.96 Other repair of joint

HCPCS Level II Supplies & Services

A4305 Disposable drug delivery system, flow rate of 50 ml or greater per hour

29847

29847 Arthroscopy, wrist, surgical; internal fixation for fracture or instability

ICD-9-CM Diagnostic

718.83 Other joint derangement, not elsewhere classified, forearm
718.93 Unspecified derangement, forearm joint ▼
733.12 Pathologic fracture of distal radius and ulna
733.81 Malunion of fracture
733.82 Nonunion of fracture
813.40 Unspecified closed fracture of lower end of forearm ▼
813.41 Closed Colles' fracture
813.42 Other closed fractures of distal end of radius (alone)
813.43 Closed fracture of distal end of ulna (alone)
813.44 Closed fracture of lower end of radius with ulna
813.45 Torus fracture of radius (alone)
813.46 Torus fracture of ulna (alone)
813.47 Torus fracture of radius and ulna
V54.12 Aftercare for healing traumatic fracture of lower arm
V54.22 Aftercare for healing pathologic fracture of lower arm

ICD-9-CM Procedural

78.59 Internal fixation of other bone, except facial bones, without fracture reduction

HCPCS Level II Supplies & Services

A4305 Disposable drug delivery system, flow rate of 50 ml or greater per hour

29848

29848 Endoscopy, wrist, surgical, with release of transverse carpal ligament

ICD-9-CM Diagnostic

354.0 Carpal tunnel syndrome

ICD-9-CM Procedural

04.43 Release of carpal tunnel

HCPCS Level II Supplies & Services

A4305 Disposable drug delivery system, flow rate of 50 ml or greater per hour

29850-29851

29850 Arthroscopically aided treatment of intercondylar spine(s) and/or tuberosity fracture(s) of the knee, with or without manipulation; without internal or external fixation (includes arthroscopy)
29851 with internal or external fixation (includes arthroscopy)

ICD-9-CM Diagnostic

717.81 Old disruption of lateral collateral ligament
717.82 Old disruption of medial collateral ligament
717.83 Old disruption of anterior cruciate ligament
717.84 Old disruption of posterior cruciate ligament
733.16 Pathologic fracture of tibia and fibula
733.93 Stress fracture of tibia or fibula — (Use additional external cause code(s) to identify the cause of the stress fracture)
823.00 Closed fracture of upper end of tibia
823.02 Closed fracture of upper end of fibula with tibia
823.10 Open fracture of upper end of tibia
823.12 Open fracture of upper end of fibula with tibia
836.2 Other tear of cartilage or meniscus of knee, current
844.9 Sprain and strain of unspecified site of knee and leg ▼

ICD-9-CM Procedural

78.17 Application of external fixator device, tibia and fibula
79.26 Open reduction of fracture of tibia and fibula without internal fixation
79.36 Open reduction of fracture of tibia and fibula with internal fixation
84.71 Application of external fixator device, monoplanar system
84.72 Application of external fixator device, ring system
84.73 Application of hybrid external fixator device

29855-29856

29855 Arthroscopically aided treatment of tibial fracture, proximal (plateau); unicondylar, includes internal fixation, when performed (includes arthroscopy)

29856 bicondylar, includes internal fixation, when performed (includes arthroscopy)

ICD-9-CM Diagnostic

733.16 Pathologic fracture of tibia and fibula
733.93 Stress fracture of tibia or fibula — (Use additional external cause code(s) to identify the cause of the stress fracture)
823.00 Closed fracture of upper end of tibia
823.02 Closed fracture of upper end of fibula with tibia
823.10 Open fracture of upper end of tibia
823.12 Open fracture of upper end of fibula with tibia

ICD-9-CM Procedural

79.26 Open reduction of fracture of tibia and fibula without internal fixation
79.36 Open reduction of fracture of tibia and fibula with internal fixation

29860

29860 Arthroscopy, hip, diagnostic with or without synovial biopsy (separate procedure)

ICD-9-CM Diagnostic

171.3 Malignant neoplasm of connective and other soft tissue of lower limb, including hip
198.89 Secondary malignant neoplasm of other specified sites
215.3 Other benign neoplasm of connective and other soft tissue of lower limb, including hip
238.1 Neoplasm of uncertain behavior of connective and other soft tissue
239.2 Neoplasms of unspecified nature of bone, soft tissue, and skin
275.40 Unspecified disorder of calcium metabolism — (Use additional code to identify any associated intellectual disabilities)
275.42 Hypercalcemia — (Use additional code to identify any associated intellectual disabilities)
275.49 Other disorders of calcium metabolism — (Use additional code to identify any associated intellectual disabilities)
275.5 Hungry bone syndrome — (Use additional code to identify any associated intellectual disabilities)
711.05 Pyogenic arthritis, pelvic region and thigh — (Use additional code to identify infectious organism: 041.0-041.8)
714.0 Rheumatoid arthritis — (Use additional code to identify manifestation: 357.1, 359.6)
715.15 Primary localized osteoarthrosis, pelvic region and thigh
716.95 Unspecified arthropathy, pelvic region and thigh
718.05 Articular cartilage disorder, pelvic region and thigh
718.15 Loose body in pelvic joint
718.35 Recurrent dislocation of pelvic region and thigh joint
718.75 Developmental dislocation of joint, pelvic region and thigh
719.25 Villonodular synovitis, pelvic region and thigh
719.45 Pain in joint, pelvic region and thigh
719.95 Unspecified disorder of joint of pelvic region and thigh
726.5 Enthesopathy of hip region
727.00 Unspecified synovitis and tenosynovitis
732.1 Juvenile osteochondrosis of hip and pelvis
732.9 Unspecified osteochondropathy
733.90 Disorder of bone and cartilage, unspecified
733.92 Chondromalacia
733.99 Other disorders of bone and cartilage
820.01 Closed fracture of epiphysis (separation) (upper) of neck of femur
835.00 Closed dislocation of hip, unspecified site
835.01 Closed posterior dislocation of hip
835.02 Closed obturator dislocation of hip
835.03 Other closed anterior dislocation of hip
843.8 Sprain and strain of other specified sites of hip and thigh
843.9 Sprain and strain of unspecified site of hip and thigh
905.6 Late effect of dislocation
908.9 Late effect of unspecified injury
959.6 Injury, other and unspecified, hip and thigh

ICD-9-CM Procedural

80.25 Arthroscopy of hip
80.35 Biopsy of joint structure of hip

29861-29862

29861 Arthroscopy, hip, surgical; with removal of loose body or foreign body

29862 with debridement/shaving of articular cartilage (chondroplasty), abrasion arthroplasty, and/or resection of labrum

ICD-9-CM Diagnostic

213.6 Benign neoplasm of pelvic bones, sacrum, and coccyx
213.7 Benign neoplasm of long bones of lower limb
215.3 Other benign neoplasm of connective and other soft tissue of lower limb, including hip
238.0 Neoplasm of uncertain behavior of bone and articular cartilage
275.40 Unspecified disorder of calcium metabolism — (Use additional code to identify any associated intellectual disabilities)
275.42 Hypercalcemia — (Use additional code to identify any associated intellectual disabilities)
275.49 Other disorders of calcium metabolism — (Use additional code to identify any associated intellectual disabilities)
275.5 Hungry bone syndrome — (Use additional code to identify any associated intellectual disabilities)
714.0 Rheumatoid arthritis — (Use additional code to identify manifestation: 357.1, 359.6)
715.15 Primary localized osteoarthrosis, pelvic region and thigh
716.95 Unspecified arthropathy, pelvic region and thigh
718.05 Articular cartilage disorder, pelvic region and thigh
718.15 Loose body in pelvic joint
718.35 Recurrent dislocation of pelvic region and thigh joint
719.45 Pain in joint, pelvic region and thigh
719.95 Unspecified disorder of joint of pelvic region and thigh
726.5 Enthesopathy of hip region
732.1 Juvenile osteochondrosis of hip and pelvis
732.9 Unspecified osteochondropathy
733.90 Disorder of bone and cartilage, unspecified
733.92 Chondromalacia
733.99 Other disorders of bone and cartilage
835.00 Closed dislocation of hip, unspecified site
835.01 Closed posterior dislocation of hip
835.02 Closed obturator dislocation of hip
835.03 Other closed anterior dislocation of hip
843.8 Sprain and strain of other specified sites of hip and thigh
843.9 Sprain and strain of unspecified site of hip and thigh
905.6 Late effect of dislocation
908.9 Late effect of unspecified injury
959.6 Injury, other and unspecified, hip and thigh

ICD-9-CM Procedural

80.25 Arthroscopy of hip
80.85 Other local excision or destruction of lesion of hip joint

29863 [29914, 29915, 29916]

29863 Arthroscopy, hip, surgical; with synovectomy
29914 with femoroplasty (ie, treatment of cam lesion)
29915 with acetabuloplasty (ie, treatment of pincer lesion)
29916 with labral repair

ICD-9-CM Diagnostic

171.3 Malignant neoplasm of connective and other soft tissue of lower limb, including hip
198.89 Secondary malignant neoplasm of other specified sites
215.3 Other benign neoplasm of connective and other soft tissue of lower limb, including hip
238.1 Neoplasm of uncertain behavior of connective and other soft tissue
239.2 Neoplasms of unspecified nature of bone, soft tissue, and skin
275.40 Unspecified disorder of calcium metabolism — (Use additional code to identify any associated intellectual disabilities) ▽
275.42 Hypercalcemia — (Use additional code to identify any associated intellectual disabilities)
275.49 Other disorders of calcium metabolism — (Use additional code to identify any associated intellectual disabilities)
275.5 Hungry bone syndrome — (Use additional code to identify any associated intellectual disabilities)
711.05 Pyogenic arthritis, pelvic region and thigh — (Use additional code to identify infectious organism: 041.0-041.8)
714.0 Rheumatoid arthritis — (Use additional code to identify manifestation: 357.1, 359.6)
715.15 Primary localized osteoarthrosis, pelvic region and thigh
716.95 Unspecified arthropathy, pelvic region and thigh ▽
718.45 Contracture of pelvic joint
718.65 Unspecified intrapelvic protrusion acetabulum, pelvic region and thigh ▽
718.85 Other joint derangement, not elsewhere classified, pelvic region and thigh
719.25 Villonodular synovitis, pelvic region and thigh
719.45 Pain in joint, pelvic region and thigh
719.55 Stiffness of joint, not elsewhere classified, pelvic region and thigh
726.5 Enthesopathy of hip region
727.00 Unspecified synovitis and tenosynovitis ▽
736.39 Other acquired deformities of hip

ICD-9-CM Procedural

78.45 Other repair or plastic operations on femur
78.49 Other repair or plastic operations on other bone, except facial bones
80.45 Division of joint capsule, ligament, or cartilage of hip
80.75 Synovectomy of hip
80.85 Other local excision or destruction of lesion of hip joint
80.95 Other excision of hip joint

29866-29867

29866 Arthroscopy, knee, surgical; osteochondral autograft(s) (eg, mosaicplasty) (includes harvesting of the autograft[s])
29867 osteochondral allograft (eg, mosaicplasty)

ICD-9-CM Diagnostic

714.30 Polyarticular juvenile rheumatoid arthritis, chronic or unspecified
715.16 Primary localized osteoarthrosis, lower leg
715.26 Secondary localized osteoarthrosis, lower leg
715.36 Localized osteoarthrosis not specified whether primary or secondary, lower leg
715.96 Osteoarthrosis, unspecified whether generalized or localized, lower leg ▽
717.7 Chondromalacia of patella
717.83 Old disruption of anterior cruciate ligament
719.96 Unspecified disorder of lower leg joint ▽
732.4 Juvenile osteochondrosis of lower extremity, excluding foot
732.7 Osteochondritis dissecans
732.9 Unspecified osteochondropathy ▽
733.90 Disorder of bone and cartilage, unspecified ▽
844.2 Sprain and strain of cruciate ligament of knee

ICD-9-CM Procedural

81.47 Other repair of knee

HCPCS Level II Supplies & Services

J7330 Autologous cultured chondrocytes, implant
S2112 Arthroscopy, knee, surgical for harvesting of cartilage (chondrocyte cells)

29868

29868 Arthroscopy, knee, surgical; meniscal transplantation (includes arthrotomy for meniscal insertion), medial or lateral

ICD-9-CM Diagnostic

717.0 Old bucket handle tear of medial meniscus
717.1 Derangement of anterior horn of medial meniscus
717.2 Derangement of posterior horn of medial meniscus
717.3 Other and unspecified derangement of medial meniscus ▽
717.40 Unspecified derangement of lateral meniscus ▽
717.41 Bucket handle tear of lateral meniscus
717.42 Derangement of anterior horn of lateral meniscus
717.43 Derangement of posterior horn of lateral meniscus
717.49 Other derangement of lateral meniscus
717.5 Derangement of meniscus, not elsewhere classified
718.36 Recurrent dislocation of lower leg joint
836.0 Tear of medial cartilage or meniscus of knee, current
836.1 Tear of lateral cartilage or meniscus of knee, current
836.2 Other tear of cartilage or meniscus of knee, current

ICD-9-CM Procedural

80.6 Excision of semilunar cartilage of knee
81.47 Other repair of knee

29870

29870 Arthroscopy, knee, diagnostic, with or without synovial biopsy (separate procedure)

ICD-9-CM Diagnostic

171.3 Malignant neoplasm of connective and other soft tissue of lower limb, including hip
198.89 Secondary malignant neoplasm of other specified sites
215.3 Other benign neoplasm of connective and other soft tissue of lower limb, including hip
238.1 Neoplasm of uncertain behavior of connective and other soft tissue
239.2 Neoplasms of unspecified nature of bone, soft tissue, and skin
275.40 Unspecified disorder of calcium metabolism — (Use additional code to identify any associated intellectual disabilities) ▽
275.41 Hypocalcemia — (Use additional code to identify any associated intellectual disabilities)
275.42 Hypercalcemia — (Use additional code to identify any associated intellectual disabilities)
275.49 Other disorders of calcium metabolism — (Use additional code to identify any associated intellectual disabilities)
275.5 Hungry bone syndrome — (Use additional code to identify any associated intellectual disabilities)
711.56 Arthropathy associated with other viral diseases, lower leg — (Code first underlying disease: 045-049, 050-079, 480, 487) ☒
712.16 Chondrocalcinosis due to dicalcium phosphate crystals, lower leg — (Code first underlying disease: 275.4) ☒
712.26 Chondrocalcinosis due to pyrophosphate crystals, lower leg — (Code first underlying disease: 275.4) ☒
713.1 Arthropathy associated with gastrointestinal conditions other than infections — (Code first underlying disease: 555.0-555.9, 556) ☒

713.2 Arthropathy associated with hematological disorders — (Code first underlying disease: 202.3, 203.0, 204.0-208.9, 282.4-282.7, 286.0-286.2) ☒
713.3 Arthropathy associated with dermatological disorders — (Code first underlying disease: 695.10-695.19, 695.2) ☒
715.09 Generalized osteoarthrosis, involving multiple sites
715.16 Primary localized osteoarthrosis, lower leg
715.96 Osteoarthrosis, unspecified whether generalized or localized, lower leg ♥
716.16 Traumatic arthropathy, lower leg
716.46 Transient arthropathy, lower leg
717.0 Old bucket handle tear of medial meniscus
717.1 Derangement of anterior horn of medial meniscus
717.2 Derangement of posterior horn of medial meniscus
717.3 Other and unspecified derangement of medial meniscus ♥
717.40 Unspecified derangement of lateral meniscus ♥
717.41 Bucket handle tear of lateral meniscus
717.42 Derangement of anterior horn of lateral meniscus
717.43 Derangement of posterior horn of lateral meniscus
717.49 Other derangement of lateral meniscus
717.5 Derangement of meniscus, not elsewhere classified
717.7 Chondromalacia of patella
717.81 Old disruption of lateral collateral ligament
717.82 Old disruption of medial collateral ligament
717.83 Old disruption of anterior cruciate ligament
717.84 Old disruption of posterior cruciate ligament
717.85 Old disruption of other ligament of knee
717.89 Other internal derangement of knee
718.36 Recurrent dislocation of lower leg joint
718.46 Contracture of lower leg joint
718.76 Developmental dislocation of joint, lower leg
718.86 Other joint derangement, not elsewhere classified, lower leg
719.06 Effusion of lower leg joint
719.16 Hemarthrosis, lower leg
719.26 Villonodular synovitis, lower leg
719.86 Other specified disorders of lower leg joint
727.00 Unspecified synovitis and tenosynovitis ♥
727.51 Synovial cyst of popliteal space
733.90 Disorder of bone and cartilage, unspecified ♥
733.92 Chondromalacia
736.6 Other acquired deformities of knee
755.64 Congenital deformity of knee (joint)
755.69 Other congenital anomaly of lower limb, including pelvic girdle
836.0 Tear of medial cartilage or meniscus of knee, current
836.1 Tear of lateral cartilage or meniscus of knee, current
836.2 Other tear of cartilage or meniscus of knee, current
836.3 Closed dislocation of patella
836.4 Open dislocation of patella
836.50 Closed dislocation of knee, unspecified part ♥
844.0 Sprain and strain of lateral collateral ligament of knee
844.1 Sprain and strain of medial collateral ligament of knee
844.2 Sprain and strain of cruciate ligament of knee

ICD-9-CM Procedural

80.26 Arthroscopy of knee
80.36 Biopsy of joint structure of knee

29871

29871 Arthroscopy, knee, surgical; for infection, lavage and drainage

ICD-9-CM Diagnostic

357.1 Polyneuropathy in collagen vascular disease — (Code first underlying disease: 446.0, 710.0, 714.0) ☒
359.6 Symptomatic inflammatory myopathy in diseases classified elsewhere — (Code first underlying disease: 135, 140.0-208.9, 277.30-277.39, 446.0, 710.0, 710.1, 710.2, 714.0) ☒
446.0 Polyarteritis nodosa
710.0 Systemic lupus erythematosus — (Use additional code to identify manifestation: 424.91, 581.81, 582.81, 583.81)
710.1 Systemic sclerosis — (Use additional code to identify manifestation: 359.6, 517.2)
710.2 Sicca syndrome
711.06 Pyogenic arthritis, lower leg — (Use additional code to identify infectious organism: 041.0-041.8)
711.46 Arthropathy associated with other bacterial diseases, lower leg — (Code first underlying disease, such as diseases classifiable to 010-040 (except 036.82), 090-099 (except 098.50)) ☒
711.56 Arthropathy associated with other viral diseases, lower leg — (Code first underlying disease: 045-049, 050-079, 480, 487) ☒
711.66 Arthropathy associated with mycoses, lower leg — (Code first underlying disease: 110.0-118) ☒
711.86 Arthropathy associated with other infectious and parasitic diseases, lower leg — (Code first underlying disease: 080-088, 100-104, 130-136) ☒
719.86 Other specified disorders of lower leg joint
727.51 Synovial cyst of popliteal space
730.06 Acute osteomyelitis, lower leg — (Use additional code to identify organism: 041.1. Use additional code to identify major osseous defect, if applicable: 731.3)
730.16 Chronic osteomyelitis, lower leg — (Use additional code to identify organism: 041.1. Use additional code to identify major osseous defect, if applicable: 731.3)
730.26 Unspecified osteomyelitis, lower leg — (Use additional code to identify organism: 041.1. Use additional code to identify major osseous defect, if applicable: 731.3) ♥
730.36 Periostitis, without mention of osteomyelitis, lower leg — (Use additional code to identify organism: 041.1)
731.3 Major osseous defects — (Code first underlying disease: 170.0-170.9, 730.00-730.29, 733.00-733.09, 733.40-733.49, 996.45)
996.66 Infection and inflammatory reaction due to internal joint prosthesis — (Use additional code to identify specified infections. Use additional code to identify infected prosthetic joint: V43.60-V43.69)
996.67 Infection and inflammatory reaction due to other internal orthopedic device, implant, and graft — (Use additional code to identify specified infections)
998.51 Infected postoperative seroma — (Use additional code to identify organism)
998.59 Other postoperative infection — (Use additional code to identify infection)

ICD-9-CM Procedural

80.26 Arthroscopy of knee

29873

29873 Arthroscopy, knee, surgical; with lateral release

ICD-9-CM Diagnostic

715.16 Primary localized osteoarthrosis, lower leg
715.96 Osteoarthrosis, unspecified whether generalized or localized, lower leg ♥
717.6 Loose body in knee
717.7 Chondromalacia of patella
717.9 Unspecified internal derangement of knee ♥
718.36 Recurrent dislocation of lower leg joint
718.46 Contracture of lower leg joint
718.56 Ankylosis of lower leg joint
718.86 Other joint derangement, not elsewhere classified, lower leg
719.26 Villonodular synovitis, lower leg

719.86 Other specified disorders of lower leg joint
733.22 Aneurysmal bone cyst
733.92 Chondromalacia
755.64 Congenital deformity of knee (joint)
836.3 Closed dislocation of patella
836.50 Closed dislocation of knee, unspecified part
836.54 Closed lateral dislocation of tibia, proximal end
844.2 Sprain and strain of cruciate ligament of knee

ICD-9-CM Procedural

80.46 Division of joint capsule, ligament, or cartilage of knee

29874

29874 Arthroscopy, knee, surgical; for removal of loose body or foreign body (eg, osteochondritis dissecans fragmentation, chondral fragmentation)

ICD-9-CM Diagnostic

275.40 Unspecified disorder of calcium metabolism — (Use additional code to identify any associated intellectual disabilities)
275.42 Hypercalcemia — (Use additional code to identify any associated intellectual disabilities)
275.49 Other disorders of calcium metabolism — (Use additional code to identify any associated intellectual disabilities)
275.5 Hungry bone syndrome — (Use additional code to identify any associated intellectual disabilities)
716.16 Traumatic arthropathy, lower leg
717.6 Loose body in knee
717.7 Chondromalacia of patella
718.18 Loose body in joint of other specified site
718.86 Other joint derangement, not elsewhere classified, lower leg
732.4 Juvenile osteochondrosis of lower extremity, excluding foot
732.6 Other juvenile osteochondrosis
732.7 Osteochondritis dissecans
732.9 Unspecified osteochondropathy
928.11 Crushing injury of knee — (Use additional code to identify any associated injuries: 800-829, 850.0-854.1, 860.0-869.1)

ICD-9-CM Procedural

80.96 Other excision of knee joint

29875-29876

29875 Arthroscopy, knee, surgical; synovectomy, limited (eg, plica or shelf resection) (separate procedure)
29876 synovectomy, major, 2 or more compartments (eg, medial or lateral)

ICD-9-CM Diagnostic

171.3 Malignant neoplasm of connective and other soft tissue of lower limb, including hip
198.89 Secondary malignant neoplasm of other specified sites
215.3 Other benign neoplasm of connective and other soft tissue of lower limb, including hip
238.1 Neoplasm of uncertain behavior of connective and other soft tissue
239.2 Neoplasms of unspecified nature of bone, soft tissue, and skin
275.41 Hypocalcemia — (Use additional code to identify any associated intellectual disabilities)
275.42 Hypercalcemia — (Use additional code to identify any associated intellectual disabilities)
275.5 Hungry bone syndrome — (Use additional code to identify any associated intellectual disabilities)
357.1 Polyneuropathy in collagen vascular disease — (Code first underlying disease: 446.0, 710.0, 714.0)
359.6 Symptomatic inflammatory myopathy in diseases classified elsewhere — (Code first underlying disease: 135, 140.0-208.9, 277.30-277.39, 446.0, 710.0, 710.1, 710.2, 714.0)
446.0 Polyarteritis nodosa
710.0 Systemic lupus erythematosus — (Use additional code to identify manifestation: 424.91, 581.81, 582.81, 583.81)
710.1 Systemic sclerosis — (Use additional code to identify manifestation: 359.6, 517.2)
710.2 Sicca syndrome
711.06 Pyogenic arthritis, lower leg — (Use additional code to identify infectious organism: 041.0-041.8)
712.16 Chondrocalcinosis due to dicalcium phosphate crystals, lower leg — (Code first underlying disease: 275.4)
712.26 Chondrocalcinosis due to pyrophosphate crystals, lower leg — (Code first underlying disease: 275.4)
714.0 Rheumatoid arthritis — (Use additional code to identify manifestation: 357.1, 359.6)
714.2 Other rheumatoid arthritis with visceral or systemic involvement
714.31 Polyarticular juvenile rheumatoid arthritis, acute
714.32 Pauciarticular juvenile rheumatoid arthritis
714.33 Monoarticular juvenile rheumatoid arthritis
715.16 Primary localized osteoarthrosis, lower leg
717.7 Chondromalacia of patella
718.36 Recurrent dislocation of lower leg joint
719.26 Villonodular synovitis, lower leg
719.56 Stiffness of joint, not elsewhere classified, lower leg
727.00 Unspecified synovitis and tenosynovitis
727.01 Synovitis and tenosynovitis in diseases classified elsewhere — (Code first underlying disease: 015.0-015.9)
727.09 Other synovitis and tenosynovitis
727.51 Synovial cyst of popliteal space
727.83 Plica syndrome
727.89 Other disorders of synovium, tendon, and bursa
755.64 Congenital deformity of knee (joint)
755.69 Other congenital anomaly of lower limb, including pelvic girdle
836.0 Tear of medial cartilage or meniscus of knee, current

ICD-9-CM Procedural

80.76 Synovectomy of knee

29877

29877 Arthroscopy, knee, surgical; debridement/shaving of articular cartilage (chondroplasty)

ICD-9-CM Diagnostic

275.40 Unspecified disorder of calcium metabolism — (Use additional code to identify any associated intellectual disabilities)
275.41 Hypocalcemia — (Use additional code to identify any associated intellectual disabilities)
275.42 Hypercalcemia — (Use additional code to identify any associated intellectual disabilities)
275.49 Other disorders of calcium metabolism — (Use additional code to identify any associated intellectual disabilities)
275.5 Hungry bone syndrome — (Use additional code to identify any associated intellectual disabilities)
357.1 Polyneuropathy in collagen vascular disease — (Code first underlying disease: 446.0, 710.0, 714.0)
359.6 Symptomatic inflammatory myopathy in diseases classified elsewhere — (Code first underlying disease: 135, 140.0-208.9, 277.30-277.39, 446.0, 710.0, 710.1, 710.2, 714.0)
446.0 Polyarteritis nodosa
710.0 Systemic lupus erythematosus — (Use additional code to identify manifestation: 424.91, 581.81, 582.81, 583.81)
710.1 Systemic sclerosis — (Use additional code to identify manifestation: 359.6, 517.2)
710.2 Sicca syndrome
712.16 Chondrocalcinosis due to dicalcium phosphate crystals, lower leg — (Code first underlying disease: 275.4)

712.26 Chondrocalcinosis due to pyrophosphate crystals, lower leg — (Code first underlying disease: 275.4) ☒
714.0 Rheumatoid arthritis — (Use additional code to identify manifestation: 357.1, 359.6)
714.1 Felty's syndrome
714.2 Other rheumatoid arthritis with visceral or systemic involvement
714.30 Polyarticular juvenile rheumatoid arthritis, chronic or unspecified
714.31 Polyarticular juvenile rheumatoid arthritis, acute
714.32 Pauciarticular juvenile rheumatoid arthritis
714.33 Monoarticular juvenile rheumatoid arthritis
715.10 Primary localized osteoarthrosis, unspecified site ▽
715.16 Primary localized osteoarthrosis, lower leg
715.26 Secondary localized osteoarthrosis, lower leg
715.36 Localized osteoarthrosis not specified whether primary or secondary, lower leg
715.96 Osteoarthrosis, unspecified whether generalized or localized, lower leg ▽
716.16 Traumatic arthropathy, lower leg
716.86 Other specified arthropathy, lower leg
717.0 Old bucket handle tear of medial meniscus
717.1 Derangement of anterior horn of medial meniscus
717.2 Derangement of posterior horn of medial meniscus
717.3 Other and unspecified derangement of medial meniscus ▽
717.40 Unspecified derangement of lateral meniscus ▽
717.7 Chondromalacia of patella
718.46 Contracture of lower leg joint
718.56 Ankylosis of lower leg joint
718.86 Other joint derangement, not elsewhere classified, lower leg
719.16 Hemarthrosis, lower leg
719.26 Villonodular synovitis, lower leg
719.86 Other specified disorders of lower leg joint
719.96 Unspecified disorder of lower leg joint ▽
732.7 Osteochondritis dissecans
732.9 Unspecified osteochondropathy ▽
733.92 Chondromalacia
733.99 Other disorders of bone and cartilage
755.64 Congenital deformity of knee (joint)
755.69 Other congenital anomaly of lower limb, including pelvic girdle
836.0 Tear of medial cartilage or meniscus of knee, current
836.1 Tear of lateral cartilage or meniscus of knee, current
836.2 Other tear of cartilage or meniscus of knee, current
844.2 Sprain and strain of cruciate ligament of knee
844.9 Sprain and strain of unspecified site of knee and leg ▽

ICD-9-CM Procedural

80.86 Other local excision or destruction of lesion of knee joint
81.47 Other repair of knee

29879

29879 Arthroscopy, knee, surgical; abrasion arthroplasty (includes chondroplasty where necessary) or multiple drilling or microfracture

ICD-9-CM Diagnostic

275.40 Unspecified disorder of calcium metabolism — (Use additional code to identify any associated intellectual disabilities) ▽
275.41 Hypocalcemia — (Use additional code to identify any associated intellectual disabilities)
275.42 Hypercalcemia — (Use additional code to identify any associated intellectual disabilities)
275.49 Other disorders of calcium metabolism — (Use additional code to identify any associated intellectual disabilities)
275.5 Hungry bone syndrome — (Use additional code to identify any associated intellectual disabilities)
357.1 Polyneuropathy in collagen vascular disease — (Code first underlying disease: 446.0, 710.0, 714.0) ☒
359.6 Symptomatic inflammatory myopathy in diseases classified elsewhere — (Code first underlying disease: 135, 140.0-208.9, 277.30-277.39, 446.0, 710.0, 710.1, 710.2, 714.0) ☒
712.16 Chondrocalcinosis due to dicalcium phosphate crystals, lower leg — (Code first underlying disease: 275.4) ☒
712.26 Chondrocalcinosis due to pyrophosphate crystals, lower leg — (Code first underlying disease: 275.4) ☒
714.0 Rheumatoid arthritis — (Use additional code to identify manifestation: 357.1, 359.6)
714.1 Felty's syndrome
714.2 Other rheumatoid arthritis with visceral or systemic involvement
714.30 Polyarticular juvenile rheumatoid arthritis, chronic or unspecified
714.31 Polyarticular juvenile rheumatoid arthritis, acute
714.32 Pauciarticular juvenile rheumatoid arthritis
714.33 Monoarticular juvenile rheumatoid arthritis
715.16 Primary localized osteoarthrosis, lower leg
715.26 Secondary localized osteoarthrosis, lower leg
715.36 Localized osteoarthrosis not specified whether primary or secondary, lower leg
715.96 Osteoarthrosis, unspecified whether generalized or localized, lower leg ▽
716.16 Traumatic arthropathy, lower leg
716.66 Unspecified monoarthritis, lower leg ▽
717.0 Old bucket handle tear of medial meniscus
717.1 Derangement of anterior horn of medial meniscus
717.2 Derangement of posterior horn of medial meniscus
717.3 Other and unspecified derangement of medial meniscus ▽
717.40 Unspecified derangement of lateral meniscus ▽
717.7 Chondromalacia of patella
717.9 Unspecified internal derangement of knee ▽
718.46 Contracture of lower leg joint
718.56 Ankylosis of lower leg joint
732.7 Osteochondritis dissecans
733.92 Chondromalacia
836.0 Tear of medial cartilage or meniscus of knee, current

ICD-9-CM Procedural

81.47 Other repair of knee

29880-29881

29880 Arthroscopy, knee, surgical; with meniscectomy (medial AND lateral, including any meniscal shaving) including debridement/shaving of articular cartilage (chondroplasty), same or separate compartment(s), when performed
29881 with meniscectomy (medial OR lateral, including any meniscal shaving) including debridement/shaving of articular cartilage (chondroplasty), same or separate compartment(s), when performed

ICD-9-CM Diagnostic

715.16 Primary localized osteoarthrosis, lower leg
715.26 Secondary localized osteoarthrosis, lower leg
715.36 Localized osteoarthrosis not specified whether primary or secondary, lower leg
715.96 Osteoarthrosis, unspecified whether generalized or localized, lower leg ▽
717.0 Old bucket handle tear of medial meniscus
717.1 Derangement of anterior horn of medial meniscus
717.2 Derangement of posterior horn of medial meniscus
717.3 Other and unspecified derangement of medial meniscus ▽
717.41 Bucket handle tear of lateral meniscus
717.42 Derangement of anterior horn of lateral meniscus
717.43 Derangement of posterior horn of lateral meniscus
717.49 Other derangement of lateral meniscus
717.5 Derangement of meniscus, not elsewhere classified
718.86 Other joint derangement, not elsewhere classified, lower leg

727.83 Plica syndrome
727.89 Other disorders of synovium, tendon, and bursa
836.0 Tear of medial cartilage or meniscus of knee, current
836.1 Tear of lateral cartilage or meniscus of knee, current
836.2 Other tear of cartilage or meniscus of knee, current

ICD-9-CM Procedural

80.6 Excision of semilunar cartilage of knee
81.42 Five-in-one repair of knee
81.43 Triad knee repair
81.47 Other repair of knee

29882-29883

29882 Arthroscopy, knee, surgical; with meniscus repair (medial OR lateral)
29883 with meniscus repair (medial AND lateral)

ICD-9-CM Diagnostic

717.0 Old bucket handle tear of medial meniscus
717.1 Derangement of anterior horn of medial meniscus
717.2 Derangement of posterior horn of medial meniscus
717.3 Other and unspecified derangement of medial meniscus ▼
717.40 Unspecified derangement of lateral meniscus ▼
717.41 Bucket handle tear of lateral meniscus
717.42 Derangement of anterior horn of lateral meniscus
717.43 Derangement of posterior horn of lateral meniscus
717.49 Other derangement of lateral meniscus
717.5 Derangement of meniscus, not elsewhere classified
836.0 Tear of medial cartilage or meniscus of knee, current
836.1 Tear of lateral cartilage or meniscus of knee, current
836.2 Other tear of cartilage or meniscus of knee, current

ICD-9-CM Procedural

81.47 Other repair of knee

29884

29884 Arthroscopy, knee, surgical; with lysis of adhesions, with or without manipulation (separate procedure)

ICD-9-CM Diagnostic

715.96 Osteoarthrosis, unspecified whether generalized or localized, lower leg ▼
717.7 Chondromalacia of patella
717.9 Unspecified internal derangement of knee ▼
718.46 Contracture of lower leg joint
718.56 Ankylosis of lower leg joint
719.56 Stiffness of joint, not elsewhere classified, lower leg
719.86 Other specified disorders of lower leg joint
726.61 Pes anserinus tendinitis or bursitis
726.62 Tibial collateral ligament bursitis
726.63 Fibular collateral ligament bursitis
726.64 Patellar tendinitis
726.65 Prepatellar bursitis
727.81 Contracture of tendon (sheath)
727.83 Plica syndrome
836.0 Tear of medial cartilage or meniscus of knee, current

ICD-9-CM Procedural

80.46 Division of joint capsule, ligament, or cartilage of knee

29885-29887

29885 Arthroscopy, knee, surgical; drilling for osteochondritis dissecans with bone grafting, with or without internal fixation (including debridement of base of lesion)
29886 drilling for intact osteochondritis dissecans lesion
29887 drilling for intact osteochondritis dissecans lesion with internal fixation

ICD-9-CM Diagnostic

717.6 Loose body in knee
732.4 Juvenile osteochondrosis of lower extremity, excluding foot
732.6 Other juvenile osteochondrosis
732.7 Osteochondritis dissecans
732.9 Unspecified osteochondropathy ▼

ICD-9-CM Procedural

78.57 Internal fixation of tibia and fibula without fracture reduction
81.47 Other repair of knee

29888-29889

29888 Arthroscopically aided anterior cruciate ligament repair/augmentation or reconstruction
29889 Arthroscopically aided posterior cruciate ligament repair/augmentation or reconstruction

ICD-9-CM Diagnostic

710.8 Other specified diffuse disease of connective tissue
717.83 Old disruption of anterior cruciate ligament
717.84 Old disruption of posterior cruciate ligament
717.9 Unspecified internal derangement of knee ▼
718.76 Developmental dislocation of joint, lower leg
718.86 Other joint derangement, not elsewhere classified, lower leg
726.64 Patellar tendinitis
728.4 Laxity of ligament
754.41 Congenital dislocation of knee (with genu recurvatum)
836.0 Tear of medial cartilage or meniscus of knee, current
836.50 Closed dislocation of knee, unspecified part ▼
836.51 Closed anterior dislocation of tibia, proximal end
836.63 Open medial dislocation of tibia, proximal end
844.0 Sprain and strain of lateral collateral ligament of knee
844.1 Sprain and strain of medial collateral ligament of knee
844.2 Sprain and strain of cruciate ligament of knee
959.7 Injury, other and unspecified, knee, leg, ankle, and foot
V15.51 Personal history of traumatic fracture
V15.59 Personal history of other injury

ICD-9-CM Procedural

81.45 Other repair of the cruciate ligaments
81.47 Other repair of knee

29891

29891 Arthroscopy, ankle, surgical, excision of osteochondral defect of talus and/or tibia, including drilling of the defect

ICD-9-CM Diagnostic

732.4 Juvenile osteochondrosis of lower extremity, excluding foot
732.5 Juvenile osteochondrosis of foot
732.7 Osteochondritis dissecans
732.9 Unspecified osteochondropathy ▼

ICD-9-CM Procedural

80.87 Other local excision or destruction of lesion of ankle joint

29892

29892 Arthroscopically aided repair of large osteochondritis dissecans lesion, talar dome fracture, or tibial plafond fracture, with or without internal fixation (includes arthroscopy)

ICD-9-CM Diagnostic

732.7 Osteochondritis dissecans
823.80 Closed fracture of unspecified part of tibia
824.0 Closed fracture of medial malleolus
825.21 Closed fracture of astragalus

ICD-9-CM Procedural

78.57 Internal fixation of tibia and fibula without fracture reduction
78.58 Internal fixation of tarsals and metatarsals without fracture reduction
79.26 Open reduction of fracture of tibia and fibula without internal fixation
79.27 Open reduction of fracture of tarsals and metatarsals without internal fixation
79.36 Open reduction of fracture of tibia and fibula with internal fixation
79.37 Open reduction of fracture of tarsals and metatarsals with internal fixation
80.87 Other local excision or destruction of lesion of ankle joint
80.90 Other excision of joint, unspecified site

29893

29893 Endoscopic plantar fasciotomy

ICD-9-CM Diagnostic

728.71 Plantar fascial fibromatosis
728.79 Other fibromatoses of muscle, ligament, and fascia
733.94 Stress fracture of the metatarsals — (Use additional external cause code(s) to identify the cause of the stress fracture)
825.25 Closed fracture of metatarsal bone(s)
825.29 Other closed fracture of tarsal and metatarsal bones
825.39 Other open fractures of tarsal and metatarsal bones
845.19 Other foot sprain and strain
892.0 Open wound of foot except toe(s) alone, without mention of complication
892.1 Open wound of foot except toe(s) alone, complicated
892.2 Open wound of foot except toe(s) alone, with tendon involvement
905.4 Late effect of fracture of lower extremities
905.8 Late effect of tendon injury
906.1 Late effect of open wound of extremities without mention of tendon injury
906.4 Late effect of crushing
928.20 Crushing injury of foot — (Use additional code to identify any associated injuries: 800-829, 850.0-854.1, 860.0-869.1)
997.99 Other complications affecting other specified body systems, NEC — (Use additional code to identify complications)

ICD-9-CM Procedural

83.14 Fasciotomy

29894

29894 Arthroscopy, ankle (tibiotalar and fibulotalar joints), surgical; with removal of loose body or foreign body

ICD-9-CM Diagnostic

275.40 Unspecified disorder of calcium metabolism — (Use additional code to identify any associated intellectual disabilities)
275.42 Hypercalcemia — (Use additional code to identify any associated intellectual disabilities)
275.49 Other disorders of calcium metabolism — (Use additional code to identify any associated intellectual disabilities)
275.5 Hungry bone syndrome — (Use additional code to identify any associated intellectual disabilities)
715.17 Primary localized osteoarthrosis, ankle and foot
715.97 Osteoarthrosis, unspecified whether generalized or localized, ankle and foot
716.17 Traumatic arthropathy, ankle and foot
718.17 Loose body in ankle and foot joint
718.87 Other joint derangement, not elsewhere classified, ankle and foot
718.97 Unspecified ankle and foot joint derangement
719.27 Villonodular synovitis, ankle and foot

ICD-9-CM Procedural

80.97 Other excision of ankle joint

HCPCS Level II Supplies & Services

A4305 Disposable drug delivery system, flow rate of 50 ml or greater per hour

29895

29895 Arthroscopy, ankle (tibiotalar and fibulotalar joints), surgical; synovectomy, partial

ICD-9-CM Diagnostic

171.3 Malignant neoplasm of connective and other soft tissue of lower limb, including hip
198.89 Secondary malignant neoplasm of other specified sites
215.3 Other benign neoplasm of connective and other soft tissue of lower limb, including hip
238.1 Neoplasm of uncertain behavior of connective and other soft tissue
239.2 Neoplasms of unspecified nature of bone, soft tissue, and skin
275.40 Unspecified disorder of calcium metabolism — (Use additional code to identify any associated intellectual disabilities)
275.42 Hypercalcemia — (Use additional code to identify any associated intellectual disabilities)
275.49 Other disorders of calcium metabolism — (Use additional code to identify any associated intellectual disabilities)
275.5 Hungry bone syndrome — (Use additional code to identify any associated intellectual disabilities)
357.1 Polyneuropathy in collagen vascular disease — (Code first underlying disease: 446.0, 710.0, 714.0)
359.6 Symptomatic inflammatory myopathy in diseases classified elsewhere — (Code first underlying disease: 135, 140.0-208.9, 277.30-277.39, 446.0, 710.0, 710.1, 710.2, 714.0)
446.0 Polyarteritis nodosa
710.0 Systemic lupus erythematosus — (Use additional code to identify manifestation: 424.91, 581.81, 582.81, 583.81)
710.1 Systemic sclerosis — (Use additional code to identify manifestation: 359.6, 517.2)
710.2 Sicca syndrome
714.0 Rheumatoid arthritis — (Use additional code to identify manifestation: 357.1, 359.6)
715.17 Primary localized osteoarthrosis, ankle and foot
715.97 Osteoarthrosis, unspecified whether generalized or localized, ankle and foot
716.17 Traumatic arthropathy, ankle and foot
718.07 Articular cartilage disorder, ankle and foot
718.87 Other joint derangement, not elsewhere classified, ankle and foot
718.97 Unspecified ankle and foot joint derangement
719.27 Villonodular synovitis, ankle and foot
719.57 Stiffness of joint, not elsewhere classified, ankle and foot
727.00 Unspecified synovitis and tenosynovitis
727.01 Synovitis and tenosynovitis in diseases classified elsewhere — (Code first underlying disease: 015.0-015.9)
727.06 Tenosynovitis of foot and ankle
959.7 Injury, other and unspecified, knee, leg, ankle, and foot

ICD-9-CM Procedural

80.77 Synovectomy of ankle

HCPCS Level II Supplies & Services

A4305 Disposable drug delivery system, flow rate of 50 ml or greater per hour

29897-29898

29897 Arthroscopy, ankle (tibiotalar and fibulotalar joints), surgical; debridement, limited
29898 debridement, extensive

ICD-9-CM Diagnostic

357.1 Polyneuropathy in collagen vascular disease — (Code first underlying disease: 446.0, 710.0, 714.0) ☒
359.6 Symptomatic inflammatory myopathy in diseases classified elsewhere — (Code first underlying disease: 135, 140.0-208.9, 277.30-277.39, 446.0, 710.0, 710.1, 710.2, 714.0) ☒
446.0 Polyarteritis nodosa
710.0 Systemic lupus erythematosus — (Use additional code to identify manifestation: 424.91, 581.81, 582.81, 583.81)
710.1 Systemic sclerosis — (Use additional code to identify manifestation: 359.6, 517.2)
710.2 Sicca syndrome
714.0 Rheumatoid arthritis — (Use additional code to identify manifestation: 357.1, 359.6)
715.17 Primary localized osteoarthrosis, ankle and foot
716.17 Traumatic arthropathy, ankle and foot
718.07 Articular cartilage disorder, ankle and foot
718.87 Other joint derangement, not elsewhere classified, ankle and foot
719.27 Villonodular synovitis, ankle and foot
726.79 Other enthesopathy of ankle and tarsus
727.06 Tenosynovitis of foot and ankle
732.7 Osteochondritis dissecans
732.9 Unspecified osteochondropathy ▽
733.92 Chondromalacia

ICD-9-CM Procedural

80.87 Other local excision or destruction of lesion of ankle joint

HCPCS Level II Supplies & Services

A4305 Disposable drug delivery system, flow rate of 50 ml or greater per hour

29899

29899 Arthroscopy, ankle (tibiotalar and fibulotalar joints), surgical; with ankle arthrodesis

ICD-9-CM Diagnostic

711.07 Pyogenic arthritis, ankle and foot — (Use additional code to identify infectious organism: 041.0-041.8)
711.67 Arthropathy associated with mycoses, ankle and foot — (Code first underlying disease: 110.0-118) ☒
712.17 Chondrocalcinosis due to dicalcium phosphate crystals, ankle and foot — (Code first underlying disease: 275.4) ☒
712.27 Chondrocalcinosis due to pyrophosphate crystals, ankle and foot — (Code first underlying disease: 275.4) ☒
713.5 Arthropathy associated with neurological disorders — (Code first underlying disease: 094.0, 249.6, 250.6, 336.0) ☒
714.0 Rheumatoid arthritis — (Use additional code to identify manifestation: 357.1, 359.6)
714.4 Chronic postrheumatic arthropathy
715.17 Primary localized osteoarthrosis, ankle and foot
715.27 Secondary localized osteoarthrosis, ankle and foot
715.97 Osteoarthrosis, unspecified whether generalized or localized, ankle and foot ▽
716.17 Traumatic arthropathy, ankle and foot
716.57 Unspecified polyarthropathy or polyarthritis, ankle and foot ▽
716.67 Unspecified monoarthritis, ankle and foot ▽
716.87 Other specified arthropathy, ankle and foot
718.87 Other joint derangement, not elsewhere classified, ankle and foot
730.17 Chronic osteomyelitis, ankle and foot — (Use additional code to identify organism: 041.1. Use additional code to identify major osseous defect, if applicable: 731.3)
731.3 Major osseous defects — (Code first underlying disease: 170.0-170.9, 730.00-730.29, 733.00-733.09, 733.40-733.49, 996.45)
733.81 Malunion of fracture
736.70 Unspecified deformity of ankle and foot, acquired ▽
754.51 Congenital talipes equinovarus
905.4 Late effect of fracture of lower extremities
906.4 Late effect of crushing
996.77 Other complications due to internal joint prosthesis — (Use additional code to identify complication: 338.18-338.19, 338.28-338.29)

ICD-9-CM Procedural

81.29 Arthrodesis of other specified joint

29900

29900 Arthroscopy, metacarpophalangeal joint, diagnostic, includes synovial biopsy

ICD-9-CM Diagnostic

357.1 Polyneuropathy in collagen vascular disease — (Code first underlying disease: 446.0, 710.0, 714.0) ☒
359.6 Symptomatic inflammatory myopathy in diseases classified elsewhere — (Code first underlying disease: 135, 140.0-208.9, 277.30-277.39, 446.0, 710.0, 710.1, 710.2, 714.0) ☒
446.0 Polyarteritis nodosa
682.4 Cellulitis and abscess of hand, except fingers and thumb — (Use additional code to identify organism, such as 041.1, etc.)
709.4 Foreign body granuloma of skin and subcutaneous tissue — (Use additional code to identify foreign body (V90.01-V90.9))
710.0 Systemic lupus erythematosus — (Use additional code to identify manifestation: 424.91, 581.81, 582.81, 583.81)
710.1 Systemic sclerosis — (Use additional code to identify manifestation: 359.6, 517.2)
710.2 Sicca syndrome
711.04 Pyogenic arthritis, hand — (Use additional code to identify infectious organism: 041.0-041.8)
714.0 Rheumatoid arthritis — (Use additional code to identify manifestation: 357.1, 359.6)
714.30 Polyarticular juvenile rheumatoid arthritis, chronic or unspecified
714.31 Polyarticular juvenile rheumatoid arthritis, acute
714.9 Unspecified inflammatory polyarthropathy ▽
716.04 Kaschin-Beck disease, hand
716.14 Traumatic arthropathy, hand
716.64 Unspecified monoarthritis, hand ▽
718.74 Developmental dislocation of joint, hand
719.24 Villonodular synovitis, hand
727.00 Unspecified synovitis and tenosynovitis ▽
727.01 Synovitis and tenosynovitis in diseases classified elsewhere — (Code first underlying disease: 015.0-015.9) ☒
727.05 Other tenosynovitis of hand and wrist
728.0 Infective myositis
728.82 Foreign body granuloma of muscle — (Use additional code to identify foreign body (V90.01-V90.9))
728.89 Other disorder of muscle, ligament, and fascia — (Use additional E code to identify drug, if drug-induced)
729.4 Unspecified fasciitis ▽
729.6 Residual foreign body in soft tissue — (Use additional code to identify foreign body (V90.01-V90.9))
730.04 Acute osteomyelitis, hand — (Use additional code to identify organism: 041.1. Use additional code to identify major osseous defect, if applicable: 731.3)
730.14 Chronic osteomyelitis, hand — (Use additional code to identify organism: 041.1. Use additional code to identify major osseous defect, if applicable: 731.3)
730.24 Unspecified osteomyelitis, hand — (Use additional code to identify organism: 041.1. Use additional code to identify major osseous defect, if applicable: 731.3) ▽
730.34 Periostitis, without mention of osteomyelitis, hand — (Use additional code to identify organism: 041.1)

730.84 Other infections involving diseases classified elsewhere, hand bone — (Use additional code to identify organism: 041.1. Code first underlying disease: 002.0, 015.0-015.9) ☒

731.3 Major osseous defects — (Code first underlying disease: 170.0-170.9, 730.00-730.29, 733.00-733.09, 733.40-733.49, 996.45)

882.1 Open wound of hand except finger(s) alone, complicated

883.1 Open wound of finger(s), complicated

ICD-9-CM Procedural

80.24 Arthroscopy of hand and finger

80.34 Biopsy of joint structure of hand and finger

29901

29901 Arthroscopy, metacarpophalangeal joint, surgical; with debridement

ICD-9-CM Diagnostic

682.4 Cellulitis and abscess of hand, except fingers and thumb — (Use additional code to identify organism, such as 041.1, etc.)

709.4 Foreign body granuloma of skin and subcutaneous tissue — (Use additional code to identify foreign body (V90.01-V90.9))

710.2 Sicca syndrome

711.04 Pyogenic arthritis, hand — (Use additional code to identify infectious organism: 041.0-041.8)

716.04 Kaschin-Beck disease, hand

716.94 Unspecified arthropathy, hand ▽

718.04 Articular cartilage disorder, hand

718.44 Contracture of hand joint

718.54 Ankylosis of hand joint

728.0 Infective myositis

728.82 Foreign body granuloma of muscle — (Use additional code to identify foreign body (V90.01-V90.9))

729.4 Unspecified fasciitis ▽

729.6 Residual foreign body in soft tissue — (Use additional code to identify foreign body (V90.01-V90.9))

730.04 Acute osteomyelitis, hand — (Use additional code to identify organism: 041.1. Use additional code to identify major osseous defect, if applicable: 731.3)

730.14 Chronic osteomyelitis, hand — (Use additional code to identify organism: 041.1. Use additional code to identify major osseous defect, if applicable: 731.3)

730.24 Unspecified osteomyelitis, hand — (Use additional code to identify organism: 041.1. Use additional code to identify major osseous defect, if applicable: 731.3) ▽

730.34 Periostitis, without mention of osteomyelitis, hand — (Use additional code to identify organism: 041.1)

730.84 Other infections involving diseases classified elsewhere, hand bone — (Use additional code to identify organism: 041.1. Code first underlying disease: 002.0, 015.0-015.9) ☒

731.3 Major osseous defects — (Code first underlying disease: 170.0-170.9, 730.00-730.29, 733.00-733.09, 733.40-733.49, 996.45)

882.1 Open wound of hand except finger(s) alone, complicated

883.1 Open wound of finger(s), complicated

ICD-9-CM Procedural

80.84 Other local excision or destruction of lesion of joint of hand and finger

29902

29902 Arthroscopy, metacarpophalangeal joint, surgical; with reduction of displaced ulnar collateral ligament (eg, Stenar lesion)

ICD-9-CM Diagnostic

815.01 Closed fracture of base of thumb (first) metacarpal bone(s)

815.11 Open fracture of base of thumb (first) metacarpal bone(s)

834.01 Closed dislocation of metacarpophalangeal (joint)

834.11 Open dislocation of metacarpophalangeal (joint)

841.1 Ulnar collateral ligament sprain and strain

842.12 Sprain and strain of metacarpophalangeal (joint) of hand

883.2 Open wound of finger(s), with tendon involvement

927.20 Crushing injury of hand(s) — (Use additional code to identify any associated injuries: 800-829, 850.0-854.1, 860.0-869.1)

927.3 Crushing injury of finger(s) — (Use additional code to identify any associated injuries: 800-829, 850.0-854.1, 860.0-869.1)

ICD-9-CM Procedural

81.96 Other repair of joint

29904-29907

29904 Arthroscopy, subtalar joint, surgical; with removal of loose body or foreign body

29905 with synovectomy

29906 with debridement

29907 with subtalar arthrodesis

ICD-9-CM Diagnostic

357.1 Polyneuropathy in collagen vascular disease — (Code first underlying disease: 446.0, 710.0, 714.0) ☒

359.6 Symptomatic inflammatory myopathy in diseases classified elsewhere — (Code first underlying disease: 135, 140.0-208.9, 277.30-277.39, 446.0, 710.0, 710.1, 710.2, 714.0) ☒

446.0 Polyarteritis nodosa

710.0 Systemic lupus erythematosus — (Use additional code to identify manifestation: 424.91, 581.81, 582.81, 583.81)

710.1 Systemic sclerosis — (Use additional code to identify manifestation: 359.6, 517.2)

710.2 Sicca syndrome

714.0 Rheumatoid arthritis — (Use additional code to identify manifestation: 357.1, 359.6)

716.17 Traumatic arthropathy, ankle and foot

731.3 Major osseous defects — (Code first underlying disease: 170.0-170.9, 730.00-730.29, 733.00-733.09, 733.40-733.49, 996.45)

733.44 Aseptic necrosis of talus — (Use additional code to identify major osseous defect, if applicable: 731.3)

733.81 Malunion of fracture

736.76 Other acquired calcaneus deformity

736.79 Other acquired deformity of ankle and foot

754.61 Congenital pes planus

754.62 Talipes calcaneovalgus

754.69 Other congenital valgus deformity of feet

755.67 Congenital anomalies of foot, not elsewhere classified

825.0 Closed fracture of calcaneus

825.1 Open fracture of calcaneus

825.20 Closed fracture of unspecified bone(s) of foot (except toes) ▽

928.20 Crushing injury of foot — (Use additional code to identify any associated injuries: 800-829, 850.0-854.1, 860.0-869.1)

928.21 Crushing injury of ankle — (Use additional code to identify any associated injuries: 800-829, 850.0-854.1, 860.0-869.1)

ICD-9-CM Procedural

80.28 Arthroscopy of foot and toe

80.78 Synovectomy of foot and toe

80.88 Other local excision or destruction of lesion of joint of foot and toe

81.13 Subtalar fusion

Respiratory System

Nose

30000-30020

30000 Drainage abscess or hematoma, nasal, internal approach
30020 Drainage abscess or hematoma, nasal septum

ICD-9-CM Diagnostic

478.19 Other diseases of nasal cavity and sinuses — (Use additional code to identify infectious organism)
729.91 Post-traumatic seroma
780.62 Postprocedural fever
784.0 Headache
802.0 Nasal bones, closed fracture
802.1 Nasal bones, open fracture
873.20 Open wound of nose, unspecified site, without mention of complication
873.21 Open wound of nasal septum, without mention of complication
873.30 Open wound of nose, unspecified site, complicated
873.31 Open wound of nasal septum, complicated
873.32 Open wound of nasal cavity, complicated
906.0 Late effect of open wound of head, neck, and trunk
920 Contusion of face, scalp, and neck except eye(s)
959.01 Head injury, unspecified
959.09 Injury of face and neck, other and unspecified
996.69 Infection and inflammatory reaction due to other internal prosthetic device, implant, and graft — (Use additional code to identify specified infections)
997.39 Other respiratory complications
998.12 Hematoma complicating a procedure
998.33 Disruption of traumatic injury wound repair
998.51 Infected postoperative seroma — (Use additional code to identify organism)
998.59 Other postoperative infection — (Use additional code to identify infection)

ICD-9-CM Procedural

21.1 Incision of nose

30100

30100 Biopsy, intranasal

ICD-9-CM Diagnostic

160.0 Malignant neoplasm of nasal cavities
195.0 Malignant neoplasm of head, face, and neck
197.3 Secondary malignant neoplasm of other respiratory organs
212.0 Benign neoplasm of nasal cavities, middle ear, and accessory sinuses
231.8 Carcinoma in situ of other specified parts of respiratory system
235.9 Neoplasm of uncertain behavior of other and unspecified respiratory organs
239.1 Neoplasm of unspecified nature of respiratory system
446.4 Wegener's granulomatosis
471.0 Polyp of nasal cavity
471.9 Unspecified nasal polyp
472.0 Chronic rhinitis — (Use additional code to identify infectious organism)
473.9 Unspecified sinusitis (chronic) — (Use additional code to identify infectious organism)
478.19 Other diseases of nasal cavity and sinuses — (Use additional code to identify infectious organism)
686.1 Pyogenic granuloma of skin and subcutaneous tissue — (Use additional code to identify any infectious organism: 041.0-041.8)
784.2 Swelling, mass, or lump in head and neck

ICD-9-CM Procedural

21.22 Biopsy of nose
22.12 Open biopsy of nasal sinus

HCPCS Level II Supplies & Services

A4305 Disposable drug delivery system, flow rate of 50 ml or greater per hour

30110-30115

30110 Excision, nasal polyp(s), simple
30115 Excision, nasal polyp(s), extensive

ICD-9-CM Diagnostic

212.0 Benign neoplasm of nasal cavities, middle ear, and accessory sinuses
471.0 Polyp of nasal cavity
471.9 Unspecified nasal polyp
478.19 Other diseases of nasal cavity and sinuses — (Use additional code to identify infectious organism)
784.7 Epistaxis

ICD-9-CM Procedural

21.31 Local excision or destruction of intranasal lesion

HCPCS Level II Supplies & Services

A4305 Disposable drug delivery system, flow rate of 50 ml or greater per hour

30117-30118

30117 Excision or destruction (eg, laser), intranasal lesion; internal approach
30118 external approach (lateral rhinotomy)

ICD-9-CM Diagnostic

147.9 Malignant neoplasm of nasopharynx, unspecified site
160.0 Malignant neoplasm of nasal cavities
171.0 Malignant neoplasm of connective and other soft tissue of head, face, and neck
195.0 Malignant neoplasm of head, face, and neck
197.3 Secondary malignant neoplasm of other respiratory organs
212.0 Benign neoplasm of nasal cavities, middle ear, and accessory sinuses
228.00 Hemangioma of unspecified site
231.8 Carcinoma in situ of other specified parts of respiratory system
235.9 Neoplasm of uncertain behavior of other and unspecified respiratory organs
239.1 Neoplasm of unspecified nature of respiratory system
471.0 Polyp of nasal cavity
471.9 Unspecified nasal polyp
478.0 Hypertrophy of nasal turbinates
478.19 Other diseases of nasal cavity and sinuses — (Use additional code to identify infectious organism)
478.26 Cyst of pharynx or nasopharynx — (Use additional code to identify infectious organism)
738.0 Acquired deformity of nose
781.1 Disturbances of sensation of smell and taste

ICD-9-CM Procedural

21.30 Excision or destruction of lesion of nose, not otherwise specified
21.31 Local excision or destruction of intranasal lesion

HCPCS Level II Supplies & Services

A4305 Disposable drug delivery system, flow rate of 50 ml or greater per hour

30120

30120 Excision or surgical planing of skin of nose for rhinophyma

ICD-9-CM Diagnostic

695.3 Rosacea

ICD-9-CM Procedural

21.32 Local excision or destruction of other lesion of nose
86.25 Dermabrasion

HCPCS Level II Supplies & Services

A4305 Disposable drug delivery system, flow rate of 50 ml or greater per hour

30124-30125

30124 Excision dermoid cyst, nose; simple, skin, subcutaneous
30125 complex, under bone or cartilage

ICD-9-CM Diagnostic

212.0 Benign neoplasm of nasal cavities, middle ear, and accessory sinuses
216.3 Benign neoplasm of skin of other and unspecified parts of face ♥
229.8 Benign neoplasm of other specified sites
709.8 Other specified disorder of skin

ICD-9-CM Procedural

21.32 Local excision or destruction of other lesion of nose

HCPCS Level II Supplies & Services

A4305 Disposable drug delivery system, flow rate of 50 ml or greater per hour

30130-30140

30130 Excision inferior turbinate, partial or complete, any method
30140 Submucous resection inferior turbinate, partial or complete, any method

ICD-9-CM Diagnostic

160.0 Malignant neoplasm of nasal cavities
170.0 Malignant neoplasm of bones of skull and face, except mandible
197.3 Secondary malignant neoplasm of other respiratory organs
198.5 Secondary malignant neoplasm of bone and bone marrow
212.0 Benign neoplasm of nasal cavities, middle ear, and accessory sinuses
213.0 Benign neoplasm of bones of skull and face
231.8 Carcinoma in situ of other specified parts of respiratory system
235.9 Neoplasm of uncertain behavior of other and unspecified respiratory organs ♥
238.0 Neoplasm of uncertain behavior of bone and articular cartilage
239.1 Neoplasm of unspecified nature of respiratory system
239.2 Neoplasms of unspecified nature of bone, soft tissue, and skin
327.20 Organic sleep apnea, unspecified ♥
327.23 Obstructive sleep apnea (adult) (pediatric)
327.29 Other organic sleep apnea
375.22 Epiphora due to insufficient drainage
461.3 Acute sphenoidal sinusitis — (Use additional code to identify infectious organism)
461.8 Other acute sinusitis — (Use additional code to identify infectious organism)
470 Deviated nasal septum
472.0 Chronic rhinitis — (Use additional code to identify infectious organism)
472.2 Chronic nasopharyngitis — (Use additional code to identify infectious organism)
473.0 Chronic maxillary sinusitis — (Use additional code to identify infectious organism)
473.1 Chronic frontal sinusitis — (Use additional code to identify infectious organism)
473.2 Chronic ethmoidal sinusitis — (Use additional code to identify infectious organism)
473.3 Chronic sphenoidal sinusitis — (Use additional code to identify infectious organism)
473.8 Other chronic sinusitis — (Use additional code to identify infectious organism)
473.9 Unspecified sinusitis (chronic) — (Use additional code to identify infectious organism) ♥
477.9 Allergic rhinitis, cause unspecified — (Use additional code to identify infectious organism) ♥
478.0 Hypertrophy of nasal turbinates
478.19 Other diseases of nasal cavity and sinuses — (Use additional code to identify infectious organism)
780.51 Insomnia with sleep apnea, unspecified ♥
780.57 Unspecified sleep apnea ♥
786.09 Other dyspnea and respiratory abnormalities
802.0 Nasal bones, closed fracture
802.1 Nasal bones, open fracture
905.0 Late effect of fracture of skull and face bones

ICD-9-CM Procedural

21.61 Turbinectomy by diathermy or cryosurgery
21.69 Other turbinectomy

HCPCS Level II Supplies & Services

A6407 Packing strips, nonimpregnated, sterile, up to 2 in in width, per linear yd

30150-30160

30150 Rhinectomy; partial
30160 total

ICD-9-CM Diagnostic

160.0 Malignant neoplasm of nasal cavities
170.0 Malignant neoplasm of bones of skull and face, except mandible
172.3 Malignant melanoma of skin of other and unspecified parts of face ♥
173.30 Unspecified malignant neoplasm of skin of other and unspecified parts of face ♥
173.31 Basal cell carcinoma of skin of other and unspecified parts of face
173.32 Squamous cell carcinoma of skin of other and unspecified parts of face
173.39 Other specified malignant neoplasm of skin of other and unspecified parts of face
195.0 Malignant neoplasm of head, face, and neck
197.3 Secondary malignant neoplasm of other respiratory organs
198.2 Secondary malignant neoplasm of skin
198.89 Secondary malignant neoplasm of other specified sites
212.0 Benign neoplasm of nasal cavities, middle ear, and accessory sinuses
228.01 Hemangioma of skin and subcutaneous tissue
231.8 Carcinoma in situ of other specified parts of respiratory system
232.3 Carcinoma in situ of skin of other and unspecified parts of face ♥
238.0 Neoplasm of uncertain behavior of bone and articular cartilage
238.2 Neoplasm of uncertain behavior of skin
478.19 Other diseases of nasal cavity and sinuses — (Use additional code to identify infectious organism)
738.0 Acquired deformity of nose
785.4 Gangrene — (Code first any associated underlying condition)
873.30 Open wound of nose, unspecified site, complicated ♥
873.31 Open wound of nasal septum, complicated
873.32 Open wound of nasal cavity, complicated
873.33 Open wound of nasal sinus, complicated
873.39 Open wound of nose, multiple sites, complicated
925.1 Crushing injury of face and scalp — (Use additional code to identify any associated injuries, such as: 800-829, 850.0-854.1, 860.0-869.1)
941.55 Deep necrosis of underlying tissues due to burn (deep third degree) of nose (septum), with loss of a body part
948.00 Burn (any degree) involving less than 10% of body surface with third degree burn of less than 10% or unspecified amount
991.0 Frostbite of face
997.39 Other respiratory complications
998.33 Disruption of traumatic injury wound repair
998.59 Other postoperative infection — (Use additional code to identify infection)
V58.42 Aftercare following surgery for neoplasm — (This code should be used in conjunction with other aftercare codes to fully identify the reason for the aftercare encounter)

ICD-9-CM Procedural

21.4 Resection of nose

30200

30200 Injection into turbinate(s), therapeutic

ICD-9-CM Diagnostic

461.0 Acute maxillary sinusitis — (Use additional code to identify infectious organism)
461.1 Acute frontal sinusitis — (Use additional code to identify infectious organism)
461.2 Acute ethmoidal sinusitis — (Use additional code to identify infectious organism)
461.3 Acute sphenoidal sinusitis — (Use additional code to identify infectious organism)
461.8 Other acute sinusitis — (Use additional code to identify infectious organism)
461.9 Acute sinusitis, unspecified — (Use additional code to identify infectious organism) ▽
470 Deviated nasal septum
472.0 Chronic rhinitis — (Use additional code to identify infectious organism)
473.0 Chronic maxillary sinusitis — (Use additional code to identify infectious organism)
473.1 Chronic frontal sinusitis — (Use additional code to identify infectious organism)
473.2 Chronic ethmoidal sinusitis — (Use additional code to identify infectious organism)
473.3 Chronic sphenoidal sinusitis — (Use additional code to identify infectious organism)
473.8 Other chronic sinusitis — (Use additional code to identify infectious organism)
473.9 Unspecified sinusitis (chronic) — (Use additional code to identify infectious organism) ▽
477.9 Allergic rhinitis, cause unspecified — (Use additional code to identify infectious organism) ▽
478.0 Hypertrophy of nasal turbinates
478.19 Other diseases of nasal cavity and sinuses — (Use additional code to identify infectious organism)

ICD-9-CM Procedural

99.29 Injection or infusion of other therapeutic or prophylactic substance
99.77 Application or administration of adhesion barrier substance

HCPCS Level II Supplies & Services

A4305 Disposable drug delivery system, flow rate of 50 ml or greater per hour

30210

30210 Displacement therapy (Proetz type)

ICD-9-CM Diagnostic

461.2 Acute ethmoidal sinusitis — (Use additional code to identify infectious organism)
461.3 Acute sphenoidal sinusitis — (Use additional code to identify infectious organism)
461.8 Other acute sinusitis — (Use additional code to identify infectious organism)
461.9 Acute sinusitis, unspecified — (Use additional code to identify infectious organism) ▽
472.0 Chronic rhinitis — (Use additional code to identify infectious organism)
473.2 Chronic ethmoidal sinusitis — (Use additional code to identify infectious organism)
473.3 Chronic sphenoidal sinusitis — (Use additional code to identify infectious organism)
473.8 Other chronic sinusitis — (Use additional code to identify infectious organism)
473.9 Unspecified sinusitis (chronic) — (Use additional code to identify infectious organism) ▽
477.9 Allergic rhinitis, cause unspecified — (Use additional code to identify infectious organism) ▽
478.0 Hypertrophy of nasal turbinates

ICD-9-CM Procedural

22.00 Aspiration and lavage of nasal sinus, not otherwise specified

HCPCS Level II Supplies & Services

A4305 Disposable drug delivery system, flow rate of 50 ml or greater per hour

30220

30220 Insertion, nasal septal prosthesis (button)

ICD-9-CM Diagnostic

160.0 Malignant neoplasm of nasal cavities
212.0 Benign neoplasm of nasal cavities, middle ear, and accessory sinuses
231.8 Carcinoma in situ of other specified parts of respiratory system
234.8 Carcinoma in situ of other specified sites
305.60 Nondependent cocaine abuse, unspecified ▽
305.61 Nondependent cocaine abuse, continuous
305.62 Nondependent cocaine abuse, episodic
305.63 Nondependent cocaine abuse, in remission
461.3 Acute sphenoidal sinusitis — (Use additional code to identify infectious organism)
470 Deviated nasal septum
473.9 Unspecified sinusitis (chronic) — (Use additional code to identify infectious organism) ▽
478.0 Hypertrophy of nasal turbinates
478.19 Other diseases of nasal cavity and sinuses — (Use additional code to identify infectious organism)
748.1 Other congenital anomaly of nose
802.0 Nasal bones, closed fracture
802.1 Nasal bones, open fracture
905.0 Late effect of fracture of skull and face bones
906.4 Late effect of crushing
906.5 Late effect of burn of eye, face, head, and neck
959.01 Head injury, unspecified ▽
959.09 Injury of face and neck, other and unspecified
997.39 Other respiratory complications
998.12 Hematoma complicating a procedure
998.33 Disruption of traumatic injury wound repair
998.59 Other postoperative infection — (Use additional code to identify infection)
V58.42 Aftercare following surgery for neoplasm — (This code should be used in conjunction with other aftercare codes to fully identify the reason for the aftercare encounter)

ICD-9-CM Procedural

21.88 Other septoplasty

30300-30320

30300 Removal foreign body, intranasal; office type procedure
30310 requiring general anesthesia
30320 by lateral rhinotomy

ICD-9-CM Diagnostic

932 Foreign body in nose

ICD-9-CM Procedural

21.1 Incision of nose
96.53 Irrigation of nasal passages
98.12 Removal of intraluminal foreign body from nose without incision

HCPCS Level II Supplies & Services

A4305 Disposable drug delivery system, flow rate of 50 ml or greater per hour

30400-30410

30400 Rhinoplasty, primary; lateral and alar cartilages and/or elevation of nasal tip
30410 complete, external parts including bony pyramid, lateral and alar cartilages, and/or elevation of nasal tip

ICD-9-CM Diagnostic

160.0 Malignant neoplasm of nasal cavities
170.0 Malignant neoplasm of bones of skull and face, except mandible
172.3 Malignant melanoma of skin of other and unspecified parts of face ▽

173.30 Unspecified malignant neoplasm of skin of other and unspecified parts of face
173.31 Basal cell carcinoma of skin of other and unspecified parts of face
173.32 Squamous cell carcinoma of skin of other and unspecified parts of face
173.39 Other specified malignant neoplasm of skin of other and unspecified parts of face
195.0 Malignant neoplasm of head, face, and neck
198.2 Secondary malignant neoplasm of skin
212.0 Benign neoplasm of nasal cavities, middle ear, and accessory sinuses
213.0 Benign neoplasm of bones of skull and face
216.3 Benign neoplasm of skin of other and unspecified parts of face
232.3 Carcinoma in situ of skin of other and unspecified parts of face
238.2 Neoplasm of uncertain behavior of skin
239.2 Neoplasms of unspecified nature of bone, soft tissue, and skin
478.19 Other diseases of nasal cavity and sinuses — (Use additional code to identify infectious organism)
738.0 Acquired deformity of nose
748.1 Other congenital anomaly of nose
754.0 Congenital musculoskeletal deformities of skull, face, and jaw
785.4 Gangrene — (Code first any associated underlying condition)
802.0 Nasal bones, closed fracture
802.1 Nasal bones, open fracture
873.32 Open wound of nasal cavity, complicated
905.0 Late effect of fracture of skull and face bones
906.0 Late effect of open wound of head, neck, and trunk
906.5 Late effect of burn of eye, face, head, and neck
925.1 Crushing injury of face and scalp — (Use additional code to identify any associated injuries, such as: 800-829, 850.0-854.1, 860.0-869.1)
991.0 Frostbite of face
V50.1 Other plastic surgery for unacceptable cosmetic appearance
V51.8 Other aftercare involving the use of plastic surgery

ICD-9-CM Procedural

21.83 Total nasal reconstruction
21.86 Limited rhinoplasty
21.87 Other rhinoplasty

30420

30420 Rhinoplasty, primary; including major septal repair

ICD-9-CM Diagnostic

160.0 Malignant neoplasm of nasal cavities
170.0 Malignant neoplasm of bones of skull and face, except mandible
172.3 Malignant melanoma of skin of other and unspecified parts of face
173.30 Unspecified malignant neoplasm of skin of other and unspecified parts of face
173.31 Basal cell carcinoma of skin of other and unspecified parts of face
173.32 Squamous cell carcinoma of skin of other and unspecified parts of face
173.39 Other specified malignant neoplasm of skin of other and unspecified parts of face
195.0 Malignant neoplasm of head, face, and neck
197.3 Secondary malignant neoplasm of other respiratory organs
198.2 Secondary malignant neoplasm of skin
198.89 Secondary malignant neoplasm of other specified sites
212.0 Benign neoplasm of nasal cavities, middle ear, and accessory sinuses
213.0 Benign neoplasm of bones of skull and face
216.3 Benign neoplasm of skin of other and unspecified parts of face
231.8 Carcinoma in situ of other specified parts of respiratory system
232.3 Carcinoma in situ of skin of other and unspecified parts of face
235.9 Neoplasm of uncertain behavior of other and unspecified respiratory organs
238.1 Neoplasm of uncertain behavior of connective and other soft tissue
238.2 Neoplasm of uncertain behavior of skin
239.1 Neoplasm of unspecified nature of respiratory system
239.2 Neoplasms of unspecified nature of bone, soft tissue, and skin
470 Deviated nasal septum
478.19 Other diseases of nasal cavity and sinuses — (Use additional code to identify infectious organism)
519.8 Other diseases of respiratory system, not elsewhere classified — (Use additional code to identify infectious organism)
738.0 Acquired deformity of nose
748.1 Other congenital anomaly of nose
754.0 Congenital musculoskeletal deformities of skull, face, and jaw
786.09 Other dyspnea and respiratory abnormalities
802.0 Nasal bones, closed fracture
802.1 Nasal bones, open fracture
802.5 Malar and maxillary bones, open fracture
873.31 Open wound of nasal septum, complicated
873.32 Open wound of nasal cavity, complicated
873.39 Open wound of nose, multiple sites, complicated
905.0 Late effect of fracture of skull and face bones
906.0 Late effect of open wound of head, neck, and trunk
906.5 Late effect of burn of eye, face, head, and neck
991.0 Frostbite of face
V50.1 Other plastic surgery for unacceptable cosmetic appearance
V51.8 Other aftercare involving the use of plastic surgery

ICD-9-CM Procedural

21.5 Submucous resection of nasal septum
21.87 Other rhinoplasty
21.88 Other septoplasty

30430-30450

30430 Rhinoplasty, secondary; minor revision (small amount of nasal tip work)
30435 intermediate revision (bony work with osteotomies)
30450 major revision (nasal tip work and osteotomies)

ICD-9-CM Diagnostic

160.0 Malignant neoplasm of nasal cavities
170.0 Malignant neoplasm of bones of skull and face, except mandible
172.3 Malignant melanoma of skin of other and unspecified parts of face
173.30 Unspecified malignant neoplasm of skin of other and unspecified parts of face
173.31 Basal cell carcinoma of skin of other and unspecified parts of face
173.32 Squamous cell carcinoma of skin of other and unspecified parts of face
173.39 Other specified malignant neoplasm of skin of other and unspecified parts of face
195.0 Malignant neoplasm of head, face, and neck
198.2 Secondary malignant neoplasm of skin
212.0 Benign neoplasm of nasal cavities, middle ear, and accessory sinuses
213.0 Benign neoplasm of bones of skull and face
216.3 Benign neoplasm of skin of other and unspecified parts of face
232.3 Carcinoma in situ of skin of other and unspecified parts of face
238.2 Neoplasm of uncertain behavior of skin
239.2 Neoplasms of unspecified nature of bone, soft tissue, and skin
738.0 Acquired deformity of nose
748.1 Other congenital anomaly of nose
754.0 Congenital musculoskeletal deformities of skull, face, and jaw
786.09 Other dyspnea and respiratory abnormalities
802.0 Nasal bones, closed fracture
802.1 Nasal bones, open fracture
905.0 Late effect of fracture of skull and face bones
906.0 Late effect of open wound of head, neck, and trunk
906.4 Late effect of crushing
906.5 Late effect of burn of eye, face, head, and neck
996.52 Mechanical complication due to other tissue graft, not elsewhere classified

996.59 Mechanical complication due to other implant and internal device, not elsewhere classified
996.69 Infection and inflammatory reaction due to other internal prosthetic device, implant, and graft — (Use additional code to identify specified infections)
996.79 Other complications due to other internal prosthetic device, implant, and graft — (Use additional code to identify complication: 338.18-338.19, 338.28-338.29)
V10.22 Personal history of malignant neoplasm of nasal cavities, middle ear, and accessory sinuses
V50.1 Other plastic surgery for unacceptable cosmetic appearance
V51.8 Other aftercare involving the use of plastic surgery

ICD-9-CM Procedural

21.84 Revision rhinoplasty
21.89 Other repair and plastic operations on nose

30460-30462

30460 Rhinoplasty for nasal deformity secondary to congenital cleft lip and/or palate, including columellar lengthening; tip only
30462 tip, septum, osteotomies

ICD-9-CM Diagnostic

470 Deviated nasal septum
748.1 Other congenital anomaly of nose
749.01 Unilateral cleft palate, complete
749.03 Bilateral cleft palate, complete
749.11 Unilateral cleft lip, complete
749.13 Bilateral cleft lip, complete
749.21 Unilateral cleft palate with cleft lip, complete
749.23 Bilateral cleft palate with cleft lip, complete
756.0 Congenital anomalies of skull and face bones
V50.1 Other plastic surgery for unacceptable cosmetic appearance
V51.8 Other aftercare involving the use of plastic surgery

ICD-9-CM Procedural

21.86 Limited rhinoplasty
21.87 Other rhinoplasty
21.88 Other septoplasty

30465

30465 Repair of nasal vestibular stenosis (eg, spreader grafting, lateral nasal wall reconstruction)

ICD-9-CM Diagnostic

478.19 Other diseases of nasal cavity and sinuses — (Use additional code to identify infectious organism)
748.0 Congenital choanal atresia

ICD-9-CM Procedural

21.89 Other repair and plastic operations on nose

30520

30520 Septoplasty or submucous resection, with or without cartilage scoring, contouring or replacement with graft

ICD-9-CM Diagnostic

160.0 Malignant neoplasm of nasal cavities
197.3 Secondary malignant neoplasm of other respiratory organs
198.89 Secondary malignant neoplasm of other specified sites
212.0 Benign neoplasm of nasal cavities, middle ear, and accessory sinuses
231.8 Carcinoma in situ of other specified parts of respiratory system
235.9 Neoplasm of uncertain behavior of other and unspecified respiratory organs ▽
239.1 Neoplasm of unspecified nature of respiratory system
305.60 Nondependent cocaine abuse, unspecified ▽
305.61 Nondependent cocaine abuse, continuous
305.62 Nondependent cocaine abuse, episodic
305.63 Nondependent cocaine abuse, in remission
461.2 Acute ethmoidal sinusitis — (Use additional code to identify infectious organism)
461.8 Other acute sinusitis — (Use additional code to identify infectious organism)
470 Deviated nasal septum
471.0 Polyp of nasal cavity
471.9 Unspecified nasal polyp ▽
472.0 Chronic rhinitis — (Use additional code to identify infectious organism)
473.0 Chronic maxillary sinusitis — (Use additional code to identify infectious organism)
473.2 Chronic ethmoidal sinusitis — (Use additional code to identify infectious organism)
473.3 Chronic sphenoidal sinusitis — (Use additional code to identify infectious organism)
473.8 Other chronic sinusitis — (Use additional code to identify infectious organism)
473.9 Unspecified sinusitis (chronic) — (Use additional code to identify infectious organism) ▽
478.19 Other diseases of nasal cavity and sinuses — (Use additional code to identify infectious organism)
738.0 Acquired deformity of nose
748.1 Other congenital anomaly of nose
754.0 Congenital musculoskeletal deformities of skull, face, and jaw
784.7 Epistaxis
786.02 Orthopnea
786.09 Other dyspnea and respiratory abnormalities
802.0 Nasal bones, closed fracture
802.1 Nasal bones, open fracture
873.31 Open wound of nasal septum, complicated
905.0 Late effect of fracture of skull and face bones
V58.42 Aftercare following surgery for neoplasm — (This code should be used in conjunction with other aftercare codes to fully identify the reason for the aftercare encounter)

ICD-9-CM Procedural

21.5 Submucous resection of nasal septum
21.88 Other septoplasty

30540-30545

30540 Repair choanal atresia; intranasal
30545 transpalatine

ICD-9-CM Diagnostic

738.0 Acquired deformity of nose
748.0 Congenital choanal atresia

ICD-9-CM Procedural

21.89 Other repair and plastic operations on nose

30560

30560 Lysis intranasal synechia

ICD-9-CM Diagnostic

470 Deviated nasal septum
471.1 Polypoid sinus degeneration
471.9 Unspecified nasal polyp ▽
473.0 Chronic maxillary sinusitis — (Use additional code to identify infectious organism)
473.1 Chronic frontal sinusitis — (Use additional code to identify infectious organism)
473.2 Chronic ethmoidal sinusitis — (Use additional code to identify infectious organism)
473.3 Chronic sphenoidal sinusitis — (Use additional code to identify infectious organism)
473.8 Other chronic sinusitis — (Use additional code to identify infectious organism)
473.9 Unspecified sinusitis (chronic) — (Use additional code to identify infectious organism) ▽
478.0 Hypertrophy of nasal turbinates
478.19 Other diseases of nasal cavity and sinuses — (Use additional code to identify infectious organism)

738.0 Acquired deformity of nose
748.0 Congenital choanal atresia
905.0 Late effect of fracture of skull and face bones
906.5 Late effect of burn of eye, face, head, and neck
V45.89 Other postprocedural status
V54.19 Aftercare for healing traumatic fracture of other bone

ICD-9-CM Procedural

21.91 Lysis of adhesions of nose

30580-30600

30580 Repair fistula; oromaxillary (combine with 31030 if antrotomy is included)
30600 oronasal

ICD-9-CM Diagnostic

473.0 Chronic maxillary sinusitis — (Use additional code to identify infectious organism)
478.19 Other diseases of nasal cavity and sinuses — (Use additional code to identify infectious organism)
526.89 Other specified disease of the jaws
528.3 Cellulitis and abscess of oral soft tissues
528.9 Other and unspecified diseases of the oral soft tissues ♥
738.19 Other specified acquired deformity of head
748.1 Other congenital anomaly of nose
749.00 Unspecified cleft palate ♥
749.01 Unilateral cleft palate, complete
749.02 Unilateral cleft palate, incomplete
749.03 Bilateral cleft palate, complete
749.04 Bilateral cleft palate, incomplete
749.20 Unspecified cleft palate with cleft lip ♥
749.21 Unilateral cleft palate with cleft lip, complete
749.22 Unilateral cleft palate with cleft lip, incomplete
749.23 Bilateral cleft palate with cleft lip, complete
749.24 Bilateral cleft palate with cleft lip, incomplete
749.25 Other combinations of cleft palate with cleft lip
905.0 Late effect of fracture of skull and face bones

ICD-9-CM Procedural

21.82 Closure of nasal fistula
22.71 Closure of nasal sinus fistula

30620

30620 Septal or other intranasal dermatoplasty (does not include obtaining graft)

ICD-9-CM Diagnostic

448.0 Hereditary hemorrhagic telangiectasia
470 Deviated nasal septum
471.0 Polyp of nasal cavity
473.0 Chronic maxillary sinusitis — (Use additional code to identify infectious organism)
473.2 Chronic ethmoidal sinusitis — (Use additional code to identify infectious organism)
473.3 Chronic sphenoidal sinusitis — (Use additional code to identify infectious organism)
473.8 Other chronic sinusitis — (Use additional code to identify infectious organism)
473.9 Unspecified sinusitis (chronic) — (Use additional code to identify infectious organism) ♥
478.0 Hypertrophy of nasal turbinates
478.19 Other diseases of nasal cavity and sinuses — (Use additional code to identify infectious organism)
519.8 Other diseases of respiratory system, not elsewhere classified — (Use additional code to identify infectious organism)
738.0 Acquired deformity of nose
748.1 Other congenital anomaly of nose
754.0 Congenital musculoskeletal deformities of skull, face, and jaw
784.7 Epistaxis
802.0 Nasal bones, closed fracture
802.1 Nasal bones, open fracture
905.0 Late effect of fracture of skull and face bones

ICD-9-CM Procedural

21.07 Control of epistaxis by excision of nasal mucosa and skin grafting of septum and lateral nasal wall
21.83 Total nasal reconstruction
21.88 Other septoplasty
21.89 Other repair and plastic operations on nose

30630

30630 Repair nasal septal perforations

ICD-9-CM Diagnostic

305.60 Nondependent cocaine abuse, unspecified ♥
305.61 Nondependent cocaine abuse, continuous
305.62 Nondependent cocaine abuse, episodic
305.63 Nondependent cocaine abuse, in remission
478.19 Other diseases of nasal cavity and sinuses — (Use additional code to identify infectious organism)
748.1 Other congenital anomaly of nose
784.7 Epistaxis
802.0 Nasal bones, closed fracture
802.1 Nasal bones, open fracture
905.0 Late effect of fracture of skull and face bones
906.4 Late effect of crushing
906.5 Late effect of burn of eye, face, head, and neck

ICD-9-CM Procedural

21.88 Other septoplasty

30801-30802

30801 Ablation, soft tissue of inferior turbinates, unilateral or bilateral, any method (eg, electrocautery, radiofrequency ablation, or tissue volume reduction); superficial
30802 intramural (ie, submucosal)

ICD-9-CM Diagnostic

327.20 Organic sleep apnea, unspecified ♥
327.23 Obstructive sleep apnea (adult) (pediatric)
327.29 Other organic sleep apnea
470 Deviated nasal septum
471.8 Other polyp of sinus
471.9 Unspecified nasal polyp ♥
472.0 Chronic rhinitis — (Use additional code to identify infectious organism)
473.0 Chronic maxillary sinusitis — (Use additional code to identify infectious organism)
473.1 Chronic frontal sinusitis — (Use additional code to identify infectious organism)
473.2 Chronic ethmoidal sinusitis — (Use additional code to identify infectious organism)
473.3 Chronic sphenoidal sinusitis — (Use additional code to identify infectious organism)
473.8 Other chronic sinusitis — (Use additional code to identify infectious organism)
473.9 Unspecified sinusitis (chronic) — (Use additional code to identify infectious organism) ♥
478.0 Hypertrophy of nasal turbinates
478.19 Other diseases of nasal cavity and sinuses — (Use additional code to identify infectious organism)
519.8 Other diseases of respiratory system, not elsewhere classified — (Use additional code to identify infectious organism)
738.0 Acquired deformity of nose
780.51 Insomnia with sleep apnea, unspecified ♥
780.57 Unspecified sleep apnea ♥
784.7 Epistaxis

786.09 Other dyspnea and respiratory abnormalities

ICD-9-CM Procedural

21.61 Turbinectomy by diathermy or cryosurgery
21.69 Other turbinectomy

HCPCS Level II Supplies & Services

A6407 Packing strips, nonimpregnated, sterile, up to 2 in in width, per linear yd

30901-30903

30901 Control nasal hemorrhage, anterior, simple (limited cautery and/or packing) any method
30903 Control nasal hemorrhage, anterior, complex (extensive cautery and/or packing) any method

ICD-9-CM Diagnostic

448.9 Other and unspecified capillary diseases ▽
478.29 Other disease of pharynx or nasopharynx — (Use additional code to identify infectious organism)
772.8 Other specified hemorrhage of fetus or newborn — (Use additional code(s) to further specify condition)
784.7 Epistaxis
904.9 Injury to blood vessels, unspecified site ▽
958.2 Secondary and recurrent hemorrhage as an early complication of trauma
998.11 Hemorrhage complicating a procedure
998.2 Accidental puncture or laceration during procedure
998.33 Disruption of traumatic injury wound repair

ICD-9-CM Procedural

21.00 Control of epistaxis, not otherwise specified
21.01 Control of epistaxis by anterior nasal packing
21.02 Control of epistaxis by posterior (and anterior) packing
21.03 Control of epistaxis by cauterization (and packing)

30905-30906

30905 Control nasal hemorrhage, posterior, with posterior nasal packs and/or cautery, any method; initial
30906 subsequent

ICD-9-CM Diagnostic

448.9 Other and unspecified capillary diseases ▽
478.29 Other disease of pharynx or nasopharynx — (Use additional code to identify infectious organism)
772.8 Other specified hemorrhage of fetus or newborn — (Use additional code(s) to further specify condition)
784.7 Epistaxis
958.2 Secondary and recurrent hemorrhage as an early complication of trauma
998.11 Hemorrhage complicating a procedure
998.2 Accidental puncture or laceration during procedure

ICD-9-CM Procedural

21.02 Control of epistaxis by posterior (and anterior) packing
21.03 Control of epistaxis by cauterization (and packing)

30915-30920

30915 Ligation arteries; ethmoidal
30920 internal maxillary artery, transantral

ICD-9-CM Diagnostic

784.7 Epistaxis
802.0 Nasal bones, closed fracture
802.1 Nasal bones, open fracture
802.8 Other facial bones, closed fracture
900.82 Injury to multiple blood vessels of head and neck
958.2 Secondary and recurrent hemorrhage as an early complication of trauma
959.01 Head injury, unspecified ▽
959.09 Injury of face and neck, other and unspecified
998.2 Accidental puncture or laceration during procedure

ICD-9-CM Procedural

21.04 Control of epistaxis by ligation of ethmoidal arteries
21.05 Control of epistaxis by (transantral) ligation of the maxillary artery

30930

30930 Fracture nasal inferior turbinate(s), therapeutic

ICD-9-CM Diagnostic

327.20 Organic sleep apnea, unspecified ▽
327.23 Obstructive sleep apnea (adult) (pediatric)
327.29 Other organic sleep apnea
375.56 Stenosis of nasolacrimal duct, acquired
461.9 Acute sinusitis, unspecified — (Use additional code to identify infectious organism) ▽
470 Deviated nasal septum
472.0 Chronic rhinitis — (Use additional code to identify infectious organism)
473.0 Chronic maxillary sinusitis — (Use additional code to identify infectious organism)
473.1 Chronic frontal sinusitis — (Use additional code to identify infectious organism)
473.2 Chronic ethmoidal sinusitis — (Use additional code to identify infectious organism)
473.3 Chronic sphenoidal sinusitis — (Use additional code to identify infectious organism)
473.8 Other chronic sinusitis — (Use additional code to identify infectious organism)
473.9 Unspecified sinusitis (chronic) — (Use additional code to identify infectious organism) ▽
477.9 Allergic rhinitis, cause unspecified — (Use additional code to identify infectious organism) ▽
478.0 Hypertrophy of nasal turbinates
478.19 Other diseases of nasal cavity and sinuses — (Use additional code to identify infectious organism)
519.8 Other diseases of respiratory system, not elsewhere classified — (Use additional code to identify infectious organism)
738.0 Acquired deformity of nose
743.65 Specified congenital anomaly of lacrimal passages
748.1 Other congenital anomaly of nose
780.51 Insomnia with sleep apnea, unspecified ▽
780.57 Unspecified sleep apnea ▽
786.09 Other dyspnea and respiratory abnormalities

ICD-9-CM Procedural

21.62 Fracture of the turbinates

HCPCS Level II Supplies & Services

A6407 Packing strips, nonimpregnated, sterile, up to 2 in in width, per linear yd

Accessory Sinuses

31000-31002

31000 Lavage by cannulation; maxillary sinus (antrum puncture or natural ostium)
31002 sphenoid sinus

ICD-9-CM Diagnostic

461.0 Acute maxillary sinusitis — (Use additional code to identify infectious organism)
461.3 Acute sphenoidal sinusitis — (Use additional code to identify infectious organism)
461.8 Other acute sinusitis — (Use additional code to identify infectious organism)
461.9 Acute sinusitis, unspecified — (Use additional code to identify infectious organism) ▽
472.0 Chronic rhinitis — (Use additional code to identify infectious organism)
473.0 Chronic maxillary sinusitis — (Use additional code to identify infectious organism)
473.3 Chronic sphenoidal sinusitis — (Use additional code to identify infectious organism)
473.8 Other chronic sinusitis — (Use additional code to identify infectious organism)

473.9 Unspecified sinusitis (chronic) — (Use additional code to identify infectious organism) ▽
478.19 Other diseases of nasal cavity and sinuses — (Use additional code to identify infectious organism)
784.0 Headache

ICD-9-CM Procedural

22.00 Aspiration and lavage of nasal sinus, not otherwise specified
22.01 Puncture of nasal sinus for aspiration or lavage
22.02 Aspiration or lavage of nasal sinus through natural ostium

31020-31032

31020 Sinusotomy, maxillary (antrotomy); intranasal
31030 radical (Caldwell-Luc) without removal of antrochoanal polyps
31032 radical (Caldwell-Luc) with removal of antrochoanal polyps

ICD-9-CM Diagnostic

160.2 Malignant neoplasm of maxillary sinus
197.3 Secondary malignant neoplasm of other respiratory organs
212.0 Benign neoplasm of nasal cavities, middle ear, and accessory sinuses
231.8 Carcinoma in situ of other specified parts of respiratory system
235.9 Neoplasm of uncertain behavior of other and unspecified respiratory organs ▽
238.0 Neoplasm of uncertain behavior of bone and articular cartilage
239.1 Neoplasm of unspecified nature of respiratory system
289.1 Chronic lymphadenitis
446.4 Wegener's granulomatosis
461.0 Acute maxillary sinusitis — (Use additional code to identify infectious organism)
461.8 Other acute sinusitis — (Use additional code to identify infectious organism)
461.9 Acute sinusitis, unspecified — (Use additional code to identify infectious organism) ▽
470 Deviated nasal septum
471.0 Polyp of nasal cavity
471.8 Other polyp of sinus
471.9 Unspecified nasal polyp ▽
473.0 Chronic maxillary sinusitis — (Use additional code to identify infectious organism)
473.8 Other chronic sinusitis — (Use additional code to identify infectious organism)
473.9 Unspecified sinusitis (chronic) — (Use additional code to identify infectious organism) ▽
478.0 Hypertrophy of nasal turbinates
478.19 Other diseases of nasal cavity and sinuses — (Use additional code to identify infectious organism)
730.18 Chronic osteomyelitis, other specified sites — (Use additional code to identify organism: 041.1. Use additional code to identify major osseous defect, if applicable: 731.3)
730.28 Unspecified osteomyelitis, other specified sites — (Use additional code to identify organism: 041.1. Use additional code to identify major osseous defect, if applicable: 731.3) ▽
748.8 Other specified congenital anomaly of respiratory system
784.0 Headache
784.2 Swelling, mass, or lump in head and neck
784.7 Epistaxis
786.09 Other dyspnea and respiratory abnormalities
905.0 Late effect of fracture of skull and face bones
996.60 Infection and inflammatory reaction due to unspecified device, implant, and graft — (Use additional code to identify specified infections) ▽
996.69 Infection and inflammatory reaction due to other internal prosthetic device, implant, and graft — (Use additional code to identify specified infections)

ICD-9-CM Procedural

22.2 Intranasal antrotomy
22.31 Radical maxillary antrotomy
22.39 Other external maxillary antrotomy
22.61 Excision of lesion of maxillary sinus with Caldwell-Luc approach

HCPCS Level II Supplies & Services

A4305 Disposable drug delivery system, flow rate of 50 ml or greater per hour

31040

31040 Pterygomaxillary fossa surgery, any approach

ICD-9-CM Diagnostic

171.0 Malignant neoplasm of connective and other soft tissue of head, face, and neck
198.89 Secondary malignant neoplasm of other specified sites
215.0 Other benign neoplasm of connective and other soft tissue of head, face, and neck
238.1 Neoplasm of uncertain behavior of connective and other soft tissue
239.1 Neoplasm of unspecified nature of respiratory system
239.2 Neoplasms of unspecified nature of bone, soft tissue, and skin
337.09 Other idiopathic peripheral autonomic neuropathy
350.1 Trigeminal neuralgia
350.2 Atypical face pain
730.18 Chronic osteomyelitis, other specified sites — (Use additional code to identify organism: 041.1. Use additional code to identify major osseous defect, if applicable: 731.3)

ICD-9-CM Procedural

22.50 Sinusotomy, not otherwise specified

31050-31051

31050 Sinusotomy, sphenoid, with or without biopsy;
31051 with mucosal stripping or removal of polyp(s)

ICD-9-CM Diagnostic

160.0 Malignant neoplasm of nasal cavities
160.5 Malignant neoplasm of sphenoidal sinus
197.3 Secondary malignant neoplasm of other respiratory organs
212.0 Benign neoplasm of nasal cavities, middle ear, and accessory sinuses
231.8 Carcinoma in situ of other specified parts of respiratory system
235.9 Neoplasm of uncertain behavior of other and unspecified respiratory organs ▽
239.1 Neoplasm of unspecified nature of respiratory system
461.3 Acute sphenoidal sinusitis — (Use additional code to identify infectious organism)
461.8 Other acute sinusitis — (Use additional code to identify infectious organism)
461.9 Acute sinusitis, unspecified — (Use additional code to identify infectious organism) ▽
471.1 Polypoid sinus degeneration
471.8 Other polyp of sinus
471.9 Unspecified nasal polyp ▽
472.0 Chronic rhinitis — (Use additional code to identify infectious organism)
473.3 Chronic sphenoidal sinusitis — (Use additional code to identify infectious organism)
473.8 Other chronic sinusitis — (Use additional code to identify infectious organism)
473.9 Unspecified sinusitis (chronic) — (Use additional code to identify infectious organism) ▽
478.0 Hypertrophy of nasal turbinates
478.19 Other diseases of nasal cavity and sinuses — (Use additional code to identify infectious organism)
730.18 Chronic osteomyelitis, other specified sites — (Use additional code to identify organism: 041.1. Use additional code to identify major osseous defect, if applicable: 731.3)
748.8 Other specified congenital anomaly of respiratory system
784.0 Headache
784.2 Swelling, mass, or lump in head and neck
905.0 Late effect of fracture of skull and face bones

ICD-9-CM Procedural

21.31 Local excision or destruction of intranasal lesion
22.12 Open biopsy of nasal sinus

22.52	Sphenoidotomy

31070

31070	Sinusotomy frontal; external, simple (trephine operation)

ICD-9-CM Diagnostic

160.0	Malignant neoplasm of nasal cavities
160.4	Malignant neoplasm of frontal sinus
160.8	Malignant neoplasm of other sites of nasal cavities, middle ear, and accessory sinuses
197.3	Secondary malignant neoplasm of other respiratory organs
212.0	Benign neoplasm of nasal cavities, middle ear, and accessory sinuses
231.8	Carcinoma in situ of other specified parts of respiratory system
235.9	Neoplasm of uncertain behavior of other and unspecified respiratory organs ▽
239.1	Neoplasm of unspecified nature of respiratory system
376.01	Orbital cellulitis
461.1	Acute frontal sinusitis — (Use additional code to identify infectious organism)
461.8	Other acute sinusitis — (Use additional code to identify infectious organism)
461.9	Acute sinusitis, unspecified — (Use additional code to identify infectious organism) ▽
471.1	Polypoid sinus degeneration
471.8	Other polyp of sinus
472.0	Chronic rhinitis — (Use additional code to identify infectious organism)
473.1	Chronic frontal sinusitis — (Use additional code to identify infectious organism)
473.8	Other chronic sinusitis — (Use additional code to identify infectious organism)
473.9	Unspecified sinusitis (chronic) — (Use additional code to identify infectious organism) ▽
478.0	Hypertrophy of nasal turbinates
478.19	Other diseases of nasal cavity and sinuses — (Use additional code to identify infectious organism)
905.0	Late effect of fracture of skull and face bones

ICD-9-CM Procedural

22.41	Frontal sinusotomy

31075

31075	Sinusotomy frontal; transorbital, unilateral (for mucocele or osteoma, Lynch type)

ICD-9-CM Diagnostic

212.0	Benign neoplasm of nasal cavities, middle ear, and accessory sinuses
213.0	Benign neoplasm of bones of skull and face
231.8	Carcinoma in situ of other specified parts of respiratory system
235.9	Neoplasm of uncertain behavior of other and unspecified respiratory organs ▽
239.1	Neoplasm of unspecified nature of respiratory system
461.1	Acute frontal sinusitis — (Use additional code to identify infectious organism)
461.8	Other acute sinusitis — (Use additional code to identify infectious organism)
461.9	Acute sinusitis, unspecified — (Use additional code to identify infectious organism) ▽
471.1	Polypoid sinus degeneration
471.8	Other polyp of sinus
472.0	Chronic rhinitis — (Use additional code to identify infectious organism)
473.1	Chronic frontal sinusitis — (Use additional code to identify infectious organism)
473.8	Other chronic sinusitis — (Use additional code to identify infectious organism)
473.9	Unspecified sinusitis (chronic) — (Use additional code to identify infectious organism) ▽
478.0	Hypertrophy of nasal turbinates
478.19	Other diseases of nasal cavity and sinuses — (Use additional code to identify infectious organism)
905.0	Late effect of fracture of skull and face bones

ICD-9-CM Procedural

22.41	Frontal sinusotomy

31080-31085

31080	Sinusotomy frontal; obliterative without osteoplastic flap, brow incision (includes ablation)
31081	obliterative, without osteoplastic flap, coronal incision (includes ablation)
31084	obliterative, with osteoplastic flap, brow incision
31085	obliterative, with osteoplastic flap, coronal incision

ICD-9-CM Diagnostic

160.0	Malignant neoplasm of nasal cavities
160.4	Malignant neoplasm of frontal sinus
160.8	Malignant neoplasm of other sites of nasal cavities, middle ear, and accessory sinuses
195.0	Malignant neoplasm of head, face, and neck
197.3	Secondary malignant neoplasm of other respiratory organs
198.89	Secondary malignant neoplasm of other specified sites
212.0	Benign neoplasm of nasal cavities, middle ear, and accessory sinuses
213.0	Benign neoplasm of bones of skull and face
231.8	Carcinoma in situ of other specified parts of respiratory system
235.9	Neoplasm of uncertain behavior of other and unspecified respiratory organs ▽
239.1	Neoplasm of unspecified nature of respiratory system
376.01	Orbital cellulitis
461.1	Acute frontal sinusitis — (Use additional code to identify infectious organism)
461.8	Other acute sinusitis — (Use additional code to identify infectious organism)
461.9	Acute sinusitis, unspecified — (Use additional code to identify infectious organism) ▽
471.1	Polypoid sinus degeneration
471.8	Other polyp of sinus
471.9	Unspecified nasal polyp ▽
472.0	Chronic rhinitis — (Use additional code to identify infectious organism)
473.1	Chronic frontal sinusitis — (Use additional code to identify infectious organism)
473.8	Other chronic sinusitis — (Use additional code to identify infectious organism)
473.9	Unspecified sinusitis (chronic) — (Use additional code to identify infectious organism) ▽
478.0	Hypertrophy of nasal turbinates
478.19	Other diseases of nasal cavity and sinuses — (Use additional code to identify infectious organism)
905.0	Late effect of fracture of skull and face bones

ICD-9-CM Procedural

22.42	Frontal sinusectomy

31086-31087

31086	Sinusotomy frontal; nonobliterative, with osteoplastic flap, brow incision
31087	nonobliterative, with osteoplastic flap, coronal incision

ICD-9-CM Diagnostic

160.0	Malignant neoplasm of nasal cavities
160.4	Malignant neoplasm of frontal sinus
160.8	Malignant neoplasm of other sites of nasal cavities, middle ear, and accessory sinuses
195.0	Malignant neoplasm of head, face, and neck
197.3	Secondary malignant neoplasm of other respiratory organs
198.89	Secondary malignant neoplasm of other specified sites
212.0	Benign neoplasm of nasal cavities, middle ear, and accessory sinuses
213.0	Benign neoplasm of bones of skull and face
231.8	Carcinoma in situ of other specified parts of respiratory system
235.9	Neoplasm of uncertain behavior of other and unspecified respiratory organs ▽
239.1	Neoplasm of unspecified nature of respiratory system
376.01	Orbital cellulitis
461.1	Acute frontal sinusitis — (Use additional code to identify infectious organism)
461.8	Other acute sinusitis — (Use additional code to identify infectious organism)
461.9	Acute sinusitis, unspecified — (Use additional code to identify infectious organism) ▽
471.1	Polypoid sinus degeneration
471.8	Other polyp of sinus

472.0 Chronic rhinitis — (Use additional code to identify infectious organism)
473.1 Chronic frontal sinusitis — (Use additional code to identify infectious organism)
473.2 Chronic ethmoidal sinusitis — (Use additional code to identify infectious organism)
473.8 Other chronic sinusitis — (Use additional code to identify infectious organism)
473.9 Unspecified sinusitis (chronic) — (Use additional code to identify infectious organism) ▽
478.0 Hypertrophy of nasal turbinates
478.19 Other diseases of nasal cavity and sinuses — (Use additional code to identify infectious organism)
905.0 Late effect of fracture of skull and face bones

ICD-9-CM Procedural

22.41 Frontal sinusotomy
22.42 Frontal sinusectomy

31090

31090 Sinusotomy, unilateral, 3 or more paranasal sinuses (frontal, maxillary, ethmoid, sphenoid)

ICD-9-CM Diagnostic

160.2 Malignant neoplasm of maxillary sinus
160.3 Malignant neoplasm of ethmoidal sinus
160.4 Malignant neoplasm of frontal sinus
160.5 Malignant neoplasm of sphenoidal sinus
160.8 Malignant neoplasm of other sites of nasal cavities, middle ear, and accessory sinuses
160.9 Malignant neoplasm of site of nasal cavities, middle ear, and accessory sinus, unspecified site ▽
195.0 Malignant neoplasm of head, face, and neck
197.3 Secondary malignant neoplasm of other respiratory organs
212.0 Benign neoplasm of nasal cavities, middle ear, and accessory sinuses
213.0 Benign neoplasm of bones of skull and face
231.8 Carcinoma in situ of other specified parts of respiratory system
235.9 Neoplasm of uncertain behavior of other and unspecified respiratory organs ▽
239.1 Neoplasm of unspecified nature of respiratory system
350.2 Atypical face pain
376.01 Orbital cellulitis
461.1 Acute frontal sinusitis — (Use additional code to identify infectious organism)
461.2 Acute ethmoidal sinusitis — (Use additional code to identify infectious organism)
461.3 Acute sphenoidal sinusitis — (Use additional code to identify infectious organism)
461.8 Other acute sinusitis — (Use additional code to identify infectious organism)
461.9 Acute sinusitis, unspecified — (Use additional code to identify infectious organism) ▽
470 Deviated nasal septum
471.1 Polypoid sinus degeneration
471.8 Other polyp of sinus
473.0 Chronic maxillary sinusitis — (Use additional code to identify infectious organism)
473.1 Chronic frontal sinusitis — (Use additional code to identify infectious organism)
473.2 Chronic ethmoidal sinusitis — (Use additional code to identify infectious organism)
473.3 Chronic sphenoidal sinusitis — (Use additional code to identify infectious organism)
473.8 Other chronic sinusitis — (Use additional code to identify infectious organism)
473.9 Unspecified sinusitis (chronic) — (Use additional code to identify infectious organism) ▽
477.9 Allergic rhinitis, cause unspecified — (Use additional code to identify infectious organism) ▽
478.0 Hypertrophy of nasal turbinates
478.19 Other diseases of nasal cavity and sinuses — (Use additional code to identify infectious organism)
786.09 Other dyspnea and respiratory abnormalities

ICD-9-CM Procedural

22.53 Incision of multiple nasal sinuses

31200-31201

31200 Ethmoidectomy; intranasal, anterior
31201 intranasal, total

ICD-9-CM Diagnostic

160.0 Malignant neoplasm of nasal cavities
160.3 Malignant neoplasm of ethmoidal sinus
160.8 Malignant neoplasm of other sites of nasal cavities, middle ear, and accessory sinuses
197.3 Secondary malignant neoplasm of other respiratory organs
212.0 Benign neoplasm of nasal cavities, middle ear, and accessory sinuses
231.8 Carcinoma in situ of other specified parts of respiratory system
235.9 Neoplasm of uncertain behavior of other and unspecified respiratory organs ▽
239.1 Neoplasm of unspecified nature of respiratory system
376.01 Orbital cellulitis
461.2 Acute ethmoidal sinusitis — (Use additional code to identify infectious organism)
461.8 Other acute sinusitis — (Use additional code to identify infectious organism)
461.9 Acute sinusitis, unspecified — (Use additional code to identify infectious organism) ▽
471.1 Polypoid sinus degeneration
471.8 Other polyp of sinus
473.2 Chronic ethmoidal sinusitis — (Use additional code to identify infectious organism)
473.8 Other chronic sinusitis — (Use additional code to identify infectious organism)
473.9 Unspecified sinusitis (chronic) — (Use additional code to identify infectious organism) ▽
478.19 Other diseases of nasal cavity and sinuses — (Use additional code to identify infectious organism)
519.8 Other diseases of respiratory system, not elsewhere classified — (Use additional code to identify infectious organism)
730.18 Chronic osteomyelitis, other specified sites — (Use additional code to identify organism: 041.1. Use additional code to identify major osseous defect, if applicable: 731.3)
784.0 Headache
802.8 Other facial bones, closed fracture
905.0 Late effect of fracture of skull and face bones

ICD-9-CM Procedural

22.63 Ethmoidectomy

31205

31205 Ethmoidectomy; extranasal, total

ICD-9-CM Diagnostic

160.0 Malignant neoplasm of nasal cavities
160.3 Malignant neoplasm of ethmoidal sinus
160.8 Malignant neoplasm of other sites of nasal cavities, middle ear, and accessory sinuses
197.3 Secondary malignant neoplasm of other respiratory organs
212.0 Benign neoplasm of nasal cavities, middle ear, and accessory sinuses
231.8 Carcinoma in situ of other specified parts of respiratory system
235.9 Neoplasm of uncertain behavior of other and unspecified respiratory organs ▽
239.1 Neoplasm of unspecified nature of respiratory system
376.01 Orbital cellulitis
461.2 Acute ethmoidal sinusitis — (Use additional code to identify infectious organism)
461.8 Other acute sinusitis — (Use additional code to identify infectious organism)
461.9 Acute sinusitis, unspecified — (Use additional code to identify infectious organism) ▽
471.1 Polypoid sinus degeneration
471.8 Other polyp of sinus
473.2 Chronic ethmoidal sinusitis — (Use additional code to identify infectious organism)
473.8 Other chronic sinusitis — (Use additional code to identify infectious organism)
473.9 Unspecified sinusitis (chronic) — (Use additional code to identify infectious organism) ▽
478.19 Other diseases of nasal cavity and sinuses — (Use additional code to identify infectious organism)

519.8 Other diseases of respiratory system, not elsewhere classified — (Use additional code to identify infectious organism)
730.18 Chronic osteomyelitis, other specified sites — (Use additional code to identify organism: 041.1. Use additional code to identify major osseous defect, if applicable: 731.3)
784.0 Headache
802.8 Other facial bones, closed fracture
905.0 Late effect of fracture of skull and face bones

ICD-9-CM Procedural

22.63 Ethmoidectomy

31225-31230

31225 Maxillectomy; without orbital exenteration
31230 with orbital exenteration (en bloc)

ICD-9-CM Diagnostic

160.0 Malignant neoplasm of nasal cavities
160.2 Malignant neoplasm of maxillary sinus
160.8 Malignant neoplasm of other sites of nasal cavities, middle ear, and accessory sinuses
170.0 Malignant neoplasm of bones of skull and face, except mandible
173.30 Unspecified malignant neoplasm of skin of other and unspecified parts of face ▽
173.31 Basal cell carcinoma of skin of other and unspecified parts of face
173.32 Squamous cell carcinoma of skin of other and unspecified parts of face
173.39 Other specified malignant neoplasm of skin of other and unspecified parts of face
190.1 Malignant neoplasm of orbit
197.3 Secondary malignant neoplasm of other respiratory organs
198.4 Secondary malignant neoplasm of other parts of nervous system
198.5 Secondary malignant neoplasm of bone and bone marrow
212.0 Benign neoplasm of nasal cavities, middle ear, and accessory sinuses
213.0 Benign neoplasm of bones of skull and face
224.1 Benign neoplasm of orbit
231.8 Carcinoma in situ of other specified parts of respiratory system
235.9 Neoplasm of uncertain behavior of other and unspecified respiratory organs ▽
238.8 Neoplasm of uncertain behavior of other specified sites
239.1 Neoplasm of unspecified nature of respiratory system
239.89 Neoplasms of unspecified nature, other specified sites
376.01 Orbital cellulitis
471.1 Polypoid sinus degeneration
471.8 Other polyp of sinus
473.0 Chronic maxillary sinusitis — (Use additional code to identify infectious organism)
478.19 Other diseases of nasal cavity and sinuses — (Use additional code to identify infectious organism)
730.18 Chronic osteomyelitis, other specified sites — (Use additional code to identify organism: 041.1. Use additional code to identify major osseous defect, if applicable: 731.3)
802.6 Orbital floor (blow-out), closed fracture
802.7 Orbital floor (blow-out), open fracture

ICD-9-CM Procedural

16.51 Exenteration of orbit with removal of adjacent structures
22.62 Excision of lesion of maxillary sinus with other approach
76.39 Partial ostectomy of other facial bone
76.45 Other total ostectomy of other facial bone

31231-31233

31231 Nasal endoscopy, diagnostic, unilateral or bilateral (separate procedure)
31233 Nasal/sinus endoscopy, diagnostic with maxillary sinusoscopy (via inferior meatus or canine fossa puncture)

ICD-9-CM Diagnostic

012.80 Other specified respiratory tuberculosis, confirmation unspecified ▽
012.81 Other specified respiratory tuberculosis, bacteriological or histological examination not done
012.82 Other specified respiratory tuberculosis, bacteriological or histological examination unknown (at present)
012.83 Other specified respiratory tuberculosis, tubercle bacilli found (in sputum) by microscopy
012.84 Other specified respiratory tuberculosis, tubercle bacilli not found (in sputum) by microscopy, but found by bacterial culture
012.85 Other specified respiratory tuberculosis, tubercle bacilli not found by bacteriological examination, but tuberculosis confirmed histologically
012.86 Other specified respiratory tuberculosis, tubercle bacilli not found by bacteriological or histological examination, but tuberculosis confirmed by other methods [inoculation of animals]
117.9 Other and unspecified mycoses — (Use additional code to identify manifestation: 321.0-321.1, 380.15, 711.6) ▽
147.0 Malignant neoplasm of superior wall of nasopharynx
147.1 Malignant neoplasm of posterior wall of nasopharynx
147.2 Malignant neoplasm of lateral wall of nasopharynx
147.3 Malignant neoplasm of anterior wall of nasopharynx
147.8 Malignant neoplasm of other specified sites of nasopharynx
147.9 Malignant neoplasm of nasopharynx, unspecified site ▽
160.0 Malignant neoplasm of nasal cavities
160.2 Malignant neoplasm of maxillary sinus
160.3 Malignant neoplasm of ethmoidal sinus
160.4 Malignant neoplasm of frontal sinus
160.5 Malignant neoplasm of sphenoidal sinus
160.8 Malignant neoplasm of other sites of nasal cavities, middle ear, and accessory sinuses
160.9 Malignant neoplasm of site of nasal cavities, middle ear, and accessory sinus, unspecified site ▽
170.0 Malignant neoplasm of bones of skull and face, except mandible
196.0 Secondary and unspecified malignant neoplasm of lymph nodes of head, face, and neck
210.7 Benign neoplasm of nasopharynx
212.0 Benign neoplasm of nasal cavities, middle ear, and accessory sinuses
228.09 Hemangioma of other sites
230.0 Carcinoma in situ of lip, oral cavity, and pharynx
231.8 Carcinoma in situ of other specified parts of respiratory system
235.1 Neoplasm of uncertain behavior of lip, oral cavity, and pharynx
235.9 Neoplasm of uncertain behavior of other and unspecified respiratory organs ▽
239.1 Neoplasm of unspecified nature of respiratory system
327.20 Organic sleep apnea, unspecified ▽
327.23 Obstructive sleep apnea (adult) (pediatric)
327.29 Other organic sleep apnea
349.81 Cerebrospinal fluid rhinorrhea
352.0 Disorders of olfactory (1st) nerve
375.56 Stenosis of nasolacrimal duct, acquired
381.81 Dysfunction of Eustachian tube
446.3 Lethal midline granuloma
446.4 Wegener's granulomatosis
461.0 Acute maxillary sinusitis — (Use additional code to identify infectious organism)
461.2 Acute ethmoidal sinusitis — (Use additional code to identify infectious organism)
461.3 Acute sphenoidal sinusitis — (Use additional code to identify infectious organism)
461.8 Other acute sinusitis — (Use additional code to identify infectious organism)
461.9 Acute sinusitis, unspecified — (Use additional code to identify infectious organism) ▽
470 Deviated nasal septum
471.0 Polyp of nasal cavity
471.1 Polypoid sinus degeneration
471.8 Other polyp of sinus
471.9 Unspecified nasal polyp ▽
472.0 Chronic rhinitis — (Use additional code to identify infectious organism)

472.2 Chronic nasopharyngitis — (Use additional code to identify infectious organism)
473.0 Chronic maxillary sinusitis — (Use additional code to identify infectious organism)
473.1 Chronic frontal sinusitis — (Use additional code to identify infectious organism)
473.2 Chronic ethmoidal sinusitis — (Use additional code to identify infectious organism)
473.3 Chronic sphenoidal sinusitis — (Use additional code to identify infectious organism)
473.8 Other chronic sinusitis — (Use additional code to identify infectious organism)
473.9 Unspecified sinusitis (chronic) — (Use additional code to identify infectious organism) ▽
477.0 Allergic rhinitis due to pollen — (Use additional code to identify infectious organism)
477.8 Allergic rhinitis due to other allergen — (Use additional code to identify infectious organism)
477.9 Allergic rhinitis, cause unspecified — (Use additional code to identify infectious organism) ▽
478.0 Hypertrophy of nasal turbinates
478.19 Other diseases of nasal cavity and sinuses — (Use additional code to identify infectious organism)
478.21 Cellulitis of pharynx or nasopharynx — (Use additional code to identify infectious organism)
478.25 Edema of pharynx or nasopharynx
478.26 Cyst of pharynx or nasopharynx — (Use additional code to identify infectious organism)
478.29 Other disease of pharynx or nasopharynx — (Use additional code to identify infectious organism)
478.9 Other and unspecified diseases of upper respiratory tract — (Use additional code to identify infectious organism) ▽
508.8 Respiratory conditions due to other specified external agents — (Use additional code to identify infectious organism. Use additional E code to identify cause. Use additional code to identify associated respiratory conditions: 518.81.)
738.0 Acquired deformity of nose
748.0 Congenital choanal atresia
748.1 Other congenital anomaly of nose
748.8 Other specified congenital anomaly of respiratory system
748.9 Unspecified congenital anomaly of respiratory system ▽
754.0 Congenital musculoskeletal deformities of skull, face, and jaw
780.51 Insomnia with sleep apnea, unspecified ▽
780.57 Unspecified sleep apnea ▽
781.1 Disturbances of sensation of smell and taste
784.0 Headache
784.2 Swelling, mass, or lump in head and neck
784.7 Epistaxis
786.00 Unspecified respiratory abnormality ▽
786.09 Other dyspnea and respiratory abnormalities
793.0 Nonspecific (abnormal) findings on radiological and other examination of skull and head
802.0 Nasal bones, closed fracture
802.1 Nasal bones, open fracture
905.0 Late effect of fracture of skull and face bones
925.1 Crushing injury of face and scalp — (Use additional code to identify any associated injuries, such as: 800-829, 850.0-854.1, 860.0-869.1)
932 Foreign body in nose
941.05 Burn of unspecified degree of nose (septum) ▽
993.1 Barotrauma, sinus
V67.09 Follow-up examination, following other surgery

ICD-9-CM Procedural

21.21 Rhinoscopy
22.19 Other diagnostic procedures on nasal sinuses

HCPCS Level II Supplies & Services

A4305 Disposable drug delivery system, flow rate of 50 ml or greater per hour

31235

31235 Nasal/sinus endoscopy, diagnostic with sphenoid sinusoscopy (via puncture of sphenoidal face or cannulation of ostium)

ICD-9-CM Diagnostic

147.0 Malignant neoplasm of superior wall of nasopharynx
147.1 Malignant neoplasm of posterior wall of nasopharynx
147.2 Malignant neoplasm of lateral wall of nasopharynx
147.3 Malignant neoplasm of anterior wall of nasopharynx
147.8 Malignant neoplasm of other specified sites of nasopharynx
147.9 Malignant neoplasm of nasopharynx, unspecified site ▽
160.0 Malignant neoplasm of nasal cavities
160.5 Malignant neoplasm of sphenoidal sinus
160.8 Malignant neoplasm of other sites of nasal cavities, middle ear, and accessory sinuses
160.9 Malignant neoplasm of site of nasal cavities, middle ear, and accessory sinus, unspecified site ▽
197.3 Secondary malignant neoplasm of other respiratory organs
212.0 Benign neoplasm of nasal cavities, middle ear, and accessory sinuses
212.9 Benign neoplasm of respiratory and intrathoracic organs, site unspecified ▽
231.8 Carcinoma in situ of other specified parts of respiratory system
235.9 Neoplasm of uncertain behavior of other and unspecified respiratory organs ▽
239.1 Neoplasm of unspecified nature of respiratory system
327.20 Organic sleep apnea, unspecified ▽
327.23 Obstructive sleep apnea (adult) (pediatric)
327.29 Other organic sleep apnea
446.4 Wegener's granulomatosis
461.3 Acute sphenoidal sinusitis — (Use additional code to identify infectious organism)
461.8 Other acute sinusitis — (Use additional code to identify infectious organism)
461.9 Acute sinusitis, unspecified — (Use additional code to identify infectious organism) ▽
470 Deviated nasal septum
471.0 Polyp of nasal cavity
471.1 Polypoid sinus degeneration
471.8 Other polyp of sinus
471.9 Unspecified nasal polyp ▽
472.0 Chronic rhinitis — (Use additional code to identify infectious organism)
472.2 Chronic nasopharyngitis — (Use additional code to identify infectious organism)
473.3 Chronic sphenoidal sinusitis — (Use additional code to identify infectious organism)
473.8 Other chronic sinusitis — (Use additional code to identify infectious organism)
473.9 Unspecified sinusitis (chronic) — (Use additional code to identify infectious organism) ▽
478.0 Hypertrophy of nasal turbinates
478.19 Other diseases of nasal cavity and sinuses — (Use additional code to identify infectious organism)
478.21 Cellulitis of pharynx or nasopharynx — (Use additional code to identify infectious organism)
478.25 Edema of pharynx or nasopharynx
478.26 Cyst of pharynx or nasopharynx — (Use additional code to identify infectious organism)
478.29 Other disease of pharynx or nasopharynx — (Use additional code to identify infectious organism)
478.9 Other and unspecified diseases of upper respiratory tract — (Use additional code to identify infectious organism) ▽
738.0 Acquired deformity of nose
748.0 Congenital choanal atresia
748.1 Other congenital anomaly of nose
748.8 Other specified congenital anomaly of respiratory system
748.9 Unspecified congenital anomaly of respiratory system ▽
780.51 Insomnia with sleep apnea, unspecified ▽
780.57 Unspecified sleep apnea ▽

784.0 Headache
784.2 Swelling, mass, or lump in head and neck
784.7 Epistaxis
786.00 Unspecified respiratory abnormality ▽
786.09 Other dyspnea and respiratory abnormalities
793.0 Nonspecific (abnormal) findings on radiological and other examination of skull and head
802.0 Nasal bones, closed fracture
802.1 Nasal bones, open fracture
905.0 Late effect of fracture of skull and face bones
925.1 Crushing injury of face and scalp — (Use additional code to identify any associated injuries, such as: 800-829, 850.0-854.1, 860.0-869.1)
V67.09 Follow-up examination, following other surgery

ICD-9-CM Procedural

22.19 Other diagnostic procedures on nasal sinuses

31237

31237 Nasal/sinus endoscopy, surgical; with biopsy, polypectomy or debridement (separate procedure)

ICD-9-CM Diagnostic

147.0 Malignant neoplasm of superior wall of nasopharynx
147.1 Malignant neoplasm of posterior wall of nasopharynx
147.2 Malignant neoplasm of lateral wall of nasopharynx
147.3 Malignant neoplasm of anterior wall of nasopharynx
147.8 Malignant neoplasm of other specified sites of nasopharynx
160.0 Malignant neoplasm of nasal cavities
160.2 Malignant neoplasm of maxillary sinus
160.3 Malignant neoplasm of ethmoidal sinus
160.4 Malignant neoplasm of frontal sinus
160.5 Malignant neoplasm of sphenoidal sinus
160.8 Malignant neoplasm of other sites of nasal cavities, middle ear, and accessory sinuses
160.9 Malignant neoplasm of site of nasal cavities, middle ear, and accessory sinus, unspecified site ▽
170.0 Malignant neoplasm of bones of skull and face, except mandible
210.7 Benign neoplasm of nasopharynx
212.0 Benign neoplasm of nasal cavities, middle ear, and accessory sinuses
228.00 Hemangioma of unspecified site ▽
228.09 Hemangioma of other sites
230.0 Carcinoma in situ of lip, oral cavity, and pharynx
231.8 Carcinoma in situ of other specified parts of respiratory system
235.9 Neoplasm of uncertain behavior of other and unspecified respiratory organs ▽
239.1 Neoplasm of unspecified nature of respiratory system
446.4 Wegener's granulomatosis
461.0 Acute maxillary sinusitis — (Use additional code to identify infectious organism)
461.1 Acute frontal sinusitis — (Use additional code to identify infectious organism)
461.2 Acute ethmoidal sinusitis — (Use additional code to identify infectious organism)
461.3 Acute sphenoidal sinusitis — (Use additional code to identify infectious organism)
461.8 Other acute sinusitis — (Use additional code to identify infectious organism)
461.9 Acute sinusitis, unspecified — (Use additional code to identify infectious organism) ▽
470 Deviated nasal septum
471.0 Polyp of nasal cavity
471.1 Polypoid sinus degeneration
471.8 Other polyp of sinus
471.9 Unspecified nasal polyp ▽
472.0 Chronic rhinitis — (Use additional code to identify infectious organism)
473.0 Chronic maxillary sinusitis — (Use additional code to identify infectious organism)
473.1 Chronic frontal sinusitis — (Use additional code to identify infectious organism)
473.2 Chronic ethmoidal sinusitis — (Use additional code to identify infectious organism)
473.3 Chronic sphenoidal sinusitis — (Use additional code to identify infectious organism)
473.8 Other chronic sinusitis — (Use additional code to identify infectious organism)
473.9 Unspecified sinusitis (chronic) — (Use additional code to identify infectious organism) ▽
478.0 Hypertrophy of nasal turbinates
478.19 Other diseases of nasal cavity and sinuses — (Use additional code to identify infectious organism)
478.20 Unspecified disease of pharynx — (Use additional code to identify infectious organism) ▽
478.21 Cellulitis of pharynx or nasopharynx — (Use additional code to identify infectious organism)
478.25 Edema of pharynx or nasopharynx
478.26 Cyst of pharynx or nasopharynx — (Use additional code to identify infectious organism)
478.29 Other disease of pharynx or nasopharynx — (Use additional code to identify infectious organism)
478.9 Other and unspecified diseases of upper respiratory tract — (Use additional code to identify infectious organism) ▽
784.0 Headache
784.2 Swelling, mass, or lump in head and neck
784.7 Epistaxis
786.00 Unspecified respiratory abnormality ▽
786.09 Other dyspnea and respiratory abnormalities
786.9 Other symptoms involving respiratory system and chest
793.0 Nonspecific (abnormal) findings on radiological and other examination of skull and head
802.0 Nasal bones, closed fracture
802.1 Nasal bones, open fracture
905.0 Late effect of fracture of skull and face bones

ICD-9-CM Procedural

21.30 Excision or destruction of lesion of nose, not otherwise specified
21.31 Local excision or destruction of intranasal lesion
21.32 Local excision or destruction of other lesion of nose
22.11 Closed (endoscopic) (needle) biopsy of nasal sinus

HCPCS Level II Supplies & Services

A4305 Disposable drug delivery system, flow rate of 50 ml or greater per hour

31238

31238 Nasal/sinus endoscopy, surgical; with control of nasal hemorrhage

ICD-9-CM Diagnostic

448.0 Hereditary hemorrhagic telangiectasia
456.8 Varices of other sites
784.7 Epistaxis
958.2 Secondary and recurrent hemorrhage as an early complication of trauma
998.11 Hemorrhage complicating a procedure

ICD-9-CM Procedural

21.00 Control of epistaxis, not otherwise specified
21.03 Control of epistaxis by cauterization (and packing)
21.07 Control of epistaxis by excision of nasal mucosa and skin grafting of septum and lateral nasal wall
21.09 Control of epistaxis by other means

HCPCS Level II Supplies & Services

A4305 Disposable drug delivery system, flow rate of 50 ml or greater per hour

31239

31239 Nasal/sinus endoscopy, surgical; with dacryocystorhinostomy

ICD-9-CM Diagnostic

375.11 Dacryops
375.21 Epiphora due to excess lacrimation
375.22 Epiphora due to insufficient drainage
375.30 Unspecified dacryocystitis ▽
375.55 Obstruction of nasolacrimal duct, neonatal
375.56 Stenosis of nasolacrimal duct, acquired
375.81 Granuloma of lacrimal passages
375.9 Unspecified disorder of lacrimal system ▽
743.65 Specified congenital anomaly of lacrimal passages
905.0 Late effect of fracture of skull and face bones

ICD-9-CM Procedural

09.81 Dacryocystorhinostomy (DCR)

31240

31240 Nasal/sinus endoscopy, surgical; with concha bullosa resection

ICD-9-CM Diagnostic

472.0 Chronic rhinitis — (Use additional code to identify infectious organism)
472.2 Chronic nasopharyngitis — (Use additional code to identify infectious organism)
473.0 Chronic maxillary sinusitis — (Use additional code to identify infectious organism)
473.8 Other chronic sinusitis — (Use additional code to identify infectious organism)
478.0 Hypertrophy of nasal turbinates
478.19 Other diseases of nasal cavity and sinuses — (Use additional code to identify infectious organism)
730.18 Chronic osteomyelitis, other specified sites — (Use additional code to identify organism: 041.1. Use additional code to identify major osseous defect, if applicable: 731.3)

ICD-9-CM Procedural

21.30 Excision or destruction of lesion of nose, not otherwise specified
21.32 Local excision or destruction of other lesion of nose
21.61 Turbinectomy by diathermy or cryosurgery
21.69 Other turbinectomy

31254-31255

31254 Nasal/sinus endoscopy, surgical; with ethmoidectomy, partial (anterior)
31255 with ethmoidectomy, total (anterior and posterior)

ICD-9-CM Diagnostic

160.0 Malignant neoplasm of nasal cavities
160.3 Malignant neoplasm of ethmoidal sinus
197.3 Secondary malignant neoplasm of other respiratory organs
212.0 Benign neoplasm of nasal cavities, middle ear, and accessory sinuses
231.8 Carcinoma in situ of other specified parts of respiratory system
235.9 Neoplasm of uncertain behavior of other and unspecified respiratory organs ▽
376.01 Orbital cellulitis
461.2 Acute ethmoidal sinusitis — (Use additional code to identify infectious organism)
461.8 Other acute sinusitis — (Use additional code to identify infectious organism)
461.9 Acute sinusitis, unspecified — (Use additional code to identify infectious organism) ▽
470 Deviated nasal septum
471.1 Polypoid sinus degeneration
471.8 Other polyp of sinus
473.2 Chronic ethmoidal sinusitis — (Use additional code to identify infectious organism)
473.8 Other chronic sinusitis — (Use additional code to identify infectious organism)
473.9 Unspecified sinusitis (chronic) — (Use additional code to identify infectious organism) ▽
478.0 Hypertrophy of nasal turbinates
478.19 Other diseases of nasal cavity and sinuses — (Use additional code to identify infectious organism)
519.8 Other diseases of respiratory system, not elsewhere classified — (Use additional code to identify infectious organism)
519.9 Unspecified disease of respiratory system — (Use additional code to identify infectious organism) ▽
730.18 Chronic osteomyelitis, other specified sites — (Use additional code to identify organism: 041.1. Use additional code to identify major osseous defect, if applicable: 731.3)
784.0 Headache
802.8 Other facial bones, closed fracture
905.0 Late effect of fracture of skull and face bones

ICD-9-CM Procedural

22.63 Ethmoidectomy

31256-31267

31256 Nasal/sinus endoscopy, surgical, with maxillary antrostomy;
31267 with removal of tissue from maxillary sinus

ICD-9-CM Diagnostic

160.2 Malignant neoplasm of maxillary sinus
197.3 Secondary malignant neoplasm of other respiratory organs
212.0 Benign neoplasm of nasal cavities, middle ear, and accessory sinuses
231.8 Carcinoma in situ of other specified parts of respiratory system
235.9 Neoplasm of uncertain behavior of other and unspecified respiratory organs ▽
238.0 Neoplasm of uncertain behavior of bone and articular cartilage
239.1 Neoplasm of unspecified nature of respiratory system
461.0 Acute maxillary sinusitis — (Use additional code to identify infectious organism)
461.8 Other acute sinusitis — (Use additional code to identify infectious organism)
461.9 Acute sinusitis, unspecified — (Use additional code to identify infectious organism) ▽
470 Deviated nasal septum
471.1 Polypoid sinus degeneration
471.8 Other polyp of sinus
473.0 Chronic maxillary sinusitis — (Use additional code to identify infectious organism)
473.8 Other chronic sinusitis — (Use additional code to identify infectious organism)
473.9 Unspecified sinusitis (chronic) — (Use additional code to identify infectious organism) ▽
478.0 Hypertrophy of nasal turbinates
478.19 Other diseases of nasal cavity and sinuses — (Use additional code to identify infectious organism)
730.18 Chronic osteomyelitis, other specified sites — (Use additional code to identify organism: 041.1. Use additional code to identify major osseous defect, if applicable: 731.3)
730.28 Unspecified osteomyelitis, other specified sites — (Use additional code to identify organism: 041.1. Use additional code to identify major osseous defect, if applicable: 731.3) ▽
748.8 Other specified congenital anomaly of respiratory system
784.0 Headache
784.2 Swelling, mass, or lump in head and neck
784.7 Epistaxis
786.09 Other dyspnea and respiratory abnormalities
802.4 Malar and maxillary bones, closed fracture
802.5 Malar and maxillary bones, open fracture
802.6 Orbital floor (blow-out), closed fracture
802.7 Orbital floor (blow-out), open fracture
905.0 Late effect of fracture of skull and face bones
996.60 Infection and inflammatory reaction due to unspecified device, implant, and graft — (Use additional code to identify specified infections) ▽
996.69 Infection and inflammatory reaction due to other internal prosthetic device, implant, and graft — (Use additional code to identify specified infections)

ICD-9-CM Procedural

22.2 Intranasal antrotomy
22.62 Excision of lesion of maxillary sinus with other approach

31276

31276 Nasal/sinus endoscopy, surgical with frontal sinus exploration, with or without removal of tissue from frontal sinus

ICD-9-CM Diagnostic

160.4 Malignant neoplasm of frontal sinus
160.8 Malignant neoplasm of other sites of nasal cavities, middle ear, and accessory sinuses
212.0 Benign neoplasm of nasal cavities, middle ear, and accessory sinuses
212.8 Benign neoplasm of other specified sites of respiratory and intrathoracic organs
212.9 Benign neoplasm of respiratory and intrathoracic organs, site unspecified ▽
231.8 Carcinoma in situ of other specified parts of respiratory system
235.9 Neoplasm of uncertain behavior of other and unspecified respiratory organs ▽
239.1 Neoplasm of unspecified nature of respiratory system
461.1 Acute frontal sinusitis — (Use additional code to identify infectious organism)
461.9 Acute sinusitis, unspecified — (Use additional code to identify infectious organism) ▽
471.1 Polypoid sinus degeneration
471.8 Other polyp of sinus
473.0 Chronic maxillary sinusitis — (Use additional code to identify infectious organism)
473.1 Chronic frontal sinusitis — (Use additional code to identify infectious organism)
473.2 Chronic ethmoidal sinusitis — (Use additional code to identify infectious organism)
473.8 Other chronic sinusitis — (Use additional code to identify infectious organism)
473.9 Unspecified sinusitis (chronic) — (Use additional code to identify infectious organism) ▽
478.0 Hypertrophy of nasal turbinates
478.19 Other diseases of nasal cavity and sinuses — (Use additional code to identify infectious organism)
730.18 Chronic osteomyelitis, other specified sites — (Use additional code to identify organism: 041.1. Use additional code to identify major osseous defect, if applicable: 731.3)
748.1 Other congenital anomaly of nose
784.0 Headache
784.2 Swelling, mass, or lump in head and neck
784.7 Epistaxis
802.8 Other facial bones, closed fracture

ICD-9-CM Procedural

22.41 Frontal sinusotomy
22.42 Frontal sinusectomy

31287-31288

31287 Nasal/sinus endoscopy, surgical, with sphenoidotomy;
31288 with removal of tissue from the sphenoid sinus

ICD-9-CM Diagnostic

160.5 Malignant neoplasm of sphenoidal sinus
160.8 Malignant neoplasm of other sites of nasal cavities, middle ear, and accessory sinuses
170.0 Malignant neoplasm of bones of skull and face, except mandible
197.3 Secondary malignant neoplasm of other respiratory organs
212.0 Benign neoplasm of nasal cavities, middle ear, and accessory sinuses
231.8 Carcinoma in situ of other specified parts of respiratory system
235.9 Neoplasm of uncertain behavior of other and unspecified respiratory organs ▽
239.1 Neoplasm of unspecified nature of respiratory system
461.3 Acute sphenoidal sinusitis — (Use additional code to identify infectious organism)
461.8 Other acute sinusitis — (Use additional code to identify infectious organism)
461.9 Acute sinusitis, unspecified — (Use additional code to identify infectious organism) ▽
471.1 Polypoid sinus degeneration
471.8 Other polyp of sinus
473.3 Chronic sphenoidal sinusitis — (Use additional code to identify infectious organism)
473.8 Other chronic sinusitis — (Use additional code to identify infectious organism)
473.9 Unspecified sinusitis (chronic) — (Use additional code to identify infectious organism) ▽
478.0 Hypertrophy of nasal turbinates
478.19 Other diseases of nasal cavity and sinuses — (Use additional code to identify infectious organism)
730.18 Chronic osteomyelitis, other specified sites — (Use additional code to identify organism: 041.1. Use additional code to identify major osseous defect, if applicable: 731.3)
748.8 Other specified congenital anomaly of respiratory system
784.0 Headache
784.2 Swelling, mass, or lump in head and neck
784.7 Epistaxis
905.0 Late effect of fracture of skull and face bones

ICD-9-CM Procedural

21.31 Local excision or destruction of intranasal lesion
22.52 Sphenoidotomy

31290-31291

31290 Nasal/sinus endoscopy, surgical, with repair of cerebrospinal fluid leak; ethmoid region
31291 sphenoid region

ICD-9-CM Diagnostic

349.1 Nervous system complications from surgically implanted device
349.31 Accidental puncture or laceration of dura during a procedure
349.39 Other dural tear
349.81 Cerebrospinal fluid rhinorrhea
473.2 Chronic ethmoidal sinusitis — (Use additional code to identify infectious organism)
473.3 Chronic sphenoidal sinusitis — (Use additional code to identify infectious organism)
748.1 Other congenital anomaly of nose
801.10 Closed fracture of base of skull with cerebral laceration and contusion, unspecified state of consciousness ▽
801.11 Closed fracture of base of skull with cerebral laceration and contusion, no loss of consciousness
801.12 Closed fracture of base of skull with cerebral laceration and contusion, brief (less than one hour) loss of consciousness
801.13 Closed fracture of base of skull with cerebral laceration and contusion, moderate (1-24 hours) loss of consciousness
801.14 Closed fracture of base of skull with cerebral laceration and contusion, prolonged (more than 24 hours) loss of consciousness and return to pre-existing conscious level
801.15 Closed fracture of base of skull with cerebral laceration and contusion, prolonged (more than 24 hours) loss of consciousness, without return to pre-existing conscious level
801.16 Closed fracture of base of skull with cerebral laceration and contusion, loss of consciousness of unspecified duration ▽
801.19 Closed fracture of base of skull with cerebral laceration and contusion, unspecified concussion ▽
802.0 Nasal bones, closed fracture
802.1 Nasal bones, open fracture
802.6 Orbital floor (blow-out), closed fracture
802.7 Orbital floor (blow-out), open fracture
802.8 Other facial bones, closed fracture
802.9 Other facial bones, open fracture
873.30 Open wound of nose, unspecified site, complicated ▽
873.31 Open wound of nasal septum, complicated
873.32 Open wound of nasal cavity, complicated
873.33 Open wound of nasal sinus, complicated
998.2 Accidental puncture or laceration during procedure

ICD-9-CM Procedural

02.12 Other repair of cerebral meninges
22.51 Ethmoidotomy
22.52 Sphenoidotomy

31292-31294

31292 Nasal/sinus endoscopy, surgical; with medial or inferior orbital wall decompression
31293 with medial orbital wall and inferior orbital wall decompression
31294 with optic nerve decompression

ICD-9-CM Diagnostic

242.00 Toxic diffuse goiter without mention of thyrotoxic crisis or storm
242.01 Toxic diffuse goiter with mention of thyrotoxic crisis or storm
376.01 Orbital cellulitis
376.11 Orbital granuloma
376.21 Thyrotoxic exophthalmos — (Code first underlying thyroid disorder: 242.00-242.9) ☒
376.30 Unspecified exophthalmos ▽
376.32 Orbital hemorrhage
376.47 Deformity of orbit due to trauma or surgery
377.49 Other disorder of optic nerve
802.6 Orbital floor (blow-out), closed fracture
802.7 Orbital floor (blow-out), open fracture
802.8 Other facial bones, closed fracture
802.9 Other facial bones, open fracture
905.0 Late effect of fracture of skull and face bones
950.0 Optic nerve injury
959.01 Head injury, unspecified ▽
959.09 Injury of face and neck, other and unspecified

ICD-9-CM Procedural

04.42 Other cranial nerve decompression
16.09 Other orbitotomy

31295-31297

31295 Nasal/sinus endoscopy, surgical; with dilation of maxillary sinus ostium (eg, balloon dilation), transnasal or via canine fossa
31296 with dilation of frontal sinus ostium (eg, balloon dilation)
31297 with dilation of sphenoid sinus ostium (eg, balloon dilation)

ICD-9-CM Diagnostic

473.0 Chronic maxillary sinusitis — (Use additional code to identify infectious organism)
473.1 Chronic frontal sinusitis — (Use additional code to identify infectious organism)
473.3 Chronic sphenoidal sinusitis — (Use additional code to identify infectious organism)
473.8 Other chronic sinusitis — (Use additional code to identify infectious organism)
473.9 Unspecified sinusitis (chronic) — (Use additional code to identify infectious organism) ▽

ICD-9-CM Procedural

22.79 Other repair of nasal sinus
22.9 Other operations on nasal sinuses

HCPCS Level II Supplies & Services

C1726 Catheter, balloon dilatation, nonvascular

Larynx

31300-31320

31300 Laryngotomy (thyrotomy, laryngofissure); with removal of tumor or laryngocele, cordectomy
31320 diagnostic

ICD-9-CM Diagnostic

148.2 Malignant neoplasm of aryepiglottic fold, hypopharyngeal aspect
161.0 Malignant neoplasm of glottis
161.1 Malignant neoplasm of supraglottis
161.2 Malignant neoplasm of subglottis
161.3 Malignant neoplasm of laryngeal cartilages
161.8 Malignant neoplasm of other specified sites of larynx
197.3 Secondary malignant neoplasm of other respiratory organs
199.1 Other malignant neoplasm of unspecified site
212.1 Benign neoplasm of larynx
231.0 Carcinoma in situ of larynx
235.6 Neoplasm of uncertain behavior of larynx
239.1 Neoplasm of unspecified nature of respiratory system
476.0 Chronic laryngitis — (Use additional code to identify infectious organism)
476.1 Chronic laryngotracheitis — (Use additional code to identify infectious organism)
478.30 Unspecified paralysis of vocal cords or larynx ▽
478.31 Unilateral partial paralysis of vocal cords or larynx
478.32 Unilateral complete paralysis of vocal cords or larynx
478.33 Bilateral partial paralysis of vocal cords or larynx
478.34 Bilateral complete paralysis of vocal cords or larynx
478.4 Polyp of vocal cord or larynx
478.5 Other diseases of vocal cords — (Use additional code to identify infectious organism)
478.6 Edema of larynx
478.71 Cellulitis and perichondritis of larynx — (Use additional code to identify infectious organism)
478.74 Stenosis of larynx
478.75 Laryngeal spasm
478.79 Other diseases of larynx — (Use additional code to identify infectious organism)
519.8 Other diseases of respiratory system, not elsewhere classified — (Use additional code to identify infectious organism)
519.9 Unspecified disease of respiratory system — (Use additional code to identify infectious organism) ▽
748.3 Other congenital anomaly of larynx, trachea, and bronchus
748.8 Other specified congenital anomaly of respiratory system
784.1 Throat pain
784.2 Swelling, mass, or lump in head and neck
784.40 Voice and resonance disorder, unspecified ▽
784.41 Aphonia
784.49 Other voice and resonance disorders
784.8 Hemorrhage from throat
785.6 Enlargement of lymph nodes
786.09 Other dyspnea and respiratory abnormalities
786.2 Cough
786.30 Hemoptysis, unspecified ▽
786.31 Acute idiopathic pulmonary hemorrhage in infants [AIPHI]
786.39 Other hemoptysis
787.20 Dysphagia, unspecified ▽
787.21 Dysphagia, oral phase
787.22 Dysphagia, oropharyngeal phase
787.23 Dysphagia, pharyngeal phase
787.24 Dysphagia, pharyngoesophageal phase
787.29 Other dysphagia

933.0 Foreign body in pharynx
933.1 Foreign body in larynx
947.1 Burn of larynx, trachea, and lung
948.00 Burn (any degree) involving less than 10% of body surface with third degree burn of less than 10% or unspecified amount

ICD-9-CM Procedural

30.09 Other excision or destruction of lesion or tissue of larynx
30.22 Vocal cordectomy
31.48 Other diagnostic procedures on larynx

31360-31365

31360 Laryngectomy; total, without radical neck dissection
31365 total, with radical neck dissection

ICD-9-CM Diagnostic

141.0 Malignant neoplasm of base of tongue
142.1 Malignant neoplasm of submandibular gland
148.2 Malignant neoplasm of aryepiglottic fold, hypopharyngeal aspect
148.9 Malignant neoplasm of hypopharynx, unspecified site
150.0 Malignant neoplasm of cervical esophagus
150.3 Malignant neoplasm of upper third of esophagus
150.8 Malignant neoplasm of other specified part of esophagus
161.0 Malignant neoplasm of glottis
161.1 Malignant neoplasm of supraglottis
161.2 Malignant neoplasm of subglottis
161.3 Malignant neoplasm of laryngeal cartilages
161.8 Malignant neoplasm of other specified sites of larynx
161.9 Malignant neoplasm of larynx, unspecified site
170.0 Malignant neoplasm of bones of skull and face, except mandible
171.0 Malignant neoplasm of connective and other soft tissue of head, face, and neck
196.0 Secondary and unspecified malignant neoplasm of lymph nodes of head, face, and neck
197.3 Secondary malignant neoplasm of other respiratory organs
197.8 Secondary malignant neoplasm of other digestive organs and spleen
198.5 Secondary malignant neoplasm of bone and bone marrow
198.89 Secondary malignant neoplasm of other specified sites
199.1 Other malignant neoplasm of unspecified site
209.20 Malignant carcinoid tumor of unknown primary site — (Code first any associated multiple endocrine neoplasia syndrome: 258.01-258.03)(Use additional code to identify associated endocrine syndrome, as: carcinoid syndrome: 259.2)
209.29 Malignant carcinoid tumor of other sites — (Code first any associated multiple endocrine neoplasia syndrome: 258.01-258.03)(Use additional code to identify associated endocrine syndrome, as: carcinoid syndrome: 259.2)
209.70 Secondary neuroendocrine tumor, unspecified site
209.71 Secondary neuroendocrine tumor of distant lymph nodes
230.0 Carcinoma in situ of lip, oral cavity, and pharynx
230.1 Carcinoma in situ of esophagus
231.0 Carcinoma in situ of larynx
235.0 Neoplasm of uncertain behavior of major salivary glands
235.1 Neoplasm of uncertain behavior of lip, oral cavity, and pharynx
235.6 Neoplasm of uncertain behavior of larynx
238.0 Neoplasm of uncertain behavior of bone and articular cartilage
238.1 Neoplasm of uncertain behavior of connective and other soft tissue
239.0 Neoplasm of unspecified nature of digestive system
239.1 Neoplasm of unspecified nature of respiratory system
239.2 Neoplasms of unspecified nature of bone, soft tissue, and skin
239.89 Neoplasms of unspecified nature, other specified sites

ICD-9-CM Procedural

30.3 Complete laryngectomy
30.4 Radical laryngectomy

31367-31368

31367 Laryngectomy; subtotal supraglottic, without radical neck dissection
31368 subtotal supraglottic, with radical neck dissection

ICD-9-CM Diagnostic

141.0 Malignant neoplasm of base of tongue
142.1 Malignant neoplasm of submandibular gland
148.2 Malignant neoplasm of aryepiglottic fold, hypopharyngeal aspect
148.9 Malignant neoplasm of hypopharynx, unspecified site
150.0 Malignant neoplasm of cervical esophagus
150.3 Malignant neoplasm of upper third of esophagus
150.8 Malignant neoplasm of other specified part of esophagus
161.0 Malignant neoplasm of glottis
161.1 Malignant neoplasm of supraglottis
161.2 Malignant neoplasm of subglottis
161.3 Malignant neoplasm of laryngeal cartilages
161.8 Malignant neoplasm of other specified sites of larynx
161.9 Malignant neoplasm of larynx, unspecified site
170.0 Malignant neoplasm of bones of skull and face, except mandible
171.0 Malignant neoplasm of connective and other soft tissue of head, face, and neck
196.0 Secondary and unspecified malignant neoplasm of lymph nodes of head, face, and neck
197.3 Secondary malignant neoplasm of other respiratory organs
197.8 Secondary malignant neoplasm of other digestive organs and spleen
198.5 Secondary malignant neoplasm of bone and bone marrow
198.89 Secondary malignant neoplasm of other specified sites
199.1 Other malignant neoplasm of unspecified site
209.20 Malignant carcinoid tumor of unknown primary site — (Code first any associated multiple endocrine neoplasia syndrome: 258.01-258.03)(Use additional code to identify associated endocrine syndrome, as: carcinoid syndrome: 259.2)
209.29 Malignant carcinoid tumor of other sites — (Code first any associated multiple endocrine neoplasia syndrome: 258.01-258.03)(Use additional code to identify associated endocrine syndrome, as: carcinoid syndrome: 259.2)
209.70 Secondary neuroendocrine tumor, unspecified site
209.71 Secondary neuroendocrine tumor of distant lymph nodes
230.0 Carcinoma in situ of lip, oral cavity, and pharynx
230.1 Carcinoma in situ of esophagus
231.0 Carcinoma in situ of larynx
235.0 Neoplasm of uncertain behavior of major salivary glands
235.1 Neoplasm of uncertain behavior of lip, oral cavity, and pharynx
235.6 Neoplasm of uncertain behavior of larynx
238.0 Neoplasm of uncertain behavior of bone and articular cartilage
238.1 Neoplasm of uncertain behavior of connective and other soft tissue
239.0 Neoplasm of unspecified nature of digestive system
239.1 Neoplasm of unspecified nature of respiratory system
239.2 Neoplasms of unspecified nature of bone, soft tissue, and skin
239.89 Neoplasms of unspecified nature, other specified sites

ICD-9-CM Procedural

30.3 Complete laryngectomy
30.4 Radical laryngectomy

31370-31382

31370 Partial laryngectomy (hemilaryngectomy); horizontal
31375 lateroverticaI
31380 anterovertical
31382 antero-latero-vertical

ICD-9-CM Diagnostic

148.2 Malignant neoplasm of aryepiglottic fold, hypopharyngeal aspect
161.0 Malignant neoplasm of glottis
161.1 Malignant neoplasm of supraglottis
161.2 Malignant neoplasm of subglottis
161.3 Malignant neoplasm of laryngeal cartilages
161.8 Malignant neoplasm of other specified sites of larynx
161.9 Malignant neoplasm of larynx, unspecified site
197.3 Secondary malignant neoplasm of other respiratory organs
198.89 Secondary malignant neoplasm of other specified sites
199.1 Other malignant neoplasm of unspecified site
209.20 Malignant carcinoid tumor of unknown primary site — (Code first any associated multiple endocrine neoplasia syndrome: 258.01-258.03)(Use additional code to identify associated endocrine syndrome, as: carcinoid syndrome: 259.2)
209.29 Malignant carcinoid tumor of other sites — (Code first any associated multiple endocrine neoplasia syndrome: 258.01-258.03)(Use additional code to identify associated endocrine syndrome, as: carcinoid syndrome: 259.2)
212.1 Benign neoplasm of larynx
230.0 Carcinoma in situ of lip, oral cavity, and pharynx
231.0 Carcinoma in situ of larynx
235.1 Neoplasm of uncertain behavior of lip, oral cavity, and pharynx
235.6 Neoplasm of uncertain behavior of larynx
239.1 Neoplasm of unspecified nature of respiratory system
478.30 Unspecified paralysis of vocal cords or larynx
478.31 Unilateral partial paralysis of vocal cords or larynx
478.32 Unilateral complete paralysis of vocal cords or larynx
478.33 Bilateral partial paralysis of vocal cords or larynx
478.34 Bilateral complete paralysis of vocal cords or larynx
478.4 Polyp of vocal cord or larynx
478.5 Other diseases of vocal cords — (Use additional code to identify infectious organism)
478.71 Cellulitis and perichondritis of larynx — (Use additional code to identify infectious organism)
478.74 Stenosis of larynx
478.79 Other diseases of larynx — (Use additional code to identify infectious organism)
748.2 Congenital web of larynx
748.3 Other congenital anomaly of larynx, trachea, and bronchus
784.8 Hemorrhage from throat
925.2 Crushing injury of neck — (Use additional code to identify any associated injuries, such as: 800-829, 850.0-854.1, 860.0-869.1)
947.1 Burn of larynx, trachea, and lung
948.00 Burn (any degree) involving less than 10% of body surface with third degree burn of less than 10% or unspecified amount
948.10 Burn (any degree) involving 10-19% of body surface with third degree burn of less than 10% or unspecified amount
948.11 Burn (any degree) involving 10-19% of body surface with third degree burn of 10-19%
949.4 Deep necrosis of underlying tissue due to burn (deep third degree), unspecified site without mention of loss of body part
949.5 Deep necrosis of underlying tissues due to burn (deep third degree, unspecified site with loss of body part

ICD-9-CM Procedural

30.1 Hemilaryngectomy
30.29 Other partial laryngectomy

31390-31395

31390 Pharyngolaryngectomy, with radical neck dissection; without reconstruction
31395 with reconstruction

ICD-9-CM Diagnostic

141.0 Malignant neoplasm of base of tongue
142.1 Malignant neoplasm of submandibular gland
146.5 Malignant neoplasm of junctional region of oropharynx
146.6 Malignant neoplasm of lateral wall of oropharynx
146.7 Malignant neoplasm of posterior wall of oropharynx
146.8 Malignant neoplasm of other specified sites of oropharynx
146.9 Malignant neoplasm of oropharynx, unspecified site
147.0 Malignant neoplasm of superior wall of nasopharynx
147.1 Malignant neoplasm of posterior wall of nasopharynx
147.2 Malignant neoplasm of lateral wall of nasopharynx
147.3 Malignant neoplasm of anterior wall of nasopharynx
147.8 Malignant neoplasm of other specified sites of nasopharynx
147.9 Malignant neoplasm of nasopharynx, unspecified site
148.0 Malignant neoplasm of postcricoid region of hypopharynx
148.1 Malignant neoplasm of pyriform sinus
148.2 Malignant neoplasm of aryepiglottic fold, hypopharyngeal aspect
148.3 Malignant neoplasm of posterior hypopharyngeal wall
148.8 Malignant neoplasm of other specified sites of hypopharynx
148.9 Malignant neoplasm of hypopharynx, unspecified site
149.0 Malignant neoplasm of pharynx, unspecified
149.1 Malignant neoplasm of Waldeyer's ring
149.8 Malignant neoplasm of other sites within the lip and oral cavity
150.0 Malignant neoplasm of cervical esophagus
150.3 Malignant neoplasm of upper third of esophagus
150.8 Malignant neoplasm of other specified part of esophagus
161.0 Malignant neoplasm of glottis
161.1 Malignant neoplasm of supraglottis
161.2 Malignant neoplasm of subglottis
161.3 Malignant neoplasm of laryngeal cartilages
161.8 Malignant neoplasm of other specified sites of larynx
161.9 Malignant neoplasm of larynx, unspecified site
171.0 Malignant neoplasm of connective and other soft tissue of head, face, and neck
196.0 Secondary and unspecified malignant neoplasm of lymph nodes of head, face, and neck
197.3 Secondary malignant neoplasm of other respiratory organs
198.5 Secondary malignant neoplasm of bone and bone marrow
198.89 Secondary malignant neoplasm of other specified sites
199.1 Other malignant neoplasm of unspecified site
209.20 Malignant carcinoid tumor of unknown primary site — (Code first any associated multiple endocrine neoplasia syndrome: 258.01-258.03)(Use additional code to identify associated endocrine syndrome, as: carcinoid syndrome: 259.2)
209.29 Malignant carcinoid tumor of other sites — (Code first any associated multiple endocrine neoplasia syndrome: 258.01-258.03)(Use additional code to identify associated endocrine syndrome, as: carcinoid syndrome: 259.2)
209.70 Secondary neuroendocrine tumor, unspecified site
209.71 Secondary neuroendocrine tumor of distant lymph nodes
230.0 Carcinoma in situ of lip, oral cavity, and pharynx
231.0 Carcinoma in situ of larynx
235.0 Neoplasm of uncertain behavior of major salivary glands
235.1 Neoplasm of uncertain behavior of lip, oral cavity, and pharynx
235.5 Neoplasm of uncertain behavior of other and unspecified digestive organs
235.6 Neoplasm of uncertain behavior of larynx
238.0 Neoplasm of uncertain behavior of bone and articular cartilage
238.1 Neoplasm of uncertain behavior of connective and other soft tissue
238.8 Neoplasm of uncertain behavior of other specified sites

239.0 Neoplasm of unspecified nature of digestive system
239.1 Neoplasm of unspecified nature of respiratory system
239.2 Neoplasms of unspecified nature of bone, soft tissue, and skin
239.89 Neoplasms of unspecified nature, other specified sites

ICD-9-CM Procedural

29.4 Plastic operation on pharynx
30.3 Complete laryngectomy
30.4 Radical laryngectomy
31.69 Other repair of larynx
31.75 Reconstruction of trachea and construction of artificial larynx

31400

31400 Arytenoidectomy or arytenoidopexy, external approach

ICD-9-CM Diagnostic

148.2 Malignant neoplasm of aryepiglottic fold, hypopharyngeal aspect
150.0 Malignant neoplasm of cervical esophagus
161.1 Malignant neoplasm of supraglottis
161.3 Malignant neoplasm of laryngeal cartilages
161.8 Malignant neoplasm of other specified sites of larynx
197.3 Secondary malignant neoplasm of other respiratory organs
198.89 Secondary malignant neoplasm of other specified sites
212.1 Benign neoplasm of larynx
231.0 Carcinoma in situ of larynx
235.6 Neoplasm of uncertain behavior of larynx
238.0 Neoplasm of uncertain behavior of bone and articular cartilage
478.33 Bilateral partial paralysis of vocal cords or larynx
478.74 Stenosis of larynx
478.79 Other diseases of larynx — (Use additional code to identify infectious organism)
748.3 Other congenital anomaly of larynx, trachea, and bronchus
784.2 Swelling, mass, or lump in head and neck

ICD-9-CM Procedural

30.29 Other partial laryngectomy
31.69 Other repair of larynx

31420

31420 Epiglottidectomy

ICD-9-CM Diagnostic

146.4 Malignant neoplasm of anterior aspect of epiglottis
146.5 Malignant neoplasm of junctional region of oropharynx
148.2 Malignant neoplasm of aryepiglottic fold, hypopharyngeal aspect
161.0 Malignant neoplasm of glottis
161.1 Malignant neoplasm of supraglottis
161.2 Malignant neoplasm of subglottis
161.3 Malignant neoplasm of laryngeal cartilages
197.3 Secondary malignant neoplasm of other respiratory organs
198.89 Secondary malignant neoplasm of other specified sites
210.6 Benign neoplasm of other parts of oropharynx
212.1 Benign neoplasm of larynx
230.0 Carcinoma in situ of lip, oral cavity, and pharynx
231.0 Carcinoma in situ of larynx
235.1 Neoplasm of uncertain behavior of lip, oral cavity, and pharynx
235.6 Neoplasm of uncertain behavior of larynx
239.0 Neoplasm of unspecified nature of digestive system
239.1 Neoplasm of unspecified nature of respiratory system
748.3 Other congenital anomaly of larynx, trachea, and bronchus

ICD-9-CM Procedural

30.21 Epiglottidectomy

31500

31500 Intubation, endotracheal, emergency procedure

ICD-9-CM Diagnostic

491.21 Obstructive chronic bronchitis, with (acute) exacerbation — (Use additional code to identify infectious organism)
491.22 Obstructive chronic bronchitis with acute bronchitis — (Use additional code to identify infectious organism)
493.01 Extrinsic asthma with status asthmaticus
493.02 Extrinsic asthma, with (acute) exacerbation
493.11 Intrinsic asthma with status asthmaticus
493.12 Intrinsic asthma, with (acute) exacerbation
493.21 Chronic obstructive asthma with status asthmaticus
493.22 Chronic obstructive asthma, with (acute) exacerbation
493.91 Asthma, unspecified with status asthmaticus ▽
493.92 Asthma, unspecified, with (acute) exacerbation ▽
507.0 Pneumonitis due to inhalation of food or vomitus — (Use additional code to identify infectious organism)
518.4 Unspecified acute edema of lung ▽
518.51 Acute respiratory failure following trauma and surgery
518.53 Acute and chronic respiratory failure following trauma and surgery
518.7 Transfusion related acute lung injury [TRALI]
518.81 Acute respiratory failure
518.84 Acute and chronic respiratory failure

ICD-9-CM Procedural

96.04 Insertion of endotracheal tube

31502

31502 Tracheotomy tube change prior to establishment of fistula tract

ICD-9-CM Diagnostic

The application of this code is too broad to adequately present ICD-9-CM diagnostic code links here. Refer to your ICD-9-CM book.

ICD-9-CM Procedural

97.23 Replacement of tracheostomy tube

HCPCS Level II Supplies & Services

A7520 Tracheostomy/laryngectomy tube, noncuffed, polyvinylchloride (PVC), silicone or equal, each

31505-31510

31505 Laryngoscopy, indirect; diagnostic (separate procedure)
31510 with biopsy

ICD-9-CM Diagnostic

148.2 Malignant neoplasm of aryepiglottic fold, hypopharyngeal aspect
161.0 Malignant neoplasm of glottis
161.1 Malignant neoplasm of supraglottis
161.2 Malignant neoplasm of subglottis
161.3 Malignant neoplasm of laryngeal cartilages
161.8 Malignant neoplasm of other specified sites of larynx
197.3 Secondary malignant neoplasm of other respiratory organs
198.89 Secondary malignant neoplasm of other specified sites
199.1 Other malignant neoplasm of unspecified site
209.20 Malignant carcinoid tumor of unknown primary site — (Code first any associated multiple endocrine neoplasia syndrome: 258.01-258.03)(Use additional code to identify associated endocrine syndrome, as: carcinoid syndrome: 259.2)
209.29 Malignant carcinoid tumor of other sites — (Code first any associated multiple endocrine neoplasia syndrome: 258.01-258.03)(Use additional code to identify associated endocrine syndrome, as: carcinoid syndrome: 259.2)
212.0 Benign neoplasm of nasal cavities, middle ear, and accessory sinuses

212.1 Benign neoplasm of larynx
231.0 Carcinoma in situ of larynx
235.6 Neoplasm of uncertain behavior of larynx
239.1 Neoplasm of unspecified nature of respiratory system
446.4 Wegener's granulomatosis
464.21 Acute laryngotracheitis with obstruction — (Use additional code to identify infectious organism)
464.31 Acute epiglottitis with obstruction — (Use additional code to identify infectious organism)
465.0 Acute laryngopharyngitis — (Use additional code to identify infectious organism)
476.0 Chronic laryngitis — (Use additional code to identify infectious organism)
476.1 Chronic laryngotracheitis — (Use additional code to identify infectious organism)
478.30 Unspecified paralysis of vocal cords or larynx ▽
478.31 Unilateral partial paralysis of vocal cords or larynx
478.32 Unilateral complete paralysis of vocal cords or larynx
478.33 Bilateral partial paralysis of vocal cords or larynx
478.34 Bilateral complete paralysis of vocal cords or larynx
478.4 Polyp of vocal cord or larynx
478.5 Other diseases of vocal cords — (Use additional code to identify infectious organism)
478.6 Edema of larynx
478.71 Cellulitis and perichondritis of larynx — (Use additional code to identify infectious organism)
478.74 Stenosis of larynx
478.75 Laryngeal spasm
478.79 Other diseases of larynx — (Use additional code to identify infectious organism)
519.8 Other diseases of respiratory system, not elsewhere classified — (Use additional code to identify infectious organism)
519.9 Unspecified disease of respiratory system — (Use additional code to identify infectious organism) ▽
748.2 Congenital web of larynx
748.3 Other congenital anomaly of larynx, trachea, and bronchus
748.8 Other specified congenital anomaly of respiratory system
784.1 Throat pain
784.2 Swelling, mass, or lump in head and neck
784.3 Aphasia
784.40 Voice and resonance disorder, unspecified ▽
784.41 Aphonia
784.49 Other voice and resonance disorders
784.59 Other speech disturbance
784.8 Hemorrhage from throat
786.09 Other dyspnea and respiratory abnormalities
786.1 Stridor
786.2 Cough
786.30 Hemoptysis, unspecified ▽
786.31 Acute idiopathic pulmonary hemorrhage in infants [AIPHI]
786.39 Other hemoptysis
787.20 Dysphagia, unspecified ▽
787.21 Dysphagia, oral phase
787.22 Dysphagia, oropharyngeal phase
787.23 Dysphagia, pharyngeal phase
787.24 Dysphagia, pharyngoesophageal phase
787.29 Other dysphagia
807.5 Closed fracture of larynx and trachea
925.2 Crushing injury of neck — (Use additional code to identify any associated injuries, such as: 800-829, 850.0-854.1, 860.0-869.1)
933.0 Foreign body in pharynx
933.1 Foreign body in larynx
947.1 Burn of larynx, trachea, and lung
948.00 Burn (any degree) involving less than 10% of body surface with third degree burn of less than 10% or unspecified amount
V67.00 Follow-up examination, following unspecified surgery ▽
V67.09 Follow-up examination, following other surgery
V71.1 Observation for suspected malignant neoplasm

ICD-9-CM Procedural

31.42 Laryngoscopy and other tracheoscopy
31.43 Closed (endoscopic) biopsy of larynx
31.48 Other diagnostic procedures on larynx

HCPCS Level II Supplies & Services

A4305 Disposable drug delivery system, flow rate of 50 ml or greater per hour

31511

31511 Laryngoscopy, indirect; with removal of foreign body

ICD-9-CM Diagnostic

787.20 Dysphagia, unspecified ▽
787.21 Dysphagia, oral phase
787.22 Dysphagia, oropharyngeal phase
787.23 Dysphagia, pharyngeal phase
787.24 Dysphagia, pharyngoesophageal phase
787.29 Other dysphagia
933.0 Foreign body in pharynx
933.1 Foreign body in larynx

ICD-9-CM Procedural

31.42 Laryngoscopy and other tracheoscopy
98.14 Removal of intraluminal foreign body from larynx without incision

HCPCS Level II Supplies & Services

A4305 Disposable drug delivery system, flow rate of 50 ml or greater per hour

31512

31512 Laryngoscopy, indirect; with removal of lesion

ICD-9-CM Diagnostic

148.2 Malignant neoplasm of aryepiglottic fold, hypopharyngeal aspect
161.0 Malignant neoplasm of glottis
161.1 Malignant neoplasm of supraglottis
161.2 Malignant neoplasm of subglottis
161.3 Malignant neoplasm of laryngeal cartilages
161.8 Malignant neoplasm of other specified sites of larynx
197.3 Secondary malignant neoplasm of other respiratory organs
198.89 Secondary malignant neoplasm of other specified sites
199.1 Other malignant neoplasm of unspecified site
209.20 Malignant carcinoid tumor of unknown primary site — (Code first any associated multiple endocrine neoplasia syndrome: 258.01-258.03)(Use additional code to identify associated endocrine syndrome, as: carcinoid syndrome: 259.2)
209.29 Malignant carcinoid tumor of other sites — (Code first any associated multiple endocrine neoplasia syndrome: 258.01-258.03)(Use additional code to identify associated endocrine syndrome, as: carcinoid syndrome: 259.2)
212.0 Benign neoplasm of nasal cavities, middle ear, and accessory sinuses
212.1 Benign neoplasm of larynx
231.0 Carcinoma in situ of larynx
235.6 Neoplasm of uncertain behavior of larynx
239.1 Neoplasm of unspecified nature of respiratory system
446.4 Wegener's granulomatosis
476.0 Chronic laryngitis — (Use additional code to identify infectious organism)
476.1 Chronic laryngotracheitis — (Use additional code to identify infectious organism)
478.4 Polyp of vocal cord or larynx
478.5 Other diseases of vocal cords — (Use additional code to identify infectious organism)

748.2 Congenital web of larynx
748.3 Other congenital anomaly of larynx, trachea, and bronchus
784.1 Throat pain
784.2 Swelling, mass, or lump in head and neck
784.3 Aphasia
784.40 Voice and resonance disorder, unspecified ▽
784.41 Aphonia
784.49 Other voice and resonance disorders
784.8 Hemorrhage from throat
786.09 Other dyspnea and respiratory abnormalities
786.1 Stridor
786.2 Cough
786.30 Hemoptysis, unspecified ▽
786.31 Acute idiopathic pulmonary hemorrhage in infants [AIPHI]
786.39 Other hemoptysis
787.20 Dysphagia, unspecified ▽
787.21 Dysphagia, oral phase
787.22 Dysphagia, oropharyngeal phase
787.23 Dysphagia, pharyngeal phase
787.24 Dysphagia, pharyngoesophageal phase
787.29 Other dysphagia
V67.09 Follow-up examination, following other surgery

ICD-9-CM Procedural

30.09 Other excision or destruction of lesion or tissue of larynx

31513

31513 Laryngoscopy, indirect; with vocal cord injection

ICD-9-CM Diagnostic

476.0 Chronic laryngitis — (Use additional code to identify infectious organism)
476.1 Chronic laryngotracheitis — (Use additional code to identify infectious organism)
478.31 Unilateral partial paralysis of vocal cords or larynx
478.32 Unilateral complete paralysis of vocal cords or larynx
478.33 Bilateral partial paralysis of vocal cords or larynx
478.34 Bilateral complete paralysis of vocal cords or larynx
478.5 Other diseases of vocal cords — (Use additional code to identify infectious organism)
478.75 Laryngeal spasm
784.41 Aphonia
784.49 Other voice and resonance disorders
786.1 Stridor

ICD-9-CM Procedural

31.0 Injection of larynx

HCPCS Level II Supplies & Services

A4305 Disposable drug delivery system, flow rate of 50 ml or greater per hour
C1878 Material for vocal cord medialization, synthetic (implantable)
J0585 Injection, onabotulinumtoxinA, 1 unit

31515

31515 Laryngoscopy direct, with or without tracheoscopy; for aspiration

ICD-9-CM Diagnostic

416.8 Other chronic pulmonary heart diseases
464.00 Acute laryngitis, without mention of obstruction — (Use additional code to identify infectious organism)
464.01 Acute laryngitis, with obstruction — (Use additional code to identify infectious organism)
478.24 Retropharyngeal abscess — (Use additional code to identify infectious organism)
478.5 Other diseases of vocal cords — (Use additional code to identify infectious organism)
478.79 Other diseases of larynx — (Use additional code to identify infectious organism)
507.0 Pneumonitis due to inhalation of food or vomitus — (Use additional code to identify infectious organism)
507.1 Pneumonitis due to inhalation of oils and essences — (Use additional code to identify infectious organism)
507.8 Pneumonitis due to other solids and liquids — (Use additional code to identify infectious organism)
519.01 Infection of tracheostomy — (Use additional code to identify type of infection: 038.0-038.9, 682.1. Use additional code to identify organism: 041.00-041.9)
519.09 Other tracheostomy complications — (Use additional code to identify infectious organism)
519.19 Other diseases of trachea and bronchus — (Use additional code to identify infectious organism)
519.8 Other diseases of respiratory system, not elsewhere classified — (Use additional code to identify infectious organism)
668.04 Pulmonary complications of the administration of anesthesia or other sedation in labor and delivery, postpartum condition or complication — (Use additional code(s) to further specify complication) ♀
729.91 Post-traumatic seroma
761.3 Fetus or newborn affected by polyhydramnios — (Use additional code(s) to further specify condition)
770.10 Fetal and newborn aspiration, unspecified — (Use additional code(s) to further specify condition) ▽
770.11 Meconium aspiration without respiratory symptoms, of fetus and newborn — (Use additional code(s) to further specify condition)
770.12 Meconium aspiration with respiratory symptoms, of fetus and newborn — (Use additional code(s) to further specify condition. Use additional code to identify any secondary pulmonary hypertension, 416.8, if applicable)
770.13 Aspiration of clear amniotic fluid without respiratory symptoms, of fetus and newborn — (Use additional code(s) to further specify condition)
770.14 Aspiration of clear amniotic fluid with respiratory symptoms, of fetus and newborn — (Use additional code(s) to further specify condition. Use additional code to identify any secondary pulmonary hypertension, 416.8, if applicable)
770.15 Aspiration of blood without respiratory symptoms, of fetus and newborn — (Use additional code(s) to further specify condition)
770.16 Aspiration of blood with respiratory symptoms, of fetus and newborn — (Use additional code(s) to further specify condition. Use additional code to identify any secondary pulmonary hypertension, 416.8, if applicable)
770.17 Other fetal and newborn aspiration without respiratory symptoms — (Use additional code(s) to further specify condition)
770.18 Other fetal and newborn aspiration with respiratory symptoms — (Use additional code(s) to further specify condition. Use additional code to identify any secondary pulmonary hypertension, 416.8, if applicable)
770.3 Pulmonary hemorrhage of fetus or newborn — (Use additional code(s) to further specify condition)
770.85 Aspiration of postnatal stomach contents without respiratory symptoms — (Use additional code(s) to further specify condition)
784.2 Swelling, mass, or lump in head and neck
784.49 Other voice and resonance disorders
784.8 Hemorrhage from throat
786.09 Other dyspnea and respiratory abnormalities
786.1 Stridor
786.30 Hemoptysis, unspecified ▽
786.31 Acute idiopathic pulmonary hemorrhage in infants [AIPHI]
786.39 Other hemoptysis
786.4 Abnormal sputum
787.20 Dysphagia, unspecified ▽
787.21 Dysphagia, oral phase
787.22 Dysphagia, oropharyngeal phase
787.23 Dysphagia, pharyngeal phase
787.24 Dysphagia, pharyngoesophageal phase
787.29 Other dysphagia

933.1 Foreign body in larynx
934.0 Foreign body in trachea
997.39 Other respiratory complications
998.51 Infected postoperative seroma — (Use additional code to identify organism)
998.59 Other postoperative infection — (Use additional code to identify infection)

ICD-9-CM Procedural

31.42 Laryngoscopy and other tracheoscopy
31.48 Other diagnostic procedures on larynx

HCPCS Level II Supplies & Services

A4305 Disposable drug delivery system, flow rate of 50 ml or greater per hour

31520-31526

31520 Laryngoscopy direct, with or without tracheoscopy; diagnostic, newborn
31525 diagnostic, except newborn
31526 diagnostic, with operating microscope or telescope

ICD-9-CM Diagnostic

032.0 Faucial diphtheria
032.1 Nasopharyngeal diphtheria
032.2 Anterior nasal diphtheria
032.3 Laryngeal diphtheria
145.2 Malignant neoplasm of hard palate
145.4 Malignant neoplasm of uvula
145.6 Malignant neoplasm of retromolar area
145.8 Malignant neoplasm of other specified parts of mouth
145.9 Malignant neoplasm of mouth, unspecified site ▽
146.0 Malignant neoplasm of tonsil
146.1 Malignant neoplasm of tonsillar fossa
146.2 Malignant neoplasm of tonsillar pillars (anterior) (posterior)
146.3 Malignant neoplasm of vallecula
146.4 Malignant neoplasm of anterior aspect of epiglottis
146.5 Malignant neoplasm of junctional region of oropharynx
146.6 Malignant neoplasm of lateral wall of oropharynx
146.7 Malignant neoplasm of posterior wall of oropharynx
146.8 Malignant neoplasm of other specified sites of oropharynx
146.9 Malignant neoplasm of oropharynx, unspecified site ▽
147.0 Malignant neoplasm of superior wall of nasopharynx
147.1 Malignant neoplasm of posterior wall of nasopharynx
147.2 Malignant neoplasm of lateral wall of nasopharynx
147.3 Malignant neoplasm of anterior wall of nasopharynx
147.8 Malignant neoplasm of other specified sites of nasopharynx
147.9 Malignant neoplasm of nasopharynx, unspecified site ▽
148.0 Malignant neoplasm of postcricoid region of hypopharynx
148.1 Malignant neoplasm of pyriform sinus
148.2 Malignant neoplasm of aryepiglottic fold, hypopharyngeal aspect
148.3 Malignant neoplasm of posterior hypopharyngeal wall
148.8 Malignant neoplasm of other specified sites of hypopharynx
148.9 Malignant neoplasm of hypopharynx, unspecified site ▽
150.0 Malignant neoplasm of cervical esophagus
161.0 Malignant neoplasm of glottis
161.1 Malignant neoplasm of supraglottis
161.2 Malignant neoplasm of subglottis
161.3 Malignant neoplasm of laryngeal cartilages
161.8 Malignant neoplasm of other specified sites of larynx
161.9 Malignant neoplasm of larynx, unspecified site ▽
162.0 Malignant neoplasm of trachea
193 Malignant neoplasm of thyroid gland — (Use additional code to identify any functional activity)
194.1 Malignant neoplasm of parathyroid gland
196.0 Secondary and unspecified malignant neoplasm of lymph nodes of head, face, and neck
197.3 Secondary malignant neoplasm of other respiratory organs
198.89 Secondary malignant neoplasm of other specified sites
199.1 Other malignant neoplasm of unspecified site
209.20 Malignant carcinoid tumor of unknown primary site — (Code first any associated multiple endocrine neoplasia syndrome: 258.01-258.03)(Use additional code to identify associated endocrine syndrome, as: carcinoid syndrome: 259.2)
209.29 Malignant carcinoid tumor of other sites — (Code first any associated multiple endocrine neoplasia syndrome: 258.01-258.03)(Use additional code to identify associated endocrine syndrome, as: carcinoid syndrome: 259.2)
209.70 Secondary neuroendocrine tumor, unspecified site ▽
209.71 Secondary neuroendocrine tumor of distant lymph nodes
210.1 Benign neoplasm of tongue
210.4 Benign neoplasm of other and unspecified parts of mouth ▽
210.6 Benign neoplasm of other parts of oropharynx
210.7 Benign neoplasm of nasopharynx
210.8 Benign neoplasm of hypopharynx
210.9 Benign neoplasm of pharynx, unspecified ▽
211.0 Benign neoplasm of esophagus
212.0 Benign neoplasm of nasal cavities, middle ear, and accessory sinuses
212.1 Benign neoplasm of larynx
212.2 Benign neoplasm of trachea
215.0 Other benign neoplasm of connective and other soft tissue of head, face, and neck
226 Benign neoplasm of thyroid glands — (Use additional code to identify any functional activity)
231.0 Carcinoma in situ of larynx
231.1 Carcinoma in situ of trachea
234.8 Carcinoma in situ of other specified sites
235.1 Neoplasm of uncertain behavior of lip, oral cavity, and pharynx
235.6 Neoplasm of uncertain behavior of larynx
235.7 Neoplasm of uncertain behavior of trachea, bronchus, and lung
239.1 Neoplasm of unspecified nature of respiratory system
240.0 Goiter, specified as simple
240.9 Goiter, unspecified ▽
241.0 Nontoxic uninodular goiter
241.1 Nontoxic multinodular goiter
241.9 Unspecified nontoxic nodular goiter ▽
242.00 Toxic diffuse goiter without mention of thyrotoxic crisis or storm
242.01 Toxic diffuse goiter with mention of thyrotoxic crisis or storm
242.10 Toxic uninodular goiter without mention of thyrotoxic crisis or storm
242.11 Toxic uninodular goiter with mention of thyrotoxic crisis or storm
242.20 Toxic multinodular goiter without mention of thyrotoxic crisis or storm
242.21 Toxic multinodular goiter with mention of thyrotoxic crisis or storm
242.30 Toxic nodular goiter, unspecified type, without mention of thyrotoxic crisis or storm ▽
242.31 Toxic nodular goiter, unspecified type, with mention of thyrotoxic crisis or storm ▽
242.40 Thyrotoxicosis from ectopic thyroid nodule without mention of thyrotoxic crisis or storm
242.41 Thyrotoxicosis from ectopic thyroid nodule with mention of thyrotoxic crisis or storm
242.80 Thyrotoxicosis of other specified origin without mention of thyrotoxic crisis or storm — (Use additional E code to identify cause, if drug-induced)
242.81 Thyrotoxicosis of other specified origin with mention of thyrotoxic crisis or storm — (Use additional E code to identify cause, if drug-induced)
242.90 Thyrotoxicosis without mention of goiter or other cause, without mention of thyrotoxic crisis or storm
242.91 Thyrotoxicosis without mention of goiter or other cause, with mention of thyrotoxic crisis or storm
243 Congenital hypothyroidism — (Use additional code to identify associated intellectual disabilities)

244.0 Postsurgical hypothyroidism
244.1 Other postablative hypothyroidism
244.2 Iodine hypothyroidism — (Use additional E code to identify drug)
244.3 Other iatrogenic hypothyroidism — (Use additional E code to identify drug)
244.8 Other specified acquired hypothyroidism
244.9 Unspecified hypothyroidism ▽
245.0 Acute thyroiditis — (Use additional code to identify organism)
245.1 Subacute thyroiditis
245.2 Chronic lymphocytic thyroiditis
245.3 Chronic fibrous thyroiditis
245.4 Iatrogenic thyroiditis — (Use additional code to identify cause)
245.8 Other and unspecified chronic thyroiditis ▽
245.9 Unspecified thyroiditis ▽
246.0 Disorders of thyrocalcitonin secretion
246.1 Dyshormonogenic goiter
246.2 Cyst of thyroid
246.3 Hemorrhage and infarction of thyroid
246.8 Other specified disorders of thyroid
246.9 Unspecified disorder of thyroid ▽
350.2 Atypical face pain
388.70 Unspecified otalgia ▽
438.82 Dysphagia due to cerebrovascular disease — (Use additional code to identify presence of hypertension)
446.4 Wegener's granulomatosis
462 Acute pharyngitis — (Use additional code to identify infectious organism)
464.00 Acute laryngitis, without mention of obstruction — (Use additional code to identify infectious organism)
464.01 Acute laryngitis, with obstruction — (Use additional code to identify infectious organism)
464.10 Acute tracheitis without mention of obstruction — (Use additional code to identify infectious organism)
464.11 Acute tracheitis with obstruction — (Use additional code to identify infectious organism)
464.20 Acute laryngotracheitis without mention of obstruction — (Use additional code to identify infectious organism)
464.21 Acute laryngotracheitis with obstruction — (Use additional code to identify infectious organism)
464.30 Acute epiglottitis without mention of obstruction — (Use additional code to identify infectious organism)
464.31 Acute epiglottitis with obstruction — (Use additional code to identify infectious organism)
464.4 Croup — (Use additional code to identify infectious organism)
465.0 Acute laryngopharyngitis — (Use additional code to identify infectious organism)
472.1 Chronic pharyngitis — (Use additional code to identify infectious organism)
476.0 Chronic laryngitis — (Use additional code to identify infectious organism)
476.1 Chronic laryngotracheitis — (Use additional code to identify infectious organism)
478.21 Cellulitis of pharynx or nasopharynx — (Use additional code to identify infectious organism)
478.22 Parapharyngeal abscess — (Use additional code to identify infectious organism)
478.24 Retropharyngeal abscess — (Use additional code to identify infectious organism)
478.31 Unilateral partial paralysis of vocal cords or larynx
478.32 Unilateral complete paralysis of vocal cords or larynx
478.33 Bilateral partial paralysis of vocal cords or larynx
478.34 Bilateral complete paralysis of vocal cords or larynx
478.4 Polyp of vocal cord or larynx
478.5 Other diseases of vocal cords — (Use additional code to identify infectious organism)
478.6 Edema of larynx
478.70 Unspecified disease of larynx ▽
478.71 Cellulitis and perichondritis of larynx — (Use additional code to identify infectious organism)
478.74 Stenosis of larynx
478.75 Laryngeal spasm
478.79 Other diseases of larynx — (Use additional code to identify infectious organism)
478.8 Upper respiratory tract hypersensitivity reaction, site unspecified — (Use additional code to identify infectious organism) ▽
507.0 Pneumonitis due to inhalation of food or vomitus — (Use additional code to identify infectious organism)
518.81 Acute respiratory failure
519.00 Unspecified tracheostomy complication — (Use additional code to identify infectious organism) ▽
519.19 Other diseases of trachea and bronchus — (Use additional code to identify infectious organism)
519.8 Other diseases of respiratory system, not elsewhere classified — (Use additional code to identify infectious organism)
530.11 Reflux esophagitis — (Use additional E code to identify cause, if induced by chemical)
530.13 Eosinophilic esophagitis
530.3 Stricture and stenosis of esophagus
530.6 Diverticulum of esophagus, acquired
530.81 Esophageal reflux
530.82 Esophageal hemorrhage
530.84 Tracheoesophageal fistula
530.86 Infection of esophagostomy — (Use additional code to specify infection)
530.87 Mechanical complication of esophagostomy
733.99 Other disorders of bone and cartilage
748.2 Congenital web of larynx
748.3 Other congenital anomaly of larynx, trachea, and bronchus
748.8 Other specified congenital anomaly of respiratory system
750.27 Congenital diverticulum of pharynx
750.29 Other specified congenital anomaly of pharynx
750.3 Congenital tracheoesophageal fistula, esophageal atresia and stenosis
763.84 Other specified complications of labor and delivery affecting fetus or newborn, Meconium passage during delivery — (Use additional code(s) to further specify condition)
768.2 Fetal distress before onset of labor, in liveborn infant — (Use additional code(s) to further specify condition. Use only when associated with newborn morbidity classifiable elsewhere)
768.3 Fetal distress first noted during labor and delivery, in liveborn infant — (Use additional code(s) to further specify condition. Use only when associated with newborn morbidity classifiable elsewhere)
768.4 Fetal distress, unspecified as to time of onset, in liveborn infant — (Use additional code(s) to further specify condition. Use only when associated with newborn morbidity classifiable elsewhere) ▽
768.5 Severe birth asphyxia — (Use additional code(s) to further specify condition. Use only when associated with newborn morbidity classifiable elsewhere)
768.6 Mild or moderate birth asphyxia — (Use additional code(s) to further specify condition. Use only when associated with newborn morbidity classifiable elsewhere)
768.70 Hypoxic-ischemic encephalopathy, unspecified ▽
768.71 Mild hypoxic-ischemic encephalopathy
768.72 Moderate hypoxic-ischemic encephalopathy
768.73 Severe hypoxic-ischemic encephalopathy
769 Respiratory distress syndrome in newborn — (Use additional code(s) to further specify condition)
770.10 Fetal and newborn aspiration, unspecified — (Use additional code(s) to further specify condition) ▽
770.11 Meconium aspiration without respiratory symptoms, of fetus and newborn — (Use additional code(s) to further specify condition)
770.12 Meconium aspiration with respiratory symptoms, of fetus and newborn — (Use additional code(s) to further specify condition. Use additional code to identify any secondary pulmonary hypertension, 416.8, if applicable)
770.13 Aspiration of clear amniotic fluid without respiratory symptoms, of fetus and newborn — (Use additional code(s) to further specify condition)

[Resequenced code]
▽ Unspecified code
♀ Female diagnosis
Manifestation code
♂ Male diagnosis

770.14 Aspiration of clear amniotic fluid with respiratory symptoms, of fetus and newborn — (Use additional code(s) to further specify condition. Use additional code to identify any secondary pulmonary hypertension, 416.8, if applicable)
770.15 Aspiration of blood without respiratory symptoms, of fetus and newborn — (Use additional code(s) to further specify condition)
770.16 Aspiration of blood with respiratory symptoms, of fetus and newborn — (Use additional code(s) to further specify condition. Use additional code to identify any secondary pulmonary hypertension, 416.8, if applicable)
770.17 Other fetal and newborn aspiration without respiratory symptoms — (Use additional code(s) to further specify condition)
770.18 Other fetal and newborn aspiration with respiratory symptoms — (Use additional code(s) to further specify condition. Use additional code to identify any secondary pulmonary hypertension, 416.8, if applicable)
770.3 Pulmonary hemorrhage of fetus or newborn — (Use additional code(s) to further specify condition)
770.81 Primary apnea of newborn — (Use additional code(s) to further specify condition)
770.82 Other apnea of newborn — (Use additional code(s) to further specify condition)
770.83 Cyanotic attacks of newborn — (Use additional code(s) to further specify condition)
770.84 Respiratory failure of newborn — (Use additional code(s) to further specify condition)
770.85 Aspiration of postnatal stomach contents without respiratory symptoms — (Use additional code(s) to further specify condition)
770.87 Respiratory arrest of newborn — (Use additional code(s) to further specify condition)
770.88 Hypoxemia of newborn — (Use additional code(s) to further specify condition)
770.89 Other respiratory problems of newborn after birth — (Use additional code(s) to further specify condition)
779.31 Feeding problems in newborn
779.32 Bilious vomiting in newborn
779.33 Other vomiting in newborn
779.34 Failure to thrive in newborn
780.51 Insomnia with sleep apnea, unspecified ▽
780.53 Hypersomnia with sleep apnea, unspecified ▽
783.3 Feeding difficulties and mismanagement
784.1 Throat pain
784.2 Swelling, mass, or lump in head and neck
784.41 Aphonia
784.42 Dysphonia
784.49 Other voice and resonance disorders
784.51 Dysarthria
784.59 Other speech disturbance
784.8 Hemorrhage from throat
786.09 Other dyspnea and respiratory abnormalities
786.1 Stridor
786.2 Cough
786.30 Hemoptysis, unspecified ▽
786.31 Acute idiopathic pulmonary hemorrhage in infants [AIPHI]
786.39 Other hemoptysis
787.20 Dysphagia, unspecified ▽
787.21 Dysphagia, oral phase
787.22 Dysphagia, oropharyngeal phase
787.23 Dysphagia, pharyngeal phase
787.24 Dysphagia, pharyngoesophageal phase
787.29 Other dysphagia
807.5 Closed fracture of larynx and trachea
807.6 Open fracture of larynx and trachea
874.10 Open wound of larynx with trachea, complicated
874.11 Open wound of larynx, complicated
925.2 Crushing injury of neck — (Use additional code to identify any associated injuries, such as: 800-829, 850.0-854.1, 860.0-869.1)
933.0 Foreign body in pharynx
933.1 Foreign body in larynx
934.0 Foreign body in trachea
934.1 Foreign body in main bronchus
934.8 Foreign body in other specified parts of trachea, bronchus, and lung
934.9 Foreign body in respiratory tree, unspecified ▽
935.1 Foreign body in esophagus
947.0 Burn of mouth and pharynx
947.1 Burn of larynx, trachea, and lung
947.2 Burn of esophagus
959.09 Injury of face and neck, other and unspecified
995.0 Other anaphylactic reaction — (Use additional E code to identify external cause, such as: E930-E949)
997.39 Other respiratory complications
V48.3 Mechanical and motor problems with neck and trunk

ICD-9-CM Procedural

31.42 Laryngoscopy and other tracheoscopy
31.48 Other diagnostic procedures on larynx

HCPCS Level II Supplies & Services

A4305 Disposable drug delivery system, flow rate of 50 ml or greater per hour

31527-31529

31527 Laryngoscopy direct, with or without tracheoscopy; with insertion of obturator
31528 with dilation, initial
31529 with dilation, subsequent

ICD-9-CM Diagnostic

148.2 Malignant neoplasm of aryepiglottic fold, hypopharyngeal aspect
161.0 Malignant neoplasm of glottis
161.1 Malignant neoplasm of supraglottis
161.2 Malignant neoplasm of subglottis
161.3 Malignant neoplasm of laryngeal cartilages
161.8 Malignant neoplasm of other specified sites of larynx
161.9 Malignant neoplasm of larynx, unspecified site ▽
197.3 Secondary malignant neoplasm of other respiratory organs
198.89 Secondary malignant neoplasm of other specified sites
199.1 Other malignant neoplasm of unspecified site
209.20 Malignant carcinoid tumor of unknown primary site — (Code first any associated multiple endocrine neoplasia syndrome: 258.01-258.03)(Use additional code to identify associated endocrine syndrome, as: carcinoid syndrome: 259.2)
209.29 Malignant carcinoid tumor of other sites — (Code first any associated multiple endocrine neoplasia syndrome: 258.01-258.03)(Use additional code to identify associated endocrine syndrome, as: carcinoid syndrome: 259.2)
212.1 Benign neoplasm of larynx
212.2 Benign neoplasm of trachea
215.0 Other benign neoplasm of connective and other soft tissue of head, face, and neck
231.0 Carcinoma in situ of larynx
231.1 Carcinoma in situ of trachea
234.8 Carcinoma in situ of other specified sites
235.6 Neoplasm of uncertain behavior of larynx
235.7 Neoplasm of uncertain behavior of trachea, bronchus, and lung
239.1 Neoplasm of unspecified nature of respiratory system
464.11 Acute tracheitis with obstruction — (Use additional code to identify infectious organism)
464.21 Acute laryngotracheitis with obstruction — (Use additional code to identify infectious organism)
464.31 Acute epiglottitis with obstruction — (Use additional code to identify infectious organism)
476.0 Chronic laryngitis — (Use additional code to identify infectious organism)
476.1 Chronic laryngotracheitis — (Use additional code to identify infectious organism)
478.31 Unilateral partial paralysis of vocal cords or larynx

478.32 Unilateral complete paralysis of vocal cords or larynx
478.33 Bilateral partial paralysis of vocal cords or larynx
478.34 Bilateral complete paralysis of vocal cords or larynx
478.4 Polyp of vocal cord or larynx
478.5 Other diseases of vocal cords — (Use additional code to identify infectious organism)
478.6 Edema of larynx
478.71 Cellulitis and perichondritis of larynx — (Use additional code to identify infectious organism)
478.74 Stenosis of larynx
478.75 Laryngeal spasm
478.79 Other diseases of larynx — (Use additional code to identify infectious organism)
518.81 Acute respiratory failure
519.19 Other diseases of trachea and bronchus — (Use additional code to identify infectious organism)
519.8 Other diseases of respiratory system, not elsewhere classified — (Use additional code to identify infectious organism)
748.2 Congenital web of larynx
748.3 Other congenital anomaly of larynx, trachea, and bronchus
748.8 Other specified congenital anomaly of respiratory system
784.1 Throat pain
784.41 Aphonia
784.49 Other voice and resonance disorders
784.8 Hemorrhage from throat
786.09 Other dyspnea and respiratory abnormalities
786.1 Stridor
786.2 Cough
787.20 Dysphagia, unspecified ▽
787.21 Dysphagia, oral phase
787.22 Dysphagia, oropharyngeal phase
787.23 Dysphagia, pharyngeal phase
787.24 Dysphagia, pharyngoesophageal phase
787.29 Other dysphagia
807.5 Closed fracture of larynx and trachea
807.6 Open fracture of larynx and trachea
933.1 Foreign body in larynx
997.39 Other respiratory complications

ICD-9-CM Procedural

31.98 Other operations on larynx

HCPCS Level II Supplies & Services

A4305 Disposable drug delivery system, flow rate of 50 ml or greater per hour

31530-31531

31530 Laryngoscopy, direct, operative, with foreign body removal;
31531 with operating microscope or telescope

ICD-9-CM Diagnostic

784.41 Aphonia
786.1 Stridor
786.2 Cough
933.1 Foreign body in larynx

ICD-9-CM Procedural

31.42 Laryngoscopy and other tracheoscopy
98.14 Removal of intraluminal foreign body from larynx without incision

31535-31536

31535 Laryngoscopy, direct, operative, with biopsy;
31536 with operating microscope or telescope

ICD-9-CM Diagnostic

150.0 Malignant neoplasm of cervical esophagus
161.0 Malignant neoplasm of glottis
161.1 Malignant neoplasm of supraglottis
161.2 Malignant neoplasm of subglottis
161.3 Malignant neoplasm of laryngeal cartilages
161.8 Malignant neoplasm of other specified sites of larynx
161.9 Malignant neoplasm of larynx, unspecified site ▽
195.0 Malignant neoplasm of head, face, and neck
196.0 Secondary and unspecified malignant neoplasm of lymph nodes of head, face, and neck
197.3 Secondary malignant neoplasm of other respiratory organs
198.89 Secondary malignant neoplasm of other specified sites
199.1 Other malignant neoplasm of unspecified site
209.20 Malignant carcinoid tumor of unknown primary site — (Code first any associated multiple endocrine neoplasia syndrome: 258.01-258.03)(Use additional code to identify associated endocrine syndrome, as: carcinoid syndrome: 259.2)
209.29 Malignant carcinoid tumor of other sites — (Code first any associated multiple endocrine neoplasia syndrome: 258.01-258.03)(Use additional code to identify associated endocrine syndrome, as: carcinoid syndrome: 259.2)
212.1 Benign neoplasm of larynx
212.2 Benign neoplasm of trachea
212.9 Benign neoplasm of respiratory and intrathoracic organs, site unspecified ▽
215.0 Other benign neoplasm of connective and other soft tissue of head, face, and neck
230.0 Carcinoma in situ of lip, oral cavity, and pharynx
231.0 Carcinoma in situ of larynx
231.1 Carcinoma in situ of trachea
234.8 Carcinoma in situ of other specified sites
235.6 Neoplasm of uncertain behavior of larynx
235.7 Neoplasm of uncertain behavior of trachea, bronchus, and lung
239.1 Neoplasm of unspecified nature of respiratory system
464.00 Acute laryngitis, without mention of obstruction — (Use additional code to identify infectious organism)
464.01 Acute laryngitis, with obstruction — (Use additional code to identify infectious organism)
464.10 Acute tracheitis without mention of obstruction — (Use additional code to identify infectious organism)
464.11 Acute tracheitis with obstruction — (Use additional code to identify infectious organism)
464.20 Acute laryngotracheitis without mention of obstruction — (Use additional code to identify infectious organism)
464.21 Acute laryngotracheitis with obstruction — (Use additional code to identify infectious organism)
464.30 Acute epiglottitis without mention of obstruction — (Use additional code to identify infectious organism)
464.31 Acute epiglottitis with obstruction — (Use additional code to identify infectious organism)
465.0 Acute laryngopharyngitis — (Use additional code to identify infectious organism)
465.8 Acute upper respiratory infections of other multiple sites — (Use additional code to identify infectious organism)
465.9 Acute upper respiratory infections of unspecified site — (Use additional code to identify infectious organism) ▽
476.0 Chronic laryngitis — (Use additional code to identify infectious organism)
476.1 Chronic laryngotracheitis — (Use additional code to identify infectious organism)
478.30 Unspecified paralysis of vocal cords or larynx ▽
478.31 Unilateral partial paralysis of vocal cords or larynx
478.32 Unilateral complete paralysis of vocal cords or larynx

478.33 Bilateral partial paralysis of vocal cords or larynx
478.4 Polyp of vocal cord or larynx
478.5 Other diseases of vocal cords — (Use additional code to identify infectious organism)
478.6 Edema of larynx
478.70 Unspecified disease of larynx ♥
478.71 Cellulitis and perichondritis of larynx — (Use additional code to identify infectious organism)
478.74 Stenosis of larynx
478.79 Other diseases of larynx — (Use additional code to identify infectious organism)
496 Chronic airway obstruction, not elsewhere classified — (Note: This code is not to be used with any code from 491-493) ♥
519.19 Other diseases of trachea and bronchus — (Use additional code to identify infectious organism)
748.2 Congenital web of larynx
748.3 Other congenital anomaly of larynx, trachea, and bronchus
748.8 Other specified congenital anomaly of respiratory system
748.9 Unspecified congenital anomaly of respiratory system ♥
784.1 Throat pain
784.2 Swelling, mass, or lump in head and neck
784.41 Aphonia
784.49 Other voice and resonance disorders
784.8 Hemorrhage from throat
785.6 Enlargement of lymph nodes
786.09 Other dyspnea and respiratory abnormalities
786.1 Stridor
786.2 Cough
786.30 Hemoptysis, unspecified ♥
786.31 Acute idiopathic pulmonary hemorrhage in infants [AIPHI]
786.39 Other hemoptysis
786.6 Swelling, mass, or lump in chest
787.20 Dysphagia, unspecified ♥
787.21 Dysphagia, oral phase
787.22 Dysphagia, oropharyngeal phase
787.23 Dysphagia, pharyngeal phase
787.24 Dysphagia, pharyngoesophageal phase
787.29 Other dysphagia
V10.20 Personal history of malignant neoplasm of unspecified respiratory organ ♥
V10.21 Personal history of malignant neoplasm of larynx
V12.60 Personal history, unspecified disease of respiratory system ♥
V12.69 Personal history, Other diseases of respiratory system
V15.82 Personal history of tobacco use, presenting hazards to health

ICD-9-CM Procedural

31.43 Closed (endoscopic) biopsy of larynx
31.44 Closed (endoscopic) biopsy of trachea

31540-31541

31540 Laryngoscopy, direct, operative, with excision of tumor and/or stripping of vocal cords or epiglottis;
31541 with operating microscope or telescope

ICD-9-CM Diagnostic

148.2 Malignant neoplasm of aryepiglottic fold, hypopharyngeal aspect
161.0 Malignant neoplasm of glottis
161.1 Malignant neoplasm of supraglottis
161.2 Malignant neoplasm of subglottis
161.3 Malignant neoplasm of laryngeal cartilages
161.8 Malignant neoplasm of other specified sites of larynx
197.3 Secondary malignant neoplasm of other respiratory organs
198.89 Secondary malignant neoplasm of other specified sites
199.1 Other malignant neoplasm of unspecified site
209.20 Malignant carcinoid tumor of unknown primary site — (Code first any associated multiple endocrine neoplasia syndrome: 258.01-258.03)(Use additional code to identify associated endocrine syndrome, as: carcinoid syndrome: 259.2)
209.29 Malignant carcinoid tumor of other sites — (Code first any associated multiple endocrine neoplasia syndrome: 258.01-258.03)(Use additional code to identify associated endocrine syndrome, as: carcinoid syndrome: 259.2)
212.1 Benign neoplasm of larynx
228.09 Hemangioma of other sites
231.0 Carcinoma in situ of larynx
235.6 Neoplasm of uncertain behavior of larynx
239.1 Neoplasm of unspecified nature of respiratory system
352.3 Disorders of pneumogastric (10th) nerve
476.0 Chronic laryngitis — (Use additional code to identify infectious organism)
478.31 Unilateral partial paralysis of vocal cords or larynx
478.32 Unilateral complete paralysis of vocal cords or larynx
478.33 Bilateral partial paralysis of vocal cords or larynx
478.34 Bilateral complete paralysis of vocal cords or larynx
478.4 Polyp of vocal cord or larynx
478.5 Other diseases of vocal cords — (Use additional code to identify infectious organism)
478.79 Other diseases of larynx — (Use additional code to identify infectious organism)
519.8 Other diseases of respiratory system, not elsewhere classified — (Use additional code to identify infectious organism)
784.2 Swelling, mass, or lump in head and neck
784.49 Other voice and resonance disorders
787.20 Dysphagia, unspecified ♥
787.21 Dysphagia, oral phase
787.22 Dysphagia, oropharyngeal phase
787.23 Dysphagia, pharyngeal phase
787.24 Dysphagia, pharyngoesophageal phase
787.29 Other dysphagia

ICD-9-CM Procedural

30.09 Other excision or destruction of lesion or tissue of larynx

31545-31546

31545 Laryngoscopy, direct, operative, with operating microscope or telescope, with submucosal removal of non-neoplastic lesion(s) of vocal cord; reconstruction with local tissue flap(s)
31546 reconstruction with graft(s) (includes obtaining autograft)

ICD-9-CM Diagnostic

212.1 Benign neoplasm of larynx
478.4 Polyp of vocal cord or larynx
478.5 Other diseases of vocal cords — (Use additional code to identify infectious organism)
478.6 Edema of larynx
478.70 Unspecified disease of larynx ♥
478.71 Cellulitis and perichondritis of larynx — (Use additional code to identify infectious organism)
478.79 Other diseases of larynx — (Use additional code to identify infectious organism)
748.2 Congenital web of larynx
748.3 Other congenital anomaly of larynx, trachea, and bronchus
784.1 Throat pain
784.2 Swelling, mass, or lump in head and neck
784.40 Voice and resonance disorder, unspecified ♥
784.49 Other voice and resonance disorders

ICD-9-CM Procedural

30.09 Other excision or destruction of lesion or tissue of larynx
31.69 Other repair of larynx

31560-31561

31560 Laryngoscopy, direct, operative, with arytenoidectomy;
31561 with operating microscope or telescope

ICD-9-CM Diagnostic

148.2 Malignant neoplasm of aryepiglottic fold, hypopharyngeal aspect
150.0 Malignant neoplasm of cervical esophagus
161.1 Malignant neoplasm of supraglottis
161.3 Malignant neoplasm of laryngeal cartilages
161.8 Malignant neoplasm of other specified sites of larynx
197.3 Secondary malignant neoplasm of other respiratory organs
198.89 Secondary malignant neoplasm of other specified sites
212.1 Benign neoplasm of larynx
231.0 Carcinoma in situ of larynx
235.6 Neoplasm of uncertain behavior of larynx
238.0 Neoplasm of uncertain behavior of bone and articular cartilage
478.79 Other diseases of larynx — (Use additional code to identify infectious organism)
748.3 Other congenital anomaly of larynx, trachea, and bronchus
784.2 Swelling, mass, or lump in head and neck

ICD-9-CM Procedural

30.29 Other partial laryngectomy

31570-31571

31570 Laryngoscopy, direct, with injection into vocal cord(s), therapeutic;
31571 with operating microscope or telescope

ICD-9-CM Diagnostic

476.0 Chronic laryngitis — (Use additional code to identify infectious organism)
476.1 Chronic laryngotracheitis — (Use additional code to identify infectious organism)
478.31 Unilateral partial paralysis of vocal cords or larynx
478.32 Unilateral complete paralysis of vocal cords or larynx
478.33 Bilateral partial paralysis of vocal cords or larynx
478.34 Bilateral complete paralysis of vocal cords or larynx
478.4 Polyp of vocal cord or larynx
478.6 Edema of larynx
478.74 Stenosis of larynx
478.75 Laryngeal spasm
784.41 Aphonia
784.49 Other voice and resonance disorders
906.0 Late effect of open wound of head, neck, and trunk
908.6 Late effect of certain complications of trauma

ICD-9-CM Procedural

31.0 Injection of larynx

HCPCS Level II Supplies & Services

C1878 Material for vocal cord medialization, synthetic (implantable)
J0585 Injection, onabotulinumtoxinA, 1 unit

31575-31576

31575 Laryngoscopy, flexible fiberoptic; diagnostic
31576 with biopsy

ICD-9-CM Diagnostic

032.0 Faucial diphtheria
032.1 Nasopharyngeal diphtheria
032.2 Anterior nasal diphtheria
032.3 Laryngeal diphtheria
145.2 Malignant neoplasm of hard palate
145.4 Malignant neoplasm of uvula
145.6 Malignant neoplasm of retromolar area
145.8 Malignant neoplasm of other specified parts of mouth
145.9 Malignant neoplasm of mouth, unspecified site ▽
146.0 Malignant neoplasm of tonsil
146.1 Malignant neoplasm of tonsillar fossa
146.2 Malignant neoplasm of tonsillar pillars (anterior) (posterior)
146.3 Malignant neoplasm of vallecula
146.4 Malignant neoplasm of anterior aspect of epiglottis
146.5 Malignant neoplasm of junctional region of oropharynx
146.6 Malignant neoplasm of lateral wall of oropharynx
146.7 Malignant neoplasm of posterior wall of oropharynx
146.8 Malignant neoplasm of other specified sites of oropharynx
146.9 Malignant neoplasm of oropharynx, unspecified site ▽
147.0 Malignant neoplasm of superior wall of nasopharynx
147.1 Malignant neoplasm of posterior wall of nasopharynx
147.2 Malignant neoplasm of lateral wall of nasopharynx
147.3 Malignant neoplasm of anterior wall of nasopharynx
147.8 Malignant neoplasm of other specified sites of nasopharynx
147.9 Malignant neoplasm of nasopharynx, unspecified site ▽
148.0 Malignant neoplasm of postcricoid region of hypopharynx
148.1 Malignant neoplasm of pyriform sinus
148.2 Malignant neoplasm of aryepiglottic fold, hypopharyngeal aspect
148.3 Malignant neoplasm of posterior hypopharyngeal wall
148.8 Malignant neoplasm of other specified sites of hypopharynx
148.9 Malignant neoplasm of hypopharynx, unspecified site ▽
150.0 Malignant neoplasm of cervical esophagus
161.0 Malignant neoplasm of glottis
161.1 Malignant neoplasm of supraglottis
161.2 Malignant neoplasm of subglottis
161.3 Malignant neoplasm of laryngeal cartilages
161.8 Malignant neoplasm of other specified sites of larynx
161.9 Malignant neoplasm of larynx, unspecified site ▽
162.0 Malignant neoplasm of trachea
193 Malignant neoplasm of thyroid gland — (Use additional code to identify any functional activity)
194.1 Malignant neoplasm of parathyroid gland
196.0 Secondary and unspecified malignant neoplasm of lymph nodes of head, face, and neck
197.3 Secondary malignant neoplasm of other respiratory organs
198.89 Secondary malignant neoplasm of other specified sites
199.1 Other malignant neoplasm of unspecified site
209.20 Malignant carcinoid tumor of unknown primary site — (Code first any associated multiple endocrine neoplasia syndrome: 258.01-258.03)(Use additional code to identify associated endocrine syndrome, as: carcinoid syndrome: 259.2)
209.29 Malignant carcinoid tumor of other sites — (Code first any associated multiple endocrine neoplasia syndrome: 258.01-258.03)(Use additional code to identify associated endocrine syndrome, as: carcinoid syndrome: 259.2)
209.70 Secondary neuroendocrine tumor, unspecified site ▽
210.1 Benign neoplasm of tongue
210.4 Benign neoplasm of other and unspecified parts of mouth ▽
210.6 Benign neoplasm of other parts of oropharynx
210.7 Benign neoplasm of nasopharynx
210.8 Benign neoplasm of hypopharynx
210.9 Benign neoplasm of pharynx, unspecified ▽
211.0 Benign neoplasm of esophagus
212.0 Benign neoplasm of nasal cavities, middle ear, and accessory sinuses
212.1 Benign neoplasm of larynx
226 Benign neoplasm of thyroid glands — (Use additional code to identify any functional activity)
231.0 Carcinoma in situ of larynx

[Resequenced code] ▽ Unspecified code ♀ Female diagnosis ◼ Manifestation code ♂ Male diagnosis

235.1 Neoplasm of uncertain behavior of lip, oral cavity, and pharynx
235.6 Neoplasm of uncertain behavior of larynx
239.1 Neoplasm of unspecified nature of respiratory system
240.0 Goiter, specified as simple
240.9 Goiter, unspecified ▽
241.0 Nontoxic uninodular goiter
241.1 Nontoxic multinodular goiter
241.9 Unspecified nontoxic nodular goiter ▽
242.00 Toxic diffuse goiter without mention of thyrotoxic crisis or storm
242.01 Toxic diffuse goiter with mention of thyrotoxic crisis or storm
242.10 Toxic uninodular goiter without mention of thyrotoxic crisis or storm
242.11 Toxic uninodular goiter with mention of thyrotoxic crisis or storm
242.20 Toxic multinodular goiter without mention of thyrotoxic crisis or storm
242.21 Toxic multinodular goiter with mention of thyrotoxic crisis or storm
242.30 Toxic nodular goiter, unspecified type, without mention of thyrotoxic crisis or storm ▽
242.31 Toxic nodular goiter, unspecified type, with mention of thyrotoxic crisis or storm ▽
242.40 Thyrotoxicosis from ectopic thyroid nodule without mention of thyrotoxic crisis or storm
242.41 Thyrotoxicosis from ectopic thyroid nodule with mention of thyrotoxic crisis or storm
242.80 Thyrotoxicosis of other specified origin without mention of thyrotoxic crisis or storm — (Use additional E code to identify cause, if drug-induced)
242.81 Thyrotoxicosis of other specified origin with mention of thyrotoxic crisis or storm — (Use additional E code to identify cause, if drug-induced)
242.90 Thyrotoxicosis without mention of goiter or other cause, without mention of thyrotoxic crisis or storm
242.91 Thyrotoxicosis without mention of goiter or other cause, with mention of thyrotoxic crisis or storm
243 Congenital hypothyroidism — (Use additional code to identify associated intellectual disabilities)
244.0 Postsurgical hypothyroidism
244.1 Other postablative hypothyroidism
244.2 Iodine hypothyroidism — (Use additional E code to identify drug)
244.3 Other iatrogenic hypothyroidism — (Use additional E code to identify drug)
244.8 Other specified acquired hypothyroidism
244.9 Unspecified hypothyroidism ▽
245.0 Acute thyroiditis — (Use additional code to identify organism)
245.1 Subacute thyroiditis
245.2 Chronic lymphocytic thyroiditis
245.3 Chronic fibrous thyroiditis
245.4 Iatrogenic thyroiditis — (Use additional code to identify cause)
245.8 Other and unspecified chronic thyroiditis ▽
245.9 Unspecified thyroiditis ▽
246.0 Disorders of thyrocalcitonin secretion
246.1 Dyshormonogenic goiter
246.2 Cyst of thyroid
246.3 Hemorrhage and infarction of thyroid
246.8 Other specified disorders of thyroid
246.9 Unspecified disorder of thyroid ▽
327.20 Organic sleep apnea, unspecified ▽
327.23 Obstructive sleep apnea (adult) (pediatric)
327.29 Other organic sleep apnea
350.2 Atypical face pain
388.70 Unspecified otalgia ▽
438.82 Dysphagia due to cerebrovascular disease — (Use additional code to identify presence of hypertension)
446.4 Wegener's granulomatosis
462 Acute pharyngitis — (Use additional code to identify infectious organism)
464.00 Acute laryngitis, without mention of obstruction — (Use additional code to identify infectious organism)
464.01 Acute laryngitis, with obstruction — (Use additional code to identify infectious organism)
464.10 Acute tracheitis without mention of obstruction — (Use additional code to identify infectious organism)
464.20 Acute laryngotracheitis without mention of obstruction — (Use additional code to identify infectious organism)
464.21 Acute laryngotracheitis with obstruction — (Use additional code to identify infectious organism)
464.30 Acute epiglottitis without mention of obstruction — (Use additional code to identify infectious organism)
464.31 Acute epiglottitis with obstruction — (Use additional code to identify infectious organism)
464.4 Croup — (Use additional code to identify infectious organism)
465.0 Acute laryngopharyngitis — (Use additional code to identify infectious organism)
472.1 Chronic pharyngitis — (Use additional code to identify infectious organism)
476.0 Chronic laryngitis — (Use additional code to identify infectious organism)
476.1 Chronic laryngotracheitis — (Use additional code to identify infectious organism)
478.21 Cellulitis of pharynx or nasopharynx — (Use additional code to identify infectious organism)
478.22 Parapharyngeal abscess — (Use additional code to identify infectious organism)
478.24 Retropharyngeal abscess — (Use additional code to identify infectious organism)
478.30 Unspecified paralysis of vocal cords or larynx ▽
478.31 Unilateral partial paralysis of vocal cords or larynx
478.32 Unilateral complete paralysis of vocal cords or larynx
478.33 Bilateral partial paralysis of vocal cords or larynx
478.34 Bilateral complete paralysis of vocal cords or larynx
478.4 Polyp of vocal cord or larynx
478.5 Other diseases of vocal cords — (Use additional code to identify infectious organism)
478.6 Edema of larynx
478.70 Unspecified disease of larynx ▽
478.75 Laryngeal spasm
478.79 Other diseases of larynx — (Use additional code to identify infectious organism)
478.8 Upper respiratory tract hypersensitivity reaction, site unspecified — (Use additional code to identify infectious organism) ▽
507.0 Pneumonitis due to inhalation of food or vomitus — (Use additional code to identify infectious organism)
519.00 Unspecified tracheostomy complication — (Use additional code to identify infectious organism) ▽
519.01 Infection of tracheostomy — (Use additional code to identify type of infection: 038.0-038.9, 682.1. Use additional code to identify organism: 041.00-041.9)
519.02 Mechanical complication of tracheostomy
519.09 Other tracheostomy complications — (Use additional code to identify infectious organism)
519.19 Other diseases of trachea and bronchus — (Use additional code to identify infectious organism)
519.8 Other diseases of respiratory system, not elsewhere classified — (Use additional code to identify infectious organism)
519.9 Unspecified disease of respiratory system — (Use additional code to identify infectious organism) ▽
530.11 Reflux esophagitis — (Use additional E code to identify cause, if induced by chemical)
530.13 Eosinophilic esophagitis
530.3 Stricture and stenosis of esophagus
530.6 Diverticulum of esophagus, acquired
530.81 Esophageal reflux
530.82 Esophageal hemorrhage
530.84 Tracheoesophageal fistula
530.86 Infection of esophagostomy — (Use additional code to specify infection)
530.87 Mechanical complication of esophagostomy

733.99 Other disorders of bone and cartilage
748.2 Congenital web of larynx
748.3 Other congenital anomaly of larynx, trachea, and bronchus
748.8 Other specified congenital anomaly of respiratory system
749.00 Unspecified cleft palate ♥
750.27 Congenital diverticulum of pharynx
750.29 Other specified congenital anomaly of pharynx
780.51 Insomnia with sleep apnea, unspecified ♥
780.53 Hypersomnia with sleep apnea, unspecified ♥
780.57 Unspecified sleep apnea ♥
783.3 Feeding difficulties and mismanagement
784.1 Throat pain
784.2 Swelling, mass, or lump in head and neck
784.41 Aphonia
784.42 Dysphonia
784.49 Other voice and resonance disorders
784.59 Other speech disturbance
784.8 Hemorrhage from throat
786.09 Other dyspnea and respiratory abnormalities
786.1 Stridor
786.2 Cough
786.30 Hemoptysis, unspecified ♥
786.31 Acute idiopathic pulmonary hemorrhage in infants [AIPHI]
786.39 Other hemoptysis
787.20 Dysphagia, unspecified ♥
787.21 Dysphagia, oral phase
787.22 Dysphagia, oropharyngeal phase
787.23 Dysphagia, pharyngeal phase
787.24 Dysphagia, pharyngoesophageal phase
787.29 Other dysphagia
807.5 Closed fracture of larynx and trachea
874.10 Open wound of larynx with trachea, complicated
874.11 Open wound of larynx, complicated
925.2 Crushing injury of neck — (Use additional code to identify any associated injuries, such as: 800-829, 850.0-854.1, 860.0-869.1)
933.0 Foreign body in pharynx
933.1 Foreign body in larynx
934.0 Foreign body in trachea
934.1 Foreign body in main bronchus
934.8 Foreign body in other specified parts of trachea, bronchus, and lung
934.9 Foreign body in respiratory tree, unspecified ♥
935.1 Foreign body in esophagus
947.0 Burn of mouth and pharynx
947.1 Burn of larynx, trachea, and lung
947.2 Burn of esophagus
959.09 Injury of face and neck, other and unspecified
995.0 Other anaphylactic reaction — (Use additional E code to identify external cause, such as: E930-E949)
V67.09 Follow-up examination, following other surgery
V71.1 Observation for suspected malignant neoplasm

ICD-9-CM Procedural

31.42 Laryngoscopy and other tracheoscopy
31.43 Closed (endoscopic) biopsy of larynx
31.48 Other diagnostic procedures on larynx

HCPCS Level II Supplies & Services

A4305 Disposable drug delivery system, flow rate of 50 ml or greater per hour

31577

31577 Laryngoscopy, flexible fiberoptic; with removal of foreign body

ICD-9-CM Diagnostic

784.1 Throat pain
786.09 Other dyspnea and respiratory abnormalities
786.1 Stridor
786.2 Cough
787.20 Dysphagia, unspecified ♥
787.21 Dysphagia, oral phase
787.22 Dysphagia, oropharyngeal phase
787.23 Dysphagia, pharyngeal phase
787.24 Dysphagia, pharyngoesophageal phase
787.29 Other dysphagia
933.0 Foreign body in pharynx
933.1 Foreign body in larynx

ICD-9-CM Procedural

31.42 Laryngoscopy and other tracheoscopy
98.14 Removal of intraluminal foreign body from larynx without incision

HCPCS Level II Supplies & Services

A4305 Disposable drug delivery system, flow rate of 50 ml or greater per hour

31578

31578 Laryngoscopy, flexible fiberoptic; with removal of lesion

ICD-9-CM Diagnostic

148.2 Malignant neoplasm of aryepiglottic fold, hypopharyngeal aspect
161.0 Malignant neoplasm of glottis
161.1 Malignant neoplasm of supraglottis
161.2 Malignant neoplasm of subglottis
161.3 Malignant neoplasm of laryngeal cartilages
161.8 Malignant neoplasm of other specified sites of larynx
197.3 Secondary malignant neoplasm of other respiratory organs
198.89 Secondary malignant neoplasm of other specified sites
199.1 Other malignant neoplasm of unspecified site
209.20 Malignant carcinoid tumor of unknown primary site — (Code first any associated multiple endocrine neoplasia syndrome: 258.01-258.03)(Use additional code to identify associated endocrine syndrome, as: carcinoid syndrome: 259.2)
209.29 Malignant carcinoid tumor of other sites — (Code first any associated multiple endocrine neoplasia syndrome: 258.01-258.03)(Use additional code to identify associated endocrine syndrome, as: carcinoid syndrome: 259.2)
212.1 Benign neoplasm of larynx
231.0 Carcinoma in situ of larynx
235.6 Neoplasm of uncertain behavior of larynx
239.1 Neoplasm of unspecified nature of respiratory system
446.4 Wegener's granulomatosis
464.21 Acute laryngotracheitis with obstruction — (Use additional code to identify infectious organism)
464.31 Acute epiglottitis with obstruction — (Use additional code to identify infectious organism)
465.0 Acute laryngopharyngitis — (Use additional code to identify infectious organism)
476.0 Chronic laryngitis — (Use additional code to identify infectious organism)
476.1 Chronic laryngotracheitis — (Use additional code to identify infectious organism)
478.30 Unspecified paralysis of vocal cords or larynx ♥
478.31 Unilateral partial paralysis of vocal cords or larynx
478.32 Unilateral complete paralysis of vocal cords or larynx
478.33 Bilateral partial paralysis of vocal cords or larynx
478.34 Bilateral complete paralysis of vocal cords or larynx
478.4 Polyp of vocal cord or larynx

478.5 Other diseases of vocal cords — (Use additional code to identify infectious organism)
478.6 Edema of larynx
478.75 Laryngeal spasm
478.79 Other diseases of larynx — (Use additional code to identify infectious organism)
519.8 Other diseases of respiratory system, not elsewhere classified — (Use additional code to identify infectious organism)
519.9 Unspecified disease of respiratory system — (Use additional code to identify infectious organism) ▽
748.2 Congenital web of larynx
748.3 Other congenital anomaly of larynx, trachea, and bronchus
748.8 Other specified congenital anomaly of respiratory system
784.1 Throat pain
784.2 Swelling, mass, or lump in head and neck
784.41 Aphonia
784.49 Other voice and resonance disorders
784.8 Hemorrhage from throat
786.09 Other dyspnea and respiratory abnormalities
786.1 Stridor
786.2 Cough
786.30 Hemoptysis, unspecified ▽
786.31 Acute idiopathic pulmonary hemorrhage in infants [AIPHI]
786.39 Other hemoptysis
787.20 Dysphagia, unspecified ▽
787.21 Dysphagia, oral phase
787.22 Dysphagia, oropharyngeal phase
787.23 Dysphagia, pharyngeal phase
787.24 Dysphagia, pharyngoesophageal phase
787.29 Other dysphagia
947.1 Burn of larynx, trachea, and lung
V67.09 Follow-up examination, following other surgery
V71.1 Observation for suspected malignant neoplasm

ICD-9-CM Procedural

30.09 Other excision or destruction of lesion or tissue of larynx

HCPCS Level II Supplies & Services

A4305 Disposable drug delivery system, flow rate of 50 ml or greater per hour

31579

31579 Laryngoscopy, flexible or rigid fiberoptic, with stroboscopy

ICD-9-CM Diagnostic

148.2 Malignant neoplasm of aryepiglottic fold, hypopharyngeal aspect
161.0 Malignant neoplasm of glottis
161.1 Malignant neoplasm of supraglottis
161.2 Malignant neoplasm of subglottis
161.3 Malignant neoplasm of laryngeal cartilages
161.8 Malignant neoplasm of other specified sites of larynx
197.3 Secondary malignant neoplasm of other respiratory organs
198.89 Secondary malignant neoplasm of other specified sites
199.1 Other malignant neoplasm of unspecified site
209.20 Malignant carcinoid tumor of unknown primary site — (Code first any associated multiple endocrine neoplasia syndrome: 258.01-258.03)(Use additional code to identify associated endocrine syndrome, as: carcinoid syndrome: 259.2)
209.29 Malignant carcinoid tumor of other sites — (Code first any associated multiple endocrine neoplasia syndrome: 258.01-258.03)(Use additional code to identify associated endocrine syndrome, as: carcinoid syndrome: 259.2)
212.1 Benign neoplasm of larynx
231.0 Carcinoma in situ of larynx
235.6 Neoplasm of uncertain behavior of larynx
239.1 Neoplasm of unspecified nature of respiratory system
315.35 Childhood onset fluency disorder
446.4 Wegener's granulomatosis
476.0 Chronic laryngitis — (Use additional code to identify infectious organism)
476.1 Chronic laryngotracheitis — (Use additional code to identify infectious organism)
478.30 Unspecified paralysis of vocal cords or larynx ▽
478.31 Unilateral partial paralysis of vocal cords or larynx
478.32 Unilateral complete paralysis of vocal cords or larynx
478.33 Bilateral partial paralysis of vocal cords or larynx
478.34 Bilateral complete paralysis of vocal cords or larynx
478.4 Polyp of vocal cord or larynx
478.5 Other diseases of vocal cords — (Use additional code to identify infectious organism)
478.6 Edema of larynx
478.75 Laryngeal spasm
478.79 Other diseases of larynx — (Use additional code to identify infectious organism)
519.8 Other diseases of respiratory system, not elsewhere classified — (Use additional code to identify infectious organism)
519.9 Unspecified disease of respiratory system — (Use additional code to identify infectious organism) ▽
748.2 Congenital web of larynx
748.3 Other congenital anomaly of larynx, trachea, and bronchus
748.8 Other specified congenital anomaly of respiratory system
784.1 Throat pain
784.2 Swelling, mass, or lump in head and neck
784.41 Aphonia
784.49 Other voice and resonance disorders
784.8 Hemorrhage from throat
786.09 Other dyspnea and respiratory abnormalities
786.1 Stridor
786.2 Cough
786.30 Hemoptysis, unspecified ▽
786.31 Acute idiopathic pulmonary hemorrhage in infants [AIPHI]
786.39 Other hemoptysis
787.20 Dysphagia, unspecified ▽
787.21 Dysphagia, oral phase
787.22 Dysphagia, oropharyngeal phase
787.23 Dysphagia, pharyngeal phase
787.24 Dysphagia, pharyngoesophageal phase
787.29 Other dysphagia
947.1 Burn of larynx, trachea, and lung
V67.09 Follow-up examination, following other surgery
V71.1 Observation for suspected malignant neoplasm

ICD-9-CM Procedural

31.42 Laryngoscopy and other tracheoscopy
31.48 Other diagnostic procedures on larynx

HCPCS Level II Supplies & Services

A4305 Disposable drug delivery system, flow rate of 50 ml or greater per hour

31580-31582

31580 Laryngoplasty; for laryngeal web, 2-stage, with keel insertion and removal
31582 for laryngeal stenosis, with graft or core mold, including tracheotomy

ICD-9-CM Diagnostic

478.74 Stenosis of larynx
748.2 Congenital web of larynx
748.3 Other congenital anomaly of larynx, trachea, and bronchus

ICD-9-CM Procedural

31.69 Other repair of larynx
31.98 Other operations on larynx

31584

31584 Laryngoplasty; with open reduction of fracture

ICD-9-CM Diagnostic

807.5 Closed fracture of larynx and trachea
807.6 Open fracture of larynx and trachea

ICD-9-CM Procedural

31.64 Repair of laryngeal fracture
31.69 Other repair of larynx

31587

31587 Laryngoplasty, cricoid split

ICD-9-CM Diagnostic

478.74 Stenosis of larynx
748.3 Other congenital anomaly of larynx, trachea, and bronchus
807.5 Closed fracture of larynx and trachea
807.6 Open fracture of larynx and trachea
874.01 Open wound of larynx, without mention of complication
874.11 Open wound of larynx, complicated
925.2 Crushing injury of neck — (Use additional code to identify any associated injuries, such as: 800-829, 850.0-854.1, 860.0-869.1)
959.01 Head injury, unspecified ▽
959.09 Injury of face and neck, other and unspecified

ICD-9-CM Procedural

31.69 Other repair of larynx

31588

31588 Laryngoplasty, not otherwise specified (eg, for burns, reconstruction after partial laryngectomy)

ICD-9-CM Diagnostic

161.0 Malignant neoplasm of glottis
161.1 Malignant neoplasm of supraglottis
161.2 Malignant neoplasm of subglottis
161.3 Malignant neoplasm of laryngeal cartilages
161.8 Malignant neoplasm of other specified sites of larynx
212.1 Benign neoplasm of larynx
231.0 Carcinoma in situ of larynx
235.6 Neoplasm of uncertain behavior of larynx
478.79 Other diseases of larynx — (Use additional code to identify infectious organism)
748.3 Other congenital anomaly of larynx, trachea, and bronchus
874.01 Open wound of larynx, without mention of complication
874.11 Open wound of larynx, complicated
906.8 Late effect of burns of other specified sites
947.1 Burn of larynx, trachea, and lung
948.00 Burn (any degree) involving less than 10% of body surface with third degree burn of less than 10% or unspecified amount
948.10 Burn (any degree) involving 10-19% of body surface with third degree burn of less than 10% or unspecified amount
948.11 Burn (any degree) involving 10-19% of body surface with third degree burn of 10-19%
949.4 Deep necrosis of underlying tissue due to burn (deep third degree), unspecified site without mention of loss of body part ▽
949.5 Deep necrosis of underlying tissues due to burn (deep third degree, unspecified site with loss of body part ▽
V58.42 Aftercare following surgery for neoplasm — (This code should be used in conjunction with other aftercare codes to fully identify the reason for the aftercare encounter)

ICD-9-CM Procedural

31.61 Suture of laceration of larynx
31.62 Closure of fistula of larynx
31.69 Other repair of larynx
31.92 Lysis of adhesions of trachea or larynx

31590

31590 Laryngeal reinnervation by neuromuscular pedicle

ICD-9-CM Diagnostic

478.30 Unspecified paralysis of vocal cords or larynx ▽
478.31 Unilateral partial paralysis of vocal cords or larynx
478.32 Unilateral complete paralysis of vocal cords or larynx
478.33 Bilateral partial paralysis of vocal cords or larynx
478.34 Bilateral complete paralysis of vocal cords or larynx
478.5 Other diseases of vocal cords — (Use additional code to identify infectious organism)
V58.42 Aftercare following surgery for neoplasm — (This code should be used in conjunction with other aftercare codes to fully identify the reason for the aftercare encounter)

ICD-9-CM Procedural

31.69 Other repair of larynx

31595

31595 Section recurrent laryngeal nerve, therapeutic (separate procedure), unilateral

ICD-9-CM Diagnostic

352.3 Disorders of pneumogastric (10th) nerve
478.30 Unspecified paralysis of vocal cords or larynx ▽
478.31 Unilateral partial paralysis of vocal cords or larynx
478.32 Unilateral complete paralysis of vocal cords or larynx
478.33 Bilateral partial paralysis of vocal cords or larynx
478.34 Bilateral complete paralysis of vocal cords or larynx
478.74 Stenosis of larynx
478.75 Laryngeal spasm
478.79 Other diseases of larynx — (Use additional code to identify infectious organism)
748.3 Other congenital anomaly of larynx, trachea, and bronchus
784.41 Aphonia
786.1 Stridor

ICD-9-CM Procedural

05.0 Division of sympathetic nerve or ganglion
31.69 Other repair of larynx
31.91 Division of laryngeal nerve

Trachea and Bronchi

31600-31601

31600 Tracheostomy, planned (separate procedure);
31601 younger than 2 years

ICD-9-CM Diagnostic

141.0 Malignant neoplasm of base of tongue
141.5 Malignant neoplasm of junctional zone of tongue
141.6 Malignant neoplasm of lingual tonsil
141.8 Malignant neoplasm of other sites of tongue
146.0 Malignant neoplasm of tonsil
146.1 Malignant neoplasm of tonsillar fossa
146.2 Malignant neoplasm of tonsillar pillars (anterior) (posterior)
146.3 Malignant neoplasm of vallecula
146.4 Malignant neoplasm of anterior aspect of epiglottis
146.5 Malignant neoplasm of junctional region of oropharynx
146.6 Malignant neoplasm of lateral wall of oropharynx
146.7 Malignant neoplasm of posterior wall of oropharynx
146.8 Malignant neoplasm of other specified sites of oropharynx
148.0 Malignant neoplasm of postcricoid region of hypopharynx

148.1 Malignant neoplasm of pyriform sinus
148.2 Malignant neoplasm of aryepiglottic fold, hypopharyngeal aspect
148.3 Malignant neoplasm of posterior hypopharyngeal wall
148.8 Malignant neoplasm of other specified sites of hypopharynx
148.9 Malignant neoplasm of hypopharynx, unspecified site
161.0 Malignant neoplasm of glottis
161.1 Malignant neoplasm of supraglottis
161.2 Malignant neoplasm of subglottis
161.3 Malignant neoplasm of laryngeal cartilages
161.8 Malignant neoplasm of other specified sites of larynx
197.3 Secondary malignant neoplasm of other respiratory organs
197.8 Secondary malignant neoplasm of other digestive organs and spleen
231.0 Carcinoma in situ of larynx
231.1 Carcinoma in situ of trachea
235.6 Neoplasm of uncertain behavior of larynx
348.1 Anoxic brain damage — (Use additional E code to identify cause)
478.74 Stenosis of larynx
518.51 Acute respiratory failure following trauma and surgery
518.52 Other pulmonary insufficiency, not elsewhere classified, following trauma and surgery
518.53 Acute and chronic respiratory failure following trauma and surgery
518.81 Acute respiratory failure
518.82 Other pulmonary insufficiency, not elsewhere classified
518.83 Chronic respiratory failure
519.00 Unspecified tracheostomy complication — (Use additional code to identify infectious organism)
519.19 Other diseases of trachea and bronchus — (Use additional code to identify infectious organism)
748.3 Other congenital anomaly of larynx, trachea, and bronchus
765.00 Extreme fetal immaturity, unspecified (weight) — (Use additional code for weeks of gestation: 765.20-765.29. Use additional code(s) to specify condition)
765.01 Extreme fetal immaturity, less than 500 grams — (Use additional code for weeks of gestation: 765.20-765.29. Use additional code(s) to specify condition)
765.02 Extreme fetal immaturity, 500-749 grams — (Use additional code for weeks of gestation: 765.20-765.29. Use additional code(s) to specify condition)
765.03 Extreme fetal immaturity, 750-999 grams — (Use additional code for weeks of gestation: 765.20-765.29. Use additional code(s) to specify condition)
765.04 Extreme fetal immaturity, 1,000-1,249 grams — (Use additional code for weeks of gestation: 765.20-765.29. Use additional code(s) to specify condition)
765.05 Extreme fetal immaturity, 1,250-1,499 grams — (Use additional code for weeks of gestation: 765.20-765.29. Use additional code(s) to specify condition)
765.06 Extreme fetal immaturity, 1,500-1,749 grams — (Use additional code for weeks of gestation: 765.20-765.29. Use additional code(s) to specify condition)
765.10 Other preterm infants, unspecified (weight) — (Use additional code for weeks of gestation: 765.20-765.29. Use additional code(s) to specify condition)
765.11 Other preterm infants, less than 500 grams — (Use additional code for weeks of gestation: 765.20-765.29. Use additional code(s) to specify condition)
765.12 Other preterm infants, 500-749 grams — (Use additional code for weeks of gestation: 765.20-765.29. Use additional code(s) to specify condition)
765.13 Other preterm infants, 750-999 grams — (Use additional code for weeks of gestation: 765.20-765.29. Use additional code(s) to specify condition)
765.14 Other preterm infants, 1,000-1,249 grams — (Use additional code for weeks of gestation: 765.20-765.29. Use additional code(s) to specify condition)
765.15 Other preterm infants, 1,250-1,499 grams — (Use additional code for weeks of gestation: 765.20-765.29. Use additional code(s) to specify condition)
765.16 Other preterm infants, 1,500-1,749 grams — (Use additional code for weeks of gestation: 765.20-765.29. Use additional code(s) to specify condition)
765.20 Unspecified weeks of gestation — (Use additional code(s) to further specify condition)
765.21 Less than 24 completed weeks of gestation — (Use additional code(s) to further specify condition)
765.22 24 completed weeks of gestation — (Use additional code(s) to further specify condition)
765.23 25-26 completed weeks of gestation — (Use additional code(s) to further specify condition)
765.24 27-28 completed weeks of gestation — (Use additional code(s) to further specify condition)
765.25 29-30 completed weeks of gestation — (Use additional code(s) to further specify condition)
765.26 31-32 completed weeks of gestation — (Use additional code(s) to further specify condition)
765.27 33-34 completed weeks of gestation — (Use additional code(s) to further specify condition)
765.28 35-36 completed weeks of gestation — (Use additional code(s) to further specify condition)
765.29 37 or more completed weeks of gestation — (Use additional code(s) to further specify condition)
769 Respiratory distress syndrome in newborn — (Use additional code(s) to further specify condition)
770.7 Chronic respiratory disease arising in the perinatal period — (Use additional code(s) to further specify condition)
770.81 Primary apnea of newborn — (Use additional code(s) to further specify condition)
770.82 Other apnea of newborn — (Use additional code(s) to further specify condition)
770.83 Cyanotic attacks of newborn — (Use additional code(s) to further specify condition)
770.84 Respiratory failure of newborn — (Use additional code(s) to further specify condition)
770.89 Other respiratory problems of newborn after birth — (Use additional code(s) to further specify condition)
786.09 Other dyspnea and respiratory abnormalities

ICD-9-CM Procedural

31.1 Temporary tracheostomy
31.21 Mediastinal tracheostomy
31.29 Other permanent tracheostomy

HCPCS Level II Supplies & Services

A7527 Tracheostomy/laryngectomy tube plug/stop, each

31603-31605

31603 Tracheostomy, emergency procedure; transtracheal
31605 cricothyroid membrane

ICD-9-CM Diagnostic

344.00 Unspecified quadriplegia
344.01 Quadriplegia and quadriparesis, C1-C4, complete
348.1 Anoxic brain damage — (Use additional E code to identify cause)
464.31 Acute epiglottitis with obstruction — (Use additional code to identify infectious organism)
478.6 Edema of larynx
478.75 Laryngeal spasm
518.51 Acute respiratory failure following trauma and surgery
518.52 Other pulmonary insufficiency, not elsewhere classified, following trauma and surgery
518.53 Acute and chronic respiratory failure following trauma and surgery
518.81 Acute respiratory failure
518.82 Other pulmonary insufficiency, not elsewhere classified
519.00 Unspecified tracheostomy complication — (Use additional code to identify infectious organism)
519.19 Other diseases of trachea and bronchus — (Use additional code to identify infectious organism)
748.3 Other congenital anomaly of larynx, trachea, and bronchus
765.00 Extreme fetal immaturity, unspecified (weight) — (Use additional code for weeks of gestation: 765.20-765.29. Use additional code(s) to specify condition)
765.01 Extreme fetal immaturity, less than 500 grams — (Use additional code for weeks of gestation: 765.20-765.29. Use additional code(s) to specify condition)

765.02 Extreme fetal immaturity, 500-749 grams — (Use additional code for weeks of gestation: 765.20-765.29. Use additional code(s) to specify condition)

765.03 Extreme fetal immaturity, 750-999 grams — (Use additional code for weeks of gestation: 765.20-765.29. Use additional code(s) to specify condition)

765.04 Extreme fetal immaturity, 1,000-1,249 grams — (Use additional code for weeks of gestation: 765.20-765.29. Use additional code(s) to specify condition)

765.05 Extreme fetal immaturity, 1,250-1,499 grams — (Use additional code for weeks of gestation: 765.20-765.29. Use additional code(s) to specify condition)

765.06 Extreme fetal immaturity, 1,500-1,749 grams — (Use additional code for weeks of gestation: 765.20-765.29. Use additional code(s) to specify condition)

765.10 Other preterm infants, unspecified (weight) — (Use additional code for weeks of gestation: 765.20-765.29. Use additional code(s) to specify condition) ▽

765.11 Other preterm infants, less than 500 grams — (Use additional code for weeks of gestation: 765.20-765.29. Use additional code(s) to specify condition)

765.12 Other preterm infants, 500-749 grams — (Use additional code for weeks of gestation: 765.20-765.29. Use additional code(s) to specify condition)

765.13 Other preterm infants, 750-999 grams — (Use additional code for weeks of gestation: 765.20-765.29. Use additional code(s) to specify condition)

765.14 Other preterm infants, 1,000-1,249 grams — (Use additional code for weeks of gestation: 765.20-765.29. Use additional code(s) to specify condition)

765.15 Other preterm infants, 1,250-1,499 grams — (Use additional code for weeks of gestation: 765.20-765.29. Use additional code(s) to specify condition)

765.16 Other preterm infants, 1,500-1,749 grams — (Use additional code for weeks of gestation: 765.20-765.29. Use additional code(s) to specify condition)

765.20 Unspecified weeks of gestation — (Use additional code(s) to further specify condition) ▽

765.21 Less than 24 completed weeks of gestation — (Use additional code(s) to further specify condition)

765.22 24 completed weeks of gestation — (Use additional code(s) to further specify condition)

765.23 25-26 completed weeks of gestation — (Use additional code(s) to further specify condition)

765.24 27-28 completed weeks of gestation — (Use additional code(s) to further specify condition)

765.25 29-30 completed weeks of gestation — (Use additional code(s) to further specify condition)

765.26 31-32 completed weeks of gestation — (Use additional code(s) to further specify condition)

765.27 33-34 completed weeks of gestation — (Use additional code(s) to further specify condition)

765.28 35-36 completed weeks of gestation — (Use additional code(s) to further specify condition)

765.29 37 or more completed weeks of gestation — (Use additional code(s) to further specify condition)

767.0 Subdural and cerebral hemorrhage, birth trauma — (Use additional code(s) to further specify condition. Use additional code to identify cause)

768.5 Severe birth asphyxia — (Use additional code(s) to further specify condition. Use only when associated with newborn morbidity classifiable elsewhere)

769 Respiratory distress syndrome in newborn — (Use additional code(s) to further specify condition)

770.83 Cyanotic attacks of newborn — (Use additional code(s) to further specify condition)

770.84 Respiratory failure of newborn — (Use additional code(s) to further specify condition)

770.89 Other respiratory problems of newborn after birth — (Use additional code(s) to further specify condition)

772.10 Intraventricular hemorrhage, unspecified grade — (Use additional code(s) to further specify condition) ▽

772.11 Intraventricular hemorrhage, Grade I — (Use additional code(s) to further specify condition)

772.12 Intraventricular hemorrhage, Grade II — (Use additional code(s) to further specify condition)

772.13 Intraventricular hemorrhage, Grade III — (Use additional code(s) to further specify condition)

772.14 Intraventricular hemorrhage, Grade IV — (Use additional code(s) to further specify condition)

772.2 Fetal and neonatal subarachnoid hemorrhage of newborn — (Use additional code(s) to further specify condition)

786.09 Other dyspnea and respiratory abnormalities

799.01 Asphyxia

799.02 Hypoxemia

799.1 Respiratory arrest

805.00 Closed fracture of cervical vertebra, unspecified level without mention of spinal cord injury ▽

805.01 Closed fracture of first cervical vertebra without mention of spinal cord injury

805.02 Closed fracture of second cervical vertebra without mention of spinal cord injury

805.03 Closed fracture of third cervical vertebra without mention of spinal cord injury

805.04 Closed fracture of fourth cervical vertebra without mention of spinal cord injury

805.10 Open fracture of cervical vertebra, unspecified level without mention of spinal cord injury ▽

805.11 Open fracture of first cervical vertebra without mention of spinal cord injury

805.12 Open fracture of second cervical vertebra without mention of spinal cord injury

805.13 Open fracture of third cervical vertebra without mention of spinal cord injury

805.14 Open fracture of fourth cervical vertebra without mention of spinal cord injury

806.00 Closed fracture of C1-C4 level with unspecified spinal cord injury ▽

806.01 Closed fracture of C1-C4 level with complete lesion of cord

806.02 Closed fracture of C1-C4 level with anterior cord syndrome

806.03 Closed fracture of C1-C4 level with central cord syndrome

806.04 Closed fracture of C1-C4 level with other specified spinal cord injury

806.05 Closed fracture of C5-C7 level with unspecified spinal cord injury ▽

806.06 Closed fracture of C5-C7 level with complete lesion of cord

806.07 Closed fracture of C5-C7 level with anterior cord syndrome

806.08 Closed fracture of C5-C7 level with central cord syndrome

806.09 Closed fracture of C5-C7 level with other specified spinal cord injury

806.10 Open fracture of C1-C4 level with unspecified spinal cord injury ▽

806.11 Open fracture of C1-C4 level with complete lesion of cord

806.12 Open fracture of C1-C4 level with anterior cord syndrome

806.13 Open fracture of C1-C4 level with central cord syndrome

806.14 Open fracture of C1-C4 level with other specified spinal cord injury

806.15 Open fracture of C5-C7 level with unspecified spinal cord injury ▽

806.16 Open fracture of C5-C7 level with complete lesion of cord

806.17 Open fracture of C5-C7 level with anterior cord syndrome

806.18 Open fracture of C5-C7 level with central cord syndrome

806.19 Open fracture of C5-C7 level with other specified spinal cord injury

807.5 Closed fracture of larynx and trachea

807.6 Open fracture of larynx and trachea

873.59 Open wound of face, other and multiple sites, complicated

873.9 Other and unspecified open wound of head, complicated ▽

874.10 Open wound of larynx with trachea, complicated

874.11 Open wound of larynx, complicated

874.12 Open wound of trachea, complicated

925.1 Crushing injury of face and scalp — (Use additional code to identify any associated injuries, such as: 800-829, 850.0-854.1, 860.0-869.1)

925.2 Crushing injury of neck — (Use additional code to identify any associated injuries, such as: 800-829, 850.0-854.1, 860.0-869.1)

933.1 Foreign body in larynx

934.0 Foreign body in trachea

934.8 Foreign body in other specified parts of trachea, bronchus, and lung

947.0 Burn of mouth and pharynx

947.1 Burn of larynx, trachea, and lung

995.0 Other anaphylactic reaction — (Use additional E code to identify external cause, such as: E930-E949)

995.1 Angioneurotic edema not elsewhere classified

997.31 Ventilator associated pneumonia — (Use additional code to identify organism)
997.39 Other respiratory complications

ICD-9-CM Procedural

31.1 Temporary tracheostomy

HCPCS Level II Supplies & Services

A4624 Tracheal suction catheter, any type other than closed system, each

31610

31610 Tracheostomy, fenestration procedure with skin flaps

ICD-9-CM Diagnostic

141.0 Malignant neoplasm of base of tongue
141.5 Malignant neoplasm of junctional zone of tongue
141.6 Malignant neoplasm of lingual tonsil
141.8 Malignant neoplasm of other sites of tongue
146.0 Malignant neoplasm of tonsil
146.1 Malignant neoplasm of tonsillar fossa
146.2 Malignant neoplasm of tonsillar pillars (anterior) (posterior)
146.3 Malignant neoplasm of vallecula
146.4 Malignant neoplasm of anterior aspect of epiglottis
146.5 Malignant neoplasm of junctional region of oropharynx
146.6 Malignant neoplasm of lateral wall of oropharynx
146.7 Malignant neoplasm of posterior wall of oropharynx
146.8 Malignant neoplasm of other specified sites of oropharynx
148.0 Malignant neoplasm of postcricoid region of hypopharynx
148.1 Malignant neoplasm of pyriform sinus
148.2 Malignant neoplasm of aryepiglottic fold, hypopharyngeal aspect
148.3 Malignant neoplasm of posterior hypopharyngeal wall
148.8 Malignant neoplasm of other specified sites of hypopharynx
148.9 Malignant neoplasm of hypopharynx, unspecified site ▽
161.0 Malignant neoplasm of glottis
161.1 Malignant neoplasm of supraglottis
161.2 Malignant neoplasm of subglottis
161.3 Malignant neoplasm of laryngeal cartilages
161.8 Malignant neoplasm of other specified sites of larynx
197.3 Secondary malignant neoplasm of other respiratory organs
197.8 Secondary malignant neoplasm of other digestive organs and spleen
231.0 Carcinoma in situ of larynx
231.1 Carcinoma in situ of trachea
235.6 Neoplasm of uncertain behavior of larynx
344.00 Unspecified quadriplegia ▽
344.01 Quadriplegia and quadriparesis, C1-C4, complete
348.1 Anoxic brain damage — (Use additional E code to identify cause)
478.74 Stenosis of larynx
518.51 Acute respiratory failure following trauma and surgery
518.52 Other pulmonary insufficiency, not elsewhere classified, following trauma and surgery
518.53 Acute and chronic respiratory failure following trauma and surgery
518.81 Acute respiratory failure
518.82 Other pulmonary insufficiency, not elsewhere classified
519.00 Unspecified tracheostomy complication — (Use additional code to identify infectious organism) ▽
519.19 Other diseases of trachea and bronchus — (Use additional code to identify infectious organism)
748.3 Other congenital anomaly of larynx, trachea, and bronchus
786.09 Other dyspnea and respiratory abnormalities
806.00 Closed fracture of C1-C4 level with unspecified spinal cord injury ▽
806.05 Closed fracture of C5-C7 level with unspecified spinal cord injury ▽
806.10 Open fracture of C1-C4 level with unspecified spinal cord injury ▽
806.15 Open fracture of C5-C7 level with unspecified spinal cord injury ▽
V10.02 Personal history of malignant neoplasm of other and unspecified parts of oral cavity and pharynx ▽
V10.21 Personal history of malignant neoplasm of larynx

ICD-9-CM Procedural

31.29 Other permanent tracheostomy

HCPCS Level II Supplies & Services

A7527 Tracheostomy/laryngectomy tube plug/stop, each

31611

31611 Construction of tracheoesophageal fistula and subsequent insertion of an alaryngeal speech prosthesis (eg, voice button, Blom-Singer prosthesis)

ICD-9-CM Diagnostic

748.3 Other congenital anomaly of larynx, trachea, and bronchus
V10.21 Personal history of malignant neoplasm of larynx

ICD-9-CM Procedural

31.75 Reconstruction of trachea and construction of artificial larynx
31.95 Tracheoesophageal fistulization

31612

31612 Tracheal puncture, percutaneous with transtracheal aspiration and/or injection

ICD-9-CM Diagnostic

162.0 Malignant neoplasm of trachea
197.3 Secondary malignant neoplasm of other respiratory organs
478.32 Unilateral complete paralysis of vocal cords or larynx
478.9 Other and unspecified diseases of upper respiratory tract — (Use additional code to identify infectious organism) ▽
482.84 Legionnaires' disease
506.0 Bronchitis and pneumonitis due to fumes and vapors — (Use additional code to identify infectious organism. Use additional E code to identify cause. Use additional code to identify associated respiratory conditions: 518.81.)
507.0 Pneumonitis due to inhalation of food or vomitus — (Use additional code to identify infectious organism)
507.8 Pneumonitis due to other solids and liquids — (Use additional code to identify infectious organism)
668.01 Pulmonary complications of the administration of anesthesia or other sedation in labor and delivery, delivered — (Use additional code(s) to further specify complication) ♀
668.02 Pulmonary complications of the administration of anesthesia or other sedation in labor and delivery, delivered, with mention of postpartum complication — (Use additional code(s) to further specify complication) ♀
668.03 Pulmonary complications of the administration of anesthesia or other sedation in labor and delivery, antepartum — (Use additional code(s) to further specify complication) ♀
668.04 Pulmonary complications of the administration of anesthesia or other sedation in labor and delivery, postpartum condition or complication — (Use additional code(s) to further specify complication) ♀
748.3 Other congenital anomaly of larynx, trachea, and bronchus
770.12 Meconium aspiration with respiratory symptoms, of fetus and newborn — (Use additional code(s) to further specify condition. Use additional code to identify any secondary pulmonary hypertension, 416.8, if applicable)
770.14 Aspiration of clear amniotic fluid with respiratory symptoms, of fetus and newborn — (Use additional code(s) to further specify condition. Use additional code to identify any secondary pulmonary hypertension, 416.8, if applicable)
770.16 Aspiration of blood with respiratory symptoms, of fetus and newborn — (Use additional code(s) to further specify condition. Use additional code to identify any secondary pulmonary hypertension, 416.8, if applicable)
770.18 Other fetal and newborn aspiration with respiratory symptoms — (Use additional code(s) to further specify condition. Use additional code to identify any secondary pulmonary hypertension, 416.8, if applicable)

770.86 Aspiration of postnatal stomach contents with respiratory symptoms — (Use additional code(s) to further specify condition. Use additional code to identify any secondary pulmonary hypertension, 416.8, if applicable)
784.2 Swelling, mass, or lump in head and neck
784.49 Other voice and resonance disorders
947.1 Burn of larynx, trachea, and lung
958.3 Posttraumatic wound infection not elsewhere classified

ICD-9-CM Procedural

31.94 Injection of locally-acting therapeutic substance into trachea
31.99 Other operations on trachea

HCPCS Level II Supplies & Services

A4305 Disposable drug delivery system, flow rate of 50 ml or greater per hour

31613-31614

31613 Tracheostoma revision; simple, without flap rotation
31614 complex, with flap rotation

ICD-9-CM Diagnostic

348.1 Anoxic brain damage — (Use additional E code to identify cause)
478.74 Stenosis of larynx
478.79 Other diseases of larynx — (Use additional code to identify infectious organism)
478.9 Other and unspecified diseases of upper respiratory tract — (Use additional code to identify infectious organism) ▽
519.00 Unspecified tracheostomy complication — (Use additional code to identify infectious organism) ▽
519.01 Infection of tracheostomy — (Use additional code to identify type of infection: 038.0-038.9, 682.1. Use additional code to identify organism: 041.00-041.9)
519.02 Mechanical complication of tracheostomy
519.09 Other tracheostomy complications — (Use additional code to identify infectious organism)
519.19 Other diseases of trachea and bronchus — (Use additional code to identify infectious organism)
750.3 Congenital tracheoesophageal fistula, esophageal atresia and stenosis
806.00 Closed fracture of C1-C4 level with unspecified spinal cord injury ▽
806.05 Closed fracture of C5-C7 level with unspecified spinal cord injury ▽
806.10 Open fracture of C1-C4 level with unspecified spinal cord injury ▽
806.15 Open fracture of C5-C7 level with unspecified spinal cord injury ▽
V10.02 Personal history of malignant neoplasm of other and unspecified parts of oral cavity and pharynx ▽
V10.21 Personal history of malignant neoplasm of larynx

ICD-9-CM Procedural

31.74 Revision of tracheostomy

31615

31615 Tracheobronchoscopy through established tracheostomy incision

ICD-9-CM Diagnostic

162.0 Malignant neoplasm of trachea
162.2 Malignant neoplasm of main bronchus
162.3 Malignant neoplasm of upper lobe, bronchus, or lung
162.4 Malignant neoplasm of middle lobe, bronchus, or lung
162.8 Malignant neoplasm of other parts of bronchus or lung
197.0 Secondary malignant neoplasm of lung
197.3 Secondary malignant neoplasm of other respiratory organs
209.21 Malignant carcinoid tumor of the bronchus and lung — (Code first any associated multiple endocrine neoplasia syndrome: 258.01-258.03)(Use additional code to identify associated endocrine syndrome, as: carcinoid syndrome: 259.2)
209.61 Benign carcinoid tumor of the bronchus and lung — (Code first any associated multiple endocrine neoplasia syndrome: 258.01-258.03)(Use additional code to identify associated endocrine syndrome, as: carcinoid syndrome: 259.2)
212.2 Benign neoplasm of trachea
212.3 Benign neoplasm of bronchus and lung
231.1 Carcinoma in situ of trachea
231.2 Carcinoma in situ of bronchus and lung
231.9 Carcinoma in situ of respiratory system, part unspecified ▽
235.7 Neoplasm of uncertain behavior of trachea, bronchus, and lung
239.1 Neoplasm of unspecified nature of respiratory system
482.42 Methicillin resistant pneumonia due to Staphylococcus aureus
486 Pneumonia, organism unspecified ▽
510.0 Empyema with fistula — (Use additional code to identify infectious organism: 041.00-041.9)
511.81 Malignant pleural effusion — (Code first malignant neoplasm, if known)
511.89 Other specified forms of effusion, except tuberculous
518.89 Other diseases of lung, not elsewhere classified — (Use additional code to identify infectious organism)
519.00 Unspecified tracheostomy complication — (Use additional code to identify infectious organism) ▽
519.01 Infection of tracheostomy — (Use additional code to identify type of infection: 038.0-038.9, 682.1. Use additional code to identify organism: 041.00-041.9)
519.02 Mechanical complication of tracheostomy
519.09 Other tracheostomy complications — (Use additional code to identify infectious organism)
519.19 Other diseases of trachea and bronchus — (Use additional code to identify infectious organism)
519.8 Other diseases of respiratory system, not elsewhere classified — (Use additional code to identify infectious organism)
786.30 Hemoptysis, unspecified ▽
786.31 Acute idiopathic pulmonary hemorrhage in infants [AIPHI]
786.39 Other hemoptysis
997.39 Other respiratory complications
V10.02 Personal history of malignant neoplasm of other and unspecified parts of oral cavity and pharynx ▽
V10.21 Personal history of malignant neoplasm of larynx

ICD-9-CM Procedural

31.41 Tracheoscopy through artificial stoma
33.21 Bronchoscopy through artificial stoma

31622-31624

31622 Bronchoscopy, rigid or flexible, including fluoroscopic guidance, when performed; diagnostic, with cell washing, when performed (separate procedure)
31623 with brushing or protected brushings
31624 with bronchial alveolar lavage

ICD-9-CM Diagnostic

135 Sarcoidosis
162.2 Malignant neoplasm of main bronchus
162.3 Malignant neoplasm of upper lobe, bronchus, or lung
162.4 Malignant neoplasm of middle lobe, bronchus, or lung
162.5 Malignant neoplasm of lower lobe, bronchus, or lung
162.8 Malignant neoplasm of other parts of bronchus or lung
162.9 Malignant neoplasm of bronchus and lung, unspecified site ▽
197.0 Secondary malignant neoplasm of lung
197.2 Secondary malignant neoplasm of pleura
198.89 Secondary malignant neoplasm of other specified sites
199.1 Other malignant neoplasm of unspecified site
209.20 Malignant carcinoid tumor of unknown primary site — (Code first any associated multiple endocrine neoplasia syndrome: 258.01-258.03)(Use additional code to identify associated endocrine syndrome, as: carcinoid syndrome: 259.2)

209.21 Malignant carcinoid tumor of the bronchus and lung — (Code first any associated multiple endocrine neoplasia syndrome: 258.01-258.03)(Use additional code to identify associated endocrine syndrome, as: carcinoid syndrome: 259.2)

209.29 Malignant carcinoid tumor of other sites — (Code first any associated multiple endocrine neoplasia syndrome: 258.01-258.03)(Use additional code to identify associated endocrine syndrome, as: carcinoid syndrome: 259.2)

209.61 Benign carcinoid tumor of the bronchus and lung — (Code first any associated multiple endocrine neoplasia syndrome: 258.01-258.03)(Use additional code to identify associated endocrine syndrome, as: carcinoid syndrome: 259.2)

212.2 Benign neoplasm of trachea

212.3 Benign neoplasm of bronchus and lung

212.4 Benign neoplasm of pleura

231.1 Carcinoma in situ of trachea

231.2 Carcinoma in situ of bronchus and lung

235.7 Neoplasm of uncertain behavior of trachea, bronchus, and lung

239.1 Neoplasm of unspecified nature of respiratory system

478.9 Other and unspecified diseases of upper respiratory tract — (Use additional code to identify infectious organism) ▽

482.42 Methicillin resistant pneumonia due to Staphylococcus aureus

485 Bronchopneumonia, organism unspecified ▽

486 Pneumonia, organism unspecified ▽

500 Coal workers' pneumoconiosis — (Use additional code to identify infectious organism)

501 Asbestosis — (Use additional code to identify infectious organism)

502 Pneumoconiosis due to other silica or silicates — (Use additional code to identify infectious organism)

503 Pneumoconiosis due to other inorganic dust — (Use additional code to identify infectious organism)

504 Pneumonopathy due to inhalation of other dust — (Use additional code to identify infectious organism)

505 Unspecified pneumoconiosis — (Use additional code to identify infectious organism) ▽

506.4 Chronic respiratory conditions due to fumes and vapors — (Use additional code to identify infectious organism. Use additional E code to identify cause. Use additional code to identify associated respiratory conditions: 518.81.)

507.0 Pneumonitis due to inhalation of food or vomitus — (Use additional code to identify infectious organism)

508.1 Chronic and other pulmonary manifestations due to radiation — (Use additional code to identify infectious organism. Use additional E code to identify cause. Use additional code to identify associated respiratory conditions: 518.81.)

508.2 Respiratory conditions due to smoke inhalation — (Use additional code to identify infectious organism. Use additional E code to identify cause. Use additional code to identify associated respiratory conditions: 518.81.)

510.0 Empyema with fistula — (Use additional code to identify infectious organism: 041.00-041.9)

510.9 Empyema without mention of fistula — (Use additional code to identify infectious organism: 041.00-041.9)

511.81 Malignant pleural effusion — (Code first malignant neoplasm, if known)

511.89 Other specified forms of effusion, except tuberculous

512.0 Spontaneous tension pneumothorax

512.1 Iatrogenic pneumothorax

512.2 Postoperative air leak

512.81 Primary spontaneous pneumothorax

512.82 Secondary spontaneous pneumothorax — (Code first underlying condition, such as: 136.3, 162.3-162.9, 197.0, 277.02, 516.4, 518.3, 530.4, 617.8, 759.82))

512.83 Chronic pneumothorax

512.84 Other air leak

512.89 Other pneumothorax

513.0 Abscess of lung — (Use additional code to identify infectious organism)

514 Pulmonary congestion and hypostasis — (Use additional code to identify infectious organism)

515 Postinflammatory pulmonary fibrosis — (Use additional code to identify infectious organism)

516.0 Pulmonary alveolar proteinosis — (Use additional code to identify infectious organism)

516.1 Idiopathic pulmonary hemosiderosis — (Use additional code to identify infectious organism. Code first underlying disease: 275.01-275.09) ☒

516.2 Pulmonary alveolar microlithiasis — (Use additional code to identify infectious organism)

516.30 Idiopathic interstitial pneumonia, not otherwise specified

516.31 Idiopathic pulmonary fibrosis

516.32 Idiopathic non-specific interstitial pneumonitis

516.33 Acute interstitial pneumonitis

516.34 Respiratory bronchiolitis interstitial lung disease

516.35 Idiopathic lymphoid interstitial pneumonia

516.36 Cryptogenic organizing pneumonia

516.37 Desquamative interstitial pneumonia

516.4 Lymphangioleiomyomatosis ♀

516.5 Adult pulmonary Langerhans cell histiocytosis

516.61 Neuroendocrine cell hyperplasia of infancy

516.62 Pulmonary interstitial glycogenosis

516.63 Surfactant mutations of the lung

516.69 Other interstitial lung diseases of childhood

516.8 Other specified alveolar and parietoalveolar pneumonopathies — (Code first, if applicable, underlying cause of pneumonopathy, if known)(Use additional code to identify infectious organism) (Use additional E code, if applicable, for drug-induced or toxic pneumonopathy)

517.3 Acute chest syndrome — (Use additional code to identify infectious organism. Code first sickle-cell disease in crisis: 282.42, 282.62, 282.64, 282.69) ☒

517.8 Lung involvement in other diseases classified elsewhere — (Use additional code to identify infectious organism. Code first underlying disease: 135, 277.30-277.39, 710.0, 710.2, 710.4) ☒

518.0 Pulmonary collapse

518.3 Pulmonary eosinophilia — (Use additional code to identify infectious organism)

518.51 Acute respiratory failure following trauma and surgery

518.52 Other pulmonary insufficiency, not elsewhere classified, following trauma and surgery

518.53 Acute and chronic respiratory failure following trauma and surgery

518.83 Chronic respiratory failure

518.84 Acute and chronic respiratory failure

518.89 Other diseases of lung, not elsewhere classified — (Use additional code to identify infectious organism)

519.8 Other diseases of respiratory system, not elsewhere classified — (Use additional code to identify infectious organism)

770.7 Chronic respiratory disease arising in the perinatal period — (Use additional code(s) to further specify condition)

786.05 Shortness of breath

786.06 Tachypnea

786.07 Wheezing

786.2 Cough

786.30 Hemoptysis, unspecified ▽

786.31 Acute idiopathic pulmonary hemorrhage in infants [AIPHI]

786.39 Other hemoptysis

862.21 Bronchus injury without mention of open wound into cavity

862.8 Injury to multiple and unspecified intrathoracic organs without mention of open wound into cavity

933.1 Foreign body in larynx

934.8 Foreign body in other specified parts of trachea, bronchus, and lung

934.9 Foreign body in respiratory tree, unspecified ▽

997.39 Other respiratory complications

V10.11 Personal history of malignant neoplasm of bronchus and lung

V10.12 Personal history of malignant neoplasm of trachea

V15.82 Personal history of tobacco use, presenting hazards to health

V15.84 Personal history of contact with and (suspected) exposure to asbestos
V16.2 Family history of malignant neoplasm of other respiratory and intrathoracic organs
V43.89 Other organ or tissue replaced by other means

ICD-9-CM Procedural

33.23 Other bronchoscopy
33.24 Closed (endoscopic) biopsy of bronchus
96.56 Other lavage of bronchus and trachea

31625-31629

31625 Bronchoscopy, rigid or flexible, including fluoroscopic guidance, when performed; with bronchial or endobronchial biopsy(s), single or multiple sites
31626 with placement of fiducial markers, single or multiple
31627 with computer-assisted, image-guided navigation (List separately in addition to code for primary procedure[s])
31628 with transbronchial lung biopsy(s), single lobe
31629 with transbronchial needle aspiration biopsy(s), trachea, main stem and/or lobar bronchus(i)

ICD-9-CM Diagnostic

135 Sarcoidosis
162.0 Malignant neoplasm of trachea
162.2 Malignant neoplasm of main bronchus
162.3 Malignant neoplasm of upper lobe, bronchus, or lung
162.4 Malignant neoplasm of middle lobe, bronchus, or lung
162.5 Malignant neoplasm of lower lobe, bronchus, or lung
162.8 Malignant neoplasm of other parts of bronchus or lung
162.9 Malignant neoplasm of bronchus and lung, unspecified site ▽
195.0 Malignant neoplasm of head, face, and neck
196.1 Secondary and unspecified malignant neoplasm of intrathoracic lymph nodes
197.0 Secondary malignant neoplasm of lung
197.2 Secondary malignant neoplasm of pleura
197.3 Secondary malignant neoplasm of other respiratory organs
198.89 Secondary malignant neoplasm of other specified sites
199.1 Other malignant neoplasm of unspecified site
209.20 Malignant carcinoid tumor of unknown primary site — (Code first any associated multiple endocrine neoplasia syndrome: 258.01-258.03)(Use additional code to identify associated endocrine syndrome, as: carcinoid syndrome: 259.2)
209.21 Malignant carcinoid tumor of the bronchus and lung — (Code first any associated multiple endocrine neoplasia syndrome: 258.01-258.03)(Use additional code to identify associated endocrine syndrome, as: carcinoid syndrome: 259.2)
209.29 Malignant carcinoid tumor of other sites — (Code first any associated multiple endocrine neoplasia syndrome: 258.01-258.03)(Use additional code to identify associated endocrine syndrome, as: carcinoid syndrome: 259.2)
209.61 Benign carcinoid tumor of the bronchus and lung — (Code first any associated multiple endocrine neoplasia syndrome: 258.01-258.03)(Use additional code to identify associated endocrine syndrome, as: carcinoid syndrome: 259.2)
212.2 Benign neoplasm of trachea
212.3 Benign neoplasm of bronchus and lung
212.4 Benign neoplasm of pleura
231.1 Carcinoma in situ of trachea
231.2 Carcinoma in situ of bronchus and lung
235.7 Neoplasm of uncertain behavior of trachea, bronchus, and lung
239.1 Neoplasm of unspecified nature of respiratory system
478.9 Other and unspecified diseases of upper respiratory tract — (Use additional code to identify infectious organism) ▽
482.42 Methicillin resistant pneumonia due to Staphylococcus aureus
485 Bronchopneumonia, organism unspecified ▽
486 Pneumonia, organism unspecified ▽
500 Coal workers' pneumoconiosis — (Use additional code to identify infectious organism)
501 Asbestosis — (Use additional code to identify infectious organism)
502 Pneumoconiosis due to other silica or silicates — (Use additional code to identify infectious organism)
503 Pneumoconiosis due to other inorganic dust — (Use additional code to identify infectious organism)
504 Pneumonopathy due to inhalation of other dust — (Use additional code to identify infectious organism)
505 Unspecified pneumoconiosis — (Use additional code to identify infectious organism) ▽
506.4 Chronic respiratory conditions due to fumes and vapors — (Use additional code to identify infectious organism. Use additional E code to identify cause. Use additional code to identify associated respiratory conditions: 518.81.)
507.0 Pneumonitis due to inhalation of food or vomitus — (Use additional code to identify infectious organism)
508.1 Chronic and other pulmonary manifestations due to radiation — (Use additional code to identify infectious organism. Use additional E code to identify cause. Use additional code to identify associated respiratory conditions: 518.81.)
510.0 Empyema with fistula — (Use additional code to identify infectious organism: 041.00-041.9)
510.9 Empyema without mention of fistula — (Use additional code to identify infectious organism: 041.00-041.9)
511.81 Malignant pleural effusion — (Code first malignant neoplasm, if known)
511.89 Other specified forms of effusion, except tuberculous
512.0 Spontaneous tension pneumothorax
512.1 Iatrogenic pneumothorax
512.2 Postoperative air leak
512.81 Primary spontaneous pneumothorax
512.82 Secondary spontaneous pneumothorax — (Code first underlying condition, such as: 136.3, 162.3-162.9, 197.0, 277.02, 516.4, 518.3, 530.4, 617.8, 759.82))
512.83 Chronic pneumothorax
512.84 Other air leak
512.89 Other pneumothorax
513.0 Abscess of lung — (Use additional code to identify infectious organism)
514 Pulmonary congestion and hypostasis — (Use additional code to identify infectious organism)
515 Postinflammatory pulmonary fibrosis — (Use additional code to identify infectious organism)
516.0 Pulmonary alveolar proteinosis — (Use additional code to identify infectious organism)
516.1 Idiopathic pulmonary hemosiderosis — (Use additional code to identify infectious organism. Code first underlying disease: 275.01-275.09) ☒
516.2 Pulmonary alveolar microlithiasis — (Use additional code to identify infectious organism)
516.30 Idiopathic interstitial pneumonia, not otherwise specified
516.31 Idiopathic pulmonary fibrosis
516.32 Idiopathic non-specific interstitial pneumonitis
516.33 Acute interstitial pneumonitis
516.34 Respiratory bronchiolitis interstitial lung disease
516.35 Idiopathic lymphoid interstitial pneumonia
516.36 Cryptogenic organizing pneumonia
516.37 Desquamative interstitial pneumonia
516.4 Lymphangioleiomyomatosis ♀
516.5 Adult pulmonary Langerhans cell histiocytosis
516.61 Neuroendocrine cell hyperplasia of infancy
516.62 Pulmonary interstitial glycogenosis
516.63 Surfactant mutations of the lung
516.69 Other interstitial lung diseases of childhood
516.8 Other specified alveolar and parietoalveolar pneumonopathies — (Code first, if applicable, underlying cause of pneumonopathy, if known)(Use additional code to identify infectious organism) (Use additional E code, if applicable, for drug-induced or toxic pneumonopathy)

517.8	Lung involvement in other diseases classified elsewhere — (Use additional code to identify infectious organism. Code first underlying disease: 135, 277.30-277.39, 710.0, 710.2, 710.4) ☒
518.0	Pulmonary collapse
518.3	Pulmonary eosinophilia — (Use additional code to identify infectious organism)
518.51	Acute respiratory failure following trauma and surgery
518.52	Other pulmonary insufficiency, not elsewhere classified, following trauma and surgery
518.53	Acute and chronic respiratory failure following trauma and surgery
518.83	Chronic respiratory failure
518.84	Acute and chronic respiratory failure
518.89	Other diseases of lung, not elsewhere classified — (Use additional code to identify infectious organism)
519.19	Other diseases of trachea and bronchus — (Use additional code to identify infectious organism)
770.7	Chronic respiratory disease arising in the perinatal period — (Use additional code(s) to further specify condition)
785.6	Enlargement of lymph nodes
786.05	Shortness of breath
786.06	Tachypnea
786.07	Wheezing
786.2	Cough
786.30	Hemoptysis, unspecified ▽
786.31	Acute idiopathic pulmonary hemorrhage in infants [AIPHI]
786.39	Other hemoptysis
997.39	Other respiratory complications
V10.11	Personal history of malignant neoplasm of bronchus and lung
V10.12	Personal history of malignant neoplasm of trachea
V10.89	Personal history of malignant neoplasm of other site
V15.82	Personal history of tobacco use, presenting hazards to health
V15.84	Personal history of contact with and (suspected) exposure to asbestos
V16.2	Family history of malignant neoplasm of other respiratory and intrathoracic organs
V43.89	Other organ or tissue replaced by other means

ICD-9-CM Procedural

00.31	Computer assisted surgery with CT/CTA
00.32	Computer assisted surgery with MR/MRA
00.33	Computer assisted surgery with fluoroscopy
00.35	Computer assisted surgery with multiple datasets
00.39	Other computer assisted surgery
31.44	Closed (endoscopic) biopsy of trachea
33.24	Closed (endoscopic) biopsy of bronchus
33.27	Closed endoscopic biopsy of lung
33.29	Other diagnostic procedures on lung or bronchus
33.79	Endoscopic insertion of other bronchial device or substances

31630-31631

31630 Bronchoscopy, rigid or flexible, including fluoroscopic guidance, when performed; with tracheal/bronchial dilation or closed reduction of fracture

31631 with placement of tracheal stent(s) (includes tracheal/bronchial dilation as required)

ICD-9-CM Diagnostic

162.0	Malignant neoplasm of trachea
162.2	Malignant neoplasm of main bronchus
162.3	Malignant neoplasm of upper lobe, bronchus, or lung
162.4	Malignant neoplasm of middle lobe, bronchus, or lung
162.5	Malignant neoplasm of lower lobe, bronchus, or lung
162.8	Malignant neoplasm of other parts of bronchus or lung
162.9	Malignant neoplasm of bronchus and lung, unspecified site ▽
197.0	Secondary malignant neoplasm of lung
197.3	Secondary malignant neoplasm of other respiratory organs
209.21	Malignant carcinoid tumor of the bronchus and lung — (Code first any associated multiple endocrine neoplasia syndrome: 258.01-258.03)(Use additional code to identify associated endocrine syndrome, as: carcinoid syndrome: 259.2)
209.61	Benign carcinoid tumor of the bronchus and lung — (Code first any associated multiple endocrine neoplasia syndrome: 258.01-258.03)(Use additional code to identify associated endocrine syndrome, as: carcinoid syndrome: 259.2)
212.2	Benign neoplasm of trachea
212.3	Benign neoplasm of bronchus and lung
231.1	Carcinoma in situ of trachea
231.2	Carcinoma in situ of bronchus and lung
235.7	Neoplasm of uncertain behavior of trachea, bronchus, and lung
239.1	Neoplasm of unspecified nature of respiratory system
476.1	Chronic laryngotracheitis — (Use additional code to identify infectious organism)
478.74	Stenosis of larynx
515	Postinflammatory pulmonary fibrosis — (Use additional code to identify infectious organism)
519.19	Other diseases of trachea and bronchus — (Use additional code to identify infectious organism)
519.3	Other diseases of mediastinum, not elsewhere classified — (Use additional code to identify infectious organism)
748.3	Other congenital anomaly of larynx, trachea, and bronchus
807.5	Closed fracture of larynx and trachea
V10.11	Personal history of malignant neoplasm of bronchus and lung
V10.12	Personal history of malignant neoplasm of trachea

ICD-9-CM Procedural

31.64	Repair of laryngeal fracture
31.93	Replacement of laryngeal or tracheal stent
31.99	Other operations on trachea
33.91	Bronchial dilation

31634

31634 Bronchoscopy, rigid or flexible, including fluoroscopic guidance, when performed; with balloon occlusion, with assessment of air leak, with administration of occlusive substance (eg, fibrin glue), if performed

ICD-9-CM Diagnostic

277.00	Cystic fibrosis without mention of meconium ileus — (Use additional code to identify any associated intellectual disabilities)
277.02	Cystic fibrosis with pulmonary manifestations — (Use additional code to identify any associated intellectual disabilities.) (Use additional code to identify any infectious organism present, such as 041.7)
277.03	Cystic fibrosis with gastrointestinal manifestations — (Use additional code to identify any associated intellectual disabilities)
277.09	Cystic fibrosis with other manifestations — (Use additional code to identify any associated intellectual disabilities)
492.0	Emphysematous bleb
510.0	Empyema with fistula — (Use additional code to identify infectious organism: 041.00-041.9)
511.0	Pleurisy without mention of effusion or current tuberculosis — (Use additional code to identify infectious organism)
511.89	Other specified forms of effusion, except tuberculous
512.0	Spontaneous tension pneumothorax
512.1	Iatrogenic pneumothorax
512.2	Postoperative air leak
512.81	Primary spontaneous pneumothorax
512.82	Secondary spontaneous pneumothorax — (Code first underlying condition, such as: 136.3, 162.3-162.9, 197.0, 277.02, 516.4, 518.3, 530.4, 617.8, 759.82))
512.83	Chronic pneumothorax
512.84	Other air leak
512.89	Other pneumothorax

518.89 Other diseases of lung, not elsewhere classified — (Use additional code to identify infectious organism)
786.09 Other dyspnea and respiratory abnormalities
860.0 Traumatic pneumothorax without mention of open wound into thorax
860.1 Traumatic pneumothorax with open wound into thorax
860.2 Traumatic hemothorax without mention of open wound into thorax
860.3 Traumatic hemothorax with open wound into thorax
860.4 Traumatic pneumohemothorax without mention of open wound into thorax
860.5 Traumatic pneumohemothorax with open wound into thorax
861.20 Unspecified lung injury without mention of open wound into thorax ▽
861.21 Lung contusion without mention of open wound into thorax
861.22 Lung laceration without mention of open wound into thorax
861.30 Unspecified lung injury with open wound into thorax ▽
861.31 Lung contusion with open wound into thorax
861.32 Lung laceration with open wound into thorax

ICD-9-CM Procedural

33.23 Other bronchoscopy
33.79 Endoscopic insertion of other bronchial device or substances

31635

31635 Bronchoscopy, rigid or flexible, including fluoroscopic guidance, when performed; with removal of foreign body

ICD-9-CM Diagnostic

934.1 Foreign body in main bronchus
934.8 Foreign body in other specified parts of trachea, bronchus, and lung
934.9 Foreign body in respiratory tree, unspecified ▽

ICD-9-CM Procedural

33.22 Fiber-optic bronchoscopy
33.23 Other bronchoscopy
98.15 Removal of intraluminal foreign body from trachea and bronchus without incision

31636-31638

31636 Bronchoscopy, rigid or flexible, including fluoroscopic guidance, when performed; with placement of bronchial stent(s) (includes tracheal/bronchial dilation as required), initial bronchus
31637 each additional major bronchus stented (List separately in addition to code for primary procedure)
31638 with revision of tracheal or bronchial stent inserted at previous session (includes tracheal/bronchial dilation as required)

ICD-9-CM Diagnostic

162.0 Malignant neoplasm of trachea
162.2 Malignant neoplasm of main bronchus
162.3 Malignant neoplasm of upper lobe, bronchus, or lung
162.4 Malignant neoplasm of middle lobe, bronchus, or lung
162.5 Malignant neoplasm of lower lobe, bronchus, or lung
162.8 Malignant neoplasm of other parts of bronchus or lung
162.9 Malignant neoplasm of bronchus and lung, unspecified site ▽
197.0 Secondary malignant neoplasm of lung
197.3 Secondary malignant neoplasm of other respiratory organs
209.21 Malignant carcinoid tumor of the bronchus and lung — (Code first any associated multiple endocrine neoplasia syndrome: 258.01-258.03)(Use additional code to identify associated endocrine syndrome, as: carcinoid syndrome: 259.2)
209.61 Benign carcinoid tumor of the bronchus and lung — (Code first any associated multiple endocrine neoplasia syndrome: 258.01-258.03)(Use additional code to identify associated endocrine syndrome, as: carcinoid syndrome: 259.2)
212.2 Benign neoplasm of trachea
212.3 Benign neoplasm of bronchus and lung
231.1 Carcinoma in situ of trachea
231.2 Carcinoma in situ of bronchus and lung
235.7 Neoplasm of uncertain behavior of trachea, bronchus, and lung
239.1 Neoplasm of unspecified nature of respiratory system
476.1 Chronic laryngotracheitis — (Use additional code to identify infectious organism)
478.74 Stenosis of larynx
515 Postinflammatory pulmonary fibrosis — (Use additional code to identify infectious organism)
519.19 Other diseases of trachea and bronchus — (Use additional code to identify infectious organism)
519.3 Other diseases of mediastinum, not elsewhere classified — (Use additional code to identify infectious organism)
748.3 Other congenital anomaly of larynx, trachea, and bronchus
807.5 Closed fracture of larynx and trachea
996.59 Mechanical complication due to other implant and internal device, not elsewhere classified
996.69 Infection and inflammatory reaction due to other internal prosthetic device, implant, and graft — (Use additional code to identify specified infections)
996.79 Other complications due to other internal prosthetic device, implant, and graft — (Use additional code to identify complication: 338.18-338.19, 338.28-338.29)
V10.11 Personal history of malignant neoplasm of bronchus and lung
V10.12 Personal history of malignant neoplasm of trachea

ICD-9-CM Procedural

31.93 Replacement of laryngeal or tracheal stent
31.99 Other operations on trachea
33.91 Bronchial dilation
96.05 Other intubation of respiratory tract

31640-31641

31640 Bronchoscopy, rigid or flexible, including fluoroscopic guidance, when performed; with excision of tumor
31641 with destruction of tumor or relief of stenosis by any method other than excision (eg, laser therapy, cryotherapy)

ICD-9-CM Diagnostic

162.2 Malignant neoplasm of main bronchus
162.3 Malignant neoplasm of upper lobe, bronchus, or lung
162.4 Malignant neoplasm of middle lobe, bronchus, or lung
162.5 Malignant neoplasm of lower lobe, bronchus, or lung
162.8 Malignant neoplasm of other parts of bronchus or lung
162.9 Malignant neoplasm of bronchus and lung, unspecified site ▽
197.0 Secondary malignant neoplasm of lung
197.3 Secondary malignant neoplasm of other respiratory organs
209.21 Malignant carcinoid tumor of the bronchus and lung — (Code first any associated multiple endocrine neoplasia syndrome: 258.01-258.03)(Use additional code to identify associated endocrine syndrome, as: carcinoid syndrome: 259.2)
209.61 Benign carcinoid tumor of the bronchus and lung — (Code first any associated multiple endocrine neoplasia syndrome: 258.01-258.03)(Use additional code to identify associated endocrine syndrome, as: carcinoid syndrome: 259.2)
212.3 Benign neoplasm of bronchus and lung
212.9 Benign neoplasm of respiratory and intrathoracic organs, site unspecified ▽
231.2 Carcinoma in situ of bronchus and lung
235.7 Neoplasm of uncertain behavior of trachea, bronchus, and lung
239.1 Neoplasm of unspecified nature of respiratory system
519.19 Other diseases of trachea and bronchus — (Use additional code to identify infectious organism)
519.8 Other diseases of respiratory system, not elsewhere classified — (Use additional code to identify infectious organism)
748.3 Other congenital anomaly of larynx, trachea, and bronchus
786.05 Shortness of breath
786.06 Tachypnea

786.07 Wheezing
786.09 Other dyspnea and respiratory abnormalities
786.6 Swelling, mass, or lump in chest
V10.11 Personal history of malignant neoplasm of bronchus and lung
V10.12 Personal history of malignant neoplasm of trachea
V15.82 Personal history of tobacco use, presenting hazards to health
V15.84 Personal history of contact with and (suspected) exposure to asbestos
V16.2 Family history of malignant neoplasm of other respiratory and intrathoracic organs

ICD-9-CM Procedural

32.01 Endoscopic excision or destruction of lesion or tissue of bronchus
32.28 Endoscopic excision or destruction of lesion or tissue of lung

31643

31643 Bronchoscopy, rigid or flexible, including fluoroscopic guidance, when performed; with placement of catheter(s) for intracavitary radioelement application

ICD-9-CM Diagnostic

162.2 Malignant neoplasm of main bronchus
162.3 Malignant neoplasm of upper lobe, bronchus, or lung
162.4 Malignant neoplasm of middle lobe, bronchus, or lung
162.5 Malignant neoplasm of lower lobe, bronchus, or lung
162.8 Malignant neoplasm of other parts of bronchus or lung
162.9 Malignant neoplasm of bronchus and lung, unspecified site ▽
197.0 Secondary malignant neoplasm of lung
197.3 Secondary malignant neoplasm of other respiratory organs
209.21 Malignant carcinoid tumor of the bronchus and lung — (Code first any associated multiple endocrine neoplasia syndrome: 258.01-258.03)(Use additional code to identify associated endocrine syndrome, as: carcinoid syndrome: 259.2)
231.2 Carcinoma in situ of bronchus and lung
235.7 Neoplasm of uncertain behavior of trachea, bronchus, and lung
239.1 Neoplasm of unspecified nature of respiratory system

ICD-9-CM Procedural

33.79 Endoscopic insertion of other bronchial device or substances
92.27 Implantation or insertion of radioactive elements

31645-31646

31645 Bronchoscopy, rigid or flexible, including fluoroscopic guidance, when performed; with therapeutic aspiration of tracheobronchial tree, initial (eg, drainage of lung abscess)
31646 with therapeutic aspiration of tracheobronchial tree, subsequent

ICD-9-CM Diagnostic

006.4 Amebic lung abscess
480.0 Pneumonia due to adenovirus
480.1 Pneumonia due to respiratory syncytial virus
480.2 Pneumonia due to parainfluenza virus
480.3 Pneumonia due to SARS-associated coronavirus
480.8 Pneumonia due to other virus not elsewhere classified
482.0 Pneumonia due to Klebsiella pneumoniae
482.1 Pneumonia due to Pseudomonas
482.2 Pneumonia due to Hemophilus influenzae (H. influenzae)
482.30 Pneumonia due to unspecified Streptococcus ▽
482.31 Pneumonia due to Streptococcus, group A
482.32 Pneumonia due to Streptococcus, group B
482.39 Pneumonia due to other Streptococcus
482.40 Pneumonia due to Staphylococcus, unspecified ▽
482.41 Methicillin susceptible pneumonia due to Staphylococcus aureus
482.42 Methicillin resistant pneumonia due to Staphylococcus aureus
482.49 Other Staphylococcus pneumonia
482.81 Pneumonia due to anaerobes
482.82 Pneumonia due to Escherichia coli (E. coli)
482.83 Pneumonia due to other gram-negative bacteria
482.89 Pneumonia due to other specified bacteria — (Use additional code to identify infectious organism)
483.0 Pneumonia due to Mycoplasma pneumoniae
483.1 Pneumonia due to Chlamydia
483.8 Pneumonia due to other specified organism — (Use additional code to identify infectious organism)
484.1 Pneumonia in cytomegalic inclusion disease — (Code first underlying disease: 078.5) ☒
484.3 Pneumonia in whooping cough — (Code first underlying disease: 033.0-033.9) ☒
484.5 Pneumonia in anthrax — (Code first underlying disease: 022.1) ☒
484.6 Pneumonia in aspergillosis — (Code first underlying disease: 117.3) ☒
484.7 Pneumonia in other systemic mycoses — (Use additional code to identify infectious organism. Code first underlying disease) ☒
484.8 Pneumonia in other infectious diseases classified elsewhere — (Code first underlying disease: 002.0, 083.0) ☒
485 Bronchopneumonia, organism unspecified ▽
486 Pneumonia, organism unspecified ▽
487.0 Influenza with pneumonia — (Use additional code to identify infectious organism. Use additional code to identify type of pneumonia: 480.0-480.9, 481, 482.0-492.9, 483.0-483.8, 485)
490 Bronchitis, not specified as acute or chronic — (Use additional code to identify infectious organism) ▽
491.0 Simple chronic bronchitis — (Use additional code to identify infectious organism)
491.1 Mucopurulent chronic bronchitis — (Use additional code to identify infectious organism)
491.20 Obstructive chronic bronchitis, without exacerbation — (Use additional code to identify infectious organism)
491.21 Obstructive chronic bronchitis, with (acute) exacerbation — (Use additional code to identify infectious organism)
491.8 Other chronic bronchitis — (Use additional code to identify infectious organism)
492.0 Emphysematous bleb
492.8 Other emphysema
494.0 Bronchiectasis without acute exacerbation — (Use additional code to identify infectious organism)
494.1 Bronchiectasis with acute exacerbation — (Use additional code to identify infectious organism)
495.0 Farmers' lung — (Use additional code to identify infectious organism)
495.1 Bagassosis — (Use additional code to identify infectious organism)
495.2 Bird-fanciers' lung — (Use additional code to identify infectious organism)
495.3 Suberosis — (Use additional code to identify infectious organism)
495.4 Malt workers' lung — (Use additional code to identify infectious organism)
495.5 Mushroom workers' lung — (Use additional code to identify infectious organism)
495.6 Maple bark-strippers' lung — (Use additional code to identify infectious organism)
495.7 Ventilation pneumonitis — (Use additional code to identify infectious organism)
495.8 Other specified allergic alveolitis and pneumonitis — (Use additional code to identify infectious organism)
495.9 Unspecified allergic alveolitis and pneumonitis — (Use additional code to identify infectious organism) ▽
496 Chronic airway obstruction, not elsewhere classified — (Note: This code is not to be used with any code from 491-493) ▽
506.1 Acute pulmonary edema due to fumes and vapors — (Use additional code to identify infectious organism. Use additional E code to identify cause. Use additional code to identify associated respiratory conditions: 518.81.)
507.0 Pneumonitis due to inhalation of food or vomitus — (Use additional code to identify infectious organism)
507.1 Pneumonitis due to inhalation of oils and essences — (Use additional code to identify infectious organism)

507.8 Pneumonitis due to other solids and liquids — (Use additional code to identify infectious organism)
508.2 Respiratory conditions due to smoke inhalation — (Use additional code to identify infectious organism. Use additional E code to identify cause. Use additional code to identify associated respiratory conditions: 518.81.)
510.0 Empyema with fistula — (Use additional code to identify infectious organism: 041.00-041.9)
510.9 Empyema without mention of fistula — (Use additional code to identify infectious organism: 041.00-041.9)
513.0 Abscess of lung — (Use additional code to identify infectious organism)
513.1 Abscess of mediastinum — (Use additional code to identify infectious organism)
514 Pulmonary congestion and hypostasis — (Use additional code to identify infectious organism)
515 Postinflammatory pulmonary fibrosis — (Use additional code to identify infectious organism)
516.0 Pulmonary alveolar proteinosis — (Use additional code to identify infectious organism)
516.1 Idiopathic pulmonary hemosiderosis — (Use additional code to identify infectious organism. Code first underlying disease: 275.01-275.09) ☒
516.2 Pulmonary alveolar microlithiasis — (Use additional code to identify infectious organism)
516.30 Idiopathic interstitial pneumonia, not otherwise specified
516.31 Idiopathic pulmonary fibrosis
516.32 Idiopathic non-specific interstitial pneumonitis
516.33 Acute interstitial pneumonitis
516.34 Respiratory bronchiolitis interstitial lung disease
516.35 Idiopathic lymphoid interstitial pneumonia
516.36 Cryptogenic organizing pneumonia
516.37 Desquamative interstitial pneumonia
516.8 Other specified alveolar and parietoalveolar pneumonopathies — (Code first, if applicable, underlying cause of pneumonopathy, if known)(Use additional code to identify infectious organism) (Use additional E code, if applicable, for drug-induced or toxic pneumonopathy)
517.1 Rheumatic pneumonia — (Use additional code to identify infectious organism. Code first underlying disease: 390) ☒
517.2 Lung involvement in systemic sclerosis — (Use additional code to identify infectious organism. Code first underlying disease: 710.1) ☒
517.8 Lung involvement in other diseases classified elsewhere — (Use additional code to identify infectious organism. Code first underlying disease: 135, 277.30-277.39, 710.0, 710.2, 710.4) ☒
518.0 Pulmonary collapse
518.3 Pulmonary eosinophilia — (Use additional code to identify infectious organism)
518.4 Unspecified acute edema of lung ▽
518.51 Acute respiratory failure following trauma and surgery
518.52 Other pulmonary insufficiency, not elsewhere classified, following trauma and surgery
518.53 Acute and chronic respiratory failure following trauma and surgery
518.81 Acute respiratory failure
518.82 Other pulmonary insufficiency, not elsewhere classified
518.89 Other diseases of lung, not elsewhere classified — (Use additional code to identify infectious organism)
519.19 Other diseases of trachea and bronchus — (Use additional code to identify infectious organism)
958.3 Posttraumatic wound infection not elsewhere classified
997.31 Ventilator associated pneumonia — (Use additional code to identify organism)
V15.82 Personal history of tobacco use, presenting hazards to health

ICD-9-CM Procedural

33.22 Fiber-optic bronchoscopy
33.23 Other bronchoscopy
96.05 Other intubation of respiratory tract

31647, 31651

31647 Bronchoscopy, rigid or flexible, including fluoroscopic guidance, when performed; with balloon occlusion, when performed, assessment of air leak, airway sizing, and insertion of bronchial valve(s), initial lobe
31651 with balloon occlusion, when performed, assessment of air leak, airway sizing, and insertion of bronchial valve(s), each additional lobe (List separately in addition to code for primary procedure[s])

ICD-9-CM Diagnostic

011.30 Tuberculosis of bronchus, confirmation unspecified — (Use additional code to identify any associated silicosis, 502) ▽
011.31 Tuberculosis of bronchus, bacteriological or histological examination not done — (Use additional code to identify any associated silicosis, 502)
011.32 Tuberculosis of bronchus, bacteriological or histological examination unknown (at present) — (Use additional code to identify any associated silicosis, 502)
011.33 Tuberculosis of bronchus, tubercle bacilli found (in sputum) by microscopy — (Use additional code to identify any associated silicosis, 502)
011.34 Tuberculosis of bronchus, tubercle bacilli not found (in sputum) by microscopy, but found in bacterial culture — (Use additional code to identify any associated silicosis, 502)
011.35 Tuberculosis of bronchus, tubercle bacilli not found by bacteriological examination, but tuberculosis confirmed histologically — (Use additional code to identify any associated silicosis, 502)
011.36 Tuberculosis of bronchus, tubercle bacilli not found by bacteriological or histological examination, but tuberculosis confirmed by other methods [inoculation of animals] — (Use additional code to identify any associated silicosis, 502)
121.2 Paragonimiasis
491.20 Obstructive chronic bronchitis, without exacerbation — (Use additional code to identify infectious organism)
492.0 Emphysematous bleb
492.8 Other emphysema
496 Chronic airway obstruction, not elsewhere classified — (Note: This code is not to be used with any code from 491-493) ▽
510.0 Empyema with fistula — (Use additional code to identify infectious organism: 041.00-041.9)
512.0 Spontaneous tension pneumothorax
512.2 Postoperative air leak
512.81 Primary spontaneous pneumothorax
512.82 Secondary spontaneous pneumothorax — (Code first underlying condition, such as: 136.3, 162.3-162.9, 197.0, 277.02, 516.4, 518.3, 530.4, 617.8, 759.82))
512.83 Chronic pneumothorax
512.84 Other air leak
512.89 Other pneumothorax
518.0 Pulmonary collapse
770.2 Interstitial emphysema and related conditions of newborn — (Use additional code(s) to further specify condition)
786.30 Hemoptysis, unspecified ▽
786.39 Other hemoptysis
860.0 Traumatic pneumothorax without mention of open wound into thorax
860.1 Traumatic pneumothorax with open wound into thorax
860.4 Traumatic pneumohemothorax without mention of open wound into thorax
860.5 Traumatic pneumohemothorax with open wound into thorax
862.21 Bronchus injury without mention of open wound into cavity
862.31 Bronchus injury with open wound into cavity
908.0 Late effect of internal injury to chest
997.39 Other respiratory complications
998.6 Persistent postoperative fistula, not elsewhere classified

ICD-9-CM Procedural

33.71 Endoscopic insertion or replacement of bronchial valve(s), single lobe
33.73 Endoscopic insertion or replacement of bronchial valve(s), multiple lobes

31648-31649

31648 Bronchoscopy, rigid or flexible, including fluoroscopic guidance, when performed; with removal of bronchial valve(s), initial lobe

31649 with removal of bronchial valve(s), each additional lobe (List separately in addition to code for primary procedure)

ICD-9-CM Diagnostic

491.21 Obstructive chronic bronchitis, with (acute) exacerbation — (Use additional code to identify infectious organism)

491.22 Obstructive chronic bronchitis with acute bronchitis — (Use additional code to identify infectious organism)

512.1 Iatrogenic pneumothorax

512.2 Postoperative air leak

512.84 Other air leak

518.0 Pulmonary collapse

519.11 Acute bronchospasm

996.59 Mechanical complication due to other implant and internal device, not elsewhere classified

996.69 Infection and inflammatory reaction due to other internal prosthetic device, implant, and graft — (Use additional code to identify specified infections)

996.79 Other complications due to other internal prosthetic device, implant, and graft — (Use additional code to identify complication: 338.18-338.19, 338.28-338.29)

997.39 Other respiratory complications

V53.99 Fitting and adjustment, Other device

V58.49 Other specified aftercare following surgery — (This code should be used in conjunction with other aftercare codes to fully identify the reason for the aftercare encounter)

V58.74 Aftercare following surgery of the respiratory system, NEC — (This code should be used in conjunction with other aftercare codes to fully identify the reason for the aftercare encounter)

ICD-9-CM Procedural

33.78 Endoscopic removal of bronchial device(s) or substances

31660-31661

31660 Bronchoscopy, rigid or flexible, including fluoroscopic guidance, when performed; with bronchial thermoplasty, 1 lobe

31661 with bronchial thermoplasty, 2 or more lobes

ICD-9-CM Diagnostic

491.20 Obstructive chronic bronchitis, without exacerbation — (Use additional code to identify infectious organism)

491.8 Other chronic bronchitis — (Use additional code to identify infectious organism)

491.9 Unspecified chronic bronchitis — (Use additional code to identify infectious organism) ▽

492.0 Emphysematous bleb

492.8 Other emphysema

493.01 Extrinsic asthma with status asthmaticus

493.11 Intrinsic asthma with status asthmaticus

493.21 Chronic obstructive asthma with status asthmaticus

493.91 Asthma, unspecified with status asthmaticus ▽

ICD-9-CM Procedural

32.27 Bronchoscopic bronchial thermoplasty, ablation of airway smooth muscle

31717

31717 Catheterization with bronchial brush biopsy

ICD-9-CM Diagnostic

135 Sarcoidosis

162.2 Malignant neoplasm of main bronchus

162.3 Malignant neoplasm of upper lobe, bronchus, or lung

162.4 Malignant neoplasm of middle lobe, bronchus, or lung

162.5 Malignant neoplasm of lower lobe, bronchus, or lung

162.8 Malignant neoplasm of other parts of bronchus or lung

162.9 Malignant neoplasm of bronchus and lung, unspecified site ▽

197.0 Secondary malignant neoplasm of lung

197.2 Secondary malignant neoplasm of pleura

198.89 Secondary malignant neoplasm of other specified sites

199.1 Other malignant neoplasm of unspecified site

209.21 Malignant carcinoid tumor of the bronchus and lung — (Code first any associated multiple endocrine neoplasia syndrome: 258.01-258.03)(Use additional code to identify associated endocrine syndrome, as: carcinoid syndrome: 259.2)

209.61 Benign carcinoid tumor of the bronchus and lung — (Code first any associated multiple endocrine neoplasia syndrome: 258.01-258.03)(Use additional code to identify associated endocrine syndrome, as: carcinoid syndrome: 259.2)

212.2 Benign neoplasm of trachea

212.3 Benign neoplasm of bronchus and lung

212.4 Benign neoplasm of pleura

231.1 Carcinoma in situ of trachea

231.2 Carcinoma in situ of bronchus and lung

235.7 Neoplasm of uncertain behavior of trachea, bronchus, and lung

239.1 Neoplasm of unspecified nature of respiratory system

482.41 Methicillin susceptible pneumonia due to Staphylococcus aureus

482.42 Methicillin resistant pneumonia due to Staphylococcus aureus

482.84 Legionnaires' disease

485 Bronchopneumonia, organism unspecified ▽

486 Pneumonia, organism unspecified ▽

495.9 Unspecified allergic alveolitis and pneumonitis — (Use additional code to identify infectious organism) ▽

500 Coal workers' pneumoconiosis — (Use additional code to identify infectious organism)

501 Asbestosis — (Use additional code to identify infectious organism)

502 Pneumoconiosis due to other silica or silicates — (Use additional code to identify infectious organism)

503 Pneumoconiosis due to other inorganic dust — (Use additional code to identify infectious organism)

504 Pneumonopathy due to inhalation of other dust — (Use additional code to identify infectious organism)

505 Unspecified pneumoconiosis — (Use additional code to identify infectious organism) ▽

506.4 Chronic respiratory conditions due to fumes and vapors — (Use additional code to identify infectious organism. Use additional E code to identify cause. Use additional code to identify associated respiratory conditions: 518.81.)

507.0 Pneumonitis due to inhalation of food or vomitus — (Use additional code to identify infectious organism)

508.1 Chronic and other pulmonary manifestations due to radiation — (Use additional code to identify infectious organism. Use additional E code to identify cause. Use additional code to identify associated respiratory conditions: 518.81.)

510.0 Empyema with fistula — (Use additional code to identify infectious organism: 041.00-041.9)

510.9 Empyema without mention of fistula — (Use additional code to identify infectious organism: 041.00-041.9)

511.81 Malignant pleural effusion — (Code first malignant neoplasm, if known)

511.89 Other specified forms of effusion, except tuberculous

512.0 Spontaneous tension pneumothorax

512.1 Iatrogenic pneumothorax

512.2 Postoperative air leak

512.81 Primary spontaneous pneumothorax

512.82 Secondary spontaneous pneumothorax — (Code first underlying condition, such as: 136.3, 162.3-162.9, 197.0, 277.02, 516.4, 518.3, 530.4, 617.8, 759.82))

512.83 Chronic pneumothorax

512.84 Other air leak

512.89 Other pneumothorax

513.0 Abscess of lung — (Use additional code to identify infectious organism)

514 Pulmonary congestion and hypostasis — (Use additional code to identify infectious organism)
515 Postinflammatory pulmonary fibrosis — (Use additional code to identify infectious organism)
516.0 Pulmonary alveolar proteinosis — (Use additional code to identify infectious organism)
516.1 Idiopathic pulmonary hemosiderosis — (Use additional code to identify infectious organism. Code first underlying disease: 275.01-275.09) ☒
516.2 Pulmonary alveolar microlithiasis — (Use additional code to identify infectious organism)
516.30 Idiopathic interstitial pneumonia, not otherwise specified
516.31 Idiopathic pulmonary fibrosis
516.32 Idiopathic non-specific interstitial pneumonitis
516.33 Acute interstitial pneumonitis
516.34 Respiratory bronchiolitis interstitial lung disease
516.35 Idiopathic lymphoid interstitial pneumonia
516.36 Cryptogenic organizing pneumonia
516.37 Desquamative interstitial pneumonia
516.8 Other specified alveolar and parietoalveolar pneumonopathies — (Code first, if applicable, underlying cause of pneumonopathy, if known)(Use additional code to identify infectious organism) (Use additional E code, if applicable, for drug-induced or toxic pneumonopathy)
517.8 Lung involvement in other diseases classified elsewhere — (Use additional code to identify infectious organism. Code first underlying disease: 135, 277.30-277.39, 710.0, 710.2, 710.4) ☒
518.0 Pulmonary collapse
518.3 Pulmonary eosinophilia — (Use additional code to identify infectious organism)
518.51 Acute respiratory failure following trauma and surgery
518.52 Other pulmonary insufficiency, not elsewhere classified, following trauma and surgery
518.53 Acute and chronic respiratory failure following trauma and surgery
518.89 Other diseases of lung, not elsewhere classified — (Use additional code to identify infectious organism)
770.7 Chronic respiratory disease arising in the perinatal period — (Use additional code(s) to further specify condition)
786.2 Cough
786.30 Hemoptysis, unspecified ▽
786.31 Acute idiopathic pulmonary hemorrhage in infants [AIPHI]
786.39 Other hemoptysis
V10.11 Personal history of malignant neoplasm of bronchus and lung
V10.12 Personal history of malignant neoplasm of trachea
V15.82 Personal history of tobacco use, presenting hazards to health
V15.84 Personal history of contact with and (suspected) exposure to asbestos
V16.2 Family history of malignant neoplasm of other respiratory and intrathoracic organs
V43.89 Other organ or tissue replaced by other means

ICD-9-CM Procedural

33.24 Closed (endoscopic) biopsy of bronchus

31720-31725

31720 Catheter aspiration (separate procedure); nasotracheal
31725 tracheobronchial with fiberscope, bedside

ICD-9-CM Diagnostic

277.00 Cystic fibrosis without mention of meconium ileus — (Use additional code to identify any associated intellectual disabilities)
277.02 Cystic fibrosis with pulmonary manifestations — (Use additional code to identify any associated intellectual disabilities.) (Use additional code to identify any infectious organism present, such as 041.7)
277.03 Cystic fibrosis with gastrointestinal manifestations — (Use additional code to identify any associated intellectual disabilities)
277.09 Cystic fibrosis with other manifestations — (Use additional code to identify any associated intellectual disabilities)
480.0 Pneumonia due to adenovirus
480.1 Pneumonia due to respiratory syncytial virus
480.2 Pneumonia due to parainfluenza virus
480.3 Pneumonia due to SARS-associated coronavirus
480.8 Pneumonia due to other virus not elsewhere classified
481 Pneumococcal pneumonia (streptococcus pneumoniae pneumonia)
482.0 Pneumonia due to Klebsiella pneumoniae
482.1 Pneumonia due to Pseudomonas
482.2 Pneumonia due to Hemophilus influenzae (H. influenzae)
482.30 Pneumonia due to unspecified Streptococcus ▽
482.31 Pneumonia due to Streptococcus, group A
482.32 Pneumonia due to Streptococcus, group B
482.39 Pneumonia due to other Streptococcus
482.41 Methicillin susceptible pneumonia due to Staphylococcus aureus
482.42 Methicillin resistant pneumonia due to Staphylococcus aureus
482.81 Pneumonia due to anaerobes
482.82 Pneumonia due to Escherichia coli (E. coli)
482.83 Pneumonia due to other gram-negative bacteria
482.89 Pneumonia due to other specified bacteria — (Use additional code to identify infectious organism)
483.0 Pneumonia due to Mycoplasma pneumoniae
483.1 Pneumonia due to Chlamydia
483.8 Pneumonia due to other specified organism — (Use additional code to identify infectious organism)
484.1 Pneumonia in cytomegalic inclusion disease — (Code first underlying disease: 078.5) ☒
484.3 Pneumonia in whooping cough — (Code first underlying disease: 033.0-033.9) ☒
484.5 Pneumonia in anthrax — (Code first underlying disease: 022.1) ☒
484.6 Pneumonia in aspergillosis — (Code first underlying disease: 117.3) ☒
484.7 Pneumonia in other systemic mycoses — (Use additional code to identify infectious organism. Code first underlying disease) ☒
484.8 Pneumonia in other infectious diseases classified elsewhere — (Code first underlying disease: 002.0, 083.0) ☒
485 Bronchopneumonia, organism unspecified ▽
487.0 Influenza with pneumonia — (Use additional code to identify infectious organism. Use additional code to identify type of pneumonia: 480.0-480.9, 481, 482.0-492.9, 483.0-483.8, 485)
490 Bronchitis, not specified as acute or chronic — (Use additional code to identify infectious organism) ▽
491.0 Simple chronic bronchitis — (Use additional code to identify infectious organism)
491.1 Mucopurulent chronic bronchitis — (Use additional code to identify infectious organism)
491.20 Obstructive chronic bronchitis, without exacerbation — (Use additional code to identify infectious organism)
491.21 Obstructive chronic bronchitis, with (acute) exacerbation — (Use additional code to identify infectious organism)
491.8 Other chronic bronchitis — (Use additional code to identify infectious organism)
492.0 Emphysematous bleb
492.8 Other emphysema
494.0 Bronchiectasis without acute exacerbation — (Use additional code to identify infectious organism)
494.1 Bronchiectasis with acute exacerbation — (Use additional code to identify infectious organism)
495.0 Farmers' lung — (Use additional code to identify infectious organism)
495.1 Bagassosis — (Use additional code to identify infectious organism)
495.2 Bird-fanciers' lung — (Use additional code to identify infectious organism)
495.3 Suberosis — (Use additional code to identify infectious organism)
495.4 Malt workers' lung — (Use additional code to identify infectious organism)
495.5 Mushroom workers' lung — (Use additional code to identify infectious organism)
495.6 Maple bark-strippers' lung — (Use additional code to identify infectious organism)

495.7	Ventilation pneumonitis — (Use additional code to identify infectious organism)
495.8	Other specified allergic alveolitis and pneumonitis — (Use additional code to identify infectious organism)
495.9	Unspecified allergic alveolitis and pneumonitis — (Use additional code to identify infectious organism)
496	Chronic airway obstruction, not elsewhere classified — (Note: This code is not to be used with any code from 491-493)
506.1	Acute pulmonary edema due to fumes and vapors — (Use additional code to identify infectious organism. Use additional E code to identify cause. Use additional code to identify associated respiratory conditions: 518.81.)
507.0	Pneumonitis due to inhalation of food or vomitus — (Use additional code to identify infectious organism)
507.1	Pneumonitis due to inhalation of oils and essences — (Use additional code to identify infectious organism)
507.8	Pneumonitis due to other solids and liquids — (Use additional code to identify infectious organism)
510.0	Empyema with fistula — (Use additional code to identify infectious organism: 041.00-041.9)
513.0	Abscess of lung — (Use additional code to identify infectious organism)
513.1	Abscess of mediastinum — (Use additional code to identify infectious organism)
514	Pulmonary congestion and hypostasis — (Use additional code to identify infectious organism)
515	Postinflammatory pulmonary fibrosis — (Use additional code to identify infectious organism)
516.0	Pulmonary alveolar proteinosis — (Use additional code to identify infectious organism)
516.1	Idiopathic pulmonary hemosiderosis — (Use additional code to identify infectious organism. Code first underlying disease: 275.01-275.09) ☒
516.2	Pulmonary alveolar microlithiasis — (Use additional code to identify infectious organism)
516.30	Idiopathic interstitial pneumonia, not otherwise specified
516.31	Idiopathic pulmonary fibrosis
516.32	Idiopathic non-specific interstitial pneumonitis
516.33	Acute interstitial pneumonitis
516.34	Respiratory bronchiolitis interstitial lung disease
516.35	Idiopathic lymphoid interstitial pneumonia
516.36	Cryptogenic organizing pneumonia
516.37	Desquamative interstitial pneumonia
516.8	Other specified alveolar and parietoalveolar pneumonopathies — (Code first, if applicable, underlying cause of pneumonopathy, if known)(Use additional code to identify infectious organism) (Use additional E code, if applicable, for drug-induced or toxic pneumonopathy)
517.1	Rheumatic pneumonia — (Use additional code to identify infectious organism. Code first underlying disease: 390) ☒
517.2	Lung involvement in systemic sclerosis — (Use additional code to identify infectious organism. Code first underlying disease: 710.1) ☒
517.8	Lung involvement in other diseases classified elsewhere — (Use additional code to identify infectious organism. Code first underlying disease: 135, 277.30-277.39, 710.0, 710.2, 710.4) ☒
518.0	Pulmonary collapse
518.3	Pulmonary eosinophilia — (Use additional code to identify infectious organism)
518.4	Unspecified acute edema of lung
518.51	Acute respiratory failure following trauma and surgery
518.52	Other pulmonary insufficiency, not elsewhere classified, following trauma and surgery
518.53	Acute and chronic respiratory failure following trauma and surgery
518.81	Acute respiratory failure
518.82	Other pulmonary insufficiency, not elsewhere classified
518.83	Chronic respiratory failure
518.84	Acute and chronic respiratory failure
518.89	Other diseases of lung, not elsewhere classified — (Use additional code to identify infectious organism)
519.19	Other diseases of trachea and bronchus — (Use additional code to identify infectious organism)
958.3	Posttraumatic wound infection not elsewhere classified
997.31	Ventilator associated pneumonia — (Use additional code to identify organism)
V15.82	Personal history of tobacco use, presenting hazards to health

ICD-9-CM Procedural

96.05	Other intubation of respiratory tract

HCPCS Level II Supplies & Services

A4305	Disposable drug delivery system, flow rate of 50 ml or greater per hour

31730

31730	Transtracheal (percutaneous) introduction of needle wire dilator/stent or indwelling tube for oxygen therapy

ICD-9-CM Diagnostic

478.6	Edema of larynx
478.71	Cellulitis and perichondritis of larynx — (Use additional code to identify infectious organism)
478.74	Stenosis of larynx
478.79	Other diseases of larynx — (Use additional code to identify infectious organism)
478.9	Other and unspecified diseases of upper respiratory tract — (Use additional code to identify infectious organism)
482.42	Methicillin resistant pneumonia due to Staphylococcus aureus
483.0	Pneumonia due to Mycoplasma pneumoniae
483.8	Pneumonia due to other specified organism — (Use additional code to identify infectious organism)
496	Chronic airway obstruction, not elsewhere classified — (Note: This code is not to be used with any code from 491-493)
518.81	Acute respiratory failure
518.82	Other pulmonary insufficiency, not elsewhere classified
518.89	Other diseases of lung, not elsewhere classified — (Use additional code to identify infectious organism)
748.2	Congenital web of larynx
770.7	Chronic respiratory disease arising in the perinatal period — (Use additional code(s) to further specify condition)

ICD-9-CM Procedural

31.99	Other operations on trachea

HCPCS Level II Supplies & Services

A4305	Disposable drug delivery system, flow rate of 50 ml or greater per hour

31750

31750	Tracheoplasty; cervical

ICD-9-CM Diagnostic

161.0	Malignant neoplasm of glottis
161.1	Malignant neoplasm of supraglottis
161.2	Malignant neoplasm of subglottis
161.3	Malignant neoplasm of laryngeal cartilages
161.8	Malignant neoplasm of other specified sites of larynx
161.9	Malignant neoplasm of larynx, unspecified site
162.0	Malignant neoplasm of trachea
197.3	Secondary malignant neoplasm of other respiratory organs
198.89	Secondary malignant neoplasm of other specified sites
212.2	Benign neoplasm of trachea
231.1	Carcinoma in situ of trachea
235.7	Neoplasm of uncertain behavior of trachea, bronchus, and lung
239.1	Neoplasm of unspecified nature of respiratory system
519.00	Unspecified tracheostomy complication — (Use additional code to identify infectious organism)

519.01 Infection of tracheostomy — (Use additional code to identify type of infection: 038.0-038.9, 682.1. Use additional code to identify organism: 041.00-041.9)
519.02 Mechanical complication of tracheostomy
519.09 Other tracheostomy complications — (Use additional code to identify infectious organism)
519.19 Other diseases of trachea and bronchus — (Use additional code to identify infectious organism)
530.84 Tracheoesophageal fistula
748.3 Other congenital anomaly of larynx, trachea, and bronchus
750.3 Congenital tracheoesophageal fistula, esophageal atresia and stenosis
874.12 Open wound of trachea, complicated
906.4 Late effect of crushing
906.8 Late effect of burns of other specified sites
925.2 Crushing injury of neck — (Use additional code to identify any associated injuries, such as: 800-829, 850.0-854.1, 860.0-869.1)
947.1 Burn of larynx, trachea, and lung
960.0 Poisoning by penicillins — (Use additional code to specify the effects of poisoning)
V10.12 Personal history of malignant neoplasm of trachea
V10.21 Personal history of malignant neoplasm of larynx
V15.82 Personal history of tobacco use, presenting hazards to health

ICD-9-CM Procedural

31.73 Closure of other fistula of trachea
31.79 Other repair and plastic operations on trachea

31755

31755 Tracheoplasty; tracheopharyngeal fistulization, each stage

ICD-9-CM Diagnostic

161.0 Malignant neoplasm of glottis
161.1 Malignant neoplasm of supraglottis
161.2 Malignant neoplasm of subglottis
161.3 Malignant neoplasm of laryngeal cartilages
161.8 Malignant neoplasm of other specified sites of larynx
161.9 Malignant neoplasm of larynx, unspecified site ▽
162.0 Malignant neoplasm of trachea
197.3 Secondary malignant neoplasm of other respiratory organs
198.89 Secondary malignant neoplasm of other specified sites
212.1 Benign neoplasm of larynx
212.2 Benign neoplasm of trachea
231.0 Carcinoma in situ of larynx
231.1 Carcinoma in situ of trachea
235.6 Neoplasm of uncertain behavior of larynx
235.7 Neoplasm of uncertain behavior of trachea, bronchus, and lung
239.1 Neoplasm of unspecified nature of respiratory system
519.00 Unspecified tracheostomy complication — (Use additional code to identify infectious organism) ▽
519.01 Infection of tracheostomy — (Use additional code to identify type of infection: 038.0-038.9, 682.1. Use additional code to identify organism: 041.00-041.9)
519.02 Mechanical complication of tracheostomy
519.09 Other tracheostomy complications — (Use additional code to identify infectious organism)
519.19 Other diseases of trachea and bronchus — (Use additional code to identify infectious organism)
530.84 Tracheoesophageal fistula
748.3 Other congenital anomaly of larynx, trachea, and bronchus
750.3 Congenital tracheoesophageal fistula, esophageal atresia and stenosis
874.12 Open wound of trachea, complicated
906.4 Late effect of crushing
906.8 Late effect of burns of other specified sites
925.2 Crushing injury of neck — (Use additional code to identify any associated injuries, such as: 800-829, 850.0-854.1, 860.0-869.1)
947.1 Burn of larynx, trachea, and lung
960.0 Poisoning by penicillins — (Use additional code to specify the effects of poisoning)
V10.12 Personal history of malignant neoplasm of trachea
V10.21 Personal history of malignant neoplasm of larynx
V15.82 Personal history of tobacco use, presenting hazards to health

ICD-9-CM Procedural

31.5 Local excision or destruction of lesion or tissue of trachea
31.79 Other repair and plastic operations on trachea

31760

31760 Tracheoplasty; intrathoracic

ICD-9-CM Diagnostic

161.0 Malignant neoplasm of glottis
161.1 Malignant neoplasm of supraglottis
161.2 Malignant neoplasm of subglottis
161.3 Malignant neoplasm of laryngeal cartilages
161.8 Malignant neoplasm of other specified sites of larynx
161.9 Malignant neoplasm of larynx, unspecified site ▽
162.0 Malignant neoplasm of trachea
197.3 Secondary malignant neoplasm of other respiratory organs
198.89 Secondary malignant neoplasm of other specified sites
212.1 Benign neoplasm of larynx
212.2 Benign neoplasm of trachea
231.0 Carcinoma in situ of larynx
231.1 Carcinoma in situ of trachea
235.6 Neoplasm of uncertain behavior of larynx
235.7 Neoplasm of uncertain behavior of trachea, bronchus, and lung
239.1 Neoplasm of unspecified nature of respiratory system
519.00 Unspecified tracheostomy complication — (Use additional code to identify infectious organism) ▽
519.01 Infection of tracheostomy — (Use additional code to identify type of infection: 038.0-038.9, 682.1. Use additional code to identify organism: 041.00-041.9)
519.02 Mechanical complication of tracheostomy
519.09 Other tracheostomy complications — (Use additional code to identify infectious organism)
519.19 Other diseases of trachea and bronchus — (Use additional code to identify infectious organism)
530.84 Tracheoesophageal fistula
748.3 Other congenital anomaly of larynx, trachea, and bronchus
750.3 Congenital tracheoesophageal fistula, esophageal atresia and stenosis
874.12 Open wound of trachea, complicated
906.4 Late effect of crushing
906.8 Late effect of burns of other specified sites
925.2 Crushing injury of neck — (Use additional code to identify any associated injuries, such as: 800-829, 850.0-854.1, 860.0-869.1)
947.1 Burn of larynx, trachea, and lung
960.0 Poisoning by penicillins — (Use additional code to specify the effects of poisoning)
V10.12 Personal history of malignant neoplasm of trachea
V10.21 Personal history of malignant neoplasm of larynx
V15.82 Personal history of tobacco use, presenting hazards to health

ICD-9-CM Procedural

31.79 Other repair and plastic operations on trachea

31766

31766 Carinal reconstruction

ICD-9-CM Diagnostic

162.0 Malignant neoplasm of trachea
162.2 Malignant neoplasm of main bronchus
197.0 Secondary malignant neoplasm of lung
197.3 Secondary malignant neoplasm of other respiratory organs
209.21 Malignant carcinoid tumor of the bronchus and lung — (Code first any associated multiple endocrine neoplasia syndrome: 258.01-258.03)(Use additional code to identify associated endocrine syndrome, as: carcinoid syndrome: 259.2)
209.61 Benign carcinoid tumor of the bronchus and lung — (Code first any associated multiple endocrine neoplasia syndrome: 258.01-258.03)(Use additional code to identify associated endocrine syndrome, as: carcinoid syndrome: 259.2)
212.2 Benign neoplasm of trachea
212.3 Benign neoplasm of bronchus and lung
231.1 Carcinoma in situ of trachea
231.2 Carcinoma in situ of bronchus and lung
235.7 Neoplasm of uncertain behavior of trachea, bronchus, and lung
239.1 Neoplasm of unspecified nature of respiratory system
515 Postinflammatory pulmonary fibrosis — (Use additional code to identify infectious organism)
519.00 Unspecified tracheostomy complication — (Use additional code to identify infectious organism) ▽
519.01 Infection of tracheostomy — (Use additional code to identify type of infection: 038.0-038.9, 682.1. Use additional code to identify organism: 041.00-041.9)
519.02 Mechanical complication of tracheostomy
519.09 Other tracheostomy complications — (Use additional code to identify infectious organism)
519.19 Other diseases of trachea and bronchus — (Use additional code to identify infectious organism)
530.84 Tracheoesophageal fistula
748.3 Other congenital anomaly of larynx, trachea, and bronchus
750.3 Congenital tracheoesophageal fistula, esophageal atresia and stenosis
862.21 Bronchus injury without mention of open wound into cavity
862.31 Bronchus injury with open wound into cavity
874.12 Open wound of trachea, complicated
906.0 Late effect of open wound of head, neck, and trunk
906.4 Late effect of crushing
906.8 Late effect of burns of other specified sites
947.1 Burn of larynx, trachea, and lung
V10.11 Personal history of malignant neoplasm of bronchus and lung
V10.12 Personal history of malignant neoplasm of trachea
V10.21 Personal history of malignant neoplasm of larynx
V15.82 Personal history of tobacco use, presenting hazards to health

ICD-9-CM Procedural

31.79 Other repair and plastic operations on trachea

31770-31775

31770 Bronchoplasty; graft repair
31775 excision stenosis and anastomosis

ICD-9-CM Diagnostic

162.2 Malignant neoplasm of main bronchus
162.3 Malignant neoplasm of upper lobe, bronchus, or lung
162.4 Malignant neoplasm of middle lobe, bronchus, or lung
162.5 Malignant neoplasm of lower lobe, bronchus, or lung
162.8 Malignant neoplasm of other parts of bronchus or lung
165.9 Malignant neoplasm of ill-defined sites within the respiratory system
171.4 Malignant neoplasm of connective and other soft tissue of thorax
197.0 Secondary malignant neoplasm of lung
197.1 Secondary malignant neoplasm of mediastinum
198.89 Secondary malignant neoplasm of other specified sites
209.21 Malignant carcinoid tumor of the bronchus and lung — (Code first any associated multiple endocrine neoplasia syndrome: 258.01-258.03)(Use additional code to identify associated endocrine syndrome, as: carcinoid syndrome: 259.2)
209.61 Benign carcinoid tumor of the bronchus and lung — (Code first any associated multiple endocrine neoplasia syndrome: 258.01-258.03)(Use additional code to identify associated endocrine syndrome, as: carcinoid syndrome: 259.2)
212.3 Benign neoplasm of bronchus and lung
231.2 Carcinoma in situ of bronchus and lung
235.7 Neoplasm of uncertain behavior of trachea, bronchus, and lung
519.19 Other diseases of trachea and bronchus — (Use additional code to identify infectious organism)
862.21 Bronchus injury without mention of open wound into cavity
862.31 Bronchus injury with open wound into cavity
906.0 Late effect of open wound of head, neck, and trunk
906.4 Late effect of crushing
906.5 Late effect of burn of eye, face, head, and neck
908.0 Late effect of internal injury to chest
934.1 Foreign body in main bronchus
947.1 Burn of larynx, trachea, and lung
V10.11 Personal history of malignant neoplasm of bronchus and lung
V10.12 Personal history of malignant neoplasm of trachea
V15.82 Personal history of tobacco use, presenting hazards to health

ICD-9-CM Procedural

32.1 Other excision of bronchus
33.48 Other repair and plastic operations on bronchus

31780

31780 Excision tracheal stenosis and anastomosis; cervical

ICD-9-CM Diagnostic

519.02 Mechanical complication of tracheostomy
519.19 Other diseases of trachea and bronchus — (Use additional code to identify infectious organism)
748.3 Other congenital anomaly of larynx, trachea, and bronchus
906.0 Late effect of open wound of head, neck, and trunk
906.4 Late effect of crushing
906.5 Late effect of burn of eye, face, head, and neck
V16.1 Family history of malignant neoplasm of trachea, bronchus, and lung

ICD-9-CM Procedural

31.5 Local excision or destruction of lesion or tissue of trachea
31.79 Other repair and plastic operations on trachea

31781

31781 Excision tracheal stenosis and anastomosis; cervicothoracic

ICD-9-CM Diagnostic

519.02 Mechanical complication of tracheostomy
519.19 Other diseases of trachea and bronchus — (Use additional code to identify infectious organism)
748.3 Other congenital anomaly of larynx, trachea, and bronchus
906.0 Late effect of open wound of head, neck, and trunk
906.4 Late effect of crushing
906.5 Late effect of burn of eye, face, head, and neck
V10.12 Personal history of malignant neoplasm of trachea
V16.1 Family history of malignant neoplasm of trachea, bronchus, and lung

ICD-9-CM Procedural

31.5 Local excision or destruction of lesion or tissue of trachea

31.79 Other repair and plastic operations on trachea

31785

31785 Excision of tracheal tumor or carcinoma; cervical

ICD-9-CM Diagnostic

162.0 Malignant neoplasm of trachea

162.2 Malignant neoplasm of main bronchus

197.0 Secondary malignant neoplasm of lung

197.3 Secondary malignant neoplasm of other respiratory organs

209.21 Malignant carcinoid tumor of the bronchus and lung — (Code first any associated multiple endocrine neoplasia syndrome: 258.01-258.03)(Use additional code to identify associated endocrine syndrome, as: carcinoid syndrome: 259.2)

209.61 Benign carcinoid tumor of the bronchus and lung — (Code first any associated multiple endocrine neoplasia syndrome: 258.01-258.03)(Use additional code to identify associated endocrine syndrome, as: carcinoid syndrome: 259.2)

212.2 Benign neoplasm of trachea

212.3 Benign neoplasm of bronchus and lung

231.1 Carcinoma in situ of trachea

231.2 Carcinoma in situ of bronchus and lung

235.7 Neoplasm of uncertain behavior of trachea, bronchus, and lung

239.1 Neoplasm of unspecified nature of respiratory system

V15.82 Personal history of tobacco use, presenting hazards to health

ICD-9-CM Procedural

31.5 Local excision or destruction of lesion or tissue of trachea

31786

31786 Excision of tracheal tumor or carcinoma; thoracic

ICD-9-CM Diagnostic

162.0 Malignant neoplasm of trachea

162.2 Malignant neoplasm of main bronchus

197.0 Secondary malignant neoplasm of lung

197.3 Secondary malignant neoplasm of other respiratory organs

209.21 Malignant carcinoid tumor of the bronchus and lung — (Code first any associated multiple endocrine neoplasia syndrome: 258.01-258.03)(Use additional code to identify associated endocrine syndrome, as: carcinoid syndrome: 259.2)

209.61 Benign carcinoid tumor of the bronchus and lung — (Code first any associated multiple endocrine neoplasia syndrome: 258.01-258.03)(Use additional code to identify associated endocrine syndrome, as: carcinoid syndrome: 259.2)

212.2 Benign neoplasm of trachea

212.3 Benign neoplasm of bronchus and lung

231.1 Carcinoma in situ of trachea

231.2 Carcinoma in situ of bronchus and lung

235.7 Neoplasm of uncertain behavior of trachea, bronchus, and lung

239.1 Neoplasm of unspecified nature of respiratory system

V15.82 Personal history of tobacco use, presenting hazards to health

ICD-9-CM Procedural

31.5 Local excision or destruction of lesion or tissue of trachea

31800

31800 Suture of tracheal wound or injury; cervical

ICD-9-CM Diagnostic

862.29 Injury to other specified intrathoracic organs without mention of open wound into cavity

862.39 Injury to other specified intrathoracic organs with open wound into cavity

874.02 Open wound of trachea, without mention of complication

874.12 Open wound of trachea, complicated

ICD-9-CM Procedural

31.71 Suture of laceration of trachea

HCPCS Level II Supplies & Services

A4305 Disposable drug delivery system, flow rate of 50 ml or greater per hour

31805

31805 Suture of tracheal wound or injury; intrathoracic

ICD-9-CM Diagnostic

862.29 Injury to other specified intrathoracic organs without mention of open wound into cavity

862.39 Injury to other specified intrathoracic organs with open wound into cavity

874.02 Open wound of trachea, without mention of complication

874.12 Open wound of trachea, complicated

ICD-9-CM Procedural

31.71 Suture of laceration of trachea

31820-31825

31820 Surgical closure tracheostomy or fistula; without plastic repair

31825 with plastic repair

ICD-9-CM Diagnostic

V44.0 Tracheostomy status

V51.8 Other aftercare involving the use of plastic surgery

V55.0 Attention to tracheostomy

ICD-9-CM Procedural

31.72 Closure of external fistula of trachea

31.79 Other repair and plastic operations on trachea

31830

31830 Revision of tracheostomy scar

ICD-9-CM Diagnostic

701.4 Keloid scar

701.5 Other abnormal granulation tissue

709.2 Scar condition and fibrosis of skin

V10.12 Personal history of malignant neoplasm of trachea

V10.21 Personal history of malignant neoplasm of larynx

V51.8 Other aftercare involving the use of plastic surgery

V58.49 Other specified aftercare following surgery — (This code should be used in conjunction with other aftercare codes to fully identify the reason for the aftercare encounter)

ICD-9-CM Procedural

86.3 Other local excision or destruction of lesion or tissue of skin and subcutaneous tissue

Lungs and Pleura

32035-32036

32035 Thoracostomy; with rib resection for empyema

32036 with open flap drainage for empyema

ICD-9-CM Diagnostic

510.0 Empyema with fistula — (Use additional code to identify infectious organism: 041.00-041.9)

510.9 Empyema without mention of fistula — (Use additional code to identify infectious organism: 041.00-041.9)

ICD-9-CM Procedural

34.09 Other incision of pleura

32096-32098

32096 Thoracotomy, with diagnostic biopsy(ies) of lung infiltrate(s) (eg, wedge, incisional), unilateral

32097 Thoracotomy, with diagnostic biopsy(ies) of lung nodule(s) or mass(es) (eg, wedge, incisional), unilateral

32098 Thoracotomy, with biopsy(ies) of pleura

ICD-9-CM Diagnostic

511.0 Pleurisy without mention of effusion or current tuberculosis — (Use additional code to identify infectious organism)

511.89 Other specified forms of effusion, except tuberculous

511.9 Unspecified pleural effusion — (Use additional code to identify infectious organism) ▽

518.89 Other diseases of lung, not elsewhere classified — (Use additional code to identify infectious organism)

786.30 Hemoptysis, unspecified ▽

786.39 Other hemoptysis

786.52 Painful respiration

786.6 Swelling, mass, or lump in chest

793.11 Solitary pulmonary nodule

793.19 Other nonspecific abnormal finding of lung field

ICD-9-CM Procedural

33.28 Open biopsy of lung

34.24 Other pleural biopsy

32100

32100 Thoracotomy; with exploration

ICD-9-CM Diagnostic

162.0 Malignant neoplasm of trachea

162.2 Malignant neoplasm of main bronchus

162.3 Malignant neoplasm of upper lobe, bronchus, or lung

162.4 Malignant neoplasm of middle lobe, bronchus, or lung

162.5 Malignant neoplasm of lower lobe, bronchus, or lung

162.8 Malignant neoplasm of other parts of bronchus or lung

162.9 Malignant neoplasm of bronchus and lung, unspecified site ▽

163.0 Malignant neoplasm of parietal pleura

163.1 Malignant neoplasm of visceral pleura

163.8 Malignant neoplasm of other specified sites of pleura

163.9 Malignant neoplasm of pleura, unspecified site ▽

164.2 Malignant neoplasm of anterior mediastinum

164.3 Malignant neoplasm of posterior mediastinum

164.8 Malignant neoplasm of other parts of mediastinum

165.8 Malignant neoplasm of other sites within the respiratory system and intrathoracic organs

165.9 Malignant neoplasm of ill-defined sites within the respiratory system

176.4 Kaposi's sarcoma of lung

195.1 Malignant neoplasm of thorax

197.0 Secondary malignant neoplasm of lung

197.1 Secondary malignant neoplasm of mediastinum

197.2 Secondary malignant neoplasm of pleura

198.89 Secondary malignant neoplasm of other specified sites

209.21 Malignant carcinoid tumor of the bronchus and lung — (Code first any associated multiple endocrine neoplasia syndrome: 258.01-258.03)(Use additional code to identify associated endocrine syndrome, as: carcinoid syndrome: 259.2)

209.61 Benign carcinoid tumor of the bronchus and lung — (Code first any associated multiple endocrine neoplasia syndrome: 258.01-258.03)(Use additional code to identify associated endocrine syndrome, as: carcinoid syndrome: 259.2)

212.3 Benign neoplasm of bronchus and lung

212.4 Benign neoplasm of pleura

212.5 Benign neoplasm of mediastinum

212.8 Benign neoplasm of other specified sites of respiratory and intrathoracic organs

231.2 Carcinoma in situ of bronchus and lung

231.9 Carcinoma in situ of respiratory system, part unspecified ▽

235.7 Neoplasm of uncertain behavior of trachea, bronchus, and lung

235.8 Neoplasm of uncertain behavior of pleura, thymus, and mediastinum

239.1 Neoplasm of unspecified nature of respiratory system

492.0 Emphysematous bleb

510.9 Empyema without mention of fistula — (Use additional code to identify infectious organism: 041.00-041.9)

511.0 Pleurisy without mention of effusion or current tuberculosis — (Use additional code to identify infectious organism)

511.1 Pleurisy with effusion, with mention of bacterial cause other than tuberculosis — (Use additional code to identify infectious organism)

511.81 Malignant pleural effusion — (Code first malignant neoplasm, if known)

511.89 Other specified forms of effusion, except tuberculous

511.9 Unspecified pleural effusion — (Use additional code to identify infectious organism) ▽

512.0 Spontaneous tension pneumothorax

512.81 Primary spontaneous pneumothorax

512.82 Secondary spontaneous pneumothorax — (Code first underlying condition, such as: 136.3, 162.3-162.9, 197.0, 277.02, 516.4, 518.3, 530.4, 617.8, 759.82))

512.83 Chronic pneumothorax

512.84 Other air leak

512.89 Other pneumothorax

513.0 Abscess of lung — (Use additional code to identify infectious organism)

515 Postinflammatory pulmonary fibrosis — (Use additional code to identify infectious organism)

516.0 Pulmonary alveolar proteinosis — (Use additional code to identify infectious organism)

516.1 Idiopathic pulmonary hemosiderosis — (Use additional code to identify infectious organism. Code first underlying disease: 275.01-275.09) ☒

516.2 Pulmonary alveolar microlithiasis — (Use additional code to identify infectious organism)

516.30 Idiopathic interstitial pneumonia, not otherwise specified

516.31 Idiopathic pulmonary fibrosis

516.32 Idiopathic non-specific interstitial pneumonitis

516.33 Acute interstitial pneumonitis

516.34 Respiratory bronchiolitis interstitial lung disease

516.35 Idiopathic lymphoid interstitial pneumonia

516.36 Cryptogenic organizing pneumonia

516.37 Desquamative interstitial pneumonia

516.4 Lymphangioleiomyomatosis ♀

516.5 Adult pulmonary Langerhans cell histiocytosis

516.61 Neuroendocrine cell hyperplasia of infancy

516.62 Pulmonary interstitial glycogenosis

516.63 Surfactant mutations of the lung

516.69 Other interstitial lung diseases of childhood

516.8 Other specified alveolar and parietoalveolar pneumonopathies — (Code first, if applicable, underlying cause of pneumonopathy, if known)(Use additional code to identify infectious organism) (Use additional E code, if applicable, for drug-induced or toxic pneumonopathy)

516.9 Unspecified alveolar and parietoalveolar pneumonopathy — (Use additional code to identify infectious organism) ▽

518.89 Other diseases of lung, not elsewhere classified — (Use additional code to identify infectious organism)

519.2 Mediastinitis — (Use additional code to identify infectious organism)

519.3 Other diseases of mediastinum, not elsewhere classified — (Use additional code to identify infectious organism)

519.8 Other diseases of respiratory system, not elsewhere classified — (Use additional code to identify infectious organism)

780.60 Fever, unspecified ▽

780.61 Fever presenting with conditions classified elsewhere — (Code first underlying condition when associated fever is present: 204-208, 282.60-282.69, 288.00-288.09) ⊠
786.09 Other dyspnea and respiratory abnormalities
786.30 Hemoptysis, unspecified ▽
786.31 Acute idiopathic pulmonary hemorrhage in infants [AIPHI]
786.39 Other hemoptysis
786.6 Swelling, mass, or lump in chest
786.9 Other symptoms involving respiratory system and chest
793.11 Solitary pulmonary nodule
793.19 Other nonspecific abnormal finding of lung field
860.2 Traumatic hemothorax without mention of open wound into thorax
860.3 Traumatic hemothorax with open wound into thorax
860.4 Traumatic pneumohemothorax without mention of open wound into thorax
860.5 Traumatic pneumohemothorax with open wound into thorax
861.22 Lung laceration without mention of open wound into thorax
861.32 Lung laceration with open wound into thorax
862.8 Injury to multiple and unspecified intrathoracic organs without mention of open wound into cavity
862.9 Injury to multiple and unspecified intrathoracic organs with open wound into cavity
908.0 Late effect of internal injury to chest

ICD-9-CM Procedural

34.02 Exploratory thoracotomy

32110

32110 Thoracotomy; with control of traumatic hemorrhage and/or repair of lung tear

ICD-9-CM Diagnostic

786.30 Hemoptysis, unspecified ▽
786.31 Acute idiopathic pulmonary hemorrhage in infants [AIPHI]
786.39 Other hemoptysis
807.10 Open fracture of rib(s), unspecified ▽
860.1 Traumatic pneumothorax with open wound into thorax
860.2 Traumatic hemothorax without mention of open wound into thorax
860.3 Traumatic hemothorax with open wound into thorax
860.4 Traumatic pneumohemothorax without mention of open wound into thorax
860.5 Traumatic pneumohemothorax with open wound into thorax
861.22 Lung laceration without mention of open wound into thorax
861.32 Lung laceration with open wound into thorax
862.1 Diaphragm injury with open wound into cavity
862.8 Injury to multiple and unspecified intrathoracic organs without mention of open wound into cavity
862.9 Injury to multiple and unspecified intrathoracic organs with open wound into cavity
901.40 Injury to unspecified pulmonary vessel(s) ▽
901.41 Pulmonary artery injury
901.42 Pulmonary vein injury
901.83 Injury to multiple blood vessels of thorax
901.89 Injury to specified blood vessels of thorax, other
926.11 Crushing injury of back — (Use additional code to identify any associated injuries: 800-829, 850.0-854.1, 860.0-869.1)
926.9 Crushing injury of unspecified site of trunk — (Use additional code to identify any associated injuries: 800-829, 850.0-854.1, 860.0-869.1) ▽
V64.42 Thorascopic surgical procedure converted to open procedure

ICD-9-CM Procedural

33.43 Closure of laceration of lung
33.49 Other repair and plastic operations on lung
33.99 Other operations on lung
34.02 Exploratory thoracotomy
34.09 Other incision of pleura
39.98 Control of hemorrhage, not otherwise specified

32120

32120 Thoracotomy; for postoperative complications

ICD-9-CM Diagnostic

199.2 Malignant neoplasm associated with transplanted organ — (Code first complication of transplanted organ (996.80-996.89) Use additional code for specific malignancy)
510.0 Empyema with fistula — (Use additional code to identify infectious organism: 041.00-041.9)
510.9 Empyema without mention of fistula — (Use additional code to identify infectious organism: 041.00-041.9)
513.0 Abscess of lung — (Use additional code to identify infectious organism)
513.1 Abscess of mediastinum — (Use additional code to identify infectious organism)
996.59 Mechanical complication due to other implant and internal device, not elsewhere classified
996.60 Infection and inflammatory reaction due to unspecified device, implant, and graft — (Use additional code to identify specified infections) ▽
996.84 Complications of transplanted lung — (Use additional code to identify nature of complication: 078.5, 199.2, 238.77, 279.50-279.53)
997.39 Other respiratory complications
998.00 Postoperative shock, unspecified ▽
998.01 Postoperative shock, cardiogenic
998.09 Postoperative shock, other
998.11 Hemorrhage complicating a procedure
998.2 Accidental puncture or laceration during procedure
998.4 Foreign body accidentally left during procedure, not elsewhere classified
998.51 Infected postoperative seroma — (Use additional code to identify organism)
998.59 Other postoperative infection — (Use additional code to identify infection)
998.6 Persistent postoperative fistula, not elsewhere classified
998.7 Acute reaction to foreign substance accidentally left during procedure, not elsewhere classified
998.9 Unspecified complication of procedure, not elsewhere classified ▽
999.2 Other vascular complications of medical care, not elsewhere classified

ICD-9-CM Procedural

34.02 Exploratory thoracotomy
34.03 Reopening of recent thoracotomy site

32124

32124 Thoracotomy; with open intrapleural pneumonolysis

ICD-9-CM Diagnostic

137.0 Late effects of respiratory or unspecified tuberculosis — (Note: This category is to be used to indicate conditions classifiable to 010-018 as the cause of late effects, which are themselves classified elsewhere. The "late effects" include those specified as such, as sequelae, or as due to old or inactive tuberculosis, without evidence of active disease.) ▽
492.8 Other emphysema
510.9 Empyema without mention of fistula — (Use additional code to identify infectious organism: 041.00-041.9)
511.0 Pleurisy without mention of effusion or current tuberculosis — (Use additional code to identify infectious organism)
512.1 Iatrogenic pneumothorax
515 Postinflammatory pulmonary fibrosis — (Use additional code to identify infectious organism)
997.39 Other respiratory complications

ICD-9-CM Procedural

33.39 Other surgical collapse of lung

32140

32140 Thoracotomy; with cyst(s) removal, includes pleural procedure when performed

ICD-9-CM Diagnostic

492.0 Emphysematous bleb
515 Postinflammatory pulmonary fibrosis — (Use additional code to identify infectious organism)
518.89 Other diseases of lung, not elsewhere classified — (Use additional code to identify infectious organism)
748.4 Congenital cystic lung

ICD-9-CM Procedural

32.23 Open ablation of lung lesion or tissue
32.26 Other and unspecified ablation of lung lesion or tissue
32.29 Other local excision or destruction of lesion or tissue of lung
33.99 Other operations on lung
34.59 Other excision of pleura

HCPCS Level II Supplies & Services

A7042 Implanted pleural catheter, each

32141

32141 Thoracotomy; with resection-plication of bullae, includes any pleural procedure when performed

ICD-9-CM Diagnostic

492.0 Emphysematous bleb
V64.42 Thorascopic surgical procedure converted to open procedure

ICD-9-CM Procedural

32.21 Plication of emphysematous bleb
32.23 Open ablation of lung lesion or tissue
32.26 Other and unspecified ablation of lung lesion or tissue
32.29 Other local excision or destruction of lesion or tissue of lung
34.59 Other excision of pleura

HCPCS Level II Supplies & Services

A7042 Implanted pleural catheter, each

32150-32151

32150 Thoracotomy; with removal of intrapleural foreign body or fibrin deposit
32151 with removal of intrapulmonary foreign body

ICD-9-CM Diagnostic

511.0 Pleurisy without mention of effusion or current tuberculosis — (Use additional code to identify infectious organism)
513.0 Abscess of lung — (Use additional code to identify infectious organism)
515 Postinflammatory pulmonary fibrosis — (Use additional code to identify infectious organism)
793.19 Other nonspecific abnormal finding of lung field
861.30 Unspecified lung injury with open wound into thorax ♥
861.31 Lung contusion with open wound into thorax
861.32 Lung laceration with open wound into thorax
862.31 Bronchus injury with open wound into cavity
862.39 Injury to other specified intrathoracic organs with open wound into cavity
934.1 Foreign body in main bronchus
934.8 Foreign body in other specified parts of trachea, bronchus, and lung
934.9 Foreign body in respiratory tree, unspecified ♥
998.4 Foreign body accidentally left during procedure, not elsewhere classified
V64.42 Thorascopic surgical procedure converted to open procedure

ICD-9-CM Procedural

33.1 Incision of lung
34.09 Other incision of pleura

32160

32160 Thoracotomy; with cardiac massage

ICD-9-CM Diagnostic

427.5 Cardiac arrest

ICD-9-CM Procedural

37.91 Open chest cardiac massage

32200

32200 Pneumonostomy, with open drainage of abscess or cyst

ICD-9-CM Diagnostic

492.0 Emphysematous bleb
510.9 Empyema without mention of fistula — (Use additional code to identify infectious organism: 041.00-041.9)
513.0 Abscess of lung — (Use additional code to identify infectious organism)
518.89 Other diseases of lung, not elsewhere classified — (Use additional code to identify infectious organism)
748.4 Congenital cystic lung
958.3 Posttraumatic wound infection not elsewhere classified
997.39 Other respiratory complications
998.59 Other postoperative infection — (Use additional code to identify infection)

ICD-9-CM Procedural

33.1 Incision of lung

32215

32215 Pleural scarification for repeat pneumothorax

ICD-9-CM Diagnostic

512.0 Spontaneous tension pneumothorax
512.1 Iatrogenic pneumothorax
512.81 Primary spontaneous pneumothorax
512.82 Secondary spontaneous pneumothorax — (Code first underlying condition, such as: 136.3, 162.3-162.9, 197.0, 277.02, 516.4, 518.3, 530.4, 617.8, 759.82))
512.83 Chronic pneumothorax
512.89 Other pneumothorax

ICD-9-CM Procedural

34.6 Scarification of pleura

HCPCS Level II Supplies & Services

A7042 Implanted pleural catheter, each

32220-32225

32220 Decortication, pulmonary (separate procedure); total
32225 partial

ICD-9-CM Diagnostic

163.0 Malignant neoplasm of parietal pleura
163.8 Malignant neoplasm of other specified sites of pleura
163.9 Malignant neoplasm of pleura, unspecified site ♥
197.2 Secondary malignant neoplasm of pleura
239.1 Neoplasm of unspecified nature of respiratory system
511.81 Malignant pleural effusion — (Code first malignant neoplasm, if known)
513.0 Abscess of lung — (Use additional code to identify infectious organism)
515 Postinflammatory pulmonary fibrosis — (Use additional code to identify infectious organism)
516.30 Idiopathic interstitial pneumonia, not otherwise specified
516.31 Idiopathic pulmonary fibrosis
516.32 Idiopathic non-specific interstitial pneumonitis
516.33 Acute interstitial pneumonitis
516.34 Respiratory bronchiolitis interstitial lung disease

516.35 Idiopathic lymphoid interstitial pneumonia
516.36 Cryptogenic organizing pneumonia
516.37 Desquamative interstitial pneumonia
V64.42 Thoracoscopic surgical procedure converted to open procedure

ICD-9-CM Procedural

34.51 Decortication of lung

32310-32320

32310 Pleurectomy, parietal (separate procedure)
32320 Decortication and parietal pleurectomy

ICD-9-CM Diagnostic

163.0 Malignant neoplasm of parietal pleura
163.8 Malignant neoplasm of other specified sites of pleura
163.9 Malignant neoplasm of pleura, unspecified site ▽
197.2 Secondary malignant neoplasm of pleura
239.1 Neoplasm of unspecified nature of respiratory system
492.0 Emphysematous bleb
510.0 Empyema with fistula — (Use additional code to identify infectious organism: 041.00-041.9)
511.0 Pleurisy without mention of effusion or current tuberculosis — (Use additional code to identify infectious organism)
511.81 Malignant pleural effusion — (Code first malignant neoplasm, if known)
512.0 Spontaneous tension pneumothorax
512.81 Primary spontaneous pneumothorax
512.82 Secondary spontaneous pneumothorax — (Code first underlying condition, such as: 136.3, 162.3-162.9, 197.0, 277.02, 516.4, 518.3, 530.4, 617.8, 759.82))
512.83 Chronic pneumothorax
512.89 Other pneumothorax
513.0 Abscess of lung — (Use additional code to identify infectious organism)
515 Postinflammatory pulmonary fibrosis — (Use additional code to identify infectious organism)
516.30 Idiopathic interstitial pneumonia, not otherwise specified
516.31 Idiopathic pulmonary fibrosis
516.32 Idiopathic non-specific interstitial pneumonitis
516.33 Acute interstitial pneumonitis
516.34 Respiratory bronchiolitis interstitial lung disease
516.35 Idiopathic lymphoid interstitial pneumonia
516.36 Cryptogenic organizing pneumonia
516.37 Desquamative interstitial pneumonia
518.89 Other diseases of lung, not elsewhere classified — (Use additional code to identify infectious organism)
V64.42 Thoracoscopic surgical procedure converted to open procedure

ICD-9-CM Procedural

34.51 Decortication of lung
34.59 Other excision of pleura

32400

32400 Biopsy, pleura; percutaneous needle

ICD-9-CM Diagnostic

163.0 Malignant neoplasm of parietal pleura
163.8 Malignant neoplasm of other specified sites of pleura
163.9 Malignant neoplasm of pleura, unspecified site ▽
197.2 Secondary malignant neoplasm of pleura
199.0 Disseminated malignant neoplasm
199.1 Other malignant neoplasm of unspecified site
199.2 Malignant neoplasm associated with transplanted organ — (Code first complication of transplanted organ (996.80-996.89) Use additional code for specific malignancy)
209.21 Malignant carcinoid tumor of the bronchus and lung — (Code first any associated multiple endocrine neoplasia syndrome: 258.01-258.03)(Use additional code to identify associated endocrine syndrome, as: carcinoid syndrome: 259.2)
209.61 Benign carcinoid tumor of the bronchus and lung — (Code first any associated multiple endocrine neoplasia syndrome: 258.01-258.03)(Use additional code to identify associated endocrine syndrome, as: carcinoid syndrome: 259.2)
212.4 Benign neoplasm of pleura
231.8 Carcinoma in situ of other specified parts of respiratory system
231.9 Carcinoma in situ of respiratory system, part unspecified ▽
235.8 Neoplasm of uncertain behavior of pleura, thymus, and mediastinum
239.1 Neoplasm of unspecified nature of respiratory system
511.81 Malignant pleural effusion — (Code first malignant neoplasm, if known)
511.89 Other specified forms of effusion, except tuberculous
518.89 Other diseases of lung, not elsewhere classified — (Use additional code to identify infectious organism)
786.09 Other dyspnea and respiratory abnormalities
786.52 Painful respiration
786.7 Abnormal chest sounds
786.9 Other symptoms involving respiratory system and chest
793.11 Solitary pulmonary nodule
793.19 Other nonspecific abnormal finding of lung field
997.39 Other respiratory complications

ICD-9-CM Procedural

34.24 Other pleural biopsy

32405

32405 Biopsy, lung or mediastinum, percutaneous needle

ICD-9-CM Diagnostic

162.2 Malignant neoplasm of main bronchus
162.3 Malignant neoplasm of upper lobe, bronchus, or lung
162.4 Malignant neoplasm of middle lobe, bronchus, or lung
162.5 Malignant neoplasm of lower lobe, bronchus, or lung
162.8 Malignant neoplasm of other parts of bronchus or lung
162.9 Malignant neoplasm of bronchus and lung, unspecified site ▽
164.2 Malignant neoplasm of anterior mediastinum
164.3 Malignant neoplasm of posterior mediastinum
164.8 Malignant neoplasm of other parts of mediastinum
164.9 Malignant neoplasm of mediastinum, part unspecified ▽
176.4 Kaposi's sarcoma of lung
195.1 Malignant neoplasm of thorax
196.1 Secondary and unspecified malignant neoplasm of intrathoracic lymph nodes
197.0 Secondary malignant neoplasm of lung
197.1 Secondary malignant neoplasm of mediastinum
209.21 Malignant carcinoid tumor of the bronchus and lung — (Code first any associated multiple endocrine neoplasia syndrome: 258.01-258.03)(Use additional code to identify associated endocrine syndrome, as: carcinoid syndrome: 259.2)
209.61 Benign carcinoid tumor of the bronchus and lung — (Code first any associated multiple endocrine neoplasia syndrome: 258.01-258.03)(Use additional code to identify associated endocrine syndrome, as: carcinoid syndrome: 259.2)
209.71 Secondary neuroendocrine tumor of distant lymph nodes
212.3 Benign neoplasm of bronchus and lung
212.5 Benign neoplasm of mediastinum
212.8 Benign neoplasm of other specified sites of respiratory and intrathoracic organs
214.2 Lipoma of intrathoracic organs
215.5 Other benign neoplasm of connective and other soft tissue of abdomen
230.1 Carcinoma in situ of esophagus
231.2 Carcinoma in situ of bronchus and lung
235.7 Neoplasm of uncertain behavior of trachea, bronchus, and lung
235.8 Neoplasm of uncertain behavior of pleura, thymus, and mediastinum

235.9 Neoplasm of uncertain behavior of other and unspecified respiratory organs ▽
239.1 Neoplasm of unspecified nature of respiratory system
239.89 Neoplasms of unspecified nature, other specified sites
482.84 Legionnaires' disease
511.0 Pleurisy without mention of effusion or current tuberculosis — (Use additional code to identify infectious organism)
516.30 Idiopathic interstitial pneumonia, not otherwise specified
516.31 Idiopathic pulmonary fibrosis
516.32 Idiopathic non-specific interstitial pneumonitis
516.33 Acute interstitial pneumonitis
516.34 Respiratory bronchiolitis interstitial lung disease
516.35 Idiopathic lymphoid interstitial pneumonia
516.36 Cryptogenic organizing pneumonia
516.37 Desquamative interstitial pneumonia
516.4 Lymphangioleiomyomatosis ♀
516.5 Adult pulmonary Langerhans cell histiocytosis
516.61 Neuroendocrine cell hyperplasia of infancy
516.62 Pulmonary interstitial glycogenosis
516.63 Surfactant mutations of the lung
516.69 Other interstitial lung diseases of childhood
518.89 Other diseases of lung, not elsewhere classified — (Use additional code to identify infectious organism)
786.09 Other dyspnea and respiratory abnormalities
786.2 Cough
786.30 Hemoptysis, unspecified ▽
786.31 Acute idiopathic pulmonary hemorrhage in infants [AIPHI]
786.39 Other hemoptysis
786.6 Swelling, mass, or lump in chest
786.7 Abnormal chest sounds
786.9 Other symptoms involving respiratory system and chest
793.11 Solitary pulmonary nodule
793.19 Other nonspecific abnormal finding of lung field
794.2 Nonspecific abnormal results of pulmonary system function study
V15.82 Personal history of tobacco use, presenting hazards to health

ICD-9-CM Procedural

33.26 Closed (percutaneous)(needle) biopsy of lung
34.25 Closed (percutaneous) (needle) biopsy of mediastinum

32440

32440 Removal of lung, pneumonectomy;

ICD-9-CM Diagnostic

162.2 Malignant neoplasm of main bronchus
162.3 Malignant neoplasm of upper lobe, bronchus, or lung
162.4 Malignant neoplasm of middle lobe, bronchus, or lung
162.5 Malignant neoplasm of lower lobe, bronchus, or lung
165.8 Malignant neoplasm of other sites within the respiratory system and intrathoracic organs
165.9 Malignant neoplasm of ill-defined sites within the respiratory system
197.0 Secondary malignant neoplasm of lung
209.21 Malignant carcinoid tumor of the bronchus and lung — (Code first any associated multiple endocrine neoplasia syndrome: 258.01-258.03)(Use additional code to identify associated endocrine syndrome, as: carcinoid syndrome: 259.2)
231.2 Carcinoma in situ of bronchus and lung
235.7 Neoplasm of uncertain behavior of trachea, bronchus, and lung
239.1 Neoplasm of unspecified nature of respiratory system
492.0 Emphysematous bleb
502 Pneumoconiosis due to other silica or silicates — (Use additional code to identify infectious organism)
513.0 Abscess of lung — (Use additional code to identify infectious organism)
514 Pulmonary congestion and hypostasis — (Use additional code to identify infectious organism)
515 Postinflammatory pulmonary fibrosis — (Use additional code to identify infectious organism)
518.89 Other diseases of lung, not elsewhere classified — (Use additional code to identify infectious organism)
786.30 Hemoptysis, unspecified ▽
786.39 Other hemoptysis

ICD-9-CM Procedural

32.59 Other and unspecified pneumonectomy

32442

32442 Removal of lung, pneumonectomy; with resection of segment of trachea followed by broncho-tracheal anastomosis (sleeve pneumonectomy)

ICD-9-CM Diagnostic

162.2 Malignant neoplasm of main bronchus
162.3 Malignant neoplasm of upper lobe, bronchus, or lung
162.4 Malignant neoplasm of middle lobe, bronchus, or lung
162.5 Malignant neoplasm of lower lobe, bronchus, or lung
162.8 Malignant neoplasm of other parts of bronchus or lung
165.8 Malignant neoplasm of other sites within the respiratory system and intrathoracic organs
165.9 Malignant neoplasm of ill-defined sites within the respiratory system
176.4 Kaposi's sarcoma of lung
197.0 Secondary malignant neoplasm of lung
198.89 Secondary malignant neoplasm of other specified sites
209.21 Malignant carcinoid tumor of the bronchus and lung — (Code first any associated multiple endocrine neoplasia syndrome: 258.01-258.03)(Use additional code to identify associated endocrine syndrome, as: carcinoid syndrome: 259.2)
231.2 Carcinoma in situ of bronchus and lung
235.7 Neoplasm of uncertain behavior of trachea, bronchus, and lung
239.1 Neoplasm of unspecified nature of respiratory system
514 Pulmonary congestion and hypostasis — (Use additional code to identify infectious organism)
515 Postinflammatory pulmonary fibrosis — (Use additional code to identify infectious organism)
V15.82 Personal history of tobacco use, presenting hazards to health

ICD-9-CM Procedural

32.59 Other and unspecified pneumonectomy
33.48 Other repair and plastic operations on bronchus

32445

32445 Removal of lung, pneumonectomy; extrapleural

ICD-9-CM Diagnostic

162.2 Malignant neoplasm of main bronchus
162.3 Malignant neoplasm of upper lobe, bronchus, or lung
162.4 Malignant neoplasm of middle lobe, bronchus, or lung
162.5 Malignant neoplasm of lower lobe, bronchus, or lung
162.8 Malignant neoplasm of other parts of bronchus or lung
165.8 Malignant neoplasm of other sites within the respiratory system and intrathoracic organs
165.9 Malignant neoplasm of ill-defined sites within the respiratory system
176.4 Kaposi's sarcoma of lung
197.0 Secondary malignant neoplasm of lung
198.89 Secondary malignant neoplasm of other specified sites

209.21 Malignant carcinoid tumor of the bronchus and lung — (Code first any associated multiple endocrine neoplasia syndrome: 258.01-258.03)(Use additional code to identify associated endocrine syndrome, as: carcinoid syndrome: 259.2)
231.2 Carcinoma in situ of bronchus and lung
235.7 Neoplasm of uncertain behavior of trachea, bronchus, and lung
239.1 Neoplasm of unspecified nature of respiratory system
514 Pulmonary congestion and hypostasis — (Use additional code to identify infectious organism)
515 Postinflammatory pulmonary fibrosis — (Use additional code to identify infectious organism)
V15.82 Personal history of tobacco use, presenting hazards to health

ICD-9-CM Procedural

32.59 Other and unspecified pneumonectomy

32480-32488

32480 Removal of lung, other than pneumonectomy; single lobe (lobectomy)
32482 2 lobes (bilobectomy)
32484 single segment (segmentectomy)
32486 with circumferential resection of segment of bronchus followed by broncho-bronchial anastomosis (sleeve lobectomy)
32488 with all remaining lung following previous removal of a portion of lung (completion pneumonectomy)

ICD-9-CM Diagnostic

162.2 Malignant neoplasm of main bronchus
162.3 Malignant neoplasm of upper lobe, bronchus, or lung
162.4 Malignant neoplasm of middle lobe, bronchus, or lung
162.5 Malignant neoplasm of lower lobe, bronchus, or lung
162.8 Malignant neoplasm of other parts of bronchus or lung
162.9 Malignant neoplasm of bronchus and lung, unspecified site ▽
176.4 Kaposi's sarcoma of lung
197.0 Secondary malignant neoplasm of lung
198.89 Secondary malignant neoplasm of other specified sites
209.21 Malignant carcinoid tumor of the bronchus and lung — (Code first any associated multiple endocrine neoplasia syndrome: 258.01-258.03)(Use additional code to identify associated endocrine syndrome, as: carcinoid syndrome: 259.2)
231.2 Carcinoma in situ of bronchus and lung
235.7 Neoplasm of uncertain behavior of trachea, bronchus, and lung
239.1 Neoplasm of unspecified nature of respiratory system
492.0 Emphysematous bleb
513.0 Abscess of lung — (Use additional code to identify infectious organism)
514 Pulmonary congestion and hypostasis — (Use additional code to identify infectious organism)
515 Postinflammatory pulmonary fibrosis — (Use additional code to identify infectious organism)
518.89 Other diseases of lung, not elsewhere classified — (Use additional code to identify infectious organism)
748.5 Congenital agenesis, hypoplasia, and dysplasia of lung
786.30 Hemoptysis, unspecified ▽
786.39 Other hemoptysis
793.11 Solitary pulmonary nodule
861.22 Lung laceration without mention of open wound into thorax
861.32 Lung laceration with open wound into thorax
862.8 Injury to multiple and unspecified intrathoracic organs without mention of open wound into cavity
862.9 Injury to multiple and unspecified intrathoracic organs with open wound into cavity
V15.82 Personal history of tobacco use, presenting hazards to health
V64.42 Thoracoscopic surgical procedure converted to open procedure

ICD-9-CM Procedural

32.1 Other excision of bronchus
32.39 Other and unspecified segmental resection of lung
32.49 Other lobectomy of lung
32.59 Other and unspecified pneumonectomy
33.48 Other repair and plastic operations on bronchus

32491

32491 Removal of lung, other than pneumonectomy; with resection-plication of emphysematous lung(s) (bullous or non-bullous) for lung volume reduction, sternal split or transthoracic approach, includes any pleural procedure, when performed

ICD-9-CM Diagnostic

492.0 Emphysematous bleb
492.8 Other emphysema

ICD-9-CM Procedural

32.21 Plication of emphysematous bleb
32.22 Lung volume reduction surgery

HCPCS Level II Supplies & Services

A7042 Implanted pleural catheter, each

32501

32501 Resection and repair of portion of bronchus (bronchoplasty) when performed at time of lobectomy or segmentectomy (List separately in addition to code for primary procedure)

ICD-9-CM Diagnostic

This is an add-on code. Refer to the corresponding primary procedure code for ICD-9-CM diagnosis code links.

ICD-9-CM Procedural

32.1 Other excision of bronchus
33.48 Other repair and plastic operations on bronchus

32503-32504

32503 Resection of apical lung tumor (eg, Pancoast tumor), including chest wall resection, rib(s) resection(s), neurovascular dissection, when performed; without chest wall reconstruction(s)
32504 with chest wall reconstruction

ICD-9-CM Diagnostic

162.3 Malignant neoplasm of upper lobe, bronchus, or lung
165.9 Malignant neoplasm of ill-defined sites within the respiratory system
195.1 Malignant neoplasm of thorax
196.1 Secondary and unspecified malignant neoplasm of intrathoracic lymph nodes
198.5 Secondary malignant neoplasm of bone and bone marrow
198.89 Secondary malignant neoplasm of other specified sites
209.21 Malignant carcinoid tumor of the bronchus and lung — (Code first any associated multiple endocrine neoplasia syndrome: 258.01-258.03)(Use additional code to identify associated endocrine syndrome, as: carcinoid syndrome: 259.2)
V15.82 Personal history of tobacco use, presenting hazards to health

ICD-9-CM Procedural

32.6 Radical dissection of thoracic structures
34.79 Other repair of chest wall

32505-32507

32505 Thoracotomy; with therapeutic wedge resection (eg, mass, nodule), initial
32506 with therapeutic wedge resection (eg, mass or nodule), each additional resection, ipsilateral (List separately in addition to code for primary procedure)
32507 with diagnostic wedge resection followed by anatomic lung resection (List separately in addition to code for primary procedure)

ICD-9-CM Diagnostic

162.3 Malignant neoplasm of upper lobe, bronchus, or lung

162.4 Malignant neoplasm of middle lobe, bronchus, or lung
162.5 Malignant neoplasm of lower lobe, bronchus, or lung
162.8 Malignant neoplasm of other parts of bronchus or lung
162.9 Malignant neoplasm of bronchus and lung, unspecified site ▽
197.0 Secondary malignant neoplasm of lung
212.3 Benign neoplasm of bronchus and lung
231.2 Carcinoma in situ of bronchus and lung
235.7 Neoplasm of uncertain behavior of trachea, bronchus, and lung
239.1 Neoplasm of unspecified nature of respiratory system
518.89 Other diseases of lung, not elsewhere classified — (Use additional code to identify infectious organism)
786.6 Swelling, mass, or lump in chest
793.11 Solitary pulmonary nodule
793.19 Other nonspecific abnormal finding of lung field

ICD-9-CM Procedural

32.29 Other local excision or destruction of lesion or tissue of lung

32540

32540 Extrapleural enucleation of empyema (empyemectomy)

ICD-9-CM Diagnostic

510.0 Empyema with fistula — (Use additional code to identify infectious organism: 041.00-041.9)
510.9 Empyema without mention of fistula — (Use additional code to identify infectious organism: 041.00-041.9)

ICD-9-CM Procedural

34.3 Excision or destruction of lesion or tissue of mediastinum

32550

32550 Insertion of indwelling tunneled pleural catheter with cuff

ICD-9-CM Diagnostic

162.2 Malignant neoplasm of main bronchus
162.3 Malignant neoplasm of upper lobe, bronchus, or lung
162.4 Malignant neoplasm of middle lobe, bronchus, or lung
162.5 Malignant neoplasm of lower lobe, bronchus, or lung
162.8 Malignant neoplasm of other parts of bronchus or lung
162.9 Malignant neoplasm of bronchus and lung, unspecified site ▽
163.0 Malignant neoplasm of parietal pleura
163.1 Malignant neoplasm of visceral pleura
163.8 Malignant neoplasm of other specified sites of pleura
163.9 Malignant neoplasm of pleura, unspecified site ▽
164.8 Malignant neoplasm of other parts of mediastinum
165.8 Malignant neoplasm of other sites within the respiratory system and intrathoracic organs
165.9 Malignant neoplasm of ill-defined sites within the respiratory system
197.0 Secondary malignant neoplasm of lung
197.1 Secondary malignant neoplasm of mediastinum
197.2 Secondary malignant neoplasm of pleura
197.3 Secondary malignant neoplasm of other respiratory organs
209.21 Malignant carcinoid tumor of the bronchus and lung — (Code first any associated multiple endocrine neoplasia syndrome: 258.01-258.03)(Use additional code to identify associated endocrine syndrome, as: carcinoid syndrome: 259.2)
231.2 Carcinoma in situ of bronchus and lung
231.8 Carcinoma in situ of other specified parts of respiratory system
231.9 Carcinoma in situ of respiratory system, part unspecified ▽
235.7 Neoplasm of uncertain behavior of trachea, bronchus, and lung
235.8 Neoplasm of uncertain behavior of pleura, thymus, and mediastinum
235.9 Neoplasm of uncertain behavior of other and unspecified respiratory organs ▽
239.1 Neoplasm of unspecified nature of respiratory system
511.81 Malignant pleural effusion — (Code first malignant neoplasm, if known)

ICD-9-CM Procedural

34.04 Insertion of intercostal catheter for drainage
34.09 Other incision of pleura

HCPCS Level II Supplies & Services

A7042 Implanted pleural catheter, each

32551

32551 Tube thoracostomy, includes connection to drainage system (eg, water seal), when performed, open (separate procedure)

ICD-9-CM Diagnostic

482.84 Legionnaires' disease
486 Pneumonia, organism unspecified ▽
510.0 Empyema with fistula — (Use additional code to identify infectious organism: 041.00-041.9)
510.9 Empyema without mention of fistula — (Use additional code to identify infectious organism: 041.00-041.9)
512.0 Spontaneous tension pneumothorax
512.1 Iatrogenic pneumothorax
512.81 Primary spontaneous pneumothorax
512.82 Secondary spontaneous pneumothorax — (Code first underlying condition, such as: 136.3, 162.3-162.9, 197.0, 277.02, 516.4, 518.3, 530.4, 617.8, 759.82))
512.83 Chronic pneumothorax
512.89 Other pneumothorax
513.0 Abscess of lung — (Use additional code to identify infectious organism)
513.1 Abscess of mediastinum — (Use additional code to identify infectious organism)
518.0 Pulmonary collapse
518.51 Acute respiratory failure following trauma and surgery
518.52 Other pulmonary insufficiency, not elsewhere classified, following trauma and surgery
518.53 Acute and chronic respiratory failure following trauma and surgery
770.3 Pulmonary hemorrhage of fetus or newborn — (Use additional code(s) to further specify condition)
770.5 Other and unspecified atelectasis of newborn — (Use additional code(s) to further specify condition) ▽
786.09 Other dyspnea and respiratory abnormalities
860.0 Traumatic pneumothorax without mention of open wound into thorax
860.1 Traumatic pneumothorax with open wound into thorax
860.2 Traumatic hemothorax without mention of open wound into thorax
860.3 Traumatic hemothorax with open wound into thorax
860.4 Traumatic pneumohemothorax without mention of open wound into thorax
862.29 Injury to other specified intrathoracic organs without mention of open wound into cavity
862.39 Injury to other specified intrathoracic organs with open wound into cavity
862.8 Injury to multiple and unspecified intrathoracic organs without mention of open wound into cavity
862.9 Injury to multiple and unspecified intrathoracic organs with open wound into cavity
958.3 Posttraumatic wound infection not elsewhere classified

ICD-9-CM Procedural

34.04 Insertion of intercostal catheter for drainage

32552

32552 Removal of indwelling tunneled pleural catheter with cuff

ICD-9-CM Diagnostic

162.2 Malignant neoplasm of main bronchus
162.3 Malignant neoplasm of upper lobe, bronchus, or lung
162.4 Malignant neoplasm of middle lobe, bronchus, or lung

162.5 Malignant neoplasm of lower lobe, bronchus, or lung
162.8 Malignant neoplasm of other parts of bronchus or lung
162.9 Malignant neoplasm of bronchus and lung, unspecified site ▽
163.0 Malignant neoplasm of parietal pleura
163.1 Malignant neoplasm of visceral pleura
163.8 Malignant neoplasm of other specified sites of pleura
163.9 Malignant neoplasm of pleura, unspecified site ▽
164.8 Malignant neoplasm of other parts of mediastinum
165.8 Malignant neoplasm of other sites within the respiratory system and intrathoracic organs
165.9 Malignant neoplasm of ill-defined sites within the respiratory system
197.0 Secondary malignant neoplasm of lung
197.1 Secondary malignant neoplasm of mediastinum
197.2 Secondary malignant neoplasm of pleura
197.3 Secondary malignant neoplasm of other respiratory organs
209.21 Malignant carcinoid tumor of the bronchus and lung — (Code first any associated multiple endocrine neoplasia syndrome: 258.01-258.03)(Use additional code to identify associated endocrine syndrome, as: carcinoid syndrome: 259.2)
231.2 Carcinoma in situ of bronchus and lung
231.8 Carcinoma in situ of other specified parts of respiratory system
231.9 Carcinoma in situ of respiratory system, part unspecified ▽
235.7 Neoplasm of uncertain behavior of trachea, bronchus, and lung
235.8 Neoplasm of uncertain behavior of pleura, thymus, and mediastinum
235.9 Neoplasm of uncertain behavior of other and unspecified respiratory organs ▽
239.1 Neoplasm of unspecified nature of respiratory system
511.81 Malignant pleural effusion — (Code first malignant neoplasm, if known)

ICD-9-CM Procedural

97.41 Removal of thoracotomy tube or pleural cavity drain

32553

32553 Placement of interstitial device(s) for radiation therapy guidance (eg, fiducial markers, dosimeter), percutaneous, intra-thoracic, single or multiple

ICD-9-CM Diagnostic

162.0 Malignant neoplasm of trachea
162.2 Malignant neoplasm of main bronchus
162.3 Malignant neoplasm of upper lobe, bronchus, or lung
162.4 Malignant neoplasm of middle lobe, bronchus, or lung
162.5 Malignant neoplasm of lower lobe, bronchus, or lung
162.8 Malignant neoplasm of other parts of bronchus or lung
162.9 Malignant neoplasm of bronchus and lung, unspecified site ▽
163.0 Malignant neoplasm of parietal pleura
163.1 Malignant neoplasm of visceral pleura
163.8 Malignant neoplasm of other specified sites of pleura
163.9 Malignant neoplasm of pleura, unspecified site ▽
165.0 Malignant neoplasm of upper respiratory tract, part unspecified ▽
165.8 Malignant neoplasm of other sites within the respiratory system and intrathoracic organs
165.9 Malignant neoplasm of ill-defined sites within the respiratory system
176.4 Kaposi's sarcoma of lung
195.1 Malignant neoplasm of thorax
197.0 Secondary malignant neoplasm of lung
197.2 Secondary malignant neoplasm of pleura
198.89 Secondary malignant neoplasm of other specified sites
209.21 Malignant carcinoid tumor of the bronchus and lung — (Code first any associated multiple endocrine neoplasia syndrome: 258.01-258.03)(Use additional code to identify associated endocrine syndrome, as: carcinoid syndrome: 259.2)
209.61 Benign carcinoid tumor of the bronchus and lung — (Code first any associated multiple endocrine neoplasia syndrome: 258.01-258.03)(Use additional code to identify associated endocrine syndrome, as: carcinoid syndrome: 259.2)
209.70 Secondary neuroendocrine tumor, unspecified site ▽
212.3 Benign neoplasm of bronchus and lung
212.4 Benign neoplasm of pleura
229.8 Benign neoplasm of other specified sites
231.2 Carcinoma in situ of bronchus and lung
234.8 Carcinoma in situ of other specified sites
235.7 Neoplasm of uncertain behavior of trachea, bronchus, and lung
235.8 Neoplasm of uncertain behavior of pleura, thymus, and mediastinum
238.8 Neoplasm of uncertain behavior of other specified sites
239.1 Neoplasm of unspecified nature of respiratory system
239.89 Neoplasms of unspecified nature, other specified sites

ICD-9-CM Procedural

34.99 Other operations on thorax

HCPCS Level II Supplies & Services

A4648 Tissue marker, implantable, any type, each
A4650 Implantable radiation dosimeter, each

32554-32555

32554 Thoracentesis, needle or catheter, aspiration of the pleural space; without imaging guidance
32555 with imaging guidance

ICD-9-CM Diagnostic

010.10 Tuberculous pleurisy in primary progressive tuberculosis, confirmation unspecified ▽
010.11 Tuberculous pleurisy in primary progressive tuberculosis, bacteriological or histological examination not done
010.12 Tuberculous pleurisy in primary progressive tuberculosis, bacteriological or histological examination results unknown (at present)
010.13 Tuberculous pleurisy in primary progressive tuberculosis, tubercle bacilli found (in sputum) by microscopy
010.14 Tuberculous pleurisy in primary progressive tuberculosis, tubercle bacilli not found (in sputum) by microscopy, but found by bacterial culture
010.15 Tuberculous pleurisy in primary progressive tuberculosis, tubercle bacilli not found by bacteriological examination, but tuberculosis confirmed histologically
010.16 Tuberculous pleurisy in primary progressive tuberculosis, tubercle bacilli not found by bacteriological or histological examination, but tuberculosis confirmed by other methods [inoculation of animals]
012.00 Tuberculous pleurisy, confirmation unspecified ▽
012.01 Tuberculous pleurisy, bacteriological or histological examination not done
012.02 Tuberculous pleurisy, bacteriological or histological examination unknown (at present)
012.03 Tuberculous pleurisy, tubercle bacilli found (in sputum) by microscopy
012.04 Tuberculous pleurisy, tubercle bacilli not found (in sputum) by microscopy, but found by bacterial culture
012.05 Tuberculous pleurisy, tubercle bacilli not found by bacteriological examination, but tuberculosis confirmed histologically
012.06 Tuberculous pleurisy, tubercle bacilli not found by bacteriological or histological examination, but tuberculosis confirmed by other methods [inoculation of animals]
457.8 Other noninfectious disorders of lymphatic channels
510.9 Empyema without mention of fistula — (Use additional code to identify infectious organism: 041.00-041.9)
511.1 Pleurisy with effusion, with mention of bacterial cause other than tuberculosis — (Use additional code to identify infectious organism)
511.81 Malignant pleural effusion — (Code first malignant neoplasm, if known)
511.89 Other specified forms of effusion, except tuberculous
511.9 Unspecified pleural effusion — (Use additional code to identify infectious organism) ▽
517.8 Lung involvement in other diseases classified elsewhere — (Use additional code to identify infectious organism. Code first underlying disease: 135, 277.30-277.39, 710.0, 710.2, 710.4) ☒
530.4 Perforation of esophagus

710.0 Systemic lupus erythematosus — (Use additional code to identify manifestation: 424.91, 581.81, 582.81, 583.81)
862.29 Injury to other specified intrathoracic organs without mention of open wound into cavity
862.39 Injury to other specified intrathoracic organs with open wound into cavity
997.39 Other respiratory complications

ICD-9-CM Procedural

34.91 Thoracentesis

32556-32557

32556 Pleural drainage, percutaneous, with insertion of indwelling catheter; without imaging guidance
32557 with imaging guidance

ICD-9-CM Diagnostic

457.8 Other noninfectious disorders of lymphatic channels
510.9 Empyema without mention of fistula — (Use additional code to identify infectious organism: 041.00-041.9)
511.1 Pleurisy with effusion, with mention of bacterial cause other than tuberculosis — (Use additional code to identify infectious organism)
511.89 Other specified forms of effusion, except tuberculous
511.9 Unspecified pleural effusion — (Use additional code to identify infectious organism) ▽
512.0 Spontaneous tension pneumothorax
512.1 Iatrogenic pneumothorax
512.81 Primary spontaneous pneumothorax
512.82 Secondary spontaneous pneumothorax — (Code first underlying condition, such as: 136.3, 162.3-162.9, 197.0, 277.02, 516.4, 518.3, 530.4, 617.8, 759.82))
512.83 Chronic pneumothorax
512.84 Other air leak
512.89 Other pneumothorax
517.8 Lung involvement in other diseases classified elsewhere — (Use additional code to identify infectious organism. Code first underlying disease: 135, 277.30-277.39, 710.0, 710.2, 710.4) ☒
710.0 Systemic lupus erythematosus — (Use additional code to identify manifestation: 424.91, 581.81, 582.81, 583.81)
860.0 Traumatic pneumothorax without mention of open wound into thorax
860.1 Traumatic pneumothorax with open wound into thorax
860.2 Traumatic hemothorax without mention of open wound into thorax
860.3 Traumatic hemothorax with open wound into thorax
860.4 Traumatic pneumohemothorax without mention of open wound into thorax
860.5 Traumatic pneumohemothorax with open wound into thorax
997.39 Other respiratory complications

ICD-9-CM Procedural

34.04 Insertion of intercostal catheter for drainage

32560

32560 Instillation, via chest tube/catheter, agent for pleurodesis (eg, talc for recurrent or persistent pneumothorax)

ICD-9-CM Diagnostic

277.00 Cystic fibrosis without mention of meconium ileus — (Use additional code to identify any associated intellectual disabilities)
277.02 Cystic fibrosis with pulmonary manifestations — (Use additional code to identify any associated intellectual disabilities.) (Use additional code to identify any infectious organism present, such as 041.7)
277.03 Cystic fibrosis with gastrointestinal manifestations — (Use additional code to identify any associated intellectual disabilities)
277.09 Cystic fibrosis with other manifestations — (Use additional code to identify any associated intellectual disabilities)
492.0 Emphysematous bleb
510.0 Empyema with fistula — (Use additional code to identify infectious organism: 041.00-041.9)
511.0 Pleurisy without mention of effusion or current tuberculosis — (Use additional code to identify infectious organism)
512.0 Spontaneous tension pneumothorax
512.1 Iatrogenic pneumothorax
512.2 Postoperative air leak
512.81 Primary spontaneous pneumothorax
512.82 Secondary spontaneous pneumothorax — (Code first underlying condition, such as: 136.3, 162.3-162.9, 197.0, 277.02, 516.4, 518.3, 530.4, 617.8, 759.82))
512.83 Chronic pneumothorax
512.84 Other air leak
512.89 Other pneumothorax
518.89 Other diseases of lung, not elsewhere classified — (Use additional code to identify infectious organism)
786.09 Other dyspnea and respiratory abnormalities
786.50 Chest pain, unspecified ▽
786.52 Painful respiration
786.7 Abnormal chest sounds

ICD-9-CM Procedural

34.92 Injection into thoracic cavity

32561-32562

32561 Instillation(s), via chest tube/catheter, agent for fibrinolysis (eg, fibrinolytic agent for break up of multiloculated effusion); initial day
32562 subsequent day

ICD-9-CM Diagnostic

012.00 Tuberculous pleurisy, confirmation unspecified ▽
012.01 Tuberculous pleurisy, bacteriological or histological examination not done
012.02 Tuberculous pleurisy, bacteriological or histological examination unknown (at present)
012.03 Tuberculous pleurisy, tubercle bacilli found (in sputum) by microscopy
012.04 Tuberculous pleurisy, tubercle bacilli not found (in sputum) by microscopy, but found by bacterial culture
012.05 Tuberculous pleurisy, tubercle bacilli not found by bacteriological examination, but tuberculosis confirmed histologically
012.06 Tuberculous pleurisy, tubercle bacilli not found by bacteriological or histological examination, but tuberculosis confirmed by other methods [inoculation of animals]
510.0 Empyema with fistula — (Use additional code to identify infectious organism: 041.00-041.9)
510.9 Empyema without mention of fistula — (Use additional code to identify infectious organism: 041.00-041.9)
511.1 Pleurisy with effusion, with mention of bacterial cause other than tuberculosis — (Use additional code to identify infectious organism)
511.81 Malignant pleural effusion — (Code first malignant neoplasm, if known)
511.89 Other specified forms of effusion, except tuberculous
511.9 Unspecified pleural effusion — (Use additional code to identify infectious organism) ▽

ICD-9-CM Procedural

34.92 Injection into thoracic cavity
99.10 Injection or infusion of thrombolytic agent

32601

32601 Thoracoscopy, diagnostic (separate procedure); lungs, pericardial sac, mediastinal or pleural space, without biopsy

ICD-9-CM Diagnostic

162.0 Malignant neoplasm of trachea
162.2 Malignant neoplasm of main bronchus
162.3 Malignant neoplasm of upper lobe, bronchus, or lung
162.4 Malignant neoplasm of middle lobe, bronchus, or lung

162.5 Malignant neoplasm of lower lobe, bronchus, or lung
162.8 Malignant neoplasm of other parts of bronchus or lung
162.9 Malignant neoplasm of bronchus and lung, unspecified site ▽
163.0 Malignant neoplasm of parietal pleura
163.1 Malignant neoplasm of visceral pleura
163.8 Malignant neoplasm of other specified sites of pleura
163.9 Malignant neoplasm of pleura, unspecified site ▽
165.0 Malignant neoplasm of upper respiratory tract, part unspecified ▽
165.8 Malignant neoplasm of other sites within the respiratory system and intrathoracic organs
165.9 Malignant neoplasm of ill-defined sites within the respiratory system
176.4 Kaposi's sarcoma of lung
195.1 Malignant neoplasm of thorax
197.0 Secondary malignant neoplasm of lung
197.2 Secondary malignant neoplasm of pleura
198.89 Secondary malignant neoplasm of other specified sites
209.21 Malignant carcinoid tumor of the bronchus and lung — (Code first any associated multiple endocrine neoplasia syndrome: 258.01-258.03)(Use additional code to identify associated endocrine syndrome, as: carcinoid syndrome: 259.2)
209.61 Benign carcinoid tumor of the bronchus and lung — (Code first any associated multiple endocrine neoplasia syndrome: 258.01-258.03)(Use additional code to identify associated endocrine syndrome, as: carcinoid syndrome: 259.2)
209.70 Secondary neuroendocrine tumor, unspecified site ▽
212.3 Benign neoplasm of bronchus and lung
212.4 Benign neoplasm of pleura
229.8 Benign neoplasm of other specified sites
231.2 Carcinoma in situ of bronchus and lung
234.8 Carcinoma in situ of other specified sites
235.7 Neoplasm of uncertain behavior of trachea, bronchus, and lung
235.8 Neoplasm of uncertain behavior of pleura, thymus, and mediastinum
238.8 Neoplasm of uncertain behavior of other specified sites
239.1 Neoplasm of unspecified nature of respiratory system
239.89 Neoplasms of unspecified nature, other specified sites
492.0 Emphysematous bleb
510.9 Empyema without mention of fistula — (Use additional code to identify infectious organism: 041.00-041.9)
511.0 Pleurisy without mention of effusion or current tuberculosis — (Use additional code to identify infectious organism)
511.1 Pleurisy with effusion, with mention of bacterial cause other than tuberculosis — (Use additional code to identify infectious organism)
511.81 Malignant pleural effusion — (Code first malignant neoplasm, if known)
511.89 Other specified forms of effusion, except tuberculous
511.9 Unspecified pleural effusion — (Use additional code to identify infectious organism) ▽
512.81 Primary spontaneous pneumothorax
512.82 Secondary spontaneous pneumothorax — (Code first underlying condition, such as: 136.3, 162.3-162.9, 197.0, 277.02, 516.4, 518.3, 530.4, 617.8, 759.82))
512.83 Chronic pneumothorax
512.84 Other air leak
512.89 Other pneumothorax
513.0 Abscess of lung — (Use additional code to identify infectious organism)
515 Postinflammatory pulmonary fibrosis — (Use additional code to identify infectious organism)
516.0 Pulmonary alveolar proteinosis — (Use additional code to identify infectious organism)
516.1 Idiopathic pulmonary hemosiderosis — (Use additional code to identify infectious organism. Code first underlying disease: 275.01-275.09) ☒
516.2 Pulmonary alveolar microlithiasis — (Use additional code to identify infectious organism)
516.30 Idiopathic interstitial pneumonia, not otherwise specified
516.31 Idiopathic pulmonary fibrosis
516.8 Other specified alveolar and parietoalveolar pneumonopathies — (Code first, if applicable, underlying cause of pneumonopathy, if known)(Use additional code to identify infectious organism) (Use additional E code, if applicable, for drug-induced or toxic pneumonopathy)
516.9 Unspecified alveolar and parietoalveolar pneumonopathy — (Use additional code to identify infectious organism) ▽
518.83 Chronic respiratory failure
518.89 Other diseases of lung, not elsewhere classified — (Use additional code to identify infectious organism)
519.8 Other diseases of respiratory system, not elsewhere classified — (Use additional code to identify infectious organism)
780.60 Fever, unspecified ▽
780.61 Fever presenting with conditions classified elsewhere — (Code first underlying condition when associated fever is present: 204-208, 282.60-282.69, 288.00-288.09) ☒
786.09 Other dyspnea and respiratory abnormalities
786.30 Hemoptysis, unspecified ▽
786.31 Acute idiopathic pulmonary hemorrhage in infants [AIPHI]
786.39 Other hemoptysis
786.59 Chest pain, other
786.6 Swelling, mass, or lump in chest
786.9 Other symptoms involving respiratory system and chest
793.11 Solitary pulmonary nodule
793.19 Other nonspecific abnormal finding of lung field
908.0 Late effect of internal injury to chest
V15.82 Personal history of tobacco use, presenting hazards to health

ICD-9-CM Procedural

34.21 Transpleural thoracoscopy

HCPCS Level II Supplies & Services

A7042 Implanted pleural catheter, each

32604

32604 Thoracoscopy, diagnostic (separate procedure); pericardial sac, with biopsy

ICD-9-CM Diagnostic

164.1 Malignant neoplasm of heart
164.8 Malignant neoplasm of other parts of mediastinum
198.89 Secondary malignant neoplasm of other specified sites
209.70 Secondary neuroendocrine tumor, unspecified site ▽
209.79 Secondary neuroendocrine tumor of other sites
212.7 Benign neoplasm of heart
238.8 Neoplasm of uncertain behavior of other specified sites
239.89 Neoplasms of unspecified nature, other specified sites
391.0 Acute rheumatic pericarditis
392.0 Rheumatic chorea with heart involvement
393 Chronic rheumatic pericarditis
411.0 Postmyocardial infarction syndrome — (Use additional code to identify presence of hypertension: 401.0-405.9)
420.0 Acute pericarditis in diseases classified elsewhere — (Code first underlying disease: 006.8, 017.9, 039.8, 585.9, 586) ☒
420.90 Unspecified acute pericarditis ▽
420.91 Acute idiopathic pericarditis
420.99 Other acute pericarditis
423.0 Hemopericardium
423.1 Adhesive pericarditis
423.2 Constrictive pericarditis
423.8 Other specified diseases of pericardium
423.9 Unspecified disease of pericardium ▽
429.3 Cardiomegaly

786.59 Chest pain, other
861.01 Heart contusion without mention of open wound into thorax

ICD-9-CM Procedural

34.21 Transpleural thoracoscopy
37.24 Biopsy of pericardium

32606

32606 Thoracoscopy, diagnostic (separate procedure); mediastinal space, with biopsy

ICD-9-CM Diagnostic

164.2 Malignant neoplasm of anterior mediastinum
164.3 Malignant neoplasm of posterior mediastinum
164.8 Malignant neoplasm of other parts of mediastinum
164.9 Malignant neoplasm of mediastinum, part unspecified ▽
195.1 Malignant neoplasm of thorax
197.1 Secondary malignant neoplasm of mediastinum
209.70 Secondary neuroendocrine tumor, unspecified site ▽
209.79 Secondary neuroendocrine tumor of other sites
212.5 Benign neoplasm of mediastinum
235.8 Neoplasm of uncertain behavior of pleura, thymus, and mediastinum
239.89 Neoplasms of unspecified nature, other specified sites
786.59 Chest pain, other
996.00 Mechanical complication of unspecified cardiac device, implant, and graft ▽

ICD-9-CM Procedural

34.22 Mediastinoscopy
34.25 Closed (percutaneous) (needle) biopsy of mediastinum

32607-32609

32607 Thoracoscopy; with diagnostic biopsy(ies) of lung infiltrate(s) (eg, wedge, incisional), unilateral
32608 with diagnostic biopsy(ies) of lung nodule(s) or mass(es) (eg, wedge, incisional), unilateral
32609 with biopsy(ies) of pleura

ICD-9-CM Diagnostic

511.0 Pleurisy without mention of effusion or current tuberculosis — (Use additional code to identify infectious organism)
511.89 Other specified forms of effusion, except tuberculous
511.9 Unspecified pleural effusion — (Use additional code to identify infectious organism) ▽
518.89 Other diseases of lung, not elsewhere classified — (Use additional code to identify infectious organism)
786.30 Hemoptysis, unspecified ▽
786.39 Other hemoptysis
786.52 Painful respiration
786.6 Swelling, mass, or lump in chest
793.11 Solitary pulmonary nodule
793.19 Other nonspecific abnormal finding of lung field

ICD-9-CM Procedural

33.20 Thoracoscopic lung biopsy
34.24 Other pleural biopsy

32650

32650 Thoracoscopy, surgical; with pleurodesis (eg, mechanical or chemical)

ICD-9-CM Diagnostic

163.0 Malignant neoplasm of parietal pleura
235.8 Neoplasm of uncertain behavior of pleura, thymus, and mediastinum
277.00 Cystic fibrosis without mention of meconium ileus — (Use additional code to identify any associated intellectual disabilities)
277.02 Cystic fibrosis with pulmonary manifestations — (Use additional code to identify any associated intellectual disabilities.) (Use additional code to identify any infectious organism present, such as 041.7)
277.03 Cystic fibrosis with gastrointestinal manifestations — (Use additional code to identify any associated intellectual disabilities)
277.09 Cystic fibrosis with other manifestations — (Use additional code to identify any associated intellectual disabilities)
492.0 Emphysematous bleb
510.0 Empyema with fistula — (Use additional code to identify infectious organism: 041.00-041.9)
511.0 Pleurisy without mention of effusion or current tuberculosis — (Use additional code to identify infectious organism)
512.0 Spontaneous tension pneumothorax
512.1 Iatrogenic pneumothorax
512.2 Postoperative air leak
512.81 Primary spontaneous pneumothorax
512.82 Secondary spontaneous pneumothorax — (Code first underlying condition, such as: 136.3, 162.3-162.9, 197.0, 277.02, 516.4, 518.3, 530.4, 617.8, 759.82))
512.83 Chronic pneumothorax
512.84 Other air leak
512.89 Other pneumothorax
518.89 Other diseases of lung, not elsewhere classified — (Use additional code to identify infectious organism)
786.09 Other dyspnea and respiratory abnormalities
786.50 Chest pain, unspecified ▽
786.52 Painful respiration
786.7 Abnormal chest sounds

ICD-9-CM Procedural

34.6 Scarification of pleura
34.92 Injection into thoracic cavity

32651-32652

32651 Thoracoscopy, surgical; with partial pulmonary decortication
32652 with total pulmonary decortication, including intrapleural pneumonolysis

ICD-9-CM Diagnostic

163.0 Malignant neoplasm of parietal pleura
163.8 Malignant neoplasm of other specified sites of pleura
163.9 Malignant neoplasm of pleura, unspecified site ▽
197.2 Secondary malignant neoplasm of pleura
239.1 Neoplasm of unspecified nature of respiratory system
492.0 Emphysematous bleb
510.0 Empyema with fistula — (Use additional code to identify infectious organism: 041.00-041.9)
511.0 Pleurisy without mention of effusion or current tuberculosis — (Use additional code to identify infectious organism)
511.81 Malignant pleural effusion — (Code first malignant neoplasm, if known)
512.0 Spontaneous tension pneumothorax
512.1 Iatrogenic pneumothorax
512.81 Primary spontaneous pneumothorax
512.82 Secondary spontaneous pneumothorax — (Code first underlying condition, such as: 136.3, 162.3-162.9, 197.0, 277.02, 516.4, 518.3, 530.4, 617.8, 759.82))
512.83 Chronic pneumothorax
512.89 Other pneumothorax
513.0 Abscess of lung — (Use additional code to identify infectious organism)
515 Postinflammatory pulmonary fibrosis — (Use additional code to identify infectious organism)
516.30 Idiopathic interstitial pneumonia, not otherwise specified
516.31 Idiopathic pulmonary fibrosis
516.32 Idiopathic non-specific interstitial pneumonitis

516.33 Acute interstitial pneumonitis

516.34 Respiratory bronchiolitis interstitial lung disease

516.35 Idiopathic lymphoid interstitial pneumonia

516.36 Cryptogenic organizing pneumonia

516.37 Desquamative interstitial pneumonia

518.89 Other diseases of lung, not elsewhere classified — (Use additional code to identify infectious organism)

ICD-9-CM Procedural

33.39 Other surgical collapse of lung

34.51 Decortication of lung

32653

32653 Thoracoscopy, surgical; with removal of intrapleural foreign body or fibrin deposit

ICD-9-CM Diagnostic

511.0 Pleurisy without mention of effusion or current tuberculosis — (Use additional code to identify infectious organism)

513.0 Abscess of lung — (Use additional code to identify infectious organism)

515 Postinflammatory pulmonary fibrosis — (Use additional code to identify infectious organism)

516.30 Idiopathic interstitial pneumonia, not otherwise specified

516.31 Idiopathic pulmonary fibrosis

516.32 Idiopathic non-specific interstitial pneumonitis

516.33 Acute interstitial pneumonitis

516.34 Respiratory bronchiolitis interstitial lung disease

516.35 Idiopathic lymphoid interstitial pneumonia

516.36 Cryptogenic organizing pneumonia

516.37 Desquamative interstitial pneumonia

793.19 Other nonspecific abnormal finding of lung field

861.30 Unspecified lung injury with open wound into thorax ▽

861.31 Lung contusion with open wound into thorax

861.32 Lung laceration with open wound into thorax

934.8 Foreign body in other specified parts of trachea, bronchus, and lung

998.4 Foreign body accidentally left during procedure, not elsewhere classified

ICD-9-CM Procedural

34.09 Other incision of pleura

32654

32654 Thoracoscopy, surgical; with control of traumatic hemorrhage

ICD-9-CM Diagnostic

786.30 Hemoptysis, unspecified ▽

786.31 Acute idiopathic pulmonary hemorrhage in infants [AIPHI]

786.39 Other hemoptysis

807.10 Open fracture of rib(s), unspecified ▽

860.1 Traumatic pneumothorax with open wound into thorax

860.3 Traumatic hemothorax with open wound into thorax

860.5 Traumatic pneumohemothorax with open wound into thorax

861.22 Lung laceration without mention of open wound into thorax

861.32 Lung laceration with open wound into thorax

862.1 Diaphragm injury with open wound into cavity

901.40 Injury to unspecified pulmonary vessel(s) ▽

901.41 Pulmonary artery injury

901.42 Pulmonary vein injury

901.83 Injury to multiple blood vessels of thorax

901.89 Injury to specified blood vessels of thorax, other

926.11 Crushing injury of back — (Use additional code to identify any associated injuries: 800-829, 850.0-854.1, 860.0-869.1)

926.9 Crushing injury of unspecified site of trunk — (Use additional code to identify any associated injuries: 800-829, 850.0-854.1, 860.0-869.1) ▽

ICD-9-CM Procedural

34.03 Reopening of recent thoracotomy site

34.09 Other incision of pleura

32655-32656

32655 Thoracoscopy, surgical; with resection-plication of bullae, includes any pleural procedure when performed

32656 with parietal pleurectomy

ICD-9-CM Diagnostic

163.0 Malignant neoplasm of parietal pleura

163.8 Malignant neoplasm of other specified sites of pleura

163.9 Malignant neoplasm of pleura, unspecified site ▽

492.0 Emphysematous bleb

515 Postinflammatory pulmonary fibrosis — (Use additional code to identify infectious organism)

518.89 Other diseases of lung, not elsewhere classified — (Use additional code to identify infectious organism)

ICD-9-CM Procedural

32.21 Plication of emphysematous bleb

32.25 Thoracoscopic ablation of lung lesion or tissue

34.59 Other excision of pleura

HCPCS Level II Supplies & Services

A7042 Implanted pleural catheter, each

32658

32658 Thoracoscopy, surgical; with removal of clot or foreign body from pericardial sac

ICD-9-CM Diagnostic

420.91 Acute idiopathic pericarditis

420.99 Other acute pericarditis

423.0 Hemopericardium

861.01 Heart contusion without mention of open wound into thorax

861.02 Heart laceration without penetration of heart chambers or mention of open wound into thorax

861.11 Heart contusion with open wound into thorax

861.12 Heart laceration without penetration of heart chambers, with open wound into thorax

862.8 Injury to multiple and unspecified intrathoracic organs without mention of open wound into cavity

908.0 Late effect of internal injury to chest

926.11 Crushing injury of back — (Use additional code to identify any associated injuries: 800-829, 850.0-854.1, 860.0-869.1)

926.8 Crushing injury of multiple sites of trunk — (Use additional code to identify any associated injuries: 800-829, 850.0-854.1, 860.0-869.1)

996.59 Mechanical complication due to other implant and internal device, not elsewhere classified

996.61 Infection and inflammatory reaction due to cardiac device, implant, and graft — (Use additional code to identify specified infections)

ICD-9-CM Procedural

37.12 Pericardiotomy

32659

32659 Thoracoscopy, surgical; with creation of pericardial window or partial resection of pericardial sac for drainage

ICD-9-CM Diagnostic

164.1 Malignant neoplasm of heart

198.89 Secondary malignant neoplasm of other specified sites

209.70 Secondary neuroendocrine tumor, unspecified site ▽
209.79 Secondary neuroendocrine tumor of other sites
212.7 Benign neoplasm of heart
234.8 Carcinoma in situ of other specified sites
238.8 Neoplasm of uncertain behavior of other specified sites
239.89 Neoplasms of unspecified nature, other specified sites
411.0 Postmyocardial infarction syndrome — (Use additional code to identify presence of hypertension: 401.0-405.9)
420.0 Acute pericarditis in diseases classified elsewhere — (Code first underlying disease: 006.8, 017.9, 039.8, 585.9, 586) ☒
420.90 Unspecified acute pericarditis ▽
420.91 Acute idiopathic pericarditis
420.99 Other acute pericarditis
423.0 Hemopericardium
423.1 Adhesive pericarditis
423.2 Constrictive pericarditis
423.3 Cardiac tamponade
423.8 Other specified diseases of pericardium
746.89 Other specified congenital anomaly of heart
786.6 Swelling, mass, or lump in chest
908.0 Late effect of internal injury to chest
909.2 Late effect of radiation
996.00 Mechanical complication of unspecified cardiac device, implant, and graft ▽
996.61 Infection and inflammatory reaction due to cardiac device, implant, and graft — (Use additional code to identify specified infections)
997.39 Other respiratory complications
998.59 Other postoperative infection — (Use additional code to identify infection)

ICD-9-CM Procedural

37.12 Pericardiotomy

32661

32661 Thoracoscopy, surgical; with excision of pericardial cyst, tumor, or mass

ICD-9-CM Diagnostic

164.1 Malignant neoplasm of heart
198.89 Secondary malignant neoplasm of other specified sites
209.21 Malignant carcinoid tumor of the bronchus and lung — (Code first any associated multiple endocrine neoplasia syndrome: 258.01-258.03)(Use additional code to identify associated endocrine syndrome, as: carcinoid syndrome: 259.2)
209.61 Benign carcinoid tumor of the bronchus and lung — (Code first any associated multiple endocrine neoplasia syndrome: 258.01-258.03)(Use additional code to identify associated endocrine syndrome, as: carcinoid syndrome: 259.2)
209.70 Secondary neuroendocrine tumor, unspecified site ▽
209.79 Secondary neuroendocrine tumor of other sites
212.7 Benign neoplasm of heart
234.8 Carcinoma in situ of other specified sites
238.8 Neoplasm of uncertain behavior of other specified sites
239.89 Neoplasms of unspecified nature, other specified sites
423.8 Other specified diseases of pericardium
746.89 Other specified congenital anomaly of heart
786.6 Swelling, mass, or lump in chest

ICD-9-CM Procedural

37.33 Excision or destruction of other lesion or tissue of heart, open approach

32662

32662 Thoracoscopy, surgical; with excision of mediastinal cyst, tumor, or mass

ICD-9-CM Diagnostic

164.2 Malignant neoplasm of anterior mediastinum
164.3 Malignant neoplasm of posterior mediastinum
164.8 Malignant neoplasm of other parts of mediastinum
164.9 Malignant neoplasm of mediastinum, part unspecified ▽
176.8 Kaposi's sarcoma of other specified sites
195.1 Malignant neoplasm of thorax
197.1 Secondary malignant neoplasm of mediastinum
199.0 Disseminated malignant neoplasm
209.21 Malignant carcinoid tumor of the bronchus and lung — (Code first any associated multiple endocrine neoplasia syndrome: 258.01-258.03)(Use additional code to identify associated endocrine syndrome, as: carcinoid syndrome: 259.2)
209.30 Malignant poorly differentiated neuroendocrine carcinoma, any site — (Code first any associated multiple endocrine neoplasia syndrome: 258.01-258.03)(Use additional code to identify associated endocrine syndrome, as: carcinoid syndrome: 259.2) ▽
209.61 Benign carcinoid tumor of the bronchus and lung — (Code first any associated multiple endocrine neoplasia syndrome: 258.01-258.03)(Use additional code to identify associated endocrine syndrome, as: carcinoid syndrome: 259.2)
209.70 Secondary neuroendocrine tumor, unspecified site ▽
209.79 Secondary neuroendocrine tumor of other sites
212.5 Benign neoplasm of mediastinum
238.8 Neoplasm of uncertain behavior of other specified sites
239.89 Neoplasms of unspecified nature, other specified sites
279.8 Other specified disorders involving the immune mechanism — (Use additional code to identify any associated intellectual disabilities) (Use additional code for associated manifestations)
748.8 Other specified congenital anomaly of respiratory system
786.6 Swelling, mass, or lump in chest

ICD-9-CM Procedural

34.3 Excision or destruction of lesion or tissue of mediastinum

32663

32663 Thoracoscopy, surgical; with lobectomy (single lobe)

ICD-9-CM Diagnostic

162.2 Malignant neoplasm of main bronchus
162.3 Malignant neoplasm of upper lobe, bronchus, or lung
162.4 Malignant neoplasm of middle lobe, bronchus, or lung
162.5 Malignant neoplasm of lower lobe, bronchus, or lung
162.8 Malignant neoplasm of other parts of bronchus or lung
176.4 Kaposi's sarcoma of lung
197.0 Secondary malignant neoplasm of lung
198.89 Secondary malignant neoplasm of other specified sites
209.21 Malignant carcinoid tumor of the bronchus and lung — (Code first any associated multiple endocrine neoplasia syndrome: 258.01-258.03)(Use additional code to identify associated endocrine syndrome, as: carcinoid syndrome: 259.2)
231.2 Carcinoma in situ of bronchus and lung
235.7 Neoplasm of uncertain behavior of trachea, bronchus, and lung
239.1 Neoplasm of unspecified nature of respiratory system
492.0 Emphysematous bleb
513.0 Abscess of lung — (Use additional code to identify infectious organism)
514 Pulmonary congestion and hypostasis — (Use additional code to identify infectious organism)
515 Postinflammatory pulmonary fibrosis — (Use additional code to identify infectious organism)
518.89 Other diseases of lung, not elsewhere classified — (Use additional code to identify infectious organism)
748.5 Congenital agenesis, hypoplasia, and dysplasia of lung
786.30 Hemoptysis, unspecified ▽
786.39 Other hemoptysis
793.11 Solitary pulmonary nodule
861.22 Lung laceration without mention of open wound into thorax
861.32 Lung laceration with open wound into thorax

862.8 Injury to multiple and unspecified intrathoracic organs without mention of open wound into cavity
862.9 Injury to multiple and unspecified intrathoracic organs with open wound into cavity
V15.82 Personal history of tobacco use, presenting hazards to health

ICD-9-CM Procedural

32.41 Thoracoscopic lobectomy of lung

32664

32664 Thoracoscopy, surgical; with thoracic sympathectomy

ICD-9-CM Diagnostic

337.20 Unspecified reflex sympathetic dystrophy ▽
337.21 Reflex sympathetic dystrophy of the upper limb
337.22 Reflex sympathetic dystrophy of the lower limb
337.29 Reflex sympathetic dystrophy of other specified site
443.0 Raynaud's syndrome — (Use additional code to identify gangrene: 785.4)
705.21 Primary focal hyperhidrosis
705.22 Secondary focal hyperhidrosis
780.8 Generalized hyperhidrosis

ICD-9-CM Procedural

05.29 Other sympathectomy and ganglionectomy

32665

32665 Thoracoscopy, surgical; with esophagomyotomy (Heller type)

ICD-9-CM Diagnostic

530.0 Achalasia and cardiospasm
530.3 Stricture and stenosis of esophagus
530.5 Dyskinesia of esophagus
750.3 Congenital tracheoesophageal fistula, esophageal atresia and stenosis

ICD-9-CM Procedural

42.7 Esophagomyotomy

32666-32667

32666 Thoracoscopy, surgical; with therapeutic wedge resection (eg, mass, nodule), initial unilateral
32667 with therapeutic wedge resection (eg, mass or nodule), each additional resection, ipsilateral (List separately in addition to code for primary procedure)

ICD-9-CM Diagnostic

162.3 Malignant neoplasm of upper lobe, bronchus, or lung
162.4 Malignant neoplasm of middle lobe, bronchus, or lung
162.5 Malignant neoplasm of lower lobe, bronchus, or lung
162.8 Malignant neoplasm of other parts of bronchus or lung
162.9 Malignant neoplasm of bronchus and lung, unspecified site ▽
197.0 Secondary malignant neoplasm of lung
212.3 Benign neoplasm of bronchus and lung
231.2 Carcinoma in situ of bronchus and lung
235.7 Neoplasm of uncertain behavior of trachea, bronchus, and lung
239.1 Neoplasm of unspecified nature of respiratory system
518.89 Other diseases of lung, not elsewhere classified — (Use additional code to identify infectious organism)
786.6 Swelling, mass, or lump in chest
793.11 Solitary pulmonary nodule
793.19 Other nonspecific abnormal finding of lung field

ICD-9-CM Procedural

32.20 Thoracoscopic excision of lesion or tissue of lung

32668

32668 Thoracoscopy, surgical; with diagnostic wedge resection followed by anatomic lung resection (List separately in addition to code for primary procedure)

ICD-9-CM Diagnostic

162.3 Malignant neoplasm of upper lobe, bronchus, or lung
162.4 Malignant neoplasm of middle lobe, bronchus, or lung
162.5 Malignant neoplasm of lower lobe, bronchus, or lung
162.8 Malignant neoplasm of other parts of bronchus or lung
162.9 Malignant neoplasm of bronchus and lung, unspecified site ▽
197.0 Secondary malignant neoplasm of lung
212.3 Benign neoplasm of bronchus and lung
231.2 Carcinoma in situ of bronchus and lung
235.7 Neoplasm of uncertain behavior of trachea, bronchus, and lung
239.1 Neoplasm of unspecified nature of respiratory system
518.89 Other diseases of lung, not elsewhere classified — (Use additional code to identify infectious organism)
786.6 Swelling, mass, or lump in chest
793.11 Solitary pulmonary nodule
793.19 Other nonspecific abnormal finding of lung field

ICD-9-CM Procedural

33.20 Thoracoscopic lung biopsy

32669-32671

32669 Thoracoscopy, surgical; with removal of a single lung segment (segmentectomy)
32670 with removal of 2 lobes (bilobectomy)
32671 with removal of lung (pneumonectomy)

ICD-9-CM Diagnostic

162.3 Malignant neoplasm of upper lobe, bronchus, or lung
162.4 Malignant neoplasm of middle lobe, bronchus, or lung
162.5 Malignant neoplasm of lower lobe, bronchus, or lung
165.8 Malignant neoplasm of other sites within the respiratory system and intrathoracic organs
165.9 Malignant neoplasm of ill-defined sites within the respiratory system
176.4 Kaposi's sarcoma of lung
197.0 Secondary malignant neoplasm of lung
209.21 Malignant carcinoid tumor of the bronchus and lung — (Code first any associated multiple endocrine neoplasia syndrome: 258.01-258.03)(Use additional code to identify associated endocrine syndrome, as: carcinoid syndrome: 259.2)
231.2 Carcinoma in situ of bronchus and lung
235.7 Neoplasm of uncertain behavior of trachea, bronchus, and lung
239.1 Neoplasm of unspecified nature of respiratory system
492.0 Emphysematous bleb
502 Pneumoconiosis due to other silica or silicates — (Use additional code to identify infectious organism)
513.0 Abscess of lung — (Use additional code to identify infectious organism)
514 Pulmonary congestion and hypostasis — (Use additional code to identify infectious organism)
515 Postinflammatory pulmonary fibrosis — (Use additional code to identify infectious organism)
518.89 Other diseases of lung, not elsewhere classified — (Use additional code to identify infectious organism)
748.5 Congenital agenesis, hypoplasia, and dysplasia of lung
786.30 Hemoptysis, unspecified ▽
786.39 Other hemoptysis

ICD-9-CM Procedural

32.30 Thoracoscopic segmental resection of lung
32.41 Thoracoscopic lobectomy of lung
32.50 Thoracoscopic pneumonectomy

32672

32672 Thoracoscopy, surgical; with resection-plication for emphysematous lung (bullous or non-bullous) for lung volume reduction (LVRS), unilateral includes any pleural procedure, when performed

ICD-9-CM Diagnostic

492.0 Emphysematous bleb
492.8 Other emphysema

ICD-9-CM Procedural

32.20 Thoracoscopic excision of lesion or tissue of lung

32673

32673 Thoracoscopy, surgical; with resection of thymus, unilateral or bilateral

ICD-9-CM Diagnostic

135 Sarcoidosis
164.0 Malignant neoplasm of thymus
198.89 Secondary malignant neoplasm of other specified sites
209.22 Malignant carcinoid tumor of the thymus — (Code first any associated multiple endocrine neoplasia syndrome: 258.01-258.03)(Use additional code to identify associated endocrine syndrome, as: carcinoid syndrome: 259.2)
209.62 Benign carcinoid tumor of the thymus — (Code first any associated multiple endocrine neoplasia syndrome: 258.01-258.03)(Use additional code to identify associated endocrine syndrome, as: carcinoid syndrome: 259.2)
212.6 Benign neoplasm of thymus
235.8 Neoplasm of uncertain behavior of pleura, thymus, and mediastinum
242.90 Thyrotoxicosis without mention of goiter or other cause, without mention of thyrotoxic crisis or storm
253.0 Acromegaly and gigantism
254.0 Persistent hyperplasia of thymus
254.8 Other specified diseases of thymus gland
255.0 Cushing's syndrome — (Use additional E code to identify cause, if drug-induced)
255.41 Glucocorticoid deficiency
358.00 Myasthenia gravis without (acute) exacerbation
358.01 Myasthenia gravis with (acute) exacerbation
710.0 Systemic lupus erythematosus — (Use additional code to identify manifestation: 424.91, 581.81, 582.81, 583.81)
714.0 Rheumatoid arthritis — (Use additional code to identify manifestation: 357.1, 359.6)

ICD-9-CM Procedural

07.83 Thoracoscopic partial excision of thymus
07.84 Thoracoscopic total excision of thymus

32674

32674 Thoracoscopy, surgical; with mediastinal and regional lymphadenectomy (List separately in addition to code for primary procedure)

ICD-9-CM Diagnostic

The ICD-9-CM diagnostic code(s) would be the same as the actual procedure performed because these are in-addition-to codes.

ICD-9-CM Procedural

40.29 Simple excision of other lymphatic structure
40.3 Regional lymph node excision
40.52 Radical excision of periaortic lymph nodes
40.59 Radical excision of other lymph nodes

32701

32701 Thoracic target(s) delineation for stereotactic body radiation therapy (SRS/SBRT), (photon or particle beam), entire course of treatment

ICD-9-CM Diagnostic

162.2 Malignant neoplasm of main bronchus
162.3 Malignant neoplasm of upper lobe, bronchus, or lung
162.4 Malignant neoplasm of middle lobe, bronchus, or lung
162.5 Malignant neoplasm of lower lobe, bronchus, or lung
162.8 Malignant neoplasm of other parts of bronchus or lung
162.9 Malignant neoplasm of bronchus and lung, unspecified site ▽
197.0 Secondary malignant neoplasm of lung

ICD-9-CM Procedural

92.29 Other radiotherapeutic procedure

32800

32800 Repair lung hernia through chest wall

ICD-9-CM Diagnostic

518.89 Other diseases of lung, not elsewhere classified — (Use additional code to identify infectious organism)
748.69 Other congenital anomaly of lung

ICD-9-CM Procedural

34.79 Other repair of chest wall

32810

32810 Closure of chest wall following open flap drainage for empyema (Clagett type procedure)

ICD-9-CM Diagnostic

510.0 Empyema with fistula — (Use additional code to identify infectious organism: 041.00-041.9)
510.9 Empyema without mention of fistula — (Use additional code to identify infectious organism: 041.00-041.9)

ICD-9-CM Procedural

34.72 Closure of thoracostomy

32815

32815 Open closure of major bronchial fistula

ICD-9-CM Diagnostic

510.0 Empyema with fistula — (Use additional code to identify infectious organism: 041.00-041.9)
530.89 Other specified disorder of the esophagus
750.3 Congenital tracheoesophageal fistula, esophageal atresia and stenosis
908.0 Late effect of internal injury to chest
998.6 Persistent postoperative fistula, not elsewhere classified

ICD-9-CM Procedural

33.42 Closure of bronchial fistula

32820

32820 Major reconstruction, chest wall (posttraumatic)

ICD-9-CM Diagnostic

807.10 Open fracture of rib(s), unspecified ▽
807.19 Open fracture of multiple ribs, unspecified ▽
807.3 Open fracture of sternum
807.4 Flail chest
809.1 Fracture of bones of trunk, open
860.0 Traumatic pneumothorax without mention of open wound into thorax
860.1 Traumatic pneumothorax with open wound into thorax
860.2 Traumatic hemothorax without mention of open wound into thorax
860.3 Traumatic hemothorax with open wound into thorax
860.4 Traumatic pneumohemothorax without mention of open wound into thorax
860.5 Traumatic pneumohemothorax with open wound into thorax
861.30 Unspecified lung injury with open wound into thorax ▽

861.32 Lung laceration with open wound into thorax
862.39 Injury to other specified intrathoracic organs with open wound into cavity
862.8 Injury to multiple and unspecified intrathoracic organs without mention of open wound into cavity
862.9 Injury to multiple and unspecified intrathoracic organs with open wound into cavity
875.1 Open wound of chest (wall), complicated
926.8 Crushing injury of multiple sites of trunk — (Use additional code to identify any associated injuries: 800-829, 850.0-854.1, 860.0-869.1)
926.9 Crushing injury of unspecified site of trunk — (Use additional code to identify any associated injuries: 800-829, 850.0-854.1, 860.0-869.1) ♥
942.22 Blisters with epidermal loss due to burn (second degree) of chest wall, excluding breast and nipple
942.32 Full-thickness skin loss due to burn (third degree NOS) of chest wall, excluding breast and nipple
942.40 Deep necrosis of underlying tissues due to burn (deep third degree) of trunk, unspecified site, without mention of loss of a body part ♥
942.42 Deep necrosis of underlying tissues due to burn (deep third degree) of chest wall, excluding breast and nipple, without mention of loss of a body part
959.11 Other injury of chest wall
998.31 Disruption of internal operation (surgical) wound
998.32 Disruption of external operation (surgical) wound

ICD-9-CM Procedural

34.79 Other repair of chest wall

32850

32850 Donor pneumonectomy(s) (including cold preservation), from cadaver donor

ICD-9-CM Diagnostic

V59.8 Donor of other specified organ or tissue

ICD-9-CM Procedural

32.50 Thoracoscopic pneumonectomy
32.59 Other and unspecified pneumonectomy

32851-32854

32851 Lung transplant, single; without cardiopulmonary bypass
32852 with cardiopulmonary bypass
32853 Lung transplant, double (bilateral sequential or en bloc); without cardiopulmonary bypass
32854 with cardiopulmonary bypass

ICD-9-CM Diagnostic

162.2 Malignant neoplasm of main bronchus
162.3 Malignant neoplasm of upper lobe, bronchus, or lung
162.4 Malignant neoplasm of middle lobe, bronchus, or lung
162.5 Malignant neoplasm of lower lobe, bronchus, or lung
162.8 Malignant neoplasm of other parts of bronchus or lung
162.9 Malignant neoplasm of bronchus and lung, unspecified site ♥
163.0 Malignant neoplasm of parietal pleura
163.1 Malignant neoplasm of visceral pleura
163.8 Malignant neoplasm of other specified sites of pleura
197.0 Secondary malignant neoplasm of lung
199.2 Malignant neoplasm associated with transplanted organ — (Code first complication of transplanted organ (996.80-996.89) Use additional code for specific malignancy)
209.21 Malignant carcinoid tumor of the bronchus and lung — (Code first any associated multiple endocrine neoplasia syndrome: 258.01-258.03)(Use additional code to identify associated endocrine syndrome, as: carcinoid syndrome: 259.2)
231.2 Carcinoma in situ of bronchus and lung
235.7 Neoplasm of uncertain behavior of trachea, bronchus, and lung
239.1 Neoplasm of unspecified nature of respiratory system
273.4 Alpha-1-antitrypsin deficiency — (Use additional code to identify any associated intellectual disabilities)
277.00 Cystic fibrosis without mention of meconium ileus — (Use additional code to identify any associated intellectual disabilities)
277.02 Cystic fibrosis with pulmonary manifestations — (Use additional code to identify any associated intellectual disabilities.) (Use additional code to identify any infectious organism present, such as 041.7)
277.03 Cystic fibrosis with gastrointestinal manifestations — (Use additional code to identify any associated intellectual disabilities)
277.09 Cystic fibrosis with other manifestations — (Use additional code to identify any associated intellectual disabilities)
500 Coal workers' pneumoconiosis — (Use additional code to identify infectious organism)
501 Asbestosis — (Use additional code to identify infectious organism)
502 Pneumoconiosis due to other silica or silicates — (Use additional code to identify infectious organism)
503 Pneumoconiosis due to other inorganic dust — (Use additional code to identify infectious organism)
506.4 Chronic respiratory conditions due to fumes and vapors — (Use additional code to identify infectious organism. Use additional E code to identify cause. Use additional code to identify associated respiratory conditions: 518.81.)
506.9 Unspecified respiratory conditions due to fumes and vapors — (Use additional code to identify infectious organism. Use additional E code to identify cause. Use additional code to identify associated respiratory conditions: 518.81.) ♥
508.1 Chronic and other pulmonary manifestations due to radiation — (Use additional code to identify infectious organism. Use additional E code to identify cause. Use additional code to identify associated respiratory conditions: 518.81.)
510.9 Empyema without mention of fistula — (Use additional code to identify infectious organism: 041.00-041.9)
513.0 Abscess of lung — (Use additional code to identify infectious organism)
515 Postinflammatory pulmonary fibrosis — (Use additional code to identify infectious organism)
516.0 Pulmonary alveolar proteinosis — (Use additional code to identify infectious organism)
516.30 Idiopathic interstitial pneumonia, not otherwise specified
516.31 Idiopathic pulmonary fibrosis
516.32 Idiopathic non-specific interstitial pneumonitis
516.33 Acute interstitial pneumonitis
516.34 Respiratory bronchiolitis interstitial lung disease
516.35 Idiopathic lymphoid interstitial pneumonia
516.36 Cryptogenic organizing pneumonia
516.37 Desquamative interstitial pneumonia
516.4 Lymphangioleiomyomatosis ♀
516.5 Adult pulmonary Langerhans cell histiocytosis
516.64 Alveolar capillary dysplasia with vein misalignment
518.51 Acute respiratory failure following trauma and surgery
518.52 Other pulmonary insufficiency, not elsewhere classified, following trauma and surgery
518.53 Acute and chronic respiratory failure following trauma and surgery
518.81 Acute respiratory failure
518.83 Chronic respiratory failure
518.89 Other diseases of lung, not elsewhere classified — (Use additional code to identify infectious organism)
519.19 Other diseases of trachea and bronchus — (Use additional code to identify infectious organism)
748.4 Congenital cystic lung
748.5 Congenital agenesis, hypoplasia, and dysplasia of lung
770.3 Pulmonary hemorrhage of fetus or newborn — (Use additional code(s) to further specify condition)
786.09 Other dyspnea and respiratory abnormalities
909.1 Late effect of toxic effects of nonmedical substances
947.1 Burn of larynx, trachea, and lung
997.39 Other respiratory complications
V15.82 Personal history of tobacco use, presenting hazards to health

ICD-9-CM Procedural

00.91 Transplant from live related donor
00.92 Transplant from live non-related donor
00.93 Transplant from cadaver
33.50 Lung transplantation, NOS
33.51 Unilateral lung transplantation
33.52 Bilateral lung transplantation
39.61 Extracorporeal circulation auxiliary to open heart surgery

32855-32856

32855 Backbench standard preparation of cadaver donor lung allograft prior to transplantation, including dissection of allograft from surrounding soft tissues to prepare pulmonary venous/atrial cuff, pulmonary artery, and bronchus; unilateral
32856 bilateral

ICD-9-CM Diagnostic

162.2 Malignant neoplasm of main bronchus
162.3 Malignant neoplasm of upper lobe, bronchus, or lung
162.4 Malignant neoplasm of middle lobe, bronchus, or lung
162.5 Malignant neoplasm of lower lobe, bronchus, or lung
162.8 Malignant neoplasm of other parts of bronchus or lung
162.9 Malignant neoplasm of bronchus and lung, unspecified site
163.0 Malignant neoplasm of parietal pleura
163.1 Malignant neoplasm of visceral pleura
163.8 Malignant neoplasm of other specified sites of pleura
197.0 Secondary malignant neoplasm of lung
199.2 Malignant neoplasm associated with transplanted organ — (Code first complication of transplanted organ (996.80-996.89) Use additional code for specific malignancy)
209.21 Malignant carcinoid tumor of the bronchus and lung — (Code first any associated multiple endocrine neoplasia syndrome: 258.01-258.03)(Use additional code to identify associated endocrine syndrome, as: carcinoid syndrome: 259.2)
231.2 Carcinoma in situ of bronchus and lung
235.7 Neoplasm of uncertain behavior of trachea, bronchus, and lung
239.1 Neoplasm of unspecified nature of respiratory system
273.4 Alpha-1-antitrypsin deficiency — (Use additional code to identify any associated intellectual disabilities)
277.00 Cystic fibrosis without mention of meconium ileus — (Use additional code to identify any associated intellectual disabilities)
277.02 Cystic fibrosis with pulmonary manifestations — (Use additional code to identify any associated intellectual disabilities.) (Use additional code to identify any infectious organism present, such as 041.7)
277.03 Cystic fibrosis with gastrointestinal manifestations — (Use additional code to identify any associated intellectual disabilities)
277.09 Cystic fibrosis with other manifestations — (Use additional code to identify any associated intellectual disabilities)
500 Coal workers' pneumoconiosis — (Use additional code to identify infectious organism)
501 Asbestosis — (Use additional code to identify infectious organism)
502 Pneumoconiosis due to other silica or silicates — (Use additional code to identify infectious organism)
503 Pneumoconiosis due to other inorganic dust — (Use additional code to identify infectious organism)
506.4 Chronic respiratory conditions due to fumes and vapors — (Use additional code to identify infectious organism. Use additional E code to identify cause. Use additional code to identify associated respiratory conditions: 518.81.)
506.9 Unspecified respiratory conditions due to fumes and vapors — (Use additional code to identify infectious organism. Use additional E code to identify cause. Use additional code to identify associated respiratory conditions: 518.81.)
508.1 Chronic and other pulmonary manifestations due to radiation — (Use additional code to identify infectious organism. Use additional E code to identify cause. Use additional code to identify associated respiratory conditions: 518.81.)
510.9 Empyema without mention of fistula — (Use additional code to identify infectious organism: 041.00-041.9)
513.0 Abscess of lung — (Use additional code to identify infectious organism)
515 Postinflammatory pulmonary fibrosis — (Use additional code to identify infectious organism)
516.0 Pulmonary alveolar proteinosis — (Use additional code to identify infectious organism)
516.30 Idiopathic interstitial pneumonia, not otherwise specified
516.31 Idiopathic pulmonary fibrosis
516.32 Idiopathic non-specific interstitial pneumonitis
516.33 Acute interstitial pneumonitis
516.34 Respiratory bronchiolitis interstitial lung disease
516.35 Idiopathic lymphoid interstitial pneumonia
516.36 Cryptogenic organizing pneumonia
516.37 Desquamative interstitial pneumonia
518.51 Acute respiratory failure following trauma and surgery
518.52 Other pulmonary insufficiency, not elsewhere classified, following trauma and surgery
518.53 Acute and chronic respiratory failure following trauma and surgery
518.81 Acute respiratory failure
518.83 Chronic respiratory failure
518.89 Other diseases of lung, not elsewhere classified — (Use additional code to identify infectious organism)
519.19 Other diseases of trachea and bronchus — (Use additional code to identify infectious organism)
748.4 Congenital cystic lung
748.5 Congenital agenesis, hypoplasia, and dysplasia of lung
770.3 Pulmonary hemorrhage of fetus or newborn — (Use additional code(s) to further specify condition)
786.09 Other dyspnea and respiratory abnormalities
909.1 Late effect of toxic effects of nonmedical substances
947.1 Burn of larynx, trachea, and lung
997.39 Other respiratory complications
V15.82 Personal history of tobacco use, presenting hazards to health

ICD-9-CM Procedural

00.93 Transplant from cadaver
33.51 Unilateral lung transplantation
33.52 Bilateral lung transplantation
33.99 Other operations on lung

32900

32900 Resection of ribs, extrapleural, all stages

ICD-9-CM Diagnostic

170.3 Malignant neoplasm of ribs, sternum, and clavicle
203.00 Multiple myeloma, without mention of having achieved remission
203.02 Multiple myeloma, in relapse
213.3 Benign neoplasm of ribs, sternum, and clavicle
238.0 Neoplasm of uncertain behavior of bone and articular cartilage
730.18 Chronic osteomyelitis, other specified sites — (Use additional code to identify organism: 041.1. Use additional code to identify major osseous defect, if applicable: 731.3)
733.20 Unspecified cyst of bone (localized)
737.34 Thoracogenic scoliosis
738.3 Acquired deformity of chest and rib
754.81 Pectus excavatum

ICD-9-CM Procedural

77.91 Total ostectomy of scapula, clavicle, and thorax (ribs and sternum)

32905-32906

32905 Thoracoplasty, Schede type or extrapleural (all stages);
32906 with closure of bronchopleural fistula

ICD-9-CM Diagnostic

510.0 Empyema with fistula — (Use additional code to identify infectious organism: 041.00-041.9)
510.9 Empyema without mention of fistula — (Use additional code to identify infectious organism: 041.00-041.9)
738.3 Acquired deformity of chest and rib
807.3 Open fracture of sternum
875.1 Open wound of chest (wall), complicated

ICD-9-CM Procedural

33.34 Thoracoplasty
34.73 Closure of other fistula of thorax

32940

32940 Pneumonolysis, extraperiosteal, including filling or packing procedures

ICD-9-CM Diagnostic

137.0 Late effects of respiratory or unspecified tuberculosis — (Note: This category is to be used to indicate conditions classifiable to 010-018 as the cause of late effects, which are themselves classified elsewhere. The "late effects" include those specified as such, as sequelae, or as due to old or inactive tuberculosis, without evidence of active disease.) ▽
492.8 Other emphysema
510.9 Empyema without mention of fistula — (Use additional code to identify infectious organism: 041.00-041.9)
511.0 Pleurisy without mention of effusion or current tuberculosis — (Use additional code to identify infectious organism)
515 Postinflammatory pulmonary fibrosis — (Use additional code to identify infectious organism)
997.39 Other respiratory complications

ICD-9-CM Procedural

33.39 Other surgical collapse of lung

32960

32960 Pneumothorax, therapeutic, intrapleural injection of air

ICD-9-CM Diagnostic

511.1 Pleurisy with effusion, with mention of bacterial cause other than tuberculosis — (Use additional code to identify infectious organism)
513.0 Abscess of lung — (Use additional code to identify infectious organism)
786.30 Hemoptysis, unspecified ▽
786.31 Acute idiopathic pulmonary hemorrhage in infants [AIPHI]
786.39 Other hemoptysis
997.39 Other respiratory complications

ICD-9-CM Procedural

33.32 Artificial pneumothorax for collapse of lung

32997

32997 Total lung lavage (unilateral)

ICD-9-CM Diagnostic

482.84 Legionnaires' disease
482.9 Unspecified bacterial pneumonia — (Use additional code to identify infectious organism) ▽
486 Pneumonia, organism unspecified ▽
506.0 Bronchitis and pneumonitis due to fumes and vapors — (Use additional code to identify infectious organism. Use additional E code to identify cause. Use additional code to identify associated respiratory conditions: 518.81.)
507.0 Pneumonitis due to inhalation of food or vomitus — (Use additional code to identify infectious organism)
507.1 Pneumonitis due to inhalation of oils and essences — (Use additional code to identify infectious organism)
507.8 Pneumonitis due to other solids and liquids — (Use additional code to identify infectious organism)
510.0 Empyema with fistula — (Use additional code to identify infectious organism: 041.00-041.9)
510.9 Empyema without mention of fistula — (Use additional code to identify infectious organism: 041.00-041.9)
513.0 Abscess of lung — (Use additional code to identify infectious organism)
860.1 Traumatic pneumothorax with open wound into thorax
860.3 Traumatic hemothorax with open wound into thorax
860.5 Traumatic pneumohemothorax with open wound into thorax
861.22 Lung laceration without mention of open wound into thorax
861.32 Lung laceration with open wound into thorax
862.8 Injury to multiple and unspecified intrathoracic organs without mention of open wound into cavity
862.9 Injury to multiple and unspecified intrathoracic organs with open wound into cavity
958.3 Posttraumatic wound infection not elsewhere classified

ICD-9-CM Procedural

33.99 Other operations on lung

32998

32998 Ablation therapy for reduction or eradication of 1 or more pulmonary tumor(s) including pleura or chest wall when involved by tumor extension, percutaneous, radiofrequency, unilateral

ICD-9-CM Diagnostic

162.2 Malignant neoplasm of main bronchus
162.3 Malignant neoplasm of upper lobe, bronchus, or lung
162.4 Malignant neoplasm of middle lobe, bronchus, or lung
162.5 Malignant neoplasm of lower lobe, bronchus, or lung
162.8 Malignant neoplasm of other parts of bronchus or lung
162.9 Malignant neoplasm of bronchus and lung, unspecified site ▽
163.0 Malignant neoplasm of parietal pleura
163.1 Malignant neoplasm of visceral pleura
163.8 Malignant neoplasm of other specified sites of pleura
163.9 Malignant neoplasm of pleura, unspecified site ▽
195.1 Malignant neoplasm of thorax
197.0 Secondary malignant neoplasm of lung
197.1 Secondary malignant neoplasm of mediastinum
197.2 Secondary malignant neoplasm of pleura
197.3 Secondary malignant neoplasm of other respiratory organs
209.21 Malignant carcinoid tumor of the bronchus and lung — (Code first any associated multiple endocrine neoplasia syndrome: 258.01-258.03)(Use additional code to identify associated endocrine syndrome, as: carcinoid syndrome: 259.2)
209.61 Benign carcinoid tumor of the bronchus and lung — (Code first any associated multiple endocrine neoplasia syndrome: 258.01-258.03)(Use additional code to identify associated endocrine syndrome, as: carcinoid syndrome: 259.2)
212.3 Benign neoplasm of bronchus and lung
212.4 Benign neoplasm of pleura
212.9 Benign neoplasm of respiratory and intrathoracic organs, site unspecified ▽
231.2 Carcinoma in situ of bronchus and lung
231.8 Carcinoma in situ of other specified parts of respiratory system
231.9 Carcinoma in situ of respiratory system, part unspecified ▽
235.7 Neoplasm of uncertain behavior of trachea, bronchus, and lung
235.8 Neoplasm of uncertain behavior of pleura, thymus, and mediastinum
235.9 Neoplasm of uncertain behavior of other and unspecified respiratory organs ▽
239.1 Neoplasm of unspecified nature of respiratory system

ICD-9-CM Procedural

32.24 Percutaneous ablation of lung lesion or tissue

Cardiovascular System

Heart and Pericardium

33010-33015

33010 Pericardiocentesis; initial
33011 subsequent
33015 Tube pericardiostomy

ICD-9-CM Diagnostic

017.90 Tuberculosis of other specified organs, confirmation unspecified — (Use additional code to identify manifestation: 420.0, 422.0, 424.91) ▽
036.41 Meningococcal pericarditis
039.8 Actinomycotic infection of other specified sites
066.8 Other specified arthropod-borne viral diseases — (Use additional code to identify any associated meningitis: 321.2)
074.21 Coxsackie pericarditis
093.81 Syphilitic pericarditis
098.83 Gonococcal pericarditis
115.03 Histoplasma capsulatum pericarditis
115.13 Histoplasma duboisii pericarditis
115.93 Unspecified Histoplasmosis pericarditis ▽
164.1 Malignant neoplasm of heart
198.89 Secondary malignant neoplasm of other specified sites
212.7 Benign neoplasm of heart
238.8 Neoplasm of uncertain behavior of other specified sites
391.0 Acute rheumatic pericarditis
393 Chronic rheumatic pericarditis
411.0 Postmyocardial infarction syndrome — (Use additional code to identify presence of hypertension: 401.0-405.9)
420.0 Acute pericarditis in diseases classified elsewhere — (Code first underlying disease: 006.8, 017.9, 039.8, 585.9, 586) ☒
420.90 Unspecified acute pericarditis ▽
420.91 Acute idiopathic pericarditis
420.99 Other acute pericarditis
423.0 Hemopericardium
423.1 Adhesive pericarditis
423.2 Constrictive pericarditis
423.3 Cardiac tamponade
423.8 Other specified diseases of pericardium
423.9 Unspecified disease of pericardium ▽
429.3 Cardiomegaly
585.1 Chronic kidney disease, Stage I — (Use additional code to identify kidney transplant status, if applicable: V42.0. Use additional code to identify manifestation: 357.4, 420.0. Code first hypertensive chronic kidney disease, if applicable: 403.00-403.91, 404.00-404.93)
585.2 Chronic kidney disease, Stage II (mild) — (Use additional code to identify kidney transplant status, if applicable: V42.0. Use additional code to identify manifestation: 357.4, 420.0. Code first hypertensive chronic kidney disease, if applicable: 403.00-403.91, 404.00-404.93)
585.3 Chronic kidney disease, Stage III (moderate) — (Use additional code to identify kidney transplant status, if applicable: V42.0. Use additional code to identify manifestation: 357.4, 420.0. Code first hypertensive chronic kidney disease, if applicable: 403.00-403.91, 404.00-404.93)
585.4 Chronic kidney disease, Stage IV (severe) — (Use additional code to identify kidney transplant status, if applicable: V42.0. Use additional code to identify manifestation: 357.4, 420.0. Code first hypertensive chronic kidney disease, if applicable: 403.00-403.91, 404.00-404.93)
585.5 Chronic kidney disease, Stage V — (Use additional code to identify kidney transplant status, if applicable: V42.0. Use additional code to identify manifestation: 357.4, 420.0. Code first hypertensive chronic kidney disease, if applicable: 403.00-403.91, 404.00-404.93)
585.6 End stage renal disease — (Use additional code to identify kidney transplant status, if applicable: V42.0. Use additional code to identify manifestation: 357.4, 420.0. Code first hypertensive chronic kidney disease, if applicable: 403.00-403.91, 404.00-404.93)
585.9 Chronic kidney disease, unspecified — (Use additional code to identify kidney transplant status, if applicable: V42.0. Use additional code to identify manifestation: 357.4, 420.0. Code first hypertensive chronic kidney disease, if applicable: 403.00-403.91, 404.00-404.93) ▽
786.50 Chest pain, unspecified ▽
786.59 Chest pain, other
861.00 Unspecified injury to heart without mention of open wound into thorax ▽
861.01 Heart contusion without mention of open wound into thorax
996.83 Complications of transplanted heart — (Use additional code to identify nature of complication: 078.5, 199.2, 238.77, 279.50-279.53)

ICD-9-CM Procedural

37.0 Pericardiocentesis
37.12 Pericardiotomy

33020

33020 Pericardiotomy for removal of clot or foreign body (primary procedure)

ICD-9-CM Diagnostic

420.91 Acute idiopathic pericarditis
420.99 Other acute pericarditis
423.0 Hemopericardium
423.2 Constrictive pericarditis
861.01 Heart contusion without mention of open wound into thorax
861.02 Heart laceration without penetration of heart chambers or mention of open wound into thorax
861.03 Heart laceration with penetration of heart chambers, without mention of open wound into thorax
861.11 Heart contusion with open wound into thorax
861.12 Heart laceration without penetration of heart chambers, with open wound into thorax
862.8 Injury to multiple and unspecified intrathoracic organs without mention of open wound into cavity
862.9 Injury to multiple and unspecified intrathoracic organs with open wound into cavity
908.0 Late effect of internal injury to chest
926.11 Crushing injury of back — (Use additional code to identify any associated injuries: 800-829, 850.0-854.1, 860.0-869.1)
926.8 Crushing injury of multiple sites of trunk — (Use additional code to identify any associated injuries: 800-829, 850.0-854.1, 860.0-869.1)
996.00 Mechanical complication of unspecified cardiac device, implant, and graft ▽
996.61 Infection and inflammatory reaction due to cardiac device, implant, and graft — (Use additional code to identify specified infections)
V64.42 Thorascopic surgical procedure converted to open procedure

ICD-9-CM Procedural

37.12 Pericardiotomy

33025

33025 Creation of pericardial window or partial resection for drainage

ICD-9-CM Diagnostic

164.1 Malignant neoplasm of heart
198.89 Secondary malignant neoplasm of other specified sites
209.70 Secondary neuroendocrine tumor, unspecified site ▽
209.79 Secondary neuroendocrine tumor of other sites
212.7 Benign neoplasm of heart
238.8 Neoplasm of uncertain behavior of other specified sites
239.89 Neoplasms of unspecified nature, other specified sites
391.0 Acute rheumatic pericarditis
411.0 Postmyocardial infarction syndrome — (Use additional code to identify presence of hypertension: 401.0-405.9)
420.0 Acute pericarditis in diseases classified elsewhere — (Code first underlying disease: 006.8, 017.9, 039.8, 585.9, 586) ☒
420.90 Unspecified acute pericarditis ▽
420.91 Acute idiopathic pericarditis
420.99 Other acute pericarditis
423.0 Hemopericardium
423.1 Adhesive pericarditis
423.2 Constrictive pericarditis
423.3 Cardiac tamponade
423.8 Other specified diseases of pericardium
423.9 Unspecified disease of pericardium ▽
908.0 Late effect of internal injury to chest
909.2 Late effect of radiation
996.00 Mechanical complication of unspecified cardiac device, implant, and graft ▽
996.61 Infection and inflammatory reaction due to cardiac device, implant, and graft — (Use additional code to identify specified infections)
998.59 Other postoperative infection — (Use additional code to identify infection)
V64.42 Thoracoscopic surgical procedure converted to open procedure

ICD-9-CM Procedural

37.12 Pericardiotomy

33030-33031

33030 Pericardiectomy, subtotal or complete; without cardiopulmonary bypass
33031 with cardiopulmonary bypass

ICD-9-CM Diagnostic

164.1 Malignant neoplasm of heart
198.89 Secondary malignant neoplasm of other specified sites
209.70 Secondary neuroendocrine tumor, unspecified site ▽
209.79 Secondary neuroendocrine tumor of other sites
212.7 Benign neoplasm of heart
238.8 Neoplasm of uncertain behavior of other specified sites
239.89 Neoplasms of unspecified nature, other specified sites
391.0 Acute rheumatic pericarditis
411.0 Postmyocardial infarction syndrome — (Use additional code to identify presence of hypertension: 401.0-405.9)
420.0 Acute pericarditis in diseases classified elsewhere — (Code first underlying disease: 006.8, 017.9, 039.8, 585.9, 586) ☒
420.90 Unspecified acute pericarditis ▽
420.91 Acute idiopathic pericarditis
420.99 Other acute pericarditis
423.0 Hemopericardium
423.1 Adhesive pericarditis
423.2 Constrictive pericarditis
423.8 Other specified diseases of pericardium
908.0 Late effect of internal injury to chest
909.2 Late effect of radiation
996.00 Mechanical complication of unspecified cardiac device, implant, and graft ▽
996.61 Infection and inflammatory reaction due to cardiac device, implant, and graft — (Use additional code to identify specified infections)
998.59 Other postoperative infection — (Use additional code to identify infection)
V64.42 Thoracoscopic surgical procedure converted to open procedure

ICD-9-CM Procedural

37.31 Pericardiectomy
39.61 Extracorporeal circulation auxiliary to open heart surgery

33050

33050 Resection of pericardial cyst or tumor

ICD-9-CM Diagnostic

164.1 Malignant neoplasm of heart
198.89 Secondary malignant neoplasm of other specified sites
209.70 Secondary neuroendocrine tumor, unspecified site ▽
209.79 Secondary neuroendocrine tumor of other sites
212.7 Benign neoplasm of heart
234.8 Carcinoma in situ of other specified sites
238.8 Neoplasm of uncertain behavior of other specified sites
239.89 Neoplasms of unspecified nature, other specified sites
423.8 Other specified diseases of pericardium
746.89 Other specified congenital anomaly of heart
V64.42 Thoracoscopic surgical procedure converted to open procedure

ICD-9-CM Procedural

37.31 Pericardiectomy

33120-33130

33120 Excision of intracardiac tumor, resection with cardiopulmonary bypass
33130 Resection of external cardiac tumor

ICD-9-CM Diagnostic

164.1 Malignant neoplasm of heart
198.89 Secondary malignant neoplasm of other specified sites
209.70 Secondary neuroendocrine tumor, unspecified site ▽
209.79 Secondary neuroendocrine tumor of other sites
212.7 Benign neoplasm of heart
234.8 Carcinoma in situ of other specified sites
238.8 Neoplasm of uncertain behavior of other specified sites
239.89 Neoplasms of unspecified nature, other specified sites

ICD-9-CM Procedural

37.33 Excision or destruction of other lesion or tissue of heart, open approach
37.37 Excision or destruction of other lesion or tissue of heart, thoracoscopic approach
39.61 Extracorporeal circulation auxiliary to open heart surgery

33140-33141

33140 Transmyocardial laser revascularization, by thoracotomy; (separate procedure)
33141 performed at the time of other open cardiac procedure(s) (List separately in addition to code for primary procedure)

ICD-9-CM Diagnostic

410.01 Acute myocardial infarction of anterolateral wall, initial episode of care — (Use additional code to identify presence of hypertension: 401.0-405.9)
410.02 Acute myocardial infarction of anterolateral wall, subsequent episode of care — (Use additional code to identify presence of hypertension: 401.0-405.9)
410.11 Acute myocardial infarction of other anterior wall, initial episode of care — (Use additional code to identify presence of hypertension: 401.0-405.9)
410.12 Acute myocardial infarction of other anterior wall, subsequent episode of care — (Use additional code to identify presence of hypertension: 401.0-405.9)

410.21 Acute myocardial infarction of inferolateral wall, initial episode of care — (Use additional code to identify presence of hypertension: 401.0-405.9)

410.22 Acute myocardial infarction of inferolateral wall, subsequent episode of care — (Use additional code to identify presence of hypertension: 401.0-405.9)

410.31 Acute myocardial infarction of inferoposterior wall, initial episode of care — (Use additional code to identify presence of hypertension: 401.0-405.9)

410.32 Acute myocardial infarction of inferoposterior wall, subsequent episode of care — (Use additional code to identify presence of hypertension: 401.0-405.9)

410.41 Acute myocardial infarction of other inferior wall, initial episode of care — (Use additional code to identify presence of hypertension: 401.0-405.9)

410.42 Acute myocardial infarction of other inferior wall, subsequent episode of care — (Use additional code to identify presence of hypertension: 401.0-405.9)

410.51 Acute myocardial infarction of other lateral wall, initial episode of care — (Use additional code to identify presence of hypertension: 401.0-405.9)

410.52 Acute myocardial infarction of other lateral wall, subsequent episode of care — (Use additional code to identify presence of hypertension: 401.0-405.9)

410.61 Acute myocardial infarction, true posterior wall infarction, initial episode of care — (Use additional code to identify presence of hypertension: 401.0-405.9)

410.62 Acute myocardial infarction, true posterior wall infarction, subsequent episode of care — (Use additional code to identify presence of hypertension: 401.0-405.9)

410.71 Acute myocardial infarction, subendocardial infarction, initial episode of care — (Use additional code to identify presence of hypertension: 401.0-405.9)

410.72 Acute myocardial infarction, subendocardial infarction, subsequent episode of care — (Use additional code to identify presence of hypertension: 401.0-405.9)

410.81 Acute myocardial infarction of other specified sites, initial episode of care — (Use additional code to identify presence of hypertension: 401.0-405.9)

410.82 Acute myocardial infarction of other specified sites, subsequent episode of care — (Use additional code to identify presence of hypertension: 401.0-405.9)

410.91 Acute myocardial infarction, unspecified site, initial episode of care — (Use additional code to identify presence of hypertension: 401.0-405.9) ▽

410.92 Acute myocardial infarction, unspecified site, subsequent episode of care — (Use additional code to identify presence of hypertension: 401.0-405.9) ▽

411.1 Intermediate coronary syndrome — (Use additional code to identify presence of hypertension: 401.0-405.9)

411.81 Acute coronary occlusion without myocardial infarction — (Use additional code to identify presence of hypertension: 401.0-405.9)

411.89 Other acute and subacute form of ischemic heart disease — (Use additional code to identify presence of hypertension: 401.0-405.9)

413.0 Angina decubitus — (Use additional code to identify presence of hypertension: 401.0-405.9)

413.1 Prinzmetal angina — (Use additional code to identify presence of hypertension: 401.0-405.9)

413.9 Other and unspecified angina pectoris — (Use additional code(s) for symptoms associated with angina equivalent)(Use additional code to identify presence of hypertension: 401.0-405.9) ▽

414.00 Coronary atherosclerosis of unspecified type of vessel, native or graft — (Use additional code to identify presence of hypertension: 401.0-405.9) ▽

414.01 Coronary atherosclerosis of native coronary artery — (Use additional code to identify presence of hypertension: 401.0-405.9)

414.02 Coronary atherosclerosis of autologous vein bypass graft — (Use additional code to identify presence of hypertension: 401.0-405.9)

414.03 Coronary atherosclerosis of nonautologous biological bypass graft — (Use additional code to identify presence of hypertension: 401.0-405.9)

414.04 Coronary atherosclerosis of artery bypass graft — (Use additional code to identify presence of hypertension: 401.0-405.9)

414.05 Coronary atherosclerosis of unspecified type of bypass graft — (Use additional code to identify presence of hypertension: 401.0-405.9) ▽

414.06 Coronary atherosclerosis, of native coronary artery of transplanted heart — (Use additional code to identify presence of hypertension: 401.0-405.9)

414.07 Coronary atherosclerosis, of bypass graft (artery) (vein) of transplanted heart — (Use additional code to identify presence of hypertension: 401.0-405.9)

414.10 Aneurysm of heart — (Use additional code to identify presence of hypertension: 401.0-405.9)

414.11 Aneurysm of coronary vessels — (Use additional code to identify presence of hypertension: 401.0-405.9)

414.12 Dissection of coronary artery — (Use additional code to identify presence of hypertension: 401.0-405.9)

414.19 Other aneurysm of heart — (Use additional code to identify presence of hypertension: 401.0-405.9)

414.2 Chronic total occlusion of coronary artery

414.3 Coronary atherosclerosis due to lipid rich plaque — (Code first coronary atherosclerosis (414.00-414.07))

414.4 Coronary atherosclerosis due to calcified coronary lesion — (Code first coronary atherosclerosis (414.00-414.07))

414.8 Other specified forms of chronic ischemic heart disease — (Use additional code to identify presence of hypertension: 401.0-405.9)

414.9 Unspecified chronic ischemic heart disease — (Use additional code to identify presence of hypertension: 401.0-405.9) ▽

746.85 Congenital coronary artery anomaly

ICD-9-CM Procedural

36.31 Open chest transmyocardial revascularization

33202-33203

33202 Insertion of epicardial electrode(s); open incision (eg, thoracotomy, median sternotomy, subxiphoid approach)

33203 endoscopic approach (eg, thoracoscopy, pericardioscopy)

ICD-9-CM Diagnostic

337.00 Idiopathic peripheral autonomic neuropathy, unspecified ▽

337.01 Carotid sinus syndrome

337.09 Other idiopathic peripheral autonomic neuropathy

426.0 Atrioventricular block, complete

426.10 Unspecified atrioventricular block ▽

426.11 First degree atrioventricular block

426.12 Mobitz (type) II atrioventricular block

426.13 Other second degree atrioventricular block

426.6 Other heart block

426.7 Anomalous atrioventricular excitation

426.82 Long QT syndrome

426.9 Unspecified conduction disorder ▽

427.0 Paroxysmal supraventricular tachycardia

427.31 Atrial fibrillation

427.81 Sinoatrial node dysfunction

427.89 Other specified cardiac dysrhythmias

746.86 Congenital heart block

996.01 Mechanical complication due to cardiac pacemaker (electrode)

996.61 Infection and inflammatory reaction due to cardiac device, implant, and graft — (Use additional code to identify specified infections)

V53.31 Fitting and adjustment of cardiac pacemaker

ICD-9-CM Procedural

37.74 Insertion or replacement of epicardial lead (electrode) into epicardium

37.95 Implantation of automatic cardioverter/defibrillator leads(s) only

37.97 Replacement of automatic cardioverter/defibrillator leads(s) only

33206-33208

33206 Insertion of new or replacement of permanent pacemaker with transvenous electrode(s); atrial
33207 ventricular
33208 atrial and ventricular

ICD-9-CM Diagnostic

426.0 Atrioventricular block, complete
426.10 Unspecified atrioventricular block
426.11 First degree atrioventricular block
426.12 Mobitz (type) II atrioventricular block
426.13 Other second degree atrioventricular block
426.2 Left bundle branch hemiblock
426.3 Other left bundle branch block
426.4 Right bundle branch block
426.50 Unspecified bundle branch block
426.51 Right bundle branch block and left posterior fascicular block
426.52 Right bundle branch block and left anterior fascicular block
426.53 Other bilateral bundle branch block
426.54 Trifascicular block
426.6 Other heart block
426.7 Anomalous atrioventricular excitation
426.82 Long QT syndrome
426.9 Unspecified conduction disorder
427.0 Paroxysmal supraventricular tachycardia
427.31 Atrial fibrillation
427.81 Sinoatrial node dysfunction
427.89 Other specified cardiac dysrhythmias
427.9 Unspecified cardiac dysrhythmia
428.0 Congestive heart failure, unspecified — (Code, if applicable, heart failure due to hypertension first: 402.0-402.9, with fifth-digit 1 or 404.0-404.9 with fifth digit 1 or 3)
428.1 Left heart failure — (Code, if applicable, heart failure due to hypertension first: 402.0-402.9, with fifth-digit 1 or 404.0-404.9 with fifth digit 1 or 3)
428.20 Unspecified systolic heart failure — (Code, if applicable, heart failure due to hypertension first: 402.0-402.9, with fifth-digit 1 or 404.0-404.9 with fifth digit 1 or 3)
428.21 Acute systolic heart failure — (Code, if applicable, heart failure due to hypertension first: 402.0-402.9, with fifth-digit 1 or 404.0-404.9 with fifth digit 1 or 3)
428.22 Chronic systolic heart failure — (Code, if applicable, heart failure due to hypertension first: 402.0-402.9, with fifth-digit 1 or 404.0-404.9 with fifth digit 1 or 3)
428.23 Acute on chronic systolic heart failure — (Code, if applicable, heart failure due to hypertension first: 402.0-402.9, with fifth-digit 1 or 404.0-404.9 with fifth digit 1 or 3)
428.30 Unspecified diastolic heart failure — (Code, if applicable, heart failure due to hypertension first: 402.0-402.9, with fifth-digit 1 or 404.0-404.9 with fifth digit 1 or 3)
428.31 Acute diastolic heart failure — (Code, if applicable, heart failure due to hypertension first: 402.0-402.9, with fifth-digit 1 or 404.0-404.9 with fifth digit 1 or 3)
428.32 Chronic diastolic heart failure — (Code, if applicable, heart failure due to hypertension first: 402.0-402.9, with fifth-digit 1 or 404.0-404.9 with fifth digit 1 or 3)
428.33 Acute on chronic diastolic heart failure — (Code, if applicable, heart failure due to hypertension first: 402.0-402.9, with fifth-digit 1 or 404.0-404.9 with fifth digit 1 or 3)
428.40 Unspecified combined systolic and diastolic heart failure — (Code, if applicable, heart failure due to hypertension first: 402.0-402.9, with fifth-digit 1 or 404.0-404.9 with fifth digit 1 or 3)
428.41 Acute combined systolic and diastolic heart failure — (Code, if applicable, heart failure due to hypertension first: 402.0-402.9, with fifth-digit 1 or 404.0-404.9 with fifth digit 1 or 3)
428.42 Chronic combined systolic and diastolic heart failure — (Code, if applicable, heart failure due to hypertension first: 402.0-402.9, with fifth-digit 1 or 404.0-404.9 with fifth digit 1 or 3)
428.43 Acute on chronic combined systolic and diastolic heart failure — (Code, if applicable, heart failure due to hypertension first: 402.0-402.9, with fifth-digit 1 or 404.0-404.9 with fifth digit 1 or 3)
428.9 Unspecified heart failure — (Code, if applicable, heart failure due to hypertension first: 402.0-402.9, with fifth-digit 1 or 404.0-404.9 with fifth digit 1 or 3)
429.3 Cardiomegaly
746.86 Congenital heart block
996.01 Mechanical complication due to cardiac pacemaker (electrode)
996.72 Other complications due to other cardiac device, implant, and graft — (Use additional code to identify complication: 338.18-338.19, 338.28-338.29)
997.1 Cardiac complications — (Use additional code to identify complications)
V45.01 Cardiac pacemaker in situ
V53.31 Fitting and adjustment of cardiac pacemaker

ICD-9-CM Procedural

00.50 Implantation of cardiac resynchronization pacemaker without mention of defibrillation, total system (CRT-P)
00.51 Implantation of cardiac resynchronization defibrillator, total system (CRT-D)
17.81 Insertion of antimicrobial envelope
37.71 Initial insertion of transvenous lead (electrode) into ventricle
37.72 Initial insertion of transvenous leads (electrodes) into atrium and ventricle
37.73 Initial insertion of transvenous lead (electrode) into atrium
37.76 Replacement of transvenous atrial and/or ventricular lead(s) (electrode(s))
37.80 Insertion of permanent pacemaker, initial or replacement, type of device not specified
37.81 Initial insertion of single-chamber device, not specified as rate responsive
37.82 Initial insertion of single-chamber device, rate responsive
37.83 Initial insertion of dual-chamber device
37.85 Replacement of any type of pacemaker device with single-chamber device, not specified as rate responsive
37.86 Replacement of any type of pacemaker device with single-chamber device, rate responsive
37.87 Replacement of any type of pacemaker device with dual-chamber device

HCPCS Level II Supplies & Services

C1779 Lead, pacemaker, transvenous VDD single pass
C1785 Pacemaker, dual chamber, rate-responsive (implantable)
C1786 Pacemaker, single chamber, rate-responsive (implantable)
C2619 Pacemaker, dual chamber, nonrate-responsive (implantable)
C2620 Pacemaker, single chamber, nonrate-responsive (implantable)

33210-33211

33210 Insertion or replacement of temporary transvenous single chamber cardiac electrode or pacemaker catheter (separate procedure)
33211 Insertion or replacement of temporary transvenous dual chamber pacing electrodes (separate procedure)

ICD-9-CM Diagnostic

337.00 Idiopathic peripheral autonomic neuropathy, unspecified
337.01 Carotid sinus syndrome
337.09 Other idiopathic peripheral autonomic neuropathy
410.00 Acute myocardial infarction of anterolateral wall, episode of care unspecified — (Use additional code to identify presence of hypertension: 401.0-405.9)
410.01 Acute myocardial infarction of anterolateral wall, initial episode of care — (Use additional code to identify presence of hypertension: 401.0-405.9)
410.02 Acute myocardial infarction of anterolateral wall, subsequent episode of care — (Use additional code to identify presence of hypertension: 401.0-405.9)
410.10 Acute myocardial infarction of other anterior wall, episode of care unspecified — (Use additional code to identify presence of hypertension: 401.0-405.9)

410.11 Acute myocardial infarction of other anterior wall, initial episode of care — (Use additional code to identify presence of hypertension: 401.0-405.9)

410.12 Acute myocardial infarction of other anterior wall, subsequent episode of care — (Use additional code to identify presence of hypertension: 401.0-405.9)

410.20 Acute myocardial infarction of inferolateral wall, episode of care unspecified — (Use additional code to identify presence of hypertension: 401.0-405.9) ▽

410.21 Acute myocardial infarction of inferolateral wall, initial episode of care — (Use additional code to identify presence of hypertension: 401.0-405.9)

410.22 Acute myocardial infarction of inferolateral wall, subsequent episode of care — (Use additional code to identify presence of hypertension: 401.0-405.9)

410.30 Acute myocardial infarction of inferoposterior wall, episode of care unspecified — (Use additional code to identify presence of hypertension: 401.0-405.9) ▽

410.31 Acute myocardial infarction of inferoposterior wall, initial episode of care — (Use additional code to identify presence of hypertension: 401.0-405.9)

410.32 Acute myocardial infarction of inferoposterior wall, subsequent episode of care — (Use additional code to identify presence of hypertension: 401.0-405.9)

410.40 Acute myocardial infarction of other inferior wall, episode of care unspecified — (Use additional code to identify presence of hypertension: 401.0-405.9) ▽

410.41 Acute myocardial infarction of other inferior wall, initial episode of care — (Use additional code to identify presence of hypertension: 401.0-405.9)

410.42 Acute myocardial infarction of other inferior wall, subsequent episode of care — (Use additional code to identify presence of hypertension: 401.0-405.9)

410.90 Acute myocardial infarction, unspecified site, episode of care unspecified — (Use additional code to identify presence of hypertension: 401.0-405.9) ▽

426.0 Atrioventricular block, complete

426.10 Unspecified atrioventricular block ▽

426.11 First degree atrioventricular block

426.12 Mobitz (type) II atrioventricular block

426.13 Other second degree atrioventricular block

426.51 Right bundle branch block and left posterior fascicular block

426.52 Right bundle branch block and left anterior fascicular block

426.53 Other bilateral bundle branch block

426.54 Trifascicular block

426.6 Other heart block

426.7 Anomalous atrioventricular excitation

426.82 Long QT syndrome

426.9 Unspecified conduction disorder ▽

427.0 Paroxysmal supraventricular tachycardia

427.31 Atrial fibrillation

427.32 Atrial flutter

427.5 Cardiac arrest

427.81 Sinoatrial node dysfunction

427.89 Other specified cardiac dysrhythmias

746.86 Congenital heart block

780.2 Syncope and collapse

785.1 Palpitations

785.51 Cardiogenic shock

785.9 Other symptoms involving cardiovascular system

972.1 Poisoning by cardiotonic glycosides and drugs of similar action — (Use additional code to specify the effects of poisoning)

996.01 Mechanical complication due to cardiac pacemaker (electrode)

996.03 Mechanical complication due to coronary bypass graft

996.09 Mechanical complication of cardiac device, implant, and graft, other

996.72 Other complications due to other cardiac device, implant, and graft — (Use additional code to identify complication: 338.18-338.19, 338.28-338.29)

997.1 Cardiac complications — (Use additional code to identify complications)

V45.01 Cardiac pacemaker in situ

V45.09 Other specified cardiac device in situ

V53.31 Fitting and adjustment of cardiac pacemaker

ICD-9-CM Procedural

00.52 Implantation or replacement of transvenous lead (electrode) into left ventricular coronary venous system

37.72 Initial insertion of transvenous leads (electrodes) into atrium and ventricle

37.76 Replacement of transvenous atrial and/or ventricular lead(s) (electrode(s))

37.78 Insertion of temporary transvenous pacemaker system

39.64 Intraoperative cardiac pacemaker

HCPCS Level II Supplies & Services

C1779 Lead, pacemaker, transvenous VDD single pass

33212-33213 [33221]

33212 Insertion of pacemaker pulse generator only; with existing single lead

33213 with existing dual leads

33221 with existing multiple leads

ICD-9-CM Diagnostic

426.0 Atrioventricular block, complete

426.10 Unspecified atrioventricular block ▽

426.11 First degree atrioventricular block

426.12 Mobitz (type) II atrioventricular block

426.13 Other second degree atrioventricular block

426.6 Other heart block

426.7 Anomalous atrioventricular excitation

426.82 Long QT syndrome

426.9 Unspecified conduction disorder ▽

427.0 Paroxysmal supraventricular tachycardia

427.31 Atrial fibrillation

427.89 Other specified cardiac dysrhythmias

427.9 Unspecified cardiac dysrhythmia ▽

746.86 Congenital heart block

996.01 Mechanical complication due to cardiac pacemaker (electrode)

996.09 Mechanical complication of cardiac device, implant, and graft, other

V45.01 Cardiac pacemaker in situ

V53.31 Fitting and adjustment of cardiac pacemaker

ICD-9-CM Procedural

00.53 Implantation or replacement of cardiac resynchronization pacemaker pulse generator only (CRT-P)

37.80 Insertion of permanent pacemaker, initial or replacement, type of device not specified

37.81 Initial insertion of single-chamber device, not specified as rate responsive

37.82 Initial insertion of single-chamber device, rate responsive

37.83 Initial insertion of dual-chamber device

37.85 Replacement of any type of pacemaker device with single-chamber device, not specified as rate responsive

37.86 Replacement of any type of pacemaker device with single-chamber device, rate responsive

37.87 Replacement of any type of pacemaker device with dual-chamber device

HCPCS Level II Supplies & Services

C1785 Pacemaker, dual chamber, rate-responsive (implantable)

33214

33214 Upgrade of implanted pacemaker system, conversion of single chamber system to dual chamber system (includes removal of previously placed pulse generator, testing of existing lead, insertion of new lead, insertion of new pulse generator)

ICD-9-CM Diagnostic

426.0 Atrioventricular block, complete

426.10 Unspecified atrioventricular block ▽

426.11 First degree atrioventricular block

426.12 Mobitz (type) II atrioventricular block

426.13 Other second degree atrioventricular block
426.2 Left bundle branch hemiblock
426.3 Other left bundle branch block
426.4 Right bundle branch block
426.50 Unspecified bundle branch block
426.51 Right bundle branch block and left posterior fascicular block
426.52 Right bundle branch block and left anterior fascicular block
426.53 Other bilateral bundle branch block
426.6 Other heart block
426.7 Anomalous atrioventricular excitation
426.82 Long QT syndrome
426.9 Unspecified conduction disorder
427.0 Paroxysmal supraventricular tachycardia
427.31 Atrial fibrillation
427.81 Sinoatrial node dysfunction
427.89 Other specified cardiac dysrhythmias
427.9 Unspecified cardiac dysrhythmia
428.0 Congestive heart failure, unspecified — (Code, if applicable, heart failure due to hypertension first: 402.0-402.9, with fifth-digit 1 or 404.0-404.9 with fifth digit 1 or 3)
428.1 Left heart failure — (Code, if applicable, heart failure due to hypertension first: 402.0-402.9, with fifth-digit 1 or 404.0-404.9 with fifth digit 1 or 3)
428.20 Unspecified systolic heart failure — (Code, if applicable, heart failure due to hypertension first: 402.0-402.9, with fifth-digit 1 or 404.0-404.9 with fifth digit 1 or 3)
428.21 Acute systolic heart failure — (Code, if applicable, heart failure due to hypertension first: 402.0-402.9, with fifth-digit 1 or 404.0-404.9 with fifth digit 1 or 3)
428.22 Chronic systolic heart failure — (Code, if applicable, heart failure due to hypertension first: 402.0-402.9, with fifth-digit 1 or 404.0-404.9 with fifth digit 1 or 3)
428.23 Acute on chronic systolic heart failure — (Code, if applicable, heart failure due to hypertension first: 402.0-402.9, with fifth-digit 1 or 404.0-404.9 with fifth digit 1 or 3)
428.30 Unspecified diastolic heart failure — (Code, if applicable, heart failure due to hypertension first: 402.0-402.9, with fifth-digit 1 or 404.0-404.9 with fifth digit 1 or 3)
428.31 Acute diastolic heart failure — (Code, if applicable, heart failure due to hypertension first: 402.0-402.9, with fifth-digit 1 or 404.0-404.9 with fifth digit 1 or 3)
428.32 Chronic diastolic heart failure — (Code, if applicable, heart failure due to hypertension first: 402.0-402.9, with fifth-digit 1 or 404.0-404.9 with fifth digit 1 or 3)
428.33 Acute on chronic diastolic heart failure — (Code, if applicable, heart failure due to hypertension first: 402.0-402.9, with fifth-digit 1 or 404.0-404.9 with fifth digit 1 or 3)
428.40 Unspecified combined systolic and diastolic heart failure — (Code, if applicable, heart failure due to hypertension first: 402.0-402.9, with fifth-digit 1 or 404.0-404.9 with fifth digit 1 or 3)
428.41 Acute combined systolic and diastolic heart failure — (Code, if applicable, heart failure due to hypertension first: 402.0-402.9, with fifth-digit 1 or 404.0-404.9 with fifth digit 1 or 3)
428.42 Chronic combined systolic and diastolic heart failure — (Code, if applicable, heart failure due to hypertension first: 402.0-402.9, with fifth-digit 1 or 404.0-404.9 with fifth digit 1 or 3)
428.43 Acute on chronic combined systolic and diastolic heart failure — (Code, if applicable, heart failure due to hypertension first: 402.0-402.9, with fifth-digit 1 or 404.0-404.9 with fifth digit 1 or 3)
428.9 Unspecified heart failure — (Code, if applicable, heart failure due to hypertension first: 402.0-402.9, with fifth-digit 1 or 404.0-404.9 with fifth digit 1 or 3)
746.86 Congenital heart block
996.01 Mechanical complication due to cardiac pacemaker (electrode)
996.09 Mechanical complication of cardiac device, implant, and graft, other
V45.01 Cardiac pacemaker in situ
V53.31 Fitting and adjustment of cardiac pacemaker

ICD-9-CM Procedural

00.50 Implantation of cardiac resynchronization pacemaker without mention of defibrillation, total system (CRT-P)
00.51 Implantation of cardiac resynchronization defibrillator, total system (CRT-D)
17.81 Insertion of antimicrobial envelope
37.76 Replacement of transvenous atrial and/or ventricular lead(s) (electrode(s))
37.87 Replacement of any type of pacemaker device with dual-chamber device

HCPCS Level II Supplies & Services

C1779 Lead, pacemaker, transvenous VDD single pass

33215-33217

33215 Repositioning of previously implanted transvenous pacemaker or pacing cardioverter-defibrillator (right atrial or right ventricular) electrode
33216 Insertion of a single transvenous electrode, permanent pacemaker or cardioverter-defibrillator
33217 Insertion of 2 transvenous electrodes, permanent pacemaker or cardioverter-defibrillator

ICD-9-CM Diagnostic

426.0 Atrioventricular block, complete
426.10 Unspecified atrioventricular block
426.11 First degree atrioventricular block
426.12 Mobitz (type) II atrioventricular block
426.13 Other second degree atrioventricular block
426.2 Left bundle branch hemiblock
426.3 Other left bundle branch block
426.4 Right bundle branch block
426.50 Unspecified bundle branch block
426.51 Right bundle branch block and left posterior fascicular block
426.52 Right bundle branch block and left anterior fascicular block
426.53 Other bilateral bundle branch block
426.6 Other heart block
426.7 Anomalous atrioventricular excitation
426.82 Long QT syndrome
426.9 Unspecified conduction disorder
427.0 Paroxysmal supraventricular tachycardia
427.31 Atrial fibrillation
427.81 Sinoatrial node dysfunction
427.89 Other specified cardiac dysrhythmias
427.9 Unspecified cardiac dysrhythmia
428.0 Congestive heart failure, unspecified — (Code, if applicable, heart failure due to hypertension first: 402.0-402.9, with fifth-digit 1 or 404.0-404.9 with fifth digit 1 or 3)
428.1 Left heart failure — (Code, if applicable, heart failure due to hypertension first: 402.0-402.9, with fifth-digit 1 or 404.0-404.9 with fifth digit 1 or 3)
428.20 Unspecified systolic heart failure — (Code, if applicable, heart failure due to hypertension first: 402.0-402.9, with fifth-digit 1 or 404.0-404.9 with fifth digit 1 or 3)
428.21 Acute systolic heart failure — (Code, if applicable, heart failure due to hypertension first: 402.0-402.9, with fifth-digit 1 or 404.0-404.9 with fifth digit 1 or 3)
428.22 Chronic systolic heart failure — (Code, if applicable, heart failure due to hypertension first: 402.0-402.9, with fifth-digit 1 or 404.0-404.9 with fifth digit 1 or 3)
428.23 Acute on chronic systolic heart failure — (Code, if applicable, heart failure due to hypertension first: 402.0-402.9, with fifth-digit 1 or 404.0-404.9 with fifth digit 1 or 3)
428.30 Unspecified diastolic heart failure — (Code, if applicable, heart failure due to hypertension first: 402.0-402.9, with fifth-digit 1 or 404.0-404.9 with fifth digit 1 or 3)
428.31 Acute diastolic heart failure — (Code, if applicable, heart failure due to hypertension first: 402.0-402.9, with fifth-digit 1 or 404.0-404.9 with fifth digit 1 or 3)

428.32 Chronic diastolic heart failure — (Code, if applicable, heart failure due to hypertension first: 402.0-402.9, with fifth-digit 1 or 404.0-404.9 with fifth digit 1 or 3)

428.33 Acute on chronic diastolic heart failure — (Code, if applicable, heart failure due to hypertension first: 402.0-402.9, with fifth-digit 1 or 404.0-404.9 with fifth digit 1 or 3)

428.40 Unspecified combined systolic and diastolic heart failure — (Code, if applicable, heart failure due to hypertension first: 402.0-402.9, with fifth-digit 1 or 404.0-404.9 with fifth digit 1 or 3) ▽

428.41 Acute combined systolic and diastolic heart failure — (Code, if applicable, heart failure due to hypertension first: 402.0-402.9, with fifth-digit 1 or 404.0-404.9 with fifth digit 1 or 3)

428.42 Chronic combined systolic and diastolic heart failure — (Code, if applicable, heart failure due to hypertension first: 402.0-402.9, with fifth-digit 1 or 404.0-404.9 with fifth digit 1 or 3)

428.43 Acute on chronic combined systolic and diastolic heart failure — (Code, if applicable, heart failure due to hypertension first: 402.0-402.9, with fifth-digit 1 or 404.0-404.9 with fifth digit 1 or 3)

428.9 Unspecified heart failure — (Code, if applicable, heart failure due to hypertension first: 402.0-402.9, with fifth-digit 1 or 404.0-404.9 with fifth digit 1 or 3) ▽

746.86 Congenital heart block

996.01 Mechanical complication due to cardiac pacemaker (electrode)

996.09 Mechanical complication of cardiac device, implant, and graft, other

V45.01 Cardiac pacemaker in situ

V53.31 Fitting and adjustment of cardiac pacemaker

ICD-9-CM Procedural

37.71 Initial insertion of transvenous lead (electrode) into ventricle

37.72 Initial insertion of transvenous leads (electrodes) into atrium and ventricle

37.73 Initial insertion of transvenous lead (electrode) into atrium

37.75 Revision of lead (electrode)

37.76 Replacement of transvenous atrial and/or ventricular lead(s) (electrode(s))

37.97 Replacement of automatic cardioverter/defibrillator leads(s) only

37.99 Other operations on heart and pericardium

HCPCS Level II Supplies & Services

C1777 Lead, cardioverter-defibrillator, endocardial single coil (implantable)

33218-33220

33218 Repair of single transvenous electrode, permanent pacemaker or pacing cardioverter-defibrillator

33220 Repair of 2 transvenous electrodes for permanent pacemaker or pacing cardioverter-defibrillator

ICD-9-CM Diagnostic

996.01 Mechanical complication due to cardiac pacemaker (electrode)

996.04 Mechanical complication due to automatic implantable cardiac defibrillator

996.09 Mechanical complication of cardiac device, implant, and graft, other

V45.01 Cardiac pacemaker in situ

V45.02 Automatic implantable cardiac defibrillator in situ

V53.31 Fitting and adjustment of cardiac pacemaker

V53.32 Fitting and adjustment of automatic implantable cardiac defibrillator

ICD-9-CM Procedural

37.75 Revision of lead (electrode)

33222-33223

33222 Relocation of skin pocket for pacemaker

33223 Relocation of skin pocket for cardioverter-defibrillator

ICD-9-CM Diagnostic

729.90 Disorders of soft tissue, unspecified ▽

729.91 Post-traumatic seroma

729.92 Nontraumatic hematoma of soft tissue

996.61 Infection and inflammatory reaction due to cardiac device, implant, and graft — (Use additional code to identify specified infections)

996.72 Other complications due to other cardiac device, implant, and graft — (Use additional code to identify complication: 338.18-338.19, 338.28-338.29)

998.51 Infected postoperative seroma — (Use additional code to identify organism)

998.59 Other postoperative infection — (Use additional code to identify infection)

998.6 Persistent postoperative fistula, not elsewhere classified

998.83 Non-healing surgical wound

998.89 Other specified complications

ICD-9-CM Procedural

37.79 Revision or relocation of cardiac device pocket

33224

33224 Insertion of pacing electrode, cardiac venous system, for left ventricular pacing, with attachment to previously placed pacemaker or pacing cardioverter-defibrillator pulse generator (including revision of pocket, removal, insertion, and/or replacement of existing generator)

ICD-9-CM Diagnostic

402.01 Malignant hypertensive heart disease with heart failure — (Use additional code to specify type of heart failure, 428.0-428.43, if known)

410.00 Acute myocardial infarction of anterolateral wall, episode of care unspecified — (Use additional code to identify presence of hypertension: 401.0-405.9) ▽

410.01 Acute myocardial infarction of anterolateral wall, initial episode of care — (Use additional code to identify presence of hypertension: 401.0-405.9)

410.02 Acute myocardial infarction of anterolateral wall, subsequent episode of care — (Use additional code to identify presence of hypertension: 401.0-405.9)

410.10 Acute myocardial infarction of other anterior wall, episode of care unspecified — (Use additional code to identify presence of hypertension: 401.0-405.9) ▽

410.11 Acute myocardial infarction of other anterior wall, initial episode of care — (Use additional code to identify presence of hypertension: 401.0-405.9)

410.12 Acute myocardial infarction of other anterior wall, subsequent episode of care — (Use additional code to identify presence of hypertension: 401.0-405.9)

410.20 Acute myocardial infarction of inferolateral wall, episode of care unspecified — (Use additional code to identify presence of hypertension: 401.0-405.9) ▽

410.21 Acute myocardial infarction of inferolateral wall, initial episode of care — (Use additional code to identify presence of hypertension: 401.0-405.9)

410.22 Acute myocardial infarction of inferolateral wall, subsequent episode of care — (Use additional code to identify presence of hypertension: 401.0-405.9)

410.30 Acute myocardial infarction of inferoposterior wall, episode of care unspecified — (Use additional code to identify presence of hypertension: 401.0-405.9) ▽

410.31 Acute myocardial infarction of inferoposterior wall, initial episode of care — (Use additional code to identify presence of hypertension: 401.0-405.9)

410.32 Acute myocardial infarction of inferoposterior wall, subsequent episode of care — (Use additional code to identify presence of hypertension: 401.0-405.9)

410.40 Acute myocardial infarction of other inferior wall, episode of care unspecified — (Use additional code to identify presence of hypertension: 401.0-405.9) ▽

410.41 Acute myocardial infarction of other inferior wall, initial episode of care — (Use additional code to identify presence of hypertension: 401.0-405.9)

410.42 Acute myocardial infarction of other inferior wall, subsequent episode of care — (Use additional code to identify presence of hypertension: 401.0-405.9)

410.50 Acute myocardial infarction of other lateral wall, episode of care unspecified — (Use additional code to identify presence of hypertension: 401.0-405.9) ▽

410.51 Acute myocardial infarction of other lateral wall, initial episode of care — (Use additional code to identify presence of hypertension: 401.0-405.9)

410.52 Acute myocardial infarction of other lateral wall, subsequent episode of care — (Use additional code to identify presence of hypertension: 401.0-405.9)

410.60 Acute myocardial infarction, true posterior wall infarction, episode of care unspecified — (Use additional code to identify presence of hypertension: 401.0-405.9) ▽

410.61 Acute myocardial infarction, true posterior wall infarction, initial episode of care — (Use additional code to identify presence of hypertension: 401.0-405.9)

410.62 Acute myocardial infarction, true posterior wall infarction, subsequent episode of care — (Use additional code to identify presence of hypertension: 401.0-405.9)
410.70 Acute myocardial infarction, subendocardial infarction, episode of care unspecified — (Use additional code to identify presence of hypertension: 401.0-405.9)
410.71 Acute myocardial infarction, subendocardial infarction, initial episode of care — (Use additional code to identify presence of hypertension: 401.0-405.9)
410.72 Acute myocardial infarction, subendocardial infarction, subsequent episode of care — (Use additional code to identify presence of hypertension: 401.0-405.9)
410.80 Acute myocardial infarction of other specified sites, episode of care unspecified — (Use additional code to identify presence of hypertension: 401.0-405.9)
410.81 Acute myocardial infarction of other specified sites, initial episode of care — (Use additional code to identify presence of hypertension: 401.0-405.9)
410.82 Acute myocardial infarction of other specified sites, subsequent episode of care — (Use additional code to identify presence of hypertension: 401.0-405.9)
410.90 Acute myocardial infarction, unspecified site, episode of care unspecified — (Use additional code to identify presence of hypertension: 401.0-405.9)
410.91 Acute myocardial infarction, unspecified site, initial episode of care — (Use additional code to identify presence of hypertension: 401.0-405.9)
410.92 Acute myocardial infarction, unspecified site, subsequent episode of care — (Use additional code to identify presence of hypertension: 401.0-405.9)
412 Old myocardial infarction — (Use additional code to identify presence of hypertension: 401.0-405.9)
414.8 Other specified forms of chronic ischemic heart disease — (Use additional code to identify presence of hypertension: 401.0-405.9)
425.0 Endomyocardial fibrosis
425.11 Hypertrophic obstructive cardiomyopathy
425.18 Other hypertrophic cardiomyopathy
425.2 Obscure cardiomyopathy of Africa
425.3 Endocardial fibroelastosis
425.4 Other primary cardiomyopathies
425.5 Alcoholic cardiomyopathy
425.7 Nutritional and metabolic cardiomyopathy — (Code first underlying disease: 242.0-242.9, 265.0, 271.0, 277.30-277.39, 277.5)
425.8 Cardiomyopathy in other diseases classified elsewhere — (Code first underlying disease: 135, 334.0, 359.1, 359.2)
425.9 Unspecified secondary cardiomyopathy
426.0 Atrioventricular block, complete
426.10 Unspecified atrioventricular block
426.11 First degree atrioventricular block
426.12 Mobitz (type) II atrioventricular block
426.13 Other second degree atrioventricular block
426.2 Left bundle branch hemiblock
426.3 Other left bundle branch block
426.4 Right bundle branch block
426.50 Unspecified bundle branch block
426.51 Right bundle branch block and left posterior fascicular block
426.52 Right bundle branch block and left anterior fascicular block
426.53 Other bilateral bundle branch block
426.54 Trifascicular block
426.6 Other heart block
426.7 Anomalous atrioventricular excitation
426.82 Long QT syndrome
426.9 Unspecified conduction disorder
427.0 Paroxysmal supraventricular tachycardia
427.1 Paroxysmal ventricular tachycardia
427.2 Unspecified paroxysmal tachycardia
427.31 Atrial fibrillation
427.41 Ventricular fibrillation
427.42 Ventricular flutter
427.5 Cardiac arrest
427.81 Sinoatrial node dysfunction
427.89 Other specified cardiac dysrhythmias
427.9 Unspecified cardiac dysrhythmia
428.0 Congestive heart failure, unspecified — (Code, if applicable, heart failure due to hypertension first: 402.0-402.9, with fifth-digit 1 or 404.0-404.9 with fifth digit 1 or 3)
428.1 Left heart failure — (Code, if applicable, heart failure due to hypertension first: 402.0-402.9, with fifth-digit 1 or 404.0-404.9 with fifth digit 1 or 3)
428.20 Unspecified systolic heart failure — (Code, if applicable, heart failure due to hypertension first: 402.0-402.9, with fifth-digit 1 or 404.0-404.9 with fifth digit 1 or 3)
428.21 Acute systolic heart failure — (Code, if applicable, heart failure due to hypertension first: 402.0-402.9, with fifth-digit 1 or 404.0-404.9 with fifth digit 1 or 3)
428.22 Chronic systolic heart failure — (Code, if applicable, heart failure due to hypertension first: 402.0-402.9, with fifth-digit 1 or 404.0-404.9 with fifth digit 1 or 3)
428.23 Acute on chronic systolic heart failure — (Code, if applicable, heart failure due to hypertension first: 402.0-402.9, with fifth-digit 1 or 404.0-404.9 with fifth digit 1 or 3)
428.30 Unspecified diastolic heart failure — (Code, if applicable, heart failure due to hypertension first: 402.0-402.9, with fifth-digit 1 or 404.0-404.9 with fifth digit 1 or 3)
428.31 Acute diastolic heart failure — (Code, if applicable, heart failure due to hypertension first: 402.0-402.9, with fifth-digit 1 or 404.0-404.9 with fifth digit 1 or 3)
428.32 Chronic diastolic heart failure — (Code, if applicable, heart failure due to hypertension first: 402.0-402.9, with fifth-digit 1 or 404.0-404.9 with fifth digit 1 or 3)
428.33 Acute on chronic diastolic heart failure — (Code, if applicable, heart failure due to hypertension first: 402.0-402.9, with fifth-digit 1 or 404.0-404.9 with fifth digit 1 or 3)
428.40 Unspecified combined systolic and diastolic heart failure — (Code, if applicable, heart failure due to hypertension first: 402.0-402.9, with fifth-digit 1 or 404.0-404.9 with fifth digit 1 or 3)
428.41 Acute combined systolic and diastolic heart failure — (Code, if applicable, heart failure due to hypertension first: 402.0-402.9, with fifth-digit 1 or 404.0-404.9 with fifth digit 1 or 3)
428.42 Chronic combined systolic and diastolic heart failure — (Code, if applicable, heart failure due to hypertension first: 402.0-402.9, with fifth-digit 1 or 404.0-404.9 with fifth digit 1 or 3)
428.43 Acute on chronic combined systolic and diastolic heart failure — (Code, if applicable, heart failure due to hypertension first: 402.0-402.9, with fifth-digit 1 or 404.0-404.9 with fifth digit 1 or 3)
428.9 Unspecified heart failure — (Code, if applicable, heart failure due to hypertension first: 402.0-402.9, with fifth-digit 1 or 404.0-404.9 with fifth digit 1 or 3)
429.3 Cardiomegaly
746.84 Congenital obstructive anomalies of heart, not elsewhere classified — (Use additional code for associated anomalies: 746.5, 746.81, 747.10)
746.86 Congenital heart block
794.30 Nonspecific abnormal unspecified cardiovascular function study
794.31 Nonspecific abnormal electrocardiogram (ECG) (EKG)
996.01 Mechanical complication due to cardiac pacemaker (electrode)
996.04 Mechanical complication due to automatic implantable cardiac defibrillator
996.09 Mechanical complication of cardiac device, implant, and graft, other
996.61 Infection and inflammatory reaction due to cardiac device, implant, and graft — (Use additional code to identify specified infections)
996.72 Other complications due to other cardiac device, implant, and graft — (Use additional code to identify complication: 338.18-338.19, 338.28-338.29)
998.89 Other specified complications
V45.01 Cardiac pacemaker in situ
V53.31 Fitting and adjustment of cardiac pacemaker
V53.32 Fitting and adjustment of automatic implantable cardiac defibrillator

ICD-9-CM Procedural

00.52 Implantation or replacement of transvenous lead (electrode) into left ventricular coronary venous system

00.53 Implantation or replacement of cardiac resynchronization pacemaker pulse generator only (CRT-P)

00.54 Implantation or replacement of cardiac resynchronization defibrillator pulse generator device only (CRT-D)

37.79 Revision or relocation of cardiac device pocket

37.98 Replacement of automatic cardioverter/defibrillator pulse generator only

HCPCS Level II Supplies & Services

C1900 Lead, left ventricular coronary venous system

33225

33225 Insertion of pacing electrode, cardiac venous system, for left ventricular pacing, at time of insertion of pacing cardioverter-defibrillator or pacemaker pulse generator (eg, for upgrade to dual chamber system) (List separately in addition to code for primary procedure)

ICD-9-CM Diagnostic

This is an add-on code. Refer to the corresponding primary procedure code for ICD-9-CM diagnosis code links.

ICD-9-CM Procedural

00.52 Implantation or replacement of transvenous lead (electrode) into left ventricular coronary venous system

HCPCS Level II Supplies & Services

The HCPCS Level II code(s) would be the same as the actual procedure performed because these are in-addition-to codes.

33226

33226 Repositioning of previously implanted cardiac venous system (left ventricular) electrode (including removal, insertion and/or replacement of existing generator)

ICD-9-CM Diagnostic

996.01 Mechanical complication due to cardiac pacemaker (electrode)

996.04 Mechanical complication due to automatic implantable cardiac defibrillator

996.09 Mechanical complication of cardiac device, implant, and graft, other

996.61 Infection and inflammatory reaction due to cardiac device, implant, and graft — (Use additional code to identify specified infections)

996.72 Other complications due to other cardiac device, implant, and graft — (Use additional code to identify complication: 338.18-338.19, 338.28-338.29)

V45.01 Cardiac pacemaker in situ

V53.32 Fitting and adjustment of automatic implantable cardiac defibrillator

ICD-9-CM Procedural

00.52 Implantation or replacement of transvenous lead (electrode) into left ventricular coronary venous system

37.99 Other operations on heart and pericardium

33233

33233 Removal of permanent pacemaker pulse generator only

ICD-9-CM Diagnostic

996.01 Mechanical complication due to cardiac pacemaker (electrode)

996.61 Infection and inflammatory reaction due to cardiac device, implant, and graft — (Use additional code to identify specified infections)

ICD-9-CM Procedural

37.89 Revision or removal of pacemaker device

[33227-33229]

33227 Removal of permanent pacemaker pulse generator with replacement of pacemaker pulse generator; single lead system

33228 dual lead system

33229 multiple lead system

ICD-9-CM Diagnostic

996.01 Mechanical complication due to cardiac pacemaker (electrode)

996.61 Infection and inflammatory reaction due to cardiac device, implant, and graft — (Use additional code to identify specified infections)

996.72 Other complications due to other cardiac device, implant, and graft — (Use additional code to identify complication: 338.18-338.19, 338.28-338.29)

V53.31 Fitting and adjustment of cardiac pacemaker

ICD-9-CM Procedural

00.53 Implantation or replacement of cardiac resynchronization pacemaker pulse generator only (CRT-P)

37.85 Replacement of any type of pacemaker device with single-chamber device, not specified as rate responsive

37.86 Replacement of any type of pacemaker device with single-chamber device, rate responsive

37.87 Replacement of any type of pacemaker device with dual-chamber device

33234-33235

33234 Removal of transvenous pacemaker electrode(s); single lead system, atrial or ventricular

33235 dual lead system

ICD-9-CM Diagnostic

996.01 Mechanical complication due to cardiac pacemaker (electrode)

996.61 Infection and inflammatory reaction due to cardiac device, implant, and graft — (Use additional code to identify specified infections)

ICD-9-CM Procedural

37.77 Removal of lead(s) (electrodes) without replacement

33236-33238

33236 Removal of permanent epicardial pacemaker and electrodes by thoracotomy; single lead system, atrial or ventricular

33237 dual lead system

33238 Removal of permanent transvenous electrode(s) by thoracotomy

ICD-9-CM Diagnostic

996.01 Mechanical complication due to cardiac pacemaker (electrode)

996.61 Infection and inflammatory reaction due to cardiac device, implant, and graft — (Use additional code to identify specified infections)

ICD-9-CM Procedural

37.77 Removal of lead(s) (electrodes) without replacement

37.89 Revision or removal of pacemaker device

33240 [33230, 33231]

33230 Insertion of pacing cardioverter-defibrillator pulse generator only; with existing dual leads

33231 with existing multiple leads

33240 Insertion of pacing cardioverter-defibrillator pulse generator only; with existing single lead

ICD-9-CM Diagnostic

402.11 Benign hypertensive heart disease with heart failure — (Use additional code to specify type of heart failure, 428.0-428.43, if known)

402.91 Hypertensive heart disease, unspecified, with heart failure — (Use additional code to specify type of heart failure, 428.0-428.43, if known) ▽

404.01 Hypertensive heart and chronic kidney disease, malignant, with heart failure and with chronic kidney disease stage I through stage IV, or unspecified — (Use additional code to specify type of heart failure, 428.0-428.43, if known. Use additional code to identify the stage of chronic kidney disease: 585.1-585.4, 585.9)

404.11 Hypertensive heart and chronic kidney disease, benign, with heart failure and with chronic kidney disease stage I through stage IV, or unspecified — (Use additional code to specify type of heart failure, 428.0-428.43, if known. Use additional code to identify the stage of chronic kidney disease: 585.1-585.4, 585.9)

404.13 Hypertensive heart and chronic kidney disease, benign, with heart failure and chronic kidney disease stage V or end stage renal disease — (Use additional code to specify type of heart failure, 428.0-428.43, if known. Use additional code to identify the stage of chronic kidney disease: 585.5-585.6)

404.91 Hypertensive heart and chronic kidney disease, unspecified, with heart failure and with chronic kidney disease stage I through stage IV, or unspecified — (Use additional code to specify type of heart failure, 428.0-428.43, if known. Use additional code to identify the stage of chronic kidney disease: 585.1-585.4, 585.9) ▽

404.93 Hypertensive heart and chronic kidney disease, unspecified, with heart failure and chronic kidney disease stage V or end stage renal disease — (Use additional code to specify type of heart failure, 428.0-428.43, if known. Use additional code to identify the stage of chronic kidney disease: 585.5-585.6) ▽

410.00 Acute myocardial infarction of anterolateral wall, episode of care unspecified — (Use additional code to identify presence of hypertension: 401.0-405.9) ▽

410.01 Acute myocardial infarction of anterolateral wall, initial episode of care — (Use additional code to identify presence of hypertension: 401.0-405.9)

410.02 Acute myocardial infarction of anterolateral wall, subsequent episode of care — (Use additional code to identify presence of hypertension: 401.0-405.9)

410.10 Acute myocardial infarction of other anterior wall, episode of care unspecified — (Use additional code to identify presence of hypertension: 401.0-405.9) ▽

410.11 Acute myocardial infarction of other anterior wall, initial episode of care — (Use additional code to identify presence of hypertension: 401.0-405.9)

410.12 Acute myocardial infarction of other anterior wall, subsequent episode of care — (Use additional code to identify presence of hypertension: 401.0-405.9)

410.20 Acute myocardial infarction of inferolateral wall, episode of care unspecified — (Use additional code to identify presence of hypertension: 401.0-405.9) ▽

410.21 Acute myocardial infarction of inferolateral wall, initial episode of care — (Use additional code to identify presence of hypertension: 401.0-405.9)

410.22 Acute myocardial infarction of inferolateral wall, subsequent episode of care — (Use additional code to identify presence of hypertension: 401.0-405.9)

410.30 Acute myocardial infarction of inferoposterior wall, episode of care unspecified — (Use additional code to identify presence of hypertension: 401.0-405.9) ▽

410.31 Acute myocardial infarction of inferoposterior wall, initial episode of care — (Use additional code to identify presence of hypertension: 401.0-405.9)

410.32 Acute myocardial infarction of inferoposterior wall, subsequent episode of care — (Use additional code to identify presence of hypertension: 401.0-405.9)

410.40 Acute myocardial infarction of other inferior wall, episode of care unspecified — (Use additional code to identify presence of hypertension: 401.0-405.9) ▽

410.41 Acute myocardial infarction of other inferior wall, initial episode of care — (Use additional code to identify presence of hypertension: 401.0-405.9)

410.42 Acute myocardial infarction of other inferior wall, subsequent episode of care — (Use additional code to identify presence of hypertension: 401.0-405.9)

410.50 Acute myocardial infarction of other lateral wall, episode of care unspecified — (Use additional code to identify presence of hypertension: 401.0-405.9) ▽

410.51 Acute myocardial infarction of other lateral wall, initial episode of care — (Use additional code to identify presence of hypertension: 401.0-405.9)

410.52 Acute myocardial infarction of other lateral wall, subsequent episode of care — (Use additional code to identify presence of hypertension: 401.0-405.9)

410.60 Acute myocardial infarction, true posterior wall infarction, episode of care unspecified — (Use additional code to identify presence of hypertension: 401.0-405.9) ▽

410.61 Acute myocardial infarction, true posterior wall infarction, initial episode of care — (Use additional code to identify presence of hypertension: 401.0-405.9)

410.62 Acute myocardial infarction, true posterior wall infarction, subsequent episode of care — (Use additional code to identify presence of hypertension: 401.0-405.9)

410.70 Acute myocardial infarction, subendocardial infarction, episode of care unspecified — (Use additional code to identify presence of hypertension: 401.0-405.9) ▽

410.71 Acute myocardial infarction, subendocardial infarction, initial episode of care — (Use additional code to identify presence of hypertension: 401.0-405.9)

410.72 Acute myocardial infarction, subendocardial infarction, subsequent episode of care — (Use additional code to identify presence of hypertension: 401.0-405.9)

410.80 Acute myocardial infarction of other specified sites, episode of care unspecified — (Use additional code to identify presence of hypertension: 401.0-405.9) ▽

410.81 Acute myocardial infarction of other specified sites, initial episode of care — (Use additional code to identify presence of hypertension: 401.0-405.9)

410.82 Acute myocardial infarction of other specified sites, subsequent episode of care — (Use additional code to identify presence of hypertension: 401.0-405.9)

410.90 Acute myocardial infarction, unspecified site, episode of care unspecified — (Use additional code to identify presence of hypertension: 401.0-405.9) ▽

410.91 Acute myocardial infarction, unspecified site, initial episode of care — (Use additional code to identify presence of hypertension: 401.0-405.9) ▽

410.92 Acute myocardial infarction, unspecified site, subsequent episode of care — (Use additional code to identify presence of hypertension: 401.0-405.9) ▽

412 Old myocardial infarction — (Use additional code to identify presence of hypertension: 401.0-405.9)

414.8 Other specified forms of chronic ischemic heart disease — (Use additional code to identify presence of hypertension: 401.0-405.9)

425.4 Other primary cardiomyopathies

426.0 Atrioventricular block, complete

426.10 Unspecified atrioventricular block ▽

426.11 First degree atrioventricular block

426.12 Mobitz (type) II atrioventricular block

426.13 Other second degree atrioventricular block

426.6 Other heart block

426.7 Anomalous atrioventricular excitation

426.82 Long QT syndrome

426.9 Unspecified conduction disorder ▽

427.0 Paroxysmal supraventricular tachycardia

427.1 Paroxysmal ventricular tachycardia

427.31 Atrial fibrillation

427.41 Ventricular fibrillation

427.42 Ventricular flutter

427.5 Cardiac arrest

427.81 Sinoatrial node dysfunction

427.89 Other specified cardiac dysrhythmias

427.9 Unspecified cardiac dysrhythmia ▽

428.0 Congestive heart failure, unspecified — (Code, if applicable, heart failure due to hypertension first: 402.0-402.9, with fifth-digit 1 or 404.0-404.9 with fifth digit 1 or 3) ▽

428.1 Left heart failure — (Code, if applicable, heart failure due to hypertension first: 402.0-402.9, with fifth-digit 1 or 404.0-404.9 with fifth digit 1 or 3)

428.20 Unspecified systolic heart failure — (Code, if applicable, heart failure due to hypertension first: 402.0-402.9, with fifth-digit 1 or 404.0-404.9 with fifth digit 1 or 3) ▽

428.21 Acute systolic heart failure — (Code, if applicable, heart failure due to hypertension first: 402.0-402.9, with fifth-digit 1 or 404.0-404.9 with fifth digit 1 or 3)

428.22 Chronic systolic heart failure — (Code, if applicable, heart failure due to hypertension first: 402.0-402.9, with fifth-digit 1 or 404.0-404.9 with fifth digit 1 or 3)

428.23 Acute on chronic systolic heart failure — (Code, if applicable, heart failure due to hypertension first: 402.0-402.9, with fifth-digit 1 or 404.0-404.9 with fifth digit 1 or 3)

428.30 Unspecified diastolic heart failure — (Code, if applicable, heart failure due to hypertension first: 402.0-402.9, with fifth-digit 1 or 404.0-404.9 with fifth digit 1 or 3) ▽

428.31 Acute diastolic heart failure — (Code, if applicable, heart failure due to hypertension first: 402.0-402.9, with fifth-digit 1 or 404.0-404.9 with fifth digit 1 or 3)

428.32 Chronic diastolic heart failure — (Code, if applicable, heart failure due to hypertension first: 402.0-402.9, with fifth-digit 1 or 404.0-404.9 with fifth digit 1 or 3)

428.33 Acute on chronic diastolic heart failure — (Code, if applicable, heart failure due to hypertension first: 402.0-402.9, with fifth-digit 1 or 404.0-404.9 with fifth digit 1 or 3)

428.40 Unspecified combined systolic and diastolic heart failure — (Code, if applicable, heart failure due to hypertension first: 402.0-402.9, with fifth-digit 1 or 404.0-404.9 with fifth digit 1 or 3) ▽

428.41 Acute combined systolic and diastolic heart failure — (Code, if applicable, heart failure due to hypertension first: 402.0-402.9, with fifth-digit 1 or 404.0-404.9 with fifth digit 1 or 3)

428.42 Chronic combined systolic and diastolic heart failure — (Code, if applicable, heart failure due to hypertension first: 402.0-402.9, with fifth-digit 1 or 404.0-404.9 with fifth digit 1 or 3)

428.43 Acute on chronic combined systolic and diastolic heart failure — (Code, if applicable, heart failure due to hypertension first: 402.0-402.9, with fifth-digit 1 or 404.0-404.9 with fifth digit 1 or 3)

428.9 Unspecified heart failure — (Code, if applicable, heart failure due to hypertension first: 402.0-402.9, with fifth-digit 1 or 404.0-404.9 with fifth digit 1 or 3) ▽

746.86 Congenital heart block

746.89 Other specified congenital anomaly of heart

996.04 Mechanical complication due to automatic implantable cardiac defibrillator

996.61 Infection and inflammatory reaction due to cardiac device, implant, and graft — (Use additional code to identify specified infections)

996.72 Other complications due to other cardiac device, implant, and graft — (Use additional code to identify complication: 338.18-338.19, 338.28-338.29)

V53.32 Fitting and adjustment of automatic implantable cardiac defibrillator

ICD-9-CM Procedural

00.54 Implantation or replacement of cardiac resynchronization defibrillator pulse generator device only (CRT-D)

37.96 Implantation of automatic cardioverter/defibrillator pulse generator only

37.98 Replacement of automatic cardioverter/defibrillator pulse generator only

HCPCS Level II Supplies & Services

C1721 Cardioverter-defibrillator, dual chamber (implantable)

C1722 Cardioverter-defibrillator, single chamber (implantable)

C1882 Cardioverter-defibrillator, other than single or dual chamber (implantable)

33241

33241 Removal of pacing cardioverter-defibrillator pulse generator only

ICD-9-CM Diagnostic

996.04 Mechanical complication due to automatic implantable cardiac defibrillator

996.61 Infection and inflammatory reaction due to cardiac device, implant, and graft — (Use additional code to identify specified infections)

996.72 Other complications due to other cardiac device, implant, and graft — (Use additional code to identify complication: 338.18-338.19, 338.28-338.29)

V53.32 Fitting and adjustment of automatic implantable cardiac defibrillator

ICD-9-CM Procedural

37.79 Revision or relocation of cardiac device pocket

[33262, 33263, 33264]

33262 Removal of pacing cardioverter-defibrillator pulse generator with replacement of pacing cardioverter-defibrillator pulse generator; single lead system

33263 dual lead system

33264 multiple lead system

ICD-9-CM Diagnostic

402.11 Benign hypertensive heart disease with heart failure — (Use additional code to specify type of heart failure, 428.0-428.43, if known)

402.91 Hypertensive heart disease, unspecified, with heart failure — (Use additional code to specify type of heart failure, 428.0-428.43, if known) ▽

404.01 Hypertensive heart and chronic kidney disease, malignant, with heart failure and with chronic kidney disease stage I through stage IV, or unspecified — (Use additional code to specify type of heart failure, 428.0-428.43, if known. Use additional code to identify the stage of chronic kidney disease: 585.1-585.4, 585.9)

404.11 Hypertensive heart and chronic kidney disease, benign, with heart failure and with chronic kidney disease stage I through stage IV, or unspecified — (Use additional code to specify type of heart failure, 428.0-428.43, if known. Use additional code to identify the stage of chronic kidney disease: 585.1-585.4, 585.9)

404.13 Hypertensive heart and chronic kidney disease, benign, with heart failure and chronic kidney disease stage V or end stage renal disease — (Use additional code to specify type of heart failure, 428.0-428.43, if known. Use additional code to identify the stage of chronic kidney disease: 585.5-585.6)

404.91 Hypertensive heart and chronic kidney disease, unspecified, with heart failure and with chronic kidney disease stage I through stage IV, or unspecified — (Use additional code to specify type of heart failure, 428.0-428.43, if known. Use additional code to identify the stage of chronic kidney disease: 585.1-585.4, 585.9) ▽

404.93 Hypertensive heart and chronic kidney disease, unspecified, with heart failure and chronic kidney disease stage V or end stage renal disease — (Use additional code to specify type of heart failure, 428.0-428.43, if known. Use additional code to identify the stage of chronic kidney disease: 585.5-585.6) ▽

410.00 Acute myocardial infarction of anterolateral wall, episode of care unspecified — (Use additional code to identify presence of hypertension: 401.0-405.9) ▽

410.01 Acute myocardial infarction of anterolateral wall, initial episode of care — (Use additional code to identify presence of hypertension: 401.0-405.9)

410.02 Acute myocardial infarction of anterolateral wall, subsequent episode of care — (Use additional code to identify presence of hypertension: 401.0-405.9)

410.10 Acute myocardial infarction of other anterior wall, episode of care unspecified — (Use additional code to identify presence of hypertension: 401.0-405.9) ▽

410.11 Acute myocardial infarction of other anterior wall, initial episode of care — (Use additional code to identify presence of hypertension: 401.0-405.9)

410.12 Acute myocardial infarction of other anterior wall, subsequent episode of care — (Use additional code to identify presence of hypertension: 401.0-405.9)

410.20 Acute myocardial infarction of inferolateral wall, episode of care unspecified — (Use additional code to identify presence of hypertension: 401.0-405.9) ▽

410.21 Acute myocardial infarction of inferolateral wall, initial episode of care — (Use additional code to identify presence of hypertension: 401.0-405.9)

410.22 Acute myocardial infarction of inferolateral wall, subsequent episode of care — (Use additional code to identify presence of hypertension: 401.0-405.9)

410.30 Acute myocardial infarction of inferoposterior wall, episode of care unspecified — (Use additional code to identify presence of hypertension: 401.0-405.9) ▽

410.31 Acute myocardial infarction of inferoposterior wall, initial episode of care — (Use additional code to identify presence of hypertension: 401.0-405.9)

410.32 Acute myocardial infarction of inferoposterior wall, subsequent episode of care — (Use additional code to identify presence of hypertension: 401.0-405.9)

410.40 Acute myocardial infarction of other inferior wall, episode of care unspecified — (Use additional code to identify presence of hypertension: 401.0-405.9) ▽

410.41 Acute myocardial infarction of other inferior wall, initial episode of care — (Use additional code to identify presence of hypertension: 401.0-405.9)

410.42 Acute myocardial infarction of other inferior wall, subsequent episode of care — (Use additional code to identify presence of hypertension: 401.0-405.9)

410.50 Acute myocardial infarction of other lateral wall, episode of care unspecified — (Use additional code to identify presence of hypertension: 401.0-405.9) ▽

410.51 Acute myocardial infarction of other lateral wall, initial episode of care — (Use additional code to identify presence of hypertension: 401.0-405.9)

410.52 Acute myocardial infarction of other lateral wall, subsequent episode of care — (Use additional code to identify presence of hypertension: 401.0-405.9)

410.60 Acute myocardial infarction, true posterior wall infarction, episode of care unspecified — (Use additional code to identify presence of hypertension: 401.0-405.9) ▽

410.61 Acute myocardial infarction, true posterior wall infarction, initial episode of care — (Use additional code to identify presence of hypertension: 401.0-405.9)

410.62 Acute myocardial infarction, true posterior wall infarction, subsequent episode of care — (Use additional code to identify presence of hypertension: 401.0-405.9)

410.70 Acute myocardial infarction, subendocardial infarction, episode of care unspecified — (Use additional code to identify presence of hypertension: 401.0-405.9) ▽

410.71 Acute myocardial infarction, subendocardial infarction, initial episode of care — (Use additional code to identify presence of hypertension: 401.0-405.9)

410.72 Acute myocardial infarction, subendocardial infarction, subsequent episode of care — (Use additional code to identify presence of hypertension: 401.0-405.9)

410.80 Acute myocardial infarction of other specified sites, episode of care unspecified — (Use additional code to identify presence of hypertension: 401.0-405.9)

410.81 Acute myocardial infarction of other specified sites, initial episode of care — (Use additional code to identify presence of hypertension: 401.0-405.9)

410.82 Acute myocardial infarction of other specified sites, subsequent episode of care — (Use additional code to identify presence of hypertension: 401.0-405.9)

410.90 Acute myocardial infarction, unspecified site, episode of care unspecified — (Use additional code to identify presence of hypertension: 401.0-405.9)

410.91 Acute myocardial infarction, unspecified site, initial episode of care — (Use additional code to identify presence of hypertension: 401.0-405.9)

410.92 Acute myocardial infarction, unspecified site, subsequent episode of care — (Use additional code to identify presence of hypertension: 401.0-405.9)

412 Old myocardial infarction — (Use additional code to identify presence of hypertension: 401.0-405.9)

414.8 Other specified forms of chronic ischemic heart disease — (Use additional code to identify presence of hypertension: 401.0-405.9)

425.4 Other primary cardiomyopathies

426.0 Atrioventricular block, complete

426.10 Unspecified atrioventricular block

426.11 First degree atrioventricular block

426.12 Mobitz (type) II atrioventricular block

426.13 Other second degree atrioventricular block

426.6 Other heart block

426.7 Anomalous atrioventricular excitation

426.82 Long QT syndrome

426.9 Unspecified conduction disorder

427.0 Paroxysmal supraventricular tachycardia

427.1 Paroxysmal ventricular tachycardia

427.31 Atrial fibrillation

427.41 Ventricular fibrillation

427.42 Ventricular flutter

427.5 Cardiac arrest

427.81 Sinoatrial node dysfunction

427.89 Other specified cardiac dysrhythmias

427.9 Unspecified cardiac dysrhythmia

428.0 Congestive heart failure, unspecified — (Code, if applicable, heart failure due to hypertension first: 402.0-402.9, with fifth-digit 1 or 404.0-404.9 with fifth digit 1 or 3)

428.1 Left heart failure — (Code, if applicable, heart failure due to hypertension first: 402.0-402.9, with fifth-digit 1 or 404.0-404.9 with fifth digit 1 or 3)

428.20 Unspecified systolic heart failure — (Code, if applicable, heart failure due to hypertension first: 402.0-402.9, with fifth-digit 1 or 404.0-404.9 with fifth digit 1 or 3)

428.21 Acute systolic heart failure — (Code, if applicable, heart failure due to hypertension first: 402.0-402.9, with fifth-digit 1 or 404.0-404.9 with fifth digit 1 or 3)

428.22 Chronic systolic heart failure — (Code, if applicable, heart failure due to hypertension first: 402.0-402.9, with fifth-digit 1 or 404.0-404.9 with fifth digit 1 or 3)

428.23 Acute on chronic systolic heart failure — (Code, if applicable, heart failure due to hypertension first: 402.0-402.9, with fifth-digit 1 or 404.0-404.9 with fifth digit 1 or 3)

428.30 Unspecified diastolic heart failure — (Code, if applicable, heart failure due to hypertension first: 402.0-402.9, with fifth-digit 1 or 404.0-404.9 with fifth digit 1 or 3)

428.31 Acute diastolic heart failure — (Code, if applicable, heart failure due to hypertension first: 402.0-402.9, with fifth-digit 1 or 404.0-404.9 with fifth digit 1 or 3)

428.32 Chronic diastolic heart failure — (Code, if applicable, heart failure due to hypertension first: 402.0-402.9, with fifth-digit 1 or 404.0-404.9 with fifth digit 1 or 3)

428.33 Acute on chronic diastolic heart failure — (Code, if applicable, heart failure due to hypertension first: 402.0-402.9, with fifth-digit 1 or 404.0-404.9 with fifth digit 1 or 3)

428.40 Unspecified combined systolic and diastolic heart failure — (Code, if applicable, heart failure due to hypertension first: 402.0-402.9, with fifth-digit 1 or 404.0-404.9 with fifth digit 1 or 3)

428.41 Acute combined systolic and diastolic heart failure — (Code, if applicable, heart failure due to hypertension first: 402.0-402.9, with fifth-digit 1 or 404.0-404.9 with fifth digit 1 or 3)

428.42 Chronic combined systolic and diastolic heart failure — (Code, if applicable, heart failure due to hypertension first: 402.0-402.9, with fifth-digit 1 or 404.0-404.9 with fifth digit 1 or 3)

428.43 Acute on chronic combined systolic and diastolic heart failure — (Code, if applicable, heart failure due to hypertension first: 402.0-402.9, with fifth-digit 1 or 404.0-404.9 with fifth digit 1 or 3)

428.9 Unspecified heart failure — (Code, if applicable, heart failure due to hypertension first: 402.0-402.9, with fifth-digit 1 or 404.0-404.9 with fifth digit 1 or 3)

746.86 Congenital heart block

746.89 Other specified congenital anomaly of heart

996.04 Mechanical complication due to automatic implantable cardiac defibrillator

996.61 Infection and inflammatory reaction due to cardiac device, implant, and graft — (Use additional code to identify specified infections)

996.72 Other complications due to other cardiac device, implant, and graft — (Use additional code to identify complication: 338.18-338.19, 338.28-338.29)

V53.32 Fitting and adjustment of automatic implantable cardiac defibrillator

ICD-9-CM Procedural

00.54 Implantation or replacement of cardiac resynchronization defibrillator pulse generator device only (CRT-D)

37.79 Revision or relocation of cardiac device pocket

37.98 Replacement of automatic cardioverter/defibrillator pulse generator only

HCPCS Level II Supplies & Services

C1721 Cardioverter-defibrillator, dual chamber (implantable)

C1722 Cardioverter-defibrillator, single chamber (implantable)

C1882 Cardioverter-defibrillator, other than single or dual chamber (implantable)

33243-33244

33243 Removal of single or dual chamber pacing cardioverter-defibrillator electrode(s); by thoracotomy

33244 by transvenous extraction

ICD-9-CM Diagnostic

996.04 Mechanical complication due to automatic implantable cardiac defibrillator

996.61 Infection and inflammatory reaction due to cardiac device, implant, and graft — (Use additional code to identify specified infections)

V53.32 Fitting and adjustment of automatic implantable cardiac defibrillator

ICD-9-CM Procedural

37.99 Other operations on heart and pericardium

33249

33249 Insertion or replacement of permanent pacing cardioverter-defibrillator system with transvenous lead(s), single or dual chamber

ICD-9-CM Diagnostic

402.01 Malignant hypertensive heart disease with heart failure — (Use additional code to specify type of heart failure, 428.0-428.43, if known)

402.11 Benign hypertensive heart disease with heart failure — (Use additional code to specify type of heart failure, 428.0-428.43, if known)

402.91 Hypertensive heart disease, unspecified, with heart failure — (Use additional code to specify type of heart failure, 428.0-428.43, if known)

404.01 Hypertensive heart and chronic kidney disease, malignant, with heart failure and with chronic kidney disease stage I through stage IV, or unspecified — (Use additional code to specify type of heart failure, 428.0-428.43, if known. Use additional code to identify the stage of chronic kidney disease: 585.1-585.4, 585.9)

404.11 Hypertensive heart and chronic kidney disease, benign, with heart failure and with chronic kidney disease stage I through stage IV, or unspecified — (Use additional code to specify type of heart failure, 428.0-428.43, if known. Use additional code to identify the stage of chronic kidney disease: 585.1-585.4, 585.9)

404.13 Hypertensive heart and chronic kidney disease, benign, with heart failure and chronic kidney disease stage V or end stage renal disease — (Use additional code to specify type of heart failure, 428.0-428.43, if known. Use additional code to identify the stage of chronic kidney disease: 585.5-585.6)

404.91 Hypertensive heart and chronic kidney disease, unspecified, with heart failure and with chronic kidney disease stage I through stage IV, or unspecified — (Use additional code to specify type of heart failure, 428.0-428.43, if known. Use additional code to identify the stage of chronic kidney disease: 585.1-585.4, 585.9) ▼

404.93 Hypertensive heart and chronic kidney disease, unspecified, with heart failure and chronic kidney disease stage V or end stage renal disease — (Use additional code to specify type of heart failure, 428.0-428.43, if known. Use additional code to identify the stage of chronic kidney disease: 585.5-585.6) ▼

410.00 Acute myocardial infarction of anterolateral wall, episode of care unspecified — (Use additional code to identify presence of hypertension: 401.0-405.9) ▼

410.01 Acute myocardial infarction of anterolateral wall, initial episode of care — (Use additional code to identify presence of hypertension: 401.0-405.9)

410.02 Acute myocardial infarction of anterolateral wall, subsequent episode of care — (Use additional code to identify presence of hypertension: 401.0-405.9)

410.10 Acute myocardial infarction of other anterior wall, episode of care unspecified — (Use additional code to identify presence of hypertension: 401.0-405.9) ▼

410.11 Acute myocardial infarction of other anterior wall, initial episode of care — (Use additional code to identify presence of hypertension: 401.0-405.9)

410.12 Acute myocardial infarction of other anterior wall, subsequent episode of care — (Use additional code to identify presence of hypertension: 401.0-405.9)

410.20 Acute myocardial infarction of inferolateral wall, episode of care unspecified — (Use additional code to identify presence of hypertension: 401.0-405.9) ▼

410.21 Acute myocardial infarction of inferolateral wall, initial episode of care — (Use additional code to identify presence of hypertension: 401.0-405.9)

410.22 Acute myocardial infarction of inferolateral wall, subsequent episode of care — (Use additional code to identify presence of hypertension: 401.0-405.9)

410.30 Acute myocardial infarction of inferoposterior wall, episode of care unspecified — (Use additional code to identify presence of hypertension: 401.0-405.9) ▼

410.31 Acute myocardial infarction of inferoposterior wall, initial episode of care — (Use additional code to identify presence of hypertension: 401.0-405.9)

410.32 Acute myocardial infarction of inferoposterior wall, subsequent episode of care — (Use additional code to identify presence of hypertension: 401.0-405.9)

410.40 Acute myocardial infarction of other inferior wall, episode of care unspecified — (Use additional code to identify presence of hypertension: 401.0-405.9) ▼

410.41 Acute myocardial infarction of other inferior wall, initial episode of care — (Use additional code to identify presence of hypertension: 401.0-405.9)

410.42 Acute myocardial infarction of other inferior wall, subsequent episode of care — (Use additional code to identify presence of hypertension: 401.0-405.9)

410.50 Acute myocardial infarction of other lateral wall, episode of care unspecified — (Use additional code to identify presence of hypertension: 401.0-405.9) ▼

410.51 Acute myocardial infarction of other lateral wall, initial episode of care — (Use additional code to identify presence of hypertension: 401.0-405.9)

410.52 Acute myocardial infarction of other lateral wall, subsequent episode of care — (Use additional code to identify presence of hypertension: 401.0-405.9)

410.60 Acute myocardial infarction, true posterior wall infarction, episode of care unspecified — (Use additional code to identify presence of hypertension: 401.0-405.9) ▼

410.61 Acute myocardial infarction, true posterior wall infarction, initial episode of care — (Use additional code to identify presence of hypertension: 401.0-405.9)

410.62 Acute myocardial infarction, true posterior wall infarction, subsequent episode of care — (Use additional code to identify presence of hypertension: 401.0-405.9)

410.70 Acute myocardial infarction, subendocardial infarction, episode of care unspecified — (Use additional code to identify presence of hypertension: 401.0-405.9) ▼

410.71 Acute myocardial infarction, subendocardial infarction, initial episode of care — (Use additional code to identify presence of hypertension: 401.0-405.9)

410.72 Acute myocardial infarction, subendocardial infarction, subsequent episode of care — (Use additional code to identify presence of hypertension: 401.0-405.9)

410.80 Acute myocardial infarction of other specified sites, episode of care unspecified — (Use additional code to identify presence of hypertension: 401.0-405.9) ▼

410.81 Acute myocardial infarction of other specified sites, initial episode of care — (Use additional code to identify presence of hypertension: 401.0-405.9)

410.82 Acute myocardial infarction of other specified sites, subsequent episode of care — (Use additional code to identify presence of hypertension: 401.0-405.9)

410.90 Acute myocardial infarction, unspecified site, episode of care unspecified — (Use additional code to identify presence of hypertension: 401.0-405.9) ▼

410.91 Acute myocardial infarction, unspecified site, initial episode of care — (Use additional code to identify presence of hypertension: 401.0-405.9) ▼

410.92 Acute myocardial infarction, unspecified site, subsequent episode of care — (Use additional code to identify presence of hypertension: 401.0-405.9) ▼

412 Old myocardial infarction — (Use additional code to identify presence of hypertension: 401.0-405.9)

414.8 Other specified forms of chronic ischemic heart disease — (Use additional code to identify presence of hypertension: 401.0-405.9)

425.11 Hypertrophic obstructive cardiomyopathy

425.18 Other hypertrophic cardiomyopathy

425.4 Other primary cardiomyopathies

426.82 Long QT syndrome

427.0 Paroxysmal supraventricular tachycardia

427.1 Paroxysmal ventricular tachycardia

427.41 Ventricular fibrillation

427.42 Ventricular flutter

427.5 Cardiac arrest

427.89 Other specified cardiac dysrhythmias

428.0 Congestive heart failure, unspecified — (Code, if applicable, heart failure due to hypertension first: 402.0-402.9, with fifth-digit 1 or 404.0-404.9 with fifth digit 1 or 3) ▼

428.1 Left heart failure — (Code, if applicable, heart failure due to hypertension first: 402.0-402.9, with fifth-digit 1 or 404.0-404.9 with fifth digit 1 or 3)

428.20 Unspecified systolic heart failure — (Code, if applicable, heart failure due to hypertension first: 402.0-402.9, with fifth-digit 1 or 404.0-404.9 with fifth digit 1 or 3) ▼

428.21 Acute systolic heart failure — (Code, if applicable, heart failure due to hypertension first: 402.0-402.9, with fifth-digit 1 or 404.0-404.9 with fifth digit 1 or 3)

428.22 Chronic systolic heart failure — (Code, if applicable, heart failure due to hypertension first: 402.0-402.9, with fifth-digit 1 or 404.0-404.9 with fifth digit 1 or 3)

428.23 Acute on chronic systolic heart failure — (Code, if applicable, heart failure due to hypertension first: 402.0-402.9, with fifth-digit 1 or 404.0-404.9 with fifth digit 1 or 3)

428.30 Unspecified diastolic heart failure — (Code, if applicable, heart failure due to hypertension first: 402.0-402.9, with fifth-digit 1 or 404.0-404.9 with fifth digit 1 or 3) ▼

428.31 Acute diastolic heart failure — (Code, if applicable, heart failure due to hypertension first: 402.0-402.9, with fifth-digit 1 or 404.0-404.9 with fifth digit 1 or 3)

428.32 Chronic diastolic heart failure — (Code, if applicable, heart failure due to hypertension first: 402.0-402.9, with fifth-digit 1 or 404.0-404.9 with fifth digit 1 or 3)

428.33 Acute on chronic diastolic heart failure — (Code, if applicable, heart failure due to hypertension first: 402.0-402.9, with fifth-digit 1 or 404.0-404.9 with fifth digit 1 or 3)

428.40 Unspecified combined systolic and diastolic heart failure — (Code, if applicable, heart failure due to hypertension first: 402.0-402.9, with fifth-digit 1 or 404.0-404.9 with fifth digit 1 or 3) ▼

428.41 Acute combined systolic and diastolic heart failure — (Code, if applicable, heart failure due to hypertension first: 402.0-402.9, with fifth-digit 1 or 404.0-404.9 with fifth digit 1 or 3)

428.42 Chronic combined systolic and diastolic heart failure — (Code, if applicable, heart failure due to hypertension first: 402.0-402.9, with fifth-digit 1 or 404.0-404.9 with fifth digit 1 or 3)

428.43 Acute on chronic combined systolic and diastolic heart failure — (Code, if applicable, heart failure due to hypertension first: 402.0-402.9, with fifth-digit 1 or 404.0-404.9 with fifth digit 1 or 3)

428.9 Unspecified heart failure — (Code, if applicable, heart failure due to hypertension first: 402.0-402.9, with fifth-digit 1 or 404.0-404.9 with fifth digit 1 or 3) ▽

746.89 Other specified congenital anomaly of heart

996.04 Mechanical complication due to automatic implantable cardiac defibrillator

996.61 Infection and inflammatory reaction due to cardiac device, implant, and graft — (Use additional code to identify specified infections)

996.72 Other complications due to other cardiac device, implant, and graft — (Use additional code to identify complication: 338.18-338.19, 338.28-338.29)

V45.02 Automatic implantable cardiac defibrillator in situ

V53.32 Fitting and adjustment of automatic implantable cardiac defibrillator

V53.39 Fitting and adjustment of other cardiac device

ICD-9-CM Procedural

00.51 Implantation of cardiac resynchronization defibrillator, total system (CRT-D)

37.94 Implantation or replacement of automatic cardioverter/ defibrillator, total system (AICD)

37.96 Implantation of automatic cardioverter/defibrillator pulse generator only

37.98 Replacement of automatic cardioverter/defibrillator pulse generator only

37.99 Other operations on heart and pericardium

HCPCS Level II Supplies & Services

C1721 Cardioverter-defibrillator, dual chamber (implantable)

C1722 Cardioverter-defibrillator, single chamber (implantable)

C1882 Cardioverter-defibrillator, other than single or dual chamber (implantable)

33250-33251

33250 Operative ablation of supraventricular arrhythmogenic focus or pathway (eg, Wolff-Parkinson-White, atrioventricular node re-entry), tract(s) and/or focus (foci); without cardiopulmonary bypass

33251 with cardiopulmonary bypass

ICD-9-CM Diagnostic

426.7 Anomalous atrioventricular excitation

426.81 Lown-Ganong-Levine syndrome

426.89 Other specified conduction disorder

427.0 Paroxysmal supraventricular tachycardia

427.1 Paroxysmal ventricular tachycardia

427.31 Atrial fibrillation

427.32 Atrial flutter

427.41 Ventricular fibrillation

427.89 Other specified cardiac dysrhythmias

ICD-9-CM Procedural

37.33 Excision or destruction of other lesion or tissue of heart, open approach

39.61 Extracorporeal circulation auxiliary to open heart surgery

33254-33256

33254 Operative tissue ablation and reconstruction of atria, limited (eg, modified maze procedure)

33255 Operative tissue ablation and reconstruction of atria, extensive (eg, maze procedure); without cardiopulmonary bypass

33256 with cardiopulmonary bypass

ICD-9-CM Diagnostic

427.0 Paroxysmal supraventricular tachycardia

427.31 Atrial fibrillation

427.32 Atrial flutter

427.89 Other specified cardiac dysrhythmias

ICD-9-CM Procedural

37.33 Excision or destruction of other lesion or tissue of heart, open approach

37.34 Excision or destruction of other lesion or tissue of heart, endovascular approach

39.61 Extracorporeal circulation auxiliary to open heart surgery

33257-33259

33257 Operative tissue ablation and reconstruction of atria, performed at the time of other cardiac procedure(s), limited (eg, modified maze procedure) (List separately in addition to code for primary procedure)

33258 Operative tissue ablation and reconstruction of atria, performed at the time of other cardiac procedure(s), extensive (eg, maze procedure), without cardiopulmonary bypass (List separately in addition to code for primary procedure)

33259 Operative tissue ablation and reconstruction of atria, performed at the time of other cardiac procedure(s), extensive (eg, maze procedure), with cardiopulmonary bypass (List separately in addition to code for primary procedure)

ICD-9-CM Diagnostic

427.0 Paroxysmal supraventricular tachycardia

427.31 Atrial fibrillation

427.32 Atrial flutter

427.89 Other specified cardiac dysrhythmias

ICD-9-CM Procedural

37.33 Excision or destruction of other lesion or tissue of heart, open approach

37.34 Excision or destruction of other lesion or tissue of heart, endovascular approach

39.61 Extracorporeal circulation auxiliary to open heart surgery

33261

33261 Operative ablation of ventricular arrhythmogenic focus with cardiopulmonary bypass

ICD-9-CM Diagnostic

426.7 Anomalous atrioventricular excitation

426.81 Lown-Ganong-Levine syndrome

426.89 Other specified conduction disorder

427.0 Paroxysmal supraventricular tachycardia

427.1 Paroxysmal ventricular tachycardia

427.31 Atrial fibrillation

427.32 Atrial flutter

427.41 Ventricular fibrillation

427.42 Ventricular flutter

427.89 Other specified cardiac dysrhythmias

ICD-9-CM Procedural

37.33 Excision or destruction of other lesion or tissue of heart, open approach

39.61 Extracorporeal circulation auxiliary to open heart surgery

33265-33266

33265 Endoscopy, surgical; operative tissue ablation and reconstruction of atria, limited (eg, modified maze procedure), without cardiopulmonary bypass

33266 operative tissue ablation and reconstruction of atria, extensive (eg, maze procedure), without cardiopulmonary bypass

ICD-9-CM Diagnostic

427.0 Paroxysmal supraventricular tachycardia

427.31 Atrial fibrillation

427.32 Atrial flutter

427.89 Other specified cardiac dysrhythmias

ICD-9-CM Procedural

37.34 Excision or destruction of other lesion or tissue of heart, endovascular approach

33282-33284

33282 Implantation of patient-activated cardiac event recorder
33284 Removal of an implantable, patient-activated cardiac event recorder

ICD-9-CM Diagnostic

337.00 Idiopathic peripheral autonomic neuropathy, unspecified ▽
337.01 Carotid sinus syndrome
337.09 Other idiopathic peripheral autonomic neuropathy
426.0 Atrioventricular block, complete
426.10 Unspecified atrioventricular block ▽
426.11 First degree atrioventricular block
426.12 Mobitz (type) II atrioventricular block
426.13 Other second degree atrioventricular block
426.6 Other heart block
426.7 Anomalous atrioventricular excitation
426.9 Unspecified conduction disorder ▽
427.0 Paroxysmal supraventricular tachycardia
427.1 Paroxysmal ventricular tachycardia
427.31 Atrial fibrillation
427.32 Atrial flutter
427.41 Ventricular fibrillation
427.42 Ventricular flutter
427.5 Cardiac arrest
427.60 Unspecified premature beats ▽
427.61 Supraventricular premature beats
427.69 Other premature beats
427.81 Sinoatrial node dysfunction
427.89 Other specified cardiac dysrhythmias
427.9 Unspecified cardiac dysrhythmia ▽
729.90 Disorders of soft tissue, unspecified ▽
729.92 Nontraumatic hematoma of soft tissue
746.86 Congenital heart block
780.2 Syncope and collapse
780.4 Dizziness and giddiness
785.0 Unspecified tachycardia ▽
785.1 Palpitations
794.31 Nonspecific abnormal electrocardiogram (ECG) (EKG)
996.09 Mechanical complication of cardiac device, implant, and graft, other
996.61 Infection and inflammatory reaction due to cardiac device, implant, and graft — (Use additional code to identify specified infections)
996.72 Other complications due to other cardiac device, implant, and graft — (Use additional code to identify complication: 338.18-338.19, 338.28-338.29)
997.1 Cardiac complications — (Use additional code to identify complications)
998.51 Infected postoperative seroma — (Use additional code to identify organism)
998.59 Other postoperative infection — (Use additional code to identify infection)
998.89 Other specified complications
V45.09 Other specified cardiac device in situ
V53.39 Fitting and adjustment of other cardiac device

ICD-9-CM Procedural

37.79 Revision or relocation of cardiac device pocket
86.05 Incision with removal of foreign body or device from skin and subcutaneous tissue
86.09 Other incision of skin and subcutaneous tissue
89.50 Ambulatory cardiac monitoring

HCPCS Level II Supplies & Services

C1764 Event recorder, cardiac (implantable)
E0616 Implantable cardiac event recorder with memory, activator, and programmer

33300-33305

33300 Repair of cardiac wound; without bypass
33305 with cardiopulmonary bypass

ICD-9-CM Diagnostic

861.00 Unspecified injury to heart without mention of open wound into thorax ▽
861.01 Heart contusion without mention of open wound into thorax
861.02 Heart laceration without penetration of heart chambers or mention of open wound into thorax
861.03 Heart laceration with penetration of heart chambers, without mention of open wound into thorax
861.10 Unspecified injury to heart with open wound into thorax ▽
861.11 Heart contusion with open wound into thorax
861.12 Heart laceration without penetration of heart chambers, with open wound into thorax
861.13 Heart laceration with penetration of heart chambers and open wound into thorax
862.8 Injury to multiple and unspecified intrathoracic organs without mention of open wound into cavity
862.9 Injury to multiple and unspecified intrathoracic organs with open wound into cavity
998.2 Accidental puncture or laceration during procedure

ICD-9-CM Procedural

35.31 Operations on papillary muscle
35.32 Operations on chordae tendineae
37.49 Other repair of heart and pericardium
39.61 Extracorporeal circulation auxiliary to open heart surgery

33310-33315

33310 Cardiotomy, exploratory (includes removal of foreign body, atrial or ventricular thrombus); without bypass
33315 with cardiopulmonary bypass

ICD-9-CM Diagnostic

410.00 Acute myocardial infarction of anterolateral wall, episode of care unspecified — (Use additional code to identify presence of hypertension: 401.0-405.9) ▽
410.01 Acute myocardial infarction of anterolateral wall, initial episode of care — (Use additional code to identify presence of hypertension: 401.0-405.9)
410.02 Acute myocardial infarction of anterolateral wall, subsequent episode of care — (Use additional code to identify presence of hypertension: 401.0-405.9)
410.10 Acute myocardial infarction of other anterior wall, episode of care unspecified — (Use additional code to identify presence of hypertension: 401.0-405.9) ▽
410.11 Acute myocardial infarction of other anterior wall, initial episode of care — (Use additional code to identify presence of hypertension: 401.0-405.9)
410.12 Acute myocardial infarction of other anterior wall, subsequent episode of care — (Use additional code to identify presence of hypertension: 401.0-405.9)
410.20 Acute myocardial infarction of inferolateral wall, episode of care unspecified — (Use additional code to identify presence of hypertension: 401.0-405.9) ▽
410.21 Acute myocardial infarction of inferolateral wall, initial episode of care — (Use additional code to identify presence of hypertension: 401.0-405.9)
410.22 Acute myocardial infarction of inferolateral wall, subsequent episode of care — (Use additional code to identify presence of hypertension: 401.0-405.9)
410.30 Acute myocardial infarction of inferoposterior wall, episode of care unspecified — (Use additional code to identify presence of hypertension: 401.0-405.9) ▽
410.31 Acute myocardial infarction of inferoposterior wall, initial episode of care — (Use additional code to identify presence of hypertension: 401.0-405.9)
410.32 Acute myocardial infarction of inferoposterior wall, subsequent episode of care — (Use additional code to identify presence of hypertension: 401.0-405.9)
410.40 Acute myocardial infarction of other inferior wall, episode of care unspecified — (Use additional code to identify presence of hypertension: 401.0-405.9) ▽
410.41 Acute myocardial infarction of other inferior wall, initial episode of care — (Use additional code to identify presence of hypertension: 401.0-405.9)
410.42 Acute myocardial infarction of other inferior wall, subsequent episode of care — (Use additional code to identify presence of hypertension: 401.0-405.9)

410.50 Acute myocardial infarction of other lateral wall, episode of care unspecified — (Use additional code to identify presence of hypertension: 401.0-405.9) ▽
410.51 Acute myocardial infarction of other lateral wall, initial episode of care — (Use additional code to identify presence of hypertension: 401.0-405.9)
410.52 Acute myocardial infarction of other lateral wall, subsequent episode of care — (Use additional code to identify presence of hypertension: 401.0-405.9)
410.60 Acute myocardial infarction, true posterior wall infarction, episode of care unspecified — (Use additional code to identify presence of hypertension: 401.0-405.9) ▽
410.61 Acute myocardial infarction, true posterior wall infarction, initial episode of care — (Use additional code to identify presence of hypertension: 401.0-405.9)
410.62 Acute myocardial infarction, true posterior wall infarction, subsequent episode of care — (Use additional code to identify presence of hypertension: 401.0-405.9)
410.70 Acute myocardial infarction, subendocardial infarction, episode of care unspecified — (Use additional code to identify presence of hypertension: 401.0-405.9) ▽
410.71 Acute myocardial infarction, subendocardial infarction, initial episode of care — (Use additional code to identify presence of hypertension: 401.0-405.9)
410.72 Acute myocardial infarction, subendocardial infarction, subsequent episode of care — (Use additional code to identify presence of hypertension: 401.0-405.9)
410.80 Acute myocardial infarction of other specified sites, episode of care unspecified — (Use additional code to identify presence of hypertension: 401.0-405.9) ▽
410.81 Acute myocardial infarction of other specified sites, initial episode of care — (Use additional code to identify presence of hypertension: 401.0-405.9)
410.82 Acute myocardial infarction of other specified sites, subsequent episode of care — (Use additional code to identify presence of hypertension: 401.0-405.9)
410.90 Acute myocardial infarction, unspecified site, episode of care unspecified — (Use additional code to identify presence of hypertension: 401.0-405.9) ▽
410.91 Acute myocardial infarction, unspecified site, initial episode of care — (Use additional code to identify presence of hypertension: 401.0-405.9) ▽
410.92 Acute myocardial infarction, unspecified site, subsequent episode of care — (Use additional code to identify presence of hypertension: 401.0-405.9) ▽
424.90 Endocarditis, valve unspecified, unspecified cause ▽
861.00 Unspecified injury to heart without mention of open wound into thorax ▽
861.01 Heart contusion without mention of open wound into thorax
861.02 Heart laceration without penetration of heart chambers or mention of open wound into thorax
861.03 Heart laceration with penetration of heart chambers, without mention of open wound into thorax
861.10 Unspecified injury to heart with open wound into thorax ▽
861.11 Heart contusion with open wound into thorax
861.12 Heart laceration without penetration of heart chambers, with open wound into thorax
861.13 Heart laceration with penetration of heart chambers and open wound into thorax
862.8 Injury to multiple and unspecified intrathoracic organs without mention of open wound into cavity
862.9 Injury to multiple and unspecified intrathoracic organs with open wound into cavity
996.01 Mechanical complication due to cardiac pacemaker (electrode)
996.1 Mechanical complication of other vascular device, implant, and graft
997.1 Cardiac complications — (Use additional code to identify complications)
998.2 Accidental puncture or laceration during procedure
998.4 Foreign body accidentally left during procedure, not elsewhere classified

ICD-9-CM Procedural

37.11 Cardiotomy
39.61 Extracorporeal circulation auxiliary to open heart surgery

33320-33322

33320 Suture repair of aorta or great vessels; without shunt or cardiopulmonary bypass
33321 with shunt bypass
33322 with cardiopulmonary bypass

ICD-9-CM Diagnostic

901.0 Thoracic aorta injury
901.2 Superior vena cava injury
901.40 Injury to unspecified pulmonary vessel(s) ▽
901.41 Pulmonary artery injury
901.42 Pulmonary vein injury
902.0 Abdominal aorta injury
902.10 Unspecified inferior vena cava injury ▽
998.2 Accidental puncture or laceration during procedure

ICD-9-CM Procedural

39.23 Other intrathoracic vascular shunt or bypass
39.31 Suture of artery
39.32 Suture of vein
39.61 Extracorporeal circulation auxiliary to open heart surgery

33330-33335

33330 Insertion of graft, aorta or great vessels; without shunt, or cardiopulmonary bypass
33332 with shunt bypass
33335 with cardiopulmonary bypass

ICD-9-CM Diagnostic

901.0 Thoracic aorta injury
901.2 Superior vena cava injury
901.40 Injury to unspecified pulmonary vessel(s) ▽
901.41 Pulmonary artery injury
901.42 Pulmonary vein injury
902.0 Abdominal aorta injury
902.10 Unspecified inferior vena cava injury ▽
998.2 Accidental puncture or laceration during procedure

ICD-9-CM Procedural

39.0 Systemic to pulmonary artery shunt
39.21 Caval-pulmonary artery anastomosis
39.23 Other intrathoracic vascular shunt or bypass
39.56 Repair of blood vessel with tissue patch graft
39.57 Repair of blood vessel with synthetic patch graft
39.58 Repair of blood vessel with unspecified type of patch graft
39.61 Extracorporeal circulation auxiliary to open heart surgery

33361-33369

33361 Transcatheter aortic valve replacement (TAVR/TAVI) with prosthetic valve; percutaneous femoral artery approach
33362 open femoral artery approach
33363 open axillary artery approach
33364 open iliac artery approach
33365 transaortic approach (eg, median sternotomy, mediastinotomy)
33367 cardiopulmonary bypass support with percutaneous peripheral arterial and venous cannulation (eg, femoral vessels) (List separately in addition to code for primary procedure)
33368 cardiopulmonary bypass support with open peripheral arterial and venous cannulation (eg, femoral, iliac, axillary vessels) (List separately in addition to code for primary procedure)
33369 cardiopulmonary bypass support with central arterial and venous cannulation (eg, aorta, right atrium, pulmonary artery) (List separately in addition to code for primary procedure)

ICD-9-CM Diagnostic

395.0 Rheumatic aortic stenosis
395.2 Rheumatic aortic stenosis with insufficiency
396.0 Mitral valve stenosis and aortic valve stenosis
396.8 Multiple involvement of mitral and aortic valves
424.1 Aortic valve disorders
746.3 Congenital stenosis of aortic valve

ICD-9-CM Procedural

35.05 Endovascular replacement of aortic valve
39.61 Extracorporeal circulation auxiliary to open heart surgery

33366

33366 Transcatheter aortic valve replacement (TAVR/TAVI) with prosthetic valve; transapical exposure (eg, left thoracotomy)

ICD-9-CM Diagnostic

395.0 Rheumatic aortic stenosis
395.2 Rheumatic aortic stenosis with insufficiency
396.0 Mitral valve stenosis and aortic valve stenosis
396.8 Multiple involvement of mitral and aortic valves
424.1 Aortic valve disorders
746.3 Congenital stenosis of aortic valve

ICD-9-CM Procedural

35.06 Transapical replacement of aortic valve
39.61 Extracorporeal circulation auxiliary to open heart surgery

33400-33401

33400 Valvuloplasty, aortic valve; open, with cardiopulmonary bypass
33401 open, with inflow occlusion

ICD-9-CM Diagnostic

395.0 Rheumatic aortic stenosis
395.1 Rheumatic aortic insufficiency
395.2 Rheumatic aortic stenosis with insufficiency
424.1 Aortic valve disorders
446.7 Takayasu's disease
746.3 Congenital stenosis of aortic valve
747.22 Congenital atresia and stenosis of aorta

ICD-9-CM Procedural

35.11 Open heart valvuloplasty of aortic valve without replacement
39.61 Extracorporeal circulation auxiliary to open heart surgery

33403

33403 Valvuloplasty, aortic valve; using transventricular dilation, with cardiopulmonary bypass

ICD-9-CM Diagnostic

395.0 Rheumatic aortic stenosis
395.1 Rheumatic aortic insufficiency
395.2 Rheumatic aortic stenosis with insufficiency
424.1 Aortic valve disorders
446.7 Takayasu's disease
746.3 Congenital stenosis of aortic valve
747.22 Congenital atresia and stenosis of aorta

ICD-9-CM Procedural

35.11 Open heart valvuloplasty of aortic valve without replacement
39.61 Extracorporeal circulation auxiliary to open heart surgery

33404

33404 Construction of apical-aortic conduit

ICD-9-CM Diagnostic

395.0 Rheumatic aortic stenosis
395.1 Rheumatic aortic insufficiency
395.2 Rheumatic aortic stenosis with insufficiency
395.9 Other and unspecified rheumatic aortic diseases ▽
424.1 Aortic valve disorders
446.7 Takayasu's disease
746.3 Congenital stenosis of aortic valve
747.22 Congenital atresia and stenosis of aorta

ICD-9-CM Procedural

35.93 Creation of conduit between left ventricle and aorta
39.61 Extracorporeal circulation auxiliary to open heart surgery

33405-33410

33405 Replacement, aortic valve, with cardiopulmonary bypass; with prosthetic valve other than homograft or stentless valve
33406 with allograft valve (freehand)
33410 with stentless tissue valve

ICD-9-CM Diagnostic

395.0 Rheumatic aortic stenosis
395.1 Rheumatic aortic insufficiency
395.2 Rheumatic aortic stenosis with insufficiency
395.9 Other and unspecified rheumatic aortic diseases ▽
396.1 Mitral valve stenosis and aortic valve insufficiency
396.2 Mitral valve insufficiency and aortic valve stenosis
396.3 Mitral valve insufficiency and aortic valve insufficiency
396.8 Multiple involvement of mitral and aortic valves
424.1 Aortic valve disorders
424.90 Endocarditis, valve unspecified, unspecified cause ▽
746.3 Congenital stenosis of aortic valve
747.22 Congenital atresia and stenosis of aorta
862.9 Injury to multiple and unspecified intrathoracic organs with open wound into cavity
996.02 Mechanical complication due to heart valve prosthesis
996.61 Infection and inflammatory reaction due to cardiac device, implant, and graft — (Use additional code to identify specified infections)
996.71 Other complications due to heart valve prosthesis — (Use additional code to identify complication: 338.18-338.19, 338.28-338.29)

ICD-9-CM Procedural

35.21 Open and other replacement of aortic valve with tissue graft
35.22 Open and other replacement of aortic valve
39.61 Extracorporeal circulation auxiliary to open heart surgery

33411-33412

33411 Replacement, aortic valve; with aortic annulus enlargement, noncoronary sinus
33412 with transventricular aortic annulus enlargement (Konno procedure)

ICD-9-CM Diagnostic

395.0 Rheumatic aortic stenosis
395.1 Rheumatic aortic insufficiency
395.2 Rheumatic aortic stenosis with insufficiency
395.9 Other and unspecified rheumatic aortic diseases ▽
396.1 Mitral valve stenosis and aortic valve insufficiency
396.2 Mitral valve insufficiency and aortic valve stenosis
396.3 Mitral valve insufficiency and aortic valve insufficiency
396.8 Multiple involvement of mitral and aortic valves
424.1 Aortic valve disorders
424.90 Endocarditis, valve unspecified, unspecified cause ▽
746.3 Congenital stenosis of aortic valve
747.22 Congenital atresia and stenosis of aorta
862.9 Injury to multiple and unspecified intrathoracic organs with open wound into cavity
996.02 Mechanical complication due to heart valve prosthesis
996.61 Infection and inflammatory reaction due to cardiac device, implant, and graft — (Use additional code to identify specified infections)
996.71 Other complications due to heart valve prosthesis — (Use additional code to identify complication: 338.18-338.19, 338.28-338.29)

ICD-9-CM Procedural

35.21 Open and other replacement of aortic valve with tissue graft
35.22 Open and other replacement of aortic valve
35.33 Annuloplasty
39.61 Extracorporeal circulation auxiliary to open heart surgery

33413

33413 Replacement, aortic valve; by translocation of autologous pulmonary valve with allograft replacement of pulmonary valve (Ross procedure)

ICD-9-CM Diagnostic

395.0 Rheumatic aortic stenosis
395.1 Rheumatic aortic insufficiency
395.2 Rheumatic aortic stenosis with insufficiency
395.9 Other and unspecified rheumatic aortic diseases ▽
396.1 Mitral valve stenosis and aortic valve insufficiency
396.2 Mitral valve insufficiency and aortic valve stenosis
396.3 Mitral valve insufficiency and aortic valve insufficiency
396.8 Multiple involvement of mitral and aortic valves
424.1 Aortic valve disorders
424.90 Endocarditis, valve unspecified, unspecified cause ▽
746.3 Congenital stenosis of aortic valve
747.22 Congenital atresia and stenosis of aorta
862.9 Injury to multiple and unspecified intrathoracic organs with open wound into cavity
996.02 Mechanical complication due to heart valve prosthesis
996.61 Infection and inflammatory reaction due to cardiac device, implant, and graft — (Use additional code to identify specified infections)
996.71 Other complications due to heart valve prosthesis — (Use additional code to identify complication: 338.18-338.19, 338.28-338.29)

ICD-9-CM Procedural

35.21 Open and other replacement of aortic valve with tissue graft
35.25 Open and other replacement of pulmonary valve with tissue graft
39.61 Extracorporeal circulation auxiliary to open heart surgery

33414

33414 Repair of left ventricular outflow tract obstruction by patch enlargement of the outflow tract

ICD-9-CM Diagnostic

395.0 Rheumatic aortic stenosis
395.1 Rheumatic aortic insufficiency
395.2 Rheumatic aortic stenosis with insufficiency
395.9 Other and unspecified rheumatic aortic diseases ▽
424.1 Aortic valve disorders
746.3 Congenital stenosis of aortic valve
747.22 Congenital atresia and stenosis of aorta

ICD-9-CM Procedural

35.35 Operations on trabeculae carneae cordis
35.98 Other operations on septa of heart
39.61 Extracorporeal circulation auxiliary to open heart surgery

33415-33416

33415 Resection or incision of subvalvular tissue for discrete subvalvular aortic stenosis
33416 Ventriculomyotomy (-myectomy) for idiopathic hypertrophic subaortic stenosis (eg, asymmetric septal hypertrophy)

ICD-9-CM Diagnostic

395.0 Rheumatic aortic stenosis
395.1 Rheumatic aortic insufficiency
395.2 Rheumatic aortic stenosis with insufficiency
395.9 Other and unspecified rheumatic aortic diseases ▽
424.1 Aortic valve disorders
746.3 Congenital stenosis of aortic valve
747.22 Congenital atresia and stenosis of aorta

ICD-9-CM Procedural

35.35 Operations on trabeculae carneae cordis
37.11 Cardiotomy
39.61 Extracorporeal circulation auxiliary to open heart surgery

33417

33417 Aortoplasty (gusset) for supravalvular stenosis

ICD-9-CM Diagnostic

395.0 Rheumatic aortic stenosis
395.1 Rheumatic aortic insufficiency
395.2 Rheumatic aortic stenosis with insufficiency
395.9 Other and unspecified rheumatic aortic diseases ▽
424.1 Aortic valve disorders
746.3 Congenital stenosis of aortic valve
747.22 Congenital atresia and stenosis of aorta

ICD-9-CM Procedural

35.11 Open heart valvuloplasty of aortic valve without replacement
39.61 Extracorporeal circulation auxiliary to open heart surgery

33420-33422

33420 Valvotomy, mitral valve; closed heart
33422 open heart, with cardiopulmonary bypass

ICD-9-CM Diagnostic

394.0 Mitral stenosis
394.1 Rheumatic mitral insufficiency
394.2 Mitral stenosis with insufficiency
394.9 Other and unspecified mitral valve diseases ▽
396.1 Mitral valve stenosis and aortic valve insufficiency
396.2 Mitral valve insufficiency and aortic valve stenosis
396.3 Mitral valve insufficiency and aortic valve insufficiency
396.8 Multiple involvement of mitral and aortic valves
424.0 Mitral valve disorders
746.5 Congenital mitral stenosis
746.6 Congenital mitral insufficiency

ICD-9-CM Procedural

35.02 Closed heart valvotomy, mitral valve
35.12 Open heart valvuloplasty of mitral valve without replacement
39.61 Extracorporeal circulation auxiliary to open heart surgery

33425-33427

33425 Valvuloplasty, mitral valve, with cardiopulmonary bypass;
33426 with prosthetic ring
33427 radical reconstruction, with or without ring

ICD-9-CM Diagnostic

394.0 Mitral stenosis
394.1 Rheumatic mitral insufficiency
394.2 Mitral stenosis with insufficiency
394.9 Other and unspecified mitral valve diseases ▽
396.1 Mitral valve stenosis and aortic valve insufficiency
396.2 Mitral valve insufficiency and aortic valve stenosis
396.3 Mitral valve insufficiency and aortic valve insufficiency
396.8 Multiple involvement of mitral and aortic valves

424.0 Mitral valve disorders
746.5 Congenital mitral stenosis
746.6 Congenital mitral insufficiency

ICD-9-CM Procedural

35.12 Open heart valvuloplasty of mitral valve without replacement
39.61 Extracorporeal circulation auxiliary to open heart surgery

33430

33430 Replacement, mitral valve, with cardiopulmonary bypass

ICD-9-CM Diagnostic

394.0 Mitral stenosis
394.1 Rheumatic mitral insufficiency
394.2 Mitral stenosis with insufficiency
394.9 Other and unspecified mitral valve diseases ▽
396.0 Mitral valve stenosis and aortic valve stenosis
396.1 Mitral valve stenosis and aortic valve insufficiency
396.2 Mitral valve insufficiency and aortic valve stenosis
396.3 Mitral valve insufficiency and aortic valve insufficiency
396.8 Multiple involvement of mitral and aortic valves
424.0 Mitral valve disorders
424.90 Endocarditis, valve unspecified, unspecified cause ▽
710.0 Systemic lupus erythematosus — (Use additional code to identify manifestation: 424.91, 581.81, 582.81, 583.81)
746.5 Congenital mitral stenosis
746.6 Congenital mitral insufficiency
996.02 Mechanical complication due to heart valve prosthesis
996.61 Infection and inflammatory reaction due to cardiac device, implant, and graft — (Use additional code to identify specified infections)
996.71 Other complications due to heart valve prosthesis — (Use additional code to identify complication: 338.18-338.19, 338.28-338.29)

ICD-9-CM Procedural

35.23 Open and other replacement of mitral valve with tissue graft
35.24 Open and other replacement of mitral valve
39.61 Extracorporeal circulation auxiliary to open heart surgery

33460-33464

33460 Valvectomy, tricuspid valve, with cardiopulmonary bypass
33463 Valvuloplasty, tricuspid valve; without ring insertion
33464 with ring insertion

ICD-9-CM Diagnostic

397.0 Diseases of tricuspid valve
424.2 Tricuspid valve disorders, specified as nonrheumatic
424.90 Endocarditis, valve unspecified, unspecified cause ▽
746.1 Congenital tricuspid atresia and stenosis
996.02 Mechanical complication due to heart valve prosthesis
996.61 Infection and inflammatory reaction due to cardiac device, implant, and graft — (Use additional code to identify specified infections)
996.71 Other complications due to heart valve prosthesis — (Use additional code to identify complication: 338.18-338.19, 338.28-338.29)

ICD-9-CM Procedural

35.14 Open heart valvuloplasty of tricuspid valve without replacement
39.61 Extracorporeal circulation auxiliary to open heart surgery

33465

33465 Replacement, tricuspid valve, with cardiopulmonary bypass

ICD-9-CM Diagnostic

397.0 Diseases of tricuspid valve
424.2 Tricuspid valve disorders, specified as nonrheumatic
424.90 Endocarditis, valve unspecified, unspecified cause ▽
746.1 Congenital tricuspid atresia and stenosis
996.02 Mechanical complication due to heart valve prosthesis
996.61 Infection and inflammatory reaction due to cardiac device, implant, and graft — (Use additional code to identify specified infections)
996.71 Other complications due to heart valve prosthesis — (Use additional code to identify complication: 338.18-338.19, 338.28-338.29)

ICD-9-CM Procedural

35.27 Open and other replacement of tricuspid valve with tissue graft
35.28 Open and other replacement of tricuspid valve
39.61 Extracorporeal circulation auxiliary to open heart surgery

33468

33468 Tricuspid valve repositioning and plication for Ebstein anomaly

ICD-9-CM Diagnostic

746.2 Ebstein's anomaly

ICD-9-CM Procedural

35.14 Open heart valvuloplasty of tricuspid valve without replacement
39.61 Extracorporeal circulation auxiliary to open heart surgery

33470-33471

33470 Valvotomy, pulmonary valve, closed heart; transventricular
33471 via pulmonary artery

ICD-9-CM Diagnostic

424.3 Pulmonary valve disorders
424.90 Endocarditis, valve unspecified, unspecified cause ▽
746.02 Congenital stenosis of pulmonary valve
996.02 Mechanical complication due to heart valve prosthesis
996.61 Infection and inflammatory reaction due to cardiac device, implant, and graft — (Use additional code to identify specified infections)
996.71 Other complications due to heart valve prosthesis — (Use additional code to identify complication: 338.18-338.19, 338.28-338.29)

ICD-9-CM Procedural

35.03 Closed heart valvotomy, pulmonary valve

33472-33474

33472 Valvotomy, pulmonary valve, open heart; with inflow occlusion
33474 with cardiopulmonary bypass

ICD-9-CM Diagnostic

424.3 Pulmonary valve disorders
424.90 Endocarditis, valve unspecified, unspecified cause ▽
746.02 Congenital stenosis of pulmonary valve
996.02 Mechanical complication due to heart valve prosthesis
996.61 Infection and inflammatory reaction due to cardiac device, implant, and graft — (Use additional code to identify specified infections)
996.71 Other complications due to heart valve prosthesis — (Use additional code to identify complication: 338.18-338.19, 338.28-338.29)

ICD-9-CM Procedural

35.13 Open heart valvuloplasty of pulmonary valve without replacement
39.61 Extracorporeal circulation auxiliary to open heart surgery

33475

33475 Replacement, pulmonary valve

ICD-9-CM Diagnostic

424.3 Pulmonary valve disorders

424.90 Endocarditis, valve unspecified, unspecified cause ▽
746.02 Congenital stenosis of pulmonary valve
996.02 Mechanical complication due to heart valve prosthesis
996.61 Infection and inflammatory reaction due to cardiac device, implant, and graft — (Use additional code to identify specified infections)
996.71 Other complications due to heart valve prosthesis — (Use additional code to identify complication: 338.18-338.19, 338.28-338.29)

ICD-9-CM Procedural
35.25 Open and other replacement of pulmonary valve with tissue graft
35.26 Open and other replacement of pulmonary valve
39.61 Extracorporeal circulation auxiliary to open heart surgery

33476-33478
33476 Right ventricular resection for infundibular stenosis, with or without commissurotomy
33478 Outflow tract augmentation (gusset), with or without commissurotomy or infundibular resection

ICD-9-CM Diagnostic
746.02 Congenital stenosis of pulmonary valve
746.83 Congenital infundibular pulmonic stenosis

ICD-9-CM Procedural
35.13 Open heart valvuloplasty of pulmonary valve without replacement
35.34 Infundibulectomy
39.61 Extracorporeal circulation auxiliary to open heart surgery

33496
33496 Repair of non-structural prosthetic valve dysfunction with cardiopulmonary bypass (separate procedure)

ICD-9-CM Diagnostic
996.02 Mechanical complication due to heart valve prosthesis
996.74 Other complications due to other vascular device, implant, and graft — (Use additional code to identify complication: 338.18-338.19, 338.28-338.29)
V43.3 Heart valve replaced by other means

ICD-9-CM Procedural
35.95 Revision of corrective procedure on heart
39.61 Extracorporeal circulation auxiliary to open heart surgery

33500-33501
33500 Repair of coronary arteriovenous or arteriocardiac chamber fistula; with cardiopulmonary bypass
33501 without cardiopulmonary bypass

ICD-9-CM Diagnostic
414.19 Other aneurysm of heart — (Use additional code to identify presence of hypertension: 401.0-405.9)
746.85 Congenital coronary artery anomaly

ICD-9-CM Procedural
36.99 Other operations on vessels of heart
39.53 Repair of arteriovenous fistula
39.61 Extracorporeal circulation auxiliary to open heart surgery

33502-33504
33502 Repair of anomalous coronary artery from pulmonary artery origin; by ligation
33503 by graft, without cardiopulmonary bypass
33504 by graft, with cardiopulmonary bypass

ICD-9-CM Diagnostic
746.85 Congenital coronary artery anomaly

ICD-9-CM Procedural
36.99 Other operations on vessels of heart
39.61 Extracorporeal circulation auxiliary to open heart surgery

33505-33506
33505 Repair of anomalous coronary artery from pulmonary artery origin; with construction of intrapulmonary artery tunnel (Takeuchi procedure)
33506 by translocation from pulmonary artery to aorta

ICD-9-CM Diagnostic
746.85 Congenital coronary artery anomaly

ICD-9-CM Procedural
36.99 Other operations on vessels of heart
39.61 Extracorporeal circulation auxiliary to open heart surgery

33507
33507 Repair of anomalous (eg, intramural) aortic origin of coronary artery by unroofing or translocation

ICD-9-CM Diagnostic
746.85 Congenital coronary artery anomaly

ICD-9-CM Procedural
36.99 Other operations on vessels of heart
39.61 Extracorporeal circulation auxiliary to open heart surgery

33508
33508 Endoscopy, surgical, including video-assisted harvest of vein(s) for coronary artery bypass procedure (List separately in addition to code for primary procedure)

ICD-9-CM Diagnostic
410.00 Acute myocardial infarction of anterolateral wall, episode of care unspecified — (Use additional code to identify presence of hypertension: 401.0-405.9) ▽
410.01 Acute myocardial infarction of anterolateral wall, initial episode of care — (Use additional code to identify presence of hypertension: 401.0-405.9)
410.02 Acute myocardial infarction of anterolateral wall, subsequent episode of care — (Use additional code to identify presence of hypertension: 401.0-405.9)
410.10 Acute myocardial infarction of other anterior wall, episode of care unspecified — (Use additional code to identify presence of hypertension: 401.0-405.9) ▽
410.11 Acute myocardial infarction of other anterior wall, initial episode of care — (Use additional code to identify presence of hypertension: 401.0-405.9)
410.12 Acute myocardial infarction of other anterior wall, subsequent episode of care — (Use additional code to identify presence of hypertension: 401.0-405.9)
410.20 Acute myocardial infarction of inferolateral wall, episode of care unspecified — (Use additional code to identify presence of hypertension: 401.0-405.9) ▽
410.21 Acute myocardial infarction of inferolateral wall, initial episode of care — (Use additional code to identify presence of hypertension: 401.0-405.9)
410.22 Acute myocardial infarction of inferolateral wall, subsequent episode of care — (Use additional code to identify presence of hypertension: 401.0-405.9)
410.30 Acute myocardial infarction of inferoposterior wall, episode of care unspecified — (Use additional code to identify presence of hypertension: 401.0-405.9) ▽
410.31 Acute myocardial infarction of inferoposterior wall, initial episode of care — (Use additional code to identify presence of hypertension: 401.0-405.9)
410.32 Acute myocardial infarction of inferoposterior wall, subsequent episode of care — (Use additional code to identify presence of hypertension: 401.0-405.9)
410.40 Acute myocardial infarction of other inferior wall, episode of care unspecified — (Use additional code to identify presence of hypertension: 401.0-405.9) ▽
410.41 Acute myocardial infarction of other inferior wall, initial episode of care — (Use additional code to identify presence of hypertension: 401.0-405.9)
410.42 Acute myocardial infarction of other inferior wall, subsequent episode of care — (Use additional code to identify presence of hypertension: 401.0-405.9)

410.50 Acute myocardial infarction of other lateral wall, episode of care unspecified — (Use additional code to identify presence of hypertension: 401.0-405.9)

410.51 Acute myocardial infarction of other lateral wall, initial episode of care — (Use additional code to identify presence of hypertension: 401.0-405.9)

410.52 Acute myocardial infarction of other lateral wall, subsequent episode of care — (Use additional code to identify presence of hypertension: 401.0-405.9)

410.60 Acute myocardial infarction, true posterior wall infarction, episode of care unspecified — (Use additional code to identify presence of hypertension: 401.0-405.9)

410.61 Acute myocardial infarction, true posterior wall infarction, initial episode of care — (Use additional code to identify presence of hypertension: 401.0-405.9)

410.62 Acute myocardial infarction, true posterior wall infarction, subsequent episode of care — (Use additional code to identify presence of hypertension: 401.0-405.9)

410.70 Acute myocardial infarction, subendocardial infarction, episode of care unspecified — (Use additional code to identify presence of hypertension: 401.0-405.9)

410.71 Acute myocardial infarction, subendocardial infarction, initial episode of care — (Use additional code to identify presence of hypertension: 401.0-405.9)

410.72 Acute myocardial infarction, subendocardial infarction, subsequent episode of care — (Use additional code to identify presence of hypertension: 401.0-405.9)

410.80 Acute myocardial infarction of other specified sites, episode of care unspecified — (Use additional code to identify presence of hypertension: 401.0-405.9)

410.81 Acute myocardial infarction of other specified sites, initial episode of care — (Use additional code to identify presence of hypertension: 401.0-405.9)

410.82 Acute myocardial infarction of other specified sites, subsequent episode of care — (Use additional code to identify presence of hypertension: 401.0-405.9)

410.90 Acute myocardial infarction, unspecified site, episode of care unspecified — (Use additional code to identify presence of hypertension: 401.0-405.9)

410.91 Acute myocardial infarction, unspecified site, initial episode of care — (Use additional code to identify presence of hypertension: 401.0-405.9)

410.92 Acute myocardial infarction, unspecified site, subsequent episode of care — (Use additional code to identify presence of hypertension: 401.0-405.9)

411.1 Intermediate coronary syndrome — (Use additional code to identify presence of hypertension: 401.0-405.9)

411.81 Acute coronary occlusion without myocardial infarction — (Use additional code to identify presence of hypertension: 401.0-405.9)

411.89 Other acute and subacute form of ischemic heart disease — (Use additional code to identify presence of hypertension: 401.0-405.9)

413.0 Angina decubitus — (Use additional code to identify presence of hypertension: 401.0-405.9)

413.1 Prinzmetal angina — (Use additional code to identify presence of hypertension: 401.0-405.9)

413.9 Other and unspecified angina pectoris — (Use additional code(s) for symptoms associated with angina equivalent)(Use additional code to identify presence of hypertension: 401.0-405.9)

414.00 Coronary atherosclerosis of unspecified type of vessel, native or graft — (Use additional code to identify presence of hypertension: 401.0-405.9)

414.01 Coronary atherosclerosis of native coronary artery — (Use additional code to identify presence of hypertension: 401.0-405.9)

414.02 Coronary atherosclerosis of autologous vein bypass graft — (Use additional code to identify presence of hypertension: 401.0-405.9)

414.03 Coronary atherosclerosis of nonautologous biological bypass graft — (Use additional code to identify presence of hypertension: 401.0-405.9)

414.04 Coronary atherosclerosis of artery bypass graft — (Use additional code to identify presence of hypertension: 401.0-405.9)

414.05 Coronary atherosclerosis of unspecified type of bypass graft — (Use additional code to identify presence of hypertension: 401.0-405.9)

414.06 Coronary atherosclerosis, of native coronary artery of transplanted heart — (Use additional code to identify presence of hypertension: 401.0-405.9)

414.07 Coronary atherosclerosis, of bypass graft (artery) (vein) of transplanted heart — (Use additional code to identify presence of hypertension: 401.0-405.9)

414.10 Aneurysm of heart — (Use additional code to identify presence of hypertension: 401.0-405.9)

414.11 Aneurysm of coronary vessels — (Use additional code to identify presence of hypertension: 401.0-405.9)

414.12 Dissection of coronary artery — (Use additional code to identify presence of hypertension: 401.0-405.9)

414.19 Other aneurysm of heart — (Use additional code to identify presence of hypertension: 401.0-405.9)

414.2 Chronic total occlusion of coronary artery

414.3 Coronary atherosclerosis due to lipid rich plaque — (Code first coronary atherosclerosis (414.00-414.07))

414.4 Coronary atherosclerosis due to calcified coronary lesion — (Code first coronary atherosclerosis (414.00-414.07))

414.8 Other specified forms of chronic ischemic heart disease — (Use additional code to identify presence of hypertension: 401.0-405.9)

414.9 Unspecified chronic ischemic heart disease — (Use additional code to identify presence of hypertension: 401.0-405.9)

426.7 Anomalous atrioventricular excitation

428.0 Congestive heart failure, unspecified — (Code, if applicable, heart failure due to hypertension first: 402.0-402.9, with fifth-digit 1 or 404.0-404.9 with fifth digit 1 or 3)

428.1 Left heart failure — (Code, if applicable, heart failure due to hypertension first: 402.0-402.9, with fifth-digit 1 or 404.0-404.9 with fifth digit 1 or 3)

428.20 Unspecified systolic heart failure — (Code, if applicable, heart failure due to hypertension first: 402.0-402.9, with fifth-digit 1 or 404.0-404.9 with fifth digit 1 or 3)

428.21 Acute systolic heart failure — (Code, if applicable, heart failure due to hypertension first: 402.0-402.9, with fifth-digit 1 or 404.0-404.9 with fifth digit 1 or 3)

428.22 Chronic systolic heart failure — (Code, if applicable, heart failure due to hypertension first: 402.0-402.9, with fifth-digit 1 or 404.0-404.9 with fifth digit 1 or 3)

428.23 Acute on chronic systolic heart failure — (Code, if applicable, heart failure due to hypertension first: 402.0-402.9, with fifth-digit 1 or 404.0-404.9 with fifth digit 1 or 3)

428.30 Unspecified diastolic heart failure — (Code, if applicable, heart failure due to hypertension first: 402.0-402.9, with fifth-digit 1 or 404.0-404.9 with fifth digit 1 or 3)

428.31 Acute diastolic heart failure — (Code, if applicable, heart failure due to hypertension first: 402.0-402.9, with fifth-digit 1 or 404.0-404.9 with fifth digit 1 or 3)

428.32 Chronic diastolic heart failure — (Code, if applicable, heart failure due to hypertension first: 402.0-402.9, with fifth-digit 1 or 404.0-404.9 with fifth digit 1 or 3)

428.33 Acute on chronic diastolic heart failure — (Code, if applicable, heart failure due to hypertension first: 402.0-402.9, with fifth-digit 1 or 404.0-404.9 with fifth digit 1 or 3)

428.40 Unspecified combined systolic and diastolic heart failure — (Code, if applicable, heart failure due to hypertension first: 402.0-402.9, with fifth-digit 1 or 404.0-404.9 with fifth digit 1 or 3)

428.41 Acute combined systolic and diastolic heart failure — (Code, if applicable, heart failure due to hypertension first: 402.0-402.9, with fifth-digit 1 or 404.0-404.9 with fifth digit 1 or 3)

428.42 Chronic combined systolic and diastolic heart failure — (Code, if applicable, heart failure due to hypertension first: 402.0-402.9, with fifth-digit 1 or 404.0-404.9 with fifth digit 1 or 3)

428.43 Acute on chronic combined systolic and diastolic heart failure — (Code, if applicable, heart failure due to hypertension first: 402.0-402.9, with fifth-digit 1 or 404.0-404.9 with fifth digit 1 or 3)

428.9 Unspecified heart failure — (Code, if applicable, heart failure due to hypertension first: 402.0-402.9, with fifth-digit 1 or 404.0-404.9 with fifth digit 1 or 3)

746.85 Congenital coronary artery anomaly

747.41 Total congenital anomalous pulmonary venous connection

996.03 Mechanical complication due to coronary bypass graft

ICD-9-CM Procedural

38.63 Other excision of upper limb vessels

HCPCS Level II Supplies & Services

The HCPCS Level II code(s) would be the same as the actual procedure performed because these are in-addition-to codes.

33510-33516

33510 Coronary artery bypass, vein only; single coronary venous graft
33511 2 coronary venous grafts
33512 3 coronary venous grafts
33513 4 coronary venous grafts
33514 5 coronary venous grafts
33516 6 or more coronary venous grafts

ICD-9-CM Diagnostic

410.00 Acute myocardial infarction of anterolateral wall, episode of care unspecified — (Use additional code to identify presence of hypertension: 401.0-405.9)
410.01 Acute myocardial infarction of anterolateral wall, initial episode of care — (Use additional code to identify presence of hypertension: 401.0-405.9)
410.02 Acute myocardial infarction of anterolateral wall, subsequent episode of care — (Use additional code to identify presence of hypertension: 401.0-405.9)
410.10 Acute myocardial infarction of other anterior wall, episode of care unspecified — (Use additional code to identify presence of hypertension: 401.0-405.9)
410.11 Acute myocardial infarction of other anterior wall, initial episode of care — (Use additional code to identify presence of hypertension: 401.0-405.9)
410.12 Acute myocardial infarction of other anterior wall, subsequent episode of care — (Use additional code to identify presence of hypertension: 401.0-405.9)
410.20 Acute myocardial infarction of inferolateral wall, episode of care unspecified — (Use additional code to identify presence of hypertension: 401.0-405.9)
410.21 Acute myocardial infarction of inferolateral wall, initial episode of care — (Use additional code to identify presence of hypertension: 401.0-405.9)
410.22 Acute myocardial infarction of inferolateral wall, subsequent episode of care — (Use additional code to identify presence of hypertension: 401.0-405.9)
410.30 Acute myocardial infarction of inferoposterior wall, episode of care unspecified — (Use additional code to identify presence of hypertension: 401.0-405.9)
410.31 Acute myocardial infarction of inferoposterior wall, initial episode of care — (Use additional code to identify presence of hypertension: 401.0-405.9)
410.32 Acute myocardial infarction of inferoposterior wall, subsequent episode of care — (Use additional code to identify presence of hypertension: 401.0-405.9)
410.40 Acute myocardial infarction of other inferior wall, episode of care unspecified — (Use additional code to identify presence of hypertension: 401.0-405.9)
410.41 Acute myocardial infarction of other inferior wall, initial episode of care — (Use additional code to identify presence of hypertension: 401.0-405.9)
410.42 Acute myocardial infarction of other inferior wall, subsequent episode of care — (Use additional code to identify presence of hypertension: 401.0-405.9)
410.50 Acute myocardial infarction of other lateral wall, episode of care unspecified — (Use additional code to identify presence of hypertension: 401.0-405.9)
410.51 Acute myocardial infarction of other lateral wall, initial episode of care — (Use additional code to identify presence of hypertension: 401.0-405.9)
410.52 Acute myocardial infarction of other lateral wall, subsequent episode of care — (Use additional code to identify presence of hypertension: 401.0-405.9)
410.60 Acute myocardial infarction, true posterior wall infarction, episode of care unspecified — (Use additional code to identify presence of hypertension: 401.0-405.9)
410.61 Acute myocardial infarction, true posterior wall infarction, initial episode of care — (Use additional code to identify presence of hypertension: 401.0-405.9)
410.62 Acute myocardial infarction, true posterior wall infarction, subsequent episode of care — (Use additional code to identify presence of hypertension: 401.0-405.9)
410.70 Acute myocardial infarction, subendocardial infarction, episode of care unspecified — (Use additional code to identify presence of hypertension: 401.0-405.9)
410.71 Acute myocardial infarction, subendocardial infarction, initial episode of care — (Use additional code to identify presence of hypertension: 401.0-405.9)
410.72 Acute myocardial infarction, subendocardial infarction, subsequent episode of care — (Use additional code to identify presence of hypertension: 401.0-405.9)
410.80 Acute myocardial infarction of other specified sites, episode of care unspecified — (Use additional code to identify presence of hypertension: 401.0-405.9)
410.81 Acute myocardial infarction of other specified sites, initial episode of care — (Use additional code to identify presence of hypertension: 401.0-405.9)
410.82 Acute myocardial infarction of other specified sites, subsequent episode of care — (Use additional code to identify presence of hypertension: 401.0-405.9)
410.90 Acute myocardial infarction, unspecified site, episode of care unspecified — (Use additional code to identify presence of hypertension: 401.0-405.9)
410.91 Acute myocardial infarction, unspecified site, initial episode of care — (Use additional code to identify presence of hypertension: 401.0-405.9)
410.92 Acute myocardial infarction, unspecified site, subsequent episode of care — (Use additional code to identify presence of hypertension: 401.0-405.9)
411.1 Intermediate coronary syndrome — (Use additional code to identify presence of hypertension: 401.0-405.9)
411.81 Acute coronary occlusion without myocardial infarction — (Use additional code to identify presence of hypertension: 401.0-405.9)
411.89 Other acute and subacute form of ischemic heart disease — (Use additional code to identify presence of hypertension: 401.0-405.9)
413.0 Angina decubitus — (Use additional code to identify presence of hypertension: 401.0-405.9)
413.1 Prinzmetal angina — (Use additional code to identify presence of hypertension: 401.0-405.9)
413.9 Other and unspecified angina pectoris — (Use additional code(s) for symptoms associated with angina equivalent)(Use additional code to identify presence of hypertension: 401.0-405.9)
414.00 Coronary atherosclerosis of unspecified type of vessel, native or graft — (Use additional code to identify presence of hypertension: 401.0-405.9)
414.01 Coronary atherosclerosis of native coronary artery — (Use additional code to identify presence of hypertension: 401.0-405.9)
414.03 Coronary atherosclerosis of nonautologous biological bypass graft — (Use additional code to identify presence of hypertension: 401.0-405.9)
414.04 Coronary atherosclerosis of artery bypass graft — (Use additional code to identify presence of hypertension: 401.0-405.9)
414.05 Coronary atherosclerosis of unspecified type of bypass graft — (Use additional code to identify presence of hypertension: 401.0-405.9)
414.06 Coronary atherosclerosis, of native coronary artery of transplanted heart — (Use additional code to identify presence of hypertension: 401.0-405.9)
414.07 Coronary atherosclerosis, of bypass graft (artery) (vein) of transplanted heart — (Use additional code to identify presence of hypertension: 401.0-405.9)
414.10 Aneurysm of heart — (Use additional code to identify presence of hypertension: 401.0-405.9)
414.11 Aneurysm of coronary vessels — (Use additional code to identify presence of hypertension: 401.0-405.9)
414.12 Dissection of coronary artery — (Use additional code to identify presence of hypertension: 401.0-405.9)
414.2 Chronic total occlusion of coronary artery
414.3 Coronary atherosclerosis due to lipid rich plaque — (Code first coronary atherosclerosis (414.00-414.07))
414.4 Coronary atherosclerosis due to calcified coronary lesion — (Code first coronary atherosclerosis (414.00-414.07))
414.8 Other specified forms of chronic ischemic heart disease — (Use additional code to identify presence of hypertension: 401.0-405.9)
414.9 Unspecified chronic ischemic heart disease — (Use additional code to identify presence of hypertension: 401.0-405.9)
426.7 Anomalous atrioventricular excitation
428.0 Congestive heart failure, unspecified — (Code, if applicable, heart failure due to hypertension first: 402.0-402.9, with fifth-digit 1 or 404.0-404.9 with fifth digit 1 or 3)
428.1 Left heart failure — (Code, if applicable, heart failure due to hypertension first: 402.0-402.9, with fifth-digit 1 or 404.0-404.9 with fifth digit 1 or 3)

428.20 Unspecified systolic heart failure — (Code, if applicable, heart failure due to hypertension first: 402.0-402.9, with fifth-digit 1 or 404.0-404.9 with fifth digit 1 or 3) ▽

428.21 Acute systolic heart failure — (Code, if applicable, heart failure due to hypertension first: 402.0-402.9, with fifth-digit 1 or 404.0-404.9 with fifth digit 1 or 3)

428.22 Chronic systolic heart failure — (Code, if applicable, heart failure due to hypertension first: 402.0-402.9, with fifth-digit 1 or 404.0-404.9 with fifth digit 1 or 3)

428.23 Acute on chronic systolic heart failure — (Code, if applicable, heart failure due to hypertension first: 402.0-402.9, with fifth-digit 1 or 404.0-404.9 with fifth digit 1 or 3)

428.30 Unspecified diastolic heart failure — (Code, if applicable, heart failure due to hypertension first: 402.0-402.9, with fifth-digit 1 or 404.0-404.9 with fifth digit 1 or 3) ▽

428.31 Acute diastolic heart failure — (Code, if applicable, heart failure due to hypertension first: 402.0-402.9, with fifth-digit 1 or 404.0-404.9 with fifth digit 1 or 3)

428.32 Chronic diastolic heart failure — (Code, if applicable, heart failure due to hypertension first: 402.0-402.9, with fifth-digit 1 or 404.0-404.9 with fifth digit 1 or 3)

428.33 Acute on chronic diastolic heart failure — (Code, if applicable, heart failure due to hypertension first: 402.0-402.9, with fifth-digit 1 or 404.0-404.9 with fifth digit 1 or 3)

428.40 Unspecified combined systolic and diastolic heart failure — (Code, if applicable, heart failure due to hypertension first: 402.0-402.9, with fifth-digit 1 or 404.0-404.9 with fifth digit 1 or 3) ▽

428.41 Acute combined systolic and diastolic heart failure — (Code, if applicable, heart failure due to hypertension first: 402.0-402.9, with fifth-digit 1 or 404.0-404.9 with fifth digit 1 or 3)

428.42 Chronic combined systolic and diastolic heart failure — (Code, if applicable, heart failure due to hypertension first: 402.0-402.9, with fifth-digit 1 or 404.0-404.9 with fifth digit 1 or 3)

428.43 Acute on chronic combined systolic and diastolic heart failure — (Code, if applicable, heart failure due to hypertension first: 402.0-402.9, with fifth-digit 1 or 404.0-404.9 with fifth digit 1 or 3)

428.9 Unspecified heart failure — (Code, if applicable, heart failure due to hypertension first: 402.0-402.9, with fifth-digit 1 or 404.0-404.9 with fifth digit 1 or 3) ▽

746.85 Congenital coronary artery anomaly

747.41 Total congenital anomalous pulmonary venous connection

996.03 Mechanical complication due to coronary bypass graft

ICD-9-CM Procedural

36.11 (Aorto)coronary bypass of one coronary artery

36.12 (Aorto)coronary bypass of two coronary arteries

36.13 (Aorto)coronary bypass of three coronary arteries

36.14 (Aorto)coronary bypass of four or more coronary arteries

39.61 Extracorporeal circulation auxiliary to open heart surgery

33517-33523

33517 Coronary artery bypass, using venous graft(s) and arterial graft(s); single vein graft (List separately in addition to code for primary procedure)

33518 2 venous grafts (List separately in addition to code for primary procedure)

33519 3 venous grafts (List separately in addition to code for primary procedure)

33521 4 venous grafts (List separately in addition to code for primary procedure)

33522 5 venous grafts (List separately in addition to code for primary procedure)

33523 6 or more venous grafts (List separately in addition to code for primary procedure)

ICD-9-CM Diagnostic

410.00 Acute myocardial infarction of anterolateral wall, episode of care unspecified — (Use additional code to identify presence of hypertension: 401.0-405.9) ▽

410.01 Acute myocardial infarction of anterolateral wall, initial episode of care — (Use additional code to identify presence of hypertension: 401.0-405.9)

410.02 Acute myocardial infarction of anterolateral wall, subsequent episode of care — (Use additional code to identify presence of hypertension: 401.0-405.9)

410.10 Acute myocardial infarction of other anterior wall, episode of care unspecified — (Use additional code to identify presence of hypertension: 401.0-405.9) ▽

410.11 Acute myocardial infarction of other anterior wall, initial episode of care — (Use additional code to identify presence of hypertension: 401.0-405.9)

410.12 Acute myocardial infarction of other anterior wall, subsequent episode of care — (Use additional code to identify presence of hypertension: 401.0-405.9)

410.20 Acute myocardial infarction of inferolateral wall, episode of care unspecified — (Use additional code to identify presence of hypertension: 401.0-405.9) ▽

410.21 Acute myocardial infarction of inferolateral wall, initial episode of care — (Use additional code to identify presence of hypertension: 401.0-405.9)

410.22 Acute myocardial infarction of inferolateral wall, subsequent episode of care — (Use additional code to identify presence of hypertension: 401.0-405.9)

410.30 Acute myocardial infarction of inferoposterior wall, episode of care unspecified — (Use additional code to identify presence of hypertension: 401.0-405.9) ▽

410.31 Acute myocardial infarction of inferoposterior wall, initial episode of care — (Use additional code to identify presence of hypertension: 401.0-405.9)

410.32 Acute myocardial infarction of inferoposterior wall, subsequent episode of care — (Use additional code to identify presence of hypertension: 401.0-405.9)

410.40 Acute myocardial infarction of other inferior wall, episode of care unspecified — (Use additional code to identify presence of hypertension: 401.0-405.9) ▽

410.41 Acute myocardial infarction of other inferior wall, initial episode of care — (Use additional code to identify presence of hypertension: 401.0-405.9)

410.42 Acute myocardial infarction of other inferior wall, subsequent episode of care — (Use additional code to identify presence of hypertension: 401.0-405.9)

410.50 Acute myocardial infarction of other lateral wall, episode of care unspecified — (Use additional code to identify presence of hypertension: 401.0-405.9) ▽

410.51 Acute myocardial infarction of other lateral wall, initial episode of care — (Use additional code to identify presence of hypertension: 401.0-405.9)

410.52 Acute myocardial infarction of other lateral wall, subsequent episode of care — (Use additional code to identify presence of hypertension: 401.0-405.9)

410.60 Acute myocardial infarction, true posterior wall infarction, episode of care unspecified — (Use additional code to identify presence of hypertension: 401.0-405.9) ▽

410.61 Acute myocardial infarction, true posterior wall infarction, initial episode of care — (Use additional code to identify presence of hypertension: 401.0-405.9)

410.62 Acute myocardial infarction, true posterior wall infarction, subsequent episode of care — (Use additional code to identify presence of hypertension: 401.0-405.9)

410.70 Acute myocardial infarction, subendocardial infarction, episode of care unspecified — (Use additional code to identify presence of hypertension: 401.0-405.9) ▽

410.71 Acute myocardial infarction, subendocardial infarction, initial episode of care — (Use additional code to identify presence of hypertension: 401.0-405.9)

410.72 Acute myocardial infarction, subendocardial infarction, subsequent episode of care — (Use additional code to identify presence of hypertension: 401.0-405.9)

410.80 Acute myocardial infarction of other specified sites, episode of care unspecified — (Use additional code to identify presence of hypertension: 401.0-405.9) ▽

410.81 Acute myocardial infarction of other specified sites, initial episode of care — (Use additional code to identify presence of hypertension: 401.0-405.9)

410.82 Acute myocardial infarction of other specified sites, subsequent episode of care — (Use additional code to identify presence of hypertension: 401.0-405.9)

410.90 Acute myocardial infarction, unspecified site, episode of care unspecified — (Use additional code to identify presence of hypertension: 401.0-405.9) ▽

410.91 Acute myocardial infarction, unspecified site, initial episode of care — (Use additional code to identify presence of hypertension: 401.0-405.9) ▽

410.92 Acute myocardial infarction, unspecified site, subsequent episode of care — (Use additional code to identify presence of hypertension: 401.0-405.9) ▽

411.1 Intermediate coronary syndrome — (Use additional code to identify presence of hypertension: 401.0-405.9)

411.81 Acute coronary occlusion without myocardial infarction — (Use additional code to identify presence of hypertension: 401.0-405.9)

411.89 Other acute and subacute form of ischemic heart disease — (Use additional code to identify presence of hypertension: 401.0-405.9)

413.0 Angina decubitus — (Use additional code to identify presence of hypertension: 401.0-405.9)

413.1 Prinzmetal angina — (Use additional code to identify presence of hypertension: 401.0-405.9)

413.9 Other and unspecified angina pectoris — (Use additional code(s) for symptoms associated with angina equivalent)(Use additional code to identify presence of hypertension: 401.0-405.9)

414.00 Coronary atherosclerosis of unspecified type of vessel, native or graft — (Use additional code to identify presence of hypertension: 401.0-405.9)

414.01 Coronary atherosclerosis of native coronary artery — (Use additional code to identify presence of hypertension: 401.0-405.9)

414.03 Coronary atherosclerosis of nonautologous biological bypass graft — (Use additional code to identify presence of hypertension: 401.0-405.9)

414.04 Coronary atherosclerosis of artery bypass graft — (Use additional code to identify presence of hypertension: 401.0-405.9)

414.05 Coronary atherosclerosis of unspecified type of bypass graft — (Use additional code to identify presence of hypertension: 401.0-405.9)

414.06 Coronary atherosclerosis, of native coronary artery of transplanted heart — (Use additional code to identify presence of hypertension: 401.0-405.9)

414.07 Coronary atherosclerosis, of bypass graft (artery) (vein) of transplanted heart — (Use additional code to identify presence of hypertension: 401.0-405.9)

414.10 Aneurysm of heart — (Use additional code to identify presence of hypertension: 401.0-405.9)

414.11 Aneurysm of coronary vessels — (Use additional code to identify presence of hypertension: 401.0-405.9)

414.12 Dissection of coronary artery — (Use additional code to identify presence of hypertension: 401.0-405.9)

414.2 Chronic total occlusion of coronary artery

414.3 Coronary atherosclerosis due to lipid rich plaque — (Code first coronary atherosclerosis (414.00-414.07))

414.4 Coronary atherosclerosis due to calcified coronary lesion — (Code first coronary atherosclerosis (414.00-414.07))

414.8 Other specified forms of chronic ischemic heart disease — (Use additional code to identify presence of hypertension: 401.0-405.9)

414.9 Unspecified chronic ischemic heart disease — (Use additional code to identify presence of hypertension: 401.0-405.9)

426.7 Anomalous atrioventricular excitation

428.0 Congestive heart failure, unspecified — (Code, if applicable, heart failure due to hypertension first: 402.0-402.9, with fifth-digit 1 or 404.0-404.9 with fifth digit 1 or 3)

428.1 Left heart failure — (Code, if applicable, heart failure due to hypertension first: 402.0-402.9, with fifth-digit 1 or 404.0-404.9 with fifth digit 1 or 3)

428.20 Unspecified systolic heart failure — (Code, if applicable, heart failure due to hypertension first: 402.0-402.9, with fifth-digit 1 or 404.0-404.9 with fifth digit 1 or 3)

428.21 Acute systolic heart failure — (Code, if applicable, heart failure due to hypertension first: 402.0-402.9, with fifth-digit 1 or 404.0-404.9 with fifth digit 1 or 3)

428.22 Chronic systolic heart failure — (Code, if applicable, heart failure due to hypertension first: 402.0-402.9, with fifth-digit 1 or 404.0-404.9 with fifth digit 1 or 3)

428.23 Acute on chronic systolic heart failure — (Code, if applicable, heart failure due to hypertension first: 402.0-402.9, with fifth-digit 1 or 404.0-404.9 with fifth digit 1 or 3)

428.30 Unspecified diastolic heart failure — (Code, if applicable, heart failure due to hypertension first: 402.0-402.9, with fifth-digit 1 or 404.0-404.9 with fifth digit 1 or 3)

428.31 Acute diastolic heart failure — (Code, if applicable, heart failure due to hypertension first: 402.0-402.9, with fifth-digit 1 or 404.0-404.9 with fifth digit 1 or 3)

428.32 Chronic diastolic heart failure — (Code, if applicable, heart failure due to hypertension first: 402.0-402.9, with fifth-digit 1 or 404.0-404.9 with fifth digit 1 or 3)

428.33 Acute on chronic diastolic heart failure — (Code, if applicable, heart failure due to hypertension first: 402.0-402.9, with fifth-digit 1 or 404.0-404.9 with fifth digit 1 or 3)

428.40 Unspecified combined systolic and diastolic heart failure — (Code, if applicable, heart failure due to hypertension first: 402.0-402.9, with fifth-digit 1 or 404.0-404.9 with fifth digit 1 or 3)

428.41 Acute combined systolic and diastolic heart failure — (Code, if applicable, heart failure due to hypertension first: 402.0-402.9, with fifth-digit 1 or 404.0-404.9 with fifth digit 1 or 3)

428.42 Chronic combined systolic and diastolic heart failure — (Code, if applicable, heart failure due to hypertension first: 402.0-402.9, with fifth-digit 1 or 404.0-404.9 with fifth digit 1 or 3)

428.43 Acute on chronic combined systolic and diastolic heart failure — (Code, if applicable, heart failure due to hypertension first: 402.0-402.9, with fifth-digit 1 or 404.0-404.9 with fifth digit 1 or 3)

428.9 Unspecified heart failure — (Code, if applicable, heart failure due to hypertension first: 402.0-402.9, with fifth-digit 1 or 404.0-404.9 with fifth digit 1 or 3)

746.85 Congenital coronary artery anomaly

747.41 Total congenital anomalous pulmonary venous connection

996.03 Mechanical complication due to coronary bypass graft

ICD-9-CM Procedural

36.11 (Aorto)coronary bypass of one coronary artery

36.12 (Aorto)coronary bypass of two coronary arteries

36.13 (Aorto)coronary bypass of three coronary arteries

36.14 (Aorto)coronary bypass of four or more coronary arteries

39.61 Extracorporeal circulation auxiliary to open heart surgery

33533-33536

33533 Coronary artery bypass, using arterial graft(s); single arterial graft

33534 2 coronary arterial grafts

33535 3 coronary arterial grafts

33536 4 or more coronary arterial grafts

ICD-9-CM Diagnostic

410.00 Acute myocardial infarction of anterolateral wall, episode of care unspecified — (Use additional code to identify presence of hypertension: 401.0-405.9)

410.01 Acute myocardial infarction of anterolateral wall, initial episode of care — (Use additional code to identify presence of hypertension: 401.0-405.9)

410.02 Acute myocardial infarction of anterolateral wall, subsequent episode of care — (Use additional code to identify presence of hypertension: 401.0-405.9)

410.10 Acute myocardial infarction of other anterior wall, episode of care unspecified — (Use additional code to identify presence of hypertension: 401.0-405.9)

410.11 Acute myocardial infarction of other anterior wall, initial episode of care — (Use additional code to identify presence of hypertension: 401.0-405.9)

410.12 Acute myocardial infarction of other anterior wall, subsequent episode of care — (Use additional code to identify presence of hypertension: 401.0-405.9)

410.20 Acute myocardial infarction of inferolateral wall, episode of care unspecified — (Use additional code to identify presence of hypertension: 401.0-405.9)

410.21 Acute myocardial infarction of inferolateral wall, initial episode of care — (Use additional code to identify presence of hypertension: 401.0-405.9)

410.22 Acute myocardial infarction of inferolateral wall, subsequent episode of care — (Use additional code to identify presence of hypertension: 401.0-405.9)

410.30 Acute myocardial infarction of inferoposterior wall, episode of care unspecified — (Use additional code to identify presence of hypertension: 401.0-405.9)

410.31 Acute myocardial infarction of inferoposterior wall, initial episode of care — (Use additional code to identify presence of hypertension: 401.0-405.9)

410.32 Acute myocardial infarction of inferoposterior wall, subsequent episode of care — (Use additional code to identify presence of hypertension: 401.0-405.9)

410.40 Acute myocardial infarction of other inferior wall, episode of care unspecified — (Use additional code to identify presence of hypertension: 401.0-405.9)

410.41 Acute myocardial infarction of other inferior wall, initial episode of care — (Use additional code to identify presence of hypertension: 401.0-405.9)

410.42 Acute myocardial infarction of other inferior wall, subsequent episode of care — (Use additional code to identify presence of hypertension: 401.0-405.9)

410.50 Acute myocardial infarction of other lateral wall, episode of care unspecified — (Use additional code to identify presence of hypertension: 401.0-405.9)

410.51 Acute myocardial infarction of other lateral wall, initial episode of care — (Use additional code to identify presence of hypertension: 401.0-405.9)

410.52 Acute myocardial infarction of other lateral wall, subsequent episode of care — (Use additional code to identify presence of hypertension: 401.0-405.9)

410.60 Acute myocardial infarction, true posterior wall infarction, episode of care unspecified — (Use additional code to identify presence of hypertension: 401.0-405.9)

410.61 Acute myocardial infarction, true posterior wall infarction, initial episode of care — (Use additional code to identify presence of hypertension: 401.0-405.9)

410.62 Acute myocardial infarction, true posterior wall infarction, subsequent episode of care — (Use additional code to identify presence of hypertension: 401.0-405.9)

410.70 Acute myocardial infarction, subendocardial infarction, episode of care unspecified — (Use additional code to identify presence of hypertension: 401.0-405.9)

410.71 Acute myocardial infarction, subendocardial infarction, initial episode of care — (Use additional code to identify presence of hypertension: 401.0-405.9)

410.72 Acute myocardial infarction, subendocardial infarction, subsequent episode of care — (Use additional code to identify presence of hypertension: 401.0-405.9)

410.80 Acute myocardial infarction of other specified sites, episode of care unspecified — (Use additional code to identify presence of hypertension: 401.0-405.9)

410.81 Acute myocardial infarction of other specified sites, initial episode of care — (Use additional code to identify presence of hypertension: 401.0-405.9)

410.82 Acute myocardial infarction of other specified sites, subsequent episode of care — (Use additional code to identify presence of hypertension: 401.0-405.9)

410.90 Acute myocardial infarction, unspecified site, episode of care unspecified — (Use additional code to identify presence of hypertension: 401.0-405.9)

410.91 Acute myocardial infarction, unspecified site, initial episode of care — (Use additional code to identify presence of hypertension: 401.0-405.9)

410.92 Acute myocardial infarction, unspecified site, subsequent episode of care — (Use additional code to identify presence of hypertension: 401.0-405.9)

411.1 Intermediate coronary syndrome — (Use additional code to identify presence of hypertension: 401.0-405.9)

411.81 Acute coronary occlusion without myocardial infarction — (Use additional code to identify presence of hypertension: 401.0-405.9)

411.89 Other acute and subacute form of ischemic heart disease — (Use additional code to identify presence of hypertension: 401.0-405.9)

413.0 Angina decubitus — (Use additional code to identify presence of hypertension: 401.0-405.9)

413.1 Prinzmetal angina — (Use additional code to identify presence of hypertension: 401.0-405.9)

413.9 Other and unspecified angina pectoris — (Use additional code(s) for symptoms associated with angina equivalent)(Use additional code to identify presence of hypertension: 401.0-405.9)

414.00 Coronary atherosclerosis of unspecified type of vessel, native or graft — (Use additional code to identify presence of hypertension: 401.0-405.9)

414.01 Coronary atherosclerosis of native coronary artery — (Use additional code to identify presence of hypertension: 401.0-405.9)

414.03 Coronary atherosclerosis of nonautologous biological bypass graft — (Use additional code to identify presence of hypertension: 401.0-405.9)

414.04 Coronary atherosclerosis of artery bypass graft — (Use additional code to identify presence of hypertension: 401.0-405.9)

414.05 Coronary atherosclerosis of unspecified type of bypass graft — (Use additional code to identify presence of hypertension: 401.0-405.9)

414.06 Coronary atherosclerosis, of native coronary artery of transplanted heart — (Use additional code to identify presence of hypertension: 401.0-405.9)

414.07 Coronary atherosclerosis, of bypass graft (artery) (vein) of transplanted heart — (Use additional code to identify presence of hypertension: 401.0-405.9)

414.10 Aneurysm of heart — (Use additional code to identify presence of hypertension: 401.0-405.9)

414.11 Aneurysm of coronary vessels — (Use additional code to identify presence of hypertension: 401.0-405.9)

414.12 Dissection of coronary artery — (Use additional code to identify presence of hypertension: 401.0-405.9)

414.2 Chronic total occlusion of coronary artery

414.3 Coronary atherosclerosis due to lipid rich plaque — (Code first coronary atherosclerosis (414.00-414.07))

414.4 Coronary atherosclerosis due to calcified coronary lesion — (Code first coronary atherosclerosis (414.00-414.07))

414.8 Other specified forms of chronic ischemic heart disease — (Use additional code to identify presence of hypertension: 401.0-405.9)

414.9 Unspecified chronic ischemic heart disease — (Use additional code to identify presence of hypertension: 401.0-405.9)

426.7 Anomalous atrioventricular excitation

428.0 Congestive heart failure, unspecified — (Code, if applicable, heart failure due to hypertension first: 402.0-402.9, with fifth-digit 1 or 404.0-404.9 with fifth digit 1 or 3)

428.1 Left heart failure — (Code, if applicable, heart failure due to hypertension first: 402.0-402.9, with fifth-digit 1 or 404.0-404.9 with fifth digit 1 or 3)

428.20 Unspecified systolic heart failure — (Code, if applicable, heart failure due to hypertension first: 402.0-402.9, with fifth-digit 1 or 404.0-404.9 with fifth digit 1 or 3)

428.21 Acute systolic heart failure — (Code, if applicable, heart failure due to hypertension first: 402.0-402.9, with fifth-digit 1 or 404.0-404.9 with fifth digit 1 or 3)

428.22 Chronic systolic heart failure — (Code, if applicable, heart failure due to hypertension first: 402.0-402.9, with fifth-digit 1 or 404.0-404.9 with fifth digit 1 or 3)

428.23 Acute on chronic systolic heart failure — (Code, if applicable, heart failure due to hypertension first: 402.0-402.9, with fifth-digit 1 or 404.0-404.9 with fifth digit 1 or 3)

428.30 Unspecified diastolic heart failure — (Code, if applicable, heart failure due to hypertension first: 402.0-402.9, with fifth-digit 1 or 404.0-404.9 with fifth digit 1 or 3)

428.31 Acute diastolic heart failure — (Code, if applicable, heart failure due to hypertension first: 402.0-402.9, with fifth-digit 1 or 404.0-404.9 with fifth digit 1 or 3)

428.32 Chronic diastolic heart failure — (Code, if applicable, heart failure due to hypertension first: 402.0-402.9, with fifth-digit 1 or 404.0-404.9 with fifth digit 1 or 3)

428.33 Acute on chronic diastolic heart failure — (Code, if applicable, heart failure due to hypertension first: 402.0-402.9, with fifth-digit 1 or 404.0-404.9 with fifth digit 1 or 3)

428.40 Unspecified combined systolic and diastolic heart failure — (Code, if applicable, heart failure due to hypertension first: 402.0-402.9, with fifth-digit 1 or 404.0-404.9 with fifth digit 1 or 3)

428.41 Acute combined systolic and diastolic heart failure — (Code, if applicable, heart failure due to hypertension first: 402.0-402.9, with fifth-digit 1 or 404.0-404.9 with fifth digit 1 or 3)

428.42 Chronic combined systolic and diastolic heart failure — (Code, if applicable, heart failure due to hypertension first: 402.0-402.9, with fifth-digit 1 or 404.0-404.9 with fifth digit 1 or 3)

428.43 Acute on chronic combined systolic and diastolic heart failure — (Code, if applicable, heart failure due to hypertension first: 402.0-402.9, with fifth-digit 1 or 404.0-404.9 with fifth digit 1 or 3)

428.9 Unspecified heart failure — (Code, if applicable, heart failure due to hypertension first: 402.0-402.9, with fifth-digit 1 or 404.0-404.9 with fifth digit 1 or 3)

746.85 Congenital coronary artery anomaly

747.41 Total congenital anomalous pulmonary venous connection

996.03 Mechanical complication due to coronary bypass graft

ICD-9-CM Procedural

36.15 Single internal mammary-coronary artery bypass

36.16 Double internal mammary-coronary artery bypass

36.17 Abdominal-coronary artery bypass

36.19 Other bypass anastomosis for heart revascularization

39.61 Extracorporeal circulation auxiliary to open heart surgery

33542

33542 Myocardial resection (eg, ventricular aneurysmectomy)

ICD-9-CM Diagnostic

414.10 Aneurysm of heart — (Use additional code to identify presence of hypertension: 401.0-405.9)

429.3 Cardiomegaly

ICD-9-CM Procedural

37.32 Excision of aneurysm of heart

37.33 Excision or destruction of other lesion or tissue of heart, open approach

39.61 Extracorporeal circulation auxiliary to open heart surgery

33545

33545 Repair of postinfarction ventricular septal defect, with or without myocardial resection

ICD-9-CM Diagnostic

410.10 Acute myocardial infarction of other anterior wall, episode of care unspecified — (Use additional code to identify presence of hypertension: 401.0-405.9) ▽

410.11 Acute myocardial infarction of other anterior wall, initial episode of care — (Use additional code to identify presence of hypertension: 401.0-405.9)

410.12 Acute myocardial infarction of other anterior wall, subsequent episode of care — (Use additional code to identify presence of hypertension: 401.0-405.9)

410.40 Acute myocardial infarction of other inferior wall, episode of care unspecified — (Use additional code to identify presence of hypertension: 401.0-405.9) ▽

410.41 Acute myocardial infarction of other inferior wall, initial episode of care — (Use additional code to identify presence of hypertension: 401.0-405.9)

410.42 Acute myocardial infarction of other inferior wall, subsequent episode of care — (Use additional code to identify presence of hypertension: 401.0-405.9)

410.90 Acute myocardial infarction, unspecified site, episode of care unspecified — (Use additional code to identify presence of hypertension: 401.0-405.9) ▽

410.92 Acute myocardial infarction, unspecified site, subsequent episode of care — (Use additional code to identify presence of hypertension: 401.0-405.9) ▽

414.00 Coronary atherosclerosis of unspecified type of vessel, native or graft — (Use additional code to identify presence of hypertension: 401.0-405.9) ▽

414.01 Coronary atherosclerosis of native coronary artery — (Use additional code to identify presence of hypertension: 401.0-405.9)

414.02 Coronary atherosclerosis of autologous vein bypass graft — (Use additional code to identify presence of hypertension: 401.0-405.9)

414.03 Coronary atherosclerosis of nonautologous biological bypass graft — (Use additional code to identify presence of hypertension: 401.0-405.9)

414.04 Coronary atherosclerosis of artery bypass graft — (Use additional code to identify presence of hypertension: 401.0-405.9)

414.05 Coronary atherosclerosis of unspecified type of bypass graft — (Use additional code to identify presence of hypertension: 401.0-405.9) ▽

414.06 Coronary atherosclerosis, of native coronary artery of transplanted heart — (Use additional code to identify presence of hypertension: 401.0-405.9)

414.07 Coronary atherosclerosis, of bypass graft (artery) (vein) of transplanted heart — (Use additional code to identify presence of hypertension: 401.0-405.9)

414.3 Coronary atherosclerosis due to lipid rich plaque — (Code first coronary atherosclerosis (414.00-414.07))

414.4 Coronary atherosclerosis due to calcified coronary lesion — (Code first coronary atherosclerosis (414.00-414.07))

429.1 Myocardial degeneration — (Use additional code to identify presence of arteriosclerosis)

ICD-9-CM Procedural

35.72 Other and unspecified repair of ventricular septal defect

39.61 Extracorporeal circulation auxiliary to open heart surgery

33548

33548 Surgical ventricular restoration procedure, includes prosthetic patch, when performed (eg, ventricular remodeling, SVR, SAVER, Dor procedures)

ICD-9-CM Diagnostic

410.01 Acute myocardial infarction of anterolateral wall, initial episode of care — (Use additional code to identify presence of hypertension: 401.0-405.9)

410.02 Acute myocardial infarction of anterolateral wall, subsequent episode of care — (Use additional code to identify presence of hypertension: 401.0-405.9)

410.11 Acute myocardial infarction of other anterior wall, initial episode of care — (Use additional code to identify presence of hypertension: 401.0-405.9)

410.12 Acute myocardial infarction of other anterior wall, subsequent episode of care — (Use additional code to identify presence of hypertension: 401.0-405.9)

410.21 Acute myocardial infarction of inferolateral wall, initial episode of care — (Use additional code to identify presence of hypertension: 401.0-405.9)

410.22 Acute myocardial infarction of inferolateral wall, subsequent episode of care — (Use additional code to identify presence of hypertension: 401.0-405.9)

410.31 Acute myocardial infarction of inferoposterior wall, initial episode of care — (Use additional code to identify presence of hypertension: 401.0-405.9)

410.32 Acute myocardial infarction of inferoposterior wall, subsequent episode of care — (Use additional code to identify presence of hypertension: 401.0-405.9)

410.41 Acute myocardial infarction of other inferior wall, initial episode of care — (Use additional code to identify presence of hypertension: 401.0-405.9)

410.42 Acute myocardial infarction of other inferior wall, subsequent episode of care — (Use additional code to identify presence of hypertension: 401.0-405.9)

410.51 Acute myocardial infarction of other lateral wall, initial episode of care — (Use additional code to identify presence of hypertension: 401.0-405.9)

410.52 Acute myocardial infarction of other lateral wall, subsequent episode of care — (Use additional code to identify presence of hypertension: 401.0-405.9)

410.61 Acute myocardial infarction, true posterior wall infarction, initial episode of care — (Use additional code to identify presence of hypertension: 401.0-405.9)

410.62 Acute myocardial infarction, true posterior wall infarction, subsequent episode of care — (Use additional code to identify presence of hypertension: 401.0-405.9)

410.71 Acute myocardial infarction, subendocardial infarction, initial episode of care — (Use additional code to identify presence of hypertension: 401.0-405.9)

410.72 Acute myocardial infarction, subendocardial infarction, subsequent episode of care — (Use additional code to identify presence of hypertension: 401.0-405.9)

410.81 Acute myocardial infarction of other specified sites, initial episode of care — (Use additional code to identify presence of hypertension: 401.0-405.9)

410.82 Acute myocardial infarction of other specified sites, subsequent episode of care — (Use additional code to identify presence of hypertension: 401.0-405.9)

410.91 Acute myocardial infarction, unspecified site, initial episode of care — (Use additional code to identify presence of hypertension: 401.0-405.9) ▽

410.92 Acute myocardial infarction, unspecified site, subsequent episode of care — (Use additional code to identify presence of hypertension: 401.0-405.9) ▽

411.1 Intermediate coronary syndrome — (Use additional code to identify presence of hypertension: 401.0-405.9)

411.81 Acute coronary occlusion without myocardial infarction — (Use additional code to identify presence of hypertension: 401.0-405.9)

411.89 Other acute and subacute form of ischemic heart disease — (Use additional code to identify presence of hypertension: 401.0-405.9)

413.9 Other and unspecified angina pectoris — (Use additional code(s) for symptoms associated with angina equivalent)(Use additional code to identify presence of hypertension: 401.0-405.9) ▽

414.00 Coronary atherosclerosis of unspecified type of vessel, native or graft — (Use additional code to identify presence of hypertension: 401.0-405.9) ▽

414.01 Coronary atherosclerosis of native coronary artery — (Use additional code to identify presence of hypertension: 401.0-405.9)

414.02 Coronary atherosclerosis of autologous vein bypass graft — (Use additional code to identify presence of hypertension: 401.0-405.9)

414.03 Coronary atherosclerosis of nonautologous biological bypass graft — (Use additional code to identify presence of hypertension: 401.0-405.9)

414.04 Coronary atherosclerosis of artery bypass graft — (Use additional code to identify presence of hypertension: 401.0-405.9)
414.05 Coronary atherosclerosis of unspecified type of bypass graft — (Use additional code to identify presence of hypertension: 401.0-405.9) ▽
414.06 Coronary atherosclerosis, of native coronary artery of transplanted heart — (Use additional code to identify presence of hypertension: 401.0-405.9)
414.07 Coronary atherosclerosis, of bypass graft (artery) (vein) of transplanted heart — (Use additional code to identify presence of hypertension: 401.0-405.9)
414.10 Aneurysm of heart — (Use additional code to identify presence of hypertension: 401.0-405.9)
414.11 Aneurysm of coronary vessels — (Use additional code to identify presence of hypertension: 401.0-405.9)
414.12 Dissection of coronary artery — (Use additional code to identify presence of hypertension: 401.0-405.9)
414.19 Other aneurysm of heart — (Use additional code to identify presence of hypertension: 401.0-405.9)
414.3 Coronary atherosclerosis due to lipid rich plaque — (Code first coronary atherosclerosis (414.00-414.07))
414.4 Coronary atherosclerosis due to calcified coronary lesion — (Code first coronary atherosclerosis (414.00-414.07))
414.8 Other specified forms of chronic ischemic heart disease — (Use additional code to identify presence of hypertension: 401.0-405.9)
414.9 Unspecified chronic ischemic heart disease — (Use additional code to identify presence of hypertension: 401.0-405.9) ▽
428.0 Congestive heart failure, unspecified — (Code, if applicable, heart failure due to hypertension first: 402.0-402.9, with fifth-digit 1 or 404.0-404.9 with fifth digit 1 or 3) ▽
428.1 Left heart failure — (Code, if applicable, heart failure due to hypertension first: 402.0-402.9, with fifth-digit 1 or 404.0-404.9 with fifth digit 1 or 3)
428.20 Unspecified systolic heart failure — (Code, if applicable, heart failure due to hypertension first: 402.0-402.9, with fifth-digit 1 or 404.0-404.9 with fifth digit 1 or 3) ▽
428.21 Acute systolic heart failure — (Code, if applicable, heart failure due to hypertension first: 402.0-402.9, with fifth-digit 1 or 404.0-404.9 with fifth digit 1 or 3)
428.22 Chronic systolic heart failure — (Code, if applicable, heart failure due to hypertension first: 402.0-402.9, with fifth-digit 1 or 404.0-404.9 with fifth digit 1 or 3)
428.23 Acute on chronic systolic heart failure — (Code, if applicable, heart failure due to hypertension first: 402.0-402.9, with fifth-digit 1 or 404.0-404.9 with fifth digit 1 or 3)
428.9 Unspecified heart failure — (Code, if applicable, heart failure due to hypertension first: 402.0-402.9, with fifth-digit 1 or 404.0-404.9 with fifth digit 1 or 3) ▽
746.85 Congenital coronary artery anomaly

ICD-9-CM Procedural

37.35 Partial ventriculectomy
37.49 Other repair of heart and pericardium
39.61 Extracorporeal circulation auxiliary to open heart surgery

33600-33602

33600 Closure of atrioventricular valve (mitral or tricuspid) by suture or patch
33602 Closure of semilunar valve (aortic or pulmonary) by suture or patch

ICD-9-CM Diagnostic

424.0 Mitral valve disorders
424.1 Aortic valve disorders
424.2 Tricuspid valve disorders, specified as nonrheumatic
424.3 Pulmonary valve disorders
745.60 Unspecified type congenital endocardial cushion defect ▽
745.61 Ostium primum defect
745.69 Other congenital endocardial cushion defect
745.7 Cor biloculare
746.00 Unspecified congenital pulmonary valve anomaly ▽
746.01 Congenital atresia of pulmonary valve
746.09 Other congenital anomalies of pulmonary valve
746.1 Congenital tricuspid atresia and stenosis
746.2 Ebstein's anomaly
746.4 Congenital insufficiency of aortic valve
746.6 Congenital mitral insufficiency
746.85 Congenital coronary artery anomaly

ICD-9-CM Procedural

35.11 Open heart valvuloplasty of aortic valve without replacement
35.12 Open heart valvuloplasty of mitral valve without replacement
35.13 Open heart valvuloplasty of pulmonary valve without replacement
35.14 Open heart valvuloplasty of tricuspid valve without replacement
39.61 Extracorporeal circulation auxiliary to open heart surgery

33606

33606 Anastomosis of pulmonary artery to aorta (Damus-Kaye-Stansel procedure)

ICD-9-CM Diagnostic

745.10 Complete transposition of great vessels
745.11 Transposition of great vessels, double outlet right ventricle
745.2 Tetralogy of Fallot
746.01 Congenital atresia of pulmonary valve
746.7 Hypoplastic left heart syndrome

ICD-9-CM Procedural

39.0 Systemic to pulmonary artery shunt
39.61 Extracorporeal circulation auxiliary to open heart surgery

33608

33608 Repair of complex cardiac anomaly other than pulmonary atresia with ventricular septal defect by construction or replacement of conduit from right or left ventricle to pulmonary artery

ICD-9-CM Diagnostic

745.10 Complete transposition of great vessels
745.11 Transposition of great vessels, double outlet right ventricle
745.2 Tetralogy of Fallot

ICD-9-CM Procedural

35.72 Other and unspecified repair of ventricular septal defect
35.82 Total repair of total anomalous pulmonary venous connection
35.83 Total repair of truncus arteriosus
35.92 Creation of conduit between right ventricle and pulmonary artery
39.61 Extracorporeal circulation auxiliary to open heart surgery

33610

33610 Repair of complex cardiac anomalies (eg, single ventricle with subaortic obstruction) by surgical enlargement of ventricular septal defect

ICD-9-CM Diagnostic

745.3 Bulbus cordis anomalies and anomalies of cardiac septal closure, common ventricle

ICD-9-CM Procedural

35.41 Enlargement of existing atrial septal defect
39.61 Extracorporeal circulation auxiliary to open heart surgery

33611-33612

33611 Repair of double outlet right ventricle with intraventricular tunnel repair;
33612 with repair of right ventricular outflow tract obstruction

ICD-9-CM Diagnostic

745.11 Transposition of great vessels, double outlet right ventricle
745.3 Bulbus cordis anomalies and anomalies of cardiac septal closure, common ventricle

746.84 Congenital obstructive anomalies of heart, not elsewhere classified — (Use additional code for associated anomalies: 746.5, 746.81, 747.10)

ICD-9-CM Procedural

35.72 Other and unspecified repair of ventricular septal defect
35.98 Other operations on septa of heart
39.61 Extracorporeal circulation auxiliary to open heart surgery

33615

33615 Repair of complex cardiac anomalies (eg, tricuspid atresia) by closure of atrial septal defect and anastomosis of atria or vena cava to pulmonary artery (simple Fontan procedure)

ICD-9-CM Diagnostic

745.5 Ostium secundum type atrial septal defect
745.61 Ostium primum defect
745.69 Other congenital endocardial cushion defect
746.01 Congenital atresia of pulmonary valve
746.1 Congenital tricuspid atresia and stenosis
746.2 Ebstein's anomaly
747.41 Total congenital anomalous pulmonary venous connection
747.42 Partial congenital anomalous pulmonary venous connection

ICD-9-CM Procedural

35.94 Creation of conduit between atrium and pulmonary artery
39.61 Extracorporeal circulation auxiliary to open heart surgery

33617

33617 Repair of complex cardiac anomalies (eg, single ventricle) by modified Fontan procedure

ICD-9-CM Diagnostic

745.3 Bulbus cordis anomalies and anomalies of cardiac septal closure, common ventricle
745.8 Other bulbus cordis anomalies and anomalies of cardiac septal closure
746.7 Hypoplastic left heart syndrome

ICD-9-CM Procedural

35.94 Creation of conduit between atrium and pulmonary artery
39.61 Extracorporeal circulation auxiliary to open heart surgery

33619

33619 Repair of single ventricle with aortic outflow obstruction and aortic arch hypoplasia (hypoplastic left heart syndrome) (eg, Norwood procedure)

ICD-9-CM Diagnostic

745.3 Bulbus cordis anomalies and anomalies of cardiac septal closure, common ventricle
745.8 Other bulbus cordis anomalies and anomalies of cardiac septal closure
746.7 Hypoplastic left heart syndrome

ICD-9-CM Procedural

39.0 Systemic to pulmonary artery shunt
39.29 Other (peripheral) vascular shunt or bypass
39.61 Extracorporeal circulation auxiliary to open heart surgery

33620-33622

33620 Application of right and left pulmonary artery bands (eg, hybrid approach stage 1)
33621 Transthoracic insertion of catheter for stent placement with catheter removal and closure (eg, hybrid approach stage 1)
33622 Reconstruction of complex cardiac anomaly (eg, single ventricle or hypoplastic left heart) with palliation of single ventricle with aortic outflow obstruction and aortic arch hypoplasia, creation of cavopulmonary anastomosis, and removal of right and left pulmonary bands (eg, hybrid approach stage 2, Norwood, bidirectional Glenn, pulmonary artery debanding)

ICD-9-CM Diagnostic

745.10 Complete transposition of great vessels
745.11 Transposition of great vessels, double outlet right ventricle
745.12 Corrected transposition of great vessels
745.19 Other transposition of great vessels
745.3 Bulbus cordis anomalies and anomalies of cardiac septal closure, common ventricle
745.4 Ventricular septal defect
745.69 Other congenital endocardial cushion defect
745.8 Other bulbus cordis anomalies and anomalies of cardiac septal closure
746.7 Hypoplastic left heart syndrome
747.10 Coarctation of aorta (preductal) (postductal)
747.11 Congenital interruption of aortic arch

ICD-9-CM Procedural

35.94 Creation of conduit between atrium and pulmonary artery
38.85 Other surgical occlusion of other thoracic vessel
39.0 Systemic to pulmonary artery shunt
39.21 Caval-pulmonary artery anastomosis
39.59 Other repair of vessel
39.61 Extracorporeal circulation auxiliary to open heart surgery

33641

33641 Repair atrial septal defect, secundum, with cardiopulmonary bypass, with or without patch

ICD-9-CM Diagnostic

410.00 Acute myocardial infarction of anterolateral wall, episode of care unspecified — (Use additional code to identify presence of hypertension: 401.0-405.9) ▽
410.01 Acute myocardial infarction of anterolateral wall, initial episode of care — (Use additional code to identify presence of hypertension: 401.0-405.9)
410.02 Acute myocardial infarction of anterolateral wall, subsequent episode of care — (Use additional code to identify presence of hypertension: 401.0-405.9)
410.10 Acute myocardial infarction of other anterior wall, episode of care unspecified — (Use additional code to identify presence of hypertension: 401.0-405.9) ▽
410.11 Acute myocardial infarction of other anterior wall, initial episode of care — (Use additional code to identify presence of hypertension: 401.0-405.9)
410.12 Acute myocardial infarction of other anterior wall, subsequent episode of care — (Use additional code to identify presence of hypertension: 401.0-405.9)
410.20 Acute myocardial infarction of inferolateral wall, episode of care unspecified — (Use additional code to identify presence of hypertension: 401.0-405.9) ▽
410.21 Acute myocardial infarction of inferolateral wall, initial episode of care — (Use additional code to identify presence of hypertension: 401.0-405.9)
410.22 Acute myocardial infarction of inferolateral wall, subsequent episode of care — (Use additional code to identify presence of hypertension: 401.0-405.9)
410.30 Acute myocardial infarction of inferoposterior wall, episode of care unspecified — (Use additional code to identify presence of hypertension: 401.0-405.9) ▽
410.31 Acute myocardial infarction of inferoposterior wall, initial episode of care — (Use additional code to identify presence of hypertension: 401.0-405.9)
410.32 Acute myocardial infarction of inferoposterior wall, subsequent episode of care — (Use additional code to identify presence of hypertension: 401.0-405.9)
410.40 Acute myocardial infarction of other inferior wall, episode of care unspecified — (Use additional code to identify presence of hypertension: 401.0-405.9) ▽

410.41 Acute myocardial infarction of other inferior wall, initial episode of care — (Use additional code to identify presence of hypertension: 401.0-405.9)

410.42 Acute myocardial infarction of other inferior wall, subsequent episode of care — (Use additional code to identify presence of hypertension: 401.0-405.9)

410.50 Acute myocardial infarction of other lateral wall, episode of care unspecified — (Use additional code to identify presence of hypertension: 401.0-405.9) ▽

410.51 Acute myocardial infarction of other lateral wall, initial episode of care — (Use additional code to identify presence of hypertension: 401.0-405.9)

410.52 Acute myocardial infarction of other lateral wall, subsequent episode of care — (Use additional code to identify presence of hypertension: 401.0-405.9)

410.60 Acute myocardial infarction, true posterior wall infarction, episode of care unspecified — (Use additional code to identify presence of hypertension: 401.0-405.9) ▽

410.61 Acute myocardial infarction, true posterior wall infarction, initial episode of care — (Use additional code to identify presence of hypertension: 401.0-405.9)

410.62 Acute myocardial infarction, true posterior wall infarction, subsequent episode of care — (Use additional code to identify presence of hypertension: 401.0-405.9)

410.70 Acute myocardial infarction, subendocardial infarction, episode of care unspecified — (Use additional code to identify presence of hypertension: 401.0-405.9) ▽

410.71 Acute myocardial infarction, subendocardial infarction, initial episode of care — (Use additional code to identify presence of hypertension: 401.0-405.9)

410.72 Acute myocardial infarction, subendocardial infarction, subsequent episode of care — (Use additional code to identify presence of hypertension: 401.0-405.9)

410.80 Acute myocardial infarction of other specified sites, episode of care unspecified — (Use additional code to identify presence of hypertension: 401.0-405.9) ▽

410.81 Acute myocardial infarction of other specified sites, initial episode of care — (Use additional code to identify presence of hypertension: 401.0-405.9)

410.82 Acute myocardial infarction of other specified sites, subsequent episode of care — (Use additional code to identify presence of hypertension: 401.0-405.9)

410.90 Acute myocardial infarction, unspecified site, episode of care unspecified — (Use additional code to identify presence of hypertension: 401.0-405.9) ▽

410.91 Acute myocardial infarction, unspecified site, initial episode of care — (Use additional code to identify presence of hypertension: 401.0-405.9) ▽

410.92 Acute myocardial infarction, unspecified site, subsequent episode of care — (Use additional code to identify presence of hypertension: 401.0-405.9) ▽

414.8 Other specified forms of chronic ischemic heart disease — (Use additional code to identify presence of hypertension: 401.0-405.9)

429.71 Acquired cardiac septal defect — (Use additional code to identify the associated myocardial infarction: with onset of 8 weeks of less, 410.00-410.92; with onset of more than 8 weeks, 414.8)

745.5 Ostium secundum type atrial septal defect

745.61 Ostium primum defect

ICD-9-CM Procedural

35.51 Repair of atrial septal defect with prosthesis, open technique

35.61 Repair of atrial septal defect with tissue graft

35.71 Other and unspecified repair of atrial septal defect

39.61 Extracorporeal circulation auxiliary to open heart surgery

33645

33645 Direct or patch closure, sinus venosus, with or without anomalous pulmonary venous drainage

ICD-9-CM Diagnostic

410.00 Acute myocardial infarction of anterolateral wall, episode of care unspecified — (Use additional code to identify presence of hypertension: 401.0-405.9) ▽

410.01 Acute myocardial infarction of anterolateral wall, initial episode of care — (Use additional code to identify presence of hypertension: 401.0-405.9)

410.02 Acute myocardial infarction of anterolateral wall, subsequent episode of care — (Use additional code to identify presence of hypertension: 401.0-405.9)

410.10 Acute myocardial infarction of other anterior wall, episode of care unspecified — (Use additional code to identify presence of hypertension: 401.0-405.9) ▽

410.11 Acute myocardial infarction of other anterior wall, initial episode of care — (Use additional code to identify presence of hypertension: 401.0-405.9)

410.12 Acute myocardial infarction of other anterior wall, subsequent episode of care — (Use additional code to identify presence of hypertension: 401.0-405.9)

410.20 Acute myocardial infarction of inferolateral wall, episode of care unspecified — (Use additional code to identify presence of hypertension: 401.0-405.9) ▽

410.21 Acute myocardial infarction of inferolateral wall, initial episode of care — (Use additional code to identify presence of hypertension: 401.0-405.9)

410.22 Acute myocardial infarction of inferolateral wall, subsequent episode of care — (Use additional code to identify presence of hypertension: 401.0-405.9)

410.30 Acute myocardial infarction of inferoposterior wall, episode of care unspecified — (Use additional code to identify presence of hypertension: 401.0-405.9) ▽

410.31 Acute myocardial infarction of inferoposterior wall, initial episode of care — (Use additional code to identify presence of hypertension: 401.0-405.9)

410.32 Acute myocardial infarction of inferoposterior wall, subsequent episode of care — (Use additional code to identify presence of hypertension: 401.0-405.9)

410.40 Acute myocardial infarction of other inferior wall, episode of care unspecified — (Use additional code to identify presence of hypertension: 401.0-405.9) ▽

410.41 Acute myocardial infarction of other inferior wall, initial episode of care — (Use additional code to identify presence of hypertension: 401.0-405.9)

410.42 Acute myocardial infarction of other inferior wall, subsequent episode of care — (Use additional code to identify presence of hypertension: 401.0-405.9)

410.50 Acute myocardial infarction of other lateral wall, episode of care unspecified — (Use additional code to identify presence of hypertension: 401.0-405.9) ▽

410.51 Acute myocardial infarction of other lateral wall, initial episode of care — (Use additional code to identify presence of hypertension: 401.0-405.9)

410.52 Acute myocardial infarction of other lateral wall, subsequent episode of care — (Use additional code to identify presence of hypertension: 401.0-405.9)

410.60 Acute myocardial infarction, true posterior wall infarction, episode of care unspecified — (Use additional code to identify presence of hypertension: 401.0-405.9) ▽

410.61 Acute myocardial infarction, true posterior wall infarction, initial episode of care — (Use additional code to identify presence of hypertension: 401.0-405.9)

410.62 Acute myocardial infarction, true posterior wall infarction, subsequent episode of care — (Use additional code to identify presence of hypertension: 401.0-405.9)

410.70 Acute myocardial infarction, subendocardial infarction, episode of care unspecified — (Use additional code to identify presence of hypertension: 401.0-405.9) ▽

410.71 Acute myocardial infarction, subendocardial infarction, initial episode of care — (Use additional code to identify presence of hypertension: 401.0-405.9)

410.72 Acute myocardial infarction, subendocardial infarction, subsequent episode of care — (Use additional code to identify presence of hypertension: 401.0-405.9)

410.80 Acute myocardial infarction of other specified sites, episode of care unspecified — (Use additional code to identify presence of hypertension: 401.0-405.9) ▽

410.81 Acute myocardial infarction of other specified sites, initial episode of care — (Use additional code to identify presence of hypertension: 401.0-405.9)

410.82 Acute myocardial infarction of other specified sites, subsequent episode of care — (Use additional code to identify presence of hypertension: 401.0-405.9)

410.90 Acute myocardial infarction, unspecified site, episode of care unspecified — (Use additional code to identify presence of hypertension: 401.0-405.9) ▽

410.91 Acute myocardial infarction, unspecified site, initial episode of care — (Use additional code to identify presence of hypertension: 401.0-405.9) ▽

410.92 Acute myocardial infarction, unspecified site, subsequent episode of care — (Use additional code to identify presence of hypertension: 401.0-405.9) ▽

414.8 Other specified forms of chronic ischemic heart disease — (Use additional code to identify presence of hypertension: 401.0-405.9)

429.71 Acquired cardiac septal defect — (Use additional code to identify the associated myocardial infarction: with onset of 8 weeks of less, 410.00-410.92; with onset of more than 8 weeks, 414.8)

745.4 Ventricular septal defect

745.5 Ostium secundum type atrial septal defect

745.61 Ostium primum defect

745.8 Other bulbus cordis anomalies and anomalies of cardiac septal closure

745.9 Unspecified congenital defect of septal closure
747.40 Congenital anomaly of great veins unspecified
747.41 Total congenital anomalous pulmonary venous connection
747.42 Partial congenital anomalous pulmonary venous connection

ICD-9-CM Procedural

35.51 Repair of atrial septal defect with prosthesis, open technique
35.61 Repair of atrial septal defect with tissue graft
35.71 Other and unspecified repair of atrial septal defect
39.61 Extracorporeal circulation auxiliary to open heart surgery

33647

33647 Repair of atrial septal defect and ventricular septal defect, with direct or patch closure

ICD-9-CM Diagnostic

410.00 Acute myocardial infarction of anterolateral wall, episode of care unspecified — (Use additional code to identify presence of hypertension: 401.0-405.9)
410.01 Acute myocardial infarction of anterolateral wall, initial episode of care — (Use additional code to identify presence of hypertension: 401.0-405.9)
410.02 Acute myocardial infarction of anterolateral wall, subsequent episode of care — (Use additional code to identify presence of hypertension: 401.0-405.9)
410.10 Acute myocardial infarction of other anterior wall, episode of care unspecified — (Use additional code to identify presence of hypertension: 401.0-405.9)
410.11 Acute myocardial infarction of other anterior wall, initial episode of care — (Use additional code to identify presence of hypertension: 401.0-405.9)
410.12 Acute myocardial infarction of other anterior wall, subsequent episode of care — (Use additional code to identify presence of hypertension: 401.0-405.9)
410.20 Acute myocardial infarction of inferolateral wall, episode of care unspecified — (Use additional code to identify presence of hypertension: 401.0-405.9)
410.21 Acute myocardial infarction of inferolateral wall, initial episode of care — (Use additional code to identify presence of hypertension: 401.0-405.9)
410.22 Acute myocardial infarction of inferolateral wall, subsequent episode of care — (Use additional code to identify presence of hypertension: 401.0-405.9)
410.30 Acute myocardial infarction of inferoposterior wall, episode of care unspecified — (Use additional code to identify presence of hypertension: 401.0-405.9)
410.31 Acute myocardial infarction of inferoposterior wall, initial episode of care — (Use additional code to identify presence of hypertension: 401.0-405.9)
410.32 Acute myocardial infarction of inferoposterior wall, subsequent episode of care — (Use additional code to identify presence of hypertension: 401.0-405.9)
410.40 Acute myocardial infarction of other inferior wall, episode of care unspecified — (Use additional code to identify presence of hypertension: 401.0-405.9)
410.41 Acute myocardial infarction of other inferior wall, initial episode of care — (Use additional code to identify presence of hypertension: 401.0-405.9)
410.42 Acute myocardial infarction of other inferior wall, subsequent episode of care — (Use additional code to identify presence of hypertension: 401.0-405.9)
410.50 Acute myocardial infarction of other lateral wall, episode of care unspecified — (Use additional code to identify presence of hypertension: 401.0-405.9)
410.51 Acute myocardial infarction of other lateral wall, initial episode of care — (Use additional code to identify presence of hypertension: 401.0-405.9)
410.52 Acute myocardial infarction of other lateral wall, subsequent episode of care — (Use additional code to identify presence of hypertension: 401.0-405.9)
410.60 Acute myocardial infarction, true posterior wall infarction, episode of care unspecified — (Use additional code to identify presence of hypertension: 401.0-405.9)
410.61 Acute myocardial infarction, true posterior wall infarction, initial episode of care — (Use additional code to identify presence of hypertension: 401.0-405.9)
410.62 Acute myocardial infarction, true posterior wall infarction, subsequent episode of care — (Use additional code to identify presence of hypertension: 401.0-405.9)
410.70 Acute myocardial infarction, subendocardial infarction, episode of care unspecified — (Use additional code to identify presence of hypertension: 401.0-405.9)
410.71 Acute myocardial infarction, subendocardial infarction, initial episode of care — (Use additional code to identify presence of hypertension: 401.0-405.9)
410.72 Acute myocardial infarction, subendocardial infarction, subsequent episode of care — (Use additional code to identify presence of hypertension: 401.0-405.9)
410.80 Acute myocardial infarction of other specified sites, episode of care unspecified — (Use additional code to identify presence of hypertension: 401.0-405.9)
410.81 Acute myocardial infarction of other specified sites, initial episode of care — (Use additional code to identify presence of hypertension: 401.0-405.9)
410.82 Acute myocardial infarction of other specified sites, subsequent episode of care — (Use additional code to identify presence of hypertension: 401.0-405.9)
410.90 Acute myocardial infarction, unspecified site, episode of care unspecified — (Use additional code to identify presence of hypertension: 401.0-405.9)
410.91 Acute myocardial infarction, unspecified site, initial episode of care — (Use additional code to identify presence of hypertension: 401.0-405.9)
410.92 Acute myocardial infarction, unspecified site, subsequent episode of care — (Use additional code to identify presence of hypertension: 401.0-405.9)
414.8 Other specified forms of chronic ischemic heart disease — (Use additional code to identify presence of hypertension: 401.0-405.9)
429.71 Acquired cardiac septal defect — (Use additional code to identify the associated myocardial infarction: with onset of 8 weeks of less, 410.00-410.92; with onset of more than 8 weeks, 414.8)
745.5 Ostium secundum type atrial septal defect
745.61 Ostium primum defect
745.69 Other congenital endocardial cushion defect
745.9 Unspecified congenital defect of septal closure
746.9 Unspecified congenital anomaly of heart
786.59 Chest pain, other

ICD-9-CM Procedural

35.51 Repair of atrial septal defect with prosthesis, open technique
35.52 Repair of atrial septal defect with prosthesis, closed technique
35.53 Repair of ventricular septal defect with prosthesis, open technique
35.61 Repair of atrial septal defect with tissue graft
35.62 Repair of ventricular septal defect with tissue graft
35.71 Other and unspecified repair of atrial septal defect
35.72 Other and unspecified repair of ventricular septal defect
39.61 Extracorporeal circulation auxiliary to open heart surgery

33660

33660 Repair of incomplete or partial atrioventricular canal (ostium primum atrial septal defect), with or without atrioventricular valve repair

ICD-9-CM Diagnostic

745.61 Ostium primum defect
745.69 Other congenital endocardial cushion defect
745.9 Unspecified congenital defect of septal closure
746.9 Unspecified congenital anomaly of heart

ICD-9-CM Procedural

35.50 Repair of unspecified septal defect of heart with prosthesis
35.54 Repair of endocardial cushion defect with prosthesis
35.60 Repair of unspecified septal defect of heart with tissue graft
35.63 Repair of endocardial cushion defect with tissue graft
35.70 Other and unspecified repair of unspecified septal defect of heart
35.73 Other and unspecified repair of endocardial cushion defect
39.61 Extracorporeal circulation auxiliary to open heart surgery

33665

33665 Repair of intermediate or transitional atrioventricular canal, with or without atrioventricular valve repair

ICD-9-CM Diagnostic

745.61 Ostium primum defect
745.69 Other congenital endocardial cushion defect

745.9 Unspecified congenital defect of septal closure
746.9 Unspecified congenital anomaly of heart

ICD-9-CM Procedural

35.50 Repair of unspecified septal defect of heart with prosthesis
35.54 Repair of endocardial cushion defect with prosthesis
35.60 Repair of unspecified septal defect of heart with tissue graft
35.63 Repair of endocardial cushion defect with tissue graft
35.70 Other and unspecified repair of unspecified septal defect of heart
35.73 Other and unspecified repair of endocardial cushion defect
39.61 Extracorporeal circulation auxiliary to open heart surgery

33670

33670 Repair of complete atrioventricular canal, with or without prosthetic valve

ICD-9-CM Diagnostic

745.61 Ostium primum defect
745.69 Other congenital endocardial cushion defect
745.9 Unspecified congenital defect of septal closure
746.9 Unspecified congenital anomaly of heart

ICD-9-CM Procedural

35.54 Repair of endocardial cushion defect with prosthesis
35.63 Repair of endocardial cushion defect with tissue graft
35.73 Other and unspecified repair of endocardial cushion defect
39.61 Extracorporeal circulation auxiliary to open heart surgery

33675

33675 Closure of multiple ventricular septal defects;

ICD-9-CM Diagnostic

410.00 Acute myocardial infarction of anterolateral wall, episode of care unspecified — (Use additional code to identify presence of hypertension: 401.0-405.9)
410.01 Acute myocardial infarction of anterolateral wall, initial episode of care — (Use additional code to identify presence of hypertension: 401.0-405.9)
410.02 Acute myocardial infarction of anterolateral wall, subsequent episode of care — (Use additional code to identify presence of hypertension: 401.0-405.9)
410.10 Acute myocardial infarction of other anterior wall, episode of care unspecified — (Use additional code to identify presence of hypertension: 401.0-405.9)
410.11 Acute myocardial infarction of other anterior wall, initial episode of care — (Use additional code to identify presence of hypertension: 401.0-405.9)
410.12 Acute myocardial infarction of other anterior wall, subsequent episode of care — (Use additional code to identify presence of hypertension: 401.0-405.9)
410.20 Acute myocardial infarction of inferolateral wall, episode of care unspecified — (Use additional code to identify presence of hypertension: 401.0-405.9)
410.21 Acute myocardial infarction of inferolateral wall, initial episode of care — (Use additional code to identify presence of hypertension: 401.0-405.9)
410.22 Acute myocardial infarction of inferolateral wall, subsequent episode of care — (Use additional code to identify presence of hypertension: 401.0-405.9)
410.30 Acute myocardial infarction of inferoposterior wall, episode of care unspecified — (Use additional code to identify presence of hypertension: 401.0-405.9)
410.31 Acute myocardial infarction of inferoposterior wall, initial episode of care — (Use additional code to identify presence of hypertension: 401.0-405.9)
410.32 Acute myocardial infarction of inferoposterior wall, subsequent episode of care — (Use additional code to identify presence of hypertension: 401.0-405.9)
410.40 Acute myocardial infarction of other inferior wall, episode of care unspecified — (Use additional code to identify presence of hypertension: 401.0-405.9)
410.41 Acute myocardial infarction of other inferior wall, initial episode of care — (Use additional code to identify presence of hypertension: 401.0-405.9)
410.42 Acute myocardial infarction of other inferior wall, subsequent episode of care — (Use additional code to identify presence of hypertension: 401.0-405.9)
410.50 Acute myocardial infarction of other lateral wall, episode of care unspecified — (Use additional code to identify presence of hypertension: 401.0-405.9)
410.51 Acute myocardial infarction of other lateral wall, initial episode of care — (Use additional code to identify presence of hypertension: 401.0-405.9)
410.52 Acute myocardial infarction of other lateral wall, subsequent episode of care — (Use additional code to identify presence of hypertension: 401.0-405.9)
410.60 Acute myocardial infarction, true posterior wall infarction, episode of care unspecified — (Use additional code to identify presence of hypertension: 401.0-405.9)
410.61 Acute myocardial infarction, true posterior wall infarction, initial episode of care — (Use additional code to identify presence of hypertension: 401.0-405.9)
410.62 Acute myocardial infarction, true posterior wall infarction, subsequent episode of care — (Use additional code to identify presence of hypertension: 401.0-405.9)
410.70 Acute myocardial infarction, subendocardial infarction, episode of care unspecified — (Use additional code to identify presence of hypertension: 401.0-405.9)
410.71 Acute myocardial infarction, subendocardial infarction, initial episode of care — (Use additional code to identify presence of hypertension: 401.0-405.9)
410.72 Acute myocardial infarction, subendocardial infarction, subsequent episode of care — (Use additional code to identify presence of hypertension: 401.0-405.9)
410.80 Acute myocardial infarction of other specified sites, episode of care unspecified — (Use additional code to identify presence of hypertension: 401.0-405.9)
410.81 Acute myocardial infarction of other specified sites, initial episode of care — (Use additional code to identify presence of hypertension: 401.0-405.9)
410.82 Acute myocardial infarction of other specified sites, subsequent episode of care — (Use additional code to identify presence of hypertension: 401.0-405.9)
410.90 Acute myocardial infarction, unspecified site, episode of care unspecified — (Use additional code to identify presence of hypertension: 401.0-405.9)
410.92 Acute myocardial infarction, unspecified site, subsequent episode of care — (Use additional code to identify presence of hypertension: 401.0-405.9)
414.8 Other specified forms of chronic ischemic heart disease — (Use additional code to identify presence of hypertension: 401.0-405.9)
429.71 Acquired cardiac septal defect — (Use additional code to identify the associated myocardial infarction: with onset of 8 weeks of less, 410.00-410.92; with onset of more than 8 weeks, 414.8)
745.4 Ventricular septal defect
745.7 Cor biloculare
745.8 Other bulbus cordis anomalies and anomalies of cardiac septal closure
745.9 Unspecified congenital defect of septal closure
746.00 Unspecified congenital pulmonary valve anomaly
746.01 Congenital atresia of pulmonary valve
746.02 Congenital stenosis of pulmonary valve
746.09 Other congenital anomalies of pulmonary valve
746.9 Unspecified congenital anomaly of heart

ICD-9-CM Procedural

35.53 Repair of ventricular septal defect with prosthesis, open technique
35.55 Repair of ventricular septal defect with prosthesis, closed technique
35.62 Repair of ventricular septal defect with tissue graft
35.70 Other and unspecified repair of unspecified septal defect of heart
35.72 Other and unspecified repair of ventricular septal defect
39.61 Extracorporeal circulation auxiliary to open heart surgery

33676

33676 Closure of multiple ventricular septal defects; with pulmonary valvotomy or infundibular resection (acyanotic)

ICD-9-CM Diagnostic

410.00 Acute myocardial infarction of anterolateral wall, episode of care unspecified — (Use additional code to identify presence of hypertension: 401.0-405.9)
410.01 Acute myocardial infarction of anterolateral wall, initial episode of care — (Use additional code to identify presence of hypertension: 401.0-405.9)
410.02 Acute myocardial infarction of anterolateral wall, subsequent episode of care — (Use additional code to identify presence of hypertension: 401.0-405.9)

410.10 Acute myocardial infarction of other anterior wall, episode of care unspecified — (Use additional code to identify presence of hypertension: 401.0-405.9)
410.11 Acute myocardial infarction of other anterior wall, initial episode of care — (Use additional code to identify presence of hypertension: 401.0-405.9)
410.12 Acute myocardial infarction of other anterior wall, subsequent episode of care — (Use additional code to identify presence of hypertension: 401.0-405.9)
410.20 Acute myocardial infarction of inferolateral wall, episode of care unspecified — (Use additional code to identify presence of hypertension: 401.0-405.9)
410.21 Acute myocardial infarction of inferolateral wall, initial episode of care — (Use additional code to identify presence of hypertension: 401.0-405.9)
410.22 Acute myocardial infarction of inferolateral wall, subsequent episode of care — (Use additional code to identify presence of hypertension: 401.0-405.9)
410.30 Acute myocardial infarction of inferoposterior wall, episode of care unspecified — (Use additional code to identify presence of hypertension: 401.0-405.9)
410.31 Acute myocardial infarction of inferoposterior wall, initial episode of care — (Use additional code to identify presence of hypertension: 401.0-405.9)
410.32 Acute myocardial infarction of inferoposterior wall, subsequent episode of care — (Use additional code to identify presence of hypertension: 401.0-405.9)
410.40 Acute myocardial infarction of other inferior wall, episode of care unspecified — (Use additional code to identify presence of hypertension: 401.0-405.9)
410.41 Acute myocardial infarction of other inferior wall, initial episode of care — (Use additional code to identify presence of hypertension: 401.0-405.9)
410.42 Acute myocardial infarction of other inferior wall, subsequent episode of care — (Use additional code to identify presence of hypertension: 401.0-405.9)
410.50 Acute myocardial infarction of other lateral wall, episode of care unspecified — (Use additional code to identify presence of hypertension: 401.0-405.9)
410.51 Acute myocardial infarction of other lateral wall, initial episode of care — (Use additional code to identify presence of hypertension: 401.0-405.9)
410.52 Acute myocardial infarction of other lateral wall, subsequent episode of care — (Use additional code to identify presence of hypertension: 401.0-405.9)
410.60 Acute myocardial infarction, true posterior wall infarction, episode of care unspecified — (Use additional code to identify presence of hypertension: 401.0-405.9)
410.61 Acute myocardial infarction, true posterior wall infarction, initial episode of care — (Use additional code to identify presence of hypertension: 401.0-405.9)
410.62 Acute myocardial infarction, true posterior wall infarction, subsequent episode of care — (Use additional code to identify presence of hypertension: 401.0-405.9)
410.70 Acute myocardial infarction, subendocardial infarction, episode of care unspecified — (Use additional code to identify presence of hypertension: 401.0-405.9)
410.71 Acute myocardial infarction, subendocardial infarction, initial episode of care — (Use additional code to identify presence of hypertension: 401.0-405.9)
410.72 Acute myocardial infarction, subendocardial infarction, subsequent episode of care — (Use additional code to identify presence of hypertension: 401.0-405.9)
410.80 Acute myocardial infarction of other specified sites, episode of care unspecified — (Use additional code to identify presence of hypertension: 401.0-405.9)
410.81 Acute myocardial infarction of other specified sites, initial episode of care — (Use additional code to identify presence of hypertension: 401.0-405.9)
410.82 Acute myocardial infarction of other specified sites, subsequent episode of care — (Use additional code to identify presence of hypertension: 401.0-405.9)
410.90 Acute myocardial infarction, unspecified site, episode of care unspecified — (Use additional code to identify presence of hypertension: 401.0-405.9)
410.91 Acute myocardial infarction, unspecified site, initial episode of care — (Use additional code to identify presence of hypertension: 401.0-405.9)
410.92 Acute myocardial infarction, unspecified site, subsequent episode of care — (Use additional code to identify presence of hypertension: 401.0-405.9)
414.8 Other specified forms of chronic ischemic heart disease — (Use additional code to identify presence of hypertension: 401.0-405.9)
429.71 Acquired cardiac septal defect — (Use additional code to identify the associated myocardial infarction: with onset of 8 weeks of less, 410.00-410.92; with onset of more than 8 weeks, 414.8)
745.4 Ventricular septal defect
745.7 Cor biloculare
745.8 Other bulbus cordis anomalies and anomalies of cardiac septal closure
745.9 Unspecified congenital defect of septal closure
746.00 Unspecified congenital pulmonary valve anomaly
746.01 Congenital atresia of pulmonary valve
746.02 Congenital stenosis of pulmonary valve
746.09 Other congenital anomalies of pulmonary valve
746.9 Unspecified congenital anomaly of heart

ICD-9-CM Procedural

35.03 Closed heart valvotomy, pulmonary valve
35.13 Open heart valvuloplasty of pulmonary valve without replacement
35.34 Infundibulectomy
35.53 Repair of ventricular septal defect with prosthesis, open technique
35.55 Repair of ventricular septal defect with prosthesis, closed technique
35.62 Repair of ventricular septal defect with tissue graft
35.72 Other and unspecified repair of ventricular septal defect
35.73 Other and unspecified repair of endocardial cushion defect
39.61 Extracorporeal circulation auxiliary to open heart surgery

33677

33677 Closure of multiple ventricular septal defects; with removal of pulmonary artery band, with or without gusset

ICD-9-CM Diagnostic

410.00 Acute myocardial infarction of anterolateral wall, episode of care unspecified — (Use additional code to identify presence of hypertension: 401.0-405.9)
410.01 Acute myocardial infarction of anterolateral wall, initial episode of care — (Use additional code to identify presence of hypertension: 401.0-405.9)
410.02 Acute myocardial infarction of anterolateral wall, subsequent episode of care — (Use additional code to identify presence of hypertension: 401.0-405.9)
410.10 Acute myocardial infarction of other anterior wall, episode of care unspecified — (Use additional code to identify presence of hypertension: 401.0-405.9)
410.11 Acute myocardial infarction of other anterior wall, initial episode of care — (Use additional code to identify presence of hypertension: 401.0-405.9)
410.12 Acute myocardial infarction of other anterior wall, subsequent episode of care — (Use additional code to identify presence of hypertension: 401.0-405.9)
410.20 Acute myocardial infarction of inferolateral wall, episode of care unspecified — (Use additional code to identify presence of hypertension: 401.0-405.9)
410.21 Acute myocardial infarction of inferolateral wall, initial episode of care — (Use additional code to identify presence of hypertension: 401.0-405.9)
410.22 Acute myocardial infarction of inferolateral wall, subsequent episode of care — (Use additional code to identify presence of hypertension: 401.0-405.9)
410.30 Acute myocardial infarction of inferoposterior wall, episode of care unspecified — (Use additional code to identify presence of hypertension: 401.0-405.9)
410.31 Acute myocardial infarction of inferoposterior wall, initial episode of care — (Use additional code to identify presence of hypertension: 401.0-405.9)
410.32 Acute myocardial infarction of inferoposterior wall, subsequent episode of care — (Use additional code to identify presence of hypertension: 401.0-405.9)
410.40 Acute myocardial infarction of other inferior wall, episode of care unspecified — (Use additional code to identify presence of hypertension: 401.0-405.9)
410.41 Acute myocardial infarction of other inferior wall, initial episode of care — (Use additional code to identify presence of hypertension: 401.0-405.9)
410.42 Acute myocardial infarction of other inferior wall, subsequent episode of care — (Use additional code to identify presence of hypertension: 401.0-405.9)
410.50 Acute myocardial infarction of other lateral wall, episode of care unspecified — (Use additional code to identify presence of hypertension: 401.0-405.9)
410.51 Acute myocardial infarction of other lateral wall, initial episode of care — (Use additional code to identify presence of hypertension: 401.0-405.9)
410.52 Acute myocardial infarction of other lateral wall, subsequent episode of care — (Use additional code to identify presence of hypertension: 401.0-405.9)

410.60 Acute myocardial infarction, true posterior wall infarction, episode of care unspecified — (Use additional code to identify presence of hypertension: 401.0-405.9)

410.61 Acute myocardial infarction, true posterior wall infarction, initial episode of care — (Use additional code to identify presence of hypertension: 401.0-405.9)

410.62 Acute myocardial infarction, true posterior wall infarction, subsequent episode of care — (Use additional code to identify presence of hypertension: 401.0-405.9)

410.70 Acute myocardial infarction, subendocardial infarction, episode of care unspecified — (Use additional code to identify presence of hypertension: 401.0-405.9)

410.71 Acute myocardial infarction, subendocardial infarction, initial episode of care — (Use additional code to identify presence of hypertension: 401.0-405.9)

410.72 Acute myocardial infarction, subendocardial infarction, subsequent episode of care — (Use additional code to identify presence of hypertension: 401.0-405.9)

410.80 Acute myocardial infarction of other specified sites, episode of care unspecified — (Use additional code to identify presence of hypertension: 401.0-405.9)

410.81 Acute myocardial infarction of other specified sites, initial episode of care — (Use additional code to identify presence of hypertension: 401.0-405.9)

410.82 Acute myocardial infarction of other specified sites, subsequent episode of care — (Use additional code to identify presence of hypertension: 401.0-405.9)

410.90 Acute myocardial infarction, unspecified site, episode of care unspecified — (Use additional code to identify presence of hypertension: 401.0-405.9)

410.91 Acute myocardial infarction, unspecified site, initial episode of care — (Use additional code to identify presence of hypertension: 401.0-405.9)

410.92 Acute myocardial infarction, unspecified site, subsequent episode of care — (Use additional code to identify presence of hypertension: 401.0-405.9)

414.8 Other specified forms of chronic ischemic heart disease — (Use additional code to identify presence of hypertension: 401.0-405.9)

429.71 Acquired cardiac septal defect — (Use additional code to identify the associated myocardial infarction: with onset of 8 weeks of less, 410.00-410.92; with onset of more than 8 weeks, 414.8)

745.4 Ventricular septal defect

745.7 Cor biloculare

745.8 Other bulbus cordis anomalies and anomalies of cardiac septal closure

745.9 Unspecified congenital defect of septal closure

746.00 Unspecified congenital pulmonary valve anomaly

746.01 Congenital atresia of pulmonary valve

746.02 Congenital stenosis of pulmonary valve

746.09 Other congenital anomalies of pulmonary valve

746.9 Unspecified congenital anomaly of heart

ICD-9-CM Procedural

35.53 Repair of ventricular septal defect with prosthesis, open technique

35.55 Repair of ventricular septal defect with prosthesis, closed technique

35.62 Repair of ventricular septal defect with tissue graft

35.72 Other and unspecified repair of ventricular septal defect

39.61 Extracorporeal circulation auxiliary to open heart surgery

33681

33681 Closure of single ventricular septal defect, with or without patch;

ICD-9-CM Diagnostic

410.00 Acute myocardial infarction of anterolateral wall, episode of care unspecified — (Use additional code to identify presence of hypertension: 401.0-405.9)

410.01 Acute myocardial infarction of anterolateral wall, initial episode of care — (Use additional code to identify presence of hypertension: 401.0-405.9)

410.02 Acute myocardial infarction of anterolateral wall, subsequent episode of care — (Use additional code to identify presence of hypertension: 401.0-405.9)

410.10 Acute myocardial infarction of other anterior wall, episode of care unspecified — (Use additional code to identify presence of hypertension: 401.0-405.9)

410.11 Acute myocardial infarction of other anterior wall, initial episode of care — (Use additional code to identify presence of hypertension: 401.0-405.9)

410.12 Acute myocardial infarction of other anterior wall, subsequent episode of care — (Use additional code to identify presence of hypertension: 401.0-405.9)

410.20 Acute myocardial infarction of inferolateral wall, episode of care unspecified — (Use additional code to identify presence of hypertension: 401.0-405.9)

410.21 Acute myocardial infarction of inferolateral wall, initial episode of care — (Use additional code to identify presence of hypertension: 401.0-405.9)

410.22 Acute myocardial infarction of inferolateral wall, subsequent episode of care — (Use additional code to identify presence of hypertension: 401.0-405.9)

410.30 Acute myocardial infarction of inferoposterior wall, episode of care unspecified — (Use additional code to identify presence of hypertension: 401.0-405.9)

410.31 Acute myocardial infarction of inferoposterior wall, initial episode of care — (Use additional code to identify presence of hypertension: 401.0-405.9)

410.32 Acute myocardial infarction of inferoposterior wall, subsequent episode of care — (Use additional code to identify presence of hypertension: 401.0-405.9)

410.40 Acute myocardial infarction of other inferior wall, episode of care unspecified — (Use additional code to identify presence of hypertension: 401.0-405.9)

410.41 Acute myocardial infarction of other inferior wall, initial episode of care — (Use additional code to identify presence of hypertension: 401.0-405.9)

410.42 Acute myocardial infarction of other inferior wall, subsequent episode of care — (Use additional code to identify presence of hypertension: 401.0-405.9)

410.50 Acute myocardial infarction of other lateral wall, episode of care unspecified — (Use additional code to identify presence of hypertension: 401.0-405.9)

410.51 Acute myocardial infarction of other lateral wall, initial episode of care — (Use additional code to identify presence of hypertension: 401.0-405.9)

410.52 Acute myocardial infarction of other lateral wall, subsequent episode of care — (Use additional code to identify presence of hypertension: 401.0-405.9)

410.60 Acute myocardial infarction, true posterior wall infarction, episode of care unspecified — (Use additional code to identify presence of hypertension: 401.0-405.9)

410.61 Acute myocardial infarction, true posterior wall infarction, initial episode of care — (Use additional code to identify presence of hypertension: 401.0-405.9)

410.62 Acute myocardial infarction, true posterior wall infarction, subsequent episode of care — (Use additional code to identify presence of hypertension: 401.0-405.9)

410.70 Acute myocardial infarction, subendocardial infarction, episode of care unspecified — (Use additional code to identify presence of hypertension: 401.0-405.9)

410.71 Acute myocardial infarction, subendocardial infarction, initial episode of care — (Use additional code to identify presence of hypertension: 401.0-405.9)

410.72 Acute myocardial infarction, subendocardial infarction, subsequent episode of care — (Use additional code to identify presence of hypertension: 401.0-405.9)

410.80 Acute myocardial infarction of other specified sites, episode of care unspecified — (Use additional code to identify presence of hypertension: 401.0-405.9)

410.81 Acute myocardial infarction of other specified sites, initial episode of care — (Use additional code to identify presence of hypertension: 401.0-405.9)

410.82 Acute myocardial infarction of other specified sites, subsequent episode of care — (Use additional code to identify presence of hypertension: 401.0-405.9)

410.90 Acute myocardial infarction, unspecified site, episode of care unspecified — (Use additional code to identify presence of hypertension: 401.0-405.9)

410.91 Acute myocardial infarction, unspecified site, initial episode of care — (Use additional code to identify presence of hypertension: 401.0-405.9)

410.92 Acute myocardial infarction, unspecified site, subsequent episode of care — (Use additional code to identify presence of hypertension: 401.0-405.9)

414.8 Other specified forms of chronic ischemic heart disease — (Use additional code to identify presence of hypertension: 401.0-405.9)

429.71 Acquired cardiac septal defect — (Use additional code to identify the associated myocardial infarction: with onset of 8 weeks of less, 410.00-410.92; with onset of more than 8 weeks, 414.8)

745.4 Ventricular septal defect

745.7 Cor biloculare

745.8 Other bulbus cordis anomalies and anomalies of cardiac septal closure

745.9 Unspecified congenital defect of septal closure

746.00 Unspecified congenital pulmonary valve anomaly

746.01 Congenital atresia of pulmonary valve

746.02 Congenital stenosis of pulmonary valve

746.09 Other congenital anomalies of pulmonary valve

746.9 Unspecified congenital anomaly of heart ▽

ICD-9-CM Procedural

35.50 Repair of unspecified septal defect of heart with prosthesis
35.53 Repair of ventricular septal defect with prosthesis, open technique
35.55 Repair of ventricular septal defect with prosthesis, closed technique
35.60 Repair of unspecified septal defect of heart with tissue graft
35.62 Repair of ventricular septal defect with tissue graft
35.70 Other and unspecified repair of unspecified septal defect of heart
35.72 Other and unspecified repair of ventricular septal defect
39.61 Extracorporeal circulation auxiliary to open heart surgery

33684

33684 Closure of single ventricular septal defect, with or without patch; with pulmonary valvotomy or infundibular resection (acyanotic)

ICD-9-CM Diagnostic

410.00 Acute myocardial infarction of anterolateral wall, episode of care unspecified — (Use additional code to identify presence of hypertension: 401.0-405.9) ▽
410.01 Acute myocardial infarction of anterolateral wall, initial episode of care — (Use additional code to identify presence of hypertension: 401.0-405.9)
410.02 Acute myocardial infarction of anterolateral wall, subsequent episode of care — (Use additional code to identify presence of hypertension: 401.0-405.9)
410.10 Acute myocardial infarction of other anterior wall, episode of care unspecified — (Use additional code to identify presence of hypertension: 401.0-405.9) ▽
410.11 Acute myocardial infarction of other anterior wall, initial episode of care — (Use additional code to identify presence of hypertension: 401.0-405.9)
410.12 Acute myocardial infarction of other anterior wall, subsequent episode of care — (Use additional code to identify presence of hypertension: 401.0-405.9)
410.20 Acute myocardial infarction of inferolateral wall, episode of care unspecified — (Use additional code to identify presence of hypertension: 401.0-405.9) ▽
410.21 Acute myocardial infarction of inferolateral wall, initial episode of care — (Use additional code to identify presence of hypertension: 401.0-405.9)
410.22 Acute myocardial infarction of inferolateral wall, subsequent episode of care — (Use additional code to identify presence of hypertension: 401.0-405.9)
410.30 Acute myocardial infarction of inferoposterior wall, episode of care unspecified — (Use additional code to identify presence of hypertension: 401.0-405.9) ▽
410.31 Acute myocardial infarction of inferoposterior wall, initial episode of care — (Use additional code to identify presence of hypertension: 401.0-405.9)
410.32 Acute myocardial infarction of inferoposterior wall, subsequent episode of care — (Use additional code to identify presence of hypertension: 401.0-405.9)
410.40 Acute myocardial infarction of other inferior wall, episode of care unspecified — (Use additional code to identify presence of hypertension: 401.0-405.9) ▽
410.41 Acute myocardial infarction of other inferior wall, initial episode of care — (Use additional code to identify presence of hypertension: 401.0-405.9)
410.42 Acute myocardial infarction of other inferior wall, subsequent episode of care — (Use additional code to identify presence of hypertension: 401.0-405.9)
410.50 Acute myocardial infarction of other lateral wall, episode of care unspecified — (Use additional code to identify presence of hypertension: 401.0-405.9) ▽
410.51 Acute myocardial infarction of other lateral wall, initial episode of care — (Use additional code to identify presence of hypertension: 401.0-405.9)
410.52 Acute myocardial infarction of other lateral wall, subsequent episode of care — (Use additional code to identify presence of hypertension: 401.0-405.9)
410.60 Acute myocardial infarction, true posterior wall infarction, episode of care unspecified — (Use additional code to identify presence of hypertension: 401.0-405.9) ▽
410.61 Acute myocardial infarction, true posterior wall infarction, initial episode of care — (Use additional code to identify presence of hypertension: 401.0-405.9)
410.62 Acute myocardial infarction, true posterior wall infarction, subsequent episode of care — (Use additional code to identify presence of hypertension: 401.0-405.9)
410.70 Acute myocardial infarction, subendocardial infarction, episode of care unspecified — (Use additional code to identify presence of hypertension: 401.0-405.9) ▽
410.71 Acute myocardial infarction, subendocardial infarction, initial episode of care — (Use additional code to identify presence of hypertension: 401.0-405.9)
410.72 Acute myocardial infarction, subendocardial infarction, subsequent episode of care — (Use additional code to identify presence of hypertension: 401.0-405.9)
410.80 Acute myocardial infarction of other specified sites, episode of care unspecified — (Use additional code to identify presence of hypertension: 401.0-405.9) ▽
410.81 Acute myocardial infarction of other specified sites, initial episode of care — (Use additional code to identify presence of hypertension: 401.0-405.9)
410.82 Acute myocardial infarction of other specified sites, subsequent episode of care — (Use additional code to identify presence of hypertension: 401.0-405.9)
410.90 Acute myocardial infarction, unspecified site, episode of care unspecified — (Use additional code to identify presence of hypertension: 401.0-405.9) ▽
410.91 Acute myocardial infarction, unspecified site, initial episode of care — (Use additional code to identify presence of hypertension: 401.0-405.9) ▽
410.92 Acute myocardial infarction, unspecified site, subsequent episode of care — (Use additional code to identify presence of hypertension: 401.0-405.9) ▽
414.8 Other specified forms of chronic ischemic heart disease — (Use additional code to identify presence of hypertension: 401.0-405.9)
429.71 Acquired cardiac septal defect — (Use additional code to identify the associated myocardial infarction: with onset of 8 weeks of less, 410.00-410.92; with onset of more than 8 weeks, 414.8)
745.4 Ventricular septal defect
745.7 Cor biloculare
745.8 Other bulbus cordis anomalies and anomalies of cardiac septal closure
745.9 Unspecified congenital defect of septal closure ▽
746.00 Unspecified congenital pulmonary valve anomaly ▽
746.01 Congenital atresia of pulmonary valve
746.02 Congenital stenosis of pulmonary valve
746.09 Other congenital anomalies of pulmonary valve
746.9 Unspecified congenital anomaly of heart ▽

ICD-9-CM Procedural

35.03 Closed heart valvotomy, pulmonary valve
35.13 Open heart valvuloplasty of pulmonary valve without replacement
35.34 Infundibulectomy
35.53 Repair of ventricular septal defect with prosthesis, open technique
35.60 Repair of unspecified septal defect of heart with tissue graft
35.62 Repair of ventricular septal defect with tissue graft
35.72 Other and unspecified repair of ventricular septal defect
39.61 Extracorporeal circulation auxiliary to open heart surgery

33688

33688 Closure of single ventricular septal defect, with or without patch; with removal of pulmonary artery band, with or without gusset

ICD-9-CM Diagnostic

410.00 Acute myocardial infarction of anterolateral wall, episode of care unspecified — (Use additional code to identify presence of hypertension: 401.0-405.9) ▽
410.01 Acute myocardial infarction of anterolateral wall, initial episode of care — (Use additional code to identify presence of hypertension: 401.0-405.9)
410.02 Acute myocardial infarction of anterolateral wall, subsequent episode of care — (Use additional code to identify presence of hypertension: 401.0-405.9)
410.10 Acute myocardial infarction of other anterior wall, episode of care unspecified — (Use additional code to identify presence of hypertension: 401.0-405.9) ▽
410.11 Acute myocardial infarction of other anterior wall, initial episode of care — (Use additional code to identify presence of hypertension: 401.0-405.9)
410.12 Acute myocardial infarction of other anterior wall, subsequent episode of care — (Use additional code to identify presence of hypertension: 401.0-405.9)
410.20 Acute myocardial infarction of inferolateral wall, episode of care unspecified — (Use additional code to identify presence of hypertension: 401.0-405.9) ▽

410.21 Acute myocardial infarction of inferolateral wall, initial episode of care — (Use additional code to identify presence of hypertension: 401.0-405.9)
410.22 Acute myocardial infarction of inferolateral wall, subsequent episode of care — (Use additional code to identify presence of hypertension: 401.0-405.9)
410.30 Acute myocardial infarction of inferoposterior wall, episode of care unspecified — (Use additional code to identify presence of hypertension: 401.0-405.9) ▽
410.31 Acute myocardial infarction of inferoposterior wall, initial episode of care — (Use additional code to identify presence of hypertension: 401.0-405.9)
410.32 Acute myocardial infarction of inferoposterior wall, subsequent episode of care — (Use additional code to identify presence of hypertension: 401.0-405.9)
410.40 Acute myocardial infarction of other inferior wall, episode of care unspecified — (Use additional code to identify presence of hypertension: 401.0-405.9) ▽
410.41 Acute myocardial infarction of other inferior wall, initial episode of care — (Use additional code to identify presence of hypertension: 401.0-405.9)
410.42 Acute myocardial infarction of other inferior wall, subsequent episode of care — (Use additional code to identify presence of hypertension: 401.0-405.9)
410.50 Acute myocardial infarction of other lateral wall, episode of care unspecified — (Use additional code to identify presence of hypertension: 401.0-405.9) ▽
410.51 Acute myocardial infarction of other lateral wall, initial episode of care — (Use additional code to identify presence of hypertension: 401.0-405.9)
410.52 Acute myocardial infarction of other lateral wall, subsequent episode of care — (Use additional code to identify presence of hypertension: 401.0-405.9)
410.60 Acute myocardial infarction, true posterior wall infarction, episode of care unspecified — (Use additional code to identify presence of hypertension: 401.0-405.9) ▽
410.61 Acute myocardial infarction, true posterior wall infarction, initial episode of care — (Use additional code to identify presence of hypertension: 401.0-405.9)
410.62 Acute myocardial infarction, true posterior wall infarction, subsequent episode of care — (Use additional code to identify presence of hypertension: 401.0-405.9)
410.70 Acute myocardial infarction, subendocardial infarction, episode of care unspecified — (Use additional code to identify presence of hypertension: 401.0-405.9) ▽
410.71 Acute myocardial infarction, subendocardial infarction, initial episode of care — (Use additional code to identify presence of hypertension: 401.0-405.9)
410.72 Acute myocardial infarction, subendocardial infarction, subsequent episode of care — (Use additional code to identify presence of hypertension: 401.0-405.9)
410.80 Acute myocardial infarction of other specified sites, episode of care unspecified — (Use additional code to identify presence of hypertension: 401.0-405.9) ▽
410.81 Acute myocardial infarction of other specified sites, initial episode of care — (Use additional code to identify presence of hypertension: 401.0-405.9)
410.82 Acute myocardial infarction of other specified sites, subsequent episode of care — (Use additional code to identify presence of hypertension: 401.0-405.9)
410.90 Acute myocardial infarction, unspecified site, episode of care unspecified — (Use additional code to identify presence of hypertension: 401.0-405.9) ▽
410.91 Acute myocardial infarction, unspecified site, initial episode of care — (Use additional code to identify presence of hypertension: 401.0-405.9) ▽
410.92 Acute myocardial infarction, unspecified site, subsequent episode of care — (Use additional code to identify presence of hypertension: 401.0-405.9) ▽
414.8 Other specified forms of chronic ischemic heart disease — (Use additional code to identify presence of hypertension: 401.0-405.9)
429.71 Acquired cardiac septal defect — (Use additional code to identify the associated myocardial infarction: with onset of 8 weeks of less, 410.00-410.92; with onset of more than 8 weeks, 414.8)
745.4 Ventricular septal defect
745.7 Cor biloculare
745.8 Other bulbus cordis anomalies and anomalies of cardiac septal closure
745.9 Unspecified congenital defect of septal closure ▽
746.00 Unspecified congenital pulmonary valve anomaly ▽
746.01 Congenital atresia of pulmonary valve
746.02 Congenital stenosis of pulmonary valve
746.09 Other congenital anomalies of pulmonary valve
746.9 Unspecified congenital anomaly of heart ▽

ICD-9-CM Procedural
35.53 Repair of ventricular septal defect with prosthesis, open technique
35.55 Repair of ventricular septal defect with prosthesis, closed technique
35.62 Repair of ventricular septal defect with tissue graft
35.72 Other and unspecified repair of ventricular septal defect
39.61 Extracorporeal circulation auxiliary to open heart surgery

33690
33690 Banding of pulmonary artery

ICD-9-CM Diagnostic
745.10 Complete transposition of great vessels
745.11 Transposition of great vessels, double outlet right ventricle
745.69 Other congenital endocardial cushion defect
746.1 Congenital tricuspid atresia and stenosis

ICD-9-CM Procedural
38.85 Other surgical occlusion of other thoracic vessel

33692-33694
33692 Complete repair tetralogy of Fallot without pulmonary atresia;
33694 with transannular patch

ICD-9-CM Diagnostic
745.2 Tetralogy of Fallot
747.39 Other anomalies of pulmonary artery and pulmonary circulation

ICD-9-CM Procedural
35.81 Total repair of tetralogy of Fallot
39.61 Extracorporeal circulation auxiliary to open heart surgery

33697
33697 Complete repair tetralogy of Fallot with pulmonary atresia including construction of conduit from right ventricle to pulmonary artery and closure of ventricular septal defect

ICD-9-CM Diagnostic
745.2 Tetralogy of Fallot
747.39 Other anomalies of pulmonary artery and pulmonary circulation

ICD-9-CM Procedural
35.81 Total repair of tetralogy of Fallot
39.61 Extracorporeal circulation auxiliary to open heart surgery

33702-33710
33702 Repair sinus of Valsalva fistula, with cardiopulmonary bypass;
33710 with repair of ventricular septal defect

ICD-9-CM Diagnostic
745.4 Ventricular septal defect
745.69 Other congenital endocardial cushion defect
747.29 Other congenital anomaly of aorta

ICD-9-CM Procedural
35.39 Operations on other structures adjacent to valves of heart
35.53 Repair of ventricular septal defect with prosthesis, open technique
35.62 Repair of ventricular septal defect with tissue graft
35.72 Other and unspecified repair of ventricular septal defect
39.61 Extracorporeal circulation auxiliary to open heart surgery

33720

33720 Repair sinus of Valsalva aneurysm, with cardiopulmonary bypass

ICD-9-CM Diagnostic

747.29 Other congenital anomaly of aorta

ICD-9-CM Procedural

35.39 Operations on other structures adjacent to valves of heart
39.61 Extracorporeal circulation auxiliary to open heart surgery

33722

33722 Closure of aortico-left ventricular tunnel

ICD-9-CM Diagnostic

745.8 Other bulbus cordis anomalies and anomalies of cardiac septal closure

ICD-9-CM Procedural

35.39 Operations on other structures adjacent to valves of heart
39.49 Other revision of vascular procedure
39.61 Extracorporeal circulation auxiliary to open heart surgery

33724

33724 Repair of isolated partial anomalous pulmonary venous return (eg, Scimitar Syndrome)

ICD-9-CM Diagnostic

747.40 Congenital anomaly of great veins unspecified ▽
747.41 Total congenital anomalous pulmonary venous connection
747.42 Partial congenital anomalous pulmonary venous connection
747.49 Other congenital anomalies of great veins

ICD-9-CM Procedural

35.82 Total repair of total anomalous pulmonary venous connection
38.35 Resection of other thoracic vessels with anastomosis
39.59 Other repair of vessel
39.61 Extracorporeal circulation auxiliary to open heart surgery

33726

33726 Repair of pulmonary venous stenosis

ICD-9-CM Diagnostic

417.8 Other specified disease of pulmonary circulation
747.40 Congenital anomaly of great veins unspecified ▽
747.41 Total congenital anomalous pulmonary venous connection
747.42 Partial congenital anomalous pulmonary venous connection
747.49 Other congenital anomalies of great veins

ICD-9-CM Procedural

39.56 Repair of blood vessel with tissue patch graft
39.57 Repair of blood vessel with synthetic patch graft
39.58 Repair of blood vessel with unspecified type of patch graft
39.59 Other repair of vessel
39.61 Extracorporeal circulation auxiliary to open heart surgery

33730

33730 Complete repair of anomalous pulmonary venous return (supracardiac, intracardiac, or infracardiac types)

ICD-9-CM Diagnostic

747.40 Congenital anomaly of great veins unspecified ▽
747.41 Total congenital anomalous pulmonary venous connection
747.42 Partial congenital anomalous pulmonary venous connection
747.49 Other congenital anomalies of great veins

ICD-9-CM Procedural

35.82 Total repair of total anomalous pulmonary venous connection
39.61 Extracorporeal circulation auxiliary to open heart surgery

33732

33732 Repair of cor triatriatum or supravalvular mitral ring by resection of left atrial membrane

ICD-9-CM Diagnostic

746.5 Congenital mitral stenosis
746.82 Cor triatriatum

ICD-9-CM Procedural

35.12 Open heart valvuloplasty of mitral valve without replacement
37.33 Excision or destruction of other lesion or tissue of heart, open approach
39.61 Extracorporeal circulation auxiliary to open heart surgery

33735-33737

33735 Atrial septectomy or septostomy; closed heart (Blalock-Hanlon type operation)
33736 open heart with cardiopulmonary bypass
33737 open heart, with inflow occlusion

ICD-9-CM Diagnostic

745.10 Complete transposition of great vessels
746.1 Congenital tricuspid atresia and stenosis
746.89 Other specified congenital anomaly of heart
747.41 Total congenital anomalous pulmonary venous connection

ICD-9-CM Procedural

35.42 Creation of septal defect in heart
39.61 Extracorporeal circulation auxiliary to open heart surgery

33750

33750 Shunt; subclavian to pulmonary artery (Blalock-Taussig type operation)

ICD-9-CM Diagnostic

424.3 Pulmonary valve disorders
745.2 Tetralogy of Fallot
746.01 Congenital atresia of pulmonary valve
746.02 Congenital stenosis of pulmonary valve
746.09 Other congenital anomalies of pulmonary valve
746.1 Congenital tricuspid atresia and stenosis
746.2 Ebstein's anomaly
746.9 Unspecified congenital anomaly of heart ▽

ICD-9-CM Procedural

39.0 Systemic to pulmonary artery shunt
39.61 Extracorporeal circulation auxiliary to open heart surgery

33755

33755 Shunt; ascending aorta to pulmonary artery (Waterston type operation)

ICD-9-CM Diagnostic

424.3 Pulmonary valve disorders
745.2 Tetralogy of Fallot
746.01 Congenital atresia of pulmonary valve
746.02 Congenital stenosis of pulmonary valve
746.09 Other congenital anomalies of pulmonary valve
746.1 Congenital tricuspid atresia and stenosis
746.2 Ebstein's anomaly
746.9 Unspecified congenital anomaly of heart ▽

ICD-9-CM Procedural

39.0 Systemic to pulmonary artery shunt
39.61 Extracorporeal circulation auxiliary to open heart surgery

33762

33762 Shunt; descending aorta to pulmonary artery (Potts-Smith type operation)

ICD-9-CM Diagnostic

424.3 Pulmonary valve disorders
745.2 Tetralogy of Fallot
746.01 Congenital atresia of pulmonary valve
746.02 Congenital stenosis of pulmonary valve
746.09 Other congenital anomalies of pulmonary valve
746.1 Congenital tricuspid atresia and stenosis
746.2 Ebstein's anomaly
746.9 Unspecified congenital anomaly of heart ▽

ICD-9-CM Procedural

39.0 Systemic to pulmonary artery shunt
39.61 Extracorporeal circulation auxiliary to open heart surgery

33764

33764 Shunt; central, with prosthetic graft

ICD-9-CM Diagnostic

745.2 Tetralogy of Fallot
745.69 Other congenital endocardial cushion defect
746.1 Congenital tricuspid atresia and stenosis
746.9 Unspecified congenital anomaly of heart ▽
747.39 Other anomalies of pulmonary artery and pulmonary circulation

ICD-9-CM Procedural

39.0 Systemic to pulmonary artery shunt
39.23 Other intrathoracic vascular shunt or bypass
39.61 Extracorporeal circulation auxiliary to open heart surgery

33766-33767

33766 Shunt; superior vena cava to pulmonary artery for flow to 1 lung (classical Glenn procedure)
33767 superior vena cava to pulmonary artery for flow to both lungs (bidirectional Glenn procedure)

ICD-9-CM Diagnostic

745.2 Tetralogy of Fallot
746.02 Congenital stenosis of pulmonary valve
746.1 Congenital tricuspid atresia and stenosis
746.2 Ebstein's anomaly
746.83 Congenital infundibular pulmonic stenosis
746.9 Unspecified congenital anomaly of heart ▽
782.5 Cyanosis

ICD-9-CM Procedural

39.21 Caval-pulmonary artery anastomosis
39.61 Extracorporeal circulation auxiliary to open heart surgery

33768

33768 Anastomosis, cavopulmonary, second superior vena cava (List separately in addition to primary procedure)

ICD-9-CM Diagnostic

This is an add-on code. Refer to the corresponding primary procedure code for ICD-9-CM diagnosis code links.

ICD-9-CM Procedural

39.21 Caval-pulmonary artery anastomosis
39.61 Extracorporeal circulation auxiliary to open heart surgery

HCPCS Level II Supplies & Services

A4641 Radiopharmaceutical, diagnostic, not otherwise classified

33770-33771

33770 Repair of transposition of the great arteries with ventricular septal defect and subpulmonary stenosis; without surgical enlargement of ventricular septal defect
33771 with surgical enlargement of ventricular septal defect

ICD-9-CM Diagnostic

745.10 Complete transposition of great vessels
745.11 Transposition of great vessels, double outlet right ventricle
745.19 Other transposition of great vessels

ICD-9-CM Procedural

35.41 Enlargement of existing atrial septal defect
35.84 Total correction of transposition of great vessels, not elsewhere classified
39.61 Extracorporeal circulation auxiliary to open heart surgery

33774-33775

33774 Repair of transposition of the great arteries, atrial baffle procedure (eg, Mustard or Senning type) with cardiopulmonary bypass;
33775 with removal of pulmonary band

ICD-9-CM Diagnostic

745.10 Complete transposition of great vessels
745.11 Transposition of great vessels, double outlet right ventricle
745.19 Other transposition of great vessels

ICD-9-CM Procedural

35.91 Interatrial transposition of venous return
39.61 Extracorporeal circulation auxiliary to open heart surgery

33776

33776 Repair of transposition of the great arteries, atrial baffle procedure (eg, Mustard or Senning type) with cardiopulmonary bypass; with closure of ventricular septal defect

ICD-9-CM Diagnostic

745.10 Complete transposition of great vessels
745.11 Transposition of great vessels, double outlet right ventricle
745.19 Other transposition of great vessels

ICD-9-CM Procedural

35.53 Repair of ventricular septal defect with prosthesis, open technique
35.62 Repair of ventricular septal defect with tissue graft
35.72 Other and unspecified repair of ventricular septal defect
35.91 Interatrial transposition of venous return
39.61 Extracorporeal circulation auxiliary to open heart surgery

33777

33777 Repair of transposition of the great arteries, atrial baffle procedure (eg, Mustard or Senning type) with cardiopulmonary bypass; with repair of subpulmonic obstruction

ICD-9-CM Diagnostic

745.10 Complete transposition of great vessels
745.11 Transposition of great vessels, double outlet right ventricle
745.19 Other transposition of great vessels

ICD-9-CM Procedural

35.91 Interatrial transposition of venous return
39.61 Extracorporeal circulation auxiliary to open heart surgery

33778-33779

33778 Repair of transposition of the great arteries, aortic pulmonary artery reconstruction (eg, Jatene type);
33779 with removal of pulmonary band

ICD-9-CM Diagnostic

745.10 Complete transposition of great vessels
745.11 Transposition of great vessels, double outlet right ventricle
745.19 Other transposition of great vessels

ICD-9-CM Procedural

35.84 Total correction of transposition of great vessels, not elsewhere classified
39.61 Extracorporeal circulation auxiliary to open heart surgery

33780

33780 Repair of transposition of the great arteries, aortic pulmonary artery reconstruction (eg, Jatene type); with closure of ventricular septal defect

ICD-9-CM Diagnostic

745.10 Complete transposition of great vessels
745.11 Transposition of great vessels, double outlet right ventricle
745.19 Other transposition of great vessels

ICD-9-CM Procedural

35.53 Repair of ventricular septal defect with prosthesis, open technique
35.62 Repair of ventricular septal defect with tissue graft
35.72 Other and unspecified repair of ventricular septal defect
35.84 Total correction of transposition of great vessels, not elsewhere classified
39.61 Extracorporeal circulation auxiliary to open heart surgery

33781

33781 Repair of transposition of the great arteries, aortic pulmonary artery reconstruction (eg, Jatene type); with repair of subpulmonic obstruction

ICD-9-CM Diagnostic

745.10 Complete transposition of great vessels
745.11 Transposition of great vessels, double outlet right ventricle
745.19 Other transposition of great vessels

ICD-9-CM Procedural

35.84 Total correction of transposition of great vessels, not elsewhere classified
39.61 Extracorporeal circulation auxiliary to open heart surgery

33782-33783

33782 Aortic root translocation with ventricular septal defect and pulmonary stenosis repair (ie, Nikaidoh procedure); without coronary ostium reimplantation
33783 with reimplantation of 1 or both coronary ostia

ICD-9-CM Diagnostic

745.0 Bulbus cordis anomalies and anomalies of cardiac septal closure, common truncus
745.19 Other transposition of great vessels
747.31 Pulmonary artery coarctation and atresia
747.39 Other anomalies of pulmonary artery and pulmonary circulation

ICD-9-CM Procedural

35.62 Repair of ventricular septal defect with tissue graft
35.84 Total correction of transposition of great vessels, not elsewhere classified
39.61 Extracorporeal circulation auxiliary to open heart surgery

33786

33786 Total repair, truncus arteriosus (Rastelli type operation)

ICD-9-CM Diagnostic

745.0 Bulbus cordis anomalies and anomalies of cardiac septal closure, common truncus
747.39 Other anomalies of pulmonary artery and pulmonary circulation

ICD-9-CM Procedural

35.83 Total repair of truncus arteriosus
39.61 Extracorporeal circulation auxiliary to open heart surgery

33788

33788 Reimplantation of an anomalous pulmonary artery

ICD-9-CM Diagnostic

747.32 Pulmonary arteriovenous malformation
747.39 Other anomalies of pulmonary artery and pulmonary circulation

ICD-9-CM Procedural

35.83 Total repair of truncus arteriosus
35.84 Total correction of transposition of great vessels, not elsewhere classified
35.92 Creation of conduit between right ventricle and pulmonary artery
39.59 Other repair of vessel
39.61 Extracorporeal circulation auxiliary to open heart surgery

33800

33800 Aortic suspension (aortopexy) for tracheal decompression (eg, for tracheomalacia) (separate procedure)

ICD-9-CM Diagnostic

519.19 Other diseases of trachea and bronchus — (Use additional code to identify infectious organism)
747.29 Other congenital anomaly of aorta
748.3 Other congenital anomaly of larynx, trachea, and bronchus

ICD-9-CM Procedural

39.59 Other repair of vessel
39.99 Other operations on vessels

33802-33803

33802 Division of aberrant vessel (vascular ring);
33803 with reanastomosis

ICD-9-CM Diagnostic

747.21 Congenital anomaly of aortic arch
747.31 Pulmonary artery coarctation and atresia
747.32 Pulmonary arteriovenous malformation
747.39 Other anomalies of pulmonary artery and pulmonary circulation

ICD-9-CM Procedural

38.35 Resection of other thoracic vessels with anastomosis
38.85 Other surgical occlusion of other thoracic vessel
39.61 Extracorporeal circulation auxiliary to open heart surgery

33813-33814

33813 Obliteration of aortopulmonary septal defect; without cardiopulmonary bypass
33814 with cardiopulmonary bypass

ICD-9-CM Diagnostic

745.0 Bulbus cordis anomalies and anomalies of cardiac septal closure, common truncus

ICD-9-CM Procedural

35.98 Other operations on septa of heart
39.59 Other repair of vessel
39.61 Extracorporeal circulation auxiliary to open heart surgery

33820-33824

33820 Repair of patent ductus arteriosus; by ligation
33822 by division, younger than 18 years
33824 by division, 18 years and older

ICD-9-CM Diagnostic

747.0 Patent ductus arteriosus

ICD-9-CM Procedural

38.85 Other surgical occlusion of other thoracic vessel
39.61 Extracorporeal circulation auxiliary to open heart surgery

33840-33851

33840 Excision of coarctation of aorta, with or without associated patent ductus arteriosus; with direct anastomosis
33845 with graft
33851 repair using either left subclavian artery or prosthetic material as gusset for enlargement

ICD-9-CM Diagnostic

747.0 Patent ductus arteriosus
747.10 Coarctation of aorta (preductal) (postductal)

ICD-9-CM Procedural

38.34 Resection of aorta with anastomosis
38.35 Resection of other thoracic vessels with anastomosis
38.45 Resection of other thoracic vessels with replacement
39.61 Extracorporeal circulation auxiliary to open heart surgery

33852-33853

33852 Repair of hypoplastic or interrupted aortic arch using autogenous or prosthetic material; without cardiopulmonary bypass
33853 with cardiopulmonary bypass

ICD-9-CM Diagnostic

747.10 Coarctation of aorta (preductal) (postductal)
747.11 Congenital interruption of aortic arch
747.22 Congenital atresia and stenosis of aorta

ICD-9-CM Procedural

38.45 Resection of other thoracic vessels with replacement
39.56 Repair of blood vessel with tissue patch graft
39.57 Repair of blood vessel with synthetic patch graft
39.61 Extracorporeal circulation auxiliary to open heart surgery

33860-33863

33860 Ascending aorta graft, with cardiopulmonary bypass, includes valve suspension, when performed
33863 Ascending aorta graft, with cardiopulmonary bypass, with aortic root replacement using valved conduit and coronary reconstruction (eg, Bentall)

ICD-9-CM Diagnostic

395.0 Rheumatic aortic stenosis
395.1 Rheumatic aortic insufficiency
395.2 Rheumatic aortic stenosis with insufficiency
441.00 Dissecting aortic aneurysm (any part), unspecified site ▽
441.01 Dissecting aortic aneurysm (any part), thoracic
441.1 Thoracic aneurysm, ruptured
441.2 Thoracic aneurysm without mention of rupture
441.9 Aortic aneurysm of unspecified site without mention of rupture ▽
861.02 Heart laceration without penetration of heart chambers or mention of open wound into thorax
861.12 Heart laceration without penetration of heart chambers, with open wound into thorax
901.0 Thoracic aorta injury

ICD-9-CM Procedural

35.11 Open heart valvuloplasty of aortic valve without replacement
38.45 Resection of other thoracic vessels with replacement
39.57 Repair of blood vessel with synthetic patch graft
39.58 Repair of blood vessel with unspecified type of patch graft
39.61 Extracorporeal circulation auxiliary to open heart surgery

33864

33864 Ascending aorta graft, with cardiopulmonary bypass with valve suspension, with coronary reconstruction and valve-sparing aortic root remodeling (eg, David Procedure, Yacoub Procedure)

ICD-9-CM Diagnostic

395.0 Rheumatic aortic stenosis
395.1 Rheumatic aortic insufficiency
395.2 Rheumatic aortic stenosis with insufficiency
441.00 Dissecting aortic aneurysm (any part), unspecified site ▽
441.01 Dissecting aortic aneurysm (any part), thoracic
441.1 Thoracic aneurysm, ruptured
441.2 Thoracic aneurysm without mention of rupture
441.9 Aortic aneurysm of unspecified site without mention of rupture ▽
861.02 Heart laceration without penetration of heart chambers or mention of open wound into thorax
861.12 Heart laceration without penetration of heart chambers, with open wound into thorax
901.0 Thoracic aorta injury

ICD-9-CM Procedural

35.11 Open heart valvuloplasty of aortic valve without replacement
38.45 Resection of other thoracic vessels with replacement
39.61 Extracorporeal circulation auxiliary to open heart surgery

33870

33870 Transverse arch graft, with cardiopulmonary bypass

ICD-9-CM Diagnostic

395.0 Rheumatic aortic stenosis
395.1 Rheumatic aortic insufficiency
395.2 Rheumatic aortic stenosis with insufficiency
441.00 Dissecting aortic aneurysm (any part), unspecified site ▽
441.01 Dissecting aortic aneurysm (any part), thoracic
441.1 Thoracic aneurysm, ruptured
441.2 Thoracic aneurysm without mention of rupture
441.9 Aortic aneurysm of unspecified site without mention of rupture ▽
861.02 Heart laceration without penetration of heart chambers or mention of open wound into thorax
861.12 Heart laceration without penetration of heart chambers, with open wound into thorax
901.0 Thoracic aorta injury

ICD-9-CM Procedural

38.45 Resection of other thoracic vessels with replacement
39.61 Extracorporeal circulation auxiliary to open heart surgery

33875-33877

33875 Descending thoracic aorta graft, with or without bypass
33877 Repair of thoracoabdominal aortic aneurysm with graft, with or without cardiopulmonary bypass

ICD-9-CM Diagnostic

395.0 Rheumatic aortic stenosis
395.1 Rheumatic aortic insufficiency
395.2 Rheumatic aortic stenosis with insufficiency
441.00 Dissecting aortic aneurysm (any part), unspecified site ▽

441.01 Dissecting aortic aneurysm (any part), thoracic
441.03 Dissecting aortic aneurysm (any part), thoracoabdominal
441.1 Thoracic aneurysm, ruptured
441.2 Thoracic aneurysm without mention of rupture
441.4 Abdominal aneurysm without mention of rupture
441.5 Aortic aneurysm of unspecified site, ruptured ▽
441.6 Thoracoabdominal aneurysm, ruptured
441.7 Thoracoabdominal aneurysm without mention of rupture
441.9 Aortic aneurysm of unspecified site without mention of rupture ▽
861.02 Heart laceration without penetration of heart chambers or mention of open wound into thorax
861.12 Heart laceration without penetration of heart chambers, with open wound into thorax
901.0 Thoracic aorta injury

ICD-9-CM Procedural

38.44 Resection of abdominal aorta with replacement
38.45 Resection of other thoracic vessels with replacement
39.61 Extracorporeal circulation auxiliary to open heart surgery
39.73 Endovascular implantation of graft in thoracic aorta

33880-33881

33880 Endovascular repair of descending thoracic aorta (eg, aneurysm, pseudoaneurysm, dissection, penetrating ulcer, intramural hematoma, or traumatic disruption); involving coverage of left subclavian artery origin, initial endoprosthesis plus descending thoracic aortic extension(s), if required, to level of celiac artery origin
33881 not involving coverage of left subclavian artery origin, initial endoprosthesis plus descending thoracic aortic extension(s), if required, to level of celiac artery origin

ICD-9-CM Diagnostic

441.01 Dissecting aortic aneurysm (any part), thoracic
441.1 Thoracic aneurysm, ruptured
441.2 Thoracic aneurysm without mention of rupture
444.1 Embolism and thrombosis of thoracic aorta
901.0 Thoracic aorta injury
901.1 Innominate and subclavian artery injury

ICD-9-CM Procedural

39.73 Endovascular implantation of graft in thoracic aorta
39.79 Other endovascular procedures on other vessels

33883-33886

33883 Placement of proximal extension prosthesis for endovascular repair of descending thoracic aorta (eg, aneurysm, pseudoaneurysm, dissection, penetrating ulcer, intramural hematoma, or traumatic disruption); initial extension
33884 each additional proximal extension (List separately in addition to code for primary procedure)
33886 Placement of distal extension prosthesis(s) delayed after endovascular repair of descending thoracic aorta

ICD-9-CM Diagnostic

441.01 Dissecting aortic aneurysm (any part), thoracic
441.1 Thoracic aneurysm, ruptured
441.2 Thoracic aneurysm without mention of rupture
444.1 Embolism and thrombosis of thoracic aorta
901.0 Thoracic aorta injury
901.1 Innominate and subclavian artery injury

ICD-9-CM Procedural

39.73 Endovascular implantation of graft in thoracic aorta
39.78 Endovascular implantation of branching or fenestrated graft(s) in aorta
39.79 Other endovascular procedures on other vessels

33889

33889 Open subclavian to carotid artery transposition performed in conjunction with endovascular repair of descending thoracic aorta, by neck incision, unilateral

ICD-9-CM Diagnostic

440.0 Atherosclerosis of aorta
440.8 Atherosclerosis of other specified arteries
441.01 Dissecting aortic aneurysm (any part), thoracic
441.2 Thoracic aneurysm without mention of rupture
443.21 Dissection of carotid artery
745.2 Tetralogy of Fallot
747.20 Unspecified congenital anomaly of aorta ▽
747.22 Congenital atresia and stenosis of aorta
747.29 Other congenital anomaly of aorta
747.81 Congenital anomaly of cerebrovascular system
900.00 Injury to carotid artery, unspecified ▽
901.1 Innominate and subclavian artery injury

ICD-9-CM Procedural

39.22 Aorta-subclavian-carotid bypass
39.59 Other repair of vessel
39.73 Endovascular implantation of graft in thoracic aorta

33891

33891 Bypass graft, with other than vein, transcervical retropharyngeal carotid-carotid, performed in conjunction with endovascular repair of descending thoracic aorta, by neck incision

ICD-9-CM Diagnostic

433.10 Occlusion and stenosis of carotid artery without mention of cerebral infarction — (Use additional code, if applicable, to identify status post administration of tPA (rtPA) in a different facility within the last 24 hours prior to admission to current facility: V45.88)
433.11 Occlusion and stenosis of carotid artery with cerebral infarction — (Use additional code, if applicable, to identify status post administration of tPA (rtPA) in a different facility within the last 24 hours prior to admission to current facility: V45.88)
433.30 Occlusion and stenosis of multiple and bilateral precerebral arteries without mention of cerebral infarction — (Use additional code, if applicable, to identify status post administration of tPA (rtPA) in a different facility within the last 24 hours prior to admission to current facility: V45.88)
433.31 Occlusion and stenosis of multiple and bilateral precerebral arteries with cerebral infarction — (Use additional code, if applicable, to identify status post administration of tPA (rtPA) in a different facility within the last 24 hours prior to admission to current facility: V45.88)
433.80 Occlusion and stenosis of other specified precerebral artery without mention of cerebral infarction — (Use additional code, if applicable, to identify status post administration of tPA (rtPA) in a different facility within the last 24 hours prior to admission to current facility: V45.88)
433.81 Occlusion and stenosis of other specified precerebral artery with cerebral infarction — (Use additional code, if applicable, to identify status post administration of tPA (rtPA) in a different facility within the last 24 hours prior to admission to current facility: V45.88)
440.0 Atherosclerosis of aorta
440.8 Atherosclerosis of other specified arteries
441.01 Dissecting aortic aneurysm (any part), thoracic
442.81 Aneurysm of artery of neck
443.21 Dissection of carotid artery
447.1 Stricture of artery
447.70 Aortic ectasia, unspecified site ▽
447.71 Thoracic aortic ectasia
745.2 Tetralogy of Fallot
747.20 Unspecified congenital anomaly of aorta ▽

747.22 Congenital atresia and stenosis of aorta
747.29 Other congenital anomaly of aorta
747.81 Congenital anomaly of cerebrovascular system
900.01 Common carotid artery injury
900.03 Internal carotid artery injury

ICD-9-CM Procedural

39.22 Aorta-subclavian-carotid bypass
39.29 Other (peripheral) vascular shunt or bypass
39.73 Endovascular implantation of graft in thoracic aorta

33910-33915

33910 Pulmonary artery embolectomy; with cardiopulmonary bypass
33915 without cardiopulmonary bypass

ICD-9-CM Diagnostic

415.11 Iatrogenic pulmonary embolism and infarction — (Use additional code for associated septic pulmonary embolism, if applicable: 415.12)
415.12 Septic pulmonary embolism
415.13 Saddle embolus of pulmonary artery
415.19 Other pulmonary embolism and infarction
416.2 Chronic pulmonary embolism — (Use additional code, if applicable, for associated long-term (current) use of anticoagulants (V58.61))
901.41 Pulmonary artery injury

ICD-9-CM Procedural

38.05 Incision of other thoracic vessels
39.61 Extracorporeal circulation auxiliary to open heart surgery

33916-33917

33916 Pulmonary endarterectomy, with or without embolectomy, with cardiopulmonary bypass
33917 Repair of pulmonary artery stenosis by reconstruction with patch or graft

ICD-9-CM Diagnostic

415.11 Iatrogenic pulmonary embolism and infarction — (Use additional code for associated septic pulmonary embolism, if applicable: 415.12)
415.12 Septic pulmonary embolism
415.13 Saddle embolus of pulmonary artery
415.19 Other pulmonary embolism and infarction
416.2 Chronic pulmonary embolism — (Use additional code, if applicable, for associated long-term (current) use of anticoagulants (V58.61))
746.83 Congenital infundibular pulmonic stenosis
747.31 Pulmonary artery coarctation and atresia
747.32 Pulmonary arteriovenous malformation
747.39 Other anomalies of pulmonary artery and pulmonary circulation
901.41 Pulmonary artery injury

ICD-9-CM Procedural

00.40 Procedure on single vessel
00.45 Insertion of one vascular stent
00.46 Insertion of two vascular stents
00.47 Insertion of three vascular stents
00.48 Insertion of four or more vascular stents
35.73 Other and unspecified repair of endocardial cushion defect
38.15 Endarterectomy of other thoracic vessels
39.56 Repair of blood vessel with tissue patch graft
39.57 Repair of blood vessel with synthetic patch graft
39.58 Repair of blood vessel with unspecified type of patch graft
39.61 Extracorporeal circulation auxiliary to open heart surgery

33920

33920 Repair of pulmonary atresia with ventricular septal defect, by construction or replacement of conduit from right or left ventricle to pulmonary artery

ICD-9-CM Diagnostic

745.4 Ventricular septal defect
746.01 Congenital atresia of pulmonary valve
746.83 Congenital infundibular pulmonic stenosis
747.31 Pulmonary artery coarctation and atresia

ICD-9-CM Procedural

35.13 Open heart valvuloplasty of pulmonary valve without replacement
35.92 Creation of conduit between right ventricle and pulmonary artery
39.61 Extracorporeal circulation auxiliary to open heart surgery

33922

33922 Transection of pulmonary artery with cardiopulmonary bypass

ICD-9-CM Diagnostic

417.8 Other specified disease of pulmonary circulation
747.31 Pulmonary artery coarctation and atresia
747.32 Pulmonary arteriovenous malformation
747.39 Other anomalies of pulmonary artery and pulmonary circulation
901.41 Pulmonary artery injury

ICD-9-CM Procedural

38.35 Resection of other thoracic vessels with anastomosis
39.56 Repair of blood vessel with tissue patch graft
39.61 Extracorporeal circulation auxiliary to open heart surgery

33925-33926

33925 Repair of pulmonary artery arborization anomalies by unifocalization; without cardiopulmonary bypass
33926 with cardiopulmonary bypass

ICD-9-CM Diagnostic

426.6 Other heart block
447.1 Stricture of artery
447.70 Aortic ectasia, unspecified site ♥
447.71 Thoracic aortic ectasia
747.31 Pulmonary artery coarctation and atresia
747.32 Pulmonary arteriovenous malformation
747.39 Other anomalies of pulmonary artery and pulmonary circulation

ICD-9-CM Procedural

38.35 Resection of other thoracic vessels with anastomosis
38.84 Other surgical occlusion of abdominal aorta
39.59 Other repair of vessel
39.61 Extracorporeal circulation auxiliary to open heart surgery

33930

33930 Donor cardiectomy-pneumonectomy (including cold preservation)

ICD-9-CM Diagnostic

V59.8 Donor of other specified organ or tissue

ICD-9-CM Procedural

32.59 Other and unspecified pneumonectomy
37.99 Other operations on heart and pericardium

33933

33933 Backbench standard preparation of cadaver donor heart/lung allograft prior to transplantation, including dissection of allograft from surrounding soft tissues to prepare aorta, superior vena cava, inferior vena cava, and trachea for implantation

ICD-9-CM Diagnostic

148.8 Malignant neoplasm of other specified sites of hypopharynx
162.2 Malignant neoplasm of main bronchus
162.3 Malignant neoplasm of upper lobe, bronchus, or lung
162.4 Malignant neoplasm of middle lobe, bronchus, or lung
162.5 Malignant neoplasm of lower lobe, bronchus, or lung
162.8 Malignant neoplasm of other parts of bronchus or lung
163.0 Malignant neoplasm of parietal pleura
163.1 Malignant neoplasm of visceral pleura
163.8 Malignant neoplasm of other specified sites of pleura
164.1 Malignant neoplasm of heart
164.8 Malignant neoplasm of other parts of mediastinum
197.0 Secondary malignant neoplasm of lung
197.1 Secondary malignant neoplasm of mediastinum
198.89 Secondary malignant neoplasm of other specified sites
209.21 Malignant carcinoid tumor of the bronchus and lung — (Code first any associated multiple endocrine neoplasia syndrome: 258.01-258.03)(Use additional code to identify associated endocrine syndrome, as: carcinoid syndrome: 259.2)
231.2 Carcinoma in situ of bronchus and lung
398.0 Rheumatic myocarditis
412 Old myocardial infarction — (Use additional code to identify presence of hypertension: 401.0-405.9)
414.00 Coronary atherosclerosis of unspecified type of vessel, native or graft — (Use additional code to identify presence of hypertension: 401.0-405.9) ▽
414.01 Coronary atherosclerosis of native coronary artery — (Use additional code to identify presence of hypertension: 401.0-405.9)
414.02 Coronary atherosclerosis of autologous vein bypass graft — (Use additional code to identify presence of hypertension: 401.0-405.9)
414.03 Coronary atherosclerosis of nonautologous biological bypass graft — (Use additional code to identify presence of hypertension: 401.0-405.9)
414.04 Coronary atherosclerosis of artery bypass graft — (Use additional code to identify presence of hypertension: 401.0-405.9)
414.05 Coronary atherosclerosis of unspecified type of bypass graft — (Use additional code to identify presence of hypertension: 401.0-405.9) ▽
414.2 Chronic total occlusion of coronary artery
414.3 Coronary atherosclerosis due to lipid rich plaque — (Code first coronary atherosclerosis (414.00-414.07))
414.4 Coronary atherosclerosis due to calcified coronary lesion — (Code first coronary atherosclerosis (414.00-414.07))
414.8 Other specified forms of chronic ischemic heart disease — (Use additional code to identify presence of hypertension: 401.0-405.9)
416.8 Other chronic pulmonary heart diseases
422.91 Idiopathic myocarditis
422.92 Septic myocarditis — (Use additional code to identify infectious organism)
422.93 Toxic myocarditis
425.0 Endomyocardial fibrosis
425.3 Endocardial fibroelastosis
425.4 Other primary cardiomyopathies
428.0 Congestive heart failure, unspecified — (Code, if applicable, heart failure due to hypertension first: 402.0-402.9, with fifth-digit 1 or 404.0-404.9 with fifth digit 1 or 3) ▽
428.1 Left heart failure — (Code, if applicable, heart failure due to hypertension first: 402.0-402.9, with fifth-digit 1 or 404.0-404.9 with fifth digit 1 or 3)
428.22 Chronic systolic heart failure — (Code, if applicable, heart failure due to hypertension first: 402.0-402.9, with fifth-digit 1 or 404.0-404.9 with fifth digit 1 or 3)
428.23 Acute on chronic systolic heart failure — (Code, if applicable, heart failure due to hypertension first: 402.0-402.9, with fifth-digit 1 or 404.0-404.9 with fifth digit 1 or 3)
428.32 Chronic diastolic heart failure — (Code, if applicable, heart failure due to hypertension first: 402.0-402.9, with fifth-digit 1 or 404.0-404.9 with fifth digit 1 or 3)
428.33 Acute on chronic diastolic heart failure — (Code, if applicable, heart failure due to hypertension first: 402.0-402.9, with fifth-digit 1 or 404.0-404.9 with fifth digit 1 or 3)
428.42 Chronic combined systolic and diastolic heart failure — (Code, if applicable, heart failure due to hypertension first: 402.0-402.9, with fifth-digit 1 or 404.0-404.9 with fifth digit 1 or 3)
428.43 Acute on chronic combined systolic and diastolic heart failure — (Code, if applicable, heart failure due to hypertension first: 402.0-402.9, with fifth-digit 1 or 404.0-404.9 with fifth digit 1 or 3)
429.0 Unspecified myocarditis — (Use additional code to identify presence of arteriosclerosis) ▽
429.1 Myocardial degeneration — (Use additional code to identify presence of arteriosclerosis)
429.2 Unspecified cardiovascular disease — (Use additional code to identify presence of arteriosclerosis) ▽
496 Chronic airway obstruction, not elsewhere classified — (Note: This code is not to be used with any code from 491-493) ▽
508.1 Chronic and other pulmonary manifestations due to radiation — (Use additional code to identify infectious organism. Use additional E code to identify cause. Use additional code to identify associated respiratory conditions: 518.81.)
514 Pulmonary congestion and hypostasis — (Use additional code to identify infectious organism)
515 Postinflammatory pulmonary fibrosis — (Use additional code to identify infectious organism)
516.30 Idiopathic interstitial pneumonia, not otherwise specified
516.31 Idiopathic pulmonary fibrosis
516.32 Idiopathic non-specific interstitial pneumonitis
516.33 Acute interstitial pneumonitis
516.34 Respiratory bronchiolitis interstitial lung disease
516.35 Idiopathic lymphoid interstitial pneumonia
516.36 Cryptogenic organizing pneumonia
516.37 Desquamative interstitial pneumonia
518.83 Chronic respiratory failure
518.89 Other diseases of lung, not elsewhere classified — (Use additional code to identify infectious organism)
746.9 Unspecified congenital anomaly of heart ▽
748.4 Congenital cystic lung
V15.82 Personal history of tobacco use, presenting hazards to health

ICD-9-CM Procedural

The ICD-9-CM procedural code(s) would be the same as the actual procedure performed because these are in-addition-to codes.

33935

33935 Heart-lung transplant with recipient cardiectomy-pneumonectomy

ICD-9-CM Diagnostic

148.8 Malignant neoplasm of other specified sites of hypopharynx
162.2 Malignant neoplasm of main bronchus
162.3 Malignant neoplasm of upper lobe, bronchus, or lung
162.4 Malignant neoplasm of middle lobe, bronchus, or lung
162.5 Malignant neoplasm of lower lobe, bronchus, or lung
162.8 Malignant neoplasm of other parts of bronchus or lung
163.0 Malignant neoplasm of parietal pleura
163.1 Malignant neoplasm of visceral pleura
163.8 Malignant neoplasm of other specified sites of pleura
164.1 Malignant neoplasm of heart

164.8	Malignant neoplasm of other parts of mediastinum
197.0	Secondary malignant neoplasm of lung
197.1	Secondary malignant neoplasm of mediastinum
198.89	Secondary malignant neoplasm of other specified sites
209.21	Malignant carcinoid tumor of the bronchus and lung — (Code first any associated multiple endocrine neoplasia syndrome: 258.01-258.03)(Use additional code to identify associated endocrine syndrome, as: carcinoid syndrome: 259.2)
231.2	Carcinoma in situ of bronchus and lung
398.0	Rheumatic myocarditis
412	Old myocardial infarction — (Use additional code to identify presence of hypertension: 401.0-405.9)
414.00	Coronary atherosclerosis of unspecified type of vessel, native or graft — (Use additional code to identify presence of hypertension: 401.0-405.9) ▽
414.01	Coronary atherosclerosis of native coronary artery — (Use additional code to identify presence of hypertension: 401.0-405.9)
414.02	Coronary atherosclerosis of autologous vein bypass graft — (Use additional code to identify presence of hypertension: 401.0-405.9)
414.03	Coronary atherosclerosis of nonautologous biological bypass graft — (Use additional code to identify presence of hypertension: 401.0-405.9)
414.04	Coronary atherosclerosis of artery bypass graft — (Use additional code to identify presence of hypertension: 401.0-405.9)
414.05	Coronary atherosclerosis of unspecified type of bypass graft — (Use additional code to identify presence of hypertension: 401.0-405.9) ▽
414.2	Chronic total occlusion of coronary artery
414.3	Coronary atherosclerosis due to lipid rich plaque — (Code first coronary atherosclerosis (414.00-414.07))
414.4	Coronary atherosclerosis due to calcified coronary lesion — (Code first coronary atherosclerosis (414.00-414.07))
414.8	Other specified forms of chronic ischemic heart disease — (Use additional code to identify presence of hypertension: 401.0-405.9)
416.8	Other chronic pulmonary heart diseases
422.91	Idiopathic myocarditis
422.92	Septic myocarditis — (Use additional code to identify infectious organism)
422.93	Toxic myocarditis
425.0	Endomyocardial fibrosis
425.3	Endocardial fibroelastosis
425.4	Other primary cardiomyopathies
428.0	Congestive heart failure, unspecified — (Code, if applicable, heart failure due to hypertension first: 402.0-402.9, with fifth-digit 1 or 404.0-404.9 with fifth digit 1 or 3) ▽
428.1	Left heart failure — (Code, if applicable, heart failure due to hypertension first: 402.0-402.9, with fifth-digit 1 or 404.0-404.9 with fifth digit 1 or 3)
428.22	Chronic systolic heart failure — (Code, if applicable, heart failure due to hypertension first: 402.0-402.9, with fifth-digit 1 or 404.0-404.9 with fifth digit 1 or 3)
428.23	Acute on chronic systolic heart failure — (Code, if applicable, heart failure due to hypertension first: 402.0-402.9, with fifth-digit 1 or 404.0-404.9 with fifth digit 1 or 3)
428.32	Chronic diastolic heart failure — (Code, if applicable, heart failure due to hypertension first: 402.0-402.9, with fifth-digit 1 or 404.0-404.9 with fifth digit 1 or 3)
428.33	Acute on chronic diastolic heart failure — (Code, if applicable, heart failure due to hypertension first: 402.0-402.9, with fifth-digit 1 or 404.0-404.9 with fifth digit 1 or 3)
428.42	Chronic combined systolic and diastolic heart failure — (Code, if applicable, heart failure due to hypertension first: 402.0-402.9, with fifth-digit 1 or 404.0-404.9 with fifth digit 1 or 3)
428.43	Acute on chronic combined systolic and diastolic heart failure — (Code, if applicable, heart failure due to hypertension first: 402.0-402.9, with fifth-digit 1 or 404.0-404.9 with fifth digit 1 or 3)
429.0	Unspecified myocarditis — (Use additional code to identify presence of arteriosclerosis) ▽
429.1	Myocardial degeneration — (Use additional code to identify presence of arteriosclerosis)
429.2	Unspecified cardiovascular disease — (Use additional code to identify presence of arteriosclerosis) ▽
496	Chronic airway obstruction, not elsewhere classified — (Note: This code is not to be used with any code from 491-493) ▽
508.1	Chronic and other pulmonary manifestations due to radiation — (Use additional code to identify infectious organism. Use additional E code to identify cause. Use additional code to identify associated respiratory conditions: 518.81.)
514	Pulmonary congestion and hypostasis — (Use additional code to identify infectious organism)
515	Postinflammatory pulmonary fibrosis — (Use additional code to identify infectious organism)
516.30	Idiopathic interstitial pneumonia, not otherwise specified
516.31	Idiopathic pulmonary fibrosis
516.32	Idiopathic non-specific interstitial pneumonitis
516.33	Acute interstitial pneumonitis
516.34	Respiratory bronchiolitis interstitial lung disease
516.35	Idiopathic lymphoid interstitial pneumonia
516.36	Cryptogenic organizing pneumonia
516.37	Desquamative interstitial pneumonia
518.83	Chronic respiratory failure
518.89	Other diseases of lung, not elsewhere classified — (Use additional code to identify infectious organism)
746.9	Unspecified congenital anomaly of heart ▽
748.4	Congenital cystic lung
V15.82	Personal history of tobacco use, presenting hazards to health

ICD-9-CM Procedural

00.93	Transplant from cadaver
33.6	Combined heart-lung transplantation
39.61	Extracorporeal circulation auxiliary to open heart surgery

33940

33940 Donor cardiectomy (including cold preservation)

ICD-9-CM Diagnostic

V59.8	Donor of other specified organ or tissue

ICD-9-CM Procedural

37.99	Other operations on heart and pericardium

33944

33944 Backbench standard preparation of cadaver donor heart allograft prior to transplantation, including dissection of allograft from surrounding soft tissues to prepare aorta, superior vena cava, inferior vena cava, pulmonary artery, and left atrium for implantation

ICD-9-CM Diagnostic

164.1	Malignant neoplasm of heart
164.8	Malignant neoplasm of other parts of mediastinum
198.89	Secondary malignant neoplasm of other specified sites
398.0	Rheumatic myocarditis
412	Old myocardial infarction — (Use additional code to identify presence of hypertension: 401.0-405.9)
414.00	Coronary atherosclerosis of unspecified type of vessel, native or graft — (Use additional code to identify presence of hypertension: 401.0-405.9) ▽
414.01	Coronary atherosclerosis of native coronary artery — (Use additional code to identify presence of hypertension: 401.0-405.9)
414.02	Coronary atherosclerosis of autologous vein bypass graft — (Use additional code to identify presence of hypertension: 401.0-405.9)

414.03 Coronary atherosclerosis of nonautologous biological bypass graft — (Use additional code to identify presence of hypertension: 401.0-405.9)
414.04 Coronary atherosclerosis of artery bypass graft — (Use additional code to identify presence of hypertension: 401.0-405.9)
414.05 Coronary atherosclerosis of unspecified type of bypass graft — (Use additional code to identify presence of hypertension: 401.0-405.9) ▽
414.2 Chronic total occlusion of coronary artery
414.3 Coronary atherosclerosis due to lipid rich plaque — (Code first coronary atherosclerosis (414.00-414.07))
414.4 Coronary atherosclerosis due to calcified coronary lesion — (Code first coronary atherosclerosis (414.00-414.07))
414.8 Other specified forms of chronic ischemic heart disease — (Use additional code to identify presence of hypertension: 401.0-405.9)
422.91 Idiopathic myocarditis
422.92 Septic myocarditis — (Use additional code to identify infectious organism)
422.93 Toxic myocarditis
425.0 Endomyocardial fibrosis
425.3 Endocardial fibroelastosis
425.4 Other primary cardiomyopathies
428.0 Congestive heart failure, unspecified — (Code, if applicable, heart failure due to hypertension first: 402.0-402.9, with fifth-digit 1 or 404.0-404.9 with fifth digit 1 or 3) ▽
428.1 Left heart failure — (Code, if applicable, heart failure due to hypertension first: 402.0-402.9, with fifth-digit 1 or 404.0-404.9 with fifth digit 1 or 3)
428.22 Chronic systolic heart failure — (Code, if applicable, heart failure due to hypertension first: 402.0-402.9, with fifth-digit 1 or 404.0-404.9 with fifth digit 1 or 3)
428.23 Acute on chronic systolic heart failure — (Code, if applicable, heart failure due to hypertension first: 402.0-402.9, with fifth-digit 1 or 404.0-404.9 with fifth digit 1 or 3)
428.32 Chronic diastolic heart failure — (Code, if applicable, heart failure due to hypertension first: 402.0-402.9, with fifth-digit 1 or 404.0-404.9 with fifth digit 1 or 3)
428.33 Acute on chronic diastolic heart failure — (Code, if applicable, heart failure due to hypertension first: 402.0-402.9, with fifth-digit 1 or 404.0-404.9 with fifth digit 1 or 3)
428.42 Chronic combined systolic and diastolic heart failure — (Code, if applicable, heart failure due to hypertension first: 402.0-402.9, with fifth-digit 1 or 404.0-404.9 with fifth digit 1 or 3)
428.43 Acute on chronic combined systolic and diastolic heart failure — (Code, if applicable, heart failure due to hypertension first: 402.0-402.9, with fifth-digit 1 or 404.0-404.9 with fifth digit 1 or 3)
428.9 Unspecified heart failure — (Code, if applicable, heart failure due to hypertension first: 402.0-402.9, with fifth-digit 1 or 404.0-404.9 with fifth digit 1 or 3) ▽
429.0 Unspecified myocarditis — (Use additional code to identify presence of arteriosclerosis) ▽
429.1 Myocardial degeneration — (Use additional code to identify presence of arteriosclerosis)
429.2 Unspecified cardiovascular disease — (Use additional code to identify presence of arteriosclerosis) ▽
429.3 Cardiomegaly
746.9 Unspecified congenital anomaly of heart ▽

ICD-9-CM Procedural

The ICD-9-CM procedural code(s) would be the same as the actual procedure performed because these are in-addition-to codes.

33945

33945 Heart transplant, with or without recipient cardiectomy

ICD-9-CM Diagnostic

164.1 Malignant neoplasm of heart
164.8 Malignant neoplasm of other parts of mediastinum
198.89 Secondary malignant neoplasm of other specified sites
398.0 Rheumatic myocarditis
412 Old myocardial infarction — (Use additional code to identify presence of hypertension: 401.0-405.9)
414.00 Coronary atherosclerosis of unspecified type of vessel, native or graft — (Use additional code to identify presence of hypertension: 401.0-405.9) ▽
414.01 Coronary atherosclerosis of native coronary artery — (Use additional code to identify presence of hypertension: 401.0-405.9)
414.02 Coronary atherosclerosis of autologous vein bypass graft — (Use additional code to identify presence of hypertension: 401.0-405.9)
414.03 Coronary atherosclerosis of nonautologous biological bypass graft — (Use additional code to identify presence of hypertension: 401.0-405.9)
414.04 Coronary atherosclerosis of artery bypass graft — (Use additional code to identify presence of hypertension: 401.0-405.9)
414.05 Coronary atherosclerosis of unspecified type of bypass graft — (Use additional code to identify presence of hypertension: 401.0-405.9) ▽
414.2 Chronic total occlusion of coronary artery
414.3 Coronary atherosclerosis due to lipid rich plaque — (Code first coronary atherosclerosis (414.00-414.07))
414.4 Coronary atherosclerosis due to calcified coronary lesion — (Code first coronary atherosclerosis (414.00-414.07))
414.8 Other specified forms of chronic ischemic heart disease — (Use additional code to identify presence of hypertension: 401.0-405.9)
422.91 Idiopathic myocarditis
422.92 Septic myocarditis — (Use additional code to identify infectious organism)
422.93 Toxic myocarditis
425.0 Endomyocardial fibrosis
425.3 Endocardial fibroelastosis
425.4 Other primary cardiomyopathies
428.0 Congestive heart failure, unspecified — (Code, if applicable, heart failure due to hypertension first: 402.0-402.9, with fifth-digit 1 or 404.0-404.9 with fifth digit 1 or 3) ▽
428.1 Left heart failure — (Code, if applicable, heart failure due to hypertension first: 402.0-402.9, with fifth-digit 1 or 404.0-404.9 with fifth digit 1 or 3)
428.22 Chronic systolic heart failure — (Code, if applicable, heart failure due to hypertension first: 402.0-402.9, with fifth-digit 1 or 404.0-404.9 with fifth digit 1 or 3)
428.23 Acute on chronic systolic heart failure — (Code, if applicable, heart failure due to hypertension first: 402.0-402.9, with fifth-digit 1 or 404.0-404.9 with fifth digit 1 or 3)
428.32 Chronic diastolic heart failure — (Code, if applicable, heart failure due to hypertension first: 402.0-402.9, with fifth-digit 1 or 404.0-404.9 with fifth digit 1 or 3)
428.33 Acute on chronic diastolic heart failure — (Code, if applicable, heart failure due to hypertension first: 402.0-402.9, with fifth-digit 1 or 404.0-404.9 with fifth digit 1 or 3)
428.42 Chronic combined systolic and diastolic heart failure — (Code, if applicable, heart failure due to hypertension first: 402.0-402.9, with fifth-digit 1 or 404.0-404.9 with fifth digit 1 or 3)
428.43 Acute on chronic combined systolic and diastolic heart failure — (Code, if applicable, heart failure due to hypertension first: 402.0-402.9, with fifth-digit 1 or 404.0-404.9 with fifth digit 1 or 3)
428.9 Unspecified heart failure — (Code, if applicable, heart failure due to hypertension first: 402.0-402.9, with fifth-digit 1 or 404.0-404.9 with fifth digit 1 or 3) ▽
429.0 Unspecified myocarditis — (Use additional code to identify presence of arteriosclerosis) ▽
429.1 Myocardial degeneration — (Use additional code to identify presence of arteriosclerosis)
429.2 Unspecified cardiovascular disease — (Use additional code to identify presence of arteriosclerosis) ▽
429.3 Cardiomegaly
746.9 Unspecified congenital anomaly of heart ▽

ICD-9-CM Procedural

00.93 Transplant from cadaver

37.51 Heart transplantation
39.61 Extracorporeal circulation auxiliary to open heart surgery

33960-33961

33960 Prolonged extracorporeal circulation for cardiopulmonary insufficiency; initial day
33961 each subsequent day

ICD-9-CM Diagnostic

086.0 Chagas' disease with heart involvement — (Use additional code to identify manifestations: 321.3, 323.2)
414.01 Coronary atherosclerosis of native coronary artery — (Use additional code to identify presence of hypertension: 401.0-405.9)
414.8 Other specified forms of chronic ischemic heart disease — (Use additional code to identify presence of hypertension: 401.0-405.9)
422.91 Idiopathic myocarditis
425.11 Hypertrophic obstructive cardiomyopathy
425.18 Other hypertrophic cardiomyopathy
425.3 Endocardial fibroelastosis
425.4 Other primary cardiomyopathies
425.5 Alcoholic cardiomyopathy
425.8 Cardiomyopathy in other diseases classified elsewhere — (Code first underlying disease: 135, 334.0, 359.1, 359.2) ☒
425.9 Unspecified secondary cardiomyopathy ▽
428.0 Congestive heart failure, unspecified — (Code, if applicable, heart failure due to hypertension first: 402.0-402.9, with fifth-digit 1 or 404.0-404.9 with fifth digit 1 or 3) ▽
428.1 Left heart failure — (Code, if applicable, heart failure due to hypertension first: 402.0-402.9, with fifth-digit 1 or 404.0-404.9 with fifth digit 1 or 3)
428.20 Unspecified systolic heart failure — (Code, if applicable, heart failure due to hypertension first: 402.0-402.9, with fifth-digit 1 or 404.0-404.9 with fifth digit 1 or 3) ▽
428.21 Acute systolic heart failure — (Code, if applicable, heart failure due to hypertension first: 402.0-402.9, with fifth-digit 1 or 404.0-404.9 with fifth digit 1 or 3)
428.22 Chronic systolic heart failure — (Code, if applicable, heart failure due to hypertension first: 402.0-402.9, with fifth-digit 1 or 404.0-404.9 with fifth digit 1 or 3)
428.23 Acute on chronic systolic heart failure — (Code, if applicable, heart failure due to hypertension first: 402.0-402.9, with fifth-digit 1 or 404.0-404.9 with fifth digit 1 or 3)
428.30 Unspecified diastolic heart failure — (Code, if applicable, heart failure due to hypertension first: 402.0-402.9, with fifth-digit 1 or 404.0-404.9 with fifth digit 1 or 3) ▽
428.31 Acute diastolic heart failure — (Code, if applicable, heart failure due to hypertension first: 402.0-402.9, with fifth-digit 1 or 404.0-404.9 with fifth digit 1 or 3)
428.32 Chronic diastolic heart failure — (Code, if applicable, heart failure due to hypertension first: 402.0-402.9, with fifth-digit 1 or 404.0-404.9 with fifth digit 1 or 3)
428.33 Acute on chronic diastolic heart failure — (Code, if applicable, heart failure due to hypertension first: 402.0-402.9, with fifth-digit 1 or 404.0-404.9 with fifth digit 1 or 3)
428.40 Unspecified combined systolic and diastolic heart failure — (Code, if applicable, heart failure due to hypertension first: 402.0-402.9, with fifth-digit 1 or 404.0-404.9 with fifth digit 1 or 3) ▽
428.41 Acute combined systolic and diastolic heart failure — (Code, if applicable, heart failure due to hypertension first: 402.0-402.9, with fifth-digit 1 or 404.0-404.9 with fifth digit 1 or 3)
428.42 Chronic combined systolic and diastolic heart failure — (Code, if applicable, heart failure due to hypertension first: 402.0-402.9, with fifth-digit 1 or 404.0-404.9 with fifth digit 1 or 3)
428.43 Acute on chronic combined systolic and diastolic heart failure — (Code, if applicable, heart failure due to hypertension first: 402.0-402.9, with fifth-digit 1 or 404.0-404.9 with fifth digit 1 or 3)
428.9 Unspecified heart failure — (Code, if applicable, heart failure due to hypertension first: 402.0-402.9, with fifth-digit 1 or 404.0-404.9 with fifth digit 1 or 3) ▽
746.84 Congenital obstructive anomalies of heart, not elsewhere classified — (Use additional code for associated anomalies: 746.5, 746.81, 747.10)

ICD-9-CM Procedural

39.61 Extracorporeal circulation auxiliary to open heart surgery
39.65 Extracorporeal membrane oxygenation (ECMO)
39.66 Percutaneous cardiopulmonary bypass

33967

33967 Insertion of intra-aortic balloon assist device, percutaneous

ICD-9-CM Diagnostic

402.01 Malignant hypertensive heart disease with heart failure — (Use additional code to specify type of heart failure, 428.0-428.43, if known)
402.11 Benign hypertensive heart disease with heart failure — (Use additional code to specify type of heart failure, 428.0-428.43, if known)
402.91 Hypertensive heart disease, unspecified, with heart failure — (Use additional code to specify type of heart failure, 428.0-428.43, if known) ▽
404.01 Hypertensive heart and chronic kidney disease, malignant, with heart failure and with chronic kidney disease stage I through stage IV, or unspecified — (Use additional code to specify type of heart failure, 428.0-428.43, if known. Use additional code to identify the stage of chronic kidney disease: 585.1-585.4, 585.9)
404.03 Hypertensive heart and chronic kidney disease, malignant, with heart failure and with chronic kidney disease stage V or end stage renal disease — (Use additional code to specify type of heart failure, 428.0-428.43, if known. Use additional code to identify the stage of chronic kidney disease: 585.5-585.6)
404.11 Hypertensive heart and chronic kidney disease, benign, with heart failure and with chronic kidney disease stage I through stage IV, or unspecified — (Use additional code to specify type of heart failure, 428.0-428.43, if known. Use additional code to identify the stage of chronic kidney disease: 585.1-585.4, 585.9)
404.13 Hypertensive heart and chronic kidney disease, benign, with heart failure and chronic kidney disease stage V or end stage renal disease — (Use additional code to specify type of heart failure, 428.0-428.43, if known. Use additional code to identify the stage of chronic kidney disease: 585.5-585.6)
404.91 Hypertensive heart and chronic kidney disease, unspecified, with heart failure and with chronic kidney disease stage I through stage IV, or unspecified — (Use additional code to specify type of heart failure, 428.0-428.43, if known. Use additional code to identify the stage of chronic kidney disease: 585.1-585.4, 585.9) ▽
404.93 Hypertensive heart and chronic kidney disease, unspecified, with heart failure and chronic kidney disease stage V or end stage renal disease — (Use additional code to specify type of heart failure, 428.0-428.43, if known. Use additional code to identify the stage of chronic kidney disease: 585.5-585.6) ▽
410.00 Acute myocardial infarction of anterolateral wall, episode of care unspecified — (Use additional code to identify presence of hypertension: 401.0-405.9) ▽
410.01 Acute myocardial infarction of anterolateral wall, initial episode of care — (Use additional code to identify presence of hypertension: 401.0-405.9)
410.02 Acute myocardial infarction of anterolateral wall, subsequent episode of care — (Use additional code to identify presence of hypertension: 401.0-405.9)
410.10 Acute myocardial infarction of other anterior wall, episode of care unspecified — (Use additional code to identify presence of hypertension: 401.0-405.9) ▽
410.11 Acute myocardial infarction of other anterior wall, initial episode of care — (Use additional code to identify presence of hypertension: 401.0-405.9)
410.12 Acute myocardial infarction of other anterior wall, subsequent episode of care — (Use additional code to identify presence of hypertension: 401.0-405.9)
410.20 Acute myocardial infarction of inferolateral wall, episode of care unspecified — (Use additional code to identify presence of hypertension: 401.0-405.9) ▽
410.21 Acute myocardial infarction of inferolateral wall, initial episode of care — (Use additional code to identify presence of hypertension: 401.0-405.9)
410.22 Acute myocardial infarction of inferolateral wall, subsequent episode of care — (Use additional code to identify presence of hypertension: 401.0-405.9)
410.30 Acute myocardial infarction of inferoposterior wall, episode of care unspecified — (Use additional code to identify presence of hypertension: 401.0-405.9) ▽

410.31 Acute myocardial infarction of inferoposterior wall, initial episode of care — (Use additional code to identify presence of hypertension: 401.0-405.9)

410.32 Acute myocardial infarction of inferoposterior wall, subsequent episode of care — (Use additional code to identify presence of hypertension: 401.0-405.9)

410.40 Acute myocardial infarction of other inferior wall, episode of care unspecified — (Use additional code to identify presence of hypertension: 401.0-405.9) ▽

410.41 Acute myocardial infarction of other inferior wall, initial episode of care — (Use additional code to identify presence of hypertension: 401.0-405.9)

410.42 Acute myocardial infarction of other inferior wall, subsequent episode of care — (Use additional code to identify presence of hypertension: 401.0-405.9)

410.50 Acute myocardial infarction of other lateral wall, episode of care unspecified — (Use additional code to identify presence of hypertension: 401.0-405.9) ▽

410.51 Acute myocardial infarction of other lateral wall, initial episode of care — (Use additional code to identify presence of hypertension: 401.0-405.9)

410.52 Acute myocardial infarction of other lateral wall, subsequent episode of care — (Use additional code to identify presence of hypertension: 401.0-405.9)

410.60 Acute myocardial infarction, true posterior wall infarction, episode of care unspecified — (Use additional code to identify presence of hypertension: 401.0-405.9) ▽

410.61 Acute myocardial infarction, true posterior wall infarction, initial episode of care — (Use additional code to identify presence of hypertension: 401.0-405.9)

410.62 Acute myocardial infarction, true posterior wall infarction, subsequent episode of care — (Use additional code to identify presence of hypertension: 401.0-405.9)

410.70 Acute myocardial infarction, subendocardial infarction, episode of care unspecified — (Use additional code to identify presence of hypertension: 401.0-405.9) ▽

410.71 Acute myocardial infarction, subendocardial infarction, initial episode of care — (Use additional code to identify presence of hypertension: 401.0-405.9)

410.72 Acute myocardial infarction, subendocardial infarction, subsequent episode of care — (Use additional code to identify presence of hypertension: 401.0-405.9)

410.80 Acute myocardial infarction of other specified sites, episode of care unspecified — (Use additional code to identify presence of hypertension: 401.0-405.9) ▽

410.81 Acute myocardial infarction of other specified sites, initial episode of care — (Use additional code to identify presence of hypertension: 401.0-405.9)

410.82 Acute myocardial infarction of other specified sites, subsequent episode of care — (Use additional code to identify presence of hypertension: 401.0-405.9)

410.90 Acute myocardial infarction, unspecified site, episode of care unspecified — (Use additional code to identify presence of hypertension: 401.0-405.9) ▽

410.91 Acute myocardial infarction, unspecified site, initial episode of care — (Use additional code to identify presence of hypertension: 401.0-405.9) ▽

410.92 Acute myocardial infarction, unspecified site, subsequent episode of care — (Use additional code to identify presence of hypertension: 401.0-405.9) ▽

411.89 Other acute and subacute form of ischemic heart disease — (Use additional code to identify presence of hypertension: 401.0-405.9)

414.9 Unspecified chronic ischemic heart disease — (Use additional code to identify presence of hypertension: 401.0-405.9) ▽

424.1 Aortic valve disorders

425.4 Other primary cardiomyopathies

427.5 Cardiac arrest

428.0 Congestive heart failure, unspecified — (Code, if applicable, heart failure due to hypertension first: 402.0-402.9, with fifth-digit 1 or 404.0-404.9 with fifth digit 1 or 3) ▽

428.1 Left heart failure — (Code, if applicable, heart failure due to hypertension first: 402.0-402.9, with fifth-digit 1 or 404.0-404.9 with fifth digit 1 or 3)

428.20 Unspecified systolic heart failure — (Code, if applicable, heart failure due to hypertension first: 402.0-402.9, with fifth-digit 1 or 404.0-404.9 with fifth digit 1 or 3) ▽

428.21 Acute systolic heart failure — (Code, if applicable, heart failure due to hypertension first: 402.0-402.9, with fifth-digit 1 or 404.0-404.9 with fifth digit 1 or 3)

428.22 Chronic systolic heart failure — (Code, if applicable, heart failure due to hypertension first: 402.0-402.9, with fifth-digit 1 or 404.0-404.9 with fifth digit 1 or 3)

428.23 Acute on chronic systolic heart failure — (Code, if applicable, heart failure due to hypertension first: 402.0-402.9, with fifth-digit 1 or 404.0-404.9 with fifth digit 1 or 3)

428.30 Unspecified diastolic heart failure — (Code, if applicable, heart failure due to hypertension first: 402.0-402.9, with fifth-digit 1 or 404.0-404.9 with fifth digit 1 or 3) ▽

428.31 Acute diastolic heart failure — (Code, if applicable, heart failure due to hypertension first: 402.0-402.9, with fifth-digit 1 or 404.0-404.9 with fifth digit 1 or 3)

428.32 Chronic diastolic heart failure — (Code, if applicable, heart failure due to hypertension first: 402.0-402.9, with fifth-digit 1 or 404.0-404.9 with fifth digit 1 or 3)

428.33 Acute on chronic diastolic heart failure — (Code, if applicable, heart failure due to hypertension first: 402.0-402.9, with fifth-digit 1 or 404.0-404.9 with fifth digit 1 or 3)

428.40 Unspecified combined systolic and diastolic heart failure — (Code, if applicable, heart failure due to hypertension first: 402.0-402.9, with fifth-digit 1 or 404.0-404.9 with fifth digit 1 or 3) ▽

428.41 Acute combined systolic and diastolic heart failure — (Code, if applicable, heart failure due to hypertension first: 402.0-402.9, with fifth-digit 1 or 404.0-404.9 with fifth digit 1 or 3)

428.42 Chronic combined systolic and diastolic heart failure — (Code, if applicable, heart failure due to hypertension first: 402.0-402.9, with fifth-digit 1 or 404.0-404.9 with fifth digit 1 or 3)

428.43 Acute on chronic combined systolic and diastolic heart failure — (Code, if applicable, heart failure due to hypertension first: 402.0-402.9, with fifth-digit 1 or 404.0-404.9 with fifth digit 1 or 3)

429.1 Myocardial degeneration — (Use additional code to identify presence of arteriosclerosis)

429.2 Unspecified cardiovascular disease — (Use additional code to identify presence of arteriosclerosis) ▽

429.4 Functional disturbances following cardiac surgery

785.51 Cardiogenic shock

997.1 Cardiac complications — (Use additional code to identify complications)

V45.81 Postprocedural aortocoronary bypass status

ICD-9-CM Procedural

37.61 Implant of pulsation balloon

33968

33968 Removal of intra-aortic balloon assist device, percutaneous

ICD-9-CM Diagnostic

996.00 Mechanical complication of unspecified cardiac device, implant, and graft ▽

996.1 Mechanical complication of other vascular device, implant, and graft

996.62 Infection and inflammatory reaction due to other vascular device, implant, and graft — (Use additional code to identify specified infections)

997.1 Cardiac complications — (Use additional code to identify complications)

V45.81 Postprocedural aortocoronary bypass status

ICD-9-CM Procedural

97.44 Nonoperative removal of heart assist system

33970-33971

33970 Insertion of intra-aortic balloon assist device through the femoral artery, open approach

33971 Removal of intra-aortic balloon assist device including repair of femoral artery, with or without graft

ICD-9-CM Diagnostic

402.01 Malignant hypertensive heart disease with heart failure — (Use additional code to specify type of heart failure, 428.0-428.43, if known)

402.11 Benign hypertensive heart disease with heart failure — (Use additional code to specify type of heart failure, 428.0-428.43, if known)

402.91 Hypertensive heart disease, unspecified, with heart failure — (Use additional code to specify type of heart failure, 428.0-428.43, if known) ▽

404.01 Hypertensive heart and chronic kidney disease, malignant, with heart failure and with chronic kidney disease stage I through stage IV, or unspecified — (Use additional code to specify type of heart failure, 428.0-428.43, if known. Use additional code to identify the stage of chronic kidney disease: 585.1-585.4, 585.9)

404.11 Hypertensive heart and chronic kidney disease, benign, with heart failure and with chronic kidney disease stage I through stage IV, or unspecified — (Use additional code to specify type of heart failure, 428.0-428.43, if known. Use additional code to identify the stage of chronic kidney disease: 585.1-585.4, 585.9)

404.13 Hypertensive heart and chronic kidney disease, benign, with heart failure and chronic kidney disease stage V or end stage renal disease — (Use additional code to specify type of heart failure, 428.0-428.43, if known. Use additional code to identify the stage of chronic kidney disease: 585.5-585.6)

404.91 Hypertensive heart and chronic kidney disease, unspecified, with heart failure and with chronic kidney disease stage I through stage IV, or unspecified — (Use additional code to specify type of heart failure, 428.0-428.43, if known. Use additional code to identify the stage of chronic kidney disease: 585.1-585.4, 585.9) ▽

404.93 Hypertensive heart and chronic kidney disease, unspecified, with heart failure and chronic kidney disease stage V or end stage renal disease — (Use additional code to specify type of heart failure, 428.0-428.43, if known. Use additional code to identify the stage of chronic kidney disease: 585.5-585.6) ▽

410.00 Acute myocardial infarction of anterolateral wall, episode of care unspecified — (Use additional code to identify presence of hypertension: 401.0-405.9) ▽

410.01 Acute myocardial infarction of anterolateral wall, initial episode of care — (Use additional code to identify presence of hypertension: 401.0-405.9)

410.02 Acute myocardial infarction of anterolateral wall, subsequent episode of care — (Use additional code to identify presence of hypertension: 401.0-405.9)

410.10 Acute myocardial infarction of other anterior wall, episode of care unspecified — (Use additional code to identify presence of hypertension: 401.0-405.9) ▽

410.11 Acute myocardial infarction of other anterior wall, initial episode of care — (Use additional code to identify presence of hypertension: 401.0-405.9)

410.12 Acute myocardial infarction of other anterior wall, subsequent episode of care — (Use additional code to identify presence of hypertension: 401.0-405.9)

410.20 Acute myocardial infarction of inferolateral wall, episode of care unspecified — (Use additional code to identify presence of hypertension: 401.0-405.9) ▽

410.21 Acute myocardial infarction of inferolateral wall, initial episode of care — (Use additional code to identify presence of hypertension: 401.0-405.9)

410.22 Acute myocardial infarction of inferolateral wall, subsequent episode of care — (Use additional code to identify presence of hypertension: 401.0-405.9)

410.30 Acute myocardial infarction of inferoposterior wall, episode of care unspecified — (Use additional code to identify presence of hypertension: 401.0-405.9) ▽

410.31 Acute myocardial infarction of inferoposterior wall, initial episode of care — (Use additional code to identify presence of hypertension: 401.0-405.9)

410.32 Acute myocardial infarction of inferoposterior wall, subsequent episode of care — (Use additional code to identify presence of hypertension: 401.0-405.9)

410.40 Acute myocardial infarction of other inferior wall, episode of care unspecified — (Use additional code to identify presence of hypertension: 401.0-405.9) ▽

410.41 Acute myocardial infarction of other inferior wall, initial episode of care — (Use additional code to identify presence of hypertension: 401.0-405.9)

410.42 Acute myocardial infarction of other inferior wall, subsequent episode of care — (Use additional code to identify presence of hypertension: 401.0-405.9)

410.50 Acute myocardial infarction of other lateral wall, episode of care unspecified — (Use additional code to identify presence of hypertension: 401.0-405.9) ▽

410.51 Acute myocardial infarction of other lateral wall, initial episode of care — (Use additional code to identify presence of hypertension: 401.0-405.9)

410.52 Acute myocardial infarction of other lateral wall, subsequent episode of care — (Use additional code to identify presence of hypertension: 401.0-405.9)

410.60 Acute myocardial infarction, true posterior wall infarction, episode of care unspecified — (Use additional code to identify presence of hypertension: 401.0-405.9) ▽

410.61 Acute myocardial infarction, true posterior wall infarction, initial episode of care — (Use additional code to identify presence of hypertension: 401.0-405.9)

410.62 Acute myocardial infarction, true posterior wall infarction, subsequent episode of care — (Use additional code to identify presence of hypertension: 401.0-405.9)

410.70 Acute myocardial infarction, subendocardial infarction, episode of care unspecified — (Use additional code to identify presence of hypertension: 401.0-405.9) ▽

410.71 Acute myocardial infarction, subendocardial infarction, initial episode of care — (Use additional code to identify presence of hypertension: 401.0-405.9)

410.72 Acute myocardial infarction, subendocardial infarction, subsequent episode of care — (Use additional code to identify presence of hypertension: 401.0-405.9)

410.80 Acute myocardial infarction of other specified sites, episode of care unspecified — (Use additional code to identify presence of hypertension: 401.0-405.9) ▽

410.81 Acute myocardial infarction of other specified sites, initial episode of care — (Use additional code to identify presence of hypertension: 401.0-405.9)

410.82 Acute myocardial infarction of other specified sites, subsequent episode of care — (Use additional code to identify presence of hypertension: 401.0-405.9)

410.90 Acute myocardial infarction, unspecified site, episode of care unspecified — (Use additional code to identify presence of hypertension: 401.0-405.9) ▽

410.91 Acute myocardial infarction, unspecified site, initial episode of care — (Use additional code to identify presence of hypertension: 401.0-405.9) ▽

410.92 Acute myocardial infarction, unspecified site, subsequent episode of care — (Use additional code to identify presence of hypertension: 401.0-405.9) ▽

411.89 Other acute and subacute form of ischemic heart disease — (Use additional code to identify presence of hypertension: 401.0-405.9)

414.9 Unspecified chronic ischemic heart disease — (Use additional code to identify presence of hypertension: 401.0-405.9) ▽

424.1 Aortic valve disorders

425.4 Other primary cardiomyopathies

427.5 Cardiac arrest

428.0 Congestive heart failure, unspecified — (Code, if applicable, heart failure due to hypertension first: 402.0-402.9, with fifth-digit 1 or 404.0-404.9 with fifth digit 1 or 3) ▽

428.1 Left heart failure — (Code, if applicable, heart failure due to hypertension first: 402.0-402.9, with fifth-digit 1 or 404.0-404.9 with fifth digit 1 or 3)

428.20 Unspecified systolic heart failure — (Code, if applicable, heart failure due to hypertension first: 402.0-402.9, with fifth-digit 1 or 404.0-404.9 with fifth digit 1 or 3) ▽

428.21 Acute systolic heart failure — (Code, if applicable, heart failure due to hypertension first: 402.0-402.9, with fifth-digit 1 or 404.0-404.9 with fifth digit 1 or 3)

428.22 Chronic systolic heart failure — (Code, if applicable, heart failure due to hypertension first: 402.0-402.9, with fifth-digit 1 or 404.0-404.9 with fifth digit 1 or 3)

428.23 Acute on chronic systolic heart failure — (Code, if applicable, heart failure due to hypertension first: 402.0-402.9, with fifth-digit 1 or 404.0-404.9 with fifth digit 1 or 3)

428.30 Unspecified diastolic heart failure — (Code, if applicable, heart failure due to hypertension first: 402.0-402.9, with fifth-digit 1 or 404.0-404.9 with fifth digit 1 or 3) ▽

428.31 Acute diastolic heart failure — (Code, if applicable, heart failure due to hypertension first: 402.0-402.9, with fifth-digit 1 or 404.0-404.9 with fifth digit 1 or 3)

428.32 Chronic diastolic heart failure — (Code, if applicable, heart failure due to hypertension first: 402.0-402.9, with fifth-digit 1 or 404.0-404.9 with fifth digit 1 or 3)

428.33 Acute on chronic diastolic heart failure — (Code, if applicable, heart failure due to hypertension first: 402.0-402.9, with fifth-digit 1 or 404.0-404.9 with fifth digit 1 or 3)

428.40 Unspecified combined systolic and diastolic heart failure — (Code, if applicable, heart failure due to hypertension first: 402.0-402.9, with fifth-digit 1 or 404.0-404.9 with fifth digit 1 or 3) ▽

428.41 Acute combined systolic and diastolic heart failure — (Code, if applicable, heart failure due to hypertension first: 402.0-402.9, with fifth-digit 1 or 404.0-404.9 with fifth digit 1 or 3)

428.42 Chronic combined systolic and diastolic heart failure — (Code, if applicable, heart failure due to hypertension first: 402.0-402.9, with fifth-digit 1 or 404.0-404.9 with fifth digit 1 or 3)

428.43 Acute on chronic combined systolic and diastolic heart failure — (Code, if applicable, heart failure due to hypertension first: 402.0-402.9, with fifth-digit 1 or 404.0-404.9 with fifth digit 1 or 3)

429.1 Myocardial degeneration — (Use additional code to identify presence of arteriosclerosis)
429.2 Unspecified cardiovascular disease — (Use additional code to identify presence of arteriosclerosis) ▽
429.4 Functional disturbances following cardiac surgery
785.51 Cardiogenic shock
996.00 Mechanical complication of unspecified cardiac device, implant, and graft ▽
996.02 Mechanical complication due to heart valve prosthesis
996.1 Mechanical complication of other vascular device, implant, and graft
996.62 Infection and inflammatory reaction due to other vascular device, implant, and graft — (Use additional code to identify specified infections)
997.1 Cardiac complications — (Use additional code to identify complications)
V45.81 Postprocedural aortocoronary bypass status
V58.81 Fitting and adjustment of vascular catheter

ICD-9-CM Procedural

37.61 Implant of pulsation balloon
37.64 Removal of external heart assist system(s) or device(s)

33973-33974

33973 Insertion of intra-aortic balloon assist device through the ascending aorta
33974 Removal of intra-aortic balloon assist device from the ascending aorta, including repair of the ascending aorta, with or without graft

ICD-9-CM Diagnostic

402.01 Malignant hypertensive heart disease with heart failure — (Use additional code to specify type of heart failure, 428.0-428.43, if known)
402.11 Benign hypertensive heart disease with heart failure — (Use additional code to specify type of heart failure, 428.0-428.43, if known)
402.91 Hypertensive heart disease, unspecified, with heart failure — (Use additional code to specify type of heart failure, 428.0-428.43, if known) ▽
404.01 Hypertensive heart and chronic kidney disease, malignant, with heart failure and with chronic kidney disease stage I through stage IV, or unspecified — (Use additional code to specify type of heart failure, 428.0-428.43, if known. Use additional code to identify the stage of chronic kidney disease: 585.1-585.4, 585.9)
404.11 Hypertensive heart and chronic kidney disease, benign, with heart failure and with chronic kidney disease stage I through stage IV, or unspecified — (Use additional code to specify type of heart failure, 428.0-428.43, if known. Use additional code to identify the stage of chronic kidney disease: 585.1-585.4, 585.9)
404.13 Hypertensive heart and chronic kidney disease, benign, with heart failure and chronic kidney disease stage V or end stage renal disease — (Use additional code to specify type of heart failure, 428.0-428.43, if known. Use additional code to identify the stage of chronic kidney disease: 585.5-585.6)
404.91 Hypertensive heart and chronic kidney disease, unspecified, with heart failure and with chronic kidney disease stage I through stage IV, or unspecified — (Use additional code to specify type of heart failure, 428.0-428.43, if known. Use additional code to identify the stage of chronic kidney disease: 585.1-585.4, 585.9) ▽
404.93 Hypertensive heart and chronic kidney disease, unspecified, with heart failure and chronic kidney disease stage V or end stage renal disease — (Use additional code to specify type of heart failure, 428.0-428.43, if known. Use additional code to identify the stage of chronic kidney disease: 585.5-585.6) ▽
410.00 Acute myocardial infarction of anterolateral wall, episode of care unspecified — (Use additional code to identify presence of hypertension: 401.0-405.9) ▽
410.01 Acute myocardial infarction of anterolateral wall, initial episode of care — (Use additional code to identify presence of hypertension: 401.0-405.9)
410.02 Acute myocardial infarction of anterolateral wall, subsequent episode of care — (Use additional code to identify presence of hypertension: 401.0-405.9)
410.10 Acute myocardial infarction of other anterior wall, episode of care unspecified — (Use additional code to identify presence of hypertension: 401.0-405.9) ▽
410.11 Acute myocardial infarction of other anterior wall, initial episode of care — (Use additional code to identify presence of hypertension: 401.0-405.9)
410.12 Acute myocardial infarction of other anterior wall, subsequent episode of care — (Use additional code to identify presence of hypertension: 401.0-405.9)
410.20 Acute myocardial infarction of inferolateral wall, episode of care unspecified — (Use additional code to identify presence of hypertension: 401.0-405.9) ▽
410.21 Acute myocardial infarction of inferolateral wall, initial episode of care — (Use additional code to identify presence of hypertension: 401.0-405.9)
410.22 Acute myocardial infarction of inferolateral wall, subsequent episode of care — (Use additional code to identify presence of hypertension: 401.0-405.9)
410.30 Acute myocardial infarction of inferoposterior wall, episode of care unspecified — (Use additional code to identify presence of hypertension: 401.0-405.9) ▽
410.31 Acute myocardial infarction of inferoposterior wall, initial episode of care — (Use additional code to identify presence of hypertension: 401.0-405.9)
410.32 Acute myocardial infarction of inferoposterior wall, subsequent episode of care — (Use additional code to identify presence of hypertension: 401.0-405.9)
410.40 Acute myocardial infarction of other inferior wall, episode of care unspecified — (Use additional code to identify presence of hypertension: 401.0-405.9) ▽
410.41 Acute myocardial infarction of other inferior wall, initial episode of care — (Use additional code to identify presence of hypertension: 401.0-405.9)
410.42 Acute myocardial infarction of other inferior wall, subsequent episode of care — (Use additional code to identify presence of hypertension: 401.0-405.9)
410.50 Acute myocardial infarction of other lateral wall, episode of care unspecified — (Use additional code to identify presence of hypertension: 401.0-405.9) ▽
410.51 Acute myocardial infarction of other lateral wall, initial episode of care — (Use additional code to identify presence of hypertension: 401.0-405.9)
410.52 Acute myocardial infarction of other lateral wall, subsequent episode of care — (Use additional code to identify presence of hypertension: 401.0-405.9)
410.60 Acute myocardial infarction, true posterior wall infarction, episode of care unspecified — (Use additional code to identify presence of hypertension: 401.0-405.9) ▽
410.61 Acute myocardial infarction, true posterior wall infarction, initial episode of care — (Use additional code to identify presence of hypertension: 401.0-405.9)
410.62 Acute myocardial infarction, true posterior wall infarction, subsequent episode of care — (Use additional code to identify presence of hypertension: 401.0-405.9)
410.70 Acute myocardial infarction, subendocardial infarction, episode of care unspecified — (Use additional code to identify presence of hypertension: 401.0-405.9) ▽
410.71 Acute myocardial infarction, subendocardial infarction, initial episode of care — (Use additional code to identify presence of hypertension: 401.0-405.9)
410.72 Acute myocardial infarction, subendocardial infarction, subsequent episode of care — (Use additional code to identify presence of hypertension: 401.0-405.9)
410.80 Acute myocardial infarction of other specified sites, episode of care unspecified — (Use additional code to identify presence of hypertension: 401.0-405.9) ▽
410.81 Acute myocardial infarction of other specified sites, initial episode of care — (Use additional code to identify presence of hypertension: 401.0-405.9)
410.82 Acute myocardial infarction of other specified sites, subsequent episode of care — (Use additional code to identify presence of hypertension: 401.0-405.9)
410.90 Acute myocardial infarction, unspecified site, episode of care unspecified — (Use additional code to identify presence of hypertension: 401.0-405.9) ▽
410.91 Acute myocardial infarction, unspecified site, initial episode of care — (Use additional code to identify presence of hypertension: 401.0-405.9) ▽
410.92 Acute myocardial infarction, unspecified site, subsequent episode of care — (Use additional code to identify presence of hypertension: 401.0-405.9) ▽
411.89 Other acute and subacute form of ischemic heart disease — (Use additional code to identify presence of hypertension: 401.0-405.9)
414.9 Unspecified chronic ischemic heart disease — (Use additional code to identify presence of hypertension: 401.0-405.9) ▽
424.1 Aortic valve disorders
425.4 Other primary cardiomyopathies
427.5 Cardiac arrest
428.0 Congestive heart failure, unspecified — (Code, if applicable, heart failure due to hypertension first: 402.0-402.9, with fifth-digit 1 or 404.0-404.9 with fifth digit 1 or 3) ▽

428.1 Left heart failure — (Code, if applicable, heart failure due to hypertension first: 402.0-402.9, with fifth-digit 1 or 404.0-404.9 with fifth digit 1 or 3)

428.20 Unspecified systolic heart failure — (Code, if applicable, heart failure due to hypertension first: 402.0-402.9, with fifth-digit 1 or 404.0-404.9 with fifth digit 1 or 3)

428.21 Acute systolic heart failure — (Code, if applicable, heart failure due to hypertension first: 402.0-402.9, with fifth-digit 1 or 404.0-404.9 with fifth digit 1 or 3)

428.22 Chronic systolic heart failure — (Code, if applicable, heart failure due to hypertension first: 402.0-402.9, with fifth-digit 1 or 404.0-404.9 with fifth digit 1 or 3)

428.23 Acute on chronic systolic heart failure — (Code, if applicable, heart failure due to hypertension first: 402.0-402.9, with fifth-digit 1 or 404.0-404.9 with fifth digit 1 or 3)

428.30 Unspecified diastolic heart failure — (Code, if applicable, heart failure due to hypertension first: 402.0-402.9, with fifth-digit 1 or 404.0-404.9 with fifth digit 1 or 3)

428.31 Acute diastolic heart failure — (Code, if applicable, heart failure due to hypertension first: 402.0-402.9, with fifth-digit 1 or 404.0-404.9 with fifth digit 1 or 3)

428.32 Chronic diastolic heart failure — (Code, if applicable, heart failure due to hypertension first: 402.0-402.9, with fifth-digit 1 or 404.0-404.9 with fifth digit 1 or 3)

428.33 Acute on chronic diastolic heart failure — (Code, if applicable, heart failure due to hypertension first: 402.0-402.9, with fifth-digit 1 or 404.0-404.9 with fifth digit 1 or 3)

428.40 Unspecified combined systolic and diastolic heart failure — (Code, if applicable, heart failure due to hypertension first: 402.0-402.9, with fifth-digit 1 or 404.0-404.9 with fifth digit 1 or 3)

428.41 Acute combined systolic and diastolic heart failure — (Code, if applicable, heart failure due to hypertension first: 402.0-402.9, with fifth-digit 1 or 404.0-404.9 with fifth digit 1 or 3)

428.42 Chronic combined systolic and diastolic heart failure — (Code, if applicable, heart failure due to hypertension first: 402.0-402.9, with fifth-digit 1 or 404.0-404.9 with fifth digit 1 or 3)

428.43 Acute on chronic combined systolic and diastolic heart failure — (Code, if applicable, heart failure due to hypertension first: 402.0-402.9, with fifth-digit 1 or 404.0-404.9 with fifth digit 1 or 3)

429.1 Myocardial degeneration — (Use additional code to identify presence of arteriosclerosis)

429.2 Unspecified cardiovascular disease — (Use additional code to identify presence of arteriosclerosis)

429.4 Functional disturbances following cardiac surgery

785.51 Cardiogenic shock

996.00 Mechanical complication of unspecified cardiac device, implant, and graft

996.02 Mechanical complication due to heart valve prosthesis

996.1 Mechanical complication of other vascular device, implant, and graft

996.62 Infection and inflammatory reaction due to other vascular device, implant, and graft — (Use additional code to identify specified infections)

997.1 Cardiac complications — (Use additional code to identify complications)

V45.81 Postprocedural aortocoronary bypass status

V58.81 Fitting and adjustment of vascular catheter

ICD-9-CM Procedural

37.61 Implant of pulsation balloon

37.64 Removal of external heart assist system(s) or device(s)

39.56 Repair of blood vessel with tissue patch graft

39.57 Repair of blood vessel with synthetic patch graft

39.58 Repair of blood vessel with unspecified type of patch graft

33975-33976

33975 Insertion of ventricular assist device; extracorporeal, single ventricle

33976 extracorporeal, biventricular

ICD-9-CM Diagnostic

402.01 Malignant hypertensive heart disease with heart failure — (Use additional code to specify type of heart failure, 428.0-428.43, if known)

402.11 Benign hypertensive heart disease with heart failure — (Use additional code to specify type of heart failure, 428.0-428.43, if known)

402.91 Hypertensive heart disease, unspecified, with heart failure — (Use additional code to specify type of heart failure, 428.0-428.43, if known)

404.01 Hypertensive heart and chronic kidney disease, malignant, with heart failure and with chronic kidney disease stage I through stage IV, or unspecified — (Use additional code to specify type of heart failure, 428.0-428.43, if known. Use additional code to identify the stage of chronic kidney disease: 585.1-585.4, 585.9)

404.03 Hypertensive heart and chronic kidney disease, malignant, with heart failure and with chronic kidney disease stage V or end stage renal disease — (Use additional code to specify type of heart failure, 428.0-428.43, if known. Use additional code to identify the stage of chronic kidney disease: 585.5-585.6)

404.11 Hypertensive heart and chronic kidney disease, benign, with heart failure and with chronic kidney disease stage I through stage IV, or unspecified — (Use additional code to specify type of heart failure, 428.0-428.43, if known. Use additional code to identify the stage of chronic kidney disease: 585.1-585.4, 585.9)

404.13 Hypertensive heart and chronic kidney disease, benign, with heart failure and chronic kidney disease stage V or end stage renal disease — (Use additional code to specify type of heart failure, 428.0-428.43, if known. Use additional code to identify the stage of chronic kidney disease: 585.5-585.6)

404.91 Hypertensive heart and chronic kidney disease, unspecified, with heart failure and with chronic kidney disease stage I through stage IV, or unspecified — (Use additional code to specify type of heart failure, 428.0-428.43, if known. Use additional code to identify the stage of chronic kidney disease: 585.1-585.4, 585.9)

404.93 Hypertensive heart and chronic kidney disease, unspecified, with heart failure and chronic kidney disease stage V or end stage renal disease — (Use additional code to specify type of heart failure, 428.0-428.43, if known. Use additional code to identify the stage of chronic kidney disease: 585.5-585.6)

410.00 Acute myocardial infarction of anterolateral wall, episode of care unspecified — (Use additional code to identify presence of hypertension: 401.0-405.9)

410.01 Acute myocardial infarction of anterolateral wall, initial episode of care — (Use additional code to identify presence of hypertension: 401.0-405.9)

410.02 Acute myocardial infarction of anterolateral wall, subsequent episode of care — (Use additional code to identify presence of hypertension: 401.0-405.9)

410.10 Acute myocardial infarction of other anterior wall, episode of care unspecified — (Use additional code to identify presence of hypertension: 401.0-405.9)

410.11 Acute myocardial infarction of other anterior wall, initial episode of care — (Use additional code to identify presence of hypertension: 401.0-405.9)

410.12 Acute myocardial infarction of other anterior wall, subsequent episode of care — (Use additional code to identify presence of hypertension: 401.0-405.9)

410.20 Acute myocardial infarction of inferolateral wall, episode of care unspecified — (Use additional code to identify presence of hypertension: 401.0-405.9)

410.21 Acute myocardial infarction of inferolateral wall, initial episode of care — (Use additional code to identify presence of hypertension: 401.0-405.9)

410.22 Acute myocardial infarction of inferolateral wall, subsequent episode of care — (Use additional code to identify presence of hypertension: 401.0-405.9)

410.30 Acute myocardial infarction of inferoposterior wall, episode of care unspecified — (Use additional code to identify presence of hypertension: 401.0-405.9)

410.31 Acute myocardial infarction of inferoposterior wall, initial episode of care — (Use additional code to identify presence of hypertension: 401.0-405.9)

410.32 Acute myocardial infarction of inferoposterior wall, subsequent episode of care — (Use additional code to identify presence of hypertension: 401.0-405.9)

410.40 Acute myocardial infarction of other inferior wall, episode of care unspecified — (Use additional code to identify presence of hypertension: 401.0-405.9)

410.41 Acute myocardial infarction of other inferior wall, initial episode of care — (Use additional code to identify presence of hypertension: 401.0-405.9)
410.42 Acute myocardial infarction of other inferior wall, subsequent episode of care — (Use additional code to identify presence of hypertension: 401.0-405.9)
410.50 Acute myocardial infarction of other lateral wall, episode of care unspecified — (Use additional code to identify presence of hypertension: 401.0-405.9) ▽
410.51 Acute myocardial infarction of other lateral wall, initial episode of care — (Use additional code to identify presence of hypertension: 401.0-405.9)
410.52 Acute myocardial infarction of other lateral wall, subsequent episode of care — (Use additional code to identify presence of hypertension: 401.0-405.9)
410.60 Acute myocardial infarction, true posterior wall infarction, episode of care unspecified — (Use additional code to identify presence of hypertension: 401.0-405.9) ▽
410.61 Acute myocardial infarction, true posterior wall infarction, initial episode of care — (Use additional code to identify presence of hypertension: 401.0-405.9)
410.62 Acute myocardial infarction, true posterior wall infarction, subsequent episode of care — (Use additional code to identify presence of hypertension: 401.0-405.9)
410.70 Acute myocardial infarction, subendocardial infarction, episode of care unspecified — (Use additional code to identify presence of hypertension: 401.0-405.9) ▽
410.71 Acute myocardial infarction, subendocardial infarction, initial episode of care — (Use additional code to identify presence of hypertension: 401.0-405.9)
410.72 Acute myocardial infarction, subendocardial infarction, subsequent episode of care — (Use additional code to identify presence of hypertension: 401.0-405.9)
410.80 Acute myocardial infarction of other specified sites, episode of care unspecified — (Use additional code to identify presence of hypertension: 401.0-405.9) ▽
410.81 Acute myocardial infarction of other specified sites, initial episode of care — (Use additional code to identify presence of hypertension: 401.0-405.9)
410.82 Acute myocardial infarction of other specified sites, subsequent episode of care — (Use additional code to identify presence of hypertension: 401.0-405.9)
410.90 Acute myocardial infarction, unspecified site, episode of care unspecified — (Use additional code to identify presence of hypertension: 401.0-405.9) ▽
410.91 Acute myocardial infarction, unspecified site, initial episode of care — (Use additional code to identify presence of hypertension: 401.0-405.9) ▽
410.92 Acute myocardial infarction, unspecified site, subsequent episode of care — (Use additional code to identify presence of hypertension: 401.0-405.9) ▽
411.89 Other acute and subacute form of ischemic heart disease — (Use additional code to identify presence of hypertension: 401.0-405.9)
425.4 Other primary cardiomyopathies
427.5 Cardiac arrest
428.0 Congestive heart failure, unspecified — (Code, if applicable, heart failure due to hypertension first: 402.0-402.9, with fifth-digit 1 or 404.0-404.9 with fifth digit 1 or 3) ▽
428.1 Left heart failure — (Code, if applicable, heart failure due to hypertension first: 402.0-402.9, with fifth-digit 1 or 404.0-404.9 with fifth digit 1 or 3)
428.20 Unspecified systolic heart failure — (Code, if applicable, heart failure due to hypertension first: 402.0-402.9, with fifth-digit 1 or 404.0-404.9 with fifth digit 1 or 3) ▽
428.21 Acute systolic heart failure — (Code, if applicable, heart failure due to hypertension first: 402.0-402.9, with fifth-digit 1 or 404.0-404.9 with fifth digit 1 or 3)
428.22 Chronic systolic heart failure — (Code, if applicable, heart failure due to hypertension first: 402.0-402.9, with fifth-digit 1 or 404.0-404.9 with fifth digit 1 or 3)
428.23 Acute on chronic systolic heart failure — (Code, if applicable, heart failure due to hypertension first: 402.0-402.9, with fifth-digit 1 or 404.0-404.9 with fifth digit 1 or 3)
428.30 Unspecified diastolic heart failure — (Code, if applicable, heart failure due to hypertension first: 402.0-402.9, with fifth-digit 1 or 404.0-404.9 with fifth digit 1 or 3) ▽
428.31 Acute diastolic heart failure — (Code, if applicable, heart failure due to hypertension first: 402.0-402.9, with fifth-digit 1 or 404.0-404.9 with fifth digit 1 or 3)
428.32 Chronic diastolic heart failure — (Code, if applicable, heart failure due to hypertension first: 402.0-402.9, with fifth-digit 1 or 404.0-404.9 with fifth digit 1 or 3)
428.33 Acute on chronic diastolic heart failure — (Code, if applicable, heart failure due to hypertension first: 402.0-402.9, with fifth-digit 1 or 404.0-404.9 with fifth digit 1 or 3)
428.40 Unspecified combined systolic and diastolic heart failure — (Code, if applicable, heart failure due to hypertension first: 402.0-402.9, with fifth-digit 1 or 404.0-404.9 with fifth digit 1 or 3) ▽
428.41 Acute combined systolic and diastolic heart failure — (Code, if applicable, heart failure due to hypertension first: 402.0-402.9, with fifth-digit 1 or 404.0-404.9 with fifth digit 1 or 3)
428.42 Chronic combined systolic and diastolic heart failure — (Code, if applicable, heart failure due to hypertension first: 402.0-402.9, with fifth-digit 1 or 404.0-404.9 with fifth digit 1 or 3)
428.43 Acute on chronic combined systolic and diastolic heart failure — (Code, if applicable, heart failure due to hypertension first: 402.0-402.9, with fifth-digit 1 or 404.0-404.9 with fifth digit 1 or 3)
428.9 Unspecified heart failure — (Code, if applicable, heart failure due to hypertension first: 402.0-402.9, with fifth-digit 1 or 404.0-404.9 with fifth digit 1 or 3) ▽
429.1 Myocardial degeneration — (Use additional code to identify presence of arteriosclerosis)
429.2 Unspecified cardiovascular disease — (Use additional code to identify presence of arteriosclerosis) ▽
429.4 Functional disturbances following cardiac surgery
785.51 Cardiogenic shock
997.1 Cardiac complications — (Use additional code to identify complications)
V45.81 Postprocedural aortocoronary bypass status

ICD-9-CM Procedural

37.60 Implantation or insertion of biventricular external heart assist system
37.62 Insertion of temporary non-implantable extracorporeal circulatory assist device
37.65 Implant of single ventricular (extracorporeal) external heart assist system

HCPCS Level II Supplies & Services

Q0506 Battery, lithium-ion, for use with electric or electric/pneumatic ventricular assist device, replacement only

33977-33978

33977 Removal of ventricular assist device; extracorporeal, single ventricle
33978 extracorporeal, biventricular

ICD-9-CM Diagnostic

996.00 Mechanical complication of unspecified cardiac device, implant, and graft ▽
996.61 Infection and inflammatory reaction due to cardiac device, implant, and graft — (Use additional code to identify specified infections)
V58.81 Fitting and adjustment of vascular catheter
V58.89 Encounter for other specified aftercare

ICD-9-CM Procedural

37.64 Removal of external heart assist system(s) or device(s)

33979

33979 Insertion of ventricular assist device, implantable intracorporeal, single ventricle

ICD-9-CM Diagnostic

402.01 Malignant hypertensive heart disease with heart failure — (Use additional code to specify type of heart failure, 428.0-428.43, if known)
402.11 Benign hypertensive heart disease with heart failure — (Use additional code to specify type of heart failure, 428.0-428.43, if known)
402.91 Hypertensive heart disease, unspecified, with heart failure — (Use additional code to specify type of heart failure, 428.0-428.43, if known) ▽
404.01 Hypertensive heart and chronic kidney disease, malignant, with heart failure and with chronic kidney disease stage I through stage IV, or unspecified — (Use additional code to specify type of heart failure, 428.0-428.43, if known. Use additional code to identify the stage of chronic kidney disease: 585.1-585.4, 585.9)

404.03 Hypertensive heart and chronic kidney disease, malignant, with heart failure and with chronic kidney disease stage V or end stage renal disease — (Use additional code to specify type of heart failure, 428.0-428.43, if known. Use additional code to identify the stage of chronic kidney disease: 585.5-585.6)

404.11 Hypertensive heart and chronic kidney disease, benign, with heart failure and with chronic kidney disease stage I through stage IV, or unspecified — (Use additional code to specify type of heart failure, 428.0-428.43, if known. Use additional code to identify the stage of chronic kidney disease: 585.1-585.4, 585.9)

404.13 Hypertensive heart and chronic kidney disease, benign, with heart failure and chronic kidney disease stage V or end stage renal disease — (Use additional code to specify type of heart failure, 428.0-428.43, if known. Use additional code to identify the stage of chronic kidney disease: 585.5-585.6)

404.91 Hypertensive heart and chronic kidney disease, unspecified, with heart failure and with chronic kidney disease stage I through stage IV, or unspecified — (Use additional code to specify type of heart failure, 428.0-428.43, if known. Use additional code to identify the stage of chronic kidney disease: 585.1-585.4, 585.9) ▼

404.93 Hypertensive heart and chronic kidney disease, unspecified, with heart failure and chronic kidney disease stage V or end stage renal disease — (Use additional code to specify type of heart failure, 428.0-428.43, if known. Use additional code to identify the stage of chronic kidney disease: 585.5-585.6) ▼

410.00 Acute myocardial infarction of anterolateral wall, episode of care unspecified — (Use additional code to identify presence of hypertension: 401.0-405.9) ▼

410.01 Acute myocardial infarction of anterolateral wall, initial episode of care — (Use additional code to identify presence of hypertension: 401.0-405.9)

410.02 Acute myocardial infarction of anterolateral wall, subsequent episode of care — (Use additional code to identify presence of hypertension: 401.0-405.9)

410.10 Acute myocardial infarction of other anterior wall, episode of care unspecified — (Use additional code to identify presence of hypertension: 401.0-405.9) ▼

410.11 Acute myocardial infarction of other anterior wall, initial episode of care — (Use additional code to identify presence of hypertension: 401.0-405.9)

410.12 Acute myocardial infarction of other anterior wall, subsequent episode of care — (Use additional code to identify presence of hypertension: 401.0-405.9)

410.20 Acute myocardial infarction of inferolateral wall, episode of care unspecified — (Use additional code to identify presence of hypertension: 401.0-405.9) ▼

410.21 Acute myocardial infarction of inferolateral wall, initial episode of care — (Use additional code to identify presence of hypertension: 401.0-405.9)

410.22 Acute myocardial infarction of inferolateral wall, subsequent episode of care — (Use additional code to identify presence of hypertension: 401.0-405.9)

410.30 Acute myocardial infarction of inferoposterior wall, episode of care unspecified — (Use additional code to identify presence of hypertension: 401.0-405.9) ▼

410.31 Acute myocardial infarction of inferoposterior wall, initial episode of care — (Use additional code to identify presence of hypertension: 401.0-405.9)

410.32 Acute myocardial infarction of inferoposterior wall, subsequent episode of care — (Use additional code to identify presence of hypertension: 401.0-405.9)

410.40 Acute myocardial infarction of other inferior wall, episode of care unspecified — (Use additional code to identify presence of hypertension: 401.0-405.9) ▼

410.41 Acute myocardial infarction of other inferior wall, initial episode of care — (Use additional code to identify presence of hypertension: 401.0-405.9)

410.42 Acute myocardial infarction of other inferior wall, subsequent episode of care — (Use additional code to identify presence of hypertension: 401.0-405.9)

410.50 Acute myocardial infarction of other lateral wall, episode of care unspecified — (Use additional code to identify presence of hypertension: 401.0-405.9) ▼

410.51 Acute myocardial infarction of other lateral wall, initial episode of care — (Use additional code to identify presence of hypertension: 401.0-405.9)

410.52 Acute myocardial infarction of other lateral wall, subsequent episode of care — (Use additional code to identify presence of hypertension: 401.0-405.9)

410.60 Acute myocardial infarction, true posterior wall infarction, episode of care unspecified — (Use additional code to identify presence of hypertension: 401.0-405.9) ▼

410.61 Acute myocardial infarction, true posterior wall infarction, initial episode of care — (Use additional code to identify presence of hypertension: 401.0-405.9)

410.62 Acute myocardial infarction, true posterior wall infarction, subsequent episode of care — (Use additional code to identify presence of hypertension: 401.0-405.9)

410.70 Acute myocardial infarction, subendocardial infarction, episode of care unspecified — (Use additional code to identify presence of hypertension: 401.0-405.9) ▼

410.71 Acute myocardial infarction, subendocardial infarction, initial episode of care — (Use additional code to identify presence of hypertension: 401.0-405.9)

410.72 Acute myocardial infarction, subendocardial infarction, subsequent episode of care — (Use additional code to identify presence of hypertension: 401.0-405.9)

410.80 Acute myocardial infarction of other specified sites, episode of care unspecified — (Use additional code to identify presence of hypertension: 401.0-405.9) ▼

410.81 Acute myocardial infarction of other specified sites, initial episode of care — (Use additional code to identify presence of hypertension: 401.0-405.9)

410.82 Acute myocardial infarction of other specified sites, subsequent episode of care — (Use additional code to identify presence of hypertension: 401.0-405.9)

410.90 Acute myocardial infarction, unspecified site, episode of care unspecified — (Use additional code to identify presence of hypertension: 401.0-405.9) ▼

410.91 Acute myocardial infarction, unspecified site, initial episode of care — (Use additional code to identify presence of hypertension: 401.0-405.9) ▼

410.92 Acute myocardial infarction, unspecified site, subsequent episode of care — (Use additional code to identify presence of hypertension: 401.0-405.9) ▼

411.89 Other acute and subacute form of ischemic heart disease — (Use additional code to identify presence of hypertension: 401.0-405.9)

425.4 Other primary cardiomyopathies

427.5 Cardiac arrest

428.0 Congestive heart failure, unspecified — (Code, if applicable, heart failure due to hypertension first: 402.0-402.9, with fifth-digit 1 or 404.0-404.9 with fifth digit 1 or 3) ▼

428.1 Left heart failure — (Code, if applicable, heart failure due to hypertension first: 402.0-402.9, with fifth-digit 1 or 404.0-404.9 with fifth digit 1 or 3)

428.20 Unspecified systolic heart failure — (Code, if applicable, heart failure due to hypertension first: 402.0-402.9, with fifth-digit 1 or 404.0-404.9 with fifth digit 1 or 3) ▼

428.21 Acute systolic heart failure — (Code, if applicable, heart failure due to hypertension first: 402.0-402.9, with fifth-digit 1 or 404.0-404.9 with fifth digit 1 or 3)

428.22 Chronic systolic heart failure — (Code, if applicable, heart failure due to hypertension first: 402.0-402.9, with fifth-digit 1 or 404.0-404.9 with fifth digit 1 or 3)

428.23 Acute on chronic systolic heart failure — (Code, if applicable, heart failure due to hypertension first: 402.0-402.9, with fifth-digit 1 or 404.0-404.9 with fifth digit 1 or 3)

428.30 Unspecified diastolic heart failure — (Code, if applicable, heart failure due to hypertension first: 402.0-402.9, with fifth-digit 1 or 404.0-404.9 with fifth digit 1 or 3) ▼

428.31 Acute diastolic heart failure — (Code, if applicable, heart failure due to hypertension first: 402.0-402.9, with fifth-digit 1 or 404.0-404.9 with fifth digit 1 or 3)

428.32 Chronic diastolic heart failure — (Code, if applicable, heart failure due to hypertension first: 402.0-402.9, with fifth-digit 1 or 404.0-404.9 with fifth digit 1 or 3)

428.33 Acute on chronic diastolic heart failure — (Code, if applicable, heart failure due to hypertension first: 402.0-402.9, with fifth-digit 1 or 404.0-404.9 with fifth digit 1 or 3)

428.40 Unspecified combined systolic and diastolic heart failure — (Code, if applicable, heart failure due to hypertension first: 402.0-402.9, with fifth-digit 1 or 404.0-404.9 with fifth digit 1 or 3) ▼

428.41 Acute combined systolic and diastolic heart failure — (Code, if applicable, heart failure due to hypertension first: 402.0-402.9, with fifth-digit 1 or 404.0-404.9 with fifth digit 1 or 3)

428.42 Chronic combined systolic and diastolic heart failure — (Code, if applicable, heart failure due to hypertension first: 402.0-402.9, with fifth-digit 1 or 404.0-404.9 with fifth digit 1 or 3)

428.43 Acute on chronic combined systolic and diastolic heart failure — (Code, if applicable, heart failure due to hypertension first: 402.0-402.9, with fifth-digit 1 or 404.0-404.9 with fifth digit 1 or 3)

428.9 Unspecified heart failure — (Code, if applicable, heart failure due to hypertension first: 402.0-402.9, with fifth-digit 1 or 404.0-404.9 with fifth digit 1 or 3) ▼

429.1 Myocardial degeneration — (Use additional code to identify presence of arteriosclerosis)
429.2 Unspecified cardiovascular disease — (Use additional code to identify presence of arteriosclerosis) ▽
429.4 Functional disturbances following cardiac surgery
785.51 Cardiogenic shock
997.1 Cardiac complications — (Use additional code to identify complications)
V45.81 Postprocedural aortocoronary bypass status

ICD-9-CM Procedural

37.66 Insertion of implantable heart assist system

HCPCS Level II Supplies & Services

Q0506 Battery, lithium-ion, for use with electric or electric/pneumatic ventricular assist device, replacement only

33980

33980 Removal of ventricular assist device, implantable intracorporeal, single ventricle

ICD-9-CM Diagnostic

996.00 Mechanical complication of unspecified cardiac device, implant, and graft ▽
996.09 Mechanical complication of cardiac device, implant, and graft, other
996.61 Infection and inflammatory reaction due to cardiac device, implant, and graft — (Use additional code to identify specified infections)
996.62 Infection and inflammatory reaction due to other vascular device, implant, and graft — (Use additional code to identify specified infections)
V58.81 Fitting and adjustment of vascular catheter
V58.89 Encounter for other specified aftercare

ICD-9-CM Procedural

37.99 Other operations on heart and pericardium

33981

33981 Replacement of extracorporeal ventricular assist device, single or biventricular, pump(s), single or each pump

ICD-9-CM Diagnostic

402.01 Malignant hypertensive heart disease with heart failure — (Use additional code to specify type of heart failure, 428.0-428.43, if known)
402.11 Benign hypertensive heart disease with heart failure — (Use additional code to specify type of heart failure, 428.0-428.43, if known)
402.91 Hypertensive heart disease, unspecified, with heart failure — (Use additional code to specify type of heart failure, 428.0-428.43, if known) ▽
404.01 Hypertensive heart and chronic kidney disease, malignant, with heart failure and with chronic kidney disease stage I through stage IV, or unspecified — (Use additional code to specify type of heart failure, 428.0-428.43, if known. Use additional code to identify the stage of chronic kidney disease: 585.1-585.4, 585.9)
404.03 Hypertensive heart and chronic kidney disease, malignant, with heart failure and with chronic kidney disease stage V or end stage renal disease — (Use additional code to specify type of heart failure, 428.0-428.43, if known. Use additional code to identify the stage of chronic kidney disease: 585.5-585.6)
404.11 Hypertensive heart and chronic kidney disease, benign, with heart failure and with chronic kidney disease stage I through stage IV, or unspecified — (Use additional code to specify type of heart failure, 428.0-428.43, if known. Use additional code to identify the stage of chronic kidney disease: 585.1-585.4, 585.9)
404.13 Hypertensive heart and chronic kidney disease, benign, with heart failure and chronic kidney disease stage V or end stage renal disease — (Use additional code to specify type of heart failure, 428.0-428.43, if known. Use additional code to identify the stage of chronic kidney disease: 585.5-585.6)
404.91 Hypertensive heart and chronic kidney disease, unspecified, with heart failure and with chronic kidney disease stage I through stage IV, or unspecified — (Use additional code to specify type of heart failure, 428.0-428.43, if known. Use additional code to identify the stage of chronic kidney disease: 585.1-585.4, 585.9) ▽
404.93 Hypertensive heart and chronic kidney disease, unspecified, with heart failure and chronic kidney disease stage V or end stage renal disease — (Use additional code to specify type of heart failure, 428.0-428.43, if known. Use additional code to identify the stage of chronic kidney disease: 585.5-585.6) ▽
410.00 Acute myocardial infarction of anterolateral wall, episode of care unspecified — (Use additional code to identify presence of hypertension: 401.0-405.9) ▽
410.01 Acute myocardial infarction of anterolateral wall, initial episode of care — (Use additional code to identify presence of hypertension: 401.0-405.9)
410.02 Acute myocardial infarction of anterolateral wall, subsequent episode of care — (Use additional code to identify presence of hypertension: 401.0-405.9)
410.10 Acute myocardial infarction of other anterior wall, episode of care unspecified — (Use additional code to identify presence of hypertension: 401.0-405.9) ▽
410.11 Acute myocardial infarction of other anterior wall, initial episode of care — (Use additional code to identify presence of hypertension: 401.0-405.9)
410.12 Acute myocardial infarction of other anterior wall, subsequent episode of care — (Use additional code to identify presence of hypertension: 401.0-405.9)
410.20 Acute myocardial infarction of inferolateral wall, episode of care unspecified — (Use additional code to identify presence of hypertension: 401.0-405.9) ▽
410.21 Acute myocardial infarction of inferolateral wall, initial episode of care — (Use additional code to identify presence of hypertension: 401.0-405.9)
410.22 Acute myocardial infarction of inferolateral wall, subsequent episode of care — (Use additional code to identify presence of hypertension: 401.0-405.9)
410.30 Acute myocardial infarction of inferoposterior wall, episode of care unspecified — (Use additional code to identify presence of hypertension: 401.0-405.9) ▽
410.31 Acute myocardial infarction of inferoposterior wall, initial episode of care — (Use additional code to identify presence of hypertension: 401.0-405.9)
410.32 Acute myocardial infarction of inferoposterior wall, subsequent episode of care — (Use additional code to identify presence of hypertension: 401.0-405.9)
410.40 Acute myocardial infarction of other inferior wall, episode of care unspecified — (Use additional code to identify presence of hypertension: 401.0-405.9) ▽
410.41 Acute myocardial infarction of other inferior wall, initial episode of care — (Use additional code to identify presence of hypertension: 401.0-405.9)
410.42 Acute myocardial infarction of other inferior wall, subsequent episode of care — (Use additional code to identify presence of hypertension: 401.0-405.9)
410.50 Acute myocardial infarction of other lateral wall, episode of care unspecified — (Use additional code to identify presence of hypertension: 401.0-405.9) ▽
410.51 Acute myocardial infarction of other lateral wall, initial episode of care — (Use additional code to identify presence of hypertension: 401.0-405.9)
410.52 Acute myocardial infarction of other lateral wall, subsequent episode of care — (Use additional code to identify presence of hypertension: 401.0-405.9)
410.60 Acute myocardial infarction, true posterior wall infarction, episode of care unspecified — (Use additional code to identify presence of hypertension: 401.0-405.9) ▽
410.61 Acute myocardial infarction, true posterior wall infarction, initial episode of care — (Use additional code to identify presence of hypertension: 401.0-405.9)
410.62 Acute myocardial infarction, true posterior wall infarction, subsequent episode of care — (Use additional code to identify presence of hypertension: 401.0-405.9)
410.70 Acute myocardial infarction, subendocardial infarction, episode of care unspecified — (Use additional code to identify presence of hypertension: 401.0-405.9) ▽
410.71 Acute myocardial infarction, subendocardial infarction, initial episode of care — (Use additional code to identify presence of hypertension: 401.0-405.9)
410.72 Acute myocardial infarction, subendocardial infarction, subsequent episode of care — (Use additional code to identify presence of hypertension: 401.0-405.9)
410.80 Acute myocardial infarction of other specified sites, episode of care unspecified — (Use additional code to identify presence of hypertension: 401.0-405.9) ▽
410.81 Acute myocardial infarction of other specified sites, initial episode of care — (Use additional code to identify presence of hypertension: 401.0-405.9)
410.82 Acute myocardial infarction of other specified sites, subsequent episode of care — (Use additional code to identify presence of hypertension: 401.0-405.9)
410.90 Acute myocardial infarction, unspecified site, episode of care unspecified — (Use additional code to identify presence of hypertension: 401.0-405.9) ▽

410.91 Acute myocardial infarction, unspecified site, initial episode of care — (Use additional code to identify presence of hypertension: 401.0-405.9) ▽

410.92 Acute myocardial infarction, unspecified site, subsequent episode of care — (Use additional code to identify presence of hypertension: 401.0-405.9) ▽

411.89 Other acute and subacute form of ischemic heart disease — (Use additional code to identify presence of hypertension: 401.0-405.9)

425.4 Other primary cardiomyopathies

427.5 Cardiac arrest

428.0 Congestive heart failure, unspecified — (Code, if applicable, heart failure due to hypertension first: 402.0-402.9, with fifth-digit 1 or 404.0-404.9 with fifth digit 1 or 3) ▽

428.1 Left heart failure — (Code, if applicable, heart failure due to hypertension first: 402.0-402.9, with fifth-digit 1 or 404.0-404.9 with fifth digit 1 or 3)

428.20 Unspecified systolic heart failure — (Code, if applicable, heart failure due to hypertension first: 402.0-402.9, with fifth-digit 1 or 404.0-404.9 with fifth digit 1 or 3) ▽

428.21 Acute systolic heart failure — (Code, if applicable, heart failure due to hypertension first: 402.0-402.9, with fifth-digit 1 or 404.0-404.9 with fifth digit 1 or 3)

428.22 Chronic systolic heart failure — (Code, if applicable, heart failure due to hypertension first: 402.0-402.9, with fifth-digit 1 or 404.0-404.9 with fifth digit 1 or 3)

428.23 Acute on chronic systolic heart failure — (Code, if applicable, heart failure due to hypertension first: 402.0-402.9, with fifth-digit 1 or 404.0-404.9 with fifth digit 1 or 3)

428.30 Unspecified diastolic heart failure — (Code, if applicable, heart failure due to hypertension first: 402.0-402.9, with fifth-digit 1 or 404.0-404.9 with fifth digit 1 or 3) ▽

428.31 Acute diastolic heart failure — (Code, if applicable, heart failure due to hypertension first: 402.0-402.9, with fifth-digit 1 or 404.0-404.9 with fifth digit 1 or 3)

428.32 Chronic diastolic heart failure — (Code, if applicable, heart failure due to hypertension first: 402.0-402.9, with fifth-digit 1 or 404.0-404.9 with fifth digit 1 or 3)

428.33 Acute on chronic diastolic heart failure — (Code, if applicable, heart failure due to hypertension first: 402.0-402.9, with fifth-digit 1 or 404.0-404.9 with fifth digit 1 or 3)

428.40 Unspecified combined systolic and diastolic heart failure — (Code, if applicable, heart failure due to hypertension first: 402.0-402.9, with fifth-digit 1 or 404.0-404.9 with fifth digit 1 or 3) ▽

428.41 Acute combined systolic and diastolic heart failure — (Code, if applicable, heart failure due to hypertension first: 402.0-402.9, with fifth-digit 1 or 404.0-404.9 with fifth digit 1 or 3)

428.42 Chronic combined systolic and diastolic heart failure — (Code, if applicable, heart failure due to hypertension first: 402.0-402.9, with fifth-digit 1 or 404.0-404.9 with fifth digit 1 or 3)

428.43 Acute on chronic combined systolic and diastolic heart failure — (Code, if applicable, heart failure due to hypertension first: 402.0-402.9, with fifth-digit 1 or 404.0-404.9 with fifth digit 1 or 3)

428.9 Unspecified heart failure — (Code, if applicable, heart failure due to hypertension first: 402.0-402.9, with fifth-digit 1 or 404.0-404.9 with fifth digit 1 or 3) ▽

429.1 Myocardial degeneration — (Use additional code to identify presence of arteriosclerosis)

429.2 Unspecified cardiovascular disease — (Use additional code to identify presence of arteriosclerosis) ▽

429.4 Functional disturbances following cardiac surgery

785.51 Cardiogenic shock

996.09 Mechanical complication of cardiac device, implant, and graft, other

996.61 Infection and inflammatory reaction due to cardiac device, implant, and graft — (Use additional code to identify specified infections)

996.72 Other complications due to other cardiac device, implant, and graft — (Use additional code to identify complication: 338.18-338.19, 338.28-338.29)

997.1 Cardiac complications — (Use additional code to identify complications)

V45.81 Postprocedural aortocoronary bypass status

ICD-9-CM Procedural

37.60 Implantation or insertion of biventricular external heart assist system

37.64 Removal of external heart assist system(s) or device(s)

37.65 Implant of single ventricular (extracorporeal) external heart assist system

33982-33983

33982 Replacement of ventricular assist device pump(s); implantable intracorporeal, single ventricle, without cardiopulmonary bypass

33983 implantable intracorporeal, single ventricle, with cardiopulmonary bypass

ICD-9-CM Diagnostic

402.01 Malignant hypertensive heart disease with heart failure — (Use additional code to specify type of heart failure, 428.0-428.43, if known)

402.11 Benign hypertensive heart disease with heart failure — (Use additional code to specify type of heart failure, 428.0-428.43, if known)

402.91 Hypertensive heart disease, unspecified, with heart failure — (Use additional code to specify type of heart failure, 428.0-428.43, if known) ▽

404.01 Hypertensive heart and chronic kidney disease, malignant, with heart failure and with chronic kidney disease stage I through stage IV, or unspecified — (Use additional code to specify type of heart failure, 428.0-428.43, if known. Use additional code to identify the stage of chronic kidney disease: 585.1-585.4, 585.9)

404.03 Hypertensive heart and chronic kidney disease, malignant, with heart failure and with chronic kidney disease stage V or end stage renal disease — (Use additional code to specify type of heart failure, 428.0-428.43, if known. Use additional code to identify the stage of chronic kidney disease: 585.5-585.6)

404.11 Hypertensive heart and chronic kidney disease, benign, with heart failure and with chronic kidney disease stage I through stage IV, or unspecified — (Use additional code to specify type of heart failure, 428.0-428.43, if known. Use additional code to identify the stage of chronic kidney disease: 585.1-585.4, 585.9)

404.13 Hypertensive heart and chronic kidney disease, benign, with heart failure and chronic kidney disease stage V or end stage renal disease — (Use additional code to specify type of heart failure, 428.0-428.43, if known. Use additional code to identify the stage of chronic kidney disease: 585.5-585.6)

404.91 Hypertensive heart and chronic kidney disease, unspecified, with heart failure and with chronic kidney disease stage I through stage IV, or unspecified — (Use additional code to specify type of heart failure, 428.0-428.43, if known. Use additional code to identify the stage of chronic kidney disease: 585.1-585.4, 585.9) ▽

404.93 Hypertensive heart and chronic kidney disease, unspecified, with heart failure and chronic kidney disease stage V or end stage renal disease — (Use additional code to specify type of heart failure, 428.0-428.43, if known. Use additional code to identify the stage of chronic kidney disease: 585.5-585.6) ▽

410.00 Acute myocardial infarction of anterolateral wall, episode of care unspecified — (Use additional code to identify presence of hypertension: 401.0-405.9) ▽

410.01 Acute myocardial infarction of anterolateral wall, initial episode of care — (Use additional code to identify presence of hypertension: 401.0-405.9)

410.02 Acute myocardial infarction of anterolateral wall, subsequent episode of care — (Use additional code to identify presence of hypertension: 401.0-405.9)

410.10 Acute myocardial infarction of other anterior wall, episode of care unspecified — (Use additional code to identify presence of hypertension: 401.0-405.9) ▽

410.11 Acute myocardial infarction of other anterior wall, initial episode of care — (Use additional code to identify presence of hypertension: 401.0-405.9)

410.12 Acute myocardial infarction of other anterior wall, subsequent episode of care — (Use additional code to identify presence of hypertension: 401.0-405.9)

410.20 Acute myocardial infarction of inferolateral wall, episode of care unspecified — (Use additional code to identify presence of hypertension: 401.0-405.9) ▽

410.21 Acute myocardial infarction of inferolateral wall, initial episode of care — (Use additional code to identify presence of hypertension: 401.0-405.9)

410.22 Acute myocardial infarction of inferolateral wall, subsequent episode of care — (Use additional code to identify presence of hypertension: 401.0-405.9)

410.30 Acute myocardial infarction of inferoposterior wall, episode of care unspecified — (Use additional code to identify presence of hypertension: 401.0-405.9) ▽

410.31 Acute myocardial infarction of inferoposterior wall, initial episode of care — (Use additional code to identify presence of hypertension: 401.0-405.9)

410.32 Acute myocardial infarction of inferoposterior wall, subsequent episode of care — (Use additional code to identify presence of hypertension: 401.0-405.9)

410.40 Acute myocardial infarction of other inferior wall, episode of care unspecified — (Use additional code to identify presence of hypertension: 401.0-405.9) ▽

410.41 Acute myocardial infarction of other inferior wall, initial episode of care — (Use additional code to identify presence of hypertension: 401.0-405.9)

410.42 Acute myocardial infarction of other inferior wall, subsequent episode of care — (Use additional code to identify presence of hypertension: 401.0-405.9)

410.50 Acute myocardial infarction of other lateral wall, episode of care unspecified — (Use additional code to identify presence of hypertension: 401.0-405.9) ▽

410.51 Acute myocardial infarction of other lateral wall, initial episode of care — (Use additional code to identify presence of hypertension: 401.0-405.9)

410.52 Acute myocardial infarction of other lateral wall, subsequent episode of care — (Use additional code to identify presence of hypertension: 401.0-405.9)

410.60 Acute myocardial infarction, true posterior wall infarction, episode of care unspecified — (Use additional code to identify presence of hypertension: 401.0-405.9) ▽

410.61 Acute myocardial infarction, true posterior wall infarction, initial episode of care — (Use additional code to identify presence of hypertension: 401.0-405.9)

410.62 Acute myocardial infarction, true posterior wall infarction, subsequent episode of care — (Use additional code to identify presence of hypertension: 401.0-405.9)

410.70 Acute myocardial infarction, subendocardial infarction, episode of care unspecified — (Use additional code to identify presence of hypertension: 401.0-405.9) ▽

410.71 Acute myocardial infarction, subendocardial infarction, initial episode of care — (Use additional code to identify presence of hypertension: 401.0-405.9)

410.72 Acute myocardial infarction, subendocardial infarction, subsequent episode of care — (Use additional code to identify presence of hypertension: 401.0-405.9)

410.80 Acute myocardial infarction of other specified sites, episode of care unspecified — (Use additional code to identify presence of hypertension: 401.0-405.9) ▽

410.81 Acute myocardial infarction of other specified sites, initial episode of care — (Use additional code to identify presence of hypertension: 401.0-405.9)

410.82 Acute myocardial infarction of other specified sites, subsequent episode of care — (Use additional code to identify presence of hypertension: 401.0-405.9)

410.90 Acute myocardial infarction, unspecified site, episode of care unspecified — (Use additional code to identify presence of hypertension: 401.0-405.9) ▽

410.91 Acute myocardial infarction, unspecified site, initial episode of care — (Use additional code to identify presence of hypertension: 401.0-405.9) ▽

410.92 Acute myocardial infarction, unspecified site, subsequent episode of care — (Use additional code to identify presence of hypertension: 401.0-405.9) ▽

411.89 Other acute and subacute form of ischemic heart disease — (Use additional code to identify presence of hypertension: 401.0-405.9)

425.4 Other primary cardiomyopathies

427.5 Cardiac arrest

428.0 Congestive heart failure, unspecified — (Code, if applicable, heart failure due to hypertension first: 402.0-402.9, with fifth-digit 1 or 404.0-404.9 with fifth digit 1 or 3) ▽

428.1 Left heart failure — (Code, if applicable, heart failure due to hypertension first: 402.0-402.9, with fifth-digit 1 or 404.0-404.9 with fifth digit 1 or 3)

428.20 Unspecified systolic heart failure — (Code, if applicable, heart failure due to hypertension first: 402.0-402.9, with fifth-digit 1 or 404.0-404.9 with fifth digit 1 or 3) ▽

428.21 Acute systolic heart failure — (Code, if applicable, heart failure due to hypertension first: 402.0-402.9, with fifth-digit 1 or 404.0-404.9 with fifth digit 1 or 3)

428.22 Chronic systolic heart failure — (Code, if applicable, heart failure due to hypertension first: 402.0-402.9, with fifth-digit 1 or 404.0-404.9 with fifth digit 1 or 3)

428.23 Acute on chronic systolic heart failure — (Code, if applicable, heart failure due to hypertension first: 402.0-402.9, with fifth-digit 1 or 404.0-404.9 with fifth digit 1 or 3)

428.30 Unspecified diastolic heart failure — (Code, if applicable, heart failure due to hypertension first: 402.0-402.9, with fifth-digit 1 or 404.0-404.9 with fifth digit 1 or 3) ▽

428.31 Acute diastolic heart failure — (Code, if applicable, heart failure due to hypertension first: 402.0-402.9, with fifth-digit 1 or 404.0-404.9 with fifth digit 1 or 3)

428.32 Chronic diastolic heart failure — (Code, if applicable, heart failure due to hypertension first: 402.0-402.9, with fifth-digit 1 or 404.0-404.9 with fifth digit 1 or 3)

428.33 Acute on chronic diastolic heart failure — (Code, if applicable, heart failure due to hypertension first: 402.0-402.9, with fifth-digit 1 or 404.0-404.9 with fifth digit 1 or 3)

428.40 Unspecified combined systolic and diastolic heart failure — (Code, if applicable, heart failure due to hypertension first: 402.0-402.9, with fifth-digit 1 or 404.0-404.9 with fifth digit 1 or 3) ▽

428.41 Acute combined systolic and diastolic heart failure — (Code, if applicable, heart failure due to hypertension first: 402.0-402.9, with fifth-digit 1 or 404.0-404.9 with fifth digit 1 or 3)

428.42 Chronic combined systolic and diastolic heart failure — (Code, if applicable, heart failure due to hypertension first: 402.0-402.9, with fifth-digit 1 or 404.0-404.9 with fifth digit 1 or 3)

428.43 Acute on chronic combined systolic and diastolic heart failure — (Code, if applicable, heart failure due to hypertension first: 402.0-402.9, with fifth-digit 1 or 404.0-404.9 with fifth digit 1 or 3)

428.9 Unspecified heart failure — (Code, if applicable, heart failure due to hypertension first: 402.0-402.9, with fifth-digit 1 or 404.0-404.9 with fifth digit 1 or 3) ▽

429.1 Myocardial degeneration — (Use additional code to identify presence of arteriosclerosis)

429.2 Unspecified cardiovascular disease — (Use additional code to identify presence of arteriosclerosis) ▽

429.4 Functional disturbances following cardiac surgery

785.51 Cardiogenic shock

996.09 Mechanical complication of cardiac device, implant, and graft, other

996.61 Infection and inflammatory reaction due to cardiac device, implant, and graft — (Use additional code to identify specified infections)

996.72 Other complications due to other cardiac device, implant, and graft — (Use additional code to identify complication: 338.18-338.19, 338.28-338.29)

997.1 Cardiac complications — (Use additional code to identify complications)

V45.81 Postprocedural aortocoronary bypass status

ICD-9-CM Procedural

37.66 Insertion of implantable heart assist system

39.61 Extracorporeal circulation auxiliary to open heart surgery

97.44 Nonoperative removal of heart assist system

33990-33991

33990 Insertion of ventricular assist device, percutaneous including radiological supervision and interpretation; arterial access only

33991 both arterial and venous access, with transseptal puncture

ICD-9-CM Diagnostic

398.91 Rheumatic heart failure (congestive)

402.01 Malignant hypertensive heart disease with heart failure — (Use additional code to specify type of heart failure, 428.0-428.43, if known)

402.11 Benign hypertensive heart disease with heart failure — (Use additional code to specify type of heart failure, 428.0-428.43, if known)

402.91 Hypertensive heart disease, unspecified, with heart failure — (Use additional code to specify type of heart failure, 428.0-428.43, if known) ▽

404.01 Hypertensive heart and chronic kidney disease, malignant, with heart failure and with chronic kidney disease stage I through stage IV, or unspecified — (Use additional code to specify type of heart failure, 428.0-428.43, if known. Use additional code to identify the stage of chronic kidney disease: 585.1-585.4, 585.9)

404.03 Hypertensive heart and chronic kidney disease, malignant, with heart failure and with chronic kidney disease stage V or end stage renal disease — (Use additional code to specify type of heart failure, 428.0-428.43, if known. Use additional code to identify the stage of chronic kidney disease: 585.5-585.6)

404.11 Hypertensive heart and chronic kidney disease, benign, with heart failure and with chronic kidney disease stage I through stage IV, or unspecified — (Use additional code to specify type of heart failure, 428.0-428.43, if known. Use additional code to identify the stage of chronic kidney disease: 585.1-585.4, 585.9)

404.13 Hypertensive heart and chronic kidney disease, benign, with heart failure and chronic kidney disease stage V or end stage renal disease — (Use additional code to specify type of heart failure, 428.0-428.43, if known. Use additional code to identify the stage of chronic kidney disease: 585.5-585.6)

404.91 Hypertensive heart and chronic kidney disease, unspecified, with heart failure and with chronic kidney disease stage I through stage IV, or unspecified — (Use additional code to specify type of heart failure, 428.0-428.43, if known. Use additional code to identify the stage of chronic kidney disease: 585.1-585.4, 585.9) ▽

404.93 Hypertensive heart and chronic kidney disease, unspecified, with heart failure and chronic kidney disease stage V or end stage renal disease — (Use additional code to specify type of heart failure, 428.0-428.43, if known. Use additional code to identify the stage of chronic kidney disease: 585.5-585.6) ▽

410.01 Acute myocardial infarction of anterolateral wall, initial episode of care — (Use additional code to identify presence of hypertension: 401.0-405.9)

410.02 Acute myocardial infarction of anterolateral wall, subsequent episode of care — (Use additional code to identify presence of hypertension: 401.0-405.9)

410.11 Acute myocardial infarction of other anterior wall, initial episode of care — (Use additional code to identify presence of hypertension: 401.0-405.9)

410.12 Acute myocardial infarction of other anterior wall, subsequent episode of care — (Use additional code to identify presence of hypertension: 401.0-405.9)

410.21 Acute myocardial infarction of inferolateral wall, initial episode of care — (Use additional code to identify presence of hypertension: 401.0-405.9)

410.22 Acute myocardial infarction of inferolateral wall, subsequent episode of care — (Use additional code to identify presence of hypertension: 401.0-405.9)

410.31 Acute myocardial infarction of inferoposterior wall, initial episode of care — (Use additional code to identify presence of hypertension: 401.0-405.9)

410.32 Acute myocardial infarction of inferoposterior wall, subsequent episode of care — (Use additional code to identify presence of hypertension: 401.0-405.9)

410.41 Acute myocardial infarction of other inferior wall, initial episode of care — (Use additional code to identify presence of hypertension: 401.0-405.9)

410.42 Acute myocardial infarction of other inferior wall, subsequent episode of care — (Use additional code to identify presence of hypertension: 401.0-405.9)

410.51 Acute myocardial infarction of other lateral wall, initial episode of care — (Use additional code to identify presence of hypertension: 401.0-405.9)

410.52 Acute myocardial infarction of other lateral wall, subsequent episode of care — (Use additional code to identify presence of hypertension: 401.0-405.9)

410.61 Acute myocardial infarction, true posterior wall infarction, initial episode of care — (Use additional code to identify presence of hypertension: 401.0-405.9)

410.62 Acute myocardial infarction, true posterior wall infarction, subsequent episode of care — (Use additional code to identify presence of hypertension: 401.0-405.9)

410.71 Acute myocardial infarction, subendocardial infarction, initial episode of care — (Use additional code to identify presence of hypertension: 401.0-405.9)

410.72 Acute myocardial infarction, subendocardial infarction, subsequent episode of care — (Use additional code to identify presence of hypertension: 401.0-405.9)

410.81 Acute myocardial infarction of other specified sites, initial episode of care — (Use additional code to identify presence of hypertension: 401.0-405.9)

410.82 Acute myocardial infarction of other specified sites, subsequent episode of care — (Use additional code to identify presence of hypertension: 401.0-405.9)

410.91 Acute myocardial infarction, unspecified site, initial episode of care — (Use additional code to identify presence of hypertension: 401.0-405.9) ▽

410.92 Acute myocardial infarction, unspecified site, subsequent episode of care — (Use additional code to identify presence of hypertension: 401.0-405.9) ▽

412 Old myocardial infarction — (Use additional code to identify presence of hypertension: 401.0-405.9)

414.8 Other specified forms of chronic ischemic heart disease — (Use additional code to identify presence of hypertension: 401.0-405.9)

422.0 Acute myocarditis in diseases classified elsewhere — (Code first underlying disease: 017.9, 487.8, 488.09, 488.19) ☒

422.90 Unspecified acute myocarditis ▽

422.91 Idiopathic myocarditis

422.92 Septic myocarditis — (Use additional code to identify infectious organism)

425.11 Hypertrophic obstructive cardiomyopathy

425.18 Other hypertrophic cardiomyopathy

425.4 Other primary cardiomyopathies

425.8 Cardiomyopathy in other diseases classified elsewhere — (Code first underlying disease: 135, 334.0, 359.1, 359.2) ☒

425.9 Unspecified secondary cardiomyopathy ▽

428.0 Congestive heart failure, unspecified — (Code, if applicable, heart failure due to hypertension first: 402.0-402.9, with fifth-digit 1 or 404.0-404.9 with fifth digit 1 or 3) ▽

428.1 Left heart failure — (Code, if applicable, heart failure due to hypertension first: 402.0-402.9, with fifth-digit 1 or 404.0-404.9 with fifth digit 1 or 3)

428.20 Unspecified systolic heart failure — (Code, if applicable, heart failure due to hypertension first: 402.0-402.9, with fifth-digit 1 or 404.0-404.9 with fifth digit 1 or 3) ▽

428.21 Acute systolic heart failure — (Code, if applicable, heart failure due to hypertension first: 402.0-402.9, with fifth-digit 1 or 404.0-404.9 with fifth digit 1 or 3)

428.22 Chronic systolic heart failure — (Code, if applicable, heart failure due to hypertension first: 402.0-402.9, with fifth-digit 1 or 404.0-404.9 with fifth digit 1 or 3)

428.23 Acute on chronic systolic heart failure — (Code, if applicable, heart failure due to hypertension first: 402.0-402.9, with fifth-digit 1 or 404.0-404.9 with fifth digit 1 or 3)

428.30 Unspecified diastolic heart failure — (Code, if applicable, heart failure due to hypertension first: 402.0-402.9, with fifth-digit 1 or 404.0-404.9 with fifth digit 1 or 3) ▽

428.31 Acute diastolic heart failure — (Code, if applicable, heart failure due to hypertension first: 402.0-402.9, with fifth-digit 1 or 404.0-404.9 with fifth digit 1 or 3)

428.32 Chronic diastolic heart failure — (Code, if applicable, heart failure due to hypertension first: 402.0-402.9, with fifth-digit 1 or 404.0-404.9 with fifth digit 1 or 3)

428.33 Acute on chronic diastolic heart failure — (Code, if applicable, heart failure due to hypertension first: 402.0-402.9, with fifth-digit 1 or 404.0-404.9 with fifth digit 1 or 3)

428.40 Unspecified combined systolic and diastolic heart failure — (Code, if applicable, heart failure due to hypertension first: 402.0-402.9, with fifth-digit 1 or 404.0-404.9 with fifth digit 1 or 3) ▽

428.41 Acute combined systolic and diastolic heart failure — (Code, if applicable, heart failure due to hypertension first: 402.0-402.9, with fifth-digit 1 or 404.0-404.9 with fifth digit 1 or 3)

428.42 Chronic combined systolic and diastolic heart failure — (Code, if applicable, heart failure due to hypertension first: 402.0-402.9, with fifth-digit 1 or 404.0-404.9 with fifth digit 1 or 3)

428.43 Acute on chronic combined systolic and diastolic heart failure — (Code, if applicable, heart failure due to hypertension first: 402.0-402.9, with fifth-digit 1 or 404.0-404.9 with fifth digit 1 or 3)

428.9 Unspecified heart failure — (Code, if applicable, heart failure due to hypertension first: 402.0-402.9, with fifth-digit 1 or 404.0-404.9 with fifth digit 1 or 3) ▽

429.4 Functional disturbances following cardiac surgery

746.84 Congenital obstructive anomalies of heart, not elsewhere classified — (Use additional code for associated anomalies: 746.5, 746.81, 747.10)

785.51 Cardiogenic shock

996.83 Complications of transplanted heart — (Use additional code to identify nature of complication: 078.5, 199.2, 238.77, 279.50-279.53)

997.1 Cardiac complications — (Use additional code to identify complications)

V43.21 Organ or tissue replaced by other means, Heart assist device

V49.83 Awaiting organ transplant status

ICD-9-CM Procedural

37.68 Insertion of percutaneous external heart assist device

33992

33992 Removal of percutaneous ventricular assist device at separate and distinct session from insertion

ICD-9-CM Diagnostic

996.09 Mechanical complication of cardiac device, implant, and graft, other

996.61 Infection and inflammatory reaction due to cardiac device, implant, and graft — (Use additional code to identify specified infections)

996.72 Other complications due to other cardiac device, implant, and graft — (Use additional code to identify complication: 338.18-338.19, 338.28-338.29)

V45.09 Other specified cardiac device in situ

V53.39 Fitting and adjustment of other cardiac device

V58.44 Aftercare following organ transplant — (This code should be used in conjunction with other aftercare codes to fully identify the reason for the aftercare encounter. Use additional code to identify the organ transplanted: V42.0-V42.9)

V58.49 Other specified aftercare following surgery — (This code should be used in conjunction with other aftercare codes to fully identify the reason for the aftercare encounter)

ICD-9-CM Procedural

97.44 Nonoperative removal of heart assist system

33993

33993 Repositioning of percutaneous ventricular assist device with imaging guidance at separate and distinct session from insertion

ICD-9-CM Diagnostic

996.09 Mechanical complication of cardiac device, implant, and graft, other

ICD-9-CM Procedural

37.99 Other operations on heart and pericardium

Arteries and Veins

34001

34001 Embolectomy or thrombectomy, with or without catheter; carotid, subclavian or innominate artery, by neck incision

ICD-9-CM Diagnostic

433.10 Occlusion and stenosis of carotid artery without mention of cerebral infarction — (Use additional code, if applicable, to identify status post administration of tPA (rtPA) in a different facility within the last 24 hours prior to admission to current facility: V45.88)

433.11 Occlusion and stenosis of carotid artery with cerebral infarction — (Use additional code, if applicable, to identify status post administration of tPA (rtPA) in a different facility within the last 24 hours prior to admission to current facility: V45.88)

433.30 Occlusion and stenosis of multiple and bilateral precerebral arteries without mention of cerebral infarction — (Use additional code, if applicable, to identify status post administration of tPA (rtPA) in a different facility within the last 24 hours prior to admission to current facility: V45.88)

433.31 Occlusion and stenosis of multiple and bilateral precerebral arteries with cerebral infarction — (Use additional code, if applicable, to identify status post administration of tPA (rtPA) in a different facility within the last 24 hours prior to admission to current facility: V45.88)

433.80 Occlusion and stenosis of other specified precerebral artery without mention of cerebral infarction — (Use additional code, if applicable, to identify status post administration of tPA (rtPA) in a different facility within the last 24 hours prior to admission to current facility: V45.88)

433.81 Occlusion and stenosis of other specified precerebral artery with cerebral infarction — (Use additional code, if applicable, to identify status post administration of tPA (rtPA) in a different facility within the last 24 hours prior to admission to current facility: V45.88)

435.0 Basilar artery syndrome — (Use additional code to identify presence of hypertension)

435.1 Vertebral artery syndrome — (Use additional code to identify presence of hypertension)

435.2 Subclavian steal syndrome — (Use additional code to identify presence of hypertension)

435.3 Vertebrobasilar artery syndrome — (Use additional code to identify presence of hypertension)

435.8 Other specified transient cerebral ischemias — (Use additional code to identify presence of hypertension)

435.9 Unspecified transient cerebral ischemia — (Use additional code to identify presence of hypertension) ▽

438.20 Hemiplegia affecting unspecified side due to cerebrovascular disease — (Use additional code to identify presence of hypertension) ▽

438.22 Hemiplegia affecting nondominant side due to cerebrovascular disease — (Use additional code to identify presence of hypertension)

438.31 Monoplegia of upper limb affecting dominant side due to cerebrovascular disease — (Use additional code to identify presence of hypertension)

438.40 Monoplegia of lower limb affecting unspecified side due to cerebrovascular disease — (Use additional code to identify presence of hypertension) ▽

438.42 Monoplegia of lower limb affecting nondominant side due to cerebrovascular disease — (Use additional code to identify presence of hypertension)

438.51 Other paralytic syndrome affecting dominant side due to cerebrovascular disease — (Use additional code to identify presence of hypertension. Use additional code to identify type of paralytic syndrome: 344.00-344.09, 344.81)

438.81 Apraxia due to cerebrovascular disease — (Use additional code to identify presence of hypertension)

438.9 Unspecified late effects of cerebrovascular disease due to cerebrovascular disease — (Use additional code to identify presence of hypertension. ▽

441.1 Thoracic aneurysm, ruptured

443.21 Dissection of carotid artery

443.29 Dissection of other artery

449 Septic arterial embolism — (Use additional code to identify the site of the embolism: 433.0-433.9, 444.01-444.9)

900.01 Common carotid artery injury

900.02 External carotid artery injury

900.03 Internal carotid artery injury

901.1 Innominate and subclavian artery injury

996.71 Other complications due to heart valve prosthesis — (Use additional code to identify complication: 338.18-338.19, 338.28-338.29)

996.72 Other complications due to other cardiac device, implant, and graft — (Use additional code to identify complication: 338.18-338.19, 338.28-338.29)

996.74 Other complications due to other vascular device, implant, and graft — (Use additional code to identify complication: 338.18-338.19, 338.28-338.29)

997.79 Vascular complications of other vessels — (Use additional code to identify complications)

ICD-9-CM Procedural

38.02 Incision of other vessels of head and neck

38.05 Incision of other thoracic vessels

34051

34051 Embolectomy or thrombectomy, with or without catheter; innominate, subclavian artery, by thoracic incision

ICD-9-CM Diagnostic

433.30 Occlusion and stenosis of multiple and bilateral precerebral arteries without mention of cerebral infarction — (Use additional code, if applicable, to identify status post administration of tPA (rtPA) in a different facility within the last 24 hours prior to admission to current facility: V45.88)

433.31 Occlusion and stenosis of multiple and bilateral precerebral arteries with cerebral infarction — (Use additional code, if applicable, to identify status post administration of tPA (rtPA) in a different facility within the last 24 hours prior to admission to current facility: V45.88)

433.80 Occlusion and stenosis of other specified precerebral artery without mention of cerebral infarction — (Use additional code, if applicable, to identify status post administration of tPA (rtPA) in a different facility within the last 24 hours prior to admission to current facility: V45.88)

433.81 Occlusion and stenosis of other specified precerebral artery with cerebral infarction — (Use additional code, if applicable, to identify status post administration of tPA (rtPA) in a different facility within the last 24 hours prior to admission to current facility: V45.88)

435.0 Basilar artery syndrome — (Use additional code to identify presence of hypertension)

435.1 Vertebral artery syndrome — (Use additional code to identify presence of hypertension)

435.2 Subclavian steal syndrome — (Use additional code to identify presence of hypertension)

435.3 Vertebrobasilar artery syndrome — (Use additional code to identify presence of hypertension)

435.8 Other specified transient cerebral ischemias — (Use additional code to identify presence of hypertension)

435.9 Unspecified transient cerebral ischemia — (Use additional code to identify presence of hypertension) ▼

438.20 Hemiplegia affecting unspecified side due to cerebrovascular disease — (Use additional code to identify presence of hypertension) ▼

438.22 Hemiplegia affecting nondominant side due to cerebrovascular disease — (Use additional code to identify presence of hypertension)

438.31 Monoplegia of upper limb affecting dominant side due to cerebrovascular disease — (Use additional code to identify presence of hypertension)

438.40 Monoplegia of lower limb affecting unspecified side due to cerebrovascular disease — (Use additional code to identify presence of hypertension) ▼

438.42 Monoplegia of lower limb affecting nondominant side due to cerebrovascular disease — (Use additional code to identify presence of hypertension)

438.51 Other paralytic syndrome affecting dominant side due to cerebrovascular disease — (Use additional code to identify presence of hypertension. Use additional code to identify type of paralytic syndrome: 344.00-344.09, 344.81)

438.81 Apraxia due to cerebrovascular disease — (Use additional code to identify presence of hypertension)

438.9 Unspecified late effects of cerebrovascular disease due to cerebrovascular disease — (Use additional code to identify presence of hypertension. ▼

443.29 Dissection of other artery

449 Septic arterial embolism — (Use additional code to identify the site of the embolism: 433.0-433.9, 444.01-444.9)

901.1 Innominate and subclavian artery injury

996.71 Other complications due to heart valve prosthesis — (Use additional code to identify complication: 338.18-338.19, 338.28-338.29)

996.72 Other complications due to other cardiac device, implant, and graft — (Use additional code to identify complication: 338.18-338.19, 338.28-338.29)

996.74 Other complications due to other vascular device, implant, and graft — (Use additional code to identify complication: 338.18-338.19, 338.28-338.29)

997.79 Vascular complications of other vessels — (Use additional code to identify complications)

ICD-9-CM Procedural

38.05 Incision of other thoracic vessels

34101-34111

34101 Embolectomy or thrombectomy, with or without catheter; axillary, brachial, innominate, subclavian artery, by arm incision

34111 radial or ulnar artery, by arm incision

ICD-9-CM Diagnostic

444.21 Embolism and thrombosis of arteries of upper extremity

444.9 Embolism and thrombosis of unspecified artery ▼

445.01 Atheroembolism of upper extremity

449 Septic arterial embolism — (Use additional code to identify the site of the embolism: 433.0-433.9, 444.01-444.9)

901.1 Innominate and subclavian artery injury

903.01 Axillary artery injury

903.1 Brachial blood vessels injury

903.2 Radial blood vessels injury

903.3 Ulnar blood vessels injury

903.8 Injury to specified blood vessels of upper extremity, other

996.62 Infection and inflammatory reaction due to other vascular device, implant, and graft — (Use additional code to identify specified infections)

996.74 Other complications due to other vascular device, implant, and graft — (Use additional code to identify complication: 338.18-338.19, 338.28-338.29)

999.2 Other vascular complications of medical care, not elsewhere classified

ICD-9-CM Procedural

38.03 Incision of upper limb vessels

38.05 Incision of other thoracic vessels

34151

34151 Embolectomy or thrombectomy, with or without catheter; renal, celiac, mesentery, aortoiliac artery, by abdominal incision

ICD-9-CM Diagnostic

440.0 Atherosclerosis of aorta

440.1 Atherosclerosis of renal artery

444.01 Saddle embolus of abdominal aorta

444.09 Other arterial embolism and thrombosis of abdominal aorta

444.81 Embolism and thrombosis of iliac artery

444.89 Embolism and thrombosis of other specified artery

445.81 Atheroembolism of kidney — (Use additional code for any associated acute kidney failure or chronic kidney disease: 584, 585)

445.89 Atheroembolism of other site

449 Septic arterial embolism — (Use additional code to identify the site of the embolism: 433.0-433.9, 444.01-444.9)

557.0 Acute vascular insufficiency of intestine

557.9 Unspecified vascular insufficiency of intestine ▼

593.81 Vascular disorders of kidney

673.24 Obstetrical blood-clot embolism, postpartum condition or complication ♀

902.24 Injury to specified branches of celiac axis, other

902.25 Superior mesenteric artery (trunk) injury

902.26 Injury to primary branches of superior mesenteric artery

902.27 Inferior mesenteric artery injury

902.41 Renal artery injury

902.49 Renal blood vessel injury, other

902.59 Injury to iliac blood vessels, other

908.4 Late effect of injury to blood vessel of thorax, abdomen, and pelvis

996.62 Infection and inflammatory reaction due to other vascular device, implant, and graft — (Use additional code to identify specified infections)

996.74 Other complications due to other vascular device, implant, and graft — (Use additional code to identify complication: 338.18-338.19, 338.28-338.29)

997.71 Vascular complications of mesenteric artery — (Use additional code to identify complications)

997.72 Vascular complications of renal artery — (Use additional code to identify complications)

997.79 Vascular complications of other vessels — (Use additional code to identify complications)

999.2 Other vascular complications of medical care, not elsewhere classified

ICD-9-CM Procedural

38.04 Incision of aorta

38.06 Incision of abdominal arteries

34201

34201 Embolectomy or thrombectomy, with or without catheter; femoropopliteal, aortoiliac artery, by leg incision

ICD-9-CM Diagnostic

444.01 Saddle embolus of abdominal aorta
444.09 Other arterial embolism and thrombosis of abdominal aorta
444.22 Embolism and thrombosis of arteries of lower extremity
445.02 Atheroembolism of lower extremity
449 Septic arterial embolism — (Use additional code to identify the site of the embolism: 433.0-433.9, 444.01-444.9)
733.93 Stress fracture of tibia or fibula — (Use additional external cause code(s) to identify the cause of the stress fracture)
733.95 Stress fracture of other bone — (Use additional external cause code(s) to identify the cause of the stress fracture)
733.97 Stress fracture of shaft of femur — (Use additional external cause code(s) to identify the cause of the stress fracture)
821.00 Closed fracture of unspecified part of femur ▽
823.80 Closed fracture of unspecified part of tibia ▽
823.81 Closed fracture of unspecified part of fibula ▽
823.82 Closed fracture of unspecified part of fibula with tibia ▽
824.8 Unspecified closed fracture of ankle ▽
902.59 Injury to iliac blood vessels, other
904.0 Common femoral artery injury
904.41 Popliteal artery injury
996.74 Other complications due to other vascular device, implant, and graft — (Use additional code to identify complication: 338.18-338.19, 338.28-338.29)
996.77 Other complications due to internal joint prosthesis — (Use additional code to identify complication: 338.18-338.19, 338.28-338.29)
996.79 Other complications due to other internal prosthetic device, implant, and graft — (Use additional code to identify complication: 338.18-338.19, 338.28-338.29)
997.79 Vascular complications of other vessels — (Use additional code to identify complications)
999.2 Other vascular complications of medical care, not elsewhere classified

ICD-9-CM Procedural

38.04 Incision of aorta
38.06 Incision of abdominal arteries
38.08 Incision of lower limb arteries

34203

34203 Embolectomy or thrombectomy, with or without catheter; popliteal-tibio-peroneal artery, by leg incision

ICD-9-CM Diagnostic

444.22 Embolism and thrombosis of arteries of lower extremity
445.02 Atheroembolism of lower extremity
449 Septic arterial embolism — (Use additional code to identify the site of the embolism: 433.0-433.9, 444.01-444.9)
733.93 Stress fracture of tibia or fibula — (Use additional external cause code(s) to identify the cause of the stress fracture)
733.95 Stress fracture of other bone — (Use additional external cause code(s) to identify the cause of the stress fracture)
733.97 Stress fracture of shaft of femur — (Use additional external cause code(s) to identify the cause of the stress fracture)
823.80 Closed fracture of unspecified part of tibia ▽
823.81 Closed fracture of unspecified part of fibula ▽
823.82 Closed fracture of unspecified part of fibula with tibia ▽
824.8 Unspecified closed fracture of ankle ▽
904.41 Popliteal artery injury
904.51 Anterior tibial artery injury
904.53 Posterior tibial artery injury
904.7 Injury to specified blood vessels of lower extremity, other
996.74 Other complications due to other vascular device, implant, and graft — (Use additional code to identify complication: 338.18-338.19, 338.28-338.29)
996.77 Other complications due to internal joint prosthesis — (Use additional code to identify complication: 338.18-338.19, 338.28-338.29)
996.79 Other complications due to other internal prosthetic device, implant, and graft — (Use additional code to identify complication: 338.18-338.19, 338.28-338.29)
999.2 Other vascular complications of medical care, not elsewhere classified

ICD-9-CM Procedural

38.08 Incision of lower limb arteries

34401

34401 Thrombectomy, direct or with catheter; vena cava, iliac vein, by abdominal incision

ICD-9-CM Diagnostic

449 Septic arterial embolism — (Use additional code to identify the site of the embolism: 433.0-433.9, 444.01-444.9)
451.81 Phlebitis and thrombophlebitis of iliac vein — (Use additional E code to identify drug, if drug-induced)
453.2 Other venous embolism and thrombosis, of inferior vena cava
453.41 Acute venous embolism and thrombosis of deep vessels of proximal lower extremity
453.51 Chronic venous embolism and thrombosis of deep vessels of proximal lower extremity — (Use additional code, if applicable, for associated long-term (current) use of anticoagulants (V58.61))
453.77 Chronic venous embolism and thrombosis of other thoracic veins — (Use additional code, if applicable, for associated long-term (current) use of anticoagulants (V58.61))
453.87 Acute venous embolism and thrombosis of other thoracic veins
671.44 Deep phlebothrombosis, postpartum condition or complication — (Use additional code to identify the deep vein thrombosis: (453.40-453.42, 453.50-453.52, 453.72-453.79, 453.82-453.89)(Use additional code for long term (current) use of anticoagulants, if applicable (V58.61)) ♀
785.9 Other symptoms involving cardiovascular system
789.00 Abdominal pain, unspecified site ▽
793.6 Nonspecific (abnormal) findings on radiological and other examination of abdominal area, including retroperitoneum
902.54 Iliac vein injury
908.4 Late effect of injury to blood vessel of thorax, abdomen, and pelvis
908.6 Late effect of certain complications of trauma
996.70 Other complications due to unspecified device, implant, and graft — (Use additional code to identify complication: 338.18-338.19, 338.28-338.29) ▽
996.74 Other complications due to other vascular device, implant, and graft — (Use additional code to identify complication: 338.18-338.19, 338.28-338.29)
996.79 Other complications due to other internal prosthetic device, implant, and graft — (Use additional code to identify complication: 338.18-338.19, 338.28-338.29)
997.2 Peripheral vascular complications — (Use additional code to identify complications)
997.79 Vascular complications of other vessels — (Use additional code to identify complications)
999.2 Other vascular complications of medical care, not elsewhere classified

ICD-9-CM Procedural

38.07 Incision of abdominal veins

34421-34451

34421 Thrombectomy, direct or with catheter; vena cava, iliac, femoropopliteal vein, by leg incision
34451 vena cava, iliac, femoropopliteal vein, by abdominal and leg incision

ICD-9-CM Diagnostic

449 Septic arterial embolism — (Use additional code to identify the site of the embolism: 433.0-433.9, 444.01-444.9)

451.0 Phlebitis and thrombophlebitis of superficial vessels of lower extremities — (Use additional E code to identify drug, if drug-induced)
451.11 Phlebitis and thrombophlebitis of femoral vein (deep) (superficial) — (Use additional E code to identify drug, if drug-induced)
451.19 Phlebitis and thrombophlebitis of other deep vessels of lower extremities — (Use additional E code to identify drug, if drug-induced)
451.81 Phlebitis and thrombophlebitis of iliac vein — (Use additional E code to identify drug, if drug-induced)
453.2 Other venous embolism and thrombosis, of inferior vena cava
453.40 Acute venous embolism and thrombosis of unspecified deep vessels of lower extremity ▽
453.41 Acute venous embolism and thrombosis of deep vessels of proximal lower extremity
453.50 Chronic venous embolism and thrombosis of unspecified deep vessels of lower extremity — (Use additional code, if applicable, for associated long-term (current) use of anticoagulants (V58.61)) ▽
453.51 Chronic venous embolism and thrombosis of deep vessels of proximal lower extremity — (Use additional code, if applicable, for associated long-term (current) use of anticoagulants (V58.61))
453.77 Chronic venous embolism and thrombosis of other thoracic veins — (Use additional code, if applicable, for associated long-term (current) use of anticoagulants (V58.61))
453.87 Acute venous embolism and thrombosis of other thoracic veins
453.89 Acute venous embolism and thrombosis of other specified veins
902.54 Iliac vein injury
904.2 Femoral vein injury
996.70 Other complications due to unspecified device, implant, and graft — (Use additional code to identify complication: 338.18-338.19, 338.28-338.29) ▽
996.74 Other complications due to other vascular device, implant, and graft — (Use additional code to identify complication: 338.18-338.19, 338.28-338.29)
997.79 Vascular complications of other vessels — (Use additional code to identify complications)
999.2 Other vascular complications of medical care, not elsewhere classified

ICD-9-CM Procedural

38.07 Incision of abdominal veins
38.09 Incision of lower limb veins

34471-34490

34471 Thrombectomy, direct or with catheter; subclavian vein, by neck incision
34490 axillary and subclavian vein, by arm incision

ICD-9-CM Diagnostic

449 Septic arterial embolism — (Use additional code to identify the site of the embolism: 433.0-433.9, 444.01-444.9)
451.89 Phlebitis and thrombophlebitis of other site — (Use additional E code to identify drug, if drug-induced)
453.74 Chronic venous embolism and thrombosis of axillary veins — (Use additional code, if applicable, for associated long-term (current) use of anticoagulants (V58.61))
453.75 Chronic venous embolism and thrombosis of subclavian veins — (Use additional code, if applicable, for associated long-term (current) use of anticoagulants (V58.61))
453.84 Acute venous embolism and thrombosis of axillary veins
453.85 Acute venous embolism and thrombosis of subclavian veins
453.9 Embolism and thrombosis of unspecified site ▽
901.3 Innominate and subclavian vein injury
903.02 Axillary vein injury
996.74 Other complications due to other vascular device, implant, and graft — (Use additional code to identify complication: 338.18-338.19, 338.28-338.29)
997.79 Vascular complications of other vessels — (Use additional code to identify complications)

ICD-9-CM Procedural

38.02 Incision of other vessels of head and neck
38.03 Incision of upper limb vessels
38.05 Incision of other thoracic vessels

34501

34501 Valvuloplasty, femoral vein

ICD-9-CM Diagnostic

454.0 Varicose veins of lower extremities with ulcer
454.1 Varicose veins of lower extremities with inflammation
454.2 Varicose veins of lower extremities with ulcer and inflammation
454.8 Varicose veins of the lower extremities with other complications
454.9 Asymptomatic varicose veins
459.10 Postphlebitic syndrome without complications
459.11 Postphlebitic syndrome with ulcer
459.12 Postphlebitic syndrome with inflammation
459.13 Postphlebitic syndrome with ulcer and inflammation
459.19 Postphlebitic syndrome with other complication
459.81 Unspecified venous (peripheral) insufficiency — (Use additional code for any associated ulceration: 707.10-707.19, 707.8, 707.9) ▽
747.60 Congenital anomaly of the peripheral vascular system, unspecified site ▽
747.64 Congenital lower limb vessel anomaly
904.2 Femoral vein injury

ICD-9-CM Procedural

39.59 Other repair of vessel

34502

34502 Reconstruction of vena cava, any method

ICD-9-CM Diagnostic

449 Septic arterial embolism — (Use additional code to identify the site of the embolism: 433.0-433.9, 444.01-444.9)
453.2 Other venous embolism and thrombosis, of inferior vena cava
453.77 Chronic venous embolism and thrombosis of other thoracic veins — (Use additional code, if applicable, for associated long-term (current) use of anticoagulants (V58.61))
453.87 Acute venous embolism and thrombosis of other thoracic veins
459.2 Compression of vein
747.41 Total congenital anomalous pulmonary venous connection
747.49 Other congenital anomalies of great veins
861.11 Heart contusion with open wound into thorax
862.9 Injury to multiple and unspecified intrathoracic organs with open wound into cavity
901.2 Superior vena cava injury
901.83 Injury to multiple blood vessels of thorax
902.10 Unspecified inferior vena cava injury ▽
902.19 Injury to specified branches of inferior vena cava, other
908.4 Late effect of injury to blood vessel of thorax, abdomen, and pelvis
997.79 Vascular complications of other vessels — (Use additional code to identify complications)

ICD-9-CM Procedural

38.47 Resection of abdominal veins with replacement
39.57 Repair of blood vessel with synthetic patch graft
39.59 Other repair of vessel

34510

34510 Venous valve transposition, any vein donor

ICD-9-CM Diagnostic

454.0 Varicose veins of lower extremities with ulcer
454.1 Varicose veins of lower extremities with inflammation
454.2 Varicose veins of lower extremities with ulcer and inflammation
454.8 Varicose veins of the lower extremities with other complications
454.9 Asymptomatic varicose veins

459.10 Postphlebitic syndrome without complications
459.11 Postphlebitic syndrome with ulcer
459.12 Postphlebitic syndrome with inflammation
459.13 Postphlebitic syndrome with ulcer and inflammation
459.19 Postphlebitic syndrome with other complication
459.81 Unspecified venous (peripheral) insufficiency — (Use additional code for any associated ulceration: 707.10-707.19, 707.8, 707.9) ▽
747.60 Congenital anomaly of the peripheral vascular system, unspecified site ▽
747.64 Congenital lower limb vessel anomaly
904.2 Femoral vein injury

ICD-9-CM Procedural

38.40 Resection of vessel with replacement, unspecified site
38.42 Resection of other vessels of head and neck with replacement
38.43 Resection of upper limb vessels with replacement
38.45 Resection of other thoracic vessels with replacement

34520

34520 Cross-over vein graft to venous system

ICD-9-CM Diagnostic

454.0 Varicose veins of lower extremities with ulcer
454.1 Varicose veins of lower extremities with inflammation
454.2 Varicose veins of lower extremities with ulcer and inflammation
454.8 Varicose veins of the lower extremities with other complications
454.9 Asymptomatic varicose veins
459.10 Postphlebitic syndrome without complications
459.11 Postphlebitic syndrome with ulcer
459.12 Postphlebitic syndrome with inflammation
459.13 Postphlebitic syndrome with ulcer and inflammation
459.19 Postphlebitic syndrome with other complication
459.2 Compression of vein
459.81 Unspecified venous (peripheral) insufficiency — (Use additional code for any associated ulceration: 707.10-707.19, 707.8, 707.9) ▽
747.49 Other congenital anomalies of great veins
747.60 Congenital anomaly of the peripheral vascular system, unspecified site ▽
747.64 Congenital lower limb vessel anomaly
904.2 Femoral vein injury

ICD-9-CM Procedural

39.23 Other intrathoracic vascular shunt or bypass
39.29 Other (peripheral) vascular shunt or bypass

34530

34530 Saphenopopliteal vein anastomosis

ICD-9-CM Diagnostic

454.0 Varicose veins of lower extremities with ulcer
454.1 Varicose veins of lower extremities with inflammation
454.2 Varicose veins of lower extremities with ulcer and inflammation
454.8 Varicose veins of the lower extremities with other complications
454.9 Asymptomatic varicose veins
459.10 Postphlebitic syndrome without complications
459.11 Postphlebitic syndrome with ulcer
459.12 Postphlebitic syndrome with inflammation
459.13 Postphlebitic syndrome with ulcer and inflammation
459.19 Postphlebitic syndrome with other complication
459.2 Compression of vein
459.81 Unspecified venous (peripheral) insufficiency — (Use additional code for any associated ulceration: 707.10-707.19, 707.8, 707.9) ▽
891.1 Open wound of knee, leg (except thigh), and ankle, complicated
904.3 Saphenous vein injury
904.42 Popliteal vein injury
904.7 Injury to specified blood vessels of lower extremity, other
998.2 Accidental puncture or laceration during procedure

ICD-9-CM Procedural

38.39 Resection of lower limb veins with anastomosis

34800-34805

34800 Endovascular repair of infrarenal abdominal aortic aneurysm or dissection; using aorto-aortic tube prosthesis
34802 using modular bifurcated prosthesis (1 docking limb)
34803 using modular bifurcated prosthesis (2 docking limbs)
34804 using unibody bifurcated prosthesis
34805 using aorto-uniiliac or aorto-unifemoral prosthesis

ICD-9-CM Diagnostic

440.0 Atherosclerosis of aorta
440.1 Atherosclerosis of renal artery
440.8 Atherosclerosis of other specified arteries
441.02 Dissecting aortic aneurysm (any part), abdominal
441.4 Abdominal aneurysm without mention of rupture
442.1 Aneurysm of renal artery
442.2 Aneurysm of iliac artery
444.01 Saddle embolus of abdominal aorta
444.09 Other arterial embolism and thrombosis of abdominal aorta
449 Septic arterial embolism — (Use additional code to identify the site of the embolism: 433.0-433.9, 444.01-444.9)
557.0 Acute vascular insufficiency of intestine
557.1 Chronic vascular insufficiency of intestine
593.81 Vascular disorders of kidney
747.89 Other specified congenital anomaly of circulatory system
902.50 Unspecified iliac vessel(s) injury ▽
902.51 Hypogastric artery injury
902.53 Iliac artery injury
908.4 Late effect of injury to blood vessel of thorax, abdomen, and pelvis
997.79 Vascular complications of other vessels — (Use additional code to identify complications)

ICD-9-CM Procedural

39.71 Endovascular implantation of other graft in abdominal aorta

34806

34806 Transcatheter placement of wireless physiologic sensor in aneurysmal sac during endovascular repair, including radiological supervision and interpretation, instrument calibration, and collection of pressure data (List separately in addition to code for primary procedure)

ICD-9-CM Diagnostic

441.01 Dissecting aortic aneurysm (any part), thoracic
441.1 Thoracic aneurysm, ruptured
441.2 Thoracic aneurysm without mention of rupture
444.1 Embolism and thrombosis of thoracic aorta
901.0 Thoracic aorta injury
901.1 Innominate and subclavian artery injury

ICD-9-CM Procedural

00.58 Insertion of intra-aneurysm sac pressure monitoring device (intraoperative)

34812

34812 Open femoral artery exposure for delivery of endovascular prosthesis, by groin incision, unilateral

ICD-9-CM Diagnostic

440.0 Atherosclerosis of aorta
440.1 Atherosclerosis of renal artery
440.8 Atherosclerosis of other specified arteries
441.02 Dissecting aortic aneurysm (any part), abdominal
441.4 Abdominal aneurysm without mention of rupture
442.1 Aneurysm of renal artery
442.2 Aneurysm of iliac artery
444.01 Saddle embolus of abdominal aorta
444.09 Other arterial embolism and thrombosis of abdominal aorta
449 Septic arterial embolism — (Use additional code to identify the site of the embolism: 433.0-433.9, 444.01-444.9)
557.0 Acute vascular insufficiency of intestine
557.1 Chronic vascular insufficiency of intestine
593.81 Vascular disorders of kidney
747.89 Other specified congenital anomaly of circulatory system
902.50 Unspecified iliac vessel(s) injury
902.51 Hypogastric artery injury
902.53 Iliac artery injury
908.4 Late effect of injury to blood vessel of thorax, abdomen, and pelvis
997.79 Vascular complications of other vessels — (Use additional code to identify complications)

ICD-9-CM Procedural

39.71 Endovascular implantation of other graft in abdominal aorta
39.78 Endovascular implantation of branching or fenestrated graft(s) in aorta

34813

34813 Placement of femoral-femoral prosthetic graft during endovascular aortic aneurysm repair (List separately in addition to code for primary procedure)

ICD-9-CM Diagnostic

440.20 Atherosclerosis of native arteries of the extremities, unspecified
440.21 Atherosclerosis of native arteries of the extremities with intermittent claudication
440.24 Atherosclerosis of native arteries of the extremities with gangrene — (Use additional code for any associated ulceration: 707.10-707.19, 707.8, 707.9)
442.3 Aneurysm of artery of lower extremity
443.29 Dissection of other artery
443.9 Unspecified peripheral vascular disease
447.1 Stricture of artery
449 Septic arterial embolism — (Use additional code to identify the site of the embolism: 433.0-433.9, 444.01-444.9)
459.9 Unspecified circulatory system disorder
747.69 Congenital anomaly of other specified site of peripheral vascular system
904.0 Common femoral artery injury
904.1 Superficial femoral artery injury
908.3 Late effect of injury to blood vessel of head, neck, and extremities
996.1 Mechanical complication of other vascular device, implant, and graft
996.74 Other complications due to other vascular device, implant, and graft — (Use additional code to identify complication: 338.18-338.19, 338.28-338.29)
997.79 Vascular complications of other vessels — (Use additional code to identify complications)

ICD-9-CM Procedural

39.79 Other endovascular procedures on other vessels

34820

34820 Open iliac artery exposure for delivery of endovascular prosthesis or iliac occlusion during endovascular therapy, by abdominal or retroperitoneal incision, unilateral

ICD-9-CM Diagnostic

440.0 Atherosclerosis of aorta
440.1 Atherosclerosis of renal artery
440.8 Atherosclerosis of other specified arteries
441.02 Dissecting aortic aneurysm (any part), abdominal
441.4 Abdominal aneurysm without mention of rupture
442.1 Aneurysm of renal artery
442.2 Aneurysm of iliac artery
443.22 Dissection of iliac artery
444.01 Saddle embolus of abdominal aorta
444.09 Other arterial embolism and thrombosis of abdominal aorta
449 Septic arterial embolism — (Use additional code to identify the site of the embolism: 433.0-433.9, 444.01-444.9)
557.0 Acute vascular insufficiency of intestine
557.1 Chronic vascular insufficiency of intestine
593.81 Vascular disorders of kidney
747.89 Other specified congenital anomaly of circulatory system
902.50 Unspecified iliac vessel(s) injury
902.51 Hypogastric artery injury
902.53 Iliac artery injury
908.4 Late effect of injury to blood vessel of thorax, abdomen, and pelvis
997.79 Vascular complications of other vessels — (Use additional code to identify complications)

ICD-9-CM Procedural

38.87 Other surgical occlusion of abdominal veins
39.79 Other endovascular procedures on other vessels

34825-34826

34825 Placement of proximal or distal extension prosthesis for endovascular repair of infrarenal abdominal aortic or iliac aneurysm, false aneurysm, or dissection; initial vessel
34826 each additional vessel (List separately in addition to code for primary procedure)

ICD-9-CM Diagnostic

440.0 Atherosclerosis of aorta
440.8 Atherosclerosis of other specified arteries
441.02 Dissecting aortic aneurysm (any part), abdominal
441.3 Abdominal aneurysm, ruptured
441.4 Abdominal aneurysm without mention of rupture
442.2 Aneurysm of iliac artery
443.22 Dissection of iliac artery
444.01 Saddle embolus of abdominal aorta
444.09 Other arterial embolism and thrombosis of abdominal aorta
444.81 Embolism and thrombosis of iliac artery
449 Septic arterial embolism — (Use additional code to identify the site of the embolism: 433.0-433.9, 444.01-444.9)
902.50 Unspecified iliac vessel(s) injury
902.53 Iliac artery injury
908.4 Late effect of injury to blood vessel of thorax, abdomen, and pelvis
997.79 Vascular complications of other vessels — (Use additional code to identify complications)

ICD-9-CM Procedural

39.71 Endovascular implantation of other graft in abdominal aorta
39.78 Endovascular implantation of branching or fenestrated graft(s) in aorta
39.79 Other endovascular procedures on other vessels

34830-34832

34830 Open repair of infrarenal aortic aneurysm or dissection, plus repair of associated arterial trauma, following unsuccessful endovascular repair; tube prosthesis

34831 aorto-bi-iliac prosthesis

34832 aorto-bifemoral prosthesis

ICD-9-CM Diagnostic

440.0 Atherosclerosis of aorta
440.1 Atherosclerosis of renal artery
440.8 Atherosclerosis of other specified arteries
441.02 Dissecting aortic aneurysm (any part), abdominal
441.4 Abdominal aneurysm without mention of rupture
442.1 Aneurysm of renal artery
442.2 Aneurysm of iliac artery
443.22 Dissection of iliac artery
444.01 Saddle embolus of abdominal aorta
444.09 Other arterial embolism and thrombosis of abdominal aorta
449 Septic arterial embolism — (Use additional code to identify the site of the embolism: 433.0-433.9, 444.01-444.9)
557.0 Acute vascular insufficiency of intestine
557.1 Chronic vascular insufficiency of intestine
593.81 Vascular disorders of kidney
747.89 Other specified congenital anomaly of circulatory system
902.50 Unspecified iliac vessel(s) injury ▽
902.51 Hypogastric artery injury
902.53 Iliac artery injury
908.4 Late effect of injury to blood vessel of thorax, abdomen, and pelvis
997.79 Vascular complications of other vessels — (Use additional code to identify complications)
998.11 Hemorrhage complicating a procedure
998.12 Hematoma complicating a procedure
998.2 Accidental puncture or laceration during procedure

ICD-9-CM Procedural

38.44 Resection of abdominal aorta with replacement

34833-34834

34833 Open iliac artery exposure with creation of conduit for delivery of aortic or iliac endovascular prosthesis, by abdominal or retroperitoneal incision, unilateral

34834 Open brachial artery exposure to assist in the deployment of aortic or iliac endovascular prosthesis by arm incision, unilateral

ICD-9-CM Diagnostic

440.0 Atherosclerosis of aorta
440.8 Atherosclerosis of other specified arteries
441.02 Dissecting aortic aneurysm (any part), abdominal
441.3 Abdominal aneurysm, ruptured
441.4 Abdominal aneurysm without mention of rupture
442.2 Aneurysm of iliac artery
444.01 Saddle embolus of abdominal aorta
444.09 Other arterial embolism and thrombosis of abdominal aorta
444.81 Embolism and thrombosis of iliac artery
444.89 Embolism and thrombosis of other specified artery
449 Septic arterial embolism — (Use additional code to identify the site of the embolism: 433.0-433.9, 444.01-444.9)
557.0 Acute vascular insufficiency of intestine
557.1 Chronic vascular insufficiency of intestine
747.89 Other specified congenital anomaly of circulatory system
902.50 Unspecified iliac vessel(s) injury ▽
902.51 Hypogastric artery injury
902.53 Iliac artery injury
908.4 Late effect of injury to blood vessel of thorax, abdomen, and pelvis
997.71 Vascular complications of mesenteric artery — (Use additional code to identify complications)
997.79 Vascular complications of other vessels — (Use additional code to identify complications)
998.11 Hemorrhage complicating a procedure
998.2 Accidental puncture or laceration during procedure

ICD-9-CM Procedural

39.78 Endovascular implantation of branching or fenestrated graft(s) in aorta
39.79 Other endovascular procedures on other vessels

34841-34844

34841 Endovascular repair of visceral aorta (eg, aneurysm, pseudoaneurysm, dissection, penetrating ulcer, intramural hematoma, or traumatic disruption) by deployment of a fenestrated visceral aortic endograft and all associated radiological supervision and interpretation, including target zone angioplasty, when performed; including one visceral artery endoprosthesis (superior mesenteric, celiac or renal artery)

34842 including two visceral artery endoprostheses (superior mesenteric, celiac and/or renal artery[s])

34843 including three visceral artery endoprostheses (superior mesenteric, celiac and/or renal artery[s])

34844 including four or more visceral artery endoprostheses (superior mesenteric, celiac and/or renal artery[s])

ICD-9-CM Diagnostic

093.0 Aneurysm of aorta, specified as syphilitic
441.02 Dissecting aortic aneurysm (any part), abdominal
441.03 Dissecting aortic aneurysm (any part), thoracoabdominal
441.3 Abdominal aneurysm, ruptured
441.4 Abdominal aneurysm without mention of rupture
441.5 Aortic aneurysm of unspecified site, ruptured ▽
441.9 Aortic aneurysm of unspecified site without mention of rupture ▽
442.1 Aneurysm of renal artery
442.84 Aneurysm of other visceral artery
443.23 Dissection of renal artery
443.29 Dissection of other artery
747.29 Other congenital anomaly of aorta
902.0 Abdominal aorta injury
902.20 Unspecified celiac and mesenteric artery injury ▽
902.23 Splenic artery injury
902.24 Injury to specified branches of celiac axis, other
902.25 Superior mesenteric artery (trunk) injury
902.26 Injury to primary branches of superior mesenteric artery
902.41 Renal artery injury
902.49 Renal blood vessel injury, other
902.87 Injury to multiple blood vessels of abdomen and pelvis
902.89 Injury to specified blood vessels of abdomen and pelvis, other
996.1 Mechanical complication of other vascular device, implant, and graft
996.62 Infection and inflammatory reaction due to other vascular device, implant, and graft — (Use additional code to identify specified infections)
996.74 Other complications due to other vascular device, implant, and graft — (Use additional code to identify complication: 338.18-338.19, 338.28-338.29)
997.71 Vascular complications of mesenteric artery — (Use additional code to identify complications)
997.72 Vascular complications of renal artery — (Use additional code to identify complications)
997.79 Vascular complications of other vessels — (Use additional code to identify complications)

ICD-9-CM Procedural

39.78 Endovascular implantation of branching or fenestrated graft(s) in aorta

34845-34848

34845 Endovascular repair of visceral aorta and infrarenal abdominal aorta (eg, aneurysm, pseudoaneurysm, dissection, penetrating ulcer, intramural hematoma, or traumatic disruption) with a fenestrated visceral aortic endograft and concomitant unibody or modular infrarenal aortic endograft and all associated radiological supervision and interpretation, including target zone angioplasty, when performed; including one visceral artery endoprosthesis (superior mesenteric, celiac or renal artery)

34846 including two visceral artery endoprostheses (superior mesenteric, celiac and/or renal artery[s])

34847 including three visceral artery endoprostheses (superior mesenteric, celiac and/or renal artery[s])

34848 including four or more visceral artery endoprostheses (superior mesenteric, celiac and/or renal artery[s])

ICD-9-CM Diagnostic

093.0 Aneurysm of aorta, specified as syphilitic
441.02 Dissecting aortic aneurysm (any part), abdominal
441.03 Dissecting aortic aneurysm (any part), thoracoabdominal
441.3 Abdominal aneurysm, ruptured
441.4 Abdominal aneurysm without mention of rupture
441.5 Aortic aneurysm of unspecified site, ruptured ▽
441.9 Aortic aneurysm of unspecified site without mention of rupture ▽
442.1 Aneurysm of renal artery
442.84 Aneurysm of other visceral artery
443.23 Dissection of renal artery
443.29 Dissection of other artery
747.29 Other congenital anomaly of aorta
902.0 Abdominal aorta injury
902.20 Unspecified celiac and mesenteric artery injury ▽
902.23 Splenic artery injury
902.24 Injury to specified branches of celiac axis, other
902.25 Superior mesenteric artery (trunk) injury
902.26 Injury to primary branches of superior mesenteric artery
902.41 Renal artery injury
902.49 Renal blood vessel injury, other
902.87 Injury to multiple blood vessels of abdomen and pelvis
902.89 Injury to specified blood vessels of abdomen and pelvis, other
996.1 Mechanical complication of other vascular device, implant, and graft
996.62 Infection and inflammatory reaction due to other vascular device, implant, and graft — (Use additional code to identify specified infections)
996.74 Other complications due to other vascular device, implant, and graft — (Use additional code to identify complication: 338.18-338.19, 338.28-338.29)
997.71 Vascular complications of mesenteric artery — (Use additional code to identify complications)
997.72 Vascular complications of renal artery — (Use additional code to identify complications)
997.79 Vascular complications of other vessels — (Use additional code to identify complications)

ICD-9-CM Procedural

39.78 Endovascular implantation of branching or fenestrated graft(s) in aorta

34900

34900 Endovascular repair of iliac artery (eg, aneurysm, pseudoaneurysm, arteriovenous malformation, trauma) using ilio-iliac tube endoprosthesis

ICD-9-CM Diagnostic

442.2 Aneurysm of iliac artery
443.22 Dissection of iliac artery
444.81 Embolism and thrombosis of iliac artery
449 Septic arterial embolism — (Use additional code to identify the site of the embolism: 433.0-433.9, 444.01-444.9)
747.64 Congenital lower limb vessel anomaly
747.89 Other specified congenital anomaly of circulatory system
902.50 Unspecified iliac vessel(s) injury ▽
902.51 Hypogastric artery injury
902.53 Iliac artery injury
908.4 Late effect of injury to blood vessel of thorax, abdomen, and pelvis
997.2 Peripheral vascular complications — (Use additional code to identify complications)
997.79 Vascular complications of other vessels — (Use additional code to identify complications)
998.11 Hemorrhage complicating a procedure
998.12 Hematoma complicating a procedure
998.2 Accidental puncture or laceration during procedure

ICD-9-CM Procedural

39.79 Other endovascular procedures on other vessels

35001-35002

35001 Direct repair of aneurysm, pseudoaneurysm, or excision (partial or total) and graft insertion, with or without patch graft; for aneurysm and associated occlusive disease, carotid, subclavian artery, by neck incision

35002 for ruptured aneurysm, carotid, subclavian artery, by neck incision

ICD-9-CM Diagnostic

433.10 Occlusion and stenosis of carotid artery without mention of cerebral infarction — (Use additional code, if applicable, to identify status post administration of tPA (rtPA) in a different facility within the last 24 hours prior to admission to current facility: V45.88)
433.11 Occlusion and stenosis of carotid artery with cerebral infarction — (Use additional code, if applicable, to identify status post administration of tPA (rtPA) in a different facility within the last 24 hours prior to admission to current facility: V45.88)
433.30 Occlusion and stenosis of multiple and bilateral precerebral arteries without mention of cerebral infarction — (Use additional code, if applicable, to identify status post administration of tPA (rtPA) in a different facility within the last 24 hours prior to admission to current facility: V45.88)
435.2 Subclavian steal syndrome — (Use additional code to identify presence of hypertension)
442.81 Aneurysm of artery of neck
442.82 Aneurysm of subclavian artery
443.21 Dissection of carotid artery
443.29 Dissection of other artery
447.1 Stricture of artery
747.89 Other specified congenital anomaly of circulatory system
900.00 Injury to carotid artery, unspecified ▽
900.01 Common carotid artery injury
900.02 External carotid artery injury
900.03 Internal carotid artery injury
900.82 Injury to multiple blood vessels of head and neck
901.1 Innominate and subclavian artery injury
908.3 Late effect of injury to blood vessel of head, neck, and extremities
996.74 Other complications due to other vascular device, implant, and graft — (Use additional code to identify complication: 338.18-338.19, 338.28-338.29)
997.2 Peripheral vascular complications — (Use additional code to identify complications)
997.79 Vascular complications of other vessels — (Use additional code to identify complications)

ICD-9-CM Procedural

38.42 Resection of other vessels of head and neck with replacement
38.45 Resection of other thoracic vessels with replacement
39.51 Clipping of aneurysm
39.52 Other repair of aneurysm

35005

35005 Direct repair of aneurysm, pseudoaneurysm, or excision (partial or total) and graft insertion, with or without patch graft; for aneurysm, pseudoaneurysm, and associated occlusive disease, vertebral artery

ICD-9-CM Diagnostic

433.20 Occlusion and stenosis of vertebral artery without mention of cerebral infarction — (Use additional code, if applicable, to identify status post administration of tPA (rtPA) in a different facility within the last 24 hours prior to admission to current facility: V45.88)

433.30 Occlusion and stenosis of multiple and bilateral precerebral arteries without mention of cerebral infarction — (Use additional code, if applicable, to identify status post administration of tPA (rtPA) in a different facility within the last 24 hours prior to admission to current facility: V45.88)

435.2 Subclavian steal syndrome — (Use additional code to identify presence of hypertension)

442.81 Aneurysm of artery of neck

442.89 Aneurysm of other specified artery

443.24 Dissection of vertebral artery

447.1 Stricture of artery

908.3 Late effect of injury to blood vessel of head, neck, and extremities

ICD-9-CM Procedural

38.32 Resection of other vessels of head and neck with anastomosis

38.42 Resection of other vessels of head and neck with replacement

39.51 Clipping of aneurysm

39.52 Other repair of aneurysm

35011-35013

35011 Direct repair of aneurysm, pseudoaneurysm, or excision (partial or total) and graft insertion, with or without patch graft; for aneurysm and associated occlusive disease, axillary-brachial artery, by arm incision

35013 for ruptured aneurysm, axillary-brachial artery, by arm incision

ICD-9-CM Diagnostic

440.20 Atherosclerosis of native arteries of the extremities, unspecified ▽

440.21 Atherosclerosis of native arteries of the extremities with intermittent claudication

440.22 Atherosclerosis of native arteries of the extremities with rest pain

442.0 Aneurysm of artery of upper extremity

443.29 Dissection of other artery

444.21 Embolism and thrombosis of arteries of upper extremity

445.01 Atheroembolism of upper extremity

447.1 Stricture of artery

747.63 Congenital upper limb vessel anomaly

903.01 Axillary artery injury

903.1 Brachial blood vessels injury

908.3 Late effect of injury to blood vessel of head, neck, and extremities

ICD-9-CM Procedural

38.33 Resection of upper limb vessels with anastomosis

38.43 Resection of upper limb vessels with replacement

39.51 Clipping of aneurysm

39.52 Other repair of aneurysm

35021-35022

35021 Direct repair of aneurysm, pseudoaneurysm, or excision (partial or total) and graft insertion, with or without patch graft; for aneurysm, pseudoaneurysm, and associated occlusive disease, innominate, subclavian artery, by thoracic incision

35022 for ruptured aneurysm, innominate, subclavian artery, by thoracic incision

ICD-9-CM Diagnostic

435.2 Subclavian steal syndrome — (Use additional code to identify presence of hypertension)

440.8 Atherosclerosis of other specified arteries

442.82 Aneurysm of subclavian artery

442.89 Aneurysm of other specified artery

443.29 Dissection of other artery

447.2 Rupture of artery

447.8 Other specified disorders of arteries and arterioles

747.89 Other specified congenital anomaly of circulatory system

901.1 Innominate and subclavian artery injury

908.3 Late effect of injury to blood vessel of head, neck, and extremities

ICD-9-CM Procedural

38.35 Resection of other thoracic vessels with anastomosis

38.45 Resection of other thoracic vessels with replacement

39.51 Clipping of aneurysm

39.52 Other repair of aneurysm

35045

35045 Direct repair of aneurysm, pseudoaneurysm, or excision (partial or total) and graft insertion, with or without patch graft; for aneurysm, pseudoaneurysm, and associated occlusive disease, radial or ulnar artery

ICD-9-CM Diagnostic

440.20 Atherosclerosis of native arteries of the extremities, unspecified ▽

440.21 Atherosclerosis of native arteries of the extremities with intermittent claudication

440.22 Atherosclerosis of native arteries of the extremities with rest pain

442.0 Aneurysm of artery of upper extremity

443.29 Dissection of other artery

444.21 Embolism and thrombosis of arteries of upper extremity

445.01 Atheroembolism of upper extremity

447.1 Stricture of artery

729.5 Pain in soft tissues of limb

747.63 Congenital upper limb vessel anomaly

785.9 Other symptoms involving cardiovascular system

903.2 Radial blood vessels injury

903.3 Ulnar blood vessels injury

903.8 Injury to specified blood vessels of upper extremity, other

908.3 Late effect of injury to blood vessel of head, neck, and extremities

ICD-9-CM Procedural

38.33 Resection of upper limb vessels with anastomosis

38.43 Resection of upper limb vessels with replacement

39.51 Clipping of aneurysm

39.52 Other repair of aneurysm

35081

35081 Direct repair of aneurysm, pseudoaneurysm, or excision (partial or total) and graft insertion, with or without patch graft; for aneurysm, pseudoaneurysm, and associated occlusive disease, abdominal aorta

ICD-9-CM Diagnostic

440.0 Atherosclerosis of aorta

441.4 Abdominal aneurysm without mention of rupture

441.7 Thoracoabdominal aneurysm without mention of rupture

444.01 Saddle embolus of abdominal aorta

444.09 Other arterial embolism and thrombosis of abdominal aorta

458.8 Other specified hypotension

458.9 Unspecified hypotension ▽

557.1 Chronic vascular insufficiency of intestine

789.07 Abdominal pain, generalized

789.09 Abdominal pain, other specified site

902.0 Abdominal aorta injury

908.4 Late effect of injury to blood vessel of thorax, abdomen, and pelvis
996.70 Other complications due to unspecified device, implant, and graft — (Use additional code to identify complication: 338.18-338.19, 338.28-338.29)
997.2 Peripheral vascular complications — (Use additional code to identify complications)
V45.89 Other postprocedural status

ICD-9-CM Procedural

38.34 Resection of aorta with anastomosis
38.44 Resection of abdominal aorta with replacement
38.64 Other excision of abdominal aorta
39.51 Clipping of aneurysm
39.52 Other repair of aneurysm

35082

35082 Direct repair of aneurysm, pseudoaneurysm, or excision (partial or total) and graft insertion, with or without patch graft; for ruptured aneurysm, abdominal aorta

ICD-9-CM Diagnostic

440.0 Atherosclerosis of aorta
441.00 Dissecting aortic aneurysm (any part), unspecified site
441.3 Abdominal aneurysm, ruptured
441.5 Aortic aneurysm of unspecified site, ruptured
557.0 Acute vascular insufficiency of intestine
785.59 Other shock without mention of trauma
788.5 Oliguria and anuria
789.00 Abdominal pain, unspecified site
789.40 Abdominal rigidity, unspecified site
793.6 Nonspecific (abnormal) findings on radiological and other examination of abdominal area, including retroperitoneum
902.0 Abdominal aorta injury
908.4 Late effect of injury to blood vessel of thorax, abdomen, and pelvis

ICD-9-CM Procedural

38.34 Resection of aorta with anastomosis
38.37 Resection of abdominal veins with anastomosis
38.44 Resection of abdominal aorta with replacement
38.64 Other excision of abdominal aorta
39.51 Clipping of aneurysm
39.52 Other repair of aneurysm

35091

35091 Direct repair of aneurysm, pseudoaneurysm, or excision (partial or total) and graft insertion, with or without patch graft; for aneurysm, pseudoaneurysm, and associated occlusive disease, abdominal aorta involving visceral vessels (mesenteric, celiac, renal)

ICD-9-CM Diagnostic

440.0 Atherosclerosis of aorta
440.1 Atherosclerosis of renal artery
440.8 Atherosclerosis of other specified arteries
441.4 Abdominal aneurysm without mention of rupture
442.1 Aneurysm of renal artery
442.83 Aneurysm of splenic artery
442.84 Aneurysm of other visceral artery
443.23 Dissection of renal artery
443.29 Dissection of other artery
444.01 Saddle embolus of abdominal aorta
444.09 Other arterial embolism and thrombosis of abdominal aorta
445.81 Atheroembolism of kidney — (Use additional code for any associated acute kidney failure or chronic kidney disease: 584, 585)
445.89 Atheroembolism of other site
557.0 Acute vascular insufficiency of intestine
557.1 Chronic vascular insufficiency of intestine
593.81 Vascular disorders of kidney
747.62 Congenital renal vessel anomaly
747.89 Other specified congenital anomaly of circulatory system
908.4 Late effect of injury to blood vessel of thorax, abdomen, and pelvis

ICD-9-CM Procedural

38.34 Resection of aorta with anastomosis
38.37 Resection of abdominal veins with anastomosis
38.44 Resection of abdominal aorta with replacement
38.64 Other excision of abdominal aorta
39.51 Clipping of aneurysm
39.52 Other repair of aneurysm

35092

35092 Direct repair of aneurysm, pseudoaneurysm, or excision (partial or total) and graft insertion, with or without patch graft; for ruptured aneurysm, abdominal aorta involving visceral vessels (mesenteric, celiac, renal)

ICD-9-CM Diagnostic

440.0 Atherosclerosis of aorta
440.1 Atherosclerosis of renal artery
440.8 Atherosclerosis of other specified arteries
441.00 Dissecting aortic aneurysm (any part), unspecified site
441.3 Abdominal aneurysm, ruptured
441.5 Aortic aneurysm of unspecified site, ruptured
441.6 Thoracoabdominal aneurysm, ruptured
442.1 Aneurysm of renal artery
442.83 Aneurysm of splenic artery
442.84 Aneurysm of other visceral artery
443.23 Dissection of renal artery
443.29 Dissection of other artery
747.89 Other specified congenital anomaly of circulatory system
902.20 Unspecified celiac and mesenteric artery injury
902.25 Superior mesenteric artery (trunk) injury
902.27 Inferior mesenteric artery injury
908.4 Late effect of injury to blood vessel of thorax, abdomen, and pelvis

ICD-9-CM Procedural

38.34 Resection of aorta with anastomosis
38.37 Resection of abdominal veins with anastomosis
38.44 Resection of abdominal aorta with replacement
38.64 Other excision of abdominal aorta
39.51 Clipping of aneurysm
39.52 Other repair of aneurysm

35102

35102 Direct repair of aneurysm, pseudoaneurysm, or excision (partial or total) and graft insertion, with or without patch graft; for aneurysm, pseudoaneurysm, and associated occlusive disease, abdominal aorta involving iliac vessels (common, hypogastric, external)

ICD-9-CM Diagnostic

440.0 Atherosclerosis of aorta
440.8 Atherosclerosis of other specified arteries
441.02 Dissecting aortic aneurysm (any part), abdominal
441.4 Abdominal aneurysm without mention of rupture
441.9 Aortic aneurysm of unspecified site without mention of rupture
442.2 Aneurysm of iliac artery
443.22 Dissection of iliac artery
747.89 Other specified congenital anomaly of circulatory system

902.50 Unspecified iliac vessel(s) injury ▽
902.51 Hypogastric artery injury
902.53 Iliac artery injury
908.4 Late effect of injury to blood vessel of thorax, abdomen, and pelvis

ICD-9-CM Procedural

38.34 Resection of aorta with anastomosis
38.37 Resection of abdominal veins with anastomosis
38.44 Resection of abdominal aorta with replacement
38.64 Other excision of abdominal aorta
39.51 Clipping of aneurysm
39.52 Other repair of aneurysm

35103

35103 Direct repair of aneurysm, pseudoaneurysm, or excision (partial or total) and graft insertion, with or without patch graft; for ruptured aneurysm, abdominal aorta involving iliac vessels (common, hypogastric, external)

ICD-9-CM Diagnostic

440.0 Atherosclerosis of aorta
440.8 Atherosclerosis of other specified arteries
441.02 Dissecting aortic aneurysm (any part), abdominal
441.3 Abdominal aneurysm, ruptured
442.2 Aneurysm of iliac artery
443.22 Dissection of iliac artery
747.89 Other specified congenital anomaly of circulatory system
902.0 Abdominal aorta injury
902.51 Hypogastric artery injury
902.53 Iliac artery injury
908.3 Late effect of injury to blood vessel of head, neck, and extremities
908.4 Late effect of injury to blood vessel of thorax, abdomen, and pelvis
996.74 Other complications due to other vascular device, implant, and graft — (Use additional code to identify complication: 338.18-338.19, 338.28-338.29)

ICD-9-CM Procedural

38.34 Resection of aorta with anastomosis
38.36 Resection of abdominal arteries with anastomosis
38.37 Resection of abdominal veins with anastomosis
38.44 Resection of abdominal aorta with replacement
38.64 Other excision of abdominal aorta
39.51 Clipping of aneurysm
39.52 Other repair of aneurysm

35111-35112

35111 Direct repair of aneurysm, pseudoaneurysm, or excision (partial or total) and graft insertion, with or without patch graft; for aneurysm, pseudoaneurysm, and associated occlusive disease, splenic artery
35112 for ruptured aneurysm, splenic artery

ICD-9-CM Diagnostic

440.8 Atherosclerosis of other specified arteries
442.83 Aneurysm of splenic artery
443.29 Dissection of other artery
747.89 Other specified congenital anomaly of circulatory system
902.23 Splenic artery injury
908.4 Late effect of injury to blood vessel of thorax, abdomen, and pelvis
996.74 Other complications due to other vascular device, implant, and graft — (Use additional code to identify complication: 338.18-338.19, 338.28-338.29)

ICD-9-CM Procedural

38.36 Resection of abdominal arteries with anastomosis
38.46 Resection of abdominal arteries with replacement
38.66 Other excision of abdominal arteries
39.51 Clipping of aneurysm
39.52 Other repair of aneurysm

35121-35122

35121 Direct repair of aneurysm, pseudoaneurysm, or excision (partial or total) and graft insertion, with or without patch graft; for aneurysm, pseudoaneurysm, and associated occlusive disease, hepatic, celiac, renal, or mesenteric artery
35122 for ruptured aneurysm, hepatic, celiac, renal, or mesenteric artery

ICD-9-CM Diagnostic

440.1 Atherosclerosis of renal artery
440.8 Atherosclerosis of other specified arteries
442.1 Aneurysm of renal artery
442.84 Aneurysm of other visceral artery
443.23 Dissection of renal artery
443.29 Dissection of other artery
447.3 Hyperplasia of renal artery
747.62 Congenital renal vessel anomaly
747.89 Other specified congenital anomaly of circulatory system
902.22 Hepatic artery injury
902.24 Injury to specified branches of celiac axis, other
902.25 Superior mesenteric artery (trunk) injury
902.26 Injury to primary branches of superior mesenteric artery
902.27 Inferior mesenteric artery injury
902.41 Renal artery injury
908.4 Late effect of injury to blood vessel of thorax, abdomen, and pelvis
997.71 Vascular complications of mesenteric artery — (Use additional code to identify complications)
997.72 Vascular complications of renal artery — (Use additional code to identify complications)
997.79 Vascular complications of other vessels — (Use additional code to identify complications)

ICD-9-CM Procedural

38.36 Resection of abdominal arteries with anastomosis
38.37 Resection of abdominal veins with anastomosis
38.46 Resection of abdominal arteries with replacement
39.51 Clipping of aneurysm
39.52 Other repair of aneurysm

35131-35132

35131 Direct repair of aneurysm, pseudoaneurysm, or excision (partial or total) and graft insertion, with or without patch graft; for aneurysm, pseudoaneurysm, and associated occlusive disease, iliac artery (common, hypogastric, external)
35132 for ruptured aneurysm, iliac artery (common, hypogastric, external)

ICD-9-CM Diagnostic

440.8 Atherosclerosis of other specified arteries
442.2 Aneurysm of iliac artery
443.22 Dissection of iliac artery
747.89 Other specified congenital anomaly of circulatory system
902.51 Hypogastric artery injury
902.53 Iliac artery injury
908.4 Late effect of injury to blood vessel of thorax, abdomen, and pelvis

ICD-9-CM Procedural

38.36 Resection of abdominal arteries with anastomosis
38.37 Resection of abdominal veins with anastomosis
39.51 Clipping of aneurysm
39.52 Other repair of aneurysm

35141-35142

35141 Direct repair of aneurysm, pseudoaneurysm, or excision (partial or total) and graft insertion, with or without patch graft; for aneurysm, pseudoaneurysm, and associated occlusive disease, common femoral artery (profunda femoris, superficial femoral)

35142 for ruptured aneurysm, common femoral artery (profunda femoris, superficial femoral)

ICD-9-CM Diagnostic

440.20 Atherosclerosis of native arteries of the extremities, unspecified ▽
440.21 Atherosclerosis of native arteries of the extremities with intermittent claudication
440.22 Atherosclerosis of native arteries of the extremities with rest pain
442.3 Aneurysm of artery of lower extremity
442.9 Other aneurysm of unspecified site ▽
443.29 Dissection of other artery
747.64 Congenital lower limb vessel anomaly
904.2 Femoral vein injury
908.3 Late effect of injury to blood vessel of head, neck, and extremities
997.2 Peripheral vascular complications — (Use additional code to identify complications)

ICD-9-CM Procedural

38.38 Resection of lower limb arteries with anastomosis
38.48 Resection of lower limb arteries with replacement
38.49 Resection of lower limb veins with replacement
39.51 Clipping of aneurysm
39.52 Other repair of aneurysm

35151-35152

35151 Direct repair of aneurysm, pseudoaneurysm, or excision (partial or total) and graft insertion, with or without patch graft; for aneurysm, pseudoaneurysm, and associated occlusive disease, popliteal artery

35152 for ruptured aneurysm, popliteal artery

ICD-9-CM Diagnostic

440.20 Atherosclerosis of native arteries of the extremities, unspecified ▽
440.21 Atherosclerosis of native arteries of the extremities with intermittent claudication
440.22 Atherosclerosis of native arteries of the extremities with rest pain
442.3 Aneurysm of artery of lower extremity
443.29 Dissection of other artery
443.9 Unspecified peripheral vascular disease ▽
444.22 Embolism and thrombosis of arteries of lower extremity
445.02 Atheroembolism of lower extremity
447.1 Stricture of artery
747.64 Congenital lower limb vessel anomaly
785.9 Other symptoms involving cardiovascular system
904.41 Popliteal artery injury
908.3 Late effect of injury to blood vessel of head, neck, and extremities

ICD-9-CM Procedural

38.38 Resection of lower limb arteries with anastomosis
38.48 Resection of lower limb arteries with replacement
38.49 Resection of lower limb veins with replacement
39.51 Clipping of aneurysm
39.52 Other repair of aneurysm

35180

35180 Repair, congenital arteriovenous fistula; head and neck

ICD-9-CM Diagnostic

430 Subarachnoid hemorrhage — (Use additional code to identify presence of hypertension)
437.3 Cerebral aneurysm, nonruptured — (Use additional code to identify presence of hypertension)
747.69 Congenital anomaly of other specified site of peripheral vascular system
747.81 Congenital anomaly of cerebrovascular system

ICD-9-CM Procedural

39.53 Repair of arteriovenous fistula

35182

35182 Repair, congenital arteriovenous fistula; thorax and abdomen

ICD-9-CM Diagnostic

746.85 Congenital coronary artery anomaly
747.32 Pulmonary arteriovenous malformation
747.49 Other congenital anomalies of great veins
747.61 Congenital gastrointestinal vessel anomaly
747.62 Congenital renal vessel anomaly

ICD-9-CM Procedural

39.53 Repair of arteriovenous fistula

35184

35184 Repair, congenital arteriovenous fistula; extremities

ICD-9-CM Diagnostic

747.63 Congenital upper limb vessel anomaly
747.64 Congenital lower limb vessel anomaly

ICD-9-CM Procedural

39.53 Repair of arteriovenous fistula

35188

35188 Repair, acquired or traumatic arteriovenous fistula; head and neck

ICD-9-CM Diagnostic

430 Subarachnoid hemorrhage — (Use additional code to identify presence of hypertension)
437.3 Cerebral aneurysm, nonruptured — (Use additional code to identify presence of hypertension)
447.0 Arteriovenous fistula, acquired
447.70 Aortic ectasia, unspecified site ▽
900.02 External carotid artery injury
908.3 Late effect of injury to blood vessel of head, neck, and extremities

ICD-9-CM Procedural

39.53 Repair of arteriovenous fistula

35189

35189 Repair, acquired or traumatic arteriovenous fistula; thorax and abdomen

ICD-9-CM Diagnostic

414.19 Other aneurysm of heart — (Use additional code to identify presence of hypertension: 401.0-405.9)
417.0 Arteriovenous fistula of pulmonary vessels
417.9 Unspecified disease of pulmonary circulation ▽
440.9 Generalized and unspecified atherosclerosis ▽
442.84 Aneurysm of other visceral artery
442.9 Other aneurysm of unspecified site ▽
444.01 Saddle embolus of abdominal aorta
444.09 Other arterial embolism and thrombosis of abdominal aorta
444.1 Embolism and thrombosis of thoracic aorta
447.0 Arteriovenous fistula, acquired
447.1 Stricture of artery
447.71 Thoracic aortic ectasia
447.72 Abdominal aortic ectasia

447.73 Thoracoabdominal aortic ectasia
901.1 Innominate and subclavian artery injury
902.22 Hepatic artery injury
908.4 Late effect of injury to blood vessel of thorax, abdomen, and pelvis

ICD-9-CM Procedural

39.53 Repair of arteriovenous fistula

35190

35190 Repair, acquired or traumatic arteriovenous fistula; extremities

ICD-9-CM Diagnostic

444.21 Embolism and thrombosis of arteries of upper extremity
444.22 Embolism and thrombosis of arteries of lower extremity
447.0 Arteriovenous fistula, acquired
903.1 Brachial blood vessels injury
904.2 Femoral vein injury
908.3 Late effect of injury to blood vessel of head, neck, and extremities

ICD-9-CM Procedural

39.53 Repair of arteriovenous fistula

35201

35201 Repair blood vessel, direct; neck

ICD-9-CM Diagnostic

433.00 Occlusion and stenosis of basilar artery without mention of cerebral infarction — (Use additional code, if applicable, to identify status post administration of tPA (rtPA) in a different facility within the last 24 hours prior to admission to current facility: V45.88)
433.10 Occlusion and stenosis of carotid artery without mention of cerebral infarction — (Use additional code, if applicable, to identify status post administration of tPA (rtPA) in a different facility within the last 24 hours prior to admission to current facility: V45.88)
433.20 Occlusion and stenosis of vertebral artery without mention of cerebral infarction — (Use additional code, if applicable, to identify status post administration of tPA (rtPA) in a different facility within the last 24 hours prior to admission to current facility: V45.88)
433.30 Occlusion and stenosis of multiple and bilateral precerebral arteries without mention of cerebral infarction — (Use additional code, if applicable, to identify status post administration of tPA (rtPA) in a different facility within the last 24 hours prior to admission to current facility: V45.88)
433.80 Occlusion and stenosis of other specified precerebral artery without mention of cerebral infarction — (Use additional code, if applicable, to identify status post administration of tPA (rtPA) in a different facility within the last 24 hours prior to admission to current facility: V45.88)
433.90 Occlusion and stenosis of unspecified precerebral artery without mention of cerebral infarction — (Use additional code, if applicable, to identify status post administration of tPA (rtPA) in a different facility within the last 24 hours prior to admission to current facility: V45.88) ▼
443.21 Dissection of carotid artery
443.29 Dissection of other artery
447.2 Rupture of artery
447.70 Aortic ectasia, unspecified site ▼
900.00 Injury to carotid artery, unspecified ▼
900.01 Common carotid artery injury
900.02 External carotid artery injury
900.03 Internal carotid artery injury
900.1 Internal jugular vein injury
900.81 External jugular vein injury
900.82 Injury to multiple blood vessels of head and neck
900.89 Injury to other specified blood vessels of head and neck
998.2 Accidental puncture or laceration during procedure

ICD-9-CM Procedural

39.30 Suture of unspecified blood vessel
39.31 Suture of artery
39.32 Suture of vein
39.59 Other repair of vessel

35206

35206 Repair blood vessel, direct; upper extremity

ICD-9-CM Diagnostic

440.20 Atherosclerosis of native arteries of the extremities, unspecified ▼
440.21 Atherosclerosis of native arteries of the extremities with intermittent claudication
440.22 Atherosclerosis of native arteries of the extremities with rest pain
440.23 Atherosclerosis of native arteries of the extremities with ulceration — (Use additional code for any associated ulceration: 707.10-707.19, 707.8, 707.9)
440.24 Atherosclerosis of native arteries of the extremities with gangrene — (Use additional code for any associated ulceration: 707.10-707.19, 707.8, 707.9)
440.30 Atherosclerosis of unspecified bypass graft of extremities ▼
440.31 Atherosclerosis of autologous vein bypass graft of extremities
440.32 Atherosclerosis of nonautologous biological bypass graft of extremities
440.4 Chronic total occlusion of artery of the extremities
447.2 Rupture of artery
903.01 Axillary artery injury
903.02 Axillary vein injury
903.1 Brachial blood vessels injury
903.2 Radial blood vessels injury
903.3 Ulnar blood vessels injury
903.8 Injury to specified blood vessels of upper extremity, other
998.2 Accidental puncture or laceration during procedure

ICD-9-CM Procedural

39.30 Suture of unspecified blood vessel
39.31 Suture of artery
39.32 Suture of vein
39.59 Other repair of vessel

35207

35207 Repair blood vessel, direct; hand, finger

ICD-9-CM Diagnostic

447.2 Rupture of artery
883.1 Open wound of finger(s), complicated
883.2 Open wound of finger(s), with tendon involvement
903.4 Palmar artery injury
903.5 Digital blood vessels injury
903.8 Injury to specified blood vessels of upper extremity, other
959.5 Injury, other and unspecified, finger
998.2 Accidental puncture or laceration during procedure

ICD-9-CM Procedural

39.30 Suture of unspecified blood vessel
39.31 Suture of artery
39.32 Suture of vein
39.59 Other repair of vessel

35211-35216

35211 Repair blood vessel, direct; intrathoracic, with bypass
35216 intrathoracic, without bypass

ICD-9-CM Diagnostic

440.0 Atherosclerosis of aorta
447.1 Stricture of artery

447.5 Necrosis of artery
447.71 Thoracic aortic ectasia
447.73 Thoracoabdominal aortic ectasia
451.89 Phlebitis and thrombophlebitis of other site — (Use additional E code to identify drug, if drug-induced)
875.1 Open wound of chest (wall), complicated
901.0 Thoracic aorta injury
901.1 Innominate and subclavian artery injury
901.2 Superior vena cava injury
901.3 Innominate and subclavian vein injury
901.40 Injury to unspecified pulmonary vessel(s) ▽
901.41 Pulmonary artery injury
901.42 Pulmonary vein injury
901.81 Intercostal artery or vein injury
901.82 Internal mammary artery or vein injury
901.83 Injury to multiple blood vessels of thorax
901.89 Injury to specified blood vessels of thorax, other
901.9 Injury to unspecified blood vessel of thorax ▽
998.2 Accidental puncture or laceration during procedure

ICD-9-CM Procedural

39.30 Suture of unspecified blood vessel
39.31 Suture of artery
39.32 Suture of vein
39.59 Other repair of vessel
39.61 Extracorporeal circulation auxiliary to open heart surgery

35221

35221 Repair blood vessel, direct; intra-abdominal

ICD-9-CM Diagnostic

440.0 Atherosclerosis of aorta
440.1 Atherosclerosis of renal artery
447.1 Stricture of artery
447.6 Unspecified arteritis ▽
447.72 Abdominal aortic ectasia
447.73 Thoracoabdominal aortic ectasia
453.0 Budd-Chiari syndrome
459.9 Unspecified circulatory system disorder ▽
557.0 Acute vascular insufficiency of intestine
902.0 Abdominal aorta injury
902.10 Unspecified inferior vena cava injury ▽
902.11 Hepatic vein injury
902.20 Unspecified celiac and mesenteric artery injury ▽
902.21 Gastric artery injury
902.22 Hepatic artery injury
902.23 Splenic artery injury
902.33 Portal vein injury
902.34 Splenic vein injury
902.39 Injury to portal and splenic veins, other
902.40 Renal vessel(s) injury, unspecified ▽
902.41 Renal artery injury
902.42 Renal vein injury
902.50 Unspecified iliac vessel(s) injury ▽
902.53 Iliac artery injury
902.55 Uterine artery injury ♀
902.56 Uterine vein injury ♀
902.59 Injury to iliac blood vessels, other
902.81 Ovarian artery injury ♀
902.82 Ovarian vein injury ♀
902.89 Injury to specified blood vessels of abdomen and pelvis, other
902.9 Injury to blood vessel of abdomen and pelvis, unspecified ▽
998.2 Accidental puncture or laceration during procedure

ICD-9-CM Procedural

39.30 Suture of unspecified blood vessel
39.31 Suture of artery
39.32 Suture of vein
39.59 Other repair of vessel

35226

35226 Repair blood vessel, direct; lower extremity

ICD-9-CM Diagnostic

440.20 Atherosclerosis of native arteries of the extremities, unspecified ▽
440.21 Atherosclerosis of native arteries of the extremities with intermittent claudication
440.22 Atherosclerosis of native arteries of the extremities with rest pain
440.23 Atherosclerosis of native arteries of the extremities with ulceration — (Use additional code for any associated ulceration: 707.10-707.19, 707.8, 707.9)
440.24 Atherosclerosis of native arteries of the extremities with gangrene — (Use additional code for any associated ulceration: 707.10-707.19, 707.8, 707.9)
440.30 Atherosclerosis of unspecified bypass graft of extremities ▽
440.31 Atherosclerosis of autologous vein bypass graft of extremities
440.32 Atherosclerosis of nonautologous biological bypass graft of extremities
440.4 Chronic total occlusion of artery of the extremities
447.2 Rupture of artery
904.0 Common femoral artery injury
904.1 Superficial femoral artery injury
904.3 Saphenous vein injury
904.41 Popliteal artery injury
904.42 Popliteal vein injury
904.51 Anterior tibial artery injury
904.52 Anterior tibial vein injury
904.53 Posterior tibial artery injury
904.54 Posterior tibial vein injury
904.7 Injury to specified blood vessels of lower extremity, other
904.8 Injury to unspecified blood vessel of lower extremity ▽
998.2 Accidental puncture or laceration during procedure

ICD-9-CM Procedural

39.30 Suture of unspecified blood vessel
39.31 Suture of artery
39.32 Suture of vein
39.59 Other repair of vessel

35231

35231 Repair blood vessel with vein graft; neck

ICD-9-CM Diagnostic

433.00 Occlusion and stenosis of basilar artery without mention of cerebral infarction — (Use additional code, if applicable, to identify status post administration of tPA (rtPA) in a different facility within the last 24 hours prior to admission to current facility: V45.88)
433.10 Occlusion and stenosis of carotid artery without mention of cerebral infarction — (Use additional code, if applicable, to identify status post administration of tPA (rtPA) in a different facility within the last 24 hours prior to admission to current facility: V45.88)
433.20 Occlusion and stenosis of vertebral artery without mention of cerebral infarction — (Use additional code, if applicable, to identify status post administration of tPA (rtPA) in a different facility within the last 24 hours prior to admission to current facility: V45.88)

433.30 Occlusion and stenosis of multiple and bilateral precerebral arteries without mention of cerebral infarction — (Use additional code, if applicable, to identify status post administration of tPA (rtPA) in a different facility within the last 24 hours prior to admission to current facility: V45.88)
433.80 Occlusion and stenosis of other specified precerebral artery without mention of cerebral infarction — (Use additional code, if applicable, to identify status post administration of tPA (rtPA) in a different facility within the last 24 hours prior to admission to current facility: V45.88)
433.90 Occlusion and stenosis of unspecified precerebral artery without mention of cerebral infarction — (Use additional code, if applicable, to identify status post administration of tPA (rtPA) in a different facility within the last 24 hours prior to admission to current facility: V45.88) ▽
443.21 Dissection of carotid artery
443.29 Dissection of other artery
447.2 Rupture of artery
447.70 Aortic ectasia, unspecified site ▽
900.00 Injury to carotid artery, unspecified ▽
900.01 Common carotid artery injury
900.02 External carotid artery injury
900.03 Internal carotid artery injury
900.1 Internal jugular vein injury
900.81 External jugular vein injury
900.82 Injury to multiple blood vessels of head and neck
900.89 Injury to other specified blood vessels of head and neck
998.2 Accidental puncture or laceration during procedure

ICD-9-CM Procedural

38.42 Resection of other vessels of head and neck with replacement
39.56 Repair of blood vessel with tissue patch graft

35236

35236 Repair blood vessel with vein graft; upper extremity

ICD-9-CM Diagnostic

440.20 Atherosclerosis of native arteries of the extremities, unspecified ▽
440.21 Atherosclerosis of native arteries of the extremities with intermittent claudication
440.22 Atherosclerosis of native arteries of the extremities with rest pain
440.23 Atherosclerosis of native arteries of the extremities with ulceration — (Use additional code for any associated ulceration: 707.10-707.19, 707.8, 707.9)
440.24 Atherosclerosis of native arteries of the extremities with gangrene — (Use additional code for any associated ulceration: 707.10-707.19, 707.8, 707.9)
440.30 Atherosclerosis of unspecified bypass graft of extremities ▽
440.31 Atherosclerosis of autologous vein bypass graft of extremities
440.32 Atherosclerosis of nonautologous biological bypass graft of extremities
440.4 Chronic total occlusion of artery of the extremities
447.2 Rupture of artery
903.01 Axillary artery injury
903.02 Axillary vein injury
903.1 Brachial blood vessels injury
903.2 Radial blood vessels injury
903.3 Ulnar blood vessels injury
903.8 Injury to specified blood vessels of upper extremity, other
998.2 Accidental puncture or laceration during procedure

ICD-9-CM Procedural

38.43 Resection of upper limb vessels with replacement
39.56 Repair of blood vessel with tissue patch graft

35241-35246

35241 Repair blood vessel with vein graft; intrathoracic, with bypass
35246 intrathoracic, without bypass

ICD-9-CM Diagnostic

171.4 Malignant neoplasm of connective and other soft tissue of thorax
215.4 Other benign neoplasm of connective and other soft tissue of thorax
239.2 Neoplasms of unspecified nature of bone, soft tissue, and skin
440.0 Atherosclerosis of aorta
441.1 Thoracic aneurysm, ruptured
447.1 Stricture of artery
447.5 Necrosis of artery
447.71 Thoracic aortic ectasia
447.73 Thoracoabdominal aortic ectasia
451.89 Phlebitis and thrombophlebitis of other site — (Use additional E code to identify drug, if drug-induced)
459.2 Compression of vein
875.1 Open wound of chest (wall), complicated
901.0 Thoracic aorta injury
901.1 Innominate and subclavian artery injury
901.2 Superior vena cava injury
901.3 Innominate and subclavian vein injury
901.40 Injury to unspecified pulmonary vessel(s) ▽
901.41 Pulmonary artery injury
901.42 Pulmonary vein injury
901.81 Intercostal artery or vein injury
901.82 Internal mammary artery or vein injury
901.83 Injury to multiple blood vessels of thorax
998.2 Accidental puncture or laceration during procedure

ICD-9-CM Procedural

38.45 Resection of other thoracic vessels with replacement
39.30 Suture of unspecified blood vessel
39.56 Repair of blood vessel with tissue patch graft
39.61 Extracorporeal circulation auxiliary to open heart surgery

35251

35251 Repair blood vessel with vein graft; intra-abdominal

ICD-9-CM Diagnostic

440.0 Atherosclerosis of aorta
440.1 Atherosclerosis of renal artery
447.1 Stricture of artery
447.72 Abdominal aortic ectasia
447.73 Thoracoabdominal aortic ectasia
453.0 Budd-Chiari syndrome
557.0 Acute vascular insufficiency of intestine
902.0 Abdominal aorta injury
902.10 Unspecified inferior vena cava injury ▽
902.11 Hepatic vein injury
902.20 Unspecified celiac and mesenteric artery injury ▽
902.21 Gastric artery injury
902.22 Hepatic artery injury
902.23 Splenic artery injury
902.33 Portal vein injury
902.34 Splenic vein injury
902.39 Injury to portal and splenic veins, other
902.40 Renal vessel(s) injury, unspecified ▽
902.41 Renal artery injury
902.42 Renal vein injury

902.50 Unspecified iliac vessel(s) injury ▽
902.53 Iliac artery injury
902.55 Uterine artery injury ♀
902.56 Uterine vein injury ♀
902.59 Injury to iliac blood vessels, other
902.81 Ovarian artery injury ♀
902.82 Ovarian vein injury ♀
902.89 Injury to specified blood vessels of abdomen and pelvis, other
902.9 Injury to blood vessel of abdomen and pelvis, unspecified ▽
998.2 Accidental puncture or laceration during procedure

ICD-9-CM Procedural

38.46 Resection of abdominal arteries with replacement
38.47 Resection of abdominal veins with replacement
39.56 Repair of blood vessel with tissue patch graft

35256

35256 Repair blood vessel with vein graft; lower extremity

ICD-9-CM Diagnostic

440.20 Atherosclerosis of native arteries of the extremities, unspecified ▽
440.21 Atherosclerosis of native arteries of the extremities with intermittent claudication
440.22 Atherosclerosis of native arteries of the extremities with rest pain
440.23 Atherosclerosis of native arteries of the extremities with ulceration — (Use additional code for any associated ulceration: 707.10-707.19, 707.8, 707.9)
440.24 Atherosclerosis of native arteries of the extremities with gangrene — (Use additional code for any associated ulceration: 707.10-707.19, 707.8, 707.9)
440.30 Atherosclerosis of unspecified bypass graft of extremities ▽
440.31 Atherosclerosis of autologous vein bypass graft of extremities
440.32 Atherosclerosis of nonautologous biological bypass graft of extremities
440.4 Chronic total occlusion of artery of the extremities
447.2 Rupture of artery
904.0 Common femoral artery injury
904.1 Superficial femoral artery injury
904.3 Saphenous vein injury
904.41 Popliteal artery injury
904.42 Popliteal vein injury
904.51 Anterior tibial artery injury
904.52 Anterior tibial vein injury
904.53 Posterior tibial artery injury
904.54 Posterior tibial vein injury
904.7 Injury to specified blood vessels of lower extremity, other
904.8 Injury to unspecified blood vessel of lower extremity ▽
998.2 Accidental puncture or laceration during procedure

ICD-9-CM Procedural

38.48 Resection of lower limb arteries with replacement
38.49 Resection of lower limb veins with replacement
39.56 Repair of blood vessel with tissue patch graft

35261

35261 Repair blood vessel with graft other than vein; neck

ICD-9-CM Diagnostic

433.00 Occlusion and stenosis of basilar artery without mention of cerebral infarction — (Use additional code, if applicable, to identify status post administration of tPA (rtPA) in a different facility within the last 24 hours prior to admission to current facility: V45.88)
433.10 Occlusion and stenosis of carotid artery without mention of cerebral infarction — (Use additional code, if applicable, to identify status post administration of tPA (rtPA) in a different facility within the last 24 hours prior to admission to current facility: V45.88)
433.20 Occlusion and stenosis of vertebral artery without mention of cerebral infarction — (Use additional code, if applicable, to identify status post administration of tPA (rtPA) in a different facility within the last 24 hours prior to admission to current facility: V45.88)
433.30 Occlusion and stenosis of multiple and bilateral precerebral arteries without mention of cerebral infarction — (Use additional code, if applicable, to identify status post administration of tPA (rtPA) in a different facility within the last 24 hours prior to admission to current facility: V45.88)
433.80 Occlusion and stenosis of other specified precerebral artery without mention of cerebral infarction — (Use additional code, if applicable, to identify status post administration of tPA (rtPA) in a different facility within the last 24 hours prior to admission to current facility: V45.88)
433.90 Occlusion and stenosis of unspecified precerebral artery without mention of cerebral infarction — (Use additional code, if applicable, to identify status post administration of tPA (rtPA) in a different facility within the last 24 hours prior to admission to current facility: V45.88) ▽
443.21 Dissection of carotid artery
443.29 Dissection of other artery
447.2 Rupture of artery
447.70 Aortic ectasia, unspecified site ▽
900.00 Injury to carotid artery, unspecified ▽
900.01 Common carotid artery injury
900.02 External carotid artery injury
900.03 Internal carotid artery injury
900.1 Internal jugular vein injury
900.81 External jugular vein injury
900.82 Injury to multiple blood vessels of head and neck
900.89 Injury to other specified blood vessels of head and neck
998.2 Accidental puncture or laceration during procedure

ICD-9-CM Procedural

38.42 Resection of other vessels of head and neck with replacement
39.57 Repair of blood vessel with synthetic patch graft
39.58 Repair of blood vessel with unspecified type of patch graft
39.72 Endovascular (total) embolization or occlusion of head and neck vessels
39.75 Endovascular embolization or occlusion of vessel(s) of head or neck using bare coils
39.76 Endovascular embolization or occlusion of vessel(s) of head or neck using bioactive coils

HCPCS Level II Supplies & Services

C1768 Graft, vascular

35266

35266 Repair blood vessel with graft other than vein; upper extremity

ICD-9-CM Diagnostic

440.20 Atherosclerosis of native arteries of the extremities, unspecified ▽
440.21 Atherosclerosis of native arteries of the extremities with intermittent claudication
440.22 Atherosclerosis of native arteries of the extremities with rest pain
440.23 Atherosclerosis of native arteries of the extremities with ulceration — (Use additional code for any associated ulceration: 707.10-707.19, 707.8, 707.9)
440.24 Atherosclerosis of native arteries of the extremities with gangrene — (Use additional code for any associated ulceration: 707.10-707.19, 707.8, 707.9)
440.30 Atherosclerosis of unspecified bypass graft of extremities ▽
440.31 Atherosclerosis of autologous vein bypass graft of extremities
440.32 Atherosclerosis of nonautologous biological bypass graft of extremities
440.4 Chronic total occlusion of artery of the extremities
447.2 Rupture of artery
903.01 Axillary artery injury
903.02 Axillary vein injury

903.1 Brachial blood vessels injury
903.2 Radial blood vessels injury
903.3 Ulnar blood vessels injury
903.8 Injury to specified blood vessels of upper extremity, other
998.2 Accidental puncture or laceration during procedure

ICD-9-CM Procedural

38.43 Resection of upper limb vessels with replacement
39.57 Repair of blood vessel with synthetic patch graft
39.58 Repair of blood vessel with unspecified type of patch graft

HCPCS Level II Supplies & Services

C1768 Graft, vascular

35271-35276

35271 Repair blood vessel with graft other than vein; intrathoracic, with bypass
35276 intrathoracic, without bypass

ICD-9-CM Diagnostic

440.0 Atherosclerosis of aorta
447.1 Stricture of artery
447.5 Necrosis of artery
447.71 Thoracic aortic ectasia
447.73 Thoracoabdominal aortic ectasia
451.89 Phlebitis and thrombophlebitis of other site — (Use additional E code to identify drug, if drug-induced)
459.2 Compression of vein
875.1 Open wound of chest (wall), complicated
901.0 Thoracic aorta injury
901.2 Superior vena cava injury
901.3 Innominate and subclavian vein injury
901.40 Injury to unspecified pulmonary vessel(s) ▽
901.41 Pulmonary artery injury
901.42 Pulmonary vein injury
901.81 Intercostal artery or vein injury
901.82 Internal mammary artery or vein injury
901.83 Injury to multiple blood vessels of thorax
901.89 Injury to specified blood vessels of thorax, other
901.9 Injury to unspecified blood vessel of thorax ▽
998.2 Accidental puncture or laceration during procedure

ICD-9-CM Procedural

38.45 Resection of other thoracic vessels with replacement
39.56 Repair of blood vessel with tissue patch graft
39.57 Repair of blood vessel with synthetic patch graft
39.58 Repair of blood vessel with unspecified type of patch graft
39.61 Extracorporeal circulation auxiliary to open heart surgery

35281

35281 Repair blood vessel with graft other than vein; intra-abdominal

ICD-9-CM Diagnostic

440.0 Atherosclerosis of aorta
440.1 Atherosclerosis of renal artery
447.2 Rupture of artery
447.72 Abdominal aortic ectasia
447.73 Thoracoabdominal aortic ectasia
451.81 Phlebitis and thrombophlebitis of iliac vein — (Use additional E code to identify drug, if drug-induced)
452 Portal vein thrombosis
453.0 Budd-Chiari syndrome
557.0 Acute vascular insufficiency of intestine
902.0 Abdominal aorta injury
902.11 Hepatic vein injury
902.20 Unspecified celiac and mesenteric artery injury ▽
902.21 Gastric artery injury
902.22 Hepatic artery injury
902.23 Splenic artery injury
902.33 Portal vein injury
902.34 Splenic vein injury
902.39 Injury to portal and splenic veins, other
902.40 Renal vessel(s) injury, unspecified ▽
902.41 Renal artery injury
902.42 Renal vein injury
902.50 Unspecified iliac vessel(s) injury ▽
902.53 Iliac artery injury
902.55 Uterine artery injury ♀
902.56 Uterine vein injury ♀
902.59 Injury to iliac blood vessels, other
902.81 Ovarian artery injury ♀
902.82 Ovarian vein injury ♀
902.89 Injury to specified blood vessels of abdomen and pelvis, other
902.9 Injury to blood vessel of abdomen and pelvis, unspecified ▽

ICD-9-CM Procedural

38.46 Resection of abdominal arteries with replacement
38.47 Resection of abdominal veins with replacement
39.30 Suture of unspecified blood vessel
39.56 Repair of blood vessel with tissue patch graft
39.57 Repair of blood vessel with synthetic patch graft
39.58 Repair of blood vessel with unspecified type of patch graft

35286

35286 Repair blood vessel with graft other than vein; lower extremity

ICD-9-CM Diagnostic

440.20 Atherosclerosis of native arteries of the extremities, unspecified ▽
440.21 Atherosclerosis of native arteries of the extremities with intermittent claudication
440.22 Atherosclerosis of native arteries of the extremities with rest pain
440.23 Atherosclerosis of native arteries of the extremities with ulceration — (Use additional code for any associated ulceration: 707.10-707.19, 707.8, 707.9)
440.24 Atherosclerosis of native arteries of the extremities with gangrene — (Use additional code for any associated ulceration: 707.10-707.19, 707.8, 707.9)
440.30 Atherosclerosis of unspecified bypass graft of extremities ▽
440.31 Atherosclerosis of autologous vein bypass graft of extremities
440.32 Atherosclerosis of nonautologous biological bypass graft of extremities
440.4 Chronic total occlusion of artery of the extremities
447.2 Rupture of artery
904.0 Common femoral artery injury
904.1 Superficial femoral artery injury
904.3 Saphenous vein injury
904.41 Popliteal artery injury
904.42 Popliteal vein injury
904.51 Anterior tibial artery injury
904.52 Anterior tibial vein injury
904.53 Posterior tibial artery injury
904.54 Posterior tibial vein injury
904.7 Injury to specified blood vessels of lower extremity, other
904.8 Injury to unspecified blood vessel of lower extremity ▽
998.2 Accidental puncture or laceration during procedure

ICD-9-CM Procedural

38.48 Resection of lower limb arteries with replacement
38.49 Resection of lower limb veins with replacement
39.30 Suture of unspecified blood vessel
39.57 Repair of blood vessel with synthetic patch graft
39.58 Repair of blood vessel with unspecified type of patch graft

HCPCS Level II Supplies & Services

C1768 Graft, vascular

35301

35301 Thromboendarterectomy, including patch graft, if performed; carotid, vertebral, subclavian, by neck incision

ICD-9-CM Diagnostic

433.00 Occlusion and stenosis of basilar artery without mention of cerebral infarction — (Use additional code, if applicable, to identify status post administration of tPA (rtPA) in a different facility within the last 24 hours prior to admission to current facility: V45.88)
433.01 Occlusion and stenosis of basilar artery with cerebral infarction — (Use additional code, if applicable, to identify status post administration of tPA (rtPA) in a different facility within the last 24 hours prior to admission to current facility: V45.88)
433.10 Occlusion and stenosis of carotid artery without mention of cerebral infarction — (Use additional code, if applicable, to identify status post administration of tPA (rtPA) in a different facility within the last 24 hours prior to admission to current facility: V45.88)
433.11 Occlusion and stenosis of carotid artery with cerebral infarction — (Use additional code, if applicable, to identify status post administration of tPA (rtPA) in a different facility within the last 24 hours prior to admission to current facility: V45.88)
433.20 Occlusion and stenosis of vertebral artery without mention of cerebral infarction — (Use additional code, if applicable, to identify status post administration of tPA (rtPA) in a different facility within the last 24 hours prior to admission to current facility: V45.88)
433.21 Occlusion and stenosis of vertebral artery with cerebral infarction — (Use additional code, if applicable, to identify status post administration of tPA (rtPA) in a different facility within the last 24 hours prior to admission to current facility: V45.88)
433.30 Occlusion and stenosis of multiple and bilateral precerebral arteries without mention of cerebral infarction — (Use additional code, if applicable, to identify status post administration of tPA (rtPA) in a different facility within the last 24 hours prior to admission to current facility: V45.88)
433.31 Occlusion and stenosis of multiple and bilateral precerebral arteries with cerebral infarction — (Use additional code, if applicable, to identify status post administration of tPA (rtPA) in a different facility within the last 24 hours prior to admission to current facility: V45.88)
433.80 Occlusion and stenosis of other specified precerebral artery without mention of cerebral infarction — (Use additional code, if applicable, to identify status post administration of tPA (rtPA) in a different facility within the last 24 hours prior to admission to current facility: V45.88)
433.81 Occlusion and stenosis of other specified precerebral artery with cerebral infarction — (Use additional code, if applicable, to identify status post administration of tPA (rtPA) in a different facility within the last 24 hours prior to admission to current facility: V45.88)
433.90 Occlusion and stenosis of unspecified precerebral artery without mention of cerebral infarction — (Use additional code, if applicable, to identify status post administration of tPA (rtPA) in a different facility within the last 24 hours prior to admission to current facility: V45.88) ▽
433.91 Occlusion and stenosis of unspecified precerebral artery with cerebral infarction — (Use additional code, if applicable, to identify status post administration of tPA (rtPA) in a different facility within the last 24 hours prior to admission to current facility: V45.88) ▽
435.0 Basilar artery syndrome — (Use additional code to identify presence of hypertension)
435.1 Vertebral artery syndrome — (Use additional code to identify presence of hypertension)
435.2 Subclavian steal syndrome — (Use additional code to identify presence of hypertension)
435.8 Other specified transient cerebral ischemias — (Use additional code to identify presence of hypertension)
435.9 Unspecified transient cerebral ischemia — (Use additional code to identify presence of hypertension) ▽
437.9 Unspecified cerebrovascular disease — (Use additional code to identify presence of hypertension) ▽
440.8 Atherosclerosis of other specified arteries
443.21 Dissection of carotid artery
443.24 Dissection of vertebral artery
443.29 Dissection of other artery
780.02 Transient alteration of awareness
780.09 Other alteration of consciousness
780.2 Syncope and collapse
780.31 Febrile convulsions (simple), unspecified ▽
780.39 Other convulsions
780.4 Dizziness and giddiness
784.0 Headache
785.9 Other symptoms involving cardiovascular system

ICD-9-CM Procedural

00.40 Procedure on single vessel
00.41 Procedure on two vessels
00.42 Procedure on three vessels
00.43 Procedure on four or more vessels
38.12 Endarterectomy of other vessels of head and neck

35302

35302 Thromboendarterectomy, including patch graft, if performed; superficial femoral artery

ICD-9-CM Diagnostic

249.70 Secondary diabetes mellitus with peripheral circulatory disorders, not stated as uncontrolled, or unspecified — (Use additional code to identify manifestation: 443.81, 785.4) (Use additional code to identify any associated insulin use: V58.67)
249.71 Secondary diabetes mellitus with peripheral circulatory disorders, uncontrolled — (Use additional code to identify manifestation: 443.81, 785.4) (Use additional code to identify any associated insulin use: V58.67)
250.70 Diabetes with peripheral circulatory disorders, type II or unspecified type, not stated as uncontrolled — (Use additional code to identify manifestation: 443.81, 785.4)
250.71 Diabetes with peripheral circulatory disorders, type I [juvenile type], not stated as uncontrolled — (Use additional code to identify manifestation: 443.81, 785.4)
250.72 Diabetes with peripheral circulatory disorders, type II or unspecified type, uncontrolled — (Use additional code to identify manifestation: 443.81, 785.4)
250.73 Diabetes with peripheral circulatory disorders, type I [juvenile type], uncontrolled — (Use additional code to identify manifestation: 443.81, 785.4)
440.20 Atherosclerosis of native arteries of the extremities, unspecified ▽
440.21 Atherosclerosis of native arteries of the extremities with intermittent claudication
440.22 Atherosclerosis of native arteries of the extremities with rest pain
440.23 Atherosclerosis of native arteries of the extremities with ulceration — (Use additional code for any associated ulceration: 707.10-707.19, 707.8, 707.9)
440.24 Atherosclerosis of native arteries of the extremities with gangrene — (Use additional code for any associated ulceration: 707.10-707.19, 707.8, 707.9)
440.29 Other atherosclerosis of native arteries of the extremities
443.29 Dissection of other artery
443.81 Peripheral angiopathy in diseases classified elsewhere — (Code first underlying disease: 249.7, 250.7) ☒
443.9 Unspecified peripheral vascular disease ▽
444.22 Embolism and thrombosis of arteries of lower extremity
444.9 Embolism and thrombosis of unspecified artery ▽

445.02 Atheroembolism of lower extremity
447.1 Stricture of artery
447.2 Rupture of artery
785.4 Gangrene — (Code first any associated underlying condition)
785.9 Other symptoms involving cardiovascular system
904.2 Femoral vein injury

ICD-9-CM Procedural

00.40 Procedure on single vessel
00.41 Procedure on two vessels
00.42 Procedure on three vessels
00.43 Procedure on four or more vessels
38.18 Endarterectomy of lower limb arteries

35303

35303 Thromboendarterectomy, including patch graft, if performed; popliteal artery

ICD-9-CM Diagnostic

249.70 Secondary diabetes mellitus with peripheral circulatory disorders, not stated as uncontrolled, or unspecified — (Use additional code to identify manifestation: 443.81, 785.4) (Use additional code to identify any associated insulin use: V58.67)
249.71 Secondary diabetes mellitus with peripheral circulatory disorders, uncontrolled — (Use additional code to identify manifestation: 443.81, 785.4) (Use additional code to identify any associated insulin use: V58.67)
250.70 Diabetes with peripheral circulatory disorders, type II or unspecified type, not stated as uncontrolled — (Use additional code to identify manifestation: 443.81, 785.4)
250.71 Diabetes with peripheral circulatory disorders, type I [juvenile type], not stated as uncontrolled — (Use additional code to identify manifestation: 443.81, 785.4)
250.72 Diabetes with peripheral circulatory disorders, type II or unspecified type, uncontrolled — (Use additional code to identify manifestation: 443.81, 785.4)
250.73 Diabetes with peripheral circulatory disorders, type I [juvenile type], uncontrolled — (Use additional code to identify manifestation: 443.81, 785.4)
440.20 Atherosclerosis of native arteries of the extremities, unspecified
440.21 Atherosclerosis of native arteries of the extremities with intermittent claudication
440.22 Atherosclerosis of native arteries of the extremities with rest pain
440.23 Atherosclerosis of native arteries of the extremities with ulceration — (Use additional code for any associated ulceration: 707.10-707.19, 707.8, 707.9)
440.24 Atherosclerosis of native arteries of the extremities with gangrene — (Use additional code for any associated ulceration: 707.10-707.19, 707.8, 707.9)
440.29 Other atherosclerosis of native arteries of the extremities
443.29 Dissection of other artery
443.81 Peripheral angiopathy in diseases classified elsewhere — (Code first underlying disease: 249.7, 250.7)
443.9 Unspecified peripheral vascular disease
444.22 Embolism and thrombosis of arteries of lower extremity
444.9 Embolism and thrombosis of unspecified artery
445.02 Atheroembolism of lower extremity
447.1 Stricture of artery
447.2 Rupture of artery
785.4 Gangrene — (Code first any associated underlying condition)
785.9 Other symptoms involving cardiovascular system
904.2 Femoral vein injury

ICD-9-CM Procedural

00.40 Procedure on single vessel
00.41 Procedure on two vessels
00.42 Procedure on three vessels
00.43 Procedure on four or more vessels
38.18 Endarterectomy of lower limb arteries

35304

35304 Thromboendarterectomy, including patch graft, if performed; tibioperoneal trunk artery

ICD-9-CM Diagnostic

249.70 Secondary diabetes mellitus with peripheral circulatory disorders, not stated as uncontrolled, or unspecified — (Use additional code to identify manifestation: 443.81, 785.4) (Use additional code to identify any associated insulin use: V58.67)
249.71 Secondary diabetes mellitus with peripheral circulatory disorders, uncontrolled — (Use additional code to identify manifestation: 443.81, 785.4) (Use additional code to identify any associated insulin use: V58.67)
250.70 Diabetes with peripheral circulatory disorders, type II or unspecified type, not stated as uncontrolled — (Use additional code to identify manifestation: 443.81, 785.4)
250.71 Diabetes with peripheral circulatory disorders, type I [juvenile type], not stated as uncontrolled — (Use additional code to identify manifestation: 443.81, 785.4)
250.72 Diabetes with peripheral circulatory disorders, type II or unspecified type, uncontrolled — (Use additional code to identify manifestation: 443.81, 785.4)
250.73 Diabetes with peripheral circulatory disorders, type I [juvenile type], uncontrolled — (Use additional code to identify manifestation: 443.81, 785.4)
440.20 Atherosclerosis of native arteries of the extremities, unspecified
440.21 Atherosclerosis of native arteries of the extremities with intermittent claudication
440.22 Atherosclerosis of native arteries of the extremities with rest pain
440.23 Atherosclerosis of native arteries of the extremities with ulceration — (Use additional code for any associated ulceration: 707.10-707.19, 707.8, 707.9)
440.24 Atherosclerosis of native arteries of the extremities with gangrene — (Use additional code for any associated ulceration: 707.10-707.19, 707.8, 707.9)
440.29 Other atherosclerosis of native arteries of the extremities
443.29 Dissection of other artery
443.81 Peripheral angiopathy in diseases classified elsewhere — (Code first underlying disease: 249.7, 250.7)
443.9 Unspecified peripheral vascular disease
444.22 Embolism and thrombosis of arteries of lower extremity
444.9 Embolism and thrombosis of unspecified artery
445.02 Atheroembolism of lower extremity
447.1 Stricture of artery
447.2 Rupture of artery
785.4 Gangrene — (Code first any associated underlying condition)
785.9 Other symptoms involving cardiovascular system
904.2 Femoral vein injury

ICD-9-CM Procedural

00.40 Procedure on single vessel
00.41 Procedure on two vessels
00.42 Procedure on three vessels
00.43 Procedure on four or more vessels
38.18 Endarterectomy of lower limb arteries

35305

35305 Thromboendarterectomy, including patch graft, if performed; tibial or peroneal artery, initial vessel

ICD-9-CM Diagnostic

249.70 Secondary diabetes mellitus with peripheral circulatory disorders, not stated as uncontrolled, or unspecified — (Use additional code to identify manifestation: 443.81, 785.4) (Use additional code to identify any associated insulin use: V58.67)
249.71 Secondary diabetes mellitus with peripheral circulatory disorders, uncontrolled — (Use additional code to identify manifestation: 443.81, 785.4) (Use additional code to identify any associated insulin use: V58.67)
250.70 Diabetes with peripheral circulatory disorders, type II or unspecified type, not stated as uncontrolled — (Use additional code to identify manifestation: 443.81, 785.4)
250.71 Diabetes with peripheral circulatory disorders, type I [juvenile type], not stated as uncontrolled — (Use additional code to identify manifestation: 443.81, 785.4)

250.72 Diabetes with peripheral circulatory disorders, type II or unspecified type, uncontrolled — (Use additional code to identify manifestation: 443.81, 785.4)

250.73 Diabetes with peripheral circulatory disorders, type I [juvenile type], uncontrolled — (Use additional code to identify manifestation: 443.81, 785.4)

440.20 Atherosclerosis of native arteries of the extremities, unspecified ▽

440.21 Atherosclerosis of native arteries of the extremities with intermittent claudication

440.22 Atherosclerosis of native arteries of the extremities with rest pain

440.23 Atherosclerosis of native arteries of the extremities with ulceration — (Use additional code for any associated ulceration: 707.10-707.19, 707.8, 707.9)

440.24 Atherosclerosis of native arteries of the extremities with gangrene — (Use additional code for any associated ulceration: 707.10-707.19, 707.8, 707.9)

440.29 Other atherosclerosis of native arteries of the extremities

443.29 Dissection of other artery

443.81 Peripheral angiopathy in diseases classified elsewhere — (Code first underlying disease: 249.7, 250.7) ☒

443.9 Unspecified peripheral vascular disease ▽

444.22 Embolism and thrombosis of arteries of lower extremity

444.9 Embolism and thrombosis of unspecified artery ▽

445.02 Atheroembolism of lower extremity

447.1 Stricture of artery

447.2 Rupture of artery

785.4 Gangrene — (Code first any associated underlying condition)

785.9 Other symptoms involving cardiovascular system

904.2 Femoral vein injury

ICD-9-CM Procedural

00.40 Procedure on single vessel

00.41 Procedure on two vessels

00.42 Procedure on three vessels

00.43 Procedure on four or more vessels

38.18 Endarterectomy of lower limb arteries

35306

35306 Thromboendarterectomy, including patch graft, if performed; each additional tibial or peroneal artery (List separately in addition to code for primary procedure)

ICD-9-CM Diagnostic

249.70 Secondary diabetes mellitus with peripheral circulatory disorders, not stated as uncontrolled, or unspecified — (Use additional code to identify manifestation: 443.81, 785.4) (Use additional code to identify any associated insulin use: V58.67)

249.71 Secondary diabetes mellitus with peripheral circulatory disorders, uncontrolled — (Use additional code to identify manifestation: 443.81, 785.4) (Use additional code to identify any associated insulin use: V58.67)

250.70 Diabetes with peripheral circulatory disorders, type II or unspecified type, not stated as uncontrolled — (Use additional code to identify manifestation: 443.81, 785.4)

250.71 Diabetes with peripheral circulatory disorders, type I [juvenile type], not stated as uncontrolled — (Use additional code to identify manifestation: 443.81, 785.4)

250.72 Diabetes with peripheral circulatory disorders, type II or unspecified type, uncontrolled — (Use additional code to identify manifestation: 443.81, 785.4)

250.73 Diabetes with peripheral circulatory disorders, type I [juvenile type], uncontrolled — (Use additional code to identify manifestation: 443.81, 785.4)

440.20 Atherosclerosis of native arteries of the extremities, unspecified ▽

440.21 Atherosclerosis of native arteries of the extremities with intermittent claudication

440.22 Atherosclerosis of native arteries of the extremities with rest pain

440.23 Atherosclerosis of native arteries of the extremities with ulceration — (Use additional code for any associated ulceration: 707.10-707.19, 707.8, 707.9)

440.24 Atherosclerosis of native arteries of the extremities with gangrene — (Use additional code for any associated ulceration: 707.10-707.19, 707.8, 707.9)

440.29 Other atherosclerosis of native arteries of the extremities

443.29 Dissection of other artery

443.81 Peripheral angiopathy in diseases classified elsewhere — (Code first underlying disease: 249.7, 250.7) ☒

443.9 Unspecified peripheral vascular disease ▽

444.22 Embolism and thrombosis of arteries of lower extremity

444.9 Embolism and thrombosis of unspecified artery ▽

445.02 Atheroembolism of lower extremity

447.1 Stricture of artery

447.2 Rupture of artery

785.4 Gangrene — (Code first any associated underlying condition)

785.9 Other symptoms involving cardiovascular system

904.2 Femoral vein injury

ICD-9-CM Procedural

00.40 Procedure on single vessel

00.41 Procedure on two vessels

00.42 Procedure on three vessels

00.43 Procedure on four or more vessels

38.18 Endarterectomy of lower limb arteries

35311

35311 Thromboendarterectomy, including patch graft, if performed; subclavian, innominate, by thoracic incision

ICD-9-CM Diagnostic

435.1 Vertebral artery syndrome — (Use additional code to identify presence of hypertension)

435.2 Subclavian steal syndrome — (Use additional code to identify presence of hypertension)

440.8 Atherosclerosis of other specified arteries

444.89 Embolism and thrombosis of other specified artery

445.89 Atheroembolism of other site

ICD-9-CM Procedural

00.40 Procedure on single vessel

00.41 Procedure on two vessels

00.42 Procedure on three vessels

00.43 Procedure on four or more vessels

38.15 Endarterectomy of other thoracic vessels

35321

35321 Thromboendarterectomy, including patch graft, if performed; axillary-brachial

ICD-9-CM Diagnostic

440.20 Atherosclerosis of native arteries of the extremities, unspecified ▽

440.21 Atherosclerosis of native arteries of the extremities with intermittent claudication

440.22 Atherosclerosis of native arteries of the extremities with rest pain

440.23 Atherosclerosis of native arteries of the extremities with ulceration — (Use additional code for any associated ulceration: 707.10-707.19, 707.8, 707.9)

440.24 Atherosclerosis of native arteries of the extremities with gangrene — (Use additional code for any associated ulceration: 707.10-707.19, 707.8, 707.9)

440.29 Other atherosclerosis of native arteries of the extremities

440.30 Atherosclerosis of unspecified bypass graft of extremities ▽

440.31 Atherosclerosis of autologous vein bypass graft of extremities

440.32 Atherosclerosis of nonautologous biological bypass graft of extremities

440.4 Chronic total occlusion of artery of the extremities

444.21 Embolism and thrombosis of arteries of upper extremity

444.9 Embolism and thrombosis of unspecified artery ▽

445.01 Atheroembolism of upper extremity

ICD-9-CM Procedural

00.40 Procedure on single vessel

00.41 Procedure on two vessels

00.42 Procedure on three vessels

00.43 Procedure on four or more vessels
38.13 Endarterectomy of upper limb vessels

35331

35331 Thromboendarterectomy, including patch graft, if performed; abdominal aorta

ICD-9-CM Diagnostic

440.0 Atherosclerosis of aorta
444.01 Saddle embolus of abdominal aorta
444.09 Other arterial embolism and thrombosis of abdominal aorta
444.9 Embolism and thrombosis of unspecified artery ▽

ICD-9-CM Procedural

00.40 Procedure on single vessel
38.14 Endarterectomy of aorta

35341

35341 Thromboendarterectomy, including patch graft, if performed; mesenteric, celiac, or renal

ICD-9-CM Diagnostic

440.1 Atherosclerosis of renal artery
440.8 Atherosclerosis of other specified arteries
557.0 Acute vascular insufficiency of intestine
557.1 Chronic vascular insufficiency of intestine
997.71 Vascular complications of mesenteric artery — (Use additional code to identify complications)
997.72 Vascular complications of renal artery — (Use additional code to identify complications)
997.79 Vascular complications of other vessels — (Use additional code to identify complications)

ICD-9-CM Procedural

00.40 Procedure on single vessel
00.41 Procedure on two vessels
00.42 Procedure on three vessels
00.43 Procedure on four or more vessels
38.16 Endarterectomy of abdominal arteries

35351

35351 Thromboendarterectomy, including patch graft, if performed; iliac

ICD-9-CM Diagnostic

440.8 Atherosclerosis of other specified arteries
444.81 Embolism and thrombosis of iliac artery
444.89 Embolism and thrombosis of other specified artery
445.89 Atheroembolism of other site
997.79 Vascular complications of other vessels — (Use additional code to identify complications)

ICD-9-CM Procedural

00.40 Procedure on single vessel
00.41 Procedure on two vessels
38.16 Endarterectomy of abdominal arteries

35355

35355 Thromboendarterectomy, including patch graft, if performed; iliofemoral

ICD-9-CM Diagnostic

440.20 Atherosclerosis of native arteries of the extremities, unspecified ▽
440.21 Atherosclerosis of native arteries of the extremities with intermittent claudication
440.22 Atherosclerosis of native arteries of the extremities with rest pain
440.23 Atherosclerosis of native arteries of the extremities with ulceration — (Use additional code for any associated ulceration: 707.10-707.19, 707.8, 707.9)
440.24 Atherosclerosis of native arteries of the extremities with gangrene — (Use additional code for any associated ulceration: 707.10-707.19, 707.8, 707.9)
440.29 Other atherosclerosis of native arteries of the extremities
440.4 Chronic total occlusion of artery of the extremities
444.22 Embolism and thrombosis of arteries of lower extremity
444.81 Embolism and thrombosis of iliac artery
445.02 Atheroembolism of lower extremity
445.89 Atheroembolism of other site
997.79 Vascular complications of other vessels — (Use additional code to identify complications)

ICD-9-CM Procedural

00.41 Procedure on two vessels
00.42 Procedure on three vessels
00.43 Procedure on four or more vessels
38.16 Endarterectomy of abdominal arteries
38.18 Endarterectomy of lower limb arteries

35361

35361 Thromboendarterectomy, including patch graft, if performed; combined aortoiliac

ICD-9-CM Diagnostic

440.8 Atherosclerosis of other specified arteries
444.01 Saddle embolus of abdominal aorta
444.09 Other arterial embolism and thrombosis of abdominal aorta
444.81 Embolism and thrombosis of iliac artery
445.89 Atheroembolism of other site
997.79 Vascular complications of other vessels — (Use additional code to identify complications)

ICD-9-CM Procedural

00.40 Procedure on single vessel
00.41 Procedure on two vessels
00.42 Procedure on three vessels
38.14 Endarterectomy of aorta
38.16 Endarterectomy of abdominal arteries
38.18 Endarterectomy of lower limb arteries

35363

35363 Thromboendarterectomy, including patch graft, if performed; combined aortoiliofemoral

ICD-9-CM Diagnostic

440.0 Atherosclerosis of aorta
440.1 Atherosclerosis of renal artery
440.21 Atherosclerosis of native arteries of the extremities with intermittent claudication
440.8 Atherosclerosis of other specified arteries
444.01 Saddle embolus of abdominal aorta
444.09 Other arterial embolism and thrombosis of abdominal aorta
444.22 Embolism and thrombosis of arteries of lower extremity
444.81 Embolism and thrombosis of iliac artery
445.02 Atheroembolism of lower extremity
445.89 Atheroembolism of other site
997.79 Vascular complications of other vessels — (Use additional code to identify complications)

ICD-9-CM Procedural

00.40 Procedure on single vessel
00.41 Procedure on two vessels
00.42 Procedure on three vessels

00.43 Procedure on four or more vessels
38.14 Endarterectomy of aorta
38.16 Endarterectomy of abdominal arteries
38.18 Endarterectomy of lower limb arteries

35371-35372

35371 Thromboendarterectomy, including patch graft, if performed; common femoral
35372 deep (profunda) femoral

ICD-9-CM Diagnostic

249.70 Secondary diabetes mellitus with peripheral circulatory disorders, not stated as uncontrolled, or unspecified — (Use additional code to identify manifestation: 443.81, 785.4) (Use additional code to identify any associated insulin use: V58.67)
249.71 Secondary diabetes mellitus with peripheral circulatory disorders, uncontrolled — (Use additional code to identify manifestation: 443.81, 785.4) (Use additional code to identify any associated insulin use: V58.67)
250.70 Diabetes with peripheral circulatory disorders, type II or unspecified type, not stated as uncontrolled — (Use additional code to identify manifestation: 443.81, 785.4)
250.71 Diabetes with peripheral circulatory disorders, type I [juvenile type], not stated as uncontrolled — (Use additional code to identify manifestation: 443.81, 785.4)
250.72 Diabetes with peripheral circulatory disorders, type II or unspecified type, uncontrolled — (Use additional code to identify manifestation: 443.81, 785.4)
250.73 Diabetes with peripheral circulatory disorders, type I [juvenile type], uncontrolled — (Use additional code to identify manifestation: 443.81, 785.4)
440.20 Atherosclerosis of native arteries of the extremities, unspecified ▼
440.21 Atherosclerosis of native arteries of the extremities with intermittent claudication
440.22 Atherosclerosis of native arteries of the extremities with rest pain
440.23 Atherosclerosis of native arteries of the extremities with ulceration — (Use additional code for any associated ulceration: 707.10-707.19, 707.8, 707.9)
440.24 Atherosclerosis of native arteries of the extremities with gangrene — (Use additional code for any associated ulceration: 707.10-707.19, 707.8, 707.9)
440.29 Other atherosclerosis of native arteries of the extremities
440.4 Chronic total occlusion of artery of the extremities
443.29 Dissection of other artery
443.81 Peripheral angiopathy in diseases classified elsewhere — (Code first underlying disease: 249.7, 250.7) ☒
443.9 Unspecified peripheral vascular disease ▼
444.22 Embolism and thrombosis of arteries of lower extremity
444.9 Embolism and thrombosis of unspecified artery ▼
445.02 Atheroembolism of lower extremity
447.1 Stricture of artery
447.2 Rupture of artery
785.9 Other symptoms involving cardiovascular system
902.53 Iliac artery injury
904.2 Femoral vein injury

ICD-9-CM Procedural

00.40 Procedure on single vessel
00.41 Procedure on two vessels
38.18 Endarterectomy of lower limb arteries

35450

35450 Transluminal balloon angioplasty, open; renal or other visceral artery

ICD-9-CM Diagnostic

405.01 Secondary renovascular hypertension, malignant
405.11 Secondary renovascular hypertension, benign
405.91 Secondary renovascular hypertension, unspecified ▼
440.1 Atherosclerosis of renal artery
440.8 Atherosclerosis of other specified arteries
447.1 Stricture of artery
447.4 Celiac artery compression syndrome
557.0 Acute vascular insufficiency of intestine
557.1 Chronic vascular insufficiency of intestine

ICD-9-CM Procedural

00.40 Procedure on single vessel
00.41 Procedure on two vessels
00.42 Procedure on three vessels
00.43 Procedure on four or more vessels
39.50 Angioplasty of other non-coronary vessel(s)

35452

35452 Transluminal balloon angioplasty, open; aortic

ICD-9-CM Diagnostic

440.0 Atherosclerosis of aorta
444.89 Embolism and thrombosis of other specified artery
747.22 Congenital atresia and stenosis of aorta

ICD-9-CM Procedural

00.40 Procedure on single vessel
39.50 Angioplasty of other non-coronary vessel(s)

35458

35458 Transluminal balloon angioplasty, open; brachiocephalic trunk or branches, each vessel

ICD-9-CM Diagnostic

249.70 Secondary diabetes mellitus with peripheral circulatory disorders, not stated as uncontrolled, or unspecified — (Use additional code to identify manifestation: 443.81, 785.4) (Use additional code to identify any associated insulin use: V58.67)
249.71 Secondary diabetes mellitus with peripheral circulatory disorders, uncontrolled — (Use additional code to identify manifestation: 443.81, 785.4) (Use additional code to identify any associated insulin use: V58.67)
250.70 Diabetes with peripheral circulatory disorders, type II or unspecified type, not stated as uncontrolled — (Use additional code to identify manifestation: 443.81, 785.4)
250.71 Diabetes with peripheral circulatory disorders, type I [juvenile type], not stated as uncontrolled — (Use additional code to identify manifestation: 443.81, 785.4)
250.72 Diabetes with peripheral circulatory disorders, type II or unspecified type, uncontrolled — (Use additional code to identify manifestation: 443.81, 785.4)
250.73 Diabetes with peripheral circulatory disorders, type I [juvenile type], uncontrolled — (Use additional code to identify manifestation: 443.81, 785.4)
433.80 Occlusion and stenosis of other specified precerebral artery without mention of cerebral infarction — (Use additional code, if applicable, to identify status post administration of tPA (rtPA) in a different facility within the last 24 hours prior to admission to current facility: V45.88)
433.81 Occlusion and stenosis of other specified precerebral artery with cerebral infarction — (Use additional code, if applicable, to identify status post administration of tPA (rtPA) in a different facility within the last 24 hours prior to admission to current facility: V45.88)
440.20 Atherosclerosis of native arteries of the extremities, unspecified ▼
440.21 Atherosclerosis of native arteries of the extremities with intermittent claudication
440.22 Atherosclerosis of native arteries of the extremities with rest pain
440.23 Atherosclerosis of native arteries of the extremities with ulceration — (Use additional code for any associated ulceration: 707.10-707.19, 707.8, 707.9)
440.24 Atherosclerosis of native arteries of the extremities with gangrene — (Use additional code for any associated ulceration: 707.10-707.19, 707.8, 707.9)
440.4 Chronic total occlusion of artery of the extremities
440.8 Atherosclerosis of other specified arteries
443.81 Peripheral angiopathy in diseases classified elsewhere — (Code first underlying disease: 249.7, 250.7) ☒
443.9 Unspecified peripheral vascular disease ▼
444.21 Embolism and thrombosis of arteries of upper extremity

444.22 Embolism and thrombosis of arteries of lower extremity
445.01 Atheroembolism of upper extremity
445.02 Atheroembolism of lower extremity
447.1 Stricture of artery
447.8 Other specified disorders of arteries and arterioles
459.2 Compression of vein
747.63 Congenital upper limb vessel anomaly
747.64 Congenital lower limb vessel anomaly
785.4 Gangrene — (Code first any associated underlying condition)
785.9 Other symptoms involving cardiovascular system
996.74 Other complications due to other vascular device, implant, and graft — (Use additional code to identify complication: 338.18-338.19, 338.28-338.29)
999.2 Other vascular complications of medical care, not elsewhere classified

ICD-9-CM Procedural

00.40 Procedure on single vessel
00.41 Procedure on two vessels
00.42 Procedure on three vessels
00.43 Procedure on four or more vessels
39.50 Angioplasty of other non-coronary vessel(s)

HCPCS Level II Supplies & Services

C1725 Catheter, transluminal angioplasty, nonlaser (may include guidance, infusion/perfusion capability)

35460

35460 Transluminal balloon angioplasty, open; venous

ICD-9-CM Diagnostic

443.89 Other peripheral vascular disease
453.2 Other venous embolism and thrombosis, of inferior vena cava
453.3 Embolism and thrombosis of renal vein
453.40 Acute venous embolism and thrombosis of unspecified deep vessels of lower extremity ▽
453.41 Acute venous embolism and thrombosis of deep vessels of proximal lower extremity
453.42 Acute venous embolism and thrombosis of deep vessels of distal lower extremity
453.50 Chronic venous embolism and thrombosis of unspecified deep vessels of lower extremity — (Use additional code, if applicable, for associated long-term (current) use of anticoagulants (V58.61)) ▽
453.51 Chronic venous embolism and thrombosis of deep vessels of proximal lower extremity — (Use additional code, if applicable, for associated long-term (current) use of anticoagulants (V58.61))
453.52 Chronic venous embolism and thrombosis of deep vessels of distal lower extremity — (Use additional code, if applicable, for associated long-term (current) use of anticoagulants (V58.61))
453.6 Venous embolism and thrombosis of superficial vessels of lower extremity — (Use additional code, if applicable, for associated long-term (current) use of anticoagulants (V58.61))
453.71 Chronic venous embolism and thrombosis of superficial veins of upper extremity — (Use additional code, if applicable, for associated long-term (current) use of anticoagulants (V58.61))
453.72 Chronic venous embolism and thrombosis of deep veins of upper extremity — (Use additional code, if applicable, for associated long-term (current) use of anticoagulants (V58.61))
453.73 Chronic venous embolism and thrombosis of upper extremity, unspecified — (Use additional code, if applicable, for associated long-term (current) use of anticoagulants (V58.61)) ▽
453.74 Chronic venous embolism and thrombosis of axillary veins — (Use additional code, if applicable, for associated long-term (current) use of anticoagulants (V58.61))
453.75 Chronic venous embolism and thrombosis of subclavian veins — (Use additional code, if applicable, for associated long-term (current) use of anticoagulants (V58.61))
453.76 Chronic venous embolism and thrombosis of internal jugular veins — (Use additional code, if applicable, for associated long-term (current) use of anticoagulants (V58.61))
453.77 Chronic venous embolism and thrombosis of other thoracic veins — (Use additional code, if applicable, for associated long-term (current) use of anticoagulants (V58.61))
453.79 Chronic venous embolism and thrombosis of other specified veins — (Use additional code, if applicable, for associated long-term (current) use of anticoagulants (V58.61))
453.81 Acute venous embolism and thrombosis of superficial veins of upper extremity
453.82 Acute venous embolism and thrombosis of deep veins of upper extremity
453.83 Acute venous embolism and thrombosis of upper extremity, unspecified ▽
453.84 Acute venous embolism and thrombosis of axillary veins
453.85 Acute venous embolism and thrombosis of subclavian veins
453.86 Acute venous embolism and thrombosis of internal jugular veins
453.87 Acute venous embolism and thrombosis of other thoracic veins
453.89 Acute venous embolism and thrombosis of other specified veins
453.9 Embolism and thrombosis of unspecified site ▽
459.2 Compression of vein
459.81 Unspecified venous (peripheral) insufficiency — (Use additional code for any associated ulceration: 707.10-707.19, 707.8, 707.9) ▽
459.89 Other specified circulatory system disorders
747.63 Congenital upper limb vessel anomaly
747.64 Congenital lower limb vessel anomaly
747.69 Congenital anomaly of other specified site of peripheral vascular system

ICD-9-CM Procedural

00.40 Procedure on single vessel
00.41 Procedure on two vessels
00.42 Procedure on three vessels
00.43 Procedure on four or more vessels
39.50 Angioplasty of other non-coronary vessel(s)

HCPCS Level II Supplies & Services

C1725 Catheter, transluminal angioplasty, nonlaser (may include guidance, infusion/perfusion capability)

35471

35471 Transluminal balloon angioplasty, percutaneous; renal or visceral artery

ICD-9-CM Diagnostic

277.1 Disorders of porphyrin metabolism — (Use additional code to identify any associated intellectual disabilities)
277.30 Amyloidosis, unspecified — (Use additional code to identify any associated intellectual disabilities) ▽
277.31 Familial Mediterranean fever — (Use additional code to identify any associated intellectual disabilities)
277.39 Other amyloidosis — (Use additional code to identify any associated intellectual disabilities)
357.4 Polyneuropathy in other diseases classified elsewhere — (Code first underlying disease, as: 032.0-032.9,135, 251.2, 265.0, 265.2, 266.0-266.9, 277.1, 277.30-277.39, 585.9, 586) ☒
405.01 Secondary renovascular hypertension, malignant
405.11 Secondary renovascular hypertension, benign
405.91 Secondary renovascular hypertension, unspecified ▽
440.1 Atherosclerosis of renal artery
440.8 Atherosclerosis of other specified arteries
440.9 Generalized and unspecified atherosclerosis ▽
443.9 Unspecified peripheral vascular disease ▽
444.01 Saddle embolus of abdominal aorta
444.09 Other arterial embolism and thrombosis of abdominal aorta
445.81 Atheroembolism of kidney — (Use additional code for any associated acute kidney failure or chronic kidney disease: 584, 585)
445.89 Atheroembolism of other site

447.1 Stricture of artery
447.4 Celiac artery compression syndrome
447.9 Unspecified disorders of arteries and arterioles
557.0 Acute vascular insufficiency of intestine
557.1 Chronic vascular insufficiency of intestine
557.9 Unspecified vascular insufficiency of intestine
585.1 Chronic kidney disease, Stage I — (Use additional code to identify kidney transplant status, if applicable: V42.0. Use additional code to identify manifestation: 357.4, 420.0. Code first hypertensive chronic kidney disease, if applicable: 403.00-403.91, 404.00-404.93)
585.2 Chronic kidney disease, Stage II (mild) — (Use additional code to identify kidney transplant status, if applicable: V42.0. Use additional code to identify manifestation: 357.4, 420.0. Code first hypertensive chronic kidney disease, if applicable: 403.00-403.91, 404.00-404.93)
585.3 Chronic kidney disease, Stage III (moderate) — (Use additional code to identify kidney transplant status, if applicable: V42.0. Use additional code to identify manifestation: 357.4, 420.0. Code first hypertensive chronic kidney disease, if applicable: 403.00-403.91, 404.00-404.93)
585.4 Chronic kidney disease, Stage IV (severe) — (Use additional code to identify kidney transplant status, if applicable: V42.0. Use additional code to identify manifestation: 357.4, 420.0. Code first hypertensive chronic kidney disease, if applicable: 403.00-403.91, 404.00-404.93)
585.5 Chronic kidney disease, Stage V — (Use additional code to identify kidney transplant status, if applicable: V42.0. Use additional code to identify manifestation: 357.4, 420.0. Code first hypertensive chronic kidney disease, if applicable: 403.00-403.91, 404.00-404.93)
585.6 End stage renal disease — (Use additional code to identify kidney transplant status, if applicable: V42.0. Use additional code to identify manifestation: 357.4, 420.0. Code first hypertensive chronic kidney disease, if applicable: 403.00-403.91, 404.00-404.93)
585.9 Chronic kidney disease, unspecified — (Use additional code to identify kidney transplant status, if applicable: V42.0. Use additional code to identify manifestation: 357.4, 420.0. Code first hypertensive chronic kidney disease, if applicable: 403.00-403.91, 404.00-404.93)
593.81 Vascular disorders of kidney
747.62 Congenital renal vessel anomaly
996.1 Mechanical complication of other vascular device, implant, and graft

ICD-9-CM Procedural

00.40 Procedure on single vessel
00.41 Procedure on two vessels
00.42 Procedure on three vessels
00.43 Procedure on four or more vessels
39.50 Angioplasty of other non-coronary vessel(s)

HCPCS Level II Supplies & Services

C1725 Catheter, transluminal angioplasty, nonlaser (may include guidance, infusion/perfusion capability)

35472

35472 Transluminal balloon angioplasty, percutaneous; aortic

ICD-9-CM Diagnostic

440.0 Atherosclerosis of aorta
444.89 Embolism and thrombosis of other specified artery
747.22 Congenital atresia and stenosis of aorta

ICD-9-CM Procedural

00.40 Procedure on single vessel
39.50 Angioplasty of other non-coronary vessel(s)

HCPCS Level II Supplies & Services

C1725 Catheter, transluminal angioplasty, nonlaser (may include guidance, infusion/perfusion capability)

35475

35475 Transluminal balloon angioplasty, percutaneous; brachiocephalic trunk or branches, each vessel

ICD-9-CM Diagnostic

249.70 Secondary diabetes mellitus with peripheral circulatory disorders, not stated as uncontrolled, or unspecified — (Use additional code to identify manifestation: 443.81, 785.4) (Use additional code to identify any associated insulin use: V58.67)
249.71 Secondary diabetes mellitus with peripheral circulatory disorders, uncontrolled — (Use additional code to identify manifestation: 443.81, 785.4) (Use additional code to identify any associated insulin use: V58.67)
250.70 Diabetes with peripheral circulatory disorders, type II or unspecified type, not stated as uncontrolled — (Use additional code to identify manifestation: 443.81, 785.4)
250.71 Diabetes with peripheral circulatory disorders, type I [juvenile type], not stated as uncontrolled — (Use additional code to identify manifestation: 443.81, 785.4)
250.72 Diabetes with peripheral circulatory disorders, type II or unspecified type, uncontrolled — (Use additional code to identify manifestation: 443.81, 785.4)
250.73 Diabetes with peripheral circulatory disorders, type I [juvenile type], uncontrolled — (Use additional code to identify manifestation: 443.81, 785.4)
433.80 Occlusion and stenosis of other specified precerebral artery without mention of cerebral infarction — (Use additional code, if applicable, to identify status post administration of tPA (rtPA) in a different facility within the last 24 hours prior to admission to current facility: V45.88)
433.81 Occlusion and stenosis of other specified precerebral artery with cerebral infarction — (Use additional code, if applicable, to identify status post administration of tPA (rtPA) in a different facility within the last 24 hours prior to admission to current facility: V45.88)
440.20 Atherosclerosis of native arteries of the extremities, unspecified
440.21 Atherosclerosis of native arteries of the extremities with intermittent claudication
440.22 Atherosclerosis of native arteries of the extremities with rest pain
440.23 Atherosclerosis of native arteries of the extremities with ulceration — (Use additional code for any associated ulceration: 707.10-707.19, 707.8, 707.9)
440.24 Atherosclerosis of native arteries of the extremities with gangrene — (Use additional code for any associated ulceration: 707.10-707.19, 707.8, 707.9)
440.29 Other atherosclerosis of native arteries of the extremities
440.30 Atherosclerosis of unspecified bypass graft of extremities
440.31 Atherosclerosis of autologous vein bypass graft of extremities
440.32 Atherosclerosis of nonautologous biological bypass graft of extremities
440.4 Chronic total occlusion of artery of the extremities
440.8 Atherosclerosis of other specified arteries
440.9 Generalized and unspecified atherosclerosis
442.3 Aneurysm of artery of lower extremity
443.81 Peripheral angiopathy in diseases classified elsewhere — (Code first underlying disease: 249.7, 250.7)
443.9 Unspecified peripheral vascular disease
444.21 Embolism and thrombosis of arteries of upper extremity
444.22 Embolism and thrombosis of arteries of lower extremity
444.89 Embolism and thrombosis of other specified artery
444.9 Embolism and thrombosis of unspecified artery
445.01 Atheroembolism of upper extremity
445.02 Atheroembolism of lower extremity
447.1 Stricture of artery
447.8 Other specified disorders of arteries and arterioles
447.9 Unspecified disorders of arteries and arterioles
747.63 Congenital upper limb vessel anomaly
747.64 Congenital lower limb vessel anomaly
785.4 Gangrene — (Code first any associated underlying condition)
785.59 Other shock without mention of trauma
785.9 Other symptoms involving cardiovascular system
996.62 Infection and inflammatory reaction due to other vascular device, implant, and graft — (Use additional code to identify specified infections)

996.73 Other complications due to renal dialysis device, implant, and graft — (Use additional code to identify complication: 338.18-338.19, 338.28-338.29)

996.74 Other complications due to other vascular device, implant, and graft — (Use additional code to identify complication: 338.18-338.19, 338.28-338.29)

ICD-9-CM Procedural

00.40 Procedure on single vessel

00.41 Procedure on two vessels

00.42 Procedure on three vessels

00.43 Procedure on four or more vessels

00.61 Percutaneous angioplasty of extracranial vessel(s)

00.62 Percutaneous angioplasty of intracranial vessel(s)

39.50 Angioplasty of other non-coronary vessel(s)

HCPCS Level II Supplies & Services

C1725 Catheter, transluminal angioplasty, nonlaser (may include guidance, infusion/perfusion capability)

35476

35476 Transluminal balloon angioplasty, percutaneous; venous

ICD-9-CM Diagnostic

440.30 Atherosclerosis of unspecified bypass graft of extremities

440.31 Atherosclerosis of autologous vein bypass graft of extremities

440.32 Atherosclerosis of nonautologous biological bypass graft of extremities

440.9 Generalized and unspecified atherosclerosis

443.89 Other peripheral vascular disease

443.9 Unspecified peripheral vascular disease

453.2 Other venous embolism and thrombosis, of inferior vena cava

453.3 Embolism and thrombosis of renal vein

453.40 Acute venous embolism and thrombosis of unspecified deep vessels of lower extremity

453.41 Acute venous embolism and thrombosis of deep vessels of proximal lower extremity

453.42 Acute venous embolism and thrombosis of deep vessels of distal lower extremity

453.50 Chronic venous embolism and thrombosis of unspecified deep vessels of lower extremity — (Use additional code, if applicable, for associated long-term (current) use of anticoagulants (V58.61))

453.51 Chronic venous embolism and thrombosis of deep vessels of proximal lower extremity — (Use additional code, if applicable, for associated long-term (current) use of anticoagulants (V58.61))

453.52 Chronic venous embolism and thrombosis of deep vessels of distal lower extremity — (Use additional code, if applicable, for associated long-term (current) use of anticoagulants (V58.61))

453.6 Venous embolism and thrombosis of superficial vessels of lower extremity — (Use additional code, if applicable, for associated long-term (current) use of anticoagulants (V58.61))

453.71 Chronic venous embolism and thrombosis of superficial veins of upper extremity — (Use additional code, if applicable, for associated long-term (current) use of anticoagulants (V58.61))

453.72 Chronic venous embolism and thrombosis of deep veins of upper extremity — (Use additional code, if applicable, for associated long-term (current) use of anticoagulants (V58.61))

453.73 Chronic venous embolism and thrombosis of upper extremity, unspecified — (Use additional code, if applicable, for associated long-term (current) use of anticoagulants (V58.61))

453.74 Chronic venous embolism and thrombosis of axillary veins — (Use additional code, if applicable, for associated long-term (current) use of anticoagulants (V58.61))

453.75 Chronic venous embolism and thrombosis of subclavian veins — (Use additional code, if applicable, for associated long-term (current) use of anticoagulants (V58.61))

453.76 Chronic venous embolism and thrombosis of internal jugular veins — (Use additional code, if applicable, for associated long-term (current) use of anticoagulants (V58.61))

453.77 Chronic venous embolism and thrombosis of other thoracic veins — (Use additional code, if applicable, for associated long-term (current) use of anticoagulants (V58.61))

453.79 Chronic venous embolism and thrombosis of other specified veins — (Use additional code, if applicable, for associated long-term (current) use of anticoagulants (V58.61))

453.81 Acute venous embolism and thrombosis of superficial veins of upper extremity

453.82 Acute venous embolism and thrombosis of deep veins of upper extremity

453.83 Acute venous embolism and thrombosis of upper extremity, unspecified

453.84 Acute venous embolism and thrombosis of axillary veins

453.85 Acute venous embolism and thrombosis of subclavian veins

453.86 Acute venous embolism and thrombosis of internal jugular veins

453.87 Acute venous embolism and thrombosis of other thoracic veins

453.89 Acute venous embolism and thrombosis of other specified veins

453.9 Embolism and thrombosis of unspecified site

459.2 Compression of vein

459.81 Unspecified venous (peripheral) insufficiency — (Use additional code for any associated ulceration: 707.10-707.19, 707.8, 707.9)

459.89 Other specified circulatory system disorders

593.81 Vascular disorders of kidney

729.81 Swelling of limb

747.63 Congenital upper limb vessel anomaly

747.64 Congenital lower limb vessel anomaly

747.69 Congenital anomaly of other specified site of peripheral vascular system

996.1 Mechanical complication of other vascular device, implant, and graft

996.62 Infection and inflammatory reaction due to other vascular device, implant, and graft — (Use additional code to identify specified infections)

996.73 Other complications due to renal dialysis device, implant, and graft — (Use additional code to identify complication: 338.18-338.19, 338.28-338.29)

996.74 Other complications due to other vascular device, implant, and graft — (Use additional code to identify complication: 338.18-338.19, 338.28-338.29)

ICD-9-CM Procedural

00.40 Procedure on single vessel

00.41 Procedure on two vessels

00.42 Procedure on three vessels

00.43 Procedure on four or more vessels

39.50 Angioplasty of other non-coronary vessel(s)

HCPCS Level II Supplies & Services

C1725 Catheter, transluminal angioplasty, nonlaser (may include guidance, infusion/perfusion capability)

35501

35501 Bypass graft, with vein; common carotid-ipsilateral internal carotid

ICD-9-CM Diagnostic

433.10 Occlusion and stenosis of carotid artery without mention of cerebral infarction — (Use additional code, if applicable, to identify status post administration of tPA (rtPA) in a different facility within the last 24 hours prior to admission to current facility: V45.88)

433.11 Occlusion and stenosis of carotid artery with cerebral infarction — (Use additional code, if applicable, to identify status post administration of tPA (rtPA) in a different facility within the last 24 hours prior to admission to current facility: V45.88)

433.30 Occlusion and stenosis of multiple and bilateral precerebral arteries without mention of cerebral infarction — (Use additional code, if applicable, to identify status post administration of tPA (rtPA) in a different facility within the last 24 hours prior to admission to current facility: V45.88)

433.31 Occlusion and stenosis of multiple and bilateral precerebral arteries with cerebral infarction — (Use additional code, if applicable, to identify status post administration of tPA (rtPA) in a different facility within the last 24 hours prior to admission to current facility: V45.88)

433.80 Occlusion and stenosis of other specified precerebral artery without mention of cerebral infarction — (Use additional code, if applicable, to identify status post administration of tPA (rtPA) in a different facility within the last 24 hours prior to admission to current facility: V45.88)

433.81 Occlusion and stenosis of other specified precerebral artery with cerebral infarction — (Use additional code, if applicable, to identify status post administration of tPA (rtPA) in a different facility within the last 24 hours prior to admission to current facility: V45.88)

435.8 Other specified transient cerebral ischemias — (Use additional code to identify presence of hypertension)

437.1 Other generalized ischemic cerebrovascular disease — (Use additional code to identify presence of hypertension)

437.3 Cerebral aneurysm, nonruptured — (Use additional code to identify presence of hypertension)

440.8 Atherosclerosis of other specified arteries

442.81 Aneurysm of artery of neck

443.21 Dissection of carotid artery

447.1 Stricture of artery

447.70 Aortic ectasia, unspecified site

747.81 Congenital anomaly of cerebrovascular system

780.2 Syncope and collapse

785.9 Other symptoms involving cardiovascular system

900.00 Injury to carotid artery, unspecified

900.01 Common carotid artery injury

900.02 External carotid artery injury

900.03 Internal carotid artery injury

906.0 Late effect of open wound of head, neck, and trunk

908.3 Late effect of injury to blood vessel of head, neck, and extremities

925.2 Crushing injury of neck — (Use additional code to identify any associated injuries, such as: 800-829, 850.0-854.1, 860.0-869.1)

996.1 Mechanical complication of other vascular device, implant, and graft

996.74 Other complications due to other vascular device, implant, and graft — (Use additional code to identify complication: 338.18-338.19, 338.28-338.29)

ICD-9-CM Procedural

39.22 Aorta-subclavian-carotid bypass

35506

35506 Bypass graft, with vein; carotid-subclavian or subclavian-carotid

ICD-9-CM Diagnostic

433.10 Occlusion and stenosis of carotid artery without mention of cerebral infarction — (Use additional code, if applicable, to identify status post administration of tPA (rtPA) in a different facility within the last 24 hours prior to admission to current facility: V45.88)

433.11 Occlusion and stenosis of carotid artery with cerebral infarction — (Use additional code, if applicable, to identify status post administration of tPA (rtPA) in a different facility within the last 24 hours prior to admission to current facility: V45.88)

433.30 Occlusion and stenosis of multiple and bilateral precerebral arteries without mention of cerebral infarction — (Use additional code, if applicable, to identify status post administration of tPA (rtPA) in a different facility within the last 24 hours prior to admission to current facility: V45.88)

433.31 Occlusion and stenosis of multiple and bilateral precerebral arteries with cerebral infarction — (Use additional code, if applicable, to identify status post administration of tPA (rtPA) in a different facility within the last 24 hours prior to admission to current facility: V45.88)

435.2 Subclavian steal syndrome — (Use additional code to identify presence of hypertension)

435.8 Other specified transient cerebral ischemias — (Use additional code to identify presence of hypertension)

440.8 Atherosclerosis of other specified arteries

442.81 Aneurysm of artery of neck

442.82 Aneurysm of subclavian artery

443.21 Dissection of carotid artery

443.29 Dissection of other artery

447.1 Stricture of artery

447.6 Unspecified arteritis

447.70 Aortic ectasia, unspecified site

447.71 Thoracic aortic ectasia

747.69 Congenital anomaly of other specified site of peripheral vascular system

785.9 Other symptoms involving cardiovascular system

874.9 Open wound of other and unspecified parts of neck, complicated

900.01 Common carotid artery injury

900.02 External carotid artery injury

900.03 Internal carotid artery injury

900.82 Injury to multiple blood vessels of head and neck

901.1 Innominate and subclavian artery injury

906.0 Late effect of open wound of head, neck, and trunk

908.3 Late effect of injury to blood vessel of head, neck, and extremities

925.2 Crushing injury of neck — (Use additional code to identify any associated injuries, such as: 800-829, 850.0-854.1, 860.0-869.1)

996.1 Mechanical complication of other vascular device, implant, and graft

996.74 Other complications due to other vascular device, implant, and graft — (Use additional code to identify complication: 338.18-338.19, 338.28-338.29)

ICD-9-CM Procedural

39.22 Aorta-subclavian-carotid bypass

35508

35508 Bypass graft, with vein; carotid-vertebral

ICD-9-CM Diagnostic

433.20 Occlusion and stenosis of vertebral artery without mention of cerebral infarction — (Use additional code, if applicable, to identify status post administration of tPA (rtPA) in a different facility within the last 24 hours prior to admission to current facility: V45.88)

433.21 Occlusion and stenosis of vertebral artery with cerebral infarction — (Use additional code, if applicable, to identify status post administration of tPA (rtPA) in a different facility within the last 24 hours prior to admission to current facility: V45.88)

435.1 Vertebral artery syndrome — (Use additional code to identify presence of hypertension)

435.8 Other specified transient cerebral ischemias — (Use additional code to identify presence of hypertension)

440.8 Atherosclerosis of other specified arteries

442.81 Aneurysm of artery of neck

443.21 Dissection of carotid artery

443.24 Dissection of vertebral artery

447.1 Stricture of artery

447.70 Aortic ectasia, unspecified site

447.71 Thoracic aortic ectasia

747.69 Congenital anomaly of other specified site of peripheral vascular system

874.9 Open wound of other and unspecified parts of neck, complicated

900.82 Injury to multiple blood vessels of head and neck

906.0 Late effect of open wound of head, neck, and trunk

ICD-9-CM Procedural

39.28 Extracranial-intracranial (EC-IC) vascular bypass

35509

35509 Bypass graft, with vein; carotid-contralateral carotid

ICD-9-CM Diagnostic

433.10 Occlusion and stenosis of carotid artery without mention of cerebral infarction — (Use additional code, if applicable, to identify status post administration of tPA (rtPA) in a different facility within the last 24 hours prior to admission to current facility: V45.88)

433.11 Occlusion and stenosis of carotid artery with cerebral infarction — (Use additional code, if applicable, to identify status post administration of tPA (rtPA) in a different facility within the last 24 hours prior to admission to current facility: V45.88)
433.30 Occlusion and stenosis of multiple and bilateral precerebral arteries without mention of cerebral infarction — (Use additional code, if applicable, to identify status post administration of tPA (rtPA) in a different facility within the last 24 hours prior to admission to current facility: V45.88)
433.31 Occlusion and stenosis of multiple and bilateral precerebral arteries with cerebral infarction — (Use additional code, if applicable, to identify status post administration of tPA (rtPA) in a different facility within the last 24 hours prior to admission to current facility: V45.88)
435.8 Other specified transient cerebral ischemias — (Use additional code to identify presence of hypertension)
442.81 Aneurysm of artery of neck
443.21 Dissection of carotid artery
447.1 Stricture of artery
447.70 Aortic ectasia, unspecified site ♡
747.69 Congenital anomaly of other specified site of peripheral vascular system
900.01 Common carotid artery injury
900.02 External carotid artery injury
900.03 Internal carotid artery injury
906.0 Late effect of open wound of head, neck, and trunk
906.4 Late effect of crushing
908.3 Late effect of injury to blood vessel of head, neck, and extremities
925.2 Crushing injury of neck — (Use additional code to identify any associated injuries, such as: 800-829, 850.0-854.1, 860.0-869.1)
996.1 Mechanical complication of other vascular device, implant, and graft
996.74 Other complications due to other vascular device, implant, and graft — (Use additional code to identify complication: 338.18-338.19, 338.28-338.29)

ICD-9-CM Procedural

39.22 Aorta-subclavian-carotid bypass

35510

35510 Bypass graft, with vein; carotid-brachial

ICD-9-CM Diagnostic

433.10 Occlusion and stenosis of carotid artery without mention of cerebral infarction — (Use additional code, if applicable, to identify status post administration of tPA (rtPA) in a different facility within the last 24 hours prior to admission to current facility: V45.88)
433.11 Occlusion and stenosis of carotid artery with cerebral infarction — (Use additional code, if applicable, to identify status post administration of tPA (rtPA) in a different facility within the last 24 hours prior to admission to current facility: V45.88)
433.30 Occlusion and stenosis of multiple and bilateral precerebral arteries without mention of cerebral infarction — (Use additional code, if applicable, to identify status post administration of tPA (rtPA) in a different facility within the last 24 hours prior to admission to current facility: V45.88)
433.31 Occlusion and stenosis of multiple and bilateral precerebral arteries with cerebral infarction — (Use additional code, if applicable, to identify status post administration of tPA (rtPA) in a different facility within the last 24 hours prior to admission to current facility: V45.88)
433.80 Occlusion and stenosis of other specified precerebral artery without mention of cerebral infarction — (Use additional code, if applicable, to identify status post administration of tPA (rtPA) in a different facility within the last 24 hours prior to admission to current facility: V45.88)
433.81 Occlusion and stenosis of other specified precerebral artery with cerebral infarction — (Use additional code, if applicable, to identify status post administration of tPA (rtPA) in a different facility within the last 24 hours prior to admission to current facility: V45.88)
435.8 Other specified transient cerebral ischemias — (Use additional code to identify presence of hypertension)
437.1 Other generalized ischemic cerebrovascular disease — (Use additional code to identify presence of hypertension)
440.20 Atherosclerosis of native arteries of the extremities, unspecified ♡
440.8 Atherosclerosis of other specified arteries
442.0 Aneurysm of artery of upper extremity
442.81 Aneurysm of artery of neck
443.21 Dissection of carotid artery
443.29 Dissection of other artery
443.9 Unspecified peripheral vascular disease ♡
444.21 Embolism and thrombosis of arteries of upper extremity
445.01 Atheroembolism of upper extremity
447.1 Stricture of artery
447.70 Aortic ectasia, unspecified site ♡
447.71 Thoracic aortic ectasia
747.81 Congenital anomaly of cerebrovascular system
780.2 Syncope and collapse
785.9 Other symptoms involving cardiovascular system
900.00 Injury to carotid artery, unspecified ♡
900.01 Common carotid artery injury
900.02 External carotid artery injury
900.03 Internal carotid artery injury
903.1 Brachial blood vessels injury
906.0 Late effect of open wound of head, neck, and trunk
908.3 Late effect of injury to blood vessel of head, neck, and extremities
925.2 Crushing injury of neck — (Use additional code to identify any associated injuries, such as: 800-829, 850.0-854.1, 860.0-869.1)
996.1 Mechanical complication of other vascular device, implant, and graft
996.74 Other complications due to other vascular device, implant, and graft — (Use additional code to identify complication: 338.18-338.19, 338.28-338.29)

ICD-9-CM Procedural

39.22 Aorta-subclavian-carotid bypass

35511

35511 Bypass graft, with vein; subclavian-subclavian

ICD-9-CM Diagnostic

435.2 Subclavian steal syndrome — (Use additional code to identify presence of hypertension)
435.8 Other specified transient cerebral ischemias — (Use additional code to identify presence of hypertension)
440.8 Atherosclerosis of other specified arteries
442.82 Aneurysm of subclavian artery
443.29 Dissection of other artery
444.89 Embolism and thrombosis of other specified artery
447.1 Stricture of artery
447.6 Unspecified arteritis ♡
447.71 Thoracic aortic ectasia
747.69 Congenital anomaly of other specified site of peripheral vascular system
785.9 Other symptoms involving cardiovascular system
874.9 Open wound of other and unspecified parts of neck, complicated ♡
900.82 Injury to multiple blood vessels of head and neck
900.89 Injury to other specified blood vessels of head and neck
901.1 Innominate and subclavian artery injury
901.89 Injury to specified blood vessels of thorax, other
906.0 Late effect of open wound of head, neck, and trunk
906.4 Late effect of crushing
908.3 Late effect of injury to blood vessel of head, neck, and extremities
996.1 Mechanical complication of other vascular device, implant, and graft

996.74 Other complications due to other vascular device, implant, and graft — (Use additional code to identify complication: 338.18-338.19, 338.28-338.29)
998.2 Accidental puncture or laceration during procedure

ICD-9-CM Procedural

39.22 Aorta-subclavian-carotid bypass

35512

35512 Bypass graft, with vein; subclavian-brachial

ICD-9-CM Diagnostic

435.2 Subclavian steal syndrome — (Use additional code to identify presence of hypertension)
435.8 Other specified transient cerebral ischemias — (Use additional code to identify presence of hypertension)
440.20 Atherosclerosis of native arteries of the extremities, unspecified ▽
440.4 Chronic total occlusion of artery of the extremities
440.8 Atherosclerosis of other specified arteries
442.0 Aneurysm of artery of upper extremity
442.82 Aneurysm of subclavian artery
443.29 Dissection of other artery
443.9 Unspecified peripheral vascular disease ▽
444.21 Embolism and thrombosis of arteries of upper extremity
444.89 Embolism and thrombosis of other specified artery
447.1 Stricture of artery
447.6 Unspecified arteritis ▽
447.70 Aortic ectasia, unspecified site ▽
447.71 Thoracic aortic ectasia
747.69 Congenital anomaly of other specified site of peripheral vascular system
785.9 Other symptoms involving cardiovascular system
874.9 Open wound of other and unspecified parts of neck, complicated ▽
900.82 Injury to multiple blood vessels of head and neck
900.89 Injury to other specified blood vessels of head and neck
901.1 Innominate and subclavian artery injury
901.89 Injury to specified blood vessels of thorax, other
903.1 Brachial blood vessels injury
906.0 Late effect of open wound of head, neck, and trunk
906.4 Late effect of crushing
908.3 Late effect of injury to blood vessel of head, neck, and extremities
996.1 Mechanical complication of other vascular device, implant, and graft
996.74 Other complications due to other vascular device, implant, and graft — (Use additional code to identify complication: 338.18-338.19, 338.28-338.29)

ICD-9-CM Procedural

39.22 Aorta-subclavian-carotid bypass

35515

35515 Bypass graft, with vein; subclavian-vertebral

ICD-9-CM Diagnostic

433.20 Occlusion and stenosis of vertebral artery without mention of cerebral infarction — (Use additional code, if applicable, to identify status post administration of tPA (rtPA) in a different facility within the last 24 hours prior to admission to current facility: V45.88)
433.21 Occlusion and stenosis of vertebral artery with cerebral infarction — (Use additional code, if applicable, to identify status post administration of tPA (rtPA) in a different facility within the last 24 hours prior to admission to current facility: V45.88)
435.1 Vertebral artery syndrome — (Use additional code to identify presence of hypertension)
435.8 Other specified transient cerebral ischemias — (Use additional code to identify presence of hypertension)
443.24 Dissection of vertebral artery
443.29 Dissection of other artery
447.1 Stricture of artery
447.6 Unspecified arteritis ▽
447.70 Aortic ectasia, unspecified site ▽
447.71 Thoracic aortic ectasia
747.69 Congenital anomaly of other specified site of peripheral vascular system
874.9 Open wound of other and unspecified parts of neck, complicated ▽
900.82 Injury to multiple blood vessels of head and neck
906.0 Late effect of open wound of head, neck, and trunk
908.3 Late effect of injury to blood vessel of head, neck, and extremities
996.1 Mechanical complication of other vascular device, implant, and graft
996.74 Other complications due to other vascular device, implant, and graft — (Use additional code to identify complication: 338.18-338.19, 338.28-338.29)
998.2 Accidental puncture or laceration during procedure

ICD-9-CM Procedural

39.22 Aorta-subclavian-carotid bypass

35516

35516 Bypass graft, with vein; subclavian-axillary

ICD-9-CM Diagnostic

435.2 Subclavian steal syndrome — (Use additional code to identify presence of hypertension)
435.8 Other specified transient cerebral ischemias — (Use additional code to identify presence of hypertension)
440.8 Atherosclerosis of other specified arteries
447.1 Stricture of artery
447.6 Unspecified arteritis ▽
447.70 Aortic ectasia, unspecified site ▽
447.71 Thoracic aortic ectasia
747.69 Congenital anomaly of other specified site of peripheral vascular system
785.9 Other symptoms involving cardiovascular system
874.9 Open wound of other and unspecified parts of neck, complicated ▽
900.82 Injury to multiple blood vessels of head and neck
901.1 Innominate and subclavian artery injury
906.0 Late effect of open wound of head, neck, and trunk
925.2 Crushing injury of neck — (Use additional code to identify any associated injuries, such as: 800-829, 850.0-854.1, 860.0-869.1)
996.1 Mechanical complication of other vascular device, implant, and graft
996.74 Other complications due to other vascular device, implant, and graft — (Use additional code to identify complication: 338.18-338.19, 338.28-338.29)
998.2 Accidental puncture or laceration during procedure

ICD-9-CM Procedural

39.29 Other (peripheral) vascular shunt or bypass

35518

35518 Bypass graft, with vein; axillary-axillary

ICD-9-CM Diagnostic

435.2 Subclavian steal syndrome — (Use additional code to identify presence of hypertension)
440.20 Atherosclerosis of native arteries of the extremities, unspecified ▽
440.4 Chronic total occlusion of artery of the extremities
440.8 Atherosclerosis of other specified arteries
442.0 Aneurysm of artery of upper extremity
442.89 Aneurysm of other specified artery
443.29 Dissection of other artery
443.9 Unspecified peripheral vascular disease ▽
444.21 Embolism and thrombosis of arteries of upper extremity
444.89 Embolism and thrombosis of other specified artery

445.01 Atheroembolism of upper extremity

447.1 Stricture of artery

447.5 Necrosis of artery

447.9 Unspecified disorders of arteries and arterioles

459.9 Unspecified circulatory system disorder

747.63 Congenital upper limb vessel anomaly

785.9 Other symptoms involving cardiovascular system

880.02 Open wound of axillary region, without mention of complication

880.12 Open wound of axillary region, complicated

901.1 Innominate and subclavian artery injury

903.01 Axillary artery injury

906.1 Late effect of open wound of extremities without mention of tendon injury

906.4 Late effect of crushing

908.3 Late effect of injury to blood vessel of head, neck, and extremities

927.02 Crushing injury of axillary region — (Use additional code to identify any associated injuries: 800-829, 850.0-854.1, 860.0-869.1)

996.1 Mechanical complication of other vascular device, implant, and graft

996.74 Other complications due to other vascular device, implant, and graft — (Use additional code to identify complication: 338.18-338.19, 338.28-338.29)

ICD-9-CM Procedural

39.29 Other (peripheral) vascular shunt or bypass

35521

35521 Bypass graft, with vein; axillary-femoral

ICD-9-CM Diagnostic

440.0 Atherosclerosis of aorta

440.4 Chronic total occlusion of artery of the extremities

440.8 Atherosclerosis of other specified arteries

440.9 Generalized and unspecified atherosclerosis

441.02 Dissecting aortic aneurysm (any part), abdominal

441.03 Dissecting aortic aneurysm (any part), thoracoabdominal

441.3 Abdominal aneurysm, ruptured

441.4 Abdominal aneurysm without mention of rupture

441.5 Aortic aneurysm of unspecified site, ruptured

441.6 Thoracoabdominal aneurysm, ruptured

441.7 Thoracoabdominal aneurysm without mention of rupture

441.9 Aortic aneurysm of unspecified site without mention of rupture

442.2 Aneurysm of iliac artery

442.3 Aneurysm of artery of lower extremity

443.22 Dissection of iliac artery

443.29 Dissection of other artery

443.9 Unspecified peripheral vascular disease

444.01 Saddle embolus of abdominal aorta

444.09 Other arterial embolism and thrombosis of abdominal aorta

444.81 Embolism and thrombosis of iliac artery

445.02 Atheroembolism of lower extremity

447.1 Stricture of artery

447.5 Necrosis of artery

447.9 Unspecified disorders of arteries and arterioles

747.22 Congenital atresia and stenosis of aorta

747.69 Congenital anomaly of other specified site of peripheral vascular system

785.4 Gangrene — (Code first any associated underlying condition)

785.9 Other symptoms involving cardiovascular system

879.5 Open wound of abdominal wall, lateral, complicated

902.0 Abdominal aorta injury

902.53 Iliac artery injury

904.7 Injury to specified blood vessels of lower extremity, other

908.3 Late effect of injury to blood vessel of head, neck, and extremities

908.4 Late effect of injury to blood vessel of thorax, abdomen, and pelvis

996.1 Mechanical complication of other vascular device, implant, and graft

996.74 Other complications due to other vascular device, implant, and graft — (Use additional code to identify complication: 338.18-338.19, 338.28-338.29)

998.2 Accidental puncture or laceration during procedure

ICD-9-CM Procedural

39.29 Other (peripheral) vascular shunt or bypass

35522

35522 Bypass graft, with vein; axillary-brachial

ICD-9-CM Diagnostic

435.2 Subclavian steal syndrome — (Use additional code to identify presence of hypertension)

440.20 Atherosclerosis of native arteries of the extremities, unspecified

440.4 Chronic total occlusion of artery of the extremities

440.8 Atherosclerosis of other specified arteries

442.0 Aneurysm of artery of upper extremity

442.89 Aneurysm of other specified artery

443.29 Dissection of other artery

443.9 Unspecified peripheral vascular disease

444.21 Embolism and thrombosis of arteries of upper extremity

444.89 Embolism and thrombosis of other specified artery

445.01 Atheroembolism of upper extremity

447.1 Stricture of artery

447.5 Necrosis of artery

447.9 Unspecified disorders of arteries and arterioles

459.9 Unspecified circulatory system disorder

747.63 Congenital upper limb vessel anomaly

785.9 Other symptoms involving cardiovascular system

880.02 Open wound of axillary region, without mention of complication

880.12 Open wound of axillary region, complicated

901.1 Innominate and subclavian artery injury

903.01 Axillary artery injury

903.1 Brachial blood vessels injury

906.1 Late effect of open wound of extremities without mention of tendon injury

906.4 Late effect of crushing

908.3 Late effect of injury to blood vessel of head, neck, and extremities

927.02 Crushing injury of axillary region — (Use additional code to identify any associated injuries: 800-829, 850.0-854.1, 860.0-869.1)

996.1 Mechanical complication of other vascular device, implant, and graft

996.74 Other complications due to other vascular device, implant, and graft — (Use additional code to identify complication: 338.18-338.19, 338.28-338.29)

ICD-9-CM Procedural

39.29 Other (peripheral) vascular shunt or bypass

35523

35523 Bypass graft, with vein; brachial-ulnar or -radial

ICD-9-CM Diagnostic

435.2 Subclavian steal syndrome — (Use additional code to identify presence of hypertension)

440.20 Atherosclerosis of native arteries of the extremities, unspecified

440.4 Chronic total occlusion of artery of the extremities

440.8 Atherosclerosis of other specified arteries

442.0 Aneurysm of artery of upper extremity

442.89 Aneurysm of other specified artery

443.29 Dissection of other artery

443.9 Unspecified peripheral vascular disease

444.21 Embolism and thrombosis of arteries of upper extremity
444.89 Embolism and thrombosis of other specified artery
445.01 Atheroembolism of upper extremity
447.1 Stricture of artery
447.5 Necrosis of artery
447.9 Unspecified disorders of arteries and arterioles ▽
459.9 Unspecified circulatory system disorder ▽
747.63 Congenital upper limb vessel anomaly
785.9 Other symptoms involving cardiovascular system
880.02 Open wound of axillary region, without mention of complication
880.12 Open wound of axillary region, complicated
901.1 Innominate and subclavian artery injury
903.01 Axillary artery injury
903.1 Brachial blood vessels injury
906.1 Late effect of open wound of extremities without mention of tendon injury
906.4 Late effect of crushing
908.3 Late effect of injury to blood vessel of head, neck, and extremities
927.02 Crushing injury of axillary region — (Use additional code to identify any associated injuries: 800-829, 850.0-854.1, 860.0-869.1)
996.1 Mechanical complication of other vascular device, implant, and graft
996.74 Other complications due to other vascular device, implant, and graft — (Use additional code to identify complication: 338.18-338.19, 338.28-338.29)

ICD-9-CM Procedural

39.29 Other (peripheral) vascular shunt or bypass

35525

35525 Bypass graft, with vein; brachial-brachial

ICD-9-CM Diagnostic

435.2 Subclavian steal syndrome — (Use additional code to identify presence of hypertension)
440.20 Atherosclerosis of native arteries of the extremities, unspecified ▽
440.4 Chronic total occlusion of artery of the extremities
440.8 Atherosclerosis of other specified arteries
442.0 Aneurysm of artery of upper extremity
442.89 Aneurysm of other specified artery
443.29 Dissection of other artery
443.9 Unspecified peripheral vascular disease ▽
444.21 Embolism and thrombosis of arteries of upper extremity
444.89 Embolism and thrombosis of other specified artery
445.01 Atheroembolism of upper extremity
447.1 Stricture of artery
447.5 Necrosis of artery
447.9 Unspecified disorders of arteries and arterioles ▽
459.9 Unspecified circulatory system disorder ▽
747.63 Congenital upper limb vessel anomaly
785.9 Other symptoms involving cardiovascular system
880.03 Open wound of upper arm, without mention of complication
880.13 Open wound of upper arm, complicated
903.1 Brachial blood vessels injury
906.1 Late effect of open wound of extremities without mention of tendon injury
906.4 Late effect of crushing
908.3 Late effect of injury to blood vessel of head, neck, and extremities
927.03 Crushing injury of upper arm — (Use additional code to identify any associated injuries: 800-829, 850.0-854.1, 860.0-869.1)
996.1 Mechanical complication of other vascular device, implant, and graft
996.74 Other complications due to other vascular device, implant, and graft — (Use additional code to identify complication: 338.18-338.19, 338.28-338.29)

ICD-9-CM Procedural

39.29 Other (peripheral) vascular shunt or bypass

35526

35526 Bypass graft, with vein; aortosubclavian, aortoinnominate, or aortocarotid

ICD-9-CM Diagnostic

433.10 Occlusion and stenosis of carotid artery without mention of cerebral infarction — (Use additional code, if applicable, to identify status post administration of tPA (rtPA) in a different facility within the last 24 hours prior to admission to current facility: V45.88)
433.11 Occlusion and stenosis of carotid artery with cerebral infarction — (Use additional code, if applicable, to identify status post administration of tPA (rtPA) in a different facility within the last 24 hours prior to admission to current facility: V45.88)
435.0 Basilar artery syndrome — (Use additional code to identify presence of hypertension)
435.2 Subclavian steal syndrome — (Use additional code to identify presence of hypertension)
437.1 Other generalized ischemic cerebrovascular disease — (Use additional code to identify presence of hypertension)
440.8 Atherosclerosis of other specified arteries
442.81 Aneurysm of artery of neck
442.82 Aneurysm of subclavian artery
443.21 Dissection of carotid artery
443.29 Dissection of other artery
901.0 Thoracic aorta injury
901.1 Innominate and subclavian artery injury
996.1 Mechanical complication of other vascular device, implant, and graft
996.74 Other complications due to other vascular device, implant, and graft — (Use additional code to identify complication: 338.18-338.19, 338.28-338.29)
997.79 Vascular complications of other vessels — (Use additional code to identify complications)
998.2 Accidental puncture or laceration during procedure

ICD-9-CM Procedural

39.22 Aorta-subclavian-carotid bypass

35531

35531 Bypass graft, with vein; aortoceliac or aortomesenteric

ICD-9-CM Diagnostic

440.0 Atherosclerosis of aorta
440.8 Atherosclerosis of other specified arteries
441.3 Abdominal aneurysm, ruptured
441.4 Abdominal aneurysm without mention of rupture
441.9 Aortic aneurysm of unspecified site without mention of rupture ▽
442.84 Aneurysm of other visceral artery
443.29 Dissection of other artery
444.89 Embolism and thrombosis of other specified artery
445.89 Atheroembolism of other site
446.0 Polyarteritis nodosa
447.1 Stricture of artery
447.4 Celiac artery compression syndrome
447.5 Necrosis of artery
447.6 Unspecified arteritis ▽
447.72 Abdominal aortic ectasia
447.73 Thoracoabdominal aortic ectasia
447.9 Unspecified disorders of arteries and arterioles ▽
459.9 Unspecified circulatory system disorder ▽
557.0 Acute vascular insufficiency of intestine
557.1 Chronic vascular insufficiency of intestine
593.81 Vascular disorders of kidney

902.0 Abdominal aorta injury
902.20 Unspecified celiac and mesenteric artery injury ▽
908.4 Late effect of injury to blood vessel of thorax, abdomen, and pelvis
996.1 Mechanical complication of other vascular device, implant, and graft
996.74 Other complications due to other vascular device, implant, and graft — (Use additional code to identify complication: 338.18-338.19, 338.28-338.29)
997.71 Vascular complications of mesenteric artery — (Use additional code to identify complications)
997.79 Vascular complications of other vessels — (Use additional code to identify complications)
998.2 Accidental puncture or laceration during procedure

ICD-9-CM Procedural

39.24 Aorta-renal bypass
39.26 Other intra-abdominal vascular shunt or bypass

35533

35533 Bypass graft, with vein; axillary-femoral-femoral

ICD-9-CM Diagnostic

249.70 Secondary diabetes mellitus with peripheral circulatory disorders, not stated as uncontrolled, or unspecified — (Use additional code to identify manifestation: 443.81, 785.4) (Use additional code to identify any associated insulin use: V58.67)
249.71 Secondary diabetes mellitus with peripheral circulatory disorders, uncontrolled — (Use additional code to identify manifestation: 443.81, 785.4) (Use additional code to identify any associated insulin use: V58.67)
250.70 Diabetes with peripheral circulatory disorders, type II or unspecified type, not stated as uncontrolled — (Use additional code to identify manifestation: 443.81, 785.4)
250.71 Diabetes with peripheral circulatory disorders, type I [juvenile type], not stated as uncontrolled — (Use additional code to identify manifestation: 443.81, 785.4)
440.0 Atherosclerosis of aorta
440.20 Atherosclerosis of native arteries of the extremities, unspecified ▽
440.21 Atherosclerosis of native arteries of the extremities with intermittent claudication
440.22 Atherosclerosis of native arteries of the extremities with rest pain
440.23 Atherosclerosis of native arteries of the extremities with ulceration — (Use additional code for any associated ulceration: 707.10-707.19, 707.8, 707.9)
440.4 Chronic total occlusion of artery of the extremities
440.8 Atherosclerosis of other specified arteries
441.00 Dissecting aortic aneurysm (any part), unspecified site ▽
441.02 Dissecting aortic aneurysm (any part), abdominal
441.03 Dissecting aortic aneurysm (any part), thoracoabdominal
441.3 Abdominal aneurysm, ruptured
441.4 Abdominal aneurysm without mention of rupture
441.5 Aortic aneurysm of unspecified site, ruptured ▽
441.6 Thoracoabdominal aneurysm, ruptured
441.7 Thoracoabdominal aneurysm without mention of rupture
441.9 Aortic aneurysm of unspecified site without mention of rupture ▽
442.2 Aneurysm of iliac artery
442.3 Aneurysm of artery of lower extremity
443.22 Dissection of iliac artery
443.29 Dissection of other artery
443.81 Peripheral angiopathy in diseases classified elsewhere — (Code first underlying disease: 249.7, 250.7) ☒
443.9 Unspecified peripheral vascular disease ▽
444.01 Saddle embolus of abdominal aorta
444.09 Other arterial embolism and thrombosis of abdominal aorta
444.22 Embolism and thrombosis of arteries of lower extremity
444.81 Embolism and thrombosis of iliac artery
445.02 Atheroembolism of lower extremity
447.1 Stricture of artery
447.5 Necrosis of artery
447.9 Unspecified disorders of arteries and arterioles ▽
747.22 Congenital atresia and stenosis of aorta
747.64 Congenital lower limb vessel anomaly
747.69 Congenital anomaly of other specified site of peripheral vascular system
785.4 Gangrene — (Code first any associated underlying condition)
785.9 Other symptoms involving cardiovascular system
902.0 Abdominal aorta injury
902.53 Iliac artery injury
904.0 Common femoral artery injury
904.1 Superficial femoral artery injury
906.0 Late effect of open wound of head, neck, and trunk
908.4 Late effect of injury to blood vessel of thorax, abdomen, and pelvis
996.1 Mechanical complication of other vascular device, implant, and graft
996.74 Other complications due to other vascular device, implant, and graft — (Use additional code to identify complication: 338.18-338.19, 338.28-338.29)
998.2 Accidental puncture or laceration during procedure

ICD-9-CM Procedural

39.29 Other (peripheral) vascular shunt or bypass

35535

35535 Bypass graft, with vein; hepatorenal

ICD-9-CM Diagnostic

405.11 Secondary renovascular hypertension, benign
405.91 Secondary renovascular hypertension, unspecified ▽
440.1 Atherosclerosis of renal artery
440.8 Atherosclerosis of other specified arteries
441.4 Abdominal aneurysm without mention of rupture
442.1 Aneurysm of renal artery
442.84 Aneurysm of other visceral artery
443.23 Dissection of renal artery
443.29 Dissection of other artery
443.9 Unspecified peripheral vascular disease ▽
445.81 Atheroembolism of kidney — (Use additional code for any associated acute kidney failure or chronic kidney disease: 584, 585)
447.1 Stricture of artery
447.3 Hyperplasia of renal artery
447.5 Necrosis of artery
447.72 Abdominal aortic ectasia
447.9 Unspecified disorders of arteries and arterioles ▽
584.9 Acute kidney failure, unspecified ▽
593.81 Vascular disorders of kidney
747.62 Congenital renal vessel anomaly
747.69 Congenital anomaly of other specified site of peripheral vascular system
902.22 Hepatic artery injury
902.39 Injury to portal and splenic veins, other
902.40 Renal vessel(s) injury, unspecified ▽
902.41 Renal artery injury
902.42 Renal vein injury
996.1 Mechanical complication of other vascular device, implant, and graft
996.74 Other complications due to other vascular device, implant, and graft — (Use additional code to identify complication: 338.18-338.19, 338.28-338.29)
997.72 Vascular complications of renal artery — (Use additional code to identify complications)

ICD-9-CM Procedural

39.26 Other intra-abdominal vascular shunt or bypass

35536

35536 Bypass graft, with vein; splenorenal

ICD-9-CM Diagnostic

405.11 Secondary renovascular hypertension, benign
405.91 Secondary renovascular hypertension, unspecified ▽
440.1 Atherosclerosis of renal artery
440.8 Atherosclerosis of other specified arteries
441.4 Abdominal aneurysm without mention of rupture
442.1 Aneurysm of renal artery
442.83 Aneurysm of splenic artery
443.23 Dissection of renal artery
443.29 Dissection of other artery
443.9 Unspecified peripheral vascular disease ▽
445.81 Atheroembolism of kidney — (Use additional code for any associated acute kidney failure or chronic kidney disease: 584, 585)
447.1 Stricture of artery
447.3 Hyperplasia of renal artery
447.5 Necrosis of artery
447.72 Abdominal aortic ectasia
447.9 Unspecified disorders of arteries and arterioles ▽
584.9 Acute kidney failure, unspecified ▽
593.81 Vascular disorders of kidney
747.62 Congenital renal vessel anomaly
747.69 Congenital anomaly of other specified site of peripheral vascular system
902.23 Splenic artery injury
902.40 Renal vessel(s) injury, unspecified ▽
902.41 Renal artery injury
996.1 Mechanical complication of other vascular device, implant, and graft
996.74 Other complications due to other vascular device, implant, and graft — (Use additional code to identify complication: 338.18-338.19, 338.28-338.29)
997.72 Vascular complications of renal artery — (Use additional code to identify complications)

ICD-9-CM Procedural

39.26 Other intra-abdominal vascular shunt or bypass

35537-35538

35537 Bypass graft, with vein; aortoiliac
35538 aortobi-iliac

ICD-9-CM Diagnostic

440.0 Atherosclerosis of aorta
440.8 Atherosclerosis of other specified arteries
441.00 Dissecting aortic aneurysm (any part), unspecified site ▽
441.02 Dissecting aortic aneurysm (any part), abdominal
441.3 Abdominal aneurysm, ruptured
441.4 Abdominal aneurysm without mention of rupture
441.5 Aortic aneurysm of unspecified site, ruptured ▽
441.9 Aortic aneurysm of unspecified site without mention of rupture ▽
442.2 Aneurysm of iliac artery
443.22 Dissection of iliac artery
443.9 Unspecified peripheral vascular disease ▽
444.01 Saddle embolus of abdominal aorta
444.09 Other arterial embolism and thrombosis of abdominal aorta
444.81 Embolism and thrombosis of iliac artery
445.89 Atheroembolism of other site
447.1 Stricture of artery
447.5 Necrosis of artery
447.72 Abdominal aortic ectasia
447.9 Unspecified disorders of arteries and arterioles ▽
747.22 Congenital atresia and stenosis of aorta
785.9 Other symptoms involving cardiovascular system
902.0 Abdominal aorta injury
902.53 Iliac artery injury
908.4 Late effect of injury to blood vessel of thorax, abdomen, and pelvis
996.1 Mechanical complication of other vascular device, implant, and graft
996.74 Other complications due to other vascular device, implant, and graft — (Use additional code to identify complication: 338.18-338.19, 338.28-338.29)
997.79 Vascular complications of other vessels — (Use additional code to identify complications)
998.2 Accidental puncture or laceration during procedure

ICD-9-CM Procedural

39.25 Aorta-iliac-femoral bypass

35539-35540

35539 Bypass graft, with vein; aortofemoral
35540 aortobifemoral

ICD-9-CM Diagnostic

249.70 Secondary diabetes mellitus with peripheral circulatory disorders, not stated as uncontrolled, or unspecified — (Use additional code to identify manifestation: 443.81, 785.4) (Use additional code to identify any associated insulin use: V58.67)
249.71 Secondary diabetes mellitus with peripheral circulatory disorders, uncontrolled — (Use additional code to identify manifestation: 443.81, 785.4) (Use additional code to identify any associated insulin use: V58.67)
250.70 Diabetes with peripheral circulatory disorders, type II or unspecified type, not stated as uncontrolled — (Use additional code to identify manifestation: 443.81, 785.4)
250.71 Diabetes with peripheral circulatory disorders, type I [juvenile type], not stated as uncontrolled — (Use additional code to identify manifestation: 443.81, 785.4)
250.72 Diabetes with peripheral circulatory disorders, type II or unspecified type, uncontrolled — (Use additional code to identify manifestation: 443.81, 785.4)
250.73 Diabetes with peripheral circulatory disorders, type I [juvenile type], uncontrolled — (Use additional code to identify manifestation: 443.81, 785.4)
440.0 Atherosclerosis of aorta
440.20 Atherosclerosis of native arteries of the extremities, unspecified ▽
440.21 Atherosclerosis of native arteries of the extremities with intermittent claudication
440.22 Atherosclerosis of native arteries of the extremities with rest pain
440.23 Atherosclerosis of native arteries of the extremities with ulceration — (Use additional code for any associated ulceration: 707.10-707.19, 707.8, 707.9)
440.4 Chronic total occlusion of artery of the extremities
440.8 Atherosclerosis of other specified arteries
440.9 Generalized and unspecified atherosclerosis ▽
441.00 Dissecting aortic aneurysm (any part), unspecified site ▽
441.02 Dissecting aortic aneurysm (any part), abdominal
441.3 Abdominal aneurysm, ruptured
441.4 Abdominal aneurysm without mention of rupture
441.5 Aortic aneurysm of unspecified site, ruptured ▽
441.6 Thoracoabdominal aneurysm, ruptured
441.9 Aortic aneurysm of unspecified site without mention of rupture ▽
442.2 Aneurysm of iliac artery
443.22 Dissection of iliac artery
443.29 Dissection of other artery
443.81 Peripheral angiopathy in diseases classified elsewhere — (Code first underlying disease: 249.7, 250.7) ☒
443.9 Unspecified peripheral vascular disease ▽
444.01 Saddle embolus of abdominal aorta
444.09 Other arterial embolism and thrombosis of abdominal aorta
444.22 Embolism and thrombosis of arteries of lower extremity
444.81 Embolism and thrombosis of iliac artery

445.02 Atheroembolism of lower extremity
447.1 Stricture of artery
447.5 Necrosis of artery
447.70 Aortic ectasia, unspecified site
447.72 Abdominal aortic ectasia
447.73 Thoracoabdominal aortic ectasia
447.9 Unspecified disorders of arteries and arterioles
707.10 Ulcer of lower limb, unspecified — (Code, if applicable, any causal condition first: 249.80-249.81, 250.80-250.83, 440.23, 459.11, 459.13, 459.31, 459.33)
707.11 Ulcer of thigh — (Code, if applicable, any causal condition first: 249.80-249.81, 250.80-250.83, 440.23, 459.11, 459.13, 459.31, 459.33)
707.12 Ulcer of calf — (Code, if applicable, any causal condition first: 249.80-249.81, 250.80-250.83, 440.23, 459.11, 459.13, 459.31, 459.33)
707.13 Ulcer of ankle — (Code, if applicable, any causal condition first: 249.80-249.81, 250.80-250.83, 440.23, 459.11, 459.13, 459.31, 459.33)
707.14 Ulcer of heel and midfoot — (Code, if applicable, any causal condition first: 249.80-249.81, 250.80-250.83, 440.23, 459.11, 459.13, 459.31, 459.33)
707.15 Ulcer of other part of foot — (Code, if applicable, any causal condition first: 249.80-249.81, 250.80-250.83, 440.23, 459.11, 459.13, 459.31, 459.33)
707.19 Ulcer of other part of lower limb — (Code, if applicable, any causal condition first: 249.80-249.81, 250.80-250.83, 440.23, 459.11, 459.13, 459.31, 459.33)
747.22 Congenital atresia and stenosis of aorta
747.64 Congenital lower limb vessel anomaly
747.69 Congenital anomaly of other specified site of peripheral vascular system
785.4 Gangrene — (Code first any associated underlying condition)
785.9 Other symptoms involving cardiovascular system
902.0 Abdominal aorta injury
904.0 Common femoral artery injury
904.1 Superficial femoral artery injury
908.3 Late effect of injury to blood vessel of head, neck, and extremities
908.4 Late effect of injury to blood vessel of thorax, abdomen, and pelvis
928.10 Crushing injury of lower leg — (Use additional code to identify any associated injuries: 800-829, 850.0-854.1, 860.0-869.1)
928.8 Crushing injury of multiple sites of lower limb — (Use additional code to identify any associated injuries: 800-829, 850.0-854.1, 860.0-869.1)
996.1 Mechanical complication of other vascular device, implant, and graft
996.74 Other complications due to other vascular device, implant, and graft — (Use additional code to identify complication: 338.18-338.19, 338.28-338.29)
997.79 Vascular complications of other vessels — (Use additional code to identify complications)
998.2 Accidental puncture or laceration during procedure

ICD-9-CM Procedural

39.25 Aorta-iliac-femoral bypass

35556

35556 Bypass graft, with vein; femoral-popliteal

ICD-9-CM Diagnostic

249.70 Secondary diabetes mellitus with peripheral circulatory disorders, not stated as uncontrolled, or unspecified — (Use additional code to identify manifestation: 443.81, 785.4) (Use additional code to identify any associated insulin use: V58.67)
249.71 Secondary diabetes mellitus with peripheral circulatory disorders, uncontrolled — (Use additional code to identify manifestation: 443.81, 785.4) (Use additional code to identify any associated insulin use: V58.67)
250.70 Diabetes with peripheral circulatory disorders, type II or unspecified type, not stated as uncontrolled — (Use additional code to identify manifestation: 443.81, 785.4)
250.71 Diabetes with peripheral circulatory disorders, type I [juvenile type], not stated as uncontrolled — (Use additional code to identify manifestation: 443.81, 785.4)
250.72 Diabetes with peripheral circulatory disorders, type II or unspecified type, uncontrolled — (Use additional code to identify manifestation: 443.81, 785.4)
250.73 Diabetes with peripheral circulatory disorders, type I [juvenile type], uncontrolled — (Use additional code to identify manifestation: 443.81, 785.4)
440.20 Atherosclerosis of native arteries of the extremities, unspecified
440.21 Atherosclerosis of native arteries of the extremities with intermittent claudication
440.22 Atherosclerosis of native arteries of the extremities with rest pain
440.23 Atherosclerosis of native arteries of the extremities with ulceration — (Use additional code for any associated ulceration: 707.10-707.19, 707.8, 707.9)
440.24 Atherosclerosis of native arteries of the extremities with gangrene — (Use additional code for any associated ulceration: 707.10-707.19, 707.8, 707.9)
440.29 Other atherosclerosis of native arteries of the extremities
440.30 Atherosclerosis of unspecified bypass graft of extremities
440.31 Atherosclerosis of autologous vein bypass graft of extremities
440.32 Atherosclerosis of nonautologous biological bypass graft of extremities
440.4 Chronic total occlusion of artery of the extremities
440.8 Atherosclerosis of other specified arteries
440.9 Generalized and unspecified atherosclerosis
442.3 Aneurysm of artery of lower extremity
442.9 Other aneurysm of unspecified site
443.0 Raynaud's syndrome — (Use additional code to identify gangrene: 785.4)
443.29 Dissection of other artery
443.81 Peripheral angiopathy in diseases classified elsewhere — (Code first underlying disease: 249.7, 250.7)
443.89 Other peripheral vascular disease
443.9 Unspecified peripheral vascular disease
444.22 Embolism and thrombosis of arteries of lower extremity
445.02 Atheroembolism of lower extremity
447.1 Stricture of artery
447.5 Necrosis of artery
459.9 Unspecified circulatory system disorder
707.10 Ulcer of lower limb, unspecified — (Code, if applicable, any causal condition first: 249.80-249.81, 250.80-250.83, 440.23, 459.11, 459.13, 459.31, 459.33)
707.11 Ulcer of thigh — (Code, if applicable, any causal condition first: 249.80-249.81, 250.80-250.83, 440.23, 459.11, 459.13, 459.31, 459.33)
707.12 Ulcer of calf — (Code, if applicable, any causal condition first: 249.80-249.81, 250.80-250.83, 440.23, 459.11, 459.13, 459.31, 459.33)
707.13 Ulcer of ankle — (Code, if applicable, any causal condition first: 249.80-249.81, 250.80-250.83, 440.23, 459.11, 459.13, 459.31, 459.33)
707.14 Ulcer of heel and midfoot — (Code, if applicable, any causal condition first: 249.80-249.81, 250.80-250.83, 440.23, 459.11, 459.13, 459.31, 459.33)
707.15 Ulcer of other part of foot — (Code, if applicable, any causal condition first: 249.80-249.81, 250.80-250.83, 440.23, 459.11, 459.13, 459.31, 459.33)
707.19 Ulcer of other part of lower limb — (Code, if applicable, any causal condition first: 249.80-249.81, 250.80-250.83, 440.23, 459.11, 459.13, 459.31, 459.33)
747.64 Congenital lower limb vessel anomaly
747.69 Congenital anomaly of other specified site of peripheral vascular system
785.4 Gangrene — (Code first any associated underlying condition)
785.9 Other symptoms involving cardiovascular system
904.1 Superficial femoral artery injury
908.3 Late effect of injury to blood vessel of head, neck, and extremities
928.10 Crushing injury of lower leg — (Use additional code to identify any associated injuries: 800-829, 850.0-854.1, 860.0-869.1)
928.8 Crushing injury of multiple sites of lower limb — (Use additional code to identify any associated injuries: 800-829, 850.0-854.1, 860.0-869.1)
996.1 Mechanical complication of other vascular device, implant, and graft
996.74 Other complications due to other vascular device, implant, and graft — (Use additional code to identify complication: 338.18-338.19, 338.28-338.29)

ICD-9-CM Procedural

39.29 Other (peripheral) vascular shunt or bypass

35558

35558 Bypass graft, with vein; femoral-femoral

ICD-9-CM Diagnostic

249.70 Secondary diabetes mellitus with peripheral circulatory disorders, not stated as uncontrolled, or unspecified — (Use additional code to identify manifestation: 443.81, 785.4) (Use additional code to identify any associated insulin use: V58.67)

249.71 Secondary diabetes mellitus with peripheral circulatory disorders, uncontrolled — (Use additional code to identify manifestation: 443.81, 785.4) (Use additional code to identify any associated insulin use: V58.67)

250.70 Diabetes with peripheral circulatory disorders, type II or unspecified type, not stated as uncontrolled — (Use additional code to identify manifestation: 443.81, 785.4)

250.71 Diabetes with peripheral circulatory disorders, type I [juvenile type], not stated as uncontrolled — (Use additional code to identify manifestation: 443.81, 785.4)

250.72 Diabetes with peripheral circulatory disorders, type II or unspecified type, uncontrolled — (Use additional code to identify manifestation: 443.81, 785.4)

250.73 Diabetes with peripheral circulatory disorders, type I [juvenile type], uncontrolled — (Use additional code to identify manifestation: 443.81, 785.4)

440.20 Atherosclerosis of native arteries of the extremities, unspecified ▽

440.21 Atherosclerosis of native arteries of the extremities with intermittent claudication

440.22 Atherosclerosis of native arteries of the extremities with rest pain

440.23 Atherosclerosis of native arteries of the extremities with ulceration — (Use additional code for any associated ulceration: 707.10-707.19, 707.8, 707.9)

440.24 Atherosclerosis of native arteries of the extremities with gangrene — (Use additional code for any associated ulceration: 707.10-707.19, 707.8, 707.9)

440.4 Chronic total occlusion of artery of the extremities

442.3 Aneurysm of artery of lower extremity

443.29 Dissection of other artery

443.81 Peripheral angiopathy in diseases classified elsewhere — (Code first underlying disease: 249.7, 250.7) ☒

443.9 Unspecified peripheral vascular disease ▽

447.1 Stricture of artery

447.5 Necrosis of artery

459.9 Unspecified circulatory system disorder ▽

707.10 Ulcer of lower limb, unspecified — (Code, if applicable, any causal condition first: 249.80-249.81, 250.80-250.83, 440.23, 459.11, 459.13, 459.31, 459.33) ▽

707.11 Ulcer of thigh — (Code, if applicable, any causal condition first: 249.80-249.81, 250.80-250.83, 440.23, 459.11, 459.13, 459.31, 459.33)

707.12 Ulcer of calf — (Code, if applicable, any causal condition first: 249.80-249.81, 250.80-250.83, 440.23, 459.11, 459.13, 459.31, 459.33)

707.13 Ulcer of ankle — (Code, if applicable, any causal condition first: 249.80-249.81, 250.80-250.83, 440.23, 459.11, 459.13, 459.31, 459.33)

707.14 Ulcer of heel and midfoot — (Code, if applicable, any causal condition first: 249.80-249.81, 250.80-250.83, 440.23, 459.11, 459.13, 459.31, 459.33)

707.15 Ulcer of other part of foot — (Code, if applicable, any causal condition first: 249.80-249.81, 250.80-250.83, 440.23, 459.11, 459.13, 459.31, 459.33)

707.19 Ulcer of other part of lower limb — (Code, if applicable, any causal condition first: 249.80-249.81, 250.80-250.83, 440.23, 459.11, 459.13, 459.31, 459.33)

747.64 Congenital lower limb vessel anomaly

747.69 Congenital anomaly of other specified site of peripheral vascular system

785.4 Gangrene — (Code first any associated underlying condition)

904.0 Common femoral artery injury

904.1 Superficial femoral artery injury

908.3 Late effect of injury to blood vessel of head, neck, and extremities

996.1 Mechanical complication of other vascular device, implant, and graft

996.74 Other complications due to other vascular device, implant, and graft — (Use additional code to identify complication: 338.18-338.19, 338.28-338.29)

ICD-9-CM Procedural

39.29 Other (peripheral) vascular shunt or bypass

35560

35560 Bypass graft, with vein; aortorenal

ICD-9-CM Diagnostic

405.11 Secondary renovascular hypertension, benign

405.91 Secondary renovascular hypertension, unspecified ▽

440.0 Atherosclerosis of aorta

440.1 Atherosclerosis of renal artery

441.00 Dissecting aortic aneurysm (any part), unspecified site ▽

441.02 Dissecting aortic aneurysm (any part), abdominal

441.3 Abdominal aneurysm, ruptured

441.4 Abdominal aneurysm without mention of rupture

441.9 Aortic aneurysm of unspecified site without mention of rupture ▽

442.1 Aneurysm of renal artery

443.23 Dissection of renal artery

444.01 Saddle embolus of abdominal aorta

444.09 Other arterial embolism and thrombosis of abdominal aorta

445.81 Atheroembolism of kidney — (Use additional code for any associated acute kidney failure or chronic kidney disease: 584, 585)

447.1 Stricture of artery

447.3 Hyperplasia of renal artery

447.5 Necrosis of artery

447.72 Abdominal aortic ectasia

447.9 Unspecified disorders of arteries and arterioles ▽

584.9 Acute kidney failure, unspecified ▽

593.81 Vascular disorders of kidney

902.0 Abdominal aorta injury

902.40 Renal vessel(s) injury, unspecified ▽

902.41 Renal artery injury

996.1 Mechanical complication of other vascular device, implant, and graft

996.74 Other complications due to other vascular device, implant, and graft — (Use additional code to identify complication: 338.18-338.19, 338.28-338.29)

997.72 Vascular complications of renal artery — (Use additional code to identify complications)

998.2 Accidental puncture or laceration during procedure

ICD-9-CM Procedural

39.24 Aorta-renal bypass

35563

35563 Bypass graft, with vein; ilioiliac

ICD-9-CM Diagnostic

440.8 Atherosclerosis of other specified arteries

442.2 Aneurysm of iliac artery

443.22 Dissection of iliac artery

443.9 Unspecified peripheral vascular disease ▽

444.81 Embolism and thrombosis of iliac artery

445.89 Atheroembolism of other site

447.1 Stricture of artery

447.5 Necrosis of artery

447.70 Aortic ectasia, unspecified site ▽

902.53 Iliac artery injury

996.1 Mechanical complication of other vascular device, implant, and graft

996.74 Other complications due to other vascular device, implant, and graft — (Use additional code to identify complication: 338.18-338.19, 338.28-338.29)

997.79 Vascular complications of other vessels — (Use additional code to identify complications)

ICD-9-CM Procedural

39.26 Other intra-abdominal vascular shunt or bypass

35565

35565 Bypass graft, with vein; iliofemoral

ICD-9-CM Diagnostic

249.70 Secondary diabetes mellitus with peripheral circulatory disorders, not stated as uncontrolled, or unspecified — (Use additional code to identify manifestation: 443.81, 785.4) (Use additional code to identify any associated insulin use: V58.67)

249.71 Secondary diabetes mellitus with peripheral circulatory disorders, uncontrolled — (Use additional code to identify manifestation: 443.81, 785.4) (Use additional code to identify any associated insulin use: V58.67)

250.70 Diabetes with peripheral circulatory disorders, type II or unspecified type, not stated as uncontrolled — (Use additional code to identify manifestation: 443.81, 785.4)

250.71 Diabetes with peripheral circulatory disorders, type I [juvenile type], not stated as uncontrolled — (Use additional code to identify manifestation: 443.81, 785.4)

250.72 Diabetes with peripheral circulatory disorders, type II or unspecified type, uncontrolled — (Use additional code to identify manifestation: 443.81, 785.4)

250.73 Diabetes with peripheral circulatory disorders, type I [juvenile type], uncontrolled — (Use additional code to identify manifestation: 443.81, 785.4)

440.21 Atherosclerosis of native arteries of the extremities with intermittent claudication

440.22 Atherosclerosis of native arteries of the extremities with rest pain

440.23 Atherosclerosis of native arteries of the extremities with ulceration — (Use additional code for any associated ulceration: 707.10-707.19, 707.8, 707.9)

440.24 Atherosclerosis of native arteries of the extremities with gangrene — (Use additional code for any associated ulceration: 707.10-707.19, 707.8, 707.9)

440.4 Chronic total occlusion of artery of the extremities

440.8 Atherosclerosis of other specified arteries

440.9 Generalized and unspecified atherosclerosis ▽

442.2 Aneurysm of iliac artery

442.3 Aneurysm of artery of lower extremity

443.22 Dissection of iliac artery

443.81 Peripheral angiopathy in diseases classified elsewhere — (Code first underlying disease: 249.7, 250.7) ☒

443.89 Other peripheral vascular disease

443.9 Unspecified peripheral vascular disease ▽

444.22 Embolism and thrombosis of arteries of lower extremity

444.81 Embolism and thrombosis of iliac artery

445.02 Atheroembolism of lower extremity

447.1 Stricture of artery

447.5 Necrosis of artery

447.70 Aortic ectasia, unspecified site ▽

459.9 Unspecified circulatory system disorder ▽

707.10 Ulcer of lower limb, unspecified — (Code, if applicable, any causal condition first: 249.80-249.81, 250.80-250.83, 440.23, 459.11, 459.13, 459.31, 459.33) ▽

707.11 Ulcer of thigh — (Code, if applicable, any causal condition first: 249.80-249.81, 250.80-250.83, 440.23, 459.11, 459.13, 459.31, 459.33)

707.12 Ulcer of calf — (Code, if applicable, any causal condition first: 249.80-249.81, 250.80-250.83, 440.23, 459.11, 459.13, 459.31, 459.33)

707.13 Ulcer of ankle — (Code, if applicable, any causal condition first: 249.80-249.81, 250.80-250.83, 440.23, 459.11, 459.13, 459.31, 459.33)

707.14 Ulcer of heel and midfoot — (Code, if applicable, any causal condition first: 249.80-249.81, 250.80-250.83, 440.23, 459.11, 459.13, 459.31, 459.33)

707.15 Ulcer of other part of foot — (Code, if applicable, any causal condition first: 249.80-249.81, 250.80-250.83, 440.23, 459.11, 459.13, 459.31, 459.33)

707.19 Ulcer of other part of lower limb — (Code, if applicable, any causal condition first: 249.80-249.81, 250.80-250.83, 440.23, 459.11, 459.13, 459.31, 459.33)

747.64 Congenital lower limb vessel anomaly

747.69 Congenital anomaly of other specified site of peripheral vascular system

785.4 Gangrene — (Code first any associated underlying condition)

785.9 Other symptoms involving cardiovascular system

894.1 Multiple and unspecified open wound of lower limb, complicated

902.53 Iliac artery injury

904.7 Injury to specified blood vessels of lower extremity, other

908.3 Late effect of injury to blood vessel of head, neck, and extremities

928.00 Crushing injury of thigh — (Use additional code to identify any associated injuries: 800-829, 850.0-854.1, 860.0-869.1)

996.74 Other complications due to other vascular device, implant, and graft — (Use additional code to identify complication: 338.18-338.19, 338.28-338.29)

997.79 Vascular complications of other vessels — (Use additional code to identify complications)

ICD-9-CM Procedural

39.25 Aorta-iliac-femoral bypass

35566

35566 Bypass graft, with vein; femoral-anterior tibial, posterior tibial, peroneal artery or other distal vessels

ICD-9-CM Diagnostic

249.70 Secondary diabetes mellitus with peripheral circulatory disorders, not stated as uncontrolled, or unspecified — (Use additional code to identify manifestation: 443.81, 785.4) (Use additional code to identify any associated insulin use: V58.67)

249.71 Secondary diabetes mellitus with peripheral circulatory disorders, uncontrolled — (Use additional code to identify manifestation: 443.81, 785.4) (Use additional code to identify any associated insulin use: V58.67)

250.70 Diabetes with peripheral circulatory disorders, type II or unspecified type, not stated as uncontrolled — (Use additional code to identify manifestation: 443.81, 785.4)

250.71 Diabetes with peripheral circulatory disorders, type I [juvenile type], not stated as uncontrolled — (Use additional code to identify manifestation: 443.81, 785.4)

250.72 Diabetes with peripheral circulatory disorders, type II or unspecified type, uncontrolled — (Use additional code to identify manifestation: 443.81, 785.4)

250.73 Diabetes with peripheral circulatory disorders, type I [juvenile type], uncontrolled — (Use additional code to identify manifestation: 443.81, 785.4)

440.21 Atherosclerosis of native arteries of the extremities with intermittent claudication

440.22 Atherosclerosis of native arteries of the extremities with rest pain

440.23 Atherosclerosis of native arteries of the extremities with ulceration — (Use additional code for any associated ulceration: 707.10-707.19, 707.8, 707.9)

440.24 Atherosclerosis of native arteries of the extremities with gangrene — (Use additional code for any associated ulceration: 707.10-707.19, 707.8, 707.9)

440.29 Other atherosclerosis of native arteries of the extremities

440.4 Chronic total occlusion of artery of the extremities

440.8 Atherosclerosis of other specified arteries

440.9 Generalized and unspecified atherosclerosis ▽

442.3 Aneurysm of artery of lower extremity

443.29 Dissection of other artery

443.9 Unspecified peripheral vascular disease ▽

447.1 Stricture of artery

459.89 Other specified circulatory system disorders

459.9 Unspecified circulatory system disorder ▽

707.10 Ulcer of lower limb, unspecified — (Code, if applicable, any causal condition first: 249.80-249.81, 250.80-250.83, 440.23, 459.11, 459.13, 459.31, 459.33) ▽

707.11 Ulcer of thigh — (Code, if applicable, any causal condition first: 249.80-249.81, 250.80-250.83, 440.23, 459.11, 459.13, 459.31, 459.33)

707.12 Ulcer of calf — (Code, if applicable, any causal condition first: 249.80-249.81, 250.80-250.83, 440.23, 459.11, 459.13, 459.31, 459.33)

707.13 Ulcer of ankle — (Code, if applicable, any causal condition first: 249.80-249.81, 250.80-250.83, 440.23, 459.11, 459.13, 459.31, 459.33)

707.14 Ulcer of heel and midfoot — (Code, if applicable, any causal condition first: 249.80-249.81, 250.80-250.83, 440.23, 459.11, 459.13, 459.31, 459.33)

707.15 Ulcer of other part of foot — (Code, if applicable, any causal condition first: 249.80-249.81, 250.80-250.83, 440.23, 459.11, 459.13, 459.31, 459.33)

707.19 Ulcer of other part of lower limb — (Code, if applicable, any causal condition first: 249.80-249.81, 250.80-250.83, 440.23, 459.11, 459.13, 459.31, 459.33)

747.64 Congenital lower limb vessel anomaly

785.4 Gangrene — (Code first any associated underlying condition)
785.9 Other symptoms involving cardiovascular system
894.1 Multiple and unspecified open wound of lower limb, complicated
904.0 Common femoral artery injury
904.1 Superficial femoral artery injury
904.41 Popliteal artery injury
904.42 Popliteal vein injury
904.51 Anterior tibial artery injury
904.52 Anterior tibial vein injury
904.53 Posterior tibial artery injury
904.54 Posterior tibial vein injury
904.7 Injury to specified blood vessels of lower extremity, other
908.3 Late effect of injury to blood vessel of head, neck, and extremities
928.10 Crushing injury of lower leg — (Use additional code to identify any associated injuries: 800-829, 850.0-854.1, 860.0-869.1)
928.8 Crushing injury of multiple sites of lower limb — (Use additional code to identify any associated injuries: 800-829, 850.0-854.1, 860.0-869.1)
996.1 Mechanical complication of other vascular device, implant, and graft
996.74 Other complications due to other vascular device, implant, and graft — (Use additional code to identify complication: 338.18-338.19, 338.28-338.29)

ICD-9-CM Procedural

39.29 Other (peripheral) vascular shunt or bypass

35570

35570 Bypass graft, with vein; tibial-tibial, peroneal-tibial, or tibial/peroneal trunk-tibial

ICD-9-CM Diagnostic

249.70 Secondary diabetes mellitus with peripheral circulatory disorders, not stated as uncontrolled, or unspecified — (Use additional code to identify manifestation: 443.81, 785.4) (Use additional code to identify any associated insulin use: V58.67)
249.71 Secondary diabetes mellitus with peripheral circulatory disorders, uncontrolled — (Use additional code to identify manifestation: 443.81, 785.4) (Use additional code to identify any associated insulin use: V58.67)
250.70 Diabetes with peripheral circulatory disorders, type II or unspecified type, not stated as uncontrolled — (Use additional code to identify manifestation: 443.81, 785.4)
250.71 Diabetes with peripheral circulatory disorders, type I [juvenile type], not stated as uncontrolled — (Use additional code to identify manifestation: 443.81, 785.4)
250.72 Diabetes with peripheral circulatory disorders, type II or unspecified type, uncontrolled — (Use additional code to identify manifestation: 443.81, 785.4)
250.73 Diabetes with peripheral circulatory disorders, type I [juvenile type], uncontrolled — (Use additional code to identify manifestation: 443.81, 785.4)
440.21 Atherosclerosis of native arteries of the extremities with intermittent claudication
440.22 Atherosclerosis of native arteries of the extremities with rest pain
440.23 Atherosclerosis of native arteries of the extremities with ulceration — (Use additional code for any associated ulceration: 707.10-707.19, 707.8, 707.9)
440.24 Atherosclerosis of native arteries of the extremities with gangrene — (Use additional code for any associated ulceration: 707.10-707.19, 707.8, 707.9)
440.29 Other atherosclerosis of native arteries of the extremities
440.4 Chronic total occlusion of artery of the extremities
440.8 Atherosclerosis of other specified arteries
440.9 Generalized and unspecified atherosclerosis ▽
442.3 Aneurysm of artery of lower extremity
443.29 Dissection of other artery
443.9 Unspecified peripheral vascular disease ▽
447.1 Stricture of artery
459.89 Other specified circulatory system disorders
459.9 Unspecified circulatory system disorder ▽
707.10 Ulcer of lower limb, unspecified — (Code, if applicable, any causal condition first: 249.80-249.81, 250.80-250.83, 440.23, 459.11, 459.13, 459.31, 459.33) ▽
707.11 Ulcer of thigh — (Code, if applicable, any causal condition first: 249.80-249.81, 250.80-250.83, 440.23, 459.11, 459.13, 459.31, 459.33)
707.12 Ulcer of calf — (Code, if applicable, any causal condition first: 249.80-249.81, 250.80-250.83, 440.23, 459.11, 459.13, 459.31, 459.33)
707.13 Ulcer of ankle — (Code, if applicable, any causal condition first: 249.80-249.81, 250.80-250.83, 440.23, 459.11, 459.13, 459.31, 459.33)
707.14 Ulcer of heel and midfoot — (Code, if applicable, any causal condition first: 249.80-249.81, 250.80-250.83, 440.23, 459.11, 459.13, 459.31, 459.33)
707.15 Ulcer of other part of foot — (Code, if applicable, any causal condition first: 249.80-249.81, 250.80-250.83, 440.23, 459.11, 459.13, 459.31, 459.33)
707.19 Ulcer of other part of lower limb — (Code, if applicable, any causal condition first: 249.80-249.81, 250.80-250.83, 440.23, 459.11, 459.13, 459.31, 459.33)
747.64 Congenital lower limb vessel anomaly
785.4 Gangrene — (Code first any associated underlying condition)
785.9 Other symptoms involving cardiovascular system
894.1 Multiple and unspecified open wound of lower limb, complicated
904.0 Common femoral artery injury
904.1 Superficial femoral artery injury
904.41 Popliteal artery injury
904.42 Popliteal vein injury
904.51 Anterior tibial artery injury
904.52 Anterior tibial vein injury
904.53 Posterior tibial artery injury
904.54 Posterior tibial vein injury
904.7 Injury to specified blood vessels of lower extremity, other
908.3 Late effect of injury to blood vessel of head, neck, and extremities
928.10 Crushing injury of lower leg — (Use additional code to identify any associated injuries: 800-829, 850.0-854.1, 860.0-869.1)
928.8 Crushing injury of multiple sites of lower limb — (Use additional code to identify any associated injuries: 800-829, 850.0-854.1, 860.0-869.1)
996.1 Mechanical complication of other vascular device, implant, and graft
996.74 Other complications due to other vascular device, implant, and graft — (Use additional code to identify complication: 338.18-338.19, 338.28-338.29)

ICD-9-CM Procedural

39.29 Other (peripheral) vascular shunt or bypass

35571

35571 Bypass graft, with vein; popliteal-tibial, -peroneal artery or other distal vessels

ICD-9-CM Diagnostic

249.70 Secondary diabetes mellitus with peripheral circulatory disorders, not stated as uncontrolled, or unspecified — (Use additional code to identify manifestation: 443.81, 785.4) (Use additional code to identify any associated insulin use: V58.67)
249.71 Secondary diabetes mellitus with peripheral circulatory disorders, uncontrolled — (Use additional code to identify manifestation: 443.81, 785.4) (Use additional code to identify any associated insulin use: V58.67)
250.70 Diabetes with peripheral circulatory disorders, type II or unspecified type, not stated as uncontrolled — (Use additional code to identify manifestation: 443.81, 785.4)
250.71 Diabetes with peripheral circulatory disorders, type I [juvenile type], not stated as uncontrolled — (Use additional code to identify manifestation: 443.81, 785.4)
250.72 Diabetes with peripheral circulatory disorders, type II or unspecified type, uncontrolled — (Use additional code to identify manifestation: 443.81, 785.4)
250.73 Diabetes with peripheral circulatory disorders, type I [juvenile type], uncontrolled — (Use additional code to identify manifestation: 443.81, 785.4)
440.20 Atherosclerosis of native arteries of the extremities, unspecified ▽
440.21 Atherosclerosis of native arteries of the extremities with intermittent claudication
440.22 Atherosclerosis of native arteries of the extremities with rest pain
440.23 Atherosclerosis of native arteries of the extremities with ulceration — (Use additional code for any associated ulceration: 707.10-707.19, 707.8, 707.9)
440.24 Atherosclerosis of native arteries of the extremities with gangrene — (Use additional code for any associated ulceration: 707.10-707.19, 707.8, 707.9)

440.4 Chronic total occlusion of artery of the extremities
440.8 Atherosclerosis of other specified arteries
442.3 Aneurysm of artery of lower extremity
443.81 Peripheral angiopathy in diseases classified elsewhere — (Code first underlying disease: 249.7, 250.7) ☒
443.9 Unspecified peripheral vascular disease ▽
444.22 Embolism and thrombosis of arteries of lower extremity
445.02 Atheroembolism of lower extremity
447.1 Stricture of artery
459.9 Unspecified circulatory system disorder ▽
707.10 Ulcer of lower limb, unspecified — (Code, if applicable, any causal condition first: 249.80-249.81, 250.80-250.83, 440.23, 459.11, 459.13, 459.31, 459.33) ▽
707.11 Ulcer of thigh — (Code, if applicable, any causal condition first: 249.80-249.81, 250.80-250.83, 440.23, 459.11, 459.13, 459.31, 459.33)
707.12 Ulcer of calf — (Code, if applicable, any causal condition first: 249.80-249.81, 250.80-250.83, 440.23, 459.11, 459.13, 459.31, 459.33)
707.13 Ulcer of ankle — (Code, if applicable, any causal condition first: 249.80-249.81, 250.80-250.83, 440.23, 459.11, 459.13, 459.31, 459.33)
707.14 Ulcer of heel and midfoot — (Code, if applicable, any causal condition first: 249.80-249.81, 250.80-250.83, 440.23, 459.11, 459.13, 459.31, 459.33)
707.15 Ulcer of other part of foot — (Code, if applicable, any causal condition first: 249.80-249.81, 250.80-250.83, 440.23, 459.11, 459.13, 459.31, 459.33)
707.19 Ulcer of other part of lower limb — (Code, if applicable, any causal condition first: 249.80-249.81, 250.80-250.83, 440.23, 459.11, 459.13, 459.31, 459.33)
747.64 Congenital lower limb vessel anomaly
785.4 Gangrene — (Code first any associated underlying condition)
785.9 Other symptoms involving cardiovascular system
894.1 Multiple and unspecified open wound of lower limb, complicated
904.41 Popliteal artery injury
904.51 Anterior tibial artery injury
904.53 Posterior tibial artery injury
904.7 Injury to specified blood vessels of lower extremity, other
908.3 Late effect of injury to blood vessel of head, neck, and extremities
928.10 Crushing injury of lower leg — (Use additional code to identify any associated injuries: 800-829, 850.0-854.1, 860.0-869.1)
928.8 Crushing injury of multiple sites of lower limb — (Use additional code to identify any associated injuries: 800-829, 850.0-854.1, 860.0-869.1)
996.1 Mechanical complication of other vascular device, implant, and graft
996.74 Other complications due to other vascular device, implant, and graft — (Use additional code to identify complication: 338.18-338.19, 338.28-338.29)

ICD-9-CM Procedural

39.29 Other (peripheral) vascular shunt or bypass

35572

35572 Harvest of femoropopliteal vein, 1 segment, for vascular reconstruction procedure (eg, aortic, vena caval, coronary, peripheral artery) (List separately in addition to code for primary procedure)

ICD-9-CM Diagnostic

This is an add-on code. Refer to the corresponding primary procedure code for ICD-9-CM diagnosis code links.

ICD-9-CM Procedural

38.69 Other excision of lower limb veins

35583

35583 In-situ vein bypass; femoral-popliteal

ICD-9-CM Diagnostic

249.70 Secondary diabetes mellitus with peripheral circulatory disorders, not stated as uncontrolled, or unspecified — (Use additional code to identify manifestation: 443.81, 785.4) (Use additional code to identify any associated insulin use: V58.67)
249.71 Secondary diabetes mellitus with peripheral circulatory disorders, uncontrolled — (Use additional code to identify manifestation: 443.81, 785.4) (Use additional code to identify any associated insulin use: V58.67)
250.70 Diabetes with peripheral circulatory disorders, type II or unspecified type, not stated as uncontrolled — (Use additional code to identify manifestation: 443.81, 785.4)
250.71 Diabetes with peripheral circulatory disorders, type I [juvenile type], not stated as uncontrolled — (Use additional code to identify manifestation: 443.81, 785.4)
250.72 Diabetes with peripheral circulatory disorders, type II or unspecified type, uncontrolled — (Use additional code to identify manifestation: 443.81, 785.4)
250.73 Diabetes with peripheral circulatory disorders, type I [juvenile type], uncontrolled — (Use additional code to identify manifestation: 443.81, 785.4)
440.21 Atherosclerosis of native arteries of the extremities with intermittent claudication
440.22 Atherosclerosis of native arteries of the extremities with rest pain
440.23 Atherosclerosis of native arteries of the extremities with ulceration — (Use additional code for any associated ulceration: 707.10-707.19, 707.8, 707.9)
440.4 Chronic total occlusion of artery of the extremities
442.3 Aneurysm of artery of lower extremity
443.0 Raynaud's syndrome — (Use additional code to identify gangrene: 785.4)
443.29 Dissection of other artery
443.81 Peripheral angiopathy in diseases classified elsewhere — (Code first underlying disease: 249.7, 250.7) ☒
443.89 Other peripheral vascular disease
443.9 Unspecified peripheral vascular disease ▽
444.22 Embolism and thrombosis of arteries of lower extremity
445.02 Atheroembolism of lower extremity
447.1 Stricture of artery
447.5 Necrosis of artery
453.9 Embolism and thrombosis of unspecified site ▽
459.81 Unspecified venous (peripheral) insufficiency — (Use additional code for any associated ulceration: 707.10-707.19, 707.8, 707.9) ▽
459.9 Unspecified circulatory system disorder ▽
707.10 Ulcer of lower limb, unspecified — (Code, if applicable, any causal condition first: 249.80-249.81, 250.80-250.83, 440.23, 459.11, 459.13, 459.31, 459.33) ▽
707.11 Ulcer of thigh — (Code, if applicable, any causal condition first: 249.80-249.81, 250.80-250.83, 440.23, 459.11, 459.13, 459.31, 459.33)
707.12 Ulcer of calf — (Code, if applicable, any causal condition first: 249.80-249.81, 250.80-250.83, 440.23, 459.11, 459.13, 459.31, 459.33)
707.13 Ulcer of ankle — (Code, if applicable, any causal condition first: 249.80-249.81, 250.80-250.83, 440.23, 459.11, 459.13, 459.31, 459.33)
707.14 Ulcer of heel and midfoot — (Code, if applicable, any causal condition first: 249.80-249.81, 250.80-250.83, 440.23, 459.11, 459.13, 459.31, 459.33)
707.15 Ulcer of other part of foot — (Code, if applicable, any causal condition first: 249.80-249.81, 250.80-250.83, 440.23, 459.11, 459.13, 459.31, 459.33)
707.19 Ulcer of other part of lower limb — (Code, if applicable, any causal condition first: 249.80-249.81, 250.80-250.83, 440.23, 459.11, 459.13, 459.31, 459.33)
747.64 Congenital lower limb vessel anomaly
747.69 Congenital anomaly of other specified site of peripheral vascular system
785.4 Gangrene — (Code first any associated underlying condition)
785.9 Other symptoms involving cardiovascular system
908.3 Late effect of injury to blood vessel of head, neck, and extremities
996.1 Mechanical complication of other vascular device, implant, and graft
996.74 Other complications due to other vascular device, implant, and graft — (Use additional code to identify complication: 338.18-338.19, 338.28-338.29)

ICD-9-CM Procedural

39.29 Other (peripheral) vascular shunt or bypass

35585

35585 In-situ vein bypass; femoral-anterior tibial, posterior tibial, or peroneal artery

ICD-9-CM Diagnostic

249.70 Secondary diabetes mellitus with peripheral circulatory disorders, not stated as uncontrolled, or unspecified — (Use additional code to identify manifestation: 443.81, 785.4) (Use additional code to identify any associated insulin use: V58.67)
249.71 Secondary diabetes mellitus with peripheral circulatory disorders, uncontrolled — (Use additional code to identify manifestation: 443.81, 785.4) (Use additional code to identify any associated insulin use: V58.67)
250.70 Diabetes with peripheral circulatory disorders, type II or unspecified type, not stated as uncontrolled — (Use additional code to identify manifestation: 443.81, 785.4)
250.71 Diabetes with peripheral circulatory disorders, type I [juvenile type], not stated as uncontrolled — (Use additional code to identify manifestation: 443.81, 785.4)
250.72 Diabetes with peripheral circulatory disorders, type II or unspecified type, uncontrolled — (Use additional code to identify manifestation: 443.81, 785.4)
250.73 Diabetes with peripheral circulatory disorders, type I [juvenile type], uncontrolled — (Use additional code to identify manifestation: 443.81, 785.4)
440.21 Atherosclerosis of native arteries of the extremities with intermittent claudication
440.22 Atherosclerosis of native arteries of the extremities with rest pain
440.23 Atherosclerosis of native arteries of the extremities with ulceration — (Use additional code for any associated ulceration: 707.10-707.19, 707.8, 707.9)
440.24 Atherosclerosis of native arteries of the extremities with gangrene — (Use additional code for any associated ulceration: 707.10-707.19, 707.8, 707.9)
440.4 Chronic total occlusion of artery of the extremities
442.3 Aneurysm of artery of lower extremity
443.81 Peripheral angiopathy in diseases classified elsewhere — (Code first underlying disease: 249.7, 250.7) ☒
443.9 Unspecified peripheral vascular disease ▽
444.22 Embolism and thrombosis of arteries of lower extremity
445.02 Atheroembolism of lower extremity
447.1 Stricture of artery
447.2 Rupture of artery
447.5 Necrosis of artery
447.6 Unspecified arteritis ▽
459.81 Unspecified venous (peripheral) insufficiency — (Use additional code for any associated ulceration: 707.10-707.19, 707.8, 707.9) ▽
459.9 Unspecified circulatory system disorder ▽
707.10 Ulcer of lower limb, unspecified — (Code, if applicable, any causal condition first: 249.80-249.81, 250.80-250.83, 440.23, 459.11, 459.13, 459.31, 459.33) ▽
707.11 Ulcer of thigh — (Code, if applicable, any causal condition first: 249.80-249.81, 250.80-250.83, 440.23, 459.11, 459.13, 459.31, 459.33)
707.12 Ulcer of calf — (Code, if applicable, any causal condition first: 249.80-249.81, 250.80-250.83, 440.23, 459.11, 459.13, 459.31, 459.33)
707.13 Ulcer of ankle — (Code, if applicable, any causal condition first: 249.80-249.81, 250.80-250.83, 440.23, 459.11, 459.13, 459.31, 459.33)
707.14 Ulcer of heel and midfoot — (Code, if applicable, any causal condition first: 249.80-249.81, 250.80-250.83, 440.23, 459.11, 459.13, 459.31, 459.33)
707.15 Ulcer of other part of foot — (Code, if applicable, any causal condition first: 249.80-249.81, 250.80-250.83, 440.23, 459.11, 459.13, 459.31, 459.33)
707.19 Ulcer of other part of lower limb — (Code, if applicable, any causal condition first: 249.80-249.81, 250.80-250.83, 440.23, 459.11, 459.13, 459.31, 459.33)
747.64 Congenital lower limb vessel anomaly
785.4 Gangrene — (Code first any associated underlying condition)
785.9 Other symptoms involving cardiovascular system
904.41 Popliteal artery injury
904.51 Anterior tibial artery injury
904.53 Posterior tibial artery injury
908.3 Late effect of injury to blood vessel of head, neck, and extremities
996.1 Mechanical complication of other vascular device, implant, and graft
996.74 Other complications due to other vascular device, implant, and graft — (Use additional code to identify complication: 338.18-338.19, 338.28-338.29)

ICD-9-CM Procedural

39.29 Other (peripheral) vascular shunt or bypass

35587

35587 In-situ vein bypass; popliteal-tibial, peroneal

ICD-9-CM Diagnostic

249.70 Secondary diabetes mellitus with peripheral circulatory disorders, not stated as uncontrolled, or unspecified — (Use additional code to identify manifestation: 443.81, 785.4) (Use additional code to identify any associated insulin use: V58.67)
249.71 Secondary diabetes mellitus with peripheral circulatory disorders, uncontrolled — (Use additional code to identify manifestation: 443.81, 785.4) (Use additional code to identify any associated insulin use: V58.67)
250.70 Diabetes with peripheral circulatory disorders, type II or unspecified type, not stated as uncontrolled — (Use additional code to identify manifestation: 443.81, 785.4)
250.71 Diabetes with peripheral circulatory disorders, type I [juvenile type], not stated as uncontrolled — (Use additional code to identify manifestation: 443.81, 785.4)
250.72 Diabetes with peripheral circulatory disorders, type II or unspecified type, uncontrolled — (Use additional code to identify manifestation: 443.81, 785.4)
250.73 Diabetes with peripheral circulatory disorders, type I [juvenile type], uncontrolled — (Use additional code to identify manifestation: 443.81, 785.4)
440.21 Atherosclerosis of native arteries of the extremities with intermittent claudication
440.22 Atherosclerosis of native arteries of the extremities with rest pain
440.4 Chronic total occlusion of artery of the extremities
443.81 Peripheral angiopathy in diseases classified elsewhere — (Code first underlying disease: 249.7, 250.7) ☒
444.22 Embolism and thrombosis of arteries of lower extremity
445.02 Atheroembolism of lower extremity
447.1 Stricture of artery
459.9 Unspecified circulatory system disorder ▽
707.10 Ulcer of lower limb, unspecified — (Code, if applicable, any causal condition first: 249.80-249.81, 250.80-250.83, 440.23, 459.11, 459.13, 459.31, 459.33) ▽
707.11 Ulcer of thigh — (Code, if applicable, any causal condition first: 249.80-249.81, 250.80-250.83, 440.23, 459.11, 459.13, 459.31, 459.33)
707.12 Ulcer of calf — (Code, if applicable, any causal condition first: 249.80-249.81, 250.80-250.83, 440.23, 459.11, 459.13, 459.31, 459.33)
707.13 Ulcer of ankle — (Code, if applicable, any causal condition first: 249.80-249.81, 250.80-250.83, 440.23, 459.11, 459.13, 459.31, 459.33)
707.14 Ulcer of heel and midfoot — (Code, if applicable, any causal condition first: 249.80-249.81, 250.80-250.83, 440.23, 459.11, 459.13, 459.31, 459.33)
707.15 Ulcer of other part of foot — (Code, if applicable, any causal condition first: 249.80-249.81, 250.80-250.83, 440.23, 459.11, 459.13, 459.31, 459.33)
707.19 Ulcer of other part of lower limb — (Code, if applicable, any causal condition first: 249.80-249.81, 250.80-250.83, 440.23, 459.11, 459.13, 459.31, 459.33)
747.64 Congenital lower limb vessel anomaly
785.4 Gangrene — (Code first any associated underlying condition)
785.9 Other symptoms involving cardiovascular system
996.1 Mechanical complication of other vascular device, implant, and graft
996.74 Other complications due to other vascular device, implant, and graft — (Use additional code to identify complication: 338.18-338.19, 338.28-338.29)

ICD-9-CM Procedural

39.29 Other (peripheral) vascular shunt or bypass

35600

35600 Harvest of upper extremity artery, 1 segment, for coronary artery bypass procedure (List separately in addition to code for primary procedure)

ICD-9-CM Diagnostic

410.00 Acute myocardial infarction of anterolateral wall, episode of care unspecified — (Use additional code to identify presence of hypertension: 401.0-405.9) ♥

410.01 Acute myocardial infarction of anterolateral wall, initial episode of care — (Use additional code to identify presence of hypertension: 401.0-405.9)

410.02 Acute myocardial infarction of anterolateral wall, subsequent episode of care — (Use additional code to identify presence of hypertension: 401.0-405.9)

410.10 Acute myocardial infarction of other anterior wall, episode of care unspecified — (Use additional code to identify presence of hypertension: 401.0-405.9) ♥

410.11 Acute myocardial infarction of other anterior wall, initial episode of care — (Use additional code to identify presence of hypertension: 401.0-405.9)

410.12 Acute myocardial infarction of other anterior wall, subsequent episode of care — (Use additional code to identify presence of hypertension: 401.0-405.9)

410.20 Acute myocardial infarction of inferolateral wall, episode of care unspecified — (Use additional code to identify presence of hypertension: 401.0-405.9) ♥

410.21 Acute myocardial infarction of inferolateral wall, initial episode of care — (Use additional code to identify presence of hypertension: 401.0-405.9)

410.22 Acute myocardial infarction of inferolateral wall, subsequent episode of care — (Use additional code to identify presence of hypertension: 401.0-405.9)

410.30 Acute myocardial infarction of inferoposterior wall, episode of care unspecified — (Use additional code to identify presence of hypertension: 401.0-405.9) ♥

410.31 Acute myocardial infarction of inferoposterior wall, initial episode of care — (Use additional code to identify presence of hypertension: 401.0-405.9)

410.32 Acute myocardial infarction of inferoposterior wall, subsequent episode of care — (Use additional code to identify presence of hypertension: 401.0-405.9)

410.40 Acute myocardial infarction of other inferior wall, episode of care unspecified — (Use additional code to identify presence of hypertension: 401.0-405.9) ♥

410.41 Acute myocardial infarction of other inferior wall, initial episode of care — (Use additional code to identify presence of hypertension: 401.0-405.9)

410.42 Acute myocardial infarction of other inferior wall, subsequent episode of care — (Use additional code to identify presence of hypertension: 401.0-405.9)

410.50 Acute myocardial infarction of other lateral wall, episode of care unspecified — (Use additional code to identify presence of hypertension: 401.0-405.9) ♥

410.51 Acute myocardial infarction of other lateral wall, initial episode of care — (Use additional code to identify presence of hypertension: 401.0-405.9)

410.52 Acute myocardial infarction of other lateral wall, subsequent episode of care — (Use additional code to identify presence of hypertension: 401.0-405.9)

410.60 Acute myocardial infarction, true posterior wall infarction, episode of care unspecified — (Use additional code to identify presence of hypertension: 401.0-405.9) ♥

410.61 Acute myocardial infarction, true posterior wall infarction, initial episode of care — (Use additional code to identify presence of hypertension: 401.0-405.9)

410.62 Acute myocardial infarction, true posterior wall infarction, subsequent episode of care — (Use additional code to identify presence of hypertension: 401.0-405.9)

410.70 Acute myocardial infarction, subendocardial infarction, episode of care unspecified — (Use additional code to identify presence of hypertension: 401.0-405.9) ♥

410.71 Acute myocardial infarction, subendocardial infarction, initial episode of care — (Use additional code to identify presence of hypertension: 401.0-405.9)

410.72 Acute myocardial infarction, subendocardial infarction, subsequent episode of care — (Use additional code to identify presence of hypertension: 401.0-405.9)

410.80 Acute myocardial infarction of other specified sites, episode of care unspecified — (Use additional code to identify presence of hypertension: 401.0-405.9) ♥

410.81 Acute myocardial infarction of other specified sites, initial episode of care — (Use additional code to identify presence of hypertension: 401.0-405.9)

410.82 Acute myocardial infarction of other specified sites, subsequent episode of care — (Use additional code to identify presence of hypertension: 401.0-405.9)

410.90 Acute myocardial infarction, unspecified site, episode of care unspecified — (Use additional code to identify presence of hypertension: 401.0-405.9) ♥

410.91 Acute myocardial infarction, unspecified site, initial episode of care — (Use additional code to identify presence of hypertension: 401.0-405.9) ♥

410.92 Acute myocardial infarction, unspecified site, subsequent episode of care — (Use additional code to identify presence of hypertension: 401.0-405.9) ♥

411.1 Intermediate coronary syndrome — (Use additional code to identify presence of hypertension: 401.0-405.9)

411.81 Acute coronary occlusion without myocardial infarction — (Use additional code to identify presence of hypertension: 401.0-405.9)

411.89 Other acute and subacute form of ischemic heart disease — (Use additional code to identify presence of hypertension: 401.0-405.9)

413.0 Angina decubitus — (Use additional code to identify presence of hypertension: 401.0-405.9)

413.1 Prinzmetal angina — (Use additional code to identify presence of hypertension: 401.0-405.9)

413.9 Other and unspecified angina pectoris — (Use additional code(s) for symptoms associated with angina equivalent)(Use additional code to identify presence of hypertension: 401.0-405.9) ♥

414.00 Coronary atherosclerosis of unspecified type of vessel, native or graft — (Use additional code to identify presence of hypertension: 401.0-405.9) ♥

414.01 Coronary atherosclerosis of native coronary artery — (Use additional code to identify presence of hypertension: 401.0-405.9)

414.03 Coronary atherosclerosis of nonautologous biological bypass graft — (Use additional code to identify presence of hypertension: 401.0-405.9)

414.04 Coronary atherosclerosis of artery bypass graft — (Use additional code to identify presence of hypertension: 401.0-405.9)

414.05 Coronary atherosclerosis of unspecified type of bypass graft — (Use additional code to identify presence of hypertension: 401.0-405.9) ♥

414.06 Coronary atherosclerosis, of native coronary artery of transplanted heart — (Use additional code to identify presence of hypertension: 401.0-405.9)

414.07 Coronary atherosclerosis, of bypass graft (artery) (vein) of transplanted heart — (Use additional code to identify presence of hypertension: 401.0-405.9)

414.10 Aneurysm of heart — (Use additional code to identify presence of hypertension: 401.0-405.9)

414.11 Aneurysm of coronary vessels — (Use additional code to identify presence of hypertension: 401.0-405.9)

414.12 Dissection of coronary artery — (Use additional code to identify presence of hypertension: 401.0-405.9)

414.2 Chronic total occlusion of coronary artery

414.3 Coronary atherosclerosis due to lipid rich plaque — (Code first coronary atherosclerosis (414.00-414.07))

414.4 Coronary atherosclerosis due to calcified coronary lesion — (Code first coronary atherosclerosis (414.00-414.07))

414.8 Other specified forms of chronic ischemic heart disease — (Use additional code to identify presence of hypertension: 401.0-405.9)

414.9 Unspecified chronic ischemic heart disease — (Use additional code to identify presence of hypertension: 401.0-405.9) ♥

426.7 Anomalous atrioventricular excitation

428.0 Congestive heart failure, unspecified — (Code, if applicable, heart failure due to hypertension first: 402.0-402.9, with fifth-digit 1 or 404.0-404.9 with fifth digit 1 or 3) ♥

428.1 Left heart failure — (Code, if applicable, heart failure due to hypertension first: 402.0-402.9, with fifth-digit 1 or 404.0-404.9 with fifth digit 1 or 3)

428.20 Unspecified systolic heart failure — (Code, if applicable, heart failure due to hypertension first: 402.0-402.9, with fifth-digit 1 or 404.0-404.9 with fifth digit 1 or 3) ♥

428.21 Acute systolic heart failure — (Code, if applicable, heart failure due to hypertension first: 402.0-402.9, with fifth-digit 1 or 404.0-404.9 with fifth digit 1 or 3)

428.22 Chronic systolic heart failure — (Code, if applicable, heart failure due to hypertension first: 402.0-402.9, with fifth-digit 1 or 404.0-404.9 with fifth digit 1 or 3)

428.23 Acute on chronic systolic heart failure — (Code, if applicable, heart failure due to hypertension first: 402.0-402.9, with fifth-digit 1 or 404.0-404.9 with fifth digit 1 or 3)

428.30 Unspecified diastolic heart failure — (Code, if applicable, heart failure due to hypertension first: 402.0-402.9, with fifth-digit 1 or 404.0-404.9 with fifth digit 1 or 3) ▽

428.31 Acute diastolic heart failure — (Code, if applicable, heart failure due to hypertension first: 402.0-402.9, with fifth-digit 1 or 404.0-404.9 with fifth digit 1 or 3)

428.32 Chronic diastolic heart failure — (Code, if applicable, heart failure due to hypertension first: 402.0-402.9, with fifth-digit 1 or 404.0-404.9 with fifth digit 1 or 3)

428.33 Acute on chronic diastolic heart failure — (Code, if applicable, heart failure due to hypertension first: 402.0-402.9, with fifth-digit 1 or 404.0-404.9 with fifth digit 1 or 3)

428.40 Unspecified combined systolic and diastolic heart failure — (Code, if applicable, heart failure due to hypertension first: 402.0-402.9, with fifth-digit 1 or 404.0-404.9 with fifth digit 1 or 3) ▽

428.41 Acute combined systolic and diastolic heart failure — (Code, if applicable, heart failure due to hypertension first: 402.0-402.9, with fifth-digit 1 or 404.0-404.9 with fifth digit 1 or 3)

428.42 Chronic combined systolic and diastolic heart failure — (Code, if applicable, heart failure due to hypertension first: 402.0-402.9, with fifth-digit 1 or 404.0-404.9 with fifth digit 1 or 3)

428.43 Acute on chronic combined systolic and diastolic heart failure — (Code, if applicable, heart failure due to hypertension first: 402.0-402.9, with fifth-digit 1 or 404.0-404.9 with fifth digit 1 or 3)

428.9 Unspecified heart failure — (Code, if applicable, heart failure due to hypertension first: 402.0-402.9, with fifth-digit 1 or 404.0-404.9 with fifth digit 1 or 3) ▽

746.85 Congenital coronary artery anomaly

747.41 Total congenital anomalous pulmonary venous connection

996.03 Mechanical complication due to coronary bypass graft

ICD-9-CM Procedural

36.10 Aortocoronary bypass for heart revascularization, not otherwise specified

36.11 (Aorto)coronary bypass of one coronary artery

36.12 (Aorto)coronary bypass of two coronary arteries

36.13 (Aorto)coronary bypass of three coronary arteries

36.14 (Aorto)coronary bypass of four or more coronary arteries

35601

35601 Bypass graft, with other than vein; common carotid-ipsilateral internal carotid

ICD-9-CM Diagnostic

433.10 Occlusion and stenosis of carotid artery without mention of cerebral infarction — (Use additional code, if applicable, to identify status post administration of tPA (rtPA) in a different facility within the last 24 hours prior to admission to current facility: V45.88)

433.11 Occlusion and stenosis of carotid artery with cerebral infarction — (Use additional code, if applicable, to identify status post administration of tPA (rtPA) in a different facility within the last 24 hours prior to admission to current facility: V45.88)

433.30 Occlusion and stenosis of multiple and bilateral precerebral arteries without mention of cerebral infarction — (Use additional code, if applicable, to identify status post administration of tPA (rtPA) in a different facility within the last 24 hours prior to admission to current facility: V45.88)

433.31 Occlusion and stenosis of multiple and bilateral precerebral arteries with cerebral infarction — (Use additional code, if applicable, to identify status post administration of tPA (rtPA) in a different facility within the last 24 hours prior to admission to current facility: V45.88)

433.80 Occlusion and stenosis of other specified precerebral artery without mention of cerebral infarction — (Use additional code, if applicable, to identify status post administration of tPA (rtPA) in a different facility within the last 24 hours prior to admission to current facility: V45.88)

433.81 Occlusion and stenosis of other specified precerebral artery with cerebral infarction — (Use additional code, if applicable, to identify status post administration of tPA (rtPA) in a different facility within the last 24 hours prior to admission to current facility: V45.88)

435.8 Other specified transient cerebral ischemias — (Use additional code to identify presence of hypertension)

440.8 Atherosclerosis of other specified arteries

442.81 Aneurysm of artery of neck

443.21 Dissection of carotid artery

447.1 Stricture of artery

447.70 Aortic ectasia, unspecified site ▽

747.81 Congenital anomaly of cerebrovascular system

780.2 Syncope and collapse

785.9 Other symptoms involving cardiovascular system

900.01 Common carotid artery injury

900.03 Internal carotid artery injury

906.0 Late effect of open wound of head, neck, and trunk

908.3 Late effect of injury to blood vessel of head, neck, and extremities

925.2 Crushing injury of neck — (Use additional code to identify any associated injuries, such as: 800-829, 850.0-854.1, 860.0-869.1)

996.1 Mechanical complication of other vascular device, implant, and graft

996.74 Other complications due to other vascular device, implant, and graft — (Use additional code to identify complication: 338.18-338.19, 338.28-338.29)

ICD-9-CM Procedural

39.22 Aorta-subclavian-carotid bypass

35606

35606 Bypass graft, with other than vein; carotid-subclavian

ICD-9-CM Diagnostic

433.10 Occlusion and stenosis of carotid artery without mention of cerebral infarction — (Use additional code, if applicable, to identify status post administration of tPA (rtPA) in a different facility within the last 24 hours prior to admission to current facility: V45.88)

433.11 Occlusion and stenosis of carotid artery with cerebral infarction — (Use additional code, if applicable, to identify status post administration of tPA (rtPA) in a different facility within the last 24 hours prior to admission to current facility: V45.88)

433.31 Occlusion and stenosis of multiple and bilateral precerebral arteries with cerebral infarction — (Use additional code, if applicable, to identify status post administration of tPA (rtPA) in a different facility within the last 24 hours prior to admission to current facility: V45.88)

435.2 Subclavian steal syndrome — (Use additional code to identify presence of hypertension)

435.8 Other specified transient cerebral ischemias — (Use additional code to identify presence of hypertension)

440.8 Atherosclerosis of other specified arteries

442.81 Aneurysm of artery of neck

443.21 Dissection of carotid artery

443.29 Dissection of other artery

447.1 Stricture of artery

447.70 Aortic ectasia, unspecified site ▽

447.71 Thoracic aortic ectasia

747.69 Congenital anomaly of other specified site of peripheral vascular system

780.2 Syncope and collapse

785.9 Other symptoms involving cardiovascular system

874.9 Open wound of other and unspecified parts of neck, complicated ▽

900.82 Injury to multiple blood vessels of head and neck

901.1 Innominate and subclavian artery injury

906.0 Late effect of open wound of head, neck, and trunk

908.3 Late effect of injury to blood vessel of head, neck, and extremities

925.2 Crushing injury of neck — (Use additional code to identify any associated injuries, such as: 800-829, 850.0-854.1, 860.0-869.1)

996.1 Mechanical complication of other vascular device, implant, and graft

996.74 Other complications due to other vascular device, implant, and graft — (Use additional code to identify complication: 338.18-338.19, 338.28-338.29)

ICD-9-CM Procedural

39.22 Aorta-subclavian-carotid bypass

35612

35612 Bypass graft, with other than vein; subclavian-subclavian

ICD-9-CM Diagnostic

435.2 Subclavian steal syndrome — (Use additional code to identify presence of hypertension)
435.8 Other specified transient cerebral ischemias — (Use additional code to identify presence of hypertension)
440.8 Atherosclerosis of other specified arteries
443.29 Dissection of other artery
447.1 Stricture of artery
447.6 Unspecified arteritis ▽
447.71 Thoracic aortic ectasia
447.73 Thoracoabdominal aortic ectasia
747.69 Congenital anomaly of other specified site of peripheral vascular system
785.9 Other symptoms involving cardiovascular system
874.9 Open wound of other and unspecified parts of neck, complicated ▽
900.82 Injury to multiple blood vessels of head and neck
900.89 Injury to other specified blood vessels of head and neck
901.1 Innominate and subclavian artery injury
901.89 Injury to specified blood vessels of thorax, other
906.0 Late effect of open wound of head, neck, and trunk
906.4 Late effect of crushing
908.3 Late effect of injury to blood vessel of head, neck, and extremities
996.1 Mechanical complication of other vascular device, implant, and graft
996.74 Other complications due to other vascular device, implant, and graft — (Use additional code to identify complication: 338.18-338.19, 338.28-338.29)

ICD-9-CM Procedural

39.22 Aorta-subclavian-carotid bypass

35616

35616 Bypass graft, with other than vein; subclavian-axillary

ICD-9-CM Diagnostic

435.2 Subclavian steal syndrome — (Use additional code to identify presence of hypertension)
435.8 Other specified transient cerebral ischemias — (Use additional code to identify presence of hypertension)
440.8 Atherosclerosis of other specified arteries
447.1 Stricture of artery
447.6 Unspecified arteritis ▽
447.70 Aortic ectasia, unspecified site ▽
447.71 Thoracic aortic ectasia
747.69 Congenital anomaly of other specified site of peripheral vascular system
785.9 Other symptoms involving cardiovascular system
874.9 Open wound of other and unspecified parts of neck, complicated ▽
900.82 Injury to multiple blood vessels of head and neck
901.1 Innominate and subclavian artery injury
906.0 Late effect of open wound of head, neck, and trunk
925.2 Crushing injury of neck — (Use additional code to identify any associated injuries, such as: 800-829, 850.0-854.1, 860.0-869.1)
996.1 Mechanical complication of other vascular device, implant, and graft
996.74 Other complications due to other vascular device, implant, and graft — (Use additional code to identify complication: 338.18-338.19, 338.28-338.29)
998.2 Accidental puncture or laceration during procedure

ICD-9-CM Procedural

38.53 Ligation and stripping of varicose veins of upper limb vessels
39.29 Other (peripheral) vascular shunt or bypass

35621

35621 Bypass graft, with other than vein; axillary-femoral

ICD-9-CM Diagnostic

440.0 Atherosclerosis of aorta
440.4 Chronic total occlusion of artery of the extremities
440.8 Atherosclerosis of other specified arteries
440.9 Generalized and unspecified atherosclerosis ▽
441.02 Dissecting aortic aneurysm (any part), abdominal
441.3 Abdominal aneurysm, ruptured
441.4 Abdominal aneurysm without mention of rupture
441.5 Aortic aneurysm of unspecified site, ruptured ▽
441.9 Aortic aneurysm of unspecified site without mention of rupture ▽
442.2 Aneurysm of iliac artery
442.3 Aneurysm of artery of lower extremity
443.22 Dissection of iliac artery
443.29 Dissection of other artery
443.9 Unspecified peripheral vascular disease ▽
444.01 Saddle embolus of abdominal aorta
444.09 Other arterial embolism and thrombosis of abdominal aorta
444.81 Embolism and thrombosis of iliac artery
445.02 Atheroembolism of lower extremity
447.1 Stricture of artery
447.5 Necrosis of artery
447.9 Unspecified disorders of arteries and arterioles ▽
747.22 Congenital atresia and stenosis of aorta
747.69 Congenital anomaly of other specified site of peripheral vascular system
785.4 Gangrene — (Code first any associated underlying condition)
785.9 Other symptoms involving cardiovascular system
879.5 Open wound of abdominal wall, lateral, complicated
902.0 Abdominal aorta injury
902.53 Iliac artery injury
904.7 Injury to specified blood vessels of lower extremity, other
908.3 Late effect of injury to blood vessel of head, neck, and extremities
908.4 Late effect of injury to blood vessel of thorax, abdomen, and pelvis
996.1 Mechanical complication of other vascular device, implant, and graft
996.74 Other complications due to other vascular device, implant, and graft — (Use additional code to identify complication: 338.18-338.19, 338.28-338.29)
998.2 Accidental puncture or laceration during procedure

ICD-9-CM Procedural

39.29 Other (peripheral) vascular shunt or bypass

35623

35623 Bypass graft, with other than vein; axillary-popliteal or -tibial

ICD-9-CM Diagnostic

249.70 Secondary diabetes mellitus with peripheral circulatory disorders, not stated as uncontrolled, or unspecified — (Use additional code to identify manifestation: 443.81, 785.4) (Use additional code to identify any associated insulin use: V58.67)
249.71 Secondary diabetes mellitus with peripheral circulatory disorders, uncontrolled — (Use additional code to identify manifestation: 443.81, 785.4) (Use additional code to identify any associated insulin use: V58.67)
250.70 Diabetes with peripheral circulatory disorders, type II or unspecified type, not stated as uncontrolled — (Use additional code to identify manifestation: 443.81, 785.4)
250.71 Diabetes with peripheral circulatory disorders, type I [juvenile type], not stated as uncontrolled — (Use additional code to identify manifestation: 443.81, 785.4)

250.72 Diabetes with peripheral circulatory disorders, type II or unspecified type, uncontrolled — (Use additional code to identify manifestation: 443.81, 785.4)

250.73 Diabetes with peripheral circulatory disorders, type I [juvenile type], uncontrolled — (Use additional code to identify manifestation: 443.81, 785.4)

440.0 Atherosclerosis of aorta

440.20 Atherosclerosis of native arteries of the extremities, unspecified ▽

440.21 Atherosclerosis of native arteries of the extremities with intermittent claudication

440.22 Atherosclerosis of native arteries of the extremities with rest pain

440.23 Atherosclerosis of native arteries of the extremities with ulceration — (Use additional code for any associated ulceration: 707.10-707.19, 707.8, 707.9)

440.4 Chronic total occlusion of artery of the extremities

440.8 Atherosclerosis of other specified arteries

440.9 Generalized and unspecified atherosclerosis ▽

441.02 Dissecting aortic aneurysm (any part), abdominal

441.03 Dissecting aortic aneurysm (any part), thoracoabdominal

441.3 Abdominal aneurysm, ruptured

441.4 Abdominal aneurysm without mention of rupture

441.5 Aortic aneurysm of unspecified site, ruptured ▽

441.6 Thoracoabdominal aneurysm, ruptured

441.7 Thoracoabdominal aneurysm without mention of rupture

441.9 Aortic aneurysm of unspecified site without mention of rupture ▽

442.2 Aneurysm of iliac artery

442.3 Aneurysm of artery of lower extremity

443.29 Dissection of other artery

443.81 Peripheral angiopathy in diseases classified elsewhere — (Code first underlying disease: 249.7, 250.7) ☒

443.9 Unspecified peripheral vascular disease ▽

444.01 Saddle embolus of abdominal aorta

444.09 Other arterial embolism and thrombosis of abdominal aorta

444.81 Embolism and thrombosis of iliac artery

445.02 Atheroembolism of lower extremity

447.1 Stricture of artery

447.5 Necrosis of artery

447.9 Unspecified disorders of arteries and arterioles ▽

707.10 Ulcer of lower limb, unspecified — (Code, if applicable, any causal condition first: 249.80-249.81, 250.80-250.83, 440.23, 459.11, 459.13, 459.31, 459.33) ▽

707.11 Ulcer of thigh — (Code, if applicable, any causal condition first: 249.80-249.81, 250.80-250.83, 440.23, 459.11, 459.13, 459.31, 459.33)

707.12 Ulcer of calf — (Code, if applicable, any causal condition first: 249.80-249.81, 250.80-250.83, 440.23, 459.11, 459.13, 459.31, 459.33)

707.13 Ulcer of ankle — (Code, if applicable, any causal condition first: 249.80-249.81, 250.80-250.83, 440.23, 459.11, 459.13, 459.31, 459.33)

707.14 Ulcer of heel and midfoot — (Code, if applicable, any causal condition first: 249.80-249.81, 250.80-250.83, 440.23, 459.11, 459.13, 459.31, 459.33)

707.15 Ulcer of other part of foot — (Code, if applicable, any causal condition first: 249.80-249.81, 250.80-250.83, 440.23, 459.11, 459.13, 459.31, 459.33)

707.19 Ulcer of other part of lower limb — (Code, if applicable, any causal condition first: 249.80-249.81, 250.80-250.83, 440.23, 459.11, 459.13, 459.31, 459.33)

747.22 Congenital atresia and stenosis of aorta

747.69 Congenital anomaly of other specified site of peripheral vascular system

785.4 Gangrene — (Code first any associated underlying condition)

785.9 Other symptoms involving cardiovascular system

879.5 Open wound of abdominal wall, lateral, complicated

902.0 Abdominal aorta injury

902.53 Iliac artery injury

904.7 Injury to specified blood vessels of lower extremity, other

908.3 Late effect of injury to blood vessel of head, neck, and extremities

908.4 Late effect of injury to blood vessel of thorax, abdomen, and pelvis

996.1 Mechanical complication of other vascular device, implant, and graft

996.74 Other complications due to other vascular device, implant, and graft — (Use additional code to identify complication: 338.18-338.19, 338.28-338.29)

ICD-9-CM Procedural

39.29 Other (peripheral) vascular shunt or bypass

35626

35626 Bypass graft, with other than vein; aortosubclavian, aortoinnominate, or aortocarotid

ICD-9-CM Diagnostic

433.10 Occlusion and stenosis of carotid artery without mention of cerebral infarction — (Use additional code, if applicable, to identify status post administration of tPA (rtPA) in a different facility within the last 24 hours prior to admission to current facility: V45.88)

433.11 Occlusion and stenosis of carotid artery with cerebral infarction — (Use additional code, if applicable, to identify status post administration of tPA (rtPA) in a different facility within the last 24 hours prior to admission to current facility: V45.88)

433.21 Occlusion and stenosis of vertebral artery with cerebral infarction — (Use additional code, if applicable, to identify status post administration of tPA (rtPA) in a different facility within the last 24 hours prior to admission to current facility: V45.88)

435.0 Basilar artery syndrome — (Use additional code to identify presence of hypertension)

435.2 Subclavian steal syndrome — (Use additional code to identify presence of hypertension)

437.1 Other generalized ischemic cerebrovascular disease — (Use additional code to identify presence of hypertension)

440.8 Atherosclerosis of other specified arteries

442.81 Aneurysm of artery of neck

442.82 Aneurysm of subclavian artery

443.21 Dissection of carotid artery

443.29 Dissection of other artery

901.0 Thoracic aorta injury

901.1 Innominate and subclavian artery injury

996.1 Mechanical complication of other vascular device, implant, and graft

996.74 Other complications due to other vascular device, implant, and graft — (Use additional code to identify complication: 338.18-338.19, 338.28-338.29)

997.79 Vascular complications of other vessels — (Use additional code to identify complications)

998.2 Accidental puncture or laceration during procedure

ICD-9-CM Procedural

39.22 Aorta-subclavian-carotid bypass

35631

35631 Bypass graft, with other than vein; aortoceliac, aortomesenteric, aortorenal

ICD-9-CM Diagnostic

440.0 Atherosclerosis of aorta

440.1 Atherosclerosis of renal artery

440.8 Atherosclerosis of other specified arteries

441.3 Abdominal aneurysm, ruptured

441.4 Abdominal aneurysm without mention of rupture

441.9 Aortic aneurysm of unspecified site without mention of rupture ▽

442.1 Aneurysm of renal artery

442.84 Aneurysm of other visceral artery

443.29 Dissection of other artery

444.89 Embolism and thrombosis of other specified artery

445.81 Atheroembolism of kidney — (Use additional code for any associated acute kidney failure or chronic kidney disease: 584, 585)

445.89 Atheroembolism of other site

446.0 Polyarteritis nodosa

447.1 Stricture of artery

447.4 Celiac artery compression syndrome

447.6 Unspecified arteritis ▽
447.72 Abdominal aortic ectasia
447.9 Unspecified disorders of arteries and arterioles ▽
557.0 Acute vascular insufficiency of intestine
557.1 Chronic vascular insufficiency of intestine
593.81 Vascular disorders of kidney
902.0 Abdominal aorta injury
902.20 Unspecified celiac and mesenteric artery injury ▽
908.4 Late effect of injury to blood vessel of thorax, abdomen, and pelvis
996.1 Mechanical complication of other vascular device, implant, and graft
996.74 Other complications due to other vascular device, implant, and graft — (Use additional code to identify complication: 338.18-338.19, 338.28-338.29)
997.71 Vascular complications of mesenteric artery — (Use additional code to identify complications)
997.72 Vascular complications of renal artery — (Use additional code to identify complications)
997.79 Vascular complications of other vessels — (Use additional code to identify complications)
998.2 Accidental puncture or laceration during procedure

ICD-9-CM Procedural

39.24 Aorta-renal bypass
39.26 Other intra-abdominal vascular shunt or bypass

35632-35634

35632 Bypass graft, with other than vein; ilio-celiac
35633 ilio-mesenteric
35634 iliorenal

ICD-9-CM Diagnostic

405.11 Secondary renovascular hypertension, benign
405.91 Secondary renovascular hypertension, unspecified ▽
440.1 Atherosclerosis of renal artery
440.8 Atherosclerosis of other specified arteries
441.4 Abdominal aneurysm without mention of rupture
442.1 Aneurysm of renal artery
442.2 Aneurysm of iliac artery
442.84 Aneurysm of other visceral artery
442.89 Aneurysm of other specified artery
443.23 Dissection of renal artery
443.29 Dissection of other artery
443.9 Unspecified peripheral vascular disease ▽
445.81 Atheroembolism of kidney — (Use additional code for any associated acute kidney failure or chronic kidney disease: 584, 585)
447.1 Stricture of artery
447.3 Hyperplasia of renal artery
447.5 Necrosis of artery
447.72 Abdominal aortic ectasia
447.9 Unspecified disorders of arteries and arterioles ▽
584.9 Acute kidney failure, unspecified ▽
593.81 Vascular disorders of kidney
747.62 Congenital renal vessel anomaly
747.69 Congenital anomaly of other specified site of peripheral vascular system
902.41 Renal artery injury
902.42 Renal vein injury
902.50 Unspecified iliac vessel(s) injury ▽
902.51 Hypogastric artery injury
902.52 Hypogastric vein injury
902.53 Iliac artery injury
902.54 Iliac vein injury
902.55 Uterine artery injury ♀
902.56 Uterine vein injury ♀
902.59 Injury to iliac blood vessels, other
996.1 Mechanical complication of other vascular device, implant, and graft
996.74 Other complications due to other vascular device, implant, and graft — (Use additional code to identify complication: 338.18-338.19, 338.28-338.29)
997.72 Vascular complications of renal artery — (Use additional code to identify complications)

ICD-9-CM Procedural

39.26 Other intra-abdominal vascular shunt or bypass

35636

35636 Bypass graft, with other than vein; splenorenal (splenic to renal arterial anastomosis)

ICD-9-CM Diagnostic

405.11 Secondary renovascular hypertension, benign
405.91 Secondary renovascular hypertension, unspecified ▽
440.1 Atherosclerosis of renal artery
440.8 Atherosclerosis of other specified arteries
441.4 Abdominal aneurysm without mention of rupture
442.1 Aneurysm of renal artery
442.83 Aneurysm of splenic artery
443.23 Dissection of renal artery
443.29 Dissection of other artery
443.9 Unspecified peripheral vascular disease ▽
445.81 Atheroembolism of kidney — (Use additional code for any associated acute kidney failure or chronic kidney disease: 584, 585)
447.1 Stricture of artery
447.3 Hyperplasia of renal artery
447.5 Necrosis of artery
447.72 Abdominal aortic ectasia
447.9 Unspecified disorders of arteries and arterioles ▽
584.9 Acute kidney failure, unspecified ▽
593.81 Vascular disorders of kidney
747.62 Congenital renal vessel anomaly
747.69 Congenital anomaly of other specified site of peripheral vascular system
902.23 Splenic artery injury
902.41 Renal artery injury
902.42 Renal vein injury
996.1 Mechanical complication of other vascular device, implant, and graft
996.74 Other complications due to other vascular device, implant, and graft — (Use additional code to identify complication: 338.18-338.19, 338.28-338.29)
997.72 Vascular complications of renal artery — (Use additional code to identify complications)

ICD-9-CM Procedural

39.26 Other intra-abdominal vascular shunt or bypass

35637-35638

35637 Bypass graft, with other than vein; aortoiliac
35638 aortobi-iliac

ICD-9-CM Diagnostic

440.0 Atherosclerosis of aorta
440.8 Atherosclerosis of other specified arteries
441.00 Dissecting aortic aneurysm (any part), unspecified site ▽
441.02 Dissecting aortic aneurysm (any part), abdominal
441.3 Abdominal aneurysm, ruptured
441.4 Abdominal aneurysm without mention of rupture
441.5 Aortic aneurysm of unspecified site, ruptured ▽

441.9 Aortic aneurysm of unspecified site without mention of rupture ▽
442.2 Aneurysm of iliac artery
443.22 Dissection of iliac artery
443.9 Unspecified peripheral vascular disease ▽
444.01 Saddle embolus of abdominal aorta
444.09 Other arterial embolism and thrombosis of abdominal aorta
444.81 Embolism and thrombosis of iliac artery
445.89 Atheroembolism of other site
447.1 Stricture of artery
447.5 Necrosis of artery
447.72 Abdominal aortic ectasia
447.9 Unspecified disorders of arteries and arterioles ▽
747.22 Congenital atresia and stenosis of aorta
785.9 Other symptoms involving cardiovascular system
902.0 Abdominal aorta injury
902.53 Iliac artery injury
908.4 Late effect of injury to blood vessel of thorax, abdomen, and pelvis
996.1 Mechanical complication of other vascular device, implant, and graft
996.74 Other complications due to other vascular device, implant, and graft — (Use additional code to identify complication: 338.18-338.19, 338.28-338.29)
997.79 Vascular complications of other vessels — (Use additional code to identify complications)
998.2 Accidental puncture or laceration during procedure

ICD-9-CM Procedural

39.25 Aorta-iliac-femoral bypass

35642-35645

35642 Bypass graft, with other than vein; carotid-vertebral
35645 subclavian-vertebral

ICD-9-CM Diagnostic

433.20 Occlusion and stenosis of vertebral artery without mention of cerebral infarction — (Use additional code, if applicable, to identify status post administration of tPA (rtPA) in a different facility within the last 24 hours prior to admission to current facility: V45.88)
433.21 Occlusion and stenosis of vertebral artery with cerebral infarction — (Use additional code, if applicable, to identify status post administration of tPA (rtPA) in a different facility within the last 24 hours prior to admission to current facility: V45.88)
435.1 Vertebral artery syndrome — (Use additional code to identify presence of hypertension)
435.2 Subclavian steal syndrome — (Use additional code to identify presence of hypertension)
435.8 Other specified transient cerebral ischemias — (Use additional code to identify presence of hypertension)
440.8 Atherosclerosis of other specified arteries
442.81 Aneurysm of artery of neck
442.82 Aneurysm of subclavian artery
443.21 Dissection of carotid artery
443.24 Dissection of vertebral artery
443.29 Dissection of other artery
447.1 Stricture of artery
447.70 Aortic ectasia, unspecified site ▽
447.71 Thoracic aortic ectasia
747.69 Congenital anomaly of other specified site of peripheral vascular system
874.9 Open wound of other and unspecified parts of neck, complicated ▽
900.82 Injury to multiple blood vessels of head and neck
901.1 Innominate and subclavian artery injury
906.0 Late effect of open wound of head, neck, and trunk
996.1 Mechanical complication of other vascular device, implant, and graft
996.74 Other complications due to other vascular device, implant, and graft — (Use additional code to identify complication: 338.18-338.19, 338.28-338.29)

ICD-9-CM Procedural

39.22 Aorta-subclavian-carotid bypass
39.28 Extracranial-intracranial (EC-IC) vascular bypass

35646

35646 Bypass graft, with other than vein; aortobifemoral

ICD-9-CM Diagnostic

249.70 Secondary diabetes mellitus with peripheral circulatory disorders, not stated as uncontrolled, or unspecified — (Use additional code to identify manifestation: 443.81, 785.4) (Use additional code to identify any associated insulin use: V58.67)
249.71 Secondary diabetes mellitus with peripheral circulatory disorders, uncontrolled — (Use additional code to identify manifestation: 443.81, 785.4) (Use additional code to identify any associated insulin use: V58.67)
250.70 Diabetes with peripheral circulatory disorders, type II or unspecified type, not stated as uncontrolled — (Use additional code to identify manifestation: 443.81, 785.4)
250.71 Diabetes with peripheral circulatory disorders, type I [juvenile type], not stated as uncontrolled — (Use additional code to identify manifestation: 443.81, 785.4)
250.72 Diabetes with peripheral circulatory disorders, type II or unspecified type, uncontrolled — (Use additional code to identify manifestation: 443.81, 785.4)
250.73 Diabetes with peripheral circulatory disorders, type I [juvenile type], uncontrolled — (Use additional code to identify manifestation: 443.81, 785.4)
440.0 Atherosclerosis of aorta
440.20 Atherosclerosis of native arteries of the extremities, unspecified ▽
440.21 Atherosclerosis of native arteries of the extremities with intermittent claudication
440.22 Atherosclerosis of native arteries of the extremities with rest pain
440.23 Atherosclerosis of native arteries of the extremities with ulceration — (Use additional code for any associated ulceration: 707.10-707.19, 707.8, 707.9)
440.4 Chronic total occlusion of artery of the extremities
440.8 Atherosclerosis of other specified arteries
440.9 Generalized and unspecified atherosclerosis ▽
441.00 Dissecting aortic aneurysm (any part), unspecified site ▽
441.02 Dissecting aortic aneurysm (any part), abdominal
441.3 Abdominal aneurysm, ruptured
441.4 Abdominal aneurysm without mention of rupture
441.5 Aortic aneurysm of unspecified site, ruptured ▽
441.6 Thoracoabdominal aneurysm, ruptured
441.9 Aortic aneurysm of unspecified site without mention of rupture ▽
442.2 Aneurysm of iliac artery
443.22 Dissection of iliac artery
443.29 Dissection of other artery
443.81 Peripheral angiopathy in diseases classified elsewhere — (Code first underlying disease: 249.7, 250.7) ☒
443.9 Unspecified peripheral vascular disease ▽
444.01 Saddle embolus of abdominal aorta
444.09 Other arterial embolism and thrombosis of abdominal aorta
444.22 Embolism and thrombosis of arteries of lower extremity
444.81 Embolism and thrombosis of iliac artery
445.02 Atheroembolism of lower extremity
447.1 Stricture of artery
447.5 Necrosis of artery
447.71 Thoracic aortic ectasia
447.72 Abdominal aortic ectasia
447.73 Thoracoabdominal aortic ectasia
447.9 Unspecified disorders of arteries and arterioles ▽
459.9 Unspecified circulatory system disorder ▽
707.10 Ulcer of lower limb, unspecified — (Code, if applicable, any causal condition first: 249.80-249.81, 250.80-250.83, 440.23, 459.11, 459.13, 459.31, 459.33) ▽
707.11 Ulcer of thigh — (Code, if applicable, any causal condition first: 249.80-249.81, 250.80-250.83, 440.23, 459.11, 459.13, 459.31, 459.33)

707.12 Ulcer of calf — (Code, if applicable, any causal condition first: 249.80-249.81, 250.80-250.83, 440.23, 459.11, 459.13, 459.31, 459.33)

707.13 Ulcer of ankle — (Code, if applicable, any causal condition first: 249.80-249.81, 250.80-250.83, 440.23, 459.11, 459.13, 459.31, 459.33)

707.14 Ulcer of heel and midfoot — (Code, if applicable, any causal condition first: 249.80-249.81, 250.80-250.83, 440.23, 459.11, 459.13, 459.31, 459.33)

707.15 Ulcer of other part of foot — (Code, if applicable, any causal condition first: 249.80-249.81, 250.80-250.83, 440.23, 459.11, 459.13, 459.31, 459.33)

707.19 Ulcer of other part of lower limb — (Code, if applicable, any causal condition first: 249.80-249.81, 250.80-250.83, 440.23, 459.11, 459.13, 459.31, 459.33)

747.22 Congenital atresia and stenosis of aorta

747.64 Congenital lower limb vessel anomaly

747.69 Congenital anomaly of other specified site of peripheral vascular system

785.4 Gangrene — (Code first any associated underlying condition)

785.9 Other symptoms involving cardiovascular system

902.0 Abdominal aorta injury

904.0 Common femoral artery injury

904.1 Superficial femoral artery injury

908.3 Late effect of injury to blood vessel of head, neck, and extremities

908.4 Late effect of injury to blood vessel of thorax, abdomen, and pelvis

928.10 Crushing injury of lower leg — (Use additional code to identify any associated injuries: 800-829, 850.0-854.1, 860.0-869.1)

928.8 Crushing injury of multiple sites of lower limb — (Use additional code to identify any associated injuries: 800-829, 850.0-854.1, 860.0-869.1)

996.1 Mechanical complication of other vascular device, implant, and graft

996.74 Other complications due to other vascular device, implant, and graft — (Use additional code to identify complication: 338.18-338.19, 338.28-338.29)

997.79 Vascular complications of other vessels — (Use additional code to identify complications)

998.2 Accidental puncture or laceration during procedure

ICD-9-CM Procedural

39.25 Aorta-iliac-femoral bypass

35647

35647 Bypass graft, with other than vein; aortofemoral

ICD-9-CM Diagnostic

249.70 Secondary diabetes mellitus with peripheral circulatory disorders, not stated as uncontrolled, or unspecified — (Use additional code to identify manifestation: 443.81, 785.4) (Use additional code to identify any associated insulin use: V58.67)

249.71 Secondary diabetes mellitus with peripheral circulatory disorders, uncontrolled — (Use additional code to identify manifestation: 443.81, 785.4) (Use additional code to identify any associated insulin use: V58.67)

250.70 Diabetes with peripheral circulatory disorders, type II or unspecified type, not stated as uncontrolled — (Use additional code to identify manifestation: 443.81, 785.4)

250.71 Diabetes with peripheral circulatory disorders, type I [juvenile type], not stated as uncontrolled — (Use additional code to identify manifestation: 443.81, 785.4)

250.72 Diabetes with peripheral circulatory disorders, type II or unspecified type, uncontrolled — (Use additional code to identify manifestation: 443.81, 785.4)

250.73 Diabetes with peripheral circulatory disorders, type I [juvenile type], uncontrolled — (Use additional code to identify manifestation: 443.81, 785.4)

440.0 Atherosclerosis of aorta

440.20 Atherosclerosis of native arteries of the extremities, unspecified ▽

440.21 Atherosclerosis of native arteries of the extremities with intermittent claudication

440.22 Atherosclerosis of native arteries of the extremities with rest pain

440.23 Atherosclerosis of native arteries of the extremities with ulceration — (Use additional code for any associated ulceration: 707.10-707.19, 707.8, 707.9)

440.4 Chronic total occlusion of artery of the extremities

440.8 Atherosclerosis of other specified arteries

440.9 Generalized and unspecified atherosclerosis ▽

441.00 Dissecting aortic aneurysm (any part), unspecified site ▽

441.02 Dissecting aortic aneurysm (any part), abdominal

441.3 Abdominal aneurysm, ruptured

441.4 Abdominal aneurysm without mention of rupture

441.5 Aortic aneurysm of unspecified site, ruptured ▽

441.6 Thoracoabdominal aneurysm, ruptured

441.9 Aortic aneurysm of unspecified site without mention of rupture ▽

442.2 Aneurysm of iliac artery

443.22 Dissection of iliac artery

443.29 Dissection of other artery

443.81 Peripheral angiopathy in diseases classified elsewhere — (Code first underlying disease: 249.7, 250.7) ☒

443.9 Unspecified peripheral vascular disease ▽

444.01 Saddle embolus of abdominal aorta

444.09 Other arterial embolism and thrombosis of abdominal aorta

444.22 Embolism and thrombosis of arteries of lower extremity

444.81 Embolism and thrombosis of iliac artery

445.02 Atheroembolism of lower extremity

447.1 Stricture of artery

447.5 Necrosis of artery

447.71 Thoracic aortic ectasia

447.72 Abdominal aortic ectasia

447.73 Thoracoabdominal aortic ectasia

447.9 Unspecified disorders of arteries and arterioles ▽

459.9 Unspecified circulatory system disorder ▽

707.10 Ulcer of lower limb, unspecified — (Code, if applicable, any causal condition first: 249.80-249.81, 250.80-250.83, 440.23, 459.11, 459.13, 459.31, 459.33) ▽

707.11 Ulcer of thigh — (Code, if applicable, any causal condition first: 249.80-249.81, 250.80-250.83, 440.23, 459.11, 459.13, 459.31, 459.33)

707.12 Ulcer of calf — (Code, if applicable, any causal condition first: 249.80-249.81, 250.80-250.83, 440.23, 459.11, 459.13, 459.31, 459.33)

707.13 Ulcer of ankle — (Code, if applicable, any causal condition first: 249.80-249.81, 250.80-250.83, 440.23, 459.11, 459.13, 459.31, 459.33)

707.14 Ulcer of heel and midfoot — (Code, if applicable, any causal condition first: 249.80-249.81, 250.80-250.83, 440.23, 459.11, 459.13, 459.31, 459.33)

707.15 Ulcer of other part of foot — (Code, if applicable, any causal condition first: 249.80-249.81, 250.80-250.83, 440.23, 459.11, 459.13, 459.31, 459.33)

707.19 Ulcer of other part of lower limb — (Code, if applicable, any causal condition first: 249.80-249.81, 250.80-250.83, 440.23, 459.11, 459.13, 459.31, 459.33)

747.22 Congenital atresia and stenosis of aorta

747.64 Congenital lower limb vessel anomaly

747.69 Congenital anomaly of other specified site of peripheral vascular system

785.4 Gangrene — (Code first any associated underlying condition)

785.9 Other symptoms involving cardiovascular system

902.0 Abdominal aorta injury

904.0 Common femoral artery injury

904.1 Superficial femoral artery injury

908.3 Late effect of injury to blood vessel of head, neck, and extremities

908.4 Late effect of injury to blood vessel of thorax, abdomen, and pelvis

928.10 Crushing injury of lower leg — (Use additional code to identify any associated injuries: 800-829, 850.0-854.1, 860.0-869.1)

928.8 Crushing injury of multiple sites of lower limb — (Use additional code to identify any associated injuries: 800-829, 850.0-854.1, 860.0-869.1)

996.1 Mechanical complication of other vascular device, implant, and graft

996.74 Other complications due to other vascular device, implant, and graft — (Use additional code to identify complication: 338.18-338.19, 338.28-338.29)

997.79 Vascular complications of other vessels — (Use additional code to identify complications)

998.2 Accidental puncture or laceration during procedure

ICD-9-CM Procedural

39.25 Aorta-iliac-femoral bypass

35650

35650 Bypass graft, with other than vein; axillary-axillary

ICD-9-CM Diagnostic

435.2 Subclavian steal syndrome — (Use additional code to identify presence of hypertension)
440.20 Atherosclerosis of native arteries of the extremities, unspecified ▽
440.4 Chronic total occlusion of artery of the extremities
440.8 Atherosclerosis of other specified arteries
442.0 Aneurysm of artery of upper extremity
442.89 Aneurysm of other specified artery
443.29 Dissection of other artery
443.9 Unspecified peripheral vascular disease ▽
444.21 Embolism and thrombosis of arteries of upper extremity
444.89 Embolism and thrombosis of other specified artery
445.01 Atheroembolism of upper extremity
447.1 Stricture of artery
447.5 Necrosis of artery
447.9 Unspecified disorders of arteries and arterioles ▽
459.9 Unspecified circulatory system disorder ▽
747.63 Congenital upper limb vessel anomaly
747.69 Congenital anomaly of other specified site of peripheral vascular system
785.9 Other symptoms involving cardiovascular system
880.02 Open wound of axillary region, without mention of complication
880.12 Open wound of axillary region, complicated
901.1 Innominate and subclavian artery injury
903.01 Axillary artery injury
906.1 Late effect of open wound of extremities without mention of tendon injury
906.4 Late effect of crushing
908.3 Late effect of injury to blood vessel of head, neck, and extremities
927.02 Crushing injury of axillary region — (Use additional code to identify any associated injuries: 800-829, 850.0-854.1, 860.0-869.1)
996.1 Mechanical complication of other vascular device, implant, and graft
996.74 Other complications due to other vascular device, implant, and graft — (Use additional code to identify complication: 338.18-338.19, 338.28-338.29)

ICD-9-CM Procedural

39.29 Other (peripheral) vascular shunt or bypass

35654

35654 Bypass graft, with other than vein; axillary-femoral-femoral

ICD-9-CM Diagnostic

249.70 Secondary diabetes mellitus with peripheral circulatory disorders, not stated as uncontrolled, or unspecified — (Use additional code to identify manifestation: 443.81, 785.4) (Use additional code to identify any associated insulin use: V58.67)
249.71 Secondary diabetes mellitus with peripheral circulatory disorders, uncontrolled — (Use additional code to identify manifestation: 443.81, 785.4) (Use additional code to identify any associated insulin use: V58.67)
250.70 Diabetes with peripheral circulatory disorders, type II or unspecified type, not stated as uncontrolled — (Use additional code to identify manifestation: 443.81, 785.4)
250.71 Diabetes with peripheral circulatory disorders, type I [juvenile type], not stated as uncontrolled — (Use additional code to identify manifestation: 443.81, 785.4)
250.72 Diabetes with peripheral circulatory disorders, type II or unspecified type, uncontrolled — (Use additional code to identify manifestation: 443.81, 785.4)
250.73 Diabetes with peripheral circulatory disorders, type I [juvenile type], uncontrolled — (Use additional code to identify manifestation: 443.81, 785.4)
440.0 Atherosclerosis of aorta
440.20 Atherosclerosis of native arteries of the extremities, unspecified ▽
440.21 Atherosclerosis of native arteries of the extremities with intermittent claudication
440.22 Atherosclerosis of native arteries of the extremities with rest pain
440.23 Atherosclerosis of native arteries of the extremities with ulceration — (Use additional code for any associated ulceration: 707.10-707.19, 707.8, 707.9)
440.4 Chronic total occlusion of artery of the extremities
440.8 Atherosclerosis of other specified arteries
441.00 Dissecting aortic aneurysm (any part), unspecified site ▽
441.02 Dissecting aortic aneurysm (any part), abdominal
441.03 Dissecting aortic aneurysm (any part), thoracoabdominal
441.3 Abdominal aneurysm, ruptured
441.4 Abdominal aneurysm without mention of rupture
441.5 Aortic aneurysm of unspecified site, ruptured ▽
441.6 Thoracoabdominal aneurysm, ruptured
441.7 Thoracoabdominal aneurysm without mention of rupture
441.9 Aortic aneurysm of unspecified site without mention of rupture ▽
442.2 Aneurysm of iliac artery
442.3 Aneurysm of artery of lower extremity
443.22 Dissection of iliac artery
443.29 Dissection of other artery
443.81 Peripheral angiopathy in diseases classified elsewhere — (Code first underlying disease: 249.7, 250.7) ☒
443.9 Unspecified peripheral vascular disease ▽
444.01 Saddle embolus of abdominal aorta
444.09 Other arterial embolism and thrombosis of abdominal aorta
444.22 Embolism and thrombosis of arteries of lower extremity
444.81 Embolism and thrombosis of iliac artery
445.02 Atheroembolism of lower extremity
447.1 Stricture of artery
447.5 Necrosis of artery
447.9 Unspecified disorders of arteries and arterioles ▽
747.22 Congenital atresia and stenosis of aorta
747.64 Congenital lower limb vessel anomaly
747.69 Congenital anomaly of other specified site of peripheral vascular system
785.4 Gangrene — (Code first any associated underlying condition)
785.9 Other symptoms involving cardiovascular system
902.0 Abdominal aorta injury
902.53 Iliac artery injury
904.0 Common femoral artery injury
904.1 Superficial femoral artery injury
906.0 Late effect of open wound of head, neck, and trunk
908.4 Late effect of injury to blood vessel of thorax, abdomen, and pelvis
996.1 Mechanical complication of other vascular device, implant, and graft
996.74 Other complications due to other vascular device, implant, and graft — (Use additional code to identify complication: 338.18-338.19, 338.28-338.29)
998.2 Accidental puncture or laceration during procedure

ICD-9-CM Procedural

39.29 Other (peripheral) vascular shunt or bypass

35656

35656 Bypass graft, with other than vein; femoral-popliteal

ICD-9-CM Diagnostic

249.70 Secondary diabetes mellitus with peripheral circulatory disorders, not stated as uncontrolled, or unspecified — (Use additional code to identify manifestation: 443.81, 785.4) (Use additional code to identify any associated insulin use: V58.67)
249.71 Secondary diabetes mellitus with peripheral circulatory disorders, uncontrolled — (Use additional code to identify manifestation: 443.81, 785.4) (Use additional code to identify any associated insulin use: V58.67)

250.70 Diabetes with peripheral circulatory disorders, type II or unspecified type, not stated as uncontrolled — (Use additional code to identify manifestation: 443.81, 785.4)
250.71 Diabetes with peripheral circulatory disorders, type I [juvenile type], not stated as uncontrolled — (Use additional code to identify manifestation: 443.81, 785.4)
250.72 Diabetes with peripheral circulatory disorders, type II or unspecified type, uncontrolled — (Use additional code to identify manifestation: 443.81, 785.4)
250.73 Diabetes with peripheral circulatory disorders, type I [juvenile type], uncontrolled — (Use additional code to identify manifestation: 443.81, 785.4)
440.20 Atherosclerosis of native arteries of the extremities, unspecified ▽
440.21 Atherosclerosis of native arteries of the extremities with intermittent claudication
440.22 Atherosclerosis of native arteries of the extremities with rest pain
440.23 Atherosclerosis of native arteries of the extremities with ulceration — (Use additional code for any associated ulceration: 707.10-707.19, 707.8, 707.9)
440.24 Atherosclerosis of native arteries of the extremities with gangrene — (Use additional code for any associated ulceration: 707.10-707.19, 707.8, 707.9)
440.29 Other atherosclerosis of native arteries of the extremities
440.30 Atherosclerosis of unspecified bypass graft of extremities ▽
440.31 Atherosclerosis of autologous vein bypass graft of extremities
440.32 Atherosclerosis of nonautologous biological bypass graft of extremities
440.4 Chronic total occlusion of artery of the extremities
440.8 Atherosclerosis of other specified arteries
440.9 Generalized and unspecified atherosclerosis ▽
442.3 Aneurysm of artery of lower extremity
443.29 Dissection of other artery
443.81 Peripheral angiopathy in diseases classified elsewhere — (Code first underlying disease: 249.7, 250.7) ☒
443.89 Other peripheral vascular disease
443.9 Unspecified peripheral vascular disease ▽
444.22 Embolism and thrombosis of arteries of lower extremity
445.02 Atheroembolism of lower extremity
447.1 Stricture of artery
447.5 Necrosis of artery
447.70 Aortic ectasia, unspecified site ▽
459.89 Other specified circulatory system disorders
459.9 Unspecified circulatory system disorder ▽
707.10 Ulcer of lower limb, unspecified — (Code, if applicable, any causal condition first: 249.80-249.81, 250.80-250.83, 440.23, 459.11, 459.13, 459.31, 459.33) ▽
707.11 Ulcer of thigh — (Code, if applicable, any causal condition first: 249.80-249.81, 250.80-250.83, 440.23, 459.11, 459.13, 459.31, 459.33)
707.12 Ulcer of calf — (Code, if applicable, any causal condition first: 249.80-249.81, 250.80-250.83, 440.23, 459.11, 459.13, 459.31, 459.33)
707.13 Ulcer of ankle — (Code, if applicable, any causal condition first: 249.80-249.81, 250.80-250.83, 440.23, 459.11, 459.13, 459.31, 459.33)
707.14 Ulcer of heel and midfoot — (Code, if applicable, any causal condition first: 249.80-249.81, 250.80-250.83, 440.23, 459.11, 459.13, 459.31, 459.33)
707.15 Ulcer of other part of foot — (Code, if applicable, any causal condition first: 249.80-249.81, 250.80-250.83, 440.23, 459.11, 459.13, 459.31, 459.33)
707.19 Ulcer of other part of lower limb — (Code, if applicable, any causal condition first: 249.80-249.81, 250.80-250.83, 440.23, 459.11, 459.13, 459.31, 459.33)
747.64 Congenital lower limb vessel anomaly
747.69 Congenital anomaly of other specified site of peripheral vascular system
785.4 Gangrene — (Code first any associated underlying condition)
785.9 Other symptoms involving cardiovascular system
894.1 Multiple and unspecified open wound of lower limb, complicated
904.1 Superficial femoral artery injury
908.3 Late effect of injury to blood vessel of head, neck, and extremities
928.10 Crushing injury of lower leg — (Use additional code to identify any associated injuries: 800-829, 850.0-854.1, 860.0-869.1)
928.8 Crushing injury of multiple sites of lower limb — (Use additional code to identify any associated injuries: 800-829, 850.0-854.1, 860.0-869.1)
996.1 Mechanical complication of other vascular device, implant, and graft
996.74 Other complications due to other vascular device, implant, and graft — (Use additional code to identify complication: 338.18-338.19, 338.28-338.29)

ICD-9-CM Procedural

39.29 Other (peripheral) vascular shunt or bypass

35661

35661 Bypass graft, with other than vein; femoral-femoral

ICD-9-CM Diagnostic

249.70 Secondary diabetes mellitus with peripheral circulatory disorders, not stated as uncontrolled, or unspecified — (Use additional code to identify manifestation: 443.81, 785.4) (Use additional code to identify any associated insulin use: V58.67)
249.71 Secondary diabetes mellitus with peripheral circulatory disorders, uncontrolled — (Use additional code to identify manifestation: 443.81, 785.4) (Use additional code to identify any associated insulin use: V58.67)
250.70 Diabetes with peripheral circulatory disorders, type II or unspecified type, not stated as uncontrolled — (Use additional code to identify manifestation: 443.81, 785.4)
250.71 Diabetes with peripheral circulatory disorders, type I [juvenile type], not stated as uncontrolled — (Use additional code to identify manifestation: 443.81, 785.4)
250.72 Diabetes with peripheral circulatory disorders, type II or unspecified type, uncontrolled — (Use additional code to identify manifestation: 443.81, 785.4)
250.73 Diabetes with peripheral circulatory disorders, type I [juvenile type], uncontrolled — (Use additional code to identify manifestation: 443.81, 785.4)
440.20 Atherosclerosis of native arteries of the extremities, unspecified ▽
440.21 Atherosclerosis of native arteries of the extremities with intermittent claudication
440.22 Atherosclerosis of native arteries of the extremities with rest pain
440.23 Atherosclerosis of native arteries of the extremities with ulceration — (Use additional code for any associated ulceration: 707.10-707.19, 707.8, 707.9)
440.24 Atherosclerosis of native arteries of the extremities with gangrene — (Use additional code for any associated ulceration: 707.10-707.19, 707.8, 707.9)
440.4 Chronic total occlusion of artery of the extremities
440.8 Atherosclerosis of other specified arteries
442.3 Aneurysm of artery of lower extremity
442.9 Other aneurysm of unspecified site ▽
443.29 Dissection of other artery
443.81 Peripheral angiopathy in diseases classified elsewhere — (Code first underlying disease: 249.7, 250.7) ☒
443.9 Unspecified peripheral vascular disease ▽
447.1 Stricture of artery
447.5 Necrosis of artery
459.9 Unspecified circulatory system disorder ▽
707.10 Ulcer of lower limb, unspecified — (Code, if applicable, any causal condition first: 249.80-249.81, 250.80-250.83, 440.23, 459.11, 459.13, 459.31, 459.33) ▽
707.11 Ulcer of thigh — (Code, if applicable, any causal condition first: 249.80-249.81, 250.80-250.83, 440.23, 459.11, 459.13, 459.31, 459.33)
707.12 Ulcer of calf — (Code, if applicable, any causal condition first: 249.80-249.81, 250.80-250.83, 440.23, 459.11, 459.13, 459.31, 459.33)
707.13 Ulcer of ankle — (Code, if applicable, any causal condition first: 249.80-249.81, 250.80-250.83, 440.23, 459.11, 459.13, 459.31, 459.33)
707.14 Ulcer of heel and midfoot — (Code, if applicable, any causal condition first: 249.80-249.81, 250.80-250.83, 440.23, 459.11, 459.13, 459.31, 459.33)
707.15 Ulcer of other part of foot — (Code, if applicable, any causal condition first: 249.80-249.81, 250.80-250.83, 440.23, 459.11, 459.13, 459.31, 459.33)
707.19 Ulcer of other part of lower limb — (Code, if applicable, any causal condition first: 249.80-249.81, 250.80-250.83, 440.23, 459.11, 459.13, 459.31, 459.33)
747.64 Congenital lower limb vessel anomaly
747.69 Congenital anomaly of other specified site of peripheral vascular system
904.0 Common femoral artery injury
904.1 Superficial femoral artery injury
908.3 Late effect of injury to blood vessel of head, neck, and extremities

996.1 Mechanical complication of other vascular device, implant, and graft
996.74 Other complications due to other vascular device, implant, and graft — (Use additional code to identify complication: 338.18-338.19, 338.28-338.29)

ICD-9-CM Procedural

39.29 Other (peripheral) vascular shunt or bypass

35663

35663 Bypass graft, with other than vein; ilioiliac

ICD-9-CM Diagnostic

440.8 Atherosclerosis of other specified arteries
443.22 Dissection of iliac artery
443.9 Unspecified peripheral vascular disease ▽
444.81 Embolism and thrombosis of iliac artery
445.89 Atheroembolism of other site
447.1 Stricture of artery
447.5 Necrosis of artery
447.70 Aortic ectasia, unspecified site ▽
902.50 Unspecified iliac vessel(s) injury ▽
902.53 Iliac artery injury
996.1 Mechanical complication of other vascular device, implant, and graft
996.74 Other complications due to other vascular device, implant, and graft — (Use additional code to identify complication: 338.18-338.19, 338.28-338.29)
997.79 Vascular complications of other vessels — (Use additional code to identify complications)

ICD-9-CM Procedural

39.26 Other intra-abdominal vascular shunt or bypass

35665

35665 Bypass graft, with other than vein; iliofemoral

ICD-9-CM Diagnostic

249.70 Secondary diabetes mellitus with peripheral circulatory disorders, not stated as uncontrolled, or unspecified — (Use additional code to identify manifestation: 443.81, 785.4) (Use additional code to identify any associated insulin use: V58.67)
249.71 Secondary diabetes mellitus with peripheral circulatory disorders, uncontrolled — (Use additional code to identify manifestation: 443.81, 785.4) (Use additional code to identify any associated insulin use: V58.67)
250.70 Diabetes with peripheral circulatory disorders, type II or unspecified type, not stated as uncontrolled — (Use additional code to identify manifestation: 443.81, 785.4)
250.71 Diabetes with peripheral circulatory disorders, type I [juvenile type], not stated as uncontrolled — (Use additional code to identify manifestation: 443.81, 785.4)
250.72 Diabetes with peripheral circulatory disorders, type II or unspecified type, uncontrolled — (Use additional code to identify manifestation: 443.81, 785.4)
250.73 Diabetes with peripheral circulatory disorders, type I [juvenile type], uncontrolled — (Use additional code to identify manifestation: 443.81, 785.4)
440.20 Atherosclerosis of native arteries of the extremities, unspecified ▽
440.21 Atherosclerosis of native arteries of the extremities with intermittent claudication
440.22 Atherosclerosis of native arteries of the extremities with rest pain
440.23 Atherosclerosis of native arteries of the extremities with ulceration — (Use additional code for any associated ulceration: 707.10-707.19, 707.8, 707.9)
440.24 Atherosclerosis of native arteries of the extremities with gangrene — (Use additional code for any associated ulceration: 707.10-707.19, 707.8, 707.9)
440.4 Chronic total occlusion of artery of the extremities
440.8 Atherosclerosis of other specified arteries
440.9 Generalized and unspecified atherosclerosis ▽
442.2 Aneurysm of iliac artery
442.3 Aneurysm of artery of lower extremity
443.22 Dissection of iliac artery
443.81 Peripheral angiopathy in diseases classified elsewhere — (Code first underlying disease: 249.7, 250.7) ☒
443.89 Other peripheral vascular disease
443.9 Unspecified peripheral vascular disease ▽
444.22 Embolism and thrombosis of arteries of lower extremity
444.81 Embolism and thrombosis of iliac artery
445.02 Atheroembolism of lower extremity
447.1 Stricture of artery
447.5 Necrosis of artery
447.70 Aortic ectasia, unspecified site ▽
459.9 Unspecified circulatory system disorder ▽
707.10 Ulcer of lower limb, unspecified — (Code, if applicable, any causal condition first: 249.80-249.81, 250.80-250.83, 440.23, 459.11, 459.13, 459.31, 459.33) ▽
707.11 Ulcer of thigh — (Code, if applicable, any causal condition first: 249.80-249.81, 250.80-250.83, 440.23, 459.11, 459.13, 459.31, 459.33)
707.12 Ulcer of calf — (Code, if applicable, any causal condition first: 249.80-249.81, 250.80-250.83, 440.23, 459.11, 459.13, 459.31, 459.33)
707.13 Ulcer of ankle — (Code, if applicable, any causal condition first: 249.80-249.81, 250.80-250.83, 440.23, 459.11, 459.13, 459.31, 459.33)
707.14 Ulcer of heel and midfoot — (Code, if applicable, any causal condition first: 249.80-249.81, 250.80-250.83, 440.23, 459.11, 459.13, 459.31, 459.33)
707.15 Ulcer of other part of foot — (Code, if applicable, any causal condition first: 249.80-249.81, 250.80-250.83, 440.23, 459.11, 459.13, 459.31, 459.33)
707.19 Ulcer of other part of lower limb — (Code, if applicable, any causal condition first: 249.80-249.81, 250.80-250.83, 440.23, 459.11, 459.13, 459.31, 459.33)
747.64 Congenital lower limb vessel anomaly
747.69 Congenital anomaly of other specified site of peripheral vascular system
785.4 Gangrene — (Code first any associated underlying condition)
785.9 Other symptoms involving cardiovascular system
894.1 Multiple and unspecified open wound of lower limb, complicated
902.53 Iliac artery injury
904.7 Injury to specified blood vessels of lower extremity, other
908.3 Late effect of injury to blood vessel of head, neck, and extremities
928.00 Crushing injury of thigh — (Use additional code to identify any associated injuries: 800-829, 850.0-854.1, 860.0-869.1)
996.74 Other complications due to other vascular device, implant, and graft — (Use additional code to identify complication: 338.18-338.19, 338.28-338.29)
997.79 Vascular complications of other vessels — (Use additional code to identify complications)

ICD-9-CM Procedural

39.25 Aorta-iliac-femoral bypass

35666

35666 Bypass graft, with other than vein; femoral-anterior tibial, posterior tibial, or peroneal artery

ICD-9-CM Diagnostic

249.70 Secondary diabetes mellitus with peripheral circulatory disorders, not stated as uncontrolled, or unspecified — (Use additional code to identify manifestation: 443.81, 785.4) (Use additional code to identify any associated insulin use: V58.67)
249.71 Secondary diabetes mellitus with peripheral circulatory disorders, uncontrolled — (Use additional code to identify manifestation: 443.81, 785.4) (Use additional code to identify any associated insulin use: V58.67)
250.70 Diabetes with peripheral circulatory disorders, type II or unspecified type, not stated as uncontrolled — (Use additional code to identify manifestation: 443.81, 785.4)
250.71 Diabetes with peripheral circulatory disorders, type I [juvenile type], not stated as uncontrolled — (Use additional code to identify manifestation: 443.81, 785.4)
250.72 Diabetes with peripheral circulatory disorders, type II or unspecified type, uncontrolled — (Use additional code to identify manifestation: 443.81, 785.4)
250.73 Diabetes with peripheral circulatory disorders, type I [juvenile type], uncontrolled — (Use additional code to identify manifestation: 443.81, 785.4)

440.20 Atherosclerosis of native arteries of the extremities, unspecified ▽
440.21 Atherosclerosis of native arteries of the extremities with intermittent claudication
440.22 Atherosclerosis of native arteries of the extremities with rest pain
440.23 Atherosclerosis of native arteries of the extremities with ulceration — (Use additional code for any associated ulceration: 707.10-707.19, 707.8, 707.9)
440.24 Atherosclerosis of native arteries of the extremities with gangrene — (Use additional code for any associated ulceration: 707.10-707.19, 707.8, 707.9)
440.29 Other atherosclerosis of native arteries of the extremities
440.4 Chronic total occlusion of artery of the extremities
440.8 Atherosclerosis of other specified arteries
440.9 Generalized and unspecified atherosclerosis ▽
442.3 Aneurysm of artery of lower extremity
443.29 Dissection of other artery
443.81 Peripheral angiopathy in diseases classified elsewhere — (Code first underlying disease: 249.7, 250.7) ☒
443.9 Unspecified peripheral vascular disease ▽
447.1 Stricture of artery
459.89 Other specified circulatory system disorders
459.9 Unspecified circulatory system disorder ▽
707.10 Ulcer of lower limb, unspecified — (Code, if applicable, any causal condition first: 249.80-249.81, 250.80-250.83, 440.23, 459.11, 459.13, 459.31, 459.33) ▽
707.11 Ulcer of thigh — (Code, if applicable, any causal condition first: 249.80-249.81, 250.80-250.83, 440.23, 459.11, 459.13, 459.31, 459.33)
707.12 Ulcer of calf — (Code, if applicable, any causal condition first: 249.80-249.81, 250.80-250.83, 440.23, 459.11, 459.13, 459.31, 459.33)
707.13 Ulcer of ankle — (Code, if applicable, any causal condition first: 249.80-249.81, 250.80-250.83, 440.23, 459.11, 459.13, 459.31, 459.33)
707.14 Ulcer of heel and midfoot — (Code, if applicable, any causal condition first: 249.80-249.81, 250.80-250.83, 440.23, 459.11, 459.13, 459.31, 459.33)
707.15 Ulcer of other part of foot — (Code, if applicable, any causal condition first: 249.80-249.81, 250.80-250.83, 440.23, 459.11, 459.13, 459.31, 459.33)
707.19 Ulcer of other part of lower limb — (Code, if applicable, any causal condition first: 249.80-249.81, 250.80-250.83, 440.23, 459.11, 459.13, 459.31, 459.33)
747.64 Congenital lower limb vessel anomaly
785.4 Gangrene — (Code first any associated underlying condition)
785.9 Other symptoms involving cardiovascular system
894.1 Multiple and unspecified open wound of lower limb, complicated
904.0 Common femoral artery injury
904.1 Superficial femoral artery injury
904.41 Popliteal artery injury
904.42 Popliteal vein injury
904.51 Anterior tibial artery injury
904.52 Anterior tibial vein injury
904.53 Posterior tibial artery injury
904.54 Posterior tibial vein injury
904.7 Injury to specified blood vessels of lower extremity, other
908.3 Late effect of injury to blood vessel of head, neck, and extremities
928.10 Crushing injury of lower leg — (Use additional code to identify any associated injuries: 800-829, 850.0-854.1, 860.0-869.1)
928.8 Crushing injury of multiple sites of lower limb — (Use additional code to identify any associated injuries: 800-829, 850.0-854.1, 860.0-869.1)
996.1 Mechanical complication of other vascular device, implant, and graft
996.74 Other complications due to other vascular device, implant, and graft — (Use additional code to identify complication: 338.18-338.19, 338.28-338.29)

ICD-9-CM Procedural

39.29 Other (peripheral) vascular shunt or bypass

35671

35671 Bypass graft, with other than vein; popliteal-tibial or -peroneal artery

ICD-9-CM Diagnostic

249.70 Secondary diabetes mellitus with peripheral circulatory disorders, not stated as uncontrolled, or unspecified — (Use additional code to identify manifestation: 443.81, 785.4) (Use additional code to identify any associated insulin use: V58.67)
249.71 Secondary diabetes mellitus with peripheral circulatory disorders, uncontrolled — (Use additional code to identify manifestation: 443.81, 785.4) (Use additional code to identify any associated insulin use: V58.67)
250.70 Diabetes with peripheral circulatory disorders, type II or unspecified type, not stated as uncontrolled — (Use additional code to identify manifestation: 443.81, 785.4)
250.71 Diabetes with peripheral circulatory disorders, type I [juvenile type], not stated as uncontrolled — (Use additional code to identify manifestation: 443.81, 785.4)
250.72 Diabetes with peripheral circulatory disorders, type II or unspecified type, uncontrolled — (Use additional code to identify manifestation: 443.81, 785.4)
250.73 Diabetes with peripheral circulatory disorders, type I [juvenile type], uncontrolled — (Use additional code to identify manifestation: 443.81, 785.4)
440.20 Atherosclerosis of native arteries of the extremities, unspecified ▽
440.21 Atherosclerosis of native arteries of the extremities with intermittent claudication
440.22 Atherosclerosis of native arteries of the extremities with rest pain
440.23 Atherosclerosis of native arteries of the extremities with ulceration — (Use additional code for any associated ulceration: 707.10-707.19, 707.8, 707.9)
440.24 Atherosclerosis of native arteries of the extremities with gangrene — (Use additional code for any associated ulceration: 707.10-707.19, 707.8, 707.9)
440.4 Chronic total occlusion of artery of the extremities
440.8 Atherosclerosis of other specified arteries
442.3 Aneurysm of artery of lower extremity
443.81 Peripheral angiopathy in diseases classified elsewhere — (Code first underlying disease: 249.7, 250.7) ☒
443.9 Unspecified peripheral vascular disease ▽
444.22 Embolism and thrombosis of arteries of lower extremity
445.02 Atheroembolism of lower extremity
447.1 Stricture of artery
459.9 Unspecified circulatory system disorder ▽
707.10 Ulcer of lower limb, unspecified — (Code, if applicable, any causal condition first: 249.80-249.81, 250.80-250.83, 440.23, 459.11, 459.13, 459.31, 459.33) ▽
707.11 Ulcer of thigh — (Code, if applicable, any causal condition first: 249.80-249.81, 250.80-250.83, 440.23, 459.11, 459.13, 459.31, 459.33)
707.12 Ulcer of calf — (Code, if applicable, any causal condition first: 249.80-249.81, 250.80-250.83, 440.23, 459.11, 459.13, 459.31, 459.33)
707.13 Ulcer of ankle — (Code, if applicable, any causal condition first: 249.80-249.81, 250.80-250.83, 440.23, 459.11, 459.13, 459.31, 459.33)
707.14 Ulcer of heel and midfoot — (Code, if applicable, any causal condition first: 249.80-249.81, 250.80-250.83, 440.23, 459.11, 459.13, 459.31, 459.33)
707.15 Ulcer of other part of foot — (Code, if applicable, any causal condition first: 249.80-249.81, 250.80-250.83, 440.23, 459.11, 459.13, 459.31, 459.33)
707.19 Ulcer of other part of lower limb — (Code, if applicable, any causal condition first: 249.80-249.81, 250.80-250.83, 440.23, 459.11, 459.13, 459.31, 459.33)
747.64 Congenital lower limb vessel anomaly
785.4 Gangrene — (Code first any associated underlying condition)
785.9 Other symptoms involving cardiovascular system
894.1 Multiple and unspecified open wound of lower limb, complicated
904.41 Popliteal artery injury
904.42 Popliteal vein injury
904.51 Anterior tibial artery injury
904.53 Posterior tibial artery injury
904.7 Injury to specified blood vessels of lower extremity, other
908.3 Late effect of injury to blood vessel of head, neck, and extremities
928.10 Crushing injury of lower leg — (Use additional code to identify any associated injuries: 800-829, 850.0-854.1, 860.0-869.1)

928.8 Crushing injury of multiple sites of lower limb — (Use additional code to identify any associated injuries: 800-829, 850.0-854.1, 860.0-869.1)
996.1 Mechanical complication of other vascular device, implant, and graft
996.74 Other complications due to other vascular device, implant, and graft — (Use additional code to identify complication: 338.18-338.19, 338.28-338.29)

ICD-9-CM Procedural

39.29 Other (peripheral) vascular shunt or bypass

35685

35685 Placement of vein patch or cuff at distal anastomosis of bypass graft, synthetic conduit (List separately in addition to code for primary procedure)

ICD-9-CM Diagnostic

This is an add-on code. Refer to the corresponding primary procedure code for ICD-9-CM diagnosis code links.

ICD-9-CM Procedural

39.56 Repair of blood vessel with tissue patch graft

35686

35686 Creation of distal arteriovenous fistula during lower extremity bypass surgery (non-hemodialysis) (List separately in addition to code for primary procedure)

ICD-9-CM Diagnostic

This is an add-on code. Refer to the corresponding primary procedure code for ICD-9-CM diagnosis code links.

ICD-9-CM Procedural

39.29 Other (peripheral) vascular shunt or bypass

35691

35691 Transposition and/or reimplantation; vertebral to carotid artery

ICD-9-CM Diagnostic

433.20 Occlusion and stenosis of vertebral artery without mention of cerebral infarction — (Use additional code, if applicable, to identify status post administration of tPA (rtPA) in a different facility within the last 24 hours prior to admission to current facility: V45.88)
433.21 Occlusion and stenosis of vertebral artery with cerebral infarction — (Use additional code, if applicable, to identify status post administration of tPA (rtPA) in a different facility within the last 24 hours prior to admission to current facility: V45.88)
435.1 Vertebral artery syndrome — (Use additional code to identify presence of hypertension)
440.8 Atherosclerosis of other specified arteries
442.81 Aneurysm of artery of neck
443.24 Dissection of vertebral artery
447.1 Stricture of artery
747.81 Congenital anomaly of cerebrovascular system
747.82 Congenital spinal vessel anomaly
900.00 Injury to carotid artery, unspecified

ICD-9-CM Procedural

39.59 Other repair of vessel

35693

35693 Transposition and/or reimplantation; vertebral to subclavian artery

ICD-9-CM Diagnostic

433.20 Occlusion and stenosis of vertebral artery without mention of cerebral infarction — (Use additional code, if applicable, to identify status post administration of tPA (rtPA) in a different facility within the last 24 hours prior to admission to current facility: V45.88)
433.21 Occlusion and stenosis of vertebral artery with cerebral infarction — (Use additional code, if applicable, to identify status post administration of tPA (rtPA) in a different facility within the last 24 hours prior to admission to current facility: V45.88)
435.1 Vertebral artery syndrome — (Use additional code to identify presence of hypertension)
435.2 Subclavian steal syndrome — (Use additional code to identify presence of hypertension)
440.8 Atherosclerosis of other specified arteries
442.82 Aneurysm of subclavian artery
443.24 Dissection of vertebral artery
447.1 Stricture of artery
747.81 Congenital anomaly of cerebrovascular system
747.82 Congenital spinal vessel anomaly
901.1 Innominate and subclavian artery injury

ICD-9-CM Procedural

39.59 Other repair of vessel

35694

35694 Transposition and/or reimplantation; subclavian to carotid artery

ICD-9-CM Diagnostic

433.10 Occlusion and stenosis of carotid artery without mention of cerebral infarction — (Use additional code, if applicable, to identify status post administration of tPA (rtPA) in a different facility within the last 24 hours prior to admission to current facility: V45.88)
433.11 Occlusion and stenosis of carotid artery with cerebral infarction — (Use additional code, if applicable, to identify status post administration of tPA (rtPA) in a different facility within the last 24 hours prior to admission to current facility: V45.88)
433.30 Occlusion and stenosis of multiple and bilateral precerebral arteries without mention of cerebral infarction — (Use additional code, if applicable, to identify status post administration of tPA (rtPA) in a different facility within the last 24 hours prior to admission to current facility: V45.88)
433.31 Occlusion and stenosis of multiple and bilateral precerebral arteries with cerebral infarction — (Use additional code, if applicable, to identify status post administration of tPA (rtPA) in a different facility within the last 24 hours prior to admission to current facility: V45.88)
435.2 Subclavian steal syndrome — (Use additional code to identify presence of hypertension)
440.8 Atherosclerosis of other specified arteries
442.81 Aneurysm of artery of neck
442.82 Aneurysm of subclavian artery
443.21 Dissection of carotid artery
443.29 Dissection of other artery
447.1 Stricture of artery
747.81 Congenital anomaly of cerebrovascular system
900.00 Injury to carotid artery, unspecified
901.1 Innominate and subclavian artery injury

ICD-9-CM Procedural

39.59 Other repair of vessel

35695

35695 Transposition and/or reimplantation; carotid to subclavian artery

ICD-9-CM Diagnostic

433.10 Occlusion and stenosis of carotid artery without mention of cerebral infarction — (Use additional code, if applicable, to identify status post administration of tPA (rtPA) in a different facility within the last 24 hours prior to admission to current facility: V45.88)
433.11 Occlusion and stenosis of carotid artery with cerebral infarction — (Use additional code, if applicable, to identify status post administration of tPA (rtPA) in a different facility within the last 24 hours prior to admission to current facility: V45.88)
433.30 Occlusion and stenosis of multiple and bilateral precerebral arteries without mention of cerebral infarction — (Use additional code, if applicable, to identify status post administration of tPA (rtPA) in a different facility within the last 24 hours prior to admission to current facility: V45.88)

433.31 Occlusion and stenosis of multiple and bilateral precerebral arteries with cerebral infarction — (Use additional code, if applicable, to identify status post administration of tPA (rtPA) in a different facility within the last 24 hours prior to admission to current facility: V45.88)
435.2 Subclavian steal syndrome — (Use additional code to identify presence of hypertension)
440.8 Atherosclerosis of other specified arteries
442.81 Aneurysm of artery of neck
442.82 Aneurysm of subclavian artery
443.21 Dissection of carotid artery
443.29 Dissection of other artery
447.1 Stricture of artery
747.81 Congenital anomaly of cerebrovascular system
900.00 Injury to carotid artery, unspecified ▽
901.1 Innominate and subclavian artery injury

ICD-9-CM Procedural

39.59 Other repair of vessel

35701

35701 Exploration (not followed by surgical repair), with or without lysis of artery; carotid artery

ICD-9-CM Diagnostic

433.10 Occlusion and stenosis of carotid artery without mention of cerebral infarction — (Use additional code, if applicable, to identify status post administration of tPA (rtPA) in a different facility within the last 24 hours prior to admission to current facility: V45.88)
433.30 Occlusion and stenosis of multiple and bilateral precerebral arteries without mention of cerebral infarction — (Use additional code, if applicable, to identify status post administration of tPA (rtPA) in a different facility within the last 24 hours prior to admission to current facility: V45.88)
435.8 Other specified transient cerebral ischemias — (Use additional code to identify presence of hypertension)
437.0 Cerebral atherosclerosis — (Use additional code to identify presence of hypertension)
443.21 Dissection of carotid artery
447.1 Stricture of artery
447.70 Aortic ectasia, unspecified site ▽
449 Septic arterial embolism — (Use additional code to identify the site of the embolism: 433.0-433.9, 444.01-444.9)
780.02 Transient alteration of awareness
780.2 Syncope and collapse
780.31 Febrile convulsions (simple), unspecified ▽
780.39 Other convulsions
780.4 Dizziness and giddiness
785.9 Other symptoms involving cardiovascular system
900.03 Internal carotid artery injury

ICD-9-CM Procedural

38.02 Incision of other vessels of head and neck
39.91 Freeing of vessel

35721

35721 Exploration (not followed by surgical repair), with or without lysis of artery; femoral artery

ICD-9-CM Diagnostic

249.70 Secondary diabetes mellitus with peripheral circulatory disorders, not stated as uncontrolled, or unspecified — (Use additional code to identify manifestation: 443.81, 785.4) (Use additional code to identify any associated insulin use: V58.67)
249.71 Secondary diabetes mellitus with peripheral circulatory disorders, uncontrolled — (Use additional code to identify manifestation: 443.81, 785.4) (Use additional code to identify any associated insulin use: V58.67)
250.70 Diabetes with peripheral circulatory disorders, type II or unspecified type, not stated as uncontrolled — (Use additional code to identify manifestation: 443.81, 785.4)
250.71 Diabetes with peripheral circulatory disorders, type I [juvenile type], not stated as uncontrolled — (Use additional code to identify manifestation: 443.81, 785.4)
250.72 Diabetes with peripheral circulatory disorders, type II or unspecified type, uncontrolled — (Use additional code to identify manifestation: 443.81, 785.4)
250.73 Diabetes with peripheral circulatory disorders, type I [juvenile type], uncontrolled — (Use additional code to identify manifestation: 443.81, 785.4)
440.20 Atherosclerosis of native arteries of the extremities, unspecified ▽
440.21 Atherosclerosis of native arteries of the extremities with intermittent claudication
440.22 Atherosclerosis of native arteries of the extremities with rest pain
440.23 Atherosclerosis of native arteries of the extremities with ulceration — (Use additional code for any associated ulceration: 707.10-707.19, 707.8, 707.9)
440.29 Other atherosclerosis of native arteries of the extremities
440.4 Chronic total occlusion of artery of the extremities
442.3 Aneurysm of artery of lower extremity
443.29 Dissection of other artery
443.81 Peripheral angiopathy in diseases classified elsewhere — (Code first underlying disease: 249.7, 250.7) ☒
443.9 Unspecified peripheral vascular disease ▽
444.22 Embolism and thrombosis of arteries of lower extremity
445.02 Atheroembolism of lower extremity
447.1 Stricture of artery
447.6 Unspecified arteritis ▽
447.8 Other specified disorders of arteries and arterioles
449 Septic arterial embolism — (Use additional code to identify the site of the embolism: 433.0-433.9, 444.01-444.9)
707.10 Ulcer of lower limb, unspecified — (Code, if applicable, any causal condition first: 249.80-249.81, 250.80-250.83, 440.23, 459.11, 459.13, 459.31, 459.33) ▽
707.11 Ulcer of thigh — (Code, if applicable, any causal condition first: 249.80-249.81, 250.80-250.83, 440.23, 459.11, 459.13, 459.31, 459.33)
707.12 Ulcer of calf — (Code, if applicable, any causal condition first: 249.80-249.81, 250.80-250.83, 440.23, 459.11, 459.13, 459.31, 459.33)
707.13 Ulcer of ankle — (Code, if applicable, any causal condition first: 249.80-249.81, 250.80-250.83, 440.23, 459.11, 459.13, 459.31, 459.33)
707.14 Ulcer of heel and midfoot — (Code, if applicable, any causal condition first: 249.80-249.81, 250.80-250.83, 440.23, 459.11, 459.13, 459.31, 459.33)
707.15 Ulcer of other part of foot — (Code, if applicable, any causal condition first: 249.80-249.81, 250.80-250.83, 440.23, 459.11, 459.13, 459.31, 459.33)
707.19 Ulcer of other part of lower limb — (Code, if applicable, any causal condition first: 249.80-249.81, 250.80-250.83, 440.23, 459.11, 459.13, 459.31, 459.33)
785.4 Gangrene — (Code first any associated underlying condition)
894.1 Multiple and unspecified open wound of lower limb, complicated
904.0 Common femoral artery injury
904.1 Superficial femoral artery injury
904.7 Injury to specified blood vessels of lower extremity, other
908.3 Late effect of injury to blood vessel of head, neck, and extremities
928.00 Crushing injury of thigh — (Use additional code to identify any associated injuries: 800-829, 850.0-854.1, 860.0-869.1)
998.9 Unspecified complication of procedure, not elsewhere classified ▽

ICD-9-CM Procedural

38.08 Incision of lower limb arteries
39.91 Freeing of vessel

35741

35741 Exploration (not followed by surgical repair), with or without lysis of artery; popliteal artery

ICD-9-CM Diagnostic

249.70 Secondary diabetes mellitus with peripheral circulatory disorders, not stated as uncontrolled, or unspecified — (Use additional code to identify manifestation: 443.81, 785.4) (Use additional code to identify any associated insulin use: V58.67)

249.71 Secondary diabetes mellitus with peripheral circulatory disorders, uncontrolled — (Use additional code to identify manifestation: 443.81, 785.4) (Use additional code to identify any associated insulin use: V58.67)

250.70 Diabetes with peripheral circulatory disorders, type II or unspecified type, not stated as uncontrolled — (Use additional code to identify manifestation: 443.81, 785.4)

250.71 Diabetes with peripheral circulatory disorders, type I [juvenile type], not stated as uncontrolled — (Use additional code to identify manifestation: 443.81, 785.4)

250.72 Diabetes with peripheral circulatory disorders, type II or unspecified type, uncontrolled — (Use additional code to identify manifestation: 443.81, 785.4)

250.73 Diabetes with peripheral circulatory disorders, type I [juvenile type], uncontrolled — (Use additional code to identify manifestation: 443.81, 785.4)

440.20 Atherosclerosis of native arteries of the extremities, unspecified ▽

440.21 Atherosclerosis of native arteries of the extremities with intermittent claudication

440.22 Atherosclerosis of native arteries of the extremities with rest pain

440.23 Atherosclerosis of native arteries of the extremities with ulceration — (Use additional code for any associated ulceration: 707.10-707.19, 707.8, 707.9)

440.24 Atherosclerosis of native arteries of the extremities with gangrene — (Use additional code for any associated ulceration: 707.10-707.19, 707.8, 707.9)

440.29 Other atherosclerosis of native arteries of the extremities

440.4 Chronic total occlusion of artery of the extremities

443.81 Peripheral angiopathy in diseases classified elsewhere — (Code first underlying disease: 249.7, 250.7) ☒

443.9 Unspecified peripheral vascular disease ▽

444.22 Embolism and thrombosis of arteries of lower extremity

444.9 Embolism and thrombosis of unspecified artery ▽

445.02 Atheroembolism of lower extremity

447.1 Stricture of artery

447.6 Unspecified arteritis ▽

447.8 Other specified disorders of arteries and arterioles

449 Septic arterial embolism — (Use additional code to identify the site of the embolism: 433.0-433.9, 444.01-444.9)

707.10 Ulcer of lower limb, unspecified — (Code, if applicable, any causal condition first: 249.80-249.81, 250.80-250.83, 440.23, 459.11, 459.13, 459.31, 459.33) ▽

707.11 Ulcer of thigh — (Code, if applicable, any causal condition first: 249.80-249.81, 250.80-250.83, 440.23, 459.11, 459.13, 459.31, 459.33)

707.12 Ulcer of calf — (Code, if applicable, any causal condition first: 249.80-249.81, 250.80-250.83, 440.23, 459.11, 459.13, 459.31, 459.33)

707.13 Ulcer of ankle — (Code, if applicable, any causal condition first: 249.80-249.81, 250.80-250.83, 440.23, 459.11, 459.13, 459.31, 459.33)

707.14 Ulcer of heel and midfoot — (Code, if applicable, any causal condition first: 249.80-249.81, 250.80-250.83, 440.23, 459.11, 459.13, 459.31, 459.33)

707.15 Ulcer of other part of foot — (Code, if applicable, any causal condition first: 249.80-249.81, 250.80-250.83, 440.23, 459.11, 459.13, 459.31, 459.33)

707.19 Ulcer of other part of lower limb — (Code, if applicable, any causal condition first: 249.80-249.81, 250.80-250.83, 440.23, 459.11, 459.13, 459.31, 459.33)

785.4 Gangrene — (Code first any associated underlying condition)

785.9 Other symptoms involving cardiovascular system

904.41 Popliteal artery injury

904.7 Injury to specified blood vessels of lower extremity, other

908.3 Late effect of injury to blood vessel of head, neck, and extremities

928.10 Crushing injury of lower leg — (Use additional code to identify any associated injuries: 800-829, 850.0-854.1, 860.0-869.1)

ICD-9-CM Procedural

38.08 Incision of lower limb arteries

39.91 Freeing of vessel

35761

35761 Exploration (not followed by surgical repair), with or without lysis of artery; other vessels

ICD-9-CM Diagnostic

440.21 Atherosclerosis of native arteries of the extremities with intermittent claudication

440.22 Atherosclerosis of native arteries of the extremities with rest pain

440.23 Atherosclerosis of native arteries of the extremities with ulceration — (Use additional code for any associated ulceration: 707.10-707.19, 707.8, 707.9)

440.24 Atherosclerosis of native arteries of the extremities with gangrene — (Use additional code for any associated ulceration: 707.10-707.19, 707.8, 707.9)

440.29 Other atherosclerosis of native arteries of the extremities

442.0 Aneurysm of artery of upper extremity

442.1 Aneurysm of renal artery

442.83 Aneurysm of splenic artery

442.84 Aneurysm of other visceral artery

443.29 Dissection of other artery

444.21 Embolism and thrombosis of arteries of upper extremity

444.22 Embolism and thrombosis of arteries of lower extremity

444.89 Embolism and thrombosis of other specified artery

445.89 Atheroembolism of other site

447.6 Unspecified arteritis ▽

447.70 Aortic ectasia, unspecified site ▽

448.1 Nevus, non-neoplastic

449 Septic arterial embolism — (Use additional code to identify the site of the embolism: 433.0-433.9, 444.01-444.9)

459.9 Unspecified circulatory system disorder ▽

557.0 Acute vascular insufficiency of intestine

729.5 Pain in soft tissues of limb

785.4 Gangrene — (Code first any associated underlying condition)

785.9 Other symptoms involving cardiovascular system

900.9 Injury to unspecified blood vessel of head and neck ▽

902.9 Injury to blood vessel of abdomen and pelvis, unspecified ▽

903.9 Injury to unspecified blood vessel of upper extremity ▽

904.8 Injury to unspecified blood vessel of lower extremity ▽

ICD-9-CM Procedural

38.00 Incision of vessel, unspecified site

39.91 Freeing of vessel

35800

35800 Exploration for postoperative hemorrhage, thrombosis or infection; neck

ICD-9-CM Diagnostic

433.10 Occlusion and stenosis of carotid artery without mention of cerebral infarction — (Use additional code, if applicable, to identify status post administration of tPA (rtPA) in a different facility within the last 24 hours prior to admission to current facility: V45.88)

433.11 Occlusion and stenosis of carotid artery with cerebral infarction — (Use additional code, if applicable, to identify status post administration of tPA (rtPA) in a different facility within the last 24 hours prior to admission to current facility: V45.88)

433.20 Occlusion and stenosis of vertebral artery without mention of cerebral infarction — (Use additional code, if applicable, to identify status post administration of tPA (rtPA) in a different facility within the last 24 hours prior to admission to current facility: V45.88)

433.21 Occlusion and stenosis of vertebral artery with cerebral infarction — (Use additional code, if applicable, to identify status post administration of tPA (rtPA) in a different facility within the last 24 hours prior to admission to current facility: V45.88)
433.30 Occlusion and stenosis of multiple and bilateral precerebral arteries without mention of cerebral infarction — (Use additional code, if applicable, to identify status post administration of tPA (rtPA) in a different facility within the last 24 hours prior to admission to current facility: V45.88)
433.31 Occlusion and stenosis of multiple and bilateral precerebral arteries with cerebral infarction — (Use additional code, if applicable, to identify status post administration of tPA (rtPA) in a different facility within the last 24 hours prior to admission to current facility: V45.88)
433.80 Occlusion and stenosis of other specified precerebral artery without mention of cerebral infarction — (Use additional code, if applicable, to identify status post administration of tPA (rtPA) in a different facility within the last 24 hours prior to admission to current facility: V45.88)
433.81 Occlusion and stenosis of other specified precerebral artery with cerebral infarction — (Use additional code, if applicable, to identify status post administration of tPA (rtPA) in a different facility within the last 24 hours prior to admission to current facility: V45.88)
958.2 Secondary and recurrent hemorrhage as an early complication of trauma
958.3 Posttraumatic wound infection not elsewhere classified
996.1 Mechanical complication of other vascular device, implant, and graft
996.60 Infection and inflammatory reaction due to unspecified device, implant, and graft — (Use additional code to identify specified infections) ▽
997.2 Peripheral vascular complications — (Use additional code to identify complications)
998.11 Hemorrhage complicating a procedure
998.12 Hematoma complicating a procedure
998.13 Seroma complicating a procedure
998.30 Disruption of wound, unspecified ▽
998.31 Disruption of internal operation (surgical) wound
998.32 Disruption of external operation (surgical) wound
998.51 Infected postoperative seroma — (Use additional code to identify organism)
998.59 Other postoperative infection — (Use additional code to identify infection)
998.83 Non-healing surgical wound
999.31 Other and unspecified infection due to central venous catheter ▽
999.32 Bloodstream infection due to central venous catheter
999.33 Local infection due to central venous catheter
999.39 Complications of medical care, NEC, infection following other infusion, injection, transfusion, or vaccination

ICD-9-CM Procedural

06.02 Reopening of wound of thyroid field
38.02 Incision of other vessels of head and neck
39.41 Control of hemorrhage following vascular surgery
39.98 Control of hemorrhage, not otherwise specified

35820

35820 Exploration for postoperative hemorrhage, thrombosis or infection; chest

ICD-9-CM Diagnostic

415.11 Iatrogenic pulmonary embolism and infarction — (Use additional code for associated septic pulmonary embolism, if applicable: 415.12)
440.0 Atherosclerosis of aorta
444.1 Embolism and thrombosis of thoracic aorta
445.89 Atheroembolism of other site
511.89 Other specified forms of effusion, except tuberculous
997.2 Peripheral vascular complications — (Use additional code to identify complications)
997.79 Vascular complications of other vessels — (Use additional code to identify complications)
998.11 Hemorrhage complicating a procedure
998.12 Hematoma complicating a procedure
998.13 Seroma complicating a procedure
998.30 Disruption of wound, unspecified ▽
998.31 Disruption of internal operation (surgical) wound
998.32 Disruption of external operation (surgical) wound
998.51 Infected postoperative seroma — (Use additional code to identify organism)
998.59 Other postoperative infection — (Use additional code to identify infection)
999.31 Other and unspecified infection due to central venous catheter ▽
999.32 Bloodstream infection due to central venous catheter
999.33 Local infection due to central venous catheter
999.39 Complications of medical care, NEC, infection following other infusion, injection, transfusion, or vaccination

ICD-9-CM Procedural

38.04 Incision of aorta
38.05 Incision of other thoracic vessels
39.41 Control of hemorrhage following vascular surgery
39.98 Control of hemorrhage, not otherwise specified

35840

35840 Exploration for postoperative hemorrhage, thrombosis or infection; abdomen

ICD-9-CM Diagnostic

338.18 Other acute postoperative pain — (Use additional code to identify pain associated with psychological factors: 307.89)
444.81 Embolism and thrombosis of iliac artery
444.89 Embolism and thrombosis of other specified artery
445.89 Atheroembolism of other site
557.0 Acute vascular insufficiency of intestine
593.81 Vascular disorders of kidney
997.2 Peripheral vascular complications — (Use additional code to identify complications)
997.49 Other digestive system complications
997.5 Urinary complications — (Use additional code to identify complications)
997.71 Vascular complications of mesenteric artery — (Use additional code to identify complications)
997.72 Vascular complications of renal artery — (Use additional code to identify complications)
997.79 Vascular complications of other vessels — (Use additional code to identify complications)
998.11 Hemorrhage complicating a procedure
998.12 Hematoma complicating a procedure
998.13 Seroma complicating a procedure
998.31 Disruption of internal operation (surgical) wound
998.32 Disruption of external operation (surgical) wound
998.51 Infected postoperative seroma — (Use additional code to identify organism)
998.59 Other postoperative infection — (Use additional code to identify infection)

ICD-9-CM Procedural

38.00 Incision of vessel, unspecified site
38.06 Incision of abdominal arteries
39.41 Control of hemorrhage following vascular surgery
39.98 Control of hemorrhage, not otherwise specified
54.19 Other laparotomy

35860

35860 Exploration for postoperative hemorrhage, thrombosis or infection; extremity

ICD-9-CM Diagnostic

440.4 Chronic total occlusion of artery of the extremities
444.21 Embolism and thrombosis of arteries of upper extremity
444.22 Embolism and thrombosis of arteries of lower extremity
445.01 Atheroembolism of upper extremity
445.02 Atheroembolism of lower extremity

997.2 Peripheral vascular complications — (Use additional code to identify complications)
998.11 Hemorrhage complicating a procedure
998.12 Hematoma complicating a procedure
998.13 Seroma complicating a procedure
998.30 Disruption of wound, unspecified
998.31 Disruption of internal operation (surgical) wound
998.32 Disruption of external operation (surgical) wound
998.33 Disruption of traumatic injury wound repair
998.51 Infected postoperative seroma — (Use additional code to identify organism)
998.59 Other postoperative infection — (Use additional code to identify infection)

ICD-9-CM Procedural

38.03 Incision of upper limb vessels
38.08 Incision of lower limb arteries
39.41 Control of hemorrhage following vascular surgery
39.98 Control of hemorrhage, not otherwise specified

35870

35870 Repair of graft-enteric fistula

ICD-9-CM Diagnostic

447.2 Rupture of artery
996.74 Other complications due to other vascular device, implant, and graft — (Use additional code to identify complication: 338.18-338.19, 338.28-338.29)

ICD-9-CM Procedural

39.49 Other revision of vascular procedure
46.72 Closure of fistula of duodenum
46.74 Closure of fistula of small intestine, except duodenum
46.76 Closure of fistula of large intestine

35875-35876

35875 Thrombectomy of arterial or venous graft (other than hemodialysis graft or fistula);
35876 with revision of arterial or venous graft

ICD-9-CM Diagnostic

996.1 Mechanical complication of other vascular device, implant, and graft
996.74 Other complications due to other vascular device, implant, and graft — (Use additional code to identify complication: 338.18-338.19, 338.28-338.29)

ICD-9-CM Procedural

38.00 Incision of vessel, unspecified site
38.01 Incision of intracranial vessels
38.02 Incision of other vessels of head and neck
38.03 Incision of upper limb vessels

35879-35881

35879 Revision, lower extremity arterial bypass, without thrombectomy, open; with vein patch angioplasty
35881 with segmental vein interposition

ICD-9-CM Diagnostic

440.30 Atherosclerosis of unspecified bypass graft of extremities
440.31 Atherosclerosis of autologous vein bypass graft of extremities
440.32 Atherosclerosis of nonautologous biological bypass graft of extremities
996.1 Mechanical complication of other vascular device, implant, and graft
996.62 Infection and inflammatory reaction due to other vascular device, implant, and graft — (Use additional code to identify specified infections)
996.74 Other complications due to other vascular device, implant, and graft — (Use additional code to identify complication: 338.18-338.19, 338.28-338.29)

ICD-9-CM Procedural

38.48 Resection of lower limb arteries with replacement
39.49 Other revision of vascular procedure
39.56 Repair of blood vessel with tissue patch graft

35883-35884

35883 Revision, femoral anastomosis of synthetic arterial bypass graft in groin, open; with nonautogenous patch graft (eg, Dacron, ePTFE, bovine pericardium)
35884 with autogenous vein patch graft

ICD-9-CM Diagnostic

996.52 Mechanical complication due to other tissue graft, not elsewhere classified
996.62 Infection and inflammatory reaction due to other vascular device, implant, and graft — (Use additional code to identify specified infections)
996.74 Other complications due to other vascular device, implant, and graft — (Use additional code to identify complication: 338.18-338.19, 338.28-338.29)
997.2 Peripheral vascular complications — (Use additional code to identify complications)
998.59 Other postoperative infection — (Use additional code to identify infection)

ICD-9-CM Procedural

39.49 Other revision of vascular procedure
39.56 Repair of blood vessel with tissue patch graft
39.57 Repair of blood vessel with synthetic patch graft
39.58 Repair of blood vessel with unspecified type of patch graft
39.59 Other repair of vessel

35901

35901 Excision of infected graft; neck

ICD-9-CM Diagnostic

996.52 Mechanical complication due to other tissue graft, not elsewhere classified
996.62 Infection and inflammatory reaction due to other vascular device, implant, and graft — (Use additional code to identify specified infections)
996.74 Other complications due to other vascular device, implant, and graft — (Use additional code to identify complication: 338.18-338.19, 338.28-338.29)
997.2 Peripheral vascular complications — (Use additional code to identify complications)
998.59 Other postoperative infection — (Use additional code to identify infection)

ICD-9-CM Procedural

38.12 Endarterectomy of other vessels of head and neck
38.62 Other excision of other vessels of head and neck
39.49 Other revision of vascular procedure

35903

35903 Excision of infected graft; extremity

ICD-9-CM Diagnostic

996.52 Mechanical complication due to other tissue graft, not elsewhere classified
996.62 Infection and inflammatory reaction due to other vascular device, implant, and graft — (Use additional code to identify specified infections)
996.74 Other complications due to other vascular device, implant, and graft — (Use additional code to identify complication: 338.18-338.19, 338.28-338.29)
997.2 Peripheral vascular complications — (Use additional code to identify complications)
998.59 Other postoperative infection — (Use additional code to identify infection)

ICD-9-CM Procedural

38.13 Endarterectomy of upper limb vessels
38.18 Endarterectomy of lower limb arteries
38.68 Other excision of lower limb arteries
39.49 Other revision of vascular procedure

35905

35905 Excision of infected graft; thorax

ICD-9-CM Diagnostic

996.52 Mechanical complication due to other tissue graft, not elsewhere classified
996.62 Infection and inflammatory reaction due to other vascular device, implant, and graft — (Use additional code to identify specified infections)
996.74 Other complications due to other vascular device, implant, and graft — (Use additional code to identify complication: 338.18-338.19, 338.28-338.29)
997.2 Peripheral vascular complications — (Use additional code to identify complications)
998.59 Other postoperative infection — (Use additional code to identify infection)

ICD-9-CM Procedural

38.15 Endarterectomy of other thoracic vessels
38.65 Other excision of other thoracic vessel
39.49 Other revision of vascular procedure

35907

35907 Excision of infected graft; abdomen

ICD-9-CM Diagnostic

996.52 Mechanical complication due to other tissue graft, not elsewhere classified
996.62 Infection and inflammatory reaction due to other vascular device, implant, and graft — (Use additional code to identify specified infections)
996.74 Other complications due to other vascular device, implant, and graft — (Use additional code to identify complication: 338.18-338.19, 338.28-338.29)
997.2 Peripheral vascular complications — (Use additional code to identify complications)
998.59 Other postoperative infection — (Use additional code to identify infection)

ICD-9-CM Procedural

38.16 Endarterectomy of abdominal arteries
38.36 Resection of abdominal arteries with anastomosis
38.66 Other excision of abdominal arteries
39.49 Other revision of vascular procedure

36000

36000 Introduction of needle or intracatheter, vein

ICD-9-CM Diagnostic

The application of this code is too broad to adequately present ICD-9-CM diagnostic code links here. Refer to your ICD-9-CM book.

ICD-9-CM Procedural

38.93 Venous catheterization, not elsewhere classified

36002

36002 Injection procedures (eg, thrombin) for percutaneous treatment of extremity pseudoaneurysm

ICD-9-CM Diagnostic

442.0 Aneurysm of artery of upper extremity
442.3 Aneurysm of artery of lower extremity
442.9 Other aneurysm of unspecified site ▽

ICD-9-CM Procedural

99.29 Injection or infusion of other therapeutic or prophylactic substance

36005

36005 Injection procedure for extremity venography (including introduction of needle or intracatheter)

ICD-9-CM Diagnostic

451.0 Phlebitis and thrombophlebitis of superficial vessels of lower extremities — (Use additional E code to identify drug, if drug-induced)
451.11 Phlebitis and thrombophlebitis of femoral vein (deep) (superficial) — (Use additional E code to identify drug, if drug-induced)
451.19 Phlebitis and thrombophlebitis of other deep vessels of lower extremities — (Use additional E code to identify drug, if drug-induced)
451.2 Phlebitis and thrombophlebitis of lower extremities, unspecified — (Use additional E code to identify drug, if drug-induced) ▽
451.81 Phlebitis and thrombophlebitis of iliac vein — (Use additional E code to identify drug, if drug-induced)
451.82 Phlebitis and thrombophlebitis of superficial veins of upper extremities — (Use additional E code to identify drug, if drug-induced)
451.83 Phlebitis and thrombophlebitis of deep veins of upper extremities — (Use additional E code to identify drug, if drug-induced)
451.84 Phlebitis and thrombophlebitis of upper extremities, unspecified — (Use additional E code to identify drug, if drug-induced) ▽
453.40 Acute venous embolism and thrombosis of unspecified deep vessels of lower extremity ▽
453.41 Acute venous embolism and thrombosis of deep vessels of proximal lower extremity
453.42 Acute venous embolism and thrombosis of deep vessels of distal lower extremity
453.50 Chronic venous embolism and thrombosis of unspecified deep vessels of lower extremity — (Use additional code, if applicable, for associated long-term (current) use of anticoagulants (V58.61)) ▽
453.51 Chronic venous embolism and thrombosis of deep vessels of proximal lower extremity — (Use additional code, if applicable, for associated long-term (current) use of anticoagulants (V58.61))
453.52 Chronic venous embolism and thrombosis of deep vessels of distal lower extremity — (Use additional code, if applicable, for associated long-term (current) use of anticoagulants (V58.61))
453.6 Venous embolism and thrombosis of superficial vessels of lower extremity — (Use additional code, if applicable, for associated long-term (current) use of anticoagulants (V58.61))
453.71 Chronic venous embolism and thrombosis of superficial veins of upper extremity — (Use additional code, if applicable, for associated long-term (current) use of anticoagulants (V58.61))
453.72 Chronic venous embolism and thrombosis of deep veins of upper extremity — (Use additional code, if applicable, for associated long-term (current) use of anticoagulants (V58.61))
453.73 Chronic venous embolism and thrombosis of upper extremity, unspecified — (Use additional code, if applicable, for associated long-term (current) use of anticoagulants (V58.61)) ▽
453.74 Chronic venous embolism and thrombosis of axillary veins — (Use additional code, if applicable, for associated long-term (current) use of anticoagulants (V58.61))
453.79 Chronic venous embolism and thrombosis of other specified veins — (Use additional code, if applicable, for associated long-term (current) use of anticoagulants (V58.61))
453.81 Acute venous embolism and thrombosis of superficial veins of upper extremity
453.82 Acute venous embolism and thrombosis of deep veins of upper extremity
453.83 Acute venous embolism and thrombosis of upper extremity, unspecified ▽
453.84 Acute venous embolism and thrombosis of axillary veins
453.89 Acute venous embolism and thrombosis of other specified veins
453.9 Embolism and thrombosis of unspecified site ▽
454.0 Varicose veins of lower extremities with ulcer
454.1 Varicose veins of lower extremities with inflammation
454.2 Varicose veins of lower extremities with ulcer and inflammation
454.8 Varicose veins of the lower extremities with other complications
454.9 Asymptomatic varicose veins
459.10 Postphlebitic syndrome without complications
459.11 Postphlebitic syndrome with ulcer
459.12 Postphlebitic syndrome with inflammation
459.13 Postphlebitic syndrome with ulcer and inflammation
459.19 Postphlebitic syndrome with other complication
459.2 Compression of vein

459.81 Unspecified venous (peripheral) insufficiency — (Use additional code for any associated ulceration: 707.10-707.19, 707.8, 707.9) ▽

996.74 Other complications due to other vascular device, implant, and graft — (Use additional code to identify complication: 338.18-338.19, 338.28-338.29)

ICD-9-CM Procedural

38.93 Venous catheterization, not elsewhere classified

88.66 Phlebography of femoral and other lower extremity veins using contrast material

88.67 Phlebography of other specified sites using contrast material

36013

36013 Introduction of catheter, right heart or main pulmonary artery

ICD-9-CM Diagnostic

414.10 Aneurysm of heart — (Use additional code to identify presence of hypertension: 401.0-405.9)

416.0 Primary pulmonary hypertension

417.0 Arteriovenous fistula of pulmonary vessels

417.1 Aneurysm of pulmonary artery

417.8 Other specified disease of pulmonary circulation

424.2 Tricuspid valve disorders, specified as nonrheumatic

424.3 Pulmonary valve disorders

745.0 Bulbus cordis anomalies and anomalies of cardiac septal closure, common truncus

745.11 Transposition of great vessels, double outlet right ventricle

745.2 Tetralogy of Fallot

745.3 Bulbus cordis anomalies and anomalies of cardiac septal closure, common ventricle

745.4 Ventricular septal defect

ICD-9-CM Procedural

37.21 Right heart cardiac catheterization

38.91 Arterial catheterization

88.43 Arteriography of pulmonary arteries

88.57 Other and unspecified coronary arteriography

36014-36015

36014 Selective catheter placement, left or right pulmonary artery

36015 Selective catheter placement, segmental or subsegmental pulmonary artery

ICD-9-CM Diagnostic

162.3 Malignant neoplasm of upper lobe, bronchus, or lung

162.4 Malignant neoplasm of middle lobe, bronchus, or lung

162.5 Malignant neoplasm of lower lobe, bronchus, or lung

162.8 Malignant neoplasm of other parts of bronchus or lung

162.9 Malignant neoplasm of bronchus and lung, unspecified site ▽

197.0 Secondary malignant neoplasm of lung

231.2 Carcinoma in situ of bronchus and lung

231.9 Carcinoma in situ of respiratory system, part unspecified ▽

415.0 Acute cor pulmonale

416.0 Primary pulmonary hypertension

416.8 Other chronic pulmonary heart diseases

416.9 Unspecified chronic pulmonary heart disease ▽

417.0 Arteriovenous fistula of pulmonary vessels

417.1 Aneurysm of pulmonary artery

417.8 Other specified disease of pulmonary circulation

417.9 Unspecified disease of pulmonary circulation ▽

424.3 Pulmonary valve disorders

425.4 Other primary cardiomyopathies

428.0 Congestive heart failure, unspecified — (Code, if applicable, heart failure due to hypertension first: 402.0-402.9, with fifth-digit 1 or 404.0-404.9 with fifth digit 1 or 3) ▽

428.1 Left heart failure — (Code, if applicable, heart failure due to hypertension first: 402.0-402.9, with fifth-digit 1 or 404.0-404.9 with fifth digit 1 or 3)

428.20 Unspecified systolic heart failure — (Code, if applicable, heart failure due to hypertension first: 402.0-402.9, with fifth-digit 1 or 404.0-404.9 with fifth digit 1 or 3) ▽

428.21 Acute systolic heart failure — (Code, if applicable, heart failure due to hypertension first: 402.0-402.9, with fifth-digit 1 or 404.0-404.9 with fifth digit 1 or 3)

428.22 Chronic systolic heart failure — (Code, if applicable, heart failure due to hypertension first: 402.0-402.9, with fifth-digit 1 or 404.0-404.9 with fifth digit 1 or 3)

428.23 Acute on chronic systolic heart failure — (Code, if applicable, heart failure due to hypertension first: 402.0-402.9, with fifth-digit 1 or 404.0-404.9 with fifth digit 1 or 3)

428.30 Unspecified diastolic heart failure — (Code, if applicable, heart failure due to hypertension first: 402.0-402.9, with fifth-digit 1 or 404.0-404.9 with fifth digit 1 or 3) ▽

428.31 Acute diastolic heart failure — (Code, if applicable, heart failure due to hypertension first: 402.0-402.9, with fifth-digit 1 or 404.0-404.9 with fifth digit 1 or 3)

428.32 Chronic diastolic heart failure — (Code, if applicable, heart failure due to hypertension first: 402.0-402.9, with fifth-digit 1 or 404.0-404.9 with fifth digit 1 or 3)

428.33 Acute on chronic diastolic heart failure — (Code, if applicable, heart failure due to hypertension first: 402.0-402.9, with fifth-digit 1 or 404.0-404.9 with fifth digit 1 or 3)

428.40 Unspecified combined systolic and diastolic heart failure — (Code, if applicable, heart failure due to hypertension first: 402.0-402.9, with fifth-digit 1 or 404.0-404.9 with fifth digit 1 or 3) ▽

428.41 Acute combined systolic and diastolic heart failure — (Code, if applicable, heart failure due to hypertension first: 402.0-402.9, with fifth-digit 1 or 404.0-404.9 with fifth digit 1 or 3)

428.42 Chronic combined systolic and diastolic heart failure — (Code, if applicable, heart failure due to hypertension first: 402.0-402.9, with fifth-digit 1 or 404.0-404.9 with fifth digit 1 or 3)

428.43 Acute on chronic combined systolic and diastolic heart failure — (Code, if applicable, heart failure due to hypertension first: 402.0-402.9, with fifth-digit 1 or 404.0-404.9 with fifth digit 1 or 3)

447.1 Stricture of artery

447.70 Aortic ectasia, unspecified site ▽

447.71 Thoracic aortic ectasia

486 Pneumonia, organism unspecified ▽

496 Chronic airway obstruction, not elsewhere classified — (Note: This code is not to be used with any code from 491-493) ▽

511.81 Malignant pleural effusion — (Code first malignant neoplasm, if known)

511.89 Other specified forms of effusion, except tuberculous

511.9 Unspecified pleural effusion — (Use additional code to identify infectious organism) ▽

514 Pulmonary congestion and hypostasis — (Use additional code to identify infectious organism)

518.0 Pulmonary collapse

518.3 Pulmonary eosinophilia — (Use additional code to identify infectious organism)

518.89 Other diseases of lung, not elsewhere classified — (Use additional code to identify infectious organism)

519.8 Other diseases of respiratory system, not elsewhere classified — (Use additional code to identify infectious organism)

673.20 Obstetrical blood-clot embolism, unspecified as to episode of care ▽ ♀

673.21 Obstetrical blood-clot embolism, with delivery, with or without mention of antepartum condition ♀

673.22 Obstetrical blood-clot embolism, with mention of postpartum complication ♀

673.24 Obstetrical blood-clot embolism, postpartum condition or complication ♀

745.0 Bulbus cordis anomalies and anomalies of cardiac septal closure, common truncus

745.10 Complete transposition of great vessels

745.11 Transposition of great vessels, double outlet right ventricle

745.2 Tetralogy of Fallot

745.3 Bulbus cordis anomalies and anomalies of cardiac septal closure, common ventricle

745.4 Ventricular septal defect

747.31 Pulmonary artery coarctation and atresia

747.32 Pulmonary arteriovenous malformation
747.39 Other anomalies of pulmonary artery and pulmonary circulation
786.09 Other dyspnea and respiratory abnormalities
786.30 Hemoptysis, unspecified ▽
786.31 Acute idiopathic pulmonary hemorrhage in infants [AIPHI]
786.39 Other hemoptysis
786.59 Chest pain, other
786.6 Swelling, mass, or lump in chest
786.9 Other symptoms involving respiratory system and chest
794.2 Nonspecific abnormal results of pulmonary system function study
794.30 Nonspecific abnormal unspecified cardiovascular function study ▽
997.31 Ventilator associated pneumonia — (Use additional code to identify organism)
997.39 Other respiratory complications

ICD-9-CM Procedural

38.91 Arterial catheterization
88.43 Arteriography of pulmonary arteries

36100

36100 Introduction of needle or intracatheter, carotid or vertebral artery

ICD-9-CM Diagnostic

337.01 Carotid sinus syndrome
430 Subarachnoid hemorrhage — (Use additional code to identify presence of hypertension)
433.10 Occlusion and stenosis of carotid artery without mention of cerebral infarction — (Use additional code, if applicable, to identify status post administration of tPA (rtPA) in a different facility within the last 24 hours prior to admission to current facility: V45.88)
433.11 Occlusion and stenosis of carotid artery with cerebral infarction — (Use additional code, if applicable, to identify status post administration of tPA (rtPA) in a different facility within the last 24 hours prior to admission to current facility: V45.88)
433.20 Occlusion and stenosis of vertebral artery without mention of cerebral infarction — (Use additional code, if applicable, to identify status post administration of tPA (rtPA) in a different facility within the last 24 hours prior to admission to current facility: V45.88)
433.21 Occlusion and stenosis of vertebral artery with cerebral infarction — (Use additional code, if applicable, to identify status post administration of tPA (rtPA) in a different facility within the last 24 hours prior to admission to current facility: V45.88)
433.30 Occlusion and stenosis of multiple and bilateral precerebral arteries without mention of cerebral infarction — (Use additional code, if applicable, to identify status post administration of tPA (rtPA) in a different facility within the last 24 hours prior to admission to current facility: V45.88)
433.31 Occlusion and stenosis of multiple and bilateral precerebral arteries with cerebral infarction — (Use additional code, if applicable, to identify status post administration of tPA (rtPA) in a different facility within the last 24 hours prior to admission to current facility: V45.88)
433.80 Occlusion and stenosis of other specified precerebral artery without mention of cerebral infarction — (Use additional code, if applicable, to identify status post administration of tPA (rtPA) in a different facility within the last 24 hours prior to admission to current facility: V45.88)
433.81 Occlusion and stenosis of other specified precerebral artery with cerebral infarction — (Use additional code, if applicable, to identify status post administration of tPA (rtPA) in a different facility within the last 24 hours prior to admission to current facility: V45.88)
433.90 Occlusion and stenosis of unspecified precerebral artery without mention of cerebral infarction — (Use additional code, if applicable, to identify status post administration of tPA (rtPA) in a different facility within the last 24 hours prior to admission to current facility: V45.88) ▽
433.91 Occlusion and stenosis of unspecified precerebral artery with cerebral infarction — (Use additional code, if applicable, to identify status post administration of tPA (rtPA) in a different facility within the last 24 hours prior to admission to current facility: V45.88) ▽
435.1 Vertebral artery syndrome — (Use additional code to identify presence of hypertension)
435.9 Unspecified transient cerebral ischemia — (Use additional code to identify presence of hypertension) ▽
436 Acute, but ill-defined, cerebrovascular disease — (Use additional code to identify presence of hypertension) ▽
437.1 Other generalized ischemic cerebrovascular disease — (Use additional code to identify presence of hypertension)
437.3 Cerebral aneurysm, nonruptured — (Use additional code to identify presence of hypertension)
437.9 Unspecified cerebrovascular disease — (Use additional code to identify presence of hypertension) ▽
442.81 Aneurysm of artery of neck
443.21 Dissection of carotid artery
443.24 Dissection of vertebral artery
682.1 Cellulitis and abscess of neck — (Use additional code to identify organism, such as 041.1, etc.)
780.02 Transient alteration of awareness
780.09 Other alteration of consciousness
780.2 Syncope and collapse
780.4 Dizziness and giddiness
784.0 Headache
784.2 Swelling, mass, or lump in head and neck
853.00 Other and unspecified intracranial hemorrhage following injury, without mention of open intracranial wound, unspecified state of consciousness ▽
V71.7 Observation for suspected cardiovascular disease
V72.5 Radiological examination, not elsewhere classified — (Use additional code(s) to identify any special screening examination(s) performed: V73.0-V82.9)

ICD-9-CM Procedural

38.91 Arterial catheterization
88.41 Arteriography of cerebral arteries

36120

36120 Introduction of needle or intracatheter; retrograde brachial artery

ICD-9-CM Diagnostic

440.20 Atherosclerosis of native arteries of the extremities, unspecified ▽
440.21 Atherosclerosis of native arteries of the extremities with intermittent claudication
442.0 Aneurysm of artery of upper extremity
442.9 Other aneurysm of unspecified site ▽
443.29 Dissection of other artery
443.9 Unspecified peripheral vascular disease ▽
444.21 Embolism and thrombosis of arteries of upper extremity
444.9 Embolism and thrombosis of unspecified artery ▽
445.01 Atheroembolism of upper extremity
447.1 Stricture of artery
447.70 Aortic ectasia, unspecified site ▽
785.4 Gangrene — (Code first any associated underlying condition)
785.9 Other symptoms involving cardiovascular system
927.02 Crushing injury of axillary region — (Use additional code to identify any associated injuries: 800-829, 850.0-854.1, 860.0-869.1)
927.03 Crushing injury of upper arm — (Use additional code to identify any associated injuries: 800-829, 850.0-854.1, 860.0-869.1)
V71.7 Observation for suspected cardiovascular disease

ICD-9-CM Procedural

38.91 Arterial catheterization
88.49 Arteriography of other specified sites

36140

36140 Introduction of needle or intracatheter; extremity artery

ICD-9-CM Diagnostic

195.4 Malignant neoplasm of upper limb
195.5 Malignant neoplasm of lower limb
228.00 Hemangioma of unspecified site ▽
249.70 Secondary diabetes mellitus with peripheral circulatory disorders, not stated as uncontrolled, or unspecified — (Use additional code to identify manifestation: 443.81, 785.4) (Use additional code to identify any associated insulin use: V58.67)
249.71 Secondary diabetes mellitus with peripheral circulatory disorders, uncontrolled — (Use additional code to identify manifestation: 443.81, 785.4) (Use additional code to identify any associated insulin use: V58.67)
250.70 Diabetes with peripheral circulatory disorders, type II or unspecified type, not stated as uncontrolled — (Use additional code to identify manifestation: 443.81, 785.4)
250.71 Diabetes with peripheral circulatory disorders, type I [juvenile type], not stated as uncontrolled — (Use additional code to identify manifestation: 443.81, 785.4)
250.72 Diabetes with peripheral circulatory disorders, type II or unspecified type, uncontrolled — (Use additional code to identify manifestation: 443.81, 785.4)
250.73 Diabetes with peripheral circulatory disorders, type I [juvenile type], uncontrolled — (Use additional code to identify manifestation: 443.81, 785.4)
354.0 Carpal tunnel syndrome
440.21 Atherosclerosis of native arteries of the extremities with intermittent claudication
440.22 Atherosclerosis of native arteries of the extremities with rest pain
440.23 Atherosclerosis of native arteries of the extremities with ulceration — (Use additional code for any associated ulceration: 707.10-707.19, 707.8, 707.9)
440.30 Atherosclerosis of unspecified bypass graft of extremities ▽
440.4 Chronic total occlusion of artery of the extremities
442.0 Aneurysm of artery of upper extremity
442.3 Aneurysm of artery of lower extremity
443.0 Raynaud's syndrome — (Use additional code to identify gangrene: 785.4)
443.1 Thromboangiitis obliterans (Buerger's disease)
443.29 Dissection of other artery
443.81 Peripheral angiopathy in diseases classified elsewhere — (Code first underlying disease: 249.7, 250.7) ☒
443.89 Other peripheral vascular disease
444.21 Embolism and thrombosis of arteries of upper extremity
444.22 Embolism and thrombosis of arteries of lower extremity
445.01 Atheroembolism of upper extremity
445.02 Atheroembolism of lower extremity
747.60 Congenital anomaly of the peripheral vascular system, unspecified site ▽
785.4 Gangrene — (Code first any associated underlying condition)

ICD-9-CM Procedural

38.91 Arterial catheterization
88.48 Arteriography of femoral and other lower extremity arteries
88.49 Arteriography of other specified sites

36147-36148

36147 Introduction of needle and/or catheter, arteriovenous shunt created for dialysis (graft/fistula); initial access with complete radiological evaluation of dialysis access, including fluoroscopy, image documentation and report (includes access of shunt, injection[s] of contrast, and all necessary imaging from the arterial anastomosis and adjacent artery through entire venous outflow including the inferior or superior vena cava)
36148 additional access for therapeutic intervention (List separately in addition to code for primary procedure)

ICD-9-CM Diagnostic

249.40 Secondary diabetes mellitus with renal manifestations, not stated as uncontrolled, or unspecified — (Use additional code to identify manifestation: 581.81, 583.81, 585.1-585.9) (Use additional code to identify any associated insulin use: V58.67)
249.41 Secondary diabetes mellitus with renal manifestations, uncontrolled — (Use additional code to identify manifestation: 581.81, 583.81, 585.1-585.9) (Use additional code to identify any associated insulin use: V58.67)
249.70 Secondary diabetes mellitus with peripheral circulatory disorders, not stated as uncontrolled, or unspecified — (Use additional code to identify manifestation: 443.81, 785.4) (Use additional code to identify any associated insulin use: V58.67)
249.71 Secondary diabetes mellitus with peripheral circulatory disorders, uncontrolled — (Use additional code to identify manifestation: 443.81, 785.4) (Use additional code to identify any associated insulin use: V58.67)
250.40 Diabetes with renal manifestations, type II or unspecified type, not stated as uncontrolled — (Use additional code to identify manifestation: 581.81, 583.81, 585.1-585.9)
250.41 Diabetes with renal manifestations, type I [juvenile type], not stated as uncontrolled — (Use additional code to identify manifestation: 581.81, 583.81, 585.1-585.9)
250.42 Diabetes with renal manifestations, type II or unspecified type, uncontrolled — (Use additional code to identify manifestation: 581.81, 583.81, 585.1-585.9)
250.43 Diabetes with renal manifestations, type I [juvenile type], uncontrolled — (Use additional code to identify manifestation: 581.81, 583.81, 585.1-585.9)
250.70 Diabetes with peripheral circulatory disorders, type II or unspecified type, not stated as uncontrolled — (Use additional code to identify manifestation: 443.81, 785.4)
445.81 Atheroembolism of kidney — (Use additional code for any associated acute kidney failure or chronic kidney disease: 584, 585)
584.5 Acute kidney failure with lesion of tubular necrosis
584.6 Acute kidney failure with lesion of renal cortical necrosis
584.7 Acute kidney failure with lesion of medullary [papillary] necrosis
584.8 Acute kidney failure with other specified pathological lesion in kidney
584.9 Acute kidney failure, unspecified ▽
585.4 Chronic kidney disease, Stage IV (severe) — (Use additional code to identify kidney transplant status, if applicable: V42.0. Use additional code to identify manifestation: 357.4, 420.0. Code first hypertensive chronic kidney disease, if applicable: 403.00-403.91, 404.00-404.93)
585.5 Chronic kidney disease, Stage V — (Use additional code to identify kidney transplant status, if applicable: V42.0. Use additional code to identify manifestation: 357.4, 420.0. Code first hypertensive chronic kidney disease, if applicable: 403.00-403.91, 404.00-404.93)
585.6 End stage renal disease — (Use additional code to identify kidney transplant status, if applicable: V42.0. Use additional code to identify manifestation: 357.4, 420.0. Code first hypertensive chronic kidney disease, if applicable: 403.00-403.91, 404.00-404.93)
585.9 Chronic kidney disease, unspecified — (Use additional code to identify kidney transplant status, if applicable: V42.0. Use additional code to identify manifestation: 357.4, 420.0. Code first hypertensive chronic kidney disease, if applicable: 403.00-403.91, 404.00-404.93) ▽
586 Unspecified renal failure ▽
728.88 Rhabdomyolysis
996.1 Mechanical complication of other vascular device, implant, and graft
996.62 Infection and inflammatory reaction due to other vascular device, implant, and graft — (Use additional code to identify specified infections)
996.73 Other complications due to renal dialysis device, implant, and graft — (Use additional code to identify complication: 338.18-338.19, 338.28-338.29)
V45.11 Renal dialysis status
V45.12 Noncompliance with renal dialysis
V72.5 Radiological examination, not elsewhere classified — (Use additional code(s) to identify any special screening examination(s) performed: V73.0-V82.9)

ICD-9-CM Procedural

38.91 Arterial catheterization
38.93 Venous catheterization, not elsewhere classified
88.49 Arteriography of other specified sites

36160

36160 Introduction of needle or intracatheter, aortic, translumbar

ICD-9-CM Diagnostic

440.0 Atherosclerosis of aorta
441.9 Aortic aneurysm of unspecified site without mention of rupture ▽
447.1 Stricture of artery
447.2 Rupture of artery
447.70 Aortic ectasia, unspecified site ▽

ICD-9-CM Procedural

38.91 Arterial catheterization
88.42 Aortography

36200

36200 Introduction of catheter, aorta

ICD-9-CM Diagnostic

440.0 Atherosclerosis of aorta
440.20 Atherosclerosis of native arteries of the extremities, unspecified ▽
440.21 Atherosclerosis of native arteries of the extremities with intermittent claudication
440.22 Atherosclerosis of native arteries of the extremities with rest pain
440.23 Atherosclerosis of native arteries of the extremities with ulceration — (Use additional code for any associated ulceration: 707.10-707.19, 707.8, 707.9)
440.24 Atherosclerosis of native arteries of the extremities with gangrene — (Use additional code for any associated ulceration: 707.10-707.19, 707.8, 707.9)
440.29 Other atherosclerosis of native arteries of the extremities
440.30 Atherosclerosis of unspecified bypass graft of extremities ▽
440.31 Atherosclerosis of autologous vein bypass graft of extremities
440.32 Atherosclerosis of nonautologous biological bypass graft of extremities
440.4 Chronic total occlusion of artery of the extremities
440.8 Atherosclerosis of other specified arteries
440.9 Generalized and unspecified atherosclerosis ▽
441.00 Dissecting aortic aneurysm (any part), unspecified site ▽
441.01 Dissecting aortic aneurysm (any part), thoracic
441.02 Dissecting aortic aneurysm (any part), abdominal
441.03 Dissecting aortic aneurysm (any part), thoracoabdominal
441.1 Thoracic aneurysm, ruptured
441.2 Thoracic aneurysm without mention of rupture
441.3 Abdominal aneurysm, ruptured
441.4 Abdominal aneurysm without mention of rupture
441.5 Aortic aneurysm of unspecified site, ruptured ▽
441.6 Thoracoabdominal aneurysm, ruptured
441.7 Thoracoabdominal aneurysm without mention of rupture
441.9 Aortic aneurysm of unspecified site without mention of rupture ▽
442.1 Aneurysm of renal artery
442.2 Aneurysm of iliac artery
442.3 Aneurysm of artery of lower extremity
443.1 Thromboangiitis obliterans (Buerger's disease)
443.22 Dissection of iliac artery
443.23 Dissection of renal artery
443.29 Dissection of other artery
443.9 Unspecified peripheral vascular disease ▽
444.01 Saddle embolus of abdominal aorta
444.09 Other arterial embolism and thrombosis of abdominal aorta
444.1 Embolism and thrombosis of thoracic aorta
444.81 Embolism and thrombosis of iliac artery
444.89 Embolism and thrombosis of other specified artery
445.02 Atheroembolism of lower extremity
445.81 Atheroembolism of kidney — (Use additional code for any associated acute kidney failure or chronic kidney disease: 584, 585)
445.89 Atheroembolism of other site
447.0 Arteriovenous fistula, acquired
447.1 Stricture of artery
447.2 Rupture of artery
447.3 Hyperplasia of renal artery
447.4 Celiac artery compression syndrome
447.5 Necrosis of artery
447.6 Unspecified arteritis ▽
447.70 Aortic ectasia, unspecified site ▽
447.71 Thoracic aortic ectasia
447.72 Abdominal aortic ectasia
447.73 Thoracoabdominal aortic ectasia
447.8 Other specified disorders of arteries and arterioles
447.9 Unspecified disorders of arteries and arterioles ▽
593.81 Vascular disorders of kidney

ICD-9-CM Procedural

38.91 Arterial catheterization
88.42 Aortography

36215-36218

36215 Selective catheter placement, arterial system; each first order thoracic or brachiocephalic branch, within a vascular family
36216 initial second order thoracic or brachiocephalic branch, within a vascular family
36217 initial third order or more selective thoracic or brachiocephalic branch, within a vascular family
36218 additional second order, third order, and beyond, thoracic or brachiocephalic branch, within a vascular family (List in addition to code for initial second or third order vessel as appropriate)

ICD-9-CM Diagnostic

162.3 Malignant neoplasm of upper lobe, bronchus, or lung
162.4 Malignant neoplasm of middle lobe, bronchus, or lung
162.5 Malignant neoplasm of lower lobe, bronchus, or lung
162.8 Malignant neoplasm of other parts of bronchus or lung
162.9 Malignant neoplasm of bronchus and lung, unspecified site ▽
191.0 Malignant neoplasm of cerebrum, except lobes and ventricles
191.1 Malignant neoplasm of frontal lobe of brain
191.2 Malignant neoplasm of temporal lobe of brain
191.3 Malignant neoplasm of parietal lobe of brain
191.4 Malignant neoplasm of occipital lobe of brain
191.5 Malignant neoplasm of ventricles of brain
191.6 Malignant neoplasm of cerebellum NOS
191.7 Malignant neoplasm of brain stem
191.8 Malignant neoplasm of other parts of brain
191.9 Malignant neoplasm of brain, unspecified site ▽
192.1 Malignant neoplasm of cerebral meninges
192.2 Malignant neoplasm of spinal cord
192.3 Malignant neoplasm of spinal meninges
192.8 Malignant neoplasm of other specified sites of nervous system
192.9 Malignant neoplasm of nervous system, part unspecified ▽
194.3 Malignant neoplasm of pituitary gland and craniopharyngeal duct
194.5 Malignant neoplasm of carotid body
197.0 Secondary malignant neoplasm of lung
198.3 Secondary malignant neoplasm of brain and spinal cord
199.1 Other malignant neoplasm of unspecified site
199.2 Malignant neoplasm associated with transplanted organ — (Code first complication of transplanted organ (996.80-996.89) Use additional code for specific malignancy)

209.20 Malignant carcinoid tumor of unknown primary site — (Code first any associated multiple endocrine neoplasia syndrome: 258.01-258.03)(Use additional code to identify associated endocrine syndrome, as: carcinoid syndrome: 259.2)

209.29 Malignant carcinoid tumor of other sites — (Code first any associated multiple endocrine neoplasia syndrome: 258.01-258.03)(Use additional code to identify associated endocrine syndrome, as: carcinoid syndrome: 259.2)

209.61 Benign carcinoid tumor of the bronchus and lung — (Code first any associated multiple endocrine neoplasia syndrome: 258.01-258.03)(Use additional code to identify associated endocrine syndrome, as: carcinoid syndrome: 259.2)

209.70 Secondary neuroendocrine tumor, unspecified site

209.79 Secondary neuroendocrine tumor of other sites

212.3 Benign neoplasm of bronchus and lung

225.0 Benign neoplasm of brain

225.2 Benign neoplasm of cerebral meninges

225.3 Benign neoplasm of spinal cord

225.4 Benign neoplasm of spinal meninges

225.8 Benign neoplasm of other specified sites of nervous system

225.9 Benign neoplasm of nervous system, part unspecified

227.3 Benign neoplasm of pituitary gland and craniopharyngeal duct (pouch) — (Use additional code to identify any functional activity)

227.5 Benign neoplasm of carotid body — (Use additional code to identify any functional activity)

228.00 Hemangioma of unspecified site

228.02 Hemangioma of intracranial structures

231.2 Carcinoma in situ of bronchus and lung

235.7 Neoplasm of uncertain behavior of trachea, bronchus, and lung

237.0 Neoplasm of uncertain behavior of pituitary gland and craniopharyngeal duct — (Use additional code to identify any functional activity)

237.3 Neoplasm of uncertain behavior of paraganglia

237.5 Neoplasm of uncertain behavior of brain and spinal cord

237.6 Neoplasm of uncertain behavior of meninges

238.9 Neoplasm of uncertain behavior, site unspecified

239.1 Neoplasm of unspecified nature of respiratory system

239.6 Neoplasm of unspecified nature of brain

239.7 Neoplasm of unspecified nature of endocrine glands and other parts of nervous system

239.89 Neoplasms of unspecified nature, other specified sites

239.9 Neoplasm of unspecified nature, site unspecified

331.4 Obstructive hydrocephalus — (Use additional code, where applicable, to identify dementia: 294.10, 294.11)

337.00 Idiopathic peripheral autonomic neuropathy, unspecified

337.01 Carotid sinus syndrome

337.09 Other idiopathic peripheral autonomic neuropathy

342.90 Unspecified hemiplegia affecting unspecified side

342.91 Unspecified hemiplegia affecting dominant side

342.92 Unspecified hemiplegia affecting nondominant side

344.9 Unspecified paralysis

348.0 Cerebral cysts

348.81 Temporal sclerosis

348.89 Other conditions of brain

348.9 Unspecified condition of brain

411.1 Intermediate coronary syndrome — (Use additional code to identify presence of hypertension: 401.0-405.9)

414.00 Coronary atherosclerosis of unspecified type of vessel, native or graft — (Use additional code to identify presence of hypertension: 401.0-405.9)

414.01 Coronary atherosclerosis of native coronary artery — (Use additional code to identify presence of hypertension: 401.0-405.9)

414.03 Coronary atherosclerosis of nonautologous biological bypass graft — (Use additional code to identify presence of hypertension: 401.0-405.9)

414.04 Coronary atherosclerosis of artery bypass graft — (Use additional code to identify presence of hypertension: 401.0-405.9)

414.05 Coronary atherosclerosis of unspecified type of bypass graft — (Use additional code to identify presence of hypertension: 401.0-405.9)

414.06 Coronary atherosclerosis, of native coronary artery of transplanted heart — (Use additional code to identify presence of hypertension: 401.0-405.9)

414.07 Coronary atherosclerosis, of bypass graft (artery) (vein) of transplanted heart — (Use additional code to identify presence of hypertension: 401.0-405.9)

414.2 Chronic total occlusion of coronary artery

414.3 Coronary atherosclerosis due to lipid rich plaque — (Code first coronary atherosclerosis (414.00-414.07))

414.4 Coronary atherosclerosis due to calcified coronary lesion — (Code first coronary atherosclerosis (414.00-414.07))

430 Subarachnoid hemorrhage — (Use additional code to identify presence of hypertension)

431 Intracerebral hemorrhage — (Use additional code to identify presence of hypertension)

432.0 Nontraumatic extradural hemorrhage — (Use additional code to identify presence of hypertension)

432.1 Subdural hemorrhage — (Use additional code to identify presence of hypertension)

432.9 Unspecified intracranial hemorrhage — (Use additional code to identify presence of hypertension)

433.00 Occlusion and stenosis of basilar artery without mention of cerebral infarction — (Use additional code, if applicable, to identify status post administration of tPA (rtPA) in a different facility within the last 24 hours prior to admission to current facility: V45.88)

433.01 Occlusion and stenosis of basilar artery with cerebral infarction — (Use additional code, if applicable, to identify status post administration of tPA (rtPA) in a different facility within the last 24 hours prior to admission to current facility: V45.88)

433.10 Occlusion and stenosis of carotid artery without mention of cerebral infarction — (Use additional code, if applicable, to identify status post administration of tPA (rtPA) in a different facility within the last 24 hours prior to admission to current facility: V45.88)

433.11 Occlusion and stenosis of carotid artery with cerebral infarction — (Use additional code, if applicable, to identify status post administration of tPA (rtPA) in a different facility within the last 24 hours prior to admission to current facility: V45.88)

433.20 Occlusion and stenosis of vertebral artery without mention of cerebral infarction — (Use additional code, if applicable, to identify status post administration of tPA (rtPA) in a different facility within the last 24 hours prior to admission to current facility: V45.88)

433.21 Occlusion and stenosis of vertebral artery with cerebral infarction — (Use additional code, if applicable, to identify status post administration of tPA (rtPA) in a different facility within the last 24 hours prior to admission to current facility: V45.88)

433.30 Occlusion and stenosis of multiple and bilateral precerebral arteries without mention of cerebral infarction — (Use additional code, if applicable, to identify status post administration of tPA (rtPA) in a different facility within the last 24 hours prior to admission to current facility: V45.88)

433.31 Occlusion and stenosis of multiple and bilateral precerebral arteries with cerebral infarction — (Use additional code, if applicable, to identify status post administration of tPA (rtPA) in a different facility within the last 24 hours prior to admission to current facility: V45.88)

433.80 Occlusion and stenosis of other specified precerebral artery without mention of cerebral infarction — (Use additional code, if applicable, to identify status post administration of tPA (rtPA) in a different facility within the last 24 hours prior to admission to current facility: V45.88)

433.81 Occlusion and stenosis of other specified precerebral artery with cerebral infarction — (Use additional code, if applicable, to identify status post administration of tPA (rtPA) in a different facility within the last 24 hours prior to admission to current facility: V45.88)

433.90 Occlusion and stenosis of unspecified precerebral artery without mention of cerebral infarction — (Use additional code, if applicable, to identify status post administration of tPA (rtPA) in a different facility within the last 24 hours prior to admission to current facility: V45.88)

433.91 Occlusion and stenosis of unspecified precerebral artery with cerebral infarction — (Use additional code, if applicable, to identify status post administration of tPA (rtPA)

in a different facility within the last 24 hours prior to admission to current facility: V45.88) ▽

434.00 Cerebral thrombosis without mention of cerebral infarction — (Use additional code, if applicable, to identify status post administration of tPA (rtPA) in a different facility within the last 24 hours prior to admission to current facility: V45.88)

434.01 Cerebral thrombosis with cerebral infarction — (Use additional code, if applicable, to identify status post administration of tPA (rtPA) in a different facility within the last 24 hours prior to admission to current facility: V45.88)

434.10 Cerebral embolism without mention of cerebral infarction — (Use additional code, if applicable, to identify status post administration of tPA (rtPA) in a different facility within the last 24 hours prior to admission to current facility: V45.88)

434.11 Cerebral embolism with cerebral infarction — (Use additional code, if applicable, to identify status post administration of tPA (rtPA) in a different facility within the last 24 hours prior to admission to current facility: V45.88)

434.90 Unspecified cerebral artery occlusion without mention of cerebral infarction — (Use additional code, if applicable, to identify status post administration of tPA (rtPA) in a different facility within the last 24 hours prior to admission to current facility: V45.88) ▽

434.91 Unspecified cerebral artery occlusion with cerebral infarction — (Use additional code, if applicable, to identify status post administration of tPA (rtPA) in a different facility within the last 24 hours prior to admission to current facility: V45.88) ▽

435.0 Basilar artery syndrome — (Use additional code to identify presence of hypertension)

435.1 Vertebral artery syndrome — (Use additional code to identify presence of hypertension)

435.2 Subclavian steal syndrome — (Use additional code to identify presence of hypertension)

435.3 Vertebrobasilar artery syndrome — (Use additional code to identify presence of hypertension)

435.8 Other specified transient cerebral ischemias — (Use additional code to identify presence of hypertension)

435.9 Unspecified transient cerebral ischemia — (Use additional code to identify presence of hypertension) ▽

436 Acute, but ill-defined, cerebrovascular disease — (Use additional code to identify presence of hypertension) ▽

437.0 Cerebral atherosclerosis — (Use additional code to identify presence of hypertension)

437.1 Other generalized ischemic cerebrovascular disease — (Use additional code to identify presence of hypertension)

437.3 Cerebral aneurysm, nonruptured — (Use additional code to identify presence of hypertension)

437.8 Other ill-defined cerebrovascular disease — (Use additional code to identify presence of hypertension)

437.9 Unspecified cerebrovascular disease — (Use additional code to identify presence of hypertension) ▽

438.0 Cognitive deficits due to cerebrovascular disease — (Use additional code to identify presence of hypertension)

438.11 Aphasia due to cerebrovascular disease — (Use additional code to identify presence of hypertension)

438.19 Other speech and language deficits due to cerebrovascular disease — (Use additional code to identify presence of hypertension)

438.21 Hemiplegia affecting dominant side due to cerebrovascular disease — (Use additional code to identify presence of hypertension)

438.30 Monoplegia of upper limb affecting unspecified side due to cerebrovascular disease — (Use additional code to identify presence of hypertension) ▽

438.32 Monoplegia of upper limb affecting nondominant side due to cerebrovascular disease — (Use additional code to identify presence of hypertension)

438.41 Monoplegia of lower limb affecting dominant side due to cerebrovascular disease — (Use additional code to identify presence of hypertension)

438.50 Other paralytic syndrome affecting unspecified side due to cerebrovascular disease — (Use additional code to identify presence of hypertension. Use additional code to identify type of paralytic syndrome: 344.00-344.09, 344.81) ▽

438.52 Other paralytic syndrome affecting nondominant side due to cerebrovascular disease — (Use additional code to identify presence of hypertension. Use additional code to identify type of paralytic syndrome: 344.00-344.09, 344.81)

438.6 Alteration of sensations as late effect of cerebrovascular disease — (Use additional code to identify presence of hypertension. Use additional code to identify the altered sensation)

438.7 Disturbance of vision as late effect of cerebrovascular disease — (Use additional code to identify presence of hypertension. Use additional code to identify the visual disturbance)

438.82 Dysphagia due to cerebrovascular disease — (Use additional code to identify presence of hypertension)

438.83 Facial weakness as late effect of cerebrovascular disease — (Use additional code to identify presence of hypertension)

438.84 Ataxia as late effect of cerebrovascular disease — (Use additional code to identify presence of hypertension)

438.85 Vertigo as late effect of cerebrovascular disease — (Use additional code to identify presence of hypertension)

438.9 Unspecified late effects of cerebrovascular disease due to cerebrovascular disease — (Use additional code to identify presence of hypertension. ▽

440.0 Atherosclerosis of aorta

440.20 Atherosclerosis of native arteries of the extremities, unspecified ▽

440.22 Atherosclerosis of native arteries of the extremities with rest pain

440.8 Atherosclerosis of other specified arteries

440.9 Generalized and unspecified atherosclerosis ▽

442.81 Aneurysm of artery of neck

442.82 Aneurysm of subclavian artery

442.9 Other aneurysm of unspecified site ▽

443.21 Dissection of carotid artery

443.29 Dissection of other artery

443.89 Other peripheral vascular disease

443.9 Unspecified peripheral vascular disease ▽

444.21 Embolism and thrombosis of arteries of upper extremity

444.9 Embolism and thrombosis of unspecified artery ▽

445.01 Atheroembolism of upper extremity

445.89 Atheroembolism of other site

447.0 Arteriovenous fistula, acquired

447.1 Stricture of artery

447.2 Rupture of artery

447.6 Unspecified arteritis ▽

447.70 Aortic ectasia, unspecified site ▽

447.9 Unspecified disorders of arteries and arterioles ▽

459.9 Unspecified circulatory system disorder ▽

729.5 Pain in soft tissues of limb

729.81 Swelling of limb

742.4 Other specified congenital anomalies of brain

747.60 Congenital anomaly of the peripheral vascular system, unspecified site ▽

747.63 Congenital upper limb vessel anomaly

747.81 Congenital anomaly of cerebrovascular system

780.02 Transient alteration of awareness

780.03 Persistent vegetative state

780.09 Other alteration of consciousness

780.1 Hallucinations

780.2 Syncope and collapse

780.31 Febrile convulsions (simple), unspecified ▽

780.39 Other convulsions

780.4 Dizziness and giddiness

780.60 Fever, unspecified ▽

780.61 Fever presenting with conditions classified elsewhere — (Code first underlying condition when associated fever is present: 204-208, 282.60-282.69, 288.00-288.09) ☒

780.79 Other malaise and fatigue

782.0 Disturbance of skin sensation

784.0 Headache
784.2 Swelling, mass, or lump in head and neck
784.3 Aphasia
785.9 Other symptoms involving cardiovascular system
786.50 Chest pain, unspecified ▽
786.59 Chest pain, other
786.6 Swelling, mass, or lump in chest
786.9 Other symptoms involving respiratory system and chest
793.0 Nonspecific (abnormal) findings on radiological and other examination of skull and head
793.2 Nonspecific (abnormal) findings on radiological and other examination of other intrathoracic organs
794.30 Nonspecific abnormal unspecified cardiovascular function study ▽
851.00 Cortex (cerebral) contusion without mention of open intracranial wound, state of consciousness unspecified ▽
851.01 Cortex (cerebral) contusion without mention of open intracranial wound, no loss of consciousness
851.02 Cortex (cerebral) contusion without mention of open intracranial wound, brief (less than 1 hour) loss of consciousness
851.03 Cortex (cerebral) contusion without mention of open intracranial wound, moderate (1-24 hours) loss of consciousness
851.04 Cortex (cerebral) contusion without mention of open intracranial wound, prolonged (more than 24 hours) loss of consciousness and return to pre-existing conscious level
851.05 Cortex (cerebral) contusion without mention of open intracranial wound, prolonged (more than 24 hours) loss of consciousness, without return to pre-existing conscious level
851.06 Cortex (cerebral) contusion without mention of open intracranial wound, loss of consciousness of unspecified duration ▽
851.09 Cortex (cerebral) contusion without mention of open intracranial wound, unspecified concussion ▽
851.10 Cortex (cerebral) contusion with open intracranial wound, unspecified state of consciousness ▽
851.11 Cortex (cerebral) contusion with open intracranial wound, no loss of consciousness
851.12 Cortex (cerebral) contusion with open intracranial wound, brief (less than 1 hour) loss of consciousness
851.13 Cortex (cerebral) contusion with open intracranial wound, moderate (1-24 hours) loss of consciousness
851.14 Cortex (cerebral) contusion with open intracranial wound, prolonged (more than 24 hours) loss of consciousness and return to pre-existing conscious level
851.15 Cortex (cerebral) contusion with open intracranial wound, prolonged (more than 24 hours) loss of consciousness, without return to pre-existing conscious level
851.16 Cortex (cerebral) contusion with open intracranial wound, loss of consciousness of unspecified duration ▽
851.19 Cortex (cerebral) contusion with open intracranial wound, unspecified concussion ▽
851.20 Cortex (cerebral) laceration without mention of open intracranial wound, unspecified state of consciousness ▽
851.21 Cortex (cerebral) laceration without mention of open intracranial wound, no loss of consciousness
851.22 Cortex (cerebral) laceration without mention of open intracranial wound, brief (less than 1 hour) loss of consciousness
851.23 Cortex (cerebral) laceration without mention of open intracranial wound, moderate (1-24 hours) loss of consciousness
851.24 Cortex (cerebral) laceration without mention of open intracranial wound, prolonged (more than 24 hours) loss of consciousness and return to pre-existing conscious level
851.25 Cortex (cerebral) laceration without mention of open intracranial wound, prolonged (more than 24 hours) loss of consciousness, without return to pre-existing conscious level
851.26 Cortex (cerebral) laceration without mention of open intracranial wound, loss of consciousness of unspecified duration ▽
851.29 Cortex (cerebral) laceration without mention of open intracranial wound, unspecified concussion ▽
851.30 Cortex (cerebral) laceration with open intracranial wound, unspecified state of consciousness ▽
851.31 Cortex (cerebral) laceration with open intracranial wound, no loss of consciousness
851.32 Cortex (cerebral) laceration with open intracranial wound, brief (less than 1 hour) loss of consciousness
851.33 Cortex (cerebral) laceration with open intracranial wound, moderate (1-24 hours) loss of consciousness
851.34 Cortex (cerebral) laceration with open intracranial wound, prolonged (more than 24 hours) loss of consciousness and return to pre-existing conscious level
851.35 Cortex (cerebral) laceration with open intracranial wound, prolonged (more than 24 hours) loss of consciousness, without return to pre-existing conscious level
851.36 Cortex (cerebral) laceration with open intracranial wound, loss of consciousness of unspecified duration ▽
851.39 Cortex (cerebral) laceration with open intracranial wound, unspecified concussion — (Use E code(s) to identify the cause and intent of the injury or poisoning: E800-E999) ▽
851.40 Cerebellar or brain stem contusion without mention of open intracranial wound, unspecified state of consciousness ▽
851.41 Cerebellar or brain stem contusion without mention of open intracranial wound, no loss of consciousness
851.42 Cerebellar or brain stem contusion without mention of open intracranial wound, brief (less than 1 hour) loss of consciousness
851.43 Cerebellar or brain stem contusion without mention of open intracranial wound, moderate (1-24 hours) loss of consciousness
851.44 Cerebellar or brain stem contusion without mention of open intracranial wound, prolonged (more than 24 hours) loss consciousness and return to pre-existing conscious level
851.45 Cerebellar or brain stem contusion without mention of open intracranial wound, prolonged (more than 24 hours) loss of consciousness, without return to pre-existing conscious level
851.46 Cerebellar or brain stem contusion without mention of open intracranial wound, loss of consciousness of unspecified duration ▽
851.49 Cerebellar or brain stem contusion without mention of open intracranial wound, unspecified concussion ▽
851.50 Cerebellar or brain stem contusion with open intracranial wound, unspecified state of consciousness ▽
851.51 Cerebellar or brain stem contusion with open intracranial wound, no loss of consciousness
851.52 Cerebellar or brain stem contusion with open intracranial wound, brief (less than 1 hour) loss of consciousness
851.53 Cerebellar or brain stem contusion with open intracranial wound, moderate (1-24 hours) loss of consciousness
851.54 Cerebellar or brain stem contusion with open intracranial wound, prolonged (more than 24 hours) loss of consciousness and return to pre-existing conscious level
851.55 Cerebellar or brain stem contusion with open intracranial wound, prolonged (more than 24 hours) loss of consciousness, without return to pre-existing conscious level
851.56 Cerebellar or brain stem contusion with open intracranial wound, loss of consciousness of unspecified duration ▽
851.59 Cerebellar or brain stem contusion with open intracranial wound, unspecified concussion ▽
851.60 Cerebellar or brain stem laceration without mention of open intracranial wound, unspecified state of consciousness ▽
851.61 Cerebellar or brain stem laceration without mention of open intracranial wound, no loss of consciousness
851.62 Cerebellar or brain stem laceration without mention of open intracranial wound, brief (less than 1 hour) loss of consciousness
851.63 Cerebellar or brain stem laceration without mention of open intracranial wound, moderate (1-24 hours) loss of consciousness
851.64 Cerebellar or brain stem laceration without mention of open intracranial wound, prolonged (more than 24 hours) loss of consciousness and return to pre-existing conscious level

851.65 Cerebellar or brain stem laceration without mention of open intracranial wound, prolonged (more than 24 hours) loss of consciousness, without return to pre-existing conscious level

851.66 Cerebellar or brain stem laceration without mention of open intracranial wound, loss of consciousness of unspecified duration

851.69 Cerebellar or brain stem laceration without mention of open intracranial wound, unspecified concussion

851.70 Cerebellar or brain stem laceration with open intracranial wound, state of consciousness unspecified

851.71 Cerebellar or brain stem laceration with open intracranial wound, no loss of consciousness

851.72 Cerebellar or brain stem laceration with open intracranial wound, brief (less than one hour) loss of consciousness

851.73 Cerebellar or brain stem laceration with open intracranial wound, moderate (1-24 hours) loss of consciousness

851.74 Cerebellar or brain stem laceration with open intracranial wound, prolonged (more than 24 hours) loss of consciousness and return to pre-existing conscious level

851.75 Cerebellar or brain stem laceration with open intracranial wound, prolonged (more than 24 hours) loss of consciousness, without return to pre-existing conscious level

851.76 Cerebellar or brain stem laceration with open intracranial wound, loss of consciousness of unspecified duration

851.79 Cerebellar or brain stem laceration with open intracranial wound, unspecified concussion

851.80 Other and unspecified cerebral laceration and contusion, without mention of open intracranial wound, unspecified state of consciousness

851.81 Other and unspecified cerebral laceration and contusion, without mention of open intracranial wound, no loss of consciousness

851.82 Other and unspecified cerebral laceration and contusion, without mention of open intracranial wound, brief (less than 1 hour) loss of consciousness

851.83 Other and unspecified cerebral laceration and contusion, without mention of open intracranial wound, moderate (1-24 hours) loss of consciousness

851.84 Other and unspecified cerebral laceration and contusion, without mention of open intracranial wound, prolonged (more than 24 hours) loss of consciousness and return to preexisting conscious level

851.85 Other and unspecified cerebral laceration and contusion, without mention of open intracranial wound, prolonged (more than 24 hours) loss of consciousness, without return to pre-existing conscious level

851.86 Other and unspecified cerebral laceration and contusion, without mention of open intracranial wound, loss of consciousness of unspecified duration

851.89 Other and unspecified cerebral laceration and contusion, without mention of open intracranial wound, unspecified concussion

851.90 Other and unspecified cerebral laceration and contusion, with open intracranial wound, unspecified state of consciousness

851.91 Other and unspecified cerebral laceration and contusion, with open intracranial wound, no loss of consciousness

851.92 Other and unspecified cerebral laceration and contusion, with open intracranial wound, brief (less than 1 hour) loss of consciousness

851.93 Other and unspecified cerebral laceration and contusion, with open intracranial wound, moderate (1-24 hours) loss of consciousness

851.94 Other and unspecified cerebral laceration and contusion, with open intracranial wound, prolonged (more than 24 hours) loss of consciousness and return to pre-existing conscious level

851.95 Other and unspecified cerebral laceration and contusion, with open intracranial wound, prolonged (more than 24 hours) loss of consciousness, without return to pre-existing conscious level

851.96 Other and unspecified cerebral laceration and contusion, with open intracranial wound, loss of consciousness of unspecified duration

851.99 Other and unspecified cerebral laceration and contusion, with open intracranial wound, unspecified concussion

852.00 Subarachnoid hemorrhage following injury, without mention of open intracranial wound, unspecified state of consciousness

852.01 Subarachnoid hemorrhage following injury, without mention of open intracranial wound, no loss of consciousness

852.02 Subarachnoid hemorrhage following injury, without mention of open intracranial wound, brief (less than 1 hour) loss of consciousness

852.03 Subarachnoid hemorrhage following injury, without mention of open intracranial wound, moderate (1-24 hours) loss of consciousness

852.04 Subarachnoid hemorrhage following injury, without mention of open intracranial wound, prolonged (more than 24 hours) loss of consciousness and return to pre-existing conscious level

852.05 Subarachnoid hemorrhage following injury, without mention of open intracranial wound, prolonged (more than 24 hours) loss of consciousness, without return to pre-existing conscious level

852.06 Subarachnoid hemorrhage following injury, without mention of open intracranial wound, loss of consciousness of unspecified duration

852.09 Subarachnoid hemorrhage following injury, without mention of open intracranial wound, unspecified concussion

852.10 Subarachnoid hemorrhage following injury, with open intracranial wound, unspecified state of consciousness

852.11 Subarachnoid hemorrhage following injury, with open intracranial wound, no loss of consciousness

852.12 Subarachnoid hemorrhage following injury, with open intracranial wound, brief (less than 1 hour) loss of consciousness

852.13 Subarachnoid hemorrhage following injury, with open intracranial wound, moderate (1-24 hours) loss of consciousness

852.14 Subarachnoid hemorrhage following injury, with open intracranial wound, prolonged (more than 24 hours) loss of consciousness and return to pre-existing conscious level

852.15 Subarachnoid hemorrhage following injury, with open intracranial wound, prolonged (more than 24 hours) loss of consciousness, without return to pre-existing conscious level

852.16 Subarachnoid hemorrhage following injury, with open intracranial wound, loss of consciousness of unspecified duration

852.19 Subarachnoid hemorrhage following injury, with open intracranial wound, unspecified concussion

852.20 Subdural hemorrhage following injury, without mention of open intracranial wound, unspecified state of consciousness

852.21 Subdural hemorrhage following injury, without mention of open intracranial wound, no loss of consciousness

852.22 Subdural hemorrhage following injury, without mention of open intracranial wound, brief (less than one hour) loss of consciousness

852.23 Subdural hemorrhage following injury, without mention of open intracranial wound, moderate (1-24 hours) loss of consciousness

852.24 Subdural hemorrhage following injury, without mention of open intracranial wound, prolonged (more than 24 hours) loss of consciousness and return to pre-existing conscious level

852.25 Subdural hemorrhage following injury, without mention of open intracranial wound, prolonged (more than 24 hours) loss of consciousness, without return to pre-existing conscious level

852.26 Subdural hemorrhage following injury, without mention of open intracranial wound, loss of consciousness of unspecified duration

852.29 Subdural hemorrhage following injury, without mention of open intracranial wound, unspecified concussion

852.30 Subdural hemorrhage following injury, with open intracranial wound, state of consciousness unspecified

852.31 Subdural hemorrhage following injury, with open intracranial wound, no loss of consciousness

852.32 Subdural hemorrhage following injury, with open intracranial wound, brief (less than 1 hour) loss of consciousness

852.33 Subdural hemorrhage following injury, with open intracranial wound, moderate (1-24 hours) loss of consciousness

852.34 Subdural hemorrhage following injury, with open intracranial wound, prolonged (more than 24 hours) loss of consciousness and return to pre-existing conscious level

852.35 Subdural hemorrhage following injury, with open intracranial wound, prolonged (more than 24 hours) loss of consciousness, without return to pre-existing conscious level
852.36 Subdural hemorrhage following injury, with open intracranial wound, loss of consciousness of unspecified duration ▽
852.39 Subdural hemorrhage following injury, with open intracranial wound, unspecified concussion ▽
852.40 Extradural hemorrhage following injury, without mention of open intracranial wound, unspecified state of consciousness ▽
852.41 Extradural hemorrhage following injury, without mention of open intracranial wound, no loss of consciousness
852.42 Extradural hemorrhage following injury, without mention of open intracranial wound, brief (less than 1 hour) loss of consciousness
852.43 Extradural hemorrhage following injury, without mention of open intracranial wound, moderate (1-24 hours) loss of consciousness
852.44 Extradural hemorrhage following injury, without mention of open intracranial wound, prolonged (more than 24 hours) loss of consciousness and return to pre-existing conscious level
852.45 Extradural hemorrhage following injury, without mention of open intracranial wound, prolonged (more than 24 hours) loss of consciousness, without return to pre-existing conscious level
852.46 Extradural hemorrhage following injury, without mention of open intracranial wound, loss of consciousness of unspecified duration ▽
852.49 Extradural hemorrhage following injury, without mention of open intracranial wound, unspecified concussion ▽
852.50 Extradural hemorrhage following injury, with open intracranial wound, state of consciousness unspecified ▽
852.51 Extradural hemorrhage following injury, with open intracranial wound, no loss of consciousness
852.52 Extradural hemorrhage following injury, with open intracranial wound, brief (less than 1 hour) loss of consciousness
852.53 Extradural hemorrhage following injury, with open intracranial wound, moderate (1-24 hours) loss of consciousness
852.54 Extradural hemorrhage following injury, with open intracranial wound, prolonged (more than 24 hours) loss of consciousness and return to pre-existing conscious level
852.55 Extradural hemorrhage following injury, with open intracranial wound, prolonged (more than 24 hours) loss of consciousness, without return to pre-existing conscious level
852.56 Extradural hemorrhage following injury, with open intracranial wound, loss of consciousness of unspecified duration ▽
852.59 Extradural hemorrhage following injury, with open intracranial wound, unspecified concussion ▽
853.00 Other and unspecified intracranial hemorrhage following injury, without mention of open intracranial wound, unspecified state of consciousness ▽
853.01 Other and unspecified intracranial hemorrhage following injury, without mention of open intracranial wound, no loss of consciousness ▽
853.02 Other and unspecified intracranial hemorrhage following injury, without mention of open intracranial wound, brief (less than 1 hour) loss of consciousness ▽
853.03 Other and unspecified intracranial hemorrhage following injury, without mention of open intracranial wound, moderate (1-24 hours) loss of consciousness ▽
853.04 Other and unspecified intracranial hemorrhage following injury, without mention of open intracranial wound, prolonged (more than 24 hours) loss of consciousness and return to preexisting conscious level ▽
853.05 Other and unspecified intracranial hemorrhage following injury. Without mention of open intracranial wound, prolonged (more than 24 hours) loss of consciousness, without return to pre-existing conscious level ▽
853.06 Other and unspecified intracranial hemorrhage following injury, without mention of open intracranial wound, loss of consciousness of unspecified duration ▽
853.09 Other and unspecified intracranial hemorrhage following injury, without mention of open intracranial wound, unspecified concussion ▽
853.10 Other and unspecified intracranial hemorrhage following injury, with open intracranial wound, unspecified state of consciousness ▽
853.11 Other and unspecified intracranial hemorrhage following injury, with open intracranial wound, no loss of consciousness ▽
853.12 Other and unspecified intracranial hemorrhage following injury, with open intracranial wound, brief (less than 1 hour) loss of consciousness ▽
853.13 Other and unspecified intracranial hemorrhage following injury, with open intracranial wound, moderate (1-24 hours) loss of consciousness ▽
853.14 Other and unspecified intracranial hemorrhage following injury, with open intracranial wound, prolonged (more than 24 hours) loss of consciousness and return to pre-existing conscious level ▽
853.15 Other and unspecified intracranial hemorrhage following injury, with open intracranial wound, prolonged (more than 24 hours) loss of consciousness, without return to pre-existing conscious level ▽
853.16 Other and unspecified intracranial hemorrhage following injury, with open intracranial wound, loss of consciousness of unspecified duration ▽
853.19 Other and unspecified intracranial hemorrhage following injury, with open intracranial wound, unspecified concussion ▽
854.00 Intracranial injury of other and unspecified nature, without mention of open intracranial wound, unspecified state of consciousness ▽
854.01 Intracranial injury of other and unspecified nature, without mention of open intracranial wound, no loss of consciousness ▽
854.02 Intracranial injury of other and unspecified nature, without mention of open intracranial wound, brief (less than 1 hour) loss of consciousness ▽
854.03 Intracranial injury of other and unspecified nature, without mention of open intracranial wound, moderate (1-24 hours) loss of consciousness ▽
854.04 Intracranial injury of other and unspecified nature, without mention of open intracranial wound, prolonged (more than 24 hours) loss of consciousness and return to pre-existing conscious level ▽
854.05 Intracranial injury of other and unspecified nature, without mention of open intracranial wound, prolonged (more than 24 hours) loss of consciousness, without return to pre-existing conscious level ▽
854.06 Intracranial injury of other and unspecified nature, without mention of open intracranial wound, loss of consciousness of unspecified duration ▽
854.09 Intracranial injury of other and unspecified nature, without mention of open intracranial wound, unspecified concussion ▽
854.10 Intracranial injury of other and unspecified nature, with open intracranial wound, unspecified state of consciousness ▽
854.11 Intracranial injury of other and unspecified nature, with open intracranial wound, no loss of consciousness ▽
854.12 Intracranial injury of other and unspecified nature, with open intracranial wound, brief (less than 1 hour) loss of consciousness ▽
854.13 Intracranial injury of other and unspecified nature, with open intracranial wound, moderate (1-24 hours) loss of consciousness ▽
854.14 Intracranial injury of other and unspecified nature, with open intracranial wound, prolonged (more than 24 hours) loss of consciousness and return to pre-existing conscious level ▽
854.15 Intracranial injury of other and unspecified nature, with open intracranial wound, prolonged (more than 24 hours) loss of consciousness, without return to pre-existing conscious level ▽
854.16 Intracranial injury of other and unspecified nature, with open intracranial wound, loss of consciousness of unspecified duration ▽
854.19 Intracranial injury of other and unspecified nature, with open intracranial wound, with unspecified concussion ▽

ICD-9-CM Procedural

38.91 Arterial catheterization
88.40 Arteriography using contrast material, unspecified site
88.41 Arteriography of cerebral arteries
88.43 Arteriography of pulmonary arteries
88.44 Arteriography of other intrathoracic vessels

88.49 Arteriography of other specified sites

36221

36221 Non-selective catheter placement, thoracic aorta, with angiography of the extracranial carotid, vertebral, and/or intracranial vessels, unilateral or bilateral, and all associated radiological supervision and interpretation, includes angiography of the cervicocerebral arch, when performed

ICD-9-CM Diagnostic

191.0 Malignant neoplasm of cerebrum, except lobes and ventricles

191.1 Malignant neoplasm of frontal lobe of brain

191.2 Malignant neoplasm of temporal lobe of brain

191.3 Malignant neoplasm of parietal lobe of brain

191.4 Malignant neoplasm of occipital lobe of brain

191.5 Malignant neoplasm of ventricles of brain

191.6 Malignant neoplasm of cerebellum NOS

191.7 Malignant neoplasm of brain stem

191.8 Malignant neoplasm of other parts of brain

191.9 Malignant neoplasm of brain, unspecified site ▽

192.1 Malignant neoplasm of cerebral meninges

194.3 Malignant neoplasm of pituitary gland and craniopharyngeal duct

194.5 Malignant neoplasm of carotid body

198.3 Secondary malignant neoplasm of brain and spinal cord

225.2 Benign neoplasm of cerebral meninges

228.02 Hemangioma of intracranial structures

237.0 Neoplasm of uncertain behavior of pituitary gland and craniopharyngeal duct — (Use additional code to identify any functional activity)

237.5 Neoplasm of uncertain behavior of brain and spinal cord

239.6 Neoplasm of unspecified nature of brain

244.9 Unspecified hypothyroidism ▽

331.4 Obstructive hydrocephalus — (Use additional code, where applicable, to identify dementia: 294.10, 294.11)

337.01 Carotid sinus syndrome

342.90 Unspecified hemiplegia affecting unspecified side ▽

342.91 Unspecified hemiplegia affecting dominant side ▽

342.92 Unspecified hemiplegia affecting nondominant side ▽

348.0 Cerebral cysts

348.81 Temporal sclerosis

348.89 Other conditions of brain

348.9 Unspecified condition of brain ▽

362.34 Transient arterial occlusion of retina

368.2 Diplopia

430 Subarachnoid hemorrhage — (Use additional code to identify presence of hypertension)

431 Intracerebral hemorrhage — (Use additional code to identify presence of hypertension)

432.0 Nontraumatic extradural hemorrhage — (Use additional code to identify presence of hypertension)

432.1 Subdural hemorrhage — (Use additional code to identify presence of hypertension)

432.9 Unspecified intracranial hemorrhage — (Use additional code to identify presence of hypertension) ▽

433.00 Occlusion and stenosis of basilar artery without mention of cerebral infarction — (Use additional code, if applicable, to identify status post administration of tPA (rtPA) in a different facility within the last 24 hours prior to admission to current facility: V45.88)

433.01 Occlusion and stenosis of basilar artery with cerebral infarction — (Use additional code, if applicable, to identify status post administration of tPA (rtPA) in a different facility within the last 24 hours prior to admission to current facility: V45.88)

433.10 Occlusion and stenosis of carotid artery without mention of cerebral infarction — (Use additional code, if applicable, to identify status post administration of tPA (rtPA) in a different facility within the last 24 hours prior to admission to current facility: V45.88)

433.11 Occlusion and stenosis of carotid artery with cerebral infarction — (Use additional code, if applicable, to identify status post administration of tPA (rtPA) in a different facility within the last 24 hours prior to admission to current facility: V45.88)

433.20 Occlusion and stenosis of vertebral artery without mention of cerebral infarction — (Use additional code, if applicable, to identify status post administration of tPA (rtPA) in a different facility within the last 24 hours prior to admission to current facility: V45.88)

433.21 Occlusion and stenosis of vertebral artery with cerebral infarction — (Use additional code, if applicable, to identify status post administration of tPA (rtPA) in a different facility within the last 24 hours prior to admission to current facility: V45.88)

433.30 Occlusion and stenosis of multiple and bilateral precerebral arteries without mention of cerebral infarction — (Use additional code, if applicable, to identify status post administration of tPA (rtPA) in a different facility within the last 24 hours prior to admission to current facility: V45.88)

433.31 Occlusion and stenosis of multiple and bilateral precerebral arteries with cerebral infarction — (Use additional code, if applicable, to identify status post administration of tPA (rtPA) in a different facility within the last 24 hours prior to admission to current facility: V45.88)

433.80 Occlusion and stenosis of other specified precerebral artery without mention of cerebral infarction — (Use additional code, if applicable, to identify status post administration of tPA (rtPA) in a different facility within the last 24 hours prior to admission to current facility: V45.88)

433.81 Occlusion and stenosis of other specified precerebral artery with cerebral infarction — (Use additional code, if applicable, to identify status post administration of tPA (rtPA) in a different facility within the last 24 hours prior to admission to current facility: V45.88)

433.90 Occlusion and stenosis of unspecified precerebral artery without mention of cerebral infarction — (Use additional code, if applicable, to identify status post administration of tPA (rtPA) in a different facility within the last 24 hours prior to admission to current facility: V45.88) ▽

433.91 Occlusion and stenosis of unspecified precerebral artery with cerebral infarction — (Use additional code, if applicable, to identify status post administration of tPA (rtPA) in a different facility within the last 24 hours prior to admission to current facility: V45.88) ▽

434.00 Cerebral thrombosis without mention of cerebral infarction — (Use additional code, if applicable, to identify status post administration of tPA (rtPA) in a different facility within the last 24 hours prior to admission to current facility: V45.88)

434.01 Cerebral thrombosis with cerebral infarction — (Use additional code, if applicable, to identify status post administration of tPA (rtPA) in a different facility within the last 24 hours prior to admission to current facility: V45.88)

434.10 Cerebral embolism without mention of cerebral infarction — (Use additional code, if applicable, to identify status post administration of tPA (rtPA) in a different facility within the last 24 hours prior to admission to current facility: V45.88)

434.11 Cerebral embolism with cerebral infarction — (Use additional code, if applicable, to identify status post administration of tPA (rtPA) in a different facility within the last 24 hours prior to admission to current facility: V45.88)

434.90 Unspecified cerebral artery occlusion without mention of cerebral infarction — (Use additional code, if applicable, to identify status post administration of tPA (rtPA) in a different facility within the last 24 hours prior to admission to current facility: V45.88) ▽

434.91 Unspecified cerebral artery occlusion with cerebral infarction — (Use additional code, if applicable, to identify status post administration of tPA (rtPA) in a different facility within the last 24 hours prior to admission to current facility: V45.88) ▽

435.0 Basilar artery syndrome — (Use additional code to identify presence of hypertension)

435.1 Vertebral artery syndrome — (Use additional code to identify presence of hypertension)

435.3 Vertebrobasilar artery syndrome — (Use additional code to identify presence of hypertension)

435.8 Other specified transient cerebral ischemias — (Use additional code to identify presence of hypertension)

435.9 Unspecified transient cerebral ischemia — (Use additional code to identify presence of hypertension) ▽

437.0 Cerebral atherosclerosis — (Use additional code to identify presence of hypertension)

437.1 Other generalized ischemic cerebrovascular disease — (Use additional code to identify presence of hypertension)
437.3 Cerebral aneurysm, nonruptured — (Use additional code to identify presence of hypertension)
442.81 Aneurysm of artery of neck
729.89 Other musculoskeletal symptoms referable to limbs
747.81 Congenital anomaly of cerebrovascular system
747.89 Other specified congenital anomaly of circulatory system
780.02 Transient alteration of awareness
780.03 Persistent vegetative state
780.09 Other alteration of consciousness
780.2 Syncope and collapse
780.39 Other convulsions
780.4 Dizziness and giddiness
780.79 Other malaise and fatigue
780.93 Memory loss
781.3 Lack of coordination
784.0 Headache
784.3 Aphasia
784.59 Other speech disturbance
900.01 Common carotid artery injury
900.02 External carotid artery injury
900.03 Internal carotid artery injury
900.82 Injury to multiple blood vessels of head and neck
900.89 Injury to other specified blood vessels of head and neck
996.74 Other complications due to other vascular device, implant, and graft — (Use additional code to identify complication: 338.18-338.19, 338.28-338.29)
997.02 Iatrogenic cerebrovascular infarction or hemorrhage — (Use additional code to identify complications)

ICD-9-CM Procedural

38.91 Arterial catheterization
88.41 Arteriography of cerebral arteries

36222-36228

36222 Selective catheter placement, common carotid or innominate artery, unilateral, any approach, with angiography of the ipsilateral extracranial carotid circulation and all associated radiological supervision and interpretation, includes angiography of the cervicocerebral arch, when performed
36223 Selective catheter placement, common carotid or innominate artery, unilateral, any approach, with angiography of the ipsilateral intracranial carotid circulation and all associated radiological supervision and interpretation, includes angiography of the extracranial carotid and cervicocerebral arch, when performed
36224 Selective catheter placement, internal carotid artery, unilateral, with angiography of the ipsilateral intracranial carotid circulation and all associated radiological supervision and interpretation, includes angiography of the extracranial carotid and cervicocerebral arch, when performed
36225 Selective catheter placement, subclavian or innominate artery, unilateral, with angiography of the ipsilateral vertebral circulation and all associated radiological supervision and interpretation, includes angiography of the cervicocerebral arch, when performed
36226 Selective catheter placement, vertebral artery, unilateral, with angiography of the ipsilateral vertebral circulation and all associated radiological supervision and interpretation, includes angiography of the cervicocerebral arch, when performed
36227 Selective catheter placement, external carotid artery, unilateral, with angiography of the ipsilateral external carotid circulation and all associated radiological supervision and interpretation (List separately in addition to code for primary procedure)
36228 Selective catheter placement, each intracranial branch of the internal carotid or vertebral arteries, unilateral, with angiography of the selected vessel circulation and all associated radiological supervision and interpretation (eg, middle cerebral artery, posterior inferior cerebellar artery) (List separately in addition to code for primary procedure)

ICD-9-CM Diagnostic

368.8 Other specified visual disturbances
433.00 Occlusion and stenosis of basilar artery without mention of cerebral infarction — (Use additional code, if applicable, to identify status post administration of tPA (rtPA) in a different facility within the last 24 hours prior to admission to current facility: V45.88)
433.01 Occlusion and stenosis of basilar artery with cerebral infarction — (Use additional code, if applicable, to identify status post administration of tPA (rtPA) in a different facility within the last 24 hours prior to admission to current facility: V45.88)
433.10 Occlusion and stenosis of carotid artery without mention of cerebral infarction — (Use additional code, if applicable, to identify status post administration of tPA (rtPA) in a different facility within the last 24 hours prior to admission to current facility: V45.88)
433.11 Occlusion and stenosis of carotid artery with cerebral infarction — (Use additional code, if applicable, to identify status post administration of tPA (rtPA) in a different facility within the last 24 hours prior to admission to current facility: V45.88)
433.20 Occlusion and stenosis of vertebral artery without mention of cerebral infarction — (Use additional code, if applicable, to identify status post administration of tPA (rtPA) in a different facility within the last 24 hours prior to admission to current facility: V45.88)
433.21 Occlusion and stenosis of vertebral artery with cerebral infarction — (Use additional code, if applicable, to identify status post administration of tPA (rtPA) in a different facility within the last 24 hours prior to admission to current facility: V45.88)
433.30 Occlusion and stenosis of multiple and bilateral precerebral arteries without mention of cerebral infarction — (Use additional code, if applicable, to identify status post administration of tPA (rtPA) in a different facility within the last 24 hours prior to admission to current facility: V45.88)
433.31 Occlusion and stenosis of multiple and bilateral precerebral arteries with cerebral infarction — (Use additional code, if applicable, to identify status post administration of tPA (rtPA) in a different facility within the last 24 hours prior to admission to current facility: V45.88)
433.80 Occlusion and stenosis of other specified precerebral artery without mention of cerebral infarction — (Use additional code, if applicable, to identify status post administration of tPA (rtPA) in a different facility within the last 24 hours prior to admission to current facility: V45.88)

433.81 Occlusion and stenosis of other specified precerebral artery with cerebral infarction — (Use additional code, if applicable, to identify status post administration of tPA (rtPA) in a different facility within the last 24 hours prior to admission to current facility: V45.88)

433.90 Occlusion and stenosis of unspecified precerebral artery without mention of cerebral infarction — (Use additional code, if applicable, to identify status post administration of tPA (rtPA) in a different facility within the last 24 hours prior to admission to current facility: V45.88) ▽

433.91 Occlusion and stenosis of unspecified precerebral artery with cerebral infarction — (Use additional code, if applicable, to identify status post administration of tPA (rtPA) in a different facility within the last 24 hours prior to admission to current facility: V45.88) ▽

434.00 Cerebral thrombosis without mention of cerebral infarction — (Use additional code, if applicable, to identify status post administration of tPA (rtPA) in a different facility within the last 24 hours prior to admission to current facility: V45.88)

434.01 Cerebral thrombosis with cerebral infarction — (Use additional code, if applicable, to identify status post administration of tPA (rtPA) in a different facility within the last 24 hours prior to admission to current facility: V45.88)

434.10 Cerebral embolism without mention of cerebral infarction — (Use additional code, if applicable, to identify status post administration of tPA (rtPA) in a different facility within the last 24 hours prior to admission to current facility: V45.88)

434.11 Cerebral embolism with cerebral infarction — (Use additional code, if applicable, to identify status post administration of tPA (rtPA) in a different facility within the last 24 hours prior to admission to current facility: V45.88)

434.90 Unspecified cerebral artery occlusion without mention of cerebral infarction — (Use additional code, if applicable, to identify status post administration of tPA (rtPA) in a different facility within the last 24 hours prior to admission to current facility: V45.88) ▽

434.91 Unspecified cerebral artery occlusion with cerebral infarction — (Use additional code, if applicable, to identify status post administration of tPA (rtPA) in a different facility within the last 24 hours prior to admission to current facility: V45.88) ▽

435.0 Basilar artery syndrome — (Use additional code to identify presence of hypertension)

435.1 Vertebral artery syndrome — (Use additional code to identify presence of hypertension)

435.3 Vertebrobasilar artery syndrome — (Use additional code to identify presence of hypertension)

435.8 Other specified transient cerebral ischemias — (Use additional code to identify presence of hypertension)

435.9 Unspecified transient cerebral ischemia — (Use additional code to identify presence of hypertension) ▽

437.1 Other generalized ischemic cerebrovascular disease — (Use additional code to identify presence of hypertension)

440.20 Atherosclerosis of native arteries of the extremities, unspecified ▽

440.21 Atherosclerosis of native arteries of the extremities with intermittent claudication

440.22 Atherosclerosis of native arteries of the extremities with rest pain

440.23 Atherosclerosis of native arteries of the extremities with ulceration — (Use additional code for any associated ulceration: 707.10-707.19, 707.8, 707.9)

440.24 Atherosclerosis of native arteries of the extremities with gangrene — (Use additional code for any associated ulceration: 707.10-707.19, 707.8, 707.9)

440.29 Other atherosclerosis of native arteries of the extremities

443.21 Dissection of carotid artery

443.24 Dissection of vertebral artery

443.29 Dissection of other artery

446.7 Takayasu's disease

447.1 Stricture of artery

447.6 Unspecified arteritis ▽

723.1 Cervicalgia

729.89 Other musculoskeletal symptoms referable to limbs

748.3 Other congenital anomaly of larynx, trachea, and bronchus

780.4 Dizziness and giddiness

782.0 Disturbance of skin sensation

785.9 Other symptoms involving cardiovascular system

901.1 Innominate and subclavian artery injury

996.74 Other complications due to other vascular device, implant, and graft — (Use additional code to identify complication: 338.18-338.19, 338.28-338.29)

997.02 Iatrogenic cerebrovascular infarction or hemorrhage — (Use additional code to identify complications)

998.2 Accidental puncture or laceration during procedure

998.6 Persistent postoperative fistula, not elsewhere classified

ICD-9-CM Procedural

38.91 Arterial catheterization

88.41 Arteriography of cerebral arteries

36245-36248

36245 Selective catheter placement, arterial system; each first order abdominal, pelvic, or lower extremity artery branch, within a vascular family

36246 initial second order abdominal, pelvic, or lower extremity artery branch, within a vascular family

36247 initial third order or more selective abdominal, pelvic, or lower extremity artery branch, within a vascular family

36248 additional second order, third order, and beyond, abdominal, pelvic, or lower extremity artery branch, within a vascular family (List in addition to code for initial second or third order vessel as appropriate)

ICD-9-CM Diagnostic

153.9 Malignant neoplasm of colon, unspecified site ▽

154.0 Malignant neoplasm of rectosigmoid junction

155.0 Malignant neoplasm of liver, primary

155.1 Malignant neoplasm of intrahepatic bile ducts

155.2 Malignant neoplasm of liver, not specified as primary or secondary ▽

157.9 Malignant neoplasm of pancreas, part unspecified ▽

195.2 Malignant neoplasm of abdomen

195.3 Malignant neoplasm of pelvis

195.5 Malignant neoplasm of lower limb

195.8 Malignant neoplasm of other specified sites

197.7 Secondary malignant neoplasm of liver

199.0 Disseminated malignant neoplasm

199.1 Other malignant neoplasm of unspecified site

199.2 Malignant neoplasm associated with transplanted organ — (Code first complication of transplanted organ (996.80-996.89) Use additional code for specific malignancy)

209.10 Malignant carcinoid tumor of the large intestine, unspecified portion — (Code first any associated multiple endocrine neoplasia syndrome: 258.01-258.03)(Use additional code to identify associated endocrine syndrome, as: carcinoid syndrome: 259.2) ▽

209.20 Malignant carcinoid tumor of unknown primary site — (Code first any associated multiple endocrine neoplasia syndrome: 258.01-258.03)(Use additional code to identify associated endocrine syndrome, as: carcinoid syndrome: 259.2)

209.25 Malignant carcinoid tumor of foregut, not otherwise specified — (Code first any associated multiple endocrine neoplasia syndrome: 258.01-258.03)(Use additional code to identify associated endocrine syndrome, as: carcinoid syndrome: 259.2)

209.26 Malignant carcinoid tumor of midgut, not otherwise specified — (Code first any associated multiple endocrine neoplasia syndrome: 258.01-258.03)(Use additional code to identify associated endocrine syndrome, as: carcinoid syndrome: 259.2)

209.27 Malignant carcinoid tumor of hindgut, not otherwise specified — (Code first any associated multiple endocrine neoplasia syndrome: 258.01-258.03)(Use additional code to identify associated endocrine syndrome, as: carcinoid syndrome: 259.2)

209.29 Malignant carcinoid tumor of other sites — (Code first any associated multiple endocrine neoplasia syndrome: 258.01-258.03)(Use additional code to identify associated endocrine syndrome, as: carcinoid syndrome: 259.2)

209.30 Malignant poorly differentiated neuroendocrine carcinoma, any site — (Code first any associated multiple endocrine neoplasia syndrome: 258.01-258.03)(Use additional code to identify associated endocrine syndrome, as: carcinoid syndrome: 259.2) ▽

211.7 Benign neoplasm of islets of Langerhans — (Use additional code to identify any functional activity)

228.04 Hemangioma of intra-abdominal structures
235.3 Neoplasm of uncertain behavior of liver and biliary passages
249.70 Secondary diabetes mellitus with peripheral circulatory disorders, not stated as uncontrolled, or unspecified — (Use additional code to identify manifestation: 443.81, 785.4) (Use additional code to identify any associated insulin use: V58.67)
249.71 Secondary diabetes mellitus with peripheral circulatory disorders, uncontrolled — (Use additional code to identify manifestation: 443.81, 785.4) (Use additional code to identify any associated insulin use: V58.67)
250.70 Diabetes with peripheral circulatory disorders, type II or unspecified type, not stated as uncontrolled — (Use additional code to identify manifestation: 443.81, 785.4)
250.71 Diabetes with peripheral circulatory disorders, type I [juvenile type], not stated as uncontrolled — (Use additional code to identify manifestation: 443.81, 785.4)
250.72 Diabetes with peripheral circulatory disorders, type II or unspecified type, uncontrolled — (Use additional code to identify manifestation: 443.81, 785.4)
250.73 Diabetes with peripheral circulatory disorders, type I [juvenile type], uncontrolled — (Use additional code to identify manifestation: 443.81, 785.4)
440.1 Atherosclerosis of renal artery
440.20 Atherosclerosis of native arteries of the extremities, unspecified
440.21 Atherosclerosis of native arteries of the extremities with intermittent claudication
440.22 Atherosclerosis of native arteries of the extremities with rest pain
440.23 Atherosclerosis of native arteries of the extremities with ulceration — (Use additional code for any associated ulceration: 707.10-707.19, 707.8, 707.9)
440.24 Atherosclerosis of native arteries of the extremities with gangrene — (Use additional code for any associated ulceration: 707.10-707.19, 707.8, 707.9)
440.29 Other atherosclerosis of native arteries of the extremities
440.30 Atherosclerosis of unspecified bypass graft of extremities
440.31 Atherosclerosis of autologous vein bypass graft of extremities
440.32 Atherosclerosis of nonautologous biological bypass graft of extremities
440.4 Chronic total occlusion of artery of the extremities
440.8 Atherosclerosis of other specified arteries
440.9 Generalized and unspecified atherosclerosis
441.4 Abdominal aneurysm without mention of rupture
442.0 Aneurysm of artery of upper extremity
442.1 Aneurysm of renal artery
442.2 Aneurysm of iliac artery
442.3 Aneurysm of artery of lower extremity
442.89 Aneurysm of other specified artery
442.9 Other aneurysm of unspecified site
443.22 Dissection of iliac artery
443.23 Dissection of renal artery
443.29 Dissection of other artery
443.81 Peripheral angiopathy in diseases classified elsewhere — (Code first underlying disease: 249.7, 250.7)
443.9 Unspecified peripheral vascular disease
444.22 Embolism and thrombosis of arteries of lower extremity
444.81 Embolism and thrombosis of iliac artery
444.89 Embolism and thrombosis of other specified artery
444.9 Embolism and thrombosis of unspecified artery
445.02 Atheroembolism of lower extremity
445.81 Atheroembolism of kidney — (Use additional code for any associated acute kidney failure or chronic kidney disease: 584, 585)
445.89 Atheroembolism of other site
447.0 Arteriovenous fistula, acquired
447.1 Stricture of artery
447.72 Abdominal aortic ectasia
447.9 Unspecified disorders of arteries and arterioles
459.9 Unspecified circulatory system disorder
593.81 Vascular disorders of kidney
729.5 Pain in soft tissues of limb
747.60 Congenital anomaly of the peripheral vascular system, unspecified site
747.64 Congenital lower limb vessel anomaly
747.89 Other specified congenital anomaly of circulatory system
780.71 Chronic fatigue syndrome
780.79 Other malaise and fatigue
782.0 Disturbance of skin sensation
782.4 Jaundice, unspecified, not of newborn
785.4 Gangrene — (Code first any associated underlying condition)
785.9 Other symptoms involving cardiovascular system
789.00 Abdominal pain, unspecified site
789.01 Abdominal pain, right upper quadrant
789.02 Abdominal pain, left upper quadrant
789.03 Abdominal pain, right lower quadrant
789.04 Abdominal pain, left lower quadrant
789.05 Abdominal pain, periumbilic
789.06 Abdominal pain, epigastric
789.07 Abdominal pain, generalized
789.09 Abdominal pain, other specified site
789.30 Abdominal or pelvic swelling, mass or lump, unspecified site
789.31 Abdominal or pelvic swelling, mass, or lump, right upper quadrant
789.32 Abdominal or pelvic swelling, mass, or lump, left upper quadrant
789.33 Abdominal or pelvic swelling, mass, or lump, right lower quadrant
789.34 Abdominal or pelvic swelling, mass, or lump, left lower quadrant
789.35 Abdominal or pelvic swelling, mass or lump, periumbilic
789.36 Abdominal or pelvic swelling, mass, or lump, epigastric
789.37 Abdominal or pelvic swelling, mass, or lump, generalized
789.39 Abdominal or pelvic swelling, mass, or lump, other specified site
794.30 Nonspecific abnormal unspecified cardiovascular function study
904.0 Common femoral artery injury
904.1 Superficial femoral artery injury
904.2 Femoral vein injury
904.3 Saphenous vein injury
904.41 Popliteal artery injury
904.42 Popliteal vein injury
904.51 Anterior tibial artery injury
904.52 Anterior tibial vein injury
904.53 Posterior tibial artery injury
904.54 Posterior tibial vein injury
904.6 Deep plantar blood vessels injury
904.7 Injury to specified blood vessels of lower extremity, other
904.8 Injury to unspecified blood vessel of lower extremity
904.9 Injury to blood vessels, unspecified site
906.4 Late effect of crushing
928.00 Crushing injury of thigh — (Use additional code to identify any associated injuries: 800-829, 850.0-854.1, 860.0-869.1)
928.01 Crushing injury of hip — (Use additional code to identify any associated injuries: 800-829, 850.0-854.1, 860.0-869.1)
928.10 Crushing injury of lower leg — (Use additional code to identify any associated injuries: 800-829, 850.0-854.1, 860.0-869.1)
928.11 Crushing injury of knee — (Use additional code to identify any associated injuries: 800-829, 850.0-854.1, 860.0-869.1)
928.20 Crushing injury of foot — (Use additional code to identify any associated injuries: 800-829, 850.0-854.1, 860.0-869.1)
928.21 Crushing injury of ankle — (Use additional code to identify any associated injuries: 800-829, 850.0-854.1, 860.0-869.1)
928.3 Crushing injury of toe(s) — (Use additional code to identify any associated injuries: 800-829, 850.0-854.1, 860.0-869.1)
928.8 Crushing injury of multiple sites of lower limb — (Use additional code to identify any associated injuries: 800-829, 850.0-854.1, 860.0-869.1)
928.9 Crushing injury of unspecified site of lower limb — (Use additional code to identify any associated injuries: 800-829, 850.0-854.1, 860.0-869.1)

[Resequenced code] Unspecified code ♀ Female diagnosis Manifestation code ♂ Male diagnosis

929.0 Crushing injury of multiple sites, not elsewhere classified — (Use additional code to identify any associated injuries: 800-829, 850.0-854.1, 860.0-869.1)
929.9 Crushing injury of unspecified site — (Use additional code to identify any associated injuries: 800-829, 850.0-854.1, 860.0-869.1) ▽
996.73 Other complications due to renal dialysis device, implant, and graft — (Use additional code to identify complication: 338.18-338.19, 338.28-338.29)
996.95 Complications of reattached foot and toe(s)
996.96 Complications of reattached lower extremity, other and unspecified ▽
996.99 Complications of other specified reattached body part
997.2 Peripheral vascular complications — (Use additional code to identify complications)
998.6 Persistent postoperative fistula, not elsewhere classified
999.2 Other vascular complications of medical care, not elsewhere classified
V82.89 Special screening for other specified conditions

ICD-9-CM Procedural

38.91 Arterial catheterization
88.48 Arteriography of femoral and other lower extremity arteries

36251-36252

36251 Selective catheter placement (first-order), main renal artery and any accessory renal artery(s) for renal angiography, including arterial puncture and catheter placement(s), fluoroscopy, contrast injection(s), image postprocessing, permanent recording of images, and radiological supervision and interpretation, including pressure gradient measurements when performed, and flush aortogram when performed; unilateral
36252 bilateral

ICD-9-CM Diagnostic

189.0 Malignant neoplasm of kidney, except pelvis
189.1 Malignant neoplasm of renal pelvis
198.0 Secondary malignant neoplasm of kidney
223.0 Benign neoplasm of kidney, except pelvis
223.1 Benign neoplasm of renal pelvis
233.9 Carcinoma in situ of other and unspecified urinary organs ▽
236.91 Neoplasm of uncertain behavior of kidney and ureter
239.5 Neoplasm of unspecified nature of other genitourinary organs
440.1 Atherosclerosis of renal artery
442.1 Aneurysm of renal artery
445.81 Atheroembolism of kidney — (Use additional code for any associated acute kidney failure or chronic kidney disease: 584, 585)
584.5 Acute kidney failure with lesion of tubular necrosis
584.6 Acute kidney failure with lesion of renal cortical necrosis
584.7 Acute kidney failure with lesion of medullary [papillary] necrosis
584.8 Acute kidney failure with other specified pathological lesion in kidney
584.9 Acute kidney failure, unspecified ▽
587 Unspecified renal sclerosis ▽
589.0 Unilateral small kidney
589.1 Bilateral small kidneys
589.9 Unspecified small kidney ▽
593.81 Vascular disorders of kidney
593.89 Other specified disorder of kidney and ureter
866.00 Unspecified kidney injury without mention of open wound into cavity ▽
866.01 Kidney hematoma without rupture of capsule or mention of open wound into cavity
866.03 Complete disruption of kidney parenchyma, without mention of open wound into cavity

ICD-9-CM Procedural

38.91 Arterial catheterization
88.45 Arteriography of renal arteries

36253-36254

36253 Superselective catheter placement (one or more second order or higher renal artery branches) renal artery and any accessory renal artery(s) for renal angiography, including arterial puncture, catheterization, fluoroscopy, contrast injection(s), image postprocessing, permanent recording of images, and radiological supervision and interpretation, including pressure gradient measurements when performed, and flush aortogram when performed; unilateral
36254 bilateral

ICD-9-CM Diagnostic

189.0 Malignant neoplasm of kidney, except pelvis
189.1 Malignant neoplasm of renal pelvis
198.0 Secondary malignant neoplasm of kidney
223.0 Benign neoplasm of kidney, except pelvis
223.1 Benign neoplasm of renal pelvis
233.9 Carcinoma in situ of other and unspecified urinary organs ▽
236.91 Neoplasm of uncertain behavior of kidney and ureter
239.5 Neoplasm of unspecified nature of other genitourinary organs
440.1 Atherosclerosis of renal artery
442.1 Aneurysm of renal artery
445.81 Atheroembolism of kidney — (Use additional code for any associated acute kidney failure or chronic kidney disease: 584, 585)
584.5 Acute kidney failure with lesion of tubular necrosis
584.6 Acute kidney failure with lesion of renal cortical necrosis
584.7 Acute kidney failure with lesion of medullary [papillary] necrosis
584.8 Acute kidney failure with other specified pathological lesion in kidney
584.9 Acute kidney failure, unspecified ▽
587 Unspecified renal sclerosis ▽
589.0 Unilateral small kidney
589.1 Bilateral small kidneys
589.9 Unspecified small kidney ▽
593.81 Vascular disorders of kidney
593.89 Other specified disorder of kidney and ureter
866.00 Unspecified kidney injury without mention of open wound into cavity ▽
866.01 Kidney hematoma without rupture of capsule or mention of open wound into cavity
866.03 Complete disruption of kidney parenchyma, without mention of open wound into cavity

ICD-9-CM Procedural

38.91 Arterial catheterization
88.45 Arteriography of renal arteries

36260-36262

36260 Insertion of implantable intra-arterial infusion pump (eg, for chemotherapy of liver)
36261 Revision of implanted intra-arterial infusion pump
36262 Removal of implanted intra-arterial infusion pump

ICD-9-CM Diagnostic

155.0 Malignant neoplasm of liver, primary
155.1 Malignant neoplasm of intrahepatic bile ducts
159.1 Malignant neoplasm of spleen, not elsewhere classified
159.8 Malignant neoplasm of other sites of digestive system and intra-abdominal organs
159.9 Malignant neoplasm of ill-defined sites of digestive organs and peritoneum ▽
171.4 Malignant neoplasm of connective and other soft tissue of thorax
197.7 Secondary malignant neoplasm of liver
197.8 Secondary malignant neoplasm of other digestive organs and spleen
230.7 Carcinoma in situ of other and unspecified parts of intestine ▽
230.8 Carcinoma in situ of liver and biliary system
230.9 Carcinoma in situ of other and unspecified digestive organs ▽
235.3 Neoplasm of uncertain behavior of liver and biliary passages
235.5 Neoplasm of uncertain behavior of other and unspecified digestive organs ▽

996.1 Mechanical complication of other vascular device, implant, and graft
996.62 Infection and inflammatory reaction due to other vascular device, implant, and graft — (Use additional code to identify specified infections)
996.74 Other complications due to other vascular device, implant, and graft — (Use additional code to identify complication: 338.18-338.19, 338.28-338.29)
V58.81 Fitting and adjustment of vascular catheter

ICD-9-CM Procedural

38.91 Arterial catheterization
39.59 Other repair of vessel
86.05 Incision with removal of foreign body or device from skin and subcutaneous tissue
86.06 Insertion of totally implantable infusion pump
86.09 Other incision of skin and subcutaneous tissue

HCPCS Level II Supplies & Services

C1772 Infusion pump, programmable (implantable)

36400-36416

36400 Venipuncture, younger than age 3 years, necessitating the skill of a physician or other qualified health care professional, not to be used for routine venipuncture; femoral or jugular vein
36405 scalp vein
36406 other vein
36410 Venipuncture, age 3 years or older, necessitating the skill of a physician or other qualified health care professional (separate procedure), for diagnostic or therapeutic purposes (not to be used for routine venipuncture)
36415 Collection of venous blood by venipuncture
36416 Collection of capillary blood specimen (eg, finger, heel, ear stick)

ICD-9-CM Diagnostic

The application of this code is too broad to adequately present ICD-9-CM diagnostic code links here. Refer to your ICD-9-CM book.

ICD-9-CM Procedural

38.99 Other puncture of vein

36420-36425

36420 Venipuncture, cutdown; younger than age 1 year
36425 age 1 or over

ICD-9-CM Diagnostic

The application of this code is too broad to adequately present ICD-9-CM diagnostic code links here. Refer to your ICD-9-CM book.

ICD-9-CM Procedural

38.94 Venous cutdown

36430

36430 Transfusion, blood or blood components

ICD-9-CM Diagnostic

The application of this code is too broad to adequately present ICD-9-CM diagnostic code links here. Refer to your ICD-9-CM book.

ICD-9-CM Procedural

99.02 Transfusion of previously collected autologous blood
99.03 Other transfusion of whole blood
99.04 Transfusion of packed cells
99.05 Transfusion of platelets
99.06 Transfusion of coagulation factors
99.07 Transfusion of other serum

HCPCS Level II Supplies & Services

A4750 Blood tubing, arterial or venous, for hemodialysis, each
P9011 Blood, split unit

36440

36440 Push transfusion, blood, 2 years or younger

ICD-9-CM Diagnostic

The application of this code is too broad to adequately present ICD-9-CM diagnostic code links here. Refer to your ICD-9-CM book.

ICD-9-CM Procedural

99.03 Other transfusion of whole blood
99.04 Transfusion of packed cells
99.05 Transfusion of platelets
99.06 Transfusion of coagulation factors
99.07 Transfusion of other serum
99.08 Transfusion of blood expander

HCPCS Level II Supplies & Services

A4750 Blood tubing, arterial or venous, for hemodialysis, each

36450-36455

36450 Exchange transfusion, blood; newborn
36455 other than newborn

ICD-9-CM Diagnostic

The application of this code is too broad to adequately present ICD-9-CM diagnostic code links here. Refer to your ICD-9-CM book.

ICD-9-CM Procedural

99.01 Exchange transfusion

HCPCS Level II Supplies & Services

A4750 Blood tubing, arterial or venous, for hemodialysis, each

36460

36460 Transfusion, intrauterine, fetal

ICD-9-CM Diagnostic

655.33 Suspected damage to fetus from viral disease in mother, affecting management of mother, antepartum condition or complication ♀
656.13 Rhesus isoimmunization affecting management of mother, antepartum condition ♀
656.23 Isoimmunization from other and unspecified blood-group incompatibility, affecting management of mother, antepartum ♀
678.03 Fetal hematologic conditions, antepartum condition or complication ♀

ICD-9-CM Procedural

75.2 Intrauterine transfusion ♀

36468

36468 Single or multiple injections of sclerosing solutions, spider veins (telangiectasia); limb or trunk

ICD-9-CM Diagnostic

448.0 Hereditary hemorrhagic telangiectasia
448.9 Other and unspecified capillary diseases ▽
V50.1 Other plastic surgery for unacceptable cosmetic appearance

ICD-9-CM Procedural

39.92 Injection of sclerosing agent into vein

36469

36469 Single or multiple injections of sclerosing solutions, spider veins (telangiectasia); face

ICD-9-CM Diagnostic

448.0 Hereditary hemorrhagic telangiectasia
448.1 Nevus, non-neoplastic
448.9 Other and unspecified capillary diseases ▽

V50.1 Other plastic surgery for unacceptable cosmetic appearance

ICD-9-CM Procedural

39.92 Injection of sclerosing agent into vein

36470-36471

36470 Injection of sclerosing solution; single vein
36471 multiple veins, same leg

ICD-9-CM Diagnostic

448.9 Other and unspecified capillary diseases
454.0 Varicose veins of lower extremities with ulcer
454.1 Varicose veins of lower extremities with inflammation
454.2 Varicose veins of lower extremities with ulcer and inflammation
454.8 Varicose veins of the lower extremities with other complications
454.9 Asymptomatic varicose veins
459.10 Postphlebitic syndrome without complications
459.11 Postphlebitic syndrome with ulcer
459.12 Postphlebitic syndrome with inflammation
459.13 Postphlebitic syndrome with ulcer and inflammation
459.19 Postphlebitic syndrome with other complication
459.81 Unspecified venous (peripheral) insufficiency — (Use additional code for any associated ulceration: 707.10-707.19, 707.8, 707.9)
459.9 Unspecified circulatory system disorder
729.5 Pain in soft tissues of limb
729.81 Swelling of limb
782.3 Edema
V50.1 Other plastic surgery for unacceptable cosmetic appearance

ICD-9-CM Procedural

39.92 Injection of sclerosing agent into vein

36475-36476

36475 Endovenous ablation therapy of incompetent vein, extremity, inclusive of all imaging guidance and monitoring, percutaneous, radiofrequency; first vein treated
36476 second and subsequent veins treated in a single extremity, each through separate access sites (List separately in addition to code for primary procedure)

ICD-9-CM Diagnostic

454.0 Varicose veins of lower extremities with ulcer
454.1 Varicose veins of lower extremities with inflammation
454.2 Varicose veins of lower extremities with ulcer and inflammation
454.8 Varicose veins of the lower extremities with other complications
454.9 Asymptomatic varicose veins
456.8 Varices of other sites

ICD-9-CM Procedural

38.83 Other surgical occlusion of upper limb vessels
38.89 Other surgical occlusion of lower limb veins
39.92 Injection of sclerosing agent into vein

36478-36479

36478 Endovenous ablation therapy of incompetent vein, extremity, inclusive of all imaging guidance and monitoring, percutaneous, laser; first vein treated
36479 second and subsequent veins treated in a single extremity, each through separate access sites (List separately in addition to code for primary procedure)

ICD-9-CM Diagnostic

454.0 Varicose veins of lower extremities with ulcer
454.1 Varicose veins of lower extremities with inflammation
454.2 Varicose veins of lower extremities with ulcer and inflammation
454.8 Varicose veins of the lower extremities with other complications
454.9 Asymptomatic varicose veins

ICD-9-CM Procedural

38.83 Other surgical occlusion of upper limb vessels
38.89 Other surgical occlusion of lower limb veins

36481

36481 Percutaneous portal vein catheterization by any method

ICD-9-CM Diagnostic

The application of this code is too broad to adequately present ICD-9-CM diagnostic code links here. Refer to your ICD-9-CM book.

ICD-9-CM Procedural

38.93 Venous catheterization, not elsewhere classified
88.64 Phlebography of the portal venous system using contrast material

36500

36500 Venous catheterization for selective organ blood sampling

ICD-9-CM Diagnostic

The application of this code is too broad to adequately present ICD-9-CM diagnostic code links here. Refer to your ICD-9-CM book.

ICD-9-CM Procedural

38.93 Venous catheterization, not elsewhere classified

HCPCS Level II Supplies & Services

A4649 Surgical supply; miscellaneous

36511-36516

36511 Therapeutic apheresis; for white blood cells
36512 for red blood cells
36513 for platelets
36514 for plasma pheresis
36515 with extracorporeal immunoadsorption and plasma reinfusion
36516 with extracorporeal selective adsorption or selective filtration and plasma reinfusion

ICD-9-CM Diagnostic

170.0 Malignant neoplasm of bones of skull and face, except mandible
170.1 Malignant neoplasm of mandible
170.2 Malignant neoplasm of vertebral column, excluding sacrum and coccyx
170.3 Malignant neoplasm of ribs, sternum, and clavicle
170.4 Malignant neoplasm of scapula and long bones of upper limb
170.5 Malignant neoplasm of short bones of upper limb
170.6 Malignant neoplasm of pelvic bones, sacrum, and coccyx
170.7 Malignant neoplasm of long bones of lower limb
170.8 Malignant neoplasm of short bones of lower limb
170.9 Malignant neoplasm of bone and articular cartilage, site unspecified
174.0 Malignant neoplasm of nipple and areola of female breast — (Use additional code to identify estrogen receptor status: V86.0-V86.1) ♀
174.1 Malignant neoplasm of central portion of female breast — (Use additional code to identify estrogen receptor status: V86.0-V86.1) ♀
174.2 Malignant neoplasm of upper-inner quadrant of female breast — (Use additional code to identify estrogen receptor status: V86.0-V86.1) ♀
174.3 Malignant neoplasm of lower-inner quadrant of female breast — (Use additional code to identify estrogen receptor status: V86.0-V86.1) ♀
174.4 Malignant neoplasm of upper-outer quadrant of female breast — (Use additional code to identify estrogen receptor status: V86.0-V86.1) ♀
174.5 Malignant neoplasm of lower-outer quadrant of female breast — (Use additional code to identify estrogen receptor status: V86.0-V86.1) ♀
174.6 Malignant neoplasm of axillary tail of female breast — (Use additional code to identify estrogen receptor status: V86.0-V86.1) ♀
174.8 Malignant neoplasm of other specified sites of female breast — (Use additional code to identify estrogen receptor status: V86.0-V86.1) ♀

174.9 Malignant neoplasm of breast (female), unspecified site — (Use additional code to identify estrogen receptor status: V86.0-V86.1) ▽ ♀
183.0 Malignant neoplasm of ovary — (Use additional code to identify any functional activity) ♀
194.0 Malignant neoplasm of adrenal gland
194.4 Malignant neoplasm of pineal gland
199.2 Malignant neoplasm associated with transplanted organ — (Code first complication of transplanted organ (996.80-996.89) Use additional code for specific malignancy)
200.10 Lymphosarcoma, unspecified site, extranodal and solid organ sites ▽
200.11 Lymphosarcoma of lymph nodes of head, face, and neck
200.12 Lymphosarcoma of intrathoracic lymph nodes
200.13 Lymphosarcoma of intra-abdominal lymph nodes
200.14 Lymphosarcoma of lymph nodes of axilla and upper limb
200.15 Lymphosarcoma of lymph nodes of inguinal region and lower limb
200.16 Lymphosarcoma of intrapelvic lymph nodes
200.17 Lymphosarcoma of spleen
200.18 Lymphosarcoma of lymph nodes of multiple sites
201.00 Hodgkin's paragranuloma, unspecified site, extranodal and solid organ sites ▽
201.01 Hodgkin's paragranuloma of lymph nodes of head, face, and neck
201.02 Hodgkin's paragranuloma of intrathoracic lymph nodes
201.03 Hodgkin's paragranuloma of intra-abdominal lymph nodes
201.04 Hodgkin's paragranuloma of lymph nodes of axilla and upper limb
201.05 Hodgkin's paragranuloma of lymph nodes of inguinal region and lower limb
201.06 Hodgkin's paragranuloma of intrapelvic lymph nodes
201.07 Hodgkin's paragranuloma of spleen
201.08 Hodgkin's paragranuloma of lymph nodes of multiple sites
201.10 Hodgkin's granuloma, unspecified site, extranodal and solid organ sites ▽
201.11 Hodgkin's granuloma of lymph nodes of head, face, and neck
201.12 Hodgkin's granuloma of intrathoracic lymph nodes
201.13 Hodgkin's granuloma of intra-abdominal lymph nodes
201.14 Hodgkin's granuloma of lymph nodes of axilla and upper limb
201.15 Hodgkin's granuloma of lymph nodes of inguinal region and lower limb
201.16 Hodgkin's granuloma of intrapelvic lymph nodes
201.17 Hodgkin's granuloma of spleen
201.18 Hodgkin's granuloma of lymph nodes of multiple sites
201.20 Hodgkin's sarcoma, unspecified site, extranodal and solid organ sites ▽
201.21 Hodgkin's sarcoma of lymph nodes of head, face, and neck
201.22 Hodgkin's sarcoma of intrathoracic lymph nodes
201.23 Hodgkin's sarcoma of intra-abdominal lymph nodes
201.24 Hodgkin's sarcoma of lymph nodes of axilla and upper limb
201.25 Hodgkin's sarcoma of lymph nodes of inguinal region and lower limb
201.26 Hodgkin's sarcoma of intrapelvic lymph nodes
201.27 Hodgkin's sarcoma of spleen
201.28 Hodgkin's sarcoma of lymph nodes of multiple sites
201.40 Hodgkin's disease, lymphocytic-histiocytic predominance, unspecified site, extranodal and solid organ sites ▽
201.41 Hodgkin's disease, lymphocytic-histiocytic predominance of lymph nodes of head, face, and neck
201.42 Hodgkin's disease, lymphocytic-histiocytic predominance of intrathoracic lymph nodes
201.43 Hodgkin's disease, lymphocytic-histiocytic predominance of intra-abdominal lymph nodes
201.44 Hodgkin's disease, lymphocytic-histiocytic predominance of lymph nodes of axilla and upper limb
201.45 Hodgkin's disease, lymphocytic-histiocytic predominance of lymph nodes of inguinal region and lower limb
201.46 Hodgkin's disease, lymphocytic-histiocytic predominance of intrapelvic lymph nodes
201.47 Hodgkin's disease, lymphocytic-histiocytic predominance of spleen
201.48 Hodgkin's disease, lymphocytic-histiocytic predominance of lymph nodes of multiple sites
201.50 Hodgkin's disease, nodular sclerosis, unspecified site, extranodal and solid organ sites ▽
201.51 Hodgkin's disease, nodular sclerosis, of lymph nodes of head, face, and neck
201.52 Hodgkin's disease, nodular sclerosis, of intrathoracic lymph nodes
201.53 Hodgkin's disease, nodular sclerosis, of intra-abdominal lymph nodes
201.54 Hodgkin's disease, nodular sclerosis, of lymph nodes of axilla and upper limb
201.55 Hodgkin's disease, nodular sclerosis, of lymph nodes of inguinal region and lower limb
201.56 Hodgkin's disease, nodular sclerosis, of intrapelvic lymph nodes
201.57 Hodgkin's disease, nodular sclerosis, of spleen
201.58 Hodgkin's disease, nodular sclerosis, of lymph nodes of multiple sites
201.60 Hodgkin's disease, mixed cellularity, unspecified site, extranodal and solid organ sites ▽
201.61 Hodgkin's disease, mixed cellularity, involving lymph nodes of head, face, and neck
201.62 Hodgkin's disease, mixed cellularity, of intrathoracic lymph nodes
201.63 Hodgkin's disease, mixed cellularity, of intra-abdominal lymph nodes
201.64 Hodgkin's disease, mixed cellularity, of lymph nodes of axilla and upper limb
201.65 Hodgkin's disease, mixed cellularity, of lymph nodes of inguinal region and lower limb
201.66 Hodgkin's disease, mixed cellularity, of intrapelvic lymph nodes
201.67 Hodgkin's disease, mixed cellularity, of spleen
201.68 Hodgkin's disease, mixed cellularity, of lymph nodes of multiple sites
201.70 Hodgkin's disease, lymphocytic depletion, unspecified site, extranodal and solid organ sites ▽
201.71 Hodgkin's disease, lymphocytic depletion, of lymph nodes of head, face, and neck
201.72 Hodgkin's disease, lymphocytic depletion, of intrathoracic lymph nodes
201.73 Hodgkin's disease, lymphocytic depletion, of intra-abdominal lymph nodes
201.74 Hodgkin's disease, lymphocytic depletion, of lymph nodes of axilla and upper limb
201.75 Hodgkin's disease, lymphocytic depletion, of lymph nodes of inguinal region and lower limb
201.76 Hodgkin's disease, lymphocytic depletion, of intrapelvic lymph nodes
201.77 Hodgkin's disease, lymphocytic depletion, of spleen
201.78 Hodgkin's disease, lymphocytic depletion, of lymph nodes of multiple sites
201.90 Hodgkin's disease, unspecified type, unspecified site, extranodal and solid organ sites ▽
201.91 Hodgkin's disease, unspecified type, of lymph nodes of head, face, and neck ▽
201.92 Hodgkin's disease, unspecified type, of intrathoracic lymph nodes ▽
201.93 Hodgkin's disease, unspecified type, of intra-abdominal lymph nodes ▽
201.94 Hodgkin's disease, unspecified type, of lymph nodes of axilla and upper limb ▽
201.95 Hodgkin's disease, unspecified type, of lymph nodes of inguinal region and lower limb ▽
201.96 Hodgkin's disease, unspecified type, of intrapelvic lymph nodes ▽
201.97 Hodgkin's disease, unspecified type, of spleen ▽
201.98 Hodgkin's disease, unspecified type, of lymph nodes of multiple sites ▽
202.00 Nodular lymphoma, unspecified site, extranodal and solid organ sites ▽
202.01 Nodular lymphoma of lymph nodes of head, face, and neck
202.02 Nodular lymphoma of intrathoracic lymph nodes
202.03 Nodular lymphoma of intra-abdominal lymph nodes
202.04 Nodular lymphoma of lymph nodes of axilla and upper limb
202.05 Nodular lymphoma of lymph nodes of inguinal region and lower limb
202.06 Nodular lymphoma of intrapelvic lymph nodes
202.07 Nodular lymphoma of spleen
202.08 Nodular lymphoma of lymph nodes of multiple sites
202.10 Mycosis fungoides, unspecified site, extranodal and solid organ sites ▽
202.11 Mycosis fungoides of lymph nodes of head, face, and neck
202.12 Mycosis fungoides of intrathoracic lymph nodes
202.13 Mycosis fungoides of intra-abdominal lymph nodes
202.14 Mycosis fungoides of lymph nodes of axilla and upper limb
202.15 Mycosis fungoides of lymph nodes of inguinal region and lower limb

202.16 Mycosis fungoides of intrapelvic lymph nodes
202.17 Mycosis fungoides of spleen
202.18 Mycosis fungoides of lymph nodes of multiple sites
202.20 Sezary's disease, unspecified site, extranodal and solid organ sites ▽
202.21 Sezary's disease of lymph nodes of head, face, and neck
202.22 Sezary's disease of intrathoracic lymph nodes
202.23 Sezary's disease of intra-abdominal lymph nodes
202.24 Sezary's disease of lymph nodes of axilla and upper limb
202.25 Sezary's disease of lymph nodes of inguinal region and lower limb
202.26 Sezary's disease of intrapelvic lymph nodes
202.27 Sezary's disease of spleen
202.28 Sezary's disease of lymph nodes of multiple sites
202.30 Malignant histiocytosis, unspecified site, extranodal and solid organ sites ▽
202.31 Malignant histiocytosis of lymph nodes of head, face, and neck
202.32 Malignant histiocytosis of intrathoracic lymph nodes
202.33 Malignant histiocytosis of intra-abdominal lymph nodes
202.34 Malignant histiocytosis of lymph nodes of axilla and upper limb
202.35 Malignant histiocytosis of lymph nodes of inguinal region and lower limb
202.36 Malignant histiocytosis of intrapelvic lymph nodes
202.37 Malignant histiocytosis of spleen
202.38 Malignant histiocytosis of lymph nodes of multiple sites
202.40 Leukemic reticuloendotheliosis, unspecified site, extranodal and solid organ sites ▽
202.41 Leukemic reticuloendotheliosis of lymph nodes of head, face, and neck
202.42 Leukemic reticuloendotheliosis of intrathoracic lymph nodes
202.43 Leukemic reticuloendotheliosis of intra-abdominal lymph nodes
202.44 Leukemic reticuloendotheliosis of lymph nodes of axilla and upper limb
202.45 Leukemic reticuloendotheliosis of lymph nodes of inguinal region and lower limb
202.46 Leukemic reticuloendotheliosis of intrapelvic lymph nodes
202.47 Leukemic reticuloendotheliosis of spleen
202.48 Leukemic reticuloendotheliosis of lymph nodes of multiple sites
202.50 Letterer-Siwe disease, unspecified site, extranodal and solid organ sites ▽
202.51 Letterer-Siwe disease of lymph nodes of head, face, and neck
202.52 Letterer-Siwe disease of intrathoracic lymph nodes
202.53 Letterer-Siwe disease of intra-abdominal lymph nodes
202.54 Letterer-Siwe disease of lymph nodes of axilla and upper limb
202.55 Letterer-Siwe disease of lymph nodes of inguinal region and lower limb
202.56 Letterer-Siwe disease of intrapelvic lymph nodes
202.57 Letterer-Siwe disease of spleen
202.58 Letterer-Siwe disease of lymph nodes of multiple sites
202.60 Malignant mast cell tumors, unspecified site, extranodal and solid organ sites ▽
202.61 Malignant mast cell tumors of lymph nodes of head, face, and neck
202.62 Malignant mast cell tumors of intrathoracic lymph nodes
202.63 Malignant mast cell tumors of intra-abdominal lymph nodes
202.64 Malignant mast cell tumors of lymph nodes of axilla and upper limb
202.65 Malignant mast cell tumors of lymph nodes of inguinal region and lower limb
202.66 Malignant mast cell tumors of intrapelvic lymph nodes
202.67 Malignant mast cell tumors of spleen
202.68 Malignant mast cell tumors of lymph nodes of multiple sites
202.80 Other malignant lymphomas, unspecified site, extranodal and solid organ sites ▽
202.81 Other malignant lymphomas of lymph nodes of head, face, and neck
202.82 Other malignant lymphomas of intrathoracic lymph nodes
202.83 Other malignant lymphomas of intra-abdominal lymph nodes
202.84 Other malignant lymphomas of lymph nodes of axilla and upper limb
202.85 Other malignant lymphomas of lymph nodes of inguinal region and lower limb
202.86 Other malignant lymphomas of intrapelvic lymph nodes
202.87 Other malignant lymphomas of spleen
202.88 Other malignant lymphomas of lymph nodes of multiple sites
202.90 Other and unspecified malignant neoplasms of lymphoid and histiocytic tissue, unspecified site, extranodal and solid organ sites ▽
202.91 Other and unspecified malignant neoplasms of lymphoid and histiocytic tissue of lymph nodes of head, face, and neck ▽
202.92 Other and unspecified malignant neoplasms of lymphoid and histiocytic tissue of intrathoracic lymph nodes ▽
202.93 Other and unspecified malignant neoplasms of lymphoid and histiocytic tissue of intra-abdominal lymph nodes ▽
202.94 Other and unspecified malignant neoplasms of lymphoid and histiocytic tissue of lymph nodes of axilla and upper limb ▽
202.95 Other and unspecified malignant neoplasms of lymphoid and histiocytic tissue of lymph nodes of inguinal region and lower limb ▽
202.96 Other and unspecified malignant neoplasms of lymphoid and histiocytic tissue of intrapelvic lymph nodes ▽
202.97 Other and unspecified malignant neoplasms of lymphoid and histiocytic tissue of spleen ▽
202.98 Other and unspecified malignant neoplasms of lymphoid and histiocytic tissue of lymph nodes of multiple sites ▽
203.00 Multiple myeloma, without mention of having achieved remission
203.02 Multiple myeloma, in relapse
203.10 Plasma cell leukemia, without mention of having achieved remission
203.12 Plasma cell leukemia, in relapse
203.80 Other immunoproliferative neoplasms, without mention of having achieved remission
203.82 Other immunoproliferative neoplasms, in relapse
204.00 Acute lymphoid leukemia, without mention of having achieved remission
204.02 Acute lymphoid leukemia, in relapse
204.12 Chronic lymphoid leukemia, in relapse
204.22 Subacute lymphoid leukemia, in relapse
204.82 Other lymphoid leukemia, in relapse
204.92 Unspecified lymphoid leukemia, in relapse
205.00 Acute myeloid leukemia, without mention of having achieved remission
205.02 Acute myeloid leukemia, in relapse
205.12 Chronic myeloid leukemia, in relapse
205.22 Subacute myeloid leukemia, in relapse
205.82 Other myeloid leukemia, in relapse
208.00 Acute leukemia of unspecified cell type, without mention of having achieved remission ▽
208.02 Acute leukemia of unspecified cell type, in relapse
208.12 Chronic leukemia of unspecified cell type, in relapse
208.22 Subacute leukemia of unspecified cell type, in relapse
208.82 Other leukemia of unspecified cell type, in relapse
208.92 Unspecified leukemia, in relapse
238.77 Post-transplant lymphoproliferative disorder [PTLD] — (Code first complications of transplant (996.80-996.89))
239.3 Neoplasm of unspecified nature of breast
242.90 Thyrotoxicosis without mention of goiter or other cause, without mention of thyrotoxic crisis or storm
273.1 Monoclonal paraproteinemia — (Use additional code to identify any associated intellectual disabilities)
273.2 Other paraproteinemias — (Use additional code to identify any associated intellectual disabilities)
274.89 Gout with other specified manifestations — (Use additional code to identify any associated intellectual disabilities.) (Use additional code to identify manifestations, as: 357.4, 364.11.)
283.0 Autoimmune hemolytic anemias — (Use additional E code to identify cause, if drug-induced)
283.11 Hemolytic-uremic syndrome — (Use additional E code to identify cause) (Use additional code to identify associated: 004.0, 041.41-041.49, 481)
287.1 Qualitative platelet defects
287.30 Primary thrombocytopenia, unspecified ▽
287.31 Immune thrombocytopenic purpura
287.32 Evans' syndrome

287.33 Congenital and hereditary thrombocytopenic purpura
287.39 Other primary thrombocytopenia
287.41 Posttransfusion purpura
287.49 Other secondary thrombocytopenia
287.5 Unspecified thrombocytopenia ▽
289.84 Heparin-induced thrombocytopenia [HIT]
340 Multiple sclerosis
341.9 Unspecified demyelinating disease of central nervous system ▽
356.3 Refsum's disease
356.9 Unspecified hereditary and idiopathic peripheral neuropathy ▽
357.1 Polyneuropathy in collagen vascular disease — (Code first underlying disease: 446.0, 710.0, 714.0) ☒
357.3 Polyneuropathy in malignant disease — (Code first underlying disease: 140.0-208.9) ☒
357.4 Polyneuropathy in other diseases classified elsewhere — (Code first underlying disease, as: 032.0-032.9,135, 251.2, 265.0, 265.2, 266.0-266.9, 277.1, 277.30-277.39, 585.9, 586) ☒
357.81 Chronic inflammatory demyelinating polyneuritis
357.82 Critical illness polyneuropathy
357.89 Other inflammatory and toxic neuropathy
358.00 Myasthenia gravis without (acute) exacerbation
358.01 Myasthenia gravis with (acute) exacerbation
358.8 Other specified myoneural disorders
358.9 Unspecified myoneural disorders ▽
446.21 Goodpasture's syndrome — (Use additional code to identify renal disease: 583.81)
446.6 Thrombotic microangiopathy
447.6 Unspecified arteritis ▽
580.4 Acute glomerulonephritis with lesion of rapidly progressive glomerulonephritis
583.0 Nephritis and nephropathy, not specified as acute or chronic, with lesion of proliferative glomerulonephritis
583.4 Nephritis and nephropathy, not specified as acute or chronic, with lesion of rapidly progressive glomerulonephritis
584.7 Acute kidney failure with lesion of medullary [papillary] necrosis
585.1 Chronic kidney disease, Stage I — (Use additional code to identify kidney transplant status, if applicable: V42.0. Use additional code to identify manifestation: 357.4, 420.0. Code first hypertensive chronic kidney disease, if applicable: 403.00-403.91, 404.00-404.93)
585.2 Chronic kidney disease, Stage II (mild) — (Use additional code to identify kidney transplant status, if applicable: V42.0. Use additional code to identify manifestation: 357.4, 420.0. Code first hypertensive chronic kidney disease, if applicable: 403.00-403.91, 404.00-404.93)
585.3 Chronic kidney disease, Stage III (moderate) — (Use additional code to identify kidney transplant status, if applicable: V42.0. Use additional code to identify manifestation: 357.4, 420.0. Code first hypertensive chronic kidney disease, if applicable: 403.00-403.91, 404.00-404.93)
585.4 Chronic kidney disease, Stage IV (severe) — (Use additional code to identify kidney transplant status, if applicable: V42.0. Use additional code to identify manifestation: 357.4, 420.0. Code first hypertensive chronic kidney disease, if applicable: 403.00-403.91, 404.00-404.93)
585.5 Chronic kidney disease, Stage V — (Use additional code to identify kidney transplant status, if applicable: V42.0. Use additional code to identify manifestation: 357.4, 420.0. Code first hypertensive chronic kidney disease, if applicable: 403.00-403.91, 404.00-404.93)
585.6 End stage renal disease — (Use additional code to identify kidney transplant status, if applicable: V42.0. Use additional code to identify manifestation: 357.4, 420.0. Code first hypertensive chronic kidney disease, if applicable: 403.00-403.91, 404.00-404.93)
585.9 Chronic kidney disease, unspecified — (Use additional code to identify kidney transplant status, if applicable: V42.0. Use additional code to identify manifestation: 357.4, 420.0. Code first hypertensive chronic kidney disease, if applicable: 403.00-403.91, 404.00-404.93) ▽
586 Unspecified renal failure ▽
694.4 Pemphigus
710.0 Systemic lupus erythematosus — (Use additional code to identify manifestation: 424.91, 581.81, 582.81, 583.81)
710.1 Systemic sclerosis — (Use additional code to identify manifestation: 359.6, 517.2)
773.0 Hemolytic disease due to Rh isoimmunization of fetus or newborn — (Use additional code(s) to further specify condition)
780.71 Chronic fatigue syndrome
780.79 Other malaise and fatigue
996.89 Complications of other transplanted organ — (Use additional code to identify nature of complication: 078.5, 199.2, 238.77, 279.50-279.53)
997.99 Other complications affecting other specified body systems, NEC — (Use additional code to identify complications)
V42.81 Bone marrow replaced by transplant
V42.82 Peripheral stem cells replaced by transplant
V42.83 Pancreas replaced by transplant
V42.89 Other organ or tissue replaced by transplant

ICD-9-CM Procedural

99.71 Therapeutic plasmapheresis
99.72 Therapeutic leukopheresis
99.73 Therapeutic erythrocytapheresis
99.74 Therapeutic plateletpheresis
99.76 Extracorporeal immunoadsorption
99.78 Aquapheresis
99.79 Other therapeutic apheresis

36555-36556

36555 Insertion of non-tunneled centrally inserted central venous catheter; younger than 5 years of age
36556 age 5 years or older

ICD-9-CM Diagnostic

The application of this code is too broad to adequately present ICD-9-CM diagnostic code links here. Refer to your ICD-9-CM book.

ICD-9-CM Procedural

38.93 Venous catheterization, not elsewhere classified
38.94 Venous cutdown
38.95 Venous catheterization for renal dialysis
38.97 Central venous catheter placement with guidance

36557-36558

36557 Insertion of tunneled centrally inserted central venous catheter, without subcutaneous port or pump; younger than 5 years of age
36558 age 5 years or older

ICD-9-CM Diagnostic

The application of this code is too broad to adequately present ICD-9-CM diagnostic code links here. Refer to your ICD-9-CM book.

ICD-9-CM Procedural

38.94 Venous cutdown
86.07 Insertion of totally implantable vascular access device (VAD)

36560-36563

36560 Insertion of tunneled centrally inserted central venous access device, with subcutaneous port; younger than 5 years of age
36561 age 5 years or older
36563 Insertion of tunneled centrally inserted central venous access device with subcutaneous pump

ICD-9-CM Diagnostic

The application of this code is too broad to adequately present ICD-9-CM diagnostic code links here. Refer to your ICD-9-CM book.

ICD-9-CM Procedural

86.06 Insertion of totally implantable infusion pump

86.07 Insertion of totally implantable vascular access device (VAD)

HCPCS Level II Supplies & Services

N/A

36565-36566

36565 Insertion of tunneled centrally inserted central venous access device, requiring 2 catheters via 2 separate venous access sites; without subcutaneous port or pump (eg, Tesio type catheter)

36566 with subcutaneous port(s)

ICD-9-CM Diagnostic

The application of this code is too broad to adequately present ICD-9-CM diagnostic code links here. Refer to your ICD-9-CM book.

ICD-9-CM Procedural

86.07 Insertion of totally implantable vascular access device (VAD)

36568-36569

36568 Insertion of peripherally inserted central venous catheter (PICC), without subcutaneous port or pump; younger than 5 years of age

36569 age 5 years or older

ICD-9-CM Diagnostic

The application of this code is too broad to adequately present ICD-9-CM diagnostic code links here. Refer to your ICD-9-CM book.

ICD-9-CM Procedural

38.93 Venous catheterization, not elsewhere classified

38.97 Central venous catheter placement with guidance

36570-36571

36570 Insertion of peripherally inserted central venous access device, with subcutaneous port; younger than 5 years of age

36571 age 5 years or older

ICD-9-CM Diagnostic

The application of this code is too broad to adequately present ICD-9-CM diagnostic code links here. Refer to your ICD-9-CM book.

ICD-9-CM Procedural

86.07 Insertion of totally implantable vascular access device (VAD)

36575-36576

36575 Repair of tunneled or non-tunneled central venous access catheter, without subcutaneous port or pump, central or peripheral insertion site

36576 Repair of central venous access device, with subcutaneous port or pump, central or peripheral insertion site

ICD-9-CM Diagnostic

996.1 Mechanical complication of other vascular device, implant, and graft

999.31 Other and unspecified infection due to central venous catheter ▽

999.32 Bloodstream infection due to central venous catheter

999.33 Local infection due to central venous catheter

ICD-9-CM Procedural

86.09 Other incision of skin and subcutaneous tissue

36578

36578 Replacement, catheter only, of central venous access device, with subcutaneous port or pump, central or peripheral insertion site

ICD-9-CM Diagnostic

996.1 Mechanical complication of other vascular device, implant, and graft

996.62 Infection and inflammatory reaction due to other vascular device, implant, and graft — (Use additional code to identify specified infections)

996.74 Other complications due to other vascular device, implant, and graft — (Use additional code to identify complication: 338.18-338.19, 338.28-338.29)

999.31 Other and unspecified infection due to central venous catheter ▽

999.32 Bloodstream infection due to central venous catheter

999.33 Local infection due to central venous catheter

V58.81 Fitting and adjustment of vascular catheter

ICD-9-CM Procedural

38.93 Venous catheterization, not elsewhere classified

86.05 Incision with removal of foreign body or device from skin and subcutaneous tissue

36580-36581

36580 Replacement, complete, of a non-tunneled centrally inserted central venous catheter, without subcutaneous port or pump, through same venous access

36581 Replacement, complete, of a tunneled centrally inserted central venous catheter, without subcutaneous port or pump, through same venous access

ICD-9-CM Diagnostic

996.1 Mechanical complication of other vascular device, implant, and graft

996.62 Infection and inflammatory reaction due to other vascular device, implant, and graft — (Use additional code to identify specified infections)

996.74 Other complications due to other vascular device, implant, and graft — (Use additional code to identify complication: 338.18-338.19, 338.28-338.29)

999.31 Other and unspecified infection due to central venous catheter ▽

999.32 Bloodstream infection due to central venous catheter

999.33 Local infection due to central venous catheter

V58.81 Fitting and adjustment of vascular catheter

ICD-9-CM Procedural

86.07 Insertion of totally implantable vascular access device (VAD)

HCPCS Level II Supplies & Services

C1750 Catheter, hemodialysis/peritoneal, long-term

36582-36583

36582 Replacement, complete, of a tunneled centrally inserted central venous access device, with subcutaneous port, through same venous access

36583 Replacement, complete, of a tunneled centrally inserted central venous access device, with subcutaneous pump, through same venous access

ICD-9-CM Diagnostic

996.1 Mechanical complication of other vascular device, implant, and graft

996.62 Infection and inflammatory reaction due to other vascular device, implant, and graft — (Use additional code to identify specified infections)

996.74 Other complications due to other vascular device, implant, and graft — (Use additional code to identify complication: 338.18-338.19, 338.28-338.29)

999.31 Other and unspecified infection due to central venous catheter ▽

999.32 Bloodstream infection due to central venous catheter

999.33 Local infection due to central venous catheter

V53.90 Fitting and adjustment of other and unspecified device, Unspecified device ▽

V53.99 Fitting and adjustment, Other device

V58.81 Fitting and adjustment of vascular catheter

ICD-9-CM Procedural

86.07 Insertion of totally implantable vascular access device (VAD)

HCPCS Level II Supplies & Services

C1751 Catheter, infusion, inserted peripherally, centrally or midline (other than hemodialysis)

36584

36584 Replacement, complete, of a peripherally inserted central venous catheter (PICC), without subcutaneous port or pump, through same venous access

ICD-9-CM Diagnostic

996.1 Mechanical complication of other vascular device, implant, and graft
996.62 Infection and inflammatory reaction due to other vascular device, implant, and graft — (Use additional code to identify specified infections)
996.74 Other complications due to other vascular device, implant, and graft — (Use additional code to identify complication: 338.18-338.19, 338.28-338.29)
999.31 Other and unspecified infection due to central venous catheter ▽
999.32 Bloodstream infection due to central venous catheter
999.33 Local infection due to central venous catheter
V53.90 Fitting and adjustment of other and unspecified device, Unspecified device ▽
V53.99 Fitting and adjustment, Other device

ICD-9-CM Procedural

38.93 Venous catheterization, not elsewhere classified
38.94 Venous cutdown
38.97 Central venous catheter placement with guidance

36585

36585 Replacement, complete, of a peripherally inserted central venous access device, with subcutaneous port, through same venous access

ICD-9-CM Diagnostic

996.1 Mechanical complication of other vascular device, implant, and graft
996.62 Infection and inflammatory reaction due to other vascular device, implant, and graft — (Use additional code to identify specified infections)
996.74 Other complications due to other vascular device, implant, and graft — (Use additional code to identify complication: 338.18-338.19, 338.28-338.29)
999.31 Other and unspecified infection due to central venous catheter ▽
999.32 Bloodstream infection due to central venous catheter
999.33 Local infection due to central venous catheter
V58.81 Fitting and adjustment of vascular catheter

ICD-9-CM Procedural

86.05 Incision with removal of foreign body or device from skin and subcutaneous tissue
86.07 Insertion of totally implantable vascular access device (VAD)

HCPCS Level II Supplies & Services

C1751 Catheter, infusion, inserted peripherally, centrally or midline (other than hemodialysis)

36589-36590

36589 Removal of tunneled central venous catheter, without subcutaneous port or pump
36590 Removal of tunneled central venous access device, with subcutaneous port or pump, central or peripheral insertion

ICD-9-CM Diagnostic

996.1 Mechanical complication of other vascular device, implant, and graft
996.62 Infection and inflammatory reaction due to other vascular device, implant, and graft — (Use additional code to identify specified infections)
996.74 Other complications due to other vascular device, implant, and graft — (Use additional code to identify complication: 338.18-338.19, 338.28-338.29)
999.31 Other and unspecified infection due to central venous catheter ▽
999.32 Bloodstream infection due to central venous catheter
999.33 Local infection due to central venous catheter
V58.81 Fitting and adjustment of vascular catheter

ICD-9-CM Procedural

86.05 Incision with removal of foreign body or device from skin and subcutaneous tissue

36591

36591 Collection of blood specimen from a completely implantable venous access device

ICD-9-CM Diagnostic

The application of this code is too broad to adequately present ICD-9-CM diagnostic code links here. Refer to your ICD-9-CM book.

ICD-9-CM Procedural

38.99 Other puncture of vein

36592

36592 Collection of blood specimen using established central or peripheral catheter, venous, not otherwise specified

ICD-9-CM Diagnostic

The application of this code is too broad to adequately present ICD-9-CM diagnostic code links here. Refer to your ICD-9-CM book.

ICD-9-CM Procedural

38.93 Venous catheterization, not elsewhere classified

HCPCS Level II Supplies & Services

A4649 Surgical supply; miscellaneous

36593

36593 Declotting by thrombolytic agent of implanted vascular access device or catheter

ICD-9-CM Diagnostic

996.74 Other complications due to other vascular device, implant, and graft — (Use additional code to identify complication: 338.18-338.19, 338.28-338.29)

ICD-9-CM Procedural

99.10 Injection or infusion of thrombolytic agent

HCPCS Level II Supplies & Services

J2995 Injection, streptokinase, per 250,000 IU

36595-36596

36595 Mechanical removal of pericatheter obstructive material (eg, fibrin sheath) from central venous device via separate venous access
36596 Mechanical removal of intraluminal (intracatheter) obstructive material from central venous device through device lumen

ICD-9-CM Diagnostic

996.1 Mechanical complication of other vascular device, implant, and graft
996.62 Infection and inflammatory reaction due to other vascular device, implant, and graft — (Use additional code to identify specified infections)
996.74 Other complications due to other vascular device, implant, and graft — (Use additional code to identify complication: 338.18-338.19, 338.28-338.29)

ICD-9-CM Procedural

86.09 Other incision of skin and subcutaneous tissue

36597

36597 Repositioning of previously placed central venous catheter under fluoroscopic guidance

ICD-9-CM Diagnostic

996.59 Mechanical complication due to other implant and internal device, not elsewhere classified
996.62 Infection and inflammatory reaction due to other vascular device, implant, and graft — (Use additional code to identify specified infections)
999.31 Other and unspecified infection due to central venous catheter ▽
999.32 Bloodstream infection due to central venous catheter
999.33 Local infection due to central venous catheter
V53.99 Fitting and adjustment, Other device

ICD-9-CM Procedural

86.09 Other incision of skin and subcutaneous tissue
88.39 X-ray, other and unspecified

36598

36598 Contrast injection(s) for radiologic evaluation of existing central venous access device, including fluoroscopy, image documentation and report

ICD-9-CM Diagnostic

444.21 Embolism and thrombosis of arteries of upper extremity
444.22 Embolism and thrombosis of arteries of lower extremity
447.1 Stricture of artery
453.2 Other venous embolism and thrombosis, of inferior vena cava
453.74 Chronic venous embolism and thrombosis of axillary veins — (Use additional code, if applicable, for associated long-term (current) use of anticoagulants (V58.61))
453.75 Chronic venous embolism and thrombosis of subclavian veins — (Use additional code, if applicable, for associated long-term (current) use of anticoagulants (V58.61))
453.76 Chronic venous embolism and thrombosis of internal jugular veins — (Use additional code, if applicable, for associated long-term (current) use of anticoagulants (V58.61))
453.77 Chronic venous embolism and thrombosis of other thoracic veins — (Use additional code, if applicable, for associated long-term (current) use of anticoagulants (V58.61))
453.79 Chronic venous embolism and thrombosis of other specified veins — (Use additional code, if applicable, for associated long-term (current) use of anticoagulants (V58.61))
453.84 Acute venous embolism and thrombosis of axillary veins
453.85 Acute venous embolism and thrombosis of subclavian veins
453.86 Acute venous embolism and thrombosis of internal jugular veins
453.87 Acute venous embolism and thrombosis of other thoracic veins
453.89 Acute venous embolism and thrombosis of other specified veins
453.9 Embolism and thrombosis of unspecified site ▽
459.2 Compression of vein
459.81 Unspecified venous (peripheral) insufficiency — (Use additional code for any associated ulceration: 707.10-707.19, 707.8, 707.9) ▽
459.89 Other specified circulatory system disorders
459.9 Unspecified circulatory system disorder ▽
901.2 Superior vena cava injury
996.1 Mechanical complication of other vascular device, implant, and graft
996.62 Infection and inflammatory reaction due to other vascular device, implant, and graft — (Use additional code to identify specified infections)
996.74 Other complications due to other vascular device, implant, and graft — (Use additional code to identify complication: 338.18-338.19, 338.28-338.29)
999.31 Other and unspecified infection due to central venous catheter ▽
999.32 Bloodstream infection due to central venous catheter
999.33 Local infection due to central venous catheter

ICD-9-CM Procedural

88.67 Phlebography of other specified sites using contrast material

36600

36600 Arterial puncture, withdrawal of blood for diagnosis

ICD-9-CM Diagnostic

The application of this code is too broad to adequately present ICD-9-CM diagnostic code links here. Refer to your ICD-9-CM book.

ICD-9-CM Procedural

38.98 Other puncture of artery

HCPCS Level II Supplies & Services

A4649 Surgical supply; miscellaneous

36620-36625

36620 Arterial catheterization or cannulation for sampling, monitoring or transfusion (separate procedure); percutaneous
36625 cutdown

ICD-9-CM Diagnostic

The application of this code is too broad to adequately present ICD-9-CM diagnostic code links here. Refer to your ICD-9-CM book.

ICD-9-CM Procedural

38.91 Arterial catheterization

HCPCS Level II Supplies & Services

A4649 Surgical supply; miscellaneous

36640

36640 Arterial catheterization for prolonged infusion therapy (chemotherapy), cutdown

ICD-9-CM Diagnostic

The application of this code is too broad to adequately present ICD-9-CM diagnostic code links here. Refer to your ICD-9-CM book.

ICD-9-CM Procedural

38.91 Arterial catheterization

HCPCS Level II Supplies & Services

A4649 Surgical supply; miscellaneous

36680

36680 Placement of needle for intraosseous infusion

ICD-9-CM Diagnostic

276.0 Hyperosmolality and/or hypernatremia — (Use additional code to identify any associated intellectual disabilities)
276.1 Hyposmolality and/or hyponatremia — (Use additional code to identify any associated intellectual disabilities)
276.50 Volume depletion, unspecified — (Use additional code to identify any associated intellectual disabilities) ▽
276.51 Dehydration — (Use additional code to identify any associated intellectual disabilities)
276.52 Hypovolemia — (Use additional code to identify any associated intellectual disabilities)

ICD-9-CM Procedural

41.92 Injection into bone marrow

36800

36800 Insertion of cannula for hemodialysis, other purpose (separate procedure); vein to vein

ICD-9-CM Diagnostic

249.40 Secondary diabetes mellitus with renal manifestations, not stated as uncontrolled, or unspecified — (Use additional code to identify manifestation: 581.81, 583.81, 585.1-585.9) (Use additional code to identify any associated insulin use: V58.67)
249.41 Secondary diabetes mellitus with renal manifestations, uncontrolled — (Use additional code to identify manifestation: 581.81, 583.81, 585.1-585.9) (Use additional code to identify any associated insulin use: V58.67)
250.40 Diabetes with renal manifestations, type II or unspecified type, not stated as uncontrolled — (Use additional code to identify manifestation: 581.81, 583.81, 585.1-585.9)
250.41 Diabetes with renal manifestations, type I [juvenile type], not stated as uncontrolled — (Use additional code to identify manifestation: 581.81, 583.81, 585.1-585.9)
250.42 Diabetes with renal manifestations, type II or unspecified type, uncontrolled — (Use additional code to identify manifestation: 581.81, 583.81, 585.1-585.9)
250.43 Diabetes with renal manifestations, type I [juvenile type], uncontrolled — (Use additional code to identify manifestation: 581.81, 583.81, 585.1-585.9)

403.91 Hypertensive chronic kidney disease, unspecified, with chronic kidney disease stage V or end stage renal disease — (Use additional code to identify the stage of chronic kidney disease: 585.5, 585.6) ▽

445.81 Atheroembolism of kidney — (Use additional code for any associated acute kidney failure or chronic kidney disease: 584, 585)

580.4 Acute glomerulonephritis with lesion of rapidly progressive glomerulonephritis

580.9 Acute glomerulonephritis with unspecified pathological lesion in kidney ▽

581.1 Nephrotic syndrome with lesion of membranous glomerulonephritis

581.81 Nephrotic syndrome with other specified pathological lesion in kidney in diseases classified elsewhere — (Code first underlying disease: 084.9, 249.4, 250.4, 277.30-277.39, 446.0, 710.0) ☒

582.0 Chronic glomerulonephritis with lesion of proliferative glomerulonephritis

582.1 Chronic glomerulonephritis with lesion of membranous glomerulonephritis

582.2 Chronic glomerulonephritis with lesion of membranoproliferative glomerulonephritis

582.4 Chronic glomerulonephritis with lesion of rapidly progressive glomerulonephritis

582.81 Chronic glomerulonephritis with other specified pathological lesion in kidney in diseases classified elsewhere — (Code first underlying disease: 277.30-277.39, 710.0) ☒

582.89 Other chronic glomerulonephritis with specified pathological lesion in kidney

582.9 Chronic glomerulonephritis with unspecified pathological lesion in kidney ▽

583.0 Nephritis and nephropathy, not specified as acute or chronic, with lesion of proliferative glomerulonephritis

583.1 Nephritis and nephropathy, not specified as acute or chronic, with lesion of membranous glomerulonephritis

583.2 Nephritis and nephropathy, not specified as acute or chronic, with lesion of membranoproliferative glomerulonephritis

583.4 Nephritis and nephropathy, not specified as acute or chronic, with lesion of rapidly progressive glomerulonephritis

583.6 Nephritis and nephropathy, not specified as acute or chronic, with lesion of renal cortical necrosis

583.7 Nephritis and nephropathy, not specified as acute or chronic, with lesion of renal medullary necrosis

583.81 Nephritis and nephropathy, not specified as acute or chronic, with other specified pathological lesion in kidney, in diseases classified elsewhere — (Code first underlying disease: 016.0, 098.19, 249.4, 250.4, 277.30-277.39, 446.21, 710.0) ☒

583.89 Other nephritis and nephropathy, not specified as acute or chronic, with specified pathological lesion in kidney

583.9 Nephritis and nephropathy, not specified as acute or chronic, with unspecified pathological lesion in kidney ▽

584.5 Acute kidney failure with lesion of tubular necrosis

584.6 Acute kidney failure with lesion of renal cortical necrosis

584.7 Acute kidney failure with lesion of medullary [papillary] necrosis

584.8 Acute kidney failure with other specified pathological lesion in kidney

584.9 Acute kidney failure, unspecified ▽

585.4 Chronic kidney disease, Stage IV (severe) — (Use additional code to identify kidney transplant status, if applicable: V42.0. Use additional code to identify manifestation: 357.4, 420.0. Code first hypertensive chronic kidney disease, if applicable: 403.00-403.91, 404.00-404.93)

585.5 Chronic kidney disease, Stage V — (Use additional code to identify kidney transplant status, if applicable: V42.0. Use additional code to identify manifestation: 357.4, 420.0. Code first hypertensive chronic kidney disease, if applicable: 403.00-403.91, 404.00-404.93)

585.6 End stage renal disease — (Use additional code to identify kidney transplant status, if applicable: V42.0. Use additional code to identify manifestation: 357.4, 420.0. Code first hypertensive chronic kidney disease, if applicable: 403.00-403.91, 404.00-404.93)

585.9 Chronic kidney disease, unspecified — (Use additional code to identify kidney transplant status, if applicable: V42.0. Use additional code to identify manifestation: 357.4, 420.0. Code first hypertensive chronic kidney disease, if applicable: 403.00-403.91, 404.00-404.93) ▽

586 Unspecified renal failure ▽

587 Unspecified renal sclerosis ▽

588.0 Renal osteodystrophy

588.81 Secondary hyperparathyroidism (of renal origin)

588.89 Other specified disorders resulting from impaired renal function

588.9 Unspecified disorder resulting from impaired renal function ▽

590.00 Chronic pyelonephritis without lesion of renal medullary necrosis — (Use additional code to identify organism, such as E. coli, 041.41-041.49. Code if applicable, any causal condition first)

590.01 Chronic pyelonephritis with lesion of renal medullary necrosis — (Use additional code to identify organism, such as E. coli, 041.41-041.49. Code if applicable, any causal condition first)

590.10 Acute pyelonephritis without lesion of renal medullary necrosis — (Use additional code to identify organism, such as E. coli, 041.40-041.49)

590.11 Acute pyelonephritis with lesion of renal medullary necrosis — (Use additional code to identify organism, such as E. coli, 041.40-041.49)

590.3 Pyeloureteritis cystica — (Use additional code to identify organism, such as E. coli, 041.41-041.49)

590.80 Unspecified pyelonephritis — (Use additional code to identify organism, such as E. coli, 041.41-041.49) ▽

590.81 Pyelitis or pyelonephritis in diseases classified elsewhere — (Use additional code to identify organism, such as E. coli, 041.41-041.49. Code first underlying disease: 016.0) ☒

590.9 Unspecified infection of kidney — (Use additional code to identify organism, such as E. coli, 041.41-041.49) ▽

593.81 Vascular disorders of kidney

728.88 Rhabdomyolysis

958.5 Traumatic anuria

996.81 Complications of transplanted kidney — (Use additional code to identify nature of complication: 078.5, 199.2, 238.77, 279.50-279.53)

ICD-9-CM Procedural

39.27 Arteriovenostomy for renal dialysis

39.93 Insertion of vessel-to-vessel cannula

HCPCS Level II Supplies & Services

A4305 Disposable drug delivery system, flow rate of 50 ml or greater per hour

36810

36810 Insertion of cannula for hemodialysis, other purpose (separate procedure); arteriovenous, external (Scribner type)

ICD-9-CM Diagnostic

249.40 Secondary diabetes mellitus with renal manifestations, not stated as uncontrolled, or unspecified — (Use additional code to identify manifestation: 581.81, 583.81, 585.1-585.9) (Use additional code to identify any associated insulin use: V58.67)

249.41 Secondary diabetes mellitus with renal manifestations, uncontrolled — (Use additional code to identify manifestation: 581.81, 583.81, 585.1-585.9) (Use additional code to identify any associated insulin use: V58.67)

250.40 Diabetes with renal manifestations, type II or unspecified type, not stated as uncontrolled — (Use additional code to identify manifestation: 581.81, 583.81, 585.1-585.9)

250.41 Diabetes with renal manifestations, type I [juvenile type], not stated as uncontrolled — (Use additional code to identify manifestation: 581.81, 583.81, 585.1-585.9)

250.42 Diabetes with renal manifestations, type II or unspecified type, uncontrolled — (Use additional code to identify manifestation: 581.81, 583.81, 585.1-585.9)

250.43 Diabetes with renal manifestations, type I [juvenile type], uncontrolled — (Use additional code to identify manifestation: 581.81, 583.81, 585.1-585.9)

403.91 Hypertensive chronic kidney disease, unspecified, with chronic kidney disease stage V or end stage renal disease — (Use additional code to identify the stage of chronic kidney disease: 585.5, 585.6) ▽

445.81 Atheroembolism of kidney — (Use additional code for any associated acute kidney failure or chronic kidney disease: 584, 585)

580.4 Acute glomerulonephritis with lesion of rapidly progressive glomerulonephritis

580.9 Acute glomerulonephritis with unspecified pathological lesion in kidney ▽

581.1 Nephrotic syndrome with lesion of membranous glomerulonephritis

581.81 Nephrotic syndrome with other specified pathological lesion in kidney in diseases classified elsewhere — (Code first underlying disease: 084.9, 249.4, 250.4, 277.30-277.39, 446.0, 710.0) ☒

582.0 Chronic glomerulonephritis with lesion of proliferative glomerulonephritis

582.1 Chronic glomerulonephritis with lesion of membranous glomerulonephritis

582.2 Chronic glomerulonephritis with lesion of membranoproliferative glomerulonephritis

582.4 Chronic glomerulonephritis with lesion of rapidly progressive glomerulonephritis

582.81 Chronic glomerulonephritis with other specified pathological lesion in kidney in diseases classified elsewhere — (Code first underlying disease: 277.30-277.39, 710.0) ☒

582.89 Other chronic glomerulonephritis with specified pathological lesion in kidney

582.9 Chronic glomerulonephritis with unspecified pathological lesion in kidney ▽

583.0 Nephritis and nephropathy, not specified as acute or chronic, with lesion of proliferative glomerulonephritis

583.1 Nephritis and nephropathy, not specified as acute or chronic, with lesion of membranous glomerulonephritis

583.2 Nephritis and nephropathy, not specified as acute or chronic, with lesion of membranoproliferative glomerulonephritis

583.4 Nephritis and nephropathy, not specified as acute or chronic, with lesion of rapidly progressive glomerulonephritis

583.6 Nephritis and nephropathy, not specified as acute or chronic, with lesion of renal cortical necrosis

583.7 Nephritis and nephropathy, not specified as acute or chronic, with lesion of renal medullary necrosis

583.81 Nephritis and nephropathy, not specified as acute or chronic, with other specified pathological lesion in kidney, in diseases classified elsewhere — (Code first underlying disease: 016.0, 098.19, 249.4, 250.4, 277.30-277.39, 446.21, 710.0) ☒

583.89 Other nephritis and nephropathy, not specified as acute or chronic, with specified pathological lesion in kidney

583.9 Nephritis and nephropathy, not specified as acute or chronic, with unspecified pathological lesion in kidney ▽

584.5 Acute kidney failure with lesion of tubular necrosis

584.6 Acute kidney failure with lesion of renal cortical necrosis

584.7 Acute kidney failure with lesion of medullary [papillary] necrosis

584.8 Acute kidney failure with other specified pathological lesion in kidney

584.9 Acute kidney failure, unspecified ▽

585.4 Chronic kidney disease, Stage IV (severe) — (Use additional code to identify kidney transplant status, if applicable: V42.0. Use additional code to identify manifestation: 357.4, 420.0. Code first hypertensive chronic kidney disease, if applicable: 403.00-403.91, 404.00-404.93)

585.5 Chronic kidney disease, Stage V — (Use additional code to identify kidney transplant status, if applicable: V42.0. Use additional code to identify manifestation: 357.4, 420.0. Code first hypertensive chronic kidney disease, if applicable: 403.00-403.91, 404.00-404.93)

585.6 End stage renal disease — (Use additional code to identify kidney transplant status, if applicable: V42.0. Use additional code to identify manifestation: 357.4, 420.0. Code first hypertensive chronic kidney disease, if applicable: 403.00-403.91, 404.00-404.93)

585.9 Chronic kidney disease, unspecified — (Use additional code to identify kidney transplant status, if applicable: V42.0. Use additional code to identify manifestation: 357.4, 420.0. Code first hypertensive chronic kidney disease, if applicable: 403.00-403.91, 404.00-404.93) ▽

586 Unspecified renal failure ▽

587 Unspecified renal sclerosis ▽

588.0 Renal osteodystrophy

588.81 Secondary hyperparathyroidism (of renal origin)

588.89 Other specified disorders resulting from impaired renal function

588.9 Unspecified disorder resulting from impaired renal function ▽

590.00 Chronic pyelonephritis without lesion of renal medullary necrosis — (Use additional code to identify organism, such as E. coli, 041.41-041.49. Code if applicable, any causal condition first)

590.01 Chronic pyelonephritis with lesion of renal medullary necrosis — (Use additional code to identify organism, such as E. coli, 041.41-041.49. Code if applicable, any causal condition first)

590.10 Acute pyelonephritis without lesion of renal medullary necrosis — (Use additional code to identify organism, such as E. coli, 041.40-041.49)

590.11 Acute pyelonephritis with lesion of renal medullary necrosis — (Use additional code to identify organism, such as E. coli, 041.40-041.49)

590.3 Pyeloureteritis cystica — (Use additional code to identify organism, such as E. coli, 041.41-041.49)

590.80 Unspecified pyelonephritis — (Use additional code to identify organism, such as E. coli, 041.41-041.49) ▽

590.81 Pyelitis or pyelonephritis in diseases classified elsewhere — (Use additional code to identify organism, such as E. coli, 041.41-041.49. Code first underlying disease: 016.0) ☒

590.9 Unspecified infection of kidney — (Use additional code to identify organism, such as E. coli, 041.41-041.49) ▽

593.81 Vascular disorders of kidney

728.88 Rhabdomyolysis

958.5 Traumatic anuria

996.81 Complications of transplanted kidney — (Use additional code to identify nature of complication: 078.5, 199.2, 238.77, 279.50-279.53)

ICD-9-CM Procedural

39.27 Arteriovenostomy for renal dialysis

39.93 Insertion of vessel-to-vessel cannula

HCPCS Level II Supplies & Services

C1750 Catheter, hemodialysis/peritoneal, long-term

36815

36815 Insertion of cannula for hemodialysis, other purpose (separate procedure); arteriovenous, external revision, or closure

ICD-9-CM Diagnostic

249.40 Secondary diabetes mellitus with renal manifestations, not stated as uncontrolled, or unspecified — (Use additional code to identify manifestation: 581.81, 583.81, 585.1-585.9) (Use additional code to identify any associated insulin use: V58.67)

249.41 Secondary diabetes mellitus with renal manifestations, uncontrolled — (Use additional code to identify manifestation: 581.81, 583.81, 585.1-585.9) (Use additional code to identify any associated insulin use: V58.67)

250.40 Diabetes with renal manifestations, type II or unspecified type, not stated as uncontrolled — (Use additional code to identify manifestation: 581.81, 583.81, 585.1-585.9)

250.41 Diabetes with renal manifestations, type I [juvenile type], not stated as uncontrolled — (Use additional code to identify manifestation: 581.81, 583.81, 585.1-585.9)

250.42 Diabetes with renal manifestations, type II or unspecified type, uncontrolled — (Use additional code to identify manifestation: 581.81, 583.81, 585.1-585.9)

250.43 Diabetes with renal manifestations, type I [juvenile type], uncontrolled — (Use additional code to identify manifestation: 581.81, 583.81, 585.1-585.9)

403.91 Hypertensive chronic kidney disease, unspecified, with chronic kidney disease stage V or end stage renal disease — (Use additional code to identify the stage of chronic kidney disease: 585.5, 585.6) ▽

445.81 Atheroembolism of kidney — (Use additional code for any associated acute kidney failure or chronic kidney disease: 584, 585)

580.4 Acute glomerulonephritis with lesion of rapidly progressive glomerulonephritis

580.9 Acute glomerulonephritis with unspecified pathological lesion in kidney ▽

581.1 Nephrotic syndrome with lesion of membranous glomerulonephritis

581.81 Nephrotic syndrome with other specified pathological lesion in kidney in diseases classified elsewhere — (Code first underlying disease: 084.9, 249.4, 250.4, 277.30-277.39, 446.0, 710.0) ☒

582.0 Chronic glomerulonephritis with lesion of proliferative glomerulonephritis

582.1 Chronic glomerulonephritis with lesion of membranous glomerulonephritis

582.2 Chronic glomerulonephritis with lesion of membranoproliferative glomerulonephritis

582.4 Chronic glomerulonephritis with lesion of rapidly progressive glomerulonephritis
582.81 Chronic glomerulonephritis with other specified pathological lesion in kidney in diseases classified elsewhere — (Code first underlying disease: 277.30-277.39, 710.0) ☒
582.89 Other chronic glomerulonephritis with specified pathological lesion in kidney
582.9 Chronic glomerulonephritis with unspecified pathological lesion in kidney ▽
583.0 Nephritis and nephropathy, not specified as acute or chronic, with lesion of proliferative glomerulonephritis
583.1 Nephritis and nephropathy, not specified as acute or chronic, with lesion of membranous glomerulonephritis
583.2 Nephritis and nephropathy, not specified as acute or chronic, with lesion of membranoproliferative glomerulonephritis
583.4 Nephritis and nephropathy, not specified as acute or chronic, with lesion of rapidly progressive glomerulonephritis
583.6 Nephritis and nephropathy, not specified as acute or chronic, with lesion of renal cortical necrosis
583.7 Nephritis and nephropathy, not specified as acute or chronic, with lesion of renal medullary necrosis
583.81 Nephritis and nephropathy, not specified as acute or chronic, with other specified pathological lesion in kidney, in diseases classified elsewhere — (Code first underlying disease: 016.0, 098.19, 249.4, 250.4, 277.30-277.39, 446.21, 710.0) ☒
583.89 Other nephritis and nephropathy, not specified as acute or chronic, with specified pathological lesion in kidney
583.9 Nephritis and nephropathy, not specified as acute or chronic, with unspecified pathological lesion in kidney ▽
584.5 Acute kidney failure with lesion of tubular necrosis
584.6 Acute kidney failure with lesion of renal cortical necrosis
584.7 Acute kidney failure with lesion of medullary [papillary] necrosis
584.8 Acute kidney failure with other specified pathological lesion in kidney
584.9 Acute kidney failure, unspecified ▽
585.4 Chronic kidney disease, Stage IV (severe) — (Use additional code to identify kidney transplant status, if applicable: V42.0. Use additional code to identify manifestation: 357.4, 420.0. Code first hypertensive chronic kidney disease, if applicable: 403.00-403.91, 404.00-404.93)
585.5 Chronic kidney disease, Stage V — (Use additional code to identify kidney transplant status, if applicable: V42.0. Use additional code to identify manifestation: 357.4, 420.0. Code first hypertensive chronic kidney disease, if applicable: 403.00-403.91, 404.00-404.93)
585.6 End stage renal disease — (Use additional code to identify kidney transplant status, if applicable: V42.0. Use additional code to identify manifestation: 357.4, 420.0. Code first hypertensive chronic kidney disease, if applicable: 403.00-403.91, 404.00-404.93)
585.9 Chronic kidney disease, unspecified — (Use additional code to identify kidney transplant status, if applicable: V42.0. Use additional code to identify manifestation: 357.4, 420.0. Code first hypertensive chronic kidney disease, if applicable: 403.00-403.91, 404.00-404.93) ▽
586 Unspecified renal failure ▽
587 Unspecified renal sclerosis ▽
588.0 Renal osteodystrophy
588.81 Secondary hyperparathyroidism (of renal origin)
588.89 Other specified disorders resulting from impaired renal function
588.9 Unspecified disorder resulting from impaired renal function ▽
590.00 Chronic pyelonephritis without lesion of renal medullary necrosis — (Use additional code to identify organism, such as E. coli, 041.41-041.49. Code if applicable, any causal condition first)
590.01 Chronic pyelonephritis with lesion of renal medullary necrosis — (Use additional code to identify organism, such as E. coli, 041.41-041.49. Code if applicable, any causal condition first)
590.10 Acute pyelonephritis without lesion of renal medullary necrosis — (Use additional code to identify organism, such as E. coli, 041.40-041.49)
590.11 Acute pyelonephritis with lesion of renal medullary necrosis — (Use additional code to identify organism, such as E. coli, 041.40-041.49)
590.3 Pyeloureteritis cystica — (Use additional code to identify organism, such as E. coli, 041.41-041.49)
590.80 Unspecified pyelonephritis — (Use additional code to identify organism, such as E. coli, 041.41-041.49) ▽
590.81 Pyelitis or pyelonephritis in diseases classified elsewhere — (Use additional code to identify organism, such as E. coli, 041.41-041.49. Code first underlying disease: 016.0) ☒
590.9 Unspecified infection of kidney — (Use additional code to identify organism, such as E. coli, 041.41-041.49) ▽
593.81 Vascular disorders of kidney
728.88 Rhabdomyolysis
958.5 Traumatic anuria
996.81 Complications of transplanted kidney — (Use additional code to identify nature of complication: 078.5, 199.2, 238.77, 279.50-279.53)

ICD-9-CM Procedural

39.27 Arteriovenostomy for renal dialysis
39.93 Insertion of vessel-to-vessel cannula

HCPCS Level II Supplies & Services

C1750 Catheter, hemodialysis/peritoneal, long-term

36818-36819

36818 Arteriovenous anastomosis, open; by upper arm cephalic vein transposition
36819 by upper arm basilic vein transposition

ICD-9-CM Diagnostic

249.40 Secondary diabetes mellitus with renal manifestations, not stated as uncontrolled, or unspecified — (Use additional code to identify manifestation: 581.81, 583.81, 585.1-585.9) (Use additional code to identify any associated insulin use: V58.67)
249.41 Secondary diabetes mellitus with renal manifestations, uncontrolled — (Use additional code to identify manifestation: 581.81, 583.81, 585.1-585.9) (Use additional code to identify any associated insulin use: V58.67)
250.40 Diabetes with renal manifestations, type II or unspecified type, not stated as uncontrolled — (Use additional code to identify manifestation: 581.81, 583.81, 585.1-585.9)
250.41 Diabetes with renal manifestations, type I [juvenile type], not stated as uncontrolled — (Use additional code to identify manifestation: 581.81, 583.81, 585.1-585.9)
250.42 Diabetes with renal manifestations, type II or unspecified type, uncontrolled — (Use additional code to identify manifestation: 581.81, 583.81, 585.1-585.9)
250.43 Diabetes with renal manifestations, type I [juvenile type], uncontrolled — (Use additional code to identify manifestation: 581.81, 583.81, 585.1-585.9)
403.91 Hypertensive chronic kidney disease, unspecified, with chronic kidney disease stage V or end stage renal disease — (Use additional code to identify the stage of chronic kidney disease: 585.5, 585.6) ▽
445.81 Atheroembolism of kidney — (Use additional code for any associated acute kidney failure or chronic kidney disease: 584, 585)
580.4 Acute glomerulonephritis with lesion of rapidly progressive glomerulonephritis
580.9 Acute glomerulonephritis with unspecified pathological lesion in kidney ▽
581.1 Nephrotic syndrome with lesion of membranous glomerulonephritis
581.81 Nephrotic syndrome with other specified pathological lesion in kidney in diseases classified elsewhere — (Code first underlying disease: 084.9, 249.4, 250.4, 277.30-277.39, 446.0, 710.0) ☒
582.0 Chronic glomerulonephritis with lesion of proliferative glomerulonephritis
582.1 Chronic glomerulonephritis with lesion of membranous glomerulonephritis
582.2 Chronic glomerulonephritis with lesion of membranoproliferative glomerulonephritis
582.4 Chronic glomerulonephritis with lesion of rapidly progressive glomerulonephritis
582.81 Chronic glomerulonephritis with other specified pathological lesion in kidney in diseases classified elsewhere — (Code first underlying disease: 277.30-277.39, 710.0) ☒
582.89 Other chronic glomerulonephritis with specified pathological lesion in kidney
582.9 Chronic glomerulonephritis with unspecified pathological lesion in kidney ▽

583.0 Nephritis and nephropathy, not specified as acute or chronic, with lesion of proliferative glomerulonephritis
583.1 Nephritis and nephropathy, not specified as acute or chronic, with lesion of membranous glomerulonephritis
583.2 Nephritis and nephropathy, not specified as acute or chronic, with lesion of membranoproliferative glomerulonephritis
583.4 Nephritis and nephropathy, not specified as acute or chronic, with lesion of rapidly progressive glomerulonephritis
583.6 Nephritis and nephropathy, not specified as acute or chronic, with lesion of renal cortical necrosis
583.7 Nephritis and nephropathy, not specified as acute or chronic, with lesion of renal medullary necrosis
583.81 Nephritis and nephropathy, not specified as acute or chronic, with other specified pathological lesion in kidney, in diseases classified elsewhere — (Code first underlying disease: 016.0, 098.19, 249.4, 250.4, 277.30-277.39, 446.21, 710.0) ☒
583.89 Other nephritis and nephropathy, not specified as acute or chronic, with specified pathological lesion in kidney
583.9 Nephritis and nephropathy, not specified as acute or chronic, with unspecified pathological lesion in kidney ▽
584.5 Acute kidney failure with lesion of tubular necrosis
584.6 Acute kidney failure with lesion of renal cortical necrosis
584.7 Acute kidney failure with lesion of medullary [papillary] necrosis
584.8 Acute kidney failure with other specified pathological lesion in kidney
584.9 Acute kidney failure, unspecified ▽
585.4 Chronic kidney disease, Stage IV (severe) — (Use additional code to identify kidney transplant status, if applicable: V42.0. Use additional code to identify manifestation: 357.4, 420.0. Code first hypertensive chronic kidney disease, if applicable: 403.00-403.91, 404.00-404.93)
585.5 Chronic kidney disease, Stage V — (Use additional code to identify kidney transplant status, if applicable: V42.0. Use additional code to identify manifestation: 357.4, 420.0. Code first hypertensive chronic kidney disease, if applicable: 403.00-403.91, 404.00-404.93)
585.6 End stage renal disease — (Use additional code to identify kidney transplant status, if applicable: V42.0. Use additional code to identify manifestation: 357.4, 420.0. Code first hypertensive chronic kidney disease, if applicable: 403.00-403.91, 404.00-404.93)
585.9 Chronic kidney disease, unspecified — (Use additional code to identify kidney transplant status, if applicable: V42.0. Use additional code to identify manifestation: 357.4, 420.0. Code first hypertensive chronic kidney disease, if applicable: 403.00-403.91, 404.00-404.93) ▽
586 Unspecified renal failure ▽
587 Unspecified renal sclerosis ▽
588.0 Renal osteodystrophy
588.81 Secondary hyperparathyroidism (of renal origin)
588.89 Other specified disorders resulting from impaired renal function
588.9 Unspecified disorder resulting from impaired renal function ▽
590.00 Chronic pyelonephritis without lesion of renal medullary necrosis — (Use additional code to identify organism, such as E. coli, 041.41-041.49. Code if applicable, any causal condition first)
590.01 Chronic pyelonephritis with lesion of renal medullary necrosis — (Use additional code to identify organism, such as E. coli, 041.41-041.49. Code if applicable, any causal condition first)
590.10 Acute pyelonephritis without lesion of renal medullary necrosis — (Use additional code to identify organism, such as E. coli, 041.40-041.49)
590.11 Acute pyelonephritis with lesion of renal medullary necrosis — (Use additional code to identify organism, such as E. coli, 041.40-041.49)
590.3 Pyeloureteritis cystica — (Use additional code to identify organism, such as E. coli, 041.41-041.49)
590.80 Unspecified pyelonephritis — (Use additional code to identify organism, such as E. coli, 041.41-041.49) ▽
590.81 Pyelitis or pyelonephritis in diseases classified elsewhere — (Use additional code to identify organism, such as E. coli, 041.41-041.49. Code first underlying disease: 016.0) ☒
590.9 Unspecified infection of kidney — (Use additional code to identify organism, such as E. coli, 041.41-041.49) ▽
593.81 Vascular disorders of kidney
728.88 Rhabdomyolysis
958.5 Traumatic anuria
996.81 Complications of transplanted kidney — (Use additional code to identify nature of complication: 078.5, 199.2, 238.77, 279.50-279.53)

ICD-9-CM Procedural

39.27 Arteriovenostomy for renal dialysis

36820

36820 Arteriovenous anastomosis, open; by forearm vein transposition

ICD-9-CM Diagnostic

249.40 Secondary diabetes mellitus with renal manifestations, not stated as uncontrolled, or unspecified — (Use additional code to identify manifestation: 581.81, 583.81, 585.1-585.9) (Use additional code to identify any associated insulin use: V58.67)
249.41 Secondary diabetes mellitus with renal manifestations, uncontrolled — (Use additional code to identify manifestation: 581.81, 583.81, 585.1-585.9) (Use additional code to identify any associated insulin use: V58.67)
250.40 Diabetes with renal manifestations, type II or unspecified type, not stated as uncontrolled — (Use additional code to identify manifestation: 581.81, 583.81, 585.1-585.9)
250.41 Diabetes with renal manifestations, type I [juvenile type], not stated as uncontrolled — (Use additional code to identify manifestation: 581.81, 583.81, 585.1-585.9)
250.42 Diabetes with renal manifestations, type II or unspecified type, uncontrolled — (Use additional code to identify manifestation: 581.81, 583.81, 585.1-585.9)
250.43 Diabetes with renal manifestations, type I [juvenile type], uncontrolled — (Use additional code to identify manifestation: 581.81, 583.81, 585.1-585.9)
403.91 Hypertensive chronic kidney disease, unspecified, with chronic kidney disease stage V or end stage renal disease — (Use additional code to identify the stage of chronic kidney disease: 585.5, 585.6) ▽
445.81 Atheroembolism of kidney — (Use additional code for any associated acute kidney failure or chronic kidney disease: 584, 585)
580.4 Acute glomerulonephritis with lesion of rapidly progressive glomerulonephritis
580.9 Acute glomerulonephritis with unspecified pathological lesion in kidney ▽
581.1 Nephrotic syndrome with lesion of membranous glomerulonephritis
581.81 Nephrotic syndrome with other specified pathological lesion in kidney in diseases classified elsewhere — (Code first underlying disease: 084.9, 249.4, 250.4, 277.30-277.39, 446.0, 710.0) ☒
582.0 Chronic glomerulonephritis with lesion of proliferative glomerulonephritis
582.1 Chronic glomerulonephritis with lesion of membranous glomerulonephritis
582.2 Chronic glomerulonephritis with lesion of membranoproliferative glomerulonephritis
582.4 Chronic glomerulonephritis with lesion of rapidly progressive glomerulonephritis
582.81 Chronic glomerulonephritis with other specified pathological lesion in kidney in diseases classified elsewhere — (Code first underlying disease: 277.30-277.39, 710.0) ☒
582.89 Other chronic glomerulonephritis with specified pathological lesion in kidney
582.9 Chronic glomerulonephritis with unspecified pathological lesion in kidney ▽
583.0 Nephritis and nephropathy, not specified as acute or chronic, with lesion of proliferative glomerulonephritis
583.1 Nephritis and nephropathy, not specified as acute or chronic, with lesion of membranous glomerulonephritis
583.2 Nephritis and nephropathy, not specified as acute or chronic, with lesion of membranoproliferative glomerulonephritis
583.4 Nephritis and nephropathy, not specified as acute or chronic, with lesion of rapidly progressive glomerulonephritis

583.6 Nephritis and nephropathy, not specified as acute or chronic, with lesion of renal cortical necrosis

583.7 Nephritis and nephropathy, not specified as acute or chronic, with lesion of renal medullary necrosis

583.81 Nephritis and nephropathy, not specified as acute or chronic, with other specified pathological lesion in kidney, in diseases classified elsewhere — (Code first underlying disease: 016.0, 098.19, 249.4, 250.4, 277.30-277.39, 446.21, 710.0) ☒

583.89 Other nephritis and nephropathy, not specified as acute or chronic, with specified pathological lesion in kidney

583.9 Nephritis and nephropathy, not specified as acute or chronic, with unspecified pathological lesion in kidney ▽

584.5 Acute kidney failure with lesion of tubular necrosis

584.6 Acute kidney failure with lesion of renal cortical necrosis

584.7 Acute kidney failure with lesion of medullary [papillary] necrosis

584.8 Acute kidney failure with other specified pathological lesion in kidney

584.9 Acute kidney failure, unspecified ▽

585.4 Chronic kidney disease, Stage IV (severe) — (Use additional code to identify kidney transplant status, if applicable: V42.0. Use additional code to identify manifestation: 357.4, 420.0. Code first hypertensive chronic kidney disease, if applicable: 403.00-403.91, 404.00-404.93)

585.5 Chronic kidney disease, Stage V — (Use additional code to identify kidney transplant status, if applicable: V42.0. Use additional code to identify manifestation: 357.4, 420.0. Code first hypertensive chronic kidney disease, if applicable: 403.00-403.91, 404.00-404.93)

585.6 End stage renal disease — (Use additional code to identify kidney transplant status, if applicable: V42.0. Use additional code to identify manifestation: 357.4, 420.0. Code first hypertensive chronic kidney disease, if applicable: 403.00-403.91, 404.00-404.93)

585.9 Chronic kidney disease, unspecified — (Use additional code to identify kidney transplant status, if applicable: V42.0. Use additional code to identify manifestation: 357.4, 420.0. Code first hypertensive chronic kidney disease, if applicable: 403.00-403.91, 404.00-404.93) ▽

586 Unspecified renal failure ▽

587 Unspecified renal sclerosis ▽

588.0 Renal osteodystrophy

588.81 Secondary hyperparathyroidism (of renal origin)

588.89 Other specified disorders resulting from impaired renal function

588.9 Unspecified disorder resulting from impaired renal function ▽

590.00 Chronic pyelonephritis without lesion of renal medullary necrosis — (Use additional code to identify organism, such as E. coli, 041.41-041.49. Code if applicable, any causal condition first)

590.01 Chronic pyelonephritis with lesion of renal medullary necrosis — (Use additional code to identify organism, such as E. coli, 041.41-041.49. Code if applicable, any causal condition first)

590.10 Acute pyelonephritis without lesion of renal medullary necrosis — (Use additional code to identify organism, such as E. coli, 041.40-041.49)

590.11 Acute pyelonephritis with lesion of renal medullary necrosis — (Use additional code to identify organism, such as E. coli, 041.40-041.49)

590.3 Pyeloureteritis cystica — (Use additional code to identify organism, such as E. coli, 041.41-041.49)

590.80 Unspecified pyelonephritis — (Use additional code to identify organism, such as E. coli, 041.41-041.49) ▽

590.81 Pyelitis or pyelonephritis in diseases classified elsewhere — (Use additional code to identify organism, such as E. coli, 041.41-041.49. Code first underlying disease: 016.0) ☒

590.9 Unspecified infection of kidney — (Use additional code to identify organism, such as E. coli, 041.41-041.49) ▽

593.81 Vascular disorders of kidney

728.88 Rhabdomyolysis

958.5 Traumatic anuria

996.81 Complications of transplanted kidney — (Use additional code to identify nature of complication: 078.5, 199.2, 238.77, 279.50-279.53)

ICD-9-CM Procedural

39.27 Arteriovenostomy for renal dialysis

36821

36821 Arteriovenous anastomosis, open; direct, any site (eg, Cimino type) (separate procedure)

ICD-9-CM Diagnostic

249.40 Secondary diabetes mellitus with renal manifestations, not stated as uncontrolled, or unspecified — (Use additional code to identify manifestation: 581.81, 583.81, 585.1-585.9) (Use additional code to identify any associated insulin use: V58.67)

249.41 Secondary diabetes mellitus with renal manifestations, uncontrolled — (Use additional code to identify manifestation: 581.81, 583.81, 585.1-585.9) (Use additional code to identify any associated insulin use: V58.67)

250.40 Diabetes with renal manifestations, type II or unspecified type, not stated as uncontrolled — (Use additional code to identify manifestation: 581.81, 583.81, 585.1-585.9)

250.41 Diabetes with renal manifestations, type I [juvenile type], not stated as uncontrolled — (Use additional code to identify manifestation: 581.81, 583.81, 585.1-585.9)

250.42 Diabetes with renal manifestations, type II or unspecified type, uncontrolled — (Use additional code to identify manifestation: 581.81, 583.81, 585.1-585.9)

250.43 Diabetes with renal manifestations, type I [juvenile type], uncontrolled — (Use additional code to identify manifestation: 581.81, 583.81, 585.1-585.9)

403.91 Hypertensive chronic kidney disease, unspecified, with chronic kidney disease stage V or end stage renal disease — (Use additional code to identify the stage of chronic kidney disease: 585.5, 585.6) ▽

445.81 Atheroembolism of kidney — (Use additional code for any associated acute kidney failure or chronic kidney disease: 584, 585)

580.4 Acute glomerulonephritis with lesion of rapidly progressive glomerulonephritis

580.9 Acute glomerulonephritis with unspecified pathological lesion in kidney ▽

581.1 Nephrotic syndrome with lesion of membranous glomerulonephritis

581.81 Nephrotic syndrome with other specified pathological lesion in kidney in diseases classified elsewhere — (Code first underlying disease: 084.9, 249.4, 250.4, 277.30-277.39, 446.0, 710.0) ☒

582.0 Chronic glomerulonephritis with lesion of proliferative glomerulonephritis

582.1 Chronic glomerulonephritis with lesion of membranous glomerulonephritis

582.2 Chronic glomerulonephritis with lesion of membranoproliferative glomerulonephritis

582.4 Chronic glomerulonephritis with lesion of rapidly progressive glomerulonephritis

582.81 Chronic glomerulonephritis with other specified pathological lesion in kidney in diseases classified elsewhere — (Code first underlying disease: 277.30-277.39, 710.0) ☒

582.89 Other chronic glomerulonephritis with specified pathological lesion in kidney

582.9 Chronic glomerulonephritis with unspecified pathological lesion in kidney ▽

583.0 Nephritis and nephropathy, not specified as acute or chronic, with lesion of proliferative glomerulonephritis

583.1 Nephritis and nephropathy, not specified as acute or chronic, with lesion of membranous glomerulonephritis

583.2 Nephritis and nephropathy, not specified as acute or chronic, with lesion of membranoproliferative glomerulonephritis

583.4 Nephritis and nephropathy, not specified as acute or chronic, with lesion of rapidly progressive glomerulonephritis

583.6 Nephritis and nephropathy, not specified as acute or chronic, with lesion of renal cortical necrosis

583.7 Nephritis and nephropathy, not specified as acute or chronic, with lesion of renal medullary necrosis

583.81 Nephritis and nephropathy, not specified as acute or chronic, with other specified pathological lesion in kidney, in diseases classified elsewhere — (Code first underlying disease: 016.0, 098.19, 249.4, 250.4, 277.30-277.39, 446.21, 710.0) ☒

583.89 Other nephritis and nephropathy, not specified as acute or chronic, with specified pathological lesion in kidney

583.9 Nephritis and nephropathy, not specified as acute or chronic, with unspecified pathological lesion in kidney ▽
584.5 Acute kidney failure with lesion of tubular necrosis
584.6 Acute kidney failure with lesion of renal cortical necrosis
584.7 Acute kidney failure with lesion of medullary [papillary] necrosis
584.8 Acute kidney failure with other specified pathological lesion in kidney
584.9 Acute kidney failure, unspecified ▽
585.4 Chronic kidney disease, Stage IV (severe) — (Use additional code to identify kidney transplant status, if applicable: V42.0. Use additional code to identify manifestation: 357.4, 420.0. Code first hypertensive chronic kidney disease, if applicable: 403.00-403.91, 404.00-404.93)
585.5 Chronic kidney disease, Stage V — (Use additional code to identify kidney transplant status, if applicable: V42.0. Use additional code to identify manifestation: 357.4, 420.0. Code first hypertensive chronic kidney disease, if applicable: 403.00-403.91, 404.00-404.93)
585.6 End stage renal disease — (Use additional code to identify kidney transplant status, if applicable: V42.0. Use additional code to identify manifestation: 357.4, 420.0. Code first hypertensive chronic kidney disease, if applicable: 403.00-403.91, 404.00-404.93)
585.9 Chronic kidney disease, unspecified — (Use additional code to identify kidney transplant status, if applicable: V42.0. Use additional code to identify manifestation: 357.4, 420.0. Code first hypertensive chronic kidney disease, if applicable: 403.00-403.91, 404.00-404.93) ▽
586 Unspecified renal failure ▽
587 Unspecified renal sclerosis ▽
588.0 Renal osteodystrophy
588.81 Secondary hyperparathyroidism (of renal origin)
588.89 Other specified disorders resulting from impaired renal function
588.9 Unspecified disorder resulting from impaired renal function ▽
590.00 Chronic pyelonephritis without lesion of renal medullary necrosis — (Use additional code to identify organism, such as E. coli, 041.41-041.49. Code if applicable, any causal condition first)
590.01 Chronic pyelonephritis with lesion of renal medullary necrosis — (Use additional code to identify organism, such as E. coli, 041.41-041.49. Code if applicable, any causal condition first)
590.10 Acute pyelonephritis without lesion of renal medullary necrosis — (Use additional code to identify organism, such as E. coli, 041.40-041.49)
590.11 Acute pyelonephritis with lesion of renal medullary necrosis — (Use additional code to identify organism, such as E. coli, 041.40-041.49)
590.3 Pyeloureteritis cystica — (Use additional code to identify organism, such as E. coli, 041.41-041.49)
590.80 Unspecified pyelonephritis — (Use additional code to identify organism, such as E. coli, 041.41-041.49) ▽
590.81 Pyelitis or pyelonephritis in diseases classified elsewhere — (Use additional code to identify organism, such as E. coli, 041.41-041.49. Code first underlying disease: 016.0) ☒
590.9 Unspecified infection of kidney — (Use additional code to identify organism, such as E. coli, 041.41-041.49) ▽
593.81 Vascular disorders of kidney
728.88 Rhabdomyolysis
958.5 Traumatic anuria
996.81 Complications of transplanted kidney — (Use additional code to identify nature of complication: 078.5, 199.2, 238.77, 279.50-279.53)

ICD-9-CM Procedural

39.27 Arteriovenostomy for renal dialysis

36822

36822 Insertion of cannula(s) for prolonged extracorporeal circulation for cardiopulmonary insufficiency (ECMO) (separate procedure)

ICD-9-CM Diagnostic

428.0 Congestive heart failure, unspecified — (Code, if applicable, heart failure due to hypertension first: 402.0-402.9, with fifth-digit 1 or 404.0-404.9 with fifth digit 1 or 3) ▽
428.20 Unspecified systolic heart failure — (Code, if applicable, heart failure due to hypertension first: 402.0-402.9, with fifth-digit 1 or 404.0-404.9 with fifth digit 1 or 3) ▽
428.21 Acute systolic heart failure — (Code, if applicable, heart failure due to hypertension first: 402.0-402.9, with fifth-digit 1 or 404.0-404.9 with fifth digit 1 or 3)
428.22 Chronic systolic heart failure — (Code, if applicable, heart failure due to hypertension first: 402.0-402.9, with fifth-digit 1 or 404.0-404.9 with fifth digit 1 or 3)
428.23 Acute on chronic systolic heart failure — (Code, if applicable, heart failure due to hypertension first: 402.0-402.9, with fifth-digit 1 or 404.0-404.9 with fifth digit 1 or 3)
428.30 Unspecified diastolic heart failure — (Code, if applicable, heart failure due to hypertension first: 402.0-402.9, with fifth-digit 1 or 404.0-404.9 with fifth digit 1 or 3) ▽
428.31 Acute diastolic heart failure — (Code, if applicable, heart failure due to hypertension first: 402.0-402.9, with fifth-digit 1 or 404.0-404.9 with fifth digit 1 or 3)
428.32 Chronic diastolic heart failure — (Code, if applicable, heart failure due to hypertension first: 402.0-402.9, with fifth-digit 1 or 404.0-404.9 with fifth digit 1 or 3)
428.33 Acute on chronic diastolic heart failure — (Code, if applicable, heart failure due to hypertension first: 402.0-402.9, with fifth-digit 1 or 404.0-404.9 with fifth digit 1 or 3)
428.40 Unspecified combined systolic and diastolic heart failure — (Code, if applicable, heart failure due to hypertension first: 402.0-402.9, with fifth-digit 1 or 404.0-404.9 with fifth digit 1 or 3) ▽
428.41 Acute combined systolic and diastolic heart failure — (Code, if applicable, heart failure due to hypertension first: 402.0-402.9, with fifth-digit 1 or 404.0-404.9 with fifth digit 1 or 3)
428.42 Chronic combined systolic and diastolic heart failure — (Code, if applicable, heart failure due to hypertension first: 402.0-402.9, with fifth-digit 1 or 404.0-404.9 with fifth digit 1 or 3)
428.43 Acute on chronic combined systolic and diastolic heart failure — (Code, if applicable, heart failure due to hypertension first: 402.0-402.9, with fifth-digit 1 or 404.0-404.9 with fifth digit 1 or 3)
429.2 Unspecified cardiovascular disease — (Use additional code to identify presence of arteriosclerosis) ▽
429.4 Functional disturbances following cardiac surgery
516.64 Alveolar capillary dysplasia with vein misalignment
518.51 Acute respiratory failure following trauma and surgery
518.52 Other pulmonary insufficiency, not elsewhere classified, following trauma and surgery
518.53 Acute and chronic respiratory failure following trauma and surgery
518.81 Acute respiratory failure
518.82 Other pulmonary insufficiency, not elsewhere classified
746.09 Other congenital anomalies of pulmonary valve
746.89 Other specified congenital anomaly of heart
769 Respiratory distress syndrome in newborn — (Use additional code(s) to further specify condition)
770.84 Respiratory failure of newborn — (Use additional code(s) to further specify condition)
770.89 Other respiratory problems of newborn after birth — (Use additional code(s) to further specify condition)
997.1 Cardiac complications — (Use additional code to identify complications)

ICD-9-CM Procedural

39.65 Extracorporeal membrane oxygenation (ECMO)

36823

36823 Insertion of arterial and venous cannula(s) for isolated extracorporeal circulation including regional chemotherapy perfusion to an extremity, with or without hyperthermia, with removal of cannula(s) and repair of arteriotomy and venotomy sites

ICD-9-CM Diagnostic

170.4 Malignant neoplasm of scapula and long bones of upper limb
170.5 Malignant neoplasm of short bones of upper limb
170.7 Malignant neoplasm of long bones of lower limb
170.8 Malignant neoplasm of short bones of lower limb
171.2 Malignant neoplasm of connective and other soft tissue of upper limb, including shoulder
171.3 Malignant neoplasm of connective and other soft tissue of lower limb, including hip
238.0 Neoplasm of uncertain behavior of bone and articular cartilage
238.1 Neoplasm of uncertain behavior of connective and other soft tissue

ICD-9-CM Procedural

38.91 Arterial catheterization
38.93 Venous catheterization, not elsewhere classified
99.25 Injection or infusion of cancer chemotherapeutic substance

36825-36830

36825 Creation of arteriovenous fistula by other than direct arteriovenous anastomosis (separate procedure); autogenous graft
36830 nonautogenous graft (eg, biological collagen, thermoplastic graft)

ICD-9-CM Diagnostic

249.40 Secondary diabetes mellitus with renal manifestations, not stated as uncontrolled, or unspecified — (Use additional code to identify manifestation: 581.81, 583.81, 585.1-585.9) (Use additional code to identify any associated insulin use: V58.67)
249.41 Secondary diabetes mellitus with renal manifestations, uncontrolled — (Use additional code to identify manifestation: 581.81, 583.81, 585.1-585.9) (Use additional code to identify any associated insulin use: V58.67)
250.40 Diabetes with renal manifestations, type II or unspecified type, not stated as uncontrolled — (Use additional code to identify manifestation: 581.81, 583.81, 585.1-585.9)
250.41 Diabetes with renal manifestations, type I [juvenile type], not stated as uncontrolled — (Use additional code to identify manifestation: 581.81, 583.81, 585.1-585.9)
250.42 Diabetes with renal manifestations, type II or unspecified type, uncontrolled — (Use additional code to identify manifestation: 581.81, 583.81, 585.1-585.9)
250.43 Diabetes with renal manifestations, type I [juvenile type], uncontrolled — (Use additional code to identify manifestation: 581.81, 583.81, 585.1-585.9)
403.01 Hypertensive chronic kidney disease, malignant, with chronic kidney disease stage V or end stage renal disease — (Use additional code to identify the stage of chronic kidney disease: 585.5, 585.6)
403.91 Hypertensive chronic kidney disease, unspecified, with chronic kidney disease stage V or end stage renal disease — (Use additional code to identify the stage of chronic kidney disease: 585.5, 585.6) ▽
404.02 Hypertensive heart and chronic kidney disease, malignant, without heart failure and with chronic kidney disease stage V or end stage renal disease — (Use additional code to identify the stage of chronic kidney disease: 585.5, 585.6)
404.03 Hypertensive heart and chronic kidney disease, malignant, with heart failure and with chronic kidney disease stage V or end stage renal disease — (Use additional code to specify type of heart failure, 428.0-428.43, if known. Use additional code to identify the stage of chronic kidney disease: 585.5-585.6)
405.01 Secondary renovascular hypertension, malignant
581.1 Nephrotic syndrome with lesion of membranous glomerulonephritis
581.81 Nephrotic syndrome with other specified pathological lesion in kidney in diseases classified elsewhere — (Code first underlying disease: 084.9, 249.4, 250.4, 277.30-277.39, 446.0, 710.0) ☒
582.0 Chronic glomerulonephritis with lesion of proliferative glomerulonephritis
582.1 Chronic glomerulonephritis with lesion of membranous glomerulonephritis
582.2 Chronic glomerulonephritis with lesion of membranoproliferative glomerulonephritis
582.4 Chronic glomerulonephritis with lesion of rapidly progressive glomerulonephritis
582.81 Chronic glomerulonephritis with other specified pathological lesion in kidney in diseases classified elsewhere — (Code first underlying disease: 277.30-277.39, 710.0) ☒
582.89 Other chronic glomerulonephritis with specified pathological lesion in kidney
582.9 Chronic glomerulonephritis with unspecified pathological lesion in kidney ▽
583.0 Nephritis and nephropathy, not specified as acute or chronic, with lesion of proliferative glomerulonephritis
583.1 Nephritis and nephropathy, not specified as acute or chronic, with lesion of membranous glomerulonephritis
583.2 Nephritis and nephropathy, not specified as acute or chronic, with lesion of membranoproliferative glomerulonephritis
583.4 Nephritis and nephropathy, not specified as acute or chronic, with lesion of rapidly progressive glomerulonephritis
583.6 Nephritis and nephropathy, not specified as acute or chronic, with lesion of renal cortical necrosis
583.7 Nephritis and nephropathy, not specified as acute or chronic, with lesion of renal medullary necrosis
583.81 Nephritis and nephropathy, not specified as acute or chronic, with other specified pathological lesion in kidney, in diseases classified elsewhere — (Code first underlying disease: 016.0, 098.19, 249.4, 250.4, 277.30-277.39, 446.21, 710.0) ☒
583.89 Other nephritis and nephropathy, not specified as acute or chronic, with specified pathological lesion in kidney
583.9 Nephritis and nephropathy, not specified as acute or chronic, with unspecified pathological lesion in kidney ▽
585.4 Chronic kidney disease, Stage IV (severe) — (Use additional code to identify kidney transplant status, if applicable: V42.0. Use additional code to identify manifestation: 357.4, 420.0. Code first hypertensive chronic kidney disease, if applicable: 403.00-403.91, 404.00-404.93)
585.5 Chronic kidney disease, Stage V — (Use additional code to identify kidney transplant status, if applicable: V42.0. Use additional code to identify manifestation: 357.4, 420.0. Code first hypertensive chronic kidney disease, if applicable: 403.00-403.91, 404.00-404.93)
585.6 End stage renal disease — (Use additional code to identify kidney transplant status, if applicable: V42.0. Use additional code to identify manifestation: 357.4, 420.0. Code first hypertensive chronic kidney disease, if applicable: 403.00-403.91, 404.00-404.93)
585.9 Chronic kidney disease, unspecified — (Use additional code to identify kidney transplant status, if applicable: V42.0. Use additional code to identify manifestation: 357.4, 420.0. Code first hypertensive chronic kidney disease, if applicable: 403.00-403.91, 404.00-404.93) ▽
586 Unspecified renal failure ▽
587 Unspecified renal sclerosis ▽
588.0 Renal osteodystrophy
588.81 Secondary hyperparathyroidism (of renal origin)
588.89 Other specified disorders resulting from impaired renal function
588.9 Unspecified disorder resulting from impaired renal function ▽
590.00 Chronic pyelonephritis without lesion of renal medullary necrosis — (Use additional code to identify organism, such as E. coli, 041.41-041.49. Code if applicable, any causal condition first)
590.01 Chronic pyelonephritis with lesion of renal medullary necrosis — (Use additional code to identify organism, such as E. coli, 041.41-041.49. Code if applicable, any causal condition first)
590.3 Pyeloureteritis cystica — (Use additional code to identify organism, such as E. coli, 041.41-041.49)
590.80 Unspecified pyelonephritis — (Use additional code to identify organism, such as E. coli, 041.41-041.49) ▽
590.81 Pyelitis or pyelonephritis in diseases classified elsewhere — (Use additional code to identify organism, such as E. coli, 041.41-041.49. Code first underlying disease: 016.0) ☒

590.9 Unspecified infection of kidney — (Use additional code to identify organism, such as E. coli, 041.41-041.49) ♈

591 Hydronephrosis

593.81 Vascular disorders of kidney

958.5 Traumatic anuria

996.1 Mechanical complication of other vascular device, implant, and graft

996.73 Other complications due to renal dialysis device, implant, and graft — (Use additional code to identify complication: 338.18-338.19, 338.28-338.29)

996.81 Complications of transplanted kidney — (Use additional code to identify nature of complication: 078.5, 199.2, 238.77, 279.50-279.53)

V42.0 Kidney replaced by transplant

ICD-9-CM Procedural

39.27 Arteriovenostomy for renal dialysis

HCPCS Level II Supplies & Services

G0365 Vessel mapping of vessels for hemodialysis access (services for preoperative vessel mapping prior to creation of hemodialysis access using an autogenous hemodialysis conduit, including arterial inflow and venous outflow)

36831

36831 Thrombectomy, open, arteriovenous fistula without revision, autogenous or nonautogenous dialysis graft (separate procedure)

ICD-9-CM Diagnostic

403.91 Hypertensive chronic kidney disease, unspecified, with chronic kidney disease stage V or end stage renal disease — (Use additional code to identify the stage of chronic kidney disease: 585.5, 585.6) ♈

585.4 Chronic kidney disease, Stage IV (severe) — (Use additional code to identify kidney transplant status, if applicable: V42.0. Use additional code to identify manifestation: 357.4, 420.0. Code first hypertensive chronic kidney disease, if applicable: 403.00-403.91, 404.00-404.93)

585.5 Chronic kidney disease, Stage V — (Use additional code to identify kidney transplant status, if applicable: V42.0. Use additional code to identify manifestation: 357.4, 420.0. Code first hypertensive chronic kidney disease, if applicable: 403.00-403.91, 404.00-404.93)

585.6 End stage renal disease — (Use additional code to identify kidney transplant status, if applicable: V42.0. Use additional code to identify manifestation: 357.4, 420.0. Code first hypertensive chronic kidney disease, if applicable: 403.00-403.91, 404.00-404.93)

585.9 Chronic kidney disease, unspecified — (Use additional code to identify kidney transplant status, if applicable: V42.0. Use additional code to identify manifestation: 357.4, 420.0. Code first hypertensive chronic kidney disease, if applicable: 403.00-403.91, 404.00-404.93) ♈

586 Unspecified renal failure ♈

996.73 Other complications due to renal dialysis device, implant, and graft — (Use additional code to identify complication: 338.18-338.19, 338.28-338.29)

V45.11 Renal dialysis status

V45.12 Noncompliance with renal dialysis

ICD-9-CM Procedural

39.49 Other revision of vascular procedure

HCPCS Level II Supplies & Services

G0365 Vessel mapping of vessels for hemodialysis access (services for preoperative vessel mapping prior to creation of hemodialysis access using an autogenous hemodialysis conduit, including arterial inflow and venous outflow)

36832-36833

36832 Revision, open, arteriovenous fistula; without thrombectomy, autogenous or nonautogenous dialysis graft (separate procedure)

36833 with thrombectomy, autogenous or nonautogenous dialysis graft (separate procedure)

ICD-9-CM Diagnostic

403.91 Hypertensive chronic kidney disease, unspecified, with chronic kidney disease stage V or end stage renal disease — (Use additional code to identify the stage of chronic kidney disease: 585.5, 585.6) ♈

585.4 Chronic kidney disease, Stage IV (severe) — (Use additional code to identify kidney transplant status, if applicable: V42.0. Use additional code to identify manifestation: 357.4, 420.0. Code first hypertensive chronic kidney disease, if applicable: 403.00-403.91, 404.00-404.93)

585.5 Chronic kidney disease, Stage V — (Use additional code to identify kidney transplant status, if applicable: V42.0. Use additional code to identify manifestation: 357.4, 420.0. Code first hypertensive chronic kidney disease, if applicable: 403.00-403.91, 404.00-404.93)

585.6 End stage renal disease — (Use additional code to identify kidney transplant status, if applicable: V42.0. Use additional code to identify manifestation: 357.4, 420.0. Code first hypertensive chronic kidney disease, if applicable: 403.00-403.91, 404.00-404.93)

585.9 Chronic kidney disease, unspecified — (Use additional code to identify kidney transplant status, if applicable: V42.0. Use additional code to identify manifestation: 357.4, 420.0. Code first hypertensive chronic kidney disease, if applicable: 403.00-403.91, 404.00-404.93) ♈

586 Unspecified renal failure ♈

996.1 Mechanical complication of other vascular device, implant, and graft

996.62 Infection and inflammatory reaction due to other vascular device, implant, and graft — (Use additional code to identify specified infections)

996.73 Other complications due to renal dialysis device, implant, and graft — (Use additional code to identify complication: 338.18-338.19, 338.28-338.29)

996.74 Other complications due to other vascular device, implant, and graft — (Use additional code to identify complication: 338.18-338.19, 338.28-338.29)

996.81 Complications of transplanted kidney — (Use additional code to identify nature of complication: 078.5, 199.2, 238.77, 279.50-279.53)

V42.0 Kidney replaced by transplant

V45.11 Renal dialysis status

V45.12 Noncompliance with renal dialysis

V53.90 Fitting and adjustment of other and unspecified device, Unspecified device ♈

V53.99 Fitting and adjustment, Other device

ICD-9-CM Procedural

39.42 Revision of arteriovenous shunt for renal dialysis

39.49 Other revision of vascular procedure

39.94 Replacement of vessel-to-vessel cannula

HCPCS Level II Supplies & Services

G0365 Vessel mapping of vessels for hemodialysis access (services for preoperative vessel mapping prior to creation of hemodialysis access using an autogenous hemodialysis conduit, including arterial inflow and venous outflow)

36835

36835 Insertion of Thomas shunt (separate procedure)

ICD-9-CM Diagnostic

249.40 Secondary diabetes mellitus with renal manifestations, not stated as uncontrolled, or unspecified — (Use additional code to identify manifestation: 581.81, 583.81, 585.1-585.9) (Use additional code to identify any associated insulin use: V58.67)

249.41 Secondary diabetes mellitus with renal manifestations, uncontrolled — (Use additional code to identify manifestation: 581.81, 583.81, 585.1-585.9) (Use additional code to identify any associated insulin use: V58.67)

250.40 Diabetes with renal manifestations, type II or unspecified type, not stated as uncontrolled — (Use additional code to identify manifestation: 581.81, 583.81, 585.1-585.9)

250.41 Diabetes with renal manifestations, type I [juvenile type], not stated as uncontrolled — (Use additional code to identify manifestation: 581.81, 583.81, 585.1-585.9)

250.42 Diabetes with renal manifestations, type II or unspecified type, uncontrolled — (Use additional code to identify manifestation: 581.81, 583.81, 585.1-585.9)

250.43 Diabetes with renal manifestations, type I [juvenile type], uncontrolled — (Use additional code to identify manifestation: 581.81, 583.81, 585.1-585.9)

403.01 Hypertensive chronic kidney disease, malignant, with chronic kidney disease stage V or end stage renal disease — (Use additional code to identify the stage of chronic kidney disease: 585.5, 585.6)

403.91 Hypertensive chronic kidney disease, unspecified, with chronic kidney disease stage V or end stage renal disease — (Use additional code to identify the stage of chronic kidney disease: 585.5, 585.6) ▽

404.02 Hypertensive heart and chronic kidney disease, malignant, without heart failure and with chronic kidney disease stage V or end stage renal disease — (Use additional code to identify the stage of chronic kidney disease: 585.5, 585.6)

404.03 Hypertensive heart and chronic kidney disease, malignant, with heart failure and with chronic kidney disease stage V or end stage renal disease — (Use additional code to specify type of heart failure, 428.0-428.43, if known. Use additional code to identify the stage of chronic kidney disease: 585.5-585.6)

405.01 Secondary renovascular hypertension, malignant

581.1 Nephrotic syndrome with lesion of membranous glomerulonephritis

581.81 Nephrotic syndrome with other specified pathological lesion in kidney in diseases classified elsewhere — (Code first underlying disease: 084.9, 249.4, 250.4, 277.30-277.39, 446.0, 710.0) ☒

582.0 Chronic glomerulonephritis with lesion of proliferative glomerulonephritis

582.1 Chronic glomerulonephritis with lesion of membranous glomerulonephritis

582.2 Chronic glomerulonephritis with lesion of membranoproliferative glomerulonephritis

582.4 Chronic glomerulonephritis with lesion of rapidly progressive glomerulonephritis

582.81 Chronic glomerulonephritis with other specified pathological lesion in kidney in diseases classified elsewhere — (Code first underlying disease: 277.30-277.39, 710.0) ☒

582.89 Other chronic glomerulonephritis with specified pathological lesion in kidney

582.9 Chronic glomerulonephritis with unspecified pathological lesion in kidney ▽

583.0 Nephritis and nephropathy, not specified as acute or chronic, with lesion of proliferative glomerulonephritis

583.1 Nephritis and nephropathy, not specified as acute or chronic, with lesion of membranous glomerulonephritis

583.2 Nephritis and nephropathy, not specified as acute or chronic, with lesion of membranoproliferative glomerulonephritis

583.4 Nephritis and nephropathy, not specified as acute or chronic, with lesion of rapidly progressive glomerulonephritis

583.6 Nephritis and nephropathy, not specified as acute or chronic, with lesion of renal cortical necrosis

583.7 Nephritis and nephropathy, not specified as acute or chronic, with lesion of renal medullary necrosis

583.81 Nephritis and nephropathy, not specified as acute or chronic, with other specified pathological lesion in kidney, in diseases classified elsewhere — (Code first underlying disease: 016.0, 098.19, 249.4, 250.4, 277.30-277.39, 446.21, 710.0) ☒

583.89 Other nephritis and nephropathy, not specified as acute or chronic, with specified pathological lesion in kidney

583.9 Nephritis and nephropathy, not specified as acute or chronic, with unspecified pathological lesion in kidney ▽

585.4 Chronic kidney disease, Stage IV (severe) — (Use additional code to identify kidney transplant status, if applicable: V42.0. Use additional code to identify manifestation: 357.4, 420.0. Code first hypertensive chronic kidney disease, if applicable: 403.00-403.91, 404.00-404.93)

585.5 Chronic kidney disease, Stage V — (Use additional code to identify kidney transplant status, if applicable: V42.0. Use additional code to identify manifestation: 357.4, 420.0. Code first hypertensive chronic kidney disease, if applicable: 403.00-403.91, 404.00-404.93)

585.6 End stage renal disease — (Use additional code to identify kidney transplant status, if applicable: V42.0. Use additional code to identify manifestation: 357.4, 420.0. Code first hypertensive chronic kidney disease, if applicable: 403.00-403.91, 404.00-404.93)

585.9 Chronic kidney disease, unspecified — (Use additional code to identify kidney transplant status, if applicable: V42.0. Use additional code to identify manifestation: 357.4, 420.0. Code first hypertensive chronic kidney disease, if applicable: 403.00-403.91, 404.00-404.93) ▽

586 Unspecified renal failure ▽

587 Unspecified renal sclerosis ▽

588.0 Renal osteodystrophy

588.81 Secondary hyperparathyroidism (of renal origin)

588.89 Other specified disorders resulting from impaired renal function

588.9 Unspecified disorder resulting from impaired renal function ▽

590.00 Chronic pyelonephritis without lesion of renal medullary necrosis — (Use additional code to identify organism, such as E. coli, 041.41-041.49. Code if applicable, any causal condition first)

590.01 Chronic pyelonephritis with lesion of renal medullary necrosis — (Use additional code to identify organism, such as E. coli, 041.41-041.49. Code if applicable, any causal condition first)

590.3 Pyeloureteritis cystica — (Use additional code to identify organism, such as E. coli, 041.41-041.49)

590.80 Unspecified pyelonephritis — (Use additional code to identify organism, such as E. coli, 041.41-041.49) ▽

590.81 Pyelitis or pyelonephritis in diseases classified elsewhere — (Use additional code to identify organism, such as E. coli, 041.41-041.49. Code first underlying disease: 016.0) ☒

590.9 Unspecified infection of kidney — (Use additional code to identify organism, such as E. coli, 041.41-041.49) ▽

591 Hydronephrosis

593.81 Vascular disorders of kidney

958.5 Traumatic anuria

996.1 Mechanical complication of other vascular device, implant, and graft

996.73 Other complications due to renal dialysis device, implant, and graft — (Use additional code to identify complication: 338.18-338.19, 338.28-338.29)

996.81 Complications of transplanted kidney — (Use additional code to identify nature of complication: 078.5, 199.2, 238.77, 279.50-279.53)

V42.0 Kidney replaced by transplant

ICD-9-CM Procedural

39.27 Arteriovenostomy for renal dialysis

HCPCS Level II Supplies & Services

C1750 Catheter, hemodialysis/peritoneal, long-term

36838

36838 Distal revascularization and interval ligation (DRIL), upper extremity hemodialysis access (steal syndrome)

ICD-9-CM Diagnostic

996.1 Mechanical complication of other vascular device, implant, and graft

996.73 Other complications due to renal dialysis device, implant, and graft — (Use additional code to identify complication: 338.18-338.19, 338.28-338.29)

996.74 Other complications due to other vascular device, implant, and graft — (Use additional code to identify complication: 338.18-338.19, 338.28-338.29)

ICD-9-CM Procedural

39.42 Revision of arteriovenous shunt for renal dialysis

39.53 Repair of arteriovenous fistula

36860-36861

36860 External cannula declotting (separate procedure); without balloon catheter
36861 with balloon catheter

ICD-9-CM Diagnostic

996.1 Mechanical complication of other vascular device, implant, and graft
996.73 Other complications due to renal dialysis device, implant, and graft — (Use additional code to identify complication: 338.18-338.19, 338.28-338.29)
996.74 Other complications due to other vascular device, implant, and graft — (Use additional code to identify complication: 338.18-338.19, 338.28-338.29)

ICD-9-CM Procedural

39.49 Other revision of vascular procedure

36870

36870 Thrombectomy, percutaneous, arteriovenous fistula, autogenous or nonautogenous graft (includes mechanical thrombus extraction and intra-graft thrombolysis)

ICD-9-CM Diagnostic

403.91 Hypertensive chronic kidney disease, unspecified, with chronic kidney disease stage V or end stage renal disease — (Use additional code to identify the stage of chronic kidney disease: 585.5, 585.6) ▽
585.4 Chronic kidney disease, Stage IV (severe) — (Use additional code to identify kidney transplant status, if applicable: V42.0. Use additional code to identify manifestation: 357.4, 420.0. Code first hypertensive chronic kidney disease, if applicable: 403.00-403.91, 404.00-404.93)
585.5 Chronic kidney disease, Stage V — (Use additional code to identify kidney transplant status, if applicable: V42.0. Use additional code to identify manifestation: 357.4, 420.0. Code first hypertensive chronic kidney disease, if applicable: 403.00-403.91, 404.00-404.93)
585.6 End stage renal disease — (Use additional code to identify kidney transplant status, if applicable: V42.0. Use additional code to identify manifestation: 357.4, 420.0. Code first hypertensive chronic kidney disease, if applicable: 403.00-403.91, 404.00-404.93)
585.9 Chronic kidney disease, unspecified — (Use additional code to identify kidney transplant status, if applicable: V42.0. Use additional code to identify manifestation: 357.4, 420.0. Code first hypertensive chronic kidney disease, if applicable: 403.00-403.91, 404.00-404.93) ▽
586 Unspecified renal failure ▽
996.73 Other complications due to renal dialysis device, implant, and graft — (Use additional code to identify complication: 338.18-338.19, 338.28-338.29)
V45.11 Renal dialysis status
V45.12 Noncompliance with renal dialysis

ICD-9-CM Procedural

39.49 Other revision of vascular procedure

HCPCS Level II Supplies & Services

C1757 Catheter, thrombectomy/embolectomy

37140

37140 Venous anastomosis, open; portocaval

ICD-9-CM Diagnostic

452 Portal vein thrombosis
453.0 Budd-Chiari syndrome
456.20 Esophageal varices with bleeding in diseases classified elsewhere — (Code first underlying disease: 571.0-571.9, 572.3) ☒
459.2 Compression of vein
572.1 Portal pyemia
572.3 Portal hypertension — (Use additional code for any associated complications, such as: portal hypertensive gastropathy (537.89))

ICD-9-CM Procedural

39.1 Intra-abdominal venous shunt

37145

37145 Venous anastomosis, open; renoportal

ICD-9-CM Diagnostic

452 Portal vein thrombosis
453.0 Budd-Chiari syndrome
453.3 Embolism and thrombosis of renal vein
578.9 Hemorrhage of gastrointestinal tract, unspecified ▽
586 Unspecified renal failure ▽
587 Unspecified renal sclerosis ▽
593.81 Vascular disorders of kidney
747.62 Congenital renal vessel anomaly
747.69 Congenital anomaly of other specified site of peripheral vascular system
902.33 Portal vein injury

ICD-9-CM Procedural

39.1 Intra-abdominal venous shunt

37160

37160 Venous anastomosis, open; caval-mesenteric

ICD-9-CM Diagnostic

453.2 Other venous embolism and thrombosis, of inferior vena cava
453.77 Chronic venous embolism and thrombosis of other thoracic veins — (Use additional code, if applicable, for associated long-term (current) use of anticoagulants (V58.61))
453.79 Chronic venous embolism and thrombosis of other specified veins — (Use additional code, if applicable, for associated long-term (current) use of anticoagulants (V58.61))
453.87 Acute venous embolism and thrombosis of other thoracic veins
453.89 Acute venous embolism and thrombosis of other specified veins
557.0 Acute vascular insufficiency of intestine
557.1 Chronic vascular insufficiency of intestine
557.9 Unspecified vascular insufficiency of intestine ▽

ICD-9-CM Procedural

39.1 Intra-abdominal venous shunt

37180

37180 Venous anastomosis, open; splenorenal, proximal

ICD-9-CM Diagnostic

453.3 Embolism and thrombosis of renal vein
453.77 Chronic venous embolism and thrombosis of other thoracic veins — (Use additional code, if applicable, for associated long-term (current) use of anticoagulants (V58.61))
453.79 Chronic venous embolism and thrombosis of other specified veins — (Use additional code, if applicable, for associated long-term (current) use of anticoagulants (V58.61))
453.87 Acute venous embolism and thrombosis of other thoracic veins
453.89 Acute venous embolism and thrombosis of other specified veins
456.20 Esophageal varices with bleeding in diseases classified elsewhere — (Code first underlying disease: 571.0-571.9, 572.3) ☒
459.2 Compression of vein
459.9 Unspecified circulatory system disorder ▽
585.1 Chronic kidney disease, Stage I — (Use additional code to identify kidney transplant status, if applicable: V42.0. Use additional code to identify manifestation: 357.4, 420.0. Code first hypertensive chronic kidney disease, if applicable: 403.00-403.91, 404.00-404.93)
585.2 Chronic kidney disease, Stage II (mild) — (Use additional code to identify kidney transplant status, if applicable: V42.0. Use additional code to identify manifestation: 357.4, 420.0. Code first hypertensive chronic kidney disease, if applicable: 403.00-403.91, 404.00-404.93)
585.3 Chronic kidney disease, Stage III (moderate) — (Use additional code to identify kidney transplant status, if applicable: V42.0. Use additional code to identify manifestation:

357.4, 420.0. Code first hypertensive chronic kidney disease, if applicable: 403.00-403.91, 404.00-404.93)

585.4 Chronic kidney disease, Stage IV (severe) — (Use additional code to identify kidney transplant status, if applicable: V42.0. Use additional code to identify manifestation: 357.4, 420.0. Code first hypertensive chronic kidney disease, if applicable: 403.00-403.91, 404.00-404.93)

585.5 Chronic kidney disease, Stage V — (Use additional code to identify kidney transplant status, if applicable: V42.0. Use additional code to identify manifestation: 357.4, 420.0. Code first hypertensive chronic kidney disease, if applicable: 403.00-403.91, 404.00-404.93)

585.6 End stage renal disease — (Use additional code to identify kidney transplant status, if applicable: V42.0. Use additional code to identify manifestation: 357.4, 420.0. Code first hypertensive chronic kidney disease, if applicable: 403.00-403.91, 404.00-404.93)

585.9 Chronic kidney disease, unspecified — (Use additional code to identify kidney transplant status, if applicable: V42.0. Use additional code to identify manifestation: 357.4, 420.0. Code first hypertensive chronic kidney disease, if applicable: 403.00-403.91, 404.00-404.93) ▽

587 Unspecified renal sclerosis ▽

865.01 Spleen hematoma, without rupture of capsule or mention of open wound into cavity

ICD-9-CM Procedural

39.1 Intra-abdominal venous shunt

37181

37181 Venous anastomosis, open; splenorenal, distal (selective decompression of esophagogastric varices, any technique)

ICD-9-CM Diagnostic

420.0 Acute pericarditis in diseases classified elsewhere — (Code first underlying disease: 006.8, 017.9, 039.8, 585.9, 586) ☒

453.3 Embolism and thrombosis of renal vein

453.77 Chronic venous embolism and thrombosis of other thoracic veins — (Use additional code, if applicable, for associated long-term (current) use of anticoagulants (V58.61))

453.79 Chronic venous embolism and thrombosis of other specified veins — (Use additional code, if applicable, for associated long-term (current) use of anticoagulants (V58.61))

453.87 Acute venous embolism and thrombosis of other thoracic veins

453.89 Acute venous embolism and thrombosis of other specified veins

456.20 Esophageal varices with bleeding in diseases classified elsewhere — (Code first underlying disease: 571.0-571.9, 572.3) ☒

459.2 Compression of vein

459.9 Unspecified circulatory system disorder ▽

578.9 Hemorrhage of gastrointestinal tract, unspecified ▽

585.1 Chronic kidney disease, Stage I — (Use additional code to identify kidney transplant status, if applicable: V42.0. Use additional code to identify manifestation: 357.4, 420.0. Code first hypertensive chronic kidney disease, if applicable: 403.00-403.91, 404.00-404.93)

585.2 Chronic kidney disease, Stage II (mild) — (Use additional code to identify kidney transplant status, if applicable: V42.0. Use additional code to identify manifestation: 357.4, 420.0. Code first hypertensive chronic kidney disease, if applicable: 403.00-403.91, 404.00-404.93)

585.3 Chronic kidney disease, Stage III (moderate) — (Use additional code to identify kidney transplant status, if applicable: V42.0. Use additional code to identify manifestation: 357.4, 420.0. Code first hypertensive chronic kidney disease, if applicable: 403.00-403.91, 404.00-404.93)

585.4 Chronic kidney disease, Stage IV (severe) — (Use additional code to identify kidney transplant status, if applicable: V42.0. Use additional code to identify manifestation: 357.4, 420.0. Code first hypertensive chronic kidney disease, if applicable: 403.00-403.91, 404.00-404.93)

585.5 Chronic kidney disease, Stage V — (Use additional code to identify kidney transplant status, if applicable: V42.0. Use additional code to identify manifestation: 357.4, 420.0. Code first hypertensive chronic kidney disease, if applicable: 403.00-403.91, 404.00-404.93)

585.6 End stage renal disease — (Use additional code to identify kidney transplant status, if applicable: V42.0. Use additional code to identify manifestation: 357.4, 420.0. Code first hypertensive chronic kidney disease, if applicable: 403.00-403.91, 404.00-404.93)

585.9 Chronic kidney disease, unspecified — (Use additional code to identify kidney transplant status, if applicable: V42.0. Use additional code to identify manifestation: 357.4, 420.0. Code first hypertensive chronic kidney disease, if applicable: 403.00-403.91, 404.00-404.93) ▽

587 Unspecified renal sclerosis ▽

865.01 Spleen hematoma, without rupture of capsule or mention of open wound into cavity

ICD-9-CM Procedural

39.1 Intra-abdominal venous shunt

37182-37183

37182 Insertion of transvenous intrahepatic portosystemic shunt(s) (TIPS) (includes venous access, hepatic and portal vein catheterization, portography with hemodynamic evaluation, intrahepatic tract formation/dilatation, stent placement and all associated imaging guidance and documentation)

37183 Revision of transvenous intrahepatic portosystemic shunt(s) (TIPS) (includes venous access, hepatic and portal vein catheterization, portography with hemodynamic evaluation, intrahepatic tract recanulization/dilatation, stent placement and all associated imaging guidance and documentation)

ICD-9-CM Diagnostic

452 Portal vein thrombosis

453.0 Budd-Chiari syndrome

456.0 Esophageal varices with bleeding

456.1 Esophageal varices without mention of bleeding

456.20 Esophageal varices with bleeding in diseases classified elsewhere — (Code first underlying disease: 571.0-571.9, 572.3) ☒

456.21 Esophageal varices without mention of bleeding in diseases classified elsewhere — (Code first underlying disease: 571.0-571.9, 572.3) ☒

459.2 Compression of vein

572.1 Portal pyemia

572.3 Portal hypertension — (Use additional code for any associated complications, such as: portal hypertensive gastropathy (537.89))

789.51 Malignant ascites

789.59 Other ascites

996.1 Mechanical complication of other vascular device, implant, and graft

996.62 Infection and inflammatory reaction due to other vascular device, implant, and graft — (Use additional code to identify specified infections)

996.74 Other complications due to other vascular device, implant, and graft — (Use additional code to identify complication: 338.18-338.19, 338.28-338.29)

997.49 Other digestive system complications

ICD-9-CM Procedural

39.1 Intra-abdominal venous shunt

37184-37185

37184 Primary percutaneous transluminal mechanical thrombectomy, noncoronary, arterial or arterial bypass graft, including fluoroscopic guidance and intraprocedural pharmacological thrombolytic injection(s); initial vessel

37185 second and all subsequent vessel(s) within the same vascular family (List separately in addition to code for primary mechanical thrombectomy procedure)

ICD-9-CM Diagnostic

433.00 Occlusion and stenosis of basilar artery without mention of cerebral infarction — (Use additional code, if applicable, to identify status post administration of tPA (rtPA) in a different facility within the last 24 hours prior to admission to current facility: V45.88)

433.01 Occlusion and stenosis of basilar artery with cerebral infarction — (Use additional code, if applicable, to identify status post administration of tPA (rtPA) in a different facility within the last 24 hours prior to admission to current facility: V45.88)

433.10 Occlusion and stenosis of carotid artery without mention of cerebral infarction — (Use additional code, if applicable, to identify status post administration of tPA (rtPA) in a different facility within the last 24 hours prior to admission to current facility: V45.88)
433.11 Occlusion and stenosis of carotid artery with cerebral infarction — (Use additional code, if applicable, to identify status post administration of tPA (rtPA) in a different facility within the last 24 hours prior to admission to current facility: V45.88)
433.20 Occlusion and stenosis of vertebral artery without mention of cerebral infarction — (Use additional code, if applicable, to identify status post administration of tPA (rtPA) in a different facility within the last 24 hours prior to admission to current facility: V45.88)
433.21 Occlusion and stenosis of vertebral artery with cerebral infarction — (Use additional code, if applicable, to identify status post administration of tPA (rtPA) in a different facility within the last 24 hours prior to admission to current facility: V45.88)
433.30 Occlusion and stenosis of multiple and bilateral precerebral arteries without mention of cerebral infarction — (Use additional code, if applicable, to identify status post administration of tPA (rtPA) in a different facility within the last 24 hours prior to admission to current facility: V45.88)
433.31 Occlusion and stenosis of multiple and bilateral precerebral arteries with cerebral infarction — (Use additional code, if applicable, to identify status post administration of tPA (rtPA) in a different facility within the last 24 hours prior to admission to current facility: V45.88)
433.80 Occlusion and stenosis of other specified precerebral artery without mention of cerebral infarction — (Use additional code, if applicable, to identify status post administration of tPA (rtPA) in a different facility within the last 24 hours prior to admission to current facility: V45.88)
433.81 Occlusion and stenosis of other specified precerebral artery with cerebral infarction — (Use additional code, if applicable, to identify status post administration of tPA (rtPA) in a different facility within the last 24 hours prior to admission to current facility: V45.88)
433.90 Occlusion and stenosis of unspecified precerebral artery without mention of cerebral infarction — (Use additional code, if applicable, to identify status post administration of tPA (rtPA) in a different facility within the last 24 hours prior to admission to current facility: V45.88) ▽
433.91 Occlusion and stenosis of unspecified precerebral artery with cerebral infarction — (Use additional code, if applicable, to identify status post administration of tPA (rtPA) in a different facility within the last 24 hours prior to admission to current facility: V45.88) ▽
444.01 Saddle embolus of abdominal aorta
444.09 Other arterial embolism and thrombosis of abdominal aorta
444.1 Embolism and thrombosis of thoracic aorta
444.21 Embolism and thrombosis of arteries of upper extremity
444.22 Embolism and thrombosis of arteries of lower extremity
444.81 Embolism and thrombosis of iliac artery
444.89 Embolism and thrombosis of other specified artery
444.9 Embolism and thrombosis of unspecified artery ▽
445.01 Atheroembolism of upper extremity
445.02 Atheroembolism of lower extremity
445.81 Atheroembolism of kidney — (Use additional code for any associated acute kidney failure or chronic kidney disease: 584, 585)
445.89 Atheroembolism of other site
447.1 Stricture of artery
447.2 Rupture of artery
557.0 Acute vascular insufficiency of intestine
557.1 Chronic vascular insufficiency of intestine
557.9 Unspecified vascular insufficiency of intestine ▽
997.71 Vascular complications of mesenteric artery — (Use additional code to identify complications)
997.72 Vascular complications of renal artery — (Use additional code to identify complications)

ICD-9-CM Procedural

38.01 Incision of intracranial vessels
38.02 Incision of other vessels of head and neck
38.03 Incision of upper limb vessels
38.04 Incision of aorta
38.05 Incision of other thoracic vessels
38.06 Incision of abdominal arteries
38.07 Incision of abdominal veins
38.08 Incision of lower limb arteries
38.09 Incision of lower limb veins
38.91 Arterial catheterization
38.98 Other puncture of artery
99.10 Injection or infusion of thrombolytic agent

37186

37186 Secondary percutaneous transluminal thrombectomy (eg, nonprimary mechanical, snare basket, suction technique), noncoronary, arterial or arterial bypass graft, including fluoroscopic guidance and intraprocedural pharmacological thrombolytic injections, provided in conjunction with another percutaneous intervention other than primary mechanical thrombectomy (List separately in addition to code for primary procedure)

ICD-9-CM Diagnostic

This is an add-on code. Refer to the corresponding primary procedure code for ICD-9-CM diagnosis code links.

37187-37188

37187 Percutaneous transluminal mechanical thrombectomy, vein(s), including intraprocedural pharmacological thrombolytic injections and fluoroscopic guidance
37188 Percutaneous transluminal mechanical thrombectomy, vein(s), including intraprocedural pharmacological thrombolytic injections and fluoroscopic guidance, repeat treatment on subsequent day during course of thrombolytic therapy

ICD-9-CM Diagnostic

451.0 Phlebitis and thrombophlebitis of superficial vessels of lower extremities — (Use additional E code to identify drug, if drug-induced)
451.11 Phlebitis and thrombophlebitis of femoral vein (deep) (superficial) — (Use additional E code to identify drug, if drug-induced)
451.19 Phlebitis and thrombophlebitis of other deep vessels of lower extremities — (Use additional E code to identify drug, if drug-induced)
451.2 Phlebitis and thrombophlebitis of lower extremities, unspecified — (Use additional E code to identify drug, if drug-induced) ▽
451.81 Phlebitis and thrombophlebitis of iliac vein — (Use additional E code to identify drug, if drug-induced)
451.82 Phlebitis and thrombophlebitis of superficial veins of upper extremities — (Use additional E code to identify drug, if drug-induced)
451.83 Phlebitis and thrombophlebitis of deep veins of upper extremities — (Use additional E code to identify drug, if drug-induced)
451.84 Phlebitis and thrombophlebitis of upper extremities, unspecified — (Use additional E code to identify drug, if drug-induced) ▽
451.89 Phlebitis and thrombophlebitis of other site — (Use additional E code to identify drug, if drug-induced)
451.9 Phlebitis and thrombophlebitis of unspecified site — (Use additional E code to identify drug, if drug-induced) ▽
453.0 Budd-Chiari syndrome
453.1 Thrombophlebitis migrans
453.2 Other venous embolism and thrombosis, of inferior vena cava
453.3 Embolism and thrombosis of renal vein
453.40 Acute venous embolism and thrombosis of unspecified deep vessels of lower extremity ▽
453.41 Acute venous embolism and thrombosis of deep vessels of proximal lower extremity
453.42 Acute venous embolism and thrombosis of deep vessels of distal lower extremity

453.50 Chronic venous embolism and thrombosis of unspecified deep vessels of lower extremity — (Use additional code, if applicable, for associated long-term (current) use of anticoagulants (V58.61)) ▽

453.51 Chronic venous embolism and thrombosis of deep vessels of proximal lower extremity — (Use additional code, if applicable, for associated long-term (current) use of anticoagulants (V58.61))

453.52 Chronic venous embolism and thrombosis of deep vessels of distal lower extremity — (Use additional code, if applicable, for associated long-term (current) use of anticoagulants (V58.61))

453.6 Venous embolism and thrombosis of superficial vessels of lower extremity — (Use additional code, if applicable, for associated long-term (current) use of anticoagulants (V58.61))

453.71 Chronic venous embolism and thrombosis of superficial veins of upper extremity — (Use additional code, if applicable, for associated long-term (current) use of anticoagulants (V58.61))

453.72 Chronic venous embolism and thrombosis of deep veins of upper extremity — (Use additional code, if applicable, for associated long-term (current) use of anticoagulants (V58.61))

453.73 Chronic venous embolism and thrombosis of upper extremity, unspecified — (Use additional code, if applicable, for associated long-term (current) use of anticoagulants (V58.61)) ▽

453.74 Chronic venous embolism and thrombosis of axillary veins — (Use additional code, if applicable, for associated long-term (current) use of anticoagulants (V58.61))

453.75 Chronic venous embolism and thrombosis of subclavian veins — (Use additional code, if applicable, for associated long-term (current) use of anticoagulants (V58.61))

453.76 Chronic venous embolism and thrombosis of internal jugular veins — (Use additional code, if applicable, for associated long-term (current) use of anticoagulants (V58.61))

453.77 Chronic venous embolism and thrombosis of other thoracic veins — (Use additional code, if applicable, for associated long-term (current) use of anticoagulants (V58.61))

453.79 Chronic venous embolism and thrombosis of other specified veins — (Use additional code, if applicable, for associated long-term (current) use of anticoagulants (V58.61))

453.81 Acute venous embolism and thrombosis of superficial veins of upper extremity

453.82 Acute venous embolism and thrombosis of deep veins of upper extremity

453.83 Acute venous embolism and thrombosis of upper extremity, unspecified ▽

453.84 Acute venous embolism and thrombosis of axillary veins

453.85 Acute venous embolism and thrombosis of subclavian veins

453.86 Acute venous embolism and thrombosis of internal jugular veins

453.87 Acute venous embolism and thrombosis of other thoracic veins

453.89 Acute venous embolism and thrombosis of other specified veins

453.9 Embolism and thrombosis of unspecified site ▽

997.79 Vascular complications of other vessels — (Use additional code to identify complications)

ICD-9-CM Procedural

38.01 Incision of intracranial vessels

38.02 Incision of other vessels of head and neck

38.03 Incision of upper limb vessels

38.04 Incision of aorta

38.05 Incision of other thoracic vessels

38.06 Incision of abdominal arteries

38.07 Incision of abdominal veins

38.08 Incision of lower limb arteries

38.09 Incision of lower limb veins

38.93 Venous catheterization, not elsewhere classified

38.99 Other puncture of vein

99.10 Injection or infusion of thrombolytic agent

HCPCS Level II Supplies & Services

A4300 Implantable access catheter, (e.g., venous, arterial, epidural subarachnoid, or peritoneal, etc.) external access

37191-37193

37191 Insertion of intravascular vena cava filter, endovascular approach including vascular access, vessel selection, and radiological supervision and interpretation, intraprocedural roadmapping, and imaging guidance (ultrasound and fluoroscopy), when performed

37192 Repositioning of intravascular vena cava filter, endovascular approach including vascular access, vessel selection, and radiological supervision and interpretation, intraprocedural roadmapping, and imaging guidance (ultrasound and fluoroscopy), when performed

37193 Retrieval (removal) of intravascular vena cava filter, endovascular approach including vascular access, vessel selection, and radiological supervision and interpretation, intraprocedural roadmapping, and imaging guidance (ultrasound and fluoroscopy), when performed

ICD-9-CM Diagnostic

415.19 Other pulmonary embolism and infarction

416.2 Chronic pulmonary embolism — (Use additional code, if applicable, for associated long-term (current) use of anticoagulants (V58.61))

453.40 Acute venous embolism and thrombosis of unspecified deep vessels of lower extremity ▽

453.41 Acute venous embolism and thrombosis of deep vessels of proximal lower extremity

453.42 Acute venous embolism and thrombosis of deep vessels of distal lower extremity

453.50 Chronic venous embolism and thrombosis of unspecified deep vessels of lower extremity — (Use additional code, if applicable, for associated long-term (current) use of anticoagulants (V58.61)) ▽

453.51 Chronic venous embolism and thrombosis of deep vessels of proximal lower extremity — (Use additional code, if applicable, for associated long-term (current) use of anticoagulants (V58.61))

453.52 Chronic venous embolism and thrombosis of deep vessels of distal lower extremity — (Use additional code, if applicable, for associated long-term (current) use of anticoagulants (V58.61))

453.6 Venous embolism and thrombosis of superficial vessels of lower extremity — (Use additional code, if applicable, for associated long-term (current) use of anticoagulants (V58.61))

996.1 Mechanical complication of other vascular device, implant, and graft

996.62 Infection and inflammatory reaction due to other vascular device, implant, and graft — (Use additional code to identify specified infections)

996.74 Other complications due to other vascular device, implant, and graft — (Use additional code to identify complication: 338.18-338.19, 338.28-338.29)

997.2 Peripheral vascular complications — (Use additional code to identify complications)

V12.51 Personal history of venous thrombosis and embolism

V12.55 Personal history of pulmonary embolism

ICD-9-CM Procedural

00.22 Intravascular imaging of intrathoracic vessels

38.7 Interruption of the vena cava

39.99 Other operations on vessels

88.51 Angiocardiography of venae cavae

HCPCS Level II Supplies & Services

C1880 Vena cava filter

37195

37195 Thrombolysis, cerebral, by intravenous infusion

ICD-9-CM Diagnostic

434.00 Cerebral thrombosis without mention of cerebral infarction — (Use additional code, if applicable, to identify status post administration of tPA (rtPA) in a different facility within the last 24 hours prior to admission to current facility: V45.88)

434.01 Cerebral thrombosis with cerebral infarction — (Use additional code, if applicable, to identify status post administration of tPA (rtPA) in a different facility within the last 24 hours prior to admission to current facility: V45.88)

434.10 Cerebral embolism without mention of cerebral infarction — (Use additional code, if applicable, to identify status post administration of tPA (rtPA) in a different facility within the last 24 hours prior to admission to current facility: V45.88)

434.11 Cerebral embolism with cerebral infarction — (Use additional code, if applicable, to identify status post administration of tPA (rtPA) in a different facility within the last 24 hours prior to admission to current facility: V45.88)

434.90 Unspecified cerebral artery occlusion without mention of cerebral infarction — (Use additional code, if applicable, to identify status post administration of tPA (rtPA) in a different facility within the last 24 hours prior to admission to current facility: V45.88) ▽

434.91 Unspecified cerebral artery occlusion with cerebral infarction — (Use additional code, if applicable, to identify status post administration of tPA (rtPA) in a different facility within the last 24 hours prior to admission to current facility: V45.88) ▽

435.9 Unspecified transient cerebral ischemia — (Use additional code to identify presence of hypertension) ▽

997.02 Iatrogenic cerebrovascular infarction or hemorrhage — (Use additional code to identify complications)

ICD-9-CM Procedural

38.93 Venous catheterization, not elsewhere classified

99.10 Injection or infusion of thrombolytic agent

37197

37197 Transcatheter retrieval, percutaneous, of intravascular foreign body (eg, fractured venous or arterial catheter), includes radiological supervision and interpretation, and imaging guidance (ultrasound or fluoroscopy), when performed

ICD-9-CM Diagnostic

996.1 Mechanical complication of other vascular device, implant, and graft

998.4 Foreign body accidentally left during procedure, not elsewhere classified

ICD-9-CM Procedural

38.91 Arterial catheterization

38.93 Venous catheterization, not elsewhere classified

[37211, 37212, 37213, 37214]

37211 Transcatheter therapy, arterial infusion for thrombolysis other than coronary, any method, including radiological supervision and interpretation, initial treatment day

37212 Transcatheter therapy, venous infusion for thrombolysis, any method, including radiological supervision and interpretation, initial treatment day

37213 Transcatheter therapy, arterial or venous infusion for thrombolysis other than coronary, any method, including radiological supervision and interpretation, continued treatment on subsequent day during course of thrombolytic therapy, including follow-up catheter contrast injection, position change, or exchange, when performed;

37214 cessation of thrombolysis including removal of catheter and vessel closure by any method

ICD-9-CM Diagnostic

362.30 Unspecified retinal vascular occlusion ▽

362.31 Central artery occlusion of retina

362.32 Arterial branch occlusion of retina

362.34 Transient arterial occlusion of retina

362.35 Central vein occlusion of retina

362.36 Venous tributary (branch) occlusion of retina

362.37 Venous engorgement of retina

415.11 Iatrogenic pulmonary embolism and infarction — (Use additional code for associated septic pulmonary embolism, if applicable: 415.12)

415.12 Septic pulmonary embolism

415.13 Saddle embolus of pulmonary artery

415.19 Other pulmonary embolism and infarction

433.00 Occlusion and stenosis of basilar artery without mention of cerebral infarction — (Use additional code, if applicable, to identify status post administration of tPA (rtPA) in a different facility within the last 24 hours prior to admission to current facility: V45.88)

433.01 Occlusion and stenosis of basilar artery with cerebral infarction — (Use additional code, if applicable, to identify status post administration of tPA (rtPA) in a different facility within the last 24 hours prior to admission to current facility: V45.88)

433.10 Occlusion and stenosis of carotid artery without mention of cerebral infarction — (Use additional code, if applicable, to identify status post administration of tPA (rtPA) in a different facility within the last 24 hours prior to admission to current facility: V45.88)

433.11 Occlusion and stenosis of carotid artery with cerebral infarction — (Use additional code, if applicable, to identify status post administration of tPA (rtPA) in a different facility within the last 24 hours prior to admission to current facility: V45.88)

433.20 Occlusion and stenosis of vertebral artery without mention of cerebral infarction — (Use additional code, if applicable, to identify status post administration of tPA (rtPA) in a different facility within the last 24 hours prior to admission to current facility: V45.88)

433.21 Occlusion and stenosis of vertebral artery with cerebral infarction — (Use additional code, if applicable, to identify status post administration of tPA (rtPA) in a different facility within the last 24 hours prior to admission to current facility: V45.88)

433.30 Occlusion and stenosis of multiple and bilateral precerebral arteries without mention of cerebral infarction — (Use additional code, if applicable, to identify status post administration of tPA (rtPA) in a different facility within the last 24 hours prior to admission to current facility: V45.88)

433.31 Occlusion and stenosis of multiple and bilateral precerebral arteries with cerebral infarction — (Use additional code, if applicable, to identify status post administration of tPA (rtPA) in a different facility within the last 24 hours prior to admission to current facility: V45.88)

433.80 Occlusion and stenosis of other specified precerebral artery without mention of cerebral infarction — (Use additional code, if applicable, to identify status post administration of tPA (rtPA) in a different facility within the last 24 hours prior to admission to current facility: V45.88)

433.81 Occlusion and stenosis of other specified precerebral artery with cerebral infarction — (Use additional code, if applicable, to identify status post administration of tPA (rtPA) in a different facility within the last 24 hours prior to admission to current facility: V45.88)

433.90 Occlusion and stenosis of unspecified precerebral artery without mention of cerebral infarction — (Use additional code, if applicable, to identify status post administration of tPA (rtPA) in a different facility within the last 24 hours prior to admission to current facility: V45.88) ▽

433.91 Occlusion and stenosis of unspecified precerebral artery with cerebral infarction — (Use additional code, if applicable, to identify status post administration of tPA (rtPA) in a different facility within the last 24 hours prior to admission to current facility: V45.88) ▽

434.00 Cerebral thrombosis without mention of cerebral infarction — (Use additional code, if applicable, to identify status post administration of tPA (rtPA) in a different facility within the last 24 hours prior to admission to current facility: V45.88)

434.01 Cerebral thrombosis with cerebral infarction — (Use additional code, if applicable, to identify status post administration of tPA (rtPA) in a different facility within the last 24 hours prior to admission to current facility: V45.88)

434.90 Unspecified cerebral artery occlusion without mention of cerebral infarction — (Use additional code, if applicable, to identify status post administration of tPA (rtPA) in a different facility within the last 24 hours prior to admission to current facility: V45.88) ▽

434.91 Unspecified cerebral artery occlusion with cerebral infarction — (Use additional code, if applicable, to identify status post administration of tPA (rtPA) in a different facility within the last 24 hours prior to admission to current facility: V45.88) ▽

444.01 Saddle embolus of abdominal aorta

444.09 Other arterial embolism and thrombosis of abdominal aorta

444.1 Embolism and thrombosis of thoracic aorta

444.21 Embolism and thrombosis of arteries of upper extremity

444.22 Embolism and thrombosis of arteries of lower extremity

444.81 Embolism and thrombosis of iliac artery

444.89 Embolism and thrombosis of other specified artery

444.9 Embolism and thrombosis of unspecified artery ▽

451.0 Phlebitis and thrombophlebitis of superficial vessels of lower extremities — (Use additional E code to identify drug, if drug-induced)

451.11 Phlebitis and thrombophlebitis of femoral vein (deep) (superficial) — (Use additional E code to identify drug, if drug-induced)

451.19 Phlebitis and thrombophlebitis of other deep vessels of lower extremities — (Use additional E code to identify drug, if drug-induced)

451.2 Phlebitis and thrombophlebitis of lower extremities, unspecified — (Use additional E code to identify drug, if drug-induced) ▽

451.81 Phlebitis and thrombophlebitis of iliac vein — (Use additional E code to identify drug, if drug-induced)

451.82 Phlebitis and thrombophlebitis of superficial veins of upper extremities — (Use additional E code to identify drug, if drug-induced)

451.83 Phlebitis and thrombophlebitis of deep veins of upper extremities — (Use additional E code to identify drug, if drug-induced)

451.84 Phlebitis and thrombophlebitis of upper extremities, unspecified — (Use additional E code to identify drug, if drug-induced) ▽

451.89 Phlebitis and thrombophlebitis of other site — (Use additional E code to identify drug, if drug-induced)

451.9 Phlebitis and thrombophlebitis of unspecified site — (Use additional E code to identify drug, if drug-induced) ▽

452 Portal vein thrombosis

453.0 Budd-Chiari syndrome

453.1 Thrombophlebitis migrans

453.2 Other venous embolism and thrombosis, of inferior vena cava

453.3 Embolism and thrombosis of renal vein

453.40 Acute venous embolism and thrombosis of unspecified deep vessels of lower extremity ▽

453.41 Acute venous embolism and thrombosis of deep vessels of proximal lower extremity

453.42 Acute venous embolism and thrombosis of deep vessels of distal lower extremity

453.50 Chronic venous embolism and thrombosis of unspecified deep vessels of lower extremity — (Use additional code, if applicable, for associated long-term (current) use of anticoagulants (V58.61)) ▽

453.51 Chronic venous embolism and thrombosis of deep vessels of proximal lower extremity — (Use additional code, if applicable, for associated long-term (current) use of anticoagulants (V58.61))

453.52 Chronic venous embolism and thrombosis of deep vessels of distal lower extremity — (Use additional code, if applicable, for associated long-term (current) use of anticoagulants (V58.61))

453.6 Venous embolism and thrombosis of superficial vessels of lower extremity — (Use additional code, if applicable, for associated long-term (current) use of anticoagulants (V58.61))

453.71 Chronic venous embolism and thrombosis of superficial veins of upper extremity — (Use additional code, if applicable, for associated long-term (current) use of anticoagulants (V58.61))

453.72 Chronic venous embolism and thrombosis of deep veins of upper extremity — (Use additional code, if applicable, for associated long-term (current) use of anticoagulants (V58.61))

453.73 Chronic venous embolism and thrombosis of upper extremity, unspecified — (Use additional code, if applicable, for associated long-term (current) use of anticoagulants (V58.61)) ▽

453.74 Chronic venous embolism and thrombosis of axillary veins — (Use additional code, if applicable, for associated long-term (current) use of anticoagulants (V58.61))

453.75 Chronic venous embolism and thrombosis of subclavian veins — (Use additional code, if applicable, for associated long-term (current) use of anticoagulants (V58.61))

453.76 Chronic venous embolism and thrombosis of internal jugular veins — (Use additional code, if applicable, for associated long-term (current) use of anticoagulants (V58.61))

453.77 Chronic venous embolism and thrombosis of other thoracic veins — (Use additional code, if applicable, for associated long-term (current) use of anticoagulants (V58.61))

453.79 Chronic venous embolism and thrombosis of other specified veins — (Use additional code, if applicable, for associated long-term (current) use of anticoagulants (V58.61))

453.81 Acute venous embolism and thrombosis of superficial veins of upper extremity

453.82 Acute venous embolism and thrombosis of deep veins of upper extremity

453.83 Acute venous embolism and thrombosis of upper extremity, unspecified ▽

453.84 Acute venous embolism and thrombosis of axillary veins

453.85 Acute venous embolism and thrombosis of subclavian veins

453.86 Acute venous embolism and thrombosis of internal jugular veins

453.87 Acute venous embolism and thrombosis of other thoracic veins

453.89 Acute venous embolism and thrombosis of other specified veins

453.9 Embolism and thrombosis of unspecified site ▽

557.0 Acute vascular insufficiency of intestine

557.1 Chronic vascular insufficiency of intestine

557.9 Unspecified vascular insufficiency of intestine ▽

593.81 Vascular disorders of kidney

671.20 Superficial thrombophlebitis complicating pregnancy and the puerperium, unspecified as to episode of care ▽ ♀

671.21 Superficial thrombophlebitis with delivery, with or without mention of antepartum condition ♀

671.22 Superficial thrombophlebitis with delivery, with mention of postpartum complication ♀

671.23 Superficial thrombophlebitis, antepartum ♀

671.24 Superficial thrombophlebitis, postpartum condition or complication ♀

671.30 Deep phlebothrombosis, antepartum, unspecified as to episode of care — (Use additional code to identify the deep vein thrombosis: (453.40-453.42, 453.50-453.52, 453.72-453.79, 453.82-453.89)Use additional code for long term (current) use of anticoagulants, if applicable (V58.61)) ▽ ♀

671.31 Deep phlebothrombosis, antepartum, with delivery — (Use additional code to identify the deep vein thrombosis: (453.40-453.42, 453.50-453.52, 453.72-453.79, 453.82-453.89)Use additional code for long term (current) use of anticoagulants, if applicable (V58.61)) ♀

671.33 Deep phlebothrombosis, antepartum — (Use additional code to identify the deep vein thrombosis: (453.40-453.42, 453.50-453.52, 453.72-453.79, 453.82-453.89)Use additional code for long term (current) use of anticoagulants, if applicable (V58.61)) ♀

671.40 Deep phlebothrombosis, postpartum, unspecified as to episode of care — (Use additional code to identify the deep vein thrombosis: (453.40-453.42, 453.50-453.52, 453.72-453.79, 453.82-453.89)(Use additional code for long term (current) use of anticoagulants, if applicable (V58.61)) ▽ ♀

671.42 Deep phlebothrombosis, postpartum, with delivery — (Use additional code to identify the deep vein thrombosis: (453.40-453.42, 453.50-453.52, 453.72-453.79, 453.82-453.89)(Use additional code for long term (current) use of anticoagulants, if applicable (V58.61)) ♀

671.44 Deep phlebothrombosis, postpartum condition or complication — (Use additional code to identify the deep vein thrombosis: (453.40-453.42, 453.50-453.52, 453.72-453.79, 453.82-453.89)(Use additional code for long term (current) use of anticoagulants, if applicable (V58.61)) ♀

671.50 Other phlebitis and thrombosis complicating pregnancy and the puerperium, unspecified as to episode of care ▽ ♀

671.51 Other phlebitis and thrombosis with delivery, with or without mention of antepartum condition ♀

671.52 Other phlebitis and thrombosis with delivery, with mention of postpartum complication ♀

671.53 Other antepartum phlebitis and thrombosis ♀

671.54 Other phlebitis and thrombosis, postpartum condition or complication ♀

673.20 Obstetrical blood-clot embolism, unspecified as to episode of care ▽ ♀

673.21 Obstetrical blood-clot embolism, with delivery, with or without mention of antepartum condition ♀

673.23 Obstetrical blood-clot embolism, antepartum ♀

673.24 Obstetrical blood-clot embolism, postpartum condition or complication ♀

996.71 Other complications due to heart valve prosthesis — (Use additional code to identify complication: 338.18-338.19, 338.28-338.29)

996.72 Other complications due to other cardiac device, implant, and graft — (Use additional code to identify complication: 338.18-338.19, 338.28-338.29)

996.73 Other complications due to renal dialysis device, implant, and graft — (Use additional code to identify complication: 338.18-338.19, 338.28-338.29)

996.74 Other complications due to other vascular device, implant, and graft — (Use additional code to identify complication: 338.18-338.19, 338.28-338.29)

996.75 Other complications due to nervous system device, implant, and graft — (Use additional code to identify complication: 338.18-338.19, 338.28-338.29)

996.77 Other complications due to internal joint prosthesis — (Use additional code to identify complication: 338.18-338.19, 338.28-338.29)

996.78 Other complications due to other internal orthopedic device, implant, and graft — (Use additional code to identify complication: 338.18-338.19, 338.28-338.29)

996.79 Other complications due to other internal prosthetic device, implant, and graft — (Use additional code to identify complication: 338.18-338.19, 338.28-338.29)

997.2 Peripheral vascular complications — (Use additional code to identify complications)

997.71 Vascular complications of mesenteric artery — (Use additional code to identify complications)

997.72 Vascular complications of renal artery — (Use additional code to identify complications)

997.79 Vascular complications of other vessels — (Use additional code to identify complications)

999.2 Other vascular complications of medical care, not elsewhere classified

ICD-9-CM Procedural

38.91 Arterial catheterization

38.93 Venous catheterization, not elsewhere classified

99.10 Injection or infusion of thrombolytic agent

37202

37202 Transcatheter therapy, infusion other than for thrombolysis, any type (eg, spasmolytic, vasoconstrictive)

ICD-9-CM Diagnostic

433.10 Occlusion and stenosis of carotid artery without mention of cerebral infarction — (Use additional code, if applicable, to identify status post administration of tPA (rtPA) in a different facility within the last 24 hours prior to admission to current facility: V45.88)

433.20 Occlusion and stenosis of vertebral artery without mention of cerebral infarction — (Use additional code, if applicable, to identify status post administration of tPA (rtPA) in a different facility within the last 24 hours prior to admission to current facility: V45.88)

433.30 Occlusion and stenosis of multiple and bilateral precerebral arteries without mention of cerebral infarction — (Use additional code, if applicable, to identify status post administration of tPA (rtPA) in a different facility within the last 24 hours prior to admission to current facility: V45.88)

433.80 Occlusion and stenosis of other specified precerebral artery without mention of cerebral infarction — (Use additional code, if applicable, to identify status post administration of tPA (rtPA) in a different facility within the last 24 hours prior to admission to current facility: V45.88)

434.00 Cerebral thrombosis without mention of cerebral infarction — (Use additional code, if applicable, to identify status post administration of tPA (rtPA) in a different facility within the last 24 hours prior to admission to current facility: V45.88)

435.0 Basilar artery syndrome — (Use additional code to identify presence of hypertension)

435.1 Vertebral artery syndrome — (Use additional code to identify presence of hypertension)

435.3 Vertebrobasilar artery syndrome — (Use additional code to identify presence of hypertension)

435.8 Other specified transient cerebral ischemias — (Use additional code to identify presence of hypertension)

435.9 Unspecified transient cerebral ischemia — (Use additional code to identify presence of hypertension) ▽

440.22 Atherosclerosis of native arteries of the extremities with rest pain

440.9 Generalized and unspecified atherosclerosis ▽

443.9 Unspecified peripheral vascular disease ▽

444.01 Saddle embolus of abdominal aorta

444.09 Other arterial embolism and thrombosis of abdominal aorta

444.21 Embolism and thrombosis of arteries of upper extremity

444.22 Embolism and thrombosis of arteries of lower extremity

444.81 Embolism and thrombosis of iliac artery

444.9 Embolism and thrombosis of unspecified artery ▽

445.01 Atheroembolism of upper extremity

445.02 Atheroembolism of lower extremity

445.81 Atheroembolism of kidney — (Use additional code for any associated acute kidney failure or chronic kidney disease: 584, 585)

445.89 Atheroembolism of other site

447.1 Stricture of artery

447.9 Unspecified disorders of arteries and arterioles ▽

453.0 Budd-Chiari syndrome

453.1 Thrombophlebitis migrans

453.2 Other venous embolism and thrombosis, of inferior vena cava

453.3 Embolism and thrombosis of renal vein

453.40 Acute venous embolism and thrombosis of unspecified deep vessels of lower extremity ▽

453.41 Acute venous embolism and thrombosis of deep vessels of proximal lower extremity

453.42 Acute venous embolism and thrombosis of deep vessels of distal lower extremity

453.50 Chronic venous embolism and thrombosis of unspecified deep vessels of lower extremity — (Use additional code, if applicable, for associated long-term (current) use of anticoagulants (V58.61)) ▽

453.51 Chronic venous embolism and thrombosis of deep vessels of proximal lower extremity — (Use additional code, if applicable, for associated long-term (current) use of anticoagulants (V58.61))

453.52 Chronic venous embolism and thrombosis of deep vessels of distal lower extremity — (Use additional code, if applicable, for associated long-term (current) use of anticoagulants (V58.61))

453.6 Venous embolism and thrombosis of superficial vessels of lower extremity — (Use additional code, if applicable, for associated long-term (current) use of anticoagulants (V58.61))

453.71 Chronic venous embolism and thrombosis of superficial veins of upper extremity — (Use additional code, if applicable, for associated long-term (current) use of anticoagulants (V58.61))

453.72 Chronic venous embolism and thrombosis of deep veins of upper extremity — (Use additional code, if applicable, for associated long-term (current) use of anticoagulants (V58.61))

453.73 Chronic venous embolism and thrombosis of upper extremity, unspecified — (Use additional code, if applicable, for associated long-term (current) use of anticoagulants (V58.61)) ▽

453.74 Chronic venous embolism and thrombosis of axillary veins — (Use additional code, if applicable, for associated long-term (current) use of anticoagulants (V58.61))

453.75 Chronic venous embolism and thrombosis of subclavian veins — (Use additional code, if applicable, for associated long-term (current) use of anticoagulants (V58.61))

453.76 Chronic venous embolism and thrombosis of internal jugular veins — (Use additional code, if applicable, for associated long-term (current) use of anticoagulants (V58.61))

453.77 Chronic venous embolism and thrombosis of other thoracic veins — (Use additional code, if applicable, for associated long-term (current) use of anticoagulants (V58.61))

453.79 Chronic venous embolism and thrombosis of other specified veins — (Use additional code, if applicable, for associated long-term (current) use of anticoagulants (V58.61))

453.81 Acute venous embolism and thrombosis of superficial veins of upper extremity

453.82 Acute venous embolism and thrombosis of deep veins of upper extremity

453.83 Acute venous embolism and thrombosis of upper extremity, unspecified ▽

453.84 Acute venous embolism and thrombosis of axillary veins

453.85 Acute venous embolism and thrombosis of subclavian veins

453.86 Acute venous embolism and thrombosis of internal jugular veins

453.87 Acute venous embolism and thrombosis of other thoracic veins

453.89 Acute venous embolism and thrombosis of other specified veins
453.9 Embolism and thrombosis of unspecified site
459.2 Compression of vein
729.5 Pain in soft tissues of limb
747.60 Congenital anomaly of the peripheral vascular system, unspecified site
780.02 Transient alteration of awareness
780.2 Syncope and collapse
780.31 Febrile convulsions (simple), unspecified
780.39 Other convulsions
780.4 Dizziness and giddiness
996.1 Mechanical complication of other vascular device, implant, and graft
996.73 Other complications due to renal dialysis device, implant, and graft — (Use additional code to identify complication: 338.18-338.19, 338.28-338.29)
996.74 Other complications due to other vascular device, implant, and graft — (Use additional code to identify complication: 338.18-338.19, 338.28-338.29)
997.2 Peripheral vascular complications — (Use additional code to identify complications)
V72.5 Radiological examination, not elsewhere classified — (Use additional code(s) to identify any special screening examination(s) performed: V73.0-V82.9)

ICD-9-CM Procedural

00.17 Infusion of vasopressor agent
99.10 Injection or infusion of thrombolytic agent
99.20 Injection or infusion of platelet inhibitor
99.29 Injection or infusion of other therapeutic or prophylactic substance

HCPCS Level II Supplies & Services

C1884 Embolization protective system

37215-37216

37215 Transcatheter placement of intravascular stent(s), cervical carotid artery, percutaneous; with distal embolic protection
37216 without distal embolic protection

ICD-9-CM Diagnostic

433.10 Occlusion and stenosis of carotid artery without mention of cerebral infarction — (Use additional code, if applicable, to identify status post administration of tPA (rtPA) in a different facility within the last 24 hours prior to admission to current facility: V45.88)
433.30 Occlusion and stenosis of multiple and bilateral precerebral arteries without mention of cerebral infarction — (Use additional code, if applicable, to identify status post administration of tPA (rtPA) in a different facility within the last 24 hours prior to admission to current facility: V45.88)
433.80 Occlusion and stenosis of other specified precerebral artery without mention of cerebral infarction — (Use additional code, if applicable, to identify status post administration of tPA (rtPA) in a different facility within the last 24 hours prior to admission to current facility: V45.88)
434.00 Cerebral thrombosis without mention of cerebral infarction — (Use additional code, if applicable, to identify status post administration of tPA (rtPA) in a different facility within the last 24 hours prior to admission to current facility: V45.88)
434.10 Cerebral embolism without mention of cerebral infarction — (Use additional code, if applicable, to identify status post administration of tPA (rtPA) in a different facility within the last 24 hours prior to admission to current facility: V45.88)
434.90 Unspecified cerebral artery occlusion without mention of cerebral infarction — (Use additional code, if applicable, to identify status post administration of tPA (rtPA) in a different facility within the last 24 hours prior to admission to current facility: V45.88)
435.8 Other specified transient cerebral ischemias — (Use additional code to identify presence of hypertension)
435.9 Unspecified transient cerebral ischemia — (Use additional code to identify presence of hypertension)
436 Acute, but ill-defined, cerebrovascular disease — (Use additional code to identify presence of hypertension)
437.0 Cerebral atherosclerosis — (Use additional code to identify presence of hypertension)
437.1 Other generalized ischemic cerebrovascular disease — (Use additional code to identify presence of hypertension)
437.3 Cerebral aneurysm, nonruptured — (Use additional code to identify presence of hypertension)
437.4 Cerebral arteritis — (Use additional code to identify presence of hypertension)
437.8 Other ill-defined cerebrovascular disease — (Use additional code to identify presence of hypertension)
438.0 Cognitive deficits due to cerebrovascular disease — (Use additional code to identify presence of hypertension)
438.20 Hemiplegia affecting unspecified side due to cerebrovascular disease — (Use additional code to identify presence of hypertension)
438.21 Hemiplegia affecting dominant side due to cerebrovascular disease — (Use additional code to identify presence of hypertension)
438.22 Hemiplegia affecting nondominant side due to cerebrovascular disease — (Use additional code to identify presence of hypertension)
438.30 Monoplegia of upper limb affecting unspecified side due to cerebrovascular disease — (Use additional code to identify presence of hypertension)
438.31 Monoplegia of upper limb affecting dominant side due to cerebrovascular disease — (Use additional code to identify presence of hypertension)
438.32 Monoplegia of upper limb affecting nondominant side due to cerebrovascular disease — (Use additional code to identify presence of hypertension)
438.40 Monoplegia of lower limb affecting unspecified side due to cerebrovascular disease — (Use additional code to identify presence of hypertension)
438.41 Monoplegia of lower limb affecting dominant side due to cerebrovascular disease — (Use additional code to identify presence of hypertension)
438.42 Monoplegia of lower limb affecting nondominant side due to cerebrovascular disease — (Use additional code to identify presence of hypertension)
438.50 Other paralytic syndrome affecting unspecified side due to cerebrovascular disease — (Use additional code to identify presence of hypertension. Use additional code to identify type of paralytic syndrome: 344.00-344.09, 344.81)
438.51 Other paralytic syndrome affecting dominant side due to cerebrovascular disease — (Use additional code to identify presence of hypertension. Use additional code to identify type of paralytic syndrome: 344.00-344.09, 344.81)
438.52 Other paralytic syndrome affecting nondominant side due to cerebrovascular disease — (Use additional code to identify presence of hypertension. Use additional code to identify type of paralytic syndrome: 344.00-344.09, 344.81)
438.53 Other paralytic syndrome, bilateral — (Use additional code to identify presence of hypertension. Use additional code to identify type of paralytic syndrome: 344.00-344.09, 344.81)
438.6 Alteration of sensations as late effect of cerebrovascular disease — (Use additional code to identify presence of hypertension. Use additional code to identify the altered sensation)
438.7 Disturbance of vision as late effect of cerebrovascular disease — (Use additional code to identify presence of hypertension. Use additional code to identify the visual disturbance)
438.81 Apraxia due to cerebrovascular disease — (Use additional code to identify presence of hypertension)
438.82 Dysphagia due to cerebrovascular disease — (Use additional code to identify presence of hypertension)
438.83 Facial weakness as late effect of cerebrovascular disease — (Use additional code to identify presence of hypertension)
438.84 Ataxia as late effect of cerebrovascular disease — (Use additional code to identify presence of hypertension)
438.85 Vertigo as late effect of cerebrovascular disease — (Use additional code to identify presence of hypertension)
438.89 Other late effects of cerebrovascular disease — (Use additional code to identify presence of hypertension. Use additional code to identify the late effect)
443.21 Dissection of carotid artery
447.1 Stricture of artery
908.3 Late effect of injury to blood vessel of head, neck, and extremities
996.1 Mechanical complication of other vascular device, implant, and graft

996.74 Other complications due to other vascular device, implant, and graft — (Use additional code to identify complication: 338.18-338.19, 338.28-338.29)

ICD-9-CM Procedural

00.45 Insertion of one vascular stent
00.46 Insertion of two vascular stents
00.47 Insertion of three vascular stents
00.48 Insertion of four or more vascular stents
00.63 Percutaneous insertion of carotid artery stent(s)

HCPCS Level II Supplies & Services

C1884 Embolization protective system

37217

37217 Transcatheter placement of an intravascular stent(s), intrathoracic common carotid artery or innominate artery by retrograde treatment, via open ipsilateral cervical carotid artery exposure, including angioplasty, when performed, and radiological supervision and interpretation

ICD-9-CM Diagnostic

433.10 Occlusion and stenosis of carotid artery without mention of cerebral infarction — (Use additional code, if applicable, to identify status post administration of tPA (rtPA) in a different facility within the last 24 hours prior to admission to current facility: V45.88)
433.30 Occlusion and stenosis of multiple and bilateral precerebral arteries without mention of cerebral infarction — (Use additional code, if applicable, to identify status post administration of tPA (rtPA) in a different facility within the last 24 hours prior to admission to current facility: V45.88)
433.80 Occlusion and stenosis of other specified precerebral artery without mention of cerebral infarction — (Use additional code, if applicable, to identify status post administration of tPA (rtPA) in a different facility within the last 24 hours prior to admission to current facility: V45.88)
447.1 Stricture of artery

ICD-9-CM Procedural

00.40 Procedure on single vessel
00.41 Procedure on two vessels
00.42 Procedure on three vessels
00.43 Procedure on four or more vessels
00.44 Procedure on vessel bifurcation
00.45 Insertion of one vascular stent
00.46 Insertion of two vascular stents
00.47 Insertion of three vascular stents
00.48 Insertion of four or more vascular stents
00.61 Percutaneous angioplasty of extracranial vessel(s)
00.63 Percutaneous insertion of carotid artery stent(s)

37220-37223

37220 Revascularization, endovascular, open or percutaneous, iliac artery, unilateral, initial vessel; with transluminal angioplasty
37221 with transluminal stent placement(s), includes angioplasty within the same vessel, when performed
37222 Revascularization, endovascular, open or percutaneous, iliac artery, each additional ipsilateral iliac vessel; with transluminal angioplasty (List separately in addition to code for primary procedure)
37223 with transluminal stent placement(s), includes angioplasty within the same vessel, when performed (List separately in addition to code for primary procedure)

ICD-9-CM Diagnostic

440.20 Atherosclerosis of native arteries of the extremities, unspecified [Unspecified code]
440.21 Atherosclerosis of native arteries of the extremities with intermittent claudication
440.22 Atherosclerosis of native arteries of the extremities with rest pain
440.23 Atherosclerosis of native arteries of the extremities with ulceration — (Use additional code for any associated ulceration: 707.10-707.19, 707.8, 707.9)
440.24 Atherosclerosis of native arteries of the extremities with gangrene — (Use additional code for any associated ulceration: 707.10-707.19, 707.8, 707.9)
440.8 Atherosclerosis of other specified arteries
440.9 Generalized and unspecified atherosclerosis [Unspecified code]
442.2 Aneurysm of iliac artery
443.9 Unspecified peripheral vascular disease [Unspecified code]
444.81 Embolism and thrombosis of iliac artery
445.89 Atheroembolism of other site
447.1 Stricture of artery
447.9 Unspecified disorders of arteries and arterioles [Unspecified code]
747.60 Congenital anomaly of the peripheral vascular system, unspecified site [Unspecified code]
747.69 Congenital anomaly of other specified site of peripheral vascular system

ICD-9-CM Procedural

00.40 Procedure on single vessel
00.41 Procedure on two vessels
00.42 Procedure on three vessels
00.43 Procedure on four or more vessels
00.45 Insertion of one vascular stent
00.46 Insertion of two vascular stents
00.47 Insertion of three vascular stents
00.48 Insertion of four or more vascular stents
00.55 Insertion of drug-eluting stent(s) of other peripheral vessel(s)
17.56 Atherectomy of other non-coronary vessel(s)
39.50 Angioplasty of other non-coronary vessel(s)
39.90 Insertion of non-drug-eluting peripheral (non-coronary) vessel stents(s)

37224-37227

37224 Revascularization, endovascular, open or percutaneous, femoral, popliteal artery(s), unilateral; with transluminal angioplasty
37225 with atherectomy, includes angioplasty within the same vessel, when performed
37226 with transluminal stent placement(s), includes angioplasty within the same vessel, when performed
37227 with transluminal stent placement(s) and atherectomy, includes angioplasty within the same vessel, when performed

ICD-9-CM Diagnostic

249.70 Secondary diabetes mellitus with peripheral circulatory disorders, not stated as uncontrolled, or unspecified — (Use additional code to identify manifestation: 443.81, 785.4) (Use additional code to identify any associated insulin use: V58.67)
249.71 Secondary diabetes mellitus with peripheral circulatory disorders, uncontrolled — (Use additional code to identify manifestation: 443.81, 785.4) (Use additional code to identify any associated insulin use: V58.67)
250.70 Diabetes with peripheral circulatory disorders, type II or unspecified type, not stated as uncontrolled — (Use additional code to identify manifestation: 443.81, 785.4)
250.71 Diabetes with peripheral circulatory disorders, type I [juvenile type], not stated as uncontrolled — (Use additional code to identify manifestation: 443.81, 785.4)
250.72 Diabetes with peripheral circulatory disorders, type II or unspecified type, uncontrolled — (Use additional code to identify manifestation: 443.81, 785.4)
250.73 Diabetes with peripheral circulatory disorders, type I [juvenile type], uncontrolled — (Use additional code to identify manifestation: 443.81, 785.4)
440.20 Atherosclerosis of native arteries of the extremities, unspecified [Unspecified code]
440.21 Atherosclerosis of native arteries of the extremities with intermittent claudication
440.22 Atherosclerosis of native arteries of the extremities with rest pain
440.23 Atherosclerosis of native arteries of the extremities with ulceration — (Use additional code for any associated ulceration: 707.10-707.19, 707.8, 707.9)
440.24 Atherosclerosis of native arteries of the extremities with gangrene — (Use additional code for any associated ulceration: 707.10-707.19, 707.8, 707.9)
440.29 Other atherosclerosis of native arteries of the extremities
440.30 Atherosclerosis of unspecified bypass graft of extremities [Unspecified code]
440.31 Atherosclerosis of autologous vein bypass graft of extremities

440.32 Atherosclerosis of nonautologous biological bypass graft of extremities
440.4 Chronic total occlusion of artery of the extremities
440.8 Atherosclerosis of other specified arteries
440.9 Generalized and unspecified atherosclerosis ▽
442.3 Aneurysm of artery of lower extremity
443.81 Peripheral angiopathy in diseases classified elsewhere — (Code first underlying disease: 249.7, 250.7) ☒
443.9 Unspecified peripheral vascular disease ▽
444.22 Embolism and thrombosis of arteries of lower extremity
444.89 Embolism and thrombosis of other specified artery
444.9 Embolism and thrombosis of unspecified artery ▽
445.02 Atheroembolism of lower extremity
447.1 Stricture of artery
447.8 Other specified disorders of arteries and arterioles
447.9 Unspecified disorders of arteries and arterioles ▽
747.64 Congenital lower limb vessel anomaly
996.62 Infection and inflammatory reaction due to other vascular device, implant, and graft — (Use additional code to identify specified infections)
996.74 Other complications due to other vascular device, implant, and graft — (Use additional code to identify complication: 338.18-338.19, 338.28-338.29)
999.2 Other vascular complications of medical care, not elsewhere classified

ICD-9-CM Procedural

00.40 Procedure on single vessel
00.41 Procedure on two vessels
00.42 Procedure on three vessels
00.43 Procedure on four or more vessels
00.45 Insertion of one vascular stent
00.46 Insertion of two vascular stents
00.47 Insertion of three vascular stents
00.48 Insertion of four or more vascular stents
00.55 Insertion of drug-eluting stent(s) of other peripheral vessel(s)
00.60 Insertion of drug-eluting stent(s) of superficial femoral artery
17.56 Atherectomy of other non-coronary vessel(s)
39.50 Angioplasty of other non-coronary vessel(s)
39.90 Insertion of non-drug-eluting peripheral (non-coronary) vessel stents(s)

37228-37235

37228 Revascularization, endovascular, open or percutaneous, tibial, peroneal artery, unilateral, initial vessel; with transluminal angioplasty
37229 with atherectomy, includes angioplasty within the same vessel, when performed
37230 with transluminal stent placement(s), includes angioplasty within the same vessel, when performed
37231 with transluminal stent placement(s) and atherectomy, includes angioplasty within the same vessel, when performed
37232 Revascularization, endovascular, open or percutaneous, tibial/peroneal artery, unilateral, each additional vessel; with transluminal angioplasty (List separately in addition to code for primary procedure)
37233 with atherectomy, includes angioplasty within the same vessel, when performed (List separately in addition to code for primary procedure)
37234 with transluminal stent placement(s), includes angioplasty within the same vessel, when performed (List separately in addition to code for primary procedure)
37235 with transluminal stent placement(s) and atherectomy, includes angioplasty within the same vessel, when performed (List separately in addition to code for primary procedure)

ICD-9-CM Diagnostic

249.70 Secondary diabetes mellitus with peripheral circulatory disorders, not stated as uncontrolled, or unspecified — (Use additional code to identify manifestation: 443.81, 785.4) (Use additional code to identify any associated insulin use: V58.67)
249.71 Secondary diabetes mellitus with peripheral circulatory disorders, uncontrolled — (Use additional code to identify manifestation: 443.81, 785.4) (Use additional code to identify any associated insulin use: V58.67)
250.70 Diabetes with peripheral circulatory disorders, type II or unspecified type, not stated as uncontrolled — (Use additional code to identify manifestation: 443.81, 785.4)
250.71 Diabetes with peripheral circulatory disorders, type I [juvenile type], not stated as uncontrolled — (Use additional code to identify manifestation: 443.81, 785.4)
250.72 Diabetes with peripheral circulatory disorders, type II or unspecified type, uncontrolled — (Use additional code to identify manifestation: 443.81, 785.4)
250.73 Diabetes with peripheral circulatory disorders, type I [juvenile type], uncontrolled — (Use additional code to identify manifestation: 443.81, 785.4)
440.20 Atherosclerosis of native arteries of the extremities, unspecified ▽
440.21 Atherosclerosis of native arteries of the extremities with intermittent claudication
440.22 Atherosclerosis of native arteries of the extremities with rest pain
440.23 Atherosclerosis of native arteries of the extremities with ulceration — (Use additional code for any associated ulceration: 707.10-707.19, 707.8, 707.9)
440.24 Atherosclerosis of native arteries of the extremities with gangrene — (Use additional code for any associated ulceration: 707.10-707.19, 707.8, 707.9)
440.29 Other atherosclerosis of native arteries of the extremities
440.30 Atherosclerosis of unspecified bypass graft of extremities ▽
440.31 Atherosclerosis of autologous vein bypass graft of extremities
440.32 Atherosclerosis of nonautologous biological bypass graft of extremities
440.4 Chronic total occlusion of artery of the extremities
440.8 Atherosclerosis of other specified arteries
440.9 Generalized and unspecified atherosclerosis ▽
442.3 Aneurysm of artery of lower extremity
443.81 Peripheral angiopathy in diseases classified elsewhere — (Code first underlying disease: 249.7, 250.7) ☒
443.9 Unspecified peripheral vascular disease ▽
444.22 Embolism and thrombosis of arteries of lower extremity
444.89 Embolism and thrombosis of other specified artery
444.9 Embolism and thrombosis of unspecified artery ▽
445.02 Atheroembolism of lower extremity
447.1 Stricture of artery
447.8 Other specified disorders of arteries and arterioles
447.9 Unspecified disorders of arteries and arterioles ▽
747.64 Congenital lower limb vessel anomaly
996.62 Infection and inflammatory reaction due to other vascular device, implant, and graft — (Use additional code to identify specified infections)
996.74 Other complications due to other vascular device, implant, and graft — (Use additional code to identify complication: 338.18-338.19, 338.28-338.29)
999.2 Other vascular complications of medical care, not elsewhere classified

ICD-9-CM Procedural

00.40 Procedure on single vessel
00.41 Procedure on two vessels
00.42 Procedure on three vessels
00.43 Procedure on four or more vessels
00.45 Insertion of one vascular stent
00.46 Insertion of two vascular stents
00.47 Insertion of three vascular stents
00.48 Insertion of four or more vascular stents
00.55 Insertion of drug-eluting stent(s) of other peripheral vessel(s)
17.56 Atherectomy of other non-coronary vessel(s)
39.50 Angioplasty of other non-coronary vessel(s)
39.90 Insertion of non-drug-eluting peripheral (non-coronary) vessel stents(s)

37236-37237

37236 Transcatheter placement of an intravascular stent(s) (except lower extremity, cervical carotid, extracranial vertebral or intrathoracic carotid, intracranial, or coronary), open or percutaneous, including radiological supervision and interpretation and including all angioplasty within the same vessel, when performed; initial artery

37237 each additional artery (List separately in addition to code for primary procedure)

ICD-9-CM Diagnostic

The application of this code is too broad to adequately present ICD-9-CM diagnostic code links here. Refer to your ICD-9-CM book.

ICD-9-CM Procedural

00.40 Procedure on single vessel
00.41 Procedure on two vessels
00.42 Procedure on three vessels
00.43 Procedure on four or more vessels
00.44 Procedure on vessel bifurcation
00.45 Insertion of one vascular stent
00.46 Insertion of two vascular stents
00.47 Insertion of three vascular stents
00.48 Insertion of four or more vascular stents
00.55 Insertion of drug-eluting stent(s) of other peripheral vessel(s)
39.50 Angioplasty of other non-coronary vessel(s)
39.90 Insertion of non-drug-eluting peripheral (non-coronary) vessel stents(s)

37238-37239

37238 Transcatheter placement of an intravascular stent(s), open or percutaneous, including radiological supervision and interpretation and including angioplasty within the same vessel, when performed; initial vein

37239 each additional vein (List separately in addition to code for primary procedure)

ICD-9-CM Diagnostic

The application of this code is too broad to adequately present ICD-9-CM diagnostic code links here. Refer to your ICD-9-CM book.

ICD-9-CM Procedural

00.40 Procedure on single vessel
00.41 Procedure on two vessels
00.42 Procedure on three vessels
00.43 Procedure on four or more vessels
00.44 Procedure on vessel bifurcation
00.45 Insertion of one vascular stent
00.46 Insertion of two vascular stents
00.47 Insertion of three vascular stents
00.48 Insertion of four or more vascular stents
00.55 Insertion of drug-eluting stent(s) of other peripheral vessel(s)
39.50 Angioplasty of other non-coronary vessel(s)
39.90 Insertion of non-drug-eluting peripheral (non-coronary) vessel stents(s)

37241-37242

37241 Vascular embolization or occlusion, inclusive of all radiological supervision and interpretation, intraprocedural roadmapping, and imaging guidance necessary to complete the intervention; venous, other than hemorrhage (eg, congenital or acquired venous malformations, venous and capillary hemangiomas, varices, varicoceles)

37242 arterial, other than hemorrhage or tumor (eg, congenital or acquired arterial malformations, arteriovenous malformations, arteriovenous fistulas, aneurysms, pseudoaneurysms)

ICD-9-CM Diagnostic

The application of this code is too broad to adequately present ICD-9-CM diagnostic code links here. Refer to your ICD-9-CM book.

ICD-9-CM Procedural

39.79 Other endovascular procedures on other vessels

37243

37243 Vascular embolization or occlusion, inclusive of all radiological supervision and interpretation, intraprocedural roadmapping, and imaging guidance necessary to complete the intervention; for tumors, organ ischemia, or infarction

ICD-9-CM Diagnostic

The application of this code is too broad to adequately present ICD-9-CM diagnostic code links here. Refer to your ICD-9-CM book.

ICD-9-CM Procedural

39.79 Other endovascular procedures on other vessels

37244

37244 Vascular embolization or occlusion, inclusive of all radiological supervision and interpretation, intraprocedural roadmapping, and imaging guidance necessary to complete the intervention; for arterial or venous hemorrhage or lymphatic extravasation

ICD-9-CM Diagnostic

The application of this code is too broad to adequately present ICD-9-CM diagnostic code links here. Refer to your ICD-9-CM book.

ICD-9-CM Procedural

39.79 Other endovascular procedures on other vessels
39.98 Control of hemorrhage, not otherwise specified

37250-37251

37250 Intravascular ultrasound (non-coronary vessel) during diagnostic evaluation and/or therapeutic intervention; initial vessel (List separately in addition to code for primary procedure)

37251 each additional vessel (List separately in addition to code for primary procedure)

ICD-9-CM Diagnostic

The ICD-9-CM diagnostic code(s) would be the same as the actual procedure performed because these are in-addition-to codes.

ICD-9-CM Procedural

00.01 Therapeutic ultrasound of vessels of head and neck
00.02 Therapeutic ultrasound of heart
00.03 Therapeutic ultrasound of peripheral vascular vessels
00.09 Other therapeutic ultrasound
00.21 Intravascular imaging of extracranial cerebral vessels
00.22 Intravascular imaging of intrathoracic vessels
00.23 Intravascular imaging of peripheral vessels
00.25 Intravascular imaging of renal vessels
00.28 Intravascular imaging, other specified vessel(s)
00.29 Intravascular imaging, unspecified vessel(s)
38.23 Intravascular spectroscopy

37500

37500 Vascular endoscopy, surgical, with ligation of perforator veins, subfascial (SEPS)

ICD-9-CM Diagnostic

454.0 Varicose veins of lower extremities with ulcer
454.1 Varicose veins of lower extremities with inflammation
454.2 Varicose veins of lower extremities with ulcer and inflammation
454.8 Varicose veins of the lower extremities with other complications
454.9 Asymptomatic varicose veins
459.10 Postphlebitic syndrome without complications
459.11 Postphlebitic syndrome with ulcer
459.12 Postphlebitic syndrome with inflammation
459.13 Postphlebitic syndrome with ulcer and inflammation
459.19 Postphlebitic syndrome with other complication
459.81 Unspecified venous (peripheral) insufficiency — (Use additional code for any associated ulceration: 707.10-707.19, 707.8, 707.9)

707.10 Ulcer of lower limb, unspecified — (Code, if applicable, any causal condition first: 249.80-249.81, 250.80-250.83, 440.23, 459.11, 459.13, 459.31, 459.33) ▽
707.11 Ulcer of thigh — (Code, if applicable, any causal condition first: 249.80-249.81, 250.80-250.83, 440.23, 459.11, 459.13, 459.31, 459.33)
707.12 Ulcer of calf — (Code, if applicable, any causal condition first: 249.80-249.81, 250.80-250.83, 440.23, 459.11, 459.13, 459.31, 459.33)
707.13 Ulcer of ankle — (Code, if applicable, any causal condition first: 249.80-249.81, 250.80-250.83, 440.23, 459.11, 459.13, 459.31, 459.33)
707.14 Ulcer of heel and midfoot — (Code, if applicable, any causal condition first: 249.80-249.81, 250.80-250.83, 440.23, 459.11, 459.13, 459.31, 459.33)
707.15 Ulcer of other part of foot — (Code, if applicable, any causal condition first: 249.80-249.81, 250.80-250.83, 440.23, 459.11, 459.13, 459.31, 459.33)
707.19 Ulcer of other part of lower limb — (Code, if applicable, any causal condition first: 249.80-249.81, 250.80-250.83, 440.23, 459.11, 459.13, 459.31, 459.33)
729.5 Pain in soft tissues of limb

ICD-9-CM Procedural

38.59 Ligation and stripping of lower limb varicose veins
38.89 Other surgical occlusion of lower limb veins

37565

37565 Ligation, internal jugular vein

ICD-9-CM Diagnostic

249.70 Secondary diabetes mellitus with peripheral circulatory disorders, not stated as uncontrolled, or unspecified — (Use additional code to identify manifestation: 443.81, 785.4) (Use additional code to identify any associated insulin use: V58.67)
249.71 Secondary diabetes mellitus with peripheral circulatory disorders, uncontrolled — (Use additional code to identify manifestation: 443.81, 785.4) (Use additional code to identify any associated insulin use: V58.67)
250.70 Diabetes with peripheral circulatory disorders, type II or unspecified type, not stated as uncontrolled — (Use additional code to identify manifestation: 443.81, 785.4)
250.71 Diabetes with peripheral circulatory disorders, type I [juvenile type], not stated as uncontrolled — (Use additional code to identify manifestation: 443.81, 785.4)
401.0 Essential hypertension, malignant
401.1 Essential hypertension, benign
401.9 Unspecified essential hypertension ▽
443.89 Other peripheral vascular disease
447.1 Stricture of artery
447.6 Unspecified arteritis ▽
447.8 Other specified disorders of arteries and arterioles
453.76 Chronic venous embolism and thrombosis of internal jugular veins — (Use additional code, if applicable, for associated long-term (current) use of anticoagulants (V58.61))
453.86 Acute venous embolism and thrombosis of internal jugular veins
459.0 Unspecified hemorrhage ▽
729.90 Disorders of soft tissue, unspecified ▽
900.1 Internal jugular vein injury
998.11 Hemorrhage complicating a procedure
998.12 Hematoma complicating a procedure
998.13 Seroma complicating a procedure
998.2 Accidental puncture or laceration during procedure
998.30 Disruption of wound, unspecified ▽
998.33 Disruption of traumatic injury wound repair

ICD-9-CM Procedural

38.82 Other surgical occlusion of other vessels of head and neck

37600

37600 Ligation; external carotid artery

ICD-9-CM Diagnostic

249.70 Secondary diabetes mellitus with peripheral circulatory disorders, not stated as uncontrolled, or unspecified — (Use additional code to identify manifestation: 443.81, 785.4) (Use additional code to identify any associated insulin use: V58.67)
249.71 Secondary diabetes mellitus with peripheral circulatory disorders, uncontrolled — (Use additional code to identify manifestation: 443.81, 785.4) (Use additional code to identify any associated insulin use: V58.67)
250.70 Diabetes with peripheral circulatory disorders, type II or unspecified type, not stated as uncontrolled — (Use additional code to identify manifestation: 443.81, 785.4)
250.71 Diabetes with peripheral circulatory disorders, type I [juvenile type], not stated as uncontrolled — (Use additional code to identify manifestation: 443.81, 785.4)
401.0 Essential hypertension, malignant
401.1 Essential hypertension, benign
401.9 Unspecified essential hypertension ▽
443.89 Other peripheral vascular disease
447.1 Stricture of artery
447.6 Unspecified arteritis ▽
447.8 Other specified disorders of arteries and arterioles
459.0 Unspecified hemorrhage ▽
478.29 Other disease of pharynx or nasopharynx — (Use additional code to identify infectious organism)
784.7 Epistaxis
900.02 External carotid artery injury
998.11 Hemorrhage complicating a procedure
998.12 Hematoma complicating a procedure
998.13 Seroma complicating a procedure
998.2 Accidental puncture or laceration during procedure

ICD-9-CM Procedural

21.06 Control of epistaxis by ligation of the external carotid artery
38.82 Other surgical occlusion of other vessels of head and neck

37605-37606

37605 Ligation; internal or common carotid artery
37606 internal or common carotid artery, with gradual occlusion, as with Selverstone or Crutchfield clamp

ICD-9-CM Diagnostic

249.70 Secondary diabetes mellitus with peripheral circulatory disorders, not stated as uncontrolled, or unspecified — (Use additional code to identify manifestation: 443.81, 785.4) (Use additional code to identify any associated insulin use: V58.67)
249.71 Secondary diabetes mellitus with peripheral circulatory disorders, uncontrolled — (Use additional code to identify manifestation: 443.81, 785.4) (Use additional code to identify any associated insulin use: V58.67)
250.70 Diabetes with peripheral circulatory disorders, type II or unspecified type, not stated as uncontrolled — (Use additional code to identify manifestation: 443.81, 785.4)
250.71 Diabetes with peripheral circulatory disorders, type I [juvenile type], not stated as uncontrolled — (Use additional code to identify manifestation: 443.81, 785.4)
401.0 Essential hypertension, malignant
401.9 Unspecified essential hypertension ▽
435.9 Unspecified transient cerebral ischemia — (Use additional code to identify presence of hypertension) ▽
442.81 Aneurysm of artery of neck
443.21 Dissection of carotid artery
443.89 Other peripheral vascular disease
447.1 Stricture of artery
447.6 Unspecified arteritis ▽
447.8 Other specified disorders of arteries and arterioles
459.0 Unspecified hemorrhage ▽

874.8 Open wound of other and unspecified parts of neck, without mention of complication ▽
900.01 Common carotid artery injury
900.03 Internal carotid artery injury
998.11 Hemorrhage complicating a procedure
998.12 Hematoma complicating a procedure
998.13 Seroma complicating a procedure
998.2 Accidental puncture or laceration during procedure

ICD-9-CM Procedural

38.82 Other surgical occlusion of other vessels of head and neck

37607

37607 Ligation or banding of angioaccess arteriovenous fistula

ICD-9-CM Diagnostic

996.73 Other complications due to renal dialysis device, implant, and graft — (Use additional code to identify complication: 338.18-338.19, 338.28-338.29)
996.74 Other complications due to other vascular device, implant, and graft — (Use additional code to identify complication: 338.18-338.19, 338.28-338.29)
V53.90 Fitting and adjustment of other and unspecified device, Unspecified device ▽
V53.99 Fitting and adjustment, Other device
V58.81 Fitting and adjustment of vascular catheter

ICD-9-CM Procedural

38.82 Other surgical occlusion of other vessels of head and neck
39.42 Revision of arteriovenous shunt for renal dialysis
39.49 Other revision of vascular procedure
39.53 Repair of arteriovenous fistula

37609

37609 Ligation or biopsy, temporal artery

ICD-9-CM Diagnostic

440.8 Atherosclerosis of other specified arteries
440.9 Generalized and unspecified atherosclerosis ▽
446.5 Giant cell arteritis
447.6 Unspecified arteritis ▽
459.9 Unspecified circulatory system disorder ▽
747.81 Congenital anomaly of cerebrovascular system
780.2 Syncope and collapse
780.4 Dizziness and giddiness
784.0 Headache
784.2 Swelling, mass, or lump in head and neck
900.89 Injury to other specified blood vessels of head and neck
V71.89 Observation for other specified suspected conditions

ICD-9-CM Procedural

38.21 Biopsy of blood vessel
38.82 Other surgical occlusion of other vessels of head and neck

37615

37615 Ligation, major artery (eg, post-traumatic, rupture); neck

ICD-9-CM Diagnostic

447.2 Rupture of artery
729.92 Nontraumatic hematoma of soft tissue
900.00 Injury to carotid artery, unspecified ▽
900.01 Common carotid artery injury
900.02 External carotid artery injury
900.03 Internal carotid artery injury
900.82 Injury to multiple blood vessels of head and neck
900.89 Injury to other specified blood vessels of head and neck
998.11 Hemorrhage complicating a procedure
998.12 Hematoma complicating a procedure
998.13 Seroma complicating a procedure
998.2 Accidental puncture or laceration during procedure

ICD-9-CM Procedural

06.92 Ligation of thyroid vessels
38.82 Other surgical occlusion of other vessels of head and neck

37616

37616 Ligation, major artery (eg, post-traumatic, rupture); chest

ICD-9-CM Diagnostic

441.1 Thoracic aneurysm, ruptured
441.5 Aortic aneurysm of unspecified site, ruptured ▽
447.2 Rupture of artery
729.92 Nontraumatic hematoma of soft tissue
901.0 Thoracic aorta injury
901.2 Superior vena cava injury
901.41 Pulmonary artery injury
908.4 Late effect of injury to blood vessel of thorax, abdomen, and pelvis
908.6 Late effect of certain complications of trauma
997.79 Vascular complications of other vessels — (Use additional code to identify complications)
998.11 Hemorrhage complicating a procedure
998.12 Hematoma complicating a procedure
998.13 Seroma complicating a procedure
998.2 Accidental puncture or laceration during procedure

ICD-9-CM Procedural

38.85 Other surgical occlusion of other thoracic vessel

37617

37617 Ligation, major artery (eg, post-traumatic, rupture); abdomen

ICD-9-CM Diagnostic

441.3 Abdominal aneurysm, ruptured
441.6 Thoracoabdominal aneurysm, ruptured
442.1 Aneurysm of renal artery
442.2 Aneurysm of iliac artery
442.84 Aneurysm of other visceral artery
729.92 Nontraumatic hematoma of soft tissue
902.0 Abdominal aorta injury
902.31 Injury to superior mesenteric vein and primary subdivisions
908.4 Late effect of injury to blood vessel of thorax, abdomen, and pelvis
908.6 Late effect of certain complications of trauma
997.71 Vascular complications of mesenteric artery — (Use additional code to identify complications)
997.72 Vascular complications of renal artery — (Use additional code to identify complications)
997.79 Vascular complications of other vessels — (Use additional code to identify complications)
998.11 Hemorrhage complicating a procedure
998.12 Hematoma complicating a procedure
998.13 Seroma complicating a procedure
998.2 Accidental puncture or laceration during procedure

ICD-9-CM Procedural

07.43 Ligation of adrenal vessels
38.86 Other surgical occlusion of abdominal arteries

37618

37618 Ligation, major artery (eg, post-traumatic, rupture); extremity

ICD-9-CM Diagnostic

881.10 Open wound of forearm, complicated
903.01 Axillary artery injury
903.1 Brachial blood vessels injury
903.2 Radial blood vessels injury
903.3 Ulnar blood vessels injury
903.5 Digital blood vessels injury
903.8 Injury to specified blood vessels of upper extremity, other
904.0 Common femoral artery injury
904.1 Superficial femoral artery injury
904.41 Popliteal artery injury
904.51 Anterior tibial artery injury
904.53 Posterior tibial artery injury
904.6 Deep plantar blood vessels injury
996.1 Mechanical complication of other vascular device, implant, and graft
998.11 Hemorrhage complicating a procedure
998.12 Hematoma complicating a procedure
998.13 Seroma complicating a procedure
998.2 Accidental puncture or laceration during procedure

ICD-9-CM Procedural

38.83 Other surgical occlusion of upper limb vessels
38.88 Other surgical occlusion of lower limb arteries
38.89 Other surgical occlusion of lower limb veins

37619

37619 Ligation of inferior vena cava

ICD-9-CM Diagnostic

415.19 Other pulmonary embolism and infarction
416.2 Chronic pulmonary embolism — (Use additional code, if applicable, for associated long-term (current) use of anticoagulants (V58.61))
453.40 Acute venous embolism and thrombosis of unspecified deep vessels of lower extremity ▽
453.41 Acute venous embolism and thrombosis of deep vessels of proximal lower extremity
453.42 Acute venous embolism and thrombosis of deep vessels of distal lower extremity
453.50 Chronic venous embolism and thrombosis of unspecified deep vessels of lower extremity — (Use additional code, if applicable, for associated long-term (current) use of anticoagulants (V58.61)) ▽
453.51 Chronic venous embolism and thrombosis of deep vessels of proximal lower extremity — (Use additional code, if applicable, for associated long-term (current) use of anticoagulants (V58.61))
453.52 Chronic venous embolism and thrombosis of deep vessels of distal lower extremity — (Use additional code, if applicable, for associated long-term (current) use of anticoagulants (V58.61))
453.6 Venous embolism and thrombosis of superficial vessels of lower extremity — (Use additional code, if applicable, for associated long-term (current) use of anticoagulants (V58.61))
V12.51 Personal history of venous thrombosis and embolism
V12.55 Personal history of pulmonary embolism

ICD-9-CM Procedural

38.7 Interruption of the vena cava

37650

37650 Ligation of femoral vein

ICD-9-CM Diagnostic

451.11 Phlebitis and thrombophlebitis of femoral vein (deep) (superficial) — (Use additional E code to identify drug, if drug-induced)
451.2 Phlebitis and thrombophlebitis of lower extremities, unspecified — (Use additional E code to identify drug, if drug-induced) ▽
454.0 Varicose veins of lower extremities with ulcer
454.1 Varicose veins of lower extremities with inflammation
454.2 Varicose veins of lower extremities with ulcer and inflammation
454.8 Varicose veins of the lower extremities with other complications
454.9 Asymptomatic varicose veins
459.10 Postphlebitic syndrome without complications
459.11 Postphlebitic syndrome with ulcer
459.12 Postphlebitic syndrome with inflammation
459.13 Postphlebitic syndrome with ulcer and inflammation
459.19 Postphlebitic syndrome with other complication
459.81 Unspecified venous (peripheral) insufficiency — (Use additional code for any associated ulceration: 707.10-707.19, 707.8, 707.9) ▽
639.6 Embolism following abortion or ectopic and molar pregnancies ♀
904.2 Femoral vein injury
997.2 Peripheral vascular complications — (Use additional code to identify complications)
998.11 Hemorrhage complicating a procedure
998.12 Hematoma complicating a procedure
998.13 Seroma complicating a procedure
998.2 Accidental puncture or laceration during procedure

ICD-9-CM Procedural

38.89 Other surgical occlusion of lower limb veins

37660

37660 Ligation of common iliac vein

ICD-9-CM Diagnostic

442.2 Aneurysm of iliac artery
443.22 Dissection of iliac artery
451.81 Phlebitis and thrombophlebitis of iliac vein — (Use additional E code to identify drug, if drug-induced)
453.41 Acute venous embolism and thrombosis of deep vessels of proximal lower extremity
453.51 Chronic venous embolism and thrombosis of deep vessels of proximal lower extremity — (Use additional code, if applicable, for associated long-term (current) use of anticoagulants (V58.61))
902.54 Iliac vein injury
902.9 Injury to blood vessel of abdomen and pelvis, unspecified ▽
997.79 Vascular complications of other vessels — (Use additional code to identify complications)
998.11 Hemorrhage complicating a procedure
998.12 Hematoma complicating a procedure
998.13 Seroma complicating a procedure
998.2 Accidental puncture or laceration during procedure

ICD-9-CM Procedural

38.87 Other surgical occlusion of abdominal veins

37700

37700 Ligation and division of long saphenous vein at saphenofemoral junction, or distal interruptions

ICD-9-CM Diagnostic

454.0 Varicose veins of lower extremities with ulcer
454.1 Varicose veins of lower extremities with inflammation

454.2 Varicose veins of lower extremities with ulcer and inflammation
454.8 Varicose veins of the lower extremities with other complications
454.9 Asymptomatic varicose veins
459.10 Postphlebitic syndrome without complications
459.11 Postphlebitic syndrome with ulcer
459.12 Postphlebitic syndrome with inflammation
459.13 Postphlebitic syndrome with ulcer and inflammation
459.19 Postphlebitic syndrome with other complication
459.81 Unspecified venous (peripheral) insufficiency — (Use additional code for any associated ulceration: 707.10-707.19, 707.8, 707.9) ▽
707.10 Ulcer of lower limb, unspecified — (Code, if applicable, any causal condition first: 249.80-249.81, 250.80-250.83, 440.23, 459.11, 459.13, 459.31, 459.33) ▽
707.11 Ulcer of thigh — (Code, if applicable, any causal condition first: 249.80-249.81, 250.80-250.83, 440.23, 459.11, 459.13, 459.31, 459.33)
707.12 Ulcer of calf — (Code, if applicable, any causal condition first: 249.80-249.81, 250.80-250.83, 440.23, 459.11, 459.13, 459.31, 459.33)
707.13 Ulcer of ankle — (Code, if applicable, any causal condition first: 249.80-249.81, 250.80-250.83, 440.23, 459.11, 459.13, 459.31, 459.33)
707.14 Ulcer of heel and midfoot — (Code, if applicable, any causal condition first: 249.80-249.81, 250.80-250.83, 440.23, 459.11, 459.13, 459.31, 459.33)
707.15 Ulcer of other part of foot — (Code, if applicable, any causal condition first: 249.80-249.81, 250.80-250.83, 440.23, 459.11, 459.13, 459.31, 459.33)
707.19 Ulcer of other part of lower limb — (Code, if applicable, any causal condition first: 249.80-249.81, 250.80-250.83, 440.23, 459.11, 459.13, 459.31, 459.33)
V50.1 Other plastic surgery for unacceptable cosmetic appearance

ICD-9-CM Procedural

38.59 Ligation and stripping of lower limb varicose veins
38.89 Other surgical occlusion of lower limb veins

37718-37722

37718 Ligation, division, and stripping, short saphenous vein
37722 Ligation, division, and stripping, long (greater) saphenous veins from saphenofemoral junction to knee or below

ICD-9-CM Diagnostic

454.0 Varicose veins of lower extremities with ulcer
454.1 Varicose veins of lower extremities with inflammation
454.2 Varicose veins of lower extremities with ulcer and inflammation
454.8 Varicose veins of the lower extremities with other complications
454.9 Asymptomatic varicose veins
459.10 Postphlebitic syndrome without complications
459.11 Postphlebitic syndrome with ulcer
459.12 Postphlebitic syndrome with inflammation
459.13 Postphlebitic syndrome with ulcer and inflammation
459.19 Postphlebitic syndrome with other complication
459.81 Unspecified venous (peripheral) insufficiency — (Use additional code for any associated ulceration: 707.10-707.19, 707.8, 707.9) ▽
707.10 Ulcer of lower limb, unspecified — (Code, if applicable, any causal condition first: 249.80-249.81, 250.80-250.83, 440.23, 459.11, 459.13, 459.31, 459.33) ▽
707.11 Ulcer of thigh — (Code, if applicable, any causal condition first: 249.80-249.81, 250.80-250.83, 440.23, 459.11, 459.13, 459.31, 459.33)
707.12 Ulcer of calf — (Code, if applicable, any causal condition first: 249.80-249.81, 250.80-250.83, 440.23, 459.11, 459.13, 459.31, 459.33)
707.13 Ulcer of ankle — (Code, if applicable, any causal condition first: 249.80-249.81, 250.80-250.83, 440.23, 459.11, 459.13, 459.31, 459.33)
707.14 Ulcer of heel and midfoot — (Code, if applicable, any causal condition first: 249.80-249.81, 250.80-250.83, 440.23, 459.11, 459.13, 459.31, 459.33)
707.15 Ulcer of other part of foot — (Code, if applicable, any causal condition first: 249.80-249.81, 250.80-250.83, 440.23, 459.11, 459.13, 459.31, 459.33)
707.19 Ulcer of other part of lower limb — (Code, if applicable, any causal condition first: 249.80-249.81, 250.80-250.83, 440.23, 459.11, 459.13, 459.31, 459.33)
V50.1 Other plastic surgery for unacceptable cosmetic appearance

ICD-9-CM Procedural

38.59 Ligation and stripping of lower limb varicose veins

37735

37735 Ligation and division and complete stripping of long or short saphenous veins with radical excision of ulcer and skin graft and/or interruption of communicating veins of lower leg, with excision of deep fascia

ICD-9-CM Diagnostic

454.0 Varicose veins of lower extremities with ulcer
454.1 Varicose veins of lower extremities with inflammation
454.2 Varicose veins of lower extremities with ulcer and inflammation
454.8 Varicose veins of the lower extremities with other complications
454.9 Asymptomatic varicose veins
459.10 Postphlebitic syndrome without complications
459.11 Postphlebitic syndrome with ulcer
459.12 Postphlebitic syndrome with inflammation
459.13 Postphlebitic syndrome with ulcer and inflammation
459.19 Postphlebitic syndrome with other complication
459.81 Unspecified venous (peripheral) insufficiency — (Use additional code for any associated ulceration: 707.10-707.19, 707.8, 707.9) ▽
707.10 Ulcer of lower limb, unspecified — (Code, if applicable, any causal condition first: 249.80-249.81, 250.80-250.83, 440.23, 459.11, 459.13, 459.31, 459.33) ▽
707.11 Ulcer of thigh — (Code, if applicable, any causal condition first: 249.80-249.81, 250.80-250.83, 440.23, 459.11, 459.13, 459.31, 459.33)
707.12 Ulcer of calf — (Code, if applicable, any causal condition first: 249.80-249.81, 250.80-250.83, 440.23, 459.11, 459.13, 459.31, 459.33)
707.13 Ulcer of ankle — (Code, if applicable, any causal condition first: 249.80-249.81, 250.80-250.83, 440.23, 459.11, 459.13, 459.31, 459.33)
707.14 Ulcer of heel and midfoot — (Code, if applicable, any causal condition first: 249.80-249.81, 250.80-250.83, 440.23, 459.11, 459.13, 459.31, 459.33)
707.15 Ulcer of other part of foot — (Code, if applicable, any causal condition first: 249.80-249.81, 250.80-250.83, 440.23, 459.11, 459.13, 459.31, 459.33)
707.19 Ulcer of other part of lower limb — (Code, if applicable, any causal condition first: 249.80-249.81, 250.80-250.83, 440.23, 459.11, 459.13, 459.31, 459.33)

ICD-9-CM Procedural

38.59 Ligation and stripping of lower limb varicose veins
86.4 Radical excision of skin lesion
86.60 Free skin graft, not otherwise specified
86.63 Full-thickness skin graft to other sites

37760-37761

37760 Ligation of perforator veins, subfascial, radical (Linton type), including skin graft, when performed, open,1 leg
37761 Ligation of perforator vein(s), subfascial, open, including ultrasound guidance, when performed, 1 leg

ICD-9-CM Diagnostic

454.0 Varicose veins of lower extremities with ulcer
454.1 Varicose veins of lower extremities with inflammation
454.2 Varicose veins of lower extremities with ulcer and inflammation
454.8 Varicose veins of the lower extremities with other complications
454.9 Asymptomatic varicose veins
459.10 Postphlebitic syndrome without complications
459.11 Postphlebitic syndrome with ulcer
459.12 Postphlebitic syndrome with inflammation
459.13 Postphlebitic syndrome with ulcer and inflammation
459.19 Postphlebitic syndrome with other complication

459.81 Unspecified venous (peripheral) insufficiency — (Use additional code for any associated ulceration: 707.10-707.19, 707.8, 707.9)

707.10 Ulcer of lower limb, unspecified — (Code, if applicable, any causal condition first: 249.80-249.81, 250.80-250.83, 440.23, 459.11, 459.13, 459.31, 459.33)

707.11 Ulcer of thigh — (Code, if applicable, any causal condition first: 249.80-249.81, 250.80-250.83, 440.23, 459.11, 459.13, 459.31, 459.33)

707.12 Ulcer of calf — (Code, if applicable, any causal condition first: 249.80-249.81, 250.80-250.83, 440.23, 459.11, 459.13, 459.31, 459.33)

707.13 Ulcer of ankle — (Code, if applicable, any causal condition first: 249.80-249.81, 250.80-250.83, 440.23, 459.11, 459.13, 459.31, 459.33)

707.14 Ulcer of heel and midfoot — (Code, if applicable, any causal condition first: 249.80-249.81, 250.80-250.83, 440.23, 459.11, 459.13, 459.31, 459.33)

707.15 Ulcer of other part of foot — (Code, if applicable, any causal condition first: 249.80-249.81, 250.80-250.83, 440.23, 459.11, 459.13, 459.31, 459.33)

707.19 Ulcer of other part of lower limb — (Code, if applicable, any causal condition first: 249.80-249.81, 250.80-250.83, 440.23, 459.11, 459.13, 459.31, 459.33)

729.5 Pain in soft tissues of limb

ICD-9-CM Procedural

38.59 Ligation and stripping of lower limb varicose veins

38.89 Other surgical occlusion of lower limb veins

86.60 Free skin graft, not otherwise specified

86.63 Full-thickness skin graft to other sites

37765-37766

37765 Stab phlebectomy of varicose veins, 1 extremity; 10-20 stab incisions

37766 more than 20 incisions

ICD-9-CM Diagnostic

454.0 Varicose veins of lower extremities with ulcer

454.1 Varicose veins of lower extremities with inflammation

454.2 Varicose veins of lower extremities with ulcer and inflammation

454.8 Varicose veins of the lower extremities with other complications

454.9 Asymptomatic varicose veins

ICD-9-CM Procedural

38.59 Ligation and stripping of lower limb varicose veins

37780

37780 Ligation and division of short saphenous vein at saphenopopliteal junction (separate procedure)

ICD-9-CM Diagnostic

454.0 Varicose veins of lower extremities with ulcer

454.1 Varicose veins of lower extremities with inflammation

454.2 Varicose veins of lower extremities with ulcer and inflammation

454.8 Varicose veins of the lower extremities with other complications

454.9 Asymptomatic varicose veins

459.10 Postphlebitic syndrome without complications

459.11 Postphlebitic syndrome with ulcer

459.12 Postphlebitic syndrome with inflammation

459.13 Postphlebitic syndrome with ulcer and inflammation

459.19 Postphlebitic syndrome with other complication

459.81 Unspecified venous (peripheral) insufficiency — (Use additional code for any associated ulceration: 707.10-707.19, 707.8, 707.9)

707.10 Ulcer of lower limb, unspecified — (Code, if applicable, any causal condition first: 249.80-249.81, 250.80-250.83, 440.23, 459.11, 459.13, 459.31, 459.33)

707.11 Ulcer of thigh — (Code, if applicable, any causal condition first: 249.80-249.81, 250.80-250.83, 440.23, 459.11, 459.13, 459.31, 459.33)

707.12 Ulcer of calf — (Code, if applicable, any causal condition first: 249.80-249.81, 250.80-250.83, 440.23, 459.11, 459.13, 459.31, 459.33)

707.13 Ulcer of ankle — (Code, if applicable, any causal condition first: 249.80-249.81, 250.80-250.83, 440.23, 459.11, 459.13, 459.31, 459.33)

707.14 Ulcer of heel and midfoot — (Code, if applicable, any causal condition first: 249.80-249.81, 250.80-250.83, 440.23, 459.11, 459.13, 459.31, 459.33)

707.15 Ulcer of other part of foot — (Code, if applicable, any causal condition first: 249.80-249.81, 250.80-250.83, 440.23, 459.11, 459.13, 459.31, 459.33)

707.19 Ulcer of other part of lower limb — (Code, if applicable, any causal condition first: 249.80-249.81, 250.80-250.83, 440.23, 459.11, 459.13, 459.31, 459.33)

729.5 Pain in soft tissues of limb

V50.1 Other plastic surgery for unacceptable cosmetic appearance

ICD-9-CM Procedural

38.59 Ligation and stripping of lower limb varicose veins

38.89 Other surgical occlusion of lower limb veins

37785

37785 Ligation, division, and/or excision of varicose vein cluster(s), 1 leg

ICD-9-CM Diagnostic

454.0 Varicose veins of lower extremities with ulcer

454.1 Varicose veins of lower extremities with inflammation

454.2 Varicose veins of lower extremities with ulcer and inflammation

454.8 Varicose veins of the lower extremities with other complications

454.9 Asymptomatic varicose veins

459.10 Postphlebitic syndrome without complications

459.11 Postphlebitic syndrome with ulcer

459.12 Postphlebitic syndrome with inflammation

459.13 Postphlebitic syndrome with ulcer and inflammation

459.19 Postphlebitic syndrome with other complication

459.81 Unspecified venous (peripheral) insufficiency — (Use additional code for any associated ulceration: 707.10-707.19, 707.8, 707.9)

ICD-9-CM Procedural

38.59 Ligation and stripping of lower limb varicose veins

37788

37788 Penile revascularization, artery, with or without vein graft

ICD-9-CM Diagnostic

249.70 Secondary diabetes mellitus with peripheral circulatory disorders, not stated as uncontrolled, or unspecified — (Use additional code to identify manifestation: 443.81, 785.4) (Use additional code to identify any associated insulin use: V58.67)

249.71 Secondary diabetes mellitus with peripheral circulatory disorders, uncontrolled — (Use additional code to identify manifestation: 443.81, 785.4) (Use additional code to identify any associated insulin use: V58.67)

249.80 Secondary diabetes mellitus with other specified manifestations, not stated as uncontrolled, or unspecified — (Use additional code to identify manifestation: 707.10-707.19, 707.8, 707.9, 731.8) (Use additional code to identify any associated insulin use: V58.67)

249.81 Secondary diabetes mellitus with other specified manifestations, uncontrolled — (Use additional code to identify manifestation: 707.10-707.19, 707.8, 707.9, 731.8) (Use additional code to identify any associated insulin use: V58.67)

250.70 Diabetes with peripheral circulatory disorders, type II or unspecified type, not stated as uncontrolled — (Use additional code to identify manifestation: 443.81, 785.4)

250.71 Diabetes with peripheral circulatory disorders, type I [juvenile type], not stated as uncontrolled — (Use additional code to identify manifestation: 443.81, 785.4)

250.72 Diabetes with peripheral circulatory disorders, type II or unspecified type, uncontrolled — (Use additional code to identify manifestation: 443.81, 785.4)

250.73 Diabetes with peripheral circulatory disorders, type I [juvenile type], uncontrolled — (Use additional code to identify manifestation: 443.81, 785.4)

250.80 Diabetes with other specified manifestations, type II or unspecified type, not stated as uncontrolled — (Use additional code to identify manifestation: 707.10-707.19, 707.8, 707.9, 731.8)

250.81 Diabetes with other specified manifestations, type I [juvenile type], not stated as uncontrolled — (Use additional code to identify manifestation: 707.10-707.19, 707.8, 707.9, 731.8)
250.82 Diabetes with other specified manifestations, type II or unspecified type, uncontrolled — (Use additional code to identify manifestation: 707.10-707.19, 707.8, 707.9, 731.8)
250.83 Diabetes with other specified manifestations, type I [juvenile type], uncontrolled — (Use additional code to identify manifestation: 707.10-707.19, 707.8, 707.9, 731.8)
443.81 Peripheral angiopathy in diseases classified elsewhere — (Code first underlying disease: 249.7, 250.7) ☒
607.82 Vascular disorders of penis ♂
607.84 Impotence of organic origin ♂
902.87 Injury to multiple blood vessels of abdomen and pelvis
902.89 Injury to specified blood vessels of abdomen and pelvis, other
908.4 Late effect of injury to blood vessel of thorax, abdomen, and pelvis

ICD-9-CM Procedural

39.29 Other (peripheral) vascular shunt or bypass
39.31 Suture of artery
64.98 Other operations on penis ♂

37790

37790 Penile venous occlusive procedure

ICD-9-CM Diagnostic

187.3 Malignant neoplasm of body of penis ♂
187.9 Malignant neoplasm of male genital organ, site unspecified ▽ ♂
249.70 Secondary diabetes mellitus with peripheral circulatory disorders, not stated as uncontrolled, or unspecified — (Use additional code to identify manifestation: 443.81, 785.4) (Use additional code to identify any associated insulin use: V58.67)
249.71 Secondary diabetes mellitus with peripheral circulatory disorders, uncontrolled — (Use additional code to identify manifestation: 443.81, 785.4) (Use additional code to identify any associated insulin use: V58.67)
249.80 Secondary diabetes mellitus with other specified manifestations, not stated as uncontrolled, or unspecified — (Use additional code to identify manifestation: 707.10-707.19, 707.8, 707.9, 731.8) (Use additional code to identify any associated insulin use: V58.67)
249.81 Secondary diabetes mellitus with other specified manifestations, uncontrolled — (Use additional code to identify manifestation: 707.10-707.19, 707.8, 707.9, 731.8) (Use additional code to identify any associated insulin use: V58.67)
250.70 Diabetes with peripheral circulatory disorders, type II or unspecified type, not stated as uncontrolled — (Use additional code to identify manifestation: 443.81, 785.4)
250.71 Diabetes with peripheral circulatory disorders, type I [juvenile type], not stated as uncontrolled — (Use additional code to identify manifestation: 443.81, 785.4)
250.72 Diabetes with peripheral circulatory disorders, type II or unspecified type, uncontrolled — (Use additional code to identify manifestation: 443.81, 785.4)
250.73 Diabetes with peripheral circulatory disorders, type I [juvenile type], uncontrolled — (Use additional code to identify manifestation: 443.81, 785.4)
250.80 Diabetes with other specified manifestations, type II or unspecified type, not stated as uncontrolled — (Use additional code to identify manifestation: 707.10-707.19, 707.8, 707.9, 731.8)
250.81 Diabetes with other specified manifestations, type I [juvenile type], not stated as uncontrolled — (Use additional code to identify manifestation: 707.10-707.19, 707.8, 707.9, 731.8)
250.82 Diabetes with other specified manifestations, type II or unspecified type, uncontrolled — (Use additional code to identify manifestation: 707.10-707.19, 707.8, 707.9, 731.8)
250.83 Diabetes with other specified manifestations, type I [juvenile type], uncontrolled — (Use additional code to identify manifestation: 707.10-707.19, 707.8, 707.9, 731.8)
443.81 Peripheral angiopathy in diseases classified elsewhere — (Code first underlying disease: 249.7, 250.7) ☒
607.82 Vascular disorders of penis ♂
607.84 Impotence of organic origin ♂
608.83 Specified vascular disorder of male genital organs ♂
878.1 Open wound of penis, complicated ♂
902.87 Injury to multiple blood vessels of abdomen and pelvis
902.89 Injury to specified blood vessels of abdomen and pelvis, other
908.4 Late effect of injury to blood vessel of thorax, abdomen, and pelvis

ICD-9-CM Procedural

39.29 Other (peripheral) vascular shunt or bypass
39.31 Suture of artery
64.98 Other operations on penis ♂

Spleen

38100-38102

38100 Splenectomy; total (separate procedure)
38101 partial (separate procedure)
38102 total, en bloc for extensive disease, in conjunction with other procedure (List in addition to code for primary procedure)

ICD-9-CM Diagnostic

159.1 Malignant neoplasm of spleen, not elsewhere classified
197.8 Secondary malignant neoplasm of other digestive organs and spleen
200.07 Reticulosarcoma of spleen
200.17 Lymphosarcoma of spleen
200.27 Burkitt's tumor or lymphoma of spleen
200.87 Other named variants of lymphosarcoma and reticulosarcoma of spleen
201.07 Hodgkin's paragranuloma of spleen
201.17 Hodgkin's granuloma of spleen
201.27 Hodgkin's sarcoma of spleen
201.47 Hodgkin's disease, lymphocytic-histiocytic predominance of spleen
201.57 Hodgkin's disease, nodular sclerosis, of spleen
201.67 Hodgkin's disease, mixed cellularity, of spleen
201.77 Hodgkin's disease, lymphocytic depletion, of spleen
201.90 Hodgkin's disease, unspecified type, unspecified site, extranodal and solid organ sites ▽
201.97 Hodgkin's disease, unspecified type, of spleen ▽
202.07 Nodular lymphoma of spleen
202.17 Mycosis fungoides of spleen
202.27 Sezary's disease of spleen
202.37 Malignant histiocytosis of spleen
202.47 Leukemic reticuloendotheliosis of spleen
202.57 Letterer-Siwe disease of spleen
202.67 Malignant mast cell tumors of spleen
202.80 Other malignant lymphomas, unspecified site, extranodal and solid organ sites ▽
202.87 Other malignant lymphomas of spleen
202.97 Other and unspecified malignant neoplasms of lymphoid and histiocytic tissue of spleen ▽
238.71 Essential thrombocythemia
238.73 High grade myelodysplastic syndrome lesions
238.74 Myelodysplastic syndrome with 5q deletion
238.75 Myelodysplastic syndrome, unspecified ▽
238.76 Myelofibrosis with myeloid metaplasia
238.77 Post-transplant lymphoproliferative disorder [PTLD] — (Code first complications of transplant (996.80-996.89))
238.79 Other lymphatic and hematopoietic tissues
238.8 Neoplasm of uncertain behavior of other specified sites
239.0 Neoplasm of unspecified nature of digestive system
279.41 Autoimmune lymphoproliferative syndrome — (Use additional code to identify any associated intellectual disabilities) (Use additional code for associated manifestations)

282.0 Hereditary spherocytosis
283.0 Autoimmune hemolytic anemias — (Use additional E code to identify cause, if drug-induced)
287.30 Primary thrombocytopenia, unspecified
287.31 Immune thrombocytopenic purpura
287.32 Evans' syndrome
287.33 Congenital and hereditary thrombocytopenic purpura
287.39 Other primary thrombocytopenia
287.5 Unspecified thrombocytopenia
289.4 Hypersplenism
289.50 Unspecified disease of spleen
289.51 Chronic congestive splenomegaly
289.52 Splenic sequestration — (Code first sickle-cell disease in crisis: 282.42, 282.62, 282.64, 282.69)
289.59 Other diseases of spleen
289.84 Heparin-induced thrombocytopenia [HIT]
442.83 Aneurysm of splenic artery
443.29 Dissection of other artery
446.6 Thrombotic microangiopathy
789.00 Abdominal pain, unspecified site
789.02 Abdominal pain, left upper quadrant
789.07 Abdominal pain, generalized
789.09 Abdominal pain, other specified site
789.2 Splenomegaly
865.01 Spleen hematoma, without rupture of capsule or mention of open wound into cavity
865.02 Capsular tears to spleen, without major disruption of parenchyma or mention of open wound into cavity
865.03 Spleen laceration extending into parenchyma without mention of open wound into cavity
865.04 Massive parenchymal disruption of spleen without mention of open wound into cavity
865.09 Other spleen injury without mention of open wound into cavity
865.10 Unspecified spleen injury with open wound into cavity
865.11 Spleen hematoma, without rupture of capsule, with open wound into cavity
865.12 Capsular tears to spleen, without major disruption of parenchyma, with open wound into cavity
865.13 Spleen laceration extending into parenchyma, with open wound into cavity
865.14 Massive parenchyma disruption of spleen with open wound into cavity
865.19 Other spleen injury with open wound into cavity
998.2 Accidental puncture or laceration during procedure
998.89 Other specified complications
998.9 Unspecified complication of procedure, not elsewhere classified
V64.41 Laparoscopic surgical procedure converted to open procedure

ICD-9-CM Procedural

41.42 Excision of lesion or tissue of spleen
41.43 Partial splenectomy
41.5 Total splenectomy

38115

38115 Repair of ruptured spleen (splenorrhaphy) with or without partial splenectomy

ICD-9-CM Diagnostic

289.59 Other diseases of spleen
767.8 Other specified birth trauma — (Use additional code(s) to further specify condition)
865.01 Spleen hematoma, without rupture of capsule or mention of open wound into cavity
865.02 Capsular tears to spleen, without major disruption of parenchyma or mention of open wound into cavity
865.03 Spleen laceration extending into parenchyma without mention of open wound into cavity
865.04 Massive parenchymal disruption of spleen without mention of open wound into cavity
865.09 Other spleen injury without mention of open wound into cavity
865.11 Spleen hematoma, without rupture of capsule, with open wound into cavity
865.12 Capsular tears to spleen, without major disruption of parenchyma, with open wound into cavity
865.13 Spleen laceration extending into parenchyma, with open wound into cavity
865.14 Massive parenchyma disruption of spleen with open wound into cavity
865.19 Other spleen injury with open wound into cavity

ICD-9-CM Procedural

41.95 Repair and plastic operations on spleen

38120

38120 Laparoscopy, surgical, splenectomy

ICD-9-CM Diagnostic

159.1 Malignant neoplasm of spleen, not elsewhere classified
197.8 Secondary malignant neoplasm of other digestive organs and spleen
200.07 Reticulosarcoma of spleen
200.17 Lymphosarcoma of spleen
200.27 Burkitt's tumor or lymphoma of spleen
200.87 Other named variants of lymphosarcoma and reticulosarcoma of spleen
201.07 Hodgkin's paragranuloma of spleen
201.17 Hodgkin's granuloma of spleen
201.27 Hodgkin's sarcoma of spleen
201.47 Hodgkin's disease, lymphocytic-histiocytic predominance of spleen
201.57 Hodgkin's disease, nodular sclerosis, of spleen
201.67 Hodgkin's disease, mixed cellularity, of spleen
201.77 Hodgkin's disease, lymphocytic depletion, of spleen
201.90 Hodgkin's disease, unspecified type, unspecified site, extranodal and solid organ sites
201.97 Hodgkin's disease, unspecified type, of spleen
202.07 Nodular lymphoma of spleen
202.17 Mycosis fungoides of spleen
202.27 Sezary's disease of spleen
202.37 Malignant histiocytosis of spleen
202.47 Leukemic reticuloendotheliosis of spleen
202.57 Letterer-Siwe disease of spleen
202.67 Malignant mast cell tumors of spleen
202.80 Other malignant lymphomas, unspecified site, extranodal and solid organ sites
202.87 Other malignant lymphomas of spleen
202.97 Other and unspecified malignant neoplasms of lymphoid and histiocytic tissue of spleen
238.71 Essential thrombocythemia
238.73 High grade myelodysplastic syndrome lesions
238.74 Myelodysplastic syndrome with 5q deletion
238.75 Myelodysplastic syndrome, unspecified
238.76 Myelofibrosis with myeloid metaplasia
238.77 Post-transplant lymphoproliferative disorder [PTLD] — (Code first complications of transplant (996.80-996.89))
238.79 Other lymphatic and hematopoietic tissues
238.8 Neoplasm of uncertain behavior of other specified sites
239.0 Neoplasm of unspecified nature of digestive system
279.41 Autoimmune lymphoproliferative syndrome — (Use additional code to identify any associated intellectual disabilities) (Use additional code for associated manifestations)
282.0 Hereditary spherocytosis
283.0 Autoimmune hemolytic anemias — (Use additional E code to identify cause, if drug-induced)
287.30 Primary thrombocytopenia, unspecified
287.31 Immune thrombocytopenic purpura
287.32 Evans' syndrome

287.33 Congenital and hereditary thrombocytopenic purpura
287.39 Other primary thrombocytopenia
287.5 Unspecified thrombocytopenia
289.4 Hypersplenism
289.50 Unspecified disease of spleen
289.51 Chronic congestive splenomegaly
289.52 Splenic sequestration — (Code first sickle-cell disease in crisis: 282.42, 282.62, 282.64, 282.69)
289.59 Other diseases of spleen
289.84 Heparin-induced thrombocytopenia [HIT]
442.83 Aneurysm of splenic artery
446.6 Thrombotic microangiopathy
789.00 Abdominal pain, unspecified site
789.02 Abdominal pain, left upper quadrant
789.07 Abdominal pain, generalized
789.09 Abdominal pain, other specified site
789.2 Splenomegaly
865.01 Spleen hematoma, without rupture of capsule or mention of open wound into cavity
865.02 Capsular tears to spleen, without major disruption of parenchyma or mention of open wound into cavity
865.03 Spleen laceration extending into parenchyma without mention of open wound into cavity
865.04 Massive parenchymal disruption of spleen without mention of open wound into cavity
865.09 Other spleen injury without mention of open wound into cavity
865.10 Unspecified spleen injury with open wound into cavity
865.11 Spleen hematoma, without rupture of capsule, with open wound into cavity
865.12 Capsular tears to spleen, without major disruption of parenchyma, with open wound into cavity
865.13 Spleen laceration extending into parenchyma, with open wound into cavity
865.14 Massive parenchyma disruption of spleen with open wound into cavity
865.19 Other spleen injury with open wound into cavity
998.2 Accidental puncture or laceration during procedure
998.89 Other specified complications

ICD-9-CM Procedural

41.43 Partial splenectomy
41.5 Total splenectomy
41.93 Excision of accessory spleen

HCPCS Level II Supplies & Services

N/A

38200

38200 Injection procedure for splenoportography

ICD-9-CM Diagnostic

230.9 Carcinoma in situ of other and unspecified digestive organs
572.3 Portal hypertension — (Use additional code for any associated complications, such as: portal hypertensive gastropathy (537.89))
865.01 Spleen hematoma, without rupture of capsule or mention of open wound into cavity
865.09 Other spleen injury without mention of open wound into cavity

ICD-9-CM Procedural

41.39 Other diagnostic procedures on spleen
41.99 Other operations on spleen
88.49 Arteriography of other specified sites

General

38204

38204 Management of recipient hematopoietic progenitor cell donor search and cell acquisition

ICD-9-CM Diagnostic

The application of this code is too broad to adequately present ICD-9-CM diagnostic code links here. Refer to your ICD-9-CM book.

38205-38206

38205 Blood-derived hematopoietic progenitor cell harvesting for transplantation, per collection; allogeneic
38206 autologous

ICD-9-CM Diagnostic

The application of this code is too broad to adequately present ICD-9-CM diagnostic code links here. Refer to your ICD-9-CM book.

ICD-9-CM Procedural

99.79 Other therapeutic apheresis

38207-38215

38207 Transplant preparation of hematopoietic progenitor cells; cryopreservation and storage
38208 thawing of previously frozen harvest, without washing, per donor
38209 thawing of previously frozen harvest, with washing, per donor
38210 specific cell depletion within harvest, T-cell depletion
38211 tumor cell depletion
38212 red blood cell removal
38213 platelet depletion
38214 plasma (volume) depletion
38215 cell concentration in plasma, mononuclear, or buffy coat layer

ICD-9-CM Diagnostic

The application of this code is too broad to adequately present ICD-9-CM diagnostic code links here. Refer to your ICD-9-CM book.

ICD-9-CM Procedural

N/A

38220-38221

38220 Bone marrow; aspiration only
38221 biopsy, needle or trocar

ICD-9-CM Diagnostic

The application of this code is too broad to adequately present ICD-9-CM diagnostic code links here. Refer to your ICD-9-CM book.

ICD-9-CM Procedural

41.31 Biopsy of bone marrow
41.98 Other operations on bone marrow

HCPCS Level II Supplies & Services

C1830 Powered bone marrow biopsy needle
G0364 Bone marrow aspiration performed with bone marrow biopsy through the same incision on the same date of service

38230-38232

38230 Bone marrow harvesting for transplantation; allogeneic
38232 autologous

ICD-9-CM Diagnostic

200.00 Reticulosarcoma, unspecified site, extranodal and solid organ sites
200.01 Reticulosarcoma of lymph nodes of head, face, and neck
200.02 Reticulosarcoma of intrathoracic lymph nodes

200.03 Reticulosarcoma of intra-abdominal lymph nodes
200.04 Reticulosarcoma of lymph nodes of axilla and upper limb
200.05 Reticulosarcoma of lymph nodes of inguinal region and lower limb
200.06 Reticulosarcoma of intrapelvic lymph nodes
200.07 Reticulosarcoma of spleen
200.08 Reticulosarcoma of lymph nodes of multiple sites
200.20 Burkitt's tumor or lymphoma, unspecified site, extranodal and solid organ sites ▽
200.21 Burkitt's tumor or lymphoma of lymph nodes of head, face, and neck
200.22 Burkitt's tumor or lymphoma of intrathoracic lymph nodes
200.23 Burkitt's tumor or lymphoma of intra-abdominal lymph nodes
200.24 Burkitt's tumor or lymphoma of lymph nodes of axilla and upper limb
200.25 Burkitt's tumor or lymphoma of lymph nodes of inguinal region and lower limb
200.26 Burkitt's tumor or lymphoma of intrapelvic lymph nodes
200.27 Burkitt's tumor or lymphoma of spleen
200.28 Burkitt's tumor or lymphoma of lymph nodes of multiple sites
202.80 Other malignant lymphomas, unspecified site, extranodal and solid organ sites ▽
202.81 Other malignant lymphomas of lymph nodes of head, face, and neck
202.82 Other malignant lymphomas of intrathoracic lymph nodes
202.83 Other malignant lymphomas of intra-abdominal lymph nodes
202.84 Other malignant lymphomas of lymph nodes of axilla and upper limb
202.85 Other malignant lymphomas of lymph nodes of inguinal region and lower limb
202.86 Other malignant lymphomas of intrapelvic lymph nodes
202.87 Other malignant lymphomas of spleen
202.88 Other malignant lymphomas of lymph nodes of multiple sites
208.01 Acute leukemia of unspecified cell type in remission ▽
208.11 Chronic leukemia of unspecified cell type in remission ▽
208.21 Subactue leukemia of unspecified cell type in remission ▽
208.81 Other leukemia of unspecified cell type in remission ▽
208.91 Unspecified leukemia in remission ▽
V59.3 Bone marrow donor

ICD-9-CM Procedural

41.91 Aspiration of bone marrow from donor for transplant

38240-38241 [38243]

38240 Hematopoietic progenitor cell (HPC); allogeneic transplantation per donor
38241 autologous transplantation
38243 Hematopoietic progenitor cell (HPC); HPC boost

ICD-9-CM Diagnostic

The application of this code is too broad to adequately present ICD-9-CM diagnostic code links here. Refer to your ICD-9-CM book.

ICD-9-CM Procedural

41.01 Autologous bone marrow transplant without purging
41.02 Allogeneic bone marrow transplant with purging
41.03 Allogeneic bone marrow transplant without purging
41.04 Autologous hematopoietic stem cell transplant without purging
41.05 Allogeneic hematopoietic stem cell transplant without purging
41.06 Cord blood stem cell transplant
41.07 Autologous hematopoietic stem cell transplant with purging
41.08 Allogeneic hematopoietic stem cell transplant with purging
41.09 Autologous bone marrow transplant with purging

Lymph Nodes and Lymphatic Channels

38230-38232

38230 Bone marrow harvesting for transplantation; allogeneic
38232 autologous

ICD-9-CM Diagnostic

200.00 Reticulosarcoma, unspecified site, extranodal and solid organ sites ▽
200.01 Reticulosarcoma of lymph nodes of head, face, and neck
200.02 Reticulosarcoma of intrathoracic lymph nodes
200.03 Reticulosarcoma of intra-abdominal lymph nodes
200.04 Reticulosarcoma of lymph nodes of axilla and upper limb
200.05 Reticulosarcoma of lymph nodes of inguinal region and lower limb
200.06 Reticulosarcoma of intrapelvic lymph nodes
200.07 Reticulosarcoma of spleen
200.08 Reticulosarcoma of lymph nodes of multiple sites
200.20 Burkitt's tumor or lymphoma, unspecified site, extranodal and solid organ sites ▽
200.21 Burkitt's tumor or lymphoma of lymph nodes of head, face, and neck
200.22 Burkitt's tumor or lymphoma of intrathoracic lymph nodes
200.23 Burkitt's tumor or lymphoma of intra-abdominal lymph nodes
200.24 Burkitt's tumor or lymphoma of lymph nodes of axilla and upper limb
200.25 Burkitt's tumor or lymphoma of lymph nodes of inguinal region and lower limb
200.26 Burkitt's tumor or lymphoma of intrapelvic lymph nodes
200.27 Burkitt's tumor or lymphoma of spleen
200.28 Burkitt's tumor or lymphoma of lymph nodes of multiple sites
202.80 Other malignant lymphomas, unspecified site, extranodal and solid organ sites ▽
202.81 Other malignant lymphomas of lymph nodes of head, face, and neck
202.82 Other malignant lymphomas of intrathoracic lymph nodes
202.83 Other malignant lymphomas of intra-abdominal lymph nodes
202.84 Other malignant lymphomas of lymph nodes of axilla and upper limb
202.85 Other malignant lymphomas of lymph nodes of inguinal region and lower limb
202.86 Other malignant lymphomas of intrapelvic lymph nodes
202.87 Other malignant lymphomas of spleen
202.88 Other malignant lymphomas of lymph nodes of multiple sites
203.01 Multiple myeloma in remission
208.01 Acute leukemia of unspecified cell type in remission ▽
208.11 Chronic leukemia of unspecified cell type in remission ▽
208.21 Subactue leukemia of unspecified cell type in remission ▽
208.81 Other leukemia of unspecified cell type in remission ▽
208.91 Unspecified leukemia in remission ▽
V59.3 Bone marrow donor

ICD-9-CM Procedural

41.91 Aspiration of bone marrow from donor for transplant

38242

38242 Allogeneic lymphocyte infusions

ICD-9-CM Diagnostic

The application of this code is too broad to adequately present ICD-9-CM diagnostic code links here. Refer to your ICD-9-CM book.

ICD-9-CM Procedural

99.09 Transfusion of other substance

38300-38305

38300 Drainage of lymph node abscess or lymphadenitis; simple
38305 extensive

ICD-9-CM Diagnostic

289.1 Chronic lymphadenitis

289.2 Nonspecific mesenteric lymphadenitis
289.3 Lymphadenitis, unspecified, except mesenteric ▽
457.2 Lymphangitis
457.8 Other noninfectious disorders of lymphatic channels
683 Acute lymphadenitis — (Use additional code to identify organism: 041.1)
784.2 Swelling, mass, or lump in head and neck

ICD-9-CM Procedural

40.0 Incision of lymphatic structures

38308

38308 Lymphangiotomy or other operations on lymphatic channels

ICD-9-CM Diagnostic

289.1 Chronic lymphadenitis
289.2 Nonspecific mesenteric lymphadenitis
289.3 Lymphadenitis, unspecified, except mesenteric ▽
457.2 Lymphangitis
457.8 Other noninfectious disorders of lymphatic channels
683 Acute lymphadenitis — (Use additional code to identify organism: 041.1)
784.2 Swelling, mass, or lump in head and neck

ICD-9-CM Procedural

40.0 Incision of lymphatic structures
40.9 Other operations on lymphatic structures

38380

38380 Suture and/or ligation of thoracic duct; cervical approach

ICD-9-CM Diagnostic

289.1 Chronic lymphadenitis
289.3 Lymphadenitis, unspecified, except mesenteric ▽
457.2 Lymphangitis
457.8 Other noninfectious disorders of lymphatic channels
908.0 Late effect of internal injury to chest

ICD-9-CM Procedural

40.63 Closure of fistula of thoracic duct
40.64 Ligation of thoracic duct

38381-38382

38381 Suture and/or ligation of thoracic duct; thoracic approach
38382 abdominal approach

ICD-9-CM Diagnostic

196.1 Secondary and unspecified malignant neoplasm of intrathoracic lymph nodes
202.82 Other malignant lymphomas of intrathoracic lymph nodes
209.71 Secondary neuroendocrine tumor of distant lymph nodes
289.1 Chronic lymphadenitis
289.3 Lymphadenitis, unspecified, except mesenteric ▽
457.2 Lymphangitis
457.8 Other noninfectious disorders of lymphatic channels
908.0 Late effect of internal injury to chest

ICD-9-CM Procedural

40.63 Closure of fistula of thoracic duct
40.64 Ligation of thoracic duct

38500-38505

38500 Biopsy or excision of lymph node(s); open, superficial
38505 by needle, superficial (eg, cervical, inguinal, axillary)

ICD-9-CM Diagnostic

135 Sarcoidosis
172.5 Malignant melanoma of skin of trunk, except scrotum
172.6 Malignant melanoma of skin of upper limb, including shoulder
172.7 Malignant melanoma of skin of lower limb, including hip
172.8 Malignant melanoma of other specified sites of skin
173.02 Squamous cell carcinoma of skin of lip
173.12 Squamous cell carcinoma of eyelid, including canthus
173.22 Squamous cell carcinoma of skin of ear and external auditory canal
173.32 Squamous cell carcinoma of skin of other and unspecified parts of face
173.42 Squamous cell carcinoma of scalp and skin of neck
173.52 Squamous cell carcinoma of skin of trunk, except scrotum
173.62 Squamous cell carcinoma of skin of upper limb, including shoulder
173.72 Squamous cell carcinoma of skin of lower limb, including hip
173.82 Squamous cell carcinoma of other specified sites of skin
173.92 Squamous cell carcinoma of skin, site unspecified
174.0 Malignant neoplasm of nipple and areola of female breast — (Use additional code to identify estrogen receptor status: V86.0-V86.1) ♀
174.1 Malignant neoplasm of central portion of female breast — (Use additional code to identify estrogen receptor status: V86.0-V86.1) ♀
174.2 Malignant neoplasm of upper-inner quadrant of female breast — (Use additional code to identify estrogen receptor status: V86.0-V86.1) ♀
174.3 Malignant neoplasm of lower-inner quadrant of female breast — (Use additional code to identify estrogen receptor status: V86.0-V86.1) ♀
174.4 Malignant neoplasm of upper-outer quadrant of female breast — (Use additional code to identify estrogen receptor status: V86.0-V86.1) ♀
174.5 Malignant neoplasm of lower-outer quadrant of female breast — (Use additional code to identify estrogen receptor status: V86.0-V86.1) ♀
174.6 Malignant neoplasm of axillary tail of female breast — (Use additional code to identify estrogen receptor status: V86.0-V86.1) ♀
174.8 Malignant neoplasm of other specified sites of female breast — (Use additional code to identify estrogen receptor status: V86.0-V86.1) ♀
174.9 Malignant neoplasm of breast (female), unspecified site — (Use additional code to identify estrogen receptor status: V86.0-V86.1) ▽ ♀
180.9 Malignant neoplasm of cervix uteri, unspecified site ▽ ♀
182.0 Malignant neoplasm of corpus uteri, except isthmus ♀
185 Malignant neoplasm of prostate ♂
188.9 Malignant neoplasm of bladder, part unspecified ▽
196.0 Secondary and unspecified malignant neoplasm of lymph nodes of head, face, and neck
196.3 Secondary and unspecified malignant neoplasm of lymph nodes of axilla and upper limb
196.5 Secondary and unspecified malignant neoplasm of lymph nodes of inguinal region and lower limb
196.8 Secondary and unspecified malignant neoplasm of lymph nodes of multiple sites
196.9 Secondary and unspecified malignant neoplasm of lymph nodes, site unspecified ▽
198.89 Secondary malignant neoplasm of other specified sites
199.0 Disseminated malignant neoplasm
199.1 Other malignant neoplasm of unspecified site
199.2 Malignant neoplasm associated with transplanted organ — (Code first complication of transplanted organ (996.80-996.89) Use additional code for specific malignancy)
200.00 Reticulosarcoma, unspecified site, extranodal and solid organ sites ▽
200.01 Reticulosarcoma of lymph nodes of head, face, and neck
200.04 Reticulosarcoma of lymph nodes of axilla and upper limb
200.05 Reticulosarcoma of lymph nodes of inguinal region and lower limb
200.08 Reticulosarcoma of lymph nodes of multiple sites

Code	Description
200.10	Lymphosarcoma, unspecified site, extranodal and solid organ sites ▽
200.14	Lymphosarcoma of lymph nodes of axilla and upper limb
200.15	Lymphosarcoma of lymph nodes of inguinal region and lower limb
200.18	Lymphosarcoma of lymph nodes of multiple sites
200.20	Burkitt's tumor or lymphoma, unspecified site, extranodal and solid organ sites ▽
200.21	Burkitt's tumor or lymphoma of lymph nodes of head, face, and neck
200.24	Burkitt's tumor or lymphoma of lymph nodes of axilla and upper limb
200.25	Burkitt's tumor or lymphoma of lymph nodes of inguinal region and lower limb
200.28	Burkitt's tumor or lymphoma of lymph nodes of multiple sites
200.30	Marginal zone lymphoma, unspecified site, extranodal and solid organ sites
200.31	Marginal zone lymphoma, lymph nodes of head, face, and neck
200.34	Marginal zone lymphoma, lymph nodes of axilla and upper limb
200.35	Marginal zone lymphoma, lymph nodes of inguinal region and lower limb
200.38	Marginal zone lymphoma, lymph nodes of multiple sites
200.40	Mantle cell lymphoma, unspecified site, extranodal and solid organ sites
200.41	Mantle cell lymphoma, lymph nodes of head, face, and neck
200.44	Mantle cell lymphoma, lymph nodes of axilla and upper limb
200.45	Mantle cell lymphoma, lymph nodes of inguinal region and lower limb
200.48	Mantle cell lymphoma, lymph nodes of multiple sites
200.50	Primary central nervous system lymphoma, unspecified site, extranodal and solid organ sites
200.51	Primary central nervous system lymphoma, lymph nodes of head, face, and neck
200.54	Primary central nervous system lymphoma, lymph nodes of axilla and upper limb
200.55	Primary central nervous system lymphoma, lymph nodes of inguinal region and lower limb
200.58	Primary central nervous system lymphoma, lymph nodes of multiple sites
200.60	Anaplastic large cell lymphoma, unspecified site, extranodal and solid organ sites
200.61	Anaplastic large cell lymphoma, lymph nodes of head, face, and neck
200.64	Anaplastic large cell lymphoma, lymph nodes of axilla and upper limb
200.65	Anaplastic large cell lymphoma, lymph nodes of inguinal region and lower limb
200.68	Anaplastic large cell lymphoma, lymph nodes of multiple sites
200.70	Large cell lymphoma, unspecified site, extranodal and solid organ sites
200.71	Large cell lymphoma, lymph nodes of head, face, and neck
200.74	Large cell lymphoma, lymph nodes of axilla and upper limb
200.75	Large cell lymphoma, lymph nodes of inguinal region and lower limb
200.78	Large cell lymphoma, lymph nodes of multiple sites
201.00	Hodgkin's paragranuloma, unspecified site, extranodal and solid organ sites ▽
201.01	Hodgkin's paragranuloma of lymph nodes of head, face, and neck
201.04	Hodgkin's paragranuloma of lymph nodes of axilla and upper limb
201.05	Hodgkin's paragranuloma of lymph nodes of inguinal region and lower limb
201.08	Hodgkin's paragranuloma of lymph nodes of multiple sites
201.10	Hodgkin's granuloma, unspecified site, extranodal and solid organ sites ▽
201.11	Hodgkin's granuloma of lymph nodes of head, face, and neck
201.14	Hodgkin's granuloma of lymph nodes of axilla and upper limb
201.15	Hodgkin's granuloma of lymph nodes of inguinal region and lower limb
201.18	Hodgkin's granuloma of lymph nodes of multiple sites
201.20	Hodgkin's sarcoma, unspecified site, extranodal and solid organ sites ▽
201.24	Hodgkin's sarcoma of lymph nodes of axilla and upper limb
201.25	Hodgkin's sarcoma of lymph nodes of inguinal region and lower limb
201.28	Hodgkin's sarcoma of lymph nodes of multiple sites
201.40	Hodgkin's disease, lymphocytic-histiocytic predominance, unspecified site, extranodal and solid organ sites ▽
201.44	Hodgkin's disease, lymphocytic-histiocytic predominance of lymph nodes of axilla and upper limb
201.45	Hodgkin's disease, lymphocytic-histiocytic predominance of lymph nodes of inguinal region and lower limb
201.48	Hodgkin's disease, lymphocytic-histiocytic predominance of lymph nodes of multiple sites
201.51	Hodgkin's disease, nodular sclerosis, of lymph nodes of head, face, and neck
201.54	Hodgkin's disease, nodular sclerosis, of lymph nodes of axilla and upper limb
201.55	Hodgkin's disease, nodular sclerosis, of lymph nodes of inguinal region and lower limb
201.58	Hodgkin's disease, nodular sclerosis, of lymph nodes of multiple sites
201.60	Hodgkin's disease, mixed cellularity, unspecified site, extranodal and solid organ sites ▽
201.61	Hodgkin's disease, mixed cellularity, involving lymph nodes of head, face, and neck
201.65	Hodgkin's disease, mixed cellularity, of lymph nodes of inguinal region and lower limb
201.68	Hodgkin's disease, mixed cellularity, of lymph nodes of multiple sites
201.70	Hodgkin's disease, lymphocytic depletion, unspecified site, extranodal and solid organ sites ▽
201.71	Hodgkin's disease, lymphocytic depletion, of lymph nodes of head, face, and neck
201.74	Hodgkin's disease, lymphocytic depletion, of lymph nodes of axilla and upper limb
201.75	Hodgkin's disease, lymphocytic depletion, of lymph nodes of inguinal region and lower limb
201.78	Hodgkin's disease, lymphocytic depletion, of lymph nodes of multiple sites
201.90	Hodgkin's disease, unspecified type, unspecified site, extranodal and solid organ sites ▽
201.91	Hodgkin's disease, unspecified type, of lymph nodes of head, face, and neck ▽
201.94	Hodgkin's disease, unspecified type, of lymph nodes of axilla and upper limb ▽
201.95	Hodgkin's disease, unspecified type, of lymph nodes of inguinal region and lower limb ▽
201.98	Hodgkin's disease, unspecified type, of lymph nodes of multiple sites ▽
202.00	Nodular lymphoma, unspecified site, extranodal and solid organ sites ▽
202.01	Nodular lymphoma of lymph nodes of head, face, and neck
202.04	Nodular lymphoma of lymph nodes of axilla and upper limb
202.05	Nodular lymphoma of lymph nodes of inguinal region and lower limb
202.08	Nodular lymphoma of lymph nodes of multiple sites
202.10	Mycosis fungoides, unspecified site, extranodal and solid organ sites ▽
202.11	Mycosis fungoides of lymph nodes of head, face, and neck
202.14	Mycosis fungoides of lymph nodes of axilla and upper limb
202.15	Mycosis fungoides of lymph nodes of inguinal region and lower limb
202.18	Mycosis fungoides of lymph nodes of multiple sites
202.20	Sezary's disease, unspecified site, extranodal and solid organ sites ▽
202.21	Sezary's disease of lymph nodes of head, face, and neck
202.28	Sezary's disease of lymph nodes of multiple sites
202.30	Malignant histiocytosis, unspecified site, extranodal and solid organ sites ▽
202.31	Malignant histiocytosis of lymph nodes of head, face, and neck
202.34	Malignant histiocytosis of lymph nodes of axilla and upper limb
202.35	Malignant histiocytosis of lymph nodes of inguinal region and lower limb
202.38	Malignant histiocytosis of lymph nodes of multiple sites
202.40	Leukemic reticuloendotheliosis, unspecified site, extranodal and solid organ sites ▽
202.41	Leukemic reticuloendotheliosis of lymph nodes of head, face, and neck
202.44	Leukemic reticuloendotheliosis of lymph nodes of axilla and upper limb
202.45	Leukemic reticuloendotheliosis of lymph nodes of inguinal region and lower limb
202.48	Leukemic reticuloendotheliosis of lymph nodes of multiple sites
202.50	Letterer-Siwe disease, unspecified site, extranodal and solid organ sites ▽
202.51	Letterer-Siwe disease of lymph nodes of head, face, and neck
202.54	Letterer-Siwe disease of lymph nodes of axilla and upper limb
202.55	Letterer-Siwe disease of lymph nodes of inguinal region and lower limb
202.58	Letterer-Siwe disease of lymph nodes of multiple sites
202.60	Malignant mast cell tumors, unspecified site, extranodal and solid organ sites ▽
202.61	Malignant mast cell tumors of lymph nodes of head, face, and neck
202.64	Malignant mast cell tumors of lymph nodes of axilla and upper limb
202.65	Malignant mast cell tumors of lymph nodes of inguinal region and lower limb
202.68	Malignant mast cell tumors of lymph nodes of multiple sites
202.70	Peripheral T-cell lymphoma, unspecified site, extranodal and solid organ sites
202.71	Peripheral T-cell lymphoma, lymph nodes of head, face, and neck

202.74 Peripheral T-cell lymphoma, lymph nodes of axilla and upper limb
202.75 Peripheral T-cell lymphoma, lymph nodes of inguinal region and lower limb
202.78 Peripheral T-cell lymphoma, lymph nodes of multiple sites
202.80 Other malignant lymphomas, unspecified site, extranodal and solid organ sites ▽
202.81 Other malignant lymphomas of lymph nodes of head, face, and neck
202.84 Other malignant lymphomas of lymph nodes of axilla and upper limb
202.85 Other malignant lymphomas of lymph nodes of inguinal region and lower limb
202.88 Other malignant lymphomas of lymph nodes of multiple sites
202.91 Other and unspecified malignant neoplasms of lymphoid and histiocytic tissue of lymph nodes of head, face, and neck ▽
202.94 Other and unspecified malignant neoplasms of lymphoid and histiocytic tissue of lymph nodes of axilla and upper limb ▽
202.95 Other and unspecified malignant neoplasms of lymphoid and histiocytic tissue of lymph nodes of inguinal region and lower limb ▽
202.98 Other and unspecified malignant neoplasms of lymphoid and histiocytic tissue of lymph nodes of multiple sites ▽
209.20 Malignant carcinoid tumor of unknown primary site — (Code first any associated multiple endocrine neoplasia syndrome: 258.01-258.03)(Use additional code to identify associated endocrine syndrome, as: carcinoid syndrome: 259.2)
209.29 Malignant carcinoid tumor of other sites — (Code first any associated multiple endocrine neoplasia syndrome: 258.01-258.03)(Use additional code to identify associated endocrine syndrome, as: carcinoid syndrome: 259.2)
209.30 Malignant poorly differentiated neuroendocrine carcinoma, any site — (Code first any associated multiple endocrine neoplasia syndrome: 258.01-258.03)(Use additional code to identify associated endocrine syndrome, as: carcinoid syndrome: 259.2) ▽
209.31 Merkel cell carcinoma of the face
209.32 Merkel cell carcinoma of the scalp and neck
209.33 Merkel cell carcinoma of the upper limb
209.34 Merkel cell carcinoma of the lower limb
209.35 Merkel cell carcinoma of the trunk
209.36 Merkel cell carcinoma of other sites
209.70 Secondary neuroendocrine tumor, unspecified site ▽
209.71 Secondary neuroendocrine tumor of distant lymph nodes
209.72 Secondary neuroendocrine tumor of liver
209.73 Secondary neuroendocrine tumor of bone
209.74 Secondary neuroendocrine tumor of peritoneum
209.75 Secondary Merkel cell carcinoma
209.79 Secondary neuroendocrine tumor of other sites
228.00 Hemangioma of unspecified site ▽
228.01 Hemangioma of skin and subcutaneous tissue
229.0 Benign neoplasm of lymph nodes
229.9 Benign neoplasm of unspecified site ▽
233.1 Carcinoma in situ of cervix uteri ♀
238.8 Neoplasm of uncertain behavior of other specified sites
239.89 Neoplasms of unspecified nature, other specified sites
239.9 Neoplasm of unspecified nature, site unspecified ▽
289.1 Chronic lymphadenitis
289.3 Lymphadenitis, unspecified, except mesenteric ▽
457.8 Other noninfectious disorders of lymphatic channels
683 Acute lymphadenitis — (Use additional code to identify organism: 041.1)
782.2 Localized superficial swelling, mass, or lump
784.2 Swelling, mass, or lump in head and neck
785.6 Enlargement of lymph nodes
V10.21 Personal history of malignant neoplasm of larynx
V10.3 Personal history of malignant neoplasm of breast
V10.41 Personal history of malignant neoplasm of cervix uteri ♀
V10.46 Personal history of malignant neoplasm of prostate ♂
V10.51 Personal history of malignant neoplasm of bladder
V10.71 Personal history of lymphosarcoma and reticulosarcoma
V10.82 Personal history of malignant melanoma of skin
V10.83 Personal history of other malignant neoplasm of skin

ICD-9-CM Procedural

40.11 Biopsy of lymphatic structure
40.23 Excision of axillary lymph node
40.24 Excision of inguinal lymph node
40.29 Simple excision of other lymphatic structure

38510-38520

38510 Biopsy or excision of lymph node(s); open, deep cervical node(s)
38520 open, deep cervical node(s) with excision scalene fat pad

ICD-9-CM Diagnostic

142.9 Malignant neoplasm of salivary gland, unspecified ▽
144.9 Malignant neoplasm of floor of mouth, part unspecified ▽
145.9 Malignant neoplasm of mouth, unspecified site ▽
146.9 Malignant neoplasm of oropharynx, unspecified site ▽
147.9 Malignant neoplasm of nasopharynx, unspecified site ▽
148.9 Malignant neoplasm of hypopharynx, unspecified site ▽
149.8 Malignant neoplasm of other sites within the lip and oral cavity
150.0 Malignant neoplasm of cervical esophagus
150.3 Malignant neoplasm of upper third of esophagus
150.9 Malignant neoplasm of esophagus, unspecified site ▽
161.9 Malignant neoplasm of larynx, unspecified site ▽
172.3 Malignant melanoma of skin of other and unspecified parts of face ▽
172.4 Malignant melanoma of skin of scalp and neck
174.8 Malignant neoplasm of other specified sites of female breast — (Use additional code to identify estrogen receptor status: V86.0-V86.1) ♀
174.9 Malignant neoplasm of breast (female), unspecified site — (Use additional code to identify estrogen receptor status: V86.0-V86.1) ▽ ♀
176.5 Kaposi's sarcoma of lymph nodes
176.9 Kaposi's sarcoma of unspecified site ▽
196.0 Secondary and unspecified malignant neoplasm of lymph nodes of head, face, and neck
196.8 Secondary and unspecified malignant neoplasm of lymph nodes of multiple sites
196.9 Secondary and unspecified malignant neoplasm of lymph nodes, site unspecified ▽
198.89 Secondary malignant neoplasm of other specified sites
199.0 Disseminated malignant neoplasm
199.1 Other malignant neoplasm of unspecified site
199.2 Malignant neoplasm associated with transplanted organ — (Code first complication of transplanted organ (996.80-996.89) Use additional code for specific malignancy)
200.00 Reticulosarcoma, unspecified site, extranodal and solid organ sites ▽
200.01 Reticulosarcoma of lymph nodes of head, face, and neck
200.10 Lymphosarcoma, unspecified site, extranodal and solid organ sites ▽
200.11 Lymphosarcoma of lymph nodes of head, face, and neck
200.20 Burkitt's tumor or lymphoma, unspecified site, extranodal and solid organ sites ▽
200.21 Burkitt's tumor or lymphoma of lymph nodes of head, face, and neck
200.30 Marginal zone lymphoma, unspecified site, extranodal and solid organ sites
200.31 Marginal zone lymphoma, lymph nodes of head, face, and neck
200.40 Mantle cell lymphoma, unspecified site, extranodal and solid organ sites
200.41 Mantle cell lymphoma, lymph nodes of head, face, and neck
200.50 Primary central nervous system lymphoma, unspecified site, extranodal and solid organ sites
200.51 Primary central nervous system lymphoma, lymph nodes of head, face, and neck
200.60 Anaplastic large cell lymphoma, unspecified site, extranodal and solid organ sites
200.61 Anaplastic large cell lymphoma, lymph nodes of head, face, and neck
200.70 Large cell lymphoma, unspecified site, extranodal and solid organ sites
200.71 Large cell lymphoma, lymph nodes of head, face, and neck
200.80 Other named variants, unspecified site, extranodal and solid organ sites ▽

200.81 Other named variants of lymphosarcoma and reticulosarcoma of lymph nodes of head, face, and neck

201.00 Hodgkin's paragranuloma, unspecified site, extranodal and solid organ sites ▽

201.01 Hodgkin's paragranuloma of lymph nodes of head, face, and neck

201.10 Hodgkin's granuloma, unspecified site, extranodal and solid organ sites ▽

201.11 Hodgkin's granuloma of lymph nodes of head, face, and neck

201.20 Hodgkin's sarcoma, unspecified site, extranodal and solid organ sites ▽

201.21 Hodgkin's sarcoma of lymph nodes of head, face, and neck

201.40 Hodgkin's disease, lymphocytic-histiocytic predominance, unspecified site, extranodal and solid organ sites ▽

201.41 Hodgkin's disease, lymphocytic-histiocytic predominance of lymph nodes of head, face, and neck

201.50 Hodgkin's disease, nodular sclerosis, unspecified site, extranodal and solid organ sites ▽

201.51 Hodgkin's disease, nodular sclerosis, of lymph nodes of head, face, and neck

201.60 Hodgkin's disease, mixed cellularity, unspecified site, extranodal and solid organ sites ▽

201.61 Hodgkin's disease, mixed cellularity, involving lymph nodes of head, face, and neck

201.70 Hodgkin's disease, lymphocytic depletion, unspecified site, extranodal and solid organ sites ▽

201.71 Hodgkin's disease, lymphocytic depletion, of lymph nodes of head, face, and neck

201.90 Hodgkin's disease, unspecified type, unspecified site, extranodal and solid organ sites ▽

201.91 Hodgkin's disease, unspecified type, of lymph nodes of head, face, and neck ▽

202.00 Nodular lymphoma, unspecified site, extranodal and solid organ sites ▽

202.01 Nodular lymphoma of lymph nodes of head, face, and neck

202.10 Mycosis fungoides, unspecified site, extranodal and solid organ sites ▽

202.11 Mycosis fungoides of lymph nodes of head, face, and neck

202.20 Sezary's disease, unspecified site, extranodal and solid organ sites ▽

202.30 Malignant histiocytosis, unspecified site, extranodal and solid organ sites ▽

202.31 Malignant histiocytosis of lymph nodes of head, face, and neck

202.40 Leukemic reticuloendotheliosis, unspecified site, extranodal and solid organ sites ▽

202.41 Leukemic reticuloendotheliosis of lymph nodes of head, face, and neck

202.50 Letterer-Siwe disease, unspecified site, extranodal and solid organ sites ▽

202.51 Letterer-Siwe disease of lymph nodes of head, face, and neck

202.60 Malignant mast cell tumors, unspecified site, extranodal and solid organ sites ▽

202.61 Malignant mast cell tumors of lymph nodes of head, face, and neck

202.70 Peripheral T-cell lymphoma, unspecified site, extranodal and solid organ sites

202.71 Peripheral T-cell lymphoma, lymph nodes of head, face, and neck

202.80 Other malignant lymphomas, unspecified site, extranodal and solid organ sites ▽

202.81 Other malignant lymphomas of lymph nodes of head, face, and neck

202.90 Other and unspecified malignant neoplasms of lymphoid and histiocytic tissue, unspecified site, extranodal and solid organ sites ▽

202.91 Other and unspecified malignant neoplasms of lymphoid and histiocytic tissue of lymph nodes of head, face, and neck ▽

209.20 Malignant carcinoid tumor of unknown primary site — (Code first any associated multiple endocrine neoplasia syndrome: 258.01-258.03)(Use additional code to identify associated endocrine syndrome, as: carcinoid syndrome: 259.2)

209.29 Malignant carcinoid tumor of other sites — (Code first any associated multiple endocrine neoplasia syndrome: 258.01-258.03)(Use additional code to identify associated endocrine syndrome, as: carcinoid syndrome: 259.2)

209.30 Malignant poorly differentiated neuroendocrine carcinoma, any site — (Code first any associated multiple endocrine neoplasia syndrome: 258.01-258.03)(Use additional code to identify associated endocrine syndrome, as: carcinoid syndrome: 259.2) ▽

209.31 Merkel cell carcinoma of the face

209.32 Merkel cell carcinoma of the scalp and neck

209.36 Merkel cell carcinoma of other sites

209.69 Benign carcinoid tumor of other sites — (Code first any associated multiple endocrine neoplasia syndrome: 258.01-258.03)(Use additional code to identify associated endocrine syndrome, as: carcinoid syndrome: 259.2)

209.70 Secondary neuroendocrine tumor, unspecified site ▽

209.71 Secondary neuroendocrine tumor of distant lymph nodes

209.75 Secondary Merkel cell carcinoma

209.79 Secondary neuroendocrine tumor of other sites

229.0 Benign neoplasm of lymph nodes

229.8 Benign neoplasm of other specified sites

229.9 Benign neoplasm of unspecified site ▽

238.2 Neoplasm of uncertain behavior of skin

238.71 Essential thrombocythemia

238.73 High grade myelodysplastic syndrome lesions

238.74 Myelodysplastic syndrome with 5q deletion

238.75 Myelodysplastic syndrome, unspecified ▽

238.76 Myelofibrosis with myeloid metaplasia

238.79 Other lymphatic and hematopoietic tissues

238.8 Neoplasm of uncertain behavior of other specified sites

239.89 Neoplasms of unspecified nature, other specified sites

239.9 Neoplasm of unspecified nature, site unspecified ▽

289.1 Chronic lymphadenitis

457.8 Other noninfectious disorders of lymphatic channels

683 Acute lymphadenitis — (Use additional code to identify organism: 041.1)

784.2 Swelling, mass, or lump in head and neck

785.6 Enlargement of lymph nodes

786.6 Swelling, mass, or lump in chest

V10.02 Personal history of malignant neoplasm of other and unspecified parts of oral cavity and pharynx ▽

V10.03 Personal history of malignant neoplasm of esophagus

V10.21 Personal history of malignant neoplasm of larynx

V10.3 Personal history of malignant neoplasm of breast

V10.82 Personal history of malignant melanoma of skin

ICD-9-CM Procedural

40.11 Biopsy of lymphatic structure

40.21 Excision of deep cervical lymph node

38525

38525 Biopsy or excision of lymph node(s); open, deep axillary node(s)

ICD-9-CM Diagnostic

172.5 Malignant melanoma of skin of trunk, except scrotum

172.6 Malignant melanoma of skin of upper limb, including shoulder

174.0 Malignant neoplasm of nipple and areola of female breast — (Use additional code to identify estrogen receptor status: V86.0-V86.1) ♀

174.3 Malignant neoplasm of lower-inner quadrant of female breast — (Use additional code to identify estrogen receptor status: V86.0-V86.1) ♀

174.4 Malignant neoplasm of upper-outer quadrant of female breast — (Use additional code to identify estrogen receptor status: V86.0-V86.1) ♀

174.5 Malignant neoplasm of lower-outer quadrant of female breast — (Use additional code to identify estrogen receptor status: V86.0-V86.1) ♀

174.6 Malignant neoplasm of axillary tail of female breast — (Use additional code to identify estrogen receptor status: V86.0-V86.1) ♀

174.8 Malignant neoplasm of other specified sites of female breast — (Use additional code to identify estrogen receptor status: V86.0-V86.1) ♀

175.9 Malignant neoplasm of other and unspecified sites of male breast — (Use additional code to identify estrogen receptor status: V86.0-V86.1) ▽ ♂

195.1 Malignant neoplasm of thorax

196.3 Secondary and unspecified malignant neoplasm of lymph nodes of axilla and upper limb

198.89 Secondary malignant neoplasm of other specified sites

199.0 Disseminated malignant neoplasm

199.1 Other malignant neoplasm of unspecified site

199.2	Malignant neoplasm associated with transplanted organ — (Code first complication of transplanted organ (996.80-996.89) Use additional code for specific malignancy)
200.00	Reticulosarcoma, unspecified site, extranodal and solid organ sites ▽
200.04	Reticulosarcoma of lymph nodes of axilla and upper limb
200.10	Lymphosarcoma, unspecified site, extranodal and solid organ sites ▽
200.14	Lymphosarcoma of lymph nodes of axilla and upper limb
200.20	Burkitt's tumor or lymphoma, unspecified site, extranodal and solid organ sites ▽
200.24	Burkitt's tumor or lymphoma of lymph nodes of axilla and upper limb
200.30	Marginal zone lymphoma, unspecified site, extranodal and solid organ sites
200.34	Marginal zone lymphoma, lymph nodes of axilla and upper limb
200.40	Mantle cell lymphoma, unspecified site, extranodal and solid organ sites
200.44	Mantle cell lymphoma, lymph nodes of axilla and upper limb
200.50	Primary central nervous system lymphoma, unspecified site, extranodal and solid organ sites
200.54	Primary central nervous system lymphoma, lymph nodes of axilla and upper limb
200.60	Anaplastic large cell lymphoma, unspecified site, extranodal and solid organ sites
200.64	Anaplastic large cell lymphoma, lymph nodes of axilla and upper limb
200.70	Large cell lymphoma, unspecified site, extranodal and solid organ sites
200.74	Large cell lymphoma, lymph nodes of axilla and upper limb
200.80	Other named variants, unspecified site, extranodal and solid organ sites ▽
200.84	Other named variants of lymphosarcoma and reticulosarcoma of lymph nodes of axilla and upper limb
201.00	Hodgkin's paragranuloma, unspecified site, extranodal and solid organ sites ▽
201.04	Hodgkin's paragranuloma of lymph nodes of axilla and upper limb
201.10	Hodgkin's granuloma, unspecified site, extranodal and solid organ sites ▽
201.14	Hodgkin's granuloma of lymph nodes of axilla and upper limb
201.20	Hodgkin's sarcoma, unspecified site, extranodal and solid organ sites ▽
201.24	Hodgkin's sarcoma of lymph nodes of axilla and upper limb
201.40	Hodgkin's disease, lymphocytic-histiocytic predominance, unspecified site, extranodal and solid organ sites ▽
201.44	Hodgkin's disease, lymphocytic-histiocytic predominance of lymph nodes of axilla and upper limb
201.50	Hodgkin's disease, nodular sclerosis, unspecified site, extranodal and solid organ sites ▽
201.54	Hodgkin's disease, nodular sclerosis, of lymph nodes of axilla and upper limb
201.60	Hodgkin's disease, mixed cellularity, unspecified site, extranodal and solid organ sites ▽
201.64	Hodgkin's disease, mixed cellularity, of lymph nodes of axilla and upper limb
201.70	Hodgkin's disease, lymphocytic depletion, unspecified site, extranodal and solid organ sites ▽
201.74	Hodgkin's disease, lymphocytic depletion, of lymph nodes of axilla and upper limb
201.90	Hodgkin's disease, unspecified type, unspecified site, extranodal and solid organ sites ▽
201.94	Hodgkin's disease, unspecified type, of lymph nodes of axilla and upper limb ▽
202.00	Nodular lymphoma, unspecified site, extranodal and solid organ sites ▽
202.04	Nodular lymphoma of lymph nodes of axilla and upper limb
202.10	Mycosis fungoides, unspecified site, extranodal and solid organ sites ▽
202.14	Mycosis fungoides of lymph nodes of axilla and upper limb
202.20	Sezary's disease, unspecified site, extranodal and solid organ sites ▽
202.24	Sezary's disease of lymph nodes of axilla and upper limb
202.30	Malignant histiocytosis, unspecified site, extranodal and solid organ sites ▽
202.34	Malignant histiocytosis of lymph nodes of axilla and upper limb
202.40	Leukemic reticuloendotheliosis, unspecified site, extranodal and solid organ sites ▽
202.44	Leukemic reticuloendotheliosis of lymph nodes of axilla and upper limb
202.50	Letterer-Siwe disease, unspecified site, extranodal and solid organ sites ▽
202.54	Letterer-Siwe disease of lymph nodes of axilla and upper limb
202.60	Malignant mast cell tumors, unspecified site, extranodal and solid organ sites ▽
202.64	Malignant mast cell tumors of lymph nodes of axilla and upper limb
202.70	Peripheral T-cell lymphoma, unspecified site, extranodal and solid organ sites
202.74	Peripheral T-cell lymphoma, lymph nodes of axilla and upper limb
202.80	Other malignant lymphomas, unspecified site, extranodal and solid organ sites ▽
202.84	Other malignant lymphomas of lymph nodes of axilla and upper limb
202.90	Other and unspecified malignant neoplasms of lymphoid and histiocytic tissue, unspecified site, extranodal and solid organ sites ▽
202.94	Other and unspecified malignant neoplasms of lymphoid and histiocytic tissue of lymph nodes of axilla and upper limb ▽
209.20	Malignant carcinoid tumor of unknown primary site — (Code first any associated multiple endocrine neoplasia syndrome: 258.01-258.03)(Use additional code to identify associated endocrine syndrome, as: carcinoid syndrome: 259.2)
209.29	Malignant carcinoid tumor of other sites — (Code first any associated multiple endocrine neoplasia syndrome: 258.01-258.03)(Use additional code to identify associated endocrine syndrome, as: carcinoid syndrome: 259.2)
209.30	Malignant poorly differentiated neuroendocrine carcinoma, any site — (Code first any associated multiple endocrine neoplasia syndrome: 258.01-258.03)(Use additional code to identify associated endocrine syndrome, as: carcinoid syndrome: 259.2) ▽
209.33	Merkel cell carcinoma of the upper limb
209.36	Merkel cell carcinoma of other sites
209.69	Benign carcinoid tumor of other sites — (Code first any associated multiple endocrine neoplasia syndrome: 258.01-258.03)(Use additional code to identify associated endocrine syndrome, as: carcinoid syndrome: 259.2)
209.70	Secondary neuroendocrine tumor, unspecified site ▽
209.71	Secondary neuroendocrine tumor of distant lymph nodes
209.75	Secondary Merkel cell carcinoma
209.79	Secondary neuroendocrine tumor of other sites
229.0	Benign neoplasm of lymph nodes
229.8	Benign neoplasm of other specified sites
229.9	Benign neoplasm of unspecified site ▽
238.71	Essential thrombocythemia
238.73	High grade myelodysplastic syndrome lesions
238.74	Myelodysplastic syndrome with 5q deletion
238.75	Myelodysplastic syndrome, unspecified ▽
238.76	Myelofibrosis with myeloid metaplasia
238.77	Post-transplant lymphoproliferative disorder [PTLD] — (Code first complications of transplant (996.80-996.89))
238.79	Other lymphatic and hematopoietic tissues
238.8	Neoplasm of uncertain behavior of other specified sites
239.89	Neoplasms of unspecified nature, other specified sites
239.9	Neoplasm of unspecified nature, site unspecified ▽
289.1	Chronic lymphadenitis
289.3	Lymphadenitis, unspecified, except mesenteric ▽
683	Acute lymphadenitis — (Use additional code to identify organism: 041.1)
785.6	Enlargement of lymph nodes
V10.3	Personal history of malignant neoplasm of breast
V10.82	Personal history of malignant melanoma of skin

ICD-9-CM Procedural

40.11	Biopsy of lymphatic structure
40.23	Excision of axillary lymph node

38530

38530 Biopsy or excision of lymph node(s); open, internal mammary node(s)

ICD-9-CM Diagnostic

170.3	Malignant neoplasm of ribs, sternum, and clavicle
171.4	Malignant neoplasm of connective and other soft tissue of thorax
174.0	Malignant neoplasm of nipple and areola of female breast — (Use additional code to identify estrogen receptor status: V86.0-V86.1) ♀
174.1	Malignant neoplasm of central portion of female breast — (Use additional code to identify estrogen receptor status: V86.0-V86.1) ♀

174.2 Malignant neoplasm of upper-inner quadrant of female breast — (Use additional code to identify estrogen receptor status: V86.0-V86.1) ♀
174.3 Malignant neoplasm of lower-inner quadrant of female breast — (Use additional code to identify estrogen receptor status: V86.0-V86.1) ♀
174.4 Malignant neoplasm of upper-outer quadrant of female breast — (Use additional code to identify estrogen receptor status: V86.0-V86.1) ♀
174.5 Malignant neoplasm of lower-outer quadrant of female breast — (Use additional code to identify estrogen receptor status: V86.0-V86.1) ♀
174.6 Malignant neoplasm of axillary tail of female breast — (Use additional code to identify estrogen receptor status: V86.0-V86.1) ♀
174.8 Malignant neoplasm of other specified sites of female breast — (Use additional code to identify estrogen receptor status: V86.0-V86.1) ♀
196.9 Secondary and unspecified malignant neoplasm of lymph nodes, site unspecified ▽
198.81 Secondary malignant neoplasm of breast
209.35 Merkel cell carcinoma of the trunk
209.70 Secondary neuroendocrine tumor, unspecified site ▽
209.71 Secondary neuroendocrine tumor of distant lymph nodes
209.75 Secondary Merkel cell carcinoma
209.79 Secondary neuroendocrine tumor of other sites
289.3 Lymphadenitis, unspecified, except mesenteric ▽
V10.3 Personal history of malignant neoplasm of breast
V10.81 Personal history of malignant neoplasm of bone

ICD-9-CM Procedural

40.22 Excision of internal mammary lymph node

38542

38542 Dissection, deep jugular node(s)

ICD-9-CM Diagnostic

142.1 Malignant neoplasm of submandibular gland
161.0 Malignant neoplasm of glottis
161.1 Malignant neoplasm of supraglottis
161.3 Malignant neoplasm of laryngeal cartilages
161.9 Malignant neoplasm of larynx, unspecified site ▽
193 Malignant neoplasm of thyroid gland — (Use additional code to identify any functional activity)
194.1 Malignant neoplasm of parathyroid gland
196.0 Secondary and unspecified malignant neoplasm of lymph nodes of head, face, and neck
200.01 Reticulosarcoma of lymph nodes of head, face, and neck
200.11 Lymphosarcoma of lymph nodes of head, face, and neck
200.31 Marginal zone lymphoma, lymph nodes of head, face, and neck
200.41 Mantle cell lymphoma, lymph nodes of head, face, and neck
200.51 Primary central nervous system lymphoma, lymph nodes of head, face, and neck
200.61 Anaplastic large cell lymphoma, lymph nodes of head, face, and neck
200.71 Large cell lymphoma, lymph nodes of head, face, and neck
201.01 Hodgkin's paragranuloma of lymph nodes of head, face, and neck
201.91 Hodgkin's disease, unspecified type, of lymph nodes of head, face, and neck ▽
202.71 Peripheral T-cell lymphoma, lymph nodes of head, face, and neck
209.32 Merkel cell carcinoma of the scalp and neck
209.70 Secondary neuroendocrine tumor, unspecified site ▽
209.71 Secondary neuroendocrine tumor of distant lymph nodes
209.75 Secondary Merkel cell carcinoma
209.79 Secondary neuroendocrine tumor of other sites
228.1 Lymphangioma, any site
784.2 Swelling, mass, or lump in head and neck
785.6 Enlargement of lymph nodes
V10.02 Personal history of malignant neoplasm of other and unspecified parts of oral cavity and pharynx ▽
V10.21 Personal history of malignant neoplasm of larynx
V10.71 Personal history of lymphosarcoma and reticulosarcoma
V10.87 Personal history of malignant neoplasm of thyroid
V10.88 Personal history of malignant neoplasm of other endocrine glands and related structures

ICD-9-CM Procedural

40.3 Regional lymph node excision
40.40 Radical neck dissection, not otherwise specified
40.41 Radical neck dissection, unilateral
40.42 Radical neck dissection, bilateral

38550-38555

38550 Excision of cystic hygroma, axillary or cervical; without deep neurovascular dissection
38555 with deep neurovascular dissection

ICD-9-CM Diagnostic

228.1 Lymphangioma, any site

ICD-9-CM Procedural

40.29 Simple excision of other lymphatic structure
40.59 Radical excision of other lymph nodes

38562-38564

38562 Limited lymphadenectomy for staging (separate procedure); pelvic and para-aortic
38564 retroperitoneal (aortic and/or splenic)

ICD-9-CM Diagnostic

151.5 Malignant neoplasm of lesser curvature of stomach, unspecified ▽
151.8 Malignant neoplasm of other specified sites of stomach
152.0 Malignant neoplasm of duodenum
153.7 Malignant neoplasm of splenic flexure
154.0 Malignant neoplasm of rectosigmoid junction
154.1 Malignant neoplasm of rectum
156.1 Malignant neoplasm of extrahepatic bile ducts
157.8 Malignant neoplasm of other specified sites of pancreas
157.9 Malignant neoplasm of pancreas, part unspecified ▽
158.0 Malignant neoplasm of retroperitoneum
158.8 Malignant neoplasm of specified parts of peritoneum
159.1 Malignant neoplasm of spleen, not elsewhere classified
180.0 Malignant neoplasm of endocervix ♀
180.1 Malignant neoplasm of exocervix ♀
180.8 Malignant neoplasm of other specified sites of cervix ♀
180.9 Malignant neoplasm of cervix uteri, unspecified site ▽ ♀
181 Malignant neoplasm of placenta ♀
182.0 Malignant neoplasm of corpus uteri, except isthmus ♀
182.1 Malignant neoplasm of isthmus ♀
182.8 Malignant neoplasm of other specified sites of body of uterus ♀
183.0 Malignant neoplasm of ovary — (Use additional code to identify any functional activity) ♀
183.2 Malignant neoplasm of fallopian tube ♀
183.3 Malignant neoplasm of broad ligament of uterus ♀
183.4 Malignant neoplasm of parametrium of uterus ♀
183.5 Malignant neoplasm of round ligament of uterus ♀
183.8 Malignant neoplasm of other specified sites of uterine adnexa ♀
183.9 Malignant neoplasm of uterine adnexa, unspecified site ▽ ♀
185 Malignant neoplasm of prostate ♂
186.9 Malignant neoplasm of other and unspecified testis — (Use additional code to identify any functional activity) ▽ ♂
187.1 Malignant neoplasm of prepuce ♂
187.2 Malignant neoplasm of glans penis ♂

187.3 Malignant neoplasm of body of penis ♂
187.4 Malignant neoplasm of penis, part unspecified ▽ ♂
187.5 Malignant neoplasm of epididymis ♂
187.6 Malignant neoplasm of spermatic cord ♂
187.7 Malignant neoplasm of scrotum ♂
187.8 Malignant neoplasm of other specified sites of male genital organs ♂
187.9 Malignant neoplasm of male genital organ, site unspecified ▽ ♂
188.0 Malignant neoplasm of trigone of urinary bladder
188.1 Malignant neoplasm of dome of urinary bladder
188.2 Malignant neoplasm of lateral wall of urinary bladder
188.3 Malignant neoplasm of anterior wall of urinary bladder
188.4 Malignant neoplasm of posterior wall of urinary bladder
188.5 Malignant neoplasm of bladder neck
188.6 Malignant neoplasm of ureteric orifice
188.8 Malignant neoplasm of other specified sites of bladder
188.9 Malignant neoplasm of bladder, part unspecified ▽
189.0 Malignant neoplasm of kidney, except pelvis
189.1 Malignant neoplasm of renal pelvis
189.2 Malignant neoplasm of ureter
189.3 Malignant neoplasm of urethra
189.4 Malignant neoplasm of paraurethral glands
189.8 Malignant neoplasm of other specified sites of urinary organs
189.9 Malignant neoplasm of urinary organ, site unspecified ▽
195.3 Malignant neoplasm of pelvis
196.2 Secondary and unspecified malignant neoplasm of intra-abdominal lymph nodes
196.6 Secondary and unspecified malignant neoplasm of intrapelvic lymph nodes
197.5 Secondary malignant neoplasm of large intestine and rectum
197.6 Secondary malignant neoplasm of retroperitoneum and peritoneum
197.8 Secondary malignant neoplasm of other digestive organs and spleen
198.89 Secondary malignant neoplasm of other specified sites
200.00 Reticulosarcoma, unspecified site, extranodal and solid organ sites ▽
200.02 Reticulosarcoma of intrathoracic lymph nodes
200.03 Reticulosarcoma of intra-abdominal lymph nodes
200.06 Reticulosarcoma of intrapelvic lymph nodes
200.07 Reticulosarcoma of spleen
200.08 Reticulosarcoma of lymph nodes of multiple sites
200.10 Lymphosarcoma, unspecified site, extranodal and solid organ sites ▽
200.12 Lymphosarcoma of intrathoracic lymph nodes
200.13 Lymphosarcoma of intra-abdominal lymph nodes
200.16 Lymphosarcoma of intrapelvic lymph nodes
200.17 Lymphosarcoma of spleen
200.18 Lymphosarcoma of lymph nodes of multiple sites
200.20 Burkitt's tumor or lymphoma, unspecified site, extranodal and solid organ sites ▽
200.22 Burkitt's tumor or lymphoma of intrathoracic lymph nodes
200.23 Burkitt's tumor or lymphoma of intra-abdominal lymph nodes
200.26 Burkitt's tumor or lymphoma of intrapelvic lymph nodes
200.27 Burkitt's tumor or lymphoma of spleen
200.28 Burkitt's tumor or lymphoma of lymph nodes of multiple sites
200.30 Marginal zone lymphoma, unspecified site, extranodal and solid organ sites
200.32 Marginal zone lymphoma, intrathoracic lymph nodes
200.33 Marginal zone lymphoma, intra-abdominal lymph nodes
200.36 Marginal zone lymphoma, intrapelvic lymph nodes
200.37 Marginal zone lymphoma, spleen
200.38 Marginal zone lymphoma, lymph nodes of multiple sites
200.40 Mantle cell lymphoma, unspecified site, extranodal and solid organ sites
200.42 Mantle cell lymphoma, intrathoracic lymph nodes
200.43 Mantle cell lymphoma, intra-abdominal lymph nodes
200.46 Mantle cell lymphoma, intrapelvic lymph nodes
200.47 Mantle cell lymphoma, spleen
200.48 Mantle cell lymphoma, lymph nodes of multiple sites
200.50 Primary central nervous system lymphoma, unspecified site, extranodal and solid organ sites
200.52 Primary central nervous system lymphoma, intrathoracic lymph nodes
200.53 Primary central nervous system lymphoma, intra-abdominal lymph nodes
200.56 Primary central nervous system lymphoma, intrapelvic lymph nodes
200.57 Primary central nervous system lymphoma, spleen
200.58 Primary central nervous system lymphoma, lymph nodes of multiple sites
200.60 Anaplastic large cell lymphoma, unspecified site, extranodal and solid organ sites
200.62 Anaplastic large cell lymphoma, intrathoracic lymph nodes
200.63 Anaplastic large cell lymphoma, intra-abdominal lymph nodes
200.66 Anaplastic large cell lymphoma, intrapelvic lymph nodes
200.67 Anaplastic large cell lymphoma, spleen
200.68 Anaplastic large cell lymphoma, lymph nodes of multiple sites
200.70 Large cell lymphoma, unspecified site, extranodal and solid organ sites
200.72 Large cell lymphoma, intrathoracic lymph nodes
200.73 Large cell lymphoma, intra-abdominal lymph nodes
200.76 Large cell lymphoma, intrapelvic lymph nodes
200.77 Large cell lymphoma, spleen
200.78 Large cell lymphoma, lymph nodes of multiple sites
200.80 Other named variants, unspecified site, extranodal and solid organ sites ▽
200.82 Other named variants of lymphosarcoma and reticulosarcoma of intrathoracic lymph nodes
200.83 Other named variants of lymphosarcoma and reticulosarcoma of intra-abdominal lymph nodes
200.86 Other named variants of lymphosarcoma and reticulosarcoma of intrapelvic lymph nodes
200.87 Other named variants of lymphosarcoma and reticulosarcoma of spleen
200.88 Other named variants of lymphosarcoma and reticulosarcoma of lymph nodes of multiple sites
201.00 Hodgkin's paragranuloma, unspecified site, extranodal and solid organ sites ▽
201.02 Hodgkin's paragranuloma of intrathoracic lymph nodes
201.03 Hodgkin's paragranuloma of intra-abdominal lymph nodes
201.06 Hodgkin's paragranuloma of intrapelvic lymph nodes
201.07 Hodgkin's paragranuloma of spleen
201.08 Hodgkin's paragranuloma of lymph nodes of multiple sites
201.10 Hodgkin's granuloma, unspecified site, extranodal and solid organ sites ▽
201.12 Hodgkin's granuloma of intrathoracic lymph nodes
201.13 Hodgkin's granuloma of intra-abdominal lymph nodes
201.16 Hodgkin's granuloma of intrapelvic lymph nodes
201.17 Hodgkin's granuloma of spleen
201.18 Hodgkin's granuloma of lymph nodes of multiple sites
201.20 Hodgkin's sarcoma, unspecified site, extranodal and solid organ sites ▽
201.22 Hodgkin's sarcoma of intrathoracic lymph nodes
201.23 Hodgkin's sarcoma of intra-abdominal lymph nodes
201.26 Hodgkin's sarcoma of intrapelvic lymph nodes
201.27 Hodgkin's sarcoma of spleen
201.28 Hodgkin's sarcoma of lymph nodes of multiple sites
201.40 Hodgkin's disease, lymphocytic-histiocytic predominance, unspecified site, extranodal and solid organ sites ▽
201.42 Hodgkin's disease, lymphocytic-histiocytic predominance of intrathoracic lymph nodes
201.43 Hodgkin's disease, lymphocytic-histiocytic predominance of intra-abdominal lymph nodes
201.46 Hodgkin's disease, lymphocytic-histiocytic predominance of intrapelvic lymph nodes
201.47 Hodgkin's disease, lymphocytic-histiocytic predominance of spleen
201.48 Hodgkin's disease, lymphocytic-histiocytic predominance of lymph nodes of multiple sites

201.50 Hodgkin's disease, nodular sclerosis, unspecified site, extranodal and solid organ sites ▽
201.52 Hodgkin's disease, nodular sclerosis, of intrathoracic lymph nodes
201.53 Hodgkin's disease, nodular sclerosis, of intra-abdominal lymph nodes
201.56 Hodgkin's disease, nodular sclerosis, of intrapelvic lymph nodes
201.57 Hodgkin's disease, nodular sclerosis, of spleen
201.58 Hodgkin's disease, nodular sclerosis, of lymph nodes of multiple sites
201.60 Hodgkin's disease, mixed cellularity, unspecified site, extranodal and solid organ sites ▽
201.62 Hodgkin's disease, mixed cellularity, of intrathoracic lymph nodes
201.63 Hodgkin's disease, mixed cellularity, of intra-abdominal lymph nodes
201.66 Hodgkin's disease, mixed cellularity, of intrapelvic lymph nodes
201.67 Hodgkin's disease, mixed cellularity, of spleen
201.68 Hodgkin's disease, mixed cellularity, of lymph nodes of multiple sites
201.70 Hodgkin's disease, lymphocytic depletion, unspecified site, extranodal and solid organ sites ▽
201.72 Hodgkin's disease, lymphocytic depletion, of intrathoracic lymph nodes
201.73 Hodgkin's disease, lymphocytic depletion, of intra-abdominal lymph nodes
201.76 Hodgkin's disease, lymphocytic depletion, of intrapelvic lymph nodes
201.77 Hodgkin's disease, lymphocytic depletion, of spleen
201.78 Hodgkin's disease, lymphocytic depletion, of lymph nodes of multiple sites
201.90 Hodgkin's disease, unspecified type, unspecified site, extranodal and solid organ sites ▽
201.92 Hodgkin's disease, unspecified type, of intrathoracic lymph nodes ▽
201.93 Hodgkin's disease, unspecified type, of intra-abdominal lymph nodes ▽
201.96 Hodgkin's disease, unspecified type, of intrapelvic lymph nodes ▽
201.97 Hodgkin's disease, unspecified type, of spleen ▽
201.98 Hodgkin's disease, unspecified type, of lymph nodes of multiple sites ▽
202.00 Nodular lymphoma, unspecified site, extranodal and solid organ sites ▽
202.02 Nodular lymphoma of intrathoracic lymph nodes
202.03 Nodular lymphoma of intra-abdominal lymph nodes
202.06 Nodular lymphoma of intrapelvic lymph nodes
202.07 Nodular lymphoma of spleen
202.08 Nodular lymphoma of lymph nodes of multiple sites
202.10 Mycosis fungoides, unspecified site, extranodal and solid organ sites ▽
202.12 Mycosis fungoides of intrathoracic lymph nodes
202.13 Mycosis fungoides of intra-abdominal lymph nodes
202.16 Mycosis fungoides of intrapelvic lymph nodes
202.17 Mycosis fungoides of spleen
202.18 Mycosis fungoides of lymph nodes of multiple sites
202.20 Sezary's disease, unspecified site, extranodal and solid organ sites ▽
202.22 Sezary's disease of intrathoracic lymph nodes
202.23 Sezary's disease of intra-abdominal lymph nodes
202.26 Sezary's disease of intrapelvic lymph nodes
202.27 Sezary's disease of spleen
202.28 Sezary's disease of lymph nodes of multiple sites
202.30 Malignant histiocytosis, unspecified site, extranodal and solid organ sites ▽
202.32 Malignant histiocytosis of intrathoracic lymph nodes
202.33 Malignant histiocytosis of intra-abdominal lymph nodes
202.36 Malignant histiocytosis of intrapelvic lymph nodes
202.37 Malignant histiocytosis of spleen
202.38 Malignant histiocytosis of lymph nodes of multiple sites
202.40 Leukemic reticuloendotheliosis, unspecified site, extranodal and solid organ sites ▽
202.42 Leukemic reticuloendotheliosis of intrathoracic lymph nodes
202.43 Leukemic reticuloendotheliosis of intra-abdominal lymph nodes
202.46 Leukemic reticuloendotheliosis of intrapelvic lymph nodes
202.47 Leukemic reticuloendotheliosis of spleen
202.48 Leukemic reticuloendotheliosis of lymph nodes of multiple sites
202.50 Letterer-Siwe disease, unspecified site, extranodal and solid organ sites ▽
202.52 Letterer-Siwe disease of intrathoracic lymph nodes
202.53 Letterer-Siwe disease of intra-abdominal lymph nodes
202.56 Letterer-Siwe disease of intrapelvic lymph nodes
202.57 Letterer-Siwe disease of spleen
202.58 Letterer-Siwe disease of lymph nodes of multiple sites
202.60 Malignant mast cell tumors, unspecified site, extranodal and solid organ sites ▽
202.62 Malignant mast cell tumors of intrathoracic lymph nodes
202.63 Malignant mast cell tumors of intra-abdominal lymph nodes
202.66 Malignant mast cell tumors of intrapelvic lymph nodes
202.67 Malignant mast cell tumors of spleen
202.68 Malignant mast cell tumors of lymph nodes of multiple sites
202.72 Peripheral T-cell lymphoma, intrathoracic lymph nodes
202.73 Peripheral T-cell lymphoma, intra-abdominal lymph nodes
202.76 Peripheral T-cell lymphoma, intrapelvic lymph nodes
202.77 Peripheral T-cell lymphoma, spleen
202.78 Peripheral T-cell lymphoma, lymph nodes of multiple sites
202.80 Other malignant lymphomas, unspecified site, extranodal and solid organ sites ▽
202.82 Other malignant lymphomas of intrathoracic lymph nodes
202.83 Other malignant lymphomas of intra-abdominal lymph nodes
202.86 Other malignant lymphomas of intrapelvic lymph nodes
202.87 Other malignant lymphomas of spleen
202.88 Other malignant lymphomas of lymph nodes of multiple sites
202.90 Other and unspecified malignant neoplasms of lymphoid and histiocytic tissue, unspecified site, extranodal and solid organ sites ▽
202.92 Other and unspecified malignant neoplasms of lymphoid and histiocytic tissue of intrathoracic lymph nodes ▽
202.93 Other and unspecified malignant neoplasms of lymphoid and histiocytic tissue of intra-abdominal lymph nodes ▽
202.96 Other and unspecified malignant neoplasms of lymphoid and histiocytic tissue of intrapelvic lymph nodes ▽
202.97 Other and unspecified malignant neoplasms of lymphoid and histiocytic tissue of spleen ▽
202.98 Other and unspecified malignant neoplasms of lymphoid and histiocytic tissue of lymph nodes of multiple sites ▽
209.01 Malignant carcinoid tumor of the duodenum — (Code first any associated multiple endocrine neoplasia syndrome: 258.01-258.03)(Use additional code to identify associated endocrine syndrome, as: carcinoid syndrome: 259.2)
209.24 Malignant carcinoid tumor of the kidney — (Code first any associated multiple endocrine neoplasia syndrome: 258.01-258.03; Use additional code to identify associated endocrine syndrome, as: carcinoid syndrome: 259.2)
209.35 Merkel cell carcinoma of the trunk
209.36 Merkel cell carcinoma of other sites
209.57 Benign carcinoid tumor of the rectum — (Code first any associated multiple endocrine neoplasia syndrome: 258.01-258.03)(Use additional code to identify associated endocrine syndrome, as: carcinoid syndrome: 259.2)
209.70 Secondary neuroendocrine tumor, unspecified site ▽
209.71 Secondary neuroendocrine tumor of distant lymph nodes
209.74 Secondary neuroendocrine tumor of peritoneum
209.75 Secondary Merkel cell carcinoma
209.79 Secondary neuroendocrine tumor of other sites
211.4 Benign neoplasm of rectum and anal canal
230.4 Carcinoma in situ of rectum
235.2 Neoplasm of uncertain behavior of stomach, intestines, and rectum
235.4 Neoplasm of uncertain behavior of retroperitoneum and peritoneum
235.5 Neoplasm of uncertain behavior of other and unspecified digestive organs ▽
238.8 Neoplasm of uncertain behavior of other specified sites
239.0 Neoplasm of unspecified nature of digestive system

ICD-9-CM Procedural

40.3 Regional lymph node excision

40.9 Other operations on lymphatic structures

38570-38572

38570 Laparoscopy, surgical; with retroperitoneal lymph node sampling (biopsy), single or multiple
38571 with bilateral total pelvic lymphadenectomy
38572 with bilateral total pelvic lymphadenectomy and peri-aortic lymph node sampling (biopsy), single or multiple

ICD-9-CM Diagnostic

153.9 Malignant neoplasm of colon, unspecified site ♥
154.0 Malignant neoplasm of rectosigmoid junction
154.1 Malignant neoplasm of rectum
180.9 Malignant neoplasm of cervix uteri, unspecified site ♥ ♀
182.0 Malignant neoplasm of corpus uteri, except isthmus ♀
183.0 Malignant neoplasm of ovary — (Use additional code to identify any functional activity) ♀
185 Malignant neoplasm of prostate ♂
196.2 Secondary and unspecified malignant neoplasm of intra-abdominal lymph nodes
196.6 Secondary and unspecified malignant neoplasm of intrapelvic lymph nodes
200.13 Lymphosarcoma of intra-abdominal lymph nodes
200.33 Marginal zone lymphoma, intra-abdominal lymph nodes
200.43 Mantle cell lymphoma, intra-abdominal lymph nodes
200.53 Primary central nervous system lymphoma, intra-abdominal lymph nodes
200.63 Anaplastic large cell lymphoma, intra-abdominal lymph nodes
200.73 Large cell lymphoma, intra-abdominal lymph nodes
201.93 Hodgkin's disease, unspecified type, of intra-abdominal lymph nodes ♥
202.03 Nodular lymphoma of intra-abdominal lymph nodes
202.73 Peripheral T-cell lymphoma, intra-abdominal lymph nodes
202.83 Other malignant lymphomas of intra-abdominal lymph nodes
209.10 Malignant carcinoid tumor of the large intestine, unspecified portion — (Code first any associated multiple endocrine neoplasia syndrome: 258.01-258.03)(Use additional code to identify associated endocrine syndrome, as: carcinoid syndrome: 259.2) ♥
209.35 Merkel cell carcinoma of the trunk
209.36 Merkel cell carcinoma of other sites
209.70 Secondary neuroendocrine tumor, unspecified site ♥
209.71 Secondary neuroendocrine tumor of distant lymph nodes
209.74 Secondary neuroendocrine tumor of peritoneum
209.75 Secondary Merkel cell carcinoma
209.79 Secondary neuroendocrine tumor of other sites
238.8 Neoplasm of uncertain behavior of other specified sites
239.89 Neoplasms of unspecified nature, other specified sites
288.8 Other specified disease of white blood cells
289.1 Chronic lymphadenitis
289.3 Lymphadenitis, unspecified, except mesenteric ♥
457.8 Other noninfectious disorders of lymphatic channels
683 Acute lymphadenitis — (Use additional code to identify organism: 041.1)
782.2 Localized superficial swelling, mass, or lump
785.6 Enlargement of lymph nodes

ICD-9-CM Procedural

40.11 Biopsy of lymphatic structure
40.3 Regional lymph node excision

38700

38700 Suprahyoid lymphadenectomy

ICD-9-CM Diagnostic

140.8 Malignant neoplasm of other sites of lip
141.9 Malignant neoplasm of tongue, unspecified site ♥
142.1 Malignant neoplasm of submandibular gland
142.2 Malignant neoplasm of sublingual gland
142.9 Malignant neoplasm of salivary gland, unspecified ♥
143.9 Malignant neoplasm of gum, unspecified site ♥
144.9 Malignant neoplasm of floor of mouth, part unspecified ♥
145.0 Malignant neoplasm of cheek mucosa
145.9 Malignant neoplasm of mouth, unspecified site ♥
146.9 Malignant neoplasm of oropharynx, unspecified site ♥
148.9 Malignant neoplasm of hypopharynx, unspecified site ♥
160.9 Malignant neoplasm of site of nasal cavities, middle ear, and accessory sinus, unspecified site ♥
161.0 Malignant neoplasm of glottis
161.1 Malignant neoplasm of supraglottis
161.3 Malignant neoplasm of laryngeal cartilages
161.8 Malignant neoplasm of other specified sites of larynx
161.9 Malignant neoplasm of larynx, unspecified site ♥
170.0 Malignant neoplasm of bones of skull and face, except mandible
170.1 Malignant neoplasm of mandible
172.9 Melanoma of skin, site unspecified ♥
196.0 Secondary and unspecified malignant neoplasm of lymph nodes of head, face, and neck
200.01 Reticulosarcoma of lymph nodes of head, face, and neck
200.11 Lymphosarcoma of lymph nodes of head, face, and neck
200.21 Burkitt's tumor or lymphoma of lymph nodes of head, face, and neck
200.31 Marginal zone lymphoma, lymph nodes of head, face, and neck
200.41 Mantle cell lymphoma, lymph nodes of head, face, and neck
200.51 Primary central nervous system lymphoma, lymph nodes of head, face, and neck
200.61 Anaplastic large cell lymphoma, lymph nodes of head, face, and neck
200.71 Large cell lymphoma, lymph nodes of head, face, and neck
200.81 Other named variants of lymphosarcoma and reticulosarcoma of lymph nodes of head, face, and neck
201.01 Hodgkin's paragranuloma of lymph nodes of head, face, and neck
201.11 Hodgkin's granuloma of lymph nodes of head, face, and neck
201.21 Hodgkin's sarcoma of lymph nodes of head, face, and neck
201.41 Hodgkin's disease, lymphocytic-histiocytic predominance of lymph nodes of head, face, and neck
201.51 Hodgkin's disease, nodular sclerosis, of lymph nodes of head, face, and neck
201.61 Hodgkin's disease, mixed cellularity, involving lymph nodes of head, face, and neck
201.71 Hodgkin's disease, lymphocytic depletion, of lymph nodes of head, face, and neck
201.91 Hodgkin's disease, unspecified type, of lymph nodes of head, face, and neck ♥
202.01 Nodular lymphoma of lymph nodes of head, face, and neck
202.11 Mycosis fungoides of lymph nodes of head, face, and neck
202.21 Sezary's disease of lymph nodes of head, face, and neck
202.31 Malignant histiocytosis of lymph nodes of head, face, and neck
202.41 Leukemic reticuloendotheliosis of lymph nodes of head, face, and neck
202.51 Letterer-Siwe disease of lymph nodes of head, face, and neck
202.61 Malignant mast cell tumors of lymph nodes of head, face, and neck
202.71 Peripheral T-cell lymphoma, lymph nodes of head, face, and neck
202.81 Other malignant lymphomas of lymph nodes of head, face, and neck
202.91 Other and unspecified malignant neoplasms of lymphoid and histiocytic tissue of lymph nodes of head, face, and neck ♥
209.31 Merkel cell carcinoma of the face
209.32 Merkel cell carcinoma of the scalp and neck
209.36 Merkel cell carcinoma of other sites
209.70 Secondary neuroendocrine tumor, unspecified site ♥
209.71 Secondary neuroendocrine tumor of distant lymph nodes
209.75 Secondary Merkel cell carcinoma
209.79 Secondary neuroendocrine tumor of other sites
238.8 Neoplasm of uncertain behavior of other specified sites

ICD-9-CM Procedural

40.3 Regional lymph node excision

38720-38724

38720 Cervical lymphadenectomy (complete)
38724 Cervical lymphadenectomy (modified radical neck dissection)

ICD-9-CM Diagnostic

141.0 Malignant neoplasm of base of tongue
141.1 Malignant neoplasm of dorsal surface of tongue
141.2 Malignant neoplasm of tip and lateral border of tongue
141.3 Malignant neoplasm of ventral surface of tongue
141.4 Malignant neoplasm of anterior two-thirds of tongue, part unspecified ▽
141.5 Malignant neoplasm of junctional zone of tongue
141.6 Malignant neoplasm of lingual tonsil
141.9 Malignant neoplasm of tongue, unspecified site ▽
142.0 Malignant neoplasm of parotid gland
142.1 Malignant neoplasm of submandibular gland
142.2 Malignant neoplasm of sublingual gland
142.8 Malignant neoplasm of other major salivary glands
142.9 Malignant neoplasm of salivary gland, unspecified ▽
144.0 Malignant neoplasm of anterior portion of floor of mouth
144.1 Malignant neoplasm of lateral portion of floor of mouth
144.8 Malignant neoplasm of other sites of floor of mouth
144.9 Malignant neoplasm of floor of mouth, part unspecified ▽
145.0 Malignant neoplasm of cheek mucosa
145.1 Malignant neoplasm of vestibule of mouth
145.2 Malignant neoplasm of hard palate
145.3 Malignant neoplasm of soft palate
145.4 Malignant neoplasm of uvula
145.5 Malignant neoplasm of palate, unspecified ▽
145.6 Malignant neoplasm of retromolar area
145.8 Malignant neoplasm of other specified parts of mouth
145.9 Malignant neoplasm of mouth, unspecified site ▽
146.9 Malignant neoplasm of oropharynx, unspecified site ▽
148.0 Malignant neoplasm of postcricoid region of hypopharynx
148.1 Malignant neoplasm of pyriform sinus
148.2 Malignant neoplasm of aryepiglottic fold, hypopharyngeal aspect
148.3 Malignant neoplasm of posterior hypopharyngeal wall
148.8 Malignant neoplasm of other specified sites of hypopharynx
148.9 Malignant neoplasm of hypopharynx, unspecified site ▽
149.0 Malignant neoplasm of pharynx, unspecified ▽
149.1 Malignant neoplasm of Waldeyer's ring
149.8 Malignant neoplasm of other sites within the lip and oral cavity
149.9 Malignant neoplasm of ill-defined sites of lip and oral cavity
150.0 Malignant neoplasm of cervical esophagus
150.1 Malignant neoplasm of thoracic esophagus
150.3 Malignant neoplasm of upper third of esophagus
150.4 Malignant neoplasm of middle third of esophagus
150.8 Malignant neoplasm of other specified part of esophagus
150.9 Malignant neoplasm of esophagus, unspecified site ▽
161.0 Malignant neoplasm of glottis
161.1 Malignant neoplasm of supraglottis
161.2 Malignant neoplasm of subglottis
161.3 Malignant neoplasm of laryngeal cartilages
161.8 Malignant neoplasm of other specified sites of larynx
161.9 Malignant neoplasm of larynx, unspecified site ▽
162.0 Malignant neoplasm of trachea
170.1 Malignant neoplasm of mandible
172.4 Malignant melanoma of skin of scalp and neck
173.40 Unspecified malignant neoplasm of scalp and skin of neck ▽
173.41 Basal cell carcinoma of scalp and skin of neck
173.42 Squamous cell carcinoma of scalp and skin of neck
173.49 Other specified malignant neoplasm of scalp and skin of neck
193 Malignant neoplasm of thyroid gland — (Use additional code to identify any functional activity)
194.1 Malignant neoplasm of parathyroid gland
194.5 Malignant neoplasm of carotid body
195.0 Malignant neoplasm of head, face, and neck
196.0 Secondary and unspecified malignant neoplasm of lymph nodes of head, face, and neck
198.89 Secondary malignant neoplasm of other specified sites
199.0 Disseminated malignant neoplasm
199.1 Other malignant neoplasm of unspecified site
209.31 Merkel cell carcinoma of the face
209.32 Merkel cell carcinoma of the scalp and neck
209.36 Merkel cell carcinoma of other sites
209.70 Secondary neuroendocrine tumor, unspecified site ▽
209.71 Secondary neuroendocrine tumor of distant lymph nodes
209.75 Secondary Merkel cell carcinoma
209.79 Secondary neuroendocrine tumor of other sites
238.8 Neoplasm of uncertain behavior of other specified sites
239.3 Neoplasm of unspecified nature of breast
239.89 Neoplasms of unspecified nature, other specified sites
784.2 Swelling, mass, or lump in head and neck
785.6 Enlargement of lymph nodes

ICD-9-CM Procedural

40.3 Regional lymph node excision
40.40 Radical neck dissection, not otherwise specified
40.41 Radical neck dissection, unilateral
40.42 Radical neck dissection, bilateral

38740-38747

38740 Axillary lymphadenectomy; superficial
38745 complete
38746 Thoracic lymphadenectomy by thoracotomy, mediastinal and regional lymphadenectomy (List separately in addition to code for primary procedure)
38747 Abdominal lymphadenectomy, regional, including celiac, gastric, portal, peripancreatic, with or without para-aortic and vena caval nodes (List separately in addition to code for primary procedure)

ICD-9-CM Diagnostic

170.4 Malignant neoplasm of scapula and long bones of upper limb
170.5 Malignant neoplasm of short bones of upper limb
171.2 Malignant neoplasm of connective and other soft tissue of upper limb, including shoulder
172.6 Malignant melanoma of skin of upper limb, including shoulder
174.1 Malignant neoplasm of central portion of female breast — (Use additional code to identify estrogen receptor status: V86.0-V86.1) ♀
174.2 Malignant neoplasm of upper-inner quadrant of female breast — (Use additional code to identify estrogen receptor status: V86.0-V86.1) ♀
174.3 Malignant neoplasm of lower-inner quadrant of female breast — (Use additional code to identify estrogen receptor status: V86.0-V86.1) ♀
174.4 Malignant neoplasm of upper-outer quadrant of female breast — (Use additional code to identify estrogen receptor status: V86.0-V86.1) ♀
174.5 Malignant neoplasm of lower-outer quadrant of female breast — (Use additional code to identify estrogen receptor status: V86.0-V86.1) ♀
174.6 Malignant neoplasm of axillary tail of female breast — (Use additional code to identify estrogen receptor status: V86.0-V86.1) ♀

174.8 Malignant neoplasm of other specified sites of female breast — (Use additional code to identify estrogen receptor status: V86.0-V86.1) ♀
174.9 Malignant neoplasm of breast (female), unspecified site — (Use additional code to identify estrogen receptor status: V86.0-V86.1) ♀
175.9 Malignant neoplasm of other and unspecified sites of male breast — (Use additional code to identify estrogen receptor status: V86.0-V86.1) ♂
176.5 Kaposi's sarcoma of lymph nodes
195.1 Malignant neoplasm of thorax
196.1 Secondary and unspecified malignant neoplasm of intrathoracic lymph nodes
196.2 Secondary and unspecified malignant neoplasm of intra-abdominal lymph nodes
196.3 Secondary and unspecified malignant neoplasm of lymph nodes of axilla and upper limb
198.89 Secondary malignant neoplasm of other specified sites
199.1 Other malignant neoplasm of unspecified site
199.2 Malignant neoplasm associated with transplanted organ — (Code first complication of transplanted organ (996.80-996.89) Use additional code for specific malignancy)
209.33 Merkel cell carcinoma of the upper limb
209.35 Merkel cell carcinoma of the trunk
209.36 Merkel cell carcinoma of other sites
209.70 Secondary neuroendocrine tumor, unspecified site
209.71 Secondary neuroendocrine tumor of distant lymph nodes
209.73 Secondary neuroendocrine tumor of bone
209.75 Secondary Merkel cell carcinoma
209.79 Secondary neuroendocrine tumor of other sites
229.0 Benign neoplasm of lymph nodes
229.8 Benign neoplasm of other specified sites
233.0 Carcinoma in situ of breast
238.8 Neoplasm of uncertain behavior of other specified sites
239.3 Neoplasm of unspecified nature of breast
239.89 Neoplasms of unspecified nature, other specified sites
611.72 Lump or mass in breast
611.89 Other specified disorders of breast
785.6 Enlargement of lymph nodes
793.80 Unspecified abnormal mammogram
793.81 Mammographic microcalcification
793.89 Other (abnormal) findings on radiological examination of breast
V10.3 Personal history of malignant neoplasm of breast
V10.79 Personal history of other lymphatic and hematopoietic neoplasm
V10.82 Personal history of malignant melanoma of skin

ICD-9-CM Procedural

40.23 Excision of axillary lymph node
40.29 Simple excision of other lymphatic structure
40.3 Regional lymph node excision
40.50 Radical excision of lymph nodes, not otherwise specified
40.51 Radical excision of axillary lymph nodes
40.52 Radical excision of periaortic lymph nodes
40.59 Radical excision of other lymph nodes

38760-38765

38760 Inguinofemoral lymphadenectomy, superficial, including Cloquets node (separate procedure)
38765 Inguinofemoral lymphadenectomy, superficial, in continuity with pelvic lymphadenectomy, including external iliac, hypogastric, and obturator nodes (separate procedure)

ICD-9-CM Diagnostic

154.0 Malignant neoplasm of rectosigmoid junction
154.1 Malignant neoplasm of rectum
172.5 Malignant melanoma of skin of trunk, except scrotum
172.7 Malignant melanoma of skin of lower limb, including hip
176.5 Kaposi's sarcoma of lymph nodes
180.0 Malignant neoplasm of endocervix ♀
180.1 Malignant neoplasm of exocervix ♀
180.8 Malignant neoplasm of other specified sites of cervix ♀
180.9 Malignant neoplasm of cervix uteri, unspecified site ♀
181 Malignant neoplasm of placenta ♀
182.0 Malignant neoplasm of corpus uteri, except isthmus ♀
182.1 Malignant neoplasm of isthmus ♀
182.8 Malignant neoplasm of other specified sites of body of uterus ♀
183.0 Malignant neoplasm of ovary — (Use additional code to identify any functional activity) ♀
183.2 Malignant neoplasm of fallopian tube ♀
183.3 Malignant neoplasm of broad ligament of uterus ♀
183.4 Malignant neoplasm of parametrium of uterus ♀
183.5 Malignant neoplasm of round ligament of uterus ♀
183.8 Malignant neoplasm of other specified sites of uterine adnexa ♀
183.9 Malignant neoplasm of uterine adnexa, unspecified site ♀
184.0 Malignant neoplasm of vagina ♀
184.1 Malignant neoplasm of labia majora ♀
184.2 Malignant neoplasm of labia minora ♀
184.3 Malignant neoplasm of clitoris ♀
184.4 Malignant neoplasm of vulva, unspecified site ♀
184.8 Malignant neoplasm of other specified sites of female genital organs ♀
184.9 Malignant neoplasm of female genital organ, site unspecified ♀
185 Malignant neoplasm of prostate ♂
186.9 Malignant neoplasm of other and unspecified testis — (Use additional code to identify any functional activity) ♂
187.1 Malignant neoplasm of prepuce ♂
187.2 Malignant neoplasm of glans penis ♂
187.3 Malignant neoplasm of body of penis ♂
187.4 Malignant neoplasm of penis, part unspecified ♂
187.5 Malignant neoplasm of epididymis ♂
187.6 Malignant neoplasm of spermatic cord ♂
187.7 Malignant neoplasm of scrotum ♂
187.8 Malignant neoplasm of other specified sites of male genital organs ♂
187.9 Malignant neoplasm of male genital organ, site unspecified ♂
188.0 Malignant neoplasm of trigone of urinary bladder
188.1 Malignant neoplasm of dome of urinary bladder
188.2 Malignant neoplasm of lateral wall of urinary bladder
188.3 Malignant neoplasm of anterior wall of urinary bladder
188.4 Malignant neoplasm of posterior wall of urinary bladder
188.5 Malignant neoplasm of bladder neck
188.6 Malignant neoplasm of ureteric orifice
188.8 Malignant neoplasm of other specified sites of bladder
188.9 Malignant neoplasm of bladder, part unspecified
189.0 Malignant neoplasm of kidney, except pelvis
189.1 Malignant neoplasm of renal pelvis
189.2 Malignant neoplasm of ureter
189.3 Malignant neoplasm of urethra
189.4 Malignant neoplasm of paraurethral glands
189.8 Malignant neoplasm of other specified sites of urinary organs
189.9 Malignant neoplasm of urinary organ, site unspecified
196.2 Secondary and unspecified malignant neoplasm of intra-abdominal lymph nodes
196.5 Secondary and unspecified malignant neoplasm of lymph nodes of inguinal region and lower limb
197.5 Secondary malignant neoplasm of large intestine and rectum

201.90 Hodgkin's disease, unspecified type, unspecified site, extranodal and solid organ sites ▽
202.85 Other malignant lymphomas of lymph nodes of inguinal region and lower limb
209.24 Malignant carcinoid tumor of the kidney — (Code first any associated multiple endocrine neoplasia syndrome: 258.01-258.03; Use additional code to identify associated endocrine syndrome, as: carcinoid syndrome: 259.2)
209.34 Merkel cell carcinoma of the lower limb
209.35 Merkel cell carcinoma of the trunk
209.36 Merkel cell carcinoma of other sites
209.57 Benign carcinoid tumor of the rectum — (Code first any associated multiple endocrine neoplasia syndrome: 258.01-258.03)(Use additional code to identify associated endocrine syndrome, as: carcinoid syndrome: 259.2)
209.70 Secondary neuroendocrine tumor, unspecified site ▽
209.71 Secondary neuroendocrine tumor of distant lymph nodes
209.75 Secondary Merkel cell carcinoma
209.79 Secondary neuroendocrine tumor of other sites
211.4 Benign neoplasm of rectum and anal canal
229.0 Benign neoplasm of lymph nodes
230.4 Carcinoma in situ of rectum
235.2 Neoplasm of uncertain behavior of stomach, intestines, and rectum
238.8 Neoplasm of uncertain behavior of other specified sites
239.0 Neoplasm of unspecified nature of digestive system
239.89 Neoplasms of unspecified nature, other specified sites
289.3 Lymphadenitis, unspecified, except mesenteric ▽
785.6 Enlargement of lymph nodes

ICD-9-CM Procedural

40.24 Excision of inguinal lymph node
40.3 Regional lymph node excision

38770

38770 Pelvic lymphadenectomy, including external iliac, hypogastric, and obturator nodes (separate procedure)

ICD-9-CM Diagnostic

154.0 Malignant neoplasm of rectosigmoid junction
154.1 Malignant neoplasm of rectum
172.5 Malignant melanoma of skin of trunk, except scrotum
172.7 Malignant melanoma of skin of lower limb, including hip
180.0 Malignant neoplasm of endocervix ♀
180.1 Malignant neoplasm of exocervix ♀
180.8 Malignant neoplasm of other specified sites of cervix ♀
180.9 Malignant neoplasm of cervix uteri, unspecified site ▽ ♀
182.0 Malignant neoplasm of corpus uteri, except isthmus ♀
182.1 Malignant neoplasm of isthmus ♀
182.8 Malignant neoplasm of other specified sites of body of uterus ♀
183.0 Malignant neoplasm of ovary — (Use additional code to identify any functional activity) ♀
183.2 Malignant neoplasm of fallopian tube ♀
183.3 Malignant neoplasm of broad ligament of uterus ♀
183.4 Malignant neoplasm of parametrium of uterus ♀
183.5 Malignant neoplasm of round ligament of uterus ♀
183.8 Malignant neoplasm of other specified sites of uterine adnexa ♀
183.9 Malignant neoplasm of uterine adnexa, unspecified site ▽ ♀
184.0 Malignant neoplasm of vagina ♀
184.1 Malignant neoplasm of labia majora ♀
184.2 Malignant neoplasm of labia minora ♀
184.3 Malignant neoplasm of clitoris ♀
184.4 Malignant neoplasm of vulva, unspecified site ▽ ♀
184.8 Malignant neoplasm of other specified sites of female genital organs ♀
184.9 Malignant neoplasm of female genital organ, site unspecified ▽ ♀
185 Malignant neoplasm of prostate ♂
186.9 Malignant neoplasm of other and unspecified testis — (Use additional code to identify any functional activity) ▽ ♂
187.1 Malignant neoplasm of prepuce ♂
187.2 Malignant neoplasm of glans penis ♂
187.3 Malignant neoplasm of body of penis ♂
187.4 Malignant neoplasm of penis, part unspecified ▽ ♂
187.5 Malignant neoplasm of epididymis ♂
187.6 Malignant neoplasm of spermatic cord ♂
187.7 Malignant neoplasm of scrotum ♂
187.8 Malignant neoplasm of other specified sites of male genital organs ♂
187.9 Malignant neoplasm of male genital organ, site unspecified ▽ ♂
188.0 Malignant neoplasm of trigone of urinary bladder
188.1 Malignant neoplasm of dome of urinary bladder
188.2 Malignant neoplasm of lateral wall of urinary bladder
188.3 Malignant neoplasm of anterior wall of urinary bladder
188.4 Malignant neoplasm of posterior wall of urinary bladder
188.5 Malignant neoplasm of bladder neck
188.6 Malignant neoplasm of ureteric orifice
188.7 Malignant neoplasm of urachus
188.8 Malignant neoplasm of other specified sites of bladder
188.9 Malignant neoplasm of bladder, part unspecified ▽
189.0 Malignant neoplasm of kidney, except pelvis
189.1 Malignant neoplasm of renal pelvis
189.2 Malignant neoplasm of ureter
189.3 Malignant neoplasm of urethra
189.4 Malignant neoplasm of paraurethral glands
189.9 Malignant neoplasm of urinary organ, site unspecified ▽
196.6 Secondary and unspecified malignant neoplasm of intrapelvic lymph nodes
198.89 Secondary malignant neoplasm of other specified sites
199.1 Other malignant neoplasm of unspecified site
199.2 Malignant neoplasm associated with transplanted organ — (Code first complication of transplanted organ (996.80-996.89) Use additional code for specific malignancy)
209.20 Malignant carcinoid tumor of unknown primary site — (Code first any associated multiple endocrine neoplasia syndrome: 258.01-258.03)(Use additional code to identify associated endocrine syndrome, as: carcinoid syndrome: 259.2)
209.24 Malignant carcinoid tumor of the kidney — (Code first any associated multiple endocrine neoplasia syndrome: 258.01-258.03; Use additional code to identify associated endocrine syndrome, as: carcinoid syndrome: 259.2)
209.29 Malignant carcinoid tumor of other sites — (Code first any associated multiple endocrine neoplasia syndrome: 258.01-258.03)(Use additional code to identify associated endocrine syndrome, as: carcinoid syndrome: 259.2)
209.34 Merkel cell carcinoma of the lower limb
209.35 Merkel cell carcinoma of the trunk
209.36 Merkel cell carcinoma of other sites
209.70 Secondary neuroendocrine tumor, unspecified site ▽
209.71 Secondary neuroendocrine tumor of distant lymph nodes
209.74 Secondary neuroendocrine tumor of peritoneum
209.75 Secondary Merkel cell carcinoma
209.79 Secondary neuroendocrine tumor of other sites
238.8 Neoplasm of uncertain behavior of other specified sites
239.89 Neoplasms of unspecified nature, other specified sites

ICD-9-CM Procedural

40.3 Regional lymph node excision
40.53 Radical excision of iliac lymph nodes

38780

38780 Retroperitoneal transabdominal lymphadenectomy, extensive, including pelvic, aortic, and renal nodes (separate procedure)

ICD-9-CM Diagnostic

Code	Description
152.0	Malignant neoplasm of duodenum
153.7	Malignant neoplasm of splenic flexure
153.9	Malignant neoplasm of colon, unspecified site ▽
154.1	Malignant neoplasm of rectum
157.0	Malignant neoplasm of head of pancreas
157.1	Malignant neoplasm of body of pancreas
157.9	Malignant neoplasm of pancreas, part unspecified ▽
158.0	Malignant neoplasm of retroperitoneum
158.8	Malignant neoplasm of specified parts of peritoneum
180.0	Malignant neoplasm of endocervix ♀
180.1	Malignant neoplasm of exocervix ♀
180.8	Malignant neoplasm of other specified sites of cervix ♀
180.9	Malignant neoplasm of cervix uteri, unspecified site ▽ ♀
182.0	Malignant neoplasm of corpus uteri, except isthmus ♀
182.1	Malignant neoplasm of isthmus ♀
182.8	Malignant neoplasm of other specified sites of body of uterus ♀
183.0	Malignant neoplasm of ovary — (Use additional code to identify any functional activity) ♀
183.2	Malignant neoplasm of fallopian tube ♀
183.3	Malignant neoplasm of broad ligament of uterus ♀
183.4	Malignant neoplasm of parametrium of uterus ♀
183.5	Malignant neoplasm of round ligament of uterus ♀
183.8	Malignant neoplasm of other specified sites of uterine adnexa ♀
183.9	Malignant neoplasm of uterine adnexa, unspecified site ▽ ♀
185	Malignant neoplasm of prostate ♂
186.9	Malignant neoplasm of other and unspecified testis — (Use additional code to identify any functional activity) ▽ ♂
188.0	Malignant neoplasm of trigone of urinary bladder
188.1	Malignant neoplasm of dome of urinary bladder
188.2	Malignant neoplasm of lateral wall of urinary bladder
188.3	Malignant neoplasm of anterior wall of urinary bladder
188.4	Malignant neoplasm of posterior wall of urinary bladder
188.5	Malignant neoplasm of bladder neck
188.6	Malignant neoplasm of ureteric orifice
188.8	Malignant neoplasm of other specified sites of bladder
188.9	Malignant neoplasm of bladder, part unspecified ▽
189.0	Malignant neoplasm of kidney, except pelvis
189.1	Malignant neoplasm of renal pelvis
189.2	Malignant neoplasm of ureter
189.3	Malignant neoplasm of urethra
189.4	Malignant neoplasm of paraurethral glands
189.8	Malignant neoplasm of other specified sites of urinary organs
189.9	Malignant neoplasm of urinary organ, site unspecified ▽
194.0	Malignant neoplasm of adrenal gland
196.2	Secondary and unspecified malignant neoplasm of intra-abdominal lymph nodes
197.5	Secondary malignant neoplasm of large intestine and rectum
197.6	Secondary malignant neoplasm of retroperitoneum and peritoneum
197.8	Secondary malignant neoplasm of other digestive organs and spleen
209.10	Malignant carcinoid tumor of the large intestine, unspecified portion — (Code first any associated multiple endocrine neoplasia syndrome: 258.01-258.03)(Use additional code to identify associated endocrine syndrome, as: carcinoid syndrome: 259.2) ▽
209.24	Malignant carcinoid tumor of the kidney — (Code first any associated multiple endocrine neoplasia syndrome: 258.01-258.03; Use additional code to identify associated endocrine syndrome, as: carcinoid syndrome: 259.2)
209.35	Merkel cell carcinoma of the trunk
209.36	Merkel cell carcinoma of other sites
209.70	Secondary neuroendocrine tumor, unspecified site ▽
209.71	Secondary neuroendocrine tumor of distant lymph nodes
209.74	Secondary neuroendocrine tumor of peritoneum
209.75	Secondary Merkel cell carcinoma
209.79	Secondary neuroendocrine tumor of other sites
235.4	Neoplasm of uncertain behavior of retroperitoneum and peritoneum
238.8	Neoplasm of uncertain behavior of other specified sites
239.89	Neoplasms of unspecified nature, other specified sites

ICD-9-CM Procedural

Code	Description
40.3	Regional lymph node excision
40.54	Radical groin dissection

38790

38790 Injection procedure; lymphangiography

ICD-9-CM Diagnostic

Code	Description
180.0	Malignant neoplasm of endocervix ♀
180.1	Malignant neoplasm of exocervix ♀
180.8	Malignant neoplasm of other specified sites of cervix ♀
180.9	Malignant neoplasm of cervix uteri, unspecified site ▽ ♀
186.0	Malignant neoplasm of undescended testis — (Use additional code to identify any functional activity) ♂
186.9	Malignant neoplasm of other and unspecified testis — (Use additional code to identify any functional activity) ▽ ♂
201.50	Hodgkin's disease, nodular sclerosis, unspecified site, extranodal and solid organ sites ▽
201.60	Hodgkin's disease, mixed cellularity, unspecified site, extranodal and solid organ sites ▽
201.70	Hodgkin's disease, lymphocytic depletion, unspecified site, extranodal and solid organ sites ▽
785.6	Enlargement of lymph nodes

ICD-9-CM Procedural

Code	Description
87.08	Cervical lymphangiogram
87.34	Intrathoracic lymphangiogram
88.04	Abdominal lymphangiogram
88.34	Lymphangiogram of upper limb
88.36	Lymphangiogram of lower limb
99.29	Injection or infusion of other therapeutic or prophylactic substance

38792

38792 Injection procedure; radioactive tracer for identification of sentinel node

ICD-9-CM Diagnostic

Code	Description
142.1	Malignant neoplasm of submandibular gland
161.0	Malignant neoplasm of glottis
161.1	Malignant neoplasm of supraglottis
161.3	Malignant neoplasm of laryngeal cartilages
161.9	Malignant neoplasm of larynx, unspecified site ▽
174.0	Malignant neoplasm of nipple and areola of female breast — (Use additional code to identify estrogen receptor status: V86.0-V86.1) ♀
174.1	Malignant neoplasm of central portion of female breast — (Use additional code to identify estrogen receptor status: V86.0-V86.1) ♀
174.2	Malignant neoplasm of upper-inner quadrant of female breast — (Use additional code to identify estrogen receptor status: V86.0-V86.1) ♀
174.3	Malignant neoplasm of lower-inner quadrant of female breast — (Use additional code to identify estrogen receptor status: V86.0-V86.1) ♀

174.4 Malignant neoplasm of upper-outer quadrant of female breast — (Use additional code to identify estrogen receptor status: V86.0-V86.1) ♀
174.5 Malignant neoplasm of lower-outer quadrant of female breast — (Use additional code to identify estrogen receptor status: V86.0-V86.1) ♀
174.6 Malignant neoplasm of axillary tail of female breast — (Use additional code to identify estrogen receptor status: V86.0-V86.1) ♀
174.8 Malignant neoplasm of other specified sites of female breast — (Use additional code to identify estrogen receptor status: V86.0-V86.1) ♀
174.9 Malignant neoplasm of breast (female), unspecified site — (Use additional code to identify estrogen receptor status: V86.0-V86.1) ▽ ♀
193 Malignant neoplasm of thyroid gland — (Use additional code to identify any functional activity)
194.1 Malignant neoplasm of parathyroid gland
196.0 Secondary and unspecified malignant neoplasm of lymph nodes of head, face, and neck
196.1 Secondary and unspecified malignant neoplasm of intrathoracic lymph nodes
196.2 Secondary and unspecified malignant neoplasm of intra-abdominal lymph nodes
196.3 Secondary and unspecified malignant neoplasm of lymph nodes of axilla and upper limb
196.5 Secondary and unspecified malignant neoplasm of lymph nodes of inguinal region and lower limb
196.6 Secondary and unspecified malignant neoplasm of intrapelvic lymph nodes
196.8 Secondary and unspecified malignant neoplasm of lymph nodes of multiple sites
196.9 Secondary and unspecified malignant neoplasm of lymph nodes, site unspecified ▽
200.01 Reticulosarcoma of lymph nodes of head, face, and neck
200.11 Lymphosarcoma of lymph nodes of head, face, and neck
201.01 Hodgkin's paragranuloma of lymph nodes of head, face, and neck
201.91 Hodgkin's disease, unspecified type, of lymph nodes of head, face, and neck ▽
202.81 Other malignant lymphomas of lymph nodes of head, face, and neck
209.71 Secondary neuroendocrine tumor of distant lymph nodes
209.79 Secondary neuroendocrine tumor of other sites
228.1 Lymphangioma, any site
784.2 Swelling, mass, or lump in head and neck
785.6 Enlargement of lymph nodes

ICD-9-CM Procedural

92.16 Scan of lymphatic system
99.29 Injection or infusion of other therapeutic or prophylactic substance

38794

38794 Cannulation, thoracic duct

ICD-9-CM Diagnostic

201.50 Hodgkin's disease, nodular sclerosis, unspecified site, extranodal and solid organ sites ▽
201.60 Hodgkin's disease, mixed cellularity, unspecified site, extranodal and solid organ sites ▽
201.70 Hodgkin's disease, lymphocytic depletion, unspecified site, extranodal and solid organ sites ▽
202.02 Nodular lymphoma of intrathoracic lymph nodes
202.22 Sezary's disease of intrathoracic lymph nodes
202.32 Malignant histiocytosis of intrathoracic lymph nodes
202.82 Other malignant lymphomas of intrathoracic lymph nodes
209.71 Secondary neuroendocrine tumor of distant lymph nodes
209.79 Secondary neuroendocrine tumor of other sites
457.1 Other noninfectious lymphedema

ICD-9-CM Procedural

40.61 Cannulation of thoracic duct
40.9 Other operations on lymphatic structures

38900

38900 Intraoperative identification (eg, mapping) of sentinel lymph node(s) includes injection of non-radioactive dye, when performed (List separately in addition to code for primary procedure)

ICD-9-CM Diagnostic

This is an add-on code. Refer to the corresponding primary procedure code for ICD-9-CM diagnosis code links.

Mediastinum

39000

39000 Mediastinotomy with exploration, drainage, removal of foreign body, or biopsy; cervical approach

ICD-9-CM Diagnostic

164.0 Malignant neoplasm of thymus
164.2 Malignant neoplasm of anterior mediastinum
164.3 Malignant neoplasm of posterior mediastinum
209.22 Malignant carcinoid tumor of the thymus — (Code first any associated multiple endocrine neoplasia syndrome: 258.01-258.03)(Use additional code to identify associated endocrine syndrome, as: carcinoid syndrome: 259.2)
209.62 Benign carcinoid tumor of the thymus — (Code first any associated multiple endocrine neoplasia syndrome: 258.01-258.03)(Use additional code to identify associated endocrine syndrome, as: carcinoid syndrome: 259.2)
212.5 Benign neoplasm of mediastinum
212.6 Benign neoplasm of thymus
235.8 Neoplasm of uncertain behavior of pleura, thymus, and mediastinum
513.1 Abscess of mediastinum — (Use additional code to identify infectious organism)
519.2 Mediastinitis — (Use additional code to identify infectious organism)
519.3 Other diseases of mediastinum, not elsewhere classified — (Use additional code to identify infectious organism)
860.2 Traumatic hemothorax without mention of open wound into thorax
860.3 Traumatic hemothorax with open wound into thorax
862.8 Injury to multiple and unspecified intrathoracic organs without mention of open wound into cavity
862.9 Injury to multiple and unspecified intrathoracic organs with open wound into cavity
901.9 Injury to unspecified blood vessel of thorax ▽
998.4 Foreign body accidentally left during procedure, not elsewhere classified

ICD-9-CM Procedural

34.1 Incision of mediastinum
34.26 Open biopsy of mediastinum

39010

39010 Mediastinotomy with exploration, drainage, removal of foreign body, or biopsy; transthoracic approach, including either transthoracic or median sternotomy

ICD-9-CM Diagnostic

164.2 Malignant neoplasm of anterior mediastinum
164.3 Malignant neoplasm of posterior mediastinum
164.9 Malignant neoplasm of mediastinum, part unspecified ▽
212.5 Benign neoplasm of mediastinum
513.1 Abscess of mediastinum — (Use additional code to identify infectious organism)
519.2 Mediastinitis — (Use additional code to identify infectious organism)
519.3 Other diseases of mediastinum, not elsewhere classified — (Use additional code to identify infectious organism)
793.11 Solitary pulmonary nodule
793.19 Other nonspecific abnormal finding of lung field
860.2 Traumatic hemothorax without mention of open wound into thorax
860.3 Traumatic hemothorax with open wound into thorax

862.8 Injury to multiple and unspecified intrathoracic organs without mention of open wound into cavity
862.9 Injury to multiple and unspecified intrathoracic organs with open wound into cavity
901.9 Injury to unspecified blood vessel of thorax ▽
998.11 Hemorrhage complicating a procedure

ICD-9-CM Procedural

34.1 Incision of mediastinum
34.26 Open biopsy of mediastinum

39200

39200 Resection of mediastinal cyst

ICD-9-CM Diagnostic

748.8 Other specified congenital anomaly of respiratory system

ICD-9-CM Procedural

34.3 Excision or destruction of lesion or tissue of mediastinum

39220

39220 Resection of mediastinal tumor

ICD-9-CM Diagnostic

164.2 Malignant neoplasm of anterior mediastinum
164.3 Malignant neoplasm of posterior mediastinum
164.8 Malignant neoplasm of other parts of mediastinum
164.9 Malignant neoplasm of mediastinum, part unspecified ▽
212.5 Benign neoplasm of mediastinum
235.8 Neoplasm of uncertain behavior of pleura, thymus, and mediastinum

ICD-9-CM Procedural

34.3 Excision or destruction of lesion or tissue of mediastinum

39400

39400 Mediastinoscopy, includes biopsy(ies), when performed

ICD-9-CM Diagnostic

162.0 Malignant neoplasm of trachea
162.2 Malignant neoplasm of main bronchus
162.3 Malignant neoplasm of upper lobe, bronchus, or lung
162.4 Malignant neoplasm of middle lobe, bronchus, or lung
162.5 Malignant neoplasm of lower lobe, bronchus, or lung
162.8 Malignant neoplasm of other parts of bronchus or lung
162.9 Malignant neoplasm of bronchus and lung, unspecified site ▽
163.0 Malignant neoplasm of parietal pleura
163.1 Malignant neoplasm of visceral pleura
163.8 Malignant neoplasm of other specified sites of pleura
163.9 Malignant neoplasm of pleura, unspecified site ▽
164.0 Malignant neoplasm of thymus
164.2 Malignant neoplasm of anterior mediastinum
164.3 Malignant neoplasm of posterior mediastinum
164.8 Malignant neoplasm of other parts of mediastinum
164.9 Malignant neoplasm of mediastinum, part unspecified ▽
165.0 Malignant neoplasm of upper respiratory tract, part unspecified ▽
165.8 Malignant neoplasm of other sites within the respiratory system and intrathoracic organs
165.9 Malignant neoplasm of ill-defined sites within the respiratory system
195.1 Malignant neoplasm of thorax
196.1 Secondary and unspecified malignant neoplasm of intrathoracic lymph nodes
197.0 Secondary malignant neoplasm of lung
197.1 Secondary malignant neoplasm of mediastinum
197.2 Secondary malignant neoplasm of pleura
197.3 Secondary malignant neoplasm of other respiratory organs
198.89 Secondary malignant neoplasm of other specified sites
199.1 Other malignant neoplasm of unspecified site
199.2 Malignant neoplasm associated with transplanted organ — (Code first complication of transplanted organ (996.80-996.89) Use additional code for specific malignancy)
200.00 Reticulosarcoma, unspecified site, extranodal and solid organ sites ▽
200.02 Reticulosarcoma of intrathoracic lymph nodes
200.08 Reticulosarcoma of lymph nodes of multiple sites
200.10 Lymphosarcoma, unspecified site, extranodal and solid organ sites ▽
200.12 Lymphosarcoma of intrathoracic lymph nodes
200.18 Lymphosarcoma of lymph nodes of multiple sites
200.20 Burkitt's tumor or lymphoma, unspecified site, extranodal and solid organ sites ▽
200.22 Burkitt's tumor or lymphoma of intrathoracic lymph nodes
200.28 Burkitt's tumor or lymphoma of lymph nodes of multiple sites
200.80 Other named variants, unspecified site, extranodal and solid organ sites ▽
200.82 Other named variants of lymphosarcoma and reticulosarcoma of intrathoracic lymph nodes
200.88 Other named variants of lymphosarcoma and reticulosarcoma of lymph nodes of multiple sites
201.00 Hodgkin's paragranuloma, unspecified site, extranodal and solid organ sites ▽
201.02 Hodgkin's paragranuloma of intrathoracic lymph nodes
201.08 Hodgkin's paragranuloma of lymph nodes of multiple sites
201.10 Hodgkin's granuloma, unspecified site, extranodal and solid organ sites ▽
201.12 Hodgkin's granuloma of intrathoracic lymph nodes
201.18 Hodgkin's granuloma of lymph nodes of multiple sites
201.20 Hodgkin's sarcoma, unspecified site, extranodal and solid organ sites ▽
201.22 Hodgkin's sarcoma of intrathoracic lymph nodes
201.28 Hodgkin's sarcoma of lymph nodes of multiple sites
201.40 Hodgkin's disease, lymphocytic-histiocytic predominance, unspecified site, extranodal and solid organ sites ▽
201.42 Hodgkin's disease, lymphocytic-histiocytic predominance of intrathoracic lymph nodes
201.48 Hodgkin's disease, lymphocytic-histiocytic predominance of lymph nodes of multiple sites
201.50 Hodgkin's disease, nodular sclerosis, unspecified site, extranodal and solid organ sites ▽
201.52 Hodgkin's disease, nodular sclerosis, of intrathoracic lymph nodes
201.58 Hodgkin's disease, nodular sclerosis, of lymph nodes of multiple sites
201.60 Hodgkin's disease, mixed cellularity, unspecified site, extranodal and solid organ sites ▽
201.62 Hodgkin's disease, mixed cellularity, of intrathoracic lymph nodes
201.68 Hodgkin's disease, mixed cellularity, of lymph nodes of multiple sites
201.70 Hodgkin's disease, lymphocytic depletion, unspecified site, extranodal and solid organ sites ▽
201.78 Hodgkin's disease, lymphocytic depletion, of lymph nodes of multiple sites
201.90 Hodgkin's disease, unspecified type, unspecified site, extranodal and solid organ sites ▽
201.92 Hodgkin's disease, unspecified type, of intrathoracic lymph nodes ▽
201.98 Hodgkin's disease, unspecified type, of lymph nodes of multiple sites ▽
202.00 Nodular lymphoma, unspecified site, extranodal and solid organ sites ▽
202.02 Nodular lymphoma of intrathoracic lymph nodes
202.08 Nodular lymphoma of lymph nodes of multiple sites
202.10 Mycosis fungoides, unspecified site, extranodal and solid organ sites ▽
202.12 Mycosis fungoides of intrathoracic lymph nodes
202.18 Mycosis fungoides of lymph nodes of multiple sites
202.20 Sezary's disease, unspecified site, extranodal and solid organ sites ▽
202.22 Sezary's disease of intrathoracic lymph nodes
202.28 Sezary's disease of lymph nodes of multiple sites
202.30 Malignant histiocytosis, unspecified site, extranodal and solid organ sites ▽

202.32 Malignant histiocytosis of intrathoracic lymph nodes
202.38 Malignant histiocytosis of lymph nodes of multiple sites
202.40 Leukemic reticuloendotheliosis, unspecified site, extranodal and solid organ sites ▽
202.42 Leukemic reticuloendotheliosis of intrathoracic lymph nodes
202.48 Leukemic reticuloendotheliosis of lymph nodes of multiple sites
202.50 Letterer-Siwe disease, unspecified site, extranodal and solid organ sites ▽
202.52 Letterer-Siwe disease of intrathoracic lymph nodes
202.58 Letterer-Siwe disease of lymph nodes of multiple sites
202.60 Malignant mast cell tumors, unspecified site, extranodal and solid organ sites ▽
202.62 Malignant mast cell tumors of intrathoracic lymph nodes
202.68 Malignant mast cell tumors of lymph nodes of multiple sites
202.80 Other malignant lymphomas, unspecified site, extranodal and solid organ sites ▽
202.82 Other malignant lymphomas of intrathoracic lymph nodes
202.88 Other malignant lymphomas of lymph nodes of multiple sites
202.90 Other and unspecified malignant neoplasms of lymphoid and histiocytic tissue, unspecified site, extranodal and solid organ sites ▽
202.92 Other and unspecified malignant neoplasms of lymphoid and histiocytic tissue of intrathoracic lymph nodes ▽
202.98 Other and unspecified malignant neoplasms of lymphoid and histiocytic tissue of lymph nodes of multiple sites ▽
209.20 Malignant carcinoid tumor of unknown primary site — (Code first any associated multiple endocrine neoplasia syndrome: 258.01-258.03)(Use additional code to identify associated endocrine syndrome, as: carcinoid syndrome: 259.2)
209.21 Malignant carcinoid tumor of the bronchus and lung — (Code first any associated multiple endocrine neoplasia syndrome: 258.01-258.03)(Use additional code to identify associated endocrine syndrome, as: carcinoid syndrome: 259.2)
209.22 Malignant carcinoid tumor of the thymus — (Code first any associated multiple endocrine neoplasia syndrome: 258.01-258.03)(Use additional code to identify associated endocrine syndrome, as: carcinoid syndrome: 259.2)
209.29 Malignant carcinoid tumor of other sites — (Code first any associated multiple endocrine neoplasia syndrome: 258.01-258.03)(Use additional code to identify associated endocrine syndrome, as: carcinoid syndrome: 259.2)
209.61 Benign carcinoid tumor of the bronchus and lung — (Code first any associated multiple endocrine neoplasia syndrome: 258.01-258.03)(Use additional code to identify associated endocrine syndrome, as: carcinoid syndrome: 259.2)
209.62 Benign carcinoid tumor of the thymus — (Code first any associated multiple endocrine neoplasia syndrome: 258.01-258.03)(Use additional code to identify associated endocrine syndrome, as: carcinoid syndrome: 259.2)
212.2 Benign neoplasm of trachea
212.3 Benign neoplasm of bronchus and lung
212.4 Benign neoplasm of pleura
212.5 Benign neoplasm of mediastinum
212.6 Benign neoplasm of thymus
231.1 Carcinoma in situ of trachea
231.2 Carcinoma in situ of bronchus and lung
231.8 Carcinoma in situ of other specified parts of respiratory system
231.9 Carcinoma in situ of respiratory system, part unspecified ▽
235.7 Neoplasm of uncertain behavior of trachea, bronchus, and lung
235.8 Neoplasm of uncertain behavior of pleura, thymus, and mediastinum
235.9 Neoplasm of uncertain behavior of other and unspecified respiratory organs ▽
238.8 Neoplasm of uncertain behavior of other specified sites
239.1 Neoplasm of unspecified nature of respiratory system
239.89 Neoplasms of unspecified nature, other specified sites
254.8 Other specified diseases of thymus gland
496 Chronic airway obstruction, not elsewhere classified — (Note: This code is not to be used with any code from 491-493) ▽
511.81 Malignant pleural effusion — (Code first malignant neoplasm, if known)
519.2 Mediastinitis — (Use additional code to identify infectious organism)
519.3 Other diseases of mediastinum, not elsewhere classified — (Use additional code to identify infectious organism)
785.6 Enlargement of lymph nodes
786.50 Chest pain, unspecified ▽
786.6 Swelling, mass, or lump in chest
793.2 Nonspecific (abnormal) findings on radiological and other examination of other intrathoracic organs

ICD-9-CM Procedural

34.22 Mediastinoscopy
34.25 Closed (percutaneous) (needle) biopsy of mediastinum
40.11 Biopsy of lymphatic structure

Diaphragm

36522

36522 Photopheresis, extracorporeal

ICD-9-CM Diagnostic

202.10 Mycosis fungoides, unspecified site, extranodal and solid organ sites ▽
202.11 Mycosis fungoides of lymph nodes of head, face, and neck
202.12 Mycosis fungoides of intrathoracic lymph nodes
202.13 Mycosis fungoides of intra-abdominal lymph nodes
202.14 Mycosis fungoides of lymph nodes of axilla and upper limb
202.15 Mycosis fungoides of lymph nodes of inguinal region and lower limb
202.16 Mycosis fungoides of intrapelvic lymph nodes
202.17 Mycosis fungoides of spleen
202.18 Mycosis fungoides of lymph nodes of multiple sites
202.20 Sezary's disease, unspecified site, extranodal and solid organ sites ▽
202.21 Sezary's disease of lymph nodes of head, face, and neck
202.22 Sezary's disease of intrathoracic lymph nodes
202.23 Sezary's disease of intra-abdominal lymph nodes
202.24 Sezary's disease of lymph nodes of axilla and upper limb
202.25 Sezary's disease of lymph nodes of inguinal region and lower limb
202.26 Sezary's disease of intrapelvic lymph nodes
202.27 Sezary's disease of spleen
202.28 Sezary's disease of lymph nodes of multiple sites
202.70 Peripheral T-cell lymphoma, unspecified site, extranodal and solid organ sites
202.71 Peripheral T-cell lymphoma, lymph nodes of head, face, and neck
202.72 Peripheral T-cell lymphoma, intrathoracic lymph nodes
202.73 Peripheral T-cell lymphoma, intra-abdominal lymph nodes
202.74 Peripheral T-cell lymphoma, lymph nodes of axilla and upper limb
202.75 Peripheral T-cell lymphoma, lymph nodes of inguinal region and lower limb
202.76 Peripheral T-cell lymphoma, intrapelvic lymph nodes
202.77 Peripheral T-cell lymphoma, spleen
202.78 Peripheral T-cell lymphoma, lymph nodes of multiple sites
710.0 Systemic lupus erythematosus — (Use additional code to identify manifestation: 424.91, 581.81, 582.81, 583.81)
710.1 Systemic sclerosis — (Use additional code to identify manifestation: 359.6, 517.2)
714.0 Rheumatoid arthritis — (Use additional code to identify manifestation: 357.1, 359.6)
714.1 Felty's syndrome
714.2 Other rheumatoid arthritis with visceral or systemic involvement
714.30 Polyarticular juvenile rheumatoid arthritis, chronic or unspecified
714.31 Polyarticular juvenile rheumatoid arthritis, acute
714.32 Pauciarticular juvenile rheumatoid arthritis
714.33 Monoarticular juvenile rheumatoid arthritis
714.4 Chronic postrheumatic arthropathy
714.81 Rheumatoid lung
714.89 Other specified inflammatory polyarthropathies
714.9 Unspecified inflammatory polyarthropathy ▽
996.80 Complications of transplanted organ, unspecified site — (Use additional code to identify nature of complication: 078.5, 199.2, 238.77, 279.50-279.53) ▽

996.81 Complications of transplanted kidney — (Use additional code to identify nature of complication: 078.5, 199.2, 238.77, 279.50-279.53)
996.82 Complications of transplanted liver — (Use additional code to identify nature of complication: 078.5, 199.2, 238.77, 279.50-279.53)
996.84 Complications of transplanted lung — (Use additional code to identify nature of complication: 078.5, 199.2, 238.77, 279.50-279.53)
996.86 Complications of transplanted pancreas — (Use additional code to identify nature of complication: 078.5, 199.2, 238.77, 279.50-279.53)
996.87 Complications of transplanted organ, intestine — (Use additional code to identify nature of complication: 078.5, 199.2, 238.77, 279.50-279.53)
996.88 Complications of transplanted organ, stem cell
996.89 Complications of other transplanted organ — (Use additional code to identify nature of complication: 078.5, 199.2, 238.77, 279.50-279.53)
999.89 Other transfusion reaction — (Use additional code to identify graft-versus-host reaction: 279.5)

ICD-9-CM Procedural

99.88 Therapeutic photopheresis

39501

39501 Repair, laceration of diaphragm, any approach

ICD-9-CM Diagnostic

862.0 Diaphragm injury without mention of open wound into cavity
862.1 Diaphragm injury with open wound into cavity
998.2 Accidental puncture or laceration during procedure

ICD-9-CM Procedural

34.82 Suture of laceration of diaphragm
34.84 Other repair of diaphragm

39503

39503 Repair, neonatal diaphragmatic hernia, with or without chest tube insertion and with or without creation of ventral hernia

ICD-9-CM Diagnostic

756.6 Congenital anomaly of diaphragm

ICD-9-CM Procedural

53.80 Repair of diaphragmatic hernia with thoracic approach, not otherwise specified
53.83 Laparoscopic repair of diaphragmatic hernia, with thoracic approach
53.84 Other and open repair of diaphragmatic hernia, with thoracic approach

39540-39541

39540 Repair, diaphragmatic hernia (other than neonatal), traumatic; acute
39541 chronic

ICD-9-CM Diagnostic

551.3 Diaphragmatic hernia with gangrene
552.3 Diaphragmatic hernia with obstruction
553.3 Diaphragmatic hernia without mention of obstruction or gangrene
862.0 Diaphragm injury without mention of open wound into cavity

ICD-9-CM Procedural

53.71 Laparoscopic repair of diaphragmatic hernia, abdominal approach
53.72 Other and open repair of diaphragmatic hernia, abdominal approach
53.75 Repair of diaphragmatic hernia, abdominal approach, not otherwise specified
53.83 Laparoscopic repair of diaphragmatic hernia, with thoracic approach
53.84 Other and open repair of diaphragmatic hernia, with thoracic approach

39545

39545 Imbrication of diaphragm for eventration, transthoracic or transabdominal, paralytic or nonparalytic

ICD-9-CM Diagnostic

519.4 Disorders of diaphragm — (Use additional code to identify infectious organism)
551.3 Diaphragmatic hernia with gangrene
552.3 Diaphragmatic hernia with obstruction
553.3 Diaphragmatic hernia without mention of obstruction or gangrene
862.0 Diaphragm injury without mention of open wound into cavity

ICD-9-CM Procedural

34.84 Other repair of diaphragm
34.89 Other operations on diaphragm
53.9 Other hernia repair

39560-39561

39560 Resection, diaphragm; with simple repair (eg, primary suture)
39561 with complex repair (eg, prosthetic material, local muscle flap)

ICD-9-CM Diagnostic

171.4 Malignant neoplasm of connective and other soft tissue of thorax
198.89 Secondary malignant neoplasm of other specified sites
215.4 Other benign neoplasm of connective and other soft tissue of thorax
238.1 Neoplasm of uncertain behavior of connective and other soft tissue
239.2 Neoplasms of unspecified nature of bone, soft tissue, and skin
519.4 Disorders of diaphragm — (Use additional code to identify infectious organism)
567.22 Peritoneal abscess
567.23 Spontaneous bacterial peritonitis
567.29 Other suppurative peritonitis
568.0 Peritoneal adhesions (postoperative) (postinfection)
568.89 Other specified disorder of peritoneum
756.6 Congenital anomaly of diaphragm
908.0 Late effect of internal injury to chest
998.31 Disruption of internal operation (surgical) wound
998.4 Foreign body accidentally left during procedure, not elsewhere classified
998.51 Infected postoperative seroma — (Use additional code to identify organism)
998.59 Other postoperative infection — (Use additional code to identify infection)
998.6 Persistent postoperative fistula, not elsewhere classified
998.83 Non-healing surgical wound

ICD-9-CM Procedural

34.81 Excision of lesion or tissue of diaphragm
83.82 Graft of muscle or fascia

Digestive System

Lips

40490

40490	Biopsy of lip

ICD-9-CM Diagnostic

140.0	Malignant neoplasm of upper lip, vermilion border
140.1	Malignant neoplasm of lower lip, vermilion border
140.3	Malignant neoplasm of upper lip, inner aspect
140.4	Malignant neoplasm of lower lip, inner aspect
140.5	Malignant neoplasm of lip, inner aspect, unspecified as to upper or lower ▽
140.6	Malignant neoplasm of commissure of lip
140.8	Malignant neoplasm of other sites of lip
140.9	Malignant neoplasm of lip, vermilion border, unspecified as to upper or lower ▽
149.8	Malignant neoplasm of other sites within the lip and oral cavity
149.9	Malignant neoplasm of ill-defined sites of lip and oral cavity
172.0	Malignant melanoma of skin of lip
173.00	Unspecified malignant neoplasm of skin of lip ▽
173.01	Basal cell carcinoma of skin of lip
173.02	Squamous cell carcinoma of skin of lip
173.09	Other specified malignant neoplasm of skin of lip
195.0	Malignant neoplasm of head, face, and neck
198.2	Secondary malignant neoplasm of skin
198.89	Secondary malignant neoplasm of other specified sites
210.0	Benign neoplasm of lip
216.0	Benign neoplasm of skin of lip
230.0	Carcinoma in situ of lip, oral cavity, and pharynx
232.0	Carcinoma in situ of skin of lip
235.1	Neoplasm of uncertain behavior of lip, oral cavity, and pharynx
239.0	Neoplasm of unspecified nature of digestive system
239.2	Neoplasms of unspecified nature of bone, soft tissue, and skin
528.5	Diseases of lips
528.6	Leukoplakia of oral mucosa, including tongue
528.9	Other and unspecified diseases of the oral soft tissues ▽
692.79	Other dermatitis due to solar radiation
782.2	Localized superficial swelling, mass, or lump
784.2	Swelling, mass, or lump in head and neck
V10.02	Personal history of malignant neoplasm of other and unspecified parts of oral cavity and pharynx ▽
V84.09	Genetic susceptibility to other malignant neoplasm — (Use additional code, if applicable, for any associated family history of the disease: V16-V19. Code first, if applicable, any current malignant neoplasms: 140.0-195.8, 200.0-208.9, 230.0-234.9. Use additional code, if applicable, for any personal history of malignant neoplasm: V10.0-V10.9)

ICD-9-CM Procedural

27.23	Biopsy of lip

HCPCS Level II Supplies & Services

A4305	Disposable drug delivery system, flow rate of 50 ml or greater per hour

40500

40500	Vermilionectomy (lip shave), with mucosal advancement

ICD-9-CM Diagnostic

140.0	Malignant neoplasm of upper lip, vermilion border
140.1	Malignant neoplasm of lower lip, vermilion border
140.3	Malignant neoplasm of upper lip, inner aspect
140.4	Malignant neoplasm of lower lip, inner aspect
140.5	Malignant neoplasm of lip, inner aspect, unspecified as to upper or lower ▽
140.6	Malignant neoplasm of commissure of lip
140.8	Malignant neoplasm of other sites of lip
140.9	Malignant neoplasm of lip, vermilion border, unspecified as to upper or lower ▽
172.0	Malignant melanoma of skin of lip
173.00	Unspecified malignant neoplasm of skin of lip ▽
173.01	Basal cell carcinoma of skin of lip
173.02	Squamous cell carcinoma of skin of lip
173.09	Other specified malignant neoplasm of skin of lip
210.0	Benign neoplasm of lip
216.0	Benign neoplasm of skin of lip
230.0	Carcinoma in situ of lip, oral cavity, and pharynx
528.5	Diseases of lips
528.6	Leukoplakia of oral mucosa, including tongue
528.9	Other and unspecified diseases of the oral soft tissues ▽
692.79	Other dermatitis due to solar radiation
709.2	Scar condition and fibrosis of skin
750.25	Congenital fistula of lip
750.9	Unspecified congenital anomaly of upper alimentary tract ▽
873.53	Open wound of lip, complicated
906.0	Late effect of open wound of head, neck, and trunk
906.5	Late effect of burn of eye, face, head, and neck
908.9	Late effect of unspecified injury ▽
941.23	Blisters, with epidermal loss due to burn (second degree) of lip(s)
941.33	Full-thickness skin loss due to burn (third degree NOS) of lip(s)
941.43	Deep necrosis of underlying tissues due to burn (deep third degree) of lip(s), without mention of loss of a body part
959.09	Injury of face and neck, other and unspecified
V50.1	Other plastic surgery for unacceptable cosmetic appearance
V51.8	Other aftercare involving the use of plastic surgery
V84.09	Genetic susceptibility to other malignant neoplasm — (Use additional code, if applicable, for any associated family history of the disease: V16-V19. Code first, if applicable, any current malignant neoplasms: 140.0-195.8, 200.0-208.9, 230.0-234.9. Use additional code, if applicable, for any personal history of malignant neoplasm: V10.0-V10.9)

ICD-9-CM Procedural

27.43	Other excision of lesion or tissue of lip
27.57	Attachment of pedicle or flap graft to lip and mouth

HCPCS Level II Supplies & Services

A4305	Disposable drug delivery system, flow rate of 50 ml or greater per hour

40510-40520

40510	Excision of lip; transverse wedge excision with primary closure
40520	V-excision with primary direct linear closure

ICD-9-CM Diagnostic

140.0	Malignant neoplasm of upper lip, vermilion border
140.1	Malignant neoplasm of lower lip, vermilion border
140.3	Malignant neoplasm of upper lip, inner aspect
140.4	Malignant neoplasm of lower lip, inner aspect
140.5	Malignant neoplasm of lip, inner aspect, unspecified as to upper or lower ▽

140.6 Malignant neoplasm of commissure of lip
140.8 Malignant neoplasm of other sites of lip
140.9 Malignant neoplasm of lip, vermilion border, unspecified as to upper or lower ▽
172.0 Malignant melanoma of skin of lip
173.00 Unspecified malignant neoplasm of skin of lip ▽
173.01 Basal cell carcinoma of skin of lip
173.02 Squamous cell carcinoma of skin of lip
173.09 Other specified malignant neoplasm of skin of lip
195.0 Malignant neoplasm of head, face, and neck
199.1 Other malignant neoplasm of unspecified site
210.0 Benign neoplasm of lip
214.0 Lipoma of skin and subcutaneous tissue of face
215.0 Other benign neoplasm of connective and other soft tissue of head, face, and neck
216.0 Benign neoplasm of skin of lip
228.00 Hemangioma of unspecified site ▽
230.0 Carcinoma in situ of lip, oral cavity, and pharynx
232.0 Carcinoma in situ of skin of lip
235.1 Neoplasm of uncertain behavior of lip, oral cavity, and pharynx
239.2 Neoplasms of unspecified nature of bone, soft tissue, and skin
528.5 Diseases of lips
692.79 Other dermatitis due to solar radiation
701.5 Other abnormal granulation tissue
709.2 Scar condition and fibrosis of skin
925.1 Crushing injury of face and scalp — (Use additional code to identify any associated injuries, such as: 800-829, 850.0-854.1, 860.0-869.1)
V51.8 Other aftercare involving the use of plastic surgery
V84.09 Genetic susceptibility to other malignant neoplasm — (Use additional code, if applicable, for any associated family history of the disease: V16-V19. Code first, if applicable, any current malignant neoplasms: 140.0-195.8, 200.0-208.9, 230.0-234.9. Use additional code, if applicable, for any personal history of malignant neoplasm: V10.0-V10.9)

ICD-9-CM Procedural

27.42 Wide excision of lesion of lip
27.43 Other excision of lesion or tissue of lip

HCPCS Level II Supplies & Services

A4305 Disposable drug delivery system, flow rate of 50 ml or greater per hour

40525-40527

40525 Excision of lip; full thickness, reconstruction with local flap (eg, Estlander or fan)
40527 full thickness, reconstruction with cross lip flap (Abbe-Estlander)

ICD-9-CM Diagnostic

140.0 Malignant neoplasm of upper lip, vermilion border
140.1 Malignant neoplasm of lower lip, vermilion border
140.3 Malignant neoplasm of upper lip, inner aspect
140.4 Malignant neoplasm of lower lip, inner aspect
140.5 Malignant neoplasm of lip, inner aspect, unspecified as to upper or lower ▽
140.6 Malignant neoplasm of commissure of lip
140.8 Malignant neoplasm of other sites of lip
140.9 Malignant neoplasm of lip, vermilion border, unspecified as to upper or lower ▽
172.0 Malignant melanoma of skin of lip
173.00 Unspecified malignant neoplasm of skin of lip ▽
173.01 Basal cell carcinoma of skin of lip
173.02 Squamous cell carcinoma of skin of lip
173.09 Other specified malignant neoplasm of skin of lip
195.0 Malignant neoplasm of head, face, and neck
199.1 Other malignant neoplasm of unspecified site
210.0 Benign neoplasm of lip
216.0 Benign neoplasm of skin of lip
228.00 Hemangioma of unspecified site ▽
230.0 Carcinoma in situ of lip, oral cavity, and pharynx
232.0 Carcinoma in situ of skin of lip
235.1 Neoplasm of uncertain behavior of lip, oral cavity, and pharynx
528.5 Diseases of lips
925.1 Crushing injury of face and scalp — (Use additional code to identify any associated injuries, such as: 800-829, 850.0-854.1, 860.0-869.1)
V84.09 Genetic susceptibility to other malignant neoplasm — (Use additional code, if applicable, for any associated family history of the disease: V16-V19. Code first, if applicable, any current malignant neoplasms: 140.0-195.8, 200.0-208.9, 230.0-234.9. Use additional code, if applicable, for any personal history of malignant neoplasm: V10.0-V10.9)

ICD-9-CM Procedural

27.42 Wide excision of lesion of lip
27.43 Other excision of lesion or tissue of lip
27.55 Full-thickness skin graft to lip and mouth
27.57 Attachment of pedicle or flap graft to lip and mouth

HCPCS Level II Supplies & Services

A4305 Disposable drug delivery system, flow rate of 50 ml or greater per hour

40530

40530 Resection of lip, more than 1/4, without reconstruction

ICD-9-CM Diagnostic

140.0 Malignant neoplasm of upper lip, vermilion border
140.1 Malignant neoplasm of lower lip, vermilion border
140.3 Malignant neoplasm of upper lip, inner aspect
140.4 Malignant neoplasm of lower lip, inner aspect
140.5 Malignant neoplasm of lip, inner aspect, unspecified as to upper or lower ▽
140.6 Malignant neoplasm of commissure of lip
140.8 Malignant neoplasm of other sites of lip
140.9 Malignant neoplasm of lip, vermilion border, unspecified as to upper or lower ▽
171.0 Malignant neoplasm of connective and other soft tissue of head, face, and neck
172.0 Malignant melanoma of skin of lip
173.00 Unspecified malignant neoplasm of skin of lip ▽
173.01 Basal cell carcinoma of skin of lip
173.02 Squamous cell carcinoma of skin of lip
173.09 Other specified malignant neoplasm of skin of lip
195.0 Malignant neoplasm of head, face, and neck
199.1 Other malignant neoplasm of unspecified site
210.0 Benign neoplasm of lip
216.0 Benign neoplasm of skin of lip
230.0 Carcinoma in situ of lip, oral cavity, and pharynx
232.0 Carcinoma in situ of skin of lip
235.1 Neoplasm of uncertain behavior of lip, oral cavity, and pharynx
528.5 Diseases of lips
V84.09 Genetic susceptibility to other malignant neoplasm — (Use additional code, if applicable, for any associated family history of the disease: V16-V19. Code first, if applicable, any current malignant neoplasms: 140.0-195.8, 200.0-208.9, 230.0-234.9. Use additional code, if applicable, for any personal history of malignant neoplasm: V10.0-V10.9)

ICD-9-CM Procedural

27.42 Wide excision of lesion of lip
27.43 Other excision of lesion or tissue of lip

HCPCS Level II Supplies & Services

A4305 Disposable drug delivery system, flow rate of 50 ml or greater per hour

40650-40654

40650 Repair lip, full thickness; vermilion only
40652 up to half vertical height
40654 over 1/2 vertical height, or complex

ICD-9-CM Diagnostic

140.0 Malignant neoplasm of upper lip, vermilion border
140.1 Malignant neoplasm of lower lip, vermilion border
140.3 Malignant neoplasm of upper lip, inner aspect
140.4 Malignant neoplasm of lower lip, inner aspect
140.9 Malignant neoplasm of lip, vermilion border, unspecified as to upper or lower ▽
172.0 Malignant melanoma of skin of lip
173.00 Unspecified malignant neoplasm of skin of lip ▽
173.01 Basal cell carcinoma of skin of lip
173.02 Squamous cell carcinoma of skin of lip
173.09 Other specified malignant neoplasm of skin of lip
195.0 Malignant neoplasm of head, face, and neck
210.0 Benign neoplasm of lip
216.0 Benign neoplasm of skin of lip
228.00 Hemangioma of unspecified site ▽
232.0 Carcinoma in situ of skin of lip
528.5 Diseases of lips
709.2 Scar condition and fibrosis of skin
744.82 Microcheilia
873.40 Open wound of face, unspecified site, without mention of complication ▽
873.43 Open wound of lip, without mention of complication
873.50 Open wound of face, unspecified site, complicated ▽
873.53 Open wound of lip, complicated
873.59 Open wound of face, other and multiple sites, complicated
906.0 Late effect of open wound of head, neck, and trunk
925.1 Crushing injury of face and scalp — (Use additional code to identify any associated injuries, such as: 800-829, 850.0-854.1, 860.0-869.1)
941.23 Blisters, with epidermal loss due to burn (second degree) of lip(s)
959.09 Injury of face and neck, other and unspecified
998.32 Disruption of external operation (surgical) wound
V51.8 Other aftercare involving the use of plastic surgery
V84.09 Genetic susceptibility to other malignant neoplasm — (Use additional code, if applicable, for any associated family history of the disease: V16-V19. Code first, if applicable, any current malignant neoplasms: 140.0-195.8, 200.0-208.9, 230.0-234.9. Use additional code, if applicable, for any personal history of malignant neoplasm: V10.0-V10.9)

ICD-9-CM Procedural

27.51 Suture of laceration of lip
27.59 Other plastic repair of mouth

HCPCS Level II Supplies & Services

A4305 Disposable drug delivery system, flow rate of 50 ml or greater per hour

40700

40700 Plastic repair of cleft lip/nasal deformity; primary, partial or complete, unilateral

ICD-9-CM Diagnostic

749.10 Unspecified cleft lip ▽
749.11 Unilateral cleft lip, complete
749.12 Unilateral cleft lip, incomplete
749.20 Unspecified cleft palate with cleft lip ▽
749.21 Unilateral cleft palate with cleft lip, complete
749.22 Unilateral cleft palate with cleft lip, incomplete

ICD-9-CM Procedural

27.54 Repair of cleft lip

40701-40702

40701 Plastic repair of cleft lip/nasal deformity; primary bilateral, 1-stage procedure
40702 primary bilateral, 1 of 2 stages

ICD-9-CM Diagnostic

749.13 Bilateral cleft lip, complete
749.14 Bilateral cleft lip, incomplete
749.23 Bilateral cleft palate with cleft lip, complete
749.24 Bilateral cleft palate with cleft lip, incomplete
749.25 Other combinations of cleft palate with cleft lip

ICD-9-CM Procedural

27.54 Repair of cleft lip

40720

40720 Plastic repair of cleft lip/nasal deformity; secondary, by recreation of defect and reclosure

ICD-9-CM Diagnostic

749.10 Unspecified cleft lip ▽
749.11 Unilateral cleft lip, complete
749.12 Unilateral cleft lip, incomplete
749.13 Bilateral cleft lip, complete
749.14 Bilateral cleft lip, incomplete
749.20 Unspecified cleft palate with cleft lip ▽
749.21 Unilateral cleft palate with cleft lip, complete
749.22 Unilateral cleft palate with cleft lip, incomplete
749.23 Bilateral cleft palate with cleft lip, complete
749.25 Other combinations of cleft palate with cleft lip

ICD-9-CM Procedural

27.54 Repair of cleft lip

40761

40761 Plastic repair of cleft lip/nasal deformity; with cross lip pedicle flap (Abbe-Estlander type), including sectioning and inserting of pedicle

ICD-9-CM Diagnostic

749.10 Unspecified cleft lip ▽
749.11 Unilateral cleft lip, complete
749.12 Unilateral cleft lip, incomplete
749.13 Bilateral cleft lip, complete
749.14 Bilateral cleft lip, incomplete
749.20 Unspecified cleft palate with cleft lip ▽
749.21 Unilateral cleft palate with cleft lip, complete
749.22 Unilateral cleft palate with cleft lip, incomplete
749.23 Bilateral cleft palate with cleft lip, complete
749.25 Other combinations of cleft palate with cleft lip

ICD-9-CM Procedural

27.54 Repair of cleft lip
27.57 Attachment of pedicle or flap graft to lip and mouth

Vestibule of Mouth

40800-40801

40800 Drainage of abscess, cyst, hematoma, vestibule of mouth; simple
40801 complicated

ICD-9-CM Diagnostic

478.24 Retropharyngeal abscess — (Use additional code to identify infectious organism)
520.6 Disturbances in tooth eruption
522.0 Pulpitis

522.5 Periapical abscess without sinus
523.30 Aggressive periodontitis, unspecified ▽
523.31 Aggressive periodontitis, localized
523.32 Aggressive periodontitis, generalized
523.33 Acute periodontitis
526.0 Developmental odontogenic cysts
526.1 Fissural cysts of jaw
528.3 Cellulitis and abscess of oral soft tissues
528.4 Cysts of oral soft tissues
682.0 Cellulitis and abscess of face — (Use additional code to identify organism, such as 041.1, etc.)
780.62 Postprocedural fever
782.2 Localized superficial swelling, mass, or lump
784.2 Swelling, mass, or lump in head and neck

ICD-9-CM Procedural

27.0 Drainage of face and floor of mouth

HCPCS Level II Supplies & Services

A4305 Disposable drug delivery system, flow rate of 50 ml or greater per hour
D7510 incision and drainage of abscess - intraoral soft tissue — Involves incision through mucosa, including periodontal origins.
D7511 incision and drainage of abscess - intraoral soft tissue - complicated (includes drainage of multiple fascial spaces) — Incision is made intraorally and dissection is extended into adjacent fascial space(s) to provide adequate drainage of abscess/cellulitis.
D7520 incision and drainage of abscess - extraoral soft tissue — Involves incision through skin.
D7521 incision and drainage of abscess - extraoral soft tissue - complicated (includes drainage of multiple fascial spaces) — Incision is made extraorally and dissection is extended into adjacent fascial space(s) to provide adequate drainage of abscess/cellulitis.

40804-40805

40804 Removal of embedded foreign body, vestibule of mouth; simple
40805 complicated

ICD-9-CM Diagnostic

709.4 Foreign body granuloma of skin and subcutaneous tissue — (Use additional code to identify foreign body (V90.01-V90.9))
728.82 Foreign body granuloma of muscle — (Use additional code to identify foreign body (V90.01-V90.9))
784.2 Swelling, mass, or lump in head and neck
873.70 Open wound of mouth, unspecified site, complicated ▽
873.71 Open wound of buccal mucosa, complicated
873.72 Open wound of gum (alveolar process), complicated
873.74 Open wound of tongue and floor of mouth, complicated
873.75 Open wound of palate, complicated
873.79 Open wound of mouth, other and multiple sites, complicated
935.0 Foreign body in mouth

ICD-9-CM Procedural

27.92 Incision of mouth, unspecified structure
98.01 Removal of intraluminal foreign body from mouth without incision

HCPCS Level II Supplies & Services

A4305 Disposable drug delivery system, flow rate of 50 ml or greater per hour

40806

40806 Incision of labial frenum (frenotomy)

ICD-9-CM Diagnostic

520.8 Other specified disorders of tooth development and eruption
523.20 Gingival recession, unspecified ▽
523.21 Gingival recession, minimal
523.22 Gingival recession, moderate
523.23 Gingival recession, severe
523.24 Gingival recession, localized
523.25 Gingival recession, generalized
524.01 Maxillary hyperplasia
524.02 Mandibular hyperplasia
524.04 Mandibular hypoplasia
524.09 Other specified major anomaly of jaw size
524.12 Other jaw asymmetry
524.39 Other anomalies of tooth position
524.71 Alveolar maxillary hyperplasia
524.72 Alveolar mandibular hyperplasia
524.74 Alveolar mandibular hypoplasia
525.20 Unspecified atrophy of edentulous alveolar ridge ▽
528.79 Other disturbances of oral epithelium, including tongue
744.9 Unspecified congenital anomaly of face and neck ▽
756.82 Accessory muscle

ICD-9-CM Procedural

27.91 Labial frenotomy

40808

40808 Biopsy, vestibule of mouth

ICD-9-CM Diagnostic

140.3 Malignant neoplasm of upper lip, inner aspect
140.4 Malignant neoplasm of lower lip, inner aspect
140.5 Malignant neoplasm of lip, inner aspect, unspecified as to upper or lower ▽
140.6 Malignant neoplasm of commissure of lip
140.8 Malignant neoplasm of other sites of lip
140.9 Malignant neoplasm of lip, vermilion border, unspecified as to upper or lower ▽
144.8 Malignant neoplasm of other sites of floor of mouth
144.9 Malignant neoplasm of floor of mouth, part unspecified ▽
145.1 Malignant neoplasm of vestibule of mouth
145.8 Malignant neoplasm of other specified parts of mouth
145.9 Malignant neoplasm of mouth, unspecified site ▽
198.89 Secondary malignant neoplasm of other specified sites
210.4 Benign neoplasm of other and unspecified parts of mouth ▽
230.0 Carcinoma in situ of lip, oral cavity, and pharynx
235.1 Neoplasm of uncertain behavior of lip, oral cavity, and pharynx
239.0 Neoplasm of unspecified nature of digestive system
239.9 Neoplasm of unspecified nature, site unspecified ▽
522.8 Radicular cyst of dental pulp
528.00 Stomatitis and mucositis, unspecified ▽
528.09 Other stomatitis and mucositis (ulcerative)
528.3 Cellulitis and abscess of oral soft tissues
528.6 Leukoplakia of oral mucosa, including tongue
528.79 Other disturbances of oral epithelium, including tongue
528.8 Oral submucosal fibrosis, including of tongue
528.9 Other and unspecified diseases of the oral soft tissues ▽
697.0 Lichen planus

ICD-9-CM Procedural

27.24 Biopsy of mouth, unspecified structure

40810-40812

40810 Excision of lesion of mucosa and submucosa, vestibule of mouth; without repair
40812 with simple repair

ICD-9-CM Diagnostic

144.9 Malignant neoplasm of floor of mouth, part unspecified ▽

145.0 Malignant neoplasm of cheek mucosa
145.1 Malignant neoplasm of vestibule of mouth
145.8 Malignant neoplasm of other specified parts of mouth
145.9 Malignant neoplasm of mouth, unspecified site
171.0 Malignant neoplasm of connective and other soft tissue of head, face, and neck
199.1 Other malignant neoplasm of unspecified site
210.0 Benign neoplasm of lip
214.8 Lipoma of other specified sites
214.9 Lipoma of unspecified site
215.0 Other benign neoplasm of connective and other soft tissue of head, face, and neck
230.0 Carcinoma in situ of lip, oral cavity, and pharynx
235.1 Neoplasm of uncertain behavior of lip, oral cavity, and pharynx
239.0 Neoplasm of unspecified nature of digestive system
239.9 Neoplasm of unspecified nature, site unspecified
527.6 Mucocele of salivary gland
528.4 Cysts of oral soft tissues
528.5 Diseases of lips
528.6 Leukoplakia of oral mucosa, including tongue
528.71 Minimal keratinized residual ridge mucosa
528.72 Excessive keratinized residual ridge mucosa
528.79 Other disturbances of oral epithelium, including tongue
528.8 Oral submucosal fibrosis, including of tongue
528.9 Other and unspecified diseases of the oral soft tissues
682.0 Cellulitis and abscess of face — (Use additional code to identify organism, such as 041.1, etc.)
697.0 Lichen planus
701.1 Acquired keratoderma
706.2 Sebaceous cyst
782.2 Localized superficial swelling, mass, or lump
784.2 Swelling, mass, or lump in head and neck

ICD-9-CM Procedural

27.49 Other excision of mouth

40814-40816

40814 Excision of lesion of mucosa and submucosa, vestibule of mouth; with complex repair
40816 complex, with excision of underlying muscle

ICD-9-CM Diagnostic

140.4 Malignant neoplasm of lower lip, inner aspect
140.5 Malignant neoplasm of lip, inner aspect, unspecified as to upper or lower
144.9 Malignant neoplasm of floor of mouth, part unspecified
145.0 Malignant neoplasm of cheek mucosa
145.1 Malignant neoplasm of vestibule of mouth
145.8 Malignant neoplasm of other specified parts of mouth
145.9 Malignant neoplasm of mouth, unspecified site
171.0 Malignant neoplasm of connective and other soft tissue of head, face, and neck
210.4 Benign neoplasm of other and unspecified parts of mouth
214.8 Lipoma of other specified sites
215.0 Other benign neoplasm of connective and other soft tissue of head, face, and neck
230.0 Carcinoma in situ of lip, oral cavity, and pharynx
235.1 Neoplasm of uncertain behavior of lip, oral cavity, and pharynx
527.6 Mucocele of salivary gland
528.4 Cysts of oral soft tissues
528.6 Leukoplakia of oral mucosa, including tongue
528.71 Minimal keratinized residual ridge mucosa
528.72 Excessive keratinized residual ridge mucosa
528.79 Other disturbances of oral epithelium, including tongue
528.8 Oral submucosal fibrosis, including of tongue
528.9 Other and unspecified diseases of the oral soft tissues
784.2 Swelling, mass, or lump in head and neck

ICD-9-CM Procedural

27.49 Other excision of mouth
27.59 Other plastic repair of mouth
83.32 Excision of lesion of muscle

HCPCS Level II Supplies & Services

A4305 Disposable drug delivery system, flow rate of 50 ml or greater per hour

40818

40818 Excision of mucosa of vestibule of mouth as donor graft

ICD-9-CM Diagnostic

140.8 Malignant neoplasm of other sites of lip
145.1 Malignant neoplasm of vestibule of mouth
210.3 Benign neoplasm of floor of mouth
230.0 Carcinoma in situ of lip, oral cavity, and pharynx
523.8 Other specified periodontal diseases
525.20 Unspecified atrophy of edentulous alveolar ridge
528.6 Leukoplakia of oral mucosa, including tongue
V10.02 Personal history of malignant neoplasm of other and unspecified parts of oral cavity and pharynx
V51.8 Other aftercare involving the use of plastic surgery

ICD-9-CM Procedural

27.49 Other excision of mouth

40819

40819 Excision of frenum, labial or buccal (frenumectomy, frenulectomy, frenectomy)

ICD-9-CM Diagnostic

140.3 Malignant neoplasm of upper lip, inner aspect
140.4 Malignant neoplasm of lower lip, inner aspect
140.5 Malignant neoplasm of lip, inner aspect, unspecified as to upper or lower
140.8 Malignant neoplasm of other sites of lip
210.0 Benign neoplasm of lip
239.0 Neoplasm of unspecified nature of digestive system
520.8 Other specified disorders of tooth development and eruption
523.8 Other specified periodontal diseases
525.20 Unspecified atrophy of edentulous alveolar ridge
528.5 Diseases of lips
744.9 Unspecified congenital anomaly of face and neck
750.26 Other specified congenital anomalies of mouth
750.8 Other specified congenital anomalies of upper alimentary tract
756.82 Accessory muscle

ICD-9-CM Procedural

27.41 Labial frenectomy

HCPCS Level II Supplies & Services

A4305 Disposable drug delivery system, flow rate of 50 ml or greater per hour

40820

40820 Destruction of lesion or scar of vestibule of mouth by physical methods (eg, laser, thermal, cryo, chemical)

ICD-9-CM Diagnostic

145.0 Malignant neoplasm of cheek mucosa
210.0 Benign neoplasm of lip
210.3 Benign neoplasm of floor of mouth
210.4 Benign neoplasm of other and unspecified parts of mouth
228.09 Hemangioma of other sites

230.0 Carcinoma in situ of lip, oral cavity, and pharynx
235.1 Neoplasm of uncertain behavior of lip, oral cavity, and pharynx
239.0 Neoplasm of unspecified nature of digestive system
239.2 Neoplasms of unspecified nature of bone, soft tissue, and skin
528.2 Oral aphthae
528.4 Cysts of oral soft tissues
528.6 Leukoplakia of oral mucosa, including tongue
528.79 Other disturbances of oral epithelium, including tongue
528.8 Oral submucosal fibrosis, including of tongue
528.9 Other and unspecified diseases of the oral soft tissues ▽
709.2 Scar condition and fibrosis of skin
784.2 Swelling, mass, or lump in head and neck

ICD-9-CM Procedural

27.49 Other excision of mouth
27.99 Other operations on oral cavity

HCPCS Level II Supplies & Services

A4305 Disposable drug delivery system, flow rate of 50 ml or greater per hour

40830-40831

40830 Closure of laceration, vestibule of mouth; 2.5 cm or less
40831 over 2.5 cm or complex

ICD-9-CM Diagnostic

873.43 Open wound of lip, without mention of complication
873.49 Open wound of face, other and multiple sites, without mention of complication
873.53 Open wound of lip, complicated
873.59 Open wound of face, other and multiple sites, complicated
873.60 Open wound of mouth, unspecified site, without mention of complication ▽
873.61 Open wound of buccal mucosa, without mention of complication
873.62 Open wound of gum (alveolar process), without mention of complication
873.64 Open wound of tongue and floor of mouth, without mention of complication
873.65 Open wound of palate, without mention of complication
873.69 Open wound of mouth, other and multiple sites, without mention of complication
873.70 Open wound of mouth, unspecified site, complicated ▽
873.71 Open wound of buccal mucosa, complicated
873.72 Open wound of gum (alveolar process), complicated
873.74 Open wound of tongue and floor of mouth, complicated
873.75 Open wound of palate, complicated
873.79 Open wound of mouth, other and multiple sites, complicated
873.8 Other and unspecified open wound of head without mention of complication ▽
873.9 Other and unspecified open wound of head, complicated ▽
959.09 Injury of face and neck, other and unspecified

ICD-9-CM Procedural

27.52 Suture of laceration of other part of mouth
27.59 Other plastic repair of mouth

40840-40844

40840 Vestibuloplasty; anterior
40842 posterior, unilateral
40843 posterior, bilateral
40844 entire arch

ICD-9-CM Diagnostic

386.12 Vestibular neuronitis
525.10 Unspecified acquired absence of teeth — (Code first class of edentulism: 525.40-525.44, 525.50-525.54) ▽ ☒
525.11 Loss of teeth due to trauma — (Code first class of edentulism: 525.40-525.44, 525.50-525.54) ☒
525.12 Loss of teeth due to periodontal disease — (Code first class of edentulism: 525.40-525.44, 525.50-525.54) ☒
525.13 Loss of teeth due to caries — (Code first class of edentulism: 525.40-525.44, 525.50-525.54) ☒
525.19 Other loss of teeth — (Code first class of edentulism: 525.40-525.44, 525.50-525.54) ☒
525.20 Unspecified atrophy of edentulous alveolar ridge ▽
525.40 Complete edentulism, unspecified — (Use additional code to identify cause of edentulism: 525.10-525.19) ▽
525.41 Complete edentulism, class I — (Use additional code to identify cause of edentulism: 525.10-525.19)
525.42 Complete edentulism, class II — (Use additional code to identify cause of edentulism: 525.10-525.19)
525.43 Complete edentulism, class III — (Use additional code to identify cause of edentulism: 525.10-525.19)
525.44 Complete edentulism, class IV — (Use additional code to identify cause of edentulism: 525.10-525.19)
525.50 Partial edentulism, unspecified — (Use additional code to identify cause of edentulism: 525.10-525.19) ▽
525.51 Partial edentulism, class I — (Use additional code to identify cause of edentulism: 525.10-525.19)
525.52 Partial edentulism, class II — (Use additional code to identify cause of edentulism: 525.10-525.19)
525.53 Partial edentulism, class III — (Use additional code to identify cause of edentulism: 525.10-525.19)
525.54 Partial edentulism, class IV — (Use additional code to identify cause of edentulism: 525.10-525.19)
525.8 Other specified disorders of the teeth and supporting structures
528.9 Other and unspecified diseases of the oral soft tissues ▽
733.7 Algoneurodystrophy
750.26 Other specified congenital anomalies of mouth
873.59 Open wound of face, other and multiple sites, complicated
905.0 Late effect of fracture of skull and face bones
906.0 Late effect of open wound of head, neck, and trunk
906.5 Late effect of burn of eye, face, head, and neck
908.9 Late effect of unspecified injury ▽
909.3 Late effect of complications of surgical and medical care
925.1 Crushing injury of face and scalp — (Use additional code to identify any associated injuries, such as: 800-829, 850.0-854.1, 860.0-869.1)
947.0 Burn of mouth and pharynx
959.09 Injury of face and neck, other and unspecified
959.9 Injury, other and unspecified, unspecified site ▽
V41.6 Problems with swallowing and mastication

ICD-9-CM Procedural

24.91 Extension or deepening of buccolabial or lingual sulcus

HCPCS Level II Supplies & Services

A4305 Disposable drug delivery system, flow rate of 50 ml or greater per hour

40845

40845 Vestibuloplasty; complex (including ridge extension, muscle repositioning)

ICD-9-CM Diagnostic

230.0 Carcinoma in situ of lip, oral cavity, and pharynx
525.10 Unspecified acquired absence of teeth — (Code first class of edentulism: 525.40-525.44, 525.50-525.54) ▽ ☒
525.11 Loss of teeth due to trauma — (Code first class of edentulism: 525.40-525.44, 525.50-525.54) ☒
525.12 Loss of teeth due to periodontal disease — (Code first class of edentulism: 525.40-525.44, 525.50-525.54) ☒

525.13 Loss of teeth due to caries — (Code first class of edentulism: 525.40-525.44, 525.50-525.54) ☒
525.19 Other loss of teeth — (Code first class of edentulism: 525.40-525.44, 525.50-525.54) ☒
525.20 Unspecified atrophy of edentulous alveolar ridge ▽
525.40 Complete edentulism, unspecified — (Use additional code to identify cause of edentulism: 525.10-525.19) ▽
525.41 Complete edentulism, class I — (Use additional code to identify cause of edentulism: 525.10-525.19)
525.42 Complete edentulism, class II — (Use additional code to identify cause of edentulism: 525.10-525.19)
525.43 Complete edentulism, class III — (Use additional code to identify cause of edentulism: 525.10-525.19)
525.44 Complete edentulism, class IV — (Use additional code to identify cause of edentulism: 525.10-525.19)
525.50 Partial edentulism, unspecified — (Use additional code to identify cause of edentulism: 525.10-525.19) ▽
525.51 Partial edentulism, class I — (Use additional code to identify cause of edentulism: 525.10-525.19)
525.52 Partial edentulism, class II — (Use additional code to identify cause of edentulism: 525.10-525.19)
525.53 Partial edentulism, class III — (Use additional code to identify cause of edentulism: 525.10-525.19)
525.54 Partial edentulism, class IV — (Use additional code to identify cause of edentulism: 525.10-525.19)
905.0 Late effect of fracture of skull and face bones
906.0 Late effect of open wound of head, neck, and trunk
906.8 Late effect of burns of other specified sites
947.0 Burn of mouth and pharynx
V10.02 Personal history of malignant neoplasm of other and unspecified parts of oral cavity and pharynx ▽
V41.6 Problems with swallowing and mastication
V50.1 Other plastic surgery for unacceptable cosmetic appearance
V51.8 Other aftercare involving the use of plastic surgery

ICD-9-CM Procedural

24.91 Extension or deepening of buccolabial or lingual sulcus

Tongue and Floor of Mouth

41000

41000 Intraoral incision and drainage of abscess, cyst, or hematoma of tongue or floor of mouth; lingual

ICD-9-CM Diagnostic

528.3 Cellulitis and abscess of oral soft tissues
528.4 Cysts of oral soft tissues
529.0 Glossitis
529.6 Glossodynia
529.8 Other specified conditions of the tongue
750.19 Other congenital anomaly of tongue
780.62 Postprocedural fever
784.2 Swelling, mass, or lump in head and neck
920 Contusion of face, scalp, and neck except eye(s)
958.3 Posttraumatic wound infection not elsewhere classified
998.12 Hematoma complicating a procedure
998.59 Other postoperative infection — (Use additional code to identify infection)

ICD-9-CM Procedural

25.94 Other glossotomy
27.0 Drainage of face and floor of mouth

HCPCS Level II Supplies & Services

A4305 Disposable drug delivery system, flow rate of 50 ml or greater per hour

41005-41007

41005 Intraoral incision and drainage of abscess, cyst, or hematoma of tongue or floor of mouth; sublingual, superficial
41006 sublingual, deep, supramylohyoid
41007 submental space

ICD-9-CM Diagnostic

523.30 Aggressive periodontitis, unspecified ▽
523.31 Aggressive periodontitis, localized
523.32 Aggressive periodontitis, generalized
523.33 Acute periodontitis
526.0 Developmental odontogenic cysts
526.4 Inflammatory conditions of jaw
527.3 Abscess of salivary gland
527.6 Mucocele of salivary gland
528.3 Cellulitis and abscess of oral soft tissues
528.4 Cysts of oral soft tissues
529.0 Glossitis
529.6 Glossodynia
529.8 Other specified conditions of the tongue
750.19 Other congenital anomaly of tongue
750.26 Other specified congenital anomalies of mouth
780.62 Postprocedural fever
784.2 Swelling, mass, or lump in head and neck
920 Contusion of face, scalp, and neck except eye(s)
958.3 Posttraumatic wound infection not elsewhere classified
998.12 Hematoma complicating a procedure
998.59 Other postoperative infection — (Use additional code to identify infection)

ICD-9-CM Procedural

25.94 Other glossotomy
27.0 Drainage of face and floor of mouth

HCPCS Level II Supplies & Services

A4305 Disposable drug delivery system, flow rate of 50 ml or greater per hour

41008

41008 Intraoral incision and drainage of abscess, cyst, or hematoma of tongue or floor of mouth; submandibular space

ICD-9-CM Diagnostic

526.4 Inflammatory conditions of jaw
528.3 Cellulitis and abscess of oral soft tissues
528.4 Cysts of oral soft tissues
528.9 Other and unspecified diseases of the oral soft tissues ▽
529.6 Glossodynia
529.8 Other specified conditions of the tongue
682.0 Cellulitis and abscess of face — (Use additional code to identify organism, such as 041.1, etc.)
750.19 Other congenital anomaly of tongue
750.26 Other specified congenital anomalies of mouth
784.2 Swelling, mass, or lump in head and neck
920 Contusion of face, scalp, and neck except eye(s)
958.3 Posttraumatic wound infection not elsewhere classified
998.12 Hematoma complicating a procedure
998.59 Other postoperative infection — (Use additional code to identify infection)

ICD-9-CM Procedural

25.94 Other glossotomy

27.0 Drainage of face and floor of mouth

HCPCS Level II Supplies & Services

A4305 Disposable drug delivery system, flow rate of 50 ml or greater per hour

41009

41009 Intraoral incision and drainage of abscess, cyst, or hematoma of tongue or floor of mouth; masticator space

ICD-9-CM Diagnostic

522.5 Periapical abscess without sinus
522.7 Periapical abscess with sinus
523.30 Aggressive periodontitis, unspecified ▽
523.31 Aggressive periodontitis, localized
523.32 Aggressive periodontitis, generalized
523.33 Acute periodontitis
528.3 Cellulitis and abscess of oral soft tissues
528.4 Cysts of oral soft tissues
528.9 Other and unspecified diseases of the oral soft tissues ▽
529.6 Glossodynia
529.8 Other specified conditions of the tongue
682.0 Cellulitis and abscess of face — (Use additional code to identify organism, such as 041.1, etc.)
750.26 Other specified congenital anomalies of mouth
784.2 Swelling, mass, or lump in head and neck
920 Contusion of face, scalp, and neck except eye(s)
958.3 Posttraumatic wound infection not elsewhere classified
998.12 Hematoma complicating a procedure
998.59 Other postoperative infection — (Use additional code to identify infection)

ICD-9-CM Procedural

25.94 Other glossotomy
27.0 Drainage of face and floor of mouth

HCPCS Level II Supplies & Services

A4305 Disposable drug delivery system, flow rate of 50 ml or greater per hour

41010

41010 Incision of lingual frenum (frenotomy)

ICD-9-CM Diagnostic

524.02 Mandibular hyperplasia
524.74 Alveolar mandibular hypoplasia
750.0 Tongue tie
750.12 Congenital adhesions of tongue

ICD-9-CM Procedural

25.91 Lingual frenotomy

41015-41016

41015 Extraoral incision and drainage of abscess, cyst, or hematoma of floor of mouth; sublingual
41016 submental

ICD-9-CM Diagnostic

526.4 Inflammatory conditions of jaw
528.3 Cellulitis and abscess of oral soft tissues
528.4 Cysts of oral soft tissues
529.0 Glossitis
529.6 Glossodynia
529.8 Other specified conditions of the tongue
682.0 Cellulitis and abscess of face — (Use additional code to identify organism, such as 041.1, etc.)
750.26 Other specified congenital anomalies of mouth
780.62 Postprocedural fever
784.2 Swelling, mass, or lump in head and neck
920 Contusion of face, scalp, and neck except eye(s)
958.3 Posttraumatic wound infection not elsewhere classified
998.12 Hematoma complicating a procedure
998.59 Other postoperative infection — (Use additional code to identify infection)

ICD-9-CM Procedural

27.0 Drainage of face and floor of mouth

HCPCS Level II Supplies & Services

A4305 Disposable drug delivery system, flow rate of 50 ml or greater per hour

41017

41017 Extraoral incision and drainage of abscess, cyst, or hematoma of floor of mouth; submandibular

ICD-9-CM Diagnostic

526.4 Inflammatory conditions of jaw
527.2 Sialoadenitis
528.3 Cellulitis and abscess of oral soft tissues
528.4 Cysts of oral soft tissues
528.9 Other and unspecified diseases of the oral soft tissues ▽
682.0 Cellulitis and abscess of face — (Use additional code to identify organism, such as 041.1, etc.)
750.26 Other specified congenital anomalies of mouth
784.2 Swelling, mass, or lump in head and neck
920 Contusion of face, scalp, and neck except eye(s)
958.3 Posttraumatic wound infection not elsewhere classified
998.12 Hematoma complicating a procedure
998.59 Other postoperative infection — (Use additional code to identify infection)

ICD-9-CM Procedural

27.0 Drainage of face and floor of mouth

HCPCS Level II Supplies & Services

A4305 Disposable drug delivery system, flow rate of 50 ml or greater per hour

41018

41018 Extraoral incision and drainage of abscess, cyst, or hematoma of floor of mouth; masticator space

ICD-9-CM Diagnostic

522.5 Periapical abscess without sinus
522.7 Periapical abscess with sinus
523.30 Aggressive periodontitis, unspecified ▽
523.31 Aggressive periodontitis, localized
523.32 Aggressive periodontitis, generalized
523.33 Acute periodontitis
528.3 Cellulitis and abscess of oral soft tissues
528.4 Cysts of oral soft tissues
528.9 Other and unspecified diseases of the oral soft tissues ▽
682.0 Cellulitis and abscess of face — (Use additional code to identify organism, such as 041.1, etc.)
750.26 Other specified congenital anomalies of mouth
784.2 Swelling, mass, or lump in head and neck
906.0 Late effect of open wound of head, neck, and trunk
920 Contusion of face, scalp, and neck except eye(s)
958.3 Posttraumatic wound infection not elsewhere classified
998.12 Hematoma complicating a procedure
998.59 Other postoperative infection — (Use additional code to identify infection)

ICD-9-CM Procedural

27.0	Drainage of face and floor of mouth
27.92	Incision of mouth, unspecified structure

HCPCS Level II Supplies & Services

A4305	Disposable drug delivery system, flow rate of 50 ml or greater per hour

41019

41019 Placement of needles, catheters, or other device(s) into the head and/or neck region (percutaneous, transoral, or transnasal) for subsequent interstitial radioelement application

ICD-9-CM Diagnostic

140.0	Malignant neoplasm of upper lip, vermilion border
140.1	Malignant neoplasm of lower lip, vermilion border
140.3	Malignant neoplasm of upper lip, inner aspect
140.4	Malignant neoplasm of lower lip, inner aspect
140.5	Malignant neoplasm of lip, inner aspect, unspecified as to upper or lower
140.6	Malignant neoplasm of commissure of lip
140.8	Malignant neoplasm of other sites of lip
140.9	Malignant neoplasm of lip, vermilion border, unspecified as to upper or lower
141.0	Malignant neoplasm of base of tongue
141.1	Malignant neoplasm of dorsal surface of tongue
141.2	Malignant neoplasm of tip and lateral border of tongue
141.3	Malignant neoplasm of ventral surface of tongue
141.4	Malignant neoplasm of anterior two-thirds of tongue, part unspecified
141.5	Malignant neoplasm of junctional zone of tongue
141.6	Malignant neoplasm of lingual tonsil
141.8	Malignant neoplasm of other sites of tongue
141.9	Malignant neoplasm of tongue, unspecified site
142.0	Malignant neoplasm of parotid gland
142.1	Malignant neoplasm of submandibular gland
142.2	Malignant neoplasm of sublingual gland
142.8	Malignant neoplasm of other major salivary glands
142.9	Malignant neoplasm of salivary gland, unspecified
143.0	Malignant neoplasm of upper gum
143.1	Malignant neoplasm of lower gum
143.8	Malignant neoplasm of other sites of gum
143.9	Malignant neoplasm of gum, unspecified site
144.0	Malignant neoplasm of anterior portion of floor of mouth
144.1	Malignant neoplasm of lateral portion of floor of mouth
144.8	Malignant neoplasm of other sites of floor of mouth
144.9	Malignant neoplasm of floor of mouth, part unspecified
145.0	Malignant neoplasm of cheek mucosa
145.1	Malignant neoplasm of vestibule of mouth
145.2	Malignant neoplasm of hard palate
145.3	Malignant neoplasm of soft palate
145.4	Malignant neoplasm of uvula
145.5	Malignant neoplasm of palate, unspecified
145.6	Malignant neoplasm of retromolar area
145.8	Malignant neoplasm of other specified parts of mouth
145.9	Malignant neoplasm of mouth, unspecified site
146.0	Malignant neoplasm of tonsil
146.1	Malignant neoplasm of tonsillar fossa
146.2	Malignant neoplasm of tonsillar pillars (anterior) (posterior)
146.3	Malignant neoplasm of vallecula
146.4	Malignant neoplasm of anterior aspect of epiglottis
146.5	Malignant neoplasm of junctional region of oropharynx
146.6	Malignant neoplasm of lateral wall of oropharynx
146.7	Malignant neoplasm of posterior wall of oropharynx
146.8	Malignant neoplasm of other specified sites of oropharynx
146.9	Malignant neoplasm of oropharynx, unspecified site
147.0	Malignant neoplasm of superior wall of nasopharynx
147.1	Malignant neoplasm of posterior wall of nasopharynx
147.2	Malignant neoplasm of lateral wall of nasopharynx
147.3	Malignant neoplasm of anterior wall of nasopharynx
147.8	Malignant neoplasm of other specified sites of nasopharynx
147.9	Malignant neoplasm of nasopharynx, unspecified site
148.0	Malignant neoplasm of postcricoid region of hypopharynx
148.1	Malignant neoplasm of pyriform sinus
148.2	Malignant neoplasm of aryepiglottic fold, hypopharyngeal aspect
148.3	Malignant neoplasm of posterior hypopharyngeal wall
148.8	Malignant neoplasm of other specified sites of hypopharynx
148.9	Malignant neoplasm of hypopharynx, unspecified site
149.0	Malignant neoplasm of pharynx, unspecified
149.1	Malignant neoplasm of Waldeyer's ring
149.8	Malignant neoplasm of other sites within the lip and oral cavity
149.9	Malignant neoplasm of ill-defined sites of lip and oral cavity
150.0	Malignant neoplasm of cervical esophagus
150.3	Malignant neoplasm of upper third of esophagus
150.4	Malignant neoplasm of middle third of esophagus
150.5	Malignant neoplasm of lower third of esophagus
150.8	Malignant neoplasm of other specified part of esophagus
150.9	Malignant neoplasm of esophagus, unspecified site
165.0	Malignant neoplasm of upper respiratory tract, part unspecified
165.8	Malignant neoplasm of other sites within the respiratory system and intrathoracic organs
165.9	Malignant neoplasm of ill-defined sites within the respiratory system
170.0	Malignant neoplasm of bones of skull and face, except mandible
170.1	Malignant neoplasm of mandible
170.9	Malignant neoplasm of bone and articular cartilage, site unspecified
171.0	Malignant neoplasm of connective and other soft tissue of head, face, and neck
171.8	Malignant neoplasm of other specified sites of connective and other soft tissue
171.9	Malignant neoplasm of connective and other soft tissue, site unspecified
172.0	Malignant melanoma of skin of lip
172.1	Malignant melanoma of skin of eyelid, including canthus
172.2	Malignant melanoma of skin of ear and external auditory canal
172.3	Malignant melanoma of skin of other and unspecified parts of face
172.4	Malignant melanoma of skin of scalp and neck
172.8	Malignant melanoma of other specified sites of skin
172.9	Melanoma of skin, site unspecified
173.00	Unspecified malignant neoplasm of skin of lip
173.01	Basal cell carcinoma of skin of lip
173.02	Squamous cell carcinoma of skin of lip
173.09	Other specified malignant neoplasm of skin of lip
173.10	Unspecified malignant neoplasm of eyelid, including canthus
173.11	Basal cell carcinoma of eyelid, including canthus
173.12	Squamous cell carcinoma of eyelid, including canthus
173.19	Other specified malignant neoplasm of eyelid, including canthus
173.20	Unspecified malignant neoplasm of skin of ear and external auditory canal
173.21	Basal cell carcinoma of skin of ear and external auditory canal
173.22	Squamous cell carcinoma of skin of ear and external auditory canal
173.29	Other specified malignant neoplasm of skin of ear and external auditory canal
173.30	Unspecified malignant neoplasm of skin of other and unspecified parts of face
173.31	Basal cell carcinoma of skin of other and unspecified parts of face
173.32	Squamous cell carcinoma of skin of other and unspecified parts of face
173.39	Other specified malignant neoplasm of skin of other and unspecified parts of face
173.40	Unspecified malignant neoplasm of scalp and skin of neck

Code	Description
173.41	Basal cell carcinoma of scalp and skin of neck
173.42	Squamous cell carcinoma of scalp and skin of neck
173.49	Other specified malignant neoplasm of scalp and skin of neck
173.80	Unspecified malignant neoplasm of other specified sites of skin
173.81	Basal cell carcinoma of other specified sites of skin
173.82	Squamous cell carcinoma of other specified sites of skin
173.89	Other specified malignant neoplasm of other specified sites of skin
173.90	Unspecified malignant neoplasm of skin, site unspecified
173.91	Basal cell carcinoma of skin, site unspecified
173.92	Squamous cell carcinoma of skin, site unspecified
173.99	Other specified malignant neoplasm of skin, site unspecified
176.0	Kaposi's sarcoma of skin
176.1	Kaposi's sarcoma of soft tissue
176.2	Kaposi's sarcoma of palate
176.8	Kaposi's sarcoma of other specified sites
176.9	Kaposi's sarcoma of unspecified site
190.0	Malignant neoplasm of eyeball, except conjunctiva, cornea, retina, and choroid
190.1	Malignant neoplasm of orbit
190.2	Malignant neoplasm of lacrimal gland
190.3	Malignant neoplasm of conjunctiva
190.4	Malignant neoplasm of cornea
190.5	Malignant neoplasm of retina
190.6	Malignant neoplasm of choroid
190.7	Malignant neoplasm of lacrimal duct
190.8	Malignant neoplasm of other specified sites of eye
190.9	Malignant neoplasm of eye, part unspecified
191.0	Malignant neoplasm of cerebrum, except lobes and ventricles
191.1	Malignant neoplasm of frontal lobe of brain
191.2	Malignant neoplasm of temporal lobe of brain
191.3	Malignant neoplasm of parietal lobe of brain
191.4	Malignant neoplasm of occipital lobe of brain
191.5	Malignant neoplasm of ventricles of brain
191.6	Malignant neoplasm of cerebellum NOS
191.7	Malignant neoplasm of brain stem
191.8	Malignant neoplasm of other parts of brain
191.9	Malignant neoplasm of brain, unspecified site
192.0	Malignant neoplasm of cranial nerves
192.1	Malignant neoplasm of cerebral meninges
192.2	Malignant neoplasm of spinal cord
192.3	Malignant neoplasm of spinal meninges
192.8	Malignant neoplasm of other specified sites of nervous system
192.9	Malignant neoplasm of nervous system, part unspecified
193	Malignant neoplasm of thyroid gland — (Use additional code to identify any functional activity)
194.0	Malignant neoplasm of adrenal gland
194.1	Malignant neoplasm of parathyroid gland
194.3	Malignant neoplasm of pituitary gland and craniopharyngeal duct
194.4	Malignant neoplasm of pineal gland
194.5	Malignant neoplasm of carotid body
194.8	Malignant neoplasm of other endocrine glands and related structures — (Note: If the sites of multiple involvements are known, they should be coded separately)
194.9	Malignant neoplasm of endocrine gland, site unspecified
195.0	Malignant neoplasm of head, face, and neck
195.8	Malignant neoplasm of other specified sites
196.0	Secondary and unspecified malignant neoplasm of lymph nodes of head, face, and neck
196.8	Secondary and unspecified malignant neoplasm of lymph nodes of multiple sites
198.3	Secondary malignant neoplasm of brain and spinal cord
200.01	Reticulosarcoma of lymph nodes of head, face, and neck
200.11	Lymphosarcoma of lymph nodes of head, face, and neck
200.31	Marginal zone lymphoma, lymph nodes of head, face, and neck
200.41	Mantle cell lymphoma, lymph nodes of head, face, and neck
200.51	Primary central nervous system lymphoma, lymph nodes of head, face, and neck
200.61	Anaplastic large cell lymphoma, lymph nodes of head, face, and neck
200.71	Large cell lymphoma, lymph nodes of head, face, and neck
201.01	Hodgkin's paragranuloma of lymph nodes of head, face, and neck
201.11	Hodgkin's granuloma of lymph nodes of head, face, and neck
201.21	Hodgkin's sarcoma of lymph nodes of head, face, and neck
201.41	Hodgkin's disease, lymphocytic-histiocytic predominance of lymph nodes of head, face, and neck
201.51	Hodgkin's disease, nodular sclerosis, of lymph nodes of head, face, and neck
201.61	Hodgkin's disease, mixed cellularity, involving lymph nodes of head, face, and neck
201.71	Hodgkin's disease, lymphocytic depletion, of lymph nodes of head, face, and neck
201.91	Hodgkin's disease, unspecified type, of lymph nodes of head, face, and neck
202.01	Nodular lymphoma of lymph nodes of head, face, and neck
202.11	Mycosis fungoides of lymph nodes of head, face, and neck
202.21	Sezary's disease of lymph nodes of head, face, and neck
202.31	Malignant histiocytosis of lymph nodes of head, face, and neck
202.41	Leukemic reticuloendotheliosis of lymph nodes of head, face, and neck
202.51	Letterer-Siwe disease of lymph nodes of head, face, and neck
202.61	Malignant mast cell tumors of lymph nodes of head, face, and neck
202.71	Peripheral T-cell lymphoma, lymph nodes of head, face, and neck
202.81	Other malignant lymphomas of lymph nodes of head, face, and neck
202.91	Other and unspecified malignant neoplasms of lymphoid and histiocytic tissue of lymph nodes of head, face, and neck
209.22	Malignant carcinoid tumor of the thymus — (Code first any associated multiple endocrine neoplasia syndrome: 258.01-258.03)(Use additional code to identify associated endocrine syndrome, as: carcinoid syndrome: 259.2)
209.30	Malignant poorly differentiated neuroendocrine carcinoma, any site — (Code first any associated multiple endocrine neoplasia syndrome: 258.01-258.03)(Use additional code to identify associated endocrine syndrome, as: carcinoid syndrome: 259.2)
209.62	Benign carcinoid tumor of the thymus — (Code first any associated multiple endocrine neoplasia syndrome: 258.01-258.03)(Use additional code to identify associated endocrine syndrome, as: carcinoid syndrome: 259.2)
209.69	Benign carcinoid tumor of other sites — (Code first any associated multiple endocrine neoplasia syndrome: 258.01-258.03)(Use additional code to identify associated endocrine syndrome, as: carcinoid syndrome: 259.2)
210.0	Benign neoplasm of lip
210.1	Benign neoplasm of tongue
210.2	Benign neoplasm of major salivary glands
210.3	Benign neoplasm of floor of mouth
210.4	Benign neoplasm of other and unspecified parts of mouth
210.5	Benign neoplasm of tonsil
210.6	Benign neoplasm of other parts of oropharynx
210.7	Benign neoplasm of nasopharynx
210.8	Benign neoplasm of hypopharynx
210.9	Benign neoplasm of pharynx, unspecified
211.0	Benign neoplasm of esophagus
212.0	Benign neoplasm of nasal cavities, middle ear, and accessory sinuses
212.1	Benign neoplasm of larynx
212.2	Benign neoplasm of trachea
213.0	Benign neoplasm of bones of skull and face
213.1	Benign neoplasm of lower jaw bone
213.2	Benign neoplasm of vertebral column, excluding sacrum and coccyx
215.0	Other benign neoplasm of connective and other soft tissue of head, face, and neck
216.0	Benign neoplasm of skin of lip
216.1	Benign neoplasm of eyelid, including canthus
216.2	Benign neoplasm of ear and external auditory canal
216.3	Benign neoplasm of skin of other and unspecified parts of face

216.4 Benign neoplasm of scalp and skin of neck
224.0 Benign neoplasm of eyeball, except conjunctiva, cornea, retina, and choroid
224.1 Benign neoplasm of orbit
224.2 Benign neoplasm of lacrimal gland
224.3 Benign neoplasm of conjunctiva
224.4 Benign neoplasm of cornea
224.5 Benign neoplasm of retina
224.6 Benign neoplasm of choroid
224.7 Benign neoplasm of lacrimal duct
224.8 Benign neoplasm of other specified parts of eye
224.9 Benign neoplasm of eye, part unspecified ▽
225.0 Benign neoplasm of brain
225.1 Benign neoplasm of cranial nerves
225.2 Benign neoplasm of cerebral meninges
225.3 Benign neoplasm of spinal cord
225.4 Benign neoplasm of spinal meninges
225.8 Benign neoplasm of other specified sites of nervous system
225.9 Benign neoplasm of nervous system, part unspecified ▽
226 Benign neoplasm of thyroid glands — (Use additional code to identify any functional activity)
227.0 Benign neoplasm of adrenal gland — (Use additional code to identify any functional activity)
227.1 Benign neoplasm of parathyroid gland — (Use additional code to identify any functional activity)
227.3 Benign neoplasm of pituitary gland and craniopharyngeal duct (pouch) — (Use additional code to identify any functional activity)
227.4 Benign neoplasm of pineal gland — (Use additional code to identify any functional activity)
227.5 Benign neoplasm of carotid body — (Use additional code to identify any functional activity)
227.6 Benign neoplasm of aortic body and other paraganglia — (Use additional code to identify any functional activity)
227.8 Benign neoplasm of other endocrine glands and related structures — (Use additional code to identify any functional activity)
227.9 Benign neoplasm of endocrine gland, site unspecified — (Use additional code to identify any functional activity) ▽
228.02 Hemangioma of intracranial structures
228.03 Hemangioma of retina
228.09 Hemangioma of other sites
228.1 Lymphangioma, any site
229.0 Benign neoplasm of lymph nodes
229.8 Benign neoplasm of other specified sites
229.9 Benign neoplasm of unspecified site ▽
230.0 Carcinoma in situ of lip, oral cavity, and pharynx
230.1 Carcinoma in situ of esophagus
231.0 Carcinoma in situ of larynx
231.1 Carcinoma in situ of trachea
231.8 Carcinoma in situ of other specified parts of respiratory system
232.0 Carcinoma in situ of skin of lip
232.1 Carcinoma in situ of eyelid, including canthus
232.2 Carcinoma in situ of skin of ear and external auditory canal
232.3 Carcinoma in situ of skin of other and unspecified parts of face ▽
232.4 Carcinoma in situ of scalp and skin of neck
234.0 Carcinoma in situ of eye
234.8 Carcinoma in situ of other specified sites
234.9 Carcinoma in situ, site unspecified ▽
235.0 Neoplasm of uncertain behavior of major salivary glands
235.1 Neoplasm of uncertain behavior of lip, oral cavity, and pharynx
235.6 Neoplasm of uncertain behavior of larynx
235.7 Neoplasm of uncertain behavior of trachea, bronchus, and lung
235.8 Neoplasm of uncertain behavior of pleura, thymus, and mediastinum
235.9 Neoplasm of uncertain behavior of other and unspecified respiratory organs ▽
237.0 Neoplasm of uncertain behavior of pituitary gland and craniopharyngeal duct — (Use additional code to identify any functional activity)
237.1 Neoplasm of uncertain behavior of pineal gland
237.2 Neoplasm of uncertain behavior of adrenal gland — (Use additional code to identify any functional activity)
237.3 Neoplasm of uncertain behavior of paraganglia
237.4 Neoplasm of uncertain behavior of other and unspecified endocrine glands ▽
237.5 Neoplasm of uncertain behavior of brain and spinal cord
237.6 Neoplasm of uncertain behavior of meninges
238.0 Neoplasm of uncertain behavior of bone and articular cartilage
242.00 Toxic diffuse goiter without mention of thyrotoxic crisis or storm
242.01 Toxic diffuse goiter with mention of thyrotoxic crisis or storm
242.90 Thyrotoxicosis without mention of goiter or other cause, without mention of thyrotoxic crisis or storm
242.91 Thyrotoxicosis without mention of goiter or other cause, with mention of thyrotoxic crisis or storm
782.2 Localized superficial swelling, mass, or lump
784.2 Swelling, mass, or lump in head and neck
785.6 Enlargement of lymph nodes

ICD-9-CM Procedural

27.92 Incision of mouth, unspecified structure
92.27 Implantation or insertion of radioactive elements

41100-41105

41100 Biopsy of tongue; anterior 2/3
41105 posterior 1/3

ICD-9-CM Diagnostic

141.0 Malignant neoplasm of base of tongue
141.1 Malignant neoplasm of dorsal surface of tongue
141.2 Malignant neoplasm of tip and lateral border of tongue
141.3 Malignant neoplasm of ventral surface of tongue
141.4 Malignant neoplasm of anterior two-thirds of tongue, part unspecified ▽
141.5 Malignant neoplasm of junctional zone of tongue
141.8 Malignant neoplasm of other sites of tongue
141.9 Malignant neoplasm of tongue, unspecified site ▽
198.89 Secondary malignant neoplasm of other specified sites
210.1 Benign neoplasm of tongue
228.00 Hemangioma of unspecified site ▽
228.09 Hemangioma of other sites
230.0 Carcinoma in situ of lip, oral cavity, and pharynx
235.1 Neoplasm of uncertain behavior of lip, oral cavity, and pharynx
239.0 Neoplasm of unspecified nature of digestive system
239.2 Neoplasms of unspecified nature of bone, soft tissue, and skin
277.30 Amyloidosis, unspecified — (Use additional code to identify any associated intellectual disabilities) ▽
277.31 Familial Mediterranean fever — (Use additional code to identify any associated intellectual disabilities)
277.39 Other amyloidosis — (Use additional code to identify any associated intellectual disabilities)
528.6 Leukoplakia of oral mucosa, including tongue
528.79 Other disturbances of oral epithelium, including tongue
528.8 Oral submucosal fibrosis, including of tongue
528.9 Other and unspecified diseases of the oral soft tissues ▽
529.0 Glossitis
529.6 Glossodynia
529.8 Other specified conditions of the tongue

697.0	Lichen planus
781.1	Disturbances of sensation of smell and taste
784.2	Swelling, mass, or lump in head and neck

ICD-9-CM Procedural

25.01	Closed (needle) biopsy of tongue
25.02	Open biopsy of tongue

41108

41108	Biopsy of floor of mouth

ICD-9-CM Diagnostic

144.0	Malignant neoplasm of anterior portion of floor of mouth
144.1	Malignant neoplasm of lateral portion of floor of mouth
144.8	Malignant neoplasm of other sites of floor of mouth
144.9	Malignant neoplasm of floor of mouth, part unspecified
145.9	Malignant neoplasm of mouth, unspecified site
198.89	Secondary malignant neoplasm of other specified sites
199.1	Other malignant neoplasm of unspecified site
210.3	Benign neoplasm of floor of mouth
210.4	Benign neoplasm of other and unspecified parts of mouth
228.00	Hemangioma of unspecified site
228.09	Hemangioma of other sites
230.0	Carcinoma in situ of lip, oral cavity, and pharynx
235.1	Neoplasm of uncertain behavior of lip, oral cavity, and pharynx
239.0	Neoplasm of unspecified nature of digestive system
528.6	Leukoplakia of oral mucosa, including tongue
528.79	Other disturbances of oral epithelium, including tongue
528.8	Oral submucosal fibrosis, including of tongue
528.9	Other and unspecified diseases of the oral soft tissues
697.0	Lichen planus

ICD-9-CM Procedural

27.24	Biopsy of mouth, unspecified structure

41110

41110	Excision of lesion of tongue without closure

ICD-9-CM Diagnostic

141.0	Malignant neoplasm of base of tongue
141.1	Malignant neoplasm of dorsal surface of tongue
141.2	Malignant neoplasm of tip and lateral border of tongue
141.3	Malignant neoplasm of ventral surface of tongue
141.4	Malignant neoplasm of anterior two-thirds of tongue, part unspecified
141.5	Malignant neoplasm of junctional zone of tongue
141.6	Malignant neoplasm of lingual tonsil
141.8	Malignant neoplasm of other sites of tongue
141.9	Malignant neoplasm of tongue, unspecified site
198.89	Secondary malignant neoplasm of other specified sites
210.1	Benign neoplasm of tongue
228.00	Hemangioma of unspecified site
228.09	Hemangioma of other sites
230.0	Carcinoma in situ of lip, oral cavity, and pharynx
235.1	Neoplasm of uncertain behavior of lip, oral cavity, and pharynx
239.0	Neoplasm of unspecified nature of digestive system
239.2	Neoplasms of unspecified nature of bone, soft tissue, and skin
528.6	Leukoplakia of oral mucosa, including tongue
528.79	Other disturbances of oral epithelium, including tongue
528.8	Oral submucosal fibrosis, including of tongue
528.9	Other and unspecified diseases of the oral soft tissues
529.0	Glossitis
529.8	Other specified conditions of the tongue
697.0	Lichen planus
784.2	Swelling, mass, or lump in head and neck

ICD-9-CM Procedural

25.1	Excision or destruction of lesion or tissue of tongue

41112-41114

41112	Excision of lesion of tongue with closure; anterior 2/3
41113	posterior 1/3
41114	with local tongue flap

ICD-9-CM Diagnostic

141.0	Malignant neoplasm of base of tongue
141.1	Malignant neoplasm of dorsal surface of tongue
141.2	Malignant neoplasm of tip and lateral border of tongue
141.3	Malignant neoplasm of ventral surface of tongue
141.4	Malignant neoplasm of anterior two-thirds of tongue, part unspecified
141.5	Malignant neoplasm of junctional zone of tongue
141.9	Malignant neoplasm of tongue, unspecified site
198.89	Secondary malignant neoplasm of other specified sites
210.1	Benign neoplasm of tongue
228.09	Hemangioma of other sites
230.0	Carcinoma in situ of lip, oral cavity, and pharynx
235.1	Neoplasm of uncertain behavior of lip, oral cavity, and pharynx
235.7	Neoplasm of uncertain behavior of trachea, bronchus, and lung
239.0	Neoplasm of unspecified nature of digestive system
528.6	Leukoplakia of oral mucosa, including tongue
528.79	Other disturbances of oral epithelium, including tongue
528.8	Oral submucosal fibrosis, including of tongue
528.9	Other and unspecified diseases of the oral soft tissues
529.0	Glossitis
529.8	Other specified conditions of the tongue
697.0	Lichen planus
784.2	Swelling, mass, or lump in head and neck

ICD-9-CM Procedural

25.1	Excision or destruction of lesion or tissue of tongue
25.59	Other repair and plastic operations on tongue

HCPCS Level II Supplies & Services

A4305	Disposable drug delivery system, flow rate of 50 ml or greater per hour

41115

41115	Excision of lingual frenum (frenectomy)

ICD-9-CM Diagnostic

141.3	Malignant neoplasm of ventral surface of tongue
145.1	Malignant neoplasm of vestibule of mouth
210.0	Benign neoplasm of lip
230.0	Carcinoma in situ of lip, oral cavity, and pharynx
235.1	Neoplasm of uncertain behavior of lip, oral cavity, and pharynx
528.9	Other and unspecified diseases of the oral soft tissues
529.6	Glossodynia
750.0	Tongue tie
750.12	Congenital adhesions of tongue

ICD-9-CM Procedural

25.92	Lingual frenectomy

HCPCS Level II Supplies & Services

A4305	Disposable drug delivery system, flow rate of 50 ml or greater per hour

41116

41116 Excision, lesion of floor of mouth

ICD-9-CM Diagnostic

144.0 Malignant neoplasm of anterior portion of floor of mouth
144.1 Malignant neoplasm of lateral portion of floor of mouth
144.8 Malignant neoplasm of other sites of floor of mouth
144.9 Malignant neoplasm of floor of mouth, part unspecified ▽
145.9 Malignant neoplasm of mouth, unspecified site ▽
149.8 Malignant neoplasm of other sites within the lip and oral cavity
198.89 Secondary malignant neoplasm of other specified sites
210.3 Benign neoplasm of floor of mouth
210.4 Benign neoplasm of other and unspecified parts of mouth ▽
228.00 Hemangioma of unspecified site ▽
228.09 Hemangioma of other sites
230.0 Carcinoma in situ of lip, oral cavity, and pharynx
235.1 Neoplasm of uncertain behavior of lip, oral cavity, and pharynx
527.6 Mucocele of salivary gland
528.6 Leukoplakia of oral mucosa, including tongue
528.79 Other disturbances of oral epithelium, including tongue
528.9 Other and unspecified diseases of the oral soft tissues ▽
784.2 Swelling, mass, or lump in head and neck

ICD-9-CM Procedural

27.49 Other excision of mouth

HCPCS Level II Supplies & Services

A4305 Disposable drug delivery system, flow rate of 50 ml or greater per hour

41120-41130

41120 Glossectomy; less than 1/2 tongue
41130 hemiglossectomy

ICD-9-CM Diagnostic

141.0 Malignant neoplasm of base of tongue
141.1 Malignant neoplasm of dorsal surface of tongue
141.2 Malignant neoplasm of tip and lateral border of tongue
141.3 Malignant neoplasm of ventral surface of tongue
141.4 Malignant neoplasm of anterior two-thirds of tongue, part unspecified ▽
141.8 Malignant neoplasm of other sites of tongue
141.9 Malignant neoplasm of tongue, unspecified site ▽
144.9 Malignant neoplasm of floor of mouth, part unspecified ▽
149.0 Malignant neoplasm of pharynx, unspecified ▽
195.0 Malignant neoplasm of head, face, and neck
198.89 Secondary malignant neoplasm of other specified sites
210.1 Benign neoplasm of tongue
230.0 Carcinoma in situ of lip, oral cavity, and pharynx
235.1 Neoplasm of uncertain behavior of lip, oral cavity, and pharynx
750.15 Macroglossia

ICD-9-CM Procedural

25.2 Partial glossectomy

41135

41135 Glossectomy; partial, with unilateral radical neck dissection

ICD-9-CM Diagnostic

141.0 Malignant neoplasm of base of tongue
141.1 Malignant neoplasm of dorsal surface of tongue
141.2 Malignant neoplasm of tip and lateral border of tongue
141.3 Malignant neoplasm of ventral surface of tongue
141.4 Malignant neoplasm of anterior two-thirds of tongue, part unspecified ▽
141.5 Malignant neoplasm of junctional zone of tongue
141.6 Malignant neoplasm of lingual tonsil
141.8 Malignant neoplasm of other sites of tongue
141.9 Malignant neoplasm of tongue, unspecified site ▽
171.0 Malignant neoplasm of connective and other soft tissue of head, face, and neck
195.0 Malignant neoplasm of head, face, and neck
196.0 Secondary and unspecified malignant neoplasm of lymph nodes of head, face, and neck
198.89 Secondary malignant neoplasm of other specified sites
238.8 Neoplasm of uncertain behavior of other specified sites

ICD-9-CM Procedural

25.2 Partial glossectomy
40.41 Radical neck dissection, unilateral

41140-41145

41140 Glossectomy; complete or total, with or without tracheostomy, without radical neck dissection
41145 complete or total, with or without tracheostomy, with unilateral radical neck dissection

ICD-9-CM Diagnostic

141.0 Malignant neoplasm of base of tongue
141.1 Malignant neoplasm of dorsal surface of tongue
141.2 Malignant neoplasm of tip and lateral border of tongue
141.3 Malignant neoplasm of ventral surface of tongue
141.4 Malignant neoplasm of anterior two-thirds of tongue, part unspecified ▽
141.5 Malignant neoplasm of junctional zone of tongue
141.6 Malignant neoplasm of lingual tonsil
141.8 Malignant neoplasm of other sites of tongue
141.9 Malignant neoplasm of tongue, unspecified site ▽
171.0 Malignant neoplasm of connective and other soft tissue of head, face, and neck
195.0 Malignant neoplasm of head, face, and neck
196.0 Secondary and unspecified malignant neoplasm of lymph nodes of head, face, and neck
198.89 Secondary malignant neoplasm of other specified sites
238.8 Neoplasm of uncertain behavior of other specified sites
239.89 Neoplasms of unspecified nature, other specified sites

ICD-9-CM Procedural

25.3 Complete glossectomy
31.1 Temporary tracheostomy
31.21 Mediastinal tracheostomy
31.29 Other permanent tracheostomy
40.41 Radical neck dissection, unilateral

HCPCS Level II Supplies & Services

A7527 Tracheostomy/laryngectomy tube plug/stop, each

41150

41150 Glossectomy; composite procedure with resection floor of mouth and mandibular resection, without radical neck dissection

ICD-9-CM Diagnostic

141.0 Malignant neoplasm of base of tongue
141.1 Malignant neoplasm of dorsal surface of tongue
141.2 Malignant neoplasm of tip and lateral border of tongue
141.3 Malignant neoplasm of ventral surface of tongue
141.4 Malignant neoplasm of anterior two-thirds of tongue, part unspecified ▽
141.5 Malignant neoplasm of junctional zone of tongue
141.6 Malignant neoplasm of lingual tonsil
141.8 Malignant neoplasm of other sites of tongue

141.9 Malignant neoplasm of tongue, unspecified site ▽

144.0 Malignant neoplasm of anterior portion of floor of mouth

144.1 Malignant neoplasm of lateral portion of floor of mouth

144.8 Malignant neoplasm of other sites of floor of mouth

144.9 Malignant neoplasm of floor of mouth, part unspecified ▽

145.8 Malignant neoplasm of other specified parts of mouth

145.9 Malignant neoplasm of mouth, unspecified site ▽

170.1 Malignant neoplasm of mandible

195.0 Malignant neoplasm of head, face, and neck

196.0 Secondary and unspecified malignant neoplasm of lymph nodes of head, face, and neck

198.5 Secondary malignant neoplasm of bone and bone marrow

198.89 Secondary malignant neoplasm of other specified sites

235.1 Neoplasm of uncertain behavior of lip, oral cavity, and pharynx

238.0 Neoplasm of uncertain behavior of bone and articular cartilage

238.8 Neoplasm of uncertain behavior of other specified sites

239.0 Neoplasm of unspecified nature of digestive system

ICD-9-CM Procedural

25.2 Partial glossectomy

25.3 Complete glossectomy

27.49 Other excision of mouth

76.31 Partial mandibulectomy

41153

41153 Glossectomy; composite procedure with resection floor of mouth, with suprahyoid neck dissection

ICD-9-CM Diagnostic

141.0 Malignant neoplasm of base of tongue

141.1 Malignant neoplasm of dorsal surface of tongue

141.2 Malignant neoplasm of tip and lateral border of tongue

141.3 Malignant neoplasm of ventral surface of tongue

141.4 Malignant neoplasm of anterior two-thirds of tongue, part unspecified ▽

141.5 Malignant neoplasm of junctional zone of tongue

141.6 Malignant neoplasm of lingual tonsil

141.8 Malignant neoplasm of other sites of tongue

141.9 Malignant neoplasm of tongue, unspecified site ▽

142.2 Malignant neoplasm of sublingual gland

144.0 Malignant neoplasm of anterior portion of floor of mouth

144.1 Malignant neoplasm of lateral portion of floor of mouth

144.8 Malignant neoplasm of other sites of floor of mouth

144.9 Malignant neoplasm of floor of mouth, part unspecified ▽

145.8 Malignant neoplasm of other specified parts of mouth

170.1 Malignant neoplasm of mandible

195.0 Malignant neoplasm of head, face, and neck

196.0 Secondary and unspecified malignant neoplasm of lymph nodes of head, face, and neck

198.5 Secondary malignant neoplasm of bone and bone marrow

198.89 Secondary malignant neoplasm of other specified sites

235.0 Neoplasm of uncertain behavior of major salivary glands

235.1 Neoplasm of uncertain behavior of lip, oral cavity, and pharynx

238.0 Neoplasm of uncertain behavior of bone and articular cartilage

238.8 Neoplasm of uncertain behavior of other specified sites

239.0 Neoplasm of unspecified nature of digestive system

ICD-9-CM Procedural

25.2 Partial glossectomy

25.3 Complete glossectomy

27.49 Other excision of mouth

40.3 Regional lymph node excision

41155

41155 Glossectomy; composite procedure with resection floor of mouth, mandibular resection, and radical neck dissection (Commando type)

ICD-9-CM Diagnostic

141.0 Malignant neoplasm of base of tongue

141.1 Malignant neoplasm of dorsal surface of tongue

141.2 Malignant neoplasm of tip and lateral border of tongue

141.3 Malignant neoplasm of ventral surface of tongue

141.4 Malignant neoplasm of anterior two-thirds of tongue, part unspecified ▽

141.5 Malignant neoplasm of junctional zone of tongue

141.6 Malignant neoplasm of lingual tonsil

141.9 Malignant neoplasm of tongue, unspecified site ▽

143.1 Malignant neoplasm of lower gum

144.0 Malignant neoplasm of anterior portion of floor of mouth

144.1 Malignant neoplasm of lateral portion of floor of mouth

144.8 Malignant neoplasm of other sites of floor of mouth

144.9 Malignant neoplasm of floor of mouth, part unspecified ▽

145.8 Malignant neoplasm of other specified parts of mouth

146.9 Malignant neoplasm of oropharynx, unspecified site ▽

170.1 Malignant neoplasm of mandible

171.0 Malignant neoplasm of connective and other soft tissue of head, face, and neck

195.0 Malignant neoplasm of head, face, and neck

196.0 Secondary and unspecified malignant neoplasm of lymph nodes of head, face, and neck

198.5 Secondary malignant neoplasm of bone and bone marrow

198.89 Secondary malignant neoplasm of other specified sites

230.0 Carcinoma in situ of lip, oral cavity, and pharynx

235.1 Neoplasm of uncertain behavior of lip, oral cavity, and pharynx

238.0 Neoplasm of uncertain behavior of bone and articular cartilage

238.8 Neoplasm of uncertain behavior of other specified sites

ICD-9-CM Procedural

25.2 Partial glossectomy

25.3 Complete glossectomy

27.49 Other excision of mouth

40.42 Radical neck dissection, bilateral

76.31 Partial mandibulectomy

41250-41252

41250 Repair of laceration 2.5 cm or less; floor of mouth and/or anterior 2/3 of tongue

41251 posterior 1/3 of tongue

41252 Repair of laceration of tongue, floor of mouth, over 2.6 cm or complex

ICD-9-CM Diagnostic

873.64 Open wound of tongue and floor of mouth, without mention of complication

873.69 Open wound of mouth, other and multiple sites, without mention of complication

873.72 Open wound of gum (alveolar process), complicated

873.74 Open wound of tongue and floor of mouth, complicated

873.79 Open wound of mouth, other and multiple sites, complicated

998.2 Accidental puncture or laceration during procedure

998.32 Disruption of external operation (surgical) wound

ICD-9-CM Procedural

25.51 Suture of laceration of tongue

25.59 Other repair and plastic operations on tongue

27.52 Suture of laceration of other part of mouth

27.59 Other plastic repair of mouth

HCPCS Level II Supplies & Services

A4305 Disposable drug delivery system, flow rate of 50 ml or greater per hour

41500

41500 Fixation of tongue, mechanical, other than suture (eg, K-wire)

ICD-9-CM Diagnostic

141.0 Malignant neoplasm of base of tongue
141.1 Malignant neoplasm of dorsal surface of tongue
141.2 Malignant neoplasm of tip and lateral border of tongue
141.3 Malignant neoplasm of ventral surface of tongue
141.4 Malignant neoplasm of anterior two-thirds of tongue, part unspecified ▼
141.5 Malignant neoplasm of junctional zone of tongue
141.9 Malignant neoplasm of tongue, unspecified site ▼
230.0 Carcinoma in situ of lip, oral cavity, and pharynx
235.1 Neoplasm of uncertain behavior of lip, oral cavity, and pharynx
529.8 Other specified conditions of the tongue
750.0 Tongue tie
750.15 Macroglossia
750.16 Microglossia
750.19 Other congenital anomaly of tongue
756.0 Congenital anomalies of skull and face bones

ICD-9-CM Procedural

25.59 Other repair and plastic operations on tongue

HCPCS Level II Supplies & Services

A4305 Disposable drug delivery system, flow rate of 50 ml or greater per hour

41510

41510 Suture of tongue to lip for micrognathia (Douglas type procedure)

ICD-9-CM Diagnostic

524.00 Unspecified major anomaly of jaw size ▼
524.03 Maxillary hypoplasia
524.04 Mandibular hypoplasia
524.06 Microgenia
524.10 Unspecified anomaly of relationship of jaw to cranial base ▼
524.73 Alveolar maxillary hypoplasia
524.74 Alveolar mandibular hypoplasia
750.15 Macroglossia

ICD-9-CM Procedural

25.59 Other repair and plastic operations on tongue

HCPCS Level II Supplies & Services

A4305 Disposable drug delivery system, flow rate of 50 ml or greater per hour

41512

41512 Tongue base suspension, permanent suture technique

ICD-9-CM Diagnostic

327.23 Obstructive sleep apnea (adult) (pediatric)
529.8 Other specified conditions of the tongue
750.15 Macroglossia
786.09 Other dyspnea and respiratory abnormalities

ICD-9-CM Procedural

93.99 Other respiratory therapy

41520

41520 Frenoplasty (surgical revision of frenum, eg, with Z-plasty)

ICD-9-CM Diagnostic

524.02 Mandibular hyperplasia
524.04 Mandibular hypoplasia
529.8 Other specified conditions of the tongue
750.0 Tongue tie
750.10 Congenital anomaly of tongue, unspecified ▼
750.12 Congenital adhesions of tongue
906.0 Late effect of open wound of head, neck, and trunk

ICD-9-CM Procedural

25.59 Other repair and plastic operations on tongue

HCPCS Level II Supplies & Services

A4305 Disposable drug delivery system, flow rate of 50 ml or greater per hour

41530

41530 Submucosal ablation of the tongue base, radiofrequency, 1 or more sites, per session

ICD-9-CM Diagnostic

327.23 Obstructive sleep apnea (adult) (pediatric)
529.8 Other specified conditions of the tongue
750.15 Macroglossia

ICD-9-CM Procedural

25.1 Excision or destruction of lesion or tissue of tongue

Dentoalveolar Structures

41800

41800 Drainage of abscess, cyst, hematoma from dentoalveolar structures

ICD-9-CM Diagnostic

522.5 Periapical abscess without sinus
522.7 Periapical abscess with sinus
522.8 Radicular cyst of dental pulp
523.30 Aggressive periodontitis, unspecified ▼
523.31 Aggressive periodontitis, localized
523.32 Aggressive periodontitis, generalized
523.33 Acute periodontitis
526.0 Developmental odontogenic cysts
526.1 Fissural cysts of jaw
526.2 Other cysts of jaws
526.4 Inflammatory conditions of jaw
528.3 Cellulitis and abscess of oral soft tissues
528.4 Cysts of oral soft tissues
784.2 Swelling, mass, or lump in head and neck
925.1 Crushing injury of face and scalp — (Use additional code to identify any associated injuries, such as: 800-829, 850.0-854.1, 860.0-869.1)
958.3 Posttraumatic wound infection not elsewhere classified
998.51 Infected postoperative seroma — (Use additional code to identify organism)
998.59 Other postoperative infection — (Use additional code to identify infection)

ICD-9-CM Procedural

24.0 Incision of gum or alveolar bone

41805-41806

41805 Removal of embedded foreign body from dentoalveolar structures; soft tissues
41806 bone

ICD-9-CM Diagnostic

522.6 Chronic apical periodontitis
523.40 Chronic periodontitis, unspecified ▼
523.41 Chronic periodontitis, localized
523.42 Chronic periodontitis, generalized
525.71 Osseointegration failure of dental implant
525.72 Post-osseointegration biological failure of dental implant
525.73 Post-osseointegration mechanical failure of dental implant

525.79 Other endosseous dental implant failure
526.4 Inflammatory conditions of jaw
873.72 Open wound of gum (alveolar process), complicated
873.73 Tooth (broken) (fractured) (due to trauma), complicated
873.79 Open wound of mouth, other and multiple sites, complicated
910.6 Face, neck, and scalp, except eye, superficial foreign body (splinter), without major open wound or mention of infection
910.7 Face, neck, and scalp except eye, superficial foreign body (splinter), without major open wound, infected
935.0 Foreign body in mouth
996.40 Unspecified mechanical complication of internal orthopedic device, implant, and graft — (Use additional code to identify prosthetic joint with mechanical complication, V43.60-V43.69)
996.49 Other mechanical complication of other internal orthopedic device, implant, and graft — (Use additional code to identify prosthetic joint with mechanical complication, V43.60-V43.69)
996.67 Infection and inflammatory reaction due to other internal orthopedic device, implant, and graft — (Use additional code to identify specified infections)
996.78 Other complications due to other internal orthopedic device, implant, and graft — (Use additional code to identify complication: 338.18-338.19, 338.28-338.29)
998.4 Foreign body accidentally left during procedure, not elsewhere classified
998.51 Infected postoperative seroma — (Use additional code to identify organism)
998.59 Other postoperative infection — (Use additional code to identify infection)

ICD-9-CM Procedural

24.0 Incision of gum or alveolar bone
98.22 Removal of other foreign body without incision from head and neck

HCPCS Level II Supplies & Services

A4305 Disposable drug delivery system, flow rate of 50 ml or greater per hour

41820

41820 Gingivectomy, excision gingiva, each quadrant

ICD-9-CM Diagnostic

143.0 Malignant neoplasm of upper gum
143.1 Malignant neoplasm of lower gum
143.8 Malignant neoplasm of other sites of gum
143.9 Malignant neoplasm of gum, unspecified site
198.89 Secondary malignant neoplasm of other specified sites
210.4 Benign neoplasm of other and unspecified parts of mouth
230.0 Carcinoma in situ of lip, oral cavity, and pharynx
235.1 Neoplasm of uncertain behavior of lip, oral cavity, and pharynx
239.0 Neoplasm of unspecified nature of digestive system
523.00 Acute gingivitis, plaque induced
523.01 Acute gingivitis, non-plaque induced
523.10 Chronic gingivitis, plaque induced
523.11 Chronic gingivitis, non-plaque induced
523.30 Aggressive periodontitis, unspecified
523.31 Aggressive periodontitis, localized
523.32 Aggressive periodontitis, generalized
523.33 Acute periodontitis
523.40 Chronic periodontitis, unspecified
523.41 Chronic periodontitis, localized
523.42 Chronic periodontitis, generalized
523.8 Other specified periodontal diseases
996.67 Infection and inflammatory reaction due to other internal orthopedic device, implant, and graft — (Use additional code to identify specified infections)

ICD-9-CM Procedural

24.31 Excision of lesion or tissue of gum

HCPCS Level II Supplies & Services

A4305 Disposable drug delivery system, flow rate of 50 ml or greater per hour

41821

41821 Operculectomy, excision pericoronal tissues

ICD-9-CM Diagnostic

520.6 Disturbances in tooth eruption
520.8 Other specified disorders of tooth development and eruption
521.6 Ankylosis of teeth
523.10 Chronic gingivitis, plaque induced
523.11 Chronic gingivitis, non-plaque induced
523.30 Aggressive periodontitis, unspecified
523.31 Aggressive periodontitis, localized
523.32 Aggressive periodontitis, generalized
523.33 Acute periodontitis
523.40 Chronic periodontitis, unspecified
523.41 Chronic periodontitis, localized
523.42 Chronic periodontitis, generalized
528.6 Leukoplakia of oral mucosa, including tongue
528.9 Other and unspecified diseases of the oral soft tissues

ICD-9-CM Procedural

24.6 Exposure of tooth

HCPCS Level II Supplies & Services

A4305 Disposable drug delivery system, flow rate of 50 ml or greater per hour

41822

41822 Excision of fibrous tuberosities, dentoalveolar structures

ICD-9-CM Diagnostic

523.30 Aggressive periodontitis, unspecified
523.31 Aggressive periodontitis, localized
523.32 Aggressive periodontitis, generalized
523.33 Acute periodontitis
523.40 Chronic periodontitis, unspecified
523.41 Chronic periodontitis, localized
523.42 Chronic periodontitis, generalized
523.8 Other specified periodontal diseases
524.70 Unspecified alveolar anomaly
524.71 Alveolar maxillary hyperplasia
524.72 Alveolar mandibular hyperplasia
524.79 Other specified alveolar anomaly
524.89 Other specified dentofacial anomalies
524.9 Unspecified dentofacial anomalies
525.8 Other specified disorders of the teeth and supporting structures
525.9 Unspecified disorder of the teeth and supporting structures
526.89 Other specified disease of the jaws

ICD-9-CM Procedural

24.4 Excision of dental lesion of jaw

HCPCS Level II Supplies & Services

A4305 Disposable drug delivery system, flow rate of 50 ml or greater per hour

41823

41823 Excision of osseous tuberosities, dentoalveolar structures

ICD-9-CM Diagnostic

210.4 Benign neoplasm of other and unspecified parts of mouth
213.0 Benign neoplasm of bones of skull and face

520.6 Disturbances in tooth eruption
523.30 Aggressive periodontitis, unspecified ▽
523.31 Aggressive periodontitis, localized
523.32 Aggressive periodontitis, generalized
523.33 Acute periodontitis
523.40 Chronic periodontitis, unspecified ▽
523.41 Chronic periodontitis, localized
523.42 Chronic periodontitis, generalized
523.8 Other specified periodontal diseases
523.9 Unspecified gingival and periodontal disease ▽
524.70 Unspecified alveolar anomaly ▽
524.71 Alveolar maxillary hyperplasia
524.72 Alveolar mandibular hyperplasia
524.79 Other specified alveolar anomaly
524.89 Other specified dentofacial anomalies
524.9 Unspecified dentofacial anomalies ▽
525.8 Other specified disorders of the teeth and supporting structures
525.9 Unspecified disorder of the teeth and supporting structures ▽
526.0 Developmental odontogenic cysts
526.81 Exostosis of jaw
526.89 Other specified disease of the jaws
528.9 Other and unspecified diseases of the oral soft tissues ▽
730.88 Other infections involving bone diseases classified elsewhere, other specified sites — (Use additional code to identify organism: 041.1. Code first underlying disease: 002.0, 015.0-015.9) ☒

ICD-9-CM Procedural

24.4 Excision of dental lesion of jaw

HCPCS Level II Supplies & Services

A4305 Disposable drug delivery system, flow rate of 50 ml or greater per hour

41825-41827

41825 Excision of lesion or tumor (except listed above), dentoalveolar structures; without repair
41826 with simple repair
41827 with complex repair

ICD-9-CM Diagnostic

143.0 Malignant neoplasm of upper gum
143.1 Malignant neoplasm of lower gum
143.8 Malignant neoplasm of other sites of gum
143.9 Malignant neoplasm of gum, unspecified site ▽
145.6 Malignant neoplasm of retromolar area
198.89 Secondary malignant neoplasm of other specified sites
210.4 Benign neoplasm of other and unspecified parts of mouth ▽
235.1 Neoplasm of uncertain behavior of lip, oral cavity, and pharynx
522.8 Radicular cyst of dental pulp
523.8 Other specified periodontal diseases
526.0 Developmental odontogenic cysts
526.1 Fissural cysts of jaw
526.2 Other cysts of jaws
526.3 Central giant cell (reparative) granuloma
528.4 Cysts of oral soft tissues
528.6 Leukoplakia of oral mucosa, including tongue
528.9 Other and unspecified diseases of the oral soft tissues ▽
784.2 Swelling, mass, or lump in head and neck

ICD-9-CM Procedural

24.2 Gingivoplasty
24.31 Excision of lesion or tissue of gum
24.4 Excision of dental lesion of jaw
24.5 Alveoloplasty

HCPCS Level II Supplies & Services

A4305 Disposable drug delivery system, flow rate of 50 ml or greater per hour

41828

41828 Excision of hyperplastic alveolar mucosa, each quadrant (specify)

ICD-9-CM Diagnostic

210.4 Benign neoplasm of other and unspecified parts of mouth ▽
523.8 Other specified periodontal diseases
528.9 Other and unspecified diseases of the oral soft tissues ▽
V54.89 Other orthopedic aftercare

ICD-9-CM Procedural

24.31 Excision of lesion or tissue of gum

41830

41830 Alveolectomy, including curettage of osteitis or sequestrectomy

ICD-9-CM Diagnostic

170.1 Malignant neoplasm of mandible
522.6 Chronic apical periodontitis
522.8 Radicular cyst of dental pulp
523.40 Chronic periodontitis, unspecified ▽
523.41 Chronic periodontitis, localized
523.42 Chronic periodontitis, generalized
523.5 Periodontosis
525.8 Other specified disorders of the teeth and supporting structures
526.4 Inflammatory conditions of jaw
526.5 Alveolitis of jaw
784.2 Swelling, mass, or lump in head and neck
906.0 Late effect of open wound of head, neck, and trunk

ICD-9-CM Procedural

24.5 Alveoloplasty

41850

41850 Destruction of lesion (except excision), dentoalveolar structures

ICD-9-CM Diagnostic

143.0 Malignant neoplasm of upper gum
143.1 Malignant neoplasm of lower gum
170.1 Malignant neoplasm of mandible
210.4 Benign neoplasm of other and unspecified parts of mouth ▽
213.1 Benign neoplasm of lower jaw bone
228.00 Hemangioma of unspecified site ▽
230.0 Carcinoma in situ of lip, oral cavity, and pharynx
235.1 Neoplasm of uncertain behavior of lip, oral cavity, and pharynx
239.2 Neoplasms of unspecified nature of bone, soft tissue, and skin
520.6 Disturbances in tooth eruption
523.8 Other specified periodontal diseases
526.0 Developmental odontogenic cysts
526.89 Other specified disease of the jaws

ICD-9-CM Procedural

24.39 Other operations on gum

41870

41870 Periodontal mucosal grafting

ICD-9-CM Diagnostic

143.0 Malignant neoplasm of upper gum
143.1 Malignant neoplasm of lower gum
210.4 Benign neoplasm of other and unspecified parts of mouth ▽
230.0 Carcinoma in situ of lip, oral cavity, and pharynx
520.6 Disturbances in tooth eruption
523.10 Chronic gingivitis, plaque induced
523.11 Chronic gingivitis, non-plaque induced
523.20 Gingival recession, unspecified ▽
523.21 Gingival recession, minimal
523.22 Gingival recession, moderate
523.23 Gingival recession, severe
523.24 Gingival recession, localized
523.25 Gingival recession, generalized
523.40 Chronic periodontitis, unspecified ▽
523.41 Chronic periodontitis, localized
523.42 Chronic periodontitis, generalized
523.5 Periodontosis
523.8 Other specified periodontal diseases
528.6 Leukoplakia of oral mucosa, including tongue
V10.02 Personal history of malignant neoplasm of other and unspecified parts of oral cavity and pharynx ▽
V51.8 Other aftercare involving the use of plastic surgery

ICD-9-CM Procedural

24.39 Other operations on gum

41872

41872 Gingivoplasty, each quadrant (specify)

ICD-9-CM Diagnostic

520.6 Disturbances in tooth eruption
523.00 Acute gingivitis, plaque induced
523.01 Acute gingivitis, non-plaque induced
523.10 Chronic gingivitis, plaque induced
523.11 Chronic gingivitis, non-plaque induced
523.20 Gingival recession, unspecified ▽
523.21 Gingival recession, minimal
523.22 Gingival recession, moderate
523.23 Gingival recession, severe
523.24 Gingival recession, localized
523.25 Gingival recession, generalized
523.5 Periodontosis
523.8 Other specified periodontal diseases
873.62 Open wound of gum (alveolar process), without mention of complication
873.72 Open wound of gum (alveolar process), complicated
906.0 Late effect of open wound of head, neck, and trunk
996.60 Infection and inflammatory reaction due to unspecified device, implant, and graft — (Use additional code to identify specified infections) ▽

ICD-9-CM Procedural

24.2 Gingivoplasty

41874

41874 Alveoloplasty, each quadrant (specify)

ICD-9-CM Diagnostic

143.0 Malignant neoplasm of upper gum
143.1 Malignant neoplasm of lower gum
143.9 Malignant neoplasm of gum, unspecified site ▽
170.1 Malignant neoplasm of mandible
198.89 Secondary malignant neoplasm of other specified sites
210.4 Benign neoplasm of other and unspecified parts of mouth ▽
213.1 Benign neoplasm of lower jaw bone
230.0 Carcinoma in situ of lip, oral cavity, and pharynx
235.1 Neoplasm of uncertain behavior of lip, oral cavity, and pharynx
238.0 Neoplasm of uncertain behavior of bone and articular cartilage
522.4 Acute apical periodontitis of pulpal origin
523.20 Gingival recession, unspecified ▽
523.21 Gingival recession, minimal
523.22 Gingival recession, moderate
523.23 Gingival recession, severe
523.24 Gingival recession, localized
523.25 Gingival recession, generalized
523.40 Chronic periodontitis, unspecified ▽
523.41 Chronic periodontitis, localized
523.42 Chronic periodontitis, generalized
524.39 Other anomalies of tooth position
524.72 Alveolar mandibular hyperplasia
524.74 Alveolar mandibular hypoplasia
524.79 Other specified alveolar anomaly
525.0 Exfoliation of teeth due to systemic causes
525.10 Unspecified acquired absence of teeth — (Code first class of edentulism: 525.40-525.44, 525.50-525.54) ▽ ☒
525.11 Loss of teeth due to trauma — (Code first class of edentulism: 525.40-525.44, 525.50-525.54) ☒
525.12 Loss of teeth due to periodontal disease — (Code first class of edentulism: 525.40-525.44, 525.50-525.54) ☒
525.13 Loss of teeth due to caries — (Code first class of edentulism: 525.40-525.44, 525.50-525.54) ☒
525.19 Other loss of teeth — (Code first class of edentulism: 525.40-525.44, 525.50-525.54) ☒
525.42 Complete edentulism, class II — (Use additional code to identify cause of edentulism: 525.10-525.19)
525.43 Complete edentulism, class III — (Use additional code to identify cause of edentulism: 525.10-525.19)
525.44 Complete edentulism, class IV — (Use additional code to identify cause of edentulism: 525.10-525.19)
525.52 Partial edentulism, class II — (Use additional code to identify cause of edentulism: 525.10-525.19)
525.53 Partial edentulism, class III — (Use additional code to identify cause of edentulism: 525.10-525.19)
525.54 Partial edentulism, class IV — (Use additional code to identify cause of edentulism: 525.10-525.19)
526.4 Inflammatory conditions of jaw
784.2 Swelling, mass, or lump in head and neck
873.72 Open wound of gum (alveolar process), complicated
996.67 Infection and inflammatory reaction due to other internal orthopedic device, implant, and graft — (Use additional code to identify specified infections)

ICD-9-CM Procedural

24.5 Alveoloplasty

Palate and Uvula

42000

42000	Drainage of abscess of palate, uvula

ICD-9-CM Diagnostic

526.4	Inflammatory conditions of jaw
528.3	Cellulitis and abscess of oral soft tissues
780.62	Postprocedural fever
958.3	Posttraumatic wound infection not elsewhere classified

ICD-9-CM Procedural

27.1	Incision of palate
27.71	Incision of uvula

42100

42100	Biopsy of palate, uvula

ICD-9-CM Diagnostic

145.2	Malignant neoplasm of hard palate
145.3	Malignant neoplasm of soft palate
145.4	Malignant neoplasm of uvula
145.5	Malignant neoplasm of palate, unspecified
145.9	Malignant neoplasm of mouth, unspecified site
147.3	Malignant neoplasm of anterior wall of nasopharynx
198.89	Secondary malignant neoplasm of other specified sites
210.4	Benign neoplasm of other and unspecified parts of mouth
210.7	Benign neoplasm of nasopharynx
210.8	Benign neoplasm of hypopharynx
213.0	Benign neoplasm of bones of skull and face
229.9	Benign neoplasm of unspecified site
230.0	Carcinoma in situ of lip, oral cavity, and pharynx
235.1	Neoplasm of uncertain behavior of lip, oral cavity, and pharynx
239.0	Neoplasm of unspecified nature of digestive system
528.00	Stomatitis and mucositis, unspecified
528.01	Mucositis (ulcerative) due to antineoplastic therapy — (Use additional E code to identify adverse effects of therapy: E879.2, E930.7, E933.1)
528.02	Mucositis (ulcerative) due to other drugs — (Use additional E code to identify drug)
528.09	Other stomatitis and mucositis (ulcerative)
528.4	Cysts of oral soft tissues
528.6	Leukoplakia of oral mucosa, including tongue
528.79	Other disturbances of oral epithelium, including tongue
528.8	Oral submucosal fibrosis, including of tongue
528.9	Other and unspecified diseases of the oral soft tissues
686.1	Pyogenic granuloma of skin and subcutaneous tissue — (Use additional code to identify any infectious organism: 041.0-041.8)
697.0	Lichen planus
784.2	Swelling, mass, or lump in head and neck
V10.89	Personal history of malignant neoplasm of other site

ICD-9-CM Procedural

27.21	Biopsy of bony palate
27.22	Biopsy of uvula and soft palate

42104-42107

42104	Excision, lesion of palate, uvula; without closure
42106	with simple primary closure
42107	with local flap closure

ICD-9-CM Diagnostic

145.2	Malignant neoplasm of hard palate
145.3	Malignant neoplasm of soft palate
145.4	Malignant neoplasm of uvula
145.5	Malignant neoplasm of palate, unspecified
147.3	Malignant neoplasm of anterior wall of nasopharynx
198.89	Secondary malignant neoplasm of other specified sites
199.1	Other malignant neoplasm of unspecified site
210.4	Benign neoplasm of other and unspecified parts of mouth
210.7	Benign neoplasm of nasopharynx
215.0	Other benign neoplasm of connective and other soft tissue of head, face, and neck
228.1	Lymphangioma, any site
230.0	Carcinoma in situ of lip, oral cavity, and pharynx
235.1	Neoplasm of uncertain behavior of lip, oral cavity, and pharynx
239.0	Neoplasm of unspecified nature of digestive system
478.26	Cyst of pharynx or nasopharynx — (Use additional code to identify infectious organism)
526.1	Fissural cysts of jaw
528.3	Cellulitis and abscess of oral soft tissues
528.4	Cysts of oral soft tissues
528.6	Leukoplakia of oral mucosa, including tongue
528.79	Other disturbances of oral epithelium, including tongue
528.9	Other and unspecified diseases of the oral soft tissues
697.0	Lichen planus
750.26	Other specified congenital anomalies of mouth
784.2	Swelling, mass, or lump in head and neck

ICD-9-CM Procedural

27.31	Local excision or destruction of lesion or tissue of bony palate
27.69	Other plastic repair of palate
27.72	Excision of uvula
27.79	Other operations on uvula

HCPCS Level II Supplies & Services

A4305	Disposable drug delivery system, flow rate of 50 ml or greater per hour

42120

42120	Resection of palate or extensive resection of lesion

ICD-9-CM Diagnostic

145.2	Malignant neoplasm of hard palate
145.3	Malignant neoplasm of soft palate
145.5	Malignant neoplasm of palate, unspecified
145.9	Malignant neoplasm of mouth, unspecified site
147.3	Malignant neoplasm of anterior wall of nasopharynx
198.89	Secondary malignant neoplasm of other specified sites
210.3	Benign neoplasm of floor of mouth
210.4	Benign neoplasm of other and unspecified parts of mouth
210.7	Benign neoplasm of nasopharynx
214.9	Lipoma of unspecified site
215.0	Other benign neoplasm of connective and other soft tissue of head, face, and neck
228.1	Lymphangioma, any site
230.0	Carcinoma in situ of lip, oral cavity, and pharynx
235.1	Neoplasm of uncertain behavior of lip, oral cavity, and pharynx
239.0	Neoplasm of unspecified nature of digestive system
478.26	Cyst of pharynx or nasopharynx — (Use additional code to identify infectious organism)
526.1	Fissural cysts of jaw
528.3	Cellulitis and abscess of oral soft tissues
528.4	Cysts of oral soft tissues
528.6	Leukoplakia of oral mucosa, including tongue
528.9	Other and unspecified diseases of the oral soft tissues

ICD-9-CM Procedural

27.31 Local excision or destruction of lesion or tissue of bony palate
27.32 Wide excision or destruction of lesion or tissue of bony palate

42140

42140 Uvulectomy, excision of uvula

ICD-9-CM Diagnostic

145.4 Malignant neoplasm of uvula
198.89 Secondary malignant neoplasm of other specified sites
210.4 Benign neoplasm of other and unspecified parts of mouth ▽
230.0 Carcinoma in situ of lip, oral cavity, and pharynx
235.1 Neoplasm of uncertain behavior of lip, oral cavity, and pharynx
239.0 Neoplasm of unspecified nature of digestive system
327.20 Organic sleep apnea, unspecified ▽
327.23 Obstructive sleep apnea (adult) (pediatric)
327.29 Other organic sleep apnea
528.9 Other and unspecified diseases of the oral soft tissues ▽
750.26 Other specified congenital anomalies of mouth
780.51 Insomnia with sleep apnea, unspecified ▽
780.53 Hypersomnia with sleep apnea, unspecified ▽
780.57 Unspecified sleep apnea ▽
786.09 Other dyspnea and respiratory abnormalities

ICD-9-CM Procedural

27.72 Excision of uvula

HCPCS Level II Supplies & Services

A4305 Disposable drug delivery system, flow rate of 50 ml or greater per hour

42145

42145 Palatopharyngoplasty (eg, uvulopalatopharyngoplasty, uvulopharyngoplasty)

ICD-9-CM Diagnostic

145.2 Malignant neoplasm of hard palate
145.3 Malignant neoplasm of soft palate
145.4 Malignant neoplasm of uvula
145.5 Malignant neoplasm of palate, unspecified ▽
146.2 Malignant neoplasm of tonsillar pillars (anterior) (posterior)
147.3 Malignant neoplasm of anterior wall of nasopharynx
149.0 Malignant neoplasm of pharynx, unspecified ▽
198.89 Secondary malignant neoplasm of other specified sites
210.4 Benign neoplasm of other and unspecified parts of mouth ▽
210.7 Benign neoplasm of nasopharynx
210.9 Benign neoplasm of pharynx, unspecified ▽
230.0 Carcinoma in situ of lip, oral cavity, and pharynx
235.1 Neoplasm of uncertain behavior of lip, oral cavity, and pharynx
239.0 Neoplasm of unspecified nature of digestive system
327.20 Organic sleep apnea, unspecified ▽
327.23 Obstructive sleep apnea (adult) (pediatric)
327.29 Other organic sleep apnea
496 Chronic airway obstruction, not elsewhere classified — (Note: This code is not to be used with any code from 491-493) ▽
528.9 Other and unspecified diseases of the oral soft tissues ▽
750.26 Other specified congenital anomalies of mouth
780.50 Unspecified sleep disturbance
780.53 Hypersomnia with sleep apnea, unspecified ▽
780.57 Unspecified sleep apnea ▽
786.09 Other dyspnea and respiratory abnormalities
786.9 Other symptoms involving respiratory system and chest

ICD-9-CM Procedural

27.69 Other plastic repair of palate
27.73 Repair of uvula
29.4 Plastic operation on pharynx

42160

42160 Destruction of lesion, palate or uvula (thermal, cryo or chemical)

ICD-9-CM Diagnostic

145.2 Malignant neoplasm of hard palate
145.3 Malignant neoplasm of soft palate
145.4 Malignant neoplasm of uvula
145.5 Malignant neoplasm of palate, unspecified ▽
147.3 Malignant neoplasm of anterior wall of nasopharynx
198.89 Secondary malignant neoplasm of other specified sites
210.4 Benign neoplasm of other and unspecified parts of mouth ▽
210.7 Benign neoplasm of nasopharynx
230.0 Carcinoma in situ of lip, oral cavity, and pharynx
235.1 Neoplasm of uncertain behavior of lip, oral cavity, and pharynx
239.0 Neoplasm of unspecified nature of digestive system
528.9 Other and unspecified diseases of the oral soft tissues ▽

ICD-9-CM Procedural

27.31 Local excision or destruction of lesion or tissue of bony palate
27.79 Other operations on uvula

HCPCS Level II Supplies & Services

A4305 Disposable drug delivery system, flow rate of 50 ml or greater per hour

42180-42182

42180 Repair, laceration of palate; up to 2 cm
42182 over 2 cm or complex

ICD-9-CM Diagnostic

873.65 Open wound of palate, without mention of complication
873.69 Open wound of mouth, other and multiple sites, without mention of complication
873.75 Open wound of palate, complicated
879.8 Open wound(s) (multiple) of unspecified site(s), without mention of complication ▽

ICD-9-CM Procedural

27.61 Suture of laceration of palate
27.69 Other plastic repair of palate

HCPCS Level II Supplies & Services

A4305 Disposable drug delivery system, flow rate of 50 ml or greater per hour

42200

42200 Palatoplasty for cleft palate, soft and/or hard palate only

ICD-9-CM Diagnostic

749.00 Unspecified cleft palate ▽
749.01 Unilateral cleft palate, complete
749.02 Unilateral cleft palate, incomplete
749.03 Bilateral cleft palate, complete
749.04 Bilateral cleft palate, incomplete
749.13 Bilateral cleft lip, complete
749.14 Bilateral cleft lip, incomplete
749.20 Unspecified cleft palate with cleft lip ▽
749.21 Unilateral cleft palate with cleft lip, complete
749.22 Unilateral cleft palate with cleft lip, incomplete
749.23 Bilateral cleft palate with cleft lip, complete
749.24 Bilateral cleft palate with cleft lip, incomplete

749.25 Other combinations of cleft palate with cleft lip

ICD-9-CM Procedural

27.62 Correction of cleft palate

42205-42210

42205 Palatoplasty for cleft palate, with closure of alveolar ridge; soft tissue only
42210 with bone graft to alveolar ridge (includes obtaining graft)

ICD-9-CM Diagnostic

749.00 Unspecified cleft palate ▼
749.01 Unilateral cleft palate, complete
749.02 Unilateral cleft palate, incomplete
749.03 Bilateral cleft palate, complete
749.04 Bilateral cleft palate, incomplete
749.13 Bilateral cleft lip, complete
749.14 Bilateral cleft lip, incomplete
749.20 Unspecified cleft palate with cleft lip ▼
749.21 Unilateral cleft palate with cleft lip, complete
749.22 Unilateral cleft palate with cleft lip, incomplete
749.23 Bilateral cleft palate with cleft lip, complete
749.24 Bilateral cleft palate with cleft lip, incomplete
749.25 Other combinations of cleft palate with cleft lip

ICD-9-CM Procedural

27.62 Correction of cleft palate
76.91 Bone graft to facial bone
77.70 Excision of bone for graft, unspecified site

42215

42215 Palatoplasty for cleft palate; major revision

ICD-9-CM Diagnostic

749.00 Unspecified cleft palate ▼
749.01 Unilateral cleft palate, complete
749.02 Unilateral cleft palate, incomplete
749.03 Bilateral cleft palate, complete
749.04 Bilateral cleft palate, incomplete
749.13 Bilateral cleft lip, complete
749.14 Bilateral cleft lip, incomplete
749.20 Unspecified cleft palate with cleft lip ▼
749.21 Unilateral cleft palate with cleft lip, complete
749.22 Unilateral cleft palate with cleft lip, incomplete
749.23 Bilateral cleft palate with cleft lip, complete
749.24 Bilateral cleft palate with cleft lip, incomplete
749.25 Other combinations of cleft palate with cleft lip
783.3 Feeding difficulties and mismanagement
784.49 Other voice and resonance disorders

ICD-9-CM Procedural

27.63 Revision of cleft palate repair

42220

42220 Palatoplasty for cleft palate; secondary lengthening procedure

ICD-9-CM Diagnostic

749.00 Unspecified cleft palate ▼
749.01 Unilateral cleft palate, complete
749.02 Unilateral cleft palate, incomplete
749.03 Bilateral cleft palate, complete
749.04 Bilateral cleft palate, incomplete
749.13 Bilateral cleft lip, complete
749.14 Bilateral cleft lip, incomplete
749.20 Unspecified cleft palate with cleft lip ▼
749.21 Unilateral cleft palate with cleft lip, complete
749.22 Unilateral cleft palate with cleft lip, incomplete
749.23 Bilateral cleft palate with cleft lip, complete
749.24 Bilateral cleft palate with cleft lip, incomplete
749.25 Other combinations of cleft palate with cleft lip
783.3 Feeding difficulties and mismanagement
784.49 Other voice and resonance disorders

ICD-9-CM Procedural

27.63 Revision of cleft palate repair

42225

42225 Palatoplasty for cleft palate; attachment pharyngeal flap

ICD-9-CM Diagnostic

749.00 Unspecified cleft palate ▼
749.01 Unilateral cleft palate, complete
749.02 Unilateral cleft palate, incomplete
749.03 Bilateral cleft palate, complete
749.04 Bilateral cleft palate, incomplete
749.13 Bilateral cleft lip, complete
749.14 Bilateral cleft lip, incomplete
749.20 Unspecified cleft palate with cleft lip ▼
749.21 Unilateral cleft palate with cleft lip, complete
749.22 Unilateral cleft palate with cleft lip, incomplete
749.23 Bilateral cleft palate with cleft lip, complete
749.24 Bilateral cleft palate with cleft lip, incomplete
749.25 Other combinations of cleft palate with cleft lip
783.3 Feeding difficulties and mismanagement
784.49 Other voice and resonance disorders

ICD-9-CM Procedural

27.63 Revision of cleft palate repair

42226

42226 Lengthening of palate, and pharyngeal flap

ICD-9-CM Diagnostic

524.10 Unspecified anomaly of relationship of jaw to cranial base ▼
524.29 Other anomalies of dental arch relationship
524.50 Dentofacial functional abnormality, unspecified ▼
524.59 Other dentofacial functional abnormalities
524.70 Unspecified alveolar anomaly ▼
524.73 Alveolar maxillary hypoplasia
524.79 Other specified alveolar anomaly
528.9 Other and unspecified diseases of the oral soft tissues ▼
750.29 Other specified congenital anomaly of pharynx
754.0 Congenital musculoskeletal deformities of skull, face, and jaw
783.3 Feeding difficulties and mismanagement

ICD-9-CM Procedural

27.62 Correction of cleft palate
27.69 Other plastic repair of palate

42227

42227 Lengthening of palate, with island flap

ICD-9-CM Diagnostic

524.10 Unspecified anomaly of relationship of jaw to cranial base ▼
524.29 Other anomalies of dental arch relationship

524.50 Dentofacial functional abnormality, unspecified ▽
524.59 Other dentofacial functional abnormalities
524.70 Unspecified alveolar anomaly ▽
524.71 Alveolar maxillary hyperplasia
524.73 Alveolar maxillary hypoplasia
524.79 Other specified alveolar anomaly
528.9 Other and unspecified diseases of the oral soft tissues ▽
750.29 Other specified congenital anomaly of pharynx
754.0 Congenital musculoskeletal deformities of skull, face, and jaw
784.49 Other voice and resonance disorders

ICD-9-CM Procedural
27.69 Other plastic repair of palate

42235
42235 Repair of anterior palate, including vomer flap

ICD-9-CM Diagnostic
145.2 Malignant neoplasm of hard palate
145.5 Malignant neoplasm of palate, unspecified ▽
147.3 Malignant neoplasm of anterior wall of nasopharynx
198.89 Secondary malignant neoplasm of other specified sites
230.0 Carcinoma in situ of lip, oral cavity, and pharynx
478.29 Other disease of pharynx or nasopharynx — (Use additional code to identify infectious organism)
526.89 Other specified disease of the jaws
749.00 Unspecified cleft palate ▽
749.22 Unilateral cleft palate with cleft lip, incomplete
749.23 Bilateral cleft palate with cleft lip, complete
783.3 Feeding difficulties and mismanagement
802.5 Malar and maxillary bones, open fracture
873.65 Open wound of palate, without mention of complication
873.75 Open wound of palate, complicated

ICD-9-CM Procedural
27.69 Other plastic repair of palate

42260
42260 Repair of nasolabial fistula

ICD-9-CM Diagnostic
473.0 Chronic maxillary sinusitis — (Use additional code to identify infectious organism)
473.2 Chronic ethmoidal sinusitis — (Use additional code to identify infectious organism)
473.3 Chronic sphenoidal sinusitis — (Use additional code to identify infectious organism)
473.8 Other chronic sinusitis — (Use additional code to identify infectious organism)
473.9 Unspecified sinusitis (chronic) — (Use additional code to identify infectious organism) ▽
478.19 Other diseases of nasal cavity and sinuses — (Use additional code to identify infectious organism)
519.8 Other diseases of respiratory system, not elsewhere classified — (Use additional code to identify infectious organism)
519.9 Unspecified disease of respiratory system — (Use additional code to identify infectious organism) ▽
528.3 Cellulitis and abscess of oral soft tissues
528.5 Diseases of lips
748.1 Other congenital anomaly of nose
750.25 Congenital fistula of lip
873.51 Open wound of cheek, complicated
873.53 Open wound of lip, complicated

ICD-9-CM Procedural
21.82 Closure of nasal fistula

42280-42281
42280 Maxillary impression for palatal prosthesis
42281 Insertion of pin-retained palatal prosthesis

ICD-9-CM Diagnostic
145.2 Malignant neoplasm of hard palate
145.5 Malignant neoplasm of palate, unspecified ▽
198.89 Secondary malignant neoplasm of other specified sites
230.0 Carcinoma in situ of lip, oral cavity, and pharynx
526.89 Other specified disease of the jaws
749.00 Unspecified cleft palate ▽
749.01 Unilateral cleft palate, complete
749.02 Unilateral cleft palate, incomplete
749.03 Bilateral cleft palate, complete
749.04 Bilateral cleft palate, incomplete
749.13 Bilateral cleft lip, complete
749.14 Bilateral cleft lip, incomplete
749.20 Unspecified cleft palate with cleft lip ▽
749.21 Unilateral cleft palate with cleft lip, complete
749.22 Unilateral cleft palate with cleft lip, incomplete
749.23 Bilateral cleft palate with cleft lip, complete
749.24 Bilateral cleft palate with cleft lip, incomplete
749.25 Other combinations of cleft palate with cleft lip
750.9 Unspecified congenital anomaly of upper alimentary tract ▽
873.65 Open wound of palate, without mention of complication
873.75 Open wound of palate, complicated
906.0 Late effect of open wound of head, neck, and trunk

ICD-9-CM Procedural
27.64 Insertion of palatal implant
27.69 Other plastic repair of palate
99.99 Other miscellaneous procedures

Salivary Gland and Ducts

42300-42305
42300 Drainage of abscess; parotid, simple
42305 parotid, complicated

ICD-9-CM Diagnostic
527.2 Sialoadenitis
527.3 Abscess of salivary gland
528.3 Cellulitis and abscess of oral soft tissues
682.0 Cellulitis and abscess of face — (Use additional code to identify organism, such as 041.1, etc.)
958.3 Posttraumatic wound infection not elsewhere classified

ICD-9-CM Procedural
26.0 Incision of salivary gland or duct

42310-42320
42310 Drainage of abscess; submaxillary or sublingual, intraoral
42320 submaxillary, external

ICD-9-CM Diagnostic
527.2 Sialoadenitis
527.3 Abscess of salivary gland
527.4 Fistula of salivary gland
527.6 Mucocele of salivary gland
528.3 Cellulitis and abscess of oral soft tissues
682.0 Cellulitis and abscess of face — (Use additional code to identify organism, such as 041.1, etc.)

958.3 Posttraumatic wound infection not elsewhere classified

ICD-9-CM Procedural

26.0 Incision of salivary gland or duct

HCPCS Level II Supplies & Services

A4305 Disposable drug delivery system, flow rate of 50 ml or greater per hour

42330-42340

42330 Sialolithotomy; submandibular (submaxillary), sublingual or parotid, uncomplicated, intraoral
42335 submandibular (submaxillary), complicated, intraoral
42340 parotid, extraoral or complicated intraoral

ICD-9-CM Diagnostic

527.2 Sialoadenitis
527.3 Abscess of salivary gland
527.5 Sialolithiasis
784.2 Swelling, mass, or lump in head and neck
793.4 Nonspecific (abnormal) findings on radiological and other examination of gastrointestinal tract

ICD-9-CM Procedural

26.0 Incision of salivary gland or duct

HCPCS Level II Supplies & Services

A4305 Disposable drug delivery system, flow rate of 50 ml or greater per hour

42400-42405

42400 Biopsy of salivary gland; needle
42405 incisional

ICD-9-CM Diagnostic

142.0 Malignant neoplasm of parotid gland
142.1 Malignant neoplasm of submandibular gland
142.2 Malignant neoplasm of sublingual gland
142.8 Malignant neoplasm of other major salivary glands
142.9 Malignant neoplasm of salivary gland, unspecified
198.89 Secondary malignant neoplasm of other specified sites
210.2 Benign neoplasm of major salivary glands
230.0 Carcinoma in situ of lip, oral cavity, and pharynx
235.0 Neoplasm of uncertain behavior of major salivary glands
238.9 Neoplasm of uncertain behavior, site unspecified
239.0 Neoplasm of unspecified nature of digestive system
239.89 Neoplasms of unspecified nature, other specified sites
359.6 Symptomatic inflammatory myopathy in diseases classified elsewhere — (Code first underlying disease: 135, 140.0-208.9, 277.30-277.39, 446.0, 710.0, 710.1, 710.2, 714.0)
517.8 Lung involvement in other diseases classified elsewhere — (Use additional code to identify infectious organism. Code first underlying disease: 135, 277.30-277.39, 710.0, 710.2, 710.4)
527.1 Hypertrophy of salivary gland
527.2 Sialoadenitis
527.3 Abscess of salivary gland
527.5 Sialolithiasis
527.8 Other specified diseases of the salivary glands
710.2 Sicca syndrome
784.2 Swelling, mass, or lump in head and neck
V41.5 Problems with smell and taste

ICD-9-CM Procedural

26.11 Closed (needle) biopsy of salivary gland or duct
26.12 Open biopsy of salivary gland or duct

HCPCS Level II Supplies & Services

A4305 Disposable drug delivery system, flow rate of 50 ml or greater per hour

42408

42408 Excision of sublingual salivary cyst (ranula)

ICD-9-CM Diagnostic

527.6 Mucocele of salivary gland
750.26 Other specified congenital anomalies of mouth

ICD-9-CM Procedural

26.29 Other excision of salivary gland lesion

HCPCS Level II Supplies & Services

A4305 Disposable drug delivery system, flow rate of 50 ml or greater per hour

42409

42409 Marsupialization of sublingual salivary cyst (ranula)

ICD-9-CM Diagnostic

527.6 Mucocele of salivary gland
750.26 Other specified congenital anomalies of mouth

ICD-9-CM Procedural

26.21 Marsupialization of salivary gland cyst

HCPCS Level II Supplies & Services

A4305 Disposable drug delivery system, flow rate of 50 ml or greater per hour

42410-42415

42410 Excision of parotid tumor or parotid gland; lateral lobe, without nerve dissection
42415 lateral lobe, with dissection and preservation of facial nerve

ICD-9-CM Diagnostic

142.0 Malignant neoplasm of parotid gland
142.9 Malignant neoplasm of salivary gland, unspecified
198.89 Secondary malignant neoplasm of other specified sites
210.2 Benign neoplasm of major salivary glands
230.0 Carcinoma in situ of lip, oral cavity, and pharynx
235.0 Neoplasm of uncertain behavior of major salivary glands
239.0 Neoplasm of unspecified nature of digestive system
527.2 Sialoadenitis
527.6 Mucocele of salivary gland
784.2 Swelling, mass, or lump in head and neck
785.6 Enlargement of lymph nodes

ICD-9-CM Procedural

26.29 Other excision of salivary gland lesion
26.31 Partial sialoadenectomy

42420-42426

42420 Excision of parotid tumor or parotid gland; total, with dissection and preservation of facial nerve
42425 total, en bloc removal with sacrifice of facial nerve
42426 total, with unilateral radical neck dissection

ICD-9-CM Diagnostic

142.0 Malignant neoplasm of parotid gland
142.9 Malignant neoplasm of salivary gland, unspecified
196.0 Secondary and unspecified malignant neoplasm of lymph nodes of head, face, and neck
198.89 Secondary malignant neoplasm of other specified sites
210.2 Benign neoplasm of major salivary glands
230.0 Carcinoma in situ of lip, oral cavity, and pharynx

235.0 Neoplasm of uncertain behavior of major salivary glands
239.0 Neoplasm of unspecified nature of digestive system
527.2 Sialoadenitis
527.6 Mucocele of salivary gland
784.2 Swelling, mass, or lump in head and neck
785.6 Enlargement of lymph nodes

ICD-9-CM Procedural

04.07 Other excision or avulsion of cranial and peripheral nerves
26.32 Complete sialoadenectomy
40.41 Radical neck dissection, unilateral

42440

42440 Excision of submandibular (submaxillary) gland

ICD-9-CM Diagnostic

142.1 Malignant neoplasm of submandibular gland
198.89 Secondary malignant neoplasm of other specified sites
210.2 Benign neoplasm of major salivary glands
230.0 Carcinoma in situ of lip, oral cavity, and pharynx
235.0 Neoplasm of uncertain behavior of major salivary glands
235.1 Neoplasm of uncertain behavior of lip, oral cavity, and pharynx
239.0 Neoplasm of unspecified nature of digestive system
527.1 Hypertrophy of salivary gland
527.2 Sialoadenitis
527.5 Sialolithiasis
527.6 Mucocele of salivary gland
527.8 Other specified diseases of the salivary glands
784.2 Swelling, mass, or lump in head and neck

ICD-9-CM Procedural

26.30 Sialoadenectomy, not otherwise specified
26.31 Partial sialoadenectomy
26.32 Complete sialoadenectomy

42450

42450 Excision of sublingual gland

ICD-9-CM Diagnostic

142.2 Malignant neoplasm of sublingual gland
144.9 Malignant neoplasm of floor of mouth, part unspecified ▽
198.89 Secondary malignant neoplasm of other specified sites
210.2 Benign neoplasm of major salivary glands
210.3 Benign neoplasm of floor of mouth
230.0 Carcinoma in situ of lip, oral cavity, and pharynx
235.0 Neoplasm of uncertain behavior of major salivary glands
235.1 Neoplasm of uncertain behavior of lip, oral cavity, and pharynx
239.0 Neoplasm of unspecified nature of digestive system
527.1 Hypertrophy of salivary gland
527.2 Sialoadenitis
527.5 Sialolithiasis
527.6 Mucocele of salivary gland
527.8 Other specified diseases of the salivary glands
784.2 Swelling, mass, or lump in head and neck
787.20 Dysphagia, unspecified ▽
787.21 Dysphagia, oral phase
787.22 Dysphagia, oropharyngeal phase
787.23 Dysphagia, pharyngeal phase
787.24 Dysphagia, pharyngoesophageal phase
787.29 Other dysphagia

ICD-9-CM Procedural

26.30 Sialoadenectomy, not otherwise specified
26.31 Partial sialoadenectomy
26.32 Complete sialoadenectomy

42500-42505

42500 Plastic repair of salivary duct, sialodochoplasty; primary or simple
42505 secondary or complicated

ICD-9-CM Diagnostic

527.2 Sialoadenitis
527.4 Fistula of salivary gland
527.5 Sialolithiasis
527.6 Mucocele of salivary gland
527.7 Disturbance of salivary secretion
527.8 Other specified diseases of the salivary glands
873.51 Open wound of cheek, complicated
873.54 Open wound of jaw, complicated
873.69 Open wound of mouth, other and multiple sites, without mention of complication
873.79 Open wound of mouth, other and multiple sites, complicated
906.0 Late effect of open wound of head, neck, and trunk
998.2 Accidental puncture or laceration during procedure

ICD-9-CM Procedural

26.49 Other repair and plastic operations on salivary gland or duct

HCPCS Level II Supplies & Services

A4305 Disposable drug delivery system, flow rate of 50 ml or greater per hour

42507-42510

42507 Parotid duct diversion, bilateral (Wilke type procedure);
42508 with excision of 1 submandibular gland
42509 with excision of both submandibular glands
42510 with ligation of both submandibular (Wharton's) ducts

ICD-9-CM Diagnostic

527.5 Sialolithiasis
527.7 Disturbance of salivary secretion
527.8 Other specified diseases of the salivary glands
873.51 Open wound of cheek, complicated
873.59 Open wound of face, other and multiple sites, complicated
873.61 Open wound of buccal mucosa, without mention of complication
873.69 Open wound of mouth, other and multiple sites, without mention of complication
873.71 Open wound of buccal mucosa, complicated
873.79 Open wound of mouth, other and multiple sites, complicated
906.0 Late effect of open wound of head, neck, and trunk

ICD-9-CM Procedural

26.31 Partial sialoadenectomy
26.32 Complete sialoadenectomy
26.49 Other repair and plastic operations on salivary gland or duct
26.99 Other operations on salivary gland or duct

42550

42550 Injection procedure for sialography

ICD-9-CM Diagnostic

142.0 Malignant neoplasm of parotid gland
142.1 Malignant neoplasm of submandibular gland
142.2 Malignant neoplasm of sublingual gland
142.8 Malignant neoplasm of other major salivary glands
142.9 Malignant neoplasm of salivary gland, unspecified ▽

144.9 Malignant neoplasm of floor of mouth, part unspecified ▽
210.2 Benign neoplasm of major salivary glands
210.3 Benign neoplasm of floor of mouth
210.4 Benign neoplasm of other and unspecified parts of mouth ▽
230.0 Carcinoma in situ of lip, oral cavity, and pharynx
235.0 Neoplasm of uncertain behavior of major salivary glands
235.1 Neoplasm of uncertain behavior of lip, oral cavity, and pharynx
239.0 Neoplasm of unspecified nature of digestive system
527.1 Hypertrophy of salivary gland
527.2 Sialoadenitis
527.5 Sialolithiasis
527.6 Mucocele of salivary gland
527.7 Disturbance of salivary secretion
527.8 Other specified diseases of the salivary glands
527.9 Unspecified disease of the salivary glands ▽
784.2 Swelling, mass, or lump in head and neck
787.20 Dysphagia, unspecified ▽
787.21 Dysphagia, oral phase
787.22 Dysphagia, oropharyngeal phase
787.23 Dysphagia, pharyngeal phase
787.24 Dysphagia, pharyngoesophageal phase
787.29 Other dysphagia
V72.5 Radiological examination, not elsewhere classified — (Use additional code(s) to identify any special screening examination(s) performed: V73.0-V82.9)

ICD-9-CM Procedural

87.09 Other soft tissue x-ray of face, head, and neck

HCPCS Level II Supplies & Services

A4305 Disposable drug delivery system, flow rate of 50 ml or greater per hour

42600

42600 Closure salivary fistula

ICD-9-CM Diagnostic

527.4 Fistula of salivary gland
750.24 Congenital fistula of salivary gland
998.6 Persistent postoperative fistula, not elsewhere classified

ICD-9-CM Procedural

26.42 Closure of salivary fistula

HCPCS Level II Supplies & Services

A4305 Disposable drug delivery system, flow rate of 50 ml or greater per hour

42650-42660

42650 Dilation salivary duct
42660 Dilation and catheterization of salivary duct, with or without injection

ICD-9-CM Diagnostic

210.2 Benign neoplasm of major salivary glands
235.0 Neoplasm of uncertain behavior of major salivary glands
527.2 Sialoadenitis
527.5 Sialolithiasis
527.7 Disturbance of salivary secretion
527.8 Other specified diseases of the salivary glands
784.2 Swelling, mass, or lump in head and neck

ICD-9-CM Procedural

26.91 Probing of salivary duct

HCPCS Level II Supplies & Services

A4305 Disposable drug delivery system, flow rate of 50 ml or greater per hour

42665

42665 Ligation salivary duct, intraoral

ICD-9-CM Diagnostic

527.2 Sialoadenitis
527.4 Fistula of salivary gland
527.5 Sialolithiasis
527.7 Disturbance of salivary secretion
527.8 Other specified diseases of the salivary glands

ICD-9-CM Procedural

26.99 Other operations on salivary gland or duct

HCPCS Level II Supplies & Services

A4305 Disposable drug delivery system, flow rate of 50 ml or greater per hour

Pharynx, Adenoids, and Tonsils

42700

42700 Incision and drainage abscess; peritonsillar

ICD-9-CM Diagnostic

034.0 Streptococcal sore throat
462 Acute pharyngitis — (Use additional code to identify infectious organism)
463 Acute tonsillitis — (Use additional code to identify infectious organism)
474.00 Chronic tonsillitis — (Use additional code to identify infectious organism)
474.01 Chronic adenoiditis — (Use additional code to identify infectious organism)
474.02 Chronic tonsillitis and adenoiditis — (Use additional code to identify infectious organism)
474.10 Hypertrophy of tonsil with adenoids — (Use additional code to identify infectious organism)
474.11 Hypertrophy of tonsils alone — (Use additional code to identify infectious organism)
474.12 Hypertrophy of adenoids alone — (Use additional code to identify infectious organism)
474.8 Other chronic disease of tonsils and adenoids — (Use additional code to identify infectious organism)
475 Peritonsillar abscess — (Use additional code to identify infectious organism)
478.24 Retropharyngeal abscess — (Use additional code to identify infectious organism)
478.29 Other disease of pharynx or nasopharynx — (Use additional code to identify infectious organism)
784.2 Swelling, mass, or lump in head and neck

ICD-9-CM Procedural

28.0 Incision and drainage of tonsil and peritonsillar structures

HCPCS Level II Supplies & Services

A4305 Disposable drug delivery system, flow rate of 50 ml or greater per hour

42720-42725

42720 Incision and drainage abscess; retropharyngeal or parapharyngeal, intraoral approach
42725 retropharyngeal or parapharyngeal, external approach

ICD-9-CM Diagnostic

475 Peritonsillar abscess — (Use additional code to identify infectious organism)
478.21 Cellulitis of pharynx or nasopharynx — (Use additional code to identify infectious organism)
478.22 Parapharyngeal abscess — (Use additional code to identify infectious organism)
478.24 Retropharyngeal abscess — (Use additional code to identify infectious organism)
478.29 Other disease of pharynx or nasopharynx — (Use additional code to identify infectious organism)

ICD-9-CM Procedural

28.0 Incision and drainage of tonsil and peritonsillar structures

HCPCS Level II Supplies & Services

A4305 Disposable drug delivery system, flow rate of 50 ml or greater per hour

42800

42800 Biopsy; oropharynx

ICD-9-CM Diagnostic

146.0 Malignant neoplasm of tonsil
146.1 Malignant neoplasm of tonsillar fossa
146.2 Malignant neoplasm of tonsillar pillars (anterior) (posterior)
146.3 Malignant neoplasm of vallecula
146.4 Malignant neoplasm of anterior aspect of epiglottis
146.6 Malignant neoplasm of lateral wall of oropharynx
146.7 Malignant neoplasm of posterior wall of oropharynx
146.8 Malignant neoplasm of other specified sites of oropharynx
146.9 Malignant neoplasm of oropharynx, unspecified site
148.0 Malignant neoplasm of postcricoid region of hypopharynx
148.1 Malignant neoplasm of pyriform sinus
148.2 Malignant neoplasm of aryepiglottic fold, hypopharyngeal aspect
148.3 Malignant neoplasm of posterior hypopharyngeal wall
148.8 Malignant neoplasm of other specified sites of hypopharynx
148.9 Malignant neoplasm of hypopharynx, unspecified site
149.0 Malignant neoplasm of pharynx, unspecified
149.8 Malignant neoplasm of other sites within the lip and oral cavity
149.9 Malignant neoplasm of ill-defined sites of lip and oral cavity
176.2 Kaposi's sarcoma of palate
176.8 Kaposi's sarcoma of other specified sites
196.0 Secondary and unspecified malignant neoplasm of lymph nodes of head, face, and neck
198.89 Secondary malignant neoplasm of other specified sites
202.81 Other malignant lymphomas of lymph nodes of head, face, and neck
210.5 Benign neoplasm of tonsil
210.6 Benign neoplasm of other parts of oropharynx
210.8 Benign neoplasm of hypopharynx
210.9 Benign neoplasm of pharynx, unspecified
230.0 Carcinoma in situ of lip, oral cavity, and pharynx
235.1 Neoplasm of uncertain behavior of lip, oral cavity, and pharynx
239.0 Neoplasm of unspecified nature of digestive system
446.4 Wegener's granulomatosis
478.21 Cellulitis of pharynx or nasopharynx — (Use additional code to identify infectious organism)
478.22 Parapharyngeal abscess — (Use additional code to identify infectious organism)
478.24 Retropharyngeal abscess — (Use additional code to identify infectious organism)
478.26 Cyst of pharynx or nasopharynx — (Use additional code to identify infectious organism)
478.29 Other disease of pharynx or nasopharynx — (Use additional code to identify infectious organism)
528.2 Oral aphthae
528.6 Leukoplakia of oral mucosa, including tongue
528.9 Other and unspecified diseases of the oral soft tissues

ICD-9-CM Procedural

29.12 Pharyngeal biopsy

HCPCS Level II Supplies & Services

A4305 Disposable drug delivery system, flow rate of 50 ml or greater per hour

42804-42806

42804 Biopsy; nasopharynx, visible lesion, simple
42806 nasopharynx, survey for unknown primary lesion

ICD-9-CM Diagnostic

147.0 Malignant neoplasm of superior wall of nasopharynx
147.1 Malignant neoplasm of posterior wall of nasopharynx
147.2 Malignant neoplasm of lateral wall of nasopharynx
147.3 Malignant neoplasm of anterior wall of nasopharynx
147.8 Malignant neoplasm of other specified sites of nasopharynx
147.9 Malignant neoplasm of nasopharynx, unspecified site
149.0 Malignant neoplasm of pharynx, unspecified
196.0 Secondary and unspecified malignant neoplasm of lymph nodes of head, face, and neck
198.89 Secondary malignant neoplasm of other specified sites
202.81 Other malignant lymphomas of lymph nodes of head, face, and neck
210.5 Benign neoplasm of tonsil
210.7 Benign neoplasm of nasopharynx
210.9 Benign neoplasm of pharynx, unspecified
229.9 Benign neoplasm of unspecified site
230.0 Carcinoma in situ of lip, oral cavity, and pharynx
235.1 Neoplasm of uncertain behavior of lip, oral cavity, and pharynx
239.0 Neoplasm of unspecified nature of digestive system
475 Peritonsillar abscess — (Use additional code to identify infectious organism)
478.0 Hypertrophy of nasal turbinates
478.21 Cellulitis of pharynx or nasopharynx — (Use additional code to identify infectious organism)
478.26 Cyst of pharynx or nasopharynx — (Use additional code to identify infectious organism)
478.29 Other disease of pharynx or nasopharynx — (Use additional code to identify infectious organism)

ICD-9-CM Procedural

29.12 Pharyngeal biopsy

HCPCS Level II Supplies & Services

A4305 Disposable drug delivery system, flow rate of 50 ml or greater per hour

42808

42808 Excision or destruction of lesion of pharynx, any method

ICD-9-CM Diagnostic

146.0 Malignant neoplasm of tonsil
147.0 Malignant neoplasm of superior wall of nasopharynx
147.1 Malignant neoplasm of posterior wall of nasopharynx
147.2 Malignant neoplasm of lateral wall of nasopharynx
147.3 Malignant neoplasm of anterior wall of nasopharynx
147.9 Malignant neoplasm of nasopharynx, unspecified site
148.0 Malignant neoplasm of postcricoid region of hypopharynx
148.1 Malignant neoplasm of pyriform sinus
148.2 Malignant neoplasm of aryepiglottic fold, hypopharyngeal aspect
148.3 Malignant neoplasm of posterior hypopharyngeal wall
148.9 Malignant neoplasm of hypopharynx, unspecified site
149.0 Malignant neoplasm of pharynx, unspecified
198.89 Secondary malignant neoplasm of other specified sites
210.5 Benign neoplasm of tonsil
210.6 Benign neoplasm of other parts of oropharynx
210.7 Benign neoplasm of nasopharynx
210.8 Benign neoplasm of hypopharynx
210.9 Benign neoplasm of pharynx, unspecified
230.0 Carcinoma in situ of lip, oral cavity, and pharynx
235.1 Neoplasm of uncertain behavior of lip, oral cavity, and pharynx
239.0 Neoplasm of unspecified nature of digestive system
478.26 Cyst of pharynx or nasopharynx — (Use additional code to identify infectious organism)
478.29 Other disease of pharynx or nasopharynx — (Use additional code to identify infectious organism)

ICD-9-CM Procedural

29.39 Other excision or destruction of lesion or tissue of pharynx

HCPCS Level II Supplies & Services

A4305 Disposable drug delivery system, flow rate of 50 ml or greater per hour

42809

42809 Removal of foreign body from pharynx

ICD-9-CM Diagnostic

784.1 Throat pain
873.70 Open wound of mouth, unspecified site, complicated ▽
873.79 Open wound of mouth, other and multiple sites, complicated
933.0 Foreign body in pharynx
998.4 Foreign body accidentally left during procedure, not elsewhere classified
998.7 Acute reaction to foreign substance accidentally left during procedure, not elsewhere classified

ICD-9-CM Procedural

29.0 Pharyngotomy
98.13 Removal of intraluminal foreign body from pharynx without incision

HCPCS Level II Supplies & Services

A4305 Disposable drug delivery system, flow rate of 50 ml or greater per hour

42810-42815

42810 Excision branchial cleft cyst or vestige, confined to skin and subcutaneous tissues
42815 Excision branchial cleft cyst, vestige, or fistula, extending beneath subcutaneous tissues and/or into pharynx

ICD-9-CM Diagnostic

744.41 Congenital branchial cleft sinus or fistula
744.42 Congenital branchial cleft cyst
744.43 Congenital cervical auricle
744.46 Congenital preauricular sinus or fistula
744.47 Congenital preauricular cyst
744.49 Other congenital branchial cleft cyst or fistula; preauricular sinus
744.89 Other specified congenital anomaly of face and neck

ICD-9-CM Procedural

29.2 Excision of branchial cleft cyst or vestige
29.52 Closure of branchial cleft fistula

HCPCS Level II Supplies & Services

A4305 Disposable drug delivery system, flow rate of 50 ml or greater per hour

42820-42821

42820 Tonsillectomy and adenoidectomy; younger than age 12
42821 age 12 or over

ICD-9-CM Diagnostic

034.0 Streptococcal sore throat
146.0 Malignant neoplasm of tonsil
210.5 Benign neoplasm of tonsil
327.20 Organic sleep apnea, unspecified ▽
327.23 Obstructive sleep apnea (adult) (pediatric)
327.29 Other organic sleep apnea
463 Acute tonsillitis — (Use additional code to identify infectious organism)
472.0 Chronic rhinitis — (Use additional code to identify infectious organism)
472.1 Chronic pharyngitis — (Use additional code to identify infectious organism)
473.0 Chronic maxillary sinusitis — (Use additional code to identify infectious organism)
473.1 Chronic frontal sinusitis — (Use additional code to identify infectious organism)
473.2 Chronic ethmoidal sinusitis — (Use additional code to identify infectious organism)
473.8 Other chronic sinusitis — (Use additional code to identify infectious organism)
474.00 Chronic tonsillitis — (Use additional code to identify infectious organism)
474.01 Chronic adenoiditis — (Use additional code to identify infectious organism)
474.02 Chronic tonsillitis and adenoiditis — (Use additional code to identify infectious organism)
474.10 Hypertrophy of tonsil with adenoids — (Use additional code to identify infectious organism)
474.11 Hypertrophy of tonsils alone — (Use additional code to identify infectious organism)
474.12 Hypertrophy of adenoids alone — (Use additional code to identify infectious organism)
474.2 Adenoid vegetations — (Use additional code to identify infectious organism)
474.8 Other chronic disease of tonsils and adenoids — (Use additional code to identify infectious organism)
474.9 Unspecified chronic disease of tonsils and adenoids — (Use additional code to identify infectious organism) ▽
475 Peritonsillar abscess — (Use additional code to identify infectious organism)
478.19 Other diseases of nasal cavity and sinuses — (Use additional code to identify infectious organism)
519.8 Other diseases of respiratory system, not elsewhere classified — (Use additional code to identify infectious organism)
780.51 Insomnia with sleep apnea, unspecified ▽
780.53 Hypersomnia with sleep apnea, unspecified ▽
780.57 Unspecified sleep apnea ▽
780.59 Other sleep disturbances
786.09 Other dyspnea and respiratory abnormalities

ICD-9-CM Procedural

28.3 Tonsillectomy with adenoidectomy

42825-42826

42825 Tonsillectomy, primary or secondary; younger than age 12
42826 age 12 or over

ICD-9-CM Diagnostic

034.0 Streptococcal sore throat
146.0 Malignant neoplasm of tonsil
210.5 Benign neoplasm of tonsil
463 Acute tonsillitis — (Use additional code to identify infectious organism)
472.1 Chronic pharyngitis — (Use additional code to identify infectious organism)
473.0 Chronic maxillary sinusitis — (Use additional code to identify infectious organism)
473.1 Chronic frontal sinusitis — (Use additional code to identify infectious organism)
473.2 Chronic ethmoidal sinusitis — (Use additional code to identify infectious organism)
473.8 Other chronic sinusitis — (Use additional code to identify infectious organism)
473.9 Unspecified sinusitis (chronic) — (Use additional code to identify infectious organism) ▽
474.00 Chronic tonsillitis — (Use additional code to identify infectious organism)
474.11 Hypertrophy of tonsils alone — (Use additional code to identify infectious organism)
474.8 Other chronic disease of tonsils and adenoids — (Use additional code to identify infectious organism)
475 Peritonsillar abscess — (Use additional code to identify infectious organism)

ICD-9-CM Procedural

28.2 Tonsillectomy without adenoidectomy

42830-42836

42830 Adenoidectomy, primary; younger than age 12
42831 age 12 or over
42835 Adenoidectomy, secondary; younger than age 12
42836 age 12 or over

ICD-9-CM Diagnostic

147.1 Malignant neoplasm of posterior wall of nasopharynx
198.89 Secondary malignant neoplasm of other specified sites
210.7 Benign neoplasm of nasopharynx

230.0 Carcinoma in situ of lip, oral cavity, and pharynx
235.1 Neoplasm of uncertain behavior of lip, oral cavity, and pharynx
239.0 Neoplasm of unspecified nature of digestive system
381.10 Simple or unspecified chronic serous otitis media ▽
382.3 Unspecified chronic suppurative otitis media ▽
382.9 Unspecified otitis media ▽
472.2 Chronic nasopharyngitis — (Use additional code to identify infectious organism)
473.0 Chronic maxillary sinusitis — (Use additional code to identify infectious organism)
473.1 Chronic frontal sinusitis — (Use additional code to identify infectious organism)
473.2 Chronic ethmoidal sinusitis — (Use additional code to identify infectious organism)
473.8 Other chronic sinusitis — (Use additional code to identify infectious organism)
473.9 Unspecified sinusitis (chronic) — (Use additional code to identify infectious organism) ▽
474.01 Chronic adenoiditis — (Use additional code to identify infectious organism)
474.12 Hypertrophy of adenoids alone — (Use additional code to identify infectious organism)
474.2 Adenoid vegetations — (Use additional code to identify infectious organism)
474.8 Other chronic disease of tonsils and adenoids — (Use additional code to identify infectious organism)
474.9 Unspecified chronic disease of tonsils and adenoids — (Use additional code to identify infectious organism) ▽
478.19 Other diseases of nasal cavity and sinuses — (Use additional code to identify infectious organism)
478.29 Other disease of pharynx or nasopharynx — (Use additional code to identify infectious organism)
519.8 Other diseases of respiratory system, not elsewhere classified — (Use additional code to identify infectious organism)
786.09 Other dyspnea and respiratory abnormalities

ICD-9-CM Procedural

28.6 Adenoidectomy without tonsillectomy

42842-42845

42842 Radical resection of tonsil, tonsillar pillars, and/or retromolar trigone; without closure
42844 closure with local flap (eg, tongue, buccal)
42845 closure with other flap

ICD-9-CM Diagnostic

141.6 Malignant neoplasm of lingual tonsil
145.6 Malignant neoplasm of retromolar area
146.0 Malignant neoplasm of tonsil
146.1 Malignant neoplasm of tonsillar fossa
146.2 Malignant neoplasm of tonsillar pillars (anterior) (posterior)
146.3 Malignant neoplasm of vallecula
146.4 Malignant neoplasm of anterior aspect of epiglottis
146.5 Malignant neoplasm of junctional region of oropharynx
146.6 Malignant neoplasm of lateral wall of oropharynx
147.1 Malignant neoplasm of posterior wall of nasopharynx
198.89 Secondary malignant neoplasm of other specified sites
210.6 Benign neoplasm of other parts of oropharynx
210.7 Benign neoplasm of nasopharynx
230.0 Carcinoma in situ of lip, oral cavity, and pharynx
235.1 Neoplasm of uncertain behavior of lip, oral cavity, and pharynx
239.0 Neoplasm of unspecified nature of digestive system

ICD-9-CM Procedural

28.2 Tonsillectomy without adenoidectomy
28.5 Excision of lingual tonsil
28.99 Other operations on tonsils and adenoids

42860

42860 Excision of tonsil tags

ICD-9-CM Diagnostic

474.8 Other chronic disease of tonsils and adenoids — (Use additional code to identify infectious organism)

ICD-9-CM Procedural

28.4 Excision of tonsil tag

42870

42870 Excision or destruction lingual tonsil, any method (separate procedure)

ICD-9-CM Diagnostic

141.6 Malignant neoplasm of lingual tonsil
198.89 Secondary malignant neoplasm of other specified sites
210.1 Benign neoplasm of tongue
230.0 Carcinoma in situ of lip, oral cavity, and pharynx
235.1 Neoplasm of uncertain behavior of lip, oral cavity, and pharynx
239.0 Neoplasm of unspecified nature of digestive system
463 Acute tonsillitis — (Use additional code to identify infectious organism)
474.00 Chronic tonsillitis — (Use additional code to identify infectious organism)
474.02 Chronic tonsillitis and adenoiditis — (Use additional code to identify infectious organism)
474.8 Other chronic disease of tonsils and adenoids — (Use additional code to identify infectious organism)
475 Peritonsillar abscess — (Use additional code to identify infectious organism)
744.89 Other specified congenital anomaly of face and neck

ICD-9-CM Procedural

28.5 Excision of lingual tonsil

42890

42890 Limited pharyngectomy

ICD-9-CM Diagnostic

146.0 Malignant neoplasm of tonsil
146.1 Malignant neoplasm of tonsillar fossa
146.2 Malignant neoplasm of tonsillar pillars (anterior) (posterior)
146.3 Malignant neoplasm of vallecula
146.4 Malignant neoplasm of anterior aspect of epiglottis
146.5 Malignant neoplasm of junctional region of oropharynx
146.6 Malignant neoplasm of lateral wall of oropharynx
146.7 Malignant neoplasm of posterior wall of oropharynx
146.8 Malignant neoplasm of other specified sites of oropharynx
147.1 Malignant neoplasm of posterior wall of nasopharynx
147.2 Malignant neoplasm of lateral wall of nasopharynx
147.3 Malignant neoplasm of anterior wall of nasopharynx
149.0 Malignant neoplasm of pharynx, unspecified ▽
198.89 Secondary malignant neoplasm of other specified sites
210.5 Benign neoplasm of tonsil
210.6 Benign neoplasm of other parts of oropharynx
210.7 Benign neoplasm of nasopharynx
210.8 Benign neoplasm of hypopharynx
230.0 Carcinoma in situ of lip, oral cavity, and pharynx
235.1 Neoplasm of uncertain behavior of lip, oral cavity, and pharynx
239.0 Neoplasm of unspecified nature of digestive system
472.1 Chronic pharyngitis — (Use additional code to identify infectious organism)
478.21 Cellulitis of pharynx or nasopharynx — (Use additional code to identify infectious organism)

ICD-9-CM Procedural

29.33 Pharyngectomy (partial)

42892-42894

42892 Resection of lateral pharyngeal wall or pyriform sinus, direct closure by advancement of lateral and posterior pharyngeal walls

42894 Resection of pharyngeal wall requiring closure with myocutaneous or fasciocutaneous flap or free muscle, skin, or fascial flap with microvascular anastomosis

ICD-9-CM Diagnostic

146.0 Malignant neoplasm of tonsil
146.1 Malignant neoplasm of tonsillar fossa
146.2 Malignant neoplasm of tonsillar pillars (anterior) (posterior)
146.3 Malignant neoplasm of vallecula
146.4 Malignant neoplasm of anterior aspect of epiglottis
146.5 Malignant neoplasm of junctional region of oropharynx
146.6 Malignant neoplasm of lateral wall of oropharynx
146.7 Malignant neoplasm of posterior wall of oropharynx
146.8 Malignant neoplasm of other specified sites of oropharynx
147.1 Malignant neoplasm of posterior wall of nasopharynx
147.2 Malignant neoplasm of lateral wall of nasopharynx
147.3 Malignant neoplasm of anterior wall of nasopharynx
148.1 Malignant neoplasm of pyriform sinus
149.0 Malignant neoplasm of pharynx, unspecified ▽
198.89 Secondary malignant neoplasm of other specified sites
210.4 Benign neoplasm of other and unspecified parts of mouth ▽
210.5 Benign neoplasm of tonsil
210.6 Benign neoplasm of other parts of oropharynx
210.7 Benign neoplasm of nasopharynx
210.8 Benign neoplasm of hypopharynx
230.0 Carcinoma in situ of lip, oral cavity, and pharynx
235.1 Neoplasm of uncertain behavior of lip, oral cavity, and pharynx
239.0 Neoplasm of unspecified nature of digestive system

ICD-9-CM Procedural

29.33 Pharyngectomy (partial)
29.4 Plastic operation on pharynx

42900

42900 Suture pharynx for wound or injury

ICD-9-CM Diagnostic

874.4 Open wound of pharynx, without mention of complication
874.5 Open wound of pharynx, complicated
959.01 Head injury, unspecified ▽
959.09 Injury of face and neck, other and unspecified
998.2 Accidental puncture or laceration during procedure

ICD-9-CM Procedural

29.51 Suture of laceration of pharynx

42950

42950 Pharyngoplasty (plastic or reconstructive operation on pharynx)

ICD-9-CM Diagnostic

146.0 Malignant neoplasm of tonsil
146.1 Malignant neoplasm of tonsillar fossa
146.2 Malignant neoplasm of tonsillar pillars (anterior) (posterior)
146.3 Malignant neoplasm of vallecula
146.4 Malignant neoplasm of anterior aspect of epiglottis
146.5 Malignant neoplasm of junctional region of oropharynx
146.6 Malignant neoplasm of lateral wall of oropharynx
146.7 Malignant neoplasm of posterior wall of oropharynx
146.8 Malignant neoplasm of other specified sites of oropharynx
147.0 Malignant neoplasm of superior wall of nasopharynx
147.1 Malignant neoplasm of posterior wall of nasopharynx
147.2 Malignant neoplasm of lateral wall of nasopharynx
147.3 Malignant neoplasm of anterior wall of nasopharynx
147.9 Malignant neoplasm of nasopharynx, unspecified site ▽
149.0 Malignant neoplasm of pharynx, unspecified ▽
198.89 Secondary malignant neoplasm of other specified sites
210.4 Benign neoplasm of other and unspecified parts of mouth ▽
210.5 Benign neoplasm of tonsil
210.6 Benign neoplasm of other parts of oropharynx
210.7 Benign neoplasm of nasopharynx
210.8 Benign neoplasm of hypopharynx
230.0 Carcinoma in situ of lip, oral cavity, and pharynx
235.1 Neoplasm of uncertain behavior of lip, oral cavity, and pharynx
239.0 Neoplasm of unspecified nature of digestive system
906.0 Late effect of open wound of head, neck, and trunk
906.5 Late effect of burn of eye, face, head, and neck
909.1 Late effect of toxic effects of nonmedical substances
909.2 Late effect of radiation
909.3 Late effect of complications of surgical and medical care
947.0 Burn of mouth and pharynx
V10.02 Personal history of malignant neoplasm of other and unspecified parts of oral cavity and pharynx ▽
V45.89 Other postprocedural status
V51.8 Other aftercare involving the use of plastic surgery

ICD-9-CM Procedural

29.4 Plastic operation on pharynx

42953

42953 Pharyngoesophageal repair

ICD-9-CM Diagnostic

862.22 Esophagus injury without mention of open wound into cavity
862.32 Esophagus injury with open wound into cavity
874.4 Open wound of pharynx, without mention of complication
874.5 Open wound of pharynx, complicated
925.2 Crushing injury of neck — (Use additional code to identify any associated injuries, such as: 800-829, 850.0-854.1, 860.0-869.1)
998.2 Accidental puncture or laceration during procedure
998.31 Disruption of internal operation (surgical) wound
998.83 Non-healing surgical wound

ICD-9-CM Procedural

29.51 Suture of laceration of pharynx
42.82 Suture of laceration of esophagus

42955

42955 Pharyngostomy (fistulization of pharynx, external for feeding)

ICD-9-CM Diagnostic

146.0 Malignant neoplasm of tonsil
146.1 Malignant neoplasm of tonsillar fossa
146.2 Malignant neoplasm of tonsillar pillars (anterior) (posterior)
146.5 Malignant neoplasm of junctional region of oropharynx
146.6 Malignant neoplasm of lateral wall of oropharynx
146.7 Malignant neoplasm of posterior wall of oropharynx
146.9 Malignant neoplasm of oropharynx, unspecified site ▽
147.0 Malignant neoplasm of superior wall of nasopharynx

147.3 Malignant neoplasm of anterior wall of nasopharynx
147.9 Malignant neoplasm of nasopharynx, unspecified site
148.0 Malignant neoplasm of postcricoid region of hypopharynx
148.1 Malignant neoplasm of pyriform sinus
148.3 Malignant neoplasm of posterior hypopharyngeal wall
148.8 Malignant neoplasm of other specified sites of hypopharynx
149.0 Malignant neoplasm of pharynx, unspecified
150.0 Malignant neoplasm of cervical esophagus
150.3 Malignant neoplasm of upper third of esophagus
150.9 Malignant neoplasm of esophagus, unspecified site
197.8 Secondary malignant neoplasm of other digestive organs and spleen
198.89 Secondary malignant neoplasm of other specified sites
210.6 Benign neoplasm of other parts of oropharynx
210.7 Benign neoplasm of nasopharynx
210.8 Benign neoplasm of hypopharynx
210.9 Benign neoplasm of pharynx, unspecified
211.0 Benign neoplasm of esophagus
874.4 Open wound of pharynx, without mention of complication
874.5 Open wound of pharynx, complicated
947.0 Burn of mouth and pharynx
V10.02 Personal history of malignant neoplasm of other and unspecified parts of oral cavity and pharynx
V45.89 Other postprocedural status

ICD-9-CM Procedural

29.99 Other operations on pharynx

42960-42962

42960 Control oropharyngeal hemorrhage, primary or secondary (eg, post-tonsillectomy); simple
42961 complicated, requiring hospitalization
42962 with secondary surgical intervention

ICD-9-CM Diagnostic

784.8 Hemorrhage from throat
998.11 Hemorrhage complicating a procedure
998.2 Accidental puncture or laceration during procedure

ICD-9-CM Procedural

28.7 Control of hemorrhage after tonsillectomy and adenoidectomy

HCPCS Level II Supplies & Services

A4305 Disposable drug delivery system, flow rate of 50 ml or greater per hour

42970-42972

42970 Control of nasopharyngeal hemorrhage, primary or secondary (eg, postadenoidectomy); simple, with posterior nasal packs, with or without anterior packs and/or cautery
42971 complicated, requiring hospitalization
42972 with secondary surgical intervention

ICD-9-CM Diagnostic

784.8 Hemorrhage from throat
998.11 Hemorrhage complicating a procedure
998.2 Accidental puncture or laceration during procedure

ICD-9-CM Procedural

28.7 Control of hemorrhage after tonsillectomy and adenoidectomy

HCPCS Level II Supplies & Services

A4305 Disposable drug delivery system, flow rate of 50 ml or greater per hour

Esophagus

43020

43020 Esophagotomy, cervical approach, with removal of foreign body

ICD-9-CM Diagnostic

729.6 Residual foreign body in soft tissue — (Use additional code to identify foreign body (V90.01-V90.9))
862.32 Esophagus injury with open wound into cavity
874.5 Open wound of pharynx, complicated
935.1 Foreign body in esophagus
998.4 Foreign body accidentally left during procedure, not elsewhere classified

ICD-9-CM Procedural

42.09 Other incision of esophagus

43030

43030 Cricopharyngeal myotomy

ICD-9-CM Diagnostic

147.1 Malignant neoplasm of posterior wall of nasopharynx
149.0 Malignant neoplasm of pharynx, unspecified
198.89 Secondary malignant neoplasm of other specified sites
210.7 Benign neoplasm of nasopharynx
210.9 Benign neoplasm of pharynx, unspecified
464.11 Acute tracheitis with obstruction — (Use additional code to identify infectious organism)
464.21 Acute laryngotracheitis with obstruction — (Use additional code to identify infectious organism)
478.29 Other disease of pharynx or nasopharynx — (Use additional code to identify infectious organism)
478.74 Stenosis of larynx

ICD-9-CM Procedural

29.31 Cricopharyngeal myotomy

43045

43045 Esophagotomy, thoracic approach, with removal of foreign body

ICD-9-CM Diagnostic

729.6 Residual foreign body in soft tissue — (Use additional code to identify foreign body (V90.01-V90.9))
862.32 Esophagus injury with open wound into cavity
935.1 Foreign body in esophagus
998.4 Foreign body accidentally left during procedure, not elsewhere classified

ICD-9-CM Procedural

42.09 Other incision of esophagus

43100

43100 Excision of lesion, esophagus, with primary repair; cervical approach

ICD-9-CM Diagnostic

150.0 Malignant neoplasm of cervical esophagus
150.1 Malignant neoplasm of thoracic esophagus
150.3 Malignant neoplasm of upper third of esophagus
150.4 Malignant neoplasm of middle third of esophagus
150.8 Malignant neoplasm of other specified part of esophagus
150.9 Malignant neoplasm of esophagus, unspecified site
197.8 Secondary malignant neoplasm of other digestive organs and spleen

209.29 Malignant carcinoid tumor of other sites — (Code first any associated multiple endocrine neoplasia syndrome: 258.01-258.03)(Use additional code to identify associated endocrine syndrome, as: carcinoid syndrome: 259.2)
209.30 Malignant poorly differentiated neuroendocrine carcinoma, any site — (Code first any associated multiple endocrine neoplasia syndrome: 258.01-258.03)(Use additional code to identify associated endocrine syndrome, as: carcinoid syndrome: 259.2) ▽
209.69 Benign carcinoid tumor of other sites — (Code first any associated multiple endocrine neoplasia syndrome: 258.01-258.03)(Use additional code to identify associated endocrine syndrome, as: carcinoid syndrome: 259.2)
211.0 Benign neoplasm of esophagus
230.1 Carcinoma in situ of esophagus
235.5 Neoplasm of uncertain behavior of other and unspecified digestive organs ▽
239.0 Neoplasm of unspecified nature of digestive system
530.89 Other specified disorder of the esophagus

ICD-9-CM Procedural

42.32 Local excision of other lesion or tissue of esophagus

43101

43101 Excision of lesion, esophagus, with primary repair; thoracic or abdominal approach

ICD-9-CM Diagnostic

150.0 Malignant neoplasm of cervical esophagus
150.1 Malignant neoplasm of thoracic esophagus
150.2 Malignant neoplasm of abdominal esophagus
150.3 Malignant neoplasm of upper third of esophagus
150.4 Malignant neoplasm of middle third of esophagus
150.5 Malignant neoplasm of lower third of esophagus
150.8 Malignant neoplasm of other specified part of esophagus
150.9 Malignant neoplasm of esophagus, unspecified site ▽
197.8 Secondary malignant neoplasm of other digestive organs and spleen
209.29 Malignant carcinoid tumor of other sites — (Code first any associated multiple endocrine neoplasia syndrome: 258.01-258.03)(Use additional code to identify associated endocrine syndrome, as: carcinoid syndrome: 259.2)
209.30 Malignant poorly differentiated neuroendocrine carcinoma, any site — (Code first any associated multiple endocrine neoplasia syndrome: 258.01-258.03)(Use additional code to identify associated endocrine syndrome, as: carcinoid syndrome: 259.2) ▽
209.69 Benign carcinoid tumor of other sites — (Code first any associated multiple endocrine neoplasia syndrome: 258.01-258.03)(Use additional code to identify associated endocrine syndrome, as: carcinoid syndrome: 259.2)
211.0 Benign neoplasm of esophagus
230.1 Carcinoma in situ of esophagus
235.5 Neoplasm of uncertain behavior of other and unspecified digestive organs ▽
239.0 Neoplasm of unspecified nature of digestive system
530.89 Other specified disorder of the esophagus

ICD-9-CM Procedural

42.32 Local excision of other lesion or tissue of esophagus

43107

43107 Total or near total esophagectomy, without thoracotomy; with pharyngogastrostomy or cervical esophagogastrostomy, with or without pyloroplasty (transhiatal)

ICD-9-CM Diagnostic

150.0 Malignant neoplasm of cervical esophagus
150.1 Malignant neoplasm of thoracic esophagus
150.2 Malignant neoplasm of abdominal esophagus
150.3 Malignant neoplasm of upper third of esophagus
150.4 Malignant neoplasm of middle third of esophagus
150.5 Malignant neoplasm of lower third of esophagus
150.8 Malignant neoplasm of other specified part of esophagus
150.9 Malignant neoplasm of esophagus, unspecified site ▽
197.8 Secondary malignant neoplasm of other digestive organs and spleen
209.29 Malignant carcinoid tumor of other sites — (Code first any associated multiple endocrine neoplasia syndrome: 258.01-258.03)(Use additional code to identify associated endocrine syndrome, as: carcinoid syndrome: 259.2)
209.30 Malignant poorly differentiated neuroendocrine carcinoma, any site — (Code first any associated multiple endocrine neoplasia syndrome: 258.01-258.03)(Use additional code to identify associated endocrine syndrome, as: carcinoid syndrome: 259.2) ▽
209.69 Benign carcinoid tumor of other sites — (Code first any associated multiple endocrine neoplasia syndrome: 258.01-258.03)(Use additional code to identify associated endocrine syndrome, as: carcinoid syndrome: 259.2)
230.1 Carcinoma in situ of esophagus
235.5 Neoplasm of uncertain behavior of other and unspecified digestive organs ▽
239.0 Neoplasm of unspecified nature of digestive system
456.0 Esophageal varices with bleeding
456.1 Esophageal varices without mention of bleeding
530.5 Dyskinesia of esophagus
530.84 Tracheoesophageal fistula
530.89 Other specified disorder of the esophagus
572.3 Portal hypertension — (Use additional code for any associated complications, such as: portal hypertensive gastropathy (537.89))
750.4 Other specified congenital anomaly of esophagus
750.9 Unspecified congenital anomaly of upper alimentary tract ▽
862.22 Esophagus injury without mention of open wound into cavity
862.32 Esophagus injury with open wound into cavity
906.8 Late effect of burns of other specified sites
909.2 Late effect of radiation
947.2 Burn of esophagus
997.49 Other digestive system complications

ICD-9-CM Procedural

42.41 Partial esophagectomy
42.42 Total esophagectomy
42.62 Antesternal esophagogastrostomy
44.29 Other pyloroplasty

43108

43108 Total or near total esophagectomy, without thoracotomy; with colon interposition or small intestine reconstruction, including intestine mobilization, preparation and anastomosis(es)

ICD-9-CM Diagnostic

150.0 Malignant neoplasm of cervical esophagus
150.1 Malignant neoplasm of thoracic esophagus
150.2 Malignant neoplasm of abdominal esophagus
150.3 Malignant neoplasm of upper third of esophagus
150.4 Malignant neoplasm of middle third of esophagus
150.5 Malignant neoplasm of lower third of esophagus
150.8 Malignant neoplasm of other specified part of esophagus
150.9 Malignant neoplasm of esophagus, unspecified site ▽
197.8 Secondary malignant neoplasm of other digestive organs and spleen
209.29 Malignant carcinoid tumor of other sites — (Code first any associated multiple endocrine neoplasia syndrome: 258.01-258.03)(Use additional code to identify associated endocrine syndrome, as: carcinoid syndrome: 259.2)
209.30 Malignant poorly differentiated neuroendocrine carcinoma, any site — (Code first any associated multiple endocrine neoplasia syndrome: 258.01-258.03)(Use additional code to identify associated endocrine syndrome, as: carcinoid syndrome: 259.2) ▽
209.69 Benign carcinoid tumor of other sites — (Code first any associated multiple endocrine neoplasia syndrome: 258.01-258.03)(Use additional code to identify associated endocrine syndrome, as: carcinoid syndrome: 259.2)
230.1 Carcinoma in situ of esophagus
235.5 Neoplasm of uncertain behavior of other and unspecified digestive organs ▽

239.0 Neoplasm of unspecified nature of digestive system
456.0 Esophageal varices with bleeding
456.1 Esophageal varices without mention of bleeding
530.5 Dyskinesia of esophagus
530.84 Tracheoesophageal fistula
530.89 Other specified disorder of the esophagus
572.3 Portal hypertension — (Use additional code for any associated complications, such as: portal hypertensive gastropathy (537.89))
750.4 Other specified congenital anomaly of esophagus
750.9 Unspecified congenital anomaly of upper alimentary tract
862.22 Esophagus injury without mention of open wound into cavity
862.32 Esophagus injury with open wound into cavity
906.8 Late effect of burns of other specified sites
909.2 Late effect of radiation
947.2 Burn of esophagus
997.49 Other digestive system complications

ICD-9-CM Procedural

42.41 Partial esophagectomy
42.42 Total esophagectomy
42.63 Antesternal esophageal anastomosis with interposition of small bowel
42.65 Antesternal esophageal anastomosis with interposition of colon

43112

43112 Total or near total esophagectomy, with thoracotomy; with pharyngogastrostomy or cervical esophagogastrostomy, with or without pyloroplasty

ICD-9-CM Diagnostic

150.0 Malignant neoplasm of cervical esophagus
150.1 Malignant neoplasm of thoracic esophagus
150.2 Malignant neoplasm of abdominal esophagus
150.3 Malignant neoplasm of upper third of esophagus
150.4 Malignant neoplasm of middle third of esophagus
150.5 Malignant neoplasm of lower third of esophagus
150.8 Malignant neoplasm of other specified part of esophagus
150.9 Malignant neoplasm of esophagus, unspecified site
197.8 Secondary malignant neoplasm of other digestive organs and spleen
209.23 Malignant carcinoid tumor of the stomach — (Code first any associated multiple endocrine neoplasia syndrome: 258.01-258.03)(Use additional code to identify associated endocrine syndrome, as: carcinoid syndrome: 259.2)
209.29 Malignant carcinoid tumor of other sites — (Code first any associated multiple endocrine neoplasia syndrome: 258.01-258.03)(Use additional code to identify associated endocrine syndrome, as: carcinoid syndrome: 259.2)
209.30 Malignant poorly differentiated neuroendocrine carcinoma, any site — (Code first any associated multiple endocrine neoplasia syndrome: 258.01-258.03)(Use additional code to identify associated endocrine syndrome, as: carcinoid syndrome: 259.2)
209.69 Benign carcinoid tumor of other sites — (Code first any associated multiple endocrine neoplasia syndrome: 258.01-258.03)(Use additional code to identify associated endocrine syndrome, as: carcinoid syndrome: 259.2)
230.1 Carcinoma in situ of esophagus
235.5 Neoplasm of uncertain behavior of other and unspecified digestive organs
239.0 Neoplasm of unspecified nature of digestive system
456.0 Esophageal varices with bleeding
456.1 Esophageal varices without mention of bleeding
530.5 Dyskinesia of esophagus
530.84 Tracheoesophageal fistula
530.89 Other specified disorder of the esophagus
572.3 Portal hypertension — (Use additional code for any associated complications, such as: portal hypertensive gastropathy (537.89))
750.4 Other specified congenital anomaly of esophagus
750.9 Unspecified congenital anomaly of upper alimentary tract
862.22 Esophagus injury without mention of open wound into cavity
862.32 Esophagus injury with open wound into cavity
906.8 Late effect of burns of other specified sites
909.1 Late effect of toxic effects of nonmedical substances
909.2 Late effect of radiation
947.2 Burn of esophagus
997.49 Other digestive system complications

ICD-9-CM Procedural

42.41 Partial esophagectomy
42.42 Total esophagectomy
42.52 Intrathoracic esophagogastrostomy
44.29 Other pyloroplasty

43113

43113 Total or near total esophagectomy, with thoracotomy; with colon interposition or small intestine reconstruction, including intestine mobilization, preparation, and anastomosis(es)

ICD-9-CM Diagnostic

150.0 Malignant neoplasm of cervical esophagus
150.1 Malignant neoplasm of thoracic esophagus
150.2 Malignant neoplasm of abdominal esophagus
150.3 Malignant neoplasm of upper third of esophagus
150.4 Malignant neoplasm of middle third of esophagus
150.5 Malignant neoplasm of lower third of esophagus
150.8 Malignant neoplasm of other specified part of esophagus
150.9 Malignant neoplasm of esophagus, unspecified site
197.8 Secondary malignant neoplasm of other digestive organs and spleen
209.29 Malignant carcinoid tumor of other sites — (Code first any associated multiple endocrine neoplasia syndrome: 258.01-258.03)(Use additional code to identify associated endocrine syndrome, as: carcinoid syndrome: 259.2)
209.30 Malignant poorly differentiated neuroendocrine carcinoma, any site — (Code first any associated multiple endocrine neoplasia syndrome: 258.01-258.03)(Use additional code to identify associated endocrine syndrome, as: carcinoid syndrome: 259.2)
209.69 Benign carcinoid tumor of other sites — (Code first any associated multiple endocrine neoplasia syndrome: 258.01-258.03)(Use additional code to identify associated endocrine syndrome, as: carcinoid syndrome: 259.2)
230.1 Carcinoma in situ of esophagus
235.5 Neoplasm of uncertain behavior of other and unspecified digestive organs
239.0 Neoplasm of unspecified nature of digestive system
456.0 Esophageal varices with bleeding
456.1 Esophageal varices without mention of bleeding
530.5 Dyskinesia of esophagus
530.84 Tracheoesophageal fistula
530.89 Other specified disorder of the esophagus
572.3 Portal hypertension — (Use additional code for any associated complications, such as: portal hypertensive gastropathy (537.89))
750.4 Other specified congenital anomaly of esophagus
750.9 Unspecified congenital anomaly of upper alimentary tract
862.22 Esophagus injury without mention of open wound into cavity
862.32 Esophagus injury with open wound into cavity
906.8 Late effect of burns of other specified sites
909.1 Late effect of toxic effects of nonmedical substances
909.2 Late effect of radiation
947.2 Burn of esophagus
997.49 Other digestive system complications

ICD-9-CM Procedural

42.41 Partial esophagectomy
42.42 Total esophagectomy

42.53 Intrathoracic esophageal anastomosis with interposition of small bowel
42.55 Intrathoracic esophageal anastomosis with interposition of colon

43116

43116 Partial esophagectomy, cervical, with free intestinal graft, including microvascular anastomosis, obtaining the graft and intestinal reconstruction

ICD-9-CM Diagnostic

150.0 Malignant neoplasm of cervical esophagus
150.1 Malignant neoplasm of thoracic esophagus
150.2 Malignant neoplasm of abdominal esophagus
150.3 Malignant neoplasm of upper third of esophagus
150.4 Malignant neoplasm of middle third of esophagus
150.5 Malignant neoplasm of lower third of esophagus
150.8 Malignant neoplasm of other specified part of esophagus
150.9 Malignant neoplasm of esophagus, unspecified site ▽
197.8 Secondary malignant neoplasm of other digestive organs and spleen
209.29 Malignant carcinoid tumor of other sites — (Code first any associated multiple endocrine neoplasia syndrome: 258.01-258.03)(Use additional code to identify associated endocrine syndrome, as: carcinoid syndrome: 259.2)
209.30 Malignant poorly differentiated neuroendocrine carcinoma, any site — (Code first any associated multiple endocrine neoplasia syndrome: 258.01-258.03)(Use additional code to identify associated endocrine syndrome, as: carcinoid syndrome: 259.2) ▽
209.69 Benign carcinoid tumor of other sites — (Code first any associated multiple endocrine neoplasia syndrome: 258.01-258.03)(Use additional code to identify associated endocrine syndrome, as: carcinoid syndrome: 259.2)
211.0 Benign neoplasm of esophagus
230.1 Carcinoma in situ of esophagus
235.5 Neoplasm of uncertain behavior of other and unspecified digestive organs ▽
239.0 Neoplasm of unspecified nature of digestive system
530.20 Ulcer of esophagus without bleeding — (Use additional E code to identify cause, if induced by chemical or drug)
530.21 Ulcer of esophagus with bleeding — (Use additional E code to identify cause, if induced by chemical or drug)
530.6 Diverticulum of esophagus, acquired
530.82 Esophageal hemorrhage
530.83 Esophageal leukoplakia
530.85 Barrett's esophagus
530.89 Other specified disorder of the esophagus

ICD-9-CM Procedural

42.41 Partial esophagectomy
42.63 Antesternal esophageal anastomosis with interposition of small bowel
42.65 Antesternal esophageal anastomosis with interposition of colon
42.69 Other antesternal anastomosis of esophagus

43117

43117 Partial esophagectomy, distal 2/3, with thoracotomy and separate abdominal incision, with or without proximal gastrectomy; with thoracic esophagogastrostomy, with or without pyloroplasty (Ivor Lewis)

ICD-9-CM Diagnostic

150.1 Malignant neoplasm of thoracic esophagus
150.2 Malignant neoplasm of abdominal esophagus
150.3 Malignant neoplasm of upper third of esophagus
150.4 Malignant neoplasm of middle third of esophagus
150.5 Malignant neoplasm of lower third of esophagus
150.8 Malignant neoplasm of other specified part of esophagus
151.0 Malignant neoplasm of cardia
151.9 Malignant neoplasm of stomach, unspecified site ▽
197.8 Secondary malignant neoplasm of other digestive organs and spleen
209.23 Malignant carcinoid tumor of the stomach — (Code first any associated multiple endocrine neoplasia syndrome: 258.01-258.03)(Use additional code to identify associated endocrine syndrome, as: carcinoid syndrome: 259.2)
209.25 Malignant carcinoid tumor of foregut, not otherwise specified — (Code first any associated multiple endocrine neoplasia syndrome: 258.01-258.03)(Use additional code to identify associated endocrine syndrome, as: carcinoid syndrome: 259.2)
209.29 Malignant carcinoid tumor of other sites — (Code first any associated multiple endocrine neoplasia syndrome: 258.01-258.03)(Use additional code to identify associated endocrine syndrome, as: carcinoid syndrome: 259.2)
209.30 Malignant poorly differentiated neuroendocrine carcinoma, any site — (Code first any associated multiple endocrine neoplasia syndrome: 258.01-258.03)(Use additional code to identify associated endocrine syndrome, as: carcinoid syndrome: 259.2) ▽
209.63 Benign carcinoid tumor of the stomach — (Code first any associated multiple endocrine neoplasia syndrome: 258.01-258.03)(Use additional code to identify associated endocrine syndrome, as: carcinoid syndrome: 259.2)
209.65 Benign carcinoid tumor of foregut, not otherwise specified — (Code first any associated multiple endocrine neoplasia syndrome: 258.01-258.03)(Use additional code to identify associated endocrine syndrome, as: carcinoid syndrome: 259.2)
209.69 Benign carcinoid tumor of other sites — (Code first any associated multiple endocrine neoplasia syndrome: 258.01-258.03)(Use additional code to identify associated endocrine syndrome, as: carcinoid syndrome: 259.2)
230.1 Carcinoma in situ of esophagus
235.5 Neoplasm of uncertain behavior of other and unspecified digestive organs ▽
239.0 Neoplasm of unspecified nature of digestive system
456.0 Esophageal varices with bleeding
456.1 Esophageal varices without mention of bleeding
530.20 Ulcer of esophagus without bleeding — (Use additional E code to identify cause, if induced by chemical or drug)
530.21 Ulcer of esophagus with bleeding — (Use additional E code to identify cause, if induced by chemical or drug)
530.6 Diverticulum of esophagus, acquired
530.82 Esophageal hemorrhage
530.85 Barrett's esophagus
530.89 Other specified disorder of the esophagus
531.20 Acute gastric ulcer with hemorrhage and perforation, without mention of obstruction — (Use additional E code to identify drug, if drug induced)

ICD-9-CM Procedural

42.41 Partial esophagectomy
42.52 Intrathoracic esophagogastrostomy
43.5 Partial gastrectomy with anastomosis to esophagus
44.29 Other pyloroplasty

43118

43118 Partial esophagectomy, distal 2/3, with thoracotomy and separate abdominal incision, with or without proximal gastrectomy; with colon interposition or small intestine reconstruction, including intestine mobilization, preparation, and anastomosis(es)

ICD-9-CM Diagnostic

150.1 Malignant neoplasm of thoracic esophagus
150.2 Malignant neoplasm of abdominal esophagus
150.3 Malignant neoplasm of upper third of esophagus
150.4 Malignant neoplasm of middle third of esophagus
150.5 Malignant neoplasm of lower third of esophagus
150.8 Malignant neoplasm of other specified part of esophagus
151.0 Malignant neoplasm of cardia
151.9 Malignant neoplasm of stomach, unspecified site ▽
197.8 Secondary malignant neoplasm of other digestive organs and spleen
209.23 Malignant carcinoid tumor of the stomach — (Code first any associated multiple endocrine neoplasia syndrome: 258.01-258.03)(Use additional code to identify associated endocrine syndrome, as: carcinoid syndrome: 259.2)

209.25 Malignant carcinoid tumor of foregut, not otherwise specified — (Code first any associated multiple endocrine neoplasia syndrome: 258.01-258.03)(Use additional code to identify associated endocrine syndrome, as: carcinoid syndrome: 259.2)
209.29 Malignant carcinoid tumor of other sites — (Code first any associated multiple endocrine neoplasia syndrome: 258.01-258.03)(Use additional code to identify associated endocrine syndrome, as: carcinoid syndrome: 259.2)
209.30 Malignant poorly differentiated neuroendocrine carcinoma, any site — (Code first any associated multiple endocrine neoplasia syndrome: 258.01-258.03)(Use additional code to identify associated endocrine syndrome, as: carcinoid syndrome: 259.2) ♥
209.63 Benign carcinoid tumor of the stomach — (Code first any associated multiple endocrine neoplasia syndrome: 258.01-258.03)(Use additional code to identify associated endocrine syndrome, as: carcinoid syndrome: 259.2)
209.65 Benign carcinoid tumor of foregut, not otherwise specified — (Code first any associated multiple endocrine neoplasia syndrome: 258.01-258.03)(Use additional code to identify associated endocrine syndrome, as: carcinoid syndrome: 259.2)
209.69 Benign carcinoid tumor of other sites — (Code first any associated multiple endocrine neoplasia syndrome: 258.01-258.03)(Use additional code to identify associated endocrine syndrome, as: carcinoid syndrome: 259.2)
230.1 Carcinoma in situ of esophagus
235.5 Neoplasm of uncertain behavior of other and unspecified digestive organs ♥
239.0 Neoplasm of unspecified nature of digestive system
530.20 Ulcer of esophagus without bleeding — (Use additional E code to identify cause, if induced by chemical or drug)
530.21 Ulcer of esophagus with bleeding — (Use additional E code to identify cause, if induced by chemical or drug)
530.6 Diverticulum of esophagus, acquired
530.82 Esophageal hemorrhage
530.85 Barrett's esophagus
530.89 Other specified disorder of the esophagus
531.00 Acute gastric ulcer with hemorrhage, without mention of obstruction — (Use additional E code to identify drug, if drug induced)
531.20 Acute gastric ulcer with hemorrhage and perforation, without mention of obstruction — (Use additional E code to identify drug, if drug induced)
531.30 Acute gastric ulcer without mention of hemorrhage, perforation, or obstruction — (Use additional E code to identify drug, if drug induced)
531.40 Chronic or unspecified gastric ulcer with hemorrhage, without mention of obstruction — (Use additional E code to identify drug, if drug induced)
531.41 Chronic or unspecified gastric ulcer with hemorrhage and obstruction — (Use additional E code to identify drug, if drug induced)

ICD-9-CM Procedural

42.41 Partial esophagectomy
42.52 Intrathoracic esophagogastrostomy
42.53 Intrathoracic esophageal anastomosis with interposition of small bowel
42.55 Intrathoracic esophageal anastomosis with interposition of colon
43.5 Partial gastrectomy with anastomosis to esophagus

43121

43121 Partial esophagectomy, distal 2/3, with thoracotomy only, with or without proximal gastrectomy, with thoracic esophagogastrostomy, with or without pyloroplasty

ICD-9-CM Diagnostic

150.1 Malignant neoplasm of thoracic esophagus
150.2 Malignant neoplasm of abdominal esophagus
150.3 Malignant neoplasm of upper third of esophagus
150.4 Malignant neoplasm of middle third of esophagus
150.5 Malignant neoplasm of lower third of esophagus
150.8 Malignant neoplasm of other specified part of esophagus
151.0 Malignant neoplasm of cardia
151.9 Malignant neoplasm of stomach, unspecified site ♥
197.8 Secondary malignant neoplasm of other digestive organs and spleen
209.23 Malignant carcinoid tumor of the stomach — (Code first any associated multiple endocrine neoplasia syndrome: 258.01-258.03)(Use additional code to identify associated endocrine syndrome, as: carcinoid syndrome: 259.2)
209.25 Malignant carcinoid tumor of foregut, not otherwise specified — (Code first any associated multiple endocrine neoplasia syndrome: 258.01-258.03)(Use additional code to identify associated endocrine syndrome, as: carcinoid syndrome: 259.2)
209.29 Malignant carcinoid tumor of other sites — (Code first any associated multiple endocrine neoplasia syndrome: 258.01-258.03)(Use additional code to identify associated endocrine syndrome, as: carcinoid syndrome: 259.2)
209.30 Malignant poorly differentiated neuroendocrine carcinoma, any site — (Code first any associated multiple endocrine neoplasia syndrome: 258.01-258.03)(Use additional code to identify associated endocrine syndrome, as: carcinoid syndrome: 259.2) ♥
209.63 Benign carcinoid tumor of the stomach — (Code first any associated multiple endocrine neoplasia syndrome: 258.01-258.03)(Use additional code to identify associated endocrine syndrome, as: carcinoid syndrome: 259.2)
209.65 Benign carcinoid tumor of foregut, not otherwise specified — (Code first any associated multiple endocrine neoplasia syndrome: 258.01-258.03)(Use additional code to identify associated endocrine syndrome, as: carcinoid syndrome: 259.2)
209.69 Benign carcinoid tumor of other sites — (Code first any associated multiple endocrine neoplasia syndrome: 258.01-258.03)(Use additional code to identify associated endocrine syndrome, as: carcinoid syndrome: 259.2)
230.1 Carcinoma in situ of esophagus
235.5 Neoplasm of uncertain behavior of other and unspecified digestive organs ♥
239.0 Neoplasm of unspecified nature of digestive system
456.0 Esophageal varices with bleeding
530.20 Ulcer of esophagus without bleeding — (Use additional E code to identify cause, if induced by chemical or drug)
530.21 Ulcer of esophagus with bleeding — (Use additional E code to identify cause, if induced by chemical or drug)
530.3 Stricture and stenosis of esophagus
530.4 Perforation of esophagus
530.5 Dyskinesia of esophagus
530.82 Esophageal hemorrhage
530.85 Barrett's esophagus
530.89 Other specified disorder of the esophagus
531.00 Acute gastric ulcer with hemorrhage, without mention of obstruction — (Use additional E code to identify drug, if drug induced)
531.20 Acute gastric ulcer with hemorrhage and perforation, without mention of obstruction — (Use additional E code to identify drug, if drug induced)
531.30 Acute gastric ulcer without mention of hemorrhage, perforation, or obstruction — (Use additional E code to identify drug, if drug induced)
531.40 Chronic or unspecified gastric ulcer with hemorrhage, without mention of obstruction — (Use additional E code to identify drug, if drug induced)
531.41 Chronic or unspecified gastric ulcer with hemorrhage and obstruction — (Use additional E code to identify drug, if drug induced)

ICD-9-CM Procedural

42.41 Partial esophagectomy
42.52 Intrathoracic esophagogastrostomy
43.5 Partial gastrectomy with anastomosis to esophagus
44.29 Other pyloroplasty

43122

43122 Partial esophagectomy, thoracoabdominal or abdominal approach, with or without proximal gastrectomy; with esophagogastrostomy, with or without pyloroplasty

ICD-9-CM Diagnostic

150.1 Malignant neoplasm of thoracic esophagus
150.2 Malignant neoplasm of abdominal esophagus
150.3 Malignant neoplasm of upper third of esophagus
150.4 Malignant neoplasm of middle third of esophagus
150.5 Malignant neoplasm of lower third of esophagus

150.8 Malignant neoplasm of other specified part of esophagus
151.0 Malignant neoplasm of cardia
151.9 Malignant neoplasm of stomach, unspecified site ▽
197.8 Secondary malignant neoplasm of other digestive organs and spleen
209.29 Malignant carcinoid tumor of other sites — (Code first any associated multiple endocrine neoplasia syndrome: 258.01-258.03)(Use additional code to identify associated endocrine syndrome, as: carcinoid syndrome: 259.2)
209.30 Malignant poorly differentiated neuroendocrine carcinoma, any site — (Code first any associated multiple endocrine neoplasia syndrome: 258.01-258.03)(Use additional code to identify associated endocrine syndrome, as: carcinoid syndrome: 259.2) ▽
209.69 Benign carcinoid tumor of other sites — (Code first any associated multiple endocrine neoplasia syndrome: 258.01-258.03)(Use additional code to identify associated endocrine syndrome, as: carcinoid syndrome: 259.2)
230.1 Carcinoma in situ of esophagus
235.5 Neoplasm of uncertain behavior of other and unspecified digestive organs ▽
239.0 Neoplasm of unspecified nature of digestive system
456.0 Esophageal varices with bleeding
530.20 Ulcer of esophagus without bleeding — (Use additional E code to identify cause, if induced by chemical or drug)
530.21 Ulcer of esophagus with bleeding — (Use additional E code to identify cause, if induced by chemical or drug)
530.3 Stricture and stenosis of esophagus
530.4 Perforation of esophagus
530.5 Dyskinesia of esophagus
530.81 Esophageal reflux
530.82 Esophageal hemorrhage
530.83 Esophageal leukoplakia
530.85 Barrett's esophagus
531.00 Acute gastric ulcer with hemorrhage, without mention of obstruction — (Use additional E code to identify drug, if drug induced)
531.20 Acute gastric ulcer with hemorrhage and perforation, without mention of obstruction — (Use additional E code to identify drug, if drug induced)
531.30 Acute gastric ulcer without mention of hemorrhage, perforation, or obstruction — (Use additional E code to identify drug, if drug induced)
531.40 Chronic or unspecified gastric ulcer with hemorrhage, without mention of obstruction — (Use additional E code to identify drug, if drug induced)
531.41 Chronic or unspecified gastric ulcer with hemorrhage and obstruction — (Use additional E code to identify drug, if drug induced)

ICD-9-CM Procedural

42.41 Partial esophagectomy
42.52 Intrathoracic esophagogastrostomy
43.5 Partial gastrectomy with anastomosis to esophagus
44.29 Other pyloroplasty

43123

43123 Partial esophagectomy, thoracoabdominal or abdominal approach, with or without proximal gastrectomy; with colon interposition or small intestine reconstruction, including intestine mobilization, preparation, and anastomosis(es)

ICD-9-CM Diagnostic

150.1 Malignant neoplasm of thoracic esophagus
150.2 Malignant neoplasm of abdominal esophagus
150.3 Malignant neoplasm of upper third of esophagus
150.4 Malignant neoplasm of middle third of esophagus
150.5 Malignant neoplasm of lower third of esophagus
150.8 Malignant neoplasm of other specified part of esophagus
150.9 Malignant neoplasm of esophagus, unspecified site ▽
151.0 Malignant neoplasm of cardia
151.9 Malignant neoplasm of stomach, unspecified site ▽
154.0 Malignant neoplasm of rectosigmoid junction
197.8 Secondary malignant neoplasm of other digestive organs and spleen
209.23 Malignant carcinoid tumor of the stomach — (Code first any associated multiple endocrine neoplasia syndrome: 258.01-258.03)(Use additional code to identify associated endocrine syndrome, as: carcinoid syndrome: 259.2)
209.25 Malignant carcinoid tumor of foregut, not otherwise specified — (Code first any associated multiple endocrine neoplasia syndrome: 258.01-258.03)(Use additional code to identify associated endocrine syndrome, as: carcinoid syndrome: 259.2)
209.29 Malignant carcinoid tumor of other sites — (Code first any associated multiple endocrine neoplasia syndrome: 258.01-258.03)(Use additional code to identify associated endocrine syndrome, as: carcinoid syndrome: 259.2)
209.30 Malignant poorly differentiated neuroendocrine carcinoma, any site — (Code first any associated multiple endocrine neoplasia syndrome: 258.01-258.03)(Use additional code to identify associated endocrine syndrome, as: carcinoid syndrome: 259.2) ▽
209.63 Benign carcinoid tumor of the stomach — (Code first any associated multiple endocrine neoplasia syndrome: 258.01-258.03)(Use additional code to identify associated endocrine syndrome, as: carcinoid syndrome: 259.2)
209.65 Benign carcinoid tumor of foregut, not otherwise specified — (Code first any associated multiple endocrine neoplasia syndrome: 258.01-258.03)(Use additional code to identify associated endocrine syndrome, as: carcinoid syndrome: 259.2)
209.69 Benign carcinoid tumor of other sites — (Code first any associated multiple endocrine neoplasia syndrome: 258.01-258.03)(Use additional code to identify associated endocrine syndrome, as: carcinoid syndrome: 259.2)
230.1 Carcinoma in situ of esophagus
235.5 Neoplasm of uncertain behavior of other and unspecified digestive organs ▽
239.0 Neoplasm of unspecified nature of digestive system
530.20 Ulcer of esophagus without bleeding — (Use additional E code to identify cause, if induced by chemical or drug)
530.21 Ulcer of esophagus with bleeding — (Use additional E code to identify cause, if induced by chemical or drug)
530.4 Perforation of esophagus
530.82 Esophageal hemorrhage
530.83 Esophageal leukoplakia
530.85 Barrett's esophagus
530.89 Other specified disorder of the esophagus
531.00 Acute gastric ulcer with hemorrhage, without mention of obstruction — (Use additional E code to identify drug, if drug induced)
531.01 Acute gastric ulcer with hemorrhage and obstruction — (Use additional E code to identify drug, if drug induced)
531.10 Acute gastric ulcer with perforation, without mention of obstruction — (Use additional E code to identify drug, if drug induced)
531.11 Acute gastric ulcer with perforation and obstruction — (Use additional E code to identify drug, if drug induced)
531.20 Acute gastric ulcer with hemorrhage and perforation, without mention of obstruction — (Use additional E code to identify drug, if drug induced)
531.21 Acute gastric ulcer with hemorrhage, perforation, and obstruction — (Use additional E code to identify drug, if drug induced)
531.30 Acute gastric ulcer without mention of hemorrhage, perforation, or obstruction — (Use additional E code to identify drug, if drug induced)
531.31 Acute gastric ulcer without mention of hemorrhage or perforation, with obstruction — (Use additional E code to identify drug, if drug induced)
531.40 Chronic or unspecified gastric ulcer with hemorrhage, without mention of obstruction — (Use additional E code to identify drug, if drug induced)
531.41 Chronic or unspecified gastric ulcer with hemorrhage and obstruction — (Use additional E code to identify drug, if drug induced)

ICD-9-CM Procedural

42.41 Partial esophagectomy
42.52 Intrathoracic esophagogastrostomy
42.53 Intrathoracic esophageal anastomosis with interposition of small bowel
42.55 Intrathoracic esophageal anastomosis with interposition of colon

43124

43124 Total or partial esophagectomy, without reconstruction (any approach), with cervical esophagostomy

ICD-9-CM Diagnostic

150.0 Malignant neoplasm of cervical esophagus
150.1 Malignant neoplasm of thoracic esophagus
150.2 Malignant neoplasm of abdominal esophagus
150.3 Malignant neoplasm of upper third of esophagus
150.4 Malignant neoplasm of middle third of esophagus
150.5 Malignant neoplasm of lower third of esophagus
150.8 Malignant neoplasm of other specified part of esophagus
150.9 Malignant neoplasm of esophagus, unspecified site
197.8 Secondary malignant neoplasm of other digestive organs and spleen
209.29 Malignant carcinoid tumor of other sites — (Code first any associated multiple endocrine neoplasia syndrome: 258.01-258.03)(Use additional code to identify associated endocrine syndrome, as: carcinoid syndrome: 259.2)
209.30 Malignant poorly differentiated neuroendocrine carcinoma, any site — (Code first any associated multiple endocrine neoplasia syndrome: 258.01-258.03)(Use additional code to identify associated endocrine syndrome, as: carcinoid syndrome: 259.2)
209.69 Benign carcinoid tumor of other sites — (Code first any associated multiple endocrine neoplasia syndrome: 258.01-258.03)(Use additional code to identify associated endocrine syndrome, as: carcinoid syndrome: 259.2)
230.1 Carcinoma in situ of esophagus
235.5 Neoplasm of uncertain behavior of other and unspecified digestive organs
239.0 Neoplasm of unspecified nature of digestive system
530.20 Ulcer of esophagus without bleeding — (Use additional E code to identify cause, if induced by chemical or drug)
530.21 Ulcer of esophagus with bleeding — (Use additional E code to identify cause, if induced by chemical or drug)
530.82 Esophageal hemorrhage
530.83 Esophageal leukoplakia
530.84 Tracheoesophageal fistula
530.85 Barrett's esophagus
530.89 Other specified disorder of the esophagus

ICD-9-CM Procedural

42.11 Cervical esophagostomy
42.41 Partial esophagectomy
42.42 Total esophagectomy
42.62 Antesternal esophagogastrostomy

43130

43130 Diverticulectomy of hypopharynx or esophagus, with or without myotomy; cervical approach

ICD-9-CM Diagnostic

530.6 Diverticulum of esophagus, acquired
750.27 Congenital diverticulum of pharynx
750.4 Other specified congenital anomaly of esophagus

ICD-9-CM Procedural

29.32 Pharyngeal diverticulectomy
42.31 Local excision of esophageal diverticulum

43135

43135 Diverticulectomy of hypopharynx or esophagus, with or without myotomy; thoracic approach

ICD-9-CM Diagnostic

530.6 Diverticulum of esophagus, acquired
750.27 Congenital diverticulum of pharynx
750.4 Other specified congenital anomaly of esophagus

ICD-9-CM Procedural

29.32 Pharyngeal diverticulectomy
42.31 Local excision of esophageal diverticulum

43191-43193

43191 Esophagoscopy, rigid, transoral; diagnostic, including collection of specimen(s) by brushing or washing when performed (separate procedure)
43192 with directed submucosal injection(s), any substance
43193 with biopsy, single or multiple

ICD-9-CM Diagnostic

112.84 Candidiasis of the esophagus — (Use additional code to identify manifestation: 321.0-321.1, 380.15, 711.6)
150.0 Malignant neoplasm of cervical esophagus
150.1 Malignant neoplasm of thoracic esophagus
150.3 Malignant neoplasm of upper third of esophagus
150.4 Malignant neoplasm of middle third of esophagus
150.5 Malignant neoplasm of lower third of esophagus
150.8 Malignant neoplasm of other specified part of esophagus
150.9 Malignant neoplasm of esophagus, unspecified site
151.0 Malignant neoplasm of cardia
211.0 Benign neoplasm of esophagus
280.8 Other specified iron deficiency anemias
300.11 Conversion disorder
306.4 Gastrointestinal malfunction arising from mental factors
456.0 Esophageal varices with bleeding
456.1 Esophageal varices without mention of bleeding
456.20 Esophageal varices with bleeding in diseases classified elsewhere — (Code first underlying disease: 571.0-571.9, 572.3)
456.21 Esophageal varices without mention of bleeding in diseases classified elsewhere — (Code first underlying disease: 571.0-571.9, 572.3)
530.0 Achalasia and cardiospasm
530.10 Unspecified esophagitis — (Use additional E code to identify cause, if induced by chemical)
530.11 Reflux esophagitis — (Use additional E code to identify cause, if induced by chemical)
530.12 Acute esophagitis — (Use additional E code to identify cause, if induced by chemical)
530.13 Eosinophilic esophagitis
530.19 Other esophagitis — (Use additional E code to identify cause, if induced by chemical)
530.20 Ulcer of esophagus without bleeding — (Use additional E code to identify cause, if induced by chemical or drug)
530.21 Ulcer of esophagus with bleeding — (Use additional E code to identify cause, if induced by chemical or drug)
530.4 Perforation of esophagus
530.5 Dyskinesia of esophagus
530.6 Diverticulum of esophagus, acquired
530.7 Gastroesophageal laceration-hemorrhage syndrome
530.81 Esophageal reflux
530.82 Esophageal hemorrhage
530.83 Esophageal leukoplakia
530.84 Tracheoesophageal fistula
530.85 Barrett's esophagus
530.86 Infection of esophagostomy — (Use additional code to specify infection)
530.87 Mechanical complication of esophagostomy
530.89 Other specified disorder of the esophagus
750.3 Congenital tracheoesophageal fistula, esophageal atresia and stenosis
750.4 Other specified congenital anomaly of esophagus
751.8 Other specified congenital anomalies of digestive system
787.20 Dysphagia, unspecified
787.21 Dysphagia, oral phase

787.22 Dysphagia, oropharyngeal phase
787.23 Dysphagia, pharyngeal phase
787.24 Dysphagia, pharyngoesophageal phase
787.29 Other dysphagia
862.22 Esophagus injury without mention of open wound into cavity
862.32 Esophagus injury with open wound into cavity
874.4 Open wound of pharynx, without mention of complication
874.5 Open wound of pharynx, complicated
996.59 Mechanical complication due to other implant and internal device, not elsewhere classified
996.79 Other complications due to other internal prosthetic device, implant, and graft — (Use additional code to identify complication: 338.18-338.19, 338.28-338.29)
997.49 Other digestive system complications
998.11 Hemorrhage complicating a procedure
998.12 Hematoma complicating a procedure
998.2 Accidental puncture or laceration during procedure
V52.8 Fitting and adjustment of other specified prosthetic device
V58.42 Aftercare following surgery for neoplasm — (This code should be used in conjunction with other aftercare codes to fully identify the reason for the aftercare encounter)
V58.75 Aftercare following surgery of the teeth, oral cavity, and digestive system, NEC — (This code should be used in conjunction with other aftercare codes to fully identify the reason for the aftercare encounter)
V67.09 Follow-up examination, following other surgery

ICD-9-CM Procedural

42.23 Other esophagoscopy
42.24 Closed (endoscopic) biopsy of esophagus
99.29 Injection or infusion of other therapeutic or prophylactic substance

43194

43194 Esophagoscopy, rigid, transoral; with removal of foreign body

ICD-9-CM Diagnostic

935.1 Foreign body in esophagus

ICD-9-CM Procedural

42.23 Other esophagoscopy
98.02 Removal of intraluminal foreign body from esophagus without incision

43195-43196

43195 Esophagoscopy, rigid, transoral; with balloon dilation (less than 30 mm diameter)
43196 with insertion of guide wire followed by dilation over guide wire

ICD-9-CM Diagnostic

530.3 Stricture and stenosis of esophagus
750.3 Congenital tracheoesophageal fistula, esophageal atresia and stenosis
787.20 Dysphagia, unspecified ▽
787.21 Dysphagia, oral phase
787.22 Dysphagia, oropharyngeal phase
787.23 Dysphagia, pharyngeal phase
787.24 Dysphagia, pharyngoesophageal phase
787.29 Other dysphagia
996.49 Other mechanical complication of other internal orthopedic device, implant, and graft — (Use additional code to identify prosthetic joint with mechanical complication, V43.60-V43.69)

ICD-9-CM Procedural

42.23 Other esophagoscopy
42.92 Dilation of esophagus

43197-43198

43197 Esophagoscopy, flexible, transnasal; diagnostic, includes collection of specimen(s) by brushing or washing when performed (separate procedure)
43198 with biopsy, single or multiple

ICD-9-CM Diagnostic

112.84 Candidiasis of the esophagus — (Use additional code to identify manifestation: 321.0-321.1, 380.15, 711.6)
150.0 Malignant neoplasm of cervical esophagus
150.1 Malignant neoplasm of thoracic esophagus
150.2 Malignant neoplasm of abdominal esophagus
150.3 Malignant neoplasm of upper third of esophagus
150.4 Malignant neoplasm of middle third of esophagus
150.5 Malignant neoplasm of lower third of esophagus
150.8 Malignant neoplasm of other specified part of esophagus
150.9 Malignant neoplasm of esophagus, unspecified site ▽
151.0 Malignant neoplasm of cardia
300.11 Conversion disorder
306.4 Gastrointestinal malfunction arising from mental factors
530.0 Achalasia and cardiospasm
530.11 Reflux esophagitis — (Use additional E code to identify cause, if induced by chemical)
530.3 Stricture and stenosis of esophagus
530.5 Dyskinesia of esophagus
530.81 Esophageal reflux
530.82 Esophageal hemorrhage
530.85 Barrett's esophagus
536.8 Dyspepsia and other specified disorders of function of stomach
750.3 Congenital tracheoesophageal fistula, esophageal atresia and stenosis
751.8 Other specified congenital anomalies of digestive system
784.42 Dysphonia
784.99 Other symptoms involving head and neck
786.2 Cough
786.39 Other hemoptysis
787.1 Heartburn
787.20 Dysphagia, unspecified ▽
787.21 Dysphagia, oral phase
787.22 Dysphagia, oropharyngeal phase
787.23 Dysphagia, pharyngeal phase
787.24 Dysphagia, pharyngoesophageal phase
787.29 Other dysphagia
935.1 Foreign body in esophagus
998.11 Hemorrhage complicating a procedure
V55.8 Attention to other specified artificial opening
V58.42 Aftercare following surgery for neoplasm — (This code should be used in conjunction with other aftercare codes to fully identify the reason for the aftercare encounter)
V58.75 Aftercare following surgery of the teeth, oral cavity, and digestive system, NEC — (This code should be used in conjunction with other aftercare codes to fully identify the reason for the aftercare encounter)
V67.09 Follow-up examination, following other surgery
V76.49 Special screening for malignant neoplasms, other sites

ICD-9-CM Procedural

42.23 Other esophagoscopy
42.24 Closed (endoscopic) biopsy of esophagus

43200-43202, 43206 [43211, 43212, 43213, 43214]

43200 Esophagoscopy, flexible, transoral; diagnostic, including collection of specimen(s) by brushing or washing, when performed (separate procedure)
43201 with directed submucosal injection(s), any substance
43202 with biopsy, single or multiple
43206 with optical endomicroscopy
43211 with endoscopic mucosal resection
43212 with placement of endoscopic stent (includes pre- and post-dilation and guide wire passage, when performed)
43213 with dilation of esophagus, by balloon or dilator, retrograde (includes fluoroscopic guidance, when performed)
43214 with dilation of esophagus with balloon (30 mm diameter or larger) (includes fluoroscopic guidance, when performed)

ICD-9-CM Diagnostic

150.0 Malignant neoplasm of cervical esophagus
150.1 Malignant neoplasm of thoracic esophagus
150.2 Malignant neoplasm of abdominal esophagus
150.3 Malignant neoplasm of upper third of esophagus
150.4 Malignant neoplasm of middle third of esophagus
150.5 Malignant neoplasm of lower third of esophagus
150.8 Malignant neoplasm of other specified part of esophagus
150.9 Malignant neoplasm of esophagus, unspecified site ▽
151.0 Malignant neoplasm of cardia
171.0 Malignant neoplasm of connective and other soft tissue of head, face, and neck
193 Malignant neoplasm of thyroid gland — (Use additional code to identify any functional activity)
195.0 Malignant neoplasm of head, face, and neck
196.0 Secondary and unspecified malignant neoplasm of lymph nodes of head, face, and neck
196.9 Secondary and unspecified malignant neoplasm of lymph nodes, site unspecified ▽
197.8 Secondary malignant neoplasm of other digestive organs and spleen
198.89 Secondary malignant neoplasm of other specified sites
199.0 Disseminated malignant neoplasm
199.1 Other malignant neoplasm of unspecified site
202.81 Other malignant lymphomas of lymph nodes of head, face, and neck
209.20 Malignant carcinoid tumor of unknown primary site — (Code first any associated multiple endocrine neoplasia syndrome: 258.01-258.03)(Use additional code to identify associated endocrine syndrome, as: carcinoid syndrome: 259.2)
209.29 Malignant carcinoid tumor of other sites — (Code first any associated multiple endocrine neoplasia syndrome: 258.01-258.03)(Use additional code to identify associated endocrine syndrome, as: carcinoid syndrome: 259.2)
209.30 Malignant poorly differentiated neuroendocrine carcinoma, any site — (Code first any associated multiple endocrine neoplasia syndrome: 258.01-258.03)(Use additional code to identify associated endocrine syndrome, as: carcinoid syndrome: 259.2) ▽
209.69 Benign carcinoid tumor of other sites — (Code first any associated multiple endocrine neoplasia syndrome: 258.01-258.03)(Use additional code to identify associated endocrine syndrome, as: carcinoid syndrome: 259.2)
211.0 Benign neoplasm of esophagus
211.9 Benign neoplasm of other and unspecified site of the digestive system ▽
230.1 Carcinoma in situ of esophagus
235.5 Neoplasm of uncertain behavior of other and unspecified digestive organs ▽
239.0 Neoplasm of unspecified nature of digestive system
263.0 Malnutrition of moderate degree
306.4 Gastrointestinal malfunction arising from mental factors
352.3 Disorders of pneumogastric (10th) nerve
448.0 Hereditary hemorrhagic telangiectasia
456.0 Esophageal varices with bleeding
456.1 Esophageal varices without mention of bleeding
530.0 Achalasia and cardiospasm
530.11 Reflux esophagitis — (Use additional E code to identify cause, if induced by chemical)
530.12 Acute esophagitis — (Use additional E code to identify cause, if induced by chemical)
530.13 Eosinophilic esophagitis
530.19 Other esophagitis — (Use additional E code to identify cause, if induced by chemical)
530.20 Ulcer of esophagus without bleeding — (Use additional E code to identify cause, if induced by chemical or drug)
530.21 Ulcer of esophagus with bleeding — (Use additional E code to identify cause, if induced by chemical or drug)
530.3 Stricture and stenosis of esophagus
530.4 Perforation of esophagus
530.5 Dyskinesia of esophagus
530.6 Diverticulum of esophagus, acquired
530.7 Gastroesophageal laceration-hemorrhage syndrome
530.81 Esophageal reflux
530.82 Esophageal hemorrhage
530.83 Esophageal leukoplakia
530.84 Tracheoesophageal fistula
530.85 Barrett's esophagus
530.89 Other specified disorder of the esophagus
530.9 Unspecified disorder of esophagus ▽
552.3 Diaphragmatic hernia with obstruction
553.3 Diaphragmatic hernia without mention of obstruction or gangrene
578.0 Hematemesis
578.1 Blood in stool
578.9 Hemorrhage of gastrointestinal tract, unspecified ▽
750.4 Other specified congenital anomaly of esophagus
750.9 Unspecified congenital anomaly of upper alimentary tract ▽
784.1 Throat pain
787.1 Heartburn
787.20 Dysphagia, unspecified ▽
787.21 Dysphagia, oral phase
787.22 Dysphagia, oropharyngeal phase
787.23 Dysphagia, pharyngeal phase
787.24 Dysphagia, pharyngoesophageal phase
787.29 Other dysphagia
793.4 Nonspecific (abnormal) findings on radiological and other examination of gastrointestinal tract
799.89 Other ill-defined conditions
862.22 Esophagus injury without mention of open wound into cavity

ICD-9-CM Procedural

42.23 Other esophagoscopy
42.24 Closed (endoscopic) biopsy of esophagus
42.33 Endoscopic excision or destruction of lesion or tissue of esophagus
42.81 Insertion of permanent tube into esophagus
42.92 Dilation of esophagus
90.89 Other microscopic examination of specimen from upper gastrointestinal tract and of vomitus
99.23 Injection of steroid
99.29 Injection or infusion of other therapeutic or prophylactic substance

HCPCS Level II Supplies & Services

A4270 Disposable endoscope sheath, each

43204-43205

43204 Esophagoscopy, flexible, transoral; with injection sclerosis of esophageal varices
43205 with band ligation of esophageal varices

ICD-9-CM Diagnostic

456.0 Esophageal varices with bleeding
456.1 Esophageal varices without mention of bleeding

456.20 Esophageal varices with bleeding in diseases classified elsewhere — (Code first underlying disease: 571.0-571.9, 572.3) ☒

456.21 Esophageal varices without mention of bleeding in diseases classified elsewhere — (Code first underlying disease: 571.0-571.9, 572.3) ☒

530.3 Stricture and stenosis of esophagus

530.82 Esophageal hemorrhage

530.89 Other specified disorder of the esophagus

571.0 Alcoholic fatty liver

571.1 Acute alcoholic hepatitis

571.2 Alcoholic cirrhosis of liver

571.3 Unspecified alcoholic liver damage ▼

571.40 Unspecified chronic hepatitis ▼

571.41 Chronic persistent hepatitis

571.42 Autoimmune hepatitis

571.49 Other chronic hepatitis

571.5 Cirrhosis of liver without mention of alcohol — (Code first, if applicable, viral hepatitis (acute) (chronic): 070.0-070.9)

571.6 Biliary cirrhosis

571.8 Other chronic nonalcoholic liver disease

571.9 Unspecified chronic liver disease without mention of alcohol ▼

572.3 Portal hypertension — (Use additional code for any associated complications, such as: portal hypertensive gastropathy (537.89))

578.0 Hematemesis

ICD-9-CM Procedural

42.33 Endoscopic excision or destruction of lesion or tissue of esophagus

43215

43215 Esophagoscopy, flexible, transoral; with removal of foreign body

ICD-9-CM Diagnostic

935.1 Foreign body in esophagus

ICD-9-CM Procedural

42.23 Other esophagoscopy

98.02 Removal of intraluminal foreign body from esophagus without incision

HCPCS Level II Supplies & Services

A4270 Disposable endoscope sheath, each

43216-43217

43216 Esophagoscopy, flexible, transoral; with removal of tumor(s), polyp(s), or other lesion(s) by hot biopsy forceps or bipolar cautery

43217 with removal of tumor(s), polyp(s), or other lesion(s) by snare technique

ICD-9-CM Diagnostic

150.0 Malignant neoplasm of cervical esophagus

150.1 Malignant neoplasm of thoracic esophagus

150.2 Malignant neoplasm of abdominal esophagus

150.3 Malignant neoplasm of upper third of esophagus

150.4 Malignant neoplasm of middle third of esophagus

150.5 Malignant neoplasm of lower third of esophagus

150.8 Malignant neoplasm of other specified part of esophagus

150.9 Malignant neoplasm of esophagus, unspecified site ▼

197.8 Secondary malignant neoplasm of other digestive organs and spleen

209.29 Malignant carcinoid tumor of other sites — (Code first any associated multiple endocrine neoplasia syndrome: 258.01-258.03)(Use additional code to identify associated endocrine syndrome, as: carcinoid syndrome: 259.2)

209.30 Malignant poorly differentiated neuroendocrine carcinoma, any site — (Code first any associated multiple endocrine neoplasia syndrome: 258.01-258.03)(Use additional code to identify associated endocrine syndrome, as: carcinoid syndrome: 259.2) ▼

209.69 Benign carcinoid tumor of other sites — (Code first any associated multiple endocrine neoplasia syndrome: 258.01-258.03)(Use additional code to identify associated endocrine syndrome, as: carcinoid syndrome: 259.2)

211.0 Benign neoplasm of esophagus

230.1 Carcinoma in situ of esophagus

235.5 Neoplasm of uncertain behavior of other and unspecified digestive organs ▼

239.0 Neoplasm of unspecified nature of digestive system

530.83 Esophageal leukoplakia

530.89 Other specified disorder of the esophagus

ICD-9-CM Procedural

42.33 Endoscopic excision or destruction of lesion or tissue of esophagus

HCPCS Level II Supplies & Services

A4270 Disposable endoscope sheath, each

43220, 43226, 43229

43220 Esophagoscopy, flexible, transoral; with transendoscopic balloon dilation (less than 30 mm diameter)

43226 with insertion of guide wire followed by passage of dilator(s) over guide wire

43229 with ablation of tumor(s), polyp(s), or other lesion(s) (includes pre- and post-dilation and guide wire passage, when performed)

ICD-9-CM Diagnostic

150.0 Malignant neoplasm of cervical esophagus

150.1 Malignant neoplasm of thoracic esophagus

150.2 Malignant neoplasm of abdominal esophagus

150.3 Malignant neoplasm of upper third of esophagus

150.4 Malignant neoplasm of middle third of esophagus

150.5 Malignant neoplasm of lower third of esophagus

150.8 Malignant neoplasm of other specified part of esophagus

151.0 Malignant neoplasm of cardia

197.8 Secondary malignant neoplasm of other digestive organs and spleen

199.1 Other malignant neoplasm of unspecified site

209.29 Malignant carcinoid tumor of other sites — (Code first any associated multiple endocrine neoplasia syndrome: 258.01-258.03)(Use additional code to identify associated endocrine syndrome, as: carcinoid syndrome: 259.2)

209.30 Malignant poorly differentiated neuroendocrine carcinoma, any site — (Code first any associated multiple endocrine neoplasia syndrome: 258.01-258.03)(Use additional code to identify associated endocrine syndrome, as: carcinoid syndrome: 259.2) ▼

209.69 Benign carcinoid tumor of other sites — (Code first any associated multiple endocrine neoplasia syndrome: 258.01-258.03)(Use additional code to identify associated endocrine syndrome, as: carcinoid syndrome: 259.2)

211.0 Benign neoplasm of esophagus

230.1 Carcinoma in situ of esophagus

235.5 Neoplasm of uncertain behavior of other and unspecified digestive organs ▼

239.0 Neoplasm of unspecified nature of digestive system

456.1 Esophageal varices without mention of bleeding

530.0 Achalasia and cardiospasm

530.11 Reflux esophagitis — (Use additional E code to identify cause, if induced by chemical)

530.12 Acute esophagitis — (Use additional E code to identify cause, if induced by chemical)

530.13 Eosinophilic esophagitis

530.19 Other esophagitis — (Use additional E code to identify cause, if induced by chemical)

530.3 Stricture and stenosis of esophagus

530.5 Dyskinesia of esophagus

530.81 Esophageal reflux

530.89 Other specified disorder of the esophagus

750.3 Congenital tracheoesophageal fistula, esophageal atresia and stenosis

ICD-9-CM Procedural

42.33 Endoscopic excision or destruction of lesion or tissue of esophagus

42.81 Insertion of permanent tube into esophagus

42.92 Dilation of esophagus

HCPCS Level II Supplies & Services

A4270 Disposable endoscope sheath, each

43227

43227 Esophagoscopy, flexible, transoral; with control of bleeding, any method

ICD-9-CM Diagnostic

150.0 Malignant neoplasm of cervical esophagus
150.1 Malignant neoplasm of thoracic esophagus
150.2 Malignant neoplasm of abdominal esophagus
150.3 Malignant neoplasm of upper third of esophagus
150.4 Malignant neoplasm of middle third of esophagus
150.5 Malignant neoplasm of lower third of esophagus
150.8 Malignant neoplasm of other specified part of esophagus
211.0 Benign neoplasm of esophagus
456.0 Esophageal varices with bleeding
456.20 Esophageal varices with bleeding in diseases classified elsewhere — (Code first underlying disease: 571.0-571.9, 572.3) ☒
530.21 Ulcer of esophagus with bleeding — (Use additional E code to identify cause, if induced by chemical or drug)
530.4 Perforation of esophagus
530.7 Gastroesophageal laceration-hemorrhage syndrome
530.81 Esophageal reflux
530.82 Esophageal hemorrhage
530.83 Esophageal leukoplakia
530.84 Tracheoesophageal fistula
530.85 Barrett's esophagus
530.89 Other specified disorder of the esophagus
571.0 Alcoholic fatty liver
571.1 Acute alcoholic hepatitis
571.2 Alcoholic cirrhosis of liver
571.3 Unspecified alcoholic liver damage ▽
571.40 Unspecified chronic hepatitis ▽
571.41 Chronic persistent hepatitis
571.9 Unspecified chronic liver disease without mention of alcohol ▽
572.3 Portal hypertension — (Use additional code for any associated complications, such as: portal hypertensive gastropathy (537.89))
998.11 Hemorrhage complicating a procedure
998.2 Accidental puncture or laceration during procedure

ICD-9-CM Procedural

42.33 Endoscopic excision or destruction of lesion or tissue of esophagus
99.29 Injection or infusion of other therapeutic or prophylactic substance

43231

43231 Esophagoscopy, flexible, transoral; with endoscopic ultrasound examination

ICD-9-CM Diagnostic

150.0 Malignant neoplasm of cervical esophagus
150.1 Malignant neoplasm of thoracic esophagus
150.2 Malignant neoplasm of abdominal esophagus
150.3 Malignant neoplasm of upper third of esophagus
150.4 Malignant neoplasm of middle third of esophagus
150.5 Malignant neoplasm of lower third of esophagus
150.8 Malignant neoplasm of other specified part of esophagus
150.9 Malignant neoplasm of esophagus, unspecified site ▽
171.0 Malignant neoplasm of connective and other soft tissue of head, face, and neck
193 Malignant neoplasm of thyroid gland — (Use additional code to identify any functional activity)
195.0 Malignant neoplasm of head, face, and neck
196.0 Secondary and unspecified malignant neoplasm of lymph nodes of head, face, and neck
196.1 Secondary and unspecified malignant neoplasm of intrathoracic lymph nodes
196.9 Secondary and unspecified malignant neoplasm of lymph nodes, site unspecified ▽
197.8 Secondary malignant neoplasm of other digestive organs and spleen
198.89 Secondary malignant neoplasm of other specified sites
199.0 Disseminated malignant neoplasm
199.1 Other malignant neoplasm of unspecified site
202.81 Other malignant lymphomas of lymph nodes of head, face, and neck
209.20 Malignant carcinoid tumor of unknown primary site — (Code first any associated multiple endocrine neoplasia syndrome: 258.01-258.03)(Use additional code to identify associated endocrine syndrome, as: carcinoid syndrome: 259.2)
209.29 Malignant carcinoid tumor of other sites — (Code first any associated multiple endocrine neoplasia syndrome: 258.01-258.03)(Use additional code to identify associated endocrine syndrome, as: carcinoid syndrome: 259.2)
209.30 Malignant poorly differentiated neuroendocrine carcinoma, any site — (Code first any associated multiple endocrine neoplasia syndrome: 258.01-258.03)(Use additional code to identify associated endocrine syndrome, as: carcinoid syndrome: 259.2) ▽
209.69 Benign carcinoid tumor of other sites — (Code first any associated multiple endocrine neoplasia syndrome: 258.01-258.03)(Use additional code to identify associated endocrine syndrome, as: carcinoid syndrome: 259.2)
211.0 Benign neoplasm of esophagus
211.9 Benign neoplasm of other and unspecified site of the digestive system ▽
230.1 Carcinoma in situ of esophagus
235.5 Neoplasm of uncertain behavior of other and unspecified digestive organs ▽
239.0 Neoplasm of unspecified nature of digestive system
263.0 Malnutrition of moderate degree
306.4 Gastrointestinal malfunction arising from mental factors
352.3 Disorders of pneumogastric (10th) nerve
448.0 Hereditary hemorrhagic telangiectasia
456.0 Esophageal varices with bleeding
456.1 Esophageal varices without mention of bleeding
530.0 Achalasia and cardiospasm
530.11 Reflux esophagitis — (Use additional E code to identify cause, if induced by chemical)
530.12 Acute esophagitis — (Use additional E code to identify cause, if induced by chemical)
530.13 Eosinophilic esophagitis
530.19 Other esophagitis — (Use additional E code to identify cause, if induced by chemical)
530.20 Ulcer of esophagus without bleeding — (Use additional E code to identify cause, if induced by chemical or drug)
530.21 Ulcer of esophagus with bleeding — (Use additional E code to identify cause, if induced by chemical or drug)
530.3 Stricture and stenosis of esophagus
530.4 Perforation of esophagus
530.5 Dyskinesia of esophagus
530.6 Diverticulum of esophagus, acquired
530.7 Gastroesophageal laceration-hemorrhage syndrome
530.81 Esophageal reflux
530.82 Esophageal hemorrhage
530.83 Esophageal leukoplakia
530.84 Tracheoesophageal fistula
530.85 Barrett's esophagus
530.89 Other specified disorder of the esophagus
530.9 Unspecified disorder of esophagus ▽
552.3 Diaphragmatic hernia with obstruction
553.3 Diaphragmatic hernia without mention of obstruction or gangrene
578.0 Hematemesis
578.9 Hemorrhage of gastrointestinal tract, unspecified ▽
750.4 Other specified congenital anomaly of esophagus
750.9 Unspecified congenital anomaly of upper alimentary tract ▽

784.1 Throat pain
787.1 Heartburn
787.20 Dysphagia, unspecified ▽
787.21 Dysphagia, oral phase
787.22 Dysphagia, oropharyngeal phase
787.23 Dysphagia, pharyngeal phase
787.24 Dysphagia, pharyngoesophageal phase
787.29 Other dysphagia
793.4 Nonspecific (abnormal) findings on radiological and other examination of gastrointestinal tract
799.89 Other ill-defined conditions
862.22 Esophagus injury without mention of open wound into cavity

ICD-9-CM Procedural

42.23 Other esophagoscopy
88.74 Diagnostic ultrasound of digestive system

43232

43232 Esophagoscopy, flexible, transoral; with transendoscopic ultrasound-guided intramural or transmural fine needle aspiration/biopsy(s)

ICD-9-CM Diagnostic

150.0 Malignant neoplasm of cervical esophagus
150.1 Malignant neoplasm of thoracic esophagus
150.2 Malignant neoplasm of abdominal esophagus
150.3 Malignant neoplasm of upper third of esophagus
150.4 Malignant neoplasm of middle third of esophagus
150.5 Malignant neoplasm of lower third of esophagus
150.8 Malignant neoplasm of other specified part of esophagus
150.9 Malignant neoplasm of esophagus, unspecified site ▽
171.0 Malignant neoplasm of connective and other soft tissue of head, face, and neck
193 Malignant neoplasm of thyroid gland — (Use additional code to identify any functional activity)
195.0 Malignant neoplasm of head, face, and neck
196.0 Secondary and unspecified malignant neoplasm of lymph nodes of head, face, and neck
196.1 Secondary and unspecified malignant neoplasm of intrathoracic lymph nodes
196.9 Secondary and unspecified malignant neoplasm of lymph nodes, site unspecified ▽
197.8 Secondary malignant neoplasm of other digestive organs and spleen
198.89 Secondary malignant neoplasm of other specified sites
199.0 Disseminated malignant neoplasm
199.1 Other malignant neoplasm of unspecified site
202.81 Other malignant lymphomas of lymph nodes of head, face, and neck
209.20 Malignant carcinoid tumor of unknown primary site — (Code first any associated multiple endocrine neoplasia syndrome: 258.01-258.03)(Use additional code to identify associated endocrine syndrome, as: carcinoid syndrome: 259.2)
209.29 Malignant carcinoid tumor of other sites — (Code first any associated multiple endocrine neoplasia syndrome: 258.01-258.03)(Use additional code to identify associated endocrine syndrome, as: carcinoid syndrome: 259.2)
209.30 Malignant poorly differentiated neuroendocrine carcinoma, any site — (Code first any associated multiple endocrine neoplasia syndrome: 258.01-258.03)(Use additional code to identify associated endocrine syndrome, as: carcinoid syndrome: 259.2) ▽
209.69 Benign carcinoid tumor of other sites — (Code first any associated multiple endocrine neoplasia syndrome: 258.01-258.03)(Use additional code to identify associated endocrine syndrome, as: carcinoid syndrome: 259.2)
209.71 Secondary neuroendocrine tumor of distant lymph nodes
211.0 Benign neoplasm of esophagus
211.9 Benign neoplasm of other and unspecified site of the digestive system ▽
230.1 Carcinoma in situ of esophagus
235.5 Neoplasm of uncertain behavior of other and unspecified digestive organs ▽
239.0 Neoplasm of unspecified nature of digestive system
239.89 Neoplasms of unspecified nature, other specified sites
448.0 Hereditary hemorrhagic telangiectasia
530.0 Achalasia and cardiospasm
530.20 Ulcer of esophagus without bleeding — (Use additional E code to identify cause, if induced by chemical or drug)
530.21 Ulcer of esophagus with bleeding — (Use additional E code to identify cause, if induced by chemical or drug)
530.6 Diverticulum of esophagus, acquired
530.83 Esophageal leukoplakia
530.85 Barrett's esophagus
530.89 Other specified disorder of the esophagus
530.9 Unspecified disorder of esophagus ▽
578.0 Hematemesis
578.9 Hemorrhage of gastrointestinal tract, unspecified ▽
786.6 Swelling, mass, or lump in chest
787.20 Dysphagia, unspecified ▽
787.21 Dysphagia, oral phase
787.22 Dysphagia, oropharyngeal phase
787.23 Dysphagia, pharyngeal phase
787.24 Dysphagia, pharyngoesophageal phase
787.29 Other dysphagia
789.36 Abdominal or pelvic swelling, mass, or lump, epigastric
793.4 Nonspecific (abnormal) findings on radiological and other examination of gastrointestinal tract
799.89 Other ill-defined conditions

ICD-9-CM Procedural

42.24 Closed (endoscopic) biopsy of esophagus
88.74 Diagnostic ultrasound of digestive system

43235-43236

43235 Esophagogastroduodenoscopy, flexible, transoral; diagnostic, including collection of specimen(s) by brushing or washing, when performed (separate procedure)
43236 with directed submucosal injection(s), any substance

ICD-9-CM Diagnostic

150.0 Malignant neoplasm of cervical esophagus
150.1 Malignant neoplasm of thoracic esophagus
150.2 Malignant neoplasm of abdominal esophagus
150.3 Malignant neoplasm of upper third of esophagus
150.4 Malignant neoplasm of middle third of esophagus
150.5 Malignant neoplasm of lower third of esophagus
150.8 Malignant neoplasm of other specified part of esophagus
150.9 Malignant neoplasm of esophagus, unspecified site ▽
151.0 Malignant neoplasm of cardia
151.1 Malignant neoplasm of pylorus
151.2 Malignant neoplasm of pyloric antrum
151.3 Malignant neoplasm of fundus of stomach
151.4 Malignant neoplasm of body of stomach
151.5 Malignant neoplasm of lesser curvature of stomach, unspecified ▽
151.6 Malignant neoplasm of greater curvature of stomach, unspecified ▽
151.8 Malignant neoplasm of other specified sites of stomach
151.9 Malignant neoplasm of stomach, unspecified site ▽
152.0 Malignant neoplasm of duodenum
152.1 Malignant neoplasm of jejunum
152.8 Malignant neoplasm of other specified sites of small intestine
152.9 Malignant neoplasm of small intestine, unspecified site ▽
159.9 Malignant neoplasm of ill-defined sites of digestive organs and peritoneum ▽
197.4 Secondary malignant neoplasm of small intestine including duodenum
197.8 Secondary malignant neoplasm of other digestive organs and spleen

199.0 Disseminated malignant neoplasm

199.1 Other malignant neoplasm of unspecified site

209.00 Malignant carcinoid tumor of the small intestine, unspecified portion — (Code first any associated multiple endocrine neoplasia syndrome: 258.01-258.03)(Use additional code to identify associated endocrine syndrome, as: carcinoid syndrome: 259.2) ♈

209.01 Malignant carcinoid tumor of the duodenum — (Code first any associated multiple endocrine neoplasia syndrome: 258.01-258.03)(Use additional code to identify associated endocrine syndrome, as: carcinoid syndrome: 259.2)

209.02 Malignant carcinoid tumor of the jejunum — (Code first any associated multiple endocrine neoplasia syndrome: 258.01-258.03)(Use additional code to identify associated endocrine syndrome, as: carcinoid syndrome: 259.2)

209.20 Malignant carcinoid tumor of unknown primary site — (Code first any associated multiple endocrine neoplasia syndrome: 258.01-258.03)(Use additional code to identify associated endocrine syndrome, as: carcinoid syndrome: 259.2)

209.23 Malignant carcinoid tumor of the stomach — (Code first any associated multiple endocrine neoplasia syndrome: 258.01-258.03)(Use additional code to identify associated endocrine syndrome, as: carcinoid syndrome: 259.2)

209.25 Malignant carcinoid tumor of foregut, not otherwise specified — (Code first any associated multiple endocrine neoplasia syndrome: 258.01-258.03)(Use additional code to identify associated endocrine syndrome, as: carcinoid syndrome: 259.2)

209.29 Malignant carcinoid tumor of other sites — (Code first any associated multiple endocrine neoplasia syndrome: 258.01-258.03)(Use additional code to identify associated endocrine syndrome, as: carcinoid syndrome: 259.2)

209.30 Malignant poorly differentiated neuroendocrine carcinoma, any site — (Code first any associated multiple endocrine neoplasia syndrome: 258.01-258.03)(Use additional code to identify associated endocrine syndrome, as: carcinoid syndrome: 259.2) ♈

209.40 Benign carcinoid tumor of the small intestine, unspecified portion — (Code first any associated multiple endocrine neoplasia syndrome: 258.01-258.03)(Use additional code to identify associated endocrine syndrome, as: carcinoid syndrome: 259.2) ♈

209.41 Benign carcinoid tumor of the duodenum — (Code first any associated multiple endocrine neoplasia syndrome: 258.01-258.03)(Use additional code to identify associated endocrine syndrome, as: carcinoid syndrome: 259.2)

209.42 Benign carcinoid tumor of the jejunum — (Code first any associated multiple endocrine neoplasia syndrome: 258.01-258.03)(Use additional code to identify associated endocrine syndrome, as: carcinoid syndrome: 259.2)

209.43 Benign carcinoid tumor of the ileum — (Code first any associated multiple endocrine neoplasia syndrome: 258.01-258.03)(Use additional code to identify associated endocrine syndrome, as: carcinoid syndrome: 259.2)

209.63 Benign carcinoid tumor of the stomach — (Code first any associated multiple endocrine neoplasia syndrome: 258.01-258.03)(Use additional code to identify associated endocrine syndrome, as: carcinoid syndrome: 259.2)

209.65 Benign carcinoid tumor of foregut, not otherwise specified — (Code first any associated multiple endocrine neoplasia syndrome: 258.01-258.03)(Use additional code to identify associated endocrine syndrome, as: carcinoid syndrome: 259.2)

209.69 Benign carcinoid tumor of other sites — (Code first any associated multiple endocrine neoplasia syndrome: 258.01-258.03)(Use additional code to identify associated endocrine syndrome, as: carcinoid syndrome: 259.2)

211.0 Benign neoplasm of esophagus

211.1 Benign neoplasm of stomach

211.2 Benign neoplasm of duodenum, jejunum, and ileum

230.1 Carcinoma in situ of esophagus

230.2 Carcinoma in situ of stomach

235.2 Neoplasm of uncertain behavior of stomach, intestines, and rectum

239.0 Neoplasm of unspecified nature of digestive system

285.9 Unspecified anemia ♈

456.21 Esophageal varices without mention of bleeding in diseases classified elsewhere — (Code first underlying disease: 571.0-571.9, 572.3) ☒

530.0 Achalasia and cardiospasm

530.10 Unspecified esophagitis — (Use additional E code to identify cause, if induced by chemical) ♈

530.11 Reflux esophagitis — (Use additional E code to identify cause, if induced by chemical)

530.12 Acute esophagitis — (Use additional E code to identify cause, if induced by chemical)

530.13 Eosinophilic esophagitis

530.19 Other esophagitis — (Use additional E code to identify cause, if induced by chemical)

530.20 Ulcer of esophagus without bleeding — (Use additional E code to identify cause, if induced by chemical or drug)

530.21 Ulcer of esophagus with bleeding — (Use additional E code to identify cause, if induced by chemical or drug)

530.3 Stricture and stenosis of esophagus

530.5 Dyskinesia of esophagus

530.6 Diverticulum of esophagus, acquired

530.7 Gastroesophageal laceration-hemorrhage syndrome

530.81 Esophageal reflux

530.82 Esophageal hemorrhage

530.83 Esophageal leukoplakia

530.84 Tracheoesophageal fistula

530.85 Barrett's esophagus

530.89 Other specified disorder of the esophagus

531.00 Acute gastric ulcer with hemorrhage, without mention of obstruction — (Use additional E code to identify drug, if drug induced)

531.01 Acute gastric ulcer with hemorrhage and obstruction — (Use additional E code to identify drug, if drug induced)

531.10 Acute gastric ulcer with perforation, without mention of obstruction — (Use additional E code to identify drug, if drug induced)

531.20 Acute gastric ulcer with hemorrhage and perforation, without mention of obstruction — (Use additional E code to identify drug, if drug induced)

531.30 Acute gastric ulcer without mention of hemorrhage, perforation, or obstruction — (Use additional E code to identify drug, if drug induced)

531.31 Acute gastric ulcer without mention of hemorrhage or perforation, with obstruction — (Use additional E code to identify drug, if drug induced)

531.40 Chronic or unspecified gastric ulcer with hemorrhage, without mention of obstruction — (Use additional E code to identify drug, if drug induced)

531.41 Chronic or unspecified gastric ulcer with hemorrhage and obstruction — (Use additional E code to identify drug, if drug induced)

531.50 Chronic or unspecified gastric ulcer with perforation, without mention of obstruction — (Use additional E code to identify drug, if drug induced)

531.51 Chronic or unspecified gastric ulcer with perforation and obstruction — (Use additional E code to identify drug, if drug induced)

531.60 Chronic or unspecified gastric ulcer with hemorrhage and perforation, without mention of obstruction — (Use additional E code to identify drug, if drug induced)

531.61 Chronic or unspecified gastric ulcer with hemorrhage, perforation, and obstruction — (Use additional E code to identify drug, if drug induced)

531.70 Chronic gastric ulcer without mention of hemorrhage, perforation, without mention of obstruction — (Use additional E code to identify drug, if drug induced)

531.71 Chronic gastric ulcer without mention of hemorrhage or perforation, with obstruction — (Use additional E code to identify drug, if drug induced)

531.90 Gastric ulcer, unspecified as acute or chronic, without mention of hemorrhage, perforation, or obstruction — (Use additional E code to identify drug, if drug induced) ♈

531.91 Gastric ulcer, unspecified as acute or chronic, without mention of hemorrhage or perforation, with obstruction — (Use additional E code to identify drug, if drug induced) ♈

532.00 Acute duodenal ulcer with hemorrhage, without mention of obstruction — (Use additional E code to identify drug, if drug induced)

532.01 Acute duodenal ulcer with hemorrhage and obstruction — (Use additional E code to identify drug, if drug induced)

532.10 Acute duodenal ulcer with perforation, without mention of obstruction — (Use additional E code to identify drug, if drug induced)

532.11 Acute duodenal ulcer with perforation and obstruction — (Use additional E code to identify drug, if drug induced)

532.20 Acute duodenal ulcer with hemorrhage and perforation, without mention of obstruction — (Use additional E code to identify drug, if drug induced)

532.21 Acute duodenal ulcer with hemorrhage, perforation, and obstruction — (Use additional E code to identify drug, if drug induced)

532.30 Acute duodenal ulcer without mention of hemorrhage, perforation, or obstruction — (Use additional E code to identify drug, if drug induced)

532.31 Acute duodenal ulcer without mention of hemorrhage or perforation, with obstruction — (Use additional E code to identify drug, if drug induced)

532.40 Duodenal ulcer, chronic or unspecified, with hemorrhage, without mention of obstruction — (Use additional E code to identify drug, if drug induced)

532.41 Chronic or unspecified duodenal ulcer with hemorrhage and obstruction — (Use additional E code to identify drug, if drug induced)

532.50 Chronic or unspecified duodenal ulcer with perforation, without mention of obstruction — (Use additional E code to identify drug, if drug induced)

532.51 Chronic or unspecified duodenal ulcer with perforation and obstruction — (Use additional E code to identify drug, if drug induced)

532.60 Chronic or unspecified duodenal ulcer with hemorrhage and perforation, without mention of obstruction — (Use additional E code to identify drug, if drug induced)

532.61 Chronic or unspecified duodenal ulcer with hemorrhage, perforation, and obstruction — (Use additional E code to identify drug, if drug induced)

532.70 Chronic duodenal ulcer without mention of hemorrhage, perforation, or obstruction — (Use additional E code to identify drug, if drug induced)

532.71 Chronic duodenal ulcer without mention of hemorrhage or perforation, with obstruction — (Use additional E code to identify drug, if drug induced)

532.90 Duodenal ulcer, unspecified as acute or chronic, without hemorrhage, perforation, or obstruction — (Use additional E code to identify drug, if drug induced)

532.91 Duodenal ulcer, unspecified as acute or chronic, without mention of hemorrhage or perforation, with obstruction — (Use additional E code to identify drug, if drug induced)

533.00 Acute peptic ulcer, unspecified site, with hemorrhage, without mention of obstruction — (Use additional E code to identify drug, if drug induced)

533.01 Acute peptic ulcer, unspecified site, with hemorrhage and obstruction — (Use additional E code to identify drug, if drug induced)

533.10 Acute peptic ulcer, unspecified site, with perforation, without mention of obstruction — (Use additional E code to identify drug, if drug induced)

533.11 Acute peptic ulcer, unspecified site, with perforation and obstruction — (Use additional E code to identify drug, if drug induced)

533.20 Acute peptic ulcer, unspecified site, with hemorrhage and perforation, without mention of obstruction — (Use additional E code to identify drug, if drug induced)

533.21 Acute peptic ulcer, unspecified site, with hemorrhage, perforation, and obstruction — (Use additional E code to identify drug, if drug induced)

533.30 Acute peptic ulcer, unspecified site, without mention of hemorrhage, perforation, or obstruction — (Use additional E code to identify drug, if drug induced)

533.31 Acute peptic ulcer, unspecified site, without mention of hemorrhage and perforation, with obstruction — (Use additional E code to identify drug, if drug induced)

533.40 Chronic or unspecified peptic ulcer, unspecified site, with hemorrhage, without mention of obstruction — (Use additional E code to identify drug, if drug induced)

533.41 Chronic or unspecified peptic ulcer, unspecified site, with hemorrhage and obstruction — (Use additional E code to identify drug, if drug induced)

533.50 Chronic or unspecified peptic ulcer, unspecified site, with perforation, without mention of obstruction — (Use additional E code to identify drug, if drug induced)

533.51 Chronic or unspecified peptic ulcer, unspecified site, with perforation and obstruction — (Use additional E code to identify drug, if drug induced)

533.60 Chronic or unspecified peptic ulcer, unspecified site, with hemorrhage and perforation, without mention of obstruction — (Use additional E code to identify drug, if drug induced)

533.61 Chronic or unspecified peptic ulcer, unspecified site, with hemorrhage, perforation, and obstruction — (Use additional E code to identify drug, if drug induced)

533.70 Chronic peptic ulcer, unspecified site, without mention of hemorrhage, perforation, or obstruction — (Use additional E code to identify drug, if drug induced)

533.71 Chronic peptic ulcer of unspecified site without mention of hemorrhage or perforation, with obstruction — (Use additional E code to identify drug, if drug induced)

533.90 Peptic ulcer, unspecified site, unspecified as acute or chronic, without mention of hemorrhage, perforation, or obstruction — (Use additional E code to identify drug, if drug induced)

533.91 Peptic ulcer, unspecified site, unspecified as acute or chronic, without mention of hemorrhage or perforation, with obstruction — (Use additional E code to identify drug, if drug induced)

534.00 Acute gastrojejunal ulcer with hemorrhage, without mention of obstruction

534.01 Acute gastrojejunal ulcer, with hemorrhage and obstruction

534.10 Acute gastrojejunal ulcer with perforation, without mention of obstruction

534.11 Acute gastrojejunal ulcer with perforation and obstruction

534.20 Acute gastrojejunal ulcer with hemorrhage and perforation, without mention of obstruction

534.21 Acute gastrojejunal ulcer with hemorrhage, perforation, and obstruction

534.30 Acute gastrojejunal ulcer without mention of hemorrhage, perforation, or obstruction

534.31 Acute gastrojejunal ulcer without mention of hemorrhage or perforation, with obstruction

534.40 Chronic or unspecified gastrojejunal ulcer with hemorrhage, without mention of obstruction

534.41 Chronic or unspecified gastrojejunal ulcer, with hemorrhage and obstruction

534.50 Chronic or unspecified gastrojejunal ulcer with perforation, without mention of obstruction

534.51 Chronic or unspecified gastrojejunal ulcer with perforation and obstruction

534.60 Chronic or unspecified gastrojejunal ulcer with hemorrhage and perforation, without mention of obstruction

534.61 Chronic or unspecified gastrojejunal ulcer with hemorrhage, perforation, and obstruction

534.70 Chronic gastrojejunal ulcer without mention of hemorrhage, perforation, or obstruction

534.71 Chronic gastrojejunal ulcer without mention of hemorrhage or perforation, with obstruction

534.90 Gastrojejunal ulcer, unspecified as acute or chronic, without mention of hemorrhage, perforation, or obstruction

534.91 Gastrojejunal ulcer, unspecified as acute or chronic, without mention of hemorrhage or perforation, with obstruction

535.00 Acute gastritis without mention of hemorrhage

535.01 Acute gastritis with hemorrhage

535.10 Atrophic gastritis without mention of hemorrhage

535.11 Atrophic gastritis with hemorrhage

535.20 Gastric mucosal hypertrophy without mention of hemorrhage

535.21 Gastric mucosal hypertrophy with hemorrhage

535.30 Alcoholic gastritis without mention of hemorrhage

535.31 Alcoholic gastritis with hemorrhage

535.40 Other specified gastritis without mention of hemorrhage

535.41 Other specified gastritis with hemorrhage

535.60 Duodenitis without mention of hemorrhage

535.61 Duodenitis with hemorrhage

535.70 Eosinophilic gastritis without mention of hemorrhage

535.71 Eosinophilic gastritis with hemorrhage

536.0 Achlorhydria

536.1 Acute dilatation of stomach

536.2 Persistent vomiting

536.3 Gastroparesis — (Code first underlying disease, if known, as: 249.6, 250.6)

536.8 Dyspepsia and other specified disorders of function of stomach

536.9 Unspecified functional disorder of stomach

537.0 Acquired hypertrophic pyloric stenosis

537.1 Gastric diverticulum

537.2 Chronic duodenal ileus

537.3 Other obstruction of duodenum

537.4 Fistula of stomach or duodenum

537.5 Gastroptosis

537.6 Hourglass stricture or stenosis of stomach

537.81 Pylorospasm
537.82 Angiodysplasia of stomach and duodenum (without mention of hemorrhage)
537.83 Angiodysplasia of stomach and duodenum with hemorrhage
537.84 Dieulafoy lesion (hemorrhagic) of stomach and duodenum
537.89 Other specified disorder of stomach and duodenum
537.9 Unspecified disorder of stomach and duodenum ▽
552.3 Diaphragmatic hernia with obstruction
553.3 Diaphragmatic hernia without mention of obstruction or gangrene
555.0 Regional enteritis of small intestine
558.1 Gastroenteritis and colitis due to radiation
558.2 Toxic gastroenteritis and colitis — (Use additional E code to identify cause)
558.3 Gastroenteritis and colitis, allergic — (Use additional code to identify type of food allergy: V15.01-V15.05)
558.41 Eosinophilic gastroenteritis
558.9 Other and unspecified noninfectious gastroenteritis and colitis ▽
569.5 Abscess of intestine
569.82 Ulceration of intestine
569.86 Dieulafoy lesion (hemorrhagic) of intestine
569.89 Other specified disorder of intestines
578.0 Hematemesis
578.1 Blood in stool
579.0 Celiac disease
579.2 Blind loop syndrome
579.3 Other and unspecified postsurgical nonabsorption ▽
579.8 Other specified intestinal malabsorption
747.61 Congenital gastrointestinal vessel anomaly
750.3 Congenital tracheoesophageal fistula, esophageal atresia and stenosis
750.4 Other specified congenital anomaly of esophagus
750.5 Congenital hypertrophic pyloric stenosis
750.6 Congenital hiatus hernia
750.7 Other specified congenital anomalies of stomach
751.8 Other specified congenital anomalies of digestive system
783.0 Anorexia
783.21 Loss of weight — (Use additional code to identify Body Mass Index (BMI), if known: V85.0-V85.54)
783.22 Underweight — (Use additional code to identify Body Mass Index (BMI), if known: V85.0-V85.54)
783.7 Adult failure to thrive
784.1 Throat pain
787.1 Heartburn
787.20 Dysphagia, unspecified ▽
787.21 Dysphagia, oral phase
787.22 Dysphagia, oropharyngeal phase
787.23 Dysphagia, pharyngeal phase
787.24 Dysphagia, pharyngoesophageal phase
787.29 Other dysphagia
787.3 Flatulence, eructation, and gas pain
787.4 Visible peristalsis
787.5 Abnormal bowel sounds
787.99 Other symptoms involving digestive system
789.09 Abdominal pain, other specified site
792.1 Nonspecific abnormal finding in stool contents
793.4 Nonspecific (abnormal) findings on radiological and other examination of gastrointestinal tract
997.49 Other digestive system complications
V10.00 Personal history of malignant neoplasm of unspecified site in gastrointestinal tract ▽
V12.71 Personal history of peptic ulcer disease
V12.79 Personal history of other diseases of digestive disease
V16.0 Family history of malignant neoplasm of gastrointestinal tract
V18.51 Family history, Colonic polyps
V18.59 Family history, other digestive disorders
V67.00 Follow-up examination, following unspecified surgery ▽
V67.09 Follow-up examination, following other surgery
V67.59 Other follow-up examination
V67.9 Unspecified follow-up examination ▽
V71.1 Observation for suspected malignant neoplasm
V71.89 Observation for other specified suspected conditions
V85.0 Body Mass Index less than 19, adult

ICD-9-CM Procedural

42.33 Endoscopic excision or destruction of lesion or tissue of esophagus
42.81 Insertion of permanent tube into esophagus
42.92 Dilation of esophagus
45.13 Other endoscopy of small intestine
45.14 Closed [endoscopic] biopsy of small intestine
45.16 Esophagogastroduodenoscopy (EGD) with closed biopsy
99.23 Injection of steroid
99.29 Injection or infusion of other therapeutic or prophylactic substance

HCPCS Level II Supplies & Services

A4270 Disposable endoscope sheath, each

43237-43238 [43270]

43237 Esophagogastroduodenoscopy, flexible, transoral; with endoscopic ultrasound examination limited to the esophagus, stomach or duodenum, and adjacent structures
43238 with transendoscopic ultrasound-guided intramural or transmural fine needle aspiration/biopsy(s), (includes endoscopic ultrasound examination limited to the esophagus, stomach or duodenum, and adjacent structures)
43270 with ablation of tumor(s), polyp(s), or other lesion(s) (includes pre- and post-dilation and guide wire passage, when performed)

ICD-9-CM Diagnostic

150.0 Malignant neoplasm of cervical esophagus
150.1 Malignant neoplasm of thoracic esophagus
150.2 Malignant neoplasm of abdominal esophagus
150.3 Malignant neoplasm of upper third of esophagus
150.4 Malignant neoplasm of middle third of esophagus
150.5 Malignant neoplasm of lower third of esophagus
150.8 Malignant neoplasm of other specified part of esophagus
150.9 Malignant neoplasm of esophagus, unspecified site ▽
171.0 Malignant neoplasm of connective and other soft tissue of head, face, and neck
193 Malignant neoplasm of thyroid gland — (Use additional code to identify any functional activity)
195.0 Malignant neoplasm of head, face, and neck
196.0 Secondary and unspecified malignant neoplasm of lymph nodes of head, face, and neck
196.9 Secondary and unspecified malignant neoplasm of lymph nodes, site unspecified ▽
197.8 Secondary malignant neoplasm of other digestive organs and spleen
198.89 Secondary malignant neoplasm of other specified sites
199.0 Disseminated malignant neoplasm
199.1 Other malignant neoplasm of unspecified site
202.81 Other malignant lymphomas of lymph nodes of head, face, and neck
209.20 Malignant carcinoid tumor of unknown primary site — (Code first any associated multiple endocrine neoplasia syndrome: 258.01-258.03)(Use additional code to identify associated endocrine syndrome, as: carcinoid syndrome: 259.2)
209.25 Malignant carcinoid tumor of foregut, not otherwise specified — (Code first any associated multiple endocrine neoplasia syndrome: 258.01-258.03)(Use additional code to identify associated endocrine syndrome, as: carcinoid syndrome: 259.2)
209.29 Malignant carcinoid tumor of other sites — (Code first any associated multiple endocrine neoplasia syndrome: 258.01-258.03)(Use additional code to identify associated endocrine syndrome, as: carcinoid syndrome: 259.2)

209.30 Malignant poorly differentiated neuroendocrine carcinoma, any site — (Code first any associated multiple endocrine neoplasia syndrome: 258.01-258.03)(Use additional code to identify associated endocrine syndrome, as: carcinoid syndrome: 259.2)

209.69 Benign carcinoid tumor of other sites — (Code first any associated multiple endocrine neoplasia syndrome: 258.01-258.03)(Use additional code to identify associated endocrine syndrome, as: carcinoid syndrome: 259.2)

211.0 Benign neoplasm of esophagus

211.9 Benign neoplasm of other and unspecified site of the digestive system

230.1 Carcinoma in situ of esophagus

235.5 Neoplasm of uncertain behavior of other and unspecified digestive organs

239.0 Neoplasm of unspecified nature of digestive system

263.0 Malnutrition of moderate degree

306.4 Gastrointestinal malfunction arising from mental factors

352.3 Disorders of pneumogastric (10th) nerve

448.0 Hereditary hemorrhagic telangiectasia

456.0 Esophageal varices with bleeding

456.1 Esophageal varices without mention of bleeding

530.0 Achalasia and cardiospasm

530.11 Reflux esophagitis — (Use additional E code to identify cause, if induced by chemical)

530.12 Acute esophagitis — (Use additional E code to identify cause, if induced by chemical)

530.13 Eosinophilic esophagitis

530.19 Other esophagitis — (Use additional E code to identify cause, if induced by chemical)

530.20 Ulcer of esophagus without bleeding — (Use additional E code to identify cause, if induced by chemical or drug)

530.21 Ulcer of esophagus with bleeding — (Use additional E code to identify cause, if induced by chemical or drug)

530.3 Stricture and stenosis of esophagus

530.4 Perforation of esophagus

530.5 Dyskinesia of esophagus

530.6 Diverticulum of esophagus, acquired

530.7 Gastroesophageal laceration-hemorrhage syndrome

530.81 Esophageal reflux

530.82 Esophageal hemorrhage

530.83 Esophageal leukoplakia

530.84 Tracheoesophageal fistula

530.85 Barrett's esophagus

530.89 Other specified disorder of the esophagus

530.9 Unspecified disorder of esophagus

552.3 Diaphragmatic hernia with obstruction

553.3 Diaphragmatic hernia without mention of obstruction or gangrene

578.0 Hematemesis

578.1 Blood in stool

578.9 Hemorrhage of gastrointestinal tract, unspecified

750.4 Other specified congenital anomaly of esophagus

750.9 Unspecified congenital anomaly of upper alimentary tract

784.1 Throat pain

787.1 Heartburn

787.20 Dysphagia, unspecified

787.21 Dysphagia, oral phase

787.22 Dysphagia, oropharyngeal phase

787.23 Dysphagia, pharyngeal phase

787.24 Dysphagia, pharyngoesophageal phase

787.29 Other dysphagia

793.4 Nonspecific (abnormal) findings on radiological and other examination of gastrointestinal tract

799.89 Other ill-defined conditions

862.22 Esophagus injury without mention of open wound into cavity

ICD-9-CM Procedural

42.33 Endoscopic excision or destruction of lesion or tissue of esophagus

45.13 Other endoscopy of small intestine

45.16 Esophagogastroduodenoscopy (EGD) with closed biopsy

88.74 Diagnostic ultrasound of digestive system

HCPCS Level II Supplies & Services

A4270 Disposable endoscope sheath, each

43239, 43252

43239 Esophagogastroduodenoscopy, flexible, transoral; with biopsy, single or multiple

43252 with optical endomicroscopy

ICD-9-CM Diagnostic

150.0 Malignant neoplasm of cervical esophagus

150.1 Malignant neoplasm of thoracic esophagus

150.2 Malignant neoplasm of abdominal esophagus

150.3 Malignant neoplasm of upper third of esophagus

150.4 Malignant neoplasm of middle third of esophagus

150.5 Malignant neoplasm of lower third of esophagus

150.8 Malignant neoplasm of other specified part of esophagus

150.9 Malignant neoplasm of esophagus, unspecified site

151.0 Malignant neoplasm of cardia

151.1 Malignant neoplasm of pylorus

151.2 Malignant neoplasm of pyloric antrum

151.3 Malignant neoplasm of fundus of stomach

151.4 Malignant neoplasm of body of stomach

151.5 Malignant neoplasm of lesser curvature of stomach, unspecified

151.6 Malignant neoplasm of greater curvature of stomach, unspecified

151.8 Malignant neoplasm of other specified sites of stomach

151.9 Malignant neoplasm of stomach, unspecified site

152.0 Malignant neoplasm of duodenum

152.1 Malignant neoplasm of jejunum

152.8 Malignant neoplasm of other specified sites of small intestine

152.9 Malignant neoplasm of small intestine, unspecified site

159.9 Malignant neoplasm of ill-defined sites of digestive organs and peritoneum

197.4 Secondary malignant neoplasm of small intestine including duodenum

197.8 Secondary malignant neoplasm of other digestive organs and spleen

199.0 Disseminated malignant neoplasm

199.1 Other malignant neoplasm of unspecified site

209.00 Malignant carcinoid tumor of the small intestine, unspecified portion — (Code first any associated multiple endocrine neoplasia syndrome: 258.01-258.03)(Use additional code to identify associated endocrine syndrome, as: carcinoid syndrome: 259.2)

209.01 Malignant carcinoid tumor of the duodenum — (Code first any associated multiple endocrine neoplasia syndrome: 258.01-258.03)(Use additional code to identify associated endocrine syndrome, as: carcinoid syndrome: 259.2)

209.02 Malignant carcinoid tumor of the jejunum — (Code first any associated multiple endocrine neoplasia syndrome: 258.01-258.03)(Use additional code to identify associated endocrine syndrome, as: carcinoid syndrome: 259.2)

209.23 Malignant carcinoid tumor of the stomach — (Code first any associated multiple endocrine neoplasia syndrome: 258.01-258.03)(Use additional code to identify associated endocrine syndrome, as: carcinoid syndrome: 259.2)

209.25 Malignant carcinoid tumor of foregut, not otherwise specified — (Code first any associated multiple endocrine neoplasia syndrome: 258.01-258.03)(Use additional code to identify associated endocrine syndrome, as: carcinoid syndrome: 259.2)

209.29 Malignant carcinoid tumor of other sites — (Code first any associated multiple endocrine neoplasia syndrome: 258.01-258.03)(Use additional code to identify associated endocrine syndrome, as: carcinoid syndrome: 259.2)

209.30 Malignant poorly differentiated neuroendocrine carcinoma, any site — (Code first any associated multiple endocrine neoplasia syndrome: 258.01-258.03)(Use additional code to identify associated endocrine syndrome, as: carcinoid syndrome: 259.2)

209.40 Benign carcinoid tumor of the small intestine, unspecified portion — (Code first any associated multiple endocrine neoplasia syndrome: 258.01-258.03)(Use additional code to identify associated endocrine syndrome, as: carcinoid syndrome: 259.2) ▽

209.41 Benign carcinoid tumor of the duodenum — (Code first any associated multiple endocrine neoplasia syndrome: 258.01-258.03)(Use additional code to identify associated endocrine syndrome, as: carcinoid syndrome: 259.2)

209.42 Benign carcinoid tumor of the jejunum — (Code first any associated multiple endocrine neoplasia syndrome: 258.01-258.03)(Use additional code to identify associated endocrine syndrome, as: carcinoid syndrome: 259.2)

209.43 Benign carcinoid tumor of the ileum — (Code first any associated multiple endocrine neoplasia syndrome: 258.01-258.03)(Use additional code to identify associated endocrine syndrome, as: carcinoid syndrome: 259.2)

209.63 Benign carcinoid tumor of the stomach — (Code first any associated multiple endocrine neoplasia syndrome: 258.01-258.03)(Use additional code to identify associated endocrine syndrome, as: carcinoid syndrome: 259.2)

209.65 Benign carcinoid tumor of foregut, not otherwise specified — (Code first any associated multiple endocrine neoplasia syndrome: 258.01-258.03)(Use additional code to identify associated endocrine syndrome, as: carcinoid syndrome: 259.2)

209.69 Benign carcinoid tumor of other sites — (Code first any associated multiple endocrine neoplasia syndrome: 258.01-258.03)(Use additional code to identify associated endocrine syndrome, as: carcinoid syndrome: 259.2)

211.0 Benign neoplasm of esophagus

211.1 Benign neoplasm of stomach

211.2 Benign neoplasm of duodenum, jejunum, and ileum

230.1 Carcinoma in situ of esophagus

230.2 Carcinoma in situ of stomach

235.2 Neoplasm of uncertain behavior of stomach, intestines, and rectum

239.0 Neoplasm of unspecified nature of digestive system

285.9 Unspecified anemia ▽

456.21 Esophageal varices without mention of bleeding in diseases classified elsewhere — (Code first underlying disease: 571.0-571.9, 572.3) ☒

530.0 Achalasia and cardiospasm

530.10 Unspecified esophagitis — (Use additional E code to identify cause, if induced by chemical) ▽

530.11 Reflux esophagitis — (Use additional E code to identify cause, if induced by chemical)

530.12 Acute esophagitis — (Use additional E code to identify cause, if induced by chemical)

530.13 Eosinophilic esophagitis

530.19 Other esophagitis — (Use additional E code to identify cause, if induced by chemical)

530.20 Ulcer of esophagus without bleeding — (Use additional E code to identify cause, if induced by chemical or drug)

530.21 Ulcer of esophagus with bleeding — (Use additional E code to identify cause, if induced by chemical or drug)

530.3 Stricture and stenosis of esophagus

530.5 Dyskinesia of esophagus

530.6 Diverticulum of esophagus, acquired

530.7 Gastroesophageal laceration-hemorrhage syndrome

530.81 Esophageal reflux

530.82 Esophageal hemorrhage

530.83 Esophageal leukoplakia

530.84 Tracheoesophageal fistula

530.85 Barrett's esophagus

530.89 Other specified disorder of the esophagus

531.00 Acute gastric ulcer with hemorrhage, without mention of obstruction — (Use additional E code to identify drug, if drug induced)

531.01 Acute gastric ulcer with hemorrhage and obstruction — (Use additional E code to identify drug, if drug induced)

531.10 Acute gastric ulcer with perforation, without mention of obstruction — (Use additional E code to identify drug, if drug induced)

531.20 Acute gastric ulcer with hemorrhage and perforation, without mention of obstruction — (Use additional E code to identify drug, if drug induced)

531.30 Acute gastric ulcer without mention of hemorrhage, perforation, or obstruction — (Use additional E code to identify drug, if drug induced)

531.31 Acute gastric ulcer without mention of hemorrhage or perforation, with obstruction — (Use additional E code to identify drug, if drug induced)

531.40 Chronic or unspecified gastric ulcer with hemorrhage, without mention of obstruction — (Use additional E code to identify drug, if drug induced)

531.41 Chronic or unspecified gastric ulcer with hemorrhage and obstruction — (Use additional E code to identify drug, if drug induced)

531.50 Chronic or unspecified gastric ulcer with perforation, without mention of obstruction — (Use additional E code to identify drug, if drug induced)

531.51 Chronic or unspecified gastric ulcer with perforation and obstruction — (Use additional E code to identify drug, if drug induced)

531.60 Chronic or unspecified gastric ulcer with hemorrhage and perforation, without mention of obstruction — (Use additional E code to identify drug, if drug induced)

531.61 Chronic or unspecified gastric ulcer with hemorrhage, perforation, and obstruction — (Use additional E code to identify drug, if drug induced)

531.70 Chronic gastric ulcer without mention of hemorrhage, perforation, without mention of obstruction — (Use additional E code to identify drug, if drug induced)

531.71 Chronic gastric ulcer without mention of hemorrhage or perforation, with obstruction — (Use additional E code to identify drug, if drug induced)

531.90 Gastric ulcer, unspecified as acute or chronic, without mention of hemorrhage, perforation, or obstruction — (Use additional E code to identify drug, if drug induced) ▽

531.91 Gastric ulcer, unspecified as acute or chronic, without mention of hemorrhage or perforation, with obstruction — (Use additional E code to identify drug, if drug induced) ▽

532.00 Acute duodenal ulcer with hemorrhage, without mention of obstruction — (Use additional E code to identify drug, if drug induced)

532.01 Acute duodenal ulcer with hemorrhage and obstruction — (Use additional E code to identify drug, if drug induced)

532.10 Acute duodenal ulcer with perforation, without mention of obstruction — (Use additional E code to identify drug, if drug induced)

532.11 Acute duodenal ulcer with perforation and obstruction — (Use additional E code to identify drug, if drug induced)

532.20 Acute duodenal ulcer with hemorrhage and perforation, without mention of obstruction — (Use additional E code to identify drug, if drug induced)

532.21 Acute duodenal ulcer with hemorrhage, perforation, and obstruction — (Use additional E code to identify drug, if drug induced)

532.30 Acute duodenal ulcer without mention of hemorrhage, perforation, or obstruction — (Use additional E code to identify drug, if drug induced)

532.31 Acute duodenal ulcer without mention of hemorrhage or perforation, with obstruction — (Use additional E code to identify drug, if drug induced)

532.40 Duodenal ulcer, chronic or unspecified, with hemorrhage, without mention of obstruction — (Use additional E code to identify drug, if drug induced)

532.41 Chronic or unspecified duodenal ulcer with hemorrhage and obstruction — (Use additional E code to identify drug, if drug induced)

532.50 Chronic or unspecified duodenal ulcer with perforation, without mention of obstruction — (Use additional E code to identify drug, if drug induced)

532.51 Chronic or unspecified duodenal ulcer with perforation and obstruction — (Use additional E code to identify drug, if drug induced)

532.60 Chronic or unspecified duodenal ulcer with hemorrhage and perforation, without mention of obstruction — (Use additional E code to identify drug, if drug induced)

532.61 Chronic or unspecified duodenal ulcer with hemorrhage, perforation, and obstruction — (Use additional E code to identify drug, if drug induced)

532.70 Chronic duodenal ulcer without mention of hemorrhage, perforation, or obstruction — (Use additional E code to identify drug, if drug induced)

532.71 Chronic duodenal ulcer without mention of hemorrhage or perforation, with obstruction — (Use additional E code to identify drug, if drug induced)

532.90 Duodenal ulcer, unspecified as acute or chronic, without hemorrhage, perforation, or obstruction — (Use additional E code to identify drug, if drug induced) ▽

532.91 Duodenal ulcer, unspecified as acute or chronic, without mention of hemorrhage or perforation, with obstruction — (Use additional E code to identify drug, if drug induced) ▽
533.00 Acute peptic ulcer, unspecified site, with hemorrhage, without mention of obstruction — (Use additional E code to identify drug, if drug induced) ▽
533.01 Acute peptic ulcer, unspecified site, with hemorrhage and obstruction — (Use additional E code to identify drug, if drug induced) ▽
533.10 Acute peptic ulcer, unspecified site, with perforation, without mention of obstruction — (Use additional E code to identify drug, if drug induced) ▽
533.11 Acute peptic ulcer, unspecified site, with perforation and obstruction — (Use additional E code to identify drug, if drug induced) ▽
533.20 Acute peptic ulcer, unspecified site, with hemorrhage and perforation, without mention of obstruction — (Use additional E code to identify drug, if drug induced) ▽
533.21 Acute peptic ulcer, unspecified site, with hemorrhage, perforation, and obstruction — (Use additional E code to identify drug, if drug induced) ▽
533.30 Acute peptic ulcer, unspecified site, without mention of hemorrhage, perforation, or obstruction — (Use additional E code to identify drug, if drug induced) ▽
533.31 Acute peptic ulcer, unspecified site, without mention of hemorrhage and perforation, with obstruction — (Use additional E code to identify drug, if drug induced) ▽
533.40 Chronic or unspecified peptic ulcer, unspecified site, with hemorrhage, without mention of obstruction — (Use additional E code to identify drug, if drug induced) ▽
533.41 Chronic or unspecified peptic ulcer, unspecified site, with hemorrhage and obstruction — (Use additional E code to identify drug, if drug induced) ▽
533.50 Chronic or unspecified peptic ulcer, unspecified site, with perforation, without mention of obstruction — (Use additional E code to identify drug, if drug induced) ▽
533.51 Chronic or unspecified peptic ulcer, unspecified site, with perforation and obstruction — (Use additional E code to identify drug, if drug induced) ▽
533.60 Chronic or unspecified peptic ulcer, unspecified site, with hemorrhage and perforation, without mention of obstruction — (Use additional E code to identify drug, if drug induced) ▽
533.61 Chronic or unspecified peptic ulcer, unspecified site, with hemorrhage, perforation, and obstruction — (Use additional E code to identify drug, if drug induced) ▽
533.70 Chronic peptic ulcer, unspecified site, without mention of hemorrhage, perforation, or obstruction — (Use additional E code to identify drug, if drug induced) ▽
533.71 Chronic peptic ulcer of unspecified site without mention of hemorrhage or perforation, with obstruction — (Use additional E code to identify drug, if drug induced) ▽
533.90 Peptic ulcer, unspecified site, unspecified as acute or chronic, without mention of hemorrhage, perforation, or obstruction — (Use additional E code to identify drug, if drug induced) ▽
533.91 Peptic ulcer, unspecified site, unspecified as acute or chronic, without mention of hemorrhage or perforation, with obstruction — (Use additional E code to identify drug, if drug induced) ▽
534.00 Acute gastrojejunal ulcer with hemorrhage, without mention of obstruction
534.01 Acute gastrojejunal ulcer, with hemorrhage and obstruction
534.10 Acute gastrojejunal ulcer with perforation, without mention of obstruction
534.11 Acute gastrojejunal ulcer with perforation and obstruction
534.20 Acute gastrojejunal ulcer with hemorrhage and perforation, without mention of obstruction
534.21 Acute gastrojejunal ulcer with hemorrhage, perforation, and obstruction
534.30 Acute gastrojejunal ulcer without mention of hemorrhage, perforation, or obstruction
534.31 Acute gastrojejunal ulcer without mention of hemorrhage or perforation, with obstruction
534.40 Chronic or unspecified gastrojejunal ulcer with hemorrhage, without mention of obstruction
534.41 Chronic or unspecified gastrojejunal ulcer, with hemorrhage and obstruction
534.50 Chronic or unspecified gastrojejunal ulcer with perforation, without mention of obstruction
534.51 Chronic or unspecified gastrojejunal ulcer with perforation and obstruction
534.60 Chronic or unspecified gastrojejunal ulcer with hemorrhage and perforation, without mention of obstruction
534.61 Chronic or unspecified gastrojejunal ulcer with hemorrhage, perforation, and obstruction
534.70 Chronic gastrojejunal ulcer without mention of hemorrhage, perforation, or obstruction
534.71 Chronic gastrojejunal ulcer without mention of hemorrhage or perforation, with obstruction
534.90 Gastrojejunal ulcer, unspecified as acute or chronic, without mention of hemorrhage, perforation, or obstruction ▽
534.91 Gastrojejunal ulcer, unspecified as acute or chronic, without mention of hemorrhage or perforation, with obstruction ▽
535.00 Acute gastritis without mention of hemorrhage
535.01 Acute gastritis with hemorrhage
535.10 Atrophic gastritis without mention of hemorrhage
535.11 Atrophic gastritis with hemorrhage
535.20 Gastric mucosal hypertrophy without mention of hemorrhage
535.21 Gastric mucosal hypertrophy with hemorrhage
535.30 Alcoholic gastritis without mention of hemorrhage
535.31 Alcoholic gastritis with hemorrhage
535.40 Other specified gastritis without mention of hemorrhage
535.41 Other specified gastritis with hemorrhage
535.50 Unspecified gastritis and gastroduodenitis without mention of hemorrhage ▽
535.51 Unspecified gastritis and gastroduodenitis with hemorrhage ▽
535.60 Duodenitis without mention of hemorrhage
535.61 Duodenitis with hemorrhage
535.70 Eosinophilic gastritis without mention of hemorrhage
535.71 Eosinophilic gastritis with hemorrhage
536.0 Achlorhydria
536.1 Acute dilatation of stomach
536.2 Persistent vomiting
536.3 Gastroparesis — (Code first underlying disease, if known, as: 249.6, 250.6)
536.8 Dyspepsia and other specified disorders of function of stomach
536.9 Unspecified functional disorder of stomach ▽
537.0 Acquired hypertrophic pyloric stenosis
537.1 Gastric diverticulum
537.2 Chronic duodenal ileus
537.3 Other obstruction of duodenum
537.4 Fistula of stomach or duodenum
537.5 Gastroptosis
537.6 Hourglass stricture or stenosis of stomach
537.81 Pylorospasm
537.82 Angiodysplasia of stomach and duodenum (without mention of hemorrhage)
537.83 Angiodysplasia of stomach and duodenum with hemorrhage
537.84 Dieulafoy lesion (hemorrhagic) of stomach and duodenum
537.89 Other specified disorder of stomach and duodenum
537.9 Unspecified disorder of stomach and duodenum ▽
552.3 Diaphragmatic hernia with obstruction
553.3 Diaphragmatic hernia without mention of obstruction or gangrene
555.0 Regional enteritis of small intestine
558.1 Gastroenteritis and colitis due to radiation
558.2 Toxic gastroenteritis and colitis — (Use additional E code to identify cause)
558.3 Gastroenteritis and colitis, allergic — (Use additional code to identify type of food allergy: V15.01-V15.05)
558.41 Eosinophilic gastroenteritis
558.9 Other and unspecified noninfectious gastroenteritis and colitis ▽
569.5 Abscess of intestine
569.82 Ulceration of intestine
569.86 Dieulafoy lesion (hemorrhagic) of intestine
569.89 Other specified disorder of intestines
571.0 Alcoholic fatty liver
571.1 Acute alcoholic hepatitis

571.2 Alcoholic cirrhosis of liver
571.3 Unspecified alcoholic liver damage ▽
571.40 Unspecified chronic hepatitis ▽
571.41 Chronic persistent hepatitis
571.42 Autoimmune hepatitis
571.49 Other chronic hepatitis
571.5 Cirrhosis of liver without mention of alcohol — (Code first, if applicable, viral hepatitis (acute) (chronic): 070.0-070.9)
571.6 Biliary cirrhosis
571.8 Other chronic nonalcoholic liver disease
572.3 Portal hypertension — (Use additional code for any associated complications, such as: portal hypertensive gastropathy (537.89))
577.0 Acute pancreatitis
577.1 Chronic pancreatitis
578.0 Hematemesis
578.1 Blood in stool
579.0 Celiac disease
579.2 Blind loop syndrome
579.3 Other and unspecified postsurgical nonabsorption ▽
579.8 Other specified intestinal malabsorption
747.61 Congenital gastrointestinal vessel anomaly
750.3 Congenital tracheoesophageal fistula, esophageal atresia and stenosis
750.4 Other specified congenital anomaly of esophagus
750.5 Congenital hypertrophic pyloric stenosis
750.6 Congenital hiatus hernia
750.7 Other specified congenital anomalies of stomach
751.8 Other specified congenital anomalies of digestive system
783.0 Anorexia
783.21 Loss of weight — (Use additional code to identify Body Mass Index (BMI), if known: V85.0-V85.54)
783.22 Underweight — (Use additional code to identify Body Mass Index (BMI), if known: V85.0-V85.54)
783.7 Adult failure to thrive
784.1 Throat pain
787.1 Heartburn
787.20 Dysphagia, unspecified ▽
787.21 Dysphagia, oral phase
787.22 Dysphagia, oropharyngeal phase
787.23 Dysphagia, pharyngeal phase
787.24 Dysphagia, pharyngoesophageal phase
787.29 Other dysphagia
787.3 Flatulence, eructation, and gas pain
787.4 Visible peristalsis
787.5 Abnormal bowel sounds
787.99 Other symptoms involving digestive system
789.09 Abdominal pain, other specified site
792.1 Nonspecific abnormal finding in stool contents
793.4 Nonspecific (abnormal) findings on radiological and other examination of gastrointestinal tract
997.49 Other digestive system complications
V10.00 Personal history of malignant neoplasm of unspecified site in gastrointestinal tract ▽
V12.71 Personal history of peptic ulcer disease
V12.79 Personal history of other diseases of digestive disease
V16.0 Family history of malignant neoplasm of gastrointestinal tract
V18.51 Family history, Colonic polyps
V18.59 Family history, other digestive disorders
V67.00 Follow-up examination, following unspecified surgery ▽
V67.09 Follow-up examination, following other surgery
V67.59 Other follow-up examination
V67.9 Unspecified follow-up examination ▽
V71.1 Observation for suspected malignant neoplasm
V71.89 Observation for other specified suspected conditions
V85.0 Body Mass Index less than 19, adult

ICD-9-CM Procedural

45.16 Esophagogastroduodenoscopy (EGD) with closed biopsy
90.89 Other microscopic examination of specimen from upper gastrointestinal tract and of vomitus

HCPCS Level II Supplies & Services

A4270 Disposable endoscope sheath, each

43240

43240 Esophagogastroduodenoscopy, flexible, transoral; with transmural drainage of pseudocyst (includes placement of transmural drainage catheter[s]/stent[s], when performed, and endoscopic ultrasound, when performed)

ICD-9-CM Diagnostic

577.2 Cyst and pseudocyst of pancreas

ICD-9-CM Procedural

52.01 Drainage of pancreatic cyst by catheter

43241

43241 Esophagogastroduodenoscopy, flexible, transoral; with insertion of intraluminal tube or catheter

ICD-9-CM Diagnostic

150.1 Malignant neoplasm of thoracic esophagus
150.2 Malignant neoplasm of abdominal esophagus
150.3 Malignant neoplasm of upper third of esophagus
150.4 Malignant neoplasm of middle third of esophagus
150.5 Malignant neoplasm of lower third of esophagus
150.8 Malignant neoplasm of other specified part of esophagus
150.9 Malignant neoplasm of esophagus, unspecified site ▽
151.0 Malignant neoplasm of cardia
151.1 Malignant neoplasm of pylorus
151.2 Malignant neoplasm of pyloric antrum
151.3 Malignant neoplasm of fundus of stomach
151.4 Malignant neoplasm of body of stomach
151.5 Malignant neoplasm of lesser curvature of stomach, unspecified ▽
151.6 Malignant neoplasm of greater curvature of stomach, unspecified ▽
151.8 Malignant neoplasm of other specified sites of stomach
151.9 Malignant neoplasm of stomach, unspecified site ▽
152.0 Malignant neoplasm of duodenum
152.1 Malignant neoplasm of jejunum
152.2 Malignant neoplasm of ileum
152.8 Malignant neoplasm of other specified sites of small intestine
161.9 Malignant neoplasm of larynx, unspecified site ▽
197.4 Secondary malignant neoplasm of small intestine including duodenum
197.8 Secondary malignant neoplasm of other digestive organs and spleen
198.89 Secondary malignant neoplasm of other specified sites
209.01 Malignant carcinoid tumor of the duodenum — (Code first any associated multiple endocrine neoplasia syndrome: 258.01-258.03)(Use additional code to identify associated endocrine syndrome, as: carcinoid syndrome: 259.2)
209.02 Malignant carcinoid tumor of the jejunum — (Code first any associated multiple endocrine neoplasia syndrome: 258.01-258.03)(Use additional code to identify associated endocrine syndrome, as: carcinoid syndrome: 259.2)
209.23 Malignant carcinoid tumor of the stomach — (Code first any associated multiple endocrine neoplasia syndrome: 258.01-258.03)(Use additional code to identify associated endocrine syndrome, as: carcinoid syndrome: 259.2)

209.25 Malignant carcinoid tumor of foregut, not otherwise specified — (Code first any associated multiple endocrine neoplasia syndrome: 258.01-258.03)(Use additional code to identify associated endocrine syndrome, as: carcinoid syndrome: 259.2)
209.63 Benign carcinoid tumor of the stomach — (Code first any associated multiple endocrine neoplasia syndrome: 258.01-258.03)(Use additional code to identify associated endocrine syndrome, as: carcinoid syndrome: 259.2)
209.65 Benign carcinoid tumor of foregut, not otherwise specified — (Code first any associated multiple endocrine neoplasia syndrome: 258.01-258.03)(Use additional code to identify associated endocrine syndrome, as: carcinoid syndrome: 259.2)
211.1 Benign neoplasm of stomach
230.1 Carcinoma in situ of esophagus
230.2 Carcinoma in situ of stomach
239.89 Neoplasms of unspecified nature, other specified sites
261 Nutritional marasmus
262 Other severe protein-calorie malnutrition
263.0 Malnutrition of moderate degree
263.1 Malnutrition of mild degree
263.2 Arrested development following protein-calorie malnutrition
263.8 Other protein-calorie malnutrition
263.9 Unspecified protein-calorie malnutrition ▽
269.8 Other nutritional deficiency
269.9 Unspecified nutritional deficiency ▽
276.50 Volume depletion, unspecified — (Use additional code to identify any associated intellectual disabilities) ▽
276.51 Dehydration — (Use additional code to identify any associated intellectual disabilities)
276.52 Hypovolemia — (Use additional code to identify any associated intellectual disabilities)
307.1 Anorexia nervosa
436 Acute, but ill-defined, cerebrovascular disease — (Use additional code to identify presence of hypertension) ▽
456.0 Esophageal varices with bleeding
519.00 Unspecified tracheostomy complication — (Use additional code to identify infectious organism) ▽
519.01 Infection of tracheostomy — (Use additional code to identify type of infection: 038.0-038.9, 682.1. Use additional code to identify organism: 041.00-041.9)
519.02 Mechanical complication of tracheostomy
519.09 Other tracheostomy complications — (Use additional code to identify infectious organism)
530.3 Stricture and stenosis of esophagus
530.4 Perforation of esophagus
530.5 Dyskinesia of esophagus
530.81 Esophageal reflux
531.00 Acute gastric ulcer with hemorrhage, without mention of obstruction — (Use additional E code to identify drug, if drug induced)
531.01 Acute gastric ulcer with hemorrhage and obstruction — (Use additional E code to identify drug, if drug induced)
531.10 Acute gastric ulcer with perforation, without mention of obstruction — (Use additional E code to identify drug, if drug induced)
531.11 Acute gastric ulcer with perforation and obstruction — (Use additional E code to identify drug, if drug induced)
531.20 Acute gastric ulcer with hemorrhage and perforation, without mention of obstruction — (Use additional E code to identify drug, if drug induced)
531.21 Acute gastric ulcer with hemorrhage, perforation, and obstruction — (Use additional E code to identify drug, if drug induced)
531.30 Acute gastric ulcer without mention of hemorrhage, perforation, or obstruction — (Use additional E code to identify drug, if drug induced)
531.31 Acute gastric ulcer without mention of hemorrhage or perforation, with obstruction — (Use additional E code to identify drug, if drug induced)
531.40 Chronic or unspecified gastric ulcer with hemorrhage, without mention of obstruction — (Use additional E code to identify drug, if drug induced)
531.41 Chronic or unspecified gastric ulcer with hemorrhage and obstruction — (Use additional E code to identify drug, if drug induced)
531.50 Chronic or unspecified gastric ulcer with perforation, without mention of obstruction — (Use additional E code to identify drug, if drug induced)
531.51 Chronic or unspecified gastric ulcer with perforation and obstruction — (Use additional E code to identify drug, if drug induced)
531.60 Chronic or unspecified gastric ulcer with hemorrhage and perforation, without mention of obstruction — (Use additional E code to identify drug, if drug induced)
531.61 Chronic or unspecified gastric ulcer with hemorrhage, perforation, and obstruction — (Use additional E code to identify drug, if drug induced)
531.70 Chronic gastric ulcer without mention of hemorrhage, perforation, without mention of obstruction — (Use additional E code to identify drug, if drug induced)
531.71 Chronic gastric ulcer without mention of hemorrhage or perforation, with obstruction — (Use additional E code to identify drug, if drug induced)
531.90 Gastric ulcer, unspecified as acute or chronic, without mention of hemorrhage, perforation, or obstruction — (Use additional E code to identify drug, if drug induced) ▽
531.91 Gastric ulcer, unspecified as acute or chronic, without mention of hemorrhage or perforation, with obstruction — (Use additional E code to identify drug, if drug induced) ▽
532.00 Acute duodenal ulcer with hemorrhage, without mention of obstruction — (Use additional E code to identify drug, if drug induced)
532.01 Acute duodenal ulcer with hemorrhage and obstruction — (Use additional E code to identify drug, if drug induced)
532.10 Acute duodenal ulcer with perforation, without mention of obstruction — (Use additional E code to identify drug, if drug induced)
532.11 Acute duodenal ulcer with perforation and obstruction — (Use additional E code to identify drug, if drug induced)
532.20 Acute duodenal ulcer with hemorrhage and perforation, without mention of obstruction — (Use additional E code to identify drug, if drug induced)
532.21 Acute duodenal ulcer with hemorrhage, perforation, and obstruction — (Use additional E code to identify drug, if drug induced)
532.30 Acute duodenal ulcer without mention of hemorrhage, perforation, or obstruction — (Use additional E code to identify drug, if drug induced)
532.31 Acute duodenal ulcer without mention of hemorrhage or perforation, with obstruction — (Use additional E code to identify drug, if drug induced)
532.40 Duodenal ulcer, chronic or unspecified, with hemorrhage, without mention of obstruction — (Use additional E code to identify drug, if drug induced)
532.41 Chronic or unspecified duodenal ulcer with hemorrhage and obstruction — (Use additional E code to identify drug, if drug induced)
532.50 Chronic or unspecified duodenal ulcer with perforation, without mention of obstruction — (Use additional E code to identify drug, if drug induced)
532.51 Chronic or unspecified duodenal ulcer with perforation and obstruction — (Use additional E code to identify drug, if drug induced)
532.60 Chronic or unspecified duodenal ulcer with hemorrhage and perforation, without mention of obstruction — (Use additional E code to identify drug, if drug induced)
532.61 Chronic or unspecified duodenal ulcer with hemorrhage, perforation, and obstruction — (Use additional E code to identify drug, if drug induced)
532.70 Chronic duodenal ulcer without mention of hemorrhage, perforation, or obstruction — (Use additional E code to identify drug, if drug induced)
532.71 Chronic duodenal ulcer without mention of hemorrhage or perforation, with obstruction — (Use additional E code to identify drug, if drug induced)
532.90 Duodenal ulcer, unspecified as acute or chronic, without hemorrhage, perforation, or obstruction — (Use additional E code to identify drug, if drug induced) ▽
532.91 Duodenal ulcer, unspecified as acute or chronic, without mention of hemorrhage or perforation, with obstruction — (Use additional E code to identify drug, if drug induced) ▽
533.00 Acute peptic ulcer, unspecified site, with hemorrhage, without mention of obstruction — (Use additional E code to identify drug, if drug induced) ▽
533.01 Acute peptic ulcer, unspecified site, with hemorrhage and obstruction — (Use additional E code to identify drug, if drug induced) ▽
533.10 Acute peptic ulcer, unspecified site, with perforation, without mention of obstruction — (Use additional E code to identify drug, if drug induced) ▽

533.11 Acute peptic ulcer, unspecified site, with perforation and obstruction — (Use additional E code to identify drug, if drug induced) ▽
533.20 Acute peptic ulcer, unspecified site, with hemorrhage and perforation, without mention of obstruction — (Use additional E code to identify drug, if drug induced) ▽
533.21 Acute peptic ulcer, unspecified site, with hemorrhage, perforation, and obstruction — (Use additional E code to identify drug, if drug induced) ▽
533.30 Acute peptic ulcer, unspecified site, without mention of hemorrhage, perforation, or obstruction — (Use additional E code to identify drug, if drug induced) ▽
533.31 Acute peptic ulcer, unspecified site, without mention of hemorrhage and perforation, with obstruction — (Use additional E code to identify drug, if drug induced) ▽
533.40 Chronic or unspecified peptic ulcer, unspecified site, with hemorrhage, without mention of obstruction — (Use additional E code to identify drug, if drug induced) ▽
533.41 Chronic or unspecified peptic ulcer, unspecified site, with hemorrhage and obstruction — (Use additional E code to identify drug, if drug induced) ▽
533.50 Chronic or unspecified peptic ulcer, unspecified site, with perforation, without mention of obstruction — (Use additional E code to identify drug, if drug induced) ▽
533.51 Chronic or unspecified peptic ulcer, unspecified site, with perforation and obstruction — (Use additional E code to identify drug, if drug induced) ▽
533.90 Peptic ulcer, unspecified site, unspecified as acute or chronic, without mention of hemorrhage, perforation, or obstruction — (Use additional E code to identify drug, if drug induced) ▽
535.50 Unspecified gastritis and gastroduodenitis without mention of hemorrhage ▽
535.60 Duodenitis without mention of hemorrhage
535.70 Eosinophilic gastritis without mention of hemorrhage
535.71 Eosinophilic gastritis with hemorrhage
536.2 Persistent vomiting
536.8 Dyspepsia and other specified disorders of function of stomach
536.9 Unspecified functional disorder of stomach ▽
537.3 Other obstruction of duodenum
537.84 Dieulafoy lesion (hemorrhagic) of stomach and duodenum
537.89 Other specified disorder of stomach and duodenum
560.1 Paralytic ileus
560.2 Volvulus
560.89 Other specified intestinal obstruction
569.84 Angiodysplasia of intestine (without mention of hemorrhage)
569.86 Dieulafoy lesion (hemorrhagic) of intestine
578.9 Hemorrhage of gastrointestinal tract, unspecified ▽
707.9 Chronic ulcer of unspecified site ▽
750.5 Congenital hypertrophic pyloric stenosis
750.7 Other specified congenital anomalies of stomach
751.1 Congenital atresia and stenosis of small intestine
783.0 Anorexia
783.3 Feeding difficulties and mismanagement
783.40 Lack of normal physiological development, unspecified ▽
783.41 Failure to thrive
783.42 Delayed milestones
783.43 Short stature
783.7 Adult failure to thrive
787.01 Nausea with vomiting
787.04 Bilious emesis
787.20 Dysphagia, unspecified ▽
787.21 Dysphagia, oral phase
787.22 Dysphagia, oropharyngeal phase
787.23 Dysphagia, pharyngeal phase
787.24 Dysphagia, pharyngoesophageal phase
787.29 Other dysphagia
854.06 Intracranial injury of other and unspecified nature, without mention of open intracranial wound, loss of consciousness of unspecified duration ▽
947.2 Burn of esophagus
959.01 Head injury, unspecified ▽
994.2 Effects of hunger
997.49 Other digestive system complications

ICD-9-CM Procedural

42.81 Insertion of permanent tube into esophagus
96.06 Insertion of Sengstaken tube

HCPCS Level II Supplies & Services

A4270 Disposable endoscope sheath, each

43242

43242 Esophagogastroduodenoscopy, flexible, transoral; with transendoscopic ultrasound-guided intramural or transmural fine needle aspiration/biopsy(s) (includes endoscopic ultrasound examination of the esophagus, stomach, and either the duodenum or a surgically altered stomach where the jejunum is examined distal to the anastomosis)

ICD-9-CM Diagnostic

150.0 Malignant neoplasm of cervical esophagus
150.1 Malignant neoplasm of thoracic esophagus
150.2 Malignant neoplasm of abdominal esophagus
150.3 Malignant neoplasm of upper third of esophagus
150.4 Malignant neoplasm of middle third of esophagus
150.5 Malignant neoplasm of lower third of esophagus
150.8 Malignant neoplasm of other specified part of esophagus
150.9 Malignant neoplasm of esophagus, unspecified site ▽
151.0 Malignant neoplasm of cardia
151.1 Malignant neoplasm of pylorus
151.2 Malignant neoplasm of pyloric antrum
151.3 Malignant neoplasm of fundus of stomach
151.4 Malignant neoplasm of body of stomach
151.5 Malignant neoplasm of lesser curvature of stomach, unspecified ▽
151.6 Malignant neoplasm of greater curvature of stomach, unspecified ▽
151.8 Malignant neoplasm of other specified sites of stomach
151.9 Malignant neoplasm of stomach, unspecified site ▽
152.0 Malignant neoplasm of duodenum
152.1 Malignant neoplasm of jejunum
152.8 Malignant neoplasm of other specified sites of small intestine
152.9 Malignant neoplasm of small intestine, unspecified site ▽
155.0 Malignant neoplasm of liver, primary
155.1 Malignant neoplasm of intrahepatic bile ducts
156.0 Malignant neoplasm of gallbladder
156.1 Malignant neoplasm of extrahepatic bile ducts
156.2 Malignant neoplasm of ampulla of Vater
156.8 Malignant neoplasm of other specified sites of gallbladder and extrahepatic bile ducts
156.9 Malignant neoplasm of biliary tract, part unspecified site ▽
157.0 Malignant neoplasm of head of pancreas
157.1 Malignant neoplasm of body of pancreas
157.2 Malignant neoplasm of tail of pancreas
157.3 Malignant neoplasm of pancreatic duct
157.4 Malignant neoplasm of islets of Langerhans — (Use additional code to identify any functional activity)
157.8 Malignant neoplasm of other specified sites of pancreas
157.9 Malignant neoplasm of pancreas, part unspecified ▽
158.8 Malignant neoplasm of specified parts of peritoneum
159.8 Malignant neoplasm of other sites of digestive system and intra-abdominal organs
159.9 Malignant neoplasm of ill-defined sites of digestive organs and peritoneum ▽
171.4 Malignant neoplasm of connective and other soft tissue of thorax
171.5 Malignant neoplasm of connective and other soft tissue of abdomen
195.1 Malignant neoplasm of thorax

195.2 Malignant neoplasm of abdomen
196.1 Secondary and unspecified malignant neoplasm of intrathoracic lymph nodes
196.2 Secondary and unspecified malignant neoplasm of intra-abdominal lymph nodes
197.4 Secondary malignant neoplasm of small intestine including duodenum
197.8 Secondary malignant neoplasm of other digestive organs and spleen
199.0 Disseminated malignant neoplasm
199.1 Other malignant neoplasm of unspecified site
209.00 Malignant carcinoid tumor of the small intestine, unspecified portion — (Code first any associated multiple endocrine neoplasia syndrome: 258.01-258.03)(Use additional code to identify associated endocrine syndrome, as: carcinoid syndrome: 259.2) ▽
209.01 Malignant carcinoid tumor of the duodenum — (Code first any associated multiple endocrine neoplasia syndrome: 258.01-258.03)(Use additional code to identify associated endocrine syndrome, as: carcinoid syndrome: 259.2)
209.02 Malignant carcinoid tumor of the jejunum — (Code first any associated multiple endocrine neoplasia syndrome: 258.01-258.03)(Use additional code to identify associated endocrine syndrome, as: carcinoid syndrome: 259.2)
209.23 Malignant carcinoid tumor of the stomach — (Code first any associated multiple endocrine neoplasia syndrome: 258.01-258.03)(Use additional code to identify associated endocrine syndrome, as: carcinoid syndrome: 259.2)
209.25 Malignant carcinoid tumor of foregut, not otherwise specified — (Code first any associated multiple endocrine neoplasia syndrome: 258.01-258.03)(Use additional code to identify associated endocrine syndrome, as: carcinoid syndrome: 259.2)
209.29 Malignant carcinoid tumor of other sites — (Code first any associated multiple endocrine neoplasia syndrome: 258.01-258.03)(Use additional code to identify associated endocrine syndrome, as: carcinoid syndrome: 259.2)
209.30 Malignant poorly differentiated neuroendocrine carcinoma, any site — (Code first any associated multiple endocrine neoplasia syndrome: 258.01-258.03)(Use additional code to identify associated endocrine syndrome, as: carcinoid syndrome: 259.2) ▽
209.40 Benign carcinoid tumor of the small intestine, unspecified portion — (Code first any associated multiple endocrine neoplasia syndrome: 258.01-258.03)(Use additional code to identify associated endocrine syndrome, as: carcinoid syndrome: 259.2) ▽
209.41 Benign carcinoid tumor of the duodenum — (Code first any associated multiple endocrine neoplasia syndrome: 258.01-258.03)(Use additional code to identify associated endocrine syndrome, as: carcinoid syndrome: 259.2)
209.42 Benign carcinoid tumor of the jejunum — (Code first any associated multiple endocrine neoplasia syndrome: 258.01-258.03)(Use additional code to identify associated endocrine syndrome, as: carcinoid syndrome: 259.2)
209.63 Benign carcinoid tumor of the stomach — (Code first any associated multiple endocrine neoplasia syndrome: 258.01-258.03)(Use additional code to identify associated endocrine syndrome, as: carcinoid syndrome: 259.2)
209.65 Benign carcinoid tumor of foregut, not otherwise specified — (Code first any associated multiple endocrine neoplasia syndrome: 258.01-258.03)(Use additional code to identify associated endocrine syndrome, as: carcinoid syndrome: 259.2)
209.71 Secondary neuroendocrine tumor of distant lymph nodes
209.72 Secondary neuroendocrine tumor of liver
211.0 Benign neoplasm of esophagus
211.1 Benign neoplasm of stomach
211.2 Benign neoplasm of duodenum, jejunum, and ileum
211.6 Benign neoplasm of pancreas, except islets of Langerhans
211.7 Benign neoplasm of islets of Langerhans — (Use additional code to identify any functional activity)
215.5 Other benign neoplasm of connective and other soft tissue of abdomen
230.1 Carcinoma in situ of esophagus
230.2 Carcinoma in situ of stomach
230.7 Carcinoma in situ of other and unspecified parts of intestine ▽
230.8 Carcinoma in situ of liver and biliary system
230.9 Carcinoma in situ of other and unspecified digestive organs ▽
235.2 Neoplasm of uncertain behavior of stomach, intestines, and rectum
235.3 Neoplasm of uncertain behavior of liver and biliary passages
235.4 Neoplasm of uncertain behavior of retroperitoneum and peritoneum
235.5 Neoplasm of uncertain behavior of other and unspecified digestive organs ▽
239.0 Neoplasm of unspecified nature of digestive system
239.89 Neoplasms of unspecified nature, other specified sites
786.6 Swelling, mass, or lump in chest
789.1 Hepatomegaly
789.30 Abdominal or pelvic swelling, mass or lump, unspecified site ▽
789.31 Abdominal or pelvic swelling, mass, or lump, right upper quadrant
789.32 Abdominal or pelvic swelling, mass, or lump, left upper quadrant
789.33 Abdominal or pelvic swelling, mass, or lump, right lower quadrant
789.34 Abdominal or pelvic swelling, mass, or lump, left lower quadrant
789.35 Abdominal or pelvic swelling, mass or lump, periumbilic
789.36 Abdominal or pelvic swelling, mass, or lump, epigastric
789.39 Abdominal or pelvic swelling, mass, or lump, other specified site

ICD-9-CM Procedural

45.16 Esophagogastroduodenoscopy (EGD) with closed biopsy
88.74 Diagnostic ultrasound of digestive system

43243-43244

43243 Esophagogastroduodenoscopy, flexible, transoral; with injection sclerosis of esophageal/gastric varices
43244 with band ligation of esophageal/gastric varices

ICD-9-CM Diagnostic

280.0 Iron deficiency anemia secondary to blood loss (chronic)
280.9 Unspecified iron deficiency anemia ▽
285.9 Unspecified anemia ▽
456.0 Esophageal varices with bleeding
456.1 Esophageal varices without mention of bleeding
456.20 Esophageal varices with bleeding in diseases classified elsewhere — (Code first underlying disease: 571.0-571.9, 572.3) ☒
456.21 Esophageal varices without mention of bleeding in diseases classified elsewhere — (Code first underlying disease: 571.0-571.9, 572.3) ☒
456.8 Varices of other sites
530.3 Stricture and stenosis of esophagus
530.7 Gastroesophageal laceration-hemorrhage syndrome
530.82 Esophageal hemorrhage
537.84 Dieulafoy lesion (hemorrhagic) of stomach and duodenum
569.86 Dieulafoy lesion (hemorrhagic) of intestine
571.0 Alcoholic fatty liver
571.1 Acute alcoholic hepatitis
571.2 Alcoholic cirrhosis of liver
571.3 Unspecified alcoholic liver damage ▽
571.40 Unspecified chronic hepatitis ▽
571.41 Chronic persistent hepatitis
571.42 Autoimmune hepatitis
571.5 Cirrhosis of liver without mention of alcohol — (Code first, if applicable, viral hepatitis (acute) (chronic): 070.0-070.9)
571.6 Biliary cirrhosis
571.8 Other chronic nonalcoholic liver disease
571.9 Unspecified chronic liver disease without mention of alcohol ▽
572.3 Portal hypertension — (Use additional code for any associated complications, such as: portal hypertensive gastropathy (537.89))
578.0 Hematemesis
578.1 Blood in stool
578.9 Hemorrhage of gastrointestinal tract, unspecified ▽
747.61 Congenital gastrointestinal vessel anomaly

ICD-9-CM Procedural

42.33 Endoscopic excision or destruction of lesion or tissue of esophagus
43.41 Endoscopic excision or destruction of lesion or tissue of stomach

HCPCS Level II Supplies & Services

A4270 Disposable endoscope sheath, each

43245

43245 Esophagogastroduodenoscopy, flexible, transoral; with dilation of gastric/duodenal stricture(s) (eg, balloon, bougie)

ICD-9-CM Diagnostic

151.4 Malignant neoplasm of body of stomach

151.9 Malignant neoplasm of stomach, unspecified site ▽

209.23 Malignant carcinoid tumor of the stomach — (Code first any associated multiple endocrine neoplasia syndrome: 258.01-258.03)(Use additional code to identify associated endocrine syndrome, as: carcinoid syndrome: 259.2)

209.25 Malignant carcinoid tumor of foregut, not otherwise specified — (Code first any associated multiple endocrine neoplasia syndrome: 258.01-258.03)(Use additional code to identify associated endocrine syndrome, as: carcinoid syndrome: 259.2)

209.63 Benign carcinoid tumor of the stomach — (Code first any associated multiple endocrine neoplasia syndrome: 258.01-258.03)(Use additional code to identify associated endocrine syndrome, as: carcinoid syndrome: 259.2)

209.65 Benign carcinoid tumor of foregut, not otherwise specified — (Code first any associated multiple endocrine neoplasia syndrome: 258.01-258.03)(Use additional code to identify associated endocrine syndrome, as: carcinoid syndrome: 259.2)

530.0 Achalasia and cardiospasm

530.10 Unspecified esophagitis — (Use additional E code to identify cause, if induced by chemical) ▽

530.11 Reflux esophagitis — (Use additional E code to identify cause, if induced by chemical)

530.12 Acute esophagitis — (Use additional E code to identify cause, if induced by chemical)

530.13 Eosinophilic esophagitis

530.19 Other esophagitis — (Use additional E code to identify cause, if induced by chemical)

530.20 Ulcer of esophagus without bleeding — (Use additional E code to identify cause, if induced by chemical or drug)

530.81 Esophageal reflux

530.85 Barrett's esophagus

531.01 Acute gastric ulcer with hemorrhage and obstruction — (Use additional E code to identify drug, if drug induced)

531.11 Acute gastric ulcer with perforation and obstruction — (Use additional E code to identify drug, if drug induced)

531.21 Acute gastric ulcer with hemorrhage, perforation, and obstruction — (Use additional E code to identify drug, if drug induced)

531.31 Acute gastric ulcer without mention of hemorrhage or perforation, with obstruction — (Use additional E code to identify drug, if drug induced)

531.41 Chronic or unspecified gastric ulcer with hemorrhage and obstruction — (Use additional E code to identify drug, if drug induced)

531.51 Chronic or unspecified gastric ulcer with perforation and obstruction — (Use additional E code to identify drug, if drug induced)

531.61 Chronic or unspecified gastric ulcer with hemorrhage, perforation, and obstruction — (Use additional E code to identify drug, if drug induced)

531.71 Chronic gastric ulcer without mention of hemorrhage or perforation, with obstruction — (Use additional E code to identify drug, if drug induced)

531.91 Gastric ulcer, unspecified as acute or chronic, without mention of hemorrhage or perforation, with obstruction — (Use additional E code to identify drug, if drug induced) ▽

533.01 Acute peptic ulcer, unspecified site, with hemorrhage and obstruction — (Use additional E code to identify drug, if drug induced) ▽

533.11 Acute peptic ulcer, unspecified site, with perforation and obstruction — (Use additional E code to identify drug, if drug induced) ▽

533.21 Acute peptic ulcer, unspecified site, with hemorrhage, perforation, and obstruction — (Use additional E code to identify drug, if drug induced) ▽

533.31 Acute peptic ulcer, unspecified site, without mention of hemorrhage and perforation, with obstruction — (Use additional E code to identify drug, if drug induced) ▽

533.41 Chronic or unspecified peptic ulcer, unspecified site, with hemorrhage and obstruction — (Use additional E code to identify drug, if drug induced) ▽

533.51 Chronic or unspecified peptic ulcer, unspecified site, with perforation and obstruction — (Use additional E code to identify drug, if drug induced) ▽

533.61 Chronic or unspecified peptic ulcer, unspecified site, with hemorrhage, perforation, and obstruction — (Use additional E code to identify drug, if drug induced) ▽

533.71 Chronic peptic ulcer of unspecified site without mention of hemorrhage or perforation, with obstruction — (Use additional E code to identify drug, if drug induced) ▽

533.91 Peptic ulcer, unspecified site, unspecified as acute or chronic, without mention of hemorrhage or perforation, with obstruction — (Use additional E code to identify drug, if drug induced) ▽

535.00 Acute gastritis without mention of hemorrhage

535.40 Other specified gastritis without mention of hemorrhage

535.70 Eosinophilic gastritis without mention of hemorrhage

535.71 Eosinophilic gastritis with hemorrhage

536.2 Persistent vomiting

537.0 Acquired hypertrophic pyloric stenosis

537.1 Gastric diverticulum

537.5 Gastroptosis

537.6 Hourglass stricture or stenosis of stomach

537.81 Pylorospasm

537.82 Angiodysplasia of stomach and duodenum (without mention of hemorrhage)

537.83 Angiodysplasia of stomach and duodenum with hemorrhage

537.89 Other specified disorder of stomach and duodenum

578.9 Hemorrhage of gastrointestinal tract, unspecified ▽

750.5 Congenital hypertrophic pyloric stenosis

750.6 Congenital hiatus hernia

750.7 Other specified congenital anomalies of stomach

750.8 Other specified congenital anomalies of upper alimentary tract

750.9 Unspecified congenital anomaly of upper alimentary tract ▽

751.8 Other specified congenital anomalies of digestive system

751.9 Unspecified congenital anomaly of digestive system ▽

787.01 Nausea with vomiting

787.04 Bilious emesis

789.00 Abdominal pain, unspecified site ▽

793.4 Nonspecific (abnormal) findings on radiological and other examination of gastrointestinal tract

997.49 Other digestive system complications

ICD-9-CM Procedural

44.22 Endoscopic dilation of pylorus

HCPCS Level II Supplies & Services

A4270 Disposable endoscope sheath, each

43246

43246 Esophagogastroduodenoscopy, flexible, transoral; with directed placement of percutaneous gastrostomy tube

ICD-9-CM Diagnostic

141.9 Malignant neoplasm of tongue, unspecified site ▽

145.0 Malignant neoplasm of cheek mucosa

145.1 Malignant neoplasm of vestibule of mouth

145.2 Malignant neoplasm of hard palate

145.3 Malignant neoplasm of soft palate

145.4 Malignant neoplasm of uvula

145.5 Malignant neoplasm of palate, unspecified ▽

145.6 Malignant neoplasm of retromolar area

145.8 Malignant neoplasm of other specified parts of mouth

145.9 Malignant neoplasm of mouth, unspecified site ▽

146.0 Malignant neoplasm of tonsil

Code	Description
146.1	Malignant neoplasm of tonsillar fossa
146.2	Malignant neoplasm of tonsillar pillars (anterior) (posterior)
146.3	Malignant neoplasm of vallecula
146.4	Malignant neoplasm of anterior aspect of epiglottis
146.5	Malignant neoplasm of junctional region of oropharynx
146.6	Malignant neoplasm of lateral wall of oropharynx
146.7	Malignant neoplasm of posterior wall of oropharynx
146.8	Malignant neoplasm of other specified sites of oropharynx
146.9	Malignant neoplasm of oropharynx, unspecified site
150.3	Malignant neoplasm of upper third of esophagus
150.4	Malignant neoplasm of middle third of esophagus
150.5	Malignant neoplasm of lower third of esophagus
150.8	Malignant neoplasm of other specified part of esophagus
150.9	Malignant neoplasm of esophagus, unspecified site
151.9	Malignant neoplasm of stomach, unspecified site
152.8	Malignant neoplasm of other specified sites of small intestine
161.9	Malignant neoplasm of larynx, unspecified site
197.8	Secondary malignant neoplasm of other digestive organs and spleen
209.23	Malignant carcinoid tumor of the stomach — (Code first any associated multiple endocrine neoplasia syndrome: 258.01-258.03)(Use additional code to identify associated endocrine syndrome, as: carcinoid syndrome: 259.2)
209.25	Malignant carcinoid tumor of foregut, not otherwise specified — (Code first any associated multiple endocrine neoplasia syndrome: 258.01-258.03)(Use additional code to identify associated endocrine syndrome, as: carcinoid syndrome: 259.2)
209.63	Benign carcinoid tumor of the stomach — (Code first any associated multiple endocrine neoplasia syndrome: 258.01-258.03)(Use additional code to identify associated endocrine syndrome, as: carcinoid syndrome: 259.2)
209.65	Benign carcinoid tumor of foregut, not otherwise specified — (Code first any associated multiple endocrine neoplasia syndrome: 258.01-258.03)(Use additional code to identify associated endocrine syndrome, as: carcinoid syndrome: 259.2)
230.1	Carcinoma in situ of esophagus
230.2	Carcinoma in situ of stomach
261	Nutritional marasmus
262	Other severe protein-calorie malnutrition
263.0	Malnutrition of moderate degree
263.1	Malnutrition of mild degree
263.2	Arrested development following protein-calorie malnutrition
263.8	Other protein-calorie malnutrition
263.9	Unspecified protein-calorie malnutrition
269.9	Unspecified nutritional deficiency
276.50	Volume depletion, unspecified — (Use additional code to identify any associated intellectual disabilities)
276.51	Dehydration — (Use additional code to identify any associated intellectual disabilities)
276.52	Hypovolemia — (Use additional code to identify any associated intellectual disabilities)
307.1	Anorexia nervosa
335.20	Amyotrophic lateral sclerosis
348.1	Anoxic brain damage — (Use additional E code to identify cause)
436	Acute, but ill-defined, cerebrovascular disease — (Use additional code to identify presence of hypertension)
530.3	Stricture and stenosis of esophagus
531.60	Chronic or unspecified gastric ulcer with hemorrhage and perforation, without mention of obstruction — (Use additional E code to identify drug, if drug induced)
532.20	Acute duodenal ulcer with hemorrhage and perforation, without mention of obstruction — (Use additional E code to identify drug, if drug induced)
536.2	Persistent vomiting
537.2	Chronic duodenal ileus
537.3	Other obstruction of duodenum
578.9	Hemorrhage of gastrointestinal tract, unspecified
579.8	Other specified intestinal malabsorption
579.9	Unspecified intestinal malabsorption
780.2	Syncope and collapse
780.31	Febrile convulsions (simple), unspecified
780.39	Other convulsions
780.4	Dizziness and giddiness
780.52	Insomnia, unspecified
780.79	Other malaise and fatigue
780.8	Generalized hyperhidrosis
783.0	Anorexia
783.21	Loss of weight — (Use additional code to identify Body Mass Index (BMI), if known: V85.0-V85.54)
783.22	Underweight — (Use additional code to identify Body Mass Index (BMI), if known: V85.0-V85.54)
783.3	Feeding difficulties and mismanagement
783.7	Adult failure to thrive
783.9	Other symptoms concerning nutrition, metabolism, and development
787.01	Nausea with vomiting
787.04	Bilious emesis
787.20	Dysphagia, unspecified
787.21	Dysphagia, oral phase
787.22	Dysphagia, oropharyngeal phase
787.23	Dysphagia, pharyngeal phase
787.24	Dysphagia, pharyngoesophageal phase
787.29	Other dysphagia
789.00	Abdominal pain, unspecified site
994.2	Effects of hunger
997.49	Other digestive system complications
V55.1	Attention to gastrostomy
V85.0	Body Mass Index less than 19, adult

ICD-9-CM Procedural

Code	Description
43.11	Percutaneous (endoscopic) gastrostomy (PEG)
44.32	Percutaneous [endoscopic] gastrojejunostomy

43247

43247 Esophagogastroduodenoscopy, flexible, transoral; with removal of foreign body

ICD-9-CM Diagnostic

Code	Description
935.1	Foreign body in esophagus
935.2	Foreign body in stomach
936	Foreign body in intestine and colon
938	Foreign body in digestive system, unspecified
996.79	Other complications due to other internal prosthetic device, implant, and graft — (Use additional code to identify complication: 338.18-338.19, 338.28-338.29)
998.4	Foreign body accidentally left during procedure, not elsewhere classified
V58.89	Encounter for other specified aftercare

ICD-9-CM Procedural

Code	Description
45.13	Other endoscopy of small intestine
97.55	Removal of T-tube, other bile duct tube, or liver tube
98.02	Removal of intraluminal foreign body from esophagus without incision
98.03	Removal of intraluminal foreign body from stomach and small intestine without incision

HCPCS Level II Supplies & Services

Code	Description
A4270	Disposable endoscope sheath, each

43248-43249 [43233]

43233 Esophagogastroduodenoscopy, flexible, transoral; with dilation of esophagus with balloon (30 mm diameter or larger) (includes fluoroscopic guidance, when performed)

43248 with insertion of guide wire followed by passage of dilator(s) through esophagus over guide wire

43249 with transendoscopic balloon dilation of esophagus (less than 30 mm diameter)

ICD-9-CM Diagnostic

150.0 Malignant neoplasm of cervical esophagus
150.1 Malignant neoplasm of thoracic esophagus
150.3 Malignant neoplasm of upper third of esophagus
150.4 Malignant neoplasm of middle third of esophagus
150.5 Malignant neoplasm of lower third of esophagus
150.8 Malignant neoplasm of other specified part of esophagus
150.9 Malignant neoplasm of esophagus, unspecified site ▽
151.0 Malignant neoplasm of cardia
151.1 Malignant neoplasm of pylorus
151.2 Malignant neoplasm of pyloric antrum
151.3 Malignant neoplasm of fundus of stomach
151.4 Malignant neoplasm of body of stomach
151.5 Malignant neoplasm of lesser curvature of stomach, unspecified ▽
151.6 Malignant neoplasm of greater curvature of stomach, unspecified ▽
151.8 Malignant neoplasm of other specified sites of stomach
151.9 Malignant neoplasm of stomach, unspecified site ▽
197.8 Secondary malignant neoplasm of other digestive organs and spleen
209.23 Malignant carcinoid tumor of the stomach — (Code first any associated multiple endocrine neoplasia syndrome: 258.01-258.03)(Use additional code to identify associated endocrine syndrome, as: carcinoid syndrome: 259.2)
209.29 Malignant carcinoid tumor of other sites — (Code first any associated multiple endocrine neoplasia syndrome: 258.01-258.03)(Use additional code to identify associated endocrine syndrome, as: carcinoid syndrome: 259.2)
209.30 Malignant poorly differentiated neuroendocrine carcinoma, any site — (Code first any associated multiple endocrine neoplasia syndrome: 258.01-258.03)(Use additional code to identify associated endocrine syndrome, as: carcinoid syndrome: 259.2) ▽
209.63 Benign carcinoid tumor of the stomach — (Code first any associated multiple endocrine neoplasia syndrome: 258.01-258.03)(Use additional code to identify associated endocrine syndrome, as: carcinoid syndrome: 259.2)
209.69 Benign carcinoid tumor of other sites — (Code first any associated multiple endocrine neoplasia syndrome: 258.01-258.03)(Use additional code to identify associated endocrine syndrome, as: carcinoid syndrome: 259.2)
211.0 Benign neoplasm of esophagus
211.1 Benign neoplasm of stomach
230.1 Carcinoma in situ of esophagus
235.5 Neoplasm of uncertain behavior of other and unspecified digestive organs ▽
239.0 Neoplasm of unspecified nature of digestive system
530.11 Reflux esophagitis — (Use additional E code to identify cause, if induced by chemical)
530.12 Acute esophagitis — (Use additional E code to identify cause, if induced by chemical)
530.13 Eosinophilic esophagitis
530.19 Other esophagitis — (Use additional E code to identify cause, if induced by chemical)
530.20 Ulcer of esophagus without bleeding — (Use additional E code to identify cause, if induced by chemical or drug)
530.3 Stricture and stenosis of esophagus
530.5 Dyskinesia of esophagus
530.81 Esophageal reflux
530.85 Barrett's esophagus
530.89 Other specified disorder of the esophagus
531.21 Acute gastric ulcer with hemorrhage, perforation, and obstruction — (Use additional E code to identify drug, if drug induced)
750.3 Congenital tracheoesophageal fistula, esophageal atresia and stenosis
787.20 Dysphagia, unspecified ▽
787.22 Dysphagia, oropharyngeal phase
787.23 Dysphagia, pharyngeal phase
787.24 Dysphagia, pharyngoesophageal phase
787.29 Other dysphagia

ICD-9-CM Procedural

42.92 Dilation of esophagus

HCPCS Level II Supplies & Services

A4270 Disposable endoscope sheath, each

43250-43251

43250 Esophagogastroduodenoscopy, flexible, transoral; with removal of tumor(s), polyp(s), or other lesion(s) by hot biopsy forceps or bipolar cautery

43251 with removal of tumor(s), polyp(s), or other lesion(s) by snare technique

ICD-9-CM Diagnostic

150.0 Malignant neoplasm of cervical esophagus
150.1 Malignant neoplasm of thoracic esophagus
150.2 Malignant neoplasm of abdominal esophagus
150.3 Malignant neoplasm of upper third of esophagus
150.4 Malignant neoplasm of middle third of esophagus
150.5 Malignant neoplasm of lower third of esophagus
150.8 Malignant neoplasm of other specified part of esophagus
151.0 Malignant neoplasm of cardia
151.1 Malignant neoplasm of pylorus
151.2 Malignant neoplasm of pyloric antrum
151.3 Malignant neoplasm of fundus of stomach
151.4 Malignant neoplasm of body of stomach
151.5 Malignant neoplasm of lesser curvature of stomach, unspecified ▽
151.6 Malignant neoplasm of greater curvature of stomach, unspecified ▽
151.8 Malignant neoplasm of other specified sites of stomach
152.0 Malignant neoplasm of duodenum
152.1 Malignant neoplasm of jejunum
152.8 Malignant neoplasm of other specified sites of small intestine
197.4 Secondary malignant neoplasm of small intestine including duodenum
197.8 Secondary malignant neoplasm of other digestive organs and spleen
209.00 Malignant carcinoid tumor of the small intestine, unspecified portion — (Code first any associated multiple endocrine neoplasia syndrome: 258.01-258.03)(Use additional code to identify associated endocrine syndrome, as: carcinoid syndrome: 259.2) ▽
209.01 Malignant carcinoid tumor of the duodenum — (Code first any associated multiple endocrine neoplasia syndrome: 258.01-258.03)(Use additional code to identify associated endocrine syndrome, as: carcinoid syndrome: 259.2)
209.02 Malignant carcinoid tumor of the jejunum — (Code first any associated multiple endocrine neoplasia syndrome: 258.01-258.03)(Use additional code to identify associated endocrine syndrome, as: carcinoid syndrome: 259.2)
209.23 Malignant carcinoid tumor of the stomach — (Code first any associated multiple endocrine neoplasia syndrome: 258.01-258.03)(Use additional code to identify associated endocrine syndrome, as: carcinoid syndrome: 259.2)
209.25 Malignant carcinoid tumor of foregut, not otherwise specified — (Code first any associated multiple endocrine neoplasia syndrome: 258.01-258.03)(Use additional code to identify associated endocrine syndrome, as: carcinoid syndrome: 259.2)
209.40 Benign carcinoid tumor of the small intestine, unspecified portion — (Code first any associated multiple endocrine neoplasia syndrome: 258.01-258.03)(Use additional code to identify associated endocrine syndrome, as: carcinoid syndrome: 259.2) ▽
209.42 Benign carcinoid tumor of the jejunum — (Code first any associated multiple endocrine neoplasia syndrome: 258.01-258.03)(Use additional code to identify associated endocrine syndrome, as: carcinoid syndrome: 259.2)
209.60 Benign carcinoid tumor of unknown primary site — (Code first any associated multiple endocrine neoplasia syndrome: 258.01-258.03)(Use additional code to identify associated endocrine syndrome, as: carcinoid syndrome: 259.2)

209.65 Benign carcinoid tumor of foregut, not otherwise specified — (Code first any associated multiple endocrine neoplasia syndrome: 258.01-258.03)(Use additional code to identify associated endocrine syndrome, as: carcinoid syndrome: 259.2)
209.69 Benign carcinoid tumor of other sites — (Code first any associated multiple endocrine neoplasia syndrome: 258.01-258.03)(Use additional code to identify associated endocrine syndrome, as: carcinoid syndrome: 259.2)
211.0 Benign neoplasm of esophagus
211.1 Benign neoplasm of stomach
211.2 Benign neoplasm of duodenum, jejunum, and ileum
211.9 Benign neoplasm of other and unspecified site of the digestive system ▽
230.2 Carcinoma in situ of stomach
230.7 Carcinoma in situ of other and unspecified parts of intestine ▽
235.2 Neoplasm of uncertain behavior of stomach, intestines, and rectum
235.5 Neoplasm of uncertain behavior of other and unspecified digestive organs ▽
530.9 Unspecified disorder of esophagus ▽
537.82 Angiodysplasia of stomach and duodenum (without mention of hemorrhage)
537.83 Angiodysplasia of stomach and duodenum with hemorrhage
537.89 Other specified disorder of stomach and duodenum

ICD-9-CM Procedural

42.33 Endoscopic excision or destruction of lesion or tissue of esophagus
43.41 Endoscopic excision or destruction of lesion or tissue of stomach
45.30 Endoscopic excision or destruction of lesion of duodenum
45.33 Local excision of lesion or tissue of small intestine, except duodenum

HCPCS Level II Supplies & Services

A4270 Disposable endoscope sheath, each

43253

43253 Esophagogastroduodenoscopy, flexible, transoral; with transendoscopic ultrasound-guided transmural injection of diagnostic or therapeutic substance(s) (eg, anesthetic, neurolytic agent) or fiducial marker(s) (includes endoscopic ultrasound examination of the esophagus, stomach, and either the duodenum or a surgically altered stomach where the jejunum is examined distal to the anastomosis)

ICD-9-CM Diagnostic

150.0 Malignant neoplasm of cervical esophagus
150.1 Malignant neoplasm of thoracic esophagus
150.2 Malignant neoplasm of abdominal esophagus
150.3 Malignant neoplasm of upper third of esophagus
150.4 Malignant neoplasm of middle third of esophagus
150.5 Malignant neoplasm of lower third of esophagus
150.8 Malignant neoplasm of other specified part of esophagus
150.9 Malignant neoplasm of esophagus, unspecified site ▽
151.0 Malignant neoplasm of cardia
151.1 Malignant neoplasm of pylorus
151.2 Malignant neoplasm of pyloric antrum
151.3 Malignant neoplasm of fundus of stomach
151.4 Malignant neoplasm of body of stomach
151.5 Malignant neoplasm of lesser curvature of stomach, unspecified ▽
151.6 Malignant neoplasm of greater curvature of stomach, unspecified ▽
151.8 Malignant neoplasm of other specified sites of stomach
151.9 Malignant neoplasm of stomach, unspecified site ▽
152.0 Malignant neoplasm of duodenum
152.1 Malignant neoplasm of jejunum
152.8 Malignant neoplasm of other specified sites of small intestine
152.9 Malignant neoplasm of small intestine, unspecified site ▽
159.9 Malignant neoplasm of ill-defined sites of digestive organs and peritoneum ▽
197.4 Secondary malignant neoplasm of small intestine including duodenum
197.8 Secondary malignant neoplasm of other digestive organs and spleen
199.0 Disseminated malignant neoplasm
199.1 Other malignant neoplasm of unspecified site
209.00 Malignant carcinoid tumor of the small intestine, unspecified portion — (Code first any associated multiple endocrine neoplasia syndrome: 258.01-258.03)(Use additional code to identify associated endocrine syndrome, as: carcinoid syndrome: 259.2) ▽
209.01 Malignant carcinoid tumor of the duodenum — (Code first any associated multiple endocrine neoplasia syndrome: 258.01-258.03)(Use additional code to identify associated endocrine syndrome, as: carcinoid syndrome: 259.2)
209.02 Malignant carcinoid tumor of the jejunum — (Code first any associated multiple endocrine neoplasia syndrome: 258.01-258.03)(Use additional code to identify associated endocrine syndrome, as: carcinoid syndrome: 259.2)
209.20 Malignant carcinoid tumor of unknown primary site — (Code first any associated multiple endocrine neoplasia syndrome: 258.01-258.03)(Use additional code to identify associated endocrine syndrome, as: carcinoid syndrome: 259.2)
209.23 Malignant carcinoid tumor of the stomach — (Code first any associated multiple endocrine neoplasia syndrome: 258.01-258.03)(Use additional code to identify associated endocrine syndrome, as: carcinoid syndrome: 259.2)
209.25 Malignant carcinoid tumor of foregut, not otherwise specified — (Code first any associated multiple endocrine neoplasia syndrome: 258.01-258.03)(Use additional code to identify associated endocrine syndrome, as: carcinoid syndrome: 259.2)
209.29 Malignant carcinoid tumor of other sites — (Code first any associated multiple endocrine neoplasia syndrome: 258.01-258.03)(Use additional code to identify associated endocrine syndrome, as: carcinoid syndrome: 259.2)
209.30 Malignant poorly differentiated neuroendocrine carcinoma, any site — (Code first any associated multiple endocrine neoplasia syndrome: 258.01-258.03)(Use additional code to identify associated endocrine syndrome, as: carcinoid syndrome: 259.2) ▽
209.40 Benign carcinoid tumor of the small intestine, unspecified portion — (Code first any associated multiple endocrine neoplasia syndrome: 258.01-258.03)(Use additional code to identify associated endocrine syndrome, as: carcinoid syndrome: 259.2) ▽
209.41 Benign carcinoid tumor of the duodenum — (Code first any associated multiple endocrine neoplasia syndrome: 258.01-258.03)(Use additional code to identify associated endocrine syndrome, as: carcinoid syndrome: 259.2)
209.42 Benign carcinoid tumor of the jejunum — (Code first any associated multiple endocrine neoplasia syndrome: 258.01-258.03)(Use additional code to identify associated endocrine syndrome, as: carcinoid syndrome: 259.2)
209.43 Benign carcinoid tumor of the ileum — (Code first any associated multiple endocrine neoplasia syndrome: 258.01-258.03)(Use additional code to identify associated endocrine syndrome, as: carcinoid syndrome: 259.2)
209.63 Benign carcinoid tumor of the stomach — (Code first any associated multiple endocrine neoplasia syndrome: 258.01-258.03)(Use additional code to identify associated endocrine syndrome, as: carcinoid syndrome: 259.2)
209.65 Benign carcinoid tumor of foregut, not otherwise specified — (Code first any associated multiple endocrine neoplasia syndrome: 258.01-258.03)(Use additional code to identify associated endocrine syndrome, as: carcinoid syndrome: 259.2)
209.69 Benign carcinoid tumor of other sites — (Code first any associated multiple endocrine neoplasia syndrome: 258.01-258.03)(Use additional code to identify associated endocrine syndrome, as: carcinoid syndrome: 259.2)
211.0 Benign neoplasm of esophagus
211.1 Benign neoplasm of stomach
211.2 Benign neoplasm of duodenum, jejunum, and ileum
230.1 Carcinoma in situ of esophagus
230.2 Carcinoma in situ of stomach
235.2 Neoplasm of uncertain behavior of stomach, intestines, and rectum
239.0 Neoplasm of unspecified nature of digestive system
285.9 Unspecified anemia ▽
456.21 Esophageal varices without mention of bleeding in diseases classified elsewhere — (Code first underlying disease: 571.0-571.9, 572.3) ☒
530.0 Achalasia and cardiospasm
530.10 Unspecified esophagitis — (Use additional E code to identify cause, if induced by chemical) ▽
530.11 Reflux esophagitis — (Use additional E code to identify cause, if induced by chemical)
530.12 Acute esophagitis — (Use additional E code to identify cause, if induced by chemical)
530.13 Eosinophilic esophagitis

530.19 Other esophagitis — (Use additional E code to identify cause, if induced by chemical)
530.20 Ulcer of esophagus without bleeding — (Use additional E code to identify cause, if induced by chemical or drug)
530.21 Ulcer of esophagus with bleeding — (Use additional E code to identify cause, if induced by chemical or drug)
530.3 Stricture and stenosis of esophagus
530.5 Dyskinesia of esophagus
530.6 Diverticulum of esophagus, acquired
530.7 Gastroesophageal laceration-hemorrhage syndrome
530.81 Esophageal reflux
530.82 Esophageal hemorrhage
530.83 Esophageal leukoplakia
530.84 Tracheoesophageal fistula
530.85 Barrett's esophagus
530.89 Other specified disorder of the esophagus
531.00 Acute gastric ulcer with hemorrhage, without mention of obstruction — (Use additional E code to identify drug, if drug induced)
531.01 Acute gastric ulcer with hemorrhage and obstruction — (Use additional E code to identify drug, if drug induced)
531.10 Acute gastric ulcer with perforation, without mention of obstruction — (Use additional E code to identify drug, if drug induced)
531.20 Acute gastric ulcer with hemorrhage and perforation, without mention of obstruction — (Use additional E code to identify drug, if drug induced)
531.30 Acute gastric ulcer without mention of hemorrhage, perforation, or obstruction — (Use additional E code to identify drug, if drug induced)
531.31 Acute gastric ulcer without mention of hemorrhage or perforation, with obstruction — (Use additional E code to identify drug, if drug induced)
531.40 Chronic or unspecified gastric ulcer with hemorrhage, without mention of obstruction — (Use additional E code to identify drug, if drug induced)
531.41 Chronic or unspecified gastric ulcer with hemorrhage and obstruction — (Use additional E code to identify drug, if drug induced)
531.50 Chronic or unspecified gastric ulcer with perforation, without mention of obstruction — (Use additional E code to identify drug, if drug induced)
531.51 Chronic or unspecified gastric ulcer with perforation and obstruction — (Use additional E code to identify drug, if drug induced)
531.60 Chronic or unspecified gastric ulcer with hemorrhage and perforation, without mention of obstruction — (Use additional E code to identify drug, if drug induced)
531.61 Chronic or unspecified gastric ulcer with hemorrhage, perforation, and obstruction — (Use additional E code to identify drug, if drug induced)
531.70 Chronic gastric ulcer without mention of hemorrhage, perforation, without mention of obstruction — (Use additional E code to identify drug, if drug induced)
531.71 Chronic gastric ulcer without mention of hemorrhage or perforation, with obstruction — (Use additional E code to identify drug, if drug induced)
531.90 Gastric ulcer, unspecified as acute or chronic, without mention of hemorrhage, perforation, or obstruction — (Use additional E code to identify drug, if drug induced) ▽
531.91 Gastric ulcer, unspecified as acute or chronic, without mention of hemorrhage or perforation, with obstruction — (Use additional E code to identify drug, if drug induced) ▽
532.00 Acute duodenal ulcer with hemorrhage, without mention of obstruction — (Use additional E code to identify drug, if drug induced)
532.01 Acute duodenal ulcer with hemorrhage and obstruction — (Use additional E code to identify drug, if drug induced)
532.10 Acute duodenal ulcer with perforation, without mention of obstruction — (Use additional E code to identify drug, if drug induced)
532.11 Acute duodenal ulcer with perforation and obstruction — (Use additional E code to identify drug, if drug induced)
532.20 Acute duodenal ulcer with hemorrhage and perforation, without mention of obstruction — (Use additional E code to identify drug, if drug induced)
532.21 Acute duodenal ulcer with hemorrhage, perforation, and obstruction — (Use additional E code to identify drug, if drug induced)
532.30 Acute duodenal ulcer without mention of hemorrhage, perforation, or obstruction — (Use additional E code to identify drug, if drug induced)
532.31 Acute duodenal ulcer without mention of hemorrhage or perforation, with obstruction — (Use additional E code to identify drug, if drug induced)
532.40 Duodenal ulcer, chronic or unspecified, with hemorrhage, without mention of obstruction — (Use additional E code to identify drug, if drug induced)
532.41 Chronic or unspecified duodenal ulcer with hemorrhage and obstruction — (Use additional E code to identify drug, if drug induced)
532.50 Chronic or unspecified duodenal ulcer with perforation, without mention of obstruction — (Use additional E code to identify drug, if drug induced)
532.51 Chronic or unspecified duodenal ulcer with perforation and obstruction — (Use additional E code to identify drug, if drug induced)
532.60 Chronic or unspecified duodenal ulcer with hemorrhage and perforation, without mention of obstruction — (Use additional E code to identify drug, if drug induced)
532.61 Chronic or unspecified duodenal ulcer with hemorrhage, perforation, and obstruction — (Use additional E code to identify drug, if drug induced)
532.70 Chronic duodenal ulcer without mention of hemorrhage, perforation, or obstruction — (Use additional E code to identify drug, if drug induced)
532.71 Chronic duodenal ulcer without mention of hemorrhage or perforation, with obstruction — (Use additional E code to identify drug, if drug induced)
532.90 Duodenal ulcer, unspecified as acute or chronic, without hemorrhage, perforation, or obstruction — (Use additional E code to identify drug, if drug induced) ▽
532.91 Duodenal ulcer, unspecified as acute or chronic, without mention of hemorrhage or perforation, with obstruction — (Use additional E code to identify drug, if drug induced) ▽
533.00 Acute peptic ulcer, unspecified site, with hemorrhage, without mention of obstruction — (Use additional E code to identify drug, if drug induced) ▽
533.01 Acute peptic ulcer, unspecified site, with hemorrhage and obstruction — (Use additional E code to identify drug, if drug induced) ▽
533.10 Acute peptic ulcer, unspecified site, with perforation, without mention of obstruction — (Use additional E code to identify drug, if drug induced) ▽
533.11 Acute peptic ulcer, unspecified site, with perforation and obstruction— (Use additional E code to identify drug, if drug induced) ▽
533.20 Acute peptic ulcer, unspecified site, with hemorrhage and perforation, without mention of obstruction — (Use additional E code to identify drug, if drug induced) ▽
533.21 Acute peptic ulcer, unspecified site, with hemorrhage, perforation, and obstruction — (Use additional E code to identify drug, if drug induced) ▽
533.30 Acute peptic ulcer, unspecified site, without mention of hemorrhage, perforation, or obstruction — (Use additional E code to identify drug, if drug induced) ▽
533.31 Acute peptic ulcer, unspecified site, without mention of hemorrhage and perforation, with obstruction — (Use additional E code to identify drug, if drug induced) ▽
533.40 Chronic or unspecified peptic ulcer, unspecified site, with hemorrhage, without mention of obstruction — (Use additional E code to identify drug, if drug induced) ▽
533.41 Chronic or unspecified peptic ulcer, unspecified site, with hemorrhage and obstruction — (Use additional E code to identify drug, if drug induced) ▽
533.50 Chronic or unspecified peptic ulcer, unspecified site, with perforation, without mention of obstruction — (Use additional E code to identify drug, if drug induced) ▽
533.51 Chronic or unspecified peptic ulcer, unspecified site, with perforation and obstruction — (Use additional E code to identify drug, if drug induced) ▽
533.60 Chronic or unspecified peptic ulcer, unspecified site, with hemorrhage and perforation, without mention of obstruction — (Use additional E code to identify drug, if drug induced) ▽
533.61 Chronic or unspecified peptic ulcer, unspecified site, with hemorrhage, perforation, and obstruction — (Use additional E code to identify drug, if drug induced) ▽
533.70 Chronic peptic ulcer, unspecified site, without mention of hemorrhage, perforation, or obstruction — (Use additional E code to identify drug, if drug induced) ▽
533.71 Chronic peptic ulcer of unspecified site without mention of hemorrhage or perforation, with obstruction — (Use additional E code to identify drug, if drug induced) ▽
533.90 Peptic ulcer, unspecified site, unspecified as acute or chronic, without mention of hemorrhage, perforation, or obstruction — (Use additional E code to identify drug, if drug induced) ▽

533.91 Peptic ulcer, unspecified site, unspecified as acute or chronic, without mention of hemorrhage or perforation, with obstruction — (Use additional E code to identify drug, if drug induced) ▽
534.00 Acute gastrojejunal ulcer with hemorrhage, without mention of obstruction
534.01 Acute gastrojejunal ulcer, with hemorrhage and obstruction
534.10 Acute gastrojejunal ulcer with perforation, without mention of obstruction
534.11 Acute gastrojejunal ulcer with perforation and obstruction
534.20 Acute gastrojejunal ulcer with hemorrhage and perforation, without mention of obstruction
534.21 Acute gastrojejunal ulcer with hemorrhage, perforation, and obstruction
534.30 Acute gastrojejunal ulcer without mention of hemorrhage, perforation, or obstruction
534.31 Acute gastrojejunal ulcer without mention of hemorrhage or perforation, with obstruction
534.40 Chronic or unspecified gastrojejunal ulcer with hemorrhage, without mention of obstruction
534.41 Chronic or unspecified gastrojejunal ulcer, with hemorrhage and obstruction
534.50 Chronic or unspecified gastrojejunal ulcer with perforation, without mention of obstruction
534.51 Chronic or unspecified gastrojejunal ulcer with perforation and obstruction
534.60 Chronic or unspecified gastrojejunal ulcer with hemorrhage and perforation, without mention of obstruction
534.61 Chronic or unspecified gastrojejunal ulcer with hemorrhage, perforation, and obstruction
534.70 Chronic gastrojejunal ulcer without mention of hemorrhage, perforation, or obstruction
534.71 Chronic gastrojejunal ulcer without mention of hemorrhage or perforation, with obstruction
534.90 Gastrojejunal ulcer, unspecified as acute or chronic, without mention of hemorrhage, perforation, or obstruction ▽
534.91 Gastrojejunal ulcer, unspecified as acute or chronic, without mention of hemorrhage or perforation, with obstruction ▽
535.00 Acute gastritis without mention of hemorrhage
535.01 Acute gastritis with hemorrhage
535.10 Atrophic gastritis without mention of hemorrhage
535.11 Atrophic gastritis with hemorrhage
535.20 Gastric mucosal hypertrophy without mention of hemorrhage
535.21 Gastric mucosal hypertrophy with hemorrhage
535.30 Alcoholic gastritis without mention of hemorrhage
535.31 Alcoholic gastritis with hemorrhage
535.40 Other specified gastritis without mention of hemorrhage
535.41 Other specified gastritis with hemorrhage
535.60 Duodenitis without mention of hemorrhage
535.61 Duodenitis with hemorrhage
535.70 Eosinophilic gastritis without mention of hemorrhage
535.71 Eosinophilic gastritis with hemorrhage
536.0 Achlorhydria
536.1 Acute dilatation of stomach
536.2 Persistent vomiting
536.3 Gastroparesis — (Code first underlying disease, if known, as: 249.6, 250.6)
536.8 Dyspepsia and other specified disorders of function of stomach
536.9 Unspecified functional disorder of stomach ▽
537.0 Acquired hypertrophic pyloric stenosis
537.1 Gastric diverticulum
537.2 Chronic duodenal ileus
537.3 Other obstruction of duodenum
537.4 Fistula of stomach or duodenum
537.5 Gastroptosis
537.6 Hourglass stricture or stenosis of stomach
537.81 Pylorospasm
537.82 Angiodysplasia of stomach and duodenum (without mention of hemorrhage)
537.83 Angiodysplasia of stomach and duodenum with hemorrhage
537.84 Dieulafoy lesion (hemorrhagic) of stomach and duodenum
537.89 Other specified disorder of stomach and duodenum
537.9 Unspecified disorder of stomach and duodenum ▽
552.3 Diaphragmatic hernia with obstruction
553.3 Diaphragmatic hernia without mention of obstruction or gangrene
555.0 Regional enteritis of small intestine
558.1 Gastroenteritis and colitis due to radiation
558.2 Toxic gastroenteritis and colitis — (Use additional E code to identify cause)
558.3 Gastroenteritis and colitis, allergic — (Use additional code to identify type of food allergy: V15.01-V15.05)
558.41 Eosinophilic gastroenteritis
558.9 Other and unspecified noninfectious gastroenteritis and colitis ▽
569.5 Abscess of intestine
569.82 Ulceration of intestine
569.86 Dieulafoy lesion (hemorrhagic) of intestine
569.89 Other specified disorder of intestines
578.0 Hematemesis
578.1 Blood in stool
579.0 Celiac disease
579.2 Blind loop syndrome
579.3 Other and unspecified postsurgical nonabsorption ▽
579.8 Other specified intestinal malabsorption
747.61 Congenital gastrointestinal vessel anomaly
750.3 Congenital tracheoesophageal fistula, esophageal atresia and stenosis
750.4 Other specified congenital anomaly of esophagus
750.5 Congenital hypertrophic pyloric stenosis
750.6 Congenital hiatus hernia
750.7 Other specified congenital anomalies of stomach
751.8 Other specified congenital anomalies of digestive system
783.0 Anorexia
783.21 Loss of weight — (Use additional code to identify Body Mass Index (BMI), if known: V85.0-V85.54)
783.22 Underweight — (Use additional code to identify Body Mass Index (BMI), if known: V85.0-V85.54)
783.7 Adult failure to thrive
784.1 Throat pain
787.1 Heartburn
787.20 Dysphagia, unspecified ▽
787.21 Dysphagia, oral phase
787.22 Dysphagia, oropharyngeal phase
787.23 Dysphagia, pharyngeal phase
787.24 Dysphagia, pharyngoesophageal phase
787.29 Other dysphagia
787.3 Flatulence, eructation, and gas pain
787.4 Visible peristalsis
787.5 Abnormal bowel sounds
787.99 Other symptoms involving digestive system
789.09 Abdominal pain, other specified site
792.1 Nonspecific abnormal finding in stool contents
793.4 Nonspecific (abnormal) findings on radiological and other examination of gastrointestinal tract
997.49 Other digestive system complications
V10.00 Personal history of malignant neoplasm of unspecified site in gastrointestinal tract ▽
V12.71 Personal history of peptic ulcer disease
V12.79 Personal history of other diseases of digestive disease
V16.0 Family history of malignant neoplasm of gastrointestinal tract
V18.51 Family history, Colonic polyps
V18.59 Family history, other digestive disorders
V67.00 Follow-up examination, following unspecified surgery ▽

V67.09 Follow-up examination, following other surgery
V67.59 Other follow-up examination
V67.9 Unspecified follow-up examination ▽
V71.1 Observation for suspected malignant neoplasm
V71.89 Observation for other specified suspected conditions
V85.0 Body Mass Index less than 19, adult

ICD-9-CM Procedural

45.13 Other endoscopy of small intestine
99.23 Injection of steroid
99.29 Injection or infusion of other therapeutic or prophylactic substance

HCPCS Level II Supplies & Services

A4270 Disposable endoscope sheath, each

43254

43254 Esophagogastroduodenoscopy, flexible, transoral; with endoscopic mucosal resection

ICD-9-CM Diagnostic

150.0 Malignant neoplasm of cervical esophagus
150.1 Malignant neoplasm of thoracic esophagus
150.2 Malignant neoplasm of abdominal esophagus
150.3 Malignant neoplasm of upper third of esophagus
150.4 Malignant neoplasm of middle third of esophagus
150.5 Malignant neoplasm of lower third of esophagus
150.8 Malignant neoplasm of other specified part of esophagus
151.0 Malignant neoplasm of cardia
197.8 Secondary malignant neoplasm of other digestive organs and spleen
199.1 Other malignant neoplasm of unspecified site
209.29 Malignant carcinoid tumor of other sites — (Code first any associated multiple endocrine neoplasia syndrome: 258.01-258.03)(Use additional code to identify associated endocrine syndrome, as: carcinoid syndrome: 259.2)
209.30 Malignant poorly differentiated neuroendocrine carcinoma, any site — (Code first any associated multiple endocrine neoplasia syndrome: 258.01-258.03)(Use additional code to identify associated endocrine syndrome, as: carcinoid syndrome: 259.2) ▽
209.69 Benign carcinoid tumor of other sites — (Code first any associated multiple endocrine neoplasia syndrome: 258.01-258.03)(Use additional code to identify associated endocrine syndrome, as: carcinoid syndrome: 259.2)
211.0 Benign neoplasm of esophagus
230.1 Carcinoma in situ of esophagus
235.5 Neoplasm of uncertain behavior of other and unspecified digestive organs ▽
239.0 Neoplasm of unspecified nature of digestive system
530.89 Other specified disorder of the esophagus

ICD-9-CM Procedural

42.33 Endoscopic excision or destruction of lesion or tissue of esophagus
43.41 Endoscopic excision or destruction of lesion or tissue of stomach
45.30 Endoscopic excision or destruction of lesion of duodenum

43255

43255 Esophagogastroduodenoscopy, flexible, transoral; with control of bleeding, any method

ICD-9-CM Diagnostic

150.5 Malignant neoplasm of lower third of esophagus
150.8 Malignant neoplasm of other specified part of esophagus
150.9 Malignant neoplasm of esophagus, unspecified site ▽
151.0 Malignant neoplasm of cardia
151.1 Malignant neoplasm of pylorus
151.2 Malignant neoplasm of pyloric antrum
151.3 Malignant neoplasm of fundus of stomach
151.4 Malignant neoplasm of body of stomach
151.5 Malignant neoplasm of lesser curvature of stomach, unspecified ▽
151.6 Malignant neoplasm of greater curvature of stomach, unspecified ▽
151.8 Malignant neoplasm of other specified sites of stomach
151.9 Malignant neoplasm of stomach, unspecified site ▽
153.3 Malignant neoplasm of sigmoid colon
209.23 Malignant carcinoid tumor of the stomach — (Code first any associated multiple endocrine neoplasia syndrome: 258.01-258.03)(Use additional code to identify associated endocrine syndrome, as: carcinoid syndrome: 259.2)
209.25 Malignant carcinoid tumor of foregut, not otherwise specified — (Code first any associated multiple endocrine neoplasia syndrome: 258.01-258.03)(Use additional code to identify associated endocrine syndrome, as: carcinoid syndrome: 259.2)
209.40 Benign carcinoid tumor of the small intestine, unspecified portion — (Code first any associated multiple endocrine neoplasia syndrome: 258.01-258.03)(Use additional code to identify associated endocrine syndrome, as: carcinoid syndrome: 259.2) ▽
209.41 Benign carcinoid tumor of the duodenum — (Code first any associated multiple endocrine neoplasia syndrome: 258.01-258.03)(Use additional code to identify associated endocrine syndrome, as: carcinoid syndrome: 259.2)
209.42 Benign carcinoid tumor of the jejunum — (Code first any associated multiple endocrine neoplasia syndrome: 258.01-258.03)(Use additional code to identify associated endocrine syndrome, as: carcinoid syndrome: 259.2)
209.63 Benign carcinoid tumor of the stomach — (Code first any associated multiple endocrine neoplasia syndrome: 258.01-258.03)(Use additional code to identify associated endocrine syndrome, as: carcinoid syndrome: 259.2)
209.65 Benign carcinoid tumor of foregut, not otherwise specified — (Code first any associated multiple endocrine neoplasia syndrome: 258.01-258.03)(Use additional code to identify associated endocrine syndrome, as: carcinoid syndrome: 259.2)
209.72 Secondary neuroendocrine tumor of liver
211.0 Benign neoplasm of esophagus
211.1 Benign neoplasm of stomach
211.2 Benign neoplasm of duodenum, jejunum, and ileum
211.3 Benign neoplasm of colon
280.0 Iron deficiency anemia secondary to blood loss (chronic)
285.1 Acute posthemorrhagic anemia
285.9 Unspecified anemia ▽
448.0 Hereditary hemorrhagic telangiectasia
448.9 Other and unspecified capillary diseases ▽
456.0 Esophageal varices with bleeding
456.20 Esophageal varices with bleeding in diseases classified elsewhere — (Code first underlying disease: 571.0-571.9, 572.3) ☒
530.21 Ulcer of esophagus with bleeding — (Use additional E code to identify cause, if induced by chemical or drug)
530.7 Gastroesophageal laceration-hemorrhage syndrome
530.81 Esophageal reflux
530.82 Esophageal hemorrhage
530.83 Esophageal leukoplakia
530.84 Tracheoesophageal fistula
530.85 Barrett's esophagus
530.89 Other specified disorder of the esophagus
530.9 Unspecified disorder of esophagus ▽
531.00 Acute gastric ulcer with hemorrhage, without mention of obstruction — (Use additional E code to identify drug, if drug induced)
531.01 Acute gastric ulcer with hemorrhage and obstruction — (Use additional E code to identify drug, if drug induced)
531.10 Acute gastric ulcer with perforation, without mention of obstruction — (Use additional E code to identify drug, if drug induced)
531.11 Acute gastric ulcer with perforation and obstruction — (Use additional E code to identify drug, if drug induced)
531.20 Acute gastric ulcer with hemorrhage and perforation, without mention of obstruction — (Use additional E code to identify drug, if drug induced)
531.21 Acute gastric ulcer with hemorrhage, perforation, and obstruction — (Use additional E code to identify drug, if drug induced)

531.30 Acute gastric ulcer without mention of hemorrhage, perforation, or obstruction — (Use additional E code to identify drug, if drug induced)
531.31 Acute gastric ulcer without mention of hemorrhage or perforation, with obstruction — (Use additional E code to identify drug, if drug induced)
531.40 Chronic or unspecified gastric ulcer with hemorrhage, without mention of obstruction — (Use additional E code to identify drug, if drug induced)
531.41 Chronic or unspecified gastric ulcer with hemorrhage and obstruction — (Use additional E code to identify drug, if drug induced)
531.50 Chronic or unspecified gastric ulcer with perforation, without mention of obstruction — (Use additional E code to identify drug, if drug induced)
531.51 Chronic or unspecified gastric ulcer with perforation and obstruction — (Use additional E code to identify drug, if drug induced)
531.60 Chronic or unspecified gastric ulcer with hemorrhage and perforation, without mention of obstruction — (Use additional E code to identify drug, if drug induced)
531.61 Chronic or unspecified gastric ulcer with hemorrhage, perforation, and obstruction — (Use additional E code to identify drug, if drug induced)
531.70 Chronic gastric ulcer without mention of hemorrhage, perforation, without mention of obstruction — (Use additional E code to identify drug, if drug induced)
531.71 Chronic gastric ulcer without mention of hemorrhage or perforation, with obstruction — (Use additional E code to identify drug, if drug induced)
531.90 Gastric ulcer, unspecified as acute or chronic, without mention of hemorrhage, perforation, or obstruction — (Use additional E code to identify drug, if drug induced) ▽
531.91 Gastric ulcer, unspecified as acute or chronic, without mention of hemorrhage or perforation, with obstruction — (Use additional E code to identify drug, if drug induced) ▽
533.00 Acute peptic ulcer, unspecified site, with hemorrhage, without mention of obstruction — (Use additional E code to identify drug, if drug induced) ▽
533.10 Acute peptic ulcer, unspecified site, with perforation, without mention of obstruction — (Use additional E code to identify drug, if drug induced) ▽
533.11 Acute peptic ulcer, unspecified site, with perforation and obstruction— (Use additional E code to identify drug, if drug induced) ▽
533.20 Acute peptic ulcer, unspecified site, with hemorrhage and perforation, without mention of obstruction — (Use additional E code to identify drug, if drug induced) ▽
533.21 Acute peptic ulcer, unspecified site, with hemorrhage, perforation, and obstruction — (Use additional E code to identify drug, if drug induced) ▽
533.30 Acute peptic ulcer, unspecified site, without mention of hemorrhage, perforation, or obstruction — (Use additional E code to identify drug, if drug induced) ▽
533.31 Acute peptic ulcer, unspecified site, without mention of hemorrhage and perforation, with obstruction — (Use additional E code to identify drug, if drug induced) ▽
533.40 Chronic or unspecified peptic ulcer, unspecified site, with hemorrhage, without mention of obstruction — (Use additional E code to identify drug, if drug induced) ▽
533.41 Chronic or unspecified peptic ulcer, unspecified site, with hemorrhage and obstruction — (Use additional E code to identify drug, if drug induced) ▽
533.50 Chronic or unspecified peptic ulcer, unspecified site, with perforation, without mention of obstruction — (Use additional E code to identify drug, if drug induced) ▽
533.51 Chronic or unspecified peptic ulcer, unspecified site, with perforation and obstruction — (Use additional E code to identify drug, if drug induced) ▽
533.60 Chronic or unspecified peptic ulcer, unspecified site, with hemorrhage and perforation, without mention of obstruction — (Use additional E code to identify drug, if drug induced) ▽
533.61 Chronic or unspecified peptic ulcer, unspecified site, with hemorrhage, perforation, and obstruction — (Use additional E code to identify drug, if drug induced) ▽
533.70 Chronic peptic ulcer, unspecified site, without mention of hemorrhage, perforation, or obstruction — (Use additional E code to identify drug, if drug induced) ▽
533.71 Chronic peptic ulcer of unspecified site without mention of hemorrhage or perforation, with obstruction — (Use additional E code to identify drug, if drug induced) ▽
533.90 Peptic ulcer, unspecified site, unspecified as acute or chronic, without mention of hemorrhage, perforation, or obstruction — (Use additional E code to identify drug, if drug induced) ▽
533.91 Peptic ulcer, unspecified site, unspecified as acute or chronic, without mention of hemorrhage or perforation, with obstruction — (Use additional E code to identify drug, if drug induced) ▽
535.11 Atrophic gastritis with hemorrhage
535.51 Unspecified gastritis and gastroduodenitis with hemorrhage ▽
537.84 Dieulafoy lesion (hemorrhagic) of stomach and duodenum
569.85 Angiodysplasia of intestine with hemorrhage
569.86 Dieulafoy lesion (hemorrhagic) of intestine
571.0 Alcoholic fatty liver
571.1 Acute alcoholic hepatitis
571.2 Alcoholic cirrhosis of liver
571.3 Unspecified alcoholic liver damage ▽
571.40 Unspecified chronic hepatitis ▽
571.41 Chronic persistent hepatitis
571.42 Autoimmune hepatitis
571.49 Other chronic hepatitis
571.5 Cirrhosis of liver without mention of alcohol — (Code first, if applicable, viral hepatitis (acute) (chronic): 070.0-070.9)
571.6 Biliary cirrhosis
571.8 Other chronic nonalcoholic liver disease
571.9 Unspecified chronic liver disease without mention of alcohol ▽
572.3 Portal hypertension — (Use additional code for any associated complications, such as: portal hypertensive gastropathy (537.89))
578.0 Hematemesis
578.1 Blood in stool
578.9 Hemorrhage of gastrointestinal tract, unspecified ▽
747.60 Congenital anomaly of the peripheral vascular system, unspecified site ▽
787.01 Nausea with vomiting
787.04 Bilious emesis
789.00 Abdominal pain, unspecified site ▽
789.30 Abdominal or pelvic swelling, mass or lump, unspecified site ▽
792.1 Nonspecific abnormal finding in stool contents
V45.89 Other postprocedural status

ICD-9-CM Procedural

42.33 Endoscopic excision or destruction of lesion or tissue of esophagus
44.43 Endoscopic control of gastric or duodenal bleeding

[43266]

43266 Esophagogastroduodenoscopy, flexible, transoral; with placement of endoscopic stent (includes pre- and post-dilation and guide wire passage, when performed)

ICD-9-CM Diagnostic

150.0 Malignant neoplasm of cervical esophagus
150.1 Malignant neoplasm of thoracic esophagus
150.2 Malignant neoplasm of abdominal esophagus
150.3 Malignant neoplasm of upper third of esophagus
150.4 Malignant neoplasm of middle third of esophagus
150.5 Malignant neoplasm of lower third of esophagus
150.8 Malignant neoplasm of other specified part of esophagus
150.9 Malignant neoplasm of esophagus, unspecified site ▽
151.0 Malignant neoplasm of cardia
151.1 Malignant neoplasm of pylorus
151.2 Malignant neoplasm of pyloric antrum
151.3 Malignant neoplasm of fundus of stomach
151.4 Malignant neoplasm of body of stomach
151.5 Malignant neoplasm of lesser curvature of stomach, unspecified ▽
151.6 Malignant neoplasm of greater curvature of stomach, unspecified ▽
151.8 Malignant neoplasm of other specified sites of stomach
151.9 Malignant neoplasm of stomach, unspecified site ▽

152.0 Malignant neoplasm of duodenum
152.1 Malignant neoplasm of jejunum
152.8 Malignant neoplasm of other specified sites of small intestine
152.9 Malignant neoplasm of small intestine, unspecified site
159.9 Malignant neoplasm of ill-defined sites of digestive organs and peritoneum
197.4 Secondary malignant neoplasm of small intestine including duodenum
197.8 Secondary malignant neoplasm of other digestive organs and spleen
199.0 Disseminated malignant neoplasm
199.1 Other malignant neoplasm of unspecified site
209.00 Malignant carcinoid tumor of the small intestine, unspecified portion — (Code first any associated multiple endocrine neoplasia syndrome: 258.01-258.03)(Use additional code to identify associated endocrine syndrome, as: carcinoid syndrome: 259.2)
209.01 Malignant carcinoid tumor of the duodenum — (Code first any associated multiple endocrine neoplasia syndrome: 258.01-258.03)(Use additional code to identify associated endocrine syndrome, as: carcinoid syndrome: 259.2)
209.02 Malignant carcinoid tumor of the jejunum — (Code first any associated multiple endocrine neoplasia syndrome: 258.01-258.03)(Use additional code to identify associated endocrine syndrome, as: carcinoid syndrome: 259.2)
209.20 Malignant carcinoid tumor of unknown primary site — (Code first any associated multiple endocrine neoplasia syndrome: 258.01-258.03)(Use additional code to identify associated endocrine syndrome, as: carcinoid syndrome: 259.2)
209.23 Malignant carcinoid tumor of the stomach — (Code first any associated multiple endocrine neoplasia syndrome: 258.01-258.03)(Use additional code to identify associated endocrine syndrome, as: carcinoid syndrome: 259.2)
209.25 Malignant carcinoid tumor of foregut, not otherwise specified — (Code first any associated multiple endocrine neoplasia syndrome: 258.01-258.03)(Use additional code to identify associated endocrine syndrome, as: carcinoid syndrome: 259.2)
209.29 Malignant carcinoid tumor of other sites — (Code first any associated multiple endocrine neoplasia syndrome: 258.01-258.03)(Use additional code to identify associated endocrine syndrome, as: carcinoid syndrome: 259.2)
209.30 Malignant poorly differentiated neuroendocrine carcinoma, any site — (Code first any associated multiple endocrine neoplasia syndrome: 258.01-258.03)(Use additional code to identify associated endocrine syndrome, as: carcinoid syndrome: 259.2)
209.40 Benign carcinoid tumor of the small intestine, unspecified portion — (Code first any associated multiple endocrine neoplasia syndrome: 258.01-258.03)(Use additional code to identify associated endocrine syndrome, as: carcinoid syndrome: 259.2)
209.41 Benign carcinoid tumor of the duodenum — (Code first any associated multiple endocrine neoplasia syndrome: 258.01-258.03)(Use additional code to identify associated endocrine syndrome, as: carcinoid syndrome: 259.2)
209.42 Benign carcinoid tumor of the jejunum — (Code first any associated multiple endocrine neoplasia syndrome: 258.01-258.03)(Use additional code to identify associated endocrine syndrome, as: carcinoid syndrome: 259.2)
209.43 Benign carcinoid tumor of the ileum — (Code first any associated multiple endocrine neoplasia syndrome: 258.01-258.03)(Use additional code to identify associated endocrine syndrome, as: carcinoid syndrome: 259.2)
209.63 Benign carcinoid tumor of the stomach — (Code first any associated multiple endocrine neoplasia syndrome: 258.01-258.03)(Use additional code to identify associated endocrine syndrome, as: carcinoid syndrome: 259.2)
209.65 Benign carcinoid tumor of foregut, not otherwise specified — (Code first any associated multiple endocrine neoplasia syndrome: 258.01-258.03)(Use additional code to identify associated endocrine syndrome, as: carcinoid syndrome: 259.2)
209.69 Benign carcinoid tumor of other sites — (Code first any associated multiple endocrine neoplasia syndrome: 258.01-258.03)(Use additional code to identify associated endocrine syndrome, as: carcinoid syndrome: 259.2)
211.0 Benign neoplasm of esophagus
211.1 Benign neoplasm of stomach
211.2 Benign neoplasm of duodenum, jejunum, and ileum
230.1 Carcinoma in situ of esophagus
230.2 Carcinoma in situ of stomach
235.2 Neoplasm of uncertain behavior of stomach, intestines, and rectum
239.0 Neoplasm of unspecified nature of digestive system
530.3 Stricture and stenosis of esophagus
530.5 Dyskinesia of esophagus
530.6 Diverticulum of esophagus, acquired
530.7 Gastroesophageal laceration-hemorrhage syndrome
530.81 Esophageal reflux
530.82 Esophageal hemorrhage
530.83 Esophageal leukoplakia
530.84 Tracheoesophageal fistula
530.85 Barrett's esophagus
530.89 Other specified disorder of the esophagus
536.3 Gastroparesis — (Code first underlying disease, if known, as: 249.6, 250.6)
536.8 Dyspepsia and other specified disorders of function of stomach
536.9 Unspecified functional disorder of stomach
537.0 Acquired hypertrophic pyloric stenosis
537.1 Gastric diverticulum
537.2 Chronic duodenal ileus
537.3 Other obstruction of duodenum
537.4 Fistula of stomach or duodenum
537.5 Gastroptosis
537.6 Hourglass stricture or stenosis of stomach
537.81 Pylorospasm
537.82 Angiodysplasia of stomach and duodenum (without mention of hemorrhage)
537.83 Angiodysplasia of stomach and duodenum with hemorrhage
537.84 Dieulafoy lesion (hemorrhagic) of stomach and duodenum
537.89 Other specified disorder of stomach and duodenum
537.9 Unspecified disorder of stomach and duodenum
569.89 Other specified disorder of intestines
579.2 Blind loop syndrome
579.3 Other and unspecified postsurgical nonabsorption
579.8 Other specified intestinal malabsorption
747.61 Congenital gastrointestinal vessel anomaly
750.3 Congenital tracheoesophageal fistula, esophageal atresia and stenosis
750.4 Other specified congenital anomaly of esophagus
750.5 Congenital hypertrophic pyloric stenosis
750.7 Other specified congenital anomalies of stomach
751.8 Other specified congenital anomalies of digestive system
783.21 Loss of weight — (Use additional code to identify Body Mass Index (BMI), if known: V85.0-V85.54)
783.22 Underweight — (Use additional code to identify Body Mass Index (BMI), if known: V85.0-V85.54)
783.7 Adult failure to thrive
787.1 Heartburn
787.3 Flatulence, eructation, and gas pain
787.4 Visible peristalsis
787.5 Abnormal bowel sounds
787.99 Other symptoms involving digestive system
789.09 Abdominal pain, other specified site
793.4 Nonspecific (abnormal) findings on radiological and other examination of gastrointestinal tract
997.49 Other digestive system complications
V10.00 Personal history of malignant neoplasm of unspecified site in gastrointestinal tract
V12.79 Personal history of other diseases of digestive disease
V16.0 Family history of malignant neoplasm of gastrointestinal tract
V18.59 Family history, other digestive disorders
V67.00 Follow-up examination, following unspecified surgery
V67.09 Follow-up examination, following other surgery
V67.59 Other follow-up examination
V67.9 Unspecified follow-up examination
V71.1 Observation for suspected malignant neoplasm
V71.89 Observation for other specified suspected conditions

V85.0 Body Mass Index less than 19, adult

ICD-9-CM Procedural

42.81 Insertion of permanent tube into esophagus
42.92 Dilation of esophagus
45.13 Other endoscopy of small intestine

HCPCS Level II Supplies & Services

A4270 Disposable endoscope sheath, each

43257

43257 Esophagogastroduodenoscopy, flexible, transoral; with delivery of thermal energy to the muscle of lower esophageal sphincter and/or gastric cardia, for treatment of gastroesophageal reflux disease

ICD-9-CM Diagnostic

530.11 Reflux esophagitis — (Use additional E code to identify cause, if induced by chemical)
530.81 Esophageal reflux

ICD-9-CM Procedural

42.33 Endoscopic excision or destruction of lesion or tissue of esophagus
43.41 Endoscopic excision or destruction of lesion or tissue of stomach

43259

43259 Esophagogastroduodenoscopy, flexible, transoral; with endoscopic ultrasound examination, including the esophagus, stomach, and either the duodenum or a surgically altered stomach where the jejunum is examined distal to the anastomosis

ICD-9-CM Diagnostic

150.0 Malignant neoplasm of cervical esophagus
150.1 Malignant neoplasm of thoracic esophagus
150.2 Malignant neoplasm of abdominal esophagus
150.3 Malignant neoplasm of upper third of esophagus
150.4 Malignant neoplasm of middle third of esophagus
150.5 Malignant neoplasm of lower third of esophagus
150.8 Malignant neoplasm of other specified part of esophagus
151.0 Malignant neoplasm of cardia
151.1 Malignant neoplasm of pylorus
151.2 Malignant neoplasm of pyloric antrum
151.3 Malignant neoplasm of fundus of stomach
151.4 Malignant neoplasm of body of stomach
151.5 Malignant neoplasm of lesser curvature of stomach, unspecified
151.6 Malignant neoplasm of greater curvature of stomach, unspecified
151.8 Malignant neoplasm of other specified sites of stomach
152.0 Malignant neoplasm of duodenum
152.1 Malignant neoplasm of jejunum
197.8 Secondary malignant neoplasm of other digestive organs and spleen
209.01 Malignant carcinoid tumor of the duodenum — (Code first any associated multiple endocrine neoplasia syndrome: 258.01-258.03)(Use additional code to identify associated endocrine syndrome, as: carcinoid syndrome: 259.2)
209.02 Malignant carcinoid tumor of the jejunum — (Code first any associated multiple endocrine neoplasia syndrome: 258.01-258.03)(Use additional code to identify associated endocrine syndrome, as: carcinoid syndrome: 259.2)
209.23 Malignant carcinoid tumor of the stomach — (Code first any associated multiple endocrine neoplasia syndrome: 258.01-258.03)(Use additional code to identify associated endocrine syndrome, as: carcinoid syndrome: 259.2)
211.1 Benign neoplasm of stomach
230.1 Carcinoma in situ of esophagus
230.2 Carcinoma in situ of stomach
230.9 Carcinoma in situ of other and unspecified digestive organs
235.2 Neoplasm of uncertain behavior of stomach, intestines, and rectum
789.30 Abdominal or pelvic swelling, mass or lump, unspecified site
789.31 Abdominal or pelvic swelling, mass, or lump, right upper quadrant
789.32 Abdominal or pelvic swelling, mass, or lump, left upper quadrant
789.33 Abdominal or pelvic swelling, mass, or lump, right lower quadrant
789.34 Abdominal or pelvic swelling, mass, or lump, left lower quadrant
789.35 Abdominal or pelvic swelling, mass or lump, periumbilic
789.36 Abdominal or pelvic swelling, mass, or lump, epigastric
789.37 Abdominal or pelvic swelling, mass, or lump, generalized
789.39 Abdominal or pelvic swelling, mass, or lump, other specified site

ICD-9-CM Procedural

45.13 Other endoscopy of small intestine
88.74 Diagnostic ultrasound of digestive system

HCPCS Level II Supplies & Services

A4270 Disposable endoscope sheath, each

43260-43261 [43274, 43275, 43276, 43277, 43278]

43260 Endoscopic retrograde cholangiopancreatography (ERCP); diagnostic, including collection of specimen(s) by brushing or washing, when performed (separate procedure)
43261 with biopsy, single or multiple
43274 with placement of endoscopic stent into biliary or pancreatic duct, including pre- and post-dilation and guide wire passage, when performed, including sphincterotomy, when performed, each stent
43275 with removal of foreign body(s) or stent(s) from biliary/pancreatic duct(s)
43276 with removal and exchange of stent(s), biliary or pancreatic duct, including pre- and post-dilation and guide wire passage, when performed, including sphincterotomy, when performed, each stent exchanged
43277 with trans-endoscopic balloon dilation of biliary/pancreatic duct(s) or of ampulla (sphincteroplasty), including sphincterotomy, when performed, each duct
43278 with ablation of tumor(s), polyp(s), or other lesion(s), including pre- and post-dilation and guide wire passage, when performed

ICD-9-CM Diagnostic

155.1 Malignant neoplasm of intrahepatic bile ducts
156.0 Malignant neoplasm of gallbladder
156.1 Malignant neoplasm of extrahepatic bile ducts
156.2 Malignant neoplasm of ampulla of Vater
156.8 Malignant neoplasm of other specified sites of gallbladder and extrahepatic bile ducts
156.9 Malignant neoplasm of biliary tract, part unspecified site
197.8 Secondary malignant neoplasm of other digestive organs and spleen
199.2 Malignant neoplasm associated with transplanted organ — (Code first complication of transplanted organ (996.80-996.89) Use additional code for specific malignancy)
209.29 Malignant carcinoid tumor of other sites — (Code first any associated multiple endocrine neoplasia syndrome: 258.01-258.03)(Use additional code to identify associated endocrine syndrome, as: carcinoid syndrome: 259.2)
209.30 Malignant poorly differentiated neuroendocrine carcinoma, any site — (Code first any associated multiple endocrine neoplasia syndrome: 258.01-258.03)(Use additional code to identify associated endocrine syndrome, as: carcinoid syndrome: 259.2)
209.69 Benign carcinoid tumor of other sites — (Code first any associated multiple endocrine neoplasia syndrome: 258.01-258.03)(Use additional code to identify associated endocrine syndrome, as: carcinoid syndrome: 259.2)
211.5 Benign neoplasm of liver and biliary passages
211.6 Benign neoplasm of pancreas, except islets of Langerhans
211.7 Benign neoplasm of islets of Langerhans — (Use additional code to identify any functional activity)
230.8 Carcinoma in situ of liver and biliary system
230.9 Carcinoma in situ of other and unspecified digestive organs
235.3 Neoplasm of uncertain behavior of liver and biliary passages
235.5 Neoplasm of uncertain behavior of other and unspecified digestive organs
239.0 Neoplasm of unspecified nature of digestive system
251.9 Unspecified disorder of pancreatic internal secretion

277.4 Disorders of bilirubin excretion — (Use additional code to identify any associated intellectual disabilities)
560.1 Paralytic ileus
560.31 Gallstone ileus
571.5 Cirrhosis of liver without mention of alcohol — (Code first, if applicable, viral hepatitis (acute) (chronic): 070.0-070.9)
571.6 Biliary cirrhosis
572.0 Abscess of liver
574.00 Calculus of gallbladder with acute cholecystitis, without mention of obstruction
574.01 Calculus of gallbladder with acute cholecystitis and obstruction
574.10 Calculus of gallbladder with other cholecystitis, without mention of obstruction
574.11 Calculus of gallbladder with other cholecystitis and obstruction
574.20 Calculus of gallbladder without mention of cholecystitis or obstruction
574.21 Calculus of gallbladder without mention of cholecystitis, with obstruction
574.30 Calculus of bile duct with acute cholecystitis without mention of obstruction
574.31 Calculus of bile duct with acute cholecystitis and obstruction
574.40 Calculus of bile duct with other cholecystitis, without mention of obstruction
574.41 Calculus of bile duct with other cholecystitis and obstruction
574.50 Calculus of bile duct without mention of cholecystitis or obstruction
574.51 Calculus of bile duct without mention of cholecystitis, with obstruction
575.0 Acute cholecystitis
575.2 Obstruction of gallbladder
575.3 Hydrops of gallbladder
575.4 Perforation of gallbladder
575.5 Fistula of gallbladder
575.6 Cholesterolosis of gallbladder
575.8 Other specified disorder of gallbladder
575.9 Unspecified disorder of gallbladder ♥
576.0 Postcholecystectomy syndrome
576.1 Cholangitis
576.2 Obstruction of bile duct
576.3 Perforation of bile duct
576.4 Fistula of bile duct
576.5 Spasm of sphincter of Oddi
576.8 Other specified disorders of biliary tract
577.0 Acute pancreatitis
577.1 Chronic pancreatitis
577.2 Cyst and pseudocyst of pancreas
577.8 Other specified disease of pancreas
578.9 Hemorrhage of gastrointestinal tract, unspecified ♥
751.60 Unspecified congenital anomaly of gallbladder, bile ducts, and liver ♥
751.61 Congenital biliary atresia
751.62 Congenital cystic disease of liver
751.69 Other congenital anomaly of gallbladder, bile ducts, and liver
751.7 Congenital anomalies of pancreas
782.4 Jaundice, unspecified, not of newborn ♥
783.0 Anorexia
783.21 Loss of weight — (Use additional code to identify Body Mass Index (BMI), if known: V85.0-V85.54)
783.22 Underweight — (Use additional code to identify Body Mass Index (BMI), if known: V85.0-V85.54)
783.7 Adult failure to thrive
790.5 Other nonspecific abnormal serum enzyme levels
793.4 Nonspecific (abnormal) findings on radiological and other examination of gastrointestinal tract
794.9 Nonspecific abnormal results of other specified function study
996.82 Complications of transplanted liver — (Use additional code to identify nature of complication: 078.5, 199.2, 238.77, 279.50-279.53)
996.86 Complications of transplanted pancreas — (Use additional code to identify nature of complication: 078.5, 199.2, 238.77, 279.50-279.53)
997.41 Retained cholelithiasis following cholecystectomy
997.49 Other digestive system complications

ICD-9-CM Procedural

51.10 Endoscopic retrograde cholangiopancreatography (ERCP)
51.14 Other closed (endoscopic) biopsy of biliary duct or sphincter of Oddi
51.83 Pancreatic sphincteroplasty
51.84 Endoscopic dilation of ampulla and biliary duct
51.85 Endoscopic sphincterotomy and papillotomy
51.87 Endoscopic insertion of stent (tube) into bile duct
51.89 Other operations on sphincter of Oddi
52.14 Closed (endoscopic) biopsy of pancreatic duct
52.93 Endoscopic insertion of stent (tube) into pancreatic duct
52.98 Endoscopic dilation of pancreatic duct
97.05 Replacement of stent (tube) in biliary or pancreatic duct
97.55 Removal of T-tube, other bile duct tube, or liver tube
97.56 Removal of pancreatic tube or drain

43262-43263

43262 Endoscopic retrograde cholangiopancreatography (ERCP); with sphincterotomy/papillotomy
43263 with pressure measurement of sphincter of Oddi

ICD-9-CM Diagnostic

155.1 Malignant neoplasm of intrahepatic bile ducts
156.0 Malignant neoplasm of gallbladder
156.1 Malignant neoplasm of extrahepatic bile ducts
156.2 Malignant neoplasm of ampulla of Vater
156.8 Malignant neoplasm of other specified sites of gallbladder and extrahepatic bile ducts
157.0 Malignant neoplasm of head of pancreas
157.1 Malignant neoplasm of body of pancreas
157.2 Malignant neoplasm of tail of pancreas
157.3 Malignant neoplasm of pancreatic duct
157.4 Malignant neoplasm of islets of Langerhans — (Use additional code to identify any functional activity)
157.8 Malignant neoplasm of other specified sites of pancreas
197.8 Secondary malignant neoplasm of other digestive organs and spleen
199.2 Malignant neoplasm associated with transplanted organ — (Code first complication of transplanted organ (996.80-996.89) Use additional code for specific malignancy)
211.5 Benign neoplasm of liver and biliary passages
230.8 Carcinoma in situ of liver and biliary system
235.3 Neoplasm of uncertain behavior of liver and biliary passages
560.31 Gallstone ileus
571.5 Cirrhosis of liver without mention of alcohol — (Code first, if applicable, viral hepatitis (acute) (chronic): 070.0-070.9)
571.6 Biliary cirrhosis
574.00 Calculus of gallbladder with acute cholecystitis, without mention of obstruction
574.01 Calculus of gallbladder with acute cholecystitis and obstruction
574.11 Calculus of gallbladder with other cholecystitis and obstruction
574.20 Calculus of gallbladder without mention of cholecystitis or obstruction
574.21 Calculus of gallbladder without mention of cholecystitis, with obstruction
574.30 Calculus of bile duct with acute cholecystitis without mention of obstruction
574.31 Calculus of bile duct with acute cholecystitis and obstruction
574.40 Calculus of bile duct with other cholecystitis, without mention of obstruction
574.41 Calculus of bile duct with other cholecystitis and obstruction
574.50 Calculus of bile duct without mention of cholecystitis or obstruction
574.51 Calculus of bile duct without mention of cholecystitis, with obstruction
575.0 Acute cholecystitis
575.11 Chronic cholecystitis

575.12 Acute and chronic cholecystitis
575.2 Obstruction of gallbladder
575.3 Hydrops of gallbladder
575.4 Perforation of gallbladder
575.5 Fistula of gallbladder
575.6 Cholesterolosis of gallbladder
575.8 Other specified disorder of gallbladder
576.0 Postcholecystectomy syndrome
576.1 Cholangitis
576.2 Obstruction of bile duct
576.3 Perforation of bile duct
576.4 Fistula of bile duct
576.5 Spasm of sphincter of Oddi
576.8 Other specified disorders of biliary tract
577.0 Acute pancreatitis
577.1 Chronic pancreatitis
577.2 Cyst and pseudocyst of pancreas
577.8 Other specified disease of pancreas
751.69 Other congenital anomaly of gallbladder, bile ducts, and liver
751.7 Congenital anomalies of pancreas
782.4 Jaundice, unspecified, not of newborn ▽
787.01 Nausea with vomiting
787.04 Bilious emesis
789.01 Abdominal pain, right upper quadrant
790.4 Nonspecific elevation of levels of transaminase or lactic acid dehydrogenase (LDH)
790.5 Other nonspecific abnormal serum enzyme levels
790.6 Other abnormal blood chemistry
793.4 Nonspecific (abnormal) findings on radiological and other examination of gastrointestinal tract
794.8 Nonspecific abnormal results of liver function study
996.82 Complications of transplanted liver — (Use additional code to identify nature of complication: 078.5, 199.2, 238.77, 279.50-279.53)
997.41 Retained cholelithiasis following cholecystectomy

ICD-9-CM Procedural

51.15 Pressure measurement of sphincter of Oddi
51.85 Endoscopic sphincterotomy and papillotomy

43264-43265

43264 Endoscopic retrograde cholangiopancreatography (ERCP); with removal of calculi/debris from biliary/pancreatic duct(s)
43265 with destruction of calculi, any method (eg, mechanical, electrohydraulic, lithotripsy)

ICD-9-CM Diagnostic

574.00 Calculus of gallbladder with acute cholecystitis, without mention of obstruction
574.01 Calculus of gallbladder with acute cholecystitis and obstruction
574.10 Calculus of gallbladder with other cholecystitis, without mention of obstruction
574.11 Calculus of gallbladder with other cholecystitis and obstruction
574.20 Calculus of gallbladder without mention of cholecystitis or obstruction
574.21 Calculus of gallbladder without mention of cholecystitis, with obstruction
574.30 Calculus of bile duct with acute cholecystitis without mention of obstruction
574.31 Calculus of bile duct with acute cholecystitis and obstruction
574.40 Calculus of bile duct with other cholecystitis, without mention of obstruction
574.41 Calculus of bile duct with other cholecystitis and obstruction
574.50 Calculus of bile duct without mention of cholecystitis or obstruction
574.51 Calculus of bile duct without mention of cholecystitis, with obstruction
576.2 Obstruction of bile duct
576.8 Other specified disorders of biliary tract
577.0 Acute pancreatitis
577.1 Chronic pancreatitis
577.2 Cyst and pseudocyst of pancreas
577.8 Other specified disease of pancreas
751.69 Other congenital anomaly of gallbladder, bile ducts, and liver
782.4 Jaundice, unspecified, not of newborn ▽
997.41 Retained cholelithiasis following cholecystectomy

ICD-9-CM Procedural

51.88 Endoscopic removal of stone(s) from biliary tract
52.94 Endoscopic removal of stone(s) from pancreatic duct
98.52 Extracorporeal shockwave lithotripsy (ESWL) of the gallbladder and/or bile duct
98.59 Extracorporeal shockwave lithotripsy (ESWL) of other sites

43273

43273 Endoscopic cannulation of papilla with direct visualization of pancreatic/common bile duct(s) (List separately in addition to code(s) for primary procedure)

ICD-9-CM Diagnostic

The ICD-9-CM diagnostic code(s) would be the same as the actual procedure performed because these are in-addition-to codes.

ICD-9-CM Procedural

51.87 Endoscopic insertion of stent (tube) into bile duct
52.93 Endoscopic insertion of stent (tube) into pancreatic duct

43279-43280

43279 Laparoscopy, surgical, esophagomyotomy (Heller type), with fundoplasty, when performed
43280 Laparoscopy, surgical, esophagogastric fundoplasty (eg, Nissen, Toupet procedures)

ICD-9-CM Diagnostic

150.4 Malignant neoplasm of middle third of esophagus
150.5 Malignant neoplasm of lower third of esophagus
150.8 Malignant neoplasm of other specified part of esophagus
150.9 Malignant neoplasm of esophagus, unspecified site ▽
151.0 Malignant neoplasm of cardia
197.8 Secondary malignant neoplasm of other digestive organs and spleen
230.1 Carcinoma in situ of esophagus
230.2 Carcinoma in situ of stomach
530.11 Reflux esophagitis — (Use additional E code to identify cause, if induced by chemical)
530.12 Acute esophagitis — (Use additional E code to identify cause, if induced by chemical)
530.13 Eosinophilic esophagitis
530.20 Ulcer of esophagus without bleeding — (Use additional E code to identify cause, if induced by chemical or drug)
530.21 Ulcer of esophagus with bleeding — (Use additional E code to identify cause, if induced by chemical or drug)
530.3 Stricture and stenosis of esophagus
530.81 Esophageal reflux
530.85 Barrett's esophagus
552.3 Diaphragmatic hernia with obstruction
553.3 Diaphragmatic hernia without mention of obstruction or gangrene
750.3 Congenital tracheoesophageal fistula, esophageal atresia and stenosis
750.4 Other specified congenital anomaly of esophagus
756.6 Congenital anomaly of diaphragm
783.3 Feeding difficulties and mismanagement
787.20 Dysphagia, unspecified ▽
787.21 Dysphagia, oral phase
787.22 Dysphagia, oropharyngeal phase
787.23 Dysphagia, pharyngeal phase
787.24 Dysphagia, pharyngoesophageal phase
787.29 Other dysphagia
789.06 Abdominal pain, epigastric

789.07 Abdominal pain, generalized
789.09 Abdominal pain, other specified site
862.22 Esophagus injury without mention of open wound into cavity
908.1 Late effect of internal injury to intra-abdominal organs
908.6 Late effect of certain complications of trauma
909.3 Late effect of complications of surgical and medical care
925.2 Crushing injury of neck — (Use additional code to identify any associated injuries, such as: 800-829, 850.0-854.1, 860.0-869.1)
997.49 Other digestive system complications
V47.3 Other digestive problems

ICD-9-CM Procedural

42.7 Esophagomyotomy
44.67 Laparoscopic procedures for creation of esophagogastric sphincteric competence

43281-43282

43281 Laparoscopy, surgical, repair of paraesophageal hernia, includes fundoplasty, when performed; without implantation of mesh
43282 with implantation of mesh

ICD-9-CM Diagnostic

553.3 Diaphragmatic hernia without mention of obstruction or gangrene
756.6 Congenital anomaly of diaphragm

ICD-9-CM Procedural

44.67 Laparoscopic procedures for creation of esophagogastric sphincteric competence
53.71 Laparoscopic repair of diaphragmatic hernia, abdominal approach
53.83 Laparoscopic repair of diaphragmatic hernia, with thoracic approach

43283

43283 Laparoscopy, surgical, esophageal lengthening procedure (eg, Collis gastroplasty or wedge gastroplasty) (List separately in addition to code for primary procedure)

ICD-9-CM Diagnostic

This is an add-on code. Refer to the corresponding primary procedure code for ICD-9-CM diagnosis code links.

ICD-9-CM Procedural

44.68 Laparoscopic gastroplasty
53.83 Laparoscopic repair of diaphragmatic hernia, with thoracic approach

43300-43305

43300 Esophagoplasty (plastic repair or reconstruction), cervical approach; without repair of tracheoesophageal fistula
43305 with repair of tracheoesophageal fistula

ICD-9-CM Diagnostic

150.0 Malignant neoplasm of cervical esophagus
150.2 Malignant neoplasm of abdominal esophagus
150.3 Malignant neoplasm of upper third of esophagus
150.4 Malignant neoplasm of middle third of esophagus
150.5 Malignant neoplasm of lower third of esophagus
150.8 Malignant neoplasm of other specified part of esophagus
209.29 Malignant carcinoid tumor of other sites — (Code first any associated multiple endocrine neoplasia syndrome: 258.01-258.03)(Use additional code to identify associated endocrine syndrome, as: carcinoid syndrome: 259.2)
209.30 Malignant poorly differentiated neuroendocrine carcinoma, any site — (Code first any associated multiple endocrine neoplasia syndrome: 258.01-258.03)(Use additional code to identify associated endocrine syndrome, as: carcinoid syndrome: 259.2) ♥
209.69 Benign carcinoid tumor of other sites — (Code first any associated multiple endocrine neoplasia syndrome: 258.01-258.03)(Use additional code to identify associated endocrine syndrome, as: carcinoid syndrome: 259.2)
211.0 Benign neoplasm of esophagus
230.1 Carcinoma in situ of esophagus
235.5 Neoplasm of uncertain behavior of other and unspecified digestive organs ♥
239.0 Neoplasm of unspecified nature of digestive system
530.0 Achalasia and cardiospasm
530.11 Reflux esophagitis — (Use additional E code to identify cause, if induced by chemical)
530.13 Eosinophilic esophagitis
530.19 Other esophagitis — (Use additional E code to identify cause, if induced by chemical)
530.20 Ulcer of esophagus without bleeding — (Use additional E code to identify cause, if induced by chemical or drug)
530.21 Ulcer of esophagus with bleeding — (Use additional E code to identify cause, if induced by chemical or drug)
530.3 Stricture and stenosis of esophagus
530.4 Perforation of esophagus
530.5 Dyskinesia of esophagus
530.6 Diverticulum of esophagus, acquired
530.7 Gastroesophageal laceration-hemorrhage syndrome
530.81 Esophageal reflux
530.82 Esophageal hemorrhage
530.83 Esophageal leukoplakia
530.84 Tracheoesophageal fistula
530.85 Barrett's esophagus
530.9 Unspecified disorder of esophagus ♥
750.3 Congenital tracheoesophageal fistula, esophageal atresia and stenosis
862.22 Esophagus injury without mention of open wound into cavity
862.32 Esophagus injury with open wound into cavity

ICD-9-CM Procedural

31.73 Closure of other fistula of trachea
42.89 Other repair of esophagus

43310-43312

43310 Esophagoplasty (plastic repair or reconstruction), thoracic approach; without repair of tracheoesophageal fistula
43312 with repair of tracheoesophageal fistula

ICD-9-CM Diagnostic

150.0 Malignant neoplasm of cervical esophagus
150.1 Malignant neoplasm of thoracic esophagus
150.2 Malignant neoplasm of abdominal esophagus
150.3 Malignant neoplasm of upper third of esophagus
150.4 Malignant neoplasm of middle third of esophagus
150.5 Malignant neoplasm of lower third of esophagus
150.8 Malignant neoplasm of other specified part of esophagus
209.29 Malignant carcinoid tumor of other sites — (Code first any associated multiple endocrine neoplasia syndrome: 258.01-258.03)(Use additional code to identify associated endocrine syndrome, as: carcinoid syndrome: 259.2)
209.30 Malignant poorly differentiated neuroendocrine carcinoma, any site — (Code first any associated multiple endocrine neoplasia syndrome: 258.01-258.03)(Use additional code to identify associated endocrine syndrome, as: carcinoid syndrome: 259.2) ♥
209.69 Benign carcinoid tumor of other sites — (Code first any associated multiple endocrine neoplasia syndrome: 258.01-258.03)(Use additional code to identify associated endocrine syndrome, as: carcinoid syndrome: 259.2)
211.0 Benign neoplasm of esophagus
230.1 Carcinoma in situ of esophagus
235.5 Neoplasm of uncertain behavior of other and unspecified digestive organs ♥
239.0 Neoplasm of unspecified nature of digestive system
530.0 Achalasia and cardiospasm
530.11 Reflux esophagitis — (Use additional E code to identify cause, if induced by chemical)
530.13 Eosinophilic esophagitis
530.19 Other esophagitis — (Use additional E code to identify cause, if induced by chemical)

530.20 Ulcer of esophagus without bleeding — (Use additional E code to identify cause, if induced by chemical or drug)
530.21 Ulcer of esophagus with bleeding — (Use additional E code to identify cause, if induced by chemical or drug)
530.3 Stricture and stenosis of esophagus
530.4 Perforation of esophagus
530.5 Dyskinesia of esophagus
530.6 Diverticulum of esophagus, acquired
530.7 Gastroesophageal laceration-hemorrhage syndrome
530.81 Esophageal reflux
530.82 Esophageal hemorrhage
530.83 Esophageal leukoplakia
530.84 Tracheoesophageal fistula
530.85 Barrett's esophagus
530.9 Unspecified disorder of esophagus
750.3 Congenital tracheoesophageal fistula, esophageal atresia and stenosis
862.22 Esophagus injury without mention of open wound into cavity
862.32 Esophagus injury with open wound into cavity

ICD-9-CM Procedural

31.73 Closure of other fistula of trachea
42.89 Other repair of esophagus

43313-43314

43313 Esophagoplasty for congenital defect (plastic repair or reconstruction), thoracic approach; without repair of congenital tracheoesophageal fistula
43314 with repair of congenital tracheoesophageal fistula

ICD-9-CM Diagnostic

750.3 Congenital tracheoesophageal fistula, esophageal atresia and stenosis
750.4 Other specified congenital anomaly of esophagus
750.6 Congenital hiatus hernia
750.7 Other specified congenital anomalies of stomach
750.8 Other specified congenital anomalies of upper alimentary tract
750.9 Unspecified congenital anomaly of upper alimentary tract

ICD-9-CM Procedural

31.73 Closure of other fistula of trachea
42.89 Other repair of esophagus

43320

43320 Esophagogastrostomy (cardioplasty), with or without vagotomy and pyloroplasty, transabdominal or transthoracic approach

ICD-9-CM Diagnostic

150.0 Malignant neoplasm of cervical esophagus
150.2 Malignant neoplasm of abdominal esophagus
150.3 Malignant neoplasm of upper third of esophagus
150.4 Malignant neoplasm of middle third of esophagus
150.5 Malignant neoplasm of lower third of esophagus
150.9 Malignant neoplasm of esophagus, unspecified site
151.0 Malignant neoplasm of cardia
197.8 Secondary malignant neoplasm of other digestive organs and spleen
209.23 Malignant carcinoid tumor of the stomach — (Code first any associated multiple endocrine neoplasia syndrome: 258.01-258.03)(Use additional code to identify associated endocrine syndrome, as: carcinoid syndrome: 259.2)
230.1 Carcinoma in situ of esophagus
230.2 Carcinoma in situ of stomach
530.0 Achalasia and cardiospasm
530.11 Reflux esophagitis — (Use additional E code to identify cause, if induced by chemical)
530.13 Eosinophilic esophagitis
530.20 Ulcer of esophagus without bleeding — (Use additional E code to identify cause, if induced by chemical or drug)
530.21 Ulcer of esophagus with bleeding — (Use additional E code to identify cause, if induced by chemical or drug)
530.3 Stricture and stenosis of esophagus
530.4 Perforation of esophagus
530.85 Barrett's esophagus
750.3 Congenital tracheoesophageal fistula, esophageal atresia and stenosis
750.4 Other specified congenital anomaly of esophagus
862.32 Esophagus injury with open wound into cavity
925.2 Crushing injury of neck — (Use additional code to identify any associated injuries, such as: 800-829, 850.0-854.1, 860.0-869.1)

ICD-9-CM Procedural

42.52 Intrathoracic esophagogastrostomy
44.02 Highly selective vagotomy
44.29 Other pyloroplasty

43325

43325 Esophagogastric fundoplasty; with fundic patch (Thal-Nissen procedure)

ICD-9-CM Diagnostic

150.4 Malignant neoplasm of middle third of esophagus
150.5 Malignant neoplasm of lower third of esophagus
150.8 Malignant neoplasm of other specified part of esophagus
150.9 Malignant neoplasm of esophagus, unspecified site
151.0 Malignant neoplasm of cardia
197.8 Secondary malignant neoplasm of other digestive organs and spleen
209.23 Malignant carcinoid tumor of the stomach — (Code first any associated multiple endocrine neoplasia syndrome: 258.01-258.03)(Use additional code to identify associated endocrine syndrome, as: carcinoid syndrome: 259.2)
230.1 Carcinoma in situ of esophagus
230.2 Carcinoma in situ of stomach
530.11 Reflux esophagitis — (Use additional E code to identify cause, if induced by chemical)
530.13 Eosinophilic esophagitis
530.20 Ulcer of esophagus without bleeding — (Use additional E code to identify cause, if induced by chemical or drug)
530.21 Ulcer of esophagus with bleeding — (Use additional E code to identify cause, if induced by chemical or drug)
530.3 Stricture and stenosis of esophagus
530.81 Esophageal reflux
530.85 Barrett's esophagus
552.3 Diaphragmatic hernia with obstruction
553.3 Diaphragmatic hernia without mention of obstruction or gangrene
750.3 Congenital tracheoesophageal fistula, esophageal atresia and stenosis
750.4 Other specified congenital anomaly of esophagus
756.6 Congenital anomaly of diaphragm
783.3 Feeding difficulties and mismanagement
787.20 Dysphagia, unspecified
787.21 Dysphagia, oral phase
787.22 Dysphagia, oropharyngeal phase
787.23 Dysphagia, pharyngeal phase
787.24 Dysphagia, pharyngoesophageal phase
787.29 Other dysphagia
789.06 Abdominal pain, epigastric
789.07 Abdominal pain, generalized
789.09 Abdominal pain, other specified site
862.22 Esophagus injury without mention of open wound into cavity
908.1 Late effect of internal injury to intra-abdominal organs
908.6 Late effect of certain complications of trauma
909.3 Late effect of complications of surgical and medical care

925.2 Crushing injury of neck — (Use additional code to identify any associated injuries, such as: 800-829, 850.0-854.1, 860.0-869.1)
997.49 Other digestive system complications
V47.3 Other digestive problems
V64.41 Laparoscopic surgical procedure converted to open procedure

ICD-9-CM Procedural

42.85 Repair of esophageal stricture
44.66 Other procedures for creation of esophagogastric sphincteric competence

43327-43328

43327 Esophagogastric fundoplasty partial or complete; laparotomy
43328 thoracotomy

ICD-9-CM Diagnostic

150.4 Malignant neoplasm of middle third of esophagus
150.5 Malignant neoplasm of lower third of esophagus
150.8 Malignant neoplasm of other specified part of esophagus
150.9 Malignant neoplasm of esophagus, unspecified site
151.0 Malignant neoplasm of cardia
197.8 Secondary malignant neoplasm of other digestive organs and spleen
209.23 Malignant carcinoid tumor of the stomach — (Code first any associated multiple endocrine neoplasia syndrome: 258.01-258.03)(Use additional code to identify associated endocrine syndrome, as: carcinoid syndrome: 259.2)
230.1 Carcinoma in situ of esophagus
230.2 Carcinoma in situ of stomach
530.11 Reflux esophagitis — (Use additional E code to identify cause, if induced by chemical)
530.13 Eosinophilic esophagitis
530.20 Ulcer of esophagus without bleeding — (Use additional E code to identify cause, if induced by chemical or drug)
530.21 Ulcer of esophagus with bleeding — (Use additional E code to identify cause, if induced by chemical or drug)
530.3 Stricture and stenosis of esophagus
530.81 Esophageal reflux
530.85 Barrett's esophagus
552.3 Diaphragmatic hernia with obstruction
553.3 Diaphragmatic hernia without mention of obstruction or gangrene
750.3 Congenital tracheoesophageal fistula, esophageal atresia and stenosis
750.4 Other specified congenital anomaly of esophagus
756.6 Congenital anomaly of diaphragm
783.3 Feeding difficulties and mismanagement
787.20 Dysphagia, unspecified
787.21 Dysphagia, oral phase
787.22 Dysphagia, oropharyngeal phase
787.23 Dysphagia, pharyngeal phase
787.24 Dysphagia, pharyngoesophageal phase
787.29 Other dysphagia
789.06 Abdominal pain, epigastric
789.07 Abdominal pain, generalized
789.09 Abdominal pain, other specified site
862.22 Esophagus injury without mention of open wound into cavity
908.1 Late effect of internal injury to intra-abdominal organs
908.6 Late effect of certain complications of trauma
909.3 Late effect of complications of surgical and medical care
925.2 Crushing injury of neck — (Use additional code to identify any associated injuries, such as: 800-829, 850.0-854.1, 860.0-869.1)
997.49 Other digestive system complications
V47.3 Other digestive problems

ICD-9-CM Procedural

44.65 Esophagogastroplasty
44.66 Other procedures for creation of esophagogastric sphincteric competence

43330-43331

43330 Esophagomyotomy (Heller type); abdominal approach
43331 thoracic approach

ICD-9-CM Diagnostic

150.0 Malignant neoplasm of cervical esophagus
150.1 Malignant neoplasm of thoracic esophagus
150.2 Malignant neoplasm of abdominal esophagus
150.3 Malignant neoplasm of upper third of esophagus
150.4 Malignant neoplasm of middle third of esophagus
150.5 Malignant neoplasm of lower third of esophagus
150.8 Malignant neoplasm of other specified part of esophagus
150.9 Malignant neoplasm of esophagus, unspecified site
530.0 Achalasia and cardiospasm
530.11 Reflux esophagitis — (Use additional E code to identify cause, if induced by chemical)
530.13 Eosinophilic esophagitis
530.19 Other esophagitis — (Use additional E code to identify cause, if induced by chemical)
530.20 Ulcer of esophagus without bleeding — (Use additional E code to identify cause, if induced by chemical or drug)
530.21 Ulcer of esophagus with bleeding — (Use additional E code to identify cause, if induced by chemical or drug)
530.3 Stricture and stenosis of esophagus
530.4 Perforation of esophagus
530.6 Diverticulum of esophagus, acquired
530.7 Gastroesophageal laceration-hemorrhage syndrome
530.81 Esophageal reflux
530.82 Esophageal hemorrhage
530.83 Esophageal leukoplakia
530.84 Tracheoesophageal fistula
530.85 Barrett's esophagus
530.89 Other specified disorder of the esophagus
552.3 Diaphragmatic hernia with obstruction
553.3 Diaphragmatic hernia without mention of obstruction or gangrene
750.4 Other specified congenital anomaly of esophagus
756.6 Congenital anomaly of diaphragm
V64.42 Thorascopic surgical procedure converted to open procedure

ICD-9-CM Procedural

42.7 Esophagomyotomy

43332-43338

43332 Repair, paraesophageal hiatal hernia (including fundoplication), via laparotomy, except neonatal; without implantation of mesh or other prosthesis
43333 with implantation of mesh or other prosthesis
43334 Repair, paraesophageal hiatal hernia (including fundoplication), via thoracotomy, except neonatal; without implantation of mesh or other prosthesis
43335 with implantation of mesh or other prosthesis
43336 Repair, paraesophageal hiatal hernia, (including fundoplication), via thoracoabdominal incision, except neonatal; without implantation of mesh or other prosthesis
43337 with implantation of mesh or other prosthesis
43338 Esophageal lengthening procedure (eg, Collis gastroplasty or wedge gastroplasty) (List separately in addition to code for primary procedure)

ICD-9-CM Diagnostic

551.3 Diaphragmatic hernia with gangrene
552.3 Diaphragmatic hernia with obstruction
553.3 Diaphragmatic hernia without mention of obstruction or gangrene
750.6 Congenital hiatus hernia

ICD-9-CM Procedural

44.00 Vagotomy, not otherwise specified
44.29 Other pyloroplasty
44.66 Other procedures for creation of esophagogastric sphincteric competence
44.69 Other repair of stomach
53.72 Other and open repair of diaphragmatic hernia, abdominal approach
53.75 Repair of diaphragmatic hernia, abdominal approach, not otherwise specified
53.80 Repair of diaphragmatic hernia with thoracic approach, not otherwise specified
53.84 Other and open repair of diaphragmatic hernia, with thoracic approach

43340-43341

43340 Esophagojejunostomy (without total gastrectomy); abdominal approach
43341 thoracic approach

ICD-9-CM Diagnostic

150.0 Malignant neoplasm of cervical esophagus
150.1 Malignant neoplasm of thoracic esophagus
150.2 Malignant neoplasm of abdominal esophagus
150.3 Malignant neoplasm of upper third of esophagus
150.4 Malignant neoplasm of middle third of esophagus
150.5 Malignant neoplasm of lower third of esophagus
150.8 Malignant neoplasm of other specified part of esophagus
150.9 Malignant neoplasm of esophagus, unspecified site ▽
151.0 Malignant neoplasm of cardia
151.3 Malignant neoplasm of fundus of stomach
151.4 Malignant neoplasm of body of stomach
209.23 Malignant carcinoid tumor of the stomach — (Code first any associated multiple endocrine neoplasia syndrome: 258.01-258.03)(Use additional code to identify associated endocrine syndrome, as: carcinoid syndrome: 259.2)
209.29 Malignant carcinoid tumor of other sites — (Code first any associated multiple endocrine neoplasia syndrome: 258.01-258.03)(Use additional code to identify associated endocrine syndrome, as: carcinoid syndrome: 259.2)
209.30 Malignant poorly differentiated neuroendocrine carcinoma, any site — (Code first any associated multiple endocrine neoplasia syndrome: 258.01-258.03)(Use additional code to identify associated endocrine syndrome, as: carcinoid syndrome: 259.2) ▽
209.69 Benign carcinoid tumor of other sites — (Code first any associated multiple endocrine neoplasia syndrome: 258.01-258.03)(Use additional code to identify associated endocrine syndrome, as: carcinoid syndrome: 259.2)
235.5 Neoplasm of uncertain behavior of other and unspecified digestive organs ▽
239.0 Neoplasm of unspecified nature of digestive system
530.11 Reflux esophagitis — (Use additional E code to identify cause, if induced by chemical)
530.13 Eosinophilic esophagitis
530.20 Ulcer of esophagus without bleeding — (Use additional E code to identify cause, if induced by chemical or drug)
530.21 Ulcer of esophagus with bleeding — (Use additional E code to identify cause, if induced by chemical or drug)
530.3 Stricture and stenosis of esophagus
530.5 Dyskinesia of esophagus
530.6 Diverticulum of esophagus, acquired
530.85 Barrett's esophagus
531.40 Chronic or unspecified gastric ulcer with hemorrhage, without mention of obstruction — (Use additional E code to identify drug, if drug induced)
531.50 Chronic or unspecified gastric ulcer with perforation, without mention of obstruction — (Use additional E code to identify drug, if drug induced)
531.60 Chronic or unspecified gastric ulcer with hemorrhage and perforation, without mention of obstruction — (Use additional E code to identify drug, if drug induced)

ICD-9-CM Procedural

42.54 Other intrathoracic esophagoenterostomy

43350-43352

43350 Esophagostomy, fistulization of esophagus, external; abdominal approach
43351 thoracic approach
43352 cervical approach

ICD-9-CM Diagnostic

148.8 Malignant neoplasm of other specified sites of hypopharynx
148.9 Malignant neoplasm of hypopharynx, unspecified site ▽
149.0 Malignant neoplasm of pharynx, unspecified ▽
150.0 Malignant neoplasm of cervical esophagus
150.1 Malignant neoplasm of thoracic esophagus
150.2 Malignant neoplasm of abdominal esophagus
150.3 Malignant neoplasm of upper third of esophagus
150.8 Malignant neoplasm of other specified part of esophagus
150.9 Malignant neoplasm of esophagus, unspecified site ▽
197.8 Secondary malignant neoplasm of other digestive organs and spleen
209.29 Malignant carcinoid tumor of other sites — (Code first any associated multiple endocrine neoplasia syndrome: 258.01-258.03)(Use additional code to identify associated endocrine syndrome, as: carcinoid syndrome: 259.2)
209.30 Malignant poorly differentiated neuroendocrine carcinoma, any site — (Code first any associated multiple endocrine neoplasia syndrome: 258.01-258.03)(Use additional code to identify associated endocrine syndrome, as: carcinoid syndrome: 259.2) ▽
209.69 Benign carcinoid tumor of other sites — (Code first any associated multiple endocrine neoplasia syndrome: 258.01-258.03)(Use additional code to identify associated endocrine syndrome, as: carcinoid syndrome: 259.2)
230.1 Carcinoma in situ of esophagus
235.5 Neoplasm of uncertain behavior of other and unspecified digestive organs ▽
239.0 Neoplasm of unspecified nature of digestive system
530.0 Achalasia and cardiospasm
530.11 Reflux esophagitis — (Use additional E code to identify cause, if induced by chemical)
530.12 Acute esophagitis — (Use additional E code to identify cause, if induced by chemical)
530.13 Eosinophilic esophagitis
530.19 Other esophagitis — (Use additional E code to identify cause, if induced by chemical)
530.20 Ulcer of esophagus without bleeding — (Use additional E code to identify cause, if induced by chemical or drug)
530.21 Ulcer of esophagus with bleeding — (Use additional E code to identify cause, if induced by chemical or drug)
530.3 Stricture and stenosis of esophagus
530.4 Perforation of esophagus
530.5 Dyskinesia of esophagus
530.6 Diverticulum of esophagus, acquired
530.7 Gastroesophageal laceration-hemorrhage syndrome
530.81 Esophageal reflux
530.82 Esophageal hemorrhage
530.83 Esophageal leukoplakia
530.84 Tracheoesophageal fistula
530.85 Barrett's esophagus
530.9 Unspecified disorder of esophagus ▽
V10.03 Personal history of malignant neoplasm of esophagus

ICD-9-CM Procedural

42.10 Esophagostomy, not otherwise specified
42.11 Cervical esophagostomy
42.19 Other external fistulization of esophagus

43360

43360 Gastrointestinal reconstruction for previous esophagectomy, for obstructing esophageal lesion or fistula, or for previous esophageal exclusion; with stomach, with or without pyloroplasty

ICD-9-CM Diagnostic

150.0 Malignant neoplasm of cervical esophagus
150.1 Malignant neoplasm of thoracic esophagus
150.2 Malignant neoplasm of abdominal esophagus
150.3 Malignant neoplasm of upper third of esophagus
150.4 Malignant neoplasm of middle third of esophagus
150.5 Malignant neoplasm of lower third of esophagus
150.8 Malignant neoplasm of other specified part of esophagus
150.9 Malignant neoplasm of esophagus, unspecified site ▽
197.8 Secondary malignant neoplasm of other digestive organs and spleen
209.29 Malignant carcinoid tumor of other sites — (Code first any associated multiple endocrine neoplasia syndrome: 258.01-258.03)(Use additional code to identify associated endocrine syndrome, as: carcinoid syndrome: 259.2)
209.30 Malignant poorly differentiated neuroendocrine carcinoma, any site — (Code first any associated multiple endocrine neoplasia syndrome: 258.01-258.03)(Use additional code to identify associated endocrine syndrome, as: carcinoid syndrome: 259.2) ▽
209.69 Benign carcinoid tumor of other sites — (Code first any associated multiple endocrine neoplasia syndrome: 258.01-258.03)(Use additional code to identify associated endocrine syndrome, as: carcinoid syndrome: 259.2)
211.0 Benign neoplasm of esophagus
230.1 Carcinoma in situ of esophagus
235.5 Neoplasm of uncertain behavior of other and unspecified digestive organs ▽
239.0 Neoplasm of unspecified nature of digestive system
530.20 Ulcer of esophagus without bleeding — (Use additional E code to identify cause, if induced by chemical or drug)
530.21 Ulcer of esophagus with bleeding — (Use additional E code to identify cause, if induced by chemical or drug)
530.3 Stricture and stenosis of esophagus
530.6 Diverticulum of esophagus, acquired
530.84 Tracheoesophageal fistula
530.85 Barrett's esophagus
530.89 Other specified disorder of the esophagus

ICD-9-CM Procedural

42.19 Other external fistulization of esophagus
42.32 Local excision of other lesion or tissue of esophagus
42.58 Intrathoracic esophageal anastomosis with other interposition
42.84 Repair of esophageal fistula, not elsewhere classified
44.29 Other pyloroplasty

43361

43361 Gastrointestinal reconstruction for previous esophagectomy, for obstructing esophageal lesion or fistula, or for previous esophageal exclusion; with colon interposition or small intestine reconstruction, including intestine mobilization, preparation, and anastomosis(es)

ICD-9-CM Diagnostic

150.0 Malignant neoplasm of cervical esophagus
150.1 Malignant neoplasm of thoracic esophagus
150.2 Malignant neoplasm of abdominal esophagus
150.3 Malignant neoplasm of upper third of esophagus
150.4 Malignant neoplasm of middle third of esophagus
150.5 Malignant neoplasm of lower third of esophagus
150.8 Malignant neoplasm of other specified part of esophagus
150.9 Malignant neoplasm of esophagus, unspecified site ▽
197.8 Secondary malignant neoplasm of other digestive organs and spleen
209.29 Malignant carcinoid tumor of other sites — (Code first any associated multiple endocrine neoplasia syndrome: 258.01-258.03)(Use additional code to identify associated endocrine syndrome, as: carcinoid syndrome: 259.2)
209.30 Malignant poorly differentiated neuroendocrine carcinoma, any site — (Code first any associated multiple endocrine neoplasia syndrome: 258.01-258.03)(Use additional code to identify associated endocrine syndrome, as: carcinoid syndrome: 259.2) ▽
209.69 Benign carcinoid tumor of other sites — (Code first any associated multiple endocrine neoplasia syndrome: 258.01-258.03)(Use additional code to identify associated endocrine syndrome, as: carcinoid syndrome: 259.2)
211.0 Benign neoplasm of esophagus
230.1 Carcinoma in situ of esophagus
235.5 Neoplasm of uncertain behavior of other and unspecified digestive organs ▽
239.0 Neoplasm of unspecified nature of digestive system
530.20 Ulcer of esophagus without bleeding — (Use additional E code to identify cause, if induced by chemical or drug)
530.21 Ulcer of esophagus with bleeding — (Use additional E code to identify cause, if induced by chemical or drug)
530.3 Stricture and stenosis of esophagus
530.6 Diverticulum of esophagus, acquired
530.84 Tracheoesophageal fistula
530.85 Barrett's esophagus
530.89 Other specified disorder of the esophagus

ICD-9-CM Procedural

42.53 Intrathoracic esophageal anastomosis with interposition of small bowel
42.55 Intrathoracic esophageal anastomosis with interposition of colon
42.63 Antesternal esophageal anastomosis with interposition of small bowel
42.65 Antesternal esophageal anastomosis with interposition of colon

43400

43400 Ligation, direct, esophageal varices

ICD-9-CM Diagnostic

456.0 Esophageal varices with bleeding
456.1 Esophageal varices without mention of bleeding
456.20 Esophageal varices with bleeding in diseases classified elsewhere — (Code first underlying disease: 571.0-571.9, 572.3) ☒
456.21 Esophageal varices without mention of bleeding in diseases classified elsewhere — (Code first underlying disease: 571.0-571.9, 572.3) ☒
530.82 Esophageal hemorrhage
530.89 Other specified disorder of the esophagus
571.0 Alcoholic fatty liver
571.1 Acute alcoholic hepatitis
571.2 Alcoholic cirrhosis of liver
571.3 Unspecified alcoholic liver damage ▽
571.40 Unspecified chronic hepatitis ▽
571.41 Chronic persistent hepatitis
571.42 Autoimmune hepatitis
571.49 Other chronic hepatitis
571.5 Cirrhosis of liver without mention of alcohol — (Code first, if applicable, viral hepatitis (acute) (chronic): 070.0-070.9)
571.6 Biliary cirrhosis
571.8 Other chronic nonalcoholic liver disease
571.9 Unspecified chronic liver disease without mention of alcohol ▽
572.3 Portal hypertension — (Use additional code for any associated complications, such as: portal hypertensive gastropathy (537.89))

ICD-9-CM Procedural

42.91 Ligation of esophageal varices

43401

43401 Transection of esophagus with repair, for esophageal varices

ICD-9-CM Diagnostic

456.0 Esophageal varices with bleeding
456.1 Esophageal varices without mention of bleeding
456.20 Esophageal varices with bleeding in diseases classified elsewhere — (Code first underlying disease: 571.0-571.9, 572.3) ☒
456.21 Esophageal varices without mention of bleeding in diseases classified elsewhere — (Code first underlying disease: 571.0-571.9, 572.3) ☒
530.82 Esophageal hemorrhage
530.89 Other specified disorder of the esophagus
571.0 Alcoholic fatty liver
571.1 Acute alcoholic hepatitis
571.2 Alcoholic cirrhosis of liver
571.3 Unspecified alcoholic liver damage ▽
571.40 Unspecified chronic hepatitis ▽
571.41 Chronic persistent hepatitis
571.42 Autoimmune hepatitis
571.49 Other chronic hepatitis
571.5 Cirrhosis of liver without mention of alcohol — (Code first, if applicable, viral hepatitis (acute) (chronic): 070.0-070.9)
571.6 Biliary cirrhosis
571.8 Other chronic nonalcoholic liver disease
571.9 Unspecified chronic liver disease without mention of alcohol ▽
572.3 Portal hypertension — (Use additional code for any associated complications, such as: portal hypertensive gastropathy (537.89))

ICD-9-CM Procedural

42.99 Other operations on esophagus

43405

43405 Ligation or stapling at gastroesophageal junction for pre-existing esophageal perforation

ICD-9-CM Diagnostic

530.4 Perforation of esophagus
530.7 Gastroesophageal laceration-hemorrhage syndrome
862.22 Esophagus injury without mention of open wound into cavity
862.32 Esophagus injury with open wound into cavity
863.0 Stomach injury without mention of open wound into cavity
863.1 Stomach injury with open wound into cavity

ICD-9-CM Procedural

42.82 Suture of laceration of esophagus
42.89 Other repair of esophagus

43410

43410 Suture of esophageal wound or injury; cervical approach

ICD-9-CM Diagnostic

530.7 Gastroesophageal laceration-hemorrhage syndrome
862.22 Esophagus injury without mention of open wound into cavity
862.32 Esophagus injury with open wound into cavity
874.4 Open wound of pharynx, without mention of complication
959.9 Injury, other and unspecified, unspecified site ▽
998.2 Accidental puncture or laceration during procedure

ICD-9-CM Procedural

42.82 Suture of laceration of esophagus

43415

43415 Suture of esophageal wound or injury; transthoracic or transabdominal approach

ICD-9-CM Diagnostic

530.7 Gastroesophageal laceration-hemorrhage syndrome
862.22 Esophagus injury without mention of open wound into cavity
862.32 Esophagus injury with open wound into cavity
959.9 Injury, other and unspecified, unspecified site ▽
998.2 Accidental puncture or laceration during procedure

ICD-9-CM Procedural

42.82 Suture of laceration of esophagus

43420

43420 Closure of esophagostomy or fistula; cervical approach

ICD-9-CM Diagnostic

530.0 Achalasia and cardiospasm
530.11 Reflux esophagitis — (Use additional E code to identify cause, if induced by chemical)
530.13 Eosinophilic esophagitis
530.20 Ulcer of esophagus without bleeding — (Use additional E code to identify cause, if induced by chemical or drug)
530.21 Ulcer of esophagus with bleeding — (Use additional E code to identify cause, if induced by chemical or drug)
530.4 Perforation of esophagus
530.5 Dyskinesia of esophagus
530.6 Diverticulum of esophagus, acquired
530.84 Tracheoesophageal fistula
530.85 Barrett's esophagus
530.89 Other specified disorder of the esophagus
750.3 Congenital tracheoesophageal fistula, esophageal atresia and stenosis
750.4 Other specified congenital anomaly of esophagus
862.32 Esophagus injury with open wound into cavity
959.9 Injury, other and unspecified, unspecified site ▽
V10.03 Personal history of malignant neoplasm of esophagus
V55.9 Attention to unspecified artificial opening ▽

ICD-9-CM Procedural

42.83 Closure of esophagostomy
42.84 Repair of esophageal fistula, not elsewhere classified

43425

43425 Closure of esophagostomy or fistula; transthoracic or transabdominal approach

ICD-9-CM Diagnostic

530.0 Achalasia and cardiospasm
530.11 Reflux esophagitis — (Use additional E code to identify cause, if induced by chemical)
530.13 Eosinophilic esophagitis
530.20 Ulcer of esophagus without bleeding — (Use additional E code to identify cause, if induced by chemical or drug)
530.21 Ulcer of esophagus with bleeding — (Use additional E code to identify cause, if induced by chemical or drug)
530.4 Perforation of esophagus
530.5 Dyskinesia of esophagus
530.6 Diverticulum of esophagus, acquired
530.84 Tracheoesophageal fistula
530.85 Barrett's esophagus
530.89 Other specified disorder of the esophagus
750.3 Congenital tracheoesophageal fistula, esophageal atresia and stenosis
750.4 Other specified congenital anomaly of esophagus
862.32 Esophagus injury with open wound into cavity
959.9 Injury, other and unspecified, unspecified site ▽

V10.03 Personal history of malignant neoplasm of esophagus
V55.9 Attention to unspecified artificial opening ▽

ICD-9-CM Procedural

42.83 Closure of esophagostomy
42.84 Repair of esophageal fistula, not elsewhere classified

43450-43453

43450 Dilation of esophagus, by unguided sound or bougie, single or multiple passes
43453 Dilation of esophagus, over guide wire

ICD-9-CM Diagnostic

150.0 Malignant neoplasm of cervical esophagus
150.1 Malignant neoplasm of thoracic esophagus
150.2 Malignant neoplasm of abdominal esophagus
150.3 Malignant neoplasm of upper third of esophagus
150.4 Malignant neoplasm of middle third of esophagus
150.5 Malignant neoplasm of lower third of esophagus
150.8 Malignant neoplasm of other specified part of esophagus
150.9 Malignant neoplasm of esophagus, unspecified site ▽
209.29 Malignant carcinoid tumor of other sites — (Code first any associated multiple endocrine neoplasia syndrome: 258.01-258.03)(Use additional code to identify associated endocrine syndrome, as: carcinoid syndrome: 259.2)
209.30 Malignant poorly differentiated neuroendocrine carcinoma, any site — (Code first any associated multiple endocrine neoplasia syndrome: 258.01-258.03)(Use additional code to identify associated endocrine syndrome, as: carcinoid syndrome: 259.2) ▽
209.69 Benign carcinoid tumor of other sites — (Code first any associated multiple endocrine neoplasia syndrome: 258.01-258.03)(Use additional code to identify associated endocrine syndrome, as: carcinoid syndrome: 259.2)
211.0 Benign neoplasm of esophagus
235.5 Neoplasm of uncertain behavior of other and unspecified digestive organs ▽
239.0 Neoplasm of unspecified nature of digestive system
530.0 Achalasia and cardiospasm
530.11 Reflux esophagitis — (Use additional E code to identify cause, if induced by chemical)
530.12 Acute esophagitis — (Use additional E code to identify cause, if induced by chemical)
530.13 Eosinophilic esophagitis
530.19 Other esophagitis — (Use additional E code to identify cause, if induced by chemical)
530.20 Ulcer of esophagus without bleeding — (Use additional E code to identify cause, if induced by chemical or drug)
530.21 Ulcer of esophagus with bleeding — (Use additional E code to identify cause, if induced by chemical or drug)
530.3 Stricture and stenosis of esophagus
530.4 Perforation of esophagus
530.5 Dyskinesia of esophagus
530.6 Diverticulum of esophagus, acquired
530.81 Esophageal reflux
530.82 Esophageal hemorrhage
530.83 Esophageal leukoplakia
530.84 Tracheoesophageal fistula
530.85 Barrett's esophagus
530.89 Other specified disorder of the esophagus
750.3 Congenital tracheoesophageal fistula, esophageal atresia and stenosis
750.4 Other specified congenital anomaly of esophagus
751.9 Unspecified congenital anomaly of digestive system ▽
784.99 Other symptoms involving head and neck
787.20 Dysphagia, unspecified ▽
787.21 Dysphagia, oral phase
787.22 Dysphagia, oropharyngeal phase
787.23 Dysphagia, pharyngeal phase
787.24 Dysphagia, pharyngoesophageal phase
787.29 Other dysphagia
793.4 Nonspecific (abnormal) findings on radiological and other examination of gastrointestinal tract
935.1 Foreign body in esophagus
V10.03 Personal history of malignant neoplasm of esophagus

ICD-9-CM Procedural

42.92 Dilation of esophagus

HCPCS Level II Supplies & Services

A4270 Disposable endoscope sheath, each

43460

43460 Esophagogastric tamponade, with balloon (Sengstaken type)

ICD-9-CM Diagnostic

456.0 Esophageal varices with bleeding
456.1 Esophageal varices without mention of bleeding
456.20 Esophageal varices with bleeding in diseases classified elsewhere — (Code first underlying disease: 571.0-571.9, 572.3) ☒
456.21 Esophageal varices without mention of bleeding in diseases classified elsewhere — (Code first underlying disease: 571.0-571.9, 572.3) ☒
530.20 Ulcer of esophagus without bleeding — (Use additional E code to identify cause, if induced by chemical or drug)
530.21 Ulcer of esophagus with bleeding — (Use additional E code to identify cause, if induced by chemical or drug)
530.4 Perforation of esophagus
530.7 Gastroesophageal laceration-hemorrhage syndrome
530.82 Esophageal hemorrhage
530.85 Barrett's esophagus
571.0 Alcoholic fatty liver
571.1 Acute alcoholic hepatitis
571.2 Alcoholic cirrhosis of liver
571.3 Unspecified alcoholic liver damage ▽
571.40 Unspecified chronic hepatitis ▽
571.41 Chronic persistent hepatitis
571.42 Autoimmune hepatitis
571.5 Cirrhosis of liver without mention of alcohol — (Code first, if applicable, viral hepatitis (acute) (chronic): 070.0-070.9)
571.8 Other chronic nonalcoholic liver disease
572.3 Portal hypertension — (Use additional code for any associated complications, such as: portal hypertensive gastropathy (537.89))

ICD-9-CM Procedural

96.06 Insertion of Sengstaken tube

HCPCS Level II Supplies & Services

A4305 Disposable drug delivery system, flow rate of 50 ml or greater per hour

43496

43496 Free jejunum transfer with microvascular anastomosis

ICD-9-CM Diagnostic

150.0 Malignant neoplasm of cervical esophagus
150.1 Malignant neoplasm of thoracic esophagus
150.2 Malignant neoplasm of abdominal esophagus
150.8 Malignant neoplasm of other specified part of esophagus
150.9 Malignant neoplasm of esophagus, unspecified site ▽
197.8 Secondary malignant neoplasm of other digestive organs and spleen
209.29 Malignant carcinoid tumor of other sites — (Code first any associated multiple endocrine neoplasia syndrome: 258.01-258.03)(Use additional code to identify associated endocrine syndrome, as: carcinoid syndrome: 259.2)

209.30 Malignant poorly differentiated neuroendocrine carcinoma, any site — (Code first any associated multiple endocrine neoplasia syndrome: 258.01-258.03)(Use additional code to identify associated endocrine syndrome, as: carcinoid syndrome: 259.2)
209.69 Benign carcinoid tumor of other sites — (Code first any associated multiple endocrine neoplasia syndrome: 258.01-258.03)(Use additional code to identify associated endocrine syndrome, as: carcinoid syndrome: 259.2)
230.1 Carcinoma in situ of esophagus
235.5 Neoplasm of uncertain behavior of other and unspecified digestive organs
239.0 Neoplasm of unspecified nature of digestive system

ICD-9-CM Procedural

45.62 Other partial resection of small intestine

Stomach

43500-43502

43500 Gastrotomy; with exploration or foreign body removal
43501 with suture repair of bleeding ulcer
43502 with suture repair of pre-existing esophagogastric laceration (eg, Mallory-Weiss)

ICD-9-CM Diagnostic

530.4 Perforation of esophagus
530.7 Gastroesophageal laceration-hemorrhage syndrome
530.89 Other specified disorder of the esophagus
531.00 Acute gastric ulcer with hemorrhage, without mention of obstruction — (Use additional E code to identify drug, if drug induced)
531.01 Acute gastric ulcer with hemorrhage and obstruction — (Use additional E code to identify drug, if drug induced)
531.20 Acute gastric ulcer with hemorrhage and perforation, without mention of obstruction — (Use additional E code to identify drug, if drug induced)
531.21 Acute gastric ulcer with hemorrhage, perforation, and obstruction — (Use additional E code to identify drug, if drug induced)
531.30 Acute gastric ulcer without mention of hemorrhage, perforation, or obstruction — (Use additional E code to identify drug, if drug induced)
531.31 Acute gastric ulcer without mention of hemorrhage or perforation, with obstruction — (Use additional E code to identify drug, if drug induced)
531.40 Chronic or unspecified gastric ulcer with hemorrhage, without mention of obstruction — (Use additional E code to identify drug, if drug induced)
531.41 Chronic or unspecified gastric ulcer with hemorrhage and obstruction — (Use additional E code to identify drug, if drug induced)
531.50 Chronic or unspecified gastric ulcer with perforation, without mention of obstruction — (Use additional E code to identify drug, if drug induced)
531.51 Chronic or unspecified gastric ulcer with perforation and obstruction — (Use additional E code to identify drug, if drug induced)
531.60 Chronic or unspecified gastric ulcer with hemorrhage and perforation, without mention of obstruction — (Use additional E code to identify drug, if drug induced)
531.61 Chronic or unspecified gastric ulcer with hemorrhage, perforation, and obstruction — (Use additional E code to identify drug, if drug induced)
531.70 Chronic gastric ulcer without mention of hemorrhage, perforation, without mention of obstruction — (Use additional E code to identify drug, if drug induced)
531.71 Chronic gastric ulcer without mention of hemorrhage or perforation, with obstruction — (Use additional E code to identify drug, if drug induced)
535.70 Eosinophilic gastritis without mention of hemorrhage
535.71 Eosinophilic gastritis with hemorrhage
537.4 Fistula of stomach or duodenum
789.06 Abdominal pain, epigastric
789.07 Abdominal pain, generalized
789.36 Abdominal or pelvic swelling, mass, or lump, epigastric
793.4 Nonspecific (abnormal) findings on radiological and other examination of gastrointestinal tract
863.0 Stomach injury without mention of open wound into cavity
935.2 Foreign body in stomach
V12.71 Personal history of peptic ulcer disease

ICD-9-CM Procedural

42.82 Suture of laceration of esophagus
43.0 Gastrotomy
44.41 Suture of gastric ulcer site
44.49 Other control of hemorrhage of stomach or duodenum

43510

43510 Gastrotomy; with esophageal dilation and insertion of permanent intraluminal tube (eg, Celestin or Mousseaux-Barbin)

ICD-9-CM Diagnostic

150.0 Malignant neoplasm of cervical esophagus
150.1 Malignant neoplasm of thoracic esophagus
150.2 Malignant neoplasm of abdominal esophagus
150.3 Malignant neoplasm of upper third of esophagus
150.4 Malignant neoplasm of middle third of esophagus
150.5 Malignant neoplasm of lower third of esophagus
150.8 Malignant neoplasm of other specified part of esophagus
150.9 Malignant neoplasm of esophagus, unspecified site
209.29 Malignant carcinoid tumor of other sites — (Code first any associated multiple endocrine neoplasia syndrome: 258.01-258.03)(Use additional code to identify associated endocrine syndrome, as: carcinoid syndrome: 259.2)
209.30 Malignant poorly differentiated neuroendocrine carcinoma, any site — (Code first any associated multiple endocrine neoplasia syndrome: 258.01-258.03)(Use additional code to identify associated endocrine syndrome, as: carcinoid syndrome: 259.2)
209.69 Benign carcinoid tumor of other sites — (Code first any associated multiple endocrine neoplasia syndrome: 258.01-258.03)(Use additional code to identify associated endocrine syndrome, as: carcinoid syndrome: 259.2)
211.1 Benign neoplasm of stomach
230.1 Carcinoma in situ of esophagus
235.5 Neoplasm of uncertain behavior of other and unspecified digestive organs
239.0 Neoplasm of unspecified nature of digestive system
530.0 Achalasia and cardiospasm
530.11 Reflux esophagitis — (Use additional E code to identify cause, if induced by chemical)
530.12 Acute esophagitis — (Use additional E code to identify cause, if induced by chemical)
530.13 Eosinophilic esophagitis
530.19 Other esophagitis — (Use additional E code to identify cause, if induced by chemical)
530.3 Stricture and stenosis of esophagus
530.5 Dyskinesia of esophagus
530.6 Diverticulum of esophagus, acquired
530.81 Esophageal reflux
530.89 Other specified disorder of the esophagus
750.3 Congenital tracheoesophageal fistula, esophageal atresia and stenosis
750.4 Other specified congenital anomaly of esophagus
751.9 Unspecified congenital anomaly of digestive system
787.20 Dysphagia, unspecified
787.21 Dysphagia, oral phase
787.22 Dysphagia, oropharyngeal phase
787.23 Dysphagia, pharyngeal phase
787.24 Dysphagia, pharyngoesophageal phase
787.29 Other dysphagia
V10.03 Personal history of malignant neoplasm of esophagus
V10.04 Personal history of malignant neoplasm of stomach

ICD-9-CM Procedural

42.81 Insertion of permanent tube into esophagus
42.92 Dilation of esophagus

43520

43520 Pyloromyotomy, cutting of pyloric muscle (Fredet-Ramstedt type operation)

ICD-9-CM Diagnostic

151.0 Malignant neoplasm of cardia
151.1 Malignant neoplasm of pylorus
151.2 Malignant neoplasm of pyloric antrum
151.3 Malignant neoplasm of fundus of stomach
209.23 Malignant carcinoid tumor of the stomach — (Code first any associated multiple endocrine neoplasia syndrome: 258.01-258.03)(Use additional code to identify associated endocrine syndrome, as: carcinoid syndrome: 259.2)
537.0 Acquired hypertrophic pyloric stenosis
537.81 Pylorospasm
537.82 Angiodysplasia of stomach and duodenum (without mention of hemorrhage)
537.83 Angiodysplasia of stomach and duodenum with hemorrhage
537.89 Other specified disorder of stomach and duodenum
537.9 Unspecified disorder of stomach and duodenum ▽
750.5 Congenital hypertrophic pyloric stenosis

ICD-9-CM Procedural

43.3 Pyloromyotomy

43605

43605 Biopsy of stomach, by laparotomy

ICD-9-CM Diagnostic

151.0 Malignant neoplasm of cardia
151.1 Malignant neoplasm of pylorus
151.2 Malignant neoplasm of pyloric antrum
151.3 Malignant neoplasm of fundus of stomach
151.4 Malignant neoplasm of body of stomach
151.5 Malignant neoplasm of lesser curvature of stomach, unspecified ▽
151.6 Malignant neoplasm of greater curvature of stomach, unspecified ▽
151.8 Malignant neoplasm of other specified sites of stomach
209.23 Malignant carcinoid tumor of the stomach — (Code first any associated multiple endocrine neoplasia syndrome: 258.01-258.03)(Use additional code to identify associated endocrine syndrome, as: carcinoid syndrome: 259.2)
209.29 Malignant carcinoid tumor of other sites — (Code first any associated multiple endocrine neoplasia syndrome: 258.01-258.03)(Use additional code to identify associated endocrine syndrome, as: carcinoid syndrome: 259.2)
209.30 Malignant poorly differentiated neuroendocrine carcinoma, any site — (Code first any associated multiple endocrine neoplasia syndrome: 258.01-258.03)(Use additional code to identify associated endocrine syndrome, as: carcinoid syndrome: 259.2) ▽
209.69 Benign carcinoid tumor of other sites — (Code first any associated multiple endocrine neoplasia syndrome: 258.01-258.03)(Use additional code to identify associated endocrine syndrome, as: carcinoid syndrome: 259.2)
209.79 Secondary neuroendocrine tumor of other sites
211.1 Benign neoplasm of stomach
230.2 Carcinoma in situ of stomach
235.2 Neoplasm of uncertain behavior of stomach, intestines, and rectum
239.0 Neoplasm of unspecified nature of digestive system
239.89 Neoplasms of unspecified nature, other specified sites
531.70 Chronic gastric ulcer without mention of hemorrhage, perforation, without mention of obstruction — (Use additional E code to identify drug, if drug induced)
535.20 Gastric mucosal hypertrophy without mention of hemorrhage
535.50 Unspecified gastritis and gastroduodenitis without mention of hemorrhage ▽
535.70 Eosinophilic gastritis without mention of hemorrhage
535.71 Eosinophilic gastritis with hemorrhage
536.1 Acute dilatation of stomach
536.2 Persistent vomiting
536.8 Dyspepsia and other specified disorders of function of stomach
537.1 Gastric diverticulum
537.81 Pylorospasm
537.82 Angiodysplasia of stomach and duodenum (without mention of hemorrhage)
537.83 Angiodysplasia of stomach and duodenum with hemorrhage
537.89 Other specified disorder of stomach and duodenum
750.5 Congenital hypertrophic pyloric stenosis
750.7 Other specified congenital anomalies of stomach
783.0 Anorexia
783.7 Adult failure to thrive
787.01 Nausea with vomiting
787.04 Bilious emesis
793.4 Nonspecific (abnormal) findings on radiological and other examination of gastrointestinal tract

ICD-9-CM Procedural

44.15 Open biopsy of stomach

HCPCS Level II Supplies & Services

A4305 Disposable drug delivery system, flow rate of 50 ml or greater per hour

43610

43610 Excision, local; ulcer or benign tumor of stomach

ICD-9-CM Diagnostic

209.63 Benign carcinoid tumor of the stomach — (Code first any associated multiple endocrine neoplasia syndrome: 258.01-258.03)(Use additional code to identify associated endocrine syndrome, as: carcinoid syndrome: 259.2)
211.1 Benign neoplasm of stomach
531.00 Acute gastric ulcer with hemorrhage, without mention of obstruction — (Use additional E code to identify drug, if drug induced)
531.01 Acute gastric ulcer with hemorrhage and obstruction — (Use additional E code to identify drug, if drug induced)
531.10 Acute gastric ulcer with perforation, without mention of obstruction — (Use additional E code to identify drug, if drug induced)
531.11 Acute gastric ulcer with perforation and obstruction — (Use additional E code to identify drug, if drug induced)
531.20 Acute gastric ulcer with hemorrhage and perforation, without mention of obstruction — (Use additional E code to identify drug, if drug induced)
531.21 Acute gastric ulcer with hemorrhage, perforation, and obstruction — (Use additional E code to identify drug, if drug induced)
531.30 Acute gastric ulcer without mention of hemorrhage, perforation, or obstruction — (Use additional E code to identify drug, if drug induced)
531.31 Acute gastric ulcer without mention of hemorrhage or perforation, with obstruction — (Use additional E code to identify drug, if drug induced)
531.40 Chronic or unspecified gastric ulcer with hemorrhage, without mention of obstruction — (Use additional E code to identify drug, if drug induced)
531.41 Chronic or unspecified gastric ulcer with hemorrhage and obstruction — (Use additional E code to identify drug, if drug induced)
531.50 Chronic or unspecified gastric ulcer with perforation, without mention of obstruction — (Use additional E code to identify drug, if drug induced)
531.51 Chronic or unspecified gastric ulcer with perforation and obstruction — (Use additional E code to identify drug, if drug induced)
531.60 Chronic or unspecified gastric ulcer with hemorrhage and perforation, without mention of obstruction — (Use additional E code to identify drug, if drug induced)
531.61 Chronic or unspecified gastric ulcer with hemorrhage, perforation, and obstruction — (Use additional E code to identify drug, if drug induced)
531.70 Chronic gastric ulcer without mention of hemorrhage, perforation, without mention of obstruction — (Use additional E code to identify drug, if drug induced)
531.71 Chronic gastric ulcer without mention of hemorrhage or perforation, with obstruction — (Use additional E code to identify drug, if drug induced)
531.90 Gastric ulcer, unspecified as acute or chronic, without mention of hemorrhage, perforation, or obstruction — (Use additional E code to identify drug, if drug induced) ▽

531.91 Gastric ulcer, unspecified as acute or chronic, without mention of hemorrhage or perforation, with obstruction — (Use additional E code to identify drug, if drug induced)

533.00 Acute peptic ulcer, unspecified site, with hemorrhage, without mention of obstruction — (Use additional E code to identify drug, if drug induced)

533.01 Acute peptic ulcer, unspecified site, with hemorrhage and obstruction — (Use additional E code to identify drug, if drug induced)

533.10 Acute peptic ulcer, unspecified site, with perforation, without mention of obstruction — (Use additional E code to identify drug, if drug induced)

533.11 Acute peptic ulcer, unspecified site, with perforation and obstruction — (Use additional E code to identify drug, if drug induced)

533.20 Acute peptic ulcer, unspecified site, with hemorrhage and perforation, without mention of obstruction — (Use additional E code to identify drug, if drug induced)

533.21 Acute peptic ulcer, unspecified site, with hemorrhage, perforation, and obstruction — (Use additional E code to identify drug, if drug induced)

533.30 Acute peptic ulcer, unspecified site, without mention of hemorrhage, perforation, or obstruction — (Use additional E code to identify drug, if drug induced)

533.31 Acute peptic ulcer, unspecified site, without mention of hemorrhage and perforation, with obstruction — (Use additional E code to identify drug, if drug induced)

533.40 Chronic or unspecified peptic ulcer, unspecified site, with hemorrhage, without mention of obstruction — (Use additional E code to identify drug, if drug induced)

533.41 Chronic or unspecified peptic ulcer, unspecified site, with hemorrhage and obstruction — (Use additional E code to identify drug, if drug induced)

533.50 Chronic or unspecified peptic ulcer, unspecified site, with perforation, without mention of obstruction — (Use additional E code to identify drug, if drug induced)

533.51 Chronic or unspecified peptic ulcer, unspecified site, with perforation and obstruction — (Use additional E code to identify drug, if drug induced)

533.60 Chronic or unspecified peptic ulcer, unspecified site, with hemorrhage and perforation, without mention of obstruction — (Use additional E code to identify drug, if drug induced)

533.61 Chronic or unspecified peptic ulcer, unspecified site, with hemorrhage, perforation, and obstruction — (Use additional E code to identify drug, if drug induced)

533.70 Chronic peptic ulcer, unspecified site, without mention of hemorrhage, perforation, or obstruction — (Use additional E code to identify drug, if drug induced)

533.71 Chronic peptic ulcer of unspecified site without mention of hemorrhage or perforation, with obstruction — (Use additional E code to identify drug, if drug induced)

533.90 Peptic ulcer, unspecified site, unspecified as acute or chronic, without mention of hemorrhage, perforation, or obstruction — (Use additional E code to identify drug, if drug induced)

533.91 Peptic ulcer, unspecified site, unspecified as acute or chronic, without mention of hemorrhage or perforation, with obstruction — (Use additional E code to identify drug, if drug induced)

ICD-9-CM Procedural

43.42 Local excision of other lesion or tissue of stomach

43611

43611 Excision, local; malignant tumor of stomach

ICD-9-CM Diagnostic

151.0 Malignant neoplasm of cardia

151.1 Malignant neoplasm of pylorus

151.2 Malignant neoplasm of pyloric antrum

151.3 Malignant neoplasm of fundus of stomach

151.4 Malignant neoplasm of body of stomach

151.5 Malignant neoplasm of lesser curvature of stomach, unspecified

151.6 Malignant neoplasm of greater curvature of stomach, unspecified

151.8 Malignant neoplasm of other specified sites of stomach

151.9 Malignant neoplasm of stomach, unspecified site

197.8 Secondary malignant neoplasm of other digestive organs and spleen

209.23 Malignant carcinoid tumor of the stomach — (Code first any associated multiple endocrine neoplasia syndrome: 258.01-258.03)(Use additional code to identify associated endocrine syndrome, as: carcinoid syndrome: 259.2)

209.29 Malignant carcinoid tumor of other sites — (Code first any associated multiple endocrine neoplasia syndrome: 258.01-258.03)(Use additional code to identify associated endocrine syndrome, as: carcinoid syndrome: 259.2)

209.30 Malignant poorly differentiated neuroendocrine carcinoma, any site — (Code first any associated multiple endocrine neoplasia syndrome: 258.01-258.03)(Use additional code to identify associated endocrine syndrome, as: carcinoid syndrome: 259.2)

209.69 Benign carcinoid tumor of other sites — (Code first any associated multiple endocrine neoplasia syndrome: 258.01-258.03)(Use additional code to identify associated endocrine syndrome, as: carcinoid syndrome: 259.2)

230.2 Carcinoma in situ of stomach

235.2 Neoplasm of uncertain behavior of stomach, intestines, and rectum

239.0 Neoplasm of unspecified nature of digestive system

ICD-9-CM Procedural

43.42 Local excision of other lesion or tissue of stomach

43620

43620 Gastrectomy, total; with esophagoenterostomy

ICD-9-CM Diagnostic

151.0 Malignant neoplasm of cardia

151.1 Malignant neoplasm of pylorus

151.2 Malignant neoplasm of pyloric antrum

151.3 Malignant neoplasm of fundus of stomach

151.4 Malignant neoplasm of body of stomach

151.5 Malignant neoplasm of lesser curvature of stomach, unspecified

151.6 Malignant neoplasm of greater curvature of stomach, unspecified

151.8 Malignant neoplasm of other specified sites of stomach

151.9 Malignant neoplasm of stomach, unspecified site

197.8 Secondary malignant neoplasm of other digestive organs and spleen

209.23 Malignant carcinoid tumor of the stomach — (Code first any associated multiple endocrine neoplasia syndrome: 258.01-258.03)(Use additional code to identify associated endocrine syndrome, as: carcinoid syndrome: 259.2)

209.25 Malignant carcinoid tumor of foregut, not otherwise specified — (Code first any associated multiple endocrine neoplasia syndrome: 258.01-258.03)(Use additional code to identify associated endocrine syndrome, as: carcinoid syndrome: 259.2)

209.29 Malignant carcinoid tumor of other sites — (Code first any associated multiple endocrine neoplasia syndrome: 258.01-258.03)(Use additional code to identify associated endocrine syndrome, as: carcinoid syndrome: 259.2)

209.30 Malignant poorly differentiated neuroendocrine carcinoma, any site — (Code first any associated multiple endocrine neoplasia syndrome: 258.01-258.03)(Use additional code to identify associated endocrine syndrome, as: carcinoid syndrome: 259.2)

209.63 Benign carcinoid tumor of the stomach — (Code first any associated multiple endocrine neoplasia syndrome: 258.01-258.03)(Use additional code to identify associated endocrine syndrome, as: carcinoid syndrome: 259.2)

209.65 Benign carcinoid tumor of foregut, not otherwise specified — (Code first any associated multiple endocrine neoplasia syndrome: 258.01-258.03)(Use additional code to identify associated endocrine syndrome, as: carcinoid syndrome: 259.2)

209.69 Benign carcinoid tumor of other sites — (Code first any associated multiple endocrine neoplasia syndrome: 258.01-258.03)(Use additional code to identify associated endocrine syndrome, as: carcinoid syndrome: 259.2)

211.1 Benign neoplasm of stomach

235.2 Neoplasm of uncertain behavior of stomach, intestines, and rectum

239.0 Neoplasm of unspecified nature of digestive system

531.00 Acute gastric ulcer with hemorrhage, without mention of obstruction — (Use additional E code to identify drug, if drug induced)

531.01 Acute gastric ulcer with hemorrhage and obstruction — (Use additional E code to identify drug, if drug induced)

531.10 Acute gastric ulcer with perforation, without mention of obstruction — (Use additional E code to identify drug, if drug induced)
531.11 Acute gastric ulcer with perforation and obstruction — (Use additional E code to identify drug, if drug induced)
531.20 Acute gastric ulcer with hemorrhage and perforation, without mention of obstruction — (Use additional E code to identify drug, if drug induced)
531.21 Acute gastric ulcer with hemorrhage, perforation, and obstruction — (Use additional E code to identify drug, if drug induced)
533.00 Acute peptic ulcer, unspecified site, with hemorrhage, without mention of obstruction — (Use additional E code to identify drug, if drug induced) ▽
533.01 Acute peptic ulcer, unspecified site, with hemorrhage and obstruction — (Use additional E code to identify drug, if drug induced) ▽
533.10 Acute peptic ulcer, unspecified site, with perforation, without mention of obstruction — (Use additional E code to identify drug, if drug induced) ▽
533.11 Acute peptic ulcer, unspecified site, with perforation and obstruction — (Use additional E code to identify drug, if drug induced) ▽
533.20 Acute peptic ulcer, unspecified site, with hemorrhage and perforation, without mention of obstruction — (Use additional E code to identify drug, if drug induced) ▽
533.21 Acute peptic ulcer, unspecified site, with hemorrhage, perforation, and obstruction — (Use additional E code to identify drug, if drug induced) ▽
533.30 Acute peptic ulcer, unspecified site, without mention of hemorrhage, perforation, or obstruction — (Use additional E code to identify drug, if drug induced) ▽
533.31 Acute peptic ulcer, unspecified site, without mention of hemorrhage and perforation, with obstruction — (Use additional E code to identify drug, if drug induced) ▽
533.40 Chronic or unspecified peptic ulcer, unspecified site, with hemorrhage, without mention of obstruction — (Use additional E code to identify drug, if drug induced) ▽
533.41 Chronic or unspecified peptic ulcer, unspecified site, with hemorrhage and obstruction — (Use additional E code to identify drug, if drug induced) ▽
533.50 Chronic or unspecified peptic ulcer, unspecified site, with perforation, without mention of obstruction — (Use additional E code to identify drug, if drug induced) ▽
533.51 Chronic or unspecified peptic ulcer, unspecified site, with perforation and obstruction — (Use additional E code to identify drug, if drug induced) ▽
533.60 Chronic or unspecified peptic ulcer, unspecified site, with hemorrhage and perforation, without mention of obstruction — (Use additional E code to identify drug, if drug induced) ▽
533.61 Chronic or unspecified peptic ulcer, unspecified site, with hemorrhage, perforation, and obstruction — (Use additional E code to identify drug, if drug induced) ▽
533.70 Chronic peptic ulcer, unspecified site, without mention of hemorrhage, perforation, or obstruction — (Use additional E code to identify drug, if drug induced) ▽
533.71 Chronic peptic ulcer of unspecified site without mention of hemorrhage or perforation, with obstruction — (Use additional E code to identify drug, if drug induced) ▽
533.90 Peptic ulcer, unspecified site, unspecified as acute or chronic, without mention of hemorrhage, perforation, or obstruction — (Use additional E code to identify drug, if drug induced) ▽
533.91 Peptic ulcer, unspecified site, unspecified as acute or chronic, without mention of hemorrhage or perforation, with obstruction — (Use additional E code to identify drug, if drug induced) ▽
863.0 Stomach injury without mention of open wound into cavity
863.1 Stomach injury with open wound into cavity

ICD-9-CM Procedural

43.91 Total gastrectomy with intestinal interposition
43.99 Other total gastrectomy

43621

43621 Gastrectomy, total; with Roux-en-Y reconstruction

ICD-9-CM Diagnostic

151.0 Malignant neoplasm of cardia
151.1 Malignant neoplasm of pylorus
151.2 Malignant neoplasm of pyloric antrum
151.3 Malignant neoplasm of fundus of stomach
151.4 Malignant neoplasm of body of stomach
151.5 Malignant neoplasm of lesser curvature of stomach, unspecified ▽
151.6 Malignant neoplasm of greater curvature of stomach, unspecified ▽
151.8 Malignant neoplasm of other specified sites of stomach
151.9 Malignant neoplasm of stomach, unspecified site ▽
197.8 Secondary malignant neoplasm of other digestive organs and spleen
209.23 Malignant carcinoid tumor of the stomach — (Code first any associated multiple endocrine neoplasia syndrome: 258.01-258.03)(Use additional code to identify associated endocrine syndrome, as: carcinoid syndrome: 259.2)
209.25 Malignant carcinoid tumor of foregut, not otherwise specified — (Code first any associated multiple endocrine neoplasia syndrome: 258.01-258.03)(Use additional code to identify associated endocrine syndrome, as: carcinoid syndrome: 259.2)
209.29 Malignant carcinoid tumor of other sites — (Code first any associated multiple endocrine neoplasia syndrome: 258.01-258.03)(Use additional code to identify associated endocrine syndrome, as: carcinoid syndrome: 259.2)
209.30 Malignant poorly differentiated neuroendocrine carcinoma, any site — (Code first any associated multiple endocrine neoplasia syndrome: 258.01-258.03)(Use additional code to identify associated endocrine syndrome, as: carcinoid syndrome: 259.2) ▽
209.63 Benign carcinoid tumor of the stomach — (Code first any associated multiple endocrine neoplasia syndrome: 258.01-258.03)(Use additional code to identify associated endocrine syndrome, as: carcinoid syndrome: 259.2)
209.65 Benign carcinoid tumor of foregut, not otherwise specified — (Code first any associated multiple endocrine neoplasia syndrome: 258.01-258.03)(Use additional code to identify associated endocrine syndrome, as: carcinoid syndrome: 259.2)
209.69 Benign carcinoid tumor of other sites — (Code first any associated multiple endocrine neoplasia syndrome: 258.01-258.03)(Use additional code to identify associated endocrine syndrome, as: carcinoid syndrome: 259.2)
211.1 Benign neoplasm of stomach
235.2 Neoplasm of uncertain behavior of stomach, intestines, and rectum
239.0 Neoplasm of unspecified nature of digestive system
531.00 Acute gastric ulcer with hemorrhage, without mention of obstruction — (Use additional E code to identify drug, if drug induced)
531.01 Acute gastric ulcer with hemorrhage and obstruction — (Use additional E code to identify drug, if drug induced)
531.10 Acute gastric ulcer with perforation, without mention of obstruction — (Use additional E code to identify drug, if drug induced)
531.11 Acute gastric ulcer with perforation and obstruction — (Use additional E code to identify drug, if drug induced)
531.20 Acute gastric ulcer with hemorrhage and perforation, without mention of obstruction — (Use additional E code to identify drug, if drug induced)
531.21 Acute gastric ulcer with hemorrhage, perforation, and obstruction — (Use additional E code to identify drug, if drug induced)
533.00 Acute peptic ulcer, unspecified site, with hemorrhage, without mention of obstruction — (Use additional E code to identify drug, if drug induced) ▽
533.01 Acute peptic ulcer, unspecified site, with hemorrhage and obstruction — (Use additional E code to identify drug, if drug induced) ▽
533.10 Acute peptic ulcer, unspecified site, with perforation, without mention of obstruction — (Use additional E code to identify drug, if drug induced) ▽
533.11 Acute peptic ulcer, unspecified site, with perforation and obstruction — (Use additional E code to identify drug, if drug induced) ▽
533.20 Acute peptic ulcer, unspecified site, with hemorrhage and perforation, without mention of obstruction — (Use additional E code to identify drug, if drug induced) ▽
533.21 Acute peptic ulcer, unspecified site, with hemorrhage, perforation, and obstruction — (Use additional E code to identify drug, if drug induced) ▽
533.30 Acute peptic ulcer, unspecified site, without mention of hemorrhage, perforation, or obstruction — (Use additional E code to identify drug, if drug induced) ▽
533.31 Acute peptic ulcer, unspecified site, without mention of hemorrhage and perforation, with obstruction — (Use additional E code to identify drug, if drug induced) ▽
533.40 Chronic or unspecified peptic ulcer, unspecified site, with hemorrhage, without mention of obstruction — (Use additional E code to identify drug, if drug induced) ▽

533.41 Chronic or unspecified peptic ulcer, unspecified site, with hemorrhage and obstruction — (Use additional E code to identify drug, if drug induced)

533.50 Chronic or unspecified peptic ulcer, unspecified site, with perforation, without mention of obstruction — (Use additional E code to identify drug, if drug induced)

533.51 Chronic or unspecified peptic ulcer, unspecified site, with perforation and obstruction — (Use additional E code to identify drug, if drug induced)

533.60 Chronic or unspecified peptic ulcer, unspecified site, with hemorrhage and perforation, without mention of obstruction — (Use additional E code to identify drug, if drug induced)

533.61 Chronic or unspecified peptic ulcer, unspecified site, with hemorrhage, perforation, and obstruction — (Use additional E code to identify drug, if drug induced)

533.70 Chronic peptic ulcer, unspecified site, without mention of hemorrhage, perforation, or obstruction — (Use additional E code to identify drug, if drug induced)

533.71 Chronic peptic ulcer of unspecified site without mention of hemorrhage or perforation, with obstruction — (Use additional E code to identify drug, if drug induced)

533.90 Peptic ulcer, unspecified site, unspecified as acute or chronic, without mention of hemorrhage, perforation, or obstruction — (Use additional E code to identify drug, if drug induced)

533.91 Peptic ulcer, unspecified site, unspecified as acute or chronic, without mention of hemorrhage or perforation, with obstruction — (Use additional E code to identify drug, if drug induced)

863.0 Stomach injury without mention of open wound into cavity

863.1 Stomach injury with open wound into cavity

ICD-9-CM Procedural

43.91 Total gastrectomy with intestinal interposition

43.99 Other total gastrectomy

43622

43622 Gastrectomy, total; with formation of intestinal pouch, any type

ICD-9-CM Diagnostic

151.0 Malignant neoplasm of cardia

151.1 Malignant neoplasm of pylorus

151.2 Malignant neoplasm of pyloric antrum

151.3 Malignant neoplasm of fundus of stomach

151.4 Malignant neoplasm of body of stomach

151.5 Malignant neoplasm of lesser curvature of stomach, unspecified

151.6 Malignant neoplasm of greater curvature of stomach, unspecified

151.8 Malignant neoplasm of other specified sites of stomach

151.9 Malignant neoplasm of stomach, unspecified site

197.8 Secondary malignant neoplasm of other digestive organs and spleen

209.23 Malignant carcinoid tumor of the stomach — (Code first any associated multiple endocrine neoplasia syndrome: 258.01-258.03)(Use additional code to identify associated endocrine syndrome, as: carcinoid syndrome: 259.2)

209.25 Malignant carcinoid tumor of foregut, not otherwise specified — (Code first any associated multiple endocrine neoplasia syndrome: 258.01-258.03)(Use additional code to identify associated endocrine syndrome, as: carcinoid syndrome: 259.2)

209.29 Malignant carcinoid tumor of other sites — (Code first any associated multiple endocrine neoplasia syndrome: 258.01-258.03)(Use additional code to identify associated endocrine syndrome, as: carcinoid syndrome: 259.2)

209.30 Malignant poorly differentiated neuroendocrine carcinoma, any site — (Code first any associated multiple endocrine neoplasia syndrome: 258.01-258.03)(Use additional code to identify associated endocrine syndrome, as: carcinoid syndrome: 259.2)

209.63 Benign carcinoid tumor of the stomach — (Code first any associated multiple endocrine neoplasia syndrome: 258.01-258.03)(Use additional code to identify associated endocrine syndrome, as: carcinoid syndrome: 259.2)

209.65 Benign carcinoid tumor of foregut, not otherwise specified — (Code first any associated multiple endocrine neoplasia syndrome: 258.01-258.03)(Use additional code to identify associated endocrine syndrome, as: carcinoid syndrome: 259.2)

209.69 Benign carcinoid tumor of other sites — (Code first any associated multiple endocrine neoplasia syndrome: 258.01-258.03)(Use additional code to identify associated endocrine syndrome, as: carcinoid syndrome: 259.2)

211.1 Benign neoplasm of stomach

235.2 Neoplasm of uncertain behavior of stomach, intestines, and rectum

239.0 Neoplasm of unspecified nature of digestive system

531.00 Acute gastric ulcer with hemorrhage, without mention of obstruction — (Use additional E code to identify drug, if drug induced)

531.01 Acute gastric ulcer with hemorrhage and obstruction — (Use additional E code to identify drug, if drug induced)

531.10 Acute gastric ulcer with perforation, without mention of obstruction — (Use additional E code to identify drug, if drug induced)

531.11 Acute gastric ulcer with perforation and obstruction — (Use additional E code to identify drug, if drug induced)

531.20 Acute gastric ulcer with hemorrhage and perforation, without mention of obstruction — (Use additional E code to identify drug, if drug induced)

531.21 Acute gastric ulcer with hemorrhage, perforation, and obstruction — (Use additional E code to identify drug, if drug induced)

533.00 Acute peptic ulcer, unspecified site, with hemorrhage, without mention of obstruction — (Use additional E code to identify drug, if drug induced)

533.01 Acute peptic ulcer, unspecified site, with hemorrhage and obstruction — (Use additional E code to identify drug, if drug induced)

533.10 Acute peptic ulcer, unspecified site, with perforation, without mention of obstruction — (Use additional E code to identify drug, if drug induced)

533.11 Acute peptic ulcer, unspecified site, with perforation and obstruction — (Use additional E code to identify drug, if drug induced)

533.20 Acute peptic ulcer, unspecified site, with hemorrhage and perforation, without mention of obstruction — (Use additional E code to identify drug, if drug induced)

533.21 Acute peptic ulcer, unspecified site, with hemorrhage, perforation, and obstruction — (Use additional E code to identify drug, if drug induced)

533.30 Acute peptic ulcer, unspecified site, without mention of hemorrhage, perforation, or obstruction — (Use additional E code to identify drug, if drug induced)

533.31 Acute peptic ulcer, unspecified site, without mention of hemorrhage and perforation, with obstruction — (Use additional E code to identify drug, if drug induced)

533.40 Chronic or unspecified peptic ulcer, unspecified site, with hemorrhage, without mention of obstruction — (Use additional E code to identify drug, if drug induced)

533.41 Chronic or unspecified peptic ulcer, unspecified site, with hemorrhage and obstruction — (Use additional E code to identify drug, if drug induced)

533.50 Chronic or unspecified peptic ulcer, unspecified site, with perforation, without mention of obstruction — (Use additional E code to identify drug, if drug induced)

533.51 Chronic or unspecified peptic ulcer, unspecified site, with perforation and obstruction — (Use additional E code to identify drug, if drug induced)

533.60 Chronic or unspecified peptic ulcer, unspecified site, with hemorrhage and perforation, without mention of obstruction — (Use additional E code to identify drug, if drug induced)

533.61 Chronic or unspecified peptic ulcer, unspecified site, with hemorrhage, perforation, and obstruction — (Use additional E code to identify drug, if drug induced)

533.70 Chronic peptic ulcer, unspecified site, without mention of hemorrhage, perforation, or obstruction — (Use additional E code to identify drug, if drug induced)

533.71 Chronic peptic ulcer of unspecified site without mention of hemorrhage or perforation, with obstruction — (Use additional E code to identify drug, if drug induced)

533.90 Peptic ulcer, unspecified site, unspecified as acute or chronic, without mention of hemorrhage, perforation, or obstruction — (Use additional E code to identify drug, if drug induced)

533.91 Peptic ulcer, unspecified site, unspecified as acute or chronic, without mention of hemorrhage or perforation, with obstruction — (Use additional E code to identify drug, if drug induced)

863.0 Stomach injury without mention of open wound into cavity

863.1 Stomach injury with open wound into cavity

ICD-9-CM Procedural

43.91 Total gastrectomy with intestinal interposition

43.99 Other total gastrectomy

43631

43631 Gastrectomy, partial, distal; with gastroduodenostomy

ICD-9-CM Diagnostic

151.1 Malignant neoplasm of pylorus
151.2 Malignant neoplasm of pyloric antrum
151.4 Malignant neoplasm of body of stomach
151.8 Malignant neoplasm of other specified sites of stomach
151.9 Malignant neoplasm of stomach, unspecified site ♡
197.8 Secondary malignant neoplasm of other digestive organs and spleen
209.23 Malignant carcinoid tumor of the stomach — (Code first any associated multiple endocrine neoplasia syndrome: 258.01-258.03)(Use additional code to identify associated endocrine syndrome, as: carcinoid syndrome: 259.2)
209.25 Malignant carcinoid tumor of foregut, not otherwise specified — (Code first any associated multiple endocrine neoplasia syndrome: 258.01-258.03)(Use additional code to identify associated endocrine syndrome, as: carcinoid syndrome: 259.2)
209.29 Malignant carcinoid tumor of other sites — (Code first any associated multiple endocrine neoplasia syndrome: 258.01-258.03)(Use additional code to identify associated endocrine syndrome, as: carcinoid syndrome: 259.2)
209.30 Malignant poorly differentiated neuroendocrine carcinoma, any site — (Code first any associated multiple endocrine neoplasia syndrome: 258.01-258.03)(Use additional code to identify associated endocrine syndrome, as: carcinoid syndrome: 259.2) ♡
209.63 Benign carcinoid tumor of the stomach — (Code first any associated multiple endocrine neoplasia syndrome: 258.01-258.03)(Use additional code to identify associated endocrine syndrome, as: carcinoid syndrome: 259.2)
209.65 Benign carcinoid tumor of foregut, not otherwise specified — (Code first any associated multiple endocrine neoplasia syndrome: 258.01-258.03)(Use additional code to identify associated endocrine syndrome, as: carcinoid syndrome: 259.2)
209.69 Benign carcinoid tumor of other sites — (Code first any associated multiple endocrine neoplasia syndrome: 258.01-258.03)(Use additional code to identify associated endocrine syndrome, as: carcinoid syndrome: 259.2)
211.1 Benign neoplasm of stomach
235.2 Neoplasm of uncertain behavior of stomach, intestines, and rectum
239.0 Neoplasm of unspecified nature of digestive system
531.00 Acute gastric ulcer with hemorrhage, without mention of obstruction — (Use additional E code to identify drug, if drug induced)
531.01 Acute gastric ulcer with hemorrhage and obstruction — (Use additional E code to identify drug, if drug induced)
531.10 Acute gastric ulcer with perforation, without mention of obstruction — (Use additional E code to identify drug, if drug induced)
531.11 Acute gastric ulcer with perforation and obstruction — (Use additional E code to identify drug, if drug induced)
531.20 Acute gastric ulcer with hemorrhage and perforation, without mention of obstruction — (Use additional E code to identify drug, if drug induced)
531.21 Acute gastric ulcer with hemorrhage, perforation, and obstruction — (Use additional E code to identify drug, if drug induced)
531.40 Chronic or unspecified gastric ulcer with hemorrhage, without mention of obstruction — (Use additional E code to identify drug, if drug induced)
531.41 Chronic or unspecified gastric ulcer with hemorrhage and obstruction — (Use additional E code to identify drug, if drug induced)
531.50 Chronic or unspecified gastric ulcer with perforation, without mention of obstruction — (Use additional E code to identify drug, if drug induced)
531.51 Chronic or unspecified gastric ulcer with perforation and obstruction — (Use additional E code to identify drug, if drug induced)
531.60 Chronic or unspecified gastric ulcer with hemorrhage and perforation, without mention of obstruction — (Use additional E code to identify drug, if drug induced)
531.61 Chronic or unspecified gastric ulcer with hemorrhage, perforation, and obstruction — (Use additional E code to identify drug, if drug induced)
531.70 Chronic gastric ulcer without mention of hemorrhage, perforation, without mention of obstruction — (Use additional E code to identify drug, if drug induced)
531.71 Chronic gastric ulcer without mention of hemorrhage or perforation, with obstruction — (Use additional E code to identify drug, if drug induced)
531.90 Gastric ulcer, unspecified as acute or chronic, without mention of hemorrhage, perforation, or obstruction — (Use additional E code to identify drug, if drug induced) ♡
531.91 Gastric ulcer, unspecified as acute or chronic, without mention of hemorrhage or perforation, with obstruction — (Use additional E code to identify drug, if drug induced) ♡
533.00 Acute peptic ulcer, unspecified site, with hemorrhage, without mention of obstruction — (Use additional E code to identify drug, if drug induced) ♡
533.01 Acute peptic ulcer, unspecified site, with hemorrhage and obstruction — (Use additional E code to identify drug, if drug induced) ♡
533.10 Acute peptic ulcer, unspecified site, with perforation, without mention of obstruction — (Use additional E code to identify drug, if drug induced) ♡
533.11 Acute peptic ulcer, unspecified site, with perforation and obstruction— (Use additional E code to identify drug, if drug induced) ♡
533.20 Acute peptic ulcer, unspecified site, with hemorrhage and perforation, without mention of obstruction — (Use additional E code to identify drug, if drug induced) ♡
533.21 Acute peptic ulcer, unspecified site, with hemorrhage, perforation, and obstruction — (Use additional E code to identify drug, if drug induced) ♡
533.30 Acute peptic ulcer, unspecified site, without mention of hemorrhage, perforation, or obstruction — (Use additional E code to identify drug, if drug induced) ♡
533.31 Acute peptic ulcer, unspecified site, without mention of hemorrhage and perforation, with obstruction — (Use additional E code to identify drug, if drug induced) ♡
533.40 Chronic or unspecified peptic ulcer, unspecified site, with hemorrhage, without mention of obstruction — (Use additional E code to identify drug, if drug induced) ♡
533.41 Chronic or unspecified peptic ulcer, unspecified site, with hemorrhage and obstruction — (Use additional E code to identify drug, if drug induced) ♡
533.50 Chronic or unspecified peptic ulcer, unspecified site, with perforation, without mention of obstruction — (Use additional E code to identify drug, if drug induced) ♡
533.51 Chronic or unspecified peptic ulcer, unspecified site, with perforation and obstruction — (Use additional E code to identify drug, if drug induced) ♡
533.60 Chronic or unspecified peptic ulcer, unspecified site, with hemorrhage and perforation, without mention of obstruction — (Use additional E code to identify drug, if drug induced) ♡
533.61 Chronic or unspecified peptic ulcer, unspecified site, with hemorrhage, perforation, and obstruction — (Use additional E code to identify drug, if drug induced) ♡
533.70 Chronic peptic ulcer, unspecified site, without mention of hemorrhage, perforation, or obstruction — (Use additional E code to identify drug, if drug induced) ♡
533.71 Chronic peptic ulcer of unspecified site without mention of hemorrhage or perforation, with obstruction — (Use additional E code to identify drug, if drug induced) ♡
533.90 Peptic ulcer, unspecified site, unspecified as acute or chronic, without mention of hemorrhage, perforation, or obstruction — (Use additional E code to identify drug, if drug induced) ♡
533.91 Peptic ulcer, unspecified site, unspecified as acute or chronic, without mention of hemorrhage or perforation, with obstruction — (Use additional E code to identify drug, if drug induced) ♡
863.0 Stomach injury without mention of open wound into cavity
863.1 Stomach injury with open wound into cavity
997.49 Other digestive system complications

ICD-9-CM Procedural

43.6 Partial gastrectomy with anastomosis to duodenum

43632

43632 Gastrectomy, partial, distal; with gastrojejunostomy

ICD-9-CM Diagnostic

151.1 Malignant neoplasm of pylorus
151.2 Malignant neoplasm of pyloric antrum
151.4 Malignant neoplasm of body of stomach
151.8 Malignant neoplasm of other specified sites of stomach

151.9 Malignant neoplasm of stomach, unspecified site
197.8 Secondary malignant neoplasm of other digestive organs and spleen
209.23 Malignant carcinoid tumor of the stomach — (Code first any associated multiple endocrine neoplasia syndrome: 258.01-258.03)(Use additional code to identify associated endocrine syndrome, as: carcinoid syndrome: 259.2)
209.25 Malignant carcinoid tumor of foregut, not otherwise specified — (Code first any associated multiple endocrine neoplasia syndrome: 258.01-258.03)(Use additional code to identify associated endocrine syndrome, as: carcinoid syndrome: 259.2)
209.29 Malignant carcinoid tumor of other sites — (Code first any associated multiple endocrine neoplasia syndrome: 258.01-258.03)(Use additional code to identify associated endocrine syndrome, as: carcinoid syndrome: 259.2)
209.30 Malignant poorly differentiated neuroendocrine carcinoma, any site — (Code first any associated multiple endocrine neoplasia syndrome: 258.01-258.03)(Use additional code to identify associated endocrine syndrome, as: carcinoid syndrome: 259.2)
209.63 Benign carcinoid tumor of the stomach — (Code first any associated multiple endocrine neoplasia syndrome: 258.01-258.03)(Use additional code to identify associated endocrine syndrome, as: carcinoid syndrome: 259.2)
209.65 Benign carcinoid tumor of foregut, not otherwise specified — (Code first any associated multiple endocrine neoplasia syndrome: 258.01-258.03)(Use additional code to identify associated endocrine syndrome, as: carcinoid syndrome: 259.2)
209.69 Benign carcinoid tumor of other sites — (Code first any associated multiple endocrine neoplasia syndrome: 258.01-258.03)(Use additional code to identify associated endocrine syndrome, as: carcinoid syndrome: 259.2)
211.1 Benign neoplasm of stomach
235.2 Neoplasm of uncertain behavior of stomach, intestines, and rectum
239.0 Neoplasm of unspecified nature of digestive system
531.00 Acute gastric ulcer with hemorrhage, without mention of obstruction — (Use additional E code to identify drug, if drug induced)
531.01 Acute gastric ulcer with hemorrhage and obstruction — (Use additional E code to identify drug, if drug induced)
531.10 Acute gastric ulcer with perforation, without mention of obstruction — (Use additional E code to identify drug, if drug induced)
531.11 Acute gastric ulcer with perforation and obstruction — (Use additional E code to identify drug, if drug induced)
531.20 Acute gastric ulcer with hemorrhage and perforation, without mention of obstruction — (Use additional E code to identify drug, if drug induced)
531.21 Acute gastric ulcer with hemorrhage, perforation, and obstruction — (Use additional E code to identify drug, if drug induced)
531.40 Chronic or unspecified gastric ulcer with hemorrhage, without mention of obstruction — (Use additional E code to identify drug, if drug induced)
531.41 Chronic or unspecified gastric ulcer with hemorrhage and obstruction — (Use additional E code to identify drug, if drug induced)
531.50 Chronic or unspecified gastric ulcer with perforation, without mention of obstruction — (Use additional E code to identify drug, if drug induced)
531.51 Chronic or unspecified gastric ulcer with perforation and obstruction — (Use additional E code to identify drug, if drug induced)
531.60 Chronic or unspecified gastric ulcer with hemorrhage and perforation, without mention of obstruction — (Use additional E code to identify drug, if drug induced)
531.61 Chronic or unspecified gastric ulcer with hemorrhage, perforation, and obstruction — (Use additional E code to identify drug, if drug induced)
531.70 Chronic gastric ulcer without mention of hemorrhage, perforation, without mention of obstruction — (Use additional E code to identify drug, if drug induced)
531.71 Chronic gastric ulcer without mention of hemorrhage or perforation, with obstruction — (Use additional E code to identify drug, if drug induced)
531.90 Gastric ulcer, unspecified as acute or chronic, without mention of hemorrhage, perforation, or obstruction — (Use additional E code to identify drug, if drug induced)
531.91 Gastric ulcer, unspecified as acute or chronic, without mention of hemorrhage or perforation, with obstruction — (Use additional E code to identify drug, if drug induced)
533.00 Acute peptic ulcer, unspecified site, with hemorrhage, without mention of obstruction — (Use additional E code to identify drug, if drug induced)
533.01 Acute peptic ulcer, unspecified site, with hemorrhage and obstruction — (Use additional E code to identify drug, if drug induced)
533.10 Acute peptic ulcer, unspecified site, with perforation, without mention of obstruction — (Use additional E code to identify drug, if drug induced)
533.11 Acute peptic ulcer, unspecified site, with perforation and obstruction — (Use additional E code to identify drug, if drug induced)
533.20 Acute peptic ulcer, unspecified site, with hemorrhage and perforation, without mention of obstruction — (Use additional E code to identify drug, if drug induced)
533.21 Acute peptic ulcer, unspecified site, with hemorrhage, perforation, and obstruction — (Use additional E code to identify drug, if drug induced)
533.30 Acute peptic ulcer, unspecified site, without mention of hemorrhage, perforation, or obstruction — (Use additional E code to identify drug, if drug induced)
533.31 Acute peptic ulcer, unspecified site, without mention of hemorrhage and perforation, with obstruction — (Use additional E code to identify drug, if drug induced)
533.40 Chronic or unspecified peptic ulcer, unspecified site, with hemorrhage, without mention of obstruction — (Use additional E code to identify drug, if drug induced)
533.41 Chronic or unspecified peptic ulcer, unspecified site, with hemorrhage and obstruction — (Use additional E code to identify drug, if drug induced)
533.50 Chronic or unspecified peptic ulcer, unspecified site, with perforation, without mention of obstruction — (Use additional E code to identify drug, if drug induced)
533.51 Chronic or unspecified peptic ulcer, unspecified site, with perforation and obstruction — (Use additional E code to identify drug, if drug induced)
533.60 Chronic or unspecified peptic ulcer, unspecified site, with hemorrhage and perforation, without mention of obstruction — (Use additional E code to identify drug, if drug induced)
533.61 Chronic or unspecified peptic ulcer, unspecified site, with hemorrhage, perforation, and obstruction — (Use additional E code to identify drug, if drug induced)
533.70 Chronic peptic ulcer, unspecified site, without mention of hemorrhage, perforation, or obstruction — (Use additional E code to identify drug, if drug induced)
533.71 Chronic peptic ulcer of unspecified site without mention of hemorrhage or perforation, with obstruction — (Use additional E code to identify drug, if drug induced)
533.90 Peptic ulcer, unspecified site, unspecified as acute or chronic, without mention of hemorrhage, perforation, or obstruction — (Use additional E code to identify drug, if drug induced)
533.91 Peptic ulcer, unspecified site, unspecified as acute or chronic, without mention of hemorrhage or perforation, with obstruction — (Use additional E code to identify drug, if drug induced)
863.0 Stomach injury without mention of open wound into cavity
863.1 Stomach injury with open wound into cavity
997.49 Other digestive system complications

ICD-9-CM Procedural

43.7 Partial gastrectomy with anastomosis to jejunum

43633-43634

43633 Gastrectomy, partial, distal; with Roux-en-Y reconstruction
43634 with formation of intestinal pouch

ICD-9-CM Diagnostic

151.1 Malignant neoplasm of pylorus
151.2 Malignant neoplasm of pyloric antrum
151.4 Malignant neoplasm of body of stomach
151.8 Malignant neoplasm of other specified sites of stomach
151.9 Malignant neoplasm of stomach, unspecified site
197.8 Secondary malignant neoplasm of other digestive organs and spleen
209.23 Malignant carcinoid tumor of the stomach — (Code first any associated multiple endocrine neoplasia syndrome: 258.01-258.03)(Use additional code to identify associated endocrine syndrome, as: carcinoid syndrome: 259.2)
209.25 Malignant carcinoid tumor of foregut, not otherwise specified — (Code first any associated multiple endocrine neoplasia syndrome: 258.01-258.03)(Use additional code to identify associated endocrine syndrome, as: carcinoid syndrome: 259.2)

209.29 Malignant carcinoid tumor of other sites — (Code first any associated multiple endocrine neoplasia syndrome: 258.01-258.03)(Use additional code to identify associated endocrine syndrome, as: carcinoid syndrome: 259.2)
209.30 Malignant poorly differentiated neuroendocrine carcinoma, any site — (Code first any associated multiple endocrine neoplasia syndrome: 258.01-258.03)(Use additional code to identify associated endocrine syndrome, as: carcinoid syndrome: 259.2) ▽
209.63 Benign carcinoid tumor of the stomach — (Code first any associated multiple endocrine neoplasia syndrome: 258.01-258.03)(Use additional code to identify associated endocrine syndrome, as: carcinoid syndrome: 259.2)
209.65 Benign carcinoid tumor of foregut, not otherwise specified — (Code first any associated multiple endocrine neoplasia syndrome: 258.01-258.03)(Use additional code to identify associated endocrine syndrome, as: carcinoid syndrome: 259.2)
209.69 Benign carcinoid tumor of other sites — (Code first any associated multiple endocrine neoplasia syndrome: 258.01-258.03)(Use additional code to identify associated endocrine syndrome, as: carcinoid syndrome: 259.2)
211.1 Benign neoplasm of stomach
235.2 Neoplasm of uncertain behavior of stomach, intestines, and rectum
239.0 Neoplasm of unspecified nature of digestive system
531.00 Acute gastric ulcer with hemorrhage, without mention of obstruction — (Use additional E code to identify drug, if drug induced)
531.01 Acute gastric ulcer with hemorrhage and obstruction — (Use additional E code to identify drug, if drug induced)
531.10 Acute gastric ulcer with perforation, without mention of obstruction — (Use additional E code to identify drug, if drug induced)
531.11 Acute gastric ulcer with perforation and obstruction — (Use additional E code to identify drug, if drug induced)
531.20 Acute gastric ulcer with hemorrhage and perforation, without mention of obstruction — (Use additional E code to identify drug, if drug induced)
531.21 Acute gastric ulcer with hemorrhage, perforation, and obstruction — (Use additional E code to identify drug, if drug induced)
531.40 Chronic or unspecified gastric ulcer with hemorrhage, without mention of obstruction — (Use additional E code to identify drug, if drug induced)
531.41 Chronic or unspecified gastric ulcer with hemorrhage and obstruction — (Use additional E code to identify drug, if drug induced)
531.50 Chronic or unspecified gastric ulcer with perforation, without mention of obstruction — (Use additional E code to identify drug, if drug induced)
531.51 Chronic or unspecified gastric ulcer with perforation and obstruction — (Use additional E code to identify drug, if drug induced)
531.60 Chronic or unspecified gastric ulcer with hemorrhage and perforation, without mention of obstruction — (Use additional E code to identify drug, if drug induced)
531.61 Chronic or unspecified gastric ulcer with hemorrhage, perforation, and obstruction — (Use additional E code to identify drug, if drug induced)
531.70 Chronic gastric ulcer without mention of hemorrhage, perforation, without mention of obstruction — (Use additional E code to identify drug, if drug induced)
531.71 Chronic gastric ulcer without mention of hemorrhage or perforation, with obstruction — (Use additional E code to identify drug, if drug induced)
531.90 Gastric ulcer, unspecified as acute or chronic, without mention of hemorrhage, perforation, or obstruction — (Use additional E code to identify drug, if drug induced) ▽
531.91 Gastric ulcer, unspecified as acute or chronic, without mention of hemorrhage or perforation, with obstruction — (Use additional E code to identify drug, if drug induced) ▽
533.00 Acute peptic ulcer, unspecified site, with hemorrhage, without mention of obstruction — (Use additional E code to identify drug, if drug induced) ▽
533.01 Acute peptic ulcer, unspecified site, with hemorrhage and obstruction — (Use additional E code to identify drug, if drug induced) ▽
533.10 Acute peptic ulcer, unspecified site, with perforation, without mention of obstruction — (Use additional E code to identify drug, if drug induced) ▽
533.11 Acute peptic ulcer, unspecified site, with perforation and obstruction — (Use additional E code to identify drug, if drug induced) ▽
533.20 Acute peptic ulcer, unspecified site, with hemorrhage and perforation, without mention of obstruction — (Use additional E code to identify drug, if drug induced) ▽
533.21 Acute peptic ulcer, unspecified site, with hemorrhage, perforation, and obstruction — (Use additional E code to identify drug, if drug induced) ▽
533.30 Acute peptic ulcer, unspecified site, without mention of hemorrhage, perforation, or obstruction — (Use additional E code to identify drug, if drug induced) ▽
533.31 Acute peptic ulcer, unspecified site, without mention of hemorrhage and perforation, with obstruction — (Use additional E code to identify drug, if drug induced) ▽
533.40 Chronic or unspecified peptic ulcer, unspecified site, with hemorrhage, without mention of obstruction — (Use additional E code to identify drug, if drug induced) ▽
533.41 Chronic or unspecified peptic ulcer, unspecified site, with hemorrhage and obstruction — (Use additional E code to identify drug, if drug induced) ▽
533.50 Chronic or unspecified peptic ulcer, unspecified site, with perforation, without mention of obstruction — (Use additional E code to identify drug, if drug induced) ▽
533.51 Chronic or unspecified peptic ulcer, unspecified site, with perforation and obstruction — (Use additional E code to identify drug, if drug induced) ▽
533.60 Chronic or unspecified peptic ulcer, unspecified site, with hemorrhage and perforation, without mention of obstruction — (Use additional E code to identify drug, if drug induced) ▽
533.61 Chronic or unspecified peptic ulcer, unspecified site, with hemorrhage, perforation, and obstruction — (Use additional E code to identify drug, if drug induced) ▽
533.70 Chronic peptic ulcer, unspecified site, without mention of hemorrhage, perforation, or obstruction — (Use additional E code to identify drug, if drug induced) ▽
533.71 Chronic peptic ulcer of unspecified site without mention of hemorrhage or perforation, with obstruction — (Use additional E code to identify drug, if drug induced) ▽
533.90 Peptic ulcer, unspecified site, unspecified as acute or chronic, without mention of hemorrhage, perforation, or obstruction — (Use additional E code to identify drug, if drug induced) ▽
533.91 Peptic ulcer, unspecified site, unspecified as acute or chronic, without mention of hemorrhage or perforation, with obstruction — (Use additional E code to identify drug, if drug induced) ▽
863.0 Stomach injury without mention of open wound into cavity
863.1 Stomach injury with open wound into cavity
997.49 Other digestive system complications

ICD-9-CM Procedural

43.6 Partial gastrectomy with anastomosis to duodenum
43.7 Partial gastrectomy with anastomosis to jejunum

43640-43641

43640 Vagotomy including pyloroplasty, with or without gastrostomy; truncal or selective
43641 parietal cell (highly selective)

ICD-9-CM Diagnostic

151.1 Malignant neoplasm of pylorus
197.8 Secondary malignant neoplasm of other digestive organs and spleen
209.23 Malignant carcinoid tumor of the stomach — (Code first any associated multiple endocrine neoplasia syndrome: 258.01-258.03)(Use additional code to identify associated endocrine syndrome, as: carcinoid syndrome: 259.2)
230.2 Carcinoma in situ of stomach
278.01 Morbid obesity — (Use additional code to identify Body Mass Index (BMI), if known: V85.0-V85.54)
531.00 Acute gastric ulcer with hemorrhage, without mention of obstruction — (Use additional E code to identify drug, if drug induced)
531.01 Acute gastric ulcer with hemorrhage and obstruction — (Use additional E code to identify drug, if drug induced)
531.10 Acute gastric ulcer with perforation, without mention of obstruction — (Use additional E code to identify drug, if drug induced)
531.11 Acute gastric ulcer with perforation and obstruction — (Use additional E code to identify drug, if drug induced)
531.20 Acute gastric ulcer with hemorrhage and perforation, without mention of obstruction — (Use additional E code to identify drug, if drug induced)
531.40 Chronic or unspecified gastric ulcer with hemorrhage, without mention of obstruction — (Use additional E code to identify drug, if drug induced)

531.41 Chronic or unspecified gastric ulcer with hemorrhage and obstruction — (Use additional E code to identify drug, if drug induced)

531.50 Chronic or unspecified gastric ulcer with perforation, without mention of obstruction — (Use additional E code to identify drug, if drug induced)

531.51 Chronic or unspecified gastric ulcer with perforation and obstruction — (Use additional E code to identify drug, if drug induced)

531.60 Chronic or unspecified gastric ulcer with hemorrhage and perforation, without mention of obstruction — (Use additional E code to identify drug, if drug induced)

531.61 Chronic or unspecified gastric ulcer with hemorrhage, perforation, and obstruction — (Use additional E code to identify drug, if drug induced)

531.70 Chronic gastric ulcer without mention of hemorrhage, perforation, without mention of obstruction — (Use additional E code to identify drug, if drug induced)

531.71 Chronic gastric ulcer without mention of hemorrhage or perforation, with obstruction — (Use additional E code to identify drug, if drug induced)

531.90 Gastric ulcer, unspecified as acute or chronic, without mention of hemorrhage, perforation, or obstruction — (Use additional E code to identify drug, if drug induced)

531.91 Gastric ulcer, unspecified as acute or chronic, without mention of hemorrhage or perforation, with obstruction — (Use additional E code to identify drug, if drug induced)

532.00 Acute duodenal ulcer with hemorrhage, without mention of obstruction — (Use additional E code to identify drug, if drug induced)

532.01 Acute duodenal ulcer with hemorrhage and obstruction — (Use additional E code to identify drug, if drug induced)

532.10 Acute duodenal ulcer with perforation, without mention of obstruction — (Use additional E code to identify drug, if drug induced)

532.11 Acute duodenal ulcer with perforation and obstruction — (Use additional E code to identify drug, if drug induced)

532.20 Acute duodenal ulcer with hemorrhage and perforation, without mention of obstruction — (Use additional E code to identify drug, if drug induced)

532.21 Acute duodenal ulcer with hemorrhage, perforation, and obstruction — (Use additional E code to identify drug, if drug induced)

532.30 Acute duodenal ulcer without mention of hemorrhage, perforation, or obstruction — (Use additional E code to identify drug, if drug induced)

532.31 Acute duodenal ulcer without mention of hemorrhage or perforation, with obstruction — (Use additional E code to identify drug, if drug induced)

532.40 Duodenal ulcer, chronic or unspecified, with hemorrhage, without mention of obstruction — (Use additional E code to identify drug, if drug induced)

532.41 Chronic or unspecified duodenal ulcer with hemorrhage and obstruction — (Use additional E code to identify drug, if drug induced)

532.50 Chronic or unspecified duodenal ulcer with perforation, without mention of obstruction — (Use additional E code to identify drug, if drug induced)

532.51 Chronic or unspecified duodenal ulcer with perforation and obstruction — (Use additional E code to identify drug, if drug induced)

532.60 Chronic or unspecified duodenal ulcer with hemorrhage and perforation, without mention of obstruction — (Use additional E code to identify drug, if drug induced)

532.61 Chronic or unspecified duodenal ulcer with hemorrhage, perforation, and obstruction — (Use additional E code to identify drug, if drug induced)

532.71 Chronic duodenal ulcer without mention of hemorrhage or perforation, with obstruction — (Use additional E code to identify drug, if drug induced)

532.90 Duodenal ulcer, unspecified as acute or chronic, without hemorrhage, perforation, or obstruction — (Use additional E code to identify drug, if drug induced)

532.91 Duodenal ulcer, unspecified as acute or chronic, without mention of hemorrhage or perforation, with obstruction — (Use additional E code to identify drug, if drug induced)

533.00 Acute peptic ulcer, unspecified site, with hemorrhage, without mention of obstruction — (Use additional E code to identify drug, if drug induced)

533.01 Acute peptic ulcer, unspecified site, with hemorrhage and obstruction — (Use additional E code to identify drug, if drug induced)

533.10 Acute peptic ulcer, unspecified site, with perforation, without mention of obstruction — (Use additional E code to identify drug, if drug induced)

533.11 Acute peptic ulcer, unspecified site, with perforation and obstruction — (Use additional E code to identify drug, if drug induced)

533.20 Acute peptic ulcer, unspecified site, with hemorrhage and perforation, without mention of obstruction — (Use additional E code to identify drug, if drug induced)

533.21 Acute peptic ulcer, unspecified site, with hemorrhage, perforation, and obstruction — (Use additional E code to identify drug, if drug induced)

533.30 Acute peptic ulcer, unspecified site, without mention of hemorrhage, perforation, or obstruction — (Use additional E code to identify drug, if drug induced)

533.31 Acute peptic ulcer, unspecified site, without mention of hemorrhage and perforation, with obstruction — (Use additional E code to identify drug, if drug induced)

533.40 Chronic or unspecified peptic ulcer, unspecified site, with hemorrhage, without mention of obstruction — (Use additional E code to identify drug, if drug induced)

533.41 Chronic or unspecified peptic ulcer, unspecified site, with hemorrhage and obstruction — (Use additional E code to identify drug, if drug induced)

533.50 Chronic or unspecified peptic ulcer, unspecified site, with perforation, without mention of obstruction — (Use additional E code to identify drug, if drug induced)

533.51 Chronic or unspecified peptic ulcer, unspecified site, with perforation and obstruction — (Use additional E code to identify drug, if drug induced)

533.60 Chronic or unspecified peptic ulcer, unspecified site, with hemorrhage and perforation, without mention of obstruction — (Use additional E code to identify drug, if drug induced)

533.61 Chronic or unspecified peptic ulcer, unspecified site, with hemorrhage, perforation, and obstruction — (Use additional E code to identify drug, if drug induced)

533.70 Chronic peptic ulcer, unspecified site, without mention of hemorrhage, perforation, or obstruction — (Use additional E code to identify drug, if drug induced)

533.71 Chronic peptic ulcer of unspecified site without mention of hemorrhage or perforation, with obstruction — (Use additional E code to identify drug, if drug induced)

533.90 Peptic ulcer, unspecified site, unspecified as acute or chronic, without mention of hemorrhage, perforation, or obstruction — (Use additional E code to identify drug, if drug induced)

533.91 Peptic ulcer, unspecified site, unspecified as acute or chronic, without mention of hemorrhage or perforation, with obstruction — (Use additional E code to identify drug, if drug induced)

536.8 Dyspepsia and other specified disorders of function of stomach

536.9 Unspecified functional disorder of stomach

537.0 Acquired hypertrophic pyloric stenosis

789.00 Abdominal pain, unspecified site

789.06 Abdominal pain, epigastric

789.9 Other symptoms involving abdomen and pelvis

ICD-9-CM Procedural

43.19 Other gastrostomy

44.01 Truncal vagotomy

44.02 Highly selective vagotomy

44.03 Other selective vagotomy

44.29 Other pyloroplasty

43644-43645

43644 Laparoscopy, surgical, gastric restrictive procedure; with gastric bypass and Roux-en-Y gastroenterostomy (roux limb 150 cm or less)

43645 with gastric bypass and small intestine reconstruction to limit absorption

ICD-9-CM Diagnostic

244.9 Unspecified hypothyroidism

253.8 Other disorders of the pituitary and other syndromes of diencephalohypophyseal origin

255.8 Other specified disorders of adrenal glands

259.9 Unspecified endocrine disorder

278.00 Obesity, unspecified — (Use additional code to identify Body Mass Index (BMI), if known: V85.0-V85.54) (Use additional code to identify any associated intellectual disabilities)

278.01 Morbid obesity — (Use additional code to identify Body Mass Index (BMI), if known: V85.0-V85.54)

ICD-9-CM Procedural

44.38 Laparoscopic gastroenterostomy

43647-43648

43647 Laparoscopy, surgical; implantation or replacement of gastric neurostimulator electrodes, antrum

43648 revision or removal of gastric neurostimulator electrodes, antrum

ICD-9-CM Diagnostic

249.60 Secondary diabetes mellitus with neurological manifestations, not stated as uncontrolled, or unspecified — (Use additional code to identify manifestation: 337.1, 353.5, 354.0-355.9, 357.2, 536.3, 713.5) (Use additional code to identify any associated insulin use: V58.67)

249.61 Secondary diabetes mellitus with neurological manifestations, uncontrolled — (Use additional code to identify manifestation: 337.1, 353.5, 354.0-355.9, 357.2, 536.3, 713.5) (Use additional code to identify any associated insulin use: V58.67)

250.60 Diabetes with neurological manifestations, type II or unspecified type, not stated as uncontrolled — (Use additional code to identify manifestation: 337.1, 353.5, 354.0-355.9, 357.2, 536.3, 713.5)

250.61 Diabetes with neurological manifestations, type I [juvenile type], not stated as uncontrolled — (Use additional code to identify manifestation: 337.1, 353.5, 354.0-355.9, 357.2, 536.3, 713.5)

250.62 Diabetes with neurological manifestations, type II or unspecified type, uncontrolled — (Use additional code to identify manifestation: 337.1, 353.5, 354.0-355.9, 357.2, 536.3, 713.5)

250.63 Diabetes with neurological manifestations, type I [juvenile type], uncontrolled — (Use additional code to identify manifestation: 337.1, 353.5, 354.0-355.9, 357.2, 536.3, 713.5)

278.00 Obesity, unspecified — (Use additional code to identify Body Mass Index (BMI), if known: V85.0-V85.54) (Use additional code to identify any associated intellectual disabilities) ▼

278.01 Morbid obesity — (Use additional code to identify Body Mass Index (BMI), if known: V85.0-V85.54)

536.3 Gastroparesis — (Code first underlying disease, if known, as: 249.6, 250.6)

996.79 Other complications due to other internal prosthetic device, implant, and graft — (Use additional code to identify complication: 338.18-338.19, 338.28-338.29)

V53.59 Fitting and adjustment of other gastrointestinal appliance and device

ICD-9-CM Procedural

04.92 Implantation or replacement of peripheral neurostimulator lead(s)

04.93 Removal of peripheral neurostimulator lead(s)

43651-43652

43651 Laparoscopy, surgical; transection of vagus nerves, truncal

43652 transection of vagus nerves, selective or highly selective

ICD-9-CM Diagnostic

150.2 Malignant neoplasm of abdominal esophagus

151.1 Malignant neoplasm of pylorus

151.2 Malignant neoplasm of pyloric antrum

151.3 Malignant neoplasm of fundus of stomach

151.4 Malignant neoplasm of body of stomach

151.5 Malignant neoplasm of lesser curvature of stomach, unspecified ▼

151.6 Malignant neoplasm of greater curvature of stomach, unspecified ▼

151.8 Malignant neoplasm of other specified sites of stomach

151.9 Malignant neoplasm of stomach, unspecified site ▼

152.0 Malignant neoplasm of duodenum

152.1 Malignant neoplasm of jejunum

155.0 Malignant neoplasm of liver, primary

209.01 Malignant carcinoid tumor of the duodenum — (Code first any associated multiple endocrine neoplasia syndrome: 258.01-258.03)(Use additional code to identify associated endocrine syndrome, as: carcinoid syndrome: 259.2)

209.02 Malignant carcinoid tumor of the jejunum — (Code first any associated multiple endocrine neoplasia syndrome: 258.01-258.03)(Use additional code to identify associated endocrine syndrome, as: carcinoid syndrome: 259.2)

209.23 Malignant carcinoid tumor of the stomach — (Code first any associated multiple endocrine neoplasia syndrome: 258.01-258.03)(Use additional code to identify associated endocrine syndrome, as: carcinoid syndrome: 259.2)

209.25 Malignant carcinoid tumor of foregut, not otherwise specified — (Code first any associated multiple endocrine neoplasia syndrome: 258.01-258.03)(Use additional code to identify associated endocrine syndrome, as: carcinoid syndrome: 259.2)

209.63 Benign carcinoid tumor of the stomach — (Code first any associated multiple endocrine neoplasia syndrome: 258.01-258.03)(Use additional code to identify associated endocrine syndrome, as: carcinoid syndrome: 259.2)

209.65 Benign carcinoid tumor of foregut, not otherwise specified — (Code first any associated multiple endocrine neoplasia syndrome: 258.01-258.03)(Use additional code to identify associated endocrine syndrome, as: carcinoid syndrome: 259.2)

278.01 Morbid obesity — (Use additional code to identify Body Mass Index (BMI), if known: V85.0-V85.54)

352.3 Disorders of pneumogastric (10th) nerve

531.70 Chronic gastric ulcer without mention of hemorrhage, perforation, without mention of obstruction — (Use additional E code to identify drug, if drug induced)

532.70 Chronic duodenal ulcer without mention of hemorrhage, perforation, or obstruction — (Use additional E code to identify drug, if drug induced)

533.70 Chronic peptic ulcer, unspecified site, without mention of hemorrhage, perforation, or obstruction — (Use additional E code to identify drug, if drug induced) ▼

536.8 Dyspepsia and other specified disorders of function of stomach

ICD-9-CM Procedural

44.01 Truncal vagotomy

44.02 Highly selective vagotomy

44.03 Other selective vagotomy

43653

43653 Laparoscopy, surgical; gastrostomy, without construction of gastric tube (eg, Stamm procedure) (separate procedure)

ICD-9-CM Diagnostic

150.1 Malignant neoplasm of thoracic esophagus

150.2 Malignant neoplasm of abdominal esophagus

150.3 Malignant neoplasm of upper third of esophagus

150.4 Malignant neoplasm of middle third of esophagus

150.5 Malignant neoplasm of lower third of esophagus

150.8 Malignant neoplasm of other specified part of esophagus

150.9 Malignant neoplasm of esophagus, unspecified site ▼

151.0 Malignant neoplasm of cardia

151.1 Malignant neoplasm of pylorus

151.2 Malignant neoplasm of pyloric antrum

151.3 Malignant neoplasm of fundus of stomach

151.4 Malignant neoplasm of body of stomach

151.5 Malignant neoplasm of lesser curvature of stomach, unspecified ▼

151.6 Malignant neoplasm of greater curvature of stomach, unspecified ▼

151.8 Malignant neoplasm of other specified sites of stomach

151.9 Malignant neoplasm of stomach, unspecified site ▼

152.0 Malignant neoplasm of duodenum

152.1 Malignant neoplasm of jejunum

152.2 Malignant neoplasm of ileum

161.9 Malignant neoplasm of larynx, unspecified site ▼

197.4 Secondary malignant neoplasm of small intestine including duodenum

197.8 Secondary malignant neoplasm of other digestive organs and spleen

198.89 Secondary malignant neoplasm of other specified sites

209.01 Malignant carcinoid tumor of the duodenum — (Code first any associated multiple endocrine neoplasia syndrome: 258.01-258.03)(Use additional code to identify associated endocrine syndrome, as: carcinoid syndrome: 259.2)

209.02 Malignant carcinoid tumor of the jejunum — (Code first any associated multiple endocrine neoplasia syndrome: 258.01-258.03)(Use additional code to identify associated endocrine syndrome, as: carcinoid syndrome: 259.2)

209.23 Malignant carcinoid tumor of the stomach — (Code first any associated multiple endocrine neoplasia syndrome: 258.01-258.03)(Use additional code to identify associated endocrine syndrome, as: carcinoid syndrome: 259.2)

209.25 Malignant carcinoid tumor of foregut, not otherwise specified — (Code first any associated multiple endocrine neoplasia syndrome: 258.01-258.03)(Use additional code to identify associated endocrine syndrome, as: carcinoid syndrome: 259.2)

209.63 Benign carcinoid tumor of the stomach — (Code first any associated multiple endocrine neoplasia syndrome: 258.01-258.03)(Use additional code to identify associated endocrine syndrome, as: carcinoid syndrome: 259.2)

209.65 Benign carcinoid tumor of foregut, not otherwise specified — (Code first any associated multiple endocrine neoplasia syndrome: 258.01-258.03)(Use additional code to identify associated endocrine syndrome, as: carcinoid syndrome: 259.2)

211.1 Benign neoplasm of stomach

230.2 Carcinoma in situ of stomach

239.89 Neoplasms of unspecified nature, other specified sites

261 Nutritional marasmus

262 Other severe protein-calorie malnutrition

263.0 Malnutrition of moderate degree

263.1 Malnutrition of mild degree

263.2 Arrested development following protein-calorie malnutrition

263.8 Other protein-calorie malnutrition

276.50 Volume depletion, unspecified — (Use additional code to identify any associated intellectual disabilities) ▽

276.51 Dehydration — (Use additional code to identify any associated intellectual disabilities)

276.52 Hypovolemia — (Use additional code to identify any associated intellectual disabilities)

307.1 Anorexia nervosa

436 Acute, but ill-defined, cerebrovascular disease — (Use additional code to identify presence of hypertension) ▽

519.00 Unspecified tracheostomy complication — (Use additional code to identify infectious organism) ▽

519.01 Infection of tracheostomy — (Use additional code to identify type of infection: 038.0-038.9, 682.1. Use additional code to identify organism: 041.00-041.9)

519.02 Mechanical complication of tracheostomy

519.09 Other tracheostomy complications — (Use additional code to identify infectious organism)

530.3 Stricture and stenosis of esophagus

530.4 Perforation of esophagus

530.5 Dyskinesia of esophagus

530.81 Esophageal reflux

531.00 Acute gastric ulcer with hemorrhage, without mention of obstruction — (Use additional E code to identify drug, if drug induced)

531.01 Acute gastric ulcer with hemorrhage and obstruction — (Use additional E code to identify drug, if drug induced)

531.10 Acute gastric ulcer with perforation, without mention of obstruction — (Use additional E code to identify drug, if drug induced)

531.11 Acute gastric ulcer with perforation and obstruction — (Use additional E code to identify drug, if drug induced)

531.20 Acute gastric ulcer with hemorrhage and perforation, without mention of obstruction — (Use additional E code to identify drug, if drug induced)

531.21 Acute gastric ulcer with hemorrhage, perforation, and obstruction — (Use additional E code to identify drug, if drug induced)

531.30 Acute gastric ulcer without mention of hemorrhage, perforation, or obstruction — (Use additional E code to identify drug, if drug induced)

531.31 Acute gastric ulcer without mention of hemorrhage or perforation, with obstruction — (Use additional E code to identify drug, if drug induced)

531.40 Chronic or unspecified gastric ulcer with hemorrhage, without mention of obstruction — (Use additional E code to identify drug, if drug induced)

531.41 Chronic or unspecified gastric ulcer with hemorrhage and obstruction — (Use additional E code to identify drug, if drug induced)

531.50 Chronic or unspecified gastric ulcer with perforation, without mention of obstruction — (Use additional E code to identify drug, if drug induced)

531.51 Chronic or unspecified gastric ulcer with perforation and obstruction — (Use additional E code to identify drug, if drug induced)

531.60 Chronic or unspecified gastric ulcer with hemorrhage and perforation, without mention of obstruction — (Use additional E code to identify drug, if drug induced)

531.61 Chronic or unspecified gastric ulcer with hemorrhage, perforation, and obstruction — (Use additional E code to identify drug, if drug induced)

531.70 Chronic gastric ulcer without mention of hemorrhage, perforation, without mention of obstruction — (Use additional E code to identify drug, if drug induced)

531.71 Chronic gastric ulcer without mention of hemorrhage or perforation, with obstruction — (Use additional E code to identify drug, if drug induced)

531.90 Gastric ulcer, unspecified as acute or chronic, without mention of hemorrhage, perforation, or obstruction — (Use additional E code to identify drug, if drug induced) ▽

531.91 Gastric ulcer, unspecified as acute or chronic, without mention of hemorrhage or perforation, with obstruction — (Use additional E code to identify drug, if drug induced) ▽

532.00 Acute duodenal ulcer with hemorrhage, without mention of obstruction — (Use additional E code to identify drug, if drug induced)

532.01 Acute duodenal ulcer with hemorrhage and obstruction — (Use additional E code to identify drug, if drug induced)

532.10 Acute duodenal ulcer with perforation, without mention of obstruction — (Use additional E code to identify drug, if drug induced)

532.11 Acute duodenal ulcer with perforation and obstruction — (Use additional E code to identify drug, if drug induced)

532.20 Acute duodenal ulcer with hemorrhage and perforation, without mention of obstruction — (Use additional E code to identify drug, if drug induced)

532.21 Acute duodenal ulcer with hemorrhage, perforation, and obstruction — (Use additional E code to identify drug, if drug induced)

532.30 Acute duodenal ulcer without mention of hemorrhage, perforation, or obstruction — (Use additional E code to identify drug, if drug induced)

532.31 Acute duodenal ulcer without mention of hemorrhage or perforation, with obstruction — (Use additional E code to identify drug, if drug induced)

532.40 Duodenal ulcer, chronic or unspecified, with hemorrhage, without mention of obstruction — (Use additional E code to identify drug, if drug induced)

532.41 Chronic or unspecified duodenal ulcer with hemorrhage and obstruction — (Use additional E code to identify drug, if drug induced)

532.50 Chronic or unspecified duodenal ulcer with perforation, without mention of obstruction — (Use additional E code to identify drug, if drug induced)

532.51 Chronic or unspecified duodenal ulcer with perforation and obstruction — (Use additional E code to identify drug, if drug induced)

532.60 Chronic or unspecified duodenal ulcer with hemorrhage and perforation, without mention of obstruction — (Use additional E code to identify drug, if drug induced)

532.61 Chronic or unspecified duodenal ulcer with hemorrhage, perforation, and obstruction — (Use additional E code to identify drug, if drug induced)

532.70 Chronic duodenal ulcer without mention of hemorrhage, perforation, or obstruction — (Use additional E code to identify drug, if drug induced)

532.71 Chronic duodenal ulcer without mention of hemorrhage or perforation, with obstruction — (Use additional E code to identify drug, if drug induced)

532.90 Duodenal ulcer, unspecified as acute or chronic, without hemorrhage, perforation, or obstruction — (Use additional E code to identify drug, if drug induced) ▽

532.91 Duodenal ulcer, unspecified as acute or chronic, without mention of hemorrhage or perforation, with obstruction — (Use additional E code to identify drug, if drug induced) ▽

533.00 Acute peptic ulcer, unspecified site, with hemorrhage, without mention of obstruction — (Use additional E code to identify drug, if drug induced) ▽
533.01 Acute peptic ulcer, unspecified site, with hemorrhage and obstruction — (Use additional E code to identify drug, if drug induced) ▽
533.10 Acute peptic ulcer, unspecified site, with perforation, without mention of obstruction — (Use additional E code to identify drug, if drug induced) ▽
533.11 Acute peptic ulcer, unspecified site, with perforation and obstruction — (Use additional E code to identify drug, if drug induced) ▽
533.20 Acute peptic ulcer, unspecified site, with hemorrhage and perforation, without mention of obstruction — (Use additional E code to identify drug, if drug induced) ▽
533.21 Acute peptic ulcer, unspecified site, with hemorrhage, perforation, and obstruction — (Use additional E code to identify drug, if drug induced) ▽
533.30 Acute peptic ulcer, unspecified site, without mention of hemorrhage, perforation, or obstruction — (Use additional E code to identify drug, if drug induced) ▽
533.40 Chronic or unspecified peptic ulcer, unspecified site, with hemorrhage, without mention of obstruction — (Use additional E code to identify drug, if drug induced) ▽
533.41 Chronic or unspecified peptic ulcer, unspecified site, with hemorrhage and obstruction — (Use additional E code to identify drug, if drug induced) ▽
533.50 Chronic or unspecified peptic ulcer, unspecified site, with perforation, without mention of obstruction — (Use additional E code to identify drug, if drug induced) ▽
533.51 Chronic or unspecified peptic ulcer, unspecified site, with perforation and obstruction — (Use additional E code to identify drug, if drug induced) ▽
535.50 Unspecified gastritis and gastroduodenitis without mention of hemorrhage ▽
535.70 Eosinophilic gastritis without mention of hemorrhage
535.71 Eosinophilic gastritis with hemorrhage
536.9 Unspecified functional disorder of stomach ▽
537.89 Other specified disorder of stomach and duodenum
578.9 Hemorrhage of gastrointestinal tract, unspecified ▽
707.9 Chronic ulcer of unspecified site ▽
750.5 Congenital hypertrophic pyloric stenosis
750.7 Other specified congenital anomalies of stomach
751.1 Congenital atresia and stenosis of small intestine
783.0 Anorexia
783.3 Feeding difficulties and mismanagement
783.7 Adult failure to thrive
787.01 Nausea with vomiting
787.04 Bilious emesis
787.20 Dysphagia, unspecified ▽
787.21 Dysphagia, oral phase
787.22 Dysphagia, oropharyngeal phase
787.23 Dysphagia, pharyngeal phase
787.24 Dysphagia, pharyngoesophageal phase
787.29 Other dysphagia
854.06 Intracranial injury of other and unspecified nature, without mention of open intracranial wound, loss of consciousness of unspecified duration ▽
994.2 Effects of hunger
997.49 Other digestive system complications

ICD-9-CM Procedural

43.19 Other gastrostomy

43752

43752 Naso- or oro-gastric tube placement, requiring physician's skill and fluoroscopic guidance (includes fluoroscopy, image documentation and report)

ICD-9-CM Diagnostic

141.0 Malignant neoplasm of base of tongue
141.1 Malignant neoplasm of dorsal surface of tongue
141.2 Malignant neoplasm of tip and lateral border of tongue
141.3 Malignant neoplasm of ventral surface of tongue
141.4 Malignant neoplasm of anterior two-thirds of tongue, part unspecified ▽
141.8 Malignant neoplasm of other sites of tongue
141.9 Malignant neoplasm of tongue, unspecified site ▽
149.0 Malignant neoplasm of pharynx, unspecified ▽
149.1 Malignant neoplasm of Waldeyer's ring
149.8 Malignant neoplasm of other sites within the lip and oral cavity
149.9 Malignant neoplasm of ill-defined sites of lip and oral cavity
150.0 Malignant neoplasm of cervical esophagus
150.1 Malignant neoplasm of thoracic esophagus
150.2 Malignant neoplasm of abdominal esophagus
150.3 Malignant neoplasm of upper third of esophagus
150.4 Malignant neoplasm of middle third of esophagus
150.5 Malignant neoplasm of lower third of esophagus
150.8 Malignant neoplasm of other specified part of esophagus
150.9 Malignant neoplasm of esophagus, unspecified site ▽
151.0 Malignant neoplasm of cardia
151.1 Malignant neoplasm of pylorus
151.2 Malignant neoplasm of pyloric antrum
151.3 Malignant neoplasm of fundus of stomach
151.4 Malignant neoplasm of body of stomach
151.5 Malignant neoplasm of lesser curvature of stomach, unspecified ▽
151.6 Malignant neoplasm of greater curvature of stomach, unspecified ▽
151.8 Malignant neoplasm of other specified sites of stomach
151.9 Malignant neoplasm of stomach, unspecified site ▽
161.9 Malignant neoplasm of larynx, unspecified site ▽
197.8 Secondary malignant neoplasm of other digestive organs and spleen
199.1 Other malignant neoplasm of unspecified site
203.00 Multiple myeloma, without mention of having achieved remission
209.23 Malignant carcinoid tumor of the stomach — (Code first any associated multiple endocrine neoplasia syndrome: 258.01-258.03)(Use additional code to identify associated endocrine syndrome, as: carcinoid syndrome: 259.2)
209.25 Malignant carcinoid tumor of foregut, not otherwise specified — (Code first any associated multiple endocrine neoplasia syndrome: 258.01-258.03)(Use additional code to identify associated endocrine syndrome, as: carcinoid syndrome: 259.2)
209.63 Benign carcinoid tumor of the stomach — (Code first any associated multiple endocrine neoplasia syndrome: 258.01-258.03)(Use additional code to identify associated endocrine syndrome, as: carcinoid syndrome: 259.2)
209.65 Benign carcinoid tumor of foregut, not otherwise specified — (Code first any associated multiple endocrine neoplasia syndrome: 258.01-258.03)(Use additional code to identify associated endocrine syndrome, as: carcinoid syndrome: 259.2)
210.9 Benign neoplasm of pharynx, unspecified ▽
235.5 Neoplasm of uncertain behavior of other and unspecified digestive organs ▽
249.30 Secondary diabetes mellitus with other coma, not stated as uncontrolled, or unspecified — (Use additional code to identify any associated insulin use: V58.67)
249.31 Secondary diabetes mellitus with other coma, uncontrolled — (Use additional code to identify any associated insulin use: V58.67)
250.30 Diabetes with other coma, type II or unspecified type, not stated as uncontrolled
250.31 Diabetes with other coma, type I [juvenile type], not stated as uncontrolled
250.32 Diabetes with other coma, type II or unspecified type, uncontrolled
250.33 Diabetes with other coma, type I [juvenile type], uncontrolled
260 Kwashiorkor
261 Nutritional marasmus
262 Other severe protein-calorie malnutrition
330.8 Other specified cerebral degenerations in childhood — (Use additional code to identify associated intellectual disabilities)
330.9 Unspecified cerebral degeneration in childhood — (Use additional code to identify associated intellectual disabilities) ▽
335.20 Amyotrophic lateral sclerosis
348.1 Anoxic brain damage — (Use additional E code to identify cause)
348.82 Brain death

436 Acute, but ill-defined, cerebrovascular disease — (Use additional code to identify presence of hypertension) ▽
478.6 Edema of larynx
530.11 Reflux esophagitis — (Use additional E code to identify cause, if induced by chemical)
530.12 Acute esophagitis — (Use additional E code to identify cause, if induced by chemical)
530.13 Eosinophilic esophagitis
530.19 Other esophagitis — (Use additional E code to identify cause, if induced by chemical)
530.20 Ulcer of esophagus without bleeding — (Use additional E code to identify cause, if induced by chemical or drug)
530.21 Ulcer of esophagus with bleeding — (Use additional E code to identify cause, if induced by chemical or drug)
530.3 Stricture and stenosis of esophagus
530.4 Perforation of esophagus
530.5 Dyskinesia of esophagus
530.6 Diverticulum of esophagus, acquired
530.7 Gastroesophageal laceration-hemorrhage syndrome
530.81 Esophageal reflux
530.82 Esophageal hemorrhage
530.83 Esophageal leukoplakia
530.84 Tracheoesophageal fistula
530.85 Barrett's esophagus
530.89 Other specified disorder of the esophagus
536.8 Dyspepsia and other specified disorders of function of stomach
750.3 Congenital tracheoesophageal fistula, esophageal atresia and stenosis
779.34 Failure to thrive in newborn
780.01 Coma
783.0 Anorexia
783.21 Loss of weight — (Use additional code to identify Body Mass Index (BMI), if known: V85.0-V85.54)
783.22 Underweight — (Use additional code to identify Body Mass Index (BMI), if known: V85.0-V85.54)
783.3 Feeding difficulties and mismanagement
783.40 Lack of normal physiological development, unspecified ▽
783.41 Failure to thrive
783.7 Adult failure to thrive
787.01 Nausea with vomiting
787.02 Nausea alone
787.03 Vomiting alone
787.04 Bilious emesis
787.20 Dysphagia, unspecified ▽
787.21 Dysphagia, oral phase
787.22 Dysphagia, oropharyngeal phase
787.23 Dysphagia, pharyngeal phase
787.24 Dysphagia, pharyngoesophageal phase
787.29 Other dysphagia
789.00 Abdominal pain, unspecified site ▽
854.00 Intracranial injury of other and unspecified nature, without mention of open intracranial wound, unspecified state of consciousness ▽
854.05 Intracranial injury of other and unspecified nature, without mention of open intracranial wound, prolonged (more than 24 hours) loss of consciousness, without return to pre-existing conscious level ▽
959.01 Head injury, unspecified ▽
998.59 Other postoperative infection — (Use additional code to identify infection)
V10.00 Personal history of malignant neoplasm of unspecified site in gastrointestinal tract ▽
V10.01 Personal history of malignant neoplasm of tongue
V10.02 Personal history of malignant neoplasm of other and unspecified parts of oral cavity and pharynx ▽
V10.03 Personal history of malignant neoplasm of esophagus
V10.21 Personal history of malignant neoplasm of larynx
V85.0 Body Mass Index less than 19, adult

ICD-9-CM Procedural

96.06 Insertion of Sengstaken tube
96.07 Insertion of other (naso-)gastric tube
96.6 Enteral infusion of concentrated nutritional substances

HCPCS Level II Supplies & Services

A4305 Disposable drug delivery system, flow rate of 50 ml or greater per hour

43753

43753 Gastric intubation and aspiration(s) therapeutic, necessitating physician's skill (eg, for gastrointestinal hemorrhage), including lavage if performed

ICD-9-CM Diagnostic

960.0 Poisoning by penicillins — (Use additional code to specify the effects of poisoning)
960.1 Poisoning by antifungal antibiotics — (Use additional code to specify the effects of poisoning)
960.2 Poisoning by chloramphenicol group — (Use additional code to specify the effects of poisoning)
960.3 Poisoning by erythromycin and other macrolides — (Use additional code to specify the effects of poisoning)
960.4 Poisoning by tetracycline group — (Use additional code to specify the effects of poisoning)
960.5 Poisoning of cephalosporin group — (Use additional code to specify the effects of poisoning)
960.6 Poisoning of antimycobacterial antibiotics — (Use additional code to specify the effects of poisoning)
960.7 Poisoning by antineoplastic antibiotics — (Use additional code to specify the effects of poisoning)
960.8 Poisoning by other specified antibiotics — (Use additional code to specify the effects of poisoning)
960.9 Poisoning by unspecified antibiotic — (Use additional code to specify the effects of poisoning) ▽
961.0 Poisoning by sulfonamides — (Use additional code to specify the effects of poisoning)
961.1 Poisoning by arsenical anti-infectives — (Use additional code to specify the effects of poisoning)
961.2 Poisoning by heavy metal anti-infectives — (Use additional code to specify the effects of poisoning)
961.3 Poisoning by quinoline and hydroxyquinoline derivatives — (Use additional code to specify the effects of poisoning)
961.4 Poisoning by antimalarials and drugs acting on other blood protozoa — (Use additional code to specify the effects of poisoning)
961.5 Poisoning by other antiprotozoal drugs — (Use additional code to specify the effects of poisoning)
961.6 Poisoning by anthelmintics — (Use additional code to specify the effects of poisoning)
961.7 Poisoning by antiviral drugs — (Use additional code to specify the effects of poisoning)
961.8 Poisoning by other antimycobacterial drugs — (Use additional code to specify the effects of poisoning)
961.9 Poisoning by other and unspecified anti-infectives — (Use additional code to specify the effects of poisoning) ▽
962.0 Poisoning by adrenal cortical steroids — (Use additional code to specify the effects of poisoning)
962.1 Poisoning by androgens and anabolic congeners — (Use additional code to specify the effects of poisoning)
962.2 Poisoning by ovarian hormones and synthetic substitutes — (Use additional code to specify the effects of poisoning)
962.3 Poisoning by insulins and antidiabetic agents — (Use additional code to specify the effects of poisoning)
962.4 Poisoning by anterior pituitary hormones — (Use additional code to specify the effects of poisoning)
962.5 Poisoning by posterior pituitary hormones — (Use additional code to specify the effects of poisoning)

962.6 Poisoning by parathyroid and parathyroid derivatives — (Use additional code to specify the effects of poisoning)

962.7 Poisoning by thyroid and thyroid derivatives — (Use additional code to specify the effects of poisoning)

962.8 Poisoning by antithyroid agents — (Use additional code to specify the effects of poisoning)

962.9 Poisoning by other and unspecified hormones and synthetic substitutes — (Use additional code to specify the effects of poisoning) ▽

963.0 Poisoning by antiallergic and antiemetic drugs — (Use additional code to specify the effects of poisoning)

963.1 Poisoning by antineoplastic and immunosuppressive drugs — (Use additional code to specify the effects of poisoning)

963.2 Poisoning by acidifying agents — (Use additional code to specify the effects of poisoning)

963.3 Poisoning by alkalizing agents — (Use additional code to specify the effects of poisoning)

963.4 Poisoning by enzymes, not elsewhere classified — (Use additional code to specify the effects of poisoning)

963.5 Poisoning by vitamins, not elsewhere classified — (Use additional code to specify the effects of poisoning)

963.8 Poisoning by other specified systemic agents — (Use additional code to specify the effects of poisoning)

963.9 Poisoning by unspecified systemic agent — (Use additional code to specify the effects of poisoning) ▽

964.0 Poisoning by iron and its compounds — (Use additional code to specify the effects of poisoning)

964.1 Poisoning by liver preparations and other antianemic agents — (Use additional code to specify the effects of poisoning)

964.2 Poisoning by anticoagulants — (Use additional code to specify the effects of poisoning)

964.3 Poisoning by vitamin K (phytonadione) — (Use additional code to specify the effects of poisoning)

964.4 Poisoning by fibrinolysis-affecting drugs — (Use additional code to specify the effects of poisoning)

964.5 Poisoning by anticoagulant antagonists and other coagulants — (Use additional code to specify the effects of poisoning)

964.6 Poisoning by gamma globulin — (Use additional code to specify the effects of poisoning)

964.7 Poisoning by natural blood and blood products — (Use additional code to specify the effects of poisoning)

964.8 Poisoning by other specified agents affecting blood constituents — (Use additional code to specify the effects of poisoning)

964.9 Poisoning by unspecified agent affecting blood constituents — (Use additional code to specify the effects of poisoning) ▽

965.00 Poisoning by opium (alkaloids), unspecified — (Use additional code to specify the effects of poisoning) ▽

965.01 Poisoning by heroin — (Use additional code to specify the effects of poisoning)

965.02 Poisoning by methadone — (Use additional code to specify the effects of poisoning)

965.09 Poisoning by opiates and related narcotics, other — (Use additional code to specify the effects of poisoning)

965.1 Poisoning by salicylates — (Use additional code to specify the effects of poisoning)

965.4 Poisoning by aromatic analgesics, not elsewhere classified — (Use additional code to specify the effects of poisoning)

965.5 Poisoning by pyrazole derivatives — (Use additional code to specify the effects of poisoning)

965.61 Poisoning by propionic acid derivatives — (Use additional code to specify the effects of poisoning)

965.69 Poisoning by other antirheumatics — (Use additional code to specify the effects of poisoning)

965.7 Poisoning by other non-narcotic analgesics — (Use additional code to specify the effects of poisoning)

965.8 Poisoning by other specified analgesics and antipyretics — (Use additional code to specify the effects of poisoning)

965.9 Poisoning by unspecified analgesic and antipyretic — (Use additional code to specify the effects of poisoning) ▽

966.0 Poisoning by oxazolidine derivatives — (Use additional code to specify the effects of poisoning)

966.1 Poisoning by hydantoin derivatives — (Use additional code to specify the effects of poisoning)

966.2 Poisoning by succinimides — (Use additional code to specify the effects of poisoning)

966.3 Poisoning by other and unspecified anticonvulsants — (Use additional code to specify the effects of poisoning) ▽

966.4 Poisoning by anti-Parkinsonism drugs — (Use additional code to specify the effects of poisoning)

967.0 Poisoning by barbiturates — (Use additional code to specify the effects of poisoning)

967.1 Poisoning by chloral hydrate group — (Use additional code to specify the effects of poisoning)

967.2 Poisoning by paraldehyde — (Use additional code to specify the effects of poisoning)

967.3 Poisoning by bromine compounds — (Use additional code to specify the effects of poisoning)

967.4 Poisoning by methaqualone compounds — (Use additional code to specify the effects of poisoning)

967.5 Poisoning by glutethimide group — (Use additional code to specify the effects of poisoning)

967.6 Poisoning by mixed sedatives, not elsewhere classified — (Use additional code to specify the effects of poisoning)

967.8 Poisoning by other sedatives and hypnotics — (Use additional code to specify the effects of poisoning)

967.9 Poisoning by unspecified sedative or hypnotic — (Use additional code to specify the effects of poisoning) ▽

968.0 Poisoning by central nervous system muscle-tone depressants — (Use additional code to specify the effects of poisoning)

968.3 Poisoning by intravenous anesthetics — (Use additional code to specify the effects of poisoning)

968.4 Poisoning by other and unspecified general anesthetics — (Use additional code to specify the effects of poisoning) ▽

969.00 Poisoning by antidepressant, unspecified ▽

969.01 Poisoning by monoamine oxidase inhibitors

969.02 Poisoning by selective serotonin and norepinephrine reuptake inhibitors

969.03 Poisoning by selective serotonin reuptake inhibitors

969.04 Poisoning by tetracyclic antidepressants

969.05 Poisoning by tricyclic antidepressants

969.09 Poisoning by other antidepressants

969.1 Poisoning by phenothiazine-based tranquilizers — (Use additional code to specify the effects of poisoning)

969.2 Poisoning by butyrophenone-based tranquilizers — (Use additional code to specify the effects of poisoning)

969.3 Poisoning by other antipsychotics, neuroleptics, and major tranquilizers — (Use additional code to specify the effects of poisoning)

969.4 Poisoning by benzodiazepine-based tranquilizers — (Use additional code to specify the effects of poisoning)

969.5 Poisoning by other tranquilizers — (Use additional code to specify the effects of poisoning)

969.6 Poisoning by psychodysleptics (hallucinogens) — (Use additional code to specify the effects of poisoning)

969.70 Poisoning by psychostimulant, unspecified ▽

969.71 Poisoning by caffeine

969.72 Poisoning by amphetamines

969.73 Poisoning by methylphenidate

969.79 Poisoning by other psychostimulants

969.8 Poisoning by other specified psychotropic agents — (Use additional code to specify the effects of poisoning)

969.9 Poisoning by unspecified psychotropic agent — (Use additional code to specify the effects of poisoning) [Unspecified code]

970.0 Poisoning by analeptics — (Use additional code to specify the effects of poisoning)

970.1 Poisoning by opiate antagonists — (Use additional code to specify the effects of poisoning)

970.81 Poisoning by cocaine

970.89 Poisoning by other central nervous system stimulants

970.9 Poisoning by unspecified central nervous system stimulant — (Use additional code to specify the effects of poisoning) [Unspecified code]

971.0 Poisoning by parasympathomimetics (cholinergics) — (Use additional code to specify the effects of poisoning)

971.1 Poisoning by parasympatholytics (anticholinergics and antimuscarinics) and spasmolytics — (Use additional code to specify the effects of poisoning)

971.2 Poisoning by sympathomimetics (adrenergics) — (Use additional code to specify the effects of poisoning)

971.3 Poisoning by sympatholytics (antiadrenergics) — (Use additional code to specify the effects of poisoning)

971.9 Poisoning by unspecified drug primarily affecting autonomic nervous system — (Use additional code to specify the effects of poisoning) [Unspecified code]

972.0 Poisoning by cardiac rhythm regulators — (Use additional code to specify the effects of poisoning)

972.1 Poisoning by cardiotonic glycosides and drugs of similar action — (Use additional code to specify the effects of poisoning)

972.2 Poisoning by antilipemic and antiarteriosclerotic drugs — (Use additional code to specify the effects of poisoning)

972.3 Poisoning by ganglion-blocking agents — (Use additional code to specify the effects of poisoning)

972.4 Poisoning by coronary vasodilators — (Use additional code to specify the effects of poisoning)

972.5 Poisoning by other vasodilators — (Use additional code to specify the effects of poisoning)

972.6 Poisoning by other antihypertensive agents — (Use additional code to specify the effects of poisoning)

972.7 Poisoning by antivaricose drugs, including sclerosing agents — (Use additional code to specify the effects of poisoning)

972.8 Poisoning by capillary-active drugs — (Use additional code to specify the effects of poisoning)

972.9 Poisoning by other and unspecified agents primarily affecting the cardiovascular system — (Use additional code to specify the effects of poisoning) [Unspecified code]

973.0 Poisoning by antacids and antigastric secretion drugs — (Use additional code to specify the effects of poisoning)

973.1 Poisoning by irritant cathartics — (Use additional code to specify the effects of poisoning)

973.2 Poisoning by emollient cathartics — (Use additional code to specify the effects of poisoning)

973.3 Poisoning by other cathartics, including intestinal atonia drugs — (Use additional code to specify the effects of poisoning)

973.4 Poisoning by digestants — (Use additional code to specify the effects of poisoning)

973.5 Poisoning by antidiarrheal drugs — (Use additional code to specify the effects of poisoning)

973.6 Poisoning by emetics — (Use additional code to specify the effects of poisoning)

973.8 Poisoning by other specified agents primarily affecting the gastrointestinal system — (Use additional code to specify the effects of poisoning)

973.9 Poisoning by unspecified agent primarily affecting the gastrointestinal system — (Use additional code to specify the effects of poisoning) [Unspecified code]

974.0 Poisoning by mercurial diuretics — (Use additional code to specify the effects of poisoning)

974.1 Poisoning by purine derivative diuretics — (Use additional code to specify the effects of poisoning)

974.2 Poisoning by carbonic acid anhydrase inhibitors — (Use additional code to specify the effects of poisoning)

974.3 Poisoning by saluretics — (Use additional code to specify the effects of poisoning)

974.4 Poisoning by other diuretics — (Use additional code to specify the effects of poisoning)

974.5 Poisoning by electrolytic, caloric, and water-balance agents — (Use additional code to specify the effects of poisoning)

974.6 Poisoning by other mineral salts, not elsewhere classified — (Use additional code to specify the effects of poisoning)

974.7 Poisoning by uric acid metabolism drugs — (Use additional code to specify the effects of poisoning)

975.0 Poisoning by oxytocic agents — (Use additional code to specify the effects of poisoning)

975.1 Poisoning by smooth muscle relaxants — (Use additional code to specify the effects of poisoning)

975.2 Poisoning by skeletal muscle relaxants — (Use additional code to specify the effects of poisoning)

975.3 Poisoning by other and unspecified drugs acting on muscles — (Use additional code to specify the effects of poisoning) [Unspecified code]

975.4 Poisoning by antitussives — (Use additional code to specify the effects of poisoning)

975.5 Poisoning by expectorants — (Use additional code to specify the effects of poisoning)

975.6 Poisoning by anti-common cold drugs — (Use additional code to specify the effects of poisoning)

975.7 Poisoning by antiasthmatics — (Use additional code to specify the effects of poisoning)

975.8 Poisoning by other and unspecified respiratory drugs — (Use additional code to specify the effects of poisoning) [Unspecified code]

976.0 Poisoning by local anti-infectives and anti-inflammatory drugs — (Use additional code to specify the effects of poisoning)

976.1 Poisoning by antipruritics — (Use additional code to specify the effects of poisoning)

976.2 Poisoning by local astringents and local detergents — (Use additional code to specify the effects of poisoning)

976.3 Poisoning by emollients, demulcents, and protectants — (Use additional code to specify the effects of poisoning)

976.4 Poisoning by keratolytics, keratoplastics, other hair treatment drugs and preparations — (Use additional code to specify the effects of poisoning)

976.5 Poisoning by eye anti-infectives and other eye drugs — (Use additional code to specify the effects of poisoning)

976.6 Poisoning by anti-infectives and other drugs and preparations for ear, nose, and throat — (Use additional code to specify the effects of poisoning)

976.7 Poisoning by dental drugs topically applied — (Use additional code to specify the effects of poisoning)

976.8 Poisoning by other agents primarily affecting skin and mucous membrane — (Use additional code to specify the effects of poisoning)

976.9 Poisoning by unspecified agent primarily affecting skin and mucous membrane — (Use additional code to specify the effects of poisoning) [Unspecified code]

977.0 Poisoning by dietetics — (Use additional code to specify the effects of poisoning)

977.1 Poisoning by lipotropic drugs — (Use additional code to specify the effects of poisoning)

977.2 Poisoning by antidotes and chelating agents, not elsewhere classified — (Use additional code to specify the effects of poisoning)

977.3 Poisoning by alcohol deterrents — (Use additional code to specify the effects of poisoning)

977.4 Poisoning by pharmaceutical excipients — (Use additional code to specify the effects of poisoning)

977.8 Poisoning by other specified drugs and medicinal substances — (Use additional code to specify the effects of poisoning)

980.0 Toxic effect of ethyl alcohol — (Use additional code to specify the nature of the toxic effect. Use additional code to identify any associated: 291.4, 303.0, 305.0)

980.1 Toxic effect of methyl alcohol — (Use additional code to specify the nature of the toxic effect)

980.2 Toxic effect of isopropyl alcohol — (Use additional code to specify the nature of the toxic effect)

980.3 Toxic effect of fusel oil — (Use additional code to specify the nature of the toxic effect)

980.8 Toxic effect of other specified alcohols — (Use additional code to specify the nature of the toxic effect)

980.9 Toxic effect of unspecified alcohol — (Use additional code to specify the nature of the toxic effect) ▽

981 Toxic effect of petroleum products — (Use additional code to specify the nature of the toxic effect)

982.0 Toxic effect of benzene and homologues — (Use additional code to specify the nature of the toxic effect)

982.1 Toxic effect of carbon tetrachloride — (Use additional code to specify the nature of the toxic effect)

982.2 Toxic effect of carbon disulfide — (Use additional code to specify the nature of the toxic effect)

982.3 Toxic effect of other chlorinated hydrocarbon solvents — (Use additional code to specify the nature of the toxic effect)

982.4 Toxic effect of nitroglycol — (Use additional code to specify the nature of the toxic effect)

982.8 Toxic effect of other nonpetroleum-based solvents — (Use additional code to specify the nature of the toxic effect)

983.0 Toxic effect of corrosive aromatics — (Use additional code to specify the nature of the toxic effect)

983.1 Toxic effect of acids — (Use additional code to specify the nature of the toxic effect)

983.2 Toxic effect of caustic alkalis — (Use additional code to specify the nature of the toxic effect)

983.9 Toxic effect of caustic, unspecified — (Use additional code to specify the nature of the toxic effect) ▽

984.0 Toxic effect of inorganic lead compounds — (Use additional code to specify the nature of the toxic effect)

984.1 Toxic effect of organic lead compounds — (Use additional code to specify the nature of the toxic effect)

984.8 Toxic effect of other lead compounds — (Use additional code to specify the nature of the toxic effect)

984.9 Toxic effect of unspecified lead compound — (Use additional code to specify the nature of the toxic effect) ▽

985.0 Toxic effect of mercury and its compounds — (Use additional code to specify the nature of the toxic effect)

985.1 Toxic effect of arsenic and its compounds — (Use additional code to specify the nature of the toxic effect)

985.2 Toxic effect of manganese and its compounds — (Use additional code to specify the nature of the toxic effect)

985.3 Toxic effect of beryllium and its compounds — (Use additional code to specify the nature of the toxic effect)

985.4 Toxic effect of antimony and its compounds — (Use additional code to specify the nature of the toxic effect)

985.5 Toxic effect of cadmium and its compounds — (Use additional code to specify the nature of the toxic effect)

985.6 Toxic effect of chromium — (Use additional code to specify the nature of the toxic effect)

985.8 Toxic effect of other specified metals — (Use additional code to specify the nature of the toxic effect)

985.9 Toxic effect of unspecified metal — (Use additional code to specify the nature of the toxic effect) ▽

988.0 Toxic effect of fish and shellfish — (Use additional code to specify the nature of the toxic effect)

988.1 Toxic effect of mushrooms — (Use additional code to specify the nature of the toxic effect)

988.2 Toxic effect of berries and other plants — (Use additional code to specify the nature of the toxic effect)

988.8 Toxic effect of other specified noxious substances — (Use additional code to specify the nature of the toxic effect)

988.9 Toxic effect of unspecified noxious substance — (Use additional code to specify the nature of the toxic effect) ▽

989.0 Toxic effect of hydrocyanic acid and cyanides — (Use additional code to specify the nature of the toxic effect)

989.1 Toxic effect of strychnine and salts — (Use additional code to specify the nature of the toxic effect)

989.2 Toxic effect of chlorinated hydrocarbons — (Use additional code to specify the nature of the toxic effect)

989.3 Toxic effect of organophosphate and carbamate — (Use additional code to specify the nature of the toxic effect)

989.4 Toxic effect of other pesticides, not elsewhere classified — (Use additional code to specify the nature of the toxic effect)

989.6 Toxic effect of soaps and detergents — (Use additional code to specify the nature of the toxic effect)

989.7 Toxic effect of aflatoxin and other mycotoxin (food contaminants) — (Use additional code to specify the nature of the toxic effect)

989.9 Toxic effect of unspecified substance, chiefly nonmedicinal as to source — (Use additional code to specify the nature of the toxic effect) ▽

ICD-9-CM Procedural

96.07 Insertion of other (naso-)gastric tube

96.33 Gastric lavage

43754-43755

43754 Gastric intubation and aspiration, diagnostic; single specimen (eg, acid analysis)

43755 collection of multiple fractional specimens with gastric stimulation, single or double lumen tube (gastric secretory study) (eg, histamine, insulin, pentagastrin, calcium, secretin), includes drug administration

ICD-9-CM Diagnostic

009.0 Infectious colitis, enteritis, and gastroenteritis

009.1 Colitis, enteritis, and gastroenteritis of presumed infectious origin

151.0 Malignant neoplasm of cardia

151.1 Malignant neoplasm of pylorus

151.2 Malignant neoplasm of pyloric antrum

151.3 Malignant neoplasm of fundus of stomach

151.4 Malignant neoplasm of body of stomach

151.5 Malignant neoplasm of lesser curvature of stomach, unspecified ▽

151.6 Malignant neoplasm of greater curvature of stomach, unspecified ▽

151.8 Malignant neoplasm of other specified sites of stomach

151.9 Malignant neoplasm of stomach, unspecified site ▽

197.8 Secondary malignant neoplasm of other digestive organs and spleen

199.0 Disseminated malignant neoplasm

199.1 Other malignant neoplasm of unspecified site

235.2 Neoplasm of uncertain behavior of stomach, intestines, and rectum

239.0 Neoplasm of unspecified nature of digestive system

531.00 Acute gastric ulcer with hemorrhage, without mention of obstruction — (Use additional E code to identify drug, if drug induced)

531.01 Acute gastric ulcer with hemorrhage and obstruction — (Use additional E code to identify drug, if drug induced)

531.10 Acute gastric ulcer with perforation, without mention of obstruction — (Use additional E code to identify drug, if drug induced)

531.11 Acute gastric ulcer with perforation and obstruction — (Use additional E code to identify drug, if drug induced)

531.20 Acute gastric ulcer with hemorrhage and perforation, without mention of obstruction — (Use additional E code to identify drug, if drug induced)

531.21 Acute gastric ulcer with hemorrhage, perforation, and obstruction — (Use additional E code to identify drug, if drug induced)

531.30 Acute gastric ulcer without mention of hemorrhage, perforation, or obstruction — (Use additional E code to identify drug, if drug induced)

531.31 Acute gastric ulcer without mention of hemorrhage or perforation, with obstruction — (Use additional E code to identify drug, if drug induced)

531.40 Chronic or unspecified gastric ulcer with hemorrhage, without mention of obstruction — (Use additional E code to identify drug, if drug induced)

531.41 Chronic or unspecified gastric ulcer with hemorrhage and obstruction — (Use additional E code to identify drug, if drug induced)

531.50 Chronic or unspecified gastric ulcer with perforation, without mention of obstruction — (Use additional E code to identify drug, if drug induced)
531.51 Chronic or unspecified gastric ulcer with perforation and obstruction — (Use additional E code to identify drug, if drug induced)
531.60 Chronic or unspecified gastric ulcer with hemorrhage and perforation, without mention of obstruction — (Use additional E code to identify drug, if drug induced)
531.61 Chronic or unspecified gastric ulcer with hemorrhage, perforation, and obstruction — (Use additional E code to identify drug, if drug induced)
531.70 Chronic gastric ulcer without mention of hemorrhage, perforation, without mention of obstruction — (Use additional E code to identify drug, if drug induced)
531.71 Chronic gastric ulcer without mention of hemorrhage or perforation, with obstruction — (Use additional E code to identify drug, if drug induced)
531.90 Gastric ulcer, unspecified as acute or chronic, without mention of hemorrhage, perforation, or obstruction — (Use additional E code to identify drug, if drug induced) ▽
531.91 Gastric ulcer, unspecified as acute or chronic, without mention of hemorrhage or perforation, with obstruction — (Use additional E code to identify drug, if drug induced) ▽
533.00 Acute peptic ulcer, unspecified site, with hemorrhage, without mention of obstruction — (Use additional E code to identify drug, if drug induced) ▽
533.01 Acute peptic ulcer, unspecified site, with hemorrhage and obstruction — (Use additional E code to identify drug, if drug induced) ▽
533.20 Acute peptic ulcer, unspecified site, with hemorrhage and perforation, without mention of obstruction — (Use additional E code to identify drug, if drug induced) ▽
533.21 Acute peptic ulcer, unspecified site, with hemorrhage, perforation, and obstruction — (Use additional E code to identify drug, if drug induced) ▽
533.40 Chronic or unspecified peptic ulcer, unspecified site, with hemorrhage, without mention of obstruction — (Use additional E code to identify drug, if drug induced) ▽
533.41 Chronic or unspecified peptic ulcer, unspecified site, with hemorrhage and obstruction — (Use additional E code to identify drug, if drug induced) ▽
533.60 Chronic or unspecified peptic ulcer, unspecified site, with hemorrhage and perforation, without mention of obstruction — (Use additional E code to identify drug, if drug induced) ▽
533.61 Chronic or unspecified peptic ulcer, unspecified site, with hemorrhage, perforation, and obstruction — (Use additional E code to identify drug, if drug induced) ▽
533.70 Chronic peptic ulcer, unspecified site, without mention of hemorrhage, perforation, or obstruction — (Use additional E code to identify drug, if drug induced) ▽
533.90 Peptic ulcer, unspecified site, unspecified as acute or chronic, without mention of hemorrhage, perforation, or obstruction — (Use additional E code to identify drug, if drug induced) ▽
534.00 Acute gastrojejunal ulcer with hemorrhage, without mention of obstruction
534.01 Acute gastrojejunal ulcer, with hemorrhage and obstruction
534.20 Acute gastrojejunal ulcer with hemorrhage and perforation, without mention of obstruction
534.21 Acute gastrojejunal ulcer with hemorrhage, perforation, and obstruction
534.40 Chronic or unspecified gastrojejunal ulcer with hemorrhage, without mention of obstruction
534.41 Chronic or unspecified gastrojejunal ulcer, with hemorrhage and obstruction
534.60 Chronic or unspecified gastrojejunal ulcer with hemorrhage and perforation, without mention of obstruction
534.61 Chronic or unspecified gastrojejunal ulcer with hemorrhage, perforation, and obstruction
535.01 Acute gastritis with hemorrhage
535.11 Atrophic gastritis with hemorrhage
535.21 Gastric mucosal hypertrophy with hemorrhage
535.31 Alcoholic gastritis with hemorrhage
535.41 Other specified gastritis with hemorrhage
535.51 Unspecified gastritis and gastroduodenitis with hemorrhage ▽
535.61 Duodenitis with hemorrhage
536.0 Achlorhydria
536.1 Acute dilatation of stomach
536.2 Persistent vomiting
536.8 Dyspepsia and other specified disorders of function of stomach
536.9 Unspecified functional disorder of stomach ▽
538 Gastrointestinal mucositis (ulcerative) — (Use additional E code to identify adverse effects of therapy: E879.2, E930.7, E933.1)
578.0 Hematemesis
578.9 Hemorrhage of gastrointestinal tract, unspecified ▽
789.00 Abdominal pain, unspecified site ▽
789.01 Abdominal pain, right upper quadrant
789.02 Abdominal pain, left upper quadrant
789.03 Abdominal pain, right lower quadrant
789.04 Abdominal pain, left lower quadrant
789.05 Abdominal pain, periumbilic
789.06 Abdominal pain, epigastric
789.07 Abdominal pain, generalized
789.09 Abdominal pain, other specified site

ICD-9-CM Procedural

89.39 Other nonoperative measurements and examinations
96.07 Insertion of other (naso-)gastric tube
96.33 Gastric lavage

43756-43757

43756 Duodenal intubation and aspiration, diagnostic, includes image guidance; single specimen (eg, bile study for crystals or afferent loop culture)
43757 collection of multiple fractional specimens with pancreatic or gallbladder stimulation, single or double lumen tube, includes drug administration

ICD-9-CM Diagnostic

531.00 Acute gastric ulcer with hemorrhage, without mention of obstruction — (Use additional E code to identify drug, if drug induced)
531.01 Acute gastric ulcer with hemorrhage and obstruction — (Use additional E code to identify drug, if drug induced)
531.10 Acute gastric ulcer with perforation, without mention of obstruction — (Use additional E code to identify drug, if drug induced)
531.11 Acute gastric ulcer with perforation and obstruction — (Use additional E code to identify drug, if drug induced)
531.20 Acute gastric ulcer with hemorrhage and perforation, without mention of obstruction — (Use additional E code to identify drug, if drug induced)
531.21 Acute gastric ulcer with hemorrhage, perforation, and obstruction — (Use additional E code to identify drug, if drug induced)
531.30 Acute gastric ulcer without mention of hemorrhage, perforation, or obstruction — (Use additional E code to identify drug, if drug induced)
531.31 Acute gastric ulcer without mention of hemorrhage or perforation, with obstruction — (Use additional E code to identify drug, if drug induced)
531.40 Chronic or unspecified gastric ulcer with hemorrhage, without mention of obstruction — (Use additional E code to identify drug, if drug induced)
531.41 Chronic or unspecified gastric ulcer with hemorrhage and obstruction — (Use additional E code to identify drug, if drug induced)
531.50 Chronic or unspecified gastric ulcer with perforation, without mention of obstruction — (Use additional E code to identify drug, if drug induced)
531.51 Chronic or unspecified gastric ulcer with perforation and obstruction — (Use additional E code to identify drug, if drug induced)
531.60 Chronic or unspecified gastric ulcer with hemorrhage and perforation, without mention of obstruction — (Use additional E code to identify drug, if drug induced)
531.61 Chronic or unspecified gastric ulcer with hemorrhage, perforation, and obstruction — (Use additional E code to identify drug, if drug induced)
531.70 Chronic gastric ulcer without mention of hemorrhage, perforation, without mention of obstruction — (Use additional E code to identify drug, if drug induced)
531.71 Chronic gastric ulcer without mention of hemorrhage or perforation, with obstruction — (Use additional E code to identify drug, if drug induced)

531.90 Gastric ulcer, unspecified as acute or chronic, without mention of hemorrhage, perforation, or obstruction — (Use additional E code to identify drug, if drug induced) ▽

531.91 Gastric ulcer, unspecified as acute or chronic, without mention of hemorrhage or perforation, with obstruction — (Use additional E code to identify drug, if drug induced) ▽

532.00 Acute duodenal ulcer with hemorrhage, without mention of obstruction — (Use additional E code to identify drug, if drug induced)

532.01 Acute duodenal ulcer with hemorrhage and obstruction — (Use additional E code to identify drug, if drug induced)

532.10 Acute duodenal ulcer with perforation, without mention of obstruction — (Use additional E code to identify drug, if drug induced)

532.11 Acute duodenal ulcer with perforation and obstruction — (Use additional E code to identify drug, if drug induced)

532.20 Acute duodenal ulcer with hemorrhage and perforation, without mention of obstruction — (Use additional E code to identify drug, if drug induced)

532.21 Acute duodenal ulcer with hemorrhage, perforation, and obstruction — (Use additional E code to identify drug, if drug induced)

532.30 Acute duodenal ulcer without mention of hemorrhage, perforation, or obstruction — (Use additional E code to identify drug, if drug induced)

532.31 Acute duodenal ulcer without mention of hemorrhage or perforation, with obstruction — (Use additional E code to identify drug, if drug induced)

532.40 Duodenal ulcer, chronic or unspecified, with hemorrhage, without mention of obstruction — (Use additional E code to identify drug, if drug induced)

532.41 Chronic or unspecified duodenal ulcer with hemorrhage and obstruction — (Use additional E code to identify drug, if drug induced)

532.50 Chronic or unspecified duodenal ulcer with perforation, without mention of obstruction — (Use additional E code to identify drug, if drug induced)

532.51 Chronic or unspecified duodenal ulcer with perforation and obstruction — (Use additional E code to identify drug, if drug induced)

532.60 Chronic or unspecified duodenal ulcer with hemorrhage and perforation, without mention of obstruction — (Use additional E code to identify drug, if drug induced)

532.61 Chronic or unspecified duodenal ulcer with hemorrhage, perforation, and obstruction — (Use additional E code to identify drug, if drug induced)

532.70 Chronic duodenal ulcer without mention of hemorrhage, perforation, or obstruction — (Use additional E code to identify drug, if drug induced)

532.71 Chronic duodenal ulcer without mention of hemorrhage or perforation, with obstruction — (Use additional E code to identify drug, if drug induced)

532.90 Duodenal ulcer, unspecified as acute or chronic, without hemorrhage, perforation, or obstruction — (Use additional E code to identify drug, if drug induced) ▽

532.91 Duodenal ulcer, unspecified as acute or chronic, without mention of hemorrhage or perforation, with obstruction — (Use additional E code to identify drug, if drug induced) ▽

533.00 Acute peptic ulcer, unspecified site, with hemorrhage, without mention of obstruction — (Use additional E code to identify drug, if drug induced) ▽

533.01 Acute peptic ulcer, unspecified site, with hemorrhage and obstruction — (Use additional E code to identify drug, if drug induced) ▽

533.20 Acute peptic ulcer, unspecified site, with hemorrhage and perforation, without mention of obstruction — (Use additional E code to identify drug, if drug induced) ▽

533.21 Acute peptic ulcer, unspecified site, with hemorrhage, perforation, and obstruction — (Use additional E code to identify drug, if drug induced) ▽

533.40 Chronic or unspecified peptic ulcer, unspecified site, with hemorrhage, without mention of obstruction — (Use additional E code to identify drug, if drug induced) ▽

533.41 Chronic or unspecified peptic ulcer, unspecified site, with hemorrhage and obstruction — (Use additional E code to identify drug, if drug induced) ▽

533.60 Chronic or unspecified peptic ulcer, unspecified site, with hemorrhage and perforation, without mention of obstruction — (Use additional E code to identify drug, if drug induced) ▽

533.61 Chronic or unspecified peptic ulcer, unspecified site, with hemorrhage, perforation, and obstruction — (Use additional E code to identify drug, if drug induced) ▽

533.70 Chronic peptic ulcer, unspecified site, without mention of hemorrhage, perforation, or obstruction — (Use additional E code to identify drug, if drug induced) ▽

533.90 Peptic ulcer, unspecified site, unspecified as acute or chronic, without mention of hemorrhage, perforation, or obstruction — (Use additional E code to identify drug, if drug induced) ▽

534.00 Acute gastrojejunal ulcer with hemorrhage, without mention of obstruction

534.01 Acute gastrojejunal ulcer, with hemorrhage and obstruction

534.20 Acute gastrojejunal ulcer with hemorrhage and perforation, without mention of obstruction

534.21 Acute gastrojejunal ulcer with hemorrhage, perforation, and obstruction

534.40 Chronic or unspecified gastrojejunal ulcer with hemorrhage, without mention of obstruction

534.41 Chronic or unspecified gastrojejunal ulcer, with hemorrhage and obstruction

534.60 Chronic or unspecified gastrojejunal ulcer with hemorrhage and perforation, without mention of obstruction

534.61 Chronic or unspecified gastrojejunal ulcer with hemorrhage, perforation, and obstruction

574.00 Calculus of gallbladder with acute cholecystitis, without mention of obstruction

574.01 Calculus of gallbladder with acute cholecystitis and obstruction

574.10 Calculus of gallbladder with other cholecystitis, without mention of obstruction

574.11 Calculus of gallbladder with other cholecystitis and obstruction

574.30 Calculus of bile duct with acute cholecystitis without mention of obstruction

574.31 Calculus of bile duct with acute cholecystitis and obstruction

574.40 Calculus of bile duct with other cholecystitis, without mention of obstruction

574.41 Calculus of bile duct with other cholecystitis and obstruction

574.60 Calculus of gallbladder and bile duct with acute cholecystitis, without mention of obstruction

574.61 Calculus of gallbladder and bile duct with acute cholecystitis, with obstruction

574.70 Calculus of gallbladder and bile duct with other cholecystitis, without mention of obstruction

574.71 Calculus of gallbladder and bile duct with other cholecystitis, with obstruction

574.80 Calculus of gallbladder and bile duct with acute and chronic cholecystitis, without mention of obstruction

574.81 Calculus of gallbladder and bile duct with acute and chronic cholecystitis, with obstruction

575.0 Acute cholecystitis

575.10 Cholecystitis, unspecified ▽

575.11 Chronic cholecystitis

575.12 Acute and chronic cholecystitis

576.1 Cholangitis

ICD-9-CM Procedural

89.39 Other nonoperative measurements and examinations

96.08 Insertion of (naso-) intestinal tube

43760

43760 Change of gastrostomy tube, percutaneous, without imaging or endoscopic guidance

ICD-9-CM Diagnostic

536.40 Unspecified gastrostomy complication ▽

536.41 Infection of gastrostomy — (Use additional code to specify type of infection: 038.0-038.9, 682.2. Use additional code to identify organism: 041.00-041.9)

536.42 Mechanical complication of gastrostomy

536.49 Other gastrostomy complications

682.2 Cellulitis and abscess of trunk — (Use additional code to identify organism, such as 041.1, etc.)

V44.1 Gastrostomy status

V53.59 Fitting and adjustment of other gastrointestinal appliance and device

V55.2 Attention to ileostomy

ICD-9-CM Procedural

97.02 Replacement of gastrostomy tube

43761

43761 Repositioning of a naso- or oro-gastric feeding tube, through the duodenum for enteric nutrition

ICD-9-CM Diagnostic

V53.50 Fitting and adjustment of intestinal appliance and device
V53.59 Fitting and adjustment of other gastrointestinal appliance and device
V55.4 Attention to other artificial opening of digestive tract

ICD-9-CM Procedural

44.99 Other operations on stomach

HCPCS Level II Supplies & Services

B4034 Enteral feeding supply kit; syringe fed, per day, includes but not limited to feeding/flushing syringe, administration set tubing, dressings, tape

43770-43775

43770 Laparoscopy, surgical, gastric restrictive procedure; placement of adjustable gastric restrictive device (eg, gastric band and subcutaneous port components)
43771 revision of adjustable gastric restrictive device component only
43772 removal of adjustable gastric restrictive device component only
43773 removal and replacement of adjustable gastric restrictive device component only
43774 removal of adjustable gastric restrictive device and subcutaneous port components
43775 longitudinal gastrectomy (ie, sleeve gastrectomy)

ICD-9-CM Diagnostic

244.9 Unspecified hypothyroidism ▽
253.8 Other disorders of the pituitary and other syndromes of diencephalohypophyseal origin
255.8 Other specified disorders of adrenal glands
259.9 Unspecified endocrine disorder ▽
278.01 Morbid obesity — (Use additional code to identify Body Mass Index (BMI), if known: V85.0-V85.54)
539.01 Infection due to gastric band procedure — (Use additional code to specify type of infection, such as: 038.0-038.9, 682.2) (Use additional code to identify organism: 041.00-041.9)
539.09 Other complications of gastric band procedure — (Use additional code(s) to further specify complication)
997.49 Other digestive system complications
998.89 Other specified complications
V53.51 Fitting and adjustment of gastric lap band

ICD-9-CM Procedural

43.82 Laparoscopic vertical (sleeve) gastrectomy
44.95 Laparoscopic gastric restrictive procedure
44.96 Laparoscopic revision of gastric restrictive procedure
44.97 Laparoscopic removal of gastric restrictive device(s)
44.98 (Laparoscopic) adjustment of size of adjustable gastric restrictive device
44.99 Other operations on stomach

43800

43800 Pyloroplasty

ICD-9-CM Diagnostic

537.0 Acquired hypertrophic pyloric stenosis
537.81 Pylorospasm
750.5 Congenital hypertrophic pyloric stenosis

ICD-9-CM Procedural

44.21 Dilation of pylorus by incision
44.22 Endoscopic dilation of pylorus
44.29 Other pyloroplasty

43810

43810 Gastroduodenostomy

ICD-9-CM Diagnostic

151.1 Malignant neoplasm of pylorus
151.5 Malignant neoplasm of lesser curvature of stomach, unspecified ▽
151.6 Malignant neoplasm of greater curvature of stomach, unspecified ▽
151.9 Malignant neoplasm of stomach, unspecified site ▽
152.0 Malignant neoplasm of duodenum
197.4 Secondary malignant neoplasm of small intestine including duodenum
209.01 Malignant carcinoid tumor of the duodenum — (Code first any associated multiple endocrine neoplasia syndrome: 258.01-258.03)(Use additional code to identify associated endocrine syndrome, as: carcinoid syndrome: 259.2)
209.23 Malignant carcinoid tumor of the stomach — (Code first any associated multiple endocrine neoplasia syndrome: 258.01-258.03)(Use additional code to identify associated endocrine syndrome, as: carcinoid syndrome: 259.2)
209.25 Malignant carcinoid tumor of foregut, not otherwise specified — (Code first any associated multiple endocrine neoplasia syndrome: 258.01-258.03)(Use additional code to identify associated endocrine syndrome, as: carcinoid syndrome: 259.2)
209.63 Benign carcinoid tumor of the stomach — (Code first any associated multiple endocrine neoplasia syndrome: 258.01-258.03)(Use additional code to identify associated endocrine syndrome, as: carcinoid syndrome: 259.2)
209.65 Benign carcinoid tumor of foregut, not otherwise specified — (Code first any associated multiple endocrine neoplasia syndrome: 258.01-258.03)(Use additional code to identify associated endocrine syndrome, as: carcinoid syndrome: 259.2)
230.7 Carcinoma in situ of other and unspecified parts of intestine ▽
235.2 Neoplasm of uncertain behavior of stomach, intestines, and rectum
531.00 Acute gastric ulcer with hemorrhage, without mention of obstruction — (Use additional E code to identify drug, if drug induced)
531.01 Acute gastric ulcer with hemorrhage and obstruction — (Use additional E code to identify drug, if drug induced)
531.10 Acute gastric ulcer with perforation, without mention of obstruction — (Use additional E code to identify drug, if drug induced)
531.11 Acute gastric ulcer with perforation and obstruction — (Use additional E code to identify drug, if drug induced)
531.20 Acute gastric ulcer with hemorrhage and perforation, without mention of obstruction — (Use additional E code to identify drug, if drug induced)
531.21 Acute gastric ulcer with hemorrhage, perforation, and obstruction — (Use additional E code to identify drug, if drug induced)
531.31 Acute gastric ulcer without mention of hemorrhage or perforation, with obstruction — (Use additional E code to identify drug, if drug induced)
531.40 Chronic or unspecified gastric ulcer with hemorrhage, without mention of obstruction — (Use additional E code to identify drug, if drug induced)
531.41 Chronic or unspecified gastric ulcer with hemorrhage and obstruction — (Use additional E code to identify drug, if drug induced)
531.50 Chronic or unspecified gastric ulcer with perforation, without mention of obstruction — (Use additional E code to identify drug, if drug induced)
531.51 Chronic or unspecified gastric ulcer with perforation and obstruction — (Use additional E code to identify drug, if drug induced)
531.60 Chronic or unspecified gastric ulcer with hemorrhage and perforation, without mention of obstruction — (Use additional E code to identify drug, if drug induced)
531.61 Chronic or unspecified gastric ulcer with hemorrhage, perforation, and obstruction — (Use additional E code to identify drug, if drug induced)
531.70 Chronic gastric ulcer without mention of hemorrhage, perforation, without mention of obstruction — (Use additional E code to identify drug, if drug induced)
531.71 Chronic gastric ulcer without mention of hemorrhage or perforation, with obstruction — (Use additional E code to identify drug, if drug induced)
531.90 Gastric ulcer, unspecified as acute or chronic, without mention of hemorrhage, perforation, or obstruction — (Use additional E code to identify drug, if drug induced) ▽

531.91 Gastric ulcer, unspecified as acute or chronic, without mention of hemorrhage or perforation, with obstruction — (Use additional E code to identify drug, if drug induced) ▽

532.00 Acute duodenal ulcer with hemorrhage, without mention of obstruction — (Use additional E code to identify drug, if drug induced)

532.01 Acute duodenal ulcer with hemorrhage and obstruction — (Use additional E code to identify drug, if drug induced)

532.10 Acute duodenal ulcer with perforation, without mention of obstruction — (Use additional E code to identify drug, if drug induced)

532.11 Acute duodenal ulcer with perforation and obstruction — (Use additional E code to identify drug, if drug induced)

532.20 Acute duodenal ulcer with hemorrhage and perforation, without mention of obstruction — (Use additional E code to identify drug, if drug induced)

532.21 Acute duodenal ulcer with hemorrhage, perforation, and obstruction — (Use additional E code to identify drug, if drug induced)

532.30 Acute duodenal ulcer without mention of hemorrhage, perforation, or obstruction — (Use additional E code to identify drug, if drug induced)

532.31 Acute duodenal ulcer without mention of hemorrhage or perforation, with obstruction — (Use additional E code to identify drug, if drug induced)

532.40 Duodenal ulcer, chronic or unspecified, with hemorrhage, without mention of obstruction — (Use additional E code to identify drug, if drug induced)

532.41 Chronic or unspecified duodenal ulcer with hemorrhage and obstruction — (Use additional E code to identify drug, if drug induced)

532.50 Chronic or unspecified duodenal ulcer with perforation, without mention of obstruction — (Use additional E code to identify drug, if drug induced)

532.51 Chronic or unspecified duodenal ulcer with perforation and obstruction — (Use additional E code to identify drug, if drug induced)

532.60 Chronic or unspecified duodenal ulcer with hemorrhage and perforation, without mention of obstruction — (Use additional E code to identify drug, if drug induced)

532.61 Chronic or unspecified duodenal ulcer with hemorrhage, perforation, and obstruction — (Use additional E code to identify drug, if drug induced)

532.70 Chronic duodenal ulcer without mention of hemorrhage, perforation, or obstruction — (Use additional E code to identify drug, if drug induced)

532.71 Chronic duodenal ulcer without mention of hemorrhage or perforation, with obstruction — (Use additional E code to identify drug, if drug induced)

532.90 Duodenal ulcer, unspecified as acute or chronic, without hemorrhage, perforation, or obstruction — (Use additional E code to identify drug, if drug induced) ▽

532.91 Duodenal ulcer, unspecified as acute or chronic, without mention of hemorrhage or perforation, with obstruction — (Use additional E code to identify drug, if drug induced) ▽

533.00 Acute peptic ulcer, unspecified site, with hemorrhage, without mention of obstruction — (Use additional E code to identify drug, if drug induced) ▽

533.01 Acute peptic ulcer, unspecified site, with hemorrhage and obstruction — (Use additional E code to identify drug, if drug induced) ▽

533.10 Acute peptic ulcer, unspecified site, with perforation, without mention of obstruction — (Use additional E code to identify drug, if drug induced) ▽

533.11 Acute peptic ulcer, unspecified site, with perforation and obstruction — (Use additional E code to identify drug, if drug induced) ▽

533.20 Acute peptic ulcer, unspecified site, with hemorrhage and perforation, without mention of obstruction — (Use additional E code to identify drug, if drug induced) ▽

533.21 Acute peptic ulcer, unspecified site, with hemorrhage, perforation, and obstruction — (Use additional E code to identify drug, if drug induced) ▽

533.30 Acute peptic ulcer, unspecified site, without mention of hemorrhage, perforation, or obstruction — (Use additional E code to identify drug, if drug induced) ▽

533.31 Acute peptic ulcer, unspecified site, without mention of hemorrhage and perforation, with obstruction — (Use additional E code to identify drug, if drug induced) ▽

533.40 Chronic or unspecified peptic ulcer, unspecified site, with hemorrhage, without mention of obstruction — (Use additional E code to identify drug, if drug induced) ▽

533.41 Chronic or unspecified peptic ulcer, unspecified site, with hemorrhage and obstruction — (Use additional E code to identify drug, if drug induced) ▽

533.50 Chronic or unspecified peptic ulcer, unspecified site, with perforation, without mention of obstruction — (Use additional E code to identify drug, if drug induced) ▽

533.51 Chronic or unspecified peptic ulcer, unspecified site, with perforation and obstruction — (Use additional E code to identify drug, if drug induced) ▽

533.60 Chronic or unspecified peptic ulcer, unspecified site, with hemorrhage and perforation, without mention of obstruction — (Use additional E code to identify drug, if drug induced) ▽

533.61 Chronic or unspecified peptic ulcer, unspecified site, with hemorrhage, perforation, and obstruction — (Use additional E code to identify drug, if drug induced) ▽

533.70 Chronic peptic ulcer, unspecified site, without mention of hemorrhage, perforation, or obstruction — (Use additional E code to identify drug, if drug induced) ▽

533.71 Chronic peptic ulcer of unspecified site without mention of hemorrhage or perforation, with obstruction — (Use additional E code to identify drug, if drug induced) ▽

533.90 Peptic ulcer, unspecified site, unspecified as acute or chronic, without mention of hemorrhage, perforation, or obstruction — (Use additional E code to identify drug, if drug induced) ▽

533.91 Peptic ulcer, unspecified site, unspecified as acute or chronic, without mention of hemorrhage or perforation, with obstruction — (Use additional E code to identify drug, if drug induced) ▽

ICD-9-CM Procedural

44.39 Other gastroenterostomy without gastrectomy

43820-43825

43820 Gastrojejunostomy; without vagotomy

43825 with vagotomy, any type

ICD-9-CM Diagnostic

151.8 Malignant neoplasm of other specified sites of stomach

151.9 Malignant neoplasm of stomach, unspecified site ▽

152.0 Malignant neoplasm of duodenum

152.1 Malignant neoplasm of jejunum

152.3 Malignant neoplasm of Meckel's diverticulum

152.8 Malignant neoplasm of other specified sites of small intestine

152.9 Malignant neoplasm of small intestine, unspecified site ▽

197.4 Secondary malignant neoplasm of small intestine including duodenum

197.8 Secondary malignant neoplasm of other digestive organs and spleen

199.0 Disseminated malignant neoplasm

209.00 Malignant carcinoid tumor of the small intestine, unspecified portion — (Code first any associated multiple endocrine neoplasia syndrome: 258.01-258.03)(Use additional code to identify associated endocrine syndrome, as: carcinoid syndrome: 259.2) ▽

209.01 Malignant carcinoid tumor of the duodenum — (Code first any associated multiple endocrine neoplasia syndrome: 258.01-258.03)(Use additional code to identify associated endocrine syndrome, as: carcinoid syndrome: 259.2)

209.02 Malignant carcinoid tumor of the jejunum — (Code first any associated multiple endocrine neoplasia syndrome: 258.01-258.03)(Use additional code to identify associated endocrine syndrome, as: carcinoid syndrome: 259.2)

209.23 Malignant carcinoid tumor of the stomach — (Code first any associated multiple endocrine neoplasia syndrome: 258.01-258.03)(Use additional code to identify associated endocrine syndrome, as: carcinoid syndrome: 259.2)

209.25 Malignant carcinoid tumor of foregut, not otherwise specified — (Code first any associated multiple endocrine neoplasia syndrome: 258.01-258.03)(Use additional code to identify associated endocrine syndrome, as: carcinoid syndrome: 259.2)

209.30 Malignant poorly differentiated neuroendocrine carcinoma, any site — (Code first any associated multiple endocrine neoplasia syndrome: 258.01-258.03)(Use additional code to identify associated endocrine syndrome, as: carcinoid syndrome: 259.2) ▽

230.7 Carcinoma in situ of other and unspecified parts of intestine ▽

235.2 Neoplasm of uncertain behavior of stomach, intestines, and rectum

531.00 Acute gastric ulcer with hemorrhage, without mention of obstruction — (Use additional E code to identify drug, if drug induced)

531.01 Acute gastric ulcer with hemorrhage and obstruction — (Use additional E code to identify drug, if drug induced)

531.10 Acute gastric ulcer with perforation, without mention of obstruction — (Use additional E code to identify drug, if drug induced)

531.11 Acute gastric ulcer with perforation and obstruction — (Use additional E code to identify drug, if drug induced)

531.20 Acute gastric ulcer with hemorrhage and perforation, without mention of obstruction — (Use additional E code to identify drug, if drug induced)

531.21 Acute gastric ulcer with hemorrhage, perforation, and obstruction — (Use additional E code to identify drug, if drug induced)

531.30 Acute gastric ulcer without mention of hemorrhage, perforation, or obstruction — (Use additional E code to identify drug, if drug induced)

531.31 Acute gastric ulcer without mention of hemorrhage or perforation, with obstruction — (Use additional E code to identify drug, if drug induced)

531.40 Chronic or unspecified gastric ulcer with hemorrhage, without mention of obstruction — (Use additional E code to identify drug, if drug induced)

531.41 Chronic or unspecified gastric ulcer with hemorrhage and obstruction — (Use additional E code to identify drug, if drug induced)

531.50 Chronic or unspecified gastric ulcer with perforation, without mention of obstruction — (Use additional E code to identify drug, if drug induced)

531.51 Chronic or unspecified gastric ulcer with perforation and obstruction — (Use additional E code to identify drug, if drug induced)

531.60 Chronic or unspecified gastric ulcer with hemorrhage and perforation, without mention of obstruction — (Use additional E code to identify drug, if drug induced)

531.61 Chronic or unspecified gastric ulcer with hemorrhage, perforation, and obstruction — (Use additional E code to identify drug, if drug induced)

531.70 Chronic gastric ulcer without mention of hemorrhage, perforation, without mention of obstruction — (Use additional E code to identify drug, if drug induced)

531.71 Chronic gastric ulcer without mention of hemorrhage or perforation, with obstruction — (Use additional E code to identify drug, if drug induced)

531.90 Gastric ulcer, unspecified as acute or chronic, without mention of hemorrhage, perforation, or obstruction — (Use additional E code to identify drug, if drug induced) ▽

531.91 Gastric ulcer, unspecified as acute or chronic, without mention of hemorrhage or perforation, with obstruction — (Use additional E code to identify drug, if drug induced) ▽

532.00 Acute duodenal ulcer with hemorrhage, without mention of obstruction — (Use additional E code to identify drug, if drug induced)

532.01 Acute duodenal ulcer with hemorrhage and obstruction — (Use additional E code to identify drug, if drug induced)

532.10 Acute duodenal ulcer with perforation, without mention of obstruction — (Use additional E code to identify drug, if drug induced)

532.11 Acute duodenal ulcer with perforation and obstruction — (Use additional E code to identify drug, if drug induced)

532.20 Acute duodenal ulcer with hemorrhage and perforation, without mention of obstruction — (Use additional E code to identify drug, if drug induced)

532.21 Acute duodenal ulcer with hemorrhage, perforation, and obstruction — (Use additional E code to identify drug, if drug induced)

532.30 Acute duodenal ulcer without mention of hemorrhage, perforation, or obstruction — (Use additional E code to identify drug, if drug induced)

532.31 Acute duodenal ulcer without mention of hemorrhage or perforation, with obstruction — (Use additional E code to identify drug, if drug induced)

532.40 Duodenal ulcer, chronic or unspecified, with hemorrhage, without mention of obstruction — (Use additional E code to identify drug, if drug induced)

532.41 Chronic or unspecified duodenal ulcer with hemorrhage and obstruction — (Use additional E code to identify drug, if drug induced)

532.50 Chronic or unspecified duodenal ulcer with perforation, without mention of obstruction — (Use additional E code to identify drug, if drug induced)

532.51 Chronic or unspecified duodenal ulcer with perforation and obstruction — (Use additional E code to identify drug, if drug induced)

532.60 Chronic or unspecified duodenal ulcer with hemorrhage and perforation, without mention of obstruction — (Use additional E code to identify drug, if drug induced)

532.61 Chronic or unspecified duodenal ulcer with hemorrhage, perforation, and obstruction — (Use additional E code to identify drug, if drug induced)

532.70 Chronic duodenal ulcer without mention of hemorrhage, perforation, or obstruction — (Use additional E code to identify drug, if drug induced)

532.71 Chronic duodenal ulcer without mention of hemorrhage or perforation, with obstruction — (Use additional E code to identify drug, if drug induced)

532.90 Duodenal ulcer, unspecified as acute or chronic, without hemorrhage, perforation, or obstruction — (Use additional E code to identify drug, if drug induced) ▽

532.91 Duodenal ulcer, unspecified as acute or chronic, without mention of hemorrhage or perforation, with obstruction — (Use additional E code to identify drug, if drug induced) ▽

533.00 Acute peptic ulcer, unspecified site, with hemorrhage, without mention of obstruction — (Use additional E code to identify drug, if drug induced) ▽

533.01 Acute peptic ulcer, unspecified site, with hemorrhage and obstruction — (Use additional E code to identify drug, if drug induced) ▽

533.10 Acute peptic ulcer, unspecified site, with perforation, without mention of obstruction — (Use additional E code to identify drug, if drug induced) ▽

533.11 Acute peptic ulcer, unspecified site, with perforation and obstruction — (Use additional E code to identify drug, if drug induced) ▽

533.20 Acute peptic ulcer, unspecified site, with hemorrhage and perforation, without mention of obstruction — (Use additional E code to identify drug, if drug induced) ▽

533.21 Acute peptic ulcer, unspecified site, with hemorrhage, perforation, and obstruction — (Use additional E code to identify drug, if drug induced) ▽

533.30 Acute peptic ulcer, unspecified site, without mention of hemorrhage, perforation, or obstruction — (Use additional E code to identify drug, if drug induced) ▽

533.31 Acute peptic ulcer, unspecified site, without mention of hemorrhage and perforation, with obstruction — (Use additional E code to identify drug, if drug induced) ▽

533.40 Chronic or unspecified peptic ulcer, unspecified site, with hemorrhage, without mention of obstruction — (Use additional E code to identify drug, if drug induced) ▽

533.41 Chronic or unspecified peptic ulcer, unspecified site, with hemorrhage and obstruction — (Use additional E code to identify drug, if drug induced) ▽

533.50 Chronic or unspecified peptic ulcer, unspecified site, with perforation, without mention of obstruction — (Use additional E code to identify drug, if drug induced) ▽

533.51 Chronic or unspecified peptic ulcer, unspecified site, with perforation and obstruction — (Use additional E code to identify drug, if drug induced) ▽

533.60 Chronic or unspecified peptic ulcer, unspecified site, with hemorrhage and perforation, without mention of obstruction — (Use additional E code to identify drug, if drug induced) ▽

533.61 Chronic or unspecified peptic ulcer, unspecified site, with hemorrhage, perforation, and obstruction — (Use additional E code to identify drug, if drug induced) ▽

533.70 Chronic peptic ulcer, unspecified site, without mention of hemorrhage, perforation, or obstruction — (Use additional E code to identify drug, if drug induced) ▽

533.71 Chronic peptic ulcer of unspecified site without mention of hemorrhage or perforation, with obstruction — (Use additional E code to identify drug, if drug induced) ▽

533.90 Peptic ulcer, unspecified site, unspecified as acute or chronic, without mention of hemorrhage, perforation, or obstruction — (Use additional E code to identify drug, if drug induced) ▽

533.91 Peptic ulcer, unspecified site, unspecified as acute or chronic, without mention of hemorrhage or perforation, with obstruction — (Use additional E code to identify drug, if drug induced) ▽

534.00 Acute gastrojejunal ulcer with hemorrhage, without mention of obstruction

534.01 Acute gastrojejunal ulcer, with hemorrhage and obstruction

534.10 Acute gastrojejunal ulcer with perforation, without mention of obstruction

534.11 Acute gastrojejunal ulcer with perforation and obstruction

534.20 Acute gastrojejunal ulcer with hemorrhage and perforation, without mention of obstruction

534.21 Acute gastrojejunal ulcer with hemorrhage, perforation, and obstruction

534.30 Acute gastrojejunal ulcer without mention of hemorrhage, perforation, or obstruction

534.31 Acute gastrojejunal ulcer without mention of hemorrhage or perforation, with obstruction

534.40 Chronic or unspecified gastrojejunal ulcer with hemorrhage, without mention of obstruction

534.41 Chronic or unspecified gastrojejunal ulcer, with hemorrhage and obstruction

537.0 Acquired hypertrophic pyloric stenosis

ICD-9-CM Procedural

44.01 Truncal vagotomy
44.02 Highly selective vagotomy
44.03 Other selective vagotomy
44.39 Other gastroenterostomy without gastrectomy

43830-43831

43830 Gastrostomy, open; without construction of gastric tube (eg, Stamm procedure) (separate procedure)
43831 neonatal, for feeding

ICD-9-CM Diagnostic

150.1 Malignant neoplasm of thoracic esophagus
150.2 Malignant neoplasm of abdominal esophagus
150.3 Malignant neoplasm of upper third of esophagus
150.4 Malignant neoplasm of middle third of esophagus
150.5 Malignant neoplasm of lower third of esophagus
150.8 Malignant neoplasm of other specified part of esophagus
150.9 Malignant neoplasm of esophagus, unspecified site ▽
151.0 Malignant neoplasm of cardia
151.1 Malignant neoplasm of pylorus
151.2 Malignant neoplasm of pyloric antrum
151.3 Malignant neoplasm of fundus of stomach
151.4 Malignant neoplasm of body of stomach
151.5 Malignant neoplasm of lesser curvature of stomach, unspecified ▽
151.6 Malignant neoplasm of greater curvature of stomach, unspecified ▽
151.8 Malignant neoplasm of other specified sites of stomach
151.9 Malignant neoplasm of stomach, unspecified site ▽
152.0 Malignant neoplasm of duodenum
152.1 Malignant neoplasm of jejunum
152.2 Malignant neoplasm of ileum
161.9 Malignant neoplasm of larynx, unspecified site ▽
197.4 Secondary malignant neoplasm of small intestine including duodenum
197.8 Secondary malignant neoplasm of other digestive organs and spleen
198.89 Secondary malignant neoplasm of other specified sites
209.01 Malignant carcinoid tumor of the duodenum — (Code first any associated multiple endocrine neoplasia syndrome: 258.01-258.03)(Use additional code to identify associated endocrine syndrome, as: carcinoid syndrome: 259.2)
209.02 Malignant carcinoid tumor of the jejunum — (Code first any associated multiple endocrine neoplasia syndrome: 258.01-258.03)(Use additional code to identify associated endocrine syndrome, as: carcinoid syndrome: 259.2)
209.03 Malignant carcinoid tumor of the ileum — (Code first any associated multiple endocrine neoplasia syndrome: 258.01-258.03)(Use additional code to identify associated endocrine syndrome, as: carcinoid syndrome: 259.2)
209.23 Malignant carcinoid tumor of the stomach — (Code first any associated multiple endocrine neoplasia syndrome: 258.01-258.03)(Use additional code to identify associated endocrine syndrome, as: carcinoid syndrome: 259.2)
209.25 Malignant carcinoid tumor of foregut, not otherwise specified — (Code first any associated multiple endocrine neoplasia syndrome: 258.01-258.03)(Use additional code to identify associated endocrine syndrome, as: carcinoid syndrome: 259.2)
211.1 Benign neoplasm of stomach
230.2 Carcinoma in situ of stomach
239.89 Neoplasms of unspecified nature, other specified sites
261 Nutritional marasmus
262 Other severe protein-calorie malnutrition
263.0 Malnutrition of moderate degree
263.1 Malnutrition of mild degree
263.2 Arrested development following protein-calorie malnutrition
263.8 Other protein-calorie malnutrition
276.50 Volume depletion, unspecified — (Use additional code to identify any associated intellectual disabilities) ▽
276.51 Dehydration — (Use additional code to identify any associated intellectual disabilities)
276.52 Hypovolemia — (Use additional code to identify any associated intellectual disabilities)
307.1 Anorexia nervosa
436 Acute, but ill-defined, cerebrovascular disease — (Use additional code to identify presence of hypertension) ▽
519.00 Unspecified tracheostomy complication — (Use additional code to identify infectious organism) ▽
519.01 Infection of tracheostomy — (Use additional code to identify type of infection: 038.0-038.9, 682.1. Use additional code to identify organism: 041.00-041.9)
519.02 Mechanical complication of tracheostomy
519.09 Other tracheostomy complications — (Use additional code to identify infectious organism)
530.3 Stricture and stenosis of esophagus
530.4 Perforation of esophagus
530.5 Dyskinesia of esophagus
530.81 Esophageal reflux
531.00 Acute gastric ulcer with hemorrhage, without mention of obstruction — (Use additional E code to identify drug, if drug induced)
531.01 Acute gastric ulcer with hemorrhage and obstruction — (Use additional E code to identify drug, if drug induced)
531.10 Acute gastric ulcer with perforation, without mention of obstruction — (Use additional E code to identify drug, if drug induced)
531.11 Acute gastric ulcer with perforation and obstruction — (Use additional E code to identify drug, if drug induced)
531.20 Acute gastric ulcer with hemorrhage and perforation, without mention of obstruction — (Use additional E code to identify drug, if drug induced)
531.21 Acute gastric ulcer with hemorrhage, perforation, and obstruction — (Use additional E code to identify drug, if drug induced)
531.30 Acute gastric ulcer without mention of hemorrhage, perforation, or obstruction — (Use additional E code to identify drug, if drug induced)
531.31 Acute gastric ulcer without mention of hemorrhage or perforation, with obstruction — (Use additional E code to identify drug, if drug induced)
531.40 Chronic or unspecified gastric ulcer with hemorrhage, without mention of obstruction — (Use additional E code to identify drug, if drug induced)
531.41 Chronic or unspecified gastric ulcer with hemorrhage and obstruction — (Use additional E code to identify drug, if drug induced)
531.50 Chronic or unspecified gastric ulcer with perforation, without mention of obstruction — (Use additional E code to identify drug, if drug induced)
531.51 Chronic or unspecified gastric ulcer with perforation and obstruction — (Use additional E code to identify drug, if drug induced)
531.60 Chronic or unspecified gastric ulcer with hemorrhage and perforation, without mention of obstruction — (Use additional E code to identify drug, if drug induced)
531.61 Chronic or unspecified gastric ulcer with hemorrhage, perforation, and obstruction — (Use additional E code to identify drug, if drug induced)
531.70 Chronic gastric ulcer without mention of hemorrhage, perforation, without mention of obstruction — (Use additional E code to identify drug, if drug induced)
531.71 Chronic gastric ulcer without mention of hemorrhage or perforation, with obstruction — (Use additional E code to identify drug, if drug induced)
531.90 Gastric ulcer, unspecified as acute or chronic, without mention of hemorrhage, perforation, or obstruction — (Use additional E code to identify drug, if drug induced) ▽
531.91 Gastric ulcer, unspecified as acute or chronic, without mention of hemorrhage or perforation, with obstruction — (Use additional E code to identify drug, if drug induced) ▽
532.00 Acute duodenal ulcer with hemorrhage, without mention of obstruction — (Use additional E code to identify drug, if drug induced)
532.01 Acute duodenal ulcer with hemorrhage and obstruction — (Use additional E code to identify drug, if drug induced)

532.10 Acute duodenal ulcer with perforation, without mention of obstruction — (Use additional E code to identify drug, if drug induced)
532.11 Acute duodenal ulcer with perforation and obstruction — (Use additional E code to identify drug, if drug induced)
532.20 Acute duodenal ulcer with hemorrhage and perforation, without mention of obstruction — (Use additional E code to identify drug, if drug induced)
532.21 Acute duodenal ulcer with hemorrhage, perforation, and obstruction — (Use additional E code to identify drug, if drug induced)
532.30 Acute duodenal ulcer without mention of hemorrhage, perforation, or obstruction — (Use additional E code to identify drug, if drug induced)
532.31 Acute duodenal ulcer without mention of hemorrhage or perforation, with obstruction — (Use additional E code to identify drug, if drug induced)
532.40 Duodenal ulcer, chronic or unspecified, with hemorrhage, without mention of obstruction — (Use additional E code to identify drug, if drug induced)
532.41 Chronic or unspecified duodenal ulcer with hemorrhage and obstruction — (Use additional E code to identify drug, if drug induced)
532.50 Chronic or unspecified duodenal ulcer with perforation, without mention of obstruction — (Use additional E code to identify drug, if drug induced)
532.51 Chronic or unspecified duodenal ulcer with perforation and obstruction — (Use additional E code to identify drug, if drug induced)
532.60 Chronic or unspecified duodenal ulcer with hemorrhage and perforation, without mention of obstruction — (Use additional E code to identify drug, if drug induced)
532.61 Chronic or unspecified duodenal ulcer with hemorrhage, perforation, and obstruction — (Use additional E code to identify drug, if drug induced)
532.70 Chronic duodenal ulcer without mention of hemorrhage, perforation, or obstruction — (Use additional E code to identify drug, if drug induced)
532.71 Chronic duodenal ulcer without mention of hemorrhage or perforation, with obstruction — (Use additional E code to identify drug, if drug induced)
532.90 Duodenal ulcer, unspecified as acute or chronic, without hemorrhage, perforation, or obstruction — (Use additional E code to identify drug, if drug induced) ▽
532.91 Duodenal ulcer, unspecified as acute or chronic, without mention of hemorrhage or perforation, with obstruction — (Use additional E code to identify drug, if drug induced) ▽
533.00 Acute peptic ulcer, unspecified site, with hemorrhage, without mention of obstruction — (Use additional E code to identify drug, if drug induced) ▽
533.01 Acute peptic ulcer, unspecified site, with hemorrhage and obstruction — (Use additional E code to identify drug, if drug induced) ▽
533.10 Acute peptic ulcer, unspecified site, with perforation, without mention of obstruction — (Use additional E code to identify drug, if drug induced) ▽
533.11 Acute peptic ulcer, unspecified site, with perforation and obstruction — (Use additional E code to identify drug, if drug induced) ▽
533.20 Acute peptic ulcer, unspecified site, with hemorrhage and perforation, without mention of obstruction — (Use additional E code to identify drug, if drug induced) ▽
533.21 Acute peptic ulcer, unspecified site, with hemorrhage, perforation, and obstruction — (Use additional E code to identify drug, if drug induced) ▽
533.30 Acute peptic ulcer, unspecified site, without mention of hemorrhage, perforation, or obstruction — (Use additional E code to identify drug, if drug induced) ▽
533.31 Acute peptic ulcer, unspecified site, without mention of hemorrhage and perforation, with obstruction — (Use additional E code to identify drug, if drug induced) ▽
533.40 Chronic or unspecified peptic ulcer, unspecified site, with hemorrhage, without mention of obstruction — (Use additional E code to identify drug, if drug induced) ▽
533.41 Chronic or unspecified peptic ulcer, unspecified site, with hemorrhage and obstruction — (Use additional E code to identify drug, if drug induced) ▽
533.50 Chronic or unspecified peptic ulcer, unspecified site, with perforation, without mention of obstruction — (Use additional E code to identify drug, if drug induced) ▽
533.51 Chronic or unspecified peptic ulcer, unspecified site, with perforation and obstruction — (Use additional E code to identify drug, if drug induced) ▽
535.50 Unspecified gastritis and gastroduodenitis without mention of hemorrhage ▽
535.70 Eosinophilic gastritis without mention of hemorrhage
535.71 Eosinophilic gastritis with hemorrhage
536.9 Unspecified functional disorder of stomach ▽
537.89 Other specified disorder of stomach and duodenum
578.9 Hemorrhage of gastrointestinal tract, unspecified ▽
707.9 Chronic ulcer of unspecified site ▽
750.5 Congenital hypertrophic pyloric stenosis
750.7 Other specified congenital anomalies of stomach
751.1 Congenital atresia and stenosis of small intestine
783.0 Anorexia
783.3 Feeding difficulties and mismanagement
783.40 Lack of normal physiological development, unspecified ▽
783.41 Failure to thrive
783.42 Delayed milestones
783.43 Short stature
783.7 Adult failure to thrive
787.01 Nausea with vomiting
787.04 Bilious emesis
787.20 Dysphagia, unspecified ▽
787.21 Dysphagia, oral phase
787.22 Dysphagia, oropharyngeal phase
787.23 Dysphagia, pharyngeal phase
787.24 Dysphagia, pharyngoesophageal phase
787.29 Other dysphagia
854.06 Intracranial injury of other and unspecified nature, without mention of open intracranial wound, loss of consciousness of unspecified duration ▽
959.01 Head injury, unspecified ▽
959.19 Other injury of other sites of trunk
994.2 Effects of hunger
997.49 Other digestive system complications
V64.41 Laparoscopic surgical procedure converted to open procedure

ICD-9-CM Procedural

43.19 Other gastrostomy

43832

43832 Gastrostomy, open; with construction of gastric tube (eg, Janeway procedure)

ICD-9-CM Diagnostic

146.2 Malignant neoplasm of tonsillar pillars (anterior) (posterior)
146.3 Malignant neoplasm of vallecula
146.5 Malignant neoplasm of junctional region of oropharynx
146.6 Malignant neoplasm of lateral wall of oropharynx
146.7 Malignant neoplasm of posterior wall of oropharynx
146.8 Malignant neoplasm of other specified sites of oropharynx
146.9 Malignant neoplasm of oropharynx, unspecified site ▽
148.0 Malignant neoplasm of postcricoid region of hypopharynx
148.1 Malignant neoplasm of pyriform sinus
148.3 Malignant neoplasm of posterior hypopharyngeal wall
148.8 Malignant neoplasm of other specified sites of hypopharynx
148.9 Malignant neoplasm of hypopharynx, unspecified site ▽
150.0 Malignant neoplasm of cervical esophagus
150.1 Malignant neoplasm of thoracic esophagus
150.2 Malignant neoplasm of abdominal esophagus
150.3 Malignant neoplasm of upper third of esophagus
150.4 Malignant neoplasm of middle third of esophagus
150.5 Malignant neoplasm of lower third of esophagus
150.8 Malignant neoplasm of other specified part of esophagus
150.9 Malignant neoplasm of esophagus, unspecified site ▽
151.0 Malignant neoplasm of cardia
151.1 Malignant neoplasm of pylorus
151.2 Malignant neoplasm of pyloric antrum
151.3 Malignant neoplasm of fundus of stomach

151.4 Malignant neoplasm of body of stomach

151.5 Malignant neoplasm of lesser curvature of stomach, unspecified ▽

151.8 Malignant neoplasm of other specified sites of stomach

151.9 Malignant neoplasm of stomach, unspecified site ▽

197.8 Secondary malignant neoplasm of other digestive organs and spleen

198.89 Secondary malignant neoplasm of other specified sites

209.23 Malignant carcinoid tumor of the stomach — (Code first any associated multiple endocrine neoplasia syndrome: 258.01-258.03)(Use additional code to identify associated endocrine syndrome, as: carcinoid syndrome: 259.2)

209.25 Malignant carcinoid tumor of foregut, not otherwise specified — (Code first any associated multiple endocrine neoplasia syndrome: 258.01-258.03)(Use additional code to identify associated endocrine syndrome, as: carcinoid syndrome: 259.2)

209.63 Benign carcinoid tumor of the stomach — (Code first any associated multiple endocrine neoplasia syndrome: 258.01-258.03)(Use additional code to identify associated endocrine syndrome, as: carcinoid syndrome: 259.2)

209.65 Benign carcinoid tumor of foregut, not otherwise specified — (Code first any associated multiple endocrine neoplasia syndrome: 258.01-258.03)(Use additional code to identify associated endocrine syndrome, as: carcinoid syndrome: 259.2)

211.1 Benign neoplasm of stomach

230.2 Carcinoma in situ of stomach

531.00 Acute gastric ulcer with hemorrhage, without mention of obstruction — (Use additional E code to identify drug, if drug induced)

531.01 Acute gastric ulcer with hemorrhage and obstruction — (Use additional E code to identify drug, if drug induced)

531.10 Acute gastric ulcer with perforation, without mention of obstruction — (Use additional E code to identify drug, if drug induced)

531.11 Acute gastric ulcer with perforation and obstruction — (Use additional E code to identify drug, if drug induced)

531.20 Acute gastric ulcer with hemorrhage and perforation, without mention of obstruction — (Use additional E code to identify drug, if drug induced)

531.21 Acute gastric ulcer with hemorrhage, perforation, and obstruction — (Use additional E code to identify drug, if drug induced)

531.30 Acute gastric ulcer without mention of hemorrhage, perforation, or obstruction — (Use additional E code to identify drug, if drug induced)

531.31 Acute gastric ulcer without mention of hemorrhage or perforation, with obstruction — (Use additional E code to identify drug, if drug induced)

531.40 Chronic or unspecified gastric ulcer with hemorrhage, without mention of obstruction — (Use additional E code to identify drug, if drug induced)

531.41 Chronic or unspecified gastric ulcer with hemorrhage and obstruction — (Use additional E code to identify drug, if drug induced)

531.50 Chronic or unspecified gastric ulcer with perforation, without mention of obstruction — (Use additional E code to identify drug, if drug induced)

531.51 Chronic or unspecified gastric ulcer with perforation and obstruction — (Use additional E code to identify drug, if drug induced)

531.60 Chronic or unspecified gastric ulcer with hemorrhage and perforation, without mention of obstruction — (Use additional E code to identify drug, if drug induced)

531.61 Chronic or unspecified gastric ulcer with hemorrhage, perforation, and obstruction — (Use additional E code to identify drug, if drug induced)

531.70 Chronic gastric ulcer without mention of hemorrhage, perforation, without mention of obstruction — (Use additional E code to identify drug, if drug induced)

531.71 Chronic gastric ulcer without mention of hemorrhage or perforation, with obstruction — (Use additional E code to identify drug, if drug induced)

531.90 Gastric ulcer, unspecified as acute or chronic, without mention of hemorrhage, perforation, or obstruction — (Use additional E code to identify drug, if drug induced) ▽

531.91 Gastric ulcer, unspecified as acute or chronic, without mention of hemorrhage or perforation, with obstruction — (Use additional E code to identify drug, if drug induced) ▽

533.00 Acute peptic ulcer, unspecified site, with hemorrhage, without mention of obstruction — (Use additional E code to identify drug, if drug induced) ▽

533.01 Acute peptic ulcer, unspecified site, with hemorrhage and obstruction — (Use additional E code to identify drug, if drug induced) ▽

533.10 Acute peptic ulcer, unspecified site, with perforation, without mention of obstruction — (Use additional E code to identify drug, if drug induced) ▽

533.11 Acute peptic ulcer, unspecified site, with perforation and obstruction — (Use additional E code to identify drug, if drug induced) ▽

533.20 Acute peptic ulcer, unspecified site, with hemorrhage and perforation, without mention of obstruction — (Use additional E code to identify drug, if drug induced) ▽

533.21 Acute peptic ulcer, unspecified site, with hemorrhage, perforation, and obstruction — (Use additional E code to identify drug, if drug induced) ▽

533.30 Acute peptic ulcer, unspecified site, without mention of hemorrhage, perforation, or obstruction — (Use additional E code to identify drug, if drug induced) ▽

533.31 Acute peptic ulcer, unspecified site, without mention of hemorrhage and perforation, with obstruction — (Use additional E code to identify drug, if drug induced) ▽

533.40 Chronic or unspecified peptic ulcer, unspecified site, with hemorrhage, without mention of obstruction — (Use additional E code to identify drug, if drug induced) ▽

533.41 Chronic or unspecified peptic ulcer, unspecified site, with hemorrhage and obstruction — (Use additional E code to identify drug, if drug induced) ▽

533.50 Chronic or unspecified peptic ulcer, unspecified site, with perforation, without mention of obstruction — (Use additional E code to identify drug, if drug induced) ▽

533.51 Chronic or unspecified peptic ulcer, unspecified site, with perforation and obstruction — (Use additional E code to identify drug, if drug induced) ▽

533.60 Chronic or unspecified peptic ulcer, unspecified site, with hemorrhage and perforation, without mention of obstruction — (Use additional E code to identify drug, if drug induced) ▽

533.61 Chronic or unspecified peptic ulcer, unspecified site, with hemorrhage, perforation, and obstruction — (Use additional E code to identify drug, if drug induced) ▽

533.70 Chronic peptic ulcer, unspecified site, without mention of hemorrhage, perforation, or obstruction — (Use additional E code to identify drug, if drug induced) ▽

533.71 Chronic peptic ulcer of unspecified site without mention of hemorrhage or perforation, with obstruction — (Use additional E code to identify drug, if drug induced) ▽

533.90 Peptic ulcer, unspecified site, unspecified as acute or chronic, without mention of hemorrhage, perforation, or obstruction — (Use additional E code to identify drug, if drug induced) ▽

533.91 Peptic ulcer, unspecified site, unspecified as acute or chronic, without mention of hemorrhage or perforation, with obstruction — (Use additional E code to identify drug, if drug induced) ▽

V64.41 Laparoscopic surgical procedure converted to open procedure

ICD-9-CM Procedural

43.19 Other gastrostomy

43840

43840 Gastrorrhaphy, suture of perforated duodenal or gastric ulcer, wound, or injury

ICD-9-CM Diagnostic

531.10 Acute gastric ulcer with perforation, without mention of obstruction — (Use additional E code to identify drug, if drug induced)

531.11 Acute gastric ulcer with perforation and obstruction — (Use additional E code to identify drug, if drug induced)

531.20 Acute gastric ulcer with hemorrhage and perforation, without mention of obstruction — (Use additional E code to identify drug, if drug induced)

531.21 Acute gastric ulcer with hemorrhage, perforation, and obstruction — (Use additional E code to identify drug, if drug induced)

531.50 Chronic or unspecified gastric ulcer with perforation, without mention of obstruction — (Use additional E code to identify drug, if drug induced)

531.51 Chronic or unspecified gastric ulcer with perforation and obstruction — (Use additional E code to identify drug, if drug induced)

531.60 Chronic or unspecified gastric ulcer with hemorrhage and perforation, without mention of obstruction — (Use additional E code to identify drug, if drug induced)

531.61 Chronic or unspecified gastric ulcer with hemorrhage, perforation, and obstruction — (Use additional E code to identify drug, if drug induced)

532.10 Acute duodenal ulcer with perforation, without mention of obstruction — (Use additional E code to identify drug, if drug induced)

532.11 Acute duodenal ulcer with perforation and obstruction — (Use additional E code to identify drug, if drug induced)

532.20 Acute duodenal ulcer with hemorrhage and perforation, without mention of obstruction — (Use additional E code to identify drug, if drug induced)

532.21 Acute duodenal ulcer with hemorrhage, perforation, and obstruction — (Use additional E code to identify drug, if drug induced)

532.50 Chronic or unspecified duodenal ulcer with perforation, without mention of obstruction — (Use additional E code to identify drug, if drug induced)

532.51 Chronic or unspecified duodenal ulcer with perforation and obstruction — (Use additional E code to identify drug, if drug induced)

532.60 Chronic or unspecified duodenal ulcer with hemorrhage and perforation, without mention of obstruction — (Use additional E code to identify drug, if drug induced)

532.61 Chronic or unspecified duodenal ulcer with hemorrhage, perforation, and obstruction — (Use additional E code to identify drug, if drug induced)

533.10 Acute peptic ulcer, unspecified site, with perforation, without mention of obstruction — (Use additional E code to identify drug, if drug induced) ▽

533.20 Acute peptic ulcer, unspecified site, with hemorrhage and perforation, without mention of obstruction — (Use additional E code to identify drug, if drug induced) ▽

533.21 Acute peptic ulcer, unspecified site, with hemorrhage, perforation, and obstruction — (Use additional E code to identify drug, if drug induced) ▽

533.50 Chronic or unspecified peptic ulcer, unspecified site, with perforation, without mention of obstruction — (Use additional E code to identify drug, if drug induced) ▽

533.51 Chronic or unspecified peptic ulcer, unspecified site, with perforation and obstruction — (Use additional E code to identify drug, if drug induced) ▽

533.60 Chronic or unspecified peptic ulcer, unspecified site, with hemorrhage and perforation, without mention of obstruction — (Use additional E code to identify drug, if drug induced) ▽

533.61 Chronic or unspecified peptic ulcer, unspecified site, with hemorrhage, perforation, and obstruction — (Use additional E code to identify drug, if drug induced) ▽

534.10 Acute gastrojejunal ulcer with perforation, without mention of obstruction

534.11 Acute gastrojejunal ulcer with perforation and obstruction

534.20 Acute gastrojejunal ulcer with hemorrhage and perforation, without mention of obstruction

534.21 Acute gastrojejunal ulcer with hemorrhage, perforation, and obstruction

534.50 Chronic or unspecified gastrojejunal ulcer with perforation, without mention of obstruction

534.51 Chronic or unspecified gastrojejunal ulcer with perforation and obstruction

534.60 Chronic or unspecified gastrojejunal ulcer with hemorrhage and perforation, without mention of obstruction

534.61 Chronic or unspecified gastrojejunal ulcer with hemorrhage, perforation, and obstruction

535.00 Acute gastritis without mention of hemorrhage

535.01 Acute gastritis with hemorrhage

535.10 Atrophic gastritis without mention of hemorrhage

535.11 Atrophic gastritis with hemorrhage

535.20 Gastric mucosal hypertrophy without mention of hemorrhage

535.21 Gastric mucosal hypertrophy with hemorrhage

535.30 Alcoholic gastritis without mention of hemorrhage

535.31 Alcoholic gastritis with hemorrhage

535.40 Other specified gastritis without mention of hemorrhage

535.41 Other specified gastritis with hemorrhage

535.60 Duodenitis without mention of hemorrhage

535.61 Duodenitis with hemorrhage

535.70 Eosinophilic gastritis without mention of hemorrhage

535.71 Eosinophilic gastritis with hemorrhage

536.0 Achlorhydria

536.1 Acute dilatation of stomach

536.2 Persistent vomiting

536.3 Gastroparesis — (Code first underlying disease, if known, as: 249.6, 250.6)

536.8 Dyspepsia and other specified disorders of function of stomach

537.4 Fistula of stomach or duodenum

537.84 Dieulafoy lesion (hemorrhagic) of stomach and duodenum

537.89 Other specified disorder of stomach and duodenum

569.83 Perforation of intestine

578.9 Hemorrhage of gastrointestinal tract, unspecified ▽

863.0 Stomach injury without mention of open wound into cavity

863.1 Stomach injury with open wound into cavity

935.2 Foreign body in stomach

996.79 Other complications due to other internal prosthetic device, implant, and graft — (Use additional code to identify complication: 338.18-338.19, 338.28-338.29)

998.4 Foreign body accidentally left during procedure, not elsewhere classified

ICD-9-CM Procedural

44.41 Suture of gastric ulcer site

44.42 Suture of duodenal ulcer site

44.61 Suture of laceration of stomach

43842-43843

43842 Gastric restrictive procedure, without gastric bypass, for morbid obesity; vertical-banded gastroplasty

43843 other than vertical-banded gastroplasty

ICD-9-CM Diagnostic

244.9 Unspecified hypothyroidism ▽

253.8 Other disorders of the pituitary and other syndromes of diencephalohypophyseal origin

255.8 Other specified disorders of adrenal glands

259.9 Unspecified endocrine disorder ▽

278.01 Morbid obesity — (Use additional code to identify Body Mass Index (BMI), if known: V85.0-V85.54)

ICD-9-CM Procedural

44.69 Other repair of stomach

43845

43845 Gastric restrictive procedure with partial gastrectomy, pylorus-preserving duodenoileostomy and ileoileostomy (50 to 100 cm common channel) to limit absorption (biliopancreatic diversion with duodenal switch)

ICD-9-CM Diagnostic

244.9 Unspecified hypothyroidism ▽

253.8 Other disorders of the pituitary and other syndromes of diencephalohypophyseal origin

255.8 Other specified disorders of adrenal glands

259.9 Unspecified endocrine disorder ▽

278.00 Obesity, unspecified — (Use additional code to identify Body Mass Index (BMI), if known: V85.0-V85.54) (Use additional code to identify any associated intellectual disabilities) ▽

278.01 Morbid obesity — (Use additional code to identify Body Mass Index (BMI), if known: V85.0-V85.54)

ICD-9-CM Procedural

43.89 Open and other partial gastrectomy

45.51 Isolation of segment of small intestine

45.91 Small-to-small intestinal anastomosis

43846-43847

43846 Gastric restrictive procedure, with gastric bypass for morbid obesity; with short limb (150 cm or less) Roux-en-Y gastroenterostomy

43847 with small intestine reconstruction to limit absorption

ICD-9-CM Diagnostic

244.9 Unspecified hypothyroidism ♥

253.8 Other disorders of the pituitary and other syndromes of diencephalohypophyseal origin

255.8 Other specified disorders of adrenal glands

259.9 Unspecified endocrine disorder ♥

278.01 Morbid obesity — (Use additional code to identify Body Mass Index (BMI), if known: V85.0-V85.54)

ICD-9-CM Procedural

44.31 High gastric bypass

43848

43848 Revision, open, of gastric restrictive procedure for morbid obesity, other than adjustable gastric restrictive device (separate procedure)

ICD-9-CM Diagnostic

278.01 Morbid obesity — (Use additional code to identify Body Mass Index (BMI), if known: V85.0-V85.54)

539.81 Infection due to other bariatric procedure — (Use additional code to specify type of infection, such as: 038.0-038.9, 682.2) (Use additional code to identify organism: 041.00-041.9)

539.89 Other complications of other bariatric procedure — (Use additional code(s) to further specify complication)

564.2 Postgastric surgery syndromes

997.49 Other digestive system complications

998.59 Other postoperative infection — (Use additional code to identify infection)

998.89 Other specified complications

ICD-9-CM Procedural

44.5 Revision of gastric anastomosis

43850-43855

43850 Revision of gastroduodenal anastomosis (gastroduodenostomy) with reconstruction; without vagotomy

43855 with vagotomy

ICD-9-CM Diagnostic

151.9 Malignant neoplasm of stomach, unspecified site ♥

152.0 Malignant neoplasm of duodenum

152.1 Malignant neoplasm of jejunum

152.2 Malignant neoplasm of ileum

152.3 Malignant neoplasm of Meckel's diverticulum

152.8 Malignant neoplasm of other specified sites of small intestine

152.9 Malignant neoplasm of small intestine, unspecified site ♥

197.8 Secondary malignant neoplasm of other digestive organs and spleen

209.00 Malignant carcinoid tumor of the small intestine, unspecified portion — (Code first any associated multiple endocrine neoplasia syndrome: 258.01-258.03)(Use additional code to identify associated endocrine syndrome, as: carcinoid syndrome: 259.2) ♥

209.01 Malignant carcinoid tumor of the duodenum — (Code first any associated multiple endocrine neoplasia syndrome: 258.01-258.03)(Use additional code to identify associated endocrine syndrome, as: carcinoid syndrome: 259.2)

209.02 Malignant carcinoid tumor of the jejunum — (Code first any associated multiple endocrine neoplasia syndrome: 258.01-258.03)(Use additional code to identify associated endocrine syndrome, as: carcinoid syndrome: 259.2)

209.03 Malignant carcinoid tumor of the ileum — (Code first any associated multiple endocrine neoplasia syndrome: 258.01-258.03)(Use additional code to identify associated endocrine syndrome, as: carcinoid syndrome: 259.2)

209.23 Malignant carcinoid tumor of the stomach — (Code first any associated multiple endocrine neoplasia syndrome: 258.01-258.03)(Use additional code to identify associated endocrine syndrome, as: carcinoid syndrome: 259.2)

209.25 Malignant carcinoid tumor of foregut, not otherwise specified — (Code first any associated multiple endocrine neoplasia syndrome: 258.01-258.03)(Use additional code to identify associated endocrine syndrome, as: carcinoid syndrome: 259.2)

211.1 Benign neoplasm of stomach

230.2 Carcinoma in situ of stomach

278.01 Morbid obesity — (Use additional code to identify Body Mass Index (BMI), if known: V85.0-V85.54)

531.00 Acute gastric ulcer with hemorrhage, without mention of obstruction — (Use additional E code to identify drug, if drug induced)

531.10 Acute gastric ulcer with perforation, without mention of obstruction — (Use additional E code to identify drug, if drug induced)

531.11 Acute gastric ulcer with perforation and obstruction — (Use additional E code to identify drug, if drug induced)

531.20 Acute gastric ulcer with hemorrhage and perforation, without mention of obstruction — (Use additional E code to identify drug, if drug induced)

531.21 Acute gastric ulcer with hemorrhage, perforation, and obstruction — (Use additional E code to identify drug, if drug induced)

531.50 Chronic or unspecified gastric ulcer with perforation, without mention of obstruction — (Use additional E code to identify drug, if drug induced)

531.51 Chronic or unspecified gastric ulcer with perforation and obstruction — (Use additional E code to identify drug, if drug induced)

531.60 Chronic or unspecified gastric ulcer with hemorrhage and perforation, without mention of obstruction — (Use additional E code to identify drug, if drug induced)

531.61 Chronic or unspecified gastric ulcer with hemorrhage, perforation, and obstruction — (Use additional E code to identify drug, if drug induced)

532.00 Acute duodenal ulcer with hemorrhage, without mention of obstruction — (Use additional E code to identify drug, if drug induced)

532.10 Acute duodenal ulcer with perforation, without mention of obstruction — (Use additional E code to identify drug, if drug induced)

532.20 Acute duodenal ulcer with hemorrhage and perforation, without mention of obstruction — (Use additional E code to identify drug, if drug induced)

533.10 Acute peptic ulcer, unspecified site, with perforation, without mention of obstruction — (Use additional E code to identify drug, if drug induced) ♥

533.11 Acute peptic ulcer, unspecified site, with perforation and obstruction — (Use additional E code to identify drug, if drug induced) ♥

533.20 Acute peptic ulcer, unspecified site, with hemorrhage and perforation, without mention of obstruction — (Use additional E code to identify drug, if drug induced) ♥

533.21 Acute peptic ulcer, unspecified site, with hemorrhage, perforation, and obstruction — (Use additional E code to identify drug, if drug induced) ♥

533.50 Chronic or unspecified peptic ulcer, unspecified site, with perforation, without mention of obstruction — (Use additional E code to identify drug, if drug induced) ♥

533.51 Chronic or unspecified peptic ulcer, unspecified site, with perforation and obstruction — (Use additional E code to identify drug, if drug induced) ♥

533.60 Chronic or unspecified peptic ulcer, unspecified site, with hemorrhage and perforation, without mention of obstruction — (Use additional E code to identify drug, if drug induced) ♥

533.61 Chronic or unspecified peptic ulcer, unspecified site, with hemorrhage, perforation, and obstruction — (Use additional E code to identify drug, if drug induced) ♥

537.2 Chronic duodenal ileus

537.3 Other obstruction of duodenum

537.81 Pylorospasm

537.82 Angiodysplasia of stomach and duodenum (without mention of hemorrhage)

537.83 Angiodysplasia of stomach and duodenum with hemorrhage

537.89 Other specified disorder of stomach and duodenum

539.81 Infection due to other bariatric procedure — (Use additional code to specify type of infection, such as: 038.0-038.9, 682.2) (Use additional code to identify organism: 041.00-041.9)

539.89 Other complications of other bariatric procedure — (Use additional code(s) to further specify complication)

564.2 Postgastric surgery syndromes

ICD-9-CM Procedural

44.00 Vagotomy, not otherwise specified

44.01 Truncal vagotomy

44.02 Highly selective vagotomy

44.03 Other selective vagotomy

44.5 Revision of gastric anastomosis

43860-43865

43860 Revision of gastrojejunal anastomosis (gastrojejunostomy) with reconstruction, with or without partial gastrectomy or intestine resection; without vagotomy

43865 with vagotomy

ICD-9-CM Diagnostic

152.0 Malignant neoplasm of duodenum

197.4 Secondary malignant neoplasm of small intestine including duodenum

209.00 Malignant carcinoid tumor of the small intestine, unspecified portion — (Code first any associated multiple endocrine neoplasia syndrome: 258.01-258.03)(Use additional code to identify associated endocrine syndrome, as: carcinoid syndrome: 259.2)

209.01 Malignant carcinoid tumor of the duodenum — (Code first any associated multiple endocrine neoplasia syndrome: 258.01-258.03)(Use additional code to identify associated endocrine syndrome, as: carcinoid syndrome: 259.2)

209.02 Malignant carcinoid tumor of the jejunum — (Code first any associated multiple endocrine neoplasia syndrome: 258.01-258.03)(Use additional code to identify associated endocrine syndrome, as: carcinoid syndrome: 259.2)

209.03 Malignant carcinoid tumor of the ileum — (Code first any associated multiple endocrine neoplasia syndrome: 258.01-258.03)(Use additional code to identify associated endocrine syndrome, as: carcinoid syndrome: 259.2)

209.40 Benign carcinoid tumor of the small intestine, unspecified portion — (Code first any associated multiple endocrine neoplasia syndrome: 258.01-258.03)(Use additional code to identify associated endocrine syndrome, as: carcinoid syndrome: 259.2)

209.41 Benign carcinoid tumor of the duodenum — (Code first any associated multiple endocrine neoplasia syndrome: 258.01-258.03)(Use additional code to identify associated endocrine syndrome, as: carcinoid syndrome: 259.2)

209.42 Benign carcinoid tumor of the jejunum — (Code first any associated multiple endocrine neoplasia syndrome: 258.01-258.03)(Use additional code to identify associated endocrine syndrome, as: carcinoid syndrome: 259.2)

209.43 Benign carcinoid tumor of the ileum — (Code first any associated multiple endocrine neoplasia syndrome: 258.01-258.03)(Use additional code to identify associated endocrine syndrome, as: carcinoid syndrome: 259.2)

211.2 Benign neoplasm of duodenum, jejunum, and ileum

230.7 Carcinoma in situ of other and unspecified parts of intestine

278.01 Morbid obesity — (Use additional code to identify Body Mass Index (BMI), if known: V85.0-V85.54)

531.10 Acute gastric ulcer with perforation, without mention of obstruction — (Use additional E code to identify drug, if drug induced)

531.11 Acute gastric ulcer with perforation and obstruction — (Use additional E code to identify drug, if drug induced)

531.20 Acute gastric ulcer with hemorrhage and perforation, without mention of obstruction — (Use additional E code to identify drug, if drug induced)

531.21 Acute gastric ulcer with hemorrhage, perforation, and obstruction — (Use additional E code to identify drug, if drug induced)

531.50 Chronic or unspecified gastric ulcer with perforation, without mention of obstruction — (Use additional E code to identify drug, if drug induced)

531.51 Chronic or unspecified gastric ulcer with perforation and obstruction — (Use additional E code to identify drug, if drug induced)

531.61 Chronic or unspecified gastric ulcer with hemorrhage, perforation, and obstruction — (Use additional E code to identify drug, if drug induced)

533.10 Acute peptic ulcer, unspecified site, with perforation, without mention of obstruction — (Use additional E code to identify drug, if drug induced)

533.11 Acute peptic ulcer, unspecified site, with perforation and obstruction — (Use additional E code to identify drug, if drug induced)

533.20 Acute peptic ulcer, unspecified site, with hemorrhage and perforation, without mention of obstruction — (Use additional E code to identify drug, if drug induced)

533.21 Acute peptic ulcer, unspecified site, with hemorrhage, perforation, and obstruction — (Use additional E code to identify drug, if drug induced)

533.50 Chronic or unspecified peptic ulcer, unspecified site, with perforation, without mention of obstruction — (Use additional E code to identify drug, if drug induced)

533.51 Chronic or unspecified peptic ulcer, unspecified site, with perforation and obstruction — (Use additional E code to identify drug, if drug induced)

533.60 Chronic or unspecified peptic ulcer, unspecified site, with hemorrhage and perforation, without mention of obstruction — (Use additional E code to identify drug, if drug induced)

533.61 Chronic or unspecified peptic ulcer, unspecified site, with hemorrhage, perforation, and obstruction — (Use additional E code to identify drug, if drug induced)

534.00 Acute gastrojejunal ulcer with hemorrhage, without mention of obstruction

534.10 Acute gastrojejunal ulcer with perforation, without mention of obstruction

534.20 Acute gastrojejunal ulcer with hemorrhage and perforation, without mention of obstruction

534.30 Acute gastrojejunal ulcer without mention of hemorrhage, perforation, or obstruction

534.50 Chronic or unspecified gastrojejunal ulcer with perforation, without mention of obstruction

534.60 Chronic or unspecified gastrojejunal ulcer with hemorrhage and perforation, without mention of obstruction

534.70 Chronic gastrojejunal ulcer without mention of hemorrhage, perforation, or obstruction

539.81 Infection due to other bariatric procedure — (Use additional code to specify type of infection, such as: 038.0-038.9, 682.2) (Use additional code to identify organism: 041.00-041.9)

539.89 Other complications of other bariatric procedure — (Use additional code(s) to further specify complication)

560.81 Intestinal or peritoneal adhesions with obstruction (postoperative) (postinfection)

564.2 Postgastric surgery syndromes

997.49 Other digestive system complications

ICD-9-CM Procedural

43.7 Partial gastrectomy with anastomosis to jejunum

44.00 Vagotomy, not otherwise specified

44.01 Truncal vagotomy

44.02 Highly selective vagotomy

44.03 Other selective vagotomy

44.39 Other gastroenterostomy without gastrectomy

44.5 Revision of gastric anastomosis

43870

43870 Closure of gastrostomy, surgical

ICD-9-CM Diagnostic

536.40 Unspecified gastrostomy complication

536.41 Infection of gastrostomy — (Use additional code to specify type of infection: 038.0-038.9, 682.2. Use additional code to identify organism: 041.00-041.9)

536.42 Mechanical complication of gastrostomy

536.49 Other gastrostomy complications

V10.00 Personal history of malignant neoplasm of unspecified site in gastrointestinal tract

V10.01 Personal history of malignant neoplasm of tongue

V10.02 Personal history of malignant neoplasm of other and unspecified parts of oral cavity and pharynx

V10.04 Personal history of malignant neoplasm of stomach

V10.21 Personal history of malignant neoplasm of larynx

V55.1 Attention to gastrostomy

ICD-9-CM Procedural

44.62 Closure of gastrostomy

43880

43880 Closure of gastrocolic fistula

ICD-9-CM Diagnostic

537.4 Fistula of stomach or duodenum

ICD-9-CM Procedural

44.63 Closure of other gastric fistula

43881-43882

43881 Implantation or replacement of gastric neurostimulator electrodes, antrum, open
43882 Revision or removal of gastric neurostimulator electrodes, antrum, open

ICD-9-CM Diagnostic

249.60 Secondary diabetes mellitus with neurological manifestations, not stated as uncontrolled, or unspecified — (Use additional code to identify manifestation: 337.1, 353.5, 354.0-355.9, 357.2, 536.3, 713.5) (Use additional code to identify any associated insulin use: V58.67)

249.61 Secondary diabetes mellitus with neurological manifestations, uncontrolled — (Use additional code to identify manifestation: 337.1, 353.5, 354.0-355.9, 357.2, 536.3, 713.5) (Use additional code to identify any associated insulin use: V58.67)

250.60 Diabetes with neurological manifestations, type II or unspecified type, not stated as uncontrolled — (Use additional code to identify manifestation: 337.1, 353.5, 354.0-355.9, 357.2, 536.3, 713.5)

250.61 Diabetes with neurological manifestations, type I [juvenile type], not stated as uncontrolled — (Use additional code to identify manifestation: 337.1, 353.5, 354.0-355.9, 357.2, 536.3, 713.5)

250.62 Diabetes with neurological manifestations, type II or unspecified type, uncontrolled — (Use additional code to identify manifestation: 337.1, 353.5, 354.0-355.9, 357.2, 536.3, 713.5)

250.63 Diabetes with neurological manifestations, type I [juvenile type], uncontrolled — (Use additional code to identify manifestation: 337.1, 353.5, 354.0-355.9, 357.2, 536.3, 713.5)

278.01 Morbid obesity — (Use additional code to identify Body Mass Index (BMI), if known: V85.0-V85.54)

536.3 Gastroparesis — (Code first underlying disease, if known, as: 249.6, 250.6)

539.81 Infection due to other bariatric procedure — (Use additional code to specify type of infection, such as: 038.0-038.9, 682.2) (Use additional code to identify organism: 041.00-041.9)

539.89 Other complications of other bariatric procedure — (Use additional code(s) to further specify complication)

996.79 Other complications due to other internal prosthetic device, implant, and graft — (Use additional code to identify complication: 338.18-338.19, 338.28-338.29)

V53.59 Fitting and adjustment of other gastrointestinal appliance and device

ICD-9-CM Procedural

04.92 Implantation or replacement of peripheral neurostimulator lead(s)
04.93 Removal of peripheral neurostimulator lead(s)

43886-43888

43886 Gastric restrictive procedure, open; revision of subcutaneous port component only
43887 removal of subcutaneous port component only
43888 removal and replacement of subcutaneous port component only

ICD-9-CM Diagnostic

539.81 Infection due to other bariatric procedure — (Use additional code to specify type of infection, such as: 038.0-038.9, 682.2) (Use additional code to identify organism: 041.00-041.9)

539.89 Other complications of other bariatric procedure — (Use additional code(s) to further specify complication)

564.2 Postgastric surgery syndromes

998.89 Other specified complications

V45.86 Bariatric surgery status

V53.51 Fitting and adjustment of gastric lap band

ICD-9-CM Procedural

44.69 Other repair of stomach
44.99 Other operations on stomach

Intestines (Except Rectum)

44005

44005 Enterolysis (freeing of intestinal adhesion) (separate procedure)

ICD-9-CM Diagnostic

537.3 Other obstruction of duodenum
560.81 Intestinal or peritoneal adhesions with obstruction (postoperative) (postinfection)
560.9 Unspecified intestinal obstruction ▽
567.82 Sclerosing mesenteritis
568.0 Peritoneal adhesions (postoperative) (postinfection)
568.81 Hemoperitoneum (nontraumatic)
569.81 Fistula of intestine, excluding rectum and anus
569.83 Perforation of intestine
569.9 Unspecified disorder of intestine ▽

614.6 Pelvic peritoneal adhesions, female (postoperative) (postinfection) — (Use additional code to identify organism: 041.00-041.09, 041.10-041.19) (Use additional code to identify any associated infertility: 628.2) ♀

628.2 Female infertility of tubal origin — (Use additional code for any associated peritubal adhesions: 614.6) ♀

789.00 Abdominal pain, unspecified site ▽
789.01 Abdominal pain, right upper quadrant
789.02 Abdominal pain, left upper quadrant
789.03 Abdominal pain, right lower quadrant
789.04 Abdominal pain, left lower quadrant
789.05 Abdominal pain, periumbilic
789.06 Abdominal pain, epigastric
789.07 Abdominal pain, generalized
789.09 Abdominal pain, other specified site
789.30 Abdominal or pelvic swelling, mass or lump, unspecified site ▽
789.31 Abdominal or pelvic swelling, mass, or lump, right upper quadrant
789.32 Abdominal or pelvic swelling, mass, or lump, left upper quadrant
789.33 Abdominal or pelvic swelling, mass, or lump, right lower quadrant
789.34 Abdominal or pelvic swelling, mass, or lump, left lower quadrant
789.35 Abdominal or pelvic swelling, mass or lump, periumbilic
789.36 Abdominal or pelvic swelling, mass, or lump, epigastric
789.37 Abdominal or pelvic swelling, mass, or lump, generalized
789.39 Abdominal or pelvic swelling, mass, or lump, other specified site
997.49 Other digestive system complications
V45.72 Acquired absence of intestine (large) (small)
V64.41 Laparoscopic surgical procedure converted to open procedure

ICD-9-CM Procedural

54.59 Other lysis of peritoneal adhesions

44010

44010 Duodenotomy, for exploration, biopsy(s), or foreign body removal

ICD-9-CM Diagnostic

152.0 Malignant neoplasm of duodenum
197.4 Secondary malignant neoplasm of small intestine including duodenum

209.01 Malignant carcinoid tumor of the duodenum — (Code first any associated multiple endocrine neoplasia syndrome: 258.01-258.03)(Use additional code to identify associated endocrine syndrome, as: carcinoid syndrome: 259.2)

209.41 Benign carcinoid tumor of the duodenum — (Code first any associated multiple endocrine neoplasia syndrome: 258.01-258.03)(Use additional code to identify associated endocrine syndrome, as: carcinoid syndrome: 259.2)

211.2 Benign neoplasm of duodenum, jejunum, and ileum

230.7 Carcinoma in situ of other and unspecified parts of intestine ▽

235.2 Neoplasm of uncertain behavior of stomach, intestines, and rectum

239.0 Neoplasm of unspecified nature of digestive system

936 Foreign body in intestine and colon

ICD-9-CM Procedural

45.01 Incision of duodenum

45.15 Open biopsy of small intestine

44020

44020 Enterotomy, small intestine, other than duodenum; for exploration, biopsy(s), or foreign body removal

ICD-9-CM Diagnostic

152.1 Malignant neoplasm of jejunum

152.2 Malignant neoplasm of ileum

197.4 Secondary malignant neoplasm of small intestine including duodenum

209.02 Malignant carcinoid tumor of the jejunum — (Code first any associated multiple endocrine neoplasia syndrome: 258.01-258.03)(Use additional code to identify associated endocrine syndrome, as: carcinoid syndrome: 259.2)

209.03 Malignant carcinoid tumor of the ileum — (Code first any associated multiple endocrine neoplasia syndrome: 258.01-258.03)(Use additional code to identify associated endocrine syndrome, as: carcinoid syndrome: 259.2)

209.29 Malignant carcinoid tumor of other sites — (Code first any associated multiple endocrine neoplasia syndrome: 258.01-258.03)(Use additional code to identify associated endocrine syndrome, as: carcinoid syndrome: 259.2)

209.42 Benign carcinoid tumor of the jejunum — (Code first any associated multiple endocrine neoplasia syndrome: 258.01-258.03)(Use additional code to identify associated endocrine syndrome, as: carcinoid syndrome: 259.2)

209.43 Benign carcinoid tumor of the ileum — (Code first any associated multiple endocrine neoplasia syndrome: 258.01-258.03)(Use additional code to identify associated endocrine syndrome, as: carcinoid syndrome: 259.2)

209.69 Benign carcinoid tumor of other sites — (Code first any associated multiple endocrine neoplasia syndrome: 258.01-258.03)(Use additional code to identify associated endocrine syndrome, as: carcinoid syndrome: 259.2)

211.2 Benign neoplasm of duodenum, jejunum, and ileum

230.7 Carcinoma in situ of other and unspecified parts of intestine ▽

235.2 Neoplasm of uncertain behavior of stomach, intestines, and rectum

239.0 Neoplasm of unspecified nature of digestive system

560.31 Gallstone ileus

936 Foreign body in intestine and colon

ICD-9-CM Procedural

45.02 Other incision of small intestine

45.15 Open biopsy of small intestine

44021

44021 Enterotomy, small intestine, other than duodenum; for decompression (eg, Baker tube)

ICD-9-CM Diagnostic

152.1 Malignant neoplasm of jejunum

152.2 Malignant neoplasm of ileum

209.02 Malignant carcinoid tumor of the jejunum — (Code first any associated multiple endocrine neoplasia syndrome: 258.01-258.03)(Use additional code to identify associated endocrine syndrome, as: carcinoid syndrome: 259.2)

209.03 Malignant carcinoid tumor of the ileum — (Code first any associated multiple endocrine neoplasia syndrome: 258.01-258.03)(Use additional code to identify associated endocrine syndrome, as: carcinoid syndrome: 259.2)

552.8 Hernia of other specified site, with obstruction

555.0 Regional enteritis of small intestine

560.1 Paralytic ileus

560.31 Gallstone ileus

560.81 Intestinal or peritoneal adhesions with obstruction (postoperative) (postinfection)

560.89 Other specified intestinal obstruction

560.9 Unspecified intestinal obstruction ▽

564.2 Postgastric surgery syndromes

ICD-9-CM Procedural

45.02 Other incision of small intestine

46.39 Other enterostomy

44025

44025 Colotomy, for exploration, biopsy(s), or foreign body removal

ICD-9-CM Diagnostic

153.0 Malignant neoplasm of hepatic flexure

153.1 Malignant neoplasm of transverse colon

153.2 Malignant neoplasm of descending colon

153.4 Malignant neoplasm of cecum

153.5 Malignant neoplasm of appendix

197.5 Secondary malignant neoplasm of large intestine and rectum

209.10 Malignant carcinoid tumor of the large intestine, unspecified portion — (Code first any associated multiple endocrine neoplasia syndrome: 258.01-258.03)(Use additional code to identify associated endocrine syndrome, as: carcinoid syndrome: 259.2) ▽

209.12 Malignant carcinoid tumor of the cecum — (Code first any associated multiple endocrine neoplasia syndrome: 258.01-258.03)(Use additional code to identify associated endocrine syndrome, as: carcinoid syndrome: 259.2)

209.14 Malignant carcinoid tumor of the transverse colon — (Code first any associated multiple endocrine neoplasia syndrome: 258.01-258.03)(Use additional code to identify associated endocrine syndrome, as: carcinoid syndrome: 259.2)

209.15 Malignant carcinoid tumor of the descending colon — (Code first any associated multiple endocrine neoplasia syndrome: 258.01-258.03)(Use additional code to identify associated endocrine syndrome, as: carcinoid syndrome: 259.2)

209.27 Malignant carcinoid tumor of hindgut, not otherwise specified — (Code first any associated multiple endocrine neoplasia syndrome: 258.01-258.03)(Use additional code to identify associated endocrine syndrome, as: carcinoid syndrome: 259.2)

209.50 Benign carcinoid tumor of the large intestine, unspecified portion — (Code first any associated multiple endocrine neoplasia syndrome: 258.01-258.03)(Use additional code to identify associated endocrine syndrome, as: carcinoid syndrome: 259.2) ▽

209.54 Benign carcinoid tumor of the transverse colon — (Code first any associated multiple endocrine neoplasia syndrome: 258.01-258.03)(Use additional code to identify associated endocrine syndrome, as: carcinoid syndrome: 259.2)

209.55 Benign carcinoid tumor of the descending colon — (Code first any associated multiple endocrine neoplasia syndrome: 258.01-258.03)(Use additional code to identify associated endocrine syndrome, as: carcinoid syndrome: 259.2)

209.56 Benign carcinoid tumor of the sigmoid colon — (Code first any associated multiple endocrine neoplasia syndrome: 258.01-258.03)(Use additional code to identify associated endocrine syndrome, as: carcinoid syndrome: 259.2)

209.57 Benign carcinoid tumor of the rectum — (Code first any associated multiple endocrine neoplasia syndrome: 258.01-258.03)(Use additional code to identify associated endocrine syndrome, as: carcinoid syndrome: 259.2)

211.3 Benign neoplasm of colon

556.0 Ulcerative (chronic) enterocolitis

556.2 Ulcerative (chronic) proctitis

556.3 Ulcerative (chronic) proctosigmoiditis

556.4 Pseudopolyposis of colon

556.5 Left sided ulcerative (chronic) colitis

556.6	Universal ulcerative (chronic) colitis
556.8	Other ulcerative colitis
556.9	Unspecified ulcerative colitis ▽
558.42	Eosinophilic colitis
560.81	Intestinal or peritoneal adhesions with obstruction (postoperative) (postinfection)
751.3	Hirschsprung's disease and other congenital functional disorders of colon
936	Foreign body in intestine and colon

ICD-9-CM Procedural

45.03	Incision of large intestine
45.26	Open biopsy of large intestine

44050-44055

44050	Reduction of volvulus, intussusception, internal hernia, by laparotomy
44055	Correction of malrotation by lysis of duodenal bands and/or reduction of midgut volvulus (eg, Ladd procedure)

ICD-9-CM Diagnostic

152.1	Malignant neoplasm of jejunum
152.2	Malignant neoplasm of ileum
152.3	Malignant neoplasm of Meckel's diverticulum
152.8	Malignant neoplasm of other specified sites of small intestine
152.9	Malignant neoplasm of small intestine, unspecified site ▽
153.0	Malignant neoplasm of hepatic flexure
153.1	Malignant neoplasm of transverse colon
153.2	Malignant neoplasm of descending colon
153.3	Malignant neoplasm of sigmoid colon
153.4	Malignant neoplasm of cecum
209.00	Malignant carcinoid tumor of the small intestine, unspecified portion — (Code first any associated multiple endocrine neoplasia syndrome: 258.01-258.03)(Use additional code to identify associated endocrine syndrome, as: carcinoid syndrome: 259.2) ▽
209.02	Malignant carcinoid tumor of the jejunum — (Code first any associated multiple endocrine neoplasia syndrome: 258.01-258.03)(Use additional code to identify associated endocrine syndrome, as: carcinoid syndrome: 259.2)
209.03	Malignant carcinoid tumor of the ileum — (Code first any associated multiple endocrine neoplasia syndrome: 258.01-258.03)(Use additional code to identify associated endocrine syndrome, as: carcinoid syndrome: 259.2)
209.12	Malignant carcinoid tumor of the cecum — (Code first any associated multiple endocrine neoplasia syndrome: 258.01-258.03)(Use additional code to identify associated endocrine syndrome, as: carcinoid syndrome: 259.2)
209.14	Malignant carcinoid tumor of the transverse colon — (Code first any associated multiple endocrine neoplasia syndrome: 258.01-258.03)(Use additional code to identify associated endocrine syndrome, as: carcinoid syndrome: 259.2)
209.15	Malignant carcinoid tumor of the descending colon — (Code first any associated multiple endocrine neoplasia syndrome: 258.01-258.03)(Use additional code to identify associated endocrine syndrome, as: carcinoid syndrome: 259.2)
209.16	Malignant carcinoid tumor of the sigmoid colon — (Code first any associated multiple endocrine neoplasia syndrome: 258.01-258.03)(Use additional code to identify associated endocrine syndrome, as: carcinoid syndrome: 259.2)
209.41	Benign carcinoid tumor of the duodenum — (Code first any associated multiple endocrine neoplasia syndrome: 258.01-258.03)(Use additional code to identify associated endocrine syndrome, as: carcinoid syndrome: 259.2)
209.42	Benign carcinoid tumor of the jejunum — (Code first any associated multiple endocrine neoplasia syndrome: 258.01-258.03)(Use additional code to identify associated endocrine syndrome, as: carcinoid syndrome: 259.2)
209.43	Benign carcinoid tumor of the ileum — (Code first any associated multiple endocrine neoplasia syndrome: 258.01-258.03)(Use additional code to identify associated endocrine syndrome, as: carcinoid syndrome: 259.2)
209.53	Benign carcinoid tumor of the ascending colon — (Code first any associated multiple endocrine neoplasia syndrome: 258.01-258.03)(Use additional code to identify associated endocrine syndrome, as: carcinoid syndrome: 259.2)
209.54	Benign carcinoid tumor of the transverse colon — (Code first any associated multiple endocrine neoplasia syndrome: 258.01-258.03)(Use additional code to identify associated endocrine syndrome, as: carcinoid syndrome: 259.2)
209.56	Benign carcinoid tumor of the sigmoid colon — (Code first any associated multiple endocrine neoplasia syndrome: 258.01-258.03)(Use additional code to identify associated endocrine syndrome, as: carcinoid syndrome: 259.2)
209.57	Benign carcinoid tumor of the rectum — (Code first any associated multiple endocrine neoplasia syndrome: 258.01-258.03)(Use additional code to identify associated endocrine syndrome, as: carcinoid syndrome: 259.2)
211.2	Benign neoplasm of duodenum, jejunum, and ileum
211.3	Benign neoplasm of colon
537.3	Other obstruction of duodenum
550.10	Inguinal hernia with obstruction, without mention of gangrene, unilateral or unspecified, (not specified as recurrent)
550.11	Inguinal hernia with obstruction, without mention of gangrene, recurrent unilateral or unspecified
550.12	Inguinal hernia with obstruction, without mention gangrene, bilateral, (not specified as recurrent)
550.90	Inguinal hernia without mention of obstruction or gangrene, unilateral or unspecified, (not specified as recurrent)
551.20	Unspecified ventral hernia with gangrene ▽
551.21	Incisional ventral hernia, with gangrene
552.00	Unilateral or unspecified femoral hernia with obstruction
552.8	Hernia of other specified site, with obstruction
552.9	Hernia of unspecified site, with obstruction ▽
553.1	Umbilical hernia without mention of obstruction or gangrene
553.8	Hernia of other specified sites of abdominal cavity without mention of obstruction or gangrene
553.9	Hernia of unspecified site of abdominal cavity without mention of obstruction or gangrene ▽
560.0	Intussusception
560.1	Paralytic ileus
560.2	Volvulus
560.81	Intestinal or peritoneal adhesions with obstruction (postoperative) (postinfection)
560.89	Other specified intestinal obstruction
560.9	Unspecified intestinal obstruction ▽
568.0	Peritoneal adhesions (postoperative) (postinfection)
569.87	Vomiting of fecal matter
751.1	Congenital atresia and stenosis of small intestine
751.4	Congenital anomalies of intestinal fixation

ICD-9-CM Procedural

46.80	Intra-abdominal manipulation of intestine, not otherwise specified
46.81	Intra-abdominal manipulation of small intestine
46.82	Intra-abdominal manipulation of large intestine
53.9	Other hernia repair
54.95	Incision of peritoneum

44100

44100	Biopsy of intestine by capsule, tube, peroral (1 or more specimens)

ICD-9-CM Diagnostic

152.0	Malignant neoplasm of duodenum
152.1	Malignant neoplasm of jejunum
152.2	Malignant neoplasm of ileum
152.8	Malignant neoplasm of other specified sites of small intestine
152.9	Malignant neoplasm of small intestine, unspecified site ▽
197.4	Secondary malignant neoplasm of small intestine including duodenum
209.00	Malignant carcinoid tumor of the small intestine, unspecified portion — (Code first any associated multiple endocrine neoplasia syndrome: 258.01-258.03)(Use additional code to identify associated endocrine syndrome, as: carcinoid syndrome: 259.2) ▽

209.01 Malignant carcinoid tumor of the duodenum — (Code first any associated multiple endocrine neoplasia syndrome: 258.01-258.03)(Use additional code to identify associated endocrine syndrome, as: carcinoid syndrome: 259.2)

209.02 Malignant carcinoid tumor of the jejunum — (Code first any associated multiple endocrine neoplasia syndrome: 258.01-258.03)(Use additional code to identify associated endocrine syndrome, as: carcinoid syndrome: 259.2)

209.03 Malignant carcinoid tumor of the ileum — (Code first any associated multiple endocrine neoplasia syndrome: 258.01-258.03)(Use additional code to identify associated endocrine syndrome, as: carcinoid syndrome: 259.2)

209.29 Malignant carcinoid tumor of other sites — (Code first any associated multiple endocrine neoplasia syndrome: 258.01-258.03)(Use additional code to identify associated endocrine syndrome, as: carcinoid syndrome: 259.2)

209.40 Benign carcinoid tumor of the small intestine, unspecified portion — (Code first any associated multiple endocrine neoplasia syndrome: 258.01-258.03)(Use additional code to identify associated endocrine syndrome, as: carcinoid syndrome: 259.2) ▽

209.41 Benign carcinoid tumor of the duodenum — (Code first any associated multiple endocrine neoplasia syndrome: 258.01-258.03)(Use additional code to identify associated endocrine syndrome, as: carcinoid syndrome: 259.2)

209.42 Benign carcinoid tumor of the jejunum — (Code first any associated multiple endocrine neoplasia syndrome: 258.01-258.03)(Use additional code to identify associated endocrine syndrome, as: carcinoid syndrome: 259.2)

209.43 Benign carcinoid tumor of the ileum — (Code first any associated multiple endocrine neoplasia syndrome: 258.01-258.03)(Use additional code to identify associated endocrine syndrome, as: carcinoid syndrome: 259.2)

209.69 Benign carcinoid tumor of other sites — (Code first any associated multiple endocrine neoplasia syndrome: 258.01-258.03)(Use additional code to identify associated endocrine syndrome, as: carcinoid syndrome: 259.2)

211.2 Benign neoplasm of duodenum, jejunum, and ileum

230.7 Carcinoma in situ of other and unspecified parts of intestine ▽

235.2 Neoplasm of uncertain behavior of stomach, intestines, and rectum

239.0 Neoplasm of unspecified nature of digestive system

556.0 Ulcerative (chronic) enterocolitis

556.2 Ulcerative (chronic) proctitis

556.3 Ulcerative (chronic) proctosigmoiditis

556.4 Pseudopolyposis of colon

556.5 Left sided ulcerative (chronic) colitis

556.6 Universal ulcerative (chronic) colitis

556.8 Other ulcerative colitis

556.9 Unspecified ulcerative colitis ▽

558.42 Eosinophilic colitis

578.1 Blood in stool

751.3 Hirschsprung's disease and other congenital functional disorders of colon

783.21 Loss of weight — (Use additional code to identify Body Mass Index (BMI), if known: V85.0-V85.54)

783.22 Underweight — (Use additional code to identify Body Mass Index (BMI), if known: V85.0-V85.54)

783.7 Adult failure to thrive

792.1 Nonspecific abnormal finding in stool contents

793.4 Nonspecific (abnormal) findings on radiological and other examination of gastrointestinal tract

V85.0 Body Mass Index less than 19, adult

ICD-9-CM Procedural

45.14 Closed [endoscopic] biopsy of small intestine

HCPCS Level II Supplies & Services

A4305 Disposable drug delivery system, flow rate of 50 ml or greater per hour

44110-44111

44110 Excision of 1 or more lesions of small or large intestine not requiring anastomosis, exteriorization, or fistulization; single enterotomy

44111 multiple enterotomies

ICD-9-CM Diagnostic

152.0 Malignant neoplasm of duodenum

152.2 Malignant neoplasm of ileum

152.8 Malignant neoplasm of other specified sites of small intestine

152.9 Malignant neoplasm of small intestine, unspecified site ▽

153.1 Malignant neoplasm of transverse colon

153.2 Malignant neoplasm of descending colon

153.3 Malignant neoplasm of sigmoid colon

197.4 Secondary malignant neoplasm of small intestine including duodenum

197.5 Secondary malignant neoplasm of large intestine and rectum

209.00 Malignant carcinoid tumor of the small intestine, unspecified portion — (Code first any associated multiple endocrine neoplasia syndrome: 258.01-258.03)(Use additional code to identify associated endocrine syndrome, as: carcinoid syndrome: 259.2) ▽

209.01 Malignant carcinoid tumor of the duodenum — (Code first any associated multiple endocrine neoplasia syndrome: 258.01-258.03)(Use additional code to identify associated endocrine syndrome, as: carcinoid syndrome: 259.2)

209.02 Malignant carcinoid tumor of the jejunum — (Code first any associated multiple endocrine neoplasia syndrome: 258.01-258.03)(Use additional code to identify associated endocrine syndrome, as: carcinoid syndrome: 259.2)

209.03 Malignant carcinoid tumor of the ileum — (Code first any associated multiple endocrine neoplasia syndrome: 258.01-258.03)(Use additional code to identify associated endocrine syndrome, as: carcinoid syndrome: 259.2)

209.10 Malignant carcinoid tumor of the large intestine, unspecified portion — (Code first any associated multiple endocrine neoplasia syndrome: 258.01-258.03)(Use additional code to identify associated endocrine syndrome, as: carcinoid syndrome: 259.2) ▽

209.12 Malignant carcinoid tumor of the cecum — (Code first any associated multiple endocrine neoplasia syndrome: 258.01-258.03)(Use additional code to identify associated endocrine syndrome, as: carcinoid syndrome: 259.2)

209.14 Malignant carcinoid tumor of the transverse colon — (Code first any associated multiple endocrine neoplasia syndrome: 258.01-258.03)(Use additional code to identify associated endocrine syndrome, as: carcinoid syndrome: 259.2)

209.15 Malignant carcinoid tumor of the descending colon — (Code first any associated multiple endocrine neoplasia syndrome: 258.01-258.03)(Use additional code to identify associated endocrine syndrome, as: carcinoid syndrome: 259.2)

209.16 Malignant carcinoid tumor of the sigmoid colon — (Code first any associated multiple endocrine neoplasia syndrome: 258.01-258.03)(Use additional code to identify associated endocrine syndrome, as: carcinoid syndrome: 259.2)

209.40 Benign carcinoid tumor of the small intestine, unspecified portion — (Code first any associated multiple endocrine neoplasia syndrome: 258.01-258.03)(Use additional code to identify associated endocrine syndrome, as: carcinoid syndrome: 259.2) ▽

209.41 Benign carcinoid tumor of the duodenum — (Code first any associated multiple endocrine neoplasia syndrome: 258.01-258.03)(Use additional code to identify associated endocrine syndrome, as: carcinoid syndrome: 259.2)

209.42 Benign carcinoid tumor of the jejunum — (Code first any associated multiple endocrine neoplasia syndrome: 258.01-258.03)(Use additional code to identify associated endocrine syndrome, as: carcinoid syndrome: 259.2)

209.43 Benign carcinoid tumor of the ileum — (Code first any associated multiple endocrine neoplasia syndrome: 258.01-258.03)(Use additional code to identify associated endocrine syndrome, as: carcinoid syndrome: 259.2)

209.50 Benign carcinoid tumor of the large intestine, unspecified portion — (Code first any associated multiple endocrine neoplasia syndrome: 258.01-258.03)(Use additional code to identify associated endocrine syndrome, as: carcinoid syndrome: 259.2) ▽

209.52 Benign carcinoid tumor of the cecum — (Code first any associated multiple endocrine neoplasia syndrome: 258.01-258.03)(Use additional code to identify associated endocrine syndrome, as: carcinoid syndrome: 259.2)

209.53 Benign carcinoid tumor of the ascending colon — (Code first any associated multiple endocrine neoplasia syndrome: 258.01-258.03)(Use additional code to identify associated endocrine syndrome, as: carcinoid syndrome: 259.2)
209.54 Benign carcinoid tumor of the transverse colon — (Code first any associated multiple endocrine neoplasia syndrome: 258.01-258.03)(Use additional code to identify associated endocrine syndrome, as: carcinoid syndrome: 259.2)
209.55 Benign carcinoid tumor of the descending colon — (Code first any associated multiple endocrine neoplasia syndrome: 258.01-258.03)(Use additional code to identify associated endocrine syndrome, as: carcinoid syndrome: 259.2)
209.56 Benign carcinoid tumor of the sigmoid colon — (Code first any associated multiple endocrine neoplasia syndrome: 258.01-258.03)(Use additional code to identify associated endocrine syndrome, as: carcinoid syndrome: 259.2)
211.2 Benign neoplasm of duodenum, jejunum, and ileum
211.3 Benign neoplasm of colon
230.3 Carcinoma in situ of colon
230.4 Carcinoma in situ of rectum
230.7 Carcinoma in situ of other and unspecified parts of intestine ▽
235.2 Neoplasm of uncertain behavior of stomach, intestines, and rectum
560.81 Intestinal or peritoneal adhesions with obstruction (postoperative) (postinfection)
617.5 Endometriosis of intestine ♀
751.3 Hirschsprung's disease and other congenital functional disorders of colon

ICD-9-CM Procedural

45.31 Other local excision of lesion of duodenum
45.33 Local excision of lesion or tissue of small intestine, except duodenum
45.41 Excision of lesion or tissue of large intestine
45.61 Multiple segmental resection of small intestine

44120-44125

44120 Enterectomy, resection of small intestine; single resection and anastomosis
44121 each additional resection and anastomosis (List separately in addition to code for primary procedure)
44125 with enterostomy

ICD-9-CM Diagnostic

152.0 Malignant neoplasm of duodenum
152.1 Malignant neoplasm of jejunum
152.2 Malignant neoplasm of ileum
152.8 Malignant neoplasm of other specified sites of small intestine
152.9 Malignant neoplasm of small intestine, unspecified site ▽
197.4 Secondary malignant neoplasm of small intestine including duodenum
209.00 Malignant carcinoid tumor of the small intestine, unspecified portion — (Code first any associated multiple endocrine neoplasia syndrome: 258.01-258.03)(Use additional code to identify associated endocrine syndrome, as: carcinoid syndrome: 259.2) ▽
209.01 Malignant carcinoid tumor of the duodenum — (Code first any associated multiple endocrine neoplasia syndrome: 258.01-258.03)(Use additional code to identify associated endocrine syndrome, as: carcinoid syndrome: 259.2)
209.02 Malignant carcinoid tumor of the jejunum — (Code first any associated multiple endocrine neoplasia syndrome: 258.01-258.03)(Use additional code to identify associated endocrine syndrome, as: carcinoid syndrome: 259.2)
209.03 Malignant carcinoid tumor of the ileum — (Code first any associated multiple endocrine neoplasia syndrome: 258.01-258.03)(Use additional code to identify associated endocrine syndrome, as: carcinoid syndrome: 259.2)
209.26 Malignant carcinoid tumor of midgut, not otherwise specified — (Code first any associated multiple endocrine neoplasia syndrome: 258.01-258.03)(Use additional code to identify associated endocrine syndrome, as: carcinoid syndrome: 259.2)
209.30 Malignant poorly differentiated neuroendocrine carcinoma, any site — (Code first any associated multiple endocrine neoplasia syndrome: 258.01-258.03)(Use additional code to identify associated endocrine syndrome, as: carcinoid syndrome: 259.2) ▽
209.41 Benign carcinoid tumor of the duodenum — (Code first any associated multiple endocrine neoplasia syndrome: 258.01-258.03)(Use additional code to identify associated endocrine syndrome, as: carcinoid syndrome: 259.2)
209.42 Benign carcinoid tumor of the jejunum — (Code first any associated multiple endocrine neoplasia syndrome: 258.01-258.03)(Use additional code to identify associated endocrine syndrome, as: carcinoid syndrome: 259.2)
209.43 Benign carcinoid tumor of the ileum — (Code first any associated multiple endocrine neoplasia syndrome: 258.01-258.03)(Use additional code to identify associated endocrine syndrome, as: carcinoid syndrome: 259.2)
209.66 Benign carcinoid tumor of midgut, not otherwise specified — (Code first any associated multiple endocrine neoplasia syndrome: 258.01-258.03)(Use additional code to identify associated endocrine syndrome, as: carcinoid syndrome: 259.2)
209.69 Benign carcinoid tumor of other sites — (Code first any associated multiple endocrine neoplasia syndrome: 258.01-258.03)(Use additional code to identify associated endocrine syndrome, as: carcinoid syndrome: 259.2)
211.2 Benign neoplasm of duodenum, jejunum, and ileum
230.7 Carcinoma in situ of other and unspecified parts of intestine ▽
230.9 Carcinoma in situ of other and unspecified digestive organs ▽
235.2 Neoplasm of uncertain behavior of stomach, intestines, and rectum
239.0 Neoplasm of unspecified nature of digestive system
551.00 Femoral hernia with gangrene, unilateral or unspecified (not specified as recurrent)
551.21 Incisional ventral hernia, with gangrene
551.8 Hernia of other specified sites, with gangrene
551.9 Hernia of unspecified site, with gangrene ▽
552.00 Unilateral or unspecified femoral hernia with obstruction
552.21 Incisional hernia with obstruction
555.0 Regional enteritis of small intestine
555.9 Regional enteritis of unspecified site ▽
556.1 Ulcerative (chronic) ileocolitis
556.8 Other ulcerative colitis
556.9 Unspecified ulcerative colitis ▽
560.0 Intussusception
560.1 Paralytic ileus
560.2 Volvulus
560.81 Intestinal or peritoneal adhesions with obstruction (postoperative) (postinfection)
560.89 Other specified intestinal obstruction
560.9 Unspecified intestinal obstruction ▽
562.00 Diverticulosis of small intestine (without mention of hemorrhage) — (Use additional code to identify any associated peritonitis: 567.0-567.9)
562.01 Diverticulitis of small intestine (without mention of hemorrhage) — (Use additional code to identify any associated peritonitis: 567.0-567.9)
562.02 Diverticulosis of small intestine with hemorrhage — (Use additional code to identify any associated peritonitis: 567.0-567.9)
562.03 Diverticulitis of small intestine with hemorrhage — (Use additional code to identify any associated peritonitis: 567.0-567.9)
567.0 Peritonitis in infectious diseases classified elsewhere — (Code first underlying disease) ☒
567.1 Pneumococcal peritonitis
567.21 Peritonitis (acute) generalized
567.22 Peritoneal abscess
567.23 Spontaneous bacterial peritonitis
567.29 Other suppurative peritonitis
567.31 Psoas muscle abscess
567.38 Other retroperitoneal abscess
567.39 Other retroperitoneal infections
567.81 Choleperitonitis
567.82 Sclerosing mesenteritis
567.89 Other specified peritonitis
567.9 Unspecified peritonitis ▽
569.5 Abscess of intestine
569.81 Fistula of intestine, excluding rectum and anus
569.82 Ulceration of intestine
569.83 Perforation of intestine

569.85 Angiodysplasia of intestine with hemorrhage
569.89 Other specified disorder of intestines
578.9 Hemorrhage of gastrointestinal tract, unspecified ▽
619.1 Digestive-genital tract fistula, female ♀
863.20 Small intestine injury, unspecified site, without mention of open wound into cavity ▽
863.21 Duodenum injury without mention of open wound into cavity
863.29 Other injury to small intestine without mention of open wound into cavity
863.30 Small intestine injury, unspecified site, with open wound into cavity ▽
863.31 Duodenum injury with open wound into cavity
863.39 Other injury to small intestine with open wound into cavity
863.80 Gastrointestinal tract injury, unspecified site, without mention of open wound into cavity ▽
863.89 Injury to other and unspecified gastrointestinal sites without mention of open wound into cavity
863.90 Gastrointestinal tract injury, unspecified site, with open wound into cavity ▽
863.99 Injury to other and unspecified gastrointestinal sites with open wound into cavity
997.49 Other digestive system complications
998.2 Accidental puncture or laceration during procedure
998.51 Infected postoperative seroma — (Use additional code to identify organism)
998.59 Other postoperative infection — (Use additional code to identify infection)
998.6 Persistent postoperative fistula, not elsewhere classified
V64.41 Laparoscopic surgical procedure converted to open procedure

ICD-9-CM Procedural

45.61 Multiple segmental resection of small intestine
45.62 Other partial resection of small intestine
46.01 Exteriorization of small intestine
46.03 Exteriorization of large intestine
46.20 Ileostomy, not otherwise specified
46.39 Other enterostomy

44126-44128

44126 Enterectomy, resection of small intestine for congenital atresia, single resection and anastomosis of proximal segment of intestine; without tapering
44127 with tapering
44128 each additional resection and anastomosis (List separately in addition to code for primary procedure)

ICD-9-CM Diagnostic

751.1 Congenital atresia and stenosis of small intestine
V64.41 Laparoscopic surgical procedure converted to open procedure

ICD-9-CM Procedural

45.62 Other partial resection of small intestine

44130

44130 Enteroenterostomy, anastomosis of intestine, with or without cutaneous enterostomy (separate procedure)

ICD-9-CM Diagnostic

152.0 Malignant neoplasm of duodenum
152.1 Malignant neoplasm of jejunum
152.2 Malignant neoplasm of ileum
152.3 Malignant neoplasm of Meckel's diverticulum
152.8 Malignant neoplasm of other specified sites of small intestine
152.9 Malignant neoplasm of small intestine, unspecified site ▽
197.4 Secondary malignant neoplasm of small intestine including duodenum
209.00 Malignant carcinoid tumor of the small intestine, unspecified portion — (Code first any associated multiple endocrine neoplasia syndrome: 258.01-258.03)(Use additional code to identify associated endocrine syndrome, as: carcinoid syndrome: 259.2) ▽
209.01 Malignant carcinoid tumor of the duodenum — (Code first any associated multiple endocrine neoplasia syndrome: 258.01-258.03)(Use additional code to identify associated endocrine syndrome, as: carcinoid syndrome: 259.2)
209.02 Malignant carcinoid tumor of the jejunum — (Code first any associated multiple endocrine neoplasia syndrome: 258.01-258.03)(Use additional code to identify associated endocrine syndrome, as: carcinoid syndrome: 259.2)
209.03 Malignant carcinoid tumor of the ileum — (Code first any associated multiple endocrine neoplasia syndrome: 258.01-258.03)(Use additional code to identify associated endocrine syndrome, as: carcinoid syndrome: 259.2)
209.20 Malignant carcinoid tumor of unknown primary site — (Code first any associated multiple endocrine neoplasia syndrome: 258.01-258.03)(Use additional code to identify associated endocrine syndrome, as: carcinoid syndrome: 259.2)
537.3 Other obstruction of duodenum
557.0 Acute vascular insufficiency of intestine
557.1 Chronic vascular insufficiency of intestine
560.0 Intussusception
560.1 Paralytic ileus
560.2 Volvulus
560.31 Gallstone ileus
560.39 Impaction of intestine, other
560.81 Intestinal or peritoneal adhesions with obstruction (postoperative) (postinfection)
560.89 Other specified intestinal obstruction
560.9 Unspecified intestinal obstruction ▽
562.00 Diverticulosis of small intestine (without mention of hemorrhage) — (Use additional code to identify any associated peritonitis: 567.0-567.9)
562.01 Diverticulitis of small intestine (without mention of hemorrhage) — (Use additional code to identify any associated peritonitis: 567.0-567.9)
562.02 Diverticulosis of small intestine with hemorrhage — (Use additional code to identify any associated peritonitis: 567.0-567.9)
562.03 Diverticulitis of small intestine with hemorrhage — (Use additional code to identify any associated peritonitis: 567.0-567.9)
564.3 Vomiting following gastrointestinal surgery
564.5 Functional diarrhea
564.81 Neurogenic bowel
564.89 Other functional disorders of intestine
567.0 Peritonitis in infectious diseases classified elsewhere — (Code first underlying disease) ☒
567.1 Pneumococcal peritonitis
567.21 Peritonitis (acute) generalized
567.22 Peritoneal abscess
567.23 Spontaneous bacterial peritonitis
567.29 Other suppurative peritonitis
567.31 Psoas muscle abscess
567.38 Other retroperitoneal abscess
567.81 Choleperitonitis
567.82 Sclerosing mesenteritis
567.89 Other specified peritonitis
567.9 Unspecified peritonitis ▽
568.0 Peritoneal adhesions (postoperative) (postinfection)
569.81 Fistula of intestine, excluding rectum and anus
569.82 Ulceration of intestine
569.83 Perforation of intestine
569.84 Angiodysplasia of intestine (without mention of hemorrhage)
569.85 Angiodysplasia of intestine with hemorrhage
569.89 Other specified disorder of intestines
569.9 Unspecified disorder of intestine ▽
578.1 Blood in stool
578.9 Hemorrhage of gastrointestinal tract, unspecified ▽
579.2 Blind loop syndrome
617.5 Endometriosis of intestine ♀

751.1 Congenital atresia and stenosis of small intestine
785.4 Gangrene — (Code first any associated underlying condition)

ICD-9-CM Procedural

45.91 Small-to-small intestinal anastomosis
45.93 Other small-to-large intestinal anastomosis
45.94 Large-to-large intestinal anastomosis
46.01 Exteriorization of small intestine
46.03 Exteriorization of large intestine
46.10 Colostomy, not otherwise specified
46.20 Ileostomy, not otherwise specified
46.39 Other enterostomy

44132-44133

44132 Donor enterectomy (including cold preservation), open; from cadaver donor
44133 partial, from living donor

ICD-9-CM Diagnostic

V59.8 Donor of other specified organ or tissue

ICD-9-CM Procedural

45.62 Other partial resection of small intestine
45.63 Total removal of small intestine

44135-44136

44135 Intestinal allotransplantation; from cadaver donor
44136 from living donor

ICD-9-CM Diagnostic

152.0 Malignant neoplasm of duodenum
152.1 Malignant neoplasm of jejunum
152.2 Malignant neoplasm of ileum
152.8 Malignant neoplasm of other specified sites of small intestine
152.9 Malignant neoplasm of small intestine, unspecified site
197.4 Secondary malignant neoplasm of small intestine including duodenum
209.00 Malignant carcinoid tumor of the small intestine, unspecified portion — (Code first any associated multiple endocrine neoplasia syndrome: 258.01-258.03)(Use additional code to identify associated endocrine syndrome, as: carcinoid syndrome: 259.2)
209.01 Malignant carcinoid tumor of the duodenum — (Code first any associated multiple endocrine neoplasia syndrome: 258.01-258.03)(Use additional code to identify associated endocrine syndrome, as: carcinoid syndrome: 259.2)
209.02 Malignant carcinoid tumor of the jejunum — (Code first any associated multiple endocrine neoplasia syndrome: 258.01-258.03)(Use additional code to identify associated endocrine syndrome, as: carcinoid syndrome: 259.2)
209.03 Malignant carcinoid tumor of the ileum — (Code first any associated multiple endocrine neoplasia syndrome: 258.01-258.03)(Use additional code to identify associated endocrine syndrome, as: carcinoid syndrome: 259.2)
551.00 Femoral hernia with gangrene, unilateral or unspecified (not specified as recurrent)
551.21 Incisional ventral hernia, with gangrene
551.8 Hernia of other specified sites, with gangrene
551.9 Hernia of unspecified site, with gangrene
552.00 Unilateral or unspecified femoral hernia with obstruction
552.21 Incisional hernia with obstruction
555.0 Regional enteritis of small intestine
555.9 Regional enteritis of unspecified site
556.1 Ulcerative (chronic) ileocolitis
556.8 Other ulcerative colitis
556.9 Unspecified ulcerative colitis
558.41 Eosinophilic gastroenteritis
558.42 Eosinophilic colitis
560.0 Intussusception
560.1 Paralytic ileus
560.2 Volvulus
560.81 Intestinal or peritoneal adhesions with obstruction (postoperative) (postinfection)
560.89 Other specified intestinal obstruction
560.9 Unspecified intestinal obstruction
562.00 Diverticulosis of small intestine (without mention of hemorrhage) — (Use additional code to identify any associated peritonitis: 567.0-567.9)
562.01 Diverticulitis of small intestine (without mention of hemorrhage) — (Use additional code to identify any associated peritonitis: 567.0-567.9)
562.02 Diverticulosis of small intestine with hemorrhage — (Use additional code to identify any associated peritonitis: 567.0-567.9)
562.03 Diverticulitis of small intestine with hemorrhage — (Use additional code to identify any associated peritonitis: 567.0-567.9)
567.0 Peritonitis in infectious diseases classified elsewhere — (Code first underlying disease)
567.1 Pneumococcal peritonitis
567.21 Peritonitis (acute) generalized
567.22 Peritoneal abscess
567.23 Spontaneous bacterial peritonitis
567.29 Other suppurative peritonitis
567.31 Psoas muscle abscess
567.38 Other retroperitoneal abscess
567.39 Other retroperitoneal infections
567.81 Choleperitonitis
567.82 Sclerosing mesenteritis
567.89 Other specified peritonitis
567.9 Unspecified peritonitis
569.85 Angiodysplasia of intestine with hemorrhage
569.89 Other specified disorder of intestines
578.9 Hemorrhage of gastrointestinal tract, unspecified
579.3 Other and unspecified postsurgical nonabsorption
751.1 Congenital atresia and stenosis of small intestine
751.5 Other congenital anomalies of intestine
863.30 Small intestine injury, unspecified site, with open wound into cavity
863.31 Duodenum injury with open wound into cavity
863.39 Other injury to small intestine with open wound into cavity
863.90 Gastrointestinal tract injury, unspecified site, with open wound into cavity
863.99 Injury to other and unspecified gastrointestinal sites with open wound into cavity
997.49 Other digestive system complications
998.51 Infected postoperative seroma — (Use additional code to identify organism)
998.59 Other postoperative infection — (Use additional code to identify infection)

ICD-9-CM Procedural

46.97 Transplant of intestine

44137

44137 Removal of transplanted intestinal allograft, complete

ICD-9-CM Diagnostic

152.0 Malignant neoplasm of duodenum
152.1 Malignant neoplasm of jejunum
152.2 Malignant neoplasm of ileum
152.8 Malignant neoplasm of other specified sites of small intestine
152.9 Malignant neoplasm of small intestine, unspecified site
197.4 Secondary malignant neoplasm of small intestine including duodenum
199.2 Malignant neoplasm associated with transplanted organ — (Code first complication of transplanted organ (996.80-996.89) Use additional code for specific malignancy)
209.00 Malignant carcinoid tumor of the small intestine, unspecified portion — (Code first any associated multiple endocrine neoplasia syndrome: 258.01-258.03)(Use additional code to identify associated endocrine syndrome, as: carcinoid syndrome: 259.2)

209.01 Malignant carcinoid tumor of the duodenum — (Code first any associated multiple endocrine neoplasia syndrome: 258.01-258.03)(Use additional code to identify associated endocrine syndrome, as: carcinoid syndrome: 259.2)
209.02 Malignant carcinoid tumor of the jejunum — (Code first any associated multiple endocrine neoplasia syndrome: 258.01-258.03)(Use additional code to identify associated endocrine syndrome, as: carcinoid syndrome: 259.2)
209.03 Malignant carcinoid tumor of the ileum — (Code first any associated multiple endocrine neoplasia syndrome: 258.01-258.03)(Use additional code to identify associated endocrine syndrome, as: carcinoid syndrome: 259.2)
551.00 Femoral hernia with gangrene, unilateral or unspecified (not specified as recurrent)
551.21 Incisional ventral hernia, with gangrene
551.8 Hernia of other specified sites, with gangrene
551.9 Hernia of unspecified site, with gangrene ▽
552.00 Unilateral or unspecified femoral hernia with obstruction
552.21 Incisional hernia with obstruction
555.0 Regional enteritis of small intestine
555.9 Regional enteritis of unspecified site ▽
556.1 Ulcerative (chronic) ileocolitis
556.8 Other ulcerative colitis
556.9 Unspecified ulcerative colitis ▽
558.41 Eosinophilic gastroenteritis
558.42 Eosinophilic colitis
560.0 Intussusception
560.1 Paralytic ileus
560.2 Volvulus
560.81 Intestinal or peritoneal adhesions with obstruction (postoperative) (postinfection)
560.89 Other specified intestinal obstruction
560.9 Unspecified intestinal obstruction ▽
562.00 Diverticulosis of small intestine (without mention of hemorrhage) — (Use additional code to identify any associated peritonitis: 567.0-567.9)
562.01 Diverticulitis of small intestine (without mention of hemorrhage) — (Use additional code to identify any associated peritonitis: 567.0-567.9)
562.02 Diverticulosis of small intestine with hemorrhage — (Use additional code to identify any associated peritonitis: 567.0-567.9)
562.03 Diverticulitis of small intestine with hemorrhage — (Use additional code to identify any associated peritonitis: 567.0-567.9)
567.0 Peritonitis in infectious diseases classified elsewhere — (Code first underlying disease) ☒
567.1 Pneumococcal peritonitis
567.21 Peritonitis (acute) generalized
567.22 Peritoneal abscess
567.23 Spontaneous bacterial peritonitis
567.29 Other suppurative peritonitis
567.31 Psoas muscle abscess
567.38 Other retroperitoneal abscess
567.39 Other retroperitoneal infections
567.81 Choleperitonitis
567.82 Sclerosing mesenteritis
567.89 Other specified peritonitis
567.9 Unspecified peritonitis ▽
569.85 Angiodysplasia of intestine with hemorrhage
569.89 Other specified disorder of intestines
578.9 Hemorrhage of gastrointestinal tract, unspecified ▽
579.3 Other and unspecified postsurgical nonabsorption ▽
729.90 Disorders of soft tissue, unspecified ▽
729.92 Nontraumatic hematoma of soft tissue
751.1 Congenital atresia and stenosis of small intestine
751.5 Other congenital anomalies of intestine
863.30 Small intestine injury, unspecified site, with open wound into cavity ▽
863.31 Duodenum injury with open wound into cavity
863.39 Other injury to small intestine with open wound into cavity
863.90 Gastrointestinal tract injury, unspecified site, with open wound into cavity ▽
863.99 Injury to other and unspecified gastrointestinal sites with open wound into cavity
996.87 Complications of transplanted organ, intestine — (Use additional code to identify nature of complication: 078.5, 199.2, 238.77, 279.50-279.53)
997.49 Other digestive system complications
998.30 Disruption of wound, unspecified ▽
998.31 Disruption of internal operation (surgical) wound
998.33 Disruption of traumatic injury wound repair
998.51 Infected postoperative seroma — (Use additional code to identify organism)
998.59 Other postoperative infection — (Use additional code to identify infection)

ICD-9-CM Procedural

46.99 Other operations on intestines

44140

44140 Colectomy, partial; with anastomosis

ICD-9-CM Diagnostic

153.0 Malignant neoplasm of hepatic flexure
153.1 Malignant neoplasm of transverse colon
153.2 Malignant neoplasm of descending colon
153.3 Malignant neoplasm of sigmoid colon
153.4 Malignant neoplasm of cecum
153.6 Malignant neoplasm of ascending colon
153.7 Malignant neoplasm of splenic flexure
153.8 Malignant neoplasm of other specified sites of large intestine
153.9 Malignant neoplasm of colon, unspecified site ▽
154.0 Malignant neoplasm of rectosigmoid junction
154.1 Malignant neoplasm of rectum
154.8 Malignant neoplasm of other sites of rectum, rectosigmoid junction, and anus
159.0 Malignant neoplasm of intestinal tract, part unspecified ▽
197.4 Secondary malignant neoplasm of small intestine including duodenum
197.5 Secondary malignant neoplasm of large intestine and rectum
209.10 Malignant carcinoid tumor of the large intestine, unspecified portion — (Code first any associated multiple endocrine neoplasia syndrome: 258.01-258.03)(Use additional code to identify associated endocrine syndrome, as: carcinoid syndrome: 259.2) ▽
209.12 Malignant carcinoid tumor of the cecum — (Code first any associated multiple endocrine neoplasia syndrome: 258.01-258.03)(Use additional code to identify associated endocrine syndrome, as: carcinoid syndrome: 259.2)
209.13 Malignant carcinoid tumor of the ascending colon — (Code first any associated multiple endocrine neoplasia syndrome: 258.01-258.03)(Use additional code to identify associated endocrine syndrome, as: carcinoid syndrome: 259.2)
209.14 Malignant carcinoid tumor of the transverse colon — (Code first any associated multiple endocrine neoplasia syndrome: 258.01-258.03)(Use additional code to identify associated endocrine syndrome, as: carcinoid syndrome: 259.2)
209.15 Malignant carcinoid tumor of the descending colon — (Code first any associated multiple endocrine neoplasia syndrome: 258.01-258.03)(Use additional code to identify associated endocrine syndrome, as: carcinoid syndrome: 259.2)
209.16 Malignant carcinoid tumor of the sigmoid colon — (Code first any associated multiple endocrine neoplasia syndrome: 258.01-258.03)(Use additional code to identify associated endocrine syndrome, as: carcinoid syndrome: 259.2)
209.29 Malignant carcinoid tumor of other sites — (Code first any associated multiple endocrine neoplasia syndrome: 258.01-258.03)(Use additional code to identify associated endocrine syndrome, as: carcinoid syndrome: 259.2)
209.30 Malignant poorly differentiated neuroendocrine carcinoma, any site — (Code first any associated multiple endocrine neoplasia syndrome: 258.01-258.03)(Use additional code to identify associated endocrine syndrome, as: carcinoid syndrome: 259.2) ▽
209.50 Benign carcinoid tumor of the large intestine, unspecified portion — (Code first any associated multiple endocrine neoplasia syndrome: 258.01-258.03)(Use additional code to identify associated endocrine syndrome, as: carcinoid syndrome: 259.2) ▽

209.52 Benign carcinoid tumor of the cecum — (Code first any associated multiple endocrine neoplasia syndrome: 258.01-258.03)(Use additional code to identify associated endocrine syndrome, as: carcinoid syndrome: 259.2)
209.53 Benign carcinoid tumor of the ascending colon — (Code first any associated multiple endocrine neoplasia syndrome: 258.01-258.03)(Use additional code to identify associated endocrine syndrome, as: carcinoid syndrome: 259.2)
209.54 Benign carcinoid tumor of the transverse colon — (Code first any associated multiple endocrine neoplasia syndrome: 258.01-258.03)(Use additional code to identify associated endocrine syndrome, as: carcinoid syndrome: 259.2)
209.55 Benign carcinoid tumor of the descending colon — (Code first any associated multiple endocrine neoplasia syndrome: 258.01-258.03)(Use additional code to identify associated endocrine syndrome, as: carcinoid syndrome: 259.2)
209.56 Benign carcinoid tumor of the sigmoid colon — (Code first any associated multiple endocrine neoplasia syndrome: 258.01-258.03)(Use additional code to identify associated endocrine syndrome, as: carcinoid syndrome: 259.2)
209.57 Benign carcinoid tumor of the rectum — (Code first any associated multiple endocrine neoplasia syndrome: 258.01-258.03)(Use additional code to identify associated endocrine syndrome, as: carcinoid syndrome: 259.2)
209.69 Benign carcinoid tumor of other sites — (Code first any associated multiple endocrine neoplasia syndrome: 258.01-258.03)(Use additional code to identify associated endocrine syndrome, as: carcinoid syndrome: 259.2)
211.3 Benign neoplasm of colon
211.4 Benign neoplasm of rectum and anal canal
211.9 Benign neoplasm of other and unspecified site of the digestive system ▽
230.3 Carcinoma in situ of colon
230.4 Carcinoma in situ of rectum
235.2 Neoplasm of uncertain behavior of stomach, intestines, and rectum
239.0 Neoplasm of unspecified nature of digestive system
550.00 Inguinal hernia with gangrene, unilateral or unspecified, (not specified as recurrent)
551.1 Umbilical hernia with gangrene
552.8 Hernia of other specified site, with obstruction
555.1 Regional enteritis of large intestine
555.2 Regional enteritis of small intestine with large intestine
555.9 Regional enteritis of unspecified site ▽
556.0 Ulcerative (chronic) enterocolitis
556.1 Ulcerative (chronic) ileocolitis
556.2 Ulcerative (chronic) proctitis
556.3 Ulcerative (chronic) proctosigmoiditis
556.4 Pseudopolyposis of colon
556.5 Left sided ulcerative (chronic) colitis
556.6 Universal ulcerative (chronic) colitis
556.8 Other ulcerative colitis
556.9 Unspecified ulcerative colitis ▽
557.0 Acute vascular insufficiency of intestine
557.1 Chronic vascular insufficiency of intestine
557.9 Unspecified vascular insufficiency of intestine ▽
558.1 Gastroenteritis and colitis due to radiation
558.2 Toxic gastroenteritis and colitis — (Use additional E code to identify cause)
558.41 Eosinophilic gastroenteritis
558.42 Eosinophilic colitis
558.9 Other and unspecified noninfectious gastroenteritis and colitis ▽
560.0 Intussusception
560.1 Paralytic ileus
560.2 Volvulus
560.81 Intestinal or peritoneal adhesions with obstruction (postoperative) (postinfection)
560.89 Other specified intestinal obstruction
560.9 Unspecified intestinal obstruction ▽
562.10 Diverticulosis of colon (without mention of hemorrhage) — (Use additional code to identify any associated peritonitis: 567.0-567.9)
562.11 Diverticulitis of colon (without mention of hemorrhage) — (Use additional code to identify any associated peritonitis: 567.0-567.9)
562.12 Diverticulosis of colon with hemorrhage — (Use additional code to identify any associated peritonitis: 567.0-567.9)
562.13 Diverticulitis of colon with hemorrhage — (Use additional code to identify any associated peritonitis: 567.0-567.9)
564.7 Megacolon, other than Hirschsprung's
567.0 Peritonitis in infectious diseases classified elsewhere — (Code first underlying disease) ☒
567.1 Pneumococcal peritonitis
567.21 Peritonitis (acute) generalized
567.22 Peritoneal abscess
567.23 Spontaneous bacterial peritonitis
567.29 Other suppurative peritonitis
567.31 Psoas muscle abscess
567.38 Other retroperitoneal abscess
567.39 Other retroperitoneal infections
567.81 Choleperitonitis
567.82 Sclerosing mesenteritis
567.89 Other specified peritonitis
567.9 Unspecified peritonitis ▽
569.44 Dysplasia of anus
569.5 Abscess of intestine
569.81 Fistula of intestine, excluding rectum and anus
569.82 Ulceration of intestine
569.83 Perforation of intestine
569.84 Angiodysplasia of intestine (without mention of hemorrhage)
569.85 Angiodysplasia of intestine with hemorrhage
569.89 Other specified disorder of intestines
569.9 Unspecified disorder of intestine ▽
578.9 Hemorrhage of gastrointestinal tract, unspecified ▽
596.1 Intestinovesical fistula — (Use additional code to identify urinary incontinence: 625.6, 788.30-788.39)
619.1 Digestive-genital tract fistula, female ♀
751.5 Other congenital anomalies of intestine
751.8 Other specified congenital anomalies of digestive system
751.9 Unspecified congenital anomaly of digestive system ▽
787.99 Other symptoms involving digestive system
V64.41 Laparoscopic surgical procedure converted to open procedure

ICD-9-CM Procedural

45.79 Other and unspecified partial excision of large intestine

44141

44141 Colectomy, partial; with skin level cecostomy or colostomy

ICD-9-CM Diagnostic

153.0 Malignant neoplasm of hepatic flexure
153.1 Malignant neoplasm of transverse colon
153.2 Malignant neoplasm of descending colon
153.3 Malignant neoplasm of sigmoid colon
153.4 Malignant neoplasm of cecum
153.5 Malignant neoplasm of appendix
153.6 Malignant neoplasm of ascending colon
153.7 Malignant neoplasm of splenic flexure
153.8 Malignant neoplasm of other specified sites of large intestine
153.9 Malignant neoplasm of colon, unspecified site ▽
154.0 Malignant neoplasm of rectosigmoid junction
154.1 Malignant neoplasm of rectum

209.10 Malignant carcinoid tumor of the large intestine, unspecified portion — (Code first any associated multiple endocrine neoplasia syndrome: 258.01-258.03)(Use additional code to identify associated endocrine syndrome, as: carcinoid syndrome: 259.2)

209.11 Malignant carcinoid tumor of the appendix — (Code first any associated multiple endocrine neoplasia syndrome: 258.01-258.03)(Use additional code to identify associated endocrine syndrome, as: carcinoid syndrome: 259.2)

209.12 Malignant carcinoid tumor of the cecum — (Code first any associated multiple endocrine neoplasia syndrome: 258.01-258.03)(Use additional code to identify associated endocrine syndrome, as: carcinoid syndrome: 259.2)

209.13 Malignant carcinoid tumor of the ascending colon — (Code first any associated multiple endocrine neoplasia syndrome: 258.01-258.03)(Use additional code to identify associated endocrine syndrome, as: carcinoid syndrome: 259.2)

209.14 Malignant carcinoid tumor of the transverse colon — (Code first any associated multiple endocrine neoplasia syndrome: 258.01-258.03)(Use additional code to identify associated endocrine syndrome, as: carcinoid syndrome: 259.2)

209.15 Malignant carcinoid tumor of the descending colon — (Code first any associated multiple endocrine neoplasia syndrome: 258.01-258.03)(Use additional code to identify associated endocrine syndrome, as: carcinoid syndrome: 259.2)

209.16 Malignant carcinoid tumor of the sigmoid colon — (Code first any associated multiple endocrine neoplasia syndrome: 258.01-258.03)(Use additional code to identify associated endocrine syndrome, as: carcinoid syndrome: 259.2)

209.29 Malignant carcinoid tumor of other sites — (Code first any associated multiple endocrine neoplasia syndrome: 258.01-258.03)(Use additional code to identify associated endocrine syndrome, as: carcinoid syndrome: 259.2)

209.30 Malignant poorly differentiated neuroendocrine carcinoma, any site — (Code first any associated multiple endocrine neoplasia syndrome: 258.01-258.03)(Use additional code to identify associated endocrine syndrome, as: carcinoid syndrome: 259.2)

209.50 Benign carcinoid tumor of the large intestine, unspecified portion — (Code first any associated multiple endocrine neoplasia syndrome: 258.01-258.03)(Use additional code to identify associated endocrine syndrome, as: carcinoid syndrome: 259.2)

209.51 Benign carcinoid tumor of the appendix — (Code first any associated multiple endocrine neoplasia syndrome: 258.01-258.03)(Use additional code to identify associated endocrine syndrome, as: carcinoid syndrome: 259.2)

209.52 Benign carcinoid tumor of the cecum — (Code first any associated multiple endocrine neoplasia syndrome: 258.01-258.03)(Use additional code to identify associated endocrine syndrome, as: carcinoid syndrome: 259.2)

209.53 Benign carcinoid tumor of the ascending colon — (Code first any associated multiple endocrine neoplasia syndrome: 258.01-258.03)(Use additional code to identify associated endocrine syndrome, as: carcinoid syndrome: 259.2)

209.54 Benign carcinoid tumor of the transverse colon — (Code first any associated multiple endocrine neoplasia syndrome: 258.01-258.03)(Use additional code to identify associated endocrine syndrome, as: carcinoid syndrome: 259.2)

209.55 Benign carcinoid tumor of the descending colon — (Code first any associated multiple endocrine neoplasia syndrome: 258.01-258.03)(Use additional code to identify associated endocrine syndrome, as: carcinoid syndrome: 259.2)

209.56 Benign carcinoid tumor of the sigmoid colon — (Code first any associated multiple endocrine neoplasia syndrome: 258.01-258.03)(Use additional code to identify associated endocrine syndrome, as: carcinoid syndrome: 259.2)

209.57 Benign carcinoid tumor of the rectum — (Code first any associated multiple endocrine neoplasia syndrome: 258.01-258.03)(Use additional code to identify associated endocrine syndrome, as: carcinoid syndrome: 259.2)

209.69 Benign carcinoid tumor of other sites — (Code first any associated multiple endocrine neoplasia syndrome: 258.01-258.03)(Use additional code to identify associated endocrine syndrome, as: carcinoid syndrome: 259.2)

211.3 Benign neoplasm of colon

211.4 Benign neoplasm of rectum and anal canal

235.2 Neoplasm of uncertain behavior of stomach, intestines, and rectum

239.0 Neoplasm of unspecified nature of digestive system

556.3 Ulcerative (chronic) proctosigmoiditis

556.4 Pseudopolyposis of colon

556.9 Unspecified ulcerative colitis

557.0 Acute vascular insufficiency of intestine

557.1 Chronic vascular insufficiency of intestine

557.9 Unspecified vascular insufficiency of intestine

560.0 Intussusception

560.1 Paralytic ileus

560.2 Volvulus

560.81 Intestinal or peritoneal adhesions with obstruction (postoperative) (postinfection)

560.89 Other specified intestinal obstruction

560.9 Unspecified intestinal obstruction

562.10 Diverticulosis of colon (without mention of hemorrhage) — (Use additional code to identify any associated peritonitis: 567.0-567.9)

562.11 Diverticulitis of colon (without mention of hemorrhage) — (Use additional code to identify any associated peritonitis: 567.0-567.9)

562.12 Diverticulosis of colon with hemorrhage — (Use additional code to identify any associated peritonitis: 567.0-567.9)

562.13 Diverticulitis of colon with hemorrhage — (Use additional code to identify any associated peritonitis: 567.0-567.9)

564.7 Megacolon, other than Hirschsprung's

567.0 Peritonitis in infectious diseases classified elsewhere — (Code first underlying disease)

567.1 Pneumococcal peritonitis

567.21 Peritonitis (acute) generalized

567.22 Peritoneal abscess

567.23 Spontaneous bacterial peritonitis

567.29 Other suppurative peritonitis

567.31 Psoas muscle abscess

567.38 Other retroperitoneal abscess

567.39 Other retroperitoneal infections

567.81 Choleperitonitis

567.82 Sclerosing mesenteritis

567.89 Other specified peritonitis

567.9 Unspecified peritonitis

569.5 Abscess of intestine

569.81 Fistula of intestine, excluding rectum and anus

569.82 Ulceration of intestine

569.83 Perforation of intestine

569.84 Angiodysplasia of intestine (without mention of hemorrhage)

569.85 Angiodysplasia of intestine with hemorrhage

569.89 Other specified disorder of intestines

569.9 Unspecified disorder of intestine

578.9 Hemorrhage of gastrointestinal tract, unspecified

614.5 Acute or unspecified pelvic peritonitis, female — (Use additional code to identify organism: 041.00-041.09, 041.10-041.19) ♀

751.5 Other congenital anomalies of intestine

785.4 Gangrene — (Code first any associated underlying condition)

863.29 Other injury to small intestine without mention of open wound into cavity

863.30 Small intestine injury, unspecified site, with open wound into cavity

863.31 Duodenum injury with open wound into cavity

863.39 Other injury to small intestine with open wound into cavity

V64.41 Laparoscopic surgical procedure converted to open procedure

ICD-9-CM Procedural

45.73 Open and other right hemicolectomy

45.74 Open and other resection of transverse colon

45.75 Open and other left hemicolectomy

45.76 Open and other sigmoidectomy

46.03 Exteriorization of large intestine

46.04 Resection of exteriorized segment of large intestine

46.10 Colostomy, not otherwise specified

46.13 Permanent colostomy

44143

44143 Colectomy, partial; with end colostomy and closure of distal segment (Hartmann type procedure)

ICD-9-CM Diagnostic

153.0 Malignant neoplasm of hepatic flexure
153.1 Malignant neoplasm of transverse colon
153.2 Malignant neoplasm of descending colon
153.3 Malignant neoplasm of sigmoid colon
153.4 Malignant neoplasm of cecum
153.5 Malignant neoplasm of appendix
153.6 Malignant neoplasm of ascending colon
153.7 Malignant neoplasm of splenic flexure
153.8 Malignant neoplasm of other specified sites of large intestine
153.9 Malignant neoplasm of colon, unspecified site ▽
154.0 Malignant neoplasm of rectosigmoid junction
154.1 Malignant neoplasm of rectum
154.8 Malignant neoplasm of other sites of rectum, rectosigmoid junction, and anus
159.0 Malignant neoplasm of intestinal tract, part unspecified ▽
197.5 Secondary malignant neoplasm of large intestine and rectum
198.89 Secondary malignant neoplasm of other specified sites
199.1 Other malignant neoplasm of unspecified site
209.10 Malignant carcinoid tumor of the large intestine, unspecified portion — (Code first any associated multiple endocrine neoplasia syndrome: 258.01-258.03)(Use additional code to identify associated endocrine syndrome, as: carcinoid syndrome: 259.2) ▽
209.11 Malignant carcinoid tumor of the appendix — (Code first any associated multiple endocrine neoplasia syndrome: 258.01-258.03)(Use additional code to identify associated endocrine syndrome, as: carcinoid syndrome: 259.2)
209.12 Malignant carcinoid tumor of the cecum — (Code first any associated multiple endocrine neoplasia syndrome: 258.01-258.03)(Use additional code to identify associated endocrine syndrome, as: carcinoid syndrome: 259.2)
209.13 Malignant carcinoid tumor of the ascending colon — (Code first any associated multiple endocrine neoplasia syndrome: 258.01-258.03)(Use additional code to identify associated endocrine syndrome, as: carcinoid syndrome: 259.2)
209.14 Malignant carcinoid tumor of the transverse colon — (Code first any associated multiple endocrine neoplasia syndrome: 258.01-258.03)(Use additional code to identify associated endocrine syndrome, as: carcinoid syndrome: 259.2)
209.15 Malignant carcinoid tumor of the descending colon — (Code first any associated multiple endocrine neoplasia syndrome: 258.01-258.03)(Use additional code to identify associated endocrine syndrome, as: carcinoid syndrome: 259.2)
209.16 Malignant carcinoid tumor of the sigmoid colon — (Code first any associated multiple endocrine neoplasia syndrome: 258.01-258.03)(Use additional code to identify associated endocrine syndrome, as: carcinoid syndrome: 259.2)
209.27 Malignant carcinoid tumor of hindgut, not otherwise specified — (Code first any associated multiple endocrine neoplasia syndrome: 258.01-258.03)(Use additional code to identify associated endocrine syndrome, as: carcinoid syndrome: 259.2)
209.29 Malignant carcinoid tumor of other sites — (Code first any associated multiple endocrine neoplasia syndrome: 258.01-258.03)(Use additional code to identify associated endocrine syndrome, as: carcinoid syndrome: 259.2)
209.30 Malignant poorly differentiated neuroendocrine carcinoma, any site — (Code first any associated multiple endocrine neoplasia syndrome: 258.01-258.03)(Use additional code to identify associated endocrine syndrome, as: carcinoid syndrome: 259.2) ▽
209.50 Benign carcinoid tumor of the large intestine, unspecified portion — (Code first any associated multiple endocrine neoplasia syndrome: 258.01-258.03)(Use additional code to identify associated endocrine syndrome, as: carcinoid syndrome: 259.2) ▽
209.51 Benign carcinoid tumor of the appendix — (Code first any associated multiple endocrine neoplasia syndrome: 258.01-258.03)(Use additional code to identify associated endocrine syndrome, as: carcinoid syndrome: 259.2)
209.52 Benign carcinoid tumor of the cecum — (Code first any associated multiple endocrine neoplasia syndrome: 258.01-258.03)(Use additional code to identify associated endocrine syndrome, as: carcinoid syndrome: 259.2)
209.53 Benign carcinoid tumor of the ascending colon — (Code first any associated multiple endocrine neoplasia syndrome: 258.01-258.03)(Use additional code to identify associated endocrine syndrome, as: carcinoid syndrome: 259.2)
209.54 Benign carcinoid tumor of the transverse colon — (Code first any associated multiple endocrine neoplasia syndrome: 258.01-258.03)(Use additional code to identify associated endocrine syndrome, as: carcinoid syndrome: 259.2)
209.55 Benign carcinoid tumor of the descending colon — (Code first any associated multiple endocrine neoplasia syndrome: 258.01-258.03)(Use additional code to identify associated endocrine syndrome, as: carcinoid syndrome: 259.2)
209.56 Benign carcinoid tumor of the sigmoid colon — (Code first any associated multiple endocrine neoplasia syndrome: 258.01-258.03)(Use additional code to identify associated endocrine syndrome, as: carcinoid syndrome: 259.2)
209.57 Benign carcinoid tumor of the rectum — (Code first any associated multiple endocrine neoplasia syndrome: 258.01-258.03)(Use additional code to identify associated endocrine syndrome, as: carcinoid syndrome: 259.2)
209.69 Benign carcinoid tumor of other sites — (Code first any associated multiple endocrine neoplasia syndrome: 258.01-258.03)(Use additional code to identify associated endocrine syndrome, as: carcinoid syndrome: 259.2)
211.3 Benign neoplasm of colon
211.4 Benign neoplasm of rectum and anal canal
230.3 Carcinoma in situ of colon
230.4 Carcinoma in situ of rectum
235.2 Neoplasm of uncertain behavior of stomach, intestines, and rectum
239.0 Neoplasm of unspecified nature of digestive system
555.1 Regional enteritis of large intestine
555.2 Regional enteritis of small intestine with large intestine
555.9 Regional enteritis of unspecified site ▽
556.0 Ulcerative (chronic) enterocolitis
556.1 Ulcerative (chronic) ileocolitis
556.2 Ulcerative (chronic) proctitis
556.3 Ulcerative (chronic) proctosigmoiditis
556.4 Pseudopolyposis of colon
556.5 Left sided ulcerative (chronic) colitis
556.6 Universal ulcerative (chronic) colitis
556.8 Other ulcerative colitis
556.9 Unspecified ulcerative colitis ▽
557.0 Acute vascular insufficiency of intestine
557.1 Chronic vascular insufficiency of intestine
557.9 Unspecified vascular insufficiency of intestine ▽
560.2 Volvulus
560.81 Intestinal or peritoneal adhesions with obstruction (postoperative) (postinfection)
560.89 Other specified intestinal obstruction
560.9 Unspecified intestinal obstruction ▽
562.10 Diverticulosis of colon (without mention of hemorrhage) — (Use additional code to identify any associated peritonitis: 567.0-567.9)
562.11 Diverticulitis of colon (without mention of hemorrhage) — (Use additional code to identify any associated peritonitis: 567.0-567.9)
562.12 Diverticulosis of colon with hemorrhage — (Use additional code to identify any associated peritonitis: 567.0-567.9)
562.13 Diverticulitis of colon with hemorrhage — (Use additional code to identify any associated peritonitis: 567.0-567.9)
564.81 Neurogenic bowel
564.89 Other functional disorders of intestine
567.0 Peritonitis in infectious diseases classified elsewhere — (Code first underlying disease) ☒
567.1 Pneumococcal peritonitis
567.21 Peritonitis (acute) generalized
567.22 Peritoneal abscess
567.23 Spontaneous bacterial peritonitis
567.29 Other suppurative peritonitis

567.31 Psoas muscle abscess
567.38 Other retroperitoneal abscess
567.39 Other retroperitoneal infections
567.81 Choleperitonitis
567.82 Sclerosing mesenteritis
567.89 Other specified peritonitis
567.9 Unspecified peritonitis ▽
569.44 Dysplasia of anus
569.5 Abscess of intestine
569.81 Fistula of intestine, excluding rectum and anus
569.82 Ulceration of intestine
569.83 Perforation of intestine
569.84 Angiodysplasia of intestine (without mention of hemorrhage)
569.85 Angiodysplasia of intestine with hemorrhage
569.89 Other specified disorder of intestines
569.9 Unspecified disorder of intestine ▽
578.1 Blood in stool
578.9 Hemorrhage of gastrointestinal tract, unspecified ▽
596.1 Intestinovesical fistula — (Use additional code to identify urinary incontinence: 625.6, 788.30-788.39)
619.1 Digestive-genital tract fistula, female ♀
751.2 Congenital atresia and stenosis of large intestine, rectum, and anal canal
751.3 Hirschsprung's disease and other congenital functional disorders of colon
751.4 Congenital anomalies of intestinal fixation
751.5 Other congenital anomalies of intestine
751.8 Other specified congenital anomalies of digestive system
751.9 Unspecified congenital anomaly of digestive system ▽
777.50 Necrotizing enterocolitis in newborn, unspecified ▽
777.51 Stage I necrotizing enterocolitis in newborn
777.52 Stage II necrotizing enterocolitis in newborn
777.53 Stage III necrotizing enterocolitis in newborn
777.6 Perinatal intestinal perforation — (Use additional code(s) to further specify condition)
777.8 Other specified perinatal disorder of digestive system — (Use additional code(s) to further specify condition)
863.40 Colon injury unspecified site, without mention of open wound into cavity ▽
863.41 Ascending (right) colon injury without mention of open wound into cavity
863.42 Transverse colon injury without mention of open wound into cavity
863.43 Descending (left) colon injury without mention of open wound into cavity
863.44 Sigmoid colon injury without mention of open wound into cavity
863.45 Rectum injury without mention of open wound into cavity
863.46 Injury to multiple sites in colon and rectum without mention of open wound into cavity
863.49 Other colon and rectum injury, without mention of open wound into cavity
863.50 Colon injury, unspecified site, with open wound into cavity ▽
863.51 Ascending (right) colon injury with open wound into cavity
863.52 Transverse colon injury with open wound into cavity
863.53 Descending (left) colon injury with open wound into cavity
863.54 Sigmoid colon injury with open wound into cavity
863.55 Rectum injury with open wound into cavity
863.56 Injury to multiple sites in colon and rectum with open wound into cavity
863.59 Other injury to colon and rectum with open wound into cavity
863.80 Gastrointestinal tract injury, unspecified site, without mention of open wound into cavity ▽
863.90 Gastrointestinal tract injury, unspecified site, with open wound into cavity ▽
869.0 Internal injury to unspecified or ill-defined organs without mention of open wound into cavity ▽
869.1 Internal injury to unspecified or ill-defined organs with open wound into cavity ▽
936 Foreign body in intestine and colon
937 Foreign body in anus and rectum
938 Foreign body in digestive system, unspecified ▽
997.49 Other digestive system complications
998.2 Accidental puncture or laceration during procedure
998.31 Disruption of internal operation (surgical) wound
998.6 Persistent postoperative fistula, not elsewhere classified
998.9 Unspecified complication of procedure, not elsewhere classified ▽
V64.41 Laparoscopic surgical procedure converted to open procedure

ICD-9-CM Procedural

45.72 Open and other cecectomy
45.73 Open and other right hemicolectomy
45.74 Open and other resection of transverse colon
45.75 Open and other left hemicolectomy

44144

44144 Colectomy, partial; with resection, with colostomy or ileostomy and creation of mucofistula

ICD-9-CM Diagnostic

153.0 Malignant neoplasm of hepatic flexure
153.1 Malignant neoplasm of transverse colon
153.2 Malignant neoplasm of descending colon
153.3 Malignant neoplasm of sigmoid colon
153.4 Malignant neoplasm of cecum
153.5 Malignant neoplasm of appendix
153.6 Malignant neoplasm of ascending colon
153.7 Malignant neoplasm of splenic flexure
153.8 Malignant neoplasm of other specified sites of large intestine
153.9 Malignant neoplasm of colon, unspecified site ▽
154.0 Malignant neoplasm of rectosigmoid junction
154.1 Malignant neoplasm of rectum
154.2 Malignant neoplasm of anal canal
159.0 Malignant neoplasm of intestinal tract, part unspecified ▽
197.5 Secondary malignant neoplasm of large intestine and rectum
198.89 Secondary malignant neoplasm of other specified sites
199.1 Other malignant neoplasm of unspecified site
209.10 Malignant carcinoid tumor of the large intestine, unspecified portion — (Code first any associated multiple endocrine neoplasia syndrome: 258.01-258.03)(Use additional code to identify associated endocrine syndrome, as: carcinoid syndrome: 259.2) ▽
209.11 Malignant carcinoid tumor of the appendix — (Code first any associated multiple endocrine neoplasia syndrome: 258.01-258.03)(Use additional code to identify associated endocrine syndrome, as: carcinoid syndrome: 259.2)
209.12 Malignant carcinoid tumor of the cecum — (Code first any associated multiple endocrine neoplasia syndrome: 258.01-258.03)(Use additional code to identify associated endocrine syndrome, as: carcinoid syndrome: 259.2)
209.13 Malignant carcinoid tumor of the ascending colon — (Code first any associated multiple endocrine neoplasia syndrome: 258.01-258.03)(Use additional code to identify associated endocrine syndrome, as: carcinoid syndrome: 259.2)
209.14 Malignant carcinoid tumor of the transverse colon — (Code first any associated multiple endocrine neoplasia syndrome: 258.01-258.03)(Use additional code to identify associated endocrine syndrome, as: carcinoid syndrome: 259.2)
209.15 Malignant carcinoid tumor of the descending colon — (Code first any associated multiple endocrine neoplasia syndrome: 258.01-258.03)(Use additional code to identify associated endocrine syndrome, as: carcinoid syndrome: 259.2)
209.16 Malignant carcinoid tumor of the sigmoid colon — (Code first any associated multiple endocrine neoplasia syndrome: 258.01-258.03)(Use additional code to identify associated endocrine syndrome, as: carcinoid syndrome: 259.2)
209.27 Malignant carcinoid tumor of hindgut, not otherwise specified — (Code first any associated multiple endocrine neoplasia syndrome: 258.01-258.03)(Use additional code to identify associated endocrine syndrome, as: carcinoid syndrome: 259.2)

209.29 Malignant carcinoid tumor of other sites — (Code first any associated multiple endocrine neoplasia syndrome: 258.01-258.03)(Use additional code to identify associated endocrine syndrome, as: carcinoid syndrome: 259.2)
209.30 Malignant poorly differentiated neuroendocrine carcinoma, any site — (Code first any associated multiple endocrine neoplasia syndrome: 258.01-258.03)(Use additional code to identify associated endocrine syndrome, as: carcinoid syndrome: 259.2) ▽
209.50 Benign carcinoid tumor of the large intestine, unspecified portion — (Code first any associated multiple endocrine neoplasia syndrome: 258.01-258.03)(Use additional code to identify associated endocrine syndrome, as: carcinoid syndrome: 259.2) ▽
209.51 Benign carcinoid tumor of the appendix — (Code first any associated multiple endocrine neoplasia syndrome: 258.01-258.03)(Use additional code to identify associated endocrine syndrome, as: carcinoid syndrome: 259.2)
209.52 Benign carcinoid tumor of the cecum — (Code first any associated multiple endocrine neoplasia syndrome: 258.01-258.03)(Use additional code to identify associated endocrine syndrome, as: carcinoid syndrome: 259.2)
209.53 Benign carcinoid tumor of the ascending colon — (Code first any associated multiple endocrine neoplasia syndrome: 258.01-258.03)(Use additional code to identify associated endocrine syndrome, as: carcinoid syndrome: 259.2)
209.54 Benign carcinoid tumor of the transverse colon — (Code first any associated multiple endocrine neoplasia syndrome: 258.01-258.03)(Use additional code to identify associated endocrine syndrome, as: carcinoid syndrome: 259.2)
209.55 Benign carcinoid tumor of the descending colon — (Code first any associated multiple endocrine neoplasia syndrome: 258.01-258.03)(Use additional code to identify associated endocrine syndrome, as: carcinoid syndrome: 259.2)
209.56 Benign carcinoid tumor of the sigmoid colon — (Code first any associated multiple endocrine neoplasia syndrome: 258.01-258.03)(Use additional code to identify associated endocrine syndrome, as: carcinoid syndrome: 259.2)
209.57 Benign carcinoid tumor of the rectum — (Code first any associated multiple endocrine neoplasia syndrome: 258.01-258.03)(Use additional code to identify associated endocrine syndrome, as: carcinoid syndrome: 259.2)
209.69 Benign carcinoid tumor of other sites — (Code first any associated multiple endocrine neoplasia syndrome: 258.01-258.03)(Use additional code to identify associated endocrine syndrome, as: carcinoid syndrome: 259.2)
211.3 Benign neoplasm of colon
211.4 Benign neoplasm of rectum and anal canal
230.3 Carcinoma in situ of colon
230.4 Carcinoma in situ of rectum
235.2 Neoplasm of uncertain behavior of stomach, intestines, and rectum
239.0 Neoplasm of unspecified nature of digestive system
550.00 Inguinal hernia with gangrene, unilateral or unspecified, (not specified as recurrent)
550.01 Inguinal hernia with gangrene, recurrent unilateral or unspecified inguinal hernia
550.02 Inguinal hernia with gangrene, bilateral
550.03 Inguinal hernia with gangrene, recurrent bilateral
550.10 Inguinal hernia with obstruction, without mention of gangrene, unilateral or unspecified, (not specified as recurrent)
550.11 Inguinal hernia with obstruction, without mention of gangrene, recurrent unilateral or unspecified
550.12 Inguinal hernia with obstruction, without mention gangrene, bilateral, (not specified as recurrent)
550.13 Inguinal hernia with obstruction, without mention of gangrene, recurrent bilateral
551.00 Femoral hernia with gangrene, unilateral or unspecified (not specified as recurrent)
551.01 Femoral hernia with gangrene, recurrent unilateral or unspecified
551.02 Femoral hernia with gangrene, bilateral, (not specified as recurrent)
551.03 Femoral hernia with gangrene, recurrent bilateral
551.1 Umbilical hernia with gangrene
551.21 Incisional ventral hernia, with gangrene
551.29 Other ventral hernia with gangrene
551.3 Diaphragmatic hernia with gangrene
551.8 Hernia of other specified sites, with gangrene
551.9 Hernia of unspecified site, with gangrene ▽
552.00 Unilateral or unspecified femoral hernia with obstruction
552.01 Recurrent unilateral or unspecified femoral hernia with obstruction
552.02 Bilateral femoral hernia with obstruction
552.03 Recurrent bilateral femoral hernia with obstruction
552.1 Umbilical hernia with obstruction
552.21 Incisional hernia with obstruction
552.29 Other ventral hernia with obstruction
552.3 Diaphragmatic hernia with obstruction
552.8 Hernia of other specified site, with obstruction
552.9 Hernia of unspecified site, with obstruction ▽
555.1 Regional enteritis of large intestine
555.9 Regional enteritis of unspecified site ▽
556.0 Ulcerative (chronic) enterocolitis
556.1 Ulcerative (chronic) ileocolitis
556.2 Ulcerative (chronic) proctitis
556.3 Ulcerative (chronic) proctosigmoiditis
556.4 Pseudopolyposis of colon
556.5 Left sided ulcerative (chronic) colitis
556.6 Universal ulcerative (chronic) colitis
556.8 Other ulcerative colitis
556.9 Unspecified ulcerative colitis ▽
557.0 Acute vascular insufficiency of intestine
557.1 Chronic vascular insufficiency of intestine
557.9 Unspecified vascular insufficiency of intestine ▽
560.2 Volvulus
560.81 Intestinal or peritoneal adhesions with obstruction (postoperative) (postinfection)
560.89 Other specified intestinal obstruction
560.9 Unspecified intestinal obstruction ▽
562.10 Diverticulosis of colon (without mention of hemorrhage) — (Use additional code to identify any associated peritonitis: 567.0-567.9)
562.11 Diverticulitis of colon (without mention of hemorrhage) — (Use additional code to identify any associated peritonitis: 567.0-567.9)
562.12 Diverticulosis of colon with hemorrhage — (Use additional code to identify any associated peritonitis: 567.0-567.9)
562.13 Diverticulitis of colon with hemorrhage — (Use additional code to identify any associated peritonitis: 567.0-567.9)
564.81 Neurogenic bowel
564.89 Other functional disorders of intestine
567.0 Peritonitis in infectious diseases classified elsewhere — (Code first underlying disease) ☒
567.1 Pneumococcal peritonitis
567.21 Peritonitis (acute) generalized
567.22 Peritoneal abscess
567.23 Spontaneous bacterial peritonitis
567.29 Other suppurative peritonitis
567.31 Psoas muscle abscess
567.38 Other retroperitoneal abscess
567.39 Other retroperitoneal infections
567.81 Choleperitonitis
567.82 Sclerosing mesenteritis
567.89 Other specified peritonitis
567.9 Unspecified peritonitis ▽
569.5 Abscess of intestine
569.81 Fistula of intestine, excluding rectum and anus
569.82 Ulceration of intestine
569.83 Perforation of intestine
569.84 Angiodysplasia of intestine (without mention of hemorrhage)
569.85 Angiodysplasia of intestine with hemorrhage
569.89 Other specified disorder of intestines
569.9 Unspecified disorder of intestine ▽

578.1 Blood in stool
578.9 Hemorrhage of gastrointestinal tract, unspecified
596.1 Intestinovesical fistula — (Use additional code to identify urinary incontinence: 625.6, 788.30-788.39)
619.1 Digestive-genital tract fistula, female ♀
751.2 Congenital atresia and stenosis of large intestine, rectum, and anal canal
751.3 Hirschsprung's disease and other congenital functional disorders of colon
751.4 Congenital anomalies of intestinal fixation
751.5 Other congenital anomalies of intestine
777.50 Necrotizing enterocolitis in newborn, unspecified
777.51 Stage I necrotizing enterocolitis in newborn
777.52 Stage II necrotizing enterocolitis in newborn
777.53 Stage III necrotizing enterocolitis in newborn
777.6 Perinatal intestinal perforation — (Use additional code(s) to further specify condition)
777.8 Other specified perinatal disorder of digestive system — (Use additional code(s) to further specify condition)
863.41 Ascending (right) colon injury without mention of open wound into cavity
863.42 Transverse colon injury without mention of open wound into cavity
863.43 Descending (left) colon injury without mention of open wound into cavity
863.44 Sigmoid colon injury without mention of open wound into cavity
863.45 Rectum injury without mention of open wound into cavity
863.46 Injury to multiple sites in colon and rectum without mention of open wound into cavity
863.49 Other colon and rectum injury, without mention of open wound into cavity
863.51 Ascending (right) colon injury with open wound into cavity
863.52 Transverse colon injury with open wound into cavity
863.53 Descending (left) colon injury with open wound into cavity
863.54 Sigmoid colon injury with open wound into cavity
863.55 Rectum injury with open wound into cavity
863.56 Injury to multiple sites in colon and rectum with open wound into cavity
863.59 Other injury to colon and rectum with open wound into cavity
869.0 Internal injury to unspecified or ill-defined organs without mention of open wound into cavity
869.1 Internal injury to unspecified or ill-defined organs with open wound into cavity
936 Foreign body in intestine and colon
937 Foreign body in anus and rectum
938 Foreign body in digestive system, unspecified
997.49 Other digestive system complications
998.2 Accidental puncture or laceration during procedure
998.31 Disruption of internal operation (surgical) wound
998.51 Infected postoperative seroma — (Use additional code to identify organism)
998.59 Other postoperative infection — (Use additional code to identify infection)
998.6 Persistent postoperative fistula, not elsewhere classified
V64.41 Laparoscopic surgical procedure converted to open procedure

ICD-9-CM Procedural

45.72 Open and other cecectomy
45.73 Open and other right hemicolectomy
45.74 Open and other resection of transverse colon
45.75 Open and other left hemicolectomy
45.76 Open and other sigmoidectomy
45.79 Other and unspecified partial excision of large intestine
46.01 Exteriorization of small intestine
46.03 Exteriorization of large intestine
46.10 Colostomy, not otherwise specified
46.11 Temporary colostomy
46.13 Permanent colostomy
46.21 Temporary ileostomy
46.22 Continent ileostomy
46.23 Other permanent ileostomy

44145-44146

44145 Colectomy, partial; with coloproctostomy (low pelvic anastomosis)
44146 with coloproctostomy (low pelvic anastomosis), with colostomy

ICD-9-CM Diagnostic

153.0 Malignant neoplasm of hepatic flexure
153.1 Malignant neoplasm of transverse colon
153.2 Malignant neoplasm of descending colon
153.3 Malignant neoplasm of sigmoid colon
153.4 Malignant neoplasm of cecum
153.5 Malignant neoplasm of appendix
153.6 Malignant neoplasm of ascending colon
153.7 Malignant neoplasm of splenic flexure
153.8 Malignant neoplasm of other specified sites of large intestine
153.9 Malignant neoplasm of colon, unspecified site
154.0 Malignant neoplasm of rectosigmoid junction
154.1 Malignant neoplasm of rectum
154.2 Malignant neoplasm of anal canal
154.8 Malignant neoplasm of other sites of rectum, rectosigmoid junction, and anus
159.0 Malignant neoplasm of intestinal tract, part unspecified
197.5 Secondary malignant neoplasm of large intestine and rectum
209.10 Malignant carcinoid tumor of the large intestine, unspecified portion — (Code first any associated multiple endocrine neoplasia syndrome: 258.01-258.03)(Use additional code to identify associated endocrine syndrome, as: carcinoid syndrome: 259.2)
209.11 Malignant carcinoid tumor of the appendix — (Code first any associated multiple endocrine neoplasia syndrome: 258.01-258.03)(Use additional code to identify associated endocrine syndrome, as: carcinoid syndrome: 259.2)
209.12 Malignant carcinoid tumor of the cecum — (Code first any associated multiple endocrine neoplasia syndrome: 258.01-258.03)(Use additional code to identify associated endocrine syndrome, as: carcinoid syndrome: 259.2)
209.13 Malignant carcinoid tumor of the ascending colon — (Code first any associated multiple endocrine neoplasia syndrome: 258.01-258.03)(Use additional code to identify associated endocrine syndrome, as: carcinoid syndrome: 259.2)
209.14 Malignant carcinoid tumor of the transverse colon — (Code first any associated multiple endocrine neoplasia syndrome: 258.01-258.03)(Use additional code to identify associated endocrine syndrome, as: carcinoid syndrome: 259.2)
209.15 Malignant carcinoid tumor of the descending colon — (Code first any associated multiple endocrine neoplasia syndrome: 258.01-258.03)(Use additional code to identify associated endocrine syndrome, as: carcinoid syndrome: 259.2)
209.16 Malignant carcinoid tumor of the sigmoid colon — (Code first any associated multiple endocrine neoplasia syndrome: 258.01-258.03)(Use additional code to identify associated endocrine syndrome, as: carcinoid syndrome: 259.2)
209.27 Malignant carcinoid tumor of hindgut, not otherwise specified — (Code first any associated multiple endocrine neoplasia syndrome: 258.01-258.03)(Use additional code to identify associated endocrine syndrome, as: carcinoid syndrome: 259.2)
209.29 Malignant carcinoid tumor of other sites — (Code first any associated multiple endocrine neoplasia syndrome: 258.01-258.03)(Use additional code to identify associated endocrine syndrome, as: carcinoid syndrome: 259.2)
209.30 Malignant poorly differentiated neuroendocrine carcinoma, any site — (Code first any associated multiple endocrine neoplasia syndrome: 258.01-258.03)(Use additional code to identify associated endocrine syndrome, as: carcinoid syndrome: 259.2)
209.50 Benign carcinoid tumor of the large intestine, unspecified portion — (Code first any associated multiple endocrine neoplasia syndrome: 258.01-258.03)(Use additional code to identify associated endocrine syndrome, as: carcinoid syndrome: 259.2)
209.51 Benign carcinoid tumor of the appendix — (Code first any associated multiple endocrine neoplasia syndrome: 258.01-258.03)(Use additional code to identify associated endocrine syndrome, as: carcinoid syndrome: 259.2)
209.52 Benign carcinoid tumor of the cecum — (Code first any associated multiple endocrine neoplasia syndrome: 258.01-258.03)(Use additional code to identify associated endocrine syndrome, as: carcinoid syndrome: 259.2)

209.53 Benign carcinoid tumor of the ascending colon — (Code first any associated multiple endocrine neoplasia syndrome: 258.01-258.03)(Use additional code to identify associated endocrine syndrome, as: carcinoid syndrome: 259.2)
209.54 Benign carcinoid tumor of the transverse colon — (Code first any associated multiple endocrine neoplasia syndrome: 258.01-258.03)(Use additional code to identify associated endocrine syndrome, as: carcinoid syndrome: 259.2)
209.55 Benign carcinoid tumor of the descending colon — (Code first any associated multiple endocrine neoplasia syndrome: 258.01-258.03)(Use additional code to identify associated endocrine syndrome, as: carcinoid syndrome: 259.2)
209.56 Benign carcinoid tumor of the sigmoid colon — (Code first any associated multiple endocrine neoplasia syndrome: 258.01-258.03)(Use additional code to identify associated endocrine syndrome, as: carcinoid syndrome: 259.2)
209.57 Benign carcinoid tumor of the rectum — (Code first any associated multiple endocrine neoplasia syndrome: 258.01-258.03)(Use additional code to identify associated endocrine syndrome, as: carcinoid syndrome: 259.2)
209.69 Benign carcinoid tumor of other sites — (Code first any associated multiple endocrine neoplasia syndrome: 258.01-258.03)(Use additional code to identify associated endocrine syndrome, as: carcinoid syndrome: 259.2)
211.3 Benign neoplasm of colon
211.4 Benign neoplasm of rectum and anal canal
230.3 Carcinoma in situ of colon
230.4 Carcinoma in situ of rectum
230.9 Carcinoma in situ of other and unspecified digestive organs ▽
235.2 Neoplasm of uncertain behavior of stomach, intestines, and rectum
239.0 Neoplasm of unspecified nature of digestive system
555.1 Regional enteritis of large intestine
555.2 Regional enteritis of small intestine with large intestine
555.9 Regional enteritis of unspecified site ▽
556.0 Ulcerative (chronic) enterocolitis
556.1 Ulcerative (chronic) ileocolitis
556.2 Ulcerative (chronic) proctitis
556.3 Ulcerative (chronic) proctosigmoiditis
556.4 Pseudopolyposis of colon
556.5 Left sided ulcerative (chronic) colitis
556.6 Universal ulcerative (chronic) colitis
556.8 Other ulcerative colitis
556.9 Unspecified ulcerative colitis ▽
557.0 Acute vascular insufficiency of intestine
557.1 Chronic vascular insufficiency of intestine
557.9 Unspecified vascular insufficiency of intestine ▽
560.39 Impaction of intestine, other
560.81 Intestinal or peritoneal adhesions with obstruction (postoperative) (postinfection)
560.89 Other specified intestinal obstruction
560.9 Unspecified intestinal obstruction ▽
562.10 Diverticulosis of colon (without mention of hemorrhage) — (Use additional code to identify any associated peritonitis: 567.0-567.9)
562.11 Diverticulitis of colon (without mention of hemorrhage) — (Use additional code to identify any associated peritonitis: 567.0-567.9)
562.12 Diverticulosis of colon with hemorrhage — (Use additional code to identify any associated peritonitis: 567.0-567.9)
562.13 Diverticulitis of colon with hemorrhage — (Use additional code to identify any associated peritonitis: 567.0-567.9)
564.7 Megacolon, other than Hirschsprung's
567.0 Peritonitis in infectious diseases classified elsewhere — (Code first underlying disease) ☒
567.1 Pneumococcal peritonitis
567.21 Peritonitis (acute) generalized
567.22 Peritoneal abscess
567.23 Spontaneous bacterial peritonitis
567.29 Other suppurative peritonitis
567.31 Psoas muscle abscess
567.38 Other retroperitoneal abscess
567.39 Other retroperitoneal infections
567.81 Choleperitonitis
567.82 Sclerosing mesenteritis
567.89 Other specified peritonitis
567.9 Unspecified peritonitis ▽
569.1 Rectal prolapse
569.44 Dysplasia of anus
569.81 Fistula of intestine, excluding rectum and anus
569.82 Ulceration of intestine
569.83 Perforation of intestine
569.84 Angiodysplasia of intestine (without mention of hemorrhage)
569.85 Angiodysplasia of intestine with hemorrhage
569.89 Other specified disorder of intestines
569.9 Unspecified disorder of intestine ▽
596.1 Intestinovesical fistula — (Use additional code to identify urinary incontinence: 625.6, 788.30-788.39)
619.1 Digestive-genital tract fistula, female ♀
751.8 Other specified congenital anomalies of digestive system
777.50 Necrotizing enterocolitis in newborn, unspecified ▽
777.51 Stage I necrotizing enterocolitis in newborn
777.52 Stage II necrotizing enterocolitis in newborn
777.53 Stage III necrotizing enterocolitis in newborn
777.6 Perinatal intestinal perforation — (Use additional code(s) to further specify condition)
777.8 Other specified perinatal disorder of digestive system — (Use additional code(s) to further specify condition)
787.99 Other symptoms involving digestive system

ICD-9-CM Procedural

45.75 Open and other left hemicolectomy
45.76 Open and other sigmoidectomy
45.94 Large-to-large intestinal anastomosis
46.03 Exteriorization of large intestine
46.10 Colostomy, not otherwise specified
46.11 Temporary colostomy
46.13 Permanent colostomy

44147

44147 Colectomy, partial; abdominal and transanal approach

ICD-9-CM Diagnostic

153.0 Malignant neoplasm of hepatic flexure
153.1 Malignant neoplasm of transverse colon
153.2 Malignant neoplasm of descending colon
153.3 Malignant neoplasm of sigmoid colon
153.4 Malignant neoplasm of cecum
153.5 Malignant neoplasm of appendix
153.6 Malignant neoplasm of ascending colon
153.7 Malignant neoplasm of splenic flexure
153.8 Malignant neoplasm of other specified sites of large intestine
153.9 Malignant neoplasm of colon, unspecified site ▽
154.0 Malignant neoplasm of rectosigmoid junction
154.1 Malignant neoplasm of rectum
154.2 Malignant neoplasm of anal canal
209.10 Malignant carcinoid tumor of the large intestine, unspecified portion — (Code first any associated multiple endocrine neoplasia syndrome: 258.01-258.03)(Use additional code to identify associated endocrine syndrome, as: carcinoid syndrome: 259.2) ▽

209.11 Malignant carcinoid tumor of the appendix — (Code first any associated multiple endocrine neoplasia syndrome: 258.01-258.03)(Use additional code to identify associated endocrine syndrome, as: carcinoid syndrome: 259.2)
209.12 Malignant carcinoid tumor of the cecum — (Code first any associated multiple endocrine neoplasia syndrome: 258.01-258.03)(Use additional code to identify associated endocrine syndrome, as: carcinoid syndrome: 259.2)
209.13 Malignant carcinoid tumor of the ascending colon — (Code first any associated multiple endocrine neoplasia syndrome: 258.01-258.03)(Use additional code to identify associated endocrine syndrome, as: carcinoid syndrome: 259.2)
209.14 Malignant carcinoid tumor of the transverse colon — (Code first any associated multiple endocrine neoplasia syndrome: 258.01-258.03)(Use additional code to identify associated endocrine syndrome, as: carcinoid syndrome: 259.2)
209.15 Malignant carcinoid tumor of the descending colon — (Code first any associated multiple endocrine neoplasia syndrome: 258.01-258.03)(Use additional code to identify associated endocrine syndrome, as: carcinoid syndrome: 259.2)
209.16 Malignant carcinoid tumor of the sigmoid colon — (Code first any associated multiple endocrine neoplasia syndrome: 258.01-258.03)(Use additional code to identify associated endocrine syndrome, as: carcinoid syndrome: 259.2)
556.9 Unspecified ulcerative colitis ▽
560.81 Intestinal or peritoneal adhesions with obstruction (postoperative) (postinfection)
562.10 Diverticulosis of colon (without mention of hemorrhage) — (Use additional code to identify any associated peritonitis: 567.0-567.9)
562.11 Diverticulitis of colon (without mention of hemorrhage) — (Use additional code to identify any associated peritonitis: 567.0-567.9)
562.12 Diverticulosis of colon with hemorrhage — (Use additional code to identify any associated peritonitis: 567.0-567.9)
562.13 Diverticulitis of colon with hemorrhage — (Use additional code to identify any associated peritonitis: 567.0-567.9)
567.0 Peritonitis in infectious diseases classified elsewhere — (Code first underlying disease) ☒
567.1 Pneumococcal peritonitis
567.21 Peritonitis (acute) generalized
567.22 Peritoneal abscess
567.23 Spontaneous bacterial peritonitis
567.29 Other suppurative peritonitis
567.31 Psoas muscle abscess
567.38 Other retroperitoneal abscess
567.39 Other retroperitoneal infections
567.81 Choleperitonitis
567.82 Sclerosing mesenteritis
567.89 Other specified peritonitis
567.9 Unspecified peritonitis ▽
569.83 Perforation of intestine
569.84 Angiodysplasia of intestine (without mention of hemorrhage)
569.89 Other specified disorder of intestines
V64.41 Laparoscopic surgical procedure converted to open procedure

ICD-9-CM Procedural

45.75 Open and other left hemicolectomy
45.76 Open and other sigmoidectomy
45.79 Other and unspecified partial excision of large intestine
45.94 Large-to-large intestinal anastomosis

44150

44150 Colectomy, total, abdominal, without proctectomy; with ileostomy or ileoproctostomy

ICD-9-CM Diagnostic

153.0 Malignant neoplasm of hepatic flexure
153.1 Malignant neoplasm of transverse colon
153.2 Malignant neoplasm of descending colon
153.3 Malignant neoplasm of sigmoid colon
153.4 Malignant neoplasm of cecum
153.5 Malignant neoplasm of appendix
153.6 Malignant neoplasm of ascending colon
153.7 Malignant neoplasm of splenic flexure
153.8 Malignant neoplasm of other specified sites of large intestine
153.9 Malignant neoplasm of colon, unspecified site ▽
154.0 Malignant neoplasm of rectosigmoid junction
154.1 Malignant neoplasm of rectum
197.5 Secondary malignant neoplasm of large intestine and rectum
209.10 Malignant carcinoid tumor of the large intestine, unspecified portion — (Code first any associated multiple endocrine neoplasia syndrome: 258.01-258.03)(Use additional code to identify associated endocrine syndrome, as: carcinoid syndrome: 259.2) ▽
209.11 Malignant carcinoid tumor of the appendix — (Code first any associated multiple endocrine neoplasia syndrome: 258.01-258.03)(Use additional code to identify associated endocrine syndrome, as: carcinoid syndrome: 259.2)
209.12 Malignant carcinoid tumor of the cecum — (Code first any associated multiple endocrine neoplasia syndrome: 258.01-258.03)(Use additional code to identify associated endocrine syndrome, as: carcinoid syndrome: 259.2)
209.13 Malignant carcinoid tumor of the ascending colon — (Code first any associated multiple endocrine neoplasia syndrome: 258.01-258.03)(Use additional code to identify associated endocrine syndrome, as: carcinoid syndrome: 259.2)
209.14 Malignant carcinoid tumor of the transverse colon — (Code first any associated multiple endocrine neoplasia syndrome: 258.01-258.03)(Use additional code to identify associated endocrine syndrome, as: carcinoid syndrome: 259.2)
209.15 Malignant carcinoid tumor of the descending colon — (Code first any associated multiple endocrine neoplasia syndrome: 258.01-258.03)(Use additional code to identify associated endocrine syndrome, as: carcinoid syndrome: 259.2)
209.16 Malignant carcinoid tumor of the sigmoid colon — (Code first any associated multiple endocrine neoplasia syndrome: 258.01-258.03)(Use additional code to identify associated endocrine syndrome, as: carcinoid syndrome: 259.2)
209.29 Malignant carcinoid tumor of other sites — (Code first any associated multiple endocrine neoplasia syndrome: 258.01-258.03)(Use additional code to identify associated endocrine syndrome, as: carcinoid syndrome: 259.2)
209.30 Malignant poorly differentiated neuroendocrine carcinoma, any site — (Code first any associated multiple endocrine neoplasia syndrome: 258.01-258.03)(Use additional code to identify associated endocrine syndrome, as: carcinoid syndrome: 259.2) ▽
209.50 Benign carcinoid tumor of the large intestine, unspecified portion — (Code first any associated multiple endocrine neoplasia syndrome: 258.01-258.03)(Use additional code to identify associated endocrine syndrome, as: carcinoid syndrome: 259.2) ▽
209.51 Benign carcinoid tumor of the appendix — (Code first any associated multiple endocrine neoplasia syndrome: 258.01-258.03)(Use additional code to identify associated endocrine syndrome, as: carcinoid syndrome: 259.2)
209.52 Benign carcinoid tumor of the cecum — (Code first any associated multiple endocrine neoplasia syndrome: 258.01-258.03)(Use additional code to identify associated endocrine syndrome, as: carcinoid syndrome: 259.2)
209.53 Benign carcinoid tumor of the ascending colon — (Code first any associated multiple endocrine neoplasia syndrome: 258.01-258.03)(Use additional code to identify associated endocrine syndrome, as: carcinoid syndrome: 259.2)
209.54 Benign carcinoid tumor of the transverse colon — (Code first any associated multiple endocrine neoplasia syndrome: 258.01-258.03)(Use additional code to identify associated endocrine syndrome, as: carcinoid syndrome: 259.2)
209.55 Benign carcinoid tumor of the descending colon — (Code first any associated multiple endocrine neoplasia syndrome: 258.01-258.03)(Use additional code to identify associated endocrine syndrome, as: carcinoid syndrome: 259.2)
209.56 Benign carcinoid tumor of the sigmoid colon — (Code first any associated multiple endocrine neoplasia syndrome: 258.01-258.03)(Use additional code to identify associated endocrine syndrome, as: carcinoid syndrome: 259.2)
209.57 Benign carcinoid tumor of the rectum — (Code first any associated multiple endocrine neoplasia syndrome: 258.01-258.03)(Use additional code to identify associated endocrine syndrome, as: carcinoid syndrome: 259.2)

209.69 Benign carcinoid tumor of other sites — (Code first any associated multiple endocrine neoplasia syndrome: 258.01-258.03)(Use additional code to identify associated endocrine syndrome, as: carcinoid syndrome: 259.2)
211.3 Benign neoplasm of colon
211.4 Benign neoplasm of rectum and anal canal
230.3 Carcinoma in situ of colon
230.4 Carcinoma in situ of rectum
230.7 Carcinoma in situ of other and unspecified parts of intestine ♥
235.2 Neoplasm of uncertain behavior of stomach, intestines, and rectum
239.0 Neoplasm of unspecified nature of digestive system
556.0 Ulcerative (chronic) enterocolitis
556.1 Ulcerative (chronic) ileocolitis
556.2 Ulcerative (chronic) proctitis
556.3 Ulcerative (chronic) proctosigmoiditis
556.4 Pseudopolyposis of colon
556.5 Left sided ulcerative (chronic) colitis
556.6 Universal ulcerative (chronic) colitis
556.8 Other ulcerative colitis
556.9 Unspecified ulcerative colitis ♥
557.0 Acute vascular insufficiency of intestine
557.1 Chronic vascular insufficiency of intestine
557.9 Unspecified vascular insufficiency of intestine ♥
558.41 Eosinophilic gastroenteritis
558.42 Eosinophilic colitis
558.9 Other and unspecified noninfectious gastroenteritis and colitis ♥
560.9 Unspecified intestinal obstruction ♥
562.10 Diverticulosis of colon (without mention of hemorrhage) — (Use additional code to identify any associated peritonitis: 567.0-567.9)
562.11 Diverticulitis of colon (without mention of hemorrhage) — (Use additional code to identify any associated peritonitis: 567.0-567.9)
562.12 Diverticulosis of colon with hemorrhage — (Use additional code to identify any associated peritonitis: 567.0-567.9)
562.13 Diverticulitis of colon with hemorrhage — (Use additional code to identify any associated peritonitis: 567.0-567.9)
564.7 Megacolon, other than Hirschsprung's
564.81 Neurogenic bowel
564.89 Other functional disorders of intestine
567.0 Peritonitis in infectious diseases classified elsewhere — (Code first underlying disease) ☒
567.1 Pneumococcal peritonitis
567.21 Peritonitis (acute) generalized
567.22 Peritoneal abscess
567.23 Spontaneous bacterial peritonitis
567.29 Other suppurative peritonitis
567.31 Psoas muscle abscess
567.38 Other retroperitoneal abscess
567.39 Other retroperitoneal infections
567.81 Choleperitonitis
567.82 Sclerosing mesenteritis
567.89 Other specified peritonitis
567.9 Unspecified peritonitis ♥
569.82 Ulceration of intestine
569.83 Perforation of intestine
569.89 Other specified disorder of intestines
569.9 Unspecified disorder of intestine ♥
578.1 Blood in stool
578.9 Hemorrhage of gastrointestinal tract, unspecified ♥
751.3 Hirschsprung's disease and other congenital functional disorders of colon
777.1 Fetal and newborn meconium obstruction — (Use additional code(s) to further specify condition)
777.50 Necrotizing enterocolitis in newborn, unspecified ♥
777.51 Stage I necrotizing enterocolitis in newborn
777.52 Stage II necrotizing enterocolitis in newborn
777.53 Stage III necrotizing enterocolitis in newborn
777.6 Perinatal intestinal perforation — (Use additional code(s) to further specify condition)
777.8 Other specified perinatal disorder of digestive system — (Use additional code(s) to further specify condition)
863.40 Colon injury unspecified site, without mention of open wound into cavity ♥
863.41 Ascending (right) colon injury without mention of open wound into cavity
863.42 Transverse colon injury without mention of open wound into cavity
863.43 Descending (left) colon injury without mention of open wound into cavity
863.44 Sigmoid colon injury without mention of open wound into cavity
863.45 Rectum injury without mention of open wound into cavity
863.46 Injury to multiple sites in colon and rectum without mention of open wound into cavity
863.49 Other colon and rectum injury, without mention of open wound into cavity
998.89 Other specified complications
V64.41 Laparoscopic surgical procedure converted to open procedure

ICD-9-CM Procedural

45.82 Open total intra-abdominal colectomy
45.83 Other and unspecified total intra-abdominal colectomy
45.92 Anastomosis of small intestine to rectal stump
46.20 Ileostomy, not otherwise specified
46.23 Other permanent ileostomy

44151

44151 Colectomy, total, abdominal, without proctectomy; with continent ileostomy

ICD-9-CM Diagnostic

153.0 Malignant neoplasm of hepatic flexure
153.1 Malignant neoplasm of transverse colon
153.2 Malignant neoplasm of descending colon
153.3 Malignant neoplasm of sigmoid colon
153.4 Malignant neoplasm of cecum
153.5 Malignant neoplasm of appendix
153.6 Malignant neoplasm of ascending colon
153.7 Malignant neoplasm of splenic flexure
153.8 Malignant neoplasm of other specified sites of large intestine
153.9 Malignant neoplasm of colon, unspecified site ♥
154.0 Malignant neoplasm of rectosigmoid junction
154.1 Malignant neoplasm of rectum
197.5 Secondary malignant neoplasm of large intestine and rectum
209.10 Malignant carcinoid tumor of the large intestine, unspecified portion — (Code first any associated multiple endocrine neoplasia syndrome: 258.01-258.03)(Use additional code to identify associated endocrine syndrome, as: carcinoid syndrome: 259.2) ♥
209.11 Malignant carcinoid tumor of the appendix — (Code first any associated multiple endocrine neoplasia syndrome: 258.01-258.03)(Use additional code to identify associated endocrine syndrome, as: carcinoid syndrome: 259.2)
209.12 Malignant carcinoid tumor of the cecum — (Code first any associated multiple endocrine neoplasia syndrome: 258.01-258.03)(Use additional code to identify associated endocrine syndrome, as: carcinoid syndrome: 259.2)
209.13 Malignant carcinoid tumor of the ascending colon — (Code first any associated multiple endocrine neoplasia syndrome: 258.01-258.03)(Use additional code to identify associated endocrine syndrome, as: carcinoid syndrome: 259.2)
209.14 Malignant carcinoid tumor of the transverse colon — (Code first any associated multiple endocrine neoplasia syndrome: 258.01-258.03)(Use additional code to identify associated endocrine syndrome, as: carcinoid syndrome: 259.2)

209.15 Malignant carcinoid tumor of the descending colon — (Code first any associated multiple endocrine neoplasia syndrome: 258.01-258.03)(Use additional code to identify associated endocrine syndrome, as: carcinoid syndrome: 259.2)

209.16 Malignant carcinoid tumor of the sigmoid colon — (Code first any associated multiple endocrine neoplasia syndrome: 258.01-258.03)(Use additional code to identify associated endocrine syndrome, as: carcinoid syndrome: 259.2)

209.29 Malignant carcinoid tumor of other sites — (Code first any associated multiple endocrine neoplasia syndrome: 258.01-258.03)(Use additional code to identify associated endocrine syndrome, as: carcinoid syndrome: 259.2)

209.30 Malignant poorly differentiated neuroendocrine carcinoma, any site — (Code first any associated multiple endocrine neoplasia syndrome: 258.01-258.03)(Use additional code to identify associated endocrine syndrome, as: carcinoid syndrome: 259.2)

209.50 Benign carcinoid tumor of the large intestine, unspecified portion — (Code first any associated multiple endocrine neoplasia syndrome: 258.01-258.03)(Use additional code to identify associated endocrine syndrome, as: carcinoid syndrome: 259.2)

209.51 Benign carcinoid tumor of the appendix — (Code first any associated multiple endocrine neoplasia syndrome: 258.01-258.03)(Use additional code to identify associated endocrine syndrome, as: carcinoid syndrome: 259.2)

209.52 Benign carcinoid tumor of the cecum — (Code first any associated multiple endocrine neoplasia syndrome: 258.01-258.03)(Use additional code to identify associated endocrine syndrome, as: carcinoid syndrome: 259.2)

209.53 Benign carcinoid tumor of the ascending colon — (Code first any associated multiple endocrine neoplasia syndrome: 258.01-258.03)(Use additional code to identify associated endocrine syndrome, as: carcinoid syndrome: 259.2)

209.54 Benign carcinoid tumor of the transverse colon — (Code first any associated multiple endocrine neoplasia syndrome: 258.01-258.03)(Use additional code to identify associated endocrine syndrome, as: carcinoid syndrome: 259.2)

209.55 Benign carcinoid tumor of the descending colon — (Code first any associated multiple endocrine neoplasia syndrome: 258.01-258.03)(Use additional code to identify associated endocrine syndrome, as: carcinoid syndrome: 259.2)

209.56 Benign carcinoid tumor of the sigmoid colon — (Code first any associated multiple endocrine neoplasia syndrome: 258.01-258.03)(Use additional code to identify associated endocrine syndrome, as: carcinoid syndrome: 259.2)

209.57 Benign carcinoid tumor of the rectum — (Code first any associated multiple endocrine neoplasia syndrome: 258.01-258.03)(Use additional code to identify associated endocrine syndrome, as: carcinoid syndrome: 259.2)

209.69 Benign carcinoid tumor of other sites — (Code first any associated multiple endocrine neoplasia syndrome: 258.01-258.03)(Use additional code to identify associated endocrine syndrome, as: carcinoid syndrome: 259.2)

211.3 Benign neoplasm of colon

211.4 Benign neoplasm of rectum and anal canal

230.3 Carcinoma in situ of colon

230.4 Carcinoma in situ of rectum

230.7 Carcinoma in situ of other and unspecified parts of intestine

235.2 Neoplasm of uncertain behavior of stomach, intestines, and rectum

239.0 Neoplasm of unspecified nature of digestive system

556.0 Ulcerative (chronic) enterocolitis

556.1 Ulcerative (chronic) ileocolitis

556.2 Ulcerative (chronic) proctitis

556.3 Ulcerative (chronic) proctosigmoiditis

556.4 Pseudopolyposis of colon

556.5 Left sided ulcerative (chronic) colitis

556.6 Universal ulcerative (chronic) colitis

556.8 Other ulcerative colitis

556.9 Unspecified ulcerative colitis

557.0 Acute vascular insufficiency of intestine

557.1 Chronic vascular insufficiency of intestine

557.9 Unspecified vascular insufficiency of intestine

558.41 Eosinophilic gastroenteritis

558.42 Eosinophilic colitis

558.9 Other and unspecified noninfectious gastroenteritis and colitis

560.9 Unspecified intestinal obstruction

562.10 Diverticulosis of colon (without mention of hemorrhage) — (Use additional code to identify any associated peritonitis: 567.0-567.9)

562.11 Diverticulitis of colon (without mention of hemorrhage) — (Use additional code to identify any associated peritonitis: 567.0-567.9)

562.12 Diverticulosis of colon with hemorrhage — (Use additional code to identify any associated peritonitis: 567.0-567.9)

562.13 Diverticulitis of colon with hemorrhage — (Use additional code to identify any associated peritonitis: 567.0-567.9)

564.7 Megacolon, other than Hirschsprung's

564.81 Neurogenic bowel

564.89 Other functional disorders of intestine

567.0 Peritonitis in infectious diseases classified elsewhere — (Code first underlying disease)

567.1 Pneumococcal peritonitis

567.21 Peritonitis (acute) generalized

567.22 Peritoneal abscess

567.23 Spontaneous bacterial peritonitis

567.29 Other suppurative peritonitis

567.31 Psoas muscle abscess

567.38 Other retroperitoneal abscess

567.39 Other retroperitoneal infections

567.81 Choleperitonitis

567.82 Sclerosing mesenteritis

567.89 Other specified peritonitis

567.9 Unspecified peritonitis

569.82 Ulceration of intestine

569.83 Perforation of intestine

569.89 Other specified disorder of intestines

569.9 Unspecified disorder of intestine

578.1 Blood in stool

578.9 Hemorrhage of gastrointestinal tract, unspecified

751.3 Hirschsprung's disease and other congenital functional disorders of colon

777.1 Fetal and newborn meconium obstruction — (Use additional code(s) to further specify condition)

777.50 Necrotizing enterocolitis in newborn, unspecified

777.51 Stage I necrotizing enterocolitis in newborn

777.52 Stage II necrotizing enterocolitis in newborn

777.53 Stage III necrotizing enterocolitis in newborn

777.6 Perinatal intestinal perforation — (Use additional code(s) to further specify condition)

777.8 Other specified perinatal disorder of digestive system — (Use additional code(s) to further specify condition)

863.40 Colon injury unspecified site, without mention of open wound into cavity

863.41 Ascending (right) colon injury without mention of open wound into cavity

863.42 Transverse colon injury without mention of open wound into cavity

863.43 Descending (left) colon injury without mention of open wound into cavity

863.44 Sigmoid colon injury without mention of open wound into cavity

863.45 Rectum injury without mention of open wound into cavity

863.46 Injury to multiple sites in colon and rectum without mention of open wound into cavity

863.49 Other colon and rectum injury, without mention of open wound into cavity

998.89 Other specified complications

V64.41 Laparoscopic surgical procedure converted to open procedure

ICD-9-CM Procedural

45.82 Open total intra-abdominal colectomy

45.83 Other and unspecified total intra-abdominal colectomy

46.22 Continent ileostomy

44155-44156

44155 Colectomy, total, abdominal, with proctectomy; with ileostomy
44156 with continent ileostomy

ICD-9-CM Diagnostic

153.0 Malignant neoplasm of hepatic flexure
153.1 Malignant neoplasm of transverse colon
153.2 Malignant neoplasm of descending colon
153.3 Malignant neoplasm of sigmoid colon
153.4 Malignant neoplasm of cecum
153.5 Malignant neoplasm of appendix
153.6 Malignant neoplasm of ascending colon
153.7 Malignant neoplasm of splenic flexure
153.8 Malignant neoplasm of other specified sites of large intestine
153.9 Malignant neoplasm of colon, unspecified site ▽
154.0 Malignant neoplasm of rectosigmoid junction
154.1 Malignant neoplasm of rectum
197.5 Secondary malignant neoplasm of large intestine and rectum
209.10 Malignant carcinoid tumor of the large intestine, unspecified portion — (Code first any associated multiple endocrine neoplasia syndrome: 258.01-258.03)(Use additional code to identify associated endocrine syndrome, as: carcinoid syndrome: 259.2) ▽
209.11 Malignant carcinoid tumor of the appendix — (Code first any associated multiple endocrine neoplasia syndrome: 258.01-258.03)(Use additional code to identify associated endocrine syndrome, as: carcinoid syndrome: 259.2)
209.12 Malignant carcinoid tumor of the cecum — (Code first any associated multiple endocrine neoplasia syndrome: 258.01-258.03)(Use additional code to identify associated endocrine syndrome, as: carcinoid syndrome: 259.2)
209.13 Malignant carcinoid tumor of the ascending colon — (Code first any associated multiple endocrine neoplasia syndrome: 258.01-258.03)(Use additional code to identify associated endocrine syndrome, as: carcinoid syndrome: 259.2)
209.14 Malignant carcinoid tumor of the transverse colon — (Code first any associated multiple endocrine neoplasia syndrome: 258.01-258.03)(Use additional code to identify associated endocrine syndrome, as: carcinoid syndrome: 259.2)
209.15 Malignant carcinoid tumor of the descending colon — (Code first any associated multiple endocrine neoplasia syndrome: 258.01-258.03)(Use additional code to identify associated endocrine syndrome, as: carcinoid syndrome: 259.2)
209.16 Malignant carcinoid tumor of the sigmoid colon — (Code first any associated multiple endocrine neoplasia syndrome: 258.01-258.03)(Use additional code to identify associated endocrine syndrome, as: carcinoid syndrome: 259.2)
209.29 Malignant carcinoid tumor of other sites — (Code first any associated multiple endocrine neoplasia syndrome: 258.01-258.03)(Use additional code to identify associated endocrine syndrome, as: carcinoid syndrome: 259.2)
209.30 Malignant poorly differentiated neuroendocrine carcinoma, any site — (Code first any associated multiple endocrine neoplasia syndrome: 258.01-258.03)(Use additional code to identify associated endocrine syndrome, as: carcinoid syndrome: 259.2) ▽
209.50 Benign carcinoid tumor of the large intestine, unspecified portion — (Code first any associated multiple endocrine neoplasia syndrome: 258.01-258.03)(Use additional code to identify associated endocrine syndrome, as: carcinoid syndrome: 259.2) ▽
209.51 Benign carcinoid tumor of the appendix — (Code first any associated multiple endocrine neoplasia syndrome: 258.01-258.03)(Use additional code to identify associated endocrine syndrome, as: carcinoid syndrome: 259.2)
209.52 Benign carcinoid tumor of the cecum — (Code first any associated multiple endocrine neoplasia syndrome: 258.01-258.03)(Use additional code to identify associated endocrine syndrome, as: carcinoid syndrome: 259.2)
209.53 Benign carcinoid tumor of the ascending colon — (Code first any associated multiple endocrine neoplasia syndrome: 258.01-258.03)(Use additional code to identify associated endocrine syndrome, as: carcinoid syndrome: 259.2)
209.54 Benign carcinoid tumor of the transverse colon — (Code first any associated multiple endocrine neoplasia syndrome: 258.01-258.03)(Use additional code to identify associated endocrine syndrome, as: carcinoid syndrome: 259.2)
209.55 Benign carcinoid tumor of the descending colon — (Code first any associated multiple endocrine neoplasia syndrome: 258.01-258.03)(Use additional code to identify associated endocrine syndrome, as: carcinoid syndrome: 259.2)
209.56 Benign carcinoid tumor of the sigmoid colon — (Code first any associated multiple endocrine neoplasia syndrome: 258.01-258.03)(Use additional code to identify associated endocrine syndrome, as: carcinoid syndrome: 259.2)
209.57 Benign carcinoid tumor of the rectum — (Code first any associated multiple endocrine neoplasia syndrome: 258.01-258.03)(Use additional code to identify associated endocrine syndrome, as: carcinoid syndrome: 259.2)
209.69 Benign carcinoid tumor of other sites — (Code first any associated multiple endocrine neoplasia syndrome: 258.01-258.03)(Use additional code to identify associated endocrine syndrome, as: carcinoid syndrome: 259.2)
211.3 Benign neoplasm of colon
211.4 Benign neoplasm of rectum and anal canal
230.3 Carcinoma in situ of colon
230.4 Carcinoma in situ of rectum
230.7 Carcinoma in situ of other and unspecified parts of intestine ▽
235.2 Neoplasm of uncertain behavior of stomach, intestines, and rectum
239.0 Neoplasm of unspecified nature of digestive system
555.1 Regional enteritis of large intestine
556.0 Ulcerative (chronic) enterocolitis
556.1 Ulcerative (chronic) ileocolitis
556.2 Ulcerative (chronic) proctitis
556.3 Ulcerative (chronic) proctosigmoiditis
556.4 Pseudopolyposis of colon
556.5 Left sided ulcerative (chronic) colitis
556.6 Universal ulcerative (chronic) colitis
556.8 Other ulcerative colitis
556.9 Unspecified ulcerative colitis ▽
557.0 Acute vascular insufficiency of intestine
557.1 Chronic vascular insufficiency of intestine
557.9 Unspecified vascular insufficiency of intestine ▽
560.9 Unspecified intestinal obstruction ▽
562.10 Diverticulosis of colon (without mention of hemorrhage) — (Use additional code to identify any associated peritonitis: 567.0-567.9)
562.11 Diverticulitis of colon (without mention of hemorrhage) — (Use additional code to identify any associated peritonitis: 567.0-567.9)
562.12 Diverticulosis of colon with hemorrhage — (Use additional code to identify any associated peritonitis: 567.0-567.9)
562.13 Diverticulitis of colon with hemorrhage — (Use additional code to identify any associated peritonitis: 567.0-567.9)
567.0 Peritonitis in infectious diseases classified elsewhere — (Code first underlying disease) ☒
567.1 Pneumococcal peritonitis
567.21 Peritonitis (acute) generalized
567.22 Peritoneal abscess
567.23 Spontaneous bacterial peritonitis
567.29 Other suppurative peritonitis
567.31 Psoas muscle abscess
567.38 Other retroperitoneal abscess
567.39 Other retroperitoneal infections
567.81 Choleperitonitis
567.82 Sclerosing mesenteritis
567.89 Other specified peritonitis
567.9 Unspecified peritonitis ▽
569.82 Ulceration of intestine
569.83 Perforation of intestine
569.89 Other specified disorder of intestines
578.1 Blood in stool
751.2 Congenital atresia and stenosis of large intestine, rectum, and anal canal

751.3 Hirschsprung's disease and other congenital functional disorders of colon
777.1 Fetal and newborn meconium obstruction — (Use additional code(s) to further specify condition)
777.50 Necrotizing enterocolitis in newborn, unspecified
777.51 Stage I necrotizing enterocolitis in newborn
777.52 Stage II necrotizing enterocolitis in newborn
777.53 Stage III necrotizing enterocolitis in newborn
777.6 Perinatal intestinal perforation — (Use additional code(s) to further specify condition)
863.40 Colon injury unspecified site, without mention of open wound into cavity
863.41 Ascending (right) colon injury without mention of open wound into cavity
863.42 Transverse colon injury without mention of open wound into cavity
863.43 Descending (left) colon injury without mention of open wound into cavity
863.44 Sigmoid colon injury without mention of open wound into cavity
863.45 Rectum injury without mention of open wound into cavity
863.46 Injury to multiple sites in colon and rectum without mention of open wound into cavity
863.49 Other colon and rectum injury, without mention of open wound into cavity
998.89 Other specified complications
V64.41 Laparoscopic surgical procedure converted to open procedure

ICD-9-CM Procedural

45.71 Open and other multiple segmental resection of large intestine
45.73 Open and other right hemicolectomy
45.82 Open total intra-abdominal colectomy
45.83 Other and unspecified total intra-abdominal colectomy
46.20 Ileostomy, not otherwise specified
46.22 Continent ileostomy
48.50 Abdominoperineal resection of the rectum, not otherwise specified
48.52 Open abdominoperineal resection of the rectum
48.59 Other abdominoperineal resection of the rectum

44157-44158

44157 Colectomy, total, abdominal, with proctectomy; with ileoanal anastomosis, includes loop ileostomy, and rectal mucosectomy, when performed
44158 with ileoanal anastomosis, creation of ileal reservoir (S or J), includes loop ileostomy, and rectal mucosectomy, when performed

ICD-9-CM Diagnostic

153.0 Malignant neoplasm of hepatic flexure
153.1 Malignant neoplasm of transverse colon
153.2 Malignant neoplasm of descending colon
153.3 Malignant neoplasm of sigmoid colon
153.4 Malignant neoplasm of cecum
153.5 Malignant neoplasm of appendix
153.6 Malignant neoplasm of ascending colon
153.7 Malignant neoplasm of splenic flexure
153.8 Malignant neoplasm of other specified sites of large intestine
153.9 Malignant neoplasm of colon, unspecified site
154.0 Malignant neoplasm of rectosigmoid junction
154.1 Malignant neoplasm of rectum
197.5 Secondary malignant neoplasm of large intestine and rectum
209.10 Malignant carcinoid tumor of the large intestine, unspecified portion — (Code first any associated multiple endocrine neoplasia syndrome: 258.01-258.03)(Use additional code to identify associated endocrine syndrome, as: carcinoid syndrome: 259.2)
209.11 Malignant carcinoid tumor of the appendix — (Code first any associated multiple endocrine neoplasia syndrome: 258.01-258.03)(Use additional code to identify associated endocrine syndrome, as: carcinoid syndrome: 259.2)
209.12 Malignant carcinoid tumor of the cecum — (Code first any associated multiple endocrine neoplasia syndrome: 258.01-258.03)(Use additional code to identify associated endocrine syndrome, as: carcinoid syndrome: 259.2)
209.13 Malignant carcinoid tumor of the ascending colon — (Code first any associated multiple endocrine neoplasia syndrome: 258.01-258.03)(Use additional code to identify associated endocrine syndrome, as: carcinoid syndrome: 259.2)
209.14 Malignant carcinoid tumor of the transverse colon — (Code first any associated multiple endocrine neoplasia syndrome: 258.01-258.03)(Use additional code to identify associated endocrine syndrome, as: carcinoid syndrome: 259.2)
209.15 Malignant carcinoid tumor of the descending colon — (Code first any associated multiple endocrine neoplasia syndrome: 258.01-258.03)(Use additional code to identify associated endocrine syndrome, as: carcinoid syndrome: 259.2)
209.16 Malignant carcinoid tumor of the sigmoid colon — (Code first any associated multiple endocrine neoplasia syndrome: 258.01-258.03)(Use additional code to identify associated endocrine syndrome, as: carcinoid syndrome: 259.2)
209.29 Malignant carcinoid tumor of other sites — (Code first any associated multiple endocrine neoplasia syndrome: 258.01-258.03)(Use additional code to identify associated endocrine syndrome, as: carcinoid syndrome: 259.2)
209.30 Malignant poorly differentiated neuroendocrine carcinoma, any site — (Code first any associated multiple endocrine neoplasia syndrome: 258.01-258.03)(Use additional code to identify associated endocrine syndrome, as: carcinoid syndrome: 259.2)
209.50 Benign carcinoid tumor of the large intestine, unspecified portion — (Code first any associated multiple endocrine neoplasia syndrome: 258.01-258.03)(Use additional code to identify associated endocrine syndrome, as: carcinoid syndrome: 259.2)
209.51 Benign carcinoid tumor of the appendix — (Code first any associated multiple endocrine neoplasia syndrome: 258.01-258.03)(Use additional code to identify associated endocrine syndrome, as: carcinoid syndrome: 259.2)
209.52 Benign carcinoid tumor of the cecum — (Code first any associated multiple endocrine neoplasia syndrome: 258.01-258.03)(Use additional code to identify associated endocrine syndrome, as: carcinoid syndrome: 259.2)
209.53 Benign carcinoid tumor of the ascending colon — (Code first any associated multiple endocrine neoplasia syndrome: 258.01-258.03)(Use additional code to identify associated endocrine syndrome, as: carcinoid syndrome: 259.2)
209.54 Benign carcinoid tumor of the transverse colon — (Code first any associated multiple endocrine neoplasia syndrome: 258.01-258.03)(Use additional code to identify associated endocrine syndrome, as: carcinoid syndrome: 259.2)
209.55 Benign carcinoid tumor of the descending colon — (Code first any associated multiple endocrine neoplasia syndrome: 258.01-258.03)(Use additional code to identify associated endocrine syndrome, as: carcinoid syndrome: 259.2)
209.56 Benign carcinoid tumor of the sigmoid colon — (Code first any associated multiple endocrine neoplasia syndrome: 258.01-258.03)(Use additional code to identify associated endocrine syndrome, as: carcinoid syndrome: 259.2)
209.57 Benign carcinoid tumor of the rectum — (Code first any associated multiple endocrine neoplasia syndrome: 258.01-258.03)(Use additional code to identify associated endocrine syndrome, as: carcinoid syndrome: 259.2)
209.69 Benign carcinoid tumor of other sites — (Code first any associated multiple endocrine neoplasia syndrome: 258.01-258.03)(Use additional code to identify associated endocrine syndrome, as: carcinoid syndrome: 259.2)
211.3 Benign neoplasm of colon
211.4 Benign neoplasm of rectum and anal canal
230.3 Carcinoma in situ of colon
230.4 Carcinoma in situ of rectum
230.7 Carcinoma in situ of other and unspecified parts of intestine
235.2 Neoplasm of uncertain behavior of stomach, intestines, and rectum
239.0 Neoplasm of unspecified nature of digestive system
556.0 Ulcerative (chronic) enterocolitis
556.1 Ulcerative (chronic) ileocolitis
556.2 Ulcerative (chronic) proctitis
556.3 Ulcerative (chronic) proctosigmoiditis
556.4 Pseudopolyposis of colon
556.5 Left sided ulcerative (chronic) colitis
556.6 Universal ulcerative (chronic) colitis
556.8 Other ulcerative colitis
556.9 Unspecified ulcerative colitis
557.0 Acute vascular insufficiency of intestine

557.1 Chronic vascular insufficiency of intestine
557.9 Unspecified vascular insufficiency of intestine ▽
558.41 Eosinophilic gastroenteritis
558.42 Eosinophilic colitis
558.9 Other and unspecified noninfectious gastroenteritis and colitis ▽
560.9 Unspecified intestinal obstruction ▽
562.10 Diverticulosis of colon (without mention of hemorrhage) — (Use additional code to identify any associated peritonitis: 567.0-567.9)
562.11 Diverticulitis of colon (without mention of hemorrhage) — (Use additional code to identify any associated peritonitis: 567.0-567.9)
562.12 Diverticulosis of colon with hemorrhage — (Use additional code to identify any associated peritonitis: 567.0-567.9)
562.13 Diverticulitis of colon with hemorrhage — (Use additional code to identify any associated peritonitis: 567.0-567.9)
564.7 Megacolon, other than Hirschsprung's
564.81 Neurogenic bowel
564.89 Other functional disorders of intestine
567.0 Peritonitis in infectious diseases classified elsewhere — (Code first underlying disease) ☒
567.1 Pneumococcal peritonitis
567.21 Peritonitis (acute) generalized
567.22 Peritoneal abscess
567.23 Spontaneous bacterial peritonitis
567.29 Other suppurative peritonitis
567.31 Psoas muscle abscess
567.38 Other retroperitoneal abscess
567.39 Other retroperitoneal infections
567.81 Choleperitonitis
567.82 Sclerosing mesenteritis
567.89 Other specified peritonitis
567.9 Unspecified peritonitis ▽
569.82 Ulceration of intestine
569.83 Perforation of intestine
569.89 Other specified disorder of intestines
569.9 Unspecified disorder of intestine ▽
578.1 Blood in stool
578.9 Hemorrhage of gastrointestinal tract, unspecified ▽
751.3 Hirschsprung's disease and other congenital functional disorders of colon
777.1 Fetal and newborn meconium obstruction — (Use additional code(s) to further specify condition)
777.50 Necrotizing enterocolitis in newborn, unspecified ▽
777.51 Stage I necrotizing enterocolitis in newborn
777.52 Stage II necrotizing enterocolitis in newborn
777.53 Stage III necrotizing enterocolitis in newborn
777.6 Perinatal intestinal perforation — (Use additional code(s) to further specify condition)
777.8 Other specified perinatal disorder of digestive system — (Use additional code(s) to further specify condition)
863.40 Colon injury unspecified site, without mention of open wound into cavity ▽
863.41 Ascending (right) colon injury without mention of open wound into cavity
863.42 Transverse colon injury without mention of open wound into cavity
863.43 Descending (left) colon injury without mention of open wound into cavity
863.44 Sigmoid colon injury without mention of open wound into cavity
863.45 Rectum injury without mention of open wound into cavity
863.46 Injury to multiple sites in colon and rectum without mention of open wound into cavity
863.49 Other colon and rectum injury, without mention of open wound into cavity
998.89 Other specified complications
V64.41 Laparoscopic surgical procedure converted to open procedure

ICD-9-CM Procedural

45.82 Open total intra-abdominal colectomy
45.83 Other and unspecified total intra-abdominal colectomy
45.95 Anastomosis to anus
46.01 Exteriorization of small intestine

44160

44160 Colectomy, partial, with removal of terminal ileum with ileocolostomy

ICD-9-CM Diagnostic

152.2 Malignant neoplasm of ileum
152.3 Malignant neoplasm of Meckel's diverticulum
152.8 Malignant neoplasm of other specified sites of small intestine
152.9 Malignant neoplasm of small intestine, unspecified site ▽
153.0 Malignant neoplasm of hepatic flexure
153.1 Malignant neoplasm of transverse colon
153.2 Malignant neoplasm of descending colon
153.3 Malignant neoplasm of sigmoid colon
153.4 Malignant neoplasm of cecum
153.6 Malignant neoplasm of ascending colon
153.7 Malignant neoplasm of splenic flexure
153.8 Malignant neoplasm of other specified sites of large intestine
153.9 Malignant neoplasm of colon, unspecified site ▽
154.0 Malignant neoplasm of rectosigmoid junction
154.1 Malignant neoplasm of rectum
154.2 Malignant neoplasm of anal canal
154.3 Malignant neoplasm of anus, unspecified site ▽
154.8 Malignant neoplasm of other sites of rectum, rectosigmoid junction, and anus
197.4 Secondary malignant neoplasm of small intestine including duodenum
197.5 Secondary malignant neoplasm of large intestine and rectum
209.00 Malignant carcinoid tumor of the small intestine, unspecified portion — (Code first any associated multiple endocrine neoplasia syndrome: 258.01-258.03)(Use additional code to identify associated endocrine syndrome, as: carcinoid syndrome: 259.2) ▽
209.03 Malignant carcinoid tumor of the ileum — (Code first any associated multiple endocrine neoplasia syndrome: 258.01-258.03)(Use additional code to identify associated endocrine syndrome, as: carcinoid syndrome: 259.2)
209.10 Malignant carcinoid tumor of the large intestine, unspecified portion — (Code first any associated multiple endocrine neoplasia syndrome: 258.01-258.03)(Use additional code to identify associated endocrine syndrome, as: carcinoid syndrome: 259.2) ▽
209.11 Malignant carcinoid tumor of the appendix — (Code first any associated multiple endocrine neoplasia syndrome: 258.01-258.03)(Use additional code to identify associated endocrine syndrome, as: carcinoid syndrome: 259.2)
209.12 Malignant carcinoid tumor of the cecum — (Code first any associated multiple endocrine neoplasia syndrome: 258.01-258.03)(Use additional code to identify associated endocrine syndrome, as: carcinoid syndrome: 259.2)
209.13 Malignant carcinoid tumor of the ascending colon — (Code first any associated multiple endocrine neoplasia syndrome: 258.01-258.03)(Use additional code to identify associated endocrine syndrome, as: carcinoid syndrome: 259.2)
209.14 Malignant carcinoid tumor of the transverse colon — (Code first any associated multiple endocrine neoplasia syndrome: 258.01-258.03)(Use additional code to identify associated endocrine syndrome, as: carcinoid syndrome: 259.2)
209.15 Malignant carcinoid tumor of the descending colon — (Code first any associated multiple endocrine neoplasia syndrome: 258.01-258.03)(Use additional code to identify associated endocrine syndrome, as: carcinoid syndrome: 259.2)
209.16 Malignant carcinoid tumor of the sigmoid colon — (Code first any associated multiple endocrine neoplasia syndrome: 258.01-258.03)(Use additional code to identify associated endocrine syndrome, as: carcinoid syndrome: 259.2)
209.29 Malignant carcinoid tumor of other sites — (Code first any associated multiple endocrine neoplasia syndrome: 258.01-258.03)(Use additional code to identify associated endocrine syndrome, as: carcinoid syndrome: 259.2)

209.30 Malignant poorly differentiated neuroendocrine carcinoma, any site — (Code first any associated multiple endocrine neoplasia syndrome: 258.01-258.03)(Use additional code to identify associated endocrine syndrome, as: carcinoid syndrome: 259.2) ▽
209.50 Benign carcinoid tumor of the large intestine, unspecified portion — (Code first any associated multiple endocrine neoplasia syndrome: 258.01-258.03)(Use additional code to identify associated endocrine syndrome, as: carcinoid syndrome: 259.2) ▽
209.51 Benign carcinoid tumor of the appendix — (Code first any associated multiple endocrine neoplasia syndrome: 258.01-258.03)(Use additional code to identify associated endocrine syndrome, as: carcinoid syndrome: 259.2)
209.52 Benign carcinoid tumor of the cecum — (Code first any associated multiple endocrine neoplasia syndrome: 258.01-258.03)(Use additional code to identify associated endocrine syndrome, as: carcinoid syndrome: 259.2)
209.53 Benign carcinoid tumor of the ascending colon — (Code first any associated multiple endocrine neoplasia syndrome: 258.01-258.03)(Use additional code to identify associated endocrine syndrome, as: carcinoid syndrome: 259.2)
209.54 Benign carcinoid tumor of the transverse colon — (Code first any associated multiple endocrine neoplasia syndrome: 258.01-258.03)(Use additional code to identify associated endocrine syndrome, as: carcinoid syndrome: 259.2)
209.55 Benign carcinoid tumor of the descending colon — (Code first any associated multiple endocrine neoplasia syndrome: 258.01-258.03)(Use additional code to identify associated endocrine syndrome, as: carcinoid syndrome: 259.2)
209.56 Benign carcinoid tumor of the sigmoid colon — (Code first any associated multiple endocrine neoplasia syndrome: 258.01-258.03)(Use additional code to identify associated endocrine syndrome, as: carcinoid syndrome: 259.2)
209.57 Benign carcinoid tumor of the rectum — (Code first any associated multiple endocrine neoplasia syndrome: 258.01-258.03)(Use additional code to identify associated endocrine syndrome, as: carcinoid syndrome: 259.2)
209.69 Benign carcinoid tumor of other sites — (Code first any associated multiple endocrine neoplasia syndrome: 258.01-258.03)(Use additional code to identify associated endocrine syndrome, as: carcinoid syndrome: 259.2)
211.2 Benign neoplasm of duodenum, jejunum, and ileum
211.3 Benign neoplasm of colon
211.4 Benign neoplasm of rectum and anal canal
211.9 Benign neoplasm of other and unspecified site of the digestive system ▽
229.9 Benign neoplasm of unspecified site ▽
230.3 Carcinoma in situ of colon
235.2 Neoplasm of uncertain behavior of stomach, intestines, and rectum
239.0 Neoplasm of unspecified nature of digestive system
550.00 Inguinal hernia with gangrene, unilateral or unspecified, (not specified as recurrent)
551.1 Umbilical hernia with gangrene
552.8 Hernia of other specified site, with obstruction
555.1 Regional enteritis of large intestine
555.2 Regional enteritis of small intestine with large intestine
556.0 Ulcerative (chronic) enterocolitis
556.1 Ulcerative (chronic) ileocolitis
556.2 Ulcerative (chronic) proctitis
556.3 Ulcerative (chronic) proctosigmoiditis
556.8 Other ulcerative colitis
557.0 Acute vascular insufficiency of intestine
557.1 Chronic vascular insufficiency of intestine
557.9 Unspecified vascular insufficiency of intestine ▽
558.1 Gastroenteritis and colitis due to radiation
558.2 Toxic gastroenteritis and colitis — (Use additional E code to identify cause)
558.41 Eosinophilic gastroenteritis
558.42 Eosinophilic colitis
558.9 Other and unspecified noninfectious gastroenteritis and colitis ▽
560.0 Intussusception
560.1 Paralytic ileus
560.2 Volvulus
560.31 Gallstone ileus
560.39 Impaction of intestine, other
560.81 Intestinal or peritoneal adhesions with obstruction (postoperative) (postinfection)
560.89 Other specified intestinal obstruction
560.9 Unspecified intestinal obstruction ▽
562.10 Diverticulosis of colon (without mention of hemorrhage) — (Use additional code to identify any associated peritonitis: 567.0-567.9)
562.11 Diverticulitis of colon (without mention of hemorrhage) — (Use additional code to identify any associated peritonitis: 567.0-567.9)
562.12 Diverticulosis of colon with hemorrhage — (Use additional code to identify any associated peritonitis: 567.0-567.9)
562.13 Diverticulitis of colon with hemorrhage — (Use additional code to identify any associated peritonitis: 567.0-567.9)
564.7 Megacolon, other than Hirschsprung's
567.0 Peritonitis in infectious diseases classified elsewhere — (Code first underlying disease) ☒
567.1 Pneumococcal peritonitis
567.21 Peritonitis (acute) generalized
567.22 Peritoneal abscess
567.23 Spontaneous bacterial peritonitis
567.29 Other suppurative peritonitis
567.31 Psoas muscle abscess
567.38 Other retroperitoneal abscess
567.39 Other retroperitoneal infections
567.81 Choleperitonitis
567.82 Sclerosing mesenteritis
567.89 Other specified peritonitis
567.9 Unspecified peritonitis ▽
569.44 Dysplasia of anus
569.81 Fistula of intestine, excluding rectum and anus
569.82 Ulceration of intestine
569.83 Perforation of intestine
569.84 Angiodysplasia of intestine (without mention of hemorrhage)
569.85 Angiodysplasia of intestine with hemorrhage
569.89 Other specified disorder of intestines
569.9 Unspecified disorder of intestine ▽
578.9 Hemorrhage of gastrointestinal tract, unspecified ▽
596.1 Intestinovesical fistula — (Use additional code to identify urinary incontinence: 625.6, 788.30-788.39)
619.1 Digestive-genital tract fistula, female ♀
751.5 Other congenital anomalies of intestine
751.8 Other specified congenital anomalies of digestive system
751.9 Unspecified congenital anomaly of digestive system ▽

ICD-9-CM Procedural

45.72 Open and other cecectomy
45.73 Open and other right hemicolectomy
45.74 Open and other resection of transverse colon
45.75 Open and other left hemicolectomy
45.93 Other small-to-large intestinal anastomosis

44180

44180 Laparoscopy, surgical, enterolysis (freeing of intestinal adhesion) (separate procedure)

ICD-9-CM Diagnostic

338.18 Other acute postoperative pain — (Use additional code to identify pain associated with psychological factors: 307.89)
338.28 Other chronic postoperative pain — (Use additional code to identify pain associated with psychological factors: 307.89)
537.3 Other obstruction of duodenum
537.4 Fistula of stomach or duodenum
560.81 Intestinal or peritoneal adhesions with obstruction (postoperative) (postinfection)

560.9 Unspecified intestinal obstruction ▽
568.0 Peritoneal adhesions (postoperative) (postinfection)
614.6 Pelvic peritoneal adhesions, female (postoperative) (postinfection) — (Use additional code to identify organism: 041.00-041.09, 041.10-041.19) (Use additional code to identify any associated infertility: 628.2) ♀
617.5 Endometriosis of intestine ♀
751.4 Congenital anomalies of intestinal fixation
789.00 Abdominal pain, unspecified site ▽
789.01 Abdominal pain, right upper quadrant
789.02 Abdominal pain, left upper quadrant
789.03 Abdominal pain, right lower quadrant
789.04 Abdominal pain, left lower quadrant
789.05 Abdominal pain, periumbilic
789.06 Abdominal pain, epigastric
789.07 Abdominal pain, generalized
789.09 Abdominal pain, other specified site
789.30 Abdominal or pelvic swelling, mass or lump, unspecified site ▽
789.31 Abdominal or pelvic swelling, mass, or lump, right upper quadrant
789.32 Abdominal or pelvic swelling, mass, or lump, left upper quadrant
789.33 Abdominal or pelvic swelling, mass, or lump, right lower quadrant
789.34 Abdominal or pelvic swelling, mass, or lump, left lower quadrant
789.35 Abdominal or pelvic swelling, mass or lump, periumbilic
789.36 Abdominal or pelvic swelling, mass, or lump, epigastric
789.37 Abdominal or pelvic swelling, mass, or lump, generalized
789.39 Abdominal or pelvic swelling, mass, or lump, other specified site
908.1 Late effect of internal injury to intra-abdominal organs
908.2 Late effect of internal injury to other internal organs
908.6 Late effect of certain complications of trauma
909.3 Late effect of complications of surgical and medical care
997.49 Other digestive system complications
V45.72 Acquired absence of intestine (large) (small)
V64.41 Laparoscopic surgical procedure converted to open procedure

ICD-9-CM Procedural

54.51 Laparoscopic lysis of peritoneal adhesions

44186-44187

44186 Laparoscopy, surgical; jejunostomy (eg, for decompression or feeding)
44187 ileostomy or jejunostomy, non-tube

ICD-9-CM Diagnostic

150.0 Malignant neoplasm of cervical esophagus
150.1 Malignant neoplasm of thoracic esophagus
150.2 Malignant neoplasm of abdominal esophagus
150.3 Malignant neoplasm of upper third of esophagus
150.4 Malignant neoplasm of middle third of esophagus
150.5 Malignant neoplasm of lower third of esophagus
150.8 Malignant neoplasm of other specified part of esophagus
150.9 Malignant neoplasm of esophagus, unspecified site ▽
151.0 Malignant neoplasm of cardia
151.1 Malignant neoplasm of pylorus
151.2 Malignant neoplasm of pyloric antrum
151.3 Malignant neoplasm of fundus of stomach
151.4 Malignant neoplasm of body of stomach
151.5 Malignant neoplasm of lesser curvature of stomach, unspecified ▽
151.6 Malignant neoplasm of greater curvature of stomach, unspecified ▽
151.8 Malignant neoplasm of other specified sites of stomach
151.9 Malignant neoplasm of stomach, unspecified site ▽
152.0 Malignant neoplasm of duodenum
152.1 Malignant neoplasm of jejunum
152.2 Malignant neoplasm of ileum
161.9 Malignant neoplasm of larynx, unspecified site ▽
197.4 Secondary malignant neoplasm of small intestine including duodenum
197.8 Secondary malignant neoplasm of other digestive organs and spleen
198.89 Secondary malignant neoplasm of other specified sites
209.01 Malignant carcinoid tumor of the duodenum — (Code first any associated multiple endocrine neoplasia syndrome: 258.01-258.03)(Use additional code to identify associated endocrine syndrome, as: carcinoid syndrome: 259.2)
209.02 Malignant carcinoid tumor of the jejunum — (Code first any associated multiple endocrine neoplasia syndrome: 258.01-258.03)(Use additional code to identify associated endocrine syndrome, as: carcinoid syndrome: 259.2)
209.03 Malignant carcinoid tumor of the ileum — (Code first any associated multiple endocrine neoplasia syndrome: 258.01-258.03)(Use additional code to identify associated endocrine syndrome, as: carcinoid syndrome: 259.2)
209.23 Malignant carcinoid tumor of the stomach — (Code first any associated multiple endocrine neoplasia syndrome: 258.01-258.03)(Use additional code to identify associated endocrine syndrome, as: carcinoid syndrome: 259.2)
209.25 Malignant carcinoid tumor of foregut, not otherwise specified — (Code first any associated multiple endocrine neoplasia syndrome: 258.01-258.03)(Use additional code to identify associated endocrine syndrome, as: carcinoid syndrome: 259.2)
209.29 Malignant carcinoid tumor of other sites — (Code first any associated multiple endocrine neoplasia syndrome: 258.01-258.03)(Use additional code to identify associated endocrine syndrome, as: carcinoid syndrome: 259.2)
209.30 Malignant poorly differentiated neuroendocrine carcinoma, any site — (Code first any associated multiple endocrine neoplasia syndrome: 258.01-258.03)(Use additional code to identify associated endocrine syndrome, as: carcinoid syndrome: 259.2) ▽
209.65 Benign carcinoid tumor of foregut, not otherwise specified — (Code first any associated multiple endocrine neoplasia syndrome: 258.01-258.03)(Use additional code to identify associated endocrine syndrome, as: carcinoid syndrome: 259.2)
209.69 Benign carcinoid tumor of other sites — (Code first any associated multiple endocrine neoplasia syndrome: 258.01-258.03)(Use additional code to identify associated endocrine syndrome, as: carcinoid syndrome: 259.2)
211.1 Benign neoplasm of stomach
211.2 Benign neoplasm of duodenum, jejunum, and ileum
211.3 Benign neoplasm of colon
230.2 Carcinoma in situ of stomach
230.3 Carcinoma in situ of colon
230.7 Carcinoma in situ of other and unspecified parts of intestine ▽
235.2 Neoplasm of uncertain behavior of stomach, intestines, and rectum
239.0 Neoplasm of unspecified nature of digestive system
261 Nutritional marasmus
262 Other severe protein-calorie malnutrition
263.0 Malnutrition of moderate degree
263.1 Malnutrition of mild degree
263.2 Arrested development following protein-calorie malnutrition
263.8 Other protein-calorie malnutrition
276.50 Volume depletion, unspecified — (Use additional code to identify any associated intellectual disabilities) ▽
276.51 Dehydration — (Use additional code to identify any associated intellectual disabilities)
276.52 Hypovolemia — (Use additional code to identify any associated intellectual disabilities)
307.1 Anorexia nervosa
436 Acute, but ill-defined, cerebrovascular disease — (Use additional code to identify presence of hypertension) ▽
438.82 Dysphagia due to cerebrovascular disease — (Use additional code to identify presence of hypertension)
530.3 Stricture and stenosis of esophagus
530.4 Perforation of esophagus
530.5 Dyskinesia of esophagus
531.00 Acute gastric ulcer with hemorrhage, without mention of obstruction — (Use additional E code to identify drug, if drug induced)

531.01 Acute gastric ulcer with hemorrhage and obstruction — (Use additional E code to identify drug, if drug induced)

531.10 Acute gastric ulcer with perforation, without mention of obstruction — (Use additional E code to identify drug, if drug induced)

531.11 Acute gastric ulcer with perforation and obstruction — (Use additional E code to identify drug, if drug induced)

531.20 Acute gastric ulcer with hemorrhage and perforation, without mention of obstruction — (Use additional E code to identify drug, if drug induced)

531.21 Acute gastric ulcer with hemorrhage, perforation, and obstruction — (Use additional E code to identify drug, if drug induced)

531.30 Acute gastric ulcer without mention of hemorrhage, perforation, or obstruction — (Use additional E code to identify drug, if drug induced)

531.31 Acute gastric ulcer without mention of hemorrhage or perforation, with obstruction — (Use additional E code to identify drug, if drug induced)

531.40 Chronic or unspecified gastric ulcer with hemorrhage, without mention of obstruction — (Use additional E code to identify drug, if drug induced)

531.41 Chronic or unspecified gastric ulcer with hemorrhage and obstruction — (Use additional E code to identify drug, if drug induced)

531.50 Chronic or unspecified gastric ulcer with perforation, without mention of obstruction — (Use additional E code to identify drug, if drug induced)

531.51 Chronic or unspecified gastric ulcer with perforation and obstruction — (Use additional E code to identify drug, if drug induced)

531.60 Chronic or unspecified gastric ulcer with hemorrhage and perforation, without mention of obstruction — (Use additional E code to identify drug, if drug induced)

531.61 Chronic or unspecified gastric ulcer with hemorrhage, perforation, and obstruction — (Use additional E code to identify drug, if drug induced)

531.70 Chronic gastric ulcer without mention of hemorrhage, perforation, without mention of obstruction — (Use additional E code to identify drug, if drug induced)

531.71 Chronic gastric ulcer without mention of hemorrhage or perforation, with obstruction — (Use additional E code to identify drug, if drug induced)

531.90 Gastric ulcer, unspecified as acute or chronic, without mention of hemorrhage, perforation, or obstruction — (Use additional E code to identify drug, if drug induced) ▽

531.91 Gastric ulcer, unspecified as acute or chronic, without mention of hemorrhage or perforation, with obstruction — (Use additional E code to identify drug, if drug induced) ▽

532.00 Acute duodenal ulcer with hemorrhage, without mention of obstruction — (Use additional E code to identify drug, if drug induced)

532.01 Acute duodenal ulcer with hemorrhage and obstruction — (Use additional E code to identify drug, if drug induced)

532.10 Acute duodenal ulcer with perforation, without mention of obstruction — (Use additional E code to identify drug, if drug induced)

532.11 Acute duodenal ulcer with perforation and obstruction — (Use additional E code to identify drug, if drug induced)

532.20 Acute duodenal ulcer with hemorrhage and perforation, without mention of obstruction — (Use additional E code to identify drug, if drug induced)

532.21 Acute duodenal ulcer with hemorrhage, perforation, and obstruction — (Use additional E code to identify drug, if drug induced)

532.30 Acute duodenal ulcer without mention of hemorrhage, perforation, or obstruction — (Use additional E code to identify drug, if drug induced)

532.31 Acute duodenal ulcer without mention of hemorrhage or perforation, with obstruction — (Use additional E code to identify drug, if drug induced)

532.40 Duodenal ulcer, chronic or unspecified, with hemorrhage, without mention of obstruction — (Use additional E code to identify drug, if drug induced)

532.41 Chronic or unspecified duodenal ulcer with hemorrhage and obstruction — (Use additional E code to identify drug, if drug induced)

532.50 Chronic or unspecified duodenal ulcer with perforation, without mention of obstruction — (Use additional E code to identify drug, if drug induced)

532.51 Chronic or unspecified duodenal ulcer with perforation and obstruction — (Use additional E code to identify drug, if drug induced)

532.60 Chronic or unspecified duodenal ulcer with hemorrhage and perforation, without mention of obstruction — (Use additional E code to identify drug, if drug induced)

532.61 Chronic or unspecified duodenal ulcer with hemorrhage, perforation, and obstruction — (Use additional E code to identify drug, if drug induced)

532.70 Chronic duodenal ulcer without mention of hemorrhage, perforation, or obstruction — (Use additional E code to identify drug, if drug induced)

532.71 Chronic duodenal ulcer without mention of hemorrhage or perforation, with obstruction — (Use additional E code to identify drug, if drug induced)

532.90 Duodenal ulcer, unspecified as acute or chronic, without hemorrhage, perforation, or obstruction — (Use additional E code to identify drug, if drug induced) ▽

532.91 Duodenal ulcer, unspecified as acute or chronic, without mention of hemorrhage or perforation, with obstruction — (Use additional E code to identify drug, if drug induced) ▽

533.00 Acute peptic ulcer, unspecified site, with hemorrhage, without mention of obstruction — (Use additional E code to identify drug, if drug induced) ▽

533.01 Acute peptic ulcer, unspecified site, with hemorrhage and obstruction — (Use additional E code to identify drug, if drug induced) ▽

533.10 Acute peptic ulcer, unspecified site, with perforation, without mention of obstruction — (Use additional E code to identify drug, if drug induced) ▽

533.11 Acute peptic ulcer, unspecified site, with perforation and obstruction — (Use additional E code to identify drug, if drug induced) ▽

533.20 Acute peptic ulcer, unspecified site, with hemorrhage and perforation, without mention of obstruction — (Use additional E code to identify drug, if drug induced) ▽

533.21 Acute peptic ulcer, unspecified site, with hemorrhage, perforation, and obstruction — (Use additional E code to identify drug, if drug induced) ▽

533.30 Acute peptic ulcer, unspecified site, without mention of hemorrhage, perforation, or obstruction — (Use additional E code to identify drug, if drug induced) ▽

533.40 Chronic or unspecified peptic ulcer, unspecified site, with hemorrhage, without mention of obstruction — (Use additional E code to identify drug, if drug induced) ▽

533.41 Chronic or unspecified peptic ulcer, unspecified site, with hemorrhage and obstruction — (Use additional E code to identify drug, if drug induced) ▽

533.50 Chronic or unspecified peptic ulcer, unspecified site, with perforation, without mention of obstruction — (Use additional E code to identify drug, if drug induced) ▽

533.51 Chronic or unspecified peptic ulcer, unspecified site, with perforation and obstruction — (Use additional E code to identify drug, if drug induced) ▽

534.00 Acute gastrojejunal ulcer with hemorrhage, without mention of obstruction

534.01 Acute gastrojejunal ulcer, with hemorrhage and obstruction

534.10 Acute gastrojejunal ulcer with perforation, without mention of obstruction

534.11 Acute gastrojejunal ulcer with perforation and obstruction

534.20 Acute gastrojejunal ulcer with hemorrhage and perforation, without mention of obstruction

534.21 Acute gastrojejunal ulcer with hemorrhage, perforation, and obstruction

534.30 Acute gastrojejunal ulcer without mention of hemorrhage, perforation, or obstruction

534.31 Acute gastrojejunal ulcer without mention of hemorrhage or perforation, with obstruction

534.40 Chronic or unspecified gastrojejunal ulcer with hemorrhage, without mention of obstruction

534.41 Chronic or unspecified gastrojejunal ulcer, with hemorrhage and obstruction

534.50 Chronic or unspecified gastrojejunal ulcer with perforation, without mention of obstruction

534.51 Chronic or unspecified gastrojejunal ulcer with perforation and obstruction

534.60 Chronic or unspecified gastrojejunal ulcer with hemorrhage and perforation, without mention of obstruction

534.61 Chronic or unspecified gastrojejunal ulcer with hemorrhage, perforation, and obstruction

534.70 Chronic gastrojejunal ulcer without mention of hemorrhage, perforation, or obstruction

534.71 Chronic gastrojejunal ulcer without mention of hemorrhage or perforation, with obstruction

534.90 Gastrojejunal ulcer, unspecified as acute or chronic, without mention of hemorrhage, perforation, or obstruction ▽

534.91 Gastrojejunal ulcer, unspecified as acute or chronic, without mention of hemorrhage or perforation, with obstruction ▽

535.50 Unspecified gastritis and gastroduodenitis without mention of hemorrhage ▽

535.70 Eosinophilic gastritis without mention of hemorrhage
535.71 Eosinophilic gastritis with hemorrhage
536.40 Unspecified gastrostomy complication ▽
536.41 Infection of gastrostomy — (Use additional code to specify type of infection: 038.0-038.9, 682.2. Use additional code to identify organism: 041.00-041.9)
536.42 Mechanical complication of gastrostomy
536.49 Other gastrostomy complications
536.9 Unspecified functional disorder of stomach ▽
537.89 Other specified disorder of stomach and duodenum
555.0 Regional enteritis of small intestine
555.2 Regional enteritis of small intestine with large intestine
556.0 Ulcerative (chronic) enterocolitis
556.1 Ulcerative (chronic) ileocolitis
557.0 Acute vascular insufficiency of intestine
557.1 Chronic vascular insufficiency of intestine
557.9 Unspecified vascular insufficiency of intestine ▽
560.2 Volvulus
564.81 Neurogenic bowel
564.89 Other functional disorders of intestine
569.82 Ulceration of intestine
569.83 Perforation of intestine
750.7 Other specified congenital anomalies of stomach
751.1 Congenital atresia and stenosis of small intestine
783.0 Anorexia
783.3 Feeding difficulties and mismanagement
783.7 Adult failure to thrive
787.01 Nausea with vomiting
787.04 Bilious emesis
787.20 Dysphagia, unspecified ▽
787.21 Dysphagia, oral phase
787.22 Dysphagia, oropharyngeal phase
787.23 Dysphagia, pharyngeal phase
787.24 Dysphagia, pharyngoesophageal phase
787.29 Other dysphagia
854.06 Intracranial injury of other and unspecified nature, without mention of open intracranial wound, loss of consciousness of unspecified duration ▽
863.20 Small intestine injury, unspecified site, without mention of open wound into cavity ▽
863.21 Duodenum injury without mention of open wound into cavity
863.29 Other injury to small intestine without mention of open wound into cavity
863.30 Small intestine injury, unspecified site, with open wound into cavity ▽
863.31 Duodenum injury with open wound into cavity
863.39 Other injury to small intestine with open wound into cavity
994.2 Effects of hunger
997.49 Other digestive system complications
998.89 Other specified complications

ICD-9-CM Procedural

46.20 Ileostomy, not otherwise specified
46.21 Temporary ileostomy
46.22 Continent ileostomy
46.23 Other permanent ileostomy
46.32 Percutaneous (endoscopic) jejunostomy (PEJ)
46.39 Other enterostomy
46.41 Revision of stoma of small intestine

44188

44188 Laparoscopy, surgical, colostomy or skin level cecostomy

ICD-9-CM Diagnostic

151.9 Malignant neoplasm of stomach, unspecified site ▽
152.0 Malignant neoplasm of duodenum
152.1 Malignant neoplasm of jejunum
152.2 Malignant neoplasm of ileum
152.3 Malignant neoplasm of Meckel's diverticulum
152.8 Malignant neoplasm of other specified sites of small intestine
152.9 Malignant neoplasm of small intestine, unspecified site ▽
153.0 Malignant neoplasm of hepatic flexure
153.1 Malignant neoplasm of transverse colon
153.2 Malignant neoplasm of descending colon
153.3 Malignant neoplasm of sigmoid colon
153.4 Malignant neoplasm of cecum
153.9 Malignant neoplasm of colon, unspecified site ▽
154.0 Malignant neoplasm of rectosigmoid junction
154.1 Malignant neoplasm of rectum
154.2 Malignant neoplasm of anal canal
197.4 Secondary malignant neoplasm of small intestine including duodenum
197.5 Secondary malignant neoplasm of large intestine and rectum
199.1 Other malignant neoplasm of unspecified site
209.00 Malignant carcinoid tumor of the small intestine, unspecified portion — (Code first any associated multiple endocrine neoplasia syndrome: 258.01-258.03)(Use additional code to identify associated endocrine syndrome, as: carcinoid syndrome: 259.2) ▽
209.01 Malignant carcinoid tumor of the duodenum — (Code first any associated multiple endocrine neoplasia syndrome: 258.01-258.03)(Use additional code to identify associated endocrine syndrome, as: carcinoid syndrome: 259.2)
209.02 Malignant carcinoid tumor of the jejunum — (Code first any associated multiple endocrine neoplasia syndrome: 258.01-258.03)(Use additional code to identify associated endocrine syndrome, as: carcinoid syndrome: 259.2)
209.03 Malignant carcinoid tumor of the ileum — (Code first any associated multiple endocrine neoplasia syndrome: 258.01-258.03)(Use additional code to identify associated endocrine syndrome, as: carcinoid syndrome: 259.2)
209.10 Malignant carcinoid tumor of the large intestine, unspecified portion — (Code first any associated multiple endocrine neoplasia syndrome: 258.01-258.03)(Use additional code to identify associated endocrine syndrome, as: carcinoid syndrome: 259.2) ▽
209.11 Malignant carcinoid tumor of the appendix — (Code first any associated multiple endocrine neoplasia syndrome: 258.01-258.03)(Use additional code to identify associated endocrine syndrome, as: carcinoid syndrome: 259.2)
209.12 Malignant carcinoid tumor of the cecum — (Code first any associated multiple endocrine neoplasia syndrome: 258.01-258.03)(Use additional code to identify associated endocrine syndrome, as: carcinoid syndrome: 259.2)
209.13 Malignant carcinoid tumor of the ascending colon — (Code first any associated multiple endocrine neoplasia syndrome: 258.01-258.03)(Use additional code to identify associated endocrine syndrome, as: carcinoid syndrome: 259.2)
209.14 Malignant carcinoid tumor of the transverse colon — (Code first any associated multiple endocrine neoplasia syndrome: 258.01-258.03)(Use additional code to identify associated endocrine syndrome, as: carcinoid syndrome: 259.2)
209.15 Malignant carcinoid tumor of the descending colon — (Code first any associated multiple endocrine neoplasia syndrome: 258.01-258.03)(Use additional code to identify associated endocrine syndrome, as: carcinoid syndrome: 259.2)
209.16 Malignant carcinoid tumor of the sigmoid colon — (Code first any associated multiple endocrine neoplasia syndrome: 258.01-258.03)(Use additional code to identify associated endocrine syndrome, as: carcinoid syndrome: 259.2)
209.17 Malignant carcinoid tumor of the rectum — (Code first any associated multiple endocrine neoplasia syndrome: 258.01-258.03)(Use additional code to identify associated endocrine syndrome, as: carcinoid syndrome: 259.2)
209.20 Malignant carcinoid tumor of unknown primary site — (Code first any associated multiple endocrine neoplasia syndrome: 258.01-258.03)(Use additional code to identify associated endocrine syndrome, as: carcinoid syndrome: 259.2)
209.23 Malignant carcinoid tumor of the stomach — (Code first any associated multiple endocrine neoplasia syndrome: 258.01-258.03)(Use additional code to identify associated endocrine syndrome, as: carcinoid syndrome: 259.2)

209.25 Malignant carcinoid tumor of foregut, not otherwise specified — (Code first any associated multiple endocrine neoplasia syndrome: 258.01-258.03)(Use additional code to identify associated endocrine syndrome, as: carcinoid syndrome: 259.2)

209.26 Malignant carcinoid tumor of midgut, not otherwise specified — (Code first any associated multiple endocrine neoplasia syndrome: 258.01-258.03)(Use additional code to identify associated endocrine syndrome, as: carcinoid syndrome: 259.2)

209.27 Malignant carcinoid tumor of hindgut, not otherwise specified — (Code first any associated multiple endocrine neoplasia syndrome: 258.01-258.03)(Use additional code to identify associated endocrine syndrome, as: carcinoid syndrome: 259.2)

209.29 Malignant carcinoid tumor of other sites — (Code first any associated multiple endocrine neoplasia syndrome: 258.01-258.03)(Use additional code to identify associated endocrine syndrome, as: carcinoid syndrome: 259.2)

209.30 Malignant poorly differentiated neuroendocrine carcinoma, any site — (Code first any associated multiple endocrine neoplasia syndrome: 258.01-258.03)(Use additional code to identify associated endocrine syndrome, as: carcinoid syndrome: 259.2) ▽

209.40 Benign carcinoid tumor of the small intestine, unspecified portion — (Code first any associated multiple endocrine neoplasia syndrome: 258.01-258.03)(Use additional code to identify associated endocrine syndrome, as: carcinoid syndrome: 259.2) ▽

209.41 Benign carcinoid tumor of the duodenum — (Code first any associated multiple endocrine neoplasia syndrome: 258.01-258.03)(Use additional code to identify associated endocrine syndrome, as: carcinoid syndrome: 259.2)

209.42 Benign carcinoid tumor of the jejunum — (Code first any associated multiple endocrine neoplasia syndrome: 258.01-258.03)(Use additional code to identify associated endocrine syndrome, as: carcinoid syndrome: 259.2)

209.43 Benign carcinoid tumor of the ileum — (Code first any associated multiple endocrine neoplasia syndrome: 258.01-258.03)(Use additional code to identify associated endocrine syndrome, as: carcinoid syndrome: 259.2)

209.50 Benign carcinoid tumor of the large intestine, unspecified portion — (Code first any associated multiple endocrine neoplasia syndrome: 258.01-258.03)(Use additional code to identify associated endocrine syndrome, as: carcinoid syndrome: 259.2) ▽

209.51 Benign carcinoid tumor of the appendix — (Code first any associated multiple endocrine neoplasia syndrome: 258.01-258.03)(Use additional code to identify associated endocrine syndrome, as: carcinoid syndrome: 259.2)

209.52 Benign carcinoid tumor of the cecum — (Code first any associated multiple endocrine neoplasia syndrome: 258.01-258.03)(Use additional code to identify associated endocrine syndrome, as: carcinoid syndrome: 259.2)

209.53 Benign carcinoid tumor of the ascending colon — (Code first any associated multiple endocrine neoplasia syndrome: 258.01-258.03)(Use additional code to identify associated endocrine syndrome, as: carcinoid syndrome: 259.2)

209.54 Benign carcinoid tumor of the transverse colon — (Code first any associated multiple endocrine neoplasia syndrome: 258.01-258.03)(Use additional code to identify associated endocrine syndrome, as: carcinoid syndrome: 259.2)

209.55 Benign carcinoid tumor of the descending colon — (Code first any associated multiple endocrine neoplasia syndrome: 258.01-258.03)(Use additional code to identify associated endocrine syndrome, as: carcinoid syndrome: 259.2)

209.56 Benign carcinoid tumor of the sigmoid colon — (Code first any associated multiple endocrine neoplasia syndrome: 258.01-258.03)(Use additional code to identify associated endocrine syndrome, as: carcinoid syndrome: 259.2)

209.57 Benign carcinoid tumor of the rectum — (Code first any associated multiple endocrine neoplasia syndrome: 258.01-258.03)(Use additional code to identify associated endocrine syndrome, as: carcinoid syndrome: 259.2)

209.65 Benign carcinoid tumor of foregut, not otherwise specified — (Code first any associated multiple endocrine neoplasia syndrome: 258.01-258.03)(Use additional code to identify associated endocrine syndrome, as: carcinoid syndrome: 259.2)

209.69 Benign carcinoid tumor of other sites — (Code first any associated multiple endocrine neoplasia syndrome: 258.01-258.03)(Use additional code to identify associated endocrine syndrome, as: carcinoid syndrome: 259.2)

211.3 Benign neoplasm of colon

230.3 Carcinoma in situ of colon

230.4 Carcinoma in situ of rectum

230.9 Carcinoma in situ of other and unspecified digestive organs ▽

235.2 Neoplasm of uncertain behavior of stomach, intestines, and rectum

239.0 Neoplasm of unspecified nature of digestive system

532.10 Acute duodenal ulcer with perforation, without mention of obstruction — (Use additional E code to identify drug, if drug induced)

555.0 Regional enteritis of small intestine

555.1 Regional enteritis of large intestine

555.2 Regional enteritis of small intestine with large intestine

555.9 Regional enteritis of unspecified site ▽

556.0 Ulcerative (chronic) enterocolitis

556.1 Ulcerative (chronic) ileocolitis

556.2 Ulcerative (chronic) proctitis

556.3 Ulcerative (chronic) proctosigmoiditis

556.4 Pseudopolyposis of colon

556.5 Left sided ulcerative (chronic) colitis

556.6 Universal ulcerative (chronic) colitis

556.8 Other ulcerative colitis

556.9 Unspecified ulcerative colitis ▽

557.0 Acute vascular insufficiency of intestine

558.1 Gastroenteritis and colitis due to radiation

558.2 Toxic gastroenteritis and colitis — (Use additional E code to identify cause)

558.3 Gastroenteritis and colitis, allergic — (Use additional code to identify type of food allergy: V15.01-V15.05)

558.41 Eosinophilic gastroenteritis

558.42 Eosinophilic colitis

558.9 Other and unspecified noninfectious gastroenteritis and colitis ▽

560.1 Paralytic ileus

560.2 Volvulus

560.31 Gallstone ileus

560.39 Impaction of intestine, other

560.81 Intestinal or peritoneal adhesions with obstruction (postoperative) (postinfection)

560.89 Other specified intestinal obstruction

560.9 Unspecified intestinal obstruction ▽

562.10 Diverticulosis of colon (without mention of hemorrhage) — (Use additional code to identify any associated peritonitis: 567.0-567.9)

562.11 Diverticulitis of colon (without mention of hemorrhage) — (Use additional code to identify any associated peritonitis: 567.0-567.9)

562.12 Diverticulosis of colon with hemorrhage — (Use additional code to identify any associated peritonitis: 567.0-567.9)

562.13 Diverticulitis of colon with hemorrhage — (Use additional code to identify any associated peritonitis: 567.0-567.9)

564.7 Megacolon, other than Hirschsprung's

564.81 Neurogenic bowel

564.89 Other functional disorders of intestine

565.1 Anal fistula

566 Abscess of anal and rectal regions

567.0 Peritonitis in infectious diseases classified elsewhere — (Code first underlying disease) ☒

567.1 Pneumococcal peritonitis

567.21 Peritonitis (acute) generalized

567.22 Peritoneal abscess

567.23 Spontaneous bacterial peritonitis

567.29 Other suppurative peritonitis

567.31 Psoas muscle abscess

567.38 Other retroperitoneal abscess

567.39 Other retroperitoneal infections

567.81 Choleperitonitis

567.82 Sclerosing mesenteritis

567.89 Other specified peritonitis

567.9 Unspecified peritonitis ▽

569.1 Rectal prolapse

569.2 Stenosis of rectum and anus
569.3 Hemorrhage of rectum and anus
569.41 Ulcer of anus and rectum
569.44 Dysplasia of anus
569.49 Other specified disorder of rectum and anus — (Use additional code for any associated fecal incontinence (787.60-787.63))
569.5 Abscess of intestine
569.61 Infection of colostomy or enterostomy — (Use additional code to identify organism: 041.00-041.9. Use additional code to specify type of infection: 038.0-038.9, 682.2)
569.69 Other complication of colostomy or enterostomy
569.81 Fistula of intestine, excluding rectum and anus
569.82 Ulceration of intestine
569.83 Perforation of intestine
569.84 Angiodysplasia of intestine (without mention of hemorrhage)
569.85 Angiodysplasia of intestine with hemorrhage
569.89 Other specified disorder of intestines
578.9 Hemorrhage of gastrointestinal tract, unspecified ▽
596.1 Intestinovesical fistula — (Use additional code to identify urinary incontinence: 625.6, 788.30-788.39)
619.1 Digestive-genital tract fistula, female ♀
625.6 Female stress incontinence ♀
751.0 Meckel's diverticulum
751.1 Congenital atresia and stenosis of small intestine
751.2 Congenital atresia and stenosis of large intestine, rectum, and anal canal
751.3 Hirschsprung's disease and other congenital functional disorders of colon
751.4 Congenital anomalies of intestinal fixation
751.5 Other congenital anomalies of intestine
787.60 Full incontinence of feces
787.61 Incomplete defecation
787.62 Fecal smearing
787.63 Fecal urgency
863.55 Rectum injury with open wound into cavity

ICD-9-CM Procedural

46.03 Exteriorization of large intestine
46.10 Colostomy, not otherwise specified
46.11 Temporary colostomy
46.13 Permanent colostomy

44202-44203

44202 Laparoscopy, surgical; enterectomy, resection of small intestine, single resection and anastomosis
44203 each additional small intestine resection and anastomosis (List separately in addition to code for primary procedure)

ICD-9-CM Diagnostic

152.0 Malignant neoplasm of duodenum
152.1 Malignant neoplasm of jejunum
152.2 Malignant neoplasm of ileum
152.8 Malignant neoplasm of other specified sites of small intestine
152.9 Malignant neoplasm of small intestine, unspecified site ▽
197.4 Secondary malignant neoplasm of small intestine including duodenum
209.00 Malignant carcinoid tumor of the small intestine, unspecified portion — (Code first any associated multiple endocrine neoplasia syndrome: 258.01-258.03)(Use additional code to identify associated endocrine syndrome, as: carcinoid syndrome: 259.2) ▽
209.01 Malignant carcinoid tumor of the duodenum — (Code first any associated multiple endocrine neoplasia syndrome: 258.01-258.03)(Use additional code to identify associated endocrine syndrome, as: carcinoid syndrome: 259.2)
209.02 Malignant carcinoid tumor of the jejunum — (Code first any associated multiple endocrine neoplasia syndrome: 258.01-258.03)(Use additional code to identify associated endocrine syndrome, as: carcinoid syndrome: 259.2)
209.03 Malignant carcinoid tumor of the ileum — (Code first any associated multiple endocrine neoplasia syndrome: 258.01-258.03)(Use additional code to identify associated endocrine syndrome, as: carcinoid syndrome: 259.2)
211.2 Benign neoplasm of duodenum, jejunum, and ileum
230.7 Carcinoma in situ of other and unspecified parts of intestine ▽
230.9 Carcinoma in situ of other and unspecified digestive organs ▽
235.2 Neoplasm of uncertain behavior of stomach, intestines, and rectum
239.0 Neoplasm of unspecified nature of digestive system
551.00 Femoral hernia with gangrene, unilateral or unspecified (not specified as recurrent)
551.01 Femoral hernia with gangrene, recurrent unilateral or unspecified
551.02 Femoral hernia with gangrene, bilateral, (not specified as recurrent)
551.03 Femoral hernia with gangrene, recurrent bilateral
551.21 Incisional ventral hernia, with gangrene
551.8 Hernia of other specified sites, with gangrene
551.9 Hernia of unspecified site, with gangrene ▽
552.00 Unilateral or unspecified femoral hernia with obstruction
552.21 Incisional hernia with obstruction
555.0 Regional enteritis of small intestine
555.9 Regional enteritis of unspecified site ▽
556.1 Ulcerative (chronic) ileocolitis
560.0 Intussusception
560.1 Paralytic ileus
560.2 Volvulus
560.81 Intestinal or peritoneal adhesions with obstruction (postoperative) (postinfection)
560.89 Other specified intestinal obstruction
560.9 Unspecified intestinal obstruction ▽
562.00 Diverticulosis of small intestine (without mention of hemorrhage) — (Use additional code to identify any associated peritonitis: 567.0-567.9)
562.01 Diverticulitis of small intestine (without mention of hemorrhage) — (Use additional code to identify any associated peritonitis: 567.0-567.9)
562.02 Diverticulosis of small intestine with hemorrhage — (Use additional code to identify any associated peritonitis: 567.0-567.9)
562.03 Diverticulitis of small intestine with hemorrhage — (Use additional code to identify any associated peritonitis: 567.0-567.9)
567.0 Peritonitis in infectious diseases classified elsewhere — (Code first underlying disease) ☒
567.1 Pneumococcal peritonitis
567.21 Peritonitis (acute) generalized
567.22 Peritoneal abscess
567.23 Spontaneous bacterial peritonitis
567.29 Other suppurative peritonitis
567.31 Psoas muscle abscess
567.38 Other retroperitoneal abscess
567.39 Other retroperitoneal infections
567.81 Choleperitonitis
567.82 Sclerosing mesenteritis
567.89 Other specified peritonitis
567.9 Unspecified peritonitis ▽
569.5 Abscess of intestine
569.81 Fistula of intestine, excluding rectum and anus
569.82 Ulceration of intestine
569.83 Perforation of intestine
569.85 Angiodysplasia of intestine with hemorrhage
569.89 Other specified disorder of intestines
578.9 Hemorrhage of gastrointestinal tract, unspecified ▽
619.1 Digestive-genital tract fistula, female ♀
863.20 Small intestine injury, unspecified site, without mention of open wound into cavity ▽
863.21 Duodenum injury without mention of open wound into cavity
863.29 Other injury to small intestine without mention of open wound into cavity

863.30 Small intestine injury, unspecified site, with open wound into cavity

863.31 Duodenum injury with open wound into cavity

863.39 Other injury to small intestine with open wound into cavity

863.80 Gastrointestinal tract injury, unspecified site, without mention of open wound into cavity

863.89 Injury to other and unspecified gastrointestinal sites without mention of open wound into cavity

863.90 Gastrointestinal tract injury, unspecified site, with open wound into cavity

863.99 Injury to other and unspecified gastrointestinal sites with open wound into cavity

997.49 Other digestive system complications

998.2 Accidental puncture or laceration during procedure

998.51 Infected postoperative seroma — (Use additional code to identify organism)

998.59 Other postoperative infection — (Use additional code to identify infection)

998.6 Persistent postoperative fistula, not elsewhere classified

ICD-9-CM Procedural

45.62 Other partial resection of small intestine

44204-44205

44204 Laparoscopy, surgical; colectomy, partial, with anastomosis

44205 colectomy, partial, with removal of terminal ileum with ileocolostomy

ICD-9-CM Diagnostic

153.0 Malignant neoplasm of hepatic flexure

153.1 Malignant neoplasm of transverse colon

153.2 Malignant neoplasm of descending colon

153.3 Malignant neoplasm of sigmoid colon

153.4 Malignant neoplasm of cecum

153.6 Malignant neoplasm of ascending colon

153.7 Malignant neoplasm of splenic flexure

153.8 Malignant neoplasm of other specified sites of large intestine

153.9 Malignant neoplasm of colon, unspecified site

154.0 Malignant neoplasm of rectosigmoid junction

154.1 Malignant neoplasm of rectum

154.2 Malignant neoplasm of anal canal

154.3 Malignant neoplasm of anus, unspecified site

154.8 Malignant neoplasm of other sites of rectum, rectosigmoid junction, and anus

197.5 Secondary malignant neoplasm of large intestine and rectum

209.10 Malignant carcinoid tumor of the large intestine, unspecified portion — (Code first any associated multiple endocrine neoplasia syndrome: 258.01-258.03)(Use additional code to identify associated endocrine syndrome, as: carcinoid syndrome: 259.2)

209.11 Malignant carcinoid tumor of the appendix — (Code first any associated multiple endocrine neoplasia syndrome: 258.01-258.03)(Use additional code to identify associated endocrine syndrome, as: carcinoid syndrome: 259.2)

209.12 Malignant carcinoid tumor of the cecum — (Code first any associated multiple endocrine neoplasia syndrome: 258.01-258.03)(Use additional code to identify associated endocrine syndrome, as: carcinoid syndrome: 259.2)

209.13 Malignant carcinoid tumor of the ascending colon — (Code first any associated multiple endocrine neoplasia syndrome: 258.01-258.03)(Use additional code to identify associated endocrine syndrome, as: carcinoid syndrome: 259.2)

209.14 Malignant carcinoid tumor of the transverse colon — (Code first any associated multiple endocrine neoplasia syndrome: 258.01-258.03)(Use additional code to identify associated endocrine syndrome, as: carcinoid syndrome: 259.2)

209.15 Malignant carcinoid tumor of the descending colon — (Code first any associated multiple endocrine neoplasia syndrome: 258.01-258.03)(Use additional code to identify associated endocrine syndrome, as: carcinoid syndrome: 259.2)

209.16 Malignant carcinoid tumor of the sigmoid colon — (Code first any associated multiple endocrine neoplasia syndrome: 258.01-258.03)(Use additional code to identify associated endocrine syndrome, as: carcinoid syndrome: 259.2)

209.29 Malignant carcinoid tumor of other sites — (Code first any associated multiple endocrine neoplasia syndrome: 258.01-258.03)(Use additional code to identify associated endocrine syndrome, as: carcinoid syndrome: 259.2)

209.30 Malignant poorly differentiated neuroendocrine carcinoma, any site — (Code first any associated multiple endocrine neoplasia syndrome: 258.01-258.03)(Use additional code to identify associated endocrine syndrome, as: carcinoid syndrome: 259.2)

209.50 Benign carcinoid tumor of the large intestine, unspecified portion — (Code first any associated multiple endocrine neoplasia syndrome: 258.01-258.03)(Use additional code to identify associated endocrine syndrome, as: carcinoid syndrome: 259.2)

209.51 Benign carcinoid tumor of the appendix — (Code first any associated multiple endocrine neoplasia syndrome: 258.01-258.03)(Use additional code to identify associated endocrine syndrome, as: carcinoid syndrome: 259.2)

209.52 Benign carcinoid tumor of the cecum — (Code first any associated multiple endocrine neoplasia syndrome: 258.01-258.03)(Use additional code to identify associated endocrine syndrome, as: carcinoid syndrome: 259.2)

209.53 Benign carcinoid tumor of the ascending colon — (Code first any associated multiple endocrine neoplasia syndrome: 258.01-258.03)(Use additional code to identify associated endocrine syndrome, as: carcinoid syndrome: 259.2)

209.54 Benign carcinoid tumor of the transverse colon — (Code first any associated multiple endocrine neoplasia syndrome: 258.01-258.03)(Use additional code to identify associated endocrine syndrome, as: carcinoid syndrome: 259.2)

209.55 Benign carcinoid tumor of the descending colon — (Code first any associated multiple endocrine neoplasia syndrome: 258.01-258.03)(Use additional code to identify associated endocrine syndrome, as: carcinoid syndrome: 259.2)

209.56 Benign carcinoid tumor of the sigmoid colon — (Code first any associated multiple endocrine neoplasia syndrome: 258.01-258.03)(Use additional code to identify associated endocrine syndrome, as: carcinoid syndrome: 259.2)

209.57 Benign carcinoid tumor of the rectum — (Code first any associated multiple endocrine neoplasia syndrome: 258.01-258.03)(Use additional code to identify associated endocrine syndrome, as: carcinoid syndrome: 259.2)

211.3 Benign neoplasm of colon

211.4 Benign neoplasm of rectum and anal canal

211.9 Benign neoplasm of other and unspecified site of the digestive system

229.9 Benign neoplasm of unspecified site

230.3 Carcinoma in situ of colon

235.2 Neoplasm of uncertain behavior of stomach, intestines, and rectum

239.0 Neoplasm of unspecified nature of digestive system

550.00 Inguinal hernia with gangrene, unilateral or unspecified, (not specified as recurrent)

551.1 Umbilical hernia with gangrene

552.8 Hernia of other specified site, with obstruction

555.1 Regional enteritis of large intestine

555.2 Regional enteritis of small intestine with large intestine

556.0 Ulcerative (chronic) enterocolitis

556.1 Ulcerative (chronic) ileocolitis

556.2 Ulcerative (chronic) proctitis

556.3 Ulcerative (chronic) proctosigmoiditis

556.8 Other ulcerative colitis

557.0 Acute vascular insufficiency of intestine

557.1 Chronic vascular insufficiency of intestine

557.9 Unspecified vascular insufficiency of intestine

558.1 Gastroenteritis and colitis due to radiation

558.2 Toxic gastroenteritis and colitis — (Use additional E code to identify cause)

558.42 Eosinophilic colitis

558.9 Other and unspecified noninfectious gastroenteritis and colitis

560.0 Intussusception

560.1 Paralytic ileus

560.2 Volvulus

560.31 Gallstone ileus

560.39 Impaction of intestine, other

560.81 Intestinal or peritoneal adhesions with obstruction (postoperative) (postinfection)

560.89 Other specified intestinal obstruction

560.9 Unspecified intestinal obstruction

562.10 Diverticulosis of colon (without mention of hemorrhage) — (Use additional code to identify any associated peritonitis: 567.0-567.9)
562.11 Diverticulitis of colon (without mention of hemorrhage) — (Use additional code to identify any associated peritonitis: 567.0-567.9)
562.12 Diverticulosis of colon with hemorrhage — (Use additional code to identify any associated peritonitis: 567.0-567.9)
562.13 Diverticulitis of colon with hemorrhage — (Use additional code to identify any associated peritonitis: 567.0-567.9)
564.7 Megacolon, other than Hirschsprung's
567.0 Peritonitis in infectious diseases classified elsewhere — (Code first underlying disease) ☒
567.1 Pneumococcal peritonitis
567.21 Peritonitis (acute) generalized
567.22 Peritoneal abscess
567.23 Spontaneous bacterial peritonitis
567.29 Other suppurative peritonitis
567.31 Psoas muscle abscess
567.38 Other retroperitoneal abscess
567.39 Other retroperitoneal infections
567.81 Choleperitonitis
567.82 Sclerosing mesenteritis
567.89 Other specified peritonitis
567.9 Unspecified peritonitis ▽
569.44 Dysplasia of anus
569.81 Fistula of intestine, excluding rectum and anus
569.82 Ulceration of intestine
569.83 Perforation of intestine
569.84 Angiodysplasia of intestine (without mention of hemorrhage)
569.85 Angiodysplasia of intestine with hemorrhage
569.89 Other specified disorder of intestines
569.9 Unspecified disorder of intestine ▽
578.9 Hemorrhage of gastrointestinal tract, unspecified ▽
596.1 Intestinovesical fistula — (Use additional code to identify urinary incontinence: 625.6, 788.30-788.39)
619.1 Digestive-genital tract fistula, female ♀
751.5 Other congenital anomalies of intestine
751.8 Other specified congenital anomalies of digestive system
751.9 Unspecified congenital anomaly of digestive system ▽

ICD-9-CM Procedural

17.31 Laparoscopic multiple segmental resection of large intestine
17.32 Laparoscopic cecectomy
17.33 Laparoscopic right hemicolectomy
17.34 Laparoscopic resection of transverse colon
17.35 Laparoscopic left hemicolectomy
17.36 Laparoscopic sigmoidectomy
17.39 Other laparoscopic partial excision of large intestine

44206

44206 Laparoscopy, surgical; colectomy, partial, with end colostomy and closure of distal segment (Hartmann type procedure)

ICD-9-CM Diagnostic

153.0 Malignant neoplasm of hepatic flexure
153.1 Malignant neoplasm of transverse colon
153.2 Malignant neoplasm of descending colon
153.3 Malignant neoplasm of sigmoid colon
153.4 Malignant neoplasm of cecum
153.5 Malignant neoplasm of appendix
153.6 Malignant neoplasm of ascending colon
153.7 Malignant neoplasm of splenic flexure
153.8 Malignant neoplasm of other specified sites of large intestine
153.9 Malignant neoplasm of colon, unspecified site ▽
154.0 Malignant neoplasm of rectosigmoid junction
154.1 Malignant neoplasm of rectum
154.8 Malignant neoplasm of other sites of rectum, rectosigmoid junction, and anus
159.0 Malignant neoplasm of intestinal tract, part unspecified ▽
197.5 Secondary malignant neoplasm of large intestine and rectum
198.89 Secondary malignant neoplasm of other specified sites
199.1 Other malignant neoplasm of unspecified site
209.10 Malignant carcinoid tumor of the large intestine, unspecified portion — (Code first any associated multiple endocrine neoplasia syndrome: 258.01-258.03)(Use additional code to identify associated endocrine syndrome, as: carcinoid syndrome: 259.2) ▽
209.11 Malignant carcinoid tumor of the appendix — (Code first any associated multiple endocrine neoplasia syndrome: 258.01-258.03)(Use additional code to identify associated endocrine syndrome, as: carcinoid syndrome: 259.2)
209.12 Malignant carcinoid tumor of the cecum — (Code first any associated multiple endocrine neoplasia syndrome: 258.01-258.03)(Use additional code to identify associated endocrine syndrome, as: carcinoid syndrome: 259.2)
209.13 Malignant carcinoid tumor of the ascending colon — (Code first any associated multiple endocrine neoplasia syndrome: 258.01-258.03)(Use additional code to identify associated endocrine syndrome, as: carcinoid syndrome: 259.2)
209.14 Malignant carcinoid tumor of the transverse colon — (Code first any associated multiple endocrine neoplasia syndrome: 258.01-258.03)(Use additional code to identify associated endocrine syndrome, as: carcinoid syndrome: 259.2)
209.15 Malignant carcinoid tumor of the descending colon — (Code first any associated multiple endocrine neoplasia syndrome: 258.01-258.03)(Use additional code to identify associated endocrine syndrome, as: carcinoid syndrome: 259.2)
209.16 Malignant carcinoid tumor of the sigmoid colon — (Code first any associated multiple endocrine neoplasia syndrome: 258.01-258.03)(Use additional code to identify associated endocrine syndrome, as: carcinoid syndrome: 259.2)
209.27 Malignant carcinoid tumor of hindgut, not otherwise specified — (Code first any associated multiple endocrine neoplasia syndrome: 258.01-258.03)(Use additional code to identify associated endocrine syndrome, as: carcinoid syndrome: 259.2)
209.29 Malignant carcinoid tumor of other sites — (Code first any associated multiple endocrine neoplasia syndrome: 258.01-258.03)(Use additional code to identify associated endocrine syndrome, as: carcinoid syndrome: 259.2)
209.30 Malignant poorly differentiated neuroendocrine carcinoma, any site — (Code first any associated multiple endocrine neoplasia syndrome: 258.01-258.03)(Use additional code to identify associated endocrine syndrome, as: carcinoid syndrome: 259.2) ▽
209.50 Benign carcinoid tumor of the large intestine, unspecified portion — (Code first any associated multiple endocrine neoplasia syndrome: 258.01-258.03)(Use additional code to identify associated endocrine syndrome, as: carcinoid syndrome: 259.2) ▽
209.51 Benign carcinoid tumor of the appendix — (Code first any associated multiple endocrine neoplasia syndrome: 258.01-258.03)(Use additional code to identify associated endocrine syndrome, as: carcinoid syndrome: 259.2)
209.52 Benign carcinoid tumor of the cecum — (Code first any associated multiple endocrine neoplasia syndrome: 258.01-258.03)(Use additional code to identify associated endocrine syndrome, as: carcinoid syndrome: 259.2)
209.53 Benign carcinoid tumor of the ascending colon — (Code first any associated multiple endocrine neoplasia syndrome: 258.01-258.03)(Use additional code to identify associated endocrine syndrome, as: carcinoid syndrome: 259.2)
209.54 Benign carcinoid tumor of the transverse colon — (Code first any associated multiple endocrine neoplasia syndrome: 258.01-258.03)(Use additional code to identify associated endocrine syndrome, as: carcinoid syndrome: 259.2)
209.55 Benign carcinoid tumor of the descending colon — (Code first any associated multiple endocrine neoplasia syndrome: 258.01-258.03)(Use additional code to identify associated endocrine syndrome, as: carcinoid syndrome: 259.2)
209.56 Benign carcinoid tumor of the sigmoid colon — (Code first any associated multiple endocrine neoplasia syndrome: 258.01-258.03)(Use additional code to identify associated endocrine syndrome, as: carcinoid syndrome: 259.2)

209.57 Benign carcinoid tumor of the rectum — (Code first any associated multiple endocrine neoplasia syndrome: 258.01-258.03)(Use additional code to identify associated endocrine syndrome, as: carcinoid syndrome: 259.2)

209.69 Benign carcinoid tumor of other sites — (Code first any associated multiple endocrine neoplasia syndrome: 258.01-258.03)(Use additional code to identify associated endocrine syndrome, as: carcinoid syndrome: 259.2)

211.3 Benign neoplasm of colon

211.4 Benign neoplasm of rectum and anal canal

230.3 Carcinoma in situ of colon

230.4 Carcinoma in situ of rectum

235.2 Neoplasm of uncertain behavior of stomach, intestines, and rectum

239.0 Neoplasm of unspecified nature of digestive system

555.1 Regional enteritis of large intestine

555.2 Regional enteritis of small intestine with large intestine

555.9 Regional enteritis of unspecified site

556.0 Ulcerative (chronic) enterocolitis

556.1 Ulcerative (chronic) ileocolitis

556.2 Ulcerative (chronic) proctitis

556.3 Ulcerative (chronic) proctosigmoiditis

556.4 Pseudopolyposis of colon

556.5 Left sided ulcerative (chronic) colitis

556.6 Universal ulcerative (chronic) colitis

556.8 Other ulcerative colitis

556.9 Unspecified ulcerative colitis

557.0 Acute vascular insufficiency of intestine

557.1 Chronic vascular insufficiency of intestine

557.9 Unspecified vascular insufficiency of intestine

560.2 Volvulus

560.81 Intestinal or peritoneal adhesions with obstruction (postoperative) (postinfection)

560.89 Other specified intestinal obstruction

560.9 Unspecified intestinal obstruction

562.10 Diverticulosis of colon (without mention of hemorrhage) — (Use additional code to identify any associated peritonitis: 567.0-567.9)

562.11 Diverticulitis of colon (without mention of hemorrhage) — (Use additional code to identify any associated peritonitis: 567.0-567.9)

562.12 Diverticulosis of colon with hemorrhage — (Use additional code to identify any associated peritonitis: 567.0-567.9)

562.13 Diverticulitis of colon with hemorrhage — (Use additional code to identify any associated peritonitis: 567.0-567.9)

564.81 Neurogenic bowel

564.89 Other functional disorders of intestine

567.0 Peritonitis in infectious diseases classified elsewhere — (Code first underlying disease)

567.1 Pneumococcal peritonitis

567.21 Peritonitis (acute) generalized

567.22 Peritoneal abscess

567.23 Spontaneous bacterial peritonitis

567.29 Other suppurative peritonitis

567.31 Psoas muscle abscess

567.38 Other retroperitoneal abscess

567.39 Other retroperitoneal infections

567.81 Choleperitonitis

567.82 Sclerosing mesenteritis

567.89 Other specified peritonitis

567.9 Unspecified peritonitis

569.44 Dysplasia of anus

569.5 Abscess of intestine

569.81 Fistula of intestine, excluding rectum and anus

569.82 Ulceration of intestine

569.83 Perforation of intestine

569.84 Angiodysplasia of intestine (without mention of hemorrhage)

569.85 Angiodysplasia of intestine with hemorrhage

569.89 Other specified disorder of intestines

569.9 Unspecified disorder of intestine

578.1 Blood in stool

578.9 Hemorrhage of gastrointestinal tract, unspecified

596.1 Intestinovesical fistula — (Use additional code to identify urinary incontinence: 625.6, 788.30-788.39)

619.1 Digestive-genital tract fistula, female ♀

751.2 Congenital atresia and stenosis of large intestine, rectum, and anal canal

751.3 Hirschsprung's disease and other congenital functional disorders of colon

751.4 Congenital anomalies of intestinal fixation

751.5 Other congenital anomalies of intestine

751.8 Other specified congenital anomalies of digestive system

751.9 Unspecified congenital anomaly of digestive system

777.50 Necrotizing enterocolitis in newborn, unspecified

777.51 Stage I necrotizing enterocolitis in newborn

777.52 Stage II necrotizing enterocolitis in newborn

777.53 Stage III necrotizing enterocolitis in newborn

777.6 Perinatal intestinal perforation — (Use additional code(s) to further specify condition)

777.8 Other specified perinatal disorder of digestive system — (Use additional code(s) to further specify condition)

793.4 Nonspecific (abnormal) findings on radiological and other examination of gastrointestinal tract

863.40 Colon injury unspecified site, without mention of open wound into cavity

863.41 Ascending (right) colon injury without mention of open wound into cavity

863.42 Transverse colon injury without mention of open wound into cavity

863.43 Descending (left) colon injury without mention of open wound into cavity

863.44 Sigmoid colon injury without mention of open wound into cavity

863.45 Rectum injury without mention of open wound into cavity

863.46 Injury to multiple sites in colon and rectum without mention of open wound into cavity

863.49 Other colon and rectum injury, without mention of open wound into cavity

863.50 Colon injury, unspecified site, with open wound into cavity

863.51 Ascending (right) colon injury with open wound into cavity

863.52 Transverse colon injury with open wound into cavity

863.53 Descending (left) colon injury with open wound into cavity

863.54 Sigmoid colon injury with open wound into cavity

863.55 Rectum injury with open wound into cavity

863.56 Injury to multiple sites in colon and rectum with open wound into cavity

863.59 Other injury to colon and rectum with open wound into cavity

863.80 Gastrointestinal tract injury, unspecified site, without mention of open wound into cavity

863.90 Gastrointestinal tract injury, unspecified site, with open wound into cavity

869.0 Internal injury to unspecified or ill-defined organs without mention of open wound into cavity

869.1 Internal injury to unspecified or ill-defined organs with open wound into cavity

936 Foreign body in intestine and colon

937 Foreign body in anus and rectum

938 Foreign body in digestive system, unspecified

997.49 Other digestive system complications

998.2 Accidental puncture or laceration during procedure

998.31 Disruption of internal operation (surgical) wound

998.6 Persistent postoperative fistula, not elsewhere classified

998.9 Unspecified complication of procedure, not elsewhere classified

ICD-9-CM Procedural

17.31 Laparoscopic multiple segmental resection of large intestine

17.32 Laparoscopic cecectomy

17.33 Laparoscopic right hemicolectomy

17.34 Laparoscopic resection of transverse colon
17.35 Laparoscopic left hemicolectomy
17.36 Laparoscopic sigmoidectomy
17.39 Other laparoscopic partial excision of large intestine

44207-44208

44207 Laparoscopy, surgical; colectomy, partial, with anastomosis, with coloproctostomy (low pelvic anastomosis)

44208 colectomy, partial, with anastomosis, with coloproctostomy (low pelvic anastomosis) with colostomy

ICD-9-CM Diagnostic

153.0 Malignant neoplasm of hepatic flexure
153.1 Malignant neoplasm of transverse colon
153.2 Malignant neoplasm of descending colon
153.3 Malignant neoplasm of sigmoid colon
153.4 Malignant neoplasm of cecum
153.5 Malignant neoplasm of appendix
153.6 Malignant neoplasm of ascending colon
153.7 Malignant neoplasm of splenic flexure
153.8 Malignant neoplasm of other specified sites of large intestine
153.9 Malignant neoplasm of colon, unspecified site ▽
154.0 Malignant neoplasm of rectosigmoid junction
154.1 Malignant neoplasm of rectum
154.2 Malignant neoplasm of anal canal
154.8 Malignant neoplasm of other sites of rectum, rectosigmoid junction, and anus
159.0 Malignant neoplasm of intestinal tract, part unspecified ▽
197.5 Secondary malignant neoplasm of large intestine and rectum
209.10 Malignant carcinoid tumor of the large intestine, unspecified portion — (Code first any associated multiple endocrine neoplasia syndrome: 258.01-258.03)(Use additional code to identify associated endocrine syndrome, as: carcinoid syndrome: 259.2) ▽
209.11 Malignant carcinoid tumor of the appendix — (Code first any associated multiple endocrine neoplasia syndrome: 258.01-258.03)(Use additional code to identify associated endocrine syndrome, as: carcinoid syndrome: 259.2)
209.12 Malignant carcinoid tumor of the cecum — (Code first any associated multiple endocrine neoplasia syndrome: 258.01-258.03)(Use additional code to identify associated endocrine syndrome, as: carcinoid syndrome: 259.2)
209.13 Malignant carcinoid tumor of the ascending colon — (Code first any associated multiple endocrine neoplasia syndrome: 258.01-258.03)(Use additional code to identify associated endocrine syndrome, as: carcinoid syndrome: 259.2)
209.14 Malignant carcinoid tumor of the transverse colon — (Code first any associated multiple endocrine neoplasia syndrome: 258.01-258.03)(Use additional code to identify associated endocrine syndrome, as: carcinoid syndrome: 259.2)
209.15 Malignant carcinoid tumor of the descending colon — (Code first any associated multiple endocrine neoplasia syndrome: 258.01-258.03)(Use additional code to identify associated endocrine syndrome, as: carcinoid syndrome: 259.2)
209.16 Malignant carcinoid tumor of the sigmoid colon — (Code first any associated multiple endocrine neoplasia syndrome: 258.01-258.03)(Use additional code to identify associated endocrine syndrome, as: carcinoid syndrome: 259.2)
209.27 Malignant carcinoid tumor of hindgut, not otherwise specified — (Code first any associated multiple endocrine neoplasia syndrome: 258.01-258.03)(Use additional code to identify associated endocrine syndrome, as: carcinoid syndrome: 259.2)
209.29 Malignant carcinoid tumor of other sites — (Code first any associated multiple endocrine neoplasia syndrome: 258.01-258.03)(Use additional code to identify associated endocrine syndrome, as: carcinoid syndrome: 259.2)
209.30 Malignant poorly differentiated neuroendocrine carcinoma, any site — (Code first any associated multiple endocrine neoplasia syndrome: 258.01-258.03)(Use additional code to identify associated endocrine syndrome, as: carcinoid syndrome: 259.2) ▽
209.50 Benign carcinoid tumor of the large intestine, unspecified portion — (Code first any associated multiple endocrine neoplasia syndrome: 258.01-258.03)(Use additional code to identify associated endocrine syndrome, as: carcinoid syndrome: 259.2) ▽
209.51 Benign carcinoid tumor of the appendix — (Code first any associated multiple endocrine neoplasia syndrome: 258.01-258.03)(Use additional code to identify associated endocrine syndrome, as: carcinoid syndrome: 259.2)
209.52 Benign carcinoid tumor of the cecum — (Code first any associated multiple endocrine neoplasia syndrome: 258.01-258.03)(Use additional code to identify associated endocrine syndrome, as: carcinoid syndrome: 259.2)
209.53 Benign carcinoid tumor of the ascending colon — (Code first any associated multiple endocrine neoplasia syndrome: 258.01-258.03)(Use additional code to identify associated endocrine syndrome, as: carcinoid syndrome: 259.2)
209.54 Benign carcinoid tumor of the transverse colon — (Code first any associated multiple endocrine neoplasia syndrome: 258.01-258.03)(Use additional code to identify associated endocrine syndrome, as: carcinoid syndrome: 259.2)
209.55 Benign carcinoid tumor of the descending colon — (Code first any associated multiple endocrine neoplasia syndrome: 258.01-258.03)(Use additional code to identify associated endocrine syndrome, as: carcinoid syndrome: 259.2)
209.56 Benign carcinoid tumor of the sigmoid colon — (Code first any associated multiple endocrine neoplasia syndrome: 258.01-258.03)(Use additional code to identify associated endocrine syndrome, as: carcinoid syndrome: 259.2)
209.57 Benign carcinoid tumor of the rectum — (Code first any associated multiple endocrine neoplasia syndrome: 258.01-258.03)(Use additional code to identify associated endocrine syndrome, as: carcinoid syndrome: 259.2)
209.69 Benign carcinoid tumor of other sites — (Code first any associated multiple endocrine neoplasia syndrome: 258.01-258.03)(Use additional code to identify associated endocrine syndrome, as: carcinoid syndrome: 259.2)
211.3 Benign neoplasm of colon
211.4 Benign neoplasm of rectum and anal canal
230.3 Carcinoma in situ of colon
230.4 Carcinoma in situ of rectum
230.9 Carcinoma in situ of other and unspecified digestive organs ▽
235.2 Neoplasm of uncertain behavior of stomach, intestines, and rectum
239.0 Neoplasm of unspecified nature of digestive system
555.1 Regional enteritis of large intestine
555.2 Regional enteritis of small intestine with large intestine
555.9 Regional enteritis of unspecified site ▽
556.0 Ulcerative (chronic) enterocolitis
556.1 Ulcerative (chronic) ileocolitis
556.2 Ulcerative (chronic) proctitis
556.3 Ulcerative (chronic) proctosigmoiditis
556.4 Pseudopolyposis of colon
556.5 Left sided ulcerative (chronic) colitis
556.6 Universal ulcerative (chronic) colitis
556.8 Other ulcerative colitis
556.9 Unspecified ulcerative colitis ▽
557.0 Acute vascular insufficiency of intestine
557.1 Chronic vascular insufficiency of intestine
557.9 Unspecified vascular insufficiency of intestine ▽
560.39 Impaction of intestine, other
560.81 Intestinal or peritoneal adhesions with obstruction (postoperative) (postinfection)
560.89 Other specified intestinal obstruction
560.9 Unspecified intestinal obstruction ▽
562.10 Diverticulosis of colon (without mention of hemorrhage) — (Use additional code to identify any associated peritonitis: 567.0-567.9)
562.11 Diverticulitis of colon (without mention of hemorrhage) — (Use additional code to identify any associated peritonitis: 567.0-567.9)
562.12 Diverticulosis of colon with hemorrhage — (Use additional code to identify any associated peritonitis: 567.0-567.9)
562.13 Diverticulitis of colon with hemorrhage — (Use additional code to identify any associated peritonitis: 567.0-567.9)
564.7 Megacolon, other than Hirschsprung's
567.0 Peritonitis in infectious diseases classified elsewhere — (Code first underlying disease) ☒

567.1 Pneumococcal peritonitis
567.21 Peritonitis (acute) generalized
567.22 Peritoneal abscess
567.23 Spontaneous bacterial peritonitis
567.29 Other suppurative peritonitis
567.31 Psoas muscle abscess
567.38 Other retroperitoneal abscess
567.39 Other retroperitoneal infections
567.81 Choleperitonitis
567.82 Sclerosing mesenteritis
567.89 Other specified peritonitis
567.9 Unspecified peritonitis
569.1 Rectal prolapse
569.44 Dysplasia of anus
569.81 Fistula of intestine, excluding rectum and anus
569.82 Ulceration of intestine
569.83 Perforation of intestine
569.84 Angiodysplasia of intestine (without mention of hemorrhage)
569.85 Angiodysplasia of intestine with hemorrhage
569.89 Other specified disorder of intestines
569.9 Unspecified disorder of intestine
596.1 Intestinovesical fistula — (Use additional code to identify urinary incontinence: 625.6, 788.30-788.39)
619.1 Digestive-genital tract fistula, female ♀
751.8 Other specified congenital anomalies of digestive system
777.50 Necrotizing enterocolitis in newborn, unspecified
777.51 Stage I necrotizing enterocolitis in newborn
777.52 Stage II necrotizing enterocolitis in newborn
777.53 Stage III necrotizing enterocolitis in newborn
777.6 Perinatal intestinal perforation — (Use additional code(s) to further specify condition)
777.8 Other specified perinatal disorder of digestive system — (Use additional code(s) to further specify condition)
787.99 Other symptoms involving digestive system

ICD-9-CM Procedural

17.31 Laparoscopic multiple segmental resection of large intestine
17.32 Laparoscopic cecectomy
17.33 Laparoscopic right hemicolectomy
17.34 Laparoscopic resection of transverse colon
17.35 Laparoscopic left hemicolectomy
17.36 Laparoscopic sigmoidectomy
17.39 Other laparoscopic partial excision of large intestine
45.94 Large-to-large intestinal anastomosis
46.03 Exteriorization of large intestine
46.11 Temporary colostomy
46.13 Permanent colostomy

44210

44210 Laparoscopy, surgical; colectomy, total, abdominal, without proctectomy, with ileostomy or ileoproctostomy

ICD-9-CM Diagnostic

153.0 Malignant neoplasm of hepatic flexure
153.1 Malignant neoplasm of transverse colon
153.2 Malignant neoplasm of descending colon
153.3 Malignant neoplasm of sigmoid colon
153.4 Malignant neoplasm of cecum
153.5 Malignant neoplasm of appendix
153.6 Malignant neoplasm of ascending colon
153.7 Malignant neoplasm of splenic flexure
153.8 Malignant neoplasm of other specified sites of large intestine
153.9 Malignant neoplasm of colon, unspecified site
154.0 Malignant neoplasm of rectosigmoid junction
154.1 Malignant neoplasm of rectum
197.5 Secondary malignant neoplasm of large intestine and rectum
209.10 Malignant carcinoid tumor of the large intestine, unspecified portion — (Code first any associated multiple endocrine neoplasia syndrome: 258.01-258.03)(Use additional code to identify associated endocrine syndrome, as: carcinoid syndrome: 259.2)
209.11 Malignant carcinoid tumor of the appendix — (Code first any associated multiple endocrine neoplasia syndrome: 258.01-258.03)(Use additional code to identify associated endocrine syndrome, as: carcinoid syndrome: 259.2)
209.12 Malignant carcinoid tumor of the cecum — (Code first any associated multiple endocrine neoplasia syndrome: 258.01-258.03)(Use additional code to identify associated endocrine syndrome, as: carcinoid syndrome: 259.2)
209.13 Malignant carcinoid tumor of the ascending colon — (Code first any associated multiple endocrine neoplasia syndrome: 258.01-258.03)(Use additional code to identify associated endocrine syndrome, as: carcinoid syndrome: 259.2)
209.14 Malignant carcinoid tumor of the transverse colon — (Code first any associated multiple endocrine neoplasia syndrome: 258.01-258.03)(Use additional code to identify associated endocrine syndrome, as: carcinoid syndrome: 259.2)
209.15 Malignant carcinoid tumor of the descending colon — (Code first any associated multiple endocrine neoplasia syndrome: 258.01-258.03)(Use additional code to identify associated endocrine syndrome, as: carcinoid syndrome: 259.2)
209.16 Malignant carcinoid tumor of the sigmoid colon — (Code first any associated multiple endocrine neoplasia syndrome: 258.01-258.03)(Use additional code to identify associated endocrine syndrome, as: carcinoid syndrome: 259.2)
209.27 Malignant carcinoid tumor of hindgut, not otherwise specified — (Code first any associated multiple endocrine neoplasia syndrome: 258.01-258.03)(Use additional code to identify associated endocrine syndrome, as: carcinoid syndrome: 259.2)
209.29 Malignant carcinoid tumor of other sites — (Code first any associated multiple endocrine neoplasia syndrome: 258.01-258.03)(Use additional code to identify associated endocrine syndrome, as: carcinoid syndrome: 259.2)
209.30 Malignant poorly differentiated neuroendocrine carcinoma, any site — (Code first any associated multiple endocrine neoplasia syndrome: 258.01-258.03)(Use additional code to identify associated endocrine syndrome, as: carcinoid syndrome: 259.2)
209.50 Benign carcinoid tumor of the large intestine, unspecified portion — (Code first any associated multiple endocrine neoplasia syndrome: 258.01-258.03)(Use additional code to identify associated endocrine syndrome, as: carcinoid syndrome: 259.2)
209.51 Benign carcinoid tumor of the appendix — (Code first any associated multiple endocrine neoplasia syndrome: 258.01-258.03)(Use additional code to identify associated endocrine syndrome, as: carcinoid syndrome: 259.2)
209.52 Benign carcinoid tumor of the cecum — (Code first any associated multiple endocrine neoplasia syndrome: 258.01-258.03)(Use additional code to identify associated endocrine syndrome, as: carcinoid syndrome: 259.2)
209.53 Benign carcinoid tumor of the ascending colon — (Code first any associated multiple endocrine neoplasia syndrome: 258.01-258.03)(Use additional code to identify associated endocrine syndrome, as: carcinoid syndrome: 259.2)
209.54 Benign carcinoid tumor of the transverse colon — (Code first any associated multiple endocrine neoplasia syndrome: 258.01-258.03)(Use additional code to identify associated endocrine syndrome, as: carcinoid syndrome: 259.2)
209.55 Benign carcinoid tumor of the descending colon — (Code first any associated multiple endocrine neoplasia syndrome: 258.01-258.03)(Use additional code to identify associated endocrine syndrome, as: carcinoid syndrome: 259.2)
209.56 Benign carcinoid tumor of the sigmoid colon — (Code first any associated multiple endocrine neoplasia syndrome: 258.01-258.03)(Use additional code to identify associated endocrine syndrome, as: carcinoid syndrome: 259.2)
209.57 Benign carcinoid tumor of the rectum — (Code first any associated multiple endocrine neoplasia syndrome: 258.01-258.03)(Use additional code to identify associated endocrine syndrome, as: carcinoid syndrome: 259.2)
209.69 Benign carcinoid tumor of other sites — (Code first any associated multiple endocrine neoplasia syndrome: 258.01-258.03)(Use additional code to identify associated endocrine syndrome, as: carcinoid syndrome: 259.2)

211.3 Benign neoplasm of colon
211.4 Benign neoplasm of rectum and anal canal
230.3 Carcinoma in situ of colon
230.4 Carcinoma in situ of rectum
230.7 Carcinoma in situ of other and unspecified parts of intestine ▽
235.2 Neoplasm of uncertain behavior of stomach, intestines, and rectum
239.0 Neoplasm of unspecified nature of digestive system
556.0 Ulcerative (chronic) enterocolitis
556.1 Ulcerative (chronic) ileocolitis
556.2 Ulcerative (chronic) proctitis
556.3 Ulcerative (chronic) proctosigmoiditis
556.4 Pseudopolyposis of colon
556.5 Left sided ulcerative (chronic) colitis
556.6 Universal ulcerative (chronic) colitis
556.8 Other ulcerative colitis
556.9 Unspecified ulcerative colitis ▽
557.0 Acute vascular insufficiency of intestine
557.1 Chronic vascular insufficiency of intestine
557.9 Unspecified vascular insufficiency of intestine ▽
558.42 Eosinophilic colitis
558.9 Other and unspecified noninfectious gastroenteritis and colitis ▽
560.9 Unspecified intestinal obstruction ▽
562.10 Diverticulosis of colon (without mention of hemorrhage) — (Use additional code to identify any associated peritonitis: 567.0-567.9)
562.11 Diverticulitis of colon (without mention of hemorrhage) — (Use additional code to identify any associated peritonitis: 567.0-567.9)
562.12 Diverticulosis of colon with hemorrhage — (Use additional code to identify any associated peritonitis: 567.0-567.9)
562.13 Diverticulitis of colon with hemorrhage — (Use additional code to identify any associated peritonitis: 567.0-567.9)
564.7 Megacolon, other than Hirschsprung's
564.81 Neurogenic bowel
564.89 Other functional disorders of intestine
567.0 Peritonitis in infectious diseases classified elsewhere — (Code first underlying disease) ☒
567.1 Pneumococcal peritonitis
567.21 Peritonitis (acute) generalized
567.22 Peritoneal abscess
567.23 Spontaneous bacterial peritonitis
567.29 Other suppurative peritonitis
567.31 Psoas muscle abscess
567.38 Other retroperitoneal abscess
567.39 Other retroperitoneal infections
567.81 Choleperitonitis
567.82 Sclerosing mesenteritis
567.89 Other specified peritonitis
567.9 Unspecified peritonitis ▽
569.82 Ulceration of intestine
569.83 Perforation of intestine
569.89 Other specified disorder of intestines
569.9 Unspecified disorder of intestine ▽
578.1 Blood in stool
578.9 Hemorrhage of gastrointestinal tract, unspecified ▽
751.3 Hirschsprung's disease and other congenital functional disorders of colon
777.1 Fetal and newborn meconium obstruction — (Use additional code(s) to further specify condition)
777.50 Necrotizing enterocolitis in newborn, unspecified ▽
777.51 Stage I necrotizing enterocolitis in newborn
777.52 Stage II necrotizing enterocolitis in newborn
777.53 Stage III necrotizing enterocolitis in newborn
777.6 Perinatal intestinal perforation — (Use additional code(s) to further specify condition)
777.8 Other specified perinatal disorder of digestive system — (Use additional code(s) to further specify condition)
863.40 Colon injury unspecified site, without mention of open wound into cavity ▽
863.41 Ascending (right) colon injury without mention of open wound into cavity
863.42 Transverse colon injury without mention of open wound into cavity
863.43 Descending (left) colon injury without mention of open wound into cavity
863.44 Sigmoid colon injury without mention of open wound into cavity
863.45 Rectum injury without mention of open wound into cavity
863.46 Injury to multiple sites in colon and rectum without mention of open wound into cavity
863.49 Other colon and rectum injury, without mention of open wound into cavity
998.89 Other specified complications

ICD-9-CM Procedural

17.32 Laparoscopic cecectomy
17.33 Laparoscopic right hemicolectomy
17.34 Laparoscopic resection of transverse colon
17.35 Laparoscopic left hemicolectomy
17.36 Laparoscopic sigmoidectomy
45.81 Laparoscopic total intra-abdominal colectomy
45.92 Anastomosis of small intestine to rectal stump
46.23 Other permanent ileostomy

44211

44211 Laparoscopy, surgical; colectomy, total, abdominal, with proctectomy, with ileoanal anastomosis, creation of ileal reservoir (S or J), with loop ileostomy, includes rectal mucosectomy, when performed

ICD-9-CM Diagnostic

153.0 Malignant neoplasm of hepatic flexure
153.1 Malignant neoplasm of transverse colon
153.2 Malignant neoplasm of descending colon
153.3 Malignant neoplasm of sigmoid colon
153.4 Malignant neoplasm of cecum
153.5 Malignant neoplasm of appendix
153.6 Malignant neoplasm of ascending colon
153.7 Malignant neoplasm of splenic flexure
153.8 Malignant neoplasm of other specified sites of large intestine
153.9 Malignant neoplasm of colon, unspecified site ▽
154.0 Malignant neoplasm of rectosigmoid junction
154.1 Malignant neoplasm of rectum
197.5 Secondary malignant neoplasm of large intestine and rectum
209.10 Malignant carcinoid tumor of the large intestine, unspecified portion — (Code first any associated multiple endocrine neoplasia syndrome: 258.01-258.03)(Use additional code to identify associated endocrine syndrome, as: carcinoid syndrome: 259.2) ▽
209.11 Malignant carcinoid tumor of the appendix — (Code first any associated multiple endocrine neoplasia syndrome: 258.01-258.03)(Use additional code to identify associated endocrine syndrome, as: carcinoid syndrome: 259.2)
209.12 Malignant carcinoid tumor of the cecum — (Code first any associated multiple endocrine neoplasia syndrome: 258.01-258.03)(Use additional code to identify associated endocrine syndrome, as: carcinoid syndrome: 259.2)
209.13 Malignant carcinoid tumor of the ascending colon — (Code first any associated multiple endocrine neoplasia syndrome: 258.01-258.03)(Use additional code to identify associated endocrine syndrome, as: carcinoid syndrome: 259.2)
209.14 Malignant carcinoid tumor of the transverse colon — (Code first any associated multiple endocrine neoplasia syndrome: 258.01-258.03)(Use additional code to identify associated endocrine syndrome, as: carcinoid syndrome: 259.2)

209.15 Malignant carcinoid tumor of the descending colon — (Code first any associated multiple endocrine neoplasia syndrome: 258.01-258.03)(Use additional code to identify associated endocrine syndrome, as: carcinoid syndrome: 259.2)
209.16 Malignant carcinoid tumor of the sigmoid colon — (Code first any associated multiple endocrine neoplasia syndrome: 258.01-258.03)(Use additional code to identify associated endocrine syndrome, as: carcinoid syndrome: 259.2)
209.27 Malignant carcinoid tumor of hindgut, not otherwise specified — (Code first any associated multiple endocrine neoplasia syndrome: 258.01-258.03)(Use additional code to identify associated endocrine syndrome, as: carcinoid syndrome: 259.2)
209.29 Malignant carcinoid tumor of other sites — (Code first any associated multiple endocrine neoplasia syndrome: 258.01-258.03)(Use additional code to identify associated endocrine syndrome, as: carcinoid syndrome: 259.2)
209.30 Malignant poorly differentiated neuroendocrine carcinoma, any site — (Code first any associated multiple endocrine neoplasia syndrome: 258.01-258.03)(Use additional code to identify associated endocrine syndrome, as: carcinoid syndrome: 259.2) ▽
209.50 Benign carcinoid tumor of the large intestine, unspecified portion — (Code first any associated multiple endocrine neoplasia syndrome: 258.01-258.03)(Use additional code to identify associated endocrine syndrome, as: carcinoid syndrome: 259.2) ▽
209.51 Benign carcinoid tumor of the appendix — (Code first any associated multiple endocrine neoplasia syndrome: 258.01-258.03)(Use additional code to identify associated endocrine syndrome, as: carcinoid syndrome: 259.2)
209.52 Benign carcinoid tumor of the cecum — (Code first any associated multiple endocrine neoplasia syndrome: 258.01-258.03)(Use additional code to identify associated endocrine syndrome, as: carcinoid syndrome: 259.2)
209.53 Benign carcinoid tumor of the ascending colon — (Code first any associated multiple endocrine neoplasia syndrome: 258.01-258.03)(Use additional code to identify associated endocrine syndrome, as: carcinoid syndrome: 259.2)
209.54 Benign carcinoid tumor of the transverse colon — (Code first any associated multiple endocrine neoplasia syndrome: 258.01-258.03)(Use additional code to identify associated endocrine syndrome, as: carcinoid syndrome: 259.2)
209.55 Benign carcinoid tumor of the descending colon — (Code first any associated multiple endocrine neoplasia syndrome: 258.01-258.03)(Use additional code to identify associated endocrine syndrome, as: carcinoid syndrome: 259.2)
209.56 Benign carcinoid tumor of the sigmoid colon — (Code first any associated multiple endocrine neoplasia syndrome: 258.01-258.03)(Use additional code to identify associated endocrine syndrome, as: carcinoid syndrome: 259.2)
209.57 Benign carcinoid tumor of the rectum — (Code first any associated multiple endocrine neoplasia syndrome: 258.01-258.03)(Use additional code to identify associated endocrine syndrome, as: carcinoid syndrome: 259.2)
209.69 Benign carcinoid tumor of other sites — (Code first any associated multiple endocrine neoplasia syndrome: 258.01-258.03)(Use additional code to identify associated endocrine syndrome, as: carcinoid syndrome: 259.2)
211.3 Benign neoplasm of colon
211.4 Benign neoplasm of rectum and anal canal
230.3 Carcinoma in situ of colon
230.4 Carcinoma in situ of rectum
230.7 Carcinoma in situ of other and unspecified parts of intestine ▽
235.2 Neoplasm of uncertain behavior of stomach, intestines, and rectum
239.0 Neoplasm of unspecified nature of digestive system
556.0 Ulcerative (chronic) enterocolitis
556.1 Ulcerative (chronic) ileocolitis
556.2 Ulcerative (chronic) proctitis
556.3 Ulcerative (chronic) proctosigmoiditis
556.4 Pseudopolyposis of colon
556.5 Left sided ulcerative (chronic) colitis
556.6 Universal ulcerative (chronic) colitis
556.8 Other ulcerative colitis
556.9 Unspecified ulcerative colitis ▽
557.0 Acute vascular insufficiency of intestine
557.1 Chronic vascular insufficiency of intestine
557.9 Unspecified vascular insufficiency of intestine ▽
558.42 Eosinophilic colitis
558.9 Other and unspecified noninfectious gastroenteritis and colitis ▽
560.9 Unspecified intestinal obstruction ▽
562.10 Diverticulosis of colon (without mention of hemorrhage) — (Use additional code to identify any associated peritonitis: 567.0-567.9)
562.11 Diverticulitis of colon (without mention of hemorrhage) — (Use additional code to identify any associated peritonitis: 567.0-567.9)
562.12 Diverticulosis of colon with hemorrhage — (Use additional code to identify any associated peritonitis: 567.0-567.9)
562.13 Diverticulitis of colon with hemorrhage — (Use additional code to identify any associated peritonitis: 567.0-567.9)
564.7 Megacolon, other than Hirschsprung's
564.81 Neurogenic bowel
564.89 Other functional disorders of intestine
567.0 Peritonitis in infectious diseases classified elsewhere — (Code first underlying disease) ☒
567.1 Pneumococcal peritonitis
567.21 Peritonitis (acute) generalized
567.22 Peritoneal abscess
567.23 Spontaneous bacterial peritonitis
567.29 Other suppurative peritonitis
567.31 Psoas muscle abscess
567.38 Other retroperitoneal abscess
567.39 Other retroperitoneal infections
567.81 Choleperitonitis
567.82 Sclerosing mesenteritis
567.89 Other specified peritonitis
567.9 Unspecified peritonitis ▽
569.82 Ulceration of intestine
569.83 Perforation of intestine
569.89 Other specified disorder of intestines
569.9 Unspecified disorder of intestine ▽
578.1 Blood in stool
578.9 Hemorrhage of gastrointestinal tract, unspecified ▽
751.3 Hirschsprung's disease and other congenital functional disorders of colon
777.1 Fetal and newborn meconium obstruction — (Use additional code(s) to further specify condition)
777.50 Necrotizing enterocolitis in newborn, unspecified ▽
777.51 Stage I necrotizing enterocolitis in newborn
777.52 Stage II necrotizing enterocolitis in newborn
777.53 Stage III necrotizing enterocolitis in newborn
777.6 Perinatal intestinal perforation — (Use additional code(s) to further specify condition)
777.8 Other specified perinatal disorder of digestive system — (Use additional code(s) to further specify condition)
863.40 Colon injury unspecified site, without mention of open wound into cavity ▽
863.41 Ascending (right) colon injury without mention of open wound into cavity
863.42 Transverse colon injury without mention of open wound into cavity
863.43 Descending (left) colon injury without mention of open wound into cavity
863.44 Sigmoid colon injury without mention of open wound into cavity
863.45 Rectum injury without mention of open wound into cavity
863.46 Injury to multiple sites in colon and rectum without mention of open wound into cavity
863.49 Other colon and rectum injury, without mention of open wound into cavity
998.89 Other specified complications

ICD-9-CM Procedural

45.81 Laparoscopic total intra-abdominal colectomy
45.95 Anastomosis to anus
46.01 Exteriorization of small intestine
46.23 Other permanent ileostomy

44212

44212 Laparoscopy, surgical; colectomy, total, abdominal, with proctectomy, with ileostomy

ICD-9-CM Diagnostic

153.0 Malignant neoplasm of hepatic flexure
153.1 Malignant neoplasm of transverse colon
153.2 Malignant neoplasm of descending colon
153.3 Malignant neoplasm of sigmoid colon
153.4 Malignant neoplasm of cecum
153.5 Malignant neoplasm of appendix
153.6 Malignant neoplasm of ascending colon
153.7 Malignant neoplasm of splenic flexure
153.8 Malignant neoplasm of other specified sites of large intestine
153.9 Malignant neoplasm of colon, unspecified site ▽
154.0 Malignant neoplasm of rectosigmoid junction
154.1 Malignant neoplasm of rectum
197.5 Secondary malignant neoplasm of large intestine and rectum
209.10 Malignant carcinoid tumor of the large intestine, unspecified portion — (Code first any associated multiple endocrine neoplasia syndrome: 258.01-258.03)(Use additional code to identify associated endocrine syndrome, as: carcinoid syndrome: 259.2) ▽
209.11 Malignant carcinoid tumor of the appendix — (Code first any associated multiple endocrine neoplasia syndrome: 258.01-258.03)(Use additional code to identify associated endocrine syndrome, as: carcinoid syndrome: 259.2)
209.12 Malignant carcinoid tumor of the cecum — (Code first any associated multiple endocrine neoplasia syndrome: 258.01-258.03)(Use additional code to identify associated endocrine syndrome, as: carcinoid syndrome: 259.2)
209.13 Malignant carcinoid tumor of the ascending colon — (Code first any associated multiple endocrine neoplasia syndrome: 258.01-258.03)(Use additional code to identify associated endocrine syndrome, as: carcinoid syndrome: 259.2)
209.14 Malignant carcinoid tumor of the transverse colon — (Code first any associated multiple endocrine neoplasia syndrome: 258.01-258.03)(Use additional code to identify associated endocrine syndrome, as: carcinoid syndrome: 259.2)
209.15 Malignant carcinoid tumor of the descending colon — (Code first any associated multiple endocrine neoplasia syndrome: 258.01-258.03)(Use additional code to identify associated endocrine syndrome, as: carcinoid syndrome: 259.2)
209.16 Malignant carcinoid tumor of the sigmoid colon — (Code first any associated multiple endocrine neoplasia syndrome: 258.01-258.03)(Use additional code to identify associated endocrine syndrome, as: carcinoid syndrome: 259.2)
209.27 Malignant carcinoid tumor of hindgut, not otherwise specified — (Code first any associated multiple endocrine neoplasia syndrome: 258.01-258.03)(Use additional code to identify associated endocrine syndrome, as: carcinoid syndrome: 259.2)
209.29 Malignant carcinoid tumor of other sites — (Code first any associated multiple endocrine neoplasia syndrome: 258.01-258.03)(Use additional code to identify associated endocrine syndrome, as: carcinoid syndrome: 259.2)
209.30 Malignant poorly differentiated neuroendocrine carcinoma, any site — (Code first any associated multiple endocrine neoplasia syndrome: 258.01-258.03)(Use additional code to identify associated endocrine syndrome, as: carcinoid syndrome: 259.2) ▽
209.50 Benign carcinoid tumor of the large intestine, unspecified portion — (Code first any associated multiple endocrine neoplasia syndrome: 258.01-258.03)(Use additional code to identify associated endocrine syndrome, as: carcinoid syndrome: 259.2) ▽
209.51 Benign carcinoid tumor of the appendix — (Code first any associated multiple endocrine neoplasia syndrome: 258.01-258.03)(Use additional code to identify associated endocrine syndrome, as: carcinoid syndrome: 259.2)
209.52 Benign carcinoid tumor of the cecum — (Code first any associated multiple endocrine neoplasia syndrome: 258.01-258.03)(Use additional code to identify associated endocrine syndrome, as: carcinoid syndrome: 259.2)
209.53 Benign carcinoid tumor of the ascending colon — (Code first any associated multiple endocrine neoplasia syndrome: 258.01-258.03)(Use additional code to identify associated endocrine syndrome, as: carcinoid syndrome: 259.2)
209.54 Benign carcinoid tumor of the transverse colon — (Code first any associated multiple endocrine neoplasia syndrome: 258.01-258.03)(Use additional code to identify associated endocrine syndrome, as: carcinoid syndrome: 259.2)
209.55 Benign carcinoid tumor of the descending colon — (Code first any associated multiple endocrine neoplasia syndrome: 258.01-258.03)(Use additional code to identify associated endocrine syndrome, as: carcinoid syndrome: 259.2)
209.56 Benign carcinoid tumor of the sigmoid colon — (Code first any associated multiple endocrine neoplasia syndrome: 258.01-258.03)(Use additional code to identify associated endocrine syndrome, as: carcinoid syndrome: 259.2)
209.57 Benign carcinoid tumor of the rectum — (Code first any associated multiple endocrine neoplasia syndrome: 258.01-258.03)(Use additional code to identify associated endocrine syndrome, as: carcinoid syndrome: 259.2)
209.69 Benign carcinoid tumor of other sites — (Code first any associated multiple endocrine neoplasia syndrome: 258.01-258.03)(Use additional code to identify associated endocrine syndrome, as: carcinoid syndrome: 259.2)
211.3 Benign neoplasm of colon
211.4 Benign neoplasm of rectum and anal canal
230.3 Carcinoma in situ of colon
230.4 Carcinoma in situ of rectum
230.7 Carcinoma in situ of other and unspecified parts of intestine ▽
235.2 Neoplasm of uncertain behavior of stomach, intestines, and rectum
239.0 Neoplasm of unspecified nature of digestive system
555.1 Regional enteritis of large intestine
556.0 Ulcerative (chronic) enterocolitis
556.1 Ulcerative (chronic) ileocolitis
556.2 Ulcerative (chronic) proctitis
556.3 Ulcerative (chronic) proctosigmoiditis
556.4 Pseudopolyposis of colon
556.5 Left sided ulcerative (chronic) colitis
556.6 Universal ulcerative (chronic) colitis
556.8 Other ulcerative colitis
556.9 Unspecified ulcerative colitis ▽
557.0 Acute vascular insufficiency of intestine
557.1 Chronic vascular insufficiency of intestine
557.9 Unspecified vascular insufficiency of intestine ▽
560.9 Unspecified intestinal obstruction ▽
562.10 Diverticulosis of colon (without mention of hemorrhage) — (Use additional code to identify any associated peritonitis: 567.0-567.9)
562.11 Diverticulitis of colon (without mention of hemorrhage) — (Use additional code to identify any associated peritonitis: 567.0-567.9)
562.12 Diverticulosis of colon with hemorrhage — (Use additional code to identify any associated peritonitis: 567.0-567.9)
562.13 Diverticulitis of colon with hemorrhage — (Use additional code to identify any associated peritonitis: 567.0-567.9)
567.0 Peritonitis in infectious diseases classified elsewhere — (Code first underlying disease) ☒
567.1 Pneumococcal peritonitis
567.21 Peritonitis (acute) generalized
567.22 Peritoneal abscess
567.23 Spontaneous bacterial peritonitis
567.29 Other suppurative peritonitis
567.31 Psoas muscle abscess
567.38 Other retroperitoneal abscess
567.39 Other retroperitoneal infections
567.81 Choleperitonitis
567.82 Sclerosing mesenteritis
567.89 Other specified peritonitis
567.9 Unspecified peritonitis ▽
569.82 Ulceration of intestine
569.83 Perforation of intestine
569.89 Other specified disorder of intestines
578.1 Blood in stool
751.2 Congenital atresia and stenosis of large intestine, rectum, and anal canal

751.3 Hirschsprung's disease and other congenital functional disorders of colon
777.1 Fetal and newborn meconium obstruction — (Use additional code(s) to further specify condition)
777.50 Necrotizing enterocolitis in newborn, unspecified
777.51 Stage I necrotizing enterocolitis in newborn
777.52 Stage II necrotizing enterocolitis in newborn
777.53 Stage III necrotizing enterocolitis in newborn
777.6 Perinatal intestinal perforation — (Use additional code(s) to further specify condition)
863.40 Colon injury unspecified site, without mention of open wound into cavity
863.41 Ascending (right) colon injury without mention of open wound into cavity
863.42 Transverse colon injury without mention of open wound into cavity
863.43 Descending (left) colon injury without mention of open wound into cavity
863.44 Sigmoid colon injury without mention of open wound into cavity
863.45 Rectum injury without mention of open wound into cavity
863.46 Injury to multiple sites in colon and rectum without mention of open wound into cavity
863.49 Other colon and rectum injury, without mention of open wound into cavity
998.89 Other specified complications

ICD-9-CM Procedural

17.32 Laparoscopic cecectomy
17.34 Laparoscopic resection of transverse colon
45.81 Laparoscopic total intra-abdominal colectomy
46.23 Other permanent ileostomy
48.51 Laparoscopic abdominoperineal resection of the rectum

44213

44213 Laparoscopy, surgical, mobilization (take-down) of splenic flexure performed in conjunction with partial colectomy (List separately in addition to primary procedure)

ICD-9-CM Diagnostic

153.0 Malignant neoplasm of hepatic flexure
153.1 Malignant neoplasm of transverse colon
153.2 Malignant neoplasm of descending colon
153.3 Malignant neoplasm of sigmoid colon
153.4 Malignant neoplasm of cecum
153.6 Malignant neoplasm of ascending colon
153.7 Malignant neoplasm of splenic flexure
153.8 Malignant neoplasm of other specified sites of large intestine
153.9 Malignant neoplasm of colon, unspecified site
154.0 Malignant neoplasm of rectosigmoid junction
154.1 Malignant neoplasm of rectum
154.2 Malignant neoplasm of anal canal
154.3 Malignant neoplasm of anus, unspecified site
154.8 Malignant neoplasm of other sites of rectum, rectosigmoid junction, and anus
197.5 Secondary malignant neoplasm of large intestine and rectum
209.10 Malignant carcinoid tumor of the large intestine, unspecified portion — (Code first any associated multiple endocrine neoplasia syndrome: 258.01-258.03)(Use additional code to identify associated endocrine syndrome, as: carcinoid syndrome: 259.2)
209.11 Malignant carcinoid tumor of the appendix — (Code first any associated multiple endocrine neoplasia syndrome: 258.01-258.03)(Use additional code to identify associated endocrine syndrome, as: carcinoid syndrome: 259.2)
209.12 Malignant carcinoid tumor of the cecum — (Code first any associated multiple endocrine neoplasia syndrome: 258.01-258.03)(Use additional code to identify associated endocrine syndrome, as: carcinoid syndrome: 259.2)
209.13 Malignant carcinoid tumor of the ascending colon — (Code first any associated multiple endocrine neoplasia syndrome: 258.01-258.03)(Use additional code to identify associated endocrine syndrome, as: carcinoid syndrome: 259.2)
209.14 Malignant carcinoid tumor of the transverse colon — (Code first any associated multiple endocrine neoplasia syndrome: 258.01-258.03)(Use additional code to identify associated endocrine syndrome, as: carcinoid syndrome: 259.2)
209.15 Malignant carcinoid tumor of the descending colon — (Code first any associated multiple endocrine neoplasia syndrome: 258.01-258.03)(Use additional code to identify associated endocrine syndrome, as: carcinoid syndrome: 259.2)
209.16 Malignant carcinoid tumor of the sigmoid colon — (Code first any associated multiple endocrine neoplasia syndrome: 258.01-258.03)(Use additional code to identify associated endocrine syndrome, as: carcinoid syndrome: 259.2)
209.27 Malignant carcinoid tumor of hindgut, not otherwise specified — (Code first any associated multiple endocrine neoplasia syndrome: 258.01-258.03)(Use additional code to identify associated endocrine syndrome, as: carcinoid syndrome: 259.2)
209.29 Malignant carcinoid tumor of other sites — (Code first any associated multiple endocrine neoplasia syndrome: 258.01-258.03)(Use additional code to identify associated endocrine syndrome, as: carcinoid syndrome: 259.2)
209.30 Malignant poorly differentiated neuroendocrine carcinoma, any site — (Code first any associated multiple endocrine neoplasia syndrome: 258.01-258.03)(Use additional code to identify associated endocrine syndrome, as: carcinoid syndrome: 259.2)
209.50 Benign carcinoid tumor of the large intestine, unspecified portion — (Code first any associated multiple endocrine neoplasia syndrome: 258.01-258.03)(Use additional code to identify associated endocrine syndrome, as: carcinoid syndrome: 259.2)
209.51 Benign carcinoid tumor of the appendix — (Code first any associated multiple endocrine neoplasia syndrome: 258.01-258.03)(Use additional code to identify associated endocrine syndrome, as: carcinoid syndrome: 259.2)
209.52 Benign carcinoid tumor of the cecum — (Code first any associated multiple endocrine neoplasia syndrome: 258.01-258.03)(Use additional code to identify associated endocrine syndrome, as: carcinoid syndrome: 259.2)
209.53 Benign carcinoid tumor of the ascending colon — (Code first any associated multiple endocrine neoplasia syndrome: 258.01-258.03)(Use additional code to identify associated endocrine syndrome, as: carcinoid syndrome: 259.2)
209.54 Benign carcinoid tumor of the transverse colon — (Code first any associated multiple endocrine neoplasia syndrome: 258.01-258.03)(Use additional code to identify associated endocrine syndrome, as: carcinoid syndrome: 259.2)
209.55 Benign carcinoid tumor of the descending colon — (Code first any associated multiple endocrine neoplasia syndrome: 258.01-258.03)(Use additional code to identify associated endocrine syndrome, as: carcinoid syndrome: 259.2)
209.56 Benign carcinoid tumor of the sigmoid colon — (Code first any associated multiple endocrine neoplasia syndrome: 258.01-258.03)(Use additional code to identify associated endocrine syndrome, as: carcinoid syndrome: 259.2)
209.57 Benign carcinoid tumor of the rectum — (Code first any associated multiple endocrine neoplasia syndrome: 258.01-258.03)(Use additional code to identify associated endocrine syndrome, as: carcinoid syndrome: 259.2)
209.69 Benign carcinoid tumor of other sites — (Code first any associated multiple endocrine neoplasia syndrome: 258.01-258.03)(Use additional code to identify associated endocrine syndrome, as: carcinoid syndrome: 259.2)
211.3 Benign neoplasm of colon
211.4 Benign neoplasm of rectum and anal canal
211.9 Benign neoplasm of other and unspecified site of the digestive system
229.9 Benign neoplasm of unspecified site
230.3 Carcinoma in situ of colon
235.2 Neoplasm of uncertain behavior of stomach, intestines, and rectum
239.0 Neoplasm of unspecified nature of digestive system
550.00 Inguinal hernia with gangrene, unilateral or unspecified, (not specified as recurrent)
551.1 Umbilical hernia with gangrene
552.8 Hernia of other specified site, with obstruction
555.1 Regional enteritis of large intestine
555.2 Regional enteritis of small intestine with large intestine
556.0 Ulcerative (chronic) enterocolitis
556.1 Ulcerative (chronic) ileocolitis
556.2 Ulcerative (chronic) proctitis
556.3 Ulcerative (chronic) proctosigmoiditis
556.8 Other ulcerative colitis
557.0 Acute vascular insufficiency of intestine
557.1 Chronic vascular insufficiency of intestine

557.9 Unspecified vascular insufficiency of intestine ▽
558.1 Gastroenteritis and colitis due to radiation
558.2 Toxic gastroenteritis and colitis — (Use additional E code to identify cause)
558.42 Eosinophilic colitis
558.9 Other and unspecified noninfectious gastroenteritis and colitis ▽
560.0 Intussusception
560.1 Paralytic ileus
560.2 Volvulus
560.31 Gallstone ileus
560.39 Impaction of intestine, other
560.81 Intestinal or peritoneal adhesions with obstruction (postoperative) (postinfection)
560.89 Other specified intestinal obstruction
560.9 Unspecified intestinal obstruction ▽
562.10 Diverticulosis of colon (without mention of hemorrhage) — (Use additional code to identify any associated peritonitis: 567.0-567.9)
562.11 Diverticulitis of colon (without mention of hemorrhage) — (Use additional code to identify any associated peritonitis: 567.0-567.9)
562.12 Diverticulosis of colon with hemorrhage — (Use additional code to identify any associated peritonitis: 567.0-567.9)
562.13 Diverticulitis of colon with hemorrhage — (Use additional code to identify any associated peritonitis: 567.0-567.9)
564.7 Megacolon, other than Hirschsprung's
567.0 Peritonitis in infectious diseases classified elsewhere — (Code first underlying disease) ☒
567.1 Pneumococcal peritonitis
567.21 Peritonitis (acute) generalized
567.22 Peritoneal abscess
567.23 Spontaneous bacterial peritonitis
567.29 Other suppurative peritonitis
567.31 Psoas muscle abscess
567.38 Other retroperitoneal abscess
567.39 Other retroperitoneal infections
567.81 Choleperitonitis
567.82 Sclerosing mesenteritis
567.89 Other specified peritonitis
567.9 Unspecified peritonitis ▽
569.44 Dysplasia of anus
569.81 Fistula of intestine, excluding rectum and anus
569.82 Ulceration of intestine
569.83 Perforation of intestine
569.84 Angiodysplasia of intestine (without mention of hemorrhage)
569.85 Angiodysplasia of intestine with hemorrhage
569.89 Other specified disorder of intestines
569.9 Unspecified disorder of intestine ▽
578.9 Hemorrhage of gastrointestinal tract, unspecified ▽
596.1 Intestinovesical fistula — (Use additional code to identify urinary incontinence: 625.6, 788.30-788.39)
619.1 Digestive-genital tract fistula, female ♀
751.5 Other congenital anomalies of intestine
751.8 Other specified congenital anomalies of digestive system
751.9 Unspecified congenital anomaly of digestive system ▽

ICD-9-CM Procedural

46.82 Intra-abdominal manipulation of large intestine

44227

44227 Laparoscopy, surgical, closure of enterostomy, large or small intestine, with resection and anastomosis

ICD-9-CM Diagnostic

560.81 Intestinal or peritoneal adhesions with obstruction (postoperative) (postinfection)
569.61 Infection of colostomy or enterostomy — (Use additional code to identify organism: 041.00-041.9. Use additional code to specify type of infection: 038.0-038.9, 682.2)
569.62 Mechanical complication of colostomy and enterostomy
569.69 Other complication of colostomy or enterostomy
V10.05 Personal history of malignant neoplasm of large intestine
V10.06 Personal history of malignant neoplasm of rectum, rectosigmoid junction, and anus
V10.09 Personal history of malignant neoplasm of other site in gastrointestinal tract
V55.2 Attention to ileostomy
V55.3 Attention to colostomy
V55.4 Attention to other artificial opening of digestive tract

ICD-9-CM Procedural

46.51 Closure of stoma of small intestine
46.52 Closure of stoma of large intestine

44300

44300 Placement, enterostomy or cecostomy, tube open (eg, for feeding or decompression) (separate procedure)

ICD-9-CM Diagnostic

150.5 Malignant neoplasm of lower third of esophagus
150.8 Malignant neoplasm of other specified part of esophagus
150.9 Malignant neoplasm of esophagus, unspecified site ▽
151.0 Malignant neoplasm of cardia
151.1 Malignant neoplasm of pylorus
151.2 Malignant neoplasm of pyloric antrum
151.3 Malignant neoplasm of fundus of stomach
151.4 Malignant neoplasm of body of stomach
151.5 Malignant neoplasm of lesser curvature of stomach, unspecified ▽
151.6 Malignant neoplasm of greater curvature of stomach, unspecified ▽
151.8 Malignant neoplasm of other specified sites of stomach
151.9 Malignant neoplasm of stomach, unspecified site ▽
152.9 Malignant neoplasm of small intestine, unspecified site ▽
153.3 Malignant neoplasm of sigmoid colon
153.4 Malignant neoplasm of cecum
153.5 Malignant neoplasm of appendix
153.6 Malignant neoplasm of ascending colon
153.7 Malignant neoplasm of splenic flexure
153.8 Malignant neoplasm of other specified sites of large intestine
153.9 Malignant neoplasm of colon, unspecified site ▽
154.0 Malignant neoplasm of rectosigmoid junction
195.2 Malignant neoplasm of abdomen
197.4 Secondary malignant neoplasm of small intestine including duodenum
197.8 Secondary malignant neoplasm of other digestive organs and spleen
209.00 Malignant carcinoid tumor of the small intestine, unspecified portion — (Code first any associated multiple endocrine neoplasia syndrome: 258.01-258.03)(Use additional code to identify associated endocrine syndrome, as: carcinoid syndrome: 259.2) ▽
209.10 Malignant carcinoid tumor of the large intestine, unspecified portion — (Code first any associated multiple endocrine neoplasia syndrome: 258.01-258.03)(Use additional code to identify associated endocrine syndrome, as: carcinoid syndrome: 259.2) ▽
209.11 Malignant carcinoid tumor of the appendix — (Code first any associated multiple endocrine neoplasia syndrome: 258.01-258.03)(Use additional code to identify associated endocrine syndrome, as: carcinoid syndrome: 259.2)

209.12 Malignant carcinoid tumor of the cecum — (Code first any associated multiple endocrine neoplasia syndrome: 258.01-258.03)(Use additional code to identify associated endocrine syndrome, as: carcinoid syndrome: 259.2)

209.13 Malignant carcinoid tumor of the ascending colon — (Code first any associated multiple endocrine neoplasia syndrome: 258.01-258.03)(Use additional code to identify associated endocrine syndrome, as: carcinoid syndrome: 259.2)

209.14 Malignant carcinoid tumor of the transverse colon — (Code first any associated multiple endocrine neoplasia syndrome: 258.01-258.03)(Use additional code to identify associated endocrine syndrome, as: carcinoid syndrome: 259.2)

209.15 Malignant carcinoid tumor of the descending colon — (Code first any associated multiple endocrine neoplasia syndrome: 258.01-258.03)(Use additional code to identify associated endocrine syndrome, as: carcinoid syndrome: 259.2)

209.16 Malignant carcinoid tumor of the sigmoid colon — (Code first any associated multiple endocrine neoplasia syndrome: 258.01-258.03)(Use additional code to identify associated endocrine syndrome, as: carcinoid syndrome: 259.2)

209.23 Malignant carcinoid tumor of the stomach — (Code first any associated multiple endocrine neoplasia syndrome: 258.01-258.03)(Use additional code to identify associated endocrine syndrome, as: carcinoid syndrome: 259.2)

209.25 Malignant carcinoid tumor of foregut, not otherwise specified — (Code first any associated multiple endocrine neoplasia syndrome: 258.01-258.03)(Use additional code to identify associated endocrine syndrome, as: carcinoid syndrome: 259.2)

209.29 Malignant carcinoid tumor of other sites — (Code first any associated multiple endocrine neoplasia syndrome: 258.01-258.03)(Use additional code to identify associated endocrine syndrome, as: carcinoid syndrome: 259.2)

209.30 Malignant poorly differentiated neuroendocrine carcinoma, any site — (Code first any associated multiple endocrine neoplasia syndrome: 258.01-258.03)(Use additional code to identify associated endocrine syndrome, as: carcinoid syndrome: 259.2) ▽

263.0 Malnutrition of moderate degree

263.1 Malnutrition of mild degree

263.2 Arrested development following protein-calorie malnutrition

263.8 Other protein-calorie malnutrition

263.9 Unspecified protein-calorie malnutrition ▽

330.8 Other specified cerebral degenerations in childhood — (Use additional code to identify associated intellectual disabilities)

348.1 Anoxic brain damage — (Use additional E code to identify cause)

436 Acute, but ill-defined, cerebrovascular disease — (Use additional code to identify presence of hypertension) ▽

530.11 Reflux esophagitis — (Use additional E code to identify cause, if induced by chemical)

530.12 Acute esophagitis — (Use additional E code to identify cause, if induced by chemical)

530.19 Other esophagitis — (Use additional E code to identify cause, if induced by chemical)

530.20 Ulcer of esophagus without bleeding — (Use additional E code to identify cause, if induced by chemical or drug)

530.21 Ulcer of esophagus with bleeding — (Use additional E code to identify cause, if induced by chemical or drug)

530.3 Stricture and stenosis of esophagus

530.4 Perforation of esophagus

530.5 Dyskinesia of esophagus

530.6 Diverticulum of esophagus, acquired

530.7 Gastroesophageal laceration-hemorrhage syndrome

530.81 Esophageal reflux

530.82 Esophageal hemorrhage

530.83 Esophageal leukoplakia

530.84 Tracheoesophageal fistula

530.85 Barrett's esophagus

530.89 Other specified disorder of the esophagus

531.00 Acute gastric ulcer with hemorrhage, without mention of obstruction — (Use additional E code to identify drug, if drug induced)

531.01 Acute gastric ulcer with hemorrhage and obstruction — (Use additional E code to identify drug, if drug induced)

531.10 Acute gastric ulcer with perforation, without mention of obstruction — (Use additional E code to identify drug, if drug induced)

531.11 Acute gastric ulcer with perforation and obstruction — (Use additional E code to identify drug, if drug induced)

531.20 Acute gastric ulcer with hemorrhage and perforation, without mention of obstruction — (Use additional E code to identify drug, if drug induced)

531.21 Acute gastric ulcer with hemorrhage, perforation, and obstruction — (Use additional E code to identify drug, if drug induced)

531.30 Acute gastric ulcer without mention of hemorrhage, perforation, or obstruction — (Use additional E code to identify drug, if drug induced)

531.31 Acute gastric ulcer without mention of hemorrhage or perforation, with obstruction — (Use additional E code to identify drug, if drug induced)

531.40 Chronic or unspecified gastric ulcer with hemorrhage, without mention of obstruction — (Use additional E code to identify drug, if drug induced)

531.41 Chronic or unspecified gastric ulcer with hemorrhage and obstruction — (Use additional E code to identify drug, if drug induced)

531.50 Chronic or unspecified gastric ulcer with perforation, without mention of obstruction — (Use additional E code to identify drug, if drug induced)

531.51 Chronic or unspecified gastric ulcer with perforation and obstruction — (Use additional E code to identify drug, if drug induced)

531.60 Chronic or unspecified gastric ulcer with hemorrhage and perforation, without mention of obstruction — (Use additional E code to identify drug, if drug induced)

531.61 Chronic or unspecified gastric ulcer with hemorrhage, perforation, and obstruction — (Use additional E code to identify drug, if drug induced)

531.70 Chronic gastric ulcer without mention of hemorrhage, perforation, without mention of obstruction — (Use additional E code to identify drug, if drug induced)

531.71 Chronic gastric ulcer without mention of hemorrhage or perforation, with obstruction — (Use additional E code to identify drug, if drug induced)

531.90 Gastric ulcer, unspecified as acute or chronic, without mention of hemorrhage, perforation, or obstruction — (Use additional E code to identify drug, if drug induced) ▽

531.91 Gastric ulcer, unspecified as acute or chronic, without mention of hemorrhage or perforation, with obstruction — (Use additional E code to identify drug, if drug induced) ▽

532.00 Acute duodenal ulcer with hemorrhage, without mention of obstruction — (Use additional E code to identify drug, if drug induced)

532.01 Acute duodenal ulcer with hemorrhage and obstruction — (Use additional E code to identify drug, if drug induced)

532.10 Acute duodenal ulcer with perforation, without mention of obstruction — (Use additional E code to identify drug, if drug induced)

532.11 Acute duodenal ulcer with perforation and obstruction — (Use additional E code to identify drug, if drug induced)

532.20 Acute duodenal ulcer with hemorrhage and perforation, without mention of obstruction — (Use additional E code to identify drug, if drug induced)

532.21 Acute duodenal ulcer with hemorrhage, perforation, and obstruction — (Use additional E code to identify drug, if drug induced)

532.30 Acute duodenal ulcer without mention of hemorrhage, perforation, or obstruction — (Use additional E code to identify drug, if drug induced)

532.31 Acute duodenal ulcer without mention of hemorrhage or perforation, with obstruction — (Use additional E code to identify drug, if drug induced)

532.40 Duodenal ulcer, chronic or unspecified, with hemorrhage, without mention of obstruction — (Use additional E code to identify drug, if drug induced)

532.41 Chronic or unspecified duodenal ulcer with hemorrhage and obstruction — (Use additional E code to identify drug, if drug induced)

532.50 Chronic or unspecified duodenal ulcer with perforation, without mention of obstruction — (Use additional E code to identify drug, if drug induced)

532.60 Chronic or unspecified duodenal ulcer with hemorrhage and perforation, without mention of obstruction — (Use additional E code to identify drug, if drug induced)

532.61 Chronic or unspecified duodenal ulcer with hemorrhage, perforation, and obstruction — (Use additional E code to identify drug, if drug induced)

532.70 Chronic duodenal ulcer without mention of hemorrhage, perforation, or obstruction — (Use additional E code to identify drug, if drug induced)

532.71 Chronic duodenal ulcer without mention of hemorrhage or perforation, with obstruction — (Use additional E code to identify drug, if drug induced)

532.90 Duodenal ulcer, unspecified as acute or chronic, without hemorrhage, perforation, or obstruction — (Use additional E code to identify drug, if drug induced) ♥

532.91 Duodenal ulcer, unspecified as acute or chronic, without mention of hemorrhage or perforation, with obstruction — (Use additional E code to identify drug, if drug induced) ♥

533.00 Acute peptic ulcer, unspecified site, with hemorrhage, without mention of obstruction — (Use additional E code to identify drug, if drug induced) ♥

533.01 Acute peptic ulcer, unspecified site, with hemorrhage and obstruction — (Use additional E code to identify drug, if drug induced) ♥

533.10 Acute peptic ulcer, unspecified site, with perforation, without mention of obstruction — (Use additional E code to identify drug, if drug induced) ♥

533.11 Acute peptic ulcer, unspecified site, with perforation and obstruction — (Use additional E code to identify drug, if drug induced) ♥

533.20 Acute peptic ulcer, unspecified site, with hemorrhage and perforation, without mention of obstruction — (Use additional E code to identify drug, if drug induced) ♥

533.21 Acute peptic ulcer, unspecified site, with hemorrhage, perforation, and obstruction — (Use additional E code to identify drug, if drug induced) ♥

533.30 Acute peptic ulcer, unspecified site, without mention of hemorrhage, perforation, or obstruction — (Use additional E code to identify drug, if drug induced) ♥

533.31 Acute peptic ulcer, unspecified site, without mention of hemorrhage and perforation, with obstruction — (Use additional E code to identify drug, if drug induced) ♥

533.40 Chronic or unspecified peptic ulcer, unspecified site, with hemorrhage, without mention of obstruction — (Use additional E code to identify drug, if drug induced) ♥

533.41 Chronic or unspecified peptic ulcer, unspecified site, with hemorrhage and obstruction — (Use additional E code to identify drug, if drug induced) ♥

533.50 Chronic or unspecified peptic ulcer, unspecified site, with perforation, without mention of obstruction — (Use additional E code to identify drug, if drug induced) ♥

533.51 Chronic or unspecified peptic ulcer, unspecified site, with perforation and obstruction — (Use additional E code to identify drug, if drug induced) ♥

533.60 Chronic or unspecified peptic ulcer, unspecified site, with hemorrhage and perforation, without mention of obstruction — (Use additional E code to identify drug, if drug induced) ♥

533.61 Chronic or unspecified peptic ulcer, unspecified site, with hemorrhage, perforation, and obstruction — (Use additional E code to identify drug, if drug induced) ♥

533.70 Chronic peptic ulcer, unspecified site, without mention of hemorrhage, perforation, or obstruction — (Use additional E code to identify drug, if drug induced) ♥

533.71 Chronic peptic ulcer of unspecified site without mention of hemorrhage or perforation, with obstruction — (Use additional E code to identify drug, if drug induced) ♥

533.90 Peptic ulcer, unspecified site, unspecified as acute or chronic, without mention of hemorrhage, perforation, or obstruction — (Use additional E code to identify drug, if drug induced) ♥

533.91 Peptic ulcer, unspecified site, unspecified as acute or chronic, without mention of hemorrhage or perforation, with obstruction — (Use additional E code to identify drug, if drug induced) ♥

537.4 Fistula of stomach or duodenum

557.0 Acute vascular insufficiency of intestine

560.1 Paralytic ileus

560.2 Volvulus

560.81 Intestinal or peritoneal adhesions with obstruction (postoperative) (postinfection)

560.9 Unspecified intestinal obstruction ♥

564.81 Neurogenic bowel

564.89 Other functional disorders of intestine

569.81 Fistula of intestine, excluding rectum and anus

569.82 Ulceration of intestine

569.83 Perforation of intestine

569.84 Angiodysplasia of intestine (without mention of hemorrhage)

569.85 Angiodysplasia of intestine with hemorrhage

569.89 Other specified disorder of intestines

783.21 Loss of weight — (Use additional code to identify Body Mass Index (BMI), if known: V85.0-V85.54)

783.22 Underweight — (Use additional code to identify Body Mass Index (BMI), if known: V85.0-V85.54)

783.3 Feeding difficulties and mismanagement

783.7 Adult failure to thrive

787.01 Nausea with vomiting

787.04 Bilious emesis

787.20 Dysphagia, unspecified ♥

787.21 Dysphagia, oral phase

787.22 Dysphagia, oropharyngeal phase

787.23 Dysphagia, pharyngeal phase

787.24 Dysphagia, pharyngoesophageal phase

787.29 Other dysphagia

793.4 Nonspecific (abnormal) findings on radiological and other examination of gastrointestinal tract

994.2 Effects of hunger

V85.0 Body Mass Index less than 19, adult

ICD-9-CM Procedural

46.10 Colostomy, not otherwise specified

46.39 Other enterostomy

44310

44310 Ileostomy or jejunostomy, non-tube

ICD-9-CM Diagnostic

153.0 Malignant neoplasm of hepatic flexure

153.1 Malignant neoplasm of transverse colon

153.2 Malignant neoplasm of descending colon

153.3 Malignant neoplasm of sigmoid colon

153.4 Malignant neoplasm of cecum

153.5 Malignant neoplasm of appendix

153.6 Malignant neoplasm of ascending colon

153.7 Malignant neoplasm of splenic flexure

153.8 Malignant neoplasm of other specified sites of large intestine

153.9 Malignant neoplasm of colon, unspecified site ♥

154.0 Malignant neoplasm of rectosigmoid junction

209.10 Malignant carcinoid tumor of the large intestine, unspecified portion — (Code first any associated multiple endocrine neoplasia syndrome: 258.01-258.03)(Use additional code to identify associated endocrine syndrome, as: carcinoid syndrome: 259.2) ♥

209.11 Malignant carcinoid tumor of the appendix — (Code first any associated multiple endocrine neoplasia syndrome: 258.01-258.03)(Use additional code to identify associated endocrine syndrome, as: carcinoid syndrome: 259.2)

209.12 Malignant carcinoid tumor of the cecum — (Code first any associated multiple endocrine neoplasia syndrome: 258.01-258.03)(Use additional code to identify associated endocrine syndrome, as: carcinoid syndrome: 259.2)

209.13 Malignant carcinoid tumor of the ascending colon — (Code first any associated multiple endocrine neoplasia syndrome: 258.01-258.03)(Use additional code to identify associated endocrine syndrome, as: carcinoid syndrome: 259.2)

209.14 Malignant carcinoid tumor of the transverse colon — (Code first any associated multiple endocrine neoplasia syndrome: 258.01-258.03)(Use additional code to identify associated endocrine syndrome, as: carcinoid syndrome: 259.2)

209.15 Malignant carcinoid tumor of the descending colon — (Code first any associated multiple endocrine neoplasia syndrome: 258.01-258.03)(Use additional code to identify associated endocrine syndrome, as: carcinoid syndrome: 259.2)

209.16 Malignant carcinoid tumor of the sigmoid colon — (Code first any associated multiple endocrine neoplasia syndrome: 258.01-258.03)(Use additional code to identify associated endocrine syndrome, as: carcinoid syndrome: 259.2)

209.29 Malignant carcinoid tumor of other sites — (Code first any associated multiple endocrine neoplasia syndrome: 258.01-258.03)(Use additional code to identify associated endocrine syndrome, as: carcinoid syndrome: 259.2)

209.30 Malignant poorly differentiated neuroendocrine carcinoma, any site — (Code first any associated multiple endocrine neoplasia syndrome: 258.01-258.03)(Use additional code to identify associated endocrine syndrome, as: carcinoid syndrome: 259.2) ▽
209.50 Benign carcinoid tumor of the large intestine, unspecified portion — (Code first any associated multiple endocrine neoplasia syndrome: 258.01-258.03)(Use additional code to identify associated endocrine syndrome, as: carcinoid syndrome: 259.2) ▽
209.51 Benign carcinoid tumor of the appendix — (Code first any associated multiple endocrine neoplasia syndrome: 258.01-258.03)(Use additional code to identify associated endocrine syndrome, as: carcinoid syndrome: 259.2)
209.52 Benign carcinoid tumor of the cecum — (Code first any associated multiple endocrine neoplasia syndrome: 258.01-258.03)(Use additional code to identify associated endocrine syndrome, as: carcinoid syndrome: 259.2)
209.53 Benign carcinoid tumor of the ascending colon — (Code first any associated multiple endocrine neoplasia syndrome: 258.01-258.03)(Use additional code to identify associated endocrine syndrome, as: carcinoid syndrome: 259.2)
209.54 Benign carcinoid tumor of the transverse colon — (Code first any associated multiple endocrine neoplasia syndrome: 258.01-258.03)(Use additional code to identify associated endocrine syndrome, as: carcinoid syndrome: 259.2)
209.55 Benign carcinoid tumor of the descending colon — (Code first any associated multiple endocrine neoplasia syndrome: 258.01-258.03)(Use additional code to identify associated endocrine syndrome, as: carcinoid syndrome: 259.2)
209.56 Benign carcinoid tumor of the sigmoid colon — (Code first any associated multiple endocrine neoplasia syndrome: 258.01-258.03)(Use additional code to identify associated endocrine syndrome, as: carcinoid syndrome: 259.2)
209.57 Benign carcinoid tumor of the rectum — (Code first any associated multiple endocrine neoplasia syndrome: 258.01-258.03)(Use additional code to identify associated endocrine syndrome, as: carcinoid syndrome: 259.2)
209.69 Benign carcinoid tumor of other sites — (Code first any associated multiple endocrine neoplasia syndrome: 258.01-258.03)(Use additional code to identify associated endocrine syndrome, as: carcinoid syndrome: 259.2)
211.2 Benign neoplasm of duodenum, jejunum, and ileum
211.3 Benign neoplasm of colon
211.4 Benign neoplasm of rectum and anal canal
230.4 Carcinoma in situ of rectum
230.7 Carcinoma in situ of other and unspecified parts of intestine ▽
235.2 Neoplasm of uncertain behavior of stomach, intestines, and rectum
239.0 Neoplasm of unspecified nature of digestive system
556.0 Ulcerative (chronic) enterocolitis
556.1 Ulcerative (chronic) ileocolitis
556.2 Ulcerative (chronic) proctitis
556.3 Ulcerative (chronic) proctosigmoiditis
556.4 Pseudopolyposis of colon
556.5 Left sided ulcerative (chronic) colitis
556.8 Other ulcerative colitis
556.9 Unspecified ulcerative colitis ▽
557.0 Acute vascular insufficiency of intestine
557.9 Unspecified vascular insufficiency of intestine ▽
560.2 Volvulus
562.10 Diverticulosis of colon (without mention of hemorrhage) — (Use additional code to identify any associated peritonitis: 567.0-567.9)
562.11 Diverticulitis of colon (without mention of hemorrhage) — (Use additional code to identify any associated peritonitis: 567.0-567.9)
562.12 Diverticulosis of colon with hemorrhage — (Use additional code to identify any associated peritonitis: 567.0-567.9)
562.13 Diverticulitis of colon with hemorrhage — (Use additional code to identify any associated peritonitis: 567.0-567.9)
564.7 Megacolon, other than Hirschsprung's
564.81 Neurogenic bowel
564.89 Other functional disorders of intestine
567.0 Peritonitis in infectious diseases classified elsewhere — (Code first underlying disease) ☒
567.1 Pneumococcal peritonitis
567.21 Peritonitis (acute) generalized
567.22 Peritoneal abscess
567.23 Spontaneous bacterial peritonitis
567.29 Other suppurative peritonitis
567.31 Psoas muscle abscess
567.38 Other retroperitoneal abscess
567.39 Other retroperitoneal infections
567.81 Choleperitonitis
567.82 Sclerosing mesenteritis
567.89 Other specified peritonitis
567.9 Unspecified peritonitis ▽
569.82 Ulceration of intestine
569.83 Perforation of intestine
569.89 Other specified disorder of intestines
777.1 Fetal and newborn meconium obstruction — (Use additional code(s) to further specify condition)
777.50 Necrotizing enterocolitis in newborn, unspecified ▽
777.51 Stage I necrotizing enterocolitis in newborn
777.52 Stage II necrotizing enterocolitis in newborn
777.53 Stage III necrotizing enterocolitis in newborn
777.6 Perinatal intestinal perforation — (Use additional code(s) to further specify condition)
863.40 Colon injury unspecified site, without mention of open wound into cavity ▽
863.41 Ascending (right) colon injury without mention of open wound into cavity
863.42 Transverse colon injury without mention of open wound into cavity
863.43 Descending (left) colon injury without mention of open wound into cavity
863.44 Sigmoid colon injury without mention of open wound into cavity
863.45 Rectum injury without mention of open wound into cavity
863.46 Injury to multiple sites in colon and rectum without mention of open wound into cavity
863.49 Other colon and rectum injury, without mention of open wound into cavity
998.89 Other specified complications
V64.41 Laparoscopic surgical procedure converted to open procedure

ICD-9-CM Procedural

46.20 Ileostomy, not otherwise specified
46.21 Temporary ileostomy

44312-44314

44312 Revision of ileostomy; simple (release of superficial scar) (separate procedure)
44314 complicated (reconstruction in-depth) (separate procedure)

ICD-9-CM Diagnostic

560.81 Intestinal or peritoneal adhesions with obstruction (postoperative) (postinfection)
569.60 Unspecified complication of colostomy or enterostomy ▽
569.61 Infection of colostomy or enterostomy — (Use additional code to identify organism: 041.00-041.9. Use additional code to specify type of infection: 038.0-038.9, 682.2)
569.62 Mechanical complication of colostomy and enterostomy
569.69 Other complication of colostomy or enterostomy
997.49 Other digestive system complications
V10.05 Personal history of malignant neoplasm of large intestine
V10.06 Personal history of malignant neoplasm of rectum, rectosigmoid junction, and anus
V44.2 Ileostomy status
V55.2 Attention to ileostomy

ICD-9-CM Procedural

46.40 Revision of intestinal stoma, not otherwise specified
46.41 Revision of stoma of small intestine

44316

44316 Continent ileostomy (Kock procedure) (separate procedure)

ICD-9-CM Diagnostic

153.0 Malignant neoplasm of hepatic flexure
153.1 Malignant neoplasm of transverse colon
153.2 Malignant neoplasm of descending colon
153.4 Malignant neoplasm of cecum
153.5 Malignant neoplasm of appendix
153.6 Malignant neoplasm of ascending colon
153.7 Malignant neoplasm of splenic flexure
153.8 Malignant neoplasm of other specified sites of large intestine
153.9 Malignant neoplasm of colon, unspecified site ▽
154.0 Malignant neoplasm of rectosigmoid junction
197.5 Secondary malignant neoplasm of large intestine and rectum
209.10 Malignant carcinoid tumor of the large intestine, unspecified portion — (Code first any associated multiple endocrine neoplasia syndrome: 258.01-258.03)(Use additional code to identify associated endocrine syndrome, as: carcinoid syndrome: 259.2) ▽
209.11 Malignant carcinoid tumor of the appendix — (Code first any associated multiple endocrine neoplasia syndrome: 258.01-258.03)(Use additional code to identify associated endocrine syndrome, as: carcinoid syndrome: 259.2)
209.12 Malignant carcinoid tumor of the cecum — (Code first any associated multiple endocrine neoplasia syndrome: 258.01-258.03)(Use additional code to identify associated endocrine syndrome, as: carcinoid syndrome: 259.2)
209.13 Malignant carcinoid tumor of the ascending colon — (Code first any associated multiple endocrine neoplasia syndrome: 258.01-258.03)(Use additional code to identify associated endocrine syndrome, as: carcinoid syndrome: 259.2)
209.14 Malignant carcinoid tumor of the transverse colon — (Code first any associated multiple endocrine neoplasia syndrome: 258.01-258.03)(Use additional code to identify associated endocrine syndrome, as: carcinoid syndrome: 259.2)
209.15 Malignant carcinoid tumor of the descending colon — (Code first any associated multiple endocrine neoplasia syndrome: 258.01-258.03)(Use additional code to identify associated endocrine syndrome, as: carcinoid syndrome: 259.2)
209.16 Malignant carcinoid tumor of the sigmoid colon — (Code first any associated multiple endocrine neoplasia syndrome: 258.01-258.03)(Use additional code to identify associated endocrine syndrome, as: carcinoid syndrome: 259.2)
209.29 Malignant carcinoid tumor of other sites — (Code first any associated multiple endocrine neoplasia syndrome: 258.01-258.03)(Use additional code to identify associated endocrine syndrome, as: carcinoid syndrome: 259.2)
209.30 Malignant poorly differentiated neuroendocrine carcinoma, any site — (Code first any associated multiple endocrine neoplasia syndrome: 258.01-258.03)(Use additional code to identify associated endocrine syndrome, as: carcinoid syndrome: 259.2) ▽
209.50 Benign carcinoid tumor of the large intestine, unspecified portion — (Code first any associated multiple endocrine neoplasia syndrome: 258.01-258.03)(Use additional code to identify associated endocrine syndrome, as: carcinoid syndrome: 259.2) ▽
209.51 Benign carcinoid tumor of the appendix — (Code first any associated multiple endocrine neoplasia syndrome: 258.01-258.03)(Use additional code to identify associated endocrine syndrome, as: carcinoid syndrome: 259.2)
209.52 Benign carcinoid tumor of the cecum — (Code first any associated multiple endocrine neoplasia syndrome: 258.01-258.03)(Use additional code to identify associated endocrine syndrome, as: carcinoid syndrome: 259.2)
209.53 Benign carcinoid tumor of the ascending colon — (Code first any associated multiple endocrine neoplasia syndrome: 258.01-258.03)(Use additional code to identify associated endocrine syndrome, as: carcinoid syndrome: 259.2)
209.54 Benign carcinoid tumor of the transverse colon — (Code first any associated multiple endocrine neoplasia syndrome: 258.01-258.03)(Use additional code to identify associated endocrine syndrome, as: carcinoid syndrome: 259.2)
209.55 Benign carcinoid tumor of the descending colon — (Code first any associated multiple endocrine neoplasia syndrome: 258.01-258.03)(Use additional code to identify associated endocrine syndrome, as: carcinoid syndrome: 259.2)
209.56 Benign carcinoid tumor of the sigmoid colon — (Code first any associated multiple endocrine neoplasia syndrome: 258.01-258.03)(Use additional code to identify associated endocrine syndrome, as: carcinoid syndrome: 259.2)
209.57 Benign carcinoid tumor of the rectum — (Code first any associated multiple endocrine neoplasia syndrome: 258.01-258.03)(Use additional code to identify associated endocrine syndrome, as: carcinoid syndrome: 259.2)
209.69 Benign carcinoid tumor of other sites — (Code first any associated multiple endocrine neoplasia syndrome: 258.01-258.03)(Use additional code to identify associated endocrine syndrome, as: carcinoid syndrome: 259.2)
211.3 Benign neoplasm of colon
211.4 Benign neoplasm of rectum and anal canal
230.3 Carcinoma in situ of colon
230.4 Carcinoma in situ of rectum
230.7 Carcinoma in situ of other and unspecified parts of intestine ▽
235.2 Neoplasm of uncertain behavior of stomach, intestines, and rectum
239.0 Neoplasm of unspecified nature of digestive system
556.0 Ulcerative (chronic) enterocolitis
556.1 Ulcerative (chronic) ileocolitis
556.2 Ulcerative (chronic) proctitis
556.3 Ulcerative (chronic) proctosigmoiditis
556.4 Pseudopolyposis of colon
556.5 Left sided ulcerative (chronic) colitis
556.6 Universal ulcerative (chronic) colitis
556.8 Other ulcerative colitis
556.9 Unspecified ulcerative colitis ▽
557.0 Acute vascular insufficiency of intestine
557.1 Chronic vascular insufficiency of intestine
557.9 Unspecified vascular insufficiency of intestine ▽
562.10 Diverticulosis of colon (without mention of hemorrhage) — (Use additional code to identify any associated peritonitis: 567.0-567.9)
562.11 Diverticulitis of colon (without mention of hemorrhage) — (Use additional code to identify any associated peritonitis: 567.0-567.9)
562.12 Diverticulosis of colon with hemorrhage — (Use additional code to identify any associated peritonitis: 567.0-567.9)
562.13 Diverticulitis of colon with hemorrhage — (Use additional code to identify any associated peritonitis: 567.0-567.9)
564.7 Megacolon, other than Hirschsprung's
564.81 Neurogenic bowel
564.89 Other functional disorders of intestine
567.0 Peritonitis in infectious diseases classified elsewhere — (Code first underlying disease) ☒
567.1 Pneumococcal peritonitis
567.21 Peritonitis (acute) generalized
567.22 Peritoneal abscess
567.23 Spontaneous bacterial peritonitis
567.29 Other suppurative peritonitis
567.31 Psoas muscle abscess
567.38 Other retroperitoneal abscess
567.39 Other retroperitoneal infections
567.81 Choleperitonitis
567.82 Sclerosing mesenteritis
567.89 Other specified peritonitis
567.9 Unspecified peritonitis ▽
569.82 Ulceration of intestine
569.83 Perforation of intestine
569.89 Other specified disorder of intestines
777.1 Fetal and newborn meconium obstruction — (Use additional code(s) to further specify condition)
777.50 Necrotizing enterocolitis in newborn, unspecified ▽
777.51 Stage I necrotizing enterocolitis in newborn

777.52 Stage II necrotizing enterocolitis in newborn
777.53 Stage III necrotizing enterocolitis in newborn
777.6 Perinatal intestinal perforation — (Use additional code(s) to further specify condition)
863.40 Colon injury unspecified site, without mention of open wound into cavity ▽
863.41 Ascending (right) colon injury without mention of open wound into cavity
863.42 Transverse colon injury without mention of open wound into cavity
863.43 Descending (left) colon injury without mention of open wound into cavity
863.44 Sigmoid colon injury without mention of open wound into cavity
863.45 Rectum injury without mention of open wound into cavity
863.46 Injury to multiple sites in colon and rectum without mention of open wound into cavity
863.49 Other colon and rectum injury, without mention of open wound into cavity
998.89 Other specified complications

ICD-9-CM Procedural

46.22 Continent ileostomy

44320-44322

44320 Colostomy or skin level cecostomy;
44322 with multiple biopsies (eg, for congenital megacolon) (separate procedure)

ICD-9-CM Diagnostic

151.9 Malignant neoplasm of stomach, unspecified site ▽
152.0 Malignant neoplasm of duodenum
152.1 Malignant neoplasm of jejunum
152.2 Malignant neoplasm of ileum
152.3 Malignant neoplasm of Meckel's diverticulum
152.8 Malignant neoplasm of other specified sites of small intestine
152.9 Malignant neoplasm of small intestine, unspecified site ▽
153.0 Malignant neoplasm of hepatic flexure
153.1 Malignant neoplasm of transverse colon
153.2 Malignant neoplasm of descending colon
153.3 Malignant neoplasm of sigmoid colon
153.4 Malignant neoplasm of cecum
153.9 Malignant neoplasm of colon, unspecified site ▽
154.0 Malignant neoplasm of rectosigmoid junction
154.1 Malignant neoplasm of rectum
154.2 Malignant neoplasm of anal canal
197.4 Secondary malignant neoplasm of small intestine including duodenum
197.5 Secondary malignant neoplasm of large intestine and rectum
199.1 Other malignant neoplasm of unspecified site
209.00 Malignant carcinoid tumor of the small intestine, unspecified portion — (Code first any associated multiple endocrine neoplasia syndrome: 258.01-258.03)(Use additional code to identify associated endocrine syndrome, as: carcinoid syndrome: 259.2) ▽
209.01 Malignant carcinoid tumor of the duodenum — (Code first any associated multiple endocrine neoplasia syndrome: 258.01-258.03)(Use additional code to identify associated endocrine syndrome, as: carcinoid syndrome: 259.2)
209.02 Malignant carcinoid tumor of the jejunum — (Code first any associated multiple endocrine neoplasia syndrome: 258.01-258.03)(Use additional code to identify associated endocrine syndrome, as: carcinoid syndrome: 259.2)
209.03 Malignant carcinoid tumor of the ileum — (Code first any associated multiple endocrine neoplasia syndrome: 258.01-258.03)(Use additional code to identify associated endocrine syndrome, as: carcinoid syndrome: 259.2)
209.10 Malignant carcinoid tumor of the large intestine, unspecified portion — (Code first any associated multiple endocrine neoplasia syndrome: 258.01-258.03)(Use additional code to identify associated endocrine syndrome, as: carcinoid syndrome: 259.2) ▽
209.12 Malignant carcinoid tumor of the cecum — (Code first any associated multiple endocrine neoplasia syndrome: 258.01-258.03)(Use additional code to identify associated endocrine syndrome, as: carcinoid syndrome: 259.2)
209.20 Malignant carcinoid tumor of unknown primary site — (Code first any associated multiple endocrine neoplasia syndrome: 258.01-258.03)(Use additional code to identify associated endocrine syndrome, as: carcinoid syndrome: 259.2)
209.25 Malignant carcinoid tumor of foregut, not otherwise specified — (Code first any associated multiple endocrine neoplasia syndrome: 258.01-258.03)(Use additional code to identify associated endocrine syndrome, as: carcinoid syndrome: 259.2)
209.26 Malignant carcinoid tumor of midgut, not otherwise specified — (Code first any associated multiple endocrine neoplasia syndrome: 258.01-258.03)(Use additional code to identify associated endocrine syndrome, as: carcinoid syndrome: 259.2)
209.27 Malignant carcinoid tumor of hindgut, not otherwise specified — (Code first any associated multiple endocrine neoplasia syndrome: 258.01-258.03)(Use additional code to identify associated endocrine syndrome, as: carcinoid syndrome: 259.2)
209.29 Malignant carcinoid tumor of other sites — (Code first any associated multiple endocrine neoplasia syndrome: 258.01-258.03)(Use additional code to identify associated endocrine syndrome, as: carcinoid syndrome: 259.2)
209.30 Malignant poorly differentiated neuroendocrine carcinoma, any site — (Code first any associated multiple endocrine neoplasia syndrome: 258.01-258.03)(Use additional code to identify associated endocrine syndrome, as: carcinoid syndrome: 259.2) ▽
209.69 Benign carcinoid tumor of other sites — (Code first any associated multiple endocrine neoplasia syndrome: 258.01-258.03)(Use additional code to identify associated endocrine syndrome, as: carcinoid syndrome: 259.2)
211.3 Benign neoplasm of colon
230.3 Carcinoma in situ of colon
230.4 Carcinoma in situ of rectum
230.9 Carcinoma in situ of other and unspecified digestive organs ▽
235.2 Neoplasm of uncertain behavior of stomach, intestines, and rectum
239.0 Neoplasm of unspecified nature of digestive system
532.10 Acute duodenal ulcer with perforation, without mention of obstruction — (Use additional E code to identify drug, if drug induced)
555.0 Regional enteritis of small intestine
555.1 Regional enteritis of large intestine
555.2 Regional enteritis of small intestine with large intestine
555.9 Regional enteritis of unspecified site ▽
556.0 Ulcerative (chronic) enterocolitis
556.1 Ulcerative (chronic) ileocolitis
556.2 Ulcerative (chronic) proctitis
556.3 Ulcerative (chronic) proctosigmoiditis
556.4 Pseudopolyposis of colon
556.5 Left sided ulcerative (chronic) colitis
556.6 Universal ulcerative (chronic) colitis
556.8 Other ulcerative colitis
556.9 Unspecified ulcerative colitis ▽
557.0 Acute vascular insufficiency of intestine
558.1 Gastroenteritis and colitis due to radiation
558.2 Toxic gastroenteritis and colitis — (Use additional E code to identify cause)
558.3 Gastroenteritis and colitis, allergic — (Use additional code to identify type of food allergy: V15.01-V15.05)
558.42 Eosinophilic colitis
558.9 Other and unspecified noninfectious gastroenteritis and colitis ▽
560.1 Paralytic ileus
560.2 Volvulus
560.31 Gallstone ileus
560.39 Impaction of intestine, other
560.81 Intestinal or peritoneal adhesions with obstruction (postoperative) (postinfection)
560.89 Other specified intestinal obstruction
560.9 Unspecified intestinal obstruction ▽
562.10 Diverticulosis of colon (without mention of hemorrhage) — (Use additional code to identify any associated peritonitis: 567.0-567.9)
562.11 Diverticulitis of colon (without mention of hemorrhage) — (Use additional code to identify any associated peritonitis: 567.0-567.9)

562.12 Diverticulosis of colon with hemorrhage — (Use additional code to identify any associated peritonitis: 567.0-567.9)
562.13 Diverticulitis of colon with hemorrhage — (Use additional code to identify any associated peritonitis: 567.0-567.9)
564.7 Megacolon, other than Hirschsprung's
564.81 Neurogenic bowel
564.89 Other functional disorders of intestine
565.1 Anal fistula
566 Abscess of anal and rectal regions
567.0 Peritonitis in infectious diseases classified elsewhere — (Code first underlying disease) ☒
567.1 Pneumococcal peritonitis
567.21 Peritonitis (acute) generalized
567.22 Peritoneal abscess
567.23 Spontaneous bacterial peritonitis
567.29 Other suppurative peritonitis
567.31 Psoas muscle abscess
567.38 Other retroperitoneal abscess
567.39 Other retroperitoneal infections
567.81 Choleperitonitis
567.82 Sclerosing mesenteritis
567.89 Other specified peritonitis
567.9 Unspecified peritonitis ▽
569.1 Rectal prolapse
569.2 Stenosis of rectum and anus
569.3 Hemorrhage of rectum and anus
569.41 Ulcer of anus and rectum
569.44 Dysplasia of anus
569.49 Other specified disorder of rectum and anus — (Use additional code for any associated fecal incontinence (787.60-787.63))
569.5 Abscess of intestine
569.61 Infection of colostomy or enterostomy — (Use additional code to identify organism: 041.00-041.9. Use additional code to specify type of infection: 038.0-038.9, 682.2)
569.69 Other complication of colostomy or enterostomy
569.81 Fistula of intestine, excluding rectum and anus
569.82 Ulceration of intestine
569.83 Perforation of intestine
569.84 Angiodysplasia of intestine (without mention of hemorrhage)
569.85 Angiodysplasia of intestine with hemorrhage
569.89 Other specified disorder of intestines
578.9 Hemorrhage of gastrointestinal tract, unspecified ▽
596.1 Intestinovesical fistula — (Use additional code to identify urinary incontinence: 625.6, 788.30-788.39)
619.1 Digestive-genital tract fistula, female ♀
625.6 Female stress incontinence ♀
751.0 Meckel's diverticulum
751.1 Congenital atresia and stenosis of small intestine
751.2 Congenital atresia and stenosis of large intestine, rectum, and anal canal
751.3 Hirschsprung's disease and other congenital functional disorders of colon
751.4 Congenital anomalies of intestinal fixation
751.5 Other congenital anomalies of intestine
787.60 Full incontinence of feces
787.61 Incomplete defecation
787.62 Fecal smearing
787.63 Fecal urgency
863.55 Rectum injury with open wound into cavity

ICD-9-CM Procedural

46.03 Exteriorization of large intestine
46.10 Colostomy, not otherwise specified
46.11 Temporary colostomy
46.13 Permanent colostomy

44340-44345

44340 Revision of colostomy; simple (release of superficial scar) (separate procedure)
44345 complicated (reconstruction in-depth) (separate procedure)

ICD-9-CM Diagnostic

560.81 Intestinal or peritoneal adhesions with obstruction (postoperative) (postinfection)
569.60 Unspecified complication of colostomy or enterostomy ▽
569.61 Infection of colostomy or enterostomy — (Use additional code to identify organism: 041.00-041.9. Use additional code to specify type of infection: 038.0-038.9, 682.2)
569.62 Mechanical complication of colostomy and enterostomy
569.69 Other complication of colostomy or enterostomy
707.8 Chronic ulcer of other specified site
997.49 Other digestive system complications
998.2 Accidental puncture or laceration during procedure
998.31 Disruption of internal operation (surgical) wound
998.32 Disruption of external operation (surgical) wound
V10.05 Personal history of malignant neoplasm of large intestine
V10.06 Personal history of malignant neoplasm of rectum, rectosigmoid junction, and anus
V44.3 Colostomy status
V55.3 Attention to colostomy

ICD-9-CM Procedural

46.40 Revision of intestinal stoma, not otherwise specified
46.43 Other revision of stoma of large intestine

44346

44346 Revision of colostomy; with repair of paracolostomy hernia (separate procedure)

ICD-9-CM Diagnostic

560.81 Intestinal or peritoneal adhesions with obstruction (postoperative) (postinfection)
569.61 Infection of colostomy or enterostomy — (Use additional code to identify organism: 041.00-041.9. Use additional code to specify type of infection: 038.0-038.9, 682.2)
569.62 Mechanical complication of colostomy and enterostomy
569.69 Other complication of colostomy or enterostomy
707.8 Chronic ulcer of other specified site
997.49 Other digestive system complications
998.2 Accidental puncture or laceration during procedure
998.31 Disruption of internal operation (surgical) wound
998.32 Disruption of external operation (surgical) wound
V10.05 Personal history of malignant neoplasm of large intestine
V10.06 Personal history of malignant neoplasm of rectum, rectosigmoid junction, and anus
V44.3 Colostomy status
V55.3 Attention to colostomy

ICD-9-CM Procedural

46.40 Revision of intestinal stoma, not otherwise specified
46.42 Repair of pericolostomy hernia
46.43 Other revision of stoma of large intestine

44360-44361

44360 Small intestinal endoscopy, enteroscopy beyond second portion of duodenum, not including ileum; diagnostic, with or without collection of specimen(s) by brushing or washing (separate procedure)
44361 with biopsy, single or multiple

ICD-9-CM Diagnostic

152.0 Malignant neoplasm of duodenum
152.1 Malignant neoplasm of jejunum
152.9 Malignant neoplasm of small intestine, unspecified site ▽

197.4 Secondary malignant neoplasm of small intestine including duodenum
209.00 Malignant carcinoid tumor of the small intestine, unspecified portion — (Code first any associated multiple endocrine neoplasia syndrome: 258.01-258.03)(Use additional code to identify associated endocrine syndrome, as: carcinoid syndrome: 259.2) ▽
209.01 Malignant carcinoid tumor of the duodenum — (Code first any associated multiple endocrine neoplasia syndrome: 258.01-258.03)(Use additional code to identify associated endocrine syndrome, as: carcinoid syndrome: 259.2)
209.02 Malignant carcinoid tumor of the jejunum — (Code first any associated multiple endocrine neoplasia syndrome: 258.01-258.03)(Use additional code to identify associated endocrine syndrome, as: carcinoid syndrome: 259.2)
211.2 Benign neoplasm of duodenum, jejunum, and ileum
532.00 Acute duodenal ulcer with hemorrhage, without mention of obstruction — (Use additional E code to identify drug, if drug induced)
532.01 Acute duodenal ulcer with hemorrhage and obstruction — (Use additional E code to identify drug, if drug induced)
532.10 Acute duodenal ulcer with perforation, without mention of obstruction — (Use additional E code to identify drug, if drug induced)
532.11 Acute duodenal ulcer with perforation and obstruction — (Use additional E code to identify drug, if drug induced)
532.20 Acute duodenal ulcer with hemorrhage and perforation, without mention of obstruction — (Use additional E code to identify drug, if drug induced)
532.21 Acute duodenal ulcer with hemorrhage, perforation, and obstruction — (Use additional E code to identify drug, if drug induced)
532.30 Acute duodenal ulcer without mention of hemorrhage, perforation, or obstruction — (Use additional E code to identify drug, if drug induced)
532.31 Acute duodenal ulcer without mention of hemorrhage or perforation, with obstruction — (Use additional E code to identify drug, if drug induced)
532.90 Duodenal ulcer, unspecified as acute or chronic, without hemorrhage, perforation, or obstruction — (Use additional E code to identify drug, if drug induced) ▽
535.50 Unspecified gastritis and gastroduodenitis without mention of hemorrhage ▽
535.51 Unspecified gastritis and gastroduodenitis with hemorrhage ▽
535.60 Duodenitis without mention of hemorrhage
535.61 Duodenitis with hemorrhage
535.70 Eosinophilic gastritis without mention of hemorrhage
535.71 Eosinophilic gastritis with hemorrhage
537.3 Other obstruction of duodenum
537.84 Dieulafoy lesion (hemorrhagic) of stomach and duodenum
555.2 Regional enteritis of small intestine with large intestine
569.86 Dieulafoy lesion (hemorrhagic) of intestine
578.0 Hematemesis
578.1 Blood in stool
578.9 Hemorrhage of gastrointestinal tract, unspecified ▽
579.9 Unspecified intestinal malabsorption ▽
751.0 Meckel's diverticulum
783.21 Loss of weight — (Use additional code to identify Body Mass Index (BMI), if known: V85.0-V85.54)
783.22 Underweight — (Use additional code to identify Body Mass Index (BMI), if known: V85.0-V85.54)
783.7 Adult failure to thrive
793.4 Nonspecific (abnormal) findings on radiological and other examination of gastrointestinal tract
V85.0 Body Mass Index less than 19, adult

ICD-9-CM Procedural

45.13 Other endoscopy of small intestine
45.14 Closed [endoscopic] biopsy of small intestine
45.16 Esophagogastroduodenoscopy (EGD) with closed biopsy

HCPCS Level II Supplies & Services

A4270 Disposable endoscope sheath, each

44363

44363 Small intestinal endoscopy, enteroscopy beyond second portion of duodenum, not including ileum; with removal of foreign body

ICD-9-CM Diagnostic

936 Foreign body in intestine and colon
998.4 Foreign body accidentally left during procedure, not elsewhere classified
998.7 Acute reaction to foreign substance accidentally left during procedure, not elsewhere classified

ICD-9-CM Procedural

98.03 Removal of intraluminal foreign body from stomach and small intestine without incision

HCPCS Level II Supplies & Services

A4270 Disposable endoscope sheath, each

44364-44365

44364 Small intestinal endoscopy, enteroscopy beyond second portion of duodenum, not including ileum; with removal of tumor(s), polyp(s), or other lesion(s) by snare technique
44365 with removal of tumor(s), polyp(s), or other lesion(s) by hot biopsy forceps or bipolar cautery

ICD-9-CM Diagnostic

152.0 Malignant neoplasm of duodenum
152.1 Malignant neoplasm of jejunum
197.4 Secondary malignant neoplasm of small intestine including duodenum
209.00 Malignant carcinoid tumor of the small intestine, unspecified portion — (Code first any associated multiple endocrine neoplasia syndrome: 258.01-258.03)(Use additional code to identify associated endocrine syndrome, as: carcinoid syndrome: 259.2) ▽
209.01 Malignant carcinoid tumor of the duodenum — (Code first any associated multiple endocrine neoplasia syndrome: 258.01-258.03)(Use additional code to identify associated endocrine syndrome, as: carcinoid syndrome: 259.2)
209.02 Malignant carcinoid tumor of the jejunum — (Code first any associated multiple endocrine neoplasia syndrome: 258.01-258.03)(Use additional code to identify associated endocrine syndrome, as: carcinoid syndrome: 259.2)
209.03 Malignant carcinoid tumor of the ileum — (Code first any associated multiple endocrine neoplasia syndrome: 258.01-258.03)(Use additional code to identify associated endocrine syndrome, as: carcinoid syndrome: 259.2)
209.29 Malignant carcinoid tumor of other sites — (Code first any associated multiple endocrine neoplasia syndrome: 258.01-258.03)(Use additional code to identify associated endocrine syndrome, as: carcinoid syndrome: 259.2)
209.30 Malignant poorly differentiated neuroendocrine carcinoma, any site — (Code first any associated multiple endocrine neoplasia syndrome: 258.01-258.03)(Use additional code to identify associated endocrine syndrome, as: carcinoid syndrome: 259.2) ▽
209.40 Benign carcinoid tumor of the small intestine, unspecified portion — (Code first any associated multiple endocrine neoplasia syndrome: 258.01-258.03)(Use additional code to identify associated endocrine syndrome, as: carcinoid syndrome: 259.2) ▽
209.41 Benign carcinoid tumor of the duodenum — (Code first any associated multiple endocrine neoplasia syndrome: 258.01-258.03)(Use additional code to identify associated endocrine syndrome, as: carcinoid syndrome: 259.2)
209.42 Benign carcinoid tumor of the jejunum — (Code first any associated multiple endocrine neoplasia syndrome: 258.01-258.03)(Use additional code to identify associated endocrine syndrome, as: carcinoid syndrome: 259.2)
209.43 Benign carcinoid tumor of the ileum — (Code first any associated multiple endocrine neoplasia syndrome: 258.01-258.03)(Use additional code to identify associated endocrine syndrome, as: carcinoid syndrome: 259.2)
209.69 Benign carcinoid tumor of other sites — (Code first any associated multiple endocrine neoplasia syndrome: 258.01-258.03)(Use additional code to identify associated endocrine syndrome, as: carcinoid syndrome: 259.2)
211.2 Benign neoplasm of duodenum, jejunum, and ileum
230.7 Carcinoma in situ of other and unspecified parts of intestine ▽

235.2 Neoplasm of uncertain behavior of stomach, intestines, and rectum
239.0 Neoplasm of unspecified nature of digestive system

ICD-9-CM Procedural

45.30 Endoscopic excision or destruction of lesion of duodenum

HCPCS Level II Supplies & Services

A4270 Disposable endoscope sheath, each

44366

44366 Small intestinal endoscopy, enteroscopy beyond second portion of duodenum, not including ileum; with control of bleeding (eg, injection, bipolar cautery, unipolar cautery, laser, heater probe, stapler, plasma coagulator)

ICD-9-CM Diagnostic

152.0 Malignant neoplasm of duodenum
152.1 Malignant neoplasm of jejunum
197.4 Secondary malignant neoplasm of small intestine including duodenum
209.00 Malignant carcinoid tumor of the small intestine, unspecified portion — (Code first any associated multiple endocrine neoplasia syndrome: 258.01-258.03)(Use additional code to identify associated endocrine syndrome, as: carcinoid syndrome: 259.2) ▽
209.01 Malignant carcinoid tumor of the duodenum — (Code first any associated multiple endocrine neoplasia syndrome: 258.01-258.03)(Use additional code to identify associated endocrine syndrome, as: carcinoid syndrome: 259.2)
209.02 Malignant carcinoid tumor of the jejunum — (Code first any associated multiple endocrine neoplasia syndrome: 258.01-258.03)(Use additional code to identify associated endocrine syndrome, as: carcinoid syndrome: 259.2)
209.03 Malignant carcinoid tumor of the ileum — (Code first any associated multiple endocrine neoplasia syndrome: 258.01-258.03)(Use additional code to identify associated endocrine syndrome, as: carcinoid syndrome: 259.2)
209.40 Benign carcinoid tumor of the small intestine, unspecified portion — (Code first any associated multiple endocrine neoplasia syndrome: 258.01-258.03)(Use additional code to identify associated endocrine syndrome, as: carcinoid syndrome: 259.2) ▽
209.41 Benign carcinoid tumor of the duodenum — (Code first any associated multiple endocrine neoplasia syndrome: 258.01-258.03)(Use additional code to identify associated endocrine syndrome, as: carcinoid syndrome: 259.2)
209.42 Benign carcinoid tumor of the jejunum — (Code first any associated multiple endocrine neoplasia syndrome: 258.01-258.03)(Use additional code to identify associated endocrine syndrome, as: carcinoid syndrome: 259.2)
209.43 Benign carcinoid tumor of the ileum — (Code first any associated multiple endocrine neoplasia syndrome: 258.01-258.03)(Use additional code to identify associated endocrine syndrome, as: carcinoid syndrome: 259.2)
211.2 Benign neoplasm of duodenum, jejunum, and ileum
532.00 Acute duodenal ulcer with hemorrhage, without mention of obstruction — (Use additional E code to identify drug, if drug induced)
532.01 Acute duodenal ulcer with hemorrhage and obstruction — (Use additional E code to identify drug, if drug induced)
532.21 Acute duodenal ulcer with hemorrhage, perforation, and obstruction — (Use additional E code to identify drug, if drug induced)
532.40 Duodenal ulcer, chronic or unspecified, with hemorrhage, without mention of obstruction — (Use additional E code to identify drug, if drug induced)
532.60 Chronic or unspecified duodenal ulcer with hemorrhage and perforation, without mention of obstruction — (Use additional E code to identify drug, if drug induced)
535.61 Duodenitis with hemorrhage
537.84 Dieulafoy lesion (hemorrhagic) of stomach and duodenum
537.89 Other specified disorder of stomach and duodenum
569.86 Dieulafoy lesion (hemorrhagic) of intestine

ICD-9-CM Procedural

44.43 Endoscopic control of gastric or duodenal bleeding

HCPCS Level II Supplies & Services

A4270 Disposable endoscope sheath, each

44369

44369 Small intestinal endoscopy, enteroscopy beyond second portion of duodenum, not including ileum; with ablation of tumor(s), polyp(s), or other lesion(s) not amenable to removal by hot biopsy forceps, bipolar cautery or snare technique

ICD-9-CM Diagnostic

152.0 Malignant neoplasm of duodenum
152.1 Malignant neoplasm of jejunum
197.4 Secondary malignant neoplasm of small intestine including duodenum
209.00 Malignant carcinoid tumor of the small intestine, unspecified portion — (Code first any associated multiple endocrine neoplasia syndrome: 258.01-258.03)(Use additional code to identify associated endocrine syndrome, as: carcinoid syndrome: 259.2) ▽
209.01 Malignant carcinoid tumor of the duodenum — (Code first any associated multiple endocrine neoplasia syndrome: 258.01-258.03)(Use additional code to identify associated endocrine syndrome, as: carcinoid syndrome: 259.2)
209.02 Malignant carcinoid tumor of the jejunum — (Code first any associated multiple endocrine neoplasia syndrome: 258.01-258.03)(Use additional code to identify associated endocrine syndrome, as: carcinoid syndrome: 259.2)
209.03 Malignant carcinoid tumor of the ileum — (Code first any associated multiple endocrine neoplasia syndrome: 258.01-258.03)(Use additional code to identify associated endocrine syndrome, as: carcinoid syndrome: 259.2)
209.29 Malignant carcinoid tumor of other sites — (Code first any associated multiple endocrine neoplasia syndrome: 258.01-258.03)(Use additional code to identify associated endocrine syndrome, as: carcinoid syndrome: 259.2)
209.30 Malignant poorly differentiated neuroendocrine carcinoma, any site — (Code first any associated multiple endocrine neoplasia syndrome: 258.01-258.03)(Use additional code to identify associated endocrine syndrome, as: carcinoid syndrome: 259.2) ▽
209.40 Benign carcinoid tumor of the small intestine, unspecified portion — (Code first any associated multiple endocrine neoplasia syndrome: 258.01-258.03)(Use additional code to identify associated endocrine syndrome, as: carcinoid syndrome: 259.2) ▽
209.41 Benign carcinoid tumor of the duodenum — (Code first any associated multiple endocrine neoplasia syndrome: 258.01-258.03)(Use additional code to identify associated endocrine syndrome, as: carcinoid syndrome: 259.2)
209.42 Benign carcinoid tumor of the jejunum — (Code first any associated multiple endocrine neoplasia syndrome: 258.01-258.03)(Use additional code to identify associated endocrine syndrome, as: carcinoid syndrome: 259.2)
209.43 Benign carcinoid tumor of the ileum — (Code first any associated multiple endocrine neoplasia syndrome: 258.01-258.03)(Use additional code to identify associated endocrine syndrome, as: carcinoid syndrome: 259.2)
209.69 Benign carcinoid tumor of other sites — (Code first any associated multiple endocrine neoplasia syndrome: 258.01-258.03)(Use additional code to identify associated endocrine syndrome, as: carcinoid syndrome: 259.2)
211.2 Benign neoplasm of duodenum, jejunum, and ileum
230.7 Carcinoma in situ of other and unspecified parts of intestine ▽
235.2 Neoplasm of uncertain behavior of stomach, intestines, and rectum
239.0 Neoplasm of unspecified nature of digestive system

ICD-9-CM Procedural

45.30 Endoscopic excision or destruction of lesion of duodenum

HCPCS Level II Supplies & Services

A4270 Disposable endoscope sheath, each

44370

44370 Small intestinal endoscopy, enteroscopy beyond second portion of duodenum, not including ileum; with transendoscopic stent placement (includes predilation)

ICD-9-CM Diagnostic

152.0 Malignant neoplasm of duodenum
152.1 Malignant neoplasm of jejunum
152.8 Malignant neoplasm of other specified sites of small intestine
152.9 Malignant neoplasm of small intestine, unspecified site ▽
196.2 Secondary and unspecified malignant neoplasm of intra-abdominal lymph nodes

197.4 Secondary malignant neoplasm of small intestine including duodenum

209.00 Malignant carcinoid tumor of the small intestine, unspecified portion — (Code first any associated multiple endocrine neoplasia syndrome: 258.01-258.03)(Use additional code to identify associated endocrine syndrome, as: carcinoid syndrome: 259.2) ▽

209.01 Malignant carcinoid tumor of the duodenum — (Code first any associated multiple endocrine neoplasia syndrome: 258.01-258.03)(Use additional code to identify associated endocrine syndrome, as: carcinoid syndrome: 259.2)

209.02 Malignant carcinoid tumor of the jejunum — (Code first any associated multiple endocrine neoplasia syndrome: 258.01-258.03)(Use additional code to identify associated endocrine syndrome, as: carcinoid syndrome: 259.2)

209.03 Malignant carcinoid tumor of the ileum — (Code first any associated multiple endocrine neoplasia syndrome: 258.01-258.03)(Use additional code to identify associated endocrine syndrome, as: carcinoid syndrome: 259.2)

209.40 Benign carcinoid tumor of the small intestine, unspecified portion — (Code first any associated multiple endocrine neoplasia syndrome: 258.01-258.03)(Use additional code to identify associated endocrine syndrome, as: carcinoid syndrome: 259.2) ▽

209.41 Benign carcinoid tumor of the duodenum — (Code first any associated multiple endocrine neoplasia syndrome: 258.01-258.03)(Use additional code to identify associated endocrine syndrome, as: carcinoid syndrome: 259.2)

209.42 Benign carcinoid tumor of the jejunum — (Code first any associated multiple endocrine neoplasia syndrome: 258.01-258.03)(Use additional code to identify associated endocrine syndrome, as: carcinoid syndrome: 259.2)

209.43 Benign carcinoid tumor of the ileum — (Code first any associated multiple endocrine neoplasia syndrome: 258.01-258.03)(Use additional code to identify associated endocrine syndrome, as: carcinoid syndrome: 259.2)

537.2 Chronic duodenal ileus

537.3 Other obstruction of duodenum

560.1 Paralytic ileus

560.2 Volvulus

560.81 Intestinal or peritoneal adhesions with obstruction (postoperative) (postinfection)

560.89 Other specified intestinal obstruction

560.9 Unspecified intestinal obstruction ▽

751.1 Congenital atresia and stenosis of small intestine

997.49 Other digestive system complications

ICD-9-CM Procedural

45.13 Other endoscopy of small intestine

46.79 Other repair of intestine

HCPCS Level II Supplies & Services

C1874 Stent, coated/covered, with delivery system

44372-44373

44372 Small intestinal endoscopy, enteroscopy beyond second portion of duodenum, not including ileum; with placement of percutaneous jejunostomy tube

44373 with conversion of percutaneous gastrostomy tube to percutaneous jejunostomy tube

ICD-9-CM Diagnostic

146.9 Malignant neoplasm of oropharynx, unspecified site ▽

148.9 Malignant neoplasm of hypopharynx, unspecified site ▽

150.9 Malignant neoplasm of esophagus, unspecified site ▽

151.9 Malignant neoplasm of stomach, unspecified site ▽

152.0 Malignant neoplasm of duodenum

152.1 Malignant neoplasm of jejunum

209.00 Malignant carcinoid tumor of the small intestine, unspecified portion — (Code first any associated multiple endocrine neoplasia syndrome: 258.01-258.03)(Use additional code to identify associated endocrine syndrome, as: carcinoid syndrome: 259.2) ▽

209.01 Malignant carcinoid tumor of the duodenum — (Code first any associated multiple endocrine neoplasia syndrome: 258.01-258.03)(Use additional code to identify associated endocrine syndrome, as: carcinoid syndrome: 259.2)

209.02 Malignant carcinoid tumor of the jejunum — (Code first any associated multiple endocrine neoplasia syndrome: 258.01-258.03)(Use additional code to identify associated endocrine syndrome, as: carcinoid syndrome: 259.2)

209.03 Malignant carcinoid tumor of the ileum — (Code first any associated multiple endocrine neoplasia syndrome: 258.01-258.03)(Use additional code to identify associated endocrine syndrome, as: carcinoid syndrome: 259.2)

209.25 Malignant carcinoid tumor of foregut, not otherwise specified — (Code first any associated multiple endocrine neoplasia syndrome: 258.01-258.03)(Use additional code to identify associated endocrine syndrome, as: carcinoid syndrome: 259.2)

209.29 Malignant carcinoid tumor of other sites — (Code first any associated multiple endocrine neoplasia syndrome: 258.01-258.03)(Use additional code to identify associated endocrine syndrome, as: carcinoid syndrome: 259.2)

209.30 Malignant poorly differentiated neuroendocrine carcinoma, any site — (Code first any associated multiple endocrine neoplasia syndrome: 258.01-258.03)(Use additional code to identify associated endocrine syndrome, as: carcinoid syndrome: 259.2) ▽

209.40 Benign carcinoid tumor of the small intestine, unspecified portion — (Code first any associated multiple endocrine neoplasia syndrome: 258.01-258.03)(Use additional code to identify associated endocrine syndrome, as: carcinoid syndrome: 259.2) ▽

209.41 Benign carcinoid tumor of the duodenum — (Code first any associated multiple endocrine neoplasia syndrome: 258.01-258.03)(Use additional code to identify associated endocrine syndrome, as: carcinoid syndrome: 259.2)

209.42 Benign carcinoid tumor of the jejunum — (Code first any associated multiple endocrine neoplasia syndrome: 258.01-258.03)(Use additional code to identify associated endocrine syndrome, as: carcinoid syndrome: 259.2)

209.43 Benign carcinoid tumor of the ileum — (Code first any associated multiple endocrine neoplasia syndrome: 258.01-258.03)(Use additional code to identify associated endocrine syndrome, as: carcinoid syndrome: 259.2)

209.69 Benign carcinoid tumor of other sites — (Code first any associated multiple endocrine neoplasia syndrome: 258.01-258.03)(Use additional code to identify associated endocrine syndrome, as: carcinoid syndrome: 259.2)

261 Nutritional marasmus

262 Other severe protein-calorie malnutrition

348.1 Anoxic brain damage — (Use additional E code to identify cause)

530.0 Achalasia and cardiospasm

530.20 Ulcer of esophagus without bleeding — (Use additional E code to identify cause, if induced by chemical or drug)

530.21 Ulcer of esophagus with bleeding — (Use additional E code to identify cause, if induced by chemical or drug)

531.00 Acute gastric ulcer with hemorrhage, without mention of obstruction — (Use additional E code to identify drug, if drug induced)

531.01 Acute gastric ulcer with hemorrhage and obstruction — (Use additional E code to identify drug, if drug induced)

535.60 Duodenitis without mention of hemorrhage

535.61 Duodenitis with hemorrhage

537.0 Acquired hypertrophic pyloric stenosis

537.4 Fistula of stomach or duodenum

579.0 Celiac disease

579.1 Tropical sprue

579.2 Blind loop syndrome

579.8 Other specified intestinal malabsorption

751.2 Congenital atresia and stenosis of large intestine, rectum, and anal canal

751.3 Hirschsprung's disease and other congenital functional disorders of colon

V10.00 Personal history of malignant neoplasm of unspecified site in gastrointestinal tract ▽

ICD-9-CM Procedural

44.32 Percutaneous [endoscopic] gastrojejunostomy

46.32 Percutaneous (endoscopic) jejunostomy (PEJ)

44376-44377

44376 Small intestinal endoscopy, enteroscopy beyond second portion of duodenum, including ileum; diagnostic, with or without collection of specimen(s) by brushing or washing (separate procedure)

44377 with biopsy, single or multiple

ICD-9-CM Diagnostic

152.0 Malignant neoplasm of duodenum

152.1 Malignant neoplasm of jejunum

152.2 Malignant neoplasm of ileum

197.4 Secondary malignant neoplasm of small intestine including duodenum

209.00 Malignant carcinoid tumor of the small intestine, unspecified portion — (Code first any associated multiple endocrine neoplasia syndrome: 258.01-258.03)(Use additional code to identify associated endocrine syndrome, as: carcinoid syndrome: 259.2) ▽

209.01 Malignant carcinoid tumor of the duodenum — (Code first any associated multiple endocrine neoplasia syndrome: 258.01-258.03)(Use additional code to identify associated endocrine syndrome, as: carcinoid syndrome: 259.2)

209.02 Malignant carcinoid tumor of the jejunum — (Code first any associated multiple endocrine neoplasia syndrome: 258.01-258.03)(Use additional code to identify associated endocrine syndrome, as: carcinoid syndrome: 259.2)

209.03 Malignant carcinoid tumor of the ileum — (Code first any associated multiple endocrine neoplasia syndrome: 258.01-258.03)(Use additional code to identify associated endocrine syndrome, as: carcinoid syndrome: 259.2)

209.29 Malignant carcinoid tumor of other sites — (Code first any associated multiple endocrine neoplasia syndrome: 258.01-258.03)(Use additional code to identify associated endocrine syndrome, as: carcinoid syndrome: 259.2)

209.30 Malignant poorly differentiated neuroendocrine carcinoma, any site — (Code first any associated multiple endocrine neoplasia syndrome: 258.01-258.03)(Use additional code to identify associated endocrine syndrome, as: carcinoid syndrome: 259.2) ▽

209.40 Benign carcinoid tumor of the small intestine, unspecified portion — (Code first any associated multiple endocrine neoplasia syndrome: 258.01-258.03)(Use additional code to identify associated endocrine syndrome, as: carcinoid syndrome: 259.2) ▽

209.41 Benign carcinoid tumor of the duodenum — (Code first any associated multiple endocrine neoplasia syndrome: 258.01-258.03)(Use additional code to identify associated endocrine syndrome, as: carcinoid syndrome: 259.2)

209.42 Benign carcinoid tumor of the jejunum — (Code first any associated multiple endocrine neoplasia syndrome: 258.01-258.03)(Use additional code to identify associated endocrine syndrome, as: carcinoid syndrome: 259.2)

209.43 Benign carcinoid tumor of the ileum — (Code first any associated multiple endocrine neoplasia syndrome: 258.01-258.03)(Use additional code to identify associated endocrine syndrome, as: carcinoid syndrome: 259.2)

209.69 Benign carcinoid tumor of other sites — (Code first any associated multiple endocrine neoplasia syndrome: 258.01-258.03)(Use additional code to identify associated endocrine syndrome, as: carcinoid syndrome: 259.2)

211.3 Benign neoplasm of colon

230.7 Carcinoma in situ of other and unspecified parts of intestine ▽

235.2 Neoplasm of uncertain behavior of stomach, intestines, and rectum

239.0 Neoplasm of unspecified nature of digestive system

532.30 Acute duodenal ulcer without mention of hemorrhage, perforation, or obstruction — (Use additional E code to identify drug, if drug induced)

532.31 Acute duodenal ulcer without mention of hemorrhage or perforation, with obstruction — (Use additional E code to identify drug, if drug induced)

532.70 Chronic duodenal ulcer without mention of hemorrhage, perforation, or obstruction — (Use additional E code to identify drug, if drug induced)

532.71 Chronic duodenal ulcer without mention of hemorrhage or perforation, with obstruction — (Use additional E code to identify drug, if drug induced)

535.60 Duodenitis without mention of hemorrhage

535.61 Duodenitis with hemorrhage

537.84 Dieulafoy lesion (hemorrhagic) of stomach and duodenum

555.0 Regional enteritis of small intestine

555.2 Regional enteritis of small intestine with large intestine

560.2 Volvulus

560.81 Intestinal or peritoneal adhesions with obstruction (postoperative) (postinfection)

560.89 Other specified intestinal obstruction

564.5 Functional diarrhea

569.82 Ulceration of intestine

569.83 Perforation of intestine

569.86 Dieulafoy lesion (hemorrhagic) of intestine

578.1 Blood in stool

793.4 Nonspecific (abnormal) findings on radiological and other examination of gastrointestinal tract

ICD-9-CM Procedural

45.14 Closed [endoscopic] biopsy of small intestine

45.16 Esophagogastroduodenoscopy (EGD) with closed biopsy

HCPCS Level II Supplies & Services

A4270 Disposable endoscope sheath, each

44378

44378 Small intestinal endoscopy, enteroscopy beyond second portion of duodenum, including ileum; with control of bleeding (eg, injection, bipolar cautery, unipolar cautery, laser, heater probe, stapler, plasma coagulator)

ICD-9-CM Diagnostic

152.0 Malignant neoplasm of duodenum

152.1 Malignant neoplasm of jejunum

152.2 Malignant neoplasm of ileum

197.4 Secondary malignant neoplasm of small intestine including duodenum

209.00 Malignant carcinoid tumor of the small intestine, unspecified portion — (Code first any associated multiple endocrine neoplasia syndrome: 258.01-258.03)(Use additional code to identify associated endocrine syndrome, as: carcinoid syndrome: 259.2) ▽

209.01 Malignant carcinoid tumor of the duodenum — (Code first any associated multiple endocrine neoplasia syndrome: 258.01-258.03)(Use additional code to identify associated endocrine syndrome, as: carcinoid syndrome: 259.2)

209.02 Malignant carcinoid tumor of the jejunum — (Code first any associated multiple endocrine neoplasia syndrome: 258.01-258.03)(Use additional code to identify associated endocrine syndrome, as: carcinoid syndrome: 259.2)

209.03 Malignant carcinoid tumor of the ileum — (Code first any associated multiple endocrine neoplasia syndrome: 258.01-258.03)(Use additional code to identify associated endocrine syndrome, as: carcinoid syndrome: 259.2)

209.40 Benign carcinoid tumor of the small intestine, unspecified portion — (Code first any associated multiple endocrine neoplasia syndrome: 258.01-258.03)(Use additional code to identify associated endocrine syndrome, as: carcinoid syndrome: 259.2) ▽

209.41 Benign carcinoid tumor of the duodenum — (Code first any associated multiple endocrine neoplasia syndrome: 258.01-258.03)(Use additional code to identify associated endocrine syndrome, as: carcinoid syndrome: 259.2)

209.42 Benign carcinoid tumor of the jejunum — (Code first any associated multiple endocrine neoplasia syndrome: 258.01-258.03)(Use additional code to identify associated endocrine syndrome, as: carcinoid syndrome: 259.2)

209.43 Benign carcinoid tumor of the ileum — (Code first any associated multiple endocrine neoplasia syndrome: 258.01-258.03)(Use additional code to identify associated endocrine syndrome, as: carcinoid syndrome: 259.2)

211.2 Benign neoplasm of duodenum, jejunum, and ileum

230.7 Carcinoma in situ of other and unspecified parts of intestine ▽

532.00 Acute duodenal ulcer with hemorrhage, without mention of obstruction — (Use additional E code to identify drug, if drug induced)

532.01 Acute duodenal ulcer with hemorrhage and obstruction — (Use additional E code to identify drug, if drug induced)

532.20 Acute duodenal ulcer with hemorrhage and perforation, without mention of obstruction — (Use additional E code to identify drug, if drug induced)

532.21 Acute duodenal ulcer with hemorrhage, perforation, and obstruction — (Use additional E code to identify drug, if drug induced)

532.40 Duodenal ulcer, chronic or unspecified, with hemorrhage, without mention of obstruction — (Use additional E code to identify drug, if drug induced)

532.41 Chronic or unspecified duodenal ulcer with hemorrhage and obstruction — (Use additional E code to identify drug, if drug induced)
532.60 Chronic or unspecified duodenal ulcer with hemorrhage and perforation, without mention of obstruction — (Use additional E code to identify drug, if drug induced)
532.61 Chronic or unspecified duodenal ulcer with hemorrhage, perforation, and obstruction — (Use additional E code to identify drug, if drug induced)
534.00 Acute gastrojejunal ulcer with hemorrhage, without mention of obstruction
534.40 Chronic or unspecified gastrojejunal ulcer with hemorrhage, without mention of obstruction
535.61 Duodenitis with hemorrhage
537.84 Dieulafoy lesion (hemorrhagic) of stomach and duodenum
537.89 Other specified disorder of stomach and duodenum
560.2 Volvulus
560.81 Intestinal or peritoneal adhesions with obstruction (postoperative) (postinfection)
564.5 Functional diarrhea
569.82 Ulceration of intestine
569.83 Perforation of intestine
569.86 Dieulafoy lesion (hemorrhagic) of intestine
578.1 Blood in stool

ICD-9-CM Procedural

44.43 Endoscopic control of gastric or duodenal bleeding
45.13 Other endoscopy of small intestine

HCPCS Level II Supplies & Services

A4270 Disposable endoscope sheath, each

44379

44379 Small intestinal endoscopy, enteroscopy beyond second portion of duodenum, including ileum; with transendoscopic stent placement (includes predilation)

ICD-9-CM Diagnostic

152.0 Malignant neoplasm of duodenum
152.1 Malignant neoplasm of jejunum
152.2 Malignant neoplasm of ileum
152.3 Malignant neoplasm of Meckel's diverticulum
152.8 Malignant neoplasm of other specified sites of small intestine
152.9 Malignant neoplasm of small intestine, unspecified site ▽
196.2 Secondary and unspecified malignant neoplasm of intra-abdominal lymph nodes
197.4 Secondary malignant neoplasm of small intestine including duodenum
209.00 Malignant carcinoid tumor of the small intestine, unspecified portion — (Code first any associated multiple endocrine neoplasia syndrome: 258.01-258.03)(Use additional code to identify associated endocrine syndrome, as: carcinoid syndrome: 259.2) ▽
209.01 Malignant carcinoid tumor of the duodenum — (Code first any associated multiple endocrine neoplasia syndrome: 258.01-258.03)(Use additional code to identify associated endocrine syndrome, as: carcinoid syndrome: 259.2)
209.02 Malignant carcinoid tumor of the jejunum — (Code first any associated multiple endocrine neoplasia syndrome: 258.01-258.03)(Use additional code to identify associated endocrine syndrome, as: carcinoid syndrome: 259.2)
209.03 Malignant carcinoid tumor of the ileum — (Code first any associated multiple endocrine neoplasia syndrome: 258.01-258.03)(Use additional code to identify associated endocrine syndrome, as: carcinoid syndrome: 259.2)
209.40 Benign carcinoid tumor of the small intestine, unspecified portion — (Code first any associated multiple endocrine neoplasia syndrome: 258.01-258.03)(Use additional code to identify associated endocrine syndrome, as: carcinoid syndrome: 259.2) ▽
209.41 Benign carcinoid tumor of the duodenum — (Code first any associated multiple endocrine neoplasia syndrome: 258.01-258.03)(Use additional code to identify associated endocrine syndrome, as: carcinoid syndrome: 259.2)
209.42 Benign carcinoid tumor of the jejunum — (Code first any associated multiple endocrine neoplasia syndrome: 258.01-258.03)(Use additional code to identify associated endocrine syndrome, as: carcinoid syndrome: 259.2)
209.43 Benign carcinoid tumor of the ileum — (Code first any associated multiple endocrine neoplasia syndrome: 258.01-258.03)(Use additional code to identify associated endocrine syndrome, as: carcinoid syndrome: 259.2)
537.2 Chronic duodenal ileus
537.3 Other obstruction of duodenum
560.1 Paralytic ileus
560.2 Volvulus
560.81 Intestinal or peritoneal adhesions with obstruction (postoperative) (postinfection)
560.89 Other specified intestinal obstruction
560.9 Unspecified intestinal obstruction ▽
751.1 Congenital atresia and stenosis of small intestine
997.49 Other digestive system complications

ICD-9-CM Procedural

45.13 Other endoscopy of small intestine
46.79 Other repair of intestine

HCPCS Level II Supplies & Services

C1874 Stent, coated/covered, with delivery system

44380-44382

44380 Ileoscopy, through stoma; diagnostic, with or without collection of specimen(s) by brushing or washing (separate procedure)
44382 with biopsy, single or multiple

ICD-9-CM Diagnostic

152.0 Malignant neoplasm of duodenum
152.1 Malignant neoplasm of jejunum
152.2 Malignant neoplasm of ileum
209.00 Malignant carcinoid tumor of the small intestine, unspecified portion — (Code first any associated multiple endocrine neoplasia syndrome: 258.01-258.03)(Use additional code to identify associated endocrine syndrome, as: carcinoid syndrome: 259.2) ▽
209.01 Malignant carcinoid tumor of the duodenum — (Code first any associated multiple endocrine neoplasia syndrome: 258.01-258.03)(Use additional code to identify associated endocrine syndrome, as: carcinoid syndrome: 259.2)
209.02 Malignant carcinoid tumor of the jejunum — (Code first any associated multiple endocrine neoplasia syndrome: 258.01-258.03)(Use additional code to identify associated endocrine syndrome, as: carcinoid syndrome: 259.2)
209.03 Malignant carcinoid tumor of the ileum — (Code first any associated multiple endocrine neoplasia syndrome: 258.01-258.03)(Use additional code to identify associated endocrine syndrome, as: carcinoid syndrome: 259.2)
209.40 Benign carcinoid tumor of the small intestine, unspecified portion — (Code first any associated multiple endocrine neoplasia syndrome: 258.01-258.03)(Use additional code to identify associated endocrine syndrome, as: carcinoid syndrome: 259.2) ▽
209.41 Benign carcinoid tumor of the duodenum — (Code first any associated multiple endocrine neoplasia syndrome: 258.01-258.03)(Use additional code to identify associated endocrine syndrome, as: carcinoid syndrome: 259.2)
209.42 Benign carcinoid tumor of the jejunum — (Code first any associated multiple endocrine neoplasia syndrome: 258.01-258.03)(Use additional code to identify associated endocrine syndrome, as: carcinoid syndrome: 259.2)
209.43 Benign carcinoid tumor of the ileum — (Code first any associated multiple endocrine neoplasia syndrome: 258.01-258.03)(Use additional code to identify associated endocrine syndrome, as: carcinoid syndrome: 259.2)
211.2 Benign neoplasm of duodenum, jejunum, and ileum
230.3 Carcinoma in situ of colon
555.0 Regional enteritis of small intestine
555.1 Regional enteritis of large intestine
555.2 Regional enteritis of small intestine with large intestine
555.9 Regional enteritis of unspecified site ▽
560.81 Intestinal or peritoneal adhesions with obstruction (postoperative) (postinfection)
564.1 Irritable bowel syndrome

569.61 Infection of colostomy or enterostomy — (Use additional code to identify organism: 041.00-041.9. Use additional code to specify type of infection: 038.0-038.9, 682.2)
569.69 Other complication of colostomy or enterostomy
578.1 Blood in stool
V10.00 Personal history of malignant neoplasm of unspecified site in gastrointestinal tract

ICD-9-CM Procedural

45.12 Endoscopy of small intestine through artificial stoma
45.14 Closed [endoscopic] biopsy of small intestine

HCPCS Level II Supplies & Services

A4270 Disposable endoscope sheath, each

44383

44383 Ileoscopy, through stoma; with transendoscopic stent placement (includes predilation)

ICD-9-CM Diagnostic

152.0 Malignant neoplasm of duodenum
152.1 Malignant neoplasm of jejunum
152.2 Malignant neoplasm of ileum
196.2 Secondary and unspecified malignant neoplasm of intra-abdominal lymph nodes
197.4 Secondary malignant neoplasm of small intestine including duodenum
209.00 Malignant carcinoid tumor of the small intestine, unspecified portion — (Code first any associated multiple endocrine neoplasia syndrome: 258.01-258.03)(Use additional code to identify associated endocrine syndrome, as: carcinoid syndrome: 259.2)
209.01 Malignant carcinoid tumor of the duodenum — (Code first any associated multiple endocrine neoplasia syndrome: 258.01-258.03)(Use additional code to identify associated endocrine syndrome, as: carcinoid syndrome: 259.2)
209.02 Malignant carcinoid tumor of the jejunum — (Code first any associated multiple endocrine neoplasia syndrome: 258.01-258.03)(Use additional code to identify associated endocrine syndrome, as: carcinoid syndrome: 259.2)
209.03 Malignant carcinoid tumor of the ileum — (Code first any associated multiple endocrine neoplasia syndrome: 258.01-258.03)(Use additional code to identify associated endocrine syndrome, as: carcinoid syndrome: 259.2)
560.81 Intestinal or peritoneal adhesions with obstruction (postoperative) (postinfection)
560.89 Other specified intestinal obstruction
560.9 Unspecified intestinal obstruction
751.1 Congenital atresia and stenosis of small intestine
997.49 Other digestive system complications

ICD-9-CM Procedural

45.12 Endoscopy of small intestine through artificial stoma
46.79 Other repair of intestine

HCPCS Level II Supplies & Services

C1874 Stent, coated/covered, with delivery system

44385-44386

44385 Endoscopic evaluation of small intestinal (abdominal or pelvic) pouch; diagnostic, with or without collection of specimen(s) by brushing or washing (separate procedure)
44386 with biopsy, single or multiple

ICD-9-CM Diagnostic

152.0 Malignant neoplasm of duodenum
152.1 Malignant neoplasm of jejunum
152.2 Malignant neoplasm of ileum
209.00 Malignant carcinoid tumor of the small intestine, unspecified portion — (Code first any associated multiple endocrine neoplasia syndrome: 258.01-258.03)(Use additional code to identify associated endocrine syndrome, as: carcinoid syndrome: 259.2)
209.01 Malignant carcinoid tumor of the duodenum — (Code first any associated multiple endocrine neoplasia syndrome: 258.01-258.03)(Use additional code to identify associated endocrine syndrome, as: carcinoid syndrome: 259.2)
209.02 Malignant carcinoid tumor of the jejunum — (Code first any associated multiple endocrine neoplasia syndrome: 258.01-258.03)(Use additional code to identify associated endocrine syndrome, as: carcinoid syndrome: 259.2)
209.03 Malignant carcinoid tumor of the ileum — (Code first any associated multiple endocrine neoplasia syndrome: 258.01-258.03)(Use additional code to identify associated endocrine syndrome, as: carcinoid syndrome: 259.2)
209.40 Benign carcinoid tumor of the small intestine, unspecified portion — (Code first any associated multiple endocrine neoplasia syndrome: 258.01-258.03)(Use additional code to identify associated endocrine syndrome, as: carcinoid syndrome: 259.2)
209.41 Benign carcinoid tumor of the duodenum — (Code first any associated multiple endocrine neoplasia syndrome: 258.01-258.03)(Use additional code to identify associated endocrine syndrome, as: carcinoid syndrome: 259.2)
209.42 Benign carcinoid tumor of the jejunum — (Code first any associated multiple endocrine neoplasia syndrome: 258.01-258.03)(Use additional code to identify associated endocrine syndrome, as: carcinoid syndrome: 259.2)
209.43 Benign carcinoid tumor of the ileum — (Code first any associated multiple endocrine neoplasia syndrome: 258.01-258.03)(Use additional code to identify associated endocrine syndrome, as: carcinoid syndrome: 259.2)
211.2 Benign neoplasm of duodenum, jejunum, and ileum
230.3 Carcinoma in situ of colon
555.0 Regional enteritis of small intestine
555.1 Regional enteritis of large intestine
555.2 Regional enteritis of small intestine with large intestine
555.9 Regional enteritis of unspecified site
560.81 Intestinal or peritoneal adhesions with obstruction (postoperative) (postinfection)
560.89 Other specified intestinal obstruction
564.1 Irritable bowel syndrome
569.61 Infection of colostomy or enterostomy — (Use additional code to identify organism: 041.00-041.9. Use additional code to specify type of infection: 038.0-038.9, 682.2)
569.69 Other complication of colostomy or enterostomy
569.71 Pouchitis
569.79 Other complications of intestinal pouch
569.81 Fistula of intestine, excluding rectum and anus
569.82 Ulceration of intestine
569.83 Perforation of intestine
569.86 Dieulafoy lesion (hemorrhagic) of intestine
578.9 Hemorrhage of gastrointestinal tract, unspecified

ICD-9-CM Procedural

45.13 Other endoscopy of small intestine
45.14 Closed [endoscopic] biopsy of small intestine

HCPCS Level II Supplies & Services

A4270 Disposable endoscope sheath, each

44388-44389

44388 Colonoscopy through stoma; diagnostic, with or without collection of specimen(s) by brushing or washing (separate procedure)
44389 with biopsy, single or multiple

ICD-9-CM Diagnostic

153.0 Malignant neoplasm of hepatic flexure
153.1 Malignant neoplasm of transverse colon
153.2 Malignant neoplasm of descending colon
153.3 Malignant neoplasm of sigmoid colon
153.4 Malignant neoplasm of cecum
153.5 Malignant neoplasm of appendix
153.6 Malignant neoplasm of ascending colon
153.7 Malignant neoplasm of splenic flexure
153.8 Malignant neoplasm of other specified sites of large intestine
153.9 Malignant neoplasm of colon, unspecified site
154.0 Malignant neoplasm of rectosigmoid junction

154.1 Malignant neoplasm of rectum
154.2 Malignant neoplasm of anal canal
154.3 Malignant neoplasm of anus, unspecified site ▽
154.8 Malignant neoplasm of other sites of rectum, rectosigmoid junction, and anus
197.5 Secondary malignant neoplasm of large intestine and rectum
209.10 Malignant carcinoid tumor of the large intestine, unspecified portion — (Code first any associated multiple endocrine neoplasia syndrome: 258.01-258.03)(Use additional code to identify associated endocrine syndrome, as: carcinoid syndrome: 259.2) ▽
209.11 Malignant carcinoid tumor of the appendix — (Code first any associated multiple endocrine neoplasia syndrome: 258.01-258.03)(Use additional code to identify associated endocrine syndrome, as: carcinoid syndrome: 259.2)
209.12 Malignant carcinoid tumor of the cecum — (Code first any associated multiple endocrine neoplasia syndrome: 258.01-258.03)(Use additional code to identify associated endocrine syndrome, as: carcinoid syndrome: 259.2)
209.13 Malignant carcinoid tumor of the ascending colon — (Code first any associated multiple endocrine neoplasia syndrome: 258.01-258.03)(Use additional code to identify associated endocrine syndrome, as: carcinoid syndrome: 259.2)
209.14 Malignant carcinoid tumor of the transverse colon — (Code first any associated multiple endocrine neoplasia syndrome: 258.01-258.03)(Use additional code to identify associated endocrine syndrome, as: carcinoid syndrome: 259.2)
209.15 Malignant carcinoid tumor of the descending colon — (Code first any associated multiple endocrine neoplasia syndrome: 258.01-258.03)(Use additional code to identify associated endocrine syndrome, as: carcinoid syndrome: 259.2)
209.16 Malignant carcinoid tumor of the sigmoid colon — (Code first any associated multiple endocrine neoplasia syndrome: 258.01-258.03)(Use additional code to identify associated endocrine syndrome, as: carcinoid syndrome: 259.2)
209.50 Benign carcinoid tumor of the large intestine, unspecified portion — (Code first any associated multiple endocrine neoplasia syndrome: 258.01-258.03)(Use additional code to identify associated endocrine syndrome, as: carcinoid syndrome: 259.2) ▽
209.51 Benign carcinoid tumor of the appendix — (Code first any associated multiple endocrine neoplasia syndrome: 258.01-258.03)(Use additional code to identify associated endocrine syndrome, as: carcinoid syndrome: 259.2)
209.52 Benign carcinoid tumor of the cecum — (Code first any associated multiple endocrine neoplasia syndrome: 258.01-258.03)(Use additional code to identify associated endocrine syndrome, as: carcinoid syndrome: 259.2)
209.53 Benign carcinoid tumor of the ascending colon — (Code first any associated multiple endocrine neoplasia syndrome: 258.01-258.03)(Use additional code to identify associated endocrine syndrome, as: carcinoid syndrome: 259.2)
209.54 Benign carcinoid tumor of the transverse colon — (Code first any associated multiple endocrine neoplasia syndrome: 258.01-258.03)(Use additional code to identify associated endocrine syndrome, as: carcinoid syndrome: 259.2)
209.55 Benign carcinoid tumor of the descending colon — (Code first any associated multiple endocrine neoplasia syndrome: 258.01-258.03)(Use additional code to identify associated endocrine syndrome, as: carcinoid syndrome: 259.2)
209.56 Benign carcinoid tumor of the sigmoid colon — (Code first any associated multiple endocrine neoplasia syndrome: 258.01-258.03)(Use additional code to identify associated endocrine syndrome, as: carcinoid syndrome: 259.2)
209.57 Benign carcinoid tumor of the rectum — (Code first any associated multiple endocrine neoplasia syndrome: 258.01-258.03)(Use additional code to identify associated endocrine syndrome, as: carcinoid syndrome: 259.2)
211.3 Benign neoplasm of colon
211.4 Benign neoplasm of rectum and anal canal
230.3 Carcinoma in situ of colon
230.4 Carcinoma in situ of rectum
230.5 Carcinoma in situ of anal canal
230.6 Carcinoma in situ of anus, unspecified ▽
230.7 Carcinoma in situ of other and unspecified parts of intestine ▽
239.9 Neoplasm of unspecified nature, site unspecified ▽
555.0 Regional enteritis of small intestine
555.2 Regional enteritis of small intestine with large intestine
555.9 Regional enteritis of unspecified site ▽
556.0 Ulcerative (chronic) enterocolitis
556.1 Ulcerative (chronic) ileocolitis
556.2 Ulcerative (chronic) proctitis
556.3 Ulcerative (chronic) proctosigmoiditis
556.4 Pseudopolyposis of colon
556.5 Left sided ulcerative (chronic) colitis
556.6 Universal ulcerative (chronic) colitis
556.8 Other ulcerative colitis
556.9 Unspecified ulcerative colitis ▽
557.0 Acute vascular insufficiency of intestine
557.1 Chronic vascular insufficiency of intestine
557.9 Unspecified vascular insufficiency of intestine ▽
558.1 Gastroenteritis and colitis due to radiation
558.2 Toxic gastroenteritis and colitis — (Use additional E code to identify cause)
558.3 Gastroenteritis and colitis, allergic — (Use additional code to identify type of food allergy: V15.01-V15.05)
558.42 Eosinophilic colitis
558.9 Other and unspecified noninfectious gastroenteritis and colitis ▽
560.81 Intestinal or peritoneal adhesions with obstruction (postoperative) (postinfection)
560.89 Other specified intestinal obstruction
560.9 Unspecified intestinal obstruction ▽
562.10 Diverticulosis of colon (without mention of hemorrhage) — (Use additional code to identify any associated peritonitis: 567.0-567.9)
562.11 Diverticulitis of colon (without mention of hemorrhage) — (Use additional code to identify any associated peritonitis: 567.0-567.9)
564.00 Unspecified constipation ▽
564.01 Slow transit constipation
564.02 Outlet dysfunction constipation
564.09 Other constipation
564.7 Megacolon, other than Hirschsprung's
567.0 Peritonitis in infectious diseases classified elsewhere — (Code first underlying disease) ☒
567.1 Pneumococcal peritonitis
567.21 Peritonitis (acute) generalized
567.22 Peritoneal abscess
567.23 Spontaneous bacterial peritonitis
567.29 Other suppurative peritonitis
567.31 Psoas muscle abscess
567.38 Other retroperitoneal abscess
567.39 Other retroperitoneal infections
567.81 Choleperitonitis
567.82 Sclerosing mesenteritis
567.89 Other specified peritonitis
567.9 Unspecified peritonitis ▽
569.1 Rectal prolapse
569.2 Stenosis of rectum and anus
569.3 Hemorrhage of rectum and anus
569.41 Ulcer of anus and rectum
569.42 Anal or rectal pain
569.44 Dysplasia of anus
569.49 Other specified disorder of rectum and anus — (Use additional code for any associated fecal incontinence (787.60-787.63))
569.5 Abscess of intestine
569.61 Infection of colostomy or enterostomy — (Use additional code to identify organism: 041.00-041.9. Use additional code to specify type of infection: 038.0-038.9, 682.2)
569.69 Other complication of colostomy or enterostomy
569.81 Fistula of intestine, excluding rectum and anus
569.82 Ulceration of intestine
569.83 Perforation of intestine

569.84 Angiodysplasia of intestine (without mention of hemorrhage)
569.85 Angiodysplasia of intestine with hemorrhage
569.86 Dieulafoy lesion (hemorrhagic) of intestine
569.89 Other specified disorder of intestines
569.9 Unspecified disorder of intestine
578.1 Blood in stool
578.9 Hemorrhage of gastrointestinal tract, unspecified
751.3 Hirschsprung's disease and other congenital functional disorders of colon
783.21 Loss of weight — (Use additional code to identify Body Mass Index (BMI), if known: V85.0-V85.54)
783.22 Underweight — (Use additional code to identify Body Mass Index (BMI), if known: V85.0-V85.54)
783.7 Adult failure to thrive
793.4 Nonspecific (abnormal) findings on radiological and other examination of gastrointestinal tract
V10.05 Personal history of malignant neoplasm of large intestine
V12.70 Personal history of unspecified digestive disease
V16.0 Family history of malignant neoplasm of gastrointestinal tract
V44.3 Colostomy status
V55.3 Attention to colostomy
V71.1 Observation for suspected malignant neoplasm
V85.0 Body Mass Index less than 19, adult

ICD-9-CM Procedural

45.22 Endoscopy of large intestine through artificial stoma
45.25 Closed [endoscopic] biopsy of large intestine

HCPCS Level II Supplies & Services

A4270 Disposable endoscope sheath, each

44390

44390 Colonoscopy through stoma; with removal of foreign body

ICD-9-CM Diagnostic

936 Foreign body in intestine and colon
998.4 Foreign body accidentally left during procedure, not elsewhere classified
998.7 Acute reaction to foreign substance accidentally left during procedure, not elsewhere classified
V44.3 Colostomy status

ICD-9-CM Procedural

98.04 Removal of intraluminal foreign body from large intestine without incision

HCPCS Level II Supplies & Services

A4270 Disposable endoscope sheath, each

44391

44391 Colonoscopy through stoma; with control of bleeding (eg, injection, bipolar cautery, unipolar cautery, laser, heater probe, stapler, plasma coagulator)

ICD-9-CM Diagnostic

152.3 Malignant neoplasm of Meckel's diverticulum
152.8 Malignant neoplasm of other specified sites of small intestine
152.9 Malignant neoplasm of small intestine, unspecified site
153.0 Malignant neoplasm of hepatic flexure
153.1 Malignant neoplasm of transverse colon
153.8 Malignant neoplasm of other specified sites of large intestine
153.9 Malignant neoplasm of colon, unspecified site
154.0 Malignant neoplasm of rectosigmoid junction
154.1 Malignant neoplasm of rectum
197.5 Secondary malignant neoplasm of large intestine and rectum
209.10 Malignant carcinoid tumor of the large intestine, unspecified portion — (Code first any associated multiple endocrine neoplasia syndrome: 258.01-258.03)(Use additional code to identify associated endocrine syndrome, as: carcinoid syndrome: 259.2)
209.11 Malignant carcinoid tumor of the appendix — (Code first any associated multiple endocrine neoplasia syndrome: 258.01-258.03)(Use additional code to identify associated endocrine syndrome, as: carcinoid syndrome: 259.2)
209.12 Malignant carcinoid tumor of the cecum — (Code first any associated multiple endocrine neoplasia syndrome: 258.01-258.03)(Use additional code to identify associated endocrine syndrome, as: carcinoid syndrome: 259.2)
209.13 Malignant carcinoid tumor of the ascending colon — (Code first any associated multiple endocrine neoplasia syndrome: 258.01-258.03)(Use additional code to identify associated endocrine syndrome, as: carcinoid syndrome: 259.2)
209.14 Malignant carcinoid tumor of the transverse colon — (Code first any associated multiple endocrine neoplasia syndrome: 258.01-258.03)(Use additional code to identify associated endocrine syndrome, as: carcinoid syndrome: 259.2)
209.15 Malignant carcinoid tumor of the descending colon — (Code first any associated multiple endocrine neoplasia syndrome: 258.01-258.03)(Use additional code to identify associated endocrine syndrome, as: carcinoid syndrome: 259.2)
209.16 Malignant carcinoid tumor of the sigmoid colon — (Code first any associated multiple endocrine neoplasia syndrome: 258.01-258.03)(Use additional code to identify associated endocrine syndrome, as: carcinoid syndrome: 259.2)
230.3 Carcinoma in situ of colon
562.12 Diverticulosis of colon with hemorrhage — (Use additional code to identify any associated peritonitis: 567.0-567.9)
562.13 Diverticulitis of colon with hemorrhage — (Use additional code to identify any associated peritonitis: 567.0-567.9)
569.69 Other complication of colostomy or enterostomy
569.82 Ulceration of intestine
569.83 Perforation of intestine
569.85 Angiodysplasia of intestine with hemorrhage
569.86 Dieulafoy lesion (hemorrhagic) of intestine
578.1 Blood in stool
578.9 Hemorrhage of gastrointestinal tract, unspecified
V44.3 Colostomy status

ICD-9-CM Procedural

45.43 Endoscopic destruction of other lesion or tissue of large intestine

HCPCS Level II Supplies & Services

A4270 Disposable endoscope sheath, each

44392-44394

44392 Colonoscopy through stoma; with removal of tumor(s), polyp(s), or other lesion(s) by hot biopsy forceps or bipolar cautery
44393 with ablation of tumor(s), polyp(s), or other lesion(s) not amenable to removal by hot biopsy forceps, bipolar cautery or snare technique
44394 with removal of tumor(s), polyp(s), or other lesion(s) by snare technique

ICD-9-CM Diagnostic

153.0 Malignant neoplasm of hepatic flexure
153.1 Malignant neoplasm of transverse colon
153.2 Malignant neoplasm of descending colon
153.3 Malignant neoplasm of sigmoid colon
153.4 Malignant neoplasm of cecum
153.5 Malignant neoplasm of appendix
153.6 Malignant neoplasm of ascending colon
153.7 Malignant neoplasm of splenic flexure
153.8 Malignant neoplasm of other specified sites of large intestine
153.9 Malignant neoplasm of colon, unspecified site
154.0 Malignant neoplasm of rectosigmoid junction
154.1 Malignant neoplasm of rectum
197.5 Secondary malignant neoplasm of large intestine and rectum

209.10 Malignant carcinoid tumor of the large intestine, unspecified portion — (Code first any associated multiple endocrine neoplasia syndrome: 258.01-258.03)(Use additional code to identify associated endocrine syndrome, as: carcinoid syndrome: 259.2) ▽
209.11 Malignant carcinoid tumor of the appendix — (Code first any associated multiple endocrine neoplasia syndrome: 258.01-258.03)(Use additional code to identify associated endocrine syndrome, as: carcinoid syndrome: 259.2)
209.12 Malignant carcinoid tumor of the cecum — (Code first any associated multiple endocrine neoplasia syndrome: 258.01-258.03)(Use additional code to identify associated endocrine syndrome, as: carcinoid syndrome: 259.2)
209.13 Malignant carcinoid tumor of the ascending colon — (Code first any associated multiple endocrine neoplasia syndrome: 258.01-258.03)(Use additional code to identify associated endocrine syndrome, as: carcinoid syndrome: 259.2)
209.14 Malignant carcinoid tumor of the transverse colon — (Code first any associated multiple endocrine neoplasia syndrome: 258.01-258.03)(Use additional code to identify associated endocrine syndrome, as: carcinoid syndrome: 259.2)
209.15 Malignant carcinoid tumor of the descending colon — (Code first any associated multiple endocrine neoplasia syndrome: 258.01-258.03)(Use additional code to identify associated endocrine syndrome, as: carcinoid syndrome: 259.2)
209.16 Malignant carcinoid tumor of the sigmoid colon — (Code first any associated multiple endocrine neoplasia syndrome: 258.01-258.03)(Use additional code to identify associated endocrine syndrome, as: carcinoid syndrome: 259.2)
209.17 Malignant carcinoid tumor of the rectum — (Code first any associated multiple endocrine neoplasia syndrome: 258.01-258.03)(Use additional code to identify associated endocrine syndrome, as: carcinoid syndrome: 259.2)
209.50 Benign carcinoid tumor of the large intestine, unspecified portion — (Code first any associated multiple endocrine neoplasia syndrome: 258.01-258.03)(Use additional code to identify associated endocrine syndrome, as: carcinoid syndrome: 259.2) ▽
209.51 Benign carcinoid tumor of the appendix — (Code first any associated multiple endocrine neoplasia syndrome: 258.01-258.03)(Use additional code to identify associated endocrine syndrome, as: carcinoid syndrome: 259.2)
209.52 Benign carcinoid tumor of the cecum — (Code first any associated multiple endocrine neoplasia syndrome: 258.01-258.03)(Use additional code to identify associated endocrine syndrome, as: carcinoid syndrome: 259.2)
209.53 Benign carcinoid tumor of the ascending colon — (Code first any associated multiple endocrine neoplasia syndrome: 258.01-258.03)(Use additional code to identify associated endocrine syndrome, as: carcinoid syndrome: 259.2)
209.54 Benign carcinoid tumor of the transverse colon — (Code first any associated multiple endocrine neoplasia syndrome: 258.01-258.03)(Use additional code to identify associated endocrine syndrome, as: carcinoid syndrome: 259.2)
209.55 Benign carcinoid tumor of the descending colon — (Code first any associated multiple endocrine neoplasia syndrome: 258.01-258.03)(Use additional code to identify associated endocrine syndrome, as: carcinoid syndrome: 259.2)
209.56 Benign carcinoid tumor of the sigmoid colon — (Code first any associated multiple endocrine neoplasia syndrome: 258.01-258.03)(Use additional code to identify associated endocrine syndrome, as: carcinoid syndrome: 259.2)
209.57 Benign carcinoid tumor of the rectum — (Code first any associated multiple endocrine neoplasia syndrome: 258.01-258.03)(Use additional code to identify associated endocrine syndrome, as: carcinoid syndrome: 259.2)
211.2 Benign neoplasm of duodenum, jejunum, and ileum
211.3 Benign neoplasm of colon
230.3 Carcinoma in situ of colon
230.7 Carcinoma in situ of other and unspecified parts of intestine ▽
235.2 Neoplasm of uncertain behavior of stomach, intestines, and rectum
560.81 Intestinal or peritoneal adhesions with obstruction (postoperative) (postinfection)
569.85 Angiodysplasia of intestine with hemorrhage
578.1 Blood in stool
V44.3 Colostomy status

ICD-9-CM Procedural

45.42 Endoscopic polypectomy of large intestine
45.43 Endoscopic destruction of other lesion or tissue of large intestine

HCPCS Level II Supplies & Services

A4270 Disposable endoscope sheath, each

44397

44397 Colonoscopy through stoma; with transendoscopic stent placement (includes predilation)

ICD-9-CM Diagnostic

153.0 Malignant neoplasm of hepatic flexure
153.1 Malignant neoplasm of transverse colon
153.2 Malignant neoplasm of descending colon
153.3 Malignant neoplasm of sigmoid colon
153.4 Malignant neoplasm of cecum
153.5 Malignant neoplasm of appendix
153.6 Malignant neoplasm of ascending colon
153.7 Malignant neoplasm of splenic flexure
153.8 Malignant neoplasm of other specified sites of large intestine
153.9 Malignant neoplasm of colon, unspecified site ▽
154.0 Malignant neoplasm of rectosigmoid junction
154.1 Malignant neoplasm of rectum
197.5 Secondary malignant neoplasm of large intestine and rectum
209.10 Malignant carcinoid tumor of the large intestine, unspecified portion — (Code first any associated multiple endocrine neoplasia syndrome: 258.01-258.03)(Use additional code to identify associated endocrine syndrome, as: carcinoid syndrome: 259.2) ▽
209.11 Malignant carcinoid tumor of the appendix — (Code first any associated multiple endocrine neoplasia syndrome: 258.01-258.03)(Use additional code to identify associated endocrine syndrome, as: carcinoid syndrome: 259.2)
209.12 Malignant carcinoid tumor of the cecum — (Code first any associated multiple endocrine neoplasia syndrome: 258.01-258.03)(Use additional code to identify associated endocrine syndrome, as: carcinoid syndrome: 259.2)
209.13 Malignant carcinoid tumor of the ascending colon — (Code first any associated multiple endocrine neoplasia syndrome: 258.01-258.03)(Use additional code to identify associated endocrine syndrome, as: carcinoid syndrome: 259.2)
209.14 Malignant carcinoid tumor of the transverse colon — (Code first any associated multiple endocrine neoplasia syndrome: 258.01-258.03)(Use additional code to identify associated endocrine syndrome, as: carcinoid syndrome: 259.2)
209.15 Malignant carcinoid tumor of the descending colon — (Code first any associated multiple endocrine neoplasia syndrome: 258.01-258.03)(Use additional code to identify associated endocrine syndrome, as: carcinoid syndrome: 259.2)
209.16 Malignant carcinoid tumor of the sigmoid colon — (Code first any associated multiple endocrine neoplasia syndrome: 258.01-258.03)(Use additional code to identify associated endocrine syndrome, as: carcinoid syndrome: 259.2)
560.81 Intestinal or peritoneal adhesions with obstruction (postoperative) (postinfection)
560.89 Other specified intestinal obstruction
560.9 Unspecified intestinal obstruction ▽
751.2 Congenital atresia and stenosis of large intestine, rectum, and anal canal
997.49 Other digestive system complications

ICD-9-CM Procedural

45.22 Endoscopy of large intestine through artificial stoma
46.86 Endoscopic insertion of colonic stent(s)

HCPCS Level II Supplies & Services

C1874 Stent, coated/covered, with delivery system

44602-44603

44602 Suture of small intestine (enterorrhaphy) for perforated ulcer, diverticulum, wound, injury or rupture; single perforation

44603 multiple perforations

ICD-9-CM Diagnostic

532.10 Acute duodenal ulcer with perforation, without mention of obstruction — (Use additional E code to identify drug, if drug induced)

532.11 Acute duodenal ulcer with perforation and obstruction — (Use additional E code to identify drug, if drug induced)

532.20 Acute duodenal ulcer with hemorrhage and perforation, without mention of obstruction — (Use additional E code to identify drug, if drug induced)

532.21 Acute duodenal ulcer with hemorrhage, perforation, and obstruction — (Use additional E code to identify drug, if drug induced)

532.50 Chronic or unspecified duodenal ulcer with perforation, without mention of obstruction — (Use additional E code to identify drug, if drug induced)

532.51 Chronic or unspecified duodenal ulcer with perforation and obstruction — (Use additional E code to identify drug, if drug induced)

532.60 Chronic or unspecified duodenal ulcer with hemorrhage and perforation, without mention of obstruction — (Use additional E code to identify drug, if drug induced)

532.61 Chronic or unspecified duodenal ulcer with hemorrhage, perforation, and obstruction — (Use additional E code to identify drug, if drug induced)

560.2 Volvulus

560.81 Intestinal or peritoneal adhesions with obstruction (postoperative) (postinfection)

560.89 Other specified intestinal obstruction

562.00 Diverticulosis of small intestine (without mention of hemorrhage) — (Use additional code to identify any associated peritonitis: 567.0-567.9)

562.01 Diverticulitis of small intestine (without mention of hemorrhage) — (Use additional code to identify any associated peritonitis: 567.0-567.9)

562.02 Diverticulosis of small intestine with hemorrhage — (Use additional code to identify any associated peritonitis: 567.0-567.9)

562.03 Diverticulitis of small intestine with hemorrhage — (Use additional code to identify any associated peritonitis: 567.0-567.9)

567.0 Peritonitis in infectious diseases classified elsewhere — (Code first underlying disease) ☒

567.1 Pneumococcal peritonitis

567.21 Peritonitis (acute) generalized

567.22 Peritoneal abscess

567.23 Spontaneous bacterial peritonitis

567.29 Other suppurative peritonitis

567.31 Psoas muscle abscess

567.38 Other retroperitoneal abscess

567.39 Other retroperitoneal infections

567.81 Choleperitonitis

567.82 Sclerosing mesenteritis

567.89 Other specified peritonitis

567.9 Unspecified peritonitis ▽

569.81 Fistula of intestine, excluding rectum and anus

569.82 Ulceration of intestine

569.83 Perforation of intestine

569.84 Angiodysplasia of intestine (without mention of hemorrhage)

569.86 Dieulafoy lesion (hemorrhagic) of intestine

569.89 Other specified disorder of intestines

596.1 Intestinovesical fistula — (Use additional code to identify urinary incontinence: 625.6, 788.30-788.39)

863.20 Small intestine injury, unspecified site, without mention of open wound into cavity ▽

863.21 Duodenum injury without mention of open wound into cavity

863.30 Small intestine injury, unspecified site, with open wound into cavity ▽

863.31 Duodenum injury with open wound into cavity

ICD-9-CM Procedural

44.42 Suture of duodenal ulcer site

46.71 Suture of laceration of duodenum

46.73 Suture of laceration of small intestine, except duodenum

46.79 Other repair of intestine

44604-44605

44604 Suture of large intestine (colorrhaphy) for perforated ulcer, diverticulum, wound, injury or rupture (single or multiple perforations); without colostomy

44605 with colostomy

ICD-9-CM Diagnostic

540.0 Acute appendicitis with generalized peritonitis

540.1 Acute appendicitis with peritoneal abscess

556.0 Ulcerative (chronic) enterocolitis

556.1 Ulcerative (chronic) ileocolitis

556.2 Ulcerative (chronic) proctitis

556.3 Ulcerative (chronic) proctosigmoiditis

556.4 Pseudopolyposis of colon

556.5 Left sided ulcerative (chronic) colitis

556.6 Universal ulcerative (chronic) colitis

556.9 Unspecified ulcerative colitis ▽

560.2 Volvulus

562.10 Diverticulosis of colon (without mention of hemorrhage) — (Use additional code to identify any associated peritonitis: 567.0-567.9)

562.11 Diverticulitis of colon (without mention of hemorrhage) — (Use additional code to identify any associated peritonitis: 567.0-567.9)

562.12 Diverticulosis of colon with hemorrhage — (Use additional code to identify any associated peritonitis: 567.0-567.9)

562.13 Diverticulitis of colon with hemorrhage — (Use additional code to identify any associated peritonitis: 567.0-567.9)

567.0 Peritonitis in infectious diseases classified elsewhere — (Code first underlying disease) ☒

567.1 Pneumococcal peritonitis

567.21 Peritonitis (acute) generalized

567.22 Peritoneal abscess

567.23 Spontaneous bacterial peritonitis

567.29 Other suppurative peritonitis

567.31 Psoas muscle abscess

567.38 Other retroperitoneal abscess

567.39 Other retroperitoneal infections

567.81 Choleperitonitis

567.82 Sclerosing mesenteritis

567.89 Other specified peritonitis

567.9 Unspecified peritonitis ▽

569.81 Fistula of intestine, excluding rectum and anus

569.82 Ulceration of intestine

569.83 Perforation of intestine

569.84 Angiodysplasia of intestine (without mention of hemorrhage)

569.85 Angiodysplasia of intestine with hemorrhage

569.86 Dieulafoy lesion (hemorrhagic) of intestine

569.89 Other specified disorder of intestines

777.6 Perinatal intestinal perforation — (Use additional code(s) to further specify condition)

863.40 Colon injury unspecified site, without mention of open wound into cavity ▽

863.41 Ascending (right) colon injury without mention of open wound into cavity

863.42 Transverse colon injury without mention of open wound into cavity

863.43 Descending (left) colon injury without mention of open wound into cavity

863.44 Sigmoid colon injury without mention of open wound into cavity

863.45 Rectum injury without mention of open wound into cavity

863.46 Injury to multiple sites in colon and rectum without mention of open wound into cavity
863.49 Other colon and rectum injury, without mention of open wound into cavity
863.50 Colon injury, unspecified site, with open wound into cavity
863.52 Transverse colon injury with open wound into cavity
863.59 Other injury to colon and rectum with open wound into cavity

ICD-9-CM Procedural

46.03 Exteriorization of large intestine
46.11 Temporary colostomy
46.13 Permanent colostomy
46.75 Suture of laceration of large intestine
46.79 Other repair of intestine

44615

44615 Intestinal stricturoplasty (enterotomy and enterorrhaphy) with or without dilation, for intestinal obstruction

ICD-9-CM Diagnostic

560.31 Gallstone ileus
560.81 Intestinal or peritoneal adhesions with obstruction (postoperative) (postinfection)
560.89 Other specified intestinal obstruction
560.9 Unspecified intestinal obstruction
751.1 Congenital atresia and stenosis of small intestine
751.2 Congenital atresia and stenosis of large intestine, rectum, and anal canal
997.49 Other digestive system complications

ICD-9-CM Procedural

45.00 Incision of intestine, not otherwise specified
45.02 Other incision of small intestine
45.03 Incision of large intestine
46.73 Suture of laceration of small intestine, except duodenum
46.79 Other repair of intestine
46.85 Dilation of intestine

44620-44626

44620 Closure of enterostomy, large or small intestine;
44625 with resection and anastomosis other than colorectal
44626 with resection and colorectal anastomosis (eg, closure of Hartmann type procedure)

ICD-9-CM Diagnostic

560.81 Intestinal or peritoneal adhesions with obstruction (postoperative) (postinfection)
569.61 Infection of colostomy or enterostomy — (Use additional code to identify organism: 041.00-041.9. Use additional code to specify type of infection: 038.0-038.9, 682.2)
569.62 Mechanical complication of colostomy and enterostomy
569.69 Other complication of colostomy or enterostomy
V10.05 Personal history of malignant neoplasm of large intestine
V10.06 Personal history of malignant neoplasm of rectum, rectosigmoid junction, and anus
V10.09 Personal history of malignant neoplasm of other site in gastrointestinal tract
V55.2 Attention to ileostomy
V55.3 Attention to colostomy
V55.4 Attention to other artificial opening of digestive tract

ICD-9-CM Procedural

45.90 Intestinal anastomosis, not otherwise specified
45.94 Large-to-large intestinal anastomosis
46.50 Closure of intestinal stoma, not otherwise specified
46.51 Closure of stoma of small intestine
46.52 Closure of stoma of large intestine

44640

44640 Closure of intestinal cutaneous fistula

ICD-9-CM Diagnostic

537.4 Fistula of stomach or duodenum
569.81 Fistula of intestine, excluding rectum and anus
576.4 Fistula of bile duct
756.71 Prune belly syndrome
756.79 Other congenital anomalies of abdominal wall
998.6 Persistent postoperative fistula, not elsewhere classified

ICD-9-CM Procedural

46.72 Closure of fistula of duodenum
46.74 Closure of fistula of small intestine, except duodenum

44650

44650 Closure of enteroenteric or enterocolic fistula

ICD-9-CM Diagnostic

537.4 Fistula of stomach or duodenum
569.81 Fistula of intestine, excluding rectum and anus
576.4 Fistula of bile duct
751.5 Other congenital anomalies of intestine
998.6 Persistent postoperative fistula, not elsewhere classified

ICD-9-CM Procedural

46.72 Closure of fistula of duodenum
46.74 Closure of fistula of small intestine, except duodenum
46.76 Closure of fistula of large intestine
47.92 Closure of appendiceal fistula

44660-44661

44660 Closure of enterovesical fistula; without intestinal or bladder resection
44661 with intestine and/or bladder resection

ICD-9-CM Diagnostic

555.0 Regional enteritis of small intestine
555.1 Regional enteritis of large intestine
555.2 Regional enteritis of small intestine with large intestine
555.9 Regional enteritis of unspecified site
562.11 Diverticulitis of colon (without mention of hemorrhage) — (Use additional code to identify any associated peritonitis: 567.0-567.9)
567.0 Peritonitis in infectious diseases classified elsewhere — (Code first underlying disease)
567.1 Pneumococcal peritonitis
567.21 Peritonitis (acute) generalized
567.22 Peritoneal abscess
567.23 Spontaneous bacterial peritonitis
567.29 Other suppurative peritonitis
567.38 Other retroperitoneal abscess
567.39 Other retroperitoneal infections
567.81 Choleperitonitis
567.82 Sclerosing mesenteritis
567.89 Other specified peritonitis
567.9 Unspecified peritonitis
596.1 Intestinovesical fistula — (Use additional code to identify urinary incontinence: 625.6, 788.30-788.39)
998.6 Persistent postoperative fistula, not elsewhere classified

ICD-9-CM Procedural

45.62 Other partial resection of small intestine
45.79 Other and unspecified partial excision of large intestine

57.6 Partial cystectomy
57.83 Repair of fistula involving bladder and intestine

44680

44680 Intestinal plication (separate procedure)

ICD-9-CM Diagnostic

560.81 Intestinal or peritoneal adhesions with obstruction (postoperative) (postinfection)
568.81 Hemoperitoneum (nontraumatic)
751.1 Congenital atresia and stenosis of small intestine
751.2 Congenital atresia and stenosis of large intestine, rectum, and anal canal
997.49 Other digestive system complications

ICD-9-CM Procedural

46.60 Fixation of intestine, not otherwise specified
46.61 Fixation of small intestine to abdominal wall
46.62 Other fixation of small intestine
46.63 Fixation of large intestine to abdominal wall

44700

44700 Exclusion of small intestine from pelvis by mesh or other prosthesis, or native tissue (eg, bladder or omentum)

ICD-9-CM Diagnostic

151.0 Malignant neoplasm of cardia
151.1 Malignant neoplasm of pylorus
151.2 Malignant neoplasm of pyloric antrum
151.3 Malignant neoplasm of fundus of stomach
151.4 Malignant neoplasm of body of stomach
151.5 Malignant neoplasm of lesser curvature of stomach, unspecified ▽
151.6 Malignant neoplasm of greater curvature of stomach, unspecified ▽
151.8 Malignant neoplasm of other specified sites of stomach
151.9 Malignant neoplasm of stomach, unspecified site ▽
152.3 Malignant neoplasm of Meckel's diverticulum
153.0 Malignant neoplasm of hepatic flexure
153.1 Malignant neoplasm of transverse colon
153.2 Malignant neoplasm of descending colon
153.3 Malignant neoplasm of sigmoid colon
153.4 Malignant neoplasm of cecum
153.5 Malignant neoplasm of appendix
153.6 Malignant neoplasm of ascending colon
153.7 Malignant neoplasm of splenic flexure
153.8 Malignant neoplasm of other specified sites of large intestine
153.9 Malignant neoplasm of colon, unspecified site ▽
154.0 Malignant neoplasm of rectosigmoid junction
155.0 Malignant neoplasm of liver, primary
157.9 Malignant neoplasm of pancreas, part unspecified ▽
158.8 Malignant neoplasm of specified parts of peritoneum
158.9 Malignant neoplasm of peritoneum, unspecified ▽
179 Malignant neoplasm of uterus, part unspecified ▽ ♀
180.0 Malignant neoplasm of endocervix ♀
180.1 Malignant neoplasm of exocervix ♀
180.8 Malignant neoplasm of other specified sites of cervix ♀
182.0 Malignant neoplasm of corpus uteri, except isthmus ♀
182.1 Malignant neoplasm of isthmus ♀
182.8 Malignant neoplasm of other specified sites of body of uterus ♀
183.0 Malignant neoplasm of ovary — (Use additional code to identify any functional activity) ♀
185 Malignant neoplasm of prostate ♂
186.0 Malignant neoplasm of undescended testis — (Use additional code to identify any functional activity) ♂
186.9 Malignant neoplasm of other and unspecified testis — (Use additional code to identify any functional activity) ▽ ♂
188.0 Malignant neoplasm of trigone of urinary bladder
188.1 Malignant neoplasm of dome of urinary bladder
188.2 Malignant neoplasm of lateral wall of urinary bladder
188.3 Malignant neoplasm of anterior wall of urinary bladder
188.4 Malignant neoplasm of posterior wall of urinary bladder
188.5 Malignant neoplasm of bladder neck
188.6 Malignant neoplasm of ureteric orifice
188.7 Malignant neoplasm of urachus
188.8 Malignant neoplasm of other specified sites of bladder
188.9 Malignant neoplasm of bladder, part unspecified ▽
189.0 Malignant neoplasm of kidney, except pelvis
189.1 Malignant neoplasm of renal pelvis
189.2 Malignant neoplasm of ureter
196.2 Secondary and unspecified malignant neoplasm of intra-abdominal lymph nodes
196.6 Secondary and unspecified malignant neoplasm of intrapelvic lymph nodes
197.4 Secondary malignant neoplasm of small intestine including duodenum
197.5 Secondary malignant neoplasm of large intestine and rectum
197.6 Secondary malignant neoplasm of retroperitoneum and peritoneum
198.82 Secondary malignant neoplasm of genital organs
199.0 Disseminated malignant neoplasm
199.1 Other malignant neoplasm of unspecified site
201.46 Hodgkin's disease, lymphocytic-histiocytic predominance of intrapelvic lymph nodes
201.96 Hodgkin's disease, unspecified type, of intrapelvic lymph nodes ▽
202.53 Letterer-Siwe disease of intra-abdominal lymph nodes
202.56 Letterer-Siwe disease of intrapelvic lymph nodes
202.63 Malignant mast cell tumors of intra-abdominal lymph nodes
202.66 Malignant mast cell tumors of intrapelvic lymph nodes
202.83 Other malignant lymphomas of intra-abdominal lymph nodes
202.86 Other malignant lymphomas of intrapelvic lymph nodes
209.00 Malignant carcinoid tumor of the small intestine, unspecified portion — (Code first any associated multiple endocrine neoplasia syndrome: 258.01-258.03)(Use additional code to identify associated endocrine syndrome, as: carcinoid syndrome: 259.2) ▽
209.01 Malignant carcinoid tumor of the duodenum — (Code first any associated multiple endocrine neoplasia syndrome: 258.01-258.03)(Use additional code to identify associated endocrine syndrome, as: carcinoid syndrome: 259.2)
209.02 Malignant carcinoid tumor of the jejunum — (Code first any associated multiple endocrine neoplasia syndrome: 258.01-258.03)(Use additional code to identify associated endocrine syndrome, as: carcinoid syndrome: 259.2)
209.03 Malignant carcinoid tumor of the ileum — (Code first any associated multiple endocrine neoplasia syndrome: 258.01-258.03)(Use additional code to identify associated endocrine syndrome, as: carcinoid syndrome: 259.2)
209.10 Malignant carcinoid tumor of the large intestine, unspecified portion — (Code first any associated multiple endocrine neoplasia syndrome: 258.01-258.03)(Use additional code to identify associated endocrine syndrome, as: carcinoid syndrome: 259.2) ▽
209.11 Malignant carcinoid tumor of the appendix — (Code first any associated multiple endocrine neoplasia syndrome: 258.01-258.03)(Use additional code to identify associated endocrine syndrome, as: carcinoid syndrome: 259.2)
209.12 Malignant carcinoid tumor of the cecum — (Code first any associated multiple endocrine neoplasia syndrome: 258.01-258.03)(Use additional code to identify associated endocrine syndrome, as: carcinoid syndrome: 259.2)
209.13 Malignant carcinoid tumor of the ascending colon — (Code first any associated multiple endocrine neoplasia syndrome: 258.01-258.03)(Use additional code to identify associated endocrine syndrome, as: carcinoid syndrome: 259.2)
209.14 Malignant carcinoid tumor of the transverse colon — (Code first any associated multiple endocrine neoplasia syndrome: 258.01-258.03)(Use additional code to identify associated endocrine syndrome, as: carcinoid syndrome: 259.2)

209.15 Malignant carcinoid tumor of the descending colon — (Code first any associated multiple endocrine neoplasia syndrome: 258.01-258.03)(Use additional code to identify associated endocrine syndrome, as: carcinoid syndrome: 259.2)

209.16 Malignant carcinoid tumor of the sigmoid colon — (Code first any associated multiple endocrine neoplasia syndrome: 258.01-258.03)(Use additional code to identify associated endocrine syndrome, as: carcinoid syndrome: 259.2)

209.17 Malignant carcinoid tumor of the rectum — (Code first any associated multiple endocrine neoplasia syndrome: 258.01-258.03)(Use additional code to identify associated endocrine syndrome, as: carcinoid syndrome: 259.2)

209.20 Malignant carcinoid tumor of unknown primary site — (Code first any associated multiple endocrine neoplasia syndrome: 258.01-258.03)(Use additional code to identify associated endocrine syndrome, as: carcinoid syndrome: 259.2)

209.23 Malignant carcinoid tumor of the stomach — (Code first any associated multiple endocrine neoplasia syndrome: 258.01-258.03)(Use additional code to identify associated endocrine syndrome, as: carcinoid syndrome: 259.2)

209.25 Malignant carcinoid tumor of foregut, not otherwise specified — (Code first any associated multiple endocrine neoplasia syndrome: 258.01-258.03)(Use additional code to identify associated endocrine syndrome, as: carcinoid syndrome: 259.2)

209.26 Malignant carcinoid tumor of midgut, not otherwise specified — (Code first any associated multiple endocrine neoplasia syndrome: 258.01-258.03)(Use additional code to identify associated endocrine syndrome, as: carcinoid syndrome: 259.2)

209.27 Malignant carcinoid tumor of hindgut, not otherwise specified — (Code first any associated multiple endocrine neoplasia syndrome: 258.01-258.03)(Use additional code to identify associated endocrine syndrome, as: carcinoid syndrome: 259.2)

209.29 Malignant carcinoid tumor of other sites — (Code first any associated multiple endocrine neoplasia syndrome: 258.01-258.03)(Use additional code to identify associated endocrine syndrome, as: carcinoid syndrome: 259.2)

209.30 Malignant poorly differentiated neuroendocrine carcinoma, any site — (Code first any associated multiple endocrine neoplasia syndrome: 258.01-258.03)(Use additional code to identify associated endocrine syndrome, as: carcinoid syndrome: 259.2) ▽

209.40 Benign carcinoid tumor of the small intestine, unspecified portion — (Code first any associated multiple endocrine neoplasia syndrome: 258.01-258.03)(Use additional code to identify associated endocrine syndrome, as: carcinoid syndrome: 259.2) ▽

209.42 Benign carcinoid tumor of the jejunum — (Code first any associated multiple endocrine neoplasia syndrome: 258.01-258.03)(Use additional code to identify associated endocrine syndrome, as: carcinoid syndrome: 259.2)

209.43 Benign carcinoid tumor of the ileum — (Code first any associated multiple endocrine neoplasia syndrome: 258.01-258.03)(Use additional code to identify associated endocrine syndrome, as: carcinoid syndrome: 259.2)

209.50 Benign carcinoid tumor of the large intestine, unspecified portion — (Code first any associated multiple endocrine neoplasia syndrome: 258.01-258.03)(Use additional code to identify associated endocrine syndrome, as: carcinoid syndrome: 259.2) ▽

209.51 Benign carcinoid tumor of the appendix — (Code first any associated multiple endocrine neoplasia syndrome: 258.01-258.03)(Use additional code to identify associated endocrine syndrome, as: carcinoid syndrome: 259.2)

209.52 Benign carcinoid tumor of the cecum — (Code first any associated multiple endocrine neoplasia syndrome: 258.01-258.03)(Use additional code to identify associated endocrine syndrome, as: carcinoid syndrome: 259.2)

209.53 Benign carcinoid tumor of the ascending colon — (Code first any associated multiple endocrine neoplasia syndrome: 258.01-258.03)(Use additional code to identify associated endocrine syndrome, as: carcinoid syndrome: 259.2)

209.54 Benign carcinoid tumor of the transverse colon — (Code first any associated multiple endocrine neoplasia syndrome: 258.01-258.03)(Use additional code to identify associated endocrine syndrome, as: carcinoid syndrome: 259.2)

209.55 Benign carcinoid tumor of the descending colon — (Code first any associated multiple endocrine neoplasia syndrome: 258.01-258.03)(Use additional code to identify associated endocrine syndrome, as: carcinoid syndrome: 259.2)

209.56 Benign carcinoid tumor of the sigmoid colon — (Code first any associated multiple endocrine neoplasia syndrome: 258.01-258.03)(Use additional code to identify associated endocrine syndrome, as: carcinoid syndrome: 259.2)

209.57 Benign carcinoid tumor of the rectum — (Code first any associated multiple endocrine neoplasia syndrome: 258.01-258.03)(Use additional code to identify associated endocrine syndrome, as: carcinoid syndrome: 259.2)

209.60 Benign carcinoid tumor of unknown primary site — (Code first any associated multiple endocrine neoplasia syndrome: 258.01-258.03)(Use additional code to identify associated endocrine syndrome, as: carcinoid syndrome: 259.2)

209.63 Benign carcinoid tumor of the stomach — (Code first any associated multiple endocrine neoplasia syndrome: 258.01-258.03)(Use additional code to identify associated endocrine syndrome, as: carcinoid syndrome: 259.2)

209.65 Benign carcinoid tumor of foregut, not otherwise specified — (Code first any associated multiple endocrine neoplasia syndrome: 258.01-258.03)(Use additional code to identify associated endocrine syndrome, as: carcinoid syndrome: 259.2)

209.66 Benign carcinoid tumor of midgut, not otherwise specified — (Code first any associated multiple endocrine neoplasia syndrome: 258.01-258.03)(Use additional code to identify associated endocrine syndrome, as: carcinoid syndrome: 259.2)

209.67 Benign carcinoid tumor of hindgut, not otherwise specified — (Code first any associated multiple endocrine neoplasia syndrome: 258.01-258.03)(Use additional code to identify associated endocrine syndrome, as: carcinoid syndrome: 259.2)

209.69 Benign carcinoid tumor of other sites — (Code first any associated multiple endocrine neoplasia syndrome: 258.01-258.03)(Use additional code to identify associated endocrine syndrome, as: carcinoid syndrome: 259.2)

209.74 Secondary neuroendocrine tumor of peritoneum

558.1 Gastroenteritis and colitis due to radiation

ICD-9-CM Procedural

46.62 Other fixation of small intestine

46.99 Other operations on intestines

44701

44701 Intraoperative colonic lavage (List separately in addition to code for primary procedure)

ICD-9-CM Diagnostic

This is an add-on code. Refer to the corresponding primary procedure code for ICD-9-CM diagnosis code links.

ICD-9-CM Procedural

46.99 Other operations on intestines

HCPCS Level II Supplies & Services

The HCPCS Level II code(s) would be the same as the actual procedure performed because these are in-addition-to codes.

44705

44705 Preparation of fecal microbiota for instillation, including assessment of donor specimen

ICD-9-CM Diagnostic

008.45 Intestinal infections due to clostridium difficile

556.0 Ulcerative (chronic) enterocolitis

556.1 Ulcerative (chronic) ileocolitis

556.2 Ulcerative (chronic) proctitis

556.3 Ulcerative (chronic) proctosigmoiditis

556.5 Left sided ulcerative (chronic) colitis

556.6 Universal ulcerative (chronic) colitis

556.8 Other ulcerative colitis

556.9 Unspecified ulcerative colitis ▽

558.9 Other and unspecified noninfectious gastroenteritis and colitis ▽

564.00 Unspecified constipation ▽

564.01 Slow transit constipation

564.02 Outlet dysfunction constipation

564.09 Other constipation

569.9 Unspecified disorder of intestine ▽

ICD-9-CM Procedural

99.99 Other miscellaneous procedures

HCPCS Level II Supplies & Services

G0455 Preparation with instillation of fecal microbiota by any method, including assessment of donor specimen

44715-44721

44715 Backbench standard preparation of cadaver or living donor intestine allograft prior to transplantation, including mobilization and fashioning of the superior mesenteric artery and vein

44720 Backbench reconstruction of cadaver or living donor intestine allograft prior to transplantation; venous anastomosis, each

44721 arterial anastomosis, each

ICD-9-CM Diagnostic

152.0 Malignant neoplasm of duodenum
152.1 Malignant neoplasm of jejunum
152.2 Malignant neoplasm of ileum
152.8 Malignant neoplasm of other specified sites of small intestine
152.9 Malignant neoplasm of small intestine, unspecified site ▽
197.4 Secondary malignant neoplasm of small intestine including duodenum
209.00 Malignant carcinoid tumor of the small intestine, unspecified portion — (Code first any associated multiple endocrine neoplasia syndrome: 258.01-258.03)(Use additional code to identify associated endocrine syndrome, as: carcinoid syndrome: 259.2) ▽
209.01 Malignant carcinoid tumor of the duodenum — (Code first any associated multiple endocrine neoplasia syndrome: 258.01-258.03)(Use additional code to identify associated endocrine syndrome, as: carcinoid syndrome: 259.2)
209.02 Malignant carcinoid tumor of the jejunum — (Code first any associated multiple endocrine neoplasia syndrome: 258.01-258.03)(Use additional code to identify associated endocrine syndrome, as: carcinoid syndrome: 259.2)
209.03 Malignant carcinoid tumor of the ileum — (Code first any associated multiple endocrine neoplasia syndrome: 258.01-258.03)(Use additional code to identify associated endocrine syndrome, as: carcinoid syndrome: 259.2)
551.00 Femoral hernia with gangrene, unilateral or unspecified (not specified as recurrent)
551.21 Incisional ventral hernia, with gangrene
551.8 Hernia of other specified sites, with gangrene
551.9 Hernia of unspecified site, with gangrene ▽
552.00 Unilateral or unspecified femoral hernia with obstruction
552.21 Incisional hernia with obstruction
555.0 Regional enteritis of small intestine
555.9 Regional enteritis of unspecified site ▽
556.1 Ulcerative (chronic) ileocolitis
556.8 Other ulcerative colitis
556.9 Unspecified ulcerative colitis ▽
560.0 Intussusception
560.1 Paralytic ileus
560.2 Volvulus
560.81 Intestinal or peritoneal adhesions with obstruction (postoperative) (postinfection)
560.89 Other specified intestinal obstruction
560.9 Unspecified intestinal obstruction ▽
562.00 Diverticulosis of small intestine (without mention of hemorrhage) — (Use additional code to identify any associated peritonitis: 567.0-567.9)
562.01 Diverticulitis of small intestine (without mention of hemorrhage) — (Use additional code to identify any associated peritonitis: 567.0-567.9)
562.02 Diverticulosis of small intestine with hemorrhage — (Use additional code to identify any associated peritonitis: 567.0-567.9)
562.03 Diverticulitis of small intestine with hemorrhage — (Use additional code to identify any associated peritonitis: 567.0-567.9)
567.0 Peritonitis in infectious diseases classified elsewhere — (Code first underlying disease) ☒
567.1 Pneumococcal peritonitis
567.21 Peritonitis (acute) generalized
567.22 Peritoneal abscess
567.23 Spontaneous bacterial peritonitis
567.29 Other suppurative peritonitis
567.31 Psoas muscle abscess
567.38 Other retroperitoneal abscess
567.39 Other retroperitoneal infections
567.81 Choleperitonitis
567.82 Sclerosing mesenteritis
567.89 Other specified peritonitis
567.9 Unspecified peritonitis ▽
569.85 Angiodysplasia of intestine with hemorrhage
569.89 Other specified disorder of intestines
578.9 Hemorrhage of gastrointestinal tract, unspecified ▽
579.3 Other and unspecified postsurgical nonabsorption ▽
751.1 Congenital atresia and stenosis of small intestine
751.5 Other congenital anomalies of intestine
863.30 Small intestine injury, unspecified site, with open wound into cavity ▽
863.31 Duodenum injury with open wound into cavity
863.39 Other injury to small intestine with open wound into cavity
863.90 Gastrointestinal tract injury, unspecified site, with open wound into cavity ▽
863.99 Injury to other and unspecified gastrointestinal sites with open wound into cavity
997.49 Other digestive system complications
998.51 Infected postoperative seroma — (Use additional code to identify organism)
998.59 Other postoperative infection — (Use additional code to identify infection)

ICD-9-CM Procedural

The ICD-9-CM procedural code(s) would be the same as the actual procedure performed because these are in-addition-to codes.

Meckel's Diverticulum and the Messentery

44800

44800 Excision of Meckel's diverticulum (diverticulectomy) or omphalomesenteric duct

ICD-9-CM Diagnostic

152.3 Malignant neoplasm of Meckel's diverticulum
197.4 Secondary malignant neoplasm of small intestine including duodenum
751.0 Meckel's diverticulum

ICD-9-CM Procedural

45.33 Local excision of lesion or tissue of small intestine, except duodenum

44820

44820 Excision of lesion of mesentery (separate procedure)

ICD-9-CM Diagnostic

153.3 Malignant neoplasm of sigmoid colon
153.4 Malignant neoplasm of cecum
153.8 Malignant neoplasm of other specified sites of large intestine
158.8 Malignant neoplasm of specified parts of peritoneum
183.4 Malignant neoplasm of parametrium of uterus ♀
197.6 Secondary malignant neoplasm of retroperitoneum and peritoneum
209.12 Malignant carcinoid tumor of the cecum — (Code first any associated multiple endocrine neoplasia syndrome: 258.01-258.03)(Use additional code to identify associated endocrine syndrome, as: carcinoid syndrome: 259.2)
209.16 Malignant carcinoid tumor of the sigmoid colon — (Code first any associated multiple endocrine neoplasia syndrome: 258.01-258.03)(Use additional code to identify associated endocrine syndrome, as: carcinoid syndrome: 259.2)
209.29 Malignant carcinoid tumor of other sites — (Code first any associated multiple endocrine neoplasia syndrome: 258.01-258.03)(Use additional code to identify associated endocrine syndrome, as: carcinoid syndrome: 259.2)

209.30 Malignant poorly differentiated neuroendocrine carcinoma, any site — (Code first any associated multiple endocrine neoplasia syndrome: 258.01-258.03)(Use additional code to identify associated endocrine syndrome, as: carcinoid syndrome: 259.2) ▽
209.69 Benign carcinoid tumor of other sites — (Code first any associated multiple endocrine neoplasia syndrome: 258.01-258.03)(Use additional code to identify associated endocrine syndrome, as: carcinoid syndrome: 259.2)
209.74 Secondary neuroendocrine tumor of peritoneum
211.8 Benign neoplasm of retroperitoneum and peritoneum
235.4 Neoplasm of uncertain behavior of retroperitoneum and peritoneum
239.0 Neoplasm of unspecified nature of digestive system
568.0 Peritoneal adhesions (postoperative) (postinfection)
568.81 Hemoperitoneum (nontraumatic)
568.82 Peritoneal effusion (chronic)
568.89 Other specified disorder of peritoneum
569.82 Ulceration of intestine

ICD-9-CM Procedural

54.4 Excision or destruction of peritoneal tissue

44850

44850 Suture of mesentery (separate procedure)

ICD-9-CM Diagnostic

560.81 Intestinal or peritoneal adhesions with obstruction (postoperative) (postinfection)
863.20 Small intestine injury, unspecified site, without mention of open wound into cavity ▽
863.30 Small intestine injury, unspecified site, with open wound into cavity ▽
863.40 Colon injury unspecified site, without mention of open wound into cavity ▽
863.50 Colon injury, unspecified site, with open wound into cavity ▽
863.89 Injury to other and unspecified gastrointestinal sites without mention of open wound into cavity
863.99 Injury to other and unspecified gastrointestinal sites with open wound into cavity

ICD-9-CM Procedural

54.75 Other repair of mesentery

Appendix

44900

44900 Incision and drainage of appendiceal abscess, open

ICD-9-CM Diagnostic

540.1 Acute appendicitis with peritoneal abscess
542 Other appendicitis

ICD-9-CM Procedural

47.2 Drainage of appendiceal abscess

44950-44955

44950 Appendectomy;
44955 when done for indicated purpose at time of other major procedure (not as separate procedure) (List separately in addition to code for primary procedure)

ICD-9-CM Diagnostic

153.5 Malignant neoplasm of appendix
209.11 Malignant carcinoid tumor of the appendix — (Code first any associated multiple endocrine neoplasia syndrome: 258.01-258.03)(Use additional code to identify associated endocrine syndrome, as: carcinoid syndrome: 259.2)
540.9 Acute appendicitis without mention of peritonitis
541 Appendicitis, unqualified
542 Other appendicitis
543.0 Hyperplasia of appendix (lymphoid)
543.9 Other and unspecified diseases of appendix ▽
617.5 Endometriosis of intestine ♀
780.60 Fever, unspecified ▽
787.01 Nausea with vomiting
787.02 Nausea alone
787.03 Vomiting alone
787.04 Bilious emesis
787.99 Other symptoms involving digestive system
789.03 Abdominal pain, right lower quadrant
789.05 Abdominal pain, periumbilic
789.06 Abdominal pain, epigastric
789.07 Abdominal pain, generalized
789.09 Abdominal pain, other specified site
789.30 Abdominal or pelvic swelling, mass or lump, unspecified site ▽
789.33 Abdominal or pelvic swelling, mass, or lump, right lower quadrant
789.35 Abdominal or pelvic swelling, mass or lump, periumbilic
789.36 Abdominal or pelvic swelling, mass, or lump, epigastric
789.37 Abdominal or pelvic swelling, mass, or lump, generalized
789.39 Abdominal or pelvic swelling, mass, or lump, other specified site
789.63 Abdominal tenderness, right lower quadrant
V50.49 Other prophylactic organ removal

ICD-9-CM Procedural

47.09 Other appendectomy
47.19 Other incidental appendectomy

44960

44960 Appendectomy; for ruptured appendix with abscess or generalized peritonitis

ICD-9-CM Diagnostic

540.0 Acute appendicitis with generalized peritonitis
540.1 Acute appendicitis with peritoneal abscess

ICD-9-CM Procedural

47.09 Other appendectomy

44970

44970 Laparoscopy, surgical, appendectomy

ICD-9-CM Diagnostic

153.5 Malignant neoplasm of appendix
197.5 Secondary malignant neoplasm of large intestine and rectum
209.11 Malignant carcinoid tumor of the appendix — (Code first any associated multiple endocrine neoplasia syndrome: 258.01-258.03)(Use additional code to identify associated endocrine syndrome, as: carcinoid syndrome: 259.2)
211.3 Benign neoplasm of colon
230.3 Carcinoma in situ of colon
235.2 Neoplasm of uncertain behavior of stomach, intestines, and rectum
239.0 Neoplasm of unspecified nature of digestive system
540.0 Acute appendicitis with generalized peritonitis
540.1 Acute appendicitis with peritoneal abscess
540.9 Acute appendicitis without mention of peritonitis
541 Appendicitis, unqualified
542 Other appendicitis
543.0 Hyperplasia of appendix (lymphoid)
543.9 Other and unspecified diseases of appendix ▽
780.60 Fever, unspecified ▽
789.03 Abdominal pain, right lower quadrant
789.05 Abdominal pain, periumbilic
789.07 Abdominal pain, generalized
789.09 Abdominal pain, other specified site
789.33 Abdominal or pelvic swelling, mass, or lump, right lower quadrant
789.35 Abdominal or pelvic swelling, mass or lump, periumbilic

789.37 Abdominal or pelvic swelling, mass, or lump, generalized
789.39 Abdominal or pelvic swelling, mass, or lump, other specified site

ICD-9-CM Procedural

47.01 Laparoscopic appendectomy
47.11 Laparoscopic incidental appendectomy

Rectum

45000

45000 Transrectal drainage of pelvic abscess

ICD-9-CM Diagnostic

540.1 Acute appendicitis with peritoneal abscess
555.1 Regional enteritis of large intestine
560.81 Intestinal or peritoneal adhesions with obstruction (postoperative) (postinfection)
562.11 Diverticulitis of colon (without mention of hemorrhage) — (Use additional code to identify any associated peritonitis: 567.0-567.9)
567.0 Peritonitis in infectious diseases classified elsewhere — (Code first underlying disease) ☒
567.1 Pneumococcal peritonitis
567.21 Peritonitis (acute) generalized
567.22 Peritoneal abscess
567.23 Spontaneous bacterial peritonitis
567.29 Other suppurative peritonitis
567.31 Psoas muscle abscess
567.38 Other retroperitoneal abscess
567.39 Other retroperitoneal infections
567.81 Choleperitonitis
567.82 Sclerosing mesenteritis
567.89 Other specified peritonitis
567.9 Unspecified peritonitis ▽
569.5 Abscess of intestine
569.82 Ulceration of intestine
569.83 Perforation of intestine
614.3 Acute parametritis and pelvic cellulitis — (Use additional code to identify organism: 041.00-041.09, 041.10-041.19) ♀
614.4 Chronic or unspecified parametritis and pelvic cellulitis — (Use additional code to identify organism: 041.00-041.09, 041.10-041.19) ♀
614.5 Acute or unspecified pelvic peritonitis, female — (Use additional code to identify organism: 041.00-041.09, 041.10-041.19) ♀
614.8 Other specified inflammatory disease of female pelvic organs and tissues — (Use additional code to identify organism: 041.00-041.09, 041.10-041.19) ♀
639.0 Genital tract and pelvic infection following abortion or ectopic and molar pregnancies ♀

ICD-9-CM Procedural

48.0 Proctotomy

45005

45005 Incision and drainage of submucosal abscess, rectum

ICD-9-CM Diagnostic

566 Abscess of anal and rectal regions
998.51 Infected postoperative seroma — (Use additional code to identify organism)
998.59 Other postoperative infection — (Use additional code to identify infection)

ICD-9-CM Procedural

48.0 Proctotomy
48.81 Incision of perirectal tissue
49.91 Incision of anal septum

45020

45020 Incision and drainage of deep supralevator, pelvirectal, or retrorectal abscess

ICD-9-CM Diagnostic

555.1 Regional enteritis of large intestine
556.1 Ulcerative (chronic) ileocolitis
556.2 Ulcerative (chronic) proctitis
556.3 Ulcerative (chronic) proctosigmoiditis
556.4 Pseudopolyposis of colon
556.5 Left sided ulcerative (chronic) colitis
556.6 Universal ulcerative (chronic) colitis
556.8 Other ulcerative colitis
566 Abscess of anal and rectal regions
567.21 Peritonitis (acute) generalized
567.22 Peritoneal abscess
567.23 Spontaneous bacterial peritonitis
567.29 Other suppurative peritonitis
567.31 Psoas muscle abscess
567.38 Other retroperitoneal abscess
567.39 Other retroperitoneal infections
567.81 Choleperitonitis
567.82 Sclerosing mesenteritis
567.89 Other specified peritonitis
614.3 Acute parametritis and pelvic cellulitis — (Use additional code to identify organism: 041.00-041.09, 041.10-041.19) ♀
614.4 Chronic or unspecified parametritis and pelvic cellulitis — (Use additional code to identify organism: 041.00-041.09, 041.10-041.19) ♀
614.8 Other specified inflammatory disease of female pelvic organs and tissues — (Use additional code to identify organism: 041.00-041.09, 041.10-041.19) ♀
639.0 Genital tract and pelvic infection following abortion or ectopic and molar pregnancies ♀
998.51 Infected postoperative seroma — (Use additional code to identify organism)
998.59 Other postoperative infection — (Use additional code to identify infection)

ICD-9-CM Procedural

48.0 Proctotomy
48.81 Incision of perirectal tissue

45100

45100 Biopsy of anorectal wall, anal approach (eg, congenital megacolon)

ICD-9-CM Diagnostic

154.1 Malignant neoplasm of rectum
154.2 Malignant neoplasm of anal canal
154.3 Malignant neoplasm of anus, unspecified site ▽
197.5 Secondary malignant neoplasm of large intestine and rectum
209.17 Malignant carcinoid tumor of the rectum — (Code first any associated multiple endocrine neoplasia syndrome: 258.01-258.03)(Use additional code to identify associated endocrine syndrome, as: carcinoid syndrome: 259.2)
209.57 Benign carcinoid tumor of the rectum — (Code first any associated multiple endocrine neoplasia syndrome: 258.01-258.03)(Use additional code to identify associated endocrine syndrome, as: carcinoid syndrome: 259.2)
211.4 Benign neoplasm of rectum and anal canal
230.4 Carcinoma in situ of rectum
239.0 Neoplasm of unspecified nature of digestive system
277.39 Other amyloidosis — (Use additional code to identify any associated intellectual disabilities)
564.00 Unspecified constipation ▽
564.01 Slow transit constipation
564.02 Outlet dysfunction constipation
564.09 Other constipation

564.1 Irritable bowel syndrome
565.0 Anal fissure
566 Abscess of anal and rectal regions
569.0 Anal and rectal polyp
569.1 Rectal prolapse
569.2 Stenosis of rectum and anus
569.41 Ulcer of anus and rectum
569.42 Anal or rectal pain
569.44 Dysplasia of anus
578.1 Blood in stool
751.3 Hirschsprung's disease and other congenital functional disorders of colon
793.4 Nonspecific (abnormal) findings on radiological and other examination of gastrointestinal tract
V10.05 Personal history of malignant neoplasm of large intestine
V10.06 Personal history of malignant neoplasm of rectum, rectosigmoid junction, and anus

ICD-9-CM Procedural

48.24 Closed (endoscopic) biopsy of rectum
48.25 Open biopsy of rectum
49.23 Biopsy of anus

HCPCS Level II Supplies & Services

A4305 Disposable drug delivery system, flow rate of 50 ml or greater per hour

45108

45108 Anorectal myomectomy

ICD-9-CM Diagnostic

154.8 Malignant neoplasm of other sites of rectum, rectosigmoid junction, and anus
209.17 Malignant carcinoid tumor of the rectum — (Code first any associated multiple endocrine neoplasia syndrome: 258.01-258.03)(Use additional code to identify associated endocrine syndrome, as: carcinoid syndrome: 259.2)
209.57 Benign carcinoid tumor of the rectum — (Code first any associated multiple endocrine neoplasia syndrome: 258.01-258.03)(Use additional code to identify associated endocrine syndrome, as: carcinoid syndrome: 259.2)
211.4 Benign neoplasm of rectum and anal canal
564.00 Unspecified constipation ▽
564.01 Slow transit constipation
564.02 Outlet dysfunction constipation
564.09 Other constipation
569.2 Stenosis of rectum and anus
569.44 Dysplasia of anus
569.49 Other specified disorder of rectum and anus — (Use additional code for any associated fecal incontinence (787.60-787.63))
787.60 Full incontinence of feces
787.61 Incomplete defecation
787.62 Fecal smearing
787.63 Fecal urgency

ICD-9-CM Procedural

48.92 Anorectal myectomy

45110-45111

45110 Proctectomy; complete, combined abdominoperineal, with colostomy
45111 partial resection of rectum, transabdominal approach

ICD-9-CM Diagnostic

153.3 Malignant neoplasm of sigmoid colon
153.9 Malignant neoplasm of colon, unspecified site ▽
154.0 Malignant neoplasm of rectosigmoid junction
154.1 Malignant neoplasm of rectum
154.2 Malignant neoplasm of anal canal
154.8 Malignant neoplasm of other sites of rectum, rectosigmoid junction, and anus
197.5 Secondary malignant neoplasm of large intestine and rectum
209.10 Malignant carcinoid tumor of the large intestine, unspecified portion — (Code first any associated multiple endocrine neoplasia syndrome: 258.01-258.03)(Use additional code to identify associated endocrine syndrome, as: carcinoid syndrome: 259.2) ▽
209.17 Malignant carcinoid tumor of the rectum — (Code first any associated multiple endocrine neoplasia syndrome: 258.01-258.03)(Use additional code to identify associated endocrine syndrome, as: carcinoid syndrome: 259.2)
209.50 Benign carcinoid tumor of the large intestine, unspecified portion — (Code first any associated multiple endocrine neoplasia syndrome: 258.01-258.03)(Use additional code to identify associated endocrine syndrome, as: carcinoid syndrome: 259.2) ▽
209.56 Benign carcinoid tumor of the sigmoid colon — (Code first any associated multiple endocrine neoplasia syndrome: 258.01-258.03)(Use additional code to identify associated endocrine syndrome, as: carcinoid syndrome: 259.2)
209.57 Benign carcinoid tumor of the rectum — (Code first any associated multiple endocrine neoplasia syndrome: 258.01-258.03)(Use additional code to identify associated endocrine syndrome, as: carcinoid syndrome: 259.2)
211.3 Benign neoplasm of colon
230.3 Carcinoma in situ of colon
230.4 Carcinoma in situ of rectum
235.2 Neoplasm of uncertain behavior of stomach, intestines, and rectum
555.1 Regional enteritis of large intestine
556.0 Ulcerative (chronic) enterocolitis
556.1 Ulcerative (chronic) ileocolitis
556.2 Ulcerative (chronic) proctitis
556.3 Ulcerative (chronic) proctosigmoiditis
556.4 Pseudopolyposis of colon
556.5 Left sided ulcerative (chronic) colitis
556.6 Universal ulcerative (chronic) colitis
556.8 Other ulcerative colitis
556.9 Unspecified ulcerative colitis ▽
557.0 Acute vascular insufficiency of intestine
557.1 Chronic vascular insufficiency of intestine
557.9 Unspecified vascular insufficiency of intestine ▽
569.1 Rectal prolapse
569.44 Dysplasia of anus
751.3 Hirschsprung's disease and other congenital functional disorders of colon

ICD-9-CM Procedural

48.50 Abdominoperineal resection of the rectum, not otherwise specified
48.52 Open abdominoperineal resection of the rectum
48.59 Other abdominoperineal resection of the rectum
48.69 Other resection of rectum

45112

45112 Proctectomy, combined abdominoperineal, pull-through procedure (eg, colo-anal anastomosis)

ICD-9-CM Diagnostic

153.3 Malignant neoplasm of sigmoid colon
153.9 Malignant neoplasm of colon, unspecified site ▽
154.0 Malignant neoplasm of rectosigmoid junction
154.1 Malignant neoplasm of rectum
209.10 Malignant carcinoid tumor of the large intestine, unspecified portion — (Code first any associated multiple endocrine neoplasia syndrome: 258.01-258.03)(Use additional code to identify associated endocrine syndrome, as: carcinoid syndrome: 259.2) ▽
209.16 Malignant carcinoid tumor of the sigmoid colon — (Code first any associated multiple endocrine neoplasia syndrome: 258.01-258.03)(Use additional code to identify associated endocrine syndrome, as: carcinoid syndrome: 259.2)

209.17 Malignant carcinoid tumor of the rectum — (Code first any associated multiple endocrine neoplasia syndrome: 258.01-258.03)(Use additional code to identify associated endocrine syndrome, as: carcinoid syndrome: 259.2)
230.3 Carcinoma in situ of colon
230.4 Carcinoma in situ of rectum
555.1 Regional enteritis of large intestine
555.9 Regional enteritis of unspecified site ▽
556.0 Ulcerative (chronic) enterocolitis
556.2 Ulcerative (chronic) proctitis
569.1 Rectal prolapse
751.3 Hirschsprung's disease and other congenital functional disorders of colon

ICD-9-CM Procedural

48.40 Pull-through resection of rectum, not otherwise specified
48.43 Open pull-through resection of rectum
48.49 Other pull-through resection of rectum
48.50 Abdominoperineal resection of the rectum, not otherwise specified
48.52 Open abdominoperineal resection of the rectum
48.59 Other abdominoperineal resection of the rectum
48.65 Duhamel resection of rectum

45113

45113 Proctectomy, partial, with rectal mucosectomy, ileoanal anastomosis, creation of ileal reservoir (S or J), with or without loop ileostomy

ICD-9-CM Diagnostic

153.9 Malignant neoplasm of colon, unspecified site ▽
154.0 Malignant neoplasm of rectosigmoid junction
154.1 Malignant neoplasm of rectum
154.2 Malignant neoplasm of anal canal
154.3 Malignant neoplasm of anus, unspecified site ▽
154.8 Malignant neoplasm of other sites of rectum, rectosigmoid junction, and anus
209.10 Malignant carcinoid tumor of the large intestine, unspecified portion — (Code first any associated multiple endocrine neoplasia syndrome: 258.01-258.03)(Use additional code to identify associated endocrine syndrome, as: carcinoid syndrome: 259.2) ▽
209.16 Malignant carcinoid tumor of the sigmoid colon — (Code first any associated multiple endocrine neoplasia syndrome: 258.01-258.03)(Use additional code to identify associated endocrine syndrome, as: carcinoid syndrome: 259.2)
209.17 Malignant carcinoid tumor of the rectum — (Code first any associated multiple endocrine neoplasia syndrome: 258.01-258.03)(Use additional code to identify associated endocrine syndrome, as: carcinoid syndrome: 259.2)
230.3 Carcinoma in situ of colon
230.4 Carcinoma in situ of rectum
235.2 Neoplasm of uncertain behavior of stomach, intestines, and rectum
555.1 Regional enteritis of large intestine
556.0 Ulcerative (chronic) enterocolitis
556.2 Ulcerative (chronic) proctitis
569.1 Rectal prolapse
569.44 Dysplasia of anus
751.3 Hirschsprung's disease and other congenital functional disorders of colon

ICD-9-CM Procedural

45.95 Anastomosis to anus
46.01 Exteriorization of small intestine
48.69 Other resection of rectum

45114-45116

45114 Proctectomy, partial, with anastomosis; abdominal and transsacral approach
45116 transsacral approach only (Kraske type)

ICD-9-CM Diagnostic

153.9 Malignant neoplasm of colon, unspecified site ▽
154.0 Malignant neoplasm of rectosigmoid junction
154.1 Malignant neoplasm of rectum
154.2 Malignant neoplasm of anal canal
154.3 Malignant neoplasm of anus, unspecified site ▽
154.8 Malignant neoplasm of other sites of rectum, rectosigmoid junction, and anus
209.10 Malignant carcinoid tumor of the large intestine, unspecified portion — (Code first any associated multiple endocrine neoplasia syndrome: 258.01-258.03)(Use additional code to identify associated endocrine syndrome, as: carcinoid syndrome: 259.2) ▽
209.16 Malignant carcinoid tumor of the sigmoid colon — (Code first any associated multiple endocrine neoplasia syndrome: 258.01-258.03)(Use additional code to identify associated endocrine syndrome, as: carcinoid syndrome: 259.2)
209.17 Malignant carcinoid tumor of the rectum — (Code first any associated multiple endocrine neoplasia syndrome: 258.01-258.03)(Use additional code to identify associated endocrine syndrome, as: carcinoid syndrome: 259.2)
230.3 Carcinoma in situ of colon
230.4 Carcinoma in situ of rectum
555.1 Regional enteritis of large intestine
556.0 Ulcerative (chronic) enterocolitis
556.2 Ulcerative (chronic) proctitis
569.1 Rectal prolapse
569.44 Dysplasia of anus
751.3 Hirschsprung's disease and other congenital functional disorders of colon

ICD-9-CM Procedural

45.92 Anastomosis of small intestine to rectal stump
48.69 Other resection of rectum

45119

45119 Proctectomy, combined abdominoperineal pull-through procedure (eg, colo-anal anastomosis), with creation of colonic reservoir (eg, J-pouch), with diverting enterostomy when performed

ICD-9-CM Diagnostic

153.9 Malignant neoplasm of colon, unspecified site ▽
154.0 Malignant neoplasm of rectosigmoid junction
154.1 Malignant neoplasm of rectum
154.2 Malignant neoplasm of anal canal
154.3 Malignant neoplasm of anus, unspecified site ▽
154.8 Malignant neoplasm of other sites of rectum, rectosigmoid junction, and anus
209.10 Malignant carcinoid tumor of the large intestine, unspecified portion — (Code first any associated multiple endocrine neoplasia syndrome: 258.01-258.03)(Use additional code to identify associated endocrine syndrome, as: carcinoid syndrome: 259.2) ▽
209.16 Malignant carcinoid tumor of the sigmoid colon — (Code first any associated multiple endocrine neoplasia syndrome: 258.01-258.03)(Use additional code to identify associated endocrine syndrome, as: carcinoid syndrome: 259.2)
209.17 Malignant carcinoid tumor of the rectum — (Code first any associated multiple endocrine neoplasia syndrome: 258.01-258.03)(Use additional code to identify associated endocrine syndrome, as: carcinoid syndrome: 259.2)
230.3 Carcinoma in situ of colon
230.4 Carcinoma in situ of rectum
235.2 Neoplasm of uncertain behavior of stomach, intestines, and rectum
555.1 Regional enteritis of large intestine
556.0 Ulcerative (chronic) enterocolitis
556.2 Ulcerative (chronic) proctitis
569.1 Rectal prolapse
569.44 Dysplasia of anus
751.3 Hirschsprung's disease and other congenital functional disorders of colon

ICD-9-CM Procedural

45.95 Anastomosis to anus
48.40 Pull-through resection of rectum, not otherwise specified
48.43 Open pull-through resection of rectum

48.49 Other pull-through resection of rectum
48.50 Abdominoperineal resection of the rectum, not otherwise specified
48.52 Open abdominoperineal resection of the rectum
48.59 Other abdominoperineal resection of the rectum
48.65 Duhamel resection of rectum

45120

45120 Proctectomy, complete (for congenital megacolon), abdominal and perineal approach; with pull-through procedure and anastomosis (eg, Swenson, Duhamel, or Soave type operation)

ICD-9-CM Diagnostic

751.3 Hirschsprung's disease and other congenital functional disorders of colon

ICD-9-CM Procedural

45.95 Anastomosis to anus
48.40 Pull-through resection of rectum, not otherwise specified
48.43 Open pull-through resection of rectum
48.49 Other pull-through resection of rectum
48.50 Abdominoperineal resection of the rectum, not otherwise specified
48.52 Open abdominoperineal resection of the rectum
48.59 Other abdominoperineal resection of the rectum
48.65 Duhamel resection of rectum

45121

45121 Proctectomy, complete (for congenital megacolon), abdominal and perineal approach; with subtotal or total colectomy, with multiple biopsies

ICD-9-CM Diagnostic

751.3 Hirschsprung's disease and other congenital functional disorders of colon

ICD-9-CM Procedural

48.40 Pull-through resection of rectum, not otherwise specified
48.43 Open pull-through resection of rectum
48.49 Other pull-through resection of rectum
48.50 Abdominoperineal resection of the rectum, not otherwise specified
48.52 Open abdominoperineal resection of the rectum
48.59 Other abdominoperineal resection of the rectum

45123

45123 Proctectomy, partial, without anastomosis, perineal approach

ICD-9-CM Diagnostic

153.9 Malignant neoplasm of colon, unspecified site ▽
154.0 Malignant neoplasm of rectosigmoid junction
154.1 Malignant neoplasm of rectum
154.2 Malignant neoplasm of anal canal
154.3 Malignant neoplasm of anus, unspecified site ▽
154.8 Malignant neoplasm of other sites of rectum, rectosigmoid junction, and anus
209.10 Malignant carcinoid tumor of the large intestine, unspecified portion — (Code first any associated multiple endocrine neoplasia syndrome: 258.01-258.03)(Use additional code to identify associated endocrine syndrome, as: carcinoid syndrome: 259.2) ▽
209.16 Malignant carcinoid tumor of the sigmoid colon — (Code first any associated multiple endocrine neoplasia syndrome: 258.01-258.03)(Use additional code to identify associated endocrine syndrome, as: carcinoid syndrome: 259.2)
209.17 Malignant carcinoid tumor of the rectum — (Code first any associated multiple endocrine neoplasia syndrome: 258.01-258.03)(Use additional code to identify associated endocrine syndrome, as: carcinoid syndrome: 259.2)
230.3 Carcinoma in situ of colon
230.4 Carcinoma in situ of rectum
235.2 Neoplasm of uncertain behavior of stomach, intestines, and rectum
555.1 Regional enteritis of large intestine
556.0 Ulcerative (chronic) enterocolitis
556.2 Ulcerative (chronic) proctitis
569.1 Rectal prolapse
569.44 Dysplasia of anus
751.3 Hirschsprung's disease and other congenital functional disorders of colon

ICD-9-CM Procedural

48.69 Other resection of rectum

45126

45126 Pelvic exenteration for colorectal malignancy, with proctectomy (with or without colostomy), with removal of bladder and ureteral transplantations, and/or hysterectomy, or cervicectomy, with or without removal of tube(s), with or without removal of ovary(s), or any combination thereof

ICD-9-CM Diagnostic

153.0 Malignant neoplasm of hepatic flexure
153.1 Malignant neoplasm of transverse colon
153.2 Malignant neoplasm of descending colon
153.3 Malignant neoplasm of sigmoid colon
153.4 Malignant neoplasm of cecum
153.5 Malignant neoplasm of appendix
153.6 Malignant neoplasm of ascending colon
153.7 Malignant neoplasm of splenic flexure
153.8 Malignant neoplasm of other specified sites of large intestine
153.9 Malignant neoplasm of colon, unspecified site ▽
154.0 Malignant neoplasm of rectosigmoid junction
154.1 Malignant neoplasm of rectum
154.2 Malignant neoplasm of anal canal
154.3 Malignant neoplasm of anus, unspecified site ▽
154.8 Malignant neoplasm of other sites of rectum, rectosigmoid junction, and anus
197.5 Secondary malignant neoplasm of large intestine and rectum
198.1 Secondary malignant neoplasm of other urinary organs
198.6 Secondary malignant neoplasm of ovary ♀
198.82 Secondary malignant neoplasm of genital organs
198.89 Secondary malignant neoplasm of other specified sites
199.0 Disseminated malignant neoplasm
199.1 Other malignant neoplasm of unspecified site
209.10 Malignant carcinoid tumor of the large intestine, unspecified portion — (Code first any associated multiple endocrine neoplasia syndrome: 258.01-258.03)(Use additional code to identify associated endocrine syndrome, as: carcinoid syndrome: 259.2) ▽
209.11 Malignant carcinoid tumor of the appendix — (Code first any associated multiple endocrine neoplasia syndrome: 258.01-258.03)(Use additional code to identify associated endocrine syndrome, as: carcinoid syndrome: 259.2)
209.12 Malignant carcinoid tumor of the cecum — (Code first any associated multiple endocrine neoplasia syndrome: 258.01-258.03)(Use additional code to identify associated endocrine syndrome, as: carcinoid syndrome: 259.2)
209.13 Malignant carcinoid tumor of the ascending colon — (Code first any associated multiple endocrine neoplasia syndrome: 258.01-258.03)(Use additional code to identify associated endocrine syndrome, as: carcinoid syndrome: 259.2)
209.14 Malignant carcinoid tumor of the transverse colon — (Code first any associated multiple endocrine neoplasia syndrome: 258.01-258.03)(Use additional code to identify associated endocrine syndrome, as: carcinoid syndrome: 259.2)
209.15 Malignant carcinoid tumor of the descending colon — (Code first any associated multiple endocrine neoplasia syndrome: 258.01-258.03)(Use additional code to identify associated endocrine syndrome, as: carcinoid syndrome: 259.2)
209.16 Malignant carcinoid tumor of the sigmoid colon — (Code first any associated multiple endocrine neoplasia syndrome: 258.01-258.03)(Use additional code to identify associated endocrine syndrome, as: carcinoid syndrome: 259.2)
209.17 Malignant carcinoid tumor of the rectum — (Code first any associated multiple endocrine neoplasia syndrome: 258.01-258.03)(Use additional code to identify associated endocrine syndrome, as: carcinoid syndrome: 259.2)

209.20 Malignant carcinoid tumor of unknown primary site — (Code first any associated multiple endocrine neoplasia syndrome: 258.01-258.03)(Use additional code to identify associated endocrine syndrome, as: carcinoid syndrome: 259.2)

209.30 Malignant poorly differentiated neuroendocrine carcinoma, any site — (Code first any associated multiple endocrine neoplasia syndrome: 258.01-258.03)(Use additional code to identify associated endocrine syndrome, as: carcinoid syndrome: 259.2) ▽

569.44 Dysplasia of anus

ICD-9-CM Procedural

46.13 Permanent colostomy

68.8 Pelvic evisceration ♀

45130-45135

45130 Excision of rectal procidentia, with anastomosis; perineal approach

45135 abdominal and perineal approach

ICD-9-CM Diagnostic

569.1 Rectal prolapse

ICD-9-CM Procedural

45.92 Anastomosis of small intestine to rectal stump

45.95 Anastomosis to anus

48.69 Other resection of rectum

45136

45136 Excision of ileoanal reservoir with ileostomy

ICD-9-CM Diagnostic

153.0 Malignant neoplasm of hepatic flexure

153.1 Malignant neoplasm of transverse colon

153.2 Malignant neoplasm of descending colon

153.3 Malignant neoplasm of sigmoid colon

153.4 Malignant neoplasm of cecum

153.5 Malignant neoplasm of appendix

153.6 Malignant neoplasm of ascending colon

153.7 Malignant neoplasm of splenic flexure

153.8 Malignant neoplasm of other specified sites of large intestine

153.9 Malignant neoplasm of colon, unspecified site ▽

154.0 Malignant neoplasm of rectosigmoid junction

154.1 Malignant neoplasm of rectum

197.5 Secondary malignant neoplasm of large intestine and rectum

209.10 Malignant carcinoid tumor of the large intestine, unspecified portion — (Code first any associated multiple endocrine neoplasia syndrome: 258.01-258.03)(Use additional code to identify associated endocrine syndrome, as: carcinoid syndrome: 259.2) ▽

209.11 Malignant carcinoid tumor of the appendix — (Code first any associated multiple endocrine neoplasia syndrome: 258.01-258.03)(Use additional code to identify associated endocrine syndrome, as: carcinoid syndrome: 259.2)

209.12 Malignant carcinoid tumor of the cecum — (Code first any associated multiple endocrine neoplasia syndrome: 258.01-258.03)(Use additional code to identify associated endocrine syndrome, as: carcinoid syndrome: 259.2)

209.13 Malignant carcinoid tumor of the ascending colon — (Code first any associated multiple endocrine neoplasia syndrome: 258.01-258.03)(Use additional code to identify associated endocrine syndrome, as: carcinoid syndrome: 259.2)

209.14 Malignant carcinoid tumor of the transverse colon — (Code first any associated multiple endocrine neoplasia syndrome: 258.01-258.03)(Use additional code to identify associated endocrine syndrome, as: carcinoid syndrome: 259.2)

209.15 Malignant carcinoid tumor of the descending colon — (Code first any associated multiple endocrine neoplasia syndrome: 258.01-258.03)(Use additional code to identify associated endocrine syndrome, as: carcinoid syndrome: 259.2)

209.16 Malignant carcinoid tumor of the sigmoid colon — (Code first any associated multiple endocrine neoplasia syndrome: 258.01-258.03)(Use additional code to identify associated endocrine syndrome, as: carcinoid syndrome: 259.2)

209.29 Malignant carcinoid tumor of other sites — (Code first any associated multiple endocrine neoplasia syndrome: 258.01-258.03)(Use additional code to identify associated endocrine syndrome, as: carcinoid syndrome: 259.2)

209.30 Malignant poorly differentiated neuroendocrine carcinoma, any site — (Code first any associated multiple endocrine neoplasia syndrome: 258.01-258.03)(Use additional code to identify associated endocrine syndrome, as: carcinoid syndrome: 259.2) ▽

209.50 Benign carcinoid tumor of the large intestine, unspecified portion — (Code first any associated multiple endocrine neoplasia syndrome: 258.01-258.03)(Use additional code to identify associated endocrine syndrome, as: carcinoid syndrome: 259.2) ▽

209.51 Benign carcinoid tumor of the appendix — (Code first any associated multiple endocrine neoplasia syndrome: 258.01-258.03)(Use additional code to identify associated endocrine syndrome, as: carcinoid syndrome: 259.2)

209.52 Benign carcinoid tumor of the cecum — (Code first any associated multiple endocrine neoplasia syndrome: 258.01-258.03)(Use additional code to identify associated endocrine syndrome, as: carcinoid syndrome: 259.2)

209.53 Benign carcinoid tumor of the ascending colon — (Code first any associated multiple endocrine neoplasia syndrome: 258.01-258.03)(Use additional code to identify associated endocrine syndrome, as: carcinoid syndrome: 259.2)

209.54 Benign carcinoid tumor of the transverse colon — (Code first any associated multiple endocrine neoplasia syndrome: 258.01-258.03)(Use additional code to identify associated endocrine syndrome, as: carcinoid syndrome: 259.2)

209.55 Benign carcinoid tumor of the descending colon — (Code first any associated multiple endocrine neoplasia syndrome: 258.01-258.03)(Use additional code to identify associated endocrine syndrome, as: carcinoid syndrome: 259.2)

209.56 Benign carcinoid tumor of the sigmoid colon — (Code first any associated multiple endocrine neoplasia syndrome: 258.01-258.03)(Use additional code to identify associated endocrine syndrome, as: carcinoid syndrome: 259.2)

209.57 Benign carcinoid tumor of the rectum — (Code first any associated multiple endocrine neoplasia syndrome: 258.01-258.03)(Use additional code to identify associated endocrine syndrome, as: carcinoid syndrome: 259.2)

209.69 Benign carcinoid tumor of other sites — (Code first any associated multiple endocrine neoplasia syndrome: 258.01-258.03)(Use additional code to identify associated endocrine syndrome, as: carcinoid syndrome: 259.2)

211.3 Benign neoplasm of colon

211.4 Benign neoplasm of rectum and anal canal

230.3 Carcinoma in situ of colon

230.4 Carcinoma in situ of rectum

230.7 Carcinoma in situ of other and unspecified parts of intestine ▽

235.2 Neoplasm of uncertain behavior of stomach, intestines, and rectum

239.0 Neoplasm of unspecified nature of digestive system

556.0 Ulcerative (chronic) enterocolitis

556.1 Ulcerative (chronic) ileocolitis

556.2 Ulcerative (chronic) proctitis

556.3 Ulcerative (chronic) proctosigmoiditis

556.4 Pseudopolyposis of colon

556.5 Left sided ulcerative (chronic) colitis

556.6 Universal ulcerative (chronic) colitis

556.8 Other ulcerative colitis

556.9 Unspecified ulcerative colitis ▽

557.0 Acute vascular insufficiency of intestine

557.1 Chronic vascular insufficiency of intestine

557.9 Unspecified vascular insufficiency of intestine ▽

558.41 Eosinophilic gastroenteritis

558.42 Eosinophilic colitis

558.9 Other and unspecified noninfectious gastroenteritis and colitis ▽

560.9 Unspecified intestinal obstruction ▽

562.10 Diverticulosis of colon (without mention of hemorrhage) — (Use additional code to identify any associated peritonitis: 567.0-567.9)

562.11 Diverticulitis of colon (without mention of hemorrhage) — (Use additional code to identify any associated peritonitis: 567.0-567.9)

562.12 Diverticulosis of colon with hemorrhage — (Use additional code to identify any associated peritonitis: 567.0-567.9)
562.13 Diverticulitis of colon with hemorrhage — (Use additional code to identify any associated peritonitis: 567.0-567.9)
564.7 Megacolon, other than Hirschsprung's
564.81 Neurogenic bowel
564.89 Other functional disorders of intestine
567.0 Peritonitis in infectious diseases classified elsewhere — (Code first underlying disease) ☒
567.1 Pneumococcal peritonitis
567.21 Peritonitis (acute) generalized
567.22 Peritoneal abscess
567.23 Spontaneous bacterial peritonitis
567.29 Other suppurative peritonitis
567.31 Psoas muscle abscess
567.38 Other retroperitoneal abscess
567.39 Other retroperitoneal infections
567.81 Choleperitonitis
567.82 Sclerosing mesenteritis
567.89 Other specified peritonitis
567.9 Unspecified peritonitis ▽
569.82 Ulceration of intestine
569.83 Perforation of intestine
569.89 Other specified disorder of intestines
569.9 Unspecified disorder of intestine ▽
578.1 Blood in stool
578.9 Hemorrhage of gastrointestinal tract, unspecified ▽
751.3 Hirschsprung's disease and other congenital functional disorders of colon
777.1 Fetal and newborn meconium obstruction — (Use additional code(s) to further specify condition)
777.50 Necrotizing enterocolitis in newborn, unspecified ▽
777.51 Stage I necrotizing enterocolitis in newborn
777.52 Stage II necrotizing enterocolitis in newborn
777.53 Stage III necrotizing enterocolitis in newborn
777.6 Perinatal intestinal perforation — (Use additional code(s) to further specify condition)
777.8 Other specified perinatal disorder of digestive system — (Use additional code(s) to further specify condition)
863.40 Colon injury unspecified site, without mention of open wound into cavity ▽
863.41 Ascending (right) colon injury without mention of open wound into cavity
863.42 Transverse colon injury without mention of open wound into cavity
863.43 Descending (left) colon injury without mention of open wound into cavity
863.44 Sigmoid colon injury without mention of open wound into cavity
863.45 Rectum injury without mention of open wound into cavity
863.46 Injury to multiple sites in colon and rectum without mention of open wound into cavity
863.49 Other colon and rectum injury, without mention of open wound into cavity
997.49 Other digestive system complications
998.59 Other postoperative infection — (Use additional code to identify infection)
998.89 Other specified complications

ICD-9-CM Procedural

46.23 Other permanent ileostomy
46.99 Other operations on intestines

45150

45150 Division of stricture of rectum

ICD-9-CM Diagnostic

569.2 Stenosis of rectum and anus
569.3 Hemorrhage of rectum and anus
569.42 Anal or rectal pain
569.44 Dysplasia of anus
569.49 Other specified disorder of rectum and anus — (Use additional code for any associated fecal incontinence (787.60-787.63))
751.2 Congenital atresia and stenosis of large intestine, rectum, and anal canal
908.1 Late effect of internal injury to intra-abdominal organs
909.3 Late effect of complications of surgical and medical care
947.3 Burn of gastrointestinal tract
997.49 Other digestive system complications

ICD-9-CM Procedural

48.91 Incision of rectal stricture

45160-45172

45160 Excision of rectal tumor by proctotomy, transsacral or transcoccygeal approach
45171 Excision of rectal tumor, transanal approach; not including muscularis propria (ie, partial thickness)
45172 including muscularis propria (ie, full thickness)

ICD-9-CM Diagnostic

154.0 Malignant neoplasm of rectosigmoid junction
154.1 Malignant neoplasm of rectum
154.8 Malignant neoplasm of other sites of rectum, rectosigmoid junction, and anus
197.5 Secondary malignant neoplasm of large intestine and rectum
209.17 Malignant carcinoid tumor of the rectum — (Code first any associated multiple endocrine neoplasia syndrome: 258.01-258.03)(Use additional code to identify associated endocrine syndrome, as: carcinoid syndrome: 259.2)
209.27 Malignant carcinoid tumor of hindgut, not otherwise specified — (Code first any associated multiple endocrine neoplasia syndrome: 258.01-258.03)(Use additional code to identify associated endocrine syndrome, as: carcinoid syndrome: 259.2)
209.29 Malignant carcinoid tumor of other sites — (Code first any associated multiple endocrine neoplasia syndrome: 258.01-258.03)(Use additional code to identify associated endocrine syndrome, as: carcinoid syndrome: 259.2)
209.30 Malignant poorly differentiated neuroendocrine carcinoma, any site — (Code first any associated multiple endocrine neoplasia syndrome: 258.01-258.03)(Use additional code to identify associated endocrine syndrome, as: carcinoid syndrome: 259.2) ▽
209.57 Benign carcinoid tumor of the rectum — (Code first any associated multiple endocrine neoplasia syndrome: 258.01-258.03)(Use additional code to identify associated endocrine syndrome, as: carcinoid syndrome: 259.2)
209.69 Benign carcinoid tumor of other sites — (Code first any associated multiple endocrine neoplasia syndrome: 258.01-258.03)(Use additional code to identify associated endocrine syndrome, as: carcinoid syndrome: 259.2)
211.4 Benign neoplasm of rectum and anal canal
228.04 Hemangioma of intra-abdominal structures
230.4 Carcinoma in situ of rectum
235.2 Neoplasm of uncertain behavior of stomach, intestines, and rectum
239.0 Neoplasm of unspecified nature of digestive system
569.3 Hemorrhage of rectum and anus
569.44 Dysplasia of anus
569.49 Other specified disorder of rectum and anus — (Use additional code for any associated fecal incontinence (787.60-787.63))
578.1 Blood in stool
751.5 Other congenital anomalies of intestine
787.99 Other symptoms involving digestive system

ICD-9-CM Procedural

48.0 Proctotomy
48.35 Local excision of rectal lesion or tissue
48.82 Excision of perirectal tissue

45190

45190 Destruction of rectal tumor (eg, electrodesiccation, electrosurgery, laser ablation, laser resection, cryosurgery) transanal approach

ICD-9-CM Diagnostic

154.0 Malignant neoplasm of rectosigmoid junction
154.1 Malignant neoplasm of rectum
154.8 Malignant neoplasm of other sites of rectum, rectosigmoid junction, and anus
197.5 Secondary malignant neoplasm of large intestine and rectum
209.17 Malignant carcinoid tumor of the rectum — (Code first any associated multiple endocrine neoplasia syndrome: 258.01-258.03)(Use additional code to identify associated endocrine syndrome, as: carcinoid syndrome: 259.2)
209.27 Malignant carcinoid tumor of hindgut, not otherwise specified — (Code first any associated multiple endocrine neoplasia syndrome: 258.01-258.03)(Use additional code to identify associated endocrine syndrome, as: carcinoid syndrome: 259.2)
209.29 Malignant carcinoid tumor of other sites — (Code first any associated multiple endocrine neoplasia syndrome: 258.01-258.03)(Use additional code to identify associated endocrine syndrome, as: carcinoid syndrome: 259.2)
209.30 Malignant poorly differentiated neuroendocrine carcinoma, any site — (Code first any associated multiple endocrine neoplasia syndrome: 258.01-258.03)(Use additional code to identify associated endocrine syndrome, as: carcinoid syndrome: 259.2) ▽
209.57 Benign carcinoid tumor of the rectum — (Code first any associated multiple endocrine neoplasia syndrome: 258.01-258.03)(Use additional code to identify associated endocrine syndrome, as: carcinoid syndrome: 259.2)
209.69 Benign carcinoid tumor of other sites — (Code first any associated multiple endocrine neoplasia syndrome: 258.01-258.03)(Use additional code to identify associated endocrine syndrome, as: carcinoid syndrome: 259.2)
211.4 Benign neoplasm of rectum and anal canal
228.04 Hemangioma of intra-abdominal structures
230.4 Carcinoma in situ of rectum
235.2 Neoplasm of uncertain behavior of stomach, intestines, and rectum
238.1 Neoplasm of uncertain behavior of connective and other soft tissue
239.0 Neoplasm of unspecified nature of digestive system
569.3 Hemorrhage of rectum and anus
569.44 Dysplasia of anus
751.5 Other congenital anomalies of intestine
780.64 Chills (without fever)
780.65 Hypothermia not associated with low environmental temperature
787.99 Other symptoms involving digestive system

ICD-9-CM Procedural

17.69 Laser interstitial thermal therapy [LITT] of lesion or tissue of other and unspecified site under guidance
48.32 Other electrocoagulation of rectal lesion or tissue
48.33 Destruction of rectal lesion or tissue by laser
48.34 Destruction of rectal lesion or tissue by cryosurgery

45300-45305

45300 Proctosigmoidoscopy, rigid; diagnostic, with or without collection of specimen(s) by brushing or washing (separate procedure)
45303 with dilation (eg, balloon, guide wire, bougie)
45305 with biopsy, single or multiple

ICD-9-CM Diagnostic

153.3 Malignant neoplasm of sigmoid colon
153.8 Malignant neoplasm of other specified sites of large intestine
154.0 Malignant neoplasm of rectosigmoid junction
154.1 Malignant neoplasm of rectum
154.2 Malignant neoplasm of anal canal
154.3 Malignant neoplasm of anus, unspecified site ▽
154.8 Malignant neoplasm of other sites of rectum, rectosigmoid junction, and anus
197.5 Secondary malignant neoplasm of large intestine and rectum
209.16 Malignant carcinoid tumor of the sigmoid colon — (Code first any associated multiple endocrine neoplasia syndrome: 258.01-258.03)(Use additional code to identify associated endocrine syndrome, as: carcinoid syndrome: 259.2)
209.17 Malignant carcinoid tumor of the rectum — (Code first any associated multiple endocrine neoplasia syndrome: 258.01-258.03)(Use additional code to identify associated endocrine syndrome, as: carcinoid syndrome: 259.2)
209.29 Malignant carcinoid tumor of other sites — (Code first any associated multiple endocrine neoplasia syndrome: 258.01-258.03)(Use additional code to identify associated endocrine syndrome, as: carcinoid syndrome: 259.2)
209.30 Malignant poorly differentiated neuroendocrine carcinoma, any site — (Code first any associated multiple endocrine neoplasia syndrome: 258.01-258.03)(Use additional code to identify associated endocrine syndrome, as: carcinoid syndrome: 259.2) ▽
209.50 Benign carcinoid tumor of the large intestine, unspecified portion — (Code first any associated multiple endocrine neoplasia syndrome: 258.01-258.03)(Use additional code to identify associated endocrine syndrome, as: carcinoid syndrome: 259.2) ▽
209.56 Benign carcinoid tumor of the sigmoid colon — (Code first any associated multiple endocrine neoplasia syndrome: 258.01-258.03)(Use additional code to identify associated endocrine syndrome, as: carcinoid syndrome: 259.2)
209.57 Benign carcinoid tumor of the rectum — (Code first any associated multiple endocrine neoplasia syndrome: 258.01-258.03)(Use additional code to identify associated endocrine syndrome, as: carcinoid syndrome: 259.2)
209.69 Benign carcinoid tumor of other sites — (Code first any associated multiple endocrine neoplasia syndrome: 258.01-258.03)(Use additional code to identify associated endocrine syndrome, as: carcinoid syndrome: 259.2)
211.3 Benign neoplasm of colon
211.4 Benign neoplasm of rectum and anal canal
230.3 Carcinoma in situ of colon
230.4 Carcinoma in situ of rectum
235.2 Neoplasm of uncertain behavior of stomach, intestines, and rectum
239.0 Neoplasm of unspecified nature of digestive system
455.0 Internal hemorrhoids without mention of complication
455.1 Internal thrombosed hemorrhoids
455.2 Internal hemorrhoids with other complication
455.3 External hemorrhoids without mention of complication
455.4 External thrombosed hemorrhoids
455.5 External hemorrhoids with other complication
455.6 Unspecified hemorrhoids without mention of complication ▽
455.7 Unspecified thrombosed hemorrhoids ▽
455.8 Unspecified hemorrhoids with other complication ▽
455.9 Residual hemorrhoidal skin tags
555.1 Regional enteritis of large intestine
555.9 Regional enteritis of unspecified site ▽
556.0 Ulcerative (chronic) enterocolitis
556.9 Unspecified ulcerative colitis ▽
557.1 Chronic vascular insufficiency of intestine
557.9 Unspecified vascular insufficiency of intestine ▽
558.1 Gastroenteritis and colitis due to radiation
558.2 Toxic gastroenteritis and colitis — (Use additional E code to identify cause)
558.3 Gastroenteritis and colitis, allergic — (Use additional code to identify type of food allergy: V15.01-V15.05)
558.42 Eosinophilic colitis
558.9 Other and unspecified noninfectious gastroenteritis and colitis ▽
560.0 Intussusception
560.1 Paralytic ileus
560.2 Volvulus
560.30 Unspecified impaction of intestine ▽
560.31 Gallstone ileus
560.32 Fecal impaction
560.39 Impaction of intestine, other

562.10 Diverticulosis of colon (without mention of hemorrhage) — (Use additional code to identify any associated peritonitis: 567.0-567.9)
562.13 Diverticulitis of colon with hemorrhage — (Use additional code to identify any associated peritonitis: 567.0-567.9)
564.00 Unspecified constipation
564.01 Slow transit constipation
564.02 Outlet dysfunction constipation
564.09 Other constipation
564.1 Irritable bowel syndrome
564.5 Functional diarrhea
564.6 Anal spasm
564.81 Neurogenic bowel
564.89 Other functional disorders of intestine
565.0 Anal fissure
565.1 Anal fistula
566 Abscess of anal and rectal regions
567.0 Peritonitis in infectious diseases classified elsewhere — (Code first underlying disease)
567.1 Pneumococcal peritonitis
567.21 Peritonitis (acute) generalized
567.22 Peritoneal abscess
567.23 Spontaneous bacterial peritonitis
567.29 Other suppurative peritonitis
567.38 Other retroperitoneal abscess
567.39 Other retroperitoneal infections
567.81 Choleperitonitis
567.82 Sclerosing mesenteritis
567.89 Other specified peritonitis
567.9 Unspecified peritonitis
569.0 Anal and rectal polyp
569.1 Rectal prolapse
569.2 Stenosis of rectum and anus
569.3 Hemorrhage of rectum and anus
569.41 Ulcer of anus and rectum
569.42 Anal or rectal pain
569.44 Dysplasia of anus
569.49 Other specified disorder of rectum and anus — (Use additional code for any associated fecal incontinence (787.60-787.63))
569.81 Fistula of intestine, excluding rectum and anus
569.82 Ulceration of intestine
569.83 Perforation of intestine
569.84 Angiodysplasia of intestine (without mention of hemorrhage)
569.85 Angiodysplasia of intestine with hemorrhage
569.89 Other specified disorder of intestines
569.9 Unspecified disorder of intestine
578.1 Blood in stool
698.0 Pruritus ani
780.99 Other general symptoms
783.21 Loss of weight — (Use additional code to identify Body Mass Index (BMI), if known: V85.0-V85.54)
783.22 Underweight — (Use additional code to identify Body Mass Index (BMI), if known: V85.0-V85.54)
783.7 Adult failure to thrive
787.3 Flatulence, eructation, and gas pain
787.60 Full incontinence of feces
787.61 Incomplete defecation
787.62 Fecal smearing
787.63 Fecal urgency
787.99 Other symptoms involving digestive system
789.00 Abdominal pain, unspecified site
789.01 Abdominal pain, right upper quadrant
789.02 Abdominal pain, left upper quadrant
789.03 Abdominal pain, right lower quadrant
789.04 Abdominal pain, left lower quadrant
789.05 Abdominal pain, periumbilic
789.06 Abdominal pain, epigastric
789.07 Abdominal pain, generalized
789.09 Abdominal pain, other specified site
789.30 Abdominal or pelvic swelling, mass or lump, unspecified site
789.31 Abdominal or pelvic swelling, mass, or lump, right upper quadrant
789.32 Abdominal or pelvic swelling, mass, or lump, left upper quadrant
789.33 Abdominal or pelvic swelling, mass, or lump, right lower quadrant
789.34 Abdominal or pelvic swelling, mass, or lump, left lower quadrant
789.35 Abdominal or pelvic swelling, mass or lump, periumbilic
789.36 Abdominal or pelvic swelling, mass, or lump, epigastric
789.37 Abdominal or pelvic swelling, mass, or lump, generalized
789.39 Abdominal or pelvic swelling, mass, or lump, other specified site
792.1 Nonspecific abnormal finding in stool contents
793.4 Nonspecific (abnormal) findings on radiological and other examination of gastrointestinal tract
863.45 Rectum injury without mention of open wound into cavity
997.49 Other digestive system complications
V76.41 Screening for malignant neoplasm of the rectum
V76.49 Special screening for malignant neoplasms, other sites

ICD-9-CM Procedural

48.23 Rigid proctosigmoidoscopy
48.24 Closed (endoscopic) biopsy of rectum
96.22 Dilation of rectum

HCPCS Level II Supplies & Services

A4270 Disposable endoscope sheath, each

45307

45307 Proctosigmoidoscopy, rigid; with removal of foreign body

ICD-9-CM Diagnostic

569.3 Hemorrhage of rectum and anus
569.42 Anal or rectal pain
569.44 Dysplasia of anus
569.49 Other specified disorder of rectum and anus — (Use additional code for any associated fecal incontinence (787.60-787.63))
578.1 Blood in stool
793.4 Nonspecific (abnormal) findings on radiological and other examination of gastrointestinal tract
936 Foreign body in intestine and colon
937 Foreign body in anus and rectum

ICD-9-CM Procedural

48.23 Rigid proctosigmoidoscopy
98.04 Removal of intraluminal foreign body from large intestine without incision

HCPCS Level II Supplies & Services

A4270 Disposable endoscope sheath, each

45308-45315

45308 Proctosigmoidoscopy, rigid; with removal of single tumor, polyp, or other lesion by hot biopsy forceps or bipolar cautery

45309 with removal of single tumor, polyp, or other lesion by snare technique

45315 with removal of multiple tumors, polyps, or other lesions by hot biopsy forceps, bipolar cautery or snare technique

ICD-9-CM Diagnostic

153.3 Malignant neoplasm of sigmoid colon

153.8 Malignant neoplasm of other specified sites of large intestine

154.0 Malignant neoplasm of rectosigmoid junction

154.1 Malignant neoplasm of rectum

209.16 Malignant carcinoid tumor of the sigmoid colon — (Code first any associated multiple endocrine neoplasia syndrome: 258.01-258.03)(Use additional code to identify associated endocrine syndrome, as: carcinoid syndrome: 259.2)

209.17 Malignant carcinoid tumor of the rectum — (Code first any associated multiple endocrine neoplasia syndrome: 258.01-258.03)(Use additional code to identify associated endocrine syndrome, as: carcinoid syndrome: 259.2)

209.29 Malignant carcinoid tumor of other sites — (Code first any associated multiple endocrine neoplasia syndrome: 258.01-258.03)(Use additional code to identify associated endocrine syndrome, as: carcinoid syndrome: 259.2)

209.50 Benign carcinoid tumor of the large intestine, unspecified portion — (Code first any associated multiple endocrine neoplasia syndrome: 258.01-258.03)(Use additional code to identify associated endocrine syndrome, as: carcinoid syndrome: 259.2) ▽

209.56 Benign carcinoid tumor of the sigmoid colon — (Code first any associated multiple endocrine neoplasia syndrome: 258.01-258.03)(Use additional code to identify associated endocrine syndrome, as: carcinoid syndrome: 259.2)

209.57 Benign carcinoid tumor of the rectum — (Code first any associated multiple endocrine neoplasia syndrome: 258.01-258.03)(Use additional code to identify associated endocrine syndrome, as: carcinoid syndrome: 259.2)

209.69 Benign carcinoid tumor of other sites — (Code first any associated multiple endocrine neoplasia syndrome: 258.01-258.03)(Use additional code to identify associated endocrine syndrome, as: carcinoid syndrome: 259.2)

211.3 Benign neoplasm of colon

211.4 Benign neoplasm of rectum and anal canal

235.2 Neoplasm of uncertain behavior of stomach, intestines, and rectum

239.0 Neoplasm of unspecified nature of digestive system

556.0 Ulcerative (chronic) enterocolitis

569.0 Anal and rectal polyp

569.3 Hemorrhage of rectum and anus

569.42 Anal or rectal pain

569.44 Dysplasia of anus

569.49 Other specified disorder of rectum and anus — (Use additional code for any associated fecal incontinence (787.60-787.63))

793.4 Nonspecific (abnormal) findings on radiological and other examination of gastrointestinal tract

ICD-9-CM Procedural

45.42 Endoscopic polypectomy of large intestine

48.32 Other electrocoagulation of rectal lesion or tissue

48.36 [Endoscopic] polypectomy of rectum

HCPCS Level II Supplies & Services

A4270 Disposable endoscope sheath, each

45317

45317 Proctosigmoidoscopy, rigid; with control of bleeding (eg, injection, bipolar cautery, unipolar cautery, laser, heater probe, stapler, plasma coagulator)

ICD-9-CM Diagnostic

154.1 Malignant neoplasm of rectum

209.17 Malignant carcinoid tumor of the rectum — (Code first any associated multiple endocrine neoplasia syndrome: 258.01-258.03)(Use additional code to identify associated endocrine syndrome, as: carcinoid syndrome: 259.2)

448.9 Other and unspecified capillary diseases ▽

455.0 Internal hemorrhoids without mention of complication

455.2 Internal hemorrhoids with other complication

556.0 Ulcerative (chronic) enterocolitis

556.3 Ulcerative (chronic) proctosigmoiditis

557.0 Acute vascular insufficiency of intestine

562.12 Diverticulosis of colon with hemorrhage — (Use additional code to identify any associated peritonitis: 567.0-567.9)

562.13 Diverticulitis of colon with hemorrhage — (Use additional code to identify any associated peritonitis: 567.0-567.9)

569.3 Hemorrhage of rectum and anus

569.44 Dysplasia of anus

569.49 Other specified disorder of rectum and anus — (Use additional code for any associated fecal incontinence (787.60-787.63))

569.85 Angiodysplasia of intestine with hemorrhage

578.1 Blood in stool

578.9 Hemorrhage of gastrointestinal tract, unspecified ▽

ICD-9-CM Procedural

45.43 Endoscopic destruction of other lesion or tissue of large intestine

48.32 Other electrocoagulation of rectal lesion or tissue

99.29 Injection or infusion of other therapeutic or prophylactic substance

HCPCS Level II Supplies & Services

A4270 Disposable endoscope sheath, each

45320

45320 Proctosigmoidoscopy, rigid; with ablation of tumor(s), polyp(s), or other lesion(s) not amenable to removal by hot biopsy forceps, bipolar cautery or snare technique (eg, laser)

ICD-9-CM Diagnostic

153.3 Malignant neoplasm of sigmoid colon

154.0 Malignant neoplasm of rectosigmoid junction

154.1 Malignant neoplasm of rectum

154.8 Malignant neoplasm of other sites of rectum, rectosigmoid junction, and anus

209.16 Malignant carcinoid tumor of the sigmoid colon — (Code first any associated multiple endocrine neoplasia syndrome: 258.01-258.03)(Use additional code to identify associated endocrine syndrome, as: carcinoid syndrome: 259.2)

209.17 Malignant carcinoid tumor of the rectum — (Code first any associated multiple endocrine neoplasia syndrome: 258.01-258.03)(Use additional code to identify associated endocrine syndrome, as: carcinoid syndrome: 259.2)

209.29 Malignant carcinoid tumor of other sites — (Code first any associated multiple endocrine neoplasia syndrome: 258.01-258.03)(Use additional code to identify associated endocrine syndrome, as: carcinoid syndrome: 259.2)

209.50 Benign carcinoid tumor of the large intestine, unspecified portion — (Code first any associated multiple endocrine neoplasia syndrome: 258.01-258.03)(Use additional code to identify associated endocrine syndrome, as: carcinoid syndrome: 259.2) ▽

209.56 Benign carcinoid tumor of the sigmoid colon — (Code first any associated multiple endocrine neoplasia syndrome: 258.01-258.03)(Use additional code to identify associated endocrine syndrome, as: carcinoid syndrome: 259.2)

209.57 Benign carcinoid tumor of the rectum — (Code first any associated multiple endocrine neoplasia syndrome: 258.01-258.03)(Use additional code to identify associated endocrine syndrome, as: carcinoid syndrome: 259.2)

209.69 Benign carcinoid tumor of other sites — (Code first any associated multiple endocrine neoplasia syndrome: 258.01-258.03)(Use additional code to identify associated endocrine syndrome, as: carcinoid syndrome: 259.2)

211.3 Benign neoplasm of colon

211.4 Benign neoplasm of rectum and anal canal

235.2 Neoplasm of uncertain behavior of stomach, intestines, and rectum
239.0 Neoplasm of unspecified nature of digestive system
569.3 Hemorrhage of rectum and anus
569.41 Ulcer of anus and rectum
569.44 Dysplasia of anus
569.49 Other specified disorder of rectum and anus — (Use additional code for any associated fecal incontinence (787.60-787.63))

ICD-9-CM Procedural

45.42 Endoscopic polypectomy of large intestine
45.43 Endoscopic destruction of other lesion or tissue of large intestine
48.33 Destruction of rectal lesion or tissue by laser
48.36 [Endoscopic] polypectomy of rectum

45321

45321 Proctosigmoidoscopy, rigid; with decompression of volvulus

ICD-9-CM Diagnostic

560.2 Volvulus
751.5 Other congenital anomalies of intestine

ICD-9-CM Procedural

46.85 Dilation of intestine
48.0 Proctotomy

45327

45327 Proctosigmoidoscopy, rigid; with transendoscopic stent placement (includes predilation)

ICD-9-CM Diagnostic

153.3 Malignant neoplasm of sigmoid colon
153.8 Malignant neoplasm of other specified sites of large intestine
153.9 Malignant neoplasm of colon, unspecified site ▽
154.0 Malignant neoplasm of rectosigmoid junction
154.1 Malignant neoplasm of rectum
197.5 Secondary malignant neoplasm of large intestine and rectum
209.10 Malignant carcinoid tumor of the large intestine, unspecified portion — (Code first any associated multiple endocrine neoplasia syndrome: 258.01-258.03)(Use additional code to identify associated endocrine syndrome, as: carcinoid syndrome: 259.2) ▽
209.16 Malignant carcinoid tumor of the sigmoid colon — (Code first any associated multiple endocrine neoplasia syndrome: 258.01-258.03)(Use additional code to identify associated endocrine syndrome, as: carcinoid syndrome: 259.2)
209.17 Malignant carcinoid tumor of the rectum — (Code first any associated multiple endocrine neoplasia syndrome: 258.01-258.03)(Use additional code to identify associated endocrine syndrome, as: carcinoid syndrome: 259.2)
209.29 Malignant carcinoid tumor of other sites — (Code first any associated multiple endocrine neoplasia syndrome: 258.01-258.03)(Use additional code to identify associated endocrine syndrome, as: carcinoid syndrome: 259.2)
560.81 Intestinal or peritoneal adhesions with obstruction (postoperative) (postinfection)
560.89 Other specified intestinal obstruction
560.9 Unspecified intestinal obstruction ▽
751.2 Congenital atresia and stenosis of large intestine, rectum, and anal canal
997.49 Other digestive system complications

ICD-9-CM Procedural

46.86 Endoscopic insertion of colonic stent(s)

HCPCS Level II Supplies & Services

C1874 Stent, coated/covered, with delivery system

45330-45331

45330 Sigmoidoscopy, flexible; diagnostic, with or without collection of specimen(s) by brushing or washing (separate procedure)
45331 with biopsy, single or multiple

ICD-9-CM Diagnostic

153.2 Malignant neoplasm of descending colon
153.3 Malignant neoplasm of sigmoid colon
153.8 Malignant neoplasm of other specified sites of large intestine
153.9 Malignant neoplasm of colon, unspecified site ▽
154.0 Malignant neoplasm of rectosigmoid junction
154.1 Malignant neoplasm of rectum
154.2 Malignant neoplasm of anal canal
154.3 Malignant neoplasm of anus, unspecified site ▽
154.8 Malignant neoplasm of other sites of rectum, rectosigmoid junction, and anus
159.0 Malignant neoplasm of intestinal tract, part unspecified ▽
159.9 Malignant neoplasm of ill-defined sites of digestive organs and peritoneum ▽
197.5 Secondary malignant neoplasm of large intestine and rectum
199.0 Disseminated malignant neoplasm
199.1 Other malignant neoplasm of unspecified site
199.2 Malignant neoplasm associated with transplanted organ — (Code first complication of transplanted organ (996.80-996.89) Use additional code for specific malignancy)
209.10 Malignant carcinoid tumor of the large intestine, unspecified portion — (Code first any associated multiple endocrine neoplasia syndrome: 258.01-258.03)(Use additional code to identify associated endocrine syndrome, as: carcinoid syndrome: 259.2) ▽
209.27 Malignant carcinoid tumor of hindgut, not otherwise specified — (Code first any associated multiple endocrine neoplasia syndrome: 258.01-258.03)(Use additional code to identify associated endocrine syndrome, as: carcinoid syndrome: 259.2)
209.29 Malignant carcinoid tumor of other sites — (Code first any associated multiple endocrine neoplasia syndrome: 258.01-258.03)(Use additional code to identify associated endocrine syndrome, as: carcinoid syndrome: 259.2)
209.30 Malignant poorly differentiated neuroendocrine carcinoma, any site — (Code first any associated multiple endocrine neoplasia syndrome: 258.01-258.03)(Use additional code to identify associated endocrine syndrome, as: carcinoid syndrome: 259.2) ▽
209.50 Benign carcinoid tumor of the large intestine, unspecified portion — (Code first any associated multiple endocrine neoplasia syndrome: 258.01-258.03)(Use additional code to identify associated endocrine syndrome, as: carcinoid syndrome: 259.2) ▽
209.56 Benign carcinoid tumor of the sigmoid colon — (Code first any associated multiple endocrine neoplasia syndrome: 258.01-258.03)(Use additional code to identify associated endocrine syndrome, as: carcinoid syndrome: 259.2)
209.57 Benign carcinoid tumor of the rectum — (Code first any associated multiple endocrine neoplasia syndrome: 258.01-258.03)(Use additional code to identify associated endocrine syndrome, as: carcinoid syndrome: 259.2)
209.69 Benign carcinoid tumor of other sites — (Code first any associated multiple endocrine neoplasia syndrome: 258.01-258.03)(Use additional code to identify associated endocrine syndrome, as: carcinoid syndrome: 259.2)
211.3 Benign neoplasm of colon
211.4 Benign neoplasm of rectum and anal canal
211.9 Benign neoplasm of other and unspecified site of the digestive system ▽
230.3 Carcinoma in situ of colon
230.4 Carcinoma in situ of rectum
230.5 Carcinoma in situ of anal canal
230.6 Carcinoma in situ of anus, unspecified ▽
230.7 Carcinoma in situ of other and unspecified parts of intestine ▽
230.9 Carcinoma in situ of other and unspecified digestive organs ▽
235.2 Neoplasm of uncertain behavior of stomach, intestines, and rectum
235.5 Neoplasm of uncertain behavior of other and unspecified digestive organs ▽
239.0 Neoplasm of unspecified nature of digestive system
280.0 Iron deficiency anemia secondary to blood loss (chronic)
285.1 Acute posthemorrhagic anemia
285.8 Other specified anemias

306.4 Gastrointestinal malfunction arising from mental factors
455.0 Internal hemorrhoids without mention of complication
455.1 Internal thrombosed hemorrhoids
455.2 Internal hemorrhoids with other complication
455.3 External hemorrhoids without mention of complication
455.4 External thrombosed hemorrhoids
455.5 External hemorrhoids with other complication
455.6 Unspecified hemorrhoids without mention of complication ▽
455.7 Unspecified thrombosed hemorrhoids ▽
455.8 Unspecified hemorrhoids with other complication ▽
455.9 Residual hemorrhoidal skin tags
555.1 Regional enteritis of large intestine
555.2 Regional enteritis of small intestine with large intestine
555.9 Regional enteritis of unspecified site ▽
556.0 Ulcerative (chronic) enterocolitis
556.2 Ulcerative (chronic) proctitis
556.3 Ulcerative (chronic) proctosigmoiditis
556.4 Pseudopolyposis of colon
556.6 Universal ulcerative (chronic) colitis
556.8 Other ulcerative colitis
556.9 Unspecified ulcerative colitis ▽
558.1 Gastroenteritis and colitis due to radiation
558.2 Toxic gastroenteritis and colitis — (Use additional E code to identify cause)
558.3 Gastroenteritis and colitis, allergic — (Use additional code to identify type of food allergy: V15.01-V15.05)
558.42 Eosinophilic colitis
558.9 Other and unspecified noninfectious gastroenteritis and colitis ▽
560.32 Fecal impaction
560.39 Impaction of intestine, other
560.9 Unspecified intestinal obstruction ▽
562.10 Diverticulosis of colon (without mention of hemorrhage) — (Use additional code to identify any associated peritonitis: 567.0-567.9)
562.11 Diverticulitis of colon (without mention of hemorrhage) — (Use additional code to identify any associated peritonitis: 567.0-567.9)
562.12 Diverticulosis of colon with hemorrhage — (Use additional code to identify any associated peritonitis: 567.0-567.9)
562.13 Diverticulitis of colon with hemorrhage — (Use additional code to identify any associated peritonitis: 567.0-567.9)
564.00 Unspecified constipation ▽
564.01 Slow transit constipation
564.02 Outlet dysfunction constipation
564.09 Other constipation
564.1 Irritable bowel syndrome
564.4 Other postoperative functional disorders
564.5 Functional diarrhea
564.6 Anal spasm
564.7 Megacolon, other than Hirschsprung's
564.81 Neurogenic bowel
564.89 Other functional disorders of intestine
565.0 Anal fissure
565.1 Anal fistula
566 Abscess of anal and rectal regions
567.0 Peritonitis in infectious diseases classified elsewhere — (Code first underlying disease) ☒
567.1 Pneumococcal peritonitis
567.21 Peritonitis (acute) generalized
567.22 Peritoneal abscess
567.23 Spontaneous bacterial peritonitis
567.29 Other suppurative peritonitis
567.38 Other retroperitoneal abscess
567.39 Other retroperitoneal infections
567.81 Choleperitonitis
567.82 Sclerosing mesenteritis
567.89 Other specified peritonitis
567.9 Unspecified peritonitis ▽
569.0 Anal and rectal polyp
569.1 Rectal prolapse
569.2 Stenosis of rectum and anus
569.3 Hemorrhage of rectum and anus
569.41 Ulcer of anus and rectum
569.42 Anal or rectal pain
569.44 Dysplasia of anus
569.49 Other specified disorder of rectum and anus — (Use additional code for any associated fecal incontinence (787.60-787.63))
569.5 Abscess of intestine
569.60 Unspecified complication of colostomy or enterostomy ▽
569.82 Ulceration of intestine
569.83 Perforation of intestine
569.84 Angiodysplasia of intestine (without mention of hemorrhage)
569.85 Angiodysplasia of intestine with hemorrhage
569.89 Other specified disorder of intestines
578.1 Blood in stool
619.0 Urinary-genital tract fistula, female ♀
619.1 Digestive-genital tract fistula, female ♀
619.2 Genital tract-skin fistula, female ♀
619.8 Other specified fistula involving female genital tract ♀
619.9 Unspecified fistula involving female genital tract ▽ ♀
747.61 Congenital gastrointestinal vessel anomaly
751.2 Congenital atresia and stenosis of large intestine, rectum, and anal canal
751.3 Hirschsprung's disease and other congenital functional disorders of colon
751.4 Congenital anomalies of intestinal fixation
751.5 Other congenital anomalies of intestine
783.21 Loss of weight — (Use additional code to identify Body Mass Index (BMI), if known: V85.0-V85.54)
783.22 Underweight — (Use additional code to identify Body Mass Index (BMI), if known: V85.0-V85.54)
783.7 Adult failure to thrive
787.3 Flatulence, eructation, and gas pain
787.4 Visible peristalsis
787.5 Abnormal bowel sounds
787.60 Full incontinence of feces
787.61 Incomplete defecation
787.62 Fecal smearing
787.63 Fecal urgency
787.7 Abnormal feces
787.91 Diarrhea
787.99 Other symptoms involving digestive system
789.00 Abdominal pain, unspecified site ▽
789.03 Abdominal pain, right lower quadrant
789.04 Abdominal pain, left lower quadrant
789.07 Abdominal pain, generalized
789.09 Abdominal pain, other specified site
789.30 Abdominal or pelvic swelling, mass or lump, unspecified site ▽
789.33 Abdominal or pelvic swelling, mass, or lump, right lower quadrant
789.34 Abdominal or pelvic swelling, mass, or lump, left lower quadrant
789.37 Abdominal or pelvic swelling, mass, or lump, generalized
789.39 Abdominal or pelvic swelling, mass, or lump, other specified site
789.51 Malignant ascites

789.59 Other ascites
792.1 Nonspecific abnormal finding in stool contents
793.4 Nonspecific (abnormal) findings on radiological and other examination of gastrointestinal tract
996.87 Complications of transplanted organ, intestine — (Use additional code to identify nature of complication: 078.5, 199.2, 238.77, 279.50-279.53)
997.49 Other digestive system complications
V67.00 Follow-up examination, following unspecified surgery ▽
V67.09 Follow-up examination, following other surgery
V76.41 Screening for malignant neoplasm of the rectum
V76.49 Special screening for malignant neoplasms, other sites

ICD-9-CM Procedural

45.24 Flexible sigmoidoscopy
45.25 Closed [endoscopic] biopsy of large intestine

HCPCS Level II Supplies & Services

A4270 Disposable endoscope sheath, each

45332

45332 Sigmoidoscopy, flexible; with removal of foreign body

ICD-9-CM Diagnostic

569.3 Hemorrhage of rectum and anus
569.42 Anal or rectal pain
578.1 Blood in stool
936 Foreign body in intestine and colon
937 Foreign body in anus and rectum

ICD-9-CM Procedural

45.24 Flexible sigmoidoscopy
98.05 Removal of intraluminal foreign body from rectum and anus without incision

HCPCS Level II Supplies & Services

A4270 Disposable endoscope sheath, each

45333

45333 Sigmoidoscopy, flexible; with removal of tumor(s), polyp(s), or other lesion(s) by hot biopsy forceps or bipolar cautery

ICD-9-CM Diagnostic

153.2 Malignant neoplasm of descending colon
153.3 Malignant neoplasm of sigmoid colon
153.8 Malignant neoplasm of other specified sites of large intestine
154.0 Malignant neoplasm of rectosigmoid junction
154.1 Malignant neoplasm of rectum
209.10 Malignant carcinoid tumor of the large intestine, unspecified portion — (Code first any associated multiple endocrine neoplasia syndrome: 258.01-258.03)(Use additional code to identify associated endocrine syndrome, as: carcinoid syndrome: 259.2) ▽
209.16 Malignant carcinoid tumor of the sigmoid colon — (Code first any associated multiple endocrine neoplasia syndrome: 258.01-258.03)(Use additional code to identify associated endocrine syndrome, as: carcinoid syndrome: 259.2)
209.17 Malignant carcinoid tumor of the rectum — (Code first any associated multiple endocrine neoplasia syndrome: 258.01-258.03)(Use additional code to identify associated endocrine syndrome, as: carcinoid syndrome: 259.2)
209.29 Malignant carcinoid tumor of other sites — (Code first any associated multiple endocrine neoplasia syndrome: 258.01-258.03)(Use additional code to identify associated endocrine syndrome, as: carcinoid syndrome: 259.2)
209.30 Malignant poorly differentiated neuroendocrine carcinoma, any site — (Code first any associated multiple endocrine neoplasia syndrome: 258.01-258.03)(Use additional code to identify associated endocrine syndrome, as: carcinoid syndrome: 259.2) ▽
209.50 Benign carcinoid tumor of the large intestine, unspecified portion — (Code first any associated multiple endocrine neoplasia syndrome: 258.01-258.03)(Use additional code to identify associated endocrine syndrome, as: carcinoid syndrome: 259.2) ▽
209.56 Benign carcinoid tumor of the sigmoid colon — (Code first any associated multiple endocrine neoplasia syndrome: 258.01-258.03)(Use additional code to identify associated endocrine syndrome, as: carcinoid syndrome: 259.2)
209.57 Benign carcinoid tumor of the rectum — (Code first any associated multiple endocrine neoplasia syndrome: 258.01-258.03)(Use additional code to identify associated endocrine syndrome, as: carcinoid syndrome: 259.2)
209.69 Benign carcinoid tumor of other sites — (Code first any associated multiple endocrine neoplasia syndrome: 258.01-258.03)(Use additional code to identify associated endocrine syndrome, as: carcinoid syndrome: 259.2)
211.3 Benign neoplasm of colon
211.4 Benign neoplasm of rectum and anal canal
211.9 Benign neoplasm of other and unspecified site of the digestive system ▽
230.3 Carcinoma in situ of colon
230.4 Carcinoma in situ of rectum
235.2 Neoplasm of uncertain behavior of stomach, intestines, and rectum
239.0 Neoplasm of unspecified nature of digestive system
455.0 Internal hemorrhoids without mention of complication
455.1 Internal thrombosed hemorrhoids
455.2 Internal hemorrhoids with other complication
455.3 External hemorrhoids without mention of complication
455.4 External thrombosed hemorrhoids
455.5 External hemorrhoids with other complication
455.6 Unspecified hemorrhoids without mention of complication ▽
455.7 Unspecified thrombosed hemorrhoids ▽
455.8 Unspecified hemorrhoids with other complication ▽
556.0 Ulcerative (chronic) enterocolitis
558.42 Eosinophilic colitis
558.9 Other and unspecified noninfectious gastroenteritis and colitis ▽
562.10 Diverticulosis of colon (without mention of hemorrhage) — (Use additional code to identify any associated peritonitis: 567.0-567.9)
562.11 Diverticulitis of colon (without mention of hemorrhage) — (Use additional code to identify any associated peritonitis: 567.0-567.9)
562.12 Diverticulosis of colon with hemorrhage — (Use additional code to identify any associated peritonitis: 567.0-567.9)
562.13 Diverticulitis of colon with hemorrhage — (Use additional code to identify any associated peritonitis: 567.0-567.9)
564.00 Unspecified constipation ▽
564.01 Slow transit constipation
564.02 Outlet dysfunction constipation
564.09 Other constipation
564.1 Irritable bowel syndrome
564.7 Megacolon, other than Hirschsprung's
569.0 Anal and rectal polyp
569.1 Rectal prolapse
569.2 Stenosis of rectum and anus
569.3 Hemorrhage of rectum and anus
569.41 Ulcer of anus and rectum
578.1 Blood in stool
578.9 Hemorrhage of gastrointestinal tract, unspecified ▽
787.3 Flatulence, eructation, and gas pain
787.4 Visible peristalsis
787.5 Abnormal bowel sounds
787.60 Full incontinence of feces
787.61 Incomplete defecation
787.62 Fecal smearing
787.63 Fecal urgency
787.7 Abnormal feces
787.91 Diarrhea
787.99 Other symptoms involving digestive system
789.00 Abdominal pain, unspecified site ▽

793.4 Nonspecific (abnormal) findings on radiological and other examination of gastrointestinal tract
V10.05 Personal history of malignant neoplasm of large intestine
V10.06 Personal history of malignant neoplasm of rectum, rectosigmoid junction, and anus
V18.51 Family history, Colonic polyps
V18.59 Family history, other digestive disorders

ICD-9-CM Procedural

45.42 Endoscopic polypectomy of large intestine
45.43 Endoscopic destruction of other lesion or tissue of large intestine

HCPCS Level II Supplies & Services

A4270 Disposable endoscope sheath, each

45334

45334 Sigmoidoscopy, flexible; with control of bleeding (eg, injection, bipolar cautery, unipolar cautery, laser, heater probe, stapler, plasma coagulator)

ICD-9-CM Diagnostic

153.3 Malignant neoplasm of sigmoid colon
154.1 Malignant neoplasm of rectum
209.16 Malignant carcinoid tumor of the sigmoid colon — (Code first any associated multiple endocrine neoplasia syndrome: 258.01-258.03)(Use additional code to identify associated endocrine syndrome, as: carcinoid syndrome: 259.2)
209.17 Malignant carcinoid tumor of the rectum — (Code first any associated multiple endocrine neoplasia syndrome: 258.01-258.03)(Use additional code to identify associated endocrine syndrome, as: carcinoid syndrome: 259.2)
448.9 Other and unspecified capillary diseases ▽
455.1 Internal thrombosed hemorrhoids
455.2 Internal hemorrhoids with other complication
556.0 Ulcerative (chronic) enterocolitis
556.2 Ulcerative (chronic) proctitis
556.3 Ulcerative (chronic) proctosigmoiditis
557.0 Acute vascular insufficiency of intestine
558.42 Eosinophilic colitis
562.12 Diverticulosis of colon with hemorrhage — (Use additional code to identify any associated peritonitis: 567.0-567.9)
562.13 Diverticulitis of colon with hemorrhage — (Use additional code to identify any associated peritonitis: 567.0-567.9)
569.3 Hemorrhage of rectum and anus
569.44 Dysplasia of anus
569.49 Other specified disorder of rectum and anus — (Use additional code for any associated fecal incontinence (787.60-787.63))
578.1 Blood in stool
578.9 Hemorrhage of gastrointestinal tract, unspecified ▽
998.11 Hemorrhage complicating a procedure

ICD-9-CM Procedural

45.43 Endoscopic destruction of other lesion or tissue of large intestine
99.29 Injection or infusion of other therapeutic or prophylactic substance

HCPCS Level II Supplies & Services

A4270 Disposable endoscope sheath, each

45335

45335 Sigmoidoscopy, flexible; with directed submucosal injection(s), any substance

ICD-9-CM Diagnostic

153.2 Malignant neoplasm of descending colon
153.3 Malignant neoplasm of sigmoid colon
153.8 Malignant neoplasm of other specified sites of large intestine
153.9 Malignant neoplasm of colon, unspecified site ▽
154.0 Malignant neoplasm of rectosigmoid junction
154.1 Malignant neoplasm of rectum
154.2 Malignant neoplasm of anal canal
154.3 Malignant neoplasm of anus, unspecified site ▽
154.8 Malignant neoplasm of other sites of rectum, rectosigmoid junction, and anus
159.0 Malignant neoplasm of intestinal tract, part unspecified ▽
159.9 Malignant neoplasm of ill-defined sites of digestive organs and peritoneum ▽
197.5 Secondary malignant neoplasm of large intestine and rectum
199.0 Disseminated malignant neoplasm
199.1 Other malignant neoplasm of unspecified site
199.2 Malignant neoplasm associated with transplanted organ — (Code first complication of transplanted organ (996.80-996.89) Use additional code for specific malignancy)
209.10 Malignant carcinoid tumor of the large intestine, unspecified portion — (Code first any associated multiple endocrine neoplasia syndrome: 258.01-258.03)(Use additional code to identify associated endocrine syndrome, as: carcinoid syndrome: 259.2) ▽
209.20 Malignant carcinoid tumor of unknown primary site — (Code first any associated multiple endocrine neoplasia syndrome: 258.01-258.03)(Use additional code to identify associated endocrine syndrome, as: carcinoid syndrome: 259.2)
209.27 Malignant carcinoid tumor of hindgut, not otherwise specified — (Code first any associated multiple endocrine neoplasia syndrome: 258.01-258.03)(Use additional code to identify associated endocrine syndrome, as: carcinoid syndrome: 259.2)
209.29 Malignant carcinoid tumor of other sites — (Code first any associated multiple endocrine neoplasia syndrome: 258.01-258.03)(Use additional code to identify associated endocrine syndrome, as: carcinoid syndrome: 259.2)
209.30 Malignant poorly differentiated neuroendocrine carcinoma, any site — (Code first any associated multiple endocrine neoplasia syndrome: 258.01-258.03)(Use additional code to identify associated endocrine syndrome, as: carcinoid syndrome: 259.2) ▽
209.50 Benign carcinoid tumor of the large intestine, unspecified portion — (Code first any associated multiple endocrine neoplasia syndrome: 258.01-258.03)(Use additional code to identify associated endocrine syndrome, as: carcinoid syndrome: 259.2) ▽
209.56 Benign carcinoid tumor of the sigmoid colon — (Code first any associated multiple endocrine neoplasia syndrome: 258.01-258.03)(Use additional code to identify associated endocrine syndrome, as: carcinoid syndrome: 259.2)
209.57 Benign carcinoid tumor of the rectum — (Code first any associated multiple endocrine neoplasia syndrome: 258.01-258.03)(Use additional code to identify associated endocrine syndrome, as: carcinoid syndrome: 259.2)
209.69 Benign carcinoid tumor of other sites — (Code first any associated multiple endocrine neoplasia syndrome: 258.01-258.03)(Use additional code to identify associated endocrine syndrome, as: carcinoid syndrome: 259.2)
211.3 Benign neoplasm of colon
211.4 Benign neoplasm of rectum and anal canal
211.9 Benign neoplasm of other and unspecified site of the digestive system ▽
230.3 Carcinoma in situ of colon
230.4 Carcinoma in situ of rectum
230.5 Carcinoma in situ of anal canal
230.6 Carcinoma in situ of anus, unspecified ▽
230.7 Carcinoma in situ of other and unspecified parts of intestine ▽
235.2 Neoplasm of uncertain behavior of stomach, intestines, and rectum
235.5 Neoplasm of uncertain behavior of other and unspecified digestive organs ▽
239.0 Neoplasm of unspecified nature of digestive system
306.4 Gastrointestinal malfunction arising from mental factors
455.0 Internal hemorrhoids without mention of complication
455.1 Internal thrombosed hemorrhoids
455.2 Internal hemorrhoids with other complication
455.6 Unspecified hemorrhoids without mention of complication ▽
455.7 Unspecified thrombosed hemorrhoids ▽
455.8 Unspecified hemorrhoids with other complication ▽
455.9 Residual hemorrhoidal skin tags
555.1 Regional enteritis of large intestine
555.2 Regional enteritis of small intestine with large intestine
555.9 Regional enteritis of unspecified site ▽

556.0	Ulcerative (chronic) enterocolitis
556.2	Ulcerative (chronic) proctitis
556.3	Ulcerative (chronic) proctosigmoiditis
556.4	Pseudopolyposis of colon
556.6	Universal ulcerative (chronic) colitis
556.8	Other ulcerative colitis
556.9	Unspecified ulcerative colitis ▽
558.1	Gastroenteritis and colitis due to radiation
558.2	Toxic gastroenteritis and colitis — (Use additional E code to identify cause)
558.3	Gastroenteritis and colitis, allergic — (Use additional code to identify type of food allergy: V15.01-V15.05)
558.9	Other and unspecified noninfectious gastroenteritis and colitis ▽
562.10	Diverticulosis of colon (without mention of hemorrhage) — (Use additional code to identify any associated peritonitis: 567.0-567.9)
562.11	Diverticulitis of colon (without mention of hemorrhage) — (Use additional code to identify any associated peritonitis: 567.0-567.9)
562.12	Diverticulosis of colon with hemorrhage — (Use additional code to identify any associated peritonitis: 567.0-567.9)
562.13	Diverticulitis of colon with hemorrhage — (Use additional code to identify any associated peritonitis: 567.0-567.9)
564.00	Unspecified constipation ▽
564.01	Slow transit constipation
564.02	Outlet dysfunction constipation
564.09	Other constipation
564.1	Irritable bowel syndrome
564.4	Other postoperative functional disorders
564.5	Functional diarrhea
564.6	Anal spasm
564.7	Megacolon, other than Hirschsprung's
564.81	Neurogenic bowel
564.89	Other functional disorders of intestine
565.0	Anal fissure
565.1	Anal fistula
566	Abscess of anal and rectal regions
569.0	Anal and rectal polyp
569.2	Stenosis of rectum and anus
569.3	Hemorrhage of rectum and anus
569.41	Ulcer of anus and rectum
569.42	Anal or rectal pain
569.44	Dysplasia of anus
569.49	Other specified disorder of rectum and anus — (Use additional code for any associated fecal incontinence (787.60-787.63))
569.5	Abscess of intestine
569.60	Unspecified complication of colostomy or enterostomy ▽
569.82	Ulceration of intestine
569.83	Perforation of intestine
569.84	Angiodysplasia of intestine (without mention of hemorrhage)
569.85	Angiodysplasia of intestine with hemorrhage
569.89	Other specified disorder of intestines
578.1	Blood in stool
619.1	Digestive-genital tract fistula, female ♀
747.61	Congenital gastrointestinal vessel anomaly
751.2	Congenital atresia and stenosis of large intestine, rectum, and anal canal
751.3	Hirschsprung's disease and other congenital functional disorders of colon
751.4	Congenital anomalies of intestinal fixation
751.5	Other congenital anomalies of intestine
787.3	Flatulence, eructation, and gas pain
787.4	Visible peristalsis
787.5	Abnormal bowel sounds
787.60	Full incontinence of feces
787.61	Incomplete defecation
787.62	Fecal smearing
787.63	Fecal urgency
787.7	Abnormal feces
787.91	Diarrhea
787.99	Other symptoms involving digestive system
789.00	Abdominal pain, unspecified site ▽
789.03	Abdominal pain, right lower quadrant
789.04	Abdominal pain, left lower quadrant
789.07	Abdominal pain, generalized
789.09	Abdominal pain, other specified site
789.51	Malignant ascites
789.59	Other ascites
792.1	Nonspecific abnormal finding in stool contents
793.4	Nonspecific (abnormal) findings on radiological and other examination of gastrointestinal tract
996.87	Complications of transplanted organ, intestine — (Use additional code to identify nature of complication: 078.5, 199.2, 238.77, 279.50-279.53)
997.49	Other digestive system complications
V47.3	Other digestive problems
V67.00	Follow-up examination, following unspecified surgery ▽
V67.09	Follow-up examination, following other surgery

ICD-9-CM Procedural

45.24	Flexible sigmoidoscopy
99.23	Injection of steroid
99.29	Injection or infusion of other therapeutic or prophylactic substance

45337

45337 Sigmoidoscopy, flexible; with decompression of volvulus, any method

ICD-9-CM Diagnostic

560.2	Volvulus

ICD-9-CM Procedural

46.85	Dilation of intestine

45338-45339

45338 Sigmoidoscopy, flexible; with removal of tumor(s), polyp(s), or other lesion(s) by snare technique

45339 with ablation of tumor(s), polyp(s), or other lesion(s) not amenable to removal by hot biopsy forceps, bipolar cautery or snare technique

ICD-9-CM Diagnostic

153.2	Malignant neoplasm of descending colon
153.3	Malignant neoplasm of sigmoid colon
153.8	Malignant neoplasm of other specified sites of large intestine
154.0	Malignant neoplasm of rectosigmoid junction
154.1	Malignant neoplasm of rectum
154.8	Malignant neoplasm of other sites of rectum, rectosigmoid junction, and anus
209.10	Malignant carcinoid tumor of the large intestine, unspecified portion — (Code first any associated multiple endocrine neoplasia syndrome: 258.01-258.03)(Use additional code to identify associated endocrine syndrome, as: carcinoid syndrome: 259.2) ▽
209.16	Malignant carcinoid tumor of the sigmoid colon — (Code first any associated multiple endocrine neoplasia syndrome: 258.01-258.03)(Use additional code to identify associated endocrine syndrome, as: carcinoid syndrome: 259.2)
209.17	Malignant carcinoid tumor of the rectum — (Code first any associated multiple endocrine neoplasia syndrome: 258.01-258.03)(Use additional code to identify associated endocrine syndrome, as: carcinoid syndrome: 259.2)

209.20 Malignant carcinoid tumor of unknown primary site — (Code first any associated multiple endocrine neoplasia syndrome: 258.01-258.03)(Use additional code to identify associated endocrine syndrome, as: carcinoid syndrome: 259.2)
209.29 Malignant carcinoid tumor of other sites — (Code first any associated multiple endocrine neoplasia syndrome: 258.01-258.03)(Use additional code to identify associated endocrine syndrome, as: carcinoid syndrome: 259.2)
209.30 Malignant poorly differentiated neuroendocrine carcinoma, any site — (Code first any associated multiple endocrine neoplasia syndrome: 258.01-258.03)(Use additional code to identify associated endocrine syndrome, as: carcinoid syndrome: 259.2) ▽
209.50 Benign carcinoid tumor of the large intestine, unspecified portion — (Code first any associated multiple endocrine neoplasia syndrome: 258.01-258.03)(Use additional code to identify associated endocrine syndrome, as: carcinoid syndrome: 259.2) ▽
209.56 Benign carcinoid tumor of the sigmoid colon — (Code first any associated multiple endocrine neoplasia syndrome: 258.01-258.03)(Use additional code to identify associated endocrine syndrome, as: carcinoid syndrome: 259.2)
209.57 Benign carcinoid tumor of the rectum — (Code first any associated multiple endocrine neoplasia syndrome: 258.01-258.03)(Use additional code to identify associated endocrine syndrome, as: carcinoid syndrome: 259.2)
209.69 Benign carcinoid tumor of other sites — (Code first any associated multiple endocrine neoplasia syndrome: 258.01-258.03)(Use additional code to identify associated endocrine syndrome, as: carcinoid syndrome: 259.2)
211.3 Benign neoplasm of colon
211.4 Benign neoplasm of rectum and anal canal
230.3 Carcinoma in situ of colon
230.4 Carcinoma in situ of rectum
235.2 Neoplasm of uncertain behavior of stomach, intestines, and rectum
239.0 Neoplasm of unspecified nature of digestive system
556.0 Ulcerative (chronic) enterocolitis
569.0 Anal and rectal polyp
569.3 Hemorrhage of rectum and anus
569.41 Ulcer of anus and rectum
569.44 Dysplasia of anus
569.49 Other specified disorder of rectum and anus — (Use additional code for any associated fecal incontinence (787.60-787.63))

ICD-9-CM Procedural

45.42 Endoscopic polypectomy of large intestine
45.43 Endoscopic destruction of other lesion or tissue of large intestine

HCPCS Level II Supplies & Services

A4270 Disposable endoscope sheath, each

45340

45340 Sigmoidoscopy, flexible; with dilation by balloon, 1 or more strictures

ICD-9-CM Diagnostic

560.81 Intestinal or peritoneal adhesions with obstruction (postoperative) (postinfection)
560.89 Other specified intestinal obstruction
560.9 Unspecified intestinal obstruction ▽
751.2 Congenital atresia and stenosis of large intestine, rectum, and anal canal
997.49 Other digestive system complications

ICD-9-CM Procedural

46.85 Dilation of intestine

45341

45341 Sigmoidoscopy, flexible; with endoscopic ultrasound examination

ICD-9-CM Diagnostic

153.3 Malignant neoplasm of sigmoid colon
153.8 Malignant neoplasm of other specified sites of large intestine
153.9 Malignant neoplasm of colon, unspecified site ▽
154.0 Malignant neoplasm of rectosigmoid junction
154.1 Malignant neoplasm of rectum
154.2 Malignant neoplasm of anal canal
154.3 Malignant neoplasm of anus, unspecified site ▽
154.8 Malignant neoplasm of other sites of rectum, rectosigmoid junction, and anus
159.0 Malignant neoplasm of intestinal tract, part unspecified ▽
159.9 Malignant neoplasm of ill-defined sites of digestive organs and peritoneum ▽
197.5 Secondary malignant neoplasm of large intestine and rectum
199.0 Disseminated malignant neoplasm
199.1 Other malignant neoplasm of unspecified site
199.2 Malignant neoplasm associated with transplanted organ — (Code first complication of transplanted organ (996.80-996.89) Use additional code for specific malignancy)
209.10 Malignant carcinoid tumor of the large intestine, unspecified portion — (Code first any associated multiple endocrine neoplasia syndrome: 258.01-258.03)(Use additional code to identify associated endocrine syndrome, as: carcinoid syndrome: 259.2) ▽
209.20 Malignant carcinoid tumor of unknown primary site — (Code first any associated multiple endocrine neoplasia syndrome: 258.01-258.03)(Use additional code to identify associated endocrine syndrome, as: carcinoid syndrome: 259.2)
209.27 Malignant carcinoid tumor of hindgut, not otherwise specified — (Code first any associated multiple endocrine neoplasia syndrome: 258.01-258.03)(Use additional code to identify associated endocrine syndrome, as: carcinoid syndrome: 259.2)
209.29 Malignant carcinoid tumor of other sites — (Code first any associated multiple endocrine neoplasia syndrome: 258.01-258.03)(Use additional code to identify associated endocrine syndrome, as: carcinoid syndrome: 259.2)
209.30 Malignant poorly differentiated neuroendocrine carcinoma, any site — (Code first any associated multiple endocrine neoplasia syndrome: 258.01-258.03)(Use additional code to identify associated endocrine syndrome, as: carcinoid syndrome: 259.2) ▽
209.50 Benign carcinoid tumor of the large intestine, unspecified portion — (Code first any associated multiple endocrine neoplasia syndrome: 258.01-258.03)(Use additional code to identify associated endocrine syndrome, as: carcinoid syndrome: 259.2) ▽
209.56 Benign carcinoid tumor of the sigmoid colon — (Code first any associated multiple endocrine neoplasia syndrome: 258.01-258.03)(Use additional code to identify associated endocrine syndrome, as: carcinoid syndrome: 259.2)
209.57 Benign carcinoid tumor of the rectum — (Code first any associated multiple endocrine neoplasia syndrome: 258.01-258.03)(Use additional code to identify associated endocrine syndrome, as: carcinoid syndrome: 259.2)
209.69 Benign carcinoid tumor of other sites — (Code first any associated multiple endocrine neoplasia syndrome: 258.01-258.03)(Use additional code to identify associated endocrine syndrome, as: carcinoid syndrome: 259.2)
211.3 Benign neoplasm of colon
211.4 Benign neoplasm of rectum and anal canal
211.9 Benign neoplasm of other and unspecified site of the digestive system ▽
230.3 Carcinoma in situ of colon
230.4 Carcinoma in situ of rectum
230.5 Carcinoma in situ of anal canal
230.6 Carcinoma in situ of anus, unspecified ▽
230.7 Carcinoma in situ of other and unspecified parts of intestine ▽
230.9 Carcinoma in situ of other and unspecified digestive organs ▽
235.2 Neoplasm of uncertain behavior of stomach, intestines, and rectum
235.5 Neoplasm of uncertain behavior of other and unspecified digestive organs ▽
239.0 Neoplasm of unspecified nature of digestive system
280.0 Iron deficiency anemia secondary to blood loss (chronic)
285.1 Acute posthemorrhagic anemia
285.8 Other specified anemias
306.4 Gastrointestinal malfunction arising from mental factors
455.0 Internal hemorrhoids without mention of complication
455.1 Internal thrombosed hemorrhoids
455.2 Internal hemorrhoids with other complication
455.3 External hemorrhoids without mention of complication
455.4 External thrombosed hemorrhoids
455.5 External hemorrhoids with other complication

455.6 Unspecified hemorrhoids without mention of complication ▽
455.7 Unspecified thrombosed hemorrhoids ▽
455.8 Unspecified hemorrhoids with other complication ▽
455.9 Residual hemorrhoidal skin tags
555.1 Regional enteritis of large intestine
555.2 Regional enteritis of small intestine with large intestine
555.9 Regional enteritis of unspecified site ▽
556.0 Ulcerative (chronic) enterocolitis
556.2 Ulcerative (chronic) proctitis
556.3 Ulcerative (chronic) proctosigmoiditis
556.4 Pseudopolyposis of colon
556.6 Universal ulcerative (chronic) colitis
556.8 Other ulcerative colitis
556.9 Unspecified ulcerative colitis ▽
558.1 Gastroenteritis and colitis due to radiation
558.2 Toxic gastroenteritis and colitis — (Use additional E code to identify cause)
558.3 Gastroenteritis and colitis, allergic — (Use additional code to identify type of food allergy: V15.01-V15.05)
558.41 Eosinophilic gastroenteritis
558.42 Eosinophilic colitis
558.9 Other and unspecified noninfectious gastroenteritis and colitis ▽
560.9 Unspecified intestinal obstruction ▽
562.10 Diverticulosis of colon (without mention of hemorrhage) — (Use additional code to identify any associated peritonitis: 567.0-567.9)
562.11 Diverticulitis of colon (without mention of hemorrhage) — (Use additional code to identify any associated peritonitis: 567.0-567.9)
562.12 Diverticulosis of colon with hemorrhage — (Use additional code to identify any associated peritonitis: 567.0-567.9)
562.13 Diverticulitis of colon with hemorrhage — (Use additional code to identify any associated peritonitis: 567.0-567.9)
564.00 Unspecified constipation ▽
564.01 Slow transit constipation
564.02 Outlet dysfunction constipation
564.09 Other constipation
564.1 Irritable bowel syndrome
564.4 Other postoperative functional disorders
564.5 Functional diarrhea
564.6 Anal spasm
564.7 Megacolon, other than Hirschsprung's
564.81 Neurogenic bowel
564.89 Other functional disorders of intestine
565.0 Anal fissure
565.1 Anal fistula
566 Abscess of anal and rectal regions
567.0 Peritonitis in infectious diseases classified elsewhere — (Code first underlying disease) ☒
567.1 Pneumococcal peritonitis
567.21 Peritonitis (acute) generalized
567.22 Peritoneal abscess
567.23 Spontaneous bacterial peritonitis
567.29 Other suppurative peritonitis
567.38 Other retroperitoneal abscess
567.39 Other retroperitoneal infections
567.81 Choleperitonitis
567.82 Sclerosing mesenteritis
567.89 Other specified peritonitis
567.9 Unspecified peritonitis ▽
569.0 Anal and rectal polyp
569.1 Rectal prolapse
569.2 Stenosis of rectum and anus
569.3 Hemorrhage of rectum and anus
569.41 Ulcer of anus and rectum
569.42 Anal or rectal pain
569.44 Dysplasia of anus
569.49 Other specified disorder of rectum and anus — (Use additional code for any associated fecal incontinence (787.60-787.63))
569.5 Abscess of intestine
569.60 Unspecified complication of colostomy or enterostomy ▽
569.82 Ulceration of intestine
569.83 Perforation of intestine
569.84 Angiodysplasia of intestine (without mention of hemorrhage)
569.85 Angiodysplasia of intestine with hemorrhage
569.89 Other specified disorder of intestines
578.1 Blood in stool
619.0 Urinary-genital tract fistula, female ♀
619.1 Digestive-genital tract fistula, female ♀
619.2 Genital tract-skin fistula, female ♀
619.8 Other specified fistula involving female genital tract ♀
619.9 Unspecified fistula involving female genital tract ▽ ♀
747.61 Congenital gastrointestinal vessel anomaly
751.2 Congenital atresia and stenosis of large intestine, rectum, and anal canal
751.3 Hirschsprung's disease and other congenital functional disorders of colon
751.4 Congenital anomalies of intestinal fixation
751.5 Other congenital anomalies of intestine
783.21 Loss of weight — (Use additional code to identify Body Mass Index (BMI), if known: V85.0-V85.54)
783.22 Underweight — (Use additional code to identify Body Mass Index (BMI), if known: V85.0-V85.54)
783.7 Adult failure to thrive
787.3 Flatulence, eructation, and gas pain
787.4 Visible peristalsis
787.5 Abnormal bowel sounds
787.60 Full incontinence of feces
787.61 Incomplete defecation
787.62 Fecal smearing
787.63 Fecal urgency
787.7 Abnormal feces
787.91 Diarrhea
787.99 Other symptoms involving digestive system
789.00 Abdominal pain, unspecified site ▽
789.03 Abdominal pain, right lower quadrant
789.04 Abdominal pain, left lower quadrant
789.07 Abdominal pain, generalized
789.09 Abdominal pain, other specified site
789.30 Abdominal or pelvic swelling, mass or lump, unspecified site ▽
789.33 Abdominal or pelvic swelling, mass, or lump, right lower quadrant
789.34 Abdominal or pelvic swelling, mass, or lump, left lower quadrant
789.37 Abdominal or pelvic swelling, mass, or lump, generalized
789.39 Abdominal or pelvic swelling, mass, or lump, other specified site
789.51 Malignant ascites
789.59 Other ascites
792.1 Nonspecific abnormal finding in stool contents
793.4 Nonspecific (abnormal) findings on radiological and other examination of gastrointestinal tract
996.87 Complications of transplanted organ, intestine — (Use additional code to identify nature of complication: 078.5, 199.2, 238.77, 279.50-279.53)
997.49 Other digestive system complications
V10.00 Personal history of malignant neoplasm of unspecified site in gastrointestinal tract ▽

V10.06 Personal history of malignant neoplasm of rectum, rectosigmoid junction, and anus
V10.09 Personal history of malignant neoplasm of other site in gastrointestinal tract
V12.70 Personal history of unspecified digestive disease ▽
V12.72 Personal history of colonic polyps
V12.79 Personal history of other diseases of digestive disease
V16.0 Family history of malignant neoplasm of gastrointestinal tract
V18.51 Family history, Colonic polyps
V18.59 Family history, other digestive disorders
V44.2 Ileostomy status
V44.3 Colostomy status
V47.3 Other digestive problems
V55.3 Attention to colostomy
V67.00 Follow-up examination, following unspecified surgery ▽
V67.09 Follow-up examination, following other surgery
V72.85 Other specified examination — (Use additional code(s) to identify any special screening examination(s) performed: V73.0-V82.9)
V76.41 Screening for malignant neoplasm of the rectum
V76.49 Special screening for malignant neoplasms, other sites
V82.9 Screening for unspecified condition ▽
V85.0 Body Mass Index less than 19, adult

ICD-9-CM Procedural

45.24 Flexible sigmoidoscopy
88.74 Diagnostic ultrasound of digestive system

45342

45342 Sigmoidoscopy, flexible; with transendoscopic ultrasound guided intramural or transmural fine needle aspiration/biopsy(s)

ICD-9-CM Diagnostic

153.3 Malignant neoplasm of sigmoid colon
153.8 Malignant neoplasm of other specified sites of large intestine
153.9 Malignant neoplasm of colon, unspecified site ▽
154.0 Malignant neoplasm of rectosigmoid junction
154.1 Malignant neoplasm of rectum
154.2 Malignant neoplasm of anal canal
154.3 Malignant neoplasm of anus, unspecified site ▽
154.8 Malignant neoplasm of other sites of rectum, rectosigmoid junction, and anus
158.8 Malignant neoplasm of specified parts of peritoneum
158.9 Malignant neoplasm of peritoneum, unspecified ▽
159.0 Malignant neoplasm of intestinal tract, part unspecified ▽
159.9 Malignant neoplasm of ill-defined sites of digestive organs and peritoneum ▽
195.2 Malignant neoplasm of abdomen
195.3 Malignant neoplasm of pelvis
196.2 Secondary and unspecified malignant neoplasm of intra-abdominal lymph nodes
196.5 Secondary and unspecified malignant neoplasm of lymph nodes of inguinal region and lower limb
196.6 Secondary and unspecified malignant neoplasm of intrapelvic lymph nodes
197.5 Secondary malignant neoplasm of large intestine and rectum
197.6 Secondary malignant neoplasm of retroperitoneum and peritoneum
199.0 Disseminated malignant neoplasm
199.1 Other malignant neoplasm of unspecified site
209.10 Malignant carcinoid tumor of the large intestine, unspecified portion — (Code first any associated multiple endocrine neoplasia syndrome: 258.01-258.03)(Use additional code to identify associated endocrine syndrome, as: carcinoid syndrome: 259.2) ▽
209.16 Malignant carcinoid tumor of the sigmoid colon — (Code first any associated multiple endocrine neoplasia syndrome: 258.01-258.03)(Use additional code to identify associated endocrine syndrome, as: carcinoid syndrome: 259.2)
209.17 Malignant carcinoid tumor of the rectum — (Code first any associated multiple endocrine neoplasia syndrome: 258.01-258.03)(Use additional code to identify associated endocrine syndrome, as: carcinoid syndrome: 259.2)
209.20 Malignant carcinoid tumor of unknown primary site — (Code first any associated multiple endocrine neoplasia syndrome: 258.01-258.03)(Use additional code to identify associated endocrine syndrome, as: carcinoid syndrome: 259.2)
209.27 Malignant carcinoid tumor of hindgut, not otherwise specified — (Code first any associated multiple endocrine neoplasia syndrome: 258.01-258.03)(Use additional code to identify associated endocrine syndrome, as: carcinoid syndrome: 259.2)
209.29 Malignant carcinoid tumor of other sites — (Code first any associated multiple endocrine neoplasia syndrome: 258.01-258.03)(Use additional code to identify associated endocrine syndrome, as: carcinoid syndrome: 259.2)
209.30 Malignant poorly differentiated neuroendocrine carcinoma, any site — (Code first any associated multiple endocrine neoplasia syndrome: 258.01-258.03)(Use additional code to identify associated endocrine syndrome, as: carcinoid syndrome: 259.2) ▽
209.50 Benign carcinoid tumor of the large intestine, unspecified portion — (Code first any associated multiple endocrine neoplasia syndrome: 258.01-258.03)(Use additional code to identify associated endocrine syndrome, as: carcinoid syndrome: 259.2) ▽
209.56 Benign carcinoid tumor of the sigmoid colon — (Code first any associated multiple endocrine neoplasia syndrome: 258.01-258.03)(Use additional code to identify associated endocrine syndrome, as: carcinoid syndrome: 259.2)
209.57 Benign carcinoid tumor of the rectum — (Code first any associated multiple endocrine neoplasia syndrome: 258.01-258.03)(Use additional code to identify associated endocrine syndrome, as: carcinoid syndrome: 259.2)
209.69 Benign carcinoid tumor of other sites — (Code first any associated multiple endocrine neoplasia syndrome: 258.01-258.03)(Use additional code to identify associated endocrine syndrome, as: carcinoid syndrome: 259.2)
209.74 Secondary neuroendocrine tumor of peritoneum
211.3 Benign neoplasm of colon
211.4 Benign neoplasm of rectum and anal canal
211.8 Benign neoplasm of retroperitoneum and peritoneum
211.9 Benign neoplasm of other and unspecified site of the digestive system ▽
230.3 Carcinoma in situ of colon
230.4 Carcinoma in situ of rectum
230.5 Carcinoma in situ of anal canal
230.6 Carcinoma in situ of anus, unspecified ▽
230.7 Carcinoma in situ of other and unspecified parts of intestine ▽
230.9 Carcinoma in situ of other and unspecified digestive organs ▽
235.2 Neoplasm of uncertain behavior of stomach, intestines, and rectum
235.4 Neoplasm of uncertain behavior of retroperitoneum and peritoneum
235.5 Neoplasm of uncertain behavior of other and unspecified digestive organs ▽
239.0 Neoplasm of unspecified nature of digestive system
555.1 Regional enteritis of large intestine
555.2 Regional enteritis of small intestine with large intestine
555.9 Regional enteritis of unspecified site ▽
556.0 Ulcerative (chronic) enterocolitis
556.2 Ulcerative (chronic) proctitis
556.3 Ulcerative (chronic) proctosigmoiditis
556.4 Pseudopolyposis of colon
556.6 Universal ulcerative (chronic) colitis
556.8 Other ulcerative colitis
556.9 Unspecified ulcerative colitis ▽
562.10 Diverticulosis of colon (without mention of hemorrhage) — (Use additional code to identify any associated peritonitis: 567.0-567.9)
562.11 Diverticulitis of colon (without mention of hemorrhage) — (Use additional code to identify any associated peritonitis: 567.0-567.9)
562.12 Diverticulosis of colon with hemorrhage — (Use additional code to identify any associated peritonitis: 567.0-567.9)
562.13 Diverticulitis of colon with hemorrhage — (Use additional code to identify any associated peritonitis: 567.0-567.9)
569.0 Anal and rectal polyp

569.41 Ulcer of anus and rectum
569.44 Dysplasia of anus
569.49 Other specified disorder of rectum and anus — (Use additional code for any associated fecal incontinence (787.60-787.63))
569.82 Ulceration of intestine
569.83 Perforation of intestine
569.89 Other specified disorder of intestines
578.1 Blood in stool
783.21 Loss of weight — (Use additional code to identify Body Mass Index (BMI), if known: V85.0-V85.54)
789.30 Abdominal or pelvic swelling, mass or lump, unspecified site ▽
789.33 Abdominal or pelvic swelling, mass, or lump, right lower quadrant
789.34 Abdominal or pelvic swelling, mass, or lump, left lower quadrant
789.39 Abdominal or pelvic swelling, mass, or lump, other specified site
793.4 Nonspecific (abnormal) findings on radiological and other examination of gastrointestinal tract
V10.00 Personal history of malignant neoplasm of unspecified site in gastrointestinal tract ▽
V10.06 Personal history of malignant neoplasm of rectum, rectosigmoid junction, and anus
V10.09 Personal history of malignant neoplasm of other site in gastrointestinal tract
V12.70 Personal history of unspecified digestive disease ▽
V12.72 Personal history of colonic polyps
V12.79 Personal history of other diseases of digestive disease
V16.0 Family history of malignant neoplasm of gastrointestinal tract
V67.09 Follow-up examination, following other surgery
V76.41 Screening for malignant neoplasm of the rectum
V76.49 Special screening for malignant neoplasms, other sites
V82.9 Screening for unspecified condition ▽
V85.0 Body Mass Index less than 19, adult

ICD-9-CM Procedural

45.25 Closed [endoscopic] biopsy of large intestine
88.74 Diagnostic ultrasound of digestive system

45345

45345 Sigmoidoscopy, flexible; with transendoscopic stent placement (includes predilation)

ICD-9-CM Diagnostic

153.3 Malignant neoplasm of sigmoid colon
153.8 Malignant neoplasm of other specified sites of large intestine
153.9 Malignant neoplasm of colon, unspecified site ▽
154.0 Malignant neoplasm of rectosigmoid junction
154.1 Malignant neoplasm of rectum
197.5 Secondary malignant neoplasm of large intestine and rectum
209.10 Malignant carcinoid tumor of the large intestine, unspecified portion — (Code first any associated multiple endocrine neoplasia syndrome: 258.01-258.03)(Use additional code to identify associated endocrine syndrome, as: carcinoid syndrome: 259.2) ▽
209.16 Malignant carcinoid tumor of the sigmoid colon — (Code first any associated multiple endocrine neoplasia syndrome: 258.01-258.03)(Use additional code to identify associated endocrine syndrome, as: carcinoid syndrome: 259.2)
209.17 Malignant carcinoid tumor of the rectum — (Code first any associated multiple endocrine neoplasia syndrome: 258.01-258.03)(Use additional code to identify associated endocrine syndrome, as: carcinoid syndrome: 259.2)
209.20 Malignant carcinoid tumor of unknown primary site — (Code first any associated multiple endocrine neoplasia syndrome: 258.01-258.03)(Use additional code to identify associated endocrine syndrome, as: carcinoid syndrome: 259.2)
209.29 Malignant carcinoid tumor of other sites — (Code first any associated multiple endocrine neoplasia syndrome: 258.01-258.03)(Use additional code to identify associated endocrine syndrome, as: carcinoid syndrome: 259.2)
209.50 Benign carcinoid tumor of the large intestine, unspecified portion — (Code first any associated multiple endocrine neoplasia syndrome: 258.01-258.03)(Use additional code to identify associated endocrine syndrome, as: carcinoid syndrome: 259.2) ▽
560.81 Intestinal or peritoneal adhesions with obstruction (postoperative) (postinfection)
560.89 Other specified intestinal obstruction
560.9 Unspecified intestinal obstruction ▽
751.2 Congenital atresia and stenosis of large intestine, rectum, and anal canal
997.49 Other digestive system complications

ICD-9-CM Procedural

46.86 Endoscopic insertion of colonic stent(s)

HCPCS Level II Supplies & Services

C1874 Stent, coated/covered, with delivery system

45355

45355 Colonoscopy, rigid or flexible, transabdominal via colotomy, single or multiple

ICD-9-CM Diagnostic

153.0 Malignant neoplasm of hepatic flexure
153.1 Malignant neoplasm of transverse colon
153.2 Malignant neoplasm of descending colon
153.3 Malignant neoplasm of sigmoid colon
153.4 Malignant neoplasm of cecum
153.5 Malignant neoplasm of appendix
153.6 Malignant neoplasm of ascending colon
153.7 Malignant neoplasm of splenic flexure
153.8 Malignant neoplasm of other specified sites of large intestine
153.9 Malignant neoplasm of colon, unspecified site ▽
154.0 Malignant neoplasm of rectosigmoid junction
154.1 Malignant neoplasm of rectum
154.2 Malignant neoplasm of anal canal
154.3 Malignant neoplasm of anus, unspecified site ▽
197.5 Secondary malignant neoplasm of large intestine and rectum
199.0 Disseminated malignant neoplasm
199.1 Other malignant neoplasm of unspecified site
209.10 Malignant carcinoid tumor of the large intestine, unspecified portion — (Code first any associated multiple endocrine neoplasia syndrome: 258.01-258.03)(Use additional code to identify associated endocrine syndrome, as: carcinoid syndrome: 259.2) ▽
209.11 Malignant carcinoid tumor of the appendix — (Code first any associated multiple endocrine neoplasia syndrome: 258.01-258.03)(Use additional code to identify associated endocrine syndrome, as: carcinoid syndrome: 259.2)
209.12 Malignant carcinoid tumor of the cecum — (Code first any associated multiple endocrine neoplasia syndrome: 258.01-258.03)(Use additional code to identify associated endocrine syndrome, as: carcinoid syndrome: 259.2)
209.13 Malignant carcinoid tumor of the ascending colon — (Code first any associated multiple endocrine neoplasia syndrome: 258.01-258.03)(Use additional code to identify associated endocrine syndrome, as: carcinoid syndrome: 259.2)
209.14 Malignant carcinoid tumor of the transverse colon — (Code first any associated multiple endocrine neoplasia syndrome: 258.01-258.03)(Use additional code to identify associated endocrine syndrome, as: carcinoid syndrome: 259.2)
209.15 Malignant carcinoid tumor of the descending colon — (Code first any associated multiple endocrine neoplasia syndrome: 258.01-258.03)(Use additional code to identify associated endocrine syndrome, as: carcinoid syndrome: 259.2)
209.16 Malignant carcinoid tumor of the sigmoid colon — (Code first any associated multiple endocrine neoplasia syndrome: 258.01-258.03)(Use additional code to identify associated endocrine syndrome, as: carcinoid syndrome: 259.2)
209.17 Malignant carcinoid tumor of the rectum — (Code first any associated multiple endocrine neoplasia syndrome: 258.01-258.03)(Use additional code to identify associated endocrine syndrome, as: carcinoid syndrome: 259.2)
209.20 Malignant carcinoid tumor of unknown primary site — (Code first any associated multiple endocrine neoplasia syndrome: 258.01-258.03)(Use additional code to identify associated endocrine syndrome, as: carcinoid syndrome: 259.2)

209.27 Malignant carcinoid tumor of hindgut, not otherwise specified — (Code first any associated multiple endocrine neoplasia syndrome: 258.01-258.03)(Use additional code to identify associated endocrine syndrome, as: carcinoid syndrome: 259.2)
209.29 Malignant carcinoid tumor of other sites — (Code first any associated multiple endocrine neoplasia syndrome: 258.01-258.03)(Use additional code to identify associated endocrine syndrome, as: carcinoid syndrome: 259.2)
209.30 Malignant poorly differentiated neuroendocrine carcinoma, any site — (Code first any associated multiple endocrine neoplasia syndrome: 258.01-258.03)(Use additional code to identify associated endocrine syndrome, as: carcinoid syndrome: 259.2) ▽
209.50 Benign carcinoid tumor of the large intestine, unspecified portion — (Code first any associated multiple endocrine neoplasia syndrome: 258.01-258.03)(Use additional code to identify associated endocrine syndrome, as: carcinoid syndrome: 259.2) ▽
209.51 Benign carcinoid tumor of the appendix — (Code first any associated multiple endocrine neoplasia syndrome: 258.01-258.03)(Use additional code to identify associated endocrine syndrome, as: carcinoid syndrome: 259.2)
209.52 Benign carcinoid tumor of the cecum — (Code first any associated multiple endocrine neoplasia syndrome: 258.01-258.03)(Use additional code to identify associated endocrine syndrome, as: carcinoid syndrome: 259.2)
209.53 Benign carcinoid tumor of the ascending colon — (Code first any associated multiple endocrine neoplasia syndrome: 258.01-258.03)(Use additional code to identify associated endocrine syndrome, as: carcinoid syndrome: 259.2)
209.54 Benign carcinoid tumor of the transverse colon — (Code first any associated multiple endocrine neoplasia syndrome: 258.01-258.03)(Use additional code to identify associated endocrine syndrome, as: carcinoid syndrome: 259.2)
209.55 Benign carcinoid tumor of the descending colon — (Code first any associated multiple endocrine neoplasia syndrome: 258.01-258.03)(Use additional code to identify associated endocrine syndrome, as: carcinoid syndrome: 259.2)
209.56 Benign carcinoid tumor of the sigmoid colon — (Code first any associated multiple endocrine neoplasia syndrome: 258.01-258.03)(Use additional code to identify associated endocrine syndrome, as: carcinoid syndrome: 259.2)
209.57 Benign carcinoid tumor of the rectum — (Code first any associated multiple endocrine neoplasia syndrome: 258.01-258.03)(Use additional code to identify associated endocrine syndrome, as: carcinoid syndrome: 259.2)
209.69 Benign carcinoid tumor of other sites — (Code first any associated multiple endocrine neoplasia syndrome: 258.01-258.03)(Use additional code to identify associated endocrine syndrome, as: carcinoid syndrome: 259.2)
211.3 Benign neoplasm of colon
230.3 Carcinoma in situ of colon
230.4 Carcinoma in situ of rectum
230.5 Carcinoma in situ of anal canal
230.6 Carcinoma in situ of anus, unspecified ▽
235.2 Neoplasm of uncertain behavior of stomach, intestines, and rectum
239.0 Neoplasm of unspecified nature of digestive system
280.0 Iron deficiency anemia secondary to blood loss (chronic)
280.9 Unspecified iron deficiency anemia ▽
455.0 Internal hemorrhoids without mention of complication
455.2 Internal hemorrhoids with other complication
455.6 Unspecified hemorrhoids without mention of complication ▽
455.8 Unspecified hemorrhoids with other complication ▽
555.1 Regional enteritis of large intestine
555.2 Regional enteritis of small intestine with large intestine
555.9 Regional enteritis of unspecified site ▽
556.0 Ulcerative (chronic) enterocolitis
556.1 Ulcerative (chronic) ileocolitis
556.2 Ulcerative (chronic) proctitis
556.3 Ulcerative (chronic) proctosigmoiditis
556.4 Pseudopolyposis of colon
556.5 Left sided ulcerative (chronic) colitis
556.6 Universal ulcerative (chronic) colitis
556.8 Other ulcerative colitis
557.0 Acute vascular insufficiency of intestine
557.1 Chronic vascular insufficiency of intestine
557.9 Unspecified vascular insufficiency of intestine ▽
558.1 Gastroenteritis and colitis due to radiation
558.2 Toxic gastroenteritis and colitis — (Use additional E code to identify cause)
558.3 Gastroenteritis and colitis, allergic — (Use additional code to identify type of food allergy: V15.01-V15.05)
558.42 Eosinophilic colitis
558.9 Other and unspecified noninfectious gastroenteritis and colitis ▽
560.0 Intussusception
560.1 Paralytic ileus
560.2 Volvulus
560.32 Fecal impaction
560.39 Impaction of intestine, other
560.89 Other specified intestinal obstruction
560.9 Unspecified intestinal obstruction ▽
562.10 Diverticulosis of colon (without mention of hemorrhage) — (Use additional code to identify any associated peritonitis: 567.0-567.9)
562.11 Diverticulitis of colon (without mention of hemorrhage) — (Use additional code to identify any associated peritonitis: 567.0-567.9)
562.13 Diverticulitis of colon with hemorrhage — (Use additional code to identify any associated peritonitis: 567.0-567.9)
564.00 Unspecified constipation ▽
564.01 Slow transit constipation
564.02 Outlet dysfunction constipation
564.09 Other constipation
564.1 Irritable bowel syndrome
564.4 Other postoperative functional disorders
564.5 Functional diarrhea
564.7 Megacolon, other than Hirschsprung's
564.81 Neurogenic bowel
564.89 Other functional disorders of intestine
565.0 Anal fissure
565.1 Anal fistula
566 Abscess of anal and rectal regions
567.0 Peritonitis in infectious diseases classified elsewhere — (Code first underlying disease) ☒
567.1 Pneumococcal peritonitis
567.21 Peritonitis (acute) generalized
567.22 Peritoneal abscess
567.23 Spontaneous bacterial peritonitis
567.29 Other suppurative peritonitis
567.31 Psoas muscle abscess
567.38 Other retroperitoneal abscess
567.39 Other retroperitoneal infections
567.81 Choleperitonitis
567.82 Sclerosing mesenteritis
567.89 Other specified peritonitis
567.9 Unspecified peritonitis ▽
569.0 Anal and rectal polyp
569.3 Hemorrhage of rectum and anus
569.42 Anal or rectal pain
569.44 Dysplasia of anus
569.49 Other specified disorder of rectum and anus — (Use additional code for any associated fecal incontinence (787.60-787.63))
569.82 Ulceration of intestine
569.89 Other specified disorder of intestines
578.1 Blood in stool
578.9 Hemorrhage of gastrointestinal tract, unspecified ▽
579.0 Celiac disease

579.1 Tropical sprue
579.2 Blind loop syndrome
579.3 Other and unspecified postsurgical nonabsorption ♥
579.4 Pancreatic steatorrhea
579.8 Other specified intestinal malabsorption
747.61 Congenital gastrointestinal vessel anomaly
751.3 Hirschsprung's disease and other congenital functional disorders of colon
751.5 Other congenital anomalies of intestine
783.21 Loss of weight — (Use additional code to identify Body Mass Index (BMI), if known: V85.0-V85.54)
783.22 Underweight — (Use additional code to identify Body Mass Index (BMI), if known: V85.0-V85.54)
783.7 Adult failure to thrive
787.3 Flatulence, eructation, and gas pain
787.7 Abnormal feces
787.91 Diarrhea
787.99 Other symptoms involving digestive system
789.00 Abdominal pain, unspecified site ♥
789.01 Abdominal pain, right upper quadrant
789.02 Abdominal pain, left upper quadrant
789.03 Abdominal pain, right lower quadrant
789.04 Abdominal pain, left lower quadrant
789.05 Abdominal pain, periumbilic
789.06 Abdominal pain, epigastric
789.07 Abdominal pain, generalized
789.09 Abdominal pain, other specified site
789.30 Abdominal or pelvic swelling, mass or lump, unspecified site ♥
789.31 Abdominal or pelvic swelling, mass, or lump, right upper quadrant
789.32 Abdominal or pelvic swelling, mass, or lump, left upper quadrant
789.33 Abdominal or pelvic swelling, mass, or lump, right lower quadrant
789.34 Abdominal or pelvic swelling, mass, or lump, left lower quadrant
789.35 Abdominal or pelvic swelling, mass or lump, periumbilic
789.36 Abdominal or pelvic swelling, mass, or lump, epigastric
789.37 Abdominal or pelvic swelling, mass, or lump, generalized
789.39 Abdominal or pelvic swelling, mass, or lump, other specified site
789.9 Other symptoms involving abdomen and pelvis
792.1 Nonspecific abnormal finding in stool contents
793.4 Nonspecific (abnormal) findings on radiological and other examination of gastrointestinal tract
997.49 Other digestive system complications
V67.00 Follow-up examination, following unspecified surgery ♥
V67.09 Follow-up examination, following other surgery
V67.51 Follow-up examination following completed treatment with high-risk medications, not elsewhere classified
V71.1 Observation for suspected malignant neoplasm
V71.89 Observation for other specified suspected conditions
V71.9 Observation for unspecified suspected condition ♥

ICD-9-CM Procedural

45.21 Transabdominal endoscopy of large intestine

45378

45378 Colonoscopy, flexible, proximal to splenic flexure; diagnostic, with or without collection of specimen(s) by brushing or washing, with or without colon decompression (separate procedure)

ICD-9-CM Diagnostic

153.0 Malignant neoplasm of hepatic flexure
153.1 Malignant neoplasm of transverse colon
153.2 Malignant neoplasm of descending colon
153.3 Malignant neoplasm of sigmoid colon
153.4 Malignant neoplasm of cecum
153.5 Malignant neoplasm of appendix
153.6 Malignant neoplasm of ascending colon
153.7 Malignant neoplasm of splenic flexure
153.8 Malignant neoplasm of other specified sites of large intestine
153.9 Malignant neoplasm of colon, unspecified site ♥
154.0 Malignant neoplasm of rectosigmoid junction
154.1 Malignant neoplasm of rectum
154.2 Malignant neoplasm of anal canal
154.3 Malignant neoplasm of anus, unspecified site ♥
197.5 Secondary malignant neoplasm of large intestine and rectum
199.0 Disseminated malignant neoplasm
199.1 Other malignant neoplasm of unspecified site
209.10 Malignant carcinoid tumor of the large intestine, unspecified portion — (Code first any associated multiple endocrine neoplasia syndrome: 258.01-258.03)(Use additional code to identify associated endocrine syndrome, as: carcinoid syndrome: 259.2) ♥
209.11 Malignant carcinoid tumor of the appendix — (Code first any associated multiple endocrine neoplasia syndrome: 258.01-258.03)(Use additional code to identify associated endocrine syndrome, as: carcinoid syndrome: 259.2)
209.12 Malignant carcinoid tumor of the cecum — (Code first any associated multiple endocrine neoplasia syndrome: 258.01-258.03)(Use additional code to identify associated endocrine syndrome, as: carcinoid syndrome: 259.2)
209.13 Malignant carcinoid tumor of the ascending colon — (Code first any associated multiple endocrine neoplasia syndrome: 258.01-258.03)(Use additional code to identify associated endocrine syndrome, as: carcinoid syndrome: 259.2)
209.14 Malignant carcinoid tumor of the transverse colon — (Code first any associated multiple endocrine neoplasia syndrome: 258.01-258.03)(Use additional code to identify associated endocrine syndrome, as: carcinoid syndrome: 259.2)
209.15 Malignant carcinoid tumor of the descending colon — (Code first any associated multiple endocrine neoplasia syndrome: 258.01-258.03)(Use additional code to identify associated endocrine syndrome, as: carcinoid syndrome: 259.2)
209.16 Malignant carcinoid tumor of the sigmoid colon — (Code first any associated multiple endocrine neoplasia syndrome: 258.01-258.03)(Use additional code to identify associated endocrine syndrome, as: carcinoid syndrome: 259.2)
209.17 Malignant carcinoid tumor of the rectum — (Code first any associated multiple endocrine neoplasia syndrome: 258.01-258.03)(Use additional code to identify associated endocrine syndrome, as: carcinoid syndrome: 259.2)
209.20 Malignant carcinoid tumor of unknown primary site — (Code first any associated multiple endocrine neoplasia syndrome: 258.01-258.03)(Use additional code to identify associated endocrine syndrome, as: carcinoid syndrome: 259.2)
209.27 Malignant carcinoid tumor of hindgut, not otherwise specified — (Code first any associated multiple endocrine neoplasia syndrome: 258.01-258.03)(Use additional code to identify associated endocrine syndrome, as: carcinoid syndrome: 259.2)
209.29 Malignant carcinoid tumor of other sites — (Code first any associated multiple endocrine neoplasia syndrome: 258.01-258.03)(Use additional code to identify associated endocrine syndrome, as: carcinoid syndrome: 259.2)
209.30 Malignant poorly differentiated neuroendocrine carcinoma, any site — (Code first any associated multiple endocrine neoplasia syndrome: 258.01-258.03)(Use additional code to identify associated endocrine syndrome, as: carcinoid syndrome: 259.2) ♥
209.50 Benign carcinoid tumor of the large intestine, unspecified portion — (Code first any associated multiple endocrine neoplasia syndrome: 258.01-258.03)(Use additional code to identify associated endocrine syndrome, as: carcinoid syndrome: 259.2) ♥
209.51 Benign carcinoid tumor of the appendix — (Code first any associated multiple endocrine neoplasia syndrome: 258.01-258.03)(Use additional code to identify associated endocrine syndrome, as: carcinoid syndrome: 259.2)
209.52 Benign carcinoid tumor of the cecum — (Code first any associated multiple endocrine neoplasia syndrome: 258.01-258.03)(Use additional code to identify associated endocrine syndrome, as: carcinoid syndrome: 259.2)
209.53 Benign carcinoid tumor of the ascending colon — (Code first any associated multiple endocrine neoplasia syndrome: 258.01-258.03)(Use additional code to identify associated endocrine syndrome, as: carcinoid syndrome: 259.2)

209.54 Benign carcinoid tumor of the transverse colon — (Code first any associated multiple endocrine neoplasia syndrome: 258.01-258.03)(Use additional code to identify associated endocrine syndrome, as: carcinoid syndrome: 259.2)
209.55 Benign carcinoid tumor of the descending colon — (Code first any associated multiple endocrine neoplasia syndrome: 258.01-258.03)(Use additional code to identify associated endocrine syndrome, as: carcinoid syndrome: 259.2)
209.56 Benign carcinoid tumor of the sigmoid colon — (Code first any associated multiple endocrine neoplasia syndrome: 258.01-258.03)(Use additional code to identify associated endocrine syndrome, as: carcinoid syndrome: 259.2)
209.57 Benign carcinoid tumor of the rectum — (Code first any associated multiple endocrine neoplasia syndrome: 258.01-258.03)(Use additional code to identify associated endocrine syndrome, as: carcinoid syndrome: 259.2)
209.69 Benign carcinoid tumor of other sites — (Code first any associated multiple endocrine neoplasia syndrome: 258.01-258.03)(Use additional code to identify associated endocrine syndrome, as: carcinoid syndrome: 259.2)
211.3 Benign neoplasm of colon
230.3 Carcinoma in situ of colon
230.4 Carcinoma in situ of rectum
230.5 Carcinoma in situ of anal canal
230.6 Carcinoma in situ of anus, unspecified ▽
235.2 Neoplasm of uncertain behavior of stomach, intestines, and rectum
239.0 Neoplasm of unspecified nature of digestive system
280.0 Iron deficiency anemia secondary to blood loss (chronic)
280.9 Unspecified iron deficiency anemia ▽
455.0 Internal hemorrhoids without mention of complication
455.2 Internal hemorrhoids with other complication
455.6 Unspecified hemorrhoids without mention of complication ▽
455.8 Unspecified hemorrhoids with other complication ▽
555.1 Regional enteritis of large intestine
555.2 Regional enteritis of small intestine with large intestine
555.9 Regional enteritis of unspecified site ▽
556.0 Ulcerative (chronic) enterocolitis
556.1 Ulcerative (chronic) ileocolitis
556.2 Ulcerative (chronic) proctitis
556.3 Ulcerative (chronic) proctosigmoiditis
556.4 Pseudopolyposis of colon
556.5 Left sided ulcerative (chronic) colitis
556.6 Universal ulcerative (chronic) colitis
556.8 Other ulcerative colitis
557.0 Acute vascular insufficiency of intestine
557.1 Chronic vascular insufficiency of intestine
557.9 Unspecified vascular insufficiency of intestine ▽
558.1 Gastroenteritis and colitis due to radiation
558.2 Toxic gastroenteritis and colitis — (Use additional E code to identify cause)
558.3 Gastroenteritis and colitis, allergic — (Use additional code to identify type of food allergy: V15.01-V15.05)
558.42 Eosinophilic colitis
558.9 Other and unspecified noninfectious gastroenteritis and colitis ▽
560.0 Intussusception
560.1 Paralytic ileus
560.2 Volvulus
560.32 Fecal impaction
560.39 Impaction of intestine, other
560.89 Other specified intestinal obstruction
560.9 Unspecified intestinal obstruction ▽
562.10 Diverticulosis of colon (without mention of hemorrhage) — (Use additional code to identify any associated peritonitis: 567.0-567.9)
562.11 Diverticulitis of colon (without mention of hemorrhage) — (Use additional code to identify any associated peritonitis: 567.0-567.9)
562.13 Diverticulitis of colon with hemorrhage — (Use additional code to identify any associated peritonitis: 567.0-567.9)
564.00 Unspecified constipation ▽
564.01 Slow transit constipation
564.02 Outlet dysfunction constipation
564.09 Other constipation
564.1 Irritable bowel syndrome
564.4 Other postoperative functional disorders
564.5 Functional diarrhea
564.7 Megacolon, other than Hirschsprung's
564.81 Neurogenic bowel
564.89 Other functional disorders of intestine
565.0 Anal fissure
565.1 Anal fistula
566 Abscess of anal and rectal regions
567.0 Peritonitis in infectious diseases classified elsewhere — (Code first underlying disease) ☒
567.1 Pneumococcal peritonitis
567.21 Peritonitis (acute) generalized
567.22 Peritoneal abscess
567.23 Spontaneous bacterial peritonitis
567.29 Other suppurative peritonitis
567.39 Other retroperitoneal infections
567.89 Other specified peritonitis
567.9 Unspecified peritonitis ▽
569.0 Anal and rectal polyp
569.3 Hemorrhage of rectum and anus
569.42 Anal or rectal pain
569.44 Dysplasia of anus
569.49 Other specified disorder of rectum and anus — (Use additional code for any associated fecal incontinence (787.60-787.63))
569.82 Ulceration of intestine
569.89 Other specified disorder of intestines
578.1 Blood in stool
578.9 Hemorrhage of gastrointestinal tract, unspecified ▽
579.0 Celiac disease
579.1 Tropical sprue
579.2 Blind loop syndrome
579.3 Other and unspecified postsurgical nonabsorption ▽
579.4 Pancreatic steatorrhea
579.8 Other specified intestinal malabsorption
747.61 Congenital gastrointestinal vessel anomaly
751.3 Hirschsprung's disease and other congenital functional disorders of colon
751.5 Other congenital anomalies of intestine
780.99 Other general symptoms
783.21 Loss of weight — (Use additional code to identify Body Mass Index (BMI), if known: V85.0-V85.54)
783.22 Underweight — (Use additional code to identify Body Mass Index (BMI), if known: V85.0-V85.54)
783.7 Adult failure to thrive
787.3 Flatulence, eructation, and gas pain
787.7 Abnormal feces
787.91 Diarrhea
787.99 Other symptoms involving digestive system
789.00 Abdominal pain, unspecified site ▽
789.01 Abdominal pain, right upper quadrant
789.02 Abdominal pain, left upper quadrant
789.03 Abdominal pain, right lower quadrant
789.04 Abdominal pain, left lower quadrant

789.05 Abdominal pain, periumbilic
789.06 Abdominal pain, epigastric
789.07 Abdominal pain, generalized
789.09 Abdominal pain, other specified site
789.30 Abdominal or pelvic swelling, mass or lump, unspecified site
789.31 Abdominal or pelvic swelling, mass, or lump, right upper quadrant
789.32 Abdominal or pelvic swelling, mass, or lump, left upper quadrant
789.33 Abdominal or pelvic swelling, mass, or lump, right lower quadrant
789.34 Abdominal or pelvic swelling, mass, or lump, left lower quadrant
789.35 Abdominal or pelvic swelling, mass or lump, periumbilic
789.36 Abdominal or pelvic swelling, mass, or lump, epigastric
789.37 Abdominal or pelvic swelling, mass, or lump, generalized
789.39 Abdominal or pelvic swelling, mass, or lump, other specified site
789.9 Other symptoms involving abdomen and pelvis
792.1 Nonspecific abnormal finding in stool contents
793.4 Nonspecific (abnormal) findings on radiological and other examination of gastrointestinal tract
997.49 Other digestive system complications
V10.05 Personal history of malignant neoplasm of large intestine
V10.06 Personal history of malignant neoplasm of rectum, rectosigmoid junction, and anus
V12.70 Personal history of unspecified digestive disease
V12.72 Personal history of colonic polyps
V12.79 Personal history of other diseases of digestive disease
V16.0 Family history of malignant neoplasm of gastrointestinal tract
V18.51 Family history, Colonic polyps
V18.59 Family history, other digestive disorders
V45.89 Other postprocedural status
V47.3 Other digestive problems
V67.00 Follow-up examination, following unspecified surgery
V67.09 Follow-up examination, following other surgery
V67.51 Follow-up examination following completed treatment with high-risk medications, not elsewhere classified
V71.1 Observation for suspected malignant neoplasm
V71.89 Observation for other specified suspected conditions
V71.9 Observation for unspecified suspected condition
V85.0 Body Mass Index less than 19, adult

ICD-9-CM Procedural

45.23 Colonoscopy
45.25 Closed [endoscopic] biopsy of large intestine
46.85 Dilation of intestine

HCPCS Level II Supplies & Services

A4270 Disposable endoscope sheath, each

45379

45379 Colonoscopy, flexible, proximal to splenic flexure; with removal of foreign body

ICD-9-CM Diagnostic

793.4 Nonspecific (abnormal) findings on radiological and other examination of gastrointestinal tract
908.5 Late effect of foreign body in orifice
936 Foreign body in intestine and colon
938 Foreign body in digestive system, unspecified
996.59 Mechanical complication due to other implant and internal device, not elsewhere classified
996.79 Other complications due to other internal prosthetic device, implant, and graft — (Use additional code to identify complication: 338.18-338.19, 338.28-338.29)
998.4 Foreign body accidentally left during procedure, not elsewhere classified

ICD-9-CM Procedural

45.23 Colonoscopy
98.04 Removal of intraluminal foreign body from large intestine without incision

HCPCS Level II Supplies & Services

A4270 Disposable endoscope sheath, each

45380

45380 Colonoscopy, flexible, proximal to splenic flexure; with biopsy, single or multiple

ICD-9-CM Diagnostic

153.1 Malignant neoplasm of transverse colon
153.2 Malignant neoplasm of descending colon
153.3 Malignant neoplasm of sigmoid colon
153.4 Malignant neoplasm of cecum
153.5 Malignant neoplasm of appendix
153.6 Malignant neoplasm of ascending colon
153.7 Malignant neoplasm of splenic flexure
153.8 Malignant neoplasm of other specified sites of large intestine
153.9 Malignant neoplasm of colon, unspecified site
154.0 Malignant neoplasm of rectosigmoid junction
154.1 Malignant neoplasm of rectum
154.8 Malignant neoplasm of other sites of rectum, rectosigmoid junction, and anus
159.0 Malignant neoplasm of intestinal tract, part unspecified
159.9 Malignant neoplasm of ill-defined sites of digestive organs and peritoneum
197.5 Secondary malignant neoplasm of large intestine and rectum
199.0 Disseminated malignant neoplasm
199.1 Other malignant neoplasm of unspecified site
209.10 Malignant carcinoid tumor of the large intestine, unspecified portion — (Code first any associated multiple endocrine neoplasia syndrome: 258.01-258.03)(Use additional code to identify associated endocrine syndrome, as: carcinoid syndrome: 259.2)
209.11 Malignant carcinoid tumor of the appendix — (Code first any associated multiple endocrine neoplasia syndrome: 258.01-258.03)(Use additional code to identify associated endocrine syndrome, as: carcinoid syndrome: 259.2)
209.12 Malignant carcinoid tumor of the cecum — (Code first any associated multiple endocrine neoplasia syndrome: 258.01-258.03)(Use additional code to identify associated endocrine syndrome, as: carcinoid syndrome: 259.2)
209.13 Malignant carcinoid tumor of the ascending colon — (Code first any associated multiple endocrine neoplasia syndrome: 258.01-258.03)(Use additional code to identify associated endocrine syndrome, as: carcinoid syndrome: 259.2)
209.14 Malignant carcinoid tumor of the transverse colon — (Code first any associated multiple endocrine neoplasia syndrome: 258.01-258.03)(Use additional code to identify associated endocrine syndrome, as: carcinoid syndrome: 259.2)
209.15 Malignant carcinoid tumor of the descending colon — (Code first any associated multiple endocrine neoplasia syndrome: 258.01-258.03)(Use additional code to identify associated endocrine syndrome, as: carcinoid syndrome: 259.2)
209.16 Malignant carcinoid tumor of the sigmoid colon — (Code first any associated multiple endocrine neoplasia syndrome: 258.01-258.03)(Use additional code to identify associated endocrine syndrome, as: carcinoid syndrome: 259.2)
209.17 Malignant carcinoid tumor of the rectum — (Code first any associated multiple endocrine neoplasia syndrome: 258.01-258.03)(Use additional code to identify associated endocrine syndrome, as: carcinoid syndrome: 259.2)
209.20 Malignant carcinoid tumor of unknown primary site — (Code first any associated multiple endocrine neoplasia syndrome: 258.01-258.03)(Use additional code to identify associated endocrine syndrome, as: carcinoid syndrome: 259.2)
209.27 Malignant carcinoid tumor of hindgut, not otherwise specified — (Code first any associated multiple endocrine neoplasia syndrome: 258.01-258.03)(Use additional code to identify associated endocrine syndrome, as: carcinoid syndrome: 259.2)
209.29 Malignant carcinoid tumor of other sites — (Code first any associated multiple endocrine neoplasia syndrome: 258.01-258.03)(Use additional code to identify associated endocrine syndrome, as: carcinoid syndrome: 259.2)
209.30 Malignant poorly differentiated neuroendocrine carcinoma, any site — (Code first any associated multiple endocrine neoplasia syndrome: 258.01-258.03)(Use additional code to identify associated endocrine syndrome, as: carcinoid syndrome: 259.2)

209.50 Benign carcinoid tumor of the large intestine, unspecified portion — (Code first any associated multiple endocrine neoplasia syndrome: 258.01-258.03)(Use additional code to identify associated endocrine syndrome, as: carcinoid syndrome: 259.2) ▽
209.51 Benign carcinoid tumor of the appendix — (Code first any associated multiple endocrine neoplasia syndrome: 258.01-258.03)(Use additional code to identify associated endocrine syndrome, as: carcinoid syndrome: 259.2)
209.52 Benign carcinoid tumor of the cecum — (Code first any associated multiple endocrine neoplasia syndrome: 258.01-258.03)(Use additional code to identify associated endocrine syndrome, as: carcinoid syndrome: 259.2)
209.53 Benign carcinoid tumor of the ascending colon — (Code first any associated multiple endocrine neoplasia syndrome: 258.01-258.03)(Use additional code to identify associated endocrine syndrome, as: carcinoid syndrome: 259.2)
209.54 Benign carcinoid tumor of the transverse colon — (Code first any associated multiple endocrine neoplasia syndrome: 258.01-258.03)(Use additional code to identify associated endocrine syndrome, as: carcinoid syndrome: 259.2)
209.55 Benign carcinoid tumor of the descending colon — (Code first any associated multiple endocrine neoplasia syndrome: 258.01-258.03)(Use additional code to identify associated endocrine syndrome, as: carcinoid syndrome: 259.2)
209.56 Benign carcinoid tumor of the sigmoid colon — (Code first any associated multiple endocrine neoplasia syndrome: 258.01-258.03)(Use additional code to identify associated endocrine syndrome, as: carcinoid syndrome: 259.2)
209.57 Benign carcinoid tumor of the rectum — (Code first any associated multiple endocrine neoplasia syndrome: 258.01-258.03)(Use additional code to identify associated endocrine syndrome, as: carcinoid syndrome: 259.2)
209.69 Benign carcinoid tumor of other sites — (Code first any associated multiple endocrine neoplasia syndrome: 258.01-258.03)(Use additional code to identify associated endocrine syndrome, as: carcinoid syndrome: 259.2)
211.3 Benign neoplasm of colon
211.4 Benign neoplasm of rectum and anal canal
228.1 Lymphangioma, any site
230.3 Carcinoma in situ of colon
230.4 Carcinoma in situ of rectum
230.5 Carcinoma in situ of anal canal
230.6 Carcinoma in situ of anus, unspecified ▽
235.2 Neoplasm of uncertain behavior of stomach, intestines, and rectum
235.5 Neoplasm of uncertain behavior of other and unspecified digestive organs ▽
239.0 Neoplasm of unspecified nature of digestive system
280.0 Iron deficiency anemia secondary to blood loss (chronic)
280.9 Unspecified iron deficiency anemia ▽
455.0 Internal hemorrhoids without mention of complication
555.1 Regional enteritis of large intestine
555.2 Regional enteritis of small intestine with large intestine
555.9 Regional enteritis of unspecified site ▽
556.0 Ulcerative (chronic) enterocolitis
556.1 Ulcerative (chronic) ileocolitis
556.2 Ulcerative (chronic) proctitis
556.3 Ulcerative (chronic) proctosigmoiditis
556.4 Pseudopolyposis of colon
556.5 Left sided ulcerative (chronic) colitis
556.6 Universal ulcerative (chronic) colitis
556.8 Other ulcerative colitis
558.1 Gastroenteritis and colitis due to radiation
558.2 Toxic gastroenteritis and colitis — (Use additional E code to identify cause)
558.3 Gastroenteritis and colitis, allergic — (Use additional code to identify type of food allergy: V15.01-V15.05)
558.42 Eosinophilic colitis
558.9 Other and unspecified noninfectious gastroenteritis and colitis ▽
560.0 Intussusception
560.1 Paralytic ileus
560.2 Volvulus
560.31 Gallstone ileus
560.32 Fecal impaction
560.39 Impaction of intestine, other
560.9 Unspecified intestinal obstruction ▽
562.10 Diverticulosis of colon (without mention of hemorrhage) — (Use additional code to identify any associated peritonitis: 567.0-567.9)
562.11 Diverticulitis of colon (without mention of hemorrhage) — (Use additional code to identify any associated peritonitis: 567.0-567.9)
564.00 Unspecified constipation ▽
564.01 Slow transit constipation
564.02 Outlet dysfunction constipation
564.09 Other constipation
564.1 Irritable bowel syndrome
564.4 Other postoperative functional disorders
564.5 Functional diarrhea
564.7 Megacolon, other than Hirschsprung's
567.0 Peritonitis in infectious diseases classified elsewhere — (Code first underlying disease) ☒
567.1 Pneumococcal peritonitis
567.21 Peritonitis (acute) generalized
567.22 Peritoneal abscess
567.23 Spontaneous bacterial peritonitis
567.29 Other suppurative peritonitis
567.31 Psoas muscle abscess
567.38 Other retroperitoneal abscess
567.39 Other retroperitoneal infections
567.81 Choleperitonitis
567.82 Sclerosing mesenteritis
567.89 Other specified peritonitis
567.9 Unspecified peritonitis ▽
569.0 Anal and rectal polyp
569.3 Hemorrhage of rectum and anus
569.44 Dysplasia of anus
569.49 Other specified disorder of rectum and anus — (Use additional code for any associated fecal incontinence (787.60-787.63))
569.82 Ulceration of intestine
569.89 Other specified disorder of intestines
578.1 Blood in stool
578.9 Hemorrhage of gastrointestinal tract, unspecified ▽
783.21 Loss of weight — (Use additional code to identify Body Mass Index (BMI), if known: V85.0-V85.54)
783.22 Underweight — (Use additional code to identify Body Mass Index (BMI), if known: V85.0-V85.54)
783.7 Adult failure to thrive
787.3 Flatulence, eructation, and gas pain
787.7 Abnormal feces
787.91 Diarrhea
787.99 Other symptoms involving digestive system
789.00 Abdominal pain, unspecified site ▽
789.01 Abdominal pain, right upper quadrant
789.02 Abdominal pain, left upper quadrant
789.03 Abdominal pain, right lower quadrant
789.04 Abdominal pain, left lower quadrant
789.05 Abdominal pain, periumbilic
789.06 Abdominal pain, epigastric
789.07 Abdominal pain, generalized
789.09 Abdominal pain, other specified site
792.1 Nonspecific abnormal finding in stool contents

793.4 Nonspecific (abnormal) findings on radiological and other examination of gastrointestinal tract
V10.05 Personal history of malignant neoplasm of large intestine
V10.06 Personal history of malignant neoplasm of rectum, rectosigmoid junction, and anus
V12.70 Personal history of unspecified digestive disease ▽
V12.72 Personal history of colonic polyps
V12.79 Personal history of other diseases of digestive disease
V16.0 Family history of malignant neoplasm of gastrointestinal tract
V18.51 Family history, Colonic polyps
V18.59 Family history, other digestive disorders
V71.1 Observation for suspected malignant neoplasm
V71.9 Observation for unspecified suspected condition ▽
V85.0 Body Mass Index less than 19, adult

ICD-9-CM Procedural

45.25 Closed [endoscopic] biopsy of large intestine

HCPCS Level II Supplies & Services

A4270 Disposable endoscope sheath, each

45381

45381 Colonoscopy, flexible, proximal to splenic flexure; with directed submucosal injection(s), any substance

ICD-9-CM Diagnostic

153.0 Malignant neoplasm of hepatic flexure
153.1 Malignant neoplasm of transverse colon
153.2 Malignant neoplasm of descending colon
153.3 Malignant neoplasm of sigmoid colon
153.4 Malignant neoplasm of cecum
153.5 Malignant neoplasm of appendix
153.6 Malignant neoplasm of ascending colon
153.7 Malignant neoplasm of splenic flexure
153.8 Malignant neoplasm of other specified sites of large intestine
153.9 Malignant neoplasm of colon, unspecified site ▽
154.0 Malignant neoplasm of rectosigmoid junction
154.1 Malignant neoplasm of rectum
154.2 Malignant neoplasm of anal canal
154.3 Malignant neoplasm of anus, unspecified site ▽
197.5 Secondary malignant neoplasm of large intestine and rectum
199.0 Disseminated malignant neoplasm
199.1 Other malignant neoplasm of unspecified site
209.10 Malignant carcinoid tumor of the large intestine, unspecified portion — (Code first any associated multiple endocrine neoplasia syndrome: 258.01-258.03)(Use additional code to identify associated endocrine syndrome, as: carcinoid syndrome: 259.2) ▽
209.11 Malignant carcinoid tumor of the appendix — (Code first any associated multiple endocrine neoplasia syndrome: 258.01-258.03)(Use additional code to identify associated endocrine syndrome, as: carcinoid syndrome: 259.2)
209.12 Malignant carcinoid tumor of the cecum — (Code first any associated multiple endocrine neoplasia syndrome: 258.01-258.03)(Use additional code to identify associated endocrine syndrome, as: carcinoid syndrome: 259.2)
209.13 Malignant carcinoid tumor of the ascending colon — (Code first any associated multiple endocrine neoplasia syndrome: 258.01-258.03)(Use additional code to identify associated endocrine syndrome, as: carcinoid syndrome: 259.2)
209.14 Malignant carcinoid tumor of the transverse colon — (Code first any associated multiple endocrine neoplasia syndrome: 258.01-258.03)(Use additional code to identify associated endocrine syndrome, as: carcinoid syndrome: 259.2)
209.15 Malignant carcinoid tumor of the descending colon — (Code first any associated multiple endocrine neoplasia syndrome: 258.01-258.03)(Use additional code to identify associated endocrine syndrome, as: carcinoid syndrome: 259.2)
209.16 Malignant carcinoid tumor of the sigmoid colon — (Code first any associated multiple endocrine neoplasia syndrome: 258.01-258.03)(Use additional code to identify associated endocrine syndrome, as: carcinoid syndrome: 259.2)
209.17 Malignant carcinoid tumor of the rectum — (Code first any associated multiple endocrine neoplasia syndrome: 258.01-258.03)(Use additional code to identify associated endocrine syndrome, as: carcinoid syndrome: 259.2)
209.20 Malignant carcinoid tumor of unknown primary site — (Code first any associated multiple endocrine neoplasia syndrome: 258.01-258.03)(Use additional code to identify associated endocrine syndrome, as: carcinoid syndrome: 259.2)
209.27 Malignant carcinoid tumor of hindgut, not otherwise specified — (Code first any associated multiple endocrine neoplasia syndrome: 258.01-258.03)(Use additional code to identify associated endocrine syndrome, as: carcinoid syndrome: 259.2)
209.29 Malignant carcinoid tumor of other sites — (Code first any associated multiple endocrine neoplasia syndrome: 258.01-258.03)(Use additional code to identify associated endocrine syndrome, as: carcinoid syndrome: 259.2)
209.30 Malignant poorly differentiated neuroendocrine carcinoma, any site — (Code first any associated multiple endocrine neoplasia syndrome: 258.01-258.03)(Use additional code to identify associated endocrine syndrome, as: carcinoid syndrome: 259.2) ▽
209.50 Benign carcinoid tumor of the large intestine, unspecified portion — (Code first any associated multiple endocrine neoplasia syndrome: 258.01-258.03)(Use additional code to identify associated endocrine syndrome, as: carcinoid syndrome: 259.2) ▽
209.51 Benign carcinoid tumor of the appendix — (Code first any associated multiple endocrine neoplasia syndrome: 258.01-258.03)(Use additional code to identify associated endocrine syndrome, as: carcinoid syndrome: 259.2)
209.52 Benign carcinoid tumor of the cecum — (Code first any associated multiple endocrine neoplasia syndrome: 258.01-258.03)(Use additional code to identify associated endocrine syndrome, as: carcinoid syndrome: 259.2)
209.53 Benign carcinoid tumor of the ascending colon — (Code first any associated multiple endocrine neoplasia syndrome: 258.01-258.03)(Use additional code to identify associated endocrine syndrome, as: carcinoid syndrome: 259.2)
209.54 Benign carcinoid tumor of the transverse colon — (Code first any associated multiple endocrine neoplasia syndrome: 258.01-258.03)(Use additional code to identify associated endocrine syndrome, as: carcinoid syndrome: 259.2)
209.55 Benign carcinoid tumor of the descending colon — (Code first any associated multiple endocrine neoplasia syndrome: 258.01-258.03)(Use additional code to identify associated endocrine syndrome, as: carcinoid syndrome: 259.2)
209.56 Benign carcinoid tumor of the sigmoid colon — (Code first any associated multiple endocrine neoplasia syndrome: 258.01-258.03)(Use additional code to identify associated endocrine syndrome, as: carcinoid syndrome: 259.2)
209.57 Benign carcinoid tumor of the rectum — (Code first any associated multiple endocrine neoplasia syndrome: 258.01-258.03)(Use additional code to identify associated endocrine syndrome, as: carcinoid syndrome: 259.2)
209.69 Benign carcinoid tumor of other sites — (Code first any associated multiple endocrine neoplasia syndrome: 258.01-258.03)(Use additional code to identify associated endocrine syndrome, as: carcinoid syndrome: 259.2)
211.3 Benign neoplasm of colon
230.3 Carcinoma in situ of colon
230.4 Carcinoma in situ of rectum
230.5 Carcinoma in situ of anal canal
230.6 Carcinoma in situ of anus, unspecified ▽
235.2 Neoplasm of uncertain behavior of stomach, intestines, and rectum
455.0 Internal hemorrhoids without mention of complication
455.1 Internal thrombosed hemorrhoids
455.2 Internal hemorrhoids with other complication
455.6 Unspecified hemorrhoids without mention of complication ▽
455.7 Unspecified thrombosed hemorrhoids ▽
455.8 Unspecified hemorrhoids with other complication ▽
555.1 Regional enteritis of large intestine
555.2 Regional enteritis of small intestine with large intestine
555.9 Regional enteritis of unspecified site ▽
556.0 Ulcerative (chronic) enterocolitis

556.1 Ulcerative (chronic) ileocolitis
556.2 Ulcerative (chronic) proctitis
556.3 Ulcerative (chronic) proctosigmoiditis
556.4 Pseudopolyposis of colon
556.5 Left sided ulcerative (chronic) colitis
556.6 Universal ulcerative (chronic) colitis
556.8 Other ulcerative colitis
558.1 Gastroenteritis and colitis due to radiation
558.2 Toxic gastroenteritis and colitis — (Use additional E code to identify cause)
558.3 Gastroenteritis and colitis, allergic — (Use additional code to identify type of food allergy: V15.01-V15.05)
558.42 Eosinophilic colitis
558.9 Other and unspecified noninfectious gastroenteritis and colitis ▽
562.10 Diverticulosis of colon (without mention of hemorrhage) — (Use additional code to identify any associated peritonitis: 567.0-567.9)
562.11 Diverticulitis of colon (without mention of hemorrhage) — (Use additional code to identify any associated peritonitis: 567.0-567.9)
562.13 Diverticulitis of colon with hemorrhage — (Use additional code to identify any associated peritonitis: 567.0-567.9)
564.00 Unspecified constipation ▽
564.01 Slow transit constipation
564.02 Outlet dysfunction constipation
564.09 Other constipation
564.1 Irritable bowel syndrome
564.4 Other postoperative functional disorders
564.5 Functional diarrhea
564.7 Megacolon, other than Hirschsprung's
564.81 Neurogenic bowel
564.89 Other functional disorders of intestine
565.0 Anal fissure
565.1 Anal fistula
566 Abscess of anal and rectal regions
569.0 Anal and rectal polyp
569.3 Hemorrhage of rectum and anus
569.42 Anal or rectal pain
569.44 Dysplasia of anus
569.49 Other specified disorder of rectum and anus — (Use additional code for any associated fecal incontinence (787.60-787.63))
569.82 Ulceration of intestine
569.89 Other specified disorder of intestines
578.1 Blood in stool
578.9 Hemorrhage of gastrointestinal tract, unspecified ▽
619.1 Digestive-genital tract fistula, female ♀
747.61 Congenital gastrointestinal vessel anomaly
751.2 Congenital atresia and stenosis of large intestine, rectum, and anal canal
751.3 Hirschsprung's disease and other congenital functional disorders of colon
751.5 Other congenital anomalies of intestine
787.3 Flatulence, eructation, and gas pain
787.7 Abnormal feces
787.91 Diarrhea
787.99 Other symptoms involving digestive system
789.00 Abdominal pain, unspecified site ▽
789.01 Abdominal pain, right upper quadrant
789.02 Abdominal pain, left upper quadrant
789.03 Abdominal pain, right lower quadrant
789.04 Abdominal pain, left lower quadrant
789.05 Abdominal pain, periumbilic
789.06 Abdominal pain, epigastric
789.07 Abdominal pain, generalized
789.09 Abdominal pain, other specified site
792.1 Nonspecific abnormal finding in stool contents
793.4 Nonspecific (abnormal) findings on radiological and other examination of gastrointestinal tract
997.49 Other digestive system complications
V47.3 Other digestive problems
V67.00 Follow-up examination, following unspecified surgery ▽
V67.09 Follow-up examination, following other surgery

ICD-9-CM Procedural

45.23 Colonoscopy
99.23 Injection of steroid
99.29 Injection or infusion of other therapeutic or prophylactic substance

45382

45382 Colonoscopy, flexible, proximal to splenic flexure; with control of bleeding (eg, injection, bipolar cautery, unipolar cautery, laser, heater probe, stapler, plasma coagulator)

ICD-9-CM Diagnostic

153.0 Malignant neoplasm of hepatic flexure
153.1 Malignant neoplasm of transverse colon
153.2 Malignant neoplasm of descending colon
153.3 Malignant neoplasm of sigmoid colon
153.4 Malignant neoplasm of cecum
153.5 Malignant neoplasm of appendix
153.6 Malignant neoplasm of ascending colon
153.7 Malignant neoplasm of splenic flexure
153.9 Malignant neoplasm of colon, unspecified site ▽
209.10 Malignant carcinoid tumor of the large intestine, unspecified portion — (Code first any associated multiple endocrine neoplasia syndrome: 258.01-258.03)(Use additional code to identify associated endocrine syndrome, as: carcinoid syndrome: 259.2) ▽
209.11 Malignant carcinoid tumor of the appendix — (Code first any associated multiple endocrine neoplasia syndrome: 258.01-258.03)(Use additional code to identify associated endocrine syndrome, as: carcinoid syndrome: 259.2)
209.12 Malignant carcinoid tumor of the cecum — (Code first any associated multiple endocrine neoplasia syndrome: 258.01-258.03)(Use additional code to identify associated endocrine syndrome, as: carcinoid syndrome: 259.2)
209.13 Malignant carcinoid tumor of the ascending colon — (Code first any associated multiple endocrine neoplasia syndrome: 258.01-258.03)(Use additional code to identify associated endocrine syndrome, as: carcinoid syndrome: 259.2)
209.14 Malignant carcinoid tumor of the transverse colon — (Code first any associated multiple endocrine neoplasia syndrome: 258.01-258.03)(Use additional code to identify associated endocrine syndrome, as: carcinoid syndrome: 259.2)
209.15 Malignant carcinoid tumor of the descending colon — (Code first any associated multiple endocrine neoplasia syndrome: 258.01-258.03)(Use additional code to identify associated endocrine syndrome, as: carcinoid syndrome: 259.2)
209.16 Malignant carcinoid tumor of the sigmoid colon — (Code first any associated multiple endocrine neoplasia syndrome: 258.01-258.03)(Use additional code to identify associated endocrine syndrome, as: carcinoid syndrome: 259.2)
209.17 Malignant carcinoid tumor of the rectum — (Code first any associated multiple endocrine neoplasia syndrome: 258.01-258.03)(Use additional code to identify associated endocrine syndrome, as: carcinoid syndrome: 259.2)
209.20 Malignant carcinoid tumor of unknown primary site — (Code first any associated multiple endocrine neoplasia syndrome: 258.01-258.03)(Use additional code to identify associated endocrine syndrome, as: carcinoid syndrome: 259.2)
209.27 Malignant carcinoid tumor of hindgut, not otherwise specified — (Code first any associated multiple endocrine neoplasia syndrome: 258.01-258.03)(Use additional code to identify associated endocrine syndrome, as: carcinoid syndrome: 259.2)
209.29 Malignant carcinoid tumor of other sites — (Code first any associated multiple endocrine neoplasia syndrome: 258.01-258.03)(Use additional code to identify associated endocrine syndrome, as: carcinoid syndrome: 259.2)

209.30 Malignant poorly differentiated neuroendocrine carcinoma, any site — (Code first any associated multiple endocrine neoplasia syndrome: 258.01-258.03)(Use additional code to identify associated endocrine syndrome, as: carcinoid syndrome: 259.2) ▽
209.50 Benign carcinoid tumor of the large intestine, unspecified portion — (Code first any associated multiple endocrine neoplasia syndrome: 258.01-258.03)(Use additional code to identify associated endocrine syndrome, as: carcinoid syndrome: 259.2) ▽
209.51 Benign carcinoid tumor of the appendix — (Code first any associated multiple endocrine neoplasia syndrome: 258.01-258.03)(Use additional code to identify associated endocrine syndrome, as: carcinoid syndrome: 259.2)
209.52 Benign carcinoid tumor of the cecum — (Code first any associated multiple endocrine neoplasia syndrome: 258.01-258.03)(Use additional code to identify associated endocrine syndrome, as: carcinoid syndrome: 259.2)
209.53 Benign carcinoid tumor of the ascending colon — (Code first any associated multiple endocrine neoplasia syndrome: 258.01-258.03)(Use additional code to identify associated endocrine syndrome, as: carcinoid syndrome: 259.2)
209.54 Benign carcinoid tumor of the transverse colon — (Code first any associated multiple endocrine neoplasia syndrome: 258.01-258.03)(Use additional code to identify associated endocrine syndrome, as: carcinoid syndrome: 259.2)
209.55 Benign carcinoid tumor of the descending colon — (Code first any associated multiple endocrine neoplasia syndrome: 258.01-258.03)(Use additional code to identify associated endocrine syndrome, as: carcinoid syndrome: 259.2)
209.56 Benign carcinoid tumor of the sigmoid colon — (Code first any associated multiple endocrine neoplasia syndrome: 258.01-258.03)(Use additional code to identify associated endocrine syndrome, as: carcinoid syndrome: 259.2)
209.57 Benign carcinoid tumor of the rectum — (Code first any associated multiple endocrine neoplasia syndrome: 258.01-258.03)(Use additional code to identify associated endocrine syndrome, as: carcinoid syndrome: 259.2)
209.69 Benign carcinoid tumor of other sites — (Code first any associated multiple endocrine neoplasia syndrome: 258.01-258.03)(Use additional code to identify associated endocrine syndrome, as: carcinoid syndrome: 259.2)
211.3 Benign neoplasm of colon
448.9 Other and unspecified capillary diseases ▽
455.2 Internal hemorrhoids with other complication
556.3 Ulcerative (chronic) proctosigmoiditis
556.9 Unspecified ulcerative colitis ▽
557.0 Acute vascular insufficiency of intestine
557.1 Chronic vascular insufficiency of intestine
558.42 Eosinophilic colitis
558.9 Other and unspecified noninfectious gastroenteritis and colitis ▽
562.12 Diverticulosis of colon with hemorrhage — (Use additional code to identify any associated peritonitis: 567.0-567.9)
562.13 Diverticulitis of colon with hemorrhage — (Use additional code to identify any associated peritonitis: 567.0-567.9)
569.82 Ulceration of intestine
569.85 Angiodysplasia of intestine with hemorrhage
578.1 Blood in stool
578.9 Hemorrhage of gastrointestinal tract, unspecified ▽
772.4 Fetal and neonatal gastrointestinal hemorrhage — (Use additional code(s) to further specify condition)
789.00 Abdominal pain, unspecified site ▽
789.01 Abdominal pain, right upper quadrant
789.02 Abdominal pain, left upper quadrant
789.03 Abdominal pain, right lower quadrant
789.04 Abdominal pain, left lower quadrant
789.05 Abdominal pain, periumbilic
789.06 Abdominal pain, epigastric
789.07 Abdominal pain, generalized
789.09 Abdominal pain, other specified site
789.30 Abdominal or pelvic swelling, mass or lump, unspecified site ▽
793.4 Nonspecific (abnormal) findings on radiological and other examination of gastrointestinal tract

ICD-9-CM Procedural

45.43 Endoscopic destruction of other lesion or tissue of large intestine
99.29 Injection or infusion of other therapeutic or prophylactic substance

HCPCS Level II Supplies & Services

A4270 Disposable endoscope sheath, each

45383-45385

45383 Colonoscopy, flexible, proximal to splenic flexure; with ablation of tumor(s), polyp(s), or other lesion(s) not amenable to removal by hot biopsy forceps, bipolar cautery or snare technique
45384 with removal of tumor(s), polyp(s), or other lesion(s) by hot biopsy forceps or bipolar cautery
45385 with removal of tumor(s), polyp(s), or other lesion(s) by snare technique

ICD-9-CM Diagnostic

153.0 Malignant neoplasm of hepatic flexure
153.1 Malignant neoplasm of transverse colon
153.2 Malignant neoplasm of descending colon
153.3 Malignant neoplasm of sigmoid colon
153.4 Malignant neoplasm of cecum
153.5 Malignant neoplasm of appendix
153.6 Malignant neoplasm of ascending colon
153.7 Malignant neoplasm of splenic flexure
153.8 Malignant neoplasm of other specified sites of large intestine
153.9 Malignant neoplasm of colon, unspecified site ▽
154.0 Malignant neoplasm of rectosigmoid junction
154.1 Malignant neoplasm of rectum
154.2 Malignant neoplasm of anal canal
154.3 Malignant neoplasm of anus, unspecified site ▽
199.1 Other malignant neoplasm of unspecified site
209.10 Malignant carcinoid tumor of the large intestine, unspecified portion — (Code first any associated multiple endocrine neoplasia syndrome: 258.01-258.03)(Use additional code to identify associated endocrine syndrome, as: carcinoid syndrome: 259.2) ▽
209.11 Malignant carcinoid tumor of the appendix — (Code first any associated multiple endocrine neoplasia syndrome: 258.01-258.03)(Use additional code to identify associated endocrine syndrome, as: carcinoid syndrome: 259.2)
209.12 Malignant carcinoid tumor of the cecum — (Code first any associated multiple endocrine neoplasia syndrome: 258.01-258.03)(Use additional code to identify associated endocrine syndrome, as: carcinoid syndrome: 259.2)
209.13 Malignant carcinoid tumor of the ascending colon — (Code first any associated multiple endocrine neoplasia syndrome: 258.01-258.03)(Use additional code to identify associated endocrine syndrome, as: carcinoid syndrome: 259.2)
209.14 Malignant carcinoid tumor of the transverse colon — (Code first any associated multiple endocrine neoplasia syndrome: 258.01-258.03)(Use additional code to identify associated endocrine syndrome, as: carcinoid syndrome: 259.2)
209.15 Malignant carcinoid tumor of the descending colon — (Code first any associated multiple endocrine neoplasia syndrome: 258.01-258.03)(Use additional code to identify associated endocrine syndrome, as: carcinoid syndrome: 259.2)
209.16 Malignant carcinoid tumor of the sigmoid colon — (Code first any associated multiple endocrine neoplasia syndrome: 258.01-258.03)(Use additional code to identify associated endocrine syndrome, as: carcinoid syndrome: 259.2)
209.17 Malignant carcinoid tumor of the rectum — (Code first any associated multiple endocrine neoplasia syndrome: 258.01-258.03)(Use additional code to identify associated endocrine syndrome, as: carcinoid syndrome: 259.2)
209.20 Malignant carcinoid tumor of unknown primary site — (Code first any associated multiple endocrine neoplasia syndrome: 258.01-258.03)(Use additional code to identify associated endocrine syndrome, as: carcinoid syndrome: 259.2)
209.27 Malignant carcinoid tumor of hindgut, not otherwise specified — (Code first any associated multiple endocrine neoplasia syndrome: 258.01-258.03)(Use additional code to identify associated endocrine syndrome, as: carcinoid syndrome: 259.2)

209.29 Malignant carcinoid tumor of other sites — (Code first any associated multiple endocrine neoplasia syndrome: 258.01-258.03)(Use additional code to identify associated endocrine syndrome, as: carcinoid syndrome: 259.2)

209.30 Malignant poorly differentiated neuroendocrine carcinoma, any site — (Code first any associated multiple endocrine neoplasia syndrome: 258.01-258.03)(Use additional code to identify associated endocrine syndrome, as: carcinoid syndrome: 259.2) ▽

209.50 Benign carcinoid tumor of the large intestine, unspecified portion — (Code first any associated multiple endocrine neoplasia syndrome: 258.01-258.03)(Use additional code to identify associated endocrine syndrome, as: carcinoid syndrome: 259.2) ▽

209.51 Benign carcinoid tumor of the appendix — (Code first any associated multiple endocrine neoplasia syndrome: 258.01-258.03)(Use additional code to identify associated endocrine syndrome, as: carcinoid syndrome: 259.2)

209.52 Benign carcinoid tumor of the cecum — (Code first any associated multiple endocrine neoplasia syndrome: 258.01-258.03)(Use additional code to identify associated endocrine syndrome, as: carcinoid syndrome: 259.2)

209.53 Benign carcinoid tumor of the ascending colon — (Code first any associated multiple endocrine neoplasia syndrome: 258.01-258.03)(Use additional code to identify associated endocrine syndrome, as: carcinoid syndrome: 259.2)

209.54 Benign carcinoid tumor of the transverse colon — (Code first any associated multiple endocrine neoplasia syndrome: 258.01-258.03)(Use additional code to identify associated endocrine syndrome, as: carcinoid syndrome: 259.2)

209.55 Benign carcinoid tumor of the descending colon — (Code first any associated multiple endocrine neoplasia syndrome: 258.01-258.03)(Use additional code to identify associated endocrine syndrome, as: carcinoid syndrome: 259.2)

209.56 Benign carcinoid tumor of the sigmoid colon — (Code first any associated multiple endocrine neoplasia syndrome: 258.01-258.03)(Use additional code to identify associated endocrine syndrome, as: carcinoid syndrome: 259.2)

209.57 Benign carcinoid tumor of the rectum — (Code first any associated multiple endocrine neoplasia syndrome: 258.01-258.03)(Use additional code to identify associated endocrine syndrome, as: carcinoid syndrome: 259.2)

209.69 Benign carcinoid tumor of other sites — (Code first any associated multiple endocrine neoplasia syndrome: 258.01-258.03)(Use additional code to identify associated endocrine syndrome, as: carcinoid syndrome: 259.2)

211.3 Benign neoplasm of colon

211.4 Benign neoplasm of rectum and anal canal

230.3 Carcinoma in situ of colon

230.4 Carcinoma in situ of rectum

230.5 Carcinoma in situ of anal canal

230.6 Carcinoma in situ of anus, unspecified ▽

235.2 Neoplasm of uncertain behavior of stomach, intestines, and rectum

235.5 Neoplasm of uncertain behavior of other and unspecified digestive organs ▽

239.0 Neoplasm of unspecified nature of digestive system

455.2 Internal hemorrhoids with other complication

556.0 Ulcerative (chronic) enterocolitis

556.1 Ulcerative (chronic) ileocolitis

556.2 Ulcerative (chronic) proctitis

556.3 Ulcerative (chronic) proctosigmoiditis

556.4 Pseudopolyposis of colon

556.5 Left sided ulcerative (chronic) colitis

556.6 Universal ulcerative (chronic) colitis

556.8 Other ulcerative colitis

556.9 Unspecified ulcerative colitis ▽

558.42 Eosinophilic colitis

558.9 Other and unspecified noninfectious gastroenteritis and colitis ▽

562.10 Diverticulosis of colon (without mention of hemorrhage) — (Use additional code to identify any associated peritonitis: 567.0-567.9)

562.11 Diverticulitis of colon (without mention of hemorrhage) — (Use additional code to identify any associated peritonitis: 567.0-567.9)

564.00 Unspecified constipation ▽

564.01 Slow transit constipation

564.02 Outlet dysfunction constipation

564.09 Other constipation

567.0 Peritonitis in infectious diseases classified elsewhere — (Code first underlying disease) ☒

567.1 Pneumococcal peritonitis

567.21 Peritonitis (acute) generalized

567.22 Peritoneal abscess

567.23 Spontaneous bacterial peritonitis

567.29 Other suppurative peritonitis

567.31 Psoas muscle abscess

567.38 Other retroperitoneal abscess

567.39 Other retroperitoneal infections

567.81 Choleperitonitis

567.82 Sclerosing mesenteritis

567.89 Other specified peritonitis

567.9 Unspecified peritonitis ▽

569.0 Anal and rectal polyp

569.3 Hemorrhage of rectum and anus

569.44 Dysplasia of anus

569.49 Other specified disorder of rectum and anus — (Use additional code for any associated fecal incontinence (787.60-787.63))

569.84 Angiodysplasia of intestine (without mention of hemorrhage)

569.85 Angiodysplasia of intestine with hemorrhage

569.89 Other specified disorder of intestines

578.1 Blood in stool

783.21 Loss of weight — (Use additional code to identify Body Mass Index (BMI), if known: V85.0-V85.54)

783.22 Underweight — (Use additional code to identify Body Mass Index (BMI), if known: V85.0-V85.54)

787.7 Abnormal feces

787.91 Diarrhea

787.99 Other symptoms involving digestive system

789.00 Abdominal pain, unspecified site ▽

789.01 Abdominal pain, right upper quadrant

789.02 Abdominal pain, left upper quadrant

789.03 Abdominal pain, right lower quadrant

789.04 Abdominal pain, left lower quadrant

789.05 Abdominal pain, periumbilic

789.06 Abdominal pain, epigastric

789.07 Abdominal pain, generalized

789.09 Abdominal pain, other specified site

789.30 Abdominal or pelvic swelling, mass or lump, unspecified site ▽

789.31 Abdominal or pelvic swelling, mass, or lump, right upper quadrant

789.32 Abdominal or pelvic swelling, mass, or lump, left upper quadrant

789.33 Abdominal or pelvic swelling, mass, or lump, right lower quadrant

789.34 Abdominal or pelvic swelling, mass, or lump, left lower quadrant

789.35 Abdominal or pelvic swelling, mass or lump, periumbilic

789.36 Abdominal or pelvic swelling, mass, or lump, epigastric

789.37 Abdominal or pelvic swelling, mass, or lump, generalized

789.39 Abdominal or pelvic swelling, mass, or lump, other specified site

792.1 Nonspecific abnormal finding in stool contents

793.4 Nonspecific (abnormal) findings on radiological and other examination of gastrointestinal tract

V10.05 Personal history of malignant neoplasm of large intestine

V10.06 Personal history of malignant neoplasm of rectum, rectosigmoid junction, and anus

V12.70 Personal history of unspecified digestive disease ▽

V12.72 Personal history of colonic polyps

V12.79 Personal history of other diseases of digestive disease

V18.51 Family history, Colonic polyps

V18.59 Family history, other digestive disorders

V71.89 Observation for other specified suspected conditions
V71.9 Observation for unspecified suspected condition
V85.0 Body Mass Index less than 19, adult

ICD-9-CM Procedural

45.42 Endoscopic polypectomy of large intestine
45.43 Endoscopic destruction of other lesion or tissue of large intestine

HCPCS Level II Supplies & Services

A4270 Disposable endoscope sheath, each

45386

45386 Colonoscopy, flexible, proximal to splenic flexure; with dilation by balloon, 1 or more strictures

ICD-9-CM Diagnostic

560.81 Intestinal or peritoneal adhesions with obstruction (postoperative) (postinfection)
560.89 Other specified intestinal obstruction
560.9 Unspecified intestinal obstruction
751.2 Congenital atresia and stenosis of large intestine, rectum, and anal canal
997.49 Other digestive system complications

ICD-9-CM Procedural

46.85 Dilation of intestine

45387

45387 Colonoscopy, flexible, proximal to splenic flexure; with transendoscopic stent placement (includes predilation)

ICD-9-CM Diagnostic

153.0 Malignant neoplasm of hepatic flexure
153.1 Malignant neoplasm of transverse colon
153.2 Malignant neoplasm of descending colon
153.3 Malignant neoplasm of sigmoid colon
153.4 Malignant neoplasm of cecum
153.5 Malignant neoplasm of appendix
153.6 Malignant neoplasm of ascending colon
153.7 Malignant neoplasm of splenic flexure
153.8 Malignant neoplasm of other specified sites of large intestine
153.9 Malignant neoplasm of colon, unspecified site
154.0 Malignant neoplasm of rectosigmoid junction
154.1 Malignant neoplasm of rectum
197.5 Secondary malignant neoplasm of large intestine and rectum
209.10 Malignant carcinoid tumor of the large intestine, unspecified portion — (Code first any associated multiple endocrine neoplasia syndrome: 258.01-258.03)(Use additional code to identify associated endocrine syndrome, as: carcinoid syndrome: 259.2)
209.11 Malignant carcinoid tumor of the appendix — (Code first any associated multiple endocrine neoplasia syndrome: 258.01-258.03)(Use additional code to identify associated endocrine syndrome, as: carcinoid syndrome: 259.2)
209.12 Malignant carcinoid tumor of the cecum — (Code first any associated multiple endocrine neoplasia syndrome: 258.01-258.03)(Use additional code to identify associated endocrine syndrome, as: carcinoid syndrome: 259.2)
209.13 Malignant carcinoid tumor of the ascending colon — (Code first any associated multiple endocrine neoplasia syndrome: 258.01-258.03)(Use additional code to identify associated endocrine syndrome, as: carcinoid syndrome: 259.2)
209.14 Malignant carcinoid tumor of the transverse colon — (Code first any associated multiple endocrine neoplasia syndrome: 258.01-258.03)(Use additional code to identify associated endocrine syndrome, as: carcinoid syndrome: 259.2)
209.15 Malignant carcinoid tumor of the descending colon — (Code first any associated multiple endocrine neoplasia syndrome: 258.01-258.03)(Use additional code to identify associated endocrine syndrome, as: carcinoid syndrome: 259.2)
209.16 Malignant carcinoid tumor of the sigmoid colon — (Code first any associated multiple endocrine neoplasia syndrome: 258.01-258.03)(Use additional code to identify associated endocrine syndrome, as: carcinoid syndrome: 259.2)
209.17 Malignant carcinoid tumor of the rectum — (Code first any associated multiple endocrine neoplasia syndrome: 258.01-258.03)(Use additional code to identify associated endocrine syndrome, as: carcinoid syndrome: 259.2)
209.20 Malignant carcinoid tumor of unknown primary site — (Code first any associated multiple endocrine neoplasia syndrome: 258.01-258.03)(Use additional code to identify associated endocrine syndrome, as: carcinoid syndrome: 259.2)
209.27 Malignant carcinoid tumor of hindgut, not otherwise specified — (Code first any associated multiple endocrine neoplasia syndrome: 258.01-258.03)(Use additional code to identify associated endocrine syndrome, as: carcinoid syndrome: 259.2)
209.29 Malignant carcinoid tumor of other sites — (Code first any associated multiple endocrine neoplasia syndrome: 258.01-258.03)(Use additional code to identify associated endocrine syndrome, as: carcinoid syndrome: 259.2)
209.30 Malignant poorly differentiated neuroendocrine carcinoma, any site — (Code first any associated multiple endocrine neoplasia syndrome: 258.01-258.03)(Use additional code to identify associated endocrine syndrome, as: carcinoid syndrome: 259.2)
209.50 Benign carcinoid tumor of the large intestine, unspecified portion — (Code first any associated multiple endocrine neoplasia syndrome: 258.01-258.03)(Use additional code to identify associated endocrine syndrome, as: carcinoid syndrome: 259.2)
209.51 Benign carcinoid tumor of the appendix — (Code first any associated multiple endocrine neoplasia syndrome: 258.01-258.03)(Use additional code to identify associated endocrine syndrome, as: carcinoid syndrome: 259.2)
209.52 Benign carcinoid tumor of the cecum — (Code first any associated multiple endocrine neoplasia syndrome: 258.01-258.03)(Use additional code to identify associated endocrine syndrome, as: carcinoid syndrome: 259.2)
209.53 Benign carcinoid tumor of the ascending colon — (Code first any associated multiple endocrine neoplasia syndrome: 258.01-258.03)(Use additional code to identify associated endocrine syndrome, as: carcinoid syndrome: 259.2)
209.54 Benign carcinoid tumor of the transverse colon — (Code first any associated multiple endocrine neoplasia syndrome: 258.01-258.03)(Use additional code to identify associated endocrine syndrome, as: carcinoid syndrome: 259.2)
209.55 Benign carcinoid tumor of the descending colon — (Code first any associated multiple endocrine neoplasia syndrome: 258.01-258.03)(Use additional code to identify associated endocrine syndrome, as: carcinoid syndrome: 259.2)
209.56 Benign carcinoid tumor of the sigmoid colon — (Code first any associated multiple endocrine neoplasia syndrome: 258.01-258.03)(Use additional code to identify associated endocrine syndrome, as: carcinoid syndrome: 259.2)
209.57 Benign carcinoid tumor of the rectum — (Code first any associated multiple endocrine neoplasia syndrome: 258.01-258.03)(Use additional code to identify associated endocrine syndrome, as: carcinoid syndrome: 259.2)
209.69 Benign carcinoid tumor of other sites — (Code first any associated multiple endocrine neoplasia syndrome: 258.01-258.03)(Use additional code to identify associated endocrine syndrome, as: carcinoid syndrome: 259.2)
560.81 Intestinal or peritoneal adhesions with obstruction (postoperative) (postinfection)
560.89 Other specified intestinal obstruction
560.9 Unspecified intestinal obstruction
751.2 Congenital atresia and stenosis of large intestine, rectum, and anal canal
997.49 Other digestive system complications

ICD-9-CM Procedural

46.86 Endoscopic insertion of colonic stent(s)

HCPCS Level II Supplies & Services

C1874 Stent, coated/covered, with delivery system

45391-45392

45391 Colonoscopy, flexible, proximal to splenic flexure; with endoscopic ultrasound examination

45392 with transendoscopic ultrasound guided intramural or transmural fine needle aspiration/biopsy(s)

ICD-9-CM Diagnostic

153.0 Malignant neoplasm of hepatic flexure

153.1 Malignant neoplasm of transverse colon

153.2 Malignant neoplasm of descending colon

153.3 Malignant neoplasm of sigmoid colon

153.4 Malignant neoplasm of cecum

153.5 Malignant neoplasm of appendix

153.6 Malignant neoplasm of ascending colon

153.7 Malignant neoplasm of splenic flexure

153.8 Malignant neoplasm of other specified sites of large intestine

153.9 Malignant neoplasm of colon, unspecified site ▽

154.0 Malignant neoplasm of rectosigmoid junction

154.1 Malignant neoplasm of rectum

154.2 Malignant neoplasm of anal canal

154.3 Malignant neoplasm of anus, unspecified site ▽

199.1 Other malignant neoplasm of unspecified site

209.10 Malignant carcinoid tumor of the large intestine, unspecified portion — (Code first any associated multiple endocrine neoplasia syndrome: 258.01-258.03)(Use additional code to identify associated endocrine syndrome, as: carcinoid syndrome: 259.2) ▽

209.11 Malignant carcinoid tumor of the appendix — (Code first any associated multiple endocrine neoplasia syndrome: 258.01-258.03)(Use additional code to identify associated endocrine syndrome, as: carcinoid syndrome: 259.2)

209.12 Malignant carcinoid tumor of the cecum — (Code first any associated multiple endocrine neoplasia syndrome: 258.01-258.03)(Use additional code to identify associated endocrine syndrome, as: carcinoid syndrome: 259.2)

209.13 Malignant carcinoid tumor of the ascending colon — (Code first any associated multiple endocrine neoplasia syndrome: 258.01-258.03)(Use additional code to identify associated endocrine syndrome, as: carcinoid syndrome: 259.2)

209.14 Malignant carcinoid tumor of the transverse colon — (Code first any associated multiple endocrine neoplasia syndrome: 258.01-258.03)(Use additional code to identify associated endocrine syndrome, as: carcinoid syndrome: 259.2)

209.15 Malignant carcinoid tumor of the descending colon — (Code first any associated multiple endocrine neoplasia syndrome: 258.01-258.03)(Use additional code to identify associated endocrine syndrome, as: carcinoid syndrome: 259.2)

209.16 Malignant carcinoid tumor of the sigmoid colon — (Code first any associated multiple endocrine neoplasia syndrome: 258.01-258.03)(Use additional code to identify associated endocrine syndrome, as: carcinoid syndrome: 259.2)

209.17 Malignant carcinoid tumor of the rectum — (Code first any associated multiple endocrine neoplasia syndrome: 258.01-258.03)(Use additional code to identify associated endocrine syndrome, as: carcinoid syndrome: 259.2)

209.20 Malignant carcinoid tumor of unknown primary site — (Code first any associated multiple endocrine neoplasia syndrome: 258.01-258.03)(Use additional code to identify associated endocrine syndrome, as: carcinoid syndrome: 259.2)

209.27 Malignant carcinoid tumor of hindgut, not otherwise specified — (Code first any associated multiple endocrine neoplasia syndrome: 258.01-258.03)(Use additional code to identify associated endocrine syndrome, as: carcinoid syndrome: 259.2)

209.29 Malignant carcinoid tumor of other sites — (Code first any associated multiple endocrine neoplasia syndrome: 258.01-258.03)(Use additional code to identify associated endocrine syndrome, as: carcinoid syndrome: 259.2)

209.30 Malignant poorly differentiated neuroendocrine carcinoma, any site — (Code first any associated multiple endocrine neoplasia syndrome: 258.01-258.03)(Use additional code to identify associated endocrine syndrome, as: carcinoid syndrome: 259.2) ▽

209.50 Benign carcinoid tumor of the large intestine, unspecified portion — (Code first any associated multiple endocrine neoplasia syndrome: 258.01-258.03)(Use additional code to identify associated endocrine syndrome, as: carcinoid syndrome: 259.2) ▽

209.51 Benign carcinoid tumor of the appendix — (Code first any associated multiple endocrine neoplasia syndrome: 258.01-258.03)(Use additional code to identify associated endocrine syndrome, as: carcinoid syndrome: 259.2)

209.52 Benign carcinoid tumor of the cecum — (Code first any associated multiple endocrine neoplasia syndrome: 258.01-258.03)(Use additional code to identify associated endocrine syndrome, as: carcinoid syndrome: 259.2)

209.53 Benign carcinoid tumor of the ascending colon — (Code first any associated multiple endocrine neoplasia syndrome: 258.01-258.03)(Use additional code to identify associated endocrine syndrome, as: carcinoid syndrome: 259.2)

209.54 Benign carcinoid tumor of the transverse colon — (Code first any associated multiple endocrine neoplasia syndrome: 258.01-258.03)(Use additional code to identify associated endocrine syndrome, as: carcinoid syndrome: 259.2)

209.55 Benign carcinoid tumor of the descending colon — (Code first any associated multiple endocrine neoplasia syndrome: 258.01-258.03)(Use additional code to identify associated endocrine syndrome, as: carcinoid syndrome: 259.2)

209.56 Benign carcinoid tumor of the sigmoid colon — (Code first any associated multiple endocrine neoplasia syndrome: 258.01-258.03)(Use additional code to identify associated endocrine syndrome, as: carcinoid syndrome: 259.2)

209.57 Benign carcinoid tumor of the rectum — (Code first any associated multiple endocrine neoplasia syndrome: 258.01-258.03)(Use additional code to identify associated endocrine syndrome, as: carcinoid syndrome: 259.2)

209.69 Benign carcinoid tumor of other sites — (Code first any associated multiple endocrine neoplasia syndrome: 258.01-258.03)(Use additional code to identify associated endocrine syndrome, as: carcinoid syndrome: 259.2)

211.3 Benign neoplasm of colon

211.4 Benign neoplasm of rectum and anal canal

230.3 Carcinoma in situ of colon

230.4 Carcinoma in situ of rectum

230.5 Carcinoma in situ of anal canal

230.6 Carcinoma in situ of anus, unspecified ▽

235.2 Neoplasm of uncertain behavior of stomach, intestines, and rectum

235.5 Neoplasm of uncertain behavior of other and unspecified digestive organs ▽

239.0 Neoplasm of unspecified nature of digestive system

277.30 Amyloidosis, unspecified — (Use additional code to identify any associated intellectual disabilities) ▽

277.31 Familial Mediterranean fever — (Use additional code to identify any associated intellectual disabilities)

277.39 Other amyloidosis — (Use additional code to identify any associated intellectual disabilities)

455.2 Internal hemorrhoids with other complication

555.9 Regional enteritis of unspecified site ▽

556.0 Ulcerative (chronic) enterocolitis

556.1 Ulcerative (chronic) ileocolitis

556.2 Ulcerative (chronic) proctitis

556.3 Ulcerative (chronic) proctosigmoiditis

556.4 Pseudopolyposis of colon

556.5 Left sided ulcerative (chronic) colitis

556.6 Universal ulcerative (chronic) colitis

556.8 Other ulcerative colitis

556.9 Unspecified ulcerative colitis ▽

558.42 Eosinophilic colitis

558.9 Other and unspecified noninfectious gastroenteritis and colitis ▽

562.10 Diverticulosis of colon (without mention of hemorrhage) — (Use additional code to identify any associated peritonitis: 567.0-567.9)

562.11 Diverticulitis of colon (without mention of hemorrhage) — (Use additional code to identify any associated peritonitis: 567.0-567.9)

564.00 Unspecified constipation ▽

564.01 Slow transit constipation

564.02 Outlet dysfunction constipation

564.09 Other constipation

564.7 Megacolon, other than Hirschsprung's

564.89 Other functional disorders of intestine
564.9 Unspecified functional disorder of intestine ▽
567.0 Peritonitis in infectious diseases classified elsewhere — (Code first underlying disease) ☒
567.1 Pneumococcal peritonitis
567.21 Peritonitis (acute) generalized
567.22 Peritoneal abscess
567.23 Spontaneous bacterial peritonitis
567.29 Other suppurative peritonitis
567.31 Psoas muscle abscess
567.38 Other retroperitoneal abscess
567.39 Other retroperitoneal infections
567.81 Choleperitonitis
567.82 Sclerosing mesenteritis
567.89 Other specified peritonitis
567.9 Unspecified peritonitis ▽
569.0 Anal and rectal polyp
569.3 Hemorrhage of rectum and anus
569.44 Dysplasia of anus
569.49 Other specified disorder of rectum and anus — (Use additional code for any associated fecal incontinence (787.60-787.63))
569.5 Abscess of intestine
569.81 Fistula of intestine, excluding rectum and anus
569.82 Ulceration of intestine
569.83 Perforation of intestine
569.84 Angiodysplasia of intestine (without mention of hemorrhage)
569.85 Angiodysplasia of intestine with hemorrhage
569.89 Other specified disorder of intestines
569.9 Unspecified disorder of intestine ▽
578.1 Blood in stool
751.3 Hirschsprung's disease and other congenital functional disorders of colon
783.21 Loss of weight — (Use additional code to identify Body Mass Index (BMI), if known: V85.0-V85.54)
783.22 Underweight — (Use additional code to identify Body Mass Index (BMI), if known: V85.0-V85.54)
787.7 Abnormal feces
787.91 Diarrhea
787.99 Other symptoms involving digestive system
789.00 Abdominal pain, unspecified site ▽
789.01 Abdominal pain, right upper quadrant
789.02 Abdominal pain, left upper quadrant
789.03 Abdominal pain, right lower quadrant
789.04 Abdominal pain, left lower quadrant
789.05 Abdominal pain, periumbilic
789.06 Abdominal pain, epigastric
789.07 Abdominal pain, generalized
789.09 Abdominal pain, other specified site
789.30 Abdominal or pelvic swelling, mass or lump, unspecified site ▽
789.31 Abdominal or pelvic swelling, mass, or lump, right upper quadrant
789.32 Abdominal or pelvic swelling, mass, or lump, left upper quadrant
789.33 Abdominal or pelvic swelling, mass, or lump, right lower quadrant
789.34 Abdominal or pelvic swelling, mass, or lump, left lower quadrant
789.35 Abdominal or pelvic swelling, mass or lump, periumbilic
789.36 Abdominal or pelvic swelling, mass, or lump, epigastric
789.37 Abdominal or pelvic swelling, mass, or lump, generalized
789.39 Abdominal or pelvic swelling, mass, or lump, other specified site
792.1 Nonspecific abnormal finding in stool contents
793.4 Nonspecific (abnormal) findings on radiological and other examination of gastrointestinal tract
V10.05 Personal history of malignant neoplasm of large intestine
V10.06 Personal history of malignant neoplasm of rectum, rectosigmoid junction, and anus
V12.70 Personal history of unspecified digestive disease ▽
V12.72 Personal history of colonic polyps
V12.79 Personal history of other diseases of digestive disease
V71.89 Observation for other specified suspected conditions
V71.9 Observation for unspecified suspected condition ▽
V85.0 Body Mass Index less than 19, adult

ICD-9-CM Procedural

45.23 Colonoscopy
45.25 Closed [endoscopic] biopsy of large intestine
88.74 Diagnostic ultrasound of digestive system

HCPCS Level II Supplies & Services

A4270 Disposable endoscope sheath, each

45395-45397

45395 Laparoscopy, surgical; proctectomy, complete, combined abdominoperineal, with colostomy

45397 proctectomy, combined abdominoperineal pull-through procedure (eg, colo-anal anastomosis), with creation of colonic reservoir (eg, J-pouch), with diverting enterostomy, when performed

ICD-9-CM Diagnostic

153.3 Malignant neoplasm of sigmoid colon
153.9 Malignant neoplasm of colon, unspecified site ▽
154.0 Malignant neoplasm of rectosigmoid junction
154.1 Malignant neoplasm of rectum
154.2 Malignant neoplasm of anal canal
154.8 Malignant neoplasm of other sites of rectum, rectosigmoid junction, and anus
197.5 Secondary malignant neoplasm of large intestine and rectum
209.10 Malignant carcinoid tumor of the large intestine, unspecified portion — (Code first any associated multiple endocrine neoplasia syndrome: 258.01-258.03)(Use additional code to identify associated endocrine syndrome, as: carcinoid syndrome: 259.2) ▽
209.11 Malignant carcinoid tumor of the appendix — (Code first any associated multiple endocrine neoplasia syndrome: 258.01-258.03)(Use additional code to identify associated endocrine syndrome, as: carcinoid syndrome: 259.2)
209.12 Malignant carcinoid tumor of the cecum — (Code first any associated multiple endocrine neoplasia syndrome: 258.01-258.03)(Use additional code to identify associated endocrine syndrome, as: carcinoid syndrome: 259.2)
209.13 Malignant carcinoid tumor of the ascending colon — (Code first any associated multiple endocrine neoplasia syndrome: 258.01-258.03)(Use additional code to identify associated endocrine syndrome, as: carcinoid syndrome: 259.2)
209.14 Malignant carcinoid tumor of the transverse colon — (Code first any associated multiple endocrine neoplasia syndrome: 258.01-258.03)(Use additional code to identify associated endocrine syndrome, as: carcinoid syndrome: 259.2)
209.15 Malignant carcinoid tumor of the descending colon — (Code first any associated multiple endocrine neoplasia syndrome: 258.01-258.03)(Use additional code to identify associated endocrine syndrome, as: carcinoid syndrome: 259.2)
209.16 Malignant carcinoid tumor of the sigmoid colon — (Code first any associated multiple endocrine neoplasia syndrome: 258.01-258.03)(Use additional code to identify associated endocrine syndrome, as: carcinoid syndrome: 259.2)
209.17 Malignant carcinoid tumor of the rectum — (Code first any associated multiple endocrine neoplasia syndrome: 258.01-258.03)(Use additional code to identify associated endocrine syndrome, as: carcinoid syndrome: 259.2)
209.20 Malignant carcinoid tumor of unknown primary site — (Code first any associated multiple endocrine neoplasia syndrome: 258.01-258.03)(Use additional code to identify associated endocrine syndrome, as: carcinoid syndrome: 259.2)
209.50 Benign carcinoid tumor of the large intestine, unspecified portion — (Code first any associated multiple endocrine neoplasia syndrome: 258.01-258.03)(Use additional code to identify associated endocrine syndrome, as: carcinoid syndrome: 259.2) ▽

209.51 Benign carcinoid tumor of the appendix — (Code first any associated multiple endocrine neoplasia syndrome: 258.01-258.03)(Use additional code to identify associated endocrine syndrome, as: carcinoid syndrome: 259.2)
209.52 Benign carcinoid tumor of the cecum — (Code first any associated multiple endocrine neoplasia syndrome: 258.01-258.03)(Use additional code to identify associated endocrine syndrome, as: carcinoid syndrome: 259.2)
209.53 Benign carcinoid tumor of the ascending colon — (Code first any associated multiple endocrine neoplasia syndrome: 258.01-258.03)(Use additional code to identify associated endocrine syndrome, as: carcinoid syndrome: 259.2)
209.54 Benign carcinoid tumor of the transverse colon — (Code first any associated multiple endocrine neoplasia syndrome: 258.01-258.03)(Use additional code to identify associated endocrine syndrome, as: carcinoid syndrome: 259.2)
209.55 Benign carcinoid tumor of the descending colon — (Code first any associated multiple endocrine neoplasia syndrome: 258.01-258.03)(Use additional code to identify associated endocrine syndrome, as: carcinoid syndrome: 259.2)
209.56 Benign carcinoid tumor of the sigmoid colon — (Code first any associated multiple endocrine neoplasia syndrome: 258.01-258.03)(Use additional code to identify associated endocrine syndrome, as: carcinoid syndrome: 259.2)
209.57 Benign carcinoid tumor of the rectum — (Code first any associated multiple endocrine neoplasia syndrome: 258.01-258.03)(Use additional code to identify associated endocrine syndrome, as: carcinoid syndrome: 259.2)
211.3 Benign neoplasm of colon
230.3 Carcinoma in situ of colon
230.4 Carcinoma in situ of rectum
235.2 Neoplasm of uncertain behavior of stomach, intestines, and rectum
555.1 Regional enteritis of large intestine
556.0 Ulcerative (chronic) enterocolitis
556.1 Ulcerative (chronic) ileocolitis
556.2 Ulcerative (chronic) proctitis
556.3 Ulcerative (chronic) proctosigmoiditis
556.4 Pseudopolyposis of colon
556.5 Left sided ulcerative (chronic) colitis
556.6 Universal ulcerative (chronic) colitis
556.8 Other ulcerative colitis
556.9 Unspecified ulcerative colitis ▽
557.0 Acute vascular insufficiency of intestine
557.1 Chronic vascular insufficiency of intestine
557.9 Unspecified vascular insufficiency of intestine ▽
569.1 Rectal prolapse
569.44 Dysplasia of anus
751.3 Hirschsprung's disease and other congenital functional disorders of colon

ICD-9-CM Procedural

48.42 Laparoscopic pull-through resection of rectum
48.51 Laparoscopic abdominoperineal resection of the rectum
48.65 Duhamel resection of rectum

45400-45402

45400 Laparoscopy, surgical; proctopexy (for prolapse)
45402 proctopexy (for prolapse), with sigmoid resection

ICD-9-CM Diagnostic

569.1 Rectal prolapse

ICD-9-CM Procedural

17.36 Laparoscopic sigmoidectomy
48.75 Abdominal proctopexy
48.76 Other proctopexy

45500

45500 Proctoplasty; for stenosis

ICD-9-CM Diagnostic

569.2 Stenosis of rectum and anus

ICD-9-CM Procedural

48.79 Other repair of rectum

45505

45505 Proctoplasty; for prolapse of mucous membrane

ICD-9-CM Diagnostic

569.1 Rectal prolapse

ICD-9-CM Procedural

48.79 Other repair of rectum

45520

45520 Perirectal injection of sclerosing solution for prolapse

ICD-9-CM Diagnostic

569.1 Rectal prolapse

ICD-9-CM Procedural

99.29 Injection or infusion of other therapeutic or prophylactic substance

HCPCS Level II Supplies & Services

A4305 Disposable drug delivery system, flow rate of 50 ml or greater per hour

45540

45540 Proctopexy (eg, for prolapse); abdominal approach

ICD-9-CM Diagnostic

569.1 Rectal prolapse

ICD-9-CM Procedural

48.75 Abdominal proctopexy

45541

45541 Proctopexy (eg, for prolapse); perineal approach

ICD-9-CM Diagnostic

569.1 Rectal prolapse

ICD-9-CM Procedural

48.76 Other proctopexy

45550

45550 Proctopexy (eg, for prolapse); with sigmoid resection, abdominal approach

ICD-9-CM Diagnostic

569.1 Rectal prolapse

ICD-9-CM Procedural

45.76 Open and other sigmoidectomy
48.75 Abdominal proctopexy

45560

45560 Repair of rectocele (separate procedure)

ICD-9-CM Diagnostic

569.1 Rectal prolapse
569.44 Dysplasia of anus
569.49 Other specified disorder of rectum and anus — (Use additional code for any associated fecal incontinence (787.60-787.63))

618.00 Unspecified prolapse of vaginal walls without mention of uterine prolapse — (Use additional code to identify urinary incontinence: 625.6, 788.31, 788.33-788.39) ▽ ♀

618.04 Rectocele without mention of uterine prolapse — (Use additional code to identify urinary incontinence: 625.6, 788.31, 788.33-788.39) (Use additional code for any associated fecal incontinence: 787.60-787.63) ♀

618.2 Uterovaginal prolapse, incomplete — (Use additional code to identify urinary incontinence: 625.6, 788.31, 788.33-788.39) ♀

618.3 Uterovaginal prolapse, complete — (Use additional code to identify urinary incontinence: 625.6, 788.31, 788.33-788.39) ♀

618.4 Uterovaginal prolapse, unspecified — (Use additional code to identify urinary incontinence: 625.6, 788.31, 788.33-788.39) ▽ ♀

618.5 Prolapse of vaginal vault after hysterectomy — (Use additional code to identify urinary incontinence: 625.6, 788.31, 788.33-788.39) ♀

618.82 Incompetence or weakening of rectovaginal tissue — (Use additional code to identify urinary incontinence: 625.6, 788.31, 788.33-788.39) ♀

618.89 Other specified genital prolapse — (Use additional code to identify urinary incontinence: 625.6, 788.31, 788.33-788.39) ♀

ICD-9-CM Procedural

48.75 Abdominal proctopexy

48.76 Other proctopexy

70.52 Repair of rectocele ♀

70.55 Repair of rectocele with graft or prosthesis ♀

70.94 Other operations on vagina and cul-de-sac, insertion of biological graft ♀

70.95 Other operations on vagina and cul-de-sac, insertion of synthetic graft or prosthesis ♀

45562-45563

45562 Exploration, repair, and presacral drainage for rectal injury;

45563 with colostomy

ICD-9-CM Diagnostic

569.42 Anal or rectal pain

863.45 Rectum injury without mention of open wound into cavity

863.46 Injury to multiple sites in colon and rectum without mention of open wound into cavity

863.55 Rectum injury with open wound into cavity

863.56 Injury to multiple sites in colon and rectum with open wound into cavity

ICD-9-CM Procedural

46.11 Temporary colostomy

46.13 Permanent colostomy

48.69 Other resection of rectum

48.71 Suture of laceration of rectum

48.79 Other repair of rectum

75.62 Repair of current obstetric laceration of rectum and sphincter ani ♀

45800-45805

45800 Closure of rectovesical fistula;

45805 with colostomy

ICD-9-CM Diagnostic

596.1 Intestinovesical fistula — (Use additional code to identify urinary incontinence: 625.6, 788.30-788.39)

625.6 Female stress incontinence ♀

753.8 Other specified congenital anomaly of bladder and urethra

788.30 Unspecified urinary incontinence — (Code, if applicable, any causal condition first: 600.0-600.9, with fifth digit 1; 618.00-618.9; 753.23) ▽

788.31 Urge incontinence — (Code, if applicable, any causal condition first: 600.0-600.9, with fifth digit 1; 618.00-618.9; 753.23)

788.32 Stress incontinence, male — (Code, if applicable, any causal condition first: 600.0-600.9, with fifth digit 1; 618.00-618.9; 753.23) ♂

788.33 Mixed incontinence urge and stress (male)(female) — (Code, if applicable, any causal condition first: 600.0-600.9, with fifth digit 1; 618.00-618.9; 753.23)

788.34 Incontinence without sensory awareness — (Code, if applicable, any causal condition first: 600.0-600.9, with fifth digit 1; 618.00-618.9; 753.23)

788.35 Post-void dribbling — (Code, if applicable, any causal condition first: 600.0-600.9, with fifth digit 1; 618.00-618.9; 753.23)

788.36 Nocturnal enuresis — (Code, if applicable, any causal condition first: 600.0-600.9, with fifth digit 1; 618.00-618.9; 753.23)

788.37 Continuous leakage — (Code, if applicable, any causal condition first: 600.0-600.9, with fifth digit 1; 618.00-618.9; 753.23)

788.39 Other urinary incontinence — (Code, if applicable, any causal condition first: 600.0-600.9, with fifth digit 1; 618.00-618.9; 753.23)

ICD-9-CM Procedural

46.11 Temporary colostomy

46.13 Permanent colostomy

57.83 Repair of fistula involving bladder and intestine

45820-45825

45820 Closure of rectourethral fistula;

45825 with colostomy

ICD-9-CM Diagnostic

599.1 Urethral fistula

625.6 Female stress incontinence ♀

753.8 Other specified congenital anomaly of bladder and urethra

788.30 Unspecified urinary incontinence — (Code, if applicable, any causal condition first: 600.0-600.9, with fifth digit 1; 618.00-618.9; 753.23) ▽

788.31 Urge incontinence — (Code, if applicable, any causal condition first: 600.0-600.9, with fifth digit 1; 618.00-618.9; 753.23)

788.32 Stress incontinence, male — (Code, if applicable, any causal condition first: 600.0-600.9, with fifth digit 1; 618.00-618.9; 753.23) ♂

788.33 Mixed incontinence urge and stress (male)(female) — (Code, if applicable, any causal condition first: 600.0-600.9, with fifth digit 1; 618.00-618.9; 753.23)

788.34 Incontinence without sensory awareness — (Code, if applicable, any causal condition first: 600.0-600.9, with fifth digit 1; 618.00-618.9; 753.23)

788.35 Post-void dribbling — (Code, if applicable, any causal condition first: 600.0-600.9, with fifth digit 1; 618.00-618.9; 753.23)

788.36 Nocturnal enuresis — (Code, if applicable, any causal condition first: 600.0-600.9, with fifth digit 1; 618.00-618.9; 753.23)

788.37 Continuous leakage — (Code, if applicable, any causal condition first: 600.0-600.9, with fifth digit 1; 618.00-618.9; 753.23)

788.39 Other urinary incontinence — (Code, if applicable, any causal condition first: 600.0-600.9, with fifth digit 1; 618.00-618.9; 753.23)

ICD-9-CM Procedural

46.03 Exteriorization of large intestine

46.10 Colostomy, not otherwise specified

46.11 Temporary colostomy

46.13 Permanent colostomy

58.43 Closure of other fistula of urethra

45900

45900 Reduction of procidentia (separate procedure) under anesthesia

ICD-9-CM Diagnostic

569.1 Rectal prolapse

ICD-9-CM Procedural

96.26 Manual reduction of rectal prolapse

HCPCS Level II Supplies & Services

A4305 Disposable drug delivery system, flow rate of 50 ml or greater per hour

45905

45905 Dilation of anal sphincter (separate procedure) under anesthesia other than local

ICD-9-CM Diagnostic

154.2 Malignant neoplasm of anal canal
209.57 Benign carcinoid tumor of the rectum — (Code first any associated multiple endocrine neoplasia syndrome: 258.01-258.03)(Use additional code to identify associated endocrine syndrome, as: carcinoid syndrome: 259.2)
211.4 Benign neoplasm of rectum and anal canal
455.2 Internal hemorrhoids with other complication
555.1 Regional enteritis of large intestine
564.6 Anal spasm
564.81 Neurogenic bowel
564.89 Other functional disorders of intestine
564.9 Unspecified functional disorder of intestine ▽
565.0 Anal fissure
565.1 Anal fistula
566 Abscess of anal and rectal regions
569.2 Stenosis of rectum and anus
569.41 Ulcer of anus and rectum
569.42 Anal or rectal pain
569.44 Dysplasia of anus
578.1 Blood in stool
751.2 Congenital atresia and stenosis of large intestine, rectum, and anal canal

ICD-9-CM Procedural

96.23 Dilation of anal sphincter

HCPCS Level II Supplies & Services

A4305 Disposable drug delivery system, flow rate of 50 ml or greater per hour

45910

45910 Dilation of rectal stricture (separate procedure) under anesthesia other than local

ICD-9-CM Diagnostic

154.2 Malignant neoplasm of anal canal
209.17 Malignant carcinoid tumor of the rectum — (Code first any associated multiple endocrine neoplasia syndrome: 258.01-258.03)(Use additional code to identify associated endocrine syndrome, as: carcinoid syndrome: 259.2)
209.57 Benign carcinoid tumor of the rectum — (Code first any associated multiple endocrine neoplasia syndrome: 258.01-258.03)(Use additional code to identify associated endocrine syndrome, as: carcinoid syndrome: 259.2)
211.3 Benign neoplasm of colon
455.2 Internal hemorrhoids with other complication
564.00 Unspecified constipation ▽
564.02 Outlet dysfunction constipation
564.09 Other constipation
565.1 Anal fistula
569.2 Stenosis of rectum and anus
569.42 Anal or rectal pain
578.1 Blood in stool
751.2 Congenital atresia and stenosis of large intestine, rectum, and anal canal

ICD-9-CM Procedural

96.22 Dilation of rectum

HCPCS Level II Supplies & Services

A4305 Disposable drug delivery system, flow rate of 50 ml or greater per hour

45915

45915 Removal of fecal impaction or foreign body (separate procedure) under anesthesia

ICD-9-CM Diagnostic

560.1 Paralytic ileus
560.32 Fecal impaction
560.39 Impaction of intestine, other
564.00 Unspecified constipation ▽
564.01 Slow transit constipation
564.02 Outlet dysfunction constipation
564.09 Other constipation
569.1 Rectal prolapse
569.2 Stenosis of rectum and anus
569.42 Anal or rectal pain
569.87 Vomiting of fecal matter
578.1 Blood in stool
787.5 Abnormal bowel sounds
937 Foreign body in anus and rectum

ICD-9-CM Procedural

96.38 Removal of impacted feces
98.05 Removal of intraluminal foreign body from rectum and anus without incision

HCPCS Level II Supplies & Services

A4305 Disposable drug delivery system, flow rate of 50 ml or greater per hour

45990

45990 Anorectal exam, surgical, requiring anesthesia (general, spinal, or epidural), diagnostic

ICD-9-CM Diagnostic

153.3 Malignant neoplasm of sigmoid colon
153.8 Malignant neoplasm of other specified sites of large intestine
154.0 Malignant neoplasm of rectosigmoid junction
154.1 Malignant neoplasm of rectum
154.2 Malignant neoplasm of anal canal
154.3 Malignant neoplasm of anus, unspecified site ▽
154.8 Malignant neoplasm of other sites of rectum, rectosigmoid junction, and anus
197.5 Secondary malignant neoplasm of large intestine and rectum
198.82 Secondary malignant neoplasm of genital organs
209.10 Malignant carcinoid tumor of the large intestine, unspecified portion — (Code first any associated multiple endocrine neoplasia syndrome: 258.01-258.03)(Use additional code to identify associated endocrine syndrome, as: carcinoid syndrome: 259.2) ▽
209.16 Malignant carcinoid tumor of the sigmoid colon — (Code first any associated multiple endocrine neoplasia syndrome: 258.01-258.03)(Use additional code to identify associated endocrine syndrome, as: carcinoid syndrome: 259.2)
209.17 Malignant carcinoid tumor of the rectum — (Code first any associated multiple endocrine neoplasia syndrome: 258.01-258.03)(Use additional code to identify associated endocrine syndrome, as: carcinoid syndrome: 259.2)
209.29 Malignant carcinoid tumor of other sites — (Code first any associated multiple endocrine neoplasia syndrome: 258.01-258.03)(Use additional code to identify associated endocrine syndrome, as: carcinoid syndrome: 259.2)
209.50 Benign carcinoid tumor of the large intestine, unspecified portion — (Code first any associated multiple endocrine neoplasia syndrome: 258.01-258.03)(Use additional code to identify associated endocrine syndrome, as: carcinoid syndrome: 259.2) ▽
209.56 Benign carcinoid tumor of the sigmoid colon — (Code first any associated multiple endocrine neoplasia syndrome: 258.01-258.03)(Use additional code to identify associated endocrine syndrome, as: carcinoid syndrome: 259.2)
209.57 Benign carcinoid tumor of the rectum — (Code first any associated multiple endocrine neoplasia syndrome: 258.01-258.03)(Use additional code to identify associated endocrine syndrome, as: carcinoid syndrome: 259.2)

209.69	Benign carcinoid tumor of other sites — (Code first any associated multiple endocrine neoplasia syndrome: 258.01-258.03)(Use additional code to identify associated endocrine syndrome, as: carcinoid syndrome: 259.2)
211.3	Benign neoplasm of colon
211.4	Benign neoplasm of rectum and anal canal
230.3	Carcinoma in situ of colon
230.4	Carcinoma in situ of rectum
230.5	Carcinoma in situ of anal canal
235.2	Neoplasm of uncertain behavior of stomach, intestines, and rectum
235.5	Neoplasm of uncertain behavior of other and unspecified digestive organs ▽
239.0	Neoplasm of unspecified nature of digestive system
455.0	Internal hemorrhoids without mention of complication
455.1	Internal thrombosed hemorrhoids
455.2	Internal hemorrhoids with other complication
455.3	External hemorrhoids without mention of complication
455.4	External thrombosed hemorrhoids
455.5	External hemorrhoids with other complication
455.6	Unspecified hemorrhoids without mention of complication ▽
455.7	Unspecified thrombosed hemorrhoids ▽
455.8	Unspecified hemorrhoids with other complication ▽
455.9	Residual hemorrhoidal skin tags
555.1	Regional enteritis of large intestine
555.9	Regional enteritis of unspecified site ▽
556.0	Ulcerative (chronic) enterocolitis
556.2	Ulcerative (chronic) proctitis
556.9	Unspecified ulcerative colitis ▽
557.1	Chronic vascular insufficiency of intestine
557.9	Unspecified vascular insufficiency of intestine ▽
558.1	Gastroenteritis and colitis due to radiation
558.2	Toxic gastroenteritis and colitis — (Use additional E code to identify cause)
558.3	Gastroenteritis and colitis, allergic — (Use additional code to identify type of food allergy: V15.01-V15.05)
558.9	Other and unspecified noninfectious gastroenteritis and colitis ▽
560.0	Intussusception
560.1	Paralytic ileus
560.2	Volvulus
560.30	Unspecified impaction of intestine ▽
560.31	Gallstone ileus
560.32	Fecal impaction
560.39	Impaction of intestine, other
560.81	Intestinal or peritoneal adhesions with obstruction (postoperative) (postinfection)
560.89	Other specified intestinal obstruction
562.10	Diverticulosis of colon (without mention of hemorrhage) — (Use additional code to identify any associated peritonitis: 567.0-567.9)
562.11	Diverticulitis of colon (without mention of hemorrhage) — (Use additional code to identify any associated peritonitis: 567.0-567.9)
562.12	Diverticulosis of colon with hemorrhage — (Use additional code to identify any associated peritonitis: 567.0-567.9)
562.13	Diverticulitis of colon with hemorrhage — (Use additional code to identify any associated peritonitis: 567.0-567.9)
564.00	Unspecified constipation ▽
564.01	Slow transit constipation
564.02	Outlet dysfunction constipation
564.09	Other constipation
564.1	Irritable bowel syndrome
564.5	Functional diarrhea
564.6	Anal spasm
564.7	Megacolon, other than Hirschsprung's
564.81	Neurogenic bowel
564.89	Other functional disorders of intestine
565.0	Anal fissure
565.1	Anal fistula
566	Abscess of anal and rectal regions
567.0	Peritonitis in infectious diseases classified elsewhere — (Code first underlying disease) ☒
567.1	Pneumococcal peritonitis
569.0	Anal and rectal polyp
569.1	Rectal prolapse
569.2	Stenosis of rectum and anus
569.3	Hemorrhage of rectum and anus
569.41	Ulcer of anus and rectum
569.42	Anal or rectal pain
569.44	Dysplasia of anus
569.49	Other specified disorder of rectum and anus — (Use additional code for any associated fecal incontinence (787.60-787.63))
569.81	Fistula of intestine, excluding rectum and anus
569.82	Ulceration of intestine
569.83	Perforation of intestine
569.84	Angiodysplasia of intestine (without mention of hemorrhage)
569.85	Angiodysplasia of intestine with hemorrhage
569.89	Other specified disorder of intestines
569.9	Unspecified disorder of intestine ▽
578.1	Blood in stool
698.0	Pruritus ani
751.2	Congenital atresia and stenosis of large intestine, rectum, and anal canal
783.21	Loss of weight — (Use additional code to identify Body Mass Index (BMI), if known: V85.0-V85.54)
783.22	Underweight — (Use additional code to identify Body Mass Index (BMI), if known: V85.0-V85.54)
783.7	Adult failure to thrive
787.3	Flatulence, eructation, and gas pain
787.60	Full incontinence of feces
787.61	Incomplete defecation
787.62	Fecal smearing
787.63	Fecal urgency
787.7	Abnormal feces
787.99	Other symptoms involving digestive system
789.00	Abdominal pain, unspecified site ▽
789.01	Abdominal pain, right upper quadrant
789.02	Abdominal pain, left upper quadrant
789.03	Abdominal pain, right lower quadrant
789.04	Abdominal pain, left lower quadrant
789.05	Abdominal pain, periumbilic
789.06	Abdominal pain, epigastric
789.07	Abdominal pain, generalized
789.09	Abdominal pain, other specified site
789.30	Abdominal or pelvic swelling, mass or lump, unspecified site ▽
789.31	Abdominal or pelvic swelling, mass, or lump, right upper quadrant
789.32	Abdominal or pelvic swelling, mass, or lump, left upper quadrant
789.33	Abdominal or pelvic swelling, mass, or lump, right lower quadrant
789.34	Abdominal or pelvic swelling, mass, or lump, left lower quadrant
789.35	Abdominal or pelvic swelling, mass or lump, periumbilic
789.36	Abdominal or pelvic swelling, mass, or lump, epigastric
789.37	Abdominal or pelvic swelling, mass, or lump, generalized
789.39	Abdominal or pelvic swelling, mass, or lump, other specified site
792.1	Nonspecific abnormal finding in stool contents
793.4	Nonspecific (abnormal) findings on radiological and other examination of gastrointestinal tract

863.45 Rectum injury without mention of open wound into cavity
863.46 Injury to multiple sites in colon and rectum without mention of open wound into cavity
863.55 Rectum injury with open wound into cavity
863.56 Injury to multiple sites in colon and rectum with open wound into cavity
997.49 Other digestive system complications
V76.41 Screening for malignant neoplasm of the rectum
V76.49 Special screening for malignant neoplasms, other sites

ICD-9-CM Procedural

49.29 Other diagnostic procedures on anus and perianal tissue
89.34 Digital examination of rectum
89.39 Other nonoperative measurements and examinations

Anus

46020

46020 Placement of seton

ICD-9-CM Diagnostic

555.1 Regional enteritis of large intestine
555.9 Regional enteritis of unspecified site ▽
565.1 Anal fistula
566 Abscess of anal and rectal regions
567.29 Other suppurative peritonitis
569.3 Hemorrhage of rectum and anus
569.42 Anal or rectal pain
569.5 Abscess of intestine
578.1 Blood in stool
751.5 Other congenital anomalies of intestine
958.3 Posttraumatic wound infection not elsewhere classified
998.51 Infected postoperative seroma — (Use additional code to identify organism)
998.59 Other postoperative infection — (Use additional code to identify infection)
998.6 Persistent postoperative fistula, not elsewhere classified

ICD-9-CM Procedural

49.99 Other operations on anus

46030

46030 Removal of anal seton, other marker

ICD-9-CM Diagnostic

555.1 Regional enteritis of large intestine
555.9 Regional enteritis of unspecified site ▽
565.1 Anal fistula
566 Abscess of anal and rectal regions
619.1 Digestive-genital tract fistula, female ♀
V58.49 Other specified aftercare following surgery — (This code should be used in conjunction with other aftercare codes to fully identify the reason for the aftercare encounter)
V58.75 Aftercare following surgery of the teeth, oral cavity, and digestive system, NEC — (This code should be used in conjunction with other aftercare codes to fully identify the reason for the aftercare encounter)

ICD-9-CM Procedural

49.93 Other incision of anus

HCPCS Level II Supplies & Services

A4305 Disposable drug delivery system, flow rate of 50 ml or greater per hour

46040

46040 Incision and drainage of ischiorectal and/or perirectal abscess (separate procedure)

ICD-9-CM Diagnostic

455.5 External hemorrhoids with other complication
555.1 Regional enteritis of large intestine
555.2 Regional enteritis of small intestine with large intestine
555.9 Regional enteritis of unspecified site ▽
562.11 Diverticulitis of colon (without mention of hemorrhage) — (Use additional code to identify any associated peritonitis: 567.0-567.9)
565.0 Anal fissure
565.1 Anal fistula
566 Abscess of anal and rectal regions
567.38 Other retroperitoneal abscess
567.39 Other retroperitoneal infections
569.41 Ulcer of anus and rectum
569.82 Ulceration of intestine
569.83 Perforation of intestine
682.5 Cellulitis and abscess of buttock — (Use additional code to identify organism, such as 041.1, etc.)
958.3 Posttraumatic wound infection not elsewhere classified
998.30 Disruption of wound, unspecified ▽
998.33 Disruption of traumatic injury wound repair
998.51 Infected postoperative seroma — (Use additional code to identify organism)
998.59 Other postoperative infection — (Use additional code to identify infection)

ICD-9-CM Procedural

48.81 Incision of perirectal tissue
49.01 Incision of perianal abscess

HCPCS Level II Supplies & Services

A4305 Disposable drug delivery system, flow rate of 50 ml or greater per hour

46045

46045 Incision and drainage of intramural, intramuscular, or submucosal abscess, transanal, under anesthesia

ICD-9-CM Diagnostic

555.1 Regional enteritis of large intestine
555.9 Regional enteritis of unspecified site ▽
562.11 Diverticulitis of colon (without mention of hemorrhage) — (Use additional code to identify any associated peritonitis: 567.0-567.9)
565.1 Anal fistula
566 Abscess of anal and rectal regions
567.0 Peritonitis in infectious diseases classified elsewhere — (Code first underlying disease) ☒
567.1 Pneumococcal peritonitis
567.21 Peritonitis (acute) generalized
567.22 Peritoneal abscess
567.23 Spontaneous bacterial peritonitis
567.29 Other suppurative peritonitis
567.31 Psoas muscle abscess
567.38 Other retroperitoneal abscess
567.39 Other retroperitoneal infections
567.81 Choleperitonitis
567.82 Sclerosing mesenteritis
567.89 Other specified peritonitis
567.9 Unspecified peritonitis ▽
680.5 Carbuncle and furuncle of buttock
682.2 Cellulitis and abscess of trunk — (Use additional code to identify organism, such as 041.1, etc.)

682.5 Cellulitis and abscess of buttock — (Use additional code to identify organism, such as 041.1, etc.)
958.3 Posttraumatic wound infection not elsewhere classified
998.51 Infected postoperative seroma — (Use additional code to identify organism)
998.59 Other postoperative infection — (Use additional code to identify infection)

ICD-9-CM Procedural

49.02 Other incision of perianal tissue
49.93 Other incision of anus

46050

46050 Incision and drainage, perianal abscess, superficial

ICD-9-CM Diagnostic

566 Abscess of anal and rectal regions
569.3 Hemorrhage of rectum and anus
680.5 Carbuncle and furuncle of buttock
958.3 Posttraumatic wound infection not elsewhere classified
998.51 Infected postoperative seroma — (Use additional code to identify organism)
998.59 Other postoperative infection — (Use additional code to identify infection)

ICD-9-CM Procedural

49.01 Incision of perianal abscess

HCPCS Level II Supplies & Services

A4305 Disposable drug delivery system, flow rate of 50 ml or greater per hour

46060

46060 Incision and drainage of ischiorectal or intramural abscess, with fistulectomy or fistulotomy, submuscular, with or without placement of seton

ICD-9-CM Diagnostic

562.11 Diverticulitis of colon (without mention of hemorrhage) — (Use additional code to identify any associated peritonitis: 567.0-567.9)
565.1 Anal fistula
566 Abscess of anal and rectal regions
567.0 Peritonitis in infectious diseases classified elsewhere — (Code first underlying disease) ☒
567.1 Pneumococcal peritonitis
567.21 Peritonitis (acute) generalized
567.22 Peritoneal abscess
567.23 Spontaneous bacterial peritonitis
567.29 Other suppurative peritonitis
567.31 Psoas muscle abscess
567.38 Other retroperitoneal abscess
567.39 Other retroperitoneal infections
567.81 Choleperitonitis
567.82 Sclerosing mesenteritis
567.89 Other specified peritonitis
567.9 Unspecified peritonitis ▽
569.42 Anal or rectal pain
569.44 Dysplasia of anus
569.49 Other specified disorder of rectum and anus — (Use additional code for any associated fecal incontinence (787.60-787.63))
569.5 Abscess of intestine
682.2 Cellulitis and abscess of trunk — (Use additional code to identify organism, such as 041.1, etc.)
682.5 Cellulitis and abscess of buttock — (Use additional code to identify organism, such as 041.1, etc.)
958.3 Posttraumatic wound infection not elsewhere classified
998.51 Infected postoperative seroma — (Use additional code to identify organism)
998.59 Other postoperative infection — (Use additional code to identify infection)

ICD-9-CM Procedural

49.01 Incision of perianal abscess
49.02 Other incision of perianal tissue
49.11 Anal fistulotomy
49.12 Anal fistulectomy

HCPCS Level II Supplies & Services

A4305 Disposable drug delivery system, flow rate of 50 ml or greater per hour

46070

46070 Incision, anal septum (infant)

ICD-9-CM Diagnostic

751.5 Other congenital anomalies of intestine

ICD-9-CM Procedural

49.91 Incision of anal septum

HCPCS Level II Supplies & Services

A4305 Disposable drug delivery system, flow rate of 50 ml or greater per hour

46080

46080 Sphincterotomy, anal, division of sphincter (separate procedure)

ICD-9-CM Diagnostic

209.57 Benign carcinoid tumor of the rectum — (Code first any associated multiple endocrine neoplasia syndrome: 258.01-258.03)(Use additional code to identify associated endocrine syndrome, as: carcinoid syndrome: 259.2)
211.4 Benign neoplasm of rectum and anal canal
455.0 Internal hemorrhoids without mention of complication
455.1 Internal thrombosed hemorrhoids
455.2 Internal hemorrhoids with other complication
455.9 Residual hemorrhoidal skin tags
564.00 Unspecified constipation ▽
564.02 Outlet dysfunction constipation
564.09 Other constipation
565.0 Anal fissure
565.1 Anal fistula
569.0 Anal and rectal polyp
569.1 Rectal prolapse
569.2 Stenosis of rectum and anus
569.3 Hemorrhage of rectum and anus
569.41 Ulcer of anus and rectum
569.42 Anal or rectal pain
569.44 Dysplasia of anus
569.49 Other specified disorder of rectum and anus — (Use additional code for any associated fecal incontinence (787.60-787.63))
578.1 Blood in stool

ICD-9-CM Procedural

49.51 Left lateral anal sphincterotomy
49.52 Posterior anal sphincterotomy
49.59 Other anal sphincterotomy

46083

46083 Incision of thrombosed hemorrhoid, external

ICD-9-CM Diagnostic

455.4 External thrombosed hemorrhoids

ICD-9-CM Procedural

49.47 Evacuation of thrombosed hemorrhoids

46200

46200 Fissurectomy, including sphincterotomy, when performed

ICD-9-CM Diagnostic

555.1 Regional enteritis of large intestine
565.0 Anal fissure
565.1 Anal fistula
566 Abscess of anal and rectal regions
569.0 Anal and rectal polyp
569.1 Rectal prolapse
569.2 Stenosis of rectum and anus
569.3 Hemorrhage of rectum and anus
569.41 Ulcer of anus and rectum
569.44 Dysplasia of anus
569.49 Other specified disorder of rectum and anus — (Use additional code for any associated fecal incontinence (787.60-787.63))
751.2 Congenital atresia and stenosis of large intestine, rectum, and anal canal
751.5 Other congenital anomalies of intestine

ICD-9-CM Procedural

49.39 Other local excision or destruction of lesion or tissue of anus
49.51 Left lateral anal sphincterotomy
49.52 Posterior anal sphincterotomy

46221

46221 Hemorrhoidectomy, internal, by rubber band ligation(s)

ICD-9-CM Diagnostic

455.0 Internal hemorrhoids without mention of complication
455.1 Internal thrombosed hemorrhoids
455.2 Internal hemorrhoids with other complication
569.1 Rectal prolapse
569.41 Ulcer of anus and rectum
569.44 Dysplasia of anus

ICD-9-CM Procedural

49.45 Ligation of hemorrhoids

[46945, 46946]

46945 Hemorrhoidectomy, internal, by ligation other than rubber band; single hemorrhoid column/group
46946 2 or more hemorrhoid columns/groups

ICD-9-CM Diagnostic

455.0 Internal hemorrhoids without mention of complication
455.1 Internal thrombosed hemorrhoids
455.2 Internal hemorrhoids with other complication

ICD-9-CM Procedural

49.45 Ligation of hemorrhoids

HCPCS Level II Supplies & Services

A4305 Disposable drug delivery system, flow rate of 50 ml or greater per hour

46230 [46220]

46220 Excision of single external papilla or tag, anus
46230 Excision of multiple external papillae or tags, anus

ICD-9-CM Diagnostic

455.3 External hemorrhoids without mention of complication
455.5 External hemorrhoids with other complication
455.9 Residual hemorrhoidal skin tags
565.0 Anal fissure
565.1 Anal fistula
569.0 Anal and rectal polyp
569.41 Ulcer of anus and rectum
569.44 Dysplasia of anus
569.49 Other specified disorder of rectum and anus — (Use additional code for any associated fecal incontinence (787.60-787.63))
787.99 Other symptoms involving digestive system

ICD-9-CM Procedural

49.03 Excision of perianal skin tags
49.39 Other local excision or destruction of lesion or tissue of anus

[46320]

46320 Excision of thrombosed hemorrhoid, external

ICD-9-CM Diagnostic

455.4 External thrombosed hemorrhoids

ICD-9-CM Procedural

49.46 Excision of hemorrhoids
49.47 Evacuation of thrombosed hemorrhoids

HCPCS Level II Supplies & Services

A4305 Disposable drug delivery system, flow rate of 50 ml or greater per hour

46250

46250 Hemorrhoidectomy, external, 2 or more columns/groups

ICD-9-CM Diagnostic

455.3 External hemorrhoids without mention of complication
455.4 External thrombosed hemorrhoids
455.5 External hemorrhoids with other complication
455.7 Unspecified thrombosed hemorrhoids ▽
455.9 Residual hemorrhoidal skin tags
569.44 Dysplasia of anus

ICD-9-CM Procedural

49.46 Excision of hemorrhoids

46255-46258

46255 Hemorrhoidectomy, internal and external, single column/group;
46257 with fissurectomy
46258 with fistulectomy, including fissurectomy, when performed

ICD-9-CM Diagnostic

209.57 Benign carcinoid tumor of the rectum — (Code first any associated multiple endocrine neoplasia syndrome: 258.01-258.03)(Use additional code to identify associated endocrine syndrome, as: carcinoid syndrome: 259.2)
211.4 Benign neoplasm of rectum and anal canal
455.0 Internal hemorrhoids without mention of complication
455.1 Internal thrombosed hemorrhoids
455.2 Internal hemorrhoids with other complication
455.3 External hemorrhoids without mention of complication
455.4 External thrombosed hemorrhoids
455.5 External hemorrhoids with other complication
455.7 Unspecified thrombosed hemorrhoids ▽
455.9 Residual hemorrhoidal skin tags
564.6 Anal spasm
565.0 Anal fissure
565.1 Anal fistula
566 Abscess of anal and rectal regions
569.3 Hemorrhage of rectum and anus
569.41 Ulcer of anus and rectum

569.42 Anal or rectal pain
569.44 Dysplasia of anus
578.1 Blood in stool
751.5 Other congenital anomalies of intestine

ICD-9-CM Procedural

49.12 Anal fistulectomy
49.39 Other local excision or destruction of lesion or tissue of anus
49.46 Excision of hemorrhoids

46260-46262

46260 Hemorrhoidectomy, internal and external, 2 or more columns/groups;
46261 with fissurectomy
46262 with fistulectomy, including fissurectomy, when performed

ICD-9-CM Diagnostic

455.0 Internal hemorrhoids without mention of complication
455.1 Internal thrombosed hemorrhoids
455.2 Internal hemorrhoids with other complication
455.3 External hemorrhoids without mention of complication
455.4 External thrombosed hemorrhoids
455.5 External hemorrhoids with other complication
455.7 Unspecified thrombosed hemorrhoids ▽
455.9 Residual hemorrhoidal skin tags
564.6 Anal spasm
565.0 Anal fissure
565.1 Anal fistula
566 Abscess of anal and rectal regions
569.3 Hemorrhage of rectum and anus
569.42 Anal or rectal pain
569.44 Dysplasia of anus
578.1 Blood in stool
751.5 Other congenital anomalies of intestine

ICD-9-CM Procedural

49.12 Anal fistulectomy
49.39 Other local excision or destruction of lesion or tissue of anus
49.46 Excision of hemorrhoids

46270-46285

46270 Surgical treatment of anal fistula (fistulectomy/fistulotomy); subcutaneous
46275 intersphincteric
46280 transsphincteric, suprasphincteric, extrasphincteric or multiple, including placement of seton, when performed
46285 second stage

ICD-9-CM Diagnostic

565.1 Anal fistula
566 Abscess of anal and rectal regions
569.3 Hemorrhage of rectum and anus
569.42 Anal or rectal pain
569.44 Dysplasia of anus
578.1 Blood in stool
751.5 Other congenital anomalies of intestine
998.6 Persistent postoperative fistula, not elsewhere classified

ICD-9-CM Procedural

49.11 Anal fistulotomy
49.12 Anal fistulectomy
49.73 Closure of anal fistula
49.93 Other incision of anus

46288

46288 Closure of anal fistula with rectal advancement flap

ICD-9-CM Diagnostic

555.9 Regional enteritis of unspecified site ▽
565.1 Anal fistula
566 Abscess of anal and rectal regions
569.3 Hemorrhage of rectum and anus
569.42 Anal or rectal pain
569.44 Dysplasia of anus
569.49 Other specified disorder of rectum and anus — (Use additional code for any associated fecal incontinence (787.60-787.63))
569.69 Other complication of colostomy or enterostomy
578.1 Blood in stool
751.5 Other congenital anomalies of intestine
998.6 Persistent postoperative fistula, not elsewhere classified

ICD-9-CM Procedural

49.73 Closure of anal fistula

46500

46500 Injection of sclerosing solution, hemorrhoids

ICD-9-CM Diagnostic

455.0 Internal hemorrhoids without mention of complication
455.1 Internal thrombosed hemorrhoids
455.2 Internal hemorrhoids with other complication
455.3 External hemorrhoids without mention of complication
455.4 External thrombosed hemorrhoids
455.5 External hemorrhoids with other complication
455.7 Unspecified thrombosed hemorrhoids ▽
569.3 Hemorrhage of rectum and anus
569.42 Anal or rectal pain
578.1 Blood in stool

ICD-9-CM Procedural

49.42 Injection of hemorrhoids

46505

46505 Chemodenervation of internal anal sphincter

ICD-9-CM Diagnostic

209.57 Benign carcinoid tumor of the rectum — (Code first any associated multiple endocrine neoplasia syndrome: 258.01-258.03)(Use additional code to identify associated endocrine syndrome, as: carcinoid syndrome: 259.2)
211.4 Benign neoplasm of rectum and anal canal
455.0 Internal hemorrhoids without mention of complication
455.1 Internal thrombosed hemorrhoids
455.2 Internal hemorrhoids with other complication
455.9 Residual hemorrhoidal skin tags
564.00 Unspecified constipation ▽
564.02 Outlet dysfunction constipation
564.09 Other constipation
565.0 Anal fissure
565.1 Anal fistula
569.0 Anal and rectal polyp
569.1 Rectal prolapse
569.2 Stenosis of rectum and anus
569.3 Hemorrhage of rectum and anus
569.41 Ulcer of anus and rectum
569.42 Anal or rectal pain
569.44 Dysplasia of anus

569.49 Other specified disorder of rectum and anus — (Use additional code for any associated fecal incontinence (787.60-787.63))
578.1 Blood in stool
751.5 Other congenital anomalies of intestine
998.6 Persistent postoperative fistula, not elsewhere classified

ICD-9-CM Procedural

48.99 Other operations on rectum and perirectal tissue
49.79 Other repair of anal sphincter
49.99 Other operations on anus
99.29 Injection or infusion of other therapeutic or prophylactic substance
99.57 Administration of botulism antitoxin

HCPCS Level II Supplies & Services

J0585 Injection, onabotulinumtoxinA, 1 unit
J0586 Injection, abobotulinumtoxinA, 5 units
J0587 Injection, rimabotulinumtoxinB, 100 units
J0588 Injection, incobotulinumtoxinA, 1 unit

46600-46606

46600 Anoscopy; diagnostic, with or without collection of specimen(s) by brushing or washing (separate procedure)
46604 with dilation (eg, balloon, guide wire, bougie)
46606 with biopsy, single or multiple

ICD-9-CM Diagnostic

154.1 Malignant neoplasm of rectum
154.2 Malignant neoplasm of anal canal
154.3 Malignant neoplasm of anus, unspecified site ▽
198.82 Secondary malignant neoplasm of genital organs
209.17 Malignant carcinoid tumor of the rectum — (Code first any associated multiple endocrine neoplasia syndrome: 258.01-258.03)(Use additional code to identify associated endocrine syndrome, as: carcinoid syndrome: 259.2)
209.29 Malignant carcinoid tumor of other sites — (Code first any associated multiple endocrine neoplasia syndrome: 258.01-258.03)(Use additional code to identify associated endocrine syndrome, as: carcinoid syndrome: 259.2)
209.57 Benign carcinoid tumor of the rectum — (Code first any associated multiple endocrine neoplasia syndrome: 258.01-258.03)(Use additional code to identify associated endocrine syndrome, as: carcinoid syndrome: 259.2)
209.69 Benign carcinoid tumor of other sites — (Code first any associated multiple endocrine neoplasia syndrome: 258.01-258.03)(Use additional code to identify associated endocrine syndrome, as: carcinoid syndrome: 259.2)
211.4 Benign neoplasm of rectum and anal canal
230.5 Carcinoma in situ of anal canal
235.5 Neoplasm of uncertain behavior of other and unspecified digestive organs ▽
239.0 Neoplasm of unspecified nature of digestive system
455.0 Internal hemorrhoids without mention of complication
455.1 Internal thrombosed hemorrhoids
455.2 Internal hemorrhoids with other complication
455.3 External hemorrhoids without mention of complication
455.4 External thrombosed hemorrhoids
455.5 External hemorrhoids with other complication
455.7 Unspecified thrombosed hemorrhoids ▽
455.9 Residual hemorrhoidal skin tags
555.1 Regional enteritis of large intestine
556.0 Ulcerative (chronic) enterocolitis
557.9 Unspecified vascular insufficiency of intestine ▽
558.3 Gastroenteritis and colitis, allergic — (Use additional code to identify type of food allergy: V15.01-V15.05)
558.42 Eosinophilic colitis
558.9 Other and unspecified noninfectious gastroenteritis and colitis ▽
560.32 Fecal impaction
560.39 Impaction of intestine, other
560.81 Intestinal or peritoneal adhesions with obstruction (postoperative) (postinfection)
560.89 Other specified intestinal obstruction
562.10 Diverticulosis of colon (without mention of hemorrhage) — (Use additional code to identify any associated peritonitis: 567.0-567.9)
562.11 Diverticulitis of colon (without mention of hemorrhage) — (Use additional code to identify any associated peritonitis: 567.0-567.9)
562.12 Diverticulosis of colon with hemorrhage — (Use additional code to identify any associated peritonitis: 567.0-567.9)
564.00 Unspecified constipation ▽
564.01 Slow transit constipation
564.02 Outlet dysfunction constipation
564.09 Other constipation
564.1 Irritable bowel syndrome
564.6 Anal spasm
564.7 Megacolon, other than Hirschsprung's
564.81 Neurogenic bowel
564.89 Other functional disorders of intestine
565.0 Anal fissure
565.1 Anal fistula
566 Abscess of anal and rectal regions
567.0 Peritonitis in infectious diseases classified elsewhere — (Code first underlying disease) ☒
567.1 Pneumococcal peritonitis
567.21 Peritonitis (acute) generalized
567.22 Peritoneal abscess
567.23 Spontaneous bacterial peritonitis
567.29 Other suppurative peritonitis
567.31 Psoas muscle abscess
567.38 Other retroperitoneal abscess
567.39 Other retroperitoneal infections
567.81 Choleperitonitis
567.82 Sclerosing mesenteritis
567.89 Other specified peritonitis
567.9 Unspecified peritonitis ▽
569.1 Rectal prolapse
569.2 Stenosis of rectum and anus
569.3 Hemorrhage of rectum and anus
569.41 Ulcer of anus and rectum
569.42 Anal or rectal pain
569.44 Dysplasia of anus
569.49 Other specified disorder of rectum and anus — (Use additional code for any associated fecal incontinence (787.60-787.63))
578.1 Blood in stool
698.0 Pruritus ani
751.2 Congenital atresia and stenosis of large intestine, rectum, and anal canal
787.3 Flatulence, eructation, and gas pain
787.60 Full incontinence of feces
787.61 Incomplete defecation
787.62 Fecal smearing
787.63 Fecal urgency

ICD-9-CM Procedural

49.21 Anoscopy
49.23 Biopsy of anus
96.23 Dilation of anal sphincter

HCPCS Level II Supplies & Services

A4270 Disposable endoscope sheath, each

46608

46608 Anoscopy; with removal of foreign body

ICD-9-CM Diagnostic

564.00 Unspecified constipation ▽
564.01 Slow transit constipation
564.02 Outlet dysfunction constipation
564.09 Other constipation
564.6 Anal spasm
569.42 Anal or rectal pain
578.1 Blood in stool
937 Foreign body in anus and rectum

ICD-9-CM Procedural

49.21 Anoscopy
98.05 Removal of intraluminal foreign body from rectum and anus without incision

HCPCS Level II Supplies & Services

A4270 Disposable endoscope sheath, each

46610-46612

46610 Anoscopy; with removal of single tumor, polyp, or other lesion by hot biopsy forceps or bipolar cautery
46611 with removal of single tumor, polyp, or other lesion by snare technique
46612 with removal of multiple tumors, polyps, or other lesions by hot biopsy forceps, bipolar cautery or snare technique

ICD-9-CM Diagnostic

154.1 Malignant neoplasm of rectum
154.2 Malignant neoplasm of anal canal
154.8 Malignant neoplasm of other sites of rectum, rectosigmoid junction, and anus
209.17 Malignant carcinoid tumor of the rectum — (Code first any associated multiple endocrine neoplasia syndrome: 258.01-258.03)(Use additional code to identify associated endocrine syndrome, as: carcinoid syndrome: 259.2)
209.29 Malignant carcinoid tumor of other sites — (Code first any associated multiple endocrine neoplasia syndrome: 258.01-258.03)(Use additional code to identify associated endocrine syndrome, as: carcinoid syndrome: 259.2)
209.57 Benign carcinoid tumor of the rectum — (Code first any associated multiple endocrine neoplasia syndrome: 258.01-258.03)(Use additional code to identify associated endocrine syndrome, as: carcinoid syndrome: 259.2)
209.69 Benign carcinoid tumor of other sites — (Code first any associated multiple endocrine neoplasia syndrome: 258.01-258.03)(Use additional code to identify associated endocrine syndrome, as: carcinoid syndrome: 259.2)
211.4 Benign neoplasm of rectum and anal canal
230.8 Carcinoma in situ of liver and biliary system
235.5 Neoplasm of uncertain behavior of other and unspecified digestive organs ▽
239.0 Neoplasm of unspecified nature of digestive system
569.0 Anal and rectal polyp
569.3 Hemorrhage of rectum and anus
569.41 Ulcer of anus and rectum
569.42 Anal or rectal pain
569.44 Dysplasia of anus
569.49 Other specified disorder of rectum and anus — (Use additional code for any associated fecal incontinence (787.60-787.63))
578.1 Blood in stool
698.0 Pruritus ani
793.4 Nonspecific (abnormal) findings on radiological and other examination of gastrointestinal tract

ICD-9-CM Procedural

49.31 Endoscopic excision or destruction of lesion or tissue of anus

HCPCS Level II Supplies & Services

A4270 Disposable endoscope sheath, each

46614

46614 Anoscopy; with control of bleeding (eg, injection, bipolar cautery, unipolar cautery, laser, heater probe, stapler, plasma coagulator)

ICD-9-CM Diagnostic

154.1 Malignant neoplasm of rectum
154.2 Malignant neoplasm of anal canal
154.8 Malignant neoplasm of other sites of rectum, rectosigmoid junction, and anus
209.17 Malignant carcinoid tumor of the rectum — (Code first any associated multiple endocrine neoplasia syndrome: 258.01-258.03)(Use additional code to identify associated endocrine syndrome, as: carcinoid syndrome: 259.2)
209.29 Malignant carcinoid tumor of other sites — (Code first any associated multiple endocrine neoplasia syndrome: 258.01-258.03)(Use additional code to identify associated endocrine syndrome, as: carcinoid syndrome: 259.2)
209.57 Benign carcinoid tumor of the rectum — (Code first any associated multiple endocrine neoplasia syndrome: 258.01-258.03)(Use additional code to identify associated endocrine syndrome, as: carcinoid syndrome: 259.2)
209.69 Benign carcinoid tumor of other sites — (Code first any associated multiple endocrine neoplasia syndrome: 258.01-258.03)(Use additional code to identify associated endocrine syndrome, as: carcinoid syndrome: 259.2)
211.4 Benign neoplasm of rectum and anal canal
455.0 Internal hemorrhoids without mention of complication
455.1 Internal thrombosed hemorrhoids
455.2 Internal hemorrhoids with other complication
455.3 External hemorrhoids without mention of complication
455.4 External thrombosed hemorrhoids
455.5 External hemorrhoids with other complication
455.8 Unspecified hemorrhoids with other complication ▽
558.42 Eosinophilic colitis
558.9 Other and unspecified noninfectious gastroenteritis and colitis ▽
569.3 Hemorrhage of rectum and anus
569.41 Ulcer of anus and rectum
569.44 Dysplasia of anus
998.11 Hemorrhage complicating a procedure

ICD-9-CM Procedural

49.95 Control of (postoperative) hemorrhage of anus
99.29 Injection or infusion of other therapeutic or prophylactic substance

HCPCS Level II Supplies & Services

A4270 Disposable endoscope sheath, each

46615

46615 Anoscopy; with ablation of tumor(s), polyp(s), or other lesion(s) not amenable to removal by hot biopsy forceps, bipolar cautery or snare technique

ICD-9-CM Diagnostic

154.1 Malignant neoplasm of rectum
154.2 Malignant neoplasm of anal canal
154.8 Malignant neoplasm of other sites of rectum, rectosigmoid junction, and anus
209.17 Malignant carcinoid tumor of the rectum — (Code first any associated multiple endocrine neoplasia syndrome: 258.01-258.03)(Use additional code to identify associated endocrine syndrome, as: carcinoid syndrome: 259.2)
209.29 Malignant carcinoid tumor of other sites — (Code first any associated multiple endocrine neoplasia syndrome: 258.01-258.03)(Use additional code to identify associated endocrine syndrome, as: carcinoid syndrome: 259.2)
209.57 Benign carcinoid tumor of the rectum — (Code first any associated multiple endocrine neoplasia syndrome: 258.01-258.03)(Use additional code to identify associated endocrine syndrome, as: carcinoid syndrome: 259.2)

209.69 Benign carcinoid tumor of other sites — (Code first any associated multiple endocrine neoplasia syndrome: 258.01-258.03)(Use additional code to identify associated endocrine syndrome, as: carcinoid syndrome: 259.2)
211.4 Benign neoplasm of rectum and anal canal
230.5 Carcinoma in situ of anal canal
239.0 Neoplasm of unspecified nature of digestive system
558.41 Eosinophilic gastroenteritis
558.42 Eosinophilic colitis
558.9 Other and unspecified noninfectious gastroenteritis and colitis ▽
569.0 Anal and rectal polyp
569.3 Hemorrhage of rectum and anus
569.41 Ulcer of anus and rectum
569.44 Dysplasia of anus
578.1 Blood in stool
787.99 Other symptoms involving digestive system

ICD-9-CM Procedural
49.31 Endoscopic excision or destruction of lesion or tissue of anus

HCPCS Level II Supplies & Services
A4270 Disposable endoscope sheath, each

46700-46705
46700 Anoplasty, plastic operation for stricture; adult
46705 infant

ICD-9-CM Diagnostic
564.00 Unspecified constipation ▽
564.02 Outlet dysfunction constipation
564.09 Other constipation
569.2 Stenosis of rectum and anus
569.42 Anal or rectal pain
751.2 Congenital atresia and stenosis of large intestine, rectum, and anal canal
908.1 Late effect of internal injury to intra-abdominal organs
908.6 Late effect of certain complications of trauma

ICD-9-CM Procedural
49.79 Other repair of anal sphincter

46706-46707
46706 Repair of anal fistula with fibrin glue
46707 Repair of anorectal fistula with plug (eg, porcine small intestine submucosa [SIS])

ICD-9-CM Diagnostic
565.1 Anal fistula
569.42 Anal or rectal pain
998.6 Persistent postoperative fistula, not elsewhere classified

ICD-9-CM Procedural
48.73 Closure of other rectal fistula
49.73 Closure of anal fistula

HCPCS Level II Supplies & Services
C1763 Connective tissue, nonhuman (includes synthetic)

46710-46712
46710 Repair of ileoanal pouch fistula/sinus (eg, perineal or vaginal), pouch advancement; transperineal approach
46712 combined transperineal and transabdominal approach

ICD-9-CM Diagnostic
565.1 Anal fistula
569.42 Anal or rectal pain
569.81 Fistula of intestine, excluding rectum and anus
599.1 Urethral fistula
619.1 Digestive-genital tract fistula, female ♀
619.2 Genital tract-skin fistula, female ♀
619.8 Other specified fistula involving female genital tract ♀
998.6 Persistent postoperative fistula, not elsewhere classified

ICD-9-CM Procedural
48.73 Closure of other rectal fistula
49.73 Closure of anal fistula
70.73 Repair of rectovaginal fistula ♀
70.74 Repair of other vaginoenteric fistula ♀
70.75 Repair of other fistula of vagina ♀
71.72 Repair of fistula of vulva or perineum ♀

46715
46715 Repair of low imperforate anus; with anoperineal fistula (cut-back procedure)

ICD-9-CM Diagnostic
751.2 Congenital atresia and stenosis of large intestine, rectum, and anal canal
751.8 Other specified congenital anomalies of digestive system

ICD-9-CM Procedural
49.11 Anal fistulotomy
49.79 Other repair of anal sphincter

46716
46716 Repair of low imperforate anus; with transposition of anoperineal or anovestibular fistula

ICD-9-CM Diagnostic
751.2 Congenital atresia and stenosis of large intestine, rectum, and anal canal
751.8 Other specified congenital anomalies of digestive system

ICD-9-CM Procedural
49.11 Anal fistulotomy
49.79 Other repair of anal sphincter

46730-46735
46730 Repair of high imperforate anus without fistula; perineal or sacroperineal approach
46735 combined transabdominal and sacroperineal approaches

ICD-9-CM Diagnostic
751.2 Congenital atresia and stenosis of large intestine, rectum, and anal canal
751.8 Other specified congenital anomalies of digestive system

ICD-9-CM Procedural
48.69 Other resection of rectum
49.79 Other repair of anal sphincter
49.99 Other operations on anus

46740-46742
46740 Repair of high imperforate anus with rectourethral or rectovaginal fistula; perineal or sacroperineal approach
46742 combined transabdominal and sacroperineal approaches

ICD-9-CM Diagnostic
751.2 Congenital atresia and stenosis of large intestine, rectum, and anal canal
753.8 Other specified congenital anomaly of bladder and urethra

ICD-9-CM Procedural
49.79 Other repair of anal sphincter
49.99 Other operations on anus
58.43 Closure of other fistula of urethra
70.73 Repair of rectovaginal fistula ♀

46744-46748

46744 Repair of cloacal anomaly by anorectovaginoplasty and urethroplasty, sacroperineal approach
46746 Repair of cloacal anomaly by anorectovaginoplasty and urethroplasty, combined abdominal and sacroperineal approach;
46748 with vaginal lengthening by intestinal graft or pedicle flaps

ICD-9-CM Diagnostic

751.5 Other congenital anomalies of intestine
752.40 Unspecified congenital anomaly of cervix, vagina, and external female genitalia ♀
752.43 Cervical agenesis ♀
752.44 Cervical duplication ♀
752.45 Vaginal agenesis ♀
752.46 Transverse vaginal septum ♀
752.47 Longitudinal vaginal septum ♀
752.49 Other congenital anomaly of cervix, vagina, and external female genitalia ♀
752.89 Other specified anomalies of genital organs
752.9 Unspecified congenital anomaly of genital organs

ICD-9-CM Procedural

48.79 Other repair of rectum
49.79 Other repair of anal sphincter
56.89 Other repair of ureter
70.73 Repair of rectovaginal fistula ♀
70.79 Other repair of vagina ♀
71.9 Other operations on female genital organs ♀

46750-46751

46750 Sphincteroplasty, anal, for incontinence or prolapse; adult
46751 child

ICD-9-CM Diagnostic

569.1 Rectal prolapse
578.1 Blood in stool
787.60 Full incontinence of feces
787.61 Incomplete defecation
787.62 Fecal smearing
787.63 Fecal urgency
863.45 Rectum injury without mention of open wound into cavity
863.55 Rectum injury with open wound into cavity

ICD-9-CM Procedural

49.79 Other repair of anal sphincter

HCPCS Level II Supplies & Services

A4520 Incontinence garment, any type, (e.g., brief, diaper), each

46753

46753 Graft (Thiersch operation) for rectal incontinence and/or prolapse

ICD-9-CM Diagnostic

569.1 Rectal prolapse
569.3 Hemorrhage of rectum and anus
578.1 Blood in stool
787.60 Full incontinence of feces
787.61 Incomplete defecation
787.62 Fecal smearing
787.63 Fecal urgency
863.45 Rectum injury without mention of open wound into cavity
863.55 Rectum injury with open wound into cavity

ICD-9-CM Procedural

49.79 Other repair of anal sphincter
49.94 Reduction of anal prolapse

HCPCS Level II Supplies & Services

A4520 Incontinence garment, any type, (e.g., brief, diaper), each

46754

46754 Removal of Thiersch wire or suture, anal canal

ICD-9-CM Diagnostic

569.1 Rectal prolapse
569.3 Hemorrhage of rectum and anus
578.1 Blood in stool
787.60 Full incontinence of feces
787.61 Incomplete defecation
787.62 Fecal smearing
787.63 Fecal urgency
863.45 Rectum injury without mention of open wound into cavity
863.55 Rectum injury with open wound into cavity
V45.89 Other postprocedural status
V58.32 Encounter for removal of sutures
V58.49 Other specified aftercare following surgery — (This code should be used in conjunction with other aftercare codes to fully identify the reason for the aftercare encounter)

ICD-9-CM Procedural

49.99 Other operations on anus

HCPCS Level II Supplies & Services

A4305 Disposable drug delivery system, flow rate of 50 ml or greater per hour

46760

46760 Sphincteroplasty, anal, for incontinence, adult; muscle transplant

ICD-9-CM Diagnostic

569.1 Rectal prolapse
787.60 Full incontinence of feces
787.61 Incomplete defecation
787.62 Fecal smearing
787.63 Fecal urgency
863.45 Rectum injury without mention of open wound into cavity
863.55 Rectum injury with open wound into cavity

ICD-9-CM Procedural

49.74 Gracilis muscle transplant for anal incontinence

HCPCS Level II Supplies & Services

A4520 Incontinence garment, any type, (e.g., brief, diaper), each

46761-46762

46761 Sphincteroplasty, anal, for incontinence, adult; levator muscle imbrication (Park posterior anal repair)
46762 implantation artificial sphincter

ICD-9-CM Diagnostic

569.1 Rectal prolapse
787.60 Full incontinence of feces
787.61 Incomplete defecation
787.62 Fecal smearing
787.63 Fecal urgency
863.45 Rectum injury without mention of open wound into cavity
863.55 Rectum injury with open wound into cavity

ICD-9-CM Procedural

49.75 Implantation or revision of artificial anal sphincter
49.79 Other repair of anal sphincter

[46947]

46947 Hemorrhoidopexy (eg, for prolapsing internal hemorrhoids) by stapling

ICD-9-CM Diagnostic

455.1 Internal thrombosed hemorrhoids
455.2 Internal hemorrhoids with other complication
569.3 Hemorrhage of rectum and anus
569.42 Anal or rectal pain
578.1 Blood in stool

ICD-9-CM Procedural

49.49 Other procedures on hemorrhoids

HCPCS Level II Supplies & Services

A4305 Disposable drug delivery system, flow rate of 50 ml or greater per hour

46900-46916

46900 Destruction of lesion(s), anus (eg, condyloma, papilloma, molluscum contagiosum, herpetic vesicle), simple; chemical
46910 electrodesiccation
46916 cryosurgery

ICD-9-CM Diagnostic

054.10 Unspecified genital herpes ▽
078.0 Molluscum contagiosum
078.10 Viral warts, unspecified ▽
078.11 Condyloma acuminatum
078.19 Other specified viral warts
154.1 Malignant neoplasm of rectum
154.2 Malignant neoplasm of anal canal
154.3 Malignant neoplasm of anus, unspecified site ▽
209.17 Malignant carcinoid tumor of the rectum — (Code first any associated multiple endocrine neoplasia syndrome: 258.01-258.03)(Use additional code to identify associated endocrine syndrome, as: carcinoid syndrome: 259.2)
209.29 Malignant carcinoid tumor of other sites — (Code first any associated multiple endocrine neoplasia syndrome: 258.01-258.03)(Use additional code to identify associated endocrine syndrome, as: carcinoid syndrome: 259.2)
209.57 Benign carcinoid tumor of the rectum — (Code first any associated multiple endocrine neoplasia syndrome: 258.01-258.03)(Use additional code to identify associated endocrine syndrome, as: carcinoid syndrome: 259.2)
209.69 Benign carcinoid tumor of other sites — (Code first any associated multiple endocrine neoplasia syndrome: 258.01-258.03)(Use additional code to identify associated endocrine syndrome, as: carcinoid syndrome: 259.2)
211.4 Benign neoplasm of rectum and anal canal
214.9 Lipoma of unspecified site ▽
216.5 Benign neoplasm of skin of trunk, except scrotum
216.9 Benign neoplasm of skin, site unspecified ▽
228.01 Hemangioma of skin and subcutaneous tissue
235.5 Neoplasm of uncertain behavior of other and unspecified digestive organs ▽
238.2 Neoplasm of uncertain behavior of skin
239.0 Neoplasm of unspecified nature of digestive system
455.2 Internal hemorrhoids with other complication
569.3 Hemorrhage of rectum and anus
569.41 Ulcer of anus and rectum
569.42 Anal or rectal pain
569.44 Dysplasia of anus
578.1 Blood in stool

ICD-9-CM Procedural

49.39 Other local excision or destruction of lesion or tissue of anus

HCPCS Level II Supplies & Services

A4305 Disposable drug delivery system, flow rate of 50 ml or greater per hour

46917-46924

46917 Destruction of lesion(s), anus (eg, condyloma, papilloma, molluscum contagiosum, herpetic vesicle), simple; laser surgery
46922 surgical excision
46924 Destruction of lesion(s), anus (eg, condyloma, papilloma, molluscum contagiosum, herpetic vesicle), extensive (eg, laser surgery, electrosurgery, cryosurgery, chemosurgery)

ICD-9-CM Diagnostic

054.10 Unspecified genital herpes ▽
078.0 Molluscum contagiosum
078.10 Viral warts, unspecified ▽
078.11 Condyloma acuminatum
078.19 Other specified viral warts
154.1 Malignant neoplasm of rectum
154.2 Malignant neoplasm of anal canal
154.3 Malignant neoplasm of anus, unspecified site ▽
209.17 Malignant carcinoid tumor of the rectum — (Code first any associated multiple endocrine neoplasia syndrome: 258.01-258.03)(Use additional code to identify associated endocrine syndrome, as: carcinoid syndrome: 259.2)
209.29 Malignant carcinoid tumor of other sites — (Code first any associated multiple endocrine neoplasia syndrome: 258.01-258.03)(Use additional code to identify associated endocrine syndrome, as: carcinoid syndrome: 259.2)
209.57 Benign carcinoid tumor of the rectum — (Code first any associated multiple endocrine neoplasia syndrome: 258.01-258.03)(Use additional code to identify associated endocrine syndrome, as: carcinoid syndrome: 259.2)
209.69 Benign carcinoid tumor of other sites — (Code first any associated multiple endocrine neoplasia syndrome: 258.01-258.03)(Use additional code to identify associated endocrine syndrome, as: carcinoid syndrome: 259.2)
211.4 Benign neoplasm of rectum and anal canal
214.9 Lipoma of unspecified site ▽
216.5 Benign neoplasm of skin of trunk, except scrotum
216.9 Benign neoplasm of skin, site unspecified ▽
228.01 Hemangioma of skin and subcutaneous tissue
235.5 Neoplasm of uncertain behavior of other and unspecified digestive organs ▽
238.2 Neoplasm of uncertain behavior of skin
239.0 Neoplasm of unspecified nature of digestive system
455.2 Internal hemorrhoids with other complication
569.3 Hemorrhage of rectum and anus
569.41 Ulcer of anus and rectum
569.42 Anal or rectal pain
569.44 Dysplasia of anus
578.1 Blood in stool

ICD-9-CM Procedural

49.39 Other local excision or destruction of lesion or tissue of anus

HCPCS Level II Supplies & Services

A4305 Disposable drug delivery system, flow rate of 50 ml or greater per hour

46930

46930 Destruction of internal hemorrhoid(s) by thermal energy (eg, infrared coagulation, cautery, radiofrequency)

ICD-9-CM Diagnostic

209.57 Benign carcinoid tumor of the rectum — (Code first any associated multiple endocrine neoplasia syndrome: 258.01-258.03)(Use additional code to identify associated endocrine syndrome, as: carcinoid syndrome: 259.2)
211.4 Benign neoplasm of rectum and anal canal
455.0 Internal hemorrhoids without mention of complication
455.1 Internal thrombosed hemorrhoids
455.2 Internal hemorrhoids with other complication

564.6 Anal spasm
565.0 Anal fissure
565.1 Anal fistula
566 Abscess of anal and rectal regions
569.3 Hemorrhage of rectum and anus
569.41 Ulcer of anus and rectum
569.42 Anal or rectal pain
569.44 Dysplasia of anus
578.1 Blood in stool
751.5 Other congenital anomalies of intestine

ICD-9-CM Procedural

49.43 Cauterization of hemorrhoids
49.49 Other procedures on hemorrhoids

46940-46942

46940 Curettage or cautery of anal fissure, including dilation of anal sphincter (separate procedure); initial
46942 subsequent

ICD-9-CM Diagnostic

564.00 Unspecified constipation ▽
564.01 Slow transit constipation
564.02 Outlet dysfunction constipation
564.09 Other constipation
565.0 Anal fissure
569.3 Hemorrhage of rectum and anus
578.1 Blood in stool

ICD-9-CM Procedural

49.39 Other local excision or destruction of lesion or tissue of anus

HCPCS Level II Supplies & Services

A4305 Disposable drug delivery system, flow rate of 50 ml or greater per hour

Liver

47000-47001

47000 Biopsy of liver, needle; percutaneous
47001 when done for indicated purpose at time of other major procedure (List separately in addition to code for primary procedure)

ICD-9-CM Diagnostic

155.0 Malignant neoplasm of liver, primary
155.1 Malignant neoplasm of intrahepatic bile ducts
155.2 Malignant neoplasm of liver, not specified as primary or secondary ▽
195.2 Malignant neoplasm of abdomen
197.7 Secondary malignant neoplasm of liver
199.2 Malignant neoplasm associated with transplanted organ — (Code first complication of transplanted organ (996.80-996.89) Use additional code for specific malignancy)
209.72 Secondary neuroendocrine tumor of liver
211.5 Benign neoplasm of liver and biliary passages
230.8 Carcinoma in situ of liver and biliary system
235.3 Neoplasm of uncertain behavior of liver and biliary passages
238.77 Post-transplant lymphoproliferative disorder [PTLD] — (Code first complications of transplant (996.80-996.89))
239.0 Neoplasm of unspecified nature of digestive system
277.30 Amyloidosis, unspecified — (Use additional code to identify any associated intellectual disabilities) ▽
277.31 Familial Mediterranean fever — (Use additional code to identify any associated intellectual disabilities)
277.39 Other amyloidosis — (Use additional code to identify any associated intellectual disabilities)
277.4 Disorders of bilirubin excretion — (Use additional code to identify any associated intellectual disabilities)
570 Acute and subacute necrosis of liver
571.0 Alcoholic fatty liver
571.1 Acute alcoholic hepatitis
571.2 Alcoholic cirrhosis of liver
571.3 Unspecified alcoholic liver damage ▽
571.41 Chronic persistent hepatitis
571.42 Autoimmune hepatitis
571.49 Other chronic hepatitis
571.5 Cirrhosis of liver without mention of alcohol — (Code first, if applicable, viral hepatitis (acute) (chronic): 070.0-070.9)
571.6 Biliary cirrhosis
571.8 Other chronic nonalcoholic liver disease
571.9 Unspecified chronic liver disease without mention of alcohol ▽
572.0 Abscess of liver
572.1 Portal pyemia
572.2 Hepatic encephalopathy
572.4 Hepatorenal syndrome
572.8 Other sequelae of chronic liver disease
573.0 Chronic passive congestion of liver
573.1 Hepatitis in viral diseases classified elsewhere — (Code first underlying disease: 074.8, 075, 078.5) ☒
573.2 Hepatitis in other infectious diseases classified elsewhere — (Code first underlying disease: 084.9) ☒
573.3 Unspecified hepatitis — (Use additional E code to identify cause) ▽
573.4 Hepatic infarction
573.8 Other specified disorders of liver
576.8 Other specified disorders of biliary tract
751.61 Congenital biliary atresia
751.62 Congenital cystic disease of liver
782.4 Jaundice, unspecified, not of newborn ▽
789.00 Abdominal pain, unspecified site ▽
789.01 Abdominal pain, right upper quadrant
789.02 Abdominal pain, left upper quadrant
789.03 Abdominal pain, right lower quadrant
789.04 Abdominal pain, left lower quadrant
789.05 Abdominal pain, periumbilic
789.06 Abdominal pain, epigastric
789.07 Abdominal pain, generalized
789.09 Abdominal pain, other specified site
789.1 Hepatomegaly
794.8 Nonspecific abnormal results of liver function study
864.01 Liver hematoma and contusion without mention of open wound into cavity
996.82 Complications of transplanted liver — (Use additional code to identify nature of complication: 078.5, 199.2, 238.77, 279.50-279.53)
V42.7 Liver replaced by transplant

ICD-9-CM Procedural

50.11 Closed (percutaneous) (needle) biopsy of liver

47010

47010 Hepatotomy, for open drainage of abscess or cyst, 1 or 2 stages

ICD-9-CM Diagnostic

572.0 Abscess of liver
573.8 Other specified disorders of liver
751.62 Congenital cystic disease of liver

ICD-9-CM Procedural

50.0 Hepatotomy

47015

47015 Laparotomy, with aspiration and/or injection of hepatic parasitic (eg, amoebic or echinococcal) cyst(s) or abscess(es)

ICD-9-CM Diagnostic

006.3 Amebic liver abscess
122.0 Echinococcus granulosus infection of liver
122.5 Echinococcus multilocularis infection of liver
122.8 Unspecified echinococcus of liver ▽
572.0 Abscess of liver
573.8 Other specified disorders of liver

ICD-9-CM Procedural

50.94 Other injection of therapeutic substance into liver
54.19 Other laparotomy

47100

47100 Biopsy of liver, wedge

ICD-9-CM Diagnostic

155.0 Malignant neoplasm of liver, primary
155.1 Malignant neoplasm of intrahepatic bile ducts
155.2 Malignant neoplasm of liver, not specified as primary or secondary ▽
156.0 Malignant neoplasm of gallbladder
156.1 Malignant neoplasm of extrahepatic bile ducts
156.2 Malignant neoplasm of ampulla of Vater
156.8 Malignant neoplasm of other specified sites of gallbladder and extrahepatic bile ducts
156.9 Malignant neoplasm of biliary tract, part unspecified site ▽
157.0 Malignant neoplasm of head of pancreas
157.2 Malignant neoplasm of tail of pancreas
157.3 Malignant neoplasm of pancreatic duct
157.4 Malignant neoplasm of islets of Langerhans — (Use additional code to identify any functional activity)
157.8 Malignant neoplasm of other specified sites of pancreas
157.9 Malignant neoplasm of pancreas, part unspecified ▽
158.0 Malignant neoplasm of retroperitoneum
197.7 Secondary malignant neoplasm of liver
199.1 Other malignant neoplasm of unspecified site
199.2 Malignant neoplasm associated with transplanted organ — (Code first complication of transplanted organ (996.80-996.89) Use additional code for specific malignancy)
209.29 Malignant carcinoid tumor of other sites — (Code first any associated multiple endocrine neoplasia syndrome: 258.01-258.03)(Use additional code to identify associated endocrine syndrome, as: carcinoid syndrome: 259.2)
209.30 Malignant poorly differentiated neuroendocrine carcinoma, any site — (Code first any associated multiple endocrine neoplasia syndrome: 258.01-258.03)(Use additional code to identify associated endocrine syndrome, as: carcinoid syndrome: 259.2) ▽
209.69 Benign carcinoid tumor of other sites — (Code first any associated multiple endocrine neoplasia syndrome: 258.01-258.03)(Use additional code to identify associated endocrine syndrome, as: carcinoid syndrome: 259.2)
209.72 Secondary neuroendocrine tumor of liver
211.5 Benign neoplasm of liver and biliary passages
211.6 Benign neoplasm of pancreas, except islets of Langerhans
230.8 Carcinoma in situ of liver and biliary system
235.3 Neoplasm of uncertain behavior of liver and biliary passages
238.77 Post-transplant lymphoproliferative disorder [PTLD] — (Code first complications of transplant (996.80-996.89))
277.30 Amyloidosis, unspecified — (Use additional code to identify any associated intellectual disabilities) ▽
277.31 Familial Mediterranean fever — (Use additional code to identify any associated intellectual disabilities)
277.39 Other amyloidosis — (Use additional code to identify any associated intellectual disabilities)
277.4 Disorders of bilirubin excretion — (Use additional code to identify any associated intellectual disabilities)
279.50 Graft-versus-host disease, unspecified — (Code first underlying cause: 996.80-996.89, 999.89)(Use additional code to identify any associated intellectual disabilities) (Use additional code to identify associated manifestations: 695.89, 704.09, 782.4, 787.91) ▽
279.51 Acute graft-versus-host disease — (Code first underlying cause: 996.80-996.89, 999.89)(Use additional code to identify any associated intellectual disabilities) (Use additional code to identify associated manifestations: 695.89, 704.09, 782.4, 787.91)
279.52 Chronic graft-versus-host disease — (Code first underlying cause: 996.80-996.89, 999.89)(Use additional code to identify any associated intellectual disabilities) (Use additional code to identify associated manifestations: 695.89, 704.09, 782.4, 787.91)
279.53 Acute on chronic graft-versus-host disease — (Code first underlying cause: 996.80-996.89, 999.89)(Use additional code to identify any associated intellectual disabilities) (Use additional code to identify associated manifestations: 695.89, 704.09, 782.4, 787.91)
287.30 Primary thrombocytopenia, unspecified ▽
287.31 Immune thrombocytopenic purpura
287.32 Evans' syndrome
287.33 Congenital and hereditary thrombocytopenic purpura
287.39 Other primary thrombocytopenia
289.84 Heparin-induced thrombocytopenia [HIT]
570 Acute and subacute necrosis of liver
571.0 Alcoholic fatty liver
571.1 Acute alcoholic hepatitis
571.2 Alcoholic cirrhosis of liver
571.3 Unspecified alcoholic liver damage ▽
571.41 Chronic persistent hepatitis
571.42 Autoimmune hepatitis
571.49 Other chronic hepatitis
571.5 Cirrhosis of liver without mention of alcohol — (Code first, if applicable, viral hepatitis (acute) (chronic): 070.0-070.9)
571.6 Biliary cirrhosis
571.8 Other chronic nonalcoholic liver disease
571.9 Unspecified chronic liver disease without mention of alcohol ▽
572.0 Abscess of liver
572.1 Portal pyemia
572.3 Portal hypertension — (Use additional code for any associated complications, such as: portal hypertensive gastropathy (537.89))
572.4 Hepatorenal syndrome
573.0 Chronic passive congestion of liver
573.1 Hepatitis in viral diseases classified elsewhere — (Code first underlying disease: 074.8, 075, 078.5) ☒
573.2 Hepatitis in other infectious diseases classified elsewhere — (Code first underlying disease: 084.9) ☒
573.3 Unspecified hepatitis — (Use additional E code to identify cause) ▽
573.4 Hepatic infarction
573.8 Other specified disorders of liver
573.9 Unspecified disorder of liver ▽
576.8 Other specified disorders of biliary tract
751.60 Unspecified congenital anomaly of gallbladder, bile ducts, and liver ▽
751.61 Congenital biliary atresia
751.62 Congenital cystic disease of liver
751.69 Other congenital anomaly of gallbladder, bile ducts, and liver
782.4 Jaundice, unspecified, not of newborn ▽
789.00 Abdominal pain, unspecified site ▽
789.01 Abdominal pain, right upper quadrant
789.02 Abdominal pain, left upper quadrant

789.03 Abdominal pain, right lower quadrant
789.04 Abdominal pain, left lower quadrant
789.05 Abdominal pain, periumbilic
789.06 Abdominal pain, epigastric
789.07 Abdominal pain, generalized
789.09 Abdominal pain, other specified site
789.1 Hepatomegaly
789.2 Splenomegaly
789.30 Abdominal or pelvic swelling, mass or lump, unspecified site
789.31 Abdominal or pelvic swelling, mass, or lump, right upper quadrant
789.36 Abdominal or pelvic swelling, mass, or lump, epigastric
789.39 Abdominal or pelvic swelling, mass, or lump, other specified site
794.8 Nonspecific abnormal results of liver function study
996.80 Complications of transplanted organ, unspecified site — (Use additional code to identify nature of complication: 078.5, 199.2, 238.77, 279.50-279.53)
996.82 Complications of transplanted liver — (Use additional code to identify nature of complication: 078.5, 199.2, 238.77, 279.50-279.53)
V42.7 Liver replaced by transplant

ICD-9-CM Procedural

50.12 Open biopsy of liver

47120-47130

47120 Hepatectomy, resection of liver; partial lobectomy
47122 trisegmentectomy
47125 total left lobectomy
47130 total right lobectomy

ICD-9-CM Diagnostic

155.0 Malignant neoplasm of liver, primary
155.2 Malignant neoplasm of liver, not specified as primary or secondary
197.7 Secondary malignant neoplasm of liver
209.29 Malignant carcinoid tumor of other sites — (Code first any associated multiple endocrine neoplasia syndrome: 258.01-258.03)(Use additional code to identify associated endocrine syndrome, as: carcinoid syndrome: 259.2)
209.30 Malignant poorly differentiated neuroendocrine carcinoma, any site — (Code first any associated multiple endocrine neoplasia syndrome: 258.01-258.03)(Use additional code to identify associated endocrine syndrome, as: carcinoid syndrome: 259.2)
209.69 Benign carcinoid tumor of other sites — (Code first any associated multiple endocrine neoplasia syndrome: 258.01-258.03)(Use additional code to identify associated endocrine syndrome, as: carcinoid syndrome: 259.2)
209.72 Secondary neuroendocrine tumor of liver
211.5 Benign neoplasm of liver and biliary passages
230.8 Carcinoma in situ of liver and biliary system
235.3 Neoplasm of uncertain behavior of liver and biliary passages
239.0 Neoplasm of unspecified nature of digestive system
277.30 Amyloidosis, unspecified — (Use additional code to identify any associated intellectual disabilities)
277.31 Familial Mediterranean fever — (Use additional code to identify any associated intellectual disabilities)
277.39 Other amyloidosis — (Use additional code to identify any associated intellectual disabilities)
277.4 Disorders of bilirubin excretion — (Use additional code to identify any associated intellectual disabilities)
571.5 Cirrhosis of liver without mention of alcohol — (Code first, if applicable, viral hepatitis (acute) (chronic): 070.0-070.9)
571.6 Biliary cirrhosis
571.8 Other chronic nonalcoholic liver disease
572.0 Abscess of liver
573.8 Other specified disorders of liver
576.8 Other specified disorders of biliary tract
751.60 Unspecified congenital anomaly of gallbladder, bile ducts, and liver
751.62 Congenital cystic disease of liver
751.69 Other congenital anomaly of gallbladder, bile ducts, and liver
782.4 Jaundice, unspecified, not of newborn
789.1 Hepatomegaly

ICD-9-CM Procedural

50.22 Partial hepatectomy
50.3 Lobectomy of liver

47133

47133 Donor hepatectomy (including cold preservation), from cadaver donor

ICD-9-CM Diagnostic

V59.6 Liver donor

ICD-9-CM Procedural

50.22 Partial hepatectomy
50.4 Total hepatectomy

47135-47136

47135 Liver allotransplantation; orthotopic, partial or whole, from cadaver or living donor, any age
47136 heterotopic, partial or whole, from cadaver or living donor, any age

ICD-9-CM Diagnostic

155.0 Malignant neoplasm of liver, primary
197.7 Secondary malignant neoplasm of liver
209.29 Malignant carcinoid tumor of other sites — (Code first any associated multiple endocrine neoplasia syndrome: 258.01-258.03)(Use additional code to identify associated endocrine syndrome, as: carcinoid syndrome: 259.2)
209.30 Malignant poorly differentiated neuroendocrine carcinoma, any site — (Code first any associated multiple endocrine neoplasia syndrome: 258.01-258.03)(Use additional code to identify associated endocrine syndrome, as: carcinoid syndrome: 259.2)
273.4 Alpha-1-antitrypsin deficiency — (Use additional code to identify any associated intellectual disabilities)
570 Acute and subacute necrosis of liver
571.42 Autoimmune hepatitis
571.49 Other chronic hepatitis
571.5 Cirrhosis of liver without mention of alcohol — (Code first, if applicable, viral hepatitis (acute) (chronic): 070.0-070.9)
571.6 Biliary cirrhosis
571.8 Other chronic nonalcoholic liver disease
571.9 Unspecified chronic liver disease without mention of alcohol
572.8 Other sequelae of chronic liver disease
573.5 Hepatopulmonary syndrome — (Code first underlying liver disease, such as: 571.2, 571.5))
573.8 Other specified disorders of liver
576.2 Obstruction of bile duct
576.8 Other specified disorders of biliary tract
751.61 Congenital biliary atresia
751.62 Congenital cystic disease of liver
751.69 Other congenital anomaly of gallbladder, bile ducts, and liver

ICD-9-CM Procedural

50.51 Auxiliary liver transplant
50.59 Other transplant of liver

47140-47142

47140 Donor hepatectomy (including cold preservation), from living donor; left lateral segment only (segments II and III)
47141 total left lobectomy (segments II, III and IV)
47142 total right lobectomy (segments V, VI, VII and VIII)

ICD-9-CM Diagnostic

V59.6 Liver donor

ICD-9-CM Procedural

The ICD-9-CM procedural code(s) would be the same as the actual procedure performed because these are in-addition-to codes.

47143-47145

47143 Backbench standard preparation of cadaver donor whole liver graft prior to allotransplantation, including cholecystectomy, if necessary, and dissection and removal of surrounding soft tissues to prepare the vena cava, portal vein, hepatic artery, and common bile duct for implantation; without trisegment or lobe split
47144 with trisegment split of whole liver graft into 2 partial liver grafts (ie, left lateral segment [segments II and III] and right trisegment [segments I and IV through VIII])
47145 with lobe split of whole liver graft into 2 partial liver grafts (ie, left lobe [segments II, III, and IV] and right lobe [segments I and V through VIII])

ICD-9-CM Diagnostic

155.0 Malignant neoplasm of liver, primary
197.7 Secondary malignant neoplasm of liver
209.72 Secondary neuroendocrine tumor of liver
273.4 Alpha-1-antitrypsin deficiency — (Use additional code to identify any associated intellectual disabilities)
570 Acute and subacute necrosis of liver
571.42 Autoimmune hepatitis
571.49 Other chronic hepatitis
571.5 Cirrhosis of liver without mention of alcohol — (Code first, if applicable, viral hepatitis (acute) (chronic): 070.0-070.9)
571.6 Biliary cirrhosis
571.8 Other chronic nonalcoholic liver disease
571.9 Unspecified chronic liver disease without mention of alcohol ▽
572.8 Other sequelae of chronic liver disease
573.8 Other specified disorders of liver
576.2 Obstruction of bile duct
576.8 Other specified disorders of biliary tract
751.61 Congenital biliary atresia
751.62 Congenital cystic disease of liver
751.69 Other congenital anomaly of gallbladder, bile ducts, and liver

ICD-9-CM Procedural

00.93 Transplant from cadaver
50.51 Auxiliary liver transplant
50.59 Other transplant of liver
50.99 Other operations on liver

47146-47147

47146 Backbench reconstruction of cadaver or living donor liver graft prior to allotransplantation; venous anastomosis, each
47147 arterial anastomosis, each

ICD-9-CM Diagnostic

155.0 Malignant neoplasm of liver, primary
197.7 Secondary malignant neoplasm of liver
209.72 Secondary neuroendocrine tumor of liver
273.4 Alpha-1-antitrypsin deficiency — (Use additional code to identify any associated intellectual disabilities)
570 Acute and subacute necrosis of liver
571.42 Autoimmune hepatitis
571.49 Other chronic hepatitis
571.5 Cirrhosis of liver without mention of alcohol — (Code first, if applicable, viral hepatitis (acute) (chronic): 070.0-070.9)
571.6 Biliary cirrhosis
571.8 Other chronic nonalcoholic liver disease
571.9 Unspecified chronic liver disease without mention of alcohol ▽
572.8 Other sequelae of chronic liver disease
573.8 Other specified disorders of liver
576.2 Obstruction of bile duct
576.8 Other specified disorders of biliary tract
751.61 Congenital biliary atresia
751.62 Congenital cystic disease of liver
751.69 Other congenital anomaly of gallbladder, bile ducts, and liver

ICD-9-CM Procedural

The ICD-9-CM procedural code(s) would be the same as the actual procedure performed because these are in-addition-to codes.

47300

47300 Marsupialization of cyst or abscess of liver

ICD-9-CM Diagnostic

571.6 Biliary cirrhosis
572.0 Abscess of liver
573.8 Other specified disorders of liver
751.62 Congenital cystic disease of liver

ICD-9-CM Procedural

50.21 Marsupialization of lesion of liver

47350-47362

47350 Management of liver hemorrhage; simple suture of liver wound or injury
47360 complex suture of liver wound or injury, with or without hepatic artery ligation
47361 exploration of hepatic wound, extensive debridement, coagulation and/or suture, with or without packing of liver
47362 re-exploration of hepatic wound for removal of packing

ICD-9-CM Diagnostic

864.02 Liver laceration, minor, without mention of open wound into cavity
864.03 Liver laceration, moderate, without mention of open wound into cavity
864.04 Liver laceration, major, without mention of open wound into cavity
864.05 Liver injury without mention of open wound into cavity, unspecified laceration ▽
864.09 Other liver injury without mention of open wound into cavity
864.12 Liver laceration, minor, with open wound into cavity
864.13 Liver laceration, moderate, with open wound into cavity
864.14 Liver laceration, major, with open wound into cavity
864.19 Other liver injury with open wound into cavity
998.11 Hemorrhage complicating a procedure
998.2 Accidental puncture or laceration during procedure
998.31 Disruption of internal operation (surgical) wound

ICD-9-CM Procedural

50.0 Hepatotomy
50.61 Closure of laceration of liver
50.69 Other repair of liver

47370-47371

47370 Laparoscopy, surgical, ablation of 1 or more liver tumor(s); radiofrequency
47371 cryosurgical

ICD-9-CM Diagnostic

155.0 Malignant neoplasm of liver, primary
155.2 Malignant neoplasm of liver, not specified as primary or secondary ▽
197.7 Secondary malignant neoplasm of liver
209.29 Malignant carcinoid tumor of other sites — (Code first any associated multiple endocrine neoplasia syndrome: 258.01-258.03)(Use additional code to identify associated endocrine syndrome, as: carcinoid syndrome: 259.2)
209.30 Malignant poorly differentiated neuroendocrine carcinoma, any site — (Code first any associated multiple endocrine neoplasia syndrome: 258.01-258.03)(Use additional code to identify associated endocrine syndrome, as: carcinoid syndrome: 259.2) ▽
209.69 Benign carcinoid tumor of other sites — (Code first any associated multiple endocrine neoplasia syndrome: 258.01-258.03)(Use additional code to identify associated endocrine syndrome, as: carcinoid syndrome: 259.2)
209.72 Secondary neuroendocrine tumor of liver
211.5 Benign neoplasm of liver and biliary passages
230.8 Carcinoma in situ of liver and biliary system
235.3 Neoplasm of uncertain behavior of liver and biliary passages
239.0 Neoplasm of unspecified nature of digestive system

ICD-9-CM Procedural

50.25 Laparoscopic ablation of liver lesion or tissue

47380-47382

47380 Ablation, open, of 1 or more liver tumor(s); radiofrequency
47381 cryosurgical
47382 Ablation, 1 or more liver tumor(s), percutaneous, radiofrequency

ICD-9-CM Diagnostic

155.0 Malignant neoplasm of liver, primary
155.2 Malignant neoplasm of liver, not specified as primary or secondary ▽
197.7 Secondary malignant neoplasm of liver
209.29 Malignant carcinoid tumor of other sites — (Code first any associated multiple endocrine neoplasia syndrome: 258.01-258.03)(Use additional code to identify associated endocrine syndrome, as: carcinoid syndrome: 259.2)
209.30 Malignant poorly differentiated neuroendocrine carcinoma, any site — (Code first any associated multiple endocrine neoplasia syndrome: 258.01-258.03)(Use additional code to identify associated endocrine syndrome, as: carcinoid syndrome: 259.2) ▽
209.69 Benign carcinoid tumor of other sites — (Code first any associated multiple endocrine neoplasia syndrome: 258.01-258.03)(Use additional code to identify associated endocrine syndrome, as: carcinoid syndrome: 259.2)
209.72 Secondary neuroendocrine tumor of liver
211.5 Benign neoplasm of liver and biliary passages
230.8 Carcinoma in situ of liver and biliary system
235.3 Neoplasm of uncertain behavior of liver and biliary passages
239.0 Neoplasm of unspecified nature of digestive system

ICD-9-CM Procedural

50.23 Open ablation of liver lesion or tissue
50.24 Percutaneous ablation of liver lesion or tissue

Biliary Tract

47400

47400 Hepaticotomy or hepaticostomy with exploration, drainage, or removal of calculus

ICD-9-CM Diagnostic

574.50 Calculus of bile duct without mention of cholecystitis or obstruction
576.8 Other specified disorders of biliary tract

ICD-9-CM Procedural

51.59 Incision of other bile duct

47420-47425

47420 Choledochotomy or choledochostomy with exploration, drainage, or removal of calculus, with or without cholecystotomy; without transduodenal sphincterotomy or sphincteroplasty
47425 with transduodenal sphincterotomy or sphincteroplasty

ICD-9-CM Diagnostic

156.0 Malignant neoplasm of gallbladder
156.9 Malignant neoplasm of biliary tract, part unspecified site ▽
574.00 Calculus of gallbladder with acute cholecystitis, without mention of obstruction
574.01 Calculus of gallbladder with acute cholecystitis and obstruction
574.10 Calculus of gallbladder with other cholecystitis, without mention of obstruction
574.11 Calculus of gallbladder with other cholecystitis and obstruction
574.20 Calculus of gallbladder without mention of cholecystitis or obstruction
574.21 Calculus of gallbladder without mention of cholecystitis, with obstruction
574.30 Calculus of bile duct with acute cholecystitis without mention of obstruction
574.31 Calculus of bile duct with acute cholecystitis and obstruction
574.40 Calculus of bile duct with other cholecystitis, without mention of obstruction
574.41 Calculus of bile duct with other cholecystitis and obstruction
574.50 Calculus of bile duct without mention of cholecystitis or obstruction
574.51 Calculus of bile duct without mention of cholecystitis, with obstruction
574.60 Calculus of gallbladder and bile duct with acute cholecystitis, without mention of obstruction
574.61 Calculus of gallbladder and bile duct with acute cholecystitis, with obstruction
574.70 Calculus of gallbladder and bile duct with other cholecystitis, without mention of obstruction
574.71 Calculus of gallbladder and bile duct with other cholecystitis, with obstruction
574.80 Calculus of gallbladder and bile duct with acute and chronic cholecystitis, without mention of obstruction
574.81 Calculus of gallbladder and bile duct with acute and chronic cholecystitis, with obstruction
574.90 Calculus of gallbladder and bile duct without cholecystitis, without mention of obstruction
574.91 Calculus of gallbladder and bile duct without cholecystitis, with obstruction
576.5 Spasm of sphincter of Oddi
576.8 Other specified disorders of biliary tract
577.0 Acute pancreatitis
577.1 Chronic pancreatitis

ICD-9-CM Procedural

51.41 Common duct exploration for removal of calculus
51.51 Exploration of common bile duct
51.82 Pancreatic sphincterotomy
51.83 Pancreatic sphincteroplasty

47460

47460 Transduodenal sphincterotomy or sphincteroplasty, with or without transduodenal extraction of calculus (separate procedure)

ICD-9-CM Diagnostic

574.40 Calculus of bile duct with other cholecystitis, without mention of obstruction
574.41 Calculus of bile duct with other cholecystitis and obstruction
574.50 Calculus of bile duct without mention of cholecystitis or obstruction
574.51 Calculus of bile duct without mention of cholecystitis, with obstruction
576.2 Obstruction of bile duct
576.5 Spasm of sphincter of Oddi
576.8 Other specified disorders of biliary tract
577.1 Chronic pancreatitis

751.69 Other congenital anomaly of gallbladder, bile ducts, and liver
782.4 Jaundice, unspecified, not of newborn ▽
789.01 Abdominal pain, right upper quadrant
789.09 Abdominal pain, other specified site

ICD-9-CM Procedural

51.82 Pancreatic sphincterotomy
51.83 Pancreatic sphincteroplasty

47480

47480 Cholecystotomy or cholecystostomy, open, with exploration, drainage, or removal of calculus (separate procedure)

ICD-9-CM Diagnostic

156.0 Malignant neoplasm of gallbladder
574.00 Calculus of gallbladder with acute cholecystitis, without mention of obstruction
574.01 Calculus of gallbladder with acute cholecystitis and obstruction
574.10 Calculus of gallbladder with other cholecystitis, without mention of obstruction
574.11 Calculus of gallbladder with other cholecystitis and obstruction
574.20 Calculus of gallbladder without mention of cholecystitis or obstruction
574.21 Calculus of gallbladder without mention of cholecystitis, with obstruction
575.0 Acute cholecystitis
575.10 Cholecystitis, unspecified ▽
575.11 Chronic cholecystitis
575.12 Acute and chronic cholecystitis
575.2 Obstruction of gallbladder
575.3 Hydrops of gallbladder
576.8 Other specified disorders of biliary tract

ICD-9-CM Procedural

51.03 Other cholecystostomy
51.04 Other cholecystotomy

47490

47490 Cholecystostomy, percutaneous, complete procedure, including imaging guidance, catheter placement, cholecystogram when performed, and radiological supervision and interpretation

ICD-9-CM Diagnostic

156.0 Malignant neoplasm of gallbladder
156.9 Malignant neoplasm of biliary tract, part unspecified site ▽
574.00 Calculus of gallbladder with acute cholecystitis, without mention of obstruction
574.20 Calculus of gallbladder without mention of cholecystitis or obstruction
575.0 Acute cholecystitis
575.11 Chronic cholecystitis
575.12 Acute and chronic cholecystitis
575.2 Obstruction of gallbladder
575.3 Hydrops of gallbladder
782.4 Jaundice, unspecified, not of newborn ▽

ICD-9-CM Procedural

51.01 Percutaneous aspiration of gallbladder
51.02 Trocar cholecystostomy

47500-47505

47500 Injection procedure for percutaneous transhepatic cholangiography
47505 Injection procedure for cholangiography through an existing catheter (eg, percutaneous transhepatic or T-tube)

ICD-9-CM Diagnostic

156.0 Malignant neoplasm of gallbladder
156.1 Malignant neoplasm of extrahepatic bile ducts
156.2 Malignant neoplasm of ampulla of Vater
156.8 Malignant neoplasm of other specified sites of gallbladder and extrahepatic bile ducts
156.9 Malignant neoplasm of biliary tract, part unspecified site ▽
157.9 Malignant neoplasm of pancreas, part unspecified ▽
195.2 Malignant neoplasm of abdomen
211.5 Benign neoplasm of liver and biliary passages
235.3 Neoplasm of uncertain behavior of liver and biliary passages
239.9 Neoplasm of unspecified nature, site unspecified ▽
573.4 Hepatic infarction
573.8 Other specified disorders of liver
574.10 Calculus of gallbladder with other cholecystitis, without mention of obstruction
574.11 Calculus of gallbladder with other cholecystitis and obstruction
574.20 Calculus of gallbladder without mention of cholecystitis or obstruction
574.21 Calculus of gallbladder without mention of cholecystitis, with obstruction
574.30 Calculus of bile duct with acute cholecystitis without mention of obstruction
574.31 Calculus of bile duct with acute cholecystitis and obstruction
574.40 Calculus of bile duct with other cholecystitis, without mention of obstruction
574.41 Calculus of bile duct with other cholecystitis and obstruction
574.50 Calculus of bile duct without mention of cholecystitis or obstruction
574.60 Calculus of gallbladder and bile duct with acute cholecystitis, without mention of obstruction
574.61 Calculus of gallbladder and bile duct with acute cholecystitis, with obstruction
574.70 Calculus of gallbladder and bile duct with other cholecystitis, without mention of obstruction
574.71 Calculus of gallbladder and bile duct with other cholecystitis, with obstruction
574.80 Calculus of gallbladder and bile duct with acute and chronic cholecystitis, without mention of obstruction
574.81 Calculus of gallbladder and bile duct with acute and chronic cholecystitis, with obstruction
574.90 Calculus of gallbladder and bile duct without cholecystitis, without mention of obstruction
574.91 Calculus of gallbladder and bile duct without cholecystitis, with obstruction
575.0 Acute cholecystitis
575.11 Chronic cholecystitis
575.12 Acute and chronic cholecystitis
575.2 Obstruction of gallbladder
575.3 Hydrops of gallbladder
575.4 Perforation of gallbladder
575.5 Fistula of gallbladder
575.6 Cholesterolosis of gallbladder
575.8 Other specified disorder of gallbladder
576.0 Postcholecystectomy syndrome
576.1 Cholangitis
576.2 Obstruction of bile duct
576.3 Perforation of bile duct
576.4 Fistula of bile duct
576.5 Spasm of sphincter of Oddi
576.8 Other specified disorders of biliary tract
751.69 Other congenital anomaly of gallbladder, bile ducts, and liver
782.4 Jaundice, unspecified, not of newborn ▽
V45.89 Other postprocedural status
V72.5 Radiological examination, not elsewhere classified — (Use additional code(s) to identify any special screening examination(s) performed: V73.0-V82.9)

ICD-9-CM Procedural

51.19 Other diagnostic procedures on biliary tract
87.51 Percutaneous hepatic cholangiogram
87.54 Other cholangiogram

47510-47511

47510 Introduction of percutaneous transhepatic catheter for biliary drainage
47511 Introduction of percutaneous transhepatic stent for internal and external biliary drainage

ICD-9-CM Diagnostic

155.0 Malignant neoplasm of liver, primary
155.1 Malignant neoplasm of intrahepatic bile ducts
155.2 Malignant neoplasm of liver, not specified as primary or secondary ▽
156.0 Malignant neoplasm of gallbladder
156.1 Malignant neoplasm of extrahepatic bile ducts
156.2 Malignant neoplasm of ampulla of Vater
156.8 Malignant neoplasm of other specified sites of gallbladder and extrahepatic bile ducts
156.9 Malignant neoplasm of biliary tract, part unspecified site ▽
211.5 Benign neoplasm of liver and biliary passages
571.42 Autoimmune hepatitis
572.0 Abscess of liver
572.1 Portal pyemia
572.2 Hepatic encephalopathy
572.3 Portal hypertension — (Use additional code for any associated complications, such as: portal hypertensive gastropathy (537.89))
572.4 Hepatorenal syndrome
573.1 Hepatitis in viral diseases classified elsewhere — (Code first underlying disease: 074.8, 075, 078.5) ☒
573.2 Hepatitis in other infectious diseases classified elsewhere — (Code first underlying disease: 084.9) ☒
573.4 Hepatic infarction
573.8 Other specified disorders of liver
574.00 Calculus of gallbladder with acute cholecystitis, without mention of obstruction
574.01 Calculus of gallbladder with acute cholecystitis and obstruction
574.10 Calculus of gallbladder with other cholecystitis, without mention of obstruction
574.11 Calculus of gallbladder with other cholecystitis and obstruction
574.20 Calculus of gallbladder without mention of cholecystitis or obstruction
574.21 Calculus of gallbladder without mention of cholecystitis, with obstruction
574.30 Calculus of bile duct with acute cholecystitis without mention of obstruction
574.31 Calculus of bile duct with acute cholecystitis and obstruction
574.40 Calculus of bile duct with other cholecystitis, without mention of obstruction
574.41 Calculus of bile duct with other cholecystitis and obstruction
574.50 Calculus of bile duct without mention of cholecystitis or obstruction
574.51 Calculus of bile duct without mention of cholecystitis, with obstruction
574.60 Calculus of gallbladder and bile duct with acute cholecystitis, without mention of obstruction
574.61 Calculus of gallbladder and bile duct with acute cholecystitis, with obstruction
574.70 Calculus of gallbladder and bile duct with other cholecystitis, without mention of obstruction
574.71 Calculus of gallbladder and bile duct with other cholecystitis, with obstruction
574.80 Calculus of gallbladder and bile duct with acute and chronic cholecystitis, without mention of obstruction
574.81 Calculus of gallbladder and bile duct with acute and chronic cholecystitis, with obstruction
574.90 Calculus of gallbladder and bile duct without cholecystitis, without mention of obstruction
574.91 Calculus of gallbladder and bile duct without cholecystitis, with obstruction
575.0 Acute cholecystitis
575.10 Cholecystitis, unspecified ▽
575.11 Chronic cholecystitis
575.12 Acute and chronic cholecystitis
575.2 Obstruction of gallbladder
575.3 Hydrops of gallbladder
575.4 Perforation of gallbladder
575.5 Fistula of gallbladder
575.6 Cholesterolosis of gallbladder
575.8 Other specified disorder of gallbladder
576.0 Postcholecystectomy syndrome
576.1 Cholangitis
576.2 Obstruction of bile duct
576.3 Perforation of bile duct
576.4 Fistula of bile duct
576.5 Spasm of sphincter of Oddi
576.8 Other specified disorders of biliary tract
782.4 Jaundice, unspecified, not of newborn ▽
868.02 Bile duct and gallbladder injury without mention of open wound into cavity
V58.82 Encounter for fitting and adjustment of non-vascular catheter NEC

ICD-9-CM Procedural

51.43 Insertion of choledochohepatic tube for decompression
51.98 Other percutaneous procedures on biliary tract
51.99 Other operations on biliary tract

47525-47530

47525 Change of percutaneous biliary drainage catheter
47530 Revision and/or reinsertion of transhepatic tube

ICD-9-CM Diagnostic

155.0 Malignant neoplasm of liver, primary
155.1 Malignant neoplasm of intrahepatic bile ducts
155.2 Malignant neoplasm of liver, not specified as primary or secondary ▽
156.0 Malignant neoplasm of gallbladder
156.1 Malignant neoplasm of extrahepatic bile ducts
156.2 Malignant neoplasm of ampulla of Vater
156.8 Malignant neoplasm of other specified sites of gallbladder and extrahepatic bile ducts
156.9 Malignant neoplasm of biliary tract, part unspecified site ▽
211.5 Benign neoplasm of liver and biliary passages
571.42 Autoimmune hepatitis
572.0 Abscess of liver
572.1 Portal pyemia
572.2 Hepatic encephalopathy
572.3 Portal hypertension — (Use additional code for any associated complications, such as: portal hypertensive gastropathy (537.89))
572.4 Hepatorenal syndrome
573.1 Hepatitis in viral diseases classified elsewhere — (Code first underlying disease: 074.8, 075, 078.5) ☒
573.2 Hepatitis in other infectious diseases classified elsewhere — (Code first underlying disease: 084.9) ☒
573.4 Hepatic infarction
573.8 Other specified disorders of liver
574.00 Calculus of gallbladder with acute cholecystitis, without mention of obstruction
574.01 Calculus of gallbladder with acute cholecystitis and obstruction
574.10 Calculus of gallbladder with other cholecystitis, without mention of obstruction
574.11 Calculus of gallbladder with other cholecystitis and obstruction
574.20 Calculus of gallbladder without mention of cholecystitis or obstruction
574.21 Calculus of gallbladder without mention of cholecystitis, with obstruction
574.30 Calculus of bile duct with acute cholecystitis without mention of obstruction
574.31 Calculus of bile duct with acute cholecystitis and obstruction
574.40 Calculus of bile duct with other cholecystitis, without mention of obstruction
574.41 Calculus of bile duct with other cholecystitis and obstruction
574.50 Calculus of bile duct without mention of cholecystitis or obstruction
574.51 Calculus of bile duct without mention of cholecystitis, with obstruction
574.60 Calculus of gallbladder and bile duct with acute cholecystitis, without mention of obstruction

574.61 Calculus of gallbladder and bile duct with acute cholecystitis, with obstruction
574.70 Calculus of gallbladder and bile duct with other cholecystitis, without mention of obstruction
574.71 Calculus of gallbladder and bile duct with other cholecystitis, with obstruction
574.80 Calculus of gallbladder and bile duct with acute and chronic cholecystitis, without mention of obstruction
574.81 Calculus of gallbladder and bile duct with acute and chronic cholecystitis, with obstruction
574.90 Calculus of gallbladder and bile duct without cholecystitis, without mention of obstruction
574.91 Calculus of gallbladder and bile duct without cholecystitis, with obstruction
575.0 Acute cholecystitis
575.10 Cholecystitis, unspecified
575.11 Chronic cholecystitis
575.12 Acute and chronic cholecystitis
575.2 Obstruction of gallbladder
575.3 Hydrops of gallbladder
575.4 Perforation of gallbladder
575.5 Fistula of gallbladder
575.6 Cholesterolosis of gallbladder
575.8 Other specified disorder of gallbladder
576.0 Postcholecystectomy syndrome
576.1 Cholangitis
576.2 Obstruction of bile duct
576.3 Perforation of bile duct
576.4 Fistula of bile duct
576.5 Spasm of sphincter of Oddi
576.8 Other specified disorders of biliary tract
782.4 Jaundice, unspecified, not of newborn
868.02 Bile duct and gallbladder injury without mention of open wound into cavity
V58.82 Encounter for fitting and adjustment of non-vascular catheter NEC

ICD-9-CM Procedural

97.05 Replacement of stent (tube) in biliary or pancreatic duct

HCPCS Level II Supplies & Services

C1729 Catheter, drainage

47552-47553

47552 Biliary endoscopy, percutaneous via T-tube or other tract; diagnostic, with collection of specimen(s) by brushing and/or washing, when performed (separate procedure)
47553 with biopsy, single or multiple

ICD-9-CM Diagnostic

156.0 Malignant neoplasm of gallbladder
156.1 Malignant neoplasm of extrahepatic bile ducts
156.8 Malignant neoplasm of other specified sites of gallbladder and extrahepatic bile ducts
156.9 Malignant neoplasm of biliary tract, part unspecified site
197.8 Secondary malignant neoplasm of other digestive organs and spleen
209.29 Malignant carcinoid tumor of other sites — (Code first any associated multiple endocrine neoplasia syndrome: 258.01-258.03)(Use additional code to identify associated endocrine syndrome, as: carcinoid syndrome: 259.2)
209.30 Malignant poorly differentiated neuroendocrine carcinoma, any site — (Code first any associated multiple endocrine neoplasia syndrome: 258.01-258.03)(Use additional code to identify associated endocrine syndrome, as: carcinoid syndrome: 259.2)
209.69 Benign carcinoid tumor of other sites — (Code first any associated multiple endocrine neoplasia syndrome: 258.01-258.03)(Use additional code to identify associated endocrine syndrome, as: carcinoid syndrome: 259.2)
211.8 Benign neoplasm of retroperitoneum and peritoneum
230.8 Carcinoma in situ of liver and biliary system
235.3 Neoplasm of uncertain behavior of liver and biliary passages
239.0 Neoplasm of unspecified nature of digestive system
575.0 Acute cholecystitis
576.8 Other specified disorders of biliary tract
782.4 Jaundice, unspecified, not of newborn

ICD-9-CM Procedural

51.14 Other closed (endoscopic) biopsy of biliary duct or sphincter of Oddi
51.98 Other percutaneous procedures on biliary tract

47554

47554 Biliary endoscopy, percutaneous via T-tube or other tract; with removal of calculus/calculi

ICD-9-CM Diagnostic

574.00 Calculus of gallbladder with acute cholecystitis, without mention of obstruction
574.01 Calculus of gallbladder with acute cholecystitis and obstruction
574.10 Calculus of gallbladder with other cholecystitis, without mention of obstruction
574.11 Calculus of gallbladder with other cholecystitis and obstruction
574.20 Calculus of gallbladder without mention of cholecystitis or obstruction
574.21 Calculus of gallbladder without mention of cholecystitis, with obstruction
574.30 Calculus of bile duct with acute cholecystitis without mention of obstruction
574.31 Calculus of bile duct with acute cholecystitis and obstruction
574.40 Calculus of bile duct with other cholecystitis, without mention of obstruction
574.41 Calculus of bile duct with other cholecystitis and obstruction
574.50 Calculus of bile duct without mention of cholecystitis or obstruction
574.51 Calculus of bile duct without mention of cholecystitis, with obstruction
574.90 Calculus of gallbladder and bile duct without cholecystitis, without mention of obstruction
574.91 Calculus of gallbladder and bile duct without cholecystitis, with obstruction

ICD-9-CM Procedural

51.96 Percutaneous extraction of common duct stones

47555-47556

47555 Biliary endoscopy, percutaneous via T-tube or other tract; with dilation of biliary duct stricture(s) without stent
47556 with dilation of biliary duct stricture(s) with stent

ICD-9-CM Diagnostic

156.1 Malignant neoplasm of extrahepatic bile ducts
156.2 Malignant neoplasm of ampulla of Vater
156.8 Malignant neoplasm of other specified sites of gallbladder and extrahepatic bile ducts
156.9 Malignant neoplasm of biliary tract, part unspecified site
209.29 Malignant carcinoid tumor of other sites — (Code first any associated multiple endocrine neoplasia syndrome: 258.01-258.03)(Use additional code to identify associated endocrine syndrome, as: carcinoid syndrome: 259.2)
209.30 Malignant poorly differentiated neuroendocrine carcinoma, any site — (Code first any associated multiple endocrine neoplasia syndrome: 258.01-258.03)(Use additional code to identify associated endocrine syndrome, as: carcinoid syndrome: 259.2)
209.69 Benign carcinoid tumor of other sites — (Code first any associated multiple endocrine neoplasia syndrome: 258.01-258.03)(Use additional code to identify associated endocrine syndrome, as: carcinoid syndrome: 259.2)
211.5 Benign neoplasm of liver and biliary passages
230.8 Carcinoma in situ of liver and biliary system
235.3 Neoplasm of uncertain behavior of liver and biliary passages
239.0 Neoplasm of unspecified nature of digestive system
574.50 Calculus of bile duct without mention of cholecystitis or obstruction
576.2 Obstruction of bile duct

ICD-9-CM Procedural

51.87 Endoscopic insertion of stent (tube) into bile duct
51.98 Other percutaneous procedures on biliary tract

47560-47561

47560 Laparoscopy, surgical; with guided transhepatic cholangiography, without biopsy
47561 with guided transhepatic cholangiography with biopsy

ICD-9-CM Diagnostic

156.0 Malignant neoplasm of gallbladder
156.1 Malignant neoplasm of extrahepatic bile ducts
156.2 Malignant neoplasm of ampulla of Vater
156.8 Malignant neoplasm of other specified sites of gallbladder and extrahepatic bile ducts
156.9 Malignant neoplasm of biliary tract, part unspecified site ▽
157.9 Malignant neoplasm of pancreas, part unspecified ▽
195.2 Malignant neoplasm of abdomen
211.5 Benign neoplasm of liver and biliary passages
235.3 Neoplasm of uncertain behavior of liver and biliary passages
239.9 Neoplasm of unspecified nature, site unspecified ▽
573.4 Hepatic infarction
573.8 Other specified disorders of liver
574.10 Calculus of gallbladder with other cholecystitis, without mention of obstruction
574.11 Calculus of gallbladder with other cholecystitis and obstruction
574.20 Calculus of gallbladder without mention of cholecystitis or obstruction
574.21 Calculus of gallbladder without mention of cholecystitis, with obstruction
574.30 Calculus of bile duct with acute cholecystitis without mention of obstruction
574.31 Calculus of bile duct with acute cholecystitis and obstruction
574.40 Calculus of bile duct with other cholecystitis, without mention of obstruction
574.41 Calculus of bile duct with other cholecystitis and obstruction
574.50 Calculus of bile duct without mention of cholecystitis or obstruction
574.60 Calculus of gallbladder and bile duct with acute cholecystitis, without mention of obstruction
574.61 Calculus of gallbladder and bile duct with acute cholecystitis, with obstruction
574.70 Calculus of gallbladder and bile duct with other cholecystitis, without mention of obstruction
574.71 Calculus of gallbladder and bile duct with other cholecystitis, with obstruction
574.80 Calculus of gallbladder and bile duct with acute and chronic cholecystitis, without mention of obstruction
574.81 Calculus of gallbladder and bile duct with acute and chronic cholecystitis, with obstruction
574.90 Calculus of gallbladder and bile duct without cholecystitis, without mention of obstruction
574.91 Calculus of gallbladder and bile duct without cholecystitis, with obstruction
575.0 Acute cholecystitis
575.11 Chronic cholecystitis
575.12 Acute and chronic cholecystitis
575.2 Obstruction of gallbladder
575.3 Hydrops of gallbladder
575.4 Perforation of gallbladder
575.5 Fistula of gallbladder
575.6 Cholesterolosis of gallbladder
575.8 Other specified disorder of gallbladder
576.0 Postcholecystectomy syndrome
576.1 Cholangitis
576.2 Obstruction of bile duct
576.3 Perforation of bile duct
576.4 Fistula of bile duct
576.5 Spasm of sphincter of Oddi
576.8 Other specified disorders of biliary tract
751.69 Other congenital anomaly of gallbladder, bile ducts, and liver
782.4 Jaundice, unspecified, not of newborn ▽
V45.89 Other postprocedural status
V72.5 Radiological examination, not elsewhere classified — (Use additional code(s) to identify any special screening examination(s) performed: V73.0-V82.9)

ICD-9-CM Procedural

50.14 Laparoscopic liver biopsy
51.14 Other closed (endoscopic) biopsy of biliary duct or sphincter of Oddi
87.53 Intraoperative cholangiogram

47562-47563

47562 Laparoscopy, surgical; cholecystectomy
47563 cholecystectomy with cholangiography

ICD-9-CM Diagnostic

156.0 Malignant neoplasm of gallbladder
156.8 Malignant neoplasm of other specified sites of gallbladder and extrahepatic bile ducts
197.8 Secondary malignant neoplasm of other digestive organs and spleen
209.29 Malignant carcinoid tumor of other sites — (Code first any associated multiple endocrine neoplasia syndrome: 258.01-258.03)(Use additional code to identify associated endocrine syndrome, as: carcinoid syndrome: 259.2)
209.30 Malignant poorly differentiated neuroendocrine carcinoma, any site — (Code first any associated multiple endocrine neoplasia syndrome: 258.01-258.03)(Use additional code to identify associated endocrine syndrome, as: carcinoid syndrome: 259.2) ▽
209.69 Benign carcinoid tumor of other sites — (Code first any associated multiple endocrine neoplasia syndrome: 258.01-258.03)(Use additional code to identify associated endocrine syndrome, as: carcinoid syndrome: 259.2)
211.5 Benign neoplasm of liver and biliary passages
230.8 Carcinoma in situ of liver and biliary system
235.3 Neoplasm of uncertain behavior of liver and biliary passages
239.0 Neoplasm of unspecified nature of digestive system
560.31 Gallstone ileus
571.5 Cirrhosis of liver without mention of alcohol — (Code first, if applicable, viral hepatitis (acute) (chronic): 070.0-070.9)
571.6 Biliary cirrhosis
574.00 Calculus of gallbladder with acute cholecystitis, without mention of obstruction
574.10 Calculus of gallbladder with other cholecystitis, without mention of obstruction
574.11 Calculus of gallbladder with other cholecystitis and obstruction
574.20 Calculus of gallbladder without mention of cholecystitis or obstruction
574.21 Calculus of gallbladder without mention of cholecystitis, with obstruction
574.30 Calculus of bile duct with acute cholecystitis without mention of obstruction
574.31 Calculus of bile duct with acute cholecystitis and obstruction
574.40 Calculus of bile duct with other cholecystitis, without mention of obstruction
574.41 Calculus of bile duct with other cholecystitis and obstruction
574.50 Calculus of bile duct without mention of cholecystitis or obstruction
574.51 Calculus of bile duct without mention of cholecystitis, with obstruction
574.60 Calculus of gallbladder and bile duct with acute cholecystitis, without mention of obstruction
574.61 Calculus of gallbladder and bile duct with acute cholecystitis, with obstruction
574.70 Calculus of gallbladder and bile duct with other cholecystitis, without mention of obstruction
574.71 Calculus of gallbladder and bile duct with other cholecystitis, with obstruction
574.80 Calculus of gallbladder and bile duct with acute and chronic cholecystitis, without mention of obstruction
574.81 Calculus of gallbladder and bile duct with acute and chronic cholecystitis, with obstruction
574.90 Calculus of gallbladder and bile duct without cholecystitis, without mention of obstruction
574.91 Calculus of gallbladder and bile duct without cholecystitis, with obstruction
575.0 Acute cholecystitis
575.11 Chronic cholecystitis
575.12 Acute and chronic cholecystitis
575.2 Obstruction of gallbladder
575.3 Hydrops of gallbladder
575.5 Fistula of gallbladder

575.6 Cholesterolosis of gallbladder
575.8 Other specified disorder of gallbladder
576.1 Cholangitis
576.8 Other specified disorders of biliary tract
782.4 Jaundice, unspecified, not of newborn ▽
789.01 Abdominal pain, right upper quadrant
789.06 Abdominal pain, epigastric
789.07 Abdominal pain, generalized
789.09 Abdominal pain, other specified site
789.30 Abdominal or pelvic swelling, mass or lump, unspecified site ▽
789.31 Abdominal or pelvic swelling, mass, or lump, right upper quadrant
789.36 Abdominal or pelvic swelling, mass, or lump, epigastric
789.37 Abdominal or pelvic swelling, mass, or lump, generalized
789.39 Abdominal or pelvic swelling, mass, or lump, other specified site
793.3 Nonspecific (abnormal) findings on radiological and other examination of biliary tract
868.02 Bile duct and gallbladder injury without mention of open wound into cavity

ICD-9-CM Procedural

51.23 Laparoscopic cholecystectomy
51.24 Laparoscopic partial cholecystectomy
87.53 Intraoperative cholangiogram

47564

47564 Laparoscopy, surgical; cholecystectomy with exploration of common duct

ICD-9-CM Diagnostic

156.0 Malignant neoplasm of gallbladder
156.8 Malignant neoplasm of other specified sites of gallbladder and extrahepatic bile ducts
197.8 Secondary malignant neoplasm of other digestive organs and spleen
209.29 Malignant carcinoid tumor of other sites — (Code first any associated multiple endocrine neoplasia syndrome: 258.01-258.03)(Use additional code to identify associated endocrine syndrome, as: carcinoid syndrome: 259.2)
209.30 Malignant poorly differentiated neuroendocrine carcinoma, any site — (Code first any associated multiple endocrine neoplasia syndrome: 258.01-258.03)(Use additional code to identify associated endocrine syndrome, as: carcinoid syndrome: 259.2) ▽
209.69 Benign carcinoid tumor of other sites — (Code first any associated multiple endocrine neoplasia syndrome: 258.01-258.03)(Use additional code to identify associated endocrine syndrome, as: carcinoid syndrome: 259.2)
211.5 Benign neoplasm of liver and biliary passages
230.8 Carcinoma in situ of liver and biliary system
235.3 Neoplasm of uncertain behavior of liver and biliary passages
239.0 Neoplasm of unspecified nature of digestive system
560.31 Gallstone ileus
571.5 Cirrhosis of liver without mention of alcohol — (Code first, if applicable, viral hepatitis (acute) (chronic): 070.0-070.9)
571.6 Biliary cirrhosis
574.00 Calculus of gallbladder with acute cholecystitis, without mention of obstruction
574.10 Calculus of gallbladder with other cholecystitis, without mention of obstruction
574.11 Calculus of gallbladder with other cholecystitis and obstruction
574.20 Calculus of gallbladder without mention of cholecystitis or obstruction
574.50 Calculus of bile duct without mention of cholecystitis or obstruction
575.0 Acute cholecystitis
575.2 Obstruction of gallbladder
575.3 Hydrops of gallbladder
575.4 Perforation of gallbladder
575.5 Fistula of gallbladder
575.6 Cholesterolosis of gallbladder
575.8 Other specified disorder of gallbladder
576.1 Cholangitis
576.2 Obstruction of bile duct
576.8 Other specified disorders of biliary tract
782.4 Jaundice, unspecified, not of newborn ▽
789.01 Abdominal pain, right upper quadrant
789.06 Abdominal pain, epigastric
789.07 Abdominal pain, generalized
789.09 Abdominal pain, other specified site
789.30 Abdominal or pelvic swelling, mass or lump, unspecified site ▽
789.31 Abdominal or pelvic swelling, mass, or lump, right upper quadrant
789.36 Abdominal or pelvic swelling, mass, or lump, epigastric
789.37 Abdominal or pelvic swelling, mass, or lump, generalized
789.39 Abdominal or pelvic swelling, mass, or lump, other specified site
793.3 Nonspecific (abnormal) findings on radiological and other examination of biliary tract
868.02 Bile duct and gallbladder injury without mention of open wound into cavity

ICD-9-CM Procedural

51.23 Laparoscopic cholecystectomy
51.41 Common duct exploration for removal of calculus
51.51 Exploration of common bile duct

47570

47570 Laparoscopy, surgical; cholecystoenterostomy

ICD-9-CM Diagnostic

155.0 Malignant neoplasm of liver, primary
155.1 Malignant neoplasm of intrahepatic bile ducts
156.0 Malignant neoplasm of gallbladder
156.9 Malignant neoplasm of biliary tract, part unspecified site ▽
157.0 Malignant neoplasm of head of pancreas
157.1 Malignant neoplasm of body of pancreas
211.5 Benign neoplasm of liver and biliary passages
571.5 Cirrhosis of liver without mention of alcohol — (Code first, if applicable, viral hepatitis (acute) (chronic): 070.0-070.9)
571.6 Biliary cirrhosis
574.00 Calculus of gallbladder with acute cholecystitis, without mention of obstruction
574.01 Calculus of gallbladder with acute cholecystitis and obstruction
574.10 Calculus of gallbladder with other cholecystitis, without mention of obstruction
574.11 Calculus of gallbladder with other cholecystitis and obstruction
574.20 Calculus of gallbladder without mention of cholecystitis or obstruction
574.21 Calculus of gallbladder without mention of cholecystitis, with obstruction
574.50 Calculus of bile duct without mention of cholecystitis or obstruction
575.2 Obstruction of gallbladder
575.8 Other specified disorder of gallbladder
576.1 Cholangitis
782.4 Jaundice, unspecified, not of newborn ▽

ICD-9-CM Procedural

51.32 Anastomosis of gallbladder to intestine

47600-47605

47600 Cholecystectomy;
47605 with cholangiography

ICD-9-CM Diagnostic

156.0 Malignant neoplasm of gallbladder
156.9 Malignant neoplasm of biliary tract, part unspecified site ▽
197.8 Secondary malignant neoplasm of other digestive organs and spleen
209.29 Malignant carcinoid tumor of other sites — (Code first any associated multiple endocrine neoplasia syndrome: 258.01-258.03)(Use additional code to identify associated endocrine syndrome, as: carcinoid syndrome: 259.2)
209.30 Malignant poorly differentiated neuroendocrine carcinoma, any site — (Code first any associated multiple endocrine neoplasia syndrome: 258.01-258.03)(Use additional code to identify associated endocrine syndrome, as: carcinoid syndrome: 259.2) ▽

209.69	Benign carcinoid tumor of other sites — (Code first any associated multiple endocrine neoplasia syndrome: 258.01-258.03)(Use additional code to identify associated endocrine syndrome, as: carcinoid syndrome: 259.2)
211.5	Benign neoplasm of liver and biliary passages
230.8	Carcinoma in situ of liver and biliary system
235.3	Neoplasm of uncertain behavior of liver and biliary passages
239.0	Neoplasm of unspecified nature of digestive system
560.31	Gallstone ileus
571.5	Cirrhosis of liver without mention of alcohol — (Code first, if applicable, viral hepatitis (acute) (chronic): 070.0-070.9)
571.6	Biliary cirrhosis
574.00	Calculus of gallbladder with acute cholecystitis, without mention of obstruction
574.01	Calculus of gallbladder with acute cholecystitis and obstruction
574.10	Calculus of gallbladder with other cholecystitis, without mention of obstruction
574.11	Calculus of gallbladder with other cholecystitis and obstruction
574.20	Calculus of gallbladder without mention of cholecystitis or obstruction
574.21	Calculus of gallbladder without mention of cholecystitis, with obstruction
574.30	Calculus of bile duct with acute cholecystitis without mention of obstruction
574.31	Calculus of bile duct with acute cholecystitis and obstruction
574.40	Calculus of bile duct with other cholecystitis, without mention of obstruction
574.41	Calculus of bile duct with other cholecystitis and obstruction
574.50	Calculus of bile duct without mention of cholecystitis or obstruction
574.51	Calculus of bile duct without mention of cholecystitis, with obstruction
574.60	Calculus of gallbladder and bile duct with acute cholecystitis, without mention of obstruction
574.61	Calculus of gallbladder and bile duct with acute cholecystitis, with obstruction
574.70	Calculus of gallbladder and bile duct with other cholecystitis, without mention of obstruction
574.71	Calculus of gallbladder and bile duct with other cholecystitis, with obstruction
574.80	Calculus of gallbladder and bile duct with acute and chronic cholecystitis, without mention of obstruction
574.81	Calculus of gallbladder and bile duct with acute and chronic cholecystitis, with obstruction
574.90	Calculus of gallbladder and bile duct without cholecystitis, without mention of obstruction
574.91	Calculus of gallbladder and bile duct without cholecystitis, with obstruction
575.0	Acute cholecystitis
575.11	Chronic cholecystitis
575.12	Acute and chronic cholecystitis
575.2	Obstruction of gallbladder
575.3	Hydrops of gallbladder
575.4	Perforation of gallbladder
575.5	Fistula of gallbladder
575.6	Cholesterolosis of gallbladder
575.8	Other specified disorder of gallbladder
576.1	Cholangitis
576.8	Other specified disorders of biliary tract
782.4	Jaundice, unspecified, not of newborn ▽
789.01	Abdominal pain, right upper quadrant
789.09	Abdominal pain, other specified site
789.31	Abdominal or pelvic swelling, mass, or lump, right upper quadrant
789.36	Abdominal or pelvic swelling, mass, or lump, epigastric
789.37	Abdominal or pelvic swelling, mass, or lump, generalized
789.39	Abdominal or pelvic swelling, mass, or lump, other specified site
793.3	Nonspecific (abnormal) findings on radiological and other examination of biliary tract
868.02	Bile duct and gallbladder injury without mention of open wound into cavity
V64.41	Laparoscopic surgical procedure converted to open procedure

ICD-9-CM Procedural

51.21	Other partial cholecystectomy
51.22	Cholecystectomy
87.53	Intraoperative cholangiogram

47610-47620

47610 Cholecystectomy with exploration of common duct;

47612 with choledochoenterostomy

47620 with transduodenal sphincterotomy or sphincteroplasty, with or without cholangiography

ICD-9-CM Diagnostic

156.0	Malignant neoplasm of gallbladder
156.9	Malignant neoplasm of biliary tract, part unspecified site ▽
560.31	Gallstone ileus
574.00	Calculus of gallbladder with acute cholecystitis, without mention of obstruction
574.01	Calculus of gallbladder with acute cholecystitis and obstruction
574.10	Calculus of gallbladder with other cholecystitis, without mention of obstruction
574.11	Calculus of gallbladder with other cholecystitis and obstruction
574.20	Calculus of gallbladder without mention of cholecystitis or obstruction
574.21	Calculus of gallbladder without mention of cholecystitis, with obstruction
574.30	Calculus of bile duct with acute cholecystitis without mention of obstruction
574.31	Calculus of bile duct with acute cholecystitis and obstruction
574.40	Calculus of bile duct with other cholecystitis, without mention of obstruction
574.41	Calculus of bile duct with other cholecystitis and obstruction
574.50	Calculus of bile duct without mention of cholecystitis or obstruction
574.51	Calculus of bile duct without mention of cholecystitis, with obstruction
575.0	Acute cholecystitis
575.10	Cholecystitis, unspecified ▽
575.11	Chronic cholecystitis
575.12	Acute and chronic cholecystitis
575.2	Obstruction of gallbladder
575.9	Unspecified disorder of gallbladder ▽
576.8	Other specified disorders of biliary tract
782.4	Jaundice, unspecified, not of newborn ▽
789.00	Abdominal pain, unspecified site ▽
789.01	Abdominal pain, right upper quadrant
789.06	Abdominal pain, epigastric
789.07	Abdominal pain, generalized
793.3	Nonspecific (abnormal) findings on radiological and other examination of biliary tract
V64.41	Laparoscopic surgical procedure converted to open procedure

ICD-9-CM Procedural

51.22	Cholecystectomy
51.36	Choledochoenterostomy
51.41	Common duct exploration for removal of calculus
51.51	Exploration of common bile duct
51.82	Pancreatic sphincterotomy
51.83	Pancreatic sphincteroplasty
87.53	Intraoperative cholangiogram

47630

47630 Biliary duct stone extraction, percutaneous via T-tube tract, basket, or snare (eg, Burhenne technique)

ICD-9-CM Diagnostic

574.50	Calculus of bile duct without mention of cholecystitis or obstruction
574.51	Calculus of bile duct without mention of cholecystitis, with obstruction
574.90	Calculus of gallbladder and bile duct without cholecystitis, without mention of obstruction
574.91	Calculus of gallbladder and bile duct without cholecystitis, with obstruction
782.4	Jaundice, unspecified, not of newborn ▽

ICD-9-CM Procedural

51.98 Other percutaneous procedures on biliary tract

47700

47700 Exploration for congenital atresia of bile ducts, without repair, with or without liver biopsy, with or without cholangiography

ICD-9-CM Diagnostic

751.61 Congenital biliary atresia

ICD-9-CM Procedural

50.12 Open biopsy of liver
51.42 Common duct exploration for relief of other obstruction
87.53 Intraoperative cholangiogram

47701

47701 Portoenterostomy (eg, Kasai procedure)

ICD-9-CM Diagnostic

156.1 Malignant neoplasm of extrahepatic bile ducts
576.2 Obstruction of bile duct
751.61 Congenital biliary atresia

ICD-9-CM Procedural

51.37 Anastomosis of hepatic duct to gastrointestinal tract

47711-47712

47711 Excision of bile duct tumor, with or without primary repair of bile duct; extrahepatic
47712 intrahepatic

ICD-9-CM Diagnostic

155.1 Malignant neoplasm of intrahepatic bile ducts
156.1 Malignant neoplasm of extrahepatic bile ducts
156.9 Malignant neoplasm of biliary tract, part unspecified site ▽
197.8 Secondary malignant neoplasm of other digestive organs and spleen
209.29 Malignant carcinoid tumor of other sites — (Code first any associated multiple endocrine neoplasia syndrome: 258.01-258.03)(Use additional code to identify associated endocrine syndrome, as: carcinoid syndrome: 259.2)
209.30 Malignant poorly differentiated neuroendocrine carcinoma, any site — (Code first any associated multiple endocrine neoplasia syndrome: 258.01-258.03)(Use additional code to identify associated endocrine syndrome, as: carcinoid syndrome: 259.2) ▽
209.69 Benign carcinoid tumor of other sites — (Code first any associated multiple endocrine neoplasia syndrome: 258.01-258.03)(Use additional code to identify associated endocrine syndrome, as: carcinoid syndrome: 259.2)
211.5 Benign neoplasm of liver and biliary passages
230.8 Carcinoma in situ of liver and biliary system
235.3 Neoplasm of uncertain behavior of liver and biliary passages
239.0 Neoplasm of unspecified nature of digestive system

ICD-9-CM Procedural

51.69 Excision of other bile duct

47715

47715 Excision of choledochal cyst

ICD-9-CM Diagnostic

576.8 Other specified disorders of biliary tract
751.62 Congenital cystic disease of liver
751.69 Other congenital anomaly of gallbladder, bile ducts, and liver

ICD-9-CM Procedural

51.63 Other excision of common duct

47720-47741

47720 Cholecystoenterostomy; direct
47721 with gastroenterostomy
47740 Roux-en-Y
47741 Roux-en-Y with gastroenterostomy

ICD-9-CM Diagnostic

156.0 Malignant neoplasm of gallbladder
156.9 Malignant neoplasm of biliary tract, part unspecified site ▽
157.0 Malignant neoplasm of head of pancreas
157.1 Malignant neoplasm of body of pancreas
211.5 Benign neoplasm of liver and biliary passages
574.20 Calculus of gallbladder without mention of cholecystitis or obstruction
575.2 Obstruction of gallbladder
782.4 Jaundice, unspecified, not of newborn ▽
V64.41 Laparoscopic surgical procedure converted to open procedure

ICD-9-CM Procedural

44.39 Other gastroenterostomy without gastrectomy
51.32 Anastomosis of gallbladder to intestine
51.36 Choledochoenterostomy

47760-47765

47760 Anastomosis, of extrahepatic biliary ducts and gastrointestinal tract
47765 Anastomosis, of intrahepatic ducts and gastrointestinal tract

ICD-9-CM Diagnostic

156.9 Malignant neoplasm of biliary tract, part unspecified site ▽
211.5 Benign neoplasm of liver and biliary passages
576.2 Obstruction of bile duct
576.8 Other specified disorders of biliary tract

ICD-9-CM Procedural

51.37 Anastomosis of hepatic duct to gastrointestinal tract
51.39 Other bile duct anastomosis

47780-47785

47780 Anastomosis, Roux-en-Y, of extrahepatic biliary ducts and gastrointestinal tract
47785 Anastomosis, Roux-en-Y, of intrahepatic biliary ducts and gastrointestinal tract

ICD-9-CM Diagnostic

156.9 Malignant neoplasm of biliary tract, part unspecified site ▽
211.5 Benign neoplasm of liver and biliary passages
576.2 Obstruction of bile duct
576.8 Other specified disorders of biliary tract

ICD-9-CM Procedural

51.36 Choledochoenterostomy
51.37 Anastomosis of hepatic duct to gastrointestinal tract
51.39 Other bile duct anastomosis

47800

47800 Reconstruction, plastic, of extrahepatic biliary ducts with end-to-end anastomosis

ICD-9-CM Diagnostic

156.9 Malignant neoplasm of biliary tract, part unspecified site ▽
157.0 Malignant neoplasm of head of pancreas
157.1 Malignant neoplasm of body of pancreas
211.5 Benign neoplasm of liver and biliary passages
576.2 Obstruction of bile duct
576.8 Other specified disorders of biliary tract

ICD-9-CM Procedural

51.63 Other excision of common duct
51.69 Excision of other bile duct

47801

47801 Placement of choledochal stent

ICD-9-CM Diagnostic

156.9 Malignant neoplasm of biliary tract, part unspecified site ▽
209.29 Malignant carcinoid tumor of other sites — (Code first any associated multiple endocrine neoplasia syndrome: 258.01-258.03)(Use additional code to identify associated endocrine syndrome, as: carcinoid syndrome: 259.2)
209.30 Malignant poorly differentiated neuroendocrine carcinoma, any site — (Code first any associated multiple endocrine neoplasia syndrome: 258.01-258.03)(Use additional code to identify associated endocrine syndrome, as: carcinoid syndrome: 259.2) ▽
209.69 Benign carcinoid tumor of other sites — (Code first any associated multiple endocrine neoplasia syndrome: 258.01-258.03)(Use additional code to identify associated endocrine syndrome, as: carcinoid syndrome: 259.2)
211.5 Benign neoplasm of liver and biliary passages
576.2 Obstruction of bile duct
576.8 Other specified disorders of biliary tract
576.9 Unspecified disorder of biliary tract ▽

ICD-9-CM Procedural

51.87 Endoscopic insertion of stent (tube) into bile duct
97.05 Replacement of stent (tube) in biliary or pancreatic duct

47802

47802 U-tube hepaticoenterostomy

ICD-9-CM Diagnostic

155.0 Malignant neoplasm of liver, primary
197.7 Secondary malignant neoplasm of liver
209.29 Malignant carcinoid tumor of other sites — (Code first any associated multiple endocrine neoplasia syndrome: 258.01-258.03)(Use additional code to identify associated endocrine syndrome, as: carcinoid syndrome: 259.2)
209.30 Malignant poorly differentiated neuroendocrine carcinoma, any site — (Code first any associated multiple endocrine neoplasia syndrome: 258.01-258.03)(Use additional code to identify associated endocrine syndrome, as: carcinoid syndrome: 259.2) ▽
571.5 Cirrhosis of liver without mention of alcohol — (Code first, if applicable, viral hepatitis (acute) (chronic): 070.0-070.9)
573.8 Other specified disorders of liver

ICD-9-CM Procedural

50.99 Other operations on liver
51.43 Insertion of choledochohepatic tube for decompression

47900

47900 Suture of extrahepatic biliary duct for pre-existing injury (separate procedure)

ICD-9-CM Diagnostic

868.02 Bile duct and gallbladder injury without mention of open wound into cavity
868.12 Bile duct and gallbladder injury, with open wound into cavity

ICD-9-CM Procedural

51.72 Choledochoplasty
51.79 Repair of other bile ducts

Pancreas

48000-48001

48000 Placement of drains, peripancreatic, for acute pancreatitis;
48001 with cholecystostomy, gastrostomy, and jejunostomy

ICD-9-CM Diagnostic

157.0 Malignant neoplasm of head of pancreas
157.1 Malignant neoplasm of body of pancreas
157.2 Malignant neoplasm of tail of pancreas
157.3 Malignant neoplasm of pancreatic duct
157.4 Malignant neoplasm of islets of Langerhans — (Use additional code to identify any functional activity)
157.8 Malignant neoplasm of other specified sites of pancreas
157.9 Malignant neoplasm of pancreas, part unspecified ▽
197.8 Secondary malignant neoplasm of other digestive organs and spleen
209.29 Malignant carcinoid tumor of other sites — (Code first any associated multiple endocrine neoplasia syndrome: 258.01-258.03)(Use additional code to identify associated endocrine syndrome, as: carcinoid syndrome: 259.2)
209.30 Malignant poorly differentiated neuroendocrine carcinoma, any site — (Code first any associated multiple endocrine neoplasia syndrome: 258.01-258.03)(Use additional code to identify associated endocrine syndrome, as: carcinoid syndrome: 259.2) ▽
209.69 Benign carcinoid tumor of other sites — (Code first any associated multiple endocrine neoplasia syndrome: 258.01-258.03)(Use additional code to identify associated endocrine syndrome, as: carcinoid syndrome: 259.2)
211.6 Benign neoplasm of pancreas, except islets of Langerhans
211.7 Benign neoplasm of islets of Langerhans — (Use additional code to identify any functional activity)
230.9 Carcinoma in situ of other and unspecified digestive organs ▽
235.5 Neoplasm of uncertain behavior of other and unspecified digestive organs ▽
239.0 Neoplasm of unspecified nature of digestive system
574.10 Calculus of gallbladder with other cholecystitis, without mention of obstruction
574.30 Calculus of bile duct with acute cholecystitis without mention of obstruction
574.40 Calculus of bile duct with other cholecystitis, without mention of obstruction
575.0 Acute cholecystitis
577.0 Acute pancreatitis
577.2 Cyst and pseudocyst of pancreas
577.8 Other specified disease of pancreas
863.81 Pancreas head injury without mention of open wound into cavity
863.82 Pancreas body injury without mention of open wound into cavity
863.84 Pancreas injury, multiple and unspecified sites, without mention of open wound into cavity
863.94 Pancreas injury, multiple and unspecified sites, with open wound into cavity
V64.41 Laparoscopic surgical procedure converted to open procedure

ICD-9-CM Procedural

43.19 Other gastrostomy
46.39 Other enterostomy
51.03 Other cholecystostomy
52.99 Other operations on pancreas

48020

48020 Removal of pancreatic calculus

ICD-9-CM Diagnostic

577.8 Other specified disease of pancreas

ICD-9-CM Procedural

52.09 Other pancreatotomy

48100-48102

48100 Biopsy of pancreas, open (eg, fine needle aspiration, needle core biopsy, wedge biopsy)
48102 Biopsy of pancreas, percutaneous needle

ICD-9-CM Diagnostic

157.0 Malignant neoplasm of head of pancreas
157.1 Malignant neoplasm of body of pancreas
157.2 Malignant neoplasm of tail of pancreas
157.3 Malignant neoplasm of pancreatic duct
157.4 Malignant neoplasm of islets of Langerhans — (Use additional code to identify any functional activity)
157.8 Malignant neoplasm of other specified sites of pancreas
157.9 Malignant neoplasm of pancreas, part unspecified ▽
197.7 Secondary malignant neoplasm of liver
197.8 Secondary malignant neoplasm of other digestive organs and spleen
209.29 Malignant carcinoid tumor of other sites — (Code first any associated multiple endocrine neoplasia syndrome: 258.01-258.03)(Use additional code to identify associated endocrine syndrome, as: carcinoid syndrome: 259.2)
209.30 Malignant poorly differentiated neuroendocrine carcinoma, any site — (Code first any associated multiple endocrine neoplasia syndrome: 258.01-258.03)(Use additional code to identify associated endocrine syndrome, as: carcinoid syndrome: 259.2) ▽
209.69 Benign carcinoid tumor of other sites — (Code first any associated multiple endocrine neoplasia syndrome: 258.01-258.03)(Use additional code to identify associated endocrine syndrome, as: carcinoid syndrome: 259.2)
211.6 Benign neoplasm of pancreas, except islets of Langerhans
211.7 Benign neoplasm of islets of Langerhans — (Use additional code to identify any functional activity)
577.0 Acute pancreatitis
577.1 Chronic pancreatitis
577.2 Cyst and pseudocyst of pancreas
577.8 Other specified disease of pancreas
579.4 Pancreatic steatorrhea

ICD-9-CM Procedural

52.11 Closed (aspiration) (needle) (percutaneous) biopsy of pancreas
52.12 Open biopsy of pancreas

48105

48105 Resection or debridement of pancreas and peripancreatic tissue for acute necrotizing pancreatitis

ICD-9-CM Diagnostic

577.0 Acute pancreatitis
577.1 Chronic pancreatitis
577.2 Cyst and pseudocyst of pancreas
577.8 Other specified disease of pancreas
998.51 Infected postoperative seroma — (Use additional code to identify organism)
998.59 Other postoperative infection — (Use additional code to identify infection)
V42.83 Pancreas replaced by transplant

ICD-9-CM Procedural

52.22 Other excision or destruction of lesion or tissue of pancreas or pancreatic duct

48120

48120 Excision of lesion of pancreas (eg, cyst, adenoma)

ICD-9-CM Diagnostic

157.0 Malignant neoplasm of head of pancreas
157.1 Malignant neoplasm of body of pancreas
157.2 Malignant neoplasm of tail of pancreas
157.3 Malignant neoplasm of pancreatic duct
157.4 Malignant neoplasm of islets of Langerhans — (Use additional code to identify any functional activity)
157.8 Malignant neoplasm of other specified sites of pancreas
157.9 Malignant neoplasm of pancreas, part unspecified ▽
197.8 Secondary malignant neoplasm of other digestive organs and spleen
209.29 Malignant carcinoid tumor of other sites — (Code first any associated multiple endocrine neoplasia syndrome: 258.01-258.03)(Use additional code to identify associated endocrine syndrome, as: carcinoid syndrome: 259.2)
209.30 Malignant poorly differentiated neuroendocrine carcinoma, any site — (Code first any associated multiple endocrine neoplasia syndrome: 258.01-258.03)(Use additional code to identify associated endocrine syndrome, as: carcinoid syndrome: 259.2) ▽
209.69 Benign carcinoid tumor of other sites — (Code first any associated multiple endocrine neoplasia syndrome: 258.01-258.03)(Use additional code to identify associated endocrine syndrome, as: carcinoid syndrome: 259.2)
211.6 Benign neoplasm of pancreas, except islets of Langerhans
211.7 Benign neoplasm of islets of Langerhans — (Use additional code to identify any functional activity)
230.9 Carcinoma in situ of other and unspecified digestive organs ▽
577.2 Cyst and pseudocyst of pancreas
V42.83 Pancreas replaced by transplant

ICD-9-CM Procedural

52.22 Other excision or destruction of lesion or tissue of pancreas or pancreatic duct

48140-48145

48140 Pancreatectomy, distal subtotal, with or without splenectomy; without pancreaticojejunostomy
48145 with pancreaticojejunostomy

ICD-9-CM Diagnostic

157.0 Malignant neoplasm of head of pancreas
157.1 Malignant neoplasm of body of pancreas
157.2 Malignant neoplasm of tail of pancreas
157.3 Malignant neoplasm of pancreatic duct
157.4 Malignant neoplasm of islets of Langerhans — (Use additional code to identify any functional activity)
157.8 Malignant neoplasm of other specified sites of pancreas
157.9 Malignant neoplasm of pancreas, part unspecified ▽
197.8 Secondary malignant neoplasm of other digestive organs and spleen
209.29 Malignant carcinoid tumor of other sites — (Code first any associated multiple endocrine neoplasia syndrome: 258.01-258.03)(Use additional code to identify associated endocrine syndrome, as: carcinoid syndrome: 259.2)
209.30 Malignant poorly differentiated neuroendocrine carcinoma, any site — (Code first any associated multiple endocrine neoplasia syndrome: 258.01-258.03)(Use additional code to identify associated endocrine syndrome, as: carcinoid syndrome: 259.2) ▽
209.69 Benign carcinoid tumor of other sites — (Code first any associated multiple endocrine neoplasia syndrome: 258.01-258.03)(Use additional code to identify associated endocrine syndrome, as: carcinoid syndrome: 259.2)
211.7 Benign neoplasm of islets of Langerhans — (Use additional code to identify any functional activity)
230.9 Carcinoma in situ of other and unspecified digestive organs ▽
577.0 Acute pancreatitis
577.1 Chronic pancreatitis
577.2 Cyst and pseudocyst of pancreas
577.8 Other specified disease of pancreas

ICD-9-CM Procedural

41.5 Total splenectomy
52.52 Distal pancreatectomy
52.96 Anastomosis of pancreas

48146

48146 Pancreatectomy, distal, near-total with preservation of duodenum (Child-type procedure)

ICD-9-CM Diagnostic

157.0 Malignant neoplasm of head of pancreas
157.1 Malignant neoplasm of body of pancreas
157.3 Malignant neoplasm of pancreatic duct
157.8 Malignant neoplasm of other specified sites of pancreas
209.29 Malignant carcinoid tumor of other sites — (Code first any associated multiple endocrine neoplasia syndrome: 258.01-258.03)(Use additional code to identify associated endocrine syndrome, as: carcinoid syndrome: 259.2)
209.30 Malignant poorly differentiated neuroendocrine carcinoma, any site — (Code first any associated multiple endocrine neoplasia syndrome: 258.01-258.03)(Use additional code to identify associated endocrine syndrome, as: carcinoid syndrome: 259.2) ▽
577.1 Chronic pancreatitis
577.2 Cyst and pseudocyst of pancreas
577.8 Other specified disease of pancreas
863.81 Pancreas head injury without mention of open wound into cavity
863.82 Pancreas body injury without mention of open wound into cavity
863.84 Pancreas injury, multiple and unspecified sites, without mention of open wound into cavity
863.94 Pancreas injury, multiple and unspecified sites, with open wound into cavity
V42.83 Pancreas replaced by transplant

ICD-9-CM Procedural

52.52 Distal pancreatectomy

48148

48148 Excision of ampulla of Vater

ICD-9-CM Diagnostic

156.2 Malignant neoplasm of ampulla of Vater
197.8 Secondary malignant neoplasm of other digestive organs and spleen
209.29 Malignant carcinoid tumor of other sites — (Code first any associated multiple endocrine neoplasia syndrome: 258.01-258.03)(Use additional code to identify associated endocrine syndrome, as: carcinoid syndrome: 259.2)
209.30 Malignant poorly differentiated neuroendocrine carcinoma, any site — (Code first any associated multiple endocrine neoplasia syndrome: 258.01-258.03)(Use additional code to identify associated endocrine syndrome, as: carcinoid syndrome: 259.2) ▽
211.5 Benign neoplasm of liver and biliary passages
230.8 Carcinoma in situ of liver and biliary system
235.3 Neoplasm of uncertain behavior of liver and biliary passages
V42.83 Pancreas replaced by transplant

ICD-9-CM Procedural

51.62 Excision of ampulla of Vater (with reimplantation of common duct)

48150-48152

48150 Pancreatectomy, proximal subtotal with total duodenectomy, partial gastrectomy, choledochoenterostomy and gastrojejunostomy (Whipple-type procedure); with pancreatojejunostomy
48152 without pancreatojejunostomy

ICD-9-CM Diagnostic

157.0 Malignant neoplasm of head of pancreas
157.1 Malignant neoplasm of body of pancreas
157.2 Malignant neoplasm of tail of pancreas
157.3 Malignant neoplasm of pancreatic duct
157.4 Malignant neoplasm of islets of Langerhans — (Use additional code to identify any functional activity)
157.8 Malignant neoplasm of other specified sites of pancreas
157.9 Malignant neoplasm of pancreas, part unspecified ▽
197.8 Secondary malignant neoplasm of other digestive organs and spleen
209.29 Malignant carcinoid tumor of other sites — (Code first any associated multiple endocrine neoplasia syndrome: 258.01-258.03)(Use additional code to identify associated endocrine syndrome, as: carcinoid syndrome: 259.2)
209.30 Malignant poorly differentiated neuroendocrine carcinoma, any site — (Code first any associated multiple endocrine neoplasia syndrome: 258.01-258.03)(Use additional code to identify associated endocrine syndrome, as: carcinoid syndrome: 259.2) ▽
209.69 Benign carcinoid tumor of other sites — (Code first any associated multiple endocrine neoplasia syndrome: 258.01-258.03)(Use additional code to identify associated endocrine syndrome, as: carcinoid syndrome: 259.2)
211.7 Benign neoplasm of islets of Langerhans — (Use additional code to identify any functional activity)
230.9 Carcinoma in situ of other and unspecified digestive organs ▽
577.1 Chronic pancreatitis
577.2 Cyst and pseudocyst of pancreas
577.8 Other specified disease of pancreas
863.81 Pancreas head injury without mention of open wound into cavity
863.82 Pancreas body injury without mention of open wound into cavity
863.84 Pancreas injury, multiple and unspecified sites, without mention of open wound into cavity
863.94 Pancreas injury, multiple and unspecified sites, with open wound into cavity

ICD-9-CM Procedural

52.7 Radical pancreaticoduodenectomy
52.96 Anastomosis of pancreas

48153-48154

48153 Pancreatectomy, proximal subtotal with near-total duodenectomy, choledochoenterostomy and duodenojejunostomy (pylorus-sparing, Whipple-type procedure); with pancreatojejunostomy
48154 without pancreatojejunostomy

ICD-9-CM Diagnostic

157.0 Malignant neoplasm of head of pancreas
157.1 Malignant neoplasm of body of pancreas
157.2 Malignant neoplasm of tail of pancreas
157.3 Malignant neoplasm of pancreatic duct
157.8 Malignant neoplasm of other specified sites of pancreas
209.29 Malignant carcinoid tumor of other sites — (Code first any associated multiple endocrine neoplasia syndrome: 258.01-258.03)(Use additional code to identify associated endocrine syndrome, as: carcinoid syndrome: 259.2)
209.30 Malignant poorly differentiated neuroendocrine carcinoma, any site — (Code first any associated multiple endocrine neoplasia syndrome: 258.01-258.03)(Use additional code to identify associated endocrine syndrome, as: carcinoid syndrome: 259.2) ▽
577.0 Acute pancreatitis
577.1 Chronic pancreatitis
577.2 Cyst and pseudocyst of pancreas
577.8 Other specified disease of pancreas
863.81 Pancreas head injury without mention of open wound into cavity
863.82 Pancreas body injury without mention of open wound into cavity
863.84 Pancreas injury, multiple and unspecified sites, without mention of open wound into cavity
863.94 Pancreas injury, multiple and unspecified sites, with open wound into cavity

ICD-9-CM Procedural

52.7 Radical pancreaticoduodenectomy
52.96 Anastomosis of pancreas

48155-48160

48155 Pancreatectomy, total
48160 Pancreatectomy, total or subtotal, with autologous transplantation of pancreas or pancreatic islet cells

ICD-9-CM Diagnostic

157.0 Malignant neoplasm of head of pancreas
157.1 Malignant neoplasm of body of pancreas
157.2 Malignant neoplasm of tail of pancreas
157.3 Malignant neoplasm of pancreatic duct
157.4 Malignant neoplasm of islets of Langerhans — (Use additional code to identify any functional activity)
157.8 Malignant neoplasm of other specified sites of pancreas
157.9 Malignant neoplasm of pancreas, part unspecified ▼
197.8 Secondary malignant neoplasm of other digestive organs and spleen
209.29 Malignant carcinoid tumor of other sites — (Code first any associated multiple endocrine neoplasia syndrome: 258.01-258.03)(Use additional code to identify associated endocrine syndrome, as: carcinoid syndrome: 259.2)
209.30 Malignant poorly differentiated neuroendocrine carcinoma, any site — (Code first any associated multiple endocrine neoplasia syndrome: 258.01-258.03)(Use additional code to identify associated endocrine syndrome, as: carcinoid syndrome: 259.2) ▼
230.9 Carcinoma in situ of other and unspecified digestive organs ▼
249.00 Secondary diabetes mellitus without mention of complication, not stated as uncontrolled, or unspecified — (Use additional code to identify any associated insulin use: V58.67)
249.01 Secondary diabetes mellitus without mention of complication, uncontrolled — (Use additional code to identify any associated insulin use: V58.67)
249.40 Secondary diabetes mellitus with renal manifestations, not stated as uncontrolled, or unspecified — (Use additional code to identify manifestation: 581.81, 583.81, 585.1-585.9) (Use additional code to identify any associated insulin use: V58.67)
249.41 Secondary diabetes mellitus with renal manifestations, uncontrolled — (Use additional code to identify manifestation: 581.81, 583.81, 585.1-585.9) (Use additional code to identify any associated insulin use: V58.67)
249.80 Secondary diabetes mellitus with other specified manifestations, not stated as uncontrolled, or unspecified — (Use additional code to identify manifestation: 707.10-707.19, 707.8, 707.9, 731.8) (Use additional code to identify any associated insulin use: V58.67)
249.81 Secondary diabetes mellitus with other specified manifestations, uncontrolled — (Use additional code to identify manifestation: 707.10-707.19, 707.8, 707.9, 731.8) (Use additional code to identify any associated insulin use: V58.67)
250.01 Diabetes mellitus without mention of complication, type I [juvenile type], not stated as uncontrolled
250.03 Diabetes mellitus without mention of complication, type I [juvenile type], uncontrolled
250.41 Diabetes with renal manifestations, type I [juvenile type], not stated as uncontrolled — (Use additional code to identify manifestation: 581.81, 583.81, 585.1-585.9)
250.43 Diabetes with renal manifestations, type I [juvenile type], uncontrolled — (Use additional code to identify manifestation: 581.81, 583.81, 585.1-585.9)
250.81 Diabetes with other specified manifestations, type I [juvenile type], not stated as uncontrolled — (Use additional code to identify manifestation: 707.10-707.19, 707.8, 707.9, 731.8)
250.83 Diabetes with other specified manifestations, type I [juvenile type], uncontrolled — (Use additional code to identify manifestation: 707.10-707.19, 707.8, 707.9, 731.8)
577.0 Acute pancreatitis
577.1 Chronic pancreatitis
577.2 Cyst and pseudocyst of pancreas
581.81 Nephrotic syndrome with other specified pathological lesion in kidney in diseases classified elsewhere — (Code first underlying disease: 084.9, 249.4, 250.4, 277.30-277.39, 446.0, 710.0) ☒
583.81 Nephritis and nephropathy, not specified as acute or chronic, with other specified pathological lesion in kidney, in diseases classified elsewhere — (Code first underlying disease: 016.0, 098.19, 249.4, 250.4, 277.30-277.39, 446.21, 710.0) ☒
V42.83 Pancreas replaced by transplant

ICD-9-CM Procedural

52.59 Other partial pancreatectomy
52.6 Total pancreatectomy
52.84 Autotransplantation of cells of islets of Langerhans

48400

48400 Injection procedure for intraoperative pancreatography (List separately in addition to code for primary procedure)

ICD-9-CM Diagnostic

This is an add-on code. Refer to the corresponding primary procedure code for ICD-9-CM diagnosis code links.

ICD-9-CM Procedural

52.19 Other diagnostic procedures on pancreas

48500

48500 Marsupialization of pancreatic cyst

ICD-9-CM Diagnostic

577.2 Cyst and pseudocyst of pancreas
751.7 Congenital anomalies of pancreas
V42.83 Pancreas replaced by transplant

ICD-9-CM Procedural

52.3 Marsupialization of pancreatic cyst

48510

48510 External drainage, pseudocyst of pancreas, open

ICD-9-CM Diagnostic

577.2 Cyst and pseudocyst of pancreas
751.7 Congenital anomalies of pancreas

ICD-9-CM Procedural

52.01 Drainage of pancreatic cyst by catheter
52.09 Other pancreatotomy

48520

48520 Internal anastomosis of pancreatic cyst to gastrointestinal tract; direct

ICD-9-CM Diagnostic

577.1 Chronic pancreatitis
577.2 Cyst and pseudocyst of pancreas
577.8 Other specified disease of pancreas
751.7 Congenital anomalies of pancreas

ICD-9-CM Procedural

52.4 Internal drainage of pancreatic cyst

48540

48540 Internal anastomosis of pancreatic cyst to gastrointestinal tract; Roux-en-Y

ICD-9-CM Diagnostic

577.1 Chronic pancreatitis
577.2 Cyst and pseudocyst of pancreas
577.8 Other specified disease of pancreas
751.7 Congenital anomalies of pancreas

ICD-9-CM Procedural

52.4 Internal drainage of pancreatic cyst

48545-48547

48545 Pancreatorrhaphy for injury

48547 Duodenal exclusion with gastrojejunostomy for pancreatic injury

ICD-9-CM Diagnostic

863.80 Gastrointestinal tract injury, unspecified site, without mention of open wound into cavity ▽

863.81 Pancreas head injury without mention of open wound into cavity

863.82 Pancreas body injury without mention of open wound into cavity

863.83 Pancreas tail injury without mention of open wound into cavity

863.84 Pancreas injury, multiple and unspecified sites, without mention of open wound into cavity

863.90 Gastrointestinal tract injury, unspecified site, with open wound into cavity ▽

863.91 Pancreas head injury with open wound into cavity

863.92 Pancreas body injury with open wound into cavity

863.93 Pancreas tail injury with open wound into cavity

863.94 Pancreas injury, multiple and unspecified sites, with open wound into cavity

ICD-9-CM Procedural

44.39 Other gastroenterostomy without gastrectomy

52.95 Other repair of pancreas

48548

48548 Pancreaticojejunostomy, side-to-side anastomosis (Puestow-type operation)

ICD-9-CM Diagnostic

577.1 Chronic pancreatitis

577.2 Cyst and pseudocyst of pancreas

577.8 Other specified disease of pancreas

V42.83 Pancreas replaced by transplant

ICD-9-CM Procedural

52.96 Anastomosis of pancreas

48550

48550 Donor pancreatectomy (including cold preservation), with or without duodenal segment for transplantation

ICD-9-CM Diagnostic

V59.8 Donor of other specified organ or tissue

ICD-9-CM Procedural

52.6 Total pancreatectomy

48551-48552

48551 Backbench standard preparation of cadaver donor pancreas allograft prior to transplantation, including dissection of allograft from surrounding soft tissues, splenectomy, duodenotomy, ligation of bile duct, ligation of mesenteric vessels, and Y-graft arterial anastomoses from iliac artery to superior mesenteric artery and to splenic artery

48552 Backbench reconstruction of cadaver donor pancreas allograft prior to transplantation, venous anastomosis, each

ICD-9-CM Diagnostic

199.2 Malignant neoplasm associated with transplanted organ — (Code first complication of transplanted organ (996.80-996.89) Use additional code for specific malignancy)

238.77 Post-transplant lymphoproliferative disorder [PTLD] — (Code first complications of transplant (996.80-996.89))

249.40 Secondary diabetes mellitus with renal manifestations, not stated as uncontrolled, or unspecified — (Use additional code to identify manifestation: 581.81, 583.81, 585.1-585.9) (Use additional code to identify any associated insulin use: V58.67)

249.41 Secondary diabetes mellitus with renal manifestations, uncontrolled — (Use additional code to identify manifestation: 581.81, 583.81, 585.1-585.9) (Use additional code to identify any associated insulin use: V58.67)

249.80 Secondary diabetes mellitus with other specified manifestations, not stated as uncontrolled, or unspecified — (Use additional code to identify manifestation: 707.10-707.19, 707.8, 707.9, 731.8) (Use additional code to identify any associated insulin use: V58.67)

249.81 Secondary diabetes mellitus with other specified manifestations, uncontrolled — (Use additional code to identify manifestation: 707.10-707.19, 707.8, 707.9, 731.8) (Use additional code to identify any associated insulin use: V58.67)

250.41 Diabetes with renal manifestations, type I [juvenile type], not stated as uncontrolled — (Use additional code to identify manifestation: 581.81, 583.81, 585.1-585.9)

250.43 Diabetes with renal manifestations, type I [juvenile type], uncontrolled — (Use additional code to identify manifestation: 581.81, 583.81, 585.1-585.9)

250.81 Diabetes with other specified manifestations, type I [juvenile type], not stated as uncontrolled — (Use additional code to identify manifestation: 707.10-707.19, 707.8, 707.9, 731.8)

250.83 Diabetes with other specified manifestations, type I [juvenile type], uncontrolled — (Use additional code to identify manifestation: 707.10-707.19, 707.8, 707.9, 731.8)

581.81 Nephrotic syndrome with other specified pathological lesion in kidney in diseases classified elsewhere — (Code first underlying disease: 084.9, 249.4, 250.4, 277.30-277.39, 446.0, 710.0) ☒

583.81 Nephritis and nephropathy, not specified as acute or chronic, with other specified pathological lesion in kidney, in diseases classified elsewhere — (Code first underlying disease: 016.0, 098.19, 249.4, 250.4, 277.30-277.39, 446.21, 710.0) ☒

586 Unspecified renal failure ▽

587 Unspecified renal sclerosis ▽

996.86 Complications of transplanted pancreas — (Use additional code to identify nature of complication: 078.5, 199.2, 238.77, 279.50-279.53)

ICD-9-CM Procedural

The ICD-9-CM procedural code(s) would be the same as the actual procedure performed because these are in-addition-to codes.

48554-48556

48554 Transplantation of pancreatic allograft

48556 Removal of transplanted pancreatic allograft

ICD-9-CM Diagnostic

199.2 Malignant neoplasm associated with transplanted organ — (Code first complication of transplanted organ (996.80-996.89) Use additional code for specific malignancy)

238.77 Post-transplant lymphoproliferative disorder [PTLD] — (Code first complications of transplant (996.80-996.89))

249.40 Secondary diabetes mellitus with renal manifestations, not stated as uncontrolled, or unspecified — (Use additional code to identify manifestation: 581.81, 583.81, 585.1-585.9) (Use additional code to identify any associated insulin use: V58.67)

249.41 Secondary diabetes mellitus with renal manifestations, uncontrolled — (Use additional code to identify manifestation: 581.81, 583.81, 585.1-585.9) (Use additional code to identify any associated insulin use: V58.67)

249.80 Secondary diabetes mellitus with other specified manifestations, not stated as uncontrolled, or unspecified — (Use additional code to identify manifestation: 707.10-707.19, 707.8, 707.9, 731.8) (Use additional code to identify any associated insulin use: V58.67)

249.81 Secondary diabetes mellitus with other specified manifestations, uncontrolled — (Use additional code to identify manifestation: 707.10-707.19, 707.8, 707.9, 731.8) (Use additional code to identify any associated insulin use: V58.67)

250.41 Diabetes with renal manifestations, type I [juvenile type], not stated as uncontrolled — (Use additional code to identify manifestation: 581.81, 583.81, 585.1-585.9)

250.43 Diabetes with renal manifestations, type I [juvenile type], uncontrolled — (Use additional code to identify manifestation: 581.81, 583.81, 585.1-585.9)

250.81 Diabetes with other specified manifestations, type I [juvenile type], not stated as uncontrolled — (Use additional code to identify manifestation: 707.10-707.19, 707.8, 707.9, 731.8)

250.83 Diabetes with other specified manifestations, type I [juvenile type], uncontrolled — (Use additional code to identify manifestation: 707.10-707.19, 707.8, 707.9, 731.8)

581.81 Nephrotic syndrome with other specified pathological lesion in kidney in diseases classified elsewhere — (Code first underlying disease: 084.9, 249.4, 250.4, 277.30-277.39, 446.0, 710.0) ⊠

583.81 Nephritis and nephropathy, not specified as acute or chronic, with other specified pathological lesion in kidney, in diseases classified elsewhere — (Code first underlying disease: 016.0, 098.19, 249.4, 250.4, 277.30-277.39, 446.21, 710.0) ⊠

586 Unspecified renal failure ▽

587 Unspecified renal sclerosis ▽

996.86 Complications of transplanted pancreas — (Use additional code to identify nature of complication: 078.5, 199.2, 238.77, 279.50-279.53)

ICD-9-CM Procedural

00.91 Transplant from live related donor

00.92 Transplant from live non-related donor

00.93 Transplant from cadaver

52.82 Homotransplant of pancreas

52.99 Other operations on pancreas

Abdomen, Peritoneum, and Omentum

49000

49000 Exploratory laparotomy, exploratory celiotomy with or without biopsy(s) (separate procedure)

ICD-9-CM Diagnostic

The application of this code is too broad to adequately present ICD-9-CM diagnostic code links here. Refer to your ICD-9-CM book.

ICD-9-CM Procedural

34.27 Biopsy of diaphragm

54.11 Exploratory laparotomy

54.23 Biopsy of peritoneum

49002

49002 Reopening of recent laparotomy

ICD-9-CM Diagnostic

338.18 Other acute postoperative pain — (Use additional code to identify pain associated with psychological factors: 307.89)

553.21 Incisional hernia without mention of obstruction or gangrene

557.0 Acute vascular insufficiency of intestine

557.1 Chronic vascular insufficiency of intestine

560.81 Intestinal or peritoneal adhesions with obstruction (postoperative) (postinfection)

560.89 Other specified intestinal obstruction

567.21 Peritonitis (acute) generalized

567.22 Peritoneal abscess

567.23 Spontaneous bacterial peritonitis

567.29 Other suppurative peritonitis

567.31 Psoas muscle abscess

567.38 Other retroperitoneal abscess

567.39 Other retroperitoneal infections

567.81 Choleperitonitis

567.82 Sclerosing mesenteritis

567.89 Other specified peritonitis

568.81 Hemoperitoneum (nontraumatic)

568.9 Unspecified disorder of peritoneum ▽

614.6 Pelvic peritoneal adhesions, female (postoperative) (postinfection) — (Use additional code to identify organism: 041.00-041.09, 041.10-041.19) (Use additional code to identify any associated infertility: 628.2) ♀

628.2 Female infertility of tubal origin — (Use additional code for any associated peritubal adhesions: 614.6) ♀

674.34 Other complications of obstetrical surgical wounds, postpartum condition or complication ♀

780.62 Postprocedural fever

789.00 Abdominal pain, unspecified site ▽

789.01 Abdominal pain, right upper quadrant

789.02 Abdominal pain, left upper quadrant

789.03 Abdominal pain, right lower quadrant

789.04 Abdominal pain, left lower quadrant

789.05 Abdominal pain, periumbilic

789.06 Abdominal pain, epigastric

789.07 Abdominal pain, generalized

789.09 Abdominal pain, other specified site

789.1 Hepatomegaly

789.2 Splenomegaly

789.30 Abdominal or pelvic swelling, mass or lump, unspecified site ▽

789.31 Abdominal or pelvic swelling, mass, or lump, right upper quadrant

789.32 Abdominal or pelvic swelling, mass, or lump, left upper quadrant

789.33 Abdominal or pelvic swelling, mass, or lump, right lower quadrant

789.34 Abdominal or pelvic swelling, mass, or lump, left lower quadrant

789.35 Abdominal or pelvic swelling, mass or lump, periumbilic

789.36 Abdominal or pelvic swelling, mass, or lump, epigastric

789.37 Abdominal or pelvic swelling, mass, or lump, generalized

789.39 Abdominal or pelvic swelling, mass, or lump, other specified site

996.80 Complications of transplanted organ, unspecified site — (Use additional code to identify nature of complication: 078.5, 199.2, 238.77, 279.50-279.53) ▽

996.81 Complications of transplanted kidney — (Use additional code to identify nature of complication: 078.5, 199.2, 238.77, 279.50-279.53)

996.82 Complications of transplanted liver — (Use additional code to identify nature of complication: 078.5, 199.2, 238.77, 279.50-279.53)

996.86 Complications of transplanted pancreas — (Use additional code to identify nature of complication: 078.5, 199.2, 238.77, 279.50-279.53)

996.87 Complications of transplanted organ, intestine — (Use additional code to identify nature of complication: 078.5, 199.2, 238.77, 279.50-279.53)

996.89 Complications of other transplanted organ — (Use additional code to identify nature of complication: 078.5, 199.2, 238.77, 279.50-279.53)

997.49 Other digestive system complications

997.5 Urinary complications — (Use additional code to identify complications)

998.11 Hemorrhage complicating a procedure

998.12 Hematoma complicating a procedure

998.13 Seroma complicating a procedure

998.31 Disruption of internal operation (surgical) wound

998.32 Disruption of external operation (surgical) wound

998.4 Foreign body accidentally left during procedure, not elsewhere classified

998.51 Infected postoperative seroma — (Use additional code to identify organism)

998.59 Other postoperative infection — (Use additional code to identify infection)

998.7 Acute reaction to foreign substance accidentally left during procedure, not elsewhere classified

ICD-9-CM Procedural

54.12 Reopening of recent laparotomy site

49010

49010 Exploration, retroperitoneal area with or without biopsy(s) (separate procedure)

ICD-9-CM Diagnostic

The application of this code is too broad to adequately present ICD-9-CM diagnostic code links here. Refer to your ICD-9-CM book.

ICD-9-CM Procedural

54.0 Incision of abdominal wall

54.23 Biopsy of peritoneum

49020

49020 Drainage of peritoneal abscess or localized peritonitis, exclusive of appendiceal abscess, open

ICD-9-CM Diagnostic

537.4 Fistula of stomach or duodenum
555.9 Regional enteritis of unspecified site
562.11 Diverticulitis of colon (without mention of hemorrhage) — (Use additional code to identify any associated peritonitis: 567.0-567.9)
562.13 Diverticulitis of colon with hemorrhage — (Use additional code to identify any associated peritonitis: 567.0-567.9)
567.0 Peritonitis in infectious diseases classified elsewhere — (Code first underlying disease)
567.1 Pneumococcal peritonitis
567.21 Peritonitis (acute) generalized
567.22 Peritoneal abscess
567.23 Spontaneous bacterial peritonitis
567.29 Other suppurative peritonitis
567.31 Psoas muscle abscess
567.38 Other retroperitoneal abscess
567.81 Choleperitonitis
567.82 Sclerosing mesenteritis
567.89 Other specified peritonitis
567.9 Unspecified peritonitis
568.81 Hemoperitoneum (nontraumatic)
568.82 Peritoneal effusion (chronic)
568.89 Other specified disorder of peritoneum
569.5 Abscess of intestine
569.83 Perforation of intestine
614.5 Acute or unspecified pelvic peritonitis, female — (Use additional code to identify organism: 041.00-041.09, 041.10-041.19) ♀
614.7 Other chronic pelvic peritonitis, female — (Use additional code to identify organism: 041.00-041.09, 041.10-041.19) ♀
670.00 Major puerperal infection, unspecified, unspecified as to episode of care or not applicable ♀
862.8 Injury to multiple and unspecified intrathoracic organs without mention of open wound into cavity
862.9 Injury to multiple and unspecified intrathoracic organs with open wound into cavity
863.95 Appendix injury with open wound into cavity
863.99 Injury to other and unspecified gastrointestinal sites with open wound into cavity
879.2 Open wound of abdominal wall, anterior, without mention of complication
998.51 Infected postoperative seroma — (Use additional code to identify organism)
998.59 Other postoperative infection — (Use additional code to identify infection)
998.7 Acute reaction to foreign substance accidentally left during procedure, not elsewhere classified

ICD-9-CM Procedural

54.19 Other laparotomy

49040

49040 Drainage of subdiaphragmatic or subphrenic abscess, open

ICD-9-CM Diagnostic

540.1 Acute appendicitis with peritoneal abscess
567.22 Peritoneal abscess
567.29 Other suppurative peritonitis
614.3 Acute parametritis and pelvic cellulitis — (Use additional code to identify organism: 041.00-041.09, 041.10-041.19) ♀
614.4 Chronic or unspecified parametritis and pelvic cellulitis — (Use additional code to identify organism: 041.00-041.09, 041.10-041.19) ♀
670.00 Major puerperal infection, unspecified, unspecified as to episode of care or not applicable ♀
670.02 Major puerperal infection, unspecified, delivered, with mention of postpartum complication ♀
670.04 Major puerperal infection, unspecified, postpartum condition or complication ♀
998.59 Other postoperative infection — (Use additional code to identify infection)

ICD-9-CM Procedural

54.19 Other laparotomy

49060

49060 Drainage of retroperitoneal abscess, open

ICD-9-CM Diagnostic

540.1 Acute appendicitis with peritoneal abscess
555.9 Regional enteritis of unspecified site
567.31 Psoas muscle abscess
567.38 Other retroperitoneal abscess
567.39 Other retroperitoneal infections
569.5 Abscess of intestine
577.0 Acute pancreatitis
590.2 Renal and perinephric abscess — (Use additional code to identify organism, such as E. coli, 041.41-041.49)
614.2 Salpingitis and oophoritis not specified as acute, subacute, or chronic — (Use additional code to identify organism: 041.00-041.09, 041.10-041.19) ♀
614.3 Acute parametritis and pelvic cellulitis — (Use additional code to identify organism: 041.00-041.09, 041.10-041.19) ♀
614.4 Chronic or unspecified parametritis and pelvic cellulitis — (Use additional code to identify organism: 041.00-041.09, 041.10-041.19) ♀
614.5 Acute or unspecified pelvic peritonitis, female — (Use additional code to identify organism: 041.00-041.09, 041.10-041.19) ♀
614.6 Pelvic peritoneal adhesions, female (postoperative) (postinfection) — (Use additional code to identify organism: 041.00-041.09, 041.10-041.19) (Use additional code to identify any associated infertility: 628.2) ♀
614.7 Other chronic pelvic peritonitis, female — (Use additional code to identify organism: 041.00-041.09, 041.10-041.19) ♀
614.8 Other specified inflammatory disease of female pelvic organs and tissues — (Use additional code to identify organism: 041.00-041.09, 041.10-041.19) ♀
670.00 Major puerperal infection, unspecified, unspecified as to episode of care or not applicable ♀
670.02 Major puerperal infection, unspecified, delivered, with mention of postpartum complication ♀
670.04 Major puerperal infection, unspecified, postpartum condition or complication ♀
998.59 Other postoperative infection — (Use additional code to identify infection)

ICD-9-CM Procedural

54.0 Incision of abdominal wall
54.19 Other laparotomy

49062

49062 Drainage of extraperitoneal lymphocele to peritoneal cavity, open

ICD-9-CM Diagnostic

457.8 Other noninfectious disorders of lymphatic channels
996.81 Complications of transplanted kidney — (Use additional code to identify nature of complication: 078.5, 199.2, 238.77, 279.50-279.53)
997.99 Other complications affecting other specified body systems, NEC — (Use additional code to identify complications)
V42.0 Kidney replaced by transplant

ICD-9-CM Procedural

40.0 Incision of lymphatic structures

54.19 Other laparotomy
54.95 Incision of peritoneum

49082-49084

49082 Abdominal paracentesis (diagnostic or therapeutic); without imaging guidance
49083 with imaging guidance
49084 Peritoneal lavage, including imaging guidance, when performed

ICD-9-CM Diagnostic

095.2 Syphilitic peritonitis
457.8 Other noninfectious disorders of lymphatic channels
567.0 Peritonitis in infectious diseases classified elsewhere — (Code first underlying disease) ☒
567.1 Pneumococcal peritonitis
567.21 Peritonitis (acute) generalized
567.22 Peritoneal abscess
567.23 Spontaneous bacterial peritonitis
567.29 Other suppurative peritonitis
567.81 Choleperitonitis
567.89 Other specified peritonitis
567.9 Unspecified peritonitis ▽
568.82 Peritoneal effusion (chronic)
789.51 Malignant ascites
789.59 Other ascites
998.4 Foreign body accidentally left during procedure, not elsewhere classified
998.7 Acute reaction to foreign substance accidentally left during procedure, not elsewhere classified

ICD-9-CM Procedural

00.31 Computer assisted surgery with CT/CTA
00.32 Computer assisted surgery with MR/MRA
00.33 Computer assisted surgery with fluoroscopy
00.34 Imageless computer assisted surgery
00.35 Computer assisted surgery with multiple datasets
00.39 Other computer assisted surgery
54.25 Peritoneal lavage
54.91 Percutaneous abdominal drainage

49180

49180 Biopsy, abdominal or retroperitoneal mass, percutaneous needle

ICD-9-CM Diagnostic

158.0 Malignant neoplasm of retroperitoneum
158.8 Malignant neoplasm of specified parts of peritoneum
158.9 Malignant neoplasm of peritoneum, unspecified ▽
159.8 Malignant neoplasm of other sites of digestive system and intra-abdominal organs
183.0 Malignant neoplasm of ovary — (Use additional code to identify any functional activity) ♀
183.8 Malignant neoplasm of other specified sites of uterine adnexa ♀
195.2 Malignant neoplasm of abdomen
196.2 Secondary and unspecified malignant neoplasm of intra-abdominal lymph nodes
196.6 Secondary and unspecified malignant neoplasm of intrapelvic lymph nodes
197.6 Secondary malignant neoplasm of retroperitoneum and peritoneum
198.89 Secondary malignant neoplasm of other specified sites
199.1 Other malignant neoplasm of unspecified site
202.80 Other malignant lymphomas, unspecified site, extranodal and solid organ sites ▽
209.20 Malignant carcinoid tumor of unknown primary site — (Code first any associated multiple endocrine neoplasia syndrome: 258.01-258.03)(Use additional code to identify associated endocrine syndrome, as: carcinoid syndrome: 259.2)
209.25 Malignant carcinoid tumor of foregut, not otherwise specified — (Code first any associated multiple endocrine neoplasia syndrome: 258.01-258.03)(Use additional code to identify associated endocrine syndrome, as: carcinoid syndrome: 259.2)
209.26 Malignant carcinoid tumor of midgut, not otherwise specified — (Code first any associated multiple endocrine neoplasia syndrome: 258.01-258.03)(Use additional code to identify associated endocrine syndrome, as: carcinoid syndrome: 259.2)
209.27 Malignant carcinoid tumor of hindgut, not otherwise specified — (Code first any associated multiple endocrine neoplasia syndrome: 258.01-258.03)(Use additional code to identify associated endocrine syndrome, as: carcinoid syndrome: 259.2)
209.29 Malignant carcinoid tumor of other sites — (Code first any associated multiple endocrine neoplasia syndrome: 258.01-258.03)(Use additional code to identify associated endocrine syndrome, as: carcinoid syndrome: 259.2)
209.30 Malignant poorly differentiated neuroendocrine carcinoma, any site — (Code first any associated multiple endocrine neoplasia syndrome: 258.01-258.03)(Use additional code to identify associated endocrine syndrome, as: carcinoid syndrome: 259.2) ▽
209.69 Benign carcinoid tumor of other sites — (Code first any associated multiple endocrine neoplasia syndrome: 258.01-258.03)(Use additional code to identify associated endocrine syndrome, as: carcinoid syndrome: 259.2)
209.71 Secondary neuroendocrine tumor of distant lymph nodes
209.74 Secondary neuroendocrine tumor of peritoneum
211.8 Benign neoplasm of retroperitoneum and peritoneum
211.9 Benign neoplasm of other and unspecified site of the digestive system ▽
220 Benign neoplasm of ovary — (Use additional code to identify any functional activity: 256.0-256.1) ♀
227.6 Benign neoplasm of aortic body and other paraganglia — (Use additional code to identify any functional activity)
228.04 Hemangioma of intra-abdominal structures
235.4 Neoplasm of uncertain behavior of retroperitoneum and peritoneum
235.5 Neoplasm of uncertain behavior of other and unspecified digestive organs ▽
236.2 Neoplasm of uncertain behavior of ovary — (Use additional code to identify any functional activity) ♀
236.3 Neoplasm of uncertain behavior of other and unspecified female genital organs ▽ ♀
237.3 Neoplasm of uncertain behavior of paraganglia
238.8 Neoplasm of uncertain behavior of other specified sites
238.9 Neoplasm of uncertain behavior, site unspecified ▽
239.0 Neoplasm of unspecified nature of digestive system
239.7 Neoplasm of unspecified nature of endocrine glands and other parts of nervous system
239.9 Neoplasm of unspecified nature, site unspecified ▽
256.0 Hyperestrogenism ♀
256.1 Other ovarian hyperfunction ♀
614.6 Pelvic peritoneal adhesions, female (postoperative) (postinfection) — (Use additional code to identify organism: 041.00-041.09, 041.10-041.19) (Use additional code to identify any associated infertility: 628.2) ♀
617.0 Endometriosis of uterus ♀
617.3 Endometriosis of pelvic peritoneum ♀
617.9 Endometriosis, site unspecified ▽ ♀
628.2 Female infertility of tubal origin — (Use additional code for any associated peritubal adhesions: 614.6) ♀
682.2 Cellulitis and abscess of trunk — (Use additional code to identify organism, such as 041.1, etc.)
785.6 Enlargement of lymph nodes
787.99 Other symptoms involving digestive system
789.09 Abdominal pain, other specified site
789.30 Abdominal or pelvic swelling, mass or lump, unspecified site ▽
789.31 Abdominal or pelvic swelling, mass, or lump, right upper quadrant
789.32 Abdominal or pelvic swelling, mass, or lump, left upper quadrant
789.33 Abdominal or pelvic swelling, mass, or lump, right lower quadrant
789.34 Abdominal or pelvic swelling, mass, or lump, left lower quadrant
789.35 Abdominal or pelvic swelling, mass or lump, periumbilic
789.36 Abdominal or pelvic swelling, mass, or lump, epigastric

789.37 Abdominal or pelvic swelling, mass, or lump, generalized
789.39 Abdominal or pelvic swelling, mass, or lump, other specified site
793.6 Nonspecific (abnormal) findings on radiological and other examination of abdominal area, including retroperitoneum
V72.5 Radiological examination, not elsewhere classified — (Use additional code(s) to identify any special screening examination(s) performed: V73.0-V82.9)

ICD-9-CM Procedural

54.24 Closed (percutaneous) (needle) biopsy of intra-abdominal mass

HCPCS Level II Supplies & Services

A4305 Disposable drug delivery system, flow rate of 50 ml or greater per hour

49203-49205

49203 Excision or destruction, open, intra-abdominal tumors, cysts or endometriomas, 1 or more peritoneal, mesenteric, or retroperitoneal primary or secondary tumors; largest tumor 5 cm diameter or less
49204 largest tumor 5.1-10.0 cm diameter
49205 largest tumor greater than 10.0 cm diameter

ICD-9-CM Diagnostic

154.0 Malignant neoplasm of rectosigmoid junction
158.0 Malignant neoplasm of retroperitoneum
158.8 Malignant neoplasm of specified parts of peritoneum
158.9 Malignant neoplasm of peritoneum, unspecified ▽
159.0 Malignant neoplasm of intestinal tract, part unspecified ▽
171.5 Malignant neoplasm of connective and other soft tissue of abdomen
171.6 Malignant neoplasm of connective and other soft tissue of pelvis
183.0 Malignant neoplasm of ovary — (Use additional code to identify any functional activity) ♀
183.3 Malignant neoplasm of broad ligament of uterus ♀
183.4 Malignant neoplasm of parametrium of uterus ♀
183.5 Malignant neoplasm of round ligament of uterus ♀
183.9 Malignant neoplasm of uterine adnexa, unspecified site ▽ ♀
194.0 Malignant neoplasm of adrenal gland
194.6 Malignant neoplasm of aortic body and other paraganglia
195.2 Malignant neoplasm of abdomen
195.3 Malignant neoplasm of pelvis
197.6 Secondary malignant neoplasm of retroperitoneum and peritoneum
198.89 Secondary malignant neoplasm of other specified sites
209.29 Malignant carcinoid tumor of other sites — (Code first any associated multiple endocrine neoplasia syndrome: 258.01-258.03)(Use additional code to identify associated endocrine syndrome, as: carcinoid syndrome: 259.2)
209.30 Malignant poorly differentiated neuroendocrine carcinoma, any site — (Code first any associated multiple endocrine neoplasia syndrome: 258.01-258.03)(Use additional code to identify associated endocrine syndrome, as: carcinoid syndrome: 259.2) ▽
209.69 Benign carcinoid tumor of other sites — (Code first any associated multiple endocrine neoplasia syndrome: 258.01-258.03)(Use additional code to identify associated endocrine syndrome, as: carcinoid syndrome: 259.2)
209.74 Secondary neuroendocrine tumor of peritoneum
211.8 Benign neoplasm of retroperitoneum and peritoneum
211.9 Benign neoplasm of other and unspecified site of the digestive system ▽
214.3 Lipoma of intra-abdominal organs
214.8 Lipoma of other specified sites
228.04 Hemangioma of intra-abdominal structures
235.2 Neoplasm of uncertain behavior of stomach, intestines, and rectum
235.4 Neoplasm of uncertain behavior of retroperitoneum and peritoneum
237.3 Neoplasm of uncertain behavior of paraganglia
238.9 Neoplasm of uncertain behavior, site unspecified ▽
239.0 Neoplasm of unspecified nature of digestive system
239.9 Neoplasm of unspecified nature, site unspecified ▽
568.89 Other specified disorder of peritoneum
614.6 Pelvic peritoneal adhesions, female (postoperative) (postinfection) — (Use additional code to identify organism: 041.00-041.09, 041.10-041.19) (Use additional code to identify any associated infertility: 628.2) ♀
617.0 Endometriosis of uterus ♀
617.1 Endometriosis of ovary ♀
617.2 Endometriosis of fallopian tube ♀
617.3 Endometriosis of pelvic peritoneum ♀
617.5 Endometriosis of intestine ♀
617.8 Endometriosis of other specified sites ♀
625.8 Other specified symptom associated with female genital organs ♀
789.00 Abdominal pain, unspecified site ▽
789.01 Abdominal pain, right upper quadrant
789.02 Abdominal pain, left upper quadrant
789.03 Abdominal pain, right lower quadrant
789.04 Abdominal pain, left lower quadrant
789.05 Abdominal pain, periumbilic
789.06 Abdominal pain, epigastric
789.07 Abdominal pain, generalized
789.09 Abdominal pain, other specified site
789.30 Abdominal or pelvic swelling, mass or lump, unspecified site ▽
789.31 Abdominal or pelvic swelling, mass, or lump, right upper quadrant
789.32 Abdominal or pelvic swelling, mass, or lump, left upper quadrant
789.33 Abdominal or pelvic swelling, mass, or lump, right lower quadrant
789.34 Abdominal or pelvic swelling, mass, or lump, left lower quadrant
789.35 Abdominal or pelvic swelling, mass or lump, periumbilic
789.36 Abdominal or pelvic swelling, mass, or lump, epigastric
789.37 Abdominal or pelvic swelling, mass, or lump, generalized
789.39 Abdominal or pelvic swelling, mass, or lump, other specified site

ICD-9-CM Procedural

54.3 Excision or destruction of lesion or tissue of abdominal wall or umbilicus
54.4 Excision or destruction of peritoneal tissue
68.23 Endometrial ablation ♀

49215

49215 Excision of presacral or sacrococcygeal tumor

ICD-9-CM Diagnostic

170.6 Malignant neoplasm of pelvic bones, sacrum, and coccyx
171.6 Malignant neoplasm of connective and other soft tissue of pelvis
195.3 Malignant neoplasm of pelvis
198.5 Secondary malignant neoplasm of bone and bone marrow
198.89 Secondary malignant neoplasm of other specified sites
209.73 Secondary neuroendocrine tumor of bone
213.6 Benign neoplasm of pelvic bones, sacrum, and coccyx
214.3 Lipoma of intra-abdominal organs
215.6 Other benign neoplasm of connective and other soft tissue of pelvis
229.8 Benign neoplasm of other specified sites
238.0 Neoplasm of uncertain behavior of bone and articular cartilage
238.1 Neoplasm of uncertain behavior of connective and other soft tissue
238.8 Neoplasm of uncertain behavior of other specified sites
239.2 Neoplasms of unspecified nature of bone, soft tissue, and skin
759.6 Other congenital hamartoses, not elsewhere classified

ICD-9-CM Procedural

54.4 Excision or destruction of peritoneal tissue
77.89 Other partial ostectomy of other bone, except facial bones
77.99 Total ostectomy of other bone, except facial bones

49220

49220 Staging laparotomy for Hodgkins disease or lymphoma (includes splenectomy, needle or open biopsies of both liver lobes, possibly also removal of abdominal nodes, abdominal node and/or bone marrow biopsies, ovarian repositioning)

ICD-9-CM Diagnostic

201.40 Hodgkin's disease, lymphocytic-histiocytic predominance, unspecified site, extranodal and solid organ sites ▽
201.41 Hodgkin's disease, lymphocytic-histiocytic predominance of lymph nodes of head, face, and neck
201.42 Hodgkin's disease, lymphocytic-histiocytic predominance of intrathoracic lymph nodes
201.43 Hodgkin's disease, lymphocytic-histiocytic predominance of intra-abdominal lymph nodes
201.44 Hodgkin's disease, lymphocytic-histiocytic predominance of lymph nodes of axilla and upper limb
201.45 Hodgkin's disease, lymphocytic-histiocytic predominance of lymph nodes of inguinal region and lower limb
201.46 Hodgkin's disease, lymphocytic-histiocytic predominance of intrapelvic lymph nodes
201.47 Hodgkin's disease, lymphocytic-histiocytic predominance of spleen
201.48 Hodgkin's disease, lymphocytic-histiocytic predominance of lymph nodes of multiple sites
201.50 Hodgkin's disease, nodular sclerosis, unspecified site, extranodal and solid organ sites ▽
201.51 Hodgkin's disease, nodular sclerosis, of lymph nodes of head, face, and neck
201.52 Hodgkin's disease, nodular sclerosis, of intrathoracic lymph nodes
201.70 Hodgkin's disease, lymphocytic depletion, unspecified site, extranodal and solid organ sites ▽
201.71 Hodgkin's disease, lymphocytic depletion, of lymph nodes of head, face, and neck
202.00 Nodular lymphoma, unspecified site, extranodal and solid organ sites ▽
202.08 Nodular lymphoma of lymph nodes of multiple sites
202.80 Other malignant lymphomas, unspecified site, extranodal and solid organ sites ▽
202.88 Other malignant lymphomas of lymph nodes of multiple sites

ICD-9-CM Procedural

40.3 Regional lymph node excision
41.31 Biopsy of bone marrow
45.19 Other diagnostic procedures on small intestine
50.11 Closed (percutaneous) (needle) biopsy of liver
50.12 Open biopsy of liver
54.11 Exploratory laparotomy

49250

49250 Umbilectomy, omphalectomy, excision of umbilicus (separate procedure)

ICD-9-CM Diagnostic

553.1 Umbilical hernia without mention of obstruction or gangrene
686.8 Other specified local infections of skin and subcutaneous tissue — (Use additional code to identify any infectious organism: 041.0-041.8)
728.84 Diastasis of muscle
771.4 Omphalitis of the newborn — (Use additional code(s) to further specify condition)

ICD-9-CM Procedural

54.3 Excision or destruction of lesion or tissue of abdominal wall or umbilicus

49255

49255 Omentectomy, epiploectomy, resection of omentum (separate procedure)

ICD-9-CM Diagnostic

158.0 Malignant neoplasm of retroperitoneum
158.8 Malignant neoplasm of specified parts of peritoneum
159.0 Malignant neoplasm of intestinal tract, part unspecified ▽
159.9 Malignant neoplasm of ill-defined sites of digestive organs and peritoneum ▽
171.5 Malignant neoplasm of connective and other soft tissue of abdomen
195.2 Malignant neoplasm of abdomen
195.8 Malignant neoplasm of other specified sites
196.2 Secondary and unspecified malignant neoplasm of intra-abdominal lymph nodes
197.4 Secondary malignant neoplasm of small intestine including duodenum
197.5 Secondary malignant neoplasm of large intestine and rectum
197.6 Secondary malignant neoplasm of retroperitoneum and peritoneum
197.7 Secondary malignant neoplasm of liver
197.8 Secondary malignant neoplasm of other digestive organs and spleen
198.82 Secondary malignant neoplasm of genital organs
198.89 Secondary malignant neoplasm of other specified sites
199.0 Disseminated malignant neoplasm
209.29 Malignant carcinoid tumor of other sites — (Code first any associated multiple endocrine neoplasia syndrome: 258.01-258.03)(Use additional code to identify associated endocrine syndrome, as: carcinoid syndrome: 259.2)
209.30 Malignant poorly differentiated neuroendocrine carcinoma, any site — (Code first any associated multiple endocrine neoplasia syndrome: 258.01-258.03)(Use additional code to identify associated endocrine syndrome, as: carcinoid syndrome: 259.2) ▽
209.69 Benign carcinoid tumor of other sites — (Code first any associated multiple endocrine neoplasia syndrome: 258.01-258.03)(Use additional code to identify associated endocrine syndrome, as: carcinoid syndrome: 259.2)
209.71 Secondary neuroendocrine tumor of distant lymph nodes
209.72 Secondary neuroendocrine tumor of liver
209.74 Secondary neuroendocrine tumor of peritoneum
211.8 Benign neoplasm of retroperitoneum and peritoneum
211.9 Benign neoplasm of other and unspecified site of the digestive system ▽
235.4 Neoplasm of uncertain behavior of retroperitoneum and peritoneum
238.1 Neoplasm of uncertain behavior of connective and other soft tissue
239.0 Neoplasm of unspecified nature of digestive system
239.89 Neoplasms of unspecified nature, other specified sites
567.21 Peritonitis (acute) generalized
567.22 Peritoneal abscess
567.23 Spontaneous bacterial peritonitis
567.29 Other suppurative peritonitis
567.39 Other retroperitoneal infections
567.89 Other specified peritonitis
568.0 Peritoneal adhesions (postoperative) (postinfection)
568.89 Other specified disorder of peritoneum
614.6 Pelvic peritoneal adhesions, female (postoperative) (postinfection) — (Use additional code to identify organism: 041.00-041.09, 041.10-041.19) (Use additional code to identify any associated infertility: 628.2) ♀
628.2 Female infertility of tubal origin — (Use additional code for any associated peritubal adhesions: 614.6) ♀
789.00 Abdominal pain, unspecified site ▽
789.30 Abdominal or pelvic swelling, mass or lump, unspecified site ▽

ICD-9-CM Procedural

54.4 Excision or destruction of peritoneal tissue

49320

49320 Laparoscopy, abdomen, peritoneum, and omentum, diagnostic, with or without collection of specimen(s) by brushing or washing (separate procedure)

ICD-9-CM Diagnostic

The application of this code is too broad to adequately present ICD-9-CM diagnostic code links here. Refer to your ICD-9-CM book.

ICD-9-CM Procedural

54.21 Laparoscopy
54.23 Biopsy of peritoneum
54.24 Closed (percutaneous) (needle) biopsy of intra-abdominal mass

65.14 Other laparoscopic diagnostic procedures on ovaries ♀

49321

49321 Laparoscopy, surgical; with biopsy (single or multiple)

ICD-9-CM Procedural

54.23 Biopsy of peritoneum
54.24 Closed (percutaneous) (needle) biopsy of intra-abdominal mass
65.14 Other laparoscopic diagnostic procedures on ovaries ♀

49322

49322 Laparoscopy, surgical; with aspiration of cavity or cyst (eg, ovarian cyst) (single or multiple)

ICD-9-CM Diagnostic

179 Malignant neoplasm of uterus, part unspecified ▽ ♀
183.0 Malignant neoplasm of ovary — (Use additional code to identify any functional activity) ♀
183.2 Malignant neoplasm of fallopian tube ♀
183.4 Malignant neoplasm of parametrium of uterus ♀
183.9 Malignant neoplasm of uterine adnexa, unspecified site ▽ ♀
184.8 Malignant neoplasm of other specified sites of female genital organs ♀
199.0 Disseminated malignant neoplasm
199.1 Other malignant neoplasm of unspecified site
209.20 Malignant carcinoid tumor of unknown primary site — (Code first any associated multiple endocrine neoplasia syndrome: 258.01-258.03)(Use additional code to identify associated endocrine syndrome, as: carcinoid syndrome: 259.2)
209.29 Malignant carcinoid tumor of other sites — (Code first any associated multiple endocrine neoplasia syndrome: 258.01-258.03)(Use additional code to identify associated endocrine syndrome, as: carcinoid syndrome: 259.2)
209.30 Malignant poorly differentiated neuroendocrine carcinoma, any site — (Code first any associated multiple endocrine neoplasia syndrome: 258.01-258.03)(Use additional code to identify associated endocrine syndrome, as: carcinoid syndrome: 259.2) ▽
220 Benign neoplasm of ovary — (Use additional code to identify any functional activity: 256.0-256.1) ♀
256.0 Hyperestrogenism ♀
614.0 Acute salpingitis and oophoritis — (Use additional code to identify organism: 041.00-041.09, 041.10-041.19) ♀
614.1 Chronic salpingitis and oophoritis — (Use additional code to identify organism: 041.00-041.09, 041.10-041.19) ♀
614.2 Salpingitis and oophoritis not specified as acute, subacute, or chronic — (Use additional code to identify organism: 041.00-041.09, 041.10-041.19) ♀
614.3 Acute parametritis and pelvic cellulitis — (Use additional code to identify organism: 041.00-041.09, 041.10-041.19) ♀
614.4 Chronic or unspecified parametritis and pelvic cellulitis — (Use additional code to identify organism: 041.00-041.09, 041.10-041.19) ♀
614.6 Pelvic peritoneal adhesions, female (postoperative) (postinfection) — (Use additional code to identify organism: 041.00-041.09, 041.10-041.19) (Use additional code to identify any associated infertility: 628.2) ♀
614.7 Other chronic pelvic peritonitis, female — (Use additional code to identify organism: 041.00-041.09, 041.10-041.19) ♀
614.8 Other specified inflammatory disease of female pelvic organs and tissues — (Use additional code to identify organism: 041.00-041.09, 041.10-041.19) ♀
617.0 Endometriosis of uterus ♀
617.1 Endometriosis of ovary ♀
617.2 Endometriosis of fallopian tube ♀
617.3 Endometriosis of pelvic peritoneum ♀
617.8 Endometriosis of other specified sites ♀
617.9 Endometriosis, site unspecified ▽ ♀
620.0 Follicular cyst of ovary ♀
620.1 Corpus luteum cyst or hematoma ♀
620.2 Other and unspecified ovarian cyst ▽ ♀
620.8 Other noninflammatory disorder of ovary, fallopian tube, and broad ligament ♀
621.0 Polyp of corpus uteri ♀
621.8 Other specified disorders of uterus, not elsewhere classified ♀
625.8 Other specified symptom associated with female genital organs ♀
625.9 Unspecified symptom associated with female genital organs ▽ ♀
627.0 Premenopausal menorrhagia ♀
628.2 Female infertility of tubal origin — (Use additional code for any associated peritubal adhesions: 614.6) ♀
789.00 Abdominal pain, unspecified site ▽
789.01 Abdominal pain, right upper quadrant
789.02 Abdominal pain, left upper quadrant
789.03 Abdominal pain, right lower quadrant
789.04 Abdominal pain, left lower quadrant
789.30 Abdominal or pelvic swelling, mass or lump, unspecified site ▽
789.31 Abdominal or pelvic swelling, mass, or lump, right upper quadrant
789.32 Abdominal or pelvic swelling, mass, or lump, left upper quadrant
789.33 Abdominal or pelvic swelling, mass, or lump, right lower quadrant
789.34 Abdominal or pelvic swelling, mass, or lump, left lower quadrant

ICD-9-CM Procedural

65.11 Aspiration biopsy of ovary ♀
65.91 Aspiration of ovary ♀
66.91 Aspiration of fallopian tube ♀

49323

49323 Laparoscopy, surgical; with drainage of lymphocele to peritoneal cavity

ICD-9-CM Diagnostic

154.0 Malignant neoplasm of rectosigmoid junction
180.9 Malignant neoplasm of cervix uteri, unspecified site ▽ ♀
182.0 Malignant neoplasm of corpus uteri, except isthmus ♀
183.0 Malignant neoplasm of ovary — (Use additional code to identify any functional activity) ♀
185 Malignant neoplasm of prostate ♂
196.2 Secondary and unspecified malignant neoplasm of intra-abdominal lymph nodes
196.6 Secondary and unspecified malignant neoplasm of intrapelvic lymph nodes
199.2 Malignant neoplasm associated with transplanted organ — (Code first complication of transplanted organ (996.80-996.89) Use additional code for specific malignancy)
200.13 Lymphosarcoma of intra-abdominal lymph nodes
201.93 Hodgkin's disease, unspecified type, of intra-abdominal lymph nodes ▽
202.03 Nodular lymphoma of intra-abdominal lymph nodes
202.83 Other malignant lymphomas of intra-abdominal lymph nodes
279.50 Graft-versus-host disease, unspecified — (Code first underlying cause: 996.80-996.89, 999.89)(Use additional code to identify any associated intellectual disabilities) (Use additional code to identify associated manifestations: 695.89, 704.09, 782.4, 787.91) ▽
279.51 Acute graft-versus-host disease — (Code first underlying cause: 996.80-996.89, 999.89)(Use additional code to identify any associated intellectual disabilities) (Use additional code to identify associated manifestations: 695.89, 704.09, 782.4, 787.91)
279.52 Chronic graft-versus-host disease — (Code first underlying cause: 996.80-996.89, 999.89)(Use additional code to identify any associated intellectual disabilities) (Use additional code to identify associated manifestations: 695.89, 704.09, 782.4, 787.91)
279.53 Acute on chronic graft-versus-host disease — (Code first underlying cause: 996.80-996.89, 999.89)(Use additional code to identify any associated intellectual disabilities) (Use additional code to identify associated manifestations: 695.89, 704.09, 782.4, 787.91)
289.1 Chronic lymphadenitis
289.3 Lymphadenitis, unspecified, except mesenteric ▽

457.8 Other noninfectious disorders of lymphatic channels
683 Acute lymphadenitis — (Use additional code to identify organism: 041.1)
782.2 Localized superficial swelling, mass, or lump
785.6 Enlargement of lymph nodes
996.81 Complications of transplanted kidney — (Use additional code to identify nature of complication: 078.5, 199.2, 238.77, 279.50-279.53)
V42.0 Kidney replaced by transplant

ICD-9-CM Procedural

40.0 Incision of lymphatic structures
54.95 Incision of peritoneum

49324-49325

49324 Laparoscopy, surgical; with insertion of tunneled intraperitoneal catheter
49325 with revision of previously placed intraperitoneal cannula or catheter, with removal of intraluminal obstructive material if performed

ICD-9-CM Diagnostic

151.0 Malignant neoplasm of cardia
151.1 Malignant neoplasm of pylorus
151.2 Malignant neoplasm of pyloric antrum
151.3 Malignant neoplasm of fundus of stomach
151.4 Malignant neoplasm of body of stomach
151.8 Malignant neoplasm of other specified sites of stomach
155.0 Malignant neoplasm of liver, primary
158.0 Malignant neoplasm of retroperitoneum
158.8 Malignant neoplasm of specified parts of peritoneum
159.8 Malignant neoplasm of other sites of digestive system and intra-abdominal organs
159.9 Malignant neoplasm of ill-defined sites of digestive organs and peritoneum ▽
182.0 Malignant neoplasm of corpus uteri, except isthmus ♀
182.1 Malignant neoplasm of isthmus ♀
182.8 Malignant neoplasm of other specified sites of body of uterus ♀
183.0 Malignant neoplasm of ovary — (Use additional code to identify any functional activity) ♀
183.2 Malignant neoplasm of fallopian tube ♀
183.5 Malignant neoplasm of round ligament of uterus ♀
183.8 Malignant neoplasm of other specified sites of uterine adnexa ♀
184.8 Malignant neoplasm of other specified sites of female genital organs ♀
197.6 Secondary malignant neoplasm of retroperitoneum and peritoneum
197.7 Secondary malignant neoplasm of liver
198.6 Secondary malignant neoplasm of ovary ♀
209.20 Malignant carcinoid tumor of unknown primary site — (Code first any associated multiple endocrine neoplasia syndrome: 258.01-258.03)(Use additional code to identify associated endocrine syndrome, as: carcinoid syndrome: 259.2)
209.23 Malignant carcinoid tumor of the stomach — (Code first any associated multiple endocrine neoplasia syndrome: 258.01-258.03)(Use additional code to identify associated endocrine syndrome, as: carcinoid syndrome: 259.2)
209.25 Malignant carcinoid tumor of foregut, not otherwise specified — (Code first any associated multiple endocrine neoplasia syndrome: 258.01-258.03)(Use additional code to identify associated endocrine syndrome, as: carcinoid syndrome: 259.2)
209.26 Malignant carcinoid tumor of midgut, not otherwise specified — (Code first any associated multiple endocrine neoplasia syndrome: 258.01-258.03)(Use additional code to identify associated endocrine syndrome, as: carcinoid syndrome: 259.2)
209.27 Malignant carcinoid tumor of hindgut, not otherwise specified — (Code first any associated multiple endocrine neoplasia syndrome: 258.01-258.03)(Use additional code to identify associated endocrine syndrome, as: carcinoid syndrome: 259.2)
209.29 Malignant carcinoid tumor of other sites — (Code first any associated multiple endocrine neoplasia syndrome: 258.01-258.03)(Use additional code to identify associated endocrine syndrome, as: carcinoid syndrome: 259.2)
209.30 Malignant poorly differentiated neuroendocrine carcinoma, any site — (Code first any associated multiple endocrine neoplasia syndrome: 258.01-258.03)(Use additional code to identify associated endocrine syndrome, as: carcinoid syndrome: 259.2) ▽
209.72 Secondary neuroendocrine tumor of liver
209.74 Secondary neuroendocrine tumor of peritoneum
209.79 Secondary neuroendocrine tumor of other sites
249.00 Secondary diabetes mellitus without mention of complication, not stated as uncontrolled, or unspecified — (Use additional code to identify any associated insulin use: V58.67)
249.01 Secondary diabetes mellitus without mention of complication, uncontrolled — (Use additional code to identify any associated insulin use: V58.67)
249.10 Secondary diabetes mellitus with ketoacidosis, not stated as uncontrolled, or unspecified — (Use additional code to identify any associated insulin use: V58.67)
249.11 Secondary diabetes mellitus with ketoacidosis, uncontrolled — (Use additional code to identify any associated insulin use: V58.67)
249.20 Secondary diabetes mellitus with hyperosmolarity, not stated as uncontrolled, or unspecified — (Use additional code to identify any associated insulin use: V58.67)
249.21 Secondary diabetes mellitus with hyperosmolarity, uncontrolled — (Use additional code to identify any associated insulin use: V58.67)
249.40 Secondary diabetes mellitus with renal manifestations, not stated as uncontrolled, or unspecified — (Use additional code to identify manifestation: 581.81, 583.81, 585.1-585.9) (Use additional code to identify any associated insulin use: V58.67)
249.41 Secondary diabetes mellitus with renal manifestations, uncontrolled — (Use additional code to identify manifestation: 581.81, 583.81, 585.1-585.9) (Use additional code to identify any associated insulin use: V58.67)
249.50 Secondary diabetes mellitus with ophthalmic manifestations, not stated as uncontrolled, or unspecified — (Use additional code to identify manifestation: 362.01-362.07, 365.44, 366.41, 369.00-369.9) (Use additional code to identify any associated insulin use: V58.67)
249.51 Secondary diabetes mellitus with ophthalmic manifestations, uncontrolled — (Use additional code to identify manifestation: 362.01-362.07, 365.44, 366.41, 369.00-369.9) (Use additional code to identify any associated insulin use: V58.67)
249.60 Secondary diabetes mellitus with neurological manifestations, not stated as uncontrolled, or unspecified — (Use additional code to identify manifestation: 337.1, 353.5, 354.0-355.9, 357.2, 536.3, 713.5) (Use additional code to identify any associated insulin use: V58.67)
249.61 Secondary diabetes mellitus with neurological manifestations, uncontrolled — (Use additional code to identify manifestation: 337.1, 353.5, 354.0-355.9, 357.2, 536.3, 713.5) (Use additional code to identify any associated insulin use: V58.67)
249.70 Secondary diabetes mellitus with peripheral circulatory disorders, not stated as uncontrolled, or unspecified — (Use additional code to identify manifestation: 443.81, 785.4) (Use additional code to identify any associated insulin use: V58.67)
249.71 Secondary diabetes mellitus with peripheral circulatory disorders, uncontrolled — (Use additional code to identify manifestation: 443.81, 785.4) (Use additional code to identify any associated insulin use: V58.67)
249.80 Secondary diabetes mellitus with other specified manifestations, not stated as uncontrolled, or unspecified — (Use additional code to identify manifestation: 707.10-707.19, 707.8, 707.9, 731.8) (Use additional code to identify any associated insulin use: V58.67)
249.81 Secondary diabetes mellitus with other specified manifestations, uncontrolled — (Use additional code to identify manifestation: 707.10-707.19, 707.8, 707.9, 731.8) (Use additional code to identify any associated insulin use: V58.67)
249.90 Secondary diabetes mellitus with unspecified complication, not stated as uncontrolled, or unspecified — (Use additional code to identify any associated insulin use: V58.67) ▽
249.91 Secondary diabetes mellitus with unspecified complication, uncontrolled — (Use additional code to identify any associated insulin use: V58.67) ▽
250.02 Diabetes mellitus without mention of complication, type II or unspecified type, uncontrolled
250.03 Diabetes mellitus without mention of complication, type I [juvenile type], uncontrolled
250.12 Diabetes with ketoacidosis, type II or unspecified type, uncontrolled
250.13 Diabetes with ketoacidosis, type I [juvenile type], uncontrolled

250.22 Diabetes with hyperosmolarity, type II or unspecified type, uncontrolled
250.23 Diabetes with hyperosmolarity, type I [juvenile type], uncontrolled
250.40 Diabetes with renal manifestations, type II or unspecified type, not stated as uncontrolled — (Use additional code to identify manifestation: 581.81, 583.81, 585.1-585.9)
250.41 Diabetes with renal manifestations, type I [juvenile type], not stated as uncontrolled — (Use additional code to identify manifestation: 581.81, 583.81, 585.1-585.9)
250.42 Diabetes with renal manifestations, type II or unspecified type, uncontrolled — (Use additional code to identify manifestation: 581.81, 583.81, 585.1-585.9)
250.43 Diabetes with renal manifestations, type I [juvenile type], uncontrolled — (Use additional code to identify manifestation: 581.81, 583.81, 585.1-585.9)
250.52 Diabetes with ophthalmic manifestations, type II or unspecified type, uncontrolled — (Use additional code to identify manifestation: 362.01-362.07, 365.44, 366.41, 369.00-369.9)
250.53 Diabetes with ophthalmic manifestations, type I [juvenile type], uncontrolled — (Use additional code to identify manifestation: 362.01-362.07, 365.44, 366.41, 369.00-369.9)
250.62 Diabetes with neurological manifestations, type II or unspecified type, uncontrolled — (Use additional code to identify manifestation: 337.1, 353.5, 354.0-355.9, 357.2, 536.3, 713.5)
250.63 Diabetes with neurological manifestations, type I [juvenile type], uncontrolled — (Use additional code to identify manifestation: 337.1, 353.5, 354.0-355.9, 357.2, 536.3, 713.5)
250.72 Diabetes with peripheral circulatory disorders, type II or unspecified type, uncontrolled — (Use additional code to identify manifestation: 443.81, 785.4)
250.73 Diabetes with peripheral circulatory disorders, type I [juvenile type], uncontrolled — (Use additional code to identify manifestation: 443.81, 785.4)
250.82 Diabetes with other specified manifestations, type II or unspecified type, uncontrolled — (Use additional code to identify manifestation: 707.10-707.19, 707.8, 707.9, 731.8)
250.83 Diabetes with other specified manifestations, type I [juvenile type], uncontrolled — (Use additional code to identify manifestation: 707.10-707.19, 707.8, 707.9, 731.8)
445.81 Atheroembolism of kidney — (Use additional code for any associated acute kidney failure or chronic kidney disease: 584, 585)
577.0 Acute pancreatitis
577.1 Chronic pancreatitis
577.2 Cyst and pseudocyst of pancreas
577.8 Other specified disease of pancreas
581.81 Nephrotic syndrome with other specified pathological lesion in kidney in diseases classified elsewhere — (Code first underlying disease: 084.9, 249.4, 250.4, 277.30-277.39, 446.0, 710.0) ☒
581.9 Nephrotic syndrome with unspecified pathological lesion in kidney ▽
583.81 Nephritis and nephropathy, not specified as acute or chronic, with other specified pathological lesion in kidney, in diseases classified elsewhere — (Code first underlying disease: 016.0, 098.19, 249.4, 250.4, 277.30-277.39, 446.21, 710.0) ☒
584.5 Acute kidney failure with lesion of tubular necrosis
584.6 Acute kidney failure with lesion of renal cortical necrosis
584.7 Acute kidney failure with lesion of medullary [papillary] necrosis
584.8 Acute kidney failure with other specified pathological lesion in kidney
584.9 Acute kidney failure, unspecified ▽
585.1 Chronic kidney disease, Stage I — (Use additional code to identify kidney transplant status, if applicable: V42.0. Use additional code to identify manifestation: 357.4, 420.0. Code first hypertensive chronic kidney disease, if applicable: 403.00-403.91, 404.00-404.93)
585.2 Chronic kidney disease, Stage II (mild) — (Use additional code to identify kidney transplant status, if applicable: V42.0. Use additional code to identify manifestation: 357.4, 420.0. Code first hypertensive chronic kidney disease, if applicable: 403.00-403.91, 404.00-404.93)
585.3 Chronic kidney disease, Stage III (moderate) — (Use additional code to identify kidney transplant status, if applicable: V42.0. Use additional code to identify manifestation: 357.4, 420.0. Code first hypertensive chronic kidney disease, if applicable: 403.00-403.91, 404.00-404.93)
585.4 Chronic kidney disease, Stage IV (severe) — (Use additional code to identify kidney transplant status, if applicable: V42.0. Use additional code to identify manifestation: 357.4, 420.0. Code first hypertensive chronic kidney disease, if applicable: 403.00-403.91, 404.00-404.93)
585.5 Chronic kidney disease, Stage V — (Use additional code to identify kidney transplant status, if applicable: V42.0. Use additional code to identify manifestation: 357.4, 420.0. Code first hypertensive chronic kidney disease, if applicable: 403.00-403.91, 404.00-404.93)
585.6 End stage renal disease — (Use additional code to identify kidney transplant status, if applicable: V42.0. Use additional code to identify manifestation: 357.4, 420.0. Code first hypertensive chronic kidney disease, if applicable: 403.00-403.91, 404.00-404.93)
585.9 Chronic kidney disease, unspecified — (Use additional code to identify kidney transplant status, if applicable: V42.0. Use additional code to identify manifestation: 357.4, 420.0. Code first hypertensive chronic kidney disease, if applicable: 403.00-403.91, 404.00-404.93) ▽
586 Unspecified renal failure ▽
728.88 Rhabdomyolysis
753.12 Congenital polycystic kidney, unspecified type ▽
789.00 Abdominal pain, unspecified site ▽
789.01 Abdominal pain, right upper quadrant
789.02 Abdominal pain, left upper quadrant
789.03 Abdominal pain, right lower quadrant
789.04 Abdominal pain, left lower quadrant
789.05 Abdominal pain, periumbilic
789.06 Abdominal pain, epigastric
789.07 Abdominal pain, generalized
789.09 Abdominal pain, other specified site
789.51 Malignant ascites
789.59 Other ascites
998.51 Infected postoperative seroma — (Use additional code to identify organism)
998.59 Other postoperative infection — (Use additional code to identify infection)
V45.11 Renal dialysis status
V45.12 Noncompliance with renal dialysis
V56.2 Fitting and adjustment of peritoneal dialysis catheter — (Use additional code to identify the associated condition. Use additional code for any concurrent peritoneal dialysis: V56.8)
V56.32 Encounter for adequacy testing for peritoneal dialysis — (Use additional code to identify the associated condition)
V56.8 Encounter other dialysis — (Use additional code to identify the associated condition)

ICD-9-CM Procedural

54.93 Creation of cutaneoperitoneal fistula
54.99 Other operations of abdominal region

49326

49326 Laparoscopy, surgical; with omentopexy (omental tacking procedure) (List separately in addition to code for primary procedure)

ICD-9-CM Diagnostic

The ICD-9-CM diagnostic code(s) would be the same as the actual procedure performed because these are in-addition-to codes.

ICD-9-CM Procedural

54.74 Other repair of omentum

49327

49327 Laparoscopy, surgical; with placement of interstitial device(s) for radiation therapy guidance (eg, fiducial markers, dosimeter), intra-abdominal, intrapelvic, and/or retroperitoneum, including imaging guidance, if performed, single or multiple (List separately in addition to code for primary procedure)

ICD-9-CM Diagnostic

This code is too broadly diagnostic to adequately present ICD-9-CM diagnostic code links here. Refer to the Neoplasm Table located in the back of this book.

ICD-9-CM Procedural

54.21 Laparoscopy
54.99 Other operations of abdominal region
92.29 Other radiotherapeutic procedure

49400

49400 Injection of air or contrast into peritoneal cavity (separate procedure)

ICD-9-CM Diagnostic

The application of this code is too broad to adequately present ICD-9-CM diagnostic code links here. Refer to your ICD-9-CM book.

ICD-9-CM Procedural

54.29 Other diagnostic procedures on abdominal region
54.96 Injection of air into peritoneal cavity
88.11 Pelvic opaque dye contrast radiography
88.12 Pelvic gas contrast radiography
88.13 Other peritoneal pneumogram

HCPCS Level II Supplies & Services

A4305 Disposable drug delivery system, flow rate of 50 ml or greater per hour

49402

49402 Removal of peritoneal foreign body from peritoneal cavity

ICD-9-CM Diagnostic

789.00 Abdominal pain, unspecified site ▽
868.10 Injury to unspecified intra-abdominal organ, with open wound into cavity ▽
868.13 Peritoneum injury with open wound into cavity
868.19 Injury to other and multiple intra-abdominal organs, with open wound into cavity
996.60 Infection and inflammatory reaction due to unspecified device, implant, and graft — (Use additional code to identify specified infections) ▽
996.62 Infection and inflammatory reaction due to other vascular device, implant, and graft — (Use additional code to identify specified infections)
996.70 Other complications due to unspecified device, implant, and graft — (Use additional code to identify complication: 338.18-338.19, 338.28-338.29) ▽
998.4 Foreign body accidentally left during procedure, not elsewhere classified

ICD-9-CM Procedural

54.92 Removal of foreign body from peritoneal cavity

49405-49407

49405 Image-guided fluid collection drainage by catheter (eg, abscess, hematoma, seroma, lymphocele, cyst); visceral (eg, kidney, liver, spleen, lung/mediastinum), percutaneous
49406 peritoneal or retroperitoneal, percutaneous
49407 peritoneal or retroperitoneal, transvaginal or transrectal

ICD-9-CM Diagnostic

289.89 Other specified diseases of blood and blood-forming organs
457.8 Other noninfectious disorders of lymphatic channels
513.0 Abscess of lung — (Use additional code to identify infectious organism)
540.1 Acute appendicitis with peritoneal abscess
572.0 Abscess of liver
573.8 Other specified disorders of liver
577.0 Acute pancreatitis
590.2 Renal and perinephric abscess — (Use additional code to identify organism, such as E. coli, 041.41-041.49)
593.81 Vascular disorders of kidney
595.89 Other specified types of cystitis — (Use additional code to identify organism, such as E. coli: 041.41-041.49)
998.12 Hematoma complicating a procedure
998.13 Seroma complicating a procedure
998.51 Infected postoperative seroma — (Use additional code to identify organism)
998.59 Other postoperative infection — (Use additional code to identify infection)

ICD-9-CM Procedural

33.1 Incision of lung
33.93 Puncture of lung
34.04 Insertion of intercostal catheter for drainage
47.2 Drainage of appendiceal abscess
50.91 Percutaneous aspiration of liver
51.01 Percutaneous aspiration of gallbladder
52.01 Drainage of pancreatic cyst by catheter
54.91 Percutaneous abdominal drainage
55.92 Percutaneous aspiration of kidney (pelvis)
57.11 Percutaneous aspiration of bladder

49411

49411 Placement of interstitial device(s) for radiation therapy guidance (eg, fiducial markers, dosimeter), percutaneous, intra-abdominal, intra-pelvic (except prostate), and/or retroperitoneum, single or multiple

ICD-9-CM Diagnostic

This code is too broadly diagnostic to adequately present ICD-9-CM diagnostic code links here. Refer to the Neoplasm Table located in the back of this book.

ICD-9-CM Procedural

54.0 Incision of abdominal wall
54.99 Other operations of abdominal region

HCPCS Level II Supplies & Services

A4648 Tissue marker, implantable, any type, each
A4650 Implantable radiation dosimeter, each

49412

49412 Placement of interstitial device(s) for radiation therapy guidance (eg, fiducial markers, dosimeter), open, intra-abdominal, intrapelvic, and/or retroperitoneum, including image guidance, if performed, single or multiple (List separately in addition to code for primary procedure)

ICD-9-CM Diagnostic

This code is too broadly diagnostic to adequately present ICD-9-CM diagnostic code links here. Refer to the Neoplasm Table located in the back of this book.

ICD-9-CM Procedural

54.0 Incision of abdominal wall
54.19 Other laparotomy
54.95 Incision of peritoneum
54.99 Other operations of abdominal region
92.29 Other radiotherapeutic procedure

49418

49418 Insertion of tunneled intraperitoneal catheter (eg, dialysis, intraperitoneal chemotherapy instillation, management of ascites), complete procedure, including imaging guidance, catheter placement, contrast injection when performed, and radiological supervision and interpretation, percutaneous

ICD-9-CM Diagnostic

151.0 Malignant neoplasm of cardia
151.1 Malignant neoplasm of pylorus
151.2 Malignant neoplasm of pyloric antrum
151.3 Malignant neoplasm of fundus of stomach
151.4 Malignant neoplasm of body of stomach
151.8 Malignant neoplasm of other specified sites of stomach
155.0 Malignant neoplasm of liver, primary
158.0 Malignant neoplasm of retroperitoneum
158.8 Malignant neoplasm of specified parts of peritoneum
159.8 Malignant neoplasm of other sites of digestive system and intra-abdominal organs
159.9 Malignant neoplasm of ill-defined sites of digestive organs and peritoneum ▽
182.0 Malignant neoplasm of corpus uteri, except isthmus ♀
182.1 Malignant neoplasm of isthmus ♀
182.8 Malignant neoplasm of other specified sites of body of uterus ♀
183.0 Malignant neoplasm of ovary — (Use additional code to identify any functional activity) ♀
183.2 Malignant neoplasm of fallopian tube ♀
183.5 Malignant neoplasm of round ligament of uterus ♀
183.8 Malignant neoplasm of other specified sites of uterine adnexa ♀
184.8 Malignant neoplasm of other specified sites of female genital organs ♀
197.6 Secondary malignant neoplasm of retroperitoneum and peritoneum
197.7 Secondary malignant neoplasm of liver
198.6 Secondary malignant neoplasm of ovary ♀
209.20 Malignant carcinoid tumor of unknown primary site — (Code first any associated multiple endocrine neoplasia syndrome: 258.01-258.03)(Use additional code to identify associated endocrine syndrome, as: carcinoid syndrome: 259.2)
209.23 Malignant carcinoid tumor of the stomach — (Code first any associated multiple endocrine neoplasia syndrome: 258.01-258.03)(Use additional code to identify associated endocrine syndrome, as: carcinoid syndrome: 259.2)
209.25 Malignant carcinoid tumor of foregut, not otherwise specified — (Code first any associated multiple endocrine neoplasia syndrome: 258.01-258.03)(Use additional code to identify associated endocrine syndrome, as: carcinoid syndrome: 259.2)
209.26 Malignant carcinoid tumor of midgut, not otherwise specified — (Code first any associated multiple endocrine neoplasia syndrome: 258.01-258.03)(Use additional code to identify associated endocrine syndrome, as: carcinoid syndrome: 259.2)
209.27 Malignant carcinoid tumor of hindgut, not otherwise specified — (Code first any associated multiple endocrine neoplasia syndrome: 258.01-258.03)(Use additional code to identify associated endocrine syndrome, as: carcinoid syndrome: 259.2)
209.29 Malignant carcinoid tumor of other sites — (Code first any associated multiple endocrine neoplasia syndrome: 258.01-258.03)(Use additional code to identify associated endocrine syndrome, as: carcinoid syndrome: 259.2)
209.30 Malignant poorly differentiated neuroendocrine carcinoma, any site — (Code first any associated multiple endocrine neoplasia syndrome: 258.01-258.03)(Use additional code to identify associated endocrine syndrome, as: carcinoid syndrome: 259.2) ▽
209.72 Secondary neuroendocrine tumor of liver
209.74 Secondary neuroendocrine tumor of peritoneum
209.79 Secondary neuroendocrine tumor of other sites
249.00 Secondary diabetes mellitus without mention of complication, not stated as uncontrolled, or unspecified — (Use additional code to identify any associated insulin use: V58.67)
249.01 Secondary diabetes mellitus without mention of complication, uncontrolled — (Use additional code to identify any associated insulin use: V58.67)
249.10 Secondary diabetes mellitus with ketoacidosis, not stated as uncontrolled, or unspecified — (Use additional code to identify any associated insulin use: V58.67)
249.11 Secondary diabetes mellitus with ketoacidosis, uncontrolled — (Use additional code to identify any associated insulin use: V58.67)
249.20 Secondary diabetes mellitus with hyperosmolarity, not stated as uncontrolled, or unspecified — (Use additional code to identify any associated insulin use: V58.67)
249.21 Secondary diabetes mellitus with hyperosmolarity, uncontrolled — (Use additional code to identify any associated insulin use: V58.67)
249.40 Secondary diabetes mellitus with renal manifestations, not stated as uncontrolled, or unspecified — (Use additional code to identify manifestation: 581.81, 583.81, 585.1-585.9) (Use additional code to identify any associated insulin use: V58.67)
249.41 Secondary diabetes mellitus with renal manifestations, uncontrolled — (Use additional code to identify manifestation: 581.81, 583.81, 585.1-585.9) (Use additional code to identify any associated insulin use: V58.67)
249.50 Secondary diabetes mellitus with ophthalmic manifestations, not stated as uncontrolled, or unspecified — (Use additional code to identify manifestation: 362.01-362.07, 365.44, 366.41, 369.00-369.9) (Use additional code to identify any associated insulin use: V58.67)
249.51 Secondary diabetes mellitus with ophthalmic manifestations, uncontrolled — (Use additional code to identify manifestation: 362.01-362.07, 365.44, 366.41, 369.00-369.9) (Use additional code to identify any associated insulin use: V58.67)
249.60 Secondary diabetes mellitus with neurological manifestations, not stated as uncontrolled, or unspecified — (Use additional code to identify manifestation: 337.1, 353.5, 354.0-355.9, 357.2, 536.3, 713.5) (Use additional code to identify any associated insulin use: V58.67)
249.61 Secondary diabetes mellitus with neurological manifestations, uncontrolled — (Use additional code to identify manifestation: 337.1, 353.5, 354.0-355.9, 357.2, 536.3, 713.5) (Use additional code to identify any associated insulin use: V58.67)
249.70 Secondary diabetes mellitus with peripheral circulatory disorders, not stated as uncontrolled, or unspecified — (Use additional code to identify manifestation: 443.81, 785.4) (Use additional code to identify any associated insulin use: V58.67)
249.71 Secondary diabetes mellitus with peripheral circulatory disorders, uncontrolled — (Use additional code to identify manifestation: 443.81, 785.4) (Use additional code to identify any associated insulin use: V58.67)
249.80 Secondary diabetes mellitus with other specified manifestations, not stated as uncontrolled, or unspecified — (Use additional code to identify manifestation: 707.10-707.19, 707.8, 707.9, 731.8) (Use additional code to identify any associated insulin use: V58.67)
249.81 Secondary diabetes mellitus with other specified manifestations, uncontrolled — (Use additional code to identify manifestation: 707.10-707.19, 707.8, 707.9, 731.8) (Use additional code to identify any associated insulin use: V58.67)
249.90 Secondary diabetes mellitus with unspecified complication, not stated as uncontrolled, or unspecified — (Use additional code to identify any associated insulin use: V58.67) ▽
249.91 Secondary diabetes mellitus with unspecified complication, uncontrolled — (Use additional code to identify any associated insulin use: V58.67) ▽
250.02 Diabetes mellitus without mention of complication, type II or unspecified type, uncontrolled
250.03 Diabetes mellitus without mention of complication, type I [juvenile type], uncontrolled
250.12 Diabetes with ketoacidosis, type II or unspecified type, uncontrolled
250.13 Diabetes with ketoacidosis, type I [juvenile type], uncontrolled
250.22 Diabetes with hyperosmolarity, type II or unspecified type, uncontrolled
250.23 Diabetes with hyperosmolarity, type I [juvenile type], uncontrolled
250.40 Diabetes with renal manifestations, type II or unspecified type, not stated as uncontrolled — (Use additional code to identify manifestation: 581.81, 583.81, 585.1-585.9)
250.41 Diabetes with renal manifestations, type I [juvenile type], not stated as uncontrolled — (Use additional code to identify manifestation: 581.81, 583.81, 585.1-585.9)
250.42 Diabetes with renal manifestations, type II or unspecified type, uncontrolled — (Use additional code to identify manifestation: 581.81, 583.81, 585.1-585.9)
250.43 Diabetes with renal manifestations, type I [juvenile type], uncontrolled — (Use additional code to identify manifestation: 581.81, 583.81, 585.1-585.9)

250.52 Diabetes with ophthalmic manifestations, type II or unspecified type, uncontrolled — (Use additional code to identify manifestation: 362.01-362.07, 365.44, 366.41, 369.00-369.9)
250.53 Diabetes with ophthalmic manifestations, type I [juvenile type], uncontrolled — (Use additional code to identify manifestation: 362.01-362.07, 365.44, 366.41, 369.00-369.9)
250.62 Diabetes with neurological manifestations, type II or unspecified type, uncontrolled — (Use additional code to identify manifestation: 337.1, 353.5, 354.0-355.9, 357.2, 536.3, 713.5)
250.63 Diabetes with neurological manifestations, type I [juvenile type], uncontrolled — (Use additional code to identify manifestation: 337.1, 353.5, 354.0-355.9, 357.2, 536.3, 713.5)
250.72 Diabetes with peripheral circulatory disorders, type II or unspecified type, uncontrolled — (Use additional code to identify manifestation: 443.81, 785.4)
250.73 Diabetes with peripheral circulatory disorders, type I [juvenile type], uncontrolled — (Use additional code to identify manifestation: 443.81, 785.4)
250.82 Diabetes with other specified manifestations, type II or unspecified type, uncontrolled — (Use additional code to identify manifestation: 707.10-707.19, 707.8, 707.9, 731.8)
250.83 Diabetes with other specified manifestations, type I [juvenile type], uncontrolled — (Use additional code to identify manifestation: 707.10-707.19, 707.8, 707.9, 731.8)
445.81 Atheroembolism of kidney — (Use additional code for any associated acute kidney failure or chronic kidney disease: 584, 585)
577.0 Acute pancreatitis
577.1 Chronic pancreatitis
577.2 Cyst and pseudocyst of pancreas
577.8 Other specified disease of pancreas
581.81 Nephrotic syndrome with other specified pathological lesion in kidney in diseases classified elsewhere — (Code first underlying disease: 084.9, 249.4, 250.4, 277.30-277.39, 446.0, 710.0) ☒
581.9 Nephrotic syndrome with unspecified pathological lesion in kidney ▽
583.81 Nephritis and nephropathy, not specified as acute or chronic, with other specified pathological lesion in kidney, in diseases classified elsewhere — (Code first underlying disease: 016.0, 098.19, 249.4, 250.4, 277.30-277.39, 446.21, 710.0) ☒
584.5 Acute kidney failure with lesion of tubular necrosis
584.6 Acute kidney failure with lesion of renal cortical necrosis
584.7 Acute kidney failure with lesion of medullary [papillary] necrosis
584.8 Acute kidney failure with other specified pathological lesion in kidney
584.9 Acute kidney failure, unspecified ▽
585.1 Chronic kidney disease, Stage I — (Use additional code to identify kidney transplant status, if applicable: V42.0. Use additional code to identify manifestation: 357.4, 420.0. Code first hypertensive chronic kidney disease, if applicable: 403.00-403.91, 404.00-404.93)
585.2 Chronic kidney disease, Stage II (mild) — (Use additional code to identify kidney transplant status, if applicable: V42.0. Use additional code to identify manifestation: 357.4, 420.0. Code first hypertensive chronic kidney disease, if applicable: 403.00-403.91, 404.00-404.93)
585.3 Chronic kidney disease, Stage III (moderate) — (Use additional code to identify kidney transplant status, if applicable: V42.0. Use additional code to identify manifestation: 357.4, 420.0. Code first hypertensive chronic kidney disease, if applicable: 403.00-403.91, 404.00-404.93)
585.4 Chronic kidney disease, Stage IV (severe) — (Use additional code to identify kidney transplant status, if applicable: V42.0. Use additional code to identify manifestation: 357.4, 420.0. Code first hypertensive chronic kidney disease, if applicable: 403.00-403.91, 404.00-404.93)
585.5 Chronic kidney disease, Stage V — (Use additional code to identify kidney transplant status, if applicable: V42.0. Use additional code to identify manifestation: 357.4, 420.0. Code first hypertensive chronic kidney disease, if applicable: 403.00-403.91, 404.00-404.93)
585.6 End stage renal disease — (Use additional code to identify kidney transplant status, if applicable: V42.0. Use additional code to identify manifestation: 357.4, 420.0. Code first hypertensive chronic kidney disease, if applicable: 403.00-403.91, 404.00-404.93)
585.9 Chronic kidney disease, unspecified — (Use additional code to identify kidney transplant status, if applicable: V42.0. Use additional code to identify manifestation: 357.4, 420.0. Code first hypertensive chronic kidney disease, if applicable: 403.00-403.91, 404.00-404.93) ▽
586 Unspecified renal failure ▽
728.88 Rhabdomyolysis
753.12 Congenital polycystic kidney, unspecified type ▽
789.00 Abdominal pain, unspecified site ▽
789.01 Abdominal pain, right upper quadrant
789.02 Abdominal pain, left upper quadrant
789.03 Abdominal pain, right lower quadrant
789.04 Abdominal pain, left lower quadrant
789.05 Abdominal pain, periumbilic
789.06 Abdominal pain, epigastric
789.07 Abdominal pain, generalized
789.09 Abdominal pain, other specified site
789.51 Malignant ascites
789.59 Other ascites
998.51 Infected postoperative seroma — (Use additional code to identify organism)
998.59 Other postoperative infection — (Use additional code to identify infection)
V45.11 Renal dialysis status
V45.12 Noncompliance with renal dialysis
V56.2 Fitting and adjustment of peritoneal dialysis catheter — (Use additional code to identify the associated condition. Use additional code for any concurrent peritoneal dialysis: V56.8)
V56.32 Encounter for adequacy testing for peritoneal dialysis — (Use additional code to identify the associated condition)
V56.8 Encounter other dialysis — (Use additional code to identify the associated condition)

ICD-9-CM Procedural

54.0 Incision of abdominal wall
54.93 Creation of cutaneoperitoneal fistula
54.95 Incision of peritoneum
54.99 Other operations of abdominal region

49419

49419 Insertion of tunneled intraperitoneal catheter, with subcutaneous port (ie, totally implantable)

ICD-9-CM Diagnostic

151.0 Malignant neoplasm of cardia
151.1 Malignant neoplasm of pylorus
151.2 Malignant neoplasm of pyloric antrum
151.3 Malignant neoplasm of fundus of stomach
151.4 Malignant neoplasm of body of stomach
151.8 Malignant neoplasm of other specified sites of stomach
155.0 Malignant neoplasm of liver, primary
158.0 Malignant neoplasm of retroperitoneum
158.8 Malignant neoplasm of specified parts of peritoneum
159.8 Malignant neoplasm of other sites of digestive system and intra-abdominal organs
159.9 Malignant neoplasm of ill-defined sites of digestive organs and peritoneum ▽
182.0 Malignant neoplasm of corpus uteri, except isthmus ♀
182.1 Malignant neoplasm of isthmus ♀
182.8 Malignant neoplasm of other specified sites of body of uterus ♀
183.0 Malignant neoplasm of ovary — (Use additional code to identify any functional activity) ♀
183.2 Malignant neoplasm of fallopian tube ♀
183.5 Malignant neoplasm of round ligament of uterus ♀
183.8 Malignant neoplasm of other specified sites of uterine adnexa ♀
184.8 Malignant neoplasm of other specified sites of female genital organs ♀

197.6 Secondary malignant neoplasm of retroperitoneum and peritoneum
197.7 Secondary malignant neoplasm of liver
198.6 Secondary malignant neoplasm of ovary ♀
209.20 Malignant carcinoid tumor of unknown primary site — (Code first any associated multiple endocrine neoplasia syndrome: 258.01-258.03)(Use additional code to identify associated endocrine syndrome, as: carcinoid syndrome: 259.2)
209.23 Malignant carcinoid tumor of the stomach — (Code first any associated multiple endocrine neoplasia syndrome: 258.01-258.03)(Use additional code to identify associated endocrine syndrome, as: carcinoid syndrome: 259.2)
209.25 Malignant carcinoid tumor of foregut, not otherwise specified — (Code first any associated multiple endocrine neoplasia syndrome: 258.01-258.03)(Use additional code to identify associated endocrine syndrome, as: carcinoid syndrome: 259.2)
209.26 Malignant carcinoid tumor of midgut, not otherwise specified — (Code first any associated multiple endocrine neoplasia syndrome: 258.01-258.03)(Use additional code to identify associated endocrine syndrome, as: carcinoid syndrome: 259.2)
209.27 Malignant carcinoid tumor of hindgut, not otherwise specified — (Code first any associated multiple endocrine neoplasia syndrome: 258.01-258.03)(Use additional code to identify associated endocrine syndrome, as: carcinoid syndrome: 259.2)
209.29 Malignant carcinoid tumor of other sites — (Code first any associated multiple endocrine neoplasia syndrome: 258.01-258.03)(Use additional code to identify associated endocrine syndrome, as: carcinoid syndrome: 259.2)
209.30 Malignant poorly differentiated neuroendocrine carcinoma, any site — (Code first any associated multiple endocrine neoplasia syndrome: 258.01-258.03)(Use additional code to identify associated endocrine syndrome, as: carcinoid syndrome: 259.2)
209.72 Secondary neuroendocrine tumor of liver
209.74 Secondary neuroendocrine tumor of peritoneum
209.79 Secondary neuroendocrine tumor of other sites
249.00 Secondary diabetes mellitus without mention of complication, not stated as uncontrolled, or unspecified — (Use additional code to identify any associated insulin use: V58.67)
249.01 Secondary diabetes mellitus without mention of complication, uncontrolled — (Use additional code to identify any associated insulin use: V58.67)
249.10 Secondary diabetes mellitus with ketoacidosis, not stated as uncontrolled, or unspecified — (Use additional code to identify any associated insulin use: V58.67)
249.11 Secondary diabetes mellitus with ketoacidosis, uncontrolled — (Use additional code to identify any associated insulin use: V58.67)
249.20 Secondary diabetes mellitus with hyperosmolarity, not stated as uncontrolled, or unspecified — (Use additional code to identify any associated insulin use: V58.67)
249.21 Secondary diabetes mellitus with hyperosmolarity, uncontrolled — (Use additional code to identify any associated insulin use: V58.67)
249.40 Secondary diabetes mellitus with renal manifestations, not stated as uncontrolled, or unspecified — (Use additional code to identify manifestation: 581.81, 583.81, 585.1-585.9) (Use additional code to identify any associated insulin use: V58.67)
249.41 Secondary diabetes mellitus with renal manifestations, uncontrolled — (Use additional code to identify manifestation: 581.81, 583.81, 585.1-585.9) (Use additional code to identify any associated insulin use: V58.67)
249.50 Secondary diabetes mellitus with ophthalmic manifestations, not stated as uncontrolled, or unspecified — (Use additional code to identify manifestation: 362.01-362.07, 365.44, 366.41, 369.00-369.9) (Use additional code to identify any associated insulin use: V58.67)
249.51 Secondary diabetes mellitus with ophthalmic manifestations, uncontrolled — (Use additional code to identify manifestation: 362.01-362.07, 365.44, 366.41, 369.00-369.9) (Use additional code to identify any associated insulin use: V58.67)
249.60 Secondary diabetes mellitus with neurological manifestations, not stated as uncontrolled, or unspecified — (Use additional code to identify manifestation: 337.1, 353.5, 354.0-355.9, 357.2, 536.3, 713.5) (Use additional code to identify any associated insulin use: V58.67)
249.61 Secondary diabetes mellitus with neurological manifestations, uncontrolled — (Use additional code to identify manifestation: 337.1, 353.5, 354.0-355.9, 357.2, 536.3, 713.5) (Use additional code to identify any associated insulin use: V58.67)
249.70 Secondary diabetes mellitus with peripheral circulatory disorders, not stated as uncontrolled, or unspecified — (Use additional code to identify manifestation: 443.81, 785.4) (Use additional code to identify any associated insulin use: V58.67)
249.71 Secondary diabetes mellitus with peripheral circulatory disorders, uncontrolled — (Use additional code to identify manifestation: 443.81, 785.4) (Use additional code to identify any associated insulin use: V58.67)
249.80 Secondary diabetes mellitus with other specified manifestations, not stated as uncontrolled, or unspecified — (Use additional code to identify manifestation: 707.10-707.19, 707.8, 707.9, 731.8) (Use additional code to identify any associated insulin use: V58.67)
249.81 Secondary diabetes mellitus with other specified manifestations, uncontrolled — (Use additional code to identify manifestation: 707.10-707.19, 707.8, 707.9, 731.8) (Use additional code to identify any associated insulin use: V58.67)
249.90 Secondary diabetes mellitus with unspecified complication, not stated as uncontrolled, or unspecified — (Use additional code to identify any associated insulin use: V58.67)
249.91 Secondary diabetes mellitus with unspecified complication, uncontrolled — (Use additional code to identify any associated insulin use: V58.67)
250.02 Diabetes mellitus without mention of complication, type II or unspecified type, uncontrolled
250.03 Diabetes mellitus without mention of complication, type I [juvenile type], uncontrolled
250.12 Diabetes with ketoacidosis, type II or unspecified type, uncontrolled
250.13 Diabetes with ketoacidosis, type I [juvenile type], uncontrolled
250.22 Diabetes with hyperosmolarity, type II or unspecified type, uncontrolled
250.23 Diabetes with hyperosmolarity, type I [juvenile type], uncontrolled
250.42 Diabetes with renal manifestations, type II or unspecified type, uncontrolled — (Use additional code to identify manifestation: 581.81, 583.81, 585.1-585.9)
250.43 Diabetes with renal manifestations, type I [juvenile type], uncontrolled — (Use additional code to identify manifestation: 581.81, 583.81, 585.1-585.9)
250.52 Diabetes with ophthalmic manifestations, type II or unspecified type, uncontrolled — (Use additional code to identify manifestation: 362.01-362.07, 365.44, 366.41, 369.00-369.9)
250.53 Diabetes with ophthalmic manifestations, type I [juvenile type], uncontrolled — (Use additional code to identify manifestation: 362.01-362.07, 365.44, 366.41, 369.00-369.9)
250.62 Diabetes with neurological manifestations, type II or unspecified type, uncontrolled — (Use additional code to identify manifestation: 337.1, 353.5, 354.0-355.9, 357.2, 536.3, 713.5)
250.63 Diabetes with neurological manifestations, type I [juvenile type], uncontrolled — (Use additional code to identify manifestation: 337.1, 353.5, 354.0-355.9, 357.2, 536.3, 713.5)
250.72 Diabetes with peripheral circulatory disorders, type II or unspecified type, uncontrolled — (Use additional code to identify manifestation: 443.81, 785.4)
250.73 Diabetes with peripheral circulatory disorders, type I [juvenile type], uncontrolled — (Use additional code to identify manifestation: 443.81, 785.4)
250.82 Diabetes with other specified manifestations, type II or unspecified type, uncontrolled — (Use additional code to identify manifestation: 707.10-707.19, 707.8, 707.9, 731.8)
250.83 Diabetes with other specified manifestations, type I [juvenile type], uncontrolled — (Use additional code to identify manifestation: 707.10-707.19, 707.8, 707.9, 731.8)
789.01 Abdominal pain, right upper quadrant
789.02 Abdominal pain, left upper quadrant
789.03 Abdominal pain, right lower quadrant
789.04 Abdominal pain, left lower quadrant
789.05 Abdominal pain, periumbilic
789.06 Abdominal pain, epigastric
789.07 Abdominal pain, generalized
789.09 Abdominal pain, other specified site

ICD-9-CM Procedural

54.0 Incision of abdominal wall
54.95 Incision of peritoneum

54.99 Other operations of abdominal region

HCPCS Level II Supplies & Services

C1788 Port, indwelling (implantable)

49421

49421 Insertion of tunneled intraperitoneal catheter for dialysis, open

ICD-9-CM Diagnostic

249.40 Secondary diabetes mellitus with renal manifestations, not stated as uncontrolled, or unspecified — (Use additional code to identify manifestation: 581.81, 583.81, 585.1-585.9) (Use additional code to identify any associated insulin use: V58.67)

249.41 Secondary diabetes mellitus with renal manifestations, uncontrolled — (Use additional code to identify manifestation: 581.81, 583.81, 585.1-585.9) (Use additional code to identify any associated insulin use: V58.67)

250.40 Diabetes with renal manifestations, type II or unspecified type, not stated as uncontrolled — (Use additional code to identify manifestation: 581.81, 583.81, 585.1-585.9)

250.41 Diabetes with renal manifestations, type I [juvenile type], not stated as uncontrolled — (Use additional code to identify manifestation: 581.81, 583.81, 585.1-585.9)

250.42 Diabetes with renal manifestations, type II or unspecified type, uncontrolled — (Use additional code to identify manifestation: 581.81, 583.81, 585.1-585.9)

250.43 Diabetes with renal manifestations, type I [juvenile type], uncontrolled — (Use additional code to identify manifestation: 581.81, 583.81, 585.1-585.9)

445.81 Atheroembolism of kidney — (Use additional code for any associated acute kidney failure or chronic kidney disease: 584, 585)

577.0 Acute pancreatitis

577.1 Chronic pancreatitis

577.2 Cyst and pseudocyst of pancreas

577.8 Other specified disease of pancreas

581.81 Nephrotic syndrome with other specified pathological lesion in kidney in diseases classified elsewhere — (Code first underlying disease: 084.9, 249.4, 250.4, 277.30-277.39, 446.0, 710.0) ☒

581.9 Nephrotic syndrome with unspecified pathological lesion in kidney ▽

583.81 Nephritis and nephropathy, not specified as acute or chronic, with other specified pathological lesion in kidney, in diseases classified elsewhere — (Code first underlying disease: 016.0, 098.19, 249.4, 250.4, 277.30-277.39, 446.21, 710.0) ☒

584.5 Acute kidney failure with lesion of tubular necrosis

584.6 Acute kidney failure with lesion of renal cortical necrosis

584.7 Acute kidney failure with lesion of medullary [papillary] necrosis

584.8 Acute kidney failure with other specified pathological lesion in kidney

584.9 Acute kidney failure, unspecified ▽

585.1 Chronic kidney disease, Stage I — (Use additional code to identify kidney transplant status, if applicable: V42.0. Use additional code to identify manifestation: 357.4, 420.0. Code first hypertensive chronic kidney disease, if applicable: 403.00-403.91, 404.00-404.93)

585.2 Chronic kidney disease, Stage II (mild) — (Use additional code to identify kidney transplant status, if applicable: V42.0. Use additional code to identify manifestation: 357.4, 420.0. Code first hypertensive chronic kidney disease, if applicable: 403.00-403.91, 404.00-404.93)

585.3 Chronic kidney disease, Stage III (moderate) — (Use additional code to identify kidney transplant status, if applicable: V42.0. Use additional code to identify manifestation: 357.4, 420.0. Code first hypertensive chronic kidney disease, if applicable: 403.00-403.91, 404.00-404.93)

585.4 Chronic kidney disease, Stage IV (severe) — (Use additional code to identify kidney transplant status, if applicable: V42.0. Use additional code to identify manifestation: 357.4, 420.0. Code first hypertensive chronic kidney disease, if applicable: 403.00-403.91, 404.00-404.93)

585.5 Chronic kidney disease, Stage V — (Use additional code to identify kidney transplant status, if applicable: V42.0. Use additional code to identify manifestation: 357.4, 420.0. Code first hypertensive chronic kidney disease, if applicable: 403.00-403.91, 404.00-404.93)

585.6 End stage renal disease — (Use additional code to identify kidney transplant status, if applicable: V42.0. Use additional code to identify manifestation: 357.4, 420.0. Code first hypertensive chronic kidney disease, if applicable: 403.00-403.91, 404.00-404.93)

585.9 Chronic kidney disease, unspecified — (Use additional code to identify kidney transplant status, if applicable: V42.0. Use additional code to identify manifestation: 357.4, 420.0. Code first hypertensive chronic kidney disease, if applicable: 403.00-403.91, 404.00-404.93) ▽

586 Unspecified renal failure ▽

728.88 Rhabdomyolysis

753.12 Congenital polycystic kidney, unspecified type ▽

789.00 Abdominal pain, unspecified site ▽

789.51 Malignant ascites

789.59 Other ascites

998.51 Infected postoperative seroma — (Use additional code to identify organism)

998.59 Other postoperative infection — (Use additional code to identify infection)

V45.11 Renal dialysis status

V45.12 Noncompliance with renal dialysis

V56.2 Fitting and adjustment of peritoneal dialysis catheter — (Use additional code to identify the associated condition. Use additional code for any concurrent peritoneal dialysis: V56.8)

V56.32 Encounter for adequacy testing for peritoneal dialysis — (Use additional code to identify the associated condition)

V56.8 Encounter other dialysis — (Use additional code to identify the associated condition)

ICD-9-CM Procedural

54.93 Creation of cutaneoperitoneal fistula

HCPCS Level II Supplies & Services

A4305 Disposable drug delivery system, flow rate of 50 ml or greater per hour

49422

49422 Removal of tunneled intraperitoneal catheter

ICD-9-CM Diagnostic

577.0 Acute pancreatitis

577.1 Chronic pancreatitis

577.2 Cyst and pseudocyst of pancreas

577.8 Other specified disease of pancreas

996.56 Mechanical complications due to peritoneal dialysis catheter

996.68 Infection and inflammatory reaction due to peritoneal dialysis catheter — (Use additional code to identify specified infections)

996.73 Other complications due to renal dialysis device, implant, and graft — (Use additional code to identify complication: 338.18-338.19, 338.28-338.29)

V56.2 Fitting and adjustment of peritoneal dialysis catheter — (Use additional code to identify the associated condition. Use additional code for any concurrent peritoneal dialysis: V56.8)

V56.32 Encounter for adequacy testing for peritoneal dialysis — (Use additional code to identify the associated condition)

ICD-9-CM Procedural

54.95 Incision of peritoneum

97.82 Removal of peritoneal drainage device

49423

49423 Exchange of previously placed abscess or cyst drainage catheter under radiological guidance (separate procedure)

ICD-9-CM Diagnostic

457.8 Other noninfectious disorders of lymphatic channels

540.1 Acute appendicitis with peritoneal abscess

567.21 Peritonitis (acute) generalized

567.22 Peritoneal abscess

567.23 Spontaneous bacterial peritonitis

567.29 Other suppurative peritonitis
567.31 Psoas muscle abscess
567.38 Other retroperitoneal abscess
567.39 Other retroperitoneal infections
567.81 Choleperitonitis
567.82 Sclerosing mesenteritis
567.89 Other specified peritonitis
568.89 Other specified disorder of peritoneum
569.5 Abscess of intestine
577.0 Acute pancreatitis
590.2 Renal and perinephric abscess — (Use additional code to identify organism, such as E. coli, 041.41-041.49)
614.2 Salpingitis and oophoritis not specified as acute, subacute, or chronic — (Use additional code to identify organism: 041.00-041.09, 041.10-041.19) ♀
614.3 Acute parametritis and pelvic cellulitis — (Use additional code to identify organism: 041.00-041.09, 041.10-041.19) ♀
614.4 Chronic or unspecified parametritis and pelvic cellulitis — (Use additional code to identify organism: 041.00-041.09, 041.10-041.19) ♀
614.5 Acute or unspecified pelvic peritonitis, female — (Use additional code to identify organism: 041.00-041.09, 041.10-041.19) ♀
751.8 Other specified congenital anomalies of digestive system
780.62 Postprocedural fever
998.59 Other postoperative infection — (Use additional code to identify infection)

ICD-9-CM Procedural

97.15 Replacement of wound catheter

49424

49424 Contrast injection for assessment of abscess or cyst via previously placed drainage catheter or tube (separate procedure)

ICD-9-CM Diagnostic

457.8 Other noninfectious disorders of lymphatic channels
540.1 Acute appendicitis with peritoneal abscess
567.21 Peritonitis (acute) generalized
567.22 Peritoneal abscess
567.23 Spontaneous bacterial peritonitis
567.29 Other suppurative peritonitis
567.31 Psoas muscle abscess
567.38 Other retroperitoneal abscess
567.39 Other retroperitoneal infections
567.81 Choleperitonitis
567.82 Sclerosing mesenteritis
567.89 Other specified peritonitis
568.89 Other specified disorder of peritoneum
569.5 Abscess of intestine
577.0 Acute pancreatitis
590.2 Renal and perinephric abscess — (Use additional code to identify organism, such as E. coli, 041.41-041.49)
614.2 Salpingitis and oophoritis not specified as acute, subacute, or chronic — (Use additional code to identify organism: 041.00-041.09, 041.10-041.19) ♀
614.3 Acute parametritis and pelvic cellulitis — (Use additional code to identify organism: 041.00-041.09, 041.10-041.19) ♀
614.4 Chronic or unspecified parametritis and pelvic cellulitis — (Use additional code to identify organism: 041.00-041.09, 041.10-041.19) ♀
614.5 Acute or unspecified pelvic peritonitis, female — (Use additional code to identify organism: 041.00-041.09, 041.10-041.19) ♀
751.8 Other specified congenital anomalies of digestive system
780.62 Postprocedural fever
998.59 Other postoperative infection — (Use additional code to identify infection)

ICD-9-CM Procedural

54.97 Injection of locally-acting therapeutic substance into peritoneal cavity

49425

49425 Insertion of peritoneal-venous shunt

ICD-9-CM Diagnostic

571.5 Cirrhosis of liver without mention of alcohol — (Code first, if applicable, viral hepatitis (acute) (chronic): 070.0-070.9)
577.0 Acute pancreatitis
577.1 Chronic pancreatitis
577.2 Cyst and pseudocyst of pancreas
577.8 Other specified disease of pancreas
789.51 Malignant ascites
789.59 Other ascites

ICD-9-CM Procedural

54.94 Creation of peritoneovascular shunt

49426

49426 Revision of peritoneal-venous shunt

ICD-9-CM Diagnostic

789.51 Malignant ascites
789.59 Other ascites
996.74 Other complications due to other vascular device, implant, and graft — (Use additional code to identify complication: 338.18-338.19, 338.28-338.29)
998.59 Other postoperative infection — (Use additional code to identify infection)
V58.81 Fitting and adjustment of vascular catheter

ICD-9-CM Procedural

54.99 Other operations of abdominal region

49427

49427 Injection procedure (eg, contrast media) for evaluation of previously placed peritoneal-venous shunt

ICD-9-CM Diagnostic

780.62 Postprocedural fever
789.51 Malignant ascites
789.59 Other ascites
996.74 Other complications due to other vascular device, implant, and graft — (Use additional code to identify complication: 338.18-338.19, 338.28-338.29)
998.59 Other postoperative infection — (Use additional code to identify infection)

ICD-9-CM Procedural

54.97 Injection of locally-acting therapeutic substance into peritoneal cavity

49428

49428 Ligation of peritoneal-venous shunt

ICD-9-CM Diagnostic

780.62 Postprocedural fever
789.51 Malignant ascites
789.59 Other ascites
996.74 Other complications due to other vascular device, implant, and graft — (Use additional code to identify complication: 338.18-338.19, 338.28-338.29)
998.59 Other postoperative infection — (Use additional code to identify infection)
V58.81 Fitting and adjustment of vascular catheter

ICD-9-CM Procedural

54.99 Other operations of abdominal region

49429

49429 Removal of peritoneal-venous shunt

ICD-9-CM Diagnostic

780.62 Postprocedural fever
789.51 Malignant ascites
789.59 Other ascites
996.74 Other complications due to other vascular device, implant, and graft — (Use additional code to identify complication: 338.18-338.19, 338.28-338.29)
998.51 Infected postoperative seroma — (Use additional code to identify organism)
998.59 Other postoperative infection — (Use additional code to identify infection)
V58.81 Fitting and adjustment of vascular catheter

ICD-9-CM Procedural

54.99 Other operations of abdominal region

49435

49435 Insertion of subcutaneous extension to intraperitoneal cannula or catheter with remote chest exit site (List separately in addition to code for primary procedure)

ICD-9-CM Diagnostic

The ICD-9-CM diagnostic code(s) would be the same as the actual procedure performed because these are in-addition-to codes.

ICD-9-CM Procedural

54.99 Other operations of abdominal region

49436

49436 Delayed creation of exit site from embedded subcutaneous segment of intraperitoneal cannula or catheter

ICD-9-CM Diagnostic

996.74 Other complications due to other vascular device, implant, and graft — (Use additional code to identify complication: 338.18-338.19, 338.28-338.29)
998.59 Other postoperative infection — (Use additional code to identify infection)

ICD-9-CM Procedural

54.99 Other operations of abdominal region

49440-49442

49440 Insertion of gastrostomy tube, percutaneous, under fluoroscopic guidance including contrast injection(s), image documentation and report
49441 Insertion of duodenostomy or jejunostomy tube, percutaneous, under fluoroscopic guidance including contrast injection(s), image documentation and report
49442 Insertion of cecostomy or other colonic tube, percutaneous, under fluoroscopic guidance including contrast injection(s), image documentation and report

ICD-9-CM Diagnostic

141.0 Malignant neoplasm of base of tongue
141.1 Malignant neoplasm of dorsal surface of tongue
141.2 Malignant neoplasm of tip and lateral border of tongue
141.3 Malignant neoplasm of ventral surface of tongue
141.4 Malignant neoplasm of anterior two-thirds of tongue, part unspecified ▽
141.8 Malignant neoplasm of other sites of tongue
141.9 Malignant neoplasm of tongue, unspecified site ▽
149.0 Malignant neoplasm of pharynx, unspecified ▽
149.1 Malignant neoplasm of Waldeyer's ring
149.8 Malignant neoplasm of other sites within the lip and oral cavity
149.9 Malignant neoplasm of ill-defined sites of lip and oral cavity
150.0 Malignant neoplasm of cervical esophagus
150.1 Malignant neoplasm of thoracic esophagus
150.2 Malignant neoplasm of abdominal esophagus
150.3 Malignant neoplasm of upper third of esophagus
150.4 Malignant neoplasm of middle third of esophagus
150.5 Malignant neoplasm of lower third of esophagus
150.8 Malignant neoplasm of other specified part of esophagus
150.9 Malignant neoplasm of esophagus, unspecified site ▽
151.0 Malignant neoplasm of cardia
151.1 Malignant neoplasm of pylorus
151.2 Malignant neoplasm of pyloric antrum
151.3 Malignant neoplasm of fundus of stomach
151.4 Malignant neoplasm of body of stomach
151.5 Malignant neoplasm of lesser curvature of stomach, unspecified ▽
151.6 Malignant neoplasm of greater curvature of stomach, unspecified ▽
151.8 Malignant neoplasm of other specified sites of stomach
151.9 Malignant neoplasm of stomach, unspecified site ▽
161.9 Malignant neoplasm of larynx, unspecified site ▽
197.8 Secondary malignant neoplasm of other digestive organs and spleen
199.1 Other malignant neoplasm of unspecified site
203.00 Multiple myeloma, without mention of having achieved remission
203.02 Multiple myeloma, in relapse
209.20 Malignant carcinoid tumor of unknown primary site — (Code first any associated multiple endocrine neoplasia syndrome: 258.01-258.03)(Use additional code to identify associated endocrine syndrome, as: carcinoid syndrome: 259.2)
209.23 Malignant carcinoid tumor of the stomach — (Code first any associated multiple endocrine neoplasia syndrome: 258.01-258.03)(Use additional code to identify associated endocrine syndrome, as: carcinoid syndrome: 259.2)
209.25 Malignant carcinoid tumor of foregut, not otherwise specified — (Code first any associated multiple endocrine neoplasia syndrome: 258.01-258.03)(Use additional code to identify associated endocrine syndrome, as: carcinoid syndrome: 259.2)
209.26 Malignant carcinoid tumor of midgut, not otherwise specified — (Code first any associated multiple endocrine neoplasia syndrome: 258.01-258.03)(Use additional code to identify associated endocrine syndrome, as: carcinoid syndrome: 259.2)
209.27 Malignant carcinoid tumor of hindgut, not otherwise specified — (Code first any associated multiple endocrine neoplasia syndrome: 258.01-258.03)(Use additional code to identify associated endocrine syndrome, as: carcinoid syndrome: 259.2)
209.29 Malignant carcinoid tumor of other sites — (Code first any associated multiple endocrine neoplasia syndrome: 258.01-258.03)(Use additional code to identify associated endocrine syndrome, as: carcinoid syndrome: 259.2)
210.9 Benign neoplasm of pharynx, unspecified ▽
235.5 Neoplasm of uncertain behavior of other and unspecified digestive organs ▽
249.30 Secondary diabetes mellitus with other coma, not stated as uncontrolled, or unspecified — (Use additional code to identify any associated insulin use: V58.67)
249.31 Secondary diabetes mellitus with other coma, uncontrolled — (Use additional code to identify any associated insulin use: V58.67)
250.30 Diabetes with other coma, type II or unspecified type, not stated as uncontrolled
250.31 Diabetes with other coma, type I [juvenile type], not stated as uncontrolled
250.32 Diabetes with other coma, type II or unspecified type, uncontrolled
250.33 Diabetes with other coma, type I [juvenile type], uncontrolled
260 Kwashiorkor
261 Nutritional marasmus
262 Other severe protein-calorie malnutrition
330.8 Other specified cerebral degenerations in childhood — (Use additional code to identify associated intellectual disabilities)
330.9 Unspecified cerebral degeneration in childhood — (Use additional code to identify associated intellectual disabilities) ▽
335.20 Amyotrophic lateral sclerosis
348.1 Anoxic brain damage — (Use additional E code to identify cause)
348.82 Brain death
436 Acute, but ill-defined, cerebrovascular disease — (Use additional code to identify presence of hypertension) ▽
478.6 Edema of larynx
530.11 Reflux esophagitis — (Use additional E code to identify cause, if induced by chemical)

530.12 Acute esophagitis — (Use additional E code to identify cause, if induced by chemical)
530.19 Other esophagitis — (Use additional E code to identify cause, if induced by chemical)
530.20 Ulcer of esophagus without bleeding — (Use additional E code to identify cause, if induced by chemical or drug)
530.21 Ulcer of esophagus with bleeding — (Use additional E code to identify cause, if induced by chemical or drug)
530.3 Stricture and stenosis of esophagus
530.4 Perforation of esophagus
530.5 Dyskinesia of esophagus
530.6 Diverticulum of esophagus, acquired
530.7 Gastroesophageal laceration-hemorrhage syndrome
530.81 Esophageal reflux
530.82 Esophageal hemorrhage
530.83 Esophageal leukoplakia
530.84 Tracheoesophageal fistula
530.85 Barrett's esophagus
530.89 Other specified disorder of the esophagus
536.8 Dyspepsia and other specified disorders of function of stomach
750.3 Congenital tracheoesophageal fistula, esophageal atresia and stenosis
780.01 Coma
783.0 Anorexia
783.21 Loss of weight — (Use additional code to identify Body Mass Index (BMI), if known: V85.0-V85.54)
783.22 Underweight — (Use additional code to identify Body Mass Index (BMI), if known: V85.0-V85.54)
783.3 Feeding difficulties and mismanagement
783.40 Lack of normal physiological development, unspecified ▽
783.41 Failure to thrive
783.7 Adult failure to thrive
787.01 Nausea with vomiting
787.02 Nausea alone
787.03 Vomiting alone
787.04 Bilious emesis
787.20 Dysphagia, unspecified ▽
787.21 Dysphagia, oral phase
787.22 Dysphagia, oropharyngeal phase
787.23 Dysphagia, pharyngeal phase
787.24 Dysphagia, pharyngoesophageal phase
787.29 Other dysphagia
789.00 Abdominal pain, unspecified site ▽
854.00 Intracranial injury of other and unspecified nature, without mention of open intracranial wound, unspecified state of consciousness ▽
854.05 Intracranial injury of other and unspecified nature, without mention of open intracranial wound, prolonged (more than 24 hours) loss of consciousness, without return to pre-existing conscious level ▽
959.01 Head injury, unspecified ▽
998.59 Other postoperative infection — (Use additional code to identify infection)
V10.00 Personal history of malignant neoplasm of unspecified site in gastrointestinal tract ▽
V10.01 Personal history of malignant neoplasm of tongue
V10.02 Personal history of malignant neoplasm of other and unspecified parts of oral cavity and pharynx ▽
V10.03 Personal history of malignant neoplasm of esophagus
V10.21 Personal history of malignant neoplasm of larynx
V53.50 Fitting and adjustment of intestinal appliance and device
V53.59 Fitting and adjustment of other gastrointestinal appliance and device
V85.0 Body Mass Index less than 19, adult

ICD-9-CM Procedural

43.11 Percutaneous (endoscopic) gastrostomy (PEG)
46.32 Percutaneous (endoscopic) jejunostomy (PEJ)
46.39 Other enterostomy

HCPCS Level II Supplies & Services

A4305 Disposable drug delivery system, flow rate of 50 ml or greater per hour

49446

49446 Conversion of gastrostomy tube to gastro-jejunostomy tube, percutaneous, under fluoroscopic guidance including contrast injection(s), image documentation and report

ICD-9-CM Diagnostic

141.0 Malignant neoplasm of base of tongue
141.1 Malignant neoplasm of dorsal surface of tongue
141.2 Malignant neoplasm of tip and lateral border of tongue
141.3 Malignant neoplasm of ventral surface of tongue
141.4 Malignant neoplasm of anterior two-thirds of tongue, part unspecified ▽
141.8 Malignant neoplasm of other sites of tongue
141.9 Malignant neoplasm of tongue, unspecified site ▽
149.0 Malignant neoplasm of pharynx, unspecified ▽
149.1 Malignant neoplasm of Waldeyer's ring
149.8 Malignant neoplasm of other sites within the lip and oral cavity
149.9 Malignant neoplasm of ill-defined sites of lip and oral cavity
150.0 Malignant neoplasm of cervical esophagus
150.1 Malignant neoplasm of thoracic esophagus
150.2 Malignant neoplasm of abdominal esophagus
150.3 Malignant neoplasm of upper third of esophagus
150.4 Malignant neoplasm of middle third of esophagus
150.5 Malignant neoplasm of lower third of esophagus
150.8 Malignant neoplasm of other specified part of esophagus
150.9 Malignant neoplasm of esophagus, unspecified site ▽
151.0 Malignant neoplasm of cardia
151.1 Malignant neoplasm of pylorus
151.2 Malignant neoplasm of pyloric antrum
151.3 Malignant neoplasm of fundus of stomach
151.4 Malignant neoplasm of body of stomach
151.5 Malignant neoplasm of lesser curvature of stomach, unspecified ▽
151.6 Malignant neoplasm of greater curvature of stomach, unspecified ▽
151.8 Malignant neoplasm of other specified sites of stomach
151.9 Malignant neoplasm of stomach, unspecified site ▽
161.9 Malignant neoplasm of larynx, unspecified site ▽
197.8 Secondary malignant neoplasm of other digestive organs and spleen
199.1 Other malignant neoplasm of unspecified site
203.00 Multiple myeloma, without mention of having achieved remission
203.02 Multiple myeloma, in relapse
209.20 Malignant carcinoid tumor of unknown primary site — (Code first any associated multiple endocrine neoplasia syndrome: 258.01-258.03)(Use additional code to identify associated endocrine syndrome, as: carcinoid syndrome: 259.2)
209.23 Malignant carcinoid tumor of the stomach — (Code first any associated multiple endocrine neoplasia syndrome: 258.01-258.03)(Use additional code to identify associated endocrine syndrome, as: carcinoid syndrome: 259.2)
209.25 Malignant carcinoid tumor of foregut, not otherwise specified — (Code first any associated multiple endocrine neoplasia syndrome: 258.01-258.03)(Use additional code to identify associated endocrine syndrome, as: carcinoid syndrome: 259.2)
209.26 Malignant carcinoid tumor of midgut, not otherwise specified — (Code first any associated multiple endocrine neoplasia syndrome: 258.01-258.03)(Use additional code to identify associated endocrine syndrome, as: carcinoid syndrome: 259.2)
209.27 Malignant carcinoid tumor of hindgut, not otherwise specified — (Code first any associated multiple endocrine neoplasia syndrome: 258.01-258.03)(Use additional code to identify associated endocrine syndrome, as: carcinoid syndrome: 259.2)
209.29 Malignant carcinoid tumor of other sites — (Code first any associated multiple endocrine neoplasia syndrome: 258.01-258.03)(Use additional code to identify associated endocrine syndrome, as: carcinoid syndrome: 259.2)

210.9 Benign neoplasm of pharynx, unspecified
235.5 Neoplasm of uncertain behavior of other and unspecified digestive organs
249.30 Secondary diabetes mellitus with other coma, not stated as uncontrolled, or unspecified — (Use additional code to identify any associated insulin use: V58.67)
249.31 Secondary diabetes mellitus with other coma, uncontrolled — (Use additional code to identify any associated insulin use: V58.67)
250.30 Diabetes with other coma, type II or unspecified type, not stated as uncontrolled
250.31 Diabetes with other coma, type I [juvenile type], not stated as uncontrolled
250.32 Diabetes with other coma, type II or unspecified type, uncontrolled
250.33 Diabetes with other coma, type I [juvenile type], uncontrolled
260 Kwashiorkor
261 Nutritional marasmus
262 Other severe protein-calorie malnutrition
330.8 Other specified cerebral degenerations in childhood — (Use additional code to identify associated intellectual disabilities)
330.9 Unspecified cerebral degeneration in childhood — (Use additional code to identify associated intellectual disabilities)
335.20 Amyotrophic lateral sclerosis
348.1 Anoxic brain damage — (Use additional E code to identify cause)
348.82 Brain death
436 Acute, but ill-defined, cerebrovascular disease — (Use additional code to identify presence of hypertension)
478.6 Edema of larynx
530.11 Reflux esophagitis — (Use additional E code to identify cause, if induced by chemical)
530.12 Acute esophagitis — (Use additional E code to identify cause, if induced by chemical)
530.19 Other esophagitis — (Use additional E code to identify cause, if induced by chemical)
530.20 Ulcer of esophagus without bleeding — (Use additional E code to identify cause, if induced by chemical or drug)
530.21 Ulcer of esophagus with bleeding — (Use additional E code to identify cause, if induced by chemical or drug)
530.3 Stricture and stenosis of esophagus
530.4 Perforation of esophagus
530.5 Dyskinesia of esophagus
530.6 Diverticulum of esophagus, acquired
530.7 Gastroesophageal laceration-hemorrhage syndrome
530.81 Esophageal reflux
530.82 Esophageal hemorrhage
530.83 Esophageal leukoplakia
530.84 Tracheoesophageal fistula
530.85 Barrett's esophagus
530.89 Other specified disorder of the esophagus
536.8 Dyspepsia and other specified disorders of function of stomach
750.3 Congenital tracheoesophageal fistula, esophageal atresia and stenosis
780.01 Coma
783.0 Anorexia
783.21 Loss of weight — (Use additional code to identify Body Mass Index (BMI), if known: V85.0-V85.54)
783.22 Underweight — (Use additional code to identify Body Mass Index (BMI), if known: V85.0-V85.54)
783.3 Feeding difficulties and mismanagement
783.40 Lack of normal physiological development, unspecified
783.41 Failure to thrive
783.7 Adult failure to thrive
787.01 Nausea with vomiting
787.02 Nausea alone
787.03 Vomiting alone
787.04 Bilious emesis
787.20 Dysphagia, unspecified
787.21 Dysphagia, oral phase
787.22 Dysphagia, oropharyngeal phase
787.23 Dysphagia, pharyngeal phase
787.24 Dysphagia, pharyngoesophageal phase
787.29 Other dysphagia
789.00 Abdominal pain, unspecified site
854.00 Intracranial injury of other and unspecified nature, without mention of open intracranial wound, unspecified state of consciousness
854.05 Intracranial injury of other and unspecified nature, without mention of open intracranial wound, prolonged (more than 24 hours) loss of consciousness, without return to pre-existing conscious level
959.01 Head injury, unspecified
998.59 Other postoperative infection — (Use additional code to identify infection)
V10.00 Personal history of malignant neoplasm of unspecified site in gastrointestinal tract
V10.01 Personal history of malignant neoplasm of tongue
V10.02 Personal history of malignant neoplasm of other and unspecified parts of oral cavity and pharynx
V10.03 Personal history of malignant neoplasm of esophagus
V10.21 Personal history of malignant neoplasm of larynx
V85.0 Body Mass Index less than 19, adult

ICD-9-CM Procedural

44.32 Percutaneous [endoscopic] gastrojejunostomy

49450-49452

49450 Replacement of gastrostomy or cecostomy (or other colonic) tube, percutaneous, under fluoroscopic guidance including contrast injection(s), image documentation and report
49451 Replacement of duodenostomy or jejunostomy tube, percutaneous, under fluoroscopic guidance including contrast injection(s), image documentation and report
49452 Replacement of gastro-jejunostomy tube, percutaneous, under fluoroscopic guidance including contrast injection(s), image documentation and report

ICD-9-CM Diagnostic

536.40 Unspecified gastrostomy complication
536.41 Infection of gastrostomy — (Use additional code to specify type of infection: 038.0-038.9, 682.2. Use additional code to identify organism: 041.00-041.9)
536.42 Mechanical complication of gastrostomy
536.49 Other gastrostomy complications
569.60 Unspecified complication of colostomy or enterostomy
569.61 Infection of colostomy or enterostomy — (Use additional code to identify organism: 041.00-041.9. Use additional code to specify type of infection: 038.0-038.9, 682.2)
569.62 Mechanical complication of colostomy and enterostomy
569.69 Other complication of colostomy or enterostomy
682.2 Cellulitis and abscess of trunk — (Use additional code to identify organism, such as 041.1, etc.)
V53.50 Fitting and adjustment of intestinal appliance and device
V53.59 Fitting and adjustment of other gastrointestinal appliance and device
V55.1 Attention to gastrostomy
V55.2 Attention to ileostomy
V55.3 Attention to colostomy
V55.4 Attention to other artificial opening of digestive tract

ICD-9-CM Procedural

97.02 Replacement of gastrostomy tube
97.03 Replacement of tube or enterostomy device of small intestine
97.04 Replacement of tube or enterostomy device of large intestine

49460

49460 Mechanical removal of obstructive material from gastrostomy, duodenostomy, jejunostomy, gastro-jejunostomy, or cecostomy (or other colonic) tube, any method, under fluoroscopic guidance including contrast injection(s), if performed, image documentation and report

ICD-9-CM Diagnostic

536.40 Unspecified gastrostomy complication
536.42 Mechanical complication of gastrostomy
536.49 Other gastrostomy complications
537.89 Other specified disorder of stomach and duodenum
569.60 Unspecified complication of colostomy or enterostomy
569.69 Other complication of colostomy or enterostomy
996.59 Mechanical complication due to other implant and internal device, not elsewhere classified
996.79 Other complications due to other internal prosthetic device, implant, and graft — (Use additional code to identify complication: 338.18-338.19, 338.28-338.29)
V55.1 Attention to gastrostomy
V55.2 Attention to ileostomy
V55.3 Attention to colostomy
V55.4 Attention to other artificial opening of digestive tract

ICD-9-CM Procedural

96.36 Irrigation of gastrostomy or enterostomy
96.43 Digestive tract instillation, except gastric gavage

49465

49465 Contrast injection(s) for radiological evaluation of existing gastrostomy, duodenostomy, jejunostomy, gastro-jejunostomy, or cecostomy (or other colonic) tube, from a percutaneous approach including image documentation and report

ICD-9-CM Diagnostic

530.87 Mechanical complication of esophagostomy
536.40 Unspecified gastrostomy complication
536.41 Infection of gastrostomy — (Use additional code to specify type of infection: 038.0-038.9, 682.2. Use additional code to identify organism: 041.00-041.9)
536.42 Mechanical complication of gastrostomy
536.49 Other gastrostomy complications
537.89 Other specified disorder of stomach and duodenum
569.60 Unspecified complication of colostomy or enterostomy
569.69 Other complication of colostomy or enterostomy
682.2 Cellulitis and abscess of trunk — (Use additional code to identify organism, such as 041.1, etc.)
996.59 Mechanical complication due to other implant and internal device, not elsewhere classified
996.79 Other complications due to other internal prosthetic device, implant, and graft — (Use additional code to identify complication: 338.18-338.19, 338.28-338.29)
V44.1 Gastrostomy status
V55.1 Attention to gastrostomy
V55.2 Attention to ileostomy
V55.3 Attention to colostomy
V55.4 Attention to other artificial opening of digestive tract

ICD-9-CM Procedural

54.29 Other diagnostic procedures on abdominal region
88.11 Pelvic opaque dye contrast radiography
88.12 Pelvic gas contrast radiography

HCPCS Level II Supplies & Services

A4305 Disposable drug delivery system, flow rate of 50 ml or greater per hour
A9576 Injection, gadoteridol, (ProHance multipack), per ml
A9577 Injection, gadobenate dimeglumine (MultiHance), per ml
A9578 Injection, gadobenate dimeglumine (MultiHance multipack), per ml
A9579 Injection, gadolinium-based magnetic resonance contrast agent, not otherwise specified (NOS), per ml
Q9953 Injection, iron-based magnetic resonance contrast agent, per ml
Q9954 Oral magnetic resonance contrast agent, per 100 ml
Q9965 Low osmolar contrast material, 100-199 mg/ml iodine concentration, per ml
Q9966 Low osmolar contrast material, 200-299 mg/ml iodine concentration, per ml
Q9967 Low osmolar contrast material, 300-399 mg/ml iodine concentration, per ml

49491-49492

49491 Repair, initial inguinal hernia, preterm infant (younger than 37 weeks gestation at birth), performed from birth up to 50 weeks postconception age, with or without hydrocelectomy; reducible
49492 incarcerated or strangulated

ICD-9-CM Diagnostic

550.00 Inguinal hernia with gangrene, unilateral or unspecified, (not specified as recurrent)
550.02 Inguinal hernia with gangrene, bilateral
550.10 Inguinal hernia with obstruction, without mention of gangrene, unilateral or unspecified, (not specified as recurrent)
550.12 Inguinal hernia with obstruction, without mention gangrene, bilateral, (not specified as recurrent)
550.90 Inguinal hernia without mention of obstruction or gangrene, unilateral or unspecified, (not specified as recurrent)
550.92 Inguinal hernia without mention of obstruction or gangrene, bilateral, (not specified as recurrent)
603.0 Encysted hydrocele ♂
603.1 Infected hydrocele — (Use additional code to identify organism) ♂
603.8 Other specified type of hydrocele ♂
603.9 Unspecified hydrocele ♂
778.6 Congenital hydrocele — (Use additional code(s) to further specify condition)
V64.41 Laparoscopic surgical procedure converted to open procedure

ICD-9-CM Procedural

53.00 Unilateral repair of inguinal hernia, not otherwise specified
53.01 Other and open repair of direct inguinal hernia
53.02 Other and open repair of indirect inguinal hernia
53.03 Other and open repair of direct inguinal hernia with graft or prosthesis
53.04 Other and open repair of indirect inguinal hernia with graft or prosthesis
53.05 Unilateral repair of inguinal hernia with graft or prosthesis, not otherwise specified
53.11 Other and open bilateral repair of direct inguinal hernia
53.12 Other and open bilateral repair of indirect inguinal hernia
53.13 Other and open bilateral repair of inguinal hernia, one direct and one indirect
53.14 Other and open bilateral repair of direct inguinal hernia with graft or prosthesis
53.15 Other and open bilateral repair of indirect inguinal hernia with graft or prosthesis
53.16 Other and open bilateral repair of inguinal hernia, one direct and one indirect, with graft or prosthesis
53.17 Bilateral inguinal hernia repair with graft or prosthesis, not otherwise specified
63.1 Excision of varicocele and hydrocele of spermatic cord ♂

49495-49496

49495 Repair, initial inguinal hernia, full term infant younger than age 6 months, or preterm infant older than 50 weeks postconception age and younger than age 6 months at the time of surgery, with or without hydrocelectomy; reducible
49496 incarcerated or strangulated

ICD-9-CM Diagnostic

550.00 Inguinal hernia with gangrene, unilateral or unspecified, (not specified as recurrent)
550.02 Inguinal hernia with gangrene, bilateral
550.10 Inguinal hernia with obstruction, without mention of gangrene, unilateral or unspecified, (not specified as recurrent)

550.12 Inguinal hernia with obstruction, without mention gangrene, bilateral, (not specified as recurrent)
550.90 Inguinal hernia without mention of obstruction or gangrene, unilateral or unspecified, (not specified as recurrent)
550.92 Inguinal hernia without mention of obstruction or gangrene, bilateral, (not specified as recurrent)
603.0 Encysted hydrocele ♂
603.1 Infected hydrocele — (Use additional code to identify organism) ♂
603.8 Other specified type of hydrocele ♂
603.9 Unspecified hydrocele ▽ ♂
778.6 Congenital hydrocele — (Use additional code(s) to further specify condition)
V64.41 Laparoscopic surgical procedure converted to open procedure

ICD-9-CM Procedural

53.00 Unilateral repair of inguinal hernia, not otherwise specified
53.01 Other and open repair of direct inguinal hernia
53.02 Other and open repair of indirect inguinal hernia
53.03 Other and open repair of direct inguinal hernia with graft or prosthesis
53.04 Other and open repair of indirect inguinal hernia with graft or prosthesis
53.05 Unilateral repair of inguinal hernia with graft or prosthesis, not otherwise specified
53.11 Other and open bilateral repair of direct inguinal hernia
53.12 Other and open bilateral repair of indirect inguinal hernia
53.13 Other and open bilateral repair of inguinal hernia, one direct and one indirect
53.14 Other and open bilateral repair of direct inguinal hernia with graft or prosthesis
53.15 Other and open bilateral repair of indirect inguinal hernia with graft or prosthesis
53.16 Other and open bilateral repair of inguinal hernia, one direct and one indirect, with graft or prosthesis
53.17 Bilateral inguinal hernia repair with graft or prosthesis, not otherwise specified
63.1 Excision of varicocele and hydrocele of spermatic cord ♂

49500-49501

49500 Repair initial inguinal hernia, age 6 months to younger than 5 years, with or without hydrocelectomy; reducible
49501 incarcerated or strangulated

ICD-9-CM Diagnostic

550.00 Inguinal hernia with gangrene, unilateral or unspecified, (not specified as recurrent)
550.02 Inguinal hernia with gangrene, bilateral
550.10 Inguinal hernia with obstruction, without mention of gangrene, unilateral or unspecified, (not specified as recurrent)
550.12 Inguinal hernia with obstruction, without mention gangrene, bilateral, (not specified as recurrent)
550.90 Inguinal hernia without mention of obstruction or gangrene, unilateral or unspecified, (not specified as recurrent)
550.92 Inguinal hernia without mention of obstruction or gangrene, bilateral, (not specified as recurrent)
603.0 Encysted hydrocele ♂
603.1 Infected hydrocele — (Use additional code to identify organism) ♂
603.8 Other specified type of hydrocele ♂
603.9 Unspecified hydrocele ▽ ♂
778.6 Congenital hydrocele — (Use additional code(s) to further specify condition)
V64.41 Laparoscopic surgical procedure converted to open procedure

ICD-9-CM Procedural

53.00 Unilateral repair of inguinal hernia, not otherwise specified
53.01 Other and open repair of direct inguinal hernia
53.02 Other and open repair of indirect inguinal hernia
53.03 Other and open repair of direct inguinal hernia with graft or prosthesis
53.04 Other and open repair of indirect inguinal hernia with graft or prosthesis
53.05 Unilateral repair of inguinal hernia with graft or prosthesis, not otherwise specified
53.11 Other and open bilateral repair of direct inguinal hernia
53.12 Other and open bilateral repair of indirect inguinal hernia
53.13 Other and open bilateral repair of inguinal hernia, one direct and one indirect
53.14 Other and open bilateral repair of direct inguinal hernia with graft or prosthesis
53.15 Other and open bilateral repair of indirect inguinal hernia with graft or prosthesis
53.16 Other and open bilateral repair of inguinal hernia, one direct and one indirect, with graft or prosthesis
53.17 Bilateral inguinal hernia repair with graft or prosthesis, not otherwise specified
53.9 Other hernia repair

49505-49507

49505 Repair initial inguinal hernia, age 5 years or older; reducible
49507 incarcerated or strangulated

ICD-9-CM Diagnostic

550.00 Inguinal hernia with gangrene, unilateral or unspecified, (not specified as recurrent)
550.02 Inguinal hernia with gangrene, bilateral
550.10 Inguinal hernia with obstruction, without mention of gangrene, unilateral or unspecified, (not specified as recurrent)
550.12 Inguinal hernia with obstruction, without mention gangrene, bilateral, (not specified as recurrent)
550.90 Inguinal hernia without mention of obstruction or gangrene, unilateral or unspecified, (not specified as recurrent)
550.92 Inguinal hernia without mention of obstruction or gangrene, bilateral, (not specified as recurrent)
V64.41 Laparoscopic surgical procedure converted to open procedure

ICD-9-CM Procedural

53.00 Unilateral repair of inguinal hernia, not otherwise specified
53.01 Other and open repair of direct inguinal hernia
53.02 Other and open repair of indirect inguinal hernia
53.03 Other and open repair of direct inguinal hernia with graft or prosthesis
53.04 Other and open repair of indirect inguinal hernia with graft or prosthesis
53.05 Unilateral repair of inguinal hernia with graft or prosthesis, not otherwise specified
53.11 Other and open bilateral repair of direct inguinal hernia
53.12 Other and open bilateral repair of indirect inguinal hernia
53.13 Other and open bilateral repair of inguinal hernia, one direct and one indirect
53.14 Other and open bilateral repair of direct inguinal hernia with graft or prosthesis
53.15 Other and open bilateral repair of indirect inguinal hernia with graft or prosthesis
53.16 Other and open bilateral repair of inguinal hernia, one direct and one indirect, with graft or prosthesis
53.17 Bilateral inguinal hernia repair with graft or prosthesis, not otherwise specified
53.9 Other hernia repair

49520-49521

49520 Repair recurrent inguinal hernia, any age; reducible
49521 incarcerated or strangulated

ICD-9-CM Diagnostic

550.01 Inguinal hernia with gangrene, recurrent unilateral or unspecified inguinal hernia
550.03 Inguinal hernia with gangrene, recurrent bilateral
550.11 Inguinal hernia with obstruction, without mention of gangrene, recurrent unilateral or unspecified
550.13 Inguinal hernia with obstruction, without mention of gangrene, recurrent bilateral
550.91 Inguinal hernia without mention of obstruction or gangrene, recurrent unilateral or unspecified
550.93 Inguinal hernia without mention of obstruction or gangrene, recurrent bilateral
V64.41 Laparoscopic surgical procedure converted to open procedure

ICD-9-CM Procedural

53.00 Unilateral repair of inguinal hernia, not otherwise specified
53.01 Other and open repair of direct inguinal hernia
53.02 Other and open repair of indirect inguinal hernia

53.03	Other and open repair of direct inguinal hernia with graft or prosthesis
53.04	Other and open repair of indirect inguinal hernia with graft or prosthesis
53.05	Unilateral repair of inguinal hernia with graft or prosthesis, not otherwise specified
53.11	Other and open bilateral repair of direct inguinal hernia
53.12	Other and open bilateral repair of indirect inguinal hernia
53.13	Other and open bilateral repair of inguinal hernia, one direct and one indirect
53.14	Other and open bilateral repair of direct inguinal hernia with graft or prosthesis
53.15	Other and open bilateral repair of indirect inguinal hernia with graft or prosthesis
53.16	Other and open bilateral repair of inguinal hernia, one direct and one indirect, with graft or prosthesis
53.17	Bilateral inguinal hernia repair with graft or prosthesis, not otherwise specified
53.9	Other hernia repair

49525

49525 Repair inguinal hernia, sliding, any age

ICD-9-CM Diagnostic

550.00	Inguinal hernia with gangrene, unilateral or unspecified, (not specified as recurrent)
550.01	Inguinal hernia with gangrene, recurrent unilateral or unspecified inguinal hernia
550.02	Inguinal hernia with gangrene, bilateral
550.03	Inguinal hernia with gangrene, recurrent bilateral
550.10	Inguinal hernia with obstruction, without mention of gangrene, unilateral or unspecified, (not specified as recurrent)
550.11	Inguinal hernia with obstruction, without mention of gangrene, recurrent unilateral or unspecified
550.12	Inguinal hernia with obstruction, without mention gangrene, bilateral, (not specified as recurrent)
550.13	Inguinal hernia with obstruction, without mention of gangrene, recurrent bilateral
550.90	Inguinal hernia without mention of obstruction or gangrene, unilateral or unspecified, (not specified as recurrent)
550.91	Inguinal hernia without mention of obstruction or gangrene, recurrent unilateral or unspecified
550.92	Inguinal hernia without mention of obstruction or gangrene, bilateral, (not specified as recurrent)
550.93	Inguinal hernia without mention of obstruction or gangrene, recurrent bilateral
V64.41	Laparoscopic surgical procedure converted to open procedure

ICD-9-CM Procedural

53.00	Unilateral repair of inguinal hernia, not otherwise specified
53.01	Other and open repair of direct inguinal hernia
53.02	Other and open repair of indirect inguinal hernia
53.03	Other and open repair of direct inguinal hernia with graft or prosthesis
53.04	Other and open repair of indirect inguinal hernia with graft or prosthesis
53.05	Unilateral repair of inguinal hernia with graft or prosthesis, not otherwise specified
53.11	Other and open bilateral repair of direct inguinal hernia
53.12	Other and open bilateral repair of indirect inguinal hernia
53.13	Other and open bilateral repair of inguinal hernia, one direct and one indirect
53.14	Other and open bilateral repair of direct inguinal hernia with graft or prosthesis
53.15	Other and open bilateral repair of indirect inguinal hernia with graft or prosthesis
53.16	Other and open bilateral repair of inguinal hernia, one direct and one indirect, with graft or prosthesis
53.17	Bilateral inguinal hernia repair with graft or prosthesis, not otherwise specified
53.9	Other hernia repair

49540

49540 Repair lumbar hernia

ICD-9-CM Diagnostic

551.8	Hernia of other specified sites, with gangrene
552.8	Hernia of other specified site, with obstruction
553.8	Hernia of other specified sites of abdominal cavity without mention of obstruction or gangrene

ICD-9-CM Procedural

53.9	Other hernia repair

49550-49553

49550 Repair initial femoral hernia, any age; reducible
49553 incarcerated or strangulated

ICD-9-CM Diagnostic

551.00	Femoral hernia with gangrene, unilateral or unspecified (not specified as recurrent)
551.02	Femoral hernia with gangrene, bilateral, (not specified as recurrent)
552.00	Unilateral or unspecified femoral hernia with obstruction
552.02	Bilateral femoral hernia with obstruction
553.00	Unilateral or unspecified femoral hernia without mention of obstruction or gangrene, unilateral or unspecified
553.02	Femoral hernia without mention of obstruction or gangrene, bilateral

ICD-9-CM Procedural

53.21	Unilateral repair of femoral hernia with graft or prosthesis
53.29	Other unilateral femoral herniorrhaphy
53.31	Bilateral repair of femoral hernia with graft or prosthesis
53.39	Other bilateral femoral herniorrhaphy

49555-49557

49555 Repair recurrent femoral hernia; reducible
49557 incarcerated or strangulated

ICD-9-CM Diagnostic

551.01	Femoral hernia with gangrene, recurrent unilateral or unspecified
551.03	Femoral hernia with gangrene, recurrent bilateral
552.01	Recurrent unilateral or unspecified femoral hernia with obstruction
552.03	Recurrent bilateral femoral hernia with obstruction
553.01	Femoral hernia without mention of obstruction or gangrene, recurrent unilateral or unspecified
553.03	Femoral hernia without mention of obstruction or gangrene, recurrent bilateral

ICD-9-CM Procedural

53.21	Unilateral repair of femoral hernia with graft or prosthesis
53.29	Other unilateral femoral herniorrhaphy
53.31	Bilateral repair of femoral hernia with graft or prosthesis
53.39	Other bilateral femoral herniorrhaphy

49560-49566

49560 Repair initial incisional or ventral hernia; reducible
49561 incarcerated or strangulated
49565 Repair recurrent incisional or ventral hernia; reducible
49566 incarcerated or strangulated

ICD-9-CM Diagnostic

551.20	Unspecified ventral hernia with gangrene ▽
551.21	Incisional ventral hernia, with gangrene
552.20	Unspecified ventral hernia with obstruction ▽
552.21	Incisional hernia with obstruction
553.20	Unspecified ventral hernia without mention of obstruction or gangrene ▽
553.21	Incisional hernia without mention of obstruction or gangrene

ICD-9-CM Procedural

53.51	Incisional hernia repair
53.59	Repair of other hernia of anterior abdominal wall
53.61	Other open incisional hernia repair with graft or prosthesis
53.69	Other and open repair of other hernia of anterior abdominal wall with graft or prosthesis

49568

49568 Implantation of mesh or other prosthesis for open incisional or ventral hernia repair or mesh for closure of debridement for necrotizing soft tissue infection (List separately in addition to code for the incisional or ventral hernia repair)

ICD-9-CM Diagnostic

The ICD-9-CM diagnostic code(s) would be the same as the actual procedure performed because these are in-addition-to codes.

ICD-9-CM Procedural

The ICD-9-CM procedural code(s) would be the same as the actual procedure performed because these are in-addition-to codes.

HCPCS Level II Supplies & Services

C1781 Mesh (implantable)

49570-49572

49570 Repair epigastric hernia (eg, preperitoneal fat); reducible (separate procedure)
49572 incarcerated or strangulated

ICD-9-CM Diagnostic

551.29 Other ventral hernia with gangrene
552.29 Other ventral hernia with obstruction
553.29 Other ventral hernia without mention of obstruction or gangrene

ICD-9-CM Procedural

53.59 Repair of other hernia of anterior abdominal wall
53.69 Other and open repair of other hernia of anterior abdominal wall with graft or prosthesis

49580-49587

49580 Repair umbilical hernia, younger than age 5 years; reducible
49582 incarcerated or strangulated
49585 Repair umbilical hernia, age 5 years or older; reducible
49587 incarcerated or strangulated

ICD-9-CM Diagnostic

551.1 Umbilical hernia with gangrene
552.1 Umbilical hernia with obstruction
553.1 Umbilical hernia without mention of obstruction or gangrene
756.79 Other congenital anomalies of abdominal wall

ICD-9-CM Procedural

53.41 Other and open repair of umbilical hernia with graft or prosthesis
53.49 Other open umbilical herniorrhaphy

49590

49590 Repair spigelian hernia

ICD-9-CM Diagnostic

551.29 Other ventral hernia with gangrene
552.29 Other ventral hernia with obstruction
553.29 Other ventral hernia without mention of obstruction or gangrene

ICD-9-CM Procedural

53.59 Repair of other hernia of anterior abdominal wall

49600

49600 Repair of small omphalocele, with primary closure

ICD-9-CM Diagnostic

756.72 Omphalocele
756.79 Other congenital anomalies of abdominal wall

ICD-9-CM Procedural

53.49 Other open umbilical herniorrhaphy

49605-49606

49605 Repair of large omphalocele or gastroschisis; with or without prosthesis
49606 with removal of prosthesis, final reduction and closure, in operating room

ICD-9-CM Diagnostic

756.72 Omphalocele
756.73 Gastroschisis
756.79 Other congenital anomalies of abdominal wall

ICD-9-CM Procedural

53.41 Other and open repair of umbilical hernia with graft or prosthesis
53.49 Other open umbilical herniorrhaphy
54.71 Repair of gastroschisis

49610-49611

49610 Repair of omphalocele (Gross type operation); first stage
49611 second stage

ICD-9-CM Diagnostic

756.72 Omphalocele
756.79 Other congenital anomalies of abdominal wall

ICD-9-CM Procedural

53.49 Other open umbilical herniorrhaphy
54.71 Repair of gastroschisis

49650-49651

49650 Laparoscopy, surgical; repair initial inguinal hernia
49651 repair recurrent inguinal hernia

ICD-9-CM Diagnostic

550.90 Inguinal hernia without mention of obstruction or gangrene, unilateral or unspecified, (not specified as recurrent)
550.91 Inguinal hernia without mention of obstruction or gangrene, recurrent unilateral or unspecified
550.92 Inguinal hernia without mention of obstruction or gangrene, bilateral, (not specified as recurrent)
550.93 Inguinal hernia without mention of obstruction or gangrene, recurrent bilateral

ICD-9-CM Procedural

17.11 Laparoscopic repair of direct inguinal hernia with graft or prosthesis
17.12 Laparoscopic repair of indirect inguinal hernia with graft or prosthesis
17.13 Laparoscopic repair of inguinal hernia with graft or prosthesis, not otherwise specified
17.21 Laparoscopic bilateral repair of direct inguinal hernia with graft or prosthesis
17.22 Laparoscopic bilateral repair of indirect inguinal hernia with graft or prosthesis
17.23 Laparoscopic bilateral repair of inguinal hernia, one direct and one indirect, with graft or prosthesis
17.24 Laparoscopic bilateral repair of inguinal hernia with graft or prosthesis, not otherwise specified
17.42 Laparoscopic robotic assisted procedure
53.00 Unilateral repair of inguinal hernia, not otherwise specified
53.01 Other and open repair of direct inguinal hernia
53.02 Other and open repair of indirect inguinal hernia
53.03 Other and open repair of direct inguinal hernia with graft or prosthesis
53.04 Other and open repair of indirect inguinal hernia with graft or prosthesis
53.05 Unilateral repair of inguinal hernia with graft or prosthesis, not otherwise specified
53.10 Bilateral repair of inguinal hernia, not otherwise specified
53.11 Other and open bilateral repair of direct inguinal hernia
53.12 Other and open bilateral repair of indirect inguinal hernia
53.13 Other and open bilateral repair of inguinal hernia, one direct and one indirect
53.14 Other and open bilateral repair of direct inguinal hernia with graft or prosthesis
53.15 Other and open bilateral repair of indirect inguinal hernia with graft or prosthesis

53.16 Other and open bilateral repair of inguinal hernia, one direct and one indirect, with graft or prosthesis
53.17 Bilateral inguinal hernia repair with graft or prosthesis, not otherwise specified

49652-49653

49652 Laparoscopy, surgical, repair, ventral, umbilical, spigelian or epigastric hernia (includes mesh insertion, when performed); reducible
49653 incarcerated or strangulated

ICD-9-CM Diagnostic

551.20 Unspecified ventral hernia with gangrene ▽
551.29 Other ventral hernia with gangrene
552.1 Umbilical hernia with obstruction
552.20 Unspecified ventral hernia with obstruction ▽
552.29 Other ventral hernia with obstruction
553.1 Umbilical hernia without mention of obstruction or gangrene
553.20 Unspecified ventral hernia without mention of obstruction or gangrene ▽
553.29 Other ventral hernia without mention of obstruction or gangrene

ICD-9-CM Procedural

53.42 Laparoscopic repair of umbilical hernia with graft or prosthesis
53.43 Other laparoscopic umbilical herniorrhaphy
53.63 Other laparoscopic repair of other hernia of anterior abdominal wall with graft or prosthesis

49654-49655

49654 Laparoscopy, surgical, repair, incisional hernia (includes mesh insertion, when performed); reducible
49655 incarcerated or strangulated

ICD-9-CM Diagnostic

551.21 Incisional ventral hernia, with gangrene
552.21 Incisional hernia with obstruction
553.21 Incisional hernia without mention of obstruction or gangrene

ICD-9-CM Procedural

53.62 Laparoscopic incisional hernia repair with graft or prosthesis

49656-49657

49656 Laparoscopy, surgical, repair, recurrent incisional hernia (includes mesh insertion, when performed); reducible
49657 incarcerated or strangulated

ICD-9-CM Diagnostic

551.21 Incisional ventral hernia, with gangrene
552.21 Incisional hernia with obstruction
553.21 Incisional hernia without mention of obstruction or gangrene

ICD-9-CM Procedural

53.62 Laparoscopic incisional hernia repair with graft or prosthesis

49900

49900 Suture, secondary, of abdominal wall for evisceration or dehiscence

ICD-9-CM Diagnostic

674.10 Disruption of cesarean wound, unspecified as to episode of care ▽ ♀
674.12 Disruption of cesarean wound, with delivery, with mention of postpartum complication ♀
674.14 Disruption of cesarean wound, postpartum condition or complication ♀
674.30 Other complication of obstetrical surgical wounds, unspecified as to episode of care ▽ ♀
674.32 Other complication of obstetrical surgical wounds, with delivery, with mention of postpartum complication ♀
674.34 Other complications of obstetrical surgical wounds, postpartum condition or complication ♀
998.30 Disruption of wound, unspecified ▽
998.31 Disruption of internal operation (surgical) wound
998.32 Disruption of external operation (surgical) wound
998.33 Disruption of traumatic injury wound repair
998.83 Non-healing surgical wound

ICD-9-CM Procedural

54.61 Reclosure of postoperative disruption of abdominal wall
54.64 Suture of peritoneum

49904

49904 Omental flap, extra-abdominal (eg, for reconstruction of sternal and chest wall defects)

ICD-9-CM Diagnostic

162.9 Malignant neoplasm of bronchus and lung, unspecified site ▽
171.4 Malignant neoplasm of connective and other soft tissue of thorax
172.5 Malignant melanoma of skin of trunk, except scrotum
174.0 Malignant neoplasm of nipple and areola of female breast — (Use additional code to identify estrogen receptor status: V86.0-V86.1) ♀
174.1 Malignant neoplasm of central portion of female breast — (Use additional code to identify estrogen receptor status: V86.0-V86.1) ♀
174.2 Malignant neoplasm of upper-inner quadrant of female breast — (Use additional code to identify estrogen receptor status: V86.0-V86.1) ♀
174.3 Malignant neoplasm of lower-inner quadrant of female breast — (Use additional code to identify estrogen receptor status: V86.0-V86.1) ♀
174.4 Malignant neoplasm of upper-outer quadrant of female breast — (Use additional code to identify estrogen receptor status: V86.0-V86.1) ♀
174.5 Malignant neoplasm of lower-outer quadrant of female breast — (Use additional code to identify estrogen receptor status: V86.0-V86.1) ♀
174.6 Malignant neoplasm of axillary tail of female breast — (Use additional code to identify estrogen receptor status: V86.0-V86.1) ♀
174.8 Malignant neoplasm of other specified sites of female breast — (Use additional code to identify estrogen receptor status: V86.0-V86.1) ♀
174.9 Malignant neoplasm of breast (female), unspecified site — (Use additional code to identify estrogen receptor status: V86.0-V86.1) ▽ ♀
756.6 Congenital anomaly of diaphragm
756.70 Unspecified congenital anomaly of abdominal wall ▽
875.0 Open wound of chest (wall), without mention of complication
875.1 Open wound of chest (wall), complicated
879.2 Open wound of abdominal wall, anterior, without mention of complication
879.3 Open wound of abdominal wall, anterior, complicated
879.4 Open wound of abdominal wall, lateral, without mention of complication
879.5 Open wound of abdominal wall, lateral, complicated
942.01 Burn of trunk, unspecified degree of breast ▽
942.02 Burn of trunk, unspecified degree of chest wall, excluding breast and nipple ▽
942.31 Full-thickness skin loss due to burn (third degree NOS) of breast
942.32 Full-thickness skin loss due to burn (third degree NOS) of chest wall, excluding breast and nipple
942.41 Deep necrosis of underlying tissues due to burn (deep third degree) of breast, without mention of loss of a body part
942.42 Deep necrosis of underlying tissues due to burn (deep third degree) of chest wall, excluding breast and nipple, without mention of loss of a body part
998.30 Disruption of wound, unspecified ▽
998.31 Disruption of internal operation (surgical) wound
998.32 Disruption of external operation (surgical) wound
998.33 Disruption of traumatic injury wound repair
998.83 Non-healing surgical wound

ICD-9-CM Procedural

34.79 Other repair of chest wall
53.9 Other hernia repair
54.74 Other repair of omentum

49905

49905 Omental flap, intra-abdominal (List separately in addition to code for primary procedure)

ICD-9-CM Diagnostic

This is an add-on code. Refer to the corresponding primary procedure code for ICD-9-CM diagnosis code links.

ICD-9-CM Procedural

53.9 Other hernia repair
54.74 Other repair of omentum

HCPCS Level II Supplies & Services

The HCPCS Level II code(s) would be the same as the actual procedure performed because these are in-addition-to codes.

49906

49906 Free omental flap with microvascular anastomosis

ICD-9-CM Diagnostic

162.9 Malignant neoplasm of bronchus and lung, unspecified site ▽
170.3 Malignant neoplasm of ribs, sternum, and clavicle
171.4 Malignant neoplasm of connective and other soft tissue of thorax
172.5 Malignant melanoma of skin of trunk, except scrotum
174.9 Malignant neoplasm of breast (female), unspecified site — (Use additional code to identify estrogen receptor status: V86.0-V86.1) ▽ ♀
701.8 Other specified hypertrophic and atrophic condition of skin
701.9 Unspecified hypertrophic and atrophic condition of skin ▽
756.3 Other congenital anomaly of ribs and sternum
756.6 Congenital anomaly of diaphragm
756.70 Unspecified congenital anomaly of abdominal wall ▽
875.0 Open wound of chest (wall), without mention of complication
875.1 Open wound of chest (wall), complicated
879.2 Open wound of abdominal wall, anterior, without mention of complication
879.3 Open wound of abdominal wall, anterior, complicated
879.4 Open wound of abdominal wall, lateral, without mention of complication
879.5 Open wound of abdominal wall, lateral, complicated
942.02 Burn of trunk, unspecified degree of chest wall, excluding breast and nipple ▽
942.32 Full-thickness skin loss due to burn (third degree NOS) of chest wall, excluding breast and nipple
942.42 Deep necrosis of underlying tissues due to burn (deep third degree) of chest wall, excluding breast and nipple, without mention of loss of a body part
998.30 Disruption of wound, unspecified ▽
998.31 Disruption of internal operation (surgical) wound
998.32 Disruption of external operation (surgical) wound
998.33 Disruption of traumatic injury wound repair
998.83 Non-healing surgical wound

ICD-9-CM Procedural

54.74 Other repair of omentum

Urinary System

Kidney

50010

50010 Renal exploration, not necessitating other specific procedures

ICD-9-CM Diagnostic

189.0 Malignant neoplasm of kidney, except pelvis
189.1 Malignant neoplasm of renal pelvis
198.0 Secondary malignant neoplasm of kidney
199.2 Malignant neoplasm associated with transplanted organ — (Code first complication of transplanted organ (996.80-996.89) Use additional code for specific malignancy)
209.24 Malignant carcinoid tumor of the kidney — (Code first any associated multiple endocrine neoplasia syndrome: 258.01-258.03; Use additional code to identify associated endocrine syndrome, as: carcinoid syndrome: 259.2)
223.1 Benign neoplasm of renal pelvis
233.9 Carcinoma in situ of other and unspecified urinary organs
236.91 Neoplasm of uncertain behavior of kidney and ureter
239.5 Neoplasm of unspecified nature of other genitourinary organs
591 Hydronephrosis
593.0 Nephroptosis
593.1 Hypertrophy of kidney
593.2 Acquired cyst of kidney
593.81 Vascular disorders of kidney
593.9 Unspecified disorder of kidney and ureter
788.99 Other symptoms involving urinary system
866.00 Unspecified kidney injury without mention of open wound into cavity
866.01 Kidney hematoma without rupture of capsule or mention of open wound into cavity
866.02 Kidney laceration without mention of open wound into cavity
866.03 Complete disruption of kidney parenchyma, without mention of open wound into cavity

ICD-9-CM Procedural

55.01 Nephrotomy
55.11 Pyelotomy

50020

50020 Drainage of perirenal or renal abscess, open

ICD-9-CM Diagnostic

199.2 Malignant neoplasm associated with transplanted organ — (Code first complication of transplanted organ (996.80-996.89) Use additional code for specific malignancy)
238.77 Post-transplant lymphoproliferative disorder [PTLD] — (Code first complications of transplant (996.80-996.89))
279.50 Graft-versus-host disease, unspecified — (Code first underlying cause: 996.80-996.89, 999.89)(Use additional code to identify any associated intellectual disabilities) (Use additional code to identify associated manifestations: 695.89, 704.09, 782.4, 787.91)
279.51 Acute graft-versus-host disease — (Code first underlying cause: 996.80-996.89, 999.89)(Use additional code to identify any associated intellectual disabilities) (Use additional code to identify associated manifestations: 695.89, 704.09, 782.4, 787.91)
279.52 Chronic graft-versus-host disease — (Code first underlying cause: 996.80-996.89, 999.89)(Use additional code to identify any associated intellectual disabilities) (Use additional code to identify associated manifestations: 695.89, 704.09, 782.4, 787.91)
279.53 Acute on chronic graft-versus-host disease — (Code first underlying cause: 996.80-996.89, 999.89)(Use additional code to identify any associated intellectual disabilities) (Use additional code to identify associated manifestations: 695.89, 704.09, 782.4, 787.91)
590.2 Renal and perinephric abscess — (Use additional code to identify organism, such as E. coli, 041.41-041.49)
785.59 Other shock without mention of trauma
788.99 Other symptoms involving urinary system
996.80 Complications of transplanted organ, unspecified site — (Use additional code to identify nature of complication: 078.5, 199.2, 238.77, 279.50-279.53)
996.81 Complications of transplanted kidney — (Use additional code to identify nature of complication: 078.5, 199.2, 238.77, 279.50-279.53)
998.51 Infected postoperative seroma — (Use additional code to identify organism)
998.59 Other postoperative infection — (Use additional code to identify infection)
V42.0 Kidney replaced by transplant

ICD-9-CM Procedural

55.01 Nephrotomy
59.09 Other incision of perirenal or periureteral tissue

50040

50040 Nephrostomy, nephrotomy with drainage

ICD-9-CM Diagnostic

252.00 Hyperparathyroidism, unspecified
252.01 Primary hyperparathyroidism
252.02 Secondary hyperparathyroidism, non-renal
252.08 Other hyperparathyroidism
588.81 Secondary hyperparathyroidism (of renal origin)
588.89 Other specified disorders resulting from impaired renal function
590.10 Acute pyelonephritis without lesion of renal medullary necrosis — (Use additional code to identify organism, such as E. coli, 041.40-041.49)
590.11 Acute pyelonephritis with lesion of renal medullary necrosis — (Use additional code to identify organism, such as E. coli, 041.40-041.49)
590.2 Renal and perinephric abscess — (Use additional code to identify organism, such as E. coli, 041.41-041.49)
590.3 Pyeloureteritis cystica — (Use additional code to identify organism, such as E. coli, 041.41-041.49)
590.80 Unspecified pyelonephritis — (Use additional code to identify organism, such as E. coli, 041.41-041.49)
592.0 Calculus of kidney
593.2 Acquired cyst of kidney
593.4 Other ureteric obstruction
593.70 Vesicoureteral reflux, unspecified or without reflex nephropathy
593.89 Other specified disorder of kidney and ureter
599.70 Hematuria, unspecified
599.71 Gross hematuria
599.72 Microscopic hematuria
753.11 Congenital single renal cyst
753.13 Congenital polycystic kidney, autosomal dominant
753.14 Congenital polycystic kidney, autosomal recessive
753.15 Congenital renal dysplasia
753.16 Congenital medullary cystic kidney
753.17 Congenital medullary sponge kidney
753.19 Other specified congenital cystic kidney disease
753.20 Unspecified obstructive defect of renal pelvis and ureter
753.21 Congenital obstruction of ureteropelvic junction
753.22 Congenital obstruction of ureterovesical junction

753.23 Congenital ureterocele
753.29 Other obstructive defect of renal pelvis and ureter
866.01 Kidney hematoma without rupture of capsule or mention of open wound into cavity
958.5 Traumatic anuria

ICD-9-CM Procedural

55.01 Nephrotomy
55.02 Nephrostomy

50045

50045 Nephrotomy, with exploration

ICD-9-CM Diagnostic

189.0 Malignant neoplasm of kidney, except pelvis
189.1 Malignant neoplasm of renal pelvis
198.0 Secondary malignant neoplasm of kidney
209.24 Malignant carcinoid tumor of the kidney — (Code first any associated multiple endocrine neoplasia syndrome: 258.01-258.03; Use additional code to identify associated endocrine syndrome, as: carcinoid syndrome: 259.2)
209.64 Benign carcinoid tumor of the kidney — (Code first any associated multiple endocrine neoplasia syndrome: 258.01-258.03; Use additional code to identify associated endocrine syndrome, as: carcinoid syndrome: 259.2)
223.0 Benign neoplasm of kidney, except pelvis
223.1 Benign neoplasm of renal pelvis
233.9 Carcinoma in situ of other and unspecified urinary organs ▽
236.91 Neoplasm of uncertain behavior of kidney and ureter
239.5 Neoplasm of unspecified nature of other genitourinary organs
593.2 Acquired cyst of kidney
593.81 Vascular disorders of kidney
958.5 Traumatic anuria

ICD-9-CM Procedural

55.01 Nephrotomy

50060-50070

50060 Nephrolithotomy; removal of calculus
50065 secondary surgical operation for calculus
50070 complicated by congenital kidney abnormality

ICD-9-CM Diagnostic

252.00 Hyperparathyroidism, unspecified ▽
252.01 Primary hyperparathyroidism
252.02 Secondary hyperparathyroidism, non-renal
252.08 Other hyperparathyroidism
588.81 Secondary hyperparathyroidism (of renal origin)
588.89 Other specified disorders resulting from impaired renal function
592.0 Calculus of kidney
592.9 Unspecified urinary calculus ▽
599.70 Hematuria, unspecified ▽
599.71 Gross hematuria
599.72 Microscopic hematuria
753.21 Congenital obstruction of ureteropelvic junction
753.22 Congenital obstruction of ureterovesical junction
753.23 Congenital ureterocele
753.29 Other obstructive defect of renal pelvis and ureter
753.3 Other specified congenital anomalies of kidney
789.00 Abdominal pain, unspecified site ▽
789.01 Abdominal pain, right upper quadrant
789.02 Abdominal pain, left upper quadrant
789.09 Abdominal pain, other specified site

ICD-9-CM Procedural

55.01 Nephrotomy

50075

50075 Nephrolithotomy; removal of large staghorn calculus filling renal pelvis and calyces (including anatrophic pyelolithotomy)

ICD-9-CM Diagnostic

252.00 Hyperparathyroidism, unspecified ▽
252.01 Primary hyperparathyroidism
252.02 Secondary hyperparathyroidism, non-renal
252.08 Other hyperparathyroidism
588.81 Secondary hyperparathyroidism (of renal origin)
592.0 Calculus of kidney
592.9 Unspecified urinary calculus ▽

ICD-9-CM Procedural

55.01 Nephrotomy
55.11 Pyelotomy

50080-50081

50080 Percutaneous nephrostolithotomy or pyelostolithotomy, with or without dilation, endoscopy, lithotripsy, stenting, or basket extraction; up to 2 cm
50081 over 2 cm

ICD-9-CM Diagnostic

252.00 Hyperparathyroidism, unspecified ▽
252.01 Primary hyperparathyroidism
252.02 Secondary hyperparathyroidism, non-renal
252.08 Other hyperparathyroidism
588.81 Secondary hyperparathyroidism (of renal origin)
588.89 Other specified disorders resulting from impaired renal function
592.0 Calculus of kidney
592.9 Unspecified urinary calculus ▽
599.70 Hematuria, unspecified ▽
599.71 Gross hematuria
599.72 Microscopic hematuria
789.00 Abdominal pain, unspecified site ▽
789.01 Abdominal pain, right upper quadrant
789.02 Abdominal pain, left upper quadrant
789.09 Abdominal pain, other specified site

ICD-9-CM Procedural

55.03 Percutaneous nephrostomy without fragmentation
55.04 Percutaneous nephrostomy with fragmentation

50100

50100 Transection or repositioning of aberrant renal vessels (separate procedure)

ICD-9-CM Diagnostic

593.3 Stricture or kinking of ureter
593.81 Vascular disorders of kidney
747.62 Congenital renal vessel anomaly
753.29 Other obstructive defect of renal pelvis and ureter
753.3 Other specified congenital anomalies of kidney

ICD-9-CM Procedural

39.55 Reimplantation of aberrant renal vessel
55.99 Other operations on kidney

50120-50135

50120 Pyelotomy; with exploration
50125 with drainage, pyelostomy
50130 with removal of calculus (pyelolithotomy, pelviolithotomy, including coagulum pyelolithotomy)
50135 complicated (eg, secondary operation, congenital kidney abnormality)

ICD-9-CM Diagnostic

189.1 Malignant neoplasm of renal pelvis
198.0 Secondary malignant neoplasm of kidney
223.1 Benign neoplasm of renal pelvis
233.9 Carcinoma in situ of other and unspecified urinary organs ▽
236.91 Neoplasm of uncertain behavior of kidney and ureter
239.5 Neoplasm of unspecified nature of other genitourinary organs
252.00 Hyperparathyroidism, unspecified ▽
252.01 Primary hyperparathyroidism
252.02 Secondary hyperparathyroidism, non-renal
252.08 Other hyperparathyroidism
588.81 Secondary hyperparathyroidism (of renal origin)
588.89 Other specified disorders resulting from impaired renal function
590.00 Chronic pyelonephritis without lesion of renal medullary necrosis — (Use additional code to identify organism, such as E. coli, 041.41-041.49. Code if applicable, any causal condition first)
590.10 Acute pyelonephritis without lesion of renal medullary necrosis — (Use additional code to identify organism, such as E. coli, 041.40-041.49)
590.11 Acute pyelonephritis with lesion of renal medullary necrosis — (Use additional code to identify organism, such as E. coli, 041.40-041.49)
590.2 Renal and perinephric abscess — (Use additional code to identify organism, such as E. coli, 041.41-041.49)
590.3 Pyeloureteritis cystica — (Use additional code to identify organism, such as E. coli, 041.41-041.49)
592.0 Calculus of kidney
592.9 Unspecified urinary calculus ▽
593.89 Other specified disorder of kidney and ureter
747.62 Congenital renal vessel anomaly
753.17 Congenital medullary sponge kidney
753.20 Unspecified obstructive defect of renal pelvis and ureter ▽
753.21 Congenital obstruction of ureteropelvic junction
753.23 Congenital ureterocele
753.29 Other obstructive defect of renal pelvis and ureter
753.3 Other specified congenital anomalies of kidney

ICD-9-CM Procedural

55.11 Pyelotomy
55.12 Pyelostomy

50200-50205

50200 Renal biopsy; percutaneous, by trocar or needle
50205 by surgical exposure of kidney

ICD-9-CM Diagnostic

189.0 Malignant neoplasm of kidney, except pelvis
189.1 Malignant neoplasm of renal pelvis
198.0 Secondary malignant neoplasm of kidney
199.2 Malignant neoplasm associated with transplanted organ — (Code first complication of transplanted organ (996.80-996.89) Use additional code for specific malignancy)
209.24 Malignant carcinoid tumor of the kidney — (Code first any associated multiple endocrine neoplasia syndrome: 258.01-258.03; Use additional code to identify associated endocrine syndrome, as: carcinoid syndrome: 259.2)
209.64 Benign carcinoid tumor of the kidney — (Code first any associated multiple endocrine neoplasia syndrome: 258.01-258.03; Use additional code to identify associated endocrine syndrome, as: carcinoid syndrome: 259.2)
223.0 Benign neoplasm of kidney, except pelvis
223.1 Benign neoplasm of renal pelvis
228.09 Hemangioma of other sites
233.9 Carcinoma in situ of other and unspecified urinary organs ▽
236.91 Neoplasm of uncertain behavior of kidney and ureter
238.77 Post-transplant lymphoproliferative disorder [PTLD] — (Code first complications of transplant (996.80-996.89))
239.5 Neoplasm of unspecified nature of other genitourinary organs
249.40 Secondary diabetes mellitus with renal manifestations, not stated as uncontrolled, or unspecified — (Use additional code to identify manifestation: 581.81, 583.81, 585.1-585.9) (Use additional code to identify any associated insulin use: V58.67)
249.41 Secondary diabetes mellitus with renal manifestations, uncontrolled — (Use additional code to identify manifestation: 581.81, 583.81, 585.1-585.9) (Use additional code to identify any associated insulin use: V58.67)
250.40 Diabetes with renal manifestations, type II or unspecified type, not stated as uncontrolled — (Use additional code to identify manifestation: 581.81, 583.81, 585.1-585.9)
250.41 Diabetes with renal manifestations, type I [juvenile type], not stated as uncontrolled — (Use additional code to identify manifestation: 581.81, 583.81, 585.1-585.9)
250.42 Diabetes with renal manifestations, type II or unspecified type, uncontrolled — (Use additional code to identify manifestation: 581.81, 583.81, 585.1-585.9)
250.43 Diabetes with renal manifestations, type I [juvenile type], uncontrolled — (Use additional code to identify manifestation: 581.81, 583.81, 585.1-585.9)
277.30 Amyloidosis, unspecified — (Use additional code to identify any associated intellectual disabilities) ▽
277.31 Familial Mediterranean fever — (Use additional code to identify any associated intellectual disabilities)
277.39 Other amyloidosis — (Use additional code to identify any associated intellectual disabilities)
279.50 Graft-versus-host disease, unspecified — (Code first underlying cause: 996.80-996.89, 999.89)(Use additional code to identify any associated intellectual disabilities) (Use additional code to identify associated manifestations: 695.89, 704.09, 782.4, 787.91) ▽
279.51 Acute graft-versus-host disease — (Code first underlying cause: 996.80-996.89, 999.89)(Use additional code to identify any associated intellectual disabilities) (Use additional code to identify associated manifestations: 695.89, 704.09, 782.4, 787.91)
279.52 Chronic graft-versus-host disease — (Code first underlying cause: 996.80-996.89, 999.89)(Use additional code to identify any associated intellectual disabilities) (Use additional code to identify associated manifestations: 695.89, 704.09, 782.4, 787.91)
279.53 Acute on chronic graft-versus-host disease — (Code first underlying cause: 996.80-996.89, 999.89)(Use additional code to identify any associated intellectual disabilities) (Use additional code to identify associated manifestations: 695.89, 704.09, 782.4, 787.91)
403.11 Hypertensive chronic kidney disease, benign, with chronic kidney disease stage V or end stage renal disease — (Use additional code to identify the stage of chronic kidney disease: 585.5, 585.6)
445.81 Atheroembolism of kidney — (Use additional code for any associated acute kidney failure or chronic kidney disease: 584, 585)
580.0 Acute glomerulonephritis with lesion of proliferative glomerulonephritis
580.89 Other acute glomerulonephritis with other specified pathological lesion in kidney
580.9 Acute glomerulonephritis with unspecified pathological lesion in kidney ▽
581.0 Nephrotic syndrome with lesion of proliferative glomerulonephritis
581.3 Nephrotic syndrome with lesion of minimal change glomerulonephritis
581.81 Nephrotic syndrome with other specified pathological lesion in kidney in diseases classified elsewhere — (Code first underlying disease: 084.9, 249.4, 250.4, 277.30-277.39, 446.0, 710.0) ☒
581.9 Nephrotic syndrome with unspecified pathological lesion in kidney ▽
582.0 Chronic glomerulonephritis with lesion of proliferative glomerulonephritis
582.2 Chronic glomerulonephritis with lesion of membranoproliferative glomerulonephritis
582.4 Chronic glomerulonephritis with lesion of rapidly progressive glomerulonephritis
582.9 Chronic glomerulonephritis with unspecified pathological lesion in kidney ▽

583.0 Nephritis and nephropathy, not specified as acute or chronic, with lesion of proliferative glomerulonephritis
583.7 Nephritis and nephropathy, not specified as acute or chronic, with lesion of renal medullary necrosis
583.81 Nephritis and nephropathy, not specified as acute or chronic, with other specified pathological lesion in kidney, in diseases classified elsewhere — (Code first underlying disease: 016.0, 098.19, 249.4, 250.4, 277.30-277.39, 446.21, 710.0) ☒
583.9 Nephritis and nephropathy, not specified as acute or chronic, with unspecified pathological lesion in kidney ▽
584.5 Acute kidney failure with lesion of tubular necrosis
584.6 Acute kidney failure with lesion of renal cortical necrosis
584.7 Acute kidney failure with lesion of medullary [papillary] necrosis
584.8 Acute kidney failure with other specified pathological lesion in kidney
584.9 Acute kidney failure, unspecified ▽
585.1 Chronic kidney disease, Stage I — (Use additional code to identify kidney transplant status, if applicable: V42.0. Use additional code to identify manifestation: 357.4, 420.0. Code first hypertensive chronic kidney disease, if applicable: 403.00-403.91, 404.00-404.93)
585.2 Chronic kidney disease, Stage II (mild) — (Use additional code to identify kidney transplant status, if applicable: V42.0. Use additional code to identify manifestation: 357.4, 420.0. Code first hypertensive chronic kidney disease, if applicable: 403.00-403.91, 404.00-404.93)
585.3 Chronic kidney disease, Stage III (moderate) — (Use additional code to identify kidney transplant status, if applicable: V42.0. Use additional code to identify manifestation: 357.4, 420.0. Code first hypertensive chronic kidney disease, if applicable: 403.00-403.91, 404.00-404.93)
585.4 Chronic kidney disease, Stage IV (severe) — (Use additional code to identify kidney transplant status, if applicable: V42.0. Use additional code to identify manifestation: 357.4, 420.0. Code first hypertensive chronic kidney disease, if applicable: 403.00-403.91, 404.00-404.93)
585.5 Chronic kidney disease, Stage V — (Use additional code to identify kidney transplant status, if applicable: V42.0. Use additional code to identify manifestation: 357.4, 420.0. Code first hypertensive chronic kidney disease, if applicable: 403.00-403.91, 404.00-404.93)
585.6 End stage renal disease — (Use additional code to identify kidney transplant status, if applicable: V42.0. Use additional code to identify manifestation: 357.4, 420.0. Code first hypertensive chronic kidney disease, if applicable: 403.00-403.91, 404.00-404.93)
585.9 Chronic kidney disease, unspecified — (Use additional code to identify kidney transplant status, if applicable: V42.0. Use additional code to identify manifestation: 357.4, 420.0. Code first hypertensive chronic kidney disease, if applicable: 403.00-403.91, 404.00-404.93) ▽
586 Unspecified renal failure ▽
588.0 Renal osteodystrophy
593.2 Acquired cyst of kidney
593.70 Vesicoureteral reflux, unspecified or without reflex nephropathy
593.9 Unspecified disorder of kidney and ureter ▽
599.70 Hematuria, unspecified ▽
599.71 Gross hematuria
599.72 Microscopic hematuria
728.88 Rhabdomyolysis
753.0 Congenital renal agenesis and dysgenesis
753.10 Unspecified congenital cystic kidney disease ▽
788.0 Renal colic
789.00 Abdominal pain, unspecified site ▽
789.09 Abdominal pain, other specified site
789.30 Abdominal or pelvic swelling, mass or lump, unspecified site ▽
789.39 Abdominal or pelvic swelling, mass, or lump, other specified site
791.0 Proteinuria
996.80 Complications of transplanted organ, unspecified site — (Use additional code to identify nature of complication: 078.5, 199.2, 238.77, 279.50-279.53) ▽
996.81 Complications of transplanted kidney — (Use additional code to identify nature of complication: 078.5, 199.2, 238.77, 279.50-279.53)
V42.0 Kidney replaced by transplant

ICD-9-CM Procedural

55.23 Closed (percutaneous) (needle) biopsy of kidney
55.24 Open biopsy of kidney

50220-50225

50220 Nephrectomy, including partial ureterectomy, any open approach including rib resection;
50225 complicated because of previous surgery on same kidney

ICD-9-CM Diagnostic

189.0 Malignant neoplasm of kidney, except pelvis
189.1 Malignant neoplasm of renal pelvis
189.2 Malignant neoplasm of ureter
189.8 Malignant neoplasm of other specified sites of urinary organs
198.0 Secondary malignant neoplasm of kidney
199.2 Malignant neoplasm associated with transplanted organ — (Code first complication of transplanted organ (996.80-996.89) Use additional code for specific malignancy)
209.24 Malignant carcinoid tumor of the kidney — (Code first any associated multiple endocrine neoplasia syndrome: 258.01-258.03; Use additional code to identify associated endocrine syndrome, as: carcinoid syndrome: 259.2)
209.64 Benign carcinoid tumor of the kidney — (Code first any associated multiple endocrine neoplasia syndrome: 258.01-258.03; Use additional code to identify associated endocrine syndrome, as: carcinoid syndrome: 259.2)
223.0 Benign neoplasm of kidney, except pelvis
223.1 Benign neoplasm of renal pelvis
223.2 Benign neoplasm of ureter
233.9 Carcinoma in situ of other and unspecified urinary organs ▽
236.91 Neoplasm of uncertain behavior of kidney and ureter
238.77 Post-transplant lymphoproliferative disorder [PTLD] — (Code first complications of transplant (996.80-996.89))
239.5 Neoplasm of unspecified nature of other genitourinary organs
403.01 Hypertensive chronic kidney disease, malignant, with chronic kidney disease stage V or end stage renal disease — (Use additional code to identify the stage of chronic kidney disease: 585.5, 585.6)
403.11 Hypertensive chronic kidney disease, benign, with chronic kidney disease stage V or end stage renal disease — (Use additional code to identify the stage of chronic kidney disease: 585.5, 585.6)
403.91 Hypertensive chronic kidney disease, unspecified, with chronic kidney disease stage V or end stage renal disease — (Use additional code to identify the stage of chronic kidney disease: 585.5, 585.6) ▽
404.02 Hypertensive heart and chronic kidney disease, malignant, without heart failure and with chronic kidney disease stage V or end stage renal disease — (Use additional code to identify the stage of chronic kidney disease: 585.5, 585.6)
404.12 Hypertensive heart and chronic kidney disease, benign, without heart failure and with chronic kidney disease stage V or end stage renal disease — (Use additional code to identify the stage of chronic kidney disease: 585.5, 585.6)
405.01 Secondary renovascular hypertension, malignant
405.91 Secondary renovascular hypertension, unspecified ▽
445.81 Atheroembolism of kidney — (Use additional code for any associated acute kidney failure or chronic kidney disease: 584, 585)
580.0 Acute glomerulonephritis with lesion of proliferative glomerulonephritis
581.0 Nephrotic syndrome with lesion of proliferative glomerulonephritis
582.0 Chronic glomerulonephritis with lesion of proliferative glomerulonephritis
584.5 Acute kidney failure with lesion of tubular necrosis
585.1 Chronic kidney disease, Stage I — (Use additional code to identify kidney transplant status, if applicable: V42.0. Use additional code to identify manifestation: 357.4, 420.0. Code first hypertensive chronic kidney disease, if applicable: 403.00-403.91, 404.00-404.93)

585.2 Chronic kidney disease, Stage II (mild) — (Use additional code to identify kidney transplant status, if applicable: V42.0. Use additional code to identify manifestation: 357.4, 420.0. Code first hypertensive chronic kidney disease, if applicable: 403.00-403.91, 404.00-404.93)

585.3 Chronic kidney disease, Stage III (moderate) — (Use additional code to identify kidney transplant status, if applicable: V42.0. Use additional code to identify manifestation: 357.4, 420.0. Code first hypertensive chronic kidney disease, if applicable: 403.00-403.91, 404.00-404.93)

585.4 Chronic kidney disease, Stage IV (severe) — (Use additional code to identify kidney transplant status, if applicable: V42.0. Use additional code to identify manifestation: 357.4, 420.0. Code first hypertensive chronic kidney disease, if applicable: 403.00-403.91, 404.00-404.93)

585.5 Chronic kidney disease, Stage V — (Use additional code to identify kidney transplant status, if applicable: V42.0. Use additional code to identify manifestation: 357.4, 420.0. Code first hypertensive chronic kidney disease, if applicable: 403.00-403.91, 404.00-404.93)

585.6 End stage renal disease — (Use additional code to identify kidney transplant status, if applicable: V42.0. Use additional code to identify manifestation: 357.4, 420.0. Code first hypertensive chronic kidney disease, if applicable: 403.00-403.91, 404.00-404.93)

585.9 Chronic kidney disease, unspecified — (Use additional code to identify kidney transplant status, if applicable: V42.0. Use additional code to identify manifestation: 357.4, 420.0. Code first hypertensive chronic kidney disease, if applicable: 403.00-403.91, 404.00-404.93) ▽

587 Unspecified renal sclerosis ▽

588.81 Secondary hyperparathyroidism (of renal origin)

588.89 Other specified disorders resulting from impaired renal function

590.00 Chronic pyelonephritis without lesion of renal medullary necrosis — (Use additional code to identify organism, such as E. coli, 041.41-041.49. Code if applicable, any causal condition first)

590.01 Chronic pyelonephritis with lesion of renal medullary necrosis — (Use additional code to identify organism, such as E. coli, 041.41-041.49. Code if applicable, any causal condition first)

591 Hydronephrosis

592.0 Calculus of kidney

593.4 Other ureteric obstruction

593.70 Vesicoureteral reflux, unspecified or without reflex nephropathy

593.71 Vesicoureteral reflux with reflux nephropathy, unilateral

593.72 Vesicoureteral reflux with reflux nephropathy, bilateral

593.73 Vesicoureteral reflux with reflux nephropathy, NOS ▽

593.81 Vascular disorders of kidney

593.89 Other specified disorder of kidney and ureter

593.9 Unspecified disorder of kidney and ureter ▽

599.60 Urinary obstruction, unspecified — (Use additional code to identify urinary incontinence: 625.6, 788.30-788.39) ▽

599.69 Urinary obstruction, not elsewhere classified — (Use additional code to identify urinary incontinence: 625.6, 788.30-788.39. Code, if applicable, any causal condition first: 600.0-600.9, with fifth-digit 1)

599.70 Hematuria, unspecified ▽

599.71 Gross hematuria

599.72 Microscopic hematuria

753.0 Congenital renal agenesis and dysgenesis

753.10 Unspecified congenital cystic kidney disease ▽

753.11 Congenital single renal cyst

753.12 Congenital polycystic kidney, unspecified type ▽

753.13 Congenital polycystic kidney, autosomal dominant

753.14 Congenital polycystic kidney, autosomal recessive

753.15 Congenital renal dysplasia

753.16 Congenital medullary cystic kidney

753.17 Congenital medullary sponge kidney

753.19 Other specified congenital cystic kidney disease

753.21 Congenital obstruction of ureteropelvic junction

753.23 Congenital ureterocele

753.29 Other obstructive defect of renal pelvis and ureter

866.02 Kidney laceration without mention of open wound into cavity

866.03 Complete disruption of kidney parenchyma, without mention of open wound into cavity

866.13 Complete disruption of kidney parenchyma, with open wound into cavity

879.3 Open wound of abdominal wall, anterior, complicated

V64.41 Laparoscopic surgical procedure converted to open procedure

ICD-9-CM Procedural

55.51 Nephroureterectomy

55.52 Nephrectomy of remaining kidney

55.54 Bilateral nephrectomy

50230

50230 Nephrectomy, including partial ureterectomy, any open approach including rib resection; radical, with regional lymphadenectomy and/or vena caval thrombectomy

ICD-9-CM Diagnostic

189.0 Malignant neoplasm of kidney, except pelvis

189.1 Malignant neoplasm of renal pelvis

189.2 Malignant neoplasm of ureter

196.2 Secondary and unspecified malignant neoplasm of intra-abdominal lymph nodes

198.0 Secondary malignant neoplasm of kidney

198.1 Secondary malignant neoplasm of other urinary organs

199.1 Other malignant neoplasm of unspecified site

199.2 Malignant neoplasm associated with transplanted organ — (Code first complication of transplanted organ (996.80-996.89) Use additional code for specific malignancy)

209.24 Malignant carcinoid tumor of the kidney — (Code first any associated multiple endocrine neoplasia syndrome: 258.01-258.03; Use additional code to identify associated endocrine syndrome, as: carcinoid syndrome: 259.2)

209.64 Benign carcinoid tumor of the kidney — (Code first any associated multiple endocrine neoplasia syndrome: 258.01-258.03; Use additional code to identify associated endocrine syndrome, as: carcinoid syndrome: 259.2)

223.0 Benign neoplasm of kidney, except pelvis

223.1 Benign neoplasm of renal pelvis

223.2 Benign neoplasm of ureter

233.9 Carcinoma in situ of other and unspecified urinary organs ▽

236.91 Neoplasm of uncertain behavior of kidney and ureter

239.5 Neoplasm of unspecified nature of other genitourinary organs

403.01 Hypertensive chronic kidney disease, malignant, with chronic kidney disease stage V or end stage renal disease — (Use additional code to identify the stage of chronic kidney disease: 585.5, 585.6)

403.11 Hypertensive chronic kidney disease, benign, with chronic kidney disease stage V or end stage renal disease — (Use additional code to identify the stage of chronic kidney disease: 585.5, 585.6)

404.02 Hypertensive heart and chronic kidney disease, malignant, without heart failure and with chronic kidney disease stage V or end stage renal disease — (Use additional code to identify the stage of chronic kidney disease: 585.5, 585.6)

404.12 Hypertensive heart and chronic kidney disease, benign, without heart failure and with chronic kidney disease stage V or end stage renal disease — (Use additional code to identify the stage of chronic kidney disease: 585.5, 585.6)

445.81 Atheroembolism of kidney — (Use additional code for any associated acute kidney failure or chronic kidney disease: 584, 585)

453.2 Other venous embolism and thrombosis, of inferior vena cava

580.0 Acute glomerulonephritis with lesion of proliferative glomerulonephritis

581.0 Nephrotic syndrome with lesion of proliferative glomerulonephritis

582.0 Chronic glomerulonephritis with lesion of proliferative glomerulonephritis

584.5 Acute kidney failure with lesion of tubular necrosis

585.1 Chronic kidney disease, Stage I — (Use additional code to identify kidney transplant status, if applicable: V42.0. Use additional code to identify manifestation: 357.4,

420.0. Code first hypertensive chronic kidney disease, if applicable: 403.00-403.91, 404.00-404.93)

585.2 Chronic kidney disease, Stage II (mild) — (Use additional code to identify kidney transplant status, if applicable: V42.0. Use additional code to identify manifestation: 357.4, 420.0. Code first hypertensive chronic kidney disease, if applicable: 403.00-403.91, 404.00-404.93)

585.3 Chronic kidney disease, Stage III (moderate) — (Use additional code to identify kidney transplant status, if applicable: V42.0. Use additional code to identify manifestation: 357.4, 420.0. Code first hypertensive chronic kidney disease, if applicable: 403.00-403.91, 404.00-404.93)

585.4 Chronic kidney disease, Stage IV (severe) — (Use additional code to identify kidney transplant status, if applicable: V42.0. Use additional code to identify manifestation: 357.4, 420.0. Code first hypertensive chronic kidney disease, if applicable: 403.00-403.91, 404.00-404.93)

585.5 Chronic kidney disease, Stage V — (Use additional code to identify kidney transplant status, if applicable: V42.0. Use additional code to identify manifestation: 357.4, 420.0. Code first hypertensive chronic kidney disease, if applicable: 403.00-403.91, 404.00-404.93)

585.6 End stage renal disease — (Use additional code to identify kidney transplant status, if applicable: V42.0. Use additional code to identify manifestation: 357.4, 420.0. Code first hypertensive chronic kidney disease, if applicable: 403.00-403.91, 404.00-404.93)

585.9 Chronic kidney disease, unspecified — (Use additional code to identify kidney transplant status, if applicable: V42.0. Use additional code to identify manifestation: 357.4, 420.0. Code first hypertensive chronic kidney disease, if applicable: 403.00-403.91, 404.00-404.93) ▽

587 Unspecified renal sclerosis ▽

588.81 Secondary hyperparathyroidism (of renal origin)

588.89 Other specified disorders resulting from impaired renal function

590.00 Chronic pyelonephritis without lesion of renal medullary necrosis — (Use additional code to identify organism, such as E. coli, 041.41-041.49. Code if applicable, any causal condition first)

590.01 Chronic pyelonephritis with lesion of renal medullary necrosis — (Use additional code to identify organism, such as E. coli, 041.41-041.49. Code if applicable, any causal condition first)

591 Hydronephrosis

592.0 Calculus of kidney

593.4 Other ureteric obstruction

593.70 Vesicoureteral reflux, unspecified or without reflex nephropathy

593.71 Vesicoureteral reflux with reflux nephropathy, unilateral

593.72 Vesicoureteral reflux with reflux nephropathy, bilateral

593.73 Vesicoureteral reflux with reflux nephropathy, NOS ▽

593.81 Vascular disorders of kidney

593.89 Other specified disorder of kidney and ureter

593.9 Unspecified disorder of kidney and ureter ▽

599.60 Urinary obstruction, unspecified — (Use additional code to identify urinary incontinence: 625.6, 788.30-788.39) ▽

599.69 Urinary obstruction, not elsewhere classified — (Use additional code to identify urinary incontinence: 625.6, 788.30-788.39. Code, if applicable, any causal condition first: 600.0-600.9, with fifth-digit 1)

599.70 Hematuria, unspecified ▽

599.71 Gross hematuria

599.72 Microscopic hematuria

753.0 Congenital renal agenesis and dysgenesis

753.10 Unspecified congenital cystic kidney disease ▽

753.11 Congenital single renal cyst

753.12 Congenital polycystic kidney, unspecified type ▽

753.13 Congenital polycystic kidney, autosomal dominant

753.14 Congenital polycystic kidney, autosomal recessive

753.15 Congenital renal dysplasia

753.16 Congenital medullary cystic kidney

753.17 Congenital medullary sponge kidney

753.19 Other specified congenital cystic kidney disease

753.21 Congenital obstruction of ureteropelvic junction

753.23 Congenital ureterocele

753.29 Other obstructive defect of renal pelvis and ureter

866.03 Complete disruption of kidney parenchyma, without mention of open wound into cavity

866.13 Complete disruption of kidney parenchyma, with open wound into cavity

V64.41 Laparoscopic surgical procedure converted to open procedure

ICD-9-CM Procedural

38.07 Incision of abdominal veins

40.3 Regional lymph node excision

55.51 Nephroureterectomy

55.52 Nephrectomy of remaining kidney

55.54 Bilateral nephrectomy

50234-50236

50234 Nephrectomy with total ureterectomy and bladder cuff; through same incision

50236 through separate incision

ICD-9-CM Diagnostic

188.6 Malignant neoplasm of ureteric orifice

189.0 Malignant neoplasm of kidney, except pelvis

189.1 Malignant neoplasm of renal pelvis

189.2 Malignant neoplasm of ureter

189.8 Malignant neoplasm of other specified sites of urinary organs

198.0 Secondary malignant neoplasm of kidney

198.1 Secondary malignant neoplasm of other urinary organs

199.2 Malignant neoplasm associated with transplanted organ — (Code first complication of transplanted organ (996.80-996.89) Use additional code for specific malignancy)

209.24 Malignant carcinoid tumor of the kidney — (Code first any associated multiple endocrine neoplasia syndrome: 258.01-258.03; Use additional code to identify associated endocrine syndrome, as: carcinoid syndrome: 259.2)

209.64 Benign carcinoid tumor of the kidney — (Code first any associated multiple endocrine neoplasia syndrome: 258.01-258.03; Use additional code to identify associated endocrine syndrome, as: carcinoid syndrome: 259.2)

223.0 Benign neoplasm of kidney, except pelvis

223.1 Benign neoplasm of renal pelvis

223.2 Benign neoplasm of ureter

233.9 Carcinoma in situ of other and unspecified urinary organs ▽

236.91 Neoplasm of uncertain behavior of kidney and ureter

239.5 Neoplasm of unspecified nature of other genitourinary organs

403.01 Hypertensive chronic kidney disease, malignant, with chronic kidney disease stage V or end stage renal disease — (Use additional code to identify the stage of chronic kidney disease: 585.5, 585.6)

403.11 Hypertensive chronic kidney disease, benign, with chronic kidney disease stage V or end stage renal disease — (Use additional code to identify the stage of chronic kidney disease: 585.5, 585.6)

403.91 Hypertensive chronic kidney disease, unspecified, with chronic kidney disease stage V or end stage renal disease — (Use additional code to identify the stage of chronic kidney disease: 585.5, 585.6) ▽

404.02 Hypertensive heart and chronic kidney disease, malignant, without heart failure and with chronic kidney disease stage V or end stage renal disease — (Use additional code to identify the stage of chronic kidney disease: 585.5, 585.6)

404.12 Hypertensive heart and chronic kidney disease, benign, without heart failure and with chronic kidney disease stage V or end stage renal disease — (Use additional code to identify the stage of chronic kidney disease: 585.5, 585.6)

405.01 Secondary renovascular hypertension, malignant

445.81 Atheroembolism of kidney — (Use additional code for any associated acute kidney failure or chronic kidney disease: 584, 585)

580.0 Acute glomerulonephritis with lesion of proliferative glomerulonephritis

581.0 Nephrotic syndrome with lesion of proliferative glomerulonephritis

582.0 Chronic glomerulonephritis with lesion of proliferative glomerulonephritis
584.5 Acute kidney failure with lesion of tubular necrosis
585.1 Chronic kidney disease, Stage I — (Use additional code to identify kidney transplant status, if applicable: V42.0. Use additional code to identify manifestation: 357.4, 420.0. Code first hypertensive chronic kidney disease, if applicable: 403.00-403.91, 404.00-404.93)
585.2 Chronic kidney disease, Stage II (mild) — (Use additional code to identify kidney transplant status, if applicable: V42.0. Use additional code to identify manifestation: 357.4, 420.0. Code first hypertensive chronic kidney disease, if applicable: 403.00-403.91, 404.00-404.93)
585.3 Chronic kidney disease, Stage III (moderate) — (Use additional code to identify kidney transplant status, if applicable: V42.0. Use additional code to identify manifestation: 357.4, 420.0. Code first hypertensive chronic kidney disease, if applicable: 403.00-403.91, 404.00-404.93)
585.4 Chronic kidney disease, Stage IV (severe) — (Use additional code to identify kidney transplant status, if applicable: V42.0. Use additional code to identify manifestation: 357.4, 420.0. Code first hypertensive chronic kidney disease, if applicable: 403.00-403.91, 404.00-404.93)
585.5 Chronic kidney disease, Stage V — (Use additional code to identify kidney transplant status, if applicable: V42.0. Use additional code to identify manifestation: 357.4, 420.0. Code first hypertensive chronic kidney disease, if applicable: 403.00-403.91, 404.00-404.93)
585.6 End stage renal disease — (Use additional code to identify kidney transplant status, if applicable: V42.0. Use additional code to identify manifestation: 357.4, 420.0. Code first hypertensive chronic kidney disease, if applicable: 403.00-403.91, 404.00-404.93)
585.9 Chronic kidney disease, unspecified — (Use additional code to identify kidney transplant status, if applicable: V42.0. Use additional code to identify manifestation: 357.4, 420.0. Code first hypertensive chronic kidney disease, if applicable: 403.00-403.91, 404.00-404.93)
587 Unspecified renal sclerosis
588.81 Secondary hyperparathyroidism (of renal origin)
588.89 Other specified disorders resulting from impaired renal function
590.00 Chronic pyelonephritis without lesion of renal medullary necrosis — (Use additional code to identify organism, such as E. coli, 041.41-041.49. Code if applicable, any causal condition first)
590.01 Chronic pyelonephritis with lesion of renal medullary necrosis — (Use additional code to identify organism, such as E. coli, 041.41-041.49. Code if applicable, any causal condition first)
591 Hydronephrosis
592.0 Calculus of kidney
593.4 Other ureteric obstruction
593.70 Vesicoureteral reflux, unspecified or without reflex nephropathy
593.71 Vesicoureteral reflux with reflux nephropathy, unilateral
593.72 Vesicoureteral reflux with reflux nephropathy, bilateral
593.73 Vesicoureteral reflux with reflux nephropathy, NOS
593.81 Vascular disorders of kidney
593.89 Other specified disorder of kidney and ureter
599.70 Hematuria, unspecified
599.71 Gross hematuria
599.72 Microscopic hematuria
753.0 Congenital renal agenesis and dysgenesis
753.10 Unspecified congenital cystic kidney disease
753.11 Congenital single renal cyst
753.12 Congenital polycystic kidney, unspecified type
753.13 Congenital polycystic kidney, autosomal dominant
753.14 Congenital polycystic kidney, autosomal recessive
753.15 Congenital renal dysplasia
753.16 Congenital medullary cystic kidney
753.17 Congenital medullary sponge kidney
753.19 Other specified congenital cystic kidney disease
753.20 Unspecified obstructive defect of renal pelvis and ureter
753.21 Congenital obstruction of ureteropelvic junction
753.22 Congenital obstruction of ureterovesical junction
753.23 Congenital ureterocele
753.29 Other obstructive defect of renal pelvis and ureter
866.02 Kidney laceration without mention of open wound into cavity
866.03 Complete disruption of kidney parenchyma, without mention of open wound into cavity
866.13 Complete disruption of kidney parenchyma, with open wound into cavity
V64.41 Laparoscopic surgical procedure converted to open procedure

ICD-9-CM Procedural

55.51 Nephroureterectomy
55.52 Nephrectomy of remaining kidney
55.54 Bilateral nephrectomy

50240

50240 Nephrectomy, partial

ICD-9-CM Diagnostic

189.0 Malignant neoplasm of kidney, except pelvis
189.1 Malignant neoplasm of renal pelvis
198.0 Secondary malignant neoplasm of kidney
199.2 Malignant neoplasm associated with transplanted organ — (Code first complication of transplanted organ (996.80-996.89) Use additional code for specific malignancy)
209.24 Malignant carcinoid tumor of the kidney — (Code first any associated multiple endocrine neoplasia syndrome: 258.01-258.03; Use additional code to identify associated endocrine syndrome, as: carcinoid syndrome: 259.2)
209.64 Benign carcinoid tumor of the kidney — (Code first any associated multiple endocrine neoplasia syndrome: 258.01-258.03; Use additional code to identify associated endocrine syndrome, as: carcinoid syndrome: 259.2)
223.0 Benign neoplasm of kidney, except pelvis
223.1 Benign neoplasm of renal pelvis
233.9 Carcinoma in situ of other and unspecified urinary organs
236.91 Neoplasm of uncertain behavior of kidney and ureter
239.5 Neoplasm of unspecified nature of other genitourinary organs
587 Unspecified renal sclerosis
591 Hydronephrosis
593.2 Acquired cyst of kidney
593.70 Vesicoureteral reflux, unspecified or without reflex nephropathy
593.71 Vesicoureteral reflux with reflux nephropathy, unilateral
593.72 Vesicoureteral reflux with reflux nephropathy, bilateral
593.73 Vesicoureteral reflux with reflux nephropathy, NOS
593.81 Vascular disorders of kidney
593.89 Other specified disorder of kidney and ureter
593.9 Unspecified disorder of kidney and ureter
599.70 Hematuria, unspecified
599.71 Gross hematuria
599.72 Microscopic hematuria
753.11 Congenital single renal cyst
753.12 Congenital polycystic kidney, unspecified type
753.13 Congenital polycystic kidney, autosomal dominant
753.14 Congenital polycystic kidney, autosomal recessive
753.15 Congenital renal dysplasia
753.16 Congenital medullary cystic kidney
753.17 Congenital medullary sponge kidney
753.19 Other specified congenital cystic kidney disease
753.20 Unspecified obstructive defect of renal pelvis and ureter
753.21 Congenital obstruction of ureteropelvic junction
753.22 Congenital obstruction of ureterovesical junction
753.23 Congenital ureterocele

753.29 Other obstructive defect of renal pelvis and ureter
866.00 Unspecified kidney injury without mention of open wound into cavity ▽
V64.41 Laparoscopic surgical procedure converted to open procedure

ICD-9-CM Procedural

55.4 Partial nephrectomy

50250

50250 Ablation, open, 1 or more renal mass lesion(s), cryosurgical, including intraoperative ultrasound guidance and monitoring, if performed

ICD-9-CM Diagnostic

189.0 Malignant neoplasm of kidney, except pelvis
189.1 Malignant neoplasm of renal pelvis
198.0 Secondary malignant neoplasm of kidney
199.2 Malignant neoplasm associated with transplanted organ — (Code first complication of transplanted organ (996.80-996.89) Use additional code for specific malignancy)
209.24 Malignant carcinoid tumor of the kidney — (Code first any associated multiple endocrine neoplasia syndrome: 258.01-258.03; Use additional code to identify associated endocrine syndrome, as: carcinoid syndrome: 259.2)
209.64 Benign carcinoid tumor of the kidney — (Code first any associated multiple endocrine neoplasia syndrome: 258.01-258.03; Use additional code to identify associated endocrine syndrome, as: carcinoid syndrome: 259.2)
223.0 Benign neoplasm of kidney, except pelvis
223.1 Benign neoplasm of renal pelvis
233.9 Carcinoma in situ of other and unspecified urinary organs ▽
236.91 Neoplasm of uncertain behavior of kidney and ureter
239.5 Neoplasm of unspecified nature of other genitourinary organs
583.9 Nephritis and nephropathy, not specified as acute or chronic, with unspecified pathological lesion in kidney ▽
593.2 Acquired cyst of kidney
593.89 Other specified disorder of kidney and ureter
753.10 Unspecified congenital cystic kidney disease ▽
753.11 Congenital single renal cyst
753.12 Congenital polycystic kidney, unspecified type ▽
753.13 Congenital polycystic kidney, autosomal dominant
753.14 Congenital polycystic kidney, autosomal recessive
753.15 Congenital renal dysplasia
753.16 Congenital medullary cystic kidney
753.17 Congenital medullary sponge kidney
753.19 Other specified congenital cystic kidney disease

ICD-9-CM Procedural

55.32 Open ablation of renal lesion or tissue

50280-50290

50280 Excision or unroofing of cyst(s) of kidney
50290 Excision of perinephric cyst

ICD-9-CM Diagnostic

593.2 Acquired cyst of kidney
593.89 Other specified disorder of kidney and ureter
753.10 Unspecified congenital cystic kidney disease ▽
753.11 Congenital single renal cyst
753.12 Congenital polycystic kidney, unspecified type ▽
753.13 Congenital polycystic kidney, autosomal dominant
753.14 Congenital polycystic kidney, autosomal recessive
753.19 Other specified congenital cystic kidney disease

ICD-9-CM Procedural

55.39 Other local destruction or excision of renal lesion or tissue
59.91 Excision of perirenal or perivesical tissue

50300-50320

50300 Donor nephrectomy (including cold preservation); from cadaver donor, unilateral or bilateral
50320 open, from living donor

ICD-9-CM Diagnostic

V59.4 Kidney donor

ICD-9-CM Procedural

55.51 Nephroureterectomy
55.54 Bilateral nephrectomy

50323-50325

50323 Backbench standard preparation of cadaver donor renal allograft prior to transplantation, including dissection and removal of perinephric fat, diaphragmatic and retroperitoneal attachments, excision of adrenal gland, and preparation of ureter(s), renal vein(s), and renal artery(s), ligating branches, as necessary
50325 Backbench standard preparation of living donor renal allograft (open or laparoscopic) prior to transplantation, including dissection and removal of perinephric fat and preparation of ureter(s), renal vein(s), and renal artery(s), ligating branches, as necessary

ICD-9-CM Diagnostic

189.0 Malignant neoplasm of kidney, except pelvis
189.1 Malignant neoplasm of renal pelvis
198.0 Secondary malignant neoplasm of kidney
199.2 Malignant neoplasm associated with transplanted organ — (Code first complication of transplanted organ (996.80-996.89) Use additional code for specific malignancy)
209.24 Malignant carcinoid tumor of the kidney — (Code first any associated multiple endocrine neoplasia syndrome: 258.01-258.03; Use additional code to identify associated endocrine syndrome, as: carcinoid syndrome: 259.2)
209.64 Benign carcinoid tumor of the kidney — (Code first any associated multiple endocrine neoplasia syndrome: 258.01-258.03; Use additional code to identify associated endocrine syndrome, as: carcinoid syndrome: 259.2)
223.0 Benign neoplasm of kidney, except pelvis
236.91 Neoplasm of uncertain behavior of kidney and ureter
238.77 Post-transplant lymphoproliferative disorder [PTLD] — (Code first complications of transplant (996.80-996.89))
249.40 Secondary diabetes mellitus with renal manifestations, not stated as uncontrolled, or unspecified — (Use additional code to identify manifestation: 581.81, 583.81, 585.1-585.9) (Use additional code to identify any associated insulin use: V58.67)
249.41 Secondary diabetes mellitus with renal manifestations, uncontrolled — (Use additional code to identify manifestation: 581.81, 583.81, 585.1-585.9) (Use additional code to identify any associated insulin use: V58.67)
250.40 Diabetes with renal manifestations, type II or unspecified type, not stated as uncontrolled — (Use additional code to identify manifestation: 581.81, 583.81, 585.1-585.9)
250.41 Diabetes with renal manifestations, type I [juvenile type], not stated as uncontrolled — (Use additional code to identify manifestation: 581.81, 583.81, 585.1-585.9)
250.42 Diabetes with renal manifestations, type II or unspecified type, uncontrolled — (Use additional code to identify manifestation: 581.81, 583.81, 585.1-585.9)
250.43 Diabetes with renal manifestations, type I [juvenile type], uncontrolled — (Use additional code to identify manifestation: 581.81, 583.81, 585.1-585.9)
279.50 Graft-versus-host disease, unspecified — (Code first underlying cause: 996.80-996.89, 999.89)(Use additional code to identify any associated intellectual disabilities) (Use additional code to identify associated manifestations: 695.89, 704.09, 782.4, 787.91) ▽
279.51 Acute graft-versus-host disease — (Code first underlying cause: 996.80-996.89, 999.89)(Use additional code to identify any associated intellectual disabilities) (Use additional code to identify associated manifestations: 695.89, 704.09, 782.4, 787.91)
279.52 Chronic graft-versus-host disease — (Code first underlying cause: 996.80-996.89, 999.89)(Use additional code to identify any associated intellectual disabilities) (Use additional code to identify associated manifestations: 695.89, 704.09, 782.4, 787.91)

279.53 Acute on chronic graft-versus-host disease — (Code first underlying cause: 996.80-996.89, 999.89)(Use additional code to identify any associated intellectual disabilities) (Use additional code to identify associated manifestations: 695.89, 704.09, 782.4, 787.91)

403.01 Hypertensive chronic kidney disease, malignant, with chronic kidney disease stage V or end stage renal disease — (Use additional code to identify the stage of chronic kidney disease: 585.5, 585.6)

403.11 Hypertensive chronic kidney disease, benign, with chronic kidney disease stage V or end stage renal disease — (Use additional code to identify the stage of chronic kidney disease: 585.5, 585.6)

403.91 Hypertensive chronic kidney disease, unspecified, with chronic kidney disease stage V or end stage renal disease — (Use additional code to identify the stage of chronic kidney disease: 585.5, 585.6) ▽

445.81 Atheroembolism of kidney — (Use additional code for any associated acute kidney failure or chronic kidney disease: 584, 585)

580.0 Acute glomerulonephritis with lesion of proliferative glomerulonephritis

581.0 Nephrotic syndrome with lesion of proliferative glomerulonephritis

581.81 Nephrotic syndrome with other specified pathological lesion in kidney in diseases classified elsewhere — (Code first underlying disease: 084.9, 249.4, 250.4, 277.30-277.39, 446.0, 710.0) ☒

582.0 Chronic glomerulonephritis with lesion of proliferative glomerulonephritis

583.81 Nephritis and nephropathy, not specified as acute or chronic, with other specified pathological lesion in kidney, in diseases classified elsewhere — (Code first underlying disease: 016.0, 098.19, 249.4, 250.4, 277.30-277.39, 446.21, 710.0) ☒

584.5 Acute kidney failure with lesion of tubular necrosis

585.5 Chronic kidney disease, Stage V — (Use additional code to identify kidney transplant status, if applicable: V42.0. Use additional code to identify manifestation: 357.4, 420.0. Code first hypertensive chronic kidney disease, if applicable: 403.00-403.91, 404.00-404.93)

585.6 End stage renal disease — (Use additional code to identify kidney transplant status, if applicable: V42.0. Use additional code to identify manifestation: 357.4, 420.0. Code first hypertensive chronic kidney disease, if applicable: 403.00-403.91, 404.00-404.93)

585.9 Chronic kidney disease, unspecified — (Use additional code to identify kidney transplant status, if applicable: V42.0. Use additional code to identify manifestation: 357.4, 420.0. Code first hypertensive chronic kidney disease, if applicable: 403.00-403.91, 404.00-404.93) ▽

586 Unspecified renal failure ▽

590.00 Chronic pyelonephritis without lesion of renal medullary necrosis — (Use additional code to identify organism, such as E. coli, 041.41-041.49. Code if applicable, any causal condition first)

590.01 Chronic pyelonephritis with lesion of renal medullary necrosis — (Use additional code to identify organism, such as E. coli, 041.41-041.49. Code if applicable, any causal condition first)

590.80 Unspecified pyelonephritis — (Use additional code to identify organism, such as E. coli, 041.41-041.49) ▽

593.70 Vesicoureteral reflux, unspecified or without reflex nephropathy

593.71 Vesicoureteral reflux with reflux nephropathy, unilateral

593.72 Vesicoureteral reflux with reflux nephropathy, bilateral

593.73 Vesicoureteral reflux with reflux nephropathy, NOS ▽

593.81 Vascular disorders of kidney

753.12 Congenital polycystic kidney, unspecified type ▽

753.17 Congenital medullary sponge kidney

866.13 Complete disruption of kidney parenchyma, with open wound into cavity

996.81 Complications of transplanted kidney — (Use additional code to identify nature of complication: 078.5, 199.2, 238.77, 279.50-279.53)

ICD-9-CM Procedural

00.91 Transplant from live related donor

00.92 Transplant from live non-related donor

00.93 Transplant from cadaver

55.69 Other kidney transplantation

55.99 Other operations on kidney

50327-50329

50327 Backbench reconstruction of cadaver or living donor renal allograft prior to transplantation; venous anastomosis, each

50328 arterial anastomosis, each

50329 ureteral anastomosis, each

ICD-9-CM Diagnostic

189.0 Malignant neoplasm of kidney, except pelvis

189.1 Malignant neoplasm of renal pelvis

198.0 Secondary malignant neoplasm of kidney

199.2 Malignant neoplasm associated with transplanted organ — (Code first complication of transplanted organ (996.80-996.89) Use additional code for specific malignancy)

209.24 Malignant carcinoid tumor of the kidney — (Code first any associated multiple endocrine neoplasia syndrome: 258.01-258.03; Use additional code to identify associated endocrine syndrome, as: carcinoid syndrome: 259.2)

209.64 Benign carcinoid tumor of the kidney — (Code first any associated multiple endocrine neoplasia syndrome: 258.01-258.03; Use additional code to identify associated endocrine syndrome, as: carcinoid syndrome: 259.2)

223.0 Benign neoplasm of kidney, except pelvis

236.91 Neoplasm of uncertain behavior of kidney and ureter

238.77 Post-transplant lymphoproliferative disorder [PTLD] — (Code first complications of transplant (996.80-996.89))

249.40 Secondary diabetes mellitus with renal manifestations, not stated as uncontrolled, or unspecified — (Use additional code to identify manifestation: 581.81, 583.81, 585.1-585.9) (Use additional code to identify any associated insulin use: V58.67)

249.41 Secondary diabetes mellitus with renal manifestations, uncontrolled — (Use additional code to identify manifestation: 581.81, 583.81, 585.1-585.9) (Use additional code to identify any associated insulin use: V58.67)

250.40 Diabetes with renal manifestations, type II or unspecified type, not stated as uncontrolled — (Use additional code to identify manifestation: 581.81, 583.81, 585.1-585.9)

250.41 Diabetes with renal manifestations, type I [juvenile type], not stated as uncontrolled — (Use additional code to identify manifestation: 581.81, 583.81, 585.1-585.9)

250.42 Diabetes with renal manifestations, type II or unspecified type, uncontrolled — (Use additional code to identify manifestation: 581.81, 583.81, 585.1-585.9)

250.43 Diabetes with renal manifestations, type I [juvenile type], uncontrolled — (Use additional code to identify manifestation: 581.81, 583.81, 585.1-585.9)

279.50 Graft-versus-host disease, unspecified — (Code first underlying cause: 996.80-996.89, 999.89)(Use additional code to identify any associated intellectual disabilities) (Use additional code to identify associated manifestations: 695.89, 704.09, 782.4, 787.91) ▽

279.51 Acute graft-versus-host disease — (Code first underlying cause: 996.80-996.89, 999.89)(Use additional code to identify any associated intellectual disabilities) (Use additional code to identify associated manifestations: 695.89, 704.09, 782.4, 787.91)

279.52 Chronic graft-versus-host disease — (Code first underlying cause: 996.80-996.89, 999.89)(Use additional code to identify any associated intellectual disabilities) (Use additional code to identify associated manifestations: 695.89, 704.09, 782.4, 787.91)

279.53 Acute on chronic graft-versus-host disease — (Code first underlying cause: 996.80-996.89, 999.89)(Use additional code to identify any associated intellectual disabilities) (Use additional code to identify associated manifestations: 695.89, 704.09, 782.4, 787.91)

403.01 Hypertensive chronic kidney disease, malignant, with chronic kidney disease stage V or end stage renal disease — (Use additional code to identify the stage of chronic kidney disease: 585.5, 585.6)

403.11 Hypertensive chronic kidney disease, benign, with chronic kidney disease stage V or end stage renal disease — (Use additional code to identify the stage of chronic kidney disease: 585.5, 585.6)

403.91 Hypertensive chronic kidney disease, unspecified, with chronic kidney disease stage V or end stage renal disease — (Use additional code to identify the stage of chronic kidney disease: 585.5, 585.6) ▽

445.81 Atheroembolism of kidney — (Use additional code for any associated acute kidney failure or chronic kidney disease: 584, 585)

580.0 Acute glomerulonephritis with lesion of proliferative glomerulonephritis
581.0 Nephrotic syndrome with lesion of proliferative glomerulonephritis
581.81 Nephrotic syndrome with other specified pathological lesion in kidney in diseases classified elsewhere — (Code first underlying disease: 084.9, 249.4, 250.4, 277.30-277.39, 446.0, 710.0) ☒
582.0 Chronic glomerulonephritis with lesion of proliferative glomerulonephritis
583.81 Nephritis and nephropathy, not specified as acute or chronic, with other specified pathological lesion in kidney, in diseases classified elsewhere — (Code first underlying disease: 016.0, 098.19, 249.4, 250.4, 277.30-277.39, 446.21, 710.0) ☒
584.5 Acute kidney failure with lesion of tubular necrosis
585.5 Chronic kidney disease, Stage V — (Use additional code to identify kidney transplant status, if applicable: V42.0. Use additional code to identify manifestation: 357.4, 420.0. Code first hypertensive chronic kidney disease, if applicable: 403.00-403.91, 404.00-404.93)
585.6 End stage renal disease — (Use additional code to identify kidney transplant status, if applicable: V42.0. Use additional code to identify manifestation: 357.4, 420.0. Code first hypertensive chronic kidney disease, if applicable: 403.00-403.91, 404.00-404.93)
585.9 Chronic kidney disease, unspecified — (Use additional code to identify kidney transplant status, if applicable: V42.0. Use additional code to identify manifestation: 357.4, 420.0. Code first hypertensive chronic kidney disease, if applicable: 403.00-403.91, 404.00-404.93) ▽
586 Unspecified renal failure ▽
590.00 Chronic pyelonephritis without lesion of renal medullary necrosis — (Use additional code to identify organism, such as E. coli, 041.41-041.49. Code if applicable, any causal condition first)
590.01 Chronic pyelonephritis with lesion of renal medullary necrosis — (Use additional code to identify organism, such as E. coli, 041.41-041.49. Code if applicable, any causal condition first)
590.80 Unspecified pyelonephritis — (Use additional code to identify organism, such as E. coli, 041.41-041.49) ▽
593.70 Vesicoureteral reflux, unspecified or without reflex nephropathy
593.71 Vesicoureteral reflux with reflux nephropathy, unilateral
593.72 Vesicoureteral reflux with reflux nephropathy, bilateral
593.73 Vesicoureteral reflux with reflux nephropathy, NOS ▽
593.81 Vascular disorders of kidney
753.12 Congenital polycystic kidney, unspecified type ▽
753.17 Congenital medullary sponge kidney
866.13 Complete disruption of kidney parenchyma, with open wound into cavity
996.81 Complications of transplanted kidney — (Use additional code to identify nature of complication: 078.5, 199.2, 238.77, 279.50-279.53)

ICD-9-CM Procedural

00.91 Transplant from live related donor
00.92 Transplant from live non-related donor
00.93 Transplant from cadaver
55.69 Other kidney transplantation
55.99 Other operations on kidney

50340

50340 Recipient nephrectomy (separate procedure)

ICD-9-CM Diagnostic

189.0 Malignant neoplasm of kidney, except pelvis
189.1 Malignant neoplasm of renal pelvis
198.0 Secondary malignant neoplasm of kidney
199.2 Malignant neoplasm associated with transplanted organ — (Code first complication of transplanted organ (996.80-996.89) Use additional code for specific malignancy)
209.24 Malignant carcinoid tumor of the kidney — (Code first any associated multiple endocrine neoplasia syndrome: 258.01-258.03; Use additional code to identify associated endocrine syndrome, as: carcinoid syndrome: 259.2)
209.64 Benign carcinoid tumor of the kidney — (Code first any associated multiple endocrine neoplasia syndrome: 258.01-258.03; Use additional code to identify associated endocrine syndrome, as: carcinoid syndrome: 259.2)
223.0 Benign neoplasm of kidney, except pelvis
236.91 Neoplasm of uncertain behavior of kidney and ureter
238.77 Post-transplant lymphoproliferative disorder [PTLD] — (Code first complications of transplant (996.80-996.89))
249.40 Secondary diabetes mellitus with renal manifestations, not stated as uncontrolled, or unspecified — (Use additional code to identify manifestation: 581.81, 583.81, 585.1-585.9) (Use additional code to identify any associated insulin use: V58.67)
249.41 Secondary diabetes mellitus with renal manifestations, uncontrolled — (Use additional code to identify manifestation: 581.81, 583.81, 585.1-585.9) (Use additional code to identify any associated insulin use: V58.67)
250.40 Diabetes with renal manifestations, type II or unspecified type, not stated as uncontrolled — (Use additional code to identify manifestation: 581.81, 583.81, 585.1-585.9)
250.41 Diabetes with renal manifestations, type I [juvenile type], not stated as uncontrolled — (Use additional code to identify manifestation: 581.81, 583.81, 585.1-585.9)
250.42 Diabetes with renal manifestations, type II or unspecified type, uncontrolled — (Use additional code to identify manifestation: 581.81, 583.81, 585.1-585.9)
250.43 Diabetes with renal manifestations, type I [juvenile type], uncontrolled — (Use additional code to identify manifestation: 581.81, 583.81, 585.1-585.9)
279.50 Graft-versus-host disease, unspecified — (Code first underlying cause: 996.80-996.89, 999.89)(Use additional code to identify any associated intellectual disabilities) (Use additional code to identify associated manifestations: 695.89, 704.09, 782.4, 787.91) ▽
279.51 Acute graft-versus-host disease — (Code first underlying cause: 996.80-996.89, 999.89)(Use additional code to identify any associated intellectual disabilities) (Use additional code to identify associated manifestations: 695.89, 704.09, 782.4, 787.91)
279.52 Chronic graft-versus-host disease — (Code first underlying cause: 996.80-996.89, 999.89)(Use additional code to identify any associated intellectual disabilities) (Use additional code to identify associated manifestations: 695.89, 704.09, 782.4, 787.91)
279.53 Acute on chronic graft-versus-host disease — (Code first underlying cause: 996.80-996.89, 999.89)(Use additional code to identify any associated intellectual disabilities) (Use additional code to identify associated manifestations: 695.89, 704.09, 782.4, 787.91)
403.01 Hypertensive chronic kidney disease, malignant, with chronic kidney disease stage V or end stage renal disease — (Use additional code to identify the stage of chronic kidney disease: 585.5, 585.6)
403.11 Hypertensive chronic kidney disease, benign, with chronic kidney disease stage V or end stage renal disease — (Use additional code to identify the stage of chronic kidney disease: 585.5, 585.6)
403.91 Hypertensive chronic kidney disease, unspecified, with chronic kidney disease stage V or end stage renal disease — (Use additional code to identify the stage of chronic kidney disease: 585.5, 585.6) ▽
445.81 Atheroembolism of kidney — (Use additional code for any associated acute kidney failure or chronic kidney disease: 584, 585)
580.0 Acute glomerulonephritis with lesion of proliferative glomerulonephritis
581.0 Nephrotic syndrome with lesion of proliferative glomerulonephritis
581.81 Nephrotic syndrome with other specified pathological lesion in kidney in diseases classified elsewhere — (Code first underlying disease: 084.9, 249.4, 250.4, 277.30-277.39, 446.0, 710.0) ☒
582.0 Chronic glomerulonephritis with lesion of proliferative glomerulonephritis
583.81 Nephritis and nephropathy, not specified as acute or chronic, with other specified pathological lesion in kidney, in diseases classified elsewhere — (Code first underlying disease: 016.0, 098.19, 249.4, 250.4, 277.30-277.39, 446.21, 710.0) ☒
584.5 Acute kidney failure with lesion of tubular necrosis
585.5 Chronic kidney disease, Stage V — (Use additional code to identify kidney transplant status, if applicable: V42.0. Use additional code to identify manifestation: 357.4, 420.0. Code first hypertensive chronic kidney disease, if applicable: 403.00-403.91, 404.00-404.93)

585.6 End stage renal disease — (Use additional code to identify kidney transplant status, if applicable: V42.0. Use additional code to identify manifestation: 357.4, 420.0. Code first hypertensive chronic kidney disease, if applicable: 403.00-403.91, 404.00-404.93)
585.9 Chronic kidney disease, unspecified — (Use additional code to identify kidney transplant status, if applicable: V42.0. Use additional code to identify manifestation: 357.4, 420.0. Code first hypertensive chronic kidney disease, if applicable: 403.00-403.91, 404.00-404.93) ▽
586 Unspecified renal failure ▽
590.00 Chronic pyelonephritis without lesion of renal medullary necrosis — (Use additional code to identify organism, such as E. coli, 041.41-041.49. Code if applicable, any causal condition first)
590.01 Chronic pyelonephritis with lesion of renal medullary necrosis — (Use additional code to identify organism, such as E. coli, 041.41-041.49. Code if applicable, any causal condition first)
590.80 Unspecified pyelonephritis — (Use additional code to identify organism, such as E. coli, 041.41-041.49) ▽
593.70 Vesicoureteral reflux, unspecified or without reflex nephropathy
593.71 Vesicoureteral reflux with reflux nephropathy, unilateral
593.72 Vesicoureteral reflux with reflux nephropathy, bilateral
593.73 Vesicoureteral reflux with reflux nephropathy, NOS ▽
593.81 Vascular disorders of kidney
753.12 Congenital polycystic kidney, unspecified type ▽
753.17 Congenital medullary sponge kidney
866.13 Complete disruption of kidney parenchyma, with open wound into cavity
996.81 Complications of transplanted kidney — (Use additional code to identify nature of complication: 078.5, 199.2, 238.77, 279.50-279.53)

ICD-9-CM Procedural

55.51 Nephroureterectomy
55.54 Bilateral nephrectomy

50360-50365

50360 Renal allotransplantation, implantation of graft; without recipient nephrectomy
50365 with recipient nephrectomy

ICD-9-CM Diagnostic

189.0 Malignant neoplasm of kidney, except pelvis
189.1 Malignant neoplasm of renal pelvis
198.0 Secondary malignant neoplasm of kidney
199.2 Malignant neoplasm associated with transplanted organ — (Code first complication of transplanted organ (996.80-996.89) Use additional code for specific malignancy)
209.24 Malignant carcinoid tumor of the kidney — (Code first any associated multiple endocrine neoplasia syndrome: 258.01-258.03; Use additional code to identify associated endocrine syndrome, as: carcinoid syndrome: 259.2)
209.64 Benign carcinoid tumor of the kidney — (Code first any associated multiple endocrine neoplasia syndrome: 258.01-258.03; Use additional code to identify associated endocrine syndrome, as: carcinoid syndrome: 259.2)
223.0 Benign neoplasm of kidney, except pelvis
236.91 Neoplasm of uncertain behavior of kidney and ureter
238.77 Post-transplant lymphoproliferative disorder [PTLD] — (Code first complications of transplant (996.80-996.89))
249.40 Secondary diabetes mellitus with renal manifestations, not stated as uncontrolled, or unspecified — (Use additional code to identify manifestation: 581.81, 583.81, 585.1-585.9) (Use additional code to identify any associated insulin use: V58.67)
249.41 Secondary diabetes mellitus with renal manifestations, uncontrolled — (Use additional code to identify manifestation: 581.81, 583.81, 585.1-585.9) (Use additional code to identify any associated insulin use: V58.67)
250.40 Diabetes with renal manifestations, type II or unspecified type, not stated as uncontrolled — (Use additional code to identify manifestation: 581.81, 583.81, 585.1-585.9)
250.41 Diabetes with renal manifestations, type I [juvenile type], not stated as uncontrolled — (Use additional code to identify manifestation: 581.81, 583.81, 585.1-585.9)
250.42 Diabetes with renal manifestations, type II or unspecified type, uncontrolled — (Use additional code to identify manifestation: 581.81, 583.81, 585.1-585.9)
250.43 Diabetes with renal manifestations, type I [juvenile type], uncontrolled — (Use additional code to identify manifestation: 581.81, 583.81, 585.1-585.9)
279.50 Graft-versus-host disease, unspecified — (Code first underlying cause: 996.80-996.89, 999.89)(Use additional code to identify any associated intellectual disabilities) (Use additional code to identify associated manifestations: 695.89, 704.09, 782.4, 787.91) ▽
279.51 Acute graft-versus-host disease — (Code first underlying cause: 996.80-996.89, 999.89)(Use additional code to identify any associated intellectual disabilities) (Use additional code to identify associated manifestations: 695.89, 704.09, 782.4, 787.91)
279.52 Chronic graft-versus-host disease — (Code first underlying cause: 996.80-996.89, 999.89)(Use additional code to identify any associated intellectual disabilities) (Use additional code to identify associated manifestations: 695.89, 704.09, 782.4, 787.91)
279.53 Acute on chronic graft-versus-host disease — (Code first underlying cause: 996.80-996.89, 999.89)(Use additional code to identify any associated intellectual disabilities) (Use additional code to identify associated manifestations: 695.89, 704.09, 782.4, 787.91)
403.01 Hypertensive chronic kidney disease, malignant, with chronic kidney disease stage V or end stage renal disease — (Use additional code to identify the stage of chronic kidney disease: 585.5, 585.6)
403.11 Hypertensive chronic kidney disease, benign, with chronic kidney disease stage V or end stage renal disease — (Use additional code to identify the stage of chronic kidney disease: 585.5, 585.6)
403.91 Hypertensive chronic kidney disease, unspecified, with chronic kidney disease stage V or end stage renal disease — (Use additional code to identify the stage of chronic kidney disease: 585.5, 585.6) ▽
445.81 Atheroembolism of kidney — (Use additional code for any associated acute kidney failure or chronic kidney disease: 584, 585)
580.0 Acute glomerulonephritis with lesion of proliferative glomerulonephritis
581.0 Nephrotic syndrome with lesion of proliferative glomerulonephritis
581.81 Nephrotic syndrome with other specified pathological lesion in kidney in diseases classified elsewhere — (Code first underlying disease: 084.9, 249.4, 250.4, 277.30-277.39, 446.0, 710.0) ☒
582.0 Chronic glomerulonephritis with lesion of proliferative glomerulonephritis
583.81 Nephritis and nephropathy, not specified as acute or chronic, with other specified pathological lesion in kidney, in diseases classified elsewhere — (Code first underlying disease: 016.0, 098.19, 249.4, 250.4, 277.30-277.39, 446.21, 710.0) ☒
584.5 Acute kidney failure with lesion of tubular necrosis
585.5 Chronic kidney disease, Stage V — (Use additional code to identify kidney transplant status, if applicable: V42.0. Use additional code to identify manifestation: 357.4, 420.0. Code first hypertensive chronic kidney disease, if applicable: 403.00-403.91, 404.00-404.93)
585.6 End stage renal disease — (Use additional code to identify kidney transplant status, if applicable: V42.0. Use additional code to identify manifestation: 357.4, 420.0. Code first hypertensive chronic kidney disease, if applicable: 403.00-403.91, 404.00-404.93)
585.9 Chronic kidney disease, unspecified — (Use additional code to identify kidney transplant status, if applicable: V42.0. Use additional code to identify manifestation: 357.4, 420.0. Code first hypertensive chronic kidney disease, if applicable: 403.00-403.91, 404.00-404.93) ▽
586 Unspecified renal failure ▽
590.00 Chronic pyelonephritis without lesion of renal medullary necrosis — (Use additional code to identify organism, such as E. coli, 041.41-041.49. Code if applicable, any causal condition first)
590.01 Chronic pyelonephritis with lesion of renal medullary necrosis — (Use additional code to identify organism, such as E. coli, 041.41-041.49. Code if applicable, any causal condition first)
590.80 Unspecified pyelonephritis — (Use additional code to identify organism, such as E. coli, 041.41-041.49) ▽
593.70 Vesicoureteral reflux, unspecified or without reflex nephropathy
593.71 Vesicoureteral reflux with reflux nephropathy, unilateral
593.72 Vesicoureteral reflux with reflux nephropathy, bilateral

593.73 Vesicoureteral reflux with reflux nephropathy, NOS ♥

593.81 Vascular disorders of kidney

753.12 Congenital polycystic kidney, unspecified type ♥

753.17 Congenital medullary sponge kidney

866.13 Complete disruption of kidney parenchyma, with open wound into cavity

996.81 Complications of transplanted kidney — (Use additional code to identify nature of complication: 078.5, 199.2, 238.77, 279.50-279.53)

ICD-9-CM Procedural

00.91 Transplant from live related donor

00.92 Transplant from live non-related donor

00.93 Transplant from cadaver

55.51 Nephroureterectomy

55.54 Bilateral nephrectomy

55.69 Other kidney transplantation

50370

50370 Removal of transplanted renal allograft

ICD-9-CM Diagnostic

199.2 Malignant neoplasm associated with transplanted organ — (Code first complication of transplanted organ (996.80-996.89) Use additional code for specific malignancy)

238.77 Post-transplant lymphoproliferative disorder [PTLD] — (Code first complications of transplant (996.80-996.89))

279.50 Graft-versus-host disease, unspecified — (Code first underlying cause: 996.80-996.89, 999.89)(Use additional code to identify any associated intellectual disabilities) (Use additional code to identify associated manifestations: 695.89, 704.09, 782.4, 787.91) ♥

279.51 Acute graft-versus-host disease — (Code first underlying cause: 996.80-996.89, 999.89)(Use additional code to identify any associated intellectual disabilities) (Use additional code to identify associated manifestations: 695.89, 704.09, 782.4, 787.91)

279.52 Chronic graft-versus-host disease — (Code first underlying cause: 996.80-996.89, 999.89)(Use additional code to identify any associated intellectual disabilities) (Use additional code to identify associated manifestations: 695.89, 704.09, 782.4, 787.91)

279.53 Acute on chronic graft-versus-host disease — (Code first underlying cause: 996.80-996.89, 999.89)(Use additional code to identify any associated intellectual disabilities) (Use additional code to identify associated manifestations: 695.89, 704.09, 782.4, 787.91)

593.81 Vascular disorders of kidney

996.81 Complications of transplanted kidney — (Use additional code to identify nature of complication: 078.5, 199.2, 238.77, 279.50-279.53)

ICD-9-CM Procedural

55.53 Removal of transplanted or rejected kidney

50380

50380 Renal autotransplantation, reimplantation of kidney

ICD-9-CM Diagnostic

238.77 Post-transplant lymphoproliferative disorder [PTLD] — (Code first complications of transplant (996.80-996.89))

279.50 Graft-versus-host disease, unspecified — (Code first underlying cause: 996.80-996.89, 999.89)(Use additional code to identify any associated intellectual disabilities) (Use additional code to identify associated manifestations: 695.89, 704.09, 782.4, 787.91) ♥

279.51 Acute graft-versus-host disease — (Code first underlying cause: 996.80-996.89, 999.89)(Use additional code to identify any associated intellectual disabilities) (Use additional code to identify associated manifestations: 695.89, 704.09, 782.4, 787.91)

279.52 Chronic graft-versus-host disease — (Code first underlying cause: 996.80-996.89, 999.89)(Use additional code to identify any associated intellectual disabilities) (Use additional code to identify associated manifestations: 695.89, 704.09, 782.4, 787.91)

279.53 Acute on chronic graft-versus-host disease — (Code first underlying cause: 996.80-996.89, 999.89)(Use additional code to identify any associated intellectual disabilities) (Use additional code to identify associated manifestations: 695.89, 704.09, 782.4, 787.91)

405.01 Secondary renovascular hypertension, malignant

405.11 Secondary renovascular hypertension, benign

593.81 Vascular disorders of kidney

902.42 Renal vein injury

902.49 Renal blood vessel injury, other

996.81 Complications of transplanted kidney — (Use additional code to identify nature of complication: 078.5, 199.2, 238.77, 279.50-279.53)

V10.52 Personal history of malignant neoplasm of kidney

V10.53 Personal history of malignant neoplasm, renal pelvis

ICD-9-CM Procedural

55.61 Renal autotransplantation

50382-50384

50382 Removal (via snare/capture) and replacement of internally dwelling ureteral stent via percutaneous approach, including radiological supervision and interpretation

50384 Removal (via snare/capture) of internally dwelling ureteral stent via percutaneous approach, including radiological supervision and interpretation

ICD-9-CM Diagnostic

188.0 Malignant neoplasm of trigone of urinary bladder

188.1 Malignant neoplasm of dome of urinary bladder

188.2 Malignant neoplasm of lateral wall of urinary bladder

188.3 Malignant neoplasm of anterior wall of urinary bladder

189.1 Malignant neoplasm of renal pelvis

189.2 Malignant neoplasm of ureter

198.0 Secondary malignant neoplasm of kidney

198.1 Secondary malignant neoplasm of other urinary organs

223.1 Benign neoplasm of renal pelvis

223.2 Benign neoplasm of ureter

223.3 Benign neoplasm of bladder

233.9 Carcinoma in situ of other and unspecified urinary organs ♥

236.7 Neoplasm of uncertain behavior of bladder

236.91 Neoplasm of uncertain behavior of kidney and ureter

238.77 Post-transplant lymphoproliferative disorder [PTLD] — (Code first complications of transplant (996.80-996.89))

239.4 Neoplasm of unspecified nature of bladder

239.5 Neoplasm of unspecified nature of other genitourinary organs

279.50 Graft-versus-host disease, unspecified — (Code first underlying cause: 996.80-996.89, 999.89)(Use additional code to identify any associated intellectual disabilities) (Use additional code to identify associated manifestations: 695.89, 704.09, 782.4, 787.91) ♥

279.51 Acute graft-versus-host disease — (Code first underlying cause: 996.80-996.89, 999.89)(Use additional code to identify any associated intellectual disabilities) (Use additional code to identify associated manifestations: 695.89, 704.09, 782.4, 787.91)

279.52 Chronic graft-versus-host disease — (Code first underlying cause: 996.80-996.89, 999.89)(Use additional code to identify any associated intellectual disabilities) (Use additional code to identify associated manifestations: 695.89, 704.09, 782.4, 787.91)

279.53 Acute on chronic graft-versus-host disease — (Code first underlying cause: 996.80-996.89, 999.89)(Use additional code to identify any associated intellectual disabilities) (Use additional code to identify associated manifestations: 695.89, 704.09, 782.4, 787.91)

588.89 Other specified disorders resulting from impaired renal function

588.9 Unspecified disorder resulting from impaired renal function ♥

590.10 Acute pyelonephritis without lesion of renal medullary necrosis — (Use additional code to identify organism, such as E. coli, 041.40-041.49)

590.11 Acute pyelonephritis with lesion of renal medullary necrosis — (Use additional code to identify organism, such as E. coli, 041.40-041.49)

590.2 Renal and perinephric abscess — (Use additional code to identify organism, such as E. coli, 041.41-041.49)

590.3 Pyeloureteritis cystica — (Use additional code to identify organism, such as E. coli, 041.41-041.49)
590.80 Unspecified pyelonephritis — (Use additional code to identify organism, such as E. coli, 041.41-041.49) ▽
590.81 Pyelitis or pyelonephritis in diseases classified elsewhere — (Use additional code to identify organism, such as E. coli, 041.41-041.49. Code first underlying disease: 016.0) ☒
590.9 Unspecified infection of kidney — (Use additional code to identify organism, such as E. coli, 041.41-041.49) ▽
591 Hydronephrosis
592.0 Calculus of kidney
592.1 Calculus of ureter
592.9 Unspecified urinary calculus ▽
593.3 Stricture or kinking of ureter
593.4 Other ureteric obstruction
593.89 Other specified disorder of kidney and ureter
599.60 Urinary obstruction, unspecified — (Use additional code to identify urinary incontinence: 625.6, 788.30-788.39) ▽
599.69 Urinary obstruction, not elsewhere classified — (Use additional code to identify urinary incontinence: 625.6, 788.30-788.39. Code, if applicable, any causal condition first: 600.0-600.9, with fifth-digit 1)
599.70 Hematuria, unspecified ▽
599.71 Gross hematuria
599.72 Microscopic hematuria
599.89 Other specified disorders of urinary tract — (Use additional code to identify urinary incontinence: 625.6, 788.30-788.39)
619.0 Urinary-genital tract fistula, female ♀
753.20 Unspecified obstructive defect of renal pelvis and ureter ▽
753.21 Congenital obstruction of ureteropelvic junction
753.22 Congenital obstruction of ureterovesical junction
753.23 Congenital ureterocele
753.29 Other obstructive defect of renal pelvis and ureter
753.4 Other specified congenital anomalies of ureter
788.0 Renal colic
867.2 Ureter injury without mention of open wound into cavity
867.3 Ureter injury with open wound into cavity
996.39 Mechanical complication of genitourinary device, implant, and graft, other
996.65 Infection and inflammatory reaction due to other genitourinary device, implant, and graft — (Use additional code to identify specified infections)
996.76 Other complications due to genitourinary device, implant, and graft — (Use additional code to identify complication: 338.18-338.19, 338.28-338.29)
996.81 Complications of transplanted kidney — (Use additional code to identify nature of complication: 078.5, 199.2, 238.77, 279.50-279.53)

ICD-9-CM Procedural

59.8 Ureteral catheterization
97.62 Removal of ureterostomy tube and ureteral catheter

50385-50386

50385 Removal (via snare/capture) and replacement of internally dwelling ureteral stent via transurethral approach, without use of cystoscopy, including radiological supervision and interpretation
50386 Removal (via snare/capture) of internally dwelling ureteral stent via transurethral approach, without use of cystoscopy, including radiological supervision and interpretation

ICD-9-CM Diagnostic

188.0 Malignant neoplasm of trigone of urinary bladder
188.1 Malignant neoplasm of dome of urinary bladder
188.2 Malignant neoplasm of lateral wall of urinary bladder
188.3 Malignant neoplasm of anterior wall of urinary bladder
189.1 Malignant neoplasm of renal pelvis
189.2 Malignant neoplasm of ureter
198.0 Secondary malignant neoplasm of kidney
198.1 Secondary malignant neoplasm of other urinary organs
223.1 Benign neoplasm of renal pelvis
223.2 Benign neoplasm of ureter
223.3 Benign neoplasm of bladder
233.9 Carcinoma in situ of other and unspecified urinary organs ▽
236.7 Neoplasm of uncertain behavior of bladder
236.91 Neoplasm of uncertain behavior of kidney and ureter
238.77 Post-transplant lymphoproliferative disorder [PTLD] — (Code first complications of transplant (996.80-996.89))
239.4 Neoplasm of unspecified nature of bladder
239.5 Neoplasm of unspecified nature of other genitourinary organs
279.50 Graft-versus-host disease, unspecified — (Code first underlying cause: 996.80-996.89, 999.89)(Use additional code to identify any associated intellectual disabilities) (Use additional code to identify associated manifestations: 695.89, 704.09, 782.4, 787.91) ▽
279.51 Acute graft-versus-host disease — (Code first underlying cause: 996.80-996.89, 999.89)(Use additional code to identify any associated intellectual disabilities) (Use additional code to identify associated manifestations: 695.89, 704.09, 782.4, 787.91)
279.52 Chronic graft-versus-host disease — (Code first underlying cause: 996.80-996.89, 999.89)(Use additional code to identify any associated intellectual disabilities) (Use additional code to identify associated manifestations: 695.89, 704.09, 782.4, 787.91)
279.53 Acute on chronic graft-versus-host disease — (Code first underlying cause: 996.80-996.89, 999.89)(Use additional code to identify any associated intellectual disabilities) (Use additional code to identify associated manifestations: 695.89, 704.09, 782.4, 787.91)
588.89 Other specified disorders resulting from impaired renal function
588.9 Unspecified disorder resulting from impaired renal function ▽
590.10 Acute pyelonephritis without lesion of renal medullary necrosis — (Use additional code to identify organism, such as E. coli, 041.40-041.49)
590.11 Acute pyelonephritis with lesion of renal medullary necrosis — (Use additional code to identify organism, such as E. coli, 041.40-041.49)
590.2 Renal and perinephric abscess — (Use additional code to identify organism, such as E. coli, 041.41-041.49)
590.3 Pyeloureteritis cystica — (Use additional code to identify organism, such as E. coli, 041.41-041.49)
590.80 Unspecified pyelonephritis — (Use additional code to identify organism, such as E. coli, 041.41-041.49) ▽
590.81 Pyelitis or pyelonephritis in diseases classified elsewhere — (Use additional code to identify organism, such as E. coli, 041.41-041.49. Code first underlying disease: 016.0) ☒
590.9 Unspecified infection of kidney — (Use additional code to identify organism, such as E. coli, 041.41-041.49) ▽
591 Hydronephrosis
592.0 Calculus of kidney
592.1 Calculus of ureter
592.9 Unspecified urinary calculus ▽
593.3 Stricture or kinking of ureter
593.4 Other ureteric obstruction
593.89 Other specified disorder of kidney and ureter
599.60 Urinary obstruction, unspecified — (Use additional code to identify urinary incontinence: 625.6, 788.30-788.39) ▽
599.69 Urinary obstruction, not elsewhere classified — (Use additional code to identify urinary incontinence: 625.6, 788.30-788.39. Code, if applicable, any causal condition first: 600.0-600.9, with fifth-digit 1)
599.70 Hematuria, unspecified ▽
599.71 Gross hematuria
599.72 Microscopic hematuria

599.89	Other specified disorders of urinary tract — (Use additional code to identify urinary incontinence: 625.6, 788.30-788.39)
619.0	Urinary-genital tract fistula, female ♀
753.20	Unspecified obstructive defect of renal pelvis and ureter ▽
753.21	Congenital obstruction of ureteropelvic junction
753.22	Congenital obstruction of ureterovesical junction
753.23	Congenital ureterocele
753.29	Other obstructive defect of renal pelvis and ureter
753.4	Other specified congenital anomalies of ureter
788.0	Renal colic
867.2	Ureter injury without mention of open wound into cavity
867.3	Ureter injury with open wound into cavity
996.39	Mechanical complication of genitourinary device, implant, and graft, other
996.65	Infection and inflammatory reaction due to other genitourinary device, implant, and graft — (Use additional code to identify specified infections)
996.76	Other complications due to genitourinary device, implant, and graft — (Use additional code to identify complication: 338.18-338.19, 338.28-338.29)
996.81	Complications of transplanted kidney — (Use additional code to identify nature of complication: 078.5, 199.2, 238.77, 279.50-279.53)

ICD-9-CM Procedural

59.8	Ureteral catheterization
97.29	Other nonoperative replacements
97.62	Removal of ureterostomy tube and ureteral catheter
97.64	Removal of other urinary drainage device
97.69	Removal of other device from urinary system

50387

50387 Removal and replacement of externally accessible transnephric ureteral stent (eg, external/internal stent) requiring fluoroscopic guidance, including radiological supervision and interpretation

ICD-9-CM Diagnostic

188.0	Malignant neoplasm of trigone of urinary bladder
188.1	Malignant neoplasm of dome of urinary bladder
188.2	Malignant neoplasm of lateral wall of urinary bladder
188.3	Malignant neoplasm of anterior wall of urinary bladder
189.1	Malignant neoplasm of renal pelvis
189.2	Malignant neoplasm of ureter
198.0	Secondary malignant neoplasm of kidney
198.1	Secondary malignant neoplasm of other urinary organs
223.1	Benign neoplasm of renal pelvis
223.2	Benign neoplasm of ureter
223.3	Benign neoplasm of bladder
233.9	Carcinoma in situ of other and unspecified urinary organs ▽
236.7	Neoplasm of uncertain behavior of bladder
236.91	Neoplasm of uncertain behavior of kidney and ureter
238.77	Post-transplant lymphoproliferative disorder [PTLD] — (Code first complications of transplant (996.80-996.89))
239.4	Neoplasm of unspecified nature of bladder
239.5	Neoplasm of unspecified nature of other genitourinary organs
279.50	Graft-versus-host disease, unspecified — (Code first underlying cause: 996.80-996.89, 999.89)(Use additional code to identify any associated intellectual disabilities) (Use additional code to identify associated manifestations: 695.89, 704.09, 782.4, 787.91) ▽
279.51	Acute graft-versus-host disease — (Code first underlying cause: 996.80-996.89, 999.89)(Use additional code to identify any associated intellectual disabilities) (Use additional code to identify associated manifestations: 695.89, 704.09, 782.4, 787.91)
279.52	Chronic graft-versus-host disease — (Code first underlying cause: 996.80-996.89, 999.89)(Use additional code to identify any associated intellectual disabilities) (Use additional code to identify associated manifestations: 695.89, 704.09, 782.4, 787.91)
279.53	Acute on chronic graft-versus-host disease — (Code first underlying cause: 996.80-996.89, 999.89)(Use additional code to identify any associated intellectual disabilities) (Use additional code to identify associated manifestations: 695.89, 704.09, 782.4, 787.91)
588.89	Other specified disorders resulting from impaired renal function
588.9	Unspecified disorder resulting from impaired renal function ▽
590.10	Acute pyelonephritis without lesion of renal medullary necrosis — (Use additional code to identify organism, such as E. coli, 041.40-041.49)
590.11	Acute pyelonephritis with lesion of renal medullary necrosis — (Use additional code to identify organism, such as E. coli, 041.40-041.49)
590.2	Renal and perinephric abscess — (Use additional code to identify organism, such as E. coli, 041.41-041.49)
590.3	Pyeloureteritis cystica — (Use additional code to identify organism, such as E. coli, 041.41-041.49)
590.80	Unspecified pyelonephritis — (Use additional code to identify organism, such as E. coli, 041.41-041.49) ▽
590.81	Pyelitis or pyelonephritis in diseases classified elsewhere — (Use additional code to identify organism, such as E. coli, 041.41-041.49. Code first underlying disease: 016.0) ☒
590.9	Unspecified infection of kidney — (Use additional code to identify organism, such as E. coli, 041.41-041.49) ▽
591	Hydronephrosis
592.0	Calculus of kidney
592.1	Calculus of ureter
592.9	Unspecified urinary calculus ▽
593.3	Stricture or kinking of ureter
593.4	Other ureteric obstruction
593.89	Other specified disorder of kidney and ureter
599.60	Urinary obstruction, unspecified — (Use additional code to identify urinary incontinence: 625.6, 788.30-788.39) ▽
599.69	Urinary obstruction, not elsewhere classified — (Use additional code to identify urinary incontinence: 625.6, 788.30-788.39. Code, if applicable, any causal condition first: 600.0-600.9, with fifth-digit 1)
599.70	Hematuria, unspecified ▽
599.71	Gross hematuria
599.72	Microscopic hematuria
599.89	Other specified disorders of urinary tract — (Use additional code to identify urinary incontinence: 625.6, 788.30-788.39)
619.0	Urinary-genital tract fistula, female ♀
753.20	Unspecified obstructive defect of renal pelvis and ureter ▽
753.21	Congenital obstruction of ureteropelvic junction
753.22	Congenital obstruction of ureterovesical junction
753.23	Congenital ureterocele
753.29	Other obstructive defect of renal pelvis and ureter
753.4	Other specified congenital anomalies of ureter
788.0	Renal colic
867.2	Ureter injury without mention of open wound into cavity
867.3	Ureter injury with open wound into cavity
996.39	Mechanical complication of genitourinary device, implant, and graft, other
996.65	Infection and inflammatory reaction due to other genitourinary device, implant, and graft — (Use additional code to identify specified infections)
996.76	Other complications due to genitourinary device, implant, and graft — (Use additional code to identify complication: 338.18-338.19, 338.28-338.29)
996.81	Complications of transplanted kidney — (Use additional code to identify nature of complication: 078.5, 199.2, 238.77, 279.50-279.53)

ICD-9-CM Procedural

59.8	Ureteral catheterization
97.62	Removal of ureterostomy tube and ureteral catheter

50389

50389 Removal of nephrostomy tube, requiring fluoroscopic guidance (eg, with concurrent indwelling ureteral stent)

ICD-9-CM Diagnostic

189.0 Malignant neoplasm of kidney, except pelvis

189.1 Malignant neoplasm of renal pelvis

189.2 Malignant neoplasm of ureter

189.9 Malignant neoplasm of urinary organ, site unspecified ▽

198.0 Secondary malignant neoplasm of kidney

198.1 Secondary malignant neoplasm of other urinary organs

199.2 Malignant neoplasm associated with transplanted organ — (Code first complication of transplanted organ (996.80-996.89) Use additional code for specific malignancy)

209.24 Malignant carcinoid tumor of the kidney — (Code first any associated multiple endocrine neoplasia syndrome: 258.01-258.03; Use additional code to identify associated endocrine syndrome, as: carcinoid syndrome: 259.2)

209.64 Benign carcinoid tumor of the kidney — (Code first any associated multiple endocrine neoplasia syndrome: 258.01-258.03; Use additional code to identify associated endocrine syndrome, as: carcinoid syndrome: 259.2)

223.0 Benign neoplasm of kidney, except pelvis

223.1 Benign neoplasm of renal pelvis

223.2 Benign neoplasm of ureter

233.9 Carcinoma in situ of other and unspecified urinary organs ▽

236.91 Neoplasm of uncertain behavior of kidney and ureter

238.77 Post-transplant lymphoproliferative disorder [PTLD] — (Code first complications of transplant (996.80-996.89))

239.5 Neoplasm of unspecified nature of other genitourinary organs

279.50 Graft-versus-host disease, unspecified — (Code first underlying cause: 996.80-996.89, 999.89)(Use additional code to identify any associated intellectual disabilities) (Use additional code to identify associated manifestations: 695.89, 704.09, 782.4, 787.91) ▽

279.51 Acute graft-versus-host disease — (Code first underlying cause: 996.80-996.89, 999.89)(Use additional code to identify any associated intellectual disabilities) (Use additional code to identify associated manifestations: 695.89, 704.09, 782.4, 787.91)

279.52 Chronic graft-versus-host disease — (Code first underlying cause: 996.80-996.89, 999.89)(Use additional code to identify any associated intellectual disabilities) (Use additional code to identify associated manifestations: 695.89, 704.09, 782.4, 787.91)

279.53 Acute on chronic graft-versus-host disease — (Code first underlying cause: 996.80-996.89, 999.89)(Use additional code to identify any associated intellectual disabilities) (Use additional code to identify associated manifestations: 695.89, 704.09, 782.4, 787.91)

586 Unspecified renal failure ▽

588.89 Other specified disorders resulting from impaired renal function

590.10 Acute pyelonephritis without lesion of renal medullary necrosis — (Use additional code to identify organism, such as E. coli, 041.40-041.49)

590.11 Acute pyelonephritis with lesion of renal medullary necrosis — (Use additional code to identify organism, such as E. coli, 041.40-041.49)

590.2 Renal and perinephric abscess — (Use additional code to identify organism, such as E. coli, 041.41-041.49)

590.3 Pyeloureteritis cystica — (Use additional code to identify organism, such as E. coli, 041.41-041.49)

590.80 Unspecified pyelonephritis — (Use additional code to identify organism, such as E. coli, 041.41-041.49) ▽

590.81 Pyelitis or pyelonephritis in diseases classified elsewhere — (Use additional code to identify organism, such as E. coli, 041.41-041.49. Code first underlying disease: 016.0) ☒

590.9 Unspecified infection of kidney — (Use additional code to identify organism, such as E. coli, 041.41-041.49) ▽

591 Hydronephrosis

592.0 Calculus of kidney

592.1 Calculus of ureter

592.9 Unspecified urinary calculus ▽

593.3 Stricture or kinking of ureter

593.4 Other ureteric obstruction

593.89 Other specified disorder of kidney and ureter

753.21 Congenital obstruction of ureteropelvic junction

753.3 Other specified congenital anomalies of kidney

996.39 Mechanical complication of genitourinary device, implant, and graft, other

996.65 Infection and inflammatory reaction due to other genitourinary device, implant, and graft — (Use additional code to identify specified infections)

996.76 Other complications due to genitourinary device, implant, and graft — (Use additional code to identify complication: 338.18-338.19, 338.28-338.29)

996.81 Complications of transplanted kidney — (Use additional code to identify nature of complication: 078.5, 199.2, 238.77, 279.50-279.53)

997.5 Urinary complications — (Use additional code to identify complications)

ICD-9-CM Procedural

97.61 Removal of pyelostomy and nephrostomy tube

50390

50390 Aspiration and/or injection of renal cyst or pelvis by needle, percutaneous

ICD-9-CM Diagnostic

189.0 Malignant neoplasm of kidney, except pelvis

189.1 Malignant neoplasm of renal pelvis

199.2 Malignant neoplasm associated with transplanted organ — (Code first complication of transplanted organ (996.80-996.89) Use additional code for specific malignancy)

209.24 Malignant carcinoid tumor of the kidney — (Code first any associated multiple endocrine neoplasia syndrome: 258.01-258.03; Use additional code to identify associated endocrine syndrome, as: carcinoid syndrome: 259.2)

209.64 Benign carcinoid tumor of the kidney — (Code first any associated multiple endocrine neoplasia syndrome: 258.01-258.03; Use additional code to identify associated endocrine syndrome, as: carcinoid syndrome: 259.2)

279.50 Graft-versus-host disease, unspecified — (Code first underlying cause: 996.80-996.89, 999.89)(Use additional code to identify any associated intellectual disabilities) (Use additional code to identify associated manifestations: 695.89, 704.09, 782.4, 787.91) ▽

279.51 Acute graft-versus-host disease — (Code first underlying cause: 996.80-996.89, 999.89)(Use additional code to identify any associated intellectual disabilities) (Use additional code to identify associated manifestations: 695.89, 704.09, 782.4, 787.91)

279.52 Chronic graft-versus-host disease — (Code first underlying cause: 996.80-996.89, 999.89)(Use additional code to identify any associated intellectual disabilities) (Use additional code to identify associated manifestations: 695.89, 704.09, 782.4, 787.91)

279.53 Acute on chronic graft-versus-host disease — (Code first underlying cause: 996.80-996.89, 999.89)(Use additional code to identify any associated intellectual disabilities) (Use additional code to identify associated manifestations: 695.89, 704.09, 782.4, 787.91)

586 Unspecified renal failure ▽

593.2 Acquired cyst of kidney

593.89 Other specified disorder of kidney and ureter

753.10 Unspecified congenital cystic kidney disease ▽

753.11 Congenital single renal cyst

753.20 Unspecified obstructive defect of renal pelvis and ureter ▽

753.21 Congenital obstruction of ureteropelvic junction

753.22 Congenital obstruction of ureterovesical junction

753.23 Congenital ureterocele

753.29 Other obstructive defect of renal pelvis and ureter

753.3 Other specified congenital anomalies of kidney

ICD-9-CM Procedural

55.92 Percutaneous aspiration of kidney (pelvis)

55.96 Other injection of therapeutic substance into kidney

50391

50391 Instillation(s) of therapeutic agent into renal pelvis and/or ureter through established nephrostomy, pyelostomy or ureterostomy tube (eg, anticarcinogenic or antifungal agent)

ICD-9-CM Diagnostic

016.00 Tuberculosis of kidney, confirmation unspecified — (Use additional code to identify manifestation: 583.81, 590.81) ▽

118 Opportunistic mycoses — (Use additional code to identify manifestation: 321.0-321.1, 370.8, 380.15, 711.6)

188.6 Malignant neoplasm of ureteric orifice

189.0 Malignant neoplasm of kidney, except pelvis

189.1 Malignant neoplasm of renal pelvis

189.2 Malignant neoplasm of ureter

198.0 Secondary malignant neoplasm of kidney

198.1 Secondary malignant neoplasm of other urinary organs

199.2 Malignant neoplasm associated with transplanted organ — (Code first complication of transplanted organ (996.80-996.89) Use additional code for specific malignancy)

209.24 Malignant carcinoid tumor of the kidney — (Code first any associated multiple endocrine neoplasia syndrome: 258.01-258.03; Use additional code to identify associated endocrine syndrome, as: carcinoid syndrome: 259.2)

233.7 Carcinoma in situ of bladder

233.9 Carcinoma in situ of other and unspecified urinary organs ▽

236.7 Neoplasm of uncertain behavior of bladder

236.91 Neoplasm of uncertain behavior of kidney and ureter

239.5 Neoplasm of unspecified nature of other genitourinary organs

583.81 Nephritis and nephropathy, not specified as acute or chronic, with other specified pathological lesion in kidney, in diseases classified elsewhere — (Code first underlying disease: 016.0, 098.19, 249.4, 250.4, 277.30-277.39, 446.21, 710.0) ☒

590.00 Chronic pyelonephritis without lesion of renal medullary necrosis — (Use additional code to identify organism, such as E. coli, 041.41-041.49. Code if applicable, any causal condition first)

590.01 Chronic pyelonephritis with lesion of renal medullary necrosis — (Use additional code to identify organism, such as E. coli, 041.41-041.49. Code if applicable, any causal condition first)

590.10 Acute pyelonephritis without lesion of renal medullary necrosis — (Use additional code to identify organism, such as E. coli, 041.40-041.49)

590.11 Acute pyelonephritis with lesion of renal medullary necrosis — (Use additional code to identify organism, such as E. coli, 041.40-041.49)

590.2 Renal and perinephric abscess — (Use additional code to identify organism, such as E. coli, 041.41-041.49)

590.3 Pyeloureteritis cystica — (Use additional code to identify organism, such as E. coli, 041.41-041.49)

590.80 Unspecified pyelonephritis — (Use additional code to identify organism, such as E. coli, 041.41-041.49) ▽

590.81 Pyelitis or pyelonephritis in diseases classified elsewhere — (Use additional code to identify organism, such as E. coli, 041.41-041.49. Code first underlying disease: 016.0) ☒

590.9 Unspecified infection of kidney — (Use additional code to identify organism, such as E. coli, 041.41-041.49) ▽

ICD-9-CM Procedural

55.96 Other injection of therapeutic substance into kidney

92.25 Teleradiotherapy using electrons

96.49 Other genitourinary instillation

99.22 Injection of other anti-infective

50392-50393

50392 Introduction of intracatheter or catheter into renal pelvis for drainage and/or injection, percutaneous

50393 Introduction of ureteral catheter or stent into ureter through renal pelvis for drainage and/or injection, percutaneous

ICD-9-CM Diagnostic

189.0 Malignant neoplasm of kidney, except pelvis

189.1 Malignant neoplasm of renal pelvis

198.0 Secondary malignant neoplasm of kidney

199.2 Malignant neoplasm associated with transplanted organ — (Code first complication of transplanted organ (996.80-996.89) Use additional code for specific malignancy)

209.24 Malignant carcinoid tumor of the kidney — (Code first any associated multiple endocrine neoplasia syndrome: 258.01-258.03; Use additional code to identify associated endocrine syndrome, as: carcinoid syndrome: 259.2)

223.1 Benign neoplasm of renal pelvis

238.77 Post-transplant lymphoproliferative disorder [PTLD] — (Code first complications of transplant (996.80-996.89))

252.00 Hyperparathyroidism, unspecified ▽

252.01 Primary hyperparathyroidism

252.02 Secondary hyperparathyroidism, non-renal

252.08 Other hyperparathyroidism

279.50 Graft-versus-host disease, unspecified — (Code first underlying cause: 996.80-996.89, 999.89)(Use additional code to identify any associated intellectual disabilities) (Use additional code to identify associated manifestations: 695.89, 704.09, 782.4, 787.91) ▽

279.51 Acute graft-versus-host disease — (Code first underlying cause: 996.80-996.89, 999.89)(Use additional code to identify any associated intellectual disabilities) (Use additional code to identify associated manifestations: 695.89, 704.09, 782.4, 787.91)

279.52 Chronic graft-versus-host disease — (Code first underlying cause: 996.80-996.89, 999.89)(Use additional code to identify any associated intellectual disabilities) (Use additional code to identify associated manifestations: 695.89, 704.09, 782.4, 787.91)

279.53 Acute on chronic graft-versus-host disease — (Code first underlying cause: 996.80-996.89, 999.89)(Use additional code to identify any associated intellectual disabilities) (Use additional code to identify associated manifestations: 695.89, 704.09, 782.4, 787.91)

586 Unspecified renal failure ▽

588.81 Secondary hyperparathyroidism (of renal origin)

588.89 Other specified disorders resulting from impaired renal function

591 Hydronephrosis

592.0 Calculus of kidney

592.1 Calculus of ureter

592.9 Unspecified urinary calculus ▽

593.4 Other ureteric obstruction

593.89 Other specified disorder of kidney and ureter

753.20 Unspecified obstructive defect of renal pelvis and ureter ▽

753.21 Congenital obstruction of ureteropelvic junction

753.22 Congenital obstruction of ureterovesical junction

753.23 Congenital ureterocele

753.29 Other obstructive defect of renal pelvis and ureter

996.65 Infection and inflammatory reaction due to other genitourinary device, implant, and graft — (Use additional code to identify specified infections)

996.81 Complications of transplanted kidney — (Use additional code to identify nature of complication: 078.5, 199.2, 238.77, 279.50-279.53)

ICD-9-CM Procedural

55.29 Other diagnostic procedures on kidney

50394

50394 Injection procedure for pyelography (as nephrostogram, pyelostogram, antegrade pyeloureterograms) through nephrostomy or pyelostomy tube, or indwelling ureteral catheter

ICD-9-CM Diagnostic

189.0 Malignant neoplasm of kidney, except pelvis
189.1 Malignant neoplasm of renal pelvis
189.2 Malignant neoplasm of ureter
189.8 Malignant neoplasm of other specified sites of urinary organs
198.0 Secondary malignant neoplasm of kidney
198.1 Secondary malignant neoplasm of other urinary organs
199.0 Disseminated malignant neoplasm
199.1 Other malignant neoplasm of unspecified site
199.2 Malignant neoplasm associated with transplanted organ — (Code first complication of transplanted organ (996.80-996.89) Use additional code for specific malignancy)
209.24 Malignant carcinoid tumor of the kidney — (Code first any associated multiple endocrine neoplasia syndrome: 258.01-258.03; Use additional code to identify associated endocrine syndrome, as: carcinoid syndrome: 259.2)
209.64 Benign carcinoid tumor of the kidney — (Code first any associated multiple endocrine neoplasia syndrome: 258.01-258.03; Use additional code to identify associated endocrine syndrome, as: carcinoid syndrome: 259.2)
223.0 Benign neoplasm of kidney, except pelvis
223.1 Benign neoplasm of renal pelvis
223.2 Benign neoplasm of ureter
233.9 Carcinoma in situ of other and unspecified urinary organs ▽
236.91 Neoplasm of uncertain behavior of kidney and ureter
238.77 Post-transplant lymphoproliferative disorder [PTLD] — (Code first complications of transplant (996.80-996.89))
239.5 Neoplasm of unspecified nature of other genitourinary organs
252.00 Hyperparathyroidism, unspecified ▽
252.01 Primary hyperparathyroidism
252.02 Secondary hyperparathyroidism, non-renal
252.08 Other hyperparathyroidism
279.50 Graft-versus-host disease, unspecified — (Code first underlying cause: 996.80-996.89, 999.89)(Use additional code to identify any associated intellectual disabilities) (Use additional code to identify associated manifestations: 695.89, 704.09, 782.4, 787.91) ▽
279.51 Acute graft-versus-host disease — (Code first underlying cause: 996.80-996.89, 999.89)(Use additional code to identify any associated intellectual disabilities) (Use additional code to identify associated manifestations: 695.89, 704.09, 782.4, 787.91)
279.52 Chronic graft-versus-host disease — (Code first underlying cause: 996.80-996.89, 999.89)(Use additional code to identify any associated intellectual disabilities) (Use additional code to identify associated manifestations: 695.89, 704.09, 782.4, 787.91)
279.53 Acute on chronic graft-versus-host disease — (Code first underlying cause: 996.80-996.89, 999.89)(Use additional code to identify any associated intellectual disabilities) (Use additional code to identify associated manifestations: 695.89, 704.09, 782.4, 787.91)
357.4 Polyneuropathy in other diseases classified elsewhere — (Code first underlying disease, as: 032.0-032.9,135, 251.2, 265.0, 265.2, 266.0-266.9, 277.1, 277.30-277.39, 585.9, 586) ☒
585.1 Chronic kidney disease, Stage I — (Use additional code to identify kidney transplant status, if applicable: V42.0. Use additional code to identify manifestation: 357.4, 420.0. Code first hypertensive chronic kidney disease, if applicable: 403.00-403.91, 404.00-404.93)
585.2 Chronic kidney disease, Stage II (mild) — (Use additional code to identify kidney transplant status, if applicable: V42.0. Use additional code to identify manifestation: 357.4, 420.0. Code first hypertensive chronic kidney disease, if applicable: 403.00-403.91, 404.00-404.93)
585.3 Chronic kidney disease, Stage III (moderate) — (Use additional code to identify kidney transplant status, if applicable: V42.0. Use additional code to identify manifestation: 357.4, 420.0. Code first hypertensive chronic kidney disease, if applicable: 403.00-403.91, 404.00-404.93)
585.4 Chronic kidney disease, Stage IV (severe) — (Use additional code to identify kidney transplant status, if applicable: V42.0. Use additional code to identify manifestation: 357.4, 420.0. Code first hypertensive chronic kidney disease, if applicable: 403.00-403.91, 404.00-404.93)
585.5 Chronic kidney disease, Stage V — (Use additional code to identify kidney transplant status, if applicable: V42.0. Use additional code to identify manifestation: 357.4, 420.0. Code first hypertensive chronic kidney disease, if applicable: 403.00-403.91, 404.00-404.93)
585.6 End stage renal disease — (Use additional code to identify kidney transplant status, if applicable: V42.0. Use additional code to identify manifestation: 357.4, 420.0. Code first hypertensive chronic kidney disease, if applicable: 403.00-403.91, 404.00-404.93)
585.9 Chronic kidney disease, unspecified — (Use additional code to identify kidney transplant status, if applicable: V42.0. Use additional code to identify manifestation: 357.4, 420.0. Code first hypertensive chronic kidney disease, if applicable: 403.00-403.91, 404.00-404.93) ▽
586 Unspecified renal failure ▽
587 Unspecified renal sclerosis ▽
588.81 Secondary hyperparathyroidism (of renal origin)
588.89 Other specified disorders resulting from impaired renal function
590.00 Chronic pyelonephritis without lesion of renal medullary necrosis — (Use additional code to identify organism, such as E. coli, 041.41-041.49. Code if applicable, any causal condition first)
590.01 Chronic pyelonephritis with lesion of renal medullary necrosis — (Use additional code to identify organism, such as E. coli, 041.41-041.49. Code if applicable, any causal condition first)
590.3 Pyeloureteritis cystica — (Use additional code to identify organism, such as E. coli, 041.41-041.49)
591 Hydronephrosis
592.0 Calculus of kidney
592.9 Unspecified urinary calculus ▽
593.2 Acquired cyst of kidney
593.3 Stricture or kinking of ureter
593.4 Other ureteric obstruction
593.70 Vesicoureteral reflux, unspecified or without reflex nephropathy
593.71 Vesicoureteral reflux with reflux nephropathy, unilateral
593.72 Vesicoureteral reflux with reflux nephropathy, bilateral
593.73 Vesicoureteral reflux with reflux nephropathy, NOS ▽
593.89 Other specified disorder of kidney and ureter
593.9 Unspecified disorder of kidney and ureter ▽
599.0 Urinary tract infection, site not specified — (Use additional code to identify organism, such as E. coli: 041.41-041.49) ▽
599.60 Urinary obstruction, unspecified — (Use additional code to identify urinary incontinence: 625.6, 788.30-788.39) ▽
599.69 Urinary obstruction, not elsewhere classified — (Use additional code to identify urinary incontinence: 625.6, 788.30-788.39. Code, if applicable, any causal condition first: 600.0-600.9, with fifth-digit 1)
599.70 Hematuria, unspecified ▽
599.71 Gross hematuria
599.72 Microscopic hematuria
601.1 Chronic prostatitis — (Use additional code to identify organism: 041.0, 041.1) ♂
625.6 Female stress incontinence ♀
753.0 Congenital renal agenesis and dysgenesis
753.11 Congenital single renal cyst
753.12 Congenital polycystic kidney, unspecified type ▽
753.13 Congenital polycystic kidney, autosomal dominant
753.14 Congenital polycystic kidney, autosomal recessive
753.15 Congenital renal dysplasia
753.16 Congenital medullary cystic kidney

753.17	Congenital medullary sponge kidney
753.19	Other specified congenital cystic kidney disease
753.20	Unspecified obstructive defect of renal pelvis and ureter ▽
753.21	Congenital obstruction of ureteropelvic junction
753.22	Congenital obstruction of ureterovesical junction
753.23	Congenital ureterocele
753.29	Other obstructive defect of renal pelvis and ureter
753.9	Unspecified congenital anomaly of urinary system ▽
788.0	Renal colic
788.21	Incomplete bladder emptying — (Code, if applicable, any causal condition first, such as: 600.0-600.9, with fifth digit 1)
788.29	Other specified retention of urine — (Code, if applicable, any causal condition first, such as: 600.0-600.9, with fifth digit 1)
788.31	Urge incontinence — (Code, if applicable, any causal condition first: 600.0-600.9, with fifth digit 1; 618.00-618.9; 753.23)
788.32	Stress incontinence, male — (Code, if applicable, any causal condition first: 600.0-600.9, with fifth digit 1; 618.00-618.9; 753.23) ♂
788.33	Mixed incontinence urge and stress (male)(female) — (Code, if applicable, any causal condition first: 600.0-600.9, with fifth digit 1; 618.00-618.9; 753.23)
788.34	Incontinence without sensory awareness — (Code, if applicable, any causal condition first: 600.0-600.9, with fifth digit 1; 618.00-618.9; 753.23)
788.35	Post-void dribbling — (Code, if applicable, any causal condition first: 600.0-600.9, with fifth digit 1; 618.00-618.9; 753.23)
788.36	Nocturnal enuresis — (Code, if applicable, any causal condition first: 600.0-600.9, with fifth digit 1; 618.00-618.9; 753.23)
788.37	Continuous leakage — (Code, if applicable, any causal condition first: 600.0-600.9, with fifth digit 1; 618.00-618.9; 753.23)
788.38	Overflow incontinence — (Code, if applicable, any causal condition first: 600.0-600.9, with fifth digit 1; 618.00-618.9; 753.23)
788.39	Other urinary incontinence — (Code, if applicable, any causal condition first: 600.0-600.9, with fifth digit 1; 618.00-618.9; 753.23)
788.41	Urinary frequency — (Code, if applicable, any causal condition first, such as: 600.0-600.9, with fifth digit 1)
788.42	Polyuria — (Code, if applicable, any causal condition first, such as: 600.0-600.9, with fifth digit 1)
788.43	Nocturia — (Code, if applicable, any causal condition first, such as: 600.0-600.9, with fifth digit 1)
788.99	Other symptoms involving urinary system
789.01	Abdominal pain, right upper quadrant
789.02	Abdominal pain, left upper quadrant
789.09	Abdominal pain, other specified site
789.31	Abdominal or pelvic swelling, mass, or lump, right upper quadrant
789.32	Abdominal or pelvic swelling, mass, or lump, left upper quadrant
789.39	Abdominal or pelvic swelling, mass, or lump, other specified site
791.9	Other nonspecific finding on examination of urine
793.5	Nonspecific (abnormal) findings on radiological and other examination of genitourinary organs
996.1	Mechanical complication of other vascular device, implant, and graft
996.59	Mechanical complication due to other implant and internal device, not elsewhere classified
996.76	Other complications due to genitourinary device, implant, and graft — (Use additional code to identify complication: 338.18-338.19, 338.28-338.29)
996.81	Complications of transplanted kidney — (Use additional code to identify nature of complication: 078.5, 199.2, 238.77, 279.50-279.53)
997.5	Urinary complications — (Use additional code to identify complications)

ICD-9-CM Procedural

55.96	Other injection of therapeutic substance into kidney
87.74	Retrograde pyelogram
87.75	Percutaneous pyelogram

50395

50395 Introduction of guide into renal pelvis and/or ureter with dilation to establish nephrostomy tract, percutaneous

ICD-9-CM Diagnostic

189.1	Malignant neoplasm of renal pelvis
189.2	Malignant neoplasm of ureter
198.0	Secondary malignant neoplasm of kidney
198.1	Secondary malignant neoplasm of other urinary organs
199.2	Malignant neoplasm associated with transplanted organ — (Code first complication of transplanted organ (996.80-996.89) Use additional code for specific malignancy)
209.24	Malignant carcinoid tumor of the kidney — (Code first any associated multiple endocrine neoplasia syndrome: 258.01-258.03; Use additional code to identify associated endocrine syndrome, as: carcinoid syndrome: 259.2)
209.64	Benign carcinoid tumor of the kidney — (Code first any associated multiple endocrine neoplasia syndrome: 258.01-258.03; Use additional code to identify associated endocrine syndrome, as: carcinoid syndrome: 259.2)
223.1	Benign neoplasm of renal pelvis
223.2	Benign neoplasm of ureter
233.9	Carcinoma in situ of other and unspecified urinary organs ▽
236.91	Neoplasm of uncertain behavior of kidney and ureter
238.77	Post-transplant lymphoproliferative disorder [PTLD] — (Code first complications of transplant (996.80-996.89))
239.5	Neoplasm of unspecified nature of other genitourinary organs
252.00	Hyperparathyroidism, unspecified ▽
252.01	Primary hyperparathyroidism
252.02	Secondary hyperparathyroidism, non-renal
252.08	Other hyperparathyroidism
279.50	Graft-versus-host disease, unspecified — (Code first underlying cause: 996.80-996.89, 999.89)(Use additional code to identify any associated intellectual disabilities) (Use additional code to identify associated manifestations: 695.89, 704.09, 782.4, 787.91) ▽
279.51	Acute graft-versus-host disease — (Code first underlying cause: 996.80-996.89, 999.89)(Use additional code to identify any associated intellectual disabilities) (Use additional code to identify associated manifestations: 695.89, 704.09, 782.4, 787.91)
279.52	Chronic graft-versus-host disease — (Code first underlying cause: 996.80-996.89, 999.89)(Use additional code to identify any associated intellectual disabilities) (Use additional code to identify associated manifestations: 695.89, 704.09, 782.4, 787.91)
279.53	Acute on chronic graft-versus-host disease — (Code first underlying cause: 996.80-996.89, 999.89)(Use additional code to identify any associated intellectual disabilities) (Use additional code to identify associated manifestations: 695.89, 704.09, 782.4, 787.91)
588.81	Secondary hyperparathyroidism (of renal origin)
588.89	Other specified disorders resulting from impaired renal function
590.3	Pyeloureteritis cystica — (Use additional code to identify organism, such as E. coli, 041.41-041.49)
591	Hydronephrosis
592.0	Calculus of kidney
592.1	Calculus of ureter
592.9	Unspecified urinary calculus ▽
593.3	Stricture or kinking of ureter
593.4	Other ureteric obstruction
593.89	Other specified disorder of kidney and ureter
593.9	Unspecified disorder of kidney and ureter ▽
599.60	Urinary obstruction, unspecified — (Use additional code to identify urinary incontinence: 625.6, 788.30-788.39) ▽
599.69	Urinary obstruction, not elsewhere classified — (Use additional code to identify urinary incontinence: 625.6, 788.30-788.39. Code, if applicable, any causal condition first: 600.0-600.9, with fifth-digit 1)
625.6	Female stress incontinence ♀
753.21	Congenital obstruction of ureteropelvic junction

753.22 Congenital obstruction of ureterovesical junction
753.23 Congenital ureterocele
753.29 Other obstructive defect of renal pelvis and ureter
788.30 Unspecified urinary incontinence — (Code, if applicable, any causal condition first: 600.0-600.9, with fifth digit 1; 618.00-618.9; 753.23) [Unspecified code]
788.31 Urge incontinence — (Code, if applicable, any causal condition first: 600.0-600.9, with fifth digit 1; 618.00-618.9; 753.23)
788.32 Stress incontinence, male — (Code, if applicable, any causal condition first: 600.0-600.9, with fifth digit 1; 618.00-618.9; 753.23) ♂
788.33 Mixed incontinence urge and stress (male)(female) — (Code, if applicable, any causal condition first: 600.0-600.9, with fifth digit 1; 618.00-618.9; 753.23)
788.38 Overflow incontinence — (Code, if applicable, any causal condition first: 600.0-600.9, with fifth digit 1; 618.00-618.9; 753.23)
788.99 Other symptoms involving urinary system
996.81 Complications of transplanted kidney — (Use additional code to identify nature of complication: 078.5, 199.2, 238.77, 279.50-279.53)

ICD-9-CM Procedural

55.03 Percutaneous nephrostomy without fragmentation

50396

50396 Manometric studies through nephrostomy or pyelostomy tube, or indwelling ureteral catheter

ICD-9-CM Diagnostic

591 Hydronephrosis
599.60 Urinary obstruction, unspecified — (Use additional code to identify urinary incontinence: 625.6, 788.30-788.39) [Unspecified code]
599.69 Urinary obstruction, not elsewhere classified — (Use additional code to identify urinary incontinence: 625.6, 788.30-788.39. Code, if applicable, any causal condition first: 600.0-600.9, with fifth-digit 1)
625.6 Female stress incontinence ♀
753.20 Unspecified obstructive defect of renal pelvis and ureter [Unspecified code]
753.21 Congenital obstruction of ureteropelvic junction
753.22 Congenital obstruction of ureterovesical junction
753.23 Congenital ureterocele
753.29 Other obstructive defect of renal pelvis and ureter
788.21 Incomplete bladder emptying — (Code, if applicable, any causal condition first, such as: 600.0-600.9, with fifth digit 1)
788.29 Other specified retention of urine — (Code, if applicable, any causal condition first, such as: 600.0-600.9, with fifth digit 1)
788.30 Unspecified urinary incontinence — (Code, if applicable, any causal condition first: 600.0-600.9, with fifth digit 1; 618.00-618.9; 753.23) [Unspecified code]
788.31 Urge incontinence — (Code, if applicable, any causal condition first: 600.0-600.9, with fifth digit 1; 618.00-618.9; 753.23)
788.32 Stress incontinence, male — (Code, if applicable, any causal condition first: 600.0-600.9, with fifth digit 1; 618.00-618.9; 753.23) ♂
788.33 Mixed incontinence urge and stress (male)(female) — (Code, if applicable, any causal condition first: 600.0-600.9, with fifth digit 1; 618.00-618.9; 753.23)
788.34 Incontinence without sensory awareness — (Code, if applicable, any causal condition first: 600.0-600.9, with fifth digit 1; 618.00-618.9; 753.23)
788.35 Post-void dribbling — (Code, if applicable, any causal condition first: 600.0-600.9, with fifth digit 1; 618.00-618.9; 753.23)
788.36 Nocturnal enuresis — (Code, if applicable, any causal condition first: 600.0-600.9, with fifth digit 1; 618.00-618.9; 753.23)
788.37 Continuous leakage — (Code, if applicable, any causal condition first: 600.0-600.9, with fifth digit 1; 618.00-618.9; 753.23)
788.38 Overflow incontinence — (Code, if applicable, any causal condition first: 600.0-600.9, with fifth digit 1; 618.00-618.9; 753.23)
788.39 Other urinary incontinence — (Code, if applicable, any causal condition first: 600.0-600.9, with fifth digit 1; 618.00-618.9; 753.23)
788.91 Functional urinary incontinence
788.99 Other symptoms involving urinary system

ICD-9-CM Procedural

89.21 Urinary manometry

50398

50398 Change of nephrostomy or pyelostomy tube

ICD-9-CM Diagnostic

185 Malignant neoplasm of prostate ♂
188.0 Malignant neoplasm of trigone of urinary bladder
188.1 Malignant neoplasm of dome of urinary bladder
188.2 Malignant neoplasm of lateral wall of urinary bladder
188.3 Malignant neoplasm of anterior wall of urinary bladder
188.4 Malignant neoplasm of posterior wall of urinary bladder
188.5 Malignant neoplasm of bladder neck
188.8 Malignant neoplasm of other specified sites of bladder
188.9 Malignant neoplasm of bladder, part unspecified [Unspecified code]
198.0 Secondary malignant neoplasm of kidney
198.1 Secondary malignant neoplasm of other urinary organs
198.82 Secondary malignant neoplasm of genital organs
199.2 Malignant neoplasm associated with transplanted organ — (Code first complication of transplanted organ (996.80-996.89) Use additional code for specific malignancy)
209.24 Malignant carcinoid tumor of the kidney — (Code first any associated multiple endocrine neoplasia syndrome: 258.01-258.03; Use additional code to identify associated endocrine syndrome, as: carcinoid syndrome: 259.2)
209.64 Benign carcinoid tumor of the kidney — (Code first any associated multiple endocrine neoplasia syndrome: 258.01-258.03; Use additional code to identify associated endocrine syndrome, as: carcinoid syndrome: 259.2)
223.0 Benign neoplasm of kidney, except pelvis
223.1 Benign neoplasm of renal pelvis
223.2 Benign neoplasm of ureter
223.3 Benign neoplasm of bladder
238.77 Post-transplant lymphoproliferative disorder [PTLD] — (Code first complications of transplant (996.80-996.89))
252.00 Hyperparathyroidism, unspecified [Unspecified code]
252.01 Primary hyperparathyroidism
252.02 Secondary hyperparathyroidism, non-renal
252.08 Other hyperparathyroidism
279.50 Graft-versus-host disease, unspecified — (Code first underlying cause: 996.80-996.89, 999.89)(Use additional code to identify any associated intellectual disabilities) (Use additional code to identify associated manifestations: 695.89, 704.09, 782.4, 787.91) [Unspecified code]
279.51 Acute graft-versus-host disease — (Code first underlying cause: 996.80-996.89, 999.89)(Use additional code to identify any associated intellectual disabilities) (Use additional code to identify associated manifestations: 695.89, 704.09, 782.4, 787.91)
279.52 Chronic graft-versus-host disease — (Code first underlying cause: 996.80-996.89, 999.89)(Use additional code to identify any associated intellectual disabilities) (Use additional code to identify associated manifestations: 695.89, 704.09, 782.4, 787.91)
279.53 Acute on chronic graft-versus-host disease — (Code first underlying cause: 996.80-996.89, 999.89)(Use additional code to identify any associated intellectual disabilities) (Use additional code to identify associated manifestations: 695.89, 704.09, 782.4, 787.91)
357.4 Polyneuropathy in other diseases classified elsewhere — (Code first underlying disease, as: 032.0-032.9,135, 251.2, 265.0, 265.2, 266.0-266.9, 277.1, 277.30-277.39, 585.9, 586) [Manifestation code]
585.1 Chronic kidney disease, Stage I — (Use additional code to identify kidney transplant status, if applicable: V42.0. Use additional code to identify manifestation: 357.4, 420.0. Code first hypertensive chronic kidney disease, if applicable: 403.00-403.91, 404.00-404.93)
585.2 Chronic kidney disease, Stage II (mild) — (Use additional code to identify kidney transplant status, if applicable: V42.0. Use additional code to identify manifestation:

357.4, 420.0. Code first hypertensive chronic kidney disease, if applicable: 403.00-403.91, 404.00-404.93)

585.3 Chronic kidney disease, Stage III (moderate) — (Use additional code to identify kidney transplant status, if applicable: V42.0. Use additional code to identify manifestation: 357.4, 420.0. Code first hypertensive chronic kidney disease, if applicable: 403.00-403.91, 404.00-404.93)

585.4 Chronic kidney disease, Stage IV (severe) — (Use additional code to identify kidney transplant status, if applicable: V42.0. Use additional code to identify manifestation: 357.4, 420.0. Code first hypertensive chronic kidney disease, if applicable: 403.00-403.91, 404.00-404.93)

585.5 Chronic kidney disease, Stage V — (Use additional code to identify kidney transplant status, if applicable: V42.0. Use additional code to identify manifestation: 357.4, 420.0. Code first hypertensive chronic kidney disease, if applicable: 403.00-403.91, 404.00-404.93)

585.6 End stage renal disease — (Use additional code to identify kidney transplant status, if applicable: V42.0. Use additional code to identify manifestation: 357.4, 420.0. Code first hypertensive chronic kidney disease, if applicable: 403.00-403.91, 404.00-404.93)

585.9 Chronic kidney disease, unspecified — (Use additional code to identify kidney transplant status, if applicable: V42.0. Use additional code to identify manifestation: 357.4, 420.0. Code first hypertensive chronic kidney disease, if applicable: 403.00-403.91, 404.00-404.93) ▽

586 Unspecified renal failure ▽

588.81 Secondary hyperparathyroidism (of renal origin)

588.89 Other specified disorders resulting from impaired renal function

590.9 Unspecified infection of kidney — (Use additional code to identify organism, such as E. coli, 041.41-041.49) ▽

591 Hydronephrosis

592.0 Calculus of kidney

593.2 Acquired cyst of kidney

593.3 Stricture or kinking of ureter

593.4 Other ureteric obstruction

593.89 Other specified disorder of kidney and ureter

593.9 Unspecified disorder of kidney and ureter ▽

599.60 Urinary obstruction, unspecified — (Use additional code to identify urinary incontinence: 625.6, 788.30-788.39) ▽

599.69 Urinary obstruction, not elsewhere classified — (Use additional code to identify urinary incontinence: 625.6, 788.30-788.39. Code, if applicable, any causal condition first: 600.0-600.9, with fifth-digit 1)

599.70 Hematuria, unspecified ▽

599.71 Gross hematuria

599.72 Microscopic hematuria

625.6 Female stress incontinence ♀

788.21 Incomplete bladder emptying — (Code, if applicable, any causal condition first, such as: 600.0-600.9, with fifth digit 1)

788.29 Other specified retention of urine — (Code, if applicable, any causal condition first, such as: 600.0-600.9, with fifth digit 1)

788.99 Other symptoms involving urinary system

996.30 Mechanical complication of unspecified genitourinary device, implant, and graft ▽

996.64 Infection and inflammatory reaction due to indwelling urinary catheter — (Use additional code to identify specified infections: 038.0-038.9, 595.0-595.9)

996.65 Infection and inflammatory reaction due to other genitourinary device, implant, and graft — (Use additional code to identify specified infections)

996.79 Other complications due to other internal prosthetic device, implant, and graft — (Use additional code to identify complication: 338.18-338.19, 338.28-338.29)

996.81 Complications of transplanted kidney — (Use additional code to identify nature of complication: 078.5, 199.2, 238.77, 279.50-279.53)

997.5 Urinary complications — (Use additional code to identify complications)

V44.6 Status of other artificial opening of urinary tract

V55.6 Attention to other artificial opening of urinary tract

ICD-9-CM Procedural

55.93 Replacement of nephrostomy tube

55.94 Replacement of pyelostomy tube

50400-50405

50400 Pyeloplasty (Foley Y-pyeloplasty), plastic operation on renal pelvis, with or without plastic operation on ureter, nephropexy, nephrostomy, pyelostomy, or ureteral splinting; simple

50405 complicated (congenital kidney abnormality, secondary pyeloplasty, solitary kidney, calycoplasty)

ICD-9-CM Diagnostic

588.81 Secondary hyperparathyroidism (of renal origin)

588.89 Other specified disorders resulting from impaired renal function

591 Hydronephrosis

592.0 Calculus of kidney

592.1 Calculus of ureter

593.3 Stricture or kinking of ureter

593.4 Other ureteric obstruction

593.5 Hydroureter

593.70 Vesicoureteral reflux, unspecified or without reflex nephropathy

593.71 Vesicoureteral reflux with reflux nephropathy, unilateral

593.72 Vesicoureteral reflux with reflux nephropathy, bilateral

593.73 Vesicoureteral reflux with reflux nephropathy, NOS ▽

593.89 Other specified disorder of kidney and ureter

599.60 Urinary obstruction, unspecified — (Use additional code to identify urinary incontinence: 625.6, 788.30-788.39) ▽

599.69 Urinary obstruction, not elsewhere classified — (Use additional code to identify urinary incontinence: 625.6, 788.30-788.39. Code, if applicable, any causal condition first: 600.0-600.9, with fifth-digit 1)

753.0 Congenital renal agenesis and dysgenesis

753.21 Congenital obstruction of ureteropelvic junction

753.22 Congenital obstruction of ureterovesical junction

753.23 Congenital ureterocele

753.29 Other obstructive defect of renal pelvis and ureter

788.99 Other symptoms involving urinary system

V64.41 Laparoscopic surgical procedure converted to open procedure

ICD-9-CM Procedural

55.12 Pyelostomy

55.7 Nephropexy

55.87 Correction of ureteropelvic junction

50500

50500 Nephrorrhaphy, suture of kidney wound or injury

ICD-9-CM Diagnostic

866.02 Kidney laceration without mention of open wound into cavity

866.03 Complete disruption of kidney parenchyma, without mention of open wound into cavity

866.12 Kidney laceration with open wound into cavity

866.13 Complete disruption of kidney parenchyma, with open wound into cavity

998.2 Accidental puncture or laceration during procedure

ICD-9-CM Procedural

55.81 Suture of laceration of kidney

50520

50520 Closure of nephrocutaneous or pyelocutaneous fistula

ICD-9-CM Diagnostic

593.89 Other specified disorder of kidney and ureter

V55.6 Attention to other artificial opening of urinary tract

ICD-9-CM Procedural

55.83 Closure of other fistula of kidney

50525-50526

50525 Closure of nephrovisceral fistula (eg, renocolic), including visceral repair; abdominal approach
50526 thoracic approach

ICD-9-CM Diagnostic

593.89 Other specified disorder of kidney and ureter
619.0 Urinary-genital tract fistula, female ♀
753.7 Congenital anomalies of urachus

ICD-9-CM Procedural

55.83 Closure of other fistula of kidney

50540

50540 Symphysiotomy for horseshoe kidney with or without pyeloplasty and/or other plastic procedure, unilateral or bilateral (1 operation)

ICD-9-CM Diagnostic

753.3 Other specified congenital anomalies of kidney

ICD-9-CM Procedural

55.85 Symphysiotomy for horseshoe kidney

50541-50542

50541 Laparoscopy, surgical; ablation of renal cysts
50542 ablation of renal mass lesion(s), including intraoperative ultrasound guidance and monitoring, when performed

ICD-9-CM Diagnostic

189.0 Malignant neoplasm of kidney, except pelvis
189.1 Malignant neoplasm of renal pelvis
198.0 Secondary malignant neoplasm of kidney
199.2 Malignant neoplasm associated with transplanted organ — (Code first complication of transplanted organ (996.80-996.89) Use additional code for specific malignancy)
209.24 Malignant carcinoid tumor of the kidney — (Code first any associated multiple endocrine neoplasia syndrome: 258.01-258.03; Use additional code to identify associated endocrine syndrome, as: carcinoid syndrome: 259.2)
209.64 Benign carcinoid tumor of the kidney — (Code first any associated multiple endocrine neoplasia syndrome: 258.01-258.03; Use additional code to identify associated endocrine syndrome, as: carcinoid syndrome: 259.2)
223.0 Benign neoplasm of kidney, except pelvis
223.1 Benign neoplasm of renal pelvis
233.9 Carcinoma in situ of other and unspecified urinary organs ▽
236.91 Neoplasm of uncertain behavior of kidney and ureter
239.5 Neoplasm of unspecified nature of other genitourinary organs
587 Unspecified renal sclerosis ▽
591 Hydronephrosis
593.2 Acquired cyst of kidney
593.89 Other specified disorder of kidney and ureter
593.9 Unspecified disorder of kidney and ureter ▽
753.10 Unspecified congenital cystic kidney disease ▽
753.11 Congenital single renal cyst
753.12 Congenital polycystic kidney, unspecified type ▽
753.13 Congenital polycystic kidney, autosomal dominant
753.14 Congenital polycystic kidney, autosomal recessive
753.15 Congenital renal dysplasia
753.16 Congenital medullary cystic kidney
753.17 Congenital medullary sponge kidney
753.19 Other specified congenital cystic kidney disease

ICD-9-CM Procedural

55.34 Laparoscopic ablation of renal lesion or tissue

50543

50543 Laparoscopy, surgical; partial nephrectomy

ICD-9-CM Diagnostic

189.0 Malignant neoplasm of kidney, except pelvis
189.1 Malignant neoplasm of renal pelvis
198.0 Secondary malignant neoplasm of kidney
199.2 Malignant neoplasm associated with transplanted organ — (Code first complication of transplanted organ (996.80-996.89) Use additional code for specific malignancy)
209.24 Malignant carcinoid tumor of the kidney — (Code first any associated multiple endocrine neoplasia syndrome: 258.01-258.03; Use additional code to identify associated endocrine syndrome, as: carcinoid syndrome: 259.2)
209.64 Benign carcinoid tumor of the kidney — (Code first any associated multiple endocrine neoplasia syndrome: 258.01-258.03; Use additional code to identify associated endocrine syndrome, as: carcinoid syndrome: 259.2)
223.0 Benign neoplasm of kidney, except pelvis
223.1 Benign neoplasm of renal pelvis
233.9 Carcinoma in situ of other and unspecified urinary organs ▽
236.91 Neoplasm of uncertain behavior of kidney and ureter
239.5 Neoplasm of unspecified nature of other genitourinary organs
587 Unspecified renal sclerosis ▽
591 Hydronephrosis
593.2 Acquired cyst of kidney
593.70 Vesicoureteral reflux, unspecified or without reflex nephropathy
593.71 Vesicoureteral reflux with reflux nephropathy, unilateral
593.72 Vesicoureteral reflux with reflux nephropathy, bilateral
593.73 Vesicoureteral reflux with reflux nephropathy, NOS ▽
593.81 Vascular disorders of kidney
593.89 Other specified disorder of kidney and ureter
593.9 Unspecified disorder of kidney and ureter ▽
599.70 Hematuria, unspecified ▽
599.71 Gross hematuria
599.72 Microscopic hematuria
753.11 Congenital single renal cyst
753.12 Congenital polycystic kidney, unspecified type ▽
753.13 Congenital polycystic kidney, autosomal dominant
753.14 Congenital polycystic kidney, autosomal recessive
753.15 Congenital renal dysplasia
753.16 Congenital medullary cystic kidney
753.17 Congenital medullary sponge kidney
753.19 Other specified congenital cystic kidney disease
753.20 Unspecified obstructive defect of renal pelvis and ureter ▽
753.21 Congenital obstruction of ureteropelvic junction
753.22 Congenital obstruction of ureterovesical junction
753.23 Congenital ureterocele
753.29 Other obstructive defect of renal pelvis and ureter
866.00 Unspecified kidney injury without mention of open wound into cavity ▽

ICD-9-CM Procedural

55.4 Partial nephrectomy

50544

50544 Laparoscopy, surgical; pyeloplasty

ICD-9-CM Diagnostic

588.81 Secondary hyperparathyroidism (of renal origin)
588.89 Other specified disorders resulting from impaired renal function

591 Hydronephrosis
592.0 Calculus of kidney
592.1 Calculus of ureter
593.3 Stricture or kinking of ureter
593.4 Other ureteric obstruction
593.5 Hydroureter
593.70 Vesicoureteral reflux, unspecified or without reflex nephropathy
593.71 Vesicoureteral reflux with reflux nephropathy, unilateral
593.72 Vesicoureteral reflux with reflux nephropathy, bilateral
593.73 Vesicoureteral reflux with reflux nephropathy, NOS
593.89 Other specified disorder of kidney and ureter
599.60 Urinary obstruction, unspecified — (Use additional code to identify urinary incontinence: 625.6, 788.30-788.39)
599.69 Urinary obstruction, not elsewhere classified — (Use additional code to identify urinary incontinence: 625.6, 788.30-788.39. Code, if applicable, any causal condition first: 600.0-600.9, with fifth-digit 1)
753.0 Congenital renal agenesis and dysgenesis
753.21 Congenital obstruction of ureteropelvic junction
753.22 Congenital obstruction of ureterovesical junction
753.23 Congenital ureterocele
753.29 Other obstructive defect of renal pelvis and ureter
788.99 Other symptoms involving urinary system

ICD-9-CM Procedural

55.87 Correction of ureteropelvic junction

50545

50545 Laparoscopy, surgical; radical nephrectomy (includes removal of Gerota's fascia and surrounding fatty tissue, removal of regional lymph nodes, and adrenalectomy)

ICD-9-CM Diagnostic

158.0 Malignant neoplasm of retroperitoneum
189.0 Malignant neoplasm of kidney, except pelvis
189.1 Malignant neoplasm of renal pelvis
194.0 Malignant neoplasm of adrenal gland
196.2 Secondary and unspecified malignant neoplasm of intra-abdominal lymph nodes
197.6 Secondary malignant neoplasm of retroperitoneum and peritoneum
198.0 Secondary malignant neoplasm of kidney
198.7 Secondary malignant neoplasm of adrenal gland
199.2 Malignant neoplasm associated with transplanted organ — (Code first complication of transplanted organ (996.80-996.89) Use additional code for specific malignancy)
209.24 Malignant carcinoid tumor of the kidney — (Code first any associated multiple endocrine neoplasia syndrome: 258.01-258.03; Use additional code to identify associated endocrine syndrome, as: carcinoid syndrome: 259.2)
209.64 Benign carcinoid tumor of the kidney — (Code first any associated multiple endocrine neoplasia syndrome: 258.01-258.03; Use additional code to identify associated endocrine syndrome, as: carcinoid syndrome: 259.2)
209.74 Secondary neuroendocrine tumor of peritoneum
223.0 Benign neoplasm of kidney, except pelvis
223.1 Benign neoplasm of renal pelvis
233.9 Carcinoma in situ of other and unspecified urinary organs
236.91 Neoplasm of uncertain behavior of kidney and ureter
239.5 Neoplasm of unspecified nature of other genitourinary organs
403.01 Hypertensive chronic kidney disease, malignant, with chronic kidney disease stage V or end stage renal disease — (Use additional code to identify the stage of chronic kidney disease: 585.5, 585.6)
403.11 Hypertensive chronic kidney disease, benign, with chronic kidney disease stage V or end stage renal disease — (Use additional code to identify the stage of chronic kidney disease: 585.5, 585.6)
403.91 Hypertensive chronic kidney disease, unspecified, with chronic kidney disease stage V or end stage renal disease — (Use additional code to identify the stage of chronic kidney disease: 585.5, 585.6)
404.02 Hypertensive heart and chronic kidney disease, malignant, without heart failure and with chronic kidney disease stage V or end stage renal disease — (Use additional code to identify the stage of chronic kidney disease: 585.5, 585.6)
404.12 Hypertensive heart and chronic kidney disease, benign, without heart failure and with chronic kidney disease stage V or end stage renal disease — (Use additional code to identify the stage of chronic kidney disease: 585.5, 585.6)
405.01 Secondary renovascular hypertension, malignant
405.91 Secondary renovascular hypertension, unspecified
445.81 Atheroembolism of kidney — (Use additional code for any associated acute kidney failure or chronic kidney disease: 584, 585)
580.0 Acute glomerulonephritis with lesion of proliferative glomerulonephritis
580.4 Acute glomerulonephritis with lesion of rapidly progressive glomerulonephritis
581.0 Nephrotic syndrome with lesion of proliferative glomerulonephritis
581.1 Nephrotic syndrome with lesion of membranous glomerulonephritis
581.2 Nephrotic syndrome with lesion of membranoproliferative glomerulonephritis
582.0 Chronic glomerulonephritis with lesion of proliferative glomerulonephritis
582.1 Chronic glomerulonephritis with lesion of membranous glomerulonephritis
582.2 Chronic glomerulonephritis with lesion of membranoproliferative glomerulonephritis
582.4 Chronic glomerulonephritis with lesion of rapidly progressive glomerulonephritis
584.5 Acute kidney failure with lesion of tubular necrosis
584.6 Acute kidney failure with lesion of renal cortical necrosis
584.7 Acute kidney failure with lesion of medullary [papillary] necrosis
585.1 Chronic kidney disease, Stage I — (Use additional code to identify kidney transplant status, if applicable: V42.0. Use additional code to identify manifestation: 357.4, 420.0. Code first hypertensive chronic kidney disease, if applicable: 403.00-403.91, 404.00-404.93)
585.2 Chronic kidney disease, Stage II (mild) — (Use additional code to identify kidney transplant status, if applicable: V42.0. Use additional code to identify manifestation: 357.4, 420.0. Code first hypertensive chronic kidney disease, if applicable: 403.00-403.91, 404.00-404.93)
585.3 Chronic kidney disease, Stage III (moderate) — (Use additional code to identify kidney transplant status, if applicable: V42.0. Use additional code to identify manifestation: 357.4, 420.0. Code first hypertensive chronic kidney disease, if applicable: 403.00-403.91, 404.00-404.93)
585.4 Chronic kidney disease, Stage IV (severe) — (Use additional code to identify kidney transplant status, if applicable: V42.0. Use additional code to identify manifestation: 357.4, 420.0. Code first hypertensive chronic kidney disease, if applicable: 403.00-403.91, 404.00-404.93)
585.5 Chronic kidney disease, Stage V — (Use additional code to identify kidney transplant status, if applicable: V42.0. Use additional code to identify manifestation: 357.4, 420.0. Code first hypertensive chronic kidney disease, if applicable: 403.00-403.91, 404.00-404.93)
585.6 End stage renal disease — (Use additional code to identify kidney transplant status, if applicable: V42.0. Use additional code to identify manifestation: 357.4, 420.0. Code first hypertensive chronic kidney disease, if applicable: 403.00-403.91, 404.00-404.93)
585.9 Chronic kidney disease, unspecified — (Use additional code to identify kidney transplant status, if applicable: V42.0. Use additional code to identify manifestation: 357.4, 420.0. Code first hypertensive chronic kidney disease, if applicable: 403.00-403.91, 404.00-404.93)
587 Unspecified renal sclerosis
588.81 Secondary hyperparathyroidism (of renal origin)
588.89 Other specified disorders resulting from impaired renal function
590.00 Chronic pyelonephritis without lesion of renal medullary necrosis — (Use additional code to identify organism, such as E. coli, 041.41-041.49. Code if applicable, any causal condition first)
590.01 Chronic pyelonephritis with lesion of renal medullary necrosis — (Use additional code to identify organism, such as E. coli, 041.41-041.49. Code if applicable, any causal condition first)
591 Hydronephrosis

592.0 Calculus of kidney

593.4 Other ureteric obstruction

593.70 Vesicoureteral reflux, unspecified or without reflex nephropathy

593.71 Vesicoureteral reflux with reflux nephropathy, unilateral

593.72 Vesicoureteral reflux with reflux nephropathy, bilateral

593.73 Vesicoureteral reflux with reflux nephropathy, NOS

593.81 Vascular disorders of kidney

593.89 Other specified disorder of kidney and ureter

593.9 Unspecified disorder of kidney and ureter

599.60 Urinary obstruction, unspecified — (Use additional code to identify urinary incontinence: 625.6, 788.30-788.39)

599.69 Urinary obstruction, not elsewhere classified — (Use additional code to identify urinary incontinence: 625.6, 788.30-788.39. Code, if applicable, any causal condition first: 600.0-600.9, with fifth-digit 1)

599.70 Hematuria, unspecified

599.71 Gross hematuria

599.72 Microscopic hematuria

728.88 Rhabdomyolysis

753.0 Congenital renal agenesis and dysgenesis

753.10 Unspecified congenital cystic kidney disease

753.11 Congenital single renal cyst

753.12 Congenital polycystic kidney, unspecified type

753.13 Congenital polycystic kidney, autosomal dominant

753.14 Congenital polycystic kidney, autosomal recessive

753.15 Congenital renal dysplasia

753.16 Congenital medullary cystic kidney

753.17 Congenital medullary sponge kidney

753.19 Other specified congenital cystic kidney disease

753.20 Unspecified obstructive defect of renal pelvis and ureter

753.21 Congenital obstruction of ureteropelvic junction

753.23 Congenital ureterocele

753.29 Other obstructive defect of renal pelvis and ureter

866.02 Kidney laceration without mention of open wound into cavity

866.03 Complete disruption of kidney parenchyma, without mention of open wound into cavity

866.13 Complete disruption of kidney parenchyma, with open wound into cavity

ICD-9-CM Procedural

40.3 Regional lymph node excision

55.51 Nephroureterectomy

50546

50546 Laparoscopy, surgical; nephrectomy, including partial ureterectomy

ICD-9-CM Diagnostic

189.0 Malignant neoplasm of kidney, except pelvis

189.1 Malignant neoplasm of renal pelvis

198.0 Secondary malignant neoplasm of kidney

199.2 Malignant neoplasm associated with transplanted organ — (Code first complication of transplanted organ (996.80-996.89) Use additional code for specific malignancy)

209.24 Malignant carcinoid tumor of the kidney — (Code first any associated multiple endocrine neoplasia syndrome: 258.01-258.03; Use additional code to identify associated endocrine syndrome, as: carcinoid syndrome: 259.2)

209.64 Benign carcinoid tumor of the kidney — (Code first any associated multiple endocrine neoplasia syndrome: 258.01-258.03; Use additional code to identify associated endocrine syndrome, as: carcinoid syndrome: 259.2)

223.0 Benign neoplasm of kidney, except pelvis

223.1 Benign neoplasm of renal pelvis

233.9 Carcinoma in situ of other and unspecified urinary organs

236.91 Neoplasm of uncertain behavior of kidney and ureter

239.5 Neoplasm of unspecified nature of other genitourinary organs

403.01 Hypertensive chronic kidney disease, malignant, with chronic kidney disease stage V or end stage renal disease — (Use additional code to identify the stage of chronic kidney disease: 585.5, 585.6)

403.11 Hypertensive chronic kidney disease, benign, with chronic kidney disease stage V or end stage renal disease — (Use additional code to identify the stage of chronic kidney disease: 585.5, 585.6)

403.91 Hypertensive chronic kidney disease, unspecified, with chronic kidney disease stage V or end stage renal disease — (Use additional code to identify the stage of chronic kidney disease: 585.5, 585.6)

404.02 Hypertensive heart and chronic kidney disease, malignant, without heart failure and with chronic kidney disease stage V or end stage renal disease — (Use additional code to identify the stage of chronic kidney disease: 585.5, 585.6)

404.12 Hypertensive heart and chronic kidney disease, benign, without heart failure and with chronic kidney disease stage V or end stage renal disease — (Use additional code to identify the stage of chronic kidney disease: 585.5, 585.6)

405.01 Secondary renovascular hypertension, malignant

405.91 Secondary renovascular hypertension, unspecified

445.81 Atheroembolism of kidney — (Use additional code for any associated acute kidney failure or chronic kidney disease: 584, 585)

580.0 Acute glomerulonephritis with lesion of proliferative glomerulonephritis

580.4 Acute glomerulonephritis with lesion of rapidly progressive glomerulonephritis

581.0 Nephrotic syndrome with lesion of proliferative glomerulonephritis

581.1 Nephrotic syndrome with lesion of membranous glomerulonephritis

581.2 Nephrotic syndrome with lesion of membranoproliferative glomerulonephritis

582.0 Chronic glomerulonephritis with lesion of proliferative glomerulonephritis

582.1 Chronic glomerulonephritis with lesion of membranous glomerulonephritis

582.2 Chronic glomerulonephritis with lesion of membranoproliferative glomerulonephritis

582.4 Chronic glomerulonephritis with lesion of rapidly progressive glomerulonephritis

584.5 Acute kidney failure with lesion of tubular necrosis

584.6 Acute kidney failure with lesion of renal cortical necrosis

584.7 Acute kidney failure with lesion of medullary [papillary] necrosis

585.1 Chronic kidney disease, Stage I — (Use additional code to identify kidney transplant status, if applicable: V42.0. Use additional code to identify manifestation: 357.4, 420.0. Code first hypertensive chronic kidney disease, if applicable: 403.00-403.91, 404.00-404.93)

585.2 Chronic kidney disease, Stage II (mild) — (Use additional code to identify kidney transplant status, if applicable: V42.0. Use additional code to identify manifestation: 357.4, 420.0. Code first hypertensive chronic kidney disease, if applicable: 403.00-403.91, 404.00-404.93)

585.3 Chronic kidney disease, Stage III (moderate) — (Use additional code to identify kidney transplant status, if applicable: V42.0. Use additional code to identify manifestation: 357.4, 420.0. Code first hypertensive chronic kidney disease, if applicable: 403.00-403.91, 404.00-404.93)

585.4 Chronic kidney disease, Stage IV (severe) — (Use additional code to identify kidney transplant status, if applicable: V42.0. Use additional code to identify manifestation: 357.4, 420.0. Code first hypertensive chronic kidney disease, if applicable: 403.00-403.91, 404.00-404.93)

585.5 Chronic kidney disease, Stage V — (Use additional code to identify kidney transplant status, if applicable: V42.0. Use additional code to identify manifestation: 357.4, 420.0. Code first hypertensive chronic kidney disease, if applicable: 403.00-403.91, 404.00-404.93)

585.6 End stage renal disease — (Use additional code to identify kidney transplant status, if applicable: V42.0. Use additional code to identify manifestation: 357.4, 420.0. Code first hypertensive chronic kidney disease, if applicable: 403.00-403.91, 404.00-404.93)

585.9 Chronic kidney disease, unspecified — (Use additional code to identify kidney transplant status, if applicable: V42.0. Use additional code to identify manifestation: 357.4, 420.0. Code first hypertensive chronic kidney disease, if applicable: 403.00-403.91, 404.00-404.93)

587 Unspecified renal sclerosis

588.81 Secondary hyperparathyroidism (of renal origin)

588.89 Other specified disorders resulting from impaired renal function

590.00 Chronic pyelonephritis without lesion of renal medullary necrosis — (Use additional code to identify organism, such as E. coli, 041.41-041.49. Code if applicable, any causal condition first)
590.01 Chronic pyelonephritis with lesion of renal medullary necrosis — (Use additional code to identify organism, such as E. coli, 041.41-041.49. Code if applicable, any causal condition first)
591 Hydronephrosis
592.0 Calculus of kidney
593.4 Other ureteric obstruction
593.70 Vesicoureteral reflux, unspecified or without reflex nephropathy
593.71 Vesicoureteral reflux with reflux nephropathy, unilateral
593.72 Vesicoureteral reflux with reflux nephropathy, bilateral
593.73 Vesicoureteral reflux with reflux nephropathy, NOS
593.81 Vascular disorders of kidney
593.89 Other specified disorder of kidney and ureter
593.9 Unspecified disorder of kidney and ureter
599.60 Urinary obstruction, unspecified — (Use additional code to identify urinary incontinence: 625.6, 788.30-788.39)
599.69 Urinary obstruction, not elsewhere classified — (Use additional code to identify urinary incontinence: 625.6, 788.30-788.39. Code, if applicable, any causal condition first: 600.0-600.9, with fifth-digit 1)
599.70 Hematuria, unspecified
599.71 Gross hematuria
599.72 Microscopic hematuria
728.88 Rhabdomyolysis
753.0 Congenital renal agenesis and dysgenesis
753.10 Unspecified congenital cystic kidney disease
753.11 Congenital single renal cyst
753.12 Congenital polycystic kidney, unspecified type
753.13 Congenital polycystic kidney, autosomal dominant
753.14 Congenital polycystic kidney, autosomal recessive
753.15 Congenital renal dysplasia
753.16 Congenital medullary cystic kidney
753.17 Congenital medullary sponge kidney
753.19 Other specified congenital cystic kidney disease
753.21 Congenital obstruction of ureteropelvic junction
753.23 Congenital ureterocele
753.29 Other obstructive defect of renal pelvis and ureter
866.02 Kidney laceration without mention of open wound into cavity
866.03 Complete disruption of kidney parenchyma, without mention of open wound into cavity
866.13 Complete disruption of kidney parenchyma, with open wound into cavity

ICD-9-CM Procedural

55.51 Nephroureterectomy

50547

50547 Laparoscopy, surgical; donor nephrectomy (including cold preservation), from living donor

ICD-9-CM Diagnostic

V59.4 Kidney donor

ICD-9-CM Procedural

55.51 Nephroureterectomy

50548

50548 Laparoscopy, surgical; nephrectomy with total ureterectomy

ICD-9-CM Diagnostic

188.6 Malignant neoplasm of ureteric orifice
189.0 Malignant neoplasm of kidney, except pelvis
189.1 Malignant neoplasm of renal pelvis
189.2 Malignant neoplasm of ureter
198.0 Secondary malignant neoplasm of kidney
198.1 Secondary malignant neoplasm of other urinary organs
199.2 Malignant neoplasm associated with transplanted organ — (Code first complication of transplanted organ (996.80-996.89) Use additional code for specific malignancy)
209.24 Malignant carcinoid tumor of the kidney — (Code first any associated multiple endocrine neoplasia syndrome: 258.01-258.03; Use additional code to identify associated endocrine syndrome, as: carcinoid syndrome: 259.2)
209.64 Benign carcinoid tumor of the kidney — (Code first any associated multiple endocrine neoplasia syndrome: 258.01-258.03; Use additional code to identify associated endocrine syndrome, as: carcinoid syndrome: 259.2)
223.0 Benign neoplasm of kidney, except pelvis
223.1 Benign neoplasm of renal pelvis
223.2 Benign neoplasm of ureter
233.9 Carcinoma in situ of other and unspecified urinary organs
236.91 Neoplasm of uncertain behavior of kidney and ureter
239.5 Neoplasm of unspecified nature of other genitourinary organs
403.01 Hypertensive chronic kidney disease, malignant, with chronic kidney disease stage V or end stage renal disease — (Use additional code to identify the stage of chronic kidney disease: 585.5, 585.6)
403.11 Hypertensive chronic kidney disease, benign, with chronic kidney disease stage V or end stage renal disease — (Use additional code to identify the stage of chronic kidney disease: 585.5, 585.6)
403.91 Hypertensive chronic kidney disease, unspecified, with chronic kidney disease stage V or end stage renal disease — (Use additional code to identify the stage of chronic kidney disease: 585.5, 585.6)
404.02 Hypertensive heart and chronic kidney disease, malignant, without heart failure and with chronic kidney disease stage V or end stage renal disease — (Use additional code to identify the stage of chronic kidney disease: 585.5, 585.6)
404.12 Hypertensive heart and chronic kidney disease, benign, without heart failure and with chronic kidney disease stage V or end stage renal disease — (Use additional code to identify the stage of chronic kidney disease: 585.5, 585.6)
405.01 Secondary renovascular hypertension, malignant
405.91 Secondary renovascular hypertension, unspecified
445.81 Atheroembolism of kidney — (Use additional code for any associated acute kidney failure or chronic kidney disease: 584, 585)
580.0 Acute glomerulonephritis with lesion of proliferative glomerulonephritis
580.4 Acute glomerulonephritis with lesion of rapidly progressive glomerulonephritis
581.0 Nephrotic syndrome with lesion of proliferative glomerulonephritis
581.1 Nephrotic syndrome with lesion of membranous glomerulonephritis
581.2 Nephrotic syndrome with lesion of membranoproliferative glomerulonephritis
582.0 Chronic glomerulonephritis with lesion of proliferative glomerulonephritis
582.1 Chronic glomerulonephritis with lesion of membranous glomerulonephritis
582.2 Chronic glomerulonephritis with lesion of membranoproliferative glomerulonephritis
582.4 Chronic glomerulonephritis with lesion of rapidly progressive glomerulonephritis
584.5 Acute kidney failure with lesion of tubular necrosis
584.6 Acute kidney failure with lesion of renal cortical necrosis
584.7 Acute kidney failure with lesion of medullary [papillary] necrosis
585.1 Chronic kidney disease, Stage I — (Use additional code to identify kidney transplant status, if applicable: V42.0. Use additional code to identify manifestation: 357.4, 420.0. Code first hypertensive chronic kidney disease, if applicable: 403.00-403.91, 404.00-404.93)
585.2 Chronic kidney disease, Stage II (mild) — (Use additional code to identify kidney transplant status, if applicable: V42.0. Use additional code to identify manifestation: 357.4, 420.0. Code first hypertensive chronic kidney disease, if applicable: 403.00-403.91, 404.00-404.93)
585.3 Chronic kidney disease, Stage III (moderate) — (Use additional code to identify kidney transplant status, if applicable: V42.0. Use additional code to identify manifestation: 357.4, 420.0. Code first hypertensive chronic kidney disease, if applicable: 403.00-403.91, 404.00-404.93)

585.4	Chronic kidney disease, Stage IV (severe) — (Use additional code to identify kidney transplant status, if applicable: V42.0. Use additional code to identify manifestation: 357.4, 420.0. Code first hypertensive chronic kidney disease, if applicable: 403.00-403.91, 404.00-404.93)
585.5	Chronic kidney disease, Stage V — (Use additional code to identify kidney transplant status, if applicable: V42.0. Use additional code to identify manifestation: 357.4, 420.0. Code first hypertensive chronic kidney disease, if applicable: 403.00-403.91, 404.00-404.93)
585.6	End stage renal disease — (Use additional code to identify kidney transplant status, if applicable: V42.0. Use additional code to identify manifestation: 357.4, 420.0. Code first hypertensive chronic kidney disease, if applicable: 403.00-403.91, 404.00-404.93)
585.9	Chronic kidney disease, unspecified — (Use additional code to identify kidney transplant status, if applicable: V42.0. Use additional code to identify manifestation: 357.4, 420.0. Code first hypertensive chronic kidney disease, if applicable: 403.00-403.91, 404.00-404.93) ▽
587	Unspecified renal sclerosis ▽
588.81	Secondary hyperparathyroidism (of renal origin)
590.00	Chronic pyelonephritis without lesion of renal medullary necrosis — (Use additional code to identify organism, such as E. coli, 041.41-041.49. Code if applicable, any causal condition first)
590.01	Chronic pyelonephritis with lesion of renal medullary necrosis — (Use additional code to identify organism, such as E. coli, 041.41-041.49. Code if applicable, any causal condition first)
591	Hydronephrosis
592.0	Calculus of kidney
593.4	Other ureteric obstruction
593.70	Vesicoureteral reflux, unspecified or without reflex nephropathy
593.71	Vesicoureteral reflux with reflux nephropathy, unilateral
593.72	Vesicoureteral reflux with reflux nephropathy, bilateral
593.73	Vesicoureteral reflux with reflux nephropathy, NOS ▽
593.81	Vascular disorders of kidney
593.89	Other specified disorder of kidney and ureter
593.9	Unspecified disorder of kidney and ureter ▽
599.60	Urinary obstruction, unspecified — (Use additional code to identify urinary incontinence: 625.6, 788.30-788.39) ▽
599.69	Urinary obstruction, not elsewhere classified — (Use additional code to identify urinary incontinence: 625.6, 788.30-788.39. Code, if applicable, any causal condition first: 600.0-600.9, with fifth-digit 1)
599.70	Hematuria, unspecified ▽
599.71	Gross hematuria
599.72	Microscopic hematuria
728.88	Rhabdomyolysis
753.0	Congenital renal agenesis and dysgenesis
753.10	Unspecified congenital cystic kidney disease ▽
753.11	Congenital single renal cyst
753.12	Congenital polycystic kidney, unspecified type ▽
753.13	Congenital polycystic kidney, autosomal dominant
753.14	Congenital polycystic kidney, autosomal recessive
753.15	Congenital renal dysplasia
753.16	Congenital medullary cystic kidney
753.17	Congenital medullary sponge kidney
753.19	Other specified congenital cystic kidney disease
753.20	Unspecified obstructive defect of renal pelvis and ureter ▽
753.21	Congenital obstruction of ureteropelvic junction
753.23	Congenital ureterocele
753.29	Other obstructive defect of renal pelvis and ureter
866.02	Kidney laceration without mention of open wound into cavity
866.03	Complete disruption of kidney parenchyma, without mention of open wound into cavity
866.13	Complete disruption of kidney parenchyma, with open wound into cavity

ICD-9-CM Procedural

55.51	Nephroureterectomy

50551-50555

50551 Renal endoscopy through established nephrostomy or pyelostomy, with or without irrigation, instillation, or ureteropyelography, exclusive of radiologic service;

50553 with ureteral catheterization, with or without dilation of ureter

50555 with biopsy

ICD-9-CM Diagnostic

189.0	Malignant neoplasm of kidney, except pelvis
189.1	Malignant neoplasm of renal pelvis
198.0	Secondary malignant neoplasm of kidney
199.2	Malignant neoplasm associated with transplanted organ — (Code first complication of transplanted organ (996.80-996.89) Use additional code for specific malignancy)
209.24	Malignant carcinoid tumor of the kidney — (Code first any associated multiple endocrine neoplasia syndrome: 258.01-258.03; Use additional code to identify associated endocrine syndrome, as: carcinoid syndrome: 259.2)
209.64	Benign carcinoid tumor of the kidney — (Code first any associated multiple endocrine neoplasia syndrome: 258.01-258.03; Use additional code to identify associated endocrine syndrome, as: carcinoid syndrome: 259.2)
223.0	Benign neoplasm of kidney, except pelvis
223.1	Benign neoplasm of renal pelvis
233.9	Carcinoma in situ of other and unspecified urinary organs ▽
236.91	Neoplasm of uncertain behavior of kidney and ureter
239.5	Neoplasm of unspecified nature of other genitourinary organs
252.00	Hyperparathyroidism, unspecified ▽
252.01	Primary hyperparathyroidism
252.02	Secondary hyperparathyroidism, non-renal
252.08	Other hyperparathyroidism
588.81	Secondary hyperparathyroidism (of renal origin)
592.0	Calculus of kidney
592.1	Calculus of ureter
593.3	Stricture or kinking of ureter
593.4	Other ureteric obstruction
593.81	Vascular disorders of kidney
593.89	Other specified disorder of kidney and ureter
599.60	Urinary obstruction, unspecified — (Use additional code to identify urinary incontinence: 625.6, 788.30-788.39) ▽
599.69	Urinary obstruction, not elsewhere classified — (Use additional code to identify urinary incontinence: 625.6, 788.30-788.39. Code, if applicable, any causal condition first: 600.0-600.9, with fifth-digit 1)
753.20	Unspecified obstructive defect of renal pelvis and ureter ▽
753.21	Congenital obstruction of ureteropelvic junction
753.22	Congenital obstruction of ureterovesical junction
753.23	Congenital ureterocele
753.29	Other obstructive defect of renal pelvis and ureter
753.3	Other specified congenital anomalies of kidney
788.0	Renal colic
958.5	Traumatic anuria

ICD-9-CM Procedural

55.21	Nephroscopy
55.22	Pyeloscopy
55.23	Closed (percutaneous) (needle) biopsy of kidney
59.8	Ureteral catheterization

HCPCS Level II Supplies & Services

A4270	Disposable endoscope sheath, each

50557-50561

50557 Renal endoscopy through established nephrostomy or pyelostomy, with or without irrigation, instillation, or ureteropyelography, exclusive of radiologic service; with fulguration and/or incision, with or without biopsy

50561 with removal of foreign body or calculus

ICD-9-CM Diagnostic

189.0 Malignant neoplasm of kidney, except pelvis
189.1 Malignant neoplasm of renal pelvis
198.0 Secondary malignant neoplasm of kidney
199.2 Malignant neoplasm associated with transplanted organ — (Code first complication of transplanted organ (996.80-996.89) Use additional code for specific malignancy)
209.24 Malignant carcinoid tumor of the kidney — (Code first any associated multiple endocrine neoplasia syndrome: 258.01-258.03; Use additional code to identify associated endocrine syndrome, as: carcinoid syndrome: 259.2)
209.64 Benign carcinoid tumor of the kidney — (Code first any associated multiple endocrine neoplasia syndrome: 258.01-258.03; Use additional code to identify associated endocrine syndrome, as: carcinoid syndrome: 259.2)
223.0 Benign neoplasm of kidney, except pelvis
223.1 Benign neoplasm of renal pelvis
233.9 Carcinoma in situ of other and unspecified urinary organs ▽
236.91 Neoplasm of uncertain behavior of kidney and ureter
239.5 Neoplasm of unspecified nature of other genitourinary organs
252.00 Hyperparathyroidism, unspecified ▽
252.01 Primary hyperparathyroidism
252.02 Secondary hyperparathyroidism, non-renal
252.08 Other hyperparathyroidism
588.81 Secondary hyperparathyroidism (of renal origin)
590.2 Renal and perinephric abscess — (Use additional code to identify organism, such as E. coli, 041.41-041.49)
592.0 Calculus of kidney
592.1 Calculus of ureter
592.9 Unspecified urinary calculus ▽
593.81 Vascular disorders of kidney
593.89 Other specified disorder of kidney and ureter
599.60 Urinary obstruction, unspecified — (Use additional code to identify urinary incontinence: 625.6, 788.30-788.39) ▽
599.69 Urinary obstruction, not elsewhere classified — (Use additional code to identify urinary incontinence: 625.6, 788.30-788.39. Code, if applicable, any causal condition first: 600.0-600.9, with fifth-digit 1)
599.70 Hematuria, unspecified ▽
599.71 Gross hematuria
599.72 Microscopic hematuria
753.3 Other specified congenital anomalies of kidney
788.0 Renal colic
958.5 Traumatic anuria
996.30 Mechanical complication of unspecified genitourinary device, implant, and graft ▽
996.39 Mechanical complication of genitourinary device, implant, and graft, other
996.65 Infection and inflammatory reaction due to other genitourinary device, implant, and graft — (Use additional code to identify specified infections)
996.76 Other complications due to genitourinary device, implant, and graft — (Use additional code to identify complication: 338.18-338.19, 338.28-338.29)
998.4 Foreign body accidentally left during procedure, not elsewhere classified

ICD-9-CM Procedural

55.03 Percutaneous nephrostomy without fragmentation
55.21 Nephroscopy
55.22 Pyeloscopy
55.23 Closed (percutaneous) (needle) biopsy of kidney
55.39 Other local destruction or excision of renal lesion or tissue

HCPCS Level II Supplies & Services

A4270 Disposable endoscope sheath, each

50562

50562 Renal endoscopy through established nephrostomy or pyelostomy, with or without irrigation, instillation, or ureteropyelography, exclusive of radiologic service; with resection of tumor

ICD-9-CM Diagnostic

189.0 Malignant neoplasm of kidney, except pelvis
189.1 Malignant neoplasm of renal pelvis
198.0 Secondary malignant neoplasm of kidney
199.2 Malignant neoplasm associated with transplanted organ — (Code first complication of transplanted organ (996.80-996.89) Use additional code for specific malignancy)
209.24 Malignant carcinoid tumor of the kidney — (Code first any associated multiple endocrine neoplasia syndrome: 258.01-258.03; Use additional code to identify associated endocrine syndrome, as: carcinoid syndrome: 259.2)
209.64 Benign carcinoid tumor of the kidney — (Code first any associated multiple endocrine neoplasia syndrome: 258.01-258.03; Use additional code to identify associated endocrine syndrome, as: carcinoid syndrome: 259.2)
223.0 Benign neoplasm of kidney, except pelvis
223.1 Benign neoplasm of renal pelvis
233.9 Carcinoma in situ of other and unspecified urinary organs ▽
236.91 Neoplasm of uncertain behavior of kidney and ureter
239.5 Neoplasm of unspecified nature of other genitourinary organs
593.2 Acquired cyst of kidney
593.89 Other specified disorder of kidney and ureter
599.70 Hematuria, unspecified ▽
599.71 Gross hematuria
599.72 Microscopic hematuria

ICD-9-CM Procedural

55.21 Nephroscopy
55.22 Pyeloscopy
55.39 Other local destruction or excision of renal lesion or tissue
55.4 Partial nephrectomy

50570-50574

50570 Renal endoscopy through nephrotomy or pyelotomy, with or without irrigation, instillation, or ureteropyelography, exclusive of radiologic service;

50572 with ureteral catheterization, with or without dilation of ureter

50574 with biopsy

ICD-9-CM Diagnostic

189.0 Malignant neoplasm of kidney, except pelvis
189.1 Malignant neoplasm of renal pelvis
198.0 Secondary malignant neoplasm of kidney
199.2 Malignant neoplasm associated with transplanted organ — (Code first complication of transplanted organ (996.80-996.89) Use additional code for specific malignancy)
209.24 Malignant carcinoid tumor of the kidney — (Code first any associated multiple endocrine neoplasia syndrome: 258.01-258.03; Use additional code to identify associated endocrine syndrome, as: carcinoid syndrome: 259.2)
209.64 Benign carcinoid tumor of the kidney — (Code first any associated multiple endocrine neoplasia syndrome: 258.01-258.03; Use additional code to identify associated endocrine syndrome, as: carcinoid syndrome: 259.2)
223.0 Benign neoplasm of kidney, except pelvis
223.1 Benign neoplasm of renal pelvis
233.9 Carcinoma in situ of other and unspecified urinary organs ▽
236.91 Neoplasm of uncertain behavior of kidney and ureter
239.5 Neoplasm of unspecified nature of other genitourinary organs
252.00 Hyperparathyroidism, unspecified ▽
252.01 Primary hyperparathyroidism

252.02 Secondary hyperparathyroidism, non-renal
252.08 Other hyperparathyroidism
588.81 Secondary hyperparathyroidism (of renal origin)
592.0 Calculus of kidney
592.1 Calculus of ureter
593.3 Stricture or kinking of ureter
593.4 Other ureteric obstruction
593.81 Vascular disorders of kidney
593.89 Other specified disorder of kidney and ureter
599.60 Urinary obstruction, unspecified — (Use additional code to identify urinary incontinence: 625.6, 788.30-788.39) ▽
599.69 Urinary obstruction, not elsewhere classified — (Use additional code to identify urinary incontinence: 625.6, 788.30-788.39. Code, if applicable, any causal condition first: 600.0-600.9, with fifth-digit 1)
599.70 Hematuria, unspecified ▽
599.71 Gross hematuria
599.72 Microscopic hematuria
753.20 Unspecified obstructive defect of renal pelvis and ureter ▽
753.21 Congenital obstruction of ureteropelvic junction
753.22 Congenital obstruction of ureterovesical junction
753.23 Congenital ureterocele
753.29 Other obstructive defect of renal pelvis and ureter
753.3 Other specified congenital anomalies of kidney
958.5 Traumatic anuria

ICD-9-CM Procedural

55.01 Nephrotomy
55.11 Pyelotomy
55.21 Nephroscopy
55.22 Pyeloscopy
55.23 Closed (percutaneous) (needle) biopsy of kidney
56.91 Dilation of ureteral meatus
59.8 Ureteral catheterization

50575

50575 Renal endoscopy through nephrotomy or pyelotomy, with or without irrigation, instillation, or ureteropyelography, exclusive of radiologic service; with endopyelotomy (includes cystoscopy, ureteroscopy, dilation of ureter and ureteral pelvic junction, incision of ureteral pelvic junction and insertion of endopyelotomy stent)

ICD-9-CM Diagnostic

189.0 Malignant neoplasm of kidney, except pelvis
189.1 Malignant neoplasm of renal pelvis
198.0 Secondary malignant neoplasm of kidney
199.2 Malignant neoplasm associated with transplanted organ — (Code first complication of transplanted organ (996.80-996.89) Use additional code for specific malignancy)
209.24 Malignant carcinoid tumor of the kidney — (Code first any associated multiple endocrine neoplasia syndrome: 258.01-258.03; Use additional code to identify associated endocrine syndrome, as: carcinoid syndrome: 259.2)
209.64 Benign carcinoid tumor of the kidney — (Code first any associated multiple endocrine neoplasia syndrome: 258.01-258.03; Use additional code to identify associated endocrine syndrome, as: carcinoid syndrome: 259.2)
223.1 Benign neoplasm of renal pelvis
593.4 Other ureteric obstruction
593.81 Vascular disorders of kidney
593.89 Other specified disorder of kidney and ureter
599.60 Urinary obstruction, unspecified — (Use additional code to identify urinary incontinence: 625.6, 788.30-788.39) ▽
599.69 Urinary obstruction, not elsewhere classified — (Use additional code to identify urinary incontinence: 625.6, 788.30-788.39. Code, if applicable, any causal condition first: 600.0-600.9, with fifth-digit 1)
753.20 Unspecified obstructive defect of renal pelvis and ureter ▽
753.21 Congenital obstruction of ureteropelvic junction
753.22 Congenital obstruction of ureterovesical junction
753.23 Congenital ureterocele
753.29 Other obstructive defect of renal pelvis and ureter
753.3 Other specified congenital anomalies of kidney
958.5 Traumatic anuria

ICD-9-CM Procedural

55.01 Nephrotomy
55.11 Pyelotomy
55.21 Nephroscopy
55.22 Pyeloscopy
56.2 Ureterotomy
56.31 Ureteroscopy
56.91 Dilation of ureteral meatus
59.8 Ureteral catheterization

50576-50580

50576 Renal endoscopy through nephrotomy or pyelotomy, with or without irrigation, instillation, or ureteropyelography, exclusive of radiologic service; with fulguration and/or incision, with or without biopsy
50580 with removal of foreign body or calculus

ICD-9-CM Diagnostic

189.0 Malignant neoplasm of kidney, except pelvis
189.1 Malignant neoplasm of renal pelvis
198.0 Secondary malignant neoplasm of kidney
199.2 Malignant neoplasm associated with transplanted organ — (Code first complication of transplanted organ (996.80-996.89) Use additional code for specific malignancy)
209.24 Malignant carcinoid tumor of the kidney — (Code first any associated multiple endocrine neoplasia syndrome: 258.01-258.03; Use additional code to identify associated endocrine syndrome, as: carcinoid syndrome: 259.2)
209.64 Benign carcinoid tumor of the kidney — (Code first any associated multiple endocrine neoplasia syndrome: 258.01-258.03; Use additional code to identify associated endocrine syndrome, as: carcinoid syndrome: 259.2)
223.0 Benign neoplasm of kidney, except pelvis
223.1 Benign neoplasm of renal pelvis
233.9 Carcinoma in situ of other and unspecified urinary organs ▽
236.91 Neoplasm of uncertain behavior of kidney and ureter
239.5 Neoplasm of unspecified nature of other genitourinary organs
252.00 Hyperparathyroidism, unspecified ▽
252.01 Primary hyperparathyroidism
252.02 Secondary hyperparathyroidism, non-renal
252.08 Other hyperparathyroidism
588.81 Secondary hyperparathyroidism (of renal origin)
590.2 Renal and perinephric abscess — (Use additional code to identify organism, such as E. coli, 041.41-041.49)
592.0 Calculus of kidney
592.1 Calculus of ureter
592.9 Unspecified urinary calculus ▽
593.4 Other ureteric obstruction
593.81 Vascular disorders of kidney
593.89 Other specified disorder of kidney and ureter
599.60 Urinary obstruction, unspecified — (Use additional code to identify urinary incontinence: 625.6, 788.30-788.39) ▽
599.69 Urinary obstruction, not elsewhere classified — (Use additional code to identify urinary incontinence: 625.6, 788.30-788.39. Code, if applicable, any causal condition first: 600.0-600.9, with fifth-digit 1)
599.70 Hematuria, unspecified ▽
599.71 Gross hematuria

599.72 Microscopic hematuria
753.3 Other specified congenital anomalies of kidney
788.0 Renal colic
958.5 Traumatic anuria
996.30 Mechanical complication of unspecified genitourinary device, implant, and graft ▽
996.39 Mechanical complication of genitourinary device, implant, and graft, other
996.65 Infection and inflammatory reaction due to other genitourinary device, implant, and graft — (Use additional code to identify specified infections)
996.76 Other complications due to genitourinary device, implant, and graft — (Use additional code to identify complication: 338.18-338.19, 338.28-338.29)
998.4 Foreign body accidentally left during procedure, not elsewhere classified

ICD-9-CM Procedural

55.01 Nephrotomy
55.03 Percutaneous nephrostomy without fragmentation
55.11 Pyelotomy
55.21 Nephroscopy
55.22 Pyeloscopy
55.23 Closed (percutaneous) (needle) biopsy of kidney
55.39 Other local destruction or excision of renal lesion or tissue

50590

50590 Lithotripsy, extracorporeal shock wave

ICD-9-CM Diagnostic

252.00 Hyperparathyroidism, unspecified ▽
252.01 Primary hyperparathyroidism
252.02 Secondary hyperparathyroidism, non-renal
252.08 Other hyperparathyroidism
588.81 Secondary hyperparathyroidism (of renal origin)
592.0 Calculus of kidney
592.1 Calculus of ureter
592.9 Unspecified urinary calculus ▽
599.70 Hematuria, unspecified ▽
599.71 Gross hematuria
599.72 Microscopic hematuria
788.0 Renal colic

ICD-9-CM Procedural

98.51 Extracorporeal shockwave lithotripsy (ESWL) of the kidney, ureter and/or bladder

50592

50592 Ablation, 1 or more renal tumor(s), percutaneous, unilateral, radiofrequency

ICD-9-CM Diagnostic

189.0 Malignant neoplasm of kidney, except pelvis
189.1 Malignant neoplasm of renal pelvis
198.0 Secondary malignant neoplasm of kidney
199.2 Malignant neoplasm associated with transplanted organ — (Code first complication of transplanted organ (996.80-996.89) Use additional code for specific malignancy)
209.24 Malignant carcinoid tumor of the kidney — (Code first any associated multiple endocrine neoplasia syndrome: 258.01-258.03; Use additional code to identify associated endocrine syndrome, as: carcinoid syndrome: 259.2)
209.64 Benign carcinoid tumor of the kidney — (Code first any associated multiple endocrine neoplasia syndrome: 258.01-258.03; Use additional code to identify associated endocrine syndrome, as: carcinoid syndrome: 259.2)
223.0 Benign neoplasm of kidney, except pelvis
223.1 Benign neoplasm of renal pelvis
233.9 Carcinoma in situ of other and unspecified urinary organs ▽
236.91 Neoplasm of uncertain behavior of kidney and ureter
239.5 Neoplasm of unspecified nature of other genitourinary organs
583.9 Nephritis and nephropathy, not specified as acute or chronic, with unspecified pathological lesion in kidney ▽
593.2 Acquired cyst of kidney
593.89 Other specified disorder of kidney and ureter
593.9 Unspecified disorder of kidney and ureter ▽
753.10 Unspecified congenital cystic kidney disease ▽
753.11 Congenital single renal cyst
753.12 Congenital polycystic kidney, unspecified type ▽
753.13 Congenital polycystic kidney, autosomal dominant
753.14 Congenital polycystic kidney, autosomal recessive
753.19 Other specified congenital cystic kidney disease

ICD-9-CM Procedural

55.33 Percutaneous ablation of renal lesion or tissue

50593

50593 Ablation, renal tumor(s), unilateral, percutaneous, cryotherapy

ICD-9-CM Diagnostic

189.0 Malignant neoplasm of kidney, except pelvis
189.1 Malignant neoplasm of renal pelvis
198.0 Secondary malignant neoplasm of kidney
199.2 Malignant neoplasm associated with transplanted organ — (Code first complication of transplanted organ (996.80-996.89) Use additional code for specific malignancy)
209.24 Malignant carcinoid tumor of the kidney — (Code first any associated multiple endocrine neoplasia syndrome: 258.01-258.03; Use additional code to identify associated endocrine syndrome, as: carcinoid syndrome: 259.2)
209.64 Benign carcinoid tumor of the kidney — (Code first any associated multiple endocrine neoplasia syndrome: 258.01-258.03; Use additional code to identify associated endocrine syndrome, as: carcinoid syndrome: 259.2)
223.0 Benign neoplasm of kidney, except pelvis
223.1 Benign neoplasm of renal pelvis
233.9 Carcinoma in situ of other and unspecified urinary organs ▽
236.91 Neoplasm of uncertain behavior of kidney and ureter
239.5 Neoplasm of unspecified nature of other genitourinary organs
583.9 Nephritis and nephropathy, not specified as acute or chronic, with unspecified pathological lesion in kidney ▽
593.89 Other specified disorder of kidney and ureter
593.9 Unspecified disorder of kidney and ureter ▽

ICD-9-CM Procedural

55.33 Percutaneous ablation of renal lesion or tissue

Ureter

50600

50600 Ureterotomy with exploration or drainage (separate procedure)

ICD-9-CM Diagnostic

189.2 Malignant neoplasm of ureter
198.1 Secondary malignant neoplasm of other urinary organs
223.2 Benign neoplasm of ureter
233.9 Carcinoma in situ of other and unspecified urinary organs ▽
236.91 Neoplasm of uncertain behavior of kidney and ureter
239.5 Neoplasm of unspecified nature of other genitourinary organs
591 Hydronephrosis
593.3 Stricture or kinking of ureter
593.4 Other ureteric obstruction
593.89 Other specified disorder of kidney and ureter
599.60 Urinary obstruction, unspecified — (Use additional code to identify urinary incontinence: 625.6, 788.30-788.39) ▽

599.69 Urinary obstruction, not elsewhere classified — (Use additional code to identify urinary incontinence: 625.6, 788.30-788.39. Code, if applicable, any causal condition first: 600.0-600.9, with fifth-digit 1)
788.29 Other specified retention of urine — (Code, if applicable, any causal condition first, such as: 600.0-600.9, with fifth digit 1)
867.2 Ureter injury without mention of open wound into cavity
867.3 Ureter injury with open wound into cavity
998.2 Accidental puncture or laceration during procedure

ICD-9-CM Procedural

56.2 Ureterotomy

50605

50605 Ureterotomy for insertion of indwelling stent, all types

ICD-9-CM Diagnostic

189.2 Malignant neoplasm of ureter
198.1 Secondary malignant neoplasm of other urinary organs
223.2 Benign neoplasm of ureter
233.9 Carcinoma in situ of other and unspecified urinary organs ▽
236.91 Neoplasm of uncertain behavior of kidney and ureter
239.5 Neoplasm of unspecified nature of other genitourinary organs
591 Hydronephrosis
592.0 Calculus of kidney
592.1 Calculus of ureter
593.3 Stricture or kinking of ureter
593.4 Other ureteric obstruction
599.70 Hematuria, unspecified ▽
599.71 Gross hematuria
599.72 Microscopic hematuria
788.29 Other specified retention of urine — (Code, if applicable, any causal condition first, such as: 600.0-600.9, with fifth digit 1)

ICD-9-CM Procedural

56.2 Ureterotomy
59.8 Ureteral catheterization

50610-50630

50610 Ureterolithotomy; upper 1/3 of ureter
50620 middle 1/3 of ureter
50630 lower 1/3 of ureter

ICD-9-CM Diagnostic

592.1 Calculus of ureter
592.9 Unspecified urinary calculus ▽
593.4 Other ureteric obstruction
599.70 Hematuria, unspecified ▽
599.71 Gross hematuria
599.72 Microscopic hematuria
V64.41 Laparoscopic surgical procedure converted to open procedure

ICD-9-CM Procedural

56.2 Ureterotomy

50650

50650 Ureterectomy, with bladder cuff (separate procedure)

ICD-9-CM Diagnostic

180.9 Malignant neoplasm of cervix uteri, unspecified site ▽ ♀
182.0 Malignant neoplasm of corpus uteri, except isthmus ♀
182.1 Malignant neoplasm of isthmus ♀
188.0 Malignant neoplasm of trigone of urinary bladder
188.1 Malignant neoplasm of dome of urinary bladder
188.2 Malignant neoplasm of lateral wall of urinary bladder
188.3 Malignant neoplasm of anterior wall of urinary bladder
188.4 Malignant neoplasm of posterior wall of urinary bladder
188.5 Malignant neoplasm of bladder neck
188.6 Malignant neoplasm of ureteric orifice
188.7 Malignant neoplasm of urachus
189.2 Malignant neoplasm of ureter
198.1 Secondary malignant neoplasm of other urinary organs
223.2 Benign neoplasm of ureter
233.9 Carcinoma in situ of other and unspecified urinary organs ▽
236.91 Neoplasm of uncertain behavior of kidney and ureter
239.5 Neoplasm of unspecified nature of other genitourinary organs
593.89 Other specified disorder of kidney and ureter
867.2 Ureter injury without mention of open wound into cavity
867.3 Ureter injury with open wound into cavity

ICD-9-CM Procedural

56.40 Ureterectomy, not otherwise specified

50660

50660 Ureterectomy, total, ectopic ureter, combination abdominal, vaginal and/or perineal approach

ICD-9-CM Diagnostic

593.3 Stricture or kinking of ureter
753.22 Congenital obstruction of ureterovesical junction
753.29 Other obstructive defect of renal pelvis and ureter
753.4 Other specified congenital anomalies of ureter

ICD-9-CM Procedural

56.42 Total ureterectomy

50684

50684 Injection procedure for ureterography or ureteropyelography through ureterostomy or indwelling ureteral catheter

ICD-9-CM Diagnostic

189.1 Malignant neoplasm of renal pelvis
189.2 Malignant neoplasm of ureter
189.9 Malignant neoplasm of urinary organ, site unspecified ▽
198.0 Secondary malignant neoplasm of kidney
198.1 Secondary malignant neoplasm of other urinary organs
198.82 Secondary malignant neoplasm of genital organs
223.0 Benign neoplasm of kidney, except pelvis
223.1 Benign neoplasm of renal pelvis
223.2 Benign neoplasm of ureter
223.3 Benign neoplasm of bladder
223.9 Benign neoplasm of urinary organ, site unspecified ▽
233.9 Carcinoma in situ of other and unspecified urinary organs ▽
236.91 Neoplasm of uncertain behavior of kidney and ureter
239.5 Neoplasm of unspecified nature of other genitourinary organs
590.9 Unspecified infection of kidney — (Use additional code to identify organism, such as E. coli, 041.41-041.49) ▽
592.0 Calculus of kidney
592.1 Calculus of ureter
592.9 Unspecified urinary calculus ▽
593.4 Other ureteric obstruction
593.70 Vesicoureteral reflux, unspecified or without reflex nephropathy
593.71 Vesicoureteral reflux with reflux nephropathy, unilateral
593.72 Vesicoureteral reflux with reflux nephropathy, bilateral

593.73 Vesicoureteral reflux with reflux nephropathy, NOS ▽
593.9 Unspecified disorder of kidney and ureter ▽
599.0 Urinary tract infection, site not specified — (Use additional code to identify organism, such as E. coli: 041.41-041.49) ▽
599.60 Urinary obstruction, unspecified — (Use additional code to identify urinary incontinence: 625.6, 788.30-788.39) ▽
599.69 Urinary obstruction, not elsewhere classified — (Use additional code to identify urinary incontinence: 625.6, 788.30-788.39. Code, if applicable, any causal condition first: 600.0-600.9, with fifth-digit 1)
599.70 Hematuria, unspecified ▽
599.71 Gross hematuria
599.72 Microscopic hematuria
619.0 Urinary-genital tract fistula, female ♀
625.6 Female stress incontinence ♀
753.8 Other specified congenital anomaly of bladder and urethra
753.9 Unspecified congenital anomaly of urinary system ▽
788.0 Renal colic
788.8 Extravasation of urine
788.99 Other symptoms involving urinary system
789.01 Abdominal pain, right upper quadrant
789.02 Abdominal pain, left upper quadrant
789.09 Abdominal pain, other specified site
789.31 Abdominal or pelvic swelling, mass, or lump, right upper quadrant
789.32 Abdominal or pelvic swelling, mass, or lump, left upper quadrant
789.39 Abdominal or pelvic swelling, mass, or lump, other specified site

ICD-9-CM Procedural

59.29 Other diagnostic procedures on perirenal tissue, perivesical tissue, and retroperitoneum
87.74 Retrograde pyelogram
87.76 Retrograde cystourethrogram

HCPCS Level II Supplies & Services

A4641 Radiopharmaceutical, diagnostic, not otherwise classified

50686

50686 Manometric studies through ureterostomy or indwelling ureteral catheter

ICD-9-CM Diagnostic

591 Hydronephrosis
593.3 Stricture or kinking of ureter
599.60 Urinary obstruction, unspecified — (Use additional code to identify urinary incontinence: 625.6, 788.30-788.39) ▽
599.69 Urinary obstruction, not elsewhere classified — (Use additional code to identify urinary incontinence: 625.6, 788.30-788.39. Code, if applicable, any causal condition first: 600.0-600.9, with fifth-digit 1)
753.21 Congenital obstruction of ureteropelvic junction
753.22 Congenital obstruction of ureterovesical junction
753.23 Congenital ureterocele
753.29 Other obstructive defect of renal pelvis and ureter

ICD-9-CM Procedural

89.21 Urinary manometry

50688

50688 Change of ureterostomy tube or externally accessible ureteral stent via ileal conduit

ICD-9-CM Diagnostic

591 Hydronephrosis
996.59 Mechanical complication due to other implant and internal device, not elsewhere classified
V55.6 Attention to other artificial opening of urinary tract

ICD-9-CM Procedural

59.93 Replacement of ureterostomy tube

50690

50690 Injection procedure for visualization of ileal conduit and/or ureteropyelography, exclusive of radiologic service

ICD-9-CM Diagnostic

189.0 Malignant neoplasm of kidney, except pelvis
189.1 Malignant neoplasm of renal pelvis
189.2 Malignant neoplasm of ureter
189.8 Malignant neoplasm of other specified sites of urinary organs
189.9 Malignant neoplasm of urinary organ, site unspecified ▽
198.0 Secondary malignant neoplasm of kidney
198.1 Secondary malignant neoplasm of other urinary organs
198.82 Secondary malignant neoplasm of genital organs
199.2 Malignant neoplasm associated with transplanted organ — (Code first complication of transplanted organ (996.80-996.89) Use additional code for specific malignancy)
209.24 Malignant carcinoid tumor of the kidney — (Code first any associated multiple endocrine neoplasia syndrome: 258.01-258.03; Use additional code to identify associated endocrine syndrome, as: carcinoid syndrome: 259.2)
209.64 Benign carcinoid tumor of the kidney — (Code first any associated multiple endocrine neoplasia syndrome: 258.01-258.03; Use additional code to identify associated endocrine syndrome, as: carcinoid syndrome: 259.2)
223.0 Benign neoplasm of kidney, except pelvis
223.1 Benign neoplasm of renal pelvis
223.2 Benign neoplasm of ureter
223.9 Benign neoplasm of urinary organ, site unspecified ▽
590.9 Unspecified infection of kidney — (Use additional code to identify organism, such as E. coli, 041.41-041.49) ▽
591 Hydronephrosis
592.0 Calculus of kidney
592.9 Unspecified urinary calculus ▽
593.4 Other ureteric obstruction
593.9 Unspecified disorder of kidney and ureter ▽
595.1 Chronic interstitial cystitis — (Use additional code to identify organism, such as E. coli: 041.41-041.49)
595.2 Other chronic cystitis — (Use additional code to identify organism, such as E. coli: 041.41-041.49)
599.0 Urinary tract infection, site not specified — (Use additional code to identify organism, such as E. coli: 041.41-041.49) ▽
599.60 Urinary obstruction, unspecified — (Use additional code to identify urinary incontinence: 625.6, 788.30-788.39) ▽
599.69 Urinary obstruction, not elsewhere classified — (Use additional code to identify urinary incontinence: 625.6, 788.30-788.39. Code, if applicable, any causal condition first: 600.0-600.9, with fifth-digit 1)
599.70 Hematuria, unspecified ▽
599.71 Gross hematuria
599.72 Microscopic hematuria
753.8 Other specified congenital anomaly of bladder and urethra
753.9 Unspecified congenital anomaly of urinary system ▽
788.0 Renal colic
789.00 Abdominal pain, unspecified site ▽
789.01 Abdominal pain, right upper quadrant
789.02 Abdominal pain, left upper quadrant
789.09 Abdominal pain, other specified site
789.30 Abdominal or pelvic swelling, mass or lump, unspecified site ▽
789.32 Abdominal or pelvic swelling, mass, or lump, left upper quadrant
789.39 Abdominal or pelvic swelling, mass, or lump, other specified site
908.2 Late effect of internal injury to other internal organs

996.30 Mechanical complication of unspecified genitourinary device, implant, and graft ▽
996.76 Other complications due to genitourinary device, implant, and graft — (Use additional code to identify complication: 338.18-338.19, 338.28-338.29)
997.5 Urinary complications — (Use additional code to identify complications)
V10.51 Personal history of malignant neoplasm of bladder
V10.52 Personal history of malignant neoplasm of kidney
V10.53 Personal history of malignant neoplasm, renal pelvis
V44.6 Status of other artificial opening of urinary tract

ICD-9-CM Procedural

59.29 Other diagnostic procedures on perirenal tissue, perivesical tissue, and retroperitoneum
87.73 Intravenous pyelogram
87.74 Retrograde pyelogram
87.75 Percutaneous pyelogram
87.78 Ileal conduitogram

HCPCS Level II Supplies & Services

A4641 Radiopharmaceutical, diagnostic, not otherwise classified

50700

50700 Ureteroplasty, plastic operation on ureter (eg, stricture)

ICD-9-CM Diagnostic

592.1 Calculus of ureter
593.3 Stricture or kinking of ureter
593.4 Other ureteric obstruction
593.89 Other specified disorder of kidney and ureter
599.60 Urinary obstruction, unspecified — (Use additional code to identify urinary incontinence: 625.6, 788.30-788.39) ▽
599.69 Urinary obstruction, not elsewhere classified — (Use additional code to identify urinary incontinence: 625.6, 788.30-788.39. Code, if applicable, any causal condition first: 600.0-600.9, with fifth-digit 1)
614.9 Unspecified inflammatory disease of female pelvic organs and tissues — (Use additional code to identify organism: 041.00-041.09, 041.10-041.19) ▽ ♀
617.9 Endometriosis, site unspecified ▽ ♀
753.21 Congenital obstruction of ureteropelvic junction
753.22 Congenital obstruction of ureterovesical junction
753.23 Congenital ureterocele
753.29 Other obstructive defect of renal pelvis and ureter
997.5 Urinary complications — (Use additional code to identify complications)

ICD-9-CM Procedural

56.89 Other repair of ureter

50715

50715 Ureterolysis, with or without repositioning of ureter for retroperitoneal fibrosis

ICD-9-CM Diagnostic

593.4 Other ureteric obstruction
593.89 Other specified disorder of kidney and ureter

ICD-9-CM Procedural

59.02 Other lysis of perirenal or periureteral adhesions

50722

50722 Ureterolysis for ovarian vein syndrome

ICD-9-CM Diagnostic

593.4 Other ureteric obstruction
593.89 Other specified disorder of kidney and ureter

ICD-9-CM Procedural

59.02 Other lysis of perirenal or periureteral adhesions

50725

50725 Ureterolysis for retrocaval ureter, with reanastomosis of upper urinary tract or vena cava

ICD-9-CM Diagnostic

753.4 Other specified congenital anomalies of ureter

ICD-9-CM Procedural

56.79 Other anastomosis or bypass of ureter
59.02 Other lysis of perirenal or periureteral adhesions

HCPCS Level II Supplies & Services

A4349 Male external catheter, with or without adhesive, disposable, each

50727-50728

50727 Revision of urinary-cutaneous anastomosis (any type urostomy);
50728 with repair of fascial defect and hernia

ICD-9-CM Diagnostic

188.0 Malignant neoplasm of trigone of urinary bladder
188.1 Malignant neoplasm of dome of urinary bladder
188.2 Malignant neoplasm of lateral wall of urinary bladder
188.3 Malignant neoplasm of anterior wall of urinary bladder
188.4 Malignant neoplasm of posterior wall of urinary bladder
188.5 Malignant neoplasm of bladder neck
188.6 Malignant neoplasm of ureteric orifice
188.8 Malignant neoplasm of other specified sites of bladder
188.9 Malignant neoplasm of bladder, part unspecified ▽
189.2 Malignant neoplasm of ureter
189.3 Malignant neoplasm of urethra
197.6 Secondary malignant neoplasm of retroperitoneum and peritoneum
560.81 Intestinal or peritoneal adhesions with obstruction (postoperative) (postinfection)
569.5 Abscess of intestine
569.60 Unspecified complication of colostomy or enterostomy ▽
569.61 Infection of colostomy or enterostomy — (Use additional code to identify organism: 041.00-041.9. Use additional code to specify type of infection: 038.0-038.9, 682.2)
569.62 Mechanical complication of colostomy and enterostomy
569.69 Other complication of colostomy or enterostomy
569.82 Ulceration of intestine
569.83 Perforation of intestine
569.89 Other specified disorder of intestines
569.9 Unspecified disorder of intestine ▽
593.3 Stricture or kinking of ureter
593.4 Other ureteric obstruction
593.89 Other specified disorder of kidney and ureter
599.60 Urinary obstruction, unspecified — (Use additional code to identify urinary incontinence: 625.6, 788.30-788.39) ▽
599.69 Urinary obstruction, not elsewhere classified — (Use additional code to identify urinary incontinence: 625.6, 788.30-788.39. Code, if applicable, any causal condition first: 600.0-600.9, with fifth-digit 1)
614.6 Pelvic peritoneal adhesions, female (postoperative) (postinfection) — (Use additional code to identify organism: 041.00-041.09, 041.10-041.19) (Use additional code to identify any associated infertility: 628.2) ♀
614.9 Unspecified inflammatory disease of female pelvic organs and tissues — (Use additional code to identify organism: 041.00-041.09, 041.10-041.19) ▽ ♀
682.2 Cellulitis and abscess of trunk — (Use additional code to identify organism, such as 041.1, etc.)
707.8 Chronic ulcer of other specified site
997.5 Urinary complications — (Use additional code to identify complications)
V10.51 Personal history of malignant neoplasm of bladder
V55.6 Attention to other artificial opening of urinary tract

ICD-9-CM Procedural

56.52 Revision of cutaneous uretero-ileostomy
56.62 Revision of other cutaneous ureterostomy
56.72 Revision of ureterointestinal anastomosis
58.44 Reanastomosis of urethra

HCPCS Level II Supplies & Services

A4349 Male external catheter, with or without adhesive, disposable, each

50740

50740 Ureteropyelostomy, anastomosis of ureter and renal pelvis

ICD-9-CM Diagnostic

189.0 Malignant neoplasm of kidney, except pelvis
189.1 Malignant neoplasm of renal pelvis
198.0 Secondary malignant neoplasm of kidney
198.1 Secondary malignant neoplasm of other urinary organs
199.2 Malignant neoplasm associated with transplanted organ — (Code first complication of transplanted organ (996.80-996.89) Use additional code for specific malignancy)
209.24 Malignant carcinoid tumor of the kidney — (Code first any associated multiple endocrine neoplasia syndrome: 258.01-258.03; Use additional code to identify associated endocrine syndrome, as: carcinoid syndrome: 259.2)
209.64 Benign carcinoid tumor of the kidney — (Code first any associated multiple endocrine neoplasia syndrome: 258.01-258.03; Use additional code to identify associated endocrine syndrome, as: carcinoid syndrome: 259.2)
223.0 Benign neoplasm of kidney, except pelvis
223.1 Benign neoplasm of renal pelvis
593.3 Stricture or kinking of ureter
593.4 Other ureteric obstruction
593.89 Other specified disorder of kidney and ureter
599.60 Urinary obstruction, unspecified — (Use additional code to identify urinary incontinence: 625.6, 788.30-788.39) ▽
599.69 Urinary obstruction, not elsewhere classified — (Use additional code to identify urinary incontinence: 625.6, 788.30-788.39. Code, if applicable, any causal condition first: 600.0-600.9, with fifth-digit 1)
753.10 Unspecified congenital cystic kidney disease ▽
753.19 Other specified congenital cystic kidney disease
753.20 Unspecified obstructive defect of renal pelvis and ureter ▽
753.21 Congenital obstruction of ureteropelvic junction
753.23 Congenital ureterocele
753.29 Other obstructive defect of renal pelvis and ureter

ICD-9-CM Procedural

55.86 Anastomosis of kidney

50750

50750 Ureterocalycostomy, anastomosis of ureter to renal calyx

ICD-9-CM Diagnostic

189.0 Malignant neoplasm of kidney, except pelvis
189.1 Malignant neoplasm of renal pelvis
198.0 Secondary malignant neoplasm of kidney
198.1 Secondary malignant neoplasm of other urinary organs
199.2 Malignant neoplasm associated with transplanted organ — (Code first complication of transplanted organ (996.80-996.89) Use additional code for specific malignancy)
209.24 Malignant carcinoid tumor of the kidney — (Code first any associated multiple endocrine neoplasia syndrome: 258.01-258.03; Use additional code to identify associated endocrine syndrome, as: carcinoid syndrome: 259.2)
209.64 Benign carcinoid tumor of the kidney — (Code first any associated multiple endocrine neoplasia syndrome: 258.01-258.03; Use additional code to identify associated endocrine syndrome, as: carcinoid syndrome: 259.2)
223.0 Benign neoplasm of kidney, except pelvis
223.1 Benign neoplasm of renal pelvis
593.3 Stricture or kinking of ureter
593.4 Other ureteric obstruction
593.89 Other specified disorder of kidney and ureter
599.60 Urinary obstruction, unspecified — (Use additional code to identify urinary incontinence: 625.6, 788.30-788.39) ▽
599.69 Urinary obstruction, not elsewhere classified — (Use additional code to identify urinary incontinence: 625.6, 788.30-788.39. Code, if applicable, any causal condition first: 600.0-600.9, with fifth-digit 1)
753.10 Unspecified congenital cystic kidney disease ▽
753.19 Other specified congenital cystic kidney disease
753.20 Unspecified obstructive defect of renal pelvis and ureter ▽
753.21 Congenital obstruction of ureteropelvic junction
753.23 Congenital ureterocele
753.29 Other obstructive defect of renal pelvis and ureter

ICD-9-CM Procedural

55.86 Anastomosis of kidney

50760

50760 Ureteroureterostomy

ICD-9-CM Diagnostic

158.0 Malignant neoplasm of retroperitoneum
189.2 Malignant neoplasm of ureter
211.8 Benign neoplasm of retroperitoneum and peritoneum
593.3 Stricture or kinking of ureter
593.4 Other ureteric obstruction
753.21 Congenital obstruction of ureteropelvic junction
753.22 Congenital obstruction of ureterovesical junction
753.23 Congenital ureterocele
753.29 Other obstructive defect of renal pelvis and ureter
753.3 Other specified congenital anomalies of kidney
867.2 Ureter injury without mention of open wound into cavity
867.3 Ureter injury with open wound into cavity

ICD-9-CM Procedural

56.41 Partial ureterectomy
56.61 Formation of other cutaneous ureterostomy
56.75 Transureteroureterostomy

50770

50770 Transureteroureterostomy, anastomosis of ureter to contralateral ureter

ICD-9-CM Diagnostic

158.0 Malignant neoplasm of retroperitoneum
189.2 Malignant neoplasm of ureter
211.8 Benign neoplasm of retroperitoneum and peritoneum
593.3 Stricture or kinking of ureter
593.4 Other ureteric obstruction
753.21 Congenital obstruction of ureteropelvic junction
753.22 Congenital obstruction of ureterovesical junction
753.23 Congenital ureterocele
753.29 Other obstructive defect of renal pelvis and ureter
753.3 Other specified congenital anomalies of kidney
867.2 Ureter injury without mention of open wound into cavity
867.3 Ureter injury with open wound into cavity

ICD-9-CM Procedural

56.75 Transureteroureterostomy

50780-50785

50780 Ureteroneocystostomy; anastomosis of single ureter to bladder
50782 anastomosis of duplicated ureter to bladder
50783 with extensive ureteral tailoring
50785 with vesico-psoas hitch or bladder flap

ICD-9-CM Diagnostic

182.8 Malignant neoplasm of other specified sites of body of uterus ♀
185 Malignant neoplasm of prostate ♂
188.0 Malignant neoplasm of trigone of urinary bladder
188.9 Malignant neoplasm of bladder, part unspecified ▽
189.2 Malignant neoplasm of ureter
197.6 Secondary malignant neoplasm of retroperitoneum and peritoneum
198.1 Secondary malignant neoplasm of other urinary organs
223.2 Benign neoplasm of ureter
223.3 Benign neoplasm of bladder
236.90 Neoplasm of uncertain behavior of urinary organ, unspecified ▽
236.91 Neoplasm of uncertain behavior of kidney and ureter
236.99 Neoplasm of uncertain behavior of other and unspecified urinary organs
238.77 Post-transplant lymphoproliferative disorder [PTLD] — (Code first complications of transplant (996.80-996.89))
239.4 Neoplasm of unspecified nature of bladder
239.5 Neoplasm of unspecified nature of other genitourinary organs
279.50 Graft-versus-host disease, unspecified — (Code first underlying cause: 996.80-996.89, 999.89)(Use additional code to identify any associated intellectual disabilities) (Use additional code to identify associated manifestations: 695.89, 704.09, 782.4, 787.91) ▽
279.51 Acute graft-versus-host disease — (Code first underlying cause: 996.80-996.89, 999.89)(Use additional code to identify any associated intellectual disabilities) (Use additional code to identify associated manifestations: 695.89, 704.09, 782.4, 787.91)
279.52 Chronic graft-versus-host disease — (Code first underlying cause: 996.80-996.89, 999.89)(Use additional code to identify any associated intellectual disabilities) (Use additional code to identify associated manifestations: 695.89, 704.09, 782.4, 787.91)
279.53 Acute on chronic graft-versus-host disease — (Code first underlying cause: 996.80-996.89, 999.89)(Use additional code to identify any associated intellectual disabilities) (Use additional code to identify associated manifestations: 695.89, 704.09, 782.4, 787.91)
344.61 Cauda equina syndrome with neurogenic bladder
591 Hydronephrosis
593.3 Stricture or kinking of ureter
593.4 Other ureteric obstruction
593.70 Vesicoureteral reflux, unspecified or without reflex nephropathy
593.71 Vesicoureteral reflux with reflux nephropathy, unilateral
593.72 Vesicoureteral reflux with reflux nephropathy, bilateral
593.73 Vesicoureteral reflux with reflux nephropathy, NOS ▽
593.89 Other specified disorder of kidney and ureter
599.0 Urinary tract infection, site not specified — (Use additional code to identify organism, such as E. coli: 041.41-041.49) ▽
614.6 Pelvic peritoneal adhesions, female (postoperative) (postinfection) — (Use additional code to identify organism: 041.00-041.09, 041.10-041.19) (Use additional code to identify any associated infertility: 628.2) ♀
614.9 Unspecified inflammatory disease of female pelvic organs and tissues — (Use additional code to identify organism: 041.00-041.09, 041.10-041.19) ▽ ♀
617.8 Endometriosis of other specified sites ♀
619.0 Urinary-genital tract fistula, female ♀
753.21 Congenital obstruction of ureteropelvic junction
753.22 Congenital obstruction of ureterovesical junction
753.23 Congenital ureterocele
753.29 Other obstructive defect of renal pelvis and ureter
753.4 Other specified congenital anomalies of ureter
753.9 Unspecified congenital anomaly of urinary system ▽
867.2 Ureter injury without mention of open wound into cavity
867.3 Ureter injury with open wound into cavity
867.7 Injury to other specified pelvic organs with open wound into cavity
867.8 Injury to unspecified pelvic organ without mention of open wound into cavity ▽
867.9 Injury to unspecified pelvic organ with open wound into cavity ▽
996.81 Complications of transplanted kidney — (Use additional code to identify nature of complication: 078.5, 199.2, 238.77, 279.50-279.53)
998.2 Accidental puncture or laceration during procedure
V64.41 Laparoscopic surgical procedure converted to open procedure

ICD-9-CM Procedural

56.74 Ureteroneocystostomy

50800

50800 Ureteroenterostomy, direct anastomosis of ureter to intestine

ICD-9-CM Diagnostic

188.0 Malignant neoplasm of trigone of urinary bladder
188.1 Malignant neoplasm of dome of urinary bladder
188.2 Malignant neoplasm of lateral wall of urinary bladder
188.3 Malignant neoplasm of anterior wall of urinary bladder
188.4 Malignant neoplasm of posterior wall of urinary bladder
188.5 Malignant neoplasm of bladder neck
188.6 Malignant neoplasm of ureteric orifice
188.8 Malignant neoplasm of other specified sites of bladder
188.9 Malignant neoplasm of bladder, part unspecified ▽
189.2 Malignant neoplasm of ureter
198.1 Secondary malignant neoplasm of other urinary organs
589.0 Unilateral small kidney
592.1 Calculus of ureter
593.3 Stricture or kinking of ureter
593.4 Other ureteric obstruction
867.0 Bladder and urethra injury without mention of open wound into cavity
867.1 Bladder and urethra injury with open wound into cavity
867.2 Ureter injury without mention of open wound into cavity
867.3 Ureter injury with open wound into cavity
997.5 Urinary complications — (Use additional code to identify complications)

ICD-9-CM Procedural

56.71 Urinary diversion to intestine

50810

50810 Ureterosigmoidostomy, with creation of sigmoid bladder and establishment of abdominal or perineal colostomy, including intestine anastomosis

ICD-9-CM Diagnostic

188.0 Malignant neoplasm of trigone of urinary bladder
188.1 Malignant neoplasm of dome of urinary bladder
188.2 Malignant neoplasm of lateral wall of urinary bladder
188.3 Malignant neoplasm of anterior wall of urinary bladder
188.4 Malignant neoplasm of posterior wall of urinary bladder
188.5 Malignant neoplasm of bladder neck
188.6 Malignant neoplasm of ureteric orifice
188.7 Malignant neoplasm of urachus
188.8 Malignant neoplasm of other specified sites of bladder
188.9 Malignant neoplasm of bladder, part unspecified ▽
189.2 Malignant neoplasm of ureter
189.3 Malignant neoplasm of urethra
198.1 Secondary malignant neoplasm of other urinary organs
593.4 Other ureteric obstruction

595.82 Irradiation cystitis — (Use additional code to identify organism, such as E. coli: 041.41-041.49. Use additional E code to identify cause)
596.54 Neurogenic bladder, NOS — (Use additional code to identify urinary incontinence: 625.6, 788.30-788.39) ▽
596.89 Other specified disorders of bladder
753.5 Exstrophy of urinary bladder
753.8 Other specified congenital anomaly of bladder and urethra
867.0 Bladder and urethra injury without mention of open wound into cavity
867.1 Bladder and urethra injury with open wound into cavity
867.2 Ureter injury without mention of open wound into cavity
867.3 Ureter injury with open wound into cavity
997.5 Urinary complications — (Use additional code to identify complications)

ICD-9-CM Procedural

56.71 Urinary diversion to intestine

50815-50820

50815 Ureterocolon conduit, including intestine anastomosis
50820 Ureteroileal conduit (ileal bladder), including intestine anastomosis (Bricker operation)

ICD-9-CM Diagnostic

188.0 Malignant neoplasm of trigone of urinary bladder
188.1 Malignant neoplasm of dome of urinary bladder
188.2 Malignant neoplasm of lateral wall of urinary bladder
188.3 Malignant neoplasm of anterior wall of urinary bladder
188.4 Malignant neoplasm of posterior wall of urinary bladder
188.5 Malignant neoplasm of bladder neck
188.6 Malignant neoplasm of ureteric orifice
188.8 Malignant neoplasm of other specified sites of bladder
188.9 Malignant neoplasm of bladder, part unspecified ▽
189.2 Malignant neoplasm of ureter
189.3 Malignant neoplasm of urethra
198.1 Secondary malignant neoplasm of other urinary organs
591 Hydronephrosis
593.4 Other ureteric obstruction
595.82 Irradiation cystitis — (Use additional code to identify organism, such as E. coli: 041.41-041.49. Use additional E code to identify cause)
596.54 Neurogenic bladder, NOS — (Use additional code to identify urinary incontinence: 625.6, 788.30-788.39) ▽
596.89 Other specified disorders of bladder
753.5 Exstrophy of urinary bladder
753.8 Other specified congenital anomaly of bladder and urethra
867.0 Bladder and urethra injury without mention of open wound into cavity
867.1 Bladder and urethra injury with open wound into cavity

ICD-9-CM Procedural

56.51 Formation of cutaneous uretero-ileostomy
56.71 Urinary diversion to intestine

50825

50825 Continent diversion, including intestine anastomosis using any segment of small and/or large intestine (Kock pouch or Camey enterocystoplasty)

ICD-9-CM Diagnostic

188.0 Malignant neoplasm of trigone of urinary bladder
188.1 Malignant neoplasm of dome of urinary bladder
188.2 Malignant neoplasm of lateral wall of urinary bladder
188.3 Malignant neoplasm of anterior wall of urinary bladder
188.4 Malignant neoplasm of posterior wall of urinary bladder
188.5 Malignant neoplasm of bladder neck
188.6 Malignant neoplasm of ureteric orifice
188.8 Malignant neoplasm of other specified sites of bladder
188.9 Malignant neoplasm of bladder, part unspecified ▽
189.2 Malignant neoplasm of ureter
189.3 Malignant neoplasm of urethra
198.1 Secondary malignant neoplasm of other urinary organs
591 Hydronephrosis
593.4 Other ureteric obstruction
595.82 Irradiation cystitis — (Use additional code to identify organism, such as E. coli: 041.41-041.49. Use additional E code to identify cause)
596.54 Neurogenic bladder, NOS — (Use additional code to identify urinary incontinence: 625.6, 788.30-788.39) ▽
596.89 Other specified disorders of bladder
753.5 Exstrophy of urinary bladder
753.8 Other specified congenital anomaly of bladder and urethra
867.0 Bladder and urethra injury without mention of open wound into cavity
867.1 Bladder and urethra injury with open wound into cavity

ICD-9-CM Procedural

56.51 Formation of cutaneous uretero-ileostomy

50830

50830 Urinary undiversion (eg, taking down of ureteroileal conduit, ureterosigmoidostomy or ureteroenterostomy with ureteroureterostomy or ureteroneocystostomy)

ICD-9-CM Diagnostic

344.61 Cauda equina syndrome with neurogenic bladder
596.54 Neurogenic bladder, NOS — (Use additional code to identify urinary incontinence: 625.6, 788.30-788.39) ▽
753.21 Congenital obstruction of ureteropelvic junction
753.22 Congenital obstruction of ureterovesical junction
753.29 Other obstructive defect of renal pelvis and ureter
V10.50 Personal history of malignant neoplasm of unspecified urinary organ ▽
V10.51 Personal history of malignant neoplasm of bladder
V10.52 Personal history of malignant neoplasm of kidney
V10.53 Personal history of malignant neoplasm, renal pelvis
V10.59 Personal history of malignant neoplasm of other urinary organ
V13.00 Personal history of unspecified urinary disorder ▽
V13.09 Personal history of other disorder of urinary system
V15.3 Personal history of irradiation, presenting hazards to health
V15.51 Personal history of traumatic fracture
V15.59 Personal history of other injury
V55.5 Attention to cystostomy
V55.6 Attention to other artificial opening of urinary tract

ICD-9-CM Procedural

56.83 Closure of ureterostomy
57.99 Other operations on bladder

HCPCS Level II Supplies & Services

A4349 Male external catheter, with or without adhesive, disposable, each

50840

50840 Replacement of all or part of ureter by intestine segment, including intestine anastomosis

ICD-9-CM Diagnostic

189.2 Malignant neoplasm of ureter
344.61 Cauda equina syndrome with neurogenic bladder
592.1 Calculus of ureter
596.54 Neurogenic bladder, NOS — (Use additional code to identify urinary incontinence: 625.6, 788.30-788.39) ▽
596.89 Other specified disorders of bladder
617.8 Endometriosis of other specified sites ♀

867.2 Ureter injury without mention of open wound into cavity
867.3 Ureter injury with open wound into cavity
997.5 Urinary complications — (Use additional code to identify complications)

ICD-9-CM Procedural

56.89 Other repair of ureter

50845

50845 Cutaneous appendico-vesicostomy

ICD-9-CM Diagnostic

154.0 Malignant neoplasm of rectosigmoid junction
154.8 Malignant neoplasm of other sites of rectum, rectosigmoid junction, and anus
180.0 Malignant neoplasm of endocervix ♀
180.8 Malignant neoplasm of other specified sites of cervix ♀
185 Malignant neoplasm of prostate ♂
187.4 Malignant neoplasm of penis, part unspecified ▽ ♂
188.3 Malignant neoplasm of anterior wall of urinary bladder
188.5 Malignant neoplasm of bladder neck
189.3 Malignant neoplasm of urethra
189.8 Malignant neoplasm of other specified sites of urinary organs
198.1 Secondary malignant neoplasm of other urinary organs
223.3 Benign neoplasm of bladder
223.81 Benign neoplasm of urethra
233.1 Carcinoma in situ of cervix uteri ♀
233.7 Carcinoma in situ of bladder
233.9 Carcinoma in situ of other and unspecified urinary organs ▽
236.7 Neoplasm of uncertain behavior of bladder
236.99 Neoplasm of uncertain behavior of other and unspecified urinary organs
239.4 Neoplasm of unspecified nature of bladder
239.5 Neoplasm of unspecified nature of other genitourinary organs
344.61 Cauda equina syndrome with neurogenic bladder
592.0 Calculus of kidney
592.1 Calculus of ureter
593.4 Other ureteric obstruction
594.1 Other calculus in bladder
594.2 Calculus in urethra
595.89 Other specified types of cystitis — (Use additional code to identify organism, such as E. coli: 041.41-041.49)
596.0 Bladder neck obstruction — (Use additional code to identify urinary incontinence: 625.6, 788.30-788.39)
596.2 Vesical fistula, not elsewhere classified — (Use additional code to identify urinary incontinence: 625.6, 788.30-788.39)
596.3 Diverticulum of bladder — (Use additional code to identify urinary incontinence: 625.6, 788.30-788.39)
596.4 Atony of bladder — (Use additional code to identify urinary incontinence: 625.6, 788.30-788.39)
596.51 Hypertonicity of bladder — (Use additional code to identify urinary incontinence: 625.6, 788.30-788.39)
596.52 Low bladder compliance — (Use additional code to identify urinary incontinence: 625.6, 788.30-788.39)
596.53 Paralysis of bladder — (Use additional code to identify urinary incontinence: 625.6, 788.30-788.39)
596.54 Neurogenic bladder, NOS — (Use additional code to identify urinary incontinence: 625.6, 788.30-788.39) ▽
596.89 Other specified disorders of bladder
598.01 Urethral stricture due to infective diseases classified elsewhere — (Use additional code to identify urinary incontinence: 625.6, 788.30-788.39. Code first underlying disease: 095.8, 098.2, 120.0-120.9) ☒
599.1 Urethral fistula
599.2 Urethral diverticulum
599.60 Urinary obstruction, unspecified — (Use additional code to identify urinary incontinence: 625.6, 788.30-788.39) ▽
599.69 Urinary obstruction, not elsewhere classified — (Use additional code to identify urinary incontinence: 625.6, 788.30-788.39. Code, if applicable, any causal condition first: 600.0-600.9, with fifth-digit 1)
599.70 Hematuria, unspecified ▽
599.71 Gross hematuria
599.72 Microscopic hematuria
599.84 Other specified disorders of urethra — (Use additional code to identify urinary incontinence: 625.6, 788.30-788.39)
600.01 Hypertrophy (benign) of prostate with urinary obstruction and other lower urinary tract symptoms [LUTS] — (Use additional code to identify symptoms: 599.69, 788.20, 788.21, 788.30-788.39, 788.41, 788.43, 788.62, 788.63, 788.64, 788.65) ♂
600.11 Nodular prostate with urinary obstruction ♂
600.21 Benign localized hyperplasia of prostate with urinary obstruction and other lower urinary tract symptoms [LUTS] — (Use additional code to identify symptoms: 599.69, 788.20, 788.21, 788.30-788.39, 788.41, 788.43, 788.62, 788.63, 788.64, 788.65) ♂
600.91 Hyperplasia of prostate, unspecified, with urinary obstruction and other lower urinary tract symptoms [LUTS] — (Use additional code to identify symptoms: 599.69, 788.20, 788.21, 788.30-788.39, 788.41, 788.43, 788.62, 788.63, 788.64, 788.65) ▽ ♂
602.1 Congestion or hemorrhage of prostate ♂
607.2 Other inflammatory disorders of penis — (Use additional code to identify organism) ♂
618.1 Uterine prolapse without mention of vaginal wall prolapse — (Use additional code to identify urinary incontinence: 625.6, 788.31, 788.33-788.39) ♀
618.2 Uterovaginal prolapse, incomplete — (Use additional code to identify urinary incontinence: 625.6, 788.31, 788.33-788.39) ♀
618.3 Uterovaginal prolapse, complete — (Use additional code to identify urinary incontinence: 625.6, 788.31, 788.33-788.39) ♀
618.4 Uterovaginal prolapse, unspecified — (Use additional code to identify urinary incontinence: 625.6, 788.31, 788.33-788.39) ▽ ♀
618.5 Prolapse of vaginal vault after hysterectomy — (Use additional code to identify urinary incontinence: 625.6, 788.31, 788.33-788.39) ♀
618.6 Vaginal enterocele, congenital or acquired — (Use additional code to identify urinary incontinence: 625.6, 788.31, 788.33-788.39) ♀
618.7 Genital prolapse, old laceration of muscles of pelvic floor — (Use additional code to identify urinary incontinence: 625.6, 788.31, 788.33-788.39) ♀
618.9 Unspecified genital prolapse — (Use additional code to identify urinary incontinence: 625.6, 788.31, 788.33-788.39) ▽ ♀
619.0 Urinary-genital tract fistula, female ♀
625.6 Female stress incontinence ♀
625.9 Unspecified symptom associated with female genital organs ▽ ♀
788.0 Renal colic
788.20 Unspecified retention of urine — (Code, if applicable, any causal condition first, such as: 600.0-600.9, with fifth digit 1) ▽
788.29 Other specified retention of urine — (Code, if applicable, any causal condition first, such as: 600.0-600.9, with fifth digit 1)
788.30 Unspecified urinary incontinence — (Code, if applicable, any causal condition first: 600.0-600.9, with fifth digit 1; 618.00-618.9; 753.23) ▽
788.31 Urge incontinence — (Code, if applicable, any causal condition first: 600.0-600.9, with fifth digit 1; 618.00-618.9; 753.23)
788.32 Stress incontinence, male — (Code, if applicable, any causal condition first: 600.0-600.9, with fifth digit 1; 618.00-618.9; 753.23) ♂
788.33 Mixed incontinence urge and stress (male)(female) — (Code, if applicable, any causal condition first: 600.0-600.9, with fifth digit 1; 618.00-618.9; 753.23)
788.38 Overflow incontinence — (Code, if applicable, any causal condition first: 600.0-600.9, with fifth digit 1; 618.00-618.9; 753.23)
788.39 Other urinary incontinence — (Code, if applicable, any causal condition first: 600.0-600.9, with fifth digit 1; 618.00-618.9; 753.23)
788.8 Extravasation of urine
788.99 Other symptoms involving urinary system

789.30 Abdominal or pelvic swelling, mass or lump, unspecified site ▽
808.8 Unspecified closed fracture of pelvis ▽
867.0 Bladder and urethra injury without mention of open wound into cavity
867.1 Bladder and urethra injury with open wound into cavity
867.2 Ureter injury without mention of open wound into cavity
867.3 Ureter injury with open wound into cavity
867.8 Injury to unspecified pelvic organ without mention of open wound into cavity ▽
867.9 Injury to unspecified pelvic organ with open wound into cavity ▽
878.0 Open wound of penis, without mention of complication ♂
878.1 Open wound of penis, complicated ♂
879.8 Open wound(s) (multiple) of unspecified site(s), without mention of complication ▽
879.9 Open wound(s) (multiple) of unspecified site(s), complicated ▽
942.05 Burn of trunk, unspecified degree of genitalia ▽
996.30 Mechanical complication of unspecified genitourinary device, implant, and graft ▽
996.31 Mechanical complication due to urethral (indwelling) catheter
996.39 Mechanical complication of genitourinary device, implant, and graft, other
996.64 Infection and inflammatory reaction due to indwelling urinary catheter — (Use additional code to identify specified infections: 038.0-038.9, 595.0-595.9)
996.65 Infection and inflammatory reaction due to other genitourinary device, implant, and graft — (Use additional code to identify specified infections)
996.76 Other complications due to genitourinary device, implant, and graft — (Use additional code to identify complication: 338.18-338.19, 338.28-338.29)
997.5 Urinary complications — (Use additional code to identify complications)
998.2 Accidental puncture or laceration during procedure
998.51 Infected postoperative seroma — (Use additional code to identify organism)
998.59 Other postoperative infection — (Use additional code to identify infection)
V55.5 Attention to cystostomy

ICD-9-CM Procedural

47.91 Appendicostomy
57.21 Vesicostomy

50860

50860 Ureterostomy, transplantation of ureter to skin

ICD-9-CM Diagnostic

188.0 Malignant neoplasm of trigone of urinary bladder
188.1 Malignant neoplasm of dome of urinary bladder
188.2 Malignant neoplasm of lateral wall of urinary bladder
188.3 Malignant neoplasm of anterior wall of urinary bladder
188.4 Malignant neoplasm of posterior wall of urinary bladder
188.5 Malignant neoplasm of bladder neck
188.6 Malignant neoplasm of ureteric orifice
188.8 Malignant neoplasm of other specified sites of bladder
344.61 Cauda equina syndrome with neurogenic bladder
592.1 Calculus of ureter
593.4 Other ureteric obstruction
596.0 Bladder neck obstruction — (Use additional code to identify urinary incontinence: 625.6, 788.30-788.39)
596.51 Hypertonicity of bladder — (Use additional code to identify urinary incontinence: 625.6, 788.30-788.39)
596.52 Low bladder compliance — (Use additional code to identify urinary incontinence: 625.6, 788.30-788.39)
596.53 Paralysis of bladder — (Use additional code to identify urinary incontinence: 625.6, 788.30-788.39)
596.54 Neurogenic bladder, NOS — (Use additional code to identify urinary incontinence: 625.6, 788.30-788.39) ▽
753.21 Congenital obstruction of ureteropelvic junction
753.22 Congenital obstruction of ureterovesical junction
753.29 Other obstructive defect of renal pelvis and ureter
753.6 Congenital atresia and stenosis of urethra and bladder neck
788.99 Other symptoms involving urinary system

ICD-9-CM Procedural

56.61 Formation of other cutaneous ureterostomy

50900

50900 Ureterorrhaphy, suture of ureter (separate procedure)

ICD-9-CM Diagnostic

867.2 Ureter injury without mention of open wound into cavity
867.3 Ureter injury with open wound into cavity
E870.0 Accidental cut, puncture, perforation, or hemorrhage during surgical operation

ICD-9-CM Procedural

56.82 Suture of laceration of ureter

50920

50920 Closure of ureterocutaneous fistula

ICD-9-CM Diagnostic

593.82 Ureteral fistula
593.9 Unspecified disorder of kidney and ureter ▽
753.4 Other specified congenital anomalies of ureter

ICD-9-CM Procedural

56.84 Closure of other fistula of ureter

50930

50930 Closure of ureterovisceral fistula (including visceral repair)

ICD-9-CM Diagnostic

593.82 Ureteral fistula
593.9 Unspecified disorder of kidney and ureter ▽
596.2 Vesical fistula, not elsewhere classified — (Use additional code to identify urinary incontinence: 625.6, 788.30-788.39)
619.0 Urinary-genital tract fistula, female ♀
753.4 Other specified congenital anomalies of ureter

ICD-9-CM Procedural

56.84 Closure of other fistula of ureter

50940

50940 Deligation of ureter

ICD-9-CM Diagnostic

238.77 Post-transplant lymphoproliferative disorder [PTLD] — (Code first complications of transplant (996.80-996.89))
279.50 Graft-versus-host disease, unspecified — (Code first underlying cause: 996.80-996.89, 999.89)(Use additional code to identify any associated intellectual disabilities) (Use additional code to identify associated manifestations: 695.89, 704.09, 782.4, 787.91) ▽
279.51 Acute graft-versus-host disease — (Code first underlying cause: 996.80-996.89, 999.89)(Use additional code to identify any associated intellectual disabilities) (Use additional code to identify associated manifestations: 695.89, 704.09, 782.4, 787.91)
279.52 Chronic graft-versus-host disease — (Code first underlying cause: 996.80-996.89, 999.89)(Use additional code to identify any associated intellectual disabilities) (Use additional code to identify associated manifestations: 695.89, 704.09, 782.4, 787.91)
279.53 Acute on chronic graft-versus-host disease — (Code first underlying cause: 996.80-996.89, 999.89)(Use additional code to identify any associated intellectual disabilities) (Use additional code to identify associated manifestations: 695.89, 704.09, 782.4, 787.91)
591 Hydronephrosis
593.4 Other ureteric obstruction

593.89 Other specified disorder of kidney and ureter
753.3 Other specified congenital anomalies of kidney
753.4 Other specified congenital anomalies of ureter
867.2 Ureter injury without mention of open wound into cavity
867.3 Ureter injury with open wound into cavity
996.81 Complications of transplanted kidney — (Use additional code to identify nature of complication: 078.5, 199.2, 238.77, 279.50-279.53)
V58.32 Encounter for removal of sutures
V58.49 Other specified aftercare following surgery — (This code should be used in conjunction with other aftercare codes to fully identify the reason for the aftercare encounter)

ICD-9-CM Procedural

56.86 Removal of ligature from ureter

50945

50945 Laparoscopy, surgical; ureterolithotomy

ICD-9-CM Diagnostic

592.1 Calculus of ureter
592.9 Unspecified urinary calculus ▽
593.4 Other ureteric obstruction
599.70 Hematuria, unspecified ▽
599.71 Gross hematuria
599.72 Microscopic hematuria

ICD-9-CM Procedural

56.2 Ureterotomy

50947-50948

50947 Laparoscopy, surgical; ureteroneocystostomy with cystoscopy and ureteral stent placement
50948 ureteroneocystostomy without cystoscopy and ureteral stent placement

ICD-9-CM Diagnostic

344.61 Cauda equina syndrome with neurogenic bladder
591 Hydronephrosis
593.3 Stricture or kinking of ureter
593.4 Other ureteric obstruction
593.5 Hydroureter
593.70 Vesicoureteral reflux, unspecified or without reflex nephropathy
593.71 Vesicoureteral reflux with reflux nephropathy, unilateral
593.72 Vesicoureteral reflux with reflux nephropathy, bilateral
593.73 Vesicoureteral reflux with reflux nephropathy, NOS ▽
593.89 Other specified disorder of kidney and ureter
593.9 Unspecified disorder of kidney and ureter ▽
599.0 Urinary tract infection, site not specified — (Use additional code to identify organism, such as E. coli: 041.41-041.49) ▽
753.21 Congenital obstruction of ureteropelvic junction
753.22 Congenital obstruction of ureterovesical junction
753.23 Congenital ureterocele
753.29 Other obstructive defect of renal pelvis and ureter
753.4 Other specified congenital anomalies of ureter
753.9 Unspecified congenital anomaly of urinary system ▽

ICD-9-CM Procedural

56.74 Ureteroneocystostomy
59.8 Ureteral catheterization

50951-50955

50951 Ureteral endoscopy through established ureterostomy, with or without irrigation, instillation, or ureteropyelography, exclusive of radiologic service;
50953 with ureteral catheterization, with or without dilation of ureter
50955 with biopsy

ICD-9-CM Diagnostic

188.6 Malignant neoplasm of ureteric orifice
189.2 Malignant neoplasm of ureter
198.0 Secondary malignant neoplasm of kidney
198.1 Secondary malignant neoplasm of other urinary organs
223.1 Benign neoplasm of renal pelvis
223.2 Benign neoplasm of ureter
233.30 Carcinoma in situ, unspecified female genital organ ▽ ♀
233.31 Carcinoma in situ, vagina ♀
233.32 Carcinoma in situ, vulva ♀
233.39 Carcinoma in situ, other female genital organ ♀
233.7 Carcinoma in situ of bladder
233.9 Carcinoma in situ of other and unspecified urinary organs ▽
236.7 Neoplasm of uncertain behavior of bladder
236.91 Neoplasm of uncertain behavior of kidney and ureter
592.1 Calculus of ureter
593.3 Stricture or kinking of ureter
593.4 Other ureteric obstruction
593.5 Hydroureter
593.82 Ureteral fistula
593.89 Other specified disorder of kidney and ureter
599.70 Hematuria, unspecified ▽
599.71 Gross hematuria
599.72 Microscopic hematuria
753.21 Congenital obstruction of ureteropelvic junction
753.22 Congenital obstruction of ureterovesical junction
753.23 Congenital ureterocele
753.29 Other obstructive defect of renal pelvis and ureter

ICD-9-CM Procedural

56.31 Ureteroscopy
56.33 Closed endoscopic biopsy of ureter
56.91 Dilation of ureteral meatus
59.8 Ureteral catheterization

HCPCS Level II Supplies & Services

A4270 Disposable endoscope sheath, each

50957-50961

50957 Ureteral endoscopy through established ureterostomy, with or without irrigation, instillation, or ureteropyelography, exclusive of radiologic service; with fulguration and/or incision, with or without biopsy
50961 with removal of foreign body or calculus

ICD-9-CM Diagnostic

188.6 Malignant neoplasm of ureteric orifice
189.2 Malignant neoplasm of ureter
198.0 Secondary malignant neoplasm of kidney
198.1 Secondary malignant neoplasm of other urinary organs
223.1 Benign neoplasm of renal pelvis
223.2 Benign neoplasm of ureter
233.30 Carcinoma in situ, unspecified female genital organ ▽ ♀
233.31 Carcinoma in situ, vagina ♀
233.32 Carcinoma in situ, vulva ♀
233.39 Carcinoma in situ, other female genital organ ♀

233.7 Carcinoma in situ of bladder
233.9 Carcinoma in situ of other and unspecified urinary organs ▽
236.7 Neoplasm of uncertain behavior of bladder
236.91 Neoplasm of uncertain behavior of kidney and ureter
252.00 Hyperparathyroidism, unspecified ▽
252.01 Primary hyperparathyroidism
252.02 Secondary hyperparathyroidism, non-renal
252.08 Other hyperparathyroidism
588.81 Secondary hyperparathyroidism (of renal origin)
592.0 Calculus of kidney
592.1 Calculus of ureter
592.9 Unspecified urinary calculus ▽
593.3 Stricture or kinking of ureter
593.4 Other ureteric obstruction
593.5 Hydroureter
593.82 Ureteral fistula
593.89 Other specified disorder of kidney and ureter
753.21 Congenital obstruction of ureteropelvic junction
753.22 Congenital obstruction of ureterovesical junction
753.23 Congenital ureterocele
753.29 Other obstructive defect of renal pelvis and ureter
996.30 Mechanical complication of unspecified genitourinary device, implant, and graft ▽
996.39 Mechanical complication of genitourinary device, implant, and graft, other
996.65 Infection and inflammatory reaction due to other genitourinary device, implant, and graft — (Use additional code to identify specified infections)
996.76 Other complications due to genitourinary device, implant, and graft — (Use additional code to identify complication: 338.18-338.19, 338.28-338.29)
998.4 Foreign body accidentally left during procedure, not elsewhere classified

ICD-9-CM Procedural

56.2 Ureterotomy
56.31 Ureteroscopy
56.33 Closed endoscopic biopsy of ureter
56.99 Other operations on ureter

HCPCS Level II Supplies & Services

A4270 Disposable endoscope sheath, each

50970-50974

50970 Ureteral endoscopy through ureterotomy, with or without irrigation, instillation, or ureteropyelography, exclusive of radiologic service;
50972 with ureteral catheterization, with or without dilation of ureter
50974 with biopsy

ICD-9-CM Diagnostic

188.6 Malignant neoplasm of ureteric orifice
189.1 Malignant neoplasm of renal pelvis
189.2 Malignant neoplasm of ureter
198.0 Secondary malignant neoplasm of kidney
198.1 Secondary malignant neoplasm of other urinary organs
223.1 Benign neoplasm of renal pelvis
223.2 Benign neoplasm of ureter
223.3 Benign neoplasm of bladder
233.7 Carcinoma in situ of bladder
233.9 Carcinoma in situ of other and unspecified urinary organs ▽
236.7 Neoplasm of uncertain behavior of bladder
236.91 Neoplasm of uncertain behavior of kidney and ureter
239.4 Neoplasm of unspecified nature of bladder
239.5 Neoplasm of unspecified nature of other genitourinary organs
592.0 Calculus of kidney
592.1 Calculus of ureter
593.3 Stricture or kinking of ureter
593.4 Other ureteric obstruction
593.5 Hydroureter
593.82 Ureteral fistula
593.89 Other specified disorder of kidney and ureter
599.70 Hematuria, unspecified ▽
599.71 Gross hematuria
599.72 Microscopic hematuria
753.21 Congenital obstruction of ureteropelvic junction
753.22 Congenital obstruction of ureterovesical junction
753.23 Congenital ureterocele
753.29 Other obstructive defect of renal pelvis and ureter
788.0 Renal colic
789.01 Abdominal pain, right upper quadrant
789.02 Abdominal pain, left upper quadrant

ICD-9-CM Procedural

56.2 Ureterotomy
56.31 Ureteroscopy
56.33 Closed endoscopic biopsy of ureter
56.91 Dilation of ureteral meatus
59.8 Ureteral catheterization

50976-50980

50976 Ureteral endoscopy through ureterotomy, with or without irrigation, instillation, or ureteropyelography, exclusive of radiologic service; with fulguration and/or incision, with or without biopsy
50980 with removal of foreign body or calculus

ICD-9-CM Diagnostic

188.6 Malignant neoplasm of ureteric orifice
189.1 Malignant neoplasm of renal pelvis
189.2 Malignant neoplasm of ureter
198.0 Secondary malignant neoplasm of kidney
198.1 Secondary malignant neoplasm of other urinary organs
223.1 Benign neoplasm of renal pelvis
223.2 Benign neoplasm of ureter
223.3 Benign neoplasm of bladder
233.7 Carcinoma in situ of bladder
233.9 Carcinoma in situ of other and unspecified urinary organs ▽
236.7 Neoplasm of uncertain behavior of bladder
236.91 Neoplasm of uncertain behavior of kidney and ureter
239.4 Neoplasm of unspecified nature of bladder
239.5 Neoplasm of unspecified nature of other genitourinary organs
252.00 Hyperparathyroidism, unspecified ▽
252.01 Primary hyperparathyroidism
252.02 Secondary hyperparathyroidism, non-renal
252.08 Other hyperparathyroidism
588.81 Secondary hyperparathyroidism (of renal origin)
592.0 Calculus of kidney
592.1 Calculus of ureter
592.9 Unspecified urinary calculus ▽
593.3 Stricture or kinking of ureter
593.4 Other ureteric obstruction
593.5 Hydroureter
593.82 Ureteral fistula
593.89 Other specified disorder of kidney and ureter
753.21 Congenital obstruction of ureteropelvic junction
753.22 Congenital obstruction of ureterovesical junction
753.23 Congenital ureterocele

753.29 Other obstructive defect of renal pelvis and ureter
996.39 Mechanical complication of genitourinary device, implant, and graft, other
996.65 Infection and inflammatory reaction due to other genitourinary device, implant, and graft — (Use additional code to identify specified infections)
996.76 Other complications due to genitourinary device, implant, and graft — (Use additional code to identify complication: 338.18-338.19, 338.28-338.29)
998.4 Foreign body accidentally left during procedure, not elsewhere classified

ICD-9-CM Procedural

56.2 Ureterotomy
56.31 Ureteroscopy
56.33 Closed endoscopic biopsy of ureter
56.99 Other operations on ureter

Bladder

51020-51030

51020 Cystotomy or cystostomy; with fulguration and/or insertion of radioactive material
51030 with cryosurgical destruction of intravesical lesion

ICD-9-CM Diagnostic

188.0 Malignant neoplasm of trigone of urinary bladder
188.1 Malignant neoplasm of dome of urinary bladder
188.2 Malignant neoplasm of lateral wall of urinary bladder
188.3 Malignant neoplasm of anterior wall of urinary bladder
188.4 Malignant neoplasm of posterior wall of urinary bladder
188.5 Malignant neoplasm of bladder neck
188.6 Malignant neoplasm of ureteric orifice
188.7 Malignant neoplasm of urachus
188.8 Malignant neoplasm of other specified sites of bladder
198.1 Secondary malignant neoplasm of other urinary organs
223.3 Benign neoplasm of bladder
233.7 Carcinoma in situ of bladder
236.7 Neoplasm of uncertain behavior of bladder
239.4 Neoplasm of unspecified nature of bladder
596.9 Unspecified disorder of bladder — (Use additional code to identify urinary incontinence: 625.6, 788.30-788.39) ▽
788.99 Other symptoms involving urinary system

ICD-9-CM Procedural

57.18 Other suprapubic cystostomy
57.19 Other cystotomy
92.27 Implantation or insertion of radioactive elements

51040

51040 Cystostomy, cystotomy with drainage

ICD-9-CM Diagnostic

185 Malignant neoplasm of prostate ♂
187.4 Malignant neoplasm of penis, part unspecified ▽ ♂
188.0 Malignant neoplasm of trigone of urinary bladder
188.2 Malignant neoplasm of lateral wall of urinary bladder
188.3 Malignant neoplasm of anterior wall of urinary bladder
188.4 Malignant neoplasm of posterior wall of urinary bladder
188.5 Malignant neoplasm of bladder neck
188.6 Malignant neoplasm of ureteric orifice
344.61 Cauda equina syndrome with neurogenic bladder
590.00 Chronic pyelonephritis without lesion of renal medullary necrosis — (Use additional code to identify organism, such as E. coli, 041.41-041.49. Code if applicable, any causal condition first)
590.3 Pyeloureteritis cystica — (Use additional code to identify organism, such as E. coli, 041.41-041.49)
590.81 Pyelitis or pyelonephritis in diseases classified elsewhere — (Use additional code to identify organism, such as E. coli, 041.41-041.49. Code first underlying disease: 016.0) ☒
593.70 Vesicoureteral reflux, unspecified or without reflex nephropathy
595.0 Acute cystitis — (Use additional code to identify organism, such as E. coli: 041.41-041.49)
595.1 Chronic interstitial cystitis — (Use additional code to identify organism, such as E. coli: 041.41-041.49)
595.3 Trigonitis — (Use additional code to identify organism, such as E. coli: 041.41-041.49)
595.4 Cystitis in diseases classified elsewhere — (Use additional code to identify organism, such as E. coli: 041.41-041.49. Code first underlying disease: 006.8, 039.8, 120.0-120.9, 122.3, 122.6) ☒
598.01 Urethral stricture due to infective diseases classified elsewhere — (Use additional code to identify urinary incontinence: 625.6, 788.30-788.39. Code first underlying disease: 095.8, 098.2, 120.0-120.9) ☒
599.0 Urinary tract infection, site not specified — (Use additional code to identify organism, such as E. coli: 041.41-041.49) ▽
599.1 Urethral fistula
599.60 Urinary obstruction, unspecified — (Use additional code to identify urinary incontinence: 625.6, 788.30-788.39) ▽
599.69 Urinary obstruction, not elsewhere classified — (Use additional code to identify urinary incontinence: 625.6, 788.30-788.39. Code, if applicable, any causal condition first: 600.0-600.9, with fifth-digit 1)
599.70 Hematuria, unspecified ▽
599.71 Gross hematuria
599.72 Microscopic hematuria
600.01 Hypertrophy (benign) of prostate with urinary obstruction and other lower urinary tract symptoms [LUTS] — (Use additional code to identify symptoms: 599.69, 788.20, 788.21, 788.30-788.39, 788.41, 788.43, 788.62, 788.63, 788.64, 788.65) ♂
600.11 Nodular prostate with urinary obstruction ♂
600.21 Benign localized hyperplasia of prostate with urinary obstruction and other lower urinary tract symptoms [LUTS] — (Use additional code to identify symptoms: 599.69, 788.20, 788.21, 788.30-788.39, 788.41, 788.43, 788.62, 788.63, 788.64, 788.65) ♂
600.91 Hyperplasia of prostate, unspecified, with urinary obstruction and other lower urinary tract symptoms [LUTS] — (Use additional code to identify symptoms: 599.69, 788.20, 788.21, 788.30-788.39, 788.41, 788.43, 788.62, 788.63, 788.64, 788.65) ▽ ♂
618.01 Cystocele without mention of uterine prolapse, midline — (Use additional code to identify urinary incontinence: 625.6, 788.31, 788.33-788.39) ♀
618.02 Cystocele without mention of uterine prolapse, lateral — (Use additional code to identify urinary incontinence: 625.6, 788.31, 788.33-788.39) ♀
618.9 Unspecified genital prolapse — (Use additional code to identify urinary incontinence: 625.6, 788.31, 788.33-788.39) ▽ ♀
625.6 Female stress incontinence ♀
752.61 Hypospadias ♂
752.62 Epispadias ♂
752.63 Congenital chordee ♂
752.64 Micropenis ♂
752.65 Hidden penis ♂
752.69 Other penile anomalies ♂
753.6 Congenital atresia and stenosis of urethra and bladder neck
771.82 Urinary tract infection of newborn — (Use additional code(s) to further specify condition. Use additional code to identify organism: 041.00-041.9)
771.89 Other infections specific to the perinatal period — (Use additional code(s) to further specify condition. Use additional code to identify organism: 041.00-041.9)
788.1 Dysuria
788.20 Unspecified retention of urine — (Code, if applicable, any causal condition first, such as: 600.0-600.9, with fifth digit 1) ▽
788.21 Incomplete bladder emptying — (Code, if applicable, any causal condition first, such as: 600.0-600.9, with fifth digit 1)

788.29 Other specified retention of urine — (Code, if applicable, any causal condition first, such as: 600.0-600.9, with fifth digit 1)
788.41 Urinary frequency — (Code, if applicable, any causal condition first, such as: 600.0-600.9, with fifth digit 1)
788.42 Polyuria — (Code, if applicable, any causal condition first, such as: 600.0-600.9, with fifth digit 1)
788.43 Nocturia — (Code, if applicable, any causal condition first, such as: 600.0-600.9, with fifth digit 1)
788.99 Other symptoms involving urinary system
867.0 Bladder and urethra injury without mention of open wound into cavity

ICD-9-CM Procedural

57.18 Other suprapubic cystostomy
57.19 Other cystotomy

51045

51045 Cystotomy, with insertion of ureteral catheter or stent (separate procedure)

ICD-9-CM Diagnostic

592.1 Calculus of ureter
593.3 Stricture or kinking of ureter
593.4 Other ureteric obstruction
593.5 Hydroureter
593.82 Ureteral fistula
599.60 Urinary obstruction, unspecified — (Use additional code to identify urinary incontinence: 625.6, 788.30-788.39) ▽
599.69 Urinary obstruction, not elsewhere classified — (Use additional code to identify urinary incontinence: 625.6, 788.30-788.39. Code, if applicable, any causal condition first: 600.0-600.9, with fifth-digit 1)
599.70 Hematuria, unspecified ▽
599.71 Gross hematuria
599.72 Microscopic hematuria
867.2 Ureter injury without mention of open wound into cavity
867.3 Ureter injury with open wound into cavity

ICD-9-CM Procedural

57.19 Other cystotomy

51050

51050 Cystolithotomy, cystotomy with removal of calculus, without vesical neck resection

ICD-9-CM Diagnostic

594.1 Other calculus in bladder
594.2 Calculus in urethra
594.8 Other lower urinary tract calculus
594.9 Unspecified calculus of lower urinary tract ▽
599.70 Hematuria, unspecified ▽
599.71 Gross hematuria
599.72 Microscopic hematuria

ICD-9-CM Procedural

57.19 Other cystotomy

51060-51065

51060 Transvesical ureterolithotomy
51065 Cystotomy, with calculus basket extraction and/or ultrasonic or electrohydraulic fragmentation of ureteral calculus

ICD-9-CM Diagnostic

592.1 Calculus of ureter
592.9 Unspecified urinary calculus ▽
594.1 Other calculus in bladder
599.70 Hematuria, unspecified ▽
599.71 Gross hematuria
599.72 Microscopic hematuria
V64.41 Laparoscopic surgical procedure converted to open procedure

ICD-9-CM Procedural

56.2 Ureterotomy
57.19 Other cystotomy

51080

51080 Drainage of perivesical or prevesical space abscess

ICD-9-CM Diagnostic

595.89 Other specified types of cystitis — (Use additional code to identify organism, such as E. coli: 041.41-041.49)
614.3 Acute parametritis and pelvic cellulitis — (Use additional code to identify organism: 041.00-041.09, 041.10-041.19) ♀
614.4 Chronic or unspecified parametritis and pelvic cellulitis — (Use additional code to identify organism: 041.00-041.09, 041.10-041.19) ♀
997.5 Urinary complications — (Use additional code to identify complications)
998.51 Infected postoperative seroma — (Use additional code to identify organism)
998.59 Other postoperative infection — (Use additional code to identify infection)

ICD-9-CM Procedural

59.19 Other incision of perivesical tissue
59.92 Other operations on perirenal or perivesical tissue

51100-51102

51100 Aspiration of bladder; by needle
51101 by trocar or intracatheter
51102 with insertion of suprapubic catheter

ICD-9-CM Diagnostic

185 Malignant neoplasm of prostate ♂
188.0 Malignant neoplasm of trigone of urinary bladder
188.2 Malignant neoplasm of lateral wall of urinary bladder
188.3 Malignant neoplasm of anterior wall of urinary bladder
188.4 Malignant neoplasm of posterior wall of urinary bladder
188.5 Malignant neoplasm of bladder neck
188.6 Malignant neoplasm of ureteric orifice
344.61 Cauda equina syndrome with neurogenic bladder
590.00 Chronic pyelonephritis without lesion of renal medullary necrosis — (Use additional code to identify organism, such as E. coli, 041.41-041.49. Code if applicable, any causal condition first)
590.3 Pyeloureteritis cystica — (Use additional code to identify organism, such as E. coli, 041.41-041.49)
590.81 Pyelitis or pyelonephritis in diseases classified elsewhere — (Use additional code to identify organism, such as E. coli, 041.41-041.49. Code first underlying disease: 016.0) ☒
593.70 Vesicoureteral reflux, unspecified or without reflex nephropathy
595.0 Acute cystitis — (Use additional code to identify organism, such as E. coli: 041.41-041.49)
595.1 Chronic interstitial cystitis — (Use additional code to identify organism, such as E. coli: 041.41-041.49)
595.3 Trigonitis — (Use additional code to identify organism, such as E. coli: 041.41-041.49)
595.4 Cystitis in diseases classified elsewhere — (Use additional code to identify organism, such as E. coli: 041.41-041.49. Code first underlying disease: 006.8, 039.8, 120.0-120.9, 122.3, 122.6) ☒
599.0 Urinary tract infection, site not specified — (Use additional code to identify organism, such as E. coli: 041.41-041.49) ▽
599.70 Hematuria, unspecified ▽
599.71 Gross hematuria
599.72 Microscopic hematuria

618.9 Unspecified genital prolapse — (Use additional code to identify urinary incontinence: 625.6, 788.31, 788.33-788.39) ♀

625.6 Female stress incontinence ♀

752.61 Hypospadias ♂

752.62 Epispadias ♂

752.63 Congenital chordee ♂

752.64 Micropenis ♂

752.65 Hidden penis ♂

752.69 Other penile anomalies ♂

753.6 Congenital atresia and stenosis of urethra and bladder neck

771.82 Urinary tract infection of newborn — (Use additional code(s) to further specify condition. Use additional code to identify organism: 041.00-041.9)

771.89 Other infections specific to the perinatal period — (Use additional code(s) to further specify condition. Use additional code to identify organism: 041.00-041.9)

783.5 Polydipsia

788.1 Dysuria

788.20 Unspecified retention of urine — (Code, if applicable, any causal condition first, such as: 600.0-600.9, with fifth digit 1)

788.21 Incomplete bladder emptying — (Code, if applicable, any causal condition first, such as: 600.0-600.9, with fifth digit 1)

788.29 Other specified retention of urine — (Code, if applicable, any causal condition first, such as: 600.0-600.9, with fifth digit 1)

788.41 Urinary frequency — (Code, if applicable, any causal condition first, such as: 600.0-600.9, with fifth digit 1)

788.42 Polyuria — (Code, if applicable, any causal condition first, such as: 600.0-600.9, with fifth digit 1)

788.43 Nocturia — (Code, if applicable, any causal condition first, such as: 600.0-600.9, with fifth digit 1)

788.63 Urgency of urination — (Code, if applicable, any causal condition first, such as: 600.0-600.9, with fifth digit 1)

867.0 Bladder and urethra injury without mention of open wound into cavity

996.30 Mechanical complication of unspecified genitourinary device, implant, and graft

996.31 Mechanical complication due to urethral (indwelling) catheter

996.39 Mechanical complication of genitourinary device, implant, and graft, other

996.76 Other complications due to genitourinary device, implant, and graft — (Use additional code to identify complication: 338.18-338.19, 338.28-338.29)

997.5 Urinary complications — (Use additional code to identify complications)

ICD-9-CM Procedural

57.11 Percutaneous aspiration of bladder

57.17 Percutaneous cystostomy

57.18 Other suprapubic cystostomy

51500

51500 Excision of urachal cyst or sinus, with or without umbilical hernia repair

ICD-9-CM Diagnostic

551.1 Umbilical hernia with gangrene

552.1 Umbilical hernia with obstruction

553.1 Umbilical hernia without mention of obstruction or gangrene

753.7 Congenital anomalies of urachus

ICD-9-CM Procedural

57.51 Excision of urachus

51520

51520 Cystotomy; for simple excision of vesical neck (separate procedure)

ICD-9-CM Diagnostic

188.5 Malignant neoplasm of bladder neck

198.1 Secondary malignant neoplasm of other urinary organs

223.3 Benign neoplasm of bladder

233.7 Carcinoma in situ of bladder

236.7 Neoplasm of uncertain behavior of bladder

239.4 Neoplasm of unspecified nature of bladder

595.1 Chronic interstitial cystitis — (Use additional code to identify organism, such as E. coli: 041.41-041.49)

598.01 Urethral stricture due to infective diseases classified elsewhere — (Use additional code to identify urinary incontinence: 625.6, 788.30-788.39. Code first underlying disease: 095.8, 098.2, 120.0-120.9)

598.1 Traumatic urethral stricture — (Use additional code to identify urinary incontinence: 625.6, 788.30-788.39)

598.2 Postoperative urethral stricture — (Use additional code to identify urinary incontinence: 625.6, 788.30-788.39)

598.9 Unspecified urethral stricture — (Use additional code to identify urinary incontinence: 625.6, 788.30-788.39)

625.6 Female stress incontinence ♀

788.30 Unspecified urinary incontinence — (Code, if applicable, any causal condition first: 600.0-600.9, with fifth digit 1; 618.00-618.9; 753.23)

788.31 Urge incontinence — (Code, if applicable, any causal condition first: 600.0-600.9, with fifth digit 1; 618.00-618.9; 753.23)

788.32 Stress incontinence, male — (Code, if applicable, any causal condition first: 600.0-600.9, with fifth digit 1; 618.00-618.9; 753.23) ♂

788.33 Mixed incontinence urge and stress (male)(female) — (Code, if applicable, any causal condition first: 600.0-600.9, with fifth digit 1; 618.00-618.9; 753.23)

788.34 Incontinence without sensory awareness — (Code, if applicable, any causal condition first: 600.0-600.9, with fifth digit 1; 618.00-618.9; 753.23)

788.35 Post-void dribbling — (Code, if applicable, any causal condition first: 600.0-600.9, with fifth digit 1; 618.00-618.9; 753.23)

788.36 Nocturnal enuresis — (Code, if applicable, any causal condition first: 600.0-600.9, with fifth digit 1; 618.00-618.9; 753.23)

788.37 Continuous leakage — (Code, if applicable, any causal condition first: 600.0-600.9, with fifth digit 1; 618.00-618.9; 753.23)

788.38 Overflow incontinence — (Code, if applicable, any causal condition first: 600.0-600.9, with fifth digit 1; 618.00-618.9; 753.23)

788.99 Other symptoms involving urinary system

ICD-9-CM Procedural

57.59 Open excision or destruction of other lesion or tissue of bladder

51525

51525 Cystotomy; for excision of bladder diverticulum, single or multiple (separate procedure)

ICD-9-CM Diagnostic

596.3 Diverticulum of bladder — (Use additional code to identify urinary incontinence: 625.6, 788.30-788.39)

625.6 Female stress incontinence ♀

788.30 Unspecified urinary incontinence — (Code, if applicable, any causal condition first: 600.0-600.9, with fifth digit 1; 618.00-618.9; 753.23)

788.31 Urge incontinence — (Code, if applicable, any causal condition first: 600.0-600.9, with fifth digit 1; 618.00-618.9; 753.23)

788.32 Stress incontinence, male — (Code, if applicable, any causal condition first: 600.0-600.9, with fifth digit 1; 618.00-618.9; 753.23) ♂

788.33 Mixed incontinence urge and stress (male)(female) — (Code, if applicable, any causal condition first: 600.0-600.9, with fifth digit 1; 618.00-618.9; 753.23)

788.34 Incontinence without sensory awareness — (Code, if applicable, any causal condition first: 600.0-600.9, with fifth digit 1; 618.00-618.9; 753.23)

788.35 Post-void dribbling — (Code, if applicable, any causal condition first: 600.0-600.9, with fifth digit 1; 618.00-618.9; 753.23)

788.36 Nocturnal enuresis — (Code, if applicable, any causal condition first: 600.0-600.9, with fifth digit 1; 618.00-618.9; 753.23)

788.37 Continuous leakage — (Code, if applicable, any causal condition first: 600.0-600.9, with fifth digit 1; 618.00-618.9; 753.23)
788.38 Overflow incontinence — (Code, if applicable, any causal condition first: 600.0-600.9, with fifth digit 1; 618.00-618.9; 753.23)
788.39 Other urinary incontinence — (Code, if applicable, any causal condition first: 600.0-600.9, with fifth digit 1; 618.00-618.9; 753.23)
788.99 Other symptoms involving urinary system

ICD-9-CM Procedural

57.59 Open excision or destruction of other lesion or tissue of bladder

51530

51530 Cystotomy; for excision of bladder tumor

ICD-9-CM Diagnostic

188.0 Malignant neoplasm of trigone of urinary bladder
188.1 Malignant neoplasm of dome of urinary bladder
188.2 Malignant neoplasm of lateral wall of urinary bladder
188.3 Malignant neoplasm of anterior wall of urinary bladder
188.4 Malignant neoplasm of posterior wall of urinary bladder
188.5 Malignant neoplasm of bladder neck
188.6 Malignant neoplasm of ureteric orifice
188.7 Malignant neoplasm of urachus
188.9 Malignant neoplasm of bladder, part unspecified ▽
198.1 Secondary malignant neoplasm of other urinary organs
223.3 Benign neoplasm of bladder
233.7 Carcinoma in situ of bladder
236.7 Neoplasm of uncertain behavior of bladder
239.4 Neoplasm of unspecified nature of bladder

ICD-9-CM Procedural

57.59 Open excision or destruction of other lesion or tissue of bladder

51535

51535 Cystotomy for excision, incision, or repair of ureterocele

ICD-9-CM Diagnostic

593.70 Vesicoureteral reflux, unspecified or without reflex nephropathy
593.71 Vesicoureteral reflux with reflux nephropathy, unilateral
593.72 Vesicoureteral reflux with reflux nephropathy, bilateral
593.73 Vesicoureteral reflux with reflux nephropathy, NOS ▽
593.89 Other specified disorder of kidney and ureter
753.23 Congenital ureterocele

ICD-9-CM Procedural

56.2 Ureterotomy
56.41 Partial ureterectomy
56.89 Other repair of ureter

51550-51555

51550 Cystectomy, partial; simple
51555 complicated (eg, postradiation, previous surgery, difficult location)

ICD-9-CM Diagnostic

188.0 Malignant neoplasm of trigone of urinary bladder
188.1 Malignant neoplasm of dome of urinary bladder
188.2 Malignant neoplasm of lateral wall of urinary bladder
188.3 Malignant neoplasm of anterior wall of urinary bladder
188.4 Malignant neoplasm of posterior wall of urinary bladder
188.5 Malignant neoplasm of bladder neck
188.6 Malignant neoplasm of ureteric orifice
188.8 Malignant neoplasm of other specified sites of bladder
188.9 Malignant neoplasm of bladder, part unspecified ▽
198.1 Secondary malignant neoplasm of other urinary organs
223.3 Benign neoplasm of bladder
233.7 Carcinoma in situ of bladder
238.8 Neoplasm of uncertain behavior of other specified sites
344.61 Cauda equina syndrome with neurogenic bladder
595.2 Other chronic cystitis — (Use additional code to identify organism, such as E. coli: 041.41-041.49)
596.1 Intestinovesical fistula — (Use additional code to identify urinary incontinence: 625.6, 788.30-788.39)
596.3 Diverticulum of bladder — (Use additional code to identify urinary incontinence: 625.6, 788.30-788.39)
625.6 Female stress incontinence ♀
788.99 Other symptoms involving urinary system
789.30 Abdominal or pelvic swelling, mass or lump, unspecified site ▽
909.2 Late effect of radiation
V45.89 Other postprocedural status

ICD-9-CM Procedural

57.6 Partial cystectomy

51565

51565 Cystectomy, partial, with reimplantation of ureter(s) into bladder (ureteroneocystostomy)

ICD-9-CM Diagnostic

188.0 Malignant neoplasm of trigone of urinary bladder
188.1 Malignant neoplasm of dome of urinary bladder
188.2 Malignant neoplasm of lateral wall of urinary bladder
188.3 Malignant neoplasm of anterior wall of urinary bladder
188.4 Malignant neoplasm of posterior wall of urinary bladder
188.5 Malignant neoplasm of bladder neck
188.6 Malignant neoplasm of ureteric orifice
188.7 Malignant neoplasm of urachus
188.8 Malignant neoplasm of other specified sites of bladder
188.9 Malignant neoplasm of bladder, part unspecified ▽
198.1 Secondary malignant neoplasm of other urinary organs
223.3 Benign neoplasm of bladder
233.7 Carcinoma in situ of bladder
238.8 Neoplasm of uncertain behavior of other specified sites
344.61 Cauda equina syndrome with neurogenic bladder
595.2 Other chronic cystitis — (Use additional code to identify organism, such as E. coli: 041.41-041.49)
596.1 Intestinovesical fistula — (Use additional code to identify urinary incontinence: 625.6, 788.30-788.39)
596.3 Diverticulum of bladder — (Use additional code to identify urinary incontinence: 625.6, 788.30-788.39)
625.6 Female stress incontinence ♀
788.99 Other symptoms involving urinary system
789.30 Abdominal or pelvic swelling, mass or lump, unspecified site ▽
909.2 Late effect of radiation
V45.89 Other postprocedural status

ICD-9-CM Procedural

56.74 Ureteroneocystostomy
57.6 Partial cystectomy

51570-51575

51570 Cystectomy, complete; (separate procedure)
51575 with bilateral pelvic lymphadenectomy, including external iliac, hypogastric, and obturator nodes

ICD-9-CM Diagnostic

185 Malignant neoplasm of prostate ♂
188.0 Malignant neoplasm of trigone of urinary bladder
188.1 Malignant neoplasm of dome of urinary bladder
188.2 Malignant neoplasm of lateral wall of urinary bladder
188.3 Malignant neoplasm of anterior wall of urinary bladder
188.4 Malignant neoplasm of posterior wall of urinary bladder
188.8 Malignant neoplasm of other specified sites of bladder
188.9 Malignant neoplasm of bladder, part unspecified ▽
196.6 Secondary and unspecified malignant neoplasm of intrapelvic lymph nodes
198.1 Secondary malignant neoplasm of other urinary organs
236.7 Neoplasm of uncertain behavior of bladder
236.99 Neoplasm of uncertain behavior of other and unspecified urinary organs
239.5 Neoplasm of unspecified nature of other genitourinary organs
595.1 Chronic interstitial cystitis — (Use additional code to identify organism, such as E. coli: 041.41-041.49)

ICD-9-CM Procedural

40.3 Regional lymph node excision
40.50 Radical excision of lymph nodes, not otherwise specified
57.71 Radical cystectomy
57.79 Other total cystectomy

51580-51585

51580 Cystectomy, complete, with ureterosigmoidostomy or ureterocutaneous transplantations;
51585 with bilateral pelvic lymphadenectomy, including external iliac, hypogastric, and obturator nodes

ICD-9-CM Diagnostic

185 Malignant neoplasm of prostate ♂
188.0 Malignant neoplasm of trigone of urinary bladder
188.1 Malignant neoplasm of dome of urinary bladder
188.2 Malignant neoplasm of lateral wall of urinary bladder
188.3 Malignant neoplasm of anterior wall of urinary bladder
188.4 Malignant neoplasm of posterior wall of urinary bladder
188.8 Malignant neoplasm of other specified sites of bladder
188.9 Malignant neoplasm of bladder, part unspecified ▽
196.6 Secondary and unspecified malignant neoplasm of intrapelvic lymph nodes
198.1 Secondary malignant neoplasm of other urinary organs
236.7 Neoplasm of uncertain behavior of bladder
239.4 Neoplasm of unspecified nature of bladder
595.1 Chronic interstitial cystitis — (Use additional code to identify organism, such as E. coli: 041.41-041.49)

ICD-9-CM Procedural

40.3 Regional lymph node excision
40.50 Radical excision of lymph nodes, not otherwise specified
56.51 Formation of cutaneous uretero-ileostomy
56.61 Formation of other cutaneous ureterostomy
56.71 Urinary diversion to intestine
57.71 Radical cystectomy

51590-51595

51590 Cystectomy, complete, with ureteroileal conduit or sigmoid bladder, including intestine anastomosis;
51595 with bilateral pelvic lymphadenectomy, including external iliac, hypogastric, and obturator nodes

ICD-9-CM Diagnostic

185 Malignant neoplasm of prostate ♂
188.0 Malignant neoplasm of trigone of urinary bladder
188.1 Malignant neoplasm of dome of urinary bladder
188.2 Malignant neoplasm of lateral wall of urinary bladder
188.3 Malignant neoplasm of anterior wall of urinary bladder
188.4 Malignant neoplasm of posterior wall of urinary bladder
188.8 Malignant neoplasm of other specified sites of bladder
188.9 Malignant neoplasm of bladder, part unspecified ▽
196.6 Secondary and unspecified malignant neoplasm of intrapelvic lymph nodes
198.1 Secondary malignant neoplasm of other urinary organs
236.7 Neoplasm of uncertain behavior of bladder
239.4 Neoplasm of unspecified nature of bladder

ICD-9-CM Procedural

40.3 Regional lymph node excision
40.50 Radical excision of lymph nodes, not otherwise specified
56.51 Formation of cutaneous uretero-ileostomy
56.71 Urinary diversion to intestine
57.71 Radical cystectomy

51596

51596 Cystectomy, complete, with continent diversion, any open technique, using any segment of small and/or large intestine to construct neobladder

ICD-9-CM Diagnostic

185 Malignant neoplasm of prostate ♂
187.8 Malignant neoplasm of other specified sites of male genital organs ♂
187.9 Malignant neoplasm of male genital organ, site unspecified ▽ ♂
188.0 Malignant neoplasm of trigone of urinary bladder
188.1 Malignant neoplasm of dome of urinary bladder
188.2 Malignant neoplasm of lateral wall of urinary bladder
188.3 Malignant neoplasm of anterior wall of urinary bladder
188.4 Malignant neoplasm of posterior wall of urinary bladder
188.8 Malignant neoplasm of other specified sites of bladder
188.9 Malignant neoplasm of bladder, part unspecified ▽
198.1 Secondary malignant neoplasm of other urinary organs
236.7 Neoplasm of uncertain behavior of bladder
239.4 Neoplasm of unspecified nature of bladder
595.1 Chronic interstitial cystitis — (Use additional code to identify organism, such as E. coli: 041.41-041.49)

ICD-9-CM Procedural

56.51 Formation of cutaneous uretero-ileostomy
57.71 Radical cystectomy

51597

51597 Pelvic exenteration, complete, for vesical, prostatic or urethral malignancy, with removal of bladder and ureteral transplantations, with or without hysterectomy and/or abdominoperineal resection of rectum and colon and colostomy, or any combination thereof

ICD-9-CM Diagnostic

185 Malignant neoplasm of prostate ♂
188.0 Malignant neoplasm of trigone of urinary bladder
188.1 Malignant neoplasm of dome of urinary bladder

188.2 Malignant neoplasm of lateral wall of urinary bladder
188.3 Malignant neoplasm of anterior wall of urinary bladder
188.4 Malignant neoplasm of posterior wall of urinary bladder
188.5 Malignant neoplasm of bladder neck
188.6 Malignant neoplasm of ureteric orifice
188.8 Malignant neoplasm of other specified sites of bladder
188.9 Malignant neoplasm of bladder, part unspecified ▽
189.3 Malignant neoplasm of urethra
197.5 Secondary malignant neoplasm of large intestine and rectum
198.1 Secondary malignant neoplasm of other urinary organs
198.6 Secondary malignant neoplasm of ovary ♀
198.82 Secondary malignant neoplasm of genital organs

ICD-9-CM Procedural

40.3 Regional lymph node excision
40.54 Radical groin dissection
46.13 Permanent colostomy
48.50 Abdominoperineal resection of the rectum, not otherwise specified
48.52 Open abdominoperineal resection of the rectum
48.59 Other abdominoperineal resection of the rectum
56.61 Formation of other cutaneous ureterostomy
56.71 Urinary diversion to intestine
57.71 Radical cystectomy
68.8 Pelvic evisceration ♀

51600-51610

51600 Injection procedure for cystography or voiding urethrocystography
51605 Injection procedure and placement of chain for contrast and/or chain urethrocystography
51610 Injection procedure for retrograde urethrocystography

ICD-9-CM Diagnostic

098.0 Gonococcal infection (acute) of lower genitourinary tract
185 Malignant neoplasm of prostate ♂
188.0 Malignant neoplasm of trigone of urinary bladder
188.1 Malignant neoplasm of dome of urinary bladder
188.2 Malignant neoplasm of lateral wall of urinary bladder
188.3 Malignant neoplasm of anterior wall of urinary bladder
188.4 Malignant neoplasm of posterior wall of urinary bladder
188.5 Malignant neoplasm of bladder neck
188.6 Malignant neoplasm of ureteric orifice
188.7 Malignant neoplasm of urachus
188.8 Malignant neoplasm of other specified sites of bladder
188.9 Malignant neoplasm of bladder, part unspecified ▽
199.0 Disseminated malignant neoplasm
199.1 Other malignant neoplasm of unspecified site
223.3 Benign neoplasm of bladder
223.81 Benign neoplasm of urethra
223.89 Benign neoplasm of other specified sites of urinary organs
239.4 Neoplasm of unspecified nature of bladder
344.61 Cauda equina syndrome with neurogenic bladder
357.4 Polyneuropathy in other diseases classified elsewhere — (Code first underlying disease, as: 032.0-032.9,135, 251.2, 265.0, 265.2, 266.0-266.9, 277.1, 277.30-277.39, 585.9, 586) ☒
585.1 Chronic kidney disease, Stage I — (Use additional code to identify kidney transplant status, if applicable: V42.0. Use additional code to identify manifestation: 357.4, 420.0. Code first hypertensive chronic kidney disease, if applicable: 403.00-403.91, 404.00-404.93)
585.2 Chronic kidney disease, Stage II (mild) — (Use additional code to identify kidney transplant status, if applicable: V42.0. Use additional code to identify manifestation: 357.4, 420.0. Code first hypertensive chronic kidney disease, if applicable: 403.00-403.91, 404.00-404.93)
585.3 Chronic kidney disease, Stage III (moderate) — (Use additional code to identify kidney transplant status, if applicable: V42.0. Use additional code to identify manifestation: 357.4, 420.0. Code first hypertensive chronic kidney disease, if applicable: 403.00-403.91, 404.00-404.93)
585.4 Chronic kidney disease, Stage IV (severe) — (Use additional code to identify kidney transplant status, if applicable: V42.0. Use additional code to identify manifestation: 357.4, 420.0. Code first hypertensive chronic kidney disease, if applicable: 403.00-403.91, 404.00-404.93)
585.5 Chronic kidney disease, Stage V — (Use additional code to identify kidney transplant status, if applicable: V42.0. Use additional code to identify manifestation: 357.4, 420.0. Code first hypertensive chronic kidney disease, if applicable: 403.00-403.91, 404.00-404.93)
585.6 End stage renal disease — (Use additional code to identify kidney transplant status, if applicable: V42.0. Use additional code to identify manifestation: 357.4, 420.0. Code first hypertensive chronic kidney disease, if applicable: 403.00-403.91, 404.00-404.93)
585.9 Chronic kidney disease, unspecified — (Use additional code to identify kidney transplant status, if applicable: V42.0. Use additional code to identify manifestation: 357.4, 420.0. Code first hypertensive chronic kidney disease, if applicable: 403.00-403.91, 404.00-404.93) ▽
586 Unspecified renal failure ▽
590.10 Acute pyelonephritis without lesion of renal medullary necrosis — (Use additional code to identify organism, such as E. coli, 041.40-041.49)
590.9 Unspecified infection of kidney — (Use additional code to identify organism, such as E. coli, 041.41-041.49) ▽
591 Hydronephrosis
592.0 Calculus of kidney
592.1 Calculus of ureter
592.9 Unspecified urinary calculus ▽
593.4 Other ureteric obstruction
593.70 Vesicoureteral reflux, unspecified or without reflex nephropathy
593.71 Vesicoureteral reflux with reflux nephropathy, unilateral
593.72 Vesicoureteral reflux with reflux nephropathy, bilateral
593.73 Vesicoureteral reflux with reflux nephropathy, NOS ▽
593.9 Unspecified disorder of kidney and ureter ▽
594.0 Calculus in diverticulum of bladder
594.1 Other calculus in bladder
594.2 Calculus in urethra
594.8 Other lower urinary tract calculus
594.9 Unspecified calculus of lower urinary tract ▽
595.0 Acute cystitis — (Use additional code to identify organism, such as E. coli: 041.41-041.49)
595.2 Other chronic cystitis — (Use additional code to identify organism, such as E. coli: 041.41-041.49)
595.3 Trigonitis — (Use additional code to identify organism, such as E. coli: 041.41-041.49)
595.4 Cystitis in diseases classified elsewhere — (Use additional code to identify organism, such as E. coli: 041.41-041.49. Code first underlying disease: 006.8, 039.8, 120.0-120.9, 122.3, 122.6) ☒
595.81 Cystitis cystica — (Use additional code to identify organism, such as E. coli: 041.41-041.49)
595.82 Irradiation cystitis — (Use additional code to identify organism, such as E. coli: 041.41-041.49. Use additional E code to identify cause)
595.89 Other specified types of cystitis — (Use additional code to identify organism, such as E. coli: 041.41-041.49)
595.9 Unspecified cystitis — (Use additional code to identify organism, such as E. coli: 041.41-041.49) ▽
596.1 Intestinovesical fistula — (Use additional code to identify urinary incontinence: 625.6, 788.30-788.39)
596.2 Vesical fistula, not elsewhere classified — (Use additional code to identify urinary incontinence: 625.6, 788.30-788.39)

596.3 Diverticulum of bladder — (Use additional code to identify urinary incontinence: 625.6, 788.30-788.39)
596.4 Atony of bladder — (Use additional code to identify urinary incontinence: 625.6, 788.30-788.39)
596.51 Hypertonicity of bladder — (Use additional code to identify urinary incontinence: 625.6, 788.30-788.39)
596.52 Low bladder compliance — (Use additional code to identify urinary incontinence: 625.6, 788.30-788.39)
596.53 Paralysis of bladder — (Use additional code to identify urinary incontinence: 625.6, 788.30-788.39)
596.54 Neurogenic bladder, NOS — (Use additional code to identify urinary incontinence: 625.6, 788.30-788.39) ▽
596.55 Detrusor sphincter dyssynergia — (Use additional code to identify urinary incontinence: 625.6, 788.30-788.39)
596.59 Other functional disorder of bladder — (Use additional code to identify urinary incontinence: 625.6, 788.30-788.39)
597.81 Urethral syndrome NOS ▽
597.89 Other urethritis
598.00 Urethral stricture due to unspecified infection — (Use additional code to identify urinary incontinence: 625.6, 788.30-788.39) ▽
598.01 Urethral stricture due to infective diseases classified elsewhere — (Use additional code to identify urinary incontinence: 625.6, 788.30-788.39. Code first underlying disease: 095.8, 098.2, 120.0-120.9) ☒
598.1 Traumatic urethral stricture — (Use additional code to identify urinary incontinence: 625.6, 788.30-788.39)
598.2 Postoperative urethral stricture — (Use additional code to identify urinary incontinence: 625.6, 788.30-788.39)
598.8 Other specified causes of urethral stricture — (Use additional code to identify urinary incontinence: 625.6, 788.30-788.39)
598.9 Unspecified urethral stricture — (Use additional code to identify urinary incontinence: 625.6, 788.30-788.39) ▽
599.0 Urinary tract infection, site not specified — (Use additional code to identify organism, such as E. coli: 041.41-041.49) ▽
599.1 Urethral fistula
599.60 Urinary obstruction, unspecified — (Use additional code to identify urinary incontinence: 625.6, 788.30-788.39) ▽
599.69 Urinary obstruction, not elsewhere classified — (Use additional code to identify urinary incontinence: 625.6, 788.30-788.39. Code, if applicable, any causal condition first: 600.0-600.9, with fifth-digit 1)
599.70 Hematuria, unspecified ▽
599.71 Gross hematuria
599.72 Microscopic hematuria
599.81 Urethral hypermobility — (Use additional code to identify urinary incontinence: 625.6, 788.30-788.39)
599.82 Intrinsic (urethral) sphincter deficiency (ISD) — (Use additional code to identify urinary incontinence: 625.6, 788.30-788.39)
599.83 Urethral instability — (Use additional code to identify urinary incontinence: 625.6, 788.30-788.39)
599.84 Other specified disorders of urethra — (Use additional code to identify urinary incontinence: 625.6, 788.30-788.39)
599.89 Other specified disorders of urinary tract — (Use additional code to identify urinary incontinence: 625.6, 788.30-788.39)
600.00 Hypertrophy (benign) of prostate without urinary obstruction and other lower urinary tract symptoms [LUTS] ♂
600.01 Hypertrophy (benign) of prostate with urinary obstruction and other lower urinary tract symptoms [LUTS] — (Use additional code to identify symptoms: 599.69, 788.20, 788.21, 788.30-788.39, 788.41, 788.43, 788.62, 788.63, 788.64, 788.65) ♂
600.10 Nodular prostate without urinary obstruction ♂
600.11 Nodular prostate with urinary obstruction ♂
600.20 Benign localized hyperplasia of prostate without urinary obstruction and other lower urinary tract symptoms [LUTS] ♂
600.21 Benign localized hyperplasia of prostate with urinary obstruction and other lower urinary tract symptoms [LUTS] — (Use additional code to identify symptoms: 599.69, 788.20, 788.21, 788.30-788.39, 788.41, 788.43, 788.62, 788.63, 788.64, 788.65) ♂
600.3 Cyst of prostate ♂
600.90 Hyperplasia of prostate, unspecified, without urinary obstruction and other lower urinary tract symptoms [LUTS] ▽ ♂
600.91 Hyperplasia of prostate, unspecified, with urinary obstruction and other lower urinary tract symptoms [LUTS] — (Use additional code to identify symptoms: 599.69, 788.20, 788.21, 788.30-788.39, 788.41, 788.43, 788.62, 788.63, 788.64, 788.65) ▽ ♂
601.1 Chronic prostatitis — (Use additional code to identify organism: 041.0, 041.1) ♂
601.9 Unspecified prostatitis — (Use additional code to identify organism: 041.0, 041.1) ▽ ♂
618.01 Cystocele without mention of uterine prolapse, midline — (Use additional code to identify urinary incontinence: 625.6, 788.31, 788.33-788.39) ♀
618.02 Cystocele without mention of uterine prolapse, lateral — (Use additional code to identify urinary incontinence: 625.6, 788.31, 788.33-788.39) ♀
618.03 Urethrocele without mention of uterine prolapse — (Use additional code to identify urinary incontinence: 625.6, 788.31, 788.33-788.39) ♀
619.0 Urinary-genital tract fistula, female ♀
625.6 Female stress incontinence ♀
753.5 Exstrophy of urinary bladder
753.6 Congenital atresia and stenosis of urethra and bladder neck
753.8 Other specified congenital anomaly of bladder and urethra
753.9 Unspecified congenital anomaly of urinary system ▽
788.0 Renal colic
788.1 Dysuria
788.21 Incomplete bladder emptying — (Code, if applicable, any causal condition first, such as: 600.0-600.9, with fifth digit 1)
788.29 Other specified retention of urine — (Code, if applicable, any causal condition first, such as: 600.0-600.9, with fifth digit 1)
788.31 Urge incontinence — (Code, if applicable, any causal condition first: 600.0-600.9, with fifth digit 1; 618.00-618.9; 753.23)
788.32 Stress incontinence, male — (Code, if applicable, any causal condition first: 600.0-600.9, with fifth digit 1; 618.00-618.9; 753.23) ♂
788.33 Mixed incontinence urge and stress (male)(female) — (Code, if applicable, any causal condition first: 600.0-600.9, with fifth digit 1; 618.00-618.9; 753.23)
788.34 Incontinence without sensory awareness — (Code, if applicable, any causal condition first: 600.0-600.9, with fifth digit 1; 618.00-618.9; 753.23)
788.35 Post-void dribbling — (Code, if applicable, any causal condition first: 600.0-600.9, with fifth digit 1; 618.00-618.9; 753.23)
788.36 Nocturnal enuresis — (Code, if applicable, any causal condition first: 600.0-600.9, with fifth digit 1; 618.00-618.9; 753.23)
788.37 Continuous leakage — (Code, if applicable, any causal condition first: 600.0-600.9, with fifth digit 1; 618.00-618.9; 753.23)
788.38 Overflow incontinence — (Code, if applicable, any causal condition first: 600.0-600.9, with fifth digit 1; 618.00-618.9; 753.23)
788.39 Other urinary incontinence — (Code, if applicable, any causal condition first: 600.0-600.9, with fifth digit 1; 618.00-618.9; 753.23)
788.41 Urinary frequency — (Code, if applicable, any causal condition first, such as: 600.0-600.9, with fifth digit 1)
788.42 Polyuria — (Code, if applicable, any causal condition first, such as: 600.0-600.9, with fifth digit 1)
788.43 Nocturia — (Code, if applicable, any causal condition first, such as: 600.0-600.9, with fifth digit 1)
788.5 Oliguria and anuria
788.61 Splitting of urinary stream — (Code, if applicable, any causal condition first, such as: 600.0-600.9, with fifth digit 1)
788.62 Slowing of urinary stream — (Code, if applicable, any causal condition first, such as: 600.0-600.9, with fifth digit 1)

788.63 Urgency of urination — (Code, if applicable, any causal condition first, such as: 600.0-600.9, with fifth digit 1)
788.64 Urinary hesitancy — (Code, if applicable, any causal condition first, such as: 600.0-600.9, with fifth digit 1)
788.65 Straining on urination — (Code, if applicable, any causal condition first, such as: 600.0-600.9, with fifth digit 1)
788.69 Other abnormality of urination — (Code, if applicable, any causal condition first, such as: 600.0-600.9, with fifth digit 1)
788.7 Urethral discharge
788.8 Extravasation of urine
788.91 Functional urinary incontinence
788.99 Other symptoms involving urinary system
789.03 Abdominal pain, right lower quadrant
789.04 Abdominal pain, left lower quadrant
789.05 Abdominal pain, periumbilic
789.07 Abdominal pain, generalized
789.09 Abdominal pain, other specified site
789.30 Abdominal or pelvic swelling, mass or lump, unspecified site ▽
789.33 Abdominal or pelvic swelling, mass, or lump, right lower quadrant
789.34 Abdominal or pelvic swelling, mass, or lump, left lower quadrant
789.35 Abdominal or pelvic swelling, mass or lump, periumbilic
789.37 Abdominal or pelvic swelling, mass, or lump, generalized
789.39 Abdominal or pelvic swelling, mass, or lump, other specified site
793.5 Nonspecific (abnormal) findings on radiological and other examination of genitourinary organs
867.0 Bladder and urethra injury without mention of open wound into cavity
867.1 Bladder and urethra injury with open wound into cavity
959.12 Other injury of abdomen
959.19 Other injury of other sites of trunk
997.5 Urinary complications — (Use additional code to identify complications)
V10.51 Personal history of malignant neoplasm of bladder
V42.0 Kidney replaced by transplant
V45.89 Other postprocedural status
V55.5 Attention to cystostomy
V55.6 Attention to other artificial opening of urinary tract
V67.00 Follow-up examination, following unspecified surgery ▽
V67.09 Follow-up examination, following other surgery
V67.1 Radiotherapy follow-up examination

ICD-9-CM Procedural

87.76 Retrograde cystourethrogram
87.77 Other cystogram

HCPCS Level II Supplies & Services

A4641 Radiopharmaceutical, diagnostic, not otherwise classified

51700

51700 Bladder irrigation, simple, lavage and/or instillation

ICD-9-CM Diagnostic

185 Malignant neoplasm of prostate ♂
188.0 Malignant neoplasm of trigone of urinary bladder
188.1 Malignant neoplasm of dome of urinary bladder
188.2 Malignant neoplasm of lateral wall of urinary bladder
188.3 Malignant neoplasm of anterior wall of urinary bladder
188.4 Malignant neoplasm of posterior wall of urinary bladder
188.5 Malignant neoplasm of bladder neck
188.6 Malignant neoplasm of ureteric orifice
188.7 Malignant neoplasm of urachus
188.8 Malignant neoplasm of other specified sites of bladder
188.9 Malignant neoplasm of bladder, part unspecified ▽
233.7 Carcinoma in situ of bladder
344.61 Cauda equina syndrome with neurogenic bladder
593.3 Stricture or kinking of ureter
595.0 Acute cystitis — (Use additional code to identify organism, such as E. coli: 041.41-041.49)
595.1 Chronic interstitial cystitis — (Use additional code to identify organism, such as E. coli: 041.41-041.49)
595.2 Other chronic cystitis — (Use additional code to identify organism, such as E. coli: 041.41-041.49)
595.3 Trigonitis — (Use additional code to identify organism, such as E. coli: 041.41-041.49)
595.4 Cystitis in diseases classified elsewhere — (Use additional code to identify organism, such as E. coli: 041.41-041.49. Code first underlying disease: 006.8, 039.8, 120.0-120.9, 122.3, 122.6) ☒
595.81 Cystitis cystica — (Use additional code to identify organism, such as E. coli: 041.41-041.49)
595.82 Irradiation cystitis — (Use additional code to identify organism, such as E. coli: 041.41-041.49. Use additional E code to identify cause)
595.89 Other specified types of cystitis — (Use additional code to identify organism, such as E. coli: 041.41-041.49)
595.9 Unspecified cystitis — (Use additional code to identify organism, such as E. coli: 041.41-041.49) ▽
596.0 Bladder neck obstruction — (Use additional code to identify urinary incontinence: 625.6, 788.30-788.39)
596.4 Atony of bladder — (Use additional code to identify urinary incontinence: 625.6, 788.30-788.39)
596.7 Hemorrhage into bladder wall — (Use additional code to identify urinary incontinence: 625.6, 788.30-788.39)
596.89 Other specified disorders of bladder
597.80 Unspecified urethritis ▽
597.81 Urethral syndrome NOS ▽
598.00 Urethral stricture due to unspecified infection — (Use additional code to identify urinary incontinence: 625.6, 788.30-788.39) ▽
598.01 Urethral stricture due to infective diseases classified elsewhere — (Use additional code to identify urinary incontinence: 625.6, 788.30-788.39. Code first underlying disease: 095.8, 098.2, 120.0-120.9) ☒
598.1 Traumatic urethral stricture — (Use additional code to identify urinary incontinence: 625.6, 788.30-788.39)
598.2 Postoperative urethral stricture — (Use additional code to identify urinary incontinence: 625.6, 788.30-788.39)
598.8 Other specified causes of urethral stricture — (Use additional code to identify urinary incontinence: 625.6, 788.30-788.39)
598.9 Unspecified urethral stricture — (Use additional code to identify urinary incontinence: 625.6, 788.30-788.39) ▽
599.0 Urinary tract infection, site not specified — (Use additional code to identify organism, such as E. coli: 041.41-041.49) ▽
599.70 Hematuria, unspecified ▽
599.71 Gross hematuria
599.72 Microscopic hematuria
600.01 Hypertrophy (benign) of prostate with urinary obstruction and other lower urinary tract symptoms [LUTS] — (Use additional code to identify symptoms: 599.69, 788.20, 788.21, 788.30-788.39, 788.41, 788.43, 788.62, 788.63, 788.64, 788.65) ♂
600.11 Nodular prostate with urinary obstruction ♂
600.21 Benign localized hyperplasia of prostate with urinary obstruction and other lower urinary tract symptoms [LUTS] — (Use additional code to identify symptoms: 599.69, 788.20, 788.21, 788.30-788.39, 788.41, 788.43, 788.62, 788.63, 788.64, 788.65) ♂
600.3 Cyst of prostate ♂
600.91 Hyperplasia of prostate, unspecified, with urinary obstruction and other lower urinary tract symptoms [LUTS] — (Use additional code to identify symptoms: 599.69, 788.20, 788.21, 788.30-788.39, 788.41, 788.43, 788.62, 788.63, 788.64, 788.65) ▽ ♂
601.1 Chronic prostatitis — (Use additional code to identify organism: 041.0, 041.1) ♂

618.01 Cystocele without mention of uterine prolapse, midline — (Use additional code to identify urinary incontinence: 625.6, 788.31, 788.33-788.39) ♀

618.02 Cystocele without mention of uterine prolapse, lateral — (Use additional code to identify urinary incontinence: 625.6, 788.31, 788.33-788.39) ♀

618.03 Urethrocele without mention of uterine prolapse — (Use additional code to identify urinary incontinence: 625.6, 788.31, 788.33-788.39) ♀

625.6 Female stress incontinence ♀

788.21 Incomplete bladder emptying — (Code, if applicable, any causal condition first, such as: 600.0-600.9, with fifth digit 1)

788.29 Other specified retention of urine — (Code, if applicable, any causal condition first, such as: 600.0-600.9, with fifth digit 1)

788.41 Urinary frequency — (Code, if applicable, any causal condition first, such as: 600.0-600.9, with fifth digit 1)

788.42 Polyuria — (Code, if applicable, any causal condition first, such as: 600.0-600.9, with fifth digit 1)

788.99 Other symptoms involving urinary system

V55.5 Attention to cystostomy

ICD-9-CM Procedural

96.47 Irrigation of cystostomy

96.49 Other genitourinary instillation

HCPCS Level II Supplies & Services

A4313 Insertion tray without drainage bag with indwelling catheter, Foley type, 3-way, for continuous irrigation

51701-51703

51701 Insertion of non-indwelling bladder catheter (eg, straight catheterization for residual urine)

51702 Insertion of temporary indwelling bladder catheter; simple (eg, Foley)

51703 complicated (eg, altered anatomy, fractured catheter/balloon)

ICD-9-CM Diagnostic

185 Malignant neoplasm of prostate ♂

188.0 Malignant neoplasm of trigone of urinary bladder

188.1 Malignant neoplasm of dome of urinary bladder

188.2 Malignant neoplasm of lateral wall of urinary bladder

188.3 Malignant neoplasm of anterior wall of urinary bladder

188.4 Malignant neoplasm of posterior wall of urinary bladder

188.5 Malignant neoplasm of bladder neck

188.6 Malignant neoplasm of ureteric orifice

188.7 Malignant neoplasm of urachus

188.8 Malignant neoplasm of other specified sites of bladder

188.9 Malignant neoplasm of bladder, part unspecified ▽

189.0 Malignant neoplasm of kidney, except pelvis

189.1 Malignant neoplasm of renal pelvis

189.2 Malignant neoplasm of ureter

189.3 Malignant neoplasm of urethra

189.4 Malignant neoplasm of paraurethral glands

189.8 Malignant neoplasm of other specified sites of urinary organs

209.24 Malignant carcinoid tumor of the kidney — (Code first any associated multiple endocrine neoplasia syndrome: 258.01-258.03; Use additional code to identify associated endocrine syndrome, as: carcinoid syndrome: 259.2)

233.7 Carcinoma in situ of bladder

344.61 Cauda equina syndrome with neurogenic bladder

589.9 Unspecified small kidney ▽

593.3 Stricture or kinking of ureter

594.0 Calculus in diverticulum of bladder

594.1 Other calculus in bladder

594.2 Calculus in urethra

594.8 Other lower urinary tract calculus

595.0 Acute cystitis — (Use additional code to identify organism, such as E. coli: 041.41-041.49)

595.1 Chronic interstitial cystitis — (Use additional code to identify organism, such as E. coli: 041.41-041.49)

595.2 Other chronic cystitis — (Use additional code to identify organism, such as E. coli: 041.41-041.49)

595.3 Trigonitis — (Use additional code to identify organism, such as E. coli: 041.41-041.49)

595.4 Cystitis in diseases classified elsewhere — (Use additional code to identify organism, such as E. coli: 041.41-041.49. Code first underlying disease: 006.8, 039.8, 120.0-120.9, 122.3, 122.6) ☒

595.81 Cystitis cystica — (Use additional code to identify organism, such as E. coli: 041.41-041.49)

595.89 Other specified types of cystitis — (Use additional code to identify organism, such as E. coli: 041.41-041.49)

596.4 Atony of bladder — (Use additional code to identify urinary incontinence: 625.6, 788.30-788.39)

596.51 Hypertonicity of bladder — (Use additional code to identify urinary incontinence: 625.6, 788.30-788.39)

596.52 Low bladder compliance — (Use additional code to identify urinary incontinence: 625.6, 788.30-788.39)

596.53 Paralysis of bladder — (Use additional code to identify urinary incontinence: 625.6, 788.30-788.39)

596.89 Other specified disorders of bladder

597.80 Unspecified urethritis ▽

597.81 Urethral syndrome NOS ▽

598.00 Urethral stricture due to unspecified infection — (Use additional code to identify urinary incontinence: 625.6, 788.30-788.39) ▽

598.01 Urethral stricture due to infective diseases classified elsewhere — (Use additional code to identify urinary incontinence: 625.6, 788.30-788.39. Code first underlying disease: 095.8, 098.2, 120.0-120.9) ☒

598.1 Traumatic urethral stricture — (Use additional code to identify urinary incontinence: 625.6, 788.30-788.39)

598.2 Postoperative urethral stricture — (Use additional code to identify urinary incontinence: 625.6, 788.30-788.39)

598.8 Other specified causes of urethral stricture — (Use additional code to identify urinary incontinence: 625.6, 788.30-788.39)

598.9 Unspecified urethral stricture — (Use additional code to identify urinary incontinence: 625.6, 788.30-788.39) ▽

599.1 Urethral fistula

599.2 Urethral diverticulum

599.3 Urethral caruncle

599.4 Urethral false passage

599.5 Prolapsed urethral mucosa

599.70 Hematuria, unspecified ▽

599.71 Gross hematuria

599.72 Microscopic hematuria

600.00 Hypertrophy (benign) of prostate without urinary obstruction and other lower urinary tract symptoms [LUTS] ♂

600.01 Hypertrophy (benign) of prostate with urinary obstruction and other lower urinary tract symptoms [LUTS] — (Use additional code to identify symptoms: 599.69, 788.20, 788.21, 788.30-788.39, 788.41, 788.43, 788.62, 788.63, 788.64, 788.65) ♂

600.10 Nodular prostate without urinary obstruction ♂

600.11 Nodular prostate with urinary obstruction ♂

600.20 Benign localized hyperplasia of prostate without urinary obstruction and other lower urinary tract symptoms [LUTS] ♂

600.21 Benign localized hyperplasia of prostate with urinary obstruction and other lower urinary tract symptoms [LUTS] — (Use additional code to identify symptoms: 599.69, 788.20, 788.21, 788.30-788.39, 788.41, 788.43, 788.62, 788.63, 788.64, 788.65) ♂

600.3 Cyst of prostate ♂

600.90 Hyperplasia of prostate, unspecified, without urinary obstruction and other lower urinary tract symptoms [LUTS] ▼ ♂

600.91 Hyperplasia of prostate, unspecified, with urinary obstruction and other lower urinary tract symptoms [LUTS] — (Use additional code to identify symptoms: 599.69, 788.20, 788.21, 788.30-788.39, 788.41, 788.43, 788.62, 788.63, 788.64, 788.65) ▼ ♂

601.1 Chronic prostatitis — (Use additional code to identify organism: 041.0, 041.1) ♂

618.00 Unspecified prolapse of vaginal walls without mention of uterine prolapse — (Use additional code to identify urinary incontinence: 625.6, 788.31, 788.33-788.39) ▼ ♀

618.01 Cystocele without mention of uterine prolapse, midline — (Use additional code to identify urinary incontinence: 625.6, 788.31, 788.33-788.39) ♀

618.02 Cystocele without mention of uterine prolapse, lateral — (Use additional code to identify urinary incontinence: 625.6, 788.31, 788.33-788.39) ♀

618.03 Urethrocele without mention of uterine prolapse — (Use additional code to identify urinary incontinence: 625.6, 788.31, 788.33-788.39) ♀

618.04 Rectocele without mention of uterine prolapse — (Use additional code to identify urinary incontinence: 625.6, 788.31, 788.33-788.39) (Use additional code for any associated fecal incontinence: 787.60-787.63) ♀

618.05 Perineocele without mention of uterine prolapse — (Use additional code to identify urinary incontinence: 625.6, 788.31, 788.33-788.39) ♀

618.09 Other prolapse of vaginal walls without mention of uterine prolapse — (Use additional code to identify urinary incontinence: 625.6, 788.31, 788.33-788.39) ♀

618.81 Incompetence or weakening of pubocervical tissue — (Use additional code to identify urinary incontinence: 625.6, 788.31, 788.33-788.39) ♀

618.82 Incompetence or weakening of rectovaginal tissue — (Use additional code to identify urinary incontinence: 625.6, 788.31, 788.33-788.39) ♀

618.83 Pelvic muscle wasting — (Use additional code to identify urinary incontinence: 625.6, 788.31, 788.33-788.39) ♀

618.89 Other specified genital prolapse — (Use additional code to identify urinary incontinence: 625.6, 788.31, 788.33-788.39) ♀

625.6 Female stress incontinence ♀

788.1 Dysuria

788.21 Incomplete bladder emptying — (Code, if applicable, any causal condition first, such as: 600.0-600.9, with fifth digit 1)

788.29 Other specified retention of urine — (Code, if applicable, any causal condition first, such as: 600.0-600.9, with fifth digit 1)

788.30 Unspecified urinary incontinence — (Code, if applicable, any causal condition first: 600.0-600.9, with fifth digit 1; 618.00-618.9; 753.23) ▼

788.37 Continuous leakage — (Code, if applicable, any causal condition first: 600.0-600.9, with fifth digit 1; 618.00-618.9; 753.23)

788.38 Overflow incontinence — (Code, if applicable, any causal condition first: 600.0-600.9, with fifth digit 1; 618.00-618.9; 753.23)

788.41 Urinary frequency — (Code, if applicable, any causal condition first, such as: 600.0-600.9, with fifth digit 1)

788.42 Polyuria — (Code, if applicable, any causal condition first, such as: 600.0-600.9, with fifth digit 1)

788.91 Functional urinary incontinence

788.99 Other symptoms involving urinary system

867.0 Bladder and urethra injury without mention of open wound into cavity

867.1 Bladder and urethra injury with open wound into cavity

952.4 Cauda equina spinal cord injury without spinal bone injury

997.5 Urinary complications — (Use additional code to identify complications)

ICD-9-CM Procedural

57.94 Insertion of indwelling urinary catheter

57.95 Replacement of indwelling urinary catheter

57.99 Other operations on bladder

HCPCS Level II Supplies & Services

A4310 Insertion tray without drainage bag and without catheter (accessories only)

51705-51710

51705 Change of cystostomy tube; simple

51710 complicated

ICD-9-CM Diagnostic

185 Malignant neoplasm of prostate ♂

188.0 Malignant neoplasm of trigone of urinary bladder

188.1 Malignant neoplasm of dome of urinary bladder

188.2 Malignant neoplasm of lateral wall of urinary bladder

188.3 Malignant neoplasm of anterior wall of urinary bladder

188.4 Malignant neoplasm of posterior wall of urinary bladder

188.5 Malignant neoplasm of bladder neck

188.6 Malignant neoplasm of ureteric orifice

188.7 Malignant neoplasm of urachus

188.8 Malignant neoplasm of other specified sites of bladder

188.9 Malignant neoplasm of bladder, part unspecified ▼

344.1 Paraplegia

344.61 Cauda equina syndrome with neurogenic bladder

555.0 Regional enteritis of small intestine

596.0 Bladder neck obstruction — (Use additional code to identify urinary incontinence: 625.6, 788.30-788.39)

596.1 Intestinovesical fistula — (Use additional code to identify urinary incontinence: 625.6, 788.30-788.39)

596.2 Vesical fistula, not elsewhere classified — (Use additional code to identify urinary incontinence: 625.6, 788.30-788.39)

596.3 Diverticulum of bladder — (Use additional code to identify urinary incontinence: 625.6, 788.30-788.39)

596.4 Atony of bladder — (Use additional code to identify urinary incontinence: 625.6, 788.30-788.39)

596.51 Hypertonicity of bladder — (Use additional code to identify urinary incontinence: 625.6, 788.30-788.39)

596.52 Low bladder compliance — (Use additional code to identify urinary incontinence: 625.6, 788.30-788.39)

596.53 Paralysis of bladder — (Use additional code to identify urinary incontinence: 625.6, 788.30-788.39)

596.54 Neurogenic bladder, NOS — (Use additional code to identify urinary incontinence: 625.6, 788.30-788.39) ▼

596.55 Detrusor sphincter dyssynergia — (Use additional code to identify urinary incontinence: 625.6, 788.30-788.39)

596.59 Other functional disorder of bladder — (Use additional code to identify urinary incontinence: 625.6, 788.30-788.39)

596.7 Hemorrhage into bladder wall — (Use additional code to identify urinary incontinence: 625.6, 788.30-788.39)

596.81 Infection of cystostomy — (Use additional code to specify type of infection, such as: 038.0-038.9, 682.2) (Use additional code to identify organism: 041.00-041.9)

596.82 Mechanical complication of cystostomy

596.83 Other complication of cystostomy

596.89 Other specified disorders of bladder

598.1 Traumatic urethral stricture — (Use additional code to identify urinary incontinence: 625.6, 788.30-788.39)

599.0 Urinary tract infection, site not specified — (Use additional code to identify organism, such as E. coli: 041.41-041.49) ▼

599.1 Urethral fistula

599.2 Urethral diverticulum

599.70 Hematuria, unspecified ▼

599.71 Gross hematuria

599.72 Microscopic hematuria

600.01 Hypertrophy (benign) of prostate with urinary obstruction and other lower urinary tract symptoms [LUTS] — (Use additional code to identify symptoms: 599.69, 788.20, 788.21, 788.30-788.39, 788.41, 788.43, 788.62, 788.63, 788.64, 788.65) ♂

600.11 Nodular prostate with urinary obstruction ♂

600.21 Benign localized hyperplasia of prostate with urinary obstruction and other lower urinary tract symptoms [LUTS] — (Use additional code to identify symptoms: 599.69, 788.20, 788.21, 788.30-788.39, 788.41, 788.43, 788.62, 788.63, 788.64, 788.65) ♂

600.3 Cyst of prostate ♂

600.91 Hyperplasia of prostate, unspecified, with urinary obstruction and other lower urinary tract symptoms [LUTS] — (Use additional code to identify symptoms: 599.69, 788.20, 788.21, 788.30-788.39, 788.41, 788.43, 788.62, 788.63, 788.64, 788.65) ▽ ♂

625.6 Female stress incontinence ♀

788.20 Unspecified retention of urine — (Code, if applicable, any causal condition first, such as: 600.0-600.9, with fifth digit 1) ▽

788.21 Incomplete bladder emptying — (Code, if applicable, any causal condition first, such as: 600.0-600.9, with fifth digit 1)

788.29 Other specified retention of urine — (Code, if applicable, any causal condition first, such as: 600.0-600.9, with fifth digit 1)

788.30 Unspecified urinary incontinence — (Code, if applicable, any causal condition first: 600.0-600.9, with fifth digit 1; 618.00-618.9; 753.23) ▽

788.31 Urge incontinence — (Code, if applicable, any causal condition first: 600.0-600.9, with fifth digit 1; 618.00-618.9; 753.23)

788.32 Stress incontinence, male — (Code, if applicable, any causal condition first: 600.0-600.9, with fifth digit 1; 618.00-618.9; 753.23) ♂

788.33 Mixed incontinence urge and stress (male)(female) — (Code, if applicable, any causal condition first: 600.0-600.9, with fifth digit 1; 618.00-618.9; 753.23)

788.38 Overflow incontinence — (Code, if applicable, any causal condition first: 600.0-600.9, with fifth digit 1; 618.00-618.9; 753.23)

788.39 Other urinary incontinence — (Code, if applicable, any causal condition first: 600.0-600.9, with fifth digit 1; 618.00-618.9; 753.23)

788.91 Functional urinary incontinence

788.99 Other symptoms involving urinary system

996.39 Mechanical complication of genitourinary device, implant, and graft, other

996.65 Infection and inflammatory reaction due to other genitourinary device, implant, and graft — (Use additional code to identify specified infections)

996.76 Other complications due to genitourinary device, implant, and graft — (Use additional code to identify complication: 338.18-338.19, 338.28-338.29)

V55.5 Attention to cystostomy

ICD-9-CM Procedural

59.94 Replacement of cystostomy tube

51715

51715 Endoscopic injection of implant material into the submucosal tissues of the urethra and/or bladder neck

ICD-9-CM Diagnostic

185 Malignant neoplasm of prostate ♂

188.9 Malignant neoplasm of bladder, part unspecified ▽

344.1 Paraplegia

596.0 Bladder neck obstruction — (Use additional code to identify urinary incontinence: 625.6, 788.30-788.39)

596.4 Atony of bladder — (Use additional code to identify urinary incontinence: 625.6, 788.30-788.39)

596.51 Hypertonicity of bladder — (Use additional code to identify urinary incontinence: 625.6, 788.30-788.39)

596.52 Low bladder compliance — (Use additional code to identify urinary incontinence: 625.6, 788.30-788.39)

596.53 Paralysis of bladder — (Use additional code to identify urinary incontinence: 625.6, 788.30-788.39)

596.54 Neurogenic bladder, NOS — (Use additional code to identify urinary incontinence: 625.6, 788.30-788.39) ▽

596.55 Detrusor sphincter dyssynergia — (Use additional code to identify urinary incontinence: 625.6, 788.30-788.39)

599.1 Urethral fistula

625.6 Female stress incontinence ♀

788.29 Other specified retention of urine — (Code, if applicable, any causal condition first, such as: 600.0-600.9, with fifth digit 1)

788.32 Stress incontinence, male — (Code, if applicable, any causal condition first: 600.0-600.9, with fifth digit 1; 618.00-618.9; 753.23) ♂

996.39 Mechanical complication of genitourinary device, implant, and graft, other

V10.46 Personal history of malignant neoplasm of prostate ♂

ICD-9-CM Procedural

59.72 Injection of implant into urethra and/or bladder neck

HCPCS Level II Supplies & Services

L8603 Injectable bulking agent, collagen implant, urinary tract, 2.5 ml syringe, includes shipping and necessary supplies

51720

51720 Bladder instillation of anticarcinogenic agent (including retention time)

ICD-9-CM Diagnostic

188.0 Malignant neoplasm of trigone of urinary bladder

188.1 Malignant neoplasm of dome of urinary bladder

188.2 Malignant neoplasm of lateral wall of urinary bladder

188.3 Malignant neoplasm of anterior wall of urinary bladder

188.4 Malignant neoplasm of posterior wall of urinary bladder

188.5 Malignant neoplasm of bladder neck

188.6 Malignant neoplasm of ureteric orifice

188.7 Malignant neoplasm of urachus

188.8 Malignant neoplasm of other specified sites of bladder

188.9 Malignant neoplasm of bladder, part unspecified ▽

198.1 Secondary malignant neoplasm of other urinary organs

233.7 Carcinoma in situ of bladder

233.9 Carcinoma in situ of other and unspecified urinary organs ▽

V58.11 Encounter for antineoplastic chemotherapy

ICD-9-CM Procedural

96.49 Other genitourinary instillation

99.25 Injection or infusion of cancer chemotherapeutic substance

HCPCS Level II Supplies & Services

J9031 BCG (intravesical) per instillation

51725-51729 [51797]

51725 Simple cystometrogram (CMG) (eg, spinal manometer)

51726 Complex cystometrogram (ie, calibrated electronic equipment);

51727 with urethral pressure profile studies (ie, urethral closure pressure profile), any technique

51728 with voiding pressure studies (ie, bladder voiding pressure), any technique

51729 with voiding pressure studies (ie, bladder voiding pressure) and urethral pressure profile studies (ie, urethral closure pressure profile), any technique

51797 Voiding pressure studies, intra-abdominal (ie, rectal, gastric, intraperitoneal) (List separately in addition to code for primary procedure)

ICD-9-CM Diagnostic

185 Malignant neoplasm of prostate ♂

344.61 Cauda equina syndrome with neurogenic bladder

595.1 Chronic interstitial cystitis — (Use additional code to identify organism, such as E. coli: 041.41-041.49)

595.2 Other chronic cystitis — (Use additional code to identify organism, such as E. coli: 041.41-041.49)

595.3 Trigonitis — (Use additional code to identify organism, such as E. coli: 041.41-041.49)

595.4 Cystitis in diseases classified elsewhere — (Use additional code to identify organism, such as E. coli: 041.41-041.49. Code first underlying disease: 006.8, 039.8, 120.0-120.9, 122.3, 122.6) ☒

595.81 Cystitis cystica — (Use additional code to identify organism, such as E. coli: 041.41-041.49)

595.82 Irradiation cystitis — (Use additional code to identify organism, such as E. coli: 041.41-041.49. Use additional E code to identify cause)

595.89 Other specified types of cystitis — (Use additional code to identify organism, such as E. coli: 041.41-041.49)

596.0 Bladder neck obstruction — (Use additional code to identify urinary incontinence: 625.6, 788.30-788.39)

596.1 Intestinovesical fistula — (Use additional code to identify urinary incontinence: 625.6, 788.30-788.39)

596.2 Vesical fistula, not elsewhere classified — (Use additional code to identify urinary incontinence: 625.6, 788.30-788.39)

596.3 Diverticulum of bladder — (Use additional code to identify urinary incontinence: 625.6, 788.30-788.39)

596.4 Atony of bladder — (Use additional code to identify urinary incontinence: 625.6, 788.30-788.39)

596.51 Hypertonicity of bladder — (Use additional code to identify urinary incontinence: 625.6, 788.30-788.39)

596.52 Low bladder compliance — (Use additional code to identify urinary incontinence: 625.6, 788.30-788.39)

596.53 Paralysis of bladder — (Use additional code to identify urinary incontinence: 625.6, 788.30-788.39)

596.54 Neurogenic bladder, NOS — (Use additional code to identify urinary incontinence: 625.6, 788.30-788.39) ▽

596.55 Detrusor sphincter dyssynergia — (Use additional code to identify urinary incontinence: 625.6, 788.30-788.39)

596.59 Other functional disorder of bladder — (Use additional code to identify urinary incontinence: 625.6, 788.30-788.39)

598.00 Urethral stricture due to unspecified infection — (Use additional code to identify urinary incontinence: 625.6, 788.30-788.39) ▽

598.1 Traumatic urethral stricture — (Use additional code to identify urinary incontinence: 625.6, 788.30-788.39)

598.2 Postoperative urethral stricture — (Use additional code to identify urinary incontinence: 625.6, 788.30-788.39)

598.8 Other specified causes of urethral stricture — (Use additional code to identify urinary incontinence: 625.6, 788.30-788.39)

598.9 Unspecified urethral stricture — (Use additional code to identify urinary incontinence: 625.6, 788.30-788.39) ▽

599.0 Urinary tract infection, site not specified — (Use additional code to identify organism, such as E. coli: 041.41-041.49) ▽

599.60 Urinary obstruction, unspecified — (Use additional code to identify urinary incontinence: 625.6, 788.30-788.39) ▽

599.69 Urinary obstruction, not elsewhere classified — (Use additional code to identify urinary incontinence: 625.6, 788.30-788.39. Code, if applicable, any causal condition first: 600.0-600.9, with fifth-digit 1)

599.70 Hematuria, unspecified ▽

599.71 Gross hematuria

599.72 Microscopic hematuria

600.00 Hypertrophy (benign) of prostate without urinary obstruction and other lower urinary tract symptoms [LUTS] ♂

600.01 Hypertrophy (benign) of prostate with urinary obstruction and other lower urinary tract symptoms [LUTS] — (Use additional code to identify symptoms: 599.69, 788.20, 788.21, 788.30-788.39, 788.41, 788.43, 788.62, 788.63, 788.64, 788.65) ♂

600.10 Nodular prostate without urinary obstruction ♂

600.11 Nodular prostate with urinary obstruction ♂

600.20 Benign localized hyperplasia of prostate without urinary obstruction and other lower urinary tract symptoms [LUTS] ♂

600.21 Benign localized hyperplasia of prostate with urinary obstruction and other lower urinary tract symptoms [LUTS] — (Use additional code to identify symptoms: 599.69, 788.20, 788.21, 788.30-788.39, 788.41, 788.43, 788.62, 788.63, 788.64, 788.65) ♂

600.3 Cyst of prostate ♂

600.90 Hyperplasia of prostate, unspecified, without urinary obstruction and other lower urinary tract symptoms [LUTS] ▽ ♂

600.91 Hyperplasia of prostate, unspecified, with urinary obstruction and other lower urinary tract symptoms [LUTS] — (Use additional code to identify symptoms: 599.69, 788.20, 788.21, 788.30-788.39, 788.41, 788.43, 788.62, 788.63, 788.64, 788.65) ▽ ♂

601.1 Chronic prostatitis — (Use additional code to identify organism: 041.0, 041.1) ♂

618.00 Unspecified prolapse of vaginal walls without mention of uterine prolapse — (Use additional code to identify urinary incontinence: 625.6, 788.31, 788.33-788.39) ▽ ♀

618.01 Cystocele without mention of uterine prolapse, midline — (Use additional code to identify urinary incontinence: 625.6, 788.31, 788.33-788.39) ♀

618.02 Cystocele without mention of uterine prolapse, lateral — (Use additional code to identify urinary incontinence: 625.6, 788.31, 788.33-788.39) ♀

618.03 Urethrocele without mention of uterine prolapse — (Use additional code to identify urinary incontinence: 625.6, 788.31, 788.33-788.39) ♀

618.09 Other prolapse of vaginal walls without mention of uterine prolapse — (Use additional code to identify urinary incontinence: 625.6, 788.31, 788.33-788.39) ♀

618.1 Uterine prolapse without mention of vaginal wall prolapse — (Use additional code to identify urinary incontinence: 625.6, 788.31, 788.33-788.39) ♀

618.2 Uterovaginal prolapse, incomplete — (Use additional code to identify urinary incontinence: 625.6, 788.31, 788.33-788.39) ♀

618.3 Uterovaginal prolapse, complete — (Use additional code to identify urinary incontinence: 625.6, 788.31, 788.33-788.39) ♀

618.4 Uterovaginal prolapse, unspecified — (Use additional code to identify urinary incontinence: 625.6, 788.31, 788.33-788.39) ▽ ♀

618.5 Prolapse of vaginal vault after hysterectomy — (Use additional code to identify urinary incontinence: 625.6, 788.31, 788.33-788.39) ♀

618.6 Vaginal enterocele, congenital or acquired — (Use additional code to identify urinary incontinence: 625.6, 788.31, 788.33-788.39) ♀

618.7 Genital prolapse, old laceration of muscles of pelvic floor — (Use additional code to identify urinary incontinence: 625.6, 788.31, 788.33-788.39) ♀

618.81 Incompetence or weakening of pubocervical tissue — (Use additional code to identify urinary incontinence: 625.6, 788.31, 788.33-788.39) ♀

618.82 Incompetence or weakening of rectovaginal tissue — (Use additional code to identify urinary incontinence: 625.6, 788.31, 788.33-788.39) ♀

618.83 Pelvic muscle wasting — (Use additional code to identify urinary incontinence: 625.6, 788.31, 788.33-788.39) ♀

618.89 Other specified genital prolapse — (Use additional code to identify urinary incontinence: 625.6, 788.31, 788.33-788.39) ♀

618.9 Unspecified genital prolapse — (Use additional code to identify urinary incontinence: 625.6, 788.31, 788.33-788.39) ▽ ♀

619.0 Urinary-genital tract fistula, female ♀

625.6 Female stress incontinence ♀

741.90 Spina bifida without mention of hydrocephalus, unspecified region ▽

753.5 Exstrophy of urinary bladder

753.6 Congenital atresia and stenosis of urethra and bladder neck

753.8 Other specified congenital anomaly of bladder and urethra

788.1 Dysuria

788.20 Unspecified retention of urine — (Code, if applicable, any causal condition first, such as: 600.0-600.9, with fifth digit 1) ▽

788.21 Incomplete bladder emptying — (Code, if applicable, any causal condition first, such as: 600.0-600.9, with fifth digit 1)

788.29 Other specified retention of urine — (Code, if applicable, any causal condition first, such as: 600.0-600.9, with fifth digit 1)

788.30 Unspecified urinary incontinence — (Code, if applicable, any causal condition first: 600.0-600.9, with fifth digit 1; 618.00-618.9; 753.23) ▽

788.31 Urge incontinence — (Code, if applicable, any causal condition first: 600.0-600.9, with fifth digit 1; 618.00-618.9; 753.23)
788.32 Stress incontinence, male — (Code, if applicable, any causal condition first: 600.0-600.9, with fifth digit 1; 618.00-618.9; 753.23) ♂
788.33 Mixed incontinence urge and stress (male)(female) — (Code, if applicable, any causal condition first: 600.0-600.9, with fifth digit 1; 618.00-618.9; 753.23)
788.34 Incontinence without sensory awareness — (Code, if applicable, any causal condition first: 600.0-600.9, with fifth digit 1; 618.00-618.9; 753.23)
788.35 Post-void dribbling — (Code, if applicable, any causal condition first: 600.0-600.9, with fifth digit 1; 618.00-618.9; 753.23)
788.36 Nocturnal enuresis — (Code, if applicable, any causal condition first: 600.0-600.9, with fifth digit 1; 618.00-618.9; 753.23)
788.37 Continuous leakage — (Code, if applicable, any causal condition first: 600.0-600.9, with fifth digit 1; 618.00-618.9; 753.23)
788.38 Overflow incontinence — (Code, if applicable, any causal condition first: 600.0-600.9, with fifth digit 1; 618.00-618.9; 753.23)
788.39 Other urinary incontinence — (Code, if applicable, any causal condition first: 600.0-600.9, with fifth digit 1; 618.00-618.9; 753.23)
788.41 Urinary frequency — (Code, if applicable, any causal condition first, such as: 600.0-600.9, with fifth digit 1)
788.42 Polyuria — (Code, if applicable, any causal condition first, such as: 600.0-600.9, with fifth digit 1)
788.43 Nocturia — (Code, if applicable, any causal condition first, such as: 600.0-600.9, with fifth digit 1)
788.61 Splitting of urinary stream — (Code, if applicable, any causal condition first, such as: 600.0-600.9, with fifth digit 1)
788.62 Slowing of urinary stream — (Code, if applicable, any causal condition first, such as: 600.0-600.9, with fifth digit 1)
788.63 Urgency of urination — (Code, if applicable, any causal condition first, such as: 600.0-600.9, with fifth digit 1)
788.64 Urinary hesitancy — (Code, if applicable, any causal condition first, such as: 600.0-600.9, with fifth digit 1)
788.65 Straining on urination — (Code, if applicable, any causal condition first, such as: 600.0-600.9, with fifth digit 1)
788.69 Other abnormality of urination — (Code, if applicable, any causal condition first, such as: 600.0-600.9, with fifth digit 1)
788.91 Functional urinary incontinence
788.99 Other symptoms involving urinary system
V67.00 Follow-up examination, following unspecified surgery ▽
V67.09 Follow-up examination, following other surgery

ICD-9-CM Procedural

89.22 Cystometrogram
89.25 Urethral pressure profile (UPP)
89.29 Other nonoperative genitourinary system measurements

51736-51741

51736 Simple uroflowmetry (UFR) (eg, stop-watch flow rate, mechanical uroflowmeter)
51741 Complex uroflowmetry (eg, calibrated electronic equipment)

ICD-9-CM Diagnostic

185 Malignant neoplasm of prostate ♂
344.61 Cauda equina syndrome with neurogenic bladder
595.1 Chronic interstitial cystitis — (Use additional code to identify organism, such as E. coli: 041.41-041.49)
595.2 Other chronic cystitis — (Use additional code to identify organism, such as E. coli: 041.41-041.49)
595.3 Trigonitis — (Use additional code to identify organism, such as E. coli: 041.41-041.49)
595.4 Cystitis in diseases classified elsewhere — (Use additional code to identify organism, such as E. coli: 041.41-041.49. Code first underlying disease: 006.8, 039.8, 120.0-120.9, 122.3, 122.6) ⊠
595.81 Cystitis cystica — (Use additional code to identify organism, such as E. coli: 041.41-041.49)
595.82 Irradiation cystitis — (Use additional code to identify organism, such as E. coli: 041.41-041.49. Use additional E code to identify cause)
595.89 Other specified types of cystitis — (Use additional code to identify organism, such as E. coli: 041.41-041.49)
595.9 Unspecified cystitis — (Use additional code to identify organism, such as E. coli: 041.41-041.49) ▽
596.0 Bladder neck obstruction — (Use additional code to identify urinary incontinence: 625.6, 788.30-788.39)
596.1 Intestinovesical fistula — (Use additional code to identify urinary incontinence: 625.6, 788.30-788.39)
596.2 Vesical fistula, not elsewhere classified — (Use additional code to identify urinary incontinence: 625.6, 788.30-788.39)
596.3 Diverticulum of bladder — (Use additional code to identify urinary incontinence: 625.6, 788.30-788.39)
596.4 Atony of bladder — (Use additional code to identify urinary incontinence: 625.6, 788.30-788.39)
596.51 Hypertonicity of bladder — (Use additional code to identify urinary incontinence: 625.6, 788.30-788.39)
596.52 Low bladder compliance — (Use additional code to identify urinary incontinence: 625.6, 788.30-788.39)
596.53 Paralysis of bladder — (Use additional code to identify urinary incontinence: 625.6, 788.30-788.39)
596.54 Neurogenic bladder, NOS — (Use additional code to identify urinary incontinence: 625.6, 788.30-788.39) ▽
596.55 Detrusor sphincter dyssynergia — (Use additional code to identify urinary incontinence: 625.6, 788.30-788.39)
596.59 Other functional disorder of bladder — (Use additional code to identify urinary incontinence: 625.6, 788.30-788.39)
596.89 Other specified disorders of bladder
598.00 Urethral stricture due to unspecified infection — (Use additional code to identify urinary incontinence: 625.6, 788.30-788.39) ▽
598.1 Traumatic urethral stricture — (Use additional code to identify urinary incontinence: 625.6, 788.30-788.39)
598.2 Postoperative urethral stricture — (Use additional code to identify urinary incontinence: 625.6, 788.30-788.39)
598.8 Other specified causes of urethral stricture — (Use additional code to identify urinary incontinence: 625.6, 788.30-788.39)
599.0 Urinary tract infection, site not specified — (Use additional code to identify organism, such as E. coli: 041.41-041.49) ▽
599.70 Hematuria, unspecified ▽
599.71 Gross hematuria
599.72 Microscopic hematuria
600.00 Hypertrophy (benign) of prostate without urinary obstruction and other lower urinary tract symptoms [LUTS] ♂
600.01 Hypertrophy (benign) of prostate with urinary obstruction and other lower urinary tract symptoms [LUTS] — (Use additional code to identify symptoms: 599.69, 788.20, 788.21, 788.30-788.39, 788.41, 788.43, 788.62, 788.63, 788.64, 788.65) ♂
600.10 Nodular prostate without urinary obstruction ♂
600.11 Nodular prostate with urinary obstruction ♂
600.20 Benign localized hyperplasia of prostate without urinary obstruction and other lower urinary tract symptoms [LUTS] ♂
600.21 Benign localized hyperplasia of prostate with urinary obstruction and other lower urinary tract symptoms [LUTS] — (Use additional code to identify symptoms: 599.69, 788.20, 788.21, 788.30-788.39, 788.41, 788.43, 788.62, 788.63, 788.64, 788.65) ♂
600.3 Cyst of prostate ♂
600.90 Hyperplasia of prostate, unspecified, without urinary obstruction and other lower urinary tract symptoms [LUTS] ▽ ♂

600.91 Hyperplasia of prostate, unspecified, with urinary obstruction and other lower urinary tract symptoms [LUTS] — (Use additional code to identify symptoms: 599.69, 788.20, 788.21, 788.30-788.39, 788.41, 788.43, 788.62, 788.63, 788.64, 788.65) ♂

601.1 Chronic prostatitis — (Use additional code to identify organism: 041.0, 041.1) ♂

618.00 Unspecified prolapse of vaginal walls without mention of uterine prolapse — (Use additional code to identify urinary incontinence: 625.6, 788.31, 788.33-788.39) ♀

618.01 Cystocele without mention of uterine prolapse, midline — (Use additional code to identify urinary incontinence: 625.6, 788.31, 788.33-788.39) ♀

618.02 Cystocele without mention of uterine prolapse, lateral — (Use additional code to identify urinary incontinence: 625.6, 788.31, 788.33-788.39) ♀

618.03 Urethrocele without mention of uterine prolapse — (Use additional code to identify urinary incontinence: 625.6, 788.31, 788.33-788.39) ♀

618.09 Other prolapse of vaginal walls without mention of uterine prolapse — (Use additional code to identify urinary incontinence: 625.6, 788.31, 788.33-788.39) ♀

618.1 Uterine prolapse without mention of vaginal wall prolapse — (Use additional code to identify urinary incontinence: 625.6, 788.31, 788.33-788.39) ♀

618.2 Uterovaginal prolapse, incomplete — (Use additional code to identify urinary incontinence: 625.6, 788.31, 788.33-788.39) ♀

618.3 Uterovaginal prolapse, complete — (Use additional code to identify urinary incontinence: 625.6, 788.31, 788.33-788.39) ♀

618.4 Uterovaginal prolapse, unspecified — (Use additional code to identify urinary incontinence: 625.6, 788.31, 788.33-788.39) ♀

618.5 Prolapse of vaginal vault after hysterectomy — (Use additional code to identify urinary incontinence: 625.6, 788.31, 788.33-788.39) ♀

618.6 Vaginal enterocele, congenital or acquired — (Use additional code to identify urinary incontinence: 625.6, 788.31, 788.33-788.39) ♀

618.7 Genital prolapse, old laceration of muscles of pelvic floor — (Use additional code to identify urinary incontinence: 625.6, 788.31, 788.33-788.39) ♀

618.81 Incompetence or weakening of pubocervical tissue — (Use additional code to identify urinary incontinence: 625.6, 788.31, 788.33-788.39) ♀

618.82 Incompetence or weakening of rectovaginal tissue — (Use additional code to identify urinary incontinence: 625.6, 788.31, 788.33-788.39) ♀

618.83 Pelvic muscle wasting — (Use additional code to identify urinary incontinence: 625.6, 788.31, 788.33-788.39) ♀

618.89 Other specified genital prolapse — (Use additional code to identify urinary incontinence: 625.6, 788.31, 788.33-788.39) ♀

618.9 Unspecified genital prolapse — (Use additional code to identify urinary incontinence: 625.6, 788.31, 788.33-788.39) ♀

619.0 Urinary-genital tract fistula, female ♀

625.6 Female stress incontinence ♀

741.90 Spina bifida without mention of hydrocephalus, unspecified region

753.5 Exstrophy of urinary bladder

753.6 Congenital atresia and stenosis of urethra and bladder neck

753.8 Other specified congenital anomaly of bladder and urethra

788.1 Dysuria

788.21 Incomplete bladder emptying — (Code, if applicable, any causal condition first, such as: 600.0-600.9, with fifth digit 1)

788.29 Other specified retention of urine — (Code, if applicable, any causal condition first, such as: 600.0-600.9, with fifth digit 1)

788.31 Urge incontinence — (Code, if applicable, any causal condition first: 600.0-600.9, with fifth digit 1; 618.00-618.9; 753.23)

788.32 Stress incontinence, male — (Code, if applicable, any causal condition first: 600.0-600.9, with fifth digit 1; 618.00-618.9; 753.23) ♂

788.33 Mixed incontinence urge and stress (male)(female) — (Code, if applicable, any causal condition first: 600.0-600.9, with fifth digit 1; 618.00-618.9; 753.23)

788.34 Incontinence without sensory awareness — (Code, if applicable, any causal condition first: 600.0-600.9, with fifth digit 1; 618.00-618.9; 753.23)

788.35 Post-void dribbling — (Code, if applicable, any causal condition first: 600.0-600.9, with fifth digit 1; 618.00-618.9; 753.23)

788.36 Nocturnal enuresis — (Code, if applicable, any causal condition first: 600.0-600.9, with fifth digit 1; 618.00-618.9; 753.23)

788.37 Continuous leakage — (Code, if applicable, any causal condition first: 600.0-600.9, with fifth digit 1; 618.00-618.9; 753.23)

788.38 Overflow incontinence — (Code, if applicable, any causal condition first: 600.0-600.9, with fifth digit 1; 618.00-618.9; 753.23)

788.39 Other urinary incontinence — (Code, if applicable, any causal condition first: 600.0-600.9, with fifth digit 1; 618.00-618.9; 753.23)

788.41 Urinary frequency — (Code, if applicable, any causal condition first, such as: 600.0-600.9, with fifth digit 1)

788.42 Polyuria — (Code, if applicable, any causal condition first, such as: 600.0-600.9, with fifth digit 1)

788.43 Nocturia — (Code, if applicable, any causal condition first, such as: 600.0-600.9, with fifth digit 1)

788.61 Splitting of urinary stream — (Code, if applicable, any causal condition first, such as: 600.0-600.9, with fifth digit 1)

788.62 Slowing of urinary stream — (Code, if applicable, any causal condition first, such as: 600.0-600.9, with fifth digit 1)

788.63 Urgency of urination — (Code, if applicable, any causal condition first, such as: 600.0-600.9, with fifth digit 1)

788.64 Urinary hesitancy — (Code, if applicable, any causal condition first, such as: 600.0-600.9, with fifth digit 1)

788.65 Straining on urination — (Code, if applicable, any causal condition first, such as: 600.0-600.9, with fifth digit 1)

788.69 Other abnormality of urination — (Code, if applicable, any causal condition first, such as: 600.0-600.9, with fifth digit 1)

788.91 Functional urinary incontinence

788.99 Other symptoms involving urinary system

V67.00 Follow-up examination, following unspecified surgery

V67.09 Follow-up examination, following other surgery

ICD-9-CM Procedural

89.24 Uroflowmetry (UFR)

51784-51785

51784 Electromyography studies (EMG) of anal or urethral sphincter, other than needle, any technique

51785 Needle electromyography studies (EMG) of anal or urethral sphincter, any technique

ICD-9-CM Diagnostic

185 Malignant neoplasm of prostate ♂

344.61 Cauda equina syndrome with neurogenic bladder

564.6 Anal spasm

595.1 Chronic interstitial cystitis — (Use additional code to identify organism, such as E. coli: 041.41-041.49)

595.2 Other chronic cystitis — (Use additional code to identify organism, such as E. coli: 041.41-041.49)

595.3 Trigonitis — (Use additional code to identify organism, such as E. coli: 041.41-041.49)

595.4 Cystitis in diseases classified elsewhere — (Use additional code to identify organism, such as E. coli: 041.41-041.49. Code first underlying disease: 006.8, 039.8, 120.0-120.9, 122.3, 122.6) ☒

595.81 Cystitis cystica — (Use additional code to identify organism, such as E. coli: 041.41-041.49)

595.82 Irradiation cystitis — (Use additional code to identify organism, such as E. coli: 041.41-041.49. Use additional E code to identify cause)

595.89 Other specified types of cystitis — (Use additional code to identify organism, such as E. coli: 041.41-041.49)

596.0 Bladder neck obstruction — (Use additional code to identify urinary incontinence: 625.6, 788.30-788.39)

596.1 Intestinovesical fistula — (Use additional code to identify urinary incontinence: 625.6, 788.30-788.39)

596.2 Vesical fistula, not elsewhere classified — (Use additional code to identify urinary incontinence: 625.6, 788.30-788.39)

596.3 Diverticulum of bladder — (Use additional code to identify urinary incontinence: 625.6, 788.30-788.39)

596.4 Atony of bladder — (Use additional code to identify urinary incontinence: 625.6, 788.30-788.39)

596.51 Hypertonicity of bladder — (Use additional code to identify urinary incontinence: 625.6, 788.30-788.39)

596.52 Low bladder compliance — (Use additional code to identify urinary incontinence: 625.6, 788.30-788.39)

596.53 Paralysis of bladder — (Use additional code to identify urinary incontinence: 625.6, 788.30-788.39)

596.54 Neurogenic bladder, NOS — (Use additional code to identify urinary incontinence: 625.6, 788.30-788.39)

596.55 Detrusor sphincter dyssynergia — (Use additional code to identify urinary incontinence: 625.6, 788.30-788.39)

596.59 Other functional disorder of bladder — (Use additional code to identify urinary incontinence: 625.6, 788.30-788.39)

596.89 Other specified disorders of bladder

598.1 Traumatic urethral stricture — (Use additional code to identify urinary incontinence: 625.6, 788.30-788.39)

598.2 Postoperative urethral stricture — (Use additional code to identify urinary incontinence: 625.6, 788.30-788.39)

598.8 Other specified causes of urethral stricture — (Use additional code to identify urinary incontinence: 625.6, 788.30-788.39)

599.0 Urinary tract infection, site not specified — (Use additional code to identify organism, such as E. coli: 041.41-041.49)

599.70 Hematuria, unspecified

599.71 Gross hematuria

599.72 Microscopic hematuria

600.00 Hypertrophy (benign) of prostate without urinary obstruction and other lower urinary tract symptoms [LUTS] ♂

600.01 Hypertrophy (benign) of prostate with urinary obstruction and other lower urinary tract symptoms [LUTS] — (Use additional code to identify symptoms: 599.69, 788.20, 788.21, 788.30-788.39, 788.41, 788.43, 788.62, 788.63, 788.64, 788.65) ♂

600.10 Nodular prostate without urinary obstruction ♂

600.11 Nodular prostate with urinary obstruction ♂

600.20 Benign localized hyperplasia of prostate without urinary obstruction and other lower urinary tract symptoms [LUTS] ♂

600.21 Benign localized hyperplasia of prostate with urinary obstruction and other lower urinary tract symptoms [LUTS] — (Use additional code to identify symptoms: 599.69, 788.20, 788.21, 788.30-788.39, 788.41, 788.43, 788.62, 788.63, 788.64, 788.65) ♂

600.3 Cyst of prostate ♂

600.90 Hyperplasia of prostate, unspecified, without urinary obstruction and other lower urinary tract symptoms [LUTS] ♂

600.91 Hyperplasia of prostate, unspecified, with urinary obstruction and other lower urinary tract symptoms [LUTS] — (Use additional code to identify symptoms: 599.69, 788.20, 788.21, 788.30-788.39, 788.41, 788.43, 788.62, 788.63, 788.64, 788.65) ♂

601.1 Chronic prostatitis — (Use additional code to identify organism: 041.0, 041.1) ♂

618.00 Unspecified prolapse of vaginal walls without mention of uterine prolapse — (Use additional code to identify urinary incontinence: 625.6, 788.31, 788.33-788.39) ♀

618.01 Cystocele without mention of uterine prolapse, midline — (Use additional code to identify urinary incontinence: 625.6, 788.31, 788.33-788.39) ♀

618.02 Cystocele without mention of uterine prolapse, lateral — (Use additional code to identify urinary incontinence: 625.6, 788.31, 788.33-788.39) ♀

618.03 Urethrocele without mention of uterine prolapse — (Use additional code to identify urinary incontinence: 625.6, 788.31, 788.33-788.39) ♀

618.04 Rectocele without mention of uterine prolapse — (Use additional code to identify urinary incontinence: 625.6, 788.31, 788.33-788.39) (Use additional code for any associated fecal incontinence: 787.60-787.63) ♀

618.05 Perineocele without mention of uterine prolapse — (Use additional code to identify urinary incontinence: 625.6, 788.31, 788.33-788.39) ♀

618.09 Other prolapse of vaginal walls without mention of uterine prolapse — (Use additional code to identify urinary incontinence: 625.6, 788.31, 788.33-788.39) ♀

618.1 Uterine prolapse without mention of vaginal wall prolapse — (Use additional code to identify urinary incontinence: 625.6, 788.31, 788.33-788.39) ♀

618.2 Uterovaginal prolapse, incomplete — (Use additional code to identify urinary incontinence: 625.6, 788.31, 788.33-788.39) ♀

618.3 Uterovaginal prolapse, complete — (Use additional code to identify urinary incontinence: 625.6, 788.31, 788.33-788.39) ♀

618.4 Uterovaginal prolapse, unspecified — (Use additional code to identify urinary incontinence: 625.6, 788.31, 788.33-788.39) ♀

618.5 Prolapse of vaginal vault after hysterectomy — (Use additional code to identify urinary incontinence: 625.6, 788.31, 788.33-788.39) ♀

618.6 Vaginal enterocele, congenital or acquired — (Use additional code to identify urinary incontinence: 625.6, 788.31, 788.33-788.39) ♀

618.7 Genital prolapse, old laceration of muscles of pelvic floor — (Use additional code to identify urinary incontinence: 625.6, 788.31, 788.33-788.39) ♀

618.81 Incompetence or weakening of pubocervical tissue — (Use additional code to identify urinary incontinence: 625.6, 788.31, 788.33-788.39) ♀

618.82 Incompetence or weakening of rectovaginal tissue — (Use additional code to identify urinary incontinence: 625.6, 788.31, 788.33-788.39) ♀

618.83 Pelvic muscle wasting — (Use additional code to identify urinary incontinence: 625.6, 788.31, 788.33-788.39) ♀

618.89 Other specified genital prolapse — (Use additional code to identify urinary incontinence: 625.6, 788.31, 788.33-788.39) ♀

618.9 Unspecified genital prolapse — (Use additional code to identify urinary incontinence: 625.6, 788.31, 788.33-788.39) ♀

625.6 Female stress incontinence ♀

728.2 Muscular wasting and disuse atrophy, not elsewhere classified

741.90 Spina bifida without mention of hydrocephalus, unspecified region

753.5 Exstrophy of urinary bladder

753.6 Congenital atresia and stenosis of urethra and bladder neck

753.8 Other specified congenital anomaly of bladder and urethra

787.60 Full incontinence of feces

787.61 Incomplete defecation

787.62 Fecal smearing

787.63 Fecal urgency

787.91 Diarrhea

787.99 Other symptoms involving digestive system

788.1 Dysuria

788.21 Incomplete bladder emptying — (Code, if applicable, any causal condition first, such as: 600.0-600.9, with fifth digit 1)

788.29 Other specified retention of urine — (Code, if applicable, any causal condition first, such as: 600.0-600.9, with fifth digit 1)

788.31 Urge incontinence — (Code, if applicable, any causal condition first: 600.0-600.9, with fifth digit 1; 618.00-618.9; 753.23)

788.32 Stress incontinence, male — (Code, if applicable, any causal condition first: 600.0-600.9, with fifth digit 1; 618.00-618.9; 753.23) ♂

788.33 Mixed incontinence urge and stress (male)(female) — (Code, if applicable, any causal condition first: 600.0-600.9, with fifth digit 1; 618.00-618.9; 753.23)

788.34 Incontinence without sensory awareness — (Code, if applicable, any causal condition first: 600.0-600.9, with fifth digit 1; 618.00-618.9; 753.23)

788.35 Post-void dribbling — (Code, if applicable, any causal condition first: 600.0-600.9, with fifth digit 1; 618.00-618.9; 753.23)

788.36 Nocturnal enuresis — (Code, if applicable, any causal condition first: 600.0-600.9, with fifth digit 1; 618.00-618.9; 753.23)

788.37 Continuous leakage — (Code, if applicable, any causal condition first: 600.0-600.9, with fifth digit 1; 618.00-618.9; 753.23)

788.38 Overflow incontinence — (Code, if applicable, any causal condition first: 600.0-600.9, with fifth digit 1; 618.00-618.9; 753.23)
788.39 Other urinary incontinence — (Code, if applicable, any causal condition first: 600.0-600.9, with fifth digit 1; 618.00-618.9; 753.23)
788.41 Urinary frequency — (Code, if applicable, any causal condition first, such as: 600.0-600.9, with fifth digit 1)
788.42 Polyuria — (Code, if applicable, any causal condition first, such as: 600.0-600.9, with fifth digit 1)
788.43 Nocturia — (Code, if applicable, any causal condition first, such as: 600.0-600.9, with fifth digit 1)
788.61 Splitting of urinary stream — (Code, if applicable, any causal condition first, such as: 600.0-600.9, with fifth digit 1)
788.62 Slowing of urinary stream — (Code, if applicable, any causal condition first, such as: 600.0-600.9, with fifth digit 1)
788.63 Urgency of urination — (Code, if applicable, any causal condition first, such as: 600.0-600.9, with fifth digit 1)
788.64 Urinary hesitancy — (Code, if applicable, any causal condition first, such as: 600.0-600.9, with fifth digit 1)
788.65 Straining on urination — (Code, if applicable, any causal condition first, such as: 600.0-600.9, with fifth digit 1)
788.69 Other abnormality of urination — (Code, if applicable, any causal condition first, such as: 600.0-600.9, with fifth digit 1)
788.91 Functional urinary incontinence
788.99 Other symptoms involving urinary system
V47.4 Other urinary problems
V67.00 Follow-up examination, following unspecified surgery ▽
V67.09 Follow-up examination, following other surgery
V71.1 Observation for suspected malignant neoplasm
V71.89 Observation for other specified suspected conditions
V71.9 Observation for unspecified suspected condition ▽

ICD-9-CM Procedural

89.23 Urethral sphincter electromyogram

51792

51792 Stimulus evoked response (eg, measurement of bulbocavernosus reflex latency time)

ICD-9-CM Diagnostic

344.61 Cauda equina syndrome with neurogenic bladder
440.9 Generalized and unspecified atherosclerosis ▽
596.51 Hypertonicity of bladder — (Use additional code to identify urinary incontinence: 625.6, 788.30-788.39)
600.00 Hypertrophy (benign) of prostate without urinary obstruction and other lower urinary tract symptoms [LUTS] ♂
600.01 Hypertrophy (benign) of prostate with urinary obstruction and other lower urinary tract symptoms [LUTS] — (Use additional code to identify symptoms: 599.69, 788.20, 788.21, 788.30-788.39, 788.41, 788.43, 788.62, 788.63, 788.64, 788.65) ♂
600.10 Nodular prostate without urinary obstruction ♂
600.11 Nodular prostate with urinary obstruction ♂
600.20 Benign localized hyperplasia of prostate without urinary obstruction and other lower urinary tract symptoms [LUTS] ♂
600.21 Benign localized hyperplasia of prostate with urinary obstruction and other lower urinary tract symptoms [LUTS] — (Use additional code to identify symptoms: 599.69, 788.20, 788.21, 788.30-788.39, 788.41, 788.43, 788.62, 788.63, 788.64, 788.65) ♂
600.3 Cyst of prostate ♂
600.90 Hyperplasia of prostate, unspecified, without urinary obstruction and other lower urinary tract symptoms [LUTS] ▽ ♂
600.91 Hyperplasia of prostate, unspecified, with urinary obstruction and other lower urinary tract symptoms [LUTS] — (Use additional code to identify symptoms: 599.69, 788.20, 788.21, 788.30-788.39, 788.41, 788.43, 788.62, 788.63, 788.64, 788.65) ▽ ♂
607.84 Impotence of organic origin ♂
608.83 Specified vascular disorder of male genital organs ♂
782.0 Disturbance of skin sensation
788.32 Stress incontinence, male — (Code, if applicable, any causal condition first: 600.0-600.9, with fifth digit 1; 618.00-618.9; 753.23) ♂
788.39 Other urinary incontinence — (Code, if applicable, any causal condition first: 600.0-600.9, with fifth digit 1; 618.00-618.9; 753.23)
788.41 Urinary frequency — (Code, if applicable, any causal condition first, such as: 600.0-600.9, with fifth digit 1)

ICD-9-CM Procedural

89.29 Other nonoperative genitourinary system measurements

51798

51798 Measurement of post-voiding residual urine and/or bladder capacity by ultrasound, non-imaging

ICD-9-CM Diagnostic

596.4 Atony of bladder — (Use additional code to identify urinary incontinence: 625.6, 788.30-788.39)
596.54 Neurogenic bladder, NOS — (Use additional code to identify urinary incontinence: 625.6, 788.30-788.39) ▽
625.6 Female stress incontinence ♀
788.0 Renal colic
788.1 Dysuria
788.20 Unspecified retention of urine — (Code, if applicable, any causal condition first, such as: 600.0-600.9, with fifth digit 1) ▽
788.21 Incomplete bladder emptying — (Code, if applicable, any causal condition first, such as: 600.0-600.9, with fifth digit 1)
788.29 Other specified retention of urine — (Code, if applicable, any causal condition first, such as: 600.0-600.9, with fifth digit 1)
788.30 Unspecified urinary incontinence — (Code, if applicable, any causal condition first: 600.0-600.9, with fifth digit 1; 618.00-618.9; 753.23) ▽
788.31 Urge incontinence — (Code, if applicable, any causal condition first: 600.0-600.9, with fifth digit 1; 618.00-618.9; 753.23)
788.32 Stress incontinence, male — (Code, if applicable, any causal condition first: 600.0-600.9, with fifth digit 1; 618.00-618.9; 753.23) ♂
788.33 Mixed incontinence urge and stress (male)(female) — (Code, if applicable, any causal condition first: 600.0-600.9, with fifth digit 1; 618.00-618.9; 753.23)
788.34 Incontinence without sensory awareness — (Code, if applicable, any causal condition first: 600.0-600.9, with fifth digit 1; 618.00-618.9; 753.23)
788.35 Post-void dribbling — (Code, if applicable, any causal condition first: 600.0-600.9, with fifth digit 1; 618.00-618.9; 753.23)
788.36 Nocturnal enuresis — (Code, if applicable, any causal condition first: 600.0-600.9, with fifth digit 1; 618.00-618.9; 753.23)
788.37 Continuous leakage — (Code, if applicable, any causal condition first: 600.0-600.9, with fifth digit 1; 618.00-618.9; 753.23)
788.38 Overflow incontinence — (Code, if applicable, any causal condition first: 600.0-600.9, with fifth digit 1; 618.00-618.9; 753.23)
788.39 Other urinary incontinence — (Code, if applicable, any causal condition first: 600.0-600.9, with fifth digit 1; 618.00-618.9; 753.23)
788.41 Urinary frequency — (Code, if applicable, any causal condition first, such as: 600.0-600.9, with fifth digit 1)
788.42 Polyuria — (Code, if applicable, any causal condition first, such as: 600.0-600.9, with fifth digit 1)
788.43 Nocturia — (Code, if applicable, any causal condition first, such as: 600.0-600.9, with fifth digit 1)
788.5 Oliguria and anuria
788.62 Slowing of urinary stream — (Code, if applicable, any causal condition first, such as: 600.0-600.9, with fifth digit 1)
788.63 Urgency of urination — (Code, if applicable, any causal condition first, such as: 600.0-600.9, with fifth digit 1)

788.64 Urinary hesitancy — (Code, if applicable, any causal condition first, such as: 600.0-600.9, with fifth digit 1)
788.65 Straining on urination — (Code, if applicable, any causal condition first, such as: 600.0-600.9, with fifth digit 1)
788.69 Other abnormality of urination — (Code, if applicable, any causal condition first, such as: 600.0-600.9, with fifth digit 1)
788.7 Urethral discharge
788.8 Extravasation of urine
788.91 Functional urinary incontinence
788.99 Other symptoms involving urinary system

ICD-9-CM Procedural

89.29 Other nonoperative genitourinary system measurements

51800

51800 Cystoplasty or cystourethroplasty, plastic operation on bladder and/or vesical neck (anterior Y-plasty, vesical fundus resection), any procedure, with or without wedge resection of posterior vesical neck

ICD-9-CM Diagnostic

185 Malignant neoplasm of prostate ♂
593.70 Vesicoureteral reflux, unspecified or without reflex nephropathy
593.71 Vesicoureteral reflux with reflux nephropathy, unilateral
593.72 Vesicoureteral reflux with reflux nephropathy, bilateral
593.73 Vesicoureteral reflux with reflux nephropathy, NOS ▽
596.2 Vesical fistula, not elsewhere classified — (Use additional code to identify urinary incontinence: 625.6, 788.30-788.39)
598.00 Urethral stricture due to unspecified infection — (Use additional code to identify urinary incontinence: 625.6, 788.30-788.39) ▽
598.01 Urethral stricture due to infective diseases classified elsewhere — (Use additional code to identify urinary incontinence: 625.6, 788.30-788.39. Code first underlying disease: 095.8, 098.2, 120.0-120.9) ☒
598.1 Traumatic urethral stricture — (Use additional code to identify urinary incontinence: 625.6, 788.30-788.39)
598.2 Postoperative urethral stricture — (Use additional code to identify urinary incontinence: 625.6, 788.30-788.39)
598.9 Unspecified urethral stricture — (Use additional code to identify urinary incontinence: 625.6, 788.30-788.39) ▽
625.6 Female stress incontinence ♀
788.30 Unspecified urinary incontinence — (Code, if applicable, any causal condition first: 600.0-600.9, with fifth digit 1; 618.00-618.9; 753.23) ▽
788.31 Urge incontinence — (Code, if applicable, any causal condition first: 600.0-600.9, with fifth digit 1; 618.00-618.9; 753.23)
788.32 Stress incontinence, male — (Code, if applicable, any causal condition first: 600.0-600.9, with fifth digit 1; 618.00-618.9; 753.23) ♂
788.33 Mixed incontinence urge and stress (male)(female) — (Code, if applicable, any causal condition first: 600.0-600.9, with fifth digit 1; 618.00-618.9; 753.23)
788.34 Incontinence without sensory awareness — (Code, if applicable, any causal condition first: 600.0-600.9, with fifth digit 1; 618.00-618.9; 753.23)

ICD-9-CM Procedural

56.74 Ureteroneocystostomy
57.85 Cystourethroplasty and plastic repair of bladder neck

51820

51820 Cystourethroplasty with unilateral or bilateral ureteroneocystostomy

ICD-9-CM Diagnostic

185 Malignant neoplasm of prostate ♂
595.1 Chronic interstitial cystitis — (Use additional code to identify organism, such as E. coli: 041.41-041.49)
595.81 Cystitis cystica — (Use additional code to identify organism, such as E. coli: 041.41-041.49)
595.89 Other specified types of cystitis — (Use additional code to identify organism, such as E. coli: 041.41-041.49)
596.2 Vesical fistula, not elsewhere classified — (Use additional code to identify urinary incontinence: 625.6, 788.30-788.39)
598.00 Urethral stricture due to unspecified infection — (Use additional code to identify urinary incontinence: 625.6, 788.30-788.39) ▽
598.01 Urethral stricture due to infective diseases classified elsewhere — (Use additional code to identify urinary incontinence: 625.6, 788.30-788.39. Code first underlying disease: 095.8, 098.2, 120.0-120.9) ☒
598.1 Traumatic urethral stricture — (Use additional code to identify urinary incontinence: 625.6, 788.30-788.39)
598.2 Postoperative urethral stricture — (Use additional code to identify urinary incontinence: 625.6, 788.30-788.39)
598.9 Unspecified urethral stricture — (Use additional code to identify urinary incontinence: 625.6, 788.30-788.39) ▽
625.6 Female stress incontinence ♀
753.5 Exstrophy of urinary bladder
788.30 Unspecified urinary incontinence — (Code, if applicable, any causal condition first: 600.0-600.9, with fifth digit 1; 618.00-618.9; 753.23) ▽
788.31 Urge incontinence — (Code, if applicable, any causal condition first: 600.0-600.9, with fifth digit 1; 618.00-618.9; 753.23)
788.32 Stress incontinence, male — (Code, if applicable, any causal condition first: 600.0-600.9, with fifth digit 1; 618.00-618.9; 753.23) ♂
788.33 Mixed incontinence urge and stress (male)(female) — (Code, if applicable, any causal condition first: 600.0-600.9, with fifth digit 1; 618.00-618.9; 753.23)
788.34 Incontinence without sensory awareness — (Code, if applicable, any causal condition first: 600.0-600.9, with fifth digit 1; 618.00-618.9; 753.23)

ICD-9-CM Procedural

56.74 Ureteroneocystostomy
57.85 Cystourethroplasty and plastic repair of bladder neck

51840-51841

51840 Anterior vesicourethropexy, or urethropexy (eg, Marshall-Marchetti-Krantz, Burch); simple
51841 complicated (eg, secondary repair)

ICD-9-CM Diagnostic

599.5 Prolapsed urethral mucosa
618.00 Unspecified prolapse of vaginal walls without mention of uterine prolapse — (Use additional code to identify urinary incontinence: 625.6, 788.31, 788.33-788.39) ▽ ♀
618.01 Cystocele without mention of uterine prolapse, midline — (Use additional code to identify urinary incontinence: 625.6, 788.31, 788.33-788.39) ♀
618.02 Cystocele without mention of uterine prolapse, lateral — (Use additional code to identify urinary incontinence: 625.6, 788.31, 788.33-788.39) ♀
618.03 Urethrocele without mention of uterine prolapse — (Use additional code to identify urinary incontinence: 625.6, 788.31, 788.33-788.39) ♀
618.1 Uterine prolapse without mention of vaginal wall prolapse — (Use additional code to identify urinary incontinence: 625.6, 788.31, 788.33-788.39) ♀
618.2 Uterovaginal prolapse, incomplete — (Use additional code to identify urinary incontinence: 625.6, 788.31, 788.33-788.39) ♀
618.3 Uterovaginal prolapse, complete — (Use additional code to identify urinary incontinence: 625.6, 788.31, 788.33-788.39) ♀
618.4 Uterovaginal prolapse, unspecified — (Use additional code to identify urinary incontinence: 625.6, 788.31, 788.33-788.39) ▽ ♀
618.5 Prolapse of vaginal vault after hysterectomy — (Use additional code to identify urinary incontinence: 625.6, 788.31, 788.33-788.39) ♀
618.6 Vaginal enterocele, congenital or acquired — (Use additional code to identify urinary incontinence: 625.6, 788.31, 788.33-788.39) ♀

618.81 Incompetence or weakening of pubocervical tissue — (Use additional code to identify urinary incontinence: 625.6, 788.31, 788.33-788.39) ♀
618.83 Pelvic muscle wasting — (Use additional code to identify urinary incontinence: 625.6, 788.31, 788.33-788.39) ♀
618.84 Cervical stump prolapse — (Use additional code to identify urinary incontinence: 625.6, 788.31, 788.33-788.39) ♀
625.5 Pelvic congestion syndrome ♀
625.6 Female stress incontinence ♀
625.8 Other specified symptom associated with female genital organs ♀
788.30 Unspecified urinary incontinence — (Code, if applicable, any causal condition first: 600.0-600.9, with fifth digit 1; 618.00-618.9; 753.23)
788.31 Urge incontinence — (Code, if applicable, any causal condition first: 600.0-600.9, with fifth digit 1; 618.00-618.9; 753.23)
788.33 Mixed incontinence urge and stress (male)(female) — (Code, if applicable, any causal condition first: 600.0-600.9, with fifth digit 1; 618.00-618.9; 753.23)
788.34 Incontinence without sensory awareness — (Code, if applicable, any causal condition first: 600.0-600.9, with fifth digit 1; 618.00-618.9; 753.23)
788.35 Post-void dribbling — (Code, if applicable, any causal condition first: 600.0-600.9, with fifth digit 1; 618.00-618.9; 753.23)
788.36 Nocturnal enuresis — (Code, if applicable, any causal condition first: 600.0-600.9, with fifth digit 1; 618.00-618.9; 753.23)
788.37 Continuous leakage — (Code, if applicable, any causal condition first: 600.0-600.9, with fifth digit 1; 618.00-618.9; 753.23)
788.38 Overflow incontinence — (Code, if applicable, any causal condition first: 600.0-600.9, with fifth digit 1; 618.00-618.9; 753.23)
788.39 Other urinary incontinence — (Code, if applicable, any causal condition first: 600.0-600.9, with fifth digit 1; 618.00-618.9; 753.23)

ICD-9-CM Procedural

59.5 Retropubic urethral suspension
59.79 Other repair of urinary stress incontinence

51845

51845 Abdomino-vaginal vesical neck suspension, with or without endoscopic control (eg, Stamey, Raz, modified Pereyra)

ICD-9-CM Diagnostic

599.5 Prolapsed urethral mucosa
618.00 Unspecified prolapse of vaginal walls without mention of uterine prolapse — (Use additional code to identify urinary incontinence: 625.6, 788.31, 788.33-788.39) ♀
618.01 Cystocele without mention of uterine prolapse, midline — (Use additional code to identify urinary incontinence: 625.6, 788.31, 788.33-788.39) ♀
618.02 Cystocele without mention of uterine prolapse, lateral — (Use additional code to identify urinary incontinence: 625.6, 788.31, 788.33-788.39) ♀
618.03 Urethrocele without mention of uterine prolapse — (Use additional code to identify urinary incontinence: 625.6, 788.31, 788.33-788.39) ♀
618.1 Uterine prolapse without mention of vaginal wall prolapse — (Use additional code to identify urinary incontinence: 625.6, 788.31, 788.33-788.39) ♀
618.2 Uterovaginal prolapse, incomplete — (Use additional code to identify urinary incontinence: 625.6, 788.31, 788.33-788.39) ♀
618.3 Uterovaginal prolapse, complete — (Use additional code to identify urinary incontinence: 625.6, 788.31, 788.33-788.39) ♀
618.4 Uterovaginal prolapse, unspecified — (Use additional code to identify urinary incontinence: 625.6, 788.31, 788.33-788.39) ♀
618.5 Prolapse of vaginal vault after hysterectomy — (Use additional code to identify urinary incontinence: 625.6, 788.31, 788.33-788.39) ♀
618.6 Vaginal enterocele, congenital or acquired — (Use additional code to identify urinary incontinence: 625.6, 788.31, 788.33-788.39) ♀
618.7 Genital prolapse, old laceration of muscles of pelvic floor — (Use additional code to identify urinary incontinence: 625.6, 788.31, 788.33-788.39) ♀
618.81 Incompetence or weakening of pubocervical tissue — (Use additional code to identify urinary incontinence: 625.6, 788.31, 788.33-788.39) ♀
618.83 Pelvic muscle wasting — (Use additional code to identify urinary incontinence: 625.6, 788.31, 788.33-788.39) ♀
618.9 Unspecified genital prolapse — (Use additional code to identify urinary incontinence: 625.6, 788.31, 788.33-788.39) ♀
625.5 Pelvic congestion syndrome ♀
625.6 Female stress incontinence ♀
753.8 Other specified congenital anomaly of bladder and urethra
788.30 Unspecified urinary incontinence — (Code, if applicable, any causal condition first: 600.0-600.9, with fifth digit 1; 618.00-618.9; 753.23)
788.32 Stress incontinence, male — (Code, if applicable, any causal condition first: 600.0-600.9, with fifth digit 1; 618.00-618.9; 753.23) ♂
788.33 Mixed incontinence urge and stress (male)(female) — (Code, if applicable, any causal condition first: 600.0-600.9, with fifth digit 1; 618.00-618.9; 753.23)
788.34 Incontinence without sensory awareness — (Code, if applicable, any causal condition first: 600.0-600.9, with fifth digit 1; 618.00-618.9; 753.23)
788.35 Post-void dribbling — (Code, if applicable, any causal condition first: 600.0-600.9, with fifth digit 1; 618.00-618.9; 753.23)
788.36 Nocturnal enuresis — (Code, if applicable, any causal condition first: 600.0-600.9, with fifth digit 1; 618.00-618.9; 753.23)
788.37 Continuous leakage — (Code, if applicable, any causal condition first: 600.0-600.9, with fifth digit 1; 618.00-618.9; 753.23)
788.38 Overflow incontinence — (Code, if applicable, any causal condition first: 600.0-600.9, with fifth digit 1; 618.00-618.9; 753.23)

ICD-9-CM Procedural

59.6 Paraurethral suspension
59.79 Other repair of urinary stress incontinence

51860-51865

51860 Cystorrhaphy, suture of bladder wound, injury or rupture; simple
51865 complicated

ICD-9-CM Diagnostic

596.6 Nontraumatic rupture of bladder — (Use additional code to identify urinary incontinence: 625.6, 788.30-788.39)
634.21 Incomplete spontaneous abortion complicated by damage to pelvic organs or tissues ♀
634.22 Complete spontaneous abortion complicated by damage to pelvic organs or tissues ♀
635.21 Legally induced abortion complicated by damage to pelvic organs or tissues, incomplete ♀
635.22 Complete legally induced abortion complicated by damage to pelvic organs or tissues ♀
636.21 Incomplete illegally induced abortion complicated by damage to pelvic organs or tissues ♀
636.22 Complete illegally induced abortion complicated by damage to pelvic organs or tissues ♀
637.21 Abortion, unspecified as to legality, incomplete, complicated by damage to pelvic organs or tissues ♀
637.22 Abortion, unspecified as to legality, complete, complicated by damage to pelvic organs or tissues ♀
638.2 Failed attempted abortion complicated by damage to pelvic organs or tissues ♀
867.0 Bladder and urethra injury without mention of open wound into cavity
867.1 Bladder and urethra injury with open wound into cavity
998.2 Accidental puncture or laceration during procedure

ICD-9-CM Procedural

57.81 Suture of laceration of bladder
75.61 Repair of current obstetric laceration of bladder and urethra ♀

51880

51880 Closure of cystostomy (separate procedure)

ICD-9-CM Diagnostic

596.81 Infection of cystostomy — (Use additional code to specify type of infection, such as: 038.0-038.9, 682.2) (Use additional code to identify organism: 041.00-041.9)
596.82 Mechanical complication of cystostomy
596.83 Other complication of cystostomy
V10.51 Personal history of malignant neoplasm of bladder
V55.5 Attention to cystostomy

ICD-9-CM Procedural

57.82 Closure of cystostomy

HCPCS Level II Supplies & Services

A4305 Disposable drug delivery system, flow rate of 50 ml or greater per hour

51900

51900 Closure of vesicovaginal fistula, abdominal approach

ICD-9-CM Diagnostic

619.0 Urinary-genital tract fistula, female ♀

ICD-9-CM Procedural

57.84 Repair of other fistula of bladder

51920-51925

51920 Closure of vesicouterine fistula;
51925 with hysterectomy

ICD-9-CM Diagnostic

182.8 Malignant neoplasm of other specified sites of body of uterus ♀
183.9 Malignant neoplasm of uterine adnexa, unspecified site ▽ ♀
615.9 Unspecified inflammatory disease of uterus — (Use additional code to identify organism: 041.00-041.09, 041.10-041.19) ▽ ♀
617.0 Endometriosis of uterus ♀
619.0 Urinary-genital tract fistula, female ♀
621.30 Endometrial hyperplasia, unspecified ▽ ♀
621.31 Simple endometrial hyperplasia without atypia ♀
621.32 Complex endometrial hyperplasia without atypia ♀
621.33 Endometrial hyperplasia with atypia ♀
621.34 Benign endometrial hyperplasia ♀
621.35 Endometrial intraepithelial neoplasia [EIN] ♀

ICD-9-CM Procedural

57.84 Repair of other fistula of bladder
68.59 Other and unspecified vaginal hysterectomy ♀

51940

51940 Closure, exstrophy of bladder

ICD-9-CM Diagnostic

753.5 Exstrophy of urinary bladder

ICD-9-CM Procedural

57.86 Repair of bladder exstrophy

51960

51960 Enterocystoplasty, including intestinal anastomosis

ICD-9-CM Diagnostic

344.61 Cauda equina syndrome with neurogenic bladder
596.51 Hypertonicity of bladder — (Use additional code to identify urinary incontinence: 625.6, 788.30-788.39)
596.52 Low bladder compliance — (Use additional code to identify urinary incontinence: 625.6, 788.30-788.39)
596.54 Neurogenic bladder, NOS — (Use additional code to identify urinary incontinence: 625.6, 788.30-788.39) ▽
596.89 Other specified disorders of bladder
753.5 Exstrophy of urinary bladder

ICD-9-CM Procedural

45.52 Isolation of segment of large intestine
57.87 Reconstruction of urinary bladder

51980

51980 Cutaneous vesicostomy

ICD-9-CM Diagnostic

233.4 Carcinoma in situ of prostate ♂
344.61 Cauda equina syndrome with neurogenic bladder
596.0 Bladder neck obstruction — (Use additional code to identify urinary incontinence: 625.6, 788.30-788.39)
596.51 Hypertonicity of bladder — (Use additional code to identify urinary incontinence: 625.6, 788.30-788.39)
596.9 Unspecified disorder of bladder — (Use additional code to identify urinary incontinence: 625.6, 788.30-788.39) ▽
598.8 Other specified causes of urethral stricture — (Use additional code to identify urinary incontinence: 625.6, 788.30-788.39)
598.9 Unspecified urethral stricture — (Use additional code to identify urinary incontinence: 625.6, 788.30-788.39) ▽
625.6 Female stress incontinence ♀
752.61 Hypospadias ♂
752.62 Epispadias ♂
752.63 Congenital chordee ♂
752.64 Micropenis ♂
752.65 Hidden penis ♂
752.69 Other penile anomalies ♂
753.6 Congenital atresia and stenosis of urethra and bladder neck

ICD-9-CM Procedural

57.21 Vesicostomy
57.22 Revision or closure of vesicostomy

51990-51992

51990 Laparoscopy, surgical; urethral suspension for stress incontinence
51992 sling operation for stress incontinence (eg, fascia or synthetic)

ICD-9-CM Diagnostic

599.5 Prolapsed urethral mucosa
618.00 Unspecified prolapse of vaginal walls without mention of uterine prolapse — (Use additional code to identify urinary incontinence: 625.6, 788.31, 788.33-788.39) ▽ ♀
618.01 Cystocele without mention of uterine prolapse, midline — (Use additional code to identify urinary incontinence: 625.6, 788.31, 788.33-788.39) ♀
618.02 Cystocele without mention of uterine prolapse, lateral — (Use additional code to identify urinary incontinence: 625.6, 788.31, 788.33-788.39) ♀
618.03 Urethrocele without mention of uterine prolapse — (Use additional code to identify urinary incontinence: 625.6, 788.31, 788.33-788.39) ♀
618.1 Uterine prolapse without mention of vaginal wall prolapse — (Use additional code to identify urinary incontinence: 625.6, 788.31, 788.33-788.39) ♀
618.2 Uterovaginal prolapse, incomplete — (Use additional code to identify urinary incontinence: 625.6, 788.31, 788.33-788.39) ♀
618.3 Uterovaginal prolapse, complete — (Use additional code to identify urinary incontinence: 625.6, 788.31, 788.33-788.39) ♀

618.4 Uterovaginal prolapse, unspecified — (Use additional code to identify urinary incontinence: 625.6, 788.31, 788.33-788.39) ▽ ♀
618.5 Prolapse of vaginal vault after hysterectomy — (Use additional code to identify urinary incontinence: 625.6, 788.31, 788.33-788.39) ♀
618.6 Vaginal enterocele, congenital or acquired — (Use additional code to identify urinary incontinence: 625.6, 788.31, 788.33-788.39) ♀
618.81 Incompetence or weakening of pubocervical tissue — (Use additional code to identify urinary incontinence: 625.6, 788.31, 788.33-788.39) ♀
618.82 Incompetence or weakening of rectovaginal tissue — (Use additional code to identify urinary incontinence: 625.6, 788.31, 788.33-788.39) ♀
625.5 Pelvic congestion syndrome ♀
625.6 Female stress incontinence ♀
625.8 Other specified symptom associated with female genital organs ♀
788.30 Unspecified urinary incontinence — (Code, if applicable, any causal condition first: 600.0-600.9, with fifth digit 1; 618.00-618.9; 753.23) ▽
788.31 Urge incontinence — (Code, if applicable, any causal condition first: 600.0-600.9, with fifth digit 1; 618.00-618.9; 753.23)
788.33 Mixed incontinence urge and stress (male)(female) — (Code, if applicable, any causal condition first: 600.0-600.9, with fifth digit 1; 618.00-618.9; 753.23)
788.34 Incontinence without sensory awareness — (Code, if applicable, any causal condition first: 600.0-600.9, with fifth digit 1; 618.00-618.9; 753.23)
788.35 Post-void dribbling — (Code, if applicable, any causal condition first: 600.0-600.9, with fifth digit 1; 618.00-618.9; 753.23)
788.36 Nocturnal enuresis — (Code, if applicable, any causal condition first: 600.0-600.9, with fifth digit 1; 618.00-618.9; 753.23)
788.37 Continuous leakage — (Code, if applicable, any causal condition first: 600.0-600.9, with fifth digit 1; 618.00-618.9; 753.23)
788.38 Overflow incontinence — (Code, if applicable, any causal condition first: 600.0-600.9, with fifth digit 1; 618.00-618.9; 753.23)
788.39 Other urinary incontinence — (Code, if applicable, any causal condition first: 600.0-600.9, with fifth digit 1; 618.00-618.9; 753.23)

ICD-9-CM Procedural

59.5 Retropubic urethral suspension

52000

52000 Cystourethroscopy (separate procedure)

ICD-9-CM Diagnostic

185 Malignant neoplasm of prostate ♂
188.0 Malignant neoplasm of trigone of urinary bladder
188.1 Malignant neoplasm of dome of urinary bladder
188.2 Malignant neoplasm of lateral wall of urinary bladder
188.3 Malignant neoplasm of anterior wall of urinary bladder
188.4 Malignant neoplasm of posterior wall of urinary bladder
188.5 Malignant neoplasm of bladder neck
188.6 Malignant neoplasm of ureteric orifice
188.8 Malignant neoplasm of other specified sites of bladder
188.9 Malignant neoplasm of bladder, part unspecified ▽
189.3 Malignant neoplasm of urethra
199.0 Disseminated malignant neoplasm
199.1 Other malignant neoplasm of unspecified site
233.4 Carcinoma in situ of prostate ♂
233.7 Carcinoma in situ of bladder
233.9 Carcinoma in situ of other and unspecified urinary organs ▽
236.5 Neoplasm of uncertain behavior of prostate ♂
236.6 Neoplasm of uncertain behavior of other and unspecified male genital organs ▽ ♂
236.7 Neoplasm of uncertain behavior of bladder
239.4 Neoplasm of unspecified nature of bladder
239.5 Neoplasm of unspecified nature of other genitourinary organs
344.61 Cauda equina syndrome with neurogenic bladder
590.00 Chronic pyelonephritis without lesion of renal medullary necrosis — (Use additional code to identify organism, such as E. coli, 041.41-041.49. Code if applicable, any causal condition first)
591 Hydronephrosis
592.9 Unspecified urinary calculus ▽
594.1 Other calculus in bladder
595.0 Acute cystitis — (Use additional code to identify organism, such as E. coli: 041.41-041.49)
595.1 Chronic interstitial cystitis — (Use additional code to identify organism, such as E. coli: 041.41-041.49)
595.2 Other chronic cystitis — (Use additional code to identify organism, such as E. coli: 041.41-041.49)
595.3 Trigonitis — (Use additional code to identify organism, such as E. coli: 041.41-041.49)
595.81 Cystitis cystica — (Use additional code to identify organism, such as E. coli: 041.41-041.49)
595.82 Irradiation cystitis — (Use additional code to identify organism, such as E. coli: 041.41-041.49. Use additional E code to identify cause)
595.89 Other specified types of cystitis — (Use additional code to identify organism, such as E. coli: 041.41-041.49)
596.0 Bladder neck obstruction — (Use additional code to identify urinary incontinence: 625.6, 788.30-788.39)
596.1 Intestinovesical fistula — (Use additional code to identify urinary incontinence: 625.6, 788.30-788.39)
596.2 Vesical fistula, not elsewhere classified — (Use additional code to identify urinary incontinence: 625.6, 788.30-788.39)
596.3 Diverticulum of bladder — (Use additional code to identify urinary incontinence: 625.6, 788.30-788.39)
596.51 Hypertonicity of bladder — (Use additional code to identify urinary incontinence: 625.6, 788.30-788.39)
596.52 Low bladder compliance — (Use additional code to identify urinary incontinence: 625.6, 788.30-788.39)
596.53 Paralysis of bladder — (Use additional code to identify urinary incontinence: 625.6, 788.30-788.39)
596.54 Neurogenic bladder, NOS — (Use additional code to identify urinary incontinence: 625.6, 788.30-788.39) ▽
596.55 Detrusor sphincter dyssynergia — (Use additional code to identify urinary incontinence: 625.6, 788.30-788.39)
596.59 Other functional disorder of bladder — (Use additional code to identify urinary incontinence: 625.6, 788.30-788.39)
596.6 Nontraumatic rupture of bladder — (Use additional code to identify urinary incontinence: 625.6, 788.30-788.39)
596.7 Hemorrhage into bladder wall — (Use additional code to identify urinary incontinence: 625.6, 788.30-788.39)
596.89 Other specified disorders of bladder
597.0 Urethral abscess
597.80 Unspecified urethritis ▽
597.81 Urethral syndrome NOS ▽
597.89 Other urethritis
598.00 Urethral stricture due to unspecified infection — (Use additional code to identify urinary incontinence: 625.6, 788.30-788.39) ▽
598.01 Urethral stricture due to infective diseases classified elsewhere — (Use additional code to identify urinary incontinence: 625.6, 788.30-788.39. Code first underlying disease: 095.8, 098.2, 120.0-120.9) ☒
598.1 Traumatic urethral stricture — (Use additional code to identify urinary incontinence: 625.6, 788.30-788.39)
598.2 Postoperative urethral stricture — (Use additional code to identify urinary incontinence: 625.6, 788.30-788.39)
598.8 Other specified causes of urethral stricture — (Use additional code to identify urinary incontinence: 625.6, 788.30-788.39)

599.0 Urinary tract infection, site not specified — (Use additional code to identify organism, such as E. coli: 041.41-041.49) ▽

599.1 Urethral fistula

599.2 Urethral diverticulum

599.3 Urethral caruncle

599.4 Urethral false passage

599.5 Prolapsed urethral mucosa

599.70 Hematuria, unspecified ▽

599.71 Gross hematuria

599.72 Microscopic hematuria

599.81 Urethral hypermobility — (Use additional code to identify urinary incontinence: 625.6, 788.30-788.39)

599.82 Intrinsic (urethral) sphincter deficiency (ISD) — (Use additional code to identify urinary incontinence: 625.6, 788.30-788.39)

599.83 Urethral instability — (Use additional code to identify urinary incontinence: 625.6, 788.30-788.39)

599.84 Other specified disorders of urethra — (Use additional code to identify urinary incontinence: 625.6, 788.30-788.39)

599.89 Other specified disorders of urinary tract — (Use additional code to identify urinary incontinence: 625.6, 788.30-788.39)

600.00 Hypertrophy (benign) of prostate without urinary obstruction and other lower urinary tract symptoms [LUTS] ♂

600.01 Hypertrophy (benign) of prostate with urinary obstruction and other lower urinary tract symptoms [LUTS] — (Use additional code to identify symptoms: 599.69, 788.20, 788.21, 788.30-788.39, 788.41, 788.43, 788.62, 788.63, 788.64, 788.65) ♂

600.10 Nodular prostate without urinary obstruction ♂

600.11 Nodular prostate with urinary obstruction ♂

600.20 Benign localized hyperplasia of prostate without urinary obstruction and other lower urinary tract symptoms [LUTS] ♂

600.21 Benign localized hyperplasia of prostate with urinary obstruction and other lower urinary tract symptoms [LUTS] — (Use additional code to identify symptoms: 599.69, 788.20, 788.21, 788.30-788.39, 788.41, 788.43, 788.62, 788.63, 788.64, 788.65) ♂

600.3 Cyst of prostate ♂

600.90 Hyperplasia of prostate, unspecified, without urinary obstruction and other lower urinary tract symptoms [LUTS] ▽ ♂

600.91 Hyperplasia of prostate, unspecified, with urinary obstruction and other lower urinary tract symptoms [LUTS] — (Use additional code to identify symptoms: 599.69, 788.20, 788.21, 788.30-788.39, 788.41, 788.43, 788.62, 788.63, 788.64, 788.65) ▽ ♂

601.0 Acute prostatitis — (Use additional code to identify organism: 041.0, 041.1) ♂

601.1 Chronic prostatitis — (Use additional code to identify organism: 041.0, 041.1) ♂

601.8 Other specified inflammatory disease of prostate — (Use additional code to identify organism: 041.0, 041.1) ♂

602.0 Calculus of prostate ♂

602.1 Congestion or hemorrhage of prostate ♂

602.3 Dysplasia of prostate ♂

602.8 Other specified disorder of prostate ♂

607.84 Impotence of organic origin ♂

619.0 Urinary-genital tract fistula, female ♀

625.6 Female stress incontinence ♀

753.5 Exstrophy of urinary bladder

753.6 Congenital atresia and stenosis of urethra and bladder neck

753.8 Other specified congenital anomaly of bladder and urethra

788.0 Renal colic

788.1 Dysuria

788.21 Incomplete bladder emptying — (Code, if applicable, any causal condition first, such as: 600.0-600.9, with fifth digit 1)

788.29 Other specified retention of urine — (Code, if applicable, any causal condition first, such as: 600.0-600.9, with fifth digit 1)

788.30 Unspecified urinary incontinence — (Code, if applicable, any causal condition first: 600.0-600.9, with fifth digit 1; 618.00-618.9; 753.23) ▽

788.31 Urge incontinence — (Code, if applicable, any causal condition first: 600.0-600.9, with fifth digit 1; 618.00-618.9; 753.23)

788.32 Stress incontinence, male — (Code, if applicable, any causal condition first: 600.0-600.9, with fifth digit 1; 618.00-618.9; 753.23) ♂

788.33 Mixed incontinence urge and stress (male)(female) — (Code, if applicable, any causal condition first: 600.0-600.9, with fifth digit 1; 618.00-618.9; 753.23)

788.34 Incontinence without sensory awareness — (Code, if applicable, any causal condition first: 600.0-600.9, with fifth digit 1; 618.00-618.9; 753.23)

788.35 Post-void dribbling — (Code, if applicable, any causal condition first: 600.0-600.9, with fifth digit 1; 618.00-618.9; 753.23)

788.36 Nocturnal enuresis — (Code, if applicable, any causal condition first: 600.0-600.9, with fifth digit 1; 618.00-618.9; 753.23)

788.37 Continuous leakage — (Code, if applicable, any causal condition first: 600.0-600.9, with fifth digit 1; 618.00-618.9; 753.23)

788.38 Overflow incontinence — (Code, if applicable, any causal condition first: 600.0-600.9, with fifth digit 1; 618.00-618.9; 753.23)

788.39 Other urinary incontinence — (Code, if applicable, any causal condition first: 600.0-600.9, with fifth digit 1; 618.00-618.9; 753.23)

788.41 Urinary frequency — (Code, if applicable, any causal condition first, such as: 600.0-600.9, with fifth digit 1)

788.42 Polyuria — (Code, if applicable, any causal condition first, such as: 600.0-600.9, with fifth digit 1)

788.43 Nocturia — (Code, if applicable, any causal condition first, such as: 600.0-600.9, with fifth digit 1)

788.5 Oliguria and anuria

788.63 Urgency of urination — (Code, if applicable, any causal condition first, such as: 600.0-600.9, with fifth digit 1)

788.64 Urinary hesitancy — (Code, if applicable, any causal condition first, such as: 600.0-600.9, with fifth digit 1)

788.65 Straining on urination — (Code, if applicable, any causal condition first, such as: 600.0-600.9, with fifth digit 1)

788.69 Other abnormality of urination — (Code, if applicable, any causal condition first, such as: 600.0-600.9, with fifth digit 1)

788.7 Urethral discharge

788.8 Extravasation of urine

789.00 Abdominal pain, unspecified site ▽

789.01 Abdominal pain, right upper quadrant

789.02 Abdominal pain, left upper quadrant

789.07 Abdominal pain, generalized

789.09 Abdominal pain, other specified site

789.30 Abdominal or pelvic swelling, mass or lump, unspecified site ▽

789.31 Abdominal or pelvic swelling, mass, or lump, right upper quadrant

789.32 Abdominal or pelvic swelling, mass, or lump, left upper quadrant

789.37 Abdominal or pelvic swelling, mass, or lump, generalized

789.39 Abdominal or pelvic swelling, mass, or lump, other specified site

793.5 Nonspecific (abnormal) findings on radiological and other examination of genitourinary organs

867.1 Bladder and urethra injury with open wound into cavity

939.0 Foreign body in bladder and urethra

V10.46 Personal history of malignant neoplasm of prostate ♂

V10.51 Personal history of malignant neoplasm of bladder

V71.1 Observation for suspected malignant neoplasm

V76.3 Screening for malignant neoplasm of the bladder

ICD-9-CM Procedural

57.32 Other cystoscopy

HCPCS Level II Supplies & Services

A4270 Disposable endoscope sheath, each

52001

52001 Cystourethroscopy with irrigation and evacuation of multiple obstructing clots

ICD-9-CM Diagnostic

Code	Description
185	Malignant neoplasm of prostate ♂
188.0	Malignant neoplasm of trigone of urinary bladder
188.1	Malignant neoplasm of dome of urinary bladder
188.2	Malignant neoplasm of lateral wall of urinary bladder
188.3	Malignant neoplasm of anterior wall of urinary bladder
188.4	Malignant neoplasm of posterior wall of urinary bladder
188.5	Malignant neoplasm of bladder neck
188.6	Malignant neoplasm of ureteric orifice
188.8	Malignant neoplasm of other specified sites of bladder
188.9	Malignant neoplasm of bladder, part unspecified ▽
189.3	Malignant neoplasm of urethra
199.0	Disseminated malignant neoplasm
199.1	Other malignant neoplasm of unspecified site
233.4	Carcinoma in situ of prostate ♂
233.7	Carcinoma in situ of bladder
233.9	Carcinoma in situ of other and unspecified urinary organs ▽
236.5	Neoplasm of uncertain behavior of prostate ♂
236.6	Neoplasm of uncertain behavior of other and unspecified male genital organs ▽ ♂
236.7	Neoplasm of uncertain behavior of bladder
239.4	Neoplasm of unspecified nature of bladder
239.5	Neoplasm of unspecified nature of other genitourinary organs
344.61	Cauda equina syndrome with neurogenic bladder
590.00	Chronic pyelonephritis without lesion of renal medullary necrosis — (Use additional code to identify organism, such as E. coli, 041.41-041.49. Code if applicable, any causal condition first)
591	Hydronephrosis
592.9	Unspecified urinary calculus ▽
594.1	Other calculus in bladder
595.0	Acute cystitis — (Use additional code to identify organism, such as E. coli: 041.41-041.49)
595.1	Chronic interstitial cystitis — (Use additional code to identify organism, such as E. coli: 041.41-041.49)
595.2	Other chronic cystitis — (Use additional code to identify organism, such as E. coli: 041.41-041.49)
595.3	Trigonitis — (Use additional code to identify organism, such as E. coli: 041.41-041.49)
595.81	Cystitis cystica — (Use additional code to identify organism, such as E. coli: 041.41-041.49)
595.82	Irradiation cystitis — (Use additional code to identify organism, such as E. coli: 041.41-041.49. Use additional E code to identify cause)
595.89	Other specified types of cystitis — (Use additional code to identify organism, such as E. coli: 041.41-041.49)
596.0	Bladder neck obstruction — (Use additional code to identify urinary incontinence: 625.6, 788.30-788.39)
596.1	Intestinovesical fistula — (Use additional code to identify urinary incontinence: 625.6, 788.30-788.39)
596.2	Vesical fistula, not elsewhere classified — (Use additional code to identify urinary incontinence: 625.6, 788.30-788.39)
596.3	Diverticulum of bladder — (Use additional code to identify urinary incontinence: 625.6, 788.30-788.39)
596.51	Hypertonicity of bladder — (Use additional code to identify urinary incontinence: 625.6, 788.30-788.39)
596.52	Low bladder compliance — (Use additional code to identify urinary incontinence: 625.6, 788.30-788.39)
596.53	Paralysis of bladder — (Use additional code to identify urinary incontinence: 625.6, 788.30-788.39)
596.54	Neurogenic bladder, NOS — (Use additional code to identify urinary incontinence: 625.6, 788.30-788.39) ▽
596.55	Detrusor sphincter dyssynergia — (Use additional code to identify urinary incontinence: 625.6, 788.30-788.39)
596.59	Other functional disorder of bladder — (Use additional code to identify urinary incontinence: 625.6, 788.30-788.39)
596.6	Nontraumatic rupture of bladder — (Use additional code to identify urinary incontinence: 625.6, 788.30-788.39)
596.7	Hemorrhage into bladder wall — (Use additional code to identify urinary incontinence: 625.6, 788.30-788.39)
596.89	Other specified disorders of bladder
597.0	Urethral abscess
597.80	Unspecified urethritis ▽
597.81	Urethral syndrome NOS ▽
597.89	Other urethritis
598.00	Urethral stricture due to unspecified infection — (Use additional code to identify urinary incontinence: 625.6, 788.30-788.39) ▽
598.01	Urethral stricture due to infective diseases classified elsewhere — (Use additional code to identify urinary incontinence: 625.6, 788.30-788.39. Code first underlying disease: 095.8, 098.2, 120.0-120.9) ☒
598.1	Traumatic urethral stricture — (Use additional code to identify urinary incontinence: 625.6, 788.30-788.39)
598.2	Postoperative urethral stricture — (Use additional code to identify urinary incontinence: 625.6, 788.30-788.39)
598.8	Other specified causes of urethral stricture — (Use additional code to identify urinary incontinence: 625.6, 788.30-788.39)
599.0	Urinary tract infection, site not specified — (Use additional code to identify organism, such as E. coli: 041.41-041.49) ▽
599.1	Urethral fistula
599.2	Urethral diverticulum
599.3	Urethral caruncle
599.4	Urethral false passage
599.5	Prolapsed urethral mucosa
599.70	Hematuria, unspecified ▽
599.71	Gross hematuria
599.72	Microscopic hematuria
599.81	Urethral hypermobility — (Use additional code to identify urinary incontinence: 625.6, 788.30-788.39)
599.82	Intrinsic (urethral) sphincter deficiency (ISD) — (Use additional code to identify urinary incontinence: 625.6, 788.30-788.39)
599.83	Urethral instability — (Use additional code to identify urinary incontinence: 625.6, 788.30-788.39)
599.84	Other specified disorders of urethra — (Use additional code to identify urinary incontinence: 625.6, 788.30-788.39)
599.89	Other specified disorders of urinary tract — (Use additional code to identify urinary incontinence: 625.6, 788.30-788.39)
600.00	Hypertrophy (benign) of prostate without urinary obstruction and other lower urinary tract symptoms [LUTS] ♂
600.01	Hypertrophy (benign) of prostate with urinary obstruction and other lower urinary tract symptoms [LUTS] — (Use additional code to identify symptoms: 599.69, 788.20, 788.21, 788.30-788.39, 788.41, 788.43, 788.62, 788.63, 788.64, 788.65) ♂
600.10	Nodular prostate without urinary obstruction ♂
600.11	Nodular prostate with urinary obstruction ♂
600.20	Benign localized hyperplasia of prostate without urinary obstruction and other lower urinary tract symptoms [LUTS] ♂
600.21	Benign localized hyperplasia of prostate with urinary obstruction and other lower urinary tract symptoms [LUTS] — (Use additional code to identify symptoms: 599.69, 788.20, 788.21, 788.30-788.39, 788.41, 788.43, 788.62, 788.63, 788.64, 788.65) ♂
600.3	Cyst of prostate ♂

600.90 Hyperplasia of prostate, unspecified, without urinary obstruction and other lower urinary tract symptoms [LUTS] ♂

600.91 Hyperplasia of prostate, unspecified, with urinary obstruction and other lower urinary tract symptoms [LUTS] — (Use additional code to identify symptoms: 599.69, 788.20, 788.21, 788.30-788.39, 788.41, 788.43, 788.62, 788.63, 788.64, 788.65) ♂

601.0 Acute prostatitis — (Use additional code to identify organism: 041.0, 041.1) ♂

601.1 Chronic prostatitis — (Use additional code to identify organism: 041.0, 041.1) ♂

601.8 Other specified inflammatory disease of prostate — (Use additional code to identify organism: 041.0, 041.1) ♂

602.0 Calculus of prostate ♂

602.1 Congestion or hemorrhage of prostate ♂

602.3 Dysplasia of prostate ♂

602.8 Other specified disorder of prostate ♂

607.84 Impotence of organic origin ♂

619.0 Urinary-genital tract fistula, female ♀

625.6 Female stress incontinence ♀

753.5 Exstrophy of urinary bladder

753.6 Congenital atresia and stenosis of urethra and bladder neck

753.8 Other specified congenital anomaly of bladder and urethra

788.0 Renal colic

788.1 Dysuria

788.21 Incomplete bladder emptying — (Code, if applicable, any causal condition first, such as: 600.0-600.9, with fifth digit 1)

788.29 Other specified retention of urine — (Code, if applicable, any causal condition first, such as: 600.0-600.9, with fifth digit 1)

788.30 Unspecified urinary incontinence — (Code, if applicable, any causal condition first: 600.0-600.9, with fifth digit 1; 618.00-618.9; 753.23)

788.31 Urge incontinence — (Code, if applicable, any causal condition first: 600.0-600.9, with fifth digit 1; 618.00-618.9; 753.23)

788.32 Stress incontinence, male — (Code, if applicable, any causal condition first: 600.0-600.9, with fifth digit 1; 618.00-618.9; 753.23) ♂

788.33 Mixed incontinence urge and stress (male)(female) — (Code, if applicable, any causal condition first: 600.0-600.9, with fifth digit 1; 618.00-618.9; 753.23)

788.34 Incontinence without sensory awareness — (Code, if applicable, any causal condition first: 600.0-600.9, with fifth digit 1; 618.00-618.9; 753.23)

788.35 Post-void dribbling — (Code, if applicable, any causal condition first: 600.0-600.9, with fifth digit 1; 618.00-618.9; 753.23)

788.36 Nocturnal enuresis — (Code, if applicable, any causal condition first: 600.0-600.9, with fifth digit 1; 618.00-618.9; 753.23)

788.37 Continuous leakage — (Code, if applicable, any causal condition first: 600.0-600.9, with fifth digit 1; 618.00-618.9; 753.23)

788.38 Overflow incontinence — (Code, if applicable, any causal condition first: 600.0-600.9, with fifth digit 1; 618.00-618.9; 753.23)

788.39 Other urinary incontinence — (Code, if applicable, any causal condition first: 600.0-600.9, with fifth digit 1; 618.00-618.9; 753.23)

788.41 Urinary frequency — (Code, if applicable, any causal condition first, such as: 600.0-600.9, with fifth digit 1)

788.42 Polyuria — (Code, if applicable, any causal condition first, such as: 600.0-600.9, with fifth digit 1)

788.43 Nocturia — (Code, if applicable, any causal condition first, such as: 600.0-600.9, with fifth digit 1)

788.5 Oliguria and anuria

788.63 Urgency of urination — (Code, if applicable, any causal condition first, such as: 600.0-600.9, with fifth digit 1)

788.64 Urinary hesitancy — (Code, if applicable, any causal condition first, such as: 600.0-600.9, with fifth digit 1)

788.65 Straining on urination — (Code, if applicable, any causal condition first, such as: 600.0-600.9, with fifth digit 1)

788.69 Other abnormality of urination — (Code, if applicable, any causal condition first, such as: 600.0-600.9, with fifth digit 1)

788.7 Urethral discharge

788.8 Extravasation of urine

789.00 Abdominal pain, unspecified site

789.01 Abdominal pain, right upper quadrant

789.02 Abdominal pain, left upper quadrant

789.07 Abdominal pain, generalized

789.09 Abdominal pain, other specified site

789.30 Abdominal or pelvic swelling, mass or lump, unspecified site

789.31 Abdominal or pelvic swelling, mass, or lump, right upper quadrant

789.32 Abdominal or pelvic swelling, mass, or lump, left upper quadrant

789.37 Abdominal or pelvic swelling, mass, or lump, generalized

789.39 Abdominal or pelvic swelling, mass, or lump, other specified site

793.5 Nonspecific (abnormal) findings on radiological and other examination of genitourinary organs

867.1 Bladder and urethra injury with open wound into cavity

939.0 Foreign body in bladder and urethra

V10.46 Personal history of malignant neoplasm of prostate ♂

V10.51 Personal history of malignant neoplasm of bladder

V71.1 Observation for suspected malignant neoplasm

V76.3 Screening for malignant neoplasm of the bladder

ICD-9-CM Procedural

57.99 Other operations on bladder

52005-52007

52005 Cystourethroscopy, with ureteral catheterization, with or without irrigation, instillation, or ureteropyelography, exclusive of radiologic service;

52007 with brush biopsy of ureter and/or renal pelvis

ICD-9-CM Diagnostic

185 Malignant neoplasm of prostate ♂

188.0 Malignant neoplasm of trigone of urinary bladder

188.1 Malignant neoplasm of dome of urinary bladder

188.2 Malignant neoplasm of lateral wall of urinary bladder

188.3 Malignant neoplasm of anterior wall of urinary bladder

188.4 Malignant neoplasm of posterior wall of urinary bladder

188.5 Malignant neoplasm of bladder neck

188.6 Malignant neoplasm of ureteric orifice

188.8 Malignant neoplasm of other specified sites of bladder

188.9 Malignant neoplasm of bladder, part unspecified

189.1 Malignant neoplasm of renal pelvis

189.2 Malignant neoplasm of ureter

189.3 Malignant neoplasm of urethra

198.0 Secondary malignant neoplasm of kidney

198.1 Secondary malignant neoplasm of other urinary organs

199.1 Other malignant neoplasm of unspecified site

222.2 Benign neoplasm of prostate ♂

223.0 Benign neoplasm of kidney, except pelvis

223.1 Benign neoplasm of renal pelvis

223.3 Benign neoplasm of bladder

223.81 Benign neoplasm of urethra

223.89 Benign neoplasm of other specified sites of urinary organs

223.9 Benign neoplasm of urinary organ, site unspecified

233.7 Carcinoma in situ of bladder

233.9 Carcinoma in situ of other and unspecified urinary organs

236.5 Neoplasm of uncertain behavior of prostate ♂

236.7 Neoplasm of uncertain behavior of bladder

239.4 Neoplasm of unspecified nature of bladder

239.5 Neoplasm of unspecified nature of other genitourinary organs

344.61 Cauda equina syndrome with neurogenic bladder

591 Hydronephrosis
592.0 Calculus of kidney
592.1 Calculus of ureter
593.0 Nephroptosis
593.1 Hypertrophy of kidney
593.2 Acquired cyst of kidney
593.3 Stricture or kinking of ureter
593.4 Other ureteric obstruction
593.5 Hydroureter
593.70 Vesicoureteral reflux, unspecified or without reflex nephropathy
593.71 Vesicoureteral reflux with reflux nephropathy, unilateral
593.72 Vesicoureteral reflux with reflux nephropathy, bilateral
593.73 Vesicoureteral reflux with reflux nephropathy, NOS ▼
593.81 Vascular disorders of kidney
593.82 Ureteral fistula
593.89 Other specified disorder of kidney and ureter
594.0 Calculus in diverticulum of bladder
594.1 Other calculus in bladder
594.2 Calculus in urethra
594.8 Other lower urinary tract calculus
595.0 Acute cystitis — (Use additional code to identify organism, such as E. coli: 041.41-041.49)
595.1 Chronic interstitial cystitis — (Use additional code to identify organism, such as E. coli: 041.41-041.49)
595.2 Other chronic cystitis — (Use additional code to identify organism, such as E. coli: 041.41-041.49)
595.3 Trigonitis — (Use additional code to identify organism, such as E. coli: 041.41-041.49)
595.81 Cystitis cystica — (Use additional code to identify organism, such as E. coli: 041.41-041.49)
595.82 Irradiation cystitis — (Use additional code to identify organism, such as E. coli: 041.41-041.49. Use additional E code to identify cause)
595.89 Other specified types of cystitis — (Use additional code to identify organism, such as E. coli: 041.41-041.49)
596.0 Bladder neck obstruction — (Use additional code to identify urinary incontinence: 625.6, 788.30-788.39)
596.1 Intestinovesical fistula — (Use additional code to identify urinary incontinence: 625.6, 788.30-788.39)
596.2 Vesical fistula, not elsewhere classified — (Use additional code to identify urinary incontinence: 625.6, 788.30-788.39)
596.3 Diverticulum of bladder — (Use additional code to identify urinary incontinence: 625.6, 788.30-788.39)
596.51 Hypertonicity of bladder — (Use additional code to identify urinary incontinence: 625.6, 788.30-788.39)
596.6 Nontraumatic rupture of bladder — (Use additional code to identify urinary incontinence: 625.6, 788.30-788.39)
596.7 Hemorrhage into bladder wall — (Use additional code to identify urinary incontinence: 625.6, 788.30-788.39)
596.89 Other specified disorders of bladder
598.00 Urethral stricture due to unspecified infection — (Use additional code to identify urinary incontinence: 625.6, 788.30-788.39) ▼
598.01 Urethral stricture due to infective diseases classified elsewhere — (Use additional code to identify urinary incontinence: 625.6, 788.30-788.39. Code first underlying disease: 095.8, 098.2, 120.0-120.9) ☒
598.1 Traumatic urethral stricture — (Use additional code to identify urinary incontinence: 625.6, 788.30-788.39)
598.2 Postoperative urethral stricture — (Use additional code to identify urinary incontinence: 625.6, 788.30-788.39)
598.8 Other specified causes of urethral stricture — (Use additional code to identify urinary incontinence: 625.6, 788.30-788.39)
599.0 Urinary tract infection, site not specified — (Use additional code to identify organism, such as E. coli: 041.41-041.49) ▼
599.70 Hematuria, unspecified ▼
599.71 Gross hematuria
599.72 Microscopic hematuria
600.00 Hypertrophy (benign) of prostate without urinary obstruction and other lower urinary tract symptoms [LUTS] ♂
600.01 Hypertrophy (benign) of prostate with urinary obstruction and other lower urinary tract symptoms [LUTS] — (Use additional code to identify symptoms: 599.69, 788.20, 788.21, 788.30-788.39, 788.41, 788.43, 788.62, 788.63, 788.64, 788.65) ♂
600.10 Nodular prostate without urinary obstruction ♂
600.11 Nodular prostate with urinary obstruction ♂
600.20 Benign localized hyperplasia of prostate without urinary obstruction and other lower urinary tract symptoms [LUTS] ♂
600.21 Benign localized hyperplasia of prostate with urinary obstruction and other lower urinary tract symptoms [LUTS] — (Use additional code to identify symptoms: 599.69, 788.20, 788.21, 788.30-788.39, 788.41, 788.43, 788.62, 788.63, 788.64, 788.65) ♂
600.3 Cyst of prostate ♂
600.90 Hyperplasia of prostate, unspecified, without urinary obstruction and other lower urinary tract symptoms [LUTS] ▼ ♂
600.91 Hyperplasia of prostate, unspecified, with urinary obstruction and other lower urinary tract symptoms [LUTS] — (Use additional code to identify symptoms: 599.69, 788.20, 788.21, 788.30-788.39, 788.41, 788.43, 788.62, 788.63, 788.64, 788.65) ▼ ♂
601.0 Acute prostatitis — (Use additional code to identify organism: 041.0, 041.1) ♂
601.1 Chronic prostatitis — (Use additional code to identify organism: 041.0, 041.1) ♂
601.8 Other specified inflammatory disease of prostate — (Use additional code to identify organism: 041.0, 041.1) ♂
625.6 Female stress incontinence ♀
625.9 Unspecified symptom associated with female genital organs ▼ ♀
753.0 Congenital renal agenesis and dysgenesis
753.11 Congenital single renal cyst
753.12 Congenital polycystic kidney, unspecified type ▼
753.13 Congenital polycystic kidney, autosomal dominant
753.14 Congenital polycystic kidney, autosomal recessive
753.15 Congenital renal dysplasia
753.16 Congenital medullary cystic kidney
753.17 Congenital medullary sponge kidney
753.19 Other specified congenital cystic kidney disease
753.21 Congenital obstruction of ureteropelvic junction
753.22 Congenital obstruction of ureterovesical junction
753.23 Congenital ureterocele
753.29 Other obstructive defect of renal pelvis and ureter
753.3 Other specified congenital anomalies of kidney
753.4 Other specified congenital anomalies of ureter
753.5 Exstrophy of urinary bladder
753.6 Congenital atresia and stenosis of urethra and bladder neck
753.8 Other specified congenital anomaly of bladder and urethra
788.0 Renal colic
788.1 Dysuria
788.21 Incomplete bladder emptying — (Code, if applicable, any causal condition first, such as: 600.0-600.9, with fifth digit 1)
788.29 Other specified retention of urine — (Code, if applicable, any causal condition first, such as: 600.0-600.9, with fifth digit 1)
788.31 Urge incontinence — (Code, if applicable, any causal condition first: 600.0-600.9, with fifth digit 1; 618.00-618.9; 753.23)
788.32 Stress incontinence, male — (Code, if applicable, any causal condition first: 600.0-600.9, with fifth digit 1; 618.00-618.9; 753.23) ♂
788.33 Mixed incontinence urge and stress (male)(female) — (Code, if applicable, any causal condition first: 600.0-600.9, with fifth digit 1; 618.00-618.9; 753.23)
788.34 Incontinence without sensory awareness — (Code, if applicable, any causal condition first: 600.0-600.9, with fifth digit 1; 618.00-618.9; 753.23)

788.35 Post-void dribbling — (Code, if applicable, any causal condition first: 600.0-600.9, with fifth digit 1; 618.00-618.9; 753.23)
788.36 Nocturnal enuresis — (Code, if applicable, any causal condition first: 600.0-600.9, with fifth digit 1; 618.00-618.9; 753.23)
788.37 Continuous leakage — (Code, if applicable, any causal condition first: 600.0-600.9, with fifth digit 1; 618.00-618.9; 753.23)
788.38 Overflow incontinence — (Code, if applicable, any causal condition first: 600.0-600.9, with fifth digit 1; 618.00-618.9; 753.23)
788.39 Other urinary incontinence — (Code, if applicable, any causal condition first: 600.0-600.9, with fifth digit 1; 618.00-618.9; 753.23)
788.41 Urinary frequency — (Code, if applicable, any causal condition first, such as: 600.0-600.9, with fifth digit 1)
788.42 Polyuria — (Code, if applicable, any causal condition first, such as: 600.0-600.9, with fifth digit 1)
788.43 Nocturia — (Code, if applicable, any causal condition first, such as: 600.0-600.9, with fifth digit 1)
788.5 Oliguria and anuria
788.61 Splitting of urinary stream — (Code, if applicable, any causal condition first, such as: 600.0-600.9, with fifth digit 1)
788.62 Slowing of urinary stream — (Code, if applicable, any causal condition first, such as: 600.0-600.9, with fifth digit 1)
788.63 Urgency of urination — (Code, if applicable, any causal condition first, such as: 600.0-600.9, with fifth digit 1)
788.64 Urinary hesitancy — (Code, if applicable, any causal condition first, such as: 600.0-600.9, with fifth digit 1)
788.65 Straining on urination — (Code, if applicable, any causal condition first, such as: 600.0-600.9, with fifth digit 1)
788.69 Other abnormality of urination — (Code, if applicable, any causal condition first, such as: 600.0-600.9, with fifth digit 1)
788.7 Urethral discharge
788.8 Extravasation of urine
788.91 Functional urinary incontinence
788.99 Other symptoms involving urinary system
789.00 Abdominal pain, unspecified site ▽
789.01 Abdominal pain, right upper quadrant
789.02 Abdominal pain, left upper quadrant
789.07 Abdominal pain, generalized
789.09 Abdominal pain, other specified site
789.30 Abdominal or pelvic swelling, mass or lump, unspecified site ▽
789.31 Abdominal or pelvic swelling, mass, or lump, right upper quadrant
789.32 Abdominal or pelvic swelling, mass, or lump, left upper quadrant
789.37 Abdominal or pelvic swelling, mass, or lump, generalized
789.39 Abdominal or pelvic swelling, mass, or lump, other specified site
793.5 Nonspecific (abnormal) findings on radiological and other examination of genitourinary organs
939.0 Foreign body in bladder and urethra

ICD-9-CM Procedural

56.33 Closed endoscopic biopsy of ureter
56.39 Other diagnostic procedures on ureter
57.32 Other cystoscopy
59.8 Ureteral catheterization
87.74 Retrograde pyelogram

HCPCS Level II Supplies & Services

A4270 Disposable endoscope sheath, each

52010

52010 Cystourethroscopy, with ejaculatory duct catheterization, with or without irrigation, instillation, or duct radiography, exclusive of radiologic service

ICD-9-CM Diagnostic

600.00 Hypertrophy (benign) of prostate without urinary obstruction and other lower urinary tract symptoms [LUTS] ♂
600.01 Hypertrophy (benign) of prostate with urinary obstruction and other lower urinary tract symptoms [LUTS] — (Use additional code to identify symptoms: 599.69, 788.20, 788.21, 788.30-788.39, 788.41, 788.43, 788.62, 788.63, 788.64, 788.65) ♂
600.10 Nodular prostate without urinary obstruction ♂
600.11 Nodular prostate with urinary obstruction ♂
600.20 Benign localized hyperplasia of prostate without urinary obstruction and other lower urinary tract symptoms [LUTS] ♂
600.21 Benign localized hyperplasia of prostate with urinary obstruction and other lower urinary tract symptoms [LUTS] — (Use additional code to identify symptoms: 599.69, 788.20, 788.21, 788.30-788.39, 788.41, 788.43, 788.62, 788.63, 788.64, 788.65) ♂
600.3 Cyst of prostate ♂
600.90 Hyperplasia of prostate, unspecified, without urinary obstruction and other lower urinary tract symptoms [LUTS] ▽ ♂
600.91 Hyperplasia of prostate, unspecified, with urinary obstruction and other lower urinary tract symptoms [LUTS] — (Use additional code to identify symptoms: 599.69, 788.20, 788.21, 788.30-788.39, 788.41, 788.43, 788.62, 788.63, 788.64, 788.65) ▽ ♂
606.8 Infertility due to extratesticular causes ♂
607.84 Impotence of organic origin ♂
608.82 Hematospermia ♂
608.83 Specified vascular disorder of male genital organs ♂
753.9 Unspecified congenital anomaly of urinary system ▽

ICD-9-CM Procedural

57.32 Other cystoscopy
87.99 Other x-ray of male genital organs ♂

HCPCS Level II Supplies & Services

A4270 Disposable endoscope sheath, each

52204

52204 Cystourethroscopy, with biopsy(s)

ICD-9-CM Diagnostic

185 Malignant neoplasm of prostate ♂
188.0 Malignant neoplasm of trigone of urinary bladder
188.1 Malignant neoplasm of dome of urinary bladder
188.2 Malignant neoplasm of lateral wall of urinary bladder
188.3 Malignant neoplasm of anterior wall of urinary bladder
188.4 Malignant neoplasm of posterior wall of urinary bladder
188.5 Malignant neoplasm of bladder neck
188.6 Malignant neoplasm of ureteric orifice
188.8 Malignant neoplasm of other specified sites of bladder
188.9 Malignant neoplasm of bladder, part unspecified ▽
189.0 Malignant neoplasm of kidney, except pelvis
189.1 Malignant neoplasm of renal pelvis
189.2 Malignant neoplasm of ureter
189.3 Malignant neoplasm of urethra
199.0 Disseminated malignant neoplasm
199.1 Other malignant neoplasm of unspecified site
223.3 Benign neoplasm of bladder
223.81 Benign neoplasm of urethra
233.4 Carcinoma in situ of prostate ♂
233.7 Carcinoma in situ of bladder

233.9 Carcinoma in situ of other and unspecified urinary organs ▽
236.5 Neoplasm of uncertain behavior of prostate ♂
236.6 Neoplasm of uncertain behavior of other and unspecified male genital organs ▽ ♂
236.7 Neoplasm of uncertain behavior of bladder
239.4 Neoplasm of unspecified nature of bladder
239.5 Neoplasm of unspecified nature of other genitourinary organs
593.89 Other specified disorder of kidney and ureter
594.1 Other calculus in bladder
595.0 Acute cystitis — (Use additional code to identify organism, such as E. coli: 041.41-041.49)
595.1 Chronic interstitial cystitis — (Use additional code to identify organism, such as E. coli: 041.41-041.49)
595.2 Other chronic cystitis — (Use additional code to identify organism, such as E. coli: 041.41-041.49)
595.3 Trigonitis — (Use additional code to identify organism, such as E. coli: 041.41-041.49)
595.4 Cystitis in diseases classified elsewhere — (Use additional code to identify organism, such as E. coli: 041.41-041.49. Code first underlying disease: 006.8, 039.8, 120.0-120.9, 122.3, 122.6) ☒
595.81 Cystitis cystica — (Use additional code to identify organism, such as E. coli: 041.41-041.49)
595.82 Irradiation cystitis — (Use additional code to identify organism, such as E. coli: 041.41-041.49. Use additional E code to identify cause)
595.89 Other specified types of cystitis — (Use additional code to identify organism, such as E. coli: 041.41-041.49)
595.9 Unspecified cystitis — (Use additional code to identify organism, such as E. coli: 041.41-041.49) ▽
596.0 Bladder neck obstruction — (Use additional code to identify urinary incontinence: 625.6, 788.30-788.39)
596.3 Diverticulum of bladder — (Use additional code to identify urinary incontinence: 625.6, 788.30-788.39)
596.9 Unspecified disorder of bladder — (Use additional code to identify urinary incontinence: 625.6, 788.30-788.39) ▽
597.0 Urethral abscess
597.81 Urethral syndrome NOS ▽
597.89 Other urethritis
598.00 Urethral stricture due to unspecified infection — (Use additional code to identify urinary incontinence: 625.6, 788.30-788.39) ▽
598.01 Urethral stricture due to infective diseases classified elsewhere — (Use additional code to identify urinary incontinence: 625.6, 788.30-788.39. Code first underlying disease: 095.8, 098.2, 120.0-120.9) ☒
598.1 Traumatic urethral stricture — (Use additional code to identify urinary incontinence: 625.6, 788.30-788.39)
598.2 Postoperative urethral stricture — (Use additional code to identify urinary incontinence: 625.6, 788.30-788.39)
598.8 Other specified causes of urethral stricture — (Use additional code to identify urinary incontinence: 625.6, 788.30-788.39)
599.0 Urinary tract infection, site not specified — (Use additional code to identify organism, such as E. coli: 041.41-041.49) ▽
599.1 Urethral fistula
599.2 Urethral diverticulum
599.3 Urethral caruncle
599.4 Urethral false passage
599.5 Prolapsed urethral mucosa
599.70 Hematuria, unspecified ▽
599.71 Gross hematuria
599.72 Microscopic hematuria
599.81 Urethral hypermobility — (Use additional code to identify urinary incontinence: 625.6, 788.30-788.39)
599.82 Intrinsic (urethral) sphincter deficiency (ISD) — (Use additional code to identify urinary incontinence: 625.6, 788.30-788.39)
599.83 Urethral instability — (Use additional code to identify urinary incontinence: 625.6, 788.30-788.39)
599.84 Other specified disorders of urethra — (Use additional code to identify urinary incontinence: 625.6, 788.30-788.39)
599.89 Other specified disorders of urinary tract — (Use additional code to identify urinary incontinence: 625.6, 788.30-788.39)
600.00 Hypertrophy (benign) of prostate without urinary obstruction and other lower urinary tract symptoms [LUTS] ♂
600.01 Hypertrophy (benign) of prostate with urinary obstruction and other lower urinary tract symptoms [LUTS] — (Use additional code to identify symptoms: 599.69, 788.20, 788.21, 788.30-788.39, 788.41, 788.43, 788.62, 788.63, 788.64, 788.65) ♂
600.10 Nodular prostate without urinary obstruction ♂
600.11 Nodular prostate with urinary obstruction ♂
600.20 Benign localized hyperplasia of prostate without urinary obstruction and other lower urinary tract symptoms [LUTS] ♂
600.21 Benign localized hyperplasia of prostate with urinary obstruction and other lower urinary tract symptoms [LUTS] — (Use additional code to identify symptoms: 599.69, 788.20, 788.21, 788.30-788.39, 788.41, 788.43, 788.62, 788.63, 788.64, 788.65) ♂
600.3 Cyst of prostate ♂
600.90 Hyperplasia of prostate, unspecified, without urinary obstruction and other lower urinary tract symptoms [LUTS] ▽ ♂
600.91 Hyperplasia of prostate, unspecified, with urinary obstruction and other lower urinary tract symptoms [LUTS] — (Use additional code to identify symptoms: 599.69, 788.20, 788.21, 788.30-788.39, 788.41, 788.43, 788.62, 788.63, 788.64, 788.65) ▽ ♂
601.0 Acute prostatitis — (Use additional code to identify organism: 041.0, 041.1) ♂
601.1 Chronic prostatitis — (Use additional code to identify organism: 041.0, 041.1) ♂
601.8 Other specified inflammatory disease of prostate — (Use additional code to identify organism: 041.0, 041.1) ♂
601.9 Unspecified prostatitis — (Use additional code to identify organism: 041.0, 041.1) ▽ ♂
602.0 Calculus of prostate ♂
602.1 Congestion or hemorrhage of prostate ♂
602.3 Dysplasia of prostate ♂
602.8 Other specified disorder of prostate ♂
602.9 Unspecified disorder of prostate ▽ ♂
607.84 Impotence of organic origin ♂
619.0 Urinary-genital tract fistula, female ♀
753.6 Congenital atresia and stenosis of urethra and bladder neck
753.8 Other specified congenital anomaly of bladder and urethra
788.1 Dysuria
788.20 Unspecified retention of urine — (Code, if applicable, any causal condition first, such as: 600.0-600.9, with fifth digit 1) ▽
788.21 Incomplete bladder emptying — (Code, if applicable, any causal condition first, such as: 600.0-600.9, with fifth digit 1)
788.29 Other specified retention of urine — (Code, if applicable, any causal condition first, such as: 600.0-600.9, with fifth digit 1)
788.30 Unspecified urinary incontinence — (Code, if applicable, any causal condition first: 600.0-600.9, with fifth digit 1; 618.00-618.9; 753.23) ▽
788.31 Urge incontinence — (Code, if applicable, any causal condition first: 600.0-600.9, with fifth digit 1; 618.00-618.9; 753.23)
788.32 Stress incontinence, male — (Code, if applicable, any causal condition first: 600.0-600.9, with fifth digit 1; 618.00-618.9; 753.23) ♂
788.33 Mixed incontinence urge and stress (male)(female) — (Code, if applicable, any causal condition first: 600.0-600.9, with fifth digit 1; 618.00-618.9; 753.23)
788.34 Incontinence without sensory awareness — (Code, if applicable, any causal condition first: 600.0-600.9, with fifth digit 1; 618.00-618.9; 753.23)
788.35 Post-void dribbling — (Code, if applicable, any causal condition first: 600.0-600.9, with fifth digit 1; 618.00-618.9; 753.23)

788.36 Nocturnal enuresis — (Code, if applicable, any causal condition first: 600.0-600.9, with fifth digit 1; 618.00-618.9; 753.23)

788.37 Continuous leakage — (Code, if applicable, any causal condition first: 600.0-600.9, with fifth digit 1; 618.00-618.9; 753.23)

788.39 Other urinary incontinence — (Code, if applicable, any causal condition first: 600.0-600.9, with fifth digit 1; 618.00-618.9; 753.23)

788.41 Urinary frequency — (Code, if applicable, any causal condition first, such as: 600.0-600.9, with fifth digit 1)

788.42 Polyuria — (Code, if applicable, any causal condition first, such as: 600.0-600.9, with fifth digit 1)

788.43 Nocturia — (Code, if applicable, any causal condition first, such as: 600.0-600.9, with fifth digit 1)

788.5 Oliguria and anuria

788.61 Splitting of urinary stream — (Code, if applicable, any causal condition first, such as: 600.0-600.9, with fifth digit 1)

788.62 Slowing of urinary stream — (Code, if applicable, any causal condition first, such as: 600.0-600.9, with fifth digit 1)

788.63 Urgency of urination — (Code, if applicable, any causal condition first, such as: 600.0-600.9, with fifth digit 1)

788.64 Urinary hesitancy — (Code, if applicable, any causal condition first, such as: 600.0-600.9, with fifth digit 1)

788.65 Straining on urination — (Code, if applicable, any causal condition first, such as: 600.0-600.9, with fifth digit 1)

788.69 Other abnormality of urination — (Code, if applicable, any causal condition first, such as: 600.0-600.9, with fifth digit 1)

788.7 Urethral discharge

788.8 Extravasation of urine

788.99 Other symptoms involving urinary system

793.5 Nonspecific (abnormal) findings on radiological and other examination of genitourinary organs

939.0 Foreign body in bladder and urethra

V10.46 Personal history of malignant neoplasm of prostate ♂

V10.51 Personal history of malignant neoplasm of bladder

V47.4 Other urinary problems

V67.59 Other follow-up examination

V71.1 Observation for suspected malignant neoplasm

V71.89 Observation for other specified suspected conditions

V76.3 Screening for malignant neoplasm of the bladder

ICD-9-CM Procedural

57.33 Closed (transurethral) biopsy of bladder

HCPCS Level II Supplies & Services

A4270 Disposable endoscope sheath, each

52214

52214 Cystourethroscopy, with fulguration (including cryosurgery or laser surgery) of trigone, bladder neck, prostatic fossa, urethra, or periurethral glands

ICD-9-CM Diagnostic

185 Malignant neoplasm of prostate ♂

188.0 Malignant neoplasm of trigone of urinary bladder

188.1 Malignant neoplasm of dome of urinary bladder

188.5 Malignant neoplasm of bladder neck

188.9 Malignant neoplasm of bladder, part unspecified

189.3 Malignant neoplasm of urethra

195.3 Malignant neoplasm of pelvis

198.1 Secondary malignant neoplasm of other urinary organs

198.89 Secondary malignant neoplasm of other specified sites

223.3 Benign neoplasm of bladder

223.81 Benign neoplasm of urethra

223.9 Benign neoplasm of urinary organ, site unspecified

229.8 Benign neoplasm of other specified sites

233.7 Carcinoma in situ of bladder

233.9 Carcinoma in situ of other and unspecified urinary organs

236.7 Neoplasm of uncertain behavior of bladder

236.99 Neoplasm of uncertain behavior of other and unspecified urinary organs

238.8 Neoplasm of uncertain behavior of other specified sites

239.4 Neoplasm of unspecified nature of bladder

239.5 Neoplasm of unspecified nature of other genitourinary organs

239.89 Neoplasms of unspecified nature, other specified sites

595.1 Chronic interstitial cystitis — (Use additional code to identify organism, such as E. coli: 041.41-041.49)

595.82 Irradiation cystitis — (Use additional code to identify organism, such as E. coli: 041.41-041.49. Use additional E code to identify cause)

596.2 Vesical fistula, not elsewhere classified — (Use additional code to identify urinary incontinence: 625.6, 788.30-788.39)

596.7 Hemorrhage into bladder wall — (Use additional code to identify urinary incontinence: 625.6, 788.30-788.39)

596.89 Other specified disorders of bladder

597.81 Urethral syndrome NOS

598.9 Unspecified urethral stricture — (Use additional code to identify urinary incontinence: 625.6, 788.30-788.39)

599.2 Urethral diverticulum

599.3 Urethral caruncle

599.70 Hematuria, unspecified

599.71 Gross hematuria

599.72 Microscopic hematuria

625.6 Female stress incontinence ♀

788.1 Dysuria

788.29 Other specified retention of urine — (Code, if applicable, any causal condition first, such as: 600.0-600.9, with fifth digit 1)

788.41 Urinary frequency — (Code, if applicable, any causal condition first, such as: 600.0-600.9, with fifth digit 1)

788.42 Polyuria — (Code, if applicable, any causal condition first, such as: 600.0-600.9, with fifth digit 1)

788.43 Nocturia — (Code, if applicable, any causal condition first, such as: 600.0-600.9, with fifth digit 1)

788.99 Other symptoms involving urinary system

ICD-9-CM Procedural

57.49 Other transurethral excision or destruction of lesion or tissue of bladder

58.31 Endoscopic excision or destruction of lesion or tissue of urethra

HCPCS Level II Supplies & Services

A4270 Disposable endoscope sheath, each

52224

52224 Cystourethroscopy, with fulguration (including cryosurgery or laser surgery) or treatment of MINOR (less than 0.5 cm) lesion(s) with or without biopsy

ICD-9-CM Diagnostic

185 Malignant neoplasm of prostate ♂

188.0 Malignant neoplasm of trigone of urinary bladder

188.1 Malignant neoplasm of dome of urinary bladder

188.2 Malignant neoplasm of lateral wall of urinary bladder

188.3 Malignant neoplasm of anterior wall of urinary bladder

188.4 Malignant neoplasm of posterior wall of urinary bladder

188.5 Malignant neoplasm of bladder neck

188.6 Malignant neoplasm of ureteric orifice

188.7 Malignant neoplasm of urachus

188.8 Malignant neoplasm of other specified sites of bladder

188.9 Malignant neoplasm of bladder, part unspecified

189.3 Malignant neoplasm of urethra
189.9 Malignant neoplasm of urinary organ, site unspecified ▽
198.1 Secondary malignant neoplasm of other urinary organs
223.3 Benign neoplasm of bladder
223.81 Benign neoplasm of urethra
223.89 Benign neoplasm of other specified sites of urinary organs
223.9 Benign neoplasm of urinary organ, site unspecified ▽
233.7 Carcinoma in situ of bladder
236.7 Neoplasm of uncertain behavior of bladder
236.99 Neoplasm of uncertain behavior of other and unspecified urinary organs
239.4 Neoplasm of unspecified nature of bladder
595.0 Acute cystitis — (Use additional code to identify organism, such as E. coli: 041.41-041.49)
595.1 Chronic interstitial cystitis — (Use additional code to identify organism, such as E. coli: 041.41-041.49)
595.3 Trigonitis — (Use additional code to identify organism, such as E. coli: 041.41-041.49)
595.4 Cystitis in diseases classified elsewhere — (Use additional code to identify organism, such as E. coli: 041.41-041.49. Code first underlying disease: 006.8, 039.8, 120.0-120.9, 122.3, 122.6) ☒
595.81 Cystitis cystica — (Use additional code to identify organism, such as E. coli: 041.41-041.49)
595.82 Irradiation cystitis — (Use additional code to identify organism, such as E. coli: 041.41-041.49. Use additional E code to identify cause)
596.3 Diverticulum of bladder — (Use additional code to identify urinary incontinence: 625.6, 788.30-788.39)
596.89 Other specified disorders of bladder
599.3 Urethral caruncle
599.70 Hematuria, unspecified ▽
599.71 Gross hematuria
599.72 Microscopic hematuria
601.1 Chronic prostatitis — (Use additional code to identify organism: 041.0, 041.1) ♂
788.29 Other specified retention of urine — (Code, if applicable, any causal condition first, such as: 600.0-600.9, with fifth digit 1)
788.43 Nocturia — (Code, if applicable, any causal condition first, such as: 600.0-600.9, with fifth digit 1)
V10.51 Personal history of malignant neoplasm of bladder

ICD-9-CM Procedural

57.49 Other transurethral excision or destruction of lesion or tissue of bladder

HCPCS Level II Supplies & Services

A4270 Disposable endoscope sheath, each

52234-52240

52234 Cystourethroscopy, with fulguration (including cryosurgery or laser surgery) and/or resection of; SMALL bladder tumor(s) (0.5 up to 2.0 cm)
52235 MEDIUM bladder tumor(s) (2.0 to 5.0 cm)
52240 LARGE bladder tumor(s)

ICD-9-CM Diagnostic

188.0 Malignant neoplasm of trigone of urinary bladder
188.1 Malignant neoplasm of dome of urinary bladder
188.2 Malignant neoplasm of lateral wall of urinary bladder
188.3 Malignant neoplasm of anterior wall of urinary bladder
188.4 Malignant neoplasm of posterior wall of urinary bladder
188.5 Malignant neoplasm of bladder neck
188.6 Malignant neoplasm of ureteric orifice
188.7 Malignant neoplasm of urachus
188.8 Malignant neoplasm of other specified sites of bladder
188.9 Malignant neoplasm of bladder, part unspecified ▽
189.8 Malignant neoplasm of other specified sites of urinary organs
198.1 Secondary malignant neoplasm of other urinary organs
223.3 Benign neoplasm of bladder
233.7 Carcinoma in situ of bladder
236.7 Neoplasm of uncertain behavior of bladder
239.4 Neoplasm of unspecified nature of bladder
595.0 Acute cystitis — (Use additional code to identify organism, such as E. coli: 041.41-041.49)
595.1 Chronic interstitial cystitis — (Use additional code to identify organism, such as E. coli: 041.41-041.49)
595.3 Trigonitis — (Use additional code to identify organism, such as E. coli: 041.41-041.49)
595.4 Cystitis in diseases classified elsewhere — (Use additional code to identify organism, such as E. coli: 041.41-041.49. Code first underlying disease: 006.8, 039.8, 120.0-120.9, 122.3, 122.6) ☒
595.81 Cystitis cystica — (Use additional code to identify organism, such as E. coli: 041.41-041.49)
595.82 Irradiation cystitis — (Use additional code to identify organism, such as E. coli: 041.41-041.49. Use additional E code to identify cause)
599.70 Hematuria, unspecified ▽
599.71 Gross hematuria
599.72 Microscopic hematuria
V10.51 Personal history of malignant neoplasm of bladder

ICD-9-CM Procedural

57.49 Other transurethral excision or destruction of lesion or tissue of bladder

HCPCS Level II Supplies & Services

A4270 Disposable endoscope sheath, each

52250

52250 Cystourethroscopy with insertion of radioactive substance, with or without biopsy or fulguration

ICD-9-CM Diagnostic

188.0 Malignant neoplasm of trigone of urinary bladder
188.1 Malignant neoplasm of dome of urinary bladder
188.2 Malignant neoplasm of lateral wall of urinary bladder
188.3 Malignant neoplasm of anterior wall of urinary bladder
188.4 Malignant neoplasm of posterior wall of urinary bladder
188.5 Malignant neoplasm of bladder neck
188.6 Malignant neoplasm of ureteric orifice
188.7 Malignant neoplasm of urachus
188.9 Malignant neoplasm of bladder, part unspecified ▽
189.3 Malignant neoplasm of urethra

ICD-9-CM Procedural

57.32 Other cystoscopy
57.33 Closed (transurethral) biopsy of bladder
57.49 Other transurethral excision or destruction of lesion or tissue of bladder
92.27 Implantation or insertion of radioactive elements

52260-52265

52260 Cystourethroscopy, with dilation of bladder for interstitial cystitis; general or conduction (spinal) anesthesia
52265 local anesthesia

ICD-9-CM Diagnostic

595.1 Chronic interstitial cystitis — (Use additional code to identify organism, such as E. coli: 041.41-041.49)
599.70 Hematuria, unspecified ▽
599.71 Gross hematuria
599.72 Microscopic hematuria
788.1 Dysuria

788.41 Urinary frequency — (Code, if applicable, any causal condition first, such as: 600.0-600.9, with fifth digit 1)

ICD-9-CM Procedural

57.92 Dilation of bladder neck

HCPCS Level II Supplies & Services

A4270 Disposable endoscope sheath, each

52270-52276

52270 Cystourethroscopy, with internal urethrotomy; female
52275 male
52276 Cystourethroscopy with direct vision internal urethrotomy

ICD-9-CM Diagnostic

185 Malignant neoplasm of prostate ♂
344.61 Cauda equina syndrome with neurogenic bladder
590.80 Unspecified pyelonephritis — (Use additional code to identify organism, such as E. coli, 041.41-041.49) ▽
595.0 Acute cystitis — (Use additional code to identify organism, such as E. coli: 041.41-041.49)
595.1 Chronic interstitial cystitis — (Use additional code to identify organism, such as E. coli: 041.41-041.49)
595.2 Other chronic cystitis — (Use additional code to identify organism, such as E. coli: 041.41-041.49)
595.3 Trigonitis — (Use additional code to identify organism, such as E. coli: 041.41-041.49)
595.4 Cystitis in diseases classified elsewhere — (Use additional code to identify organism, such as E. coli: 041.41-041.49. Code first underlying disease: 006.8, 039.8, 120.0-120.9, 122.3, 122.6) ☒
595.81 Cystitis cystica — (Use additional code to identify organism, such as E. coli: 041.41-041.49)
595.82 Irradiation cystitis — (Use additional code to identify organism, such as E. coli: 041.41-041.49. Use additional E code to identify cause)
595.89 Other specified types of cystitis — (Use additional code to identify organism, such as E. coli: 041.41-041.49)
595.9 Unspecified cystitis — (Use additional code to identify organism, such as E. coli: 041.41-041.49) ▽
596.89 Other specified disorders of bladder
597.0 Urethral abscess
598.00 Urethral stricture due to unspecified infection — (Use additional code to identify urinary incontinence: 625.6, 788.30-788.39) ▽
598.01 Urethral stricture due to infective diseases classified elsewhere — (Use additional code to identify urinary incontinence: 625.6, 788.30-788.39. Code first underlying disease: 095.8, 098.2, 120.0-120.9) ☒
598.1 Traumatic urethral stricture — (Use additional code to identify urinary incontinence: 625.6, 788.30-788.39)
598.2 Postoperative urethral stricture — (Use additional code to identify urinary incontinence: 625.6, 788.30-788.39)
598.8 Other specified causes of urethral stricture — (Use additional code to identify urinary incontinence: 625.6, 788.30-788.39)
598.9 Unspecified urethral stricture — (Use additional code to identify urinary incontinence: 625.6, 788.30-788.39) ▽
599.1 Urethral fistula
599.2 Urethral diverticulum
599.3 Urethral caruncle
599.60 Urinary obstruction, unspecified — (Use additional code to identify urinary incontinence: 625.6, 788.30-788.39) ▽
599.69 Urinary obstruction, not elsewhere classified — (Use additional code to identify urinary incontinence: 625.6, 788.30-788.39. Code, if applicable, any causal condition first: 600.0-600.9, with fifth-digit 1)
599.70 Hematuria, unspecified ▽
599.71 Gross hematuria
599.72 Microscopic hematuria
600.00 Hypertrophy (benign) of prostate without urinary obstruction and other lower urinary tract symptoms [LUTS] ♂
600.01 Hypertrophy (benign) of prostate with urinary obstruction and other lower urinary tract symptoms [LUTS] — (Use additional code to identify symptoms: 599.69, 788.20, 788.21, 788.30-788.39, 788.41, 788.43, 788.62, 788.63, 788.64, 788.65) ♂
600.10 Nodular prostate without urinary obstruction ♂
600.11 Nodular prostate with urinary obstruction ♂
600.20 Benign localized hyperplasia of prostate without urinary obstruction and other lower urinary tract symptoms [LUTS] ♂
600.21 Benign localized hyperplasia of prostate with urinary obstruction and other lower urinary tract symptoms [LUTS] — (Use additional code to identify symptoms: 599.69, 788.20, 788.21, 788.30-788.39, 788.41, 788.43, 788.62, 788.63, 788.64, 788.65) ♂
600.3 Cyst of prostate ♂
600.90 Hyperplasia of prostate, unspecified, without urinary obstruction and other lower urinary tract symptoms [LUTS] ▽ ♂
600.91 Hyperplasia of prostate, unspecified, with urinary obstruction and other lower urinary tract symptoms [LUTS] — (Use additional code to identify symptoms: 599.69, 788.20, 788.21, 788.30-788.39, 788.41, 788.43, 788.62, 788.63, 788.64, 788.65) ▽ ♂
605 Redundant prepuce and phimosis ♂
625.6 Female stress incontinence ♀
753.6 Congenital atresia and stenosis of urethra and bladder neck
788.99 Other symptoms involving urinary system
867.0 Bladder and urethra injury without mention of open wound into cavity
996.76 Other complications due to genitourinary device, implant, and graft — (Use additional code to identify complication: 338.18-338.19, 338.28-338.29)

ICD-9-CM Procedural

57.32 Other cystoscopy
58.5 Release of urethral stricture

HCPCS Level II Supplies & Services

A4270 Disposable endoscope sheath, each

52277

52277 Cystourethroscopy, with resection of external sphincter (sphincterotomy)

ICD-9-CM Diagnostic

344.61 Cauda equina syndrome with neurogenic bladder
596.51 Hypertonicity of bladder — (Use additional code to identify urinary incontinence: 625.6, 788.30-788.39)
596.54 Neurogenic bladder, NOS — (Use additional code to identify urinary incontinence: 625.6, 788.30-788.39) ▽
625.6 Female stress incontinence ♀

ICD-9-CM Procedural

57.32 Other cystoscopy
57.91 Sphincterotomy of bladder

HCPCS Level II Supplies & Services

A4270 Disposable endoscope sheath, each

52281-52282

52281 Cystourethroscopy, with calibration and/or dilation of urethral stricture or stenosis, with or without meatotomy, with or without injection procedure for cystography, male or female
52282 Cystourethroscopy, with insertion of permanent urethral stent

ICD-9-CM Diagnostic

185 Malignant neoplasm of prostate ♂
222.2 Benign neoplasm of prostate ♂
233.4 Carcinoma in situ of prostate ♂

236.5 Neoplasm of uncertain behavior of prostate ♂
596.0 Bladder neck obstruction — (Use additional code to identify urinary incontinence: 625.6, 788.30-788.39)
597.89 Other urethritis
598.00 Urethral stricture due to unspecified infection — (Use additional code to identify urinary incontinence: 625.6, 788.30-788.39) ▽
598.01 Urethral stricture due to infective diseases classified elsewhere — (Use additional code to identify urinary incontinence: 625.6, 788.30-788.39. Code first underlying disease: 095.8, 098.2, 120.0-120.9) ☒
598.1 Traumatic urethral stricture — (Use additional code to identify urinary incontinence: 625.6, 788.30-788.39)
598.2 Postoperative urethral stricture — (Use additional code to identify urinary incontinence: 625.6, 788.30-788.39)
598.8 Other specified causes of urethral stricture — (Use additional code to identify urinary incontinence: 625.6, 788.30-788.39)
598.9 Unspecified urethral stricture — (Use additional code to identify urinary incontinence: 625.6, 788.30-788.39) ▽
599.1 Urethral fistula
599.2 Urethral diverticulum
599.3 Urethral caruncle
599.4 Urethral false passage
599.5 Prolapsed urethral mucosa
599.60 Urinary obstruction, unspecified — (Use additional code to identify urinary incontinence: 625.6, 788.30-788.39) ▽
599.69 Urinary obstruction, not elsewhere classified — (Use additional code to identify urinary incontinence: 625.6, 788.30-788.39. Code, if applicable, any causal condition first: 600.0-600.9, with fifth-digit 1)
600.00 Hypertrophy (benign) of prostate without urinary obstruction and other lower urinary tract symptoms [LUTS] ♂
600.01 Hypertrophy (benign) of prostate with urinary obstruction and other lower urinary tract symptoms [LUTS] — (Use additional code to identify symptoms: 599.69, 788.20, 788.21, 788.30-788.39, 788.41, 788.43, 788.62, 788.63, 788.64, 788.65) ♂
600.10 Nodular prostate without urinary obstruction ♂
600.11 Nodular prostate with urinary obstruction ♂
600.20 Benign localized hyperplasia of prostate without urinary obstruction and other lower urinary tract symptoms [LUTS] ♂
600.21 Benign localized hyperplasia of prostate with urinary obstruction and other lower urinary tract symptoms [LUTS] — (Use additional code to identify symptoms: 599.69, 788.20, 788.21, 788.30-788.39, 788.41, 788.43, 788.62, 788.63, 788.64, 788.65) ♂
600.3 Cyst of prostate ♂
600.90 Hyperplasia of prostate, unspecified, without urinary obstruction and other lower urinary tract symptoms [LUTS] ▽ ♂
600.91 Hyperplasia of prostate, unspecified, with urinary obstruction and other lower urinary tract symptoms [LUTS] — (Use additional code to identify symptoms: 599.69, 788.20, 788.21, 788.30-788.39, 788.41, 788.43, 788.62, 788.63, 788.64, 788.65) ▽ ♂
601.1 Chronic prostatitis — (Use additional code to identify organism: 041.0, 041.1) ♂
601.9 Unspecified prostatitis — (Use additional code to identify organism: 041.0, 041.1) ▽ ♂
602.3 Dysplasia of prostate ♂
753.6 Congenital atresia and stenosis of urethra and bladder neck
788.29 Other specified retention of urine — (Code, if applicable, any causal condition first, such as: 600.0-600.9, with fifth digit 1)

ICD-9-CM Procedural

57.32 Other cystoscopy
57.94 Insertion of indwelling urinary catheter
58.5 Release of urethral stricture
58.99 Other operations on urethra and periurethral tissue
87.77 Other cystogram

HCPCS Level II Supplies & Services

A4270 Disposable endoscope sheath, each

52283

52283 Cystourethroscopy, with steroid injection into stricture

ICD-9-CM Diagnostic

596.0 Bladder neck obstruction — (Use additional code to identify urinary incontinence: 625.6, 788.30-788.39)
598.00 Urethral stricture due to unspecified infection — (Use additional code to identify urinary incontinence: 625.6, 788.30-788.39) ▽
598.01 Urethral stricture due to infective diseases classified elsewhere — (Use additional code to identify urinary incontinence: 625.6, 788.30-788.39. Code first underlying disease: 095.8, 098.2, 120.0-120.9) ☒
598.1 Traumatic urethral stricture — (Use additional code to identify urinary incontinence: 625.6, 788.30-788.39)
598.2 Postoperative urethral stricture — (Use additional code to identify urinary incontinence: 625.6, 788.30-788.39)
598.8 Other specified causes of urethral stricture — (Use additional code to identify urinary incontinence: 625.6, 788.30-788.39)
598.9 Unspecified urethral stricture — (Use additional code to identify urinary incontinence: 625.6, 788.30-788.39) ▽
599.60 Urinary obstruction, unspecified — (Use additional code to identify urinary incontinence: 625.6, 788.30-788.39) ▽
599.69 Urinary obstruction, not elsewhere classified — (Use additional code to identify urinary incontinence: 625.6, 788.30-788.39. Code, if applicable, any causal condition first: 600.0-600.9, with fifth-digit 1)

ICD-9-CM Procedural

57.32 Other cystoscopy
99.23 Injection of steroid

HCPCS Level II Supplies & Services

A4270 Disposable endoscope sheath, each

52285

52285 Cystourethroscopy for treatment of the female urethral syndrome with any or all of the following: urethral meatotomy, urethral dilation, internal urethrotomy, lysis of urethrovaginal septal fibrosis, lateral incisions of the bladder neck, and fulguration of polyp(s) of urethra, bladder neck, and/or trigone

ICD-9-CM Diagnostic

595.0 Acute cystitis — (Use additional code to identify organism, such as E. coli: 041.41-041.49)
595.1 Chronic interstitial cystitis — (Use additional code to identify organism, such as E. coli: 041.41-041.49)
595.2 Other chronic cystitis — (Use additional code to identify organism, such as E. coli: 041.41-041.49)
595.3 Trigonitis — (Use additional code to identify organism, such as E. coli: 041.41-041.49)
595.4 Cystitis in diseases classified elsewhere — (Use additional code to identify organism, such as E. coli: 041.41-041.49. Code first underlying disease: 006.8, 039.8, 120.0-120.9, 122.3, 122.6) ☒
595.89 Other specified types of cystitis — (Use additional code to identify organism, such as E. coli: 041.41-041.49)
595.9 Unspecified cystitis — (Use additional code to identify organism, such as E. coli: 041.41-041.49) ▽
596.0 Bladder neck obstruction — (Use additional code to identify urinary incontinence: 625.6, 788.30-788.39)
597.0 Urethral abscess
597.80 Unspecified urethritis ▽
597.81 Urethral syndrome NOS ▽
597.89 Other urethritis

598.1 Traumatic urethral stricture — (Use additional code to identify urinary incontinence: 625.6, 788.30-788.39)
598.2 Postoperative urethral stricture — (Use additional code to identify urinary incontinence: 625.6, 788.30-788.39)
599.0 Urinary tract infection, site not specified — (Use additional code to identify organism, such as E. coli: 041.41-041.49) ▽
599.1 Urethral fistula
599.3 Urethral caruncle
599.70 Hematuria, unspecified ▽
599.71 Gross hematuria
599.72 Microscopic hematuria
599.89 Other specified disorders of urinary tract — (Use additional code to identify urinary incontinence: 625.6, 788.30-788.39)
625.6 Female stress incontinence ♀
780.64 Chills (without fever)
780.65 Hypothermia not associated with low environmental temperature
780.99 Other general symptoms
788.29 Other specified retention of urine — (Code, if applicable, any causal condition first, such as: 600.0-600.9, with fifth digit 1)
788.99 Other symptoms involving urinary system

ICD-9-CM Procedural

57.32 Other cystoscopy
58.31 Endoscopic excision or destruction of lesion or tissue of urethra
58.5 Release of urethral stricture
58.6 Dilation of urethra

52287

52287 Cystourethroscopy, with injection(s) for chemodenervation of the bladder

ICD-9-CM Diagnostic

596.51 Hypertonicity of bladder — (Use additional code to identify urinary incontinence: 625.6, 788.30-788.39)
596.54 Neurogenic bladder, NOS — (Use additional code to identify urinary incontinence: 625.6, 788.30-788.39) ▽
596.55 Detrusor sphincter dyssynergia — (Use additional code to identify urinary incontinence: 625.6, 788.30-788.39)
596.59 Other functional disorder of bladder — (Use additional code to identify urinary incontinence: 625.6, 788.30-788.39)
788.31 Urge incontinence — (Code, if applicable, any causal condition first: 600.0-600.9, with fifth digit 1; 618.00-618.9; 753.23)
788.39 Other urinary incontinence — (Code, if applicable, any causal condition first: 600.0-600.9, with fifth digit 1; 618.00-618.9; 753.23)
788.41 Urinary frequency — (Code, if applicable, any causal condition first, such as: 600.0-600.9, with fifth digit 1)

ICD-9-CM Procedural

57.32 Other cystoscopy
99.29 Injection or infusion of other therapeutic or prophylactic substance

HCPCS Level II Supplies & Services

J0585 Injection, onabotulinumtoxinA, 1 unit
J0586 Injection, abobotulinumtoxinA, 5 units
J0587 Injection, rimabotulinumtoxinB, 100 units
J0588 Injection, incobotulinumtoxinA, 1 unit

52290

52290 Cystourethroscopy; with ureteral meatotomy, unilateral or bilateral

ICD-9-CM Diagnostic

593.3 Stricture or kinking of ureter
593.4 Other ureteric obstruction
753.22 Congenital obstruction of ureterovesical junction
753.23 Congenital ureterocele
753.29 Other obstructive defect of renal pelvis and ureter

ICD-9-CM Procedural

56.1 Ureteral meatotomy
56.39 Other diagnostic procedures on ureter
57.32 Other cystoscopy

52300-52301

52300 Cystourethroscopy; with resection or fulguration of orthotopic ureterocele(s), unilateral or bilateral
52301 with resection or fulguration of ectopic ureterocele(s), unilateral or bilateral

ICD-9-CM Diagnostic

593.89 Other specified disorder of kidney and ureter
753.23 Congenital ureterocele

ICD-9-CM Procedural

56.41 Partial ureterectomy
57.49 Other transurethral excision or destruction of lesion or tissue of bladder

52305

52305 Cystourethroscopy; with incision or resection of orifice of bladder diverticulum, single or multiple

ICD-9-CM Diagnostic

596.3 Diverticulum of bladder — (Use additional code to identify urinary incontinence: 625.6, 788.30-788.39)

ICD-9-CM Procedural

57.32 Other cystoscopy
57.49 Other transurethral excision or destruction of lesion or tissue of bladder

52310-52315

52310 Cystourethroscopy, with removal of foreign body, calculus, or ureteral stent from urethra or bladder (separate procedure); simple
52315 complicated

ICD-9-CM Diagnostic

594.1 Other calculus in bladder
594.2 Calculus in urethra
594.9 Unspecified calculus of lower urinary tract ▽
939.0 Foreign body in bladder and urethra
939.9 Foreign body in unspecified site in genitourinary tract ▽
996.39 Mechanical complication of genitourinary device, implant, and graft, other
996.65 Infection and inflammatory reaction due to other genitourinary device, implant, and graft — (Use additional code to identify specified infections)
996.76 Other complications due to genitourinary device, implant, and graft — (Use additional code to identify complication: 338.18-338.19, 338.28-338.29)

ICD-9-CM Procedural

57.0 Transurethral clearance of bladder
57.32 Other cystoscopy
57.99 Other operations on bladder
97.62 Removal of ureterostomy tube and ureteral catheter
98.19 Removal of intraluminal foreign body from urethra without incision

HCPCS Level II Supplies & Services

A4270 Disposable endoscope sheath, each

52317-52318

52317 Litholapaxy: crushing or fragmentation of calculus by any means in bladder and removal of fragments; simple or small (less than 2.5 cm)
52318 complicated or large (over 2.5 cm)

ICD-9-CM Diagnostic

594.0 Calculus in diverticulum of bladder
594.1 Other calculus in bladder

ICD-9-CM Procedural

57.0 Transurethral clearance of bladder
57.19 Other cystotomy
57.99 Other operations on bladder
59.95 Ultrasonic fragmentation of urinary stones
98.19 Removal of intraluminal foreign body from urethra without incision

52320-52330

52320 Cystourethroscopy (including ureteral catheterization); with removal of ureteral calculus
52325 with fragmentation of ureteral calculus (eg, ultrasonic or electro-hydraulic technique)
52327 with subureteric injection of implant material
52330 with manipulation, without removal of ureteral calculus

ICD-9-CM Diagnostic

591 Hydronephrosis
592.1 Calculus of ureter
593.3 Stricture or kinking of ureter
593.4 Other ureteric obstruction
593.5 Hydroureter
593.89 Other specified disorder of kidney and ureter
599.70 Hematuria, unspecified ▽
599.71 Gross hematuria
599.72 Microscopic hematuria
788.0 Renal colic

ICD-9-CM Procedural

56.0 Transurethral removal of obstruction from ureter and renal pelvis
57.32 Other cystoscopy
59.95 Ultrasonic fragmentation of urinary stones

52332

52332 Cystourethroscopy, with insertion of indwelling ureteral stent (eg, Gibbons or double-J type)

ICD-9-CM Diagnostic

188.0 Malignant neoplasm of trigone of urinary bladder
188.1 Malignant neoplasm of dome of urinary bladder
188.2 Malignant neoplasm of lateral wall of urinary bladder
188.3 Malignant neoplasm of anterior wall of urinary bladder
189.2 Malignant neoplasm of ureter
198.1 Secondary malignant neoplasm of other urinary organs
223.2 Benign neoplasm of ureter
223.3 Benign neoplasm of bladder
223.9 Benign neoplasm of urinary organ, site unspecified ▽
236.7 Neoplasm of uncertain behavior of bladder
236.91 Neoplasm of uncertain behavior of kidney and ureter
239.4 Neoplasm of unspecified nature of bladder
239.5 Neoplasm of unspecified nature of other genitourinary organs
591 Hydronephrosis
592.0 Calculus of kidney
592.1 Calculus of ureter
593.3 Stricture or kinking of ureter
593.4 Other ureteric obstruction
593.89 Other specified disorder of kidney and ureter
599.60 Urinary obstruction, unspecified — (Use additional code to identify urinary incontinence: 625.6, 788.30-788.39) ▽
599.69 Urinary obstruction, not elsewhere classified — (Use additional code to identify urinary incontinence: 625.6, 788.30-788.39. Code, if applicable, any causal condition first: 600.0-600.9, with fifth-digit 1)
599.70 Hematuria, unspecified ▽
599.71 Gross hematuria
599.72 Microscopic hematuria
599.89 Other specified disorders of urinary tract — (Use additional code to identify urinary incontinence: 625.6, 788.30-788.39)
619.0 Urinary-genital tract fistula, female ♀
753.4 Other specified congenital anomalies of ureter
788.0 Renal colic
867.2 Ureter injury without mention of open wound into cavity
867.3 Ureter injury with open wound into cavity
996.59 Mechanical complication due to other implant and internal device, not elsewhere classified

ICD-9-CM Procedural

57.32 Other cystoscopy
59.8 Ureteral catheterization

HCPCS Level II Supplies & Services

A4270 Disposable endoscope sheath, each

52334

52334 Cystourethroscopy with insertion of ureteral guide wire through kidney to establish a percutaneous nephrostomy, retrograde

ICD-9-CM Diagnostic

188.0 Malignant neoplasm of trigone of urinary bladder
188.1 Malignant neoplasm of dome of urinary bladder
188.2 Malignant neoplasm of lateral wall of urinary bladder
188.3 Malignant neoplasm of anterior wall of urinary bladder
188.4 Malignant neoplasm of posterior wall of urinary bladder
188.5 Malignant neoplasm of bladder neck
188.6 Malignant neoplasm of ureteric orifice
188.8 Malignant neoplasm of other specified sites of bladder
188.9 Malignant neoplasm of bladder, part unspecified ▽
189.0 Malignant neoplasm of kidney, except pelvis
189.1 Malignant neoplasm of renal pelvis
189.2 Malignant neoplasm of ureter
209.24 Malignant carcinoid tumor of the kidney — (Code first any associated multiple endocrine neoplasia syndrome: 258.01-258.03; Use additional code to identify associated endocrine syndrome, as: carcinoid syndrome: 259.2)
236.7 Neoplasm of uncertain behavior of bladder
590.2 Renal and perinephric abscess — (Use additional code to identify organism, such as E. coli, 041.41-041.49)
590.3 Pyeloureteritis cystica — (Use additional code to identify organism, such as E. coli, 041.41-041.49)
591 Hydronephrosis
592.0 Calculus of kidney
592.1 Calculus of ureter
593.3 Stricture or kinking of ureter
593.4 Other ureteric obstruction
593.89 Other specified disorder of kidney and ureter
596.89 Other specified disorders of bladder

599.60 Urinary obstruction, unspecified — (Use additional code to identify urinary incontinence: 625.6, 788.30-788.39) ▽
599.69 Urinary obstruction, not elsewhere classified — (Use additional code to identify urinary incontinence: 625.6, 788.30-788.39. Code, if applicable, any causal condition first: 600.0-600.9, with fifth-digit 1)
599.70 Hematuria, unspecified ▽
599.71 Gross hematuria
599.72 Microscopic hematuria
753.21 Congenital obstruction of ureteropelvic junction
753.22 Congenital obstruction of ureterovesical junction
753.29 Other obstructive defect of renal pelvis and ureter
788.0 Renal colic

ICD-9-CM Procedural

55.03 Percutaneous nephrostomy without fragmentation
57.32 Other cystoscopy

52341-52343

52341 Cystourethroscopy; with treatment of ureteral stricture (eg, balloon dilation, laser, electrocautery, and incision)
52342 with treatment of ureteropelvic junction stricture (eg, balloon dilation, laser, electrocautery, and incision)
52343 with treatment of intra-renal stricture (eg, balloon dilation, laser, electrocautery, and incision)

ICD-9-CM Diagnostic

591 Hydronephrosis
593.3 Stricture or kinking of ureter
593.5 Hydroureter
593.89 Other specified disorder of kidney and ureter
753.20 Unspecified obstructive defect of renal pelvis and ureter ▽
753.21 Congenital obstruction of ureteropelvic junction
753.22 Congenital obstruction of ureterovesical junction
753.29 Other obstructive defect of renal pelvis and ureter
753.3 Other specified congenital anomalies of kidney

ICD-9-CM Procedural

56.2 Ureterotomy
57.32 Other cystoscopy
59.8 Ureteral catheterization

52344-52346

52344 Cystourethroscopy with ureteroscopy; with treatment of ureteral stricture (eg, balloon dilation, laser, electrocautery, and incision)
52345 with treatment of ureteropelvic junction stricture (eg, balloon dilation, laser, electrocautery, and incision)
52346 with treatment of intra-renal stricture (eg, balloon dilation, laser, electrocautery, and incision)

ICD-9-CM Diagnostic

591 Hydronephrosis
593.3 Stricture or kinking of ureter
593.5 Hydroureter
593.89 Other specified disorder of kidney and ureter
753.20 Unspecified obstructive defect of renal pelvis and ureter ▽
753.21 Congenital obstruction of ureteropelvic junction
753.22 Congenital obstruction of ureterovesical junction
753.29 Other obstructive defect of renal pelvis and ureter
753.3 Other specified congenital anomalies of kidney

ICD-9-CM Procedural

56.2 Ureterotomy
56.31 Ureteroscopy
57.32 Other cystoscopy
59.8 Ureteral catheterization

52351 [52356]

52351 Cystourethroscopy, with ureteroscopy and/or pyeloscopy; diagnostic
52356 with lithotripsy including insertion of indwelling ureteral stent (eg, Gibbons or double-J type)

ICD-9-CM Diagnostic

188.0 Malignant neoplasm of trigone of urinary bladder
188.1 Malignant neoplasm of dome of urinary bladder
188.2 Malignant neoplasm of lateral wall of urinary bladder
188.3 Malignant neoplasm of anterior wall of urinary bladder
188.4 Malignant neoplasm of posterior wall of urinary bladder
188.5 Malignant neoplasm of bladder neck
188.6 Malignant neoplasm of ureteric orifice
188.7 Malignant neoplasm of urachus
188.8 Malignant neoplasm of other specified sites of bladder
188.9 Malignant neoplasm of bladder, part unspecified ▽
189.0 Malignant neoplasm of kidney, except pelvis
189.1 Malignant neoplasm of renal pelvis
189.2 Malignant neoplasm of ureter
198.0 Secondary malignant neoplasm of kidney
198.1 Secondary malignant neoplasm of other urinary organs
209.24 Malignant carcinoid tumor of the kidney — (Code first any associated multiple endocrine neoplasia syndrome: 258.01-258.03; Use additional code to identify associated endocrine syndrome, as: carcinoid syndrome: 259.2)
209.64 Benign carcinoid tumor of the kidney — (Code first any associated multiple endocrine neoplasia syndrome: 258.01-258.03; Use additional code to identify associated endocrine syndrome, as: carcinoid syndrome: 259.2)
223.0 Benign neoplasm of kidney, except pelvis
233.7 Carcinoma in situ of bladder
233.9 Carcinoma in situ of other and unspecified urinary organs ▽
236.7 Neoplasm of uncertain behavior of bladder
236.90 Neoplasm of uncertain behavior of urinary organ, unspecified ▽
236.91 Neoplasm of uncertain behavior of kidney and ureter
236.99 Neoplasm of uncertain behavior of other and unspecified urinary organs
239.5 Neoplasm of unspecified nature of other genitourinary organs
591 Hydronephrosis
592.0 Calculus of kidney
592.1 Calculus of ureter
593.3 Stricture or kinking of ureter
593.4 Other ureteric obstruction
593.5 Hydroureter
593.89 Other specified disorder of kidney and ureter
599.60 Urinary obstruction, unspecified — (Use additional code to identify urinary incontinence: 625.6, 788.30-788.39) ▽
599.69 Urinary obstruction, not elsewhere classified — (Use additional code to identify urinary incontinence: 625.6, 788.30-788.39. Code, if applicable, any causal condition first: 600.0-600.9, with fifth-digit 1)
599.70 Hematuria, unspecified ▽
599.71 Gross hematuria
599.72 Microscopic hematuria
753.20 Unspecified obstructive defect of renal pelvis and ureter ▽
753.21 Congenital obstruction of ureteropelvic junction
753.22 Congenital obstruction of ureterovesical junction
753.23 Congenital ureterocele
753.29 Other obstructive defect of renal pelvis and ureter
788.0 Renal colic
788.1 Dysuria

789.00 Abdominal pain, unspecified site ♥
789.01 Abdominal pain, right upper quadrant
789.02 Abdominal pain, left upper quadrant
793.5 Nonspecific (abnormal) findings on radiological and other examination of genitourinary organs

ICD-9-CM Procedural

55.22 Pyeloscopy
56.0 Transurethral removal of obstruction from ureter and renal pelvis
56.31 Ureteroscopy
57.32 Other cystoscopy
59.8 Ureteral catheterization

52352-52353

52352 Cystourethroscopy, with ureteroscopy and/or pyeloscopy; with removal or manipulation of calculus (ureteral catheterization is included)
52353 with lithotripsy (ureteral catheterization is included)

ICD-9-CM Diagnostic

591 Hydronephrosis
592.0 Calculus of kidney
592.1 Calculus of ureter
593.5 Hydroureter
594.1 Other calculus in bladder
599.70 Hematuria, unspecified ♥
599.71 Gross hematuria
599.72 Microscopic hematuria
788.0 Renal colic
789.01 Abdominal pain, right upper quadrant
789.02 Abdominal pain, left upper quadrant

ICD-9-CM Procedural

55.22 Pyeloscopy
56.0 Transurethral removal of obstruction from ureter and renal pelvis
56.31 Ureteroscopy

52354-52355

52354 Cystourethroscopy, with ureteroscopy and/or pyeloscopy; with biopsy and/or fulguration of ureteral or renal pelvic lesion
52355 with resection of ureteral or renal pelvic tumor

ICD-9-CM Diagnostic

188.6 Malignant neoplasm of ureteric orifice
189.1 Malignant neoplasm of renal pelvis
189.2 Malignant neoplasm of ureter
198.0 Secondary malignant neoplasm of kidney
198.1 Secondary malignant neoplasm of other urinary organs
209.24 Malignant carcinoid tumor of the kidney — (Code first any associated multiple endocrine neoplasia syndrome: 258.01-258.03; Use additional code to identify associated endocrine syndrome, as: carcinoid syndrome: 259.2)
209.64 Benign carcinoid tumor of the kidney — (Code first any associated multiple endocrine neoplasia syndrome: 258.01-258.03; Use additional code to identify associated endocrine syndrome, as: carcinoid syndrome: 259.2)
223.1 Benign neoplasm of renal pelvis
223.2 Benign neoplasm of ureter
233.9 Carcinoma in situ of other and unspecified urinary organs ♥
236.7 Neoplasm of uncertain behavior of bladder
236.91 Neoplasm of uncertain behavior of kidney and ureter
239.4 Neoplasm of unspecified nature of bladder
239.5 Neoplasm of unspecified nature of other genitourinary organs
590.3 Pyeloureteritis cystica — (Use additional code to identify organism, such as E. coli, 041.41-041.49)
593.4 Other ureteric obstruction
593.89 Other specified disorder of kidney and ureter
599.70 Hematuria, unspecified ♥
599.71 Gross hematuria
599.72 Microscopic hematuria
788.1 Dysuria
793.5 Nonspecific (abnormal) findings on radiological and other examination of genitourinary organs

ICD-9-CM Procedural

55.22 Pyeloscopy
55.23 Closed (percutaneous) (needle) biopsy of kidney
55.39 Other local destruction or excision of renal lesion or tissue
55.4 Partial nephrectomy
56.31 Ureteroscopy
56.33 Closed endoscopic biopsy of ureter
56.99 Other operations on ureter
57.32 Other cystoscopy
57.33 Closed (transurethral) biopsy of bladder
57.49 Other transurethral excision or destruction of lesion or tissue of bladder
58.23 Biopsy of urethra
58.31 Endoscopic excision or destruction of lesion or tissue of urethra
58.39 Other local excision or destruction of lesion or tissue of urethra

52400

52400 Cystourethroscopy with incision, fulguration, or resection of congenital posterior urethral valves, or congenital obstructive hypertrophic mucosal folds

ICD-9-CM Diagnostic

596.4 Atony of bladder — (Use additional code to identify urinary incontinence: 625.6, 788.30-788.39)
596.89 Other specified disorders of bladder
753.6 Congenital atresia and stenosis of urethra and bladder neck
753.8 Other specified congenital anomaly of bladder and urethra
753.9 Unspecified congenital anomaly of urinary system ♥
788.20 Unspecified retention of urine — (Code, if applicable, any causal condition first, such as: 600.0-600.9, with fifth digit 1) ♥

ICD-9-CM Procedural

57.19 Other cystotomy
57.32 Other cystoscopy
57.49 Other transurethral excision or destruction of lesion or tissue of bladder
58.0 Urethrotomy
58.31 Endoscopic excision or destruction of lesion or tissue of urethra

52402

52402 Cystourethroscopy with transurethral resection or incision of ejaculatory ducts

ICD-9-CM Diagnostic

187.8 Malignant neoplasm of other specified sites of male genital organs ♂
198.82 Secondary malignant neoplasm of genital organs
222.8 Benign neoplasm of other specified sites of male genital organs ♂
233.6 Carcinoma in situ of other and unspecified male genital organs ♥ ♂
236.6 Neoplasm of uncertain behavior of other and unspecified male genital organs ♥ ♂
239.5 Neoplasm of unspecified nature of other genitourinary organs
600.00 Hypertrophy (benign) of prostate without urinary obstruction and other lower urinary tract symptoms [LUTS] ♂
600.01 Hypertrophy (benign) of prostate with urinary obstruction and other lower urinary tract symptoms [LUTS] — (Use additional code to identify symptoms: 599.69, 788.20, 788.21, 788.30-788.39, 788.41, 788.43, 788.62, 788.63, 788.64, 788.65) ♂
600.10 Nodular prostate without urinary obstruction ♂

600.11 Nodular prostate with urinary obstruction ♂

600.20 Benign localized hyperplasia of prostate without urinary obstruction and other lower urinary tract symptoms [LUTS] ♂

600.21 Benign localized hyperplasia of prostate with urinary obstruction and other lower urinary tract symptoms [LUTS] — (Use additional code to identify symptoms: 599.69, 788.20, 788.21, 788.30-788.39, 788.41, 788.43, 788.62, 788.63, 788.64, 788.65) ♂

600.90 Hyperplasia of prostate, unspecified, without urinary obstruction and other lower urinary tract symptoms [LUTS] ▽ ♂

600.91 Hyperplasia of prostate, unspecified, with urinary obstruction and other lower urinary tract symptoms [LUTS] — (Use additional code to identify symptoms: 599.69, 788.20, 788.21, 788.30-788.39, 788.41, 788.43, 788.62, 788.63, 788.64, 788.65) ▽ ♂

606.0 Azoospermia ♂

606.1 Oligospermia ♂

606.8 Infertility due to extratesticular causes ♂

607.84 Impotence of organic origin ♂

608.4 Other inflammatory disorder of male genital organs — (Use additional code to identify organism) ♂

608.81 Specified disorder of male genital organs in diseases classified elsewhere — (Code first underlying disease: 016.5, 125.0-125.9) ☒ ♂

608.82 Hematospermia ♂

608.83 Specified vascular disorder of male genital organs ♂

608.85 Stricture of male genital organs ♂

608.89 Other specified disorder of male genital organs ♂

752.9 Unspecified congenital anomaly of genital organs ▽

V26.21 Fertility testing

V26.29 Other investigation and testing

ICD-9-CM Procedural

57.32 Other cystoscopy

60.72 Incision of seminal vesicle ♂

60.73 Excision of seminal vesicle ♂

60.79 Other operations on seminal vesicles ♂

52450

52450 Transurethral incision of prostate

ICD-9-CM Diagnostic

185 Malignant neoplasm of prostate ♂

596.0 Bladder neck obstruction — (Use additional code to identify urinary incontinence: 625.6, 788.30-788.39)

600.00 Hypertrophy (benign) of prostate without urinary obstruction and other lower urinary tract symptoms [LUTS] ♂

600.01 Hypertrophy (benign) of prostate with urinary obstruction and other lower urinary tract symptoms [LUTS] — (Use additional code to identify symptoms: 599.69, 788.20, 788.21, 788.30-788.39, 788.41, 788.43, 788.62, 788.63, 788.64, 788.65) ♂

600.10 Nodular prostate without urinary obstruction ♂

600.11 Nodular prostate with urinary obstruction ♂

600.20 Benign localized hyperplasia of prostate without urinary obstruction and other lower urinary tract symptoms [LUTS] ♂

600.21 Benign localized hyperplasia of prostate with urinary obstruction and other lower urinary tract symptoms [LUTS] — (Use additional code to identify symptoms: 599.69, 788.20, 788.21, 788.30-788.39, 788.41, 788.43, 788.62, 788.63, 788.64, 788.65) ♂

600.3 Cyst of prostate ♂

600.90 Hyperplasia of prostate, unspecified, without urinary obstruction and other lower urinary tract symptoms [LUTS] ▽ ♂

600.91 Hyperplasia of prostate, unspecified, with urinary obstruction and other lower urinary tract symptoms [LUTS] — (Use additional code to identify symptoms: 599.69, 788.20, 788.21, 788.30-788.39, 788.41, 788.43, 788.62, 788.63, 788.64, 788.65) ▽ ♂

601.1 Chronic prostatitis — (Use additional code to identify organism: 041.0, 041.1) ♂

601.9 Unspecified prostatitis — (Use additional code to identify organism: 041.0, 041.1) ▽ ♂

788.20 Unspecified retention of urine — (Code, if applicable, any causal condition first, such as: 600.0-600.9, with fifth digit 1) ▽

788.21 Incomplete bladder emptying — (Code, if applicable, any causal condition first, such as: 600.0-600.9, with fifth digit 1)

788.29 Other specified retention of urine — (Code, if applicable, any causal condition first, such as: 600.0-600.9, with fifth digit 1)

788.30 Unspecified urinary incontinence — (Code, if applicable, any causal condition first: 600.0-600.9, with fifth digit 1; 618.00-618.9; 753.23) ▽

788.31 Urge incontinence — (Code, if applicable, any causal condition first: 600.0-600.9, with fifth digit 1; 618.00-618.9; 753.23)

788.32 Stress incontinence, male — (Code, if applicable, any causal condition first: 600.0-600.9, with fifth digit 1; 618.00-618.9; 753.23) ♂

788.33 Mixed incontinence urge and stress (male)(female) — (Code, if applicable, any causal condition first: 600.0-600.9, with fifth digit 1; 618.00-618.9; 753.23)

788.34 Incontinence without sensory awareness — (Code, if applicable, any causal condition first: 600.0-600.9, with fifth digit 1; 618.00-618.9; 753.23)

788.35 Post-void dribbling — (Code, if applicable, any causal condition first: 600.0-600.9, with fifth digit 1; 618.00-618.9; 753.23)

788.36 Nocturnal enuresis — (Code, if applicable, any causal condition first: 600.0-600.9, with fifth digit 1; 618.00-618.9; 753.23)

788.37 Continuous leakage — (Code, if applicable, any causal condition first: 600.0-600.9, with fifth digit 1; 618.00-618.9; 753.23)

788.39 Other urinary incontinence — (Code, if applicable, any causal condition first: 600.0-600.9, with fifth digit 1; 618.00-618.9; 753.23)

788.99 Other symptoms involving urinary system

ICD-9-CM Procedural

60.0 Incision of prostate ♂

52500

52500 Transurethral resection of bladder neck (separate procedure)

ICD-9-CM Diagnostic

185 Malignant neoplasm of prostate ♂

223.3 Benign neoplasm of bladder

236.7 Neoplasm of uncertain behavior of bladder

596.0 Bladder neck obstruction — (Use additional code to identify urinary incontinence: 625.6, 788.30-788.39)

596.4 Atony of bladder — (Use additional code to identify urinary incontinence: 625.6, 788.30-788.39)

596.89 Other specified disorders of bladder

599.1 Urethral fistula

599.2 Urethral diverticulum

599.3 Urethral caruncle

599.4 Urethral false passage

599.70 Hematuria, unspecified ▽

599.71 Gross hematuria

599.72 Microscopic hematuria

599.81 Urethral hypermobility — (Use additional code to identify urinary incontinence: 625.6, 788.30-788.39)

600.00 Hypertrophy (benign) of prostate without urinary obstruction and other lower urinary tract symptoms [LUTS] ♂

600.01 Hypertrophy (benign) of prostate with urinary obstruction and other lower urinary tract symptoms [LUTS] — (Use additional code to identify symptoms: 599.69, 788.20, 788.21, 788.30-788.39, 788.41, 788.43, 788.62, 788.63, 788.64, 788.65) ♂

600.10 Nodular prostate without urinary obstruction ♂

600.11 Nodular prostate with urinary obstruction ♂

600.20 Benign localized hyperplasia of prostate without urinary obstruction and other lower urinary tract symptoms [LUTS] ♂

600.21 Benign localized hyperplasia of prostate with urinary obstruction and other lower urinary tract symptoms [LUTS] — (Use additional code to identify symptoms: 599.69, 788.20, 788.21, 788.30-788.39, 788.41, 788.43, 788.62, 788.63, 788.64, 788.65) ♂

600.3 Cyst of prostate ♂

600.90 Hyperplasia of prostate, unspecified, without urinary obstruction and other lower urinary tract symptoms [LUTS] ♂

600.91 Hyperplasia of prostate, unspecified, with urinary obstruction and other lower urinary tract symptoms [LUTS] — (Use additional code to identify symptoms: 599.69, 788.20, 788.21, 788.30-788.39, 788.41, 788.43, 788.62, 788.63, 788.64, 788.65) ♂

753.6 Congenital atresia and stenosis of urethra and bladder neck

753.9 Unspecified congenital anomaly of urinary system

788.1 Dysuria

788.21 Incomplete bladder emptying — (Code, if applicable, any causal condition first, such as: 600.0-600.9, with fifth digit 1)

788.29 Other specified retention of urine — (Code, if applicable, any causal condition first, such as: 600.0-600.9, with fifth digit 1)

ICD-9-CM Procedural

57.49 Other transurethral excision or destruction of lesion or tissue of bladder

52601

52601 Transurethral electrosurgical resection of prostate, including control of postoperative bleeding, complete (vasectomy, meatotomy, cystourethroscopy, urethral calibration and/or dilation, and internal urethrotomy are included)

ICD-9-CM Diagnostic

185 Malignant neoplasm of prostate ♂

222.2 Benign neoplasm of prostate ♂

233.4 Carcinoma in situ of prostate ♂

236.5 Neoplasm of uncertain behavior of prostate ♂

591 Hydronephrosis

596.0 Bladder neck obstruction — (Use additional code to identify urinary incontinence: 625.6, 788.30-788.39)

598.9 Unspecified urethral stricture — (Use additional code to identify urinary incontinence: 625.6, 788.30-788.39)

599.60 Urinary obstruction, unspecified — (Use additional code to identify urinary incontinence: 625.6, 788.30-788.39)

599.69 Urinary obstruction, not elsewhere classified — (Use additional code to identify urinary incontinence: 625.6, 788.30-788.39. Code, if applicable, any causal condition first: 600.0-600.9, with fifth-digit 1)

599.70 Hematuria, unspecified

599.71 Gross hematuria

599.72 Microscopic hematuria

600.00 Hypertrophy (benign) of prostate without urinary obstruction and other lower urinary tract symptoms [LUTS] ♂

600.01 Hypertrophy (benign) of prostate with urinary obstruction and other lower urinary tract symptoms [LUTS] — (Use additional code to identify symptoms: 599.69, 788.20, 788.21, 788.30-788.39, 788.41, 788.43, 788.62, 788.63, 788.64, 788.65) ♂

600.10 Nodular prostate without urinary obstruction ♂

600.11 Nodular prostate with urinary obstruction ♂

600.20 Benign localized hyperplasia of prostate without urinary obstruction and other lower urinary tract symptoms [LUTS] ♂

600.21 Benign localized hyperplasia of prostate with urinary obstruction and other lower urinary tract symptoms [LUTS] — (Use additional code to identify symptoms: 599.69, 788.20, 788.21, 788.30-788.39, 788.41, 788.43, 788.62, 788.63, 788.64, 788.65) ♂

600.3 Cyst of prostate ♂

600.90 Hyperplasia of prostate, unspecified, without urinary obstruction and other lower urinary tract symptoms [LUTS] ♂

600.91 Hyperplasia of prostate, unspecified, with urinary obstruction and other lower urinary tract symptoms [LUTS] — (Use additional code to identify symptoms: 599.69, 788.20, 788.21, 788.30-788.39, 788.41, 788.43, 788.62, 788.63, 788.64, 788.65) ♂

601.0 Acute prostatitis — (Use additional code to identify organism: 041.0, 041.1) ♂

601.1 Chronic prostatitis — (Use additional code to identify organism: 041.0, 041.1) ♂

601.9 Unspecified prostatitis — (Use additional code to identify organism: 041.0, 041.1) ♂

602.3 Dysplasia of prostate ♂

602.9 Unspecified disorder of prostate ♂

788.20 Unspecified retention of urine — (Code, if applicable, any causal condition first, such as: 600.0-600.9, with fifth digit 1)

788.21 Incomplete bladder emptying — (Code, if applicable, any causal condition first, such as: 600.0-600.9, with fifth digit 1)

788.29 Other specified retention of urine — (Code, if applicable, any causal condition first, such as: 600.0-600.9, with fifth digit 1)

788.39 Other urinary incontinence — (Code, if applicable, any causal condition first: 600.0-600.9, with fifth digit 1; 618.00-618.9; 753.23)

V84.03 Genetic susceptibility to malignant neoplasm of prostate — (Use additional code, if applicable, for any associated family history of the disease: V16-V19. Code first, if applicable, any current malignant neoplasms: 140.0-195.8, 200.0-208.9, 230.0-234.9. Use additional code, if applicable, for any personal history of malignant neoplasm: V10.0-V10.9) ♂

V84.09 Genetic susceptibility to other malignant neoplasm — (Use additional code, if applicable, for any associated family history of the disease: V16-V19. Code first, if applicable, any current malignant neoplasms: 140.0-195.8, 200.0-208.9, 230.0-234.9. Use additional code, if applicable, for any personal history of malignant neoplasm: V10.0-V10.9)

ICD-9-CM Procedural

60.21 Transurethral (ultrasound) guided laser induced prostatectomy (TULIP) ♂

60.29 Other transurethral prostatectomy ♂

52630

52630 Transurethral resection; residual or regrowth of obstructive prostate tissue including control of postoperative bleeding, complete (vasectomy, meatotomy, cystourethroscopy, urethral calibration and/or dilation, and internal urethrotomy are included)

ICD-9-CM Diagnostic

185 Malignant neoplasm of prostate ♂

188.9 Malignant neoplasm of bladder, part unspecified

222.2 Benign neoplasm of prostate ♂

233.4 Carcinoma in situ of prostate ♂

236.5 Neoplasm of uncertain behavior of prostate ♂

591 Hydronephrosis

596.0 Bladder neck obstruction — (Use additional code to identify urinary incontinence: 625.6, 788.30-788.39)

598.9 Unspecified urethral stricture — (Use additional code to identify urinary incontinence: 625.6, 788.30-788.39)

599.60 Urinary obstruction, unspecified — (Use additional code to identify urinary incontinence: 625.6, 788.30-788.39)

599.69 Urinary obstruction, not elsewhere classified — (Use additional code to identify urinary incontinence: 625.6, 788.30-788.39. Code, if applicable, any causal condition first: 600.0-600.9, with fifth-digit 1)

600.00 Hypertrophy (benign) of prostate without urinary obstruction and other lower urinary tract symptoms [LUTS] ♂

600.01 Hypertrophy (benign) of prostate with urinary obstruction and other lower urinary tract symptoms [LUTS] — (Use additional code to identify symptoms: 599.69, 788.20, 788.21, 788.30-788.39, 788.41, 788.43, 788.62, 788.63, 788.64, 788.65) ♂

600.10 Nodular prostate without urinary obstruction ♂

600.11 Nodular prostate with urinary obstruction ♂

600.20 Benign localized hyperplasia of prostate without urinary obstruction and other lower urinary tract symptoms [LUTS] ♂

600.21 Benign localized hyperplasia of prostate with urinary obstruction and other lower urinary tract symptoms [LUTS] — (Use additional code to identify symptoms: 599.69, 788.20, 788.21, 788.30-788.39, 788.41, 788.43, 788.62, 788.63, 788.64, 788.65) ♂

600.3 Cyst of prostate ♂

600.90 Hyperplasia of prostate, unspecified, without urinary obstruction and other lower urinary tract symptoms [LUTS] ♂

600.91 Hyperplasia of prostate, unspecified, with urinary obstruction and other lower urinary tract symptoms [LUTS] — (Use additional code to identify symptoms: 599.69, 788.20, 788.21, 788.30-788.39, 788.41, 788.43, 788.62, 788.63, 788.64, 788.65) ♂

601.0 Acute prostatitis — (Use additional code to identify organism: 041.0, 041.1) ♂

601.1 Chronic prostatitis — (Use additional code to identify organism: 041.0, 041.1) ♂

601.9 Unspecified prostatitis — (Use additional code to identify organism: 041.0, 041.1) ♂

602.3 Dysplasia of prostate ♂

602.9 Unspecified disorder of prostate ♂

788.20 Unspecified retention of urine — (Code, if applicable, any causal condition first, such as: 600.0-600.9, with fifth digit 1)

788.21 Incomplete bladder emptying — (Code, if applicable, any causal condition first, such as: 600.0-600.9, with fifth digit 1)

788.29 Other specified retention of urine — (Code, if applicable, any causal condition first, such as: 600.0-600.9, with fifth digit 1)

788.39 Other urinary incontinence — (Code, if applicable, any causal condition first: 600.0-600.9, with fifth digit 1; 618.00-618.9; 753.23)

ICD-9-CM Procedural

60.29 Other transurethral prostatectomy ♂

52640

52640 Transurethral resection; of postoperative bladder neck contracture

ICD-9-CM Diagnostic

596.0 Bladder neck obstruction — (Use additional code to identify urinary incontinence: 625.6, 788.30-788.39)

598.2 Postoperative urethral stricture — (Use additional code to identify urinary incontinence: 625.6, 788.30-788.39)

599.60 Urinary obstruction, unspecified — (Use additional code to identify urinary incontinence: 625.6, 788.30-788.39)

599.69 Urinary obstruction, not elsewhere classified — (Use additional code to identify urinary incontinence: 625.6, 788.30-788.39. Code, if applicable, any causal condition first: 600.0-600.9, with fifth-digit 1)

788.20 Unspecified retention of urine — (Code, if applicable, any causal condition first, such as: 600.0-600.9, with fifth digit 1)

788.21 Incomplete bladder emptying — (Code, if applicable, any causal condition first, such as: 600.0-600.9, with fifth digit 1)

788.29 Other specified retention of urine — (Code, if applicable, any causal condition first, such as: 600.0-600.9, with fifth digit 1)

788.30 Unspecified urinary incontinence — (Code, if applicable, any causal condition first: 600.0-600.9, with fifth digit 1; 618.00-618.9; 753.23)

788.31 Urge incontinence — (Code, if applicable, any causal condition first: 600.0-600.9, with fifth digit 1; 618.00-618.9; 753.23)

788.32 Stress incontinence, male — (Code, if applicable, any causal condition first: 600.0-600.9, with fifth digit 1; 618.00-618.9; 753.23) ♂

788.33 Mixed incontinence urge and stress (male)(female) — (Code, if applicable, any causal condition first: 600.0-600.9, with fifth digit 1; 618.00-618.9; 753.23)

788.34 Incontinence without sensory awareness — (Code, if applicable, any causal condition first: 600.0-600.9, with fifth digit 1; 618.00-618.9; 753.23)

788.35 Post-void dribbling — (Code, if applicable, any causal condition first: 600.0-600.9, with fifth digit 1; 618.00-618.9; 753.23)

788.36 Nocturnal enuresis — (Code, if applicable, any causal condition first: 600.0-600.9, with fifth digit 1; 618.00-618.9; 753.23)

788.37 Continuous leakage — (Code, if applicable, any causal condition first: 600.0-600.9, with fifth digit 1; 618.00-618.9; 753.23)

788.38 Overflow incontinence — (Code, if applicable, any causal condition first: 600.0-600.9, with fifth digit 1; 618.00-618.9; 753.23)

788.39 Other urinary incontinence — (Code, if applicable, any causal condition first: 600.0-600.9, with fifth digit 1; 618.00-618.9; 753.23)

ICD-9-CM Procedural

57.49 Other transurethral excision or destruction of lesion or tissue of bladder

52647-52648

52647 Laser coagulation of prostate, including control of postoperative bleeding, complete (vasectomy, meatotomy, cystourethroscopy, urethral calibration and/or dilation, and internal urethrotomy are included if performed)

52648 Laser vaporization of prostate, including control of postoperative bleeding, complete (vasectomy, meatotomy, cystourethroscopy, urethral calibration and/or dilation, internal urethrotomy and transurethral resection of prostate are included if performed)

ICD-9-CM Diagnostic

185 Malignant neoplasm of prostate ♂

188.9 Malignant neoplasm of bladder, part unspecified

198.82 Secondary malignant neoplasm of genital organs

222.2 Benign neoplasm of prostate ♂

233.4 Carcinoma in situ of prostate ♂

236.5 Neoplasm of uncertain behavior of prostate ♂

239.5 Neoplasm of unspecified nature of other genitourinary organs

591 Hydronephrosis

596.0 Bladder neck obstruction — (Use additional code to identify urinary incontinence: 625.6, 788.30-788.39)

600.00 Hypertrophy (benign) of prostate without urinary obstruction and other lower urinary tract symptoms [LUTS] ♂

600.01 Hypertrophy (benign) of prostate with urinary obstruction and other lower urinary tract symptoms [LUTS] — (Use additional code to identify symptoms: 599.69, 788.20, 788.21, 788.30-788.39, 788.41, 788.43, 788.62, 788.63, 788.64, 788.65) ♂

600.10 Nodular prostate without urinary obstruction ♂

600.11 Nodular prostate with urinary obstruction ♂

600.20 Benign localized hyperplasia of prostate without urinary obstruction and other lower urinary tract symptoms [LUTS] ♂

600.21 Benign localized hyperplasia of prostate with urinary obstruction and other lower urinary tract symptoms [LUTS] — (Use additional code to identify symptoms: 599.69, 788.20, 788.21, 788.30-788.39, 788.41, 788.43, 788.62, 788.63, 788.64, 788.65) ♂

600.3 Cyst of prostate ♂

600.90 Hyperplasia of prostate, unspecified, without urinary obstruction and other lower urinary tract symptoms [LUTS] ♂

600.91 Hyperplasia of prostate, unspecified, with urinary obstruction and other lower urinary tract symptoms [LUTS] — (Use additional code to identify symptoms: 599.69, 788.20, 788.21, 788.30-788.39, 788.41, 788.43, 788.62, 788.63, 788.64, 788.65) ♂

601.0 Acute prostatitis — (Use additional code to identify organism: 041.0, 041.1) ♂

601.1 Chronic prostatitis — (Use additional code to identify organism: 041.0, 041.1) ♂

601.2 Abscess of prostate — (Use additional code to identify organism: 041.0, 041.1) ♂

601.3 Prostatocystitis — (Use additional code to identify organism: 041.0, 041.1) ♂

601.4 Prostatitis in diseases classified elsewhere — (Use additional code to identify organism: 041.0, 041.1. Code first underlying disease: 016.5, 039.8, 095.8, 116.0) ☒ ♂

601.8 Other specified inflammatory disease of prostate — (Use additional code to identify organism: 041.0, 041.1) ♂

602.3 Dysplasia of prostate ♂

788.20 Unspecified retention of urine — (Code, if applicable, any causal condition first, such as: 600.0-600.9, with fifth digit 1)

ICD-9-CM Procedural

60.21 Transurethral (ultrasound) guided laser induced prostatectomy (TULIP) ♂

60.61 Local excision of lesion of prostate ♂

60.93 Repair of prostate ♂

60.94 Control of (postoperative) hemorrhage of prostate ♂

52649

52649 Laser enucleation of the prostate with morcellation, including control of postoperative bleeding, complete (vasectomy, meatotomy, cystourethroscopy, urethral calibration and/or dilation, internal urethrotomy and transurethral resection of prostate are included if performed)

ICD-9-CM Diagnostic

185 Malignant neoplasm of prostate ♂

188.9 Malignant neoplasm of bladder, part unspecified ▽

198.82 Secondary malignant neoplasm of genital organs

222.2 Benign neoplasm of prostate ♂

233.4 Carcinoma in situ of prostate ♂

236.5 Neoplasm of uncertain behavior of prostate ♂

239.5 Neoplasm of unspecified nature of other genitourinary organs

591 Hydronephrosis

596.0 Bladder neck obstruction — (Use additional code to identify urinary incontinence: 625.6, 788.30-788.39)

600.00 Hypertrophy (benign) of prostate without urinary obstruction and other lower urinary tract symptoms [LUTS] ♂

600.01 Hypertrophy (benign) of prostate with urinary obstruction and other lower urinary tract symptoms [LUTS] — (Use additional code to identify symptoms: 599.69, 788.20, 788.21, 788.30-788.39, 788.41, 788.43, 788.62, 788.63, 788.64, 788.65) ♂

600.10 Nodular prostate without urinary obstruction ♂

600.11 Nodular prostate with urinary obstruction ♂

600.20 Benign localized hyperplasia of prostate without urinary obstruction and other lower urinary tract symptoms [LUTS] ♂

600.21 Benign localized hyperplasia of prostate with urinary obstruction and other lower urinary tract symptoms [LUTS] — (Use additional code to identify symptoms: 599.69, 788.20, 788.21, 788.30-788.39, 788.41, 788.43, 788.62, 788.63, 788.64, 788.65) ♂

600.3 Cyst of prostate ♂

600.90 Hyperplasia of prostate, unspecified, without urinary obstruction and other lower urinary tract symptoms [LUTS] ▽ ♂

600.91 Hyperplasia of prostate, unspecified, with urinary obstruction and other lower urinary tract symptoms [LUTS] — (Use additional code to identify symptoms: 599.69, 788.20, 788.21, 788.30-788.39, 788.41, 788.43, 788.62, 788.63, 788.64, 788.65) ▽ ♂

601.0 Acute prostatitis — (Use additional code to identify organism: 041.0, 041.1) ♂

601.1 Chronic prostatitis — (Use additional code to identify organism: 041.0, 041.1) ♂

601.2 Abscess of prostate — (Use additional code to identify organism: 041.0, 041.1) ♂

601.3 Prostatocystitis — (Use additional code to identify organism: 041.0, 041.1) ♂

601.4 Prostatitis in diseases classified elsewhere — (Use additional code to identify organism: 041.0, 041.1. Code first underlying disease: 016.5, 039.8, 095.8, 116.0) ☒ ♂

601.8 Other specified inflammatory disease of prostate — (Use additional code to identify organism: 041.0, 041.1) ♂

602.3 Dysplasia of prostate ♂

788.20 Unspecified retention of urine — (Code, if applicable, any causal condition first, such as: 600.0-600.9, with fifth digit 1) ▽

ICD-9-CM Procedural

60.21 Transurethral (ultrasound) guided laser induced prostatectomy (TULIP) ♂

60.29 Other transurethral prostatectomy ♂

60.5 Radical prostatectomy ♂

60.61 Local excision of lesion of prostate ♂

60.62 Perineal prostatectomy ♂

60.69 Other prostatectomy ♂

60.93 Repair of prostate ♂

60.94 Control of (postoperative) hemorrhage of prostate ♂

52700

52700 Transurethral drainage of prostatic abscess

ICD-9-CM Diagnostic

601.0 Acute prostatitis — (Use additional code to identify organism: 041.0, 041.1) ♂

601.1 Chronic prostatitis — (Use additional code to identify organism: 041.0, 041.1) ♂

601.2 Abscess of prostate — (Use additional code to identify organism: 041.0, 041.1) ♂

601.3 Prostatocystitis — (Use additional code to identify organism: 041.0, 041.1) ♂

601.4 Prostatitis in diseases classified elsewhere — (Use additional code to identify organism: 041.0, 041.1. Code first underlying disease: 016.5, 039.8, 095.8, 116.0) ☒ ♂

601.8 Other specified inflammatory disease of prostate — (Use additional code to identify organism: 041.0, 041.1) ♂

601.9 Unspecified prostatitis — (Use additional code to identify organism: 041.0, 041.1) ▽ ♂

ICD-9-CM Procedural

60.0 Incision of prostate ♂

Urethra

53000-53010

53000 Urethrotomy or urethrostomy, external (separate procedure); pendulous urethra
53010 perineal urethra, external

ICD-9-CM Diagnostic

597.81 Urethral syndrome NOS ▽

598.00 Urethral stricture due to unspecified infection — (Use additional code to identify urinary incontinence: 625.6, 788.30-788.39) ▽

598.01 Urethral stricture due to infective diseases classified elsewhere — (Use additional code to identify urinary incontinence: 625.6, 788.30-788.39. Code first underlying disease: 095.8, 098.2, 120.0-120.9) ☒

598.1 Traumatic urethral stricture — (Use additional code to identify urinary incontinence: 625.6, 788.30-788.39)

598.2 Postoperative urethral stricture — (Use additional code to identify urinary incontinence: 625.6, 788.30-788.39)

598.8 Other specified causes of urethral stricture — (Use additional code to identify urinary incontinence: 625.6, 788.30-788.39)

598.9 Unspecified urethral stricture — (Use additional code to identify urinary incontinence: 625.6, 788.30-788.39) ▽

599.84 Other specified disorders of urethra — (Use additional code to identify urinary incontinence: 625.6, 788.30-788.39)

600.00 Hypertrophy (benign) of prostate without urinary obstruction and other lower urinary tract symptoms [LUTS] ♂

600.01 Hypertrophy (benign) of prostate with urinary obstruction and other lower urinary tract symptoms [LUTS] — (Use additional code to identify symptoms: 599.69, 788.20, 788.21, 788.30-788.39, 788.41, 788.43, 788.62, 788.63, 788.64, 788.65) ♂

600.10 Nodular prostate without urinary obstruction ♂

600.11 Nodular prostate with urinary obstruction ♂

600.20 Benign localized hyperplasia of prostate without urinary obstruction and other lower urinary tract symptoms [LUTS] ♂

600.21 Benign localized hyperplasia of prostate with urinary obstruction and other lower urinary tract symptoms [LUTS] — (Use additional code to identify symptoms: 599.69, 788.20, 788.21, 788.30-788.39, 788.41, 788.43, 788.62, 788.63, 788.64, 788.65) ♂

600.3 Cyst of prostate ♂

600.90 Hyperplasia of prostate, unspecified, without urinary obstruction and other lower urinary tract symptoms [LUTS] ♂

600.91 Hyperplasia of prostate, unspecified, with urinary obstruction and other lower urinary tract symptoms [LUTS] — (Use additional code to identify symptoms: 599.69, 788.20, 788.21, 788.30-788.39, 788.41, 788.43, 788.62, 788.63, 788.64, 788.65) ♂

ICD-9-CM Procedural

58.0 Urethrotomy

53020-53025

53020 Meatotomy, cutting of meatus (separate procedure); except infant
53025 infant

ICD-9-CM Diagnostic

598.00 Urethral stricture due to unspecified infection — (Use additional code to identify urinary incontinence: 625.6, 788.30-788.39)

598.01 Urethral stricture due to infective diseases classified elsewhere — (Use additional code to identify urinary incontinence: 625.6, 788.30-788.39. Code first underlying disease: 095.8, 098.2, 120.0-120.9)

598.1 Traumatic urethral stricture — (Use additional code to identify urinary incontinence: 625.6, 788.30-788.39)

598.2 Postoperative urethral stricture — (Use additional code to identify urinary incontinence: 625.6, 788.30-788.39)

598.8 Other specified causes of urethral stricture — (Use additional code to identify urinary incontinence: 625.6, 788.30-788.39)

607.1 Balanoposthitis — (Use additional code to identify organism) ♂

608.89 Other specified disorder of male genital organs ♂

752.61 Hypospadias ♂

752.62 Epispadias ♂

752.63 Congenital chordee ♂

752.64 Micropenis ♂

752.69 Other penile anomalies ♂

752.81 Scrotal transposition ♂

753.6 Congenital atresia and stenosis of urethra and bladder neck

788.29 Other specified retention of urine — (Code, if applicable, any causal condition first, such as: 600.0-600.9, with fifth digit 1)

ICD-9-CM Procedural

58.1 Urethral meatotomy

HCPCS Level II Supplies & Services

A4305 Disposable drug delivery system, flow rate of 50 ml or greater per hour

53040-53060

53040 Drainage of deep periurethral abscess
53060 Drainage of Skene's gland abscess or cyst

ICD-9-CM Diagnostic

597.0 Urethral abscess

599.89 Other specified disorders of urinary tract — (Use additional code to identify urinary incontinence: 625.6, 788.30-788.39)

ICD-9-CM Procedural

58.91 Incision of periurethral tissue

71.09 Other incision of vulva and perineum ♀

HCPCS Level II Supplies & Services

A4305 Disposable drug delivery system, flow rate of 50 ml or greater per hour

53080-53085

53080 Drainage of perineal urinary extravasation; uncomplicated (separate procedure)
53085 complicated

ICD-9-CM Diagnostic

788.8 Extravasation of urine

ICD-9-CM Procedural

59.92 Other operations on perirenal or perivesical tissue

HCPCS Level II Supplies & Services

A4305 Disposable drug delivery system, flow rate of 50 ml or greater per hour

53200

53200 Biopsy of urethra

ICD-9-CM Diagnostic

188.5 Malignant neoplasm of bladder neck

188.9 Malignant neoplasm of bladder, part unspecified

189.3 Malignant neoplasm of urethra

198.1 Secondary malignant neoplasm of other urinary organs

233.9 Carcinoma in situ of other and unspecified urinary organs

239.5 Neoplasm of unspecified nature of other genitourinary organs

597.0 Urethral abscess

597.81 Urethral syndrome NOS

598.01 Urethral stricture due to infective diseases classified elsewhere — (Use additional code to identify urinary incontinence: 625.6, 788.30-788.39. Code first underlying disease: 095.8, 098.2, 120.0-120.9)

598.2 Postoperative urethral stricture — (Use additional code to identify urinary incontinence: 625.6, 788.30-788.39)

598.8 Other specified causes of urethral stricture — (Use additional code to identify urinary incontinence: 625.6, 788.30-788.39)

598.9 Unspecified urethral stricture — (Use additional code to identify urinary incontinence: 625.6, 788.30-788.39)

599.70 Hematuria, unspecified

599.71 Gross hematuria

599.72 Microscopic hematuria

625.6 Female stress incontinence ♀

ICD-9-CM Procedural

58.23 Biopsy of urethra

53210-53220

53210 Urethrectomy, total, including cystostomy; female
53215 male
53220 Excision or fulguration of carcinoma of urethra

ICD-9-CM Diagnostic

185 Malignant neoplasm of prostate ♂

188.5 Malignant neoplasm of bladder neck

189.3 Malignant neoplasm of urethra

198.1 Secondary malignant neoplasm of other urinary organs

233.7 Carcinoma in situ of bladder

233.9 Carcinoma in situ of other and unspecified urinary organs

236.7 Neoplasm of uncertain behavior of bladder

236.99 Neoplasm of uncertain behavior of other and unspecified urinary organs

239.4 Neoplasm of unspecified nature of bladder

239.5 Neoplasm of unspecified nature of other genitourinary organs

ICD-9-CM Procedural

58.39 Other local excision or destruction of lesion or tissue of urethra

53230-53240

53230 Excision of urethral diverticulum (separate procedure); female
53235 male
53240 Marsupialization of urethral diverticulum, male or female

ICD-9-CM Diagnostic

599.2 Urethral diverticulum

ICD-9-CM Procedural

58.39 Other local excision or destruction of lesion or tissue of urethra

53250

53250 Excision of bulbourethral gland (Cowper's gland)

ICD-9-CM Diagnostic

597.0 Urethral abscess
597.89 Other urethritis

ICD-9-CM Procedural

58.92 Excision of periurethral tissue

53260-53275

53260 Excision or fulguration; urethral polyp(s), distal urethra
53265 urethral caruncle
53270 Skene's glands
53275 urethral prolapse

ICD-9-CM Diagnostic

597.89 Other urethritis
599.3 Urethral caruncle
599.5 Prolapsed urethral mucosa
599.81 Urethral hypermobility — (Use additional code to identify urinary incontinence: 625.6, 788.30-788.39)
599.89 Other specified disorders of urinary tract — (Use additional code to identify urinary incontinence: 625.6, 788.30-788.39)
599.9 Unspecified disorder of urethra and urinary tract ▽
753.8 Other specified congenital anomaly of bladder and urethra

ICD-9-CM Procedural

58.39 Other local excision or destruction of lesion or tissue of urethra
71.3 Other local excision or destruction of vulva and perineum ♀

53400-53405

53400 Urethroplasty; first stage, for fistula, diverticulum, or stricture (eg, Johannsen type)
53405 second stage (formation of urethra), including urinary diversion

ICD-9-CM Diagnostic

597.81 Urethral syndrome NOS ▽
598.00 Urethral stricture due to unspecified infection — (Use additional code to identify urinary incontinence: 625.6, 788.30-788.39) ▽
598.01 Urethral stricture due to infective diseases classified elsewhere — (Use additional code to identify urinary incontinence: 625.6, 788.30-788.39. Code first underlying disease: 095.8, 098.2, 120.0-120.9) ☒
598.1 Traumatic urethral stricture — (Use additional code to identify urinary incontinence: 625.6, 788.30-788.39)
598.2 Postoperative urethral stricture — (Use additional code to identify urinary incontinence: 625.6, 788.30-788.39)
598.8 Other specified causes of urethral stricture — (Use additional code to identify urinary incontinence: 625.6, 788.30-788.39)
598.9 Unspecified urethral stricture — (Use additional code to identify urinary incontinence: 625.6, 788.30-788.39) ▽
599.1 Urethral fistula
599.2 Urethral diverticulum
788.99 Other symptoms involving urinary system

ICD-9-CM Procedural

58.46 Other reconstruction of urethra

HCPCS Level II Supplies & Services

A4349 Male external catheter, with or without adhesive, disposable, each

53410

53410 Urethroplasty, 1-stage reconstruction of male anterior urethra

ICD-9-CM Diagnostic

188.5 Malignant neoplasm of bladder neck
189.3 Malignant neoplasm of urethra
597.0 Urethral abscess
597.81 Urethral syndrome NOS ▽
597.89 Other urethritis
598.00 Urethral stricture due to unspecified infection — (Use additional code to identify urinary incontinence: 625.6, 788.30-788.39) ▽
598.01 Urethral stricture due to infective diseases classified elsewhere — (Use additional code to identify urinary incontinence: 625.6, 788.30-788.39. Code first underlying disease: 095.8, 098.2, 120.0-120.9) ☒
598.1 Traumatic urethral stricture — (Use additional code to identify urinary incontinence: 625.6, 788.30-788.39)
598.2 Postoperative urethral stricture — (Use additional code to identify urinary incontinence: 625.6, 788.30-788.39)
598.8 Other specified causes of urethral stricture — (Use additional code to identify urinary incontinence: 625.6, 788.30-788.39)
598.9 Unspecified urethral stricture — (Use additional code to identify urinary incontinence: 625.6, 788.30-788.39) ▽
599.1 Urethral fistula
599.2 Urethral diverticulum
752.61 Hypospadias ♂
752.62 Epispadias ♂
752.63 Congenital chordee ♂
752.64 Micropenis ♂
752.65 Hidden penis ♂
752.69 Other penile anomalies ♂
752.81 Scrotal transposition ♂

ICD-9-CM Procedural

58.46 Other reconstruction of urethra

53415

53415 Urethroplasty, transpubic or perineal, 1-stage, for reconstruction or repair of prostatic or membranous urethra

ICD-9-CM Diagnostic

185 Malignant neoplasm of prostate ♂
188.5 Malignant neoplasm of bladder neck
189.3 Malignant neoplasm of urethra
598.00 Urethral stricture due to unspecified infection — (Use additional code to identify urinary incontinence: 625.6, 788.30-788.39) ▽
598.01 Urethral stricture due to infective diseases classified elsewhere — (Use additional code to identify urinary incontinence: 625.6, 788.30-788.39. Code first underlying disease: 095.8, 098.2, 120.0-120.9) ☒
598.1 Traumatic urethral stricture — (Use additional code to identify urinary incontinence: 625.6, 788.30-788.39)
598.2 Postoperative urethral stricture — (Use additional code to identify urinary incontinence: 625.6, 788.30-788.39)
598.8 Other specified causes of urethral stricture — (Use additional code to identify urinary incontinence: 625.6, 788.30-788.39)

598.9 Unspecified urethral stricture — (Use additional code to identify urinary incontinence: 625.6, 788.30-788.39) ▽
599.1 Urethral fistula
599.2 Urethral diverticulum
599.84 Other specified disorders of urethra — (Use additional code to identify urinary incontinence: 625.6, 788.30-788.39)
600.00 Hypertrophy (benign) of prostate without urinary obstruction and other lower urinary tract symptoms [LUTS] ♂
600.01 Hypertrophy (benign) of prostate with urinary obstruction and other lower urinary tract symptoms [LUTS] — (Use additional code to identify symptoms: 599.69, 788.20, 788.21, 788.30-788.39, 788.41, 788.43, 788.62, 788.63, 788.64, 788.65) ♂
600.10 Nodular prostate without urinary obstruction ♂
600.11 Nodular prostate with urinary obstruction ♂
600.20 Benign localized hyperplasia of prostate without urinary obstruction and other lower urinary tract symptoms [LUTS] ♂
600.21 Benign localized hyperplasia of prostate with urinary obstruction and other lower urinary tract symptoms [LUTS] — (Use additional code to identify symptoms: 599.69, 788.20, 788.21, 788.30-788.39, 788.41, 788.43, 788.62, 788.63, 788.64, 788.65) ♂
600.3 Cyst of prostate ♂
600.90 Hyperplasia of prostate, unspecified, without urinary obstruction and other lower urinary tract symptoms [LUTS] ▽ ♂
600.91 Hyperplasia of prostate, unspecified, with urinary obstruction and other lower urinary tract symptoms [LUTS] — (Use additional code to identify symptoms: 599.69, 788.20, 788.21, 788.30-788.39, 788.41, 788.43, 788.62, 788.63, 788.64, 788.65) ▽ ♂
752.61 Hypospadias ♂
752.62 Epispadias ♂
752.63 Congenital chordee ♂
752.64 Micropenis ♂
752.65 Hidden penis ♂
752.69 Other penile anomalies ♂
752.81 Scrotal transposition ♂

ICD-9-CM Procedural

58.46 Other reconstruction of urethra

53420-53425

53420 Urethroplasty, 2-stage reconstruction or repair of prostatic or membranous urethra; first stage
53425 second stage

ICD-9-CM Diagnostic

185 Malignant neoplasm of prostate ♂
188.5 Malignant neoplasm of bladder neck
189.3 Malignant neoplasm of urethra
598.00 Urethral stricture due to unspecified infection — (Use additional code to identify urinary incontinence: 625.6, 788.30-788.39) ▽
598.01 Urethral stricture due to infective diseases classified elsewhere — (Use additional code to identify urinary incontinence: 625.6, 788.30-788.39. Code first underlying disease: 095.8, 098.2, 120.0-120.9) ☒
598.1 Traumatic urethral stricture — (Use additional code to identify urinary incontinence: 625.6, 788.30-788.39)
598.2 Postoperative urethral stricture — (Use additional code to identify urinary incontinence: 625.6, 788.30-788.39)
598.8 Other specified causes of urethral stricture — (Use additional code to identify urinary incontinence: 625.6, 788.30-788.39)
598.9 Unspecified urethral stricture — (Use additional code to identify urinary incontinence: 625.6, 788.30-788.39) ▽
599.1 Urethral fistula
599.2 Urethral diverticulum
599.5 Prolapsed urethral mucosa
599.84 Other specified disorders of urethra — (Use additional code to identify urinary incontinence: 625.6, 788.30-788.39)
600.00 Hypertrophy (benign) of prostate without urinary obstruction and other lower urinary tract symptoms [LUTS] ♂
600.01 Hypertrophy (benign) of prostate with urinary obstruction and other lower urinary tract symptoms [LUTS] — (Use additional code to identify symptoms: 599.69, 788.20, 788.21, 788.30-788.39, 788.41, 788.43, 788.62, 788.63, 788.64, 788.65) ♂
600.10 Nodular prostate without urinary obstruction ♂
600.11 Nodular prostate with urinary obstruction ♂
600.20 Benign localized hyperplasia of prostate without urinary obstruction and other lower urinary tract symptoms [LUTS] ♂
600.21 Benign localized hyperplasia of prostate with urinary obstruction and other lower urinary tract symptoms [LUTS] — (Use additional code to identify symptoms: 599.69, 788.20, 788.21, 788.30-788.39, 788.41, 788.43, 788.62, 788.63, 788.64, 788.65) ♂
600.3 Cyst of prostate ♂
600.90 Hyperplasia of prostate, unspecified, without urinary obstruction and other lower urinary tract symptoms [LUTS] ▽ ♂
600.91 Hyperplasia of prostate, unspecified, with urinary obstruction and other lower urinary tract symptoms [LUTS] — (Use additional code to identify symptoms: 599.69, 788.20, 788.21, 788.30-788.39, 788.41, 788.43, 788.62, 788.63, 788.64, 788.65) ▽ ♂
752.61 Hypospadias ♂
752.62 Epispadias ♂
752.63 Congenital chordee ♂
752.64 Micropenis ♂
752.65 Hidden penis ♂
752.69 Other penile anomalies ♂
752.81 Scrotal transposition ♂

ICD-9-CM Procedural

58.46 Other reconstruction of urethra

53430

53430 Urethroplasty, reconstruction of female urethra

ICD-9-CM Diagnostic

188.5 Malignant neoplasm of bladder neck
189.3 Malignant neoplasm of urethra
598.01 Urethral stricture due to infective diseases classified elsewhere — (Use additional code to identify urinary incontinence: 625.6, 788.30-788.39. Code first underlying disease: 095.8, 098.2, 120.0-120.9) ☒
598.1 Traumatic urethral stricture — (Use additional code to identify urinary incontinence: 625.6, 788.30-788.39)
598.2 Postoperative urethral stricture — (Use additional code to identify urinary incontinence: 625.6, 788.30-788.39)
598.8 Other specified causes of urethral stricture — (Use additional code to identify urinary incontinence: 625.6, 788.30-788.39)
598.9 Unspecified urethral stricture — (Use additional code to identify urinary incontinence: 625.6, 788.30-788.39) ▽
599.89 Other specified disorders of urinary tract — (Use additional code to identify urinary incontinence: 625.6, 788.30-788.39)
625.6 Female stress incontinence ♀

ICD-9-CM Procedural

58.46 Other reconstruction of urethra

53431

53431 Urethroplasty with tubularization of posterior urethra and/or lower bladder for incontinence (eg, Tenago, Leadbetter procedure)

ICD-9-CM Diagnostic

598.8 Other specified causes of urethral stricture — (Use additional code to identify urinary incontinence: 625.6, 788.30-788.39)

625.6 Female stress incontinence ♀

788.30 Unspecified urinary incontinence — (Code, if applicable, any causal condition first: 600.0-600.9, with fifth digit 1; 618.00-618.9; 753.23)

788.31 Urge incontinence — (Code, if applicable, any causal condition first: 600.0-600.9, with fifth digit 1; 618.00-618.9; 753.23)

788.32 Stress incontinence, male — (Code, if applicable, any causal condition first: 600.0-600.9, with fifth digit 1; 618.00-618.9; 753.23) ♂

788.33 Mixed incontinence urge and stress (male)(female) — (Code, if applicable, any causal condition first: 600.0-600.9, with fifth digit 1; 618.00-618.9; 753.23)

788.34 Incontinence without sensory awareness — (Code, if applicable, any causal condition first: 600.0-600.9, with fifth digit 1; 618.00-618.9; 753.23)

788.35 Post-void dribbling — (Code, if applicable, any causal condition first: 600.0-600.9, with fifth digit 1; 618.00-618.9; 753.23)

788.36 Nocturnal enuresis — (Code, if applicable, any causal condition first: 600.0-600.9, with fifth digit 1; 618.00-618.9; 753.23)

788.37 Continuous leakage — (Code, if applicable, any causal condition first: 600.0-600.9, with fifth digit 1; 618.00-618.9; 753.23)

788.38 Overflow incontinence — (Code, if applicable, any causal condition first: 600.0-600.9, with fifth digit 1; 618.00-618.9; 753.23)

788.39 Other urinary incontinence — (Code, if applicable, any causal condition first: 600.0-600.9, with fifth digit 1; 618.00-618.9; 753.23)

788.99 Other symptoms involving urinary system

ICD-9-CM Procedural

58.49 Other repair of urethra

53440

53440 Sling operation for correction of male urinary incontinence (eg, fascia or synthetic)

ICD-9-CM Diagnostic

598.8 Other specified causes of urethral stricture — (Use additional code to identify urinary incontinence: 625.6, 788.30-788.39)

788.30 Unspecified urinary incontinence — (Code, if applicable, any causal condition first: 600.0-600.9, with fifth digit 1; 618.00-618.9; 753.23)

788.31 Urge incontinence — (Code, if applicable, any causal condition first: 600.0-600.9, with fifth digit 1; 618.00-618.9; 753.23)

788.32 Stress incontinence, male — (Code, if applicable, any causal condition first: 600.0-600.9, with fifth digit 1; 618.00-618.9; 753.23) ♂

788.33 Mixed incontinence urge and stress (male)(female) — (Code, if applicable, any causal condition first: 600.0-600.9, with fifth digit 1; 618.00-618.9; 753.23)

788.34 Incontinence without sensory awareness — (Code, if applicable, any causal condition first: 600.0-600.9, with fifth digit 1; 618.00-618.9; 753.23)

788.35 Post-void dribbling — (Code, if applicable, any causal condition first: 600.0-600.9, with fifth digit 1; 618.00-618.9; 753.23)

788.36 Nocturnal enuresis — (Code, if applicable, any causal condition first: 600.0-600.9, with fifth digit 1; 618.00-618.9; 753.23)

788.37 Continuous leakage — (Code, if applicable, any causal condition first: 600.0-600.9, with fifth digit 1; 618.00-618.9; 753.23)

788.38 Overflow incontinence — (Code, if applicable, any causal condition first: 600.0-600.9, with fifth digit 1; 618.00-618.9; 753.23)

788.39 Other urinary incontinence — (Code, if applicable, any causal condition first: 600.0-600.9, with fifth digit 1; 618.00-618.9; 753.23)

788.99 Other symptoms involving urinary system

ICD-9-CM Procedural

57.99 Other operations on bladder

HCPCS Level II Supplies & Services

A4349 Male external catheter, with or without adhesive, disposable, each

53442

53442 Removal or revision of sling for male urinary incontinence (eg, fascia or synthetic)

ICD-9-CM Diagnostic

598.8 Other specified causes of urethral stricture — (Use additional code to identify urinary incontinence: 625.6, 788.30-788.39)

788.31 Urge incontinence — (Code, if applicable, any causal condition first: 600.0-600.9, with fifth digit 1; 618.00-618.9; 753.23)

788.32 Stress incontinence, male — (Code, if applicable, any causal condition first: 600.0-600.9, with fifth digit 1; 618.00-618.9; 753.23) ♂

788.33 Mixed incontinence urge and stress (male)(female) — (Code, if applicable, any causal condition first: 600.0-600.9, with fifth digit 1; 618.00-618.9; 753.23)

788.34 Incontinence without sensory awareness — (Code, if applicable, any causal condition first: 600.0-600.9, with fifth digit 1; 618.00-618.9; 753.23)

788.35 Post-void dribbling — (Code, if applicable, any causal condition first: 600.0-600.9, with fifth digit 1; 618.00-618.9; 753.23)

788.36 Nocturnal enuresis — (Code, if applicable, any causal condition first: 600.0-600.9, with fifth digit 1; 618.00-618.9; 753.23)

788.37 Continuous leakage — (Code, if applicable, any causal condition first: 600.0-600.9, with fifth digit 1; 618.00-618.9; 753.23)

788.38 Overflow incontinence — (Code, if applicable, any causal condition first: 600.0-600.9, with fifth digit 1; 618.00-618.9; 753.23)

788.39 Other urinary incontinence — (Code, if applicable, any causal condition first: 600.0-600.9, with fifth digit 1; 618.00-618.9; 753.23)

788.99 Other symptoms involving urinary system

996.39 Mechanical complication of genitourinary device, implant, and graft, other

996.76 Other complications due to genitourinary device, implant, and graft — (Use additional code to identify complication: 338.18-338.19, 338.28-338.29)

ICD-9-CM Procedural

58.99 Other operations on urethra and periurethral tissue

HCPCS Level II Supplies & Services

A4349 Male external catheter, with or without adhesive, disposable, each

53444

53444 Insertion of tandem cuff (dual cuff)

ICD-9-CM Diagnostic

598.8 Other specified causes of urethral stricture — (Use additional code to identify urinary incontinence: 625.6, 788.30-788.39)

625.6 Female stress incontinence ♀

753.6 Congenital atresia and stenosis of urethra and bladder neck

788.30 Unspecified urinary incontinence — (Code, if applicable, any causal condition first: 600.0-600.9, with fifth digit 1; 618.00-618.9; 753.23)

788.31 Urge incontinence — (Code, if applicable, any causal condition first: 600.0-600.9, with fifth digit 1; 618.00-618.9; 753.23)

788.32 Stress incontinence, male — (Code, if applicable, any causal condition first: 600.0-600.9, with fifth digit 1; 618.00-618.9; 753.23) ♂

788.33 Mixed incontinence urge and stress (male)(female) — (Code, if applicable, any causal condition first: 600.0-600.9, with fifth digit 1; 618.00-618.9; 753.23)

788.34 Incontinence without sensory awareness — (Code, if applicable, any causal condition first: 600.0-600.9, with fifth digit 1; 618.00-618.9; 753.23)

788.35 Post-void dribbling — (Code, if applicable, any causal condition first: 600.0-600.9, with fifth digit 1; 618.00-618.9; 753.23)

788.36 Nocturnal enuresis — (Code, if applicable, any causal condition first: 600.0-600.9, with fifth digit 1; 618.00-618.9; 753.23)

788.37 Continuous leakage — (Code, if applicable, any causal condition first: 600.0-600.9, with fifth digit 1; 618.00-618.9; 753.23)

788.38 Overflow incontinence — (Code, if applicable, any causal condition first: 600.0-600.9, with fifth digit 1; 618.00-618.9; 753.23)

788.39 Other urinary incontinence — (Code, if applicable, any causal condition first: 600.0-600.9, with fifth digit 1; 618.00-618.9; 753.23)

788.99 Other symptoms involving urinary system

ICD-9-CM Procedural

58.93 Implantation of artificial urinary sphincter (AUS)

HCPCS Level II Supplies & Services

C1815 Prosthesis, urinary sphincter (implantable)

53445

53445 Insertion of inflatable urethral/bladder neck sphincter, including placement of pump, reservoir, and cuff

ICD-9-CM Diagnostic

598.8 Other specified causes of urethral stricture — (Use additional code to identify urinary incontinence: 625.6, 788.30-788.39)

625.6 Female stress incontinence ♀

753.5 Exstrophy of urinary bladder

753.6 Congenital atresia and stenosis of urethra and bladder neck

788.30 Unspecified urinary incontinence — (Code, if applicable, any causal condition first: 600.0-600.9, with fifth digit 1; 618.00-618.9; 753.23) ▽

788.31 Urge incontinence — (Code, if applicable, any causal condition first: 600.0-600.9, with fifth digit 1; 618.00-618.9; 753.23)

788.32 Stress incontinence, male — (Code, if applicable, any causal condition first: 600.0-600.9, with fifth digit 1; 618.00-618.9; 753.23) ♂

788.33 Mixed incontinence urge and stress (male)(female) — (Code, if applicable, any causal condition first: 600.0-600.9, with fifth digit 1; 618.00-618.9; 753.23)

788.34 Incontinence without sensory awareness — (Code, if applicable, any causal condition first: 600.0-600.9, with fifth digit 1; 618.00-618.9; 753.23)

788.35 Post-void dribbling — (Code, if applicable, any causal condition first: 600.0-600.9, with fifth digit 1; 618.00-618.9; 753.23)

788.36 Nocturnal enuresis — (Code, if applicable, any causal condition first: 600.0-600.9, with fifth digit 1; 618.00-618.9; 753.23)

788.37 Continuous leakage — (Code, if applicable, any causal condition first: 600.0-600.9, with fifth digit 1; 618.00-618.9; 753.23)

788.38 Overflow incontinence — (Code, if applicable, any causal condition first: 600.0-600.9, with fifth digit 1; 618.00-618.9; 753.23)

788.39 Other urinary incontinence — (Code, if applicable, any causal condition first: 600.0-600.9, with fifth digit 1; 618.00-618.9; 753.23)

788.99 Other symptoms involving urinary system

V10.46 Personal history of malignant neoplasm of prostate ♂

ICD-9-CM Procedural

58.93 Implantation of artificial urinary sphincter (AUS)

HCPCS Level II Supplies & Services

C1815 Prosthesis, urinary sphincter (implantable)

53446

53446 Removal of inflatable urethral/bladder neck sphincter, including pump, reservoir, and cuff

ICD-9-CM Diagnostic

996.39 Mechanical complication of genitourinary device, implant, and graft, other

996.65 Infection and inflammatory reaction due to other genitourinary device, implant, and graft — (Use additional code to identify specified infections)

996.76 Other complications due to genitourinary device, implant, and graft — (Use additional code to identify complication: 338.18-338.19, 338.28-338.29)

997.5 Urinary complications — (Use additional code to identify complications)

ICD-9-CM Procedural

58.99 Other operations on urethra and periurethral tissue

53447

53447 Removal and replacement of inflatable urethral/bladder neck sphincter including pump, reservoir, and cuff at the same operative session

ICD-9-CM Diagnostic

625.6 Female stress incontinence ♀

788.30 Unspecified urinary incontinence — (Code, if applicable, any causal condition first: 600.0-600.9, with fifth digit 1; 618.00-618.9; 753.23) ▽

788.31 Urge incontinence — (Code, if applicable, any causal condition first: 600.0-600.9, with fifth digit 1; 618.00-618.9; 753.23)

788.32 Stress incontinence, male — (Code, if applicable, any causal condition first: 600.0-600.9, with fifth digit 1; 618.00-618.9; 753.23) ♂

788.33 Mixed incontinence urge and stress (male)(female) — (Code, if applicable, any causal condition first: 600.0-600.9, with fifth digit 1; 618.00-618.9; 753.23)

788.34 Incontinence without sensory awareness — (Code, if applicable, any causal condition first: 600.0-600.9, with fifth digit 1; 618.00-618.9; 753.23)

788.35 Post-void dribbling — (Code, if applicable, any causal condition first: 600.0-600.9, with fifth digit 1; 618.00-618.9; 753.23)

788.36 Nocturnal enuresis — (Code, if applicable, any causal condition first: 600.0-600.9, with fifth digit 1; 618.00-618.9; 753.23)

788.37 Continuous leakage — (Code, if applicable, any causal condition first: 600.0-600.9, with fifth digit 1; 618.00-618.9; 753.23)

788.38 Overflow incontinence — (Code, if applicable, any causal condition first: 600.0-600.9, with fifth digit 1; 618.00-618.9; 753.23)

788.39 Other urinary incontinence — (Code, if applicable, any causal condition first: 600.0-600.9, with fifth digit 1; 618.00-618.9; 753.23)

788.99 Other symptoms involving urinary system

996.39 Mechanical complication of genitourinary device, implant, and graft, other

996.65 Infection and inflammatory reaction due to other genitourinary device, implant, and graft — (Use additional code to identify specified infections)

996.76 Other complications due to genitourinary device, implant, and graft — (Use additional code to identify complication: 338.18-338.19, 338.28-338.29)

997.5 Urinary complications — (Use additional code to identify complications)

V53.6 Fitting and adjustment of urinary device

ICD-9-CM Procedural

58.99 Other operations on urethra and periurethral tissue

HCPCS Level II Supplies & Services

C1815 Prosthesis, urinary sphincter (implantable)

53448

53448 Removal and replacement of inflatable urethral/bladder neck sphincter including pump, reservoir, and cuff through an infected field at the same operative session including irrigation and debridement of infected tissue

ICD-9-CM Diagnostic

595.89 Other specified types of cystitis — (Use additional code to identify organism, such as E. coli: 041.41-041.49)

596.89 Other specified disorders of bladder

597.0 Urethral abscess

597.80 Unspecified urethritis ▽

597.89 Other urethritis

625.6 Female stress incontinence ♀

788.30 Unspecified urinary incontinence — (Code, if applicable, any causal condition first: 600.0-600.9, with fifth digit 1; 618.00-618.9; 753.23) ▽

788.31 Urge incontinence — (Code, if applicable, any causal condition first: 600.0-600.9, with fifth digit 1; 618.00-618.9; 753.23)

788.32 Stress incontinence, male — (Code, if applicable, any causal condition first: 600.0-600.9, with fifth digit 1; 618.00-618.9; 753.23) ♂
788.33 Mixed incontinence urge and stress (male)(female) — (Code, if applicable, any causal condition first: 600.0-600.9, with fifth digit 1; 618.00-618.9; 753.23)
788.34 Incontinence without sensory awareness — (Code, if applicable, any causal condition first: 600.0-600.9, with fifth digit 1; 618.00-618.9; 753.23)
788.35 Post-void dribbling — (Code, if applicable, any causal condition first: 600.0-600.9, with fifth digit 1; 618.00-618.9; 753.23)
788.36 Nocturnal enuresis — (Code, if applicable, any causal condition first: 600.0-600.9, with fifth digit 1; 618.00-618.9; 753.23)
788.37 Continuous leakage — (Code, if applicable, any causal condition first: 600.0-600.9, with fifth digit 1; 618.00-618.9; 753.23)
788.38 Overflow incontinence — (Code, if applicable, any causal condition first: 600.0-600.9, with fifth digit 1; 618.00-618.9; 753.23)
788.39 Other urinary incontinence — (Code, if applicable, any causal condition first: 600.0-600.9, with fifth digit 1; 618.00-618.9; 753.23)
788.99 Other symptoms involving urinary system
996.65 Infection and inflammatory reaction due to other genitourinary device, implant, and graft — (Use additional code to identify specified infections)
996.76 Other complications due to genitourinary device, implant, and graft — (Use additional code to identify complication: 338.18-338.19, 338.28-338.29)
997.5 Urinary complications — (Use additional code to identify complications)
998.59 Other postoperative infection — (Use additional code to identify infection)

ICD-9-CM Procedural

58.93 Implantation of artificial urinary sphincter (AUS)

53449

53449 Repair of inflatable urethral/bladder neck sphincter, including pump, reservoir, and cuff

ICD-9-CM Diagnostic

996.39 Mechanical complication of genitourinary device, implant, and graft, other

ICD-9-CM Procedural

58.99 Other operations on urethra and periurethral tissue

53450-53460

53450 Urethromeatoplasty, with mucosal advancement
53460 Urethromeatoplasty, with partial excision of distal urethral segment (Richardson type procedure)

ICD-9-CM Diagnostic

598.00 Urethral stricture due to unspecified infection — (Use additional code to identify urinary incontinence: 625.6, 788.30-788.39) ▽
598.01 Urethral stricture due to infective diseases classified elsewhere — (Use additional code to identify urinary incontinence: 625.6, 788.30-788.39. Code first underlying disease: 095.8, 098.2, 120.0-120.9) ☒
598.1 Traumatic urethral stricture — (Use additional code to identify urinary incontinence: 625.6, 788.30-788.39)
598.2 Postoperative urethral stricture — (Use additional code to identify urinary incontinence: 625.6, 788.30-788.39)
598.8 Other specified causes of urethral stricture — (Use additional code to identify urinary incontinence: 625.6, 788.30-788.39)
598.9 Unspecified urethral stricture — (Use additional code to identify urinary incontinence: 625.6, 788.30-788.39) ▽
599.1 Urethral fistula
599.2 Urethral diverticulum
599.3 Urethral caruncle
599.4 Urethral false passage
599.5 Prolapsed urethral mucosa
599.9 Unspecified disorder of urethra and urinary tract ▽
607.1 Balanoposthitis — (Use additional code to identify organism) ♂
607.81 Balanitis xerotica obliterans ♂
752.61 Hypospadias ♂
752.62 Epispadias ♂
752.81 Scrotal transposition ♂
753.6 Congenital atresia and stenosis of urethra and bladder neck
788.99 Other symptoms involving urinary system

ICD-9-CM Procedural

58.39 Other local excision or destruction of lesion or tissue of urethra
58.47 Urethral meatoplasty
58.49 Other repair of urethra

53500

53500 Urethrolysis, transvaginal, secondary, open, including cystourethroscopy (eg, postsurgical obstruction, scarring)

ICD-9-CM Diagnostic

597.81 Urethral syndrome NOS ▽
598.00 Urethral stricture due to unspecified infection — (Use additional code to identify urinary incontinence: 625.6, 788.30-788.39) ▽
598.01 Urethral stricture due to infective diseases classified elsewhere — (Use additional code to identify urinary incontinence: 625.6, 788.30-788.39. Code first underlying disease: 095.8, 098.2, 120.0-120.9) ☒
598.1 Traumatic urethral stricture — (Use additional code to identify urinary incontinence: 625.6, 788.30-788.39)
598.2 Postoperative urethral stricture — (Use additional code to identify urinary incontinence: 625.6, 788.30-788.39)
598.8 Other specified causes of urethral stricture — (Use additional code to identify urinary incontinence: 625.6, 788.30-788.39)
598.9 Unspecified urethral stricture — (Use additional code to identify urinary incontinence: 625.6, 788.30-788.39) ▽

ICD-9-CM Procedural

58.5 Release of urethral stricture

53502-53515

53502 Urethrorrhaphy, suture of urethral wound or injury, female
53505 Urethrorrhaphy, suture of urethral wound or injury; penile
53510 perineal
53515 prostatomembranous

ICD-9-CM Diagnostic

599.84 Other specified disorders of urethra — (Use additional code to identify urinary incontinence: 625.6, 788.30-788.39)
634.22 Complete spontaneous abortion complicated by damage to pelvic organs or tissues ♀
635.21 Legally induced abortion complicated by damage to pelvic organs or tissues, incomplete ♀
635.22 Complete legally induced abortion complicated by damage to pelvic organs or tissues ♀
636.21 Incomplete illegally induced abortion complicated by damage to pelvic organs or tissues ♀
636.22 Complete illegally induced abortion complicated by damage to pelvic organs or tissues ♀
637.21 Abortion, unspecified as to legality, incomplete, complicated by damage to pelvic organs or tissues ♀
637.22 Abortion, unspecified as to legality, complete, complicated by damage to pelvic organs or tissues ♀
638.2 Failed attempted abortion complicated by damage to pelvic organs or tissues ♀
639.2 Damage to pelvic organs and tissues following abortion or ectopic and molar pregnancies ♀
665.51 Other injury to pelvic organs, with delivery ♀
665.54 Other injury to pelvic organs, postpartum condition or complication ♀

867.0 Bladder and urethra injury without mention of open wound into cavity
867.1 Bladder and urethra injury with open wound into cavity
878.0 Open wound of penis, without mention of complication ♂
878.1 Open wound of penis, complicated ♂
998.2 Accidental puncture or laceration during procedure

ICD-9-CM Procedural

58.41 Suture of laceration of urethra
75.61 Repair of current obstetric laceration of bladder and urethra ♀

HCPCS Level II Supplies & Services

A4305 Disposable drug delivery system, flow rate of 50 ml or greater per hour

53520

53520 Closure of urethrostomy or urethrocutaneous fistula, male (separate procedure)

ICD-9-CM Diagnostic

599.1 Urethral fistula
V10.51 Personal history of malignant neoplasm of bladder
V10.59 Personal history of malignant neoplasm of other urinary organ
V13.09 Personal history of other disorder of urinary system
V15.3 Personal history of irradiation, presenting hazards to health
V15.51 Personal history of traumatic fracture
V15.59 Personal history of other injury
V55.5 Attention to cystostomy
V55.6 Attention to other artificial opening of urinary tract

ICD-9-CM Procedural

58.42 Closure of urethrostomy

53600-53605

53600 Dilation of urethral stricture by passage of sound or urethral dilator, male; initial
53601 subsequent
53605 Dilation of urethral stricture or vesical neck by passage of sound or urethral dilator, male, general or conduction (spinal) anesthesia

ICD-9-CM Diagnostic

185 Malignant neoplasm of prostate ♂
596.0 Bladder neck obstruction — (Use additional code to identify urinary incontinence: 625.6, 788.30-788.39)
597.81 Urethral syndrome NOS ▽
598.00 Urethral stricture due to unspecified infection — (Use additional code to identify urinary incontinence: 625.6, 788.30-788.39) ▽
598.01 Urethral stricture due to infective diseases classified elsewhere — (Use additional code to identify urinary incontinence: 625.6, 788.30-788.39. Code first underlying disease: 095.8, 098.2, 120.0-120.9) ☒
598.1 Traumatic urethral stricture — (Use additional code to identify urinary incontinence: 625.6, 788.30-788.39)
598.2 Postoperative urethral stricture — (Use additional code to identify urinary incontinence: 625.6, 788.30-788.39)
598.8 Other specified causes of urethral stricture — (Use additional code to identify urinary incontinence: 625.6, 788.30-788.39)
598.9 Unspecified urethral stricture — (Use additional code to identify urinary incontinence: 625.6, 788.30-788.39) ▽
600.00 Hypertrophy (benign) of prostate without urinary obstruction and other lower urinary tract symptoms [LUTS] ♂
600.01 Hypertrophy (benign) of prostate with urinary obstruction and other lower urinary tract symptoms [LUTS] — (Use additional code to identify symptoms: 599.69, 788.20, 788.21, 788.30-788.39, 788.41, 788.43, 788.62, 788.63, 788.64, 788.65) ♂
600.10 Nodular prostate without urinary obstruction ♂
600.11 Nodular prostate with urinary obstruction ♂
600.20 Benign localized hyperplasia of prostate without urinary obstruction and other lower urinary tract symptoms [LUTS] ♂
600.21 Benign localized hyperplasia of prostate with urinary obstruction and other lower urinary tract symptoms [LUTS] — (Use additional code to identify symptoms: 599.69, 788.20, 788.21, 788.30-788.39, 788.41, 788.43, 788.62, 788.63, 788.64, 788.65) ♂
600.3 Cyst of prostate ♂
600.90 Hyperplasia of prostate, unspecified, without urinary obstruction and other lower urinary tract symptoms [LUTS] ▽ ♂
600.91 Hyperplasia of prostate, unspecified, with urinary obstruction and other lower urinary tract symptoms [LUTS] — (Use additional code to identify symptoms: 599.69, 788.20, 788.21, 788.30-788.39, 788.41, 788.43, 788.62, 788.63, 788.64, 788.65) ▽ ♂
601.1 Chronic prostatitis — (Use additional code to identify organism: 041.0, 041.1) ♂
601.9 Unspecified prostatitis — (Use additional code to identify organism: 041.0, 041.1) ▽ ♂
753.6 Congenital atresia and stenosis of urethra and bladder neck
788.29 Other specified retention of urine — (Code, if applicable, any causal condition first, such as: 600.0-600.9, with fifth digit 1)

ICD-9-CM Procedural

57.92 Dilation of bladder neck
58.6 Dilation of urethra

53620-53621

53620 Dilation of urethral stricture by passage of filiform and follower, male; initial
53621 subsequent

ICD-9-CM Diagnostic

185 Malignant neoplasm of prostate ♂
596.0 Bladder neck obstruction — (Use additional code to identify urinary incontinence: 625.6, 788.30-788.39)
596.89 Other specified disorders of bladder
597.81 Urethral syndrome NOS ▽
598.00 Urethral stricture due to unspecified infection — (Use additional code to identify urinary incontinence: 625.6, 788.30-788.39) ▽
598.01 Urethral stricture due to infective diseases classified elsewhere — (Use additional code to identify urinary incontinence: 625.6, 788.30-788.39. Code first underlying disease: 095.8, 098.2, 120.0-120.9) ☒
598.1 Traumatic urethral stricture — (Use additional code to identify urinary incontinence: 625.6, 788.30-788.39)
598.2 Postoperative urethral stricture — (Use additional code to identify urinary incontinence: 625.6, 788.30-788.39)
598.8 Other specified causes of urethral stricture — (Use additional code to identify urinary incontinence: 625.6, 788.30-788.39)
598.9 Unspecified urethral stricture — (Use additional code to identify urinary incontinence: 625.6, 788.30-788.39) ▽
599.60 Urinary obstruction, unspecified — (Use additional code to identify urinary incontinence: 625.6, 788.30-788.39) ▽
599.69 Urinary obstruction, not elsewhere classified — (Use additional code to identify urinary incontinence: 625.6, 788.30-788.39. Code, if applicable, any causal condition first: 600.0-600.9, with fifth-digit 1)
599.70 Hematuria, unspecified ▽
599.71 Gross hematuria
599.72 Microscopic hematuria
600.00 Hypertrophy (benign) of prostate without urinary obstruction and other lower urinary tract symptoms [LUTS] ♂
600.01 Hypertrophy (benign) of prostate with urinary obstruction and other lower urinary tract symptoms [LUTS] — (Use additional code to identify symptoms: 599.69, 788.20, 788.21, 788.30-788.39, 788.41, 788.43, 788.62, 788.63, 788.64, 788.65) ♂
600.10 Nodular prostate without urinary obstruction ♂
600.11 Nodular prostate with urinary obstruction ♂

600.20 Benign localized hyperplasia of prostate without urinary obstruction and other lower urinary tract symptoms [LUTS] ♂

600.21 Benign localized hyperplasia of prostate with urinary obstruction and other lower urinary tract symptoms [LUTS] — (Use additional code to identify symptoms: 599.69, 788.20, 788.21, 788.30-788.39, 788.41, 788.43, 788.62, 788.63, 788.64, 788.65) ♂

600.3 Cyst of prostate ♂

600.90 Hyperplasia of prostate, unspecified, without urinary obstruction and other lower urinary tract symptoms [LUTS] ▽ ♂

600.91 Hyperplasia of prostate, unspecified, with urinary obstruction and other lower urinary tract symptoms [LUTS] — (Use additional code to identify symptoms: 599.69, 788.20, 788.21, 788.30-788.39, 788.41, 788.43, 788.62, 788.63, 788.64, 788.65) ▽ ♂

601.0 Acute prostatitis — (Use additional code to identify organism: 041.0, 041.1) ♂

601.1 Chronic prostatitis — (Use additional code to identify organism: 041.0, 041.1) ♂

601.9 Unspecified prostatitis — (Use additional code to identify organism: 041.0, 041.1) ▽ ♂

753.6 Congenital atresia and stenosis of urethra and bladder neck

788.20 Unspecified retention of urine — (Code, if applicable, any causal condition first, such as: 600.0-600.9, with fifth digit 1) ▽

788.29 Other specified retention of urine — (Code, if applicable, any causal condition first, such as: 600.0-600.9, with fifth digit 1)

ICD-9-CM Procedural

58.6 Dilation of urethra

53660-53665

53660 Dilation of female urethra including suppository and/or instillation; initial

53661 subsequent

53665 Dilation of female urethra, general or conduction (spinal) anesthesia

ICD-9-CM Diagnostic

595.1 Chronic interstitial cystitis — (Use additional code to identify organism, such as E. coli: 041.41-041.49)

595.2 Other chronic cystitis — (Use additional code to identify organism, such as E. coli: 041.41-041.49)

595.3 Trigonitis — (Use additional code to identify organism, such as E. coli: 041.41-041.49)

597.80 Unspecified urethritis ▽

597.81 Urethral syndrome NOS ▽

597.89 Other urethritis

598.00 Urethral stricture due to unspecified infection — (Use additional code to identify urinary incontinence: 625.6, 788.30-788.39) ▽

598.01 Urethral stricture due to infective diseases classified elsewhere — (Use additional code to identify urinary incontinence: 625.6, 788.30-788.39. Code first underlying disease: 095.8, 098.2, 120.0-120.9) ☒

598.1 Traumatic urethral stricture — (Use additional code to identify urinary incontinence: 625.6, 788.30-788.39)

598.2 Postoperative urethral stricture — (Use additional code to identify urinary incontinence: 625.6, 788.30-788.39)

598.8 Other specified causes of urethral stricture — (Use additional code to identify urinary incontinence: 625.6, 788.30-788.39)

599.82 Intrinsic (urethral) sphincter deficiency (ISD) — (Use additional code to identify urinary incontinence: 625.6, 788.30-788.39)

599.83 Urethral instability — (Use additional code to identify urinary incontinence: 625.6, 788.30-788.39)

599.89 Other specified disorders of urinary tract — (Use additional code to identify urinary incontinence: 625.6, 788.30-788.39)

599.9 Unspecified disorder of urethra and urinary tract ▽

625.6 Female stress incontinence ♀

753.6 Congenital atresia and stenosis of urethra and bladder neck

788.1 Dysuria

788.20 Unspecified retention of urine — (Code, if applicable, any causal condition first, such as: 600.0-600.9, with fifth digit 1) ▽

788.21 Incomplete bladder emptying — (Code, if applicable, any causal condition first, such as: 600.0-600.9, with fifth digit 1)

788.29 Other specified retention of urine — (Code, if applicable, any causal condition first, such as: 600.0-600.9, with fifth digit 1)

788.99 Other symptoms involving urinary system

ICD-9-CM Procedural

58.6 Dilation of urethra

96.49 Other genitourinary instillation

53850-53852

53850 Transurethral destruction of prostate tissue; by microwave thermotherapy

53852 by radiofrequency thermotherapy

ICD-9-CM Diagnostic

185 Malignant neoplasm of prostate ♂

198.82 Secondary malignant neoplasm of genital organs

222.2 Benign neoplasm of prostate ♂

233.4 Carcinoma in situ of prostate ♂

236.5 Neoplasm of uncertain behavior of prostate ♂

239.5 Neoplasm of unspecified nature of other genitourinary organs

600.00 Hypertrophy (benign) of prostate without urinary obstruction and other lower urinary tract symptoms [LUTS] ♂

600.01 Hypertrophy (benign) of prostate with urinary obstruction and other lower urinary tract symptoms [LUTS] — (Use additional code to identify symptoms: 599.69, 788.20, 788.21, 788.30-788.39, 788.41, 788.43, 788.62, 788.63, 788.64, 788.65) ♂

600.10 Nodular prostate without urinary obstruction ♂

600.11 Nodular prostate with urinary obstruction ♂

600.20 Benign localized hyperplasia of prostate without urinary obstruction and other lower urinary tract symptoms [LUTS] ♂

600.21 Benign localized hyperplasia of prostate with urinary obstruction and other lower urinary tract symptoms [LUTS] — (Use additional code to identify symptoms: 599.69, 788.20, 788.21, 788.30-788.39, 788.41, 788.43, 788.62, 788.63, 788.64, 788.65) ♂

600.3 Cyst of prostate ♂

600.90 Hyperplasia of prostate, unspecified, without urinary obstruction and other lower urinary tract symptoms [LUTS] ▽ ♂

600.91 Hyperplasia of prostate, unspecified, with urinary obstruction and other lower urinary tract symptoms [LUTS] — (Use additional code to identify symptoms: 599.69, 788.20, 788.21, 788.30-788.39, 788.41, 788.43, 788.62, 788.63, 788.64, 788.65) ▽ ♂

602.3 Dysplasia of prostate ♂

ICD-9-CM Procedural

60.29 Other transurethral prostatectomy ♂

60.97 Other transurethral destruction of prostate tissue by other thermotherapy ♂

HCPCS Level II Supplies & Services

A4305 Disposable drug delivery system, flow rate of 50 ml or greater per hour

53855

53855 Insertion of a temporary prostatic urethral stent, including urethral measurement

ICD-9-CM Diagnostic

185 Malignant neoplasm of prostate ♂

222.2 Benign neoplasm of prostate ♂

233.4 Carcinoma in situ of prostate ♂

236.5 Neoplasm of uncertain behavior of prostate ♂

596.0 Bladder neck obstruction — (Use additional code to identify urinary incontinence: 625.6, 788.30-788.39)

597.89 Other urethritis

598.00 Urethral stricture due to unspecified infection — (Use additional code to identify urinary incontinence: 625.6, 788.30-788.39) ▽

598.01 Urethral stricture due to infective diseases classified elsewhere — (Use additional code to identify urinary incontinence: 625.6, 788.30-788.39. Code first underlying disease: 095.8, 098.2, 120.0-120.9) ☒

598.1 Traumatic urethral stricture — (Use additional code to identify urinary incontinence: 625.6, 788.30-788.39)

598.2 Postoperative urethral stricture — (Use additional code to identify urinary incontinence: 625.6, 788.30-788.39)

598.8 Other specified causes of urethral stricture — (Use additional code to identify urinary incontinence: 625.6, 788.30-788.39)

598.9 Unspecified urethral stricture — (Use additional code to identify urinary incontinence: 625.6, 788.30-788.39) ▽

599.1 Urethral fistula

599.2 Urethral diverticulum

599.3 Urethral caruncle

599.4 Urethral false passage

599.5 Prolapsed urethral mucosa

599.60 Urinary obstruction, unspecified — (Use additional code to identify urinary incontinence: 625.6, 788.30-788.39) ▽

599.69 Urinary obstruction, not elsewhere classified — (Use additional code to identify urinary incontinence: 625.6, 788.30-788.39. Code, if applicable, any causal condition first: 600.0-600.9, with fifth-digit 1)

600.00 Hypertrophy (benign) of prostate without urinary obstruction and other lower urinary tract symptoms [LUTS] ♂

600.01 Hypertrophy (benign) of prostate with urinary obstruction and other lower urinary tract symptoms [LUTS] — (Use additional code to identify symptoms: 599.69, 788.20, 788.21, 788.30-788.39, 788.41, 788.43, 788.62, 788.63, 788.64, 788.65) ♂

600.10 Nodular prostate without urinary obstruction ♂

600.11 Nodular prostate with urinary obstruction ♂

600.20 Benign localized hyperplasia of prostate without urinary obstruction and other lower urinary tract symptoms [LUTS] ♂

600.21 Benign localized hyperplasia of prostate with urinary obstruction and other lower urinary tract symptoms [LUTS] — (Use additional code to identify symptoms: 599.69, 788.20, 788.21, 788.30-788.39, 788.41, 788.43, 788.62, 788.63, 788.64, 788.65) ♂

600.3 Cyst of prostate ♂

600.90 Hyperplasia of prostate, unspecified, without urinary obstruction and other lower urinary tract symptoms [LUTS] ▽ ♂

600.91 Hyperplasia of prostate, unspecified, with urinary obstruction and other lower urinary tract symptoms [LUTS] — (Use additional code to identify symptoms: 599.69, 788.20, 788.21, 788.30-788.39, 788.41, 788.43, 788.62, 788.63, 788.64, 788.65) ▽ ♂

601.1 Chronic prostatitis — (Use additional code to identify organism: 041.0, 041.1) ♂

601.9 Unspecified prostatitis — (Use additional code to identify organism: 041.0, 041.1) ▽ ♂

602.3 Dysplasia of prostate ♂

753.6 Congenital atresia and stenosis of urethra and bladder neck

788.29 Other specified retention of urine — (Code, if applicable, any causal condition first, such as: 600.0-600.9, with fifth digit 1)

ICD-9-CM Procedural

58.99 Other operations on urethra and periurethral tissue

89.29 Other nonoperative genitourinary system measurements

53860

53860 Transurethral radiofrequency micro-remodeling of the female bladder neck and proximal urethra for stress urinary incontinence

ICD-9-CM Diagnostic

625.6 Female stress incontinence ♀

788.33 Mixed incontinence urge and stress (male)(female) — (Code, if applicable, any causal condition first: 600.0-600.9, with fifth digit 1; 618.00-618.9; 753.23)

ICD-9-CM Procedural

59.79 Other repair of urinary stress incontinence

Male Genital System

Penis

54000-54001

54000 Slitting of prepuce, dorsal or lateral (separate procedure); newborn
54001 except newborn

ICD-9-CM Diagnostic

605 Redundant prepuce and phimosis ♂

ICD-9-CM Procedural

64.91 Dorsal or lateral slit of prepuce ♂

54015

54015 Incision and drainage of penis, deep

ICD-9-CM Diagnostic

098.0 Gonococcal infection (acute) of lower genitourinary tract
098.2 Gonococcal infections, chronic, of lower genitourinary tract
607.2 Other inflammatory disorders of penis — (Use additional code to identify organism) ♂
607.82 Vascular disorders of penis ♂
607.85 Peyronie's disease ♂
607.89 Other specified disorder of penis ♂

ICD-9-CM Procedural

64.92 Incision of penis ♂

54050-54056

54050 Destruction of lesion(s), penis (eg, condyloma, papilloma, molluscum contagiosum, herpetic vesicle), simple; chemical
54055 electrodesiccation
54056 cryosurgery

ICD-9-CM Diagnostic

054.13 Herpetic infection of penis ♂
078.0 Molluscum contagiosum
078.11 Condyloma acuminatum
078.19 Other specified viral warts
091.0 Genital syphilis (primary)
187.8 Malignant neoplasm of other specified sites of male genital organs ♂
198.82 Secondary malignant neoplasm of genital organs
222.1 Benign neoplasm of penis ♂
233.6 Carcinoma in situ of other and unspecified male genital organs ▽ ♂
239.5 Neoplasm of unspecified nature of other genitourinary organs
709.8 Other specified disorder of skin
709.9 Unspecified disorder of skin and subcutaneous tissue ▽

ICD-9-CM Procedural

64.2 Local excision or destruction of lesion of penis ♂

54057-54065

54057 Destruction of lesion(s), penis (eg, condyloma, papilloma, molluscum contagiosum, herpetic vesicle), simple; laser surgery
54060 surgical excision
54065 Destruction of lesion(s), penis (eg, condyloma, papilloma, molluscum contagiosum, herpetic vesicle), extensive (eg, laser surgery, electrosurgery, cryosurgery, chemosurgery)

ICD-9-CM Diagnostic

054.13 Herpetic infection of penis ♂
078.0 Molluscum contagiosum
078.11 Condyloma acuminatum
078.19 Other specified viral warts
091.0 Genital syphilis (primary)
187.8 Malignant neoplasm of other specified sites of male genital organs ♂
198.82 Secondary malignant neoplasm of genital organs
222.1 Benign neoplasm of penis ♂
233.6 Carcinoma in situ of other and unspecified male genital organs ▽ ♂
239.5 Neoplasm of unspecified nature of other genitourinary organs
709.8 Other specified disorder of skin
709.9 Unspecified disorder of skin and subcutaneous tissue ▽

ICD-9-CM Procedural

64.2 Local excision or destruction of lesion of penis ♂

54100-54105

54100 Biopsy of penis; (separate procedure)
54105 deep structures

ICD-9-CM Diagnostic

187.1 Malignant neoplasm of prepuce ♂
187.2 Malignant neoplasm of glans penis ♂
187.3 Malignant neoplasm of body of penis ♂
187.4 Malignant neoplasm of penis, part unspecified ▽ ♂
187.9 Malignant neoplasm of male genital organ, site unspecified ▽ ♂
198.82 Secondary malignant neoplasm of genital organs
222.1 Benign neoplasm of penis ♂
233.5 Carcinoma in situ of penis ♂
236.6 Neoplasm of uncertain behavior of other and unspecified male genital organs ▽ ♂
239.5 Neoplasm of unspecified nature of other genitourinary organs
607.0 Leukoplakia of penis ♂
607.85 Peyronie's disease ♂
607.89 Other specified disorder of penis ♂
686.1 Pyogenic granuloma of skin and subcutaneous tissue — (Use additional code to identify any infectious organism: 041.0-041.8)

ICD-9-CM Procedural

64.11 Biopsy of penis ♂

54110-54112

54110 Excision of penile plaque (Peyronie disease);
54111 with graft to 5 cm in length
54112 with graft greater than 5 cm in length

ICD-9-CM Diagnostic

607.85 Peyronie's disease ♂

ICD-9-CM Procedural

64.2 Local excision or destruction of lesion of penis ♂
64.49 Other repair of penis ♂

54115

54115 Removal foreign body from deep penile tissue (eg, plastic implant)

ICD-9-CM Diagnostic

939.3 Foreign body in penis ♂
996.39 Mechanical complication of genitourinary device, implant, and graft, other
996.65 Infection and inflammatory reaction due to other genitourinary device, implant, and graft — (Use additional code to identify specified infections)

ICD-9-CM Procedural

64.92 Incision of penis ♂
64.96 Removal of internal prosthesis of penis ♂

54120-54125

54120 Amputation of penis; partial
54125 complete

ICD-9-CM Diagnostic

187.1 Malignant neoplasm of prepuce ♂
187.2 Malignant neoplasm of glans penis ♂
187.3 Malignant neoplasm of body of penis ♂
187.4 Malignant neoplasm of penis, part unspecified ▽ ♂
187.9 Malignant neoplasm of male genital organ, site unspecified ▽ ♂
198.89 Secondary malignant neoplasm of other specified sites
222.1 Benign neoplasm of penis ♂
233.5 Carcinoma in situ of penis ♂
878.0 Open wound of penis, without mention of complication ♂
878.1 Open wound of penis, complicated ♂
942.35 Full-thickness skin loss due to burn (third degree NOS) of genitalia
942.45 Deep necrosis of underlying tissues due to burn (deep third degree) of genitalia, without mention of loss of a body part
948.00 Burn (any degree) involving less than 10% of body surface with third degree burn of less than 10% or unspecified amount

ICD-9-CM Procedural

64.3 Amputation of penis ♂

54130-54135

54130 Amputation of penis, radical; with bilateral inguinofemoral lymphadenectomy
54135 in continuity with bilateral pelvic lymphadenectomy, including external iliac, hypogastric and obturator nodes

ICD-9-CM Diagnostic

187.1 Malignant neoplasm of prepuce ♂
187.2 Malignant neoplasm of glans penis ♂
187.3 Malignant neoplasm of body of penis ♂
187.4 Malignant neoplasm of penis, part unspecified ▽ ♂
187.9 Malignant neoplasm of male genital organ, site unspecified ▽ ♂
196.2 Secondary and unspecified malignant neoplasm of intra-abdominal lymph nodes
196.5 Secondary and unspecified malignant neoplasm of lymph nodes of inguinal region and lower limb
196.6 Secondary and unspecified malignant neoplasm of intrapelvic lymph nodes
198.82 Secondary malignant neoplasm of genital organs
233.5 Carcinoma in situ of penis ♂
236.6 Neoplasm of uncertain behavior of other and unspecified male genital organs ▽ ♂
238.8 Neoplasm of uncertain behavior of other specified sites
239.5 Neoplasm of unspecified nature of other genitourinary organs
239.89 Neoplasms of unspecified nature, other specified sites

ICD-9-CM Procedural

40.50 Radical excision of lymph nodes, not otherwise specified
40.53 Radical excision of iliac lymph nodes
64.3 Amputation of penis ♂

54150-54161

54150 Circumcision, using clamp or other device with regional dorsal penile or ring block
54160 Circumcision, surgical excision other than clamp, device, or dorsal slit; neonate (28 days of age or less)
54161 older than 28 days of age

ICD-9-CM Diagnostic

187.1 Malignant neoplasm of prepuce ♂
187.2 Malignant neoplasm of glans penis ♂
187.3 Malignant neoplasm of body of penis ♂
187.4 Malignant neoplasm of penis, part unspecified ▽ ♂
187.5 Malignant neoplasm of epididymis ♂
187.8 Malignant neoplasm of other specified sites of male genital organs ♂
187.9 Malignant neoplasm of male genital organ, site unspecified ▽ ♂
198.82 Secondary malignant neoplasm of genital organs
222.1 Benign neoplasm of penis ♂
233.5 Carcinoma in situ of penis ♂
236.6 Neoplasm of uncertain behavior of other and unspecified male genital organs ▽ ♂
239.5 Neoplasm of unspecified nature of other genitourinary organs
605 Redundant prepuce and phimosis ♂
607.0 Leukoplakia of penis ♂
607.1 Balanoposthitis — (Use additional code to identify organism) ♂
607.2 Other inflammatory disorders of penis — (Use additional code to identify organism) ♂
607.81 Balanitis xerotica obliterans ♂
607.82 Vascular disorders of penis ♂
607.83 Edema of penis ♂
607.84 Impotence of organic origin ♂
607.85 Peyronie's disease ♂
607.89 Other specified disorder of penis ♂
607.9 Unspecified disorder of penis ▽ ♂
752.61 Hypospadias ♂
752.62 Epispadias ♂
752.63 Congenital chordee ♂
752.64 Micropenis ♂
752.65 Hidden penis ♂
752.69 Other penile anomalies ♂
753.8 Other specified congenital anomaly of bladder and urethra
V13.61 Personal history of (corrected) hypospadias ♂
V50.2 Routine or ritual circumcision ♂

ICD-9-CM Procedural

64.0 Circumcision ♂

54162

54162 Lysis or excision of penile post-circumcision adhesions

ICD-9-CM Diagnostic

605 Redundant prepuce and phimosis ♂
709.2 Scar condition and fibrosis of skin
998.9 Unspecified complication of procedure, not elsewhere classified

ICD-9-CM Procedural

64.93 Division of penile adhesions ♂

54163

54163 Repair incomplete circumcision

ICD-9-CM Diagnostic

605 Redundant prepuce and phimosis ♂
V50.1 Other plastic surgery for unacceptable cosmetic appearance
V50.2 Routine or ritual circumcision ♂

ICD-9-CM Procedural

64.0 Circumcision ♂

54164

54164 Frenulotomy of penis

ICD-9-CM Diagnostic

607.85 Peyronie's disease ♂
607.89 Other specified disorder of penis ♂
752.63 Congenital chordee ♂
752.69 Other penile anomalies ♂

ICD-9-CM Procedural

64.98 Other operations on penis ♂

54200-54205

54200 Injection procedure for Peyronie disease;
54205 with surgical exposure of plaque

ICD-9-CM Diagnostic

607.85 Peyronie's disease ♂

ICD-9-CM Procedural

64.92 Incision of penis ♂
64.98 Other operations on penis ♂
99.29 Injection or infusion of other therapeutic or prophylactic substance
99.77 Application or administration of adhesion barrier substance

54220

54220 Irrigation of corpora cavernosa for priapism

ICD-9-CM Diagnostic

607.3 Priapism ♂

ICD-9-CM Procedural

64.98 Other operations on penis ♂

54230-54235

54230 Injection procedure for corpora cavernosography
54231 Dynamic cavernosometry, including intracavernosal injection of vasoactive drugs (eg, papaverine, phentolamine)
54235 Injection of corpora cavernosa with pharmacologic agent(s) (eg, papaverine, phentolamine)

ICD-9-CM Diagnostic

257.2 Other testicular hypofunction
302.72 Psychosexual dysfunction with inhibited sexual excitement
607.3 Priapism ♂
607.82 Vascular disorders of penis ♂
607.84 Impotence of organic origin ♂
607.85 Peyronie's disease ♂
607.89 Other specified disorder of penis ♂
V41.7 Problems with sexual function

ICD-9-CM Procedural

64.19 Other diagnostic procedures on penis ♂
87.99 Other x-ray of male genital organs ♂
99.29 Injection or infusion of other therapeutic or prophylactic substance
99.77 Application or administration of adhesion barrier substance

54240-54250

54240 Penile plethysmography
54250 Nocturnal penile tumescence and/or rigidity test

ICD-9-CM Diagnostic

257.2 Other testicular hypofunction
302.72 Psychosexual dysfunction with inhibited sexual excitement
607.2 Other inflammatory disorders of penis — (Use additional code to identify organism) ♂
607.3 Priapism ♂
607.81 Balanitis xerotica obliterans ♂
607.82 Vascular disorders of penis ♂
607.83 Edema of penis ♂
607.84 Impotence of organic origin ♂
607.85 Peyronie's disease ♂
607.89 Other specified disorder of penis ♂
V41.7 Problems with sexual function

ICD-9-CM Procedural

89.29 Other nonoperative genitourinary system measurements
89.58 Plethysmogram

54300-54304

54300 Plastic operation of penis for straightening of chordee (eg, hypospadias), with or without mobilization of urethra
54304 Plastic operation on penis for correction of chordee or for first stage hypospadias repair with or without transplantation of prepuce and/or skin flaps

ICD-9-CM Diagnostic

607.89 Other specified disorder of penis ♂
752.61 Hypospadias ♂
752.63 Congenital chordee ♂
752.69 Other penile anomalies ♂
752.81 Scrotal transposition ♂

ICD-9-CM Procedural

58.45 Repair of hypospadias or epispadias
64.42 Release of chordee ♂
64.49 Other repair of penis ♂

54308-54312

54308 Urethroplasty for second stage hypospadias repair (including urinary diversion); less than 3 cm

54312 greater than 3 cm

ICD-9-CM Diagnostic

607.89 Other specified disorder of penis ♂
752.61 Hypospadias ♂
752.63 Congenital chordee ♂
752.69 Other penile anomalies ♂
752.81 Scrotal transposition ♂

ICD-9-CM Procedural

58.45 Repair of hypospadias or epispadias

HCPCS Level II Supplies & Services

A4349 Male external catheter, with or without adhesive, disposable, each

54316

54316 Urethroplasty for second stage hypospadias repair (including urinary diversion) with free skin graft obtained from site other than genitalia

ICD-9-CM Diagnostic

607.89 Other specified disorder of penis ♂
752.61 Hypospadias ♂
752.63 Congenital chordee ♂
752.69 Other penile anomalies ♂
752.81 Scrotal transposition ♂

ICD-9-CM Procedural

58.45 Repair of hypospadias or epispadias

HCPCS Level II Supplies & Services

A4349 Male external catheter, with or without adhesive, disposable, each

54318

54318 Urethroplasty for third stage hypospadias repair to release penis from scrotum (eg, third stage Cecil repair)

ICD-9-CM Diagnostic

607.89 Other specified disorder of penis ♂
752.61 Hypospadias ♂
752.63 Congenital chordee ♂
752.64 Micropenis ♂
752.65 Hidden penis ♂
752.69 Other penile anomalies ♂
752.81 Scrotal transposition ♂

ICD-9-CM Procedural

58.46 Other reconstruction of urethra

54322-54328

54322 1-stage distal hypospadias repair (with or without chordee or circumcision); with simple meatal advancement (eg, Magpi, V-flap)

54324 with urethroplasty by local skin flaps (eg, flip-flap, prepucial flap)

54326 with urethroplasty by local skin flaps and mobilization of urethra

54328 with extensive dissection to correct chordee and urethroplasty with local skin flaps, skin graft patch, and/or island flap

ICD-9-CM Diagnostic

607.89 Other specified disorder of penis ♂
752.61 Hypospadias ♂
752.63 Congenital chordee ♂
752.69 Other penile anomalies ♂
752.81 Scrotal transposition ♂

ICD-9-CM Procedural

58.45 Repair of hypospadias or epispadias
64.42 Release of chordee ♂

54332-54336

54332 1-stage proximal penile or penoscrotal hypospadias repair requiring extensive dissection to correct chordee and urethroplasty by use of skin graft tube and/or island flap

54336 1-stage perineal hypospadias repair requiring extensive dissection to correct chordee and urethroplasty by use of skin graft tube and/or island flap

ICD-9-CM Diagnostic

607.89 Other specified disorder of penis ♂
752.61 Hypospadias ♂
752.63 Congenital chordee ♂
752.69 Other penile anomalies ♂
752.81 Scrotal transposition ♂

ICD-9-CM Procedural

58.45 Repair of hypospadias or epispadias
64.42 Release of chordee ♂

54340-54348

54340 Repair of hypospadias complications (ie, fistula, stricture, diverticula); by closure, incision, or excision, simple

54344 requiring mobilization of skin flaps and urethroplasty with flap or patch graft

54348 requiring extensive dissection and urethroplasty with flap, patch or tubed graft (includes urinary diversion)

ICD-9-CM Diagnostic

598.2 Postoperative urethral stricture — (Use additional code to identify urinary incontinence: 625.6, 788.30-788.39)
599.1 Urethral fistula
599.2 Urethral diverticulum
605 Redundant prepuce and phimosis ♂
607.89 Other specified disorder of penis ♂
752.61 Hypospadias ♂
752.63 Congenital chordee ♂
752.81 Scrotal transposition ♂
753.8 Other specified congenital anomaly of bladder and urethra
788.29 Other specified retention of urine — (Code, if applicable, any causal condition first, such as: 600.0-600.9, with fifth digit 1)
996.39 Mechanical complication of genitourinary device, implant, and graft, other
996.65 Infection and inflammatory reaction due to other genitourinary device, implant, and graft — (Use additional code to identify specified infections)
997.5 Urinary complications — (Use additional code to identify complications)
997.99 Other complications affecting other specified body systems, NEC — (Use additional code to identify complications)
998.59 Other postoperative infection — (Use additional code to identify infection)
998.6 Persistent postoperative fistula, not elsewhere classified
998.83 Non-healing surgical wound
998.89 Other specified complications
V13.61 Personal history of (corrected) hypospadias ♂

ICD-9-CM Procedural

58.0 Urethrotomy
58.39 Other local excision or destruction of lesion or tissue of urethra
58.43 Closure of other fistula of urethra

58.6 Dilation of urethra

HCPCS Level II Supplies & Services

A4305 Disposable drug delivery system, flow rate of 50 ml or greater per hour

54352

54352 Repair of hypospadias cripple requiring extensive dissection and excision of previously constructed structures including re-release of chordee and reconstruction of urethra and penis by use of local skin as grafts and island flaps and skin brought in as flaps or grafts

ICD-9-CM Diagnostic

598.2 Postoperative urethral stricture — (Use additional code to identify urinary incontinence: 625.6, 788.30-788.39)
599.1 Urethral fistula
599.2 Urethral diverticulum
605 Redundant prepuce and phimosis ♂
752.61 Hypospadias ♂
752.63 Congenital chordee ♂
752.81 Scrotal transposition ♂
753.8 Other specified congenital anomaly of bladder and urethra
788.29 Other specified retention of urine — (Code, if applicable, any causal condition first, such as: 600.0-600.9, with fifth digit 1)
996.39 Mechanical complication of genitourinary device, implant, and graft, other
996.65 Infection and inflammatory reaction due to other genitourinary device, implant, and graft — (Use additional code to identify specified infections)
997.5 Urinary complications — (Use additional code to identify complications)
998.59 Other postoperative infection — (Use additional code to identify infection)
998.6 Persistent postoperative fistula, not elsewhere classified
998.83 Non-healing surgical wound
998.89 Other specified complications

ICD-9-CM Procedural

58.0 Urethrotomy
58.39 Other local excision or destruction of lesion or tissue of urethra
58.43 Closure of other fistula of urethra
58.45 Repair of hypospadias or epispadias
58.49 Other repair of urethra
58.6 Dilation of urethra
64.42 Release of chordee ♂

54360

54360 Plastic operation on penis to correct angulation

ICD-9-CM Diagnostic

098.2 Gonococcal infections, chronic, of lower genitourinary tract
607.85 Peyronie's disease ♂
607.89 Other specified disorder of penis ♂
752.62 Epispadias ♂
752.63 Congenital chordee ♂
752.69 Other penile anomalies ♂
996.39 Mechanical complication of genitourinary device, implant, and graft, other
996.65 Infection and inflammatory reaction due to other genitourinary device, implant, and graft — (Use additional code to identify specified infections)

ICD-9-CM Procedural

64.49 Other repair of penis ♂

54380-54390

54380 Plastic operation on penis for epispadias distal to external sphincter;
54385 with incontinence
54390 with exstrophy of bladder

ICD-9-CM Diagnostic

752.62 Epispadias ♂
753.5 Exstrophy of urinary bladder
788.37 Continuous leakage — (Code, if applicable, any causal condition first: 600.0-600.9, with fifth digit 1; 618.00-618.9; 753.23)
788.39 Other urinary incontinence — (Code, if applicable, any causal condition first: 600.0-600.9, with fifth digit 1; 618.00-618.9; 753.23)
788.99 Other symptoms involving urinary system

ICD-9-CM Procedural

57.86 Repair of bladder exstrophy
58.45 Repair of hypospadias or epispadias
64.49 Other repair of penis ♂

54400-54401

54400 Insertion of penile prosthesis; non-inflatable (semi-rigid)
54401 inflatable (self-contained)

ICD-9-CM Diagnostic

227.3 Benign neoplasm of pituitary gland and craniopharyngeal duct (pouch) — (Use additional code to identify any functional activity)
249.60 Secondary diabetes mellitus with neurological manifestations, not stated as uncontrolled, or unspecified — (Use additional code to identify manifestation: 337.1, 353.5, 354.0-355.9, 357.2, 536.3, 713.5) (Use additional code to identify any associated insulin use: V58.67)
249.61 Secondary diabetes mellitus with neurological manifestations, uncontrolled — (Use additional code to identify manifestation: 337.1, 353.5, 354.0-355.9, 357.2, 536.3, 713.5) (Use additional code to identify any associated insulin use: V58.67)
249.70 Secondary diabetes mellitus with peripheral circulatory disorders, not stated as uncontrolled, or unspecified — (Use additional code to identify manifestation: 443.81, 785.4) (Use additional code to identify any associated insulin use: V58.67)
249.71 Secondary diabetes mellitus with peripheral circulatory disorders, uncontrolled — (Use additional code to identify manifestation: 443.81, 785.4) (Use additional code to identify any associated insulin use: V58.67)
250.60 Diabetes with neurological manifestations, type II or unspecified type, not stated as uncontrolled — (Use additional code to identify manifestation: 337.1, 353.5, 354.0-355.9, 357.2, 536.3, 713.5)
250.61 Diabetes with neurological manifestations, type I [juvenile type], not stated as uncontrolled — (Use additional code to identify manifestation: 337.1, 353.5, 354.0-355.9, 357.2, 536.3, 713.5)
250.62 Diabetes with neurological manifestations, type II or unspecified type, uncontrolled — (Use additional code to identify manifestation: 337.1, 353.5, 354.0-355.9, 357.2, 536.3, 713.5)
250.63 Diabetes with neurological manifestations, type I [juvenile type], uncontrolled — (Use additional code to identify manifestation: 337.1, 353.5, 354.0-355.9, 357.2, 536.3, 713.5)
250.70 Diabetes with peripheral circulatory disorders, type II or unspecified type, not stated as uncontrolled — (Use additional code to identify manifestation: 443.81, 785.4)
250.71 Diabetes with peripheral circulatory disorders, type I [juvenile type], not stated as uncontrolled — (Use additional code to identify manifestation: 443.81, 785.4)
250.72 Diabetes with peripheral circulatory disorders, type II or unspecified type, uncontrolled — (Use additional code to identify manifestation: 443.81, 785.4)
250.73 Diabetes with peripheral circulatory disorders, type I [juvenile type], uncontrolled — (Use additional code to identify manifestation: 443.81, 785.4)
253.1 Other and unspecified anterior pituitary hyperfunction ▽
257.2 Other testicular hypofunction
302.72 Psychosexual dysfunction with inhibited sexual excitement

337.1 Peripheral autonomic neuropathy in disorders classified elsewhere — (Code first underlying disease: 249.6, 250.6, 277.30-277.39) ☒

443.81 Peripheral angiopathy in diseases classified elsewhere — (Code first underlying disease: 249.7, 250.7) ☒

600.00 Hypertrophy (benign) of prostate without urinary obstruction and other lower urinary tract symptoms [LUTS] ♂

600.10 Nodular prostate without urinary obstruction ♂

600.20 Benign localized hyperplasia of prostate without urinary obstruction and other lower urinary tract symptoms [LUTS] ♂

600.3 Cyst of prostate ♂

600.90 Hyperplasia of prostate, unspecified, without urinary obstruction and other lower urinary tract symptoms [LUTS] ▽ ♂

607.81 Balanitis xerotica obliterans ♂

607.82 Vascular disorders of penis ♂

607.84 Impotence of organic origin ♂

607.89 Other specified disorder of penis ♂

608.83 Specified vascular disorder of male genital organs ♂

608.89 Other specified disorder of male genital organs ♂

752.89 Other specified anomalies of genital organs

907.2 Late effect of spinal cord injury

V10.46 Personal history of malignant neoplasm of prostate ♂

V52.8 Fitting and adjustment of other specified prosthetic device

ICD-9-CM Procedural

64.95 Insertion or replacement of non-inflatable penile prosthesis ♂

64.97 Insertion or replacement of inflatable penile prosthesis ♂

HCPCS Level II Supplies & Services

C1813 Prosthesis, penile, inflatable

C2622 Prosthesis, penile, noninflatable

54405

54405 Insertion of multi-component, inflatable penile prosthesis, including placement of pump, cylinders, and reservoir

ICD-9-CM Diagnostic

227.3 Benign neoplasm of pituitary gland and craniopharyngeal duct (pouch) — (Use additional code to identify any functional activity)

249.60 Secondary diabetes mellitus with neurological manifestations, not stated as uncontrolled, or unspecified — (Use additional code to identify manifestation: 337.1, 353.5, 354.0-355.9, 357.2, 536.3, 713.5) (Use additional code to identify any associated insulin use: V58.67)

249.61 Secondary diabetes mellitus with neurological manifestations, uncontrolled — (Use additional code to identify manifestation: 337.1, 353.5, 354.0-355.9, 357.2, 536.3, 713.5) (Use additional code to identify any associated insulin use: V58.67)

249.70 Secondary diabetes mellitus with peripheral circulatory disorders, not stated as uncontrolled, or unspecified — (Use additional code to identify manifestation: 443.81, 785.4) (Use additional code to identify any associated insulin use: V58.67)

249.71 Secondary diabetes mellitus with peripheral circulatory disorders, uncontrolled — (Use additional code to identify manifestation: 443.81, 785.4) (Use additional code to identify any associated insulin use: V58.67)

250.60 Diabetes with neurological manifestations, type II or unspecified type, not stated as uncontrolled — (Use additional code to identify manifestation: 337.1, 353.5, 354.0-355.9, 357.2, 536.3, 713.5)

250.61 Diabetes with neurological manifestations, type I [juvenile type], not stated as uncontrolled — (Use additional code to identify manifestation: 337.1, 353.5, 354.0-355.9, 357.2, 536.3, 713.5)

250.62 Diabetes with neurological manifestations, type II or unspecified type, uncontrolled — (Use additional code to identify manifestation: 337.1, 353.5, 354.0-355.9, 357.2, 536.3, 713.5)

250.63 Diabetes with neurological manifestations, type I [juvenile type], uncontrolled — (Use additional code to identify manifestation: 337.1, 353.5, 354.0-355.9, 357.2, 536.3, 713.5)

250.70 Diabetes with peripheral circulatory disorders, type II or unspecified type, not stated as uncontrolled — (Use additional code to identify manifestation: 443.81, 785.4)

250.71 Diabetes with peripheral circulatory disorders, type I [juvenile type], not stated as uncontrolled — (Use additional code to identify manifestation: 443.81, 785.4)

250.72 Diabetes with peripheral circulatory disorders, type II or unspecified type, uncontrolled — (Use additional code to identify manifestation: 443.81, 785.4)

250.73 Diabetes with peripheral circulatory disorders, type I [juvenile type], uncontrolled — (Use additional code to identify manifestation: 443.81, 785.4)

253.1 Other and unspecified anterior pituitary hyperfunction ▽

257.2 Other testicular hypofunction

302.72 Psychosexual dysfunction with inhibited sexual excitement

337.1 Peripheral autonomic neuropathy in disorders classified elsewhere — (Code first underlying disease: 249.6, 250.6, 277.30-277.39) ☒

443.81 Peripheral angiopathy in diseases classified elsewhere — (Code first underlying disease: 249.7, 250.7) ☒

600.00 Hypertrophy (benign) of prostate without urinary obstruction and other lower urinary tract symptoms [LUTS] ♂

600.10 Nodular prostate without urinary obstruction ♂

600.20 Benign localized hyperplasia of prostate without urinary obstruction and other lower urinary tract symptoms [LUTS] ♂

600.3 Cyst of prostate ♂

600.90 Hyperplasia of prostate, unspecified, without urinary obstruction and other lower urinary tract symptoms [LUTS] ▽ ♂

607.81 Balanitis xerotica obliterans ♂

607.82 Vascular disorders of penis ♂

607.84 Impotence of organic origin ♂

607.89 Other specified disorder of penis ♂

608.83 Specified vascular disorder of male genital organs ♂

608.89 Other specified disorder of male genital organs ♂

752.89 Other specified anomalies of genital organs

907.2 Late effect of spinal cord injury

V10.46 Personal history of malignant neoplasm of prostate ♂

V52.8 Fitting and adjustment of other specified prosthetic device

ICD-9-CM Procedural

64.97 Insertion or replacement of inflatable penile prosthesis ♂

HCPCS Level II Supplies & Services

C1813 Prosthesis, penile, inflatable

54406

54406 Removal of all components of a multi-component, inflatable penile prosthesis without replacement of prosthesis

ICD-9-CM Diagnostic

187.5 Malignant neoplasm of epididymis ♂

187.6 Malignant neoplasm of spermatic cord ♂

187.8 Malignant neoplasm of other specified sites of male genital organs ♂

233.6 Carcinoma in situ of other and unspecified male genital organs ▽ ♂

597.0 Urethral abscess

597.80 Unspecified urethritis ▽

597.89 Other urethritis

603.1 Infected hydrocele — (Use additional code to identify organism) ♂

604.0 Orchitis, epididymitis, and epididymo-orchitis, with abscess — (Use additional code to identify organism: 041.00-041.09, 041.10-041.19, 041.41-041.49) ♂

604.90 Unspecified orchitis and epididymitis — (Use additional code to identify organism: 041.00-041.09, 041.10-041.19, 041.41-041.49) ▽ ♂

604.91 Orchitis and epididymitis in disease classified elsewhere — (Use additional code to identify organism: 041.00-041.09, 041.10-041.19, 041.41-041.49. Code first underlying disease: 032.89, 095.8, 125.0-125.9) ☒ ♂
607.1 Balanoposthitis — (Use additional code to identify organism) ♂
607.2 Other inflammatory disorders of penis — (Use additional code to identify organism) ♂
607.81 Balanitis xerotica obliterans ♂
607.83 Edema of penis ♂
608.0 Seminal vesiculitis — (Use additional code to identify organism) ♂
608.1 Spermatocele ♂
608.4 Other inflammatory disorder of male genital organs — (Use additional code to identify organism) ♂
608.81 Specified disorder of male genital organs in diseases classified elsewhere — (Code first underlying disease: 016.5, 125.0-125.9) ☒ ♂
608.86 Edema of male genital organs ♂
867.1 Bladder and urethra injury with open wound into cavity
867.7 Injury to other specified pelvic organs with open wound into cavity
878.1 Open wound of penis, complicated ♂
878.3 Open wound of scrotum and testes, complicated ♂
996.39 Mechanical complication of genitourinary device, implant, and graft, other
996.65 Infection and inflammatory reaction due to other genitourinary device, implant, and graft — (Use additional code to identify specified infections)
996.76 Other complications due to genitourinary device, implant, and graft — (Use additional code to identify complication: 338.18-338.19, 338.28-338.29)
998.59 Other postoperative infection — (Use additional code to identify infection)
V52.8 Fitting and adjustment of other specified prosthetic device

ICD-9-CM Procedural

64.96 Removal of internal prosthesis of penis ♂

54408

54408 Repair of component(s) of a multi-component, inflatable penile prosthesis

ICD-9-CM Diagnostic

996.39 Mechanical complication of genitourinary device, implant, and graft, other

ICD-9-CM Procedural

64.99 Other operations on male genital organs ♂

54410

54410 Removal and replacement of all component(s) of a multi-component, inflatable penile prosthesis at the same operative session

ICD-9-CM Diagnostic

227.3 Benign neoplasm of pituitary gland and craniopharyngeal duct (pouch) — (Use additional code to identify any functional activity)
249.60 Secondary diabetes mellitus with neurological manifestations, not stated as uncontrolled, or unspecified — (Use additional code to identify manifestation: 337.1, 353.5, 354.0-355.9, 357.2, 536.3, 713.5) (Use additional code to identify any associated insulin use: V58.67)
249.61 Secondary diabetes mellitus with neurological manifestations, uncontrolled — (Use additional code to identify manifestation: 337.1, 353.5, 354.0-355.9, 357.2, 536.3, 713.5) (Use additional code to identify any associated insulin use: V58.67)
249.70 Secondary diabetes mellitus with peripheral circulatory disorders, not stated as uncontrolled, or unspecified — (Use additional code to identify manifestation: 443.81, 785.4) (Use additional code to identify any associated insulin use: V58.67)
249.71 Secondary diabetes mellitus with peripheral circulatory disorders, uncontrolled — (Use additional code to identify manifestation: 443.81, 785.4) (Use additional code to identify any associated insulin use: V58.67)
250.60 Diabetes with neurological manifestations, type II or unspecified type, not stated as uncontrolled — (Use additional code to identify manifestation: 337.1, 353.5, 354.0-355.9, 357.2, 536.3, 713.5)
250.61 Diabetes with neurological manifestations, type I [juvenile type], not stated as uncontrolled — (Use additional code to identify manifestation: 337.1, 353.5, 354.0-355.9, 357.2, 536.3, 713.5)
250.62 Diabetes with neurological manifestations, type II or unspecified type, uncontrolled — (Use additional code to identify manifestation: 337.1, 353.5, 354.0-355.9, 357.2, 536.3, 713.5)
250.63 Diabetes with neurological manifestations, type I [juvenile type], uncontrolled — (Use additional code to identify manifestation: 337.1, 353.5, 354.0-355.9, 357.2, 536.3, 713.5)
250.70 Diabetes with peripheral circulatory disorders, type II or unspecified type, not stated as uncontrolled — (Use additional code to identify manifestation: 443.81, 785.4)
250.71 Diabetes with peripheral circulatory disorders, type I [juvenile type], not stated as uncontrolled — (Use additional code to identify manifestation: 443.81, 785.4)
250.72 Diabetes with peripheral circulatory disorders, type II or unspecified type, uncontrolled — (Use additional code to identify manifestation: 443.81, 785.4)
250.73 Diabetes with peripheral circulatory disorders, type I [juvenile type], uncontrolled — (Use additional code to identify manifestation: 443.81, 785.4)
253.1 Other and unspecified anterior pituitary hyperfunction ▽
257.2 Other testicular hypofunction
302.72 Psychosexual dysfunction with inhibited sexual excitement
337.1 Peripheral autonomic neuropathy in disorders classified elsewhere — (Code first underlying disease: 249.6, 250.6, 277.30-277.39) ☒
443.81 Peripheral angiopathy in diseases classified elsewhere — (Code first underlying disease: 249.7, 250.7) ☒
607.82 Vascular disorders of penis ♂
607.84 Impotence of organic origin ♂
607.89 Other specified disorder of penis ♂
608.83 Specified vascular disorder of male genital organs ♂
608.89 Other specified disorder of male genital organs ♂
752.89 Other specified anomalies of genital organs
907.2 Late effect of spinal cord injury
996.39 Mechanical complication of genitourinary device, implant, and graft, other
996.65 Infection and inflammatory reaction due to other genitourinary device, implant, and graft — (Use additional code to identify specified infections)
996.76 Other complications due to genitourinary device, implant, and graft — (Use additional code to identify complication: 338.18-338.19, 338.28-338.29)
V10.46 Personal history of malignant neoplasm of prostate ♂
V45.77 Acquired absence of organ, genital organs
V52.8 Fitting and adjustment of other specified prosthetic device

ICD-9-CM Procedural

64.97 Insertion or replacement of inflatable penile prosthesis ♂

HCPCS Level II Supplies & Services

C1813 Prosthesis, penile, inflatable

54411

54411 Removal and replacement of all components of a multi-component inflatable penile prosthesis through an infected field at the same operative session, including irrigation and debridement of infected tissue

ICD-9-CM Diagnostic

227.3 Benign neoplasm of pituitary gland and craniopharyngeal duct (pouch) — (Use additional code to identify any functional activity)
249.60 Secondary diabetes mellitus with neurological manifestations, not stated as uncontrolled, or unspecified — (Use additional code to identify manifestation: 337.1, 353.5, 354.0-355.9, 357.2, 536.3, 713.5) (Use additional code to identify any associated insulin use: V58.67)
249.61 Secondary diabetes mellitus with neurological manifestations, uncontrolled — (Use additional code to identify manifestation: 337.1, 353.5, 354.0-355.9, 357.2, 536.3, 713.5) (Use additional code to identify any associated insulin use: V58.67)

249.70 Secondary diabetes mellitus with peripheral circulatory disorders, not stated as uncontrolled, or unspecified — (Use additional code to identify manifestation: 443.81, 785.4) (Use additional code to identify any associated insulin use: V58.67)
249.71 Secondary diabetes mellitus with peripheral circulatory disorders, uncontrolled — (Use additional code to identify manifestation: 443.81, 785.4) (Use additional code to identify any associated insulin use: V58.67)
250.60 Diabetes with neurological manifestations, type II or unspecified type, not stated as uncontrolled — (Use additional code to identify manifestation: 337.1, 353.5, 354.0-355.9, 357.2, 536.3, 713.5)
250.61 Diabetes with neurological manifestations, type I [juvenile type], not stated as uncontrolled — (Use additional code to identify manifestation: 337.1, 353.5, 354.0-355.9, 357.2, 536.3, 713.5)
250.62 Diabetes with neurological manifestations, type II or unspecified type, uncontrolled — (Use additional code to identify manifestation: 337.1, 353.5, 354.0-355.9, 357.2, 536.3, 713.5)
250.63 Diabetes with neurological manifestations, type I [juvenile type], uncontrolled — (Use additional code to identify manifestation: 337.1, 353.5, 354.0-355.9, 357.2, 536.3, 713.5)
250.70 Diabetes with peripheral circulatory disorders, type II or unspecified type, not stated as uncontrolled — (Use additional code to identify manifestation: 443.81, 785.4)
250.71 Diabetes with peripheral circulatory disorders, type I [juvenile type], not stated as uncontrolled — (Use additional code to identify manifestation: 443.81, 785.4)
250.72 Diabetes with peripheral circulatory disorders, type II or unspecified type, uncontrolled — (Use additional code to identify manifestation: 443.81, 785.4)
250.73 Diabetes with peripheral circulatory disorders, type I [juvenile type], uncontrolled — (Use additional code to identify manifestation: 443.81, 785.4)
253.1 Other and unspecified anterior pituitary hyperfunction ▽
257.2 Other testicular hypofunction
302.72 Psychosexual dysfunction with inhibited sexual excitement
337.1 Peripheral autonomic neuropathy in disorders classified elsewhere — (Code first underlying disease: 249.6, 250.6, 277.30-277.39) ☒
443.81 Peripheral angiopathy in diseases classified elsewhere — (Code first underlying disease: 249.7, 250.7) ☒
597.0 Urethral abscess
597.80 Unspecified urethritis ▽
597.89 Other urethritis
603.1 Infected hydrocele — (Use additional code to identify organism) ♂
604.0 Orchitis, epididymitis, and epididymo-orchitis, with abscess — (Use additional code to identify organism: 041.00-041.09, 041.10-041.19, 041.41-041.49) ♂
604.90 Unspecified orchitis and epididymitis — (Use additional code to identify organism: 041.00-041.09, 041.10-041.19, 041.41-041.49) ▽ ♂
604.91 Orchitis and epididymitis in disease classified elsewhere — (Use additional code to identify organism: 041.00-041.09, 041.10-041.19, 041.41-041.49. Code first underlying disease: 032.89, 095.8, 125.0-125.9) ☒ ♂
607.1 Balanoposthitis — (Use additional code to identify organism) ♂
607.2 Other inflammatory disorders of penis — (Use additional code to identify organism) ♂
607.81 Balanitis xerotica obliterans ♂
607.82 Vascular disorders of penis ♂
607.84 Impotence of organic origin ♂
607.89 Other specified disorder of penis ♂
608.0 Seminal vesiculitis — (Use additional code to identify organism) ♂
608.4 Other inflammatory disorder of male genital organs — (Use additional code to identify organism) ♂
608.81 Specified disorder of male genital organs in diseases classified elsewhere — (Code first underlying disease: 016.5, 125.0-125.9) ☒ ♂
608.83 Specified vascular disorder of male genital organs ♂
608.89 Other specified disorder of male genital organs ♂
752.89 Other specified anomalies of genital organs
907.2 Late effect of spinal cord injury
996.65 Infection and inflammatory reaction due to other genitourinary device, implant, and graft — (Use additional code to identify specified infections)
996.76 Other complications due to genitourinary device, implant, and graft — (Use additional code to identify complication: 338.18-338.19, 338.28-338.29)
998.59 Other postoperative infection — (Use additional code to identify infection)
V10.46 Personal history of malignant neoplasm of prostate ♂
V52.8 Fitting and adjustment of other specified prosthetic device

ICD-9-CM Procedural

64.96 Removal of internal prosthesis of penis ♂
64.97 Insertion or replacement of inflatable penile prosthesis ♂
86.22 Excisional debridement of wound, infection, or burn

HCPCS Level II Supplies & Services

C1813 Prosthesis, penile, inflatable

54415

54415 Removal of non-inflatable (semi-rigid) or inflatable (self-contained) penile prosthesis, without replacement of prosthesis

ICD-9-CM Diagnostic

187.5 Malignant neoplasm of epididymis ♂
187.6 Malignant neoplasm of spermatic cord ♂
187.8 Malignant neoplasm of other specified sites of male genital organs ♂
233.6 Carcinoma in situ of other and unspecified male genital organs ▽ ♂
597.0 Urethral abscess
597.80 Unspecified urethritis ▽
597.89 Other urethritis
603.1 Infected hydrocele — (Use additional code to identify organism) ♂
604.0 Orchitis, epididymitis, and epididymo-orchitis, with abscess — (Use additional code to identify organism: 041.00-041.09, 041.10-041.19, 041.41-041.49) ♂
604.90 Unspecified orchitis and epididymitis — (Use additional code to identify organism: 041.00-041.09, 041.10-041.19, 041.41-041.49) ▽ ♂
604.91 Orchitis and epididymitis in disease classified elsewhere — (Use additional code to identify organism: 041.00-041.09, 041.10-041.19, 041.41-041.49. Code first underlying disease: 032.89, 095.8, 125.0-125.9) ☒ ♂
607.1 Balanoposthitis — (Use additional code to identify organism) ♂
607.2 Other inflammatory disorders of penis — (Use additional code to identify organism) ♂
607.81 Balanitis xerotica obliterans ♂
607.83 Edema of penis ♂
608.0 Seminal vesiculitis — (Use additional code to identify organism) ♂
608.1 Spermatocele ♂
608.4 Other inflammatory disorder of male genital organs — (Use additional code to identify organism) ♂
608.81 Specified disorder of male genital organs in diseases classified elsewhere — (Code first underlying disease: 016.5, 125.0-125.9) ☒ ♂
608.86 Edema of male genital organs ♂
867.1 Bladder and urethra injury with open wound into cavity
867.7 Injury to other specified pelvic organs with open wound into cavity
878.1 Open wound of penis, complicated ♂
878.3 Open wound of scrotum and testes, complicated ♂
996.39 Mechanical complication of genitourinary device, implant, and graft, other
996.65 Infection and inflammatory reaction due to other genitourinary device, implant, and graft — (Use additional code to identify specified infections)
996.76 Other complications due to genitourinary device, implant, and graft — (Use additional code to identify complication: 338.18-338.19, 338.28-338.29)
998.59 Other postoperative infection — (Use additional code to identify infection)
V52.8 Fitting and adjustment of other specified prosthetic device

ICD-9-CM Procedural

64.96 Removal of internal prosthesis of penis ♂

54416

54416 Removal and replacement of non-inflatable (semi-rigid) or inflatable (self-contained) penile prosthesis at the same operative session

ICD-9-CM Diagnostic

227.3 Benign neoplasm of pituitary gland and craniopharyngeal duct (pouch) — (Use additional code to identify any functional activity)

249.60 Secondary diabetes mellitus with neurological manifestations, not stated as uncontrolled, or unspecified — (Use additional code to identify manifestation: 337.1, 353.5, 354.0-355.9, 357.2, 536.3, 713.5) (Use additional code to identify any associated insulin use: V58.67)

249.61 Secondary diabetes mellitus with neurological manifestations, uncontrolled — (Use additional code to identify manifestation: 337.1, 353.5, 354.0-355.9, 357.2, 536.3, 713.5) (Use additional code to identify any associated insulin use: V58.67)

249.70 Secondary diabetes mellitus with peripheral circulatory disorders, not stated as uncontrolled, or unspecified — (Use additional code to identify manifestation: 443.81, 785.4) (Use additional code to identify any associated insulin use: V58.67)

249.71 Secondary diabetes mellitus with peripheral circulatory disorders, uncontrolled — (Use additional code to identify manifestation: 443.81, 785.4) (Use additional code to identify any associated insulin use: V58.67)

250.60 Diabetes with neurological manifestations, type II or unspecified type, not stated as uncontrolled — (Use additional code to identify manifestation: 337.1, 353.5, 354.0-355.9, 357.2, 536.3, 713.5)

250.61 Diabetes with neurological manifestations, type I [juvenile type], not stated as uncontrolled — (Use additional code to identify manifestation: 337.1, 353.5, 354.0-355.9, 357.2, 536.3, 713.5)

250.62 Diabetes with neurological manifestations, type II or unspecified type, uncontrolled — (Use additional code to identify manifestation: 337.1, 353.5, 354.0-355.9, 357.2, 536.3, 713.5)

250.63 Diabetes with neurological manifestations, type I [juvenile type], uncontrolled — (Use additional code to identify manifestation: 337.1, 353.5, 354.0-355.9, 357.2, 536.3, 713.5)

250.70 Diabetes with peripheral circulatory disorders, type II or unspecified type, not stated as uncontrolled — (Use additional code to identify manifestation: 443.81, 785.4)

250.71 Diabetes with peripheral circulatory disorders, type I [juvenile type], not stated as uncontrolled — (Use additional code to identify manifestation: 443.81, 785.4)

250.72 Diabetes with peripheral circulatory disorders, type II or unspecified type, uncontrolled — (Use additional code to identify manifestation: 443.81, 785.4)

250.73 Diabetes with peripheral circulatory disorders, type I [juvenile type], uncontrolled — (Use additional code to identify manifestation: 443.81, 785.4)

253.1 Other and unspecified anterior pituitary hyperfunction ▽

257.2 Other testicular hypofunction

302.72 Psychosexual dysfunction with inhibited sexual excitement

337.1 Peripheral autonomic neuropathy in disorders classified elsewhere — (Code first underlying disease: 249.6, 250.6, 277.30-277.39) ☒

443.81 Peripheral angiopathy in diseases classified elsewhere — (Code first underlying disease: 249.7, 250.7) ☒

607.82 Vascular disorders of penis ♂

607.84 Impotence of organic origin ♂

607.89 Other specified disorder of penis ♂

608.83 Specified vascular disorder of male genital organs ♂

608.89 Other specified disorder of male genital organs ♂

752.89 Other specified anomalies of genital organs

907.2 Late effect of spinal cord injury

996.39 Mechanical complication of genitourinary device, implant, and graft, other

996.65 Infection and inflammatory reaction due to other genitourinary device, implant, and graft — (Use additional code to identify specified infections)

996.76 Other complications due to genitourinary device, implant, and graft — (Use additional code to identify complication: 338.18-338.19, 338.28-338.29)

V10.46 Personal history of malignant neoplasm of prostate ♂

V52.8 Fitting and adjustment of other specified prosthetic device

ICD-9-CM Procedural

64.95 Insertion or replacement of non-inflatable penile prosthesis ♂

64.97 Insertion or replacement of inflatable penile prosthesis ♂

HCPCS Level II Supplies & Services

C1813 Prosthesis, penile, inflatable

C2622 Prosthesis, penile, noninflatable

54417

54417 Removal and replacement of non-inflatable (semi-rigid) or inflatable (self-contained) penile prosthesis through an infected field at the same operative session, including irrigation and debridement of infected tissue

ICD-9-CM Diagnostic

227.3 Benign neoplasm of pituitary gland and craniopharyngeal duct (pouch) — (Use additional code to identify any functional activity)

249.60 Secondary diabetes mellitus with neurological manifestations, not stated as uncontrolled, or unspecified — (Use additional code to identify manifestation: 337.1, 353.5, 354.0-355.9, 357.2, 536.3, 713.5) (Use additional code to identify any associated insulin use: V58.67)

249.61 Secondary diabetes mellitus with neurological manifestations, uncontrolled — (Use additional code to identify manifestation: 337.1, 353.5, 354.0-355.9, 357.2, 536.3, 713.5) (Use additional code to identify any associated insulin use: V58.67)

249.70 Secondary diabetes mellitus with peripheral circulatory disorders, not stated as uncontrolled, or unspecified — (Use additional code to identify manifestation: 443.81, 785.4) (Use additional code to identify any associated insulin use: V58.67)

249.71 Secondary diabetes mellitus with peripheral circulatory disorders, uncontrolled — (Use additional code to identify manifestation: 443.81, 785.4) (Use additional code to identify any associated insulin use: V58.67)

250.60 Diabetes with neurological manifestations, type II or unspecified type, not stated as uncontrolled — (Use additional code to identify manifestation: 337.1, 353.5, 354.0-355.9, 357.2, 536.3, 713.5)

250.61 Diabetes with neurological manifestations, type I [juvenile type], not stated as uncontrolled — (Use additional code to identify manifestation: 337.1, 353.5, 354.0-355.9, 357.2, 536.3, 713.5)

250.62 Diabetes with neurological manifestations, type II or unspecified type, uncontrolled — (Use additional code to identify manifestation: 337.1, 353.5, 354.0-355.9, 357.2, 536.3, 713.5)

250.63 Diabetes with neurological manifestations, type I [juvenile type], uncontrolled — (Use additional code to identify manifestation: 337.1, 353.5, 354.0-355.9, 357.2, 536.3, 713.5)

250.70 Diabetes with peripheral circulatory disorders, type II or unspecified type, not stated as uncontrolled — (Use additional code to identify manifestation: 443.81, 785.4)

250.71 Diabetes with peripheral circulatory disorders, type I [juvenile type], not stated as uncontrolled — (Use additional code to identify manifestation: 443.81, 785.4)

250.72 Diabetes with peripheral circulatory disorders, type II or unspecified type, uncontrolled — (Use additional code to identify manifestation: 443.81, 785.4)

250.73 Diabetes with peripheral circulatory disorders, type I [juvenile type], uncontrolled — (Use additional code to identify manifestation: 443.81, 785.4)

253.1 Other and unspecified anterior pituitary hyperfunction ▽

257.2 Other testicular hypofunction

302.72 Psychosexual dysfunction with inhibited sexual excitement

337.1 Peripheral autonomic neuropathy in disorders classified elsewhere — (Code first underlying disease: 249.6, 250.6, 277.30-277.39) ☒

443.81 Peripheral angiopathy in diseases classified elsewhere — (Code first underlying disease: 249.7, 250.7) ☒

597.0 Urethral abscess

597.80 Unspecified urethritis ▽

597.89 Other urethritis
603.1 Infected hydrocele — (Use additional code to identify organism) ♂
604.0 Orchitis, epididymitis, and epididymo-orchitis, with abscess — (Use additional code to identify organism: 041.00-041.09, 041.10-041.19, 041.41-041.49) ♂
604.90 Unspecified orchitis and epididymitis — (Use additional code to identify organism: 041.00-041.09, 041.10-041.19, 041.41-041.49) ♂
604.91 Orchitis and epididymitis in disease classified elsewhere — (Use additional code to identify organism: 041.00-041.09, 041.10-041.19, 041.41-041.49. Code first underlying disease: 032.89, 095.8, 125.0-125.9) ♂
607.1 Balanoposthitis — (Use additional code to identify organism) ♂
607.2 Other inflammatory disorders of penis — (Use additional code to identify organism) ♂
607.81 Balanitis xerotica obliterans ♂
607.82 Vascular disorders of penis ♂
607.84 Impotence of organic origin ♂
607.89 Other specified disorder of penis ♂
608.0 Seminal vesiculitis — (Use additional code to identify organism) ♂
608.4 Other inflammatory disorder of male genital organs — (Use additional code to identify organism) ♂
608.81 Specified disorder of male genital organs in diseases classified elsewhere — (Code first underlying disease: 016.5, 125.0-125.9) ♂
608.83 Specified vascular disorder of male genital organs ♂
608.89 Other specified disorder of male genital organs ♂
752.89 Other specified anomalies of genital organs
907.2 Late effect of spinal cord injury
996.65 Infection and inflammatory reaction due to other genitourinary device, implant, and graft — (Use additional code to identify specified infections)
996.76 Other complications due to genitourinary device, implant, and graft — (Use additional code to identify complication: 338.18-338.19, 338.28-338.29)
998.59 Other postoperative infection — (Use additional code to identify infection)
V10.46 Personal history of malignant neoplasm of prostate ♂
V45.77 Acquired absence of organ, genital organs
V52.8 Fitting and adjustment of other specified prosthetic device

ICD-9-CM Procedural

64.95 Insertion or replacement of non-inflatable penile prosthesis ♂
64.97 Insertion or replacement of inflatable penile prosthesis ♂
86.22 Excisional debridement of wound, infection, or burn

54420-54435

54420 Corpora cavernosa-saphenous vein shunt (priapism operation), unilateral or bilateral
54430 Corpora cavernosa-corpus spongiosum shunt (priapism operation), unilateral or bilateral
54435 Corpora cavernosa-glans penis fistulization (eg, biopsy needle, Winter procedure, rongeur, or punch) for priapism

ICD-9-CM Diagnostic

607.3 Priapism ♂

ICD-9-CM Procedural

64.98 Other operations on penis ♂

HCPCS Level II Supplies & Services

A4305 Disposable drug delivery system, flow rate of 50 ml or greater per hour

54440

54440 Plastic operation of penis for injury

ICD-9-CM Diagnostic

878.0 Open wound of penis, without mention of complication ♂
878.1 Open wound of penis, complicated ♂
959.13 Fracture of corpus cavernosum penis ♂
959.14 Other injury of external genitals

ICD-9-CM Procedural

64.41 Suture of laceration of penis ♂
64.43 Construction of penis ♂
64.44 Reconstruction of penis ♂
64.49 Other repair of penis ♂

54450

54450 Foreskin manipulation including lysis of preputial adhesions and stretching

ICD-9-CM Diagnostic

605 Redundant prepuce and phimosis ♂
752.89 Other specified anomalies of genital organs

ICD-9-CM Procedural

64.93 Division of penile adhesions ♂
64.98 Other operations on penis ♂
99.95 Stretching of foreskin ♂

Testis

54500-54505

54500 Biopsy of testis, needle (separate procedure)
54505 Biopsy of testis, incisional (separate procedure)

ICD-9-CM Diagnostic

186.0 Malignant neoplasm of undescended testis — (Use additional code to identify any functional activity) ♂
186.9 Malignant neoplasm of other and unspecified testis — (Use additional code to identify any functional activity) ♂
198.82 Secondary malignant neoplasm of genital organs
222.0 Benign neoplasm of testis — (Use additional code to identify any functional activity) ♂
233.6 Carcinoma in situ of other and unspecified male genital organs ♂
236.4 Neoplasm of uncertain behavior of testis — (Use additional code to identify any functional activity) ♂
239.5 Neoplasm of unspecified nature of other genitourinary organs
257.2 Other testicular hypofunction
606.0 Azoospermia ♂
606.1 Oligospermia ♂
608.20 Torsion of testis, unspecified ♂
608.21 Extravaginal torsion of spermatic cord ♂
608.22 Intravaginal torsion of spermatic cord ♂
608.23 Torsion of appendix testis ♂
608.24 Torsion of appendix epididymis ♂
608.3 Atrophy of testis ♂
608.81 Specified disorder of male genital organs in diseases classified elsewhere — (Code first underlying disease: 016.5, 125.0-125.9) ♂
608.82 Hematospermia ♂
608.89 Other specified disorder of male genital organs ♂

ICD-9-CM Procedural

62.11 Closed (percutaneous) (needle) biopsy of testis ♂
62.12 Open biopsy of testis ♂

54512

54512 Excision of extraparenchymal lesion of testis

ICD-9-CM Diagnostic

186.0 Malignant neoplasm of undescended testis — (Use additional code to identify any functional activity) ♂

186.9 Malignant neoplasm of other and unspecified testis — (Use additional code to identify any functional activity) ▽ ♂

198.82 Secondary malignant neoplasm of genital organs

222.0 Benign neoplasm of testis — (Use additional code to identify any functional activity) ♂

233.6 Carcinoma in situ of other and unspecified male genital organs ▽ ♂

236.4 Neoplasm of uncertain behavior of testis — (Use additional code to identify any functional activity) ♂

239.5 Neoplasm of unspecified nature of other genitourinary organs

608.4 Other inflammatory disorder of male genital organs — (Use additional code to identify organism) ♂

608.89 Other specified disorder of male genital organs ♂

608.9 Unspecified disorder of male genital organs ▽ ♂

ICD-9-CM Procedural

62.2 Excision or destruction of testicular lesion ♂

54520

54520 Orchiectomy, simple (including subcapsular), with or without testicular prosthesis, scrotal or inguinal approach

ICD-9-CM Diagnostic

185 Malignant neoplasm of prostate ♂

186.0 Malignant neoplasm of undescended testis — (Use additional code to identify any functional activity) ♂

186.9 Malignant neoplasm of other and unspecified testis — (Use additional code to identify any functional activity) ▽ ♂

198.82 Secondary malignant neoplasm of genital organs

222.0 Benign neoplasm of testis — (Use additional code to identify any functional activity) ♂

233.6 Carcinoma in situ of other and unspecified male genital organs ▽ ♂

239.5 Neoplasm of unspecified nature of other genitourinary organs

604.0 Orchitis, epididymitis, and epididymo-orchitis, with abscess — (Use additional code to identify organism: 041.00-041.09, 041.10-041.19, 041.41-041.49) ♂

604.91 Orchitis and epididymitis in disease classified elsewhere — (Use additional code to identify organism: 041.00-041.09, 041.10-041.19, 041.41-041.49. Code first underlying disease: 032.89, 095.8, 125.0-125.9) ☒ ♂

604.99 Other orchitis, epididymitis, and epididymo-orchitis, without mention of abscess — (Use additional code to identify organism: 041.00-041.09, 041.10-041.19, 041.41-041.49) ♂

608.20 Torsion of testis, unspecified ▽ ♂

608.21 Extravaginal torsion of spermatic cord ♂

608.22 Intravaginal torsion of spermatic cord ♂

608.23 Torsion of appendix testis ♂

608.24 Torsion of appendix epididymis ♂

608.3 Atrophy of testis ♂

608.4 Other inflammatory disorder of male genital organs — (Use additional code to identify organism) ♂

608.81 Specified disorder of male genital organs in diseases classified elsewhere — (Code first underlying disease: 016.5, 125.0-125.9) ☒ ♂

608.83 Specified vascular disorder of male genital organs ♂

608.89 Other specified disorder of male genital organs ♂

752.51 Undescended testis ♂

752.52 Retractile testis ♂

752.81 Scrotal transposition ♂

878.2 Open wound of scrotum and testes, without mention of complication ♂

878.3 Open wound of scrotum and testes, complicated ♂

926.0 Crushing injury of external genitalia — (Use additional code to identify any associated injuries: 800-829, 850.0-854.1, 860.0-869.1)

V50.49 Other prophylactic organ removal

V64.41 Laparoscopic surgical procedure converted to open procedure

ICD-9-CM Procedural

62.3 Unilateral orchiectomy ♂

62.41 Removal of both testes at same operative episode ♂

62.42 Removal of remaining testis ♂

62.7 Insertion of testicular prosthesis ♂

54522

54522 Orchiectomy, partial

ICD-9-CM Diagnostic

186.0 Malignant neoplasm of undescended testis — (Use additional code to identify any functional activity) ♂

186.9 Malignant neoplasm of other and unspecified testis — (Use additional code to identify any functional activity) ▽ ♂

198.82 Secondary malignant neoplasm of genital organs

222.0 Benign neoplasm of testis — (Use additional code to identify any functional activity) ♂

233.6 Carcinoma in situ of other and unspecified male genital organs ▽ ♂

239.5 Neoplasm of unspecified nature of other genitourinary organs

604.0 Orchitis, epididymitis, and epididymo-orchitis, with abscess — (Use additional code to identify organism: 041.00-041.09, 041.10-041.19, 041.41-041.49) ♂

604.91 Orchitis and epididymitis in disease classified elsewhere — (Use additional code to identify organism: 041.00-041.09, 041.10-041.19, 041.41-041.49. Code first underlying disease: 032.89, 095.8, 125.0-125.9) ☒ ♂

604.99 Other orchitis, epididymitis, and epididymo-orchitis, without mention of abscess — (Use additional code to identify organism: 041.00-041.09, 041.10-041.19, 041.41-041.49) ♂

608.20 Torsion of testis, unspecified ▽ ♂

608.21 Extravaginal torsion of spermatic cord ♂

608.22 Intravaginal torsion of spermatic cord ♂

608.23 Torsion of appendix testis ♂

608.24 Torsion of appendix epididymis ♂

608.4 Other inflammatory disorder of male genital organs — (Use additional code to identify organism) ♂

608.81 Specified disorder of male genital organs in diseases classified elsewhere — (Code first underlying disease: 016.5, 125.0-125.9) ☒ ♂

608.83 Specified vascular disorder of male genital organs ♂

608.89 Other specified disorder of male genital organs ♂

878.2 Open wound of scrotum and testes, without mention of complication ♂

878.3 Open wound of scrotum and testes, complicated ♂

926.0 Crushing injury of external genitalia — (Use additional code to identify any associated injuries: 800-829, 850.0-854.1, 860.0-869.1)

V64.41 Laparoscopic surgical procedure converted to open procedure

ICD-9-CM Procedural

62.3 Unilateral orchiectomy ♂

54530-54535

54530 Orchiectomy, radical, for tumor; inguinal approach
54535 with abdominal exploration

ICD-9-CM Diagnostic

186.0 Malignant neoplasm of undescended testis — (Use additional code to identify any functional activity) ♂
186.9 Malignant neoplasm of other and unspecified testis — (Use additional code to identify any functional activity) ▽ ♂
187.5 Malignant neoplasm of epididymis ♂
187.8 Malignant neoplasm of other specified sites of male genital organs ♂
198.82 Secondary malignant neoplasm of genital organs
233.6 Carcinoma in situ of other and unspecified male genital organs ▽ ♂
236.4 Neoplasm of uncertain behavior of testis — (Use additional code to identify any functional activity) ♂
239.5 Neoplasm of unspecified nature of other genitourinary organs
V64.41 Laparoscopic surgical procedure converted to open procedure

ICD-9-CM Procedural

62.3 Unilateral orchiectomy ♂
62.41 Removal of both testes at same operative episode ♂
62.42 Removal of remaining testis ♂

54550-54560

54550 Exploration for undescended testis (inguinal or scrotal area)
54560 Exploration for undescended testis with abdominal exploration

ICD-9-CM Diagnostic

752.51 Undescended testis ♂
752.52 Retractile testis ♂
752.81 Scrotal transposition ♂

ICD-9-CM Procedural

62.0 Incision of testis ♂

54600

54600 Reduction of torsion of testis, surgical, with or without fixation of contralateral testis

ICD-9-CM Diagnostic

608.20 Torsion of testis, unspecified ▽ ♂
608.21 Extravaginal torsion of spermatic cord ♂
608.22 Intravaginal torsion of spermatic cord ♂
608.23 Torsion of appendix testis ♂
608.24 Torsion of appendix epididymis ♂

ICD-9-CM Procedural

63.52 Reduction of torsion of testis or spermatic cord ♂

54620

54620 Fixation of contralateral testis (separate procedure)

ICD-9-CM Diagnostic

608.20 Torsion of testis, unspecified ▽ ♂
608.81 Specified disorder of male genital organs in diseases classified elsewhere — (Code first underlying disease: 016.5, 125.0-125.9) ☒ ♂
608.89 Other specified disorder of male genital organs ♂

ICD-9-CM Procedural

62.5 Orchiopexy ♂

54640-54650

54640 Orchiopexy, inguinal approach, with or without hernia repair
54650 Orchiopexy, abdominal approach, for intra-abdominal testis (eg, Fowler-Stephens)

ICD-9-CM Diagnostic

550.90 Inguinal hernia without mention of obstruction or gangrene, unilateral or unspecified, (not specified as recurrent)
608.20 Torsion of testis, unspecified ▽ ♂
608.21 Extravaginal torsion of spermatic cord ♂
608.22 Intravaginal torsion of spermatic cord ♂
608.23 Torsion of appendix testis ♂
608.24 Torsion of appendix epididymis ♂
608.89 Other specified disorder of male genital organs ♂
752.51 Undescended testis ♂
752.52 Retractile testis ♂
752.81 Scrotal transposition ♂
752.89 Other specified anomalies of genital organs
V64.41 Laparoscopic surgical procedure converted to open procedure

ICD-9-CM Procedural

62.5 Orchiopexy ♂

54660

54660 Insertion of testicular prosthesis (separate procedure)

ICD-9-CM Diagnostic

608.89 Other specified disorder of male genital organs ♂
752.51 Undescended testis ♂
752.52 Retractile testis ♂
752.9 Unspecified congenital anomaly of genital organs ▽
V10.47 Personal history of malignant neoplasm of testis ♂
V45.89 Other postprocedural status
V52.8 Fitting and adjustment of other specified prosthetic device

ICD-9-CM Procedural

62.7 Insertion of testicular prosthesis ♂

54670

54670 Suture or repair of testicular injury

ICD-9-CM Diagnostic

878.2 Open wound of scrotum and testes, without mention of complication ♂
878.3 Open wound of scrotum and testes, complicated ♂
926.0 Crushing injury of external genitalia — (Use additional code to identify any associated injuries: 800-829, 850.0-854.1, 860.0-869.1)

ICD-9-CM Procedural

62.61 Suture of laceration of testis ♂

54680

54680 Transplantation of testis(es) to thigh (because of scrotal destruction)

ICD-9-CM Diagnostic

187.7 Malignant neoplasm of scrotum ♂
198.82 Secondary malignant neoplasm of genital organs
222.4 Benign neoplasm of scrotum ♂
233.6 Carcinoma in situ of other and unspecified male genital organs ▽ ♂
878.2 Open wound of scrotum and testes, without mention of complication ♂
878.3 Open wound of scrotum and testes, complicated ♂

926.0 Crushing injury of external genitalia — (Use additional code to identify any associated injuries: 800-829, 850.0-854.1, 860.0-869.1)
942.35 Full-thickness skin loss due to burn (third degree NOS) of genitalia
959.14 Other injury of external genitals

ICD-9-CM Procedural

62.99 Other operations on testes ♂

54690

54690 Laparoscopy, surgical; orchiectomy

ICD-9-CM Diagnostic

186.0 Malignant neoplasm of undescended testis — (Use additional code to identify any functional activity) ♂
186.9 Malignant neoplasm of other and unspecified testis — (Use additional code to identify any functional activity) ▽ ♂
198.82 Secondary malignant neoplasm of genital organs
222.0 Benign neoplasm of testis — (Use additional code to identify any functional activity) ♂
233.6 Carcinoma in situ of other and unspecified male genital organs ▽ ♂
236.4 Neoplasm of uncertain behavior of testis — (Use additional code to identify any functional activity) ♂
239.5 Neoplasm of unspecified nature of other genitourinary organs
608.20 Torsion of testis, unspecified ▽ ♂
608.21 Extravaginal torsion of spermatic cord ♂
608.22 Intravaginal torsion of spermatic cord ♂
608.23 Torsion of appendix testis ♂
608.24 Torsion of appendix epididymis ♂
608.3 Atrophy of testis ♂
608.83 Specified vascular disorder of male genital organs ♂
608.89 Other specified disorder of male genital organs ♂
V50.49 Other prophylactic organ removal

ICD-9-CM Procedural

62.3 Unilateral orchiectomy ♂
62.41 Removal of both testes at same operative episode ♂
62.42 Removal of remaining testis ♂

54692

54692 Laparoscopy, surgical; orchiopexy for intra-abdominal testis

ICD-9-CM Diagnostic

752.51 Undescended testis ♂
752.52 Retractile testis ♂
752.81 Scrotal transposition ♂

ICD-9-CM Procedural

62.5 Orchiopexy ♂

Epididymis

54700

54700 Incision and drainage of epididymis, testis and/or scrotal space (eg, abscess or hematoma)

ICD-9-CM Diagnostic

604.0 Orchitis, epididymitis, and epididymo-orchitis, with abscess — (Use additional code to identify organism: 041.00-041.09, 041.10-041.19, 041.41-041.49) ♂
608.82 Hematospermia ♂
608.83 Specified vascular disorder of male genital organs ♂
922.4 Contusion of genital organs
998.12 Hematoma complicating a procedure

ICD-9-CM Procedural

61.0 Incision and drainage of scrotum and tunica vaginalis ♂
62.0 Incision of testis ♂

54800

54800 Biopsy of epididymis, needle

ICD-9-CM Diagnostic

187.5 Malignant neoplasm of epididymis ♂
198.82 Secondary malignant neoplasm of genital organs
222.3 Benign neoplasm of epididymis ♂
233.6 Carcinoma in situ of other and unspecified male genital organs ▽ ♂
236.6 Neoplasm of uncertain behavior of other and unspecified male genital organs ▽ ♂
239.5 Neoplasm of unspecified nature of other genitourinary organs
604.90 Unspecified orchitis and epididymitis — (Use additional code to identify organism: 041.00-041.09, 041.10-041.19, 041.41-041.49) ▽ ♂
604.91 Orchitis and epididymitis in disease classified elsewhere — (Use additional code to identify organism: 041.00-041.09, 041.10-041.19, 041.41-041.49. Code first underlying disease: 032.89, 095.8, 125.0-125.9) ☒ ♂

ICD-9-CM Procedural

63.01 Biopsy of spermatic cord, epididymis, or vas deferens ♂
63.92 Epididymotomy ♂

54830

54830 Excision of local lesion of epididymis

ICD-9-CM Diagnostic

187.5 Malignant neoplasm of epididymis ♂
198.82 Secondary malignant neoplasm of genital organs
222.3 Benign neoplasm of epididymis ♂
233.6 Carcinoma in situ of other and unspecified male genital organs ▽ ♂
236.6 Neoplasm of uncertain behavior of other and unspecified male genital organs ▽ ♂
239.5 Neoplasm of unspecified nature of other genitourinary organs
608.89 Other specified disorder of male genital organs ♂

ICD-9-CM Procedural

63.2 Excision of cyst of epididymis ♂
63.3 Excision of other lesion or tissue of spermatic cord and epididymis ♂

54840

54840 Excision of spermatocele, with or without epididymectomy

ICD-9-CM Diagnostic

608.1 Spermatocele ♂

ICD-9-CM Procedural

63.3 Excision of other lesion or tissue of spermatic cord and epididymis ♂
63.4 Epididymectomy ♂

54860-54861

54860 Epididymectomy; unilateral
54861 bilateral

ICD-9-CM Diagnostic

187.5 Malignant neoplasm of epididymis ♂
198.82 Secondary malignant neoplasm of genital organs
214.8 Lipoma of other specified sites
222.3 Benign neoplasm of epididymis ♂

233.6 Carcinoma in situ of other and unspecified male genital organs ▽ ♂

236.6 Neoplasm of uncertain behavior of other and unspecified male genital organs ▽ ♂

239.5 Neoplasm of unspecified nature of other genitourinary organs

604.90 Unspecified orchitis and epididymitis — (Use additional code to identify organism: 041.00-041.09, 041.10-041.19, 041.41-041.49) ▽ ♂

604.91 Orchitis and epididymitis in disease classified elsewhere — (Use additional code to identify organism: 041.00-041.09, 041.10-041.19, 041.41-041.49. Code first underlying disease: 032.89, 095.8, 125.0-125.9) ⊠ ♂

604.99 Other orchitis, epididymitis, and epididymo-orchitis, without mention of abscess — (Use additional code to identify organism: 041.00-041.09, 041.10-041.19, 041.41-041.49) ♂

608.81 Specified disorder of male genital organs in diseases classified elsewhere — (Code first underlying disease: 016.5, 125.0-125.9) ⊠ ♂

608.89 Other specified disorder of male genital organs ♂

ICD-9-CM Procedural

63.4 Epididymectomy ♂

54865

54865 Exploration of epididymis, with or without biopsy

ICD-9-CM Diagnostic

187.5 Malignant neoplasm of epididymis ♂

198.82 Secondary malignant neoplasm of genital organs

222.3 Benign neoplasm of epididymis ♂

233.6 Carcinoma in situ of other and unspecified male genital organs ▽ ♂

236.6 Neoplasm of uncertain behavior of other and unspecified male genital organs ▽ ♂

239.5 Neoplasm of unspecified nature of other genitourinary organs

604.90 Unspecified orchitis and epididymitis — (Use additional code to identify organism: 041.00-041.09, 041.10-041.19, 041.41-041.49) ▽ ♂

604.91 Orchitis and epididymitis in disease classified elsewhere — (Use additional code to identify organism: 041.00-041.09, 041.10-041.19, 041.41-041.49. Code first underlying disease: 032.89, 095.8, 125.0-125.9) ⊠ ♂

ICD-9-CM Procedural

63.01 Biopsy of spermatic cord, epididymis, or vas deferens ♂

63.92 Epididymotomy ♂

54900-54901

54900 Epididymovasostomy, anastomosis of epididymis to vas deferens; unilateral

54901 bilateral

ICD-9-CM Diagnostic

606.0 Azoospermia ♂

606.1 Oligospermia ♂

606.8 Infertility due to extratesticular causes ♂

752.9 Unspecified congenital anomaly of genital organs ▽

ICD-9-CM Procedural

63.83 Epididymovasostomy ♂

Tunica Vaginalis

55000

55000 Puncture aspiration of hydrocele, tunica vaginalis, with or without injection of medication

ICD-9-CM Diagnostic

603.0 Encysted hydrocele ♂

603.1 Infected hydrocele — (Use additional code to identify organism) ♂

603.8 Other specified type of hydrocele ♂

603.9 Unspecified hydrocele ▽ ♂

608.84 Chylocele of tunica vaginalis ♂

778.6 Congenital hydrocele — (Use additional code(s) to further specify condition)

ICD-9-CM Procedural

61.91 Percutaneous aspiration of tunica vaginalis ♂

55040-55041

55040 Excision of hydrocele; unilateral

55041 bilateral

ICD-9-CM Diagnostic

603.0 Encysted hydrocele ♂

603.1 Infected hydrocele — (Use additional code to identify organism) ♂

603.8 Other specified type of hydrocele ♂

603.9 Unspecified hydrocele ▽ ♂

778.6 Congenital hydrocele — (Use additional code(s) to further specify condition)

ICD-9-CM Procedural

61.2 Excision of hydrocele (of tunica vaginalis) ♂

55060

55060 Repair of tunica vaginalis hydrocele (Bottle type)

ICD-9-CM Diagnostic

603.0 Encysted hydrocele ♂

603.1 Infected hydrocele — (Use additional code to identify organism) ♂

603.8 Other specified type of hydrocele ♂

603.9 Unspecified hydrocele ▽ ♂

608.84 Chylocele of tunica vaginalis ♂

778.6 Congenital hydrocele — (Use additional code(s) to further specify condition)

ICD-9-CM Procedural

61.2 Excision of hydrocele (of tunica vaginalis) ♂

Scrotum

55100

55100 Drainage of scrotal wall abscess

ICD-9-CM Diagnostic

608.4 Other inflammatory disorder of male genital organs — (Use additional code to identify organism) ♂

ICD-9-CM Procedural

61.0 Incision and drainage of scrotum and tunica vaginalis ♂

55110

55110 Scrotal exploration

ICD-9-CM Diagnostic

187.7 Malignant neoplasm of scrotum ♂

198.82 Secondary malignant neoplasm of genital organs

222.4 Benign neoplasm of scrotum ♂

233.6 Carcinoma in situ of other and unspecified male genital organs ▽ ♂

236.6 Neoplasm of uncertain behavior of other and unspecified male genital organs ▽ ♂

239.5 Neoplasm of unspecified nature of other genitourinary organs

257.2 Other testicular hypofunction

456.4 Scrotal varices ♂

604.0 Orchitis, epididymitis, and epididymo-orchitis, with abscess — (Use additional code to identify organism: 041.00-041.09, 041.10-041.19, 041.41-041.49) ♂

604.91 Orchitis and epididymitis in disease classified elsewhere — (Use additional code to identify organism: 041.00-041.09, 041.10-041.19, 041.41-041.49. Code first underlying disease: 032.89, 095.8, 125.0-125.9) ☒ ♂
604.99 Other orchitis, epididymitis, and epididymo-orchitis, without mention of abscess — (Use additional code to identify organism: 041.00-041.09, 041.10-041.19, 041.41-041.49) ♂
608.20 Torsion of testis, unspecified ▽ ♂
608.21 Extravaginal torsion of spermatic cord ♂
608.22 Intravaginal torsion of spermatic cord ♂
608.23 Torsion of appendix testis ♂
608.24 Torsion of appendix epididymis ♂
608.4 Other inflammatory disorder of male genital organs — (Use additional code to identify organism) ♂
608.81 Specified disorder of male genital organs in diseases classified elsewhere — (Code first underlying disease: 016.5, 125.0-125.9) ☒ ♂
608.82 Hematospermia ♂
608.83 Specified vascular disorder of male genital organs ♂
608.84 Chylocele of tunica vaginalis ♂
608.85 Stricture of male genital organs ♂
608.89 Other specified disorder of male genital organs ♂
729.91 Post-traumatic seroma
752.81 Scrotal transposition ♂
752.89 Other specified anomalies of genital organs
996.39 Mechanical complication of genitourinary device, implant, and graft, other
996.65 Infection and inflammatory reaction due to other genitourinary device, implant, and graft — (Use additional code to identify specified infections)
996.76 Other complications due to genitourinary device, implant, and graft — (Use additional code to identify complication: 338.18-338.19, 338.28-338.29)
998.2 Accidental puncture or laceration during procedure
998.51 Infected postoperative seroma — (Use additional code to identify organism)
998.59 Other postoperative infection — (Use additional code to identify infection)
998.89 Other specified complications

ICD-9-CM Procedural

61.0 Incision and drainage of scrotum and tunica vaginalis ♂

55120

55120 Removal of foreign body in scrotum

ICD-9-CM Diagnostic

709.4 Foreign body granuloma of skin and subcutaneous tissue — (Use additional code to identify foreign body (V90.01-V90.9))
729.6 Residual foreign body in soft tissue — (Use additional code to identify foreign body (V90.01-V90.9))
878.2 Open wound of scrotum and testes, without mention of complication ♂
878.3 Open wound of scrotum and testes, complicated ♂
911.6 Trunk, superficial foreign body (splinter), without major open wound and without mention of infection
911.7 Trunk, superficial foreign body (splinter), without major open wound, infected
998.4 Foreign body accidentally left during procedure, not elsewhere classified

ICD-9-CM Procedural

61.0 Incision and drainage of scrotum and tunica vaginalis ♂

55150

55150 Resection of scrotum

ICD-9-CM Diagnostic

187.7 Malignant neoplasm of scrotum ♂
198.82 Secondary malignant neoplasm of genital organs
222.4 Benign neoplasm of scrotum ♂
233.6 Carcinoma in situ of other and unspecified male genital organs ▽ ♂
236.6 Neoplasm of uncertain behavior of other and unspecified male genital organs ▽ ♂
239.5 Neoplasm of unspecified nature of other genitourinary organs
608.89 Other specified disorder of male genital organs ♂
878.2 Open wound of scrotum and testes, without mention of complication ♂
878.3 Open wound of scrotum and testes, complicated ♂

ICD-9-CM Procedural

61.3 Excision or destruction of lesion or tissue of scrotum ♂
61.41 Suture of laceration of scrotum and tunica vaginalis ♂

55175-55180

55175 Scrotoplasty; simple
55180 complicated

ICD-9-CM Diagnostic

187.7 Malignant neoplasm of scrotum ♂
198.82 Secondary malignant neoplasm of genital organs
222.4 Benign neoplasm of scrotum ♂
233.6 Carcinoma in situ of other and unspecified male genital organs ▽ ♂
236.6 Neoplasm of uncertain behavior of other and unspecified male genital organs ▽ ♂
239.5 Neoplasm of unspecified nature of other genitourinary organs
608.89 Other specified disorder of male genital organs ♂
878.2 Open wound of scrotum and testes, without mention of complication ♂
878.3 Open wound of scrotum and testes, complicated ♂

ICD-9-CM Procedural

61.3 Excision or destruction of lesion or tissue of scrotum ♂
61.41 Suture of laceration of scrotum and tunica vaginalis ♂
61.49 Other repair of scrotum and tunica vaginalis ♂

Vas Deferens

55200

55200 Vasotomy, cannulization with or without incision of vas, unilateral or bilateral (separate procedure)

ICD-9-CM Diagnostic

302.72 Psychosexual dysfunction with inhibited sexual excitement
606.0 Azoospermia ♂
606.1 Oligospermia ♂
606.8 Infertility due to extratesticular causes ♂
607.84 Impotence of organic origin ♂
608.4 Other inflammatory disorder of male genital organs — (Use additional code to identify organism) ♂
608.81 Specified disorder of male genital organs in diseases classified elsewhere — (Code first underlying disease: 016.5, 125.0-125.9) ☒ ♂
608.82 Hematospermia ♂
608.83 Specified vascular disorder of male genital organs ♂
608.85 Stricture of male genital organs ♂
608.89 Other specified disorder of male genital organs ♂
V26.21 Fertility testing
V26.22 Aftercare following sterilization reversal
V26.29 Other investigation and testing

ICD-9-CM Procedural

63.6 Vasotomy ♂

55250

55250 Vasectomy, unilateral or bilateral (separate procedure), including postoperative semen examination(s)

ICD-9-CM Diagnostic

V25.2 Sterilization

ICD-9-CM Procedural

63.73 Vasectomy ♂

55300

55300 Vasotomy for vasograms, seminal vesiculograms, or epididymograms, unilateral or bilateral

ICD-9-CM Diagnostic

187.6 Malignant neoplasm of spermatic cord ♂
198.82 Secondary malignant neoplasm of genital organs
222.8 Benign neoplasm of other specified sites of male genital organs ♂
233.6 Carcinoma in situ of other and unspecified male genital organs ▽ ♂
302.72 Psychosexual dysfunction with inhibited sexual excitement
606.0 Azoospermia ♂
606.1 Oligospermia ♂
606.8 Infertility due to extratesticular causes ♂
607.84 Impotence of organic origin ♂
608.4 Other inflammatory disorder of male genital organs — (Use additional code to identify organism) ♂
608.81 Specified disorder of male genital organs in diseases classified elsewhere — (Code first underlying disease: 016.5, 125.0-125.9) ☒ ♂
608.82 Hematospermia ♂
608.83 Specified vascular disorder of male genital organs ♂
608.85 Stricture of male genital organs ♂
608.89 Other specified disorder of male genital organs ♂
V26.21 Fertility testing
V26.22 Aftercare following sterilization reversal
V26.29 Other investigation and testing

ICD-9-CM Procedural

63.6 Vasotomy ♂
87.91 Contrast seminal vesiculogram ♂
87.92 Other x-ray of prostate and seminal vesicles ♂
87.93 Contrast epididymogram ♂
87.94 Contrast vasogram ♂
87.95 Other x-ray of epididymis and vas deferens ♂

55400

55400 Vasovasostomy, vasovasorrhaphy

ICD-9-CM Diagnostic

V26.0 Tuboplasty or vasoplasty after previous sterilization
V26.52 Vasectomy sterilization status ♂

ICD-9-CM Procedural

63.81 Suture of laceration of vas deferens and epididymis ♂
63.82 Reconstruction of surgically divided vas deferens ♂
63.89 Other repair of vas deferens and epididymis ♂

55450

55450 Ligation (percutaneous) of vas deferens, unilateral or bilateral (separate procedure)

ICD-9-CM Diagnostic

V25.2 Sterilization

ICD-9-CM Procedural

63.71 Ligation of vas deferens ♂

Spermatic Cord

55500

55500 Excision of hydrocele of spermatic cord, unilateral (separate procedure)

ICD-9-CM Diagnostic

603.0 Encysted hydrocele ♂
603.1 Infected hydrocele — (Use additional code to identify organism) ♂
603.8 Other specified type of hydrocele ♂
603.9 Unspecified hydrocele ▽ ♂
778.6 Congenital hydrocele — (Use additional code(s) to further specify condition)

ICD-9-CM Procedural

63.1 Excision of varicocele and hydrocele of spermatic cord ♂

HCPCS Level II Supplies & Services

A4305 Disposable drug delivery system, flow rate of 50 ml or greater per hour

55520

55520 Excision of lesion of spermatic cord (separate procedure)

ICD-9-CM Diagnostic

187.6 Malignant neoplasm of spermatic cord ♂
198.82 Secondary malignant neoplasm of genital organs
214.4 Lipoma of spermatic cord ♂
222.8 Benign neoplasm of other specified sites of male genital organs ♂
233.6 Carcinoma in situ of other and unspecified male genital organs ▽ ♂
236.6 Neoplasm of uncertain behavior of other and unspecified male genital organs ▽ ♂
239.5 Neoplasm of unspecified nature of other genitourinary organs
608.4 Other inflammatory disorder of male genital organs — (Use additional code to identify organism) ♂
608.89 Other specified disorder of male genital organs ♂

ICD-9-CM Procedural

63.3 Excision of other lesion or tissue of spermatic cord and epididymis ♂

HCPCS Level II Supplies & Services

A4305 Disposable drug delivery system, flow rate of 50 ml or greater per hour

55530-55535

55530 Excision of varicocele or ligation of spermatic veins for varicocele; (separate procedure)
55535 abdominal approach

ICD-9-CM Diagnostic

456.4 Scrotal varices ♂
V64.41 Laparoscopic surgical procedure converted to open procedure

ICD-9-CM Procedural

63.1 Excision of varicocele and hydrocele of spermatic cord ♂
63.72 Ligation of spermatic cord ♂

55540

55540 Excision of varicocele or ligation of spermatic veins for varicocele; with hernia repair

ICD-9-CM Diagnostic

456.4 Scrotal varices ♂

V64.41 Laparoscopic surgical procedure converted to open procedure

ICD-9-CM Procedural

53.01 Other and open repair of direct inguinal hernia

53.02 Other and open repair of indirect inguinal hernia

53.03 Other and open repair of direct inguinal hernia with graft or prosthesis

63.1 Excision of varicocele and hydrocele of spermatic cord ♂

63.72 Ligation of spermatic cord ♂

55550

55550 Laparoscopy, surgical, with ligation of spermatic veins for varicocele

ICD-9-CM Diagnostic

456.4 Scrotal varices ♂

606.8 Infertility due to extratesticular causes ♂

ICD-9-CM Procedural

63.1 Excision of varicocele and hydrocele of spermatic cord ♂

Seminal Vesicles

55600-55605

55600 Vesiculotomy;
55605 complicated

ICD-9-CM Diagnostic

187.8 Malignant neoplasm of other specified sites of male genital organs ♂

198.82 Secondary malignant neoplasm of genital organs

222.8 Benign neoplasm of other specified sites of male genital organs ♂

233.6 Carcinoma in situ of other and unspecified male genital organs ▽ ♂

236.6 Neoplasm of uncertain behavior of other and unspecified male genital organs ▽ ♂

239.5 Neoplasm of unspecified nature of other genitourinary organs

608.0 Seminal vesiculitis — (Use additional code to identify organism) ♂

608.82 Hematospermia ♂

608.83 Specified vascular disorder of male genital organs ♂

608.85 Stricture of male genital organs ♂

608.89 Other specified disorder of male genital organs ♂

ICD-9-CM Procedural

60.72 Incision of seminal vesicle ♂

55650

55650 Vesiculectomy, any approach

ICD-9-CM Diagnostic

187.8 Malignant neoplasm of other specified sites of male genital organs ♂

198.82 Secondary malignant neoplasm of genital organs

222.8 Benign neoplasm of other specified sites of male genital organs ♂

233.6 Carcinoma in situ of other and unspecified male genital organs ▽ ♂

236.6 Neoplasm of uncertain behavior of other and unspecified male genital organs ▽ ♂

239.5 Neoplasm of unspecified nature of other genitourinary organs

608.0 Seminal vesiculitis — (Use additional code to identify organism) ♂

608.83 Specified vascular disorder of male genital organs ♂

608.85 Stricture of male genital organs ♂

608.89 Other specified disorder of male genital organs ♂

ICD-9-CM Procedural

60.73 Excision of seminal vesicle ♂

55680

55680 Excision of Mullerian duct cyst

ICD-9-CM Diagnostic

752.89 Other specified anomalies of genital organs

ICD-9-CM Procedural

60.73 Excision of seminal vesicle ♂

Prostate

55700-55705

55700 Biopsy, prostate; needle or punch, single or multiple, any approach
55705 incisional, any approach

ICD-9-CM Diagnostic

185 Malignant neoplasm of prostate ♂

198.82 Secondary malignant neoplasm of genital organs

222.2 Benign neoplasm of prostate ♂

233.4 Carcinoma in situ of prostate ♂

236.5 Neoplasm of uncertain behavior of prostate ♂

239.5 Neoplasm of unspecified nature of other genitourinary organs

600.00 Hypertrophy (benign) of prostate without urinary obstruction and other lower urinary tract symptoms [LUTS] ♂

600.01 Hypertrophy (benign) of prostate with urinary obstruction and other lower urinary tract symptoms [LUTS] — (Use additional code to identify symptoms: 599.69, 788.20, 788.21, 788.30-788.39, 788.41, 788.43, 788.62, 788.63, 788.64, 788.65) ♂

600.10 Nodular prostate without urinary obstruction ♂

600.11 Nodular prostate with urinary obstruction ♂

600.20 Benign localized hyperplasia of prostate without urinary obstruction and other lower urinary tract symptoms [LUTS] ♂

600.21 Benign localized hyperplasia of prostate with urinary obstruction and other lower urinary tract symptoms [LUTS] — (Use additional code to identify symptoms: 599.69, 788.20, 788.21, 788.30-788.39, 788.41, 788.43, 788.62, 788.63, 788.64, 788.65) ♂

600.3 Cyst of prostate ♂

600.90 Hyperplasia of prostate, unspecified, without urinary obstruction and other lower urinary tract symptoms [LUTS] ▽ ♂

600.91 Hyperplasia of prostate, unspecified, with urinary obstruction and other lower urinary tract symptoms [LUTS] — (Use additional code to identify symptoms: 599.69, 788.20, 788.21, 788.30-788.39, 788.41, 788.43, 788.62, 788.63, 788.64, 788.65) ▽ ♂

601.0 Acute prostatitis — (Use additional code to identify organism: 041.0, 041.1) ♂

601.1 Chronic prostatitis — (Use additional code to identify organism: 041.0, 041.1) ♂

601.2 Abscess of prostate — (Use additional code to identify organism: 041.0, 041.1) ♂

601.3 Prostatocystitis — (Use additional code to identify organism: 041.0, 041.1) ♂

601.4 Prostatitis in diseases classified elsewhere — (Use additional code to identify organism: 041.0, 041.1. Code first underlying disease: 016.5, 039.8, 095.8, 116.0) ☒ ♂

601.8 Other specified inflammatory disease of prostate — (Use additional code to identify organism: 041.0, 041.1) ♂

602.0 Calculus of prostate ♂

602.1 Congestion or hemorrhage of prostate ♂

602.2 Atrophy of prostate ♂

602.3 Dysplasia of prostate ♂

602.8 Other specified disorder of prostate ♂

788.29 Other specified retention of urine — (Code, if applicable, any causal condition first, such as: 600.0-600.9, with fifth digit 1)

788.41 Urinary frequency — (Code, if applicable, any causal condition first, such as: 600.0-600.9, with fifth digit 1)
788.42 Polyuria — (Code, if applicable, any causal condition first, such as: 600.0-600.9, with fifth digit 1)
788.43 Nocturia — (Code, if applicable, any causal condition first, such as: 600.0-600.9, with fifth digit 1)
790.93 Elevated prostate specific antigen (PSA) ♂
793.5 Nonspecific (abnormal) findings on radiological and other examination of genitourinary organs
V10.46 Personal history of malignant neoplasm of prostate ♂
V71.1 Observation for suspected malignant neoplasm

ICD-9-CM Procedural

60.11 Closed (percutaneous) (needle) biopsy of prostate ♂
60.12 Open biopsy of prostate ♂
60.91 Percutaneous aspiration of prostate ♂

55706

55706 Biopsies, prostate, needle, transperineal, stereotactic template guided saturation sampling, including imaging guidance

ICD-9-CM Diagnostic

185 Malignant neoplasm of prostate ♂
198.82 Secondary malignant neoplasm of genital organs
222.2 Benign neoplasm of prostate ♂
233.4 Carcinoma in situ of prostate ♂
236.5 Neoplasm of uncertain behavior of prostate ♂
239.5 Neoplasm of unspecified nature of other genitourinary organs
600.00 Hypertrophy (benign) of prostate without urinary obstruction and other lower urinary tract symptoms [LUTS] ♂
600.01 Hypertrophy (benign) of prostate with urinary obstruction and other lower urinary tract symptoms [LUTS] — (Use additional code to identify symptoms: 599.69, 788.20, 788.21, 788.30-788.39, 788.41, 788.43, 788.62, 788.63, 788.64, 788.65) ♂
600.10 Nodular prostate without urinary obstruction ♂
600.11 Nodular prostate with urinary obstruction ♂
600.20 Benign localized hyperplasia of prostate without urinary obstruction and other lower urinary tract symptoms [LUTS] ♂
600.21 Benign localized hyperplasia of prostate with urinary obstruction and other lower urinary tract symptoms [LUTS] — (Use additional code to identify symptoms: 599.69, 788.20, 788.21, 788.30-788.39, 788.41, 788.43, 788.62, 788.63, 788.64, 788.65) ♂
600.3 Cyst of prostate ♂
600.90 Hyperplasia of prostate, unspecified, without urinary obstruction and other lower urinary tract symptoms [LUTS] ▽ ♂
600.91 Hyperplasia of prostate, unspecified, with urinary obstruction and other lower urinary tract symptoms [LUTS] — (Use additional code to identify symptoms: 599.69, 788.20, 788.21, 788.30-788.39, 788.41, 788.43, 788.62, 788.63, 788.64, 788.65) ▽ ♂
601.0 Acute prostatitis — (Use additional code to identify organism: 041.0, 041.1) ♂
601.1 Chronic prostatitis — (Use additional code to identify organism: 041.0, 041.1) ♂
601.2 Abscess of prostate — (Use additional code to identify organism: 041.0, 041.1) ♂
601.3 Prostatocystitis — (Use additional code to identify organism: 041.0, 041.1) ♂
601.4 Prostatitis in diseases classified elsewhere — (Use additional code to identify organism: 041.0, 041.1. Code first underlying disease: 016.5, 039.8, 095.8, 116.0) ☒ ♂
601.8 Other specified inflammatory disease of prostate — (Use additional code to identify organism: 041.0, 041.1) ♂
602.0 Calculus of prostate ♂
602.1 Congestion or hemorrhage of prostate ♂
602.2 Atrophy of prostate ♂
602.3 Dysplasia of prostate ♂
602.8 Other specified disorder of prostate ♂
788.29 Other specified retention of urine — (Code, if applicable, any causal condition first, such as: 600.0-600.9, with fifth digit 1)
788.41 Urinary frequency — (Code, if applicable, any causal condition first, such as: 600.0-600.9, with fifth digit 1)
788.42 Polyuria — (Code, if applicable, any causal condition first, such as: 600.0-600.9, with fifth digit 1)
788.43 Nocturia — (Code, if applicable, any causal condition first, such as: 600.0-600.9, with fifth digit 1)
790.93 Elevated prostate specific antigen (PSA) ♂
793.5 Nonspecific (abnormal) findings on radiological and other examination of genitourinary organs
V10.46 Personal history of malignant neoplasm of prostate ♂
V71.1 Observation for suspected malignant neoplasm

ICD-9-CM Procedural

60.11 Closed (percutaneous) (needle) biopsy of prostate ♂
92.39 Stereotactic radiosurgery, not elsewhere classified

55720-55725

55720 Prostatotomy, external drainage of prostatic abscess, any approach; simple
55725 complicated

ICD-9-CM Diagnostic

098.12 Gonococcal prostatitis (acute) ♂
098.32 Gonococcal prostatitis, chronic ♂
601.2 Abscess of prostate — (Use additional code to identify organism: 041.0, 041.1) ♂

ICD-9-CM Procedural

60.0 Incision of prostate ♂
60.81 Incision of periprostatic tissue ♂

HCPCS Level II Supplies & Services

A4305 Disposable drug delivery system, flow rate of 50 ml or greater per hour

55801

55801 Prostatectomy, perineal, subtotal (including control of postoperative bleeding, vasectomy, meatotomy, urethral calibration and/or dilation, and internal urethrotomy)

ICD-9-CM Diagnostic

185 Malignant neoplasm of prostate ♂
198.82 Secondary malignant neoplasm of genital organs
222.2 Benign neoplasm of prostate ♂
233.4 Carcinoma in situ of prostate ♂
236.5 Neoplasm of uncertain behavior of prostate ♂
239.5 Neoplasm of unspecified nature of other genitourinary organs
600.00 Hypertrophy (benign) of prostate without urinary obstruction and other lower urinary tract symptoms [LUTS] ♂
600.01 Hypertrophy (benign) of prostate with urinary obstruction and other lower urinary tract symptoms [LUTS] — (Use additional code to identify symptoms: 599.69, 788.20, 788.21, 788.30-788.39, 788.41, 788.43, 788.62, 788.63, 788.64, 788.65) ♂
600.10 Nodular prostate without urinary obstruction ♂
600.11 Nodular prostate with urinary obstruction ♂
600.20 Benign localized hyperplasia of prostate without urinary obstruction and other lower urinary tract symptoms [LUTS] ♂
600.21 Benign localized hyperplasia of prostate with urinary obstruction and other lower urinary tract symptoms [LUTS] — (Use additional code to identify symptoms: 599.69, 788.20, 788.21, 788.30-788.39, 788.41, 788.43, 788.62, 788.63, 788.64, 788.65) ♂
600.3 Cyst of prostate ♂
600.90 Hyperplasia of prostate, unspecified, without urinary obstruction and other lower urinary tract symptoms [LUTS] ▽ ♂

600.91 Hyperplasia of prostate, unspecified, with urinary obstruction and other lower urinary tract symptoms [LUTS] — (Use additional code to identify symptoms: 599.69, 788.20, 788.21, 788.30-788.39, 788.41, 788.43, 788.62, 788.63, 788.64, 788.65) ♂

601.0 Acute prostatitis — (Use additional code to identify organism: 041.0, 041.1) ♂

601.1 Chronic prostatitis — (Use additional code to identify organism: 041.0, 041.1) ♂

601.2 Abscess of prostate — (Use additional code to identify organism: 041.0, 041.1) ♂

601.3 Prostatocystitis — (Use additional code to identify organism: 041.0, 041.1) ♂

601.4 Prostatitis in diseases classified elsewhere — (Use additional code to identify organism: 041.0, 041.1. Code first underlying disease: 016.5, 039.8, 095.8, 116.0) ♂

601.8 Other specified inflammatory disease of prostate — (Use additional code to identify organism: 041.0, 041.1) ♂

602.0 Calculus of prostate ♂

602.2 Atrophy of prostate ♂

602.3 Dysplasia of prostate ♂

602.8 Other specified disorder of prostate ♂

V84.03 Genetic susceptibility to malignant neoplasm of prostate — (Use additional code, if applicable, for any associated family history of the disease: V16-V19. Code first, if applicable, any current malignant neoplasms: 140.0-195.8, 200.0-208.9, 230.0-234.9. Use additional code, if applicable, for any personal history of malignant neoplasm: V10.0-V10.9) ♂

V84.09 Genetic susceptibility to other malignant neoplasm — (Use additional code, if applicable, for any associated family history of the disease: V16-V19. Code first, if applicable, any current malignant neoplasms: 140.0-195.8, 200.0-208.9, 230.0-234.9. Use additional code, if applicable, for any personal history of malignant neoplasm: V10.0-V10.9)

ICD-9-CM Procedural

60.62 Perineal prostatectomy ♂

60.82 Excision of periprostatic tissue ♂

55810-55812

55810 Prostatectomy, perineal radical;

55812 with lymph node biopsy(s) (limited pelvic lymphadenectomy)

ICD-9-CM Diagnostic

185 Malignant neoplasm of prostate ♂

196.6 Secondary and unspecified malignant neoplasm of intrapelvic lymph nodes

198.82 Secondary malignant neoplasm of genital organs

233.4 Carcinoma in situ of prostate ♂

236.5 Neoplasm of uncertain behavior of prostate ♂

239.5 Neoplasm of unspecified nature of other genitourinary organs

601.0 Acute prostatitis — (Use additional code to identify organism: 041.0, 041.1) ♂

601.1 Chronic prostatitis — (Use additional code to identify organism: 041.0, 041.1) ♂

601.2 Abscess of prostate — (Use additional code to identify organism: 041.0, 041.1) ♂

601.3 Prostatocystitis — (Use additional code to identify organism: 041.0, 041.1) ♂

601.4 Prostatitis in diseases classified elsewhere — (Use additional code to identify organism: 041.0, 041.1. Code first underlying disease: 016.5, 039.8, 095.8, 116.0) ♂

601.8 Other specified inflammatory disease of prostate — (Use additional code to identify organism: 041.0, 041.1) ♂

602.0 Calculus of prostate ♂

602.2 Atrophy of prostate ♂

602.3 Dysplasia of prostate ♂

602.8 Other specified disorder of prostate ♂

V84.03 Genetic susceptibility to malignant neoplasm of prostate — (Use additional code, if applicable, for any associated family history of the disease: V16-V19. Code first, if applicable, any current malignant neoplasms: 140.0-195.8, 200.0-208.9, 230.0-234.9. Use additional code, if applicable, for any personal history of malignant neoplasm: V10.0-V10.9) ♂

V84.09 Genetic susceptibility to other malignant neoplasm — (Use additional code, if applicable, for any associated family history of the disease: V16-V19. Code first, if applicable, any current malignant neoplasms: 140.0-195.8, 200.0-208.9, 230.0-234.9. Use additional code, if applicable, for any personal history of malignant neoplasm: V10.0-V10.9)

ICD-9-CM Procedural

40.11 Biopsy of lymphatic structure

40.3 Regional lymph node excision

60.5 Radical prostatectomy ♂

55815

55815 Prostatectomy, perineal radical; with bilateral pelvic lymphadenectomy, including external iliac, hypogastric and obturator nodes

ICD-9-CM Diagnostic

185 Malignant neoplasm of prostate ♂

196.6 Secondary and unspecified malignant neoplasm of intrapelvic lymph nodes

198.82 Secondary malignant neoplasm of genital organs

233.4 Carcinoma in situ of prostate ♂

236.5 Neoplasm of uncertain behavior of prostate ♂

239.5 Neoplasm of unspecified nature of other genitourinary organs

601.0 Acute prostatitis — (Use additional code to identify organism: 041.0, 041.1) ♂

601.1 Chronic prostatitis — (Use additional code to identify organism: 041.0, 041.1) ♂

601.2 Abscess of prostate — (Use additional code to identify organism: 041.0, 041.1) ♂

601.3 Prostatocystitis — (Use additional code to identify organism: 041.0, 041.1) ♂

601.4 Prostatitis in diseases classified elsewhere — (Use additional code to identify organism: 041.0, 041.1. Code first underlying disease: 016.5, 039.8, 095.8, 116.0) ♂

601.8 Other specified inflammatory disease of prostate — (Use additional code to identify organism: 041.0, 041.1) ♂

602.0 Calculus of prostate ♂

602.2 Atrophy of prostate ♂

602.3 Dysplasia of prostate ♂

602.8 Other specified disorder of prostate ♂

V84.03 Genetic susceptibility to malignant neoplasm of prostate — (Use additional code, if applicable, for any associated family history of the disease: V16-V19. Code first, if applicable, any current malignant neoplasms: 140.0-195.8, 200.0-208.9, 230.0-234.9. Use additional code, if applicable, for any personal history of malignant neoplasm: V10.0-V10.9) ♂

V84.09 Genetic susceptibility to other malignant neoplasm — (Use additional code, if applicable, for any associated family history of the disease: V16-V19. Code first, if applicable, any current malignant neoplasms: 140.0-195.8, 200.0-208.9, 230.0-234.9. Use additional code, if applicable, for any personal history of malignant neoplasm: V10.0-V10.9)

ICD-9-CM Procedural

40.53 Radical excision of iliac lymph nodes

40.59 Radical excision of other lymph nodes

60.5 Radical prostatectomy ♂

55821-55831

55821 Prostatectomy (including control of postoperative bleeding, vasectomy, meatotomy, urethral calibration and/or dilation, and internal urethrotomy); suprapubic, subtotal, 1 or 2 stages

55831 retropubic, subtotal

ICD-9-CM Diagnostic

185 Malignant neoplasm of prostate ♂

198.82 Secondary malignant neoplasm of genital organs

222.2 Benign neoplasm of prostate ♂

233.4 Carcinoma in situ of prostate ♂

236.5 Neoplasm of uncertain behavior of prostate ♂

239.5 Neoplasm of unspecified nature of other genitourinary organs

600.00 Hypertrophy (benign) of prostate without urinary obstruction and other lower urinary tract symptoms [LUTS] ♂

600.01 Hypertrophy (benign) of prostate with urinary obstruction and other lower urinary tract symptoms [LUTS] — (Use additional code to identify symptoms: 599.69, 788.20, 788.21, 788.30-788.39, 788.41, 788.43, 788.62, 788.63, 788.64, 788.65) ♂

600.10 Nodular prostate without urinary obstruction ♂

600.11 Nodular prostate with urinary obstruction ♂

600.20 Benign localized hyperplasia of prostate without urinary obstruction and other lower urinary tract symptoms [LUTS] ♂

600.21 Benign localized hyperplasia of prostate with urinary obstruction and other lower urinary tract symptoms [LUTS] — (Use additional code to identify symptoms: 599.69, 788.20, 788.21, 788.30-788.39, 788.41, 788.43, 788.62, 788.63, 788.64, 788.65) ♂

600.3 Cyst of prostate ♂

600.90 Hyperplasia of prostate, unspecified, without urinary obstruction and other lower urinary tract symptoms [LUTS] ▽ ♂

600.91 Hyperplasia of prostate, unspecified, with urinary obstruction and other lower urinary tract symptoms [LUTS] — (Use additional code to identify symptoms: 599.69, 788.20, 788.21, 788.30-788.39, 788.41, 788.43, 788.62, 788.63, 788.64, 788.65) ▽ ♂

601.0 Acute prostatitis — (Use additional code to identify organism: 041.0, 041.1) ♂

601.1 Chronic prostatitis — (Use additional code to identify organism: 041.0, 041.1) ♂

601.2 Abscess of prostate — (Use additional code to identify organism: 041.0, 041.1) ♂

601.3 Prostatocystitis — (Use additional code to identify organism: 041.0, 041.1) ♂

601.4 Prostatitis in diseases classified elsewhere — (Use additional code to identify organism: 041.0, 041.1. Code first underlying disease: 016.5, 039.8, 095.8, 116.0) ☒ ♂

601.8 Other specified inflammatory disease of prostate — (Use additional code to identify organism: 041.0, 041.1) ♂

602.0 Calculus of prostate ♂

602.2 Atrophy of prostate ♂

602.3 Dysplasia of prostate ♂

602.8 Other specified disorder of prostate ♂

788.20 Unspecified retention of urine — (Code, if applicable, any causal condition first, such as: 600.0-600.9, with fifth digit 1) ▽

788.21 Incomplete bladder emptying — (Code, if applicable, any causal condition first, such as: 600.0-600.9, with fifth digit 1)

788.29 Other specified retention of urine — (Code, if applicable, any causal condition first, such as: 600.0-600.9, with fifth digit 1)

V84.03 Genetic susceptibility to malignant neoplasm of prostate — (Use additional code, if applicable, for any associated family history of the disease: V16-V19. Code first, if applicable, any current malignant neoplasms: 140.0-195.8, 200.0-208.9, 230.0-234.9. Use additional code, if applicable, for any personal history of malignant neoplasm: V10.0-V10.9) ♂

V84.09 Genetic susceptibility to other malignant neoplasm — (Use additional code, if applicable, for any associated family history of the disease: V16-V19. Code first, if applicable, any current malignant neoplasms: 140.0-195.8, 200.0-208.9, 230.0-234.9. Use additional code, if applicable, for any personal history of malignant neoplasm: V10.0-V10.9)

ICD-9-CM Procedural

60.3 Suprapubic prostatectomy ♂

60.4 Retropubic prostatectomy ♂

55840-55842

55840 Prostatectomy, retropubic radical, with or without nerve sparing;

55842 with lymph node biopsy(s) (limited pelvic lymphadenectomy)

ICD-9-CM Diagnostic

185 Malignant neoplasm of prostate ♂

196.6 Secondary and unspecified malignant neoplasm of intrapelvic lymph nodes

198.82 Secondary malignant neoplasm of genital organs

233.4 Carcinoma in situ of prostate ♂

236.5 Neoplasm of uncertain behavior of prostate ♂

239.5 Neoplasm of unspecified nature of other genitourinary organs

V64.41 Laparoscopic surgical procedure converted to open procedure

V84.03 Genetic susceptibility to malignant neoplasm of prostate — (Use additional code, if applicable, for any associated family history of the disease: V16-V19. Code first, if applicable, any current malignant neoplasms: 140.0-195.8, 200.0-208.9, 230.0-234.9. Use additional code, if applicable, for any personal history of malignant neoplasm: V10.0-V10.9) ♂

V84.09 Genetic susceptibility to other malignant neoplasm — (Use additional code, if applicable, for any associated family history of the disease: V16-V19. Code first, if applicable, any current malignant neoplasms: 140.0-195.8, 200.0-208.9, 230.0-234.9. Use additional code, if applicable, for any personal history of malignant neoplasm: V10.0-V10.9)

ICD-9-CM Procedural

40.11 Biopsy of lymphatic structure

40.3 Regional lymph node excision

60.5 Radical prostatectomy ♂

55845

55845 Prostatectomy, retropubic radical, with or without nerve sparing; with bilateral pelvic lymphadenectomy, including external iliac, hypogastric, and obturator nodes

ICD-9-CM Diagnostic

185 Malignant neoplasm of prostate ♂

196.6 Secondary and unspecified malignant neoplasm of intrapelvic lymph nodes

198.82 Secondary malignant neoplasm of genital organs

233.4 Carcinoma in situ of prostate ♂

236.5 Neoplasm of uncertain behavior of prostate ♂

239.5 Neoplasm of unspecified nature of other genitourinary organs

V64.41 Laparoscopic surgical procedure converted to open procedure

V84.03 Genetic susceptibility to malignant neoplasm of prostate — (Use additional code, if applicable, for any associated family history of the disease: V16-V19. Code first, if applicable, any current malignant neoplasms: 140.0-195.8, 200.0-208.9, 230.0-234.9. Use additional code, if applicable, for any personal history of malignant neoplasm: V10.0-V10.9) ♂

V84.09 Genetic susceptibility to other malignant neoplasm — (Use additional code, if applicable, for any associated family history of the disease: V16-V19. Code first, if applicable, any current malignant neoplasms: 140.0-195.8, 200.0-208.9, 230.0-234.9. Use additional code, if applicable, for any personal history of malignant neoplasm: V10.0-V10.9)

ICD-9-CM Procedural

40.3 Regional lymph node excision

40.53 Radical excision of iliac lymph nodes

40.59 Radical excision of other lymph nodes

60.5 Radical prostatectomy ♂

55860-55865

55860 Exposure of prostate, any approach, for insertion of radioactive substance;

55862 with lymph node biopsy(s) (limited pelvic lymphadenectomy)

55865 with bilateral pelvic lymphadenectomy, including external iliac, hypogastric and obturator nodes

ICD-9-CM Diagnostic

185 Malignant neoplasm of prostate ♂

196.6 Secondary and unspecified malignant neoplasm of intrapelvic lymph nodes

198.82 Secondary malignant neoplasm of genital organs

233.4 Carcinoma in situ of prostate ♂

236.5 Neoplasm of uncertain behavior of prostate ♂

239.5 Neoplasm of unspecified nature of other genitourinary organs

V84.03 Genetic susceptibility to malignant neoplasm of prostate — (Use additional code, if applicable, for any associated family history of the disease: V16-V19. Code first, if applicable, any current malignant neoplasms: 140.0-195.8, 200.0-208.9, 230.0-234.9. Use additional code, if applicable, for any personal history of malignant neoplasm: V10.0-V10.9) ♂

V84.09 Genetic susceptibility to other malignant neoplasm — (Use additional code, if applicable, for any associated family history of the disease: V16-V19. Code first, if applicable, any current malignant neoplasms: 140.0-195.8, 200.0-208.9, 230.0-234.9. Use additional code, if applicable, for any personal history of malignant neoplasm: V10.0-V10.9)

ICD-9-CM Procedural

40.11 Biopsy of lymphatic structure

40.3 Regional lymph node excision

40.53 Radical excision of iliac lymph nodes

60.0 Incision of prostate ♂

55866

55866 Laparoscopy, surgical prostatectomy, retropubic radical, including nerve sparing, includes robotic assistance, when performed

ICD-9-CM Diagnostic

185 Malignant neoplasm of prostate ♂

196.6 Secondary and unspecified malignant neoplasm of intrapelvic lymph nodes

198.82 Secondary malignant neoplasm of genital organs

233.4 Carcinoma in situ of prostate ♂

236.5 Neoplasm of uncertain behavior of prostate ♂

239.5 Neoplasm of unspecified nature of other genitourinary organs

V84.03 Genetic susceptibility to malignant neoplasm of prostate — (Use additional code, if applicable, for any associated family history of the disease: V16-V19. Code first, if applicable, any current malignant neoplasms: 140.0-195.8, 200.0-208.9, 230.0-234.9. Use additional code, if applicable, for any personal history of malignant neoplasm: V10.0-V10.9) ♂

V84.09 Genetic susceptibility to other malignant neoplasm — (Use additional code, if applicable, for any associated family history of the disease: V16-V19. Code first, if applicable, any current malignant neoplasms: 140.0-195.8, 200.0-208.9, 230.0-234.9. Use additional code, if applicable, for any personal history of malignant neoplasm: V10.0-V10.9)

ICD-9-CM Procedural

17.42 Laparoscopic robotic assisted procedure

60.5 Radical prostatectomy ♂

55870

55870 Electroejaculation

ICD-9-CM Diagnostic

302.72 Psychosexual dysfunction with inhibited sexual excitement

344.00 Unspecified quadriplegia ▽

344.01 Quadriplegia and quadriparesis, C1-C4, complete

344.02 Quadriplegia and quadriparesis, C1-C4, incomplete

344.03 Quadriplegia and quadriparesis, C5-C7, complete

344.04 C5-C7, incomplete

344.09 Other quadriplegia and quadriparesis

344.1 Paraplegia

607.84 Impotence of organic origin ♂

608.87 Retrograde ejaculation ♂

V26.82 Encounter for fertility preservation procedure

ICD-9-CM Procedural

99.96 Collection of sperm for artificial insemination ♂

55873

55873 Cryosurgical ablation of the prostate (includes ultrasonic guidance and monitoring)

ICD-9-CM Diagnostic

185 Malignant neoplasm of prostate ♂

198.82 Secondary malignant neoplasm of genital organs

222.2 Benign neoplasm of prostate ♂

233.4 Carcinoma in situ of prostate ♂

236.5 Neoplasm of uncertain behavior of prostate ♂

239.5 Neoplasm of unspecified nature of other genitourinary organs

600.00 Hypertrophy (benign) of prostate without urinary obstruction and other lower urinary tract symptoms [LUTS] ♂

600.01 Hypertrophy (benign) of prostate with urinary obstruction and other lower urinary tract symptoms [LUTS] — (Use additional code to identify symptoms: 599.69, 788.20, 788.21, 788.30-788.39, 788.41, 788.43, 788.62, 788.63, 788.64, 788.65) ♂

600.10 Nodular prostate without urinary obstruction ♂

600.11 Nodular prostate with urinary obstruction ♂

600.20 Benign localized hyperplasia of prostate without urinary obstruction and other lower urinary tract symptoms [LUTS] ♂

600.21 Benign localized hyperplasia of prostate with urinary obstruction and other lower urinary tract symptoms [LUTS] — (Use additional code to identify symptoms: 599.69, 788.20, 788.21, 788.30-788.39, 788.41, 788.43, 788.62, 788.63, 788.64, 788.65) ♂

600.3 Cyst of prostate ♂

600.90 Hyperplasia of prostate, unspecified, without urinary obstruction and other lower urinary tract symptoms [LUTS] ▽ ♂

600.91 Hyperplasia of prostate, unspecified, with urinary obstruction and other lower urinary tract symptoms [LUTS] — (Use additional code to identify symptoms: 599.69, 788.20, 788.21, 788.30-788.39, 788.41, 788.43, 788.62, 788.63, 788.64, 788.65) ▽ ♂

601.0 Acute prostatitis — (Use additional code to identify organism: 041.0, 041.1) ♂

601.1 Chronic prostatitis — (Use additional code to identify organism: 041.0, 041.1) ♂

601.2 Abscess of prostate — (Use additional code to identify organism: 041.0, 041.1) ♂

601.3 Prostatocystitis — (Use additional code to identify organism: 041.0, 041.1) ♂

601.4 Prostatitis in diseases classified elsewhere — (Use additional code to identify organism: 041.0, 041.1. Code first underlying disease: 016.5, 039.8, 095.8, 116.0) ☒ ♂

601.8 Other specified inflammatory disease of prostate — (Use additional code to identify organism: 041.0, 041.1) ♂

602.0 Calculus of prostate ♂

602.2 Atrophy of prostate ♂

602.3 Dysplasia of prostate ♂

602.8 Other specified disorder of prostate ♂

V84.03 Genetic susceptibility to malignant neoplasm of prostate — (Use additional code, if applicable, for any associated family history of the disease: V16-V19. Code first, if applicable, any current malignant neoplasms: 140.0-195.8, 200.0-208.9, 230.0-234.9. Use additional code, if applicable, for any personal history of malignant neoplasm: V10.0-V10.9) ♂

V84.09 Genetic susceptibility to other malignant neoplasm — (Use additional code, if applicable, for any associated family history of the disease: V16-V19. Code first, if applicable, any current malignant neoplasms: 140.0-195.8, 200.0-208.9, 230.0-234.9. Use additional code, if applicable, for any personal history of malignant neoplasm: V10.0-V10.9)

ICD-9-CM Procedural

60.62 Perineal prostatectomy ♂

HCPCS Level II Supplies & Services

C2618 Probe, cryoablation

55875

55875 Transperineal placement of needles or catheters into prostate for interstitial radioelement application, with or without cystoscopy

ICD-9-CM Diagnostic

185 Malignant neoplasm of prostate ♂

198.82 Secondary malignant neoplasm of genital organs

233.4 Carcinoma in situ of prostate ♂

236.5 Neoplasm of uncertain behavior of prostate ♂

239.5 Neoplasm of unspecified nature of other genitourinary organs

V84.03 Genetic susceptibility to malignant neoplasm of prostate — (Use additional code, if applicable, for any associated family history of the disease: V16-V19. Code first, if applicable, any current malignant neoplasms: 140.0-195.8, 200.0-208.9, 230.0-234.9. Use additional code, if applicable, for any personal history of malignant neoplasm: V10.0-V10.9) ♂

V84.09 Genetic susceptibility to other malignant neoplasm — (Use additional code, if applicable, for any associated family history of the disease: V16-V19. Code first, if applicable, any current malignant neoplasms: 140.0-195.8, 200.0-208.9, 230.0-234.9. Use additional code, if applicable, for any personal history of malignant neoplasm: V10.0-V10.9)

ICD-9-CM Procedural

60.99 Other operations on prostate ♂

92.27 Implantation or insertion of radioactive elements

55876

55876 Placement of interstitial device(s) for radiation therapy guidance (eg, fiducial markers, dosimeter), prostate (via needle, any approach), single or multiple

ICD-9-CM Diagnostic

185 Malignant neoplasm of prostate ♂

198.82 Secondary malignant neoplasm of genital organs

233.4 Carcinoma in situ of prostate ♂

236.5 Neoplasm of uncertain behavior of prostate ♂

239.5 Neoplasm of unspecified nature of other genitourinary organs

V84.03 Genetic susceptibility to malignant neoplasm of prostate — (Use additional code, if applicable, for any associated family history of the disease: V16-V19. Code first, if applicable, any current malignant neoplasms: 140.0-195.8, 200.0-208.9, 230.0-234.9. Use additional code, if applicable, for any personal history of malignant neoplasm: V10.0-V10.9) ♂

V84.09 Genetic susceptibility to other malignant neoplasm — (Use additional code, if applicable, for any associated family history of the disease: V16-V19. Code first, if applicable, any current malignant neoplasms: 140.0-195.8, 200.0-208.9, 230.0-234.9. Use additional code, if applicable, for any personal history of malignant neoplasm: V10.0-V10.9)

ICD-9-CM Procedural

60.99 Other operations on prostate ♂

92.27 Implantation or insertion of radioactive elements

92.29 Other radiotherapeutic procedure

HCPCS Level II Supplies & Services

A4648 Tissue marker, implantable, any type, each

A4650 Implantable radiation dosimeter, each

Reproductive System Procedures

55920

55920 Placement of needles or catheters into pelvic organs and/or genitalia (except prostate) for subsequent interstitial radioelement application

ICD-9-CM Diagnostic

158.8	Malignant neoplasm of specified parts of peritoneum
158.9	Malignant neoplasm of peritoneum, unspecified ▽
180.0	Malignant neoplasm of endocervix ♀
180.1	Malignant neoplasm of exocervix ♀
180.8	Malignant neoplasm of other specified sites of cervix ♀
180.9	Malignant neoplasm of cervix uteri, unspecified site ▽ ♀
183.0	Malignant neoplasm of ovary — (Use additional code to identify any functional activity) ♀
183.8	Malignant neoplasm of other specified sites of uterine adnexa ♀
186.0	Malignant neoplasm of undescended testis — (Use additional code to identify any functional activity) ♂
186.9	Malignant neoplasm of other and unspecified testis — (Use additional code to identify any functional activity) ▽ ♂
196.6	Secondary and unspecified malignant neoplasm of intrapelvic lymph nodes
197.6	Secondary malignant neoplasm of retroperitoneum and peritoneum
198.6	Secondary malignant neoplasm of ovary ♀
198.89	Secondary malignant neoplasm of other specified sites
201.50	Hodgkin's disease, nodular sclerosis, unspecified site, extranodal and solid organ sites ▽
201.60	Hodgkin's disease, mixed cellularity, unspecified site, extranodal and solid organ sites ▽
201.70	Hodgkin's disease, lymphocytic depletion, unspecified site, extranodal and solid organ sites ▽
209.74	Secondary neuroendocrine tumor of peritoneum
209.79	Secondary neuroendocrine tumor of other sites
236.2	Neoplasm of uncertain behavior of ovary — (Use additional code to identify any functional activity) ♀
785.6	Enlargement of lymph nodes
V10.43	Personal history of malignant neoplasm of ovary ♀
V10.90	Personal history of unspecified malignant neoplasm ▽
V10.91	Personal history of malignant neuroendocrine tumor — (Code first any continuing functional activity, such as: carcinoid syndrome (259.2))
V84.02	Genetic susceptibility to malignant neoplasm of ovary — (Use additional code, if applicable, for any associated family history of the disease: V16-V19. Code first, if applicable, any current malignant neoplasms: 140.0-195.8, 200.0-208.9, 230.0-234.9. Use additional code, if applicable, for any personal history of malignant neoplasm: V10.0-V10.9) ♀
V84.04	Genetic susceptibility to malignant neoplasm of endometrium — (Use additional code, if applicable, for any associated family history of the disease: V16-V19. Code first, if applicable, any current malignant neoplasms: 140.0-195.8, 200.0-208.9, 230.0-234.9. Use additional code, if applicable, for any personal history of malignant neoplasm: V10.0-V10.9) ♀
V84.09	Genetic susceptibility to other malignant neoplasm — (Use additional code, if applicable, for any associated family history of the disease: V16-V19. Code first, if applicable, any current malignant neoplasms: 140.0-195.8, 200.0-208.9, 230.0-234.9. Use additional code, if applicable, for any personal history of malignant neoplasm: V10.0-V10.9)
V87.41	Personal history of antineoplastic chemotherapy
V87.42	Personal history of monoclonal drug therapy
V88.01	Acquired absence of both cervix and uterus ♀
V88.02	Acquired absence of uterus with remaining cervical stump ♀
V88.03	Acquired absence of cervix with remaining uterus ♀

ICD-9-CM Procedural

54.12	Reopening of recent laparotomy site
54.19	Other laparotomy
62.0	Incision of testis ♂
65.09	Other oophorotomy ♀
68.0	Hysterotomy ♀
69.95	Incision of cervix ♀
70.12	Culdotomy ♀
70.14	Other vaginotomy ♀
71.09	Other incision of vulva and perineum ♀
92.27	Implantation or insertion of radioactive elements

Intersex Surgery

55970

55970 Intersex surgery; male to female

ICD-9-CM Diagnostic

259.50 Androgen insensitivity, unspecified ▽
259.51 Androgen insensitivity syndrome
259.52 Partial androgen insensitivity
302.50 Trans-sexualism with unspecified sexual history ▽
302.51 Trans-sexualism with asexual history
302.52 Trans-sexualism with homosexual history
302.53 Trans-sexualism with heterosexual history
302.6 Gender identity disorder in children
302.85 Gender identity disorder in adolescents or adults
752.7 Indeterminate sex and pseudohermaphroditism
752.89 Other specified anomalies of genital organs
758.81 Other conditions due to sex chromosome anomalies — (Use additional codes for conditions associated with the chromosomal anomalies)

ICD-9-CM Procedural

62.41 Removal of both testes at same operative episode ♂
64.3 Amputation of penis ♂
64.5 Operations for sex transformation, not elsewhere classified ♂
64.99 Other operations on male genital organs ♂
70.61 Vaginal construction ♀

55980

55980 Intersex surgery; female to male

ICD-9-CM Diagnostic

259.50 Androgen insensitivity, unspecified ▽
259.51 Androgen insensitivity syndrome
259.52 Partial androgen insensitivity
302.50 Trans-sexualism with unspecified sexual history ▽
302.51 Trans-sexualism with asexual history
302.52 Trans-sexualism with homosexual history
302.53 Trans-sexualism with heterosexual history
302.6 Gender identity disorder in children
302.85 Gender identity disorder in adolescents or adults
752.7 Indeterminate sex and pseudohermaphroditism
752.89 Other specified anomalies of genital organs
758.81 Other conditions due to sex chromosome anomalies — (Use additional codes for conditions associated with the chromosomal anomalies)

ICD-9-CM Procedural

62.7 Insertion of testicular prosthesis ♂
64.43 Construction of penis ♂
64.5 Operations for sex transformation, not elsewhere classified ♂
64.97 Insertion or replacement of inflatable penile prosthesis ♂
70.4 Obliteration and total excision of vagina ♀

Female Genital System

Vulva, Perineum, and Introitus

56405

56405 Incision and drainage of vulva or perineal abscess

ICD-9-CM Diagnostic

597.0 Urethral abscess
614.4 Chronic or unspecified parametritis and pelvic cellulitis — (Use additional code to identify organism: 041.00-041.09, 041.10-041.19) ♀
616.4 Other abscess of vulva — (Use additional code to identify organism: 041.00-041.09, 041.10-041.19) ♀
616.9 Unspecified inflammatory disease of cervix, vagina, and vulva — (Use additional code to identify organism: 041.00-041.09, 041.10-041.19) ♀
682.2 Cellulitis and abscess of trunk — (Use additional code to identify organism, such as 041.1, etc.)
752.49 Other congenital anomaly of cervix, vagina, and external female genitalia ♀

ICD-9-CM Procedural

71.09 Other incision of vulva and perineum ♀

56420

56420 Incision and drainage of Bartholin's gland abscess

ICD-9-CM Diagnostic

616.3 Abscess of Bartholin's gland — (Use additional code to identify organism: 041.00-041.09, 041.10-041.19) ♀

ICD-9-CM Procedural

71.22 Incision of Bartholin's gland (cyst) ♀

56440

56440 Marsupialization of Bartholin's gland cyst

ICD-9-CM Diagnostic

616.2 Cyst of Bartholin's gland — (Use additional code to identify organism: 041.00-041.09, 041.10-041.19) ♀
616.3 Abscess of Bartholin's gland — (Use additional code to identify organism: 041.00-041.09, 041.10-041.19) ♀

ICD-9-CM Procedural

71.23 Marsupialization of Bartholin's gland (cyst) ♀

56441

56441 Lysis of labial adhesions

ICD-9-CM Diagnostic

624.4 Old laceration or scarring of vulva ♀
629.29 Other female genital mutilation status ♀
752.49 Other congenital anomaly of cervix, vagina, and external female genitalia ♀

ICD-9-CM Procedural

71.01 Lysis of vulvar adhesions ♀

56442

56442 Hymenotomy, simple incision

ICD-9-CM Diagnostic

623.3 Tight hymenal ring ♀
752.42 Imperforate hymen ♀
752.49 Other congenital anomaly of cervix, vagina, and external female genitalia ♀

ICD-9-CM Procedural

70.11 Hymenotomy ♀

56501-56515

56501 Destruction of lesion(s), vulva; simple (eg, laser surgery, electrosurgery, cryosurgery, chemosurgery)
56515 extensive (eg, laser surgery, electrosurgery, cryosurgery, chemosurgery)

ICD-9-CM Diagnostic

054.11 Herpetic vulvovaginitis ♀
054.12 Herpetic ulceration of vulva ♀
078.11 Condyloma acuminatum
078.19 Other specified viral warts
184.4 Malignant neoplasm of vulva, unspecified site ♀
198.82 Secondary malignant neoplasm of genital organs
221.2 Benign neoplasm of vulva ♀
228.01 Hemangioma of skin and subcutaneous tissue
233.30 Carcinoma in situ, unspecified female genital organ ♀
233.31 Carcinoma in situ, vagina ♀
233.32 Carcinoma in situ, vulva ♀
233.39 Carcinoma in situ, other female genital organ ♀
236.3 Neoplasm of uncertain behavior of other and unspecified female genital organs ♀
239.5 Neoplasm of unspecified nature of other genitourinary organs
456.6 Vulval varices ♀
616.81 Mucositis (ulcerative) of cervix, vagina, and vulva — (Use additional code to identify organism: 041.00-041.09, 041.10-041.19) (Use additional E code to identify adverse effects of therapy: E879.2, E930.7, E933.1) ♀
616.89 Other inflammatory disease of cervix, vagina and vulva — (Use additional code to identify organism: 041.00-041.09, 041.10-041.19) ♀
624.01 Vulvar intraepithelial neoplasia I [VIN I] ♀
624.02 Vulvar intraepithelial neoplasia II [VIN II] ♀
624.09 Other dystrophy of vulva ♀
624.6 Polyp of labia and vulva ♀
624.8 Other specified noninflammatory disorder of vulva and perineum ♀
625.8 Other specified symptom associated with female genital organs ♀
698.1 Pruritus of genital organs
701.0 Circumscribed scleroderma
701.5 Other abnormal granulation tissue
709.9 Unspecified disorder of skin and subcutaneous tissue
752.49 Other congenital anomaly of cervix, vagina, and external female genitalia ♀

ICD-9-CM Procedural

71.3 Other local excision or destruction of vulva and perineum ♀

HCPCS Level II Supplies & Services

A4305 Disposable drug delivery system, flow rate of 50 ml or greater per hour

56605-56606

56605 Biopsy of vulva or perineum (separate procedure); 1 lesion
56606 each separate additional lesion (List separately in addition to code for primary procedure)

ICD-9-CM Diagnostic

054.11 Herpetic vulvovaginitis ♀

054.12 Herpetic ulceration of vulva ♀
078.11 Condyloma acuminatum
078.19 Other specified viral warts
172.5 Malignant melanoma of skin of trunk, except scrotum
173.50 Unspecified malignant neoplasm of skin of trunk, except scrotum ▽
173.51 Basal cell carcinoma of skin of trunk, except scrotum
173.52 Squamous cell carcinoma of skin of trunk, except scrotum
173.59 Other specified malignant neoplasm of skin of trunk, except scrotum
184.4 Malignant neoplasm of vulva, unspecified site ▽ ♀
195.3 Malignant neoplasm of pelvis
198.2 Secondary malignant neoplasm of skin
198.82 Secondary malignant neoplasm of genital organs
198.89 Secondary malignant neoplasm of other specified sites
214.9 Lipoma of unspecified site ▽
216.5 Benign neoplasm of skin of trunk, except scrotum
221.2 Benign neoplasm of vulva ♀
232.5 Carcinoma in situ of skin of trunk, except scrotum
233.30 Carcinoma in situ, unspecified female genital organ ▽ ♀
233.31 Carcinoma in situ, vagina ♀
233.32 Carcinoma in situ, vulva ♀
233.39 Carcinoma in situ, other female genital organ ♀
234.8 Carcinoma in situ of other specified sites
236.3 Neoplasm of uncertain behavior of other and unspecified female genital organs ▽ ♀
238.2 Neoplasm of uncertain behavior of skin
239.2 Neoplasms of unspecified nature of bone, soft tissue, and skin
239.5 Neoplasm of unspecified nature of other genitourinary organs
567.9 Unspecified peritonitis ▽
616.10 Unspecified vaginitis and vulvovaginitis — (Use additional code to identify organism, such as: 041.00-041.09, 041.10-041.19, 041.41-041.49) ▽ ♀
616.81 Mucositis (ulcerative) of cervix, vagina, and vulva — (Use additional code to identify organism: 041.00-041.09, 041.10-041.19) (Use additional E code to identify adverse effects of therapy: E879.2, E930.7, E933.1) ♀
616.89 Other inflammatory disease of cervix, vagina and vulva — (Use additional code to identify organism: 041.00-041.09, 041.10-041.19) ♀
624.01 Vulvar intraepithelial neoplasia I [VIN I] ♀
624.02 Vulvar intraepithelial neoplasia II [VIN II] ♀
624.09 Other dystrophy of vulva ♀
624.8 Other specified noninflammatory disorder of vulva and perineum ♀
625.8 Other specified symptom associated with female genital organs ♀
629.89 Other specified disorders of female genital organs ♀
709.9 Unspecified disorder of skin and subcutaneous tissue ▽
752.49 Other congenital anomaly of cervix, vagina, and external female genitalia ♀

ICD-9-CM Procedural

71.11 Biopsy of vulva ♀
86.11 Closed biopsy of skin and subcutaneous tissue

56620-56625

56620 Vulvectomy simple; partial
56625 complete

ICD-9-CM Diagnostic

171.6 Malignant neoplasm of connective and other soft tissue of pelvis
172.5 Malignant melanoma of skin of trunk, except scrotum
173.50 Unspecified malignant neoplasm of skin of trunk, except scrotum ▽
173.51 Basal cell carcinoma of skin of trunk, except scrotum
173.52 Squamous cell carcinoma of skin of trunk, except scrotum
173.59 Other specified malignant neoplasm of skin of trunk, except scrotum
184.4 Malignant neoplasm of vulva, unspecified site ▽ ♀
198.82 Secondary malignant neoplasm of genital organs
199.1 Other malignant neoplasm of unspecified site
221.2 Benign neoplasm of vulva ♀
233.30 Carcinoma in situ, unspecified female genital organ ▽ ♀
233.31 Carcinoma in situ, vagina ♀
233.32 Carcinoma in situ, vulva ♀
233.39 Carcinoma in situ, other female genital organ ♀
236.3 Neoplasm of uncertain behavior of other and unspecified female genital organs ▽ ♀
239.5 Neoplasm of unspecified nature of other genitourinary organs
278.1 Localized adiposity — (Use additional code to identify any associated intellectual disabilities.)
616.4 Other abscess of vulva — (Use additional code to identify organism: 041.00-041.09, 041.10-041.19) ♀
623.0 Dysplasia of vagina ♀
623.8 Other specified noninflammatory disorder of vagina ♀
624.3 Hypertrophy of labia ♀
624.8 Other specified noninflammatory disorder of vulva and perineum ♀
624.9 Unspecified noninflammatory disorder of vulva and perineum ▽ ♀
625.0 Dyspareunia ♀
625.70 Vulvodynia, unspecified ▽ ♀
625.71 Vulvar vestibulitis ♀
625.79 Other vulvodynia ♀
698.1 Pruritus of genital organs
701.0 Circumscribed scleroderma
752.40 Unspecified congenital anomaly of cervix, vagina, and external female genitalia ▽ ♀
752.41 Embryonic cyst of cervix, vagina, and external female genitalia ♀
752.49 Other congenital anomaly of cervix, vagina, and external female genitalia ♀
752.89 Other specified anomalies of genital organs
752.9 Unspecified congenital anomaly of genital organs ▽
V50.1 Other plastic surgery for unacceptable cosmetic appearance
V50.8 Other elective surgery for purposes other than remedying health states
V50.9 Unspecified elective surgery for purposes other than remedying health states ▽
V84.09 Genetic susceptibility to other malignant neoplasm — (Use additional code, if applicable, for any associated family history of the disease: V16-V19. Code first, if applicable, any current malignant neoplasms: 140.0-195.8, 200.0-208.9, 230.0-234.9. Use additional code, if applicable, for any personal history of malignant neoplasm: V10.0-V10.9)

ICD-9-CM Procedural

71.61 Unilateral vulvectomy ♀
71.62 Bilateral vulvectomy ♀

HCPCS Level II Supplies & Services

A4305 Disposable drug delivery system, flow rate of 50 ml or greater per hour

56630-56632

56630 Vulvectomy, radical, partial;
56631 with unilateral inguinofemoral lymphadenectomy
56632 with bilateral inguinofemoral lymphadenectomy

ICD-9-CM Diagnostic

171.6 Malignant neoplasm of connective and other soft tissue of pelvis
172.5 Malignant melanoma of skin of trunk, except scrotum
173.50 Unspecified malignant neoplasm of skin of trunk, except scrotum ▽
173.51 Basal cell carcinoma of skin of trunk, except scrotum
173.52 Squamous cell carcinoma of skin of trunk, except scrotum
173.59 Other specified malignant neoplasm of skin of trunk, except scrotum
184.4 Malignant neoplasm of vulva, unspecified site ▽ ♀
196.5 Secondary and unspecified malignant neoplasm of lymph nodes of inguinal region and lower limb

198.82 Secondary malignant neoplasm of genital organs
209.36 Merkel cell carcinoma of other sites
209.71 Secondary neuroendocrine tumor of distant lymph nodes
209.79 Secondary neuroendocrine tumor of other sites
233.30 Carcinoma in situ, unspecified female genital organ ▽ ♀
233.31 Carcinoma in situ, vagina ♀
233.32 Carcinoma in situ, vulva ♀
233.39 Carcinoma in situ, other female genital organ ♀
236.3 Neoplasm of uncertain behavior of other and unspecified female genital organs ▽ ♀
239.5 Neoplasm of unspecified nature of other genitourinary organs
239.89 Neoplasms of unspecified nature, other specified sites
278.1 Localized adiposity — (Use additional code to identify any associated intellectual disabilities.)
623.8 Other specified noninflammatory disorder of vagina ♀
624.9 Unspecified noninflammatory disorder of vulva and perineum ▽ ♀
625.0 Dyspareunia ♀
625.70 Vulvodynia, unspecified ▽ ♀
625.71 Vulvar vestibulitis ♀
625.79 Other vulvodynia ♀
752.40 Unspecified congenital anomaly of cervix, vagina, and external female genitalia ▽ ♀
752.41 Embryonic cyst of cervix, vagina, and external female genitalia ♀
752.49 Other congenital anomaly of cervix, vagina, and external female genitalia ♀
752.89 Other specified anomalies of genital organs
752.9 Unspecified congenital anomaly of genital organs ▽
V50.1 Other plastic surgery for unacceptable cosmetic appearance
V50.8 Other elective surgery for purposes other than remedying health states
V50.9 Unspecified elective surgery for purposes other than remedying health states ▽
V84.09 Genetic susceptibility to other malignant neoplasm — (Use additional code, if applicable, for any associated family history of the disease: V16-V19. Code first, if applicable, any current malignant neoplasms: 140.0-195.8, 200.0-208.9, 230.0-234.9. Use additional code, if applicable, for any personal history of malignant neoplasm: V10.0-V10.9)

ICD-9-CM Procedural

40.3 Regional lymph node excision
71.5 Radical vulvectomy ♀

56633-56637

56633 Vulvectomy, radical, complete;
56634 with unilateral inguinofemoral lymphadenectomy
56637 with bilateral inguinofemoral lymphadenectomy

ICD-9-CM Diagnostic

171.6 Malignant neoplasm of connective and other soft tissue of pelvis
172.5 Malignant melanoma of skin of trunk, except scrotum
173.50 Unspecified malignant neoplasm of skin of trunk, except scrotum ▽
173.51 Basal cell carcinoma of skin of trunk, except scrotum
173.52 Squamous cell carcinoma of skin of trunk, except scrotum
173.59 Other specified malignant neoplasm of skin of trunk, except scrotum
184.4 Malignant neoplasm of vulva, unspecified site ▽ ♀
196.5 Secondary and unspecified malignant neoplasm of lymph nodes of inguinal region and lower limb
198.82 Secondary malignant neoplasm of genital organs
209.36 Merkel cell carcinoma of other sites
209.71 Secondary neuroendocrine tumor of distant lymph nodes
209.79 Secondary neuroendocrine tumor of other sites
233.30 Carcinoma in situ, unspecified female genital organ ▽ ♀
233.31 Carcinoma in situ, vagina ♀
233.32 Carcinoma in situ, vulva ♀
233.39 Carcinoma in situ, other female genital organ ♀
236.3 Neoplasm of uncertain behavior of other and unspecified female genital organs ▽ ♀
239.5 Neoplasm of unspecified nature of other genitourinary organs
239.89 Neoplasms of unspecified nature, other specified sites
752.40 Unspecified congenital anomaly of cervix, vagina, and external female genitalia ▽ ♀
752.41 Embryonic cyst of cervix, vagina, and external female genitalia ♀
752.49 Other congenital anomaly of cervix, vagina, and external female genitalia ♀
752.89 Other specified anomalies of genital organs
V84.09 Genetic susceptibility to other malignant neoplasm — (Use additional code, if applicable, for any associated family history of the disease: V16-V19. Code first, if applicable, any current malignant neoplasms: 140.0-195.8, 200.0-208.9, 230.0-234.9. Use additional code, if applicable, for any personal history of malignant neoplasm: V10.0-V10.9)

ICD-9-CM Procedural

40.3 Regional lymph node excision
71.5 Radical vulvectomy ♀

56640

56640 Vulvectomy, radical, complete, with inguinofemoral, iliac, and pelvic lymphadenectomy

ICD-9-CM Diagnostic

171.6 Malignant neoplasm of connective and other soft tissue of pelvis
172.5 Malignant melanoma of skin of trunk, except scrotum
173.50 Unspecified malignant neoplasm of skin of trunk, except scrotum ▽
173.51 Basal cell carcinoma of skin of trunk, except scrotum
173.52 Squamous cell carcinoma of skin of trunk, except scrotum
173.59 Other specified malignant neoplasm of skin of trunk, except scrotum
184.4 Malignant neoplasm of vulva, unspecified site ▽ ♀
196.5 Secondary and unspecified malignant neoplasm of lymph nodes of inguinal region and lower limb
196.6 Secondary and unspecified malignant neoplasm of intrapelvic lymph nodes
198.82 Secondary malignant neoplasm of genital organs
209.36 Merkel cell carcinoma of other sites
209.71 Secondary neuroendocrine tumor of distant lymph nodes
209.79 Secondary neuroendocrine tumor of other sites
233.30 Carcinoma in situ, unspecified female genital organ ▽ ♀
233.31 Carcinoma in situ, vagina ♀
233.32 Carcinoma in situ, vulva ♀
233.39 Carcinoma in situ, other female genital organ ♀
236.3 Neoplasm of uncertain behavior of other and unspecified female genital organs ▽ ♀
239.5 Neoplasm of unspecified nature of other genitourinary organs
239.89 Neoplasms of unspecified nature, other specified sites
V84.09 Genetic susceptibility to other malignant neoplasm — (Use additional code, if applicable, for any associated family history of the disease: V16-V19. Code first, if applicable, any current malignant neoplasms: 140.0-195.8, 200.0-208.9, 230.0-234.9. Use additional code, if applicable, for any personal history of malignant neoplasm: V10.0-V10.9)

ICD-9-CM Procedural

40.59 Radical excision of other lymph nodes
71.5 Radical vulvectomy ♀

56700

56700 Partial hymenectomy or revision of hymenal ring

ICD-9-CM Diagnostic

184.0 Malignant neoplasm of vagina ♀
198.82 Secondary malignant neoplasm of genital organs
221.1 Benign neoplasm of vagina ♀
233.30 Carcinoma in situ, unspecified female genital organ ▽ ♀

233.31 Carcinoma in situ, vagina ♀

233.32 Carcinoma in situ, vulva ♀

233.39 Carcinoma in situ, other female genital organ ♀

236.3 Neoplasm of uncertain behavior of other and unspecified female genital organs ▼ ♀

614.9 Unspecified inflammatory disease of female pelvic organs and tissues — (Use additional code to identify organism: 041.00-041.09, 041.10-041.19) ▼ ♀

623.3 Tight hymenal ring ♀

625.0 Dyspareunia ♀

629.89 Other specified disorders of female genital organs ♀

752.40 Unspecified congenital anomaly of cervix, vagina, and external female genitalia ▼ ♀

752.41 Embryonic cyst of cervix, vagina, and external female genitalia ♀

752.42 Imperforate hymen ♀

752.49 Other congenital anomaly of cervix, vagina, and external female genitalia ♀

752.89 Other specified anomalies of genital organs

752.9 Unspecified congenital anomaly of genital organs ▼

ICD-9-CM Procedural

70.31 Hymenectomy ♀

70.76 Hymenorrhaphy ♀

56740

56740 Excision of Bartholin's gland or cyst

ICD-9-CM Diagnostic

616.2 Cyst of Bartholin's gland — (Use additional code to identify organism: 041.00-041.09, 041.10-041.19) ♀

616.3 Abscess of Bartholin's gland — (Use additional code to identify organism: 041.00-041.09, 041.10-041.19) ♀

ICD-9-CM Procedural

71.24 Excision or other destruction of Bartholin's gland (cyst) ♀

56800

56800 Plastic repair of introitus

ICD-9-CM Diagnostic

623.2 Stricture or atresia of vagina — (Use additional E code to identify any external cause) ♀

624.4 Old laceration or scarring of vulva ♀

629.20 Female genital mutilation status, unspecified ▼ ♀

629.21 Female genital mutilation, Type I status ♀

629.22 Female genital mutilation, Type II status ♀

629.23 Female genital mutilation, Type III status ♀

629.29 Other female genital mutilation status ♀

677 Late effect of complication of pregnancy, childbirth, and the puerperium — (Code first any sequelae) ♀

752.40 Unspecified congenital anomaly of cervix, vagina, and external female genitalia ▼ ♀

752.42 Imperforate hymen ♀

752.49 Other congenital anomaly of cervix, vagina, and external female genitalia ♀

752.81 Scrotal transposition ♂

759.9 Unspecified congenital anomaly ▼

ICD-9-CM Procedural

71.79 Other repair of vulva and perineum ♀

56805

56805 Clitoroplasty for intersex state

ICD-9-CM Diagnostic

255.2 Adrenogenital disorders

259.50 Androgen insensitivity, unspecified ▼

259.51 Androgen insensitivity syndrome

259.52 Partial androgen insensitivity

752.49 Other congenital anomaly of cervix, vagina, and external female genitalia ♀

752.7 Indeterminate sex and pseudohermaphroditism

ICD-9-CM Procedural

71.4 Operations on clitoris ♀

56810

56810 Perineoplasty, repair of perineum, nonobstetrical (separate procedure)

ICD-9-CM Diagnostic

184.8 Malignant neoplasm of other specified sites of female genital organs ♀

195.3 Malignant neoplasm of pelvis

198.89 Secondary malignant neoplasm of other specified sites

209.36 Merkel cell carcinoma of other sites

209.79 Secondary neuroendocrine tumor of other sites

229.8 Benign neoplasm of other specified sites

234.8 Carcinoma in situ of other specified sites

238.8 Neoplasm of uncertain behavior of other specified sites

239.89 Neoplasms of unspecified nature, other specified sites

618.05 Perineocele without mention of uterine prolapse — (Use additional code to identify urinary incontinence: 625.6, 788.31, 788.33-788.39) ♀

618.7 Genital prolapse, old laceration of muscles of pelvic floor — (Use additional code to identify urinary incontinence: 625.6, 788.31, 788.33-788.39) ♀

618.81 Incompetence or weakening of pubocervical tissue — (Use additional code to identify urinary incontinence: 625.6, 788.31, 788.33-788.39) ♀

618.82 Incompetence or weakening of rectovaginal tissue — (Use additional code to identify urinary incontinence: 625.6, 788.31, 788.33-788.39) ♀

618.83 Pelvic muscle wasting — (Use additional code to identify urinary incontinence: 625.6, 788.31, 788.33-788.39) ♀

618.9 Unspecified genital prolapse — (Use additional code to identify urinary incontinence: 625.6, 788.31, 788.33-788.39) ▼ ♀

625.0 Dyspareunia ♀

625.6 Female stress incontinence ♀

629.20 Female genital mutilation status, unspecified ▼ ♀

629.21 Female genital mutilation, Type I status ♀

629.22 Female genital mutilation, Type II status ♀

629.23 Female genital mutilation, Type III status ♀

629.29 Other female genital mutilation status ♀

701.0 Circumscribed scleroderma

752.40 Unspecified congenital anomaly of cervix, vagina, and external female genitalia ▼ ♀

752.41 Embryonic cyst of cervix, vagina, and external female genitalia ♀

752.49 Other congenital anomaly of cervix, vagina, and external female genitalia ♀

879.6 Open wound of other and unspecified parts of trunk, without mention of complication ▼

879.7 Open wound of other and unspecified parts of trunk, complicated ▼

959.14 Other injury of external genitals

959.19 Other injury of other sites of trunk

ICD-9-CM Procedural

71.79 Other repair of vulva and perineum ♀

56820-56821

56820 Colposcopy of the vulva;

56821 with biopsy(s)

ICD-9-CM Diagnostic

054.11 Herpetic vulvovaginitis ♀

054.12 Herpetic ulceration of vulva ♀

078.11 Condyloma acuminatum

078.19 Other specified viral warts

184.1 Malignant neoplasm of labia majora ♀
184.2 Malignant neoplasm of labia minora ♀
184.3 Malignant neoplasm of clitoris ♀
184.4 Malignant neoplasm of vulva, unspecified site ▽ ♀
198.82 Secondary malignant neoplasm of genital organs
221.2 Benign neoplasm of vulva ♀
228.01 Hemangioma of skin and subcutaneous tissue
233.30 Carcinoma in situ, unspecified female genital organ ▽ ♀
233.31 Carcinoma in situ, vagina ♀
233.32 Carcinoma in situ, vulva ♀
236.3 Neoplasm of uncertain behavior of other and unspecified female genital organs ▽ ♀
239.5 Neoplasm of unspecified nature of other genitourinary organs
456.6 Vulval varices ♀
616.10 Unspecified vaginitis and vulvovaginitis — (Use additional code to identify organism, such as: 041.00-041.09, 041.10-041.19, 041.41-041.49) ▽ ♀
616.11 Vaginitis and vulvovaginitis in diseases classified elsewhere — (Use additional code to identify organism: 041.00-041.09, 041.10-041.19) (Code first underlying disease: 127.4) ☒ ♀
616.2 Cyst of Bartholin's gland — (Use additional code to identify organism: 041.00-041.09, 041.10-041.19) ♀
616.3 Abscess of Bartholin's gland — (Use additional code to identify organism: 041.00-041.09, 041.10-041.19) ♀
616.4 Other abscess of vulva — (Use additional code to identify organism: 041.00-041.09, 041.10-041.19) ♀
616.50 Unspecified ulceration of vulva — (Use additional code to identify organism: 041.00-041.09, 041.10-041.19) ▽ ♀
616.51 Ulceration of vulva in disease classified elsewhere — (Use additional code to identify organism: 041.00-041.09, 041.10-041.19) (Code first underlying disease: 016.7, 136.1) ☒ ♀
616.81 Mucositis (ulcerative) of cervix, vagina, and vulva — (Use additional code to identify organism: 041.00-041.09, 041.10-041.19) (Use additional E code to identify adverse effects of therapy: E879.2, E930.7, E933.1) ♀
616.89 Other inflammatory disease of cervix, vagina and vulva — (Use additional code to identify organism: 041.00-041.09, 041.10-041.19) ♀
616.9 Unspecified inflammatory disease of cervix, vagina, and vulva — (Use additional code to identify organism: 041.00-041.09, 041.10-041.19) ▽ ♀
617.8 Endometriosis of other specified sites ♀
624.01 Vulvar intraepithelial neoplasia I [VIN I] ♀
624.02 Vulvar intraepithelial neoplasia II [VIN II] ♀
624.09 Other dystrophy of vulva ♀
624.1 Atrophy of vulva ♀
624.2 Hypertrophy of clitoris ♀
624.3 Hypertrophy of labia ♀
624.4 Old laceration or scarring of vulva ♀
624.5 Hematoma of vulva ♀
624.6 Polyp of labia and vulva ♀
624.8 Other specified noninflammatory disorder of vulva and perineum ♀
624.9 Unspecified noninflammatory disorder of vulva and perineum ▽ ♀
625.8 Other specified symptom associated with female genital organs ♀
625.9 Unspecified symptom associated with female genital organs ▽ ♀
654.80 Congenital or acquired abnormality of vulva, unspecified as to episode of care in pregnancy — (Code first any associated obstructed labor: 660.2) ▽ ♀
654.81 Congenital or acquired abnormality of vulva, with delivery — (Code first any associated obstructed labor, 660.2) ♀
654.82 Congenital or acquired abnormality of vulva, delivered, with mention of postpartum complication — (Code first any associated obstructed labor: 660.2) ♀
654.83 Congenital or acquired abnormality of vulva, antepartum condition or complication — (Code first any associated obstructed labor: 660.2) ♀
654.84 Congenital or acquired abnormality of vulva, postpartum condition or complication — (Code first any associated obstructed labor: 660.2) ♀
698.1 Pruritus of genital organs
701.0 Circumscribed scleroderma
701.5 Other abnormal granulation tissue
709.9 Unspecified disorder of skin and subcutaneous tissue ▽
752.40 Unspecified congenital anomaly of cervix, vagina, and external female genitalia ▽ ♀
752.41 Embryonic cyst of cervix, vagina, and external female genitalia ♀
752.42 Imperforate hymen ♀
752.49 Other congenital anomaly of cervix, vagina, and external female genitalia ♀
V13.29 Personal history of other genital system and obstetric disorders ♀
V67.00 Follow-up examination, following unspecified surgery ▽
V67.09 Follow-up examination, following other surgery
V71.5 Observation following alleged rape or seduction
V71.6 Observation following other inflicted injury

ICD-9-CM Procedural

71.11 Biopsy of vulva ♀
71.19 Other diagnostic procedures on vulva ♀

Vagina

57000

57000 Colpotomy; with exploration

ICD-9-CM Diagnostic

158.8 Malignant neoplasm of specified parts of peritoneum
184.0 Malignant neoplasm of vagina ♀
197.6 Secondary malignant neoplasm of retroperitoneum and peritoneum
198.82 Secondary malignant neoplasm of genital organs
209.74 Secondary neuroendocrine tumor of peritoneum
209.79 Secondary neuroendocrine tumor of other sites
211.8 Benign neoplasm of retroperitoneum and peritoneum
221.1 Benign neoplasm of vagina ♀
235.4 Neoplasm of uncertain behavior of retroperitoneum and peritoneum
236.3 Neoplasm of uncertain behavior of other and unspecified female genital organs ▽ ♀
239.0 Neoplasm of unspecified nature of digestive system
239.5 Neoplasm of unspecified nature of other genitourinary organs
616.10 Unspecified vaginitis and vulvovaginitis — (Use additional code to identify organism, such as: 041.00-041.09, 041.10-041.19, 041.41-041.49) ▽ ♀
623.8 Other specified noninflammatory disorder of vagina ♀
623.9 Unspecified noninflammatory disorder of vagina ▽ ♀
625.3 Dysmenorrhea ♀

ICD-9-CM Procedural

70.12 Culdotomy ♀

57010

57010 Colpotomy; with drainage of pelvic abscess

ICD-9-CM Diagnostic

614.3 Acute parametritis and pelvic cellulitis — (Use additional code to identify organism: 041.00-041.09, 041.10-041.19) ♀
614.4 Chronic or unspecified parametritis and pelvic cellulitis — (Use additional code to identify organism: 041.00-041.09, 041.10-041.19) ♀
616.10 Unspecified vaginitis and vulvovaginitis — (Use additional code to identify organism, such as: 041.00-041.09, 041.10-041.19, 041.41-041.49) ▽ ♀
998.51 Infected postoperative seroma — (Use additional code to identify organism)
998.59 Other postoperative infection — (Use additional code to identify infection)

ICD-9-CM Procedural

70.14 Other vaginotomy ♀

HCPCS Level II Supplies & Services

A4305 Disposable drug delivery system, flow rate of 50 ml or greater per hour

57020

57020 Colpocentesis (separate procedure)

ICD-9-CM Diagnostic

184.0 Malignant neoplasm of vagina ♀
198.82 Secondary malignant neoplasm of genital organs
221.1 Benign neoplasm of vagina ♀
233.30 Carcinoma in situ, unspecified female genital organ ♀
233.31 Carcinoma in situ, vagina ♀
233.32 Carcinoma in situ, vulva ♀
233.39 Carcinoma in situ, other female genital organ ♀
236.3 Neoplasm of uncertain behavior of other and unspecified female genital organs ♀
239.5 Neoplasm of unspecified nature of other genitourinary organs
614.3 Acute parametritis and pelvic cellulitis — (Use additional code to identify organism: 041.00-041.09, 041.10-041.19) ♀
614.4 Chronic or unspecified parametritis and pelvic cellulitis — (Use additional code to identify organism: 041.00-041.09, 041.10-041.19) ♀
614.5 Acute or unspecified pelvic peritonitis, female — (Use additional code to identify organism: 041.00-041.09, 041.10-041.19) ♀
614.7 Other chronic pelvic peritonitis, female — (Use additional code to identify organism: 041.00-041.09, 041.10-041.19) ♀
614.8 Other specified inflammatory disease of female pelvic organs and tissues — (Use additional code to identify organism: 041.00-041.09, 041.10-041.19) ♀
614.9 Unspecified inflammatory disease of female pelvic organs and tissues — (Use additional code to identify organism: 041.00-041.09, 041.10-041.19) ♀
752.40 Unspecified congenital anomaly of cervix, vagina, and external female genitalia ♀
752.41 Embryonic cyst of cervix, vagina, and external female genitalia ♀
752.49 Other congenital anomaly of cervix, vagina, and external female genitalia ♀
878.6 Open wound of vagina, without mention of complication ♀
878.7 Open wound of vagina, complicated ♀

ICD-9-CM Procedural

70.0 Culdocentesis ♀

HCPCS Level II Supplies & Services

A4305 Disposable drug delivery system, flow rate of 50 ml or greater per hour

57022-57023

57022 Incision and drainage of vaginal hematoma; obstetrical/postpartum
57023 non-obstetrical (eg, post-trauma, spontaneous bleeding)

ICD-9-CM Diagnostic

623.6 Vaginal hematoma ♀
665.70 Pelvic hematoma, unspecified as to episode of care ♀
665.71 Pelvic hematoma, with delivery ♀
665.72 Pelvic hematoma, delivered with postpartum complication ♀
665.74 Pelvic hematoma, postpartum condition or complication ♀
922.4 Contusion of genital organs

ICD-9-CM Procedural

70.14 Other vaginotomy ♀
75.91 Evacuation of obstetrical incisional hematoma of perineum ♀
75.92 Evacuation of other hematoma of vulva or vagina ♀

57061-57065

57061 Destruction of vaginal lesion(s); simple (eg, laser surgery, electrosurgery, cryosurgery, chemosurgery)
57065 extensive (eg, laser surgery, electrosurgery, cryosurgery, chemosurgery)

ICD-9-CM Diagnostic

078.11 Condyloma acuminatum
078.19 Other specified viral warts
184.0 Malignant neoplasm of vagina ♀
198.82 Secondary malignant neoplasm of genital organs
221.1 Benign neoplasm of vagina ♀
236.3 Neoplasm of uncertain behavior of other and unspecified female genital organs ♀
239.5 Neoplasm of unspecified nature of other genitourinary organs
616.81 Mucositis (ulcerative) of cervix, vagina, and vulva — (Use additional code to identify organism: 041.00-041.09, 041.10-041.19) (Use additional E code to identify adverse effects of therapy: E879.2, E930.7, E933.1) ♀
616.89 Other inflammatory disease of cervix, vagina and vulva — (Use additional code to identify organism: 041.00-041.09, 041.10-041.19) ♀
616.9 Unspecified inflammatory disease of cervix, vagina, and vulva — (Use additional code to identify organism: 041.00-041.09, 041.10-041.19) ♀
623.0 Dysplasia of vagina ♀
623.1 Leukoplakia of vagina ♀
623.5 Leukorrhea, not specified as infective ♀
623.7 Polyp of vagina ♀
623.8 Other specified noninflammatory disorder of vagina ♀
624.01 Vulvar intraepithelial neoplasia I [VIN I] ♀
624.02 Vulvar intraepithelial neoplasia II [VIN II] ♀
624.09 Other dystrophy of vulva ♀
624.8 Other specified noninflammatory disorder of vulva and perineum ♀
701.5 Other abnormal granulation tissue
795.05 Cervical high risk human papillomavirus (HPV) DNA test positive ♀

ICD-9-CM Procedural

70.13 Lysis of intraluminal adhesions of vagina ♀
70.32 Excision or destruction of lesion of cul-de-sac ♀
70.33 Excision or destruction of lesion of vagina ♀

HCPCS Level II Supplies & Services

A4305 Disposable drug delivery system, flow rate of 50 ml or greater per hour

57100-57105

57100 Biopsy of vaginal mucosa; simple (separate procedure)
57105 extensive, requiring suture (including cysts)

ICD-9-CM Diagnostic

054.11 Herpetic vulvovaginitis ♀
078.11 Condyloma acuminatum
078.19 Other specified viral warts
098.0 Gonococcal infection (acute) of lower genitourinary tract
184.0 Malignant neoplasm of vagina ♀
198.82 Secondary malignant neoplasm of genital organs
221.1 Benign neoplasm of vagina ♀
236.3 Neoplasm of uncertain behavior of other and unspecified female genital organs ♀
239.5 Neoplasm of unspecified nature of other genitourinary organs
616.10 Unspecified vaginitis and vulvovaginitis — (Use additional code to identify organism, such as: 041.00-041.09, 041.10-041.19, 041.41-041.49) ♀
616.81 Mucositis (ulcerative) of cervix, vagina, and vulva — (Use additional code to identify organism: 041.00-041.09, 041.10-041.19) (Use additional E code to identify adverse effects of therapy: E879.2, E930.7, E933.1) ♀
616.89 Other inflammatory disease of cervix, vagina and vulva — (Use additional code to identify organism: 041.00-041.09, 041.10-041.19) ♀

623.0 Dysplasia of vagina ♀
623.1 Leukoplakia of vagina ♀
623.5 Leukorrhea, not specified as infective ♀
623.7 Polyp of vagina ♀
623.8 Other specified noninflammatory disorder of vagina ♀
625.8 Other specified symptom associated with female genital organs ♀
627.3 Postmenopausal atrophic vaginitis ♀
698.1 Pruritus of genital organs
701.5 Other abnormal granulation tissue
752.41 Embryonic cyst of cervix, vagina, and external female genitalia ♀
752.49 Other congenital anomaly of cervix, vagina, and external female genitalia ♀
795.00 Abnormal glandular Papanicolaou smear of cervix ♀
795.01 Papanicolaou smear of cervix with atypical squamous cells of undetermined significance (ASC-US) ♀
795.02 Papanicolaou smear of cervix with atypical squamous cells cannot exclude high grade squamous intraepithelial lesion (ASC-H) ♀
795.03 Papanicolaou smear of cervix with low grade squamous intraepithelial lesion (LGSIL) ♀
795.04 Papanicolaou smear of cervix with high grade squamous intraepithelial lesion (HGSIL) ♀
795.05 Cervical high risk human papillomavirus (HPV) DNA test positive ♀
795.07 Satisfactory cervical smear but lacking transformation zone ♀
795.08 Unsatisfactory cervical cytology smear ♀
795.09 Other abnormal Papanicolaou smear of cervix and cervical HPV — (Use additional code for associated human papillomavirus: 079.4) ♀
795.10 Abnormal glandular Papanicolaou smear of vagina — (Use additional code to identify acquired absence of uterus and cervix, if applicable: V88.01-V88.03) ♀
795.11 Papanicolaou smear of vagina with atypical squamous cells of undetermined significance (ASC-US) — (Use additional code to identify acquired absence of uterus and cervix, if applicable: V88.01-V88.03) ♀
795.12 Papanicolaou smear of vagina with atypical squamous cells cannot exclude high grade squamous intraepithelial lesion (ASC-H) — (Use additional code to identify acquired absence of uterus and cervix, if applicable: V88.01-V88.03) ♀
795.13 Papanicolaou smear of vagina with low grade squamous intraepithelial lesion (LGSIL) — (Use additional code to identify acquired absence of uterus and cervix, if applicable: V88.01-V88.03) ♀
795.14 Papanicolaou smear of vagina with high grade squamous intraepithelial lesion (HGSIL) — (Use additional code to identify acquired absence of uterus and cervix, if applicable: V88.01-V88.03) ♀
795.15 Vaginal high risk human papillomavirus (HPV) DNA test positive — (Use additional code to identify acquired absence of uterus and cervix, if applicable: V88.01-V88.03) ♀
795.16 Papanicolaou smear of vagina with cytologic evidence of malignancy — (Use additional code to identify acquired absence of uterus and cervix, if applicable: V88.01-V88.03) ♀
795.18 Unsatisfactory vaginal cytology smear — (Use additional code to identify acquired absence of uterus and cervix, if applicable: V88.01-V88.03) ♀
795.19 Other abnormal Papanicolaou smear of vagina and vaginal HPV — (Use additional code to identify acquired absence of uterus and cervix, if applicable: V88.01-V88.03) (Use additional code for associated human papillomavirus: 079.4) ♀
V67.1 Radiotherapy follow-up examination

ICD-9-CM Procedural

70.23 Biopsy of cul-de-sac ♀
70.24 Vaginal biopsy ♀

57106-57109

57106 Vaginectomy, partial removal of vaginal wall;
57107 with removal of paravaginal tissue (radical vaginectomy)
57109 with removal of paravaginal tissue (radical vaginectomy) with bilateral total pelvic lymphadenectomy and para-aortic lymph node sampling (biopsy)

ICD-9-CM Diagnostic

184.0 Malignant neoplasm of vagina ♀
184.1 Malignant neoplasm of labia majora ♀
184.2 Malignant neoplasm of labia minora ♀
184.4 Malignant neoplasm of vulva, unspecified site ▽ ♀
184.8 Malignant neoplasm of other specified sites of female genital organs ♀
184.9 Malignant neoplasm of female genital organ, site unspecified ▽ ♀
196.2 Secondary and unspecified malignant neoplasm of intra-abdominal lymph nodes
198.82 Secondary malignant neoplasm of genital organs
221.1 Benign neoplasm of vagina ♀
233.30 Carcinoma in situ, unspecified female genital organ ▽ ♀
233.31 Carcinoma in situ, vagina ♀
233.32 Carcinoma in situ, vulva ♀
233.39 Carcinoma in situ, other female genital organ ♀
236.3 Neoplasm of uncertain behavior of other and unspecified female genital organs ▽ ♀
239.5 Neoplasm of unspecified nature of other genitourinary organs
616.10 Unspecified vaginitis and vulvovaginitis — (Use additional code to identify organism, such as: 041.00-041.09, 041.10-041.19, 041.41-041.49) ▽ ♀
616.11 Vaginitis and vulvovaginitis in diseases classified elsewhere — (Use additional code to identify organism: 041.00-041.09, 041.10-041.19) (Code first underlying disease: 127.4) ☒ ♀
616.89 Other inflammatory disease of cervix, vagina and vulva — (Use additional code to identify organism: 041.00-041.09, 041.10-041.19) ♀
616.9 Unspecified inflammatory disease of cervix, vagina, and vulva — (Use additional code to identify organism: 041.00-041.09, 041.10-041.19) ▽ ♀
618.00 Unspecified prolapse of vaginal walls without mention of uterine prolapse — (Use additional code to identify urinary incontinence: 625.6, 788.31, 788.33-788.39) ▽ ♀
618.09 Other prolapse of vaginal walls without mention of uterine prolapse — (Use additional code to identify urinary incontinence: 625.6, 788.31, 788.33-788.39) ♀
618.4 Uterovaginal prolapse, unspecified — (Use additional code to identify urinary incontinence: 625.6, 788.31, 788.33-788.39) ▽ ♀
618.84 Cervical stump prolapse — (Use additional code to identify urinary incontinence: 625.6, 788.31, 788.33-788.39) ♀
618.89 Other specified genital prolapse — (Use additional code to identify urinary incontinence: 625.6, 788.31, 788.33-788.39) ♀
623.2 Stricture or atresia of vagina — (Use additional E code to identify any external cause) ♀
752.49 Other congenital anomaly of cervix, vagina, and external female genitalia ♀
V84.02 Genetic susceptibility to malignant neoplasm of ovary — (Use additional code, if applicable, for any associated family history of the disease: V16-V19. Code first, if applicable, any current malignant neoplasms: 140.0-195.8, 200.0-208.9, 230.0-234.9. Use additional code, if applicable, for any personal history of malignant neoplasm: V10.0-V10.9) ♀
V84.04 Genetic susceptibility to malignant neoplasm of endometrium — (Use additional code, if applicable, for any associated family history of the disease: V16-V19. Code first, if applicable, any current malignant neoplasms: 140.0-195.8, 200.0-208.9, 230.0-234.9. Use additional code, if applicable, for any personal history of malignant neoplasm: V10.0-V10.9) ♀
V84.09 Genetic susceptibility to other malignant neoplasm — (Use additional code, if applicable, for any associated family history of the disease: V16-V19. Code first, if applicable, any current malignant neoplasms: 140.0-195.8, 200.0-208.9, 230.0-234.9. Use additional code, if applicable, for any personal history of malignant neoplasm: V10.0-V10.9)

ICD-9-CM Procedural

40.3 Regional lymph node excision
70.4 Obliteration and total excision of vagina ♀

57110-57112

57110 Vaginectomy, complete removal of vaginal wall;
57111 with removal of paravaginal tissue (radical vaginectomy)
57112 with removal of paravaginal tissue (radical vaginectomy) with bilateral total pelvic lymphadenectomy and para-aortic lymph node sampling (biopsy)

ICD-9-CM Diagnostic

184.0 Malignant neoplasm of vagina ♀
184.1 Malignant neoplasm of labia majora ♀
184.2 Malignant neoplasm of labia minora ♀
184.4 Malignant neoplasm of vulva, unspecified site ▽ ♀
184.8 Malignant neoplasm of other specified sites of female genital organs ♀
184.9 Malignant neoplasm of female genital organ, site unspecified ▽ ♀
196.2 Secondary and unspecified malignant neoplasm of intra-abdominal lymph nodes
198.82 Secondary malignant neoplasm of genital organs
221.1 Benign neoplasm of vagina ♀
233.30 Carcinoma in situ, unspecified female genital organ ▽ ♀
233.31 Carcinoma in situ, vagina ♀
233.32 Carcinoma in situ, vulva ♀
233.39 Carcinoma in situ, other female genital organ ♀
236.3 Neoplasm of uncertain behavior of other and unspecified female genital organs ▽ ♀
239.5 Neoplasm of unspecified nature of other genitourinary organs
616.10 Unspecified vaginitis and vulvovaginitis — (Use additional code to identify organism, such as: 041.00-041.09, 041.10-041.19, 041.41-041.49) ▽ ♀
616.11 Vaginitis and vulvovaginitis in diseases classified elsewhere — (Use additional code to identify organism: 041.00-041.09, 041.10-041.19) (Code first underlying disease: 127.4) ☒ ♀
616.89 Other inflammatory disease of cervix, vagina and vulva — (Use additional code to identify organism: 041.00-041.09, 041.10-041.19) ♀
616.9 Unspecified inflammatory disease of cervix, vagina, and vulva — (Use additional code to identify organism: 041.00-041.09, 041.10-041.19) ▽ ♀
618.00 Unspecified prolapse of vaginal walls without mention of uterine prolapse — (Use additional code to identify urinary incontinence: 625.6, 788.31, 788.33-788.39) ▽ ♀
618.05 Perineocele without mention of uterine prolapse — (Use additional code to identify urinary incontinence: 625.6, 788.31, 788.33-788.39) ♀
618.09 Other prolapse of vaginal walls without mention of uterine prolapse — (Use additional code to identify urinary incontinence: 625.6, 788.31, 788.33-788.39) ♀
618.4 Uterovaginal prolapse, unspecified — (Use additional code to identify urinary incontinence: 625.6, 788.31, 788.33-788.39) ▽ ♀
618.84 Cervical stump prolapse — (Use additional code to identify urinary incontinence: 625.6, 788.31, 788.33-788.39) ♀
623.2 Stricture or atresia of vagina — (Use additional E code to identify any external cause) ♀
752.49 Other congenital anomaly of cervix, vagina, and external female genitalia ♀
V84.01 Genetic susceptibility to malignant neoplasm of breast — (Use additional code, if applicable, for any associated family history of the disease: V16-V19. Code first, if applicable, any current malignant neoplasms: 140.0-195.8, 200.0-208.9, 230.0-234.9. Use additional code, if applicable, for any personal history of malignant neoplasm: V10.0-V10.9)
V84.02 Genetic susceptibility to malignant neoplasm of ovary — (Use additional code, if applicable, for any associated family history of the disease: V16-V19. Code first, if applicable, any current malignant neoplasms: 140.0-195.8, 200.0-208.9, 230.0-234.9. Use additional code, if applicable, for any personal history of malignant neoplasm: V10.0-V10.9) ♀
V84.04 Genetic susceptibility to malignant neoplasm of endometrium — (Use additional code, if applicable, for any associated family history of the disease: V16-V19. Code first, if applicable, any current malignant neoplasms: 140.0-195.8, 200.0-208.9, 230.0-234.9. Use additional code, if applicable, for any personal history of malignant neoplasm: V10.0-V10.9) ♀
V84.09 Genetic susceptibility to other malignant neoplasm — (Use additional code, if applicable, for any associated family history of the disease: V16-V19. Code first, if applicable, any current malignant neoplasms: 140.0-195.8, 200.0-208.9, 230.0-234.9. Use additional code, if applicable, for any personal history of malignant neoplasm: V10.0-V10.9)

ICD-9-CM Procedural

40.3 Regional lymph node excision
70.4 Obliteration and total excision of vagina ♀

57120

57120 Colpocleisis (Le Fort type)

ICD-9-CM Diagnostic

184.0 Malignant neoplasm of vagina ♀
198.82 Secondary malignant neoplasm of genital organs
221.1 Benign neoplasm of vagina ♀
233.30 Carcinoma in situ, unspecified female genital organ ▽ ♀
233.31 Carcinoma in situ, vagina ♀
233.32 Carcinoma in situ, vulva ♀
233.39 Carcinoma in situ, other female genital organ ♀
236.3 Neoplasm of uncertain behavior of other and unspecified female genital organs ▽ ♀
239.5 Neoplasm of unspecified nature of other genitourinary organs
618.00 Unspecified prolapse of vaginal walls without mention of uterine prolapse — (Use additional code to identify urinary incontinence: 625.6, 788.31, 788.33-788.39) ▽ ♀
618.01 Cystocele without mention of uterine prolapse, midline — (Use additional code to identify urinary incontinence: 625.6, 788.31, 788.33-788.39) ♀
618.02 Cystocele without mention of uterine prolapse, lateral — (Use additional code to identify urinary incontinence: 625.6, 788.31, 788.33-788.39) ♀
618.05 Perineocele without mention of uterine prolapse — (Use additional code to identify urinary incontinence: 625.6, 788.31, 788.33-788.39) ♀
618.09 Other prolapse of vaginal walls without mention of uterine prolapse — (Use additional code to identify urinary incontinence: 625.6, 788.31, 788.33-788.39) ♀
618.4 Uterovaginal prolapse, unspecified — (Use additional code to identify urinary incontinence: 625.6, 788.31, 788.33-788.39) ▽ ♀
618.84 Cervical stump prolapse — (Use additional code to identify urinary incontinence: 625.6, 788.31, 788.33-788.39) ♀
752.49 Other congenital anomaly of cervix, vagina, and external female genitalia ♀

ICD-9-CM Procedural

70.8 Obliteration of vaginal vault ♀

57130

57130 Excision of vaginal septum

ICD-9-CM Diagnostic

752.49 Other congenital anomaly of cervix, vagina, and external female genitalia ♀

ICD-9-CM Procedural

70.33 Excision or destruction of lesion of vagina ♀

HCPCS Level II Supplies & Services

A4305 Disposable drug delivery system, flow rate of 50 ml or greater per hour

57135

57135 Excision of vaginal cyst or tumor

ICD-9-CM Diagnostic

184.0 Malignant neoplasm of vagina ♀
198.82 Secondary malignant neoplasm of genital organs
221.1 Benign neoplasm of vagina ♀
233.30 Carcinoma in situ, unspecified female genital organ ▽ ♀
233.31 Carcinoma in situ, vagina ♀
233.32 Carcinoma in situ, vulva ♀
233.39 Carcinoma in situ, other female genital organ ♀

236.3 Neoplasm of uncertain behavior of other and unspecified female genital organs ♀
239.5 Neoplasm of unspecified nature of other genitourinary organs
623.7 Polyp of vagina ♀
623.8 Other specified noninflammatory disorder of vagina ♀
752.41 Embryonic cyst of cervix, vagina, and external female genitalia ♀

ICD-9-CM Procedural

70.33 Excision or destruction of lesion of vagina ♀

HCPCS Level II Supplies & Services

A4305 Disposable drug delivery system, flow rate of 50 ml or greater per hour

57150

57150 Irrigation of vagina and/or application of medicament for treatment of bacterial, parasitic, or fungoid disease

ICD-9-CM Diagnostic

054.11 Herpetic vulvovaginitis ♀
112.1 Candidiasis of vulva and vagina — (Use additional code to identify manifestation: 321.0-321.1, 380.15, 711.6) ♀
127.4 Enterobiasis
131.01 Trichomonal vulvovaginitis ♀
616.0 Cervicitis and endocervicitis — (Use additional code to identify organism: 041.00-041.09, 041.10-041.19) ♀
616.10 Unspecified vaginitis and vulvovaginitis — (Use additional code to identify organism, such as: 041.00-041.09, 041.10-041.19, 041.41-041.49) ♀
616.11 Vaginitis and vulvovaginitis in diseases classified elsewhere — (Use additional code to identify organism: 041.00-041.09, 041.10-041.19) (Code first underlying disease: 127.4) ♀
616.81 Mucositis (ulcerative) of cervix, vagina, and vulva — (Use additional code to identify organism: 041.00-041.09, 041.10-041.19) (Use additional E code to identify adverse effects of therapy: E879.2, E930.7, E933.1) ♀
623.5 Leukorrhea, not specified as infective ♀

ICD-9-CM Procedural

96.44 Vaginal douche ♀
96.49 Other genitourinary instillation

57155

57155 Insertion of uterine tandem and/or vaginal ovoids for clinical brachytherapy

ICD-9-CM Diagnostic

179 Malignant neoplasm of uterus, part unspecified ♀
180.0 Malignant neoplasm of endocervix ♀
180.1 Malignant neoplasm of exocervix ♀
180.8 Malignant neoplasm of other specified sites of cervix ♀
180.9 Malignant neoplasm of cervix uteri, unspecified site ♀
182.0 Malignant neoplasm of corpus uteri, except isthmus ♀
182.1 Malignant neoplasm of isthmus ♀
182.8 Malignant neoplasm of other specified sites of body of uterus ♀
184.0 Malignant neoplasm of vagina ♀
184.8 Malignant neoplasm of other specified sites of female genital organs ♀
184.9 Malignant neoplasm of female genital organ, site unspecified ♀
198.82 Secondary malignant neoplasm of genital organs
233.1 Carcinoma in situ of cervix uteri ♀
233.2 Carcinoma in situ of other and unspecified parts of uterus ♀
233.30 Carcinoma in situ, unspecified female genital organ ♀
233.31 Carcinoma in situ, vagina ♀
233.32 Carcinoma in situ, vulva ♀
233.39 Carcinoma in situ, other female genital organ ♀
236.0 Neoplasm of uncertain behavior of uterus ♀
236.3 Neoplasm of uncertain behavior of other and unspecified female genital organs ♀

ICD-9-CM Procedural

92.27 Implantation or insertion of radioactive elements

57156

57156 Insertion of a vaginal radiation afterloading apparatus for clinical brachytherapy

ICD-9-CM Diagnostic

179 Malignant neoplasm of uterus, part unspecified ♀
180.0 Malignant neoplasm of endocervix ♀
180.1 Malignant neoplasm of exocervix ♀
180.8 Malignant neoplasm of other specified sites of cervix ♀
180.9 Malignant neoplasm of cervix uteri, unspecified site ♀
182.0 Malignant neoplasm of corpus uteri, except isthmus ♀
182.1 Malignant neoplasm of isthmus ♀
182.8 Malignant neoplasm of other specified sites of body of uterus ♀
184.0 Malignant neoplasm of vagina ♀
184.8 Malignant neoplasm of other specified sites of female genital organs ♀
184.9 Malignant neoplasm of female genital organ, site unspecified ♀
198.82 Secondary malignant neoplasm of genital organs
233.1 Carcinoma in situ of cervix uteri ♀
233.2 Carcinoma in situ of other and unspecified parts of uterus ♀
233.30 Carcinoma in situ, unspecified female genital organ ♀
233.31 Carcinoma in situ, vagina ♀
233.32 Carcinoma in situ, vulva ♀
233.39 Carcinoma in situ, other female genital organ ♀
236.0 Neoplasm of uncertain behavior of uterus ♀
236.3 Neoplasm of uncertain behavior of other and unspecified female genital organs ♀

ICD-9-CM Procedural

92.27 Implantation or insertion of radioactive elements

57160

57160 Fitting and insertion of pessary or other intravaginal support device

ICD-9-CM Diagnostic

618.00 Unspecified prolapse of vaginal walls without mention of uterine prolapse — (Use additional code to identify urinary incontinence: 625.6, 788.31, 788.33-788.39) ♀
618.01 Cystocele without mention of uterine prolapse, midline — (Use additional code to identify urinary incontinence: 625.6, 788.31, 788.33-788.39) ♀
618.02 Cystocele without mention of uterine prolapse, lateral — (Use additional code to identify urinary incontinence: 625.6, 788.31, 788.33-788.39) ♀
618.03 Urethrocele without mention of uterine prolapse — (Use additional code to identify urinary incontinence: 625.6, 788.31, 788.33-788.39) ♀
618.04 Rectocele without mention of uterine prolapse — (Use additional code to identify urinary incontinence: 625.6, 788.31, 788.33-788.39) (Use additional code for any associated fecal incontinence: 787.60-787.63) ♀
618.05 Perineocele without mention of uterine prolapse — (Use additional code to identify urinary incontinence: 625.6, 788.31, 788.33-788.39) ♀
618.09 Other prolapse of vaginal walls without mention of uterine prolapse — (Use additional code to identify urinary incontinence: 625.6, 788.31, 788.33-788.39) ♀
618.1 Uterine prolapse without mention of vaginal wall prolapse — (Use additional code to identify urinary incontinence: 625.6, 788.31, 788.33-788.39) ♀
618.2 Uterovaginal prolapse, incomplete — (Use additional code to identify urinary incontinence: 625.6, 788.31, 788.33-788.39) ♀
618.3 Uterovaginal prolapse, complete — (Use additional code to identify urinary incontinence: 625.6, 788.31, 788.33-788.39) ♀
618.4 Uterovaginal prolapse, unspecified — (Use additional code to identify urinary incontinence: 625.6, 788.31, 788.33-788.39) ♀

618.5 Prolapse of vaginal vault after hysterectomy — (Use additional code to identify urinary incontinence: 625.6, 788.31, 788.33-788.39) ♀

618.6 Vaginal enterocele, congenital or acquired — (Use additional code to identify urinary incontinence: 625.6, 788.31, 788.33-788.39) ♀

618.81 Incompetence or weakening of pubocervical tissue — (Use additional code to identify urinary incontinence: 625.6, 788.31, 788.33-788.39) ♀

618.82 Incompetence or weakening of rectovaginal tissue — (Use additional code to identify urinary incontinence: 625.6, 788.31, 788.33-788.39) ♀

618.83 Pelvic muscle wasting — (Use additional code to identify urinary incontinence: 625.6, 788.31, 788.33-788.39) ♀

618.84 Cervical stump prolapse — (Use additional code to identify urinary incontinence: 625.6, 788.31, 788.33-788.39) ♀

618.89 Other specified genital prolapse — (Use additional code to identify urinary incontinence: 625.6, 788.31, 788.33-788.39) ♀

618.9 Unspecified genital prolapse — (Use additional code to identify urinary incontinence: 625.6, 788.31, 788.33-788.39) ▽ ♀

625.6 Female stress incontinence ♀

878.6 Open wound of vagina, without mention of complication ♀

878.7 Open wound of vagina, complicated ♀

ICD-9-CM Procedural

96.18 Insertion of other vaginal pessary ♀

97.25 Replacement of other vaginal pessary ♀

57170

57170 Diaphragm or cervical cap fitting with instructions

ICD-9-CM Diagnostic

V24.2 Routine postpartum follow-up ♀

V25.02 General counseling for initiation of other contraceptive measures

V25.09 Other general counseling and advice for contraceptive management

V25.49 Surveillance of other previously prescribed contraceptive method

ICD-9-CM Procedural

96.17 Insertion of vaginal diaphragm ♀

97.24 Replacement and refitting of vaginal diaphragm ♀

HCPCS Level II Supplies & Services

A4261 Cervical cap for contraceptive use

57180

57180 Introduction of any hemostatic agent or pack for spontaneous or traumatic nonobstetrical vaginal hemorrhage (separate procedure)

ICD-9-CM Diagnostic

623.8 Other specified noninflammatory disorder of vagina ♀

626.9 Unspecified disorder of menstruation and other abnormal bleeding from female genital tract ▽ ♀

867.4 Uterus injury without mention of open wound into cavity ♀

878.6 Open wound of vagina, without mention of complication ♀

878.7 Open wound of vagina, complicated ♀

996.32 Mechanical complication due to intrauterine contraceptive device ♀

996.76 Other complications due to genitourinary device, implant, and graft — (Use additional code to identify complication: 338.18-338.19, 338.28-338.29)

998.11 Hemorrhage complicating a procedure

ICD-9-CM Procedural

96.14 Vaginal packing ♀

97.26 Replacement of vaginal or vulvar packing or drain ♀

57200-57210

57200 Colporrhaphy, suture of injury of vagina (nonobstetrical)

57210 Colpoperineorrhaphy, suture of injury of vagina and/or perineum (nonobstetrical)

ICD-9-CM Diagnostic

629.20 Female genital mutilation status, unspecified ▽ ♀

629.21 Female genital mutilation, Type I status ♀

629.22 Female genital mutilation, Type II status ♀

629.23 Female genital mutilation, Type III status ♀

629.29 Other female genital mutilation status ♀

878.4 Open wound of vulva, without mention of complication ♀

878.5 Open wound of vulva, complicated ♀

878.6 Open wound of vagina, without mention of complication ♀

878.7 Open wound of vagina, complicated ♀

878.8 Open wound of other and unspecified parts of genital organs, without mention of complication ▽

878.9 Open wound of other and unspecified parts of genital organs, complicated ▽

911.6 Trunk, superficial foreign body (splinter), without major open wound and without mention of infection

911.7 Trunk, superficial foreign body (splinter), without major open wound, infected

926.0 Crushing injury of external genitalia — (Use additional code to identify any associated injuries: 800-829, 850.0-854.1, 860.0-869.1)

939.2 Foreign body in vulva and vagina ♀

939.9 Foreign body in unspecified site in genitourinary tract ▽

959.14 Other injury of external genitals

995.53 Child sexual abuse — (Use additional code, if applicable, to identify any associated injuries. Use additional E code to identify nature of abuse, E960-E968, and perpetrator, E967.0-E967.9)

995.83 Adult sexual abuse — (Use additional code to identify any associated injury and perpetrator, E967.0-E967.9)

ICD-9-CM Procedural

70.71 Suture of laceration of vagina ♀

HCPCS Level II Supplies & Services

A4305 Disposable drug delivery system, flow rate of 50 ml or greater per hour

57220

57220 Plastic operation on urethral sphincter, vaginal approach (eg, Kelly urethral plication)

ICD-9-CM Diagnostic

599.81 Urethral hypermobility — (Use additional code to identify urinary incontinence: 625.6, 788.30-788.39)

599.82 Intrinsic (urethral) sphincter deficiency (ISD) — (Use additional code to identify urinary incontinence: 625.6, 788.30-788.39)

599.83 Urethral instability — (Use additional code to identify urinary incontinence: 625.6, 788.30-788.39)

599.84 Other specified disorders of urethra — (Use additional code to identify urinary incontinence: 625.6, 788.30-788.39)

599.89 Other specified disorders of urinary tract — (Use additional code to identify urinary incontinence: 625.6, 788.30-788.39)

625.6 Female stress incontinence ♀

ICD-9-CM Procedural

59.3 Plication of urethrovesical junction

57230

57230 Plastic repair of urethrocele

ICD-9-CM Diagnostic

618.00 Unspecified prolapse of vaginal walls without mention of uterine prolapse — (Use additional code to identify urinary incontinence: 625.6, 788.31, 788.33-788.39) ▽ ♀

618.01 Cystocele without mention of uterine prolapse, midline — (Use additional code to identify urinary incontinence: 625.6, 788.31, 788.33-788.39) ♀

618.02 Cystocele without mention of uterine prolapse, lateral — (Use additional code to identify urinary incontinence: 625.6, 788.31, 788.33-788.39) ♀

618.03 Urethrocele without mention of uterine prolapse — (Use additional code to identify urinary incontinence: 625.6, 788.31, 788.33-788.39) ♀

618.09 Other prolapse of vaginal walls without mention of uterine prolapse — (Use additional code to identify urinary incontinence: 625.6, 788.31, 788.33-788.39) ♀

618.2 Uterovaginal prolapse, incomplete — (Use additional code to identify urinary incontinence: 625.6, 788.31, 788.33-788.39) ♀

618.3 Uterovaginal prolapse, complete — (Use additional code to identify urinary incontinence: 625.6, 788.31, 788.33-788.39) ♀

618.4 Uterovaginal prolapse, unspecified — (Use additional code to identify urinary incontinence: 625.6, 788.31, 788.33-788.39) ▽ ♀

ICD-9-CM Procedural

70.51 Repair of cystocele ♀

57240

57240 Anterior colporrhaphy, repair of cystocele with or without repair of urethrocele

ICD-9-CM Diagnostic

618.00 Unspecified prolapse of vaginal walls without mention of uterine prolapse — (Use additional code to identify urinary incontinence: 625.6, 788.31, 788.33-788.39) ▽ ♀

618.01 Cystocele without mention of uterine prolapse, midline — (Use additional code to identify urinary incontinence: 625.6, 788.31, 788.33-788.39) ♀

618.02 Cystocele without mention of uterine prolapse, lateral — (Use additional code to identify urinary incontinence: 625.6, 788.31, 788.33-788.39) ♀

618.03 Urethrocele without mention of uterine prolapse — (Use additional code to identify urinary incontinence: 625.6, 788.31, 788.33-788.39) ♀

618.09 Other prolapse of vaginal walls without mention of uterine prolapse — (Use additional code to identify urinary incontinence: 625.6, 788.31, 788.33-788.39) ♀

618.2 Uterovaginal prolapse, incomplete — (Use additional code to identify urinary incontinence: 625.6, 788.31, 788.33-788.39) ♀

618.3 Uterovaginal prolapse, complete — (Use additional code to identify urinary incontinence: 625.6, 788.31, 788.33-788.39) ♀

618.4 Uterovaginal prolapse, unspecified — (Use additional code to identify urinary incontinence: 625.6, 788.31, 788.33-788.39) ▽ ♀

618.81 Incompetence or weakening of pubocervical tissue — (Use additional code to identify urinary incontinence: 625.6, 788.31, 788.33-788.39) ♀

618.82 Incompetence or weakening of rectovaginal tissue — (Use additional code to identify urinary incontinence: 625.6, 788.31, 788.33-788.39) ♀

618.83 Pelvic muscle wasting — (Use additional code to identify urinary incontinence: 625.6, 788.31, 788.33-788.39) ♀

618.89 Other specified genital prolapse — (Use additional code to identify urinary incontinence: 625.6, 788.31, 788.33-788.39) ♀

625.6 Female stress incontinence ♀

ICD-9-CM Procedural

70.51 Repair of cystocele ♀

57250

57250 Posterior colporrhaphy, repair of rectocele with or without perineorrhaphy

ICD-9-CM Diagnostic

618.00 Unspecified prolapse of vaginal walls without mention of uterine prolapse — (Use additional code to identify urinary incontinence: 625.6, 788.31, 788.33-788.39) ▽ ♀

618.04 Rectocele without mention of uterine prolapse — (Use additional code to identify urinary incontinence: 625.6, 788.31, 788.33-788.39) (Use additional code for any associated fecal incontinence: 787.60-787.63) ♀

618.05 Perineocele without mention of uterine prolapse — (Use additional code to identify urinary incontinence: 625.6, 788.31, 788.33-788.39) ♀

618.2 Uterovaginal prolapse, incomplete — (Use additional code to identify urinary incontinence: 625.6, 788.31, 788.33-788.39) ♀

618.3 Uterovaginal prolapse, complete — (Use additional code to identify urinary incontinence: 625.6, 788.31, 788.33-788.39) ♀

618.4 Uterovaginal prolapse, unspecified — (Use additional code to identify urinary incontinence: 625.6, 788.31, 788.33-788.39) ▽ ♀

618.5 Prolapse of vaginal vault after hysterectomy — (Use additional code to identify urinary incontinence: 625.6, 788.31, 788.33-788.39) ♀

618.6 Vaginal enterocele, congenital or acquired — (Use additional code to identify urinary incontinence: 625.6, 788.31, 788.33-788.39) ♀

618.7 Genital prolapse, old laceration of muscles of pelvic floor — (Use additional code to identify urinary incontinence: 625.6, 788.31, 788.33-788.39) ♀

618.82 Incompetence or weakening of rectovaginal tissue — (Use additional code to identify urinary incontinence: 625.6, 788.31, 788.33-788.39) ♀

625.6 Female stress incontinence ♀

788.33 Mixed incontinence urge and stress (male)(female) — (Code, if applicable, any causal condition first: 600.0-600.9, with fifth digit 1; 618.00-618.9; 753.23)

ICD-9-CM Procedural

70.52 Repair of rectocele ♀

57260-57265

57260 Combined anteroposterior colporrhaphy;
57265 with enterocele repair

ICD-9-CM Diagnostic

618.00 Unspecified prolapse of vaginal walls without mention of uterine prolapse — (Use additional code to identify urinary incontinence: 625.6, 788.31, 788.33-788.39) ▽ ♀

618.03 Urethrocele without mention of uterine prolapse — (Use additional code to identify urinary incontinence: 625.6, 788.31, 788.33-788.39) ♀

618.04 Rectocele without mention of uterine prolapse — (Use additional code to identify urinary incontinence: 625.6, 788.31, 788.33-788.39) (Use additional code for any associated fecal incontinence: 787.60-787.63) ♀

618.05 Perineocele without mention of uterine prolapse — (Use additional code to identify urinary incontinence: 625.6, 788.31, 788.33-788.39) ♀

618.09 Other prolapse of vaginal walls without mention of uterine prolapse — (Use additional code to identify urinary incontinence: 625.6, 788.31, 788.33-788.39) ♀

618.2 Uterovaginal prolapse, incomplete — (Use additional code to identify urinary incontinence: 625.6, 788.31, 788.33-788.39) ♀

618.3 Uterovaginal prolapse, complete — (Use additional code to identify urinary incontinence: 625.6, 788.31, 788.33-788.39) ♀

618.4 Uterovaginal prolapse, unspecified — (Use additional code to identify urinary incontinence: 625.6, 788.31, 788.33-788.39) ▽ ♀

618.5 Prolapse of vaginal vault after hysterectomy — (Use additional code to identify urinary incontinence: 625.6, 788.31, 788.33-788.39) ♀

618.6 Vaginal enterocele, congenital or acquired — (Use additional code to identify urinary incontinence: 625.6, 788.31, 788.33-788.39) ♀

618.7 Genital prolapse, old laceration of muscles of pelvic floor — (Use additional code to identify urinary incontinence: 625.6, 788.31, 788.33-788.39) ♀

618.81 Incompetence or weakening of pubocervical tissue — (Use additional code to identify urinary incontinence: 625.6, 788.31, 788.33-788.39) ♀

618.82 Incompetence or weakening of rectovaginal tissue — (Use additional code to identify urinary incontinence: 625.6, 788.31, 788.33-788.39) ♀

618.84 Cervical stump prolapse — (Use additional code to identify urinary incontinence: 625.6, 788.31, 788.33-788.39) ♀

618.89 Other specified genital prolapse — (Use additional code to identify urinary incontinence: 625.6, 788.31, 788.33-788.39) ♀

625.6 Female stress incontinence ♀

788.33 Mixed incontinence urge and stress (male)(female) — (Code, if applicable, any causal condition first: 600.0-600.9, with fifth digit 1; 618.00-618.9; 753.23)

ICD-9-CM Procedural

70.50 Repair of cystocele and rectocele ♀
70.92 Other operations on cul-de-sac ♀

57268-57270

57268 Repair of enterocele, vaginal approach (separate procedure)
57270 Repair of enterocele, abdominal approach (separate procedure)

ICD-9-CM Diagnostic

618.6 Vaginal enterocele, congenital or acquired — (Use additional code to identify urinary incontinence: 625.6, 788.31, 788.33-788.39) ♀
625.6 Female stress incontinence ♀

ICD-9-CM Procedural

70.92 Other operations on cul-de-sac ♀

57280

57280 Colpopexy, abdominal approach

ICD-9-CM Diagnostic

618.00 Unspecified prolapse of vaginal walls without mention of uterine prolapse — (Use additional code to identify urinary incontinence: 625.6, 788.31, 788.33-788.39) ▽ ♀
618.01 Cystocele without mention of uterine prolapse, midline — (Use additional code to identify urinary incontinence: 625.6, 788.31, 788.33-788.39) ♀
618.02 Cystocele without mention of uterine prolapse, lateral — (Use additional code to identify urinary incontinence: 625.6, 788.31, 788.33-788.39) ♀
618.03 Urethrocele without mention of uterine prolapse — (Use additional code to identify urinary incontinence: 625.6, 788.31, 788.33-788.39) ♀
618.04 Rectocele without mention of uterine prolapse — (Use additional code to identify urinary incontinence: 625.6, 788.31, 788.33-788.39) (Use additional code for any associated fecal incontinence: 787.60-787.63) ♀
618.05 Perineocele without mention of uterine prolapse — (Use additional code to identify urinary incontinence: 625.6, 788.31, 788.33-788.39) ♀
618.09 Other prolapse of vaginal walls without mention of uterine prolapse — (Use additional code to identify urinary incontinence: 625.6, 788.31, 788.33-788.39) ♀
618.1 Uterine prolapse without mention of vaginal wall prolapse — (Use additional code to identify urinary incontinence: 625.6, 788.31, 788.33-788.39) ♀
618.2 Uterovaginal prolapse, incomplete — (Use additional code to identify urinary incontinence: 625.6, 788.31, 788.33-788.39) ♀
618.3 Uterovaginal prolapse, complete — (Use additional code to identify urinary incontinence: 625.6, 788.31, 788.33-788.39) ♀
618.4 Uterovaginal prolapse, unspecified — (Use additional code to identify urinary incontinence: 625.6, 788.31, 788.33-788.39) ▽ ♀
618.5 Prolapse of vaginal vault after hysterectomy — (Use additional code to identify urinary incontinence: 625.6, 788.31, 788.33-788.39) ♀
618.81 Incompetence or weakening of pubocervical tissue — (Use additional code to identify urinary incontinence: 625.6, 788.31, 788.33-788.39) ♀
618.82 Incompetence or weakening of rectovaginal tissue — (Use additional code to identify urinary incontinence: 625.6, 788.31, 788.33-788.39) ♀
618.83 Pelvic muscle wasting — (Use additional code to identify urinary incontinence: 625.6, 788.31, 788.33-788.39) ♀
618.84 Cervical stump prolapse — (Use additional code to identify urinary incontinence: 625.6, 788.31, 788.33-788.39) ♀
618.89 Other specified genital prolapse — (Use additional code to identify urinary incontinence: 625.6, 788.31, 788.33-788.39) ♀
625.6 Female stress incontinence ♀

ICD-9-CM Procedural

70.77 Vaginal suspension and fixation ♀

57282-57283

57282 Colpopexy, vaginal; extra-peritoneal approach (sacrospinous, iliococcygeus)
57283 intra-peritoneal approach (uterosacral, levator myorrhaphy)

ICD-9-CM Diagnostic

618.00 Unspecified prolapse of vaginal walls without mention of uterine prolapse — (Use additional code to identify urinary incontinence: 625.6, 788.31, 788.33-788.39) ▽ ♀
618.01 Cystocele without mention of uterine prolapse, midline — (Use additional code to identify urinary incontinence: 625.6, 788.31, 788.33-788.39) ♀
618.02 Cystocele without mention of uterine prolapse, lateral — (Use additional code to identify urinary incontinence: 625.6, 788.31, 788.33-788.39) ♀
618.03 Urethrocele without mention of uterine prolapse — (Use additional code to identify urinary incontinence: 625.6, 788.31, 788.33-788.39) ♀
618.04 Rectocele without mention of uterine prolapse — (Use additional code to identify urinary incontinence: 625.6, 788.31, 788.33-788.39) (Use additional code for any associated fecal incontinence: 787.60-787.63) ♀
618.05 Perineocele without mention of uterine prolapse — (Use additional code to identify urinary incontinence: 625.6, 788.31, 788.33-788.39) ♀
618.09 Other prolapse of vaginal walls without mention of uterine prolapse — (Use additional code to identify urinary incontinence: 625.6, 788.31, 788.33-788.39) ♀
618.1 Uterine prolapse without mention of vaginal wall prolapse — (Use additional code to identify urinary incontinence: 625.6, 788.31, 788.33-788.39) ♀
618.2 Uterovaginal prolapse, incomplete — (Use additional code to identify urinary incontinence: 625.6, 788.31, 788.33-788.39) ♀
618.3 Uterovaginal prolapse, complete — (Use additional code to identify urinary incontinence: 625.6, 788.31, 788.33-788.39) ♀
618.4 Uterovaginal prolapse, unspecified — (Use additional code to identify urinary incontinence: 625.6, 788.31, 788.33-788.39) ▽ ♀
618.5 Prolapse of vaginal vault after hysterectomy — (Use additional code to identify urinary incontinence: 625.6, 788.31, 788.33-788.39) ♀
618.7 Genital prolapse, old laceration of muscles of pelvic floor — (Use additional code to identify urinary incontinence: 625.6, 788.31, 788.33-788.39) ♀
618.81 Incompetence or weakening of pubocervical tissue — (Use additional code to identify urinary incontinence: 625.6, 788.31, 788.33-788.39) ♀
618.82 Incompetence or weakening of rectovaginal tissue — (Use additional code to identify urinary incontinence: 625.6, 788.31, 788.33-788.39) ♀
618.83 Pelvic muscle wasting — (Use additional code to identify urinary incontinence: 625.6, 788.31, 788.33-788.39) ♀
618.84 Cervical stump prolapse — (Use additional code to identify urinary incontinence: 625.6, 788.31, 788.33-788.39) ♀
618.89 Other specified genital prolapse — (Use additional code to identify urinary incontinence: 625.6, 788.31, 788.33-788.39) ♀
625.6 Female stress incontinence ♀
788.30 Unspecified urinary incontinence — (Code, if applicable, any causal condition first: 600.0-600.9, with fifth digit 1; 618.00-618.9; 753.23) ▽
788.33 Mixed incontinence urge and stress (male)(female) — (Code, if applicable, any causal condition first: 600.0-600.9, with fifth digit 1; 618.00-618.9; 753.23)
788.38 Overflow incontinence — (Code, if applicable, any causal condition first: 600.0-600.9, with fifth digit 1; 618.00-618.9; 753.23)

ICD-9-CM Procedural

70.77 Vaginal suspension and fixation ♀

57284-57285

57284 Paravaginal defect repair (including repair of cystocele, if performed); open abdominal approach
57285 vaginal approach

ICD-9-CM Diagnostic

618.00 Unspecified prolapse of vaginal walls without mention of uterine prolapse — (Use additional code to identify urinary incontinence: 625.6, 788.31, 788.33-788.39) ▽ ♀

618.01 Cystocele without mention of uterine prolapse, midline — (Use additional code to identify urinary incontinence: 625.6, 788.31, 788.33-788.39) ♀

618.02 Cystocele without mention of uterine prolapse, lateral — (Use additional code to identify urinary incontinence: 625.6, 788.31, 788.33-788.39) ♀

618.03 Urethrocele without mention of uterine prolapse — (Use additional code to identify urinary incontinence: 625.6, 788.31, 788.33-788.39) ♀

618.04 Rectocele without mention of uterine prolapse — (Use additional code to identify urinary incontinence: 625.6, 788.31, 788.33-788.39) (Use additional code for any associated fecal incontinence: 787.60-787.63) ♀

618.05 Perineocele without mention of uterine prolapse — (Use additional code to identify urinary incontinence: 625.6, 788.31, 788.33-788.39) ♀

618.09 Other prolapse of vaginal walls without mention of uterine prolapse — (Use additional code to identify urinary incontinence: 625.6, 788.31, 788.33-788.39) ♀

618.1 Uterine prolapse without mention of vaginal wall prolapse — (Use additional code to identify urinary incontinence: 625.6, 788.31, 788.33-788.39) ♀

618.2 Uterovaginal prolapse, incomplete — (Use additional code to identify urinary incontinence: 625.6, 788.31, 788.33-788.39) ♀

618.3 Uterovaginal prolapse, complete — (Use additional code to identify urinary incontinence: 625.6, 788.31, 788.33-788.39) ♀

618.4 Uterovaginal prolapse, unspecified — (Use additional code to identify urinary incontinence: 625.6, 788.31, 788.33-788.39) ▽ ♀

618.5 Prolapse of vaginal vault after hysterectomy — (Use additional code to identify urinary incontinence: 625.6, 788.31, 788.33-788.39) ♀

618.82 Incompetence or weakening of rectovaginal tissue — (Use additional code to identify urinary incontinence: 625.6, 788.31, 788.33-788.39) ♀

618.83 Pelvic muscle wasting — (Use additional code to identify urinary incontinence: 625.6, 788.31, 788.33-788.39) ♀

618.84 Cervical stump prolapse — (Use additional code to identify urinary incontinence: 625.6, 788.31, 788.33-788.39) ♀

618.89 Other specified genital prolapse — (Use additional code to identify urinary incontinence: 625.6, 788.31, 788.33-788.39) ♀

625.6 Female stress incontinence ♀

ICD-9-CM Procedural

70.51 Repair of cystocele ♀

70.54 Repair of cystocele with graft or prosthesis ♀

70.77 Vaginal suspension and fixation ♀

70.78 Vaginal suspension and fixation with graft or prosthesis ♀

57287

57287 Removal or revision of sling for stress incontinence (eg, fascia or synthetic)

ICD-9-CM Diagnostic

625.6 Female stress incontinence ♀

996.39 Mechanical complication of genitourinary device, implant, and graft, other

996.65 Infection and inflammatory reaction due to other genitourinary device, implant, and graft — (Use additional code to identify specified infections)

996.76 Other complications due to genitourinary device, implant, and graft — (Use additional code to identify complication: 338.18-338.19, 338.28-338.29)

V53.6 Fitting and adjustment of urinary device

ICD-9-CM Procedural

59.79 Other repair of urinary stress incontinence

57288

57288 Sling operation for stress incontinence (eg, fascia or synthetic)

ICD-9-CM Diagnostic

625.6 Female stress incontinence ♀

ICD-9-CM Procedural

59.4 Suprapubic sling operation

59.71 Levator muscle operation for urethrovesical suspension

70.77 Vaginal suspension and fixation ♀

HCPCS Level II Supplies & Services

C1762 Connective tissue, human (includes fascia lata)

57289

57289 Pereyra procedure, including anterior colporrhaphy

ICD-9-CM Diagnostic

618.00 Unspecified prolapse of vaginal walls without mention of uterine prolapse — (Use additional code to identify urinary incontinence: 625.6, 788.31, 788.33-788.39) ▽ ♀

618.01 Cystocele without mention of uterine prolapse, midline — (Use additional code to identify urinary incontinence: 625.6, 788.31, 788.33-788.39) ♀

618.02 Cystocele without mention of uterine prolapse, lateral — (Use additional code to identify urinary incontinence: 625.6, 788.31, 788.33-788.39) ♀

618.03 Urethrocele without mention of uterine prolapse — (Use additional code to identify urinary incontinence: 625.6, 788.31, 788.33-788.39) ♀

618.05 Perineocele without mention of uterine prolapse — (Use additional code to identify urinary incontinence: 625.6, 788.31, 788.33-788.39) ♀

618.09 Other prolapse of vaginal walls without mention of uterine prolapse — (Use additional code to identify urinary incontinence: 625.6, 788.31, 788.33-788.39) ♀

618.1 Uterine prolapse without mention of vaginal wall prolapse — (Use additional code to identify urinary incontinence: 625.6, 788.31, 788.33-788.39) ♀

618.2 Uterovaginal prolapse, incomplete — (Use additional code to identify urinary incontinence: 625.6, 788.31, 788.33-788.39) ♀

618.3 Uterovaginal prolapse, complete — (Use additional code to identify urinary incontinence: 625.6, 788.31, 788.33-788.39) ♀

618.4 Uterovaginal prolapse, unspecified — (Use additional code to identify urinary incontinence: 625.6, 788.31, 788.33-788.39) ▽ ♀

618.84 Cervical stump prolapse — (Use additional code to identify urinary incontinence: 625.6, 788.31, 788.33-788.39) ♀

625.6 Female stress incontinence ♀

ICD-9-CM Procedural

59.6 Paraurethral suspension

70.51 Repair of cystocele ♀

57291-57292

57291 Construction of artificial vagina; without graft

57292 with graft

ICD-9-CM Diagnostic

184.0 Malignant neoplasm of vagina ♀

198.82 Secondary malignant neoplasm of genital organs

221.1 Benign neoplasm of vagina ♀

233.30 Carcinoma in situ, unspecified female genital organ ▽ ♀

233.31 Carcinoma in situ, vagina ♀

233.32 Carcinoma in situ, vulva ♀

233.39 Carcinoma in situ, other female genital organ ♀

236.3 Neoplasm of uncertain behavior of other and unspecified female genital organs ▽ ♀

239.5 Neoplasm of unspecified nature of other genitourinary organs

752.49 Other congenital anomaly of cervix, vagina, and external female genitalia ♀

959.12 Other injury of abdomen

959.19 Other injury of other sites of trunk

V51.8 Other aftercare involving the use of plastic surgery

ICD-9-CM Procedural

70.61 Vaginal construction ♀

70.63 Vaginal construction with graft or prosthesis

86.63 Full-thickness skin graft to other sites

86.69 Other skin graft to other sites

57295

57295 Revision (including removal) of prosthetic vaginal graft; vaginal approach

ICD-9-CM Diagnostic

054.11 Herpetic vulvovaginitis ♀
098.0 Gonococcal infection (acute) of lower genitourinary tract
098.2 Gonococcal infections, chronic, of lower genitourinary tract
099.53 Chlamydia trachomatis infection of lower genitourinary sites — (Use additional code to specify site of infection: 595.4, 616.0, 616.11)
112.1 Candidiasis of vulva and vagina — (Use additional code to identify manifestation: 321.0-321.1, 380.15, 711.6) ♀
184.0 Malignant neoplasm of vagina ♀
198.82 Secondary malignant neoplasm of genital organs
221.1 Benign neoplasm of vagina ♀
233.30 Carcinoma in situ, unspecified female genital organ ▽ ♀
233.31 Carcinoma in situ, vagina ♀
233.32 Carcinoma in situ, vulva ♀
233.39 Carcinoma in situ, other female genital organ ♀
236.3 Neoplasm of uncertain behavior of other and unspecified female genital organs ▽ ♀
239.5 Neoplasm of unspecified nature of other genitourinary organs
616.10 Unspecified vaginitis and vulvovaginitis — (Use additional code to identify organism, such as: 041.00-041.09, 041.10-041.19, 041.41-041.49) ▽ ♀
616.11 Vaginitis and vulvovaginitis in diseases classified elsewhere — (Use additional code to identify organism: 041.00-041.09, 041.10-041.19) (Code first underlying disease: 127.4) ☒ ♀
629.31 Erosion of implanted vaginal mesh and other prosthetic materials to surrounding organ or tissue ♀
629.32 Exposure of implanted vaginal mesh and other prosthetic materials into vagina ♀
752.49 Other congenital anomaly of cervix, vagina, and external female genitalia ♀
996.30 Mechanical complication of unspecified genitourinary device, implant, and graft ▽
996.39 Mechanical complication of genitourinary device, implant, and graft, other
996.52 Mechanical complication due to other tissue graft, not elsewhere classified
996.59 Mechanical complication due to other implant and internal device, not elsewhere classified
996.60 Infection and inflammatory reaction due to unspecified device, implant, and graft — (Use additional code to identify specified infections) ▽
996.65 Infection and inflammatory reaction due to other genitourinary device, implant, and graft — (Use additional code to identify specified infections)
996.70 Other complications due to unspecified device, implant, and graft — (Use additional code to identify complication: 338.18-338.19, 338.28-338.29) ▽
996.76 Other complications due to genitourinary device, implant, and graft — (Use additional code to identify complication: 338.18-338.19, 338.28-338.29)
V51.8 Other aftercare involving the use of plastic surgery

ICD-9-CM Procedural

70.14 Other vaginotomy ♀
70.62 Vaginal reconstruction ♀
70.64 Vaginal reconstruction with graft or prosthesis ♀
70.79 Other repair of vagina ♀
70.91 Other operations on vagina ♀

57296

57296 Revision (including removal) of prosthetic vaginal graft; open abdominal approach

ICD-9-CM Diagnostic

054.11 Herpetic vulvovaginitis ♀
098.0 Gonococcal infection (acute) of lower genitourinary tract
098.2 Gonococcal infections, chronic, of lower genitourinary tract
099.53 Chlamydia trachomatis infection of lower genitourinary sites — (Use additional code to specify site of infection: 595.4, 616.0, 616.11)
112.1 Candidiasis of vulva and vagina — (Use additional code to identify manifestation: 321.0-321.1, 380.15, 711.6) ♀
616.10 Unspecified vaginitis and vulvovaginitis — (Use additional code to identify organism, such as: 041.00-041.09, 041.10-041.19, 041.41-041.49) ▽ ♀
616.11 Vaginitis and vulvovaginitis in diseases classified elsewhere — (Use additional code to identify organism: 041.00-041.09, 041.10-041.19) (Code first underlying disease: 127.4) ☒ ♀
629.31 Erosion of implanted vaginal mesh and other prosthetic materials to surrounding organ or tissue ♀
629.32 Exposure of implanted vaginal mesh and other prosthetic materials into vagina ♀
752.49 Other congenital anomaly of cervix, vagina, and external female genitalia ♀
996.30 Mechanical complication of unspecified genitourinary device, implant, and graft ▽
996.39 Mechanical complication of genitourinary device, implant, and graft, other
996.52 Mechanical complication due to other tissue graft, not elsewhere classified
996.59 Mechanical complication due to other implant and internal device, not elsewhere classified
996.60 Infection and inflammatory reaction due to unspecified device, implant, and graft — (Use additional code to identify specified infections) ▽
996.65 Infection and inflammatory reaction due to other genitourinary device, implant, and graft — (Use additional code to identify specified infections)
996.70 Other complications due to unspecified device, implant, and graft — (Use additional code to identify complication: 338.18-338.19, 338.28-338.29) ▽
996.76 Other complications due to genitourinary device, implant, and graft — (Use additional code to identify complication: 338.18-338.19, 338.28-338.29)
V51.8 Other aftercare involving the use of plastic surgery

ICD-9-CM Procedural

70.79 Other repair of vagina ♀
70.91 Other operations on vagina ♀

57300

57300 Closure of rectovaginal fistula; vaginal or transanal approach

ICD-9-CM Diagnostic

619.1 Digestive-genital tract fistula, female ♀
677 Late effect of complication of pregnancy, childbirth, and the puerperium — (Code first any sequelae) ♀

ICD-9-CM Procedural

70.73 Repair of rectovaginal fistula ♀

57305-57307

57305 Closure of rectovaginal fistula; abdominal approach
57307 abdominal approach, with concomitant colostomy

ICD-9-CM Diagnostic

619.1 Digestive-genital tract fistula, female ♀
677 Late effect of complication of pregnancy, childbirth, and the puerperium — (Code first any sequelae) ♀

ICD-9-CM Procedural

46.10 Colostomy, not otherwise specified
70.73 Repair of rectovaginal fistula ♀

57308

57308 Closure of rectovaginal fistula; transperineal approach, with perineal body reconstruction, with or without levator plication

ICD-9-CM Diagnostic

619.1 Digestive-genital tract fistula, female ♀
677 Late effect of complication of pregnancy, childbirth, and the puerperium — (Code first any sequelae) ♀

ICD-9-CM Procedural

70.73 Repair of rectovaginal fistula ♀

57310-57311

57310 Closure of urethrovaginal fistula;
57311 with bulbocavernosus transplant

ICD-9-CM Diagnostic

619.0 Urinary-genital tract fistula, female ♀
677 Late effect of complication of pregnancy, childbirth, and the puerperium — (Code first any sequelae) ♀

ICD-9-CM Procedural

58.43 Closure of other fistula of urethra

57320-57330

57320 Closure of vesicovaginal fistula; vaginal approach
57330 transvesical and vaginal approach

ICD-9-CM Diagnostic

619.0 Urinary-genital tract fistula, female ♀
677 Late effect of complication of pregnancy, childbirth, and the puerperium — (Code first any sequelae) ♀

ICD-9-CM Procedural

57.84 Repair of other fistula of bladder

57335

57335 Vaginoplasty for intersex state

ICD-9-CM Diagnostic

255.2 Adrenogenital disorders
259.50 Androgen insensitivity, unspecified ▽
259.51 Androgen insensitivity syndrome
259.52 Partial androgen insensitivity
752.40 Unspecified congenital anomaly of cervix, vagina, and external female genitalia ▽ ♀
752.49 Other congenital anomaly of cervix, vagina, and external female genitalia ♀

ICD-9-CM Procedural

70.79 Other repair of vagina ♀

57400

57400 Dilation of vagina under anesthesia (other than local)

ICD-9-CM Diagnostic

616.81 Mucositis (ulcerative) of cervix, vagina, and vulva — (Use additional code to identify organism: 041.00-041.09, 041.10-041.19) (Use additional E code to identify adverse effects of therapy: E879.2, E930.7, E933.1) ♀
616.89 Other inflammatory disease of cervix, vagina and vulva — (Use additional code to identify organism: 041.00-041.09, 041.10-041.19) ♀
623.2 Stricture or atresia of vagina — (Use additional E code to identify any external cause) ♀
752.49 Other congenital anomaly of cervix, vagina, and external female genitalia ♀

ICD-9-CM Procedural

96.16 Other vaginal dilation ♀

HCPCS Level II Supplies & Services

A4305 Disposable drug delivery system, flow rate of 50 ml or greater per hour

57410

57410 Pelvic examination under anesthesia (other than local)

ICD-9-CM Diagnostic

179 Malignant neoplasm of uterus, part unspecified ▽ ♀
180.0 Malignant neoplasm of endocervix ♀
180.1 Malignant neoplasm of exocervix ♀
180.8 Malignant neoplasm of other specified sites of cervix ♀
182.0 Malignant neoplasm of corpus uteri, except isthmus ♀
182.1 Malignant neoplasm of isthmus ♀
182.8 Malignant neoplasm of other specified sites of body of uterus ♀
183.0 Malignant neoplasm of ovary — (Use additional code to identify any functional activity) ♀
183.8 Malignant neoplasm of other specified sites of uterine adnexa ♀
198.82 Secondary malignant neoplasm of genital organs
218.0 Submucous leiomyoma of uterus ♀
218.1 Intramural leiomyoma of uterus ♀
218.2 Subserous leiomyoma of uterus ♀
219.0 Benign neoplasm of cervix uteri ♀
219.1 Benign neoplasm of corpus uteri ♀
219.8 Benign neoplasm of other specified parts of uterus ♀
219.9 Benign neoplasm of uterus, part unspecified ▽ ♀
220 Benign neoplasm of ovary — (Use additional code to identify any functional activity: 256.0-256.1) ♀
233.1 Carcinoma in situ of cervix uteri ♀
233.2 Carcinoma in situ of other and unspecified parts of uterus ▽ ♀
236.0 Neoplasm of uncertain behavior of uterus ♀
236.2 Neoplasm of uncertain behavior of ovary — (Use additional code to identify any functional activity) ♀
239.5 Neoplasm of unspecified nature of other genitourinary organs
256.0 Hyperestrogenism ♀
614.1 Chronic salpingitis and oophoritis — (Use additional code to identify organism: 041.00-041.09, 041.10-041.19) ♀
614.6 Pelvic peritoneal adhesions, female (postoperative) (postinfection) — (Use additional code to identify organism: 041.00-041.09, 041.10-041.19) (Use additional code to identify any associated infertility: 628.2) ♀
614.9 Unspecified inflammatory disease of female pelvic organs and tissues — (Use additional code to identify organism: 041.00-041.09, 041.10-041.19) ▽ ♀
616.0 Cervicitis and endocervicitis — (Use additional code to identify organism: 041.00-041.09, 041.10-041.19) ♀
616.10 Unspecified vaginitis and vulvovaginitis — (Use additional code to identify organism, such as: 041.00-041.09, 041.10-041.19, 041.41-041.49) ▽ ♀
617.0 Endometriosis of uterus ♀
617.1 Endometriosis of ovary ♀
617.3 Endometriosis of pelvic peritoneum ♀
617.4 Endometriosis of rectovaginal septum and vagina ♀
617.5 Endometriosis of intestine ♀
618.00 Unspecified prolapse of vaginal walls without mention of uterine prolapse — (Use additional code to identify urinary incontinence: 625.6, 788.31, 788.33-788.39) ▽ ♀
618.09 Other prolapse of vaginal walls without mention of uterine prolapse — (Use additional code to identify urinary incontinence: 625.6, 788.31, 788.33-788.39) ♀
618.1 Uterine prolapse without mention of vaginal wall prolapse — (Use additional code to identify urinary incontinence: 625.6, 788.31, 788.33-788.39) ♀
618.81 Incompetence or weakening of pubocervical tissue — (Use additional code to identify urinary incontinence: 625.6, 788.31, 788.33-788.39) ♀
618.83 Pelvic muscle wasting — (Use additional code to identify urinary incontinence: 625.6, 788.31, 788.33-788.39) ♀
618.84 Cervical stump prolapse — (Use additional code to identify urinary incontinence: 625.6, 788.31, 788.33-788.39) ♀
618.89 Other specified genital prolapse — (Use additional code to identify urinary incontinence: 625.6, 788.31, 788.33-788.39) ♀
620.0 Follicular cyst of ovary ♀
620.1 Corpus luteum cyst or hematoma ♀
620.2 Other and unspecified ovarian cyst ▽ ♀

620.4 Prolapse or hernia of ovary and fallopian tube ♀
620.5 Torsion of ovary, ovarian pedicle, or fallopian tube ♀
620.8 Other noninflammatory disorder of ovary, fallopian tube, and broad ligament ♀
621.0 Polyp of corpus uteri ♀
621.1 Chronic subinvolution of uterus ♀
621.2 Hypertrophy of uterus ♀
621.30 Endometrial hyperplasia, unspecified ♀
621.31 Simple endometrial hyperplasia without atypia ♀
621.32 Complex endometrial hyperplasia without atypia ♀
621.33 Endometrial hyperplasia with atypia ♀
621.34 Benign endometrial hyperplasia ♀
621.35 Endometrial intraepithelial neoplasia [EIN] ♀
621.5 Intrauterine synechiae ♀
621.6 Malposition of uterus ♀
621.7 Chronic inversion of uterus ♀
621.8 Other specified disorders of uterus, not elsewhere classified ♀
622.10 Dysplasia of cervix, unspecified ♀
622.11 Mild dysplasia of cervix ♀
622.12 Moderate dysplasia of cervix ♀
622.4 Stricture and stenosis of cervix ♀
622.7 Mucous polyp of cervix ♀
623.5 Leukorrhea, not specified as infective ♀
623.7 Polyp of vagina ♀
623.8 Other specified noninflammatory disorder of vagina ♀
625.0 Dyspareunia ♀
625.1 Vaginismus ♀
625.3 Dysmenorrhea ♀
625.5 Pelvic congestion syndrome ♀
625.6 Female stress incontinence ♀
625.70 Vulvodynia, unspecified ♀
625.71 Vulvar vestibulitis ♀
625.79 Other vulvodynia ♀
625.8 Other specified symptom associated with female genital organs ♀
626.0 Absence of menstruation ♀
626.1 Scanty or infrequent menstruation ♀
626.2 Excessive or frequent menstruation ♀
626.4 Irregular menstrual cycle ♀
626.6 Metrorrhagia ♀
626.8 Other disorder of menstruation and other abnormal bleeding from female genital tract ♀
627.1 Postmenopausal bleeding ♀
627.9 Unspecified menopausal and postmenopausal disorder ♀
628.2 Female infertility of tubal origin — (Use additional code for any associated peritubal adhesions: 614.6) ♀
631.8 Other abnormal products of conception ♀
632 Missed abortion — (Use additional code from category 639 to identify any associated complications) ♀
633.10 Tubal pregnancy without intrauterine pregnancy — (Use additional code from category 639 to identify any associated complications) ♀
633.11 Tubal pregnancy with intrauterine pregnancy — (Use additional code from category 639 to identify any associated complications) ♀
752.11 Embryonic cyst of fallopian tubes and broad ligaments ♀
788.91 Functional urinary incontinence
789.03 Abdominal pain, right lower quadrant
789.04 Abdominal pain, left lower quadrant
789.05 Abdominal pain, periumbilic
789.07 Abdominal pain, generalized
789.09 Abdominal pain, other specified site
789.30 Abdominal or pelvic swelling, mass or lump, unspecified site
789.31 Abdominal or pelvic swelling, mass, or lump, right upper quadrant
789.32 Abdominal or pelvic swelling, mass, or lump, left upper quadrant
789.33 Abdominal or pelvic swelling, mass, or lump, right lower quadrant
789.34 Abdominal or pelvic swelling, mass, or lump, left lower quadrant
795.00 Abnormal glandular Papanicolaou smear of cervix ♀
795.01 Papanicolaou smear of cervix with atypical squamous cells of undetermined significance (ASC-US) ♀
795.02 Papanicolaou smear of cervix with atypical squamous cells cannot exclude high grade squamous intraepithelial lesion (ASC-H) ♀
795.03 Papanicolaou smear of cervix with low grade squamous intraepithelial lesion (LGSIL) ♀
795.04 Papanicolaou smear of cervix with high grade squamous intraepithelial lesion (HGSIL) ♀
795.05 Cervical high risk human papillomavirus (HPV) DNA test positive ♀
795.07 Satisfactory cervical smear but lacking transformation zone ♀
795.08 Unsatisfactory cervical cytology smear ♀
795.09 Other abnormal Papanicolaou smear of cervix and cervical HPV — (Use additional code for associated human papillomavirus: 079.4) ♀
795.10 Abnormal glandular Papanicolaou smear of vagina — (Use additional code to identify acquired absence of uterus and cervix, if applicable: V88.01-V88.03) ♀
795.11 Papanicolaou smear of vagina with atypical squamous cells of undetermined significance (ASC-US) — (Use additional code to identify acquired absence of uterus and cervix, if applicable: V88.01-V88.03) ♀
795.12 Papanicolaou smear of vagina with atypical squamous cells cannot exclude high grade squamous intraepithelial lesion (ASC-H) — (Use additional code to identify acquired absence of uterus and cervix, if applicable: V88.01-V88.03) ♀
795.13 Papanicolaou smear of vagina with low grade squamous intraepithelial lesion (LGSIL) — (Use additional code to identify acquired absence of uterus and cervix, if applicable: V88.01-V88.03) ♀
795.14 Papanicolaou smear of vagina with high grade squamous intraepithelial lesion (HGSIL) — (Use additional code to identify acquired absence of uterus and cervix, if applicable: V88.01-V88.03) ♀
795.15 Vaginal high risk human papillomavirus (HPV) DNA test positive — (Use additional code to identify acquired absence of uterus and cervix, if applicable: V88.01-V88.03) ♀
795.16 Papanicolaou smear of vagina with cytologic evidence of malignancy — (Use additional code to identify acquired absence of uterus and cervix, if applicable: V88.01-V88.03) ♀
795.18 Unsatisfactory vaginal cytology smear — (Use additional code to identify acquired absence of uterus and cervix, if applicable: V88.01-V88.03) ♀
795.19 Other abnormal Papanicolaou smear of vagina and vaginal HPV — (Use additional code to identify acquired absence of uterus and cervix, if applicable: V88.01-V88.03) (Use additional code for associated human papillomavirus: 079.4) ♀
V25.2 Sterilization
V71.5 Observation following alleged rape or seduction
V72.31 Routine gynecological examination — (Use additional code(s) to identify any special screening examination(s) performed: V73.0-V82.9) ♀
V72.32 Encounter for Papanicolaou cervical smear to confirm findings of recent normal smear following initial abnormal smear — (Use additional code(s) to identify any special screening examination(s) performed: V73.0-V82.9) ♀

ICD-9-CM Procedural

70.29 Other diagnostic procedures on vagina and cul-de-sac ♀
89.26 Gynecological examination ♀

HCPCS Level II Supplies & Services

A4305 Disposable drug delivery system, flow rate of 50 ml or greater per hour

57415

57415 Removal of impacted vaginal foreign body (separate procedure) under anesthesia (other than local)

ICD-9-CM Diagnostic

939.2 Foreign body in vulva and vagina ♀

ICD-9-CM Procedural

98.17 Removal of intraluminal foreign body from vagina without incision ♀

HCPCS Level II Supplies & Services

A4305 Disposable drug delivery system, flow rate of 50 ml or greater per hour

57420-57421

57420 Colposcopy of the entire vagina, with cervix if present;
57421 with biopsy(s) of vagina/cervix

ICD-9-CM Diagnostic

054.11 Herpetic vulvovaginitis ♀
180.0 Malignant neoplasm of endocervix ♀
180.1 Malignant neoplasm of exocervix ♀
180.8 Malignant neoplasm of other specified sites of cervix ♀
180.9 Malignant neoplasm of cervix uteri, unspecified site ▽ ♀
184.0 Malignant neoplasm of vagina ♀
184.8 Malignant neoplasm of other specified sites of female genital organs ♀
184.9 Malignant neoplasm of female genital organ, site unspecified ▽ ♀
198.82 Secondary malignant neoplasm of genital organs
199.1 Other malignant neoplasm of unspecified site
221.1 Benign neoplasm of vagina ♀
221.8 Benign neoplasm of other specified sites of female genital organs ♀
221.9 Benign neoplasm of female genital organ, site unspecified ▽ ♀
233.30 Carcinoma in situ, unspecified female genital organ ▽ ♀
233.31 Carcinoma in situ, vagina ♀
233.32 Carcinoma in situ, vulva ♀
233.39 Carcinoma in situ, other female genital organ ♀
236.0 Neoplasm of uncertain behavior of uterus ♀
236.3 Neoplasm of uncertain behavior of other and unspecified female genital organs ▽ ♀
238.9 Neoplasm of uncertain behavior, site unspecified ▽
239.5 Neoplasm of unspecified nature of other genitourinary organs
616.0 Cervicitis and endocervicitis — (Use additional code to identify organism: 041.00-041.09, 041.10-041.19) ♀
616.10 Unspecified vaginitis and vulvovaginitis — (Use additional code to identify organism, such as: 041.00-041.09, 041.10-041.19, 041.41-041.49) ▽ ♀
616.11 Vaginitis and vulvovaginitis in diseases classified elsewhere — (Use additional code to identify organism: 041.00-041.09, 041.10-041.19) (Code first underlying disease: 127.4) ☒ ♀
616.2 Cyst of Bartholin's gland — (Use additional code to identify organism: 041.00-041.09, 041.10-041.19) ♀
616.3 Abscess of Bartholin's gland — (Use additional code to identify organism: 041.00-041.09, 041.10-041.19) ♀
616.81 Mucositis (ulcerative) of cervix, vagina, and vulva — (Use additional code to identify organism: 041.00-041.09, 041.10-041.19) (Use additional E code to identify adverse effects of therapy: E879.2, E930.7, E933.1) ♀
616.89 Other inflammatory disease of cervix, vagina and vulva — (Use additional code to identify organism: 041.00-041.09, 041.10-041.19) ♀
617.4 Endometriosis of rectovaginal septum and vagina ♀
617.9 Endometriosis, site unspecified ▽ ♀
623.0 Dysplasia of vagina ♀
623.1 Leukoplakia of vagina ♀
623.2 Stricture or atresia of vagina — (Use additional E code to identify any external cause) ♀
623.4 Old vaginal laceration ♀
623.5 Leukorrhea, not specified as infective ♀
623.6 Vaginal hematoma ♀
623.7 Polyp of vagina ♀
623.8 Other specified noninflammatory disorder of vagina ♀
623.9 Unspecified noninflammatory disorder of vagina ▽ ♀
625.0 Dyspareunia ♀
625.1 Vaginismus ♀
625.3 Dysmenorrhea ♀
625.8 Other specified symptom associated with female genital organs ♀
625.9 Unspecified symptom associated with female genital organs ▽ ♀
626.0 Absence of menstruation ♀
626.1 Scanty or infrequent menstruation ♀
626.2 Excessive or frequent menstruation ♀
626.3 Puberty bleeding ♀
626.4 Irregular menstrual cycle ♀
626.5 Ovulation bleeding ♀
626.6 Metrorrhagia ♀
626.7 Postcoital bleeding ♀
626.8 Other disorder of menstruation and other abnormal bleeding from female genital tract ♀
626.9 Unspecified disorder of menstruation and other abnormal bleeding from female genital tract ▽ ♀
627.0 Premenopausal menorrhagia ♀
627.1 Postmenopausal bleeding ♀
627.2 Symptomatic menopausal or female climacteric states ♀
627.3 Postmenopausal atrophic vaginitis ♀
627.4 Symptomatic states associated with artificial menopause ♀
760.76 Noxious influences affecting fetus or newborn via placenta or breast milk, diethylstilbestrol [DES] — (Use additional code(s) to further specify condition)
789.00 Abdominal pain, unspecified site ▽
789.01 Abdominal pain, right upper quadrant
789.02 Abdominal pain, left upper quadrant
789.03 Abdominal pain, right lower quadrant
789.04 Abdominal pain, left lower quadrant
789.30 Abdominal or pelvic swelling, mass or lump, unspecified site ▽
789.31 Abdominal or pelvic swelling, mass, or lump, right upper quadrant
789.32 Abdominal or pelvic swelling, mass, or lump, left upper quadrant
789.33 Abdominal or pelvic swelling, mass, or lump, right lower quadrant
789.34 Abdominal or pelvic swelling, mass, or lump, left lower quadrant
795.04 Papanicolaou smear of cervix with high grade squamous intraepithelial lesion (HGSIL) ♀
795.06 Papanicolaou smear of cervix with cytologic evidence of malignancy ♀
795.07 Satisfactory cervical smear but lacking transformation zone ♀
795.10 Abnormal glandular Papanicolaou smear of vagina — (Use additional code to identify acquired absence of uterus and cervix, if applicable: V88.01-V88.03) ♀
795.11 Papanicolaou smear of vagina with atypical squamous cells of undetermined significance (ASC-US) — (Use additional code to identify acquired absence of uterus and cervix, if applicable: V88.01-V88.03) ♀
795.12 Papanicolaou smear of vagina with atypical squamous cells cannot exclude high grade squamous intraepithelial lesion (ASC-H) — (Use additional code to identify acquired absence of uterus and cervix, if applicable: V88.01-V88.03) ♀
795.13 Papanicolaou smear of vagina with low grade squamous intraepithelial lesion (LGSIL) — (Use additional code to identify acquired absence of uterus and cervix, if applicable: V88.01-V88.03) ♀
795.14 Papanicolaou smear of vagina with high grade squamous intraepithelial lesion (HGSIL) — (Use additional code to identify acquired absence of uterus and cervix, if applicable: V88.01-V88.03) ♀
795.15 Vaginal high risk human papillomavirus (HPV) DNA test positive — (Use additional code to identify acquired absence of uterus and cervix, if applicable: V88.01-V88.03) ♀
795.16 Papanicolaou smear of vagina with cytologic evidence of malignancy — (Use additional code to identify acquired absence of uterus and cervix, if applicable: V88.01-V88.03) ♀
795.18 Unsatisfactory vaginal cytology smear — (Use additional code to identify acquired absence of uterus and cervix, if applicable: V88.01-V88.03) ♀

795.19 Other abnormal Papanicolaou smear of vagina and vaginal HPV — (Use additional code to identify acquired absence of uterus and cervix, if applicable: V88.01-V88.03) (Use additional code for associated human papillomavirus: 079.4) ♀

795.39 Other nonspecific positive culture findings

796.0 Nonspecific abnormal toxicological findings — (Use additional code for retained foreign body, if applicable, (V90.01-V90.9))

ICD-9-CM Procedural

70.21 Vaginoscopy ♀

70.23 Biopsy of cul-de-sac ♀

70.24 Vaginal biopsy ♀

57423

57423 Paravaginal defect repair (including repair of cystocele, if performed), laparoscopic approach

ICD-9-CM Diagnostic

618.00 Unspecified prolapse of vaginal walls without mention of uterine prolapse — (Use additional code to identify urinary incontinence: 625.6, 788.31, 788.33-788.39) 🔽 ♀

618.01 Cystocele without mention of uterine prolapse, midline — (Use additional code to identify urinary incontinence: 625.6, 788.31, 788.33-788.39) ♀

618.02 Cystocele without mention of uterine prolapse, lateral — (Use additional code to identify urinary incontinence: 625.6, 788.31, 788.33-788.39) ♀

618.03 Urethrocele without mention of uterine prolapse — (Use additional code to identify urinary incontinence: 625.6, 788.31, 788.33-788.39) ♀

618.04 Rectocele without mention of uterine prolapse — (Use additional code to identify urinary incontinence: 625.6, 788.31, 788.33-788.39) (Use additional code for any associated fecal incontinence: 787.60-787.63) ♀

618.05 Perineocele without mention of uterine prolapse — (Use additional code to identify urinary incontinence: 625.6, 788.31, 788.33-788.39) ♀

618.09 Other prolapse of vaginal walls without mention of uterine prolapse — (Use additional code to identify urinary incontinence: 625.6, 788.31, 788.33-788.39) ♀

618.1 Uterine prolapse without mention of vaginal wall prolapse — (Use additional code to identify urinary incontinence: 625.6, 788.31, 788.33-788.39) ♀

618.2 Uterovaginal prolapse, incomplete — (Use additional code to identify urinary incontinence: 625.6, 788.31, 788.33-788.39) ♀

618.3 Uterovaginal prolapse, complete — (Use additional code to identify urinary incontinence: 625.6, 788.31, 788.33-788.39) ♀

618.4 Uterovaginal prolapse, unspecified — (Use additional code to identify urinary incontinence: 625.6, 788.31, 788.33-788.39) 🔽 ♀

618.5 Prolapse of vaginal vault after hysterectomy — (Use additional code to identify urinary incontinence: 625.6, 788.31, 788.33-788.39) ♀

618.82 Incompetence or weakening of rectovaginal tissue — (Use additional code to identify urinary incontinence: 625.6, 788.31, 788.33-788.39) ♀

618.83 Pelvic muscle wasting — (Use additional code to identify urinary incontinence: 625.6, 788.31, 788.33-788.39) ♀

618.84 Cervical stump prolapse — (Use additional code to identify urinary incontinence: 625.6, 788.31, 788.33-788.39) ♀

618.89 Other specified genital prolapse — (Use additional code to identify urinary incontinence: 625.6, 788.31, 788.33-788.39) ♀

625.6 Female stress incontinence ♀

ICD-9-CM Procedural

70.51 Repair of cystocele ♀

70.54 Repair of cystocele with graft or prosthesis ♀

70.77 Vaginal suspension and fixation ♀

70.78 Vaginal suspension and fixation with graft or prosthesis ♀

57425

57425 Laparoscopy, surgical, colpopexy (suspension of vaginal apex)

ICD-9-CM Diagnostic

618.00 Unspecified prolapse of vaginal walls without mention of uterine prolapse — (Use additional code to identify urinary incontinence: 625.6, 788.31, 788.33-788.39) 🔽 ♀

618.01 Cystocele without mention of uterine prolapse, midline — (Use additional code to identify urinary incontinence: 625.6, 788.31, 788.33-788.39) ♀

618.02 Cystocele without mention of uterine prolapse, lateral — (Use additional code to identify urinary incontinence: 625.6, 788.31, 788.33-788.39) ♀

618.03 Urethrocele without mention of uterine prolapse — (Use additional code to identify urinary incontinence: 625.6, 788.31, 788.33-788.39) ♀

618.04 Rectocele without mention of uterine prolapse — (Use additional code to identify urinary incontinence: 625.6, 788.31, 788.33-788.39) (Use additional code for any associated fecal incontinence: 787.60-787.63) ♀

618.05 Perineocele without mention of uterine prolapse — (Use additional code to identify urinary incontinence: 625.6, 788.31, 788.33-788.39) ♀

618.09 Other prolapse of vaginal walls without mention of uterine prolapse — (Use additional code to identify urinary incontinence: 625.6, 788.31, 788.33-788.39) ♀

618.1 Uterine prolapse without mention of vaginal wall prolapse — (Use additional code to identify urinary incontinence: 625.6, 788.31, 788.33-788.39) ♀

618.2 Uterovaginal prolapse, incomplete — (Use additional code to identify urinary incontinence: 625.6, 788.31, 788.33-788.39) ♀

618.3 Uterovaginal prolapse, complete — (Use additional code to identify urinary incontinence: 625.6, 788.31, 788.33-788.39) ♀

618.4 Uterovaginal prolapse, unspecified — (Use additional code to identify urinary incontinence: 625.6, 788.31, 788.33-788.39) 🔽 ♀

618.5 Prolapse of vaginal vault after hysterectomy — (Use additional code to identify urinary incontinence: 625.6, 788.31, 788.33-788.39) ♀

618.81 Incompetence or weakening of pubocervical tissue — (Use additional code to identify urinary incontinence: 625.6, 788.31, 788.33-788.39) ♀

618.82 Incompetence or weakening of rectovaginal tissue — (Use additional code to identify urinary incontinence: 625.6, 788.31, 788.33-788.39) ♀

618.83 Pelvic muscle wasting — (Use additional code to identify urinary incontinence: 625.6, 788.31, 788.33-788.39) ♀

618.84 Cervical stump prolapse — (Use additional code to identify urinary incontinence: 625.6, 788.31, 788.33-788.39) ♀

618.89 Other specified genital prolapse — (Use additional code to identify urinary incontinence: 625.6, 788.31, 788.33-788.39) ♀

625.6 Female stress incontinence ♀

ICD-9-CM Procedural

70.77 Vaginal suspension and fixation ♀

57426

57426 Revision (including removal) of prosthetic vaginal graft, laparoscopic approach

ICD-9-CM Diagnostic

054.11 Herpetic vulvovaginitis ♀

098.0 Gonococcal infection (acute) of lower genitourinary tract

098.2 Gonococcal infections, chronic, of lower genitourinary tract

099.53 Chlamydia trachomatis infection of lower genitourinary sites — (Use additional code to specify site of infection: 595.4, 616.0, 616.11)

112.1 Candidiasis of vulva and vagina — (Use additional code to identify manifestation: 321.0-321.1, 380.15, 711.6) ♀

616.10 Unspecified vaginitis and vulvovaginitis — (Use additional code to identify organism, such as: 041.00-041.09, 041.10-041.19, 041.41-041.49) 🔽 ♀

616.11 Vaginitis and vulvovaginitis in diseases classified elsewhere — (Use additional code to identify organism: 041.00-041.09, 041.10-041.19) (Code first underlying disease: 127.4) ☒ ♀

629.31 Erosion of implanted vaginal mesh and other prosthetic materials to surrounding organ or tissue ♀

629.32 Exposure of implanted vaginal mesh and other prosthetic materials into vagina ♀
752.49 Other congenital anomaly of cervix, vagina, and external female genitalia ♀
996.30 Mechanical complication of unspecified genitourinary device, implant, and graft ▽
996.39 Mechanical complication of genitourinary device, implant, and graft, other
996.52 Mechanical complication due to other tissue graft, not elsewhere classified
996.59 Mechanical complication due to other implant and internal device, not elsewhere classified
996.60 Infection and inflammatory reaction due to unspecified device, implant, and graft — (Use additional code to identify specified infections) ▽
996.65 Infection and inflammatory reaction due to other genitourinary device, implant, and graft — (Use additional code to identify specified infections)
996.70 Other complications due to unspecified device, implant, and graft — (Use additional code to identify complication: 338.18-338.19, 338.28-338.29) ▽
996.76 Other complications due to genitourinary device, implant, and graft — (Use additional code to identify complication: 338.18-338.19, 338.28-338.29)
V51.8 Other aftercare involving the use of plastic surgery

ICD-9-CM Procedural

70.62 Vaginal reconstruction ♀
70.79 Other repair of vagina ♀
70.91 Other operations on vagina ♀

Cervix Uteri

57452-57461

57452 Colposcopy of the cervix including upper/adjacent vagina;
57454 with biopsy(s) of the cervix and endocervical curettage
57455 with biopsy(s) of the cervix
57456 with endocervical curettage
57460 with loop electrode biopsy(s) of the cervix
57461 with loop electrode conization of the cervix

ICD-9-CM Diagnostic

079.4 Human papilloma virus in conditions classified elsewhere and of unspecified site — (Note: This code is to be used as an additional code to identify the viral agent in diseases classifiable elsewhere and viral infection of unspecified nature or site)
180.0 Malignant neoplasm of endocervix ♀
180.1 Malignant neoplasm of exocervix ♀
180.8 Malignant neoplasm of other specified sites of cervix ♀
180.9 Malignant neoplasm of cervix uteri, unspecified site ▽ ♀
182.0 Malignant neoplasm of corpus uteri, except isthmus ♀
182.1 Malignant neoplasm of isthmus ♀
182.8 Malignant neoplasm of other specified sites of body of uterus ♀
184.0 Malignant neoplasm of vagina ♀
198.82 Secondary malignant neoplasm of genital organs
199.1 Other malignant neoplasm of unspecified site
219.0 Benign neoplasm of cervix uteri ♀
221.2 Benign neoplasm of vulva ♀
221.8 Benign neoplasm of other specified sites of female genital organs ♀
233.1 Carcinoma in situ of cervix uteri ♀
233.30 Carcinoma in situ, unspecified female genital organ ▽ ♀
233.31 Carcinoma in situ, vagina ♀
233.32 Carcinoma in situ, vulva ♀
233.39 Carcinoma in situ, other female genital organ ♀
236.0 Neoplasm of uncertain behavior of uterus ♀
236.3 Neoplasm of uncertain behavior of other and unspecified female genital organs ▽ ♀
239.5 Neoplasm of unspecified nature of other genitourinary organs
616.0 Cervicitis and endocervicitis — (Use additional code to identify organism: 041.00-041.09, 041.10-041.19) ♀
616.10 Unspecified vaginitis and vulvovaginitis — (Use additional code to identify organism, such as: 041.00-041.09, 041.10-041.19, 041.41-041.49) ▽ ♀
616.11 Vaginitis and vulvovaginitis in diseases classified elsewhere — (Use additional code to identify organism: 041.00-041.09, 041.10-041.19) (Code first underlying disease: 127.4) ☒ ♀
616.81 Mucositis (ulcerative) of cervix, vagina, and vulva — (Use additional code to identify organism: 041.00-041.09, 041.10-041.19) (Use additional E code to identify adverse effects of therapy: E879.2, E930.7, E933.1) ♀
616.89 Other inflammatory disease of cervix, vagina and vulva — (Use additional code to identify organism: 041.00-041.09, 041.10-041.19) ♀
616.9 Unspecified inflammatory disease of cervix, vagina, and vulva — (Use additional code to identify organism: 041.00-041.09, 041.10-041.19) ▽ ♀
617.4 Endometriosis of rectovaginal septum and vagina ♀
617.9 Endometriosis, site unspecified ▽ ♀
622.0 Erosion and ectropion of cervix ♀
622.10 Dysplasia of cervix, unspecified ▽ ♀
622.11 Mild dysplasia of cervix ♀
622.12 Moderate dysplasia of cervix ♀
622.2 Leukoplakia of cervix (uteri) ♀
622.3 Old laceration of cervix ♀
622.4 Stricture and stenosis of cervix ♀
622.5 Incompetence of cervix ♀
622.6 Hypertrophic elongation of cervix ♀
622.7 Mucous polyp of cervix ♀
622.8 Other specified noninflammatory disorder of cervix ♀
622.9 Unspecified noninflammatory disorder of cervix ▽ ♀
625.0 Dyspareunia ♀
625.3 Dysmenorrhea ♀
625.8 Other specified symptom associated with female genital organs ♀
625.9 Unspecified symptom associated with female genital organs ▽ ♀
626.0 Absence of menstruation ♀
626.1 Scanty or infrequent menstruation ♀
626.2 Excessive or frequent menstruation ♀
626.3 Puberty bleeding ♀
626.4 Irregular menstrual cycle ♀
626.5 Ovulation bleeding ♀
626.6 Metrorrhagia ♀
626.7 Postcoital bleeding ♀
626.8 Other disorder of menstruation and other abnormal bleeding from female genital tract ♀
626.9 Unspecified disorder of menstruation and other abnormal bleeding from female genital tract ▽ ♀
627.0 Premenopausal menorrhagia ♀
627.1 Postmenopausal bleeding ♀
627.4 Symptomatic states associated with artificial menopause ♀
752.40 Unspecified congenital anomaly of cervix, vagina, and external female genitalia ▽ ♀
752.49 Other congenital anomaly of cervix, vagina, and external female genitalia ♀
760.76 Noxious influences affecting fetus or newborn via placenta or breast milk, diethylstilbestrol [DES] — (Use additional code(s) to further specify condition)
789.00 Abdominal pain, unspecified site ▽
789.01 Abdominal pain, right upper quadrant
789.02 Abdominal pain, left upper quadrant
789.03 Abdominal pain, right lower quadrant
789.04 Abdominal pain, left lower quadrant
789.30 Abdominal or pelvic swelling, mass or lump, unspecified site ▽
789.31 Abdominal or pelvic swelling, mass, or lump, right upper quadrant
789.32 Abdominal or pelvic swelling, mass, or lump, left upper quadrant
789.33 Abdominal or pelvic swelling, mass, or lump, right lower quadrant

789.34 Abdominal or pelvic swelling, mass, or lump, left lower quadrant
795.00 Abnormal glandular Papanicolaou smear of cervix ♀
795.01 Papanicolaou smear of cervix with atypical squamous cells of undetermined significance (ASC-US) ♀
795.02 Papanicolaou smear of cervix with atypical squamous cells cannot exclude high grade squamous intraepithelial lesion (ASC-H) ♀
795.03 Papanicolaou smear of cervix with low grade squamous intraepithelial lesion (LGSIL) ♀
795.04 Papanicolaou smear of cervix with high grade squamous intraepithelial lesion (HGSIL) ♀
795.05 Cervical high risk human papillomavirus (HPV) DNA test positive ♀
795.06 Papanicolaou smear of cervix with cytologic evidence of malignancy ♀
795.07 Satisfactory cervical smear but lacking transformation zone ♀
795.08 Unsatisfactory cervical cytology smear ♀
795.09 Other abnormal Papanicolaou smear of cervix and cervical HPV — (Use additional code for associated human papillomavirus: 079.4) ♀
795.10 Abnormal glandular Papanicolaou smear of vagina — (Use additional code to identify acquired absence of uterus and cervix, if applicable: V88.01-V88.03) ♀
795.11 Papanicolaou smear of vagina with atypical squamous cells of undetermined significance (ASC-US) — (Use additional code to identify acquired absence of uterus and cervix, if applicable: V88.01-V88.03) ♀
795.12 Papanicolaou smear of vagina with atypical squamous cells cannot exclude high grade squamous intraepithelial lesion (ASC-H) — (Use additional code to identify acquired absence of uterus and cervix, if applicable: V88.01-V88.03) ♀
795.13 Papanicolaou smear of vagina with low grade squamous intraepithelial lesion (LGSIL) — (Use additional code to identify acquired absence of uterus and cervix, if applicable: V88.01-V88.03) ♀
795.14 Papanicolaou smear of vagina with high grade squamous intraepithelial lesion (HGSIL) — (Use additional code to identify acquired absence of uterus and cervix, if applicable: V88.01-V88.03) ♀
795.15 Vaginal high risk human papillomavirus (HPV) DNA test positive — (Use additional code to identify acquired absence of uterus and cervix, if applicable: V88.01-V88.03) ♀
795.16 Papanicolaou smear of vagina with cytologic evidence of malignancy — (Use additional code to identify acquired absence of uterus and cervix, if applicable: V88.01-V88.03) ♀
795.18 Unsatisfactory vaginal cytology smear — (Use additional code to identify acquired absence of uterus and cervix, if applicable: V88.01-V88.03) ♀
795.19 Other abnormal Papanicolaou smear of vagina and vaginal HPV — (Use additional code to identify acquired absence of uterus and cervix, if applicable: V88.01-V88.03) (Use additional code for associated human papillomavirus: 079.4) ♀
795.39 Other nonspecific positive culture findings
796.0 Nonspecific abnormal toxicological findings — (Use additional code for retained foreign body, if applicable, (V90.01-V90.9))
V10.40 Personal history of malignant neoplasm of unspecified female genital organ ▽ ♀
V10.41 Personal history of malignant neoplasm of cervix uteri ♀
V10.42 Personal history of malignant neoplasm of other parts of uterus ♀
V13.29 Personal history of other genital system and obstetric disorders ♀
V67.00 Follow-up examination, following unspecified surgery ▽
V67.09 Follow-up examination, following other surgery
V71.5 Observation following alleged rape or seduction
V71.6 Observation following other inflicted injury
V76.2 Screening for malignant neoplasm of the cervix ♀

ICD-9-CM Procedural

67.11 Endocervical biopsy ♀
67.12 Other cervical biopsy ♀
67.19 Other diagnostic procedures on cervix ♀
67.32 Destruction of lesion of cervix by cauterization ♀
70.21 Vaginoscopy ♀

HCPCS Level II Supplies & Services

A4305 Disposable drug delivery system, flow rate of 50 ml or greater per hour

57500

57500 Biopsy of cervix, single or multiple, or local excision of lesion, with or without fulguration (separate procedure)

ICD-9-CM Diagnostic

180.0 Malignant neoplasm of endocervix ♀
180.1 Malignant neoplasm of exocervix ♀
180.8 Malignant neoplasm of other specified sites of cervix ♀
180.9 Malignant neoplasm of cervix uteri, unspecified site ▽ ♀
182.0 Malignant neoplasm of corpus uteri, except isthmus ♀
198.82 Secondary malignant neoplasm of genital organs
219.0 Benign neoplasm of cervix uteri ♀
221.8 Benign neoplasm of other specified sites of female genital organs ♀
221.9 Benign neoplasm of female genital organ, site unspecified ▽ ♀
228.00 Hemangioma of unspecified site ▽
229.8 Benign neoplasm of other specified sites
233.1 Carcinoma in situ of cervix uteri ♀
239.5 Neoplasm of unspecified nature of other genitourinary organs
616.0 Cervicitis and endocervicitis — (Use additional code to identify organism: 041.00-041.09, 041.10-041.19) ♀
616.81 Mucositis (ulcerative) of cervix, vagina, and vulva — (Use additional code to identify organism: 041.00-041.09, 041.10-041.19) (Use additional E code to identify adverse effects of therapy: E879.2, E930.7, E933.1) ♀
622.0 Erosion and ectropion of cervix ♀
622.10 Dysplasia of cervix, unspecified ▽ ♀
622.11 Mild dysplasia of cervix ♀
622.12 Moderate dysplasia of cervix ♀
622.2 Leukoplakia of cervix (uteri) ♀
622.7 Mucous polyp of cervix ♀
622.8 Other specified noninflammatory disorder of cervix ♀
623.5 Leukorrhea, not specified as infective ♀
623.8 Other specified noninflammatory disorder of vagina ♀
625.3 Dysmenorrhea ♀
625.8 Other specified symptom associated with female genital organs ♀
626.2 Excessive or frequent menstruation ♀
626.4 Irregular menstrual cycle ♀
626.6 Metrorrhagia ♀
626.8 Other disorder of menstruation and other abnormal bleeding from female genital tract ♀
795.00 Abnormal glandular Papanicolaou smear of cervix ♀
795.01 Papanicolaou smear of cervix with atypical squamous cells of undetermined significance (ASC-US) ♀
795.02 Papanicolaou smear of cervix with atypical squamous cells cannot exclude high grade squamous intraepithelial lesion (ASC-H) ♀
795.03 Papanicolaou smear of cervix with low grade squamous intraepithelial lesion (LGSIL) ♀
795.04 Papanicolaou smear of cervix with high grade squamous intraepithelial lesion (HGSIL) ♀
795.05 Cervical high risk human papillomavirus (HPV) DNA test positive ♀
795.07 Satisfactory cervical smear but lacking transformation zone ♀
795.08 Unsatisfactory cervical cytology smear ♀
795.09 Other abnormal Papanicolaou smear of cervix and cervical HPV — (Use additional code for associated human papillomavirus: 079.4) ♀
V76.2 Screening for malignant neoplasm of the cervix ♀
V84.09 Genetic susceptibility to other malignant neoplasm — (Use additional code, if applicable, for any associated family history of the disease: V16-V19. Code first, if applicable, any current malignant neoplasms: 140.0-195.8, 200.0-208.9, 230.0-234.9. Use additional code, if applicable, for any personal history of malignant neoplasm: V10.0-V10.9)

ICD-9-CM Procedural

67.11 Endocervical biopsy ♀
67.12 Other cervical biopsy ♀
67.31 Marsupialization of cervical cyst ♀
67.39 Other excision or destruction of lesion or tissue of cervix ♀

57505

57505 Endocervical curettage (not done as part of a dilation and curettage)

ICD-9-CM Diagnostic

180.0 Malignant neoplasm of endocervix ♀
180.8 Malignant neoplasm of other specified sites of cervix ♀
218.0 Submucous leiomyoma of uterus ♀
218.2 Subserous leiomyoma of uterus ♀
218.9 Leiomyoma of uterus, unspecified ▽ ♀
219.0 Benign neoplasm of cervix uteri ♀
233.1 Carcinoma in situ of cervix uteri ♀
236.0 Neoplasm of uncertain behavior of uterus ♀
616.0 Cervicitis and endocervicitis — (Use additional code to identify organism: 041.00-041.09, 041.10-041.19) ♀
616.81 Mucositis (ulcerative) of cervix, vagina, and vulva — (Use additional code to identify organism: 041.00-041.09, 041.10-041.19) (Use additional E code to identify adverse effects of therapy: E879.2, E930.7, E933.1) ♀
616.89 Other inflammatory disease of cervix, vagina and vulva — (Use additional code to identify organism: 041.00-041.09, 041.10-041.19) ♀
617.0 Endometriosis of uterus ♀
622.0 Erosion and ectropion of cervix ♀
622.10 Dysplasia of cervix, unspecified ▽ ♀
622.11 Mild dysplasia of cervix ♀
622.12 Moderate dysplasia of cervix ♀
622.2 Leukoplakia of cervix (uteri) ♀
622.7 Mucous polyp of cervix ♀
622.8 Other specified noninflammatory disorder of cervix ♀
623.0 Dysplasia of vagina ♀
623.1 Leukoplakia of vagina ♀
623.5 Leukorrhea, not specified as infective ♀
623.8 Other specified noninflammatory disorder of vagina ♀
625.3 Dysmenorrhea ♀
626.0 Absence of menstruation ♀
626.2 Excessive or frequent menstruation ♀
626.4 Irregular menstrual cycle ♀
626.6 Metrorrhagia ♀
626.8 Other disorder of menstruation and other abnormal bleeding from female genital tract ♀
627.1 Postmenopausal bleeding ♀
752.49 Other congenital anomaly of cervix, vagina, and external female genitalia ♀
789.00 Abdominal pain, unspecified site ▽
789.30 Abdominal or pelvic swelling, mass or lump, unspecified site ▽
795.00 Abnormal glandular Papanicolaou smear of cervix ♀
795.01 Papanicolaou smear of cervix with atypical squamous cells of undetermined significance (ASC-US) ♀
795.02 Papanicolaou smear of cervix with atypical squamous cells cannot exclude high grade squamous intraepithelial lesion (ASC-H) ♀
795.03 Papanicolaou smear of cervix with low grade squamous intraepithelial lesion (LGSIL) ♀
795.04 Papanicolaou smear of cervix with high grade squamous intraepithelial lesion (HGSIL) ♀
795.05 Cervical high risk human papillomavirus (HPV) DNA test positive ♀
795.07 Satisfactory cervical smear but lacking transformation zone ♀
795.08 Unsatisfactory cervical cytology smear ♀
795.09 Other abnormal Papanicolaou smear of cervix and cervical HPV — (Use additional code for associated human papillomavirus: 079.4) ♀
795.11 Papanicolaou smear of vagina with atypical squamous cells of undetermined significance (ASC-US) — (Use additional code to identify acquired absence of uterus and cervix, if applicable: V88.01-V88.03) ♀
795.12 Papanicolaou smear of vagina with atypical squamous cells cannot exclude high grade squamous intraepithelial lesion (ASC-H) — (Use additional code to identify acquired absence of uterus and cervix, if applicable: V88.01-V88.03) ♀
795.13 Papanicolaou smear of vagina with low grade squamous intraepithelial lesion (LGSIL) — (Use additional code to identify acquired absence of uterus and cervix, if applicable: V88.01-V88.03) ♀
795.14 Papanicolaou smear of vagina with high grade squamous intraepithelial lesion (HGSIL) — (Use additional code to identify acquired absence of uterus and cervix, if applicable: V88.01-V88.03) ♀
795.15 Vaginal high risk human papillomavirus (HPV) DNA test positive — (Use additional code to identify acquired absence of uterus and cervix, if applicable: V88.01-V88.03) ♀
795.16 Papanicolaou smear of vagina with cytologic evidence of malignancy — (Use additional code to identify acquired absence of uterus and cervix, if applicable: V88.01-V88.03) ♀
795.18 Unsatisfactory vaginal cytology smear — (Use additional code to identify acquired absence of uterus and cervix, if applicable: V88.01-V88.03) ♀
795.19 Other abnormal Papanicolaou smear of vagina and vaginal HPV — (Use additional code to identify acquired absence of uterus and cervix, if applicable: V88.01-V88.03) (Use additional code for associated human papillomavirus: 079.4) ♀
795.39 Other nonspecific positive culture findings
V84.02 Genetic susceptibility to malignant neoplasm of ovary — (Use additional code, if applicable, for any associated family history of the disease: V16-V19. Code first, if applicable, any current malignant neoplasms: 140.0-195.8, 200.0-208.9, 230.0-234.9. Use additional code, if applicable, for any personal history of malignant neoplasm: V10.0-V10.9) ♀
V84.04 Genetic susceptibility to malignant neoplasm of endometrium — (Use additional code, if applicable, for any associated family history of the disease: V16-V19. Code first, if applicable, any current malignant neoplasms: 140.0-195.8, 200.0-208.9, 230.0-234.9. Use additional code, if applicable, for any personal history of malignant neoplasm: V10.0-V10.9) ♀
V84.09 Genetic susceptibility to other malignant neoplasm — (Use additional code, if applicable, for any associated family history of the disease: V16-V19. Code first, if applicable, any current malignant neoplasms: 140.0-195.8, 200.0-208.9, 230.0-234.9. Use additional code, if applicable, for any personal history of malignant neoplasm: V10.0-V10.9)

ICD-9-CM Procedural

69.09 Other dilation and curettage of uterus ♀

HCPCS Level II Supplies & Services

A4305 Disposable drug delivery system, flow rate of 50 ml or greater per hour

57510-57513

57510 Cautery of cervix; electro or thermal
57511 cryocautery, initial or repeat
57513 laser ablation

ICD-9-CM Diagnostic

180.1 Malignant neoplasm of exocervix ♀
180.8 Malignant neoplasm of other specified sites of cervix ♀
219.0 Benign neoplasm of cervix uteri ♀
233.1 Carcinoma in situ of cervix uteri ♀
236.0 Neoplasm of uncertain behavior of uterus ♀
239.5 Neoplasm of unspecified nature of other genitourinary organs
616.0 Cervicitis and endocervicitis — (Use additional code to identify organism: 041.00-041.09, 041.10-041.19) ♀

616.81 Mucositis (ulcerative) of cervix, vagina, and vulva — (Use additional code to identify organism: 041.00-041.09, 041.10-041.19) (Use additional E code to identify adverse effects of therapy: E879.2, E930.7, E933.1) ♀
616.89 Other inflammatory disease of cervix, vagina and vulva — (Use additional code to identify organism: 041.00-041.09, 041.10-041.19) ♀
617.0 Endometriosis of uterus ♀
622.0 Erosion and ectropion of cervix ♀
622.10 Dysplasia of cervix, unspecified ♀
622.11 Mild dysplasia of cervix ♀
622.12 Moderate dysplasia of cervix ♀
622.2 Leukoplakia of cervix (uteri) ♀
622.6 Hypertrophic elongation of cervix ♀
622.7 Mucous polyp of cervix ♀
622.8 Other specified noninflammatory disorder of cervix ♀
625.0 Dyspareunia ♀
625.3 Dysmenorrhea ♀
626.2 Excessive or frequent menstruation ♀
626.6 Metrorrhagia ♀
626.7 Postcoital bleeding ♀
626.8 Other disorder of menstruation and other abnormal bleeding from female genital tract ♀
627.1 Postmenopausal bleeding ♀
752.40 Unspecified congenital anomaly of cervix, vagina, and external female genitalia ♀
752.49 Other congenital anomaly of cervix, vagina, and external female genitalia ♀
795.00 Abnormal glandular Papanicolaou smear of cervix ♀
795.01 Papanicolaou smear of cervix with atypical squamous cells of undetermined significance (ASC-US) ♀
795.02 Papanicolaou smear of cervix with atypical squamous cells cannot exclude high grade squamous intraepithelial lesion (ASC-H) ♀
795.03 Papanicolaou smear of cervix with low grade squamous intraepithelial lesion (LGSIL) ♀
795.04 Papanicolaou smear of cervix with high grade squamous intraepithelial lesion (HGSIL) ♀
795.05 Cervical high risk human papillomavirus (HPV) DNA test positive ♀
795.06 Papanicolaou smear of cervix with cytologic evidence of malignancy ♀
795.07 Satisfactory cervical smear but lacking transformation zone ♀
795.08 Unsatisfactory cervical cytology smear ♀
795.09 Other abnormal Papanicolaou smear of cervix and cervical HPV — (Use additional code for associated human papillomavirus: 079.4) ♀
V84.02 Genetic susceptibility to malignant neoplasm of ovary — (Use additional code, if applicable, for any associated family history of the disease: V16-V19. Code first, if applicable, any current malignant neoplasms: 140.0-195.8, 200.0-208.9, 230.0-234.9. Use additional code, if applicable, for any personal history of malignant neoplasm: V10.0-V10.9) ♀
V84.04 Genetic susceptibility to malignant neoplasm of endometrium — (Use additional code, if applicable, for any associated family history of the disease: V16-V19. Code first, if applicable, any current malignant neoplasms: 140.0-195.8, 200.0-208.9, 230.0-234.9. Use additional code, if applicable, for any personal history of malignant neoplasm: V10.0-V10.9) ♀
V84.09 Genetic susceptibility to other malignant neoplasm — (Use additional code, if applicable, for any associated family history of the disease: V16-V19. Code first, if applicable, any current malignant neoplasms: 140.0-195.8, 200.0-208.9, 230.0-234.9. Use additional code, if applicable, for any personal history of malignant neoplasm: V10.0-V10.9)

ICD-9-CM Procedural

67.32 Destruction of lesion of cervix by cauterization ♀
67.33 Destruction of lesion of cervix by cryosurgery ♀
67.39 Other excision or destruction of lesion or tissue of cervix ♀

HCPCS Level II Supplies & Services

A4305 Disposable drug delivery system, flow rate of 50 ml or greater per hour

57520-57522

57520 Conization of cervix, with or without fulguration, with or without dilation and curettage, with or without repair; cold knife or laser
57522 loop electrode excision

ICD-9-CM Diagnostic

180.0 Malignant neoplasm of endocervix ♀
180.1 Malignant neoplasm of exocervix ♀
180.8 Malignant neoplasm of other specified sites of cervix ♀
180.9 Malignant neoplasm of cervix uteri, unspecified site ♀
198.82 Secondary malignant neoplasm of genital organs
199.1 Other malignant neoplasm of unspecified site
219.0 Benign neoplasm of cervix uteri ♀
233.1 Carcinoma in situ of cervix uteri ♀
233.30 Carcinoma in situ, unspecified female genital organ ♀
233.31 Carcinoma in situ, vagina ♀
233.32 Carcinoma in situ, vulva ♀
233.39 Carcinoma in situ, other female genital organ ♀
236.0 Neoplasm of uncertain behavior of uterus ♀
239.5 Neoplasm of unspecified nature of other genitourinary organs
616.0 Cervicitis and endocervicitis — (Use additional code to identify organism: 041.00-041.09, 041.10-041.19) ♀
622.0 Erosion and ectropion of cervix ♀
622.10 Dysplasia of cervix, unspecified ♀
622.11 Mild dysplasia of cervix ♀
622.12 Moderate dysplasia of cervix ♀
622.6 Hypertrophic elongation of cervix ♀
622.7 Mucous polyp of cervix ♀
622.8 Other specified noninflammatory disorder of cervix ♀
623.0 Dysplasia of vagina ♀
625.3 Dysmenorrhea ♀
625.9 Unspecified symptom associated with female genital organs ♀
626.2 Excessive or frequent menstruation ♀
626.4 Irregular menstrual cycle ♀
626.6 Metrorrhagia ♀
626.8 Other disorder of menstruation and other abnormal bleeding from female genital tract ♀
627.1 Postmenopausal bleeding ♀
795.00 Abnormal glandular Papanicolaou smear of cervix ♀
795.01 Papanicolaou smear of cervix with atypical squamous cells of undetermined significance (ASC-US) ♀
795.02 Papanicolaou smear of cervix with atypical squamous cells cannot exclude high grade squamous intraepithelial lesion (ASC-H) ♀
795.03 Papanicolaou smear of cervix with low grade squamous intraepithelial lesion (LGSIL) ♀
795.04 Papanicolaou smear of cervix with high grade squamous intraepithelial lesion (HGSIL) ♀
795.05 Cervical high risk human papillomavirus (HPV) DNA test positive ♀
795.07 Satisfactory cervical smear but lacking transformation zone ♀
795.08 Unsatisfactory cervical cytology smear ♀
795.09 Other abnormal Papanicolaou smear of cervix and cervical HPV — (Use additional code for associated human papillomavirus: 079.4) ♀
V84.02 Genetic susceptibility to malignant neoplasm of ovary — (Use additional code, if applicable, for any associated family history of the disease: V16-V19. Code first, if applicable, any current malignant neoplasms: 140.0-195.8, 200.0-208.9, 230.0-234.9. Use additional code, if applicable, for any personal history of malignant neoplasm: V10.0-V10.9) ♀
V84.04 Genetic susceptibility to malignant neoplasm of endometrium — (Use additional code, if applicable, for any associated family history of the disease: V16-V19. Code first, if applicable, any current malignant neoplasms: 140.0-195.8, 200.0-208.9,

230.0-234.9. Use additional code, if applicable, for any personal history of malignant neoplasm: V10.0-V10.9) ♀

V84.09 Genetic susceptibility to other malignant neoplasm — (Use additional code, if applicable, for any associated family history of the disease: V16-V19. Code first, if applicable, any current malignant neoplasms: 140.0-195.8, 200.0-208.9, 230.0-234.9. Use additional code, if applicable, for any personal history of malignant neoplasm: V10.0-V10.9)

ICD-9-CM Procedural

67.2 Conization of cervix ♀

67.32 Destruction of lesion of cervix by cauterization ♀

67.39 Other excision or destruction of lesion or tissue of cervix ♀

69.09 Other dilation and curettage of uterus ♀

HCPCS Level II Supplies & Services

A4305 Disposable drug delivery system, flow rate of 50 ml or greater per hour

57530-57531

57530 Trachelectomy (cervicectomy), amputation of cervix (separate procedure)

57531 Radical trachelectomy, with bilateral total pelvic lymphadenectomy and para-aortic lymph node sampling biopsy, with or without removal of tube(s), with or without removal of ovary(s)

ICD-9-CM Diagnostic

180.0 Malignant neoplasm of endocervix ♀

180.1 Malignant neoplasm of exocervix ♀

180.8 Malignant neoplasm of other specified sites of cervix ♀

196.2 Secondary and unspecified malignant neoplasm of intra-abdominal lymph nodes

196.6 Secondary and unspecified malignant neoplasm of intrapelvic lymph nodes

219.0 Benign neoplasm of cervix uteri ♀

233.1 Carcinoma in situ of cervix uteri ♀

236.0 Neoplasm of uncertain behavior of uterus ♀

239.5 Neoplasm of unspecified nature of other genitourinary organs

622.10 Dysplasia of cervix, unspecified ♀

622.11 Mild dysplasia of cervix ♀

622.12 Moderate dysplasia of cervix ♀

795.00 Abnormal glandular Papanicolaou smear of cervix ♀

795.01 Papanicolaou smear of cervix with atypical squamous cells of undetermined significance (ASC-US) ♀

795.02 Papanicolaou smear of cervix with atypical squamous cells cannot exclude high grade squamous intraepithelial lesion (ASC-H) ♀

795.03 Papanicolaou smear of cervix with low grade squamous intraepithelial lesion (LGSIL) ♀

795.07 Satisfactory cervical smear but lacking transformation zone ♀

795.09 Other abnormal Papanicolaou smear of cervix and cervical HPV — (Use additional code for associated human papillomavirus: 079.4) ♀

V10.42 Personal history of malignant neoplasm of other parts of uterus ♀

V84.01 Genetic susceptibility to malignant neoplasm of breast — (Use additional code, if applicable, for any associated family history of the disease: V16-V19. Code first, if applicable, any current malignant neoplasms: 140.0-195.8, 200.0-208.9, 230.0-234.9. Use additional code, if applicable, for any personal history of malignant neoplasm: V10.0-V10.9)

V84.02 Genetic susceptibility to malignant neoplasm of ovary — (Use additional code, if applicable, for any associated family history of the disease: V16-V19. Code first, if applicable, any current malignant neoplasms: 140.0-195.8, 200.0-208.9, 230.0-234.9. Use additional code, if applicable, for any personal history of malignant neoplasm: V10.0-V10.9) ♀

V84.04 Genetic susceptibility to malignant neoplasm of endometrium — (Use additional code, if applicable, for any associated family history of the disease: V16-V19. Code first, if applicable, any current malignant neoplasms: 140.0-195.8, 200.0-208.9, 230.0-234.9. Use additional code, if applicable, for any personal history of malignant neoplasm: V10.0-V10.9) ♀

V84.09 Genetic susceptibility to other malignant neoplasm — (Use additional code, if applicable, for any associated family history of the disease: V16-V19. Code first, if applicable, any current malignant neoplasms: 140.0-195.8, 200.0-208.9, 230.0-234.9. Use additional code, if applicable, for any personal history of malignant neoplasm: V10.0-V10.9)

ICD-9-CM Procedural

40.53 Radical excision of iliac lymph nodes

40.59 Radical excision of other lymph nodes

65.39 Other unilateral oophorectomy ♀

65.49 Other unilateral salpingo-oophorectomy ♀

65.51 Other removal of both ovaries at same operative episode ♀

65.61 Other removal of both ovaries and tubes at same operative episode ♀

65.62 Other removal of remaining ovary and tube ♀

66.4 Total unilateral salpingectomy ♀

66.51 Removal of both fallopian tubes at same operative episode ♀

66.52 Removal of remaining fallopian tube ♀

67.4 Amputation of cervix ♀

57540-57545

57540 Excision of cervical stump, abdominal approach;

57545 with pelvic floor repair

ICD-9-CM Diagnostic

180.0 Malignant neoplasm of endocervix ♀

180.1 Malignant neoplasm of exocervix ♀

180.8 Malignant neoplasm of other specified sites of cervix ♀

219.0 Benign neoplasm of cervix uteri ♀

233.1 Carcinoma in situ of cervix uteri ♀

236.0 Neoplasm of uncertain behavior of uterus ♀

239.5 Neoplasm of unspecified nature of other genitourinary organs

618.7 Genital prolapse, old laceration of muscles of pelvic floor — (Use additional code to identify urinary incontinence: 625.6, 788.31, 788.33-788.39) ♀

618.81 Incompetence or weakening of pubocervical tissue — (Use additional code to identify urinary incontinence: 625.6, 788.31, 788.33-788.39) ♀

618.82 Incompetence or weakening of rectovaginal tissue — (Use additional code to identify urinary incontinence: 625.6, 788.31, 788.33-788.39) ♀

618.83 Pelvic muscle wasting — (Use additional code to identify urinary incontinence: 625.6, 788.31, 788.33-788.39) ♀

618.84 Cervical stump prolapse — (Use additional code to identify urinary incontinence: 625.6, 788.31, 788.33-788.39) ♀

622.0 Erosion and ectropion of cervix ♀

622.10 Dysplasia of cervix, unspecified ♀

622.11 Mild dysplasia of cervix ♀

622.12 Moderate dysplasia of cervix ♀

625.6 Female stress incontinence ♀

795.00 Abnormal glandular Papanicolaou smear of cervix ♀

795.01 Papanicolaou smear of cervix with atypical squamous cells of undetermined significance (ASC-US) ♀

795.02 Papanicolaou smear of cervix with atypical squamous cells cannot exclude high grade squamous intraepithelial lesion (ASC-H) ♀

795.04 Papanicolaou smear of cervix with high grade squamous intraepithelial lesion (HGSIL) ♀

795.05 Cervical high risk human papillomavirus (HPV) DNA test positive ♀

795.07 Satisfactory cervical smear but lacking transformation zone ♀

795.08 Unsatisfactory cervical cytology smear ♀

795.09 Other abnormal Papanicolaou smear of cervix and cervical HPV — (Use additional code for associated human papillomavirus: 079.4) ♀

V84.02 Genetic susceptibility to malignant neoplasm of ovary — (Use additional code, if applicable, for any associated family history of the disease: V16-V19. Code first, if applicable, any current malignant neoplasms: 140.0-195.8, 200.0-208.9, 230.0-234.9. Use additional code, if applicable, for any personal history of malignant neoplasm: V10.0-V10.9) ♀

V84.04 Genetic susceptibility to malignant neoplasm of endometrium — (Use additional code, if applicable, for any associated family history of the disease: V16-V19. Code first, if applicable, any current malignant neoplasms: 140.0-195.8, 200.0-208.9, 230.0-234.9. Use additional code, if applicable, for any personal history of malignant neoplasm: V10.0-V10.9) ♀

V84.09 Genetic susceptibility to other malignant neoplasm — (Use additional code, if applicable, for any associated family history of the disease: V16-V19. Code first, if applicable, any current malignant neoplasms: 140.0-195.8, 200.0-208.9, 230.0-234.9. Use additional code, if applicable, for any personal history of malignant neoplasm: V10.0-V10.9)

ICD-9-CM Procedural

67.4 Amputation of cervix ♀

70.79 Other repair of vagina ♀

57550

57550 Excision of cervical stump, vaginal approach;

ICD-9-CM Diagnostic

180.0 Malignant neoplasm of endocervix ♀

180.1 Malignant neoplasm of exocervix ♀

180.8 Malignant neoplasm of other specified sites of cervix ♀

219.0 Benign neoplasm of cervix uteri ♀

233.1 Carcinoma in situ of cervix uteri ♀

236.0 Neoplasm of uncertain behavior of uterus ♀

239.5 Neoplasm of unspecified nature of other genitourinary organs

618.84 Cervical stump prolapse — (Use additional code to identify urinary incontinence: 625.6, 788.31, 788.33-788.39) ♀

622.0 Erosion and ectropion of cervix ♀

622.10 Dysplasia of cervix, unspecified ♥ ♀

622.11 Mild dysplasia of cervix ♀

622.12 Moderate dysplasia of cervix ♀

795.00 Abnormal glandular Papanicolaou smear of cervix ♀

795.01 Papanicolaou smear of cervix with atypical squamous cells of undetermined significance (ASC-US) ♀

795.02 Papanicolaou smear of cervix with atypical squamous cells cannot exclude high grade squamous intraepithelial lesion (ASC-H) ♀

795.03 Papanicolaou smear of cervix with low grade squamous intraepithelial lesion (LGSIL) ♀

795.04 Papanicolaou smear of cervix with high grade squamous intraepithelial lesion (HGSIL) ♀

795.05 Cervical high risk human papillomavirus (HPV) DNA test positive ♀

795.07 Satisfactory cervical smear but lacking transformation zone ♀

795.08 Unsatisfactory cervical cytology smear ♀

795.09 Other abnormal Papanicolaou smear of cervix and cervical HPV — (Use additional code for associated human papillomavirus: 079.4) ♀

V84.02 Genetic susceptibility to malignant neoplasm of ovary — (Use additional code, if applicable, for any associated family history of the disease: V16-V19. Code first, if applicable, any current malignant neoplasms: 140.0-195.8, 200.0-208.9, 230.0-234.9. Use additional code, if applicable, for any personal history of malignant neoplasm: V10.0-V10.9) ♀

V84.04 Genetic susceptibility to malignant neoplasm of endometrium — (Use additional code, if applicable, for any associated family history of the disease: V16-V19. Code first, if applicable, any current malignant neoplasms: 140.0-195.8, 200.0-208.9, 230.0-234.9. Use additional code, if applicable, for any personal history of malignant neoplasm: V10.0-V10.9) ♀

V84.09 Genetic susceptibility to other malignant neoplasm — (Use additional code, if applicable, for any associated family history of the disease: V16-V19. Code first, if applicable, any current malignant neoplasms: 140.0-195.8, 200.0-208.9, 230.0-234.9. Use additional code, if applicable, for any personal history of malignant neoplasm: V10.0-V10.9)

ICD-9-CM Procedural

67.4 Amputation of cervix ♀

57555-57556

57555 Excision of cervical stump, vaginal approach; with anterior and/or posterior repair

57556 with repair of enterocele

ICD-9-CM Diagnostic

180.0 Malignant neoplasm of endocervix ♀

180.1 Malignant neoplasm of exocervix ♀

180.8 Malignant neoplasm of other specified sites of cervix ♀

219.0 Benign neoplasm of cervix uteri ♀

233.1 Carcinoma in situ of cervix uteri ♀

236.0 Neoplasm of uncertain behavior of uterus ♀

239.5 Neoplasm of unspecified nature of other genitourinary organs

617.0 Endometriosis of uterus ♀

618.00 Unspecified prolapse of vaginal walls without mention of uterine prolapse — (Use additional code to identify urinary incontinence: 625.6, 788.31, 788.33-788.39) ♥ ♀

618.03 Urethrocele without mention of uterine prolapse — (Use additional code to identify urinary incontinence: 625.6, 788.31, 788.33-788.39) ♀

618.04 Rectocele without mention of uterine prolapse — (Use additional code to identify urinary incontinence: 625.6, 788.31, 788.33-788.39) (Use additional code for any associated fecal incontinence: 787.60-787.63) ♀

618.05 Perineocele without mention of uterine prolapse — (Use additional code to identify urinary incontinence: 625.6, 788.31, 788.33-788.39) ♀

618.1 Uterine prolapse without mention of vaginal wall prolapse — (Use additional code to identify urinary incontinence: 625.6, 788.31, 788.33-788.39) ♀

618.2 Uterovaginal prolapse, incomplete — (Use additional code to identify urinary incontinence: 625.6, 788.31, 788.33-788.39) ♀

618.5 Prolapse of vaginal vault after hysterectomy — (Use additional code to identify urinary incontinence: 625.6, 788.31, 788.33-788.39) ♀

618.6 Vaginal enterocele, congenital or acquired — (Use additional code to identify urinary incontinence: 625.6, 788.31, 788.33-788.39) ♀

618.81 Incompetence or weakening of pubocervical tissue — (Use additional code to identify urinary incontinence: 625.6, 788.31, 788.33-788.39) ♀

618.82 Incompetence or weakening of rectovaginal tissue — (Use additional code to identify urinary incontinence: 625.6, 788.31, 788.33-788.39) ♀

618.84 Cervical stump prolapse — (Use additional code to identify urinary incontinence: 625.6, 788.31, 788.33-788.39) ♀

622.0 Erosion and ectropion of cervix ♀

622.10 Dysplasia of cervix, unspecified ♥ ♀

622.11 Mild dysplasia of cervix ♀

622.12 Moderate dysplasia of cervix ♀

622.2 Leukoplakia of cervix (uteri) ♀

622.8 Other specified noninflammatory disorder of cervix ♀

625.6 Female stress incontinence ♀

795.00 Abnormal glandular Papanicolaou smear of cervix ♀

795.01 Papanicolaou smear of cervix with atypical squamous cells of undetermined significance (ASC-US) ♀

795.02 Papanicolaou smear of cervix with atypical squamous cells cannot exclude high grade squamous intraepithelial lesion (ASC-H) ♀

795.03 Papanicolaou smear of cervix with low grade squamous intraepithelial lesion (LGSIL) ♀

795.04 Papanicolaou smear of cervix with high grade squamous intraepithelial lesion (HGSIL) ♀

795.05 Cervical high risk human papillomavirus (HPV) DNA test positive ♀

795.07 Satisfactory cervical smear but lacking transformation zone ♀

795.08 Unsatisfactory cervical cytology smear ♀

795.09 Other abnormal Papanicolaou smear of cervix and cervical HPV — (Use additional code for associated human papillomavirus: 079.4) ♀
V84.02 Genetic susceptibility to malignant neoplasm of ovary — (Use additional code, if applicable, for any associated family history of the disease: V16-V19. Code first, if applicable, any current malignant neoplasms: 140.0-195.8, 200.0-208.9, 230.0-234.9. Use additional code, if applicable, for any personal history of malignant neoplasm: V10.0-V10.9) ♀
V84.04 Genetic susceptibility to malignant neoplasm of endometrium — (Use additional code, if applicable, for any associated family history of the disease: V16-V19. Code first, if applicable, any current malignant neoplasms: 140.0-195.8, 200.0-208.9, 230.0-234.9. Use additional code, if applicable, for any personal history of malignant neoplasm: V10.0-V10.9) ♀
V84.09 Genetic susceptibility to other malignant neoplasm — (Use additional code, if applicable, for any associated family history of the disease: V16-V19. Code first, if applicable, any current malignant neoplasms: 140.0-195.8, 200.0-208.9, 230.0-234.9. Use additional code, if applicable, for any personal history of malignant neoplasm: V10.0-V10.9)

ICD-9-CM Procedural
67.4 Amputation of cervix ♀
70.50 Repair of cystocele and rectocele ♀
70.92 Other operations on cul-de-sac ♀

57558
57558 Dilation and curettage of cervical stump

ICD-9-CM Diagnostic
180.0 Malignant neoplasm of endocervix ♀
180.8 Malignant neoplasm of other specified sites of cervix ♀
233.1 Carcinoma in situ of cervix uteri ♀
236.0 Neoplasm of uncertain behavior of uterus ♀
239.5 Neoplasm of unspecified nature of other genitourinary organs
616.0 Cervicitis and endocervicitis — (Use additional code to identify organism: 041.00-041.09, 041.10-041.19) ♀
617.0 Endometriosis of uterus ♀
622.0 Erosion and ectropion of cervix ♀
622.10 Dysplasia of cervix, unspecified ▽ ♀
622.11 Mild dysplasia of cervix ♀
622.12 Moderate dysplasia of cervix ♀
622.2 Leukoplakia of cervix (uteri) ♀
622.4 Stricture and stenosis of cervix ♀
622.7 Mucous polyp of cervix ♀
622.8 Other specified noninflammatory disorder of cervix ♀
627.1 Postmenopausal bleeding ♀

ICD-9-CM Procedural
69.09 Other dilation and curettage of uterus ♀

57700
57700 Cerclage of uterine cervix, nonobstetrical

ICD-9-CM Diagnostic
622.5 Incompetence of cervix ♀
654.54 Cervical incompetence, postpartum condition or complication — (Code first any associated obstructed labor, 660.2) ♀
867.4 Uterus injury without mention of open wound into cavity ♀

ICD-9-CM Procedural
67.59 Other repair of cervical os ♀

57720
57720 Trachelorrhaphy, plastic repair of uterine cervix, vaginal approach

ICD-9-CM Diagnostic
622.3 Old laceration of cervix ♀
622.5 Incompetence of cervix ♀
665.31 Laceration of cervix, with delivery ♀
665.34 Laceration of cervix, postpartum condition or complication ♀
867.4 Uterus injury without mention of open wound into cavity ♀

ICD-9-CM Procedural
67.69 Other repair of cervix ♀

57800
57800 Dilation of cervical canal, instrumental (separate procedure)

ICD-9-CM Diagnostic
622.4 Stricture and stenosis of cervix ♀
622.8 Other specified noninflammatory disorder of cervix ♀
626.8 Other disorder of menstruation and other abnormal bleeding from female genital tract ♀
628.4 Female infertility of cervical or vaginal origin ♀
789.00 Abdominal pain, unspecified site ▽

ICD-9-CM Procedural
67.0 Dilation of cervical canal ♀

Corpus Uteri

58100-58110
58100 Endometrial sampling (biopsy) with or without endocervical sampling (biopsy), without cervical dilation, any method (separate procedure)
58110 Endometrial sampling (biopsy) performed in conjunction with colposcopy (List separately in addition to code for primary procedure)

ICD-9-CM Diagnostic
179 Malignant neoplasm of uterus, part unspecified ▽ ♀
180.0 Malignant neoplasm of endocervix ♀
180.1 Malignant neoplasm of exocervix ♀
180.8 Malignant neoplasm of other specified sites of cervix ♀
180.9 Malignant neoplasm of cervix uteri, unspecified site ▽ ♀
182.0 Malignant neoplasm of corpus uteri, except isthmus ♀
182.8 Malignant neoplasm of other specified sites of body of uterus ♀
184.9 Malignant neoplasm of female genital organ, site unspecified ▽ ♀
198.82 Secondary malignant neoplasm of genital organs
198.89 Secondary malignant neoplasm of other specified sites
199.1 Other malignant neoplasm of unspecified site
218.0 Submucous leiomyoma of uterus ♀
218.1 Intramural leiomyoma of uterus ♀
219.0 Benign neoplasm of cervix uteri ♀
219.1 Benign neoplasm of corpus uteri ♀
219.8 Benign neoplasm of other specified parts of uterus ♀
219.9 Benign neoplasm of uterus, part unspecified ▽ ♀
221.8 Benign neoplasm of other specified sites of female genital organs ♀
221.9 Benign neoplasm of female genital organ, site unspecified ▽ ♀
233.1 Carcinoma in situ of cervix uteri ♀
233.2 Carcinoma in situ of other and unspecified parts of uterus ▽ ♀
233.30 Carcinoma in situ, unspecified female genital organ ▽ ♀
233.31 Carcinoma in situ, vagina ♀
233.32 Carcinoma in situ, vulva ♀

233.39 Carcinoma in situ, other female genital organ ♀
238.8 Neoplasm of uncertain behavior of other specified sites
239.5 Neoplasm of unspecified nature of other genitourinary organs
256.31 Premature menopause — (Use additional code for states associated with natural menopause: 627.2) ♀
256.39 Other ovarian failure — (Use additional code for states associated with natural menopause: 627.2) ♀
256.4 Polycystic ovaries ♀
615.0 Acute inflammatory disease of uterus, except cervix — (Use additional code to identify organism: 041.00-041.09, 041.10-041.19) ♀
615.1 Chronic inflammatory disease of uterus, except cervix — (Use additional code to identify organism: 041.00-041.09, 041.10-041.19) ♀
615.9 Unspecified inflammatory disease of uterus — (Use additional code to identify organism: 041.00-041.09, 041.10-041.19) ▽ ♀
616.0 Cervicitis and endocervicitis — (Use additional code to identify organism: 041.00-041.09, 041.10-041.19) ♀
617.0 Endometriosis of uterus ♀
617.8 Endometriosis of other specified sites ♀
617.9 Endometriosis, site unspecified ▽ ♀
621.0 Polyp of corpus uteri ♀
621.2 Hypertrophy of uterus ♀
621.30 Endometrial hyperplasia, unspecified ▽ ♀
621.31 Simple endometrial hyperplasia without atypia ♀
621.32 Complex endometrial hyperplasia without atypia ♀
621.33 Endometrial hyperplasia with atypia ♀
621.34 Benign endometrial hyperplasia ♀
621.35 Endometrial intraepithelial neoplasia [EIN] ♀
621.4 Hematometra ♀
621.5 Intrauterine synechiae ♀
621.8 Other specified disorders of uterus, not elsewhere classified ♀
622.10 Dysplasia of cervix, unspecified ▽ ♀
622.11 Mild dysplasia of cervix ♀
622.12 Moderate dysplasia of cervix ♀
622.4 Stricture and stenosis of cervix ♀
622.7 Mucous polyp of cervix ♀
623.5 Leukorrhea, not specified as infective ♀
623.7 Polyp of vagina ♀
625.1 Vaginismus ♀
625.3 Dysmenorrhea ♀
625.8 Other specified symptom associated with female genital organs ♀
626.0 Absence of menstruation ♀
626.1 Scanty or infrequent menstruation ♀
626.2 Excessive or frequent menstruation ♀
626.3 Puberty bleeding ♀
626.4 Irregular menstrual cycle ♀
626.5 Ovulation bleeding ♀
626.6 Metrorrhagia ♀
626.8 Other disorder of menstruation and other abnormal bleeding from female genital tract ♀
627.1 Postmenopausal bleeding ♀
627.2 Symptomatic menopausal or female climacteric states ♀
627.3 Postmenopausal atrophic vaginitis ♀
627.8 Other specified menopausal and postmenopausal disorder ♀
628.0 Female infertility associated with anovulation — (Use additional code for any associated Stein-Leventhal syndrome: 256.4) ♀
628.3 Female infertility of uterine origin — (Use additional code for any associated tuberculous endometriosis: 016.7) ♀
628.4 Female infertility of cervical or vaginal origin ♀
628.8 Female infertility of other specified origin ♀
629.0 Hematocele, female, not elsewhere classified ♀
646.30 Pregnancy complication, recurrent pregnancy loss, unspecified as to episode of care — (Use additional code to further specify complication) ▽ ♀
677 Late effect of complication of pregnancy, childbirth, and the puerperium — (Code first any sequelae) ♀
789.30 Abdominal or pelvic swelling, mass or lump, unspecified site ▽
795.00 Abnormal glandular Papanicolaou smear of cervix ♀
795.01 Papanicolaou smear of cervix with atypical squamous cells of undetermined significance (ASC-US) ♀
795.02 Papanicolaou smear of cervix with atypical squamous cells cannot exclude high grade squamous intraepithelial lesion (ASC-H) ♀
795.03 Papanicolaou smear of cervix with low grade squamous intraepithelial lesion (LGSIL) ♀
795.04 Papanicolaou smear of cervix with high grade squamous intraepithelial lesion (HGSIL) ♀
795.05 Cervical high risk human papillomavirus (HPV) DNA test positive ♀
795.07 Satisfactory cervical smear but lacking transformation zone ♀
795.08 Unsatisfactory cervical cytology smear ♀
795.09 Other abnormal Papanicolaou smear of cervix and cervical HPV — (Use additional code for associated human papillomavirus: 079.4) ♀
795.10 Abnormal glandular Papanicolaou smear of vagina — (Use additional code to identify acquired absence of uterus and cervix, if applicable: V88.01-V88.03) ♀
795.11 Papanicolaou smear of vagina with atypical squamous cells of undetermined significance (ASC-US) — (Use additional code to identify acquired absence of uterus and cervix, if applicable: V88.01-V88.03) ♀
795.12 Papanicolaou smear of vagina with atypical squamous cells cannot exclude high grade squamous intraepithelial lesion (ASC-H) — (Use additional code to identify acquired absence of uterus and cervix, if applicable: V88.01-V88.03) ♀
795.13 Papanicolaou smear of vagina with low grade squamous intraepithelial lesion (LGSIL) — (Use additional code to identify acquired absence of uterus and cervix, if applicable: V88.01-V88.03) ♀
795.14 Papanicolaou smear of vagina with high grade squamous intraepithelial lesion (HGSIL) — (Use additional code to identify acquired absence of uterus and cervix, if applicable: V88.01-V88.03) ♀
795.15 Vaginal high risk human papillomavirus (HPV) DNA test positive — (Use additional code to identify acquired absence of uterus and cervix, if applicable: V88.01-V88.03) ♀
795.16 Papanicolaou smear of vagina with cytologic evidence of malignancy — (Use additional code to identify acquired absence of uterus and cervix, if applicable: V88.01-V88.03) ♀
795.18 Unsatisfactory vaginal cytology smear — (Use additional code to identify acquired absence of uterus and cervix, if applicable: V88.01-V88.03) ♀
795.19 Other abnormal Papanicolaou smear of vagina and vaginal HPV — (Use additional code to identify acquired absence of uterus and cervix, if applicable: V88.01-V88.03) (Use additional code for associated human papillomavirus: 079.4) ♀
795.39 Other nonspecific positive culture findings
795.4 Other nonspecific abnormal histological findings
V84.02 Genetic susceptibility to malignant neoplasm of ovary — (Use additional code, if applicable, for any associated family history of the disease: V16-V19. Code first, if applicable, any current malignant neoplasms: 140.0-195.8, 200.0-208.9, 230.0-234.9. Use additional code, if applicable, for any personal history of malignant neoplasm: V10.0-V10.9) ♀
V84.04 Genetic susceptibility to malignant neoplasm of endometrium — (Use additional code, if applicable, for any associated family history of the disease: V16-V19. Code first, if applicable, any current malignant neoplasms: 140.0-195.8, 200.0-208.9, 230.0-234.9. Use additional code, if applicable, for any personal history of malignant neoplasm: V10.0-V10.9) ♀
V84.09 Genetic susceptibility to other malignant neoplasm — (Use additional code, if applicable, for any associated family history of the disease: V16-V19. Code first, if applicable, any current malignant neoplasms: 140.0-195.8, 200.0-208.9, 230.0-234.9. Use additional code, if applicable, for any personal history of malignant neoplasm: V10.0-V10.9)

ICD-9-CM Procedural

67.11 Endocervical biopsy ♀
67.12 Other cervical biopsy ♀
68.16 Closed biopsy of uterus ♀

58120

58120 Dilation and curettage, diagnostic and/or therapeutic (nonobstetrical)

ICD-9-CM Diagnostic

179 Malignant neoplasm of uterus, part unspecified ▽ ♀
180.0 Malignant neoplasm of endocervix ♀
180.1 Malignant neoplasm of exocervix ♀
180.8 Malignant neoplasm of other specified sites of cervix ♀
180.9 Malignant neoplasm of cervix uteri, unspecified site ▽ ♀
182.0 Malignant neoplasm of corpus uteri, except isthmus ♀
182.1 Malignant neoplasm of isthmus ♀
182.8 Malignant neoplasm of other specified sites of body of uterus ♀
184.0 Malignant neoplasm of vagina ♀
198.82 Secondary malignant neoplasm of genital organs
218.0 Submucous leiomyoma of uterus ♀
218.1 Intramural leiomyoma of uterus ♀
218.9 Leiomyoma of uterus, unspecified ▽ ♀
233.1 Carcinoma in situ of cervix uteri ♀
233.2 Carcinoma in situ of other and unspecified parts of uterus ▽ ♀
233.30 Carcinoma in situ, unspecified female genital organ ▽ ♀
233.31 Carcinoma in situ, vagina ♀
233.32 Carcinoma in situ, vulva ♀
233.39 Carcinoma in situ, other female genital organ ♀
236.0 Neoplasm of uncertain behavior of uterus ♀
239.5 Neoplasm of unspecified nature of other genitourinary organs
615.1 Chronic inflammatory disease of uterus, except cervix — (Use additional code to identify organism: 041.00-041.09, 041.10-041.19) ♀
616.0 Cervicitis and endocervicitis — (Use additional code to identify organism: 041.00-041.09, 041.10-041.19) ♀
616.10 Unspecified vaginitis and vulvovaginitis — (Use additional code to identify organism, such as: 041.00-041.09, 041.10-041.19, 041.41-041.49) ▽ ♀
617.0 Endometriosis of uterus ♀
617.9 Endometriosis, site unspecified ▽ ♀
621.0 Polyp of corpus uteri ♀
621.2 Hypertrophy of uterus ♀
621.30 Endometrial hyperplasia, unspecified ▽ ♀
621.31 Simple endometrial hyperplasia without atypia ♀
621.32 Complex endometrial hyperplasia without atypia ♀
621.33 Endometrial hyperplasia with atypia ♀
621.34 Benign endometrial hyperplasia ♀
621.35 Endometrial intraepithelial neoplasia [EIN] ♀
621.8 Other specified disorders of uterus, not elsewhere classified ♀
622.10 Dysplasia of cervix, unspecified ▽ ♀
622.11 Mild dysplasia of cervix ♀
622.12 Moderate dysplasia of cervix ♀
622.4 Stricture and stenosis of cervix ♀
622.7 Mucous polyp of cervix ♀
623.8 Other specified noninflammatory disorder of vagina ♀
625.0 Dyspareunia ♀
625.3 Dysmenorrhea ♀
625.8 Other specified symptom associated with female genital organs ♀
626.0 Absence of menstruation ♀
626.1 Scanty or infrequent menstruation ♀
626.2 Excessive or frequent menstruation ♀
626.3 Puberty bleeding ♀
626.4 Irregular menstrual cycle ♀
626.6 Metrorrhagia ♀
626.8 Other disorder of menstruation and other abnormal bleeding from female genital tract ♀
627.0 Premenopausal menorrhagia ♀
627.1 Postmenopausal bleeding ♀
628.9 Female infertility of unspecified origin ▽ ♀
677 Late effect of complication of pregnancy, childbirth, and the puerperium — (Code first any sequelae) ♀
V84.02 Genetic susceptibility to malignant neoplasm of ovary — (Use additional code, if applicable, for any associated family history of the disease: V16-V19. Code first, if applicable, any current malignant neoplasms: 140.0-195.8, 200.0-208.9, 230.0-234.9. Use additional code, if applicable, for any personal history of malignant neoplasm: V10.0-V10.9) ♀
V84.04 Genetic susceptibility to malignant neoplasm of endometrium — (Use additional code, if applicable, for any associated family history of the disease: V16-V19. Code first, if applicable, any current malignant neoplasms: 140.0-195.8, 200.0-208.9, 230.0-234.9. Use additional code, if applicable, for any personal history of malignant neoplasm: V10.0-V10.9) ♀
V84.09 Genetic susceptibility to other malignant neoplasm — (Use additional code, if applicable, for any associated family history of the disease: V16-V19. Code first, if applicable, any current malignant neoplasms: 140.0-195.8, 200.0-208.9, 230.0-234.9. Use additional code, if applicable, for any personal history of malignant neoplasm: V10.0-V10.9)

ICD-9-CM Procedural

69.09 Other dilation and curettage of uterus ♀

HCPCS Level II Supplies & Services

A4305 Disposable drug delivery system, flow rate of 50 ml or greater per hour

58140-58146

58140 Myomectomy, excision of fibroid tumor(s) of uterus, 1 to 4 intramural myoma(s) with total weight of 250 g or less and/or removal of surface myomas; abdominal approach
58145 vaginal approach
58146 Myomectomy, excision of fibroid tumor(s) of uterus, 5 or more intramural myomas and/or intramural myomas with total weight greater than 250 g, abdominal approach

ICD-9-CM Diagnostic

218.0 Submucous leiomyoma of uterus ♀
218.1 Intramural leiomyoma of uterus ♀
218.2 Subserous leiomyoma of uterus ♀
218.9 Leiomyoma of uterus, unspecified ▽ ♀
V64.41 Laparoscopic surgical procedure converted to open procedure

ICD-9-CM Procedural

68.29 Other excision or destruction of lesion of uterus ♀

58150-58152

58150 Total abdominal hysterectomy (corpus and cervix), with or without removal of tube(s), with or without removal of ovary(s);
58152 with colpo-urethrocystopexy (eg, Marshall-Marchetti-Krantz, Burch)

ICD-9-CM Diagnostic

179 Malignant neoplasm of uterus, part unspecified ▽ ♀
180.0 Malignant neoplasm of endocervix ♀
180.9 Malignant neoplasm of cervix uteri, unspecified site ▽ ♀
182.0 Malignant neoplasm of corpus uteri, except isthmus ♀
182.1 Malignant neoplasm of isthmus ♀
182.8 Malignant neoplasm of other specified sites of body of uterus ♀

183.0 Malignant neoplasm of ovary — (Use additional code to identify any functional activity) ♀
183.2 Malignant neoplasm of fallopian tube ♀
183.8 Malignant neoplasm of other specified sites of uterine adnexa ♀
183.9 Malignant neoplasm of uterine adnexa, unspecified site ♀
184.9 Malignant neoplasm of female genital organ, site unspecified ♀
198.6 Secondary malignant neoplasm of ovary ♀
198.82 Secondary malignant neoplasm of genital organs
199.1 Other malignant neoplasm of unspecified site
209.74 Secondary neuroendocrine tumor of peritoneum
209.79 Secondary neuroendocrine tumor of other sites
218.0 Submucous leiomyoma of uterus ♀
218.1 Intramural leiomyoma of uterus ♀
218.2 Subserous leiomyoma of uterus ♀
233.1 Carcinoma in situ of cervix uteri ♀
233.2 Carcinoma in situ of other and unspecified parts of uterus ♀
233.30 Carcinoma in situ, unspecified female genital organ ♀
233.31 Carcinoma in situ, vagina ♀
233.32 Carcinoma in situ, vulva ♀
233.39 Carcinoma in situ, other female genital organ ♀
236.0 Neoplasm of uncertain behavior of uterus ♀
236.1 Neoplasm of uncertain behavior of placenta ♀
236.2 Neoplasm of uncertain behavior of ovary — (Use additional code to identify any functional activity) ♀
236.3 Neoplasm of uncertain behavior of other and unspecified female genital organs ♀
239.5 Neoplasm of unspecified nature of other genitourinary organs
256.0 Hyperestrogenism ♀
614.1 Chronic salpingitis and oophoritis — (Use additional code to identify organism: 041.00-041.09, 041.10-041.19) ♀
614.2 Salpingitis and oophoritis not specified as acute, subacute, or chronic — (Use additional code to identify organism: 041.00-041.09, 041.10-041.19) ♀
614.3 Acute parametritis and pelvic cellulitis — (Use additional code to identify organism: 041.00-041.09, 041.10-041.19) ♀
614.4 Chronic or unspecified parametritis and pelvic cellulitis — (Use additional code to identify organism: 041.00-041.09, 041.10-041.19) ♀
614.5 Acute or unspecified pelvic peritonitis, female — (Use additional code to identify organism: 041.00-041.09, 041.10-041.19) ♀
614.6 Pelvic peritoneal adhesions, female (postoperative) (postinfection) — (Use additional code to identify organism: 041.00-041.09, 041.10-041.19) (Use additional code to identify any associated infertility: 628.2) ♀
617.0 Endometriosis of uterus ♀
617.1 Endometriosis of ovary ♀
617.2 Endometriosis of fallopian tube ♀
617.3 Endometriosis of pelvic peritoneum ♀
617.9 Endometriosis, site unspecified ♀
618.01 Cystocele without mention of uterine prolapse, midline — (Use additional code to identify urinary incontinence: 625.6, 788.31, 788.33-788.39) ♀
618.02 Cystocele without mention of uterine prolapse, lateral — (Use additional code to identify urinary incontinence: 625.6, 788.31, 788.33-788.39) ♀
618.03 Urethrocele without mention of uterine prolapse — (Use additional code to identify urinary incontinence: 625.6, 788.31, 788.33-788.39) ♀
618.09 Other prolapse of vaginal walls without mention of uterine prolapse — (Use additional code to identify urinary incontinence: 625.6, 788.31, 788.33-788.39) ♀
618.1 Uterine prolapse without mention of vaginal wall prolapse — (Use additional code to identify urinary incontinence: 625.6, 788.31, 788.33-788.39) ♀
618.2 Uterovaginal prolapse, incomplete — (Use additional code to identify urinary incontinence: 625.6, 788.31, 788.33-788.39) ♀
618.3 Uterovaginal prolapse, complete — (Use additional code to identify urinary incontinence: 625.6, 788.31, 788.33-788.39) ♀
618.4 Uterovaginal prolapse, unspecified — (Use additional code to identify urinary incontinence: 625.6, 788.31, 788.33-788.39) ♀
620.0 Follicular cyst of ovary ♀
620.1 Corpus luteum cyst or hematoma ♀
620.2 Other and unspecified ovarian cyst ♀
620.8 Other noninflammatory disorder of ovary, fallopian tube, and broad ligament ♀
621.0 Polyp of corpus uteri ♀
621.2 Hypertrophy of uterus ♀
621.30 Endometrial hyperplasia, unspecified ♀
621.31 Simple endometrial hyperplasia without atypia ♀
621.32 Complex endometrial hyperplasia without atypia ♀
621.33 Endometrial hyperplasia with atypia ♀
621.34 Benign endometrial hyperplasia ♀
621.35 Endometrial intraepithelial neoplasia [EIN] ♀
621.8 Other specified disorders of uterus, not elsewhere classified ♀
622.10 Dysplasia of cervix, unspecified ♀
622.11 Mild dysplasia of cervix ♀
622.12 Moderate dysplasia of cervix ♀
625.3 Dysmenorrhea ♀
625.5 Pelvic congestion syndrome ♀
625.6 Female stress incontinence ♀
625.8 Other specified symptom associated with female genital organs ♀
626.2 Excessive or frequent menstruation ♀
626.6 Metrorrhagia ♀
626.8 Other disorder of menstruation and other abnormal bleeding from female genital tract ♀
627.1 Postmenopausal bleeding ♀
627.2 Symptomatic menopausal or female climacteric states ♀
677 Late effect of complication of pregnancy, childbirth, and the puerperium — (Code first any sequelae) ♀
789.00 Abdominal pain, unspecified site
789.30 Abdominal or pelvic swelling, mass or lump, unspecified site
V84.02 Genetic susceptibility to malignant neoplasm of ovary — (Use additional code, if applicable, for any associated family history of the disease: V16-V19. Code first, if applicable, any current malignant neoplasms: 140.0-195.8, 200.0-208.9, 230.0-234.9. Use additional code, if applicable, for any personal history of malignant neoplasm: V10.0-V10.9) ♀
V84.04 Genetic susceptibility to malignant neoplasm of endometrium — (Use additional code, if applicable, for any associated family history of the disease: V16-V19. Code first, if applicable, any current malignant neoplasms: 140.0-195.8, 200.0-208.9, 230.0-234.9. Use additional code, if applicable, for any personal history of malignant neoplasm: V10.0-V10.9) ♀
V84.09 Genetic susceptibility to other malignant neoplasm — (Use additional code, if applicable, for any associated family history of the disease: V16-V19. Code first, if applicable, any current malignant neoplasms: 140.0-195.8, 200.0-208.9, 230.0-234.9. Use additional code, if applicable, for any personal history of malignant neoplasm: V10.0-V10.9)

ICD-9-CM Procedural

59.5 Retropubic urethral suspension
65.39 Other unilateral oophorectomy ♀
65.49 Other unilateral salpingo-oophorectomy ♀
65.51 Other removal of both ovaries at same operative episode ♀
65.52 Other removal of remaining ovary ♀
65.61 Other removal of both ovaries and tubes at same operative episode ♀
65.62 Other removal of remaining ovary and tube ♀
68.49 Other and unspecified total abdominal hysterectomy ♀

58180

58180 Supracervical abdominal hysterectomy (subtotal hysterectomy), with or without removal of tube(s), with or without removal of ovary(s)

ICD-9-CM Diagnostic

182.0 Malignant neoplasm of corpus uteri, except isthmus ♀
182.1 Malignant neoplasm of isthmus ♀
182.8 Malignant neoplasm of other specified sites of body of uterus ♀
183.8 Malignant neoplasm of other specified sites of uterine adnexa ♀
183.9 Malignant neoplasm of uterine adnexa, unspecified site ♀
184.8 Malignant neoplasm of other specified sites of female genital organs ♀
218.0 Submucous leiomyoma of uterus ♀
218.1 Intramural leiomyoma of uterus ♀
218.2 Subserous leiomyoma of uterus ♀
219.1 Benign neoplasm of corpus uteri ♀
219.9 Benign neoplasm of uterus, part unspecified ♀
236.0 Neoplasm of uncertain behavior of uterus ♀
236.3 Neoplasm of uncertain behavior of other and unspecified female genital organs ♀
239.5 Neoplasm of unspecified nature of other genitourinary organs
617.0 Endometriosis of uterus ♀
617.1 Endometriosis of ovary ♀
617.2 Endometriosis of fallopian tube ♀
618.1 Uterine prolapse without mention of vaginal wall prolapse — (Use additional code to identify urinary incontinence: 625.6, 788.31, 788.33-788.39) ♀
625.3 Dysmenorrhea ♀
626.8 Other disorder of menstruation and other abnormal bleeding from female genital tract ♀
677 Late effect of complication of pregnancy, childbirth, and the puerperium — (Code first any sequelae) ♀
V84.02 Genetic susceptibility to malignant neoplasm of ovary — (Use additional code, if applicable, for any associated family history of the disease: V16-V19. Code first, if applicable, any current malignant neoplasms: 140.0-195.8, 200.0-208.9, 230.0-234.9. Use additional code, if applicable, for any personal history of malignant neoplasm: V10.0-V10.9) ♀
V84.04 Genetic susceptibility to malignant neoplasm of endometrium — (Use additional code, if applicable, for any associated family history of the disease: V16-V19. Code first, if applicable, any current malignant neoplasms: 140.0-195.8, 200.0-208.9, 230.0-234.9. Use additional code, if applicable, for any personal history of malignant neoplasm: V10.0-V10.9) ♀
V84.09 Genetic susceptibility to other malignant neoplasm — (Use additional code, if applicable, for any associated family history of the disease: V16-V19. Code first, if applicable, any current malignant neoplasms: 140.0-195.8, 200.0-208.9, 230.0-234.9. Use additional code, if applicable, for any personal history of malignant neoplasm: V10.0-V10.9)

ICD-9-CM Procedural

65.39 Other unilateral oophorectomy ♀
65.49 Other unilateral salpingo-oophorectomy ♀
65.51 Other removal of both ovaries at same operative episode ♀
65.52 Other removal of remaining ovary ♀
65.61 Other removal of both ovaries and tubes at same operative episode ♀
65.62 Other removal of remaining ovary and tube ♀
68.39 Other and unspecified subtotal abdominal hysterectomy ♀

58200

58200 Total abdominal hysterectomy, including partial vaginectomy, with para-aortic and pelvic lymph node sampling, with or without removal of tube(s), with or without removal of ovary(s)

ICD-9-CM Diagnostic

179 Malignant neoplasm of uterus, part unspecified ♀
180.0 Malignant neoplasm of endocervix ♀
180.1 Malignant neoplasm of exocervix ♀
180.8 Malignant neoplasm of other specified sites of cervix ♀
182.0 Malignant neoplasm of corpus uteri, except isthmus ♀
182.1 Malignant neoplasm of isthmus ♀
182.8 Malignant neoplasm of other specified sites of body of uterus ♀
183.0 Malignant neoplasm of ovary — (Use additional code to identify any functional activity) ♀
183.2 Malignant neoplasm of fallopian tube ♀
183.3 Malignant neoplasm of broad ligament of uterus ♀
183.4 Malignant neoplasm of parametrium of uterus ♀
183.5 Malignant neoplasm of round ligament of uterus ♀
183.8 Malignant neoplasm of other specified sites of uterine adnexa ♀
183.9 Malignant neoplasm of uterine adnexa, unspecified site ♀
184.0 Malignant neoplasm of vagina ♀
184.8 Malignant neoplasm of other specified sites of female genital organs ♀
196.2 Secondary and unspecified malignant neoplasm of intra-abdominal lymph nodes
196.6 Secondary and unspecified malignant neoplasm of intrapelvic lymph nodes
196.8 Secondary and unspecified malignant neoplasm of lymph nodes of multiple sites
198.82 Secondary malignant neoplasm of genital organs
209.71 Secondary neuroendocrine tumor of distant lymph nodes
209.74 Secondary neuroendocrine tumor of peritoneum
209.79 Secondary neuroendocrine tumor of other sites
233.1 Carcinoma in situ of cervix uteri ♀
236.0 Neoplasm of uncertain behavior of uterus ♀
236.2 Neoplasm of uncertain behavior of ovary — (Use additional code to identify any functional activity) ♀
238.8 Neoplasm of uncertain behavior of other specified sites
239.5 Neoplasm of unspecified nature of other genitourinary organs
239.89 Neoplasms of unspecified nature, other specified sites
V84.02 Genetic susceptibility to malignant neoplasm of ovary — (Use additional code, if applicable, for any associated family history of the disease: V16-V19. Code first, if applicable, any current malignant neoplasms: 140.0-195.8, 200.0-208.9, 230.0-234.9. Use additional code, if applicable, for any personal history of malignant neoplasm: V10.0-V10.9) ♀
V84.04 Genetic susceptibility to malignant neoplasm of endometrium — (Use additional code, if applicable, for any associated family history of the disease: V16-V19. Code first, if applicable, any current malignant neoplasms: 140.0-195.8, 200.0-208.9, 230.0-234.9. Use additional code, if applicable, for any personal history of malignant neoplasm: V10.0-V10.9) ♀
V84.09 Genetic susceptibility to other malignant neoplasm — (Use additional code, if applicable, for any associated family history of the disease: V16-V19. Code first, if applicable, any current malignant neoplasms: 140.0-195.8, 200.0-208.9, 230.0-234.9. Use additional code, if applicable, for any personal history of malignant neoplasm: V10.0-V10.9)

ICD-9-CM Procedural

40.11 Biopsy of lymphatic structure
65.39 Other unilateral oophorectomy ♀
65.49 Other unilateral salpingo-oophorectomy ♀
65.51 Other removal of both ovaries at same operative episode ♀
65.52 Other removal of remaining ovary ♀
65.61 Other removal of both ovaries and tubes at same operative episode ♀
65.62 Other removal of remaining ovary and tube ♀
68.49 Other and unspecified total abdominal hysterectomy ♀
70.8 Obliteration of vaginal vault ♀

58210

58210 Radical abdominal hysterectomy, with bilateral total pelvic lymphadenectomy and para-aortic lymph node sampling (biopsy), with or without removal of tube(s), with or without removal of ovary(s)

ICD-9-CM Diagnostic

179 Malignant neoplasm of uterus, part unspecified ▽ ♀
180.0 Malignant neoplasm of endocervix ♀
180.1 Malignant neoplasm of exocervix ♀
180.8 Malignant neoplasm of other specified sites of cervix ♀
182.0 Malignant neoplasm of corpus uteri, except isthmus ♀
182.1 Malignant neoplasm of isthmus ♀
182.8 Malignant neoplasm of other specified sites of body of uterus ♀
183.0 Malignant neoplasm of ovary — (Use additional code to identify any functional activity) ♀
183.2 Malignant neoplasm of fallopian tube ♀
183.3 Malignant neoplasm of broad ligament of uterus ♀
183.4 Malignant neoplasm of parametrium of uterus ♀
183.5 Malignant neoplasm of round ligament of uterus ♀
183.8 Malignant neoplasm of other specified sites of uterine adnexa ♀
183.9 Malignant neoplasm of uterine adnexa, unspecified site ▽ ♀
184.0 Malignant neoplasm of vagina ♀
184.8 Malignant neoplasm of other specified sites of female genital organs ♀
196.2 Secondary and unspecified malignant neoplasm of intra-abdominal lymph nodes
196.6 Secondary and unspecified malignant neoplasm of intrapelvic lymph nodes
196.8 Secondary and unspecified malignant neoplasm of lymph nodes of multiple sites
198.82 Secondary malignant neoplasm of genital organs
209.71 Secondary neuroendocrine tumor of distant lymph nodes
209.74 Secondary neuroendocrine tumor of peritoneum
209.79 Secondary neuroendocrine tumor of other sites
233.1 Carcinoma in situ of cervix uteri ♀
236.0 Neoplasm of uncertain behavior of uterus ♀
236.2 Neoplasm of uncertain behavior of ovary — (Use additional code to identify any functional activity) ♀
238.8 Neoplasm of uncertain behavior of other specified sites
239.5 Neoplasm of unspecified nature of other genitourinary organs
239.89 Neoplasms of unspecified nature, other specified sites
V84.02 Genetic susceptibility to malignant neoplasm of ovary — (Use additional code, if applicable, for any associated family history of the disease: V16-V19. Code first, if applicable, any current malignant neoplasms: 140.0-195.8, 200.0-208.9, 230.0-234.9. Use additional code, if applicable, for any personal history of malignant neoplasm: V10.0-V10.9) ♀
V84.04 Genetic susceptibility to malignant neoplasm of endometrium — (Use additional code, if applicable, for any associated family history of the disease: V16-V19. Code first, if applicable, any current malignant neoplasms: 140.0-195.8, 200.0-208.9, 230.0-234.9. Use additional code, if applicable, for any personal history of malignant neoplasm: V10.0-V10.9) ♀
V84.09 Genetic susceptibility to other malignant neoplasm — (Use additional code, if applicable, for any associated family history of the disease: V16-V19. Code first, if applicable, any current malignant neoplasms: 140.0-195.8, 200.0-208.9, 230.0-234.9. Use additional code, if applicable, for any personal history of malignant neoplasm: V10.0-V10.9)

ICD-9-CM Procedural

40.11 Biopsy of lymphatic structure
40.3 Regional lymph node excision
40.59 Radical excision of other lymph nodes
65.39 Other unilateral oophorectomy ♀
65.49 Other unilateral salpingo-oophorectomy ♀
65.51 Other removal of both ovaries at same operative episode ♀
65.52 Other removal of remaining ovary ♀
65.61 Other removal of both ovaries and tubes at same operative episode ♀
65.62 Other removal of remaining ovary and tube ♀
68.69 Other and unspecified radical abdominal hysterectomy ♀

58240

58240 Pelvic exenteration for gynecologic malignancy, with total abdominal hysterectomy or cervicectomy, with or without removal of tube(s), with or without removal of ovary(s), with removal of bladder and ureteral transplantations, and/or abdominoperineal resection of rectum and colon and colostomy, or any combination thereof

ICD-9-CM Diagnostic

179 Malignant neoplasm of uterus, part unspecified ▽ ♀
180.0 Malignant neoplasm of endocervix ♀
180.1 Malignant neoplasm of exocervix ♀
180.8 Malignant neoplasm of other specified sites of cervix ♀
182.0 Malignant neoplasm of corpus uteri, except isthmus ♀
182.1 Malignant neoplasm of isthmus ♀
182.8 Malignant neoplasm of other specified sites of body of uterus ♀
183.0 Malignant neoplasm of ovary — (Use additional code to identify any functional activity) ♀
183.2 Malignant neoplasm of fallopian tube ♀
183.3 Malignant neoplasm of broad ligament of uterus ♀
183.4 Malignant neoplasm of parametrium of uterus ♀
183.5 Malignant neoplasm of round ligament of uterus ♀
183.8 Malignant neoplasm of other specified sites of uterine adnexa ♀
183.9 Malignant neoplasm of uterine adnexa, unspecified site ▽ ♀
184.0 Malignant neoplasm of vagina ♀
184.8 Malignant neoplasm of other specified sites of female genital organs ♀
184.9 Malignant neoplasm of female genital organ, site unspecified ▽ ♀
197.5 Secondary malignant neoplasm of large intestine and rectum
198.1 Secondary malignant neoplasm of other urinary organs
198.6 Secondary malignant neoplasm of ovary ♀
198.82 Secondary malignant neoplasm of genital organs
199.0 Disseminated malignant neoplasm
199.1 Other malignant neoplasm of unspecified site
V84.02 Genetic susceptibility to malignant neoplasm of ovary — (Use additional code, if applicable, for any associated family history of the disease: V16-V19. Code first, if applicable, any current malignant neoplasms: 140.0-195.8, 200.0-208.9, 230.0-234.9. Use additional code, if applicable, for any personal history of malignant neoplasm: V10.0-V10.9) ♀
V84.04 Genetic susceptibility to malignant neoplasm of endometrium — (Use additional code, if applicable, for any associated family history of the disease: V16-V19. Code first, if applicable, any current malignant neoplasms: 140.0-195.8, 200.0-208.9, 230.0-234.9. Use additional code, if applicable, for any personal history of malignant neoplasm: V10.0-V10.9) ♀
V84.09 Genetic susceptibility to other malignant neoplasm — (Use additional code, if applicable, for any associated family history of the disease: V16-V19. Code first, if applicable, any current malignant neoplasms: 140.0-195.8, 200.0-208.9, 230.0-234.9. Use additional code, if applicable, for any personal history of malignant neoplasm: V10.0-V10.9)

ICD-9-CM Procedural

40.3 Regional lymph node excision
40.59 Radical excision of other lymph nodes
46.13 Permanent colostomy
56.61 Formation of other cutaneous ureterostomy
68.8 Pelvic evisceration ♀

58260-58263

58260 Vaginal hysterectomy, for uterus 250 g or less;
58262 with removal of tube(s), and/or ovary(s)
58263 with removal of tube(s), and/or ovary(s), with repair of enterocele

ICD-9-CM Diagnostic

180.0 Malignant neoplasm of endocervix ♀
180.1 Malignant neoplasm of exocervix ♀
180.8 Malignant neoplasm of other specified sites of cervix ♀
180.9 Malignant neoplasm of cervix uteri, unspecified site ♀
181 Malignant neoplasm of placenta ♀
182.0 Malignant neoplasm of corpus uteri, except isthmus ♀
182.1 Malignant neoplasm of isthmus ♀
182.8 Malignant neoplasm of other specified sites of body of uterus ♀
183.0 Malignant neoplasm of ovary — (Use additional code to identify any functional activity) ♀
183.8 Malignant neoplasm of other specified sites of uterine adnexa ♀
183.9 Malignant neoplasm of uterine adnexa, unspecified site ♀
198.6 Secondary malignant neoplasm of ovary ♀
199.1 Other malignant neoplasm of unspecified site
218.0 Submucous leiomyoma of uterus ♀
218.1 Intramural leiomyoma of uterus ♀
218.2 Subserous leiomyoma of uterus ♀
218.9 Leiomyoma of uterus, unspecified ♀
233.1 Carcinoma in situ of cervix uteri ♀
233.2 Carcinoma in situ of other and unspecified parts of uterus ♀
233.30 Carcinoma in situ, unspecified female genital organ ♀
233.31 Carcinoma in situ, vagina ♀
233.32 Carcinoma in situ, vulva ♀
233.39 Carcinoma in situ, other female genital organ ♀
236.0 Neoplasm of uncertain behavior of uterus ♀
236.2 Neoplasm of uncertain behavior of ovary — (Use additional code to identify any functional activity) ♀
236.3 Neoplasm of uncertain behavior of other and unspecified female genital organs ♀
239.5 Neoplasm of unspecified nature of other genitourinary organs
553.9 Hernia of unspecified site of abdominal cavity without mention of obstruction or gangrene
614.4 Chronic or unspecified parametritis and pelvic cellulitis — (Use additional code to identify organism: 041.00-041.09, 041.10-041.19) ♀
614.9 Unspecified inflammatory disease of female pelvic organs and tissues — (Use additional code to identify organism: 041.00-041.09, 041.10-041.19) ♀
617.0 Endometriosis of uterus ♀
617.9 Endometriosis, site unspecified ♀
618.00 Unspecified prolapse of vaginal walls without mention of uterine prolapse — (Use additional code to identify urinary incontinence: 625.6, 788.31, 788.33-788.39) ♀
618.1 Uterine prolapse without mention of vaginal wall prolapse — (Use additional code to identify urinary incontinence: 625.6, 788.31, 788.33-788.39) ♀
618.2 Uterovaginal prolapse, incomplete — (Use additional code to identify urinary incontinence: 625.6, 788.31, 788.33-788.39) ♀
618.3 Uterovaginal prolapse, complete — (Use additional code to identify urinary incontinence: 625.6, 788.31, 788.33-788.39) ♀
618.4 Uterovaginal prolapse, unspecified — (Use additional code to identify urinary incontinence: 625.6, 788.31, 788.33-788.39) ♀
618.6 Vaginal enterocele, congenital or acquired — (Use additional code to identify urinary incontinence: 625.6, 788.31, 788.33-788.39) ♀
618.9 Unspecified genital prolapse — (Use additional code to identify urinary incontinence: 625.6, 788.31, 788.33-788.39) ♀
621.0 Polyp of corpus uteri ♀
621.2 Hypertrophy of uterus ♀
621.30 Endometrial hyperplasia, unspecified ♀
621.31 Simple endometrial hyperplasia without atypia ♀
621.32 Complex endometrial hyperplasia without atypia ♀
621.33 Endometrial hyperplasia with atypia ♀
621.34 Benign endometrial hyperplasia ♀
621.35 Endometrial intraepithelial neoplasia [EIN] ♀
621.6 Malposition of uterus ♀
621.8 Other specified disorders of uterus, not elsewhere classified ♀
621.9 Unspecified disorder of uterus ♀
622.10 Dysplasia of cervix, unspecified ♀
622.11 Mild dysplasia of cervix ♀
622.12 Moderate dysplasia of cervix ♀
625.3 Dysmenorrhea ♀
625.6 Female stress incontinence ♀
625.8 Other specified symptom associated with female genital organs ♀
626.2 Excessive or frequent menstruation ♀
626.6 Metrorrhagia ♀
626.8 Other disorder of menstruation and other abnormal bleeding from female genital tract ♀
626.9 Unspecified disorder of menstruation and other abnormal bleeding from female genital tract ♀
627.1 Postmenopausal bleeding ♀
677 Late effect of complication of pregnancy, childbirth, and the puerperium — (Code first any sequelae) ♀
788.33 Mixed incontinence urge and stress (male)(female) — (Code, if applicable, any causal condition first: 600.0-600.9, with fifth digit 1; 618.00-618.9; 753.23)
789.30 Abdominal or pelvic swelling, mass or lump, unspecified site
795.05 Cervical high risk human papillomavirus (HPV) DNA test positive ♀
V50.49 Other prophylactic organ removal
V84.02 Genetic susceptibility to malignant neoplasm of ovary — (Use additional code, if applicable, for any associated family history of the disease: V16-V19. Code first, if applicable, any current malignant neoplasms: 140.0-195.8, 200.0-208.9, 230.0-234.9. Use additional code, if applicable, for any personal history of malignant neoplasm: V10.0-V10.9) ♀
V84.04 Genetic susceptibility to malignant neoplasm of endometrium — (Use additional code, if applicable, for any associated family history of the disease: V16-V19. Code first, if applicable, any current malignant neoplasms: 140.0-195.8, 200.0-208.9, 230.0-234.9. Use additional code, if applicable, for any personal history of malignant neoplasm: V10.0-V10.9) ♀
V84.09 Genetic susceptibility to other malignant neoplasm — (Use additional code, if applicable, for any associated family history of the disease: V16-V19. Code first, if applicable, any current malignant neoplasms: 140.0-195.8, 200.0-208.9, 230.0-234.9. Use additional code, if applicable, for any personal history of malignant neoplasm: V10.0-V10.9)

ICD-9-CM Procedural

65.39 Other unilateral oophorectomy ♀
65.49 Other unilateral salpingo-oophorectomy ♀
65.51 Other removal of both ovaries at same operative episode ♀
65.52 Other removal of remaining ovary ♀
65.61 Other removal of both ovaries and tubes at same operative episode ♀
65.62 Other removal of remaining ovary and tube ♀
68.59 Other and unspecified vaginal hysterectomy ♀
68.79 Other and unspecified radical vaginal hysterectomy ♀
70.92 Other operations on cul-de-sac ♀

58267

58267 Vaginal hysterectomy, for uterus 250 g or less; with colpo-urethrocystopexy (Marshall-Marchetti-Krantz type, Pereyra type) with or without endoscopic control

ICD-9-CM Diagnostic

180.0 Malignant neoplasm of endocervix ♀
180.1 Malignant neoplasm of exocervix ♀
180.8 Malignant neoplasm of other specified sites of cervix ♀
182.0 Malignant neoplasm of corpus uteri, except isthmus ♀
182.1 Malignant neoplasm of isthmus ♀
182.8 Malignant neoplasm of other specified sites of body of uterus ♀
218.0 Submucous leiomyoma of uterus ♀
218.1 Intramural leiomyoma of uterus ♀
218.2 Subserous leiomyoma of uterus ♀
218.9 Leiomyoma of uterus, unspecified ♀
614.4 Chronic or unspecified parametritis and pelvic cellulitis — (Use additional code to identify organism: 041.00-041.09, 041.10-041.19) ♀
614.9 Unspecified inflammatory disease of female pelvic organs and tissues — (Use additional code to identify organism: 041.00-041.09, 041.10-041.19) ♀
617.0 Endometriosis of uterus ♀
618.00 Unspecified prolapse of vaginal walls without mention of uterine prolapse — (Use additional code to identify urinary incontinence: 625.6, 788.31, 788.33-788.39) ♀
618.01 Cystocele without mention of uterine prolapse, midline — (Use additional code to identify urinary incontinence: 625.6, 788.31, 788.33-788.39) ♀
618.02 Cystocele without mention of uterine prolapse, lateral — (Use additional code to identify urinary incontinence: 625.6, 788.31, 788.33-788.39) ♀
618.03 Urethrocele without mention of uterine prolapse — (Use additional code to identify urinary incontinence: 625.6, 788.31, 788.33-788.39) ♀
618.05 Perineocele without mention of uterine prolapse — (Use additional code to identify urinary incontinence: 625.6, 788.31, 788.33-788.39) ♀
618.09 Other prolapse of vaginal walls without mention of uterine prolapse — (Use additional code to identify urinary incontinence: 625.6, 788.31, 788.33-788.39) ♀
618.1 Uterine prolapse without mention of vaginal wall prolapse — (Use additional code to identify urinary incontinence: 625.6, 788.31, 788.33-788.39) ♀
618.2 Uterovaginal prolapse, incomplete — (Use additional code to identify urinary incontinence: 625.6, 788.31, 788.33-788.39) ♀
618.3 Uterovaginal prolapse, complete — (Use additional code to identify urinary incontinence: 625.6, 788.31, 788.33-788.39) ♀
618.4 Uterovaginal prolapse, unspecified — (Use additional code to identify urinary incontinence: 625.6, 788.31, 788.33-788.39) ♀
625.3 Dysmenorrhea ♀
625.6 Female stress incontinence ♀
626.2 Excessive or frequent menstruation ♀
626.8 Other disorder of menstruation and other abnormal bleeding from female genital tract ♀
788.33 Mixed incontinence urge and stress (male)(female) — (Code, if applicable, any causal condition first: 600.0-600.9, with fifth digit 1; 618.00-618.9; 753.23)
795.05 Cervical high risk human papillomavirus (HPV) DNA test positive ♀
V84.02 Genetic susceptibility to malignant neoplasm of ovary — (Use additional code, if applicable, for any associated family history of the disease: V16-V19. Code first, if applicable, any current malignant neoplasms: 140.0-195.8, 200.0-208.9, 230.0-234.9. Use additional code, if applicable, for any personal history of malignant neoplasm: V10.0-V10.9) ♀
V84.04 Genetic susceptibility to malignant neoplasm of endometrium — (Use additional code, if applicable, for any associated family history of the disease: V16-V19. Code first, if applicable, any current malignant neoplasms: 140.0-195.8, 200.0-208.9, 230.0-234.9. Use additional code, if applicable, for any personal history of malignant neoplasm: V10.0-V10.9) ♀
V84.09 Genetic susceptibility to other malignant neoplasm — (Use additional code, if applicable, for any associated family history of the disease: V16-V19. Code first, if applicable, any current malignant neoplasms: 140.0-195.8, 200.0-208.9, 230.0-234.9. Use additional code, if applicable, for any personal history of malignant neoplasm: V10.0-V10.9)

ICD-9-CM Procedural

59.5 Retropubic urethral suspension
68.59 Other and unspecified vaginal hysterectomy ♀

58270

58270 Vaginal hysterectomy, for uterus 250 g or less; with repair of enterocele

ICD-9-CM Diagnostic

180.0 Malignant neoplasm of endocervix ♀
180.1 Malignant neoplasm of exocervix ♀
182.0 Malignant neoplasm of corpus uteri, except isthmus ♀
182.1 Malignant neoplasm of isthmus ♀
182.8 Malignant neoplasm of other specified sites of body of uterus ♀
218.0 Submucous leiomyoma of uterus ♀
218.1 Intramural leiomyoma of uterus ♀
218.2 Subserous leiomyoma of uterus ♀
218.9 Leiomyoma of uterus, unspecified ♀
233.1 Carcinoma in situ of cervix uteri ♀
618.04 Rectocele without mention of uterine prolapse — (Use additional code to identify urinary incontinence: 625.6, 788.31, 788.33-788.39) (Use additional code for any associated fecal incontinence: 787.60-787.63) ♀
618.1 Uterine prolapse without mention of vaginal wall prolapse — (Use additional code to identify urinary incontinence: 625.6, 788.31, 788.33-788.39) ♀
618.2 Uterovaginal prolapse, incomplete — (Use additional code to identify urinary incontinence: 625.6, 788.31, 788.33-788.39) ♀
618.3 Uterovaginal prolapse, complete — (Use additional code to identify urinary incontinence: 625.6, 788.31, 788.33-788.39) ♀
618.4 Uterovaginal prolapse, unspecified — (Use additional code to identify urinary incontinence: 625.6, 788.31, 788.33-788.39) ♀
618.6 Vaginal enterocele, congenital or acquired — (Use additional code to identify urinary incontinence: 625.6, 788.31, 788.33-788.39) ♀
618.83 Pelvic muscle wasting — (Use additional code to identify urinary incontinence: 625.6, 788.31, 788.33-788.39) ♀
618.9 Unspecified genital prolapse — (Use additional code to identify urinary incontinence: 625.6, 788.31, 788.33-788.39) ♀
621.30 Endometrial hyperplasia, unspecified ♀
621.31 Simple endometrial hyperplasia without atypia ♀
621.32 Complex endometrial hyperplasia without atypia ♀
621.33 Endometrial hyperplasia with atypia ♀
621.34 Benign endometrial hyperplasia ♀
621.35 Endometrial intraepithelial neoplasia [EIN] ♀
622.10 Dysplasia of cervix, unspecified ♀
622.11 Mild dysplasia of cervix ♀
622.12 Moderate dysplasia of cervix ♀
625.3 Dysmenorrhea ♀
625.6 Female stress incontinence ♀
626.2 Excessive or frequent menstruation ♀
626.6 Metrorrhagia ♀
626.8 Other disorder of menstruation and other abnormal bleeding from female genital tract ♀
627.1 Postmenopausal bleeding ♀
788.33 Mixed incontinence urge and stress (male)(female) — (Code, if applicable, any causal condition first: 600.0-600.9, with fifth digit 1; 618.00-618.9; 753.23)
V84.02 Genetic susceptibility to malignant neoplasm of ovary — (Use additional code, if applicable, for any associated family history of the disease: V16-V19. Code first, if applicable, any current malignant neoplasms: 140.0-195.8, 200.0-208.9, 230.0-234.9.

Use additional code, if applicable, for any personal history of malignant neoplasm: V10.0-V10.9) ♀

V84.04 Genetic susceptibility to malignant neoplasm of endometrium — (Use additional code, if applicable, for any associated family history of the disease: V16-V19. Code first, if applicable, any current malignant neoplasms: 140.0-195.8, 200.0-208.9, 230.0-234.9. Use additional code, if applicable, for any personal history of malignant neoplasm: V10.0-V10.9) ♀

V84.09 Genetic susceptibility to other malignant neoplasm — (Use additional code, if applicable, for any associated family history of the disease: V16-V19. Code first, if applicable, any current malignant neoplasms: 140.0-195.8, 200.0-208.9, 230.0-234.9. Use additional code, if applicable, for any personal history of malignant neoplasm: V10.0-V10.9)

ICD-9-CM Procedural

68.59 Other and unspecified vaginal hysterectomy ♀

70.92 Other operations on cul-de-sac ♀

58275-58280

58275 Vaginal hysterectomy, with total or partial vaginectomy;

58280 with repair of enterocele

ICD-9-CM Diagnostic

180.0 Malignant neoplasm of endocervix ♀

180.1 Malignant neoplasm of exocervix ♀

180.8 Malignant neoplasm of other specified sites of cervix ♀

182.0 Malignant neoplasm of corpus uteri, except isthmus ♀

182.1 Malignant neoplasm of isthmus ♀

182.8 Malignant neoplasm of other specified sites of body of uterus ♀

184.0 Malignant neoplasm of vagina ♀

218.0 Submucous leiomyoma of uterus ♀

218.1 Intramural leiomyoma of uterus ♀

218.2 Subserous leiomyoma of uterus ♀

618.00 Unspecified prolapse of vaginal walls without mention of uterine prolapse — (Use additional code to identify urinary incontinence: 625.6, 788.31, 788.33-788.39) ♀

618.09 Other prolapse of vaginal walls without mention of uterine prolapse — (Use additional code to identify urinary incontinence: 625.6, 788.31, 788.33-788.39) ♀

618.1 Uterine prolapse without mention of vaginal wall prolapse — (Use additional code to identify urinary incontinence: 625.6, 788.31, 788.33-788.39) ♀

618.2 Uterovaginal prolapse, incomplete — (Use additional code to identify urinary incontinence: 625.6, 788.31, 788.33-788.39) ♀

618.3 Uterovaginal prolapse, complete — (Use additional code to identify urinary incontinence: 625.6, 788.31, 788.33-788.39) ♀

618.6 Vaginal enterocele, congenital or acquired — (Use additional code to identify urinary incontinence: 625.6, 788.31, 788.33-788.39) ♀

618.82 Incompetence or weakening of rectovaginal tissue — (Use additional code to identify urinary incontinence: 625.6, 788.31, 788.33-788.39) ♀

621.2 Hypertrophy of uterus ♀

625.3 Dysmenorrhea ♀

625.6 Female stress incontinence ♀

626.2 Excessive or frequent menstruation ♀

626.6 Metrorrhagia ♀

626.8 Other disorder of menstruation and other abnormal bleeding from female genital tract ♀

788.33 Mixed incontinence urge and stress (male)(female) — (Code, if applicable, any causal condition first: 600.0-600.9, with fifth digit 1; 618.00-618.9; 753.23)

V84.02 Genetic susceptibility to malignant neoplasm of ovary — (Use additional code, if applicable, for any associated family history of the disease: V16-V19. Code first, if applicable, any current malignant neoplasms: 140.0-195.8, 200.0-208.9, 230.0-234.9. Use additional code, if applicable, for any personal history of malignant neoplasm: V10.0-V10.9) ♀

V84.04 Genetic susceptibility to malignant neoplasm of endometrium — (Use additional code, if applicable, for any associated family history of the disease: V16-V19. Code first, if applicable, any current malignant neoplasms: 140.0-195.8, 200.0-208.9, 230.0-234.9. Use additional code, if applicable, for any personal history of malignant neoplasm: V10.0-V10.9) ♀

V84.09 Genetic susceptibility to other malignant neoplasm — (Use additional code, if applicable, for any associated family history of the disease: V16-V19. Code first, if applicable, any current malignant neoplasms: 140.0-195.8, 200.0-208.9, 230.0-234.9. Use additional code, if applicable, for any personal history of malignant neoplasm: V10.0-V10.9)

ICD-9-CM Procedural

68.59 Other and unspecified vaginal hysterectomy ♀

70.4 Obliteration and total excision of vagina ♀

70.8 Obliteration of vaginal vault ♀

70.92 Other operations on cul-de-sac ♀

58285

58285 Vaginal hysterectomy, radical (Schauta type operation)

ICD-9-CM Diagnostic

180.0 Malignant neoplasm of endocervix ♀

180.1 Malignant neoplasm of exocervix ♀

180.8 Malignant neoplasm of other specified sites of cervix ♀

182.0 Malignant neoplasm of corpus uteri, except isthmus ♀

182.1 Malignant neoplasm of isthmus ♀

182.8 Malignant neoplasm of other specified sites of body of uterus ♀

183.2 Malignant neoplasm of fallopian tube ♀

183.3 Malignant neoplasm of broad ligament of uterus ♀

183.4 Malignant neoplasm of parametrium of uterus ♀

183.5 Malignant neoplasm of round ligament of uterus ♀

183.8 Malignant neoplasm of other specified sites of uterine adnexa ♀

198.82 Secondary malignant neoplasm of genital organs

236.0 Neoplasm of uncertain behavior of uterus ♀

239.5 Neoplasm of unspecified nature of other genitourinary organs

618.1 Uterine prolapse without mention of vaginal wall prolapse — (Use additional code to identify urinary incontinence: 625.6, 788.31, 788.33-788.39) ♀

618.2 Uterovaginal prolapse, incomplete — (Use additional code to identify urinary incontinence: 625.6, 788.31, 788.33-788.39) ♀

618.3 Uterovaginal prolapse, complete — (Use additional code to identify urinary incontinence: 625.6, 788.31, 788.33-788.39) ♀

618.4 Uterovaginal prolapse, unspecified — (Use additional code to identify urinary incontinence: 625.6, 788.31, 788.33-788.39) ♀

618.83 Pelvic muscle wasting — (Use additional code to identify urinary incontinence: 625.6, 788.31, 788.33-788.39) ♀

618.89 Other specified genital prolapse — (Use additional code to identify urinary incontinence: 625.6, 788.31, 788.33-788.39) ♀

625.6 Female stress incontinence ♀

V84.02 Genetic susceptibility to malignant neoplasm of ovary — (Use additional code, if applicable, for any associated family history of the disease: V16-V19. Code first, if applicable, any current malignant neoplasms: 140.0-195.8, 200.0-208.9, 230.0-234.9. Use additional code, if applicable, for any personal history of malignant neoplasm: V10.0-V10.9) ♀

V84.04 Genetic susceptibility to malignant neoplasm of endometrium — (Use additional code, if applicable, for any associated family history of the disease: V16-V19. Code first, if applicable, any current malignant neoplasms: 140.0-195.8, 200.0-208.9, 230.0-234.9. Use additional code, if applicable, for any personal history of malignant neoplasm: V10.0-V10.9) ♀

V84.09 Genetic susceptibility to other malignant neoplasm — (Use additional code, if applicable, for any associated family history of the disease: V16-V19. Code first, if applicable, any current malignant neoplasms: 140.0-195.8, 200.0-208.9, 230.0-234.9.

Use additional code, if applicable, for any personal history of malignant neoplasm: V10.0-V10.9)

ICD-9-CM Procedural

68.79 Other and unspecified radical vaginal hysterectomy ♀

58290-58292

58290 Vaginal hysterectomy, for uterus greater than 250 g;
58291 with removal of tube(s) and/or ovary(s)
58292 with removal of tube(s) and/or ovary(s), with repair of enterocele

ICD-9-CM Diagnostic

180.0 Malignant neoplasm of endocervix ♀
180.1 Malignant neoplasm of exocervix ♀
180.8 Malignant neoplasm of other specified sites of cervix ♀
180.9 Malignant neoplasm of cervix uteri, unspecified site ▽ ♀
181 Malignant neoplasm of placenta ♀
182.0 Malignant neoplasm of corpus uteri, except isthmus ♀
182.1 Malignant neoplasm of isthmus ♀
182.8 Malignant neoplasm of other specified sites of body of uterus ♀
183.0 Malignant neoplasm of ovary — (Use additional code to identify any functional activity) ♀
183.8 Malignant neoplasm of other specified sites of uterine adnexa ♀
183.9 Malignant neoplasm of uterine adnexa, unspecified site ▽ ♀
198.6 Secondary malignant neoplasm of ovary ♀
199.1 Other malignant neoplasm of unspecified site
218.0 Submucous leiomyoma of uterus ♀
218.1 Intramural leiomyoma of uterus ♀
218.2 Subserous leiomyoma of uterus ♀
218.9 Leiomyoma of uterus, unspecified ▽ ♀
233.1 Carcinoma in situ of cervix uteri ♀
233.2 Carcinoma in situ of other and unspecified parts of uterus ▽ ♀
233.30 Carcinoma in situ, unspecified female genital organ ▽ ♀
233.31 Carcinoma in situ, vagina ♀
233.32 Carcinoma in situ, vulva ♀
233.39 Carcinoma in situ, other female genital organ ♀
236.0 Neoplasm of uncertain behavior of uterus ♀
236.2 Neoplasm of uncertain behavior of ovary — (Use additional code to identify any functional activity) ♀
236.3 Neoplasm of uncertain behavior of other and unspecified female genital organs ▽ ♀
239.5 Neoplasm of unspecified nature of other genitourinary organs
553.9 Hernia of unspecified site of abdominal cavity without mention of obstruction or gangrene ▽
614.4 Chronic or unspecified parametritis and pelvic cellulitis — (Use additional code to identify organism: 041.00-041.09, 041.10-041.19) ♀
614.9 Unspecified inflammatory disease of female pelvic organs and tissues — (Use additional code to identify organism: 041.00-041.09, 041.10-041.19) ▽ ♀
617.0 Endometriosis of uterus ♀
617.9 Endometriosis, site unspecified ▽ ♀
618.1 Uterine prolapse without mention of vaginal wall prolapse — (Use additional code to identify urinary incontinence: 625.6, 788.31, 788.33-788.39) ♀
618.2 Uterovaginal prolapse, incomplete — (Use additional code to identify urinary incontinence: 625.6, 788.31, 788.33-788.39) ♀
618.3 Uterovaginal prolapse, complete — (Use additional code to identify urinary incontinence: 625.6, 788.31, 788.33-788.39) ♀
618.4 Uterovaginal prolapse, unspecified — (Use additional code to identify urinary incontinence: 625.6, 788.31, 788.33-788.39) ▽ ♀
618.6 Vaginal enterocele, congenital or acquired — (Use additional code to identify urinary incontinence: 625.6, 788.31, 788.33-788.39) ♀
618.82 Incompetence or weakening of rectovaginal tissue — (Use additional code to identify urinary incontinence: 625.6, 788.31, 788.33-788.39) ♀
618.9 Unspecified genital prolapse — (Use additional code to identify urinary incontinence: 625.6, 788.31, 788.33-788.39) ▽ ♀
621.0 Polyp of corpus uteri ♀
621.2 Hypertrophy of uterus ♀
621.30 Endometrial hyperplasia, unspecified ▽ ♀
621.31 Simple endometrial hyperplasia without atypia ♀
621.32 Complex endometrial hyperplasia without atypia ♀
621.33 Endometrial hyperplasia with atypia ♀
621.34 Benign endometrial hyperplasia ♀
621.35 Endometrial intraepithelial neoplasia [EIN] ♀
621.6 Malposition of uterus ♀
621.8 Other specified disorders of uterus, not elsewhere classified ♀
621.9 Unspecified disorder of uterus ▽ ♀
622.10 Dysplasia of cervix, unspecified ▽ ♀
622.11 Mild dysplasia of cervix ♀
622.12 Moderate dysplasia of cervix ♀
625.3 Dysmenorrhea ♀
625.6 Female stress incontinence ♀
625.8 Other specified symptom associated with female genital organs ♀
625.9 Unspecified symptom associated with female genital organs ▽ ♀
626.2 Excessive or frequent menstruation ♀
626.6 Metrorrhagia ♀
626.8 Other disorder of menstruation and other abnormal bleeding from female genital tract ♀
626.9 Unspecified disorder of menstruation and other abnormal bleeding from female genital tract ▽ ♀
627.1 Postmenopausal bleeding ♀
677 Late effect of complication of pregnancy, childbirth, and the puerperium — (Code first any sequelae) ♀
788.33 Mixed incontinence urge and stress (male)(female) — (Code, if applicable, any causal condition first: 600.0-600.9, with fifth digit 1; 618.00-618.9; 753.23)
789.30 Abdominal or pelvic swelling, mass or lump, unspecified site ▽
V50.49 Other prophylactic organ removal
V84.02 Genetic susceptibility to malignant neoplasm of ovary — (Use additional code, if applicable, for any associated family history of the disease: V16-V19. Code first, if applicable, any current malignant neoplasms: 140.0-195.8, 200.0-208.9, 230.0-234.9. Use additional code, if applicable, for any personal history of malignant neoplasm: V10.0-V10.9) ♀
V84.04 Genetic susceptibility to malignant neoplasm of endometrium — (Use additional code, if applicable, for any associated family history of the disease: V16-V19. Code first, if applicable, any current malignant neoplasms: 140.0-195.8, 200.0-208.9, 230.0-234.9. Use additional code, if applicable, for any personal history of malignant neoplasm: V10.0-V10.9) ♀
V84.09 Genetic susceptibility to other malignant neoplasm — (Use additional code, if applicable, for any associated family history of the disease: V16-V19. Code first, if applicable, any current malignant neoplasms: 140.0-195.8, 200.0-208.9, 230.0-234.9. Use additional code, if applicable, for any personal history of malignant neoplasm: V10.0-V10.9)

ICD-9-CM Procedural

65.39 Other unilateral oophorectomy ♀
65.49 Other unilateral salpingo-oophorectomy ♀
65.51 Other removal of both ovaries at same operative episode ♀
65.52 Other removal of remaining ovary ♀
65.61 Other removal of both ovaries and tubes at same operative episode ♀
65.62 Other removal of remaining ovary and tube ♀
68.59 Other and unspecified vaginal hysterectomy ♀
68.79 Other and unspecified radical vaginal hysterectomy ♀

70.92 Other operations on cul-de-sac ♀

58293

58293 Vaginal hysterectomy, for uterus greater than 250 g; with colpo-urethrocystopexy (Marshall-Marchetti-Krantz type, Pereyra type) with or without endoscopic control

ICD-9-CM Diagnostic

180.0 Malignant neoplasm of endocervix ♀
180.1 Malignant neoplasm of exocervix ♀
180.8 Malignant neoplasm of other specified sites of cervix ♀
182.0 Malignant neoplasm of corpus uteri, except isthmus ♀
182.1 Malignant neoplasm of isthmus ♀
182.8 Malignant neoplasm of other specified sites of body of uterus ♀
218.0 Submucous leiomyoma of uterus ♀
218.1 Intramural leiomyoma of uterus ♀
218.2 Subserous leiomyoma of uterus ♀
218.9 Leiomyoma of uterus, unspecified ▽ ♀
614.4 Chronic or unspecified parametritis and pelvic cellulitis — (Use additional code to identify organism: 041.00-041.09, 041.10-041.19) ♀
614.9 Unspecified inflammatory disease of female pelvic organs and tissues — (Use additional code to identify organism: 041.00-041.09, 041.10-041.19) ▽ ♀
617.0 Endometriosis of uterus ♀
618.00 Unspecified prolapse of vaginal walls without mention of uterine prolapse — (Use additional code to identify urinary incontinence: 625.6, 788.31, 788.33-788.39) ▽ ♀
618.01 Cystocele without mention of uterine prolapse, midline — (Use additional code to identify urinary incontinence: 625.6, 788.31, 788.33-788.39) ♀
618.02 Cystocele without mention of uterine prolapse, lateral — (Use additional code to identify urinary incontinence: 625.6, 788.31, 788.33-788.39) ♀
618.03 Urethrocele without mention of uterine prolapse — (Use additional code to identify urinary incontinence: 625.6, 788.31, 788.33-788.39) ♀
618.09 Other prolapse of vaginal walls without mention of uterine prolapse — (Use additional code to identify urinary incontinence: 625.6, 788.31, 788.33-788.39) ♀
618.1 Uterine prolapse without mention of vaginal wall prolapse — (Use additional code to identify urinary incontinence: 625.6, 788.31, 788.33-788.39) ♀
618.2 Uterovaginal prolapse, incomplete — (Use additional code to identify urinary incontinence: 625.6, 788.31, 788.33-788.39) ♀
618.3 Uterovaginal prolapse, complete — (Use additional code to identify urinary incontinence: 625.6, 788.31, 788.33-788.39) ♀
618.4 Uterovaginal prolapse, unspecified — (Use additional code to identify urinary incontinence: 625.6, 788.31, 788.33-788.39) ▽ ♀
618.81 Incompetence or weakening of pubocervical tissue — (Use additional code to identify urinary incontinence: 625.6, 788.31, 788.33-788.39) ♀
618.82 Incompetence or weakening of rectovaginal tissue — (Use additional code to identify urinary incontinence: 625.6, 788.31, 788.33-788.39) ♀
618.83 Pelvic muscle wasting — (Use additional code to identify urinary incontinence: 625.6, 788.31, 788.33-788.39) ♀
625.3 Dysmenorrhea ♀
625.6 Female stress incontinence ♀
626.2 Excessive or frequent menstruation ♀
626.8 Other disorder of menstruation and other abnormal bleeding from female genital tract ♀
788.33 Mixed incontinence urge and stress (male)(female) — (Code, if applicable, any causal condition first: 600.0-600.9, with fifth digit 1; 618.00-618.9; 753.23)
V84.02 Genetic susceptibility to malignant neoplasm of ovary — (Use additional code, if applicable, for any associated family history of the disease: V16-V19. Code first, if applicable, any current malignant neoplasms: 140.0-195.8, 200.0-208.9, 230.0-234.9. Use additional code, if applicable, for any personal history of malignant neoplasm: V10.0-V10.9) ♀
V84.04 Genetic susceptibility to malignant neoplasm of endometrium — (Use additional code, if applicable, for any associated family history of the disease: V16-V19. Code first, if applicable, any current malignant neoplasms: 140.0-195.8, 200.0-208.9, 230.0-234.9. Use additional code, if applicable, for any personal history of malignant neoplasm: V10.0-V10.9) ♀
V84.09 Genetic susceptibility to other malignant neoplasm — (Use additional code, if applicable, for any associated family history of the disease: V16-V19. Code first, if applicable, any current malignant neoplasms: 140.0-195.8, 200.0-208.9, 230.0-234.9. Use additional code, if applicable, for any personal history of malignant neoplasm: V10.0-V10.9)

ICD-9-CM Procedural

59.5 Retropubic urethral suspension
68.59 Other and unspecified vaginal hysterectomy ♀

58294

58294 Vaginal hysterectomy, for uterus greater than 250 g; with repair of enterocele

ICD-9-CM Diagnostic

180.0 Malignant neoplasm of endocervix ♀
180.1 Malignant neoplasm of exocervix ♀
182.0 Malignant neoplasm of corpus uteri, except isthmus ♀
182.1 Malignant neoplasm of isthmus ♀
182.8 Malignant neoplasm of other specified sites of body of uterus ♀
218.0 Submucous leiomyoma of uterus ♀
218.1 Intramural leiomyoma of uterus ♀
218.2 Subserous leiomyoma of uterus ♀
218.9 Leiomyoma of uterus, unspecified ▽ ♀
233.1 Carcinoma in situ of cervix uteri ♀
618.00 Unspecified prolapse of vaginal walls without mention of uterine prolapse — (Use additional code to identify urinary incontinence: 625.6, 788.31, 788.33-788.39) ▽ ♀
618.1 Uterine prolapse without mention of vaginal wall prolapse — (Use additional code to identify urinary incontinence: 625.6, 788.31, 788.33-788.39) ♀
618.2 Uterovaginal prolapse, incomplete — (Use additional code to identify urinary incontinence: 625.6, 788.31, 788.33-788.39) ♀
618.3 Uterovaginal prolapse, complete — (Use additional code to identify urinary incontinence: 625.6, 788.31, 788.33-788.39) ♀
618.4 Uterovaginal prolapse, unspecified — (Use additional code to identify urinary incontinence: 625.6, 788.31, 788.33-788.39) ▽ ♀
618.6 Vaginal enterocele, congenital or acquired — (Use additional code to identify urinary incontinence: 625.6, 788.31, 788.33-788.39) ♀
618.82 Incompetence or weakening of rectovaginal tissue — (Use additional code to identify urinary incontinence: 625.6, 788.31, 788.33-788.39) ♀
618.9 Unspecified genital prolapse — (Use additional code to identify urinary incontinence: 625.6, 788.31, 788.33-788.39) ▽ ♀
621.30 Endometrial hyperplasia, unspecified ▽ ♀
621.31 Simple endometrial hyperplasia without atypia ♀
621.32 Complex endometrial hyperplasia without atypia ♀
621.33 Endometrial hyperplasia with atypia ♀
621.34 Benign endometrial hyperplasia ♀
621.35 Endometrial intraepithelial neoplasia [EIN] ♀
622.10 Dysplasia of cervix, unspecified ▽ ♀
622.11 Mild dysplasia of cervix ♀
622.12 Moderate dysplasia of cervix ♀
625.3 Dysmenorrhea ♀
625.6 Female stress incontinence ♀
626.2 Excessive or frequent menstruation ♀
626.6 Metrorrhagia ♀
626.8 Other disorder of menstruation and other abnormal bleeding from female genital tract ♀
627.1 Postmenopausal bleeding ♀

788.33 Mixed incontinence urge and stress (male)(female) — (Code, if applicable, any causal condition first: 600.0-600.9, with fifth digit 1; 618.00-618.9; 753.23)

V84.02 Genetic susceptibility to malignant neoplasm of ovary — (Use additional code, if applicable, for any associated family history of the disease: V16-V19. Code first, if applicable, any current malignant neoplasms: 140.0-195.8, 200.0-208.9, 230.0-234.9. Use additional code, if applicable, for any personal history of malignant neoplasm: V10.0-V10.9) ♀

V84.04 Genetic susceptibility to malignant neoplasm of endometrium — (Use additional code, if applicable, for any associated family history of the disease: V16-V19. Code first, if applicable, any current malignant neoplasms: 140.0-195.8, 200.0-208.9, 230.0-234.9. Use additional code, if applicable, for any personal history of malignant neoplasm: V10.0-V10.9) ♀

V84.09 Genetic susceptibility to other malignant neoplasm — (Use additional code, if applicable, for any associated family history of the disease: V16-V19. Code first, if applicable, any current malignant neoplasms: 140.0-195.8, 200.0-208.9, 230.0-234.9. Use additional code, if applicable, for any personal history of malignant neoplasm: V10.0-V10.9)

ICD-9-CM Procedural

68.59 Other and unspecified vaginal hysterectomy ♀

70.92 Other operations on cul-de-sac ♀

58300-58301

58300 Insertion of intrauterine device (IUD)

58301 Removal of intrauterine device (IUD)

ICD-9-CM Diagnostic

996.32 Mechanical complication due to intrauterine contraceptive device ♀

996.65 Infection and inflammatory reaction due to other genitourinary device, implant, and graft — (Use additional code to identify specified infections)

996.76 Other complications due to genitourinary device, implant, and graft — (Use additional code to identify complication: 338.18-338.19, 338.28-338.29)

V25.11 Encounter for insertion of intrauterine contraceptive device ♀

V25.12 Encounter for removal of intrauterine contraceptive device ♀

V25.13 Encounter for removal and reinsertion of intrauterine contraceptive device ♀

V25.42 Surveillance of previously prescribed intrauterine contraceptive device ♀

ICD-9-CM Procedural

69.7 Insertion of intrauterine contraceptive device ♀

97.71 Removal of intrauterine contraceptive device ♀

58321-58322

58321 Artificial insemination; intra-cervical

58322 intra-uterine

ICD-9-CM Diagnostic

606.0 Azoospermia ♂

606.1 Oligospermia ♂

606.8 Infertility due to extratesticular causes ♂

606.9 Unspecified male infertility ▽ ♂

617.0 Endometriosis of uterus ♀

622.4 Stricture and stenosis of cervix ♀

628.0 Female infertility associated with anovulation — (Use additional code for any associated Stein-Leventhal syndrome: 256.4) ♀

628.1 Female infertility of pituitary-hypothalamic origin — (Code first underlying cause: 253.0-253.4, 253.8) ☒ ♀

628.3 Female infertility of uterine origin — (Use additional code for any associated tuberculous endometriosis: 016.7) ♀

628.4 Female infertility of cervical or vaginal origin ♀

628.8 Female infertility of other specified origin ♀

628.9 Female infertility of unspecified origin ▽ ♀

V26.1 Artificial insemination ♀

ICD-9-CM Procedural

69.92 Artificial insemination ♀

58323

58323 Sperm washing for artificial insemination

ICD-9-CM Diagnostic

606.0 Azoospermia ♂

606.1 Oligospermia ♂

606.8 Infertility due to extratesticular causes ♂

606.9 Unspecified male infertility ▽ ♂

622.4 Stricture and stenosis of cervix ♀

628.0 Female infertility associated with anovulation — (Use additional code for any associated Stein-Leventhal syndrome: 256.4) ♀

628.1 Female infertility of pituitary-hypothalamic origin — (Code first underlying cause: 253.0-253.4, 253.8) ☒ ♀

628.4 Female infertility of cervical or vaginal origin ♀

628.8 Female infertility of other specified origin ♀

628.9 Female infertility of unspecified origin ▽ ♀

V26.1 Artificial insemination ♀

ICD-9-CM Procedural

99.99 Other miscellaneous procedures

HCPCS Level II Supplies & Services

A4649 Surgical supply; miscellaneous

58340

58340 Catheterization and introduction of saline or contrast material for saline infusion sonohysterography (SIS) or hysterosalpingography

ICD-9-CM Diagnostic

218.0 Submucous leiomyoma of uterus ♀

218.1 Intramural leiomyoma of uterus ♀

218.2 Subserous leiomyoma of uterus ♀

218.9 Leiomyoma of uterus, unspecified ▽ ♀

256.31 Premature menopause — (Use additional code for states associated with natural menopause: 627.2) ♀

256.39 Other ovarian failure — (Use additional code for states associated with natural menopause: 627.2) ♀

256.4 Polycystic ovaries ♀

256.8 Other ovarian dysfunction ♀

259.9 Unspecified endocrine disorder ▽

614.1 Chronic salpingitis and oophoritis — (Use additional code to identify organism: 041.00-041.09, 041.10-041.19) ♀

614.2 Salpingitis and oophoritis not specified as acute, subacute, or chronic — (Use additional code to identify organism: 041.00-041.09, 041.10-041.19) ♀

614.6 Pelvic peritoneal adhesions, female (postoperative) (postinfection) — (Use additional code to identify organism: 041.00-041.09, 041.10-041.19) (Use additional code to identify any associated infertility: 628.2) ♀

614.9 Unspecified inflammatory disease of female pelvic organs and tissues — (Use additional code to identify organism: 041.00-041.09, 041.10-041.19) ▽ ♀

617.0 Endometriosis of uterus ♀

617.1 Endometriosis of ovary ♀

617.2 Endometriosis of fallopian tube ♀

617.3 Endometriosis of pelvic peritoneum ♀

617.9 Endometriosis, site unspecified ▽ ♀

620.5 Torsion of ovary, ovarian pedicle, or fallopian tube ♀

620.8 Other noninflammatory disorder of ovary, fallopian tube, and broad ligament ♀

621.1 Chronic subinvolution of uterus ♀

621.2 Hypertrophy of uterus ♀
625.3 Dysmenorrhea ♀
625.5 Pelvic congestion syndrome ♀
626.0 Absence of menstruation ♀
626.1 Scanty or infrequent menstruation ♀
626.2 Excessive or frequent menstruation ♀
626.4 Irregular menstrual cycle ♀
626.6 Metrorrhagia ♀
628.0 Female infertility associated with anovulation — (Use additional code for any associated Stein-Leventhal syndrome: 256.4) ♀
628.2 Female infertility of tubal origin — (Use additional code for any associated peritubal adhesions: 614.6) ♀
628.3 Female infertility of uterine origin — (Use additional code for any associated tuberculous endometriosis: 016.7) ♀
628.8 Female infertility of other specified origin ♀
628.9 Female infertility of unspecified origin ▽ ♀
629.0 Hematocele, female, not elsewhere classified ♀
752.2 Congenital doubling of uterus ♀
752.31 Agenesis of uterus ♀
752.32 Hypoplasia of uterus ♀
752.33 Unicornuate uterus ♀
752.34 Bicornuate uterus ♀
752.35 Septate uterus ♀
752.36 Arcuate uterus ♀
752.39 Other anomalies of uterus ♀
789.00 Abdominal pain, unspecified site ▽
789.30 Abdominal or pelvic swelling, mass or lump, unspecified site ▽
793.5 Nonspecific (abnormal) findings on radiological and other examination of genitourinary organs
998.2 Accidental puncture or laceration during procedure
V13.29 Personal history of other genital system and obstetric disorders ♀
V26.0 Tuboplasty or vasoplasty after previous sterilization
V26.21 Fertility testing
V26.22 Aftercare following sterilization reversal
V26.29 Other investigation and testing
V71.89 Observation for other specified suspected conditions
V72.5 Radiological examination, not elsewhere classified — (Use additional code(s) to identify any special screening examination(s) performed: V73.0-V82.9)

ICD-9-CM Procedural

68.19 Other diagnostic procedures on uterus and supporting structures ♀
87.82 Gas contrast hysterosalpingogram ♀
87.83 Opaque dye contrast hysterosalpingogram ♀
87.84 Percutaneous hysterogram ♀

58345

58345 Transcervical introduction of fallopian tube catheter for diagnosis and/or re-establishing patency (any method), with or without hysterosalpingography

ICD-9-CM Diagnostic

256.4 Polycystic ovaries ♀
256.8 Other ovarian dysfunction ♀
614.1 Chronic salpingitis and oophoritis — (Use additional code to identify organism: 041.00-041.09, 041.10-041.19) ♀
614.2 Salpingitis and oophoritis not specified as acute, subacute, or chronic — (Use additional code to identify organism: 041.00-041.09, 041.10-041.19) ♀
614.6 Pelvic peritoneal adhesions, female (postoperative) (postinfection) — (Use additional code to identify organism: 041.00-041.09, 041.10-041.19) (Use additional code to identify any associated infertility: 628.2) ♀
617.2 Endometriosis of fallopian tube ♀
620.8 Other noninflammatory disorder of ovary, fallopian tube, and broad ligament ♀
621.1 Chronic subinvolution of uterus ♀
621.2 Hypertrophy of uterus ♀
621.30 Endometrial hyperplasia, unspecified ▽ ♀
621.31 Simple endometrial hyperplasia without atypia ♀
621.32 Complex endometrial hyperplasia without atypia ♀
621.33 Endometrial hyperplasia with atypia ♀
621.34 Benign endometrial hyperplasia ♀
621.35 Endometrial intraepithelial neoplasia [EIN] ♀
621.7 Chronic inversion of uterus ♀
622.4 Stricture and stenosis of cervix ♀
622.8 Other specified noninflammatory disorder of cervix ♀
628.2 Female infertility of tubal origin — (Use additional code for any associated peritubal adhesions: 614.6) ♀
628.8 Female infertility of other specified origin ♀
628.9 Female infertility of unspecified origin ▽ ♀
752.19 Other congenital anomaly of fallopian tubes and broad ligaments ♀
V26.21 Fertility testing
V26.22 Aftercare following sterilization reversal
V26.29 Other investigation and testing

ICD-9-CM Procedural

66.79 Other repair of fallopian tube ♀
66.8 Insufflation of fallopian tube ♀
66.95 Insufflation of therapeutic agent into fallopian tubes ♀
66.96 Dilation of fallopian tube ♀
87.85 Other x-ray of fallopian tubes and uterus ♀

58346

58346 Insertion of Heyman capsules for clinical brachytherapy

ICD-9-CM Diagnostic

179 Malignant neoplasm of uterus, part unspecified ▽ ♀
180.0 Malignant neoplasm of endocervix ♀
180.1 Malignant neoplasm of exocervix ♀
180.8 Malignant neoplasm of other specified sites of cervix ♀
180.9 Malignant neoplasm of cervix uteri, unspecified site ▽ ♀
182.0 Malignant neoplasm of corpus uteri, except isthmus ♀
182.1 Malignant neoplasm of isthmus ♀
182.8 Malignant neoplasm of other specified sites of body of uterus ♀
198.82 Secondary malignant neoplasm of genital organs
233.1 Carcinoma in situ of cervix uteri ♀
233.2 Carcinoma in situ of other and unspecified parts of uterus ▽ ♀
233.30 Carcinoma in situ, unspecified female genital organ ▽ ♀
233.31 Carcinoma in situ, vagina ♀
233.32 Carcinoma in situ, vulva ♀
233.39 Carcinoma in situ, other female genital organ ♀
236.0 Neoplasm of uncertain behavior of uterus ♀
236.3 Neoplasm of uncertain behavior of other and unspecified female genital organs ▽ ♀

ICD-9-CM Procedural

68.0 Hysterotomy ♀
92.27 Implantation or insertion of radioactive elements

58350

58350 Chromotubation of oviduct, including materials

ICD-9-CM Diagnostic

614.1 Chronic salpingitis and oophoritis — (Use additional code to identify organism: 041.00-041.09, 041.10-041.19) ♀

614.2 Salpingitis and oophoritis not specified as acute, subacute, or chronic — (Use additional code to identify organism: 041.00-041.09, 041.10-041.19) ♀
614.3 Acute parametritis and pelvic cellulitis — (Use additional code to identify organism: 041.00-041.09, 041.10-041.19) ♀
614.4 Chronic or unspecified parametritis and pelvic cellulitis — (Use additional code to identify organism: 041.00-041.09, 041.10-041.19) ♀
614.5 Acute or unspecified pelvic peritonitis, female — (Use additional code to identify organism: 041.00-041.09, 041.10-041.19) ♀
614.6 Pelvic peritoneal adhesions, female (postoperative) (postinfection) — (Use additional code to identify organism: 041.00-041.09, 041.10-041.19) (Use additional code to identify any associated infertility: 628.2) ♀
617.0 Endometriosis of uterus ♀
617.2 Endometriosis of fallopian tube ♀
617.3 Endometriosis of pelvic peritoneum ♀
617.8 Endometriosis of other specified sites ♀
620.0 Follicular cyst of ovary ♀
620.2 Other and unspecified ovarian cyst ▽ ♀
620.3 Acquired atrophy of ovary and fallopian tube ♀
620.8 Other noninflammatory disorder of ovary, fallopian tube, and broad ligament ♀
625.3 Dysmenorrhea ♀
628.2 Female infertility of tubal origin — (Use additional code for any associated peritubal adhesions: 614.6) ♀
628.8 Female infertility of other specified origin ♀
628.9 Female infertility of unspecified origin ▽ ♀
752.19 Other congenital anomaly of fallopian tubes and broad ligaments ♀
V26.21 Fertility testing
V26.22 Aftercare following sterilization reversal
V26.29 Other investigation and testing

ICD-9-CM Procedural

66.8 Insufflation of fallopian tube ♀
66.95 Insufflation of therapeutic agent into fallopian tubes ♀

58353-58356

58353 Endometrial ablation, thermal, without hysteroscopic guidance
58356 Endometrial cryoablation with ultrasonic guidance, including endometrial curettage, when performed

ICD-9-CM Diagnostic

617.0 Endometriosis of uterus ♀
617.9 Endometriosis, site unspecified ▽ ♀
626.2 Excessive or frequent menstruation ♀
626.6 Metrorrhagia ♀
626.8 Other disorder of menstruation and other abnormal bleeding from female genital tract ♀
627.1 Postmenopausal bleeding ♀

ICD-9-CM Procedural

68.23 Endometrial ablation ♀
69.09 Other dilation and curettage of uterus ♀
69.59 Other aspiration curettage of uterus ♀
88.79 Other diagnostic ultrasound

58400-58410

58400 Uterine suspension, with or without shortening of round ligaments, with or without shortening of sacrouterine ligaments; (separate procedure)
58410 with presacral sympathectomy

ICD-9-CM Diagnostic

618.00 Unspecified prolapse of vaginal walls without mention of uterine prolapse — (Use additional code to identify urinary incontinence: 625.6, 788.31, 788.33-788.39) ▽ ♀
618.01 Cystocele without mention of uterine prolapse, midline — (Use additional code to identify urinary incontinence: 625.6, 788.31, 788.33-788.39) ♀
618.02 Cystocele without mention of uterine prolapse, lateral — (Use additional code to identify urinary incontinence: 625.6, 788.31, 788.33-788.39) ♀
618.03 Urethrocele without mention of uterine prolapse — (Use additional code to identify urinary incontinence: 625.6, 788.31, 788.33-788.39) ♀
618.04 Rectocele without mention of uterine prolapse — (Use additional code to identify urinary incontinence: 625.6, 788.31, 788.33-788.39) (Use additional code for any associated fecal incontinence: 787.60-787.63) ♀
618.05 Perineocele without mention of uterine prolapse — (Use additional code to identify urinary incontinence: 625.6, 788.31, 788.33-788.39) ♀
618.1 Uterine prolapse without mention of vaginal wall prolapse — (Use additional code to identify urinary incontinence: 625.6, 788.31, 788.33-788.39) ♀
618.2 Uterovaginal prolapse, incomplete — (Use additional code to identify urinary incontinence: 625.6, 788.31, 788.33-788.39) ♀
618.3 Uterovaginal prolapse, complete — (Use additional code to identify urinary incontinence: 625.6, 788.31, 788.33-788.39) ♀
618.81 Incompetence or weakening of pubocervical tissue — (Use additional code to identify urinary incontinence: 625.6, 788.31, 788.33-788.39) ♀
618.82 Incompetence or weakening of rectovaginal tissue — (Use additional code to identify urinary incontinence: 625.6, 788.31, 788.33-788.39) ♀
618.83 Pelvic muscle wasting — (Use additional code to identify urinary incontinence: 625.6, 788.31, 788.33-788.39) ♀
618.89 Other specified genital prolapse — (Use additional code to identify urinary incontinence: 625.6, 788.31, 788.33-788.39) ♀
621.6 Malposition of uterus ♀
621.7 Chronic inversion of uterus ♀
625.0 Dyspareunia ♀
625.3 Dysmenorrhea ♀
625.6 Female stress incontinence ♀
625.8 Other specified symptom associated with female genital organs ♀
625.9 Unspecified symptom associated with female genital organs ▽ ♀

ICD-9-CM Procedural

05.24 Presacral sympathectomy
69.21 Interposition operation of uterine supporting structures ♀
69.22 Other uterine suspension ♀
69.29 Other repair of uterus and supporting structures ♀
69.98 Other operations on supporting structures of uterus ♀

58520

58520 Hysterorrhaphy, repair of ruptured uterus (nonobstetrical)

ICD-9-CM Diagnostic

621.8 Other specified disorders of uterus, not elsewhere classified ♀
867.4 Uterus injury without mention of open wound into cavity ♀
867.5 Uterus injury with open wound into cavity ♀

ICD-9-CM Procedural

69.29 Other repair of uterus and supporting structures ♀
69.49 Other repair of uterus ♀

58540

58540 Hysteroplasty, repair of uterine anomaly (Strassman type)

ICD-9-CM Diagnostic

621.5 Intrauterine synechiae ♀
621.8 Other specified disorders of uterus, not elsewhere classified ♀
752.2 Congenital doubling of uterus ♀
752.31 Agenesis of uterus ♀
752.32 Hypoplasia of uterus ♀

752.33 Unicornuate uterus ♀

752.34 Bicornuate uterus ♀

752.35 Septate uterus ♀

752.36 Arcuate uterus ♀

752.39 Other anomalies of uterus ♀

ICD-9-CM Procedural

68.22 Incision or excision of congenital septum of uterus ♀

69.23 Vaginal repair of chronic inversion of uterus ♀

69.49 Other repair of uterus ♀

58541-58542

58541 Laparoscopy, surgical, supracervical hysterectomy, for uterus 250 g or less;
58542 with removal of tube(s) and/or ovary(s)

ICD-9-CM Diagnostic

180.0 Malignant neoplasm of endocervix ♀

180.1 Malignant neoplasm of exocervix ♀

180.8 Malignant neoplasm of other specified sites of cervix ♀

180.9 Malignant neoplasm of cervix uteri, unspecified site ▽ ♀

181 Malignant neoplasm of placenta ♀

182.0 Malignant neoplasm of corpus uteri, except isthmus ♀

182.1 Malignant neoplasm of isthmus ♀

182.8 Malignant neoplasm of other specified sites of body of uterus ♀

183.0 Malignant neoplasm of ovary — (Use additional code to identify any functional activity) ♀

183.8 Malignant neoplasm of other specified sites of uterine adnexa ♀

183.9 Malignant neoplasm of uterine adnexa, unspecified site ▽ ♀

198.6 Secondary malignant neoplasm of ovary ♀

199.1 Other malignant neoplasm of unspecified site

218.0 Submucous leiomyoma of uterus ♀

218.1 Intramural leiomyoma of uterus ♀

218.2 Subserous leiomyoma of uterus ♀

218.9 Leiomyoma of uterus, unspecified ▽ ♀

233.1 Carcinoma in situ of cervix uteri ♀

233.2 Carcinoma in situ of other and unspecified parts of uterus ▽ ♀

233.30 Carcinoma in situ, unspecified female genital organ ▽ ♀

233.31 Carcinoma in situ, vagina ♀

233.32 Carcinoma in situ, vulva ♀

233.39 Carcinoma in situ, other female genital organ ♀

236.0 Neoplasm of uncertain behavior of uterus ♀

236.2 Neoplasm of uncertain behavior of ovary — (Use additional code to identify any functional activity) ♀

236.3 Neoplasm of uncertain behavior of other and unspecified female genital organs ▽ ♀

239.5 Neoplasm of unspecified nature of other genitourinary organs

553.9 Hernia of unspecified site of abdominal cavity without mention of obstruction or gangrene ▽

614.4 Chronic or unspecified parametritis and pelvic cellulitis — (Use additional code to identify organism: 041.00-041.09, 041.10-041.19) ♀

614.9 Unspecified inflammatory disease of female pelvic organs and tissues — (Use additional code to identify organism: 041.00-041.09, 041.10-041.19) ▽ ♀

617.0 Endometriosis of uterus ♀

617.9 Endometriosis, site unspecified ▽ ♀

618.00 Unspecified prolapse of vaginal walls without mention of uterine prolapse — (Use additional code to identify urinary incontinence: 625.6, 788.31, 788.33-788.39) ▽ ♀

618.1 Uterine prolapse without mention of vaginal wall prolapse — (Use additional code to identify urinary incontinence: 625.6, 788.31, 788.33-788.39) ♀

618.2 Uterovaginal prolapse, incomplete — (Use additional code to identify urinary incontinence: 625.6, 788.31, 788.33-788.39) ♀

618.3 Uterovaginal prolapse, complete — (Use additional code to identify urinary incontinence: 625.6, 788.31, 788.33-788.39) ♀

618.4 Uterovaginal prolapse, unspecified — (Use additional code to identify urinary incontinence: 625.6, 788.31, 788.33-788.39) ▽ ♀

618.89 Other specified genital prolapse — (Use additional code to identify urinary incontinence: 625.6, 788.31, 788.33-788.39) ♀

618.9 Unspecified genital prolapse — (Use additional code to identify urinary incontinence: 625.6, 788.31, 788.33-788.39) ▽ ♀

621.0 Polyp of corpus uteri ♀

621.2 Hypertrophy of uterus ♀

621.30 Endometrial hyperplasia, unspecified ▽ ♀

621.31 Simple endometrial hyperplasia without atypia ♀

621.32 Complex endometrial hyperplasia without atypia ♀

621.33 Endometrial hyperplasia with atypia ♀

621.34 Benign endometrial hyperplasia ♀

621.35 Endometrial intraepithelial neoplasia [EIN] ♀

621.6 Malposition of uterus ♀

621.8 Other specified disorders of uterus, not elsewhere classified ♀

621.9 Unspecified disorder of uterus ▽ ♀

622.10 Dysplasia of cervix, unspecified ▽ ♀

622.11 Mild dysplasia of cervix ♀

622.12 Moderate dysplasia of cervix ♀

625.3 Dysmenorrhea ♀

625.6 Female stress incontinence ♀

625.8 Other specified symptom associated with female genital organs ♀

625.9 Unspecified symptom associated with female genital organs ▽ ♀

626.2 Excessive or frequent menstruation ♀

626.6 Metrorrhagia ♀

626.8 Other disorder of menstruation and other abnormal bleeding from female genital tract ♀

626.9 Unspecified disorder of menstruation and other abnormal bleeding from female genital tract ▽ ♀

627.1 Postmenopausal bleeding ♀

677 Late effect of complication of pregnancy, childbirth, and the puerperium — (Code first any sequelae) ♀

788.33 Mixed incontinence urge and stress (male)(female) — (Code, if applicable, any causal condition first: 600.0-600.9, with fifth digit 1; 618.00-618.9; 753.23)

789.30 Abdominal or pelvic swelling, mass or lump, unspecified site ▽

V50.49 Other prophylactic organ removal

V84.02 Genetic susceptibility to malignant neoplasm of ovary — (Use additional code, if applicable, for any associated family history of the disease: V16-V19. Code first, if applicable, any current malignant neoplasms: 140.0-195.8, 200.0-208.9, 230.0-234.9. Use additional code, if applicable, for any personal history of malignant neoplasm: V10.0-V10.9) ♀

V84.04 Genetic susceptibility to malignant neoplasm of endometrium — (Use additional code, if applicable, for any associated family history of the disease: V16-V19. Code first, if applicable, any current malignant neoplasms: 140.0-195.8, 200.0-208.9, 230.0-234.9. Use additional code, if applicable, for any personal history of malignant neoplasm: V10.0-V10.9) ♀

V84.09 Genetic susceptibility to other malignant neoplasm — (Use additional code, if applicable, for any associated family history of the disease: V16-V19. Code first, if applicable, any current malignant neoplasms: 140.0-195.8, 200.0-208.9, 230.0-234.9. Use additional code, if applicable, for any personal history of malignant neoplasm: V10.0-V10.9)

ICD-9-CM Procedural

65.31 Laparoscopic unilateral oophorectomy ♀

65.41 Laparoscopic unilateral salpingo-oophorectomy ♀

65.53 Laparoscopic removal of both ovaries at same operative episode ♀

65.54 Laparoscopic removal of remaining ovary ♀

65.63 Laparoscopic removal of both ovaries and tubes at same operative episode ♀
65.64 Laparoscopic removal of remaining ovary and tube ♀
68.31 Laparoscopic supracervical hysterectomy [LSH] ♀

58543-58544

58543 Laparoscopy, surgical, supracervical hysterectomy, for uterus greater than 250 g;
58544 with removal of tube(s) and/or ovary(s)

ICD-9-CM Diagnostic

180.0 Malignant neoplasm of endocervix ♀
180.1 Malignant neoplasm of exocervix ♀
180.8 Malignant neoplasm of other specified sites of cervix ♀
180.9 Malignant neoplasm of cervix uteri, unspecified site ▽ ♀
181 Malignant neoplasm of placenta ♀
182.0 Malignant neoplasm of corpus uteri, except isthmus ♀
182.1 Malignant neoplasm of isthmus ♀
182.8 Malignant neoplasm of other specified sites of body of uterus ♀
183.0 Malignant neoplasm of ovary — (Use additional code to identify any functional activity) ♀
183.8 Malignant neoplasm of other specified sites of uterine adnexa ♀
183.9 Malignant neoplasm of uterine adnexa, unspecified site ▽ ♀
198.6 Secondary malignant neoplasm of ovary ♀
199.1 Other malignant neoplasm of unspecified site
218.0 Submucous leiomyoma of uterus ♀
218.1 Intramural leiomyoma of uterus ♀
218.2 Subserous leiomyoma of uterus ♀
218.9 Leiomyoma of uterus, unspecified ▽ ♀
233.1 Carcinoma in situ of cervix uteri ♀
233.2 Carcinoma in situ of other and unspecified parts of uterus ▽ ♀
233.30 Carcinoma in situ, unspecified female genital organ ▽ ♀
233.31 Carcinoma in situ, vagina ♀
233.32 Carcinoma in situ, vulva ♀
233.39 Carcinoma in situ, other female genital organ ♀
236.0 Neoplasm of uncertain behavior of uterus ♀
236.2 Neoplasm of uncertain behavior of ovary — (Use additional code to identify any functional activity) ♀
236.3 Neoplasm of uncertain behavior of other and unspecified female genital organs ▽ ♀
239.5 Neoplasm of unspecified nature of other genitourinary organs
553.9 Hernia of unspecified site of abdominal cavity without mention of obstruction or gangrene ▽
614.4 Chronic or unspecified parametritis and pelvic cellulitis — (Use additional code to identify organism: 041.00-041.09, 041.10-041.19) ♀
614.9 Unspecified inflammatory disease of female pelvic organs and tissues — (Use additional code to identify organism: 041.00-041.09, 041.10-041.19) ▽ ♀
617.0 Endometriosis of uterus ♀
617.9 Endometriosis, site unspecified ▽ ♀
618.00 Unspecified prolapse of vaginal walls without mention of uterine prolapse — (Use additional code to identify urinary incontinence: 625.6, 788.31, 788.33-788.39) ▽ ♀
618.1 Uterine prolapse without mention of vaginal wall prolapse — (Use additional code to identify urinary incontinence: 625.6, 788.31, 788.33-788.39) ♀
618.2 Uterovaginal prolapse, incomplete — (Use additional code to identify urinary incontinence: 625.6, 788.31, 788.33-788.39) ♀
618.3 Uterovaginal prolapse, complete — (Use additional code to identify urinary incontinence: 625.6, 788.31, 788.33-788.39) ♀
618.4 Uterovaginal prolapse, unspecified — (Use additional code to identify urinary incontinence: 625.6, 788.31, 788.33-788.39) ▽ ♀
618.89 Other specified genital prolapse — (Use additional code to identify urinary incontinence: 625.6, 788.31, 788.33-788.39) ♀
618.9 Unspecified genital prolapse — (Use additional code to identify urinary incontinence: 625.6, 788.31, 788.33-788.39) ▽ ♀
621.0 Polyp of corpus uteri ♀
621.2 Hypertrophy of uterus ♀
621.30 Endometrial hyperplasia, unspecified ▽ ♀
621.31 Simple endometrial hyperplasia without atypia ♀
621.32 Complex endometrial hyperplasia without atypia ♀
621.33 Endometrial hyperplasia with atypia ♀
621.34 Benign endometrial hyperplasia ♀
621.35 Endometrial intraepithelial neoplasia [EIN] ♀
621.6 Malposition of uterus ♀
621.8 Other specified disorders of uterus, not elsewhere classified ♀
621.9 Unspecified disorder of uterus ▽ ♀
622.10 Dysplasia of cervix, unspecified ▽ ♀
622.11 Mild dysplasia of cervix ♀
622.12 Moderate dysplasia of cervix ♀
625.3 Dysmenorrhea ♀
625.6 Female stress incontinence ♀
625.8 Other specified symptom associated with female genital organs ♀
625.9 Unspecified symptom associated with female genital organs ▽ ♀
626.2 Excessive or frequent menstruation ♀
626.6 Metrorrhagia ♀
626.8 Other disorder of menstruation and other abnormal bleeding from female genital tract ♀
626.9 Unspecified disorder of menstruation and other abnormal bleeding from female genital tract ▽ ♀
627.1 Postmenopausal bleeding ♀
677 Late effect of complication of pregnancy, childbirth, and the puerperium — (Code first any sequelae) ♀
788.33 Mixed incontinence urge and stress (male)(female) — (Code, if applicable, any causal condition first: 600.0-600.9, with fifth digit 1; 618.00-618.9; 753.23)
789.30 Abdominal or pelvic swelling, mass or lump, unspecified site ▽
V50.49 Other prophylactic organ removal
V84.02 Genetic susceptibility to malignant neoplasm of ovary — (Use additional code, if applicable, for any associated family history of the disease: V16-V19. Code first, if applicable, any current malignant neoplasms: 140.0-195.8, 200.0-208.9, 230.0-234.9. Use additional code, if applicable, for any personal history of malignant neoplasm: V10.0-V10.9) ♀
V84.04 Genetic susceptibility to malignant neoplasm of endometrium — (Use additional code, if applicable, for any associated family history of the disease: V16-V19. Code first, if applicable, any current malignant neoplasms: 140.0-195.8, 200.0-208.9, 230.0-234.9. Use additional code, if applicable, for any personal history of malignant neoplasm: V10.0-V10.9) ♀
V84.09 Genetic susceptibility to other malignant neoplasm — (Use additional code, if applicable, for any associated family history of the disease: V16-V19. Code first, if applicable, any current malignant neoplasms: 140.0-195.8, 200.0-208.9, 230.0-234.9. Use additional code, if applicable, for any personal history of malignant neoplasm: V10.0-V10.9)

ICD-9-CM Procedural

65.31 Laparoscopic unilateral oophorectomy ♀
65.41 Laparoscopic unilateral salpingo-oophorectomy ♀
65.53 Laparoscopic removal of both ovaries at same operative episode ♀
65.54 Laparoscopic removal of remaining ovary ♀
65.63 Laparoscopic removal of both ovaries and tubes at same operative episode ♀
65.64 Laparoscopic removal of remaining ovary and tube ♀
68.31 Laparoscopic supracervical hysterectomy [LSH] ♀

58545-58546

58545 Laparoscopy, surgical, myomectomy, excision; 1 to 4 intramural myomas with total weight of 250 g or less and/or removal of surface myomas

58546 5 or more intramural myomas and/or intramural myomas with total weight greater than 250 g

ICD-9-CM Diagnostic

218.0 Submucous leiomyoma of uterus ♀

218.1 Intramural leiomyoma of uterus ♀

218.2 Subserous leiomyoma of uterus ♀

218.9 Leiomyoma of uterus, unspecified ▽ ♀

ICD-9-CM Procedural

68.29 Other excision or destruction of lesion of uterus ♀

58548

58548 Laparoscopy, surgical, with radical hysterectomy, with bilateral total pelvic lymphadenectomy and para-aortic lymph node sampling (biopsy), with removal of tube(s) and ovary(s), if performed

ICD-9-CM Diagnostic

179 Malignant neoplasm of uterus, part unspecified ▽ ♀

180.0 Malignant neoplasm of endocervix ♀

180.1 Malignant neoplasm of exocervix ♀

180.8 Malignant neoplasm of other specified sites of cervix ♀

182.0 Malignant neoplasm of corpus uteri, except isthmus ♀

182.1 Malignant neoplasm of isthmus ♀

182.8 Malignant neoplasm of other specified sites of body of uterus ♀

183.0 Malignant neoplasm of ovary — (Use additional code to identify any functional activity) ♀

183.2 Malignant neoplasm of fallopian tube ♀

183.3 Malignant neoplasm of broad ligament of uterus ♀

183.4 Malignant neoplasm of parametrium of uterus ♀

183.5 Malignant neoplasm of round ligament of uterus ♀

183.8 Malignant neoplasm of other specified sites of uterine adnexa ♀

183.9 Malignant neoplasm of uterine adnexa, unspecified site ▽ ♀

184.0 Malignant neoplasm of vagina ♀

184.8 Malignant neoplasm of other specified sites of female genital organs ♀

196.2 Secondary and unspecified malignant neoplasm of intra-abdominal lymph nodes

196.6 Secondary and unspecified malignant neoplasm of intrapelvic lymph nodes

196.8 Secondary and unspecified malignant neoplasm of lymph nodes of multiple sites

198.82 Secondary malignant neoplasm of genital organs

209.71 Secondary neuroendocrine tumor of distant lymph nodes

209.74 Secondary neuroendocrine tumor of peritoneum

209.79 Secondary neuroendocrine tumor of other sites

233.1 Carcinoma in situ of cervix uteri ♀

236.0 Neoplasm of uncertain behavior of uterus ♀

236.2 Neoplasm of uncertain behavior of ovary — (Use additional code to identify any functional activity) ♀

238.8 Neoplasm of uncertain behavior of other specified sites

239.5 Neoplasm of unspecified nature of other genitourinary organs

239.89 Neoplasms of unspecified nature, other specified sites

V84.02 Genetic susceptibility to malignant neoplasm of ovary — (Use additional code, if applicable, for any associated family history of the disease: V16-V19. Code first, if applicable, any current malignant neoplasms: 140.0-195.8, 200.0-208.9, 230.0-234.9. Use additional code, if applicable, for any personal history of malignant neoplasm: V10.0-V10.9) ♀

V84.04 Genetic susceptibility to malignant neoplasm of endometrium — (Use additional code, if applicable, for any associated family history of the disease: V16-V19. Code first, if applicable, any current malignant neoplasms: 140.0-195.8, 200.0-208.9, 230.0-234.9. Use additional code, if applicable, for any personal history of malignant neoplasm: V10.0-V10.9) ♀

V84.09 Genetic susceptibility to other malignant neoplasm — (Use additional code, if applicable, for any associated family history of the disease: V16-V19. Code first, if applicable, any current malignant neoplasms: 140.0-195.8, 200.0-208.9, 230.0-234.9. Use additional code, if applicable, for any personal history of malignant neoplasm: V10.0-V10.9)

ICD-9-CM Procedural

40.11 Biopsy of lymphatic structure

40.3 Regional lymph node excision

40.59 Radical excision of other lymph nodes

65.31 Laparoscopic unilateral oophorectomy ♀

65.41 Laparoscopic unilateral salpingo-oophorectomy ♀

65.53 Laparoscopic removal of both ovaries at same operative episode ♀

65.54 Laparoscopic removal of remaining ovary ♀

65.63 Laparoscopic removal of both ovaries and tubes at same operative episode ♀

65.64 Laparoscopic removal of remaining ovary and tube ♀

68.61 Laparoscopic radical abdominal hysterectomy ♀

68.71 Laparoscopic radical vaginal hysterectomy [LRVH] ♀

58550-58554

58550 Laparoscopy, surgical, with vaginal hysterectomy, for uterus 250 g or less;

58552 with removal of tube(s) and/or ovary(s)

58553 Laparoscopy, surgical, with vaginal hysterectomy, for uterus greater than 250 g;

58554 with removal of tube(s) and/or ovary(s)

ICD-9-CM Diagnostic

180.0 Malignant neoplasm of endocervix ♀

180.1 Malignant neoplasm of exocervix ♀

180.8 Malignant neoplasm of other specified sites of cervix ♀

180.9 Malignant neoplasm of cervix uteri, unspecified site ▽ ♀

181 Malignant neoplasm of placenta ♀

182.0 Malignant neoplasm of corpus uteri, except isthmus ♀

182.1 Malignant neoplasm of isthmus ♀

182.8 Malignant neoplasm of other specified sites of body of uterus ♀

183.0 Malignant neoplasm of ovary — (Use additional code to identify any functional activity) ♀

183.8 Malignant neoplasm of other specified sites of uterine adnexa ♀

183.9 Malignant neoplasm of uterine adnexa, unspecified site ▽ ♀

198.6 Secondary malignant neoplasm of ovary ♀

199.1 Other malignant neoplasm of unspecified site

218.0 Submucous leiomyoma of uterus ♀

218.1 Intramural leiomyoma of uterus ♀

218.2 Subserous leiomyoma of uterus ♀

218.9 Leiomyoma of uterus, unspecified ▽ ♀

233.1 Carcinoma in situ of cervix uteri ♀

233.2 Carcinoma in situ of other and unspecified parts of uterus ▽ ♀

233.30 Carcinoma in situ, unspecified female genital organ ▽ ♀

233.31 Carcinoma in situ, vagina ♀

233.32 Carcinoma in situ, vulva ♀

233.39 Carcinoma in situ, other female genital organ ♀

236.0 Neoplasm of uncertain behavior of uterus ♀

236.2 Neoplasm of uncertain behavior of ovary — (Use additional code to identify any functional activity) ♀

236.3 Neoplasm of uncertain behavior of other and unspecified female genital organs ▽ ♀

239.5 Neoplasm of unspecified nature of other genitourinary organs

553.9 Hernia of unspecified site of abdominal cavity without mention of obstruction or gangrene ▽

614.4 Chronic or unspecified parametritis and pelvic cellulitis — (Use additional code to identify organism: 041.00-041.09, 041.10-041.19) ♀

614.9 Unspecified inflammatory disease of female pelvic organs and tissues — (Use additional code to identify organism: 041.00-041.09, 041.10-041.19) ▽ ♀

617.0 Endometriosis of uterus ♀

617.9 Endometriosis, site unspecified ▽ ♀

618.00 Unspecified prolapse of vaginal walls without mention of uterine prolapse — (Use additional code to identify urinary incontinence: 625.6, 788.31, 788.33-788.39) ▽ ♀

618.1 Uterine prolapse without mention of vaginal wall prolapse — (Use additional code to identify urinary incontinence: 625.6, 788.31, 788.33-788.39) ♀

618.2 Uterovaginal prolapse, incomplete — (Use additional code to identify urinary incontinence: 625.6, 788.31, 788.33-788.39) ♀

618.3 Uterovaginal prolapse, complete — (Use additional code to identify urinary incontinence: 625.6, 788.31, 788.33-788.39) ♀

618.4 Uterovaginal prolapse, unspecified — (Use additional code to identify urinary incontinence: 625.6, 788.31, 788.33-788.39) ▽ ♀

618.89 Other specified genital prolapse — (Use additional code to identify urinary incontinence: 625.6, 788.31, 788.33-788.39) ♀

618.9 Unspecified genital prolapse — (Use additional code to identify urinary incontinence: 625.6, 788.31, 788.33-788.39) ▽ ♀

621.0 Polyp of corpus uteri ♀

621.2 Hypertrophy of uterus ♀

621.30 Endometrial hyperplasia, unspecified ▽ ♀

621.31 Simple endometrial hyperplasia without atypia ♀

621.32 Complex endometrial hyperplasia without atypia ♀

621.33 Endometrial hyperplasia with atypia ♀

621.34 Benign endometrial hyperplasia ♀

621.35 Endometrial intraepithelial neoplasia [EIN] ♀

621.6 Malposition of uterus ♀

621.8 Other specified disorders of uterus, not elsewhere classified ♀

621.9 Unspecified disorder of uterus ▽ ♀

622.10 Dysplasia of cervix, unspecified ▽ ♀

622.11 Mild dysplasia of cervix ♀

622.12 Moderate dysplasia of cervix ♀

625.3 Dysmenorrhea ♀

625.6 Female stress incontinence ♀

625.8 Other specified symptom associated with female genital organs ♀

625.9 Unspecified symptom associated with female genital organs ▽ ♀

626.2 Excessive or frequent menstruation ♀

626.6 Metrorrhagia ♀

626.8 Other disorder of menstruation and other abnormal bleeding from female genital tract ♀

626.9 Unspecified disorder of menstruation and other abnormal bleeding from female genital tract ▽ ♀

627.1 Postmenopausal bleeding ♀

677 Late effect of complication of pregnancy, childbirth, and the puerperium — (Code first any sequelae) ♀

788.33 Mixed incontinence urge and stress (male)(female) — (Code, if applicable, any causal condition first: 600.0-600.9, with fifth digit 1; 618.00-618.9; 753.23)

789.30 Abdominal or pelvic swelling, mass or lump, unspecified site ▽

V50.49 Other prophylactic organ removal

V84.02 Genetic susceptibility to malignant neoplasm of ovary — (Use additional code, if applicable, for any associated family history of the disease: V16-V19. Code first, if applicable, any current malignant neoplasms: 140.0-195.8, 200.0-208.9, 230.0-234.9. Use additional code, if applicable, for any personal history of malignant neoplasm: V10.0-V10.9) ♀

V84.04 Genetic susceptibility to malignant neoplasm of endometrium — (Use additional code, if applicable, for any associated family history of the disease: V16-V19. Code first, if applicable, any current malignant neoplasms: 140.0-195.8, 200.0-208.9, 230.0-234.9. Use additional code, if applicable, for any personal history of malignant neoplasm: V10.0-V10.9) ♀

V84.09 Genetic susceptibility to other malignant neoplasm — (Use additional code, if applicable, for any associated family history of the disease: V16-V19. Code first, if applicable, any current malignant neoplasms: 140.0-195.8, 200.0-208.9, 230.0-234.9. Use additional code, if applicable, for any personal history of malignant neoplasm: V10.0-V10.9)

ICD-9-CM Procedural

65.31 Laparoscopic unilateral oophorectomy ♀

65.41 Laparoscopic unilateral salpingo-oophorectomy ♀

65.53 Laparoscopic removal of both ovaries at same operative episode ♀

65.54 Laparoscopic removal of remaining ovary ♀

65.63 Laparoscopic removal of both ovaries and tubes at same operative episode ♀

65.64 Laparoscopic removal of remaining ovary and tube ♀

68.51 Laparoscopically assisted vaginal hysterectomy (LAVH) ♀

68.71 Laparoscopic radical vaginal hysterectomy [LRVH] ♀

58555

58555 Hysteroscopy, diagnostic (separate procedure)

ICD-9-CM Diagnostic

179 Malignant neoplasm of uterus, part unspecified ▽ ♀

180.0 Malignant neoplasm of endocervix ♀

180.1 Malignant neoplasm of exocervix ♀

180.8 Malignant neoplasm of other specified sites of cervix ♀

180.9 Malignant neoplasm of cervix uteri, unspecified site ▽ ♀

182.0 Malignant neoplasm of corpus uteri, except isthmus ♀

182.1 Malignant neoplasm of isthmus ♀

183.2 Malignant neoplasm of fallopian tube ♀

183.3 Malignant neoplasm of broad ligament of uterus ♀

183.4 Malignant neoplasm of parametrium of uterus ♀

183.5 Malignant neoplasm of round ligament of uterus ♀

183.8 Malignant neoplasm of other specified sites of uterine adnexa ♀

183.9 Malignant neoplasm of uterine adnexa, unspecified site ▽ ♀

198.82 Secondary malignant neoplasm of genital organs

218.0 Submucous leiomyoma of uterus ♀

218.1 Intramural leiomyoma of uterus ♀

218.2 Subserous leiomyoma of uterus ♀

218.9 Leiomyoma of uterus, unspecified ▽ ♀

219.0 Benign neoplasm of cervix uteri ♀

219.1 Benign neoplasm of corpus uteri ♀

219.8 Benign neoplasm of other specified parts of uterus ♀

219.9 Benign neoplasm of uterus, part unspecified ▽ ♀

221.0 Benign neoplasm of fallopian tube and uterine ligaments ♀

221.8 Benign neoplasm of other specified sites of female genital organs ♀

233.1 Carcinoma in situ of cervix uteri ♀

233.2 Carcinoma in situ of other and unspecified parts of uterus ▽ ♀

233.30 Carcinoma in situ, unspecified female genital organ ▽ ♀

233.31 Carcinoma in situ, vagina ♀

233.32 Carcinoma in situ, vulva ♀

233.39 Carcinoma in situ, other female genital organ ♀

236.0 Neoplasm of uncertain behavior of uterus ♀

236.3 Neoplasm of uncertain behavior of other and unspecified female genital organs ▽ ♀

239.5 Neoplasm of unspecified nature of other genitourinary organs

614.4 Chronic or unspecified parametritis and pelvic cellulitis — (Use additional code to identify organism: 041.00-041.09, 041.10-041.19) ♀

615.0 Acute inflammatory disease of uterus, except cervix — (Use additional code to identify organism: 041.00-041.09, 041.10-041.19) ♀

615.1 Chronic inflammatory disease of uterus, except cervix — (Use additional code to identify organism: 041.00-041.09, 041.10-041.19) ♀
616.0 Cervicitis and endocervicitis — (Use additional code to identify organism: 041.00-041.09, 041.10-041.19) ♀
617.0 Endometriosis of uterus ♀
618.1 Uterine prolapse without mention of vaginal wall prolapse — (Use additional code to identify urinary incontinence: 625.6, 788.31, 788.33-788.39) ♀
621.0 Polyp of corpus uteri ♀
621.2 Hypertrophy of uterus ♀
621.30 Endometrial hyperplasia, unspecified ♀
621.31 Simple endometrial hyperplasia without atypia ♀
621.32 Complex endometrial hyperplasia without atypia ♀
621.33 Endometrial hyperplasia with atypia ♀
621.34 Benign endometrial hyperplasia ♀
621.35 Endometrial intraepithelial neoplasia [EIN] ♀
621.4 Hematometra ♀
621.5 Intrauterine synechiae ♀
621.8 Other specified disorders of uterus, not elsewhere classified ♀
622.10 Dysplasia of cervix, unspecified ♀
622.11 Mild dysplasia of cervix ♀
622.12 Moderate dysplasia of cervix ♀
623.8 Other specified noninflammatory disorder of vagina ♀
625.3 Dysmenorrhea ♀
626.0 Absence of menstruation ♀
626.2 Excessive or frequent menstruation ♀
626.4 Irregular menstrual cycle ♀
626.6 Metrorrhagia ♀
626.8 Other disorder of menstruation and other abnormal bleeding from female genital tract ♀
627.0 Premenopausal menorrhagia ♀
627.1 Postmenopausal bleeding ♀
628.3 Female infertility of uterine origin — (Use additional code for any associated tuberculous endometriosis: 016.7) ♀
628.9 Female infertility of unspecified origin ♀
629.0 Hematocele, female, not elsewhere classified ♀
629.1 Hydrocele, canal of Nuck ♀
629.81 Recurrent pregnancy loss without current pregnancy ♀
629.89 Other specified disorders of female genital organs ♀
789.00 Abdominal pain, unspecified site
789.01 Abdominal pain, right upper quadrant
789.02 Abdominal pain, left upper quadrant
789.03 Abdominal pain, right lower quadrant
789.04 Abdominal pain, left lower quadrant
789.30 Abdominal or pelvic swelling, mass or lump, unspecified site
789.31 Abdominal or pelvic swelling, mass, or lump, right upper quadrant
789.32 Abdominal or pelvic swelling, mass, or lump, left upper quadrant
789.33 Abdominal or pelvic swelling, mass, or lump, right lower quadrant
789.34 Abdominal or pelvic swelling, mass, or lump, left lower quadrant
V26.21 Fertility testing
V26.29 Other investigation and testing
V84.02 Genetic susceptibility to malignant neoplasm of ovary — (Use additional code, if applicable, for any associated family history of the disease: V16-V19. Code first, if applicable, any current malignant neoplasms: 140.0-195.8, 200.0-208.9, 230.0-234.9. Use additional code, if applicable, for any personal history of malignant neoplasm: V10.0-V10.9) ♀
V84.04 Genetic susceptibility to malignant neoplasm of endometrium — (Use additional code, if applicable, for any associated family history of the disease: V16-V19. Code first, if applicable, any current malignant neoplasms: 140.0-195.8, 200.0-208.9, 230.0-234.9. Use additional code, if applicable, for any personal history of malignant neoplasm: V10.0-V10.9) ♀
V84.09 Genetic susceptibility to other malignant neoplasm — (Use additional code, if applicable, for any associated family history of the disease: V16-V19. Code first, if applicable, any current malignant neoplasms: 140.0-195.8, 200.0-208.9, 230.0-234.9. Use additional code, if applicable, for any personal history of malignant neoplasm: V10.0-V10.9)

ICD-9-CM Procedural

68.12 Hysteroscopy ♀

58558

58558 Hysteroscopy, surgical; with sampling (biopsy) of endometrium and/or polypectomy, with or without D & C

ICD-9-CM Diagnostic

179 Malignant neoplasm of uterus, part unspecified ♀
180.0 Malignant neoplasm of endocervix ♀
180.1 Malignant neoplasm of exocervix ♀
180.8 Malignant neoplasm of other specified sites of cervix ♀
180.9 Malignant neoplasm of cervix uteri, unspecified site ♀
182.0 Malignant neoplasm of corpus uteri, except isthmus ♀
182.1 Malignant neoplasm of isthmus ♀
182.8 Malignant neoplasm of other specified sites of body of uterus ♀
199.1 Other malignant neoplasm of unspecified site
218.0 Submucous leiomyoma of uterus ♀
218.1 Intramural leiomyoma of uterus ♀
218.2 Subserous leiomyoma of uterus ♀
219.0 Benign neoplasm of cervix uteri ♀
219.1 Benign neoplasm of corpus uteri ♀
219.8 Benign neoplasm of other specified parts of uterus ♀
219.9 Benign neoplasm of uterus, part unspecified ♀
233.1 Carcinoma in situ of cervix uteri ♀
233.2 Carcinoma in situ of other and unspecified parts of uterus ♀
233.30 Carcinoma in situ, unspecified female genital organ ♀
233.31 Carcinoma in situ, vagina ♀
233.32 Carcinoma in situ, vulva ♀
233.39 Carcinoma in situ, other female genital organ ♀
236.0 Neoplasm of uncertain behavior of uterus ♀
236.3 Neoplasm of uncertain behavior of other and unspecified female genital organs ♀
239.5 Neoplasm of unspecified nature of other genitourinary organs
256.9 Unspecified ovarian dysfunction ♀
614.6 Pelvic peritoneal adhesions, female (postoperative) (postinfection) — (Use additional code to identify organism: 041.00-041.09, 041.10-041.19) (Use additional code to identify any associated infertility: 628.2) ♀
617.0 Endometriosis of uterus ♀
617.1 Endometriosis of ovary ♀
617.3 Endometriosis of pelvic peritoneum ♀
617.9 Endometriosis, site unspecified ♀
618.1 Uterine prolapse without mention of vaginal wall prolapse — (Use additional code to identify urinary incontinence: 625.6, 788.31, 788.33-788.39) ♀
621.0 Polyp of corpus uteri ♀
621.2 Hypertrophy of uterus ♀
621.30 Endometrial hyperplasia, unspecified ♀
621.31 Simple endometrial hyperplasia without atypia ♀
621.32 Complex endometrial hyperplasia without atypia ♀
621.33 Endometrial hyperplasia with atypia ♀
621.34 Benign endometrial hyperplasia ♀
621.35 Endometrial intraepithelial neoplasia [EIN] ♀

622.10 Dysplasia of cervix, unspecified ♀
622.11 Mild dysplasia of cervix ♀
622.12 Moderate dysplasia of cervix ♀
622.4 Stricture and stenosis of cervix ♀
622.7 Mucous polyp of cervix ♀
625.3 Dysmenorrhea ♀
625.6 Female stress incontinence ♀
625.8 Other specified symptom associated with female genital organs ♀
626.0 Absence of menstruation ♀
626.2 Excessive or frequent menstruation ♀
626.4 Irregular menstrual cycle ♀
626.6 Metrorrhagia ♀
626.8 Other disorder of menstruation and other abnormal bleeding from female genital tract ♀
627.0 Premenopausal menorrhagia ♀
627.1 Postmenopausal bleeding ♀
628.2 Female infertility of tubal origin — (Use additional code for any associated peritubal adhesions: 614.6) ♀
628.3 Female infertility of uterine origin — (Use additional code for any associated tuberculous endometriosis: 016.7) ♀
628.4 Female infertility of cervical or vaginal origin ♀
628.8 Female infertility of other specified origin ♀
628.9 Female infertility of unspecified origin ♀
789.30 Abdominal or pelvic swelling, mass or lump, unspecified site
789.31 Abdominal or pelvic swelling, mass, or lump, right upper quadrant
789.32 Abdominal or pelvic swelling, mass, or lump, left upper quadrant
789.33 Abdominal or pelvic swelling, mass, or lump, right lower quadrant
789.34 Abdominal or pelvic swelling, mass, or lump, left lower quadrant
795.00 Abnormal glandular Papanicolaou smear of cervix ♀
795.01 Papanicolaou smear of cervix with atypical squamous cells of undetermined significance (ASC-US) ♀
795.02 Papanicolaou smear of cervix with atypical squamous cells cannot exclude high grade squamous intraepithelial lesion (ASC-H) ♀
795.03 Papanicolaou smear of cervix with low grade squamous intraepithelial lesion (LGSIL) ♀
795.04 Papanicolaou smear of cervix with high grade squamous intraepithelial lesion (HGSIL) ♀
795.05 Cervical high risk human papillomavirus (HPV) DNA test positive ♀
795.07 Satisfactory cervical smear but lacking transformation zone ♀
795.08 Unsatisfactory cervical cytology smear ♀
795.09 Other abnormal Papanicolaou smear of cervix and cervical HPV — (Use additional code for associated human papillomavirus: 079.4) ♀
795.10 Abnormal glandular Papanicolaou smear of vagina — (Use additional code to identify acquired absence of uterus and cervix, if applicable: V88.01-V88.03) ♀
795.11 Papanicolaou smear of vagina with atypical squamous cells of undetermined significance (ASC-US) — (Use additional code to identify acquired absence of uterus and cervix, if applicable: V88.01-V88.03) ♀
795.12 Papanicolaou smear of vagina with atypical squamous cells cannot exclude high grade squamous intraepithelial lesion (ASC-H) — (Use additional code to identify acquired absence of uterus and cervix, if applicable: V88.01-V88.03) ♀
795.13 Papanicolaou smear of vagina with low grade squamous intraepithelial lesion (LGSIL) — (Use additional code to identify acquired absence of uterus and cervix, if applicable: V88.01-V88.03) ♀
795.14 Papanicolaou smear of vagina with high grade squamous intraepithelial lesion (HGSIL) — (Use additional code to identify acquired absence of uterus and cervix, if applicable: V88.01-V88.03) ♀
795.15 Vaginal high risk human papillomavirus (HPV) DNA test positive — (Use additional code to identify acquired absence of uterus and cervix, if applicable: V88.01-V88.03) ♀
795.16 Papanicolaou smear of vagina with cytologic evidence of malignancy — (Use additional code to identify acquired absence of uterus and cervix, if applicable: V88.01-V88.03) ♀
795.18 Unsatisfactory vaginal cytology smear — (Use additional code to identify acquired absence of uterus and cervix, if applicable: V88.01-V88.03) ♀
795.19 Other abnormal Papanicolaou smear of vagina and vaginal HPV — (Use additional code to identify acquired absence of uterus and cervix, if applicable: V88.01-V88.03) (Use additional code for associated human papillomavirus: 079.4) ♀
795.39 Other nonspecific positive culture findings
V26.21 Fertility testing
V84.02 Genetic susceptibility to malignant neoplasm of ovary — (Use additional code, if applicable, for any associated family history of the disease: V16-V19. Code first, if applicable, any current malignant neoplasms: 140.0-195.8, 200.0-208.9, 230.0-234.9. Use additional code, if applicable, for any personal history of malignant neoplasm: V10.0-V10.9) ♀
V84.04 Genetic susceptibility to malignant neoplasm of endometrium — (Use additional code, if applicable, for any associated family history of the disease: V16-V19. Code first, if applicable, any current malignant neoplasms: 140.0-195.8, 200.0-208.9, 230.0-234.9. Use additional code, if applicable, for any personal history of malignant neoplasm: V10.0-V10.9) ♀
V84.09 Genetic susceptibility to other malignant neoplasm — (Use additional code, if applicable, for any associated family history of the disease: V16-V19. Code first, if applicable, any current malignant neoplasms: 140.0-195.8, 200.0-208.9, 230.0-234.9. Use additional code, if applicable, for any personal history of malignant neoplasm: V10.0-V10.9)

ICD-9-CM Procedural

68.16 Closed biopsy of uterus ♀
68.29 Other excision or destruction of lesion of uterus ♀
69.09 Other dilation and curettage of uterus ♀

58559-58560

58559 Hysteroscopy, surgical; with lysis of intrauterine adhesions (any method)
58560 with division or resection of intrauterine septum (any method)

ICD-9-CM Diagnostic

621.5 Intrauterine synechiae ♀
626.2 Excessive or frequent menstruation ♀
752.2 Congenital doubling of uterus ♀
752.31 Agenesis of uterus ♀
752.32 Hypoplasia of uterus ♀
752.33 Unicornuate uterus ♀
752.34 Bicornuate uterus ♀
752.35 Septate uterus ♀
752.36 Arcuate uterus ♀
752.39 Other anomalies of uterus ♀
908.1 Late effect of internal injury to intra-abdominal organs
908.2 Late effect of internal injury to other internal organs
908.6 Late effect of certain complications of trauma
909.3 Late effect of complications of surgical and medical care

ICD-9-CM Procedural

68.21 Division of endometrial synechiae ♀
68.22 Incision or excision of congenital septum of uterus ♀

58561

58561 Hysteroscopy, surgical; with removal of leiomyomata

ICD-9-CM Diagnostic

218.0 Submucous leiomyoma of uterus ♀
218.1 Intramural leiomyoma of uterus ♀
218.2 Subserous leiomyoma of uterus ♀
218.9 Leiomyoma of uterus, unspecified ♀
626.2 Excessive or frequent menstruation ♀
626.6 Metrorrhagia ♀

ICD-9-CM Procedural

68.29 Other excision or destruction of lesion of uterus ♀

58562

58562 Hysteroscopy, surgical; with removal of impacted foreign body

ICD-9-CM Diagnostic

939.1 Foreign body in uterus, any part ♀

996.32 Mechanical complication due to intrauterine contraceptive device ♀

996.65 Infection and inflammatory reaction due to other genitourinary device, implant, and graft — (Use additional code to identify specified infections)

ICD-9-CM Procedural

97.71 Removal of intrauterine contraceptive device ♀

98.16 Removal of intraluminal foreign body from uterus without incision ♀

58563

58563 Hysteroscopy, surgical; with endometrial ablation (eg, endometrial resection, electrosurgical ablation, thermoablation)

ICD-9-CM Diagnostic

617.0 Endometriosis of uterus ♀

617.9 Endometriosis, site unspecified ▽ ♀

626.2 Excessive or frequent menstruation ♀

626.6 Metrorrhagia ♀

626.8 Other disorder of menstruation and other abnormal bleeding from female genital tract ♀

627.1 Postmenopausal bleeding ♀

ICD-9-CM Procedural

68.23 Endometrial ablation ♀

58565

58565 Hysteroscopy, surgical; with bilateral fallopian tube cannulation to induce occlusion by placement of permanent implants

ICD-9-CM Diagnostic

659.41 Grand multiparity, delivered, with or without mention of antepartum condition ♀

V25.2 Sterilization

V61.5 Multiparity

ICD-9-CM Procedural

66.29 Other bilateral endoscopic destruction or occlusion of fallopian tubes ♀

58570-58573

58570 Laparoscopy, surgical, with total hysterectomy, for uterus 250 g or less;

58571 with removal of tube(s) and/or ovary(s)

58572 Laparoscopy, surgical, with total hysterectomy, for uterus greater than 250 g;

58573 with removal of tube(s) and/or ovary(s)

ICD-9-CM Diagnostic

179 Malignant neoplasm of uterus, part unspecified ▽ ♀

180.0 Malignant neoplasm of endocervix ♀

180.1 Malignant neoplasm of exocervix ♀

180.8 Malignant neoplasm of other specified sites of cervix ♀

180.9 Malignant neoplasm of cervix uteri, unspecified site ▽ ♀

181 Malignant neoplasm of placenta ♀

182.0 Malignant neoplasm of corpus uteri, except isthmus ♀

182.1 Malignant neoplasm of isthmus ♀

182.8 Malignant neoplasm of other specified sites of body of uterus ♀

183.0 Malignant neoplasm of ovary — (Use additional code to identify any functional activity) ♀

183.8 Malignant neoplasm of other specified sites of uterine adnexa ♀

183.9 Malignant neoplasm of uterine adnexa, unspecified site ▽ ♀

198.6 Secondary malignant neoplasm of ovary ♀

198.82 Secondary malignant neoplasm of genital organs

199.1 Other malignant neoplasm of unspecified site

218.0 Submucous leiomyoma of uterus ♀

218.1 Intramural leiomyoma of uterus ♀

218.2 Subserous leiomyoma of uterus ♀

218.9 Leiomyoma of uterus, unspecified ▽ ♀

233.1 Carcinoma in situ of cervix uteri ♀

233.2 Carcinoma in situ of other and unspecified parts of uterus ▽ ♀

233.30 Carcinoma in situ, unspecified female genital organ ▽ ♀

233.31 Carcinoma in situ, vagina ♀

233.32 Carcinoma in situ, vulva ♀

233.39 Carcinoma in situ, other female genital organ ♀

236.0 Neoplasm of uncertain behavior of uterus ♀

236.2 Neoplasm of uncertain behavior of ovary — (Use additional code to identify any functional activity) ♀

236.3 Neoplasm of uncertain behavior of other and unspecified female genital organs ▽ ♀

239.5 Neoplasm of unspecified nature of other genitourinary organs

553.9 Hernia of unspecified site of abdominal cavity without mention of obstruction or gangrene ▽

614.3 Acute parametritis and pelvic cellulitis — (Use additional code to identify organism: 041.00-041.09, 041.10-041.19) ♀

614.4 Chronic or unspecified parametritis and pelvic cellulitis — (Use additional code to identify organism: 041.00-041.09, 041.10-041.19) ♀

614.5 Acute or unspecified pelvic peritonitis, female — (Use additional code to identify organism: 041.00-041.09, 041.10-041.19) ♀

614.6 Pelvic peritoneal adhesions, female (postoperative) (postinfection) — (Use additional code to identify organism: 041.00-041.09, 041.10-041.19) (Use additional code to identify any associated infertility: 628.2) ♀

614.7 Other chronic pelvic peritonitis, female — (Use additional code to identify organism: 041.00-041.09, 041.10-041.19) ♀

614.8 Other specified inflammatory disease of female pelvic organs and tissues — (Use additional code to identify organism: 041.00-041.09, 041.10-041.19) ♀

614.9 Unspecified inflammatory disease of female pelvic organs and tissues — (Use additional code to identify organism: 041.00-041.09, 041.10-041.19) ▽ ♀

617.0 Endometriosis of uterus ♀

617.1 Endometriosis of ovary ♀

617.2 Endometriosis of fallopian tube ♀

617.3 Endometriosis of pelvic peritoneum ♀

617.9 Endometriosis, site unspecified ▽ ♀

618.00 Unspecified prolapse of vaginal walls without mention of uterine prolapse — (Use additional code to identify urinary incontinence: 625.6, 788.31, 788.33-788.39) ▽ ♀

618.1 Uterine prolapse without mention of vaginal wall prolapse — (Use additional code to identify urinary incontinence: 625.6, 788.31, 788.33-788.39) ♀

618.2 Uterovaginal prolapse, incomplete — (Use additional code to identify urinary incontinence: 625.6, 788.31, 788.33-788.39) ♀

618.3 Uterovaginal prolapse, complete — (Use additional code to identify urinary incontinence: 625.6, 788.31, 788.33-788.39) ♀

618.4 Uterovaginal prolapse, unspecified — (Use additional code to identify urinary incontinence: 625.6, 788.31, 788.33-788.39) ▽ ♀

618.89 Other specified genital prolapse — (Use additional code to identify urinary incontinence: 625.6, 788.31, 788.33-788.39) ♀

618.9 Unspecified genital prolapse — (Use additional code to identify urinary incontinence: 625.6, 788.31, 788.33-788.39) ▽ ♀

621.0 Polyp of corpus uteri ♀

621.2 Hypertrophy of uterus ♀

621.30 Endometrial hyperplasia, unspecified ▽ ♀

621.31 Simple endometrial hyperplasia without atypia ♀
621.32 Complex endometrial hyperplasia without atypia ♀
621.33 Endometrial hyperplasia with atypia ♀
621.34 Benign endometrial hyperplasia ♀
621.35 Endometrial intraepithelial neoplasia [EIN] ♀
621.6 Malposition of uterus ♀
621.8 Other specified disorders of uterus, not elsewhere classified ♀
621.9 Unspecified disorder of uterus ♀
622.10 Dysplasia of cervix, unspecified ♀
622.11 Mild dysplasia of cervix ♀
622.12 Moderate dysplasia of cervix ♀
625.3 Dysmenorrhea ♀
625.5 Pelvic congestion syndrome ♀
625.6 Female stress incontinence ♀
625.8 Other specified symptom associated with female genital organs ♀
625.9 Unspecified symptom associated with female genital organs ♀
626.2 Excessive or frequent menstruation ♀
626.6 Metrorrhagia ♀
626.8 Other disorder of menstruation and other abnormal bleeding from female genital tract ♀
626.9 Unspecified disorder of menstruation and other abnormal bleeding from female genital tract ♀
627.1 Postmenopausal bleeding ♀
627.2 Symptomatic menopausal or female climacteric states ♀
677 Late effect of complication of pregnancy, childbirth, and the puerperium — (Code first any sequelae) ♀
788.33 Mixed incontinence urge and stress (male)(female) — (Code, if applicable, any causal condition first: 600.0-600.9, with fifth digit 1; 618.00-618.9; 753.23)
789.30 Abdominal or pelvic swelling, mass or lump, unspecified site

ICD-9-CM Procedural

65.31 Laparoscopic unilateral oophorectomy ♀
65.41 Laparoscopic unilateral salpingo-oophorectomy ♀
65.53 Laparoscopic removal of both ovaries at same operative episode ♀
65.54 Laparoscopic removal of remaining ovary ♀
65.63 Laparoscopic removal of both ovaries and tubes at same operative episode ♀
65.64 Laparoscopic removal of remaining ovary and tube ♀
68.41 Laparoscopic total abdominal hysterectomy ♀
68.51 Laparoscopically assisted vaginal hysterectomy (LAVH) ♀
68.61 Laparoscopic radical abdominal hysterectomy ♀
68.71 Laparoscopic radical vaginal hysterectomy [LRVH] ♀

Oviduct/Ovary

58600-58605

58600 Ligation or transection of fallopian tube(s), abdominal or vaginal approach, unilateral or bilateral
58605 Ligation or transection of fallopian tube(s), abdominal or vaginal approach, postpartum, unilateral or bilateral, during same hospitalization (separate procedure)

ICD-9-CM Diagnostic

659.41 Grand multiparity, delivered, with or without mention of antepartum condition ♀
V25.2 Sterilization

ICD-9-CM Procedural

66.32 Other bilateral ligation and division of fallopian tubes ♀

58611

58611 Ligation or transection of fallopian tube(s) when done at the time of cesarean delivery or intra-abdominal surgery (not a separate procedure) (List separately in addition to code for primary procedure)

ICD-9-CM Diagnostic

V25.2 Sterilization

ICD-9-CM Procedural

66.32 Other bilateral ligation and division of fallopian tubes ♀

58615

58615 Occlusion of fallopian tube(s) by device (eg, band, clip, Falope ring) vaginal or suprapubic approach

ICD-9-CM Diagnostic

V25.2 Sterilization

ICD-9-CM Procedural

66.31 Other bilateral ligation and crushing of fallopian tubes ♀
66.39 Other bilateral destruction or occlusion of fallopian tubes ♀
66.92 Unilateral destruction or occlusion of fallopian tube ♀

58660

58660 Laparoscopy, surgical; with lysis of adhesions (salpingolysis, ovariolysis) (separate procedure)

ICD-9-CM Diagnostic

568.0 Peritoneal adhesions (postoperative) (postinfection)
568.89 Other specified disorder of peritoneum
614.1 Chronic salpingitis and oophoritis — (Use additional code to identify organism: 041.00-041.09, 041.10-041.19) ♀
614.2 Salpingitis and oophoritis not specified as acute, subacute, or chronic — (Use additional code to identify organism: 041.00-041.09, 041.10-041.19) ♀
614.5 Acute or unspecified pelvic peritonitis, female — (Use additional code to identify organism: 041.00-041.09, 041.10-041.19) ♀
614.6 Pelvic peritoneal adhesions, female (postoperative) (postinfection) — (Use additional code to identify organism: 041.00-041.09, 041.10-041.19) (Use additional code to identify any associated infertility: 628.2) ♀
614.9 Unspecified inflammatory disease of female pelvic organs and tissues — (Use additional code to identify organism: 041.00-041.09, 041.10-041.19) ♀
617.0 Endometriosis of uterus ♀
617.1 Endometriosis of ovary ♀
617.2 Endometriosis of fallopian tube ♀
617.3 Endometriosis of pelvic peritoneum ♀
617.8 Endometriosis of other specified sites ♀
625.3 Dysmenorrhea ♀
625.8 Other specified symptom associated with female genital organs ♀
628.2 Female infertility of tubal origin — (Use additional code for any associated peritubal adhesions: 614.6) ♀
628.3 Female infertility of uterine origin — (Use additional code for any associated tuberculous endometriosis: 016.7) ♀
628.8 Female infertility of other specified origin ♀
628.9 Female infertility of unspecified origin ♀
789.00 Abdominal pain, unspecified site
789.01 Abdominal pain, right upper quadrant
789.02 Abdominal pain, left upper quadrant
789.03 Abdominal pain, right lower quadrant
789.04 Abdominal pain, left lower quadrant
789.05 Abdominal pain, periumbilic
789.30 Abdominal or pelvic swelling, mass or lump, unspecified site
789.31 Abdominal or pelvic swelling, mass, or lump, right upper quadrant

789.32 Abdominal or pelvic swelling, mass, or lump, left upper quadrant
789.33 Abdominal or pelvic swelling, mass, or lump, right lower quadrant
789.34 Abdominal or pelvic swelling, mass, or lump, left lower quadrant

ICD-9-CM Procedural

65.81 Laparoscopic lysis of adhesions of ovary and fallopian tube ♀

58661

58661 Laparoscopy, surgical; with removal of adnexal structures (partial or total oophorectomy and/or salpingectomy)

ICD-9-CM Diagnostic

183.0 Malignant neoplasm of ovary — (Use additional code to identify any functional activity) ♀
183.2 Malignant neoplasm of fallopian tube ♀
183.8 Malignant neoplasm of other specified sites of uterine adnexa ♀
198.6 Secondary malignant neoplasm of ovary ♀
220 Benign neoplasm of ovary — (Use additional code to identify any functional activity: 256.0-256.1) ♀
221.0 Benign neoplasm of fallopian tube and uterine ligaments ♀
221.8 Benign neoplasm of other specified sites of female genital organs ♀
233.30 Carcinoma in situ, unspecified female genital organ ▽ ♀
233.31 Carcinoma in situ, vagina ♀
233.32 Carcinoma in situ, vulva ♀
233.39 Carcinoma in situ, other female genital organ ♀
236.2 Neoplasm of uncertain behavior of ovary — (Use additional code to identify any functional activity) ♀
236.3 Neoplasm of uncertain behavior of other and unspecified female genital organs ▽ ♀
239.5 Neoplasm of unspecified nature of other genitourinary organs
256.0 Hyperestrogenism ♀
614.1 Chronic salpingitis and oophoritis — (Use additional code to identify organism: 041.00-041.09, 041.10-041.19) ♀
614.2 Salpingitis and oophoritis not specified as acute, subacute, or chronic — (Use additional code to identify organism: 041.00-041.09, 041.10-041.19) ♀
614.6 Pelvic peritoneal adhesions, female (postoperative) (postinfection) — (Use additional code to identify organism: 041.00-041.09, 041.10-041.19) (Use additional code to identify any associated infertility: 628.2) ♀
617.1 Endometriosis of ovary ♀
617.2 Endometriosis of fallopian tube ♀
617.3 Endometriosis of pelvic peritoneum ♀
617.9 Endometriosis, site unspecified ▽ ♀
620.0 Follicular cyst of ovary ♀
620.1 Corpus luteum cyst or hematoma ♀
620.2 Other and unspecified ovarian cyst ▽ ♀
620.5 Torsion of ovary, ovarian pedicle, or fallopian tube ♀
628.2 Female infertility of tubal origin — (Use additional code for any associated peritubal adhesions: 614.6) ♀
789.00 Abdominal pain, unspecified site ▽
789.01 Abdominal pain, right upper quadrant
789.02 Abdominal pain, left upper quadrant
789.03 Abdominal pain, right lower quadrant
789.04 Abdominal pain, left lower quadrant
789.30 Abdominal or pelvic swelling, mass or lump, unspecified site ▽
789.31 Abdominal or pelvic swelling, mass, or lump, right upper quadrant
789.32 Abdominal or pelvic swelling, mass, or lump, left upper quadrant
789.33 Abdominal or pelvic swelling, mass, or lump, right lower quadrant
789.34 Abdominal or pelvic swelling, mass, or lump, left lower quadrant
V84.02 Genetic susceptibility to malignant neoplasm of ovary — (Use additional code, if applicable, for any associated family history of the disease: V16-V19. Code first, if applicable, any current malignant neoplasms: 140.0-195.8, 200.0-208.9, 230.0-234.9. Use additional code, if applicable, for any personal history of malignant neoplasm: V10.0-V10.9) ♀
V84.04 Genetic susceptibility to malignant neoplasm of endometrium — (Use additional code, if applicable, for any associated family history of the disease: V16-V19. Code first, if applicable, any current malignant neoplasms: 140.0-195.8, 200.0-208.9, 230.0-234.9. Use additional code, if applicable, for any personal history of malignant neoplasm: V10.0-V10.9) ♀
V84.09 Genetic susceptibility to other malignant neoplasm — (Use additional code, if applicable, for any associated family history of the disease: V16-V19. Code first, if applicable, any current malignant neoplasms: 140.0-195.8, 200.0-208.9, 230.0-234.9. Use additional code, if applicable, for any personal history of malignant neoplasm: V10.0-V10.9)

ICD-9-CM Procedural

65.24 Laparoscopic wedge resection of ovary ♀
65.31 Laparoscopic unilateral oophorectomy ♀
65.41 Laparoscopic unilateral salpingo-oophorectomy ♀
65.53 Laparoscopic removal of both ovaries at same operative episode ♀
65.54 Laparoscopic removal of remaining ovary ♀
65.63 Laparoscopic removal of both ovaries and tubes at same operative episode ♀
65.64 Laparoscopic removal of remaining ovary and tube ♀
66.4 Total unilateral salpingectomy ♀
66.51 Removal of both fallopian tubes at same operative episode ♀
66.52 Removal of remaining fallopian tube ♀
66.62 Salpingectomy with removal of tubal pregnancy ♀
66.63 Bilateral partial salpingectomy, not otherwise specified ♀
66.69 Other partial salpingectomy ♀

58662

58662 Laparoscopy, surgical; with fulguration or excision of lesions of the ovary, pelvic viscera, or peritoneal surface by any method

ICD-9-CM Diagnostic

158.8 Malignant neoplasm of specified parts of peritoneum
158.9 Malignant neoplasm of peritoneum, unspecified ▽
159.8 Malignant neoplasm of other sites of digestive system and intra-abdominal organs
197.6 Secondary malignant neoplasm of retroperitoneum and peritoneum
209.74 Secondary neuroendocrine tumor of peritoneum
211.8 Benign neoplasm of retroperitoneum and peritoneum
219.1 Benign neoplasm of corpus uteri ♀
220 Benign neoplasm of ovary — (Use additional code to identify any functional activity: 256.0-256.1) ♀
221.0 Benign neoplasm of fallopian tube and uterine ligaments ♀
235.4 Neoplasm of uncertain behavior of retroperitoneum and peritoneum
256.4 Polycystic ovaries ♀
568.89 Other specified disorder of peritoneum
614.6 Pelvic peritoneal adhesions, female (postoperative) (postinfection) — (Use additional code to identify organism: 041.00-041.09, 041.10-041.19) (Use additional code to identify any associated infertility: 628.2) ♀
617.0 Endometriosis of uterus ♀
617.1 Endometriosis of ovary ♀
617.2 Endometriosis of fallopian tube ♀
617.3 Endometriosis of pelvic peritoneum ♀
617.8 Endometriosis of other specified sites ♀
617.9 Endometriosis, site unspecified ▽ ♀
620.0 Follicular cyst of ovary ♀
620.1 Corpus luteum cyst or hematoma ♀
620.2 Other and unspecified ovarian cyst ▽ ♀
620.8 Other noninflammatory disorder of ovary, fallopian tube, and broad ligament ♀
621.0 Polyp of corpus uteri ♀

621.30 Endometrial hyperplasia, unspecified ♀
621.31 Simple endometrial hyperplasia without atypia ♀
621.32 Complex endometrial hyperplasia without atypia ♀
621.33 Endometrial hyperplasia with atypia ♀
621.34 Benign endometrial hyperplasia ♀
621.35 Endometrial intraepithelial neoplasia [EIN] ♀
625.3 Dysmenorrhea ♀
625.8 Other specified symptom associated with female genital organs ♀
628.0 Female infertility associated with anovulation — (Use additional code for any associated Stein-Leventhal syndrome: 256.4) ♀
628.2 Female infertility of tubal origin — (Use additional code for any associated peritubal adhesions: 614.6) ♀
628.3 Female infertility of uterine origin — (Use additional code for any associated tuberculous endometriosis: 016.7) ♀
628.8 Female infertility of other specified origin ♀
752.11 Embryonic cyst of fallopian tubes and broad ligaments ♀
789.00 Abdominal pain, unspecified site
789.01 Abdominal pain, right upper quadrant
789.02 Abdominal pain, left upper quadrant
789.03 Abdominal pain, right lower quadrant
789.04 Abdominal pain, left lower quadrant
789.30 Abdominal or pelvic swelling, mass or lump, unspecified site
789.31 Abdominal or pelvic swelling, mass, or lump, right upper quadrant
789.32 Abdominal or pelvic swelling, mass, or lump, left upper quadrant
789.33 Abdominal or pelvic swelling, mass, or lump, right lower quadrant
789.34 Abdominal or pelvic swelling, mass, or lump, left lower quadrant
V84.02 Genetic susceptibility to malignant neoplasm of ovary — (Use additional code, if applicable, for any associated family history of the disease: V16-V19. Code first, if applicable, any current malignant neoplasms: 140.0-195.8, 200.0-208.9, 230.0-234.9. Use additional code, if applicable, for any personal history of malignant neoplasm: V10.0-V10.9) ♀
V84.04 Genetic susceptibility to malignant neoplasm of endometrium — (Use additional code, if applicable, for any associated family history of the disease: V16-V19. Code first, if applicable, any current malignant neoplasms: 140.0-195.8, 200.0-208.9, 230.0-234.9. Use additional code, if applicable, for any personal history of malignant neoplasm: V10.0-V10.9) ♀
V84.09 Genetic susceptibility to other malignant neoplasm — (Use additional code, if applicable, for any associated family history of the disease: V16-V19. Code first, if applicable, any current malignant neoplasms: 140.0-195.8, 200.0-208.9, 230.0-234.9. Use additional code, if applicable, for any personal history of malignant neoplasm: V10.0-V10.9)

ICD-9-CM Procedural

54.4 Excision or destruction of peritoneal tissue
65.25 Other laparoscopic local excision or destruction of ovary ♀
69.19 Other excision or destruction of uterus and supporting structures ♀

58670-58671

58670 Laparoscopy, surgical; with fulguration of oviducts (with or without transection)
58671 with occlusion of oviducts by device (eg, band, clip, or Falope ring)

ICD-9-CM Diagnostic

V25.2 Sterilization
V61.5 Multiparity

ICD-9-CM Procedural

66.21 Bilateral endoscopic ligation and crushing of fallopian tubes ♀
66.22 Bilateral endoscopic ligation and division of fallopian tubes ♀
66.29 Other bilateral endoscopic destruction or occlusion of fallopian tubes ♀

58672

58672 Laparoscopy, surgical; with fimbrioplasty

ICD-9-CM Diagnostic

614.1 Chronic salpingitis and oophoritis — (Use additional code to identify organism: 041.00-041.09, 041.10-041.19) ♀
614.2 Salpingitis and oophoritis not specified as acute, subacute, or chronic — (Use additional code to identify organism: 041.00-041.09, 041.10-041.19) ♀
614.4 Chronic or unspecified parametritis and pelvic cellulitis — (Use additional code to identify organism: 041.00-041.09, 041.10-041.19) ♀
614.6 Pelvic peritoneal adhesions, female (postoperative) (postinfection) — (Use additional code to identify organism: 041.00-041.09, 041.10-041.19) (Use additional code to identify any associated infertility: 628.2) ♀
614.8 Other specified inflammatory disease of female pelvic organs and tissues — (Use additional code to identify organism: 041.00-041.09, 041.10-041.19) ♀
617.2 Endometriosis of fallopian tube ♀
628.2 Female infertility of tubal origin — (Use additional code for any associated peritubal adhesions: 614.6) ♀
752.19 Other congenital anomaly of fallopian tubes and broad ligaments ♀

ICD-9-CM Procedural

66.79 Other repair of fallopian tube ♀

58673

58673 Laparoscopy, surgical; with salpingostomy (salpingoneostomy)

ICD-9-CM Diagnostic

139.8 Late effects of other and unspecified infectious and parasitic diseases — (Note: This category is to be used to indicate conditions classifiable to categories 001-009, 020-041, 046-136 as the cause of late effects, which are themselves classified elsewhere. The "late effects" include conditions specified as such, as sequelae of diseases classifiable to the above categories if there is evidence that the disease itself is no longer present.)
614.1 Chronic salpingitis and oophoritis — (Use additional code to identify organism: 041.00-041.09, 041.10-041.19) ♀
614.2 Salpingitis and oophoritis not specified as acute, subacute, or chronic — (Use additional code to identify organism: 041.00-041.09, 041.10-041.19) ♀
614.4 Chronic or unspecified parametritis and pelvic cellulitis — (Use additional code to identify organism: 041.00-041.09, 041.10-041.19) ♀
614.6 Pelvic peritoneal adhesions, female (postoperative) (postinfection) — (Use additional code to identify organism: 041.00-041.09, 041.10-041.19) (Use additional code to identify any associated infertility: 628.2) ♀
614.8 Other specified inflammatory disease of female pelvic organs and tissues — (Use additional code to identify organism: 041.00-041.09, 041.10-041.19) ♀
617.2 Endometriosis of fallopian tube ♀
628.2 Female infertility of tubal origin — (Use additional code for any associated peritubal adhesions: 614.6) ♀
908.2 Late effect of internal injury to other internal organs
V51.8 Other aftercare involving the use of plastic surgery

ICD-9-CM Procedural

66.02 Salpingostomy ♀

58700

58700 Salpingectomy, complete or partial, unilateral or bilateral (separate procedure)

ICD-9-CM Diagnostic

183.2 Malignant neoplasm of fallopian tube ♀
198.82 Secondary malignant neoplasm of genital organs
221.0 Benign neoplasm of fallopian tube and uterine ligaments ♀
233.30 Carcinoma in situ, unspecified female genital organ ♀
233.31 Carcinoma in situ, vagina ♀

233.32 Carcinoma in situ, vulva ♀

233.39 Carcinoma in situ, other female genital organ ♀

236.3 Neoplasm of uncertain behavior of other and unspecified female genital organs ▼ ♀

239.5 Neoplasm of unspecified nature of other genitourinary organs

614.1 Chronic salpingitis and oophoritis — (Use additional code to identify organism: 041.00-041.09, 041.10-041.19) ♀

614.2 Salpingitis and oophoritis not specified as acute, subacute, or chronic — (Use additional code to identify organism: 041.00-041.09, 041.10-041.19) ♀

617.2 Endometriosis of fallopian tube ♀

620.4 Prolapse or hernia of ovary and fallopian tube ♀

620.5 Torsion of ovary, ovarian pedicle, or fallopian tube ♀

789.00 Abdominal pain, unspecified site ▼

V50.49 Other prophylactic organ removal

V84.02 Genetic susceptibility to malignant neoplasm of ovary — (Use additional code, if applicable, for any associated family history of the disease: V16-V19. Code first, if applicable, any current malignant neoplasms: 140.0-195.8, 200.0-208.9, 230.0-234.9. Use additional code, if applicable, for any personal history of malignant neoplasm: V10.0-V10.9) ♀

V84.04 Genetic susceptibility to malignant neoplasm of endometrium — (Use additional code, if applicable, for any associated family history of the disease: V16-V19. Code first, if applicable, any current malignant neoplasms: 140.0-195.8, 200.0-208.9, 230.0-234.9. Use additional code, if applicable, for any personal history of malignant neoplasm: V10.0-V10.9) ♀

V84.09 Genetic susceptibility to other malignant neoplasm — (Use additional code, if applicable, for any associated family history of the disease: V16-V19. Code first, if applicable, any current malignant neoplasms: 140.0-195.8, 200.0-208.9, 230.0-234.9. Use additional code, if applicable, for any personal history of malignant neoplasm: V10.0-V10.9)

ICD-9-CM Procedural

66.4 Total unilateral salpingectomy ♀

66.51 Removal of both fallopian tubes at same operative episode ♀

66.52 Removal of remaining fallopian tube ♀

66.63 Bilateral partial salpingectomy, not otherwise specified ♀

66.69 Other partial salpingectomy ♀

58720

58720 Salpingo-oophorectomy, complete or partial, unilateral or bilateral (separate procedure)

ICD-9-CM Diagnostic

183.0 Malignant neoplasm of ovary — (Use additional code to identify any functional activity) ♀

183.2 Malignant neoplasm of fallopian tube ♀

198.6 Secondary malignant neoplasm of ovary ♀

198.89 Secondary malignant neoplasm of other specified sites

199.1 Other malignant neoplasm of unspecified site

220 Benign neoplasm of ovary — (Use additional code to identify any functional activity: 256.0-256.1) ♀

221.0 Benign neoplasm of fallopian tube and uterine ligaments ♀

233.30 Carcinoma in situ, unspecified female genital organ ▼ ♀

233.31 Carcinoma in situ, vagina ♀

233.32 Carcinoma in situ, vulva ♀

233.39 Carcinoma in situ, other female genital organ ♀

236.2 Neoplasm of uncertain behavior of ovary — (Use additional code to identify any functional activity) ♀

236.3 Neoplasm of uncertain behavior of other and unspecified female genital organs ▼ ♀

239.5 Neoplasm of unspecified nature of other genitourinary organs

256.0 Hyperestrogenism ♀

256.4 Polycystic ovaries ♀

614.0 Acute salpingitis and oophoritis — (Use additional code to identify organism: 041.00-041.09, 041.10-041.19) ♀

614.1 Chronic salpingitis and oophoritis — (Use additional code to identify organism: 041.00-041.09, 041.10-041.19) ♀

614.2 Salpingitis and oophoritis not specified as acute, subacute, or chronic — (Use additional code to identify organism: 041.00-041.09, 041.10-041.19) ♀

614.6 Pelvic peritoneal adhesions, female (postoperative) (postinfection) — (Use additional code to identify organism: 041.00-041.09, 041.10-041.19) (Use additional code to identify any associated infertility: 628.2) ♀

617.1 Endometriosis of ovary ♀

617.2 Endometriosis of fallopian tube ♀

620.0 Follicular cyst of ovary ♀

620.1 Corpus luteum cyst or hematoma ♀

620.2 Other and unspecified ovarian cyst ▼ ♀

620.4 Prolapse or hernia of ovary and fallopian tube ♀

620.5 Torsion of ovary, ovarian pedicle, or fallopian tube ♀

620.8 Other noninflammatory disorder of ovary, fallopian tube, and broad ligament ♀

625.3 Dysmenorrhea ♀

625.8 Other specified symptom associated with female genital organs ♀

626.2 Excessive or frequent menstruation ♀

626.8 Other disorder of menstruation and other abnormal bleeding from female genital tract ♀

628.2 Female infertility of tubal origin — (Use additional code for any associated peritubal adhesions: 614.6) ♀

752.0 Congenital anomalies of ovaries ♀

752.10 Unspecified congenital anomaly of fallopian tubes and broad ligaments ▼ ♀

752.11 Embryonic cyst of fallopian tubes and broad ligaments ♀

V84.02 Genetic susceptibility to malignant neoplasm of ovary — (Use additional code, if applicable, for any associated family history of the disease: V16-V19. Code first, if applicable, any current malignant neoplasms: 140.0-195.8, 200.0-208.9, 230.0-234.9. Use additional code, if applicable, for any personal history of malignant neoplasm: V10.0-V10.9) ♀

V84.04 Genetic susceptibility to malignant neoplasm of endometrium — (Use additional code, if applicable, for any associated family history of the disease: V16-V19. Code first, if applicable, any current malignant neoplasms: 140.0-195.8, 200.0-208.9, 230.0-234.9. Use additional code, if applicable, for any personal history of malignant neoplasm: V10.0-V10.9) ♀

V84.09 Genetic susceptibility to other malignant neoplasm — (Use additional code, if applicable, for any associated family history of the disease: V16-V19. Code first, if applicable, any current malignant neoplasms: 140.0-195.8, 200.0-208.9, 230.0-234.9. Use additional code, if applicable, for any personal history of malignant neoplasm: V10.0-V10.9)

ICD-9-CM Procedural

65.49 Other unilateral salpingo-oophorectomy ♀

65.61 Other removal of both ovaries and tubes at same operative episode ♀

65.62 Other removal of remaining ovary and tube ♀

58740

58740 Lysis of adhesions (salpingolysis, ovariolysis)

ICD-9-CM Diagnostic

614.1 Chronic salpingitis and oophoritis — (Use additional code to identify organism: 041.00-041.09, 041.10-041.19) ♀

614.2 Salpingitis and oophoritis not specified as acute, subacute, or chronic — (Use additional code to identify organism: 041.00-041.09, 041.10-041.19) ♀

614.5 Acute or unspecified pelvic peritonitis, female — (Use additional code to identify organism: 041.00-041.09, 041.10-041.19) ♀

614.6 Pelvic peritoneal adhesions, female (postoperative) (postinfection) — (Use additional code to identify organism: 041.00-041.09, 041.10-041.19) (Use additional code to identify any associated infertility: 628.2) ♀

617.0 Endometriosis of uterus ♀
617.1 Endometriosis of ovary ♀
617.2 Endometriosis of fallopian tube ♀
617.3 Endometriosis of pelvic peritoneum ♀
625.3 Dysmenorrhea ♀
625.8 Other specified symptom associated with female genital organs ♀
626.2 Excessive or frequent menstruation ♀
628.2 Female infertility of tubal origin — (Use additional code for any associated peritubal adhesions: 614.6) ♀
628.8 Female infertility of other specified origin ♀
752.19 Other congenital anomaly of fallopian tubes and broad ligaments ♀
789.01 Abdominal pain, right upper quadrant
789.02 Abdominal pain, left upper quadrant
789.03 Abdominal pain, right lower quadrant
789.04 Abdominal pain, left lower quadrant
789.31 Abdominal or pelvic swelling, mass, or lump, right upper quadrant
789.32 Abdominal or pelvic swelling, mass, or lump, left upper quadrant
789.33 Abdominal or pelvic swelling, mass, or lump, right lower quadrant
789.34 Abdominal or pelvic swelling, mass, or lump, left lower quadrant
V64.41 Laparoscopic surgical procedure converted to open procedure

ICD-9-CM Procedural

65.89 Other lysis of adhesions of ovary and fallopian tube ♀

58750

58750 Tubotubal anastomosis

ICD-9-CM Diagnostic

221.0 Benign neoplasm of fallopian tube and uterine ligaments ♀
614.1 Chronic salpingitis and oophoritis — (Use additional code to identify organism: 041.00-041.09, 041.10-041.19) ♀
614.2 Salpingitis and oophoritis not specified as acute, subacute, or chronic — (Use additional code to identify organism: 041.00-041.09, 041.10-041.19) ♀
614.6 Pelvic peritoneal adhesions, female (postoperative) (postinfection) — (Use additional code to identify organism: 041.00-041.09, 041.10-041.19) (Use additional code to identify any associated infertility: 628.2) ♀
614.7 Other chronic pelvic peritonitis, female — (Use additional code to identify organism: 041.00-041.09, 041.10-041.19) ♀
614.8 Other specified inflammatory disease of female pelvic organs and tissues — (Use additional code to identify organism: 041.00-041.09, 041.10-041.19) ♀
628.2 Female infertility of tubal origin — (Use additional code for any associated peritubal adhesions: 614.6) ♀
628.8 Female infertility of other specified origin ♀
628.9 Female infertility of unspecified origin ▽ ♀
752.19 Other congenital anomaly of fallopian tubes and broad ligaments ♀
V26.0 Tuboplasty or vasoplasty after previous sterilization

ICD-9-CM Procedural

66.73 Salpingo-salpingostomy ♀

58752

58752 Tubouterine implantation

ICD-9-CM Diagnostic

221.0 Benign neoplasm of fallopian tube and uterine ligaments ♀
614.1 Chronic salpingitis and oophoritis — (Use additional code to identify organism: 041.00-041.09, 041.10-041.19) ♀
614.2 Salpingitis and oophoritis not specified as acute, subacute, or chronic — (Use additional code to identify organism: 041.00-041.09, 041.10-041.19) ♀
614.6 Pelvic peritoneal adhesions, female (postoperative) (postinfection) — (Use additional code to identify organism: 041.00-041.09, 041.10-041.19) (Use additional code to identify any associated infertility: 628.2) ♀
614.7 Other chronic pelvic peritonitis, female — (Use additional code to identify organism: 041.00-041.09, 041.10-041.19) ♀
614.8 Other specified inflammatory disease of female pelvic organs and tissues — (Use additional code to identify organism: 041.00-041.09, 041.10-041.19) ♀
628.2 Female infertility of tubal origin — (Use additional code for any associated peritubal adhesions: 614.6) ♀
752.19 Other congenital anomaly of fallopian tubes and broad ligaments ♀
V26.0 Tuboplasty or vasoplasty after previous sterilization

ICD-9-CM Procedural

66.74 Salpingo-uterostomy ♀

58760

58760 Fimbrioplasty

ICD-9-CM Diagnostic

614.1 Chronic salpingitis and oophoritis — (Use additional code to identify organism: 041.00-041.09, 041.10-041.19) ♀
614.2 Salpingitis and oophoritis not specified as acute, subacute, or chronic — (Use additional code to identify organism: 041.00-041.09, 041.10-041.19) ♀
614.3 Acute parametritis and pelvic cellulitis — (Use additional code to identify organism: 041.00-041.09, 041.10-041.19) ♀
614.4 Chronic or unspecified parametritis and pelvic cellulitis — (Use additional code to identify organism: 041.00-041.09, 041.10-041.19) ♀
614.5 Acute or unspecified pelvic peritonitis, female — (Use additional code to identify organism: 041.00-041.09, 041.10-041.19) ♀
614.6 Pelvic peritoneal adhesions, female (postoperative) (postinfection) — (Use additional code to identify organism: 041.00-041.09, 041.10-041.19) (Use additional code to identify any associated infertility: 628.2) ♀
614.8 Other specified inflammatory disease of female pelvic organs and tissues — (Use additional code to identify organism: 041.00-041.09, 041.10-041.19) ♀
617.2 Endometriosis of fallopian tube ♀
628.2 Female infertility of tubal origin — (Use additional code for any associated peritubal adhesions: 614.6) ♀
752.19 Other congenital anomaly of fallopian tubes and broad ligaments ♀
909.3 Late effect of complications of surgical and medical care
V64.41 Laparoscopic surgical procedure converted to open procedure

ICD-9-CM Procedural

66.79 Other repair of fallopian tube ♀

58770

58770 Salpingostomy (salpingoneostomy)

ICD-9-CM Diagnostic

221.0 Benign neoplasm of fallopian tube and uterine ligaments ♀
256.9 Unspecified ovarian dysfunction ▽ ♀
614.1 Chronic salpingitis and oophoritis — (Use additional code to identify organism: 041.00-041.09, 041.10-041.19) ♀
614.2 Salpingitis and oophoritis not specified as acute, subacute, or chronic — (Use additional code to identify organism: 041.00-041.09, 041.10-041.19) ♀
614.3 Acute parametritis and pelvic cellulitis — (Use additional code to identify organism: 041.00-041.09, 041.10-041.19) ♀
614.4 Chronic or unspecified parametritis and pelvic cellulitis — (Use additional code to identify organism: 041.00-041.09, 041.10-041.19) ♀
614.5 Acute or unspecified pelvic peritonitis, female — (Use additional code to identify organism: 041.00-041.09, 041.10-041.19) ♀

614.6 Pelvic peritoneal adhesions, female (postoperative) (postinfection) — (Use additional code to identify organism: 041.00-041.09, 041.10-041.19) (Use additional code to identify any associated infertility: 628.2) ♀

614.8 Other specified inflammatory disease of female pelvic organs and tissues — (Use additional code to identify organism: 041.00-041.09, 041.10-041.19) ♀

617.2 Endometriosis of fallopian tube ♀

620.9 Unspecified noninflammatory disorder of ovary, fallopian tube, and broad ligament ♀

625.9 Unspecified symptom associated with female genital organs ♀

628.2 Female infertility of tubal origin — (Use additional code for any associated peritubal adhesions: 614.6) ♀

908.2 Late effect of internal injury to other internal organs

909.3 Late effect of complications of surgical and medical care

V64.41 Laparoscopic surgical procedure converted to open procedure

ICD-9-CM Procedural

66.02 Salpingostomy ♀

66.72 Salpingo-oophorostomy ♀

Ovary

58800-58805

58800 Drainage of ovarian cyst(s), unilateral or bilateral (separate procedure); vaginal approach

58805 abdominal approach

ICD-9-CM Diagnostic

220 Benign neoplasm of ovary — (Use additional code to identify any functional activity: 256.0-256.1) ♀

256.4 Polycystic ovaries ♀

620.0 Follicular cyst of ovary ♀

620.1 Corpus luteum cyst or hematoma ♀

620.2 Other and unspecified ovarian cyst ♀

789.31 Abdominal or pelvic swelling, mass, or lump, right upper quadrant

789.32 Abdominal or pelvic swelling, mass, or lump, left upper quadrant

789.33 Abdominal or pelvic swelling, mass, or lump, right lower quadrant

789.34 Abdominal or pelvic swelling, mass, or lump, left lower quadrant

V84.02 Genetic susceptibility to malignant neoplasm of ovary — (Use additional code, if applicable, for any associated family history of the disease: V16-V19. Code first, if applicable, any current malignant neoplasms: 140.0-195.8, 200.0-208.9, 230.0-234.9. Use additional code, if applicable, for any personal history of malignant neoplasm: V10.0-V10.9) ♀

V84.04 Genetic susceptibility to malignant neoplasm of endometrium — (Use additional code, if applicable, for any associated family history of the disease: V16-V19. Code first, if applicable, any current malignant neoplasms: 140.0-195.8, 200.0-208.9, 230.0-234.9. Use additional code, if applicable, for any personal history of malignant neoplasm: V10.0-V10.9) ♀

V84.09 Genetic susceptibility to other malignant neoplasm — (Use additional code, if applicable, for any associated family history of the disease: V16-V19. Code first, if applicable, any current malignant neoplasms: 140.0-195.8, 200.0-208.9, 230.0-234.9. Use additional code, if applicable, for any personal history of malignant neoplasm: V10.0-V10.9)

ICD-9-CM Procedural

65.09 Other oophorotomy ♀

65.91 Aspiration of ovary ♀

65.93 Manual rupture of ovarian cyst ♀

58820-58822

58820 Drainage of ovarian abscess; vaginal approach, open

58822 abdominal approach

ICD-9-CM Diagnostic

614.0 Acute salpingitis and oophoritis — (Use additional code to identify organism: 041.00-041.09, 041.10-041.19) ♀

614.1 Chronic salpingitis and oophoritis — (Use additional code to identify organism: 041.00-041.09, 041.10-041.19) ♀

614.2 Salpingitis and oophoritis not specified as acute, subacute, or chronic — (Use additional code to identify organism: 041.00-041.09, 041.10-041.19) ♀

614.3 Acute parametritis and pelvic cellulitis — (Use additional code to identify organism: 041.00-041.09, 041.10-041.19) ♀

614.4 Chronic or unspecified parametritis and pelvic cellulitis — (Use additional code to identify organism: 041.00-041.09, 041.10-041.19) ♀

780.60 Fever, unspecified

789.01 Abdominal pain, right upper quadrant

789.02 Abdominal pain, left upper quadrant

789.03 Abdominal pain, right lower quadrant

789.04 Abdominal pain, left lower quadrant

789.31 Abdominal or pelvic swelling, mass, or lump, right upper quadrant

789.32 Abdominal or pelvic swelling, mass, or lump, left upper quadrant

789.33 Abdominal or pelvic swelling, mass, or lump, right lower quadrant

789.34 Abdominal or pelvic swelling, mass, or lump, left lower quadrant

998.51 Infected postoperative seroma — (Use additional code to identify organism)

998.59 Other postoperative infection — (Use additional code to identify infection)

ICD-9-CM Procedural

65.09 Other oophorotomy ♀

65.11 Aspiration biopsy of ovary ♀

65.91 Aspiration of ovary ♀

58825

58825 Transposition, ovary(s)

ICD-9-CM Diagnostic

153.3 Malignant neoplasm of sigmoid colon

153.8 Malignant neoplasm of other specified sites of large intestine

154.0 Malignant neoplasm of rectosigmoid junction

154.1 Malignant neoplasm of rectum

154.8 Malignant neoplasm of other sites of rectum, rectosigmoid junction, and anus

158.0 Malignant neoplasm of retroperitoneum

158.8 Malignant neoplasm of specified parts of peritoneum

188.0 Malignant neoplasm of trigone of urinary bladder

188.1 Malignant neoplasm of dome of urinary bladder

188.2 Malignant neoplasm of lateral wall of urinary bladder

188.3 Malignant neoplasm of anterior wall of urinary bladder

188.4 Malignant neoplasm of posterior wall of urinary bladder

188.5 Malignant neoplasm of bladder neck

189.2 Malignant neoplasm of ureter

189.3 Malignant neoplasm of urethra

752.0 Congenital anomalies of ovaries ♀

ICD-9-CM Procedural

65.99 Other operations on ovary ♀

58900

58900 Biopsy of ovary, unilateral or bilateral (separate procedure)

ICD-9-CM Diagnostic

183.0 Malignant neoplasm of ovary — (Use additional code to identify any functional activity) ♀

183.8 Malignant neoplasm of other specified sites of uterine adnexa ♀
198.82 Secondary malignant neoplasm of genital organs
220 Benign neoplasm of ovary — (Use additional code to identify any functional activity: 256.0-256.1) ♀
236.2 Neoplasm of uncertain behavior of ovary — (Use additional code to identify any functional activity) ♀
239.5 Neoplasm of unspecified nature of other genitourinary organs
256.0 Hyperestrogenism ♀
617.1 Endometriosis of ovary ♀
620.0 Follicular cyst of ovary ♀
620.1 Corpus luteum cyst or hematoma ♀
620.2 Other and unspecified ovarian cyst ♀
620.8 Other noninflammatory disorder of ovary, fallopian tube, and broad ligament ♀
789.01 Abdominal pain, right upper quadrant
789.02 Abdominal pain, left upper quadrant
789.03 Abdominal pain, right lower quadrant
789.04 Abdominal pain, left lower quadrant
789.30 Abdominal or pelvic swelling, mass or lump, unspecified site
789.31 Abdominal or pelvic swelling, mass, or lump, right upper quadrant
789.32 Abdominal or pelvic swelling, mass, or lump, left upper quadrant
789.33 Abdominal or pelvic swelling, mass, or lump, right lower quadrant
789.34 Abdominal or pelvic swelling, mass, or lump, left lower quadrant
V84.02 Genetic susceptibility to malignant neoplasm of ovary — (Use additional code, if applicable, for any associated family history of the disease: V16-V19. Code first, if applicable, any current malignant neoplasms: 140.0-195.8, 200.0-208.9, 230.0-234.9. Use additional code, if applicable, for any personal history of malignant neoplasm: V10.0-V10.9) ♀
V84.04 Genetic susceptibility to malignant neoplasm of endometrium — (Use additional code, if applicable, for any associated family history of the disease: V16-V19. Code first, if applicable, any current malignant neoplasms: 140.0-195.8, 200.0-208.9, 230.0-234.9. Use additional code, if applicable, for any personal history of malignant neoplasm: V10.0-V10.9) ♀
V84.09 Genetic susceptibility to other malignant neoplasm — (Use additional code, if applicable, for any associated family history of the disease: V16-V19. Code first, if applicable, any current malignant neoplasms: 140.0-195.8, 200.0-208.9, 230.0-234.9. Use additional code, if applicable, for any personal history of malignant neoplasm: V10.0-V10.9)

ICD-9-CM Procedural

65.11 Aspiration biopsy of ovary ♀
65.12 Other biopsy of ovary ♀

58920

58920 Wedge resection or bisection of ovary, unilateral or bilateral

ICD-9-CM Diagnostic

220 Benign neoplasm of ovary — (Use additional code to identify any functional activity: 256.0-256.1) ♀
256.0 Hyperestrogenism ♀
256.1 Other ovarian hyperfunction ♀
256.4 Polycystic ovaries ♀
256.8 Other ovarian dysfunction ♀
620.0 Follicular cyst of ovary ♀
620.1 Corpus luteum cyst or hematoma ♀
620.2 Other and unspecified ovarian cyst ♀
789.31 Abdominal or pelvic swelling, mass, or lump, right upper quadrant
789.32 Abdominal or pelvic swelling, mass, or lump, left upper quadrant
789.33 Abdominal or pelvic swelling, mass, or lump, right lower quadrant
789.34 Abdominal or pelvic swelling, mass, or lump, left lower quadrant

ICD-9-CM Procedural

65.22 Wedge resection of ovary ♀
65.29 Other local excision or destruction of ovary ♀

58925

58925 Ovarian cystectomy, unilateral or bilateral

ICD-9-CM Diagnostic

220 Benign neoplasm of ovary — (Use additional code to identify any functional activity: 256.0-256.1) ♀
236.2 Neoplasm of uncertain behavior of ovary — (Use additional code to identify any functional activity) ♀
256.0 Hyperestrogenism ♀
256.4 Polycystic ovaries ♀
620.0 Follicular cyst of ovary ♀
620.1 Corpus luteum cyst or hematoma ♀
620.2 Other and unspecified ovarian cyst ♀
625.8 Other specified symptom associated with female genital organs ♀
625.9 Unspecified symptom associated with female genital organs ♀
752.11 Embryonic cyst of fallopian tubes and broad ligaments ♀
789.01 Abdominal pain, right upper quadrant
789.02 Abdominal pain, left upper quadrant
789.03 Abdominal pain, right lower quadrant
789.04 Abdominal pain, left lower quadrant
789.31 Abdominal or pelvic swelling, mass, or lump, right upper quadrant
789.32 Abdominal or pelvic swelling, mass, or lump, left upper quadrant
789.33 Abdominal or pelvic swelling, mass, or lump, right lower quadrant
789.34 Abdominal or pelvic swelling, mass, or lump, left lower quadrant

ICD-9-CM Procedural

65.21 Marsupialization of ovarian cyst ♀
65.29 Other local excision or destruction of ovary ♀

58940

58940 Oophorectomy, partial or total, unilateral or bilateral;

ICD-9-CM Diagnostic

183.0 Malignant neoplasm of ovary — (Use additional code to identify any functional activity) ♀
198.6 Secondary malignant neoplasm of ovary ♀
220 Benign neoplasm of ovary — (Use additional code to identify any functional activity: 256.0-256.1) ♀
233.30 Carcinoma in situ, unspecified female genital organ ♀
233.31 Carcinoma in situ, vagina ♀
233.32 Carcinoma in situ, vulva ♀
233.39 Carcinoma in situ, other female genital organ ♀
236.2 Neoplasm of uncertain behavior of ovary — (Use additional code to identify any functional activity) ♀
239.5 Neoplasm of unspecified nature of other genitourinary organs
256.0 Hyperestrogenism ♀
617.1 Endometriosis of ovary ♀
620.0 Follicular cyst of ovary ♀
620.1 Corpus luteum cyst or hematoma ♀
620.2 Other and unspecified ovarian cyst ♀
620.5 Torsion of ovary, ovarian pedicle, or fallopian tube ♀
620.8 Other noninflammatory disorder of ovary, fallopian tube, and broad ligament ♀
625.8 Other specified symptom associated with female genital organs ♀
625.9 Unspecified symptom associated with female genital organs ♀
752.11 Embryonic cyst of fallopian tubes and broad ligaments ♀

789.01 Abdominal pain, right upper quadrant
789.02 Abdominal pain, left upper quadrant
789.03 Abdominal pain, right lower quadrant
789.04 Abdominal pain, left lower quadrant
789.31 Abdominal or pelvic swelling, mass, or lump, right upper quadrant
789.32 Abdominal or pelvic swelling, mass, or lump, left upper quadrant
789.33 Abdominal or pelvic swelling, mass, or lump, right lower quadrant
789.34 Abdominal or pelvic swelling, mass, or lump, left lower quadrant
V50.42 Prophylactic ovary removal ♀
V64.41 Laparoscopic surgical procedure converted to open procedure
V84.02 Genetic susceptibility to malignant neoplasm of ovary — (Use additional code, if applicable, for any associated family history of the disease: V16-V19. Code first, if applicable, any current malignant neoplasms: 140.0-195.8, 200.0-208.9, 230.0-234.9. Use additional code, if applicable, for any personal history of malignant neoplasm: V10.0-V10.9) ♀
V84.04 Genetic susceptibility to malignant neoplasm of endometrium — (Use additional code, if applicable, for any associated family history of the disease: V16-V19. Code first, if applicable, any current malignant neoplasms: 140.0-195.8, 200.0-208.9, 230.0-234.9. Use additional code, if applicable, for any personal history of malignant neoplasm: V10.0-V10.9) ♀
V84.09 Genetic susceptibility to other malignant neoplasm — (Use additional code, if applicable, for any associated family history of the disease: V16-V19. Code first, if applicable, any current malignant neoplasms: 140.0-195.8, 200.0-208.9, 230.0-234.9. Use additional code, if applicable, for any personal history of malignant neoplasm: V10.0-V10.9)

ICD-9-CM Procedural

65.21 Marsupialization of ovarian cyst ♀
65.29 Other local excision or destruction of ovary ♀
65.39 Other unilateral oophorectomy ♀
65.51 Other removal of both ovaries at same operative episode ♀
65.52 Other removal of remaining ovary ♀

58943

58943 Oophorectomy, partial or total, unilateral or bilateral; for ovarian, tubal or primary peritoneal malignancy, with para-aortic and pelvic lymph node biopsies, peritoneal washings, peritoneal biopsies, diaphragmatic assessments, with or without salpingectomy(s), with or without omentectomy

ICD-9-CM Diagnostic

183.0 Malignant neoplasm of ovary — (Use additional code to identify any functional activity) ♀
183.8 Malignant neoplasm of other specified sites of uterine adnexa ♀
196.6 Secondary and unspecified malignant neoplasm of intrapelvic lymph nodes
197.6 Secondary malignant neoplasm of retroperitoneum and peritoneum
198.6 Secondary malignant neoplasm of ovary ♀
209.71 Secondary neuroendocrine tumor of distant lymph nodes
209.74 Secondary neuroendocrine tumor of peritoneum
236.2 Neoplasm of uncertain behavior of ovary — (Use additional code to identify any functional activity) ♀
V84.02 Genetic susceptibility to malignant neoplasm of ovary — (Use additional code, if applicable, for any associated family history of the disease: V16-V19. Code first, if applicable, any current malignant neoplasms: 140.0-195.8, 200.0-208.9, 230.0-234.9. Use additional code, if applicable, for any personal history of malignant neoplasm: V10.0-V10.9) ♀
V84.04 Genetic susceptibility to malignant neoplasm of endometrium — (Use additional code, if applicable, for any associated family history of the disease: V16-V19. Code first, if applicable, any current malignant neoplasms: 140.0-195.8, 200.0-208.9, 230.0-234.9. Use additional code, if applicable, for any personal history of malignant neoplasm: V10.0-V10.9) ♀
V84.09 Genetic susceptibility to other malignant neoplasm — (Use additional code, if applicable, for any associated family history of the disease: V16-V19. Code first, if applicable, any current malignant neoplasms: 140.0-195.8, 200.0-208.9, 230.0-234.9. Use additional code, if applicable, for any personal history of malignant neoplasm: V10.0-V10.9)

ICD-9-CM Procedural

40.11 Biopsy of lymphatic structure
54.23 Biopsy of peritoneum
54.4 Excision or destruction of peritoneal tissue
65.29 Other local excision or destruction of ovary ♀
65.39 Other unilateral oophorectomy ♀
65.49 Other unilateral salpingo-oophorectomy ♀
65.51 Other removal of both ovaries at same operative episode ♀
65.52 Other removal of remaining ovary ♀
65.61 Other removal of both ovaries and tubes at same operative episode ♀
65.62 Other removal of remaining ovary and tube ♀

58950

58950 Resection (initial) of ovarian, tubal or primary peritoneal malignancy with bilateral salpingo-oophorectomy and omentectomy;

ICD-9-CM Diagnostic

158.8 Malignant neoplasm of specified parts of peritoneum
158.9 Malignant neoplasm of peritoneum, unspecified ▽
183.0 Malignant neoplasm of ovary — (Use additional code to identify any functional activity) ♀
183.2 Malignant neoplasm of fallopian tube ♀
183.8 Malignant neoplasm of other specified sites of uterine adnexa ♀
198.6 Secondary malignant neoplasm of ovary ♀
198.82 Secondary malignant neoplasm of genital organs
209.74 Secondary neuroendocrine tumor of peritoneum
235.4 Neoplasm of uncertain behavior of retroperitoneum and peritoneum
236.2 Neoplasm of uncertain behavior of ovary — (Use additional code to identify any functional activity) ♀
236.3 Neoplasm of uncertain behavior of other and unspecified female genital organs ▽ ♀
V84.02 Genetic susceptibility to malignant neoplasm of ovary — (Use additional code, if applicable, for any associated family history of the disease: V16-V19. Code first, if applicable, any current malignant neoplasms: 140.0-195.8, 200.0-208.9, 230.0-234.9. Use additional code, if applicable, for any personal history of malignant neoplasm: V10.0-V10.9) ♀
V84.04 Genetic susceptibility to malignant neoplasm of endometrium — (Use additional code, if applicable, for any associated family history of the disease: V16-V19. Code first, if applicable, any current malignant neoplasms: 140.0-195.8, 200.0-208.9, 230.0-234.9. Use additional code, if applicable, for any personal history of malignant neoplasm: V10.0-V10.9) ♀
V84.09 Genetic susceptibility to other malignant neoplasm — (Use additional code, if applicable, for any associated family history of the disease: V16-V19. Code first, if applicable, any current malignant neoplasms: 140.0-195.8, 200.0-208.9, 230.0-234.9. Use additional code, if applicable, for any personal history of malignant neoplasm: V10.0-V10.9)

ICD-9-CM Procedural

54.4 Excision or destruction of peritoneal tissue
65.61 Other removal of both ovaries and tubes at same operative episode ♀

58951

58951 Resection (initial) of ovarian, tubal or primary peritoneal malignancy with bilateral salpingo-oophorectomy and omentectomy; with total abdominal hysterectomy, pelvic and limited para-aortic lymphadenectomy

ICD-9-CM Diagnostic

158.8 Malignant neoplasm of specified parts of peritoneum
158.9 Malignant neoplasm of peritoneum, unspecified ▽

183.0 Malignant neoplasm of ovary — (Use additional code to identify any functional activity) ♀
183.2 Malignant neoplasm of fallopian tube ♀
183.8 Malignant neoplasm of other specified sites of uterine adnexa ♀
196.2 Secondary and unspecified malignant neoplasm of intra-abdominal lymph nodes
196.6 Secondary and unspecified malignant neoplasm of intrapelvic lymph nodes
198.6 Secondary malignant neoplasm of ovary ♀
198.82 Secondary malignant neoplasm of genital organs
209.71 Secondary neuroendocrine tumor of distant lymph nodes
209.74 Secondary neuroendocrine tumor of peritoneum
235.4 Neoplasm of uncertain behavior of retroperitoneum and peritoneum
236.2 Neoplasm of uncertain behavior of ovary — (Use additional code to identify any functional activity) ♀
236.3 Neoplasm of uncertain behavior of other and unspecified female genital organs ▽ ♀
V84.02 Genetic susceptibility to malignant neoplasm of ovary — (Use additional code, if applicable, for any associated family history of the disease: V16-V19. Code first, if applicable, any current malignant neoplasms: 140.0-195.8, 200.0-208.9, 230.0-234.9. Use additional code, if applicable, for any personal history of malignant neoplasm: V10.0-V10.9) ♀
V84.04 Genetic susceptibility to malignant neoplasm of endometrium — (Use additional code, if applicable, for any associated family history of the disease: V16-V19. Code first, if applicable, any current malignant neoplasms: 140.0-195.8, 200.0-208.9, 230.0-234.9. Use additional code, if applicable, for any personal history of malignant neoplasm: V10.0-V10.9) ♀
V84.09 Genetic susceptibility to other malignant neoplasm — (Use additional code, if applicable, for any associated family history of the disease: V16-V19. Code first, if applicable, any current malignant neoplasms: 140.0-195.8, 200.0-208.9, 230.0-234.9. Use additional code, if applicable, for any personal history of malignant neoplasm: V10.0-V10.9)

ICD-9-CM Procedural

40.3 Regional lymph node excision
54.4 Excision or destruction of peritoneal tissue
65.61 Other removal of both ovaries and tubes at same operative episode ♀
68.49 Other and unspecified total abdominal hysterectomy ♀

58952

58952 Resection (initial) of ovarian, tubal or primary peritoneal malignancy with bilateral salpingo-oophorectomy and omentectomy; with radical dissection for debulking (ie, radical excision or destruction, intra-abdominal or retroperitoneal tumors)

ICD-9-CM Diagnostic

158.8 Malignant neoplasm of specified parts of peritoneum
158.9 Malignant neoplasm of peritoneum, unspecified ▽
183.0 Malignant neoplasm of ovary — (Use additional code to identify any functional activity) ♀
183.2 Malignant neoplasm of fallopian tube ♀
183.8 Malignant neoplasm of other specified sites of uterine adnexa ♀
197.6 Secondary malignant neoplasm of retroperitoneum and peritoneum
198.6 Secondary malignant neoplasm of ovary ♀
198.82 Secondary malignant neoplasm of genital organs
198.89 Secondary malignant neoplasm of other specified sites
199.0 Disseminated malignant neoplasm
199.1 Other malignant neoplasm of unspecified site
209.74 Secondary neuroendocrine tumor of peritoneum
235.4 Neoplasm of uncertain behavior of retroperitoneum and peritoneum
236.2 Neoplasm of uncertain behavior of ovary — (Use additional code to identify any functional activity) ♀
236.3 Neoplasm of uncertain behavior of other and unspecified female genital organs ▽ ♀
V84.02 Genetic susceptibility to malignant neoplasm of ovary — (Use additional code, if applicable, for any associated family history of the disease: V16-V19. Code first, if applicable, any current malignant neoplasms: 140.0-195.8, 200.0-208.9, 230.0-234.9. Use additional code, if applicable, for any personal history of malignant neoplasm: V10.0-V10.9) ♀
V84.04 Genetic susceptibility to malignant neoplasm of endometrium — (Use additional code, if applicable, for any associated family history of the disease: V16-V19. Code first, if applicable, any current malignant neoplasms: 140.0-195.8, 200.0-208.9, 230.0-234.9. Use additional code, if applicable, for any personal history of malignant neoplasm: V10.0-V10.9) ♀
V84.09 Genetic susceptibility to other malignant neoplasm — (Use additional code, if applicable, for any associated family history of the disease: V16-V19. Code first, if applicable, any current malignant neoplasms: 140.0-195.8, 200.0-208.9, 230.0-234.9. Use additional code, if applicable, for any personal history of malignant neoplasm: V10.0-V10.9)

ICD-9-CM Procedural

54.4 Excision or destruction of peritoneal tissue
65.61 Other removal of both ovaries and tubes at same operative episode ♀

58953

58953 Bilateral salpingo-oophorectomy with omentectomy, total abdominal hysterectomy and radical dissection for debulking;

ICD-9-CM Diagnostic

158.8 Malignant neoplasm of specified parts of peritoneum
158.9 Malignant neoplasm of peritoneum, unspecified ▽
183.0 Malignant neoplasm of ovary — (Use additional code to identify any functional activity) ♀
183.2 Malignant neoplasm of fallopian tube ♀
183.8 Malignant neoplasm of other specified sites of uterine adnexa ♀
197.6 Secondary malignant neoplasm of retroperitoneum and peritoneum
198.6 Secondary malignant neoplasm of ovary ♀
198.82 Secondary malignant neoplasm of genital organs
198.89 Secondary malignant neoplasm of other specified sites
209.74 Secondary neuroendocrine tumor of peritoneum
235.4 Neoplasm of uncertain behavior of retroperitoneum and peritoneum
236.2 Neoplasm of uncertain behavior of ovary — (Use additional code to identify any functional activity) ♀
236.3 Neoplasm of uncertain behavior of other and unspecified female genital organs ▽ ♀
V84.02 Genetic susceptibility to malignant neoplasm of ovary — (Use additional code, if applicable, for any associated family history of the disease: V16-V19. Code first, if applicable, any current malignant neoplasms: 140.0-195.8, 200.0-208.9, 230.0-234.9. Use additional code, if applicable, for any personal history of malignant neoplasm: V10.0-V10.9) ♀
V84.04 Genetic susceptibility to malignant neoplasm of endometrium — (Use additional code, if applicable, for any associated family history of the disease: V16-V19. Code first, if applicable, any current malignant neoplasms: 140.0-195.8, 200.0-208.9, 230.0-234.9. Use additional code, if applicable, for any personal history of malignant neoplasm: V10.0-V10.9) ♀
V84.09 Genetic susceptibility to other malignant neoplasm — (Use additional code, if applicable, for any associated family history of the disease: V16-V19. Code first, if applicable, any current malignant neoplasms: 140.0-195.8, 200.0-208.9, 230.0-234.9. Use additional code, if applicable, for any personal history of malignant neoplasm: V10.0-V10.9)

ICD-9-CM Procedural

54.4 Excision or destruction of peritoneal tissue
68.69 Other and unspecified radical abdominal hysterectomy ♀

58954

58954 Bilateral salpingo-oophorectomy with omentectomy, total abdominal hysterectomy and radical dissection for debulking; with pelvic lymphadenectomy and limited para-aortic lymphadenectomy

ICD-9-CM Diagnostic

158.8 Malignant neoplasm of specified parts of peritoneum
158.9 Malignant neoplasm of peritoneum, unspecified ▽
183.0 Malignant neoplasm of ovary — (Use additional code to identify any functional activity) ♀
183.2 Malignant neoplasm of fallopian tube ♀
183.8 Malignant neoplasm of other specified sites of uterine adnexa ♀
196.2 Secondary and unspecified malignant neoplasm of intra-abdominal lymph nodes
196.6 Secondary and unspecified malignant neoplasm of intrapelvic lymph nodes
197.6 Secondary malignant neoplasm of retroperitoneum and peritoneum
198.6 Secondary malignant neoplasm of ovary ♀
198.82 Secondary malignant neoplasm of genital organs
198.89 Secondary malignant neoplasm of other specified sites
209.71 Secondary neuroendocrine tumor of distant lymph nodes
209.74 Secondary neuroendocrine tumor of peritoneum
209.79 Secondary neuroendocrine tumor of other sites
235.4 Neoplasm of uncertain behavior of retroperitoneum and peritoneum
236.2 Neoplasm of uncertain behavior of ovary — (Use additional code to identify any functional activity) ♀
236.3 Neoplasm of uncertain behavior of other and unspecified female genital organs ▽ ♀
V84.02 Genetic susceptibility to malignant neoplasm of ovary — (Use additional code, if applicable, for any associated family history of the disease: V16-V19. Code first, if applicable, any current malignant neoplasms: 140.0-195.8, 200.0-208.9, 230.0-234.9. Use additional code, if applicable, for any personal history of malignant neoplasm: V10.0-V10.9) ♀
V84.04 Genetic susceptibility to malignant neoplasm of endometrium — (Use additional code, if applicable, for any associated family history of the disease: V16-V19. Code first, if applicable, any current malignant neoplasms: 140.0-195.8, 200.0-208.9, 230.0-234.9. Use additional code, if applicable, for any personal history of malignant neoplasm: V10.0-V10.9) ♀
V84.09 Genetic susceptibility to other malignant neoplasm — (Use additional code, if applicable, for any associated family history of the disease: V16-V19. Code first, if applicable, any current malignant neoplasms: 140.0-195.8, 200.0-208.9, 230.0-234.9. Use additional code, if applicable, for any personal history of malignant neoplasm: V10.0-V10.9)

ICD-9-CM Procedural

40.3 Regional lymph node excision
54.4 Excision or destruction of peritoneal tissue
65.61 Other removal of both ovaries and tubes at same operative episode ♀
68.49 Other and unspecified total abdominal hysterectomy ♀
68.69 Other and unspecified radical abdominal hysterectomy ♀

58956

58956 Bilateral salpingo-oophorectomy with total omentectomy, total abdominal hysterectomy for malignancy

ICD-9-CM Diagnostic

158.8 Malignant neoplasm of specified parts of peritoneum
179 Malignant neoplasm of uterus, part unspecified ▽ ♀
180.0 Malignant neoplasm of endocervix ♀
180.1 Malignant neoplasm of exocervix ♀
180.8 Malignant neoplasm of other specified sites of cervix ♀
180.9 Malignant neoplasm of cervix uteri, unspecified site ▽ ♀
182.0 Malignant neoplasm of corpus uteri, except isthmus ♀
182.1 Malignant neoplasm of isthmus ♀
182.8 Malignant neoplasm of other specified sites of body of uterus ♀
183.0 Malignant neoplasm of ovary — (Use additional code to identify any functional activity) ♀
183.2 Malignant neoplasm of fallopian tube ♀
183.3 Malignant neoplasm of broad ligament of uterus ♀
183.4 Malignant neoplasm of parametrium of uterus ♀
183.5 Malignant neoplasm of round ligament of uterus ♀
183.8 Malignant neoplasm of other specified sites of uterine adnexa ♀
183.9 Malignant neoplasm of uterine adnexa, unspecified site ▽ ♀
184.0 Malignant neoplasm of vagina ♀
184.8 Malignant neoplasm of other specified sites of female genital organs ♀
184.9 Malignant neoplasm of female genital organ, site unspecified ▽ ♀
197.5 Secondary malignant neoplasm of large intestine and rectum
197.6 Secondary malignant neoplasm of retroperitoneum and peritoneum
198.1 Secondary malignant neoplasm of other urinary organs
198.6 Secondary malignant neoplasm of ovary ♀
198.82 Secondary malignant neoplasm of genital organs
199.0 Disseminated malignant neoplasm
199.1 Other malignant neoplasm of unspecified site
209.74 Secondary neuroendocrine tumor of peritoneum
V84.02 Genetic susceptibility to malignant neoplasm of ovary — (Use additional code, if applicable, for any associated family history of the disease: V16-V19. Code first, if applicable, any current malignant neoplasms: 140.0-195.8, 200.0-208.9, 230.0-234.9. Use additional code, if applicable, for any personal history of malignant neoplasm: V10.0-V10.9) ♀
V84.04 Genetic susceptibility to malignant neoplasm of endometrium — (Use additional code, if applicable, for any associated family history of the disease: V16-V19. Code first, if applicable, any current malignant neoplasms: 140.0-195.8, 200.0-208.9, 230.0-234.9. Use additional code, if applicable, for any personal history of malignant neoplasm: V10.0-V10.9) ♀
V84.09 Genetic susceptibility to other malignant neoplasm — (Use additional code, if applicable, for any associated family history of the disease: V16-V19. Code first, if applicable, any current malignant neoplasms: 140.0-195.8, 200.0-208.9, 230.0-234.9. Use additional code, if applicable, for any personal history of malignant neoplasm: V10.0-V10.9)

ICD-9-CM Procedural

54.4 Excision or destruction of peritoneal tissue
65.61 Other removal of both ovaries and tubes at same operative episode ♀
68.49 Other and unspecified total abdominal hysterectomy ♀

58957-58958

58957 Resection (tumor debulking) of recurrent ovarian, tubal, primary peritoneal, uterine malignancy (intra-abdominal, retroperitoneal tumors), with omentectomy, if performed;
58958 with pelvic lymphadenectomy and limited para-aortic lymphadenectomy

ICD-9-CM Diagnostic

158.8 Malignant neoplasm of specified parts of peritoneum
158.9 Malignant neoplasm of peritoneum, unspecified ▽
183.0 Malignant neoplasm of ovary — (Use additional code to identify any functional activity) ♀
183.2 Malignant neoplasm of fallopian tube ♀
183.8 Malignant neoplasm of other specified sites of uterine adnexa ♀
196.2 Secondary and unspecified malignant neoplasm of intra-abdominal lymph nodes
196.6 Secondary and unspecified malignant neoplasm of intrapelvic lymph nodes
198.6 Secondary malignant neoplasm of ovary ♀
198.82 Secondary malignant neoplasm of genital organs
209.71 Secondary neuroendocrine tumor of distant lymph nodes
209.74 Secondary neuroendocrine tumor of peritoneum
209.79 Secondary neuroendocrine tumor of other sites

235.4 Neoplasm of uncertain behavior of retroperitoneum and peritoneum

236.2 Neoplasm of uncertain behavior of ovary — (Use additional code to identify any functional activity) ♀

236.3 Neoplasm of uncertain behavior of other and unspecified female genital organs ▽ ♀

V84.02 Genetic susceptibility to malignant neoplasm of ovary — (Use additional code, if applicable, for any associated family history of the disease: V16-V19. Code first, if applicable, any current malignant neoplasms: 140.0-195.8, 200.0-208.9, 230.0-234.9. Use additional code, if applicable, for any personal history of malignant neoplasm: V10.0-V10.9) ♀

V84.04 Genetic susceptibility to malignant neoplasm of endometrium — (Use additional code, if applicable, for any associated family history of the disease: V16-V19. Code first, if applicable, any current malignant neoplasms: 140.0-195.8, 200.0-208.9, 230.0-234.9. Use additional code, if applicable, for any personal history of malignant neoplasm: V10.0-V10.9) ♀

V84.09 Genetic susceptibility to other malignant neoplasm — (Use additional code, if applicable, for any associated family history of the disease: V16-V19. Code first, if applicable, any current malignant neoplasms: 140.0-195.8, 200.0-208.9, 230.0-234.9. Use additional code, if applicable, for any personal history of malignant neoplasm: V10.0-V10.9)

ICD-9-CM Procedural

40.3 Regional lymph node excision

54.4 Excision or destruction of peritoneal tissue

58960

58960 Laparotomy, for staging or restaging of ovarian, tubal, or primary peritoneal malignancy (second look), with or without omentectomy, peritoneal washing, biopsy of abdominal and pelvic peritoneum, diaphragmatic assessment with pelvic and limited para-aortic lymphadenectomy

ICD-9-CM Diagnostic

183.0 Malignant neoplasm of ovary — (Use additional code to identify any functional activity) ♀

183.8 Malignant neoplasm of other specified sites of uterine adnexa ♀

196.6 Secondary and unspecified malignant neoplasm of intrapelvic lymph nodes

197.6 Secondary malignant neoplasm of retroperitoneum and peritoneum

198.6 Secondary malignant neoplasm of ovary ♀

198.89 Secondary malignant neoplasm of other specified sites

209.71 Secondary neuroendocrine tumor of distant lymph nodes

209.74 Secondary neuroendocrine tumor of peritoneum

209.79 Secondary neuroendocrine tumor of other sites

236.2 Neoplasm of uncertain behavior of ovary — (Use additional code to identify any functional activity) ♀

V10.43 Personal history of malignant neoplasm of ovary ♀

V84.02 Genetic susceptibility to malignant neoplasm of ovary — (Use additional code, if applicable, for any associated family history of the disease: V16-V19. Code first, if applicable, any current malignant neoplasms: 140.0-195.8, 200.0-208.9, 230.0-234.9. Use additional code, if applicable, for any personal history of malignant neoplasm: V10.0-V10.9) ♀

V84.04 Genetic susceptibility to malignant neoplasm of endometrium — (Use additional code, if applicable, for any associated family history of the disease: V16-V19. Code first, if applicable, any current malignant neoplasms: 140.0-195.8, 200.0-208.9, 230.0-234.9. Use additional code, if applicable, for any personal history of malignant neoplasm: V10.0-V10.9) ♀

V84.09 Genetic susceptibility to other malignant neoplasm — (Use additional code, if applicable, for any associated family history of the disease: V16-V19. Code first, if applicable, any current malignant neoplasms: 140.0-195.8, 200.0-208.9, 230.0-234.9. Use additional code, if applicable, for any personal history of malignant neoplasm: V10.0-V10.9)

ICD-9-CM Procedural

40.3 Regional lymph node excision

54.11 Exploratory laparotomy

54.12 Reopening of recent laparotomy site

54.23 Biopsy of peritoneum

In Vitro Fertilization

58970

58970 Follicle puncture for oocyte retrieval, any method

ICD-9-CM Diagnostic

256.4 Polycystic ovaries ♀

614.5 Acute or unspecified pelvic peritonitis, female — (Use additional code to identify organism: 041.00-041.09, 041.10-041.19) ♀

614.6 Pelvic peritoneal adhesions, female (postoperative) (postinfection) — (Use additional code to identify organism: 041.00-041.09, 041.10-041.19) (Use additional code to identify any associated infertility: 628.2) ♀

617.0 Endometriosis of uterus ♀

617.3 Endometriosis of pelvic peritoneum ♀

628.0 Female infertility associated with anovulation — (Use additional code for any associated Stein-Leventhal syndrome: 256.4) ♀

628.1 Female infertility of pituitary-hypothalamic origin — (Code first underlying cause: 253.0-253.4, 253.8) ☒ ♀

628.2 Female infertility of tubal origin — (Use additional code for any associated peritubal adhesions: 614.6) ♀

628.3 Female infertility of uterine origin — (Use additional code for any associated tuberculous endometriosis: 016.7) ♀

628.4 Female infertility of cervical or vaginal origin ♀

628.8 Female infertility of other specified origin ♀

628.9 Female infertility of unspecified origin ▽ ♀

V26.81 Encounter for assisted reproductive fertility procedure cycle ♀

V26.82 Encounter for fertility preservation procedure

V26.89 Other specified procreative management

V59.70 Egg (oocyte) (ovum) donor, unspecified ▽ ♀

V59.71 Egg (oocyte) (ovum) donor, under age 35, anonymous recipient ♀

V59.72 Egg (oocyte) (ovum) donor, under age 35, designated recipient ♀

V59.73 Egg (oocyte) (ovum) donor, age 35 and over, anonymous recipient ♀

V59.74 Egg (oocyte) (ovum) donor, age 35 and over, designated recipient ♀

ICD-9-CM Procedural

65.99 Other operations on ovary ♀

HCPCS Level II Supplies & Services

A4305 Disposable drug delivery system, flow rate of 50 ml or greater per hour

58974

58974 Embryo transfer, intrauterine

ICD-9-CM Diagnostic

256.39 Other ovarian failure — (Use additional code for states associated with natural menopause: 627.2) ♀

256.4 Polycystic ovaries ♀

256.8 Other ovarian dysfunction ♀

614.6 Pelvic peritoneal adhesions, female (postoperative) (postinfection) — (Use additional code to identify organism: 041.00-041.09, 041.10-041.19) (Use additional code to identify any associated infertility: 628.2) ♀

628.0 Female infertility associated with anovulation — (Use additional code for any associated Stein-Leventhal syndrome: 256.4) ♀

628.1 Female infertility of pituitary-hypothalamic origin — (Code first underlying cause: 253.0-253.4, 253.8) ☒ ♀

628.2 Female infertility of tubal origin — (Use additional code for any associated peritubal adhesions: 614.6) ♀

628.3 Female infertility of uterine origin — (Use additional code for any associated tuberculous endometriosis: 016.7) ♀

628.4 Female infertility of cervical or vaginal origin ♀

628.8 Female infertility of other specified origin ♀

628.9 Female infertility of unspecified origin ♀

V26.81 Encounter for assisted reproductive fertility procedure cycle ♀

V26.89 Other specified procreative management

ICD-9-CM Procedural

71.9 Other operations on female genital organs ♀

HCPCS Level II Supplies & Services

A4305 Disposable drug delivery system, flow rate of 50 ml or greater per hour

58976

58976 Gamete, zygote, or embryo intrafallopian transfer, any method

ICD-9-CM Diagnostic

256.39 Other ovarian failure — (Use additional code for states associated with natural menopause: 627.2) ♀

256.4 Polycystic ovaries ♀

617.1 Endometriosis of ovary ♀

628.0 Female infertility associated with anovulation — (Use additional code for any associated Stein-Leventhal syndrome: 256.4) ♀

628.1 Female infertility of pituitary-hypothalamic origin — (Code first underlying cause: 253.0-253.4, 253.8) ☒ ♀

628.2 Female infertility of tubal origin — (Use additional code for any associated peritubal adhesions: 614.6) ♀

628.8 Female infertility of other specified origin ♀

628.9 Female infertility of unspecified origin ♀

V26.81 Encounter for assisted reproductive fertility procedure cycle ♀

V26.89 Other specified procreative management

ICD-9-CM Procedural

71.9 Other operations on female genital organs ♀

HCPCS Level II Supplies & Services

A4305 Disposable drug delivery system, flow rate of 50 ml or greater per hour

Maternity Care and Delivery

59000

59000 Amniocentesis; diagnostic

ICD-9-CM Diagnostic

642.03 Benign essential hypertension antepartum ♀
644.03 Threatened premature labor, antepartum ♀
645.13 Post term pregnancy, antepartum condition or complication ♀
645.23 Prolonged pregnancy, antepartum condition or complication ♀
646.03 Papyraceous fetus, antepartum — (Use additional code to further specify complication) ♀
646.13 Edema or excessive weight gain, antepartum — (Use additional code to further specify complication) ♀
646.83 Other specified complication, antepartum — (Use additional code to further specify complication) ♀
648.03 Maternal diabetes mellitus, antepartum — (Use additional code(s) to identify the condition) ♀
648.93 Other current maternal conditions classifiable elsewhere, antepartum — (Use additional code(s) to identify the condition) ♀
649.03 Tobacco use disorder complicating pregnancy, childbirth, or the puerperium, antepartum condition or complication ♀
649.13 Obesity complicating pregnancy, childbirth, or the puerperium, antepartum condition or complication — (Use additional code to identify the obesity: 278.00-278.01) ♀
649.23 Bariatric surgery status complicating pregnancy, childbirth, or the puerperium, antepartum condition or complication ♀
649.33 Coagulation defects complicating pregnancy, childbirth, or the puerperium, antepartum condition or complication — (Use additional code to identify the specific coagulation defect: 286.0-286.9, 287.0-287.9, 289.0-289.9) ♀
649.43 Epilepsy complicating pregnancy, childbirth, or the puerperium, antepartum condition or complication — (Use additional code to identify the specific type of epilepsy: 345.00-345.91) ♀
649.53 Spotting complicating pregnancy, antepartum condition or complication ♀
649.63 Uterine size date discrepancy, antepartum condition or complication ♀
651.03 Twin pregnancy, antepartum ♀
651.13 Triplet pregnancy, antepartum ♀
651.23 Quadruplet pregnancy, antepartum ♀
651.33 Twin pregnancy with fetal loss and retention of one fetus, antepartum ♀
651.43 Triplet pregnancy with fetal loss and retention of one or more, antepartum ♀
651.53 Quadruplet pregnancy with fetal loss and retention of one or more, antepartum ♀
651.63 Other multiple pregnancy with fetal loss and retention of one or more fetus(es), antepartum ♀
651.73 Multiple gestation following (elective) fetal reduction, antepartum condition or complication ♀
651.83 Other specified multiple gestation, antepartum ♀
655.03 Central nervous system malformation in fetus, antepartum ♀
655.13 Chromosomal abnormality in fetus, affecting management of mother, antepartum ♀
655.23 Hereditary disease in family possibly affecting fetus, affecting management of mother, antepartum condition or complication ♀
655.33 Suspected damage to fetus from viral disease in mother, affecting management of mother, antepartum condition or complication ♀
655.43 Suspected damage to fetus from other disease in mother, affecting management of mother, antepartum condition or complication ♀
655.53 Suspected damage to fetus from drugs, affecting management of mother, antepartum ♀
655.63 Suspected damage to fetus from radiation, affecting management of mother, antepartum condition or complication ♀
655.73 Decreased fetal movements, affecting management of mother, antepartum condition or complication ♀
655.83 Other known or suspected fetal abnormality, not elsewhere classified, affecting management of mother, antepartum condition or complication ♀
655.93 Unspecified fetal abnormality affecting management of mother, antepartum condition or complication ▽ ♀
656.03 Fetal-maternal hemorrhage, antepartum condition or complication ♀
656.13 Rhesus isoimmunization affecting management of mother, antepartum condition ♀
656.23 Isoimmunization from other and unspecified blood-group incompatibility, affecting management of mother, antepartum ♀
656.53 Poor fetal growth, affecting management of mother, antepartum condition or complication ♀
656.83 Other specified fetal and placental problems affecting management of mother, antepartum ♀
657.03 Polyhydramnios, antepartum complication ♀
658.03 Oligohydramnios, antepartum ♀
658.43 Infection of amniotic cavity, antepartum ♀
658.83 Other problem associated with amniotic cavity and membranes, antepartum ♀
659.53 Elderly primigravida, antepartum ♀
659.63 Elderly multigravida, with antepartum condition or complication ♀
678.03 Fetal hematologic conditions, antepartum condition or complication ♀
678.13 Fetal conjoined twins, antepartum condition or complication ♀
679.03 Maternal complications from in utero procedure, antepartum condition or complication ♀
741.90 Spina bifida without mention of hydrocephalus, unspecified region ▽
758.0 Down's syndrome — (Use additional codes for conditions associated with the chromosomal anomalies)
758.1 Patau's syndrome — (Use additional codes for conditions associated with the chromosomal anomalies)
758.2 Edwards' syndrome — (Use additional codes for conditions associated with the chromosomal anomalies)
758.31 Cri-du-chat syndrome — (Use additional codes for conditions associated with the chromosomal anomalies)
758.32 Velo-cardio-facial syndrome — (Use additional codes for conditions associated with the chromosomal anomalies)
758.33 Autosomal deletion syndromes, other microdeletions — (Use additional codes for conditions associated with the chromosomal anomalies)
758.39 Autosomal deletion syndromes, other autosomal deletions — (Use additional codes for conditions associated with the chromosomal anomalies)
758.4 Balanced autosomal translocation in normal individual — (Use additional codes for conditions associated with the chromosomal anomalies)
758.5 Other conditions due to autosomal anomalies — (Use additional codes for conditions associated with the chromosomal anomalies)
758.6 Gonadal dysgenesis — (Use additional codes for conditions associated with the chromosomal anomalies)
758.7 Klinefelter's syndrome — (Use additional codes for conditions associated with the chromosomal anomalies) ♂
758.9 Conditions due to anomaly of unspecified chromosome — (Use additional codes for conditions associated with the chromosomal anomalies) ▽
762.7 Fetus or newborn affected by chorioamnionitis — (Use additional code(s) to further specify condition)
762.8 Fetus or newborn affected by other specified abnormalities of chorion and amnion — (Use additional code(s) to further specify condition)
792.3 Nonspecific abnormal finding in amniotic fluid ♀
795.2 Nonspecific abnormal findings on chromosomal analysis

V13.29 Personal history of other genital system and obstetric disorders ♀
V15.21 Personal history of undergoing in utero procedure during pregnancy ♀
V15.29 Personal history of surgery to other organs
V18.4 Family history of intellectual disabilities
V19.5 Family history of congenital anomalies
V19.7 Family history of consanguinity
V23.41 Supervision of pregnancy with history of pre-term labor ♀
V23.49 Supervision of pregnancy with other poor obstetric history ♀
V23.81 Supervision of high-risk pregnancy of elderly primigravida ♀
V23.82 Supervision of high-risk pregnancy of elderly multigravida ♀
V23.85 Supervision of high risk pregnancy, pregnancy resulting from assisted reproductive technology ♀
V23.86 Supervision of high risk pregnancy, pregnancy with history of in utero procedure during previous pregnancy ♀
V23.89 Supervision of other high-risk pregnancy ♀
V28.0 Screening for chromosomal anomalies by amniocentesis ♀
V28.1 Screening for raised alpha-fetoprotein levels in amniotic fluid ♀
V28.2 Other antenatal screening based on amniocentesis ♀
V28.5 Antenatal screening for isoimmunization ♀
V28.81 Encounter for fetal anatomic survey ♀
V28.82 Encounter for screening for risk of pre-term labor ♀
V28.89 Other specified antenatal screening ♀
V89.01 Suspected problem with amniotic cavity and membrane not found ♀
V89.02 Suspected placental problem not found ♀
V89.03 Suspected fetal anomaly not found ♀
V89.04 Suspected problem with fetal growth not found ♀
V89.09 Other suspected maternal and fetal condition not found ♀

ICD-9-CM Procedural

75.1 Diagnostic amniocentesis ♀

HCPCS Level II Supplies & Services

A4305 Disposable drug delivery system, flow rate of 50 ml or greater per hour

59001

59001 Amniocentesis; therapeutic amniotic fluid reduction (includes ultrasound guidance)

ICD-9-CM Diagnostic

657.00 Polyhydramnios, unspecified as to episode of care ▽ ♀
657.01 Polyhydramnios, with delivery ♀
657.03 Polyhydramnios, antepartum complication ♀

ICD-9-CM Procedural

75.99 Other obstetric operations ♀

59012

59012 Cordocentesis (intrauterine), any method

ICD-9-CM Diagnostic

646.13 Edema or excessive weight gain, antepartum — (Use additional code to further specify complication) ♀
646.83 Other specified complication, antepartum — (Use additional code to further specify complication) ♀
655.13 Chromosomal abnormality in fetus, affecting management of mother, antepartum ♀
655.23 Hereditary disease in family possibly affecting fetus, affecting management of mother, antepartum condition or complication ♀
655.33 Suspected damage to fetus from viral disease in mother, affecting management of mother, antepartum condition or complication ♀
655.43 Suspected damage to fetus from other disease in mother, affecting management of mother, antepartum condition or complication ♀
656.03 Fetal-maternal hemorrhage, antepartum condition or complication ♀
658.43 Infection of amniotic cavity, antepartum ♀
659.53 Elderly primigravida, antepartum ♀
678.03 Fetal hematologic conditions, antepartum condition or complication ♀
678.13 Fetal conjoined twins, antepartum condition or complication ♀
679.03 Maternal complications from in utero procedure, antepartum condition or complication ♀
759.83 Fragile X syndrome
762.7 Fetus or newborn affected by chorioamnionitis — (Use additional code(s) to further specify condition)
762.8 Fetus or newborn affected by other specified abnormalities of chorion and amnion — (Use additional code(s) to further specify condition)
772.0 Fetal blood loss affecting newborn — (Use additional code(s) to further specify condition)
V15.21 Personal history of undergoing in utero procedure during pregnancy ♀
V15.29 Personal history of surgery to other organs
V23.81 Supervision of high-risk pregnancy of elderly primigravida ♀
V23.82 Supervision of high-risk pregnancy of elderly multigravida ♀
V23.85 Supervision of high risk pregnancy, pregnancy resulting from assisted reproductive technology ♀
V23.86 Supervision of high risk pregnancy, pregnancy with history of in utero procedure during previous pregnancy ♀
V89.01 Suspected problem with amniotic cavity and membrane not found ♀
V89.02 Suspected placental problem not found ♀
V89.03 Suspected fetal anomaly not found ♀
V89.04 Suspected problem with fetal growth not found ♀
V89.09 Other suspected maternal and fetal condition not found ♀

ICD-9-CM Procedural

75.35 Other diagnostic procedures on fetus and amnion ♀

59015

59015 Chorionic villus sampling, any method

ICD-9-CM Diagnostic

646.03 Papyraceous fetus, antepartum — (Use additional code to further specify complication) ♀
655.13 Chromosomal abnormality in fetus, affecting management of mother, antepartum ♀
655.23 Hereditary disease in family possibly affecting fetus, affecting management of mother, antepartum condition or complication ♀
655.33 Suspected damage to fetus from viral disease in mother, affecting management of mother, antepartum condition or complication ♀
655.43 Suspected damage to fetus from other disease in mother, affecting management of mother, antepartum condition or complication ♀
655.83 Other known or suspected fetal abnormality, not elsewhere classified, affecting management of mother, antepartum condition or complication ♀
655.93 Unspecified fetal abnormality affecting management of mother, antepartum condition or complication ▽ ♀
659.53 Elderly primigravida, antepartum ♀
659.63 Elderly multigravida, with antepartum condition or complication ♀
678.03 Fetal hematologic conditions, antepartum condition or complication ♀
678.13 Fetal conjoined twins, antepartum condition or complication ♀
V28.81 Encounter for fetal anatomic survey ♀

ICD-9-CM Procedural

75.35 Other diagnostic procedures on fetus and amnion ♀

59020

59020 Fetal contraction stress test

ICD-9-CM Diagnostic

642.03 Benign essential hypertension antepartum ♀

642.13 Hypertension secondary to renal disease, antepartum ♀
642.23 Other pre-existing hypertension, antepartum ♀
642.33 Transient hypertension of pregnancy, antepartum ♀
642.43 Mild or unspecified pre-eclampsia, antepartum ♀
642.53 Severe pre-eclampsia, antepartum ♀
642.73 Pre-eclampsia or eclampsia superimposed on pre-existing hypertension, antepartum ♀
642.93 Unspecified hypertension antepartum ♀
643.13 Hyperemesis gravidarum with metabolic disturbance, antepartum ♀
643.23 Late vomiting of pregnancy, antepartum ♀
643.83 Other vomiting complicating pregnancy, antepartum — (Use additional code to specify cause) ♀
643.93 Unspecified vomiting of pregnancy, antepartum ♀
645.13 Post term pregnancy, antepartum condition or complication ♀
645.23 Prolonged pregnancy, antepartum condition or complication ♀
646.13 Edema or excessive weight gain, antepartum — (Use additional code to further specify complication) ♀
646.23 Unspecified antepartum renal disease — (Use additional code to further specify complication) ♀
646.83 Other specified complication, antepartum — (Use additional code to further specify complication) ♀
646.93 Unspecified complication of pregnancy, antepartum — (Use additional code to further specify complication) ♀
648.03 Maternal diabetes mellitus, antepartum — (Use additional code(s) to identify the condition) ♀
648.33 Maternal drug dependence, antepartum — (Use additional code(s) to identify the condition) ♀
648.53 Maternal congenital cardiovascular disorders, antepartum — (Use additional code(s) to identify the condition) ♀
648.63 Other maternal cardiovascular diseases, antepartum — (Use additional code(s) to identify the condition) ♀
648.83 Abnormal maternal glucose tolerance, antepartum — (Use additional code(s) to identify the condition. Use additional code, if applicable, for associated long-term (current) insulin use: V58.67) ♀
648.93 Other current maternal conditions classifiable elsewhere, antepartum — (Use additional code(s) to identify the condition) ♀
649.03 Tobacco use disorder complicating pregnancy, childbirth, or the puerperium, antepartum condition or complication ♀
649.13 Obesity complicating pregnancy, childbirth, or the puerperium, antepartum condition or complication — (Use additional code to identify the obesity: 278.00-278.01) ♀
649.23 Bariatric surgery status complicating pregnancy, childbirth, or the puerperium, antepartum condition or complication ♀
649.33 Coagulation defects complicating pregnancy, childbirth, or the puerperium, antepartum condition or complication — (Use additional code to identify the specific coagulation defect: 286.0-286.9, 287.0-287.9, 289.0-289.9) ♀
649.43 Epilepsy complicating pregnancy, childbirth, or the puerperium, antepartum condition or complication — (Use additional code to identify the specific type of epilepsy: 345.00-345.91) ♀
649.53 Spotting complicating pregnancy, antepartum condition or complication ♀
649.63 Uterine size date discrepancy, antepartum condition or complication ♀
649.70 Cervical shortening, unspecified as to episode of care or not applicable ♀
649.71 Cervical shortening, delivered, with or without mention of antepartum condition ♀
649.73 Cervical shortening, antepartum condition or complication ♀
651.03 Twin pregnancy, antepartum ♀
651.13 Triplet pregnancy, antepartum ♀
651.23 Quadruplet pregnancy, antepartum ♀
651.33 Twin pregnancy with fetal loss and retention of one fetus, antepartum ♀
651.43 Triplet pregnancy with fetal loss and retention of one or more, antepartum ♀
651.53 Quadruplet pregnancy with fetal loss and retention of one or more, antepartum ♀
651.63 Other multiple pregnancy with fetal loss and retention of one or more fetus(es), antepartum ♀
651.73 Multiple gestation following (elective) fetal reduction, antepartum condition or complication ♀
651.83 Other specified multiple gestation, antepartum ♀
651.93 Unspecified multiple gestation, antepartum ♀
654.23 Previous cesarean delivery, antepartum condition or complication — (Code first any associated obstructed labor, 660.2) ♀
655.03 Central nervous system malformation in fetus, antepartum ♀
655.13 Chromosomal abnormality in fetus, affecting management of mother, antepartum ♀
655.23 Hereditary disease in family possibly affecting fetus, affecting management of mother, antepartum condition or complication ♀
655.33 Suspected damage to fetus from viral disease in mother, affecting management of mother, antepartum condition or complication ♀
655.43 Suspected damage to fetus from other disease in mother, affecting management of mother, antepartum condition or complication ♀
655.53 Suspected damage to fetus from drugs, affecting management of mother, antepartum ♀
655.63 Suspected damage to fetus from radiation, affecting management of mother, antepartum condition or complication ♀
655.83 Other known or suspected fetal abnormality, not elsewhere classified, affecting management of mother, antepartum condition or complication ♀
655.93 Unspecified fetal abnormality affecting management of mother, antepartum condition or complication ♀
656.03 Fetal-maternal hemorrhage, antepartum condition or complication ♀
656.13 Rhesus isoimmunization affecting management of mother, antepartum condition ♀
656.23 Isoimmunization from other and unspecified blood-group incompatibility, affecting management of mother, antepartum ♀
656.33 Fetal distress affecting management of mother, antepartum ♀
656.53 Poor fetal growth, affecting management of mother, antepartum condition or complication ♀
656.63 Excessive fetal growth affecting management of mother, antepartum ♀
656.83 Other specified fetal and placental problems affecting management of mother, antepartum ♀
656.93 Unspecified fetal and placental problem affecting management of mother, antepartum ♀
657.03 Polyhydramnios, antepartum complication ♀
658.03 Oligohydramnios, antepartum ♀
659.53 Elderly primigravida, antepartum ♀
659.63 Elderly multigravida, with antepartum condition or complication ♀
659.73 Abnormality in fetal heart rate or rhythm, antepartum condition or complication ♀
V15.29 Personal history of surgery to other organs
V22.0 Supervision of normal first pregnancy ♀
V22.1 Supervision of other normal pregnancy ♀
V23.0 Pregnancy with history of infertility ♀
V23.1 Pregnancy with history of trophoblastic disease ♀
V23.2 Pregnancy with history of abortion ♀
V23.3 Pregnancy with grand multiparity ♀
V23.41 Supervision of pregnancy with history of pre-term labor ♀
V23.49 Supervision of pregnancy with other poor obstetric history ♀
V23.5 Pregnancy with other poor reproductive history ♀
V23.7 Insufficient prenatal care ♀
V23.81 Supervision of high-risk pregnancy of elderly primigravida ♀
V23.82 Supervision of high-risk pregnancy of elderly multigravida ♀
V23.83 Supervision of high-risk pregnancy of young primigravida ♀
V23.84 Supervision of high-risk pregnancy of young multigravida ♀
V23.85 Supervision of high risk pregnancy, pregnancy resulting from assisted reproductive technology ♀
V23.86 Supervision of high risk pregnancy, pregnancy with history of in utero procedure during previous pregnancy ♀

[Resequenced code] Unspecified code ■ Manifestation code ♀ Female diagnosis ♂ Male diagnosis

V23.89 Supervision of other high-risk pregnancy ♀
V71.89 Observation for other specified suspected conditions
V89.09 Other suspected maternal and fetal condition not found ♀

ICD-9-CM Procedural

75.34 Other fetal monitoring ♀

HCPCS Level II Supplies & Services

A4649 Surgical supply; miscellaneous

59025

59025 Fetal non-stress test

ICD-9-CM Diagnostic

641.03 Placenta previa without hemorrhage, antepartum ♀
641.83 Other antepartum hemorrhage, antepartum ♀
642.03 Benign essential hypertension antepartum ♀
642.13 Hypertension secondary to renal disease, antepartum ♀
642.23 Other pre-existing hypertension, antepartum ♀
642.33 Transient hypertension of pregnancy, antepartum ♀
642.43 Mild or unspecified pre-eclampsia, antepartum ♀
642.53 Severe pre-eclampsia, antepartum ♀
642.63 Eclampsia, antepartum ♀
642.73 Pre-eclampsia or eclampsia superimposed on pre-existing hypertension, antepartum ♀
642.93 Unspecified hypertension antepartum ▽ ♀
643.13 Hyperemesis gravidarum with metabolic disturbance, antepartum ♀
643.23 Late vomiting of pregnancy, antepartum ♀
643.83 Other vomiting complicating pregnancy, antepartum — (Use additional code to specify cause) ♀
643.93 Unspecified vomiting of pregnancy, antepartum ▽ ♀
644.03 Threatened premature labor, antepartum ♀
644.13 Other threatened labor, antepartum ♀
645.13 Post term pregnancy, antepartum condition or complication ♀
645.23 Prolonged pregnancy, antepartum condition or complication ♀
646.13 Edema or excessive weight gain, antepartum — (Use additional code to further specify complication) ♀
646.23 Unspecified antepartum renal disease — (Use additional code to further specify complication) ▽ ♀
646.73 Liver and biliary tract disorders in pregnancy, antepartum condition or complication — (Use additional code to further specify complication) ♀
646.83 Other specified complication, antepartum — (Use additional code to further specify complication) ♀
646.93 Unspecified complication of pregnancy, antepartum — (Use additional code to further specify complication) ▽ ♀
647.23 Other maternal venereal diseases, antepartum condition or complication — (Use additional code to further specify complication) ♀
647.53 Maternal rubella, antepartum — (Use additional code to further specify complication) ♀
647.63 Other maternal viral disease, antepartum — (Use additional code to further specify complication) ♀
647.83 Other specified maternal infectious and parasitic disease, antepartum — (Use additional code to further specify complication) ♀
647.93 Unspecified maternal infection or infestation, antepartum — (Use additional code to further specify complication) ▽ ♀
648.03 Maternal diabetes mellitus, antepartum — (Use additional code(s) to identify the condition) ♀
648.13 Maternal thyroid dysfunction, antepartum condition or complication — (Use additional code(s) to identify the condition) ♀
648.23 Maternal anemia, antepartum — (Use additional code(s) to identify the condition) ♀
648.33 Maternal drug dependence, antepartum — (Use additional code(s) to identify the condition) ♀
648.43 Maternal mental disorders, antepartum — (Use additional code(s) to identify the condition) ♀
648.53 Maternal congenital cardiovascular disorders, antepartum — (Use additional code(s) to identify the condition) ♀
648.63 Other maternal cardiovascular diseases, antepartum — (Use additional code(s) to identify the condition) ♀
648.83 Abnormal maternal glucose tolerance, antepartum — (Use additional code(s) to identify the condition. Use additional code, if applicable, for associated long-term (current) insulin use: V58.67) ♀
648.93 Other current maternal conditions classifiable elsewhere, antepartum — (Use additional code(s) to identify the condition) ♀
649.13 Obesity complicating pregnancy, childbirth, or the puerperium, antepartum condition or complication — (Use additional code to identify the obesity: 278.00-278.01) ♀
649.23 Bariatric surgery status complicating pregnancy, childbirth, or the puerperium, antepartum condition or complication ♀
649.63 Uterine size date discrepancy, antepartum condition or complication ♀
649.70 Cervical shortening, unspecified as to episode of care or not applicable ♀
649.71 Cervical shortening, delivered, with or without mention of antepartum condition ♀
649.73 Cervical shortening, antepartum condition or complication ♀
651.03 Twin pregnancy, antepartum ♀
651.13 Triplet pregnancy, antepartum ♀
651.23 Quadruplet pregnancy, antepartum ♀
651.33 Twin pregnancy with fetal loss and retention of one fetus, antepartum ♀
651.43 Triplet pregnancy with fetal loss and retention of one or more, antepartum ♀
651.53 Quadruplet pregnancy with fetal loss and retention of one or more, antepartum ♀
651.63 Other multiple pregnancy with fetal loss and retention of one or more fetus(es), antepartum ♀
651.73 Multiple gestation following (elective) fetal reduction, antepartum condition or complication ♀
651.83 Other specified multiple gestation, antepartum ♀
651.93 Unspecified multiple gestation, antepartum ▽ ♀
655.03 Central nervous system malformation in fetus, antepartum ♀
655.13 Chromosomal abnormality in fetus, affecting management of mother, antepartum ♀
655.23 Hereditary disease in family possibly affecting fetus, affecting management of mother, antepartum condition or complication ♀
655.33 Suspected damage to fetus from viral disease in mother, affecting management of mother, antepartum condition or complication ♀
655.43 Suspected damage to fetus from other disease in mother, affecting management of mother, antepartum condition or complication ♀
655.53 Suspected damage to fetus from drugs, affecting management of mother, antepartum ♀
655.63 Suspected damage to fetus from radiation, affecting management of mother, antepartum condition or complication ♀
655.83 Other known or suspected fetal abnormality, not elsewhere classified, affecting management of mother, antepartum condition or complication ♀
655.93 Unspecified fetal abnormality affecting management of mother, antepartum condition or complication ▽ ♀
656.23 Isoimmunization from other and unspecified blood-group incompatibility, affecting management of mother, antepartum ♀
656.33 Fetal distress affecting management of mother, antepartum ♀
656.53 Poor fetal growth, affecting management of mother, antepartum condition or complication ♀
656.63 Excessive fetal growth affecting management of mother, antepartum ♀
656.73 Other placental conditions affecting management of mother, antepartum ♀
656.83 Other specified fetal and placental problems affecting management of mother, antepartum ♀
656.93 Unspecified fetal and placental problem affecting management of mother, antepartum ▽ ♀

657.03 Polyhydramnios, antepartum complication ♀

658.03 Oligohydramnios, antepartum ♀

658.13 Premature rupture of membranes in pregnancy, antepartum ♀

658.23 Delayed delivery after spontaneous or unspecified rupture of membranes, antepartum ♀

658.33 Delayed delivery after artificial rupture of membranes, antepartum ♀

658.43 Infection of amniotic cavity, antepartum ♀

659.03 Failed mechanical induction of labor, antepartum ♀

659.13 Failed medical or unspecified induction of labor, antepartum ♀

659.23 Unspecified maternal pyrexia, antepartum ♀

659.43 Grand multiparity with current pregnancy, antepartum ♀

659.53 Elderly primigravida, antepartum ♀

659.63 Elderly multigravida, with antepartum condition or complication ♀

659.73 Abnormality in fetal heart rate or rhythm, antepartum condition or complication ♀

V15.21 Personal history of undergoing in utero procedure during pregnancy ♀

V15.29 Personal history of surgery to other organs

V22.0 Supervision of normal first pregnancy ♀

V22.1 Supervision of other normal pregnancy ♀

V23.0 Pregnancy with history of infertility ♀

V23.1 Pregnancy with history of trophoblastic disease ♀

V23.2 Pregnancy with history of abortion ♀

V23.3 Pregnancy with grand multiparity ♀

V23.41 Supervision of pregnancy with history of pre-term labor ♀

V23.49 Supervision of pregnancy with other poor obstetric history ♀

V23.5 Pregnancy with other poor reproductive history ♀

V23.7 Insufficient prenatal care ♀

V23.81 Supervision of high-risk pregnancy of elderly primigravida ♀

V23.82 Supervision of high-risk pregnancy of elderly multigravida ♀

V23.83 Supervision of high-risk pregnancy of young primigravida ♀

V23.84 Supervision of high-risk pregnancy of young multigravida ♀

V23.85 Supervision of high risk pregnancy, pregnancy resulting from assisted reproductive technology ♀

V23.86 Supervision of high risk pregnancy, pregnancy with history of in utero procedure during previous pregnancy ♀

V23.89 Supervision of other high-risk pregnancy ♀

V23.9 Unspecified high-risk pregnancy ♀

V89.09 Other suspected maternal and fetal condition not found ♀

ICD-9-CM Procedural

75.34 Other fetal monitoring ♀

HCPCS Level II Supplies & Services

A4649 Surgical supply; miscellaneous

59030

59030 Fetal scalp blood sampling

ICD-9-CM Diagnostic

642.41 Mild or unspecified pre-eclampsia, with delivery ♀

642.43 Mild or unspecified pre-eclampsia, antepartum ♀

642.51 Severe pre-eclampsia, with delivery ♀

642.53 Severe pre-eclampsia, antepartum ♀

642.61 Eclampsia, with delivery ♀

642.63 Eclampsia, antepartum ♀

642.71 Pre-eclampsia or eclampsia superimposed on pre-existing hypertension, with delivery ♀

642.73 Pre-eclampsia or eclampsia superimposed on pre-existing hypertension, antepartum ♀

648.01 Maternal diabetes mellitus with delivery — (Use additional code(s) to identify the condition) ♀

648.03 Maternal diabetes mellitus, antepartum — (Use additional code(s) to identify the condition) ♀

649.23 Bariatric surgery status complicating pregnancy, childbirth, or the puerperium, antepartum condition or complication ♀

649.33 Coagulation defects complicating pregnancy, childbirth, or the puerperium, antepartum condition or complication — (Use additional code to identify the specific coagulation defect: 286.0-286.9, 287.0-287.9, 289.0-289.9) ♀

649.43 Epilepsy complicating pregnancy, childbirth, or the puerperium, antepartum condition or complication — (Use additional code to identify the specific type of epilepsy: 345.00-345.91) ♀

649.53 Spotting complicating pregnancy, antepartum condition or complication ♀

656.11 Rhesus isoimmunization affecting management of mother, delivered ♀

656.13 Rhesus isoimmunization affecting management of mother, antepartum condition ♀

656.31 Fetal distress affecting management of mother, delivered ♀

656.33 Fetal distress affecting management of mother, antepartum ♀

656.71 Other placental conditions affecting management of mother, delivered ♀

656.73 Other placental conditions affecting management of mother, antepartum ♀

658.31 Delayed delivery after artificial rupture of membranes, delivered ♀

658.33 Delayed delivery after artificial rupture of membranes, antepartum ♀

659.71 Abnormality in fetal heart rate or rhythm, delivered, with or without mention of antepartum condition ♀

659.73 Abnormality in fetal heart rate or rhythm, antepartum condition or complication ♀

661.01 Primary uterine inertia, with delivery ♀

661.03 Primary uterine inertia, antepartum ♀

661.11 Secondary uterine inertia, with delivery ♀

661.13 Secondary uterine inertia, antepartum ♀

661.21 Other and unspecified uterine inertia, with delivery ♀

661.23 Other and unspecified uterine inertia, antepartum ♀

661.41 Hypertonic, incoordinate, or prolonged uterine contractions, with delivery ♀

661.43 Hypertonic, incoordinate, or prolonged uterine contractions, antepartum ♀

662.01 Prolonged first stage of labor, delivered ♀

662.03 Prolonged first stage of labor, antepartum ♀

662.11 Unspecified prolonged labor, delivered ♀

662.13 Unspecified prolonged labor, antepartum ♀

662.21 Prolonged second stage of labor, delivered ♀

662.23 Prolonged second stage of labor, antepartum ♀

ICD-9-CM Procedural

75.33 Fetal blood sampling and biopsy ♀

HCPCS Level II Supplies & Services

A4649 Surgical supply; miscellaneous

59050-59051

59050 Fetal monitoring during labor by consulting physician (ie, non-attending physician) with written report; supervision and interpretation

59051 interpretation only

ICD-9-CM Diagnostic

641.01 Placenta previa without hemorrhage, with delivery ♀

641.03 Placenta previa without hemorrhage, antepartum ♀

641.11 Hemorrhage from placenta previa, with delivery ♀

641.13 Hemorrhage from placenta previa, antepartum ♀

641.21 Premature separation of placenta, with delivery ♀

641.23 Premature separation of placenta, antepartum ♀

641.31 Antepartum hemorrhage associated with coagulation defects, with delivery ♀

641.33 Antepartum hemorrhage associated with coagulation defect, antepartum ♀

641.81 Other antepartum hemorrhage, with delivery ♀

641.83 Other antepartum hemorrhage, antepartum ♀

642.01 Benign essential hypertension with delivery ♀

[Resequenced code] Unspecified code ☒ Manifestation code ♀ Female diagnosis ♂ Male diagnosis

642.03 Benign essential hypertension antepartum ♀
642.11 Hypertension secondary to renal disease, with delivery ♀
642.13 Hypertension secondary to renal disease, antepartum ♀
642.21 Other pre-existing hypertension, with delivery ♀
642.23 Other pre-existing hypertension, antepartum ♀
642.31 Transient hypertension of pregnancy, with delivery ♀
642.33 Transient hypertension of pregnancy, antepartum ♀
642.41 Mild or unspecified pre-eclampsia, with delivery ♀
642.43 Mild or unspecified pre-eclampsia, antepartum ♀
642.51 Severe pre-eclampsia, with delivery ♀
642.53 Severe pre-eclampsia, antepartum ♀
642.61 Eclampsia, with delivery ♀
642.63 Eclampsia, antepartum ♀
642.71 Pre-eclampsia or eclampsia superimposed on pre-existing hypertension, with delivery ♀
642.73 Pre-eclampsia or eclampsia superimposed on pre-existing hypertension, antepartum ♀
642.91 Unspecified hypertension, with delivery ♀
642.93 Unspecified hypertension antepartum ♀
643.11 Hyperemesis gravidarum with metabolic disturbance, delivered ♀
643.13 Hyperemesis gravidarum with metabolic disturbance, antepartum ♀
643.21 Late vomiting of pregnancy, delivered ♀
643.23 Late vomiting of pregnancy, antepartum ♀
643.81 Other vomiting complicating pregnancy, delivered — (Use additional code to specify cause) ♀
643.83 Other vomiting complicating pregnancy, antepartum — (Use additional code to specify cause) ♀
643.91 Unspecified vomiting of pregnancy, delivered ♀
643.93 Unspecified vomiting of pregnancy, antepartum ♀
645.11 Post term pregnancy, delivered, with or without mention of antepartum condition ♀
645.13 Post term pregnancy, antepartum condition or complication ♀
645.21 Prolonged pregnancy, delivered, with or without mention of antepartum condition ♀
645.23 Prolonged pregnancy, antepartum condition or complication ♀
646.11 Edema or excessive weight gain in pregnancy, with delivery, with or without mention of antepartum complication — (Use additional code to further specify complication) ♀
646.13 Edema or excessive weight gain, antepartum — (Use additional code to further specify complication) ♀
646.21 Unspecified renal disease in pregnancy, with delivery — (Use additional code to further specify complication) ♀
646.23 Unspecified antepartum renal disease — (Use additional code to further specify complication) ♀
646.31 Pregnancy complication, recurrent pregnancy loss, with or without mention of antepartum condition — (Use additional code to further specify complication) ♀
646.33 Pregnancy complication, recurrent pregnancy loss, antepartum condition or complication — (Use additional code to further specify complication) ♀
646.71 Liver and biliary tract disorders in pregnancy, delivered, with or without mention of antepartum condition — (Use additional code to further specify complication) ♀
646.73 Liver and biliary tract disorders in pregnancy, antepartum condition or complication — (Use additional code to further specify complication) ♀
646.81 Other specified complication of pregnancy, with delivery — (Use additional code to further specify complication) ♀
646.83 Other specified complication, antepartum — (Use additional code to further specify complication) ♀
646.91 Unspecified complication of pregnancy, with delivery — (Use additional code to further specify complication) ♀
646.93 Unspecified complication of pregnancy, antepartum — (Use additional code to further specify complication) ♀
647.01 Maternal syphilis, complicating pregnancy, with delivery — (Use additional code to further specify complication) ♀
647.03 Maternal syphilis, antepartum — (Use additional code to further specify complication) ♀
647.11 Maternal gonorrhea with delivery — (Use additional code to further specify complication) ♀
647.13 Maternal gonorrhea, antepartum — (Use additional code to further specify complication) ♀
647.21 Other maternal venereal diseases with delivery — (Use additional code to further specify complication) ♀
647.23 Other maternal venereal diseases, antepartum condition or complication — (Use additional code to further specify complication) ♀
647.31 Maternal tuberculosis with delivery — (Use additional code to further specify complication) ♀
647.33 Maternal tuberculosis, antepartum — (Use additional code to further specify complication) ♀
647.51 Maternal rubella with delivery — (Use additional code to further specify complication) ♀
647.53 Maternal rubella, antepartum — (Use additional code to further specify complication) ♀
647.61 Other maternal viral disease with delivery — (Use additional code to further specify complication) ♀
647.63 Other maternal viral disease, antepartum — (Use additional code to further specify complication) ♀
647.81 Other specified maternal infectious and parasitic disease with delivery — (Use additional code to further specify complication) ♀
647.83 Other specified maternal infectious and parasitic disease, antepartum — (Use additional code to further specify complication) ♀
647.91 Unspecified maternal infection or infestation with delivery — (Use additional code to further specify complication) ♀
647.93 Unspecified maternal infection or infestation, antepartum — (Use additional code to further specify complication) ♀
648.01 Maternal diabetes mellitus with delivery — (Use additional code(s) to identify the condition) ♀
648.03 Maternal diabetes mellitus, antepartum — (Use additional code(s) to identify the condition) ♀
648.11 Maternal thyroid dysfunction with delivery, with or without mention of antepartum condition — (Use additional code(s) to identify the condition) ♀
648.13 Maternal thyroid dysfunction, antepartum condition or complication — (Use additional code(s) to identify the condition) ♀
648.21 Maternal anemia, with delivery — (Use additional code(s) to identify the condition) ♀
648.23 Maternal anemia, antepartum — (Use additional code(s) to identify the condition) ♀
648.31 Maternal drug dependence, with delivery — (Use additional code(s) to identify the condition) ♀
648.33 Maternal drug dependence, antepartum — (Use additional code(s) to identify the condition) ♀
648.51 Maternal congenital cardiovascular disorders, with delivery — (Use additional code(s) to identify the condition) ♀
648.53 Maternal congenital cardiovascular disorders, antepartum — (Use additional code(s) to identify the condition) ♀
648.61 Other maternal cardiovascular diseases, with delivery — (Use additional code(s) to identify the condition) ♀
648.63 Other maternal cardiovascular diseases, antepartum — (Use additional code(s) to identify the condition) ♀
648.81 Abnormal maternal glucose tolerance, with delivery — (Use additional code(s) to identify the condition. Use additional code, if applicable, for associated long-term (current) insulin use: V58.67) ♀
648.83 Abnormal maternal glucose tolerance, antepartum — (Use additional code(s) to identify the condition. Use additional code, if applicable, for associated long-term (current) insulin use: V58.67) ♀
648.91 Other current maternal conditions classifiable elsewhere, with delivery — (Use additional code(s) to identify the condition) ♀

648.93 Other current maternal conditions classifiable elsewhere, antepartum — (Use additional code(s) to identify the condition) ♀
649.70 Cervical shortening, unspecified as to episode of care or not applicable ♀
649.71 Cervical shortening, delivered, with or without mention of antepartum condition ♀
649.73 Cervical shortening, antepartum condition or complication ♀
651.01 Twin pregnancy, delivered ♀
651.03 Twin pregnancy, antepartum ♀
651.11 Triplet pregnancy, delivered ♀
651.13 Triplet pregnancy, antepartum ♀
651.21 Quadruplet pregnancy, delivered ♀
651.23 Quadruplet pregnancy, antepartum ♀
651.31 Twin pregnancy with fetal loss and retention of one fetus, delivered ♀
651.33 Twin pregnancy with fetal loss and retention of one fetus, antepartum ♀
651.41 Triplet pregnancy with fetal loss and retention of one or more, delivered ♀
651.43 Triplet pregnancy with fetal loss and retention of one or more, antepartum ♀
651.51 Quadruplet pregnancy with fetal loss and retention of one or more, delivered ♀
651.53 Quadruplet pregnancy with fetal loss and retention of one or more, antepartum ♀
651.61 Other multiple pregnancy with fetal loss and retention of one or more fetus(es), delivered ♀
651.63 Other multiple pregnancy with fetal loss and retention of one or more fetus(es), antepartum ♀
651.73 Multiple gestation following (elective) fetal reduction, antepartum condition or complication ♀
651.81 Other specified multiple gestation, delivered ♀
651.83 Other specified multiple gestation, antepartum ♀
651.91 Unspecified multiple gestation, delivered ▽ ♀
651.93 Unspecified multiple gestation, antepartum ▽ ♀
654.41 Other abnormalities in shape or position of gravid uterus and of neighboring structures, delivered — (Code first any associated obstructed labor: 660.2) ♀
655.01 Central nervous system malformation in fetus, with delivery ♀
655.03 Central nervous system malformation in fetus, antepartum ♀
655.11 Chromosomal abnormality in fetus, affecting management of mother, with delivery ♀
655.13 Chromosomal abnormality in fetus, affecting management of mother, antepartum ♀
655.21 Hereditary disease in family possibly affecting fetus, affecting management of mother, with delivery ♀
655.23 Hereditary disease in family possibly affecting fetus, affecting management of mother, antepartum condition or complication ♀
655.31 Suspected damage to fetus from viral disease in mother, affecting management of mother, with delivery ♀
655.33 Suspected damage to fetus from viral disease in mother, affecting management of mother, antepartum condition or complication ♀
655.41 Suspected damage to fetus from other disease in mother, affecting management of mother, with delivery ♀
655.43 Suspected damage to fetus from other disease in mother, affecting management of mother, antepartum condition or complication ♀
655.51 Suspected damage to fetus from drugs, affecting management of mother, delivered ♀
655.53 Suspected damage to fetus from drugs, affecting management of mother, antepartum ♀
655.61 Suspected damage to fetus from radiation, affecting management of mother, delivered ♀
655.63 Suspected damage to fetus from radiation, affecting management of mother, antepartum condition or complication ♀
655.81 Other known or suspected fetal abnormality, not elsewhere classified, affecting management of mother, delivery ♀
655.83 Other known or suspected fetal abnormality, not elsewhere classified, affecting management of mother, antepartum condition or complication ♀
655.91 Unspecified fetal abnormality affecting management of mother, delivery ▽ ♀
655.93 Unspecified fetal abnormality affecting management of mother, antepartum condition or complication ▽ ♀
656.01 Fetal-maternal hemorrhage, with delivery ♀
656.11 Rhesus isoimmunization affecting management of mother, delivered ♀
656.13 Rhesus isoimmunization affecting management of mother, antepartum condition ♀
656.21 Isoimmunization from other and unspecified blood-group incompatibility, affecting management of mother, delivered ♀
656.23 Isoimmunization from other and unspecified blood-group incompatibility, affecting management of mother, antepartum ♀
656.31 Fetal distress affecting management of mother, delivered ♀
656.33 Fetal distress affecting management of mother, antepartum ♀
656.51 Poor fetal growth, affecting management of mother, delivered ♀
656.53 Poor fetal growth, affecting management of mother, antepartum condition or complication ♀
656.61 Excessive fetal growth affecting management of mother, delivered ♀
656.63 Excessive fetal growth affecting management of mother, antepartum ♀
656.71 Other placental conditions affecting management of mother, delivered ♀
656.73 Other placental conditions affecting management of mother, antepartum ♀
656.81 Other specified fetal and placental problems affecting management of mother, delivered ♀
656.83 Other specified fetal and placental problems affecting management of mother, antepartum ♀
656.91 Unspecified fetal and placental problem affecting management of mother, delivered ▽ ♀
656.93 Unspecified fetal and placental problem affecting management of mother, antepartum ▽ ♀
657.01 Polyhydramnios, with delivery ♀
657.03 Polyhydramnios, antepartum complication ♀
658.01 Oligohydramnios, delivered ♀
658.03 Oligohydramnios, antepartum ♀
658.11 Premature rupture of membranes in pregnancy, delivered ♀
658.13 Premature rupture of membranes in pregnancy, antepartum ♀
658.21 Delayed delivery after spontaneous or unspecified rupture of membranes, delivered ♀
658.23 Delayed delivery after spontaneous or unspecified rupture of membranes, antepartum ♀
658.31 Delayed delivery after artificial rupture of membranes, delivered ♀
658.33 Delayed delivery after artificial rupture of membranes, antepartum ♀
658.41 Infection of amniotic cavity, delivered ♀
658.43 Infection of amniotic cavity, antepartum ♀
659.01 Failed mechanical induction of labor, delivered ♀
659.03 Failed mechanical induction of labor, antepartum ♀
659.11 Failed medical or unspecified induction of labor, delivered ♀
659.13 Failed medical or unspecified induction of labor, antepartum ♀
659.21 Unspecified maternal pyrexia during labor, delivered ▽ ♀
659.23 Unspecified maternal pyrexia, antepartum ▽ ♀
659.31 Generalized infection during labor, delivered ♀
659.33 Generalized infection during labor, antepartum ♀
659.41 Grand multiparity, delivered, with or without mention of antepartum condition ♀
659.43 Grand multiparity with current pregnancy, antepartum ♀
659.51 Elderly primigravida, delivered ♀
659.53 Elderly primigravida, antepartum ♀
659.61 Elderly multigravida, delivered, with mention of antepartum condition ♀
659.63 Elderly multigravida, with antepartum condition or complication ♀
659.71 Abnormality in fetal heart rate or rhythm, delivered, with or without mention of antepartum condition ♀
659.73 Abnormality in fetal heart rate or rhythm, antepartum condition or complication ♀
660.61 Unspecified failed trial of labor, delivered ▽ ♀
660.63 Unspecified failed trial of labor, antepartum ▽ ♀
661.11 Secondary uterine inertia, with delivery ♀
661.13 Secondary uterine inertia, antepartum ♀
661.21 Other and unspecified uterine inertia, with delivery ▽ ♀

661.23 Other and unspecified uterine inertia, antepartum ♀
661.41 Hypertonic, incoordinate, or prolonged uterine contractions, with delivery ♀
661.43 Hypertonic, incoordinate, or prolonged uterine contractions, antepartum ♀
662.01 Prolonged first stage of labor, delivered ♀
662.03 Prolonged first stage of labor, antepartum ♀
662.11 Unspecified prolonged labor, delivered ♀
662.13 Unspecified prolonged labor, antepartum ♀
662.21 Prolonged second stage of labor, delivered ♀
662.23 Prolonged second stage of labor, antepartum ♀
678.03 Fetal hematologic conditions, antepartum condition or complication ♀
678.13 Fetal conjoined twins, antepartum condition or complication ♀
679.03 Maternal complications from in utero procedure, antepartum condition or complication ♀
V15.21 Personal history of undergoing in utero procedure during pregnancy ♀
V15.29 Personal history of surgery to other organs
V23.3 Pregnancy with grand multiparity ♀
V23.41 Supervision of pregnancy with history of pre-term labor ♀
V23.49 Supervision of pregnancy with other poor obstetric history ♀
V23.5 Pregnancy with other poor reproductive history ♀
V23.7 Insufficient prenatal care ♀
V23.81 Supervision of high-risk pregnancy of elderly primigravida ♀
V23.82 Supervision of high-risk pregnancy of elderly multigravida ♀
V23.83 Supervision of high-risk pregnancy of young primigravida ♀
V23.84 Supervision of high-risk pregnancy of young multigravida ♀
V23.85 Supervision of high risk pregnancy, pregnancy resulting from assisted reproductive technology ♀
V23.86 Supervision of high risk pregnancy, pregnancy with history of in utero procedure during previous pregnancy ♀
V23.89 Supervision of other high-risk pregnancy ♀
V23.9 Unspecified high-risk pregnancy ♀
V89.09 Other suspected maternal and fetal condition not found ♀

ICD-9-CM Procedural

75.34 Other fetal monitoring ♀

HCPCS Level II Supplies & Services

A4649 Surgical supply; miscellaneous

59070

59070 Transabdominal amnioinfusion, including ultrasound guidance

ICD-9-CM Diagnostic

656.83 Other specified fetal and placental problems affecting management of mother, antepartum ♀
658.03 Oligohydramnios, antepartum ♀
658.43 Infection of amniotic cavity, antepartum ♀
659.73 Abnormality in fetal heart rate or rhythm, antepartum condition or complication ♀
663.13 Cord around neck, with compression, complicating labor and delivery, antepartum ♀
663.23 Other and unspecified cord entanglement, with compression, complicating labor and delivery, antepartum ♀
V89.01 Suspected problem with amniotic cavity and membrane not found ♀
V89.09 Other suspected maternal and fetal condition not found ♀

ICD-9-CM Procedural

75.37 Amnioinfusion ♀

59072

59072 Fetal umbilical cord occlusion, including ultrasound guidance

ICD-9-CM Diagnostic

649.70 Cervical shortening, unspecified as to episode of care or not applicable ♀
649.71 Cervical shortening, delivered, with or without mention of antepartum condition ♀
649.73 Cervical shortening, antepartum condition or complication ♀
651.03 Twin pregnancy, antepartum ♀
651.13 Triplet pregnancy, antepartum ♀
651.23 Quadruplet pregnancy, antepartum ♀
651.73 Multiple gestation following (elective) fetal reduction, antepartum condition or complication ♀
651.83 Other specified multiple gestation, antepartum ♀
653.73 Other fetal abnormality causing disproportion, antepartum — (Code first any associated obstructed labor, 660.1) ♀
657.03 Polyhydramnios, antepartum complication ♀
658.03 Oligohydramnios, antepartum ♀
658.83 Other problem associated with amniotic cavity and membranes, antepartum ♀
678.03 Fetal hematologic conditions, antepartum condition or complication ♀
678.13 Fetal conjoined twins, antepartum condition or complication ♀
679.03 Maternal complications from in utero procedure, antepartum condition or complication ♀
V15.29 Personal history of surgery to other organs
V23.85 Supervision of high risk pregnancy, pregnancy resulting from assisted reproductive technology ♀
V23.86 Supervision of high risk pregnancy, pregnancy with history of in utero procedure during previous pregnancy ♀
V89.03 Suspected fetal anomaly not found ♀
V89.09 Other suspected maternal and fetal condition not found ♀

ICD-9-CM Procedural

75.35 Other diagnostic procedures on fetus and amnion ♀

59074-59076

59074 Fetal fluid drainage (eg, vesicocentesis, thoracocentesis, paracentesis), including ultrasound guidance
59076 Fetal shunt placement, including ultrasound guidance

ICD-9-CM Diagnostic

078.5 Cytomegaloviral disease — (Use additional code to identify manifestation: 484.1, 573.1)
647.63 Other maternal viral disease, antepartum — (Use additional code to further specify complication) ♀
653.73 Other fetal abnormality causing disproportion, antepartum — (Code first any associated obstructed labor, 660.1) ♀
655.33 Suspected damage to fetus from viral disease in mother, affecting management of mother, antepartum condition or complication ♀
655.83 Other known or suspected fetal abnormality, not elsewhere classified, affecting management of mother, antepartum condition or complication ♀
656.83 Other specified fetal and placental problems affecting management of mother, antepartum ♀
657.03 Polyhydramnios, antepartum complication ♀
679.03 Maternal complications from in utero procedure, antepartum condition or complication ♀
V15.21 Personal history of undergoing in utero procedure during pregnancy ♀
V15.29 Personal history of surgery to other organs
V23.85 Supervision of high risk pregnancy, pregnancy resulting from assisted reproductive technology ♀
V23.86 Supervision of high risk pregnancy, pregnancy with history of in utero procedure during previous pregnancy ♀
V89.01 Suspected problem with amniotic cavity and membrane not found ♀
V89.03 Suspected fetal anomaly not found ♀
V89.09 Other suspected maternal and fetal condition not found ♀

ICD-9-CM Procedural

75.35 Other diagnostic procedures on fetus and amnion ♀

59100

59100 Hysterotomy, abdominal (eg, for hydatidiform mole, abortion)

ICD-9-CM Diagnostic

630 Hydatidiform mole — (Use additional code from category 639 to identify any associated complications) ♀

631.8 Other abnormal products of conception ♀

632 Missed abortion — (Use additional code from category 639 to identify any associated complications) ♀

655.01 Central nervous system malformation in fetus, with delivery ♀

655.03 Central nervous system malformation in fetus, antepartum ♀

655.11 Chromosomal abnormality in fetus, affecting management of mother, with delivery ♀

655.13 Chromosomal abnormality in fetus, affecting management of mother, antepartum ♀

655.21 Hereditary disease in family possibly affecting fetus, affecting management of mother, with delivery ♀

655.23 Hereditary disease in family possibly affecting fetus, affecting management of mother, antepartum condition or complication ♀

655.31 Suspected damage to fetus from viral disease in mother, affecting management of mother, with delivery ♀

655.33 Suspected damage to fetus from viral disease in mother, affecting management of mother, antepartum condition or complication ♀

655.41 Suspected damage to fetus from other disease in mother, affecting management of mother, with delivery ♀

655.43 Suspected damage to fetus from other disease in mother, affecting management of mother, antepartum condition or complication ♀

655.51 Suspected damage to fetus from drugs, affecting management of mother, delivered ♀

655.53 Suspected damage to fetus from drugs, affecting management of mother, antepartum ♀

655.61 Suspected damage to fetus from radiation, affecting management of mother, delivered ♀

655.63 Suspected damage to fetus from radiation, affecting management of mother, antepartum condition or complication ♀

655.71 Decreased fetal movements, affecting management of mother, delivered ♀

655.73 Decreased fetal movements, affecting management of mother, antepartum condition or complication ♀

655.81 Other known or suspected fetal abnormality, not elsewhere classified, affecting management of mother, delivery ♀

655.83 Other known or suspected fetal abnormality, not elsewhere classified, affecting management of mother, antepartum condition or complication ♀

655.91 Unspecified fetal abnormality affecting management of mother, delivery ▽ ♀

655.93 Unspecified fetal abnormality affecting management of mother, antepartum condition or complication ▽ ♀

656.41 Intrauterine death affecting management of mother, delivered ♀

656.43 Intrauterine death affecting management of mother, antepartum ♀

659.51 Elderly primigravida, delivered ♀

659.53 Elderly primigravida, antepartum ♀

659.61 Elderly multigravida, delivered, with mention of antepartum condition ♀

659.63 Elderly multigravida, with antepartum condition or complication ♀

678.13 Fetal conjoined twins, antepartum condition or complication ♀

V13.1 Personal history of trophoblastic disease ♀

V15.29 Personal history of surgery to other organs

V19.5 Family history of congenital anomalies

V23.1 Pregnancy with history of trophoblastic disease ♀

V61.7 Other unwanted pregnancy ♀

ICD-9-CM Procedural

68.0 Hysterotomy ♀

74.91 Hysterotomy to terminate pregnancy ♀

75.33 Fetal blood sampling and biopsy ♀

59120-59121

59120 Surgical treatment of ectopic pregnancy; tubal or ovarian, requiring salpingectomy and/or oophorectomy, abdominal or vaginal approach

59121 tubal or ovarian, without salpingectomy and/or oophorectomy

ICD-9-CM Diagnostic

633.10 Tubal pregnancy without intrauterine pregnancy — (Use additional code from category 639 to identify any associated complications) ♀

633.11 Tubal pregnancy with intrauterine pregnancy — (Use additional code from category 639 to identify any associated complications) ♀

633.20 Ovarian pregnancy without intrauterine pregnancy — (Use additional code from category 639 to identify any associated complications) ♀

633.21 Ovarian pregnancy with intrauterine pregnancy — (Use additional code from category 639 to identify any associated complications) ♀

633.80 Other ectopic pregnancy without intrauterine pregnancy — (Use additional code from category 639 to identify any associated complications) ♀

633.81 Other ectopic pregnancy with intrauterine pregnancy — (Use additional code from category 639 to identify any associated complications) ♀

633.90 Unspecified ectopic pregnancy without intrauterine pregnancy — (Use additional code from category 639 to identify any associated complications) ▽ ♀

633.91 Unspecified ectopic pregnancy with intrauterine pregnancy — (Use additional code from category 639 to identify any associated complications) ▽ ♀

639.0 Genital tract and pelvic infection following abortion or ectopic and molar pregnancies ♀

639.1 Delayed or excessive hemorrhage following abortion or ectopic and molar pregnancies ♀

639.2 Damage to pelvic organs and tissues following abortion or ectopic and molar pregnancies ♀

639.8 Other specified complication following abortion or ectopic and molar pregnancies ♀

639.9 Unspecified complication following abortion or ectopic and molar pregnancies ▽ ♀

789.00 Abdominal pain, unspecified site ▽

789.03 Abdominal pain, right lower quadrant

789.04 Abdominal pain, left lower quadrant

V64.41 Laparoscopic surgical procedure converted to open procedure

ICD-9-CM Procedural

65.22 Wedge resection of ovary ♀

65.39 Other unilateral oophorectomy ♀

65.49 Other unilateral salpingo-oophorectomy ♀

66.01 Salpingotomy ♀

66.62 Salpingectomy with removal of tubal pregnancy ♀

59130

59130 Surgical treatment of ectopic pregnancy; abdominal pregnancy

ICD-9-CM Diagnostic

633.00 Abdominal pregnancy without intrauterine pregnancy — (Use additional code from category 639 to identify any associated complications) ♀

633.01 Abdominal pregnancy with intrauterine pregnancy — (Use additional code from category 639 to identify any associated complications) ♀

633.80 Other ectopic pregnancy without intrauterine pregnancy — (Use additional code from category 639 to identify any associated complications) ♀

633.81 Other ectopic pregnancy with intrauterine pregnancy — (Use additional code from category 639 to identify any associated complications) ♀

639.0 Genital tract and pelvic infection following abortion or ectopic and molar pregnancies ♀

639.1 Delayed or excessive hemorrhage following abortion or ectopic and molar pregnancies ♀

639.2 Damage to pelvic organs and tissues following abortion or ectopic and molar pregnancies ♀

639.8 Other specified complication following abortion or ectopic and molar pregnancies ♀

[Resequenced code] ▽ Unspecified code ☒ Manifestation code
♀ Female diagnosis ♂ Male diagnosis

639.9 Unspecified complication following abortion or ectopic and molar pregnancies ♀

ICD-9-CM Procedural

74.3 Removal of extratubal ectopic pregnancy ♀

75.99 Other obstetric operations ♀

59135-59140

59135 Surgical treatment of ectopic pregnancy; interstitial, uterine pregnancy requiring total hysterectomy

59136 interstitial, uterine pregnancy with partial resection of uterus

59140 cervical, with evacuation

ICD-9-CM Diagnostic

633.80 Other ectopic pregnancy without intrauterine pregnancy — (Use additional code from category 639 to identify any associated complications) ♀

633.81 Other ectopic pregnancy with intrauterine pregnancy — (Use additional code from category 639 to identify any associated complications) ♀

633.90 Unspecified ectopic pregnancy without intrauterine pregnancy — (Use additional code from category 639 to identify any associated complications) ♀

633.91 Unspecified ectopic pregnancy with intrauterine pregnancy — (Use additional code from category 639 to identify any associated complications) ♀

639.0 Genital tract and pelvic infection following abortion or ectopic and molar pregnancies ♀

639.1 Delayed or excessive hemorrhage following abortion or ectopic and molar pregnancies ♀

639.2 Damage to pelvic organs and tissues following abortion or ectopic and molar pregnancies ♀

639.8 Other specified complication following abortion or ectopic and molar pregnancies ♀

639.9 Unspecified complication following abortion or ectopic and molar pregnancies ♀

ICD-9-CM Procedural

68.39 Other and unspecified subtotal abdominal hysterectomy ♀

68.49 Other and unspecified total abdominal hysterectomy ♀

74.3 Removal of extratubal ectopic pregnancy ♀

59150-59151

59150 Laparoscopic treatment of ectopic pregnancy; without salpingectomy and/or oophorectomy

59151 with salpingectomy and/or oophorectomy

ICD-9-CM Diagnostic

633.00 Abdominal pregnancy without intrauterine pregnancy — (Use additional code from category 639 to identify any associated complications) ♀

633.01 Abdominal pregnancy with intrauterine pregnancy — (Use additional code from category 639 to identify any associated complications) ♀

633.10 Tubal pregnancy without intrauterine pregnancy — (Use additional code from category 639 to identify any associated complications) ♀

633.11 Tubal pregnancy with intrauterine pregnancy — (Use additional code from category 639 to identify any associated complications) ♀

633.20 Ovarian pregnancy without intrauterine pregnancy — (Use additional code from category 639 to identify any associated complications) ♀

633.21 Ovarian pregnancy with intrauterine pregnancy — (Use additional code from category 639 to identify any associated complications) ♀

633.80 Other ectopic pregnancy without intrauterine pregnancy — (Use additional code from category 639 to identify any associated complications) ♀

633.81 Other ectopic pregnancy with intrauterine pregnancy — (Use additional code from category 639 to identify any associated complications) ♀

633.90 Unspecified ectopic pregnancy without intrauterine pregnancy — (Use additional code from category 639 to identify any associated complications) ♀

633.91 Unspecified ectopic pregnancy with intrauterine pregnancy — (Use additional code from category 639 to identify any associated complications) ♀

639.0 Genital tract and pelvic infection following abortion or ectopic and molar pregnancies ♀

639.1 Delayed or excessive hemorrhage following abortion or ectopic and molar pregnancies ♀

639.2 Damage to pelvic organs and tissues following abortion or ectopic and molar pregnancies ♀

639.8 Other specified complication following abortion or ectopic and molar pregnancies ♀

639.9 Unspecified complication following abortion or ectopic and molar pregnancies ♀

789.00 Abdominal pain, unspecified site

789.03 Abdominal pain, right lower quadrant

789.04 Abdominal pain, left lower quadrant

ICD-9-CM Procedural

65.01 Laparoscopic oophorotomy ♀

65.31 Laparoscopic unilateral oophorectomy ♀

65.41 Laparoscopic unilateral salpingo-oophorectomy ♀

65.54 Laparoscopic removal of remaining ovary ♀

65.63 Laparoscopic removal of both ovaries and tubes at same operative episode ♀

65.64 Laparoscopic removal of remaining ovary and tube ♀

66.01 Salpingotomy ♀

66.4 Total unilateral salpingectomy ♀

66.62 Salpingectomy with removal of tubal pregnancy ♀

74.3 Removal of extratubal ectopic pregnancy ♀

59160

59160 Curettage, postpartum

ICD-9-CM Diagnostic

666.00 Third-stage postpartum hemorrhage, unspecified as to episode of care ♀

666.02 Third-stage postpartum hemorrhage, with delivery ♀

666.04 Third-stage postpartum hemorrhage, postpartum condition or complication ♀

666.10 Other immediate postpartum hemorrhage, unspecified as to episode of care ♀

666.12 Other immediate postpartum hemorrhage, with delivery ♀

666.14 Other immediate postpartum hemorrhage, postpartum condition or complication ♀

666.20 Delayed and secondary postpartum hemorrhage, unspecified as to episode of care ♀

666.22 Delayed and secondary postpartum hemorrhage, with delivery ♀

666.24 Delayed and secondary postpartum hemorrhage, postpartum condition or complication ♀

666.30 Postpartum coagulation defects, unspecified as to episode of care ♀

666.32 Postpartum coagulation defects, with delivery ♀

666.34 Postpartum coagulation defects, postpartum condition or complication ♀

667.00 Retained placenta without hemorrhage, unspecified as to episode of care ♀

667.02 Retained placenta without hemorrhage, with delivery, with mention of postpartum complication ♀

667.04 Retained placenta without hemorrhage, postpartum condition or complication ♀

667.10 Retained portions of placenta or membranes, without hemorrhage, unspecified as to episode of care ♀

667.12 Retained portions of placenta or membranes, without hemorrhage, delivered, with mention of postpartum complication ♀

667.14 Retained portions of placenta or membranes, without hemorrhage, postpartum condition or complication ♀

ICD-9-CM Procedural

69.02 Dilation and curettage following delivery or abortion ♀

69.52 Aspiration curettage following delivery or abortion ♀

HCPCS Level II Supplies & Services

A4305 Disposable drug delivery system, flow rate of 50 ml or greater per hour

59200

59200 Insertion of cervical dilator (eg, laminaria, prostaglandin) (separate procedure)

ICD-9-CM Diagnostic

645.11 Post term pregnancy, delivered, with or without mention of antepartum condition ♀
645.13 Post term pregnancy, antepartum condition or complication ♀
645.21 Prolonged pregnancy, delivered, with or without mention of antepartum condition ♀
645.23 Prolonged pregnancy, antepartum condition or complication ♀
656.40 Intrauterine death affecting management of mother, unspecified as to episode of care ▽ ♀
656.41 Intrauterine death affecting management of mother, delivered ♀
656.43 Intrauterine death affecting management of mother, antepartum ♀
658.10 Premature rupture of membranes in pregnancy, unspecified as to episode of care ▽ ♀
658.11 Premature rupture of membranes in pregnancy, delivered ♀
658.13 Premature rupture of membranes in pregnancy, antepartum ♀
658.20 Delayed delivery after spontaneous or unspecified rupture of membranes, unspecified as to episode of care ▽ ♀
658.21 Delayed delivery after spontaneous or unspecified rupture of membranes, delivered ♀
658.23 Delayed delivery after spontaneous or unspecified rupture of membranes, antepartum ♀
658.30 Delayed delivery after artificial rupture of membranes, unspecified as to episode of care ▽ ♀
658.31 Delayed delivery after artificial rupture of membranes, delivered ♀
658.33 Delayed delivery after artificial rupture of membranes, antepartum ♀
658.90 Unspecified problem associated with amniotic cavity and membranes, unspecified as to episode of care ▽ ♀
658.91 Unspecified problem associated with amniotic cavity and membranes, delivered ▽ ♀
658.93 Unspecified problem associated with amniotic cavity and membranes, antepartum ▽ ♀
659.10 Failed medical or unspecified induction of labor, unspecified as to episode of care ▽ ♀
659.11 Failed medical or unspecified induction of labor, delivered ♀
659.13 Failed medical or unspecified induction of labor, antepartum ♀
661.00 Primary uterine inertia, unspecified as to episode of care ▽ ♀
661.01 Primary uterine inertia, with delivery ♀
661.03 Primary uterine inertia, antepartum ♀
661.10 Secondary uterine inertia, unspecified as to episode of care ▽ ♀
661.13 Secondary uterine inertia, antepartum ♀
661.20 Other and unspecified uterine inertia, unspecified as to episode of care ▽ ♀
661.23 Other and unspecified uterine inertia, antepartum ▽ ♀
661.40 Hypertonic, incoordinate, or prolonged uterine contractions, unspecified as to episode of care ▽ ♀
661.41 Hypertonic, incoordinate, or prolonged uterine contractions, with delivery ♀
661.43 Hypertonic, incoordinate, or prolonged uterine contractions, antepartum ♀
661.90 Unspecified abnormality of labor, unspecified as to episode of care ▽ ♀
661.91 Unspecified abnormality of labor, with delivery ▽ ♀
661.93 Unspecified abnormality of labor, antepartum ▽ ♀
662.00 Prolonged first stage of labor, unspecified as to episode of care ▽ ♀
662.03 Prolonged first stage of labor, antepartum ♀

ICD-9-CM Procedural

69.93 Insertion of laminaria ♀
73.1 Other surgical induction of labor ♀

HCPCS Level II Supplies & Services

A4649 Surgical supply; miscellaneous

59300

59300 Episiotomy or vaginal repair, by other than attending

ICD-9-CM Diagnostic

664.01 First-degree perineal laceration, with delivery ♀
664.04 First-degree perineal laceration, postpartum condition or complication ♀
664.11 Second-degree perineal laceration, with delivery ♀
664.14 Second-degree perineal laceration, postpartum condition or complication ♀
664.21 Third-degree perineal laceration, with delivery ♀
664.24 Third-degree perineal laceration, postpartum condition or complication ♀
664.31 Fourth-degree perineal laceration, with delivery ♀
664.34 Fourth-degree perineal laceration, postpartum condition or complication ♀
664.41 Unspecified perineal laceration, with delivery ▽ ♀
664.44 Unspecified perineal laceration, postpartum condition or complication ▽ ♀
665.41 High vaginal laceration, with delivery ♀
665.44 High vaginal laceration, postpartum condition or complication ♀

ICD-9-CM Procedural

73.6 Episiotomy ♀
75.69 Repair of other current obstetric laceration ♀

59320-59325

59320 Cerclage of cervix, during pregnancy; vaginal
59325 abdominal

ICD-9-CM Diagnostic

622.3 Old laceration of cervix ♀
654.50 Cervical incompetence, unspecified as to episode of care in pregnancy — (Code first any associated obstructed labor, 660.2) ▽ ♀
654.53 Cervical incompetence, antepartum condition or complication — (Code first any associated obstructed labor, 660.2) ♀
654.60 Other congenital or acquired abnormality of cervix, unspecified as to episode of care in pregnancy — (Code first any associated obstructed labor, 660.2) ▽ ♀
654.63 Other congenital or acquired abnormality of cervix, antepartum condition or complication — (Code first any associated obstructed labor, 660.2) ♀
654.90 Other and unspecified abnormality of organs and soft tissues of pelvis, unspecified as to episode of care in pregnancy — (Code first any associated obstructed labor, 660.2) ▽ ♀
654.93 Other and unspecified abnormality of organs and soft tissues of pelvis, antepartum condition or complication — (Code first any associated obstructed labor, 660.2) ▽ ♀
V23.2 Pregnancy with history of abortion ♀
V23.81 Supervision of high-risk pregnancy of elderly primigravida ♀
V23.82 Supervision of high-risk pregnancy of elderly multigravida ♀
V23.83 Supervision of high-risk pregnancy of young primigravida ♀
V23.84 Supervision of high-risk pregnancy of young multigravida ♀
V23.89 Supervision of other high-risk pregnancy ♀

ICD-9-CM Procedural

67.51 Transabdominal cerclage of cervix ♀
67.59 Other repair of cervical os ♀

HCPCS Level II Supplies & Services

A4305 Disposable drug delivery system, flow rate of 50 ml or greater per hour

59350

59350 Hysterorrhaphy of ruptured uterus

ICD-9-CM Diagnostic

654.20 Previous cesarean delivery, unspecified as to episode of care or not applicable — (Code first any associated obstructed labor, 660.2) ▽ ♀
654.21 Previous cesarean delivery, delivered, with or without mention of antepartum condition — (Code first any associated obstructed labor, 660.2) ♀

654.23 Previous cesarean delivery, antepartum condition or complication — (Code first any associated obstructed labor, 660.2) ♀
665.00 Rupture of uterus before onset of labor, unspecified as to episode of care ▽ ♀
665.01 Rupture of uterus before onset of labor, with delivery ♀
665.03 Rupture of uterus before onset of labor, antepartum ♀
665.10 Rupture of uterus during labor, unspecified as to episode ▽ ♀
665.11 Rupture of uterus during labor, with delivery ♀

ICD-9-CM Procedural

69.41 Suture of laceration of uterus ♀
75.50 Repair of current obstetric laceration of uterus, not otherwise specified ♀
75.52 Repair of current obstetric laceration of corpus uteri ♀

59400-59410

59400 Routine obstetric care including antepartum care, vaginal delivery (with or without episiotomy, and/or forceps) and postpartum care
59409 Vaginal delivery only (with or without episiotomy and/or forceps);
59410 including postpartum care

ICD-9-CM Diagnostic

640.01 Threatened abortion, delivered ♀
641.01 Placenta previa without hemorrhage, with delivery ♀
641.11 Hemorrhage from placenta previa, with delivery ♀
641.21 Premature separation of placenta, with delivery ♀
641.31 Antepartum hemorrhage associated with coagulation defects, with delivery ♀
641.81 Other antepartum hemorrhage, with delivery ♀
641.91 Unspecified antepartum hemorrhage, with delivery ▽ ♀
642.01 Benign essential hypertension with delivery ♀
642.11 Hypertension secondary to renal disease, with delivery ♀
642.21 Other pre-existing hypertension, with delivery ♀
642.31 Transient hypertension of pregnancy, with delivery ♀
642.41 Mild or unspecified pre-eclampsia, with delivery ♀
642.51 Severe pre-eclampsia, with delivery ♀
642.61 Eclampsia, with delivery ♀
642.71 Pre-eclampsia or eclampsia superimposed on pre-existing hypertension, with delivery ♀
642.91 Unspecified hypertension, with delivery ▽ ♀
643.01 Mild hyperemesis gravidarum, delivered ♀
643.11 Hyperemesis gravidarum with metabolic disturbance, delivered ♀
643.21 Late vomiting of pregnancy, delivered ♀
643.81 Other vomiting complicating pregnancy, delivered — (Use additional code to specify cause) ♀
644.21 Early onset of delivery, delivered, with or without mention of antepartum condition ♀
645.11 Post term pregnancy, delivered, with or without mention of antepartum condition ♀
645.21 Prolonged pregnancy, delivered, with or without mention of antepartum condition ♀
646.01 Papyraceous fetus, delivered, with or without mention of antepartum condition — (Use additional code to further specify complication) ♀
646.11 Edema or excessive weight gain in pregnancy, with delivery, with or without mention of antepartum complication — (Use additional code to further specify complication) ♀
646.21 Unspecified renal disease in pregnancy, with delivery — (Use additional code to further specify complication) ▽ ♀
646.31 Pregnancy complication, recurrent pregnancy loss, with or without mention of antepartum condition — (Use additional code to further specify complication) ♀
646.41 Peripheral neuritis in pregnancy, with delivery — (Use additional code to further specify complication) ♀
646.51 Asymptomatic bacteriuria in pregnancy, with delivery — (Use additional code to further specify complication) ♀
646.61 Infections of genitourinary tract in pregnancy, with delivery — (Use additional code to further specify complication) ♀
646.71 Liver and biliary tract disorders in pregnancy, delivered, with or without mention of antepartum condition — (Use additional code to further specify complication) ♀
646.81 Other specified complication of pregnancy, with delivery — (Use additional code to further specify complication) ♀
646.91 Unspecified complication of pregnancy, with delivery — (Use additional code to further specify complication) ▽ ♀
647.01 Maternal syphilis, complicating pregnancy, with delivery — (Use additional code to further specify complication) ♀
647.11 Maternal gonorrhea with delivery — (Use additional code to further specify complication) ♀
647.21 Other maternal venereal diseases with delivery — (Use additional code to further specify complication) ♀
647.31 Maternal tuberculosis with delivery — (Use additional code to further specify complication) ♀
647.41 Maternal malaria with delivery — (Use additional code to further specify complication) ♀
647.51 Maternal rubella with delivery — (Use additional code to further specify complication) ♀
647.61 Other maternal viral disease with delivery — (Use additional code to further specify complication) ♀
647.81 Other specified maternal infectious and parasitic disease with delivery — (Use additional code to further specify complication) ♀
647.91 Unspecified maternal infection or infestation with delivery — (Use additional code to further specify complication) ▽ ♀
648.01 Maternal diabetes mellitus with delivery — (Use additional code(s) to identify the condition) ♀
648.11 Maternal thyroid dysfunction with delivery, with or without mention of antepartum condition — (Use additional code(s) to identify the condition) ♀
648.21 Maternal anemia, with delivery — (Use additional code(s) to identify the condition) ♀
648.31 Maternal drug dependence, with delivery — (Use additional code(s) to identify the condition) ♀
648.41 Maternal mental disorders, with delivery — (Use additional code(s) to identify the condition) ♀
648.51 Maternal congenital cardiovascular disorders, with delivery — (Use additional code(s) to identify the condition) ♀
648.61 Other maternal cardiovascular diseases, with delivery — (Use additional code(s) to identify the condition) ♀
648.71 Bone and joint disorders of maternal back, pelvis, and lower limbs, with delivery — (Use additional code(s) to identify the condition) ♀
648.81 Abnormal maternal glucose tolerance, with delivery — (Use additional code(s) to identify the condition. Use additional code, if applicable, for associated long-term (current) insulin use: V58.67) ♀
648.91 Other current maternal conditions classifiable elsewhere, with delivery — (Use additional code(s) to identify the condition) ♀
649.01 Tobacco use disorder complicating pregnancy, childbirth, or the puerperium, delivered, with or without mention of antepartum condition ♀
649.11 Obesity complicating pregnancy, childbirth, or the puerperium, delivered, with or without mention of antepartum condition — (Use additional code to identify the obesity: 278.00-278.01) ♀
649.21 Bariatric surgery status complicating pregnancy, childbirth, or the puerperium, delivered, with or without mention of antepartum condition ♀
649.31 Coagulation defects complicating pregnancy, childbirth, or the puerperium, delivered, with or without mention of antepartum condition — (Use additional code to identify the specific coagulation defect: 286.0-286.9, 287.0-287.9, 289.0-289.9) ♀
649.41 Epilepsy complicating pregnancy, childbirth, or the puerperium, delivered, with or without mention of antepartum condition — (Use additional code to identify the specific type of epilepsy: 345.00-345.91) ♀
649.51 Spotting complicating pregnancy, delivered, with or without mention of antepartum condition ♀
649.61 Uterine size date discrepancy, delivered, with or without mention of antepartum condition ♀

649.71 Cervical shortening, delivered, with or without mention of antepartum condition ♀

650 Normal delivery — (This code is for use as a single diagnosis code and is not to be used with any other code in the range 630-676. Use additional code to indicate outcome of delivery: V27.0.) ♀

651.01 Twin pregnancy, delivered ♀

651.11 Triplet pregnancy, delivered ♀

651.21 Quadruplet pregnancy, delivered ♀

651.31 Twin pregnancy with fetal loss and retention of one fetus, delivered ♀

651.41 Triplet pregnancy with fetal loss and retention of one or more, delivered ♀

651.51 Quadruplet pregnancy with fetal loss and retention of one or more, delivered ♀

651.61 Other multiple pregnancy with fetal loss and retention of one or more fetus(es), delivered ♀

651.71 Multiple gestation following (elective) fetal reduction, delivered, with or without mention of antepartum condition ♀

651.81 Other specified multiple gestation, delivered ♀

651.91 Unspecified multiple gestation, delivered ▼ ♀

652.11 Breech or other malpresentation successfully converted to cephalic presentation, delivered — (Code first any associated obstructed labor, 660.0) ♀

652.21 Breech presentation without mention of version, delivered — (Code first any associated obstructed labor, 660.0) ♀

652.41 Fetal face or brow presentation, delivered — (Code first any associated obstructed labor: 660.0) ♀

652.71 Prolapsed arm of fetus, delivered — (Code first any associated obstructed labor: 660.0) ♀

652.81 Other specified malposition or malpresentation of fetus, delivered — (Code first any associated obstructed labor: 660.0) ♀

652.91 Unspecified malposition or malpresentation of fetus, delivered — (Code first any associated obstructed labor: 660.0) ▼ ♀

654.01 Congenital abnormalities of pregnant uterus, delivered — (Code first any associated obstructed labor: 660.2) ♀

654.11 Tumors of body of uterus, delivered — (Code first any associated obstructed labor, 660.2) ♀

654.31 Retroverted and incarcerated gravid uterus, delivered — (Code first any associated obstructed labor, 660.2) ♀

654.41 Other abnormalities in shape or position of gravid uterus and of neighboring structures, delivered — (Code first any associated obstructed labor: 660.2) ♀

654.51 Cervical incompetence, delivered — (Code first any associated obstructed labor: 660.2) ♀

654.61 Other congenital or acquired abnormality of cervix, with delivery — (Code first any associated obstructed labor: 660.2) ♀

654.71 Congenital or acquired abnormality of vagina, with delivery — (Code first any associated obstructed labor: 660.2) ♀

654.81 Congenital or acquired abnormality of vulva, with delivery — (Code first any associated obstructed labor, 660.2) ♀

654.91 Other and unspecified abnormality of organs and soft tissues of pelvis, with delivery — (Code first any associated obstructed labor: 660.2) ▼ ♀

655.01 Central nervous system malformation in fetus, with delivery ♀

655.11 Chromosomal abnormality in fetus, affecting management of mother, with delivery ♀

655.21 Hereditary disease in family possibly affecting fetus, affecting management of mother, with delivery ♀

655.31 Suspected damage to fetus from viral disease in mother, affecting management of mother, with delivery ♀

655.41 Suspected damage to fetus from other disease in mother, affecting management of mother, with delivery ♀

655.81 Other known or suspected fetal abnormality, not elsewhere classified, affecting management of mother, delivery ♀

655.91 Unspecified fetal abnormality affecting management of mother, delivery ▼ ♀

656.01 Fetal-maternal hemorrhage, with delivery ♀

656.11 Rhesus isoimmunization affecting management of mother, delivered ♀

656.21 Isoimmunization from other and unspecified blood-group incompatibility, affecting management of mother, delivered ♀

656.31 Fetal distress affecting management of mother, delivered ♀

656.41 Intrauterine death affecting management of mother, delivered ♀

656.51 Poor fetal growth, affecting management of mother, delivered ♀

656.61 Excessive fetal growth affecting management of mother, delivered ♀

656.71 Other placental conditions affecting management of mother, delivered ♀

656.81 Other specified fetal and placental problems affecting management of mother, delivered ♀

656.91 Unspecified fetal and placental problem affecting management of mother, delivered ▼ ♀

657.01 Polyhydramnios, with delivery ♀

658.01 Oligohydramnios, delivered ♀

658.11 Premature rupture of membranes in pregnancy, delivered ♀

658.21 Delayed delivery after spontaneous or unspecified rupture of membranes, delivered ♀

658.31 Delayed delivery after artificial rupture of membranes, delivered ♀

658.41 Infection of amniotic cavity, delivered ♀

658.81 Other problem associated with amniotic cavity and membranes, delivered ♀

658.91 Unspecified problem associated with amniotic cavity and membranes, delivered ▼ ♀

659.21 Unspecified maternal pyrexia during labor, delivered ▼ ♀

659.31 Generalized infection during labor, delivered ♀

659.41 Grand multiparity, delivered, with or without mention of antepartum condition ♀

659.51 Elderly primigravida, delivered ♀

659.61 Elderly multigravida, delivered, with mention of antepartum condition ♀

659.81 Other specified indication for care or intervention related to labor and delivery, delivered ♀

659.91 Unspecified indication for care or intervention related to labor and delivery, delivered ▼ ♀

660.81 Other causes of obstructed labor, delivered — (Use additional code to identify condition) ♀

661.31 Precipitate labor, with delivery ♀

662.01 Prolonged first stage of labor, delivered ♀

662.21 Prolonged second stage of labor, delivered ♀

662.31 Delayed delivery of second twin, triplet, etc., delivered ♀

663.11 Cord around neck, with compression, complicating labor and delivery, delivered ♀

663.31 Other and unspecified cord entanglement, without mention of compression, complicating labor and delivery, delivered ▼ ♀

663.41 Short cord complicating labor and delivery, delivered ♀

663.61 Vascular lesions of cord complicating labor and delivery, delivered ♀

663.81 Other umbilical cord complications during labor and delivery, delivered ♀

663.91 Unspecified umbilical cord complication during labor and delivery, delivered ▼ ♀

664.01 First-degree perineal laceration, with delivery ♀

664.11 Second-degree perineal laceration, with delivery ♀

664.21 Third-degree perineal laceration, with delivery ♀

664.31 Fourth-degree perineal laceration, with delivery ♀

664.41 Unspecified perineal laceration, with delivery ▼ ♀

664.51 Vulvar and perineal hematoma, with delivery ♀

664.61 Anal sphincter tear complicating delivery, not associated with third-degree perineal laceration, delivered, with or without mention of antepartum condition ♀

664.80 Other specified trauma to perineum and vulva, unspecified as to episode of care in pregnancy ▼ ♀

664.81 Other specified trauma to perineum and vulva, with delivery ♀

664.91 Unspecified trauma to perineum and vulva, with delivery ▼ ♀

665.31 Laceration of cervix, with delivery ♀

665.41 High vaginal laceration, with delivery ♀

665.51 Other injury to pelvic organs, with delivery ♀

665.61 Damage to pelvic joints and ligaments, with delivery ♀

665.71 Pelvic hematoma, with delivery ♀

665.81 Other specified obstetrical trauma, with delivery ♀

665.91 Unspecified obstetrical trauma, with delivery ▽ ♀

666.02 Third-stage postpartum hemorrhage, with delivery ♀

666.12 Other immediate postpartum hemorrhage, with delivery ♀

666.22 Delayed and secondary postpartum hemorrhage, with delivery ♀

667.02 Retained placenta without hemorrhage, with delivery, with mention of postpartum complication ♀

668.01 Pulmonary complications of the administration of anesthesia or other sedation in labor and delivery, delivered — (Use additional code(s) to further specify complication) ♀

668.11 Cardiac complications of the administration of anesthesia or other sedation in labor and delivery, delivered — (Use additional code(s) to further specify complication) ♀

668.21 Central nervous system complications of the administration of anesthesia or other sedation in labor and delivery, delivered — (Use additional code(s) to further specify complication) ♀

668.81 Other complications of the administration of anesthesia or other sedation in labor and delivery, delivered — (Use additional code(s) to further specify complication) ♀

668.91 Unspecified complication of the administration of anesthesia or other sedation in labor and delivery, delivered — (Use additional code(s) to further specify complication) ▽ ♀

669.01 Maternal distress, with delivery, with or without mention of antepartum condition ♀

669.11 Shock during or following labor and delivery, with delivery, with or without mention of antepartum condition ♀

669.21 Maternal hypotension syndrome, with delivery, with or without mention of antepartum condition ♀

669.51 Forceps or vacuum extractor delivery without mention of indication, delivered, with or without mention of antepartum condition ♀

669.81 Other complication of labor and delivery, delivered, with or without mention of antepartum condition ♀

671.01 Varicose veins of legs, with delivery, with or without mention of antepartum condition ♀

671.81 Other venous complication, with delivery, with or without mention of antepartum condition ♀

671.82 Other venous complication, with delivery, with mention of postpartum complication ♀

676.01 Retracted nipple, delivered, with or without mention of antepartum condition ♀

676.02 Retracted nipple, delivered, with mention of postpartum complication ♀

676.21 Engorgement of breasts, delivered, with or without mention of antepartum condition ♀

676.22 Engorgement of breasts, delivered, with mention of postpartum complication ♀

676.31 Other and unspecified disorder of breast associated with childbirth, delivered, with or without mention of antepartum condition ▽ ♀

676.32 Other and unspecified disorder of breast associated with childbirth, delivered, with mention of postpartum complication ▽ ♀

676.41 Failure of lactation, with delivery, with or without mention of antepartum condition ♀

676.42 Failure of lactation, with delivery, with mention of postpartum complication ♀

676.51 Suppressed lactation, with delivery, with or without mention of antepartum condition ♀

676.52 Suppressed lactation, with delivery, with mention of postpartum complication ♀

676.91 Unspecified disorder of lactation, with delivery, with or without mention of antepartum condition ▽ ♀

676.92 Unspecified disorder of lactation, with delivery, with mention of postpartum complication ▽ ♀

678.01 Fetal hematologic conditions, delivered, with or without mention of antepartum condition ♀

678.11 Fetal conjoined twins, delivered, with or without mention of antepartum condition ♀

679.01 Maternal complications from in utero procedure, delivered, with or without mention of antepartum condition ♀

679.02 Maternal complications from in utero procedure, delivered, with mention of postpartum complication ♀

ICD-9-CM Procedural

72.0 Low forceps operation ♀

72.1 Low forceps operation with episiotomy ♀

72.21 Mid forceps operation with episiotomy ♀

72.29 Other mid forceps operation ♀

72.31 High forceps operation with episiotomy ♀

72.39 Other high forceps operation ♀

72.4 Forceps rotation of fetal head ♀

72.51 Partial breech extraction with forceps to aftercoming head ♀

72.52 Other partial breech extraction ♀

72.53 Total breech extraction with forceps to aftercoming head ♀

72.54 Other total breech extraction ♀

72.6 Forceps application to aftercoming head ♀

72.71 Vacuum extraction with episiotomy ♀

72.79 Other vacuum extraction ♀

72.8 Other specified instrumental delivery ♀

72.9 Unspecified instrumental delivery ♀

73.01 Induction of labor by artificial rupture of membranes ♀

73.09 Other artificial rupture of membranes ♀

73.4 Medical induction of labor ♀

73.59 Other manually assisted delivery ♀

73.6 Episiotomy ♀

59412

59412 External cephalic version, with or without tocolysis

ICD-9-CM Diagnostic

652.10 Breech or other malpresentation successfully converted to cephalic presentation, unspecified as to episode of care — (Code first any associated obstructed labor, 660.0) ▽ ♀

652.11 Breech or other malpresentation successfully converted to cephalic presentation, delivered — (Code first any associated obstructed labor, 660.0) ♀

652.13 Breech or other malpresentation successfully converted to cephalic presentation, antepartum — (Code first any associated obstructed labor, 660.0) ♀

652.21 Breech presentation without mention of version, delivered — (Code first any associated obstructed labor, 660.0) ♀

652.23 Breech presentation without mention of version, antepartum — (Code first any associated obstructed labor, 660.0) ♀

ICD-9-CM Procedural

72.51 Partial breech extraction with forceps to aftercoming head ♀

73.21 Internal and combined version without extraction ♀

73.22 Internal and combined version with extraction ♀

73.51 Manual rotation of fetal head ♀

73.59 Other manually assisted delivery ♀

73.6 Episiotomy ♀

73.91 External version to assist delivery ♀

59414

59414 Delivery of placenta (separate procedure)

ICD-9-CM Diagnostic

666.02 Third-stage postpartum hemorrhage, with delivery ♀

666.04 Third-stage postpartum hemorrhage, postpartum condition or complication ♀

666.22 Delayed and secondary postpartum hemorrhage, with delivery ♀

666.24 Delayed and secondary postpartum hemorrhage, postpartum condition or complication ♀

667.02 Retained placenta without hemorrhage, with delivery, with mention of postpartum complication ♀

667.04 Retained placenta without hemorrhage, postpartum condition or complication ♀

667.12 Retained portions of placenta or membranes, without hemorrhage, delivered, with mention of postpartum complication ♀

667.14 Retained portions of placenta or membranes, without hemorrhage, postpartum condition or complication ♀

V27.0 Outcome of delivery, single liveborn — (This code is intended for the coding of the outcome of delivery on the mother's record) ♀

V27.1 Outcome of delivery, single stillborn — (This code is intended for the coding of the outcome of delivery on the mother's record) ♀

V27.2 Outcome of delivery, twins, both liveborn — (This code is intended for the coding of the outcome of delivery on the mother's record) ♀

V27.3 Outcome of delivery, twins, one liveborn and one stillborn — (This code is intended for the coding of the outcome of delivery on the mother's record) ♀

V27.4 Outcome of delivery, twins, both stillborn — (This code is intended for the coding of the outcome of delivery on the mother's record) ♀

ICD-9-CM Procedural

73.59 Other manually assisted delivery ♀

75.4 Manual removal of retained placenta ♀

59425-59426

59425 Antepartum care only; 4-6 visits

59426 7 or more visits

ICD-9-CM Diagnostic

632 Missed abortion — (Use additional code from category 639 to identify any associated complications) ♀

634.00 Unspecified spontaneous abortion complicated by genital tract and pelvic infection ▽ ♀

634.01 Incomplete spontaneous abortion complicated by genital tract and pelvic infection ♀

634.02 Complete spontaneous abortion complicated by genital tract and pelvic infection ♀

634.10 Unspecified spontaneous abortion complicated by delayed or excessive hemorrhage ▽ ♀

634.11 Incomplete spontaneous abortion complicated by delayed or excessive hemorrhage ♀

634.12 Complete spontaneous abortion complicated by delayed or excessive hemorrhage ♀

634.20 Unspecified spontaneous abortion complicated by damage to pelvic organs or tissues ▽ ♀

634.21 Incomplete spontaneous abortion complicated by damage to pelvic organs or tissues ♀

634.22 Complete spontaneous abortion complicated by damage to pelvic organs or tissues ♀

634.30 Unspecified spontaneous abortion complicated by renal failure ▽ ♀

634.31 Incomplete spontaneous abortion complicated by renal failure ♀

634.32 Complete spontaneous abortion complicated by renal failure ♀

634.40 Unspecified spontaneous abortion complicated by metabolic disorder ▽ ♀

634.41 Incomplete spontaneous abortion complicated by metabolic disorder ♀

634.42 Complete spontaneous abortion complicated by metabolic disorder ♀

634.50 Unspecified spontaneous abortion complicated by shock ▽ ♀

634.51 Incomplete spontaneous abortion complicated by shock ♀

634.52 Complete spontaneous abortion complicated by shock ♀

634.60 Unspecified spontaneous abortion complicated by embolism ▽ ♀

634.61 Incomplete spontaneous abortion complicated by embolism ♀

634.62 Complete spontaneous abortion complicated by embolism ♀

634.70 Unspecified spontaneous abortion with other specified complications ▽ ♀

634.71 Incomplete spontaneous abortion with other specified complications ♀

634.72 Complete spontaneous abortion with other specified complications ♀

634.80 Unspecified spontaneous abortion with unspecified complication ▽ ♀

634.81 Incomplete spontaneous abortion with unspecified complication ▽ ♀

634.82 Complete spontaneous abortion with unspecified complication ▽ ♀

634.90 Unspecified spontaneous abortion without mention of complication ▽ ♀

634.91 Incomplete spontaneous abortion without mention of complication ♀

634.92 Complete spontaneous abortion without mention of complication ♀

635.00 Unspecified legally induced abortion complicated by genital tract and pelvic infection ▽ ♀

635.01 Incomplete legally induced abortion complicated by genital tract and pelvic infection ♀

635.02 Complete legally induced abortion complicated by genital tract and pelvic infection ♀

635.10 Unspecified legally induced abortion complicated by delayed or excessive hemorrhage ▽ ♀

635.11 Incomplete legally induced abortion complicated by delayed or excessive hemorrhage ♀

635.12 Complete legally induced abortion complicated by delayed or excessive hemorrhage ♀

635.20 Unspecified legally induced abortion complicated by damage to pelvic organs or tissues ▽ ♀

635.21 Legally induced abortion complicated by damage to pelvic organs or tissues, incomplete ♀

635.22 Complete legally induced abortion complicated by damage to pelvic organs or tissues ♀

635.30 Unspecified legally induced abortion complicated by renal failure ▽ ♀

635.31 Incomplete legally induced abortion complicated by renal failure ♀

635.32 Complete legally induced abortion complicated by renal failure ♀

635.40 Unspecified legally induced abortion complicated by metabolic disorder ▽ ♀

635.41 Incomplete legally induced abortion complicated by metabolic disorder ♀

635.42 Complete legally induced abortion complicated by metabolic disorder ♀

635.50 Unspecified legally induced abortion complicated by shock ▽ ♀

635.51 Legally induced abortion, complicated by shock, incomplete ♀

635.52 Complete legally induced abortion complicated by shock ♀

635.60 Unspecified legally induced abortion complicated by embolism ▽ ♀

635.61 Incomplete legally induced abortion complicated by embolism ♀

635.62 Complete legally induced abortion complicated by embolism ♀

635.70 Unspecified legally induced abortion with other specified complications ▽ ♀

635.71 Incomplete legally induced abortion with other specified complications ♀

635.72 Complete legally induced abortion with other specified complications ♀

635.80 Unspecified legally induced abortion with unspecified complication ▽ ♀

635.81 Incomplete legally induced abortion with unspecified complication ▽ ♀

635.82 Complete legally induced abortion with unspecified complication ▽ ♀

635.90 Unspecified legally induced abortion without mention of complication ▽ ♀

635.91 Incomplete legally induced abortion without mention of complication ♀

635.92 Complete legally induced abortion without mention of complication ♀

642.03 Benign essential hypertension antepartum ♀

642.13 Hypertension secondary to renal disease, antepartum ♀

642.23 Other pre-existing hypertension, antepartum ♀

642.33 Transient hypertension of pregnancy, antepartum ♀

642.43 Mild or unspecified pre-eclampsia, antepartum ♀

642.53 Severe pre-eclampsia, antepartum ♀

642.63 Eclampsia, antepartum ♀

642.73 Pre-eclampsia or eclampsia superimposed on pre-existing hypertension, antepartum ♀

642.93 Unspecified hypertension antepartum ▽ ♀

643.03 Mild hyperemesis gravidarum, antepartum ♀

643.13 Hyperemesis gravidarum with metabolic disturbance, antepartum ♀

643.23 Late vomiting of pregnancy, antepartum ♀

643.83 Other vomiting complicating pregnancy, antepartum — (Use additional code to specify cause) ♀

643.93 Unspecified vomiting of pregnancy, antepartum ▽ ♀

646.53 Asymptomatic bacteriuria antepartum — (Use additional code to further specify complication) ♀

648.13 Maternal thyroid dysfunction, antepartum condition or complication — (Use additional code(s) to identify the condition) ♀

648.83 Abnormal maternal glucose tolerance, antepartum — (Use additional code(s) to identify the condition. Use additional code, if applicable, for associated long-term (current) insulin use: V58.67) ♀

649.73 Cervical shortening, antepartum condition or complication ♀
652.23 Breech presentation without mention of version, antepartum — (Code first any associated obstructed labor, 660.0) ♀
654.13 Tumors of body of uterus, antepartum condition or complication — (Code first any associated obstructed labor: 660.2) ♀
654.43 Other abnormalities in shape or position of gravid uterus and of neighboring structures, antepartum — (Code first any associated obstructed labor: 660.2) ♀
654.53 Cervical incompetence, antepartum condition or complication — (Code first any associated obstructed labor, 660.2) ♀
654.73 Congenital or acquired abnormality of vagina, antepartum condition or complication — (Code first any associated obstructed labor: 660.2) ♀
654.83 Congenital or acquired abnormality of vulva, antepartum condition or complication — (Code first any associated obstructed labor: 660.2) ♀
654.93 Other and unspecified abnormality of organs and soft tissues of pelvis, antepartum condition or complication — (Code first any associated obstructed labor, 660.2) ▽ ♀
655.13 Chromosomal abnormality in fetus, affecting management of mother, antepartum ♀
655.23 Hereditary disease in family possibly affecting fetus, affecting management of mother, antepartum condition or complication ♀
655.33 Suspected damage to fetus from viral disease in mother, affecting management of mother, antepartum condition or complication ♀
655.43 Suspected damage to fetus from other disease in mother, affecting management of mother, antepartum condition or complication ♀
655.63 Suspected damage to fetus from radiation, affecting management of mother, antepartum condition or complication ♀
655.83 Other known or suspected fetal abnormality, not elsewhere classified, affecting management of mother, antepartum condition or complication ♀
655.93 Unspecified fetal abnormality affecting management of mother, antepartum condition or complication ▽ ♀
656.43 Intrauterine death affecting management of mother, antepartum ♀
656.53 Poor fetal growth, affecting management of mother, antepartum condition or complication ♀
656.63 Excessive fetal growth affecting management of mother, antepartum ♀
657.03 Polyhydramnios, antepartum complication ♀
658.03 Oligohydramnios, antepartum ♀
658.13 Premature rupture of membranes in pregnancy, antepartum ♀
659.43 Grand multiparity with current pregnancy, antepartum ♀
659.53 Elderly primigravida, antepartum ♀
659.63 Elderly multigravida, with antepartum condition or complication ♀
669.23 Maternal hypotension syndrome, antepartum ♀
671.03 Varicose veins of legs, antepartum ♀
671.83 Other venous complication, antepartum ♀
676.03 Retracted nipple, antepartum condition or complication ♀
676.23 Engorgement of breast, antepartum ♀
676.33 Other and unspecified disorder of breast associated with childbirth, antepartum condition or complication ▽ ♀
V22.0 Supervision of normal first pregnancy ♀
V22.1 Supervision of other normal pregnancy ♀
V23.81 Supervision of high-risk pregnancy of elderly primigravida ♀
V23.82 Supervision of high-risk pregnancy of elderly multigravida ♀
V23.83 Supervision of high-risk pregnancy of young primigravida ♀
V23.84 Supervision of high-risk pregnancy of young multigravida ♀
V23.89 Supervision of other high-risk pregnancy ♀

ICD-9-CM Procedural

89.04 Other interview and evaluation
89.26 Gynecological examination ♀

HCPCS Level II Supplies & Services

A4649 Surgical supply; miscellaneous

59430

59430 Postpartum care only (separate procedure)

ICD-9-CM Diagnostic

V24.0 Postpartum care and examination immediately after delivery ♀
V24.1 Postpartum care and examination of lactating mother ♀
V24.2 Routine postpartum follow-up ♀
V72.31 Routine gynecological examination — (Use additional code(s) to identify any special screening examination(s) performed: V73.0-V82.9) ♀

ICD-9-CM Procedural

89.04 Other interview and evaluation
89.26 Gynecological examination ♀

HCPCS Level II Supplies & Services

A4649 Surgical supply; miscellaneous

59510-59515

59510 Routine obstetric care including antepartum care, cesarean delivery, and postpartum care
59514 Cesarean delivery only;
59515 including postpartum care

ICD-9-CM Diagnostic

640.01 Threatened abortion, delivered ♀
640.91 Unspecified hemorrhage in early pregnancy, delivered ▽ ♀
641.01 Placenta previa without hemorrhage, with delivery ♀
641.11 Hemorrhage from placenta previa, with delivery ♀
641.21 Premature separation of placenta, with delivery ♀
641.31 Antepartum hemorrhage associated with coagulation defects, with delivery ♀
641.81 Other antepartum hemorrhage, with delivery ♀
641.91 Unspecified antepartum hemorrhage, with delivery ▽ ♀
642.01 Benign essential hypertension with delivery ♀
642.11 Hypertension secondary to renal disease, with delivery ♀
642.21 Other pre-existing hypertension, with delivery ♀
642.31 Transient hypertension of pregnancy, with delivery ♀
642.41 Mild or unspecified pre-eclampsia, with delivery ♀
642.51 Severe pre-eclampsia, with delivery ♀
642.61 Eclampsia, with delivery ♀
642.71 Pre-eclampsia or eclampsia superimposed on pre-existing hypertension, with delivery ♀
642.91 Unspecified hypertension, with delivery ▽ ♀
643.01 Mild hyperemesis gravidarum, delivered ♀
643.11 Hyperemesis gravidarum with metabolic disturbance, delivered ♀
643.21 Late vomiting of pregnancy, delivered ♀
643.81 Other vomiting complicating pregnancy, delivered — (Use additional code to specify cause) ♀
643.91 Unspecified vomiting of pregnancy, delivered ▽ ♀
644.21 Early onset of delivery, delivered, with or without mention of antepartum condition ♀
645.11 Post term pregnancy, delivered, with or without mention of antepartum condition ♀
645.21 Prolonged pregnancy, delivered, with or without mention of antepartum condition ♀
646.01 Papyraceous fetus, delivered, with or without mention of antepartum condition — (Use additional code to further specify complication) ♀
646.11 Edema or excessive weight gain in pregnancy, with delivery, with or without mention of antepartum complication — (Use additional code to further specify complication) ♀
646.21 Unspecified renal disease in pregnancy, with delivery — (Use additional code to further specify complication) ▽ ♀
646.23 Unspecified antepartum renal disease — (Use additional code to further specify complication) ▽ ♀

646.41 Peripheral neuritis in pregnancy, with delivery — (Use additional code to further specify complication) ♀

646.51 Asymptomatic bacteriuria in pregnancy, with delivery — (Use additional code to further specify complication) ♀

646.61 Infections of genitourinary tract in pregnancy, with delivery — (Use additional code to further specify complication) ♀

646.71 Liver and biliary tract disorders in pregnancy, delivered, with or without mention of antepartum condition — (Use additional code to further specify complication) ♀

646.81 Other specified complication of pregnancy, with delivery — (Use additional code to further specify complication) ♀

646.91 Unspecified complication of pregnancy, with delivery — (Use additional code to further specify complication) ♀

647.01 Maternal syphilis, complicating pregnancy, with delivery — (Use additional code to further specify complication) ♀

647.11 Maternal gonorrhea with delivery — (Use additional code to further specify complication) ♀

647.21 Other maternal venereal diseases with delivery — (Use additional code to further specify complication) ♀

647.31 Maternal tuberculosis with delivery — (Use additional code to further specify complication) ♀

647.41 Maternal malaria with delivery — (Use additional code to further specify complication) ♀

647.51 Maternal rubella with delivery — (Use additional code to further specify complication) ♀

647.61 Other maternal viral disease with delivery — (Use additional code to further specify complication) ♀

647.81 Other specified maternal infectious and parasitic disease with delivery — (Use additional code to further specify complication) ♀

647.91 Unspecified maternal infection or infestation with delivery — (Use additional code to further specify complication) ♀

648.01 Maternal diabetes mellitus with delivery — (Use additional code(s) to identify the condition) ♀

648.11 Maternal thyroid dysfunction with delivery, with or without mention of antepartum condition — (Use additional code(s) to identify the condition) ♀

648.21 Maternal anemia, with delivery — (Use additional code(s) to identify the condition) ♀

648.31 Maternal drug dependence, with delivery — (Use additional code(s) to identify the condition) ♀

648.41 Maternal mental disorders, with delivery — (Use additional code(s) to identify the condition) ♀

648.51 Maternal congenital cardiovascular disorders, with delivery — (Use additional code(s) to identify the condition) ♀

648.61 Other maternal cardiovascular diseases, with delivery — (Use additional code(s) to identify the condition) ♀

648.71 Bone and joint disorders of maternal back, pelvis, and lower limbs, with delivery — (Use additional code(s) to identify the condition) ♀

648.81 Abnormal maternal glucose tolerance, with delivery — (Use additional code(s) to identify the condition. Use additional code, if applicable, for associated long-term (current) insulin use: V58.67) ♀

648.91 Other current maternal conditions classifiable elsewhere, with delivery — (Use additional code(s) to identify the condition) ♀

649.01 Tobacco use disorder complicating pregnancy, childbirth, or the puerperium, delivered, with or without mention of antepartum condition ♀

649.11 Obesity complicating pregnancy, childbirth, or the puerperium, delivered, with or without mention of antepartum condition — (Use additional code to identify the obesity: 278.00-278.01) ♀

649.21 Bariatric surgery status complicating pregnancy, childbirth, or the puerperium, delivered, with or without mention of antepartum condition ♀

649.31 Coagulation defects complicating pregnancy, childbirth, or the puerperium, delivered, with or without mention of antepartum condition — (Use additional code to identify the specific coagulation defect: 286.0-286.9, 287.0-287.9, 289.0-289.9) ♀

649.41 Epilepsy complicating pregnancy, childbirth, or the puerperium, delivered, with or without mention of antepartum condition — (Use additional code to identify the specific type of epilepsy: 345.00-345.91) ♀

649.51 Spotting complicating pregnancy, delivered, with or without mention of antepartum condition ♀

649.61 Uterine size date discrepancy, delivered, with or without mention of antepartum condition ♀

649.71 Cervical shortening, delivered, with or without mention of antepartum condition ♀

649.81 Onset (spontaneous) of labor after 37 completed weeks of gestation but before 39 completed weeks gestation, with delivery by (planned) cesarean section, delivered, with or without mention of antepartum condition — (Use additional code to specify reason for planned cesarean section: 653.4, 654.2) ♀

649.82 Onset (spontaneous) of labor after 37 completed weeks of gestation but before 39 completed weeks gestation, with delivery by (planned) cesarean section, delivered, with mention of postpartum complication — (Use additional code to specify reason for planned cesarean section: 653.4, 654.2) ♀

651.01 Twin pregnancy, delivered ♀

651.11 Triplet pregnancy, delivered ♀

651.21 Quadruplet pregnancy, delivered ♀

651.31 Twin pregnancy with fetal loss and retention of one fetus, delivered ♀

651.41 Triplet pregnancy with fetal loss and retention of one or more, delivered ♀

651.51 Quadruplet pregnancy with fetal loss and retention of one or more, delivered ♀

651.61 Other multiple pregnancy with fetal loss and retention of one or more fetus(es), delivered ♀

651.71 Multiple gestation following (elective) fetal reduction, delivered, with or without mention of antepartum condition ♀

651.81 Other specified multiple gestation, delivered ♀

651.91 Unspecified multiple gestation, delivered ♀

652.01 Unstable lie of fetus, delivered — (Code first any associated obstructed labor: 660.0) ♀

652.11 Breech or other malpresentation successfully converted to cephalic presentation, delivered — (Code first any associated obstructed labor, 660.0) ♀

652.21 Breech presentation without mention of version, delivered — (Code first any associated obstructed labor, 660.0) ♀

652.31 Transverse or oblique fetal presentation, delivered — (Code first any associated obstructed labor: 660.0) ♀

652.41 Fetal face or brow presentation, delivered — (Code first any associated obstructed labor: 660.0) ♀

652.51 High fetal head at term, delivered — (Code first any associated obstructed labor: 660.0) ♀

652.61 Multiple gestation with malpresentation of one fetus or more, delivered — (Code first any associated obstructed labor: 660.0) ♀

652.71 Prolapsed arm of fetus, delivered — (Code first any associated obstructed labor: 660.0) ♀

652.81 Other specified malposition or malpresentation of fetus, delivered — (Code first any associated obstructed labor: 660.0) ♀

652.91 Unspecified malposition or malpresentation of fetus, delivered — (Code first any associated obstructed labor: 660.0) ♀

653.01 Major abnormality of bony pelvis, not further specified, delivered — (Code first any associated obstructed labor: 660.1) ♀

653.11 Generally contracted pelvis in pregnancy, delivered — (Code first any associated obstructed labor: 660.1) ♀

653.21 Inlet contraction of pelvis in pregnancy, delivered — (Code first any associated obstructed labor: 660.1) ♀

653.31 Outlet contraction of pelvis in pregnancy, delivered — (Code first any associated obstructed labor: 660.1) ♀

653.41 Fetopelvic disproportion, delivered — (Code first any associated obstructed labor: 660.1) ♀

653.51 Unusually large fetus causing disproportion, delivered — (Code first any associated obstructed labor: 660.1) ♀

653.61 Hydrocephalic fetus causing disproportion, delivered — (Code first any associated obstructed labor: 660.1) ♀
653.71 Other fetal abnormality causing disproportion, delivered — (Code first any associated obstructed labor: 660.1) ♀
654.01 Congenital abnormalities of pregnant uterus, delivered — (Code first any associated obstructed labor: 660.2) ♀
654.11 Tumors of body of uterus, delivered — (Code first any associated obstructed labor, 660.2) ♀
654.21 Previous cesarean delivery, delivered, with or without mention of antepartum condition — (Code first any associated obstructed labor, 660.2) ♀
654.31 Retroverted and incarcerated gravid uterus, delivered — (Code first any associated obstructed labor, 660.2) ♀
654.41 Other abnormalities in shape or position of gravid uterus and of neighboring structures, delivered — (Code first any associated obstructed labor: 660.2) ♀
654.51 Cervical incompetence, delivered — (Code first any associated obstructed labor: 660.2) ♀
654.61 Other congenital or acquired abnormality of cervix, with delivery — (Code first any associated obstructed labor: 660.2) ♀
654.71 Congenital or acquired abnormality of vagina, with delivery — (Code first any associated obstructed labor: 660.2) ♀
654.81 Congenital or acquired abnormality of vulva, with delivery — (Code first any associated obstructed labor, 660.2) ♀
654.84 Congenital or acquired abnormality of vulva, postpartum condition or complication — (Code first any associated obstructed labor: 660.2) ♀
654.91 Other and unspecified abnormality of organs and soft tissues of pelvis, with delivery — (Code first any associated obstructed labor: 660.2) ▽ ♀
655.01 Central nervous system malformation in fetus, with delivery ♀
655.11 Chromosomal abnormality in fetus, affecting management of mother, with delivery ♀
655.21 Hereditary disease in family possibly affecting fetus, affecting management of mother, with delivery ♀
655.31 Suspected damage to fetus from viral disease in mother, affecting management of mother, with delivery ♀
655.41 Suspected damage to fetus from other disease in mother, affecting management of mother, with delivery ♀
655.51 Suspected damage to fetus from drugs, affecting management of mother, delivered ♀
655.61 Suspected damage to fetus from radiation, affecting management of mother, delivered ♀
655.81 Other known or suspected fetal abnormality, not elsewhere classified, affecting management of mother, delivery ♀
655.91 Unspecified fetal abnormality affecting management of mother, delivery ▽ ♀
656.01 Fetal-maternal hemorrhage, with delivery ♀
656.11 Rhesus isoimmunization affecting management of mother, delivered ♀
656.21 Isoimmunization from other and unspecified blood-group incompatibility, affecting management of mother, delivered ♀
656.31 Fetal distress affecting management of mother, delivered ♀
656.41 Intrauterine death affecting management of mother, delivered ♀
656.51 Poor fetal growth, affecting management of mother, delivered ♀
656.61 Excessive fetal growth affecting management of mother, delivered ♀
656.71 Other placental conditions affecting management of mother, delivered ♀
656.81 Other specified fetal and placental problems affecting management of mother, delivered ♀
656.91 Unspecified fetal and placental problem affecting management of mother, delivered ▽ ♀
657.01 Polyhydramnios, with delivery ♀
658.01 Oligohydramnios, delivered ♀
658.11 Premature rupture of membranes in pregnancy, delivered ♀
658.21 Delayed delivery after spontaneous or unspecified rupture of membranes, delivered ♀
658.31 Delayed delivery after artificial rupture of membranes, delivered ♀
658.41 Infection of amniotic cavity, delivered ♀
658.81 Other problem associated with amniotic cavity and membranes, delivered ♀
658.91 Unspecified problem associated with amniotic cavity and membranes, delivered ▽ ♀
659.01 Failed mechanical induction of labor, delivered ♀
659.11 Failed medical or unspecified induction of labor, delivered ♀
659.21 Unspecified maternal pyrexia during labor, delivered ▽ ♀
659.31 Generalized infection during labor, delivered ♀
659.41 Grand multiparity, delivered, with or without mention of antepartum condition ♀
659.51 Elderly primigravida, delivered ♀
659.61 Elderly multigravida, delivered, with mention of antepartum condition ♀
659.81 Other specified indication for care or intervention related to labor and delivery, delivered ♀
659.91 Unspecified indication for care or intervention related to labor and delivery, delivered ▽ ♀
660.01 Obstruction caused by malposition of fetus at onset of labor, delivered — (Use additional code from 652.0-652.9 to identify condition) ♀
660.11 Obstruction by bony pelvis during labor and delivery, delivered — (Use additional code from 653.0-653.9 to identify condition) ♀
660.21 Obstruction by abnormal pelvic soft tissues during labor and delivery, delivered — (Use additional code from 654.0-654.9 to identify condition) ♀
660.31 Deep transverse arrest and persistent occipitoposterior position during labor and deliver, delivered ♀
660.41 Shoulder (girdle) dystocia during labor and deliver, delivered ♀
660.51 Locked twins, delivered ♀
660.61 Unspecified failed trial of labor, delivered ▽ ♀
660.71 Unspecified failed forceps or vacuum extractor, delivered ▽ ♀
660.81 Other causes of obstructed labor, delivered — (Use additional code to identify condition) ♀
660.91 Unspecified obstructed labor, with delivery ▽ ♀
661.01 Primary uterine inertia, with delivery ♀
661.11 Secondary uterine inertia, with delivery ♀
661.21 Other and unspecified uterine inertia, with delivery ▽ ♀
662.01 Prolonged first stage of labor, delivered ♀
662.21 Prolonged second stage of labor, delivered ♀
662.31 Delayed delivery of second twin, triplet, etc., delivered ♀
663.01 Prolapse of cord, complicating labor and delivery, delivered ♀
663.11 Cord around neck, with compression, complicating labor and delivery, delivered ♀
663.21 Other and unspecified cord entanglement, with compression, complicating labor and delivery, delivered ▽ ♀
663.31 Other and unspecified cord entanglement, without mention of compression, complicating labor and delivery, delivered ▽ ♀
663.41 Short cord complicating labor and delivery, delivered ♀
663.51 Vasa previa complicating labor and delivery, delivered ♀
663.61 Vascular lesions of cord complicating labor and delivery, delivered ♀
663.81 Other umbilical cord complications during labor and delivery, delivered ♀
663.91 Unspecified umbilical cord complication during labor and delivery, delivered ▽ ♀
665.01 Rupture of uterus before onset of labor, with delivery ♀
665.11 Rupture of uterus during labor, with delivery ♀
665.22 Inversion of uterus, delivered with postpartum complication ♀
665.81 Other specified obstetrical trauma, with delivery ♀
665.82 Other specified obstetrical trauma, delivered, with postpartum ♀
665.91 Unspecified obstetrical trauma, with delivery ▽ ♀
665.92 Unspecified obstetrical trauma, delivered, with postpartum complication ▽ ♀
666.02 Third-stage postpartum hemorrhage, with delivery ♀
666.12 Other immediate postpartum hemorrhage, with delivery ♀
667.02 Retained placenta without hemorrhage, with delivery, with mention of postpartum complication ♀
667.12 Retained portions of placenta or membranes, without hemorrhage, delivered, with mention of postpartum complication ♀

668.01 Pulmonary complications of the administration of anesthesia or other sedation in labor and delivery, delivered — (Use additional code(s) to further specify complication) ♀
668.11 Cardiac complications of the administration of anesthesia or other sedation in labor and delivery, delivered — (Use additional code(s) to further specify complication) ♀
668.21 Central nervous system complications of the administration of anesthesia or other sedation in labor and delivery, delivered — (Use additional code(s) to further specify complication) ♀
668.81 Other complications of the administration of anesthesia or other sedation in labor and delivery, delivered — (Use additional code(s) to further specify complication) ♀
668.91 Unspecified complication of the administration of anesthesia or other sedation in labor and delivery, delivered — (Use additional code(s) to further specify complication) ♀
669.01 Maternal distress, with delivery, with or without mention of antepartum condition ♀
669.02 Maternal distress, with delivery, with mention of postpartum complication ♀
669.11 Shock during or following labor and delivery, with delivery, with or without mention of antepartum condition ♀
669.12 Shock during or following labor and delivery, with delivery, with mention of postpartum complication ♀
669.21 Maternal hypotension syndrome, with delivery, with or without mention of antepartum condition ♀
669.32 Acute kidney failure following labor and delivery, delivered, with mention of postpartum complication ♀
669.41 Other complications of obstetrical surgery and procedures, with delivery, with or without mention of antepartum condition ♀
669.42 Other complications of obstetrical surgery and procedures, with delivery, with mention of postpartum complication ♀
669.51 Forceps or vacuum extractor delivery without mention of indication, delivered, with or without mention of antepartum condition ♀
669.61 Breech extraction, without mention of indication, delivered, with or without mention of antepartum condition ♀
669.71 Cesarean delivery, without mention of indication, delivered, with or without mention of antepartum condition ♀
669.81 Other complication of labor and delivery, delivered, with or without mention of antepartum condition ♀
669.91 Unspecified complication of labor and delivery, with delivery, with or without mention of antepartum condition ♀
671.01 Varicose veins of legs, with delivery, with or without mention of antepartum condition ♀
671.81 Other venous complication, with delivery, with or without mention of antepartum condition ♀
671.82 Other venous complication, with delivery, with mention of postpartum complication ♀
676.01 Retracted nipple, delivered, with or without mention of antepartum condition ♀
676.02 Retracted nipple, delivered, with mention of postpartum complication ♀
676.21 Engorgement of breasts, delivered, with or without mention of antepartum condition ♀
676.22 Engorgement of breasts, delivered, with mention of postpartum complication ♀
676.31 Other and unspecified disorder of breast associated with childbirth, delivered, with or without mention of antepartum condition ♀
676.32 Other and unspecified disorder of breast associated with childbirth, delivered, with mention of postpartum complication ♀
676.41 Failure of lactation, with delivery, with or without mention of antepartum condition ♀
676.42 Failure of lactation, with delivery, with mention of postpartum complication ♀
676.51 Suppressed lactation, with delivery, with or without mention of antepartum condition ♀
676.52 Suppressed lactation, with delivery, with mention of postpartum complication ♀
676.91 Unspecified disorder of lactation, with delivery, with or without mention of antepartum condition ♀
676.92 Unspecified disorder of lactation, with delivery, with mention of postpartum complication ♀
678.01 Fetal hematologic conditions, delivered, with or without mention of antepartum condition ♀
678.11 Fetal conjoined twins, delivered, with or without mention of antepartum condition ♀
679.01 Maternal complications from in utero procedure, delivered, with or without mention of antepartum condition ♀
679.02 Maternal complications from in utero procedure, delivered, with mention of postpartum complication ♀
V23.0 Pregnancy with history of infertility ♀
V23.1 Pregnancy with history of trophoblastic disease ♀
V23.2 Pregnancy with history of abortion ♀
V23.3 Pregnancy with grand multiparity ♀
V23.41 Supervision of pregnancy with history of pre-term labor ♀
V23.49 Supervision of pregnancy with other poor obstetric history ♀
V23.5 Pregnancy with other poor reproductive history ♀
V23.7 Insufficient prenatal care ♀
V23.81 Supervision of high-risk pregnancy of elderly primigravida ♀
V23.82 Supervision of high-risk pregnancy of elderly multigravida ♀
V23.83 Supervision of high-risk pregnancy of young primigravida ♀
V23.84 Supervision of high-risk pregnancy of young multigravida ♀
V23.89 Supervision of other high-risk pregnancy ♀
V23.9 Unspecified high-risk pregnancy ♀
V24.0 Postpartum care and examination immediately after delivery ♀
V24.1 Postpartum care and examination of lactating mother ♀
V24.2 Routine postpartum follow-up ♀
V27.0 Outcome of delivery, single liveborn — (This code is intended for the coding of the outcome of delivery on the mother's record) ♀
V27.1 Outcome of delivery, single stillborn — (This code is intended for the coding of the outcome of delivery on the mother's record) ♀
V27.2 Outcome of delivery, twins, both liveborn — (This code is intended for the coding of the outcome of delivery on the mother's record) ♀
V27.3 Outcome of delivery, twins, one liveborn and one stillborn — (This code is intended for the coding of the outcome of delivery on the mother's record) ♀
V27.4 Outcome of delivery, twins, both stillborn — (This code is intended for the coding of the outcome of delivery on the mother's record) ♀
V27.5 Outcome of delivery, other multiple birth, all liveborn — (This code is intended for the coding of the outcome of delivery on the mother's record) ♀
V27.6 Outcome of delivery, other multiple birth, some liveborn — (This code is intended for the coding of the outcome of delivery on the mother's record) ♀
V27.7 Outcome of delivery, other multiple birth, all stillborn — (This code is intended for the coding of the outcome of delivery on the mother's record) ♀
V27.9 Outcome of delivery, unspecified — (This code is intended for the coding of the outcome of delivery on the mother's record) ♀
V89.01 Suspected problem with amniotic cavity and membrane not found ♀

ICD-9-CM Procedural

73.3 Failed forceps ♀
74.0 Classical cesarean section ♀
74.1 Low cervical cesarean section ♀
74.2 Extraperitoneal cesarean section ♀
74.4 Cesarean section of other specified type ♀

59525

59525 Subtotal or total hysterectomy after cesarean delivery (List separately in addition to code for primary procedure)

ICD-9-CM Diagnostic

180.0 Malignant neoplasm of endocervix ♀
180.1 Malignant neoplasm of exocervix ♀
182.0 Malignant neoplasm of corpus uteri, except isthmus ♀
182.8 Malignant neoplasm of other specified sites of body of uterus ♀

183.2 Malignant neoplasm of fallopian tube ♀
183.3 Malignant neoplasm of broad ligament of uterus ♀
183.4 Malignant neoplasm of parametrium of uterus ♀
614.7 Other chronic pelvic peritonitis, female — (Use additional code to identify organism: 041.00-041.09, 041.10-041.19) ♀
614.8 Other specified inflammatory disease of female pelvic organs and tissues — (Use additional code to identify organism: 041.00-041.09, 041.10-041.19) ♀
615.0 Acute inflammatory disease of uterus, except cervix — (Use additional code to identify organism: 041.00-041.09, 041.10-041.19) ♀
615.1 Chronic inflammatory disease of uterus, except cervix — (Use additional code to identify organism: 041.00-041.09, 041.10-041.19) ♀
615.9 Unspecified inflammatory disease of uterus — (Use additional code to identify organism: 041.00-041.09, 041.10-041.19) ▽ ♀
617.0 Endometriosis of uterus ♀
626.8 Other disorder of menstruation and other abnormal bleeding from female genital tract ♀
654.11 Tumors of body of uterus, delivered — (Code first any associated obstructed labor, 660.2) ♀
654.31 Retroverted and incarcerated gravid uterus, delivered — (Code first any associated obstructed labor, 660.2) ♀
665.01 Rupture of uterus before onset of labor, with delivery ♀
665.11 Rupture of uterus during labor, with delivery ♀
666.12 Other immediate postpartum hemorrhage, with delivery ♀

ICD-9-CM Procedural

68.39 Other and unspecified subtotal abdominal hysterectomy ♀
68.49 Other and unspecified total abdominal hysterectomy ♀
68.9 Other and unspecified hysterectomy ♀

59610-59614

59610 Routine obstetric care including antepartum care, vaginal delivery (with or without episiotomy, and/or forceps) and postpartum care, after previous cesarean delivery
59612 Vaginal delivery only, after previous cesarean delivery (with or without episiotomy and/or forceps);
59614 including postpartum care

ICD-9-CM Diagnostic

640.01 Threatened abortion, delivered ♀
640.91 Unspecified hemorrhage in early pregnancy, delivered ▽ ♀
641.01 Placenta previa without hemorrhage, with delivery ♀
641.11 Hemorrhage from placenta previa, with delivery ♀
641.21 Premature separation of placenta, with delivery ♀
641.31 Antepartum hemorrhage associated with coagulation defects, with delivery ♀
641.81 Other antepartum hemorrhage, with delivery ♀
641.91 Unspecified antepartum hemorrhage, with delivery ▽ ♀
642.01 Benign essential hypertension with delivery ♀
642.11 Hypertension secondary to renal disease, with delivery ♀
642.21 Other pre-existing hypertension, with delivery ♀
642.31 Transient hypertension of pregnancy, with delivery ♀
642.41 Mild or unspecified pre-eclampsia, with delivery ♀
642.51 Severe pre-eclampsia, with delivery ♀
642.61 Eclampsia, with delivery ♀
642.71 Pre-eclampsia or eclampsia superimposed on pre-existing hypertension, with delivery ♀
642.91 Unspecified hypertension, with delivery ▽ ♀
643.01 Mild hyperemesis gravidarum, delivered ♀
643.11 Hyperemesis gravidarum with metabolic disturbance, delivered ♀
643.21 Late vomiting of pregnancy, delivered ♀
643.81 Other vomiting complicating pregnancy, delivered — (Use additional code to specify cause) ♀
643.91 Unspecified vomiting of pregnancy, delivered ▽ ♀
644.21 Early onset of delivery, delivered, with or without mention of antepartum condition ♀
645.11 Post term pregnancy, delivered, with or without mention of antepartum condition ♀
645.21 Prolonged pregnancy, delivered, with or without mention of antepartum condition ♀
646.01 Papyraceous fetus, delivered, with or without mention of antepartum condition — (Use additional code to further specify complication) ♀
646.11 Edema or excessive weight gain in pregnancy, with delivery, with or without mention of antepartum complication — (Use additional code to further specify complication) ♀
646.21 Unspecified renal disease in pregnancy, with delivery — (Use additional code to further specify complication) ▽ ♀
646.31 Pregnancy complication, recurrent pregnancy loss, with or without mention of antepartum condition — (Use additional code to further specify complication) ♀
646.41 Peripheral neuritis in pregnancy, with delivery — (Use additional code to further specify complication) ♀
646.51 Asymptomatic bacteriuria in pregnancy, with delivery — (Use additional code to further specify complication) ♀
646.61 Infections of genitourinary tract in pregnancy, with delivery — (Use additional code to further specify complication) ♀
646.71 Liver and biliary tract disorders in pregnancy, delivered, with or without mention of antepartum condition — (Use additional code to further specify complication) ♀
646.81 Other specified complication of pregnancy, with delivery — (Use additional code to further specify complication) ♀
646.91 Unspecified complication of pregnancy, with delivery — (Use additional code to further specify complication) ▽ ♀
647.01 Maternal syphilis, complicating pregnancy, with delivery — (Use additional code to further specify complication) ♀
647.11 Maternal gonorrhea with delivery — (Use additional code to further specify complication) ♀
647.21 Other maternal venereal diseases with delivery — (Use additional code to further specify complication) ♀
647.31 Maternal tuberculosis with delivery — (Use additional code to further specify complication) ♀
647.41 Maternal malaria with delivery — (Use additional code to further specify complication) ♀
647.51 Maternal rubella with delivery — (Use additional code to further specify complication) ♀
647.61 Other maternal viral disease with delivery — (Use additional code to further specify complication) ♀
647.81 Other specified maternal infectious and parasitic disease with delivery — (Use additional code to further specify complication) ♀
647.91 Unspecified maternal infection or infestation with delivery — (Use additional code to further specify complication) ▽ ♀
648.01 Maternal diabetes mellitus with delivery — (Use additional code(s) to identify the condition) ♀
648.11 Maternal thyroid dysfunction with delivery, with or without mention of antepartum condition — (Use additional code(s) to identify the condition) ♀
648.21 Maternal anemia, with delivery — (Use additional code(s) to identify the condition) ♀
648.31 Maternal drug dependence, with delivery — (Use additional code(s) to identify the condition) ♀
648.41 Maternal mental disorders, with delivery — (Use additional code(s) to identify the condition) ♀
648.51 Maternal congenital cardiovascular disorders, with delivery — (Use additional code(s) to identify the condition) ♀
648.61 Other maternal cardiovascular diseases, with delivery — (Use additional code(s) to identify the condition) ♀
648.71 Bone and joint disorders of maternal back, pelvis, and lower limbs, with delivery — (Use additional code(s) to identify the condition) ♀
648.81 Abnormal maternal glucose tolerance, with delivery — (Use additional code(s) to identify the condition. Use additional code, if applicable, for associated long-term (current) insulin use: V58.67) ♀

648.91 Other current maternal conditions classifiable elsewhere, with delivery — (Use additional code(s) to identify the condition) ♀

649.01 Tobacco use disorder complicating pregnancy, childbirth, or the puerperium, delivered, with or without mention of antepartum condition ♀

649.11 Obesity complicating pregnancy, childbirth, or the puerperium, delivered, with or without mention of antepartum condition — (Use additional code to identify the obesity: 278.00-278.01) ♀

649.21 Bariatric surgery status complicating pregnancy, childbirth, or the puerperium, delivered, with or without mention of antepartum condition ♀

649.31 Coagulation defects complicating pregnancy, childbirth, or the puerperium, delivered, with or without mention of antepartum condition — (Use additional code to identify the specific coagulation defect: 286.0-286.9, 287.0-287.9, 289.0-289.9) ♀

649.41 Epilepsy complicating pregnancy, childbirth, or the puerperium, delivered, with or without mention of antepartum condition — (Use additional code to identify the specific type of epilepsy: 345.00-345.91) ♀

649.51 Spotting complicating pregnancy, delivered, with or without mention of antepartum condition ♀

649.61 Uterine size date discrepancy, delivered, with or without mention of antepartum condition ♀

649.71 Cervical shortening, delivered, with or without mention of antepartum condition ♀

651.01 Twin pregnancy, delivered ♀

651.21 Quadruplet pregnancy, delivered ♀

651.31 Twin pregnancy with fetal loss and retention of one fetus, delivered ♀

651.41 Triplet pregnancy with fetal loss and retention of one or more, delivered ♀

651.51 Quadruplet pregnancy with fetal loss and retention of one or more, delivered ♀

651.61 Other multiple pregnancy with fetal loss and retention of one or more fetus(es), delivered ♀

651.71 Multiple gestation following (elective) fetal reduction, delivered, with or without mention of antepartum condition ♀

651.81 Other specified multiple gestation, delivered ♀

651.91 Unspecified multiple gestation, delivered ▽ ♀

652.11 Breech or other malpresentation successfully converted to cephalic presentation, delivered — (Code first any associated obstructed labor, 660.0) ♀

652.21 Breech presentation without mention of version, delivered — (Code first any associated obstructed labor, 660.0) ♀

652.41 Fetal face or brow presentation, delivered — (Code first any associated obstructed labor: 660.0) ♀

652.71 Prolapsed arm of fetus, delivered — (Code first any associated obstructed labor: 660.0) ♀

652.81 Other specified malposition or malpresentation of fetus, delivered — (Code first any associated obstructed labor: 660.0) ♀

652.91 Unspecified malposition or malpresentation of fetus, delivered — (Code first any associated obstructed labor: 660.0) ▽ ♀

654.01 Congenital abnormalities of pregnant uterus, delivered — (Code first any associated obstructed labor: 660.2) ♀

654.11 Tumors of body of uterus, delivered — (Code first any associated obstructed labor, 660.2) ♀

654.21 Previous cesarean delivery, delivered, with or without mention of antepartum condition — (Code first any associated obstructed labor, 660.2) ♀

654.31 Retroverted and incarcerated gravid uterus, delivered — (Code first any associated obstructed labor, 660.2) ♀

654.41 Other abnormalities in shape or position of gravid uterus and of neighboring structures, delivered — (Code first any associated obstructed labor: 660.2) ♀

654.51 Cervical incompetence, delivered — (Code first any associated obstructed labor: 660.2) ♀

654.61 Other congenital or acquired abnormality of cervix, with delivery — (Code first any associated obstructed labor: 660.2) ♀

654.71 Congenital or acquired abnormality of vagina, with delivery — (Code first any associated obstructed labor: 660.2) ♀

654.81 Congenital or acquired abnormality of vulva, with delivery — (Code first any associated obstructed labor, 660.2) ♀

654.91 Other and unspecified abnormality of organs and soft tissues of pelvis, with delivery — (Code first any associated obstructed labor: 660.2) ▽ ♀

655.01 Central nervous system malformation in fetus, with delivery ♀

655.11 Chromosomal abnormality in fetus, affecting management of mother, with delivery ♀

655.21 Hereditary disease in family possibly affecting fetus, affecting management of mother, with delivery ♀

655.31 Suspected damage to fetus from viral disease in mother, affecting management of mother, with delivery ♀

655.41 Suspected damage to fetus from other disease in mother, affecting management of mother, with delivery ♀

655.81 Other known or suspected fetal abnormality, not elsewhere classified, affecting management of mother, delivery ♀

655.91 Unspecified fetal abnormality affecting management of mother, delivery ▽ ♀

656.01 Fetal-maternal hemorrhage, with delivery ♀

656.11 Rhesus isoimmunization affecting management of mother, delivered ♀

656.21 Isoimmunization from other and unspecified blood-group incompatibility, affecting management of mother, delivered ♀

656.31 Fetal distress affecting management of mother, delivered ♀

656.41 Intrauterine death affecting management of mother, delivered ♀

656.51 Poor fetal growth, affecting management of mother, delivered ♀

656.61 Excessive fetal growth affecting management of mother, delivered ♀

656.71 Other placental conditions affecting management of mother, delivered ♀

656.81 Other specified fetal and placental problems affecting management of mother, delivered ♀

656.91 Unspecified fetal and placental problem affecting management of mother, delivered ▽ ♀

657.01 Polyhydramnios, with delivery ♀

658.01 Oligohydramnios, delivered ♀

658.11 Premature rupture of membranes in pregnancy, delivered ♀

658.21 Delayed delivery after spontaneous or unspecified rupture of membranes, delivered ♀

658.31 Delayed delivery after artificial rupture of membranes, delivered ♀

658.41 Infection of amniotic cavity, delivered ♀

658.81 Other problem associated with amniotic cavity and membranes, delivered ♀

658.91 Unspecified problem associated with amniotic cavity and membranes, delivered ▽ ♀

659.21 Unspecified maternal pyrexia during labor, delivered ▽ ♀

659.31 Generalized infection during labor, delivered ♀

659.41 Grand multiparity, delivered, with or without mention of antepartum condition ♀

659.51 Elderly primigravida, delivered ♀

659.61 Elderly multigravida, delivered, with mention of antepartum condition ♀

659.81 Other specified indication for care or intervention related to labor and delivery, delivered ♀

659.91 Unspecified indication for care or intervention related to labor and delivery, delivered ▽ ♀

660.81 Other causes of obstructed labor, delivered — (Use additional code to identify condition) ♀

661.31 Precipitate labor, with delivery ♀

662.01 Prolonged first stage of labor, delivered ♀

662.21 Prolonged second stage of labor, delivered ♀

662.31 Delayed delivery of second twin, triplet, etc., delivered ♀

663.11 Cord around neck, with compression, complicating labor and delivery, delivered ♀

663.31 Other and unspecified cord entanglement, without mention of compression, complicating labor and delivery, delivered ▽ ♀

663.41 Short cord complicating labor and delivery, delivered ♀

663.61 Vascular lesions of cord complicating labor and delivery, delivered ♀

663.81 Other umbilical cord complications during labor and delivery, delivered ♀

663.91 Unspecified umbilical cord complication during labor and delivery, delivered ▽ ♀

664.01 First-degree perineal laceration, with delivery ♀
664.11 Second-degree perineal laceration, with delivery ♀
664.21 Third-degree perineal laceration, with delivery ♀
664.31 Fourth-degree perineal laceration, with delivery ♀
664.41 Unspecified perineal laceration, with delivery ▽ ♀
664.51 Vulvar and perineal hematoma, with delivery ♀
664.61 Anal sphincter tear complicating delivery, not associated with third-degree perineal laceration, delivered, with or without mention of antepartum condition ♀
664.81 Other specified trauma to perineum and vulva, with delivery ♀
664.91 Unspecified trauma to perineum and vulva, with delivery ▽ ♀
665.31 Laceration of cervix, with delivery ♀
665.41 High vaginal laceration, with delivery ♀
665.51 Other injury to pelvic organs, with delivery ♀
665.61 Damage to pelvic joints and ligaments, with delivery ♀
665.71 Pelvic hematoma, with delivery ♀
665.81 Other specified obstetrical trauma, with delivery ♀
665.91 Unspecified obstetrical trauma, with delivery ▽ ♀
666.02 Third-stage postpartum hemorrhage, with delivery ♀
666.12 Other immediate postpartum hemorrhage, with delivery ♀
666.22 Delayed and secondary postpartum hemorrhage, with delivery ♀
667.02 Retained placenta without hemorrhage, with delivery, with mention of postpartum complication ♀
668.01 Pulmonary complications of the administration of anesthesia or other sedation in labor and delivery, delivered — (Use additional code(s) to further specify complication) ♀
668.11 Cardiac complications of the administration of anesthesia or other sedation in labor and delivery, delivered — (Use additional code(s) to further specify complication) ♀
668.21 Central nervous system complications of the administration of anesthesia or other sedation in labor and delivery, delivered — (Use additional code(s) to further specify complication) ♀
668.81 Other complications of the administration of anesthesia or other sedation in labor and delivery, delivered — (Use additional code(s) to further specify complication) ♀
668.91 Unspecified complication of the administration of anesthesia or other sedation in labor and delivery, delivered — (Use additional code(s) to further specify complication) ▽ ♀
669.01 Maternal distress, with delivery, with or without mention of antepartum condition ♀
669.11 Shock during or following labor and delivery, with delivery, with or without mention of antepartum condition ♀
669.21 Maternal hypotension syndrome, with delivery, with or without mention of antepartum condition ♀
669.41 Other complications of obstetrical surgery and procedures, with delivery, with or without mention of antepartum condition ♀
669.51 Forceps or vacuum extractor delivery without mention of indication, delivered, with or without mention of antepartum condition ♀
669.61 Breech extraction, without mention of indication, delivered, with or without mention of antepartum condition ♀
669.81 Other complication of labor and delivery, delivered, with or without mention of antepartum condition ♀
669.91 Unspecified complication of labor and delivery, with delivery, with or without mention of antepartum condition ▽ ♀
671.01 Varicose veins of legs, with delivery, with or without mention of antepartum condition ♀
671.81 Other venous complication, with delivery, with or without mention of antepartum condition ♀
671.82 Other venous complication, with delivery, with mention of postpartum complication ♀
676.01 Retracted nipple, delivered, with or without mention of antepartum condition ♀
676.02 Retracted nipple, delivered, with mention of postpartum complication ♀
676.04 Retracted nipple, postpartum condition or complication ♀
676.21 Engorgement of breasts, delivered, with or without mention of antepartum condition ♀
676.22 Engorgement of breasts, delivered, with mention of postpartum complication ♀
676.31 Other and unspecified disorder of breast associated with childbirth, delivered, with or without mention of antepartum condition ▽ ♀
676.32 Other and unspecified disorder of breast associated with childbirth, delivered, with mention of postpartum complication ▽ ♀
676.41 Failure of lactation, with delivery, with or without mention of antepartum condition ♀
676.42 Failure of lactation, with delivery, with mention of postpartum complication ♀
676.51 Suppressed lactation, with delivery, with or without mention of antepartum condition ♀
676.52 Suppressed lactation, with delivery, with mention of postpartum complication ♀
676.91 Unspecified disorder of lactation, with delivery, with or without mention of antepartum condition ▽ ♀
676.92 Unspecified disorder of lactation, with delivery, with mention of postpartum complication ▽ ♀
678.01 Fetal hematologic conditions, delivered, with or without mention of antepartum condition ♀
679.01 Maternal complications from in utero procedure, delivered, with or without mention of antepartum condition ♀
679.02 Maternal complications from in utero procedure, delivered, with mention of postpartum complication ♀
V22.1 Supervision of other normal pregnancy ♀
V23.0 Pregnancy with history of infertility ♀
V23.2 Pregnancy with history of abortion ♀
V23.41 Supervision of pregnancy with history of pre-term labor ♀
V23.49 Supervision of pregnancy with other poor obstetric history ♀
V23.82 Supervision of high-risk pregnancy of elderly multigravida ♀
V23.84 Supervision of high-risk pregnancy of young multigravida ♀
V23.89 Supervision of other high-risk pregnancy ♀
V24.0 Postpartum care and examination immediately after delivery ♀
V24.1 Postpartum care and examination of lactating mother ♀
V24.2 Routine postpartum follow-up ♀
V27.0 Outcome of delivery, single liveborn — (This code is intended for the coding of the outcome of delivery on the mother's record) ♀
V27.1 Outcome of delivery, single stillborn — (This code is intended for the coding of the outcome of delivery on the mother's record) ♀
V27.2 Outcome of delivery, twins, both liveborn — (This code is intended for the coding of the outcome of delivery on the mother's record) ♀
V27.3 Outcome of delivery, twins, one liveborn and one stillborn — (This code is intended for the coding of the outcome of delivery on the mother's record) ♀
V27.4 Outcome of delivery, twins, both stillborn — (This code is intended for the coding of the outcome of delivery on the mother's record) ♀
V27.5 Outcome of delivery, other multiple birth, all liveborn — (This code is intended for the coding of the outcome of delivery on the mother's record) ♀
V27.6 Outcome of delivery, other multiple birth, some liveborn — (This code is intended for the coding of the outcome of delivery on the mother's record) ♀
V27.7 Outcome of delivery, other multiple birth, all stillborn — (This code is intended for the coding of the outcome of delivery on the mother's record) ♀
V89.01 Suspected problem with amniotic cavity and membrane not found ♀

ICD-9-CM Procedural

72.0 Low forceps operation ♀
72.1 Low forceps operation with episiotomy ♀
72.21 Mid forceps operation with episiotomy ♀
72.29 Other mid forceps operation ♀
72.31 High forceps operation with episiotomy ♀
72.39 Other high forceps operation ♀
72.4 Forceps rotation of fetal head ♀
72.51 Partial breech extraction with forceps to aftercoming head ♀
72.52 Other partial breech extraction ♀

72.53 Total breech extraction with forceps to aftercoming head ♀
72.54 Other total breech extraction ♀
72.6 Forceps application to aftercoming head ♀
72.71 Vacuum extraction with episiotomy ♀
72.79 Other vacuum extraction ♀
72.8 Other specified instrumental delivery ♀
72.9 Unspecified instrumental delivery ♀
73.01 Induction of labor by artificial rupture of membranes ♀
73.09 Other artificial rupture of membranes ♀
73.4 Medical induction of labor ♀
73.59 Other manually assisted delivery ♀
73.6 Episiotomy ♀

59618-59622

59618 Routine obstetric care including antepartum care, cesarean delivery, and postpartum care, following attempted vaginal delivery after previous cesarean delivery
59620 Cesarean delivery only, following attempted vaginal delivery after previous cesarean delivery;
59622 including postpartum care

ICD-9-CM Diagnostic

640.01 Threatened abortion, delivered ♀
640.91 Unspecified hemorrhage in early pregnancy, delivered ♀
641.01 Placenta previa without hemorrhage, with delivery ♀
641.11 Hemorrhage from placenta previa, with delivery ♀
641.21 Premature separation of placenta, with delivery ♀
641.31 Antepartum hemorrhage associated with coagulation defects, with delivery ♀
641.81 Other antepartum hemorrhage, with delivery ♀
641.91 Unspecified antepartum hemorrhage, with delivery ♀
642.01 Benign essential hypertension with delivery ♀
642.11 Hypertension secondary to renal disease, with delivery ♀
642.21 Other pre-existing hypertension, with delivery ♀
642.31 Transient hypertension of pregnancy, with delivery ♀
642.41 Mild or unspecified pre-eclampsia, with delivery ♀
642.51 Severe pre-eclampsia, with delivery ♀
642.61 Eclampsia, with delivery ♀
642.71 Pre-eclampsia or eclampsia superimposed on pre-existing hypertension, with delivery ♀
642.91 Unspecified hypertension, with delivery ♀
643.01 Mild hyperemesis gravidarum, delivered ♀
643.11 Hyperemesis gravidarum with metabolic disturbance, delivered ♀
643.21 Late vomiting of pregnancy, delivered ♀
643.81 Other vomiting complicating pregnancy, delivered — (Use additional code to specify cause) ♀
643.91 Unspecified vomiting of pregnancy, delivered ♀
644.21 Early onset of delivery, delivered, with or without mention of antepartum condition ♀
645.11 Post term pregnancy, delivered, with or without mention of antepartum condition ♀
645.21 Prolonged pregnancy, delivered, with or without mention of antepartum condition ♀
646.01 Papyraceous fetus, delivered, with or without mention of antepartum condition — (Use additional code to further specify complication) ♀
646.11 Edema or excessive weight gain in pregnancy, with delivery, with or without mention of antepartum complication — (Use additional code to further specify complication) ♀
646.21 Unspecified renal disease in pregnancy, with delivery — (Use additional code to further specify complication) ♀
646.31 Pregnancy complication, recurrent pregnancy loss, with or without mention of antepartum condition — (Use additional code to further specify complication) ♀
646.41 Peripheral neuritis in pregnancy, with delivery — (Use additional code to further specify complication) ♀
646.51 Asymptomatic bacteriuria in pregnancy, with delivery — (Use additional code to further specify complication) ♀
646.61 Infections of genitourinary tract in pregnancy, with delivery — (Use additional code to further specify complication) ♀
646.71 Liver and biliary tract disorders in pregnancy, delivered, with or without mention of antepartum condition — (Use additional code to further specify complication) ♀
646.81 Other specified complication of pregnancy, with delivery — (Use additional code to further specify complication) ♀
646.91 Unspecified complication of pregnancy, with delivery — (Use additional code to further specify complication) ♀
647.01 Maternal syphilis, complicating pregnancy, with delivery — (Use additional code to further specify complication) ♀
647.11 Maternal gonorrhea with delivery — (Use additional code to further specify complication) ♀
647.21 Other maternal venereal diseases with delivery — (Use additional code to further specify complication) ♀
647.31 Maternal tuberculosis with delivery — (Use additional code to further specify complication) ♀
647.41 Maternal malaria with delivery — (Use additional code to further specify complication) ♀
647.51 Maternal rubella with delivery — (Use additional code to further specify complication) ♀
647.61 Other maternal viral disease with delivery — (Use additional code to further specify complication) ♀
647.81 Other specified maternal infectious and parasitic disease with delivery — (Use additional code to further specify complication) ♀
647.91 Unspecified maternal infection or infestation with delivery — (Use additional code to further specify complication) ♀
648.01 Maternal diabetes mellitus with delivery — (Use additional code(s) to identify the condition) ♀
648.11 Maternal thyroid dysfunction with delivery, with or without mention of antepartum condition — (Use additional code(s) to identify the condition) ♀
648.21 Maternal anemia, with delivery — (Use additional code(s) to identify the condition) ♀
648.31 Maternal drug dependence, with delivery — (Use additional code(s) to identify the condition) ♀
648.41 Maternal mental disorders, with delivery — (Use additional code(s) to identify the condition) ♀
648.51 Maternal congenital cardiovascular disorders, with delivery — (Use additional code(s) to identify the condition) ♀
648.61 Other maternal cardiovascular diseases, with delivery — (Use additional code(s) to identify the condition) ♀
648.71 Bone and joint disorders of maternal back, pelvis, and lower limbs, with delivery — (Use additional code(s) to identify the condition) ♀
648.81 Abnormal maternal glucose tolerance, with delivery — (Use additional code(s) to identify the condition. Use additional code, if applicable, for associated long-term (current) insulin use: V58.67) ♀
648.91 Other current maternal conditions classifiable elsewhere, with delivery — (Use additional code(s) to identify the condition) ♀
649.01 Tobacco use disorder complicating pregnancy, childbirth, or the puerperium, delivered, with or without mention of antepartum condition ♀
649.11 Obesity complicating pregnancy, childbirth, or the puerperium, delivered, with or without mention of antepartum condition — (Use additional code to identify the obesity: 278.00-278.01) ♀
649.21 Bariatric surgery status complicating pregnancy, childbirth, or the puerperium, delivered, with or without mention of antepartum condition ♀
649.31 Coagulation defects complicating pregnancy, childbirth, or the puerperium, delivered, with or without mention of antepartum condition — (Use additional code to identify the specific coagulation defect: 286.0-286.9, 287.0-287.9, 289.0-289.9) ♀
649.41 Epilepsy complicating pregnancy, childbirth, or the puerperium, delivered, with or without mention of antepartum condition — (Use additional code to identify the specific type of epilepsy: 345.00-345.91) ♀

649.51 Spotting complicating pregnancy, delivered, with or without mention of antepartum condition ♀
649.61 Uterine size date discrepancy, delivered, with or without mention of antepartum condition ♀
649.71 Cervical shortening, delivered, with or without mention of antepartum condition ♀
651.01 Twin pregnancy, delivered ♀
651.11 Triplet pregnancy, delivered ♀
651.21 Quadruplet pregnancy, delivered ♀
651.31 Twin pregnancy with fetal loss and retention of one fetus, delivered ♀
651.41 Triplet pregnancy with fetal loss and retention of one or more, delivered ♀
651.51 Quadruplet pregnancy with fetal loss and retention of one or more, delivered ♀
651.61 Other multiple pregnancy with fetal loss and retention of one or more fetus(es), delivered ♀
651.71 Multiple gestation following (elective) fetal reduction, delivered, with or without mention of antepartum condition ♀
651.81 Other specified multiple gestation, delivered ♀
651.91 Unspecified multiple gestation, delivered ▽ ♀
652.01 Unstable lie of fetus, delivered — (Code first any associated obstructed labor: 660.0) ♀
652.11 Breech or other malpresentation successfully converted to cephalic presentation, delivered — (Code first any associated obstructed labor, 660.0) ♀
652.21 Breech presentation without mention of version, delivered — (Code first any associated obstructed labor, 660.0) ♀
652.31 Transverse or oblique fetal presentation, delivered — (Code first any associated obstructed labor: 660.0) ♀
652.41 Fetal face or brow presentation, delivered — (Code first any associated obstructed labor: 660.0) ♀
652.51 High fetal head at term, delivered — (Code first any associated obstructed labor: 660.0) ♀
652.61 Multiple gestation with malpresentation of one fetus or more, delivered — (Code first any associated obstructed labor: 660.0) ♀
652.71 Prolapsed arm of fetus, delivered — (Code first any associated obstructed labor: 660.0) ♀
652.81 Other specified malposition or malpresentation of fetus, delivered — (Code first any associated obstructed labor: 660.0) ♀
652.91 Unspecified malposition or malpresentation of fetus, delivered — (Code first any associated obstructed labor: 660.0) ▽ ♀
653.01 Major abnormality of bony pelvis, not further specified, delivered — (Code first any associated obstructed labor: 660.1) ♀
653.11 Generally contracted pelvis in pregnancy, delivered — (Code first any associated obstructed labor: 660.1) ♀
653.21 Inlet contraction of pelvis in pregnancy, delivered — (Code first any associated obstructed labor: 660.1) ♀
653.31 Outlet contraction of pelvis in pregnancy, delivered — (Code first any associated obstructed labor: 660.1) ♀
653.41 Fetopelvic disproportion, delivered — (Code first any associated obstructed labor: 660.1) ♀
653.51 Unusually large fetus causing disproportion, delivered — (Code first any associated obstructed labor: 660.1) ♀
653.61 Hydrocephalic fetus causing disproportion, delivered — (Code first any associated obstructed labor: 660.1) ♀
653.71 Other fetal abnormality causing disproportion, delivered — (Code first any associated obstructed labor: 660.1) ♀
654.01 Congenital abnormalities of pregnant uterus, delivered — (Code first any associated obstructed labor: 660.2) ♀
654.11 Tumors of body of uterus, delivered — (Code first any associated obstructed labor, 660.2) ♀
654.21 Previous cesarean delivery, delivered, with or without mention of antepartum condition — (Code first any associated obstructed labor, 660.2) ♀
654.31 Retroverted and incarcerated gravid uterus, delivered — (Code first any associated obstructed labor, 660.2) ♀
654.41 Other abnormalities in shape or position of gravid uterus and of neighboring structures, delivered — (Code first any associated obstructed labor: 660.2) ♀
654.51 Cervical incompetence, delivered — (Code first any associated obstructed labor: 660.2) ♀
654.61 Other congenital or acquired abnormality of cervix, with delivery — (Code first any associated obstructed labor: 660.2) ♀
654.71 Congenital or acquired abnormality of vagina, with delivery — (Code first any associated obstructed labor: 660.2) ♀
654.81 Congenital or acquired abnormality of vulva, with delivery — (Code first any associated obstructed labor, 660.2) ♀
654.91 Other and unspecified abnormality of organs and soft tissues of pelvis, with delivery — (Code first any associated obstructed labor: 660.2) ▽ ♀
655.01 Central nervous system malformation in fetus, with delivery ♀
655.11 Chromosomal abnormality in fetus, affecting management of mother, with delivery ♀
655.21 Hereditary disease in family possibly affecting fetus, affecting management of mother, with delivery ♀
655.31 Suspected damage to fetus from viral disease in mother, affecting management of mother, with delivery ♀
655.41 Suspected damage to fetus from other disease in mother, affecting management of mother, with delivery ♀
655.51 Suspected damage to fetus from drugs, affecting management of mother, delivered ♀
655.61 Suspected damage to fetus from radiation, affecting management of mother, delivered ♀
655.81 Other known or suspected fetal abnormality, not elsewhere classified, affecting management of mother, delivery ♀
655.91 Unspecified fetal abnormality affecting management of mother, delivery ▽ ♀
656.01 Fetal-maternal hemorrhage, with delivery ♀
656.11 Rhesus isoimmunization affecting management of mother, delivered ♀
656.21 Isoimmunization from other and unspecified blood-group incompatibility, affecting management of mother, delivered ♀
656.31 Fetal distress affecting management of mother, delivered ♀
656.41 Intrauterine death affecting management of mother, delivered ♀
656.51 Poor fetal growth, affecting management of mother, delivered ♀
656.61 Excessive fetal growth affecting management of mother, delivered ♀
656.71 Other placental conditions affecting management of mother, delivered ♀
656.81 Other specified fetal and placental problems affecting management of mother, delivered ♀
656.91 Unspecified fetal and placental problem affecting management of mother, delivered ▽ ♀
657.01 Polyhydramnios, with delivery ♀
658.01 Oligohydramnios, delivered ♀
658.11 Premature rupture of membranes in pregnancy, delivered ♀
658.21 Delayed delivery after spontaneous or unspecified rupture of membranes, delivered ♀
658.31 Delayed delivery after artificial rupture of membranes, delivered ♀
658.41 Infection of amniotic cavity, delivered ♀
658.81 Other problem associated with amniotic cavity and membranes, delivered ♀
658.91 Unspecified problem associated with amniotic cavity and membranes, delivered ▽ ♀
659.01 Failed mechanical induction of labor, delivered ♀
659.11 Failed medical or unspecified induction of labor, delivered ♀
659.21 Unspecified maternal pyrexia during labor, delivered ▽ ♀
659.31 Generalized infection during labor, delivered ♀
659.41 Grand multiparity, delivered, with or without mention of antepartum condition ♀
659.51 Elderly primigravida, delivered ♀
659.61 Elderly multigravida, delivered, with mention of antepartum condition ♀
659.81 Other specified indication for care or intervention related to labor and delivery, delivered ♀
659.91 Unspecified indication for care or intervention related to labor and delivery, delivered ▽ ♀

660.01 Obstruction caused by malposition of fetus at onset of labor, delivered — (Use additional code from 652.0-652.9 to identify condition) ♀
660.11 Obstruction by bony pelvis during labor and delivery, delivered — (Use additional code from 653.0-653.9 to identify condition) ♀
660.21 Obstruction by abnormal pelvic soft tissues during labor and delivery, delivered — (Use additional code from 654.0-654.9 to identify condition) ♀
660.31 Deep transverse arrest and persistent occipitoposterior position during labor and deliver, delivered ♀
660.41 Shoulder (girdle) dystocia during labor and deliver, delivered ♀
660.51 Locked twins, delivered ♀
660.61 Unspecified failed trial of labor, delivered ▽ ♀
660.71 Unspecified failed forceps or vacuum extractor, delivered ▽ ♀
660.81 Other causes of obstructed labor, delivered — (Use additional code to identify condition) ♀
660.91 Unspecified obstructed labor, with delivery ▽ ♀
661.01 Primary uterine inertia, with delivery ♀
661.11 Secondary uterine inertia, with delivery ♀
661.21 Other and unspecified uterine inertia, with delivery ▽ ♀
662.01 Prolonged first stage of labor, delivered ♀
662.21 Prolonged second stage of labor, delivered ♀
662.31 Delayed delivery of second twin, triplet, etc., delivered ♀
663.01 Prolapse of cord, complicating labor and delivery, delivered ♀
663.11 Cord around neck, with compression, complicating labor and delivery, delivered ♀
663.21 Other and unspecified cord entanglement, with compression, complicating labor and delivery, delivered ▽ ♀
663.31 Other and unspecified cord entanglement, without mention of compression, complicating labor and delivery, delivered ▽ ♀
663.41 Short cord complicating labor and delivery, delivered ♀
663.51 Vasa previa complicating labor and delivery, delivered ♀
663.61 Vascular lesions of cord complicating labor and delivery, delivered ♀
663.81 Other umbilical cord complications during labor and delivery, delivered ♀
663.91 Unspecified umbilical cord complication during labor and delivery, delivered ▽ ♀
665.01 Rupture of uterus before onset of labor, with delivery ♀
665.11 Rupture of uterus during labor, with delivery ♀
665.22 Inversion of uterus, delivered with postpartum complication ♀
665.81 Other specified obstetrical trauma, with delivery ♀
665.82 Other specified obstetrical trauma, delivered, with postpartum ♀
665.91 Unspecified obstetrical trauma, with delivery ▽ ♀
665.92 Unspecified obstetrical trauma, delivered, with postpartum complication ▽ ♀
666.02 Third-stage postpartum hemorrhage, with delivery ♀
666.12 Other immediate postpartum hemorrhage, with delivery ♀
667.02 Retained placenta without hemorrhage, with delivery, with mention of postpartum complication ♀
667.12 Retained portions of placenta or membranes, without hemorrhage, delivered, with mention of postpartum complication ♀
668.01 Pulmonary complications of the administration of anesthesia or other sedation in labor and delivery, delivered — (Use additional code(s) to further specify complication) ♀
668.11 Cardiac complications of the administration of anesthesia or other sedation in labor and delivery, delivered — (Use additional code(s) to further specify complication) ♀
668.21 Central nervous system complications of the administration of anesthesia or other sedation in labor and delivery, delivered — (Use additional code(s) to further specify complication) ♀
668.81 Other complications of the administration of anesthesia or other sedation in labor and delivery, delivered — (Use additional code(s) to further specify complication) ♀
668.91 Unspecified complication of the administration of anesthesia or other sedation in labor and delivery, delivered — (Use additional code(s) to further specify complication) ▽ ♀
669.01 Maternal distress, with delivery, with or without mention of antepartum condition ♀
669.02 Maternal distress, with delivery, with mention of postpartum complication ♀
669.11 Shock during or following labor and delivery, with delivery, with or without mention of antepartum condition ♀
669.12 Shock during or following labor and delivery, with delivery, with mention of postpartum complication ♀
669.21 Maternal hypotension syndrome, with delivery, with or without mention of antepartum condition ♀
669.32 Acute kidney failure following labor and delivery, delivered, with mention of postpartum complication ♀
669.41 Other complications of obstetrical surgery and procedures, with delivery, with or without mention of antepartum condition ♀
669.42 Other complications of obstetrical surgery and procedures, with delivery, with mention of postpartum complication ♀
669.51 Forceps or vacuum extractor delivery without mention of indication, delivered, with or without mention of antepartum condition ♀
669.61 Breech extraction, without mention of indication, delivered, with or without mention of antepartum condition ♀
669.71 Cesarean delivery, without mention of indication, delivered, with or without mention of antepartum condition ♀
669.81 Other complication of labor and delivery, delivered, with or without mention of antepartum condition ♀
669.91 Unspecified complication of labor and delivery, with delivery, with or without mention of antepartum condition ▽ ♀
671.01 Varicose veins of legs, with delivery, with or without mention of antepartum condition ♀
671.81 Other venous complication, with delivery, with or without mention of antepartum condition ♀
671.82 Other venous complication, with delivery, with mention of postpartum complication ♀
676.01 Retracted nipple, delivered, with or without mention of antepartum condition ♀
676.02 Retracted nipple, delivered, with mention of postpartum complication ♀
676.21 Engorgement of breasts, delivered, with or without mention of antepartum condition ♀
676.22 Engorgement of breasts, delivered, with mention of postpartum complication ♀
676.31 Other and unspecified disorder of breast associated with childbirth, delivered, with or without mention of antepartum condition ▽ ♀
676.32 Other and unspecified disorder of breast associated with childbirth, delivered, with mention of postpartum complication ▽ ♀
676.41 Failure of lactation, with delivery, with or without mention of antepartum condition ♀
676.42 Failure of lactation, with delivery, with mention of postpartum complication ♀
676.51 Suppressed lactation, with delivery, with or without mention of antepartum condition ♀
676.52 Suppressed lactation, with delivery, with mention of postpartum complication ♀
676.91 Unspecified disorder of lactation, with delivery, with or without mention of antepartum condition ▽ ♀
676.92 Unspecified disorder of lactation, with delivery, with mention of postpartum complication ▽ ♀
678.01 Fetal hematologic conditions, delivered, with or without mention of antepartum condition ♀
678.11 Fetal conjoined twins, delivered, with or without mention of antepartum condition ♀
679.01 Maternal complications from in utero procedure, delivered, with or without mention of antepartum condition ♀
679.02 Maternal complications from in utero procedure, delivered, with mention of postpartum complication ♀
V23.0 Pregnancy with history of infertility ♀
V23.1 Pregnancy with history of trophoblastic disease ♀
V23.2 Pregnancy with history of abortion ♀
V23.3 Pregnancy with grand multiparity ♀
V23.41 Supervision of pregnancy with history of pre-term labor ♀
V23.49 Supervision of pregnancy with other poor obstetric history ♀
V23.5 Pregnancy with other poor reproductive history ♀

[Resequenced code] ▽ Unspecified code ⊠ Manifestation code ♀ Female diagnosis ♂ Male diagnosis

V23.7 Insufficient prenatal care ♀

V23.82 Supervision of high-risk pregnancy of elderly multigravida ♀

V23.84 Supervision of high-risk pregnancy of young multigravida ♀

V23.89 Supervision of other high-risk pregnancy ♀

V23.9 Unspecified high-risk pregnancy ▽ ♀

V24.0 Postpartum care and examination immediately after delivery ♀

V24.1 Postpartum care and examination of lactating mother ♀

V24.2 Routine postpartum follow-up ♀

V27.0 Outcome of delivery, single liveborn — (This code is intended for the coding of the outcome of delivery on the mother's record) ♀

V27.1 Outcome of delivery, single stillborn — (This code is intended for the coding of the outcome of delivery on the mother's record) ♀

V27.2 Outcome of delivery, twins, both liveborn — (This code is intended for the coding of the outcome of delivery on the mother's record) ♀

V27.3 Outcome of delivery, twins, one liveborn and one stillborn — (This code is intended for the coding of the outcome of delivery on the mother's record) ♀

V27.4 Outcome of delivery, twins, both stillborn — (This code is intended for the coding of the outcome of delivery on the mother's record) ♀

ICD-9-CM Procedural

73.3 Failed forceps ♀

74.0 Classical cesarean section ♀

74.1 Low cervical cesarean section ♀

74.4 Cesarean section of other specified type ♀

59812

59812 Treatment of incomplete abortion, any trimester, completed surgically

ICD-9-CM Diagnostic

631.8 Other abnormal products of conception ♀

634.01 Incomplete spontaneous abortion complicated by genital tract and pelvic infection ♀

634.11 Incomplete spontaneous abortion complicated by delayed or excessive hemorrhage ♀

634.21 Incomplete spontaneous abortion complicated by damage to pelvic organs or tissues ♀

634.31 Incomplete spontaneous abortion complicated by renal failure ♀

634.41 Incomplete spontaneous abortion complicated by metabolic disorder ♀

634.51 Incomplete spontaneous abortion complicated by shock ♀

634.61 Incomplete spontaneous abortion complicated by embolism ♀

634.71 Incomplete spontaneous abortion with other specified complications ♀

634.81 Incomplete spontaneous abortion with unspecified complication ▽ ♀

634.91 Incomplete spontaneous abortion without mention of complication ♀

635.01 Incomplete legally induced abortion complicated by genital tract and pelvic infection ♀

635.11 Incomplete legally induced abortion complicated by delayed or excessive hemorrhage ♀

635.21 Legally induced abortion complicated by damage to pelvic organs or tissues, incomplete ♀

635.31 Incomplete legally induced abortion complicated by renal failure ♀

635.41 Incomplete legally induced abortion complicated by metabolic disorder ♀

635.51 Legally induced abortion, complicated by shock, incomplete ♀

635.61 Incomplete legally induced abortion complicated by embolism ♀

635.71 Incomplete legally induced abortion with other specified complications ♀

635.81 Incomplete legally induced abortion with unspecified complication ▽ ♀

635.91 Incomplete legally induced abortion without mention of complication ♀

636.01 Incomplete illegally induced abortion complicated by genital tract and pelvic infection ♀

636.11 Incomplete illegally induced abortion complicated by delayed or excessive hemorrhage ♀

636.21 Incomplete illegally induced abortion complicated by damage to pelvic organs or tissues ♀

636.31 Incomplete illegally induced abortion complicated by renal failure ♀

636.41 Incomplete illegally induced abortion complicated by metabolic disorder ♀

636.51 Incomplete illegally induced abortion complicated by shock ♀

636.61 Incomplete illegally induced abortion complicated by embolism ♀

636.71 Incomplete illegally induced abortion with other specified complications ♀

636.81 Incomplete illegally induced abortion with unspecified complication ▽ ♀

636.91 Incomplete illegally induced abortion without mention of complication ♀

637.01 Abortion, unspecified as to legality, incomplete, complicated by genital tract and pelvic infection ♀

637.11 Abortion, unspecified as to legality, incomplete, complicated by delayed or excessive hemorrhage ♀

637.21 Abortion, unspecified as to legality, incomplete, complicated by damage to pelvic organs or tissues ♀

637.31 Abortion, unspecified as to legality, incomplete, complicated by renal failure ♀

637.41 Abortion, unspecified as to legality, incomplete, complicated by metabolic disorder ♀

637.51 Abortion, unspecified as to legality, incomplete, complicated by shock ♀

637.61 Abortion, unspecified as to legality, incomplete, complicated by embolism ♀

637.71 Abortion, unspecified as to legality, incomplete, with other specified complications ♀

637.81 Abortion, unspecified as to legality, incomplete, with unspecified complication ▽ ♀

637.91 Abortion, unspecified as to legality, incomplete, without mention of complication ♀

639.0 Genital tract and pelvic infection following abortion or ectopic and molar pregnancies ♀

639.1 Delayed or excessive hemorrhage following abortion or ectopic and molar pregnancies ♀

639.2 Damage to pelvic organs and tissues following abortion or ectopic and molar pregnancies ♀

639.3 Complications following abortion and ectopic and molar pregnancies, kidney failure ♀

639.4 Metabolic disorders following abortion or ectopic and molar pregnancies ♀

639.5 Shock following abortion or ectopic and molar pregnancies ♀

639.6 Embolism following abortion or ectopic and molar pregnancies ♀

639.8 Other specified complication following abortion or ectopic and molar pregnancies ♀

639.9 Unspecified complication following abortion or ectopic and molar pregnancies ▽ ♀

ICD-9-CM Procedural

69.02 Dilation and curettage following delivery or abortion ♀

69.52 Aspiration curettage following delivery or abortion ♀

HCPCS Level II Supplies & Services

A4305 Disposable drug delivery system, flow rate of 50 ml or greater per hour

59820-59821

59820 Treatment of missed abortion, completed surgically; first trimester

59821 second trimester

ICD-9-CM Diagnostic

631.8 Other abnormal products of conception ♀

632 Missed abortion — (Use additional code from category 639 to identify any associated complications) ♀

656.41 Intrauterine death affecting management of mother, delivered ♀

656.43 Intrauterine death affecting management of mother, antepartum ♀

ICD-9-CM Procedural

69.02 Dilation and curettage following delivery or abortion ♀

69.52 Aspiration curettage following delivery or abortion ♀

HCPCS Level II Supplies & Services

A4305 Disposable drug delivery system, flow rate of 50 ml or greater per hour

59830

59830 Treatment of septic abortion, completed surgically

ICD-9-CM Diagnostic

634.01 Incomplete spontaneous abortion complicated by genital tract and pelvic infection ♀

634.71 Incomplete spontaneous abortion with other specified complications ♀
634.81 Incomplete spontaneous abortion with unspecified complication ▼ ♀
634.91 Incomplete spontaneous abortion without mention of complication ♀
635.01 Incomplete legally induced abortion complicated by genital tract and pelvic infection ♀
635.81 Incomplete legally induced abortion with unspecified complication ▼ ♀
635.91 Incomplete legally induced abortion without mention of complication ♀
636.01 Incomplete illegally induced abortion complicated by genital tract and pelvic infection ♀
636.71 Incomplete illegally induced abortion with other specified complications ♀
636.81 Incomplete illegally induced abortion with unspecified complication ▼ ♀
636.91 Incomplete illegally induced abortion without mention of complication ♀
637.01 Abortion, unspecified as to legality, incomplete, complicated by genital tract and pelvic infection ♀
637.71 Abortion, unspecified as to legality, incomplete, with other specified complications ♀
637.81 Abortion, unspecified as to legality, incomplete, with unspecified complication ▼ ♀
638.0 Failed attempted abortion complicated by genital tract and pelvic infection ♀
638.7 Failed attempted abortion with other specified complication ♀
656.41 Intrauterine death affecting management of mother, delivered ♀
656.43 Intrauterine death affecting management of mother, antepartum ♀

ICD-9-CM Procedural

69.02 Dilation and curettage following delivery or abortion ♀

59840-59841

59840 Induced abortion, by dilation and curettage
59841 Induced abortion, by dilation and evacuation

ICD-9-CM Diagnostic

631.8 Other abnormal products of conception ♀
635.00 Unspecified legally induced abortion complicated by genital tract and pelvic infection ▼ ♀
635.01 Incomplete legally induced abortion complicated by genital tract and pelvic infection ♀
635.02 Complete legally induced abortion complicated by genital tract and pelvic infection ♀
635.10 Unspecified legally induced abortion complicated by delayed or excessive hemorrhage ▼ ♀
635.11 Incomplete legally induced abortion complicated by delayed or excessive hemorrhage ♀
635.12 Complete legally induced abortion complicated by delayed or excessive hemorrhage ♀
635.20 Unspecified legally induced abortion complicated by damage to pelvic organs or tissues ▼ ♀
635.21 Legally induced abortion complicated by damage to pelvic organs or tissues, incomplete ♀
635.22 Complete legally induced abortion complicated by damage to pelvic organs or tissues ♀
635.30 Unspecified legally induced abortion complicated by renal failure ▼ ♀
635.31 Incomplete legally induced abortion complicated by renal failure ♀
635.32 Complete legally induced abortion complicated by renal failure ♀
635.40 Unspecified legally induced abortion complicated by metabolic disorder ▼ ♀
635.41 Incomplete legally induced abortion complicated by metabolic disorder ♀
635.42 Complete legally induced abortion complicated by metabolic disorder ♀
635.50 Unspecified legally induced abortion complicated by shock ▼ ♀
635.51 Legally induced abortion, complicated by shock, incomplete ♀
635.52 Complete legally induced abortion complicated by shock ♀
635.60 Unspecified legally induced abortion complicated by embolism ▼ ♀
635.61 Incomplete legally induced abortion complicated by embolism ♀
635.62 Complete legally induced abortion complicated by embolism ♀
635.70 Unspecified legally induced abortion with other specified complications ▼ ♀
635.71 Incomplete legally induced abortion with other specified complications ♀
635.72 Complete legally induced abortion with other specified complications ♀
635.80 Unspecified legally induced abortion with unspecified complication ▼ ♀
635.81 Incomplete legally induced abortion with unspecified complication ▼ ♀
635.82 Complete legally induced abortion with unspecified complication ▼ ♀
635.90 Unspecified legally induced abortion without mention of complication ▼ ♀
635.91 Incomplete legally induced abortion without mention of complication ♀
635.92 Complete legally induced abortion without mention of complication ♀
646.03 Papyraceous fetus, antepartum — (Use additional code to further specify complication) ♀
646.23 Unspecified antepartum renal disease — (Use additional code to further specify complication) ▼ ♀
655.00 Central nervous system malformation in fetus, unspecified as to episode of care in pregnancy ▼ ♀
655.03 Central nervous system malformation in fetus, antepartum ♀
655.10 Chromosomal abnormality in fetus, affecting management of mother, unspecified as to episode of care in pregnancy ▼ ♀
655.13 Chromosomal abnormality in fetus, affecting management of mother, antepartum ♀
655.20 Hereditary disease in family possibly affecting fetus, affecting management of mother, unspecified as to episode of care in pregnancy ▼ ♀
655.30 Suspected damage to fetus from viral disease in mother, affecting management of mother, unspecified as to episode of care in pregnancy ▼ ♀
655.33 Suspected damage to fetus from viral disease in mother, affecting management of mother, antepartum condition or complication ♀
655.40 Suspected damage to fetus from other disease in mother, affecting management of mother, unspecified as to episode of care in pregnancy ▼ ♀
655.43 Suspected damage to fetus from other disease in mother, affecting management of mother, antepartum condition or complication ♀
655.50 Suspected damage to fetus from drugs, affecting management of mother, unspecified as to episode of care ▼ ♀
655.53 Suspected damage to fetus from drugs, affecting management of mother, antepartum ♀
655.60 Suspected damage to fetus from radiation, affecting management of mother, unspecified as to episode of care ▼ ♀
655.63 Suspected damage to fetus from radiation, affecting management of mother, antepartum condition or complication ♀
655.80 Other known or suspected fetal abnormality, not elsewhere classified, affecting management of mother, unspecified as to episode of care ▼ ♀
655.83 Other known or suspected fetal abnormality, not elsewhere classified, affecting management of mother, antepartum condition or complication ♀
655.90 Unspecified fetal abnormality affecting management of mother, unspecified as to episode of care ▼ ♀
655.93 Unspecified fetal abnormality affecting management of mother, antepartum condition or complication ▼ ♀
656.23 Isoimmunization from other and unspecified blood-group incompatibility, affecting management of mother, antepartum ♀
656.43 Intrauterine death affecting management of mother, antepartum ♀
659.63 Elderly multigravida, with antepartum condition or complication ♀
V61.7 Other unwanted pregnancy ♀

ICD-9-CM Procedural

69.01 Dilation and curettage for termination of pregnancy ♀
69.51 Aspiration curettage of uterus for termination of pregnancy ♀
69.99 Other operations on cervix and uterus ♀

HCPCS Level II Supplies & Services

A4305 Disposable drug delivery system, flow rate of 50 ml or greater per hour

59850-59852

59850 Induced abortion, by 1 or more intra-amniotic injections (amniocentesis-injections), including hospital admission and visits, delivery of fetus and secundines;
59851 with dilation and curettage and/or evacuation
59852 with hysterotomy (failed intra-amniotic injection)

ICD-9-CM Diagnostic

631.8 Other abnormal products of conception ♀
635.00 Unspecified legally induced abortion complicated by genital tract and pelvic infection ▼ ♀
635.01 Incomplete legally induced abortion complicated by genital tract and pelvic infection ♀
635.02 Complete legally induced abortion complicated by genital tract and pelvic infection ♀
635.10 Unspecified legally induced abortion complicated by delayed or excessive hemorrhage ▼ ♀
635.11 Incomplete legally induced abortion complicated by delayed or excessive hemorrhage ♀
635.12 Complete legally induced abortion complicated by delayed or excessive hemorrhage ♀
635.20 Unspecified legally induced abortion complicated by damage to pelvic organs or tissues ▼ ♀
635.21 Legally induced abortion complicated by damage to pelvic organs or tissues, incomplete ♀
635.22 Complete legally induced abortion complicated by damage to pelvic organs or tissues ♀
635.30 Unspecified legally induced abortion complicated by renal failure ▼ ♀
635.31 Incomplete legally induced abortion complicated by renal failure ♀
635.32 Complete legally induced abortion complicated by renal failure ♀
635.40 Unspecified legally induced abortion complicated by metabolic disorder ▼ ♀
635.41 Incomplete legally induced abortion complicated by metabolic disorder ♀
635.42 Complete legally induced abortion complicated by metabolic disorder ♀
635.50 Unspecified legally induced abortion complicated by shock ▼ ♀
635.51 Legally induced abortion, complicated by shock, incomplete ♀
635.52 Complete legally induced abortion complicated by shock ♀
635.60 Unspecified legally induced abortion complicated by embolism ▼ ♀
635.61 Incomplete legally induced abortion complicated by embolism ♀
635.62 Complete legally induced abortion complicated by embolism ♀
635.70 Unspecified legally induced abortion with other specified complications ▼ ♀
635.71 Incomplete legally induced abortion with other specified complications ♀
635.72 Complete legally induced abortion with other specified complications ♀
635.80 Unspecified legally induced abortion with unspecified complication ▼ ♀
635.81 Incomplete legally induced abortion with unspecified complication ▼ ♀
635.82 Complete legally induced abortion with unspecified complication ▼ ♀
635.90 Unspecified legally induced abortion without mention of complication ▼ ♀
635.91 Incomplete legally induced abortion without mention of complication ♀
635.92 Complete legally induced abortion without mention of complication ♀
638.0 Failed attempted abortion complicated by genital tract and pelvic infection ♀
638.1 Failed attempted abortion complicated by delayed or excessive hemorrhage ♀
638.2 Failed attempted abortion complicated by damage to pelvic organs or tissues ♀
638.3 Failed attempted abortion complicated by renal failure ♀
638.4 Failed attempted abortion complicated by metabolic disorder ♀
638.5 Failed attempted abortion complicated by shock ♀
638.6 Failed attempted abortion complicated by embolism ♀
638.7 Failed attempted abortion with other specified complication ♀
638.8 Failed attempted abortion with unspecified complication ▼ ♀
638.9 Failed attempted abortion without mention of complication ♀
646.03 Papyraceous fetus, antepartum — (Use additional code to further specify complication) ♀
646.23 Unspecified antepartum renal disease — (Use additional code to further specify complication) ▼ ♀
648.40 Maternal mental disorders, complicating pregnancy, childbirth, or the puerperium, unspecified as to episode of care — (Use additional code(s) to identify the condition) ▼ ♀
648.41 Maternal mental disorders, with delivery — (Use additional code(s) to identify the condition) ♀
648.43 Maternal mental disorders, antepartum — (Use additional code(s) to identify the condition) ♀
655.00 Central nervous system malformation in fetus, unspecified as to episode of care in pregnancy ▼ ♀
655.01 Central nervous system malformation in fetus, with delivery ♀
655.03 Central nervous system malformation in fetus, antepartum ♀
655.10 Chromosomal abnormality in fetus, affecting management of mother, unspecified as to episode of care in pregnancy ▼ ♀
655.13 Chromosomal abnormality in fetus, affecting management of mother, antepartum ♀
655.20 Hereditary disease in family possibly affecting fetus, affecting management of mother, unspecified as to episode of care in pregnancy ▼ ♀
655.21 Hereditary disease in family possibly affecting fetus, affecting management of mother, with delivery ♀
655.23 Hereditary disease in family possibly affecting fetus, affecting management of mother, antepartum condition or complication ♀
655.80 Other known or suspected fetal abnormality, not elsewhere classified, affecting management of mother, unspecified as to episode of care ▼ ♀
655.81 Other known or suspected fetal abnormality, not elsewhere classified, affecting management of mother, delivery ♀
655.83 Other known or suspected fetal abnormality, not elsewhere classified, affecting management of mother, antepartum condition or complication ♀
655.90 Unspecified fetal abnormality affecting management of mother, unspecified as to episode of care ▼ ♀
655.91 Unspecified fetal abnormality affecting management of mother, delivery ▼ ♀
655.93 Unspecified fetal abnormality affecting management of mother, antepartum condition or complication ▼ ♀
656.40 Intrauterine death affecting management of mother, unspecified as to episode of care ▼ ♀
656.41 Intrauterine death affecting management of mother, delivered ♀
656.43 Intrauterine death affecting management of mother, antepartum ♀
659.63 Elderly multigravida, with antepartum condition or complication ♀
V19.5 Family history of congenital anomalies
V61.7 Other unwanted pregnancy ♀

ICD-9-CM Procedural

69.01 Dilation and curettage for termination of pregnancy ♀
69.51 Aspiration curettage of uterus for termination of pregnancy ♀
74.91 Hysterotomy to terminate pregnancy ♀
75.0 Intra-amniotic injection for abortion ♀

59855-59857

59855 Induced abortion, by 1 or more vaginal suppositories (eg, prostaglandin) with or without cervical dilation (eg, laminaria), including hospital admission and visits, delivery of fetus and secundines;
59856 with dilation and curettage and/or evacuation
59857 with hysterotomy (failed medical evacuation)

ICD-9-CM Diagnostic

631.8 Other abnormal products of conception ♀
635.00 Unspecified legally induced abortion complicated by genital tract and pelvic infection ▼ ♀
635.01 Incomplete legally induced abortion complicated by genital tract and pelvic infection ♀
635.02 Complete legally induced abortion complicated by genital tract and pelvic infection ♀
635.10 Unspecified legally induced abortion complicated by delayed or excessive hemorrhage ▼ ♀

635.11 Incomplete legally induced abortion complicated by delayed or excessive hemorrhage ♀
635.12 Complete legally induced abortion complicated by delayed or excessive hemorrhage ♀
635.20 Unspecified legally induced abortion complicated by damage to pelvic organs or tissues ♀
635.21 Legally induced abortion complicated by damage to pelvic organs or tissues, incomplete ♀
635.22 Complete legally induced abortion complicated by damage to pelvic organs or tissues ♀
635.30 Unspecified legally induced abortion complicated by renal failure ♀
635.31 Incomplete legally induced abortion complicated by renal failure ♀
635.32 Complete legally induced abortion complicated by renal failure ♀
635.40 Unspecified legally induced abortion complicated by metabolic disorder ♀
635.41 Incomplete legally induced abortion complicated by metabolic disorder ♀
635.42 Complete legally induced abortion complicated by metabolic disorder ♀
635.50 Unspecified legally induced abortion complicated by shock ♀
635.51 Legally induced abortion, complicated by shock, incomplete ♀
635.52 Complete legally induced abortion complicated by shock ♀
635.60 Unspecified legally induced abortion complicated by embolism ♀
635.61 Incomplete legally induced abortion complicated by embolism ♀
635.62 Complete legally induced abortion complicated by embolism ♀
635.70 Unspecified legally induced abortion with other specified complications ♀
635.71 Incomplete legally induced abortion with other specified complications ♀
635.72 Complete legally induced abortion with other specified complications ♀
635.80 Unspecified legally induced abortion with unspecified complication ♀
635.81 Incomplete legally induced abortion with unspecified complication ♀
635.82 Complete legally induced abortion with unspecified complication ♀
635.90 Unspecified legally induced abortion without mention of complication ♀
635.91 Incomplete legally induced abortion without mention of complication ♀
635.92 Complete legally induced abortion without mention of complication ♀
638.0 Failed attempted abortion complicated by genital tract and pelvic infection ♀
638.1 Failed attempted abortion complicated by delayed or excessive hemorrhage ♀
638.2 Failed attempted abortion complicated by damage to pelvic organs or tissues ♀
638.3 Failed attempted abortion complicated by renal failure ♀
638.4 Failed attempted abortion complicated by metabolic disorder ♀
638.5 Failed attempted abortion complicated by shock ♀
638.6 Failed attempted abortion complicated by embolism ♀
638.7 Failed attempted abortion with other specified complication ♀
638.8 Failed attempted abortion with unspecified complication ♀
638.9 Failed attempted abortion without mention of complication ♀
646.03 Papyraceous fetus, antepartum — (Use additional code to further specify complication) ♀
646.23 Unspecified antepartum renal disease — (Use additional code to further specify complication) ♀
648.40 Maternal mental disorders, complicating pregnancy, childbirth, or the puerperium, unspecified as to episode of care — (Use additional code(s) to identify the condition) ♀
648.41 Maternal mental disorders, with delivery — (Use additional code(s) to identify the condition) ♀
648.43 Maternal mental disorders, antepartum — (Use additional code(s) to identify the condition) ♀
655.00 Central nervous system malformation in fetus, unspecified as to episode of care in pregnancy ♀
655.01 Central nervous system malformation in fetus, with delivery ♀
655.03 Central nervous system malformation in fetus, antepartum ♀
655.10 Chromosomal abnormality in fetus, affecting management of mother, unspecified as to episode of care in pregnancy ♀
655.13 Chromosomal abnormality in fetus, affecting management of mother, antepartum ♀
655.20 Hereditary disease in family possibly affecting fetus, affecting management of mother, unspecified as to episode of care in pregnancy ♀
655.21 Hereditary disease in family possibly affecting fetus, affecting management of mother, with delivery ♀
655.23 Hereditary disease in family possibly affecting fetus, affecting management of mother, antepartum condition or complication ♀
655.80 Other known or suspected fetal abnormality, not elsewhere classified, affecting management of mother, unspecified as to episode of care ♀
655.81 Other known or suspected fetal abnormality, not elsewhere classified, affecting management of mother, delivery ♀
655.83 Other known or suspected fetal abnormality, not elsewhere classified, affecting management of mother, antepartum condition or complication ♀
655.90 Unspecified fetal abnormality affecting management of mother, unspecified as to episode of care ♀
655.91 Unspecified fetal abnormality affecting management of mother, delivery ♀
655.93 Unspecified fetal abnormality affecting management of mother, antepartum condition or complication ♀
656.40 Intrauterine death affecting management of mother, unspecified as to episode of care ♀
656.41 Intrauterine death affecting management of mother, delivered ♀
656.43 Intrauterine death affecting management of mother, antepartum ♀
659.63 Elderly multigravida, with antepartum condition or complication ♀
V19.5 Family history of congenital anomalies
V61.7 Other unwanted pregnancy ♀

ICD-9-CM Procedural

69.01 Dilation and curettage for termination of pregnancy ♀
69.51 Aspiration curettage of uterus for termination of pregnancy ♀
69.93 Insertion of laminaria ♀
74.91 Hysterotomy to terminate pregnancy ♀
96.49 Other genitourinary instillation

59866

59866 Multifetal pregnancy reduction(s) (MPR)

ICD-9-CM Diagnostic

651.13 Triplet pregnancy, antepartum ♀
651.23 Quadruplet pregnancy, antepartum ♀
651.73 Multiple gestation following (elective) fetal reduction, antepartum condition or complication ♀
651.83 Other specified multiple gestation, antepartum ♀
651.93 Unspecified multiple gestation, antepartum ♀
V23.0 Pregnancy with history of infertility ♀
V23.41 Supervision of pregnancy with history of pre-term labor ♀
V23.49 Supervision of pregnancy with other poor obstetric history ♀
V23.5 Pregnancy with other poor reproductive history ♀
V23.81 Supervision of high-risk pregnancy of elderly primigravida ♀
V23.82 Supervision of high-risk pregnancy of elderly multigravida ♀
V23.83 Supervision of high-risk pregnancy of young primigravida ♀
V23.84 Supervision of high-risk pregnancy of young multigravida ♀
V23.89 Supervision of other high-risk pregnancy ♀

ICD-9-CM Procedural

75.0 Intra-amniotic injection for abortion ♀
75.99 Other obstetric operations ♀

59870

59870 Uterine evacuation and curettage for hydatidiform mole

ICD-9-CM Diagnostic

630 Hydatidiform mole — (Use additional code from category 639 to identify any associated complications) ♀

ICD-9-CM Procedural

69.01 Dilation and curettage for termination of pregnancy ♀

69.02 Dilation and curettage following delivery or abortion ♀

69.59 Other aspiration curettage of uterus ♀

HCPCS Level II Supplies & Services

A4305 Disposable drug delivery system, flow rate of 50 ml or greater per hour

59871

59871 Removal of cerclage suture under anesthesia (other than local)

ICD-9-CM Diagnostic

622.3 Old laceration of cervix ♀

654.53 Cervical incompetence, antepartum condition or complication — (Code first any associated obstructed labor, 660.2) ♀

654.63 Other congenital or acquired abnormality of cervix, antepartum condition or complication — (Code first any associated obstructed labor, 660.2) ♀

654.93 Other and unspecified abnormality of organs and soft tissues of pelvis, antepartum condition or complication — (Code first any associated obstructed labor, 660.2) ▽ ♀

V23.2 Pregnancy with history of abortion ♀

V23.81 Supervision of high-risk pregnancy of elderly primigravida ♀

V23.82 Supervision of high-risk pregnancy of elderly multigravida ♀

V23.83 Supervision of high-risk pregnancy of young primigravida ♀

V23.84 Supervision of high-risk pregnancy of young multigravida ♀

V23.89 Supervision of other high-risk pregnancy ♀

ICD-9-CM Procedural

69.96 Removal of cerclage material from cervix ♀

Endocrine System

Thyroid Gland

60000

60000 Incision and drainage of thyroglossal duct cyst, infected

ICD-9-CM Diagnostic

759.2 Congenital anomalies of other endocrine glands
780.60 Fever, unspecified ▼
780.62 Postprocedural fever
784.2 Swelling, mass, or lump in head and neck

ICD-9-CM Procedural

06.02 Reopening of wound of thyroid field
06.09 Other incision of thyroid field

HCPCS Level II Supplies & Services

A4305 Disposable drug delivery system, flow rate of 50 ml or greater per hour

60100

60100 Biopsy thyroid, percutaneous core needle

ICD-9-CM Diagnostic

193 Malignant neoplasm of thyroid gland — (Use additional code to identify any functional activity)
198.89 Secondary malignant neoplasm of other specified sites
226 Benign neoplasm of thyroid glands — (Use additional code to identify any functional activity)
234.8 Carcinoma in situ of other specified sites
237.4 Neoplasm of uncertain behavior of other and unspecified endocrine glands ▼
239.7 Neoplasm of unspecified nature of endocrine glands and other parts of nervous system
240.0 Goiter, specified as simple
240.9 Goiter, unspecified ▼
241.0 Nontoxic uninodular goiter
241.1 Nontoxic multinodular goiter
241.9 Unspecified nontoxic nodular goiter ▼
242.10 Toxic uninodular goiter without mention of thyrotoxic crisis or storm
242.11 Toxic uninodular goiter with mention of thyrotoxic crisis or storm
242.20 Toxic multinodular goiter without mention of thyrotoxic crisis or storm
242.21 Toxic multinodular goiter with mention of thyrotoxic crisis or storm
242.30 Toxic nodular goiter, unspecified type, without mention of thyrotoxic crisis or storm ▼
242.31 Toxic nodular goiter, unspecified type, with mention of thyrotoxic crisis or storm ▼
242.40 Thyrotoxicosis from ectopic thyroid nodule without mention of thyrotoxic crisis or storm
242.41 Thyrotoxicosis from ectopic thyroid nodule with mention of thyrotoxic crisis or storm
245.0 Acute thyroiditis — (Use additional code to identify organism)
245.1 Subacute thyroiditis
245.2 Chronic lymphocytic thyroiditis
245.3 Chronic fibrous thyroiditis
245.4 Iatrogenic thyroiditis — (Use additional code to identify cause)
245.8 Other and unspecified chronic thyroiditis ▼
245.9 Unspecified thyroiditis ▼
246.2 Cyst of thyroid
246.8 Other specified disorders of thyroid
648.10 Maternal thyroid dysfunction complicating pregnancy, childbirth, or the puerperium, unspecified as to episode of care or not applicable — (Use additional code(s) to identify the condition) ▼ ♀
648.11 Maternal thyroid dysfunction with delivery, with or without mention of antepartum condition — (Use additional code(s) to identify the condition) ♀
648.12 Maternal thyroid dysfunction with delivery, with current postpartum complication — (Use additional code(s) to identify the condition) ♀
648.13 Maternal thyroid dysfunction, antepartum condition or complication — (Use additional code(s) to identify the condition) ♀
648.14 Maternal thyroid dysfunction complicating pregnancy, childbirth, or the puerperium, postpartum condition or complication — (Use additional code(s) to identify the condition) ♀
759.2 Congenital anomalies of other endocrine glands
784.2 Swelling, mass, or lump in head and neck
794.5 Nonspecific abnormal results of thyroid function study
794.6 Nonspecific abnormal results of other endocrine function study
V10.29 Personal history of malignant neoplasm of other respiratory and intrathoracic organs

ICD-9-CM Procedural

06.11 Closed (percutaneous) (needle) biopsy of thyroid gland

HCPCS Level II Supplies & Services

A4305 Disposable drug delivery system, flow rate of 50 ml or greater per hour

60200

60200 Excision of cyst or adenoma of thyroid, or transection of isthmus

ICD-9-CM Diagnostic

226 Benign neoplasm of thyroid glands — (Use additional code to identify any functional activity)
237.4 Neoplasm of uncertain behavior of other and unspecified endocrine glands ▼
240.9 Goiter, unspecified ▼
241.0 Nontoxic uninodular goiter
241.1 Nontoxic multinodular goiter
241.9 Unspecified nontoxic nodular goiter ▼
242.00 Toxic diffuse goiter without mention of thyrotoxic crisis or storm
242.01 Toxic diffuse goiter with mention of thyrotoxic crisis or storm
242.10 Toxic uninodular goiter without mention of thyrotoxic crisis or storm
242.11 Toxic uninodular goiter with mention of thyrotoxic crisis or storm
242.20 Toxic multinodular goiter without mention of thyrotoxic crisis or storm
242.21 Toxic multinodular goiter with mention of thyrotoxic crisis or storm
242.30 Toxic nodular goiter, unspecified type, without mention of thyrotoxic crisis or storm ▼
242.31 Toxic nodular goiter, unspecified type, with mention of thyrotoxic crisis or storm ▼
242.40 Thyrotoxicosis from ectopic thyroid nodule without mention of thyrotoxic crisis or storm
242.41 Thyrotoxicosis from ectopic thyroid nodule with mention of thyrotoxic crisis or storm
242.80 Thyrotoxicosis of other specified origin without mention of thyrotoxic crisis or storm — (Use additional E code to identify cause, if drug-induced)
242.81 Thyrotoxicosis of other specified origin with mention of thyrotoxic crisis or storm — (Use additional E code to identify cause, if drug-induced)
242.90 Thyrotoxicosis without mention of goiter or other cause, without mention of thyrotoxic crisis or storm
242.91 Thyrotoxicosis without mention of goiter or other cause, with mention of thyrotoxic crisis or storm
245.8 Other and unspecified chronic thyroiditis ▼
246.2 Cyst of thyroid

784.2 Swelling, mass, or lump in head and neck

ICD-9-CM Procedural

06.31 Excision of lesion of thyroid
06.39 Other partial thyroidectomy
06.91 Division of thyroid isthmus

HCPCS Level II Supplies & Services

A4305 Disposable drug delivery system, flow rate of 50 ml or greater per hour

60210-60212

60210 Partial thyroid lobectomy, unilateral; with or without isthmusectomy
60212 with contralateral subtotal lobectomy, including isthmusectomy

ICD-9-CM Diagnostic

193 Malignant neoplasm of thyroid gland — (Use additional code to identify any functional activity)
198.89 Secondary malignant neoplasm of other specified sites
226 Benign neoplasm of thyroid glands — (Use additional code to identify any functional activity)
234.8 Carcinoma in situ of other specified sites
237.4 Neoplasm of uncertain behavior of other and unspecified endocrine glands ▽
239.7 Neoplasm of unspecified nature of endocrine glands and other parts of nervous system
240.0 Goiter, specified as simple
240.9 Goiter, unspecified ▽
241.0 Nontoxic uninodular goiter
241.1 Nontoxic multinodular goiter
241.9 Unspecified nontoxic nodular goiter ▽
242.10 Toxic uninodular goiter without mention of thyrotoxic crisis or storm
242.11 Toxic uninodular goiter with mention of thyrotoxic crisis or storm
242.20 Toxic multinodular goiter without mention of thyrotoxic crisis or storm
242.21 Toxic multinodular goiter with mention of thyrotoxic crisis or storm
242.30 Toxic nodular goiter, unspecified type, without mention of thyrotoxic crisis or storm ▽
242.31 Toxic nodular goiter, unspecified type, with mention of thyrotoxic crisis or storm ▽
242.40 Thyrotoxicosis from ectopic thyroid nodule without mention of thyrotoxic crisis or storm
242.41 Thyrotoxicosis from ectopic thyroid nodule with mention of thyrotoxic crisis or storm
245.0 Acute thyroiditis — (Use additional code to identify organism)
245.1 Subacute thyroiditis
245.2 Chronic lymphocytic thyroiditis
245.3 Chronic fibrous thyroiditis
245.4 Iatrogenic thyroiditis — (Use additional code to identify cause)
245.8 Other and unspecified chronic thyroiditis ▽
245.9 Unspecified thyroiditis ▽
246.2 Cyst of thyroid
246.8 Other specified disorders of thyroid
648.10 Maternal thyroid dysfunction complicating pregnancy, childbirth, or the puerperium, unspecified as to episode of care or not applicable — (Use additional code(s) to identify the condition) ▽ ♀
648.11 Maternal thyroid dysfunction with delivery, with or without mention of antepartum condition — (Use additional code(s) to identify the condition) ♀
648.12 Maternal thyroid dysfunction with delivery, with current postpartum complication — (Use additional code(s) to identify the condition) ♀
648.13 Maternal thyroid dysfunction, antepartum condition or complication — (Use additional code(s) to identify the condition) ♀
648.14 Maternal thyroid dysfunction complicating pregnancy, childbirth, or the puerperium, postpartum condition or complication — (Use additional code(s) to identify the condition) ♀
759.2 Congenital anomalies of other endocrine glands
784.2 Swelling, mass, or lump in head and neck
794.5 Nonspecific abnormal results of thyroid function study

ICD-9-CM Procedural

06.2 Unilateral thyroid lobectomy
06.39 Other partial thyroidectomy

60220-60225

60220 Total thyroid lobectomy, unilateral; with or without isthmusectomy
60225 with contralateral subtotal lobectomy, including isthmusectomy

ICD-9-CM Diagnostic

193 Malignant neoplasm of thyroid gland — (Use additional code to identify any functional activity)
195.0 Malignant neoplasm of head, face, and neck
198.89 Secondary malignant neoplasm of other specified sites
226 Benign neoplasm of thyroid glands — (Use additional code to identify any functional activity)
234.8 Carcinoma in situ of other specified sites
237.4 Neoplasm of uncertain behavior of other and unspecified endocrine glands ▽
239.7 Neoplasm of unspecified nature of endocrine glands and other parts of nervous system
240.0 Goiter, specified as simple
240.9 Goiter, unspecified ▽
241.0 Nontoxic uninodular goiter
241.1 Nontoxic multinodular goiter
241.9 Unspecified nontoxic nodular goiter ▽
242.10 Toxic uninodular goiter without mention of thyrotoxic crisis or storm
242.20 Toxic multinodular goiter without mention of thyrotoxic crisis or storm
245.2 Chronic lymphocytic thyroiditis
245.3 Chronic fibrous thyroiditis
245.4 Iatrogenic thyroiditis — (Use additional code to identify cause)
245.8 Other and unspecified chronic thyroiditis ▽
245.9 Unspecified thyroiditis ▽
648.10 Maternal thyroid dysfunction complicating pregnancy, childbirth, or the puerperium, unspecified as to episode of care or not applicable — (Use additional code(s) to identify the condition) ▽ ♀
648.11 Maternal thyroid dysfunction with delivery, with or without mention of antepartum condition — (Use additional code(s) to identify the condition) ♀
648.12 Maternal thyroid dysfunction with delivery, with current postpartum complication — (Use additional code(s) to identify the condition) ♀
648.13 Maternal thyroid dysfunction, antepartum condition or complication — (Use additional code(s) to identify the condition) ♀
648.14 Maternal thyroid dysfunction complicating pregnancy, childbirth, or the puerperium, postpartum condition or complication — (Use additional code(s) to identify the condition) ♀
784.2 Swelling, mass, or lump in head and neck

ICD-9-CM Procedural

06.2 Unilateral thyroid lobectomy
06.39 Other partial thyroidectomy

60240

60240 Thyroidectomy, total or complete

ICD-9-CM Diagnostic

193 Malignant neoplasm of thyroid gland — (Use additional code to identify any functional activity)
198.89 Secondary malignant neoplasm of other specified sites
226 Benign neoplasm of thyroid glands — (Use additional code to identify any functional activity)
234.8 Carcinoma in situ of other specified sites
237.4 Neoplasm of uncertain behavior of other and unspecified endocrine glands ▽
239.1 Neoplasm of unspecified nature of respiratory system

239.7 Neoplasm of unspecified nature of endocrine glands and other parts of nervous system
240.9 Goiter, unspecified ▼
241.0 Nontoxic uninodular goiter
241.1 Nontoxic multinodular goiter
241.9 Unspecified nontoxic nodular goiter ▼
242.00 Toxic diffuse goiter without mention of thyrotoxic crisis or storm
242.01 Toxic diffuse goiter with mention of thyrotoxic crisis or storm
242.10 Toxic uninodular goiter without mention of thyrotoxic crisis or storm
242.20 Toxic multinodular goiter without mention of thyrotoxic crisis or storm
242.21 Toxic multinodular goiter with mention of thyrotoxic crisis or storm
242.90 Thyrotoxicosis without mention of goiter or other cause, without mention of thyrotoxic crisis or storm
242.91 Thyrotoxicosis without mention of goiter or other cause, with mention of thyrotoxic crisis or storm
245.2 Chronic lymphocytic thyroiditis
245.8 Other and unspecified chronic thyroiditis ▼
245.9 Unspecified thyroiditis ▼
784.2 Swelling, mass, or lump in head and neck

ICD-9-CM Procedural

06.4 Complete thyroidectomy

60252-60254

60252 Thyroidectomy, total or subtotal for malignancy; with limited neck dissection
60254 with radical neck dissection

ICD-9-CM Diagnostic

161.0 Malignant neoplasm of glottis
161.1 Malignant neoplasm of supraglottis
161.2 Malignant neoplasm of subglottis
161.3 Malignant neoplasm of laryngeal cartilages
161.8 Malignant neoplasm of other specified sites of larynx
193 Malignant neoplasm of thyroid gland — (Use additional code to identify any functional activity)
196.0 Secondary and unspecified malignant neoplasm of lymph nodes of head, face, and neck
198.89 Secondary malignant neoplasm of other specified sites
200.01 Reticulosarcoma of lymph nodes of head, face, and neck
234.8 Carcinoma in situ of other specified sites
237.4 Neoplasm of uncertain behavior of other and unspecified endocrine glands ▼
238.8 Neoplasm of uncertain behavior of other specified sites
239.7 Neoplasm of unspecified nature of endocrine glands and other parts of nervous system
239.89 Neoplasms of unspecified nature, other specified sites

ICD-9-CM Procedural

06.39 Other partial thyroidectomy
06.4 Complete thyroidectomy
40.3 Regional lymph node excision
40.41 Radical neck dissection, unilateral

60260

60260 Thyroidectomy, removal of all remaining thyroid tissue following previous removal of a portion of thyroid

ICD-9-CM Diagnostic

161.3 Malignant neoplasm of laryngeal cartilages
193 Malignant neoplasm of thyroid gland — (Use additional code to identify any functional activity)
197.3 Secondary malignant neoplasm of other respiratory organs
198.89 Secondary malignant neoplasm of other specified sites
231.0 Carcinoma in situ of larynx
234.8 Carcinoma in situ of other specified sites
237.4 Neoplasm of uncertain behavior of other and unspecified endocrine glands ▼
239.7 Neoplasm of unspecified nature of endocrine glands and other parts of nervous system

ICD-9-CM Procedural

06.4 Complete thyroidectomy

60270-60271

60270 Thyroidectomy, including substernal thyroid; sternal split or transthoracic approach
60271 cervical approach

ICD-9-CM Diagnostic

193 Malignant neoplasm of thyroid gland — (Use additional code to identify any functional activity)
202.00 Nodular lymphoma, unspecified site, extranodal and solid organ sites ▼
226 Benign neoplasm of thyroid glands — (Use additional code to identify any functional activity)
237.4 Neoplasm of uncertain behavior of other and unspecified endocrine glands ▼
239.7 Neoplasm of unspecified nature of endocrine glands and other parts of nervous system
240.0 Goiter, specified as simple
240.9 Goiter, unspecified ▼
241.9 Unspecified nontoxic nodular goiter ▼
242.00 Toxic diffuse goiter without mention of thyrotoxic crisis or storm
242.01 Toxic diffuse goiter with mention of thyrotoxic crisis or storm
242.10 Toxic uninodular goiter without mention of thyrotoxic crisis or storm
242.11 Toxic uninodular goiter with mention of thyrotoxic crisis or storm
242.20 Toxic multinodular goiter without mention of thyrotoxic crisis or storm
242.40 Thyrotoxicosis from ectopic thyroid nodule without mention of thyrotoxic crisis or storm

ICD-9-CM Procedural

06.50 Substernal thyroidectomy, not otherwise specified
06.51 Partial substernal thyroidectomy
06.52 Complete substernal thyroidectomy

60280-60281

60280 Excision of thyroglossal duct cyst or sinus;
60281 recurrent

ICD-9-CM Diagnostic

759.2 Congenital anomalies of other endocrine glands

ICD-9-CM Procedural

06.7 Excision of thyroglossal duct or tract

60300

60300 Aspiration and/or injection, thyroid cyst

ICD-9-CM Diagnostic

193 Malignant neoplasm of thyroid gland — (Use additional code to identify any functional activity)
198.89 Secondary malignant neoplasm of other specified sites
226 Benign neoplasm of thyroid glands — (Use additional code to identify any functional activity)
234.8 Carcinoma in situ of other specified sites
237.4 Neoplasm of uncertain behavior of other and unspecified endocrine glands ▼
239.7 Neoplasm of unspecified nature of endocrine glands and other parts of nervous system
246.2 Cyst of thyroid
246.8 Other specified disorders of thyroid
246.9 Unspecified disorder of thyroid ▼
648.11 Maternal thyroid dysfunction with delivery, with or without mention of antepartum condition — (Use additional code(s) to identify the condition) ♀
648.12 Maternal thyroid dysfunction with delivery, with current postpartum complication — (Use additional code(s) to identify the condition) ♀

648.13 Maternal thyroid dysfunction, antepartum condition or complication — (Use additional code(s) to identify the condition) ♀
648.14 Maternal thyroid dysfunction complicating pregnancy, childbirth, or the puerperium, postpartum condition or complication — (Use additional code(s) to identify the condition) ♀
V10.29 Personal history of malignant neoplasm of other respiratory and intrathoracic organs
V18.11 Family history of multiple endocrine neoplasia [MEN] syndrome
V18.19 Family history of other endocrine and metabolic diseases

ICD-9-CM Procedural

06.01 Aspiration of thyroid field
06.98 Other operations on thyroid glands
99.29 Injection or infusion of other therapeutic or prophylactic substance

HCPCS Level II Supplies & Services

A4305 Disposable drug delivery system, flow rate of 50 ml or greater per hour

Parathyroid, Thymus, Adrenal Glands, Pancreas, and Carotid Body

60500-60505

60500 Parathyroidectomy or exploration of parathyroid(s);
60502 re-exploration
60505 with mediastinal exploration, sternal split or transthoracic approach

ICD-9-CM Diagnostic

194.1 Malignant neoplasm of parathyroid gland
196.1 Secondary and unspecified malignant neoplasm of intrathoracic lymph nodes
198.89 Secondary malignant neoplasm of other specified sites
227.1 Benign neoplasm of parathyroid gland — (Use additional code to identify any functional activity)
234.8 Carcinoma in situ of other specified sites
237.4 Neoplasm of uncertain behavior of other and unspecified endocrine glands ▽
238.8 Neoplasm of uncertain behavior of other specified sites
239.7 Neoplasm of unspecified nature of endocrine glands and other parts of nervous system
239.89 Neoplasms of unspecified nature, other specified sites
252.00 Hyperparathyroidism, unspecified ▽
252.01 Primary hyperparathyroidism
252.02 Secondary hyperparathyroidism, non-renal
252.08 Other hyperparathyroidism
252.1 Hypoparathyroidism
275.40 Unspecified disorder of calcium metabolism — (Use additional code to identify any associated intellectual disabilities) ▽
275.41 Hypocalcemia — (Use additional code to identify any associated intellectual disabilities)
275.42 Hypercalcemia — (Use additional code to identify any associated intellectual disabilities)
275.49 Other disorders of calcium metabolism — (Use additional code to identify any associated intellectual disabilities)
275.5 Hungry bone syndrome — (Use additional code to identify any associated intellectual disabilities)

ICD-9-CM Procedural

06.02 Reopening of wound of thyroid field
06.09 Other incision of thyroid field
06.81 Complete parathyroidectomy
06.89 Other parathyroidectomy
06.99 Other operations on parathyroid glands

60512

60512 Parathyroid autotransplantation (List separately in addition to code for primary procedure)

ICD-9-CM Diagnostic

The application of this code is too broad to adequately present ICD-9-CM diagnostic code links here. Refer to your ICD-9-CM book.

ICD-9-CM Procedural

06.95 Parathyroid tissue reimplantation

60520

60520 Thymectomy, partial or total; transcervical approach (separate procedure)

ICD-9-CM Diagnostic

164.0 Malignant neoplasm of thymus
196.1 Secondary and unspecified malignant neoplasm of intrathoracic lymph nodes
198.89 Secondary malignant neoplasm of other specified sites
209.22 Malignant carcinoid tumor of the thymus — (Code first any associated multiple endocrine neoplasia syndrome: 258.01-258.03)(Use additional code to identify associated endocrine syndrome, as: carcinoid syndrome: 259.2)
209.62 Benign carcinoid tumor of the thymus — (Code first any associated multiple endocrine neoplasia syndrome: 258.01-258.03)(Use additional code to identify associated endocrine syndrome, as: carcinoid syndrome: 259.2)
212.6 Benign neoplasm of thymus
235.8 Neoplasm of uncertain behavior of pleura, thymus, and mediastinum
238.8 Neoplasm of uncertain behavior of other specified sites
239.89 Neoplasms of unspecified nature, other specified sites
279.2 Combined immunity deficiency — (Use additional code to identify any associated intellectual disabilities) (Use additional code for associated manifestations)
358.00 Myasthenia gravis without (acute) exacerbation
358.01 Myasthenia gravis with (acute) exacerbation
759.2 Congenital anomalies of other endocrine glands
786.6 Swelling, mass, or lump in chest

ICD-9-CM Procedural

07.80 Thymectomy, not otherwise specified
07.81 Other partial excision of thymus
07.82 Other total excision of thymus

60521-60522

60521 Thymectomy, partial or total; sternal split or transthoracic approach, without radical mediastinal dissection (separate procedure)
60522 sternal split or transthoracic approach, with radical mediastinal dissection (separate procedure)

ICD-9-CM Diagnostic

164.0 Malignant neoplasm of thymus
196.1 Secondary and unspecified malignant neoplasm of intrathoracic lymph nodes
198.89 Secondary malignant neoplasm of other specified sites
209.22 Malignant carcinoid tumor of the thymus — (Code first any associated multiple endocrine neoplasia syndrome: 258.01-258.03)(Use additional code to identify associated endocrine syndrome, as: carcinoid syndrome: 259.2)
209.62 Benign carcinoid tumor of the thymus — (Code first any associated multiple endocrine neoplasia syndrome: 258.01-258.03)(Use additional code to identify associated endocrine syndrome, as: carcinoid syndrome: 259.2)
212.6 Benign neoplasm of thymus
235.8 Neoplasm of uncertain behavior of pleura, thymus, and mediastinum
238.8 Neoplasm of uncertain behavior of other specified sites
239.89 Neoplasms of unspecified nature, other specified sites
279.2 Combined immunity deficiency — (Use additional code to identify any associated intellectual disabilities) (Use additional code for associated manifestations)
358.00 Myasthenia gravis without (acute) exacerbation

358.01 Myasthenia gravis with (acute) exacerbation
759.2 Congenital anomalies of other endocrine glands
786.6 Swelling, mass, or lump in chest

ICD-9-CM Procedural

07.80 Thymectomy, not otherwise specified
07.81 Other partial excision of thymus
07.82 Other total excision of thymus
07.83 Thoracoscopic partial excision of thymus
07.84 Thoracoscopic total excision of thymus
07.95 Thoracoscopic incision of thymus
07.98 Other and unspecified thoracoscopic operations on thymus
40.59 Radical excision of other lymph nodes

60540-60545

60540 Adrenalectomy, partial or complete, or exploration of adrenal gland with or without biopsy, transabdominal, lumbar or dorsal (separate procedure);
60545 with excision of adjacent retroperitoneal tumor

ICD-9-CM Diagnostic

189.0 Malignant neoplasm of kidney, except pelvis
189.1 Malignant neoplasm of renal pelvis
194.0 Malignant neoplasm of adrenal gland
197.6 Secondary malignant neoplasm of retroperitoneum and peritoneum
197.7 Secondary malignant neoplasm of liver
198.7 Secondary malignant neoplasm of adrenal gland
209.24 Malignant carcinoid tumor of the kidney — (Code first any associated multiple endocrine neoplasia syndrome: 258.01-258.03; Use additional code to identify associated endocrine syndrome, as: carcinoid syndrome: 259.2)
211.8 Benign neoplasm of retroperitoneum and peritoneum
227.0 Benign neoplasm of adrenal gland — (Use additional code to identify any functional activity)
234.8 Carcinoma in situ of other specified sites
235.4 Neoplasm of uncertain behavior of retroperitoneum and peritoneum
237.2 Neoplasm of uncertain behavior of adrenal gland — (Use additional code to identify any functional activity)
239.0 Neoplasm of unspecified nature of digestive system
239.7 Neoplasm of unspecified nature of endocrine glands and other parts of nervous system
255.0 Cushing's syndrome — (Use additional E code to identify cause, if drug-induced)
255.10 Hyperaldosteronism, unspecified
255.11 Glucocorticoid-remediable aldosteronism
255.12 Conn's syndrome
255.13 Bartter's syndrome
255.14 Other secondary aldosteronism
255.2 Adrenogenital disorders
255.3 Other corticoadrenal overactivity
255.41 Glucocorticoid deficiency
255.42 Mineralocorticoid deficiency
255.5 Other adrenal hypofunction
255.6 Medulloadrenal hyperfunction
V64.41 Laparoscopic surgical procedure converted to open procedure

ICD-9-CM Procedural

07.00 Exploration of adrenal field, not otherwise specified
07.01 Unilateral exploration of adrenal field
07.02 Bilateral exploration of adrenal field
07.12 Open biopsy of adrenal gland
07.21 Excision of lesion of adrenal gland
07.22 Unilateral adrenalectomy
07.29 Other partial adrenalectomy
07.3 Bilateral adrenalectomy
54.4 Excision or destruction of peritoneal tissue

60600-60605

60600 Excision of carotid body tumor; without excision of carotid artery
60605 with excision of carotid artery

ICD-9-CM Diagnostic

194.5 Malignant neoplasm of carotid body
198.89 Secondary malignant neoplasm of other specified sites
227.5 Benign neoplasm of carotid body — (Use additional code to identify any functional activity)
239.7 Neoplasm of unspecified nature of endocrine glands and other parts of nervous system

ICD-9-CM Procedural

39.89 Other operations on carotid body, carotid sinus and other vascular bodies

60650

60650 Laparoscopy, surgical, with adrenalectomy, partial or complete, or exploration of adrenal gland with or without biopsy, transabdominal, lumbar or dorsal

ICD-9-CM Diagnostic

189.0 Malignant neoplasm of kidney, except pelvis
189.1 Malignant neoplasm of renal pelvis
194.0 Malignant neoplasm of adrenal gland
197.7 Secondary malignant neoplasm of liver
198.7 Secondary malignant neoplasm of adrenal gland
209.24 Malignant carcinoid tumor of the kidney — (Code first any associated multiple endocrine neoplasia syndrome: 258.01-258.03; Use additional code to identify associated endocrine syndrome, as: carcinoid syndrome: 259.2)
227.0 Benign neoplasm of adrenal gland — (Use additional code to identify any functional activity)
234.8 Carcinoma in situ of other specified sites
237.2 Neoplasm of uncertain behavior of adrenal gland — (Use additional code to identify any functional activity)
239.7 Neoplasm of unspecified nature of endocrine glands and other parts of nervous system
255.0 Cushing's syndrome — (Use additional E code to identify cause, if drug-induced)
255.10 Hyperaldosteronism, unspecified
255.11 Glucocorticoid-remediable aldosteronism
255.12 Conn's syndrome
255.13 Bartter's syndrome
255.14 Other secondary aldosteronism
255.2 Adrenogenital disorders
255.3 Other corticoadrenal overactivity
255.41 Glucocorticoid deficiency
255.42 Mineralocorticoid deficiency
255.5 Other adrenal hypofunction
255.6 Medulloadrenal hyperfunction

ICD-9-CM Procedural

07.00 Exploration of adrenal field, not otherwise specified
07.01 Unilateral exploration of adrenal field
07.02 Bilateral exploration of adrenal field
07.11 Closed (percutaneous) (needle) biopsy of adrenal gland
07.22 Unilateral adrenalectomy
07.29 Other partial adrenalectomy
07.3 Bilateral adrenalectomy

Nervous System

Skull, Meninges, and Brain

61000-61001

61000 Subdural tap through fontanelle, or suture, infant, unilateral or bilateral; initial
61001 subsequent taps

ICD-9-CM Diagnostic

322.9 Unspecified meningitis ▽
324.0 Intracranial abscess
331.3 Communicating hydrocephalus — (Use additional code, where applicable, to identify dementia: 294.10, 294.11)
331.4 Obstructive hydrocephalus — (Use additional code, where applicable, to identify dementia: 294.10, 294.11)
432.1 Subdural hemorrhage — (Use additional code to identify presence of hypertension)
741.01 Spina bifida with hydrocephalus, cervical region
742.3 Congenital hydrocephalus
742.4 Other specified congenital anomalies of brain
767.0 Subdural and cerebral hemorrhage, birth trauma — (Use additional code(s) to further specify condition. Use additional code to identify cause)
771.2 Other congenital infection specific to the perinatal period — (Use additional code(s) to further specify condition)
854.00 Intracranial injury of other and unspecified nature, without mention of open intracranial wound, unspecified state of consciousness ▽
907.0 Late effect of intracranial injury without mention of skull fracture
995.54 Child physical abuse — (Use additional code, if applicable, to identify any associated injuries. Use additional E code to identify nature of abuse, E960-E968, and perpetrator, E967.0-E967.9)
995.55 Shaken infant syndrome — (Use additional code, if applicable, to identify any associated injuries. Use additional E code to identify nature of abuse, E960-E968, and perpetrator, E967.0-E967.9)

ICD-9-CM Procedural

01.09 Other cranial puncture

61020-61026

61020 Ventricular puncture through previous burr hole, fontanelle, suture, or implanted ventricular catheter/reservoir; without injection
61026 with injection of medication or other substance for diagnosis or treatment

ICD-9-CM Diagnostic

324.0 Intracranial abscess
331.3 Communicating hydrocephalus — (Use additional code, where applicable, to identify dementia: 294.10, 294.11)
331.4 Obstructive hydrocephalus — (Use additional code, where applicable, to identify dementia: 294.10, 294.11)
331.5 Idiopathic normal pressure hydrocephalus [INPH] — (Use additional code, where applicable, to identify dementia: 294.10, 294.11)
348.5 Cerebral edema
772.12 Intraventricular hemorrhage, Grade II — (Use additional code(s) to further specify condition)
772.13 Intraventricular hemorrhage, Grade III — (Use additional code(s) to further specify condition)
854.00 Intracranial injury of other and unspecified nature, without mention of open intracranial wound, unspecified state of consciousness ▽
907.0 Late effect of intracranial injury without mention of skull fracture

ICD-9-CM Procedural

01.02 Ventriculopuncture through previously implanted catheter
01.09 Other cranial puncture
99.29 Injection or infusion of other therapeutic or prophylactic substance

61050-61055

61050 Cisternal or lateral cervical (C1-C2) puncture; without injection (separate procedure)
61055 with injection of medication or other substance for diagnosis or treatment (eg, C1-C2)

ICD-9-CM Diagnostic

321.1 Meningitis in other fungal diseases — (Code first underlying disease: 110.0-118) ☒
321.2 Meningitis due to viruses not elsewhere classified — (Code first underlying disease: 060.0-066.9) ☒
321.3 Meningitis due to trypanosomiasis — (Code first underlying disease: 086.0-086.9) ☒
321.4 Meningitis in sarcoidosis — (Code first underlying disease: 135) ☒
321.8 Meningitis due to other nonbacterial organisms classified elsewhere — (Code first underlying disease) ☒
324.1 Intraspinal abscess
324.9 Intracranial and intraspinal abscess of unspecified site ▽
331.3 Communicating hydrocephalus — (Use additional code, where applicable, to identify dementia: 294.10, 294.11)
331.4 Obstructive hydrocephalus — (Use additional code, where applicable, to identify dementia: 294.10, 294.11)
331.5 Idiopathic normal pressure hydrocephalus [INPH] — (Use additional code, where applicable, to identify dementia: 294.10, 294.11)
349.31 Accidental puncture or laceration of dura during a procedure
349.39 Other dural tear
349.81 Cerebrospinal fluid rhinorrhea
368.2 Diplopia
722.71 Intervertebral cervical disc disorder with myelopathy, cervical region
723.0 Spinal stenosis in cervical region
723.1 Cervicalgia
723.3 Cervicobrachial syndrome (diffuse)
723.8 Other syndromes affecting cervical region
780.2 Syncope and collapse
780.4 Dizziness and giddiness
784.0 Headache
996.2 Mechanical complication of nervous system device, implant, and graft
996.63 Infection and inflammatory reaction due to nervous system device, implant, and graft — (Use additional code to identify specified infections)
996.75 Other complications due to nervous system device, implant, and graft — (Use additional code to identify complication: 338.18-338.19, 338.28-338.29)
997.01 Central nervous system complication — (Use additional code to identify complications)
998.2 Accidental puncture or laceration during procedure
V45.2 Presence of cerebrospinal fluid drainage device
V67.00 Follow-up examination, following unspecified surgery ▽
V67.09 Follow-up examination, following other surgery
V67.1 Radiotherapy follow-up examination
V67.2 Chemotherapy follow-up examination
V67.51 Follow-up examination following completed treatment with high-risk medications, not elsewhere classified
V67.59 Other follow-up examination
V67.6 Combined treatment follow-up examination

ICD-9-CM Procedural

01.01 Cisternal puncture
99.29 Injection or infusion of other therapeutic or prophylactic substance

61070

61070 Puncture of shunt tubing or reservoir for aspiration or injection procedure

ICD-9-CM Diagnostic

191.5 Malignant neoplasm of ventricles of brain
191.8 Malignant neoplasm of other parts of brain
198.3 Secondary malignant neoplasm of brain and spinal cord
322.0 Nonpyogenic meningitis
324.9 Intracranial and intraspinal abscess of unspecified site
331.3 Communicating hydrocephalus — (Use additional code, where applicable, to identify dementia: 294.10, 294.11)
331.4 Obstructive hydrocephalus — (Use additional code, where applicable, to identify dementia: 294.10, 294.11)
331.5 Idiopathic normal pressure hydrocephalus [INPH] — (Use additional code, where applicable, to identify dementia: 294.10, 294.11)
996.2 Mechanical complication of nervous system device, implant, and graft
996.63 Infection and inflammatory reaction due to nervous system device, implant, and graft — (Use additional code to identify specified infections)
996.75 Other complications due to nervous system device, implant, and graft — (Use additional code to identify complication: 338.18-338.19, 338.28-338.29)
V45.89 Other postprocedural status
V67.00 Follow-up examination, following unspecified surgery
V67.09 Follow-up examination, following other surgery
V67.1 Radiotherapy follow-up examination
V67.2 Chemotherapy follow-up examination
V67.51 Follow-up examination following completed treatment with high-risk medications, not elsewhere classified
V67.59 Other follow-up examination

ICD-9-CM Procedural

01.02 Ventriculopuncture through previously implanted catheter
02.41 Irrigation and exploration of ventricular shunt
99.29 Injection or infusion of other therapeutic or prophylactic substance

61105-61108

61105 Twist drill hole for subdural or ventricular puncture
61107 Twist drill hole(s) for subdural, intracerebral, or ventricular puncture; for implanting ventricular catheter, pressure recording device, or other intracerebral monitoring device
61108 for evacuation and/or drainage of subdural hematoma

ICD-9-CM Diagnostic

191.1 Malignant neoplasm of frontal lobe of brain
191.2 Malignant neoplasm of temporal lobe of brain
191.3 Malignant neoplasm of parietal lobe of brain
191.4 Malignant neoplasm of occipital lobe of brain
191.5 Malignant neoplasm of ventricles of brain
191.6 Malignant neoplasm of cerebellum NOS
191.7 Malignant neoplasm of brain stem
191.8 Malignant neoplasm of other parts of brain
191.9 Malignant neoplasm of brain, unspecified site
192.1 Malignant neoplasm of cerebral meninges
198.3 Secondary malignant neoplasm of brain and spinal cord
225.0 Benign neoplasm of brain
225.2 Benign neoplasm of cerebral meninges
237.5 Neoplasm of uncertain behavior of brain and spinal cord
239.6 Neoplasm of unspecified nature of brain
324.0 Intracranial abscess
331.3 Communicating hydrocephalus — (Use additional code, where applicable, to identify dementia: 294.10, 294.11)
331.4 Obstructive hydrocephalus — (Use additional code, where applicable, to identify dementia: 294.10, 294.11)
331.5 Idiopathic normal pressure hydrocephalus [INPH] — (Use additional code, where applicable, to identify dementia: 294.10, 294.11)
348.5 Cerebral edema
430 Subarachnoid hemorrhage — (Use additional code to identify presence of hypertension)
431 Intracerebral hemorrhage — (Use additional code to identify presence of hypertension)
432.1 Subdural hemorrhage — (Use additional code to identify presence of hypertension)
432.9 Unspecified intracranial hemorrhage — (Use additional code to identify presence of hypertension)
437.3 Cerebral aneurysm, nonruptured — (Use additional code to identify presence of hypertension)
742.3 Congenital hydrocephalus
747.81 Congenital anomaly of cerebrovascular system
767.0 Subdural and cerebral hemorrhage, birth trauma — (Use additional code(s) to further specify condition. Use additional code to identify cause)
800.24 Closed fracture of vault of skull with subarachnoid, subdural, and extradural hemorrhage, prolonged (more than 24 hours) loss of consciousness and return to pre-existing conscious level
851.05 Cortex (cerebral) contusion without mention of open intracranial wound, prolonged (more than 24 hours) loss of consciousness, without return to pre-existing conscious level
852.00 Subarachnoid hemorrhage following injury, without mention of open intracranial wound, unspecified state of consciousness
852.01 Subarachnoid hemorrhage following injury, without mention of open intracranial wound, no loss of consciousness
852.02 Subarachnoid hemorrhage following injury, without mention of open intracranial wound, brief (less than 1 hour) loss of consciousness
852.03 Subarachnoid hemorrhage following injury, without mention of open intracranial wound, moderate (1-24 hours) loss of consciousness
852.04 Subarachnoid hemorrhage following injury, without mention of open intracranial wound, prolonged (more than 24 hours) loss of consciousness and return to pre-existing conscious level
852.05 Subarachnoid hemorrhage following injury, without mention of open intracranial wound, prolonged (more than 24 hours) loss of consciousness, without return to pre-existing conscious level
852.06 Subarachnoid hemorrhage following injury, without mention of open intracranial wound, loss of consciousness of unspecified duration
852.09 Subarachnoid hemorrhage following injury, without mention of open intracranial wound, unspecified concussion
852.10 Subarachnoid hemorrhage following injury, with open intracranial wound, unspecified state of consciousness
852.11 Subarachnoid hemorrhage following injury, with open intracranial wound, no loss of consciousness
852.12 Subarachnoid hemorrhage following injury, with open intracranial wound, brief (less than 1 hour) loss of consciousness
852.13 Subarachnoid hemorrhage following injury, with open intracranial wound, moderate (1-24 hours) loss of consciousness
852.14 Subarachnoid hemorrhage following injury, with open intracranial wound, prolonged (more than 24 hours) loss of consciousness and return to pre-existing conscious level
852.15 Subarachnoid hemorrhage following injury, with open intracranial wound, prolonged (more than 24 hours) loss of consciousness, without return to pre-existing conscious level
852.16 Subarachnoid hemorrhage following injury, with open intracranial wound, loss of consciousness of unspecified duration
852.19 Subarachnoid hemorrhage following injury, with open intracranial wound, unspecified concussion

852.20 Subdural hemorrhage following injury, without mention of open intracranial wound, unspecified state of consciousness ▽

852.21 Subdural hemorrhage following injury, without mention of open intracranial wound, no loss of consciousness

852.22 Subdural hemorrhage following injury, without mention of open intracranial wound, brief (less than one hour) loss of consciousness

852.23 Subdural hemorrhage following injury, without mention of open intracranial wound, moderate (1-24 hours) loss of consciousness

852.24 Subdural hemorrhage following injury, without mention of open intracranial wound, prolonged (more than 24 hours) loss of consciousness and return to pre-existing conscious level

852.25 Subdural hemorrhage following injury, without mention of open intracranial wound, prolonged (more than 24 hours) loss of consciousness, without return to pre-existing conscious level

852.26 Subdural hemorrhage following injury, without mention of open intracranial wound, loss of consciousness of unspecified duration ▽

852.29 Subdural hemorrhage following injury, without mention of open intracranial wound, unspecified concussion ▽

852.30 Subdural hemorrhage following injury, with open intracranial wound, state of consciousness unspecified ▽

852.31 Subdural hemorrhage following injury, with open intracranial wound, no loss of consciousness

852.32 Subdural hemorrhage following injury, with open intracranial wound, brief (less than 1 hour) loss of consciousness

852.33 Subdural hemorrhage following injury, with open intracranial wound, moderate (1-24 hours) loss of consciousness

852.34 Subdural hemorrhage following injury, with open intracranial wound, prolonged (more than 24 hours) loss of consciousness and return to pre-existing conscious level

852.35 Subdural hemorrhage following injury, with open intracranial wound, prolonged (more than 24 hours) loss of consciousness, without return to pre-existing conscious level

852.36 Subdural hemorrhage following injury, with open intracranial wound, loss of consciousness of unspecified duration ▽

852.39 Subdural hemorrhage following injury, with open intracranial wound, unspecified concussion ▽

852.40 Extradural hemorrhage following injury, without mention of open intracranial wound, unspecified state of consciousness ▽

852.41 Extradural hemorrhage following injury, without mention of open intracranial wound, no loss of consciousness

852.42 Extradural hemorrhage following injury, without mention of open intracranial wound, brief (less than 1 hour) loss of consciousness

852.43 Extradural hemorrhage following injury, without mention of open intracranial wound, moderate (1-24 hours) loss of consciousness

852.44 Extradural hemorrhage following injury, without mention of open intracranial wound, prolonged (more than 24 hours) loss of consciousness and return to pre-existing conscious level

852.45 Extradural hemorrhage following injury, without mention of open intracranial wound, prolonged (more than 24 hours) loss of consciousness, without return to pre-existing conscious level

852.46 Extradural hemorrhage following injury, without mention of open intracranial wound, loss of consciousness of unspecified duration ▽

852.49 Extradural hemorrhage following injury, without mention of open intracranial wound, unspecified concussion ▽

852.50 Extradural hemorrhage following injury, with open intracranial wound, state of consciousness unspecified ▽

852.51 Extradural hemorrhage following injury, with open intracranial wound, no loss of consciousness

852.52 Extradural hemorrhage following injury, with open intracranial wound, brief (less than 1 hour) loss of consciousness

852.53 Extradural hemorrhage following injury, with open intracranial wound, moderate (1-24 hours) loss of consciousness

852.54 Extradural hemorrhage following injury, with open intracranial wound, prolonged (more than 24 hours) loss of consciousness and return to pre-existing conscious level

852.55 Extradural hemorrhage following injury, with open intracranial wound, prolonged (more than 24 hours) loss of consciousness, without return to pre-existing conscious level

852.56 Extradural hemorrhage following injury, with open intracranial wound, loss of consciousness of unspecified duration ▽

852.59 Extradural hemorrhage following injury, with open intracranial wound, unspecified concussion ▽

853.00 Other and unspecified intracranial hemorrhage following injury, without mention of open intracranial wound, unspecified state of consciousness ▽

853.01 Other and unspecified intracranial hemorrhage following injury, without mention of open intracranial wound, no loss of consciousness ▽

853.02 Other and unspecified intracranial hemorrhage following injury, without mention of open intracranial wound, brief (less than 1 hour) loss of consciousness ▽

853.03 Other and unspecified intracranial hemorrhage following injury, without mention of open intracranial wound, moderate (1-24 hours) loss of consciousness ▽

853.04 Other and unspecified intracranial hemorrhage following injury, without mention of open intracranial wound, prolonged (more than 24 hours) loss of consciousness and return to preexisting conscious level ▽

853.05 Other and unspecified intracranial hemorrhage following injury. Without mention of open intracranial wound, prolonged (more than 24 hours) loss of consciousness, without return to pre-existing conscious level ▽

853.06 Other and unspecified intracranial hemorrhage following injury, without mention of open intracranial wound, loss of consciousness of unspecified duration ▽

853.09 Other and unspecified intracranial hemorrhage following injury, without mention of open intracranial wound, unspecified concussion ▽

853.10 Other and unspecified intracranial hemorrhage following injury, with open intracranial wound, unspecified state of consciousness ▽

853.11 Other and unspecified intracranial hemorrhage following injury, with open intracranial wound, no loss of consciousness ▽

853.12 Other and unspecified intracranial hemorrhage following injury, with open intracranial wound, brief (less than 1 hour) loss of consciousness ▽

853.13 Other and unspecified intracranial hemorrhage following injury, with open intracranial wound, moderate (1-24 hours) loss of consciousness ▽

853.14 Other and unspecified intracranial hemorrhage following injury, with open intracranial wound, prolonged (more than 24 hours) loss of consciousness and return to pre-existing conscious level ▽

853.15 Other and unspecified intracranial hemorrhage following injury, with open intracranial wound, prolonged (more than 24 hours) loss of consciousness, without return to pre-existing conscious level ▽

853.16 Other and unspecified intracranial hemorrhage following injury, with open intracranial wound, loss of consciousness of unspecified duration ▽

853.19 Other and unspecified intracranial hemorrhage following injury, with open intracranial wound, unspecified concussion ▽

854.00 Intracranial injury of other and unspecified nature, without mention of open intracranial wound, unspecified state of consciousness ▽

854.01 Intracranial injury of other and unspecified nature, without mention of open intracranial wound, no loss of consciousness ▽

854.02 Intracranial injury of other and unspecified nature, without mention of open intracranial wound, brief (less than 1 hour) loss of consciousness ▽

854.03 Intracranial injury of other and unspecified nature, without mention of open intracranial wound, moderate (1-24 hours) loss of consciousness ▽

854.04 Intracranial injury of other and unspecified nature, without mention of open intracranial wound, prolonged (more than 24 hours) loss of consciousness and return to pre-existing conscious level ▽

854.05 Intracranial injury of other and unspecified nature, without mention of open intracranial wound, prolonged (more than 24 hours) loss of consciousness, without return to pre-existing conscious level ▽

854.06 Intracranial injury of other and unspecified nature, without mention of open intracranial wound, loss of consciousness of unspecified duration ▽

854.09 Intracranial injury of other and unspecified nature, without mention of open intracranial wound, unspecified concussion

854.10 Intracranial injury of other and unspecified nature, with open intracranial wound, unspecified state of consciousness

854.11 Intracranial injury of other and unspecified nature, with open intracranial wound, no loss of consciousness

854.12 Intracranial injury of other and unspecified nature, with open intracranial wound, brief (less than 1 hour) loss of consciousness

854.13 Intracranial injury of other and unspecified nature, with open intracranial wound, moderate (1-24 hours) loss of consciousness

854.14 Intracranial injury of other and unspecified nature, with open intracranial wound, prolonged (more than 24 hours) loss of consciousness and return to pre-existing conscious level

854.15 Intracranial injury of other and unspecified nature, with open intracranial wound, prolonged (more than 24 hours) loss of consciousness, without return to pre-existing conscious level

854.16 Intracranial injury of other and unspecified nature, with open intracranial wound, loss of consciousness of unspecified duration

854.19 Intracranial injury of other and unspecified nature, with open intracranial wound, with unspecified concussion

958.2 Secondary and recurrent hemorrhage as an early complication of trauma

996.63 Infection and inflammatory reaction due to nervous system device, implant, and graft — (Use additional code to identify specified infections)

ICD-9-CM Procedural

01.09 Other cranial puncture

01.18 Other diagnostic procedures on brain and cerebral meninges

01.31 Incision of cerebral meninges

02.21 Insertion or replacement of external ventricular drain [EVD]

02.31 Ventricular shunt to structure in head and neck

02.39 Ventricular shunt to extracranial site NEC

61120

61120 Burr hole(s) for ventricular puncture (including injection of gas, contrast media, dye, or radioactive material)

ICD-9-CM Diagnostic

191.9 Malignant neoplasm of brain, unspecified site

225.0 Benign neoplasm of brain

239.6 Neoplasm of unspecified nature of brain

331.3 Communicating hydrocephalus — (Use additional code, where applicable, to identify dementia: 294.10, 294.11)

331.4 Obstructive hydrocephalus — (Use additional code, where applicable, to identify dementia: 294.10, 294.11)

331.5 Idiopathic normal pressure hydrocephalus [INPH] — (Use additional code, where applicable, to identify dementia: 294.10, 294.11)

349.89 Other specified disorder of nervous system

349.9 Unspecified disorders of nervous system

388.61 Cerebrospinal fluid otorrhea

430 Subarachnoid hemorrhage — (Use additional code to identify presence of hypertension)

431 Intracerebral hemorrhage — (Use additional code to identify presence of hypertension)

803.10 Other closed skull fracture with cerebral laceration and contusion, unspecified state of consciousness

803.20 Other closed skull fracture with subarachnoid, subdural, and extradural hemorrhage, unspecified state of consciousness

803.60 Other open skull fracture with cerebral laceration and contusion, unspecified state of consciousness

ICD-9-CM Procedural

01.18 Other diagnostic procedures on brain and cerebral meninges

01.24 Other craniotomy

61140

61140 Burr hole(s) or trephine; with biopsy of brain or intracranial lesion

ICD-9-CM Diagnostic

191.0 Malignant neoplasm of cerebrum, except lobes and ventricles

191.1 Malignant neoplasm of frontal lobe of brain

191.2 Malignant neoplasm of temporal lobe of brain

191.3 Malignant neoplasm of parietal lobe of brain

191.4 Malignant neoplasm of occipital lobe of brain

191.5 Malignant neoplasm of ventricles of brain

191.6 Malignant neoplasm of cerebellum NOS

191.7 Malignant neoplasm of brain stem

191.8 Malignant neoplasm of other parts of brain

191.9 Malignant neoplasm of brain, unspecified site

192.1 Malignant neoplasm of cerebral meninges

198.3 Secondary malignant neoplasm of brain and spinal cord

198.4 Secondary malignant neoplasm of other parts of nervous system

199.1 Other malignant neoplasm of unspecified site

225.0 Benign neoplasm of brain

237.5 Neoplasm of uncertain behavior of brain and spinal cord

239.6 Neoplasm of unspecified nature of brain

239.7 Neoplasm of unspecified nature of endocrine glands and other parts of nervous system

324.0 Intracranial abscess

348.0 Cerebral cysts

ICD-9-CM Procedural

01.11 Closed (percutaneous) (needle) biopsy of cerebral meninges

01.12 Open biopsy of cerebral meninges

01.13 Closed (percutaneous) (needle) biopsy of brain

01.14 Open biopsy of brain

61150-61151

61150 Burr hole(s) or trephine; with drainage of brain abscess or cyst

61151 with subsequent tapping (aspiration) of intracranial abscess or cyst

ICD-9-CM Diagnostic

324.0 Intracranial abscess

324.9 Intracranial and intraspinal abscess of unspecified site

348.0 Cerebral cysts

349.1 Nervous system complications from surgically implanted device

742.4 Other specified congenital anomalies of brain

ICD-9-CM Procedural

01.09 Other cranial puncture

01.21 Incision and drainage of cranial sinus

01.24 Other craniotomy

01.31 Incision of cerebral meninges

01.39 Other incision of brain

61154

61154 Burr hole(s) with evacuation and/or drainage of hematoma, extradural or subdural

ICD-9-CM Diagnostic

432.0 Nontraumatic extradural hemorrhage — (Use additional code to identify presence of hypertension)

432.1 Subdural hemorrhage — (Use additional code to identify presence of hypertension)

852.04 Subarachnoid hemorrhage following injury, without mention of open intracranial wound, prolonged (more than 24 hours) loss of consciousness and return to pre-existing conscious level

852.20 Subdural hemorrhage following injury, without mention of open intracranial wound, unspecified state of consciousness

852.21 Subdural hemorrhage following injury, without mention of open intracranial wound, no loss of consciousness
852.22 Subdural hemorrhage following injury, without mention of open intracranial wound, brief (less than one hour) loss of consciousness
852.23 Subdural hemorrhage following injury, without mention of open intracranial wound, moderate (1-24 hours) loss of consciousness
852.24 Subdural hemorrhage following injury, without mention of open intracranial wound, prolonged (more than 24 hours) loss of consciousness and return to pre-existing conscious level
852.25 Subdural hemorrhage following injury, without mention of open intracranial wound, prolonged (more than 24 hours) loss of consciousness, without return to pre-existing conscious level
852.26 Subdural hemorrhage following injury, without mention of open intracranial wound, loss of consciousness of unspecified duration
852.29 Subdural hemorrhage following injury, without mention of open intracranial wound, unspecified concussion
852.30 Subdural hemorrhage following injury, with open intracranial wound, state of consciousness unspecified
852.31 Subdural hemorrhage following injury, with open intracranial wound, no loss of consciousness
852.32 Subdural hemorrhage following injury, with open intracranial wound, brief (less than 1 hour) loss of consciousness
852.33 Subdural hemorrhage following injury, with open intracranial wound, moderate (1-24 hours) loss of consciousness
852.34 Subdural hemorrhage following injury, with open intracranial wound, prolonged (more than 24 hours) loss of consciousness and return to pre-existing conscious level
852.35 Subdural hemorrhage following injury, with open intracranial wound, prolonged (more than 24 hours) loss of consciousness, without return to pre-existing conscious level
852.36 Subdural hemorrhage following injury, with open intracranial wound, loss of consciousness of unspecified duration
852.39 Subdural hemorrhage following injury, with open intracranial wound, unspecified concussion
852.40 Extradural hemorrhage following injury, without mention of open intracranial wound, unspecified state of consciousness
852.41 Extradural hemorrhage following injury, without mention of open intracranial wound, no loss of consciousness
852.42 Extradural hemorrhage following injury, without mention of open intracranial wound, brief (less than 1 hour) loss of consciousness
852.43 Extradural hemorrhage following injury, without mention of open intracranial wound, moderate (1-24 hours) loss of consciousness
852.44 Extradural hemorrhage following injury, without mention of open intracranial wound, prolonged (more than 24 hours) loss of consciousness and return to pre-existing conscious level
852.45 Extradural hemorrhage following injury, without mention of open intracranial wound, prolonged (more than 24 hours) loss of consciousness, without return to pre-existing conscious level
852.46 Extradural hemorrhage following injury, without mention of open intracranial wound, loss of consciousness of unspecified duration
852.49 Extradural hemorrhage following injury, without mention of open intracranial wound, unspecified concussion
852.50 Extradural hemorrhage following injury, with open intracranial wound, state of consciousness unspecified
852.51 Extradural hemorrhage following injury, with open intracranial wound, no loss of consciousness
852.52 Extradural hemorrhage following injury, with open intracranial wound, brief (less than 1 hour) loss of consciousness
852.53 Extradural hemorrhage following injury, with open intracranial wound, moderate (1-24 hours) loss of consciousness
852.54 Extradural hemorrhage following injury, with open intracranial wound, prolonged (more than 24 hours) loss of consciousness and return to pre-existing conscious level
852.55 Extradural hemorrhage following injury, with open intracranial wound, prolonged (more than 24 hours) loss of consciousness, without return to pre-existing conscious level
852.56 Extradural hemorrhage following injury, with open intracranial wound, loss of consciousness of unspecified duration
852.59 Extradural hemorrhage following injury, with open intracranial wound, unspecified concussion
854.00 Intracranial injury of other and unspecified nature, without mention of open intracranial wound, unspecified state of consciousness
854.01 Intracranial injury of other and unspecified nature, without mention of open intracranial wound, no loss of consciousness
854.02 Intracranial injury of other and unspecified nature, without mention of open intracranial wound, brief (less than 1 hour) loss of consciousness
854.03 Intracranial injury of other and unspecified nature, without mention of open intracranial wound, moderate (1-24 hours) loss of consciousness
854.04 Intracranial injury of other and unspecified nature, without mention of open intracranial wound, prolonged (more than 24 hours) loss of consciousness and return to pre-existing conscious level
854.05 Intracranial injury of other and unspecified nature, without mention of open intracranial wound, prolonged (more than 24 hours) loss of consciousness, without return to pre-existing conscious level
854.06 Intracranial injury of other and unspecified nature, without mention of open intracranial wound, loss of consciousness of unspecified duration
854.09 Intracranial injury of other and unspecified nature, without mention of open intracranial wound, unspecified concussion
854.10 Intracranial injury of other and unspecified nature, with open intracranial wound, unspecified state of consciousness
854.11 Intracranial injury of other and unspecified nature, with open intracranial wound, no loss of consciousness
854.12 Intracranial injury of other and unspecified nature, with open intracranial wound, brief (less than 1 hour) loss of consciousness
854.13 Intracranial injury of other and unspecified nature, with open intracranial wound, moderate (1-24 hours) loss of consciousness
854.14 Intracranial injury of other and unspecified nature, with open intracranial wound, prolonged (more than 24 hours) loss of consciousness and return to pre-existing conscious level
854.15 Intracranial injury of other and unspecified nature, with open intracranial wound, prolonged (more than 24 hours) loss of consciousness, without return to pre-existing conscious level
854.16 Intracranial injury of other and unspecified nature, with open intracranial wound, loss of consciousness of unspecified duration
854.19 Intracranial injury of other and unspecified nature, with open intracranial wound, with unspecified concussion
997.02 Iatrogenic cerebrovascular infarction or hemorrhage — (Use additional code to identify complications)

ICD-9-CM Procedural

01.24 Other craniotomy
01.31 Incision of cerebral meninges

61156-61210

61156 Burr hole(s); with aspiration of hematoma or cyst, intracerebral
61210 for implanting ventricular catheter, reservoir, EEG electrode(s), pressure recording device, or other cerebral monitoring device (separate procedure)

ICD-9-CM Diagnostic

191.1 Malignant neoplasm of frontal lobe of brain
191.2 Malignant neoplasm of temporal lobe of brain
191.3 Malignant neoplasm of parietal lobe of brain
191.4 Malignant neoplasm of occipital lobe of brain
191.5 Malignant neoplasm of ventricles of brain
191.6 Malignant neoplasm of cerebellum NOS

191.7 Malignant neoplasm of brain stem

191.8 Malignant neoplasm of other parts of brain

191.9 Malignant neoplasm of brain, unspecified site ▼

192.1 Malignant neoplasm of cerebral meninges

198.3 Secondary malignant neoplasm of brain and spinal cord

225.0 Benign neoplasm of brain

225.2 Benign neoplasm of cerebral meninges

239.6 Neoplasm of unspecified nature of brain

324.0 Intracranial abscess

331.3 Communicating hydrocephalus — (Use additional code, where applicable, to identify dementia: 294.10, 294.11)

331.4 Obstructive hydrocephalus — (Use additional code, where applicable, to identify dementia: 294.10, 294.11)

331.5 Idiopathic normal pressure hydrocephalus [INPH] — (Use additional code, where applicable, to identify dementia: 294.10, 294.11)

345.01 Generalized nonconvulsive epilepsy with intractable epilepsy

345.10 Generalized convulsive epilepsy without mention of intractable epilepsy

345.11 Generalized convulsive epilepsy with intractable epilepsy

345.2 Epileptic petit mal status

345.40 Localization-related (focal) (partial) epilepsy and epileptic syndromes with complex partial seizures, without mention of intractable epilepsy

345.41 Localization-related (focal) (partial) epilepsy and epileptic syndromes with complex partial seizures, with intractable epilepsy

345.50 Localization-related (focal) (partial) epilepsy and epileptic syndromes with simple partial seizures, without mention of intractable epilepsy

345.51 Localization-related (focal) (partial) epilepsy and epileptic syndromes with simple partial seizures, with intractable epilepsy

345.60 Infantile spasms without mention of intractable epilepsy

345.61 Infantile spasms with intractable epilepsy

345.70 Epilepsia partialis continua without mention of intractable epilepsy

345.71 Epilepsia partialis continua with intractable epilepsy

345.80 Other forms of epilepsy and recurrent seizures, without mention of intractable epilepsy

345.81 Other forms of epilepsy and recurrent seizures, with intractable epilepsy

345.90 Unspecified epilepsy without mention of intractable epilepsy ▼

345.91 Unspecified epilepsy with intractable epilepsy ▼

348.0 Cerebral cysts

348.5 Cerebral edema

430 Subarachnoid hemorrhage — (Use additional code to identify presence of hypertension)

431 Intracerebral hemorrhage — (Use additional code to identify presence of hypertension)

432.1 Subdural hemorrhage — (Use additional code to identify presence of hypertension)

432.9 Unspecified intracranial hemorrhage — (Use additional code to identify presence of hypertension) ▼

742.4 Other specified congenital anomalies of brain

767.0 Subdural and cerebral hemorrhage, birth trauma — (Use additional code(s) to further specify condition. Use additional code to identify cause)

780.33 Post traumatic seizures

800.24 Closed fracture of vault of skull with subarachnoid, subdural, and extradural hemorrhage, prolonged (more than 24 hours) loss of consciousness and return to pre-existing conscious level

803.30 Other closed skull fracture with other and unspecified intracranial hemorrhage, unspecified state of unconsciousness ▼

803.31 Other closed skull fracture with other and unspecified intracranial hemorrhage, no loss of consciousness ▼

803.32 Other closed skull fracture with other and unspecified intracranial hemorrhage, brief (less than one hour) loss of consciousness ▼

803.33 Other closed skull fracture with other and unspecified intracranial hemorrhage, moderate (1-24 hours) loss of consciousness ▼

803.34 Other closed skull fracture with other and unspecified intracranial hemorrhage, prolonged (more than 24 hours) loss of consciousness and return to pre-existing conscious level ▼

803.35 Other closed skull fracture with other and unspecified intracranial hemorrhage, prolonged (more than 24 hours) loss of consciousness, without return to pre-existing conscious level ▼

803.36 Other closed skull fracture with other and unspecified intracranial hemorrhage, loss of consciousness of unspecified duration ▼

803.39 Other closed skull fracture with other and unspecified intracranial hemorrhage, unspecified concussion ▼

852.00 Subarachnoid hemorrhage following injury, without mention of open intracranial wound, unspecified state of consciousness ▼

852.01 Subarachnoid hemorrhage following injury, without mention of open intracranial wound, no loss of consciousness

852.02 Subarachnoid hemorrhage following injury, without mention of open intracranial wound, brief (less than 1 hour) loss of consciousness

852.03 Subarachnoid hemorrhage following injury, without mention of open intracranial wound, moderate (1-24 hours) loss of consciousness

852.04 Subarachnoid hemorrhage following injury, without mention of open intracranial wound, prolonged (more than 24 hours) loss of consciousness and return to pre-existing conscious level

852.05 Subarachnoid hemorrhage following injury, without mention of open intracranial wound, prolonged (more than 24 hours) loss of consciousness, without return to pre-existing conscious level

852.06 Subarachnoid hemorrhage following injury, without mention of open intracranial wound, loss of consciousness of unspecified duration ▼

852.09 Subarachnoid hemorrhage following injury, without mention of open intracranial wound, unspecified concussion ▼

852.10 Subarachnoid hemorrhage following injury, with open intracranial wound, unspecified state of consciousness ▼

852.11 Subarachnoid hemorrhage following injury, with open intracranial wound, no loss of consciousness

852.12 Subarachnoid hemorrhage following injury, with open intracranial wound, brief (less than 1 hour) loss of consciousness

852.13 Subarachnoid hemorrhage following injury, with open intracranial wound, moderate (1-24 hours) loss of consciousness

852.14 Subarachnoid hemorrhage following injury, with open intracranial wound, prolonged (more than 24 hours) loss of consciousness and return to pre-existing conscious level

852.15 Subarachnoid hemorrhage following injury, with open intracranial wound, prolonged (more than 24 hours) loss of consciousness, without return to pre-existing conscious level

852.16 Subarachnoid hemorrhage following injury, with open intracranial wound, loss of consciousness of unspecified duration ▼

852.19 Subarachnoid hemorrhage following injury, with open intracranial wound, unspecified concussion ▼

852.20 Subdural hemorrhage following injury, without mention of open intracranial wound, unspecified state of consciousness ▼

852.21 Subdural hemorrhage following injury, without mention of open intracranial wound, no loss of consciousness

852.22 Subdural hemorrhage following injury, without mention of open intracranial wound, brief (less than one hour) loss of consciousness

852.23 Subdural hemorrhage following injury, without mention of open intracranial wound, moderate (1-24 hours) loss of consciousness

852.24 Subdural hemorrhage following injury, without mention of open intracranial wound, prolonged (more than 24 hours) loss of consciousness and return to pre-existing conscious level

852.25 Subdural hemorrhage following injury, without mention of open intracranial wound, prolonged (more than 24 hours) loss of consciousness, without return to pre-existing conscious level

852.26 Subdural hemorrhage following injury, without mention of open intracranial wound, loss of consciousness of unspecified duration ▼

852.29 Subdural hemorrhage following injury, without mention of open intracranial wound, unspecified concussion ▼
852.30 Subdural hemorrhage following injury, with open intracranial wound, state of consciousness unspecified ▼
852.31 Subdural hemorrhage following injury, with open intracranial wound, no loss of consciousness
852.32 Subdural hemorrhage following injury, with open intracranial wound, brief (less than 1 hour) loss of consciousness
852.33 Subdural hemorrhage following injury, with open intracranial wound, moderate (1-24 hours) loss of consciousness
852.34 Subdural hemorrhage following injury, with open intracranial wound, prolonged (more than 24 hours) loss of consciousness and return to pre-existing conscious level
852.35 Subdural hemorrhage following injury, with open intracranial wound, prolonged (more than 24 hours) loss of consciousness, without return to pre-existing conscious level
852.36 Subdural hemorrhage following injury, with open intracranial wound, loss of consciousness of unspecified duration ▼
852.39 Subdural hemorrhage following injury, with open intracranial wound, unspecified concussion ▼
852.40 Extradural hemorrhage following injury, without mention of open intracranial wound, unspecified state of consciousness ▼
852.41 Extradural hemorrhage following injury, without mention of open intracranial wound, no loss of consciousness
852.42 Extradural hemorrhage following injury, without mention of open intracranial wound, brief (less than 1 hour) loss of consciousness
852.43 Extradural hemorrhage following injury, without mention of open intracranial wound, moderate (1-24 hours) loss of consciousness
852.44 Extradural hemorrhage following injury, without mention of open intracranial wound, prolonged (more than 24 hours) loss of consciousness and return to pre-existing conscious level
852.45 Extradural hemorrhage following injury, without mention of open intracranial wound, prolonged (more than 24 hours) loss of consciousness, without return to pre-existing conscious level
852.46 Extradural hemorrhage following injury, without mention of open intracranial wound, loss of consciousness of unspecified duration ▼
852.49 Extradural hemorrhage following injury, without mention of open intracranial wound, unspecified concussion ▼
852.50 Extradural hemorrhage following injury, with open intracranial wound, state of consciousness unspecified ▼
852.51 Extradural hemorrhage following injury, with open intracranial wound, no loss of consciousness
852.52 Extradural hemorrhage following injury, with open intracranial wound, brief (less than 1 hour) loss of consciousness
852.53 Extradural hemorrhage following injury, with open intracranial wound, moderate (1-24 hours) loss of consciousness
852.54 Extradural hemorrhage following injury, with open intracranial wound, prolonged (more than 24 hours) loss of consciousness and return to pre-existing conscious level
852.55 Extradural hemorrhage following injury, with open intracranial wound, prolonged (more than 24 hours) loss of consciousness, without return to pre-existing conscious level
852.56 Extradural hemorrhage following injury, with open intracranial wound, loss of consciousness of unspecified duration ▼
852.59 Extradural hemorrhage following injury, with open intracranial wound, unspecified concussion ▼
996.2 Mechanical complication of nervous system device, implant, and graft
996.63 Infection and inflammatory reaction due to nervous system device, implant, and graft — (Use additional code to identify specified infections)
997.09 Other nervous system complications — (Use additional code to identify complications)

ICD-9-CM Procedural

01.18 Other diagnostic procedures on brain and cerebral meninges
01.24 Other craniotomy
01.28 Placement of intracerebral catheter(s) via burr hole(s)
02.21 Insertion or replacement of external ventricular drain [EVD]
02.93 Implantation or replacement of intracranial neurostimulator lead(s)

61215

61215 Insertion of subcutaneous reservoir, pump or continuous infusion system for connection to ventricular catheter

ICD-9-CM Diagnostic

191.3 Malignant neoplasm of parietal lobe of brain
191.9 Malignant neoplasm of brain, unspecified site ▼
198.3 Secondary malignant neoplasm of brain and spinal cord
198.4 Secondary malignant neoplasm of other parts of nervous system
199.1 Other malignant neoplasm of unspecified site
202.81 Other malignant lymphomas of lymph nodes of head, face, and neck
237.5 Neoplasm of uncertain behavior of brain and spinal cord

ICD-9-CM Procedural

02.21 Insertion or replacement of external ventricular drain [EVD]
86.06 Insertion of totally implantable infusion pump

61250-61253

61250 Burr hole(s) or trephine, supratentorial, exploratory, not followed by other surgery
61253 Burr hole(s) or trephine, infratentorial, unilateral or bilateral

ICD-9-CM Diagnostic

326 Late effects of intracranial abscess or pyogenic infection — (Use additional code to identify condition: 331.4, 342.0-342.9, 344.0-344.9)
348.4 Compression of brain
430 Subarachnoid hemorrhage — (Use additional code to identify presence of hypertension)
432.1 Subdural hemorrhage — (Use additional code to identify presence of hypertension)
742.9 Unspecified congenital anomaly of brain, spinal cord, and nervous system ▼
747.81 Congenital anomaly of cerebrovascular system
767.0 Subdural and cerebral hemorrhage, birth trauma — (Use additional code(s) to further specify condition. Use additional code to identify cause)
803.30 Other closed skull fracture with other and unspecified intracranial hemorrhage, unspecified state of unconsciousness ▼
803.31 Other closed skull fracture with other and unspecified intracranial hemorrhage, no loss of consciousness ▼
803.32 Other closed skull fracture with other and unspecified intracranial hemorrhage, brief (less than one hour) loss of consciousness ▼
803.33 Other closed skull fracture with other and unspecified intracranial hemorrhage, moderate (1-24 hours) loss of consciousness ▼
803.34 Other closed skull fracture with other and unspecified intracranial hemorrhage, prolonged (more than 24 hours) loss of consciousness and return to pre-existing conscious level ▼
803.35 Other closed skull fracture with other and unspecified intracranial hemorrhage, prolonged (more than 24 hours) loss of consciousness, without return to pre-existing conscious level ▼
803.36 Other closed skull fracture with other and unspecified intracranial hemorrhage, loss of consciousness of unspecified duration ▼
803.39 Other closed skull fracture with other and unspecified intracranial hemorrhage, unspecified concussion ▼
852.20 Subdural hemorrhage following injury, without mention of open intracranial wound, unspecified state of consciousness ▼
853.10 Other and unspecified intracranial hemorrhage following injury, with open intracranial wound, unspecified state of consciousness ▼

ICD-9-CM Procedural

01.24 Other craniotomy
07.51 Exploration of pineal field

07.52 Incision of pineal gland
07.71 Exploration of pituitary fossa
07.72 Incision of pituitary gland

61304-61305

61304 Craniectomy or craniotomy, exploratory; supratentorial
61305 infratentorial (posterior fossa)

ICD-9-CM Diagnostic

191.0 Malignant neoplasm of cerebrum, except lobes and ventricles
191.1 Malignant neoplasm of frontal lobe of brain
191.2 Malignant neoplasm of temporal lobe of brain
191.3 Malignant neoplasm of parietal lobe of brain
191.4 Malignant neoplasm of occipital lobe of brain
191.5 Malignant neoplasm of ventricles of brain
191.6 Malignant neoplasm of cerebellum NOS
191.7 Malignant neoplasm of brain stem
191.8 Malignant neoplasm of other parts of brain
198.3 Secondary malignant neoplasm of brain and spinal cord
225.0 Benign neoplasm of brain
225.1 Benign neoplasm of cranial nerves
225.2 Benign neoplasm of cerebral meninges
239.6 Neoplasm of unspecified nature of brain
239.7 Neoplasm of unspecified nature of endocrine glands and other parts of nervous system
324.0 Intracranial abscess
348.4 Compression of brain
349.81 Cerebrospinal fluid rhinorrhea
388.61 Cerebrospinal fluid otorrhea
430 Subarachnoid hemorrhage — (Use additional code to identify presence of hypertension)
431 Intracerebral hemorrhage — (Use additional code to identify presence of hypertension)
432.0 Nontraumatic extradural hemorrhage — (Use additional code to identify presence of hypertension)
432.1 Subdural hemorrhage — (Use additional code to identify presence of hypertension)
432.9 Unspecified intracranial hemorrhage — (Use additional code to identify presence of hypertension) ▽
437.3 Cerebral aneurysm, nonruptured — (Use additional code to identify presence of hypertension)
767.0 Subdural and cerebral hemorrhage, birth trauma — (Use additional code(s) to further specify condition. Use additional code to identify cause)
784.0 Headache
800.00 Closed fracture of vault of skull without mention of intracranial injury, unspecified state of consciousness ▽
800.01 Closed fracture of vault of skull without mention of intracranial injury, no loss of consciousness
800.02 Closed fracture of vault of skull without mention of intracranial injury, brief (less than one hour) loss of consciousness
800.03 Closed fracture of vault of skull without mention of intracranial injury, moderate (1-24 hours) loss of consciousness
800.04 Closed fracture of vault of skull without mention of intracranial injury, prolonged (more than 24 hours) loss of consciousness and return to pre-existing conscious level
800.05 Closed fracture of vault of skull without mention of intracranial injury, prolonged (more than 24 hours) loss of consciousness, without return to pre-existing conscious level
800.06 Closed fracture of vault of skull without mention of intracranial injury, loss of consciousness of unspecified duration ▽
800.09 Closed fracture of vault of skull without mention of intracranial injury, unspecified concussion ▽
800.10 Closed fracture of vault of skull with cerebral laceration and contusion, unspecified state of consciousness ▽
800.11 Closed fracture of vault of skull with cerebral laceration and contusion, no loss of consciousness
800.12 Closed fracture of vault of skull with cerebral laceration and contusion, brief (less than one hour) loss of consciousness
800.13 Closed fracture of vault of skull with cerebral laceration and contusion, moderate (1-24 hours) loss of consciousness
800.14 Closed fracture of vault of skull with cerebral laceration and contusion, prolonged (more than 24 hours) loss of consciousness and return to pre-existing conscious level
800.15 Closed fracture of vault of skull with cerebral laceration and contusion, prolonged (more than 24 hours) loss of consciousness, without return to pre-existing conscious level
800.16 Closed fracture of vault of skull with cerebral laceration and contusion, loss of consciousness of unspecified duration ▽
800.19 Closed fracture of vault of skull with cerebral laceration and contusion, unspecified concussion ▽
800.20 Closed fracture of vault of skull with subarachnoid, subdural, and extradural hemorrhage, unspecified state of consciousness ▽
800.21 Closed fracture of vault of skull with subarachnoid, subdural, and extradural hemorrhage, no loss of consciousness
800.22 Closed fracture of vault of skull with subarachnoid, subdural, and extradural hemorrhage, brief (less than one hour) loss of consciousness
800.23 Closed fracture of vault of skull with subarachnoid, subdural, and extradural hemorrhage, moderate (1-24 hours) loss of consciousness
800.24 Closed fracture of vault of skull with subarachnoid, subdural, and extradural hemorrhage, prolonged (more than 24 hours) loss of consciousness and return to pre-existing conscious level
800.25 Closed fracture of vault of skull with subarachnoid, subdural, and extradural hemorrhage, prolonged (more than 24 hours) loss of consciousness, without return to pre-existing conscious level
800.26 Closed fracture of vault of skull with subarachnoid, subdural, and extradural hemorrhage, loss of consciousness of unspecified duration ▽
800.29 Closed fracture of vault of skull with subarachnoid, subdural, and extradural hemorrhage, unspecified concussion ▽
800.30 Closed fracture of vault of skull with other and unspecified intracranial hemorrhage, unspecified state of consciousness ▽
800.31 Closed fracture of vault of skull with other and unspecified intracranial hemorrhage, no loss of consciousness ▽
800.32 Closed fracture of vault of skull with other and unspecified intracranial hemorrhage, brief (less than one hour) loss of consciousness ▽
800.33 Closed fracture of vault of skull with other and unspecified intracranial hemorrhage, moderate (1-24 hours) loss of consciousness ▽
800.34 Closed fracture of vault of skull with other and unspecified intracranial hemorrhage, prolonged (more than 24 hours) loss of consciousness and return to pre-existing conscious level ▽
800.35 Closed fracture of vault of skull with other and unspecified intracranial hemorrhage, prolonged (more than 24 hours) loss of consciousness, without return to pre-existing conscious level ▽
800.36 Closed fracture of vault of skull with other and unspecified intracranial hemorrhage, loss of consciousness of unspecified duration ▽
800.40 Closed fracture of vault of skull with intracranial injury of other and unspecified nature, unspecified state of consciousness ▽
800.41 Closed fracture of vault of skull with intracranial injury of other and unspecified nature, no loss of consciousness ▽
800.42 Closed fracture of vault of skull with intracranial injury of other and unspecified nature, brief (less than one hour) loss of consciousness ▽
800.43 Closed fracture of vault of skull with intracranial injury of other and unspecified nature, moderate (1-24 hours) loss of consciousness ▽
800.44 Closed fracture of vault of skull with intracranial injury of other and unspecified nature, prolonged (more than 24 hours) loss of consciousness and return to pre-existing conscious level ▽

800.45 Closed fracture of vault of skull with intracranial injury of other and unspecified nature, prolonged (more than 24 hours) loss of consciousness, without return to pre-existing conscious level ▽

800.46 Closed fracture of vault of skull with intracranial injury of other and unspecified nature, loss of consciousness of unspecified duration ▽

800.49 Closed fracture of vault of skull with intracranial injury of other and unspecified nature, unspecified concussion ▽

800.50 Open fracture of vault of skull without mention of intracranial injury, unspecified state of consciousness ▽

800.51 Open fracture of vault of skull without mention of intracranial injury, no loss of consciousness

800.52 Open fracture of vault of skull without mention of intracranial injury, brief (less than one hour) loss of consciousness

800.53 Open fracture of vault of skull without mention of intracranial injury, moderate (1-24 hours) loss of consciousness

800.54 Open fracture of vault of skull without mention of intracranial injury, prolonged (more than 24 hours) loss of consciousness and return to pre-existing conscious level

800.55 Open fracture of vault of skull without mention of intracranial injury, prolonged (more than 24 hours) loss of consciousness, without return to pre-existing conscious level

800.56 Open fracture of vault of skull without mention of intracranial injury, loss of consciousness of unspecified duration ▽

800.59 Open fracture of vault of skull without mention of intracranial injury, unspecified concussion ▽

800.60 Open fracture of vault of skull with cerebral laceration and contusion, unspecified state of consciousness ▽

800.61 Open fracture of vault of skull with cerebral laceration and contusion, no loss of consciousness

800.62 Open fracture of vault of skull with cerebral laceration and contusion, brief (less than one hour) loss of consciousness

800.63 Open fracture of vault of skull with cerebral laceration and contusion, moderate (1-24 hours) loss of consciousness

800.64 Open fracture of vault of skull with cerebral laceration and contusion, prolonged (more than 24 hours) loss of consciousness and return to pre-existing conscious level

800.65 Open fracture of vault of skull with cerebral laceration and contusion, prolonged (more than 24 hours) loss of consciousness, without return to pre-existing conscious level

800.66 Open fracture of vault of skull with cerebral laceration and contusion, loss of consciousness of unspecified duration ▽

800.69 Open fracture of vault of skull with cerebral laceration and contusion, unspecified concussion ▽

800.70 Open fracture of vault of skull with subarachnoid, subdural, and extradural hemorrhage, unspecified state of consciousness ▽

800.71 Open fracture of vault of skull with subarachnoid, subdural, and extradural hemorrhage, no loss of consciousness

800.72 Open fracture of vault of skull with subarachnoid, subdural, and extradural hemorrhage, brief (less than one hour) loss of consciousness

800.73 Open fracture of vault of skull with subarachnoid, subdural, and extradural hemorrhage, moderate (1-24 hours) loss of consciousness

800.74 Open fracture of vault of skull with subarachnoid, subdural, and extradural hemorrhage, prolonged (more than 24 hours) loss of consciousness and return to pre-existing conscious level

800.75 Open fracture of vault of skull with subarachnoid, subdural, and extradural hemorrhage, prolonged (more than 24 hours) loss of consciousness, without return to pre-existing conscious level

800.76 Open fracture of vault of skull with subarachnoid, subdural, and extradural hemorrhage, loss of consciousness of unspecified duration ▽

800.79 Open fracture of vault of skull with subarachnoid, subdural, and extradural hemorrhage, unspecified concussion ▽

800.80 Open fracture of vault of skull with other and unspecified intracranial hemorrhage, unspecified state of consciousness ▽

800.81 Open fracture of vault of skull with other and unspecified intracranial hemorrhage, no loss of consciousness ▽

800.82 Open fracture of vault of skull with other and unspecified intracranial hemorrhage, brief (less than one hour) loss of consciousness ▽

800.83 Open fracture of vault of skull with other and unspecified intracranial hemorrhage, moderate (1-24 hours) loss of consciousness ▽

800.84 Open fracture of vault of skull with other and unspecified intracranial hemorrhage, prolonged (more than 24 hours) loss of consciousness and return to pre-existing conscious level ▽

800.85 Open fracture of vault of skull with other and unspecified intracranial hemorrhage, prolonged (more than 24 hours) loss of consciousness, without return to pre-existing conscious level ▽

800.86 Open fracture of vault of skull with other and unspecified intracranial hemorrhage, loss of consciousness of unspecified duration ▽

800.89 Open fracture of vault of skull with other and unspecified intracranial hemorrhage, unspecified concussion ▽

800.90 Open fracture of vault of skull with intracranial injury of other and unspecified nature, unspecified state of consciousness ▽

800.91 Open fracture of vault of skull with intracranial injury of other and unspecified nature, no loss of consciousness ▽

800.92 Open fracture of vault of skull with intracranial injury of other and unspecified nature, brief (less than one hour) loss of consciousness ▽

800.93 Open fracture of vault of skull with intracranial injury of other and unspecified nature, moderate (1-24 hours) loss of consciousness ▽

800.94 Open fracture of vault of skull with intracranial injury of other and unspecified nature, prolonged (more than 24 hours) loss of consciousness and return to pre-existing conscious level ▽

800.95 Open fracture of vault of skull with intracranial injury of other and unspecified nature, prolonged (more than 24 hours) loss of consciousness, without return to pre-existing conscious level ▽

800.96 Open fracture of vault of skull with intracranial injury of other and unspecified nature, loss of consciousness of unspecified duration ▽

800.99 Open fracture of vault of skull with intracranial injury of other and unspecified nature, unspecified concussion ▽

801.00 Closed fracture of base of skull without mention of intracranial injury, unspecified state of consciousness ▽

801.01 Closed fracture of base of skull without mention of intracranial injury, no loss of consciousness

801.02 Closed fracture of base of skull without mention of intracranial injury, brief (less than one hour) loss of consciousness

801.03 Closed fracture of base of skull without mention of intracranial injury, moderate (1-24 hours) loss of consciousness

801.04 Closed fracture of base of skull without mention of intracranial injury, prolonged (more than 24 hours) loss of consciousness and return to pre-existing conscious level

801.05 Closed fracture of base of skull without mention of intracranial injury, prolonged (more than 24 hours) loss of consciousness, without return to pre-existing conscious level

801.06 Closed fracture of base of skull without mention of intracranial injury, loss of consciousness of unspecified duration ▽

801.09 Closed fracture of base of skull without mention of intracranial injury, unspecified concussion ▽

801.10 Closed fracture of base of skull with cerebral laceration and contusion, unspecified state of consciousness ▽

801.11 Closed fracture of base of skull with cerebral laceration and contusion, no loss of consciousness

801.12 Closed fracture of base of skull with cerebral laceration and contusion, brief (less than one hour) loss of consciousness

801.13 Closed fracture of base of skull with cerebral laceration and contusion, moderate (1-24 hours) loss of consciousness

801.14 Closed fracture of base of skull with cerebral laceration and contusion, prolonged (more than 24 hours) loss of consciousness and return to pre-existing conscious level

801.15 Closed fracture of base of skull with cerebral laceration and contusion, prolonged (more than 24 hours) loss of consciousness, without return to pre-existing conscious level

801.16 Closed fracture of base of skull with cerebral laceration and contusion, loss of consciousness of unspecified duration ▼

801.19 Closed fracture of base of skull with cerebral laceration and contusion, unspecified concussion ▼

801.20 Closed fracture of base of skull with subarachnoid, subdural, and extradural hemorrhage, unspecified state of consciousness ▼

801.21 Closed fracture of base of skull with subarachnoid, subdural, and extradural hemorrhage, no loss of consciousness

801.22 Closed fracture of base of skull with subarachnoid, subdural, and extradural hemorrhage, brief (less than one hour) loss of consciousness

801.23 Closed fracture of base of skull with subarachnoid, subdural, and extradural hemorrhage, moderate (1-24 hours) loss of consciousness

801.24 Closed fracture of base of skull with subarachnoid, subdural, and extradural hemorrhage, prolonged (more than 24 hours) loss of consciousness and return to pre-existing conscious level

801.25 Closed fracture of base of skull with subarachnoid, subdural, and extradural hemorrhage, prolonged (more than 24 hours) loss of consciousness, without return to pre-existing conscious level

801.26 Closed fracture of base of skull with subarachnoid, subdural, and extradural hemorrhage, loss of consciousness of unspecified duration ▼

801.29 Closed fracture of base of skull with subarachnoid, subdural, and extradural hemorrhage, unspecified concussion ▼

801.30 Closed fracture of base of skull with other and unspecified intracranial hemorrhage, unspecified state of consciousness ▼

801.31 Closed fracture of base of skull with other and unspecified intracranial hemorrhage, no loss of consciousness ▼

801.32 Closed fracture of base of skull with other and unspecified intracranial hemorrhage, brief (less than one hour) loss of consciousness ▼

801.33 Closed fracture of base of skull with other and unspecified intracranial hemorrhage, moderate (1-24 hours) loss of consciousness ▼

801.34 Closed fracture of base of skull with other and unspecified intracranial hemorrhage, prolonged (more than 24 hours) loss of consciousness and return to pre-existing conscious level ▼

801.35 Closed fracture of base of skull with other and unspecified intracranial hemorrhage, prolonged (more than 24 hours) loss of consciousness, without return to pre-existing conscious level ▼

801.36 Closed fracture of base of skull with other and unspecified intracranial hemorrhage, loss of consciousness of unspecified duration ▼

801.39 Closed fracture of base of skull with other and unspecified intracranial hemorrhage, unspecified concussion ▼

801.40 Closed fracture of base of skull with intracranial injury of other and unspecified nature, unspecified state of consciousness ▼

801.41 Closed fracture of base of skull with intracranial injury of other and unspecified nature, no loss of consciousness ▼

801.42 Closed fracture of base of skull with intracranial injury of other and unspecified nature, brief (less than one hour) loss of consciousness ▼

801.43 Closed fracture of base of skull with intracranial injury of other and unspecified nature, moderate (1-24 hours) loss of consciousness ▼

801.44 Closed fracture of base of skull with intracranial injury of other and unspecified nature, prolonged (more than 24 hours) loss of consciousness and return to pre-existing conscious level ▼

801.45 Closed fracture of base of skull with intracranial injury of other and unspecified nature, prolonged (more than 24 hours) loss of consciousness, without return to pre-existing conscious level ▼

801.46 Closed fracture of base of skull with intracranial injury of other and unspecified nature, loss of consciousness of unspecified duration ▼

801.49 Closed fracture of base of skull with intracranial injury of other and unspecified nature, unspecified concussion ▼

801.50 Open fracture of base of skull without mention of intracranial injury, unspecified state of consciousness ▼

801.51 Open fracture of base of skull without mention of intracranial injury, no loss of consciousness

801.52 Open fracture of base of skull without mention of intracranial injury, brief (less than one hour) loss of consciousness

801.53 Open fracture of base of skull without mention of intracranial injury, moderate (1-24 hours) loss of consciousness

801.54 Open fracture of base of skull without mention of intracranial injury, prolonged (more than 24 hours) loss of consciousness and return to pre-existing conscious level

801.55 Open fracture of base of skull without mention of intracranial injury, prolonged (more than 24 hours) loss of consciousness, without return to pre-existing conscious level

801.56 Open fracture of base of skull without mention of intracranial injury, loss of consciousness of unspecified duration ▼

801.59 Open fracture of base of skull without mention of intracranial injury, unspecified concussion ▼

801.60 Open fracture of base of skull with cerebral laceration and contusion, unspecified state of consciousness ▼

801.61 Open fracture of base of skull with cerebral laceration and contusion, no loss of consciousness

801.62 Open fracture of base of skull with cerebral laceration and contusion, brief (less than one hour) loss of consciousness

801.63 Open fracture of base of skull with cerebral laceration and contusion, moderate (1-24 hours) loss of consciousness

801.64 Open fracture of base of skull with cerebral laceration and contusion, prolonged (more than 24 hours) loss of consciousness and return to pre-existing conscious level

801.65 Open fracture of base of skull with cerebral laceration and contusion, prolonged (more than 24 hours) loss of consciousness, without return to pre-existing conscious level

801.66 Open fracture of base of skull with cerebral laceration and contusion, loss of consciousness of unspecified duration ▼

801.69 Open fracture of base of skull with cerebral laceration and contusion, unspecified concussion ▼

801.70 Open fracture of base of skull with subarachnoid, subdural, and extradural hemorrhage, unspecified state of consciousness ▼

801.71 Open fracture of base of skull with subarachnoid, subdural, and extradural hemorrhage, no loss of consciousness

801.72 Open fracture of base of skull with subarachnoid, subdural, and extradural hemorrhage, brief (less than one hour) loss of consciousness

801.73 Open fracture of base of skull with subarachnoid, subdural, and extradural hemorrhage, moderate (1-24 hours) loss of consciousness

801.74 Open fracture of base of skull with subarachnoid, subdural, and extradural hemorrhage, prolonged (more than 24 hours) loss of consciousness and return to pre-existing conscious level

801.75 Open fracture of base of skull with subarachnoid, subdural, and extradural hemorrhage, prolonged (more than 24 hours) loss of consciousness, without return to pre-existing conscious level

801.76 Open fracture of base of skull with subarachnoid, subdural, and extradural hemorrhage, loss of consciousness of unspecified duration ▼

801.79 Open fracture of base of skull with subarachnoid, subdural, and extradural hemorrhage, unspecified concussion ▼

801.80 Open fracture of base of skull with other and unspecified intracranial hemorrhage, unspecified state of consciousness ▼

801.81 Open fracture of base of skull with other and unspecified intracranial hemorrhage, no loss of consciousness ▼

801.82 Open fracture of base of skull with other and unspecified intracranial hemorrhage, brief (less than one hour) loss of consciousness ▼

801.83 Open fracture of base of skull with other and unspecified intracranial hemorrhage, moderate (1-24 hours) loss of consciousness ▼

801.84 Open fracture of base of skull with other and unspecified intracranial hemorrhage, prolonged (more than 24 hours) loss of consciousness and return to pre-existing conscious level ▼

801.85 Open fracture of base of skull with other and unspecified intracranial hemorrhage, prolonged (more than 24 hours) loss of consciousness, without return to pre-existing conscious level ▽

801.86 Open fracture of base of skull with other and unspecified intracranial hemorrhage, loss of consciousness of unspecified duration ▽

801.89 Open fracture of base of skull with other and unspecified intracranial hemorrhage, unspecified concussion ▽

801.90 Open fracture of base of skull with intracranial injury of other and unspecified nature, unspecified state of consciousness ▽

801.91 Open fracture of base of skull with intracranial injury of other and unspecified nature, no loss of consciousness ▽

801.92 Open fracture of base of skull with intracranial injury of other and unspecified nature, brief (less than one hour) loss of consciousness ▽

801.93 Open fracture of base of skull with intracranial injury of other and unspecified nature, moderate (1-24 hours) loss of consciousness ▽

801.94 Open fracture of base of skull with intracranial injury of other and unspecified nature, prolonged (more than 24 hours) loss of consciousness and return to pre-existing conscious level ▽

801.95 Open fracture of base of skull with intracranial injury of other and unspecified nature, prolonged (more than 24 hours) loss of consciousness, without return to pre-existing conscious level ▽

801.96 Open fracture of base of skull with intracranial injury of other and unspecified nature, loss of consciousness of unspecified duration ▽

801.99 Open fracture of base of skull with intracranial injury of other and unspecified nature, unspecified concussion ▽

803.00 Other closed skull fracture without mention of intracranial injury, unspecified state of consciousness ▽

803.01 Other closed skull fracture without mention of intracranial injury, no loss of consciousness

803.02 Other closed skull fracture without mention of intracranial injury, brief (less than one hour) loss of consciousness

803.03 Other closed skull fracture without mention of intracranial injury, moderate (1-24 hours) loss of consciousness

803.04 Other closed skull fracture without mention of intracranial injury, prolonged (more than 24 hours) loss of consciousness and return to pre-existing conscious level

803.05 Other closed skull fracture without mention of intracranial injury, prolonged (more than 24 hours) loss of consciousness, without return to pre-existing conscious level

803.06 Other closed skull fracture without mention of intracranial injury, loss of consciousness of unspecified duration ▽

803.09 Other closed skull fracture without mention of intracranial injury, unspecified concussion ▽

803.10 Other closed skull fracture with cerebral laceration and contusion, unspecified state of consciousness ▽

803.11 Other closed skull fracture with cerebral laceration and contusion, no loss of consciousness

803.12 Other closed skull fracture with cerebral laceration and contusion, brief (less than one hour) loss of consciousness

803.13 Other closed skull fracture with cerebral laceration and contusion, moderate (1-24 hours) loss of consciousness

803.14 Other closed skull fracture with cerebral laceration and contusion, prolonged (more than 24 hours) loss of consciousness and return to pre-existing conscious level

803.15 Other closed skull fracture with cerebral laceration and contusion, prolonged (more than 24 hours) loss of consciousness, without return to pre-existing conscious level

803.16 Other closed skull fracture with cerebral laceration and contusion, loss of consciousness of unspecified duration ▽

803.19 Other closed skull fracture with cerebral laceration and contusion, unspecified concussion ▽

803.20 Other closed skull fracture with subarachnoid, subdural, and extradural hemorrhage, unspecified state of consciousness ▽

803.21 Other closed skull fracture with subarachnoid, subdural, and extradural hemorrhage, no loss of consciousness

803.22 Other closed skull fracture with subarachnoid, subdural, and extradural hemorrhage, brief (less than one hour) loss of consciousness

803.23 Other closed skull fracture with subarachnoid, subdural, and extradural hemorrhage, moderate (1-24 hours) loss of consciousness

803.24 Other closed skull fracture with subarachnoid, subdural, and extradural hemorrhage, prolonged (more than 24 hours) loss of consciousness and return to pre-existing conscious level

803.25 Other closed skull fracture with subarachnoid, subdural, and extradural hemorrhage, prolonged (more than 24 hours) loss of consciousness, without return to pre-existing conscious level

803.26 Other closed skull fracture with subarachnoid, subdural, and extradural hemorrhage, loss of consciousness of unspecified duration ▽

803.29 Other closed skull fracture with subarachnoid, subdural, and extradural hemorrhage, unspecified concussion ▽

803.30 Other closed skull fracture with other and unspecified intracranial hemorrhage, unspecified state of unconsciousness ▽

803.31 Other closed skull fracture with other and unspecified intracranial hemorrhage, no loss of consciousness ▽

803.32 Other closed skull fracture with other and unspecified intracranial hemorrhage, brief (less than one hour) loss of consciousness ▽

803.33 Other closed skull fracture with other and unspecified intracranial hemorrhage, moderate (1-24 hours) loss of consciousness ▽

803.34 Other closed skull fracture with other and unspecified intracranial hemorrhage, prolonged (more than 24 hours) loss of consciousness and return to pre-existing conscious level ▽

803.35 Other closed skull fracture with other and unspecified intracranial hemorrhage, prolonged (more than 24 hours) loss of consciousness, without return to pre-existing conscious level ▽

803.36 Other closed skull fracture with other and unspecified intracranial hemorrhage, loss of consciousness of unspecified duration ▽

803.39 Other closed skull fracture with other and unspecified intracranial hemorrhage, unspecified concussion ▽

803.40 Other closed skull fracture with intracranial injury of other and unspecified nature, unspecified state of consciousness ▽

803.41 Other closed skull fracture with intracranial injury of other and unspecified nature, no loss of consciousness ▽

803.42 Other closed skull fracture with intracranial injury of other and unspecified nature, brief (less than one hour) loss of consciousness ▽

803.43 Other closed skull fracture with intracranial injury of other and unspecified nature, moderate (1-24 hours) loss of consciousness ▽

803.44 Other closed skull fracture with intracranial injury of other and unspecified nature, prolonged (more than 24 hours) loss of consciousness and return to pre-existing conscious level ▽

803.45 Other closed skull fracture with intracranial injury of other and unspecified nature, prolonged (more than 24 hours) loss of consciousness, without return to pre-existing conscious level ▽

803.46 Other closed skull fracture with intracranial injury of other and unspecified nature, loss of consciousness of unspecified duration ▽

803.49 Other closed skull fracture with intracranial injury of other and unspecified nature, unspecified concussion ▽

803.50 Other open skull fracture without mention of injury, state of consciousness unspecified ▽

803.51 Other open skull fracture without mention of intracranial injury, no loss of consciousness

803.52 Other open skull fracture without mention of intracranial injury, brief (less than one hour) loss of consciousness

803.53 Other open skull fracture without mention of intracranial injury, moderate (1-24 hours) loss of consciousness

803.54 Other open skull fracture without mention of intracranial injury, prolonged (more than 24 hours) loss of consciousness and return to pre-existing conscious level

803.55 Other open skull fracture without mention of intracranial injury, prolonged (more than 24 hours) loss of consciousness, without return to pre-existing conscious level

803.56 Other open skull fracture without mention of intracranial injury, loss of consciousness of unspecified duration

803.59 Other open skull fracture without mention of intracranial injury, unspecified concussion

803.60 Other open skull fracture with cerebral laceration and contusion, unspecified state of consciousness

803.61 Other open skull fracture with cerebral laceration and contusion, no loss of consciousness

803.62 Other open skull fracture with cerebral laceration and contusion, brief (less than one hour) loss of consciousness

803.63 Other open skull fracture with cerebral laceration and contusion, moderate (1-24 hours) loss of consciousness

803.64 Other open skull fracture with cerebral laceration and contusion, prolonged (more than 24 hours) loss of consciousness and return to pre-existing conscious level

803.65 Other open skull fracture with cerebral laceration and contusion, prolonged (more than 24 hours) loss of consciousness, without return to pre-existing conscious level

803.66 Other open skull fracture with cerebral laceration and contusion, loss of consciousness of unspecified duration

803.69 Other open skull fracture with cerebral laceration and contusion, unspecified concussion

803.70 Other open skull fracture with subarachnoid, subdural, and extradural hemorrhage, unspecified state of consciousness

803.71 Other open skull fracture with subarachnoid, subdural, and extradural hemorrhage, no loss of consciousness

803.72 Other open skull fracture with subarachnoid, subdural, and extradural hemorrhage, brief (less than one hour) loss of consciousness

803.73 Other open skull fracture with subarachnoid, subdural, and extradural hemorrhage, moderate (1-24 hours) loss of consciousness

803.74 Other open skull fracture with subarachnoid, subdural, and extradural hemorrhage, prolonged (more than 24 hours) loss of consciousness and return to pre-existing conscious level

803.75 Other open skull fracture with subarachnoid, subdural, and extradural hemorrhage, prolonged (more than 24 hours) loss of consciousness, without return to pre-existing conscious level

803.76 Other open skull fracture with subarachnoid, subdural, and extradural hemorrhage, loss of consciousness of unspecified duration

803.79 Other open skull fracture with subarachnoid, subdural, and extradural hemorrhage, unspecified concussion

803.80 Other open skull fracture with other and unspecified intracranial hemorrhage, unspecified state of consciousness

803.81 Other open skull fracture with other and unspecified intracranial hemorrhage, no loss of consciousness

803.82 Other open skull fracture with other and unspecified intracranial hemorrhage, brief (less than one hour) loss of consciousness

803.83 Other open skull fracture with other and unspecified intracranial hemorrhage, moderate (1-24 hours) loss of consciousness

803.84 Other open skull fracture with other and unspecified intracranial hemorrhage, prolonged (more than 24 hours) loss of consciousness and return to pre-existing conscious level

803.85 Other open skull fracture with other and unspecified intracranial hemorrhage, prolonged (more than 24 hours) loss of consciousness, without return to pre-existing conscious level

803.86 Other open skull fracture with other and unspecified intracranial hemorrhage, loss of consciousness of unspecified duration

803.89 Other open skull fracture with other and unspecified intracranial hemorrhage, unspecified concussion

803.90 Other open skull fracture with intracranial injury of other and unspecified nature, unspecified state of consciousness

803.91 Other open skull fracture with intracranial injury of other and unspecified nature, no loss of consciousness

803.92 Other open skull fracture with intracranial injury of other and unspecified nature, brief (less than one hour) loss of consciousness

803.93 Other open skull fracture with intracranial injury of other and unspecified nature, moderate (1-24 hours) loss of consciousness

803.94 Other open skull fracture with intracranial injury of other and unspecified nature, prolonged (more than 24 hours) loss of consciousness and return to pre-existing conscious level

803.95 Other open skull fracture with intracranial injury of other and unspecified nature, prolonged (more than 24 hours) loss of consciousness, without return to pre-existing conscious level

803.96 Other open skull fracture with intracranial injury of other and unspecified nature, loss of consciousness of unspecified duration

803.99 Other open skull fracture with intracranial injury of other and unspecified nature, unspecified concussion

804.00 Closed fractures involving skull or face with other bones, without mention of intracranial injury, unspecified state of consciousness

804.01 Closed fractures involving skull or face with other bones, without mention of intracranial injury, no loss of consciousness

804.02 Closed fractures involving skull or face with other bones, without mention of intracranial injury, brief (less than one hour) loss of consciousness

804.03 Closed fractures involving skull or face with other bones, without mention of intracranial injury, moderate (1-24 hours) loss of consciousness

804.04 Closed fractures involving skull or face with other bones, without mention or intracranial injury, prolonged (more than 24 hours) loss of consciousness and return to pre-existing conscious level

804.05 Closed fractures involving skull of face with other bones, without mention of intracranial injury, prolonged (more than 24 hours) loss of consciousness, without return to pre-existing conscious level

804.06 Closed fractures involving skull of face with other bones, without mention of intracranial injury, loss of consciousness of unspecified duration

804.09 Closed fractures involving skull of face with other bones, without mention of intracranial injury, unspecified concussion

804.10 Closed fractures involving skull or face with other bones, with cerebral laceration and contusion, unspecified state of consciousness

804.11 Closed fractures involving skull or face with other bones, with cerebral laceration and contusion, no loss of consciousness

804.12 Closed fractures involving skull or face with other bones, with cerebral laceration and contusion, brief (less than one hour) loss of consciousness

804.13 Closed fractures involving skull or face with other bones, with cerebral laceration and contusion, moderate (1-24 hours) loss of consciousness

804.14 Closed fractures involving skull or face with other bones, with cerebral laceration and contusion, prolonged (more than 24 hours) loss of consciousness and return to pre-existing conscious level

804.15 Closed fractures involving skull or face with other bones, with cerebral laceration and contusion, prolonged (more than 24 hours) loss of consciousness, without return to pre-existing conscious level

804.16 Closed fractures involving skull or face with other bones, with cerebral laceration and contusion, loss of consciousness of unspecified duration

804.19 Closed fractures involving skull or face with other bones, with cerebral laceration and contusion, unspecified concussion

804.20 Closed fractures involving skull or face with other bones with subarachnoid, subdural, and extradural hemorrhage, unspecified state of consciousness

804.21 Closed fractures involving skull or face with other bones with subarachnoid, subdural, and extradural hemorrhage, no loss of consciousness

804.22 Closed fractures involving skull or face with other bones with subarachnoid, subdural, and extradural hemorrhage, brief (less than one hour) loss of consciousness

804.23 Closed fractures involving skull or face with other bones with subarachnoid, subdural, and extradural hemorrhage, moderate (1-24 hours) loss of consciousness

804.24 Closed fractures involving skull or face with other bones with subarachnoid, subdural, and extradural hemorrhage, prolonged (more than 24 hours) loss of consciousness and return to pre-existing conscious level

804.25 Closed fractures involving skull or face with other bones with subarachnoid, subdural, and extradural hemorrhage, prolonged (more than 24 hours) loss of consciousness, without return to pre-existing conscious level

804.26 Closed fractures involving skull or face with other bones with subarachnoid, subdural, and extradural hemorrhage, loss of consciousness of unspecified duration ▽

804.29 Closed fractures involving skull or face with other bones with subarachnoid, subdural, and extradural hemorrhage, unspecified concussion ▽

804.30 Closed fractures involving skull or face with other bones, with other and unspecified intracranial hemorrhage, unspecified state of consciousness ▽

804.31 Closed fractures involving skull or face with other bones, with other and unspecified intracranial hemorrhage, no loss of consciousness ▽

804.32 Closed fractures involving skull or face with other bones, with other and unspecified intracranial hemorrhage, brief (less than one hour) loss of consciousness ▽

804.33 Closed fractures involving skull or face with other bones, with other and unspecified intracranial hemorrhage, moderate (1-24 hours) loss of consciousness ▽

804.34 Closed fractures involving skull or face with other bones, with other and unspecified intracranial hemorrhage, prolonged (more than 24 hours) loss of consciousness and return to preexisting conscious level ▽

804.35 Closed fractures involving skull or face with other bones, with other and unspecified intracranial hemorrhage, prolonged (more than 24 hours) loss of consciousness, without return to pre-existing conscious level ▽

804.36 Closed fractures involving skull or face with other bones, with other and unspecified intracranial hemorrhage, loss of consciousness of unspecified duration ▽

804.39 Closed fractures involving skull or face with other bones, with other and unspecified intracranial hemorrhage, unspecified concussion ▽

804.40 Closed fractures involving skull or face with other bones, with intracranial injury of other and unspecified nature, unspecified state of consciousness ▽

804.41 Closed fractures involving skull or face with other bones, with intracranial injury of other and unspecified nature, no loss of consciousness ▽

804.42 Closed fractures involving skull or face with other bones, with intracranial injury of other and unspecified nature, brief (less than one hour) loss of consciousness ▽

804.43 Closed fractures involving skull or face with other bones, with intracranial injury of other and unspecified nature, moderate (1-24 hours) loss of consciousness ▽

804.44 Closed fractures involving skull or face with other bones, with intracranial injury of other and unspecified nature, prolonged (more than 24 hours) loss of consciousness and return to pre-existing conscious level ▽

804.45 Closed fractures involving skull or face with other bones, with intracranial injury of other and unspecified nature, prolonged (more than 24 hours) loss of consciousness, without return to pre-existing conscious level ▽

804.46 Closed fractures involving skull or face with other bones, with intracranial injury of other and unspecified nature, loss of consciousness of unspecified duration ▽

804.49 Closed fractures involving skull or face with other bones, with intracranial injury of other and unspecified nature, unspecified concussion ▽

804.50 Open fractures involving skull or face with other bones, without mention of intracranial injury, unspecified state of consciousness ▽

804.51 Open fractures involving skull or face with other bones, without mention of intracranial injury, no loss of consciousness

804.52 Open fractures involving skull or face with other bones, without mention of intracranial injury, brief (less than one hour) loss of consciousness

804.54 Open fractures involving skull or face with other bones, without mention of intracranial injury, prolonged (more than 24 hours) loss of consciousness and return to pre-existing conscious level

804.55 Open fractures involving skull or face with other bones, without mention of intracranial injury, prolonged (more than 24 hours) loss of consciousness, without return to pre-existing conscious level

804.56 Open fractures involving skull or face with other bones, without mention of intracranial injury, loss of consciousness of unspecified duration ▽

804.59 Open fractures involving skull or face with other bones, without mention of intracranial injury, unspecified concussion ▽

804.60 Open fractures involving skull or face with other bones, with cerebral laceration and contusion, unspecified state of consciousness ▽

804.61 Open fractures involving skull or face with other bones, with cerebral laceration and contusion, no loss of consciousness

804.62 Open fractures involving skull or face with other bones, with cerebral laceration and contusion, brief (less than one hour) loss of consciousness

804.63 Open fractures involving skull or face with other bones, with cerebral laceration and contusion, moderate (1-24 hours) loss of consciousness

804.64 Open fractures involving skull or face with other bones, with cerebral laceration and contusion, prolonged (more than 24 hours) loss of consciousness and return to pre-existing conscious level

804.65 Open fractures involving skull or face with other bones, with cerebral laceration and contusion, prolonged (more than 24 hours) loss of consciousness, without return to pre-existing conscious level

804.66 Open fractures involving skull or face with other bones, with cerebral laceration and contusion, loss of consciousness of unspecified duration ▽

804.69 Open fractures involving skull or face with other bones, with cerebral laceration and contusion, unspecified concussion ▽

804.70 Open fractures involving skull or face with other bones with subarachnoid, subdural, and extradural hemorrhage, unspecified state of consciousness ▽

804.71 Open fractures involving skull or face with other bones with subarachnoid, subdural, and extradural hemorrhage, no loss of consciousness

804.72 Open fractures involving skull or face with other bones with subarachnoid, subdural, and extradural hemorrhage, brief (less than one hour) loss of consciousness

804.73 Open fractures involving skull or face with other bones with subarachnoid, subdural, and extradural hemorrhage, moderate (1-24 hours) loss of consciousness

804.74 Open fractures involving skull or face with other bones with subarachnoid, subdural, and extradural hemorrhage, prolonged (more than 24 hours) loss of consciousness and return to pre-existing conscious level

804.75 Open fractures involving skull or face with other bones with subarachnoid, subdural, and extradural hemorrhage, prolonged (more than 24 hours) loss of consciousness, without return to pre-existing conscious level

804.76 Open fractures involving skull or face with other bones with subarachnoid, subdural, and extradural hemorrhage, loss of consciousness of unspecified duration ▽

804.79 Open fractures involving skull or face with other bones with subarachnoid, subdural, and extradural hemorrhage, unspecified concussion ▽

804.80 Open fractures involving skull or face with other bones, with other and unspecified intracranial hemorrhage, unspecified state of consciousness ▽

804.81 Open fractures involving skull or face with other bones, with other and unspecified intracranial hemorrhage, no loss of consciousness ▽

804.82 Open fractures involving skull or face with other bones, with other and unspecified intracranial hemorrhage, brief (less than one hour) loss of consciousness ▽

804.83 Open fractures involving skull or face with other bones, with other and unspecified intracranial hemorrhage, moderate (1-24 hours) loss of consciousness ▽

804.84 Open fractures involving skull or face with other bones, with other and unspecified intracranial hemorrhage, prolonged (more than 24 hours) loss of consciousness and return to pre-existing conscious level ▽

804.85 Open fractures involving skull or face with other bones, with other and unspecified intracranial hemorrhage, prolonged (more than 24 hours) loss of consciousness, without return to pre-existing conscious level ▽

804.86 Open fractures involving skull or face with other bones, with other and unspecified intracranial hemorrhage, loss of consciousness of unspecified duration ▽

804.89 Open fractures involving skull or face with other bones, with other and unspecified intracranial hemorrhage, unspecified concussion ▽

804.90 Open fractures involving skull or face with other bones, with intracranial injury of other and unspecified nature, unspecified state of consciousness ▽

804.91 Open fractures involving skull or face with other bones, with intracranial injury of other and unspecified nature, no loss of consciousness ▽

804.92 Open fractures involving skull or face with other bones, with intracranial injury of other and unspecified nature, brief (less than one hour) loss of consciousness

804.93 Open fractures involving skull or face with other bones, with intracranial injury of other and unspecified nature, moderate (1-24 hours) loss of consciousness

804.94 Open fractures involving skull or face with other bones, with intracranial injury of other and unspecified nature, prolonged (more than 24 hours) loss of consciousness and return to pre-existing conscious level

804.95 Open fractures involving skull or face with other bones, with intracranial injury of other and unspecified nature, prolonged (more than 24 hours) loss of consciousness, without return to pre-existing level

804.96 Open fractures involving skull or face with other bones, with intracranial injury of other and unspecified nature, loss of consciousness of unspecified duration

804.99 Open fractures involving skull or face with other bones, with intracranial injury of other and unspecified nature, unspecified concussion

854.05 Intracranial injury of other and unspecified nature, without mention of open intracranial wound, prolonged (more than 24 hours) loss of consciousness, without return to pre-existing conscious level

854.06 Intracranial injury of other and unspecified nature, without mention of open intracranial wound, loss of consciousness of unspecified duration

854.09 Intracranial injury of other and unspecified nature, without mention of open intracranial wound, unspecified concussion

854.10 Intracranial injury of other and unspecified nature, with open intracranial wound, unspecified state of consciousness

854.11 Intracranial injury of other and unspecified nature, with open intracranial wound, no loss of consciousness

854.12 Intracranial injury of other and unspecified nature, with open intracranial wound, brief (less than 1 hour) loss of consciousness

854.13 Intracranial injury of other and unspecified nature, with open intracranial wound, moderate (1-24 hours) loss of consciousness

854.14 Intracranial injury of other and unspecified nature, with open intracranial wound, prolonged (more than 24 hours) loss of consciousness and return to pre-existing conscious level

854.15 Intracranial injury of other and unspecified nature, with open intracranial wound, prolonged (more than 24 hours) loss of consciousness, without return to pre-existing conscious level

854.16 Intracranial injury of other and unspecified nature, with open intracranial wound, loss of consciousness of unspecified duration

854.19 Intracranial injury of other and unspecified nature, with open intracranial wound, with unspecified concussion

ICD-9-CM Procedural

01.24 Other craniotomy

01.25 Other craniectomy

07.51 Exploration of pineal field

07.52 Incision of pineal gland

07.71 Exploration of pituitary fossa

07.72 Incision of pituitary gland

61312-61313

61312 Craniectomy or craniotomy for evacuation of hematoma, supratentorial; extradural or subdural

61313 intracerebral

ICD-9-CM Diagnostic

348.4 Compression of brain

431 Intracerebral hemorrhage — (Use additional code to identify presence of hypertension)

432.0 Nontraumatic extradural hemorrhage — (Use additional code to identify presence of hypertension)

432.1 Subdural hemorrhage — (Use additional code to identify presence of hypertension)

432.9 Unspecified intracranial hemorrhage — (Use additional code to identify presence of hypertension)

747.81 Congenital anomaly of cerebrovascular system

800.20 Closed fracture of vault of skull with subarachnoid, subdural, and extradural hemorrhage, unspecified state of consciousness

800.21 Closed fracture of vault of skull with subarachnoid, subdural, and extradural hemorrhage, no loss of consciousness

800.22 Closed fracture of vault of skull with subarachnoid, subdural, and extradural hemorrhage, brief (less than one hour) loss of consciousness

800.23 Closed fracture of vault of skull with subarachnoid, subdural, and extradural hemorrhage, moderate (1-24 hours) loss of consciousness

800.24 Closed fracture of vault of skull with subarachnoid, subdural, and extradural hemorrhage, prolonged (more than 24 hours) loss of consciousness and return to pre-existing conscious level

800.25 Closed fracture of vault of skull with subarachnoid, subdural, and extradural hemorrhage, prolonged (more than 24 hours) loss of consciousness, without return to pre-existing conscious level

800.26 Closed fracture of vault of skull with subarachnoid, subdural, and extradural hemorrhage, loss of consciousness of unspecified duration

800.29 Closed fracture of vault of skull with subarachnoid, subdural, and extradural hemorrhage, unspecified concussion

800.30 Closed fracture of vault of skull with other and unspecified intracranial hemorrhage, unspecified state of consciousness

800.70 Open fracture of vault of skull with subarachnoid, subdural, and extradural hemorrhage, unspecified state of consciousness

800.71 Open fracture of vault of skull with subarachnoid, subdural, and extradural hemorrhage, no loss of consciousness

800.72 Open fracture of vault of skull with subarachnoid, subdural, and extradural hemorrhage, brief (less than one hour) loss of consciousness

800.73 Open fracture of vault of skull with subarachnoid, subdural, and extradural hemorrhage, moderate (1-24 hours) loss of consciousness

800.74 Open fracture of vault of skull with subarachnoid, subdural, and extradural hemorrhage, prolonged (more than 24 hours) loss of consciousness and return to pre-existing conscious level

800.75 Open fracture of vault of skull with subarachnoid, subdural, and extradural hemorrhage, prolonged (more than 24 hours) loss of consciousness, without return to pre-existing conscious level

800.76 Open fracture of vault of skull with subarachnoid, subdural, and extradural hemorrhage, loss of consciousness of unspecified duration

800.79 Open fracture of vault of skull with subarachnoid, subdural, and extradural hemorrhage, unspecified concussion

851.00 Cortex (cerebral) contusion without mention of open intracranial wound, state of consciousness unspecified

851.02 Cortex (cerebral) contusion without mention of open intracranial wound, brief (less than 1 hour) loss of consciousness

851.03 Cortex (cerebral) contusion without mention of open intracranial wound, moderate (1-24 hours) loss of consciousness

851.04 Cortex (cerebral) contusion without mention of open intracranial wound, prolonged (more than 24 hours) loss of consciousness and return to pre-existing conscious level

851.05 Cortex (cerebral) contusion without mention of open intracranial wound, prolonged (more than 24 hours) loss of consciousness, without return to pre-existing conscious level

851.06 Cortex (cerebral) contusion without mention of open intracranial wound, loss of consciousness of unspecified duration

851.09 Cortex (cerebral) contusion without mention of open intracranial wound, unspecified concussion

851.80 Other and unspecified cerebral laceration and contusion, without mention of open intracranial wound, unspecified state of consciousness

851.81 Other and unspecified cerebral laceration and contusion, without mention of open intracranial wound, no loss of consciousness

851.82 Other and unspecified cerebral laceration and contusion, without mention of open intracranial wound, brief (less than 1 hour) loss of consciousness

851.83 Other and unspecified cerebral laceration and contusion, without mention of open intracranial wound, moderate (1-24 hours) loss of consciousness

851.84 Other and unspecified cerebral laceration and contusion, without mention of open intracranial wound, prolonged (more than 24 hours) loss of consciousness and return to preexisting conscious level ▽

851.85 Other and unspecified cerebral laceration and contusion, without mention of open intracranial wound, prolonged (more than 24 hours) loss of consciousness, without return to pre-existing conscious level ▽

851.86 Other and unspecified cerebral laceration and contusion, without mention of open intracranial wound, loss of consciousness of unspecified duration ▽

851.89 Other and unspecified cerebral laceration and contusion, without mention of open intracranial wound, unspecified concussion ▽

852.20 Subdural hemorrhage following injury, without mention of open intracranial wound, unspecified state of consciousness ▽

852.21 Subdural hemorrhage following injury, without mention of open intracranial wound, no loss of consciousness

852.22 Subdural hemorrhage following injury, without mention of open intracranial wound, brief (less than one hour) loss of consciousness

852.23 Subdural hemorrhage following injury, without mention of open intracranial wound, moderate (1-24 hours) loss of consciousness

852.24 Subdural hemorrhage following injury, without mention of open intracranial wound, prolonged (more than 24 hours) loss of consciousness and return to pre-existing conscious level

852.25 Subdural hemorrhage following injury, without mention of open intracranial wound, prolonged (more than 24 hours) loss of consciousness, without return to pre-existing conscious level

852.26 Subdural hemorrhage following injury, without mention of open intracranial wound, loss of consciousness of unspecified duration ▽

852.29 Subdural hemorrhage following injury, without mention of open intracranial wound, unspecified concussion ▽

852.40 Extradural hemorrhage following injury, without mention of open intracranial wound, unspecified state of consciousness ▽

852.41 Extradural hemorrhage following injury, without mention of open intracranial wound, no loss of consciousness

852.42 Extradural hemorrhage following injury, without mention of open intracranial wound, brief (less than 1 hour) loss of consciousness

852.43 Extradural hemorrhage following injury, without mention of open intracranial wound, moderate (1-24 hours) loss of consciousness

852.44 Extradural hemorrhage following injury, without mention of open intracranial wound, prolonged (more than 24 hours) loss of consciousness and return to pre-existing conscious level

852.45 Extradural hemorrhage following injury, without mention of open intracranial wound, prolonged (more than 24 hours) loss of consciousness, without return to pre-existing conscious level

852.46 Extradural hemorrhage following injury, without mention of open intracranial wound, loss of consciousness of unspecified duration ▽

852.49 Extradural hemorrhage following injury, without mention of open intracranial wound, unspecified concussion ▽

853.00 Other and unspecified intracranial hemorrhage following injury, without mention of open intracranial wound, unspecified state of consciousness ▽

853.01 Other and unspecified intracranial hemorrhage following injury, without mention of open intracranial wound, no loss of consciousness ▽

853.02 Other and unspecified intracranial hemorrhage following injury, without mention of open intracranial wound, brief (less than 1 hour) loss of consciousness ▽

853.03 Other and unspecified intracranial hemorrhage following injury, without mention of open intracranial wound, moderate (1-24 hours) loss of consciousness ▽

853.04 Other and unspecified intracranial hemorrhage following injury, without mention of open intracranial wound, prolonged (more than 24 hours) loss of consciousness and return to preexisting conscious level ▽

853.05 Other and unspecified intracranial hemorrhage following injury. Without mention of open intracranial wound, prolonged (more than 24 hours) loss of consciousness, without return to pre-existing conscious level ▽

853.06 Other and unspecified intracranial hemorrhage following injury, without mention of open intracranial wound, loss of consciousness of unspecified duration ▽

853.09 Other and unspecified intracranial hemorrhage following injury, without mention of open intracranial wound, unspecified concussion ▽

853.10 Other and unspecified intracranial hemorrhage following injury, with open intracranial wound, unspecified state of consciousness ▽

853.11 Other and unspecified intracranial hemorrhage following injury, with open intracranial wound, no loss of consciousness ▽

853.12 Other and unspecified intracranial hemorrhage following injury, with open intracranial wound, brief (less than 1 hour) loss of consciousness ▽

853.13 Other and unspecified intracranial hemorrhage following injury, with open intracranial wound, moderate (1-24 hours) loss of consciousness ▽

853.14 Other and unspecified intracranial hemorrhage following injury, with open intracranial wound, prolonged (more than 24 hours) loss of consciousness and return to pre-existing conscious level ▽

853.15 Other and unspecified intracranial hemorrhage following injury, with open intracranial wound, prolonged (more than 24 hours) loss of consciousness, without return to pre-existing conscious level ▽

853.16 Other and unspecified intracranial hemorrhage following injury, with open intracranial wound, loss of consciousness of unspecified duration ▽

853.19 Other and unspecified intracranial hemorrhage following injury, with open intracranial wound, unspecified concussion ▽

ICD-9-CM Procedural

01.24 Other craniotomy

01.31 Incision of cerebral meninges

01.39 Other incision of brain

61314-61315

61314 Craniectomy or craniotomy for evacuation of hematoma, infratentorial; extradural or subdural

61315 intracerebellar

ICD-9-CM Diagnostic

348.4 Compression of brain

431 Intracerebral hemorrhage — (Use additional code to identify presence of hypertension)

432.0 Nontraumatic extradural hemorrhage — (Use additional code to identify presence of hypertension)

432.1 Subdural hemorrhage — (Use additional code to identify presence of hypertension)

432.9 Unspecified intracranial hemorrhage — (Use additional code to identify presence of hypertension) ▽

747.81 Congenital anomaly of cerebrovascular system

801.20 Closed fracture of base of skull with subarachnoid, subdural, and extradural hemorrhage, unspecified state of consciousness ▽

801.21 Closed fracture of base of skull with subarachnoid, subdural, and extradural hemorrhage, no loss of consciousness

801.22 Closed fracture of base of skull with subarachnoid, subdural, and extradural hemorrhage, brief (less than one hour) loss of consciousness

801.23 Closed fracture of base of skull with subarachnoid, subdural, and extradural hemorrhage, moderate (1-24 hours) loss of consciousness

801.24 Closed fracture of base of skull with subarachnoid, subdural, and extradural hemorrhage, prolonged (more than 24 hours) loss of consciousness and return to pre-existing conscious level

801.25 Closed fracture of base of skull with subarachnoid, subdural, and extradural hemorrhage, prolonged (more than 24 hours) loss of consciousness, without return to pre-existing conscious level

801.26 Closed fracture of base of skull with subarachnoid, subdural, and extradural hemorrhage, loss of consciousness of unspecified duration ▽

801.29 Closed fracture of base of skull with subarachnoid, subdural, and extradural hemorrhage, unspecified concussion ▽

801.70 Open fracture of base of skull with subarachnoid, subdural, and extradural hemorrhage, unspecified state of consciousness ▽

801.72 Open fracture of base of skull with subarachnoid, subdural, and extradural hemorrhage, brief (less than one hour) loss of consciousness

801.73 Open fracture of base of skull with subarachnoid, subdural, and extradural hemorrhage, moderate (1-24 hours) loss of consciousness

801.74 Open fracture of base of skull with subarachnoid, subdural, and extradural hemorrhage, prolonged (more than 24 hours) loss of consciousness and return to pre-existing conscious level

801.75 Open fracture of base of skull with subarachnoid, subdural, and extradural hemorrhage, prolonged (more than 24 hours) loss of consciousness, without return to pre-existing conscious level

801.76 Open fracture of base of skull with subarachnoid, subdural, and extradural hemorrhage, loss of consciousness of unspecified duration

801.79 Open fracture of base of skull with subarachnoid, subdural, and extradural hemorrhage, unspecified concussion

851.03 Cortex (cerebral) contusion without mention of open intracranial wound, moderate (1-24 hours) loss of consciousness

851.40 Cerebellar or brain stem contusion without mention of open intracranial wound, unspecified state of consciousness

851.41 Cerebellar or brain stem contusion without mention of open intracranial wound, no loss of consciousness

851.42 Cerebellar or brain stem contusion without mention of open intracranial wound, brief (less than 1 hour) loss of consciousness

851.43 Cerebellar or brain stem contusion without mention of open intracranial wound, moderate (1-24 hours) loss of consciousness

851.44 Cerebellar or brain stem contusion without mention of open intracranial wound, prolonged (more than 24 hours) loss consciousness and return to pre-existing conscious level

851.45 Cerebellar or brain stem contusion without mention of open intracranial wound, prolonged (more than 24 hours) loss of consciousness, without return to pre-existing conscious level

851.46 Cerebellar or brain stem contusion without mention of open intracranial wound, loss of consciousness of unspecified duration

851.49 Cerebellar or brain stem contusion without mention of open intracranial wound, unspecified concussion

851.50 Cerebellar or brain stem contusion with open intracranial wound, unspecified state of consciousness

851.51 Cerebellar or brain stem contusion with open intracranial wound, no loss of consciousness

851.52 Cerebellar or brain stem contusion with open intracranial wound, brief (less than 1 hour) loss of consciousness

851.53 Cerebellar or brain stem contusion with open intracranial wound, moderate (1-24 hours) loss of consciousness

851.54 Cerebellar or brain stem contusion with open intracranial wound, prolonged (more than 24 hours) loss of consciousness and return to pre-existing conscious level

851.55 Cerebellar or brain stem contusion with open intracranial wound, prolonged (more than 24 hours) loss of consciousness, without return to pre-existing conscious level

851.56 Cerebellar or brain stem contusion with open intracranial wound, loss of consciousness of unspecified duration

851.59 Cerebellar or brain stem contusion with open intracranial wound, unspecified concussion

852.20 Subdural hemorrhage following injury, without mention of open intracranial wound, unspecified state of consciousness

852.21 Subdural hemorrhage following injury, without mention of open intracranial wound, no loss of consciousness

852.22 Subdural hemorrhage following injury, without mention of open intracranial wound, brief (less than one hour) loss of consciousness

852.23 Subdural hemorrhage following injury, without mention of open intracranial wound, moderate (1-24 hours) loss of consciousness

852.24 Subdural hemorrhage following injury, without mention of open intracranial wound, prolonged (more than 24 hours) loss of consciousness and return to pre-existing conscious level

852.25 Subdural hemorrhage following injury, without mention of open intracranial wound, prolonged (more than 24 hours) loss of consciousness, without return to pre-existing conscious level

852.26 Subdural hemorrhage following injury, without mention of open intracranial wound, loss of consciousness of unspecified duration

852.29 Subdural hemorrhage following injury, without mention of open intracranial wound, unspecified concussion

852.30 Subdural hemorrhage following injury, with open intracranial wound, state of consciousness unspecified

852.31 Subdural hemorrhage following injury, with open intracranial wound, no loss of consciousness

852.32 Subdural hemorrhage following injury, with open intracranial wound, brief (less than 1 hour) loss of consciousness

852.33 Subdural hemorrhage following injury, with open intracranial wound, moderate (1-24 hours) loss of consciousness

852.34 Subdural hemorrhage following injury, with open intracranial wound, prolonged (more than 24 hours) loss of consciousness and return to pre-existing conscious level

852.35 Subdural hemorrhage following injury, with open intracranial wound, prolonged (more than 24 hours) loss of consciousness, without return to pre-existing conscious level

852.36 Subdural hemorrhage following injury, with open intracranial wound, loss of consciousness of unspecified duration

852.39 Subdural hemorrhage following injury, with open intracranial wound, unspecified concussion

852.40 Extradural hemorrhage following injury, without mention of open intracranial wound, unspecified state of consciousness

852.41 Extradural hemorrhage following injury, without mention of open intracranial wound, no loss of consciousness

852.42 Extradural hemorrhage following injury, without mention of open intracranial wound, brief (less than 1 hour) loss of consciousness

852.43 Extradural hemorrhage following injury, without mention of open intracranial wound, moderate (1-24 hours) loss of consciousness

852.44 Extradural hemorrhage following injury, without mention of open intracranial wound, prolonged (more than 24 hours) loss of consciousness and return to pre-existing conscious level

852.45 Extradural hemorrhage following injury, without mention of open intracranial wound, prolonged (more than 24 hours) loss of consciousness, without return to pre-existing conscious level

852.46 Extradural hemorrhage following injury, without mention of open intracranial wound, loss of consciousness of unspecified duration

852.49 Extradural hemorrhage following injury, without mention of open intracranial wound, unspecified concussion

852.50 Extradural hemorrhage following injury, with open intracranial wound, state of consciousness unspecified

852.51 Extradural hemorrhage following injury, with open intracranial wound, no loss of consciousness

852.52 Extradural hemorrhage following injury, with open intracranial wound, brief (less than 1 hour) loss of consciousness

852.53 Extradural hemorrhage following injury, with open intracranial wound, moderate (1-24 hours) loss of consciousness

852.54 Extradural hemorrhage following injury, with open intracranial wound, prolonged (more than 24 hours) loss of consciousness and return to pre-existing conscious level

852.55 Extradural hemorrhage following injury, with open intracranial wound, prolonged (more than 24 hours) loss of consciousness, without return to pre-existing conscious level

852.56 Extradural hemorrhage following injury, with open intracranial wound, loss of consciousness of unspecified duration

852.59 Extradural hemorrhage following injury, with open intracranial wound, unspecified concussion

853.00 Other and unspecified intracranial hemorrhage following injury, without mention of open intracranial wound, unspecified state of consciousness

853.10 Other and unspecified intracranial hemorrhage following injury, with open intracranial wound, unspecified state of consciousness ▽

ICD-9-CM Procedural

01.24 Other craniotomy
01.31 Incision of cerebral meninges
01.39 Other incision of brain

61316

61316 Incision and subcutaneous placement of cranial bone graft (List separately in addition to code for primary procedure)

ICD-9-CM Diagnostic

This is an add-on code. Refer to the corresponding primary procedure code for ICD-9-CM diagnosis code links.

ICD-9-CM Procedural

02.03 Formation of cranial bone flap

61320-61321

61320 Craniectomy or craniotomy, drainage of intracranial abscess; supratentorial
61321 infratentorial

ICD-9-CM Diagnostic

324.0 Intracranial abscess
324.9 Intracranial and intraspinal abscess of unspecified site ▽
998.59 Other postoperative infection — (Use additional code to identify infection)

ICD-9-CM Procedural

01.24 Other craniotomy
01.31 Incision of cerebral meninges
01.39 Other incision of brain

61322-61323

61322 Craniectomy or craniotomy, decompressive, with or without duraplasty, for treatment of intracranial hypertension, without evacuation of associated intraparenchymal hematoma; without lobectomy
61323 with lobectomy

ICD-9-CM Diagnostic

191.0 Malignant neoplasm of cerebrum, except lobes and ventricles
191.1 Malignant neoplasm of frontal lobe of brain
191.2 Malignant neoplasm of temporal lobe of brain
191.3 Malignant neoplasm of parietal lobe of brain
191.4 Malignant neoplasm of occipital lobe of brain
191.5 Malignant neoplasm of ventricles of brain
191.9 Malignant neoplasm of brain, unspecified site ▽
225.0 Benign neoplasm of brain
227.3 Benign neoplasm of pituitary gland and craniopharyngeal duct (pouch) — (Use additional code to identify any functional activity)
237.5 Neoplasm of uncertain behavior of brain and spinal cord
239.6 Neoplasm of unspecified nature of brain
323.01 Encephalitis and encephalomyelitis in viral diseases classified elsewhere — (Code first underlying disease: 042, 073.7, 075, 078.3) ☒
323.02 Myelitis in viral diseases classified elsewhere — (Code first underlying disease: 042, 073.7, 075, 078.3) ☒
324.0 Intracranial abscess
331.3 Communicating hydrocephalus — (Use additional code, where applicable, to identify dementia: 294.10, 294.11)
331.4 Obstructive hydrocephalus — (Use additional code, where applicable, to identify dementia: 294.10, 294.11)
331.5 Idiopathic normal pressure hydrocephalus [INPH] — (Use additional code, where applicable, to identify dementia: 294.10, 294.11)
348.2 Benign intracranial hypertension
348.30 Encephalopathy, unspecified ▽
348.4 Compression of brain
348.5 Cerebral edema
348.9 Unspecified condition of brain ▽
430 Subarachnoid hemorrhage — (Use additional code to identify presence of hypertension)
431 Intracerebral hemorrhage — (Use additional code to identify presence of hypertension)
432.0 Nontraumatic extradural hemorrhage — (Use additional code to identify presence of hypertension)
432.1 Subdural hemorrhage — (Use additional code to identify presence of hypertension)
432.9 Unspecified intracranial hemorrhage — (Use additional code to identify presence of hypertension) ▽
741.00 Spina bifida with hydrocephalus, unspecified region ▽
742.3 Congenital hydrocephalus
800.10 Closed fracture of vault of skull with cerebral laceration and contusion, unspecified state of consciousness ▽
800.11 Closed fracture of vault of skull with cerebral laceration and contusion, no loss of consciousness
800.12 Closed fracture of vault of skull with cerebral laceration and contusion, brief (less than one hour) loss of consciousness
800.13 Closed fracture of vault of skull with cerebral laceration and contusion, moderate (1-24 hours) loss of consciousness
800.14 Closed fracture of vault of skull with cerebral laceration and contusion, prolonged (more than 24 hours) loss of consciousness and return to pre-existing conscious level
800.15 Closed fracture of vault of skull with cerebral laceration and contusion, prolonged (more than 24 hours) loss of consciousness, without return to pre-existing conscious level
800.16 Closed fracture of vault of skull with cerebral laceration and contusion, loss of consciousness of unspecified duration ▽
800.19 Closed fracture of vault of skull with cerebral laceration and contusion, unspecified concussion ▽
800.20 Closed fracture of vault of skull with subarachnoid, subdural, and extradural hemorrhage, unspecified state of consciousness ▽
800.21 Closed fracture of vault of skull with subarachnoid, subdural, and extradural hemorrhage, no loss of consciousness
800.22 Closed fracture of vault of skull with subarachnoid, subdural, and extradural hemorrhage, brief (less than one hour) loss of consciousness
800.23 Closed fracture of vault of skull with subarachnoid, subdural, and extradural hemorrhage, moderate (1-24 hours) loss of consciousness
800.24 Closed fracture of vault of skull with subarachnoid, subdural, and extradural hemorrhage, prolonged (more than 24 hours) loss of consciousness and return to pre-existing conscious level
800.25 Closed fracture of vault of skull with subarachnoid, subdural, and extradural hemorrhage, prolonged (more than 24 hours) loss of consciousness, without return to pre-existing conscious level
800.26 Closed fracture of vault of skull with subarachnoid, subdural, and extradural hemorrhage, loss of consciousness of unspecified duration ▽
800.29 Closed fracture of vault of skull with subarachnoid, subdural, and extradural hemorrhage, unspecified concussion ▽
800.30 Closed fracture of vault of skull with other and unspecified intracranial hemorrhage, unspecified state of consciousness ▽
800.31 Closed fracture of vault of skull with other and unspecified intracranial hemorrhage, no loss of consciousness ▽
800.32 Closed fracture of vault of skull with other and unspecified intracranial hemorrhage, brief (less than one hour) loss of consciousness ▽
800.33 Closed fracture of vault of skull with other and unspecified intracranial hemorrhage, moderate (1-24 hours) loss of consciousness ▽
800.34 Closed fracture of vault of skull with other and unspecified intracranial hemorrhage, prolonged (more than 24 hours) loss of consciousness and return to pre-existing conscious level ▽

800.35 Closed fracture of vault of skull with other and unspecified intracranial hemorrhage, prolonged (more than 24 hours) loss of consciousness, without return to pre-existing conscious level ▽

800.36 Closed fracture of vault of skull with other and unspecified intracranial hemorrhage, loss of consciousness of unspecified duration ▽

800.39 Closed fracture of vault of skull with other and unspecified intracranial hemorrhage, unspecified concussion ▽

801.10 Closed fracture of base of skull with cerebral laceration and contusion, unspecified state of consciousness ▽

801.11 Closed fracture of base of skull with cerebral laceration and contusion, no loss of consciousness

801.12 Closed fracture of base of skull with cerebral laceration and contusion, brief (less than one hour) loss of consciousness

801.13 Closed fracture of base of skull with cerebral laceration and contusion, moderate (1-24 hours) loss of consciousness

801.14 Closed fracture of base of skull with cerebral laceration and contusion, prolonged (more than 24 hours) loss of consciousness and return to pre-existing conscious level

801.15 Closed fracture of base of skull with cerebral laceration and contusion, prolonged (more than 24 hours) loss of consciousness, without return to pre-existing conscious level

801.16 Closed fracture of base of skull with cerebral laceration and contusion, loss of consciousness of unspecified duration ▽

801.19 Closed fracture of base of skull with cerebral laceration and contusion, unspecified concussion ▽

801.20 Closed fracture of base of skull with subarachnoid, subdural, and extradural hemorrhage, unspecified state of consciousness ▽

801.21 Closed fracture of base of skull with subarachnoid, subdural, and extradural hemorrhage, no loss of consciousness

801.22 Closed fracture of base of skull with subarachnoid, subdural, and extradural hemorrhage, brief (less than one hour) loss of consciousness

801.23 Closed fracture of base of skull with subarachnoid, subdural, and extradural hemorrhage, moderate (1-24 hours) loss of consciousness

801.24 Closed fracture of base of skull with subarachnoid, subdural, and extradural hemorrhage, prolonged (more than 24 hours) loss of consciousness and return to pre-existing conscious level

801.25 Closed fracture of base of skull with subarachnoid, subdural, and extradural hemorrhage, prolonged (more than 24 hours) loss of consciousness, without return to pre-existing conscious level

801.26 Closed fracture of base of skull with subarachnoid, subdural, and extradural hemorrhage, loss of consciousness of unspecified duration ▽

801.29 Closed fracture of base of skull with subarachnoid, subdural, and extradural hemorrhage, unspecified concussion ▽

801.30 Closed fracture of base of skull with other and unspecified intracranial hemorrhage, unspecified state of consciousness ▽

801.31 Closed fracture of base of skull with other and unspecified intracranial hemorrhage, no loss of consciousness ▽

801.32 Closed fracture of base of skull with other and unspecified intracranial hemorrhage, brief (less than one hour) loss of consciousness ▽

801.33 Closed fracture of base of skull with other and unspecified intracranial hemorrhage, moderate (1-24 hours) loss of consciousness ▽

801.34 Closed fracture of base of skull with other and unspecified intracranial hemorrhage, prolonged (more than 24 hours) loss of consciousness and return to pre-existing conscious level ▽

801.35 Closed fracture of base of skull with other and unspecified intracranial hemorrhage, prolonged (more than 24 hours) loss of consciousness, without return to pre-existing conscious level ▽

801.36 Closed fracture of base of skull with other and unspecified intracranial hemorrhage, loss of consciousness of unspecified duration ▽

801.39 Closed fracture of base of skull with other and unspecified intracranial hemorrhage, unspecified concussion ▽

851.00 Cortex (cerebral) contusion without mention of open intracranial wound, state of consciousness unspecified ▽

851.01 Cortex (cerebral) contusion without mention of open intracranial wound, no loss of consciousness

851.02 Cortex (cerebral) contusion without mention of open intracranial wound, brief (less than 1 hour) loss of consciousness

851.03 Cortex (cerebral) contusion without mention of open intracranial wound, moderate (1-24 hours) loss of consciousness

851.04 Cortex (cerebral) contusion without mention of open intracranial wound, prolonged (more than 24 hours) loss of consciousness and return to pre-existing conscious level

851.05 Cortex (cerebral) contusion without mention of open intracranial wound, prolonged (more than 24 hours) loss of consciousness, without return to pre-existing conscious level

851.06 Cortex (cerebral) contusion without mention of open intracranial wound, loss of consciousness of unspecified duration ▽

851.09 Cortex (cerebral) contusion without mention of open intracranial wound, unspecified concussion ▽

851.40 Cerebellar or brain stem contusion without mention of open intracranial wound, unspecified state of consciousness ▽

851.41 Cerebellar or brain stem contusion without mention of open intracranial wound, no loss of consciousness

851.42 Cerebellar or brain stem contusion without mention of open intracranial wound, brief (less than 1 hour) loss of consciousness

851.43 Cerebellar or brain stem contusion without mention of open intracranial wound, moderate (1-24 hours) loss of consciousness

851.44 Cerebellar or brain stem contusion without mention of open intracranial wound, prolonged (more than 24 hours) loss consciousness and return to pre-existing conscious level

851.45 Cerebellar or brain stem contusion without mention of open intracranial wound, prolonged (more than 24 hours) loss of consciousness, without return to pre-existing conscious level

851.46 Cerebellar or brain stem contusion without mention of open intracranial wound, loss of consciousness of unspecified duration ▽

851.49 Cerebellar or brain stem contusion without mention of open intracranial wound, unspecified concussion ▽

852.00 Subarachnoid hemorrhage following injury, without mention of open intracranial wound, unspecified state of consciousness ▽

852.01 Subarachnoid hemorrhage following injury, without mention of open intracranial wound, no loss of consciousness

852.02 Subarachnoid hemorrhage following injury, without mention of open intracranial wound, brief (less than 1 hour) loss of consciousness

852.03 Subarachnoid hemorrhage following injury, without mention of open intracranial wound, moderate (1-24 hours) loss of consciousness

852.04 Subarachnoid hemorrhage following injury, without mention of open intracranial wound, prolonged (more than 24 hours) loss of consciousness and return to pre-existing conscious level

852.05 Subarachnoid hemorrhage following injury, without mention of open intracranial wound, prolonged (more than 24 hours) loss of consciousness, without return to pre-existing conscious level

852.06 Subarachnoid hemorrhage following injury, without mention of open intracranial wound, loss of consciousness of unspecified duration ▽

852.09 Subarachnoid hemorrhage following injury, without mention of open intracranial wound, unspecified concussion ▽

852.20 Subdural hemorrhage following injury, without mention of open intracranial wound, unspecified state of consciousness ▽

852.21 Subdural hemorrhage following injury, without mention of open intracranial wound, no loss of consciousness

852.22 Subdural hemorrhage following injury, without mention of open intracranial wound, brief (less than one hour) loss of consciousness

852.23 Subdural hemorrhage following injury, without mention of open intracranial wound, moderate (1-24 hours) loss of consciousness

852.24 Subdural hemorrhage following injury, without mention of open intracranial wound, prolonged (more than 24 hours) loss of consciousness and return to pre-existing conscious level
852.25 Subdural hemorrhage following injury, without mention of open intracranial wound, prolonged (more than 24 hours) loss of consciousness, without return to pre-existing conscious level
852.26 Subdural hemorrhage following injury, without mention of open intracranial wound, loss of consciousness of unspecified duration ▽
852.29 Subdural hemorrhage following injury, without mention of open intracranial wound, unspecified concussion ▽
852.40 Extradural hemorrhage following injury, without mention of open intracranial wound, unspecified state of consciousness ▽
852.41 Extradural hemorrhage following injury, without mention of open intracranial wound, no loss of consciousness
852.42 Extradural hemorrhage following injury, without mention of open intracranial wound, brief (less than 1 hour) loss of consciousness
852.43 Extradural hemorrhage following injury, without mention of open intracranial wound, moderate (1-24 hours) loss of consciousness
852.44 Extradural hemorrhage following injury, without mention of open intracranial wound, prolonged (more than 24 hours) loss of consciousness and return to pre-existing conscious level
852.45 Extradural hemorrhage following injury, without mention of open intracranial wound, prolonged (more than 24 hours) loss of consciousness, without return to pre-existing conscious level
852.46 Extradural hemorrhage following injury, without mention of open intracranial wound, loss of consciousness of unspecified duration ▽
852.49 Extradural hemorrhage following injury, without mention of open intracranial wound, unspecified concussion ▽

ICD-9-CM Procedural

01.24 Other craniotomy
01.25 Other craniectomy
01.53 Lobectomy of brain
01.59 Other excision or destruction of lesion or tissue of brain

61330

61330 Decompression of orbit only, transcranial approach

ICD-9-CM Diagnostic

191.9 Malignant neoplasm of brain, unspecified site ▽
202.81 Other malignant lymphomas of lymph nodes of head, face, and neck
213.0 Benign neoplasm of bones of skull and face
224.0 Benign neoplasm of eyeball, except conjunctiva, cornea, retina, and choroid
239.6 Neoplasm of unspecified nature of brain
348.2 Benign intracranial hypertension
348.5 Cerebral edema
377.39 Other optic neuritis
747.81 Congenital anomaly of cerebrovascular system
756.0 Congenital anomalies of skull and face bones
854.05 Intracranial injury of other and unspecified nature, without mention of open intracranial wound, prolonged (more than 24 hours) loss of consciousness, without return to pre-existing conscious level ▽

ICD-9-CM Procedural

01.24 Other craniotomy
16.09 Other orbitotomy

61332-61333

61332 Exploration of orbit (transcranial approach); with biopsy
61333 with removal of lesion

ICD-9-CM Diagnostic

170.0 Malignant neoplasm of bones of skull and face, except mandible
190.1 Malignant neoplasm of orbit
190.9 Malignant neoplasm of eye, part unspecified ▽
198.4 Secondary malignant neoplasm of other parts of nervous system
198.5 Secondary malignant neoplasm of bone and bone marrow
209.73 Secondary neuroendocrine tumor of bone
213.0 Benign neoplasm of bones of skull and face
224.1 Benign neoplasm of orbit
228.02 Hemangioma of intracranial structures
234.0 Carcinoma in situ of eye
238.0 Neoplasm of uncertain behavior of bone and articular cartilage
238.8 Neoplasm of uncertain behavior of other specified sites
239.2 Neoplasms of unspecified nature of bone, soft tissue, and skin
239.89 Neoplasms of unspecified nature, other specified sites
341.0 Neuromyelitis optica
367.52 Total or complete internal ophthalmoplegia
378.72 Progressive external ophthalmoplegia
743.66 Specified congenital anomaly of orbit

ICD-9-CM Procedural

01.24 Other craniotomy
16.09 Other orbitotomy
16.23 Biopsy of eyeball and orbit
16.92 Excision of lesion of orbit

61334

61334 Exploration of orbit (transcranial approach); with removal of foreign body

ICD-9-CM Diagnostic

870.4 Penetrating wound of orbit with foreign body
871.5 Penetration of eyeball with magnetic foreign body

ICD-9-CM Procedural

16.09 Other orbitotomy
16.1 Removal of penetrating foreign body from eye, not otherwise specified

61340

61340 Subtemporal cranial decompression (pseudotumor cerebri, slit ventricle syndrome)

ICD-9-CM Diagnostic

331.3 Communicating hydrocephalus — (Use additional code, where applicable, to identify dementia: 294.10, 294.11)
331.4 Obstructive hydrocephalus — (Use additional code, where applicable, to identify dementia: 294.10, 294.11)
331.5 Idiopathic normal pressure hydrocephalus [INPH] — (Use additional code, where applicable, to identify dementia: 294.10, 294.11)
348.2 Benign intracranial hypertension
741.00 Spina bifida with hydrocephalus, unspecified region ▽
741.01 Spina bifida with hydrocephalus, cervical region
741.02 Spina bifida with hydrocephalus, dorsal (thoracic) region
741.03 Spina bifida with hydrocephalus, lumbar region
742.3 Congenital hydrocephalus
996.75 Other complications due to nervous system device, implant, and graft — (Use additional code to identify complication: 338.18-338.19, 338.28-338.29)

ICD-9-CM Procedural

01.24 Other craniotomy

61343

61343 Craniectomy, suboccipital with cervical laminectomy for decompression of medulla and spinal cord, with or without dural graft (eg, Arnold-Chiari malformation)

ICD-9-CM Diagnostic

336.0 Syringomyelia and syringobulbia

336.9	Unspecified disease of spinal cord ▽
348.4	Compression of brain
741.01	Spina bifida with hydrocephalus, cervical region
742.0	Encephalocele
742.2	Congenital reduction deformities of brain
742.59	Other specified congenital anomaly of spinal cord
742.9	Unspecified congenital anomaly of brain, spinal cord, and nervous system ▽
756.10	Congenital anomaly of spine, unspecified ▽
756.4	Chondrodystrophy
784.0	Headache

ICD-9-CM Procedural

03.09	Other exploration and decompression of spinal canal

61345

61345 Other cranial decompression, posterior fossa

ICD-9-CM Diagnostic

191.9	Malignant neoplasm of brain, unspecified site ▽
202.81	Other malignant lymphomas of lymph nodes of head, face, and neck
237.5	Neoplasm of uncertain behavior of brain and spinal cord
323.01	Encephalitis and encephalomyelitis in viral diseases classified elsewhere — (Code first underlying disease: 042, 073.7, 075, 078.3) ☒
323.02	Myelitis in viral diseases classified elsewhere — (Code first underlying disease: 042, 073.7, 075, 078.3) ☒
437.0	Cerebral atherosclerosis — (Use additional code to identify presence of hypertension)
437.3	Cerebral aneurysm, nonruptured — (Use additional code to identify presence of hypertension)
741.00	Spina bifida with hydrocephalus, unspecified region ▽
742.53	Hydromyelia
850.4	Concussion with prolonged (more than 24 hours) loss of consciousness, without return to pre-existing conscious level

ICD-9-CM Procedural

01.24	Other craniotomy

61440

61440 Craniotomy for section of tentorium cerebelli (separate procedure)

ICD-9-CM Diagnostic

148.3	Malignant neoplasm of posterior hypopharyngeal wall
191.6	Malignant neoplasm of cerebellum NOS
191.9	Malignant neoplasm of brain, unspecified site ▽
192.1	Malignant neoplasm of cerebral meninges
198.3	Secondary malignant neoplasm of brain and spinal cord
225.0	Benign neoplasm of brain
225.1	Benign neoplasm of cranial nerves
225.2	Benign neoplasm of cerebral meninges
237.5	Neoplasm of uncertain behavior of brain and spinal cord
239.6	Neoplasm of unspecified nature of brain
322.2	Chronic meningitis
324.0	Intracranial abscess
326	Late effects of intracranial abscess or pyogenic infection — (Use additional code to identify condition: 331.4, 342.0-342.9, 344.0-344.9)
331.4	Obstructive hydrocephalus — (Use additional code, where applicable, to identify dementia: 294.10, 294.11)
348.0	Cerebral cysts
747.81	Congenital anomaly of cerebrovascular system

ICD-9-CM Procedural

01.32	Lobotomy and tractotomy

61450

61450 Craniectomy, subtemporal, for section, compression, or decompression of sensory root of gasserian ganglion

ICD-9-CM Diagnostic

192.0	Malignant neoplasm of cranial nerves
195.0	Malignant neoplasm of head, face, and neck
350.1	Trigeminal neuralgia
350.2	Atypical face pain
738.19	Other specified acquired deformity of head
756.0	Congenital anomalies of skull and face bones

ICD-9-CM Procedural

04.05	Gasserian ganglionectomy
04.42	Other cranial nerve decompression

61458

61458 Craniectomy, suboccipital; for exploration or decompression of cranial nerves

ICD-9-CM Diagnostic

225.1	Benign neoplasm of cranial nerves
350.1	Trigeminal neuralgia
350.8	Other specified trigeminal nerve disorders
351.8	Other facial nerve disorders
352.1	Glossopharyngeal neuralgia
386.01	Active Meniere's disease, cochleovestibular

ICD-9-CM Procedural

04.42	Other cranial nerve decompression

61460

61460 Craniectomy, suboccipital; for section of 1 or more cranial nerves

ICD-9-CM Diagnostic

350.1	Trigeminal neuralgia
351.8	Other facial nerve disorders
352.1	Glossopharyngeal neuralgia
355.9	Mononeuritis of unspecified site ▽
386.01	Active Meniere's disease, cochleovestibular
386.19	Other and unspecified peripheral vertigo
386.2	Vertigo of central origin

ICD-9-CM Procedural

04.02	Division of trigeminal nerve
04.03	Division or crushing of other cranial and peripheral nerves

61470

61470 Craniectomy, suboccipital; for medullary tractotomy

ICD-9-CM Diagnostic

350.1	Trigeminal neuralgia
352.1	Glossopharyngeal neuralgia
352.6	Multiple cranial nerve palsies
386.03	Active Meniere's disease, vestibular
723.1	Cervicalgia

ICD-9-CM Procedural

01.32	Lobotomy and tractotomy

61480

61480 Craniectomy, suboccipital; for mesencephalic tractotomy or pedunculotomy

ICD-9-CM Diagnostic

350.1	Trigeminal neuralgia

350.2 Atypical face pain
352.1 Glossopharyngeal neuralgia
352.6 Multiple cranial nerve palsies
386.03 Active Meniere's disease, vestibular
723.1 Cervicalgia

ICD-9-CM Procedural

01.32 Lobotomy and tractotomy

61490

61490 Craniotomy for lobotomy, including cingulotomy

ICD-9-CM Diagnostic

191.1 Malignant neoplasm of frontal lobe of brain
191.2 Malignant neoplasm of temporal lobe of brain
191.3 Malignant neoplasm of parietal lobe of brain
191.4 Malignant neoplasm of occipital lobe of brain
198.3 Secondary malignant neoplasm of brain and spinal cord
225.0 Benign neoplasm of brain
237.5 Neoplasm of uncertain behavior of brain and spinal cord
239.6 Neoplasm of unspecified nature of brain
296.33 Major depressive disorder, recurrent episode, severe, without mention of psychotic behavior — (Use additional code to identify any associated physical disease, injury, or condition affecting the brain with psychoses classifiable to 295-298)
300.09 Other anxiety states
300.3 Obsessive-compulsive disorders
723.1 Cervicalgia

ICD-9-CM Procedural

01.32 Lobotomy and tractotomy

61500-61501

61500 Craniectomy; with excision of tumor or other bone lesion of skull
61501 for osteomyelitis

ICD-9-CM Diagnostic

170.0 Malignant neoplasm of bones of skull and face, except mandible
198.5 Secondary malignant neoplasm of bone and bone marrow
213.0 Benign neoplasm of bones of skull and face
238.0 Neoplasm of uncertain behavior of bone and articular cartilage
239.2 Neoplasms of unspecified nature of bone, soft tissue, and skin
730.18 Chronic osteomyelitis, other specified sites — (Use additional code to identify organism: 041.1. Use additional code to identify major osseous defect, if applicable: 731.3)
730.28 Unspecified osteomyelitis, other specified sites — (Use additional code to identify organism: 041.1. Use additional code to identify major osseous defect, if applicable: 731.3) ▽
733.21 Solitary bone cyst
733.22 Aneurysmal bone cyst
733.29 Other cyst of bone
733.3 Hyperostosis of skull

ICD-9-CM Procedural

01.6 Excision of lesion of skull
77.09 Sequestrectomy of other bone, except facial bones

61510

61510 Craniectomy, trephination, bone flap craniotomy; for excision of brain tumor, supratentorial, except meningioma

ICD-9-CM Diagnostic

191.0 Malignant neoplasm of cerebrum, except lobes and ventricles
191.1 Malignant neoplasm of frontal lobe of brain
191.2 Malignant neoplasm of temporal lobe of brain
191.3 Malignant neoplasm of parietal lobe of brain
191.4 Malignant neoplasm of occipital lobe of brain
191.5 Malignant neoplasm of ventricles of brain
191.8 Malignant neoplasm of other parts of brain
198.3 Secondary malignant neoplasm of brain and spinal cord
198.4 Secondary malignant neoplasm of other parts of nervous system
225.0 Benign neoplasm of brain
225.1 Benign neoplasm of cranial nerves
228.02 Hemangioma of intracranial structures
237.5 Neoplasm of uncertain behavior of brain and spinal cord
238.1 Neoplasm of uncertain behavior of connective and other soft tissue
239.6 Neoplasm of unspecified nature of brain

ICD-9-CM Procedural

01.59 Other excision or destruction of lesion or tissue of brain
07.59 Other operations on pineal gland

61512

61512 Craniectomy, trephination, bone flap craniotomy; for excision of meningioma, supratentorial

ICD-9-CM Diagnostic

192.1 Malignant neoplasm of cerebral meninges
225.2 Benign neoplasm of cerebral meninges
237.6 Neoplasm of uncertain behavior of meninges

ICD-9-CM Procedural

01.51 Excision of lesion or tissue of cerebral meninges

61514

61514 Craniectomy, trephination, bone flap craniotomy; for excision of brain abscess, supratentorial

ICD-9-CM Diagnostic

324.0 Intracranial abscess

ICD-9-CM Procedural

01.59 Other excision or destruction of lesion or tissue of brain

61516

61516 Craniectomy, trephination, bone flap craniotomy; for excision or fenestration of cyst, supratentorial

ICD-9-CM Diagnostic

331.4 Obstructive hydrocephalus — (Use additional code, where applicable, to identify dementia: 294.10, 294.11)
348.0 Cerebral cysts
742.4 Other specified congenital anomalies of brain

ICD-9-CM Procedural

01.59 Other excision or destruction of lesion or tissue of brain

61517

61517 Implantation of brain intracavitary chemotherapy agent (List separately in addition to code for primary procedure)

ICD-9-CM Diagnostic

This is an add-on code. Refer to the corresponding primary procedure code for ICD-9-CM diagnosis code links.

ICD-9-CM Procedural

00.10 Implantation of chemotherapeutic agent

61518

61518 Craniectomy for excision of brain tumor, infratentorial or posterior fossa; except meningioma, cerebellopontine angle tumor, or midline tumor at base of skull

ICD-9-CM Diagnostic

191.6 Malignant neoplasm of cerebellum NOS
191.7 Malignant neoplasm of brain stem
191.9 Malignant neoplasm of brain, unspecified site ▽
192.8 Malignant neoplasm of other specified sites of nervous system
198.3 Secondary malignant neoplasm of brain and spinal cord
225.0 Benign neoplasm of brain
225.1 Benign neoplasm of cranial nerves
237.5 Neoplasm of uncertain behavior of brain and spinal cord
239.6 Neoplasm of unspecified nature of brain

ICD-9-CM Procedural

01.59 Other excision or destruction of lesion or tissue of brain

61519

61519 Craniectomy for excision of brain tumor, infratentorial or posterior fossa; meningioma

ICD-9-CM Diagnostic

192.1 Malignant neoplasm of cerebral meninges
225.2 Benign neoplasm of cerebral meninges
237.6 Neoplasm of uncertain behavior of meninges

ICD-9-CM Procedural

01.51 Excision of lesion or tissue of cerebral meninges

61520

61520 Craniectomy for excision of brain tumor, infratentorial or posterior fossa; cerebellopontine angle tumor

ICD-9-CM Diagnostic

191.6 Malignant neoplasm of cerebellum NOS
198.3 Secondary malignant neoplasm of brain and spinal cord
225.0 Benign neoplasm of brain
225.1 Benign neoplasm of cranial nerves
228.02 Hemangioma of intracranial structures
237.3 Neoplasm of uncertain behavior of paraganglia
237.5 Neoplasm of uncertain behavior of brain and spinal cord
237.70 Neurofibromatosis, unspecified ▽
237.71 Neurofibromatosis, Type 1 (von Recklinghausen's disease)
237.72 Neurofibromatosis, Type 2 (acoustic neurofibromatosis)
237.79 Other neurofibromatosis
239.6 Neoplasm of unspecified nature of brain

ICD-9-CM Procedural

01.59 Other excision or destruction of lesion or tissue of brain
04.01 Excision of acoustic neuroma

61521

61521 Craniectomy for excision of brain tumor, infratentorial or posterior fossa; midline tumor at base of skull

ICD-9-CM Diagnostic

191.7 Malignant neoplasm of brain stem
191.8 Malignant neoplasm of other parts of brain
198.3 Secondary malignant neoplasm of brain and spinal cord
225.0 Benign neoplasm of brain
225.1 Benign neoplasm of cranial nerves
225.2 Benign neoplasm of cerebral meninges
225.8 Benign neoplasm of other specified sites of nervous system
225.9 Benign neoplasm of nervous system, part unspecified ▽
237.5 Neoplasm of uncertain behavior of brain and spinal cord
239.6 Neoplasm of unspecified nature of brain

ICD-9-CM Procedural

01.59 Other excision or destruction of lesion or tissue of brain

61522

61522 Craniectomy, infratentorial or posterior fossa; for excision of brain abscess

ICD-9-CM Diagnostic

324.0 Intracranial abscess

ICD-9-CM Procedural

01.59 Other excision or destruction of lesion or tissue of brain

61524

61524 Craniectomy, infratentorial or posterior fossa; for excision or fenestration of cyst

ICD-9-CM Diagnostic

348.0 Cerebral cysts
742.4 Other specified congenital anomalies of brain

ICD-9-CM Procedural

01.59 Other excision or destruction of lesion or tissue of brain

61526-61530

61526 Craniectomy, bone flap craniotomy, transtemporal (mastoid) for excision of cerebellopontine angle tumor;
61530 combined with middle/posterior fossa craniotomy/craniectomy

ICD-9-CM Diagnostic

191.6 Malignant neoplasm of cerebellum NOS
198.3 Secondary malignant neoplasm of brain and spinal cord
225.0 Benign neoplasm of brain
225.1 Benign neoplasm of cranial nerves
228.02 Hemangioma of intracranial structures
237.3 Neoplasm of uncertain behavior of paraganglia
237.5 Neoplasm of uncertain behavior of brain and spinal cord
237.70 Neurofibromatosis, unspecified ▽
237.71 Neurofibromatosis, Type 1 (von Recklinghausen's disease)
237.72 Neurofibromatosis, Type 2 (acoustic neurofibromatosis)
237.79 Other neurofibromatosis
239.6 Neoplasm of unspecified nature of brain

ICD-9-CM Procedural

01.59 Other excision or destruction of lesion or tissue of brain
04.01 Excision of acoustic neuroma

61531

61531 Subdural implantation of strip electrodes through 1 or more burr or trephine hole(s) for long-term seizure monitoring

ICD-9-CM Diagnostic

345.00 Generalized nonconvulsive epilepsy without mention of intractable epilepsy
345.01 Generalized nonconvulsive epilepsy with intractable epilepsy
345.10 Generalized convulsive epilepsy without mention of intractable epilepsy
345.11 Generalized convulsive epilepsy with intractable epilepsy
345.2 Epileptic petit mal status
345.3 Epileptic grand mal status
345.40 Localization-related (focal) (partial) epilepsy and epileptic syndromes with complex partial seizures, without mention of intractable epilepsy
345.41 Localization-related (focal) (partial) epilepsy and epileptic syndromes with complex partial seizures, with intractable epilepsy

345.50 Localization-related (focal) (partial) epilepsy and epileptic syndromes with simple partial seizures, without mention of intractable epilepsy
345.51 Localization-related (focal) (partial) epilepsy and epileptic syndromes with simple partial seizures, with intractable epilepsy
345.70 Epilepsia partialis continua without mention of intractable epilepsy
345.71 Epilepsia partialis continua with intractable epilepsy
345.80 Other forms of epilepsy and recurrent seizures, without mention of intractable epilepsy
345.81 Other forms of epilepsy and recurrent seizures, with intractable epilepsy
345.90 Unspecified epilepsy without mention of intractable epilepsy ▽
345.91 Unspecified epilepsy with intractable epilepsy ▽
780.33 Post traumatic seizures

ICD-9-CM Procedural

02.93 Implantation or replacement of intracranial neurostimulator lead(s)

61533

61533 Craniotomy with elevation of bone flap; for subdural implantation of an electrode array, for long-term seizure monitoring

ICD-9-CM Diagnostic

345.00 Generalized nonconvulsive epilepsy without mention of intractable epilepsy
345.01 Generalized nonconvulsive epilepsy with intractable epilepsy
345.10 Generalized convulsive epilepsy without mention of intractable epilepsy
345.11 Generalized convulsive epilepsy with intractable epilepsy
345.2 Epileptic petit mal status
345.3 Epileptic grand mal status
345.40 Localization-related (focal) (partial) epilepsy and epileptic syndromes with complex partial seizures, without mention of intractable epilepsy
345.41 Localization-related (focal) (partial) epilepsy and epileptic syndromes with complex partial seizures, with intractable epilepsy
345.50 Localization-related (focal) (partial) epilepsy and epileptic syndromes with simple partial seizures, without mention of intractable epilepsy
345.51 Localization-related (focal) (partial) epilepsy and epileptic syndromes with simple partial seizures, with intractable epilepsy
345.70 Epilepsia partialis continua without mention of intractable epilepsy
345.71 Epilepsia partialis continua with intractable epilepsy
345.80 Other forms of epilepsy and recurrent seizures, without mention of intractable epilepsy
345.81 Other forms of epilepsy and recurrent seizures, with intractable epilepsy
345.90 Unspecified epilepsy without mention of intractable epilepsy ▽
345.91 Unspecified epilepsy with intractable epilepsy ▽
780.33 Post traumatic seizures

ICD-9-CM Procedural

02.93 Implantation or replacement of intracranial neurostimulator lead(s)

61534

61534 Craniotomy with elevation of bone flap; for excision of epileptogenic focus without electrocorticography during surgery

ICD-9-CM Diagnostic

345.00 Generalized nonconvulsive epilepsy without mention of intractable epilepsy
345.01 Generalized nonconvulsive epilepsy with intractable epilepsy
345.10 Generalized convulsive epilepsy without mention of intractable epilepsy
345.11 Generalized convulsive epilepsy with intractable epilepsy
345.2 Epileptic petit mal status
345.3 Epileptic grand mal status
345.40 Localization-related (focal) (partial) epilepsy and epileptic syndromes with complex partial seizures, without mention of intractable epilepsy
345.41 Localization-related (focal) (partial) epilepsy and epileptic syndromes with complex partial seizures, with intractable epilepsy
345.50 Localization-related (focal) (partial) epilepsy and epileptic syndromes with simple partial seizures, without mention of intractable epilepsy
345.51 Localization-related (focal) (partial) epilepsy and epileptic syndromes with simple partial seizures, with intractable epilepsy
345.70 Epilepsia partialis continua without mention of intractable epilepsy
345.71 Epilepsia partialis continua with intractable epilepsy
345.80 Other forms of epilepsy and recurrent seizures, without mention of intractable epilepsy
345.81 Other forms of epilepsy and recurrent seizures, with intractable epilepsy
345.90 Unspecified epilepsy without mention of intractable epilepsy ▽
345.91 Unspecified epilepsy with intractable epilepsy ▽

ICD-9-CM Procedural

01.59 Other excision or destruction of lesion or tissue of brain

61535

61535 Craniotomy with elevation of bone flap; for removal of epidural or subdural electrode array, without excision of cerebral tissue (separate procedure)

ICD-9-CM Diagnostic

345.00 Generalized nonconvulsive epilepsy without mention of intractable epilepsy
345.01 Generalized nonconvulsive epilepsy with intractable epilepsy
345.10 Generalized convulsive epilepsy without mention of intractable epilepsy
345.11 Generalized convulsive epilepsy with intractable epilepsy
345.2 Epileptic petit mal status
345.3 Epileptic grand mal status
345.40 Localization-related (focal) (partial) epilepsy and epileptic syndromes with complex partial seizures, without mention of intractable epilepsy
345.41 Localization-related (focal) (partial) epilepsy and epileptic syndromes with complex partial seizures, with intractable epilepsy
345.50 Localization-related (focal) (partial) epilepsy and epileptic syndromes with simple partial seizures, without mention of intractable epilepsy
345.51 Localization-related (focal) (partial) epilepsy and epileptic syndromes with simple partial seizures, with intractable epilepsy
345.70 Epilepsia partialis continua without mention of intractable epilepsy
345.71 Epilepsia partialis continua with intractable epilepsy
345.80 Other forms of epilepsy and recurrent seizures, without mention of intractable epilepsy
345.81 Other forms of epilepsy and recurrent seizures, with intractable epilepsy
345.90 Unspecified epilepsy without mention of intractable epilepsy ▽
345.91 Unspecified epilepsy with intractable epilepsy ▽
996.2 Mechanical complication of nervous system device, implant, and graft
996.63 Infection and inflammatory reaction due to nervous system device, implant, and graft — (Use additional code to identify specified infections)
996.75 Other complications due to nervous system device, implant, and graft — (Use additional code to identify complication: 338.18-338.19, 338.28-338.29)
V53.02 Neuropacemaker (brain) (peripheral nerve) (spinal cord)

ICD-9-CM Procedural

01.22 Removal of intracranial neurostimulator lead(s)

61536

61536 Craniotomy with elevation of bone flap; for excision of cerebral epileptogenic focus, with electrocorticography during surgery (includes removal of electrode array)

ICD-9-CM Diagnostic

345.00 Generalized nonconvulsive epilepsy without mention of intractable epilepsy
345.01 Generalized nonconvulsive epilepsy with intractable epilepsy
345.10 Generalized convulsive epilepsy without mention of intractable epilepsy
345.11 Generalized convulsive epilepsy with intractable epilepsy
345.2 Epileptic petit mal status
345.3 Epileptic grand mal status
345.40 Localization-related (focal) (partial) epilepsy and epileptic syndromes with complex partial seizures, without mention of intractable epilepsy
345.41 Localization-related (focal) (partial) epilepsy and epileptic syndromes with complex partial seizures, with intractable epilepsy

345.50 Localization-related (focal) (partial) epilepsy and epileptic syndromes with simple partial seizures, without mention of intractable epilepsy
345.51 Localization-related (focal) (partial) epilepsy and epileptic syndromes with simple partial seizures, with intractable epilepsy
345.70 Epilepsia partialis continua without mention of intractable epilepsy
345.71 Epilepsia partialis continua with intractable epilepsy
345.80 Other forms of epilepsy and recurrent seizures, without mention of intractable epilepsy
345.81 Other forms of epilepsy and recurrent seizures, with intractable epilepsy
345.90 Unspecified epilepsy without mention of intractable epilepsy
345.91 Unspecified epilepsy with intractable epilepsy

ICD-9-CM Procedural

01.24 Other craniotomy
01.59 Other excision or destruction of lesion or tissue of brain

61537-61540

61537 Craniotomy with elevation of bone flap; for lobectomy, temporal lobe, without electrocorticography during surgery
61538 for lobectomy, temporal lobe, with electrocorticography during surgery
61539 for lobectomy, other than temporal lobe, partial or total, with electrocorticography during surgery
61540 for lobectomy, other than temporal lobe, partial or total, without electrocorticography during surgery

ICD-9-CM Diagnostic

191.1 Malignant neoplasm of frontal lobe of brain
191.2 Malignant neoplasm of temporal lobe of brain
191.3 Malignant neoplasm of parietal lobe of brain
191.4 Malignant neoplasm of occipital lobe of brain
191.9 Malignant neoplasm of brain, unspecified site
198.3 Secondary malignant neoplasm of brain and spinal cord
225.0 Benign neoplasm of brain
228.02 Hemangioma of intracranial structures
237.5 Neoplasm of uncertain behavior of brain and spinal cord
239.6 Neoplasm of unspecified nature of brain
345.00 Generalized nonconvulsive epilepsy without mention of intractable epilepsy
345.01 Generalized nonconvulsive epilepsy with intractable epilepsy
345.10 Generalized convulsive epilepsy without mention of intractable epilepsy
345.11 Generalized convulsive epilepsy with intractable epilepsy
345.2 Epileptic petit mal status
345.3 Epileptic grand mal status
345.40 Localization-related (focal) (partial) epilepsy and epileptic syndromes with complex partial seizures, without mention of intractable epilepsy
345.41 Localization-related (focal) (partial) epilepsy and epileptic syndromes with complex partial seizures, with intractable epilepsy
345.50 Localization-related (focal) (partial) epilepsy and epileptic syndromes with simple partial seizures, without mention of intractable epilepsy
345.51 Localization-related (focal) (partial) epilepsy and epileptic syndromes with simple partial seizures, with intractable epilepsy
345.70 Epilepsia partialis continua without mention of intractable epilepsy
345.71 Epilepsia partialis continua with intractable epilepsy
345.80 Other forms of epilepsy and recurrent seizures, without mention of intractable epilepsy
345.81 Other forms of epilepsy and recurrent seizures, with intractable epilepsy
345.90 Unspecified epilepsy without mention of intractable epilepsy
345.91 Unspecified epilepsy with intractable epilepsy

ICD-9-CM Procedural

01.53 Lobectomy of brain
01.59 Other excision or destruction of lesion or tissue of brain

61541

61541 Craniotomy with elevation of bone flap; for transection of corpus callosum

ICD-9-CM Diagnostic

198.3 Secondary malignant neoplasm of brain and spinal cord
225.0 Benign neoplasm of brain
237.5 Neoplasm of uncertain behavior of brain and spinal cord
239.6 Neoplasm of unspecified nature of brain
345.00 Generalized nonconvulsive epilepsy without mention of intractable epilepsy
345.01 Generalized nonconvulsive epilepsy with intractable epilepsy
345.10 Generalized convulsive epilepsy without mention of intractable epilepsy
345.11 Generalized convulsive epilepsy with intractable epilepsy
345.2 Epileptic petit mal status
345.3 Epileptic grand mal status
345.40 Localization-related (focal) (partial) epilepsy and epileptic syndromes with complex partial seizures, without mention of intractable epilepsy
345.41 Localization-related (focal) (partial) epilepsy and epileptic syndromes with complex partial seizures, with intractable epilepsy
345.50 Localization-related (focal) (partial) epilepsy and epileptic syndromes with simple partial seizures, without mention of intractable epilepsy
345.51 Localization-related (focal) (partial) epilepsy and epileptic syndromes with simple partial seizures, with intractable epilepsy
345.70 Epilepsia partialis continua without mention of intractable epilepsy
345.71 Epilepsia partialis continua with intractable epilepsy
345.80 Other forms of epilepsy and recurrent seizures, without mention of intractable epilepsy
345.81 Other forms of epilepsy and recurrent seizures, with intractable epilepsy
345.90 Unspecified epilepsy without mention of intractable epilepsy
345.91 Unspecified epilepsy with intractable epilepsy
348.0 Cerebral cysts
742.4 Other specified congenital anomalies of brain

ICD-9-CM Procedural

01.32 Lobotomy and tractotomy

61542-61543

61542 Craniotomy with elevation of bone flap; for total hemispherectomy
61543 for partial or subtotal (functional) hemispherectomy

ICD-9-CM Diagnostic

191.2 Malignant neoplasm of temporal lobe of brain
198.3 Secondary malignant neoplasm of brain and spinal cord
225.0 Benign neoplasm of brain
237.5 Neoplasm of uncertain behavior of brain and spinal cord
239.6 Neoplasm of unspecified nature of brain
345.00 Generalized nonconvulsive epilepsy without mention of intractable epilepsy
345.01 Generalized nonconvulsive epilepsy with intractable epilepsy
345.10 Generalized convulsive epilepsy without mention of intractable epilepsy
345.11 Generalized convulsive epilepsy with intractable epilepsy
345.2 Epileptic petit mal status
345.3 Epileptic grand mal status
345.40 Localization-related (focal) (partial) epilepsy and epileptic syndromes with complex partial seizures, without mention of intractable epilepsy
345.41 Localization-related (focal) (partial) epilepsy and epileptic syndromes with complex partial seizures, with intractable epilepsy
345.50 Localization-related (focal) (partial) epilepsy and epileptic syndromes with simple partial seizures, without mention of intractable epilepsy
345.51 Localization-related (focal) (partial) epilepsy and epileptic syndromes with simple partial seizures, with intractable epilepsy
345.70 Epilepsia partialis continua without mention of intractable epilepsy
345.71 Epilepsia partialis continua with intractable epilepsy
345.80 Other forms of epilepsy and recurrent seizures, without mention of intractable epilepsy

345.81 Other forms of epilepsy and recurrent seizures, with intractable epilepsy
345.90 Unspecified epilepsy without mention of intractable epilepsy ▽
345.91 Unspecified epilepsy with intractable epilepsy ▽

ICD-9-CM Procedural

01.52 Hemispherectomy

61544

61544 Craniotomy with elevation of bone flap; for excision or coagulation of choroid plexus

ICD-9-CM Diagnostic

191.5 Malignant neoplasm of ventricles of brain
198.3 Secondary malignant neoplasm of brain and spinal cord
225.0 Benign neoplasm of brain
237.5 Neoplasm of uncertain behavior of brain and spinal cord
239.6 Neoplasm of unspecified nature of brain
331.3 Communicating hydrocephalus — (Use additional code, where applicable, to identify dementia: 294.10, 294.11)
741.00 Spina bifida with hydrocephalus, unspecified region ▽
742.3 Congenital hydrocephalus

ICD-9-CM Procedural

02.14 Choroid plexectomy

61545

61545 Craniotomy with elevation of bone flap; for excision of craniopharyngioma

ICD-9-CM Diagnostic

237.0 Neoplasm of uncertain behavior of pituitary gland and craniopharyngeal duct — (Use additional code to identify any functional activity)

ICD-9-CM Procedural

01.59 Other excision or destruction of lesion or tissue of brain

61546-61548

61546 Craniotomy for hypophysectomy or excision of pituitary tumor, intracranial approach
61548 Hypophysectomy or excision of pituitary tumor, transnasal or transseptal approach, nonstereotactic

ICD-9-CM Diagnostic

194.3 Malignant neoplasm of pituitary gland and craniopharyngeal duct
227.3 Benign neoplasm of pituitary gland and craniopharyngeal duct (pouch) — (Use additional code to identify any functional activity)
237.0 Neoplasm of uncertain behavior of pituitary gland and craniopharyngeal duct — (Use additional code to identify any functional activity)
239.7 Neoplasm of unspecified nature of endocrine glands and other parts of nervous system
253.0 Acromegaly and gigantism
253.1 Other and unspecified anterior pituitary hyperfunction ▽
253.2 Panhypopituitarism
253.3 Pituitary dwarfism
253.4 Other anterior pituitary disorders
253.5 Diabetes insipidus
253.6 Other disorders of neurohypophysis
253.7 Iatrogenic pituitary disorders — (Use additional E code to identify cause)
253.8 Other disorders of the pituitary and other syndromes of diencephalohypophyseal origin
253.9 Unspecified disorder of the pituitary gland and its hypothalamic control ▽

ICD-9-CM Procedural

07.61 Partial excision of pituitary gland, transfrontal approach
07.62 Partial excision of pituitary gland, transsphenoidal approach
07.63 Partial excision of pituitary gland, unspecified approach
07.64 Total excision of pituitary gland, transfrontal approach
07.65 Total excision of pituitary gland, transsphenoidal approach
07.68 Total excision of pituitary gland, other specified approach
07.69 Total excision of pituitary gland, unspecified approach

61550-61552

61550 Craniectomy for craniosynostosis; single cranial suture
61552 multiple cranial sutures

ICD-9-CM Diagnostic

756.0 Congenital anomalies of skull and face bones

ICD-9-CM Procedural

02.01 Opening of cranial suture

61556-61557

61556 Craniotomy for craniosynostosis; frontal or parietal bone flap
61557 bifrontal bone flap

ICD-9-CM Diagnostic

756.0 Congenital anomalies of skull and face bones

ICD-9-CM Procedural

01.24 Other craniotomy

61558-61559

61558 Extensive craniectomy for multiple cranial suture craniosynostosis (eg, cloverleaf skull); not requiring bone grafts
61559 recontouring with multiple osteotomies and bone autografts (eg, barrel-stave procedure) (includes obtaining grafts)

ICD-9-CM Diagnostic

756.0 Congenital anomalies of skull and face bones
756.59 Other congenital osteodystrophy

ICD-9-CM Procedural

02.01 Opening of cranial suture
02.04 Bone graft to skull

61563-61564

61563 Excision, intra and extracranial, benign tumor of cranial bone (eg, fibrous dysplasia); without optic nerve decompression
61564 with optic nerve decompression

ICD-9-CM Diagnostic

213.0 Benign neoplasm of bones of skull and face

ICD-9-CM Procedural

01.6 Excision of lesion of skull
04.42 Other cranial nerve decompression

61566-61567

61566 Craniotomy with elevation of bone flap; for selective amygdalohippocampectomy
61567 for multiple subpial transections, with electrocorticography during surgery

ICD-9-CM Diagnostic

345.41 Localization-related (focal) (partial) epilepsy and epileptic syndromes with complex partial seizures, with intractable epilepsy
348.81 Temporal sclerosis
348.89 Other conditions of brain

ICD-9-CM Procedural

01.59 Other excision or destruction of lesion or tissue of brain

61570-61571

61570 Craniectomy or craniotomy; with excision of foreign body from brain
61571 with treatment of penetrating wound of brain

ICD-9-CM Diagnostic

800.61 Open fracture of vault of skull with cerebral laceration and contusion, no loss of consciousness
800.62 Open fracture of vault of skull with cerebral laceration and contusion, brief (less than one hour) loss of consciousness
800.63 Open fracture of vault of skull with cerebral laceration and contusion, moderate (1-24 hours) loss of consciousness
800.64 Open fracture of vault of skull with cerebral laceration and contusion, prolonged (more than 24 hours) loss of consciousness and return to pre-existing conscious level
800.65 Open fracture of vault of skull with cerebral laceration and contusion, prolonged (more than 24 hours) loss of consciousness, without return to pre-existing conscious level
800.66 Open fracture of vault of skull with cerebral laceration and contusion, loss of consciousness of unspecified duration ▽
800.69 Open fracture of vault of skull with cerebral laceration and contusion, unspecified concussion ▽
800.71 Open fracture of vault of skull with subarachnoid, subdural, and extradural hemorrhage, no loss of consciousness
800.74 Open fracture of vault of skull with subarachnoid, subdural, and extradural hemorrhage, prolonged (more than 24 hours) loss of consciousness and return to pre-existing conscious level
801.61 Open fracture of base of skull with cerebral laceration and contusion, no loss of consciousness
801.62 Open fracture of base of skull with cerebral laceration and contusion, brief (less than one hour) loss of consciousness
801.63 Open fracture of base of skull with cerebral laceration and contusion, moderate (1-24 hours) loss of consciousness
801.64 Open fracture of base of skull with cerebral laceration and contusion, prolonged (more than 24 hours) loss of consciousness and return to pre-existing conscious level
801.65 Open fracture of base of skull with cerebral laceration and contusion, prolonged (more than 24 hours) loss of consciousness, without return to pre-existing conscious level
801.66 Open fracture of base of skull with cerebral laceration and contusion, loss of consciousness of unspecified duration ▽
801.69 Open fracture of base of skull with cerebral laceration and contusion, unspecified concussion ▽
851.12 Cortex (cerebral) contusion with open intracranial wound, brief (less than 1 hour) loss of consciousness
851.16 Cortex (cerebral) contusion with open intracranial wound, loss of consciousness of unspecified duration ▽
851.31 Cortex (cerebral) laceration with open intracranial wound, no loss of consciousness
851.32 Cortex (cerebral) laceration with open intracranial wound, brief (less than 1 hour) loss of consciousness
851.33 Cortex (cerebral) laceration with open intracranial wound, moderate (1-24 hours) loss of consciousness
851.36 Cortex (cerebral) laceration with open intracranial wound, loss of consciousness of unspecified duration ▽
851.90 Other and unspecified cerebral laceration and contusion, with open intracranial wound, unspecified state of consciousness ▽
852.34 Subdural hemorrhage following injury, with open intracranial wound, prolonged (more than 24 hours) loss of consciousness and return to pre-existing conscious level
852.51 Extradural hemorrhage following injury, with open intracranial wound, no loss of consciousness
852.52 Extradural hemorrhage following injury, with open intracranial wound, brief (less than 1 hour) loss of consciousness
852.56 Extradural hemorrhage following injury, with open intracranial wound, loss of consciousness of unspecified duration ▽
853.11 Other and unspecified intracranial hemorrhage following injury, with open intracranial wound, no loss of consciousness ▽
853.12 Other and unspecified intracranial hemorrhage following injury, with open intracranial wound, brief (less than 1 hour) loss of consciousness ▽
854.10 Intracranial injury of other and unspecified nature, with open intracranial wound, unspecified state of consciousness ▽
854.11 Intracranial injury of other and unspecified nature, with open intracranial wound, no loss of consciousness ▽
854.12 Intracranial injury of other and unspecified nature, with open intracranial wound, brief (less than 1 hour) loss of consciousness ▽
854.13 Intracranial injury of other and unspecified nature, with open intracranial wound, moderate (1-24 hours) loss of consciousness ▽
854.14 Intracranial injury of other and unspecified nature, with open intracranial wound, prolonged (more than 24 hours) loss of consciousness and return to pre-existing conscious level ▽
854.15 Intracranial injury of other and unspecified nature, with open intracranial wound, prolonged (more than 24 hours) loss of consciousness, without return to pre-existing conscious level ▽
854.16 Intracranial injury of other and unspecified nature, with open intracranial wound, loss of consciousness of unspecified duration ▽
854.19 Intracranial injury of other and unspecified nature, with open intracranial wound, with unspecified concussion ▽

ICD-9-CM Procedural

01.39 Other incision of brain
02.92 Repair of brain

61575-61576

61575 Transoral approach to skull base, brain stem or upper spinal cord for biopsy, decompression or excision of lesion;
61576 requiring splitting of tongue and/or mandible (including tracheostomy)

ICD-9-CM Diagnostic

170.0 Malignant neoplasm of bones of skull and face, except mandible
191.7 Malignant neoplasm of brain stem
192.2 Malignant neoplasm of spinal cord
198.3 Secondary malignant neoplasm of brain and spinal cord
198.5 Secondary malignant neoplasm of bone and bone marrow
213.0 Benign neoplasm of bones of skull and face
225.0 Benign neoplasm of brain
225.2 Benign neoplasm of cerebral meninges
237.5 Neoplasm of uncertain behavior of brain and spinal cord
238.0 Neoplasm of uncertain behavior of bone and articular cartilage
239.6 Neoplasm of unspecified nature of brain
721.0 Cervical spondylosis without myelopathy
721.1 Cervical spondylosis with myelopathy
756.12 Congenital spondylolisthesis
756.15 Congenital fusion of spine (vertebra)

ICD-9-CM Procedural

01.14 Open biopsy of brain
01.59 Other excision or destruction of lesion or tissue of brain
03.32 Biopsy of spinal cord or spinal meninges

HCPCS Level II Supplies & Services

A7527 Tracheostomy/laryngectomy tube plug/stop, each

61580

61580 Craniofacial approach to anterior cranial fossa; extradural, including lateral rhinotomy, ethmoidectomy, sphenoidectomy, without maxillectomy or orbital exenteration

ICD-9-CM Diagnostic

160.0 Malignant neoplasm of nasal cavities
160.3 Malignant neoplasm of ethmoidal sinus
160.5 Malignant neoplasm of sphenoidal sinus

160.8 Malignant neoplasm of other sites of nasal cavities, middle ear, and accessory sinuses
170.0 Malignant neoplasm of bones of skull and face, except mandible
190.0 Malignant neoplasm of eyeball, except conjunctiva, cornea, retina, and choroid
191.0 Malignant neoplasm of cerebrum, except lobes and ventricles
192.0 Malignant neoplasm of cranial nerves
192.1 Malignant neoplasm of cerebral meninges
196.0 Secondary and unspecified malignant neoplasm of lymph nodes of head, face, and neck
197.3 Secondary malignant neoplasm of other respiratory organs
198.4 Secondary malignant neoplasm of other parts of nervous system
225.1 Benign neoplasm of cranial nerves
225.2 Benign neoplasm of cerebral meninges
237.6 Neoplasm of uncertain behavior of meninges
239.7 Neoplasm of unspecified nature of endocrine glands and other parts of nervous system
324.0 Intracranial abscess
349.81 Cerebrospinal fluid rhinorrhea
430 Subarachnoid hemorrhage — (Use additional code to identify presence of hypertension)
437.3 Cerebral aneurysm, nonruptured — (Use additional code to identify presence of hypertension)
747.81 Congenital anomaly of cerebrovascular system

ICD-9-CM Procedural

01.24 Other craniotomy
21.1 Incision of nose
22.63 Ethmoidectomy
22.64 Sphenoidectomy

61581

61581 Craniofacial approach to anterior cranial fossa; extradural, including lateral rhinotomy, orbital exenteration, ethmoidectomy, sphenoidectomy and/or maxillectomy

ICD-9-CM Diagnostic

160.0 Malignant neoplasm of nasal cavities
160.3 Malignant neoplasm of ethmoidal sinus
160.5 Malignant neoplasm of sphenoidal sinus
160.8 Malignant neoplasm of other sites of nasal cavities, middle ear, and accessory sinuses
170.0 Malignant neoplasm of bones of skull and face, except mandible
190.0 Malignant neoplasm of eyeball, except conjunctiva, cornea, retina, and choroid
191.0 Malignant neoplasm of cerebrum, except lobes and ventricles
192.0 Malignant neoplasm of cranial nerves
192.1 Malignant neoplasm of cerebral meninges
196.0 Secondary and unspecified malignant neoplasm of lymph nodes of head, face, and neck
197.3 Secondary malignant neoplasm of other respiratory organs
198.4 Secondary malignant neoplasm of other parts of nervous system
225.1 Benign neoplasm of cranial nerves
225.2 Benign neoplasm of cerebral meninges
237.6 Neoplasm of uncertain behavior of meninges
239.7 Neoplasm of unspecified nature of endocrine glands and other parts of nervous system
324.0 Intracranial abscess
349.81 Cerebrospinal fluid rhinorrhea
430 Subarachnoid hemorrhage — (Use additional code to identify presence of hypertension)
437.3 Cerebral aneurysm, nonruptured — (Use additional code to identify presence of hypertension)
747.81 Congenital anomaly of cerebrovascular system

ICD-9-CM Procedural

01.24 Other craniotomy
16.59 Other exenteration of orbit
21.1 Incision of nose
22.62 Excision of lesion of maxillary sinus with other approach
22.63 Ethmoidectomy
22.64 Sphenoidectomy

61582

61582 Craniofacial approach to anterior cranial fossa; extradural, including unilateral or bifrontal craniotomy, elevation of frontal lobe(s), osteotomy of base of anterior cranial fossa

ICD-9-CM Diagnostic

170.0 Malignant neoplasm of bones of skull and face, except mandible
191.0 Malignant neoplasm of cerebrum, except lobes and ventricles
191.1 Malignant neoplasm of frontal lobe of brain
191.8 Malignant neoplasm of other parts of brain
192.0 Malignant neoplasm of cranial nerves
192.1 Malignant neoplasm of cerebral meninges
198.3 Secondary malignant neoplasm of brain and spinal cord
198.4 Secondary malignant neoplasm of other parts of nervous system
225.0 Benign neoplasm of brain
225.1 Benign neoplasm of cranial nerves
225.2 Benign neoplasm of cerebral meninges
237.0 Neoplasm of uncertain behavior of pituitary gland and craniopharyngeal duct — (Use additional code to identify any functional activity)
237.5 Neoplasm of uncertain behavior of brain and spinal cord
237.6 Neoplasm of uncertain behavior of meninges
239.6 Neoplasm of unspecified nature of brain
239.7 Neoplasm of unspecified nature of endocrine glands and other parts of nervous system
324.0 Intracranial abscess
349.81 Cerebrospinal fluid rhinorrhea
430 Subarachnoid hemorrhage — (Use additional code to identify presence of hypertension)
437.3 Cerebral aneurysm, nonruptured — (Use additional code to identify presence of hypertension)
747.81 Congenital anomaly of cerebrovascular system

ICD-9-CM Procedural

01.24 Other craniotomy

61583

61583 Craniofacial approach to anterior cranial fossa; intradural, including unilateral or bifrontal craniotomy, elevation or resection of frontal lobe, osteotomy of base of anterior cranial fossa

ICD-9-CM Diagnostic

170.0 Malignant neoplasm of bones of skull and face, except mandible
191.0 Malignant neoplasm of cerebrum, except lobes and ventricles
191.1 Malignant neoplasm of frontal lobe of brain
191.8 Malignant neoplasm of other parts of brain
192.0 Malignant neoplasm of cranial nerves
192.1 Malignant neoplasm of cerebral meninges
198.3 Secondary malignant neoplasm of brain and spinal cord
198.4 Secondary malignant neoplasm of other parts of nervous system
225.0 Benign neoplasm of brain
225.2 Benign neoplasm of cerebral meninges
237.0 Neoplasm of uncertain behavior of pituitary gland and craniopharyngeal duct — (Use additional code to identify any functional activity)
237.5 Neoplasm of uncertain behavior of brain and spinal cord
239.6 Neoplasm of unspecified nature of brain
324.0 Intracranial abscess
349.81 Cerebrospinal fluid rhinorrhea

430 Subarachnoid hemorrhage — (Use additional code to identify presence of hypertension)
437.3 Cerebral aneurysm, nonruptured — (Use additional code to identify presence of hypertension)
747.81 Congenital anomaly of cerebrovascular system

ICD-9-CM Procedural

01.24 Other craniotomy

61584

61584 Orbitocranial approach to anterior cranial fossa, extradural, including supraorbital ridge osteotomy and elevation of frontal and/or temporal lobe(s); without orbital exenteration

ICD-9-CM Diagnostic

160.8 Malignant neoplasm of other sites of nasal cavities, middle ear, and accessory sinuses
170.0 Malignant neoplasm of bones of skull and face, except mandible
190.0 Malignant neoplasm of eyeball, except conjunctiva, cornea, retina, and choroid
190.1 Malignant neoplasm of orbit
190.8 Malignant neoplasm of other specified sites of eye
191.0 Malignant neoplasm of cerebrum, except lobes and ventricles
191.1 Malignant neoplasm of frontal lobe of brain
191.2 Malignant neoplasm of temporal lobe of brain
191.8 Malignant neoplasm of other parts of brain
192.0 Malignant neoplasm of cranial nerves
192.1 Malignant neoplasm of cerebral meninges
192.3 Malignant neoplasm of spinal meninges
198.3 Secondary malignant neoplasm of brain and spinal cord
198.4 Secondary malignant neoplasm of other parts of nervous system
213.0 Benign neoplasm of bones of skull and face
225.0 Benign neoplasm of brain
225.2 Benign neoplasm of cerebral meninges
237.5 Neoplasm of uncertain behavior of brain and spinal cord
324.0 Intracranial abscess
430 Subarachnoid hemorrhage — (Use additional code to identify presence of hypertension)
437.3 Cerebral aneurysm, nonruptured — (Use additional code to identify presence of hypertension)
747.81 Congenital anomaly of cerebrovascular system

ICD-9-CM Procedural

01.24 Other craniotomy
77.30 Other division of bone, unspecified site

61585

61585 Orbitocranial approach to anterior cranial fossa, extradural, including supraorbital ridge osteotomy and elevation of frontal and/or temporal lobe(s); with orbital exenteration

ICD-9-CM Diagnostic

160.8 Malignant neoplasm of other sites of nasal cavities, middle ear, and accessory sinuses
170.0 Malignant neoplasm of bones of skull and face, except mandible
190.0 Malignant neoplasm of eyeball, except conjunctiva, cornea, retina, and choroid
190.1 Malignant neoplasm of orbit
190.8 Malignant neoplasm of other specified sites of eye
191.0 Malignant neoplasm of cerebrum, except lobes and ventricles
191.1 Malignant neoplasm of frontal lobe of brain
191.2 Malignant neoplasm of temporal lobe of brain
191.8 Malignant neoplasm of other parts of brain
191.9 Malignant neoplasm of brain, unspecified site ▽
192.0 Malignant neoplasm of cranial nerves
192.1 Malignant neoplasm of cerebral meninges
196.0 Secondary and unspecified malignant neoplasm of lymph nodes of head, face, and neck
198.3 Secondary malignant neoplasm of brain and spinal cord
198.4 Secondary malignant neoplasm of other parts of nervous system
225.0 Benign neoplasm of brain
225.2 Benign neoplasm of cerebral meninges
237.5 Neoplasm of uncertain behavior of brain and spinal cord
324.0 Intracranial abscess
430 Subarachnoid hemorrhage — (Use additional code to identify presence of hypertension)
437.3 Cerebral aneurysm, nonruptured — (Use additional code to identify presence of hypertension)
747.81 Congenital anomaly of cerebrovascular system

ICD-9-CM Procedural

01.24 Other craniotomy

61586

61586 Bicoronal, transzygomatic and/or LeFort I osteotomy approach to anterior cranial fossa with or without internal fixation, without bone graft

ICD-9-CM Diagnostic

160.8 Malignant neoplasm of other sites of nasal cavities, middle ear, and accessory sinuses
170.0 Malignant neoplasm of bones of skull and face, except mandible
190.0 Malignant neoplasm of eyeball, except conjunctiva, cornea, retina, and choroid
190.1 Malignant neoplasm of orbit
190.8 Malignant neoplasm of other specified sites of eye
191.0 Malignant neoplasm of cerebrum, except lobes and ventricles
191.1 Malignant neoplasm of frontal lobe of brain
191.2 Malignant neoplasm of temporal lobe of brain
191.8 Malignant neoplasm of other parts of brain
192.0 Malignant neoplasm of cranial nerves
192.1 Malignant neoplasm of cerebral meninges
196.0 Secondary and unspecified malignant neoplasm of lymph nodes of head, face, and neck
198.3 Secondary malignant neoplasm of brain and spinal cord
198.4 Secondary malignant neoplasm of other parts of nervous system
225.0 Benign neoplasm of brain
225.2 Benign neoplasm of cerebral meninges
237.5 Neoplasm of uncertain behavior of brain and spinal cord
324.0 Intracranial abscess

ICD-9-CM Procedural

01.24 Other craniotomy

61590-61591

61590 Infratemporal pre-auricular approach to middle cranial fossa (parapharyngeal space, infratemporal and midline skull base, nasopharynx), with or without disarticulation of the mandible, including parotidectomy, craniotomy, decompression and/or mobilization of the facial nerve and/or petrous carotid artery

61591 Infratemporal post-auricular approach to middle cranial fossa (internal auditory meatus, petrous apex, tentorium, cavernous sinus, parasellar area, infratemporal fossa) including mastoidectomy, resection of sigmoid sinus, with or without decompression and/or mobilization of contents of auditory canal or petrous carotid artery

ICD-9-CM Diagnostic

160.1 Malignant neoplasm of auditory tube, middle ear, and mastoid air cells
170.0 Malignant neoplasm of bones of skull and face, except mandible
191.2 Malignant neoplasm of temporal lobe of brain
191.3 Malignant neoplasm of parietal lobe of brain
191.9 Malignant neoplasm of brain, unspecified site ▽
194.3 Malignant neoplasm of pituitary gland and craniopharyngeal duct

196.0 Secondary and unspecified malignant neoplasm of lymph nodes of head, face, and neck
198.3 Secondary malignant neoplasm of brain and spinal cord
198.4 Secondary malignant neoplasm of other parts of nervous system
198.5 Secondary malignant neoplasm of bone and bone marrow
198.89 Secondary malignant neoplasm of other specified sites
212.0 Benign neoplasm of nasal cavities, middle ear, and accessory sinuses
213.0 Benign neoplasm of bones of skull and face
225.0 Benign neoplasm of brain
225.1 Benign neoplasm of cranial nerves
225.2 Benign neoplasm of cerebral meninges
237.0 Neoplasm of uncertain behavior of pituitary gland and craniopharyngeal duct — (Use additional code to identify any functional activity)
237.3 Neoplasm of uncertain behavior of paraganglia
237.5 Neoplasm of uncertain behavior of brain and spinal cord
239.6 Neoplasm of unspecified nature of brain
324.0 Intracranial abscess
430 Subarachnoid hemorrhage — (Use additional code to identify presence of hypertension)
437.3 Cerebral aneurysm, nonruptured — (Use additional code to identify presence of hypertension)
747.81 Congenital anomaly of cerebrovascular system

ICD-9-CM Procedural

01.24 Other craniotomy
04.42 Other cranial nerve decompression
20.49 Other mastoidectomy
26.30 Sialoadenectomy, not otherwise specified

61592

61592 Orbitocranial zygomatic approach to middle cranial fossa (cavernous sinus and carotid artery, clivus, basilar artery or petrous apex) including osteotomy of zygoma, craniotomy, extra- or intradural elevation of temporal lobe

ICD-9-CM Diagnostic

147.0 Malignant neoplasm of superior wall of nasopharynx
147.8 Malignant neoplasm of other specified sites of nasopharynx
170.0 Malignant neoplasm of bones of skull and face, except mandible
191.2 Malignant neoplasm of temporal lobe of brain
191.3 Malignant neoplasm of parietal lobe of brain
191.7 Malignant neoplasm of brain stem
191.8 Malignant neoplasm of other parts of brain
191.9 Malignant neoplasm of brain, unspecified site
198.3 Secondary malignant neoplasm of brain and spinal cord
198.4 Secondary malignant neoplasm of other parts of nervous system
210.7 Benign neoplasm of nasopharynx
225.0 Benign neoplasm of brain
225.2 Benign neoplasm of cerebral meninges
237.5 Neoplasm of uncertain behavior of brain and spinal cord
239.6 Neoplasm of unspecified nature of brain
324.0 Intracranial abscess
430 Subarachnoid hemorrhage — (Use additional code to identify presence of hypertension)
437.3 Cerebral aneurysm, nonruptured — (Use additional code to identify presence of hypertension)
747.81 Congenital anomaly of cerebrovascular system

ICD-9-CM Procedural

01.24 Other craniotomy
77.30 Other division of bone, unspecified site

61595

61595 Transtemporal approach to posterior cranial fossa, jugular foramen or midline skull base, including mastoidectomy, decompression of sigmoid sinus and/or facial nerve, with or without mobilization

ICD-9-CM Diagnostic

191.7 Malignant neoplasm of brain stem
191.8 Malignant neoplasm of other parts of brain
192.0 Malignant neoplasm of cranial nerves
198.3 Secondary malignant neoplasm of brain and spinal cord
198.5 Secondary malignant neoplasm of bone and bone marrow
213.0 Benign neoplasm of bones of skull and face
225.0 Benign neoplasm of brain
225.1 Benign neoplasm of cranial nerves
225.2 Benign neoplasm of cerebral meninges
237.5 Neoplasm of uncertain behavior of brain and spinal cord
238.0 Neoplasm of uncertain behavior of bone and articular cartilage
239.6 Neoplasm of unspecified nature of brain
239.7 Neoplasm of unspecified nature of endocrine glands and other parts of nervous system
324.0 Intracranial abscess
430 Subarachnoid hemorrhage — (Use additional code to identify presence of hypertension)
437.3 Cerebral aneurysm, nonruptured — (Use additional code to identify presence of hypertension)
747.81 Congenital anomaly of cerebrovascular system

ICD-9-CM Procedural

01.59 Other excision or destruction of lesion or tissue of brain
04.42 Other cranial nerve decompression
20.49 Other mastoidectomy

61596

61596 Transcochlear approach to posterior cranial fossa, jugular foramen or midline skull base, including labyrinthectomy, decompression, with or without mobilization of facial nerve and/or petrous carotid artery

ICD-9-CM Diagnostic

170.0 Malignant neoplasm of bones of skull and face, except mandible
191.7 Malignant neoplasm of brain stem
191.8 Malignant neoplasm of other parts of brain
191.9 Malignant neoplasm of brain, unspecified site
192.0 Malignant neoplasm of cranial nerves
198.3 Secondary malignant neoplasm of brain and spinal cord
198.4 Secondary malignant neoplasm of other parts of nervous system
198.5 Secondary malignant neoplasm of bone and bone marrow
213.0 Benign neoplasm of bones of skull and face
225.0 Benign neoplasm of brain
225.1 Benign neoplasm of cranial nerves
225.2 Benign neoplasm of cerebral meninges
237.3 Neoplasm of uncertain behavior of paraganglia
237.5 Neoplasm of uncertain behavior of brain and spinal cord
238.0 Neoplasm of uncertain behavior of bone and articular cartilage
239.6 Neoplasm of unspecified nature of brain
239.7 Neoplasm of unspecified nature of endocrine glands and other parts of nervous system
324.0 Intracranial abscess
430 Subarachnoid hemorrhage — (Use additional code to identify presence of hypertension)
437.3 Cerebral aneurysm, nonruptured — (Use additional code to identify presence of hypertension)
747.81 Congenital anomaly of cerebrovascular system

ICD-9-CM Procedural

04.42 Other cranial nerve decompression
20.79 Other incision, excision, and destruction of inner ear

61597

61597 Transcondylar (far lateral) approach to posterior cranial fossa, jugular foramen or midline skull base, including occipital condylectomy, mastoidectomy, resection of C1-C3 vertebral body(s), decompression of vertebral artery, with or without mobilization

ICD-9-CM Diagnostic

170.2 Malignant neoplasm of vertebral column, excluding sacrum and coccyx
191.6 Malignant neoplasm of cerebellum NOS
191.7 Malignant neoplasm of brain stem
192.0 Malignant neoplasm of cranial nerves
198.3 Secondary malignant neoplasm of brain and spinal cord
198.4 Secondary malignant neoplasm of other parts of nervous system
198.5 Secondary malignant neoplasm of bone and bone marrow
213.0 Benign neoplasm of bones of skull and face
225.0 Benign neoplasm of brain
225.1 Benign neoplasm of cranial nerves
225.2 Benign neoplasm of cerebral meninges
228.02 Hemangioma of intracranial structures
237.5 Neoplasm of uncertain behavior of brain and spinal cord
238.0 Neoplasm of uncertain behavior of bone and articular cartilage
239.2 Neoplasms of unspecified nature of bone, soft tissue, and skin
239.6 Neoplasm of unspecified nature of brain
324.0 Intracranial abscess
430 Subarachnoid hemorrhage — (Use additional code to identify presence of hypertension)
437.3 Cerebral aneurysm, nonruptured — (Use additional code to identify presence of hypertension)
747.81 Congenital anomaly of cerebrovascular system

ICD-9-CM Procedural

20.49 Other mastoidectomy
77.89 Other partial ostectomy of other bone, except facial bones

61598

61598 Transpetrosal approach to posterior cranial fossa, clivus or foramen magnum, including ligation of superior petrosal sinus and/or sigmoid sinus

ICD-9-CM Diagnostic

170.0 Malignant neoplasm of bones of skull and face, except mandible
170.2 Malignant neoplasm of vertebral column, excluding sacrum and coccyx
191.7 Malignant neoplasm of brain stem
192.0 Malignant neoplasm of cranial nerves
198.3 Secondary malignant neoplasm of brain and spinal cord
198.4 Secondary malignant neoplasm of other parts of nervous system
198.5 Secondary malignant neoplasm of bone and bone marrow
213.0 Benign neoplasm of bones of skull and face
225.0 Benign neoplasm of brain
225.1 Benign neoplasm of cranial nerves
225.2 Benign neoplasm of cerebral meninges
228.02 Hemangioma of intracranial structures
237.3 Neoplasm of uncertain behavior of paraganglia
237.5 Neoplasm of uncertain behavior of brain and spinal cord
238.0 Neoplasm of uncertain behavior of bone and articular cartilage
239.6 Neoplasm of unspecified nature of brain
430 Subarachnoid hemorrhage — (Use additional code to identify presence of hypertension)
437.3 Cerebral aneurysm, nonruptured — (Use additional code to identify presence of hypertension)
747.81 Congenital anomaly of cerebrovascular system

ICD-9-CM Procedural

01.59 Other excision or destruction of lesion or tissue of brain

61600-61601

61600 Resection or excision of neoplastic, vascular or infectious lesion of base of anterior cranial fossa; extradural
61601 intradural, including dural repair, with or without graft

ICD-9-CM Diagnostic

170.0 Malignant neoplasm of bones of skull and face, except mandible
191.0 Malignant neoplasm of cerebrum, except lobes and ventricles
191.1 Malignant neoplasm of frontal lobe of brain
191.8 Malignant neoplasm of other parts of brain
192.0 Malignant neoplasm of cranial nerves
192.1 Malignant neoplasm of cerebral meninges
198.3 Secondary malignant neoplasm of brain and spinal cord
198.4 Secondary malignant neoplasm of other parts of nervous system
198.5 Secondary malignant neoplasm of bone and bone marrow
225.0 Benign neoplasm of brain
225.1 Benign neoplasm of cranial nerves
225.2 Benign neoplasm of cerebral meninges
237.0 Neoplasm of uncertain behavior of pituitary gland and craniopharyngeal duct — (Use additional code to identify any functional activity)
237.5 Neoplasm of uncertain behavior of brain and spinal cord
237.6 Neoplasm of uncertain behavior of meninges
239.6 Neoplasm of unspecified nature of brain
239.7 Neoplasm of unspecified nature of endocrine glands and other parts of nervous system
324.0 Intracranial abscess
349.81 Cerebrospinal fluid rhinorrhea
430 Subarachnoid hemorrhage — (Use additional code to identify presence of hypertension)
437.3 Cerebral aneurysm, nonruptured — (Use additional code to identify presence of hypertension)
437.8 Other ill-defined cerebrovascular disease — (Use additional code to identify presence of hypertension)
437.9 Unspecified cerebrovascular disease — (Use additional code to identify presence of hypertension) ▼
747.81 Congenital anomaly of cerebrovascular system

ICD-9-CM Procedural

01.24 Other craniotomy
01.51 Excision of lesion or tissue of cerebral meninges

61605-61606

61605 Resection or excision of neoplastic, vascular or infectious lesion of infratemporal fossa, parapharyngeal space, petrous apex; extradural
61606 intradural, including dural repair, with or without graft

ICD-9-CM Diagnostic

170.0 Malignant neoplasm of bones of skull and face, except mandible
191.2 Malignant neoplasm of temporal lobe of brain
191.3 Malignant neoplasm of parietal lobe of brain
191.9 Malignant neoplasm of brain, unspecified site ▼
192.0 Malignant neoplasm of cranial nerves
194.3 Malignant neoplasm of pituitary gland and craniopharyngeal duct
198.3 Secondary malignant neoplasm of brain and spinal cord
198.4 Secondary malignant neoplasm of other parts of nervous system
225.0 Benign neoplasm of brain

225.1	Benign neoplasm of cranial nerves
225.2	Benign neoplasm of cerebral meninges
237.5	Neoplasm of uncertain behavior of brain and spinal cord
239.6	Neoplasm of unspecified nature of brain
324.0	Intracranial abscess
430	Subarachnoid hemorrhage — (Use additional code to identify presence of hypertension)
437.3	Cerebral aneurysm, nonruptured — (Use additional code to identify presence of hypertension)
437.8	Other ill-defined cerebrovascular disease — (Use additional code to identify presence of hypertension)
747.81	Congenital anomaly of cerebrovascular system

ICD-9-CM Procedural

01.24	Other craniotomy
01.51	Excision of lesion or tissue of cerebral meninges

61607-61608

61607 Resection or excision of neoplastic, vascular or infectious lesion of parasellar area, cavernous sinus, clivus or midline skull base; extradural

61608 intradural, including dural repair, with or without graft

ICD-9-CM Diagnostic

170.0	Malignant neoplasm of bones of skull and face, except mandible
191.7	Malignant neoplasm of brain stem
191.8	Malignant neoplasm of other parts of brain
192.0	Malignant neoplasm of cranial nerves
194.3	Malignant neoplasm of pituitary gland and craniopharyngeal duct
198.3	Secondary malignant neoplasm of brain and spinal cord
198.5	Secondary malignant neoplasm of bone and bone marrow
225.0	Benign neoplasm of brain
225.1	Benign neoplasm of cranial nerves
225.2	Benign neoplasm of cerebral meninges
237.0	Neoplasm of uncertain behavior of pituitary gland and craniopharyngeal duct — (Use additional code to identify any functional activity)
237.5	Neoplasm of uncertain behavior of brain and spinal cord
239.7	Neoplasm of unspecified nature of endocrine glands and other parts of nervous system
324.0	Intracranial abscess
325	Phlebitis and thrombophlebitis of intracranial venous sinuses
430	Subarachnoid hemorrhage — (Use additional code to identify presence of hypertension)
437.3	Cerebral aneurysm, nonruptured — (Use additional code to identify presence of hypertension)
437.8	Other ill-defined cerebrovascular disease — (Use additional code to identify presence of hypertension)
478.19	Other diseases of nasal cavity and sinuses — (Use additional code to identify infectious organism)
747.81	Congenital anomaly of cerebrovascular system

ICD-9-CM Procedural

01.51	Excision of lesion or tissue of cerebral meninges
01.6	Excision of lesion of skull

61613

61613 Obliteration of carotid aneurysm, arteriovenous malformation, or carotid-cavernous fistula by dissection within cavernous sinus

ICD-9-CM Diagnostic

430	Subarachnoid hemorrhage — (Use additional code to identify presence of hypertension)
437.3	Cerebral aneurysm, nonruptured — (Use additional code to identify presence of hypertension)
747.81	Congenital anomaly of cerebrovascular system
853.00	Other and unspecified intracranial hemorrhage following injury, without mention of open intracranial wound, unspecified state of consciousness ▽
900.82	Injury to multiple blood vessels of head and neck

ICD-9-CM Procedural

38.60	Other excision of vessels, unspecified site
38.82	Other surgical occlusion of other vessels of head and neck
39.52	Other repair of aneurysm
39.53	Repair of arteriovenous fistula

61615-61616

61615 Resection or excision of neoplastic, vascular or infectious lesion of base of posterior cranial fossa, jugular foramen, foramen magnum, or C1-C3 vertebral bodies; extradural

61616 intradural, including dural repair, with or without graft

ICD-9-CM Diagnostic

170.0	Malignant neoplasm of bones of skull and face, except mandible
170.2	Malignant neoplasm of vertebral column, excluding sacrum and coccyx
191.7	Malignant neoplasm of brain stem
191.8	Malignant neoplasm of other parts of brain
191.9	Malignant neoplasm of brain, unspecified site ▽
192.0	Malignant neoplasm of cranial nerves
198.3	Secondary malignant neoplasm of brain and spinal cord
198.5	Secondary malignant neoplasm of bone and bone marrow
213.2	Benign neoplasm of vertebral column, excluding sacrum and coccyx
225.0	Benign neoplasm of brain
225.1	Benign neoplasm of cranial nerves
225.2	Benign neoplasm of cerebral meninges
228.02	Hemangioma of intracranial structures
237.3	Neoplasm of uncertain behavior of paraganglia
237.5	Neoplasm of uncertain behavior of brain and spinal cord
238.0	Neoplasm of uncertain behavior of bone and articular cartilage
239.2	Neoplasms of unspecified nature of bone, soft tissue, and skin
239.6	Neoplasm of unspecified nature of brain
239.7	Neoplasm of unspecified nature of endocrine glands and other parts of nervous system
324.0	Intracranial abscess
348.0	Cerebral cysts
437.1	Other generalized ischemic cerebrovascular disease — (Use additional code to identify presence of hypertension)
437.8	Other ill-defined cerebrovascular disease — (Use additional code to identify presence of hypertension)
437.9	Unspecified cerebrovascular disease — (Use additional code to identify presence of hypertension) ▽
747.81	Congenital anomaly of cerebrovascular system

ICD-9-CM Procedural

01.24	Other craniotomy
01.51	Excision of lesion or tissue of cerebral meninges
01.6	Excision of lesion of skull
77.69	Local excision of lesion or tissue of other bone, except facial bones

61618-61619

61618 Secondary repair of dura for cerebrospinal fluid leak, anterior, middle or posterior cranial fossa following surgery of the skull base; by free tissue graft (eg, pericranium, fascia, tensor fascia lata, adipose tissue, homologous or synthetic grafts)

61619 by local or regionalized vascularized pedicle flap or myocutaneous flap (including galea, temporalis, frontalis or occipitalis muscle)

ICD-9-CM Diagnostic

349.31	Accidental puncture or laceration of dura during a procedure
349.39	Other dural tear

349.81 Cerebrospinal fluid rhinorrhea
388.61 Cerebrospinal fluid otorrhea
997.00 Unspecified nervous system complication — (Use additional code to identify complications) ▽
998.2 Accidental puncture or laceration during procedure

ICD-9-CM Procedural

02.12 Other repair of cerebral meninges

61623

61623 Endovascular temporary balloon arterial occlusion, head or neck (extracranial/intracranial) including selective catheterization of vessel to be occluded, positioning and inflation of occlusion balloon, concomitant neurological monitoring, and radiologic supervision and interpretation of all angiography required for balloon occlusion and to exclude vascular injury post occlusion

ICD-9-CM Diagnostic

171.0 Malignant neoplasm of connective and other soft tissue of head, face, and neck
198.89 Secondary malignant neoplasm of other specified sites
215.0 Other benign neoplasm of connective and other soft tissue of head, face, and neck
228.00 Hemangioma of unspecified site ▽
228.09 Hemangioma of other sites
238.1 Neoplasm of uncertain behavior of connective and other soft tissue
239.2 Neoplasms of unspecified nature of bone, soft tissue, and skin
442.81 Aneurysm of artery of neck
447.0 Arteriovenous fistula, acquired
747.60 Congenital anomaly of the peripheral vascular system, unspecified site ▽
747.69 Congenital anomaly of other specified site of peripheral vascular system
900.02 External carotid artery injury

ICD-9-CM Procedural

38.82 Other surgical occlusion of other vessels of head and neck
39.77 Temporary (partial) therapeutic endovascular occlusion of vessel

61624

61624 Transcatheter permanent occlusion or embolization (eg, for tumor destruction, to achieve hemostasis, to occlude a vascular malformation), percutaneous, any method; central nervous system (intracranial, spinal cord)

ICD-9-CM Diagnostic

191.0 Malignant neoplasm of cerebrum, except lobes and ventricles
191.1 Malignant neoplasm of frontal lobe of brain
191.2 Malignant neoplasm of temporal lobe of brain
191.3 Malignant neoplasm of parietal lobe of brain
191.4 Malignant neoplasm of occipital lobe of brain
191.5 Malignant neoplasm of ventricles of brain
191.6 Malignant neoplasm of cerebellum NOS
191.8 Malignant neoplasm of other parts of brain
191.9 Malignant neoplasm of brain, unspecified site ▽
192.1 Malignant neoplasm of cerebral meninges
192.2 Malignant neoplasm of spinal cord
198.3 Secondary malignant neoplasm of brain and spinal cord
198.4 Secondary malignant neoplasm of other parts of nervous system
225.0 Benign neoplasm of brain
225.2 Benign neoplasm of cerebral meninges
225.3 Benign neoplasm of spinal cord
225.4 Benign neoplasm of spinal meninges
225.8 Benign neoplasm of other specified sites of nervous system
228.02 Hemangioma of intracranial structures
237.5 Neoplasm of uncertain behavior of brain and spinal cord
237.6 Neoplasm of uncertain behavior of meninges
239.6 Neoplasm of unspecified nature of brain
239.7 Neoplasm of unspecified nature of endocrine glands and other parts of nervous system
430 Subarachnoid hemorrhage — (Use additional code to identify presence of hypertension)
431 Intracerebral hemorrhage — (Use additional code to identify presence of hypertension)
437.3 Cerebral aneurysm, nonruptured — (Use additional code to identify presence of hypertension)
747.81 Congenital anomaly of cerebrovascular system
747.82 Congenital spinal vessel anomaly

ICD-9-CM Procedural

38.81 Other surgical occlusion of intracranial vessels
38.82 Other surgical occlusion of other vessels of head and neck
39.75 Endovascular embolization or occlusion of vessel(s) of head or neck using bare coils
39.76 Endovascular embolization or occlusion of vessel(s) of head or neck using bioactive coils

61626

61626 Transcatheter permanent occlusion or embolization (eg, for tumor destruction, to achieve hemostasis, to occlude a vascular malformation), percutaneous, any method; non-central nervous system, head or neck (extracranial, brachiocephalic branch)

ICD-9-CM Diagnostic

171.0 Malignant neoplasm of connective and other soft tissue of head, face, and neck
198.89 Secondary malignant neoplasm of other specified sites
215.0 Other benign neoplasm of connective and other soft tissue of head, face, and neck
228.00 Hemangioma of unspecified site ▽
228.09 Hemangioma of other sites
238.1 Neoplasm of uncertain behavior of connective and other soft tissue
239.2 Neoplasms of unspecified nature of bone, soft tissue, and skin
442.81 Aneurysm of artery of neck
447.0 Arteriovenous fistula, acquired
747.60 Congenital anomaly of the peripheral vascular system, unspecified site ▽
747.69 Congenital anomaly of other specified site of peripheral vascular system
900.02 External carotid artery injury

ICD-9-CM Procedural

38.82 Other surgical occlusion of other vessels of head and neck
39.75 Endovascular embolization or occlusion of vessel(s) of head or neck using bare coils
39.76 Endovascular embolization or occlusion of vessel(s) of head or neck using bioactive coils

HCPCS Level II Supplies & Services

C1887 Catheter, guiding (may include infusion/perfusion capability)

61630-61635

61630 Balloon angioplasty, intracranial (eg, atherosclerotic stenosis), percutaneous
61635 Transcatheter placement of intravascular stent(s), intracranial (eg, atherosclerotic stenosis), including balloon angioplasty, if performed

ICD-9-CM Diagnostic

434.00 Cerebral thrombosis without mention of cerebral infarction — (Use additional code, if applicable, to identify status post administration of tPA (rtPA) in a different facility within the last 24 hours prior to admission to current facility: V45.88)
434.01 Cerebral thrombosis with cerebral infarction — (Use additional code, if applicable, to identify status post administration of tPA (rtPA) in a different facility within the last 24 hours prior to admission to current facility: V45.88)
434.10 Cerebral embolism without mention of cerebral infarction — (Use additional code, if applicable, to identify status post administration of tPA (rtPA) in a different facility within the last 24 hours prior to admission to current facility: V45.88)
434.11 Cerebral embolism with cerebral infarction — (Use additional code, if applicable, to identify status post administration of tPA (rtPA) in a different facility within the last 24 hours prior to admission to current facility: V45.88)

434.90 Unspecified cerebral artery occlusion without mention of cerebral infarction — (Use additional code, if applicable, to identify status post administration of tPA (rtPA) in a different facility within the last 24 hours prior to admission to current facility: V45.88) ▽

434.91 Unspecified cerebral artery occlusion with cerebral infarction — (Use additional code, if applicable, to identify status post administration of tPA (rtPA) in a different facility within the last 24 hours prior to admission to current facility: V45.88) ▽

435.0 Basilar artery syndrome — (Use additional code to identify presence of hypertension)

435.8 Other specified transient cerebral ischemias — (Use additional code to identify presence of hypertension)

435.9 Unspecified transient cerebral ischemia — (Use additional code to identify presence of hypertension) ▽

436 Acute, but ill-defined, cerebrovascular disease — (Use additional code to identify presence of hypertension) ▽

437.0 Cerebral atherosclerosis — (Use additional code to identify presence of hypertension)

437.1 Other generalized ischemic cerebrovascular disease — (Use additional code to identify presence of hypertension)

437.8 Other ill-defined cerebrovascular disease — (Use additional code to identify presence of hypertension)

437.9 Unspecified cerebrovascular disease — (Use additional code to identify presence of hypertension) ▽

674.00 Cerebrovascular disorder occurring in pregnancy, childbirth, or the puerperium, unspecified as to episode of care ▽ ♀

674.01 Cerebrovascular disorder, with delivery, with or without mention of antepartum condition ♀

674.02 Cerebrovascular disorder, with delivery, with mention of postpartum complication ♀

674.03 Cerebrovascular disorder, antepartum ♀

674.04 Cerebrovascular disorders in the puerperium, postpartum condition or complication ♀

747.89 Other specified congenital anomaly of circulatory system

997.02 Iatrogenic cerebrovascular infarction or hemorrhage — (Use additional code to identify complications)

ICD-9-CM Procedural

00.40 Procedure on single vessel

00.41 Procedure on two vessels

00.42 Procedure on three vessels

00.43 Procedure on four or more vessels

00.45 Insertion of one vascular stent

00.46 Insertion of two vascular stents

00.47 Insertion of three vascular stents

00.48 Insertion of four or more vascular stents

00.62 Percutaneous angioplasty of intracranial vessel(s)

00.65 Percutaneous insertion of intracranial vascular stent(s)

61640-61642

61640 Balloon dilatation of intracranial vasospasm, percutaneous; initial vessel

61641 each additional vessel in same vascular family (List separately in addition to code for primary procedure)

61642 each additional vessel in different vascular family (List separately in addition to code for primary procedure)

ICD-9-CM Diagnostic

434.00 Cerebral thrombosis without mention of cerebral infarction — (Use additional code, if applicable, to identify status post administration of tPA (rtPA) in a different facility within the last 24 hours prior to admission to current facility: V45.88)

434.01 Cerebral thrombosis with cerebral infarction — (Use additional code, if applicable, to identify status post administration of tPA (rtPA) in a different facility within the last 24 hours prior to admission to current facility: V45.88)

434.10 Cerebral embolism without mention of cerebral infarction — (Use additional code, if applicable, to identify status post administration of tPA (rtPA) in a different facility within the last 24 hours prior to admission to current facility: V45.88)

434.11 Cerebral embolism with cerebral infarction — (Use additional code, if applicable, to identify status post administration of tPA (rtPA) in a different facility within the last 24 hours prior to admission to current facility: V45.88)

434.90 Unspecified cerebral artery occlusion without mention of cerebral infarction — (Use additional code, if applicable, to identify status post administration of tPA (rtPA) in a different facility within the last 24 hours prior to admission to current facility: V45.88) ▽

434.91 Unspecified cerebral artery occlusion with cerebral infarction — (Use additional code, if applicable, to identify status post administration of tPA (rtPA) in a different facility within the last 24 hours prior to admission to current facility: V45.88) ▽

435.0 Basilar artery syndrome — (Use additional code to identify presence of hypertension)

435.8 Other specified transient cerebral ischemias — (Use additional code to identify presence of hypertension)

435.9 Unspecified transient cerebral ischemia — (Use additional code to identify presence of hypertension) ▽

436 Acute, but ill-defined, cerebrovascular disease — (Use additional code to identify presence of hypertension) ▽

437.0 Cerebral atherosclerosis — (Use additional code to identify presence of hypertension)

437.1 Other generalized ischemic cerebrovascular disease — (Use additional code to identify presence of hypertension)

437.9 Unspecified cerebrovascular disease — (Use additional code to identify presence of hypertension) ▽

674.00 Cerebrovascular disorder occurring in pregnancy, childbirth, or the puerperium, unspecified as to episode of care ▽ ♀

674.01 Cerebrovascular disorder, with delivery, with or without mention of antepartum condition ♀

674.02 Cerebrovascular disorder, with delivery, with mention of postpartum complication ♀

674.03 Cerebrovascular disorder, antepartum ♀

674.04 Cerebrovascular disorders in the puerperium, postpartum condition or complication ♀

747.89 Other specified congenital anomaly of circulatory system

997.02 Iatrogenic cerebrovascular infarction or hemorrhage — (Use additional code to identify complications)

ICD-9-CM Procedural

00.62 Percutaneous angioplasty of intracranial vessel(s)

61680-61682

61680 Surgery of intracranial arteriovenous malformation; supratentorial, simple

61682 supratentorial, complex

ICD-9-CM Diagnostic

228.02 Hemangioma of intracranial structures

437.3 Cerebral aneurysm, nonruptured — (Use additional code to identify presence of hypertension)

437.8 Other ill-defined cerebrovascular disease — (Use additional code to identify presence of hypertension)

747.81 Congenital anomaly of cerebrovascular system

ICD-9-CM Procedural

38.31 Resection of intracranial vessels with anastomosis

38.41 Resection of intracranial vessels with replacement

61684-61686

61684 Surgery of intracranial arteriovenous malformation; infratentorial, simple

61686 infratentorial, complex

ICD-9-CM Diagnostic

228.02 Hemangioma of intracranial structures

437.3 Cerebral aneurysm, nonruptured — (Use additional code to identify presence of hypertension)

437.8 Other ill-defined cerebrovascular disease — (Use additional code to identify presence of hypertension)

747.81 Congenital anomaly of cerebrovascular system

ICD-9-CM Procedural

38.31 Resection of intracranial vessels with anastomosis
38.41 Resection of intracranial vessels with replacement
38.42 Resection of other vessels of head and neck with replacement

61690-61692

61690 Surgery of intracranial arteriovenous malformation; dural, simple
61692 dural, complex

ICD-9-CM Diagnostic

228.02 Hemangioma of intracranial structures
437.8 Other ill-defined cerebrovascular disease — (Use additional code to identify presence of hypertension)
747.81 Congenital anomaly of cerebrovascular system
900.9 Injury to unspecified blood vessel of head and neck ▽

ICD-9-CM Procedural

02.13 Ligation of meningeal vessel
38.31 Resection of intracranial vessels with anastomosis
38.41 Resection of intracranial vessels with replacement
38.42 Resection of other vessels of head and neck with replacement

61697-61698

61697 Surgery of complex intracranial aneurysm, intracranial approach; carotid circulation
61698 vertebrobasilar circulation

ICD-9-CM Diagnostic

437.3 Cerebral aneurysm, nonruptured — (Use additional code to identify presence of hypertension)
747.81 Congenital anomaly of cerebrovascular system
900.01 Common carotid artery injury
900.82 Injury to multiple blood vessels of head and neck
900.89 Injury to other specified blood vessels of head and neck

ICD-9-CM Procedural

38.31 Resection of intracranial vessels with anastomosis
38.41 Resection of intracranial vessels with replacement

61700

61700 Surgery of simple intracranial aneurysm, intracranial approach; carotid circulation

ICD-9-CM Diagnostic

437.3 Cerebral aneurysm, nonruptured — (Use additional code to identify presence of hypertension)
747.81 Congenital anomaly of cerebrovascular system
900.01 Common carotid artery injury
900.82 Injury to multiple blood vessels of head and neck

ICD-9-CM Procedural

38.31 Resection of intracranial vessels with anastomosis
38.41 Resection of intracranial vessels with replacement

61702

61702 Surgery of simple intracranial aneurysm, intracranial approach; vertebrobasilar circulation

ICD-9-CM Diagnostic

437.3 Cerebral aneurysm, nonruptured — (Use additional code to identify presence of hypertension)
747.81 Congenital anomaly of cerebrovascular system
900.89 Injury to other specified blood vessels of head and neck

ICD-9-CM Procedural

38.31 Resection of intracranial vessels with anastomosis
38.41 Resection of intracranial vessels with replacement

61703

61703 Surgery of intracranial aneurysm, cervical approach by application of occluding clamp to cervical carotid artery (Selverstone-Crutchfield type)

ICD-9-CM Diagnostic

437.3 Cerebral aneurysm, nonruptured — (Use additional code to identify presence of hypertension)
747.81 Congenital anomaly of cerebrovascular system

ICD-9-CM Procedural

38.31 Resection of intracranial vessels with anastomosis
38.32 Resection of other vessels of head and neck with anastomosis
38.81 Other surgical occlusion of intracranial vessels

61705-61710

61705 Surgery of aneurysm, vascular malformation or carotid-cavernous fistula; by intracranial and cervical occlusion of carotid artery
61708 by intracranial electrothrombosis
61710 by intra-arterial embolization, injection procedure, or balloon catheter

ICD-9-CM Diagnostic

437.3 Cerebral aneurysm, nonruptured — (Use additional code to identify presence of hypertension)
442.81 Aneurysm of artery of neck
443.21 Dissection of carotid artery
747.69 Congenital anomaly of other specified site of peripheral vascular system
747.81 Congenital anomaly of cerebrovascular system
853.00 Other and unspecified intracranial hemorrhage following injury, without mention of open intracranial wound, unspecified state of consciousness ▽
900.82 Injury to multiple blood vessels of head and neck

ICD-9-CM Procedural

38.31 Resection of intracranial vessels with anastomosis
38.32 Resection of other vessels of head and neck with anastomosis
38.81 Other surgical occlusion of intracranial vessels

61711

61711 Anastomosis, arterial, extracranial-intracranial (eg, middle cerebral/cortical) arteries

ICD-9-CM Diagnostic

433.10 Occlusion and stenosis of carotid artery without mention of cerebral infarction — (Use additional code, if applicable, to identify status post administration of tPA (rtPA) in a different facility within the last 24 hours prior to admission to current facility: V45.88)
437.0 Cerebral atherosclerosis — (Use additional code to identify presence of hypertension)
437.3 Cerebral aneurysm, nonruptured — (Use additional code to identify presence of hypertension)
442.9 Other aneurysm of unspecified site ▽
747.81 Congenital anomaly of cerebrovascular system

ICD-9-CM Procedural

38.31 Resection of intracranial vessels with anastomosis
38.32 Resection of other vessels of head and neck with anastomosis

61720-61735

61720 Creation of lesion by stereotactic method, including burr hole(s) and localizing and recording techniques, single or multiple stages; globus pallidus or thalamus
61735 subcortical structure(s) other than globus pallidus or thalamus

ICD-9-CM Diagnostic

239.6 Neoplasm of unspecified nature of brain
300.3 Obsessive-compulsive disorders

332.0 Paralysis agitans
333.0 Other degenerative diseases of the basal ganglia
333.5 Other choreas — (Use additional E code to identify drug, if drug-induced)
340 Multiple sclerosis
343.1 Hemiplegic infantile cerebral palsy
729.2 Unspecified neuralgia, neuritis, and radiculitis
782.0 Disturbance of skin sensation
854.00 Intracranial injury of other and unspecified nature, without mention of open intracranial wound, unspecified state of consciousness
854.19 Intracranial injury of other and unspecified nature, with open intracranial wound, with unspecified concussion

ICD-9-CM Procedural

01.39 Other incision of brain
01.41 Operations on thalamus
01.42 Operations on globus pallidus
07.61 Partial excision of pituitary gland, transfrontal approach

61750-61751

61750 Stereotactic biopsy, aspiration, or excision, including burr hole(s), for intracranial lesion;
61751 with computed tomography and/or magnetic resonance guidance

ICD-9-CM Diagnostic

191.1 Malignant neoplasm of frontal lobe of brain
191.2 Malignant neoplasm of temporal lobe of brain
191.3 Malignant neoplasm of parietal lobe of brain
191.4 Malignant neoplasm of occipital lobe of brain
191.7 Malignant neoplasm of brain stem
191.9 Malignant neoplasm of brain, unspecified site
198.3 Secondary malignant neoplasm of brain and spinal cord
225.0 Benign neoplasm of brain
237.5 Neoplasm of uncertain behavior of brain and spinal cord
239.6 Neoplasm of unspecified nature of brain
324.0 Intracranial abscess
330.0 Leukodystrophy — (Use additional code to identify associated intellectual disabilities)
340 Multiple sclerosis
431 Intracerebral hemorrhage — (Use additional code to identify presence of hypertension)

ICD-9-CM Procedural

01.09 Other cranial puncture
01.13 Closed (percutaneous) (needle) biopsy of brain
87.03 Computerized axial tomography of head
88.91 Magnetic resonance imaging of brain and brain stem
88.96 Other intraoperative magnetic resonance imaging
92.30 Stereotactic radiosurgery, not otherwise specified

61760

61760 Stereotactic implantation of depth electrodes into the cerebrum for long-term seizure monitoring

ICD-9-CM Diagnostic

345.10 Generalized convulsive epilepsy without mention of intractable epilepsy
345.11 Generalized convulsive epilepsy with intractable epilepsy
345.3 Epileptic grand mal status
345.40 Localization-related (focal) (partial) epilepsy and epileptic syndromes with complex partial seizures, without mention of intractable epilepsy
345.41 Localization-related (focal) (partial) epilepsy and epileptic syndromes with complex partial seizures, with intractable epilepsy
345.80 Other forms of epilepsy and recurrent seizures, without mention of intractable epilepsy
345.81 Other forms of epilepsy and recurrent seizures, with intractable epilepsy

ICD-9-CM Procedural

02.93 Implantation or replacement of intracranial neurostimulator lead(s)

61770

61770 Stereotactic localization, including burr hole(s), with insertion of catheter(s) or probe(s) for placement of radiation source

ICD-9-CM Diagnostic

191.0 Malignant neoplasm of cerebrum, except lobes and ventricles
191.1 Malignant neoplasm of frontal lobe of brain
191.2 Malignant neoplasm of temporal lobe of brain
191.3 Malignant neoplasm of parietal lobe of brain
191.4 Malignant neoplasm of occipital lobe of brain
191.5 Malignant neoplasm of ventricles of brain
191.6 Malignant neoplasm of cerebellum NOS
191.7 Malignant neoplasm of brain stem
191.8 Malignant neoplasm of other parts of brain
194.3 Malignant neoplasm of pituitary gland and craniopharyngeal duct
198.3 Secondary malignant neoplasm of brain and spinal cord
198.89 Secondary malignant neoplasm of other specified sites
234.8 Carcinoma in situ of other specified sites
237.0 Neoplasm of uncertain behavior of pituitary gland and craniopharyngeal duct — (Use additional code to identify any functional activity)

ICD-9-CM Procedural

01.24 Other craniotomy
01.28 Placement of intracerebral catheter(s) via burr hole(s)
87.03 Computerized axial tomography of head
93.59 Other immobilization, pressure, and attention to wound

61781-61783

61781 Stereotactic computer-assisted (navigational) procedure; cranial, intradural (List separately in addition to code for primary procedure)
61782 cranial, extradural (List separately in addition to code for primary procedure)
61783 spinal (List separately in addition to code for primary procedure)

ICD-9-CM Diagnostic

The ICD-9-CM diagnostic code(s) would be the same as the actual procedure performed because these are in-addition-to codes.

ICD-9-CM Procedural

00.31 Computer assisted surgery with CT/CTA
00.32 Computer assisted surgery with MR/MRA
00.33 Computer assisted surgery with fluoroscopy
00.34 Imageless computer assisted surgery
00.35 Computer assisted surgery with multiple datasets
00.39 Other computer assisted surgery

61790-61791

61790 Creation of lesion by stereotactic method, percutaneous, by neurolytic agent (eg, alcohol, thermal, electrical, radiofrequency); gasserian ganglion
61791 trigeminal medullary tract

ICD-9-CM Diagnostic

192.0 Malignant neoplasm of cranial nerves
195.0 Malignant neoplasm of head, face, and neck
198.4 Secondary malignant neoplasm of other parts of nervous system
350.1 Trigeminal neuralgia
350.2 Atypical face pain
350.8 Other specified trigeminal nerve disorders

ICD-9-CM Procedural

04.05 Gasserian ganglionectomy

04.2 Destruction of cranial and peripheral nerves

61796-61797

61796 Stereotactic radiosurgery (particle beam, gamma ray, or linear accelerator); 1 simple cranial lesion

61797 each additional cranial lesion, simple (List separately in addition to code for primary procedure)

ICD-9-CM Diagnostic

191.0 Malignant neoplasm of cerebrum, except lobes and ventricles
191.1 Malignant neoplasm of frontal lobe of brain
191.2 Malignant neoplasm of temporal lobe of brain
191.3 Malignant neoplasm of parietal lobe of brain
191.4 Malignant neoplasm of occipital lobe of brain
191.5 Malignant neoplasm of ventricles of brain
191.6 Malignant neoplasm of cerebellum NOS
191.7 Malignant neoplasm of brain stem
192.1 Malignant neoplasm of cerebral meninges
194.3 Malignant neoplasm of pituitary gland and craniopharyngeal duct
198.3 Secondary malignant neoplasm of brain and spinal cord
225.0 Benign neoplasm of brain
225.1 Benign neoplasm of cranial nerves
225.2 Benign neoplasm of cerebral meninges
227.3 Benign neoplasm of pituitary gland and craniopharyngeal duct (pouch) — (Use additional code to identify any functional activity)
237.0 Neoplasm of uncertain behavior of pituitary gland and craniopharyngeal duct — (Use additional code to identify any functional activity)
237.5 Neoplasm of uncertain behavior of brain and spinal cord
239.6 Neoplasm of unspecified nature of brain

ICD-9-CM Procedural

92.31 Single source photon radiosurgery
92.32 Multi-source photon radiosurgery
92.33 Particulate radiosurgery

61798-61799

61798 Stereotactic radiosurgery (particle beam, gamma ray, or linear accelerator); 1 complex cranial lesion

61799 each additional cranial lesion, complex (List separately in addition to code for primary procedure)

ICD-9-CM Diagnostic

191.0 Malignant neoplasm of cerebrum, except lobes and ventricles
191.1 Malignant neoplasm of frontal lobe of brain
191.2 Malignant neoplasm of temporal lobe of brain
191.3 Malignant neoplasm of parietal lobe of brain
191.4 Malignant neoplasm of occipital lobe of brain
191.5 Malignant neoplasm of ventricles of brain
191.6 Malignant neoplasm of cerebellum NOS
191.7 Malignant neoplasm of brain stem
192.1 Malignant neoplasm of cerebral meninges
194.3 Malignant neoplasm of pituitary gland and craniopharyngeal duct
198.3 Secondary malignant neoplasm of brain and spinal cord
225.0 Benign neoplasm of brain
225.1 Benign neoplasm of cranial nerves
225.2 Benign neoplasm of cerebral meninges
227.3 Benign neoplasm of pituitary gland and craniopharyngeal duct (pouch) — (Use additional code to identify any functional activity)
237.0 Neoplasm of uncertain behavior of pituitary gland and craniopharyngeal duct — (Use additional code to identify any functional activity)
237.5 Neoplasm of uncertain behavior of brain and spinal cord
239.6 Neoplasm of unspecified nature of brain

ICD-9-CM Procedural

92.31 Single source photon radiosurgery
92.32 Multi-source photon radiosurgery
92.33 Particulate radiosurgery

61800

61800 Application of stereotactic headframe for stereotactic radiosurgery (List separately in addition to code for primary procedure)

ICD-9-CM Diagnostic

The ICD-9-CM diagnostic code(s) would be the same as the actual procedure performed because these are in-addition-to codes.

ICD-9-CM Procedural

93.59 Other immobilization, pressure, and attention to wound

61850

61850 Twist drill or burr hole(s) for implantation of neurostimulator electrodes, cortical

ICD-9-CM Diagnostic

296.33 Major depressive disorder, recurrent episode, severe, without mention of psychotic behavior — (Use additional code to identify any associated physical disease, injury, or condition affecting the brain with psychoses classifiable to 295-298)
300.3 Obsessive-compulsive disorders
345.11 Generalized convulsive epilepsy with intractable epilepsy
350.2 Atypical face pain
723.1 Cervicalgia
729.2 Unspecified neuralgia, neuritis, and radiculitis ▽
782.0 Disturbance of skin sensation
784.0 Headache

ICD-9-CM Procedural

02.93 Implantation or replacement of intracranial neurostimulator lead(s)

61860

61860 Craniectomy or craniotomy for implantation of neurostimulator electrodes, cerebral, cortical

ICD-9-CM Diagnostic

296.33 Major depressive disorder, recurrent episode, severe, without mention of psychotic behavior — (Use additional code to identify any associated physical disease, injury, or condition affecting the brain with psychoses classifiable to 295-298)
300.3 Obsessive-compulsive disorders
307.48 Repetitive intrusions of sleep
343.3 Monoplegic infantile cerebral palsy
344.40 Monoplegia of upper limb affecting unspecified side ▽
344.41 Monoplegia of upper limb affecting dominant side
344.42 Monoplegia of upper limb affecting nondominant side
345.11 Generalized convulsive epilepsy with intractable epilepsy
345.40 Localization-related (focal) (partial) epilepsy and epileptic syndromes with complex partial seizures, without mention of intractable epilepsy
346.01 Migraine with aura, with intractable migraine, so stated, without mention of status migrainosus
346.02 Migraine with aura, without mention of intractable migraine with status migrainosus
346.03 Migraine with aura, with intractable migraine, so stated, with status migrainosus
346.11 Migraine without aura, with intractable migraine, so stated, without mention of status migrainosus
346.12 Migraine without aura, without mention of intractable migraine with status migrainosus
346.13 Migraine without aura, with intractable migraine, so stated, with status migrainosus
346.20 Variants of migraine, not elsewhere classified, without mention of intractable migraine without mention of status migrainosus

346.50 Persistent migraine aura without cerebral infarction, without mention of intractable migraine without mention of status migrainosus
346.51 Persistent migraine aura without cerebral infarction, with intractable migraine, so stated, without mention of status migrainosus
346.52 Persistent migraine aura without cerebral infarction, without mention of intractable migraine with status migrainosus
346.53 Persistent migraine aura without cerebral infarction, with intractable migraine, so stated, with status migrainosus
346.60 Persistent migraine aura with cerebral infarction, without mention of intractable migraine without mention of status migrainosus
346.61 Persistent migraine aura with cerebral infarction, with intractable migraine, so stated, without mention of status migrainosus
346.62 Persistent migraine aura with cerebral infarction, without mention of intractable migraine with status migrainosus
348.1 Anoxic brain damage — (Use additional E code to identify cause)
350.1 Trigeminal neuralgia
350.2 Atypical face pain
433.21 Occlusion and stenosis of vertebral artery with cerebral infarction — (Use additional code, if applicable, to identify status post administration of tPA (rtPA) in a different facility within the last 24 hours prior to admission to current facility: V45.88)
723.1 Cervicalgia
729.2 Unspecified neuralgia, neuritis, and radiculitis
782.4 Jaundice, unspecified, not of newborn
784.0 Headache

ICD-9-CM Procedural

02.93 Implantation or replacement of intracranial neurostimulator lead(s)

61863-61864

61863 Twist drill, burr hole, craniotomy, or craniectomy with stereotactic implantation of neurostimulator electrode array in subcortical site (eg, thalamus, globus pallidus, subthalamic nucleus, periventricular, periaqueductal gray), without use of intraoperative microelectrode recording; first array
61864 each additional array (List separately in addition to primary procedure)

ICD-9-CM Diagnostic

296.33 Major depressive disorder, recurrent episode, severe, without mention of psychotic behavior — (Use additional code to identify any associated physical disease, injury, or condition affecting the brain with psychoses classifiable to 295-298)
300.3 Obsessive-compulsive disorders
307.48 Repetitive intrusions of sleep
332.0 Paralysis agitans
333.1 Essential and other specified forms of tremor — (Use additional E code to identify drug, if drug-induced)
343.3 Monoplegic infantile cerebral palsy
344.41 Monoplegia of upper limb affecting dominant side
344.42 Monoplegia of upper limb affecting nondominant side
345.11 Generalized convulsive epilepsy with intractable epilepsy
346.01 Migraine with aura, with intractable migraine, so stated, without mention of status migrainosus
346.02 Migraine with aura, without mention of intractable migraine with status migrainosus
346.03 Migraine with aura, with intractable migraine, so stated, with status migrainosus
346.11 Migraine without aura, with intractable migraine, so stated, without mention of status migrainosus
346.12 Migraine without aura, without mention of intractable migraine with status migrainosus
346.13 Migraine without aura, with intractable migraine, so stated, with status migrainosus
346.50 Persistent migraine aura without cerebral infarction, without mention of intractable migraine without mention of status migrainosus
346.51 Persistent migraine aura without cerebral infarction, with intractable migraine, so stated, without mention of status migrainosus
346.52 Persistent migraine aura without cerebral infarction, without mention of intractable migraine with status migrainosus
346.53 Persistent migraine aura without cerebral infarction, with intractable migraine, so stated, with status migrainosus
346.60 Persistent migraine aura with cerebral infarction, without mention of intractable migraine without mention of status migrainosus
346.61 Persistent migraine aura with cerebral infarction, with intractable migraine, so stated, without mention of status migrainosus
346.62 Persistent migraine aura with cerebral infarction, without mention of intractable migraine with status migrainosus
346.63 Persistent migraine aura with cerebral infarction, with intractable migraine, so stated, with status migrainosus
348.1 Anoxic brain damage — (Use additional E code to identify cause)
350.1 Trigeminal neuralgia

ICD-9-CM Procedural

02.93 Implantation or replacement of intracranial neurostimulator lead(s)

61867-61868

61867 Twist drill, burr hole, craniotomy, or craniectomy with stereotactic implantation of neurostimulator electrode array in subcortical site (eg, thalamus, globus pallidus, subthalamic nucleus, periventricular, periaqueductal gray), with use of intraoperative microelectrode recording; first array
61868 each additional array (List separately in addition to primary procedure)

ICD-9-CM Diagnostic

296.33 Major depressive disorder, recurrent episode, severe, without mention of psychotic behavior — (Use additional code to identify any associated physical disease, injury, or condition affecting the brain with psychoses classifiable to 295-298)
300.3 Obsessive-compulsive disorders
307.48 Repetitive intrusions of sleep
332.0 Paralysis agitans
333.1 Essential and other specified forms of tremor — (Use additional E code to identify drug, if drug-induced)
343.3 Monoplegic infantile cerebral palsy
344.41 Monoplegia of upper limb affecting dominant side
344.42 Monoplegia of upper limb affecting nondominant side
345.11 Generalized convulsive epilepsy with intractable epilepsy
346.01 Migraine with aura, with intractable migraine, so stated, without mention of status migrainosus
346.02 Migraine with aura, without mention of intractable migraine with status migrainosus
346.03 Migraine with aura, with intractable migraine, so stated, with status migrainosus
346.11 Migraine without aura, with intractable migraine, so stated, without mention of status migrainosus
346.12 Migraine without aura, without mention of intractable migraine with status migrainosus
346.13 Migraine without aura, with intractable migraine, so stated, with status migrainosus
346.50 Persistent migraine aura without cerebral infarction, without mention of intractable migraine without mention of status migrainosus
346.51 Persistent migraine aura without cerebral infarction, with intractable migraine, so stated, without mention of status migrainosus
346.52 Persistent migraine aura without cerebral infarction, without mention of intractable migraine with status migrainosus
346.53 Persistent migraine aura without cerebral infarction, with intractable migraine, so stated, with status migrainosus
346.60 Persistent migraine aura with cerebral infarction, without mention of intractable migraine without mention of status migrainosus
346.61 Persistent migraine aura with cerebral infarction, with intractable migraine, so stated, without mention of status migrainosus
346.62 Persistent migraine aura with cerebral infarction, without mention of intractable migraine with status migrainosus
346.63 Persistent migraine aura with cerebral infarction, with intractable migraine, so stated, with status migrainosus
348.1 Anoxic brain damage — (Use additional E code to identify cause)
350.1 Trigeminal neuralgia

ICD-9-CM Procedural

02.93 Implantation or replacement of intracranial neurostimulator lead(s)

61870-61875

61870 Craniectomy for implantation of neurostimulator electrodes, cerebellar; cortical
61875 subcortical

ICD-9-CM Diagnostic

332.0 Paralysis agitans
333.1 Essential and other specified forms of tremor — (Use additional E code to identify drug, if drug-induced)
339.00 Cluster headache syndrome, unspecified
339.01 Episodic cluster headache
339.02 Chronic cluster headache
343.3 Monoplegic infantile cerebral palsy
344.41 Monoplegia of upper limb affecting dominant side
344.42 Monoplegia of upper limb affecting nondominant side
345.11 Generalized convulsive epilepsy with intractable epilepsy
346.01 Migraine with aura, with intractable migraine, so stated, without mention of status migrainosus
346.02 Migraine with aura, without mention of intractable migraine with status migrainosus
346.03 Migraine with aura, with intractable migraine, so stated, with status migrainosus
346.11 Migraine without aura, with intractable migraine, so stated, without mention of status migrainosus
346.12 Migraine without aura, without mention of intractable migraine with status migrainosus
346.13 Migraine without aura, with intractable migraine, so stated, with status migrainosus
346.20 Variants of migraine, not elsewhere classified, without mention of intractable migraine without mention of status migrainosus
346.50 Persistent migraine aura without cerebral infarction, without mention of intractable migraine without mention of status migrainosus
346.51 Persistent migraine aura without cerebral infarction, with intractable migraine, so stated, without mention of status migrainosus
346.52 Persistent migraine aura without cerebral infarction, without mention of intractable migraine with status migrainosus
346.53 Persistent migraine aura without cerebral infarction, with intractable migraine, so stated, with status migrainosus
346.60 Persistent migraine aura with cerebral infarction, without mention of intractable migraine without mention of status migrainosus
346.61 Persistent migraine aura with cerebral infarction, with intractable migraine, so stated, without mention of status migrainosus
346.62 Persistent migraine aura with cerebral infarction, without mention of intractable migraine with status migrainosus
346.63 Persistent migraine aura with cerebral infarction, with intractable migraine, so stated, with status migrainosus
350.1 Trigeminal neuralgia
350.2 Atypical face pain
433.21 Occlusion and stenosis of vertebral artery with cerebral infarction — (Use additional code, if applicable, to identify status post administration of tPA (rtPA) in a different facility within the last 24 hours prior to admission to current facility: V45.88)

ICD-9-CM Procedural

02.93 Implantation or replacement of intracranial neurostimulator lead(s)

61880

61880 Revision or removal of intracranial neurostimulator electrodes

ICD-9-CM Diagnostic

307.81 Tension headache
307.89 Other pain disorder related to psychological factors — (Code first to type or site of pain)
332.0 Paralysis agitans
345.10 Generalized convulsive epilepsy without mention of intractable epilepsy
345.2 Epileptic petit mal status
345.3 Epileptic grand mal status
345.40 Localization-related (focal) (partial) epilepsy and epileptic syndromes with complex partial seizures, without mention of intractable epilepsy
350.1 Trigeminal neuralgia
996.2 Mechanical complication of nervous system device, implant, and graft
996.63 Infection and inflammatory reaction due to nervous system device, implant, and graft — (Use additional code to identify specified infections)
996.75 Other complications due to nervous system device, implant, and graft — (Use additional code to identify complication: 338.18-338.19, 338.28-338.29)
998.51 Infected postoperative seroma — (Use additional code to identify organism)
998.59 Other postoperative infection — (Use additional code to identify infection)
V53.02 Neuropacemaker (brain) (peripheral nerve) (spinal cord)

ICD-9-CM Procedural

01.22 Removal of intracranial neurostimulator lead(s)
02.99 Other operations on skull, brain, and cerebral meninges

61885-61886

61885 Insertion or replacement of cranial neurostimulator pulse generator or receiver, direct or inductive coupling; with connection to a single electrode array
61886 with connection to 2 or more electrode arrays

ICD-9-CM Diagnostic

296.33 Major depressive disorder, recurrent episode, severe, without mention of psychotic behavior — (Use additional code to identify any associated physical disease, injury, or condition affecting the brain with psychoses classifiable to 295-298)
300.3 Obsessive-compulsive disorders
332.0 Paralysis agitans
333.1 Essential and other specified forms of tremor — (Use additional E code to identify drug, if drug-induced)
345.01 Generalized nonconvulsive epilepsy with intractable epilepsy
345.11 Generalized convulsive epilepsy with intractable epilepsy
345.41 Localization-related (focal) (partial) epilepsy and epileptic syndromes with complex partial seizures, with intractable epilepsy
345.51 Localization-related (focal) (partial) epilepsy and epileptic syndromes with simple partial seizures, with intractable epilepsy
345.91 Unspecified epilepsy with intractable epilepsy
350.2 Atypical face pain
723.1 Cervicalgia
729.2 Unspecified neuralgia, neuritis, and radiculitis
780.33 Post traumatic seizures
780.39 Other convulsions
996.2 Mechanical complication of nervous system device, implant, and graft
996.63 Infection and inflammatory reaction due to nervous system device, implant, and graft — (Use additional code to identify specified infections)
996.75 Other complications due to nervous system device, implant, and graft — (Use additional code to identify complication: 338.18-338.19, 338.28-338.29)
997.00 Unspecified nervous system complication — (Use additional code to identify complications)

ICD-9-CM Procedural

01.20 Cranial implantation or replacement of neurostimulator pulse generator
86.94 Insertion or replacement of single array neurostimulator pulse generator, not specified as rechargeable
86.95 Insertion or replacement of multiple array neurostimulator pulse generator, not specified as rechargeable

HCPCS Level II Supplies & Services

C1767 Generator, neurostimulator (implantable), nonrechargeable

61888

61888 Revision or removal of cranial neurostimulator pulse generator or receiver

ICD-9-CM Diagnostic

307.81 Tension headache
307.89 Other pain disorder related to psychological factors — (Code first to type or site of pain)
332.0 Paralysis agitans
345.10 Generalized convulsive epilepsy without mention of intractable epilepsy
345.2 Epileptic petit mal status
345.3 Epileptic grand mal status
350.1 Trigeminal neuralgia
996.2 Mechanical complication of nervous system device, implant, and graft
996.63 Infection and inflammatory reaction due to nervous system device, implant, and graft — (Use additional code to identify specified infections)
996.75 Other complications due to nervous system device, implant, and graft — (Use additional code to identify complication: 338.18-338.19, 338.28-338.29)
998.51 Infected postoperative seroma — (Use additional code to identify organism)
998.59 Other postoperative infection — (Use additional code to identify infection)
V53.02 Neuropacemaker (brain) (peripheral nerve) (spinal cord)

ICD-9-CM Procedural

01.29 Removal of cranial neurostimulator pulse generator
02.99 Other operations on skull, brain, and cerebral meninges
86.05 Incision with removal of foreign body or device from skin and subcutaneous tissue

62000-62010

62000 Elevation of depressed skull fracture; simple, extradural
62005 compound or comminuted, extradural
62010 with repair of dura and/or debridement of brain

ICD-9-CM Diagnostic

800.02 Closed fracture of vault of skull without mention of intracranial injury, brief (less than one hour) loss of consciousness
800.10 Closed fracture of vault of skull with cerebral laceration and contusion, unspecified state of consciousness ▽
800.13 Closed fracture of vault of skull with cerebral laceration and contusion, moderate (1-24 hours) loss of consciousness
800.16 Closed fracture of vault of skull with cerebral laceration and contusion, loss of consciousness of unspecified duration ▽
800.21 Closed fracture of vault of skull with subarachnoid, subdural, and extradural hemorrhage, no loss of consciousness
800.26 Closed fracture of vault of skull with subarachnoid, subdural, and extradural hemorrhage, loss of consciousness of unspecified duration ▽
800.41 Closed fracture of vault of skull with intracranial injury of other and unspecified nature, no loss of consciousness ▽
800.46 Closed fracture of vault of skull with intracranial injury of other and unspecified nature, loss of consciousness of unspecified duration ▽
800.50 Open fracture of vault of skull without mention of intracranial injury, unspecified state of consciousness ▽
800.56 Open fracture of vault of skull without mention of intracranial injury, loss of consciousness of unspecified duration ▽
800.60 Open fracture of vault of skull with cerebral laceration and contusion, unspecified state of consciousness ▽
800.63 Open fracture of vault of skull with cerebral laceration and contusion, moderate (1-24 hours) loss of consciousness
800.65 Open fracture of vault of skull with cerebral laceration and contusion, prolonged (more than 24 hours) loss of consciousness, without return to pre-existing conscious level
800.66 Open fracture of vault of skull with cerebral laceration and contusion, loss of consciousness of unspecified duration ▽
800.76 Open fracture of vault of skull with subarachnoid, subdural, and extradural hemorrhage, loss of consciousness of unspecified duration ▽
801.01 Closed fracture of base of skull without mention of intracranial injury, no loss of consciousness
801.23 Closed fracture of base of skull with subarachnoid, subdural, and extradural hemorrhage, moderate (1-24 hours) loss of consciousness
801.46 Closed fracture of base of skull with intracranial injury of other and unspecified nature, loss of consciousness of unspecified duration ▽
801.50 Open fracture of base of skull without mention of intracranial injury, unspecified state of consciousness ▽
801.51 Open fracture of base of skull without mention of intracranial injury, no loss of consciousness
801.56 Open fracture of base of skull without mention of intracranial injury, loss of consciousness of unspecified duration ▽
801.66 Open fracture of base of skull with cerebral laceration and contusion, loss of consciousness of unspecified duration ▽
801.76 Open fracture of base of skull with subarachnoid, subdural, and extradural hemorrhage, loss of consciousness of unspecified duration ▽
803.11 Other closed skull fracture with cerebral laceration and contusion, no loss of consciousness
803.21 Other closed skull fracture with subarachnoid, subdural, and extradural hemorrhage, no loss of consciousness
803.26 Other closed skull fracture with subarachnoid, subdural, and extradural hemorrhage, loss of consciousness of unspecified duration ▽
803.50 Other open skull fracture without mention of injury, state of consciousness unspecified ▽
803.51 Other open skull fracture without mention of intracranial injury, no loss of consciousness
803.56 Other open skull fracture without mention of intracranial injury, loss of consciousness of unspecified duration ▽
803.61 Other open skull fracture with cerebral laceration and contusion, no loss of consciousness
803.66 Other open skull fracture with cerebral laceration and contusion, loss of consciousness of unspecified duration ▽
804.12 Closed fractures involving skull or face with other bones, with cerebral laceration and contusion, brief (less than one hour) loss of consciousness
804.56 Open fractures involving skull or face with other bones, without mention of intracranial injury, loss of consciousness of unspecified duration ▽
804.66 Open fractures involving skull or face with other bones, with cerebral laceration and contusion, loss of consciousness of unspecified duration ▽

ICD-9-CM Procedural

01.59 Other excision or destruction of lesion or tissue of brain
02.02 Elevation of skull fracture fragments

62100

62100 Craniotomy for repair of dural/cerebrospinal fluid leak, including surgery for rhinorrhea/otorrhea

ICD-9-CM Diagnostic

349.31 Accidental puncture or laceration of dura during a procedure
349.39 Other dural tear
349.81 Cerebrospinal fluid rhinorrhea
388.61 Cerebrospinal fluid otorrhea
800.43 Closed fracture of vault of skull with intracranial injury of other and unspecified nature, moderate (1-24 hours) loss of consciousness ▽
800.56 Open fracture of vault of skull without mention of intracranial injury, loss of consciousness of unspecified duration ▽
800.66 Open fracture of vault of skull with cerebral laceration and contusion, loss of consciousness of unspecified duration ▽
801.22 Closed fracture of base of skull with subarachnoid, subdural, and extradural hemorrhage, brief (less than one hour) loss of consciousness

801.41 Closed fracture of base of skull with intracranial injury of other and unspecified nature, no loss of consciousness ▽
801.46 Closed fracture of base of skull with intracranial injury of other and unspecified nature, loss of consciousness of unspecified duration ▽
997.01 Central nervous system complication — (Use additional code to identify complications)
998.2 Accidental puncture or laceration during procedure

ICD-9-CM Procedural

02.11 Simple suture of dura mater of brain
02.12 Other repair of cerebral meninges

62115-62117

62115 Reduction of craniomegalic skull (eg, treated hydrocephalus); not requiring bone grafts or cranioplasty
62116 with simple cranioplasty
62117 requiring craniotomy and reconstruction with or without bone graft (includes obtaining grafts)

ICD-9-CM Diagnostic

331.3 Communicating hydrocephalus — (Use additional code, where applicable, to identify dementia: 294.10, 294.11)
331.4 Obstructive hydrocephalus — (Use additional code, where applicable, to identify dementia: 294.10, 294.11)
331.5 Idiopathic normal pressure hydrocephalus [INPH] — (Use additional code, where applicable, to identify dementia: 294.10, 294.11)
733.3 Hyperostosis of skull
738.12 Zygomatic hypoplasia
738.19 Other specified acquired deformity of head
741.00 Spina bifida with hydrocephalus, unspecified region ▽
742.3 Congenital hydrocephalus

ICD-9-CM Procedural

02.01 Opening of cranial suture
02.04 Bone graft to skull
02.06 Other cranial osteoplasty

62120-62121

62120 Repair of encephalocele, skull vault, including cranioplasty
62121 Craniotomy for repair of encephalocele, skull base

ICD-9-CM Diagnostic

742.0 Encephalocele
742.3 Congenital hydrocephalus
905.0 Late effect of fracture of skull and face bones

ICD-9-CM Procedural

02.12 Other repair of cerebral meninges

62140-62141

62140 Cranioplasty for skull defect; up to 5 cm diameter
62141 larger than 5 cm diameter

ICD-9-CM Diagnostic

738.11 Zygomatic hyperplasia
740.0 Anencephalus
741.00 Spina bifida with hydrocephalus, unspecified region ▽
742.1 Microcephalus
742.3 Congenital hydrocephalus
754.0 Congenital musculoskeletal deformities of skull, face, and jaw
756.0 Congenital anomalies of skull and face bones
800.65 Open fracture of vault of skull with cerebral laceration and contusion, prolonged (more than 24 hours) loss of consciousness, without return to pre-existing conscious level
800.75 Open fracture of vault of skull with subarachnoid, subdural, and extradural hemorrhage, prolonged (more than 24 hours) loss of consciousness, without return to pre-existing conscious level
905.0 Late effect of fracture of skull and face bones

ICD-9-CM Procedural

02.06 Other cranial osteoplasty

62142

62142 Removal of bone flap or prosthetic plate of skull

ICD-9-CM Diagnostic

170.0 Malignant neoplasm of bones of skull and face, except mandible
738.19 Other specified acquired deformity of head
996.60 Infection and inflammatory reaction due to unspecified device, implant, and graft — (Use additional code to identify specified infections) ▽
996.63 Infection and inflammatory reaction due to nervous system device, implant, and graft — (Use additional code to identify specified infections)

ICD-9-CM Procedural

02.06 Other cranial osteoplasty
02.07 Removal of skull plate

62143

62143 Replacement of bone flap or prosthetic plate of skull

ICD-9-CM Diagnostic

170.0 Malignant neoplasm of bones of skull and face, except mandible
738.19 Other specified acquired deformity of head
800.65 Open fracture of vault of skull with cerebral laceration and contusion, prolonged (more than 24 hours) loss of consciousness, without return to pre-existing conscious level
800.75 Open fracture of vault of skull with subarachnoid, subdural, and extradural hemorrhage, prolonged (more than 24 hours) loss of consciousness, without return to pre-existing conscious level
905.0 Late effect of fracture of skull and face bones
907.0 Late effect of intracranial injury without mention of skull fracture
996.60 Infection and inflammatory reaction due to unspecified device, implant, and graft — (Use additional code to identify specified infections) ▽
996.63 Infection and inflammatory reaction due to nervous system device, implant, and graft — (Use additional code to identify specified infections)

ICD-9-CM Procedural

02.05 Insertion of skull plate
02.06 Other cranial osteoplasty

62145

62145 Cranioplasty for skull defect with reparative brain surgery

ICD-9-CM Diagnostic

170.0 Malignant neoplasm of bones of skull and face, except mandible
738.19 Other specified acquired deformity of head
742.4 Other specified congenital anomalies of brain
756.0 Congenital anomalies of skull and face bones
800.66 Open fracture of vault of skull with cerebral laceration and contusion, loss of consciousness of unspecified duration ▽
801.06 Closed fracture of base of skull without mention of intracranial injury, loss of consciousness of unspecified duration ▽
801.66 Open fracture of base of skull with cerebral laceration and contusion, loss of consciousness of unspecified duration ▽
803.66 Other open skull fracture with cerebral laceration and contusion, loss of consciousness of unspecified duration ▽

ICD-9-CM Procedural

02.06 Other cranial osteoplasty

62146-62147

62146 Cranioplasty with autograft (includes obtaining bone grafts); up to 5 cm diameter
62147 larger than 5 cm diameter

ICD-9-CM Diagnostic

170.0 Malignant neoplasm of bones of skull and face, except mandible
738.19 Other specified acquired deformity of head
742.4 Other specified congenital anomalies of brain
756.0 Congenital anomalies of skull and face bones
800.66 Open fracture of vault of skull with cerebral laceration and contusion, loss of consciousness of unspecified duration
801.06 Closed fracture of base of skull without mention of intracranial injury, loss of consciousness of unspecified duration
801.66 Open fracture of base of skull with cerebral laceration and contusion, loss of consciousness of unspecified duration
803.61 Other open skull fracture with cerebral laceration and contusion, no loss of consciousness
854.06 Intracranial injury of other and unspecified nature, without mention of open intracranial wound, loss of consciousness of unspecified duration

ICD-9-CM Procedural

02.04 Bone graft to skull
02.06 Other cranial osteoplasty

62148

62148 Incision and retrieval of subcutaneous cranial bone graft for cranioplasty (List separately in addition to code for primary procedure)

ICD-9-CM Diagnostic

This is an add-on code. Refer to the corresponding primary procedure code for ICD-9-CM diagnosis code links.

ICD-9-CM Procedural

02.03 Formation of cranial bone flap
02.06 Other cranial osteoplasty

62160

62160 Neuroendoscopy, intracranial, for placement or replacement of ventricular catheter and attachment to shunt system or external drainage (List separately in addition to code for primary procedure)

ICD-9-CM Diagnostic

This is an add-on code. Refer to the corresponding primary procedure code for ICD-9-CM diagnosis code links.

ICD-9-CM Procedural

02.21 Insertion or replacement of external ventricular drain [EVD]
02.31 Ventricular shunt to structure in head and neck
02.32 Ventricular shunt to circulatory system
02.33 Ventricular shunt to thoracic cavity
02.34 Ventricular shunt to abdominal cavity and organs
02.35 Ventricular shunt to urinary system
02.39 Ventricular shunt to extracranial site NEC
02.42 Replacement of ventricular shunt

62161-62162

62161 Neuroendoscopy, intracranial; with dissection of adhesions, fenestration of septum pellucidum or intraventricular cysts (including placement, replacement, or removal of ventricular catheter)
62162 with fenestration or excision of colloid cyst, including placement of external ventricular catheter for drainage

ICD-9-CM Diagnostic

348.0 Cerebral cysts
349.2 Disorders of meninges, not elsewhere classified
742.4 Other specified congenital anomalies of brain

ICD-9-CM Procedural

01.59 Other excision or destruction of lesion or tissue of brain
02.21 Insertion or replacement of external ventricular drain [EVD]

62163

62163 Neuroendoscopy, intracranial; with retrieval of foreign body

ICD-9-CM Diagnostic

851.10 Cortex (cerebral) contusion with open intracranial wound, unspecified state of consciousness
851.11 Cortex (cerebral) contusion with open intracranial wound, no loss of consciousness
851.12 Cortex (cerebral) contusion with open intracranial wound, brief (less than 1 hour) loss of consciousness
851.13 Cortex (cerebral) contusion with open intracranial wound, moderate (1-24 hours) loss of consciousness
851.14 Cortex (cerebral) contusion with open intracranial wound, prolonged (more than 24 hours) loss of consciousness and return to pre-existing conscious level
851.15 Cortex (cerebral) contusion with open intracranial wound, prolonged (more than 24 hours) loss of consciousness, without return to pre-existing conscious level
851.16 Cortex (cerebral) contusion with open intracranial wound, loss of consciousness of unspecified duration
851.19 Cortex (cerebral) contusion with open intracranial wound, unspecified concussion
851.30 Cortex (cerebral) laceration with open intracranial wound, unspecified state of consciousness
851.31 Cortex (cerebral) laceration with open intracranial wound, no loss of consciousness
851.32 Cortex (cerebral) laceration with open intracranial wound, brief (less than 1 hour) loss of consciousness
851.33 Cortex (cerebral) laceration with open intracranial wound, moderate (1-24 hours) loss of consciousness
851.34 Cortex (cerebral) laceration with open intracranial wound, prolonged (more than 24 hours) loss of consciousness and return to pre-existing conscious level
851.35 Cortex (cerebral) laceration with open intracranial wound, prolonged (more than 24 hours) loss of consciousness, without return to pre-existing conscious level
851.36 Cortex (cerebral) laceration with open intracranial wound, loss of consciousness of unspecified duration
851.39 Cortex (cerebral) laceration with open intracranial wound, unspecified concussion — (Use E code(s) to identify the cause and intent of the injury or poisoning: E800-E999)
851.50 Cerebellar or brain stem contusion with open intracranial wound, unspecified state of consciousness
851.51 Cerebellar or brain stem contusion with open intracranial wound, no loss of consciousness
851.52 Cerebellar or brain stem contusion with open intracranial wound, brief (less than 1 hour) loss of consciousness
851.53 Cerebellar or brain stem contusion with open intracranial wound, moderate (1-24 hours) loss of consciousness
851.54 Cerebellar or brain stem contusion with open intracranial wound, prolonged (more than 24 hours) loss of consciousness and return to pre-existing conscious level
851.55 Cerebellar or brain stem contusion with open intracranial wound, prolonged (more than 24 hours) loss of consciousness, without return to pre-existing conscious level

851.56 Cerebellar or brain stem contusion with open intracranial wound, loss of consciousness of unspecified duration

851.59 Cerebellar or brain stem contusion with open intracranial wound, unspecified concussion

851.70 Cerebellar or brain stem laceration with open intracranial wound, state of consciousness unspecified

851.71 Cerebellar or brain stem laceration with open intracranial wound, no loss of consciousness

851.72 Cerebellar or brain stem laceration with open intracranial wound, brief (less than one hour) loss of consciousness

851.73 Cerebellar or brain stem laceration with open intracranial wound, moderate (1-24 hours) loss of consciousness

851.74 Cerebellar or brain stem laceration with open intracranial wound, prolonged (more than 24 hours) loss of consciousness and return to pre-existing conscious level

851.75 Cerebellar or brain stem laceration with open intracranial wound, prolonged (more than 24 hours) loss of consciousness, without return to pre-existing conscious level

851.76 Cerebellar or brain stem laceration with open intracranial wound, loss of consciousness of unspecified duration

851.79 Cerebellar or brain stem laceration with open intracranial wound, unspecified concussion

851.90 Other and unspecified cerebral laceration and contusion, with open intracranial wound, unspecified state of consciousness

851.91 Other and unspecified cerebral laceration and contusion, with open intracranial wound, no loss of consciousness

851.92 Other and unspecified cerebral laceration and contusion, with open intracranial wound, brief (less than 1 hour) loss of consciousness

851.93 Other and unspecified cerebral laceration and contusion, with open intracranial wound, moderate (1-24 hours) loss of consciousness

851.94 Other and unspecified cerebral laceration and contusion, with open intracranial wound, prolonged (more than 24 hours) loss of consciousness and return to pre-existing conscious level

851.95 Other and unspecified cerebral laceration and contusion, with open intracranial wound, prolonged (more than 24 hours) loss of consciousness, without return to pre-existing conscious level

851.96 Other and unspecified cerebral laceration and contusion, with open intracranial wound, loss of consciousness of unspecified duration

851.99 Other and unspecified cerebral laceration and contusion, with open intracranial wound, unspecified concussion

852.10 Subarachnoid hemorrhage following injury, with open intracranial wound, unspecified state of consciousness

852.11 Subarachnoid hemorrhage following injury, with open intracranial wound, no loss of consciousness

852.12 Subarachnoid hemorrhage following injury, with open intracranial wound, brief (less than 1 hour) loss of consciousness

852.13 Subarachnoid hemorrhage following injury, with open intracranial wound, moderate (1-24 hours) loss of consciousness

852.14 Subarachnoid hemorrhage following injury, with open intracranial wound, prolonged (more than 24 hours) loss of consciousness and return to pre-existing conscious level

852.15 Subarachnoid hemorrhage following injury, with open intracranial wound, prolonged (more than 24 hours) loss of consciousness, without return to pre-existing conscious level

852.16 Subarachnoid hemorrhage following injury, with open intracranial wound, loss of consciousness of unspecified duration

852.19 Subarachnoid hemorrhage following injury, with open intracranial wound, unspecified concussion

852.30 Subdural hemorrhage following injury, with open intracranial wound, state of consciousness unspecified

852.31 Subdural hemorrhage following injury, with open intracranial wound, no loss of consciousness

852.32 Subdural hemorrhage following injury, with open intracranial wound, brief (less than 1 hour) loss of consciousness

852.33 Subdural hemorrhage following injury, with open intracranial wound, moderate (1-24 hours) loss of consciousness

852.34 Subdural hemorrhage following injury, with open intracranial wound, prolonged (more than 24 hours) loss of consciousness and return to pre-existing conscious level

852.35 Subdural hemorrhage following injury, with open intracranial wound, prolonged (more than 24 hours) loss of consciousness, without return to pre-existing conscious level

852.36 Subdural hemorrhage following injury, with open intracranial wound, loss of consciousness of unspecified duration

852.39 Subdural hemorrhage following injury, with open intracranial wound, unspecified concussion

852.50 Extradural hemorrhage following injury, with open intracranial wound, state of consciousness unspecified

852.51 Extradural hemorrhage following injury, with open intracranial wound, no loss of consciousness

852.52 Extradural hemorrhage following injury, with open intracranial wound, brief (less than 1 hour) loss of consciousness

852.53 Extradural hemorrhage following injury, with open intracranial wound, moderate (1-24 hours) loss of consciousness

852.54 Extradural hemorrhage following injury, with open intracranial wound, prolonged (more than 24 hours) loss of consciousness and return to pre-existing conscious level

852.55 Extradural hemorrhage following injury, with open intracranial wound, prolonged (more than 24 hours) loss of consciousness, without return to pre-existing conscious level

852.56 Extradural hemorrhage following injury, with open intracranial wound, loss of consciousness of unspecified duration

852.59 Extradural hemorrhage following injury, with open intracranial wound, unspecified concussion

853.10 Other and unspecified intracranial hemorrhage following injury, with open intracranial wound, unspecified state of consciousness

853.11 Other and unspecified intracranial hemorrhage following injury, with open intracranial wound, no loss of consciousness

853.12 Other and unspecified intracranial hemorrhage following injury, with open intracranial wound, brief (less than 1 hour) loss of consciousness

853.13 Other and unspecified intracranial hemorrhage following injury, with open intracranial wound, moderate (1-24 hours) loss of consciousness

853.14 Other and unspecified intracranial hemorrhage following injury, with open intracranial wound, prolonged (more than 24 hours) loss of consciousness and return to pre-existing conscious level

853.15 Other and unspecified intracranial hemorrhage following injury, with open intracranial wound, prolonged (more than 24 hours) loss of consciousness, without return to pre-existing conscious level

853.16 Other and unspecified intracranial hemorrhage following injury, with open intracranial wound, loss of consciousness of unspecified duration

853.19 Other and unspecified intracranial hemorrhage following injury, with open intracranial wound, unspecified concussion

854.10 Intracranial injury of other and unspecified nature, with open intracranial wound, unspecified state of consciousness

854.11 Intracranial injury of other and unspecified nature, with open intracranial wound, no loss of consciousness

854.12 Intracranial injury of other and unspecified nature, with open intracranial wound, brief (less than 1 hour) loss of consciousness

854.13 Intracranial injury of other and unspecified nature, with open intracranial wound, moderate (1-24 hours) loss of consciousness

854.14 Intracranial injury of other and unspecified nature, with open intracranial wound, prolonged (more than 24 hours) loss of consciousness and return to pre-existing conscious level

854.15 Intracranial injury of other and unspecified nature, with open intracranial wound, prolonged (more than 24 hours) loss of consciousness, without return to pre-existing conscious level

854.16 Intracranial injury of other and unspecified nature, with open intracranial wound, loss of consciousness of unspecified duration ▽
854.19 Intracranial injury of other and unspecified nature, with open intracranial wound, with unspecified concussion ▽

ICD-9-CM Procedural
01.24 Other craniotomy
01.39 Other incision of brain

62164
62164 Neuroendoscopy, intracranial; with excision of brain tumor, including placement of external ventricular catheter for drainage

ICD-9-CM Diagnostic
191.0 Malignant neoplasm of cerebrum, except lobes and ventricles
191.1 Malignant neoplasm of frontal lobe of brain
191.2 Malignant neoplasm of temporal lobe of brain
191.3 Malignant neoplasm of parietal lobe of brain
191.4 Malignant neoplasm of occipital lobe of brain
191.5 Malignant neoplasm of ventricles of brain
191.6 Malignant neoplasm of cerebellum NOS
191.7 Malignant neoplasm of brain stem
191.8 Malignant neoplasm of other parts of brain
191.9 Malignant neoplasm of brain, unspecified site ▽
192.0 Malignant neoplasm of cranial nerves
192.1 Malignant neoplasm of cerebral meninges
192.8 Malignant neoplasm of other specified sites of nervous system
198.3 Secondary malignant neoplasm of brain and spinal cord
225.0 Benign neoplasm of brain
225.1 Benign neoplasm of cranial nerves
237.5 Neoplasm of uncertain behavior of brain and spinal cord
239.6 Neoplasm of unspecified nature of brain

ICD-9-CM Procedural
01.59 Other excision or destruction of lesion or tissue of brain
02.21 Insertion or replacement of external ventricular drain [EVD]

62165
62165 Neuroendoscopy, intracranial; with excision of pituitary tumor, transnasal or trans-sphenoidal approach

ICD-9-CM Diagnostic
194.3 Malignant neoplasm of pituitary gland and craniopharyngeal duct
227.3 Benign neoplasm of pituitary gland and craniopharyngeal duct (pouch) — (Use additional code to identify any functional activity)
237.0 Neoplasm of uncertain behavior of pituitary gland and craniopharyngeal duct — (Use additional code to identify any functional activity)
239.7 Neoplasm of unspecified nature of endocrine glands and other parts of nervous system
253.0 Acromegaly and gigantism
253.1 Other and unspecified anterior pituitary hyperfunction ▽
253.2 Panhypopituitarism
253.3 Pituitary dwarfism
253.4 Other anterior pituitary disorders
253.5 Diabetes insipidus
253.6 Other disorders of neurohypophysis
253.7 Iatrogenic pituitary disorders — (Use additional E code to identify cause)
253.8 Other disorders of the pituitary and other syndromes of diencephalohypophyseal origin
253.9 Unspecified disorder of the pituitary gland and its hypothalamic control ▽

ICD-9-CM Procedural
07.62 Partial excision of pituitary gland, transsphenoidal approach
07.63 Partial excision of pituitary gland, unspecified approach
07.68 Total excision of pituitary gland, other specified approach

62180
62180 Ventriculocisternostomy (Torkildsen type operation)

ICD-9-CM Diagnostic
191.5 Malignant neoplasm of ventricles of brain
237.5 Neoplasm of uncertain behavior of brain and spinal cord
331.3 Communicating hydrocephalus — (Use additional code, where applicable, to identify dementia: 294.10, 294.11)
331.4 Obstructive hydrocephalus — (Use additional code, where applicable, to identify dementia: 294.10, 294.11)
331.5 Idiopathic normal pressure hydrocephalus [INPH] — (Use additional code, where applicable, to identify dementia: 294.10, 294.11)
348.2 Benign intracranial hypertension
741.01 Spina bifida with hydrocephalus, cervical region
742.3 Congenital hydrocephalus

ICD-9-CM Procedural
02.22 Intracranial ventricular shunt or anastomosis
02.31 Ventricular shunt to structure in head and neck

62190
62190 Creation of shunt; subarachnoid/subdural-atrial, -jugular, -auricular

ICD-9-CM Diagnostic
331.3 Communicating hydrocephalus — (Use additional code, where applicable, to identify dementia: 294.10, 294.11)
331.4 Obstructive hydrocephalus — (Use additional code, where applicable, to identify dementia: 294.10, 294.11)
331.5 Idiopathic normal pressure hydrocephalus [INPH] — (Use additional code, where applicable, to identify dementia: 294.10, 294.11)
741.01 Spina bifida with hydrocephalus, cervical region
742.3 Congenital hydrocephalus
905.0 Late effect of fracture of skull and face bones

ICD-9-CM Procedural
02.32 Ventricular shunt to circulatory system

62192
62192 Creation of shunt; subarachnoid/subdural-peritoneal, -pleural, other terminus

ICD-9-CM Diagnostic
331.3 Communicating hydrocephalus — (Use additional code, where applicable, to identify dementia: 294.10, 294.11)
331.4 Obstructive hydrocephalus — (Use additional code, where applicable, to identify dementia: 294.10, 294.11)
331.5 Idiopathic normal pressure hydrocephalus [INPH] — (Use additional code, where applicable, to identify dementia: 294.10, 294.11)
741.03 Spina bifida with hydrocephalus, lumbar region
742.3 Congenital hydrocephalus
905.0 Late effect of fracture of skull and face bones

ICD-9-CM Procedural
02.31 Ventricular shunt to structure in head and neck
02.33 Ventricular shunt to thoracic cavity
02.34 Ventricular shunt to abdominal cavity and organs
02.35 Ventricular shunt to urinary system
02.39 Ventricular shunt to extracranial site NEC

62194

62194 Replacement or irrigation, subarachnoid/subdural catheter

ICD-9-CM Diagnostic

331.3 Communicating hydrocephalus — (Use additional code, where applicable, to identify dementia: 294.10, 294.11)

331.4 Obstructive hydrocephalus — (Use additional code, where applicable, to identify dementia: 294.10, 294.11)

331.5 Idiopathic normal pressure hydrocephalus [INPH] — (Use additional code, where applicable, to identify dementia: 294.10, 294.11)

741.03 Spina bifida with hydrocephalus, lumbar region

742.3 Congenital hydrocephalus

905.0 Late effect of fracture of skull and face bones

996.2 Mechanical complication of nervous system device, implant, and graft

996.63 Infection and inflammatory reaction due to nervous system device, implant, and graft — (Use additional code to identify specified infections)

V53.01 Fitting and adjustment of cerebral ventricular (communicating) shunt

ICD-9-CM Procedural

02.41 Irrigation and exploration of ventricular shunt

02.42 Replacement of ventricular shunt

62200-62201

62200 Ventriculocisternostomy, third ventricle;

62201 stereotactic, neuroendoscopic method

ICD-9-CM Diagnostic

331.3 Communicating hydrocephalus — (Use additional code, where applicable, to identify dementia: 294.10, 294.11)

331.4 Obstructive hydrocephalus — (Use additional code, where applicable, to identify dementia: 294.10, 294.11)

331.5 Idiopathic normal pressure hydrocephalus [INPH] — (Use additional code, where applicable, to identify dementia: 294.10, 294.11)

741.01 Spina bifida with hydrocephalus, cervical region

741.03 Spina bifida with hydrocephalus, lumbar region

742.3 Congenital hydrocephalus

772.10 Intraventricular hemorrhage, unspecified grade — (Use additional code(s) to further specify condition)

772.11 Intraventricular hemorrhage, Grade I — (Use additional code(s) to further specify condition)

772.12 Intraventricular hemorrhage, Grade II — (Use additional code(s) to further specify condition)

772.13 Intraventricular hemorrhage, Grade III — (Use additional code(s) to further specify condition)

772.14 Intraventricular hemorrhage, Grade IV — (Use additional code(s) to further specify condition)

996.2 Mechanical complication of nervous system device, implant, and graft

996.63 Infection and inflammatory reaction due to nervous system device, implant, and graft — (Use additional code to identify specified infections)

ICD-9-CM Procedural

02.22 Intracranial ventricular shunt or anastomosis

62220

62220 Creation of shunt; ventriculo-atrial, -jugular, -auricular

ICD-9-CM Diagnostic

225.2 Benign neoplasm of cerebral meninges

331.3 Communicating hydrocephalus — (Use additional code, where applicable, to identify dementia: 294.10, 294.11)

331.4 Obstructive hydrocephalus — (Use additional code, where applicable, to identify dementia: 294.10, 294.11)

331.5 Idiopathic normal pressure hydrocephalus [INPH] — (Use additional code, where applicable, to identify dementia: 294.10, 294.11)

741.03 Spina bifida with hydrocephalus, lumbar region

742.3 Congenital hydrocephalus

907.0 Late effect of intracranial injury without mention of skull fracture

996.2 Mechanical complication of nervous system device, implant, and graft

996.63 Infection and inflammatory reaction due to nervous system device, implant, and graft — (Use additional code to identify specified infections)

ICD-9-CM Procedural

02.31 Ventricular shunt to structure in head and neck

02.32 Ventricular shunt to circulatory system

62223

62223 Creation of shunt; ventriculo-peritoneal, -pleural, other terminus

ICD-9-CM Diagnostic

191.5 Malignant neoplasm of ventricles of brain

191.6 Malignant neoplasm of cerebellum NOS

198.3 Secondary malignant neoplasm of brain and spinal cord

225.0 Benign neoplasm of brain

225.2 Benign neoplasm of cerebral meninges

225.8 Benign neoplasm of other specified sites of nervous system

225.9 Benign neoplasm of nervous system, part unspecified

239.6 Neoplasm of unspecified nature of brain

331.3 Communicating hydrocephalus — (Use additional code, where applicable, to identify dementia: 294.10, 294.11)

331.4 Obstructive hydrocephalus — (Use additional code, where applicable, to identify dementia: 294.10, 294.11)

331.5 Idiopathic normal pressure hydrocephalus [INPH] — (Use additional code, where applicable, to identify dementia: 294.10, 294.11)

348.0 Cerebral cysts

348.2 Benign intracranial hypertension

741.01 Spina bifida with hydrocephalus, cervical region

741.03 Spina bifida with hydrocephalus, lumbar region

742.3 Congenital hydrocephalus

772.10 Intraventricular hemorrhage, unspecified grade — (Use additional code(s) to further specify condition)

772.11 Intraventricular hemorrhage, Grade I — (Use additional code(s) to further specify condition)

772.12 Intraventricular hemorrhage, Grade II — (Use additional code(s) to further specify condition)

772.13 Intraventricular hemorrhage, Grade III — (Use additional code(s) to further specify condition)

772.14 Intraventricular hemorrhage, Grade IV — (Use additional code(s) to further specify condition)

907.0 Late effect of intracranial injury without mention of skull fracture

996.2 Mechanical complication of nervous system device, implant, and graft

ICD-9-CM Procedural

02.33 Ventricular shunt to thoracic cavity

02.34 Ventricular shunt to abdominal cavity and organs

02.35 Ventricular shunt to urinary system

02.39 Ventricular shunt to extracranial site NEC

62225-62230

62225 Replacement or irrigation, ventricular catheter
62230 Replacement or revision of cerebrospinal fluid shunt, obstructed valve, or distal catheter in shunt system

ICD-9-CM Diagnostic

331.3 Communicating hydrocephalus — (Use additional code, where applicable, to identify dementia: 294.10, 294.11)
331.4 Obstructive hydrocephalus — (Use additional code, where applicable, to identify dementia: 294.10, 294.11)
331.5 Idiopathic normal pressure hydrocephalus [INPH] — (Use additional code, where applicable, to identify dementia: 294.10, 294.11)
741.03 Spina bifida with hydrocephalus, lumbar region
742.3 Congenital hydrocephalus
772.10 Intraventricular hemorrhage, unspecified grade — (Use additional code(s) to further specify condition)
772.11 Intraventricular hemorrhage, Grade I — (Use additional code(s) to further specify condition)
772.12 Intraventricular hemorrhage, Grade II — (Use additional code(s) to further specify condition)
772.13 Intraventricular hemorrhage, Grade III — (Use additional code(s) to further specify condition)
772.14 Intraventricular hemorrhage, Grade IV — (Use additional code(s) to further specify condition)
907.0 Late effect of intracranial injury without mention of skull fracture
996.2 Mechanical complication of nervous system device, implant, and graft
996.63 Infection and inflammatory reaction due to nervous system device, implant, and graft — (Use additional code to identify specified infections)
996.75 Other complications due to nervous system device, implant, and graft — (Use additional code to identify complication: 338.18-338.19, 338.28-338.29)
V53.01 Fitting and adjustment of cerebral ventricular (communicating) shunt

ICD-9-CM Procedural

02.21 Insertion or replacement of external ventricular drain [EVD]
02.41 Irrigation and exploration of ventricular shunt
02.42 Replacement of ventricular shunt

62252

62252 Reprogramming of programmable cerebrospinal shunt

ICD-9-CM Diagnostic

331.3 Communicating hydrocephalus — (Use additional code, where applicable, to identify dementia: 294.10, 294.11)
331.4 Obstructive hydrocephalus — (Use additional code, where applicable, to identify dementia: 294.10, 294.11)
331.5 Idiopathic normal pressure hydrocephalus [INPH] — (Use additional code, where applicable, to identify dementia: 294.10, 294.11)
741.03 Spina bifida with hydrocephalus, lumbar region
742.3 Congenital hydrocephalus
772.10 Intraventricular hemorrhage, unspecified grade — (Use additional code(s) to further specify condition)
772.11 Intraventricular hemorrhage, Grade I — (Use additional code(s) to further specify condition)
772.12 Intraventricular hemorrhage, Grade II — (Use additional code(s) to further specify condition)
772.13 Intraventricular hemorrhage, Grade III — (Use additional code(s) to further specify condition)
772.14 Intraventricular hemorrhage, Grade IV — (Use additional code(s) to further specify condition)
907.0 Late effect of intracranial injury without mention of skull fracture
V53.01 Fitting and adjustment of cerebral ventricular (communicating) shunt

ICD-9-CM Procedural

02.41 Irrigation and exploration of ventricular shunt

62256-62258

62256 Removal of complete cerebrospinal fluid shunt system; without replacement
62258 with replacement by similar or other shunt at same operation

ICD-9-CM Diagnostic

331.3 Communicating hydrocephalus — (Use additional code, where applicable, to identify dementia: 294.10, 294.11)
331.4 Obstructive hydrocephalus — (Use additional code, where applicable, to identify dementia: 294.10, 294.11)
331.5 Idiopathic normal pressure hydrocephalus [INPH] — (Use additional code, where applicable, to identify dementia: 294.10, 294.11)
348.2 Benign intracranial hypertension
741.01 Spina bifida with hydrocephalus, cervical region
741.03 Spina bifida with hydrocephalus, lumbar region
742.3 Congenital hydrocephalus
772.10 Intraventricular hemorrhage, unspecified grade — (Use additional code(s) to further specify condition)
772.11 Intraventricular hemorrhage, Grade I — (Use additional code(s) to further specify condition)
772.12 Intraventricular hemorrhage, Grade II — (Use additional code(s) to further specify condition)
772.13 Intraventricular hemorrhage, Grade III — (Use additional code(s) to further specify condition)
772.14 Intraventricular hemorrhage, Grade IV — (Use additional code(s) to further specify condition)
996.2 Mechanical complication of nervous system device, implant, and graft
996.63 Infection and inflammatory reaction due to nervous system device, implant, and graft — (Use additional code to identify specified infections)
V53.01 Fitting and adjustment of cerebral ventricular (communicating) shunt

ICD-9-CM Procedural

02.42 Replacement of ventricular shunt
02.43 Removal of ventricular shunt

Spine and Spinal Cord

62263-62264

62263 Percutaneous lysis of epidural adhesions using solution injection (eg, hypertonic saline, enzyme) or mechanical means (eg, catheter) including radiologic localization (includes contrast when administered), multiple adhesiolysis sessions; 2 or more days
62264 1 day

ICD-9-CM Diagnostic

349.2 Disorders of meninges, not elsewhere classified
742.59 Other specified congenital anomaly of spinal cord

ICD-9-CM Procedural

03.6 Lysis of adhesions of spinal cord and nerve roots
03.90 Insertion of catheter into spinal canal for infusion of therapeutic or palliative substances
03.91 Injection of anesthetic into spinal canal for analgesia
03.92 Injection of other agent into spinal canal
03.96 Percutaneous denervation of facet
86.09 Other incision of skin and subcutaneous tissue

62267

62267 Percutaneous aspiration within the nucleus pulposus, intervertebral disc, or paravertebral tissue for diagnostic purposes

ICD-9-CM Diagnostic

324.1 Intraspinal abscess

336.0 Syringomyelia and syringobulbia
711.08 Pyogenic arthritis, other specified sites — (Use additional code to identify infectious organism: 041.0-041.8)
722.90 Other and unspecified disc disorder of unspecified region
722.91 Other and unspecified disc disorder of cervical region
722.92 Other and unspecified disc disorder of thoracic region
722.93 Other and unspecified disc disorder of lumbar region
730.08 Acute osteomyelitis, other specified site — (Use additional code to identify organism: 041.1. Use additional code to identify major osseous defect, if applicable: 731.3)
730.18 Chronic osteomyelitis, other specified sites — (Use additional code to identify organism: 041.1. Use additional code to identify major osseous defect, if applicable: 731.3)
730.28 Unspecified osteomyelitis, other specified sites — (Use additional code to identify organism: 041.1. Use additional code to identify major osseous defect, if applicable: 731.3)

ICD-9-CM Procedural

80.39 Biopsy of joint structure of other specified site

62268

62268 Percutaneous aspiration, spinal cord cyst or syrinx

ICD-9-CM Diagnostic

324.1 Intraspinal abscess
336.0 Syringomyelia and syringobulbia
349.2 Disorders of meninges, not elsewhere classified

ICD-9-CM Procedural

03.99 Other operations on spinal cord and spinal canal structures

62269

62269 Biopsy of spinal cord, percutaneous needle

ICD-9-CM Diagnostic

192.2 Malignant neoplasm of spinal cord
198.3 Secondary malignant neoplasm of brain and spinal cord
225.3 Benign neoplasm of spinal cord
237.5 Neoplasm of uncertain behavior of brain and spinal cord
324.1 Intraspinal abscess
336.0 Syringomyelia and syringobulbia
340 Multiple sclerosis
349.2 Disorders of meninges, not elsewhere classified

ICD-9-CM Procedural

03.32 Biopsy of spinal cord or spinal meninges

62270

62270 Spinal puncture, lumbar, diagnostic

ICD-9-CM Diagnostic

052.2 Postvaricella myelitis
053.14 Herpes zoster myelitis
054.74 Herpes simplex myelitis
170.2 Malignant neoplasm of vertebral column, excluding sacrum and coccyx
191.5 Malignant neoplasm of ventricles of brain
191.8 Malignant neoplasm of other parts of brain
191.9 Malignant neoplasm of brain, unspecified site
192.2 Malignant neoplasm of spinal cord
192.3 Malignant neoplasm of spinal meninges
192.8 Malignant neoplasm of other specified sites of nervous system
192.9 Malignant neoplasm of nervous system, part unspecified
198.3 Secondary malignant neoplasm of brain and spinal cord
198.4 Secondary malignant neoplasm of other parts of nervous system
198.5 Secondary malignant neoplasm of bone and bone marrow
199.0 Disseminated malignant neoplasm
199.1 Other malignant neoplasm of unspecified site
225.0 Benign neoplasm of brain
225.2 Benign neoplasm of cerebral meninges
225.3 Benign neoplasm of spinal cord
225.4 Benign neoplasm of spinal meninges
225.8 Benign neoplasm of other specified sites of nervous system
225.9 Benign neoplasm of nervous system, part unspecified
237.5 Neoplasm of uncertain behavior of brain and spinal cord
237.6 Neoplasm of uncertain behavior of meninges
238.71 Essential thrombocythemia
238.72 Low grade myelodysplastic syndrome lesions
238.73 High grade myelodysplastic syndrome lesions
238.74 Myelodysplastic syndrome with 5q deletion
238.75 Myelodysplastic syndrome, unspecified
238.76 Myelofibrosis with myeloid metaplasia
238.79 Other lymphatic and hematopoietic tissues
239.6 Neoplasm of unspecified nature of brain
239.7 Neoplasm of unspecified nature of endocrine glands and other parts of nervous system
293.0 Delirium due to conditions classified elsewhere — (Code first the associated physical or neurological condition)
293.1 Subacute delirium — (Code first the associated physical or neurological condition)
303.00 Acute alcoholic intoxication, unspecified — (Use additional code to identify any associated condition: 291.0-291.9, 304.0-304.9, 331.7, 345.0-345.9, 535.3, 571.1, 571.2, 571.3)
303.01 Acute alcoholic intoxication, continuous — (Use additional code to identify any associated condition: 291.0-291.9, 304.0-304.9, 331.7, 345.0-345.9, 535.3, 571.1, 571.2, 571.3)
303.02 Acute alcoholic intoxication, episodic — (Use additional code to identify any associated condition: 291.0-291.9, 304.0-304.9, 331.7, 345.0-345.9, 535.3, 571.1, 571.2, 571.3)
303.03 Acute alcoholic intoxication, in remission — (Use additional code to identify any associated condition: 291.0-291.9, 304.0-304.9, 331.7, 345.0-345.9, 535.3, 571.1, 571.2, 571.3)
303.90 Other and unspecified alcohol dependence, unspecified — (Use additional code to identify any associated condition: 291.0-291.9, 304.0-304.9, 331.7, 345.0-345.9, 535.3, 571.1, 571.2, 571.3)
303.91 Other and unspecified alcohol dependence, continuous — (Use additional code to identify any associated condition: 291.0-291.9, 304.0-304.9, 331.7, 345.0-345.9, 535.3, 571.1, 571.2, 571.3)
303.92 Other and unspecified alcohol dependence, episodic — (Use additional code to identify any associated condition: 291.0-291.9, 304.0-304.9, 331.7, 345.0-345.9, 535.3, 571.1, 571.2, 571.3)
303.93 Other and unspecified alcohol dependence, in remission — (Use additional code to identify any associated condition: 291.0-291.9, 304.0-304.9, 331.7, 345.0-345.9, 535.3, 571.1, 571.2, 571.3)
320.0 Hemophilus meningitis
320.1 Pneumococcal meningitis
320.2 Streptococcal meningitis
320.3 Staphylococcal meningitis
320.7 Meningitis in other bacterial diseases classified elsewhere — (Code first underlying disease: 002.0, 027.0, 033.0-033.9, 039.8)
320.81 Anaerobic meningitis
320.82 Meningitis due to gram-negative bacteria, not elsewhere classified
320.89 Meningitis due to other specified bacteria
320.9 Meningitis due to unspecified bacterium
321.0 Cryptococcal meningitis — (Code first underlying disease: 117.5)
321.1 Meningitis in other fungal diseases — (Code first underlying disease: 110.0-118)

321.2 Meningitis due to viruses not elsewhere classified — (Code first underlying disease: 060.0-066.9) ☒

321.3 Meningitis due to trypanosomiasis — (Code first underlying disease: 086.0-086.9) ☒

321.4 Meningitis in sarcoidosis — (Code first underlying disease: 135) ☒

321.8 Meningitis due to other nonbacterial organisms classified elsewhere — (Code first underlying disease) ☒

322.0 Nonpyogenic meningitis

322.1 Eosinophilic meningitis

322.2 Chronic meningitis

322.9 Unspecified meningitis ▼

323.01 Encephalitis and encephalomyelitis in viral diseases classified elsewhere — (Code first underlying disease: 042, 073.7, 075, 078.3) ☒

323.02 Myelitis in viral diseases classified elsewhere — (Code first underlying disease: 042, 073.7, 075, 078.3) ☒

323.1 Encephalitis, myelitis, and encephalomyelitis in rickettsial diseases classified elsewhere — (Code first underlying disease: 080-083.9) ☒

323.2 Encephalitis, myelitis, and encephalomyelitis in protozoal diseases classified elsewhere — (Code first underlying disease: 084.0-084.9, 086.0-086.9) ☒

323.41 Other encephalitis and encephalomyelitis due to other infections classified elsewhere — (Code first underlying disease) ☒

323.42 Other myelitis due to other infections classified elsewhere — (Code first underlying disease) ☒

323.51 Encephalitis and encephalomyelitis following immunization procedures — (Use additional E code to identify vaccine)

323.52 Myelitis following immunization procedures — (Use additional E code to identify vaccine)

323.61 Infectious acute disseminated encephalomyelitis [ADEM] — (Code first underlying disease) ☒

323.62 Other postinfectious encephalitis and encephalomyelitis — (Code first underlying disease) ☒

323.63 Postinfectious myelitis — (Code first underlying disease) ☒

323.71 Toxic encephalitis and encephalomyelitis — (Code first underlying cause: 961.3, 982.1, 984.0-984.9, 985.0, 985.8) ☒

323.72 Toxic myelitis — (Code first underlying cause: 961.3, 982.1, 984.0-984.9, 985.0, 985.8) ☒

323.81 Other causes of encephalitis and encephalomyelitis

323.82 Other causes of myelitis

323.9 Unspecified causes of encephalitis, myelitis, and encephalomyelitis ▼

324.0 Intracranial abscess

324.1 Intraspinal abscess

324.9 Intracranial and intraspinal abscess of unspecified site ▼

331.3 Communicating hydrocephalus — (Use additional code, where applicable, to identify dementia: 294.10, 294.11)

331.4 Obstructive hydrocephalus — (Use additional code, where applicable, to identify dementia: 294.10, 294.11)

331.5 Idiopathic normal pressure hydrocephalus [INPH] — (Use additional code, where applicable, to identify dementia: 294.10, 294.11)

331.83 Mild cognitive impairment, so stated — (Use additional code, where applicable, to identify dementia: 294.10, 294.11)

332.0 Paralysis agitans

333.6 Genetic torsion dystonia

334.0 Friedreich's ataxia

334.1 Hereditary spastic paraplegia

334.2 Primary cerebellar degeneration

334.3 Other cerebellar ataxia — (Use additional E code to identify drug, if drug-induced)

334.4 Cerebellar ataxia in diseases classified elsewhere — (Code first underlying disease: 140.0-239.9, 244.0-244.9, 303.0-303.9) ☒

334.8 Other spinocerebellar diseases

334.9 Unspecified spinocerebellar disease ▼

335.0 Werdnig-Hoffmann disease

335.10 Unspecified spinal muscular atrophy ▼

335.11 Kugelberg-Welander disease

335.19 Other spinal muscular atrophy

335.20 Amyotrophic lateral sclerosis

335.21 Progressive muscular atrophy

335.22 Progressive bulbar palsy

335.23 Pseudobulbar palsy

335.24 Primary lateral sclerosis

335.29 Other motor neuron diseases

335.8 Other anterior horn cell diseases

335.9 Unspecified anterior horn cell disease ▼

336.0 Syringomyelia and syringobulbia

336.2 Subacute combined degeneration of spinal cord in diseases classified elsewhere — (Code first underlying disease: 266.2, 281.0, 281.1) ☒

336.3 Myelopathy in other diseases classified elsewhere — (Code first underlying disease: 140.0-239.9) ☒

336.8 Other myelopathy — (Use additional E code to identify cause)

336.9 Unspecified disease of spinal cord ▼

339.05 Short lasting unilateral neuralgiform headache with conjunctival injection and tearing

339.09 Other trigeminal autonomic cephalgias

339.20 Post-traumatic headache, unspecified ▼

339.21 Acute post-traumatic headache

339.22 Chronic post-traumatic headache

339.3 Drug induced headache, not elsewhere classified

339.41 Hemicrania continua

339.42 New daily persistent headache

339.43 Primary thunderclap headache

339.44 Other complicated headache syndrome

339.81 Hypnic headache

339.82 Headache associated with sexual activity

339.83 Primary cough headache

339.84 Primary exertional headache

339.85 Primary stabbing headache

339.89 Other specified headache syndromes

340 Multiple sclerosis

341.20 Acute (transverse) myelitis NOS

341.21 Acute (transverse) myelitis in conditions classified elsewhere — (Code first underlying condition) ☒

341.22 Idiopathic transverse myelitis

341.8 Other demyelinating diseases of central nervous system

341.9 Unspecified demyelinating disease of central nervous system ▼

342.90 Unspecified hemiplegia affecting unspecified side ▼

342.91 Unspecified hemiplegia affecting dominant side ▼

342.92 Unspecified hemiplegia affecting nondominant side ▼

344.00 Unspecified quadriplegia ▼

344.30 Monoplegia of lower limb affecting unspecified side ▼

344.31 Monoplegia of lower limb affecting dominant side

344.32 Monoplegia of lower limb affecting nondominant side

344.9 Unspecified paralysis ▼

348.2 Benign intracranial hypertension

348.30 Encephalopathy, unspecified ▼

348.82 Brain death

348.9 Unspecified condition of brain ▼

349.82 Toxic encephalopathy — (Use additional E code to identify cause)

349.89 Other specified disorder of nervous system

357.0 Acute infective polyneuritis

430 Subarachnoid hemorrhage — (Use additional code to identify presence of hypertension)

432.1 Subdural hemorrhage — (Use additional code to identify presence of hypertension)

432.9 Unspecified intracranial hemorrhage — (Use additional code to identify presence of hypertension) ▽
434.91 Unspecified cerebral artery occlusion with cerebral infarction — (Use additional code, if applicable, to identify status post administration of tPA (rtPA) in a different facility within the last 24 hours prior to admission to current facility: V45.88) ▽
435.9 Unspecified transient cerebral ischemia — (Use additional code to identify presence of hypertension) ▽
436 Acute, but ill-defined, cerebrovascular disease — (Use additional code to identify presence of hypertension) ▽
437.2 Hypertensive encephalopathy — (Use additional code to identify presence of hypertension)
437.3 Cerebral aneurysm, nonruptured — (Use additional code to identify presence of hypertension)
437.4 Cerebral arteritis — (Use additional code to identify presence of hypertension)
437.5 Moyamoya disease — (Use additional code to identify presence of hypertension)
437.6 Nonpyogenic thrombosis of intracranial venous sinus — (Use additional code to identify presence of hypertension)
437.7 Transient global amnesia — (Use additional code to identify presence of hypertension)
437.8 Other ill-defined cerebrovascular disease — (Use additional code to identify presence of hypertension)
437.9 Unspecified cerebrovascular disease — (Use additional code to identify presence of hypertension) ▽
724.2 Lumbago
724.5 Unspecified backache ▽
747.81 Congenital anomaly of cerebrovascular system
771.81 Septicemia (sepsis) of newborn — (Use additional code to identify organism: 041.00-041.9) (Use additional codes to identify severe sepsis (995.92) and any associated acute organ dysfunction, if applicable)
771.83 Bacteremia of newborn — (Use additional code(s) to further specify condition. Use additional code to identify organism: 041.00-041.9)
771.89 Other infections specific to the perinatal period — (Use additional code(s) to further specify condition. Use additional code to identify organism: 041.00-041.9)
777.2 Neonatal intestinal obstruction due to inspissated milk — (Use additional code(s) to further specify condition)
779.0 Convulsions in newborn — (Use additional code(s) to further specify condition)
779.1 Other and unspecified cerebral irritability in newborn — (Use additional code(s) to further specify condition) ▽
780.01 Coma
780.02 Transient alteration of awareness
780.03 Persistent vegetative state
780.09 Other alteration of consciousness
780.2 Syncope and collapse
780.31 Febrile convulsions (simple), unspecified ▽
780.39 Other convulsions
780.4 Dizziness and giddiness
780.60 Fever, unspecified ▽
780.62 Postprocedural fever
781.3 Lack of coordination
781.6 Meningismus
782.0 Disturbance of skin sensation
784.0 Headache
785.52 Septic shock — (Code first underlying infection) (Use additional code, if applicable, to identify systemic inflammatory response syndrome due to infectious process with organ dysfunction (995.92)) ☒
790.7 Bacteremia — (Use additional code to identify organism: 041)
792.0 Nonspecific abnormal finding in cerebrospinal fluid
901.89 Injury to specified blood vessels of thorax, other
961.3 Poisoning by quinoline and hydroxyquinoline derivatives — (Use additional code to specify the effects of poisoning)
982.1 Toxic effect of carbon tetrachloride — (Use additional code to specify the nature of the toxic effect)
984.0 Toxic effect of inorganic lead compounds — (Use additional code to specify the nature of the toxic effect)
984.1 Toxic effect of organic lead compounds — (Use additional code to specify the nature of the toxic effect)
984.8 Toxic effect of other lead compounds — (Use additional code to specify the nature of the toxic effect)
984.9 Toxic effect of unspecified lead compound — (Use additional code to specify the nature of the toxic effect) ▽
985.0 Toxic effect of mercury and its compounds — (Use additional code to specify the nature of the toxic effect)
985.8 Toxic effect of other specified metals — (Use additional code to specify the nature of the toxic effect)
997.01 Central nervous system complication — (Use additional code to identify complications)
997.02 Iatrogenic cerebrovascular infarction or hemorrhage — (Use additional code to identify complications)
997.09 Other nervous system complications — (Use additional code to identify complications)
V71.89 Observation for other specified suspected conditions
V71.9 Observation for unspecified suspected condition ▽

ICD-9-CM Procedural

03.31 Spinal tap

62272

62272 Spinal puncture, therapeutic, for drainage of cerebrospinal fluid (by needle or catheter)

ICD-9-CM Diagnostic

191.0 Malignant neoplasm of cerebrum, except lobes and ventricles
225.2 Benign neoplasm of cerebral meninges
225.3 Benign neoplasm of spinal cord
322.9 Unspecified meningitis ▽
324.0 Intracranial abscess
324.1 Intraspinal abscess
325 Phlebitis and thrombophlebitis of intracranial venous sinuses
340 Multiple sclerosis
348.4 Compression of brain
742.0 Encephalocele
781.6 Meningismus
997.09 Other nervous system complications — (Use additional code to identify complications)

ICD-9-CM Procedural

03.31 Spinal tap

62273

62273 Injection, epidural, of blood or clot patch

ICD-9-CM Diagnostic

349.0 Reaction to spinal or lumbar puncture
668.82 Other complications of the administration of anesthesia or other sedation in labor and delivery, delivered, with mention of postpartum complication — (Use additional code(s) to further specify complication) ♀
668.84 Other complications of the administration of anesthesia or other sedation in labor and delivery, postpartum condition or complication — (Use additional code(s) to further specify complication) ♀
784.0 Headache
997.09 Other nervous system complications — (Use additional code to identify complications)

ICD-9-CM Procedural

03.95 Spinal blood patch

62280-62282

62280 Injection/infusion of neurolytic substance (eg, alcohol, phenol, iced saline solutions), with or without other therapeutic substance; subarachnoid
62281 epidural, cervical or thoracic
62282 epidural, lumbar, sacral (caudal)

ICD-9-CM Diagnostic

333.83 Spasmodic torticollis — (Use additional E code to identify drug, if drug-induced)
337.22 Reflex sympathetic dystrophy of the lower limb
337.9 Unspecified disorder of autonomic nervous system ▽
340 Multiple sclerosis
353.1 Lumbosacral plexus lesions
353.4 Lumbosacral root lesions, not elsewhere classified
354.4 Causalgia of upper limb
354.5 Mononeuritis multiplex
355.71 Causalgia of lower limb
715.98 Osteoarthrosis, unspecified whether generalized or localized, other specified sites ▽
722.52 Degeneration of lumbar or lumbosacral intervertebral disc
722.83 Postlaminectomy syndrome, lumbar region
724.01 Spinal stenosis of thoracic region
724.02 Spinal stenosis of lumbar region, without neurogenic claudication
724.03 Spinal stenosis of lumbar region, with neurogenic claudication
724.2 Lumbago
724.3 Sciatica
724.4 Thoracic or lumbosacral neuritis or radiculitis, unspecified ▽
724.6 Disorders of sacrum
729.2 Unspecified neuralgia, neuritis, and radiculitis ▽

ICD-9-CM Procedural

03.8 Injection of destructive agent into spinal canal
03.92 Injection of other agent into spinal canal

62284

62284 Injection procedure for myelography and/or computed tomography, spinal (other than C1-C2 and posterior fossa)

ICD-9-CM Diagnostic

170.2 Malignant neoplasm of vertebral column, excluding sacrum and coccyx
191.5 Malignant neoplasm of ventricles of brain
191.8 Malignant neoplasm of other parts of brain
192.2 Malignant neoplasm of spinal cord
192.3 Malignant neoplasm of spinal meninges
192.8 Malignant neoplasm of other specified sites of nervous system
198.3 Secondary malignant neoplasm of brain and spinal cord
198.4 Secondary malignant neoplasm of other parts of nervous system
198.5 Secondary malignant neoplasm of bone and bone marrow
199.0 Disseminated malignant neoplasm
209.73 Secondary neuroendocrine tumor of bone
213.2 Benign neoplasm of vertebral column, excluding sacrum and coccyx
225.3 Benign neoplasm of spinal cord
225.4 Benign neoplasm of spinal meninges
225.8 Benign neoplasm of other specified sites of nervous system
237.5 Neoplasm of uncertain behavior of brain and spinal cord
237.6 Neoplasm of uncertain behavior of meninges
237.70 Neurofibromatosis, unspecified ▽
237.71 Neurofibromatosis, Type 1 (von Recklinghausen's disease)
237.72 Neurofibromatosis, Type 2 (acoustic neurofibromatosis)
237.73 Schwannomatosis
237.79 Other neurofibromatosis
238.0 Neoplasm of uncertain behavior of bone and articular cartilage
239.2 Neoplasms of unspecified nature of bone, soft tissue, and skin
239.89 Neoplasms of unspecified nature, other specified sites
324.1 Intraspinal abscess
336.0 Syringomyelia and syringobulbia
344.01 Quadriplegia and quadriparesis, C1-C4, complete
344.02 Quadriplegia and quadriparesis, C1-C4, incomplete
344.03 Quadriplegia and quadriparesis, C5-C7, complete
344.04 C5-C7, incomplete
344.09 Other quadriplegia and quadriparesis
344.1 Paraplegia
344.60 Cauda equina syndrome without mention of neurogenic bladder
349.1 Nervous system complications from surgically implanted device
349.2 Disorders of meninges, not elsewhere classified
349.89 Other specified disorder of nervous system
353.1 Lumbosacral plexus lesions
359.1 Hereditary progressive muscular dystrophy
721.0 Cervical spondylosis without myelopathy
721.1 Cervical spondylosis with myelopathy
721.2 Thoracic spondylosis without myelopathy
721.3 Lumbosacral spondylosis without myelopathy
721.41 Spondylosis with myelopathy, thoracic region
721.42 Spondylosis with myelopathy, lumbar region
721.5 Kissing spine
721.6 Ankylosing vertebral hyperostosis
721.7 Traumatic spondylopathy
721.8 Other allied disorders of spine
722.0 Displacement of cervical intervertebral disc without myelopathy
722.10 Displacement of lumbar intervertebral disc without myelopathy
722.11 Displacement of thoracic intervertebral disc without myelopathy
722.4 Degeneration of cervical intervertebral disc
722.51 Degeneration of thoracic or thoracolumbar intervertebral disc
722.52 Degeneration of lumbar or lumbosacral intervertebral disc
722.6 Degeneration of intervertebral disc, site unspecified ▽
722.71 Intervertebral cervical disc disorder with myelopathy, cervical region
722.72 Intervertebral thoracic disc disorder with myelopathy, thoracic region
722.73 Intervertebral lumbar disc disorder with myelopathy, lumbar region
722.81 Postlaminectomy syndrome, cervical region
722.82 Postlaminectomy syndrome, thoracic region
722.83 Postlaminectomy syndrome, lumbar region
722.91 Other and unspecified disc disorder of cervical region ▽
722.92 Other and unspecified disc disorder of thoracic region ▽
722.93 Other and unspecified disc disorder of lumbar region ▽
723.0 Spinal stenosis in cervical region
723.1 Cervicalgia
723.4 Brachial neuritis or radiculitis NOS ▽
723.5 Torticollis, unspecified ▽
723.6 Panniculitis specified as affecting neck
723.7 Ossification of posterior longitudinal ligament in cervical region
723.9 Unspecified musculoskeletal disorders and symptoms referable to neck ▽
724.02 Spinal stenosis of lumbar region, without neurogenic claudication
724.03 Spinal stenosis of lumbar region, with neurogenic claudication
724.09 Spinal stenosis, other region other than cervical
724.1 Pain in thoracic spine
724.2 Lumbago
724.3 Sciatica
724.4 Thoracic or lumbosacral neuritis or radiculitis, unspecified ▽
724.5 Unspecified backache ▽
724.6 Disorders of sacrum
724.70 Unspecified disorder of coccyx ▽

Code	Description
724.71	Hypermobility of coccyx
724.79	Other disorder of coccyx
724.8	Other symptoms referable to back
724.9	Other unspecified back disorder
729.2	Unspecified neuralgia, neuritis, and radiculitis
729.5	Pain in soft tissues of limb
733.13	Pathologic fracture of vertebrae
733.90	Disorder of bone and cartilage, unspecified
733.95	Stress fracture of other bone — (Use additional external cause code(s) to identify the cause of the stress fracture)
738.4	Acquired spondylolisthesis
738.5	Other acquired deformity of back or spine
739.1	Nonallopathic lesion of cervical region, not elsewhere classified
739.2	Nonallopathic lesion of thoracic region, not elsewhere classified
739.3	Nonallopathic lesion of lumbar region, not elsewhere classified
741.01	Spina bifida with hydrocephalus, cervical region
741.02	Spina bifida with hydrocephalus, dorsal (thoracic) region
741.03	Spina bifida with hydrocephalus, lumbar region
741.92	Spina bifida without mention of hydrocephalus, dorsal (thoracic) region
741.93	Spina bifida without mention of hydrocephalus, lumbar region
756.10	Congenital anomaly of spine, unspecified
756.11	Congenital spondylolysis, lumbosacral region
756.12	Congenital spondylolisthesis
756.13	Congenital absence of vertebra
756.14	Hemivertebra
756.15	Congenital fusion of spine (vertebra)
756.16	Klippel-Feil syndrome
756.17	Spina bifida occulta
756.19	Other congenital anomaly of spine
784.99	Other symptoms involving head and neck
793.7	Nonspecific (abnormal) findings on radiological and other examination of musculoskeletal system
805.10	Open fracture of cervical vertebra, unspecified level without mention of spinal cord injury
805.11	Open fracture of first cervical vertebra without mention of spinal cord injury
805.12	Open fracture of second cervical vertebra without mention of spinal cord injury
805.13	Open fracture of third cervical vertebra without mention of spinal cord injury
805.14	Open fracture of fourth cervical vertebra without mention of spinal cord injury
805.15	Open fracture of fifth cervical vertebra without mention of spinal cord injury
805.16	Open fracture of sixth cervical vertebra without mention of spinal cord injury
805.17	Open fracture of seventh cervical vertebra without mention of spinal cord injury
805.18	Open fracture of multiple cervical vertebrae without mention of spinal cord injury
805.2	Closed fracture of dorsal (thoracic) vertebra without mention of spinal cord injury
805.3	Open fracture of dorsal (thoracic) vertebra without mention of spinal cord injury
805.4	Closed fracture of lumbar vertebra without mention of spinal cord injury
805.5	Open fracture of lumbar vertebra without mention of spinal cord injury
805.6	Closed fracture of sacrum and coccyx without mention of spinal cord injury
805.7	Open fracture of sacrum and coccyx without mention of spinal cord injury
806.00	Closed fracture of C1-C4 level with unspecified spinal cord injury
806.01	Closed fracture of C1-C4 level with complete lesion of cord
806.02	Closed fracture of C1-C4 level with anterior cord syndrome
806.03	Closed fracture of C1-C4 level with central cord syndrome
806.04	Closed fracture of C1-C4 level with other specified spinal cord injury
806.05	Closed fracture of C5-C7 level with unspecified spinal cord injury
806.06	Closed fracture of C5-C7 level with complete lesion of cord
806.07	Closed fracture of C5-C7 level with anterior cord syndrome
806.08	Closed fracture of C5-C7 level with central cord syndrome
806.09	Closed fracture of C5-C7 level with other specified spinal cord injury
806.10	Open fracture of C1-C4 level with unspecified spinal cord injury
806.11	Open fracture of C1-C4 level with complete lesion of cord
806.12	Open fracture of C1-C4 level with anterior cord syndrome
806.13	Open fracture of C1-C4 level with central cord syndrome
806.14	Open fracture of C1-C4 level with other specified spinal cord injury
806.15	Open fracture of C5-C7 level with unspecified spinal cord injury
806.16	Open fracture of C5-C7 level with complete lesion of cord
806.17	Open fracture of C5-C7 level with anterior cord syndrome
806.18	Open fracture of C5-C7 level with central cord syndrome
806.19	Open fracture of C5-C7 level with other specified spinal cord injury
806.20	Closed fracture of T1-T6 level with unspecified spinal cord injury
806.21	Closed fracture of T1-T6 level with complete lesion of cord
806.22	Closed fracture of T1-T6 level with anterior cord syndrome
806.23	Closed fracture of T1-T6 level with central cord syndrome
806.24	Closed fracture of T1-T6 level with other specified spinal cord injury
806.25	Closed fracture of T7-T12 level with unspecified spinal cord injury
806.26	Closed fracture of T7-T12 level with complete lesion of cord
806.27	Closed fracture of T7-T12 level with anterior cord syndrome
806.28	Closed fracture of T7-T12 level with central cord syndrome
806.29	Closed fracture of T7-T12 level with other specified spinal cord injury
806.30	Open fracture of T1-T6 level with unspecified spinal cord injury
806.31	Open fracture of T1-T6 level with complete lesion of cord
806.32	Open fracture of T1-T6 level with anterior cord syndrome
806.33	Open fracture of T1-T6 level with central cord syndrome
806.34	Open fracture of T1-T6 level with other specified spinal cord injury
806.35	Open fracture of T7-T12 level with unspecified spinal cord injury
806.36	Open fracture of T7-T12 level with complete lesion of cord
806.37	Open fracture of T7-T12 level with anterior cord syndrome
806.38	Open fracture of T7-T12 level with central cord syndrome
806.39	Open fracture of T7-T12 level with other specified spinal cord injury
806.4	Closed fracture of lumbar spine with spinal cord injury
806.5	Open fracture of lumbar spine with spinal cord injury
839.01	Closed dislocation, first cervical vertebra
839.02	Closed dislocation, second cervical vertebra
839.03	Closed dislocation, third cervical vertebra
839.04	Closed dislocation, fourth cervical vertebra
839.05	Closed dislocation, fifth cervical vertebra
839.06	Closed dislocation, sixth cervical vertebra
839.07	Closed dislocation, seventh cervical vertebra
839.08	Closed dislocation, multiple cervical vertebrae
839.11	Open dislocation, first cervical vertebra
839.12	Open dislocation, second cervical vertebra
839.13	Open dislocation, third cervical vertebra
839.14	Open dislocation, fourth cervical vertebra
839.15	Open dislocation, fifth cervical vertebra
839.16	Open dislocation, sixth cervical vertebra
839.17	Open dislocation, seventh cervical vertebra
839.18	Open dislocation, multiple cervical vertebrae
839.20	Closed dislocation, lumbar vertebra
839.21	Closed dislocation, thoracic vertebra
839.30	Open dislocation, lumbar vertebra
839.31	Open dislocation, thoracic vertebra
846.0	Sprain and strain of lumbosacral (joint) (ligament)
846.9	Unspecified site of sacroiliac region sprain and strain
847.0	Neck sprain and strain
847.1	Thoracic sprain and strain
847.2	Lumbar sprain and strain
847.9	Sprain and strain of unspecified site of back
905.1	Late effect of fracture of spine and trunk without mention of spinal cord lesion
907.2	Late effect of spinal cord injury

952.00 C1-C4 level spinal cord injury, unspecified ♥
952.01 C1-C4 level with complete lesion of spinal cord
952.02 C1-C4 level with anterior cord syndrome
952.03 C1-C4 level with central cord syndrome
952.04 C1-C4 level with other specified spinal cord injury
952.05 C5-C7 level spinal cord injury, unspecified ♥
952.06 C5-C7 level with complete lesion of spinal cord
952.07 C5-C7 level with anterior cord syndrome
952.08 C5-C7 level with central cord syndrome
952.09 C5-C7 level with other specified spinal cord injury
952.10 T1-T6 level spinal cord injury, unspecified ♥
952.11 T1-T6 level with complete lesion of spinal cord
952.12 T1-T6 level with anterior cord syndrome
952.13 T1-T6 level with central cord syndrome
952.14 T1-T6 level with other specified spinal cord injury
952.15 T7-T12 level spinal cord injury, unspecified ♥
952.16 T7-T12 level with complete lesion of spinal cord
952.17 T7-T12 level with anterior cord syndrome
952.18 T7-T12 level with central cord syndrome
952.19 T7-T12 level with other specified spinal cord injury
952.2 Lumbar spinal cord injury without spinal bone injury
952.3 Sacral spinal cord injury without spinal bone injury
952.4 Cauda equina spinal cord injury without spinal bone injury
952.8 Multiple sites of spinal cord injury without spinal bone injury
953.0 Injury to cervical nerve root
953.1 Injury to dorsal nerve root
953.2 Injury to lumbar nerve root
953.3 Injury to sacral nerve root
953.4 Injury to brachial plexus
953.5 Injury to lumbosacral plexus
953.8 Injury to multiple sites of nerve roots and spinal plexus
959.09 Injury of face and neck, other and unspecified
959.19 Other injury of other sites of trunk
996.40 Unspecified mechanical complication of internal orthopedic device, implant, and graft — (Use additional code to identify prosthetic joint with mechanical complication, V43.60-V43.69) ♥
996.49 Other mechanical complication of other internal orthopedic device, implant, and graft — (Use additional code to identify prosthetic joint with mechanical complication, V43.60-V43.69)
996.63 Infection and inflammatory reaction due to nervous system device, implant, and graft — (Use additional code to identify specified infections)
996.67 Infection and inflammatory reaction due to other internal orthopedic device, implant, and graft — (Use additional code to identify specified infections)
996.75 Other complications due to nervous system device, implant, and graft — (Use additional code to identify complication: 338.18-338.19, 338.28-338.29)
996.78 Other complications due to other internal orthopedic device, implant, and graft — (Use additional code to identify complication: 338.18-338.19, 338.28-338.29)

ICD-9-CM Procedural

03.92 Injection of other agent into spinal canal
87.21 Contrast myelogram
88.38 Other computerized axial tomography

62287

62287 Decompression procedure, percutaneous, of nucleus pulposus of intervertebral disc, any method utilizing needle based technique to remove disc material under fluoroscopic imaging or other form of indirect visualization, with the use of an endoscope, with discography and/or epidural injection(s) at the treated level(s), when performed, single or multiple levels, lumbar

ICD-9-CM Diagnostic

722.10 Displacement of lumbar intervertebral disc without myelopathy
722.73 Intervertebral lumbar disc disorder with myelopathy, lumbar region
722.93 Other and unspecified disc disorder of lumbar region ♥
724.2 Lumbago
724.4 Thoracic or lumbosacral neuritis or radiculitis, unspecified ♥
724.5 Unspecified backache ♥

ICD-9-CM Procedural

80.59 Other destruction of intervertebral disc

HCPCS Level II Supplies & Services

C2614 Probe, percutaneous lumbar discectomy

62290-62291

62290 Injection procedure for discography, each level; lumbar
62291 cervical or thoracic

ICD-9-CM Diagnostic

719.48 Pain in joint, other specified sites
721.0 Cervical spondylosis without myelopathy
721.1 Cervical spondylosis with myelopathy
721.2 Thoracic spondylosis without myelopathy
721.3 Lumbosacral spondylosis without myelopathy
721.41 Spondylosis with myelopathy, thoracic region
721.42 Spondylosis with myelopathy, lumbar region
722.0 Displacement of cervical intervertebral disc without myelopathy
722.10 Displacement of lumbar intervertebral disc without myelopathy
722.11 Displacement of thoracic intervertebral disc without myelopathy
722.31 Schmorl's nodes, thoracic region
722.32 Schmorl's nodes, lumbar region
722.4 Degeneration of cervical intervertebral disc
722.51 Degeneration of thoracic or thoracolumbar intervertebral disc
722.52 Degeneration of lumbar or lumbosacral intervertebral disc
722.71 Intervertebral cervical disc disorder with myelopathy, cervical region
722.72 Intervertebral thoracic disc disorder with myelopathy, thoracic region
722.73 Intervertebral lumbar disc disorder with myelopathy, lumbar region
722.82 Postlaminectomy syndrome, thoracic region
722.83 Postlaminectomy syndrome, lumbar region
722.91 Other and unspecified disc disorder of cervical region ♥
722.92 Other and unspecified disc disorder of thoracic region ♥
722.93 Other and unspecified disc disorder of lumbar region ♥
723.1 Cervicalgia
723.4 Brachial neuritis or radiculitis NOS ♥
724.01 Spinal stenosis of thoracic region
724.02 Spinal stenosis of lumbar region, without neurogenic claudication
724.03 Spinal stenosis of lumbar region, with neurogenic claudication
724.1 Pain in thoracic spine
724.2 Lumbago
724.4 Thoracic or lumbosacral neuritis or radiculitis, unspecified ♥
724.5 Unspecified backache ♥
724.9 Other unspecified back disorder
729.5 Pain in soft tissues of limb
756.10 Congenital anomaly of spine, unspecified ♥

756.19 Other congenital anomaly of spine

ICD-9-CM Procedural

03.92 Injection of other agent into spinal canal
87.22 Other x-ray of cervical spine
87.24 Other x-ray of lumbosacral spine

62292

62292 Injection procedure for chemonucleolysis, including discography, intervertebral disc, single or multiple levels, lumbar

ICD-9-CM Diagnostic

722.10 Displacement of lumbar intervertebral disc without myelopathy
722.51 Degeneration of thoracic or thoracolumbar intervertebral disc
722.73 Intervertebral lumbar disc disorder with myelopathy, lumbar region
722.93 Other and unspecified disc disorder of lumbar region ▽
724.2 Lumbago
724.4 Thoracic or lumbosacral neuritis or radiculitis, unspecified ▽
724.5 Unspecified backache ▽

ICD-9-CM Procedural

03.6 Lysis of adhesions of spinal cord and nerve roots
80.52 Intervertebral chemonucleolysis
80.59 Other destruction of intervertebral disc
87.29 Other x-ray of spine

62294

62294 Injection procedure, arterial, for occlusion of arteriovenous malformation, spinal

ICD-9-CM Diagnostic

442.89 Aneurysm of other specified artery
747.82 Congenital spinal vessel anomaly

ICD-9-CM Procedural

03.99 Other operations on spinal cord and spinal canal structures

62310

62310 Injection(s), of diagnostic or therapeutic substance(s) (including anesthetic, antispasmodic, opioid, steroid, other solution), not including neurolytic substances, including needle or catheter placement, includes contrast for localization when performed, epidural or subarachnoid; cervical or thoracic

ICD-9-CM Diagnostic

340 Multiple sclerosis
721.0 Cervical spondylosis without myelopathy
721.1 Cervical spondylosis with myelopathy
721.2 Thoracic spondylosis without myelopathy
721.41 Spondylosis with myelopathy, thoracic region
722.0 Displacement of cervical intervertebral disc without myelopathy
722.11 Displacement of thoracic intervertebral disc without myelopathy
722.31 Schmorl's nodes, thoracic region
722.4 Degeneration of cervical intervertebral disc
722.51 Degeneration of thoracic or thoracolumbar intervertebral disc
722.71 Intervertebral cervical disc disorder with myelopathy, cervical region
722.72 Intervertebral thoracic disc disorder with myelopathy, thoracic region
722.81 Postlaminectomy syndrome, cervical region
722.82 Postlaminectomy syndrome, thoracic region
722.91 Other and unspecified disc disorder of cervical region ▽
722.92 Other and unspecified disc disorder of thoracic region ▽
723.0 Spinal stenosis in cervical region
723.1 Cervicalgia
723.2 Cervicocranial syndrome
723.3 Cervicobrachial syndrome (diffuse)
723.4 Brachial neuritis or radiculitis NOS ▽
723.8 Other syndromes affecting cervical region
724.01 Spinal stenosis of thoracic region
724.4 Thoracic or lumbosacral neuritis or radiculitis, unspecified ▽
733.20 Unspecified cyst of bone (localized) ▽
847.0 Neck sprain and strain
847.1 Thoracic sprain and strain

ICD-9-CM Procedural

03.91 Injection of anesthetic into spinal canal for analgesia
03.92 Injection of other agent into spinal canal
99.23 Injection of steroid
99.29 Injection or infusion of other therapeutic or prophylactic substance

62311

62311 Injection(s), of diagnostic or therapeutic substance(s) (including anesthetic, antispasmodic, opioid, steroid, other solution), not including neurolytic substances, including needle or catheter placement, includes contrast for localization when performed, epidural or subarachnoid; lumbar or sacral (caudal)

ICD-9-CM Diagnostic

340 Multiple sclerosis
721.3 Lumbosacral spondylosis without myelopathy
721.42 Spondylosis with myelopathy, lumbar region
722.10 Displacement of lumbar intervertebral disc without myelopathy
722.32 Schmorl's nodes, lumbar region
722.51 Degeneration of thoracic or thoracolumbar intervertebral disc
722.52 Degeneration of lumbar or lumbosacral intervertebral disc
722.73 Intervertebral lumbar disc disorder with myelopathy, lumbar region
722.83 Postlaminectomy syndrome, lumbar region
722.93 Other and unspecified disc disorder of lumbar region ▽
724.02 Spinal stenosis of lumbar region, without neurogenic claudication
724.03 Spinal stenosis of lumbar region, with neurogenic claudication
724.2 Lumbago
724.3 Sciatica
724.4 Thoracic or lumbosacral neuritis or radiculitis, unspecified ▽
724.5 Unspecified backache ▽
724.6 Disorders of sacrum
733.20 Unspecified cyst of bone (localized) ▽
733.21 Solitary bone cyst
846.0 Sprain and strain of lumbosacral (joint) (ligament)
847.2 Lumbar sprain and strain
847.3 Sprain and strain of sacrum

ICD-9-CM Procedural

03.91 Injection of anesthetic into spinal canal for analgesia
03.92 Injection of other agent into spinal canal
99.23 Injection of steroid
99.29 Injection or infusion of other therapeutic or prophylactic substance

62318

62318 Injection(s), including indwelling catheter placement, continuous infusion or intermittent bolus, of diagnostic or therapeutic substance(s) (including anesthetic, antispasmodic, opioid, steroid, other solution), not including neurolytic substances, includes contrast for localization when performed, epidural or subarachnoid; cervical or thoracic

ICD-9-CM Diagnostic

340 Multiple sclerosis
721.0 Cervical spondylosis without myelopathy

721.1 Cervical spondylosis with myelopathy
721.2 Thoracic spondylosis without myelopathy
721.41 Spondylosis with myelopathy, thoracic region
722.0 Displacement of cervical intervertebral disc without myelopathy
722.11 Displacement of thoracic intervertebral disc without myelopathy
722.31 Schmorl's nodes, thoracic region
722.4 Degeneration of cervical intervertebral disc
722.51 Degeneration of thoracic or thoracolumbar intervertebral disc
722.71 Intervertebral cervical disc disorder with myelopathy, cervical region
722.72 Intervertebral thoracic disc disorder with myelopathy, thoracic region
722.81 Postlaminectomy syndrome, cervical region
722.82 Postlaminectomy syndrome, thoracic region
722.91 Other and unspecified disc disorder of cervical region ▽
722.92 Other and unspecified disc disorder of thoracic region ▽
723.0 Spinal stenosis in cervical region
723.1 Cervicalgia
723.2 Cervicocranial syndrome
723.3 Cervicobrachial syndrome (diffuse)
723.4 Brachial neuritis or radiculitis NOS ▽
723.8 Other syndromes affecting cervical region
724.01 Spinal stenosis of thoracic region
724.4 Thoracic or lumbosacral neuritis or radiculitis, unspecified ▽
733.20 Unspecified cyst of bone (localized) ▽
733.21 Solitary bone cyst
847.0 Neck sprain and strain
847.1 Thoracic sprain and strain

ICD-9-CM Procedural

03.90 Insertion of catheter into spinal canal for infusion of therapeutic or palliative substances
03.91 Injection of anesthetic into spinal canal for analgesia
03.92 Injection of other agent into spinal canal
99.23 Injection of steroid
99.29 Injection or infusion of other therapeutic or prophylactic substance

62319

62319 Injection(s), including indwelling catheter placement, continuous infusion or intermittent bolus, of diagnostic or therapeutic substance(s) (including anesthetic, antispasmodic, opioid, steroid, other solution), not including neurolytic substances, includes contrast for localization when performed, epidural or subarachnoid; lumbar or sacral (caudal)

ICD-9-CM Diagnostic

340 Multiple sclerosis
721.3 Lumbosacral spondylosis without myelopathy
721.42 Spondylosis with myelopathy, lumbar region
722.10 Displacement of lumbar intervertebral disc without myelopathy
722.32 Schmorl's nodes, lumbar region
722.51 Degeneration of thoracic or thoracolumbar intervertebral disc
722.52 Degeneration of lumbar or lumbosacral intervertebral disc
722.73 Intervertebral lumbar disc disorder with myelopathy, lumbar region
722.83 Postlaminectomy syndrome, lumbar region
722.93 Other and unspecified disc disorder of lumbar region ▽
724.02 Spinal stenosis of lumbar region, without neurogenic claudication
724.03 Spinal stenosis of lumbar region, with neurogenic claudication
724.2 Lumbago
724.3 Sciatica
724.4 Thoracic or lumbosacral neuritis or radiculitis, unspecified ▽
724.5 Unspecified backache ▽
724.6 Disorders of sacrum
733.20 Unspecified cyst of bone (localized) ▽
733.21 Solitary bone cyst
846.0 Sprain and strain of lumbosacral (joint) (ligament)
847.2 Lumbar sprain and strain
847.3 Sprain and strain of sacrum

ICD-9-CM Procedural

03.90 Insertion of catheter into spinal canal for infusion of therapeutic or palliative substances
03.91 Injection of anesthetic into spinal canal for analgesia
03.92 Injection of other agent into spinal canal
99.23 Injection of steroid
99.29 Injection or infusion of other therapeutic or prophylactic substance

62350-62355

62350 Implantation, revision or repositioning of tunneled intrathecal or epidural catheter, for long-term medication administration via an external pump or implantable reservoir/infusion pump; without laminectomy
62351 with laminectomy
62355 Removal of previously implanted intrathecal or epidural catheter

ICD-9-CM Diagnostic

191.7 Malignant neoplasm of brain stem
192.2 Malignant neoplasm of spinal cord
192.3 Malignant neoplasm of spinal meninges
198.3 Secondary malignant neoplasm of brain and spinal cord
199.0 Disseminated malignant neoplasm
199.1 Other malignant neoplasm of unspecified site
202.80 Other malignant lymphomas, unspecified site, extranodal and solid organ sites ▽
202.90 Other and unspecified malignant neoplasms of lymphoid and histiocytic tissue, unspecified site, extranodal and solid organ sites ▽
722.81 Postlaminectomy syndrome, cervical region
722.82 Postlaminectomy syndrome, thoracic region
722.83 Postlaminectomy syndrome, lumbar region
723.1 Cervicalgia
724.1 Pain in thoracic spine
724.2 Lumbago
996.2 Mechanical complication of nervous system device, implant, and graft
996.63 Infection and inflammatory reaction due to nervous system device, implant, and graft — (Use additional code to identify specified infections)
996.75 Other complications due to nervous system device, implant, and graft — (Use additional code to identify complication: 338.18-338.19, 338.28-338.29)
V53.09 Fitting and adjustment of other devices related to nervous system and special senses

ICD-9-CM Procedural

03.02 Reopening of laminectomy site
03.09 Other exploration and decompression of spinal canal
03.90 Insertion of catheter into spinal canal for infusion of therapeutic or palliative substances
03.99 Other operations on spinal cord and spinal canal structures
80.53 Repair of the anulus fibrosus with graft or prosthesis
80.54 Other and unspecified repair of the anulus fibrosus

62360-62365

62360 Implantation or replacement of device for intrathecal or epidural drug infusion; subcutaneous reservoir
62361 nonprogrammable pump
62362 programmable pump, including preparation of pump, with or without programming
62365 Removal of subcutaneous reservoir or pump, previously implanted for intrathecal or epidural infusion

ICD-9-CM Diagnostic

191.7 Malignant neoplasm of brain stem
192.2 Malignant neoplasm of spinal cord

192.3 Malignant neoplasm of spinal meninges

198.3 Secondary malignant neoplasm of brain and spinal cord

202.80 Other malignant lymphomas, unspecified site, extranodal and solid organ sites

202.90 Other and unspecified malignant neoplasms of lymphoid and histiocytic tissue, unspecified site, extranodal and solid organ sites

722.81 Postlaminectomy syndrome, cervical region

722.82 Postlaminectomy syndrome, thoracic region

722.83 Postlaminectomy syndrome, lumbar region

723.1 Cervicalgia

724.1 Pain in thoracic spine

724.2 Lumbago

996.2 Mechanical complication of nervous system device, implant, and graft

996.63 Infection and inflammatory reaction due to nervous system device, implant, and graft — (Use additional code to identify specified infections)

996.75 Other complications due to nervous system device, implant, and graft — (Use additional code to identify complication: 338.18-338.19, 338.28-338.29)

V53.09 Fitting and adjustment of other devices related to nervous system and special senses

ICD-9-CM Procedural

86.06 Insertion of totally implantable infusion pump

86.09 Other incision of skin and subcutaneous tissue

62367-62370

62367 Electronic analysis of programmable, implanted pump for intrathecal or epidural drug infusion (includes evaluation of reservoir status, alarm status, drug prescription status); without reprogramming or refill

62368 with reprogramming

62369 with reprogramming and refill

62370 with reprogramming and refill (requiring skill of a physician or other qualified health care professional)

ICD-9-CM Diagnostic

191.7 Malignant neoplasm of brain stem

192.2 Malignant neoplasm of spinal cord

192.3 Malignant neoplasm of spinal meninges

198.3 Secondary malignant neoplasm of brain and spinal cord

202.80 Other malignant lymphomas, unspecified site, extranodal and solid organ sites

202.90 Other and unspecified malignant neoplasms of lymphoid and histiocytic tissue, unspecified site, extranodal and solid organ sites

722.81 Postlaminectomy syndrome, cervical region

722.82 Postlaminectomy syndrome, thoracic region

722.83 Postlaminectomy syndrome, lumbar region

723.1 Cervicalgia

724.1 Pain in thoracic spine

724.2 Lumbago

996.2 Mechanical complication of nervous system device, implant, and graft

996.63 Infection and inflammatory reaction due to nervous system device, implant, and graft — (Use additional code to identify specified infections)

996.75 Other complications due to nervous system device, implant, and graft — (Use additional code to identify complication: 338.18-338.19, 338.28-338.29)

V53.09 Fitting and adjustment of other devices related to nervous system and special senses

ICD-9-CM Procedural

89.39 Other nonoperative measurements and examinations

63001-63011

63001 Laminectomy with exploration and/or decompression of spinal cord and/or cauda equina, without facetectomy, foraminotomy or discectomy (eg, spinal stenosis), 1 or 2 vertebral segments; cervical

63003 thoracic

63005 lumbar, except for spondylolisthesis

63011 sacral

ICD-9-CM Diagnostic

344.60 Cauda equina syndrome without mention of neurogenic bladder

353.1 Lumbosacral plexus lesions

355.0 Lesion of sciatic nerve

715.98 Osteoarthrosis, unspecified whether generalized or localized, other specified sites

719.48 Pain in joint, other specified sites

720.0 Ankylosing spondylitis

720.2 Sacroiliitis, not elsewhere classified

721.0 Cervical spondylosis without myelopathy

721.1 Cervical spondylosis with myelopathy

721.2 Thoracic spondylosis without myelopathy

721.3 Lumbosacral spondylosis without myelopathy

721.41 Spondylosis with myelopathy, thoracic region

721.42 Spondylosis with myelopathy, lumbar region

722.0 Displacement of cervical intervertebral disc without myelopathy

722.10 Displacement of lumbar intervertebral disc without myelopathy

722.52 Degeneration of lumbar or lumbosacral intervertebral disc

722.71 Intervertebral cervical disc disorder with myelopathy, cervical region

722.73 Intervertebral lumbar disc disorder with myelopathy, lumbar region

722.83 Postlaminectomy syndrome, lumbar region

722.91 Other and unspecified disc disorder of cervical region

722.93 Other and unspecified disc disorder of lumbar region

723.0 Spinal stenosis in cervical region

723.1 Cervicalgia

723.4 Brachial neuritis or radiculitis NOS

724.01 Spinal stenosis of thoracic region

724.02 Spinal stenosis of lumbar region, without neurogenic claudication

724.03 Spinal stenosis of lumbar region, with neurogenic claudication

724.09 Spinal stenosis, other region other than cervical

724.1 Pain in thoracic spine

724.2 Lumbago

724.3 Sciatica

724.4 Thoracic or lumbosacral neuritis or radiculitis, unspecified

724.6 Disorders of sacrum

728.5 Hypermobility syndrome

729.2 Unspecified neuralgia, neuritis, and radiculitis

729.4 Unspecified fasciitis

738.2 Acquired deformity of neck

738.4 Acquired spondylolisthesis

756.10 Congenital anomaly of spine, unspecified

756.11 Congenital spondylolysis, lumbosacral region

805.10 Open fracture of cervical vertebra, unspecified level without mention of spinal cord injury

805.2 Closed fracture of dorsal (thoracic) vertebra without mention of spinal cord injury

805.3 Open fracture of dorsal (thoracic) vertebra without mention of spinal cord injury

805.4 Closed fracture of lumbar vertebra without mention of spinal cord injury

805.5 Open fracture of lumbar vertebra without mention of spinal cord injury

805.6 Closed fracture of sacrum and coccyx without mention of spinal cord injury

805.7 Open fracture of sacrum and coccyx without mention of spinal cord injury

806.00 Closed fracture of C1-C4 level with unspecified spinal cord injury

806.20 Closed fracture of T1-T6 level with unspecified spinal cord injury

806.4 Closed fracture of lumbar spine with spinal cord injury
806.5 Open fracture of lumbar spine with spinal cord injury
806.60 Closed fracture of sacrum and coccyx with unspecified spinal cord injury ▽
806.69 Closed fracture of sacrum and coccyx with other spinal cord injury
806.70 Open fracture of sacrum and coccyx with unspecified spinal cord injury ▽
806.79 Open fracture of sacrum and coccyx with other spinal cord injury
839.00 Closed dislocation, unspecified cervical vertebra ▽
839.10 Open dislocation, unspecified cervical vertebra ▽
905.1 Late effect of fracture of spine and trunk without mention of spinal cord lesion
907.2 Late effect of spinal cord injury
952.2 Lumbar spinal cord injury without spinal bone injury
952.3 Sacral spinal cord injury without spinal bone injury
953.3 Injury to sacral nerve root
953.5 Injury to lumbosacral plexus

ICD-9-CM Procedural

03.09 Other exploration and decompression of spinal canal

63012

63012 Laminectomy with removal of abnormal facets and/or pars inter-articularis with decompression of cauda equina and nerve roots for spondylolisthesis, lumbar (Gill type procedure)

ICD-9-CM Diagnostic

721.3 Lumbosacral spondylosis without myelopathy
721.42 Spondylosis with myelopathy, lumbar region
724.2 Lumbago
724.4 Thoracic or lumbosacral neuritis or radiculitis, unspecified ▽
724.5 Unspecified backache ▽
738.4 Acquired spondylolisthesis
756.11 Congenital spondylolysis, lumbosacral region
756.12 Congenital spondylolisthesis

ICD-9-CM Procedural

03.09 Other exploration and decompression of spinal canal

63015-63017

63015 Laminectomy with exploration and/or decompression of spinal cord and/or cauda equina, without facetectomy, foraminotomy or discectomy (eg, spinal stenosis), more than 2 vertebral segments; cervical
63016 thoracic
63017 lumbar

ICD-9-CM Diagnostic

720.0 Ankylosing spondylitis
721.0 Cervical spondylosis without myelopathy
721.1 Cervical spondylosis with myelopathy
721.2 Thoracic spondylosis without myelopathy
721.3 Lumbosacral spondylosis without myelopathy
721.41 Spondylosis with myelopathy, thoracic region
721.42 Spondylosis with myelopathy, lumbar region
722.10 Displacement of lumbar intervertebral disc without myelopathy
722.83 Postlaminectomy syndrome, lumbar region
722.93 Other and unspecified disc disorder of lumbar region ▽
723.0 Spinal stenosis in cervical region
723.4 Brachial neuritis or radiculitis NOS ▽
723.7 Ossification of posterior longitudinal ligament in cervical region
724.01 Spinal stenosis of thoracic region
724.02 Spinal stenosis of lumbar region, without neurogenic claudication
724.03 Spinal stenosis of lumbar region, with neurogenic claudication
724.1 Pain in thoracic spine
724.2 Lumbago
724.3 Sciatica
724.4 Thoracic or lumbosacral neuritis or radiculitis, unspecified ▽
724.5 Unspecified backache ▽
724.9 Other unspecified back disorder
729.2 Unspecified neuralgia, neuritis, and radiculitis ▽
738.4 Acquired spondylolisthesis
756.11 Congenital spondylolysis, lumbosacral region
756.12 Congenital spondylolisthesis
756.19 Other congenital anomaly of spine
805.00 Closed fracture of cervical vertebra, unspecified level without mention of spinal cord injury ▽
805.10 Open fracture of cervical vertebra, unspecified level without mention of spinal cord injury ▽
805.2 Closed fracture of dorsal (thoracic) vertebra without mention of spinal cord injury
805.3 Open fracture of dorsal (thoracic) vertebra without mention of spinal cord injury
805.4 Closed fracture of lumbar vertebra without mention of spinal cord injury
805.5 Open fracture of lumbar vertebra without mention of spinal cord injury
806.00 Closed fracture of C1-C4 level with unspecified spinal cord injury ▽
806.19 Open fracture of C5-C7 level with other specified spinal cord injury
806.20 Closed fracture of T1-T6 level with unspecified spinal cord injury ▽
806.30 Open fracture of T1-T6 level with unspecified spinal cord injury ▽
806.4 Closed fracture of lumbar spine with spinal cord injury
806.5 Open fracture of lumbar spine with spinal cord injury
846.0 Sprain and strain of lumbosacral (joint) (ligament)
905.1 Late effect of fracture of spine and trunk without mention of spinal cord lesion
905.6 Late effect of dislocation
907.2 Late effect of spinal cord injury
907.3 Late effect of injury to nerve root(s), spinal plexus(es), and other nerves of trunk
952.2 Lumbar spinal cord injury without spinal bone injury
953.0 Injury to cervical nerve root
953.1 Injury to dorsal nerve root
953.2 Injury to lumbar nerve root
953.5 Injury to lumbosacral plexus

ICD-9-CM Procedural

03.09 Other exploration and decompression of spinal canal

63020-63035

63020 Laminotomy (hemilaminectomy), with decompression of nerve root(s), including partial facetectomy, foraminotomy and/or excision of herniated intervertebral disc; 1 interspace, cervical
63030 1 interspace, lumbar
63035 each additional interspace, cervical or lumbar (List separately in addition to code for primary procedure)

ICD-9-CM Diagnostic

721.0 Cervical spondylosis without myelopathy
721.1 Cervical spondylosis with myelopathy
721.3 Lumbosacral spondylosis without myelopathy
721.42 Spondylosis with myelopathy, lumbar region
722.0 Displacement of cervical intervertebral disc without myelopathy
722.10 Displacement of lumbar intervertebral disc without myelopathy
722.51 Degeneration of thoracic or thoracolumbar intervertebral disc
722.52 Degeneration of lumbar or lumbosacral intervertebral disc
722.71 Intervertebral cervical disc disorder with myelopathy, cervical region
722.73 Intervertebral lumbar disc disorder with myelopathy, lumbar region
723.0 Spinal stenosis in cervical region
723.1 Cervicalgia
723.4 Brachial neuritis or radiculitis NOS ▽

723.7 Ossification of posterior longitudinal ligament in cervical region
724.02 Spinal stenosis of lumbar region, without neurogenic claudication
724.03 Spinal stenosis of lumbar region, with neurogenic claudication
724.2 Lumbago
724.3 Sciatica
724.4 Thoracic or lumbosacral neuritis or radiculitis, unspecified
724.9 Other unspecified back disorder
738.4 Acquired spondylolisthesis
756.10 Congenital anomaly of spine, unspecified
756.11 Congenital spondylolysis, lumbosacral region
756.12 Congenital spondylolisthesis
756.19 Other congenital anomaly of spine
805.4 Closed fracture of lumbar vertebra without mention of spinal cord injury
805.5 Open fracture of lumbar vertebra without mention of spinal cord injury
806.00 Closed fracture of C1-C4 level with unspecified spinal cord injury
806.10 Open fracture of C1-C4 level with unspecified spinal cord injury
806.19 Open fracture of C5-C7 level with other specified spinal cord injury
806.4 Closed fracture of lumbar spine with spinal cord injury
806.5 Open fracture of lumbar spine with spinal cord injury
839.03 Closed dislocation, third cervical vertebra
839.04 Closed dislocation, fourth cervical vertebra
839.05 Closed dislocation, fifth cervical vertebra
839.06 Closed dislocation, sixth cervical vertebra
839.07 Closed dislocation, seventh cervical vertebra
839.08 Closed dislocation, multiple cervical vertebrae
839.10 Open dislocation, unspecified cervical vertebra
839.11 Open dislocation, first cervical vertebra
839.12 Open dislocation, second cervical vertebra
839.13 Open dislocation, third cervical vertebra
839.14 Open dislocation, fourth cervical vertebra
839.15 Open dislocation, fifth cervical vertebra
839.16 Open dislocation, sixth cervical vertebra
839.17 Open dislocation, seventh cervical vertebra
839.18 Open dislocation, multiple cervical vertebrae
839.20 Closed dislocation, lumbar vertebra
905.1 Late effect of fracture of spine and trunk without mention of spinal cord lesion
907.2 Late effect of spinal cord injury
952.00 C1-C4 level spinal cord injury, unspecified
952.2 Lumbar spinal cord injury without spinal bone injury
953.2 Injury to lumbar nerve root

ICD-9-CM Procedural

03.09 Other exploration and decompression of spinal canal
80.51 Excision of intervertebral disc

63040-63044

63040 Laminotomy (hemilaminectomy), with decompression of nerve root(s), including partial facetectomy, foraminotomy and/or excision of herniated intervertebral disc, reexploration, single interspace; cervical
63042 lumbar
63043 each additional cervical interspace (List separately in addition to code for primary procedure)
63044 each additional lumbar interspace (List separately in addition to code for primary procedure)

ICD-9-CM Diagnostic

721.0 Cervical spondylosis without myelopathy
721.1 Cervical spondylosis with myelopathy
721.3 Lumbosacral spondylosis without myelopathy
721.42 Spondylosis with myelopathy, lumbar region
722.0 Displacement of cervical intervertebral disc without myelopathy
722.10 Displacement of lumbar intervertebral disc without myelopathy
722.4 Degeneration of cervical intervertebral disc
722.52 Degeneration of lumbar or lumbosacral intervertebral disc
722.71 Intervertebral cervical disc disorder with myelopathy, cervical region
722.73 Intervertebral lumbar disc disorder with myelopathy, lumbar region
722.81 Postlaminectomy syndrome, cervical region
722.83 Postlaminectomy syndrome, lumbar region
722.93 Other and unspecified disc disorder of lumbar region
723.0 Spinal stenosis in cervical region
723.1 Cervicalgia
723.4 Brachial neuritis or radiculitis NOS
724.02 Spinal stenosis of lumbar region, without neurogenic claudication
724.03 Spinal stenosis of lumbar region, with neurogenic claudication
724.4 Thoracic or lumbosacral neuritis or radiculitis, unspecified
756.11 Congenital spondylolysis, lumbosacral region
756.12 Congenital spondylolisthesis
805.00 Closed fracture of cervical vertebra, unspecified level without mention of spinal cord injury
805.10 Open fracture of cervical vertebra, unspecified level without mention of spinal cord injury
806.00 Closed fracture of C1-C4 level with unspecified spinal cord injury
806.10 Open fracture of C1-C4 level with unspecified spinal cord injury
806.4 Closed fracture of lumbar spine with spinal cord injury
806.5 Open fracture of lumbar spine with spinal cord injury
839.00 Closed dislocation, unspecified cervical vertebra
839.10 Open dislocation, unspecified cervical vertebra
907.3 Late effect of injury to nerve root(s), spinal plexus(es), and other nerves of trunk
909.3 Late effect of complications of surgical and medical care
952.2 Lumbar spinal cord injury without spinal bone injury
953.2 Injury to lumbar nerve root
953.5 Injury to lumbosacral plexus

ICD-9-CM Procedural

03.02 Reopening of laminectomy site
80.51 Excision of intervertebral disc

63045-63048

63045 Laminectomy, facetectomy and foraminotomy (unilateral or bilateral with decompression of spinal cord, cauda equina and/or nerve root[s], [eg, spinal or lateral recess stenosis]), single vertebral segment; cervical
63046 thoracic
63047 lumbar
63048 each additional segment, cervical, thoracic, or lumbar (List separately in addition to code for primary procedure)

ICD-9-CM Diagnostic

721.0 Cervical spondylosis without myelopathy
721.1 Cervical spondylosis with myelopathy
721.2 Thoracic spondylosis without myelopathy
721.3 Lumbosacral spondylosis without myelopathy
721.41 Spondylosis with myelopathy, thoracic region
721.42 Spondylosis with myelopathy, lumbar region
722.10 Displacement of lumbar intervertebral disc without myelopathy
722.51 Degeneration of thoracic or thoracolumbar intervertebral disc
722.52 Degeneration of lumbar or lumbosacral intervertebral disc
722.71 Intervertebral cervical disc disorder with myelopathy, cervical region
722.72 Intervertebral thoracic disc disorder with myelopathy, thoracic region
722.73 Intervertebral lumbar disc disorder with myelopathy, lumbar region
722.83 Postlaminectomy syndrome, lumbar region

722.93	Other and unspecified disc disorder of lumbar region
723.0	Spinal stenosis in cervical region
723.1	Cervicalgia
723.4	Brachial neuritis or radiculitis NOS
723.7	Ossification of posterior longitudinal ligament in cervical region
724.01	Spinal stenosis of thoracic region
724.02	Spinal stenosis of lumbar region, without neurogenic claudication
724.03	Spinal stenosis of lumbar region, with neurogenic claudication
724.1	Pain in thoracic spine
724.4	Thoracic or lumbosacral neuritis or radiculitis, unspecified
724.9	Other unspecified back disorder
729.2	Unspecified neuralgia, neuritis, and radiculitis
738.4	Acquired spondylolisthesis
756.11	Congenital spondylolysis, lumbosacral region
756.12	Congenital spondylolisthesis
805.2	Closed fracture of dorsal (thoracic) vertebra without mention of spinal cord injury
805.3	Open fracture of dorsal (thoracic) vertebra without mention of spinal cord injury
805.4	Closed fracture of lumbar vertebra without mention of spinal cord injury
805.5	Open fracture of lumbar vertebra without mention of spinal cord injury
806.00	Closed fracture of C1-C4 level with unspecified spinal cord injury
806.10	Open fracture of C1-C4 level with unspecified spinal cord injury
806.20	Closed fracture of T1-T6 level with unspecified spinal cord injury
806.30	Open fracture of T1-T6 level with unspecified spinal cord injury
806.4	Closed fracture of lumbar spine with spinal cord injury
806.5	Open fracture of lumbar spine with spinal cord injury
839.00	Closed dislocation, unspecified cervical vertebra
839.10	Open dislocation, unspecified cervical vertebra
839.21	Closed dislocation, thoracic vertebra
839.31	Open dislocation, thoracic vertebra
952.00	C1-C4 level spinal cord injury, unspecified
952.10	T1-T6 level spinal cord injury, unspecified
952.2	Lumbar spinal cord injury without spinal bone injury
953.1	Injury to dorsal nerve root
953.2	Injury to lumbar nerve root

ICD-9-CM Procedural

03.09	Other exploration and decompression of spinal canal

63050-63051

63050 Laminoplasty, cervical, with decompression of the spinal cord, 2 or more vertebral segments;

63051 with reconstruction of the posterior bony elements (including the application of bridging bone graft and non-segmental fixation devices [eg, wire, suture, mini-plates], when performed)

ICD-9-CM Diagnostic

720.0	Ankylosing spondylitis
721.1	Cervical spondylosis with myelopathy
722.71	Intervertebral cervical disc disorder with myelopathy, cervical region
723.0	Spinal stenosis in cervical region
723.1	Cervicalgia
723.4	Brachial neuritis or radiculitis NOS
756.10	Congenital anomaly of spine, unspecified
756.19	Other congenital anomaly of spine
905.1	Late effect of fracture of spine and trunk without mention of spinal cord lesion

ICD-9-CM Procedural

03.09	Other exploration and decompression of spinal canal
03.59	Other repair and plastic operations on spinal cord structures

63055-63057

63055 Transpedicular approach with decompression of spinal cord, equina and/or nerve root(s) (eg, herniated intervertebral disc), single segment; thoracic

63056 lumbar (including transfacet, or lateral extraforaminal approach) (eg, far lateral herniated intervertebral disc)

63057 each additional segment, thoracic or lumbar (List separately in addition to code for primary procedure)

ICD-9-CM Diagnostic

722.10	Displacement of lumbar intervertebral disc without myelopathy
722.11	Displacement of thoracic intervertebral disc without myelopathy
722.51	Degeneration of thoracic or thoracolumbar intervertebral disc
722.52	Degeneration of lumbar or lumbosacral intervertebral disc
722.72	Intervertebral thoracic disc disorder with myelopathy, thoracic region
722.73	Intervertebral lumbar disc disorder with myelopathy, lumbar region
724.01	Spinal stenosis of thoracic region
724.02	Spinal stenosis of lumbar region, without neurogenic claudication
724.03	Spinal stenosis of lumbar region, with neurogenic claudication
724.3	Sciatica
724.4	Thoracic or lumbosacral neuritis or radiculitis, unspecified
729.2	Unspecified neuralgia, neuritis, and radiculitis
729.5	Pain in soft tissues of limb
733.13	Pathologic fracture of vertebrae
733.95	Stress fracture of other bone — (Use additional external cause code(s) to identify the cause of the stress fracture)
805.2	Closed fracture of dorsal (thoracic) vertebra without mention of spinal cord injury
805.3	Open fracture of dorsal (thoracic) vertebra without mention of spinal cord injury
805.4	Closed fracture of lumbar vertebra without mention of spinal cord injury
805.5	Open fracture of lumbar vertebra without mention of spinal cord injury
806.20	Closed fracture of T1-T6 level with unspecified spinal cord injury
806.30	Open fracture of T1-T6 level with unspecified spinal cord injury
806.4	Closed fracture of lumbar spine with spinal cord injury
806.5	Open fracture of lumbar spine with spinal cord injury

ICD-9-CM Procedural

03.09	Other exploration and decompression of spinal canal

63064-63066

63064 Costovertebral approach with decompression of spinal cord or nerve root(s) (eg, herniated intervertebral disc), thoracic; single segment

63066 each additional segment (List separately in addition to code for primary procedure)

ICD-9-CM Diagnostic

722.11	Displacement of thoracic intervertebral disc without myelopathy
722.51	Degeneration of thoracic or thoracolumbar intervertebral disc
722.72	Intervertebral thoracic disc disorder with myelopathy, thoracic region
722.92	Other and unspecified disc disorder of thoracic region
724.01	Spinal stenosis of thoracic region
738.4	Acquired spondylolisthesis
756.12	Congenital spondylolisthesis
805.2	Closed fracture of dorsal (thoracic) vertebra without mention of spinal cord injury
805.3	Open fracture of dorsal (thoracic) vertebra without mention of spinal cord injury
806.20	Closed fracture of T1-T6 level with unspecified spinal cord injury
806.21	Closed fracture of T1-T6 level with complete lesion of cord
806.30	Open fracture of T1-T6 level with unspecified spinal cord injury
952.19	T7-T12 level with other specified spinal cord injury

ICD-9-CM Procedural

03.09	Other exploration and decompression of spinal canal

63075-63076

63075 Discectomy, anterior, with decompression of spinal cord and/or nerve root(s), including osteophytectomy; cervical, single interspace

63076 cervical, each additional interspace (List separately in addition to code for primary procedure)

ICD-9-CM Diagnostic

721.0 Cervical spondylosis without myelopathy

721.1 Cervical spondylosis with myelopathy

721.8 Other allied disorders of spine

722.0 Displacement of cervical intervertebral disc without myelopathy

722.4 Degeneration of cervical intervertebral disc

722.71 Intervertebral cervical disc disorder with myelopathy, cervical region

722.91 Other and unspecified disc disorder of cervical region

723.0 Spinal stenosis in cervical region

723.1 Cervicalgia

723.2 Cervicocranial syndrome

723.3 Cervicobrachial syndrome (diffuse)

723.4 Brachial neuritis or radiculitis NOS

723.7 Ossification of posterior longitudinal ligament in cervical region

729.5 Pain in soft tissues of limb

738.4 Acquired spondylolisthesis

738.5 Other acquired deformity of back or spine

756.10 Congenital anomaly of spine, unspecified

756.19 Other congenital anomaly of spine

839.03 Closed dislocation, third cervical vertebra

839.04 Closed dislocation, fourth cervical vertebra

839.05 Closed dislocation, fifth cervical vertebra

839.06 Closed dislocation, sixth cervical vertebra

839.07 Closed dislocation, seventh cervical vertebra

839.08 Closed dislocation, multiple cervical vertebrae

839.11 Open dislocation, first cervical vertebra

839.12 Open dislocation, second cervical vertebra

839.13 Open dislocation, third cervical vertebra

839.14 Open dislocation, fourth cervical vertebra

839.15 Open dislocation, fifth cervical vertebra

839.16 Open dislocation, sixth cervical vertebra

839.17 Open dislocation, seventh cervical vertebra

839.18 Open dislocation, multiple cervical vertebrae

905.1 Late effect of fracture of spine and trunk without mention of spinal cord lesion

907.2 Late effect of spinal cord injury

952.00 C1-C4 level spinal cord injury, unspecified

952.09 C5-C7 level with other specified spinal cord injury

ICD-9-CM Procedural

80.51 Excision of intervertebral disc

63077-63078

63077 Discectomy, anterior, with decompression of spinal cord and/or nerve root(s), including osteophytectomy; thoracic, single interspace

63078 thoracic, each additional interspace (List separately in addition to code for primary procedure)

ICD-9-CM Diagnostic

721.2 Thoracic spondylosis without myelopathy

721.41 Spondylosis with myelopathy, thoracic region

721.8 Other allied disorders of spine

722.11 Displacement of thoracic intervertebral disc without myelopathy

722.51 Degeneration of thoracic or thoracolumbar intervertebral disc

722.72 Intervertebral thoracic disc disorder with myelopathy, thoracic region

722.92 Other and unspecified disc disorder of thoracic region

724.01 Spinal stenosis of thoracic region

724.1 Pain in thoracic spine

729.2 Unspecified neuralgia, neuritis, and radiculitis

754.2 Congenital musculoskeletal deformity of spine

952.10 T1-T6 level spinal cord injury, unspecified

ICD-9-CM Procedural

80.51 Excision of intervertebral disc

63081-63082

63081 Vertebral corpectomy (vertebral body resection), partial or complete, anterior approach with decompression of spinal cord and/or nerve root(s); cervical, single segment

63082 cervical, each additional segment (List separately in addition to code for primary procedure)

ICD-9-CM Diagnostic

170.2 Malignant neoplasm of vertebral column, excluding sacrum and coccyx

721.0 Cervical spondylosis without myelopathy

721.1 Cervical spondylosis with myelopathy

722.0 Displacement of cervical intervertebral disc without myelopathy

722.4 Degeneration of cervical intervertebral disc

722.71 Intervertebral cervical disc disorder with myelopathy, cervical region

722.91 Other and unspecified disc disorder of cervical region

723.0 Spinal stenosis in cervical region

723.1 Cervicalgia

723.4 Brachial neuritis or radiculitis NOS

730.28 Unspecified osteomyelitis, other specified sites — (Use additional code to identify organism: 041.1. Use additional code to identify major osseous defect, if applicable: 731.3)

756.10 Congenital anomaly of spine, unspecified

756.12 Congenital spondylolisthesis

806.00 Closed fracture of C1-C4 level with unspecified spinal cord injury

806.10 Open fracture of C1-C4 level with unspecified spinal cord injury

ICD-9-CM Procedural

03.09 Other exploration and decompression of spinal canal

03.59 Other repair and plastic operations on spinal cord structures

63085-63086

63085 Vertebral corpectomy (vertebral body resection), partial or complete, transthoracic approach with decompression of spinal cord and/or nerve root(s); thoracic, single segment

63086 thoracic, each additional segment (List separately in addition to code for primary procedure)

ICD-9-CM Diagnostic

170.2 Malignant neoplasm of vertebral column, excluding sacrum and coccyx

721.2 Thoracic spondylosis without myelopathy

721.41 Spondylosis with myelopathy, thoracic region

722.11 Displacement of thoracic intervertebral disc without myelopathy

722.51 Degeneration of thoracic or thoracolumbar intervertebral disc

722.72 Intervertebral thoracic disc disorder with myelopathy, thoracic region

724.1 Pain in thoracic spine

724.4 Thoracic or lumbosacral neuritis or radiculitis, unspecified

729.2 Unspecified neuralgia, neuritis, and radiculitis

730.28 Unspecified osteomyelitis, other specified sites — (Use additional code to identify organism: 041.1. Use additional code to identify major osseous defect, if applicable: 731.3)

805.2 Closed fracture of dorsal (thoracic) vertebra without mention of spinal cord injury

805.3 Open fracture of dorsal (thoracic) vertebra without mention of spinal cord injury

806.20 Closed fracture of T1-T6 level with unspecified spinal cord injury

806.30 Open fracture of T1-T6 level with unspecified spinal cord injury

ICD-9-CM Procedural

03.09 Other exploration and decompression of spinal canal
03.59 Other repair and plastic operations on spinal cord structures

63087-63088

63087 Vertebral corpectomy (vertebral body resection), partial or complete, combined thoracolumbar approach with decompression of spinal cord, cauda equina or nerve root(s), lower thoracic or lumbar; single segment
63088 each additional segment (List separately in addition to code for primary procedure)

ICD-9-CM Diagnostic

170.2 Malignant neoplasm of vertebral column, excluding sacrum and coccyx
721.2 Thoracic spondylosis without myelopathy
721.41 Spondylosis with myelopathy, thoracic region
722.10 Displacement of lumbar intervertebral disc without myelopathy
722.11 Displacement of thoracic intervertebral disc without myelopathy
722.51 Degeneration of thoracic or thoracolumbar intervertebral disc
722.52 Degeneration of lumbar or lumbosacral intervertebral disc
722.72 Intervertebral thoracic disc disorder with myelopathy, thoracic region
722.73 Intervertebral lumbar disc disorder with myelopathy, lumbar region
722.93 Other and unspecified disc disorder of lumbar region ▽
724.02 Spinal stenosis of lumbar region, without neurogenic claudication
724.03 Spinal stenosis of lumbar region, with neurogenic claudication
724.4 Thoracic or lumbosacral neuritis or radiculitis, unspecified ▽
730.28 Unspecified osteomyelitis, other specified sites — (Use additional code to identify organism: 041.1. Use additional code to identify major osseous defect, if applicable: 731.3) ▽
805.2 Closed fracture of dorsal (thoracic) vertebra without mention of spinal cord injury
805.3 Open fracture of dorsal (thoracic) vertebra without mention of spinal cord injury
805.4 Closed fracture of lumbar vertebra without mention of spinal cord injury
805.5 Open fracture of lumbar vertebra without mention of spinal cord injury
806.25 Closed fracture of T7-T12 level with unspecified spinal cord injury ▽
806.35 Open fracture of T7-T12 level with unspecified spinal cord injury ▽
806.4 Closed fracture of lumbar spine with spinal cord injury
806.5 Open fracture of lumbar spine with spinal cord injury

ICD-9-CM Procedural

03.09 Other exploration and decompression of spinal canal
03.59 Other repair and plastic operations on spinal cord structures

63090-63091

63090 Vertebral corpectomy (vertebral body resection), partial or complete, transperitoneal or retroperitoneal approach with decompression of spinal cord, cauda equina or nerve root(s), lower thoracic, lumbar, or sacral; single segment
63091 each additional segment (List separately in addition to code for primary procedure)

ICD-9-CM Diagnostic

170.2 Malignant neoplasm of vertebral column, excluding sacrum and coccyx
170.6 Malignant neoplasm of pelvic bones, sacrum, and coccyx
721.2 Thoracic spondylosis without myelopathy
721.3 Lumbosacral spondylosis without myelopathy
721.41 Spondylosis with myelopathy, thoracic region
722.10 Displacement of lumbar intervertebral disc without myelopathy
722.11 Displacement of thoracic intervertebral disc without myelopathy
722.51 Degeneration of thoracic or thoracolumbar intervertebral disc
722.52 Degeneration of lumbar or lumbosacral intervertebral disc
722.72 Intervertebral thoracic disc disorder with myelopathy, thoracic region
722.73 Intervertebral lumbar disc disorder with myelopathy, lumbar region
722.93 Other and unspecified disc disorder of lumbar region ▽
724.02 Spinal stenosis of lumbar region, without neurogenic claudication
724.03 Spinal stenosis of lumbar region, with neurogenic claudication
724.4 Thoracic or lumbosacral neuritis or radiculitis, unspecified ▽
724.6 Disorders of sacrum
730.28 Unspecified osteomyelitis, other specified sites — (Use additional code to identify organism: 041.1. Use additional code to identify major osseous defect, if applicable: 731.3) ▽
738.4 Acquired spondylolisthesis
805.2 Closed fracture of dorsal (thoracic) vertebra without mention of spinal cord injury
805.3 Open fracture of dorsal (thoracic) vertebra without mention of spinal cord injury
805.4 Closed fracture of lumbar vertebra without mention of spinal cord injury
805.5 Open fracture of lumbar vertebra without mention of spinal cord injury
806.25 Closed fracture of T7-T12 level with unspecified spinal cord injury ▽
806.35 Open fracture of T7-T12 level with unspecified spinal cord injury ▽
806.4 Closed fracture of lumbar spine with spinal cord injury
806.5 Open fracture of lumbar spine with spinal cord injury

ICD-9-CM Procedural

03.09 Other exploration and decompression of spinal canal
03.59 Other repair and plastic operations on spinal cord structures

63101-63103

63101 Vertebral corpectomy (vertebral body resection), partial or complete, lateral extracavitary approach with decompression of spinal cord and/or nerve root(s) (eg, for tumor or retropulsed bone fragments); thoracic, single segment
63102 lumbar, single segment
63103 thoracic or lumbar, each additional segment (List separately in addition to code for primary procedure)

ICD-9-CM Diagnostic

170.2 Malignant neoplasm of vertebral column, excluding sacrum and coccyx
721.2 Thoracic spondylosis without myelopathy
721.41 Spondylosis with myelopathy, thoracic region
722.10 Displacement of lumbar intervertebral disc without myelopathy
722.11 Displacement of thoracic intervertebral disc without myelopathy
722.51 Degeneration of thoracic or thoracolumbar intervertebral disc
722.52 Degeneration of lumbar or lumbosacral intervertebral disc
722.72 Intervertebral thoracic disc disorder with myelopathy, thoracic region
722.73 Intervertebral lumbar disc disorder with myelopathy, lumbar region
722.93 Other and unspecified disc disorder of lumbar region ▽
724.02 Spinal stenosis of lumbar region, without neurogenic claudication
724.03 Spinal stenosis of lumbar region, with neurogenic claudication
724.1 Pain in thoracic spine
724.4 Thoracic or lumbosacral neuritis or radiculitis, unspecified ▽
730.28 Unspecified osteomyelitis, other specified sites — (Use additional code to identify organism: 041.1. Use additional code to identify major osseous defect, if applicable: 731.3) ▽
805.2 Closed fracture of dorsal (thoracic) vertebra without mention of spinal cord injury
805.3 Open fracture of dorsal (thoracic) vertebra without mention of spinal cord injury
805.4 Closed fracture of lumbar vertebra without mention of spinal cord injury
805.5 Open fracture of lumbar vertebra without mention of spinal cord injury
806.20 Closed fracture of T1-T6 level with unspecified spinal cord injury ▽
806.25 Closed fracture of T7-T12 level with unspecified spinal cord injury ▽
806.30 Open fracture of T1-T6 level with unspecified spinal cord injury ▽
806.35 Open fracture of T7-T12 level with unspecified spinal cord injury ▽
806.4 Closed fracture of lumbar spine with spinal cord injury
806.5 Open fracture of lumbar spine with spinal cord injury

ICD-9-CM Procedural

03.09 Other exploration and decompression of spinal canal
03.59 Other repair and plastic operations on spinal cord structures

63170

63170 Laminectomy with myelotomy (eg, Bischof or DREZ type), cervical, thoracic, or thoracolumbar

ICD-9-CM Diagnostic

336.0 Syringomyelia and syringobulbia
353.6 Phantom limb (syndrome)
724.1 Pain in thoracic spine
724.2 Lumbago
724.4 Thoracic or lumbosacral neuritis or radiculitis, unspecified
724.5 Unspecified backache
741.01 Spina bifida with hydrocephalus, cervical region
741.02 Spina bifida with hydrocephalus, dorsal (thoracic) region
741.03 Spina bifida with hydrocephalus, lumbar region
741.91 Spina bifida without mention of hydrocephalus, cervical region
741.92 Spina bifida without mention of hydrocephalus, dorsal (thoracic) region
741.93 Spina bifida without mention of hydrocephalus, lumbar region

ICD-9-CM Procedural

03.09 Other exploration and decompression of spinal canal
03.29 Other chordotomy

63172-63173

63172 Laminectomy with drainage of intramedullary cyst/syrinx; to subarachnoid space
63173 to peritoneal or pleural space

ICD-9-CM Diagnostic

336.0 Syringomyelia and syringobulbia
349.2 Disorders of meninges, not elsewhere classified

ICD-9-CM Procedural

03.09 Other exploration and decompression of spinal canal
03.79 Other shunt of spinal theca

63180-63182

63180 Laminectomy and section of dentate ligaments, with or without dural graft, cervical; 1 or 2 segments
63182 more than 2 segments

ICD-9-CM Diagnostic

353.2 Cervical root lesions, not elsewhere classified
354.5 Mononeuritis multiplex
723.1 Cervicalgia
723.4 Brachial neuritis or radiculitis NOS

ICD-9-CM Procedural

03.09 Other exploration and decompression of spinal canal

63185-63190

63185 Laminectomy with rhizotomy; 1 or 2 segments
63190 more than 2 segments

ICD-9-CM Diagnostic

343.9 Unspecified infantile cerebral palsy
720.2 Sacroiliitis, not elsewhere classified
723.1 Cervicalgia
723.4 Brachial neuritis or radiculitis NOS
724.1 Pain in thoracic spine
724.2 Lumbago
724.3 Sciatica
724.4 Thoracic or lumbosacral neuritis or radiculitis, unspecified
724.6 Disorders of sacrum
729.1 Unspecified myalgia and myositis
729.2 Unspecified neuralgia, neuritis, and radiculitis
729.5 Pain in soft tissues of limb
786.52 Painful respiration

ICD-9-CM Procedural

03.09 Other exploration and decompression of spinal canal
03.1 Division of intraspinal nerve root

63191

63191 Laminectomy with section of spinal accessory nerve

ICD-9-CM Diagnostic

334.1 Hereditary spastic paraplegia
343.0 Diplegic infantile cerebral palsy
343.8 Other specified infantile cerebral palsy
343.9 Unspecified infantile cerebral palsy
724.1 Pain in thoracic spine
724.3 Sciatica
724.4 Thoracic or lumbosacral neuritis or radiculitis, unspecified
724.6 Disorders of sacrum
729.1 Unspecified myalgia and myositis
729.2 Unspecified neuralgia, neuritis, and radiculitis
739.4 Nonallopathic lesion of sacral region, not elsewhere classified
781.0 Abnormal involuntary movements
786.52 Painful respiration

ICD-9-CM Procedural

03.09 Other exploration and decompression of spinal canal
03.59 Other repair and plastic operations on spinal cord structures
04.04 Other incision of cranial and peripheral nerves

63194-63195

63194 Laminectomy with cordotomy, with section of 1 spinothalamic tract, 1 stage; cervical
63195 thoracic

ICD-9-CM Diagnostic

334.1 Hereditary spastic paraplegia
343.0 Diplegic infantile cerebral palsy
343.8 Other specified infantile cerebral palsy
343.9 Unspecified infantile cerebral palsy
724.1 Pain in thoracic spine
724.4 Thoracic or lumbosacral neuritis or radiculitis, unspecified
729.1 Unspecified myalgia and myositis
729.2 Unspecified neuralgia, neuritis, and radiculitis
781.0 Abnormal involuntary movements
781.7 Tetany

ICD-9-CM Procedural

03.09 Other exploration and decompression of spinal canal
03.29 Other chordotomy

63196-63199

63196 Laminectomy with cordotomy, with section of both spinothalamic tracts, 1 stage; cervical
63197 thoracic
63198 Laminectomy with cordotomy with section of both spinothalamic tracts, 2 stages within 14 days; cervical
63199 thoracic

ICD-9-CM Diagnostic

334.1 Hereditary spastic paraplegia
343.0 Diplegic infantile cerebral palsy

343.8	Other specified infantile cerebral palsy
343.9	Unspecified infantile cerebral palsy ▽
724.1	Pain in thoracic spine
724.4	Thoracic or lumbosacral neuritis or radiculitis, unspecified ▽
729.1	Unspecified myalgia and myositis ▽
729.2	Unspecified neuralgia, neuritis, and radiculitis ▽
781.0	Abnormal involuntary movements
781.7	Tetany

ICD-9-CM Procedural

03.09	Other exploration and decompression of spinal canal
03.29	Other chordotomy

63200

63200 Laminectomy, with release of tethered spinal cord, lumbar

ICD-9-CM Diagnostic

741.01	Spina bifida with hydrocephalus, cervical region
741.02	Spina bifida with hydrocephalus, dorsal (thoracic) region
741.03	Spina bifida with hydrocephalus, lumbar region
741.91	Spina bifida without mention of hydrocephalus, cervical region
741.92	Spina bifida without mention of hydrocephalus, dorsal (thoracic) region
741.93	Spina bifida without mention of hydrocephalus, lumbar region
742.53	Hydromyelia
742.59	Other specified congenital anomaly of spinal cord
756.10	Congenital anomaly of spine, unspecified ▽
756.11	Congenital spondylolysis, lumbosacral region
756.12	Congenital spondylolisthesis
756.13	Congenital absence of vertebra
756.15	Congenital fusion of spine (vertebra)

ICD-9-CM Procedural

03.09	Other exploration and decompression of spinal canal
03.29	Other chordotomy

63250-63252

63250 Laminectomy for excision or occlusion of arteriovenous malformation of spinal cord; cervical
63251 thoracic
63252 thoracolumbar

ICD-9-CM Diagnostic

747.82	Congenital spinal vessel anomaly

ICD-9-CM Procedural

03.09	Other exploration and decompression of spinal canal
03.39	Other diagnostic procedures on spinal cord and spinal canal structures
03.59	Other repair and plastic operations on spinal cord structures

63265-63268

63265 Laminectomy for excision or evacuation of intraspinal lesion other than neoplasm, extradural; cervical
63266 thoracic
63267 lumbar
63268 sacral

ICD-9-CM Diagnostic

324.1	Intraspinal abscess
336.1	Vascular myelopathies

ICD-9-CM Procedural

03.4	Excision or destruction of lesion of spinal cord or spinal meninges

63270-63273

63270 Laminectomy for excision of intraspinal lesion other than neoplasm, intradural; cervical
63271 thoracic
63272 lumbar
63273 sacral

ICD-9-CM Diagnostic

324.1	Intraspinal abscess
349.2	Disorders of meninges, not elsewhere classified

ICD-9-CM Procedural

03.4	Excision or destruction of lesion of spinal cord or spinal meninges

63275-63278

63275 Laminectomy for biopsy/excision of intraspinal neoplasm; extradural, cervical
63276 extradural, thoracic
63277 extradural, lumbar
63278 extradural, sacral

ICD-9-CM Diagnostic

192.2	Malignant neoplasm of spinal cord
192.3	Malignant neoplasm of spinal meninges
198.3	Secondary malignant neoplasm of brain and spinal cord
199.0	Disseminated malignant neoplasm
225.3	Benign neoplasm of spinal cord
237.5	Neoplasm of uncertain behavior of brain and spinal cord
237.6	Neoplasm of uncertain behavior of meninges
239.7	Neoplasm of unspecified nature of endocrine glands and other parts of nervous system

ICD-9-CM Procedural

03.32	Biopsy of spinal cord or spinal meninges
03.4	Excision or destruction of lesion of spinal cord or spinal meninges

63280-63283

63280 Laminectomy for biopsy/excision of intraspinal neoplasm; intradural, extramedullary, cervical
63281 intradural, extramedullary, thoracic
63282 intradural, extramedullary, lumbar
63283 intradural, sacral

ICD-9-CM Diagnostic

192.2	Malignant neoplasm of spinal cord
192.3	Malignant neoplasm of spinal meninges
198.3	Secondary malignant neoplasm of brain and spinal cord
199.0	Disseminated malignant neoplasm
225.3	Benign neoplasm of spinal cord
225.4	Benign neoplasm of spinal meninges
237.5	Neoplasm of uncertain behavior of brain and spinal cord
237.6	Neoplasm of uncertain behavior of meninges
239.7	Neoplasm of unspecified nature of endocrine glands and other parts of nervous system

ICD-9-CM Procedural

03.32	Biopsy of spinal cord or spinal meninges
03.4	Excision or destruction of lesion of spinal cord or spinal meninges

63285-63290

63285 Laminectomy for biopsy/excision of intraspinal neoplasm; intradural, intramedullary, cervical
63286 intradural, intramedullary, thoracic
63287 intradural, intramedullary, thoracolumbar
63290 combined extradural-intradural lesion, any level

ICD-9-CM Diagnostic

192.2	Malignant neoplasm of spinal cord

192.3	Malignant neoplasm of spinal meninges
198.3	Secondary malignant neoplasm of brain and spinal cord
199.0	Disseminated malignant neoplasm
225.3	Benign neoplasm of spinal cord
225.4	Benign neoplasm of spinal meninges
237.5	Neoplasm of uncertain behavior of brain and spinal cord
237.6	Neoplasm of uncertain behavior of meninges
239.7	Neoplasm of unspecified nature of endocrine glands and other parts of nervous system

ICD-9-CM Procedural

03.32	Biopsy of spinal cord or spinal meninges
03.4	Excision or destruction of lesion of spinal cord or spinal meninges

63300-63303

63300 Vertebral corpectomy (vertebral body resection), partial or complete, for excision of intraspinal lesion, single segment; extradural, cervical

63301 extradural, thoracic by transthoracic approach

63302 extradural, thoracic by thoracolumbar approach

63303 extradural, lumbar or sacral by transperitoneal or retroperitoneal approach

ICD-9-CM Diagnostic

192.2	Malignant neoplasm of spinal cord
192.3	Malignant neoplasm of spinal meninges
198.3	Secondary malignant neoplasm of brain and spinal cord
199.0	Disseminated malignant neoplasm
225.3	Benign neoplasm of spinal cord
225.4	Benign neoplasm of spinal meninges
237.5	Neoplasm of uncertain behavior of brain and spinal cord
237.6	Neoplasm of uncertain behavior of meninges
239.7	Neoplasm of unspecified nature of endocrine glands and other parts of nervous system
324.1	Intraspinal abscess
336.1	Vascular myelopathies

ICD-9-CM Procedural

03.39	Other diagnostic procedures on spinal cord and spinal canal structures
03.4	Excision or destruction of lesion of spinal cord or spinal meninges
03.6	Lysis of adhesions of spinal cord and nerve roots

63304-63307

63304 Vertebral corpectomy (vertebral body resection), partial or complete, for excision of intraspinal lesion, single segment; intradural, cervical

63305 intradural, thoracic by transthoracic approach

63306 intradural, thoracic by thoracolumbar approach

63307 intradural, lumbar or sacral by transperitoneal or retroperitoneal approach

ICD-9-CM Diagnostic

192.2	Malignant neoplasm of spinal cord
192.3	Malignant neoplasm of spinal meninges
198.3	Secondary malignant neoplasm of brain and spinal cord
199.0	Disseminated malignant neoplasm
225.3	Benign neoplasm of spinal cord
225.4	Benign neoplasm of spinal meninges
237.5	Neoplasm of uncertain behavior of brain and spinal cord
237.6	Neoplasm of uncertain behavior of meninges
239.7	Neoplasm of unspecified nature of endocrine glands and other parts of nervous system
324.1	Intraspinal abscess
336.1	Vascular myelopathies

ICD-9-CM Procedural

03.39	Other diagnostic procedures on spinal cord and spinal canal structures
03.4	Excision or destruction of lesion of spinal cord or spinal meninges
03.6	Lysis of adhesions of spinal cord and nerve roots

63600-63615

63600 Creation of lesion of spinal cord by stereotactic method, percutaneous, any modality (including stimulation and/or recording)

63610 Stereotactic stimulation of spinal cord, percutaneous, separate procedure not followed by other surgery

63615 Stereotactic biopsy, aspiration, or excision of lesion, spinal cord

ICD-9-CM Diagnostic

192.2	Malignant neoplasm of spinal cord
192.3	Malignant neoplasm of spinal meninges
198.3	Secondary malignant neoplasm of brain and spinal cord
225.3	Benign neoplasm of spinal cord
237.5	Neoplasm of uncertain behavior of brain and spinal cord
239.7	Neoplasm of unspecified nature of endocrine glands and other parts of nervous system
332.0	Paralysis agitans
332.1	Secondary Parkinsonism — (Use additional E code to identify drug, if drug-induced)
336.1	Vascular myelopathies
722.2	Displacement of intervertebral disc, site unspecified, without myelopathy ▽
722.52	Degeneration of lumbar or lumbosacral intervertebral disc
722.73	Intervertebral lumbar disc disorder with myelopathy, lumbar region
722.82	Postlaminectomy syndrome, thoracic region
724.02	Spinal stenosis of lumbar region, without neurogenic claudication
724.03	Spinal stenosis of lumbar region, with neurogenic claudication
724.4	Thoracic or lumbosacral neuritis or radiculitis, unspecified ▽
729.5	Pain in soft tissues of limb
781.2	Abnormality of gait
781.3	Lack of coordination
953.2	Injury to lumbar nerve root

ICD-9-CM Procedural

03.21	Percutaneous chordotomy
03.32	Biopsy of spinal cord or spinal meninges
03.39	Other diagnostic procedures on spinal cord and spinal canal structures
03.4	Excision or destruction of lesion of spinal cord or spinal meninges
03.92	Injection of other agent into spinal canal

63620-63621

63620 Stereotactic radiosurgery (particle beam, gamma ray, or linear accelerator); 1 spinal lesion

63621 each additional spinal lesion (List separately in addition to code for primary procedure)

ICD-9-CM Diagnostic

171.9	Malignant neoplasm of connective and other soft tissue, site unspecified ▽
191.7	Malignant neoplasm of brain stem
192.2	Malignant neoplasm of spinal cord
192.3	Malignant neoplasm of spinal meninges
192.8	Malignant neoplasm of other specified sites of nervous system
198.3	Secondary malignant neoplasm of brain and spinal cord
198.4	Secondary malignant neoplasm of other parts of nervous system
198.89	Secondary malignant neoplasm of other specified sites
215.8	Other benign neoplasm of connective and other soft tissue of other specified sites
225.3	Benign neoplasm of spinal cord
225.4	Benign neoplasm of spinal meninges
225.8	Benign neoplasm of other specified sites of nervous system
237.5	Neoplasm of uncertain behavior of brain and spinal cord
237.6	Neoplasm of uncertain behavior of meninges
238.1	Neoplasm of uncertain behavior of connective and other soft tissue
239.89	Neoplasms of unspecified nature, other specified sites

ICD-9-CM Procedural

92.31 Single source photon radiosurgery
92.32 Multi-source photon radiosurgery
92.33 Particulate radiosurgery

63650

63650 Percutaneous implantation of neurostimulator electrode array, epidural

ICD-9-CM Diagnostic

337.00 Idiopathic peripheral autonomic neuropathy, unspecified ▽
337.09 Other idiopathic peripheral autonomic neuropathy
337.20 Unspecified reflex sympathetic dystrophy ▽
337.21 Reflex sympathetic dystrophy of the upper limb
337.22 Reflex sympathetic dystrophy of the lower limb
337.29 Reflex sympathetic dystrophy of other specified site
337.9 Unspecified disorder of autonomic nervous system ▽
344.1 Paraplegia
353.0 Brachial plexus lesions
353.1 Lumbosacral plexus lesions
353.2 Cervical root lesions, not elsewhere classified
353.3 Thoracic root lesions, not elsewhere classified
353.4 Lumbosacral root lesions, not elsewhere classified
353.5 Neuralgic amyotrophy — (Code first any associated underlying disease as: 249.6, 250.6)
353.6 Phantom limb (syndrome)
353.8 Other nerve root and plexus disorders
354.4 Causalgia of upper limb
354.5 Mononeuritis multiplex
354.8 Other mononeuritis of upper limb
354.9 Unspecified mononeuritis of upper limb ▽
355.0 Lesion of sciatic nerve
355.1 Meralgia paresthetica
355.2 Other lesion of femoral nerve
355.3 Lesion of lateral popliteal nerve
355.4 Lesion of medial popliteal nerve
355.6 Lesion of plantar nerve
355.71 Causalgia of lower limb
355.8 Unspecified mononeuritis of lower limb ▽
577.0 Acute pancreatitis
577.1 Chronic pancreatitis
577.9 Unspecified disease of pancreas ▽
721.3 Lumbosacral spondylosis without myelopathy
722.52 Degeneration of lumbar or lumbosacral intervertebral disc
722.73 Intervertebral lumbar disc disorder with myelopathy, lumbar region
722.81 Postlaminectomy syndrome, cervical region
722.82 Postlaminectomy syndrome, thoracic region
722.83 Postlaminectomy syndrome, lumbar region
723.1 Cervicalgia
723.4 Brachial neuritis or radiculitis NOS ▽
723.9 Unspecified musculoskeletal disorders and symptoms referable to neck ▽
724.02 Spinal stenosis of lumbar region, without neurogenic claudication
724.03 Spinal stenosis of lumbar region, with neurogenic claudication
724.1 Pain in thoracic spine
724.2 Lumbago
724.3 Sciatica
724.4 Thoracic or lumbosacral neuritis or radiculitis, unspecified ▽
724.79 Other disorder of coccyx
729.2 Unspecified neuralgia, neuritis, and radiculitis ▽
729.5 Pain in soft tissues of limb
731.0 Osteitis deformans without mention of bone tumor
905.1 Late effect of fracture of spine and trunk without mention of spinal cord lesion
905.2 Late effect of fracture of upper extremities
905.3 Late effect of fracture of neck of femur
905.4 Late effect of fracture of lower extremities
905.5 Late effect of fracture of multiple and unspecified bones
907.2 Late effect of spinal cord injury
907.3 Late effect of injury to nerve root(s), spinal plexus(es), and other nerves of trunk
907.4 Late effect of injury to peripheral nerve of shoulder girdle and upper limb
907.5 Late effect of injury to peripheral nerve of pelvic girdle and lower limb
907.9 Late effect of injury to other and unspecified nerve ▽
908.6 Late effect of certain complications of trauma
908.9 Late effect of unspecified injury ▽
953.2 Injury to lumbar nerve root

ICD-9-CM Procedural

03.93 Implantation or replacement of spinal neurostimulator lead(s)

HCPCS Level II Supplies & Services

C1778 Lead, neurostimulator (implantable)

63655

63655 Laminectomy for implantation of neurostimulator electrodes, plate/paddle, epidural

ICD-9-CM Diagnostic

337.00 Idiopathic peripheral autonomic neuropathy, unspecified ▽
337.09 Other idiopathic peripheral autonomic neuropathy
337.20 Unspecified reflex sympathetic dystrophy ▽
337.21 Reflex sympathetic dystrophy of the upper limb
337.22 Reflex sympathetic dystrophy of the lower limb
337.29 Reflex sympathetic dystrophy of other specified site
337.9 Unspecified disorder of autonomic nervous system ▽
344.1 Paraplegia
353.0 Brachial plexus lesions
353.1 Lumbosacral plexus lesions
353.2 Cervical root lesions, not elsewhere classified
353.3 Thoracic root lesions, not elsewhere classified
353.4 Lumbosacral root lesions, not elsewhere classified
353.5 Neuralgic amyotrophy — (Code first any associated underlying disease as: 249.6, 250.6)
353.6 Phantom limb (syndrome)
353.8 Other nerve root and plexus disorders
354.4 Causalgia of upper limb
354.5 Mononeuritis multiplex
354.8 Other mononeuritis of upper limb
354.9 Unspecified mononeuritis of upper limb ▽
355.0 Lesion of sciatic nerve
355.1 Meralgia paresthetica
355.2 Other lesion of femoral nerve
355.3 Lesion of lateral popliteal nerve
355.4 Lesion of medial popliteal nerve
355.6 Lesion of plantar nerve
355.71 Causalgia of lower limb
355.8 Unspecified mononeuritis of lower limb ▽
577.0 Acute pancreatitis
577.1 Chronic pancreatitis
577.9 Unspecified disease of pancreas ▽
721.3 Lumbosacral spondylosis without myelopathy
722.52 Degeneration of lumbar or lumbosacral intervertebral disc
722.73 Intervertebral lumbar disc disorder with myelopathy, lumbar region

722.81 Postlaminectomy syndrome, cervical region
722.82 Postlaminectomy syndrome, thoracic region
722.83 Postlaminectomy syndrome, lumbar region
723.1 Cervicalgia
723.4 Brachial neuritis or radiculitis NOS
723.9 Unspecified musculoskeletal disorders and symptoms referable to neck
724.02 Spinal stenosis of lumbar region, without neurogenic claudication
724.03 Spinal stenosis of lumbar region, with neurogenic claudication
724.1 Pain in thoracic spine
724.2 Lumbago
724.3 Sciatica
724.4 Thoracic or lumbosacral neuritis or radiculitis, unspecified
724.79 Other disorder of coccyx
729.2 Unspecified neuralgia, neuritis, and radiculitis
729.5 Pain in soft tissues of limb
731.0 Osteitis deformans without mention of bone tumor
905.1 Late effect of fracture of spine and trunk without mention of spinal cord lesion
905.2 Late effect of fracture of upper extremities
905.3 Late effect of fracture of neck of femur
905.4 Late effect of fracture of lower extremities
905.5 Late effect of fracture of multiple and unspecified bones
907.2 Late effect of spinal cord injury
907.3 Late effect of injury to nerve root(s), spinal plexus(es), and other nerves of trunk
907.4 Late effect of injury to peripheral nerve of shoulder girdle and upper limb
907.5 Late effect of injury to peripheral nerve of pelvic girdle and lower limb
907.9 Late effect of injury to other and unspecified nerve
908.6 Late effect of certain complications of trauma
908.9 Late effect of unspecified injury
953.2 Injury to lumbar nerve root

ICD-9-CM Procedural

03.09 Other exploration and decompression of spinal canal
03.93 Implantation or replacement of spinal neurostimulator lead(s)

HCPCS Level II Supplies & Services

C1778 Lead, neurostimulator (implantable)

63661-63664

63661 Removal of spinal neurostimulator electrode percutaneous array(s), including fluoroscopy, when performed
63662 Removal of spinal neurostimulator electrode plate/paddle(s) placed via laminotomy or laminectomy, including fluoroscopy, when performed
63663 Revision including replacement, when performed, of spinal neurostimulator electrode percutaneous array(s), including fluoroscopy, when performed
63664 Revision including replacement, when performed, of spinal neurostimulator electrode plate/paddle(s) placed via laminotomy or laminectomy, including fluoroscopy, when performed

ICD-9-CM Diagnostic

349.1 Nervous system complications from surgically implanted device
353.8 Other nerve root and plexus disorders
443.9 Unspecified peripheral vascular disease
722.2 Displacement of intervertebral disc, site unspecified, without myelopathy
722.83 Postlaminectomy syndrome, lumbar region
724.2 Lumbago
724.4 Thoracic or lumbosacral neuritis or radiculitis, unspecified
729.5 Pain in soft tissues of limb
953.2 Injury to lumbar nerve root
996.2 Mechanical complication of nervous system device, implant, and graft
996.63 Infection and inflammatory reaction due to nervous system device, implant, and graft — (Use additional code to identify specified infections)
996.75 Other complications due to nervous system device, implant, and graft — (Use additional code to identify complication: 338.18-338.19, 338.28-338.29)
V53.02 Neuropacemaker (brain) (peripheral nerve) (spinal cord)

ICD-9-CM Procedural

03.93 Implantation or replacement of spinal neurostimulator lead(s)
03.94 Removal of spinal neurostimulator lead(s)

63685

63685 Insertion or replacement of spinal neurostimulator pulse generator or receiver, direct or inductive coupling

ICD-9-CM Diagnostic

053.19 Other herpes zoster with nervous system complications
322.9 Unspecified meningitis
337.21 Reflex sympathetic dystrophy of the upper limb
337.22 Reflex sympathetic dystrophy of the lower limb
337.29 Reflex sympathetic dystrophy of other specified site
353.3 Thoracic root lesions, not elsewhere classified
353.4 Lumbosacral root lesions, not elsewhere classified
353.6 Phantom limb (syndrome)
353.8 Other nerve root and plexus disorders
354.4 Causalgia of upper limb
355.71 Causalgia of lower limb
440.22 Atherosclerosis of native arteries of the extremities with rest pain
721.2 Thoracic spondylosis without myelopathy
721.3 Lumbosacral spondylosis without myelopathy
722.10 Displacement of lumbar intervertebral disc without myelopathy
722.11 Displacement of thoracic intervertebral disc without myelopathy
722.2 Displacement of intervertebral disc, site unspecified, without myelopathy
722.51 Degeneration of thoracic or thoracolumbar intervertebral disc
722.52 Degeneration of lumbar or lumbosacral intervertebral disc
722.81 Postlaminectomy syndrome, cervical region
722.82 Postlaminectomy syndrome, thoracic region
722.83 Postlaminectomy syndrome, lumbar region
723.4 Brachial neuritis or radiculitis NOS
724.2 Lumbago
724.4 Thoracic or lumbosacral neuritis or radiculitis, unspecified
729.2 Unspecified neuralgia, neuritis, and radiculitis
952.4 Cauda equina spinal cord injury without spinal bone injury
953.2 Injury to lumbar nerve root
996.2 Mechanical complication of nervous system device, implant, and graft
996.63 Infection and inflammatory reaction due to nervous system device, implant, and graft — (Use additional code to identify specified infections)
996.75 Other complications due to nervous system device, implant, and graft — (Use additional code to identify complication: 338.18-338.19, 338.28-338.29)

ICD-9-CM Procedural

86.94 Insertion or replacement of single array neurostimulator pulse generator, not specified as rechargeable
86.95 Insertion or replacement of multiple array neurostimulator pulse generator, not specified as rechargeable
86.96 Insertion or replacement of other neurostimulator pulse generator

HCPCS Level II Supplies & Services

C1767 Generator, neurostimulator (implantable), nonrechargeable

63688

63688 Revision or removal of implanted spinal neurostimulator pulse generator or receiver

ICD-9-CM Diagnostic

349.1 Nervous system complications from surgically implanted device

353.8 Other nerve root and plexus disorders
721.3 Lumbosacral spondylosis without myelopathy
722.2 Displacement of intervertebral disc, site unspecified, without myelopathy
722.83 Postlaminectomy syndrome, lumbar region
724.2 Lumbago
724.4 Thoracic or lumbosacral neuritis or radiculitis, unspecified
729.5 Pain in soft tissues of limb
953.2 Injury to lumbar nerve root
996.2 Mechanical complication of nervous system device, implant, and graft
996.63 Infection and inflammatory reaction due to nervous system device, implant, and graft — (Use additional code to identify specified infections)

ICD-9-CM Procedural

86.05 Incision with removal of foreign body or device from skin and subcutaneous tissue

63700-63702

63700 Repair of meningocele; less than 5 cm diameter
63702 larger than 5 cm diameter

ICD-9-CM Diagnostic

331.4 Obstructive hydrocephalus — (Use additional code, where applicable, to identify dementia: 294.10, 294.11)
741.01 Spina bifida with hydrocephalus, cervical region
741.02 Spina bifida with hydrocephalus, dorsal (thoracic) region
741.03 Spina bifida with hydrocephalus, lumbar region
741.91 Spina bifida without mention of hydrocephalus, cervical region
741.92 Spina bifida without mention of hydrocephalus, dorsal (thoracic) region
741.93 Spina bifida without mention of hydrocephalus, lumbar region

ICD-9-CM Procedural

03.51 Repair of spinal meningocele

63704-63706

63704 Repair of myelomeningocele; less than 5 cm diameter
63706 larger than 5 cm diameter

ICD-9-CM Diagnostic

741.01 Spina bifida with hydrocephalus, cervical region
741.02 Spina bifida with hydrocephalus, dorsal (thoracic) region
741.03 Spina bifida with hydrocephalus, lumbar region
741.91 Spina bifida without mention of hydrocephalus, cervical region
741.92 Spina bifida without mention of hydrocephalus, dorsal (thoracic) region
741.93 Spina bifida without mention of hydrocephalus, lumbar region

ICD-9-CM Procedural

03.52 Repair of spinal myelomeningocele
03.59 Other repair and plastic operations on spinal cord structures

63707-63709

63707 Repair of dural/cerebrospinal fluid leak, not requiring laminectomy
63709 Repair of dural/cerebrospinal fluid leak or pseudomeningocele, with laminectomy

ICD-9-CM Diagnostic

349.31 Accidental puncture or laceration of dura during a procedure
349.39 Other dural tear
996.75 Other complications due to nervous system device, implant, and graft — (Use additional code to identify complication: 338.18-338.19, 338.28-338.29)
997.09 Other nervous system complications — (Use additional code to identify complications)
998.2 Accidental puncture or laceration during procedure
998.30 Disruption of wound, unspecified
998.31 Disruption of internal operation (surgical) wound
998.33 Disruption of traumatic injury wound repair
998.6 Persistent postoperative fistula, not elsewhere classified

ICD-9-CM Procedural

03.09 Other exploration and decompression of spinal canal
03.59 Other repair and plastic operations on spinal cord structures

63710

63710 Dural graft, spinal

ICD-9-CM Diagnostic

225.2 Benign neoplasm of cerebral meninges
237.5 Neoplasm of uncertain behavior of brain and spinal cord
349.31 Accidental puncture or laceration of dura during a procedure
349.39 Other dural tear
996.75 Other complications due to nervous system device, implant, and graft — (Use additional code to identify complication: 338.18-338.19, 338.28-338.29)
998.31 Disruption of internal operation (surgical) wound

ICD-9-CM Procedural

03.09 Other exploration and decompression of spinal canal
03.59 Other repair and plastic operations on spinal cord structures

63740-63741

63740 Creation of shunt, lumbar, subarachnoid-peritoneal, -pleural, or other; including laminectomy
63741 percutaneous, not requiring laminectomy

ICD-9-CM Diagnostic

331.3 Communicating hydrocephalus — (Use additional code, where applicable, to identify dementia: 294.10, 294.11)
331.4 Obstructive hydrocephalus — (Use additional code, where applicable, to identify dementia: 294.10, 294.11)
331.5 Idiopathic normal pressure hydrocephalus [INPH] — (Use additional code, where applicable, to identify dementia: 294.10, 294.11)
348.2 Benign intracranial hypertension
742.3 Congenital hydrocephalus

ICD-9-CM Procedural

03.09 Other exploration and decompression of spinal canal
03.71 Spinal subarachnoid-peritoneal shunt
03.72 Spinal subarachnoid-ureteral shunt
03.79 Other shunt of spinal theca

63744

63744 Replacement, irrigation or revision of lumbosubarachnoid shunt

ICD-9-CM Diagnostic

331.3 Communicating hydrocephalus — (Use additional code, where applicable, to identify dementia: 294.10, 294.11)
331.4 Obstructive hydrocephalus — (Use additional code, where applicable, to identify dementia: 294.10, 294.11)
331.5 Idiopathic normal pressure hydrocephalus [INPH] — (Use additional code, where applicable, to identify dementia: 294.10, 294.11)
348.2 Benign intracranial hypertension
742.3 Congenital hydrocephalus
996.1 Mechanical complication of other vascular device, implant, and graft
996.2 Mechanical complication of nervous system device, implant, and graft
996.63 Infection and inflammatory reaction due to nervous system device, implant, and graft — (Use additional code to identify specified infections)
996.75 Other complications due to nervous system device, implant, and graft — (Use additional code to identify complication: 338.18-338.19, 338.28-338.29)

ICD-9-CM Procedural

03.97 Revision of spinal thecal shunt
03.99 Other operations on spinal cord and spinal canal structures

HCPCS Level II Supplies & Services

A4305 Disposable drug delivery system, flow rate of 50 ml or greater per hour

63746

63746 Removal of entire lumbosubarachnoid shunt system without replacement

ICD-9-CM Diagnostic

331.3 Communicating hydrocephalus — (Use additional code, where applicable, to identify dementia: 294.10, 294.11)
331.4 Obstructive hydrocephalus — (Use additional code, where applicable, to identify dementia: 294.10, 294.11)
331.5 Idiopathic normal pressure hydrocephalus [INPH] — (Use additional code, where applicable, to identify dementia: 294.10, 294.11)
348.2 Benign intracranial hypertension
742.3 Congenital hydrocephalus
996.2 Mechanical complication of nervous system device, implant, and graft
996.63 Infection and inflammatory reaction due to nervous system device, implant, and graft — (Use additional code to identify specified infections)
996.75 Other complications due to nervous system device, implant, and graft — (Use additional code to identify complication: 338.18-338.19, 338.28-338.29)

ICD-9-CM Procedural

03.98 Removal of spinal thecal shunt
03.99 Other operations on spinal cord and spinal canal structures

Extracranial Nerves, Peripheral Nerves, and Autonomic Nervous System

64400

64400 Injection, anesthetic agent; trigeminal nerve, any division or branch

ICD-9-CM Diagnostic

350.1 Trigeminal neuralgia
350.2 Atypical face pain
729.1 Unspecified myalgia and myositis ▽

ICD-9-CM Procedural

04.81 Injection of anesthetic into peripheral nerve for analgesia

HCPCS Level II Supplies & Services

J2400 Injection, chloroprocaine HCl, per 30 ml

64402

64402 Injection, anesthetic agent; facial nerve

ICD-9-CM Diagnostic

333.81 Blepharospasm — (Use additional E code to identify drug, if drug-induced)
339.05 Short lasting unilateral neuralgiform headache with conjunctival injection and tearing
339.09 Other trigeminal autonomic cephalgias
339.20 Post-traumatic headache, unspecified ▽
339.21 Acute post-traumatic headache
339.22 Chronic post-traumatic headache
339.3 Drug induced headache, not elsewhere classified
339.41 Hemicrania continua
339.42 New daily persistent headache
339.43 Primary thunderclap headache
339.44 Other complicated headache syndrome
339.81 Hypnic headache
339.82 Headache associated with sexual activity
339.83 Primary cough headache
339.84 Primary exertional headache
339.85 Primary stabbing headache
339.89 Other specified headache syndromes
350.2 Atypical face pain
351.0 Bell's palsy
351.1 Geniculate ganglionitis
351.8 Other facial nerve disorders
352.9 Unspecified disorder of cranial nerves ▽
525.3 Retained dental root
526.4 Inflammatory conditions of jaw
691.8 Other atopic dermatitis and related conditions
784.0 Headache
873.41 Open wound of cheek, without mention of complication
873.42 Open wound of forehead, without mention of complication
873.43 Open wound of lip, without mention of complication
873.44 Open wound of jaw, without mention of complication

ICD-9-CM Procedural

04.81 Injection of anesthetic into peripheral nerve for analgesia

HCPCS Level II Supplies & Services

J2400 Injection, chloroprocaine HCl, per 30 ml

64405

64405 Injection, anesthetic agent; greater occipital nerve

ICD-9-CM Diagnostic

353.2 Cervical root lesions, not elsewhere classified
353.8 Other nerve root and plexus disorders
723.8 Other syndromes affecting cervical region
729.2 Unspecified neuralgia, neuritis, and radiculitis ▽

ICD-9-CM Procedural

04.81 Injection of anesthetic into peripheral nerve for analgesia

HCPCS Level II Supplies & Services

J2400 Injection, chloroprocaine HCl, per 30 ml

64408

64408 Injection, anesthetic agent; vagus nerve

ICD-9-CM Diagnostic

352.3 Disorders of pneumogastric (10th) nerve
536.1 Acute dilatation of stomach

ICD-9-CM Procedural

04.81 Injection of anesthetic into peripheral nerve for analgesia

HCPCS Level II Supplies & Services

J2400 Injection, chloroprocaine HCl, per 30 ml

64410

64410 Injection, anesthetic agent; phrenic nerve

ICD-9-CM Diagnostic

353.2 Cervical root lesions, not elsewhere classified
519.4 Disorders of diaphragm — (Use additional code to identify infectious organism)
786.8 Hiccough

ICD-9-CM Procedural

04.81 Injection of anesthetic into peripheral nerve for analgesia

HCPCS Level II Supplies & Services

J2400 Injection, chloroprocaine HCl, per 30 ml

64412

64412 Injection, anesthetic agent; spinal accessory nerve

ICD-9-CM Diagnostic

333.83 Spasmodic torticollis — (Use additional E code to identify drug, if drug-induced)
352.4 Disorders of accessory (11th) nerve

ICD-9-CM Procedural

03.91 Injection of anesthetic into spinal canal for analgesia
04.81 Injection of anesthetic into peripheral nerve for analgesia

HCPCS Level II Supplies & Services

J2400 Injection, chloroprocaine HCl, per 30 ml

64413

64413 Injection, anesthetic agent; cervical plexus

ICD-9-CM Diagnostic

721.0 Cervical spondylosis without myelopathy
721.1 Cervical spondylosis with myelopathy
722.0 Displacement of cervical intervertebral disc without myelopathy
722.4 Degeneration of cervical intervertebral disc
723.1 Cervicalgia
723.2 Cervicocranial syndrome
723.3 Cervicobrachial syndrome (diffuse)
723.4 Brachial neuritis or radiculitis NOS ▽
847.0 Neck sprain and strain
847.1 Thoracic sprain and strain

ICD-9-CM Procedural

04.81 Injection of anesthetic into peripheral nerve for analgesia

HCPCS Level II Supplies & Services

J2400 Injection, chloroprocaine HCl, per 30 ml

64415-64417

64415 Injection, anesthetic agent; brachial plexus, single
64416 brachial plexus, continuous infusion by catheter (including catheter placement)
64417 axillary nerve

ICD-9-CM Diagnostic

337.21 Reflex sympathetic dystrophy of the upper limb
353.0 Brachial plexus lesions
354.4 Causalgia of upper limb
357.81 Chronic inflammatory demyelinating polyneuritis
357.89 Other inflammatory and toxic neuropathy
716.11 Traumatic arthropathy, shoulder region
719.41 Pain in joint, shoulder region
719.42 Pain in joint, upper arm
723.4 Brachial neuritis or radiculitis NOS ▽
729.1 Unspecified myalgia and myositis ▽
729.5 Pain in soft tissues of limb
840.4 Rotator cuff (capsule) sprain and strain
953.4 Injury to brachial plexus

ICD-9-CM Procedural

04.81 Injection of anesthetic into peripheral nerve for analgesia

HCPCS Level II Supplies & Services

J2400 Injection, chloroprocaine HCl, per 30 ml

64418

64418 Injection, anesthetic agent; suprascapular nerve

ICD-9-CM Diagnostic

357.81 Chronic inflammatory demyelinating polyneuritis
357.89 Other inflammatory and toxic neuropathy
718.31 Recurrent dislocation of shoulder joint
719.41 Pain in joint, shoulder region
723.1 Cervicalgia
723.4 Brachial neuritis or radiculitis NOS ▽
726.11 Calcifying tendinitis of shoulder
728.85 Spasm of muscle
729.1 Unspecified myalgia and myositis ▽
729.2 Unspecified neuralgia, neuritis, and radiculitis ▽
729.5 Pain in soft tissues of limb

ICD-9-CM Procedural

04.81 Injection of anesthetic into peripheral nerve for analgesia

HCPCS Level II Supplies & Services

J2400 Injection, chloroprocaine HCl, per 30 ml

64420-64421

64420 Injection, anesthetic agent; intercostal nerve, single
64421 intercostal nerves, multiple, regional block

ICD-9-CM Diagnostic

162.4 Malignant neoplasm of middle lobe, bronchus, or lung
162.9 Malignant neoplasm of bronchus and lung, unspecified site ▽
174.0 Malignant neoplasm of nipple and areola of female breast — (Use additional code to identify estrogen receptor status: V86.0-V86.1) ♀
174.1 Malignant neoplasm of central portion of female breast — (Use additional code to identify estrogen receptor status: V86.0-V86.1) ♀
174.2 Malignant neoplasm of upper-inner quadrant of female breast — (Use additional code to identify estrogen receptor status: V86.0-V86.1) ♀
174.3 Malignant neoplasm of lower-inner quadrant of female breast — (Use additional code to identify estrogen receptor status: V86.0-V86.1) ♀
174.4 Malignant neoplasm of upper-outer quadrant of female breast — (Use additional code to identify estrogen receptor status: V86.0-V86.1) ♀
174.5 Malignant neoplasm of lower-outer quadrant of female breast — (Use additional code to identify estrogen receptor status: V86.0-V86.1) ♀
174.6 Malignant neoplasm of axillary tail of female breast — (Use additional code to identify estrogen receptor status: V86.0-V86.1) ♀
174.8 Malignant neoplasm of other specified sites of female breast — (Use additional code to identify estrogen receptor status: V86.0-V86.1) ♀
174.9 Malignant neoplasm of breast (female), unspecified site — (Use additional code to identify estrogen receptor status: V86.0-V86.1) ▽ ♀
175.0 Malignant neoplasm of nipple and areola of male breast — (Use additional code to identify estrogen receptor status: V86.0-V86.1) ♂
197.0 Secondary malignant neoplasm of lung
197.1 Secondary malignant neoplasm of mediastinum
197.2 Secondary malignant neoplasm of pleura
198.5 Secondary malignant neoplasm of bone and bone marrow
353.8 Other nerve root and plexus disorders
354.8 Other mononeuritis of upper limb
357.81 Chronic inflammatory demyelinating polyneuritis
357.89 Other inflammatory and toxic neuropathy
357.9 Unspecified inflammatory and toxic neuropathy ▽
724.1 Pain in thoracic spine
729.1 Unspecified myalgia and myositis ▽
729.2 Unspecified neuralgia, neuritis, and radiculitis ▽

733.99 Other disorders of bone and cartilage
786.52 Painful respiration
807.00 Closed fracture of rib(s), unspecified ▽
807.01 Closed fracture of one rib
807.02 Closed fracture of two ribs
807.03 Closed fracture of three ribs
807.04 Closed fracture of four ribs
807.05 Closed fracture of five ribs
807.06 Closed fracture of six ribs
807.07 Closed fracture of seven ribs
807.08 Closed fracture of eight or more ribs
807.09 Closed fracture of multiple ribs, unspecified ▽
807.10 Open fracture of rib(s), unspecified ▽
807.11 Open fracture of one rib
807.12 Open fracture of two ribs
807.13 Open fracture of three ribs
807.14 Open fracture of four ribs
807.15 Open fracture of five ribs
807.16 Open fracture of six ribs
807.17 Open fracture of seven ribs
807.18 Open fracture of eight or more ribs
807.19 Open fracture of multiple ribs, unspecified ▽
807.2 Closed fracture of sternum
807.3 Open fracture of sternum
922.1 Contusion of chest wall
957.9 Injury to nerves, unspecified site ▽

ICD-9-CM Procedural

04.81 Injection of anesthetic into peripheral nerve for analgesia

HCPCS Level II Supplies & Services

J2400 Injection, chloroprocaine HCl, per 30 ml

64425

64425 Injection, anesthetic agent; ilioinguinal, iliohypogastric nerves

ICD-9-CM Diagnostic

185 Malignant neoplasm of prostate ♂
195.2 Malignant neoplasm of abdomen
337.9 Unspecified disorder of autonomic nervous system ▽
355.1 Meralgia paresthetica
355.2 Other lesion of femoral nerve
355.3 Lesion of lateral popliteal nerve
355.4 Lesion of medial popliteal nerve
355.5 Tarsal tunnel syndrome
355.6 Lesion of plantar nerve
355.79 Other mononeuritis of lower limb
355.8 Unspecified mononeuritis of lower limb ▽
355.9 Mononeuritis of unspecified site ▽
550.90 Inguinal hernia without mention of obstruction or gangrene, unilateral or unspecified, (not specified as recurrent)
603.8 Other specified type of hydrocele ♂
607.1 Balanoposthitis — (Use additional code to identify organism) ♂
608.1 Spermatocele ♂
721.42 Spondylosis with myelopathy, lumbar region
724.2 Lumbago
729.2 Unspecified neuralgia, neuritis, and radiculitis ▽
729.5 Pain in soft tissues of limb

ICD-9-CM Procedural

04.81 Injection of anesthetic into peripheral nerve for analgesia

HCPCS Level II Supplies & Services

J2400 Injection, chloroprocaine HCl, per 30 ml

64430-64435

64430 Injection, anesthetic agent; pudendal nerve
64435 paracervical (uterine) nerve

ICD-9-CM Diagnostic

218.0 Submucous leiomyoma of uterus ♀
218.1 Intramural leiomyoma of uterus ♀
218.2 Subserous leiomyoma of uterus ♀
218.9 Leiomyoma of uterus, unspecified ▽ ♀
219.0 Benign neoplasm of cervix uteri ♀
219.1 Benign neoplasm of corpus uteri ♀
219.8 Benign neoplasm of other specified parts of uterus ♀
219.9 Benign neoplasm of uterus, part unspecified ▽ ♀
221.0 Benign neoplasm of fallopian tube and uterine ligaments ♀
239.5 Neoplasm of unspecified nature of other genitourinary organs
616.0 Cervicitis and endocervicitis — (Use additional code to identify organism: 041.00-041.09, 041.10-041.19) ♀
616.2 Cyst of Bartholin's gland — (Use additional code to identify organism: 041.00-041.09, 041.10-041.19) ♀
622.10 Dysplasia of cervix, unspecified ▽ ♀
622.11 Mild dysplasia of cervix ♀
622.12 Moderate dysplasia of cervix ♀
622.7 Mucous polyp of cervix ♀
625.3 Dysmenorrhea ♀
626.2 Excessive or frequent menstruation ♀
626.4 Irregular menstrual cycle ♀
626.6 Metrorrhagia ♀
626.8 Other disorder of menstruation and other abnormal bleeding from female genital tract ♀
626.9 Unspecified disorder of menstruation and other abnormal bleeding from female genital tract ▽ ♀
627.0 Premenopausal menorrhagia ♀
627.1 Postmenopausal bleeding ♀
628.3 Female infertility of uterine origin — (Use additional code for any associated tuberculous endometriosis: 016.7) ♀
632 Missed abortion — (Use additional code from category 639 to identify any associated complications) ♀
635.00 Unspecified legally induced abortion complicated by genital tract and pelvic infection ▽ ♀
635.01 Incomplete legally induced abortion complicated by genital tract and pelvic infection ♀
635.02 Complete legally induced abortion complicated by genital tract and pelvic infection ♀
635.10 Unspecified legally induced abortion complicated by delayed or excessive hemorrhage ▽ ♀
635.11 Incomplete legally induced abortion complicated by delayed or excessive hemorrhage ♀
635.12 Complete legally induced abortion complicated by delayed or excessive hemorrhage ♀
635.20 Unspecified legally induced abortion complicated by damage to pelvic organs or tissues ▽ ♀
635.21 Legally induced abortion complicated by damage to pelvic organs or tissues, incomplete ♀
635.22 Complete legally induced abortion complicated by damage to pelvic organs or tissues ♀
635.30 Unspecified legally induced abortion complicated by renal failure ▽ ♀
635.31 Incomplete legally induced abortion complicated by renal failure ♀
635.32 Complete legally induced abortion complicated by renal failure ♀
635.40 Unspecified legally induced abortion complicated by metabolic disorder ▽ ♀

635.41 Incomplete legally induced abortion complicated by metabolic disorder ♀

635.42 Complete legally induced abortion complicated by metabolic disorder ♀

635.50 Unspecified legally induced abortion complicated by shock ▼ ♀

635.51 Legally induced abortion, complicated by shock, incomplete ♀

635.52 Complete legally induced abortion complicated by shock ♀

635.60 Unspecified legally induced abortion complicated by embolism ▼ ♀

635.61 Incomplete legally induced abortion complicated by embolism ♀

635.62 Complete legally induced abortion complicated by embolism ♀

635.70 Unspecified legally induced abortion with other specified complications ▼ ♀

635.71 Incomplete legally induced abortion with other specified complications ♀

635.72 Complete legally induced abortion with other specified complications ♀

635.80 Unspecified legally induced abortion with unspecified complication ▼ ♀

635.81 Incomplete legally induced abortion with unspecified complication ▼ ♀

635.82 Complete legally induced abortion with unspecified complication ▼ ♀

635.90 Unspecified legally induced abortion without mention of complication ▼ ♀

635.91 Incomplete legally induced abortion without mention of complication ♀

635.92 Complete legally induced abortion without mention of complication ♀

637.00 Abortion, unspecified as to completion or legality, complicated by genital tract and pelvic infection ▼ ♀

637.01 Abortion, unspecified as to legality, incomplete, complicated by genital tract and pelvic infection ♀

637.02 Abortion, unspecified as to legality, complete, complicated by genital tract and pelvic infection ♀

637.10 Abortion, unspecified as to completion or legality, complicated by delayed or excessive hemorrhage ▼ ♀

637.11 Abortion, unspecified as to legality, incomplete, complicated by delayed or excessive hemorrhage ♀

637.12 Abortion, unspecified as to legality, complete, complicated by delayed or excessive hemorrhage ♀

637.20 Abortion, unspecified as to completion or legality, complicated by damage to pelvic organs or tissues ▼ ♀

637.21 Abortion, unspecified as to legality, incomplete, complicated by damage to pelvic organs or tissues ♀

637.22 Abortion, unspecified as to legality, complete, complicated by damage to pelvic organs or tissues ♀

637.30 Abortion, unspecified as to completion or legality, complicated by renal failure ▼ ♀

637.31 Abortion, unspecified as to legality, incomplete, complicated by renal failure ♀

637.32 Abortion, unspecified as to legality, complete, complicated by renal failure ♀

637.40 Abortion, unspecified as to completion or legality, complicated by metabolic disorder ▼ ♀

637.41 Abortion, unspecified as to legality, incomplete, complicated by metabolic disorder ♀

637.42 Abortion, unspecified as to legality, complete, complicated by metabolic disorder ♀

637.50 Abortion, unspecified as to completion or legality, complicated by shock ▼ ♀

637.51 Abortion, unspecified as to legality, incomplete, complicated by shock ♀

637.52 Abortion, unspecified as to legality, complete, complicated by shock ♀

637.60 Abortion, unspecified as to completion or legality, complicated by embolism ▼ ♀

637.61 Abortion, unspecified as to legality, incomplete, complicated by embolism ♀

637.62 Abortion, unspecified as to legality, complete, complicated by embolism ♀

637.70 Abortion, unspecified as to completion or legality, with other specified complications ▼ ♀

637.71 Abortion, unspecified as to legality, incomplete, with other specified complications ♀

637.72 Abortion, unspecified as to legality, complete, with other specified complications ♀

637.80 Abortion, unspecified as to completion or legality, with unspecified complication ▼ ♀

637.81 Abortion, unspecified as to legality, incomplete, with unspecified complication ▼ ♀

637.82 Abortion, unspecified as to legality, complete, with unspecified complication ▼ ♀

637.90 Unspecified type of abortion, unspecified as to completion or legality, without mention of complication ▼ ♀

637.91 Abortion, unspecified as to legality, incomplete, without mention of complication ♀

637.92 Abortion, unspecified as to legality, complete, without mention of complication ♀

638.0 Failed attempted abortion complicated by genital tract and pelvic infection ♀

638.1 Failed attempted abortion complicated by delayed or excessive hemorrhage ♀

638.2 Failed attempted abortion complicated by damage to pelvic organs or tissues ♀

638.3 Failed attempted abortion complicated by renal failure ♀

638.4 Failed attempted abortion complicated by metabolic disorder ♀

638.5 Failed attempted abortion complicated by shock ♀

638.6 Failed attempted abortion complicated by embolism ♀

638.7 Failed attempted abortion with other specified complication ♀

638.8 Failed attempted abortion with unspecified complication ▼ ♀

638.9 Failed attempted abortion without mention of complication ♀

646.31 Pregnancy complication, recurrent pregnancy loss, with or without mention of antepartum condition — (Use additional code to further specify complication) ♀

650 Normal delivery — (This code is for use as a single diagnosis code and is not to be used with any other code in the range 630-676. Use additional code to indicate outcome of delivery: V27.0.) ♀

652.11 Breech or other malpresentation successfully converted to cephalic presentation, delivered — (Code first any associated obstructed labor, 660.0) ♀

652.13 Breech or other malpresentation successfully converted to cephalic presentation, antepartum — (Code first any associated obstructed labor, 660.0) ♀

656.31 Fetal distress affecting management of mother, delivered ♀

658.11 Premature rupture of membranes in pregnancy, delivered ♀

658.31 Delayed delivery after artificial rupture of membranes, delivered ♀

660.01 Obstruction caused by malposition of fetus at onset of labor, delivered — (Use additional code from 652.0-652.9 to identify condition) ♀

660.03 Obstruction caused by malposition of fetus at onset of labor, antepartum — (Use additional code from 652.0-652.9 to identify condition) ♀

664.01 First-degree perineal laceration, with delivery ♀

ICD-9-CM Procedural

04.81 Injection of anesthetic into peripheral nerve for analgesia

64445-64446

64445 Injection, anesthetic agent; sciatic nerve, single

64446 sciatic nerve, continuous infusion by catheter (including catheter placement)

ICD-9-CM Diagnostic

355.0 Lesion of sciatic nerve

355.79 Other mononeuritis of lower limb

357.81 Chronic inflammatory demyelinating polyneuritis

357.89 Other inflammatory and toxic neuropathy

719.45 Pain in joint, pelvic region and thigh

720.2 Sacroiliitis, not elsewhere classified

721.42 Spondylosis with myelopathy, lumbar region

722.10 Displacement of lumbar intervertebral disc without myelopathy

722.52 Degeneration of lumbar or lumbosacral intervertebral disc

722.83 Postlaminectomy syndrome, lumbar region

724.02 Spinal stenosis of lumbar region, without neurogenic claudication

724.03 Spinal stenosis of lumbar region, with neurogenic claudication

724.2 Lumbago

724.3 Sciatica

724.4 Thoracic or lumbosacral neuritis or radiculitis, unspecified ▼

729.1 Unspecified myalgia and myositis ▼

729.2 Unspecified neuralgia, neuritis, and radiculitis ▼

729.5 Pain in soft tissues of limb

ICD-9-CM Procedural

04.81 Injection of anesthetic into peripheral nerve for analgesia

HCPCS Level II Supplies & Services

J2400 Injection, chloroprocaine HCl, per 30 ml

64447-64448

64447 Injection, anesthetic agent; femoral nerve, single
64448 femoral nerve, continuous infusion by catheter (including catheter placement)

ICD-9-CM Diagnostic

355.1 Meralgia paresthetica
355.2 Other lesion of femoral nerve
355.71 Causalgia of lower limb
355.79 Other mononeuritis of lower limb
719.45 Pain in joint, pelvic region and thigh
726.5 Enthesopathy of hip region
726.61 Pes anserinus tendinitis or bursitis
726.62 Tibial collateral ligament bursitis
726.63 Fibular collateral ligament bursitis
726.65 Prepatellar bursitis
726.69 Other enthesopathy of knee
729.1 Unspecified myalgia and myositis ▽
729.2 Unspecified neuralgia, neuritis, and radiculitis ▽
729.5 Pain in soft tissues of limb

ICD-9-CM Procedural

04.81 Injection of anesthetic into peripheral nerve for analgesia

64449

64449 Injection, anesthetic agent; lumbar plexus, posterior approach, continuous infusion by catheter (including catheter placement)

ICD-9-CM Diagnostic

353.1 Lumbosacral plexus lesions
353.4 Lumbosacral root lesions, not elsewhere classified
353.6 Phantom limb (syndrome)
353.8 Other nerve root and plexus disorders
355.0 Lesion of sciatic nerve
355.79 Other mononeuritis of lower limb
719.45 Pain in joint, pelvic region and thigh
719.48 Pain in joint, other specified sites
720.0 Ankylosing spondylitis
720.1 Spinal enthesopathy
721.3 Lumbosacral spondylosis without myelopathy
721.42 Spondylosis with myelopathy, lumbar region
721.6 Ankylosing vertebral hyperostosis
721.7 Traumatic spondylopathy
722.10 Displacement of lumbar intervertebral disc without myelopathy
722.32 Schmorl's nodes, lumbar region
722.52 Degeneration of lumbar or lumbosacral intervertebral disc
722.73 Intervertebral lumbar disc disorder with myelopathy, lumbar region
722.83 Postlaminectomy syndrome, lumbar region
722.93 Other and unspecified disc disorder of lumbar region ▽
724.02 Spinal stenosis of lumbar region, without neurogenic claudication
724.03 Spinal stenosis of lumbar region, with neurogenic claudication
724.2 Lumbago
724.3 Sciatica
724.4 Thoracic or lumbosacral neuritis or radiculitis, unspecified ▽
724.5 Unspecified backache ▽
724.6 Disorders of sacrum
724.8 Other symptoms referable to back
724.9 Other unspecified back disorder
729.2 Unspecified neuralgia, neuritis, and radiculitis ▽
739.3 Nonallopathic lesion of lumbar region, not elsewhere classified
739.4 Nonallopathic lesion of sacral region, not elsewhere classified
756.12 Congenital spondylolisthesis
847.2 Lumbar sprain and strain
847.3 Sprain and strain of sacrum

ICD-9-CM Procedural

04.81 Injection of anesthetic into peripheral nerve for analgesia

64450

64450 Injection, anesthetic agent; other peripheral nerve or branch

ICD-9-CM Diagnostic

The application of this code is too broad to adequately present ICD-9-CM diagnostic code links here. Refer to your ICD-9-CM book.

ICD-9-CM Procedural

04.81 Injection of anesthetic into peripheral nerve for analgesia

HCPCS Level II Supplies & Services

J2400 Injection, chloroprocaine HCl, per 30 ml

64455

64455 Injection(s), anesthetic agent and/or steroid, plantar common digital nerve(s) (eg, Morton's neuroma)

ICD-9-CM Diagnostic

355.6 Lesion of plantar nerve
355.71 Causalgia of lower limb
355.79 Other mononeuritis of lower limb
355.8 Unspecified mononeuritis of lower limb ▽
719.47 Pain in joint, ankle and foot
727.06 Tenosynovitis of foot and ankle
729.1 Unspecified myalgia and myositis ▽
729.2 Unspecified neuralgia, neuritis, and radiculitis ▽
729.5 Pain in soft tissues of limb

ICD-9-CM Procedural

04.81 Injection of anesthetic into peripheral nerve for analgesia

64479-64480

64479 Injection(s), anesthetic agent and/or steroid, transforaminal epidural, with imaging guidance (fluoroscopy or CT); cervical or thoracic, single level
64480 cervical or thoracic, each additional level (List separately in addition to code for primary procedure)

ICD-9-CM Diagnostic

353.2 Cervical root lesions, not elsewhere classified
353.3 Thoracic root lesions, not elsewhere classified
353.5 Neuralgic amyotrophy — (Code first any associated underlying disease as: 249.6, 250.6)
353.6 Phantom limb (syndrome)
353.8 Other nerve root and plexus disorders
720.0 Ankylosing spondylitis
720.1 Spinal enthesopathy
721.0 Cervical spondylosis without myelopathy
721.1 Cervical spondylosis with myelopathy
721.2 Thoracic spondylosis without myelopathy
721.41 Spondylosis with myelopathy, thoracic region
721.6 Ankylosing vertebral hyperostosis
721.7 Traumatic spondylopathy
722.0 Displacement of cervical intervertebral disc without myelopathy
722.11 Displacement of thoracic intervertebral disc without myelopathy
722.31 Schmorl's nodes, thoracic region
722.4 Degeneration of cervical intervertebral disc

722.51 Degeneration of thoracic or thoracolumbar intervertebral disc
722.71 Intervertebral cervical disc disorder with myelopathy, cervical region
722.72 Intervertebral thoracic disc disorder with myelopathy, thoracic region
722.81 Postlaminectomy syndrome, cervical region
722.82 Postlaminectomy syndrome, thoracic region
722.91 Other and unspecified disc disorder of cervical region
722.92 Other and unspecified disc disorder of thoracic region
723.0 Spinal stenosis in cervical region
723.1 Cervicalgia
723.2 Cervicocranial syndrome
723.3 Cervicobrachial syndrome (diffuse)
723.4 Brachial neuritis or radiculitis NOS
723.6 Panniculitis specified as affecting neck
723.8 Other syndromes affecting cervical region
723.9 Unspecified musculoskeletal disorders and symptoms referable to neck
724.01 Spinal stenosis of thoracic region
724.1 Pain in thoracic spine
724.4 Thoracic or lumbosacral neuritis or radiculitis, unspecified
729.2 Unspecified neuralgia, neuritis, and radiculitis
739.0 Nonallopathic lesion of head region, not elsewhere classified
847.0 Neck sprain and strain
847.1 Thoracic sprain and strain

ICD-9-CM Procedural

03.91 Injection of anesthetic into spinal canal for analgesia
03.92 Injection of other agent into spinal canal

HCPCS Level II Supplies & Services

J2400 Injection, chloroprocaine HCl, per 30 ml

64483-64484

64483 Injection(s), anesthetic agent and/or steroid, transforaminal epidural, with imaging guidance (fluoroscopy or CT); lumbar or sacral, single level
64484 lumbar or sacral, each additional level (List separately in addition to code for primary procedure)

ICD-9-CM Diagnostic

353.1 Lumbosacral plexus lesions
353.4 Lumbosacral root lesions, not elsewhere classified
353.6 Phantom limb (syndrome)
353.8 Other nerve root and plexus disorders
355.0 Lesion of sciatic nerve
355.79 Other mononeuritis of lower limb
719.45 Pain in joint, pelvic region and thigh
719.48 Pain in joint, other specified sites
720.0 Ankylosing spondylitis
720.1 Spinal enthesopathy
721.3 Lumbosacral spondylosis without myelopathy
721.42 Spondylosis with myelopathy, lumbar region
721.6 Ankylosing vertebral hyperostosis
721.7 Traumatic spondylopathy
722.10 Displacement of lumbar intervertebral disc without myelopathy
722.32 Schmorl's nodes, lumbar region
722.52 Degeneration of lumbar or lumbosacral intervertebral disc
722.73 Intervertebral lumbar disc disorder with myelopathy, lumbar region
722.83 Postlaminectomy syndrome, lumbar region
722.93 Other and unspecified disc disorder of lumbar region
724.02 Spinal stenosis of lumbar region, without neurogenic claudication
724.03 Spinal stenosis of lumbar region, with neurogenic claudication
724.2 Lumbago
724.3 Sciatica
724.4 Thoracic or lumbosacral neuritis or radiculitis, unspecified
724.5 Unspecified backache
724.6 Disorders of sacrum
724.8 Other symptoms referable to back
724.9 Other unspecified back disorder
729.2 Unspecified neuralgia, neuritis, and radiculitis
739.3 Nonallopathic lesion of lumbar region, not elsewhere classified
739.4 Nonallopathic lesion of sacral region, not elsewhere classified
756.12 Congenital spondylolisthesis
847.2 Lumbar sprain and strain
847.3 Sprain and strain of sacrum

ICD-9-CM Procedural

03.91 Injection of anesthetic into spinal canal for analgesia
03.92 Injection of other agent into spinal canal

HCPCS Level II Supplies & Services

J2400 Injection, chloroprocaine HCl, per 30 ml

64490-64492

64490 Injection(s), diagnostic or therapeutic agent, paravertebral facet (zygapophyseal) joint (or nerves innervating that joint) with image guidance (fluoroscopy or CT), cervical or thoracic; single level
64491 second level (List separately in addition to code for primary procedure)
64492 third and any additional level(s) (List separately in addition to code for primary procedure)

ICD-9-CM Diagnostic

353.2 Cervical root lesions, not elsewhere classified
353.3 Thoracic root lesions, not elsewhere classified
353.5 Neuralgic amyotrophy — (Code first any associated underlying disease as: 249.6, 250.6)
353.6 Phantom limb (syndrome)
353.8 Other nerve root and plexus disorders
720.0 Ankylosing spondylitis
720.1 Spinal enthesopathy
721.0 Cervical spondylosis without myelopathy
721.1 Cervical spondylosis with myelopathy
721.2 Thoracic spondylosis without myelopathy
721.41 Spondylosis with myelopathy, thoracic region
721.6 Ankylosing vertebral hyperostosis
721.7 Traumatic spondylopathy
722.0 Displacement of cervical intervertebral disc without myelopathy
722.11 Displacement of thoracic intervertebral disc without myelopathy
722.31 Schmorl's nodes, thoracic region
722.4 Degeneration of cervical intervertebral disc
722.51 Degeneration of thoracic or thoracolumbar intervertebral disc
722.71 Intervertebral cervical disc disorder with myelopathy, cervical region
722.72 Intervertebral thoracic disc disorder with myelopathy, thoracic region
722.81 Postlaminectomy syndrome, cervical region
722.82 Postlaminectomy syndrome, thoracic region
722.91 Other and unspecified disc disorder of cervical region
722.92 Other and unspecified disc disorder of thoracic region
723.0 Spinal stenosis in cervical region
723.1 Cervicalgia
723.2 Cervicocranial syndrome
723.3 Cervicobrachial syndrome (diffuse)
723.4 Brachial neuritis or radiculitis NOS
723.6 Panniculitis specified as affecting neck
723.8 Other syndromes affecting cervical region
723.9 Unspecified musculoskeletal disorders and symptoms referable to neck

724.01 Spinal stenosis of thoracic region
724.1 Pain in thoracic spine
724.4 Thoracic or lumbosacral neuritis or radiculitis, unspecified
729.2 Unspecified neuralgia, neuritis, and radiculitis
739.0 Nonallopathic lesion of head region, not elsewhere classified
847.0 Neck sprain and strain
847.1 Thoracic sprain and strain

ICD-9-CM Procedural

81.92 Injection of therapeutic substance into joint or ligament

HCPCS Level II Supplies & Services

J2400 Injection, chloroprocaine HCl, per 30 ml

64493-64495

64493 Injection(s), diagnostic or therapeutic agent, paravertebral facet (zygapophyseal) joint (or nerves innervating that joint) with image guidance (fluoroscopy or CT), lumbar or sacral; single level
64494 second level (List separately in addition to code for primary procedure)
64495 third and any additional level(s) (List separately in addition to code for primary procedure)

ICD-9-CM Diagnostic

353.1 Lumbosacral plexus lesions
353.4 Lumbosacral root lesions, not elsewhere classified
353.6 Phantom limb (syndrome)
353.8 Other nerve root and plexus disorders
355.0 Lesion of sciatic nerve
355.79 Other mononeuritis of lower limb
719.45 Pain in joint, pelvic region and thigh
719.48 Pain in joint, other specified sites
720.0 Ankylosing spondylitis
720.1 Spinal enthesopathy
721.3 Lumbosacral spondylosis without myelopathy
721.42 Spondylosis with myelopathy, lumbar region
721.6 Ankylosing vertebral hyperostosis
721.7 Traumatic spondylopathy
722.10 Displacement of lumbar intervertebral disc without myelopathy
722.32 Schmorl's nodes, lumbar region
722.52 Degeneration of lumbar or lumbosacral intervertebral disc
722.73 Intervertebral lumbar disc disorder with myelopathy, lumbar region
722.83 Postlaminectomy syndrome, lumbar region
722.93 Other and unspecified disc disorder of lumbar region
724.02 Spinal stenosis of lumbar region, without neurogenic claudication
724.03 Spinal stenosis of lumbar region, with neurogenic claudication
724.2 Lumbago
724.3 Sciatica
724.4 Thoracic or lumbosacral neuritis or radiculitis, unspecified
724.5 Unspecified backache
724.6 Disorders of sacrum
724.8 Other symptoms referable to back
724.9 Other unspecified back disorder
729.2 Unspecified neuralgia, neuritis, and radiculitis
739.3 Nonallopathic lesion of lumbar region, not elsewhere classified
739.4 Nonallopathic lesion of sacral region, not elsewhere classified
756.12 Congenital spondylolisthesis
847.2 Lumbar sprain and strain
847.3 Sprain and strain of sacrum

ICD-9-CM Procedural

81.92 Injection of therapeutic substance into joint or ligament

HCPCS Level II Supplies & Services

J2400 Injection, chloroprocaine HCl, per 30 ml

64505

64505 Injection, anesthetic agent; sphenopalatine ganglion

ICD-9-CM Diagnostic

350.2 Atypical face pain
524.62 Arthralgia of temporomandibular joint
784.0 Headache
830.1 Open dislocation of jaw
848.1 Sprain and strain of jaw

ICD-9-CM Procedural

05.31 Injection of anesthetic into sympathetic nerve for analgesia

HCPCS Level II Supplies & Services

J2400 Injection, chloroprocaine HCl, per 30 ml

64508

64508 Injection, anesthetic agent; carotid sinus (separate procedure)

ICD-9-CM Diagnostic

333.0 Other degenerative diseases of the basal ganglia
337.00 Idiopathic peripheral autonomic neuropathy, unspecified
337.01 Carotid sinus syndrome
337.09 Other idiopathic peripheral autonomic neuropathy

ICD-9-CM Procedural

05.31 Injection of anesthetic into sympathetic nerve for analgesia

HCPCS Level II Supplies & Services

J2400 Injection, chloroprocaine HCl, per 30 ml

64510-64520

64510 Injection, anesthetic agent; stellate ganglion (cervical sympathetic)
64517 superior hypogastric plexus
64520 lumbar or thoracic (paravertebral sympathetic)

ICD-9-CM Diagnostic

337.00 Idiopathic peripheral autonomic neuropathy, unspecified
337.09 Other idiopathic peripheral autonomic neuropathy
337.21 Reflex sympathetic dystrophy of the upper limb
337.22 Reflex sympathetic dystrophy of the lower limb
337.29 Reflex sympathetic dystrophy of other specified site
338.11 Acute pain due to trauma — (Use additional code to identify pain associated with psychological factors: 307.89)
338.12 Acute post-thoracotomy pain — (Use additional code to identify pain associated with psychological factors: 307.89)
338.18 Other acute postoperative pain — (Use additional code to identify pain associated with psychological factors: 307.89)
338.19 Other acute pain — (Use additional code to identify pain associated with psychological factors: 307.89)
338.21 Chronic pain due to trauma — (Use additional code to identify pain associated with psychological factors: 307.89)
338.22 Chronic post-thoracotomy pain — (Use additional code to identify pain associated with psychological factors: 307.89)
338.28 Other chronic postoperative pain — (Use additional code to identify pain associated with psychological factors: 307.89)
338.29 Other chronic pain — (Use additional code to identify pain associated with psychological factors: 307.89)
346.01 Migraine with aura, with intractable migraine, so stated, without mention of status migrainosus
346.02 Migraine with aura, without mention of intractable migraine with status migrainosus

346.03 Migraine with aura, with intractable migraine, so stated, with status migrainosus
346.11 Migraine without aura, with intractable migraine, so stated, without mention of status migrainosus
346.12 Migraine without aura, without mention of intractable migraine with status migrainosus
346.13 Migraine without aura, with intractable migraine, so stated, with status migrainosus
346.21 Variants of migraine, not elsewhere classified, with intractable migraine, so stated, without mention of status migrainosus
346.22 Variants of migraine, not elsewhere classified, without mention of intractable migraine with status migrainosus
346.23 Variants of migraine, not elsewhere classified, with intractable migraine, so stated, with status migrainosus
346.31 Hemiplegic migraine, with intractable migraine, so stated, without mention of status migrainosus
346.32 Hemiplegic migraine, without mention of intractable migraine with status migrainosus
346.33 Hemiplegic migraine, with intractable migraine, so stated, with status migrainosus
346.41 Menstrual migraine, with intractable migraine, so stated, without mention of status migrainosus ♀
346.42 Menstrual migraine, without mention of intractable migraine with status migrainosus ♀
346.43 Menstrual migraine, with intractable migraine, so stated, with status migrainosus ♀
346.51 Persistent migraine aura without cerebral infarction, with intractable migraine, so stated, without mention of status migrainosus
346.52 Persistent migraine aura without cerebral infarction, without mention of intractable migraine with status migrainosus
346.53 Persistent migraine aura without cerebral infarction, with intractable migraine, so stated, with status migrainosus
346.61 Persistent migraine aura with cerebral infarction, with intractable migraine, so stated, without mention of status migrainosus
346.62 Persistent migraine aura with cerebral infarction, without mention of intractable migraine with status migrainosus
346.63 Persistent migraine aura with cerebral infarction, with intractable migraine, so stated, with status migrainosus
346.71 Chronic migraine without aura, with intractable migraine, so stated, without mention of status migrainosus
346.72 Chronic migraine without aura, without mention of intractable migraine with status migrainosus
346.73 Chronic migraine without aura, with intractable migraine, so stated, with status migrainosus
346.81 Other forms of migraine, with intractable migraine, so stated, without mention of status migrainosus
346.82 Other forms of migraine, without mention of intractable migraine with status migrainosus
346.83 Other forms of migraine, with intractable migraine, so stated, with status migrainosus
346.91 Migraine, unspecified, with intractable migraine, so stated, without mention of status migrainosus ▽
346.92 Migraine, unspecified, without mention of intractable migraine with status migrainosus ▽
346.93 Migraine, unspecified, with intractable migraine, so stated, with status migrainosus ▽
350.1 Trigeminal neuralgia
350.8 Other specified trigeminal nerve disorders
350.9 Unspecified trigeminal nerve disorder ▽
353.6 Phantom limb (syndrome)
354.4 Causalgia of upper limb
354.5 Mononeuritis multiplex
354.9 Unspecified mononeuritis of upper limb ▽
355.8 Unspecified mononeuritis of lower limb ▽
355.9 Mononeuritis of unspecified site ▽
443.0 Raynaud's syndrome — (Use additional code to identify gangrene: 785.4)
443.9 Unspecified peripheral vascular disease ▽
617.0 Endometriosis of uterus ♀
617.1 Endometriosis of ovary ♀
617.2 Endometriosis of fallopian tube ♀
617.3 Endometriosis of pelvic peritoneum ♀
617.4 Endometriosis of rectovaginal septum and vagina ♀
617.5 Endometriosis of intestine ♀
617.8 Endometriosis of other specified sites ♀
617.9 Endometriosis, site unspecified ▽ ♀
625.0 Dyspareunia ♀
625.2 Mittelschmerz ♀
625.3 Dysmenorrhea ♀
625.9 Unspecified symptom associated with female genital organs ▽ ♀
719.41 Pain in joint, shoulder region
719.42 Pain in joint, upper arm
719.44 Pain in joint, hand
719.45 Pain in joint, pelvic region and thigh
719.46 Pain in joint, lower leg
723.1 Cervicalgia
723.2 Cervicocranial syndrome
723.3 Cervicobrachial syndrome (diffuse)
723.4 Brachial neuritis or radiculitis NOS ▽
724.2 Lumbago
724.5 Unspecified backache ▽
729.2 Unspecified neuralgia, neuritis, and radiculitis ▽
729.5 Pain in soft tissues of limb

ICD-9-CM Procedural

05.31 Injection of anesthetic into sympathetic nerve for analgesia

HCPCS Level II Supplies & Services

J2400 Injection, chloroprocaine HCl, per 30 ml

64530

64530 Injection, anesthetic agent; celiac plexus, with or without radiologic monitoring

ICD-9-CM Diagnostic

157.0 Malignant neoplasm of head of pancreas
157.1 Malignant neoplasm of body of pancreas
157.2 Malignant neoplasm of tail of pancreas
157.3 Malignant neoplasm of pancreatic duct
157.4 Malignant neoplasm of islets of Langerhans — (Use additional code to identify any functional activity)
157.8 Malignant neoplasm of other specified sites of pancreas
157.9 Malignant neoplasm of pancreas, part unspecified ▽
577.0 Acute pancreatitis
577.1 Chronic pancreatitis
786.51 Precordial pain
789.00 Abdominal pain, unspecified site ▽
789.01 Abdominal pain, right upper quadrant
789.02 Abdominal pain, left upper quadrant
789.06 Abdominal pain, epigastric
789.07 Abdominal pain, generalized
789.09 Abdominal pain, other specified site

ICD-9-CM Procedural

05.31 Injection of anesthetic into sympathetic nerve for analgesia

64550

64550 Application of surface (transcutaneous) neurostimulator

ICD-9-CM Diagnostic

338.11 Acute pain due to trauma — (Use additional code to identify pain associated with psychological factors: 307.89)

338.19 Other acute pain — (Use additional code to identify pain associated with psychological factors: 307.89)
338.21 Chronic pain due to trauma — (Use additional code to identify pain associated with psychological factors: 307.89)
338.28 Other chronic postoperative pain — (Use additional code to identify pain associated with psychological factors: 307.89)
338.29 Other chronic pain — (Use additional code to identify pain associated with psychological factors: 307.89)
344.60 Cauda equina syndrome without mention of neurogenic bladder
354.4 Causalgia of upper limb
719.46 Pain in joint, lower leg
722.11 Displacement of thoracic intervertebral disc without myelopathy
723.1 Cervicalgia
723.4 Brachial neuritis or radiculitis NOS
724.02 Spinal stenosis of lumbar region, without neurogenic claudication
724.03 Spinal stenosis of lumbar region, with neurogenic claudication
724.2 Lumbago
724.3 Sciatica
729.1 Unspecified myalgia and myositis
729.2 Unspecified neuralgia, neuritis, and radiculitis
846.0 Sprain and strain of lumbosacral (joint) (ligament)

ICD-9-CM Procedural

93.09 Other diagnostic physical therapy procedure
93.39 Other physical therapy

HCPCS Level II Supplies & Services

A4558 Conductive gel or paste, for use with electrical device (e.g., TENS, NMES), per oz
E0720 Transcutaneous electrical nerve stimulation (TENS) device, 2 lead, localized stimulation

64553-64565

64553 Percutaneous implantation of neurostimulator electrode array; cranial nerve
64555 peripheral nerve (excludes sacral nerve)
64561 sacral nerve (transforaminal placement) including image guidance, if performed
64565 neuromuscular

ICD-9-CM Diagnostic

296.33 Major depressive disorder, recurrent episode, severe, without mention of psychotic behavior — (Use additional code to identify any associated physical disease, injury, or condition affecting the brain with psychoses classifiable to 295-298)
300.3 Obsessive-compulsive disorders
332.0 Paralysis agitans
333.1 Essential and other specified forms of tremor — (Use additional E code to identify drug, if drug-induced)
338.0 Central pain syndrome — (Use additional code to identify pain associated with psychological factors: 307.89)
338.21 Chronic pain due to trauma — (Use additional code to identify pain associated with psychological factors: 307.89)
338.22 Chronic post-thoracotomy pain — (Use additional code to identify pain associated with psychological factors: 307.89)
338.28 Other chronic postoperative pain — (Use additional code to identify pain associated with psychological factors: 307.89)
338.29 Other chronic pain — (Use additional code to identify pain associated with psychological factors: 307.89)
338.4 Chronic pain syndrome — (Use additional code to identify pain associated with psychological factors: 307.89)
345.01 Generalized nonconvulsive epilepsy with intractable epilepsy
345.11 Generalized convulsive epilepsy with intractable epilepsy
345.41 Localization-related (focal) (partial) epilepsy and epileptic syndromes with complex partial seizures, with intractable epilepsy
345.51 Localization-related (focal) (partial) epilepsy and epileptic syndromes with simple partial seizures, with intractable epilepsy
345.91 Unspecified epilepsy with intractable epilepsy
780.33 Post traumatic seizures
780.39 Other convulsions
787.60 Full incontinence of feces
788.20 Unspecified retention of urine — (Code, if applicable, any causal condition first, such as: 600.0-600.9, with fifth digit 1)
788.21 Incomplete bladder emptying — (Code, if applicable, any causal condition first, such as: 600.0-600.9, with fifth digit 1)
788.31 Urge incontinence — (Code, if applicable, any causal condition first: 600.0-600.9, with fifth digit 1; 618.00-618.9; 753.23)
788.41 Urinary frequency — (Code, if applicable, any causal condition first, such as: 600.0-600.9, with fifth digit 1)

ICD-9-CM Procedural

04.92 Implantation or replacement of peripheral neurostimulator lead(s)

64566

64566 Posterior tibial neurostimulation, percutaneous needle electrode, single treatment, includes programming

ICD-9-CM Diagnostic

595.1 Chronic interstitial cystitis — (Use additional code to identify organism, such as E. coli: 041.41-041.49)
596.51 Hypertonicity of bladder — (Use additional code to identify urinary incontinence: 625.6, 788.30-788.39)
788.31 Urge incontinence — (Code, if applicable, any causal condition first: 600.0-600.9, with fifth digit 1; 618.00-618.9; 753.23)
788.33 Mixed incontinence urge and stress (male)(female) — (Code, if applicable, any causal condition first: 600.0-600.9, with fifth digit 1; 618.00-618.9; 753.23)
788.41 Urinary frequency — (Code, if applicable, any causal condition first, such as: 600.0-600.9, with fifth digit 1)
788.63 Urgency of urination — (Code, if applicable, any causal condition first, such as: 600.0-600.9, with fifth digit 1)

ICD-9-CM Procedural

04.99 Other operations on cranial and peripheral nerves

64568-64570

64568 Incision for implantation of cranial nerve (eg, vagus nerve) neurostimulator electrode array and pulse generator
64569 Revision or replacement of cranial nerve (eg, vagus nerve) neurostimulator electrode array, including connection to existing pulse generator
64570 Removal of cranial nerve (eg, vagus nerve) neurostimulator electrode array and pulse generator

ICD-9-CM Diagnostic

296.33 Major depressive disorder, recurrent episode, severe, without mention of psychotic behavior — (Use additional code to identify any associated physical disease, injury, or condition affecting the brain with psychoses classifiable to 295-298)
300.3 Obsessive-compulsive disorders
332.0 Paralysis agitans
333.1 Essential and other specified forms of tremor — (Use additional E code to identify drug, if drug-induced)
345.01 Generalized nonconvulsive epilepsy with intractable epilepsy
345.11 Generalized convulsive epilepsy with intractable epilepsy
345.41 Localization-related (focal) (partial) epilepsy and epileptic syndromes with complex partial seizures, with intractable epilepsy
345.51 Localization-related (focal) (partial) epilepsy and epileptic syndromes with simple partial seizures, with intractable epilepsy
345.91 Unspecified epilepsy with intractable epilepsy
350.2 Atypical face pain
723.1 Cervicalgia
729.2 Unspecified neuralgia, neuritis, and radiculitis

780.33 Post traumatic seizures
780.39 Other convulsions
996.2 Mechanical complication of nervous system device, implant, and graft
996.63 Infection and inflammatory reaction due to nervous system device, implant, and graft — (Use additional code to identify specified infections)
996.75 Other complications due to nervous system device, implant, and graft — (Use additional code to identify complication: 338.18-338.19, 338.28-338.29)
997.00 Unspecified nervous system complication — (Use additional code to identify complications) ♥

ICD-9-CM Procedural

04.92 Implantation or replacement of peripheral neurostimulator lead(s)
86.94 Insertion or replacement of single array neurostimulator pulse generator, not specified as rechargeable
86.95 Insertion or replacement of multiple array neurostimulator pulse generator, not specified as rechargeable
86.96 Insertion or replacement of other neurostimulator pulse generator
86.97 Insertion or replacement of single array rechargeable neurostimulator pulse generator
86.98 Insertion or replacement of multiple array (two or more) rechargeable neurostimulator pulse generator

64575-64581

64575 Incision for implantation of neurostimulator electrode array; peripheral nerve (excludes sacral nerve)
64580 neuromuscular
64581 sacral nerve (transforaminal placement)

ICD-9-CM Diagnostic

296.33 Major depressive disorder, recurrent episode, severe, without mention of psychotic behavior — (Use additional code to identify any associated physical disease, injury, or condition affecting the brain with psychoses classifiable to 295-298)
300.3 Obsessive-compulsive disorders
332.0 Paralysis agitans
333.1 Essential and other specified forms of tremor — (Use additional E code to identify drug, if drug-induced)
338.0 Central pain syndrome — (Use additional code to identify pain associated with psychological factors: 307.89)
338.21 Chronic pain due to trauma — (Use additional code to identify pain associated with psychological factors: 307.89)
338.22 Chronic post-thoracotomy pain — (Use additional code to identify pain associated with psychological factors: 307.89)
338.28 Other chronic postoperative pain — (Use additional code to identify pain associated with psychological factors: 307.89)
338.29 Other chronic pain — (Use additional code to identify pain associated with psychological factors: 307.89)
338.4 Chronic pain syndrome — (Use additional code to identify pain associated with psychological factors: 307.89)
345.01 Generalized nonconvulsive epilepsy with intractable epilepsy
345.11 Generalized convulsive epilepsy with intractable epilepsy
345.41 Localization-related (focal) (partial) epilepsy and epileptic syndromes with complex partial seizures, with intractable epilepsy
345.51 Localization-related (focal) (partial) epilepsy and epileptic syndromes with simple partial seizures, with intractable epilepsy
345.91 Unspecified epilepsy with intractable epilepsy ♥
780.33 Post traumatic seizures
780.39 Other convulsions
787.60 Full incontinence of feces
788.20 Unspecified retention of urine — (Code, if applicable, any causal condition first, such as: 600.0-600.9, with fifth digit 1) ♥
788.21 Incomplete bladder emptying — (Code, if applicable, any causal condition first, such as: 600.0-600.9, with fifth digit 1)
788.31 Urge incontinence — (Code, if applicable, any causal condition first: 600.0-600.9, with fifth digit 1; 618.00-618.9; 753.23)
788.41 Urinary frequency — (Code, if applicable, any causal condition first, such as: 600.0-600.9, with fifth digit 1)

ICD-9-CM Procedural

04.92 Implantation or replacement of peripheral neurostimulator lead(s)

64585

64585 Revision or removal of peripheral neurostimulator electrode array

ICD-9-CM Diagnostic

996.2 Mechanical complication of nervous system device, implant, and graft
996.63 Infection and inflammatory reaction due to nervous system device, implant, and graft — (Use additional code to identify specified infections)
996.75 Other complications due to nervous system device, implant, and graft — (Use additional code to identify complication: 338.18-338.19, 338.28-338.29)

ICD-9-CM Procedural

04.93 Removal of peripheral neurostimulator lead(s)

64590-64595

64590 Insertion or replacement of peripheral or gastric neurostimulator pulse generator or receiver, direct or inductive coupling
64595 Revision or removal of peripheral or gastric neurostimulator pulse generator or receiver

ICD-9-CM Diagnostic

249.60 Secondary diabetes mellitus with neurological manifestations, not stated as uncontrolled, or unspecified — (Use additional code to identify manifestation: 337.1, 353.5, 354.0-355.9, 357.2, 536.3, 713.5) (Use additional code to identify any associated insulin use: V58.67)
249.61 Secondary diabetes mellitus with neurological manifestations, uncontrolled — (Use additional code to identify manifestation: 337.1, 353.5, 354.0-355.9, 357.2, 536.3, 713.5) (Use additional code to identify any associated insulin use: V58.67)
250.60 Diabetes with neurological manifestations, type II or unspecified type, not stated as uncontrolled — (Use additional code to identify manifestation: 337.1, 353.5, 354.0-355.9, 357.2, 536.3, 713.5)
250.61 Diabetes with neurological manifestations, type I [juvenile type], not stated as uncontrolled — (Use additional code to identify manifestation: 337.1, 353.5, 354.0-355.9, 357.2, 536.3, 713.5)
250.62 Diabetes with neurological manifestations, type II or unspecified type, uncontrolled — (Use additional code to identify manifestation: 337.1, 353.5, 354.0-355.9, 357.2, 536.3, 713.5)
250.63 Diabetes with neurological manifestations, type I [juvenile type], uncontrolled — (Use additional code to identify manifestation: 337.1, 353.5, 354.0-355.9, 357.2, 536.3, 713.5)
278.01 Morbid obesity — (Use additional code to identify Body Mass Index (BMI), if known: V85.0-V85.54)
337.1 Peripheral autonomic neuropathy in disorders classified elsewhere — (Code first underlying disease: 249.6, 250.6, 277.30-277.39) ☒
337.20 Unspecified reflex sympathetic dystrophy ♥
337.22 Reflex sympathetic dystrophy of the lower limb
337.29 Reflex sympathetic dystrophy of other specified site
354.5 Mononeuritis multiplex
355.1 Meralgia paresthetica
355.2 Other lesion of femoral nerve
355.3 Lesion of lateral popliteal nerve
355.4 Lesion of medial popliteal nerve
355.71 Causalgia of lower limb
355.79 Other mononeuritis of lower limb
355.8 Unspecified mononeuritis of lower limb ♥
356.0 Hereditary peripheral neuropathy
356.3 Refsum's disease

356.4 Idiopathic progressive polyneuropathy
356.8 Other specified idiopathic peripheral neuropathy
357.2 Polyneuropathy in diabetes — (Code first underlying disease: 249.6, 250.6) ☒
357.3 Polyneuropathy in malignant disease — (Code first underlying disease: 140.0-208.9) ☒
536.3 Gastroparesis — (Code first underlying disease, if known, as: 249.6, 250.6)
595.1 Chronic interstitial cystitis — (Use additional code to identify organism, such as E. coli: 041.41-041.49)
596.55 Detrusor sphincter dyssynergia — (Use additional code to identify urinary incontinence: 625.6, 788.30-788.39)
596.59 Other functional disorder of bladder — (Use additional code to identify urinary incontinence: 625.6, 788.30-788.39)
787.60 Full incontinence of feces
788.20 Unspecified retention of urine — (Code, if applicable, any causal condition first, such as: 600.0-600.9, with fifth digit 1) ▽
788.21 Incomplete bladder emptying — (Code, if applicable, any causal condition first, such as: 600.0-600.9, with fifth digit 1)
788.31 Urge incontinence — (Code, if applicable, any causal condition first: 600.0-600.9, with fifth digit 1; 618.00-618.9; 753.23)
788.33 Mixed incontinence urge and stress (male)(female) — (Code, if applicable, any causal condition first: 600.0-600.9, with fifth digit 1; 618.00-618.9; 753.23)
788.34 Incontinence without sensory awareness — (Code, if applicable, any causal condition first: 600.0-600.9, with fifth digit 1; 618.00-618.9; 753.23)
788.41 Urinary frequency — (Code, if applicable, any causal condition first, such as: 600.0-600.9, with fifth digit 1)
996.2 Mechanical complication of nervous system device, implant, and graft
996.63 Infection and inflammatory reaction due to nervous system device, implant, and graft — (Use additional code to identify specified infections)
996.75 Other complications due to nervous system device, implant, and graft — (Use additional code to identify complication: 338.18-338.19, 338.28-338.29)
996.76 Other complications due to genitourinary device, implant, and graft — (Use additional code to identify complication: 338.18-338.19, 338.28-338.29)
V53.59 Fitting and adjustment of other gastrointestinal appliance and device
V53.99 Fitting and adjustment, Other device

ICD-9-CM Procedural

86.05 Incision with removal of foreign body or device from skin and subcutaneous tissue
86.94 Insertion or replacement of single array neurostimulator pulse generator, not specified as rechargeable
86.95 Insertion or replacement of multiple array neurostimulator pulse generator, not specified as rechargeable
86.96 Insertion or replacement of other neurostimulator pulse generator

HCPCS Level II Supplies & Services

C1767 Generator, neurostimulator (implantable), nonrechargeable

64600

64600 Destruction by neurolytic agent, trigeminal nerve; supraorbital, infraorbital, mental, or inferior alveolar branch

ICD-9-CM Diagnostic

171.0 Malignant neoplasm of connective and other soft tissue of head, face, and neck
225.1 Benign neoplasm of cranial nerves
238.1 Neoplasm of uncertain behavior of connective and other soft tissue
239.2 Neoplasms of unspecified nature of bone, soft tissue, and skin
350.1 Trigeminal neuralgia
350.2 Atypical face pain
350.8 Other specified trigeminal nerve disorders
907.1 Late effect of injury to cranial nerve
951.2 Injury to trigeminal nerve

ICD-9-CM Procedural

04.2 Destruction of cranial and peripheral nerves

64605-64610

64605 Destruction by neurolytic agent, trigeminal nerve; second and third division branches at foramen ovale
64610 second and third division branches at foramen ovale under radiologic monitoring

ICD-9-CM Diagnostic

171.0 Malignant neoplasm of connective and other soft tissue of head, face, and neck
225.1 Benign neoplasm of cranial nerves
238.1 Neoplasm of uncertain behavior of connective and other soft tissue
239.2 Neoplasms of unspecified nature of bone, soft tissue, and skin
350.1 Trigeminal neuralgia
350.2 Atypical face pain
350.8 Other specified trigeminal nerve disorders
907.1 Late effect of injury to cranial nerve
951.2 Injury to trigeminal nerve

ICD-9-CM Procedural

04.2 Destruction of cranial and peripheral nerves

64611

64611 Chemodenervation of parotid and submandibular salivary glands, bilateral

ICD-9-CM Diagnostic

318.0 Moderate intellectual disabilities — (Use additional code(s) to identify any associated psychiatric or physical condition(s))
318.1 Severe intellectual disabilities — (Use additional code(s) to identify any associated psychiatric or physical condition(s))
318.2 Profound intellectual disabilities — (Use additional code(s) to identify any associated psychiatric or physical condition(s))
332.0 Paralysis agitans
335.22 Progressive bulbar palsy
335.23 Pseudobulbar palsy
343.9 Unspecified infantile cerebral palsy ▽
438.82 Dysphagia due to cerebrovascular disease — (Use additional code to identify presence of hypertension)
438.89 Other late effects of cerebrovascular disease — (Use additional code to identify presence of hypertension. Use additional code to identify the late effect)
527.7 Disturbance of salivary secretion
527.8 Other specified diseases of the salivary glands
528.3 Cellulitis and abscess of oral soft tissues
528.9 Other and unspecified diseases of the oral soft tissues ▽
530.81 Esophageal reflux
750.15 Macroglossia
985.0 Toxic effect of mercury and its compounds — (Use additional code to specify the nature of the toxic effect)
V13.64 Personal history of (corrected) congenital malformations of eye, ear, face and neck
V13.67 Personal history of (corrected) congenital malformations of digestive system
V47.3 Other digestive problems

ICD-9-CM Procedural

04.2 Destruction of cranial and peripheral nerves

64612, 64616-64617

64612 Chemodenervation of muscle(s); muscle(s) innervated by facial nerve, unilateral (eg, for blepharospasm, hemifacial spasm)
64616 neck muscle(s), excluding muscles of the larynx, unilateral (eg, for cervical dystonia, spasmodic torticollis)
64617 larynx, unilateral, percutaneous (eg, for spasmodic dysphonia), includes guidance by needle electromyography, when performed

ICD-9-CM Diagnostic

333.3 Tics of organic origin — (Use additional E code to identify drug, if drug-induced)
333.6 Genetic torsion dystonia

333.79	Other acquired torsion dystonia
333.81	Blepharospasm — (Use additional E code to identify drug, if drug-induced)
333.82	Orofacial dyskinesia — (Use additional E code to identify drug, if drug-induced)
333.83	Spasmodic torticollis — (Use additional E code to identify drug, if drug-induced)
333.89	Other fragments of torsion dystonia — (Use additional E code to identify drug, if drug-induced)
340	Multiple sclerosis
350.2	Atypical face pain
351.8	Other facial nerve disorders
478.79	Other diseases of larynx — (Use additional code to identify infectious organism)
781.0	Abnormal involuntary movements

ICD-9-CM Procedural

04.2	Destruction of cranial and peripheral nerves
93.08	Electromyography

HCPCS Level II Supplies & Services

J0585	Injection, onabotulinumtoxinA, 1 unit
J0587	Injection, rimabotulinumtoxinB, 100 units

64615

64615 Chemodenervation of muscle(s); muscle(s) innervated by facial, trigeminal, cervical spinal and accessory nerves, bilateral (eg, for chronic migraine)

ICD-9-CM Diagnostic

307.81	Tension headache
333.81	Blepharospasm — (Use additional E code to identify drug, if drug-induced)
333.82	Orofacial dyskinesia — (Use additional E code to identify drug, if drug-induced)
333.83	Spasmodic torticollis — (Use additional E code to identify drug, if drug-induced)
339.02	Chronic cluster headache
339.09	Other trigeminal autonomic cephalgias
339.12	Chronic tension type headache
346.01	Migraine with aura, with intractable migraine, so stated, without mention of status migrainosus
346.02	Migraine with aura, without mention of intractable migraine with status migrainosus
346.03	Migraine with aura, with intractable migraine, so stated, with status migrainosus
346.11	Migraine without aura, with intractable migraine, so stated, without mention of status migrainosus
346.12	Migraine without aura, without mention of intractable migraine with status migrainosus
346.13	Migraine without aura, with intractable migraine, so stated, with status migrainosus
346.21	Variants of migraine, not elsewhere classified, with intractable migraine, so stated, without mention of status migrainosus
346.22	Variants of migraine, not elsewhere classified, without mention of intractable migraine with status migrainosus
346.23	Variants of migraine, not elsewhere classified, with intractable migraine, so stated, with status migrainosus
346.31	Hemiplegic migraine, with intractable migraine, so stated, without mention of status migrainosus
346.32	Hemiplegic migraine, without mention of intractable migraine with status migrainosus
346.33	Hemiplegic migraine, with intractable migraine, so stated, with status migrainosus
346.41	Menstrual migraine, with intractable migraine, so stated, without mention of status migrainosus ♀
346.42	Menstrual migraine, without mention of intractable migraine with status migrainosus ♀
346.43	Menstrual migraine, with intractable migraine, so stated, with status migrainosus ♀
346.51	Persistent migraine aura without cerebral infarction, with intractable migraine, so stated, without mention of status migrainosus
346.52	Persistent migraine aura without cerebral infarction, without mention of intractable migraine with status migrainosus
346.53	Persistent migraine aura without cerebral infarction, with intractable migraine, so stated, with status migrainosus
346.61	Persistent migraine aura with cerebral infarction, with intractable migraine, so stated, without mention of status migrainosus
346.62	Persistent migraine aura with cerebral infarction, without mention of intractable migraine with status migrainosus
346.63	Persistent migraine aura with cerebral infarction, with intractable migraine, so stated, with status migrainosus
346.71	Chronic migraine without aura, with intractable migraine, so stated, without mention of status migrainosus
346.72	Chronic migraine without aura, without mention of intractable migraine with status migrainosus
346.73	Chronic migraine without aura, with intractable migraine, so stated, with status migrainosus
346.81	Other forms of migraine, with intractable migraine, so stated, without mention of status migrainosus
346.82	Other forms of migraine, without mention of intractable migraine with status migrainosus
346.83	Other forms of migraine, with intractable migraine, so stated, with status migrainosus
346.91	Migraine, unspecified, with intractable migraine, so stated, without mention of status migrainosus ▽
346.92	Migraine, unspecified, without mention of intractable migraine with status migrainosus ▽
346.93	Migraine, unspecified, with intractable migraine, so stated, with status migrainosus ▽
350.8	Other specified trigeminal nerve disorders
351.8	Other facial nerve disorders
351.9	Unspecified facial nerve disorder ▽
352.4	Disorders of accessory (11th) nerve
353.2	Cervical root lesions, not elsewhere classified
374.03	Spastic entropion
720.1	Spinal enthesopathy
724.9	Other unspecified back disorder
784.0	Headache

ICD-9-CM Procedural

04.2	Destruction of cranial and peripheral nerves

HCPCS Level II Supplies & Services

J0585	Injection, onabotulinumtoxinA, 1 unit
J0586	Injection, abobotulinumtoxinA, 5 units
J0587	Injection, rimabotulinumtoxinB, 100 units
J0588	Injection, incobotulinumtoxinA, 1 unit

64620

64620 Destruction by neurolytic agent, intercostal nerve

ICD-9-CM Diagnostic

355.9	Mononeuritis of unspecified site ▽
729.2	Unspecified neuralgia, neuritis, and radiculitis ▽
786.52	Painful respiration

ICD-9-CM Procedural

04.2	Destruction of cranial and peripheral nerves

[64633-64636]

64633 Destruction by neurolytic agent, paravertebral facet joint nerve(s), with imaging guidance (fluoroscopy or CT); cervical or thoracic, single facet joint

64634 cervical or thoracic, each additional facet joint (List separately in addition to code for primary procedure)

64635 lumbar or sacral, single facet joint

64636 lumbar or sacral, each additional facet joint (List separately in addition to code for primary procedure)

ICD-9-CM Diagnostic

720.1	Spinal enthesopathy
721.0	Cervical spondylosis without myelopathy
721.2	Thoracic spondylosis without myelopathy

721.3 Lumbosacral spondylosis without myelopathy
721.41 Spondylosis with myelopathy, thoracic region
721.42 Spondylosis with myelopathy, lumbar region
721.90 Spondylosis of unspecified site without mention of myelopathy ▽
722.10 Displacement of lumbar intervertebral disc without myelopathy
722.11 Displacement of thoracic intervertebral disc without myelopathy
722.4 Degeneration of cervical intervertebral disc
722.51 Degeneration of thoracic or thoracolumbar intervertebral disc
722.52 Degeneration of lumbar or lumbosacral intervertebral disc
722.71 Intervertebral cervical disc disorder with myelopathy, cervical region
722.72 Intervertebral thoracic disc disorder with myelopathy, thoracic region
722.73 Intervertebral lumbar disc disorder with myelopathy, lumbar region
722.81 Postlaminectomy syndrome, cervical region
722.82 Postlaminectomy syndrome, thoracic region
722.83 Postlaminectomy syndrome, lumbar region
723.1 Cervicalgia
724.00 Spinal stenosis, unspecified region other than cervical ▽
724.01 Spinal stenosis of thoracic region
724.02 Spinal stenosis of lumbar region, without neurogenic claudication
724.03 Spinal stenosis of lumbar region, with neurogenic claudication
724.09 Spinal stenosis, other region other than cervical
724.1 Pain in thoracic spine
724.2 Lumbago
724.3 Sciatica
733.13 Pathologic fracture of vertebrae
738.4 Acquired spondylolisthesis

ICD-9-CM Procedural

03.96 Percutaneous denervation of facet

64630

64630 Destruction by neurolytic agent; pudendal nerve

ICD-9-CM Diagnostic

154.0 Malignant neoplasm of rectosigmoid junction
154.1 Malignant neoplasm of rectum
154.8 Malignant neoplasm of other sites of rectum, rectosigmoid junction, and anus
180.0 Malignant neoplasm of endocervix ♀
180.1 Malignant neoplasm of exocervix ♀
180.9 Malignant neoplasm of cervix uteri, unspecified site ▽ ♀
184.0 Malignant neoplasm of vagina ♀
184.1 Malignant neoplasm of labia majora ♀
184.2 Malignant neoplasm of labia minora ♀
184.4 Malignant neoplasm of vulva, unspecified site ▽ ♀
185 Malignant neoplasm of prostate ♂
197.5 Secondary malignant neoplasm of large intestine and rectum
198.82 Secondary malignant neoplasm of genital organs
729.2 Unspecified neuralgia, neuritis, and radiculitis ▽

ICD-9-CM Procedural

04.2 Destruction of cranial and peripheral nerves

64632

64632 Destruction by neurolytic agent; plantar common digital nerve

ICD-9-CM Diagnostic

355.6 Lesion of plantar nerve
355.71 Causalgia of lower limb
355.79 Other mononeuritis of lower limb
355.8 Unspecified mononeuritis of lower limb ▽
719.47 Pain in joint, ankle and foot
727.06 Tenosynovitis of foot and ankle
729.1 Unspecified myalgia and myositis ▽
729.2 Unspecified neuralgia, neuritis, and radiculitis ▽
729.5 Pain in soft tissues of limb

ICD-9-CM Procedural

04.2 Destruction of cranial and peripheral nerves

64640

64640 Destruction by neurolytic agent; other peripheral nerve or branch

ICD-9-CM Diagnostic

The application of this code is too broad to adequately present ICD-9-CM diagnostic code links here. Refer to your ICD-9-CM book.

ICD-9-CM Procedural

04.2 Destruction of cranial and peripheral nerves
69.3 Paracervical uterine denervation ♀

64642-64645

64642 Chemodenervation of one extremity; 1-4 muscle(s)
64643 each additional extremity, 1-4 muscle(s) (List separately in addition to code for primary procedure)
64644 Chemodenervation of one extremity; 5 or more muscle(s)
64645 each additional extremity, 5 or more muscle(s) (List separately in addition to code for primary procedure)

ICD-9-CM Diagnostic

333.6 Genetic torsion dystonia
333.79 Other acquired torsion dystonia
333.84 Organic writers' cramp — (Use additional E code to identify drug, if drug-induced)
338.11 Acute pain due to trauma — (Use additional code to identify pain associated with psychological factors: 307.89)
338.18 Other acute postoperative pain — (Use additional code to identify pain associated with psychological factors: 307.89)
338.19 Other acute pain — (Use additional code to identify pain associated with psychological factors: 307.89)
338.21 Chronic pain due to trauma — (Use additional code to identify pain associated with psychological factors: 307.89)
338.28 Other chronic postoperative pain — (Use additional code to identify pain associated with psychological factors: 307.89)
338.29 Other chronic pain — (Use additional code to identify pain associated with psychological factors: 307.89)
340 Multiple sclerosis
344.89 Other specified paralytic syndrome
729.1 Unspecified myalgia and myositis ▽
729.5 Pain in soft tissues of limb
729.82 Cramp of limb
781.0 Abnormal involuntary movements

ICD-9-CM Procedural

04.2 Destruction of cranial and peripheral nerves

HCPCS Level II Supplies & Services

J0585 Injection, onabotulinumtoxinA, 1 unit
J0586 Injection, abobotulinumtoxinA, 5 units
J0587 Injection, rimabotulinumtoxinB, 100 units
J0588 Injection, incobotulinumtoxinA, 1 unit

64646-64647

64646 Chemodenervation of trunk muscle(s); 1-5 muscle(s)
64647 6 or more muscle(s)

ICD-9-CM Diagnostic

333.6 Genetic torsion dystonia
333.79 Other acquired torsion dystonia
338.11 Acute pain due to trauma — (Use additional code to identify pain associated with psychological factors: 307.89)
338.12 Acute post-thoracotomy pain — (Use additional code to identify pain associated with psychological factors: 307.89)
338.18 Other acute postoperative pain — (Use additional code to identify pain associated with psychological factors: 307.89)
338.19 Other acute pain — (Use additional code to identify pain associated with psychological factors: 307.89)
338.21 Chronic pain due to trauma — (Use additional code to identify pain associated with psychological factors: 307.89)
338.22 Chronic post-thoracotomy pain — (Use additional code to identify pain associated with psychological factors: 307.89)
338.28 Other chronic postoperative pain — (Use additional code to identify pain associated with psychological factors: 307.89)
338.29 Other chronic pain — (Use additional code to identify pain associated with psychological factors: 307.89)
340 Multiple sclerosis
344.89 Other specified paralytic syndrome
729.1 Unspecified myalgia and myositis ▽
781.0 Abnormal involuntary movements

ICD-9-CM Procedural

04.2 Destruction of cranial and peripheral nerves

HCPCS Level II Supplies & Services

J0585 Injection, onabotulinumtoxinA, 1 unit
J0586 Injection, abobotulinumtoxinA, 5 units
J0587 Injection, rimabotulinumtoxinB, 100 units
J0588 Injection, incobotulinumtoxinA, 1 unit

64650-64653

64650 Chemodenervation of eccrine glands; both axillae
64653 other area(s) (eg, scalp, face, neck), per day

ICD-9-CM Diagnostic

705.0 Anhidrosis
705.21 Primary focal hyperhidrosis
705.22 Secondary focal hyperhidrosis
705.81 Dyshidrosis
705.83 Hidradenitis
705.89 Other specified disorder of sweat glands
780.8 Generalized hyperhidrosis

ICD-9-CM Procedural

99.29 Injection or infusion of other therapeutic or prophylactic substance
99.57 Administration of botulism antitoxin

HCPCS Level II Supplies & Services

J0585 Injection, onabotulinumtoxinA, 1 unit
J0587 Injection, rimabotulinumtoxinB, 100 units

64680

64680 Destruction by neurolytic agent, with or without radiologic monitoring; celiac plexus

ICD-9-CM Diagnostic

157.0 Malignant neoplasm of head of pancreas
157.1 Malignant neoplasm of body of pancreas
157.2 Malignant neoplasm of tail of pancreas
157.3 Malignant neoplasm of pancreatic duct
157.4 Malignant neoplasm of islets of Langerhans — (Use additional code to identify any functional activity)
577.1 Chronic pancreatitis
577.8 Other specified disease of pancreas

ICD-9-CM Procedural

05.32 Injection of neurolytic agent into sympathetic nerve

64681

64681 Destruction by neurolytic agent, with or without radiologic monitoring; superior hypogastric plexus

ICD-9-CM Diagnostic

617.0 Endometriosis of uterus ♀
617.1 Endometriosis of ovary ♀
617.2 Endometriosis of fallopian tube ♀
617.3 Endometriosis of pelvic peritoneum ♀
617.4 Endometriosis of rectovaginal septum and vagina ♀
617.5 Endometriosis of intestine ♀
617.8 Endometriosis of other specified sites ♀
617.9 Endometriosis, site unspecified ▽ ♀
625.0 Dyspareunia ♀
625.2 Mittelschmerz ♀
625.3 Dysmenorrhea ♀
625.9 Unspecified symptom associated with female genital organs ▽ ♀

ICD-9-CM Procedural

05.32 Injection of neurolytic agent into sympathetic nerve

64702-64704

64702 Neuroplasty; digital, 1 or both, same digit
64704 nerve of hand or foot

ICD-9-CM Diagnostic

354.2 Lesion of ulnar nerve
354.3 Lesion of radial nerve
354.4 Causalgia of upper limb
355.4 Lesion of medial popliteal nerve
355.5 Tarsal tunnel syndrome
355.6 Lesion of plantar nerve
355.71 Causalgia of lower limb
355.79 Other mononeuritis of lower limb
355.8 Unspecified mononeuritis of lower limb ▽
709.2 Scar condition and fibrosis of skin
711.44 Arthropathy, associated with other bacterial diseases, hand — (Code first underlying disease, such as diseases classifiable to 010-040 (except 036.82), 090-099 (except 098.50)) ☒
718.54 Ankylosis of hand joint
719.44 Pain in joint, hand
719.47 Pain in joint, ankle and foot
719.64 Other symptoms referable to hand joint
727.03 Trigger finger (acquired)
727.05 Other tenosynovitis of hand and wrist
727.42 Ganglion of tendon sheath
727.81 Contracture of tendon (sheath)
728.6 Contracture of palmar fascia
728.71 Plantar fascial fibromatosis
729.2 Unspecified neuralgia, neuritis, and radiculitis ▽
729.5 Pain in soft tissues of limb

736.21 Boutonniere deformity
736.22 Swan-neck deformity
755.12 Syndactyly of fingers with fusion of bone
755.13 Syndactyly of toes without fusion of bone
755.14 Syndactyly of toes with fusion of bone
782.0 Disturbance of skin sensation
906.1 Late effect of open wound of extremities without mention of tendon injury
907.4 Late effect of injury to peripheral nerve of shoulder girdle and upper limb
907.5 Late effect of injury to peripheral nerve of pelvic girdle and lower limb
907.9 Late effect of injury to other and unspecified nerve
908.6 Late effect of certain complications of trauma
908.9 Late effect of unspecified injury
909.3 Late effect of complications of surgical and medical care
955.6 Injury to digital nerve, upper limb
955.7 Injury to other specified nerve(s) of shoulder girdle and upper limb
955.8 Injury to multiple nerves of shoulder girdle and upper limb
955.9 Injury to unspecified nerve of shoulder girdle and upper limb
957.8 Injury to multiple nerves in several parts

ICD-9-CM Procedural

04.49 Other peripheral nerve or ganglion decompression or lysis of adhesions
04.79 Other neuroplasty

64708-64712

64708 Neuroplasty, major peripheral nerve, arm or leg, open; other than specified
64712 sciatic nerve

ICD-9-CM Diagnostic

353.9 Unspecified nerve root and plexus disorder
354.3 Lesion of radial nerve
354.4 Causalgia of upper limb
354.9 Unspecified mononeuritis of upper limb
355.0 Lesion of sciatic nerve
355.71 Causalgia of lower limb
355.79 Other mononeuritis of lower limb
355.8 Unspecified mononeuritis of lower limb
729.5 Pain in soft tissues of limb
782.0 Disturbance of skin sensation
906.1 Late effect of open wound of extremities without mention of tendon injury
907.4 Late effect of injury to peripheral nerve of shoulder girdle and upper limb
907.5 Late effect of injury to peripheral nerve of pelvic girdle and lower limb
907.9 Late effect of injury to other and unspecified nerve
908.6 Late effect of certain complications of trauma
908.9 Late effect of unspecified injury
909.3 Late effect of complications of surgical and medical care
955.0 Injury to axillary nerve
955.1 Injury to median nerve
955.2 Injury to ulnar nerve
955.3 Injury to radial nerve
955.4 Injury to musculocutaneous nerve
955.7 Injury to other specified nerve(s) of shoulder girdle and upper limb
955.8 Injury to multiple nerves of shoulder girdle and upper limb
955.9 Injury to unspecified nerve of shoulder girdle and upper limb
956.0 Injury to sciatic nerve
956.1 Injury to femoral nerve
956.2 Injury to posterior tibial nerve
956.3 Injury to peroneal nerve
956.4 Injury to cutaneous sensory nerve, lower limb
956.5 Injury to other specified nerve(s) of pelvic girdle and lower limb
956.8 Injury to multiple nerves of pelvic girdle and lower limb
956.9 Injury to unspecified nerve of pelvic girdle and lower limb
957.8 Injury to multiple nerves in several parts
996.75 Other complications due to nervous system device, implant, and graft — (Use additional code to identify complication: 338.18-338.19, 338.28-338.29)
998.2 Accidental puncture or laceration during procedure

ICD-9-CM Procedural

04.49 Other peripheral nerve or ganglion decompression or lysis of adhesions
04.79 Other neuroplasty

64713

64713 Neuroplasty, major peripheral nerve, arm or leg, open; brachial plexus

ICD-9-CM Diagnostic

353.0 Brachial plexus lesions
723.4 Brachial neuritis or radiculitis NOS
953.4 Injury to brachial plexus
996.75 Other complications due to nervous system device, implant, and graft — (Use additional code to identify complication: 338.18-338.19, 338.28-338.29)

ICD-9-CM Procedural

04.79 Other neuroplasty

64714

64714 Neuroplasty, major peripheral nerve, arm or leg, open; lumbar plexus

ICD-9-CM Diagnostic

353.1 Lumbosacral plexus lesions
724.2 Lumbago
724.4 Thoracic or lumbosacral neuritis or radiculitis, unspecified
729.5 Pain in soft tissues of limb
953.5 Injury to lumbosacral plexus
996.75 Other complications due to nervous system device, implant, and graft — (Use additional code to identify complication: 338.18-338.19, 338.28-338.29)

ICD-9-CM Procedural

04.79 Other neuroplasty

64716

64716 Neuroplasty and/or transposition; cranial nerve (specify)

ICD-9-CM Diagnostic

171.0 Malignant neoplasm of connective and other soft tissue of head, face, and neck
225.1 Benign neoplasm of cranial nerves
350.1 Trigeminal neuralgia
350.2 Atypical face pain
350.8 Other specified trigeminal nerve disorders
350.9 Unspecified trigeminal nerve disorder
351.0 Bell's palsy
352.1 Glossopharyngeal neuralgia
352.6 Multiple cranial nerve palsies
907.1 Late effect of injury to cranial nerve
951.2 Injury to trigeminal nerve
951.4 Injury to facial nerve
998.2 Accidental puncture or laceration during procedure

ICD-9-CM Procedural

04.41 Decompression of trigeminal nerve root
04.6 Transposition of cranial and peripheral nerves
04.79 Other neuroplasty

64718

64718 Neuroplasty and/or transposition; ulnar nerve at elbow

ICD-9-CM Diagnostic

354.2 Lesion of ulnar nerve
354.5 Mononeuritis multiplex
356.8 Other specified idiopathic peripheral neuropathy
718.42 Contracture of upper arm joint
719.42 Pain in joint, upper arm
723.4 Brachial neuritis or radiculitis NOS
727.41 Ganglion of joint
729.5 Pain in soft tissues of limb
782.0 Disturbance of skin sensation
906.1 Late effect of open wound of extremities without mention of tendon injury
907.4 Late effect of injury to peripheral nerve of shoulder girdle and upper limb
908.9 Late effect of unspecified injury
909.3 Late effect of complications of surgical and medical care
955.2 Injury to ulnar nerve
955.9 Injury to unspecified nerve of shoulder girdle and upper limb
996.75 Other complications due to nervous system device, implant, and graft — (Use additional code to identify complication: 338.18-338.19, 338.28-338.29)

ICD-9-CM Procedural

04.49 Other peripheral nerve or ganglion decompression or lysis of adhesions
04.6 Transposition of cranial and peripheral nerves
04.79 Other neuroplasty

64719-64721

64719 Neuroplasty and/or transposition; ulnar nerve at wrist
64721 median nerve at carpal tunnel

ICD-9-CM Diagnostic

354.0 Carpal tunnel syndrome
354.2 Lesion of ulnar nerve
354.5 Mononeuritis multiplex
357.1 Polyneuropathy in collagen vascular disease — (Code first underlying disease: 446.0, 710.0, 714.0)
359.6 Symptomatic inflammatory myopathy in diseases classified elsewhere — (Code first underlying disease: 135, 140.0-208.9, 277.30-277.39, 446.0, 710.0, 710.1, 710.2, 714.0)
714.0 Rheumatoid arthritis — (Use additional code to identify manifestation: 357.1, 359.6)
715.94 Osteoarthrosis, unspecified whether generalized or localized, hand
716.14 Traumatic arthropathy, hand
719.44 Pain in joint, hand
723.4 Brachial neuritis or radiculitis NOS
726.4 Enthesopathy of wrist and carpus
727.04 Radial styloid tenosynovitis
727.41 Ganglion of joint
728.6 Contracture of palmar fascia
729.5 Pain in soft tissues of limb
782.0 Disturbance of skin sensation
794.17 Nonspecific abnormal electromyogram (EMG)
906.1 Late effect of open wound of extremities without mention of tendon injury
907.4 Late effect of injury to peripheral nerve of shoulder girdle and upper limb
908.9 Late effect of unspecified injury
909.3 Late effect of complications of surgical and medical care
955.1 Injury to median nerve
955.2 Injury to ulnar nerve

ICD-9-CM Procedural

04.43 Release of carpal tunnel
04.49 Other peripheral nerve or ganglion decompression or lysis of adhesions
04.6 Transposition of cranial and peripheral nerves
04.79 Other neuroplasty

64726

64726 Decompression; plantar digital nerve

ICD-9-CM Diagnostic

355.5 Tarsal tunnel syndrome
355.6 Lesion of plantar nerve
355.71 Causalgia of lower limb

ICD-9-CM Procedural

04.49 Other peripheral nerve or ganglion decompression or lysis of adhesions

64732

64732 Transection or avulsion of; supraorbital nerve

ICD-9-CM Diagnostic

190.1 Malignant neoplasm of orbit
238.8 Neoplasm of uncertain behavior of other specified sites
802.6 Orbital floor (blow-out), closed fracture
870.3 Penetrating wound of orbit, without mention of foreign body
871.1 Ocular laceration with prolapse or exposure of intraocular tissue
873.52 Open wound of forehead, complicated
925.1 Crushing injury of face and scalp — (Use additional code to identify any associated injuries, such as: 800-829, 850.0-854.1, 860.0-869.1)
959.01 Head injury, unspecified
959.09 Injury of face and neck, other and unspecified

ICD-9-CM Procedural

04.07 Other excision or avulsion of cranial and peripheral nerves

64734

64734 Transection or avulsion of; infraorbital nerve

ICD-9-CM Diagnostic

171.0 Malignant neoplasm of connective and other soft tissue of head, face, and neck
225.1 Benign neoplasm of cranial nerves
238.1 Neoplasm of uncertain behavior of connective and other soft tissue
239.2 Neoplasms of unspecified nature of bone, soft tissue, and skin
350.1 Trigeminal neuralgia
350.2 Atypical face pain
350.8 Other specified trigeminal nerve disorders
729.6 Residual foreign body in soft tissue — (Use additional code to identify foreign body (V90.01-V90.9))
784.2 Swelling, mass, or lump in head and neck
907.1 Late effect of injury to cranial nerve
925.1 Crushing injury of face and scalp — (Use additional code to identify any associated injuries, such as: 800-829, 850.0-854.1, 860.0-869.1)
951.2 Injury to trigeminal nerve

ICD-9-CM Procedural

04.07 Other excision or avulsion of cranial and peripheral nerves

64736

64736 Transection or avulsion of; mental nerve

ICD-9-CM Diagnostic

171.0 Malignant neoplasm of connective and other soft tissue of head, face, and neck
225.1 Benign neoplasm of cranial nerves
238.1 Neoplasm of uncertain behavior of connective and other soft tissue
239.2 Neoplasms of unspecified nature of bone, soft tissue, and skin

350.1 Trigeminal neuralgia

350.2 Atypical face pain

350.8 Other specified trigeminal nerve disorders

784.0 Headache

907.1 Late effect of injury to cranial nerve

951.2 Injury to trigeminal nerve

951.8 Injury to other specified cranial nerves

ICD-9-CM Procedural

04.07 Other excision or avulsion of cranial and peripheral nerves

64738

64738 Transection or avulsion of; inferior alveolar nerve by osteotomy

ICD-9-CM Diagnostic

171.0 Malignant neoplasm of connective and other soft tissue of head, face, and neck

225.1 Benign neoplasm of cranial nerves

238.1 Neoplasm of uncertain behavior of connective and other soft tissue

239.2 Neoplasms of unspecified nature of bone, soft tissue, and skin

350.1 Trigeminal neuralgia

350.2 Atypical face pain

907.1 Late effect of injury to cranial nerve

951.2 Injury to trigeminal nerve

ICD-9-CM Procedural

04.07 Other excision or avulsion of cranial and peripheral nerves

64740

64740 Transection or avulsion of; lingual nerve

ICD-9-CM Diagnostic

171.0 Malignant neoplasm of connective and other soft tissue of head, face, and neck

225.1 Benign neoplasm of cranial nerves

238.1 Neoplasm of uncertain behavior of connective and other soft tissue

239.2 Neoplasms of unspecified nature of bone, soft tissue, and skin

350.1 Trigeminal neuralgia

350.8 Other specified trigeminal nerve disorders

729.6 Residual foreign body in soft tissue — (Use additional code to identify foreign body (V90.01-V90.9))

907.1 Late effect of injury to cranial nerve

951.2 Injury to trigeminal nerve

ICD-9-CM Procedural

04.07 Other excision or avulsion of cranial and peripheral nerves

64742

64742 Transection or avulsion of; facial nerve, differential or complete

ICD-9-CM Diagnostic

192.0 Malignant neoplasm of cranial nerves

237.9 Neoplasm of uncertain behavior of other and unspecified parts of nervous system ▽

350.2 Atypical face pain

351.1 Geniculate ganglionitis

729.2 Unspecified neuralgia, neuritis, and radiculitis ▽

784.2 Swelling, mass, or lump in head and neck

802.8 Other facial bones, closed fracture

873.51 Open wound of cheek, complicated

925.1 Crushing injury of face and scalp — (Use additional code to identify any associated injuries, such as: 800-829, 850.0-854.1, 860.0-869.1)

959.01 Head injury, unspecified ▽

959.09 Injury of face and neck, other and unspecified

ICD-9-CM Procedural

04.07 Other excision or avulsion of cranial and peripheral nerves

64744

64744 Transection or avulsion of; greater occipital nerve

ICD-9-CM Diagnostic

237.5 Neoplasm of uncertain behavior of brain and spinal cord

339.00 Cluster headache syndrome, unspecified ▽

339.01 Episodic cluster headache

339.02 Chronic cluster headache

346.21 Variants of migraine, not elsewhere classified, with intractable migraine, so stated, without mention of status migrainosus

346.22 Variants of migraine, not elsewhere classified, without mention of intractable migraine with status migrainosus

346.23 Variants of migraine, not elsewhere classified, with intractable migraine, so stated, with status migrainosus

353.2 Cervical root lesions, not elsewhere classified

729.2 Unspecified neuralgia, neuritis, and radiculitis ▽

805.01 Closed fracture of first cervical vertebra without mention of spinal cord injury

847.0 Neck sprain and strain

925.2 Crushing injury of neck — (Use additional code to identify any associated injuries, such as: 800-829, 850.0-854.1, 860.0-869.1)

959.01 Head injury, unspecified ▽

959.09 Injury of face and neck, other and unspecified

ICD-9-CM Procedural

04.07 Other excision or avulsion of cranial and peripheral nerves

64746

64746 Transection or avulsion of; phrenic nerve

ICD-9-CM Diagnostic

519.4 Disorders of diaphragm — (Use additional code to identify infectious organism)

786.8 Hiccough

ICD-9-CM Procedural

04.07 Other excision or avulsion of cranial and peripheral nerves

33.31 Destruction of phrenic nerve for collapse of lung

64752-64760

64752 Transection or avulsion of; vagus nerve (vagotomy), transthoracic

64755 vagus nerves limited to proximal stomach (selective proximal vagotomy, proximal gastric vagotomy, parietal cell vagotomy, supra- or highly selective vagotomy)

64760 vagus nerve (vagotomy), abdominal

ICD-9-CM Diagnostic

150.2 Malignant neoplasm of abdominal esophagus

155.0 Malignant neoplasm of liver, primary

159.1 Malignant neoplasm of spleen, not elsewhere classified

192.0 Malignant neoplasm of cranial nerves

235.2 Neoplasm of uncertain behavior of stomach, intestines, and rectum

237.70 Neurofibromatosis, unspecified ▽

237.79 Other neurofibromatosis

237.9 Neoplasm of uncertain behavior of other and unspecified parts of nervous system ▽

352.3 Disorders of pneumogastric (10th) nerve

531.70 Chronic gastric ulcer without mention of hemorrhage, perforation, without mention of obstruction — (Use additional E code to identify drug, if drug induced)

533.40 Chronic or unspecified peptic ulcer, unspecified site, with hemorrhage, without mention of obstruction — (Use additional E code to identify drug, if drug induced) ▽

750.3 Congenital tracheoesophageal fistula, esophageal atresia and stenosis

951.8 Injury to other specified cranial nerves

V64.41 Laparoscopic surgical procedure converted to open procedure

ICD-9-CM Procedural

04.07 Other excision or avulsion of cranial and peripheral nerves
44.00 Vagotomy, not otherwise specified
44.01 Truncal vagotomy
44.02 Highly selective vagotomy
44.03 Other selective vagotomy

64761

64761 Transection or avulsion of; pudendal nerve

ICD-9-CM Diagnostic

198.82 Secondary malignant neoplasm of genital organs
236.3 Neoplasm of uncertain behavior of other and unspecified female genital organs ▽ ♀
623.2 Stricture or atresia of vagina — (Use additional E code to identify any external cause) ♀
625.0 Dyspareunia ♀
669.81 Other complication of labor and delivery, delivered, with or without mention of antepartum condition ♀
956.5 Injury to other specified nerve(s) of pelvic girdle and lower limb

ICD-9-CM Procedural

04.07 Other excision or avulsion of cranial and peripheral nerves

64763-64766

64763 Transection or avulsion of obturator nerve, extrapelvic, with or without adductor tenotomy
64766 Transection or avulsion of obturator nerve, intrapelvic, with or without adductor tenotomy

ICD-9-CM Diagnostic

171.3 Malignant neoplasm of connective and other soft tissue of lower limb, including hip
198.89 Secondary malignant neoplasm of other specified sites
215.3 Other benign neoplasm of connective and other soft tissue of lower limb, including hip
225.8 Benign neoplasm of other specified sites of nervous system
237.70 Neurofibromatosis, unspecified ▽
237.79 Other neurofibromatosis
238.1 Neoplasm of uncertain behavior of connective and other soft tissue
239.2 Neoplasms of unspecified nature of bone, soft tissue, and skin
351.1 Geniculate ganglionitis
353.6 Phantom limb (syndrome)
355.71 Causalgia of lower limb
355.9 Mononeuritis of unspecified site ▽
729.2 Unspecified neuralgia, neuritis, and radiculitis ▽
907.5 Late effect of injury to peripheral nerve of pelvic girdle and lower limb
956.5 Injury to other specified nerve(s) of pelvic girdle and lower limb

ICD-9-CM Procedural

04.07 Other excision or avulsion of cranial and peripheral nerves
83.12 Adductor tenotomy of hip

64771

64771 Transection or avulsion of other cranial nerve, extradural

ICD-9-CM Diagnostic

171.0 Malignant neoplasm of connective and other soft tissue of head, face, and neck
192.0 Malignant neoplasm of cranial nerves
350.2 Atypical face pain
351.1 Geniculate ganglionitis
352.0 Disorders of olfactory (1st) nerve
729.2 Unspecified neuralgia, neuritis, and radiculitis ▽
784.2 Swelling, mass, or lump in head and neck
803.09 Other closed skull fracture without mention of intracranial injury, unspecified concussion ▽
925.1 Crushing injury of face and scalp — (Use additional code to identify any associated injuries, such as: 800-829, 850.0-854.1, 860.0-869.1)
951.2 Injury to trigeminal nerve
959.01 Head injury, unspecified ▽
959.09 Injury of face and neck, other and unspecified

ICD-9-CM Procedural

04.07 Other excision or avulsion of cranial and peripheral nerves

64772

64772 Transection or avulsion of other spinal nerve, extradural

ICD-9-CM Diagnostic

237.70 Neurofibromatosis, unspecified ▽
237.71 Neurofibromatosis, Type 1 (von Recklinghausen's disease)
237.72 Neurofibromatosis, Type 2 (acoustic neurofibromatosis)
237.73 Schwannomatosis
237.79 Other neurofibromatosis
353.6 Phantom limb (syndrome)
354.4 Causalgia of upper limb
355.1 Meralgia paresthetica
716.15 Traumatic arthropathy, pelvic region and thigh
729.2 Unspecified neuralgia, neuritis, and radiculitis ▽
879.4 Open wound of abdominal wall, lateral, without mention of complication
926.11 Crushing injury of back — (Use additional code to identify any associated injuries: 800-829, 850.0-854.1, 860.0-869.1)
953.4 Injury to brachial plexus
954.1 Injury to other sympathetic nerve, excluding shoulder and pelvic girdles
955.3 Injury to radial nerve

ICD-9-CM Procedural

03.1 Division of intraspinal nerve root
04.07 Other excision or avulsion of cranial and peripheral nerves
07.42 Division of nerves to adrenal glands

64774

64774 Excision of neuroma; cutaneous nerve, surgically identifiable

ICD-9-CM Diagnostic

The application of this code is too broad to adequately present ICD-9-CM diagnostic code links here. Refer to your ICD-9-CM book.

ICD-9-CM Procedural

04.07 Other excision or avulsion of cranial and peripheral nerves

64776-64778

64776 Excision of neuroma; digital nerve, 1 or both, same digit
64778 digital nerve, each additional digit (List separately in addition to code for primary procedure)

ICD-9-CM Diagnostic

237.70 Neurofibromatosis, unspecified ▽
237.71 Neurofibromatosis, Type 1 (von Recklinghausen's disease)
237.72 Neurofibromatosis, Type 2 (acoustic neurofibromatosis)
237.73 Schwannomatosis
237.79 Other neurofibromatosis
354.9 Unspecified mononeuritis of upper limb ▽
355.6 Lesion of plantar nerve
356.4 Idiopathic progressive polyneuropathy
782.2 Localized superficial swelling, mass, or lump

ICD-9-CM Procedural

04.07 Other excision or avulsion of cranial and peripheral nerves

64782-64783

64782 Excision of neuroma; hand or foot, except digital nerve

64783 hand or foot, each additional nerve, except same digit (List separately in addition to code for primary procedure)

ICD-9-CM Diagnostic

215.2 Other benign neoplasm of connective and other soft tissue of upper limb, including shoulder

215.3 Other benign neoplasm of connective and other soft tissue of lower limb, including hip

354.8 Other mononeuritis of upper limb

355.8 Unspecified mononeuritis of lower limb ▽

729.2 Unspecified neuralgia, neuritis, and radiculitis ▽

729.5 Pain in soft tissues of limb

782.0 Disturbance of skin sensation

782.2 Localized superficial swelling, mass, or lump

955.7 Injury to other specified nerve(s) of shoulder girdle and upper limb

955.8 Injury to multiple nerves of shoulder girdle and upper limb

955.9 Injury to unspecified nerve of shoulder girdle and upper limb ▽

956.5 Injury to other specified nerve(s) of pelvic girdle and lower limb

956.8 Injury to multiple nerves of pelvic girdle and lower limb

956.9 Injury to unspecified nerve of pelvic girdle and lower limb ▽

ICD-9-CM Procedural

04.07 Other excision or avulsion of cranial and peripheral nerves

64784

64784 Excision of neuroma; major peripheral nerve, except sciatic

ICD-9-CM Diagnostic

215.2 Other benign neoplasm of connective and other soft tissue of upper limb, including shoulder

215.3 Other benign neoplasm of connective and other soft tissue of lower limb, including hip

353.6 Phantom limb (syndrome)

729.5 Pain in soft tissues of limb

907.4 Late effect of injury to peripheral nerve of shoulder girdle and upper limb

907.5 Late effect of injury to peripheral nerve of pelvic girdle and lower limb

997.61 Neuroma of amputation stump — (Use additional code to identify complications)

ICD-9-CM Procedural

04.06 Other cranial or peripheral ganglionectomy

04.07 Other excision or avulsion of cranial and peripheral nerves

64786

64786 Excision of neuroma; sciatic nerve

ICD-9-CM Diagnostic

215.3 Other benign neoplasm of connective and other soft tissue of lower limb, including hip

237.70 Neurofibromatosis, unspecified ▽

237.79 Other neurofibromatosis

355.0 Lesion of sciatic nerve

355.71 Causalgia of lower limb

724.3 Sciatica

729.5 Pain in soft tissues of limb

ICD-9-CM Procedural

04.06 Other cranial or peripheral ganglionectomy

04.07 Other excision or avulsion of cranial and peripheral nerves

64788-64792

64788 Excision of neurofibroma or neurolemmoma; cutaneous nerve

64790 major peripheral nerve

64792 extensive (including malignant type)

ICD-9-CM Diagnostic

171.0 Malignant neoplasm of connective and other soft tissue of head, face, and neck

171.2 Malignant neoplasm of connective and other soft tissue of upper limb, including shoulder

171.3 Malignant neoplasm of connective and other soft tissue of lower limb, including hip

171.4 Malignant neoplasm of connective and other soft tissue of thorax

171.5 Malignant neoplasm of connective and other soft tissue of abdomen

171.6 Malignant neoplasm of connective and other soft tissue of pelvis

171.7 Malignant neoplasm of connective and other soft tissue of trunk, unspecified site ▽

171.9 Malignant neoplasm of connective and other soft tissue, site unspecified ▽

215.0 Other benign neoplasm of connective and other soft tissue of head, face, and neck

215.2 Other benign neoplasm of connective and other soft tissue of upper limb, including shoulder

215.3 Other benign neoplasm of connective and other soft tissue of lower limb, including hip

215.4 Other benign neoplasm of connective and other soft tissue of thorax

215.5 Other benign neoplasm of connective and other soft tissue of abdomen

215.6 Other benign neoplasm of connective and other soft tissue of pelvis

215.7 Other benign neoplasm of connective and other soft tissue of trunk, unspecified ▽

215.9 Other benign neoplasm of connective and other soft tissue of unspecified site ▽

237.70 Neurofibromatosis, unspecified ▽

237.71 Neurofibromatosis, Type 1 (von Recklinghausen's disease)

237.72 Neurofibromatosis, Type 2 (acoustic neurofibromatosis)

237.73 Schwannomatosis

237.79 Other neurofibromatosis

238.1 Neoplasm of uncertain behavior of connective and other soft tissue

353.9 Unspecified nerve root and plexus disorder ▽

354.3 Lesion of radial nerve

354.8 Other mononeuritis of upper limb

354.9 Unspecified mononeuritis of upper limb ▽

355.6 Lesion of plantar nerve

355.71 Causalgia of lower limb

355.9 Mononeuritis of unspecified site ▽

729.5 Pain in soft tissues of limb

ICD-9-CM Procedural

04.07 Other excision or avulsion of cranial and peripheral nerves

64795

64795 Biopsy of nerve

ICD-9-CM Diagnostic

171.0 Malignant neoplasm of connective and other soft tissue of head, face, and neck

195.0 Malignant neoplasm of head, face, and neck

198.4 Secondary malignant neoplasm of other parts of nervous system

215.0 Other benign neoplasm of connective and other soft tissue of head, face, and neck

234.8 Carcinoma in situ of other specified sites

237.70 Neurofibromatosis, unspecified ▽

237.71 Neurofibromatosis, Type 1 (von Recklinghausen's disease)

237.72 Neurofibromatosis, Type 2 (acoustic neurofibromatosis)

237.73 Schwannomatosis

237.79 Other neurofibromatosis

238.1 Neoplasm of uncertain behavior of connective and other soft tissue

239.2 Neoplasms of unspecified nature of bone, soft tissue, and skin

277.30 Amyloidosis, unspecified — (Use additional code to identify any associated intellectual disabilities) ▽
277.31 Familial Mediterranean fever — (Use additional code to identify any associated intellectual disabilities)
277.39 Other amyloidosis — (Use additional code to identify any associated intellectual disabilities)
350.8 Other specified trigeminal nerve disorders

ICD-9-CM Procedural

04.12 Open biopsy of cranial or peripheral nerve or ganglion
04.19 Other diagnostic procedures on cranial and peripheral nerves and ganglia
05.11 Biopsy of sympathetic nerve or ganglion

HCPCS Level II Supplies & Services

A4305 Disposable drug delivery system, flow rate of 50 ml or greater per hour

64802-64804

64802 Sympathectomy, cervical
64804 Sympathectomy, cervicothoracic

ICD-9-CM Diagnostic

198.89 Secondary malignant neoplasm of other specified sites
238.1 Neoplasm of uncertain behavior of connective and other soft tissue
239.2 Neoplasms of unspecified nature of bone, soft tissue, and skin
277.30 Amyloidosis, unspecified — (Use additional code to identify any associated intellectual disabilities) ▽
277.31 Familial Mediterranean fever — (Use additional code to identify any associated intellectual disabilities)
277.39 Other amyloidosis — (Use additional code to identify any associated intellectual disabilities)
337.1 Peripheral autonomic neuropathy in disorders classified elsewhere — (Code first underlying disease: 249.6, 250.6, 277.30-277.39) ☒
353.2 Cervical root lesions, not elsewhere classified
353.3 Thoracic root lesions, not elsewhere classified
354.4 Causalgia of upper limb
354.5 Mononeuritis multiplex
780.8 Generalized hyperhidrosis

ICD-9-CM Procedural

05.22 Cervical sympathectomy

64809

64809 Sympathectomy, thoracolumbar

ICD-9-CM Diagnostic

198.89 Secondary malignant neoplasm of other specified sites
238.1 Neoplasm of uncertain behavior of connective and other soft tissue
239.2 Neoplasms of unspecified nature of bone, soft tissue, and skin
353.1 Lumbosacral plexus lesions
353.3 Thoracic root lesions, not elsewhere classified
355.71 Causalgia of lower limb
724.4 Thoracic or lumbosacral neuritis or radiculitis, unspecified ▽

ICD-9-CM Procedural

05.23 Lumbar sympathectomy

64818

64818 Sympathectomy, lumbar

ICD-9-CM Diagnostic

238.1 Neoplasm of uncertain behavior of connective and other soft tissue
239.2 Neoplasms of unspecified nature of bone, soft tissue, and skin
337.9 Unspecified disorder of autonomic nervous system ▽
353.1 Lumbosacral plexus lesions
353.4 Lumbosacral root lesions, not elsewhere classified
354.4 Causalgia of upper limb
724.4 Thoracic or lumbosacral neuritis or radiculitis, unspecified ▽
729.5 Pain in soft tissues of limb
736.71 Acquired equinovarus deformity

ICD-9-CM Procedural

05.23 Lumbar sympathectomy

64820-64823

64820 Sympathectomy; digital arteries, each digit
64821 radial artery
64822 ulnar artery
64823 superficial palmar arch

ICD-9-CM Diagnostic

277.30 Amyloidosis, unspecified — (Use additional code to identify any associated intellectual disabilities) ▽
277.31 Familial Mediterranean fever — (Use additional code to identify any associated intellectual disabilities)
277.39 Other amyloidosis — (Use additional code to identify any associated intellectual disabilities)
337.1 Peripheral autonomic neuropathy in disorders classified elsewhere — (Code first underlying disease: 249.6, 250.6, 277.30-277.39) ☒
354.2 Lesion of ulnar nerve
354.3 Lesion of radial nerve
354.4 Causalgia of upper limb
354.5 Mononeuritis multiplex
354.8 Other mononeuritis of upper limb
354.9 Unspecified mononeuritis of upper limb ▽
443.0 Raynaud's syndrome — (Use additional code to identify gangrene: 785.4)
710.1 Systemic sclerosis — (Use additional code to identify manifestation: 359.6, 517.2)
729.5 Pain in soft tissues of limb

ICD-9-CM Procedural

05.25 Periarterial sympathectomy

64831-64832

64831 Suture of digital nerve, hand or foot; 1 nerve
64832 each additional digital nerve (List separately in addition to code for primary procedure)

ICD-9-CM Diagnostic

816.11 Open fracture of middle or proximal phalanx or phalanges of hand
882.2 Open wound of hand except finger(s) alone, with tendon involvement
883.0 Open wound of finger(s), without mention of complication
883.2 Open wound of finger(s), with tendon involvement
892.1 Open wound of foot except toe(s) alone, complicated
893.0 Open wound of toe(s), without mention of complication
893.2 Open wound of toe(s), with tendon involvement
927.20 Crushing injury of hand(s) — (Use additional code to identify any associated injuries: 800-829, 850.0-854.1, 860.0-869.1)
927.3 Crushing injury of finger(s) — (Use additional code to identify any associated injuries: 800-829, 850.0-854.1, 860.0-869.1)
928.3 Crushing injury of toe(s) — (Use additional code to identify any associated injuries: 800-829, 850.0-854.1, 860.0-869.1)
955.6 Injury to digital nerve, upper limb
956.5 Injury to other specified nerve(s) of pelvic girdle and lower limb
959.5 Injury, other and unspecified, finger

ICD-9-CM Procedural

04.3 Suture of cranial and peripheral nerves

64834-64837

64834 Suture of 1 nerve; hand or foot, common sensory nerve
64835 median motor thenar
64836 ulnar motor
64837 Suture of each additional nerve, hand or foot (List separately in addition to code for primary procedure)

ICD-9-CM Diagnostic

881.02 Open wound of wrist, without mention of complication
881.22 Open wound of wrist, with tendon involvement
882.0 Open wound of hand except finger(s) alone, without mention of complication
883.0 Open wound of finger(s), without mention of complication
892.0 Open wound of foot except toe(s) alone, without mention of complication
893.0 Open wound of toe(s), without mention of complication
927.21 Crushing injury of wrist — (Use additional code to identify any associated injuries: 800-829, 850.0-854.1, 860.0-869.1)
928.20 Crushing injury of foot — (Use additional code to identify any associated injuries: 800-829, 850.0-854.1, 860.0-869.1)
955.1 Injury to median nerve
955.2 Injury to ulnar nerve
955.5 Injury to cutaneous sensory nerve, upper limb
956.4 Injury to cutaneous sensory nerve, lower limb
956.5 Injury to other specified nerve(s) of pelvic girdle and lower limb
959.4 Injury, other and unspecified, hand, except finger

ICD-9-CM Procedural

04.3 Suture of cranial and peripheral nerves

64840

64840 Suture of posterior tibial nerve

ICD-9-CM Diagnostic

891.0 Open wound of knee, leg (except thigh), and ankle, without mention of complication
928.10 Crushing injury of lower leg — (Use additional code to identify any associated injuries: 800-829, 850.0-854.1, 860.0-869.1)
928.11 Crushing injury of knee — (Use additional code to identify any associated injuries: 800-829, 850.0-854.1, 860.0-869.1)
956.2 Injury to posterior tibial nerve

ICD-9-CM Procedural

04.3 Suture of cranial and peripheral nerves

64856-64859

64856 Suture of major peripheral nerve, arm or leg, except sciatic; including transposition
64857 without transposition
64858 Suture of sciatic nerve
64859 Suture of each additional major peripheral nerve (List separately in addition to code for primary procedure)

ICD-9-CM Diagnostic

880.03 Open wound of upper arm, without mention of complication
880.23 Open wound of upper arm, with tendon involvement
881.02 Open wound of wrist, without mention of complication
881.22 Open wound of wrist, with tendon involvement
884.0 Multiple and unspecified open wound of upper limb, without mention of complication
890.0 Open wound of hip and thigh, without mention of complication
890.2 Open wound of hip and thigh, with tendon involvement
891.0 Open wound of knee, leg (except thigh), and ankle, without mention of complication
891.2 Open wound of knee, leg (except thigh), and ankle, with tendon involvement
927.8 Crushing injury of multiple sites of upper limb — (Use additional code to identify any associated injuries: 800-829, 850.0-854.1, 860.0-869.1)
928.00 Crushing injury of thigh — (Use additional code to identify any associated injuries: 800-829, 850.0-854.1, 860.0-869.1)
928.10 Crushing injury of lower leg — (Use additional code to identify any associated injuries: 800-829, 850.0-854.1, 860.0-869.1)
955.0 Injury to axillary nerve
955.1 Injury to median nerve
955.2 Injury to ulnar nerve
955.3 Injury to radial nerve
955.7 Injury to other specified nerve(s) of shoulder girdle and upper limb
956.0 Injury to sciatic nerve
956.1 Injury to femoral nerve
956.3 Injury to peroneal nerve
956.5 Injury to other specified nerve(s) of pelvic girdle and lower limb

ICD-9-CM Procedural

04.3 Suture of cranial and peripheral nerves
04.6 Transposition of cranial and peripheral nerves

64861

64861 Suture of; brachial plexus

ICD-9-CM Diagnostic

880.03 Open wound of upper arm, without mention of complication
927.00 Crushing injury of shoulder region — (Use additional code to identify any associated injuries: 800-829, 850.0-854.1, 860.0-869.1)
953.4 Injury to brachial plexus

ICD-9-CM Procedural

04.3 Suture of cranial and peripheral nerves

64862

64862 Suture of; lumbar plexus

ICD-9-CM Diagnostic

876.0 Open wound of back, without mention of complication
876.1 Open wound of back, complicated
877.0 Open wound of buttock, without mention of complication
877.1 Open wound of buttock, complicated
926.11 Crushing injury of back — (Use additional code to identify any associated injuries: 800-829, 850.0-854.1, 860.0-869.1)
953.5 Injury to lumbosacral plexus

ICD-9-CM Procedural

04.3 Suture of cranial and peripheral nerves

64864-64865

64864 Suture of facial nerve; extracranial
64865 infratemporal, with or without grafting

ICD-9-CM Diagnostic

872.8 Open wound of ear, part unspecified, without mention of complication ▽
873.40 Open wound of face, unspecified site, without mention of complication ▽
873.42 Open wound of forehead, without mention of complication
873.50 Open wound of face, unspecified site, complicated ▽
925.1 Crushing injury of face and scalp — (Use additional code to identify any associated injuries, such as: 800-829, 850.0-854.1, 860.0-869.1)
951.4 Injury to facial nerve

ICD-9-CM Procedural

04.3 Suture of cranial and peripheral nerves
04.5 Cranial or peripheral nerve graft

64866-64870

64866 Anastomosis; facial-spinal accessory
64868 facial-hypoglossal
64870 facial-phrenic

ICD-9-CM Diagnostic

277.30 Amyloidosis, unspecified — (Use additional code to identify any associated intellectual disabilities) ▽
277.31 Familial Mediterranean fever — (Use additional code to identify any associated intellectual disabilities)
277.39 Other amyloidosis — (Use additional code to identify any associated intellectual disabilities)
307.0 Adult onset fluency disorder
351.0 Bell's palsy
352.4 Disorders of accessory (11th) nerve
352.5 Disorders of hypoglossal (12th) nerve
352.6 Multiple cranial nerve palsies
355.9 Mononeuritis of unspecified site ▽
357.4 Polyneuropathy in other diseases classified elsewhere — (Code first underlying disease, as: 032.0-032.9,135, 251.2, 265.0, 265.2, 266.0-266.9, 277.1, 277.30-277.39, 585.9, 586) ☒
527.8 Other specified diseases of the salivary glands
529.8 Other specified conditions of the tongue
782.62 Flushing
784.51 Dysarthria
784.59 Other speech disturbance
803.90 Other open skull fracture with intracranial injury of other and unspecified nature, unspecified state of consciousness ▽
951.4 Injury to facial nerve
951.6 Injury to accessory nerve
951.7 Injury to hypoglossal nerve

ICD-9-CM Procedural

04.71 Hypoglossal-facial anastomosis
04.72 Accessory-facial anastomosis
04.74 Other anastomosis of cranial or peripheral nerve

64872-64876

64872 Suture of nerve; requiring secondary or delayed suture (List separately in addition to code for primary neurorrhaphy)
64874 requiring extensive mobilization, or transposition of nerve (List separately in addition to code for nerve suture)
64876 requiring shortening of bone of extremity (List separately in addition to code for nerve suture)

ICD-9-CM Diagnostic

The ICD-9-CM diagnostic code(s) would be the same as the actual procedure performed because these are in-addition-to codes.

ICD-9-CM Procedural

04.3 Suture of cranial and peripheral nerves
04.6 Transposition of cranial and peripheral nerves
04.76 Repair of old traumatic injury of cranial and peripheral nerves
05.81 Repair of sympathetic nerve or ganglion
78.29 Limb shortening procedures, other

64885-64886

64885 Nerve graft (includes obtaining graft), head or neck; up to 4 cm in length
64886 more than 4 cm length

ICD-9-CM Diagnostic

171.0 Malignant neoplasm of connective and other soft tissue of head, face, and neck
225.1 Benign neoplasm of cranial nerves
873.54 Open wound of jaw, complicated
905.0 Late effect of fracture of skull and face bones
906.0 Late effect of open wound of head, neck, and trunk
907.1 Late effect of injury to cranial nerve
951.2 Injury to trigeminal nerve
951.4 Injury to facial nerve
951.7 Injury to hypoglossal nerve
951.8 Injury to other specified cranial nerves

ICD-9-CM Procedural

04.5 Cranial or peripheral nerve graft

64890-64891

64890 Nerve graft (includes obtaining graft), single strand, hand or foot; up to 4 cm length
64891 more than 4 cm length

ICD-9-CM Diagnostic

171.2 Malignant neoplasm of connective and other soft tissue of upper limb, including shoulder
171.3 Malignant neoplasm of connective and other soft tissue of lower limb, including hip
215.2 Other benign neoplasm of connective and other soft tissue of upper limb, including shoulder
215.3 Other benign neoplasm of connective and other soft tissue of lower limb, including hip
238.1 Neoplasm of uncertain behavior of connective and other soft tissue
239.2 Neoplasms of unspecified nature of bone, soft tissue, and skin
277.30 Amyloidosis, unspecified — (Use additional code to identify any associated intellectual disabilities) ▽
277.31 Familial Mediterranean fever — (Use additional code to identify any associated intellectual disabilities)
277.39 Other amyloidosis — (Use additional code to identify any associated intellectual disabilities)
354.0 Carpal tunnel syndrome
354.5 Mononeuritis multiplex
355.6 Lesion of plantar nerve
356.0 Hereditary peripheral neuropathy
356.4 Idiopathic progressive polyneuropathy
357.81 Chronic inflammatory demyelinating polyneuritis
357.82 Critical illness polyneuropathy
357.89 Other inflammatory and toxic neuropathy
359.6 Symptomatic inflammatory myopathy in diseases classified elsewhere — (Code first underlying disease: 135, 140.0-208.9, 277.30-277.39, 446.0, 710.0, 710.1, 710.2, 714.0) ☒
446.0 Polyarteritis nodosa
710.0 Systemic lupus erythematosus — (Use additional code to identify manifestation: 424.91, 581.81, 582.81, 583.81)
710.1 Systemic sclerosis — (Use additional code to identify manifestation: 359.6, 517.2)
710.2 Sicca syndrome
714.0 Rheumatoid arthritis — (Use additional code to identify manifestation: 357.1, 359.6)
882.1 Open wound of hand except finger(s) alone, complicated
883.1 Open wound of finger(s), complicated
892.1 Open wound of foot except toe(s) alone, complicated
893.1 Open wound of toe(s), complicated
927.20 Crushing injury of hand(s) — (Use additional code to identify any associated injuries: 800-829, 850.0-854.1, 860.0-869.1)
927.3 Crushing injury of finger(s) — (Use additional code to identify any associated injuries: 800-829, 850.0-854.1, 860.0-869.1)
928.20 Crushing injury of foot — (Use additional code to identify any associated injuries: 800-829, 850.0-854.1, 860.0-869.1)
928.3 Crushing injury of toe(s) — (Use additional code to identify any associated injuries: 800-829, 850.0-854.1, 860.0-869.1)

ICD-9-CM Procedural

04.5 Cranial or peripheral nerve graft

64892-64893

64892 Nerve graft (includes obtaining graft), single strand, arm or leg; up to 4 cm length
64893 more than 4 cm length

ICD-9-CM Diagnostic

171.2 Malignant neoplasm of connective and other soft tissue of upper limb, including shoulder
171.3 Malignant neoplasm of connective and other soft tissue of lower limb, including hip
215.2 Other benign neoplasm of connective and other soft tissue of upper limb, including shoulder
215.3 Other benign neoplasm of connective and other soft tissue of lower limb, including hip
238.1 Neoplasm of uncertain behavior of connective and other soft tissue
239.2 Neoplasms of unspecified nature of bone, soft tissue, and skin
354.3 Lesion of radial nerve
355.0 Lesion of sciatic nerve
880.13 Open wound of upper arm, complicated
881.10 Open wound of forearm, complicated
890.1 Open wound of hip and thigh, complicated
891.1 Open wound of knee, leg (except thigh), and ankle, complicated
927.03 Crushing injury of upper arm — (Use additional code to identify any associated injuries: 800-829, 850.0-854.1, 860.0-869.1)
927.10 Crushing injury of forearm — (Use additional code to identify any associated injuries: 800-829, 850.0-854.1, 860.0-869.1)
928.00 Crushing injury of thigh — (Use additional code to identify any associated injuries: 800-829, 850.0-854.1, 860.0-869.1)
928.10 Crushing injury of lower leg — (Use additional code to identify any associated injuries: 800-829, 850.0-854.1, 860.0-869.1)
956.0 Injury to sciatic nerve

ICD-9-CM Procedural

04.5 Cranial or peripheral nerve graft

64895-64896

64895 Nerve graft (includes obtaining graft), multiple strands (cable), hand or foot; up to 4 cm length
64896 more than 4 cm length

ICD-9-CM Diagnostic

171.2 Malignant neoplasm of connective and other soft tissue of upper limb, including shoulder
171.3 Malignant neoplasm of connective and other soft tissue of lower limb, including hip
215.2 Other benign neoplasm of connective and other soft tissue of upper limb, including shoulder
215.3 Other benign neoplasm of connective and other soft tissue of lower limb, including hip
238.1 Neoplasm of uncertain behavior of connective and other soft tissue
239.2 Neoplasms of unspecified nature of bone, soft tissue, and skin
277.30 Amyloidosis, unspecified — (Use additional code to identify any associated intellectual disabilities) ▽
277.31 Familial Mediterranean fever — (Use additional code to identify any associated intellectual disabilities)
277.39 Other amyloidosis — (Use additional code to identify any associated intellectual disabilities)
354.5 Mononeuritis multiplex
356.0 Hereditary peripheral neuropathy
356.4 Idiopathic progressive polyneuropathy
357.81 Chronic inflammatory demyelinating polyneuritis
357.82 Critical illness polyneuropathy
357.89 Other inflammatory and toxic neuropathy
359.6 Symptomatic inflammatory myopathy in diseases classified elsewhere — (Code first underlying disease: 135, 140.0-208.9, 277.30-277.39, 446.0, 710.0, 710.1, 710.2, 714.0) ☒
446.0 Polyarteritis nodosa
710.0 Systemic lupus erythematosus — (Use additional code to identify manifestation: 424.91, 581.81, 582.81, 583.81)
710.1 Systemic sclerosis — (Use additional code to identify manifestation: 359.6, 517.2)
710.2 Sicca syndrome
714.0 Rheumatoid arthritis — (Use additional code to identify manifestation: 357.1, 359.6)
882.1 Open wound of hand except finger(s) alone, complicated
883.1 Open wound of finger(s), complicated
892.1 Open wound of foot except toe(s) alone, complicated
893.1 Open wound of toe(s), complicated
927.20 Crushing injury of hand(s) — (Use additional code to identify any associated injuries: 800-829, 850.0-854.1, 860.0-869.1)
927.3 Crushing injury of finger(s) — (Use additional code to identify any associated injuries: 800-829, 850.0-854.1, 860.0-869.1)
928.20 Crushing injury of foot — (Use additional code to identify any associated injuries: 800-829, 850.0-854.1, 860.0-869.1)
928.3 Crushing injury of toe(s) — (Use additional code to identify any associated injuries: 800-829, 850.0-854.1, 860.0-869.1)
955.8 Injury to multiple nerves of shoulder girdle and upper limb
956.8 Injury to multiple nerves of pelvic girdle and lower limb

ICD-9-CM Procedural

04.5 Cranial or peripheral nerve graft

64897-64898

64897 Nerve graft (includes obtaining graft), multiple strands (cable), arm or leg; up to 4 cm length
64898 more than 4 cm length

ICD-9-CM Diagnostic

171.2 Malignant neoplasm of connective and other soft tissue of upper limb, including shoulder
171.3 Malignant neoplasm of connective and other soft tissue of lower limb, including hip
215.2 Other benign neoplasm of connective and other soft tissue of upper limb, including shoulder
215.3 Other benign neoplasm of connective and other soft tissue of lower limb, including hip
238.1 Neoplasm of uncertain behavior of connective and other soft tissue
239.2 Neoplasms of unspecified nature of bone, soft tissue, and skin
277.30 Amyloidosis, unspecified — (Use additional code to identify any associated intellectual disabilities) ▽
277.31 Familial Mediterranean fever — (Use additional code to identify any associated intellectual disabilities)
277.39 Other amyloidosis — (Use additional code to identify any associated intellectual disabilities)
354.5 Mononeuritis multiplex
356.0 Hereditary peripheral neuropathy
356.4 Idiopathic progressive polyneuropathy
357.81 Chronic inflammatory demyelinating polyneuritis
357.82 Critical illness polyneuropathy
357.89 Other inflammatory and toxic neuropathy
359.6 Symptomatic inflammatory myopathy in diseases classified elsewhere — (Code first underlying disease: 135, 140.0-208.9, 277.30-277.39, 446.0, 710.0, 710.1, 710.2, 714.0) ☒
446.0 Polyarteritis nodosa
710.0 Systemic lupus erythematosus — (Use additional code to identify manifestation: 424.91, 581.81, 582.81, 583.81)
710.1 Systemic sclerosis — (Use additional code to identify manifestation: 359.6, 517.2)

710.2 Sicca syndrome
714.0 Rheumatoid arthritis — (Use additional code to identify manifestation: 357.1, 359.6)
881.10 Open wound of forearm, complicated
891.0 Open wound of knee, leg (except thigh), and ankle, without mention of complication
927.03 Crushing injury of upper arm — (Use additional code to identify any associated injuries: 800-829, 850.0-854.1, 860.0-869.1)
928.10 Crushing injury of lower leg — (Use additional code to identify any associated injuries: 800-829, 850.0-854.1, 860.0-869.1)
955.7 Injury to other specified nerve(s) of shoulder girdle and upper limb
956.5 Injury to other specified nerve(s) of pelvic girdle and lower limb

ICD-9-CM Procedural

04.5 Cranial or peripheral nerve graft

64910

64910 Nerve repair; with synthetic conduit or vein allograft (eg, nerve tube), each nerve

ICD-9-CM Diagnostic

816.11 Open fracture of middle or proximal phalanx or phalanges of hand
872.8 Open wound of ear, part unspecified, without mention of complication ▽
873.40 Open wound of face, unspecified site, without mention of complication ▽
873.42 Open wound of forehead, without mention of complication
873.50 Open wound of face, unspecified site, complicated ▽
876.0 Open wound of back, without mention of complication
876.1 Open wound of back, complicated
877.0 Open wound of buttock, without mention of complication
877.1 Open wound of buttock, complicated
880.03 Open wound of upper arm, without mention of complication
880.23 Open wound of upper arm, with tendon involvement
881.02 Open wound of wrist, without mention of complication
881.22 Open wound of wrist, with tendon involvement
882.0 Open wound of hand except finger(s) alone, without mention of complication
882.1 Open wound of hand except finger(s) alone, complicated
882.2 Open wound of hand except finger(s) alone, with tendon involvement
883.0 Open wound of finger(s), without mention of complication
883.1 Open wound of finger(s), complicated
883.2 Open wound of finger(s), with tendon involvement
884.0 Multiple and unspecified open wound of upper limb, without mention of complication
890.0 Open wound of hip and thigh, without mention of complication
890.2 Open wound of hip and thigh, with tendon involvement
891.0 Open wound of knee, leg (except thigh), and ankle, without mention of complication
891.2 Open wound of knee, leg (except thigh), and ankle, with tendon involvement
892.0 Open wound of foot except toe(s) alone, without mention of complication
892.1 Open wound of foot except toe(s) alone, complicated
893.0 Open wound of toe(s), without mention of complication
893.1 Open wound of toe(s), complicated
893.2 Open wound of toe(s), with tendon involvement
925.1 Crushing injury of face and scalp — (Use additional code to identify any associated injuries, such as: 800-829, 850.0-854.1, 860.0-869.1)
926.11 Crushing injury of back — (Use additional code to identify any associated injuries: 800-829, 850.0-854.1, 860.0-869.1)
927.00 Crushing injury of shoulder region — (Use additional code to identify any associated injuries: 800-829, 850.0-854.1, 860.0-869.1)
927.20 Crushing injury of hand(s) — (Use additional code to identify any associated injuries: 800-829, 850.0-854.1, 860.0-869.1)
927.21 Crushing injury of wrist — (Use additional code to identify any associated injuries: 800-829, 850.0-854.1, 860.0-869.1)
927.3 Crushing injury of finger(s) — (Use additional code to identify any associated injuries: 800-829, 850.0-854.1, 860.0-869.1)
927.8 Crushing injury of multiple sites of upper limb — (Use additional code to identify any associated injuries: 800-829, 850.0-854.1, 860.0-869.1)
928.00 Crushing injury of thigh — (Use additional code to identify any associated injuries: 800-829, 850.0-854.1, 860.0-869.1)
928.10 Crushing injury of lower leg — (Use additional code to identify any associated injuries: 800-829, 850.0-854.1, 860.0-869.1)
928.11 Crushing injury of knee — (Use additional code to identify any associated injuries: 800-829, 850.0-854.1, 860.0-869.1)
928.20 Crushing injury of foot — (Use additional code to identify any associated injuries: 800-829, 850.0-854.1, 860.0-869.1)
928.3 Crushing injury of toe(s) — (Use additional code to identify any associated injuries: 800-829, 850.0-854.1, 860.0-869.1)
951.4 Injury to facial nerve
953.4 Injury to brachial plexus
953.5 Injury to lumbosacral plexus
955.0 Injury to axillary nerve
955.1 Injury to median nerve
955.2 Injury to ulnar nerve
955.3 Injury to radial nerve
955.5 Injury to cutaneous sensory nerve, upper limb
955.6 Injury to digital nerve, upper limb
955.7 Injury to other specified nerve(s) of shoulder girdle and upper limb
955.8 Injury to multiple nerves of shoulder girdle and upper limb
956.0 Injury to sciatic nerve
956.1 Injury to femoral nerve
956.2 Injury to posterior tibial nerve
956.3 Injury to peroneal nerve
956.4 Injury to cutaneous sensory nerve, lower limb
956.5 Injury to other specified nerve(s) of pelvic girdle and lower limb
956.8 Injury to multiple nerves of pelvic girdle and lower limb
959.4 Injury, other and unspecified, hand, except finger
959.5 Injury, other and unspecified, finger

ICD-9-CM Procedural

04.3 Suture of cranial and peripheral nerves
04.5 Cranial or peripheral nerve graft
04.6 Transposition of cranial and peripheral nerves
04.75 Revision of previous repair of cranial and peripheral nerves
04.76 Repair of old traumatic injury of cranial and peripheral nerves
04.79 Other neuroplasty

HCPCS Level II Supplies & Services

C9361 Collagen matrix nerve wrap (NeuroMend Collagen Nerve Wrap), per 0.5 cm length

64911

64911 Nerve repair; with autogenous vein graft (includes harvest of vein graft), each nerve

ICD-9-CM Diagnostic

816.11 Open fracture of middle or proximal phalanx or phalanges of hand
872.8 Open wound of ear, part unspecified, without mention of complication ▽
873.40 Open wound of face, unspecified site, without mention of complication ▽
873.42 Open wound of forehead, without mention of complication
873.50 Open wound of face, unspecified site, complicated ▽
876.0 Open wound of back, without mention of complication
876.1 Open wound of back, complicated
877.0 Open wound of buttock, without mention of complication
877.1 Open wound of buttock, complicated
880.03 Open wound of upper arm, without mention of complication
880.23 Open wound of upper arm, with tendon involvement
881.02 Open wound of wrist, without mention of complication
881.22 Open wound of wrist, with tendon involvement
882.0 Open wound of hand except finger(s) alone, without mention of complication
882.1 Open wound of hand except finger(s) alone, complicated

882.2 Open wound of hand except finger(s) alone, with tendon involvement
883.0 Open wound of finger(s), without mention of complication
883.1 Open wound of finger(s), complicated
883.2 Open wound of finger(s), with tendon involvement
884.0 Multiple and unspecified open wound of upper limb, without mention of complication
890.0 Open wound of hip and thigh, without mention of complication
890.2 Open wound of hip and thigh, with tendon involvement
891.0 Open wound of knee, leg (except thigh), and ankle, without mention of complication
891.2 Open wound of knee, leg (except thigh), and ankle, with tendon involvement
892.0 Open wound of foot except toe(s) alone, without mention of complication
892.1 Open wound of foot except toe(s) alone, complicated
893.0 Open wound of toe(s), without mention of complication
893.1 Open wound of toe(s), complicated
893.2 Open wound of toe(s), with tendon involvement
925.1 Crushing injury of face and scalp — (Use additional code to identify any associated injuries, such as: 800-829, 850.0-854.1, 860.0-869.1)
926.11 Crushing injury of back — (Use additional code to identify any associated injuries: 800-829, 850.0-854.1, 860.0-869.1)
927.00 Crushing injury of shoulder region — (Use additional code to identify any associated injuries: 800-829, 850.0-854.1, 860.0-869.1)
927.20 Crushing injury of hand(s) — (Use additional code to identify any associated injuries: 800-829, 850.0-854.1, 860.0-869.1)
927.21 Crushing injury of wrist — (Use additional code to identify any associated injuries: 800-829, 850.0-854.1, 860.0-869.1)
927.3 Crushing injury of finger(s) — (Use additional code to identify any associated injuries: 800-829, 850.0-854.1, 860.0-869.1)
927.8 Crushing injury of multiple sites of upper limb — (Use additional code to identify any associated injuries: 800-829, 850.0-854.1, 860.0-869.1)
928.00 Crushing injury of thigh — (Use additional code to identify any associated injuries: 800-829, 850.0-854.1, 860.0-869.1)
928.10 Crushing injury of lower leg — (Use additional code to identify any associated injuries: 800-829, 850.0-854.1, 860.0-869.1)
928.11 Crushing injury of knee — (Use additional code to identify any associated injuries: 800-829, 850.0-854.1, 860.0-869.1)
928.20 Crushing injury of foot — (Use additional code to identify any associated injuries: 800-829, 850.0-854.1, 860.0-869.1)
928.3 Crushing injury of toe(s) — (Use additional code to identify any associated injuries: 800-829, 850.0-854.1, 860.0-869.1)
951.4 Injury to facial nerve
953.4 Injury to brachial plexus
953.5 Injury to lumbosacral plexus
955.0 Injury to axillary nerve
955.1 Injury to median nerve
955.2 Injury to ulnar nerve
955.3 Injury to radial nerve
955.5 Injury to cutaneous sensory nerve, upper limb
955.6 Injury to digital nerve, upper limb
955.7 Injury to other specified nerve(s) of shoulder girdle and upper limb
955.8 Injury to multiple nerves of shoulder girdle and upper limb
956.0 Injury to sciatic nerve
956.1 Injury to femoral nerve
956.2 Injury to posterior tibial nerve
956.3 Injury to peroneal nerve
956.4 Injury to cutaneous sensory nerve, lower limb
956.5 Injury to other specified nerve(s) of pelvic girdle and lower limb
956.8 Injury to multiple nerves of pelvic girdle and lower limb
959.4 Injury, other and unspecified, hand, except finger
959.5 Injury, other and unspecified, finger

ICD-9-CM Procedural

04.3 Suture of cranial and peripheral nerves
04.5 Cranial or peripheral nerve graft
04.6 Transposition of cranial and peripheral nerves
04.75 Revision of previous repair of cranial and peripheral nerves
04.76 Repair of old traumatic injury of cranial and peripheral nerves
04.79 Other neuroplasty

Eye and Ocular Adnexa

Eyeball

65091-65093

65091 Evisceration of ocular contents; without implant
65093 with implant

ICD-9-CM Diagnostic

360.00 Unspecified purulent endophthalmitis
360.01 Acute endophthalmitis
360.02 Panophthalmitis
360.13 Parasitic endophthalmitis NOS
360.41 Blind hypotensive eye
360.42 Blind hypertensive eye
871.1 Ocular laceration with prolapse or exposure of intraocular tissue
871.2 Rupture of eye with partial loss of intraocular tissue
871.5 Penetration of eyeball with magnetic foreign body
871.6 Penetration of eyeball with (nonmagnetic) foreign body
V43.0 Eye globe replaced by other means
V52.2 Fitting and adjustment of artificial eye

ICD-9-CM Procedural

16.31 Removal of ocular contents with synchronous implant into scleral shell
16.39 Other evisceration of eyeball

HCPCS Level II Supplies & Services

V2623 Prosthetic eye, plastic, custom

65101-65105

65101 Enucleation of eye; without implant
65103 with implant, muscles not attached to implant
65105 with implant, muscles attached to implant

ICD-9-CM Diagnostic

190.0 Malignant neoplasm of eyeball, except conjunctiva, cornea, retina, and choroid
190.3 Malignant neoplasm of conjunctiva
190.4 Malignant neoplasm of cornea
190.5 Malignant neoplasm of retina
190.6 Malignant neoplasm of choroid
190.8 Malignant neoplasm of other specified sites of eye
234.0 Carcinoma in situ of eye
360.41 Blind hypotensive eye
360.42 Blind hypertensive eye
376.51 Enophthalmos due to atrophy of orbital tissue
376.52 Enophthalmos due to trauma or surgery
871.2 Rupture of eye with partial loss of intraocular tissue
871.3 Avulsion of eye
871.5 Penetration of eyeball with magnetic foreign body
871.6 Penetration of eyeball with (nonmagnetic) foreign body
V43.0 Eye globe replaced by other means
V52.2 Fitting and adjustment of artificial eye

ICD-9-CM Procedural

16.41 Enucleation of eyeball with synchronous implant into Tenon's capsule with attachment of muscles
16.42 Enucleation of eyeball with other synchronous implant
16.49 Other enucleation of eyeball

65110-65114

65110 Exenteration of orbit (does not include skin graft), removal of orbital contents; only
65112 with therapeutic removal of bone
65114 with muscle or myocutaneous flap

ICD-9-CM Diagnostic

170.0 Malignant neoplasm of bones of skull and face, except mandible
172.1 Malignant melanoma of skin of eyelid, including canthus
173.10 Unspecified malignant neoplasm of eyelid, including canthus
173.11 Basal cell carcinoma of eyelid, including canthus
173.12 Squamous cell carcinoma of eyelid, including canthus
173.19 Other specified malignant neoplasm of eyelid, including canthus
190.0 Malignant neoplasm of eyeball, except conjunctiva, cornea, retina, and choroid
190.1 Malignant neoplasm of orbit
190.2 Malignant neoplasm of lacrimal gland
190.3 Malignant neoplasm of conjunctiva
190.4 Malignant neoplasm of cornea
190.5 Malignant neoplasm of retina
190.6 Malignant neoplasm of choroid
190.8 Malignant neoplasm of other specified sites of eye

ICD-9-CM Procedural

16.51 Exenteration of orbit with removal of adjacent structures
16.52 Exenteration of orbit with therapeutic removal of orbital bone
16.59 Other exenteration of orbit
83.82 Graft of muscle or fascia

65125

65125 Modification of ocular implant with placement or replacement of pegs (eg, drilling receptacle for prosthesis appendage) (separate procedure)

ICD-9-CM Diagnostic

338.28 Other chronic postoperative pain — (Use additional code to identify pain associated with psychological factors: 307.89)
360.89 Other disorders of globe
996.59 Mechanical complication due to other implant and internal device, not elsewhere classified
V10.84 Personal history of malignant neoplasm of eye
V52.2 Fitting and adjustment of artificial eye

ICD-9-CM Procedural

16.69 Other secondary procedures after removal of eyeball
95.34 Ocular prosthetics

HCPCS Level II Supplies & Services

V2623 Prosthetic eye, plastic, custom

65130-65140

65130 Insertion of ocular implant secondary; after evisceration, in scleral shell
65135 after enucleation, muscles not attached to implant
65140 after enucleation, muscles attached to implant

ICD-9-CM Diagnostic

360.89 Other disorders of globe
V10.84 Personal history of malignant neoplasm of eye
V43.0 Eye globe replaced by other means
V52.2 Fitting and adjustment of artificial eye

ICD-9-CM Procedural

16.61 Secondary insertion of ocular implant

HCPCS Level II Supplies & Services

V2623 Prosthetic eye, plastic, custom

65150-65155

65150 Reinsertion of ocular implant; with or without conjunctival graft
65155 with use of foreign material for reinforcement and/or attachment of muscles to implant

ICD-9-CM Diagnostic

360.89 Other disorders of globe
996.59 Mechanical complication due to other implant and internal device, not elsewhere classified
998.30 Disruption of wound, unspecified ▽
998.33 Disruption of traumatic injury wound repair
998.51 Infected postoperative seroma — (Use additional code to identify organism)
998.59 Other postoperative infection — (Use additional code to identify infection)
V10.84 Personal history of malignant neoplasm of eye
V52.2 Fitting and adjustment of artificial eye

ICD-9-CM Procedural

10.42 Reconstruction of conjunctival cul-de-sac with free graft
10.43 Other reconstruction of conjunctival cul-de-sac
10.44 Other free graft to conjunctiva
16.62 Revision and reinsertion of ocular implant

HCPCS Level II Supplies & Services

V2623 Prosthetic eye, plastic, custom

65175

65175 Removal of ocular implant

ICD-9-CM Diagnostic

338.18 Other acute postoperative pain — (Use additional code to identify pain associated with psychological factors: 307.89)
338.28 Other chronic postoperative pain — (Use additional code to identify pain associated with psychological factors: 307.89)
376.00 Unspecified acute inflammation of orbit ▽
376.10 Unspecified chronic inflammation of orbit ▽
379.91 Pain in or around eye
996.59 Mechanical complication due to other implant and internal device, not elsewhere classified
996.69 Infection and inflammatory reaction due to other internal prosthetic device, implant, and graft — (Use additional code to identify specified infections)
998.30 Disruption of wound, unspecified ▽
998.31 Disruption of internal operation (surgical) wound
998.33 Disruption of traumatic injury wound repair
998.51 Infected postoperative seroma — (Use additional code to identify organism)
998.59 Other postoperative infection — (Use additional code to identify infection)

ICD-9-CM Procedural

16.71 Removal of ocular implant
97.31 Removal of eye prosthesis

HCPCS Level II Supplies & Services

V2623 Prosthetic eye, plastic, custom

65205-65210

65205 Removal of foreign body, external eye; conjunctival superficial
65210 conjunctival embedded (includes concretions), subconjunctival, or scleral nonperforating

ICD-9-CM Diagnostic

918.2 Superficial injury of conjunctiva
918.9 Other and unspecified superficial injuries of eye ▽
930.1 Foreign body in conjunctival sac
930.8 Foreign body in other and combined sites on external eye
930.9 Foreign body in unspecified site on external eye ▽

ICD-9-CM Procedural

10.0 Removal of embedded foreign body from conjunctiva by incision
98.21 Removal of superficial foreign body from eye without incision
98.22 Removal of other foreign body without incision from head and neck

65220-65222

65220 Removal of foreign body, external eye; corneal, without slit lamp
65222 corneal, with slit lamp

ICD-9-CM Diagnostic

918.1 Superficial injury of cornea
918.9 Other and unspecified superficial injuries of eye ▽
930.0 Foreign body in cornea
930.8 Foreign body in other and combined sites on external eye

ICD-9-CM Procedural

11.1 Incision of cornea
98.21 Removal of superficial foreign body from eye without incision

65235

65235 Removal of foreign body, intraocular; from anterior chamber of eye or lens

ICD-9-CM Diagnostic

360.51 Retained (old) foreign body, magnetic, in anterior chamber of eye
360.52 Retained (old) foreign body, magnetic, in iris or ciliary body
360.53 Retained (old) foreign body, magnetic, in lens
360.59 Retained (old) intraocular foreign body, magnetic, in other or multiple sites
360.60 Retained (old) foreign body, intraocular, unspecified ▽
360.61 Retained (old) foreign body in anterior chamber
360.62 Retained (old) foreign body in iris or ciliary body
360.63 Retained (old) foreign body in lens
360.69 Retained (old) foreign body in other or multiple sites of eye
871.5 Penetration of eyeball with magnetic foreign body
871.6 Penetration of eyeball with (nonmagnetic) foreign body

ICD-9-CM Procedural

12.00 Removal of intraocular foreign body from anterior segment of eye, not otherwise specified
12.01 Removal of intraocular foreign body from anterior segment of eye with use of magnet
12.02 Removal of intraocular foreign body from anterior segment of eye without use of magnet
13.01 Removal of foreign body from lens with use of magnet
13.02 Removal of foreign body from lens without use of magnet

65260

65260 Removal of foreign body, intraocular; from posterior segment, magnetic extraction, anterior or posterior route

ICD-9-CM Diagnostic

360.50 Retained (old) foreign body, magnetic, intraocular, unspecified ▽
360.54 Retained (old) foreign body, magnetic, in vitreous

360.55 Retained (old) foreign body, magnetic, in posterior wall
360.59 Retained (old) intraocular foreign body, magnetic, in other or multiple sites
871.5 Penetration of eyeball with magnetic foreign body

ICD-9-CM Procedural

14.00 Removal of foreign body from posterior segment of eye, not otherwise specified
14.01 Removal of foreign body from posterior segment of eye with use of magnet

65265

65265 Removal of foreign body, intraocular; from posterior segment, nonmagnetic extraction

ICD-9-CM Diagnostic

360.60 Retained (old) foreign body, intraocular, unspecified ▽
360.64 Retained (old) foreign body in vitreous
360.65 Retained (old) foreign body in posterior wall of eye
360.69 Retained (old) foreign body in other or multiple sites of eye
870.4 Penetrating wound of orbit with foreign body
871.6 Penetration of eyeball with (nonmagnetic) foreign body

ICD-9-CM Procedural

14.00 Removal of foreign body from posterior segment of eye, not otherwise specified
14.02 Removal of foreign body from posterior segment of eye without use of magnet

65270-65273

65270 Repair of laceration; conjunctiva, with or without nonperforating laceration sclera, direct closure
65272 conjunctiva, by mobilization and rearrangement, without hospitalization
65273 conjunctiva, by mobilization and rearrangement, with hospitalization

ICD-9-CM Diagnostic

871.0 Ocular laceration without prolapse of intraocular tissue
871.4 Unspecified laceration of eye ▽
871.9 Unspecified open wound of eyeball ▽
918.2 Superficial injury of conjunctiva

ICD-9-CM Procedural

10.6 Repair of laceration of conjunctiva
12.81 Suture of laceration of sclera

65275-65285

65275 Repair of laceration; cornea, nonperforating, with or without removal foreign body
65280 cornea and/or sclera, perforating, not involving uveal tissue
65285 cornea and/or sclera, perforating, with reposition or resection of uveal tissue

ICD-9-CM Diagnostic

871.0 Ocular laceration without prolapse of intraocular tissue
871.1 Ocular laceration with prolapse or exposure of intraocular tissue
871.2 Rupture of eye with partial loss of intraocular tissue
871.4 Unspecified laceration of eye ▽
871.7 Unspecified ocular penetration ▽
871.9 Unspecified open wound of eyeball ▽
918.1 Superficial injury of cornea
930.0 Foreign body in cornea
930.1 Foreign body in conjunctival sac
930.8 Foreign body in other and combined sites on external eye

ICD-9-CM Procedural

11.51 Suture of corneal laceration
12.81 Suture of laceration of sclera
12.97 Other operations on iris
12.98 Other operations on ciliary body

HCPCS Level II Supplies & Services

A4305 Disposable drug delivery system, flow rate of 50 ml or greater per hour

65286

65286 Repair of laceration; application of tissue glue, wounds of cornea and/or sclera

ICD-9-CM Diagnostic

871.0 Ocular laceration without prolapse of intraocular tissue
871.1 Ocular laceration with prolapse or exposure of intraocular tissue
871.2 Rupture of eye with partial loss of intraocular tissue
871.4 Unspecified laceration of eye ▽
871.7 Unspecified ocular penetration ▽
871.9 Unspecified open wound of eyeball ▽
918.1 Superficial injury of cornea

ICD-9-CM Procedural

11.59 Other repair of cornea
12.89 Other operations on sclera
16.82 Repair of rupture of eyeball

HCPCS Level II Supplies & Services

A4305 Disposable drug delivery system, flow rate of 50 ml or greater per hour

65290

65290 Repair of wound, extraocular muscle, tendon and/or Tenon's capsule

ICD-9-CM Diagnostic

802.6 Orbital floor (blow-out), closed fracture
802.7 Orbital floor (blow-out), open fracture
802.8 Other facial bones, closed fracture
802.9 Other facial bones, open fracture
870.3 Penetrating wound of orbit, without mention of foreign body
870.4 Penetrating wound of orbit with foreign body
870.8 Other specified open wound of ocular adnexa
871.1 Ocular laceration with prolapse or exposure of intraocular tissue
871.2 Rupture of eye with partial loss of intraocular tissue
871.3 Avulsion of eye
871.4 Unspecified laceration of eye ▽
871.5 Penetration of eyeball with magnetic foreign body
871.6 Penetration of eyeball with (nonmagnetic) foreign body
871.7 Unspecified ocular penetration ▽
871.9 Unspecified open wound of eyeball ▽
921.0 Black eye, not otherwise specified
921.1 Contusion of eyelids and periocular area
921.2 Contusion of orbital tissues
921.3 Contusion of eyeball
921.9 Unspecified contusion of eye ▽
998.33 Disruption of traumatic injury wound repair

ICD-9-CM Procedural

16.81 Repair of wound of orbit
16.89 Other repair of injury of eyeball or orbit

Anterior Segment

65400-65410

65400 Excision of lesion, cornea (keratectomy, lamellar, partial), except pterygium
65410 Biopsy of cornea

ICD-9-CM Diagnostic

190.4 Malignant neoplasm of cornea
198.4 Secondary malignant neoplasm of other parts of nervous system
224.4 Benign neoplasm of cornea
234.0 Carcinoma in situ of eye
238.8 Neoplasm of uncertain behavior of other specified sites

239.89 Neoplasms of unspecified nature, other specified sites
370.01 Marginal corneal ulcer
370.03 Central corneal ulcer
370.55 Corneal abscess
371.00 Unspecified corneal opacity ▽
371.10 Unspecified corneal deposit ▽
371.11 Anterior pigmentations of cornea
371.12 Stromal pigmentations of cornea
371.13 Posterior pigmentations of cornea
371.14 Kayser-Fleischer ring
371.15 Other deposits of cornea associated with metabolic disorders
371.16 Argentous deposits of cornea
371.70 Unspecified corneal deformity ▽
371.89 Other corneal disorder

ICD-9-CM Procedural

11.22 Biopsy of cornea
11.49 Other removal or destruction of corneal lesion

65420-65426

65420 Excision or transposition of pterygium; without graft
65426 with graft

ICD-9-CM Diagnostic

372.40 Unspecified pterygium ▽
372.41 Peripheral pterygium, stationary
372.42 Peripheral pterygium, progressive
372.43 Central pterygium
372.44 Double pterygium
372.45 Recurrent pterygium
372.52 Pseudopterygium

ICD-9-CM Procedural

11.31 Transposition of pterygium
11.32 Excision of pterygium with corneal graft
11.39 Other excision of pterygium

HCPCS Level II Supplies & Services

A4305 Disposable drug delivery system, flow rate of 50 ml or greater per hour
J7315 Mitomycin, opthalmic, 0.2 mg

65430

65430 Scraping of cornea, diagnostic, for smear and/or culture

ICD-9-CM Diagnostic

017.30 Tuberculosis of eye, confirmation unspecified — (Use additional code to identify manifestation: 363.13, 364.11, 370.31, 370.59, 379.09) ▽
017.32 Tuberculosis of eye, bacteriological or histological examination unknown (at present) — (Use additional code to identify manifestation: 363.13, 364.11, 370.31, 370.59, 379.09)
017.33 Tuberculosis of eye, tubercle bacilli found (in sputum) by microscopy — (Use additional code to identify manifestation: 363.13, 364.11, 370.31, 370.59, 379.09)
017.34 Tuberculosis of eye, tubercle bacilli not found (in sputum) by microscopy, but found by bacterial culture — (Use additional code to identify manifestation: 363.13, 364.11, 370.31, 370.59, 379.09)
017.35 Tuberculosis of eye, tubercle bacilli not found by bacteriological examination, but tuberculosis confirmed histologically — (Use additional code to identify manifestation: 363.13, 364.11, 370.31, 370.59, 379.09)
017.36 Tuberculosis of eye, tubercle bacilli not found by bacteriological or histological examination, but tuberculosis confirmed by other methods [inoculation of animals] — (Use additional code to identify manifestation: 363.13, 364.11, 370.31, 370.59, 379.09)
053.21 Herpes zoster keratoconjunctivitis
054.42 Dendritic keratitis
054.43 Herpes simplex disciform keratitis
077.1 Epidemic keratoconjunctivitis
090.3 Syphilitic interstitial keratitis
098.43 Gonococcal keratitis
370.00 Unspecified corneal ulcer ▽
370.01 Marginal corneal ulcer
370.03 Central corneal ulcer
370.21 Punctate keratitis
370.22 Macular keratitis
370.23 Filamentary keratitis
370.31 Phlyctenular keratoconjunctivitis — (Use additional code for any associated tuberculosis: 017.3)
370.40 Unspecified keratoconjunctivitis ▽
370.44 Keratitis or keratoconjunctivitis in exanthema — (Code first underlying condition: 050.0-052.9) ☒
370.49 Other unspecified keratoconjunctivitis
370.52 Diffuse interstitial keratitis
370.54 Sclerosing keratitis
370.55 Corneal abscess
370.8 Other forms of keratitis — (Code first underlying condition: 118, 136.21)
371.00 Unspecified corneal opacity ▽
371.10 Unspecified corneal deposit ▽
371.70 Unspecified corneal deformity ▽
371.89 Other corneal disorder

ICD-9-CM Procedural

11.21 Scraping of cornea for smear or culture

HCPCS Level II Supplies & Services

A4305 Disposable drug delivery system, flow rate of 50 ml or greater per hour

65435-65436

65435 Removal of corneal epithelium; with or without chemocauterization (abrasion, curettage)
65436 with application of chelating agent (eg, EDTA)

ICD-9-CM Diagnostic

053.29 Other ophthalmic herpes zoster complications
054.43 Herpes simplex disciform keratitis
364.10 Unspecified chronic iridocyclitis ▽
371.40 Unspecified corneal degeneration ▽
371.41 Senile corneal changes
371.42 Recurrent erosion of cornea
371.43 Band-shaped keratopathy
371.44 Other calcerous degenerations of cornea
371.45 Keratomalacia NOS
371.46 Nodular degeneration of cornea
371.48 Peripheral degenerations of cornea
371.49 Other corneal degenerations
940.2 Alkaline chemical burn of cornea and conjunctival sac
940.3 Acid chemical burn of cornea and conjunctival sac
940.4 Other burn of cornea and conjunctival sac

ICD-9-CM Procedural

11.31 Transposition of pterygium
11.41 Mechanical removal of corneal epithelium
11.49 Other removal or destruction of corneal lesion

HCPCS Level II Supplies & Services

A4305 Disposable drug delivery system, flow rate of 50 ml or greater per hour
J7315 Mitomycin, opthalmic, 0.2 mg

65450

65450 Destruction of lesion of cornea by cryotherapy, photocoagulation or thermocauterization

ICD-9-CM Diagnostic

054.43 Herpes simplex disciform keratitis
090.3 Syphilitic interstitial keratitis
190.4 Malignant neoplasm of cornea
224.4 Benign neoplasm of cornea
234.0 Carcinoma in situ of eye
238.8 Neoplasm of uncertain behavior of other specified sites
238.9 Neoplasm of uncertain behavior, site unspecified ▽
370.00 Unspecified corneal ulcer ▽
370.55 Corneal abscess
371.70 Unspecified corneal deformity ▽
371.89 Other corneal disorder

ICD-9-CM Procedural

11.42 Thermocauterization of corneal lesion
11.43 Cryotherapy of corneal lesion
11.49 Other removal or destruction of corneal lesion

HCPCS Level II Supplies & Services

A4305 Disposable drug delivery system, flow rate of 50 ml or greater per hour

65600

65600 Multiple punctures of anterior cornea (eg, for corneal erosion, tattoo)

ICD-9-CM Diagnostic

054.43 Herpes simplex disciform keratitis
090.3 Syphilitic interstitial keratitis
370.00 Unspecified corneal ulcer ▽
370.20 Unspecified superficial keratitis ▽
370.23 Filamentary keratitis
370.34 Exposure keratoconjunctivitis
370.35 Neurotrophic keratoconjunctivitis
370.50 Unspecified interstitial keratitis ▽
370.55 Corneal abscess
371.40 Unspecified corneal degeneration ▽
371.41 Senile corneal changes
371.42 Recurrent erosion of cornea
371.43 Band-shaped keratopathy
371.44 Other calcerous degenerations of cornea
371.45 Keratomalacia NOS
371.46 Nodular degeneration of cornea
371.48 Peripheral degenerations of cornea
371.49 Other corneal degenerations
371.52 Other anterior corneal dystrophies
371.70 Unspecified corneal deformity ▽
371.89 Other corneal disorder

ICD-9-CM Procedural

11.91 Tattooing of cornea

65710

65710 Keratoplasty (corneal transplant); anterior lamellar

ICD-9-CM Diagnostic

371.01 Minor opacity of cornea
371.02 Peripheral opacity of cornea
371.03 Central opacity of cornea
371.11 Anterior pigmentations of cornea
371.12 Stromal pigmentations of cornea
371.13 Posterior pigmentations of cornea
371.30 Unspecified corneal membrane change ▽
371.41 Senile corneal changes
371.60 Unspecified keratoconus ▽
371.61 Keratoconus, stable condition
371.62 Keratoconus, acute hydrops
743.41 Congenital anomaly of corneal size and shape
998.32 Disruption of external operation (surgical) wound

ICD-9-CM Procedural

11.61 Lamellar keratoplasty with autograft
11.62 Other lamellar keratoplasty

HCPCS Level II Supplies & Services

C1818 Integrated keratoprosthesis
J7315 Mitomycin, opthalmic, 0.2 mg

65730-65757

65730 Keratoplasty (corneal transplant); penetrating (except in aphakia or pseudophakia)
65750 penetrating (in aphakia)
65755 penetrating (in pseudophakia)
65756 endothelial
65757 Backbench preparation of corneal endothelial allograft prior to transplantation (List separately in addition to code for primary procedure)

ICD-9-CM Diagnostic

264.6 Vitamin A deficiency with xerophthalmic scars of cornea
370.06 Perforated corneal ulcer
370.63 Deep vascularization of cornea
370.8 Other forms of keratitis — (Code first underlying condition: 118, 136.21)
371.02 Peripheral opacity of cornea
371.03 Central opacity of cornea
371.04 Adherent leucoma
371.11 Anterior pigmentations of cornea
371.16 Argentous deposits of cornea
371.20 Unspecified corneal edema ▽
371.23 Bullous keratopathy
371.31 Folds and rupture of Bowman's membrane
371.46 Nodular degeneration of cornea
371.53 Granular corneal dystrophy
371.57 Endothelial corneal dystrophy
371.60 Unspecified keratoconus ▽
371.62 Keratoconus, acute hydrops
379.31 Aphakia
743.35 Congenital aphakia
743.41 Congenital anomaly of corneal size and shape
743.42 Congenital corneal opacity, interfering with vision
871.0 Ocular laceration without prolapse of intraocular tissue
871.1 Ocular laceration with prolapse or exposure of intraocular tissue
871.5 Penetration of eyeball with magnetic foreign body
871.6 Penetration of eyeball with (nonmagnetic) foreign body
871.9 Unspecified open wound of eyeball ▽
940.2 Alkaline chemical burn of cornea and conjunctival sac
996.51 Mechanical complication due to corneal graft
996.53 Mechanical complication due to ocular lens prosthesis
V43.1 Lens replaced by other means

ICD-9-CM Procedural

11.63 Penetrating keratoplasty with autograft
11.64 Other penetrating keratoplasty
11.69 Other corneal transplant

HCPCS Level II Supplies & Services

C1818 Integrated keratoprosthesis
J7315 Mitomycin, opthalmic, 0.2 mg

65760

65760 Keratomileusis

ICD-9-CM Diagnostic

367.1 Myopia
367.20 Unspecified astigmatism
367.21 Regular astigmatism
367.22 Irregular astigmatism
367.89 Other disorders of refraction and accommodation
367.9 Unspecified disorder of refraction and accommodation
371.61 Keratoconus, stable condition
371.62 Keratoconus, acute hydrops
371.70 Unspecified corneal deformity

ICD-9-CM Procedural

11.71 Keratomileusis

HCPCS Level II Supplies & Services

C1818 Integrated keratoprosthesis
J7315 Mitomycin, opthalmic, 0.2 mg

65765

65765 Keratophakia

ICD-9-CM Diagnostic

367.0 Hypermetropia
367.1 Myopia
367.89 Other disorders of refraction and accommodation
367.9 Unspecified disorder of refraction and accommodation

ICD-9-CM Procedural

11.72 Keratophakia

HCPCS Level II Supplies & Services

J7315 Mitomycin, opthalmic, 0.2 mg

65767

65767 Epikeratoplasty

ICD-9-CM Diagnostic

367.0 Hypermetropia
367.1 Myopia
367.20 Unspecified astigmatism
367.21 Regular astigmatism
367.22 Irregular astigmatism
367.31 Anisometropia
367.32 Aniseikonia
367.89 Other disorders of refraction and accommodation
367.9 Unspecified disorder of refraction and accommodation
371.61 Keratoconus, stable condition
379.31 Aphakia
743.35 Congenital aphakia
996.51 Mechanical complication due to corneal graft
996.53 Mechanical complication due to ocular lens prosthesis
V43.1 Lens replaced by other means

ICD-9-CM Procedural

11.76 Epikeratophakia

HCPCS Level II Supplies & Services

J7315 Mitomycin, opthalmic, 0.2 mg

65770

65770 Keratoprosthesis

ICD-9-CM Diagnostic

076.1 Active stage trachoma
694.61 Benign mucous membrane pemphigoid with ocular involvement
871.0 Ocular laceration without prolapse of intraocular tissue
871.2 Rupture of eye with partial loss of intraocular tissue
906.5 Late effect of burn of eye, face, head, and neck
940.2 Alkaline chemical burn of cornea and conjunctival sac
940.3 Acid chemical burn of cornea and conjunctival sac
940.4 Other burn of cornea and conjunctival sac
996.51 Mechanical complication due to corneal graft

ICD-9-CM Procedural

11.73 Keratoprosthesis

HCPCS Level II Supplies & Services

C1818 Integrated keratoprosthesis
J7315 Mitomycin, opthalmic, 0.2 mg

65771

65771 Radial keratotomy

ICD-9-CM Diagnostic

367.1 Myopia
367.20 Unspecified astigmatism
367.21 Regular astigmatism
367.22 Irregular astigmatism

ICD-9-CM Procedural

11.75 Radial keratotomy

HCPCS Level II Supplies & Services

A4305 Disposable drug delivery system, flow rate of 50 ml or greater per hour
J7315 Mitomycin, opthalmic, 0.2 mg

65772-65775

65772 Corneal relaxing incision for correction of surgically induced astigmatism
65775 Corneal wedge resection for correction of surgically induced astigmatism

ICD-9-CM Diagnostic

367.0 Hypermetropia
367.1 Myopia
367.20 Unspecified astigmatism
367.21 Regular astigmatism
367.22 Irregular astigmatism
367.31 Anisometropia
367.32 Aniseikonia
379.31 Aphakia
743.35 Congenital aphakia
996.51 Mechanical complication due to corneal graft
V42.5 Cornea replaced by transplant
V43.1 Lens replaced by other means
V45.69 Other states following surgery of eye and adnexa

ICD-9-CM Procedural

11.79 Other reconstructive surgery on cornea

HCPCS Level II Supplies & Services

A4305 Disposable drug delivery system, flow rate of 50 ml or greater per hour

J7315 Mitomycin, opthalmic, 0.2 mg

65778-65779

65778 Placement of amniotic membrane on the ocular surface; without sutures
65779 single layer, sutured

ICD-9-CM Diagnostic

190.3 Malignant neoplasm of conjunctiva
198.4 Secondary malignant neoplasm of other parts of nervous system
224.3 Benign neoplasm of conjunctiva
234.0 Carcinoma in situ of eye
238.8 Neoplasm of uncertain behavior of other specified sites
239.89 Neoplasms of unspecified nature, other specified sites
370.00 Unspecified corneal ulcer ▽
370.01 Marginal corneal ulcer
370.02 Ring corneal ulcer
370.03 Central corneal ulcer
370.04 Hypopyon ulcer
370.05 Mycotic corneal ulcer
370.06 Perforated corneal ulcer
370.07 Mooren's ulcer
370.40 Unspecified keratoconjunctivitis ▽
370.49 Other unspecified keratoconjunctivitis
370.62 Pannus (corneal)
371.23 Bullous keratopathy
371.32 Folds in Descemet's membrane
371.33 Rupture in Descemet's membrane
371.40 Unspecified corneal degeneration ▽
372.50 Unspecified conjunctival degeneration ▽
372.52 Pseudopterygium
372.53 Conjunctival xerosis
372.54 Conjunctival concretions
372.63 Symblepharon
695.13 Stevens-Johnson syndrome
940.2 Alkaline chemical burn of cornea and conjunctival sac
940.3 Acid chemical burn of cornea and conjunctival sac
940.4 Other burn of cornea and conjunctival sac
940.9 Unspecified burn of eye and adnexa ▽
941.12 Erythema due to burn (first degree) of eye (with other parts face, head, and neck)
941.22 Blisters, with epidermal loss due to burn (second degree) of eye (with other parts of face, head, and neck)
941.32 Full-thickness skin loss due to burn (third degree NOS) of eye (with other parts of face, head, and neck)
996.51 Mechanical complication due to corneal graft
996.53 Mechanical complication due to ocular lens prosthesis
996.63 Infection and inflammatory reaction due to nervous system device, implant, and graft — (Use additional code to identify specified infections)
996.75 Other complications due to nervous system device, implant, and graft — (Use additional code to identify complication: 338.18-338.19, 338.28-338.29)
997.99 Other complications affecting other specified body systems, NEC — (Use additional code to identify complications)
998.32 Disruption of external operation (surgical) wound
998.83 Non-healing surgical wound
V45.69 Other states following surgery of eye and adnexa

ICD-9-CM Procedural

11.52 Repair of postoperative wound dehiscence of cornea
11.59 Other repair of cornea
11.79 Other reconstructive surgery on cornea
11.99 Other operations on cornea

65780-65782

65780 Ocular surface reconstruction; amniotic membrane transplantation, multiple layers
65781 limbal stem cell allograft (eg, cadaveric or living donor)
65782 limbal conjunctival autograft (includes obtaining graft)

ICD-9-CM Diagnostic

190.3 Malignant neoplasm of conjunctiva
198.4 Secondary malignant neoplasm of other parts of nervous system
224.3 Benign neoplasm of conjunctiva
234.0 Carcinoma in situ of eye
238.8 Neoplasm of uncertain behavior of other specified sites
239.89 Neoplasms of unspecified nature, other specified sites
370.00 Unspecified corneal ulcer ▽
370.01 Marginal corneal ulcer
370.02 Ring corneal ulcer
370.03 Central corneal ulcer
370.07 Mooren's ulcer
371.23 Bullous keratopathy
371.24 Corneal edema due to wearing of contact lenses
371.40 Unspecified corneal degeneration ▽
371.42 Recurrent erosion of cornea
371.43 Band-shaped keratopathy
371.48 Peripheral degenerations of cornea
371.49 Other corneal degenerations
371.82 Corneal disorder due to contact lens
372.40 Unspecified pterygium ▽
372.41 Peripheral pterygium, stationary
372.42 Peripheral pterygium, progressive
372.43 Central pterygium
372.44 Double pterygium
372.45 Recurrent pterygium
372.50 Unspecified conjunctival degeneration ▽
372.52 Pseudopterygium
372.53 Conjunctival xerosis
372.54 Conjunctival concretions
372.63 Symblepharon
374.44 Sensory disorders of eyelid
743.45 Aniridia
940.0 Chemical burn of eyelids and periocular area
940.1 Other burns of eyelids and periocular area
940.2 Alkaline chemical burn of cornea and conjunctival sac
940.3 Acid chemical burn of cornea and conjunctival sac
940.4 Other burn of cornea and conjunctival sac
940.9 Unspecified burn of eye and adnexa ▽
941.03 Burn of unspecified degree of lip(s) ▽
941.12 Erythema due to burn (first degree) of eye (with other parts face, head, and neck)
941.22 Blisters, with epidermal loss due to burn (second degree) of eye (with other parts of face, head, and neck)
941.32 Full-thickness skin loss due to burn (third degree NOS) of eye (with other parts of face, head, and neck)

ICD-9-CM Procedural

11.79 Other reconstructive surgery on cornea

65800

65800 Paracentesis of anterior chamber of eye (separate procedure); with removal of aqueous

ICD-9-CM Diagnostic

054.44 Herpes simplex iridocyclitis
091.50 Early syphilis, syphilitic uveitis, unspecified ▽

091.52 Early syphilis, syphilitic iridocyclitis (secondary)
098.41 Gonococcal iridocyclitis
360.00 Unspecified purulent endophthalmitis ▽
360.01 Acute endophthalmitis
360.03 Chronic endophthalmitis
360.19 Other endophthalmitis
362.30 Unspecified retinal vascular occlusion ▽
362.31 Central artery occlusion of retina
362.81 Retinal hemorrhage
364.00 Unspecified acute and subacute iridocyclitis ▽
364.01 Primary iridocyclitis
364.02 Recurrent iridocyclitis
364.03 Secondary iridocyclitis, infectious
364.04 Secondary iridocyclitis, noninfectious
364.05 Hypopyon
364.41 Hyphema
364.74 Adhesions and disruptions of pupillary membranes
364.82 Plateau iris syndrome
365.06 Primary angle closure without glaucoma damage
365.20 Unspecified primary angle-closure glaucoma — (Use additional code to identify glaucoma stage: 365.70-365.74) ▽
365.21 Intermittent angle-closure glaucoma
365.22 Acute angle-closure glaucoma
365.23 Chronic angle-closure glaucoma — (Use additional code to identify glaucoma stage: 365.70-365.74)
365.59 Glaucoma associated with other lens disorders
365.61 Glaucoma associated with pupillary block
365.62 Glaucoma associated with ocular inflammations — (Use additional code to identify glaucoma stage: 365.70-365.74)
365.64 Glaucoma associated with tumors or cysts
365.65 Glaucoma associated with ocular trauma — (Use additional code to identify glaucoma stage: 365.70-365.74)
365.70 Glaucoma stage, unspecified — (Code first associated type of glaucoma (365.10-365.13, 365.20, 365.23, 365.31, 365.52, 365.62-365.63, 365.65)) ▽
365.71 Mild stage glaucoma — (Code first associated type of glaucoma (365.10-365.13, 365.20, 365.23, 365.31, 365.52, 365.62-365.63, 365.65))
365.72 Moderate stage glaucoma — (Code first associated type of glaucoma (365.10-365.13, 365.20, 365.23, 365.31, 365.52, 365.62-365.63, 365.65))
365.73 Severe stage glaucoma — (Code first associated type of glaucoma (365.10-365.13, 365.20, 365.23, 365.31, 365.52, 365.62-365.63, 365.65))
365.74 Indeterminate stage glaucoma — (Code first associated type of glaucoma (365.10-365.13, 365.20, 365.23, 365.31, 365.52, 365.62-365.63, 365.65))
365.83 Aqueous misdirection
365.89 Other specified glaucoma
371.20 Unspecified corneal edema ▽

ICD-9-CM Procedural

12.21 Diagnostic aspiration of anterior chamber of eye
12.91 Therapeutic evacuation of anterior chamber

HCPCS Level II Supplies & Services

A4305 Disposable drug delivery system, flow rate of 50 ml or greater per hour

65810

65810 Paracentesis of anterior chamber of eye (separate procedure); with removal of vitreous and/or discission of anterior hyaloid membrane, with or without air injection

ICD-9-CM Diagnostic

364.74 Adhesions and disruptions of pupillary membranes
365.61 Glaucoma associated with pupillary block
365.83 Aqueous misdirection
379.26 Vitreous prolapse

ICD-9-CM Procedural

12.91 Therapeutic evacuation of anterior chamber

65815

65815 Paracentesis of anterior chamber of eye (separate procedure); with removal of blood, with or without irrigation and/or air injection

ICD-9-CM Diagnostic

190.0 Malignant neoplasm of eyeball, except conjunctiva, cornea, retina, and choroid
190.3 Malignant neoplasm of conjunctiva
190.4 Malignant neoplasm of cornea
224.0 Benign neoplasm of eyeball, except conjunctiva, cornea, retina, and choroid
364.41 Hyphema
364.61 Implantation cysts of iris, ciliary body, and anterior chamber
365.64 Glaucoma associated with tumors or cysts
365.83 Aqueous misdirection
921.3 Contusion of eyeball

ICD-9-CM Procedural

12.91 Therapeutic evacuation of anterior chamber

HCPCS Level II Supplies & Services

A4305 Disposable drug delivery system, flow rate of 50 ml or greater per hour

65820

65820 Goniotomy

ICD-9-CM Diagnostic

237.70 Neurofibromatosis, unspecified ▽
237.71 Neurofibromatosis, Type 1 (von Recklinghausen's disease)
237.72 Neurofibromatosis, Type 2 (acoustic neurofibromatosis)
237.73 Schwannomatosis
237.79 Other neurofibromatosis
364.82 Plateau iris syndrome
365.14 Open-angle glaucoma of childhood
365.41 Glaucoma associated with chamber angle anomalies
365.44 Glaucoma associated with systemic syndromes — (Code first associated disease: 237.70-237.79, 759.6) ☒
365.83 Aqueous misdirection
743.20 Unspecified buphthalmos ▽
743.21 Simple buphthalmos
743.22 Buphthalmos associated with other ocular anomaly
743.44 Specified congenital anomaly of anterior chamber, chamber angle, and related structures
759.6 Other congenital hamartoses, not elsewhere classified

ICD-9-CM Procedural

12.52 Goniotomy without goniopuncture
12.53 Goniotomy with goniopuncture

HCPCS Level II Supplies & Services

A4305 Disposable drug delivery system, flow rate of 50 ml or greater per hour

65850

65850 Trabeculotomy ab externo

ICD-9-CM Diagnostic

237.70 Neurofibromatosis, unspecified ▽
237.71 Neurofibromatosis, Type 1 (von Recklinghausen's disease)
237.72 Neurofibromatosis, Type 2 (acoustic neurofibromatosis)
237.73 Schwannomatosis
237.79 Other neurofibromatosis

364.82	Plateau iris syndrome
365.05	Open angle with borderline findings, high risk
365.10	Unspecified open-angle glaucoma — (Use additional code to identify glaucoma stage: 365.70-365.74) ▽
365.11	Primary open-angle glaucoma — (Use additional code to identify glaucoma stage: 365.70-365.74)
365.12	Low tension open-angle glaucoma — (Use additional code to identify glaucoma stage: 365.70-365.74)
365.13	Pigmentary open-angle glaucoma — (Use additional code to identify glaucoma stage: 365.70-365.74)
365.14	Open-angle glaucoma of childhood
365.15	Residual stage of open angle glaucoma
365.41	Glaucoma associated with chamber angle anomalies
365.44	Glaucoma associated with systemic syndromes — (Code first associated disease: 237.70-237.79, 759.6) ☒
365.60	Glaucoma associated with unspecified ocular disorder ▽
365.83	Aqueous misdirection
371.11	Anterior pigmentations of cornea
371.12	Stromal pigmentations of cornea
743.20	Unspecified buphthalmos ▽
743.21	Simple buphthalmos
743.22	Buphthalmos associated with other ocular anomaly
743.44	Specified congenital anomaly of anterior chamber, chamber angle, and related structures
759.6	Other congenital hamartoses, not elsewhere classified

ICD-9-CM Procedural

12.54 Trabeculotomy ab externo

HCPCS Level II Supplies & Services

A4305 Disposable drug delivery system, flow rate of 50 ml or greater per hour

J7315 Mitomycin, opthalmic, 0.2 mg

65855

65855 Trabeculoplasty by laser surgery, 1 or more sessions (defined treatment series)

ICD-9-CM Diagnostic

364.82	Plateau iris syndrome
365.01	Borderline glaucoma, open angle with borderline findings, low risk
365.05	Open angle with borderline findings, high risk
365.10	Unspecified open-angle glaucoma — (Use additional code to identify glaucoma stage: 365.70-365.74) ▽
365.11	Primary open-angle glaucoma — (Use additional code to identify glaucoma stage: 365.70-365.74)
365.13	Pigmentary open-angle glaucoma — (Use additional code to identify glaucoma stage: 365.70-365.74)
365.15	Residual stage of open angle glaucoma
365.52	Pseudoexfoliation glaucoma — (Use additional code to identify glaucoma stage: 365.70-365.74)
365.60	Glaucoma associated with unspecified ocular disorder ▽
365.70	Glaucoma stage, unspecified — (Code first associated type of glaucoma (365.10-365.13, 365.20, 365.23, 365.31, 365.52, 365.62-365.63, 365.65)) ▽
365.71	Mild stage glaucoma — (Code first associated type of glaucoma (365.10-365.13, 365.20, 365.23, 365.31, 365.52, 365.62-365.63, 365.65))
365.72	Moderate stage glaucoma — (Code first associated type of glaucoma (365.10-365.13, 365.20, 365.23, 365.31, 365.52, 365.62-365.63, 365.65))
365.73	Severe stage glaucoma — (Code first associated type of glaucoma (365.10-365.13, 365.20, 365.23, 365.31, 365.52, 365.62-365.63, 365.65))
365.74	Indeterminate stage glaucoma — (Code first associated type of glaucoma (365.10-365.13, 365.20, 365.23, 365.31, 365.52, 365.62-365.63, 365.65))
365.83	Aqueous misdirection
365.9	Unspecified glaucoma ▽
366.11	Pseudoexfoliation of lens capsule

ICD-9-CM Procedural

12.59 Other facilitation of intraocular circulation

HCPCS Level II Supplies & Services

A4305 Disposable drug delivery system, flow rate of 50 ml or greater per hour

65860

65860 Severing adhesions of anterior segment, laser technique (separate procedure)

ICD-9-CM Diagnostic

364.70	Unspecified adhesions of iris ▽
364.72	Anterior synechiae
364.73	Goniosynechiae

ICD-9-CM Procedural

12.39 Other iridoplasty

HCPCS Level II Supplies & Services

A4305 Disposable drug delivery system, flow rate of 50 ml or greater per hour

65865

65865 Severing adhesions of anterior segment of eye, incisional technique (with or without injection of air or liquid) (separate procedure); goniosynechiae

ICD-9-CM Diagnostic

364.73 Goniosynechiae

ICD-9-CM Procedural

12.31 Lysis of goniosynechiae

HCPCS Level II Supplies & Services

A4305 Disposable drug delivery system, flow rate of 50 ml or greater per hour

65870-65875

65870 Severing adhesions of anterior segment of eye, incisional technique (with or without injection of air or liquid) (separate procedure); anterior synechiae, except goniosynechiae

65875 posterior synechiae

ICD-9-CM Diagnostic

364.70	Unspecified adhesions of iris ▽
364.71	Posterior synechiae
364.72	Anterior synechiae
379.27	Vitreomacular adhesion

ICD-9-CM Procedural

12.32 Lysis of other anterior synechiae

12.33 Lysis of posterior synechiae

HCPCS Level II Supplies & Services

A4305 Disposable drug delivery system, flow rate of 50 ml or greater per hour

65880

65880 Severing adhesions of anterior segment of eye, incisional technique (with or without injection of air or liquid) (separate procedure); corneovitreal adhesions

ICD-9-CM Diagnostic

362.53	Cystoid macular degeneration of retina
364.70	Unspecified adhesions of iris ▽
371.00	Unspecified corneal opacity ▽
371.01	Minor opacity of cornea
371.02	Peripheral opacity of cornea
371.03	Central opacity of cornea
371.04	Adherent leucoma

379.29 Other disorders of vitreous
379.31 Aphakia

ICD-9-CM Procedural
12.34 Lysis of corneovitreal adhesions

HCPCS Level II Supplies & Services
A4305 Disposable drug delivery system, flow rate of 50 ml or greater per hour

65900
65900 Removal of epithelial downgrowth, anterior chamber of eye

ICD-9-CM Diagnostic
364.61 Implantation cysts of iris, ciliary body, and anterior chamber
906.0 Late effect of open wound of head, neck, and trunk
996.51 Mechanical complication due to corneal graft
996.53 Mechanical complication due to ocular lens prosthesis
996.69 Infection and inflammatory reaction due to other internal prosthetic device, implant, and graft — (Use additional code to identify specified infections)
996.79 Other complications due to other internal prosthetic device, implant, and graft — (Use additional code to identify complication: 338.18-338.19, 338.28-338.29)
998.89 Other specified complications

ICD-9-CM Procedural
12.93 Removal or destruction of epithelial downgrowth from anterior chamber

HCPCS Level II Supplies & Services
A4305 Disposable drug delivery system, flow rate of 50 ml or greater per hour

65920
65920 Removal of implanted material, anterior segment of eye

ICD-9-CM Diagnostic
364.04 Secondary iridocyclitis, noninfectious
364.23 Lens-induced iridocyclitis
364.41 Hyphema
365.9 Unspecified glaucoma ♥
996.53 Mechanical complication due to ocular lens prosthesis
996.69 Infection and inflammatory reaction due to other internal prosthetic device, implant, and graft — (Use additional code to identify specified infections)
996.79 Other complications due to other internal prosthetic device, implant, and graft — (Use additional code to identify complication: 338.18-338.19, 338.28-338.29)

ICD-9-CM Procedural
13.8 Removal of implanted lens

HCPCS Level II Supplies & Services
A4305 Disposable drug delivery system, flow rate of 50 ml or greater per hour

65930
65930 Removal of blood clot, anterior segment of eye

ICD-9-CM Diagnostic
364.41 Hyphema
364.42 Rubeosis iridis
364.77 Recession of chamber angle of eye
365.65 Glaucoma associated with ocular trauma — (Use additional code to identify glaucoma stage: 365.70-365.74)
372.72 Conjunctival hemorrhage
871.4 Unspecified laceration of eye ♥
871.5 Penetration of eyeball with magnetic foreign body
871.6 Penetration of eyeball with (nonmagnetic) foreign body
871.7 Unspecified ocular penetration ♥
871.9 Unspecified open wound of eyeball ♥
921.3 Contusion of eyeball
996.79 Other complications due to other internal prosthetic device, implant, and graft — (Use additional code to identify complication: 338.18-338.19, 338.28-338.29)
998.11 Hemorrhage complicating a procedure
998.12 Hematoma complicating a procedure

ICD-9-CM Procedural
12.91 Therapeutic evacuation of anterior chamber

HCPCS Level II Supplies & Services
A4305 Disposable drug delivery system, flow rate of 50 ml or greater per hour

66020-66030
66020 Injection, anterior chamber of eye (separate procedure); air or liquid
66030 medication

ICD-9-CM Diagnostic
360.00 Unspecified purulent endophthalmitis ♥
360.01 Acute endophthalmitis
360.34 Flat anterior chamber of eye
364.01 Primary iridocyclitis
364.3 Unspecified iridocyclitis ♥
364.73 Goniosynechiae
364.82 Plateau iris syndrome
365.22 Acute angle-closure glaucoma
365.83 Aqueous misdirection
379.60 Inflammation (infection) of postprocedural bleb, unspecified ♥
379.61 Inflammation (infection) of postprocedural bleb, stage 1
379.62 Inflammation (infection) of postprocedural bleb, stage 2

ICD-9-CM Procedural
12.92 Injection into anterior chamber

66130
66130 Excision of lesion, sclera

ICD-9-CM Diagnostic
190.0 Malignant neoplasm of eyeball, except conjunctiva, cornea, retina, and choroid
198.4 Secondary malignant neoplasm of other parts of nervous system
224.0 Benign neoplasm of eyeball, except conjunctiva, cornea, retina, and choroid
234.0 Carcinoma in situ of eye
238.8 Neoplasm of uncertain behavior of other specified sites
239.89 Neoplasms of unspecified nature, other specified sites
379.19 Other scleral disorder

ICD-9-CM Procedural
12.84 Excision or destruction of lesion of sclera

HCPCS Level II Supplies & Services
A4305 Disposable drug delivery system, flow rate of 50 ml or greater per hour

66150-66155
66150 Fistulization of sclera for glaucoma; trephination with iridectomy
66155 thermocauterization with iridectomy

ICD-9-CM Diagnostic
364.51 Essential or progressive iris atrophy
364.82 Plateau iris syndrome
365.20 Unspecified primary angle-closure glaucoma — (Use additional code to identify glaucoma stage: 365.70-365.74) ♥
365.21 Intermittent angle-closure glaucoma
365.22 Acute angle-closure glaucoma
365.23 Chronic angle-closure glaucoma — (Use additional code to identify glaucoma stage: 365.70-365.74)

365.24 Residual stage of angle-closure glaucoma
365.42 Glaucoma associated with anomalies of iris
365.51 Phacolytic glaucoma
365.52 Pseudoexfoliation glaucoma — (Use additional code to identify glaucoma stage: 365.70-365.74)
365.70 Glaucoma stage, unspecified — (Code first associated type of glaucoma (365.10-365.13, 365.20, 365.23, 365.31, 365.52, 365.62-365.63, 365.65))
365.71 Mild stage glaucoma — (Code first associated type of glaucoma (365.10-365.13, 365.20, 365.23, 365.31, 365.52, 365.62-365.63, 365.65))
365.72 Moderate stage glaucoma — (Code first associated type of glaucoma (365.10-365.13, 365.20, 365.23, 365.31, 365.52, 365.62-365.63, 365.65))
365.73 Severe stage glaucoma — (Code first associated type of glaucoma (365.10-365.13, 365.20, 365.23, 365.31, 365.52, 365.62-365.63, 365.65))
365.74 Indeterminate stage glaucoma — (Code first associated type of glaucoma (365.10-365.13, 365.20, 365.23, 365.31, 365.52, 365.62-365.63, 365.65))
365.83 Aqueous misdirection
366.11 Pseudoexfoliation of lens capsule
366.18 Hypermature senile cataract
743.45 Aniridia

ICD-9-CM Procedural

12.61 Trephination of sclera with iridectomy
12.62 Thermocauterization of sclera with iridectomy

66160

66160 Fistulization of sclera for glaucoma; sclerectomy with punch or scissors, with iridectomy

ICD-9-CM Diagnostic

364.51 Essential or progressive iris atrophy
364.82 Plateau iris syndrome
365.11 Primary open-angle glaucoma — (Use additional code to identify glaucoma stage: 365.70-365.74)
365.20 Unspecified primary angle-closure glaucoma — (Use additional code to identify glaucoma stage: 365.70-365.74)
365.21 Intermittent angle-closure glaucoma
365.22 Acute angle-closure glaucoma
365.23 Chronic angle-closure glaucoma — (Use additional code to identify glaucoma stage: 365.70-365.74)
365.24 Residual stage of angle-closure glaucoma
365.42 Glaucoma associated with anomalies of iris
365.51 Phacolytic glaucoma
365.52 Pseudoexfoliation glaucoma — (Use additional code to identify glaucoma stage: 365.70-365.74)
365.70 Glaucoma stage, unspecified — (Code first associated type of glaucoma (365.10-365.13, 365.20, 365.23, 365.31, 365.52, 365.62-365.63, 365.65))
365.71 Mild stage glaucoma — (Code first associated type of glaucoma (365.10-365.13, 365.20, 365.23, 365.31, 365.52, 365.62-365.63, 365.65))
365.72 Moderate stage glaucoma — (Code first associated type of glaucoma (365.10-365.13, 365.20, 365.23, 365.31, 365.52, 365.62-365.63, 365.65))
365.73 Severe stage glaucoma — (Code first associated type of glaucoma (365.10-365.13, 365.20, 365.23, 365.31, 365.52, 365.62-365.63, 365.65))
365.74 Indeterminate stage glaucoma — (Code first associated type of glaucoma (365.10-365.13, 365.20, 365.23, 365.31, 365.52, 365.62-365.63, 365.65))
365.83 Aqueous misdirection
366.11 Pseudoexfoliation of lens capsule
366.18 Hypermature senile cataract
743.45 Aniridia

ICD-9-CM Procedural

12.65 Other scleral fistulization with iridectomy

66165

66165 Fistulization of sclera for glaucoma; iridencleisis or iridotasis

ICD-9-CM Diagnostic

364.51 Essential or progressive iris atrophy
364.82 Plateau iris syndrome
365.11 Primary open-angle glaucoma — (Use additional code to identify glaucoma stage: 365.70-365.74)
365.20 Unspecified primary angle-closure glaucoma — (Use additional code to identify glaucoma stage: 365.70-365.74)
365.21 Intermittent angle-closure glaucoma
365.22 Acute angle-closure glaucoma
365.23 Chronic angle-closure glaucoma — (Use additional code to identify glaucoma stage: 365.70-365.74)
365.24 Residual stage of angle-closure glaucoma
365.42 Glaucoma associated with anomalies of iris
365.51 Phacolytic glaucoma
365.52 Pseudoexfoliation glaucoma — (Use additional code to identify glaucoma stage: 365.70-365.74)
365.70 Glaucoma stage, unspecified — (Code first associated type of glaucoma (365.10-365.13, 365.20, 365.23, 365.31, 365.52, 365.62-365.63, 365.65))
365.71 Mild stage glaucoma — (Code first associated type of glaucoma (365.10-365.13, 365.20, 365.23, 365.31, 365.52, 365.62-365.63, 365.65))
365.72 Moderate stage glaucoma — (Code first associated type of glaucoma (365.10-365.13, 365.20, 365.23, 365.31, 365.52, 365.62-365.63, 365.65))
365.73 Severe stage glaucoma — (Code first associated type of glaucoma (365.10-365.13, 365.20, 365.23, 365.31, 365.52, 365.62-365.63, 365.65))
365.74 Indeterminate stage glaucoma — (Code first associated type of glaucoma (365.10-365.13, 365.20, 365.23, 365.31, 365.52, 365.62-365.63, 365.65))
365.83 Aqueous misdirection
366.11 Pseudoexfoliation of lens capsule
366.18 Hypermature senile cataract
743.45 Aniridia

ICD-9-CM Procedural

12.63 Iridencleisis and iridotasis
12.79 Other glaucoma procedures

66170-66172

66170 Fistulization of sclera for glaucoma; trabeculectomy ab externo in absence of previous surgery
66172 trabeculectomy ab externo with scarring from previous ocular surgery or trauma (includes injection of antifibrotic agents)

ICD-9-CM Diagnostic

364.82 Plateau iris syndrome
365.10 Unspecified open-angle glaucoma — (Use additional code to identify glaucoma stage: 365.70-365.74)
365.11 Primary open-angle glaucoma — (Use additional code to identify glaucoma stage: 365.70-365.74)
365.12 Low tension open-angle glaucoma — (Use additional code to identify glaucoma stage: 365.70-365.74)
365.13 Pigmentary open-angle glaucoma — (Use additional code to identify glaucoma stage: 365.70-365.74)
365.14 Open-angle glaucoma of childhood
365.15 Residual stage of open angle glaucoma
365.20 Unspecified primary angle-closure glaucoma — (Use additional code to identify glaucoma stage: 365.70-365.74)
365.21 Intermittent angle-closure glaucoma
365.23 Chronic angle-closure glaucoma — (Use additional code to identify glaucoma stage: 365.70-365.74)
365.24 Residual stage of angle-closure glaucoma

365.42 Glaucoma associated with anomalies of iris
365.52 Pseudoexfoliation glaucoma — (Use additional code to identify glaucoma stage: 365.70-365.74)
365.60 Glaucoma associated with unspecified ocular disorder ▽
365.70 Glaucoma stage, unspecified — (Code first associated type of glaucoma (365.10-365.13, 365.20, 365.23, 365.31, 365.52, 365.62-365.63, 365.65)) ▽
365.71 Mild stage glaucoma — (Code first associated type of glaucoma (365.10-365.13, 365.20, 365.23, 365.31, 365.52, 365.62-365.63, 365.65))
365.72 Moderate stage glaucoma — (Code first associated type of glaucoma (365.10-365.13, 365.20, 365.23, 365.31, 365.52, 365.62-365.63, 365.65))
365.73 Severe stage glaucoma — (Code first associated type of glaucoma (365.10-365.13, 365.20, 365.23, 365.31, 365.52, 365.62-365.63, 365.65))
365.74 Indeterminate stage glaucoma — (Code first associated type of glaucoma (365.10-365.13, 365.20, 365.23, 365.31, 365.52, 365.62-365.63, 365.65))
365.83 Aqueous misdirection
365.9 Unspecified glaucoma ▽
366.11 Pseudoexfoliation of lens capsule
379.63 Inflammation (infection) of postprocedural bleb, stage 3
743.45 Aniridia

ICD-9-CM Procedural

12.64 Trabeculectomy ab externo

66174-66175

66174 Transluminal dilation of aqueous outflow canal; without retention of device or stent
66175 with retention of device or stent

ICD-9-CM Diagnostic

365.10 Unspecified open-angle glaucoma — (Use additional code to identify glaucoma stage: 365.70-365.74) ▽
365.11 Primary open-angle glaucoma — (Use additional code to identify glaucoma stage: 365.70-365.74)
365.12 Low tension open-angle glaucoma — (Use additional code to identify glaucoma stage: 365.70-365.74)
365.13 Pigmentary open-angle glaucoma — (Use additional code to identify glaucoma stage: 365.70-365.74)
365.14 Open-angle glaucoma of childhood
365.15 Residual stage of open angle glaucoma
365.20 Unspecified primary angle-closure glaucoma — (Use additional code to identify glaucoma stage: 365.70-365.74) ▽
365.21 Intermittent angle-closure glaucoma
365.22 Acute angle-closure glaucoma
365.23 Chronic angle-closure glaucoma — (Use additional code to identify glaucoma stage: 365.70-365.74)
365.24 Residual stage of angle-closure glaucoma
365.70 Glaucoma stage, unspecified — (Code first associated type of glaucoma (365.10-365.13, 365.20, 365.23, 365.31, 365.52, 365.62-365.63, 365.65)) ▽
365.71 Mild stage glaucoma — (Code first associated type of glaucoma (365.10-365.13, 365.20, 365.23, 365.31, 365.52, 365.62-365.63, 365.65))
365.72 Moderate stage glaucoma — (Code first associated type of glaucoma (365.10-365.13, 365.20, 365.23, 365.31, 365.52, 365.62-365.63, 365.65))
365.73 Severe stage glaucoma — (Code first associated type of glaucoma (365.10-365.13, 365.20, 365.23, 365.31, 365.52, 365.62-365.63, 365.65))
365.74 Indeterminate stage glaucoma — (Code first associated type of glaucoma (365.10-365.13, 365.20, 365.23, 365.31, 365.52, 365.62-365.63, 365.65))

ICD-9-CM Procedural

12.67 Insertion of aqueous drainage device
12.69 Other scleral fistulizing procedure
12.79 Other glaucoma procedures

66180

66180 Aqueous shunt to extraocular reservoir (eg, Molteno, Schocket, Denver-Krupin)

ICD-9-CM Diagnostic

237.70 Neurofibromatosis, unspecified ▽
237.71 Neurofibromatosis, Type 1 (von Recklinghausen's disease)
237.72 Neurofibromatosis, Type 2 (acoustic neurofibromatosis)
237.73 Schwannomatosis
237.79 Other neurofibromatosis
362.35 Central vein occlusion of retina
364.41 Hyphema
364.51 Essential or progressive iris atrophy
365.00 Unspecified preglaucoma ▽
365.10 Unspecified open-angle glaucoma — (Use additional code to identify glaucoma stage: 365.70-365.74) ▽
365.11 Primary open-angle glaucoma — (Use additional code to identify glaucoma stage: 365.70-365.74)
365.12 Low tension open-angle glaucoma — (Use additional code to identify glaucoma stage: 365.70-365.74)
365.13 Pigmentary open-angle glaucoma — (Use additional code to identify glaucoma stage: 365.70-365.74)
365.14 Open-angle glaucoma of childhood
365.15 Residual stage of open angle glaucoma
365.20 Unspecified primary angle-closure glaucoma — (Use additional code to identify glaucoma stage: 365.70-365.74) ▽
365.21 Intermittent angle-closure glaucoma
365.22 Acute angle-closure glaucoma
365.23 Chronic angle-closure glaucoma — (Use additional code to identify glaucoma stage: 365.70-365.74)
365.24 Residual stage of angle-closure glaucoma
365.31 Corticosteroid-induced glaucoma, glaucomatous stage — (Use additional code to identify glaucoma stage: 365.70-365.74)
365.32 Corticosteroid-induced glaucoma, residual stage
365.41 Glaucoma associated with chamber angle anomalies
365.42 Glaucoma associated with anomalies of iris
365.43 Glaucoma associated with other anterior segment anomalies
365.44 Glaucoma associated with systemic syndromes — (Code first associated disease: 237.70-237.79, 759.6) ☒
365.51 Phacolytic glaucoma
365.52 Pseudoexfoliation glaucoma — (Use additional code to identify glaucoma stage: 365.70-365.74)
365.59 Glaucoma associated with other lens disorders
365.60 Glaucoma associated with unspecified ocular disorder ▽
365.61 Glaucoma associated with pupillary block
365.62 Glaucoma associated with ocular inflammations — (Use additional code to identify glaucoma stage: 365.70-365.74)
365.63 Glaucoma associated with vascular disorders of eye — (Use additional code to identify glaucoma stage: 365.70-365.74)
365.64 Glaucoma associated with tumors or cysts
365.65 Glaucoma associated with ocular trauma — (Use additional code to identify glaucoma stage: 365.70-365.74)
365.70 Glaucoma stage, unspecified — (Code first associated type of glaucoma (365.10-365.13, 365.20, 365.23, 365.31, 365.52, 365.62-365.63, 365.65)) ▽
365.71 Mild stage glaucoma — (Code first associated type of glaucoma (365.10-365.13, 365.20, 365.23, 365.31, 365.52, 365.62-365.63, 365.65))
365.72 Moderate stage glaucoma — (Code first associated type of glaucoma (365.10-365.13, 365.20, 365.23, 365.31, 365.52, 365.62-365.63, 365.65))
365.73 Severe stage glaucoma — (Code first associated type of glaucoma (365.10-365.13, 365.20, 365.23, 365.31, 365.52, 365.62-365.63, 365.65))
365.74 Indeterminate stage glaucoma — (Code first associated type of glaucoma (365.10-365.13, 365.20, 365.23, 365.31, 365.52, 365.62-365.63, 365.65))

365.81 Hypersecretion glaucoma
365.82 Glaucoma with increased episcleral venous pressure
365.83 Aqueous misdirection
365.89 Other specified glaucoma
365.9 Unspecified glaucoma ▽
743.20 Unspecified buphthalmos ▽
743.21 Simple buphthalmos
743.22 Buphthalmos associated with other ocular anomaly
743.45 Aniridia
759.6 Other congenital hamartoses, not elsewhere classified
767.8 Other specified birth trauma — (Use additional code(s) to further specify condition)
996.59 Mechanical complication due to other implant and internal device, not elsewhere classified
996.69 Infection and inflammatory reaction due to other internal prosthetic device, implant, and graft — (Use additional code to identify specified infections)
996.79 Other complications due to other internal prosthetic device, implant, and graft — (Use additional code to identify complication: 338.18-338.19, 338.28-338.29)

ICD-9-CM Procedural

12.67 Insertion of aqueous drainage device

HCPCS Level II Supplies & Services

C1783 Ocular implant, aqueous drainage assist device

66183

66183 Insertion of anterior segment aqueous drainage device, without extraocular reservoir, external approach

ICD-9-CM Diagnostic

237.70 Neurofibromatosis, unspecified ▽
237.71 Neurofibromatosis, Type 1 (von Recklinghausen's disease)
237.72 Neurofibromatosis, Type 2 (acoustic neurofibromatosis)
237.73 Schwannomatosis
237.79 Other neurofibromatosis
362.35 Central vein occlusion of retina
364.41 Hyphema
364.51 Essential or progressive iris atrophy
365.00 Unspecified preglaucoma ▽
365.10 Unspecified open-angle glaucoma — (Use additional code to identify glaucoma stage: 365.70-365.74) ▽
365.11 Primary open-angle glaucoma — (Use additional code to identify glaucoma stage: 365.70-365.74)
365.12 Low tension open-angle glaucoma — (Use additional code to identify glaucoma stage: 365.70-365.74)
365.13 Pigmentary open-angle glaucoma — (Use additional code to identify glaucoma stage: 365.70-365.74)
365.14 Open-angle glaucoma of childhood
365.15 Residual stage of open angle glaucoma
365.20 Unspecified primary angle-closure glaucoma — (Use additional code to identify glaucoma stage: 365.70-365.74) ▽
365.21 Intermittent angle-closure glaucoma
365.22 Acute angle-closure glaucoma
365.23 Chronic angle-closure glaucoma — (Use additional code to identify glaucoma stage: 365.70-365.74)
365.24 Residual stage of angle-closure glaucoma
365.31 Corticosteroid-induced glaucoma, glaucomatous stage — (Use additional code to identify glaucoma stage: 365.70-365.74)
365.32 Corticosteroid-induced glaucoma, residual stage
365.41 Glaucoma associated with chamber angle anomalies
365.42 Glaucoma associated with anomalies of iris
365.43 Glaucoma associated with other anterior segment anomalies
365.44 Glaucoma associated with systemic syndromes — (Code first associated disease: 237.70-237.79, 759.6) ☒
365.51 Phacolytic glaucoma
365.52 Pseudoexfoliation glaucoma — (Use additional code to identify glaucoma stage: 365.70-365.74)
365.59 Glaucoma associated with other lens disorders
365.60 Glaucoma associated with unspecified ocular disorder ▽
365.61 Glaucoma associated with pupillary block
365.62 Glaucoma associated with ocular inflammations — (Use additional code to identify glaucoma stage: 365.70-365.74)
365.63 Glaucoma associated with vascular disorders of eye — (Use additional code to identify glaucoma stage: 365.70-365.74)
365.64 Glaucoma associated with tumors or cysts
365.65 Glaucoma associated with ocular trauma — (Use additional code to identify glaucoma stage: 365.70-365.74)
365.70 Glaucoma stage, unspecified — (Code first associated type of glaucoma (365.10-365.13, 365.20, 365.23, 365.31, 365.52, 365.62-365.63, 365.65)) ▽
365.71 Mild stage glaucoma — (Code first associated type of glaucoma (365.10-365.13, 365.20, 365.23, 365.31, 365.52, 365.62-365.63, 365.65))
365.72 Moderate stage glaucoma — (Code first associated type of glaucoma (365.10-365.13, 365.20, 365.23, 365.31, 365.52, 365.62-365.63, 365.65))
365.73 Severe stage glaucoma — (Code first associated type of glaucoma (365.10-365.13, 365.20, 365.23, 365.31, 365.52, 365.62-365.63, 365.65))
365.74 Indeterminate stage glaucoma — (Code first associated type of glaucoma (365.10-365.13, 365.20, 365.23, 365.31, 365.52, 365.62-365.63, 365.65))
365.81 Hypersecretion glaucoma
365.82 Glaucoma with increased episcleral venous pressure
365.83 Aqueous misdirection
365.89 Other specified glaucoma
365.9 Unspecified glaucoma ▽
743.20 Unspecified buphthalmos ▽
743.21 Simple buphthalmos
743.22 Buphthalmos associated with other ocular anomaly
743.45 Aniridia
759.6 Other congenital hamartoses, not elsewhere classified
767.8 Other specified birth trauma — (Use additional code(s) to further specify condition)
996.59 Mechanical complication due to other implant and internal device, not elsewhere classified
996.69 Infection and inflammatory reaction due to other internal prosthetic device, implant, and graft — (Use additional code to identify specified infections)
996.79 Other complications due to other internal prosthetic device, implant, and graft — (Use additional code to identify complication: 338.18-338.19, 338.28-338.29)

ICD-9-CM Procedural

12.67 Insertion of aqueous drainage device

HCPCS Level II Supplies & Services

C1783 Ocular implant, aqueous drainage assist device

66185

66185 Revision of aqueous shunt to extraocular reservoir

ICD-9-CM Diagnostic

996.59 Mechanical complication due to other implant and internal device, not elsewhere classified
996.79 Other complications due to other internal prosthetic device, implant, and graft — (Use additional code to identify complication: 338.18-338.19, 338.28-338.29)
997.99 Other complications affecting other specified body systems, NEC — (Use additional code to identify complications)

ICD-9-CM Procedural

12.66 Postoperative revision of scleral fistulization procedure

66220-66225

66220 Repair of scleral staphyloma; without graft
66225 with graft

ICD-9-CM Diagnostic

379.11 Scleral ectasia
379.12 Staphyloma posticum
379.13 Equatorial staphyloma
379.14 Anterior staphyloma, localized
379.15 Ring staphyloma

ICD-9-CM Procedural

12.85 Repair of scleral staphyloma with graft
12.86 Other repair of scleral staphyloma

HCPCS Level II Supplies & Services

A4305 Disposable drug delivery system, flow rate of 50 ml or greater per hour

66250

66250 Revision or repair of operative wound of anterior segment, any type, early or late, major or minor procedure

ICD-9-CM Diagnostic

996.59 Mechanical complication due to other implant and internal device, not elsewhere classified
996.69 Infection and inflammatory reaction due to other internal prosthetic device, implant, and graft — (Use additional code to identify specified infections)
996.79 Other complications due to other internal prosthetic device, implant, and graft — (Use additional code to identify complication: 338.18-338.19, 338.28-338.29)
998.30 Disruption of wound, unspecified
998.31 Disruption of internal operation (surgical) wound
998.33 Disruption of traumatic injury wound repair
998.59 Other postoperative infection — (Use additional code to identify infection)

ICD-9-CM Procedural

11.52 Repair of postoperative wound dehiscence of cornea
12.82 Repair of scleral fistula
12.83 Revision of operative wound of anterior segment, not elsewhere classified
12.99 Other operations on anterior chamber

66500-66505

66500 Iridotomy by stab incision (separate procedure); except transfixion
66505 with transfixion as for iris bombe

ICD-9-CM Diagnostic

364.51 Essential or progressive iris atrophy
364.74 Adhesions and disruptions of pupillary membranes
364.82 Plateau iris syndrome
365.20 Unspecified primary angle-closure glaucoma — (Use additional code to identify glaucoma stage: 365.70-365.74)
365.21 Intermittent angle-closure glaucoma
365.22 Acute angle-closure glaucoma
365.23 Chronic angle-closure glaucoma — (Use additional code to identify glaucoma stage: 365.70-365.74)
365.24 Residual stage of angle-closure glaucoma
365.42 Glaucoma associated with anomalies of iris
365.61 Glaucoma associated with pupillary block
365.70 Glaucoma stage, unspecified — (Code first associated type of glaucoma (365.10-365.13, 365.20, 365.23, 365.31, 365.52, 365.62-365.63, 365.65))
365.71 Mild stage glaucoma — (Code first associated type of glaucoma (365.10-365.13, 365.20, 365.23, 365.31, 365.52, 365.62-365.63, 365.65))
365.72 Moderate stage glaucoma — (Code first associated type of glaucoma (365.10-365.13, 365.20, 365.23, 365.31, 365.52, 365.62-365.63, 365.65))
365.73 Severe stage glaucoma — (Code first associated type of glaucoma (365.10-365.13, 365.20, 365.23, 365.31, 365.52, 365.62-365.63, 365.65))
365.74 Indeterminate stage glaucoma — (Code first associated type of glaucoma (365.10-365.13, 365.20, 365.23, 365.31, 365.52, 365.62-365.63, 365.65))
365.83 Aqueous misdirection
743.45 Aniridia

ICD-9-CM Procedural

12.11 Iridotomy with transfixion
12.12 Other iridotomy

HCPCS Level II Supplies & Services

A4305 Disposable drug delivery system, flow rate of 50 ml or greater per hour

66600-66605

66600 Iridectomy, with corneoscleral or corneal section; for removal of lesion
66605 with cyclectomy

ICD-9-CM Diagnostic

190.0 Malignant neoplasm of eyeball, except conjunctiva, cornea, retina, and choroid
198.4 Secondary malignant neoplasm of other parts of nervous system
224.0 Benign neoplasm of eyeball, except conjunctiva, cornea, retina, and choroid
224.4 Benign neoplasm of cornea
234.0 Carcinoma in situ of eye
238.8 Neoplasm of uncertain behavior of other specified sites
239.89 Neoplasms of unspecified nature, other specified sites
364.60 Idiopathic cysts of iris, ciliary body, and anterior chamber
364.62 Exudative cysts of iris or anterior chamber

ICD-9-CM Procedural

12.14 Other iridectomy
12.40 Removal of lesion of anterior segment of eye, not otherwise specified
12.42 Excision of lesion of iris
12.44 Excision of lesion of ciliary body

66625

66625 Iridectomy, with corneoscleral or corneal section; peripheral for glaucoma (separate procedure)

ICD-9-CM Diagnostic

364.82 Plateau iris syndrome
365.02 Borderline glaucoma with anatomical narrow angle
365.20 Unspecified primary angle-closure glaucoma — (Use additional code to identify glaucoma stage: 365.70-365.74)
365.21 Intermittent angle-closure glaucoma
365.22 Acute angle-closure glaucoma
365.23 Chronic angle-closure glaucoma — (Use additional code to identify glaucoma stage: 365.70-365.74)
365.24 Residual stage of angle-closure glaucoma
365.42 Glaucoma associated with anomalies of iris
365.61 Glaucoma associated with pupillary block
365.70 Glaucoma stage, unspecified — (Code first associated type of glaucoma (365.10-365.13, 365.20, 365.23, 365.31, 365.52, 365.62-365.63, 365.65))
365.71 Mild stage glaucoma — (Code first associated type of glaucoma (365.10-365.13, 365.20, 365.23, 365.31, 365.52, 365.62-365.63, 365.65))
365.72 Moderate stage glaucoma — (Code first associated type of glaucoma (365.10-365.13, 365.20, 365.23, 365.31, 365.52, 365.62-365.63, 365.65))
365.73 Severe stage glaucoma — (Code first associated type of glaucoma (365.10-365.13, 365.20, 365.23, 365.31, 365.52, 365.62-365.63, 365.65))
365.74 Indeterminate stage glaucoma — (Code first associated type of glaucoma (365.10-365.13, 365.20, 365.23, 365.31, 365.52, 365.62-365.63, 365.65))
365.83 Aqueous misdirection

ICD-9-CM Procedural

12.14 Other iridectomy

66630

66630 Iridectomy, with corneoscleral or corneal section; sector for glaucoma (separate procedure)

ICD-9-CM Diagnostic

364.82 Plateau iris syndrome
365.20 Unspecified primary angle-closure glaucoma — (Use additional code to identify glaucoma stage: 365.70-365.74) ♥
365.21 Intermittent angle-closure glaucoma
365.22 Acute angle-closure glaucoma
365.23 Chronic angle-closure glaucoma — (Use additional code to identify glaucoma stage: 365.70-365.74)
365.24 Residual stage of angle-closure glaucoma
365.42 Glaucoma associated with anomalies of iris
365.61 Glaucoma associated with pupillary block
365.70 Glaucoma stage, unspecified — (Code first associated type of glaucoma (365.10-365.13, 365.20, 365.23, 365.31, 365.52, 365.62-365.63, 365.65)) ♥
365.71 Mild stage glaucoma — (Code first associated type of glaucoma (365.10-365.13, 365.20, 365.23, 365.31, 365.52, 365.62-365.63, 365.65))
365.72 Moderate stage glaucoma — (Code first associated type of glaucoma (365.10-365.13, 365.20, 365.23, 365.31, 365.52, 365.62-365.63, 365.65))
365.73 Severe stage glaucoma — (Code first associated type of glaucoma (365.10-365.13, 365.20, 365.23, 365.31, 365.52, 365.62-365.63, 365.65))
365.74 Indeterminate stage glaucoma — (Code first associated type of glaucoma (365.10-365.13, 365.20, 365.23, 365.31, 365.52, 365.62-365.63, 365.65))
365.83 Aqueous misdirection
365.9 Unspecified glaucoma ♥

ICD-9-CM Procedural

12.14 Other iridectomy
12.39 Other iridoplasty

66635

66635 Iridectomy, with corneoscleral or corneal section; optical (separate procedure)

ICD-9-CM Diagnostic

364.75 Pupillary abnormalities
379.40 Unspecified abnormal pupillary function ♥
379.42 Miosis (persistent), not due to miotics
379.45 Argyll Robertson pupil, atypical

ICD-9-CM Procedural

12.14 Other iridectomy
12.39 Other iridoplasty

66680

66680 Repair of iris, ciliary body (as for iridodialysis)

ICD-9-CM Diagnostic

364.51 Essential or progressive iris atrophy
364.52 Iridoschisis
364.53 Pigmentary iris degeneration
364.54 Degeneration of pupillary margin
364.55 Miotic cysts of pupillary margin
364.56 Degenerative changes of chamber angle
364.57 Degenerative changes of ciliary body
364.75 Pupillary abnormalities
364.76 Iridodialysis
364.81 Floppy iris syndrome
364.89 Other disorders of iris and ciliary body
871.1 Ocular laceration with prolapse or exposure of intraocular tissue

ICD-9-CM Procedural

12.39 Other iridoplasty

66682

66682 Suture of iris, ciliary body (separate procedure) with retrieval of suture through small incision (eg, McCannel suture)

ICD-9-CM Diagnostic

364.51 Essential or progressive iris atrophy
364.52 Iridoschisis
364.53 Pigmentary iris degeneration
364.54 Degeneration of pupillary margin
364.55 Miotic cysts of pupillary margin
364.56 Degenerative changes of chamber angle
364.57 Degenerative changes of ciliary body
364.75 Pupillary abnormalities
364.76 Iridodialysis
364.81 Floppy iris syndrome
364.89 Other disorders of iris and ciliary body
871.1 Ocular laceration with prolapse or exposure of intraocular tissue

ICD-9-CM Procedural

12.39 Other iridoplasty

HCPCS Level II Supplies & Services

A4305 Disposable drug delivery system, flow rate of 50 ml or greater per hour

66700-66711

66700 Ciliary body destruction; diathermy
66710 cyclophotocoagulation, transscleral
66711 cyclophotocoagulation, endoscopic

ICD-9-CM Diagnostic

362.35 Central vein occlusion of retina
364.41 Hyphema
364.82 Plateau iris syndrome
365.05 Open angle with borderline findings, high risk
365.10 Unspecified open-angle glaucoma — (Use additional code to identify glaucoma stage: 365.70-365.74) ♥
365.11 Primary open-angle glaucoma — (Use additional code to identify glaucoma stage: 365.70-365.74)
365.12 Low tension open-angle glaucoma — (Use additional code to identify glaucoma stage: 365.70-365.74)
365.13 Pigmentary open-angle glaucoma — (Use additional code to identify glaucoma stage: 365.70-365.74)
365.14 Open-angle glaucoma of childhood
365.15 Residual stage of open angle glaucoma
365.20 Unspecified primary angle-closure glaucoma — (Use additional code to identify glaucoma stage: 365.70-365.74) ♥
365.21 Intermittent angle-closure glaucoma
365.22 Acute angle-closure glaucoma
365.23 Chronic angle-closure glaucoma — (Use additional code to identify glaucoma stage: 365.70-365.74)
365.24 Residual stage of angle-closure glaucoma
365.41 Glaucoma associated with chamber angle anomalies
365.60 Glaucoma associated with unspecified ocular disorder ♥
365.63 Glaucoma associated with vascular disorders of eye — (Use additional code to identify glaucoma stage: 365.70-365.74)
365.70 Glaucoma stage, unspecified — (Code first associated type of glaucoma (365.10-365.13, 365.20, 365.23, 365.31, 365.52, 365.62-365.63, 365.65)) ♥

365.71 Mild stage glaucoma — (Code first associated type of glaucoma (365.10-365.13, 365.20, 365.23, 365.31, 365.52, 365.62-365.63, 365.65))
365.72 Moderate stage glaucoma — (Code first associated type of glaucoma (365.10-365.13, 365.20, 365.23, 365.31, 365.52, 365.62-365.63, 365.65))
365.73 Severe stage glaucoma — (Code first associated type of glaucoma (365.10-365.13, 365.20, 365.23, 365.31, 365.52, 365.62-365.63, 365.65))
365.74 Indeterminate stage glaucoma — (Code first associated type of glaucoma (365.10-365.13, 365.20, 365.23, 365.31, 365.52, 365.62-365.63, 365.65))
365.83 Aqueous misdirection
365.9 Unspecified glaucoma ▼
743.44 Specified congenital anomaly of anterior chamber, chamber angle, and related structures

ICD-9-CM Procedural

12.71 Cyclodiathermy
12.73 Cyclophotocoagulation

HCPCS Level II Supplies & Services

A4305 Disposable drug delivery system, flow rate of 50 ml or greater per hour

66720

66720 Ciliary body destruction; cryotherapy

ICD-9-CM Diagnostic

360.42 Blind hypertensive eye
364.82 Plateau iris syndrome
365.02 Borderline glaucoma with anatomical narrow angle
365.04 Borderline glaucoma with ocular hypertension
365.05 Open angle with borderline findings, high risk
365.10 Unspecified open-angle glaucoma — (Use additional code to identify glaucoma stage: 365.70-365.74) ▼
365.11 Primary open-angle glaucoma — (Use additional code to identify glaucoma stage: 365.70-365.74)
365.12 Low tension open-angle glaucoma — (Use additional code to identify glaucoma stage: 365.70-365.74)
365.13 Pigmentary open-angle glaucoma — (Use additional code to identify glaucoma stage: 365.70-365.74)
365.14 Open-angle glaucoma of childhood
365.15 Residual stage of open angle glaucoma
365.20 Unspecified primary angle-closure glaucoma — (Use additional code to identify glaucoma stage: 365.70-365.74) ▼
365.21 Intermittent angle-closure glaucoma
365.22 Acute angle-closure glaucoma
365.23 Chronic angle-closure glaucoma — (Use additional code to identify glaucoma stage: 365.70-365.74)
365.24 Residual stage of angle-closure glaucoma
365.63 Glaucoma associated with vascular disorders of eye — (Use additional code to identify glaucoma stage: 365.70-365.74)
365.70 Glaucoma stage, unspecified — (Code first associated type of glaucoma (365.10-365.13, 365.20, 365.23, 365.31, 365.52, 365.62-365.63, 365.65)) ▼
365.71 Mild stage glaucoma — (Code first associated type of glaucoma (365.10-365.13, 365.20, 365.23, 365.31, 365.52, 365.62-365.63, 365.65))
365.72 Moderate stage glaucoma — (Code first associated type of glaucoma (365.10-365.13, 365.20, 365.23, 365.31, 365.52, 365.62-365.63, 365.65))
365.73 Severe stage glaucoma — (Code first associated type of glaucoma (365.10-365.13, 365.20, 365.23, 365.31, 365.52, 365.62-365.63, 365.65))
365.74 Indeterminate stage glaucoma — (Code first associated type of glaucoma (365.10-365.13, 365.20, 365.23, 365.31, 365.52, 365.62-365.63, 365.65))
365.83 Aqueous misdirection

ICD-9-CM Procedural

12.72 Cyclocryotherapy

HCPCS Level II Supplies & Services

A4305 Disposable drug delivery system, flow rate of 50 ml or greater per hour

66740

66740 Ciliary body destruction; cyclodialysis

ICD-9-CM Diagnostic

364.51 Essential or progressive iris atrophy
364.82 Plateau iris syndrome
365.02 Borderline glaucoma with anatomical narrow angle
365.04 Borderline glaucoma with ocular hypertension
365.10 Unspecified open-angle glaucoma — (Use additional code to identify glaucoma stage: 365.70-365.74) ▼
365.11 Primary open-angle glaucoma — (Use additional code to identify glaucoma stage: 365.70-365.74)
365.12 Low tension open-angle glaucoma — (Use additional code to identify glaucoma stage: 365.70-365.74)
365.13 Pigmentary open-angle glaucoma — (Use additional code to identify glaucoma stage: 365.70-365.74)
365.14 Open-angle glaucoma of childhood
365.15 Residual stage of open angle glaucoma
365.20 Unspecified primary angle-closure glaucoma — (Use additional code to identify glaucoma stage: 365.70-365.74) ▼
365.21 Intermittent angle-closure glaucoma
365.22 Acute angle-closure glaucoma
365.23 Chronic angle-closure glaucoma — (Use additional code to identify glaucoma stage: 365.70-365.74)
365.24 Residual stage of angle-closure glaucoma
365.42 Glaucoma associated with anomalies of iris
365.43 Glaucoma associated with other anterior segment anomalies
365.44 Glaucoma associated with systemic syndromes — (Code first associated disease: 237.70-237.79, 759.6) ☒
365.70 Glaucoma stage, unspecified — (Code first associated type of glaucoma (365.10-365.13, 365.20, 365.23, 365.31, 365.52, 365.62-365.63, 365.65)) ▼
365.71 Mild stage glaucoma — (Code first associated type of glaucoma (365.10-365.13, 365.20, 365.23, 365.31, 365.52, 365.62-365.63, 365.65))
365.72 Moderate stage glaucoma — (Code first associated type of glaucoma (365.10-365.13, 365.20, 365.23, 365.31, 365.52, 365.62-365.63, 365.65))
365.73 Severe stage glaucoma — (Code first associated type of glaucoma (365.10-365.13, 365.20, 365.23, 365.31, 365.52, 365.62-365.63, 365.65))
365.74 Indeterminate stage glaucoma — (Code first associated type of glaucoma (365.10-365.13, 365.20, 365.23, 365.31, 365.52, 365.62-365.63, 365.65))
365.83 Aqueous misdirection
743.41 Congenital anomaly of corneal size and shape
743.45 Aniridia

ICD-9-CM Procedural

12.55 Cyclodialysis

HCPCS Level II Supplies & Services

A4305 Disposable drug delivery system, flow rate of 50 ml or greater per hour

66761

66761 Iridotomy/iridectomy by laser surgery (eg, for glaucoma) (per session)

ICD-9-CM Diagnostic

364.51 Essential or progressive iris atrophy
364.82 Plateau iris syndrome
365.02 Borderline glaucoma with anatomical narrow angle
365.20 Unspecified primary angle-closure glaucoma — (Use additional code to identify glaucoma stage: 365.70-365.74) ▼
365.21 Intermittent angle-closure glaucoma

365.22 Acute angle-closure glaucoma
365.23 Chronic angle-closure glaucoma — (Use additional code to identify glaucoma stage: 365.70-365.74)
365.24 Residual stage of angle-closure glaucoma
365.42 Glaucoma associated with anomalies of iris
365.43 Glaucoma associated with other anterior segment anomalies
365.70 Glaucoma stage, unspecified — (Code first associated type of glaucoma (365.10-365.13, 365.20, 365.23, 365.31, 365.52, 365.62-365.63, 365.65)) ▽
365.71 Mild stage glaucoma — (Code first associated type of glaucoma (365.10-365.13, 365.20, 365.23, 365.31, 365.52, 365.62-365.63, 365.65))
365.72 Moderate stage glaucoma — (Code first associated type of glaucoma (365.10-365.13, 365.20, 365.23, 365.31, 365.52, 365.62-365.63, 365.65))
365.73 Severe stage glaucoma — (Code first associated type of glaucoma (365.10-365.13, 365.20, 365.23, 365.31, 365.52, 365.62-365.63, 365.65))
365.74 Indeterminate stage glaucoma — (Code first associated type of glaucoma (365.10-365.13, 365.20, 365.23, 365.31, 365.52, 365.62-365.63, 365.65))
365.83 Aqueous misdirection
743.41 Congenital anomaly of corneal size and shape
743.45 Aniridia

ICD-9-CM Procedural

12.12 Other iridotomy
12.59 Other facilitation of intraocular circulation

HCPCS Level II Supplies & Services

A4305 Disposable drug delivery system, flow rate of 50 ml or greater per hour

66762

66762 Iridoplasty by photocoagulation (1 or more sessions) (eg, for improvement of vision, for widening of anterior chamber angle)

ICD-9-CM Diagnostic

364.75 Pupillary abnormalities
364.76 Iridodialysis
364.77 Recession of chamber angle of eye
364.82 Plateau iris syndrome
365.11 Primary open-angle glaucoma — (Use additional code to identify glaucoma stage: 365.70-365.74)
365.83 Aqueous misdirection
379.42 Miosis (persistent), not due to miotics
871.1 Ocular laceration with prolapse or exposure of intraocular tissue

ICD-9-CM Procedural

12.35 Coreoplasty
12.39 Other iridoplasty

HCPCS Level II Supplies & Services

A4305 Disposable drug delivery system, flow rate of 50 ml or greater per hour

66770

66770 Destruction of cyst or lesion iris or ciliary body (nonexcisional procedure)

ICD-9-CM Diagnostic

190.0 Malignant neoplasm of eyeball, except conjunctiva, cornea, retina, and choroid
198.4 Secondary malignant neoplasm of other parts of nervous system
224.0 Benign neoplasm of eyeball, except conjunctiva, cornea, retina, and choroid
234.0 Carcinoma in situ of eye
238.8 Neoplasm of uncertain behavior of other specified sites
239.89 Neoplasms of unspecified nature, other specified sites
364.55 Miotic cysts of pupillary margin
364.60 Idiopathic cysts of iris, ciliary body, and anterior chamber
364.61 Implantation cysts of iris, ciliary body, and anterior chamber
364.62 Exudative cysts of iris or anterior chamber
364.64 Exudative cyst of pars plana

ICD-9-CM Procedural

12.41 Destruction of lesion of iris, nonexcisional
12.43 Destruction of lesion of ciliary body, nonexcisional

HCPCS Level II Supplies & Services

A4305 Disposable drug delivery system, flow rate of 50 ml or greater per hour

66820

66820 Discission of secondary membranous cataract (opacified posterior lens capsule and/or anterior hyaloid); stab incision technique (Ziegler or Wheeler knife)

ICD-9-CM Diagnostic

366.50 Unspecified after-cataract ▽
366.51 Soemmering's ring
366.52 Other after-cataract, not obscuring vision
366.53 After-cataract, obscuring vision
996.53 Mechanical complication due to ocular lens prosthesis

ICD-9-CM Procedural

13.64 Discission of secondary membrane (after cataract)
13.66 Mechanical fragmentation of secondary membrane (after cataract)

HCPCS Level II Supplies & Services

A4305 Disposable drug delivery system, flow rate of 50 ml or greater per hour

66821

66821 Discission of secondary membranous cataract (opacified posterior lens capsule and/or anterior hyaloid); laser surgery (eg, YAG laser) (1 or more stages)

ICD-9-CM Diagnostic

366.50 Unspecified after-cataract ▽
366.51 Soemmering's ring
366.52 Other after-cataract, not obscuring vision
366.53 After-cataract, obscuring vision
996.53 Mechanical complication due to ocular lens prosthesis

ICD-9-CM Procedural

13.64 Discission of secondary membrane (after cataract)

HCPCS Level II Supplies & Services

A4305 Disposable drug delivery system, flow rate of 50 ml or greater per hour

66825

66825 Repositioning of intraocular lens prosthesis, requiring an incision (separate procedure)

ICD-9-CM Diagnostic

996.53 Mechanical complication due to ocular lens prosthesis
V43.1 Lens replaced by other means
V45.61 Cataract extraction status — (Use additional code for associated artificial lens status: V43.1)
V45.69 Other states following surgery of eye and adnexa

ICD-9-CM Procedural

13.90 Operation on lens, not elsewhere classified

66830

66830 Removal of secondary membranous cataract (opacified posterior lens capsule and/or anterior hyaloid) with corneo-scleral section, with or without iridectomy (iridocapsulotomy, iridocapsulectomy)

ICD-9-CM Diagnostic

366.50 Unspecified after-cataract ▽
366.51 Soemmering's ring

366.52 Other after-cataract, not obscuring vision
366.53 After-cataract, obscuring vision

ICD-9-CM Procedural

13.65 Excision of secondary membrane (after cataract)

HCPCS Level II Supplies & Services

A4305 Disposable drug delivery system, flow rate of 50 ml or greater per hour

66840

66840 Removal of lens material; aspiration technique, 1 or more stages

ICD-9-CM Diagnostic

366.00 Unspecified nonsenile cataract ▽
366.20 Unspecified traumatic cataract ▽
366.46 Cataract associated with radiation and other physical influences — (Use additional E code to identify cause)

ICD-9-CM Procedural

13.3 Extracapsular extraction of lens by simple aspiration (and irrigation) technique
13.41 Phacoemulsification and aspiration of cataract

HCPCS Level II Supplies & Services

A4305 Disposable drug delivery system, flow rate of 50 ml or greater per hour

66850

66850 Removal of lens material; phacofragmentation technique (mechanical or ultrasonic) (eg, phacoemulsification), with aspiration

ICD-9-CM Diagnostic

366.00 Unspecified nonsenile cataract ▽
366.04 Nuclear cataract, nonsenile
366.10 Unspecified senile cataract ▽
366.12 Incipient cataract
366.13 Anterior subcapsular polar senile cataract
366.19 Other and combined forms of senile cataract
366.21 Localized traumatic opacities of cataract
366.22 Total traumatic cataract
366.46 Cataract associated with radiation and other physical influences — (Use additional E code to identify cause)
366.8 Other cataract

ICD-9-CM Procedural

13.41 Phacoemulsification and aspiration of cataract
13.43 Mechanical phacofragmentation and other aspiration of cataract

HCPCS Level II Supplies & Services

A4305 Disposable drug delivery system, flow rate of 50 ml or greater per hour

66852

66852 Removal of lens material; pars plana approach, with or without vitrectomy

ICD-9-CM Diagnostic

366.00 Unspecified nonsenile cataract ▽
366.04 Nuclear cataract, nonsenile
366.10 Unspecified senile cataract ▽
366.12 Incipient cataract
366.13 Anterior subcapsular polar senile cataract
366.14 Posterior subcapsular polar senile cataract
366.15 Cortical senile cataract
366.16 Nuclear sclerosis
366.17 Total or mature senile cataract
366.18 Hypermature senile cataract
366.19 Other and combined forms of senile cataract
366.20 Unspecified traumatic cataract ▽
366.21 Localized traumatic opacities of cataract
366.22 Total traumatic cataract
366.46 Cataract associated with radiation and other physical influences — (Use additional E code to identify cause)
366.8 Other cataract

ICD-9-CM Procedural

13.42 Mechanical phacofragmentation and aspiration of cataract by posterior route
14.74 Other mechanical vitrectomy

66920

66920 Removal of lens material; intracapsular

ICD-9-CM Diagnostic

366.00 Unspecified nonsenile cataract ▽
366.04 Nuclear cataract, nonsenile
366.10 Unspecified senile cataract ▽
366.11 Pseudoexfoliation of lens capsule
366.12 Incipient cataract
366.13 Anterior subcapsular polar senile cataract
366.14 Posterior subcapsular polar senile cataract
366.15 Cortical senile cataract
366.16 Nuclear sclerosis
366.17 Total or mature senile cataract
366.18 Hypermature senile cataract
366.19 Other and combined forms of senile cataract
366.20 Unspecified traumatic cataract ▽
366.21 Localized traumatic opacities of cataract
366.22 Total traumatic cataract
366.46 Cataract associated with radiation and other physical influences — (Use additional E code to identify cause)
366.8 Other cataract
379.32 Subluxation of lens
379.33 Anterior dislocation of lens
379.34 Posterior dislocation of lens
379.39 Other disorders of lens

ICD-9-CM Procedural

13.11 Intracapsular extraction of lens by temporal inferior route
13.19 Other intracapsular extraction of lens

66930

66930 Removal of lens material; intracapsular, for dislocated lens

ICD-9-CM Diagnostic

379.32 Subluxation of lens
379.33 Anterior dislocation of lens
379.34 Posterior dislocation of lens
743.37 Congenital ectopic lens
921.3 Contusion of eyeball

ICD-9-CM Procedural

13.11 Intracapsular extraction of lens by temporal inferior route
13.19 Other intracapsular extraction of lens

66940

66940 Removal of lens material; extracapsular (other than 66840, 66850, 66852)

ICD-9-CM Diagnostic

366.00 Unspecified nonsenile cataract ▽
366.04 Nuclear cataract, nonsenile

366.10 Unspecified senile cataract ▽
366.12 Incipient cataract
366.13 Anterior subcapsular polar senile cataract
366.14 Posterior subcapsular polar senile cataract
366.15 Cortical senile cataract
366.16 Nuclear sclerosis
366.17 Total or mature senile cataract
366.18 Hypermature senile cataract
366.19 Other and combined forms of senile cataract
366.20 Unspecified traumatic cataract ▽
366.21 Localized traumatic opacities of cataract
366.22 Total traumatic cataract
366.46 Cataract associated with radiation and other physical influences — (Use additional E code to identify cause)
366.8 Other cataract

ICD-9-CM Procedural

13.2 Extracapsular extraction of lens by linear extraction technique
13.51 Extracapsular extraction of lens by temporal inferior route
13.59 Other extracapsular extraction of lens

66982

66982 Extracapsular cataract removal with insertion of intraocular lens prosthesis (1-stage procedure), manual or mechanical technique (eg, irrigation and aspiration or phacoemulsification), complex, requiring devices or techniques not generally used in routine cataract surgery (eg, iris expansion device, suture support for intraocular lens, or primary posterior capsulorrhexis) or performed on patients in the amblyogenic developmental stage

ICD-9-CM Diagnostic

364.81 Floppy iris syndrome
366.00 Unspecified nonsenile cataract ▽
366.04 Nuclear cataract, nonsenile
366.10 Unspecified senile cataract ▽
366.12 Incipient cataract
366.13 Anterior subcapsular polar senile cataract
366.14 Posterior subcapsular polar senile cataract
366.15 Cortical senile cataract
366.16 Nuclear sclerosis
366.17 Total or mature senile cataract
366.18 Hypermature senile cataract
366.19 Other and combined forms of senile cataract
366.20 Unspecified traumatic cataract ▽
366.21 Localized traumatic opacities of cataract
366.22 Total traumatic cataract
366.46 Cataract associated with radiation and other physical influences — (Use additional E code to identify cause)
366.8 Other cataract
743.30 Unspecified congenital cataract ▽
743.31 Congenital capsular and subcapsular cataract
743.32 Congenital cortical and zonular cataract
743.33 Congenital nuclear cataract

ICD-9-CM Procedural

13.3 Extracapsular extraction of lens by simple aspiration (and irrigation) technique
13.41 Phacoemulsification and aspiration of cataract
13.43 Mechanical phacofragmentation and other aspiration of cataract
13.71 Insertion of intraocular lens prosthesis at time of cataract extraction, one-stage

66983

66983 Intracapsular cataract extraction with insertion of intraocular lens prosthesis (1 stage procedure)

ICD-9-CM Diagnostic

366.00 Unspecified nonsenile cataract ▽
366.04 Nuclear cataract, nonsenile
366.10 Unspecified senile cataract ▽
366.12 Incipient cataract
366.13 Anterior subcapsular polar senile cataract
366.14 Posterior subcapsular polar senile cataract
366.15 Cortical senile cataract
366.16 Nuclear sclerosis
366.17 Total or mature senile cataract
366.18 Hypermature senile cataract
366.19 Other and combined forms of senile cataract
366.20 Unspecified traumatic cataract ▽
366.21 Localized traumatic opacities of cataract
366.22 Total traumatic cataract
366.46 Cataract associated with radiation and other physical influences — (Use additional E code to identify cause)
366.8 Other cataract

ICD-9-CM Procedural

13.11 Intracapsular extraction of lens by temporal inferior route
13.19 Other intracapsular extraction of lens
13.71 Insertion of intraocular lens prosthesis at time of cataract extraction, one-stage

66984

66984 Extracapsular cataract removal with insertion of intraocular lens prosthesis (1 stage procedure), manual or mechanical technique (eg, irrigation and aspiration or phacoemulsification)

ICD-9-CM Diagnostic

366.00 Unspecified nonsenile cataract ▽
366.04 Nuclear cataract, nonsenile
366.10 Unspecified senile cataract ▽
366.12 Incipient cataract
366.13 Anterior subcapsular polar senile cataract
366.14 Posterior subcapsular polar senile cataract
366.15 Cortical senile cataract
366.16 Nuclear sclerosis
366.17 Total or mature senile cataract
366.18 Hypermature senile cataract
366.19 Other and combined forms of senile cataract
366.20 Unspecified traumatic cataract ▽
366.21 Localized traumatic opacities of cataract
366.22 Total traumatic cataract
366.46 Cataract associated with radiation and other physical influences — (Use additional E code to identify cause)
366.8 Other cataract
743.30 Unspecified congenital cataract ▽
743.31 Congenital capsular and subcapsular cataract
743.32 Congenital cortical and zonular cataract
743.33 Congenital nuclear cataract

ICD-9-CM Procedural

13.3 Extracapsular extraction of lens by simple aspiration (and irrigation) technique
13.41 Phacoemulsification and aspiration of cataract
13.43 Mechanical phacofragmentation and other aspiration of cataract
13.71 Insertion of intraocular lens prosthesis at time of cataract extraction, one-stage

HCPCS Level II Supplies & Services

V2630 Anterior chamber intraocular lens

66985

66985 Insertion of intraocular lens prosthesis (secondary implant), not associated with concurrent cataract removal

ICD-9-CM Diagnostic

379.31 Aphakia
743.35 Congenital aphakia
V43.1 Lens replaced by other means
V45.61 Cataract extraction status — (Use additional code for associated artificial lens status: V43.1)
V45.69 Other states following surgery of eye and adnexa

ICD-9-CM Procedural

13.70 Insertion of pseudophakos, not otherwise specified
13.72 Secondary insertion of intraocular lens prosthesis

66986

66986 Exchange of intraocular lens

ICD-9-CM Diagnostic

364.10 Unspecified chronic iridocyclitis
379.32 Subluxation of lens
379.33 Anterior dislocation of lens
379.34 Posterior dislocation of lens
996.53 Mechanical complication due to ocular lens prosthesis
V43.1 Lens replaced by other means
V45.61 Cataract extraction status — (Use additional code for associated artificial lens status: V43.1)
V45.69 Other states following surgery of eye and adnexa

ICD-9-CM Procedural

13.70 Insertion of pseudophakos, not otherwise specified
13.8 Removal of implanted lens

66990

66990 Use of ophthalmic endoscope (List separately in addition to code for primary procedure)

ICD-9-CM Diagnostic

This is an add-on code. Refer to the corresponding primary procedure code for ICD-9-CM diagnosis code links.

ICD-9-CM Procedural

16.21 Ophthalmoscopy
16.29 Other diagnostic procedures on orbit and eyeball

Posterior Segment

67005-67010

67005 Removal of vitreous, anterior approach (open sky technique or limbal incision); partial removal
67010 subtotal removal with mechanical vitrectomy

ICD-9-CM Diagnostic

360.19 Other endophthalmitis
379.21 Vitreous degeneration
379.22 Crystalline deposits in vitreous
379.23 Vitreous hemorrhage
379.25 Vitreous membranes and strands
379.26 Vitreous prolapse
379.29 Other disorders of vitreous
379.62 Inflammation (infection) of postprocedural bleb, stage 2
379.63 Inflammation (infection) of postprocedural bleb, stage 3
729.91 Post-traumatic seroma
871.1 Ocular laceration with prolapse or exposure of intraocular tissue
997.99 Other complications affecting other specified body systems, NEC — (Use additional code to identify complications)
998.30 Disruption of wound, unspecified
998.31 Disruption of internal operation (surgical) wound
998.33 Disruption of traumatic injury wound repair
998.9 Unspecified complication of procedure, not elsewhere classified

ICD-9-CM Procedural

14.71 Removal of vitreous, anterior approach
14.73 Mechanical vitrectomy by anterior approach
14.74 Other mechanical vitrectomy

HCPCS Level II Supplies & Services

A4305 Disposable drug delivery system, flow rate of 50 ml or greater per hour

67015

67015 Aspiration or release of vitreous, subretinal or choroidal fluid, pars plana approach (posterior sclerotomy)

ICD-9-CM Diagnostic

360.01 Acute endophthalmitis
360.02 Panophthalmitis
360.03 Chronic endophthalmitis
360.04 Vitreous abscess
362.40 Unspecified retinal layer separation
363.61 Unspecified choroidal hemorrhage
363.62 Expulsive choroidal hemorrhage
363.63 Choroidal rupture
363.70 Unspecified choroidal detachment
363.71 Serous choroidal detachment
363.72 Hemorrhagic choroidal detachment
379.62 Inflammation (infection) of postprocedural bleb, stage 2
379.63 Inflammation (infection) of postprocedural bleb, stage 3

ICD-9-CM Procedural

14.11 Diagnostic aspiration of vitreous
14.19 Other diagnostic procedures on retina, choroid, vitreous, and posterior chamber
14.71 Removal of vitreous, anterior approach
14.72 Other removal of vitreous

HCPCS Level II Supplies & Services

A4305 Disposable drug delivery system, flow rate of 50 ml or greater per hour

67025-67028

67025 Injection of vitreous substitute, pars plana or limbal approach (fluid-gas exchange), with or without aspiration (separate procedure)
67027 Implantation of intravitreal drug delivery system (eg, ganciclovir implant), includes concomitant removal of vitreous
67028 Intravitreal injection of a pharmacologic agent (separate procedure)

ICD-9-CM Diagnostic

042 Human immunodeficiency virus [HIV] — (Use additional code(s) to identify all manifestations of HIV. Use additional code to identify HIV-2 infection: 079.53)
078.5 Cytomegaloviral disease — (Use additional code to identify manifestation: 484.1, 573.1)
153.0 Malignant neoplasm of hepatic flexure
153.1 Malignant neoplasm of transverse colon
153.2 Malignant neoplasm of descending colon

153.3 Malignant neoplasm of sigmoid colon
153.4 Malignant neoplasm of cecum
153.5 Malignant neoplasm of appendix
153.6 Malignant neoplasm of ascending colon
153.7 Malignant neoplasm of splenic flexure
153.8 Malignant neoplasm of other specified sites of large intestine
153.9 Malignant neoplasm of colon, unspecified site ▽
154.0 Malignant neoplasm of rectosigmoid junction
154.1 Malignant neoplasm of rectum
154.8 Malignant neoplasm of other sites of rectum, rectosigmoid junction, and anus
360.00 Unspecified purulent endophthalmitis ▽
360.01 Acute endophthalmitis
360.02 Panophthalmitis
360.03 Chronic endophthalmitis
360.04 Vitreous abscess
361.00 Retinal detachment with retinal defect, unspecified ▽
361.01 Recent retinal detachment, partial, with single defect
361.02 Recent retinal detachment, partial, with multiple defects
361.03 Recent retinal detachment, partial, with giant tear
361.04 Recent retinal detachment, partial, with retinal dialysis
361.05 Recent retinal detachment, total or subtotal
361.06 Old retinal detachment, partial
361.07 Old retinal detachment, total or subtotal
361.81 Traction detachment of retina
362.02 Proliferative diabetic retinopathy — (Code first diabetes, 249.5, 250.5) ☒
362.35 Central vein occlusion of retina
362.36 Venous tributary (branch) occlusion of retina
362.42 Serous detachment of retinal pigment epithelium
362.50 Macular degeneration (senile) of retina, unspecified ▽
362.51 Nonexudative senile macular degeneration of retina
362.52 Exudative senile macular degeneration of retina
362.53 Cystoid macular degeneration of retina
362.54 Macular cyst, hole, or pseudohole of retina
362.55 Toxic maculopathy of retina — (Use additional E code to identify drug, if drug induced)
362.56 Macular puckering of retina
362.57 Drusen (degenerative) of retina
362.83 Retinal edema
363.00 Unspecified focal chorioretinitis ▽
363.01 Focal choroiditis and chorioretinitis, juxtapapillary
363.03 Focal choroiditis and chorioretinitis of other posterior pole
363.04 Focal choroiditis and chorioretinitis, peripheral
363.05 Focal retinitis and retinochoroiditis, juxtapapillary
363.06 Focal retinitis and retinochoroiditis, macular or paramacular
363.07 Focal retinitis and retinochoroiditis of other posterior pole
363.08 Focal retinitis and retinochoroiditis, peripheral
363.10 Unspecified disseminated chorioretinitis ▽
363.11 Disseminated choroiditis and chorioretinitis, posterior pole
363.12 Disseminated choroiditis and chorioretinitis, peripheral
363.13 Disseminated choroiditis and chorioretinitis, generalized — (Code first any underlying disease: 017.3)
363.14 Disseminated retinitis and retinochoroiditis, metastatic
363.20 Unspecified chorioretinitis ▽
364.42 Rubeosis iridis
365.63 Glaucoma associated with vascular disorders of eye — (Use additional code to identify glaucoma stage: 365.70-365.74)
369.8 Unqualified visual loss, one eye
379.27 Vitreomacular adhesion

ICD-9-CM Procedural

14.75 Injection of vitreous substitute
14.79 Other operations on vitreous
14.9 Other operations on retina, choroid, and posterior chamber

HCPCS Level II Supplies & Services

A4305 Disposable drug delivery system, flow rate of 50 ml or greater per hour
J7312 Injection, dexamethasone, intravitreal implant, 0.1 mg

67030-67031

67030 Discission of vitreous strands (without removal), pars plana approach
67031 Severing of vitreous strands, vitreous face adhesions, sheets, membranes or opacities, laser surgery (1 or more stages)

ICD-9-CM Diagnostic

379.24 Other vitreous opacities
379.25 Vitreous membranes and strands
379.27 Vitreomacular adhesion
379.29 Other disorders of vitreous

ICD-9-CM Procedural

14.74 Other mechanical vitrectomy
14.79 Other operations on vitreous

HCPCS Level II Supplies & Services

A4305 Disposable drug delivery system, flow rate of 50 ml or greater per hour

67036

67036 Vitrectomy, mechanical, pars plana approach;

ICD-9-CM Diagnostic

249.50 Secondary diabetes mellitus with ophthalmic manifestations, not stated as uncontrolled, or unspecified — (Use additional code to identify manifestation: 362.01-362.07, 365.44, 366.41, 369.00-369.9) (Use additional code to identify any associated insulin use: V58.67)
249.51 Secondary diabetes mellitus with ophthalmic manifestations, uncontrolled — (Use additional code to identify manifestation: 362.01-362.07, 365.44, 366.41, 369.00-369.9) (Use additional code to identify any associated insulin use: V58.67)
250.52 Diabetes with ophthalmic manifestations, type II or unspecified type, uncontrolled — (Use additional code to identify manifestation: 362.01-362.07, 365.44, 366.41, 369.00-369.9)
250.53 Diabetes with ophthalmic manifestations, type I [juvenile type], uncontrolled — (Use additional code to identify manifestation: 362.01-362.07, 365.44, 366.41, 369.00-369.9)
360.00 Unspecified purulent endophthalmitis ▽
360.01 Acute endophthalmitis
360.02 Panophthalmitis
360.03 Chronic endophthalmitis
360.04 Vitreous abscess
360.13 Parasitic endophthalmitis NOS ▽
360.19 Other endophthalmitis
361.30 Unspecified retinal defect ▽
361.33 Multiple defects of retina without detachment
362.01 Background diabetic retinopathy — (Code first diabetes, 249.5, 250.5) ☒
362.02 Proliferative diabetic retinopathy — (Code first diabetes, 249.5, 250.5) ☒
362.03 Nonproliferative diabetic retinopathy NOS — (Code first diabetes, 249.5, 250.5) ▽ ☒
362.04 Mild nonproliferative diabetic retinopathy — (Code first diabetes, 249.5, 250.5) ☒
362.05 Moderate nonproliferative diabetic retinopathy — (Code first diabetes, 249.5, 250.5) ☒
362.06 Severe nonproliferative diabetic retinopathy — (Code first diabetes, 249.5, 250.5) ☒

362.07 Diabetic macular edema — (Code first diabetes, 249.5, 250.5 Code 362.07 must be used with a code for diabetic retinopathy: 362.01-362.06) ☒

362.20 Retinopathy of prematurity, unspecified ▽

362.22 Retinopathy of prematurity, stage 0

362.23 Retinopathy of prematurity, stage 1

362.24 Retinopathy of prematurity, stage 2

362.25 Retinopathy of prematurity, stage 3

362.26 Retinopathy of prematurity, stage 4

362.27 Retinopathy of prematurity, stage 5

362.54 Macular cyst, hole, or pseudohole of retina

362.56 Macular puckering of retina

362.83 Retinal edema

363.32 Other macular chorioretinal scars

365.44 Glaucoma associated with systemic syndromes — (Code first associated disease: 237.70-237.79, 759.6) ☒

365.83 Aqueous misdirection

366.41 Diabetic cataract — (Code first diabetes: 249.5, 250.5) ☒

369.00 Blindness of both eyes, impairment level not further specified ▽

369.01 Better eye: total vision impairment; lesser eye: total vision impairment

369.02 Better eye: near-total vision impairment; lesser eye: not further specified ▽

369.03 Better eye: near-total vision impairment; lesser eye: total vision impairment

369.04 Better eye: near-total vision impairment; lesser eye: near-total vision impairment

369.05 Better eye: profound vision impairment; lesser eye: not further specified ▽

369.06 Better eye: profound vision impairment; lesser eye: total vision impairment

369.07 Better eye: profound vision impairment; lesser eye: near-total vision impairment

369.08 Better eye: profound vision impairment; lesser eye: profound vision impairment

369.10 Profound, moderate or severe vision impairment, not further specified ▽

369.11 Better eye: severe vision impairment; lesser eye: blind, not further specified ▽

369.12 Better eye: severe vision impairment; lesser eye: total vision impairment

369.13 Better eye: severe vision impairment; lesser eye: near-total vision impairment

369.14 Better eye: severe vision impairment; lesser eye: profound vision impairment

369.15 Better eye: moderate vision impairment; lesser eye: blind, not further specified ▽

369.16 Better eye: moderate vision impairment; lesser eye: total vision impairment

369.17 Better eye: moderate vision impairment; lesser eye: near-total vision impairment

369.18 Better eye: moderate vision impairment; lesser eye: profound vision impairment

369.20 Vision impairment, both eyes, impairment level not further specified ▽

369.21 Better eye: severe vision impairment; lesser eye; impairment not further specified ▽

369.22 Better eye: severe vision impairment; lesser eye: severe vision impairment

369.23 Better eye: moderate vision impairment; lesser eye: impairment not further specified ▽

369.24 Better eye: moderate vision impairment; lesser eye: severe vision impairment

369.25 Better eye: moderate vision impairment; lesser eye: moderate vision impairment

369.3 Unqualified visual loss, both eyes

369.4 Legal blindness, as defined in USA

369.60 Impairment level not further specified ▽

369.61 One eye: total vision impairment; other eye: not specified ▽

369.62 One eye: total vision impairment; other eye: near-normal vision

369.64 One eye: near-total vision impairment; other eye: vision not specified ▽

369.65 One eye: near-total vision impairment; other eye: near-normal vision

369.66 One eye: near-total vision impairment; other eye: normal vision

369.67 One eye: profound vision impairment; other eye: vision not specified ▽

369.68 One eye: profound vision impairment; other eye: near-normal vision

369.69 One eye: profound vision impairment; other eye: normal vision

369.70 Low vision, one eye, not otherwise specified ▽

369.71 One eye: severe vision impairment; other eye: vision not specified ▽

369.72 One eye: severe vision impairment; other eye: near-normal vision

369.73 One eye: severe vision impairment; other eye: normal vision

369.74 One eye: moderate vision impairment; other eye: vision not specified ▽

369.75 One eye: moderate vision impairment; other eye: near-normal vision

369.76 One eye: moderate vision impairment; other eye: normal vision

369.8 Unqualified visual loss, one eye

369.9 Unspecified visual loss ▽

379.22 Crystalline deposits in vitreous

379.23 Vitreous hemorrhage

379.24 Other vitreous opacities

379.25 Vitreous membranes and strands

379.26 Vitreous prolapse

743.51 Vitreous anomaly, congenital

997.99 Other complications affecting other specified body systems, NEC — (Use additional code to identify complications)

ICD-9-CM Procedural

14.74 Other mechanical vitrectomy

14.9 Other operations on retina, choroid, and posterior chamber

HCPCS Level II Supplies & Services

A4305 Disposable drug delivery system, flow rate of 50 ml or greater per hour

67039-67040

67039 Vitrectomy, mechanical, pars plana approach; with focal endolaser photocoagulation

67040 with endolaser panretinal photocoagulation

ICD-9-CM Diagnostic

249.50 Secondary diabetes mellitus with ophthalmic manifestations, not stated as uncontrolled, or unspecified — (Use additional code to identify manifestation: 362.01-362.07, 365.44, 366.41, 369.00-369.9) (Use additional code to identify any associated insulin use: V58.67)

249.51 Secondary diabetes mellitus with ophthalmic manifestations, uncontrolled — (Use additional code to identify manifestation: 362.01-362.07, 365.44, 366.41, 369.00-369.9) (Use additional code to identify any associated insulin use: V58.67)

250.50 Diabetes with ophthalmic manifestations, type II or unspecified type, not stated as uncontrolled — (Use additional code to identify manifestation: 362.01-362.07, 365.44, 366.41, 369.00-369.9)

250.51 Diabetes with ophthalmic manifestations, type I [juvenile type], not stated as uncontrolled — (Use additional code to identify manifestation: 362.01-362.07, 365.44, 366.41, 369.00-369.9)

250.52 Diabetes with ophthalmic manifestations, type II or unspecified type, uncontrolled — (Use additional code to identify manifestation: 362.01-362.07, 365.44, 366.41, 369.00-369.9)

250.53 Diabetes with ophthalmic manifestations, type I [juvenile type], uncontrolled — (Use additional code to identify manifestation: 362.01-362.07, 365.44, 366.41, 369.00-369.9)

361.30 Unspecified retinal defect ▽

361.33 Multiple defects of retina without detachment

361.81 Traction detachment of retina

362.01 Background diabetic retinopathy — (Code first diabetes, 249.5, 250.5) ☒

362.02 Proliferative diabetic retinopathy — (Code first diabetes, 249.5, 250.5) ☒

362.03 Nonproliferative diabetic retinopathy NOS — (Code first diabetes, 249.5, 250.5) ▽ ☒

362.04 Mild nonproliferative diabetic retinopathy — (Code first diabetes, 249.5, 250.5) ☒

362.05 Moderate nonproliferative diabetic retinopathy — (Code first diabetes, 249.5, 250.5) ☒

362.06 Severe nonproliferative diabetic retinopathy — (Code first diabetes, 249.5, 250.5) ☒

362.07 Diabetic macular edema — (Code first diabetes, 249.5, 250.5 Code 362.07 must be used with a code for diabetic retinopathy: 362.01-362.06) ☒

362.14 Retinal microaneurysms NOS ▽

362.20 Retinopathy of prematurity, unspecified ▽

362.22 Retinopathy of prematurity, stage 0

362.23 Retinopathy of prematurity, stage 1

362.24 Retinopathy of prematurity, stage 2

362.25 Retinopathy of prematurity, stage 3

362.26 Retinopathy of prematurity, stage 4
362.27 Retinopathy of prematurity, stage 5
362.54 Macular cyst, hole, or pseudohole of retina
362.56 Macular puckering of retina
362.83 Retinal edema
363.32 Other macular chorioretinal scars
365.44 Glaucoma associated with systemic syndromes — (Code first associated disease: 237.70-237.79, 759.6) ☒
365.83 Aqueous misdirection
366.41 Diabetic cataract — (Code first diabetes: 249.5, 250.5) ☒
369.00 Blindness of both eyes, impairment level not further specified ▽
369.01 Better eye: total vision impairment; lesser eye: total vision impairment
369.02 Better eye: near-total vision impairment; lesser eye: not further specified ▽
369.03 Better eye: near-total vision impairment; lesser eye: total vision impairment
369.04 Better eye: near-total vision impairment; lesser eye: near-total vision impairment
369.05 Better eye: profound vision impairment; lesser eye: not further specified ▽
369.06 Better eye: profound vision impairment; lesser eye: total vision impairment
369.07 Better eye: profound vision impairment; lesser eye: near-total vision impairment
369.08 Better eye: profound vision impairment; lesser eye: profound vision impairment
369.10 Profound, moderate or severe vision impairment, not further specified ▽
369.11 Better eye: severe vision impairment; lesser eye: blind, not further specified ▽
369.12 Better eye: severe vision impairment; lesser eye: total vision impairment
369.13 Better eye: severe vision impairment; lesser eye: near-total vision impairment
369.14 Better eye: severe vision impairment; lesser eye: profound vision impairment
369.15 Better eye: moderate vision impairment; lesser eye: blind, not further specified ▽
369.16 Better eye: moderate vision impairment; lesser eye: total vision impairment
369.17 Better eye: moderate vision impairment; lesser eye: near-total vision impairment
369.18 Better eye: moderate vision impairment; lesser eye: profound vision impairment
369.20 Vision impairment, both eyes, impairment level not further specified ▽
369.21 Better eye: severe vision impairment; lesser eye; impairment not further specified ▽
369.22 Better eye: severe vision impairment; lesser eye: severe vision impairment
369.23 Better eye: moderate vision impairment; lesser eye: impairment not further specified ▽
369.24 Better eye: moderate vision impairment; lesser eye: severe vision impairment
369.25 Better eye: moderate vision impairment; lesser eye: moderate vision impairment
369.3 Unqualified visual loss, both eyes
369.4 Legal blindness, as defined in USA
369.60 Impairment level not further specified ▽
369.61 One eye: total vision impairment; other eye: not specified ▽
369.62 One eye: total vision impairment; other eye: near-normal vision
369.64 One eye: near-total vision impairment; other eye: vision not specified ▽
369.65 One eye: near-total vision impairment; other eye: near-normal vision
369.66 One eye: near-total vision impairment; other eye: normal vision
369.67 One eye: profound vision impairment; other eye: vision not specified ▽
369.68 One eye: profound vision impairment; other eye: near-normal vision
369.69 One eye: profound vision impairment; other eye: normal vision
369.70 Low vision, one eye, not otherwise specified ▽
369.71 One eye: severe vision impairment; other eye: vision not specified ▽
369.72 One eye: severe vision impairment; other eye: near-normal vision
369.73 One eye: severe vision impairment; other eye: normal vision
369.74 One eye: moderate vision impairment; other eye: vision not specified ▽
369.75 One eye: moderate vision impairment; other eye: near-normal vision
369.76 One eye: moderate vision impairment; other eye: normal vision
369.8 Unqualified visual loss, one eye
379.24 Other vitreous opacities

ICD-9-CM Procedural

14.33 Repair of retinal tear by xenon arc photocoagulation
14.34 Repair of retinal tear by laser photocoagulation
14.53 Repair of retinal detachment with xenon arc photocoagulation
14.54 Repair of retinal detachment with laser photocoagulation

HCPCS Level II Supplies & Services

A4305 Disposable drug delivery system, flow rate of 50 ml or greater per hour

67041-67043

67041 Vitrectomy, mechanical, pars plana approach; with removal of preretinal cellular membrane (eg, macular pucker)
67042 with removal of internal limiting membrane of retina (eg, for repair of macular hole, diabetic macular edema), includes, if performed, intraocular tamponade (ie, air, gas or silicone oil)
67043 with removal of subretinal membrane (eg, choroidal neovascularization), includes, if performed, intraocular tamponade (ie, air, gas or silicone oil) and laser photocoagulation

ICD-9-CM Diagnostic

249.50 Secondary diabetes mellitus with ophthalmic manifestations, not stated as uncontrolled, or unspecified — (Use additional code to identify manifestation: 362.01-362.07, 365.44, 366.41, 369.00-369.9) (Use additional code to identify any associated insulin use: V58.67)
249.51 Secondary diabetes mellitus with ophthalmic manifestations, uncontrolled — (Use additional code to identify manifestation: 362.01-362.07, 365.44, 366.41, 369.00-369.9) (Use additional code to identify any associated insulin use: V58.67)
250.50 Diabetes with ophthalmic manifestations, type II or unspecified type, not stated as uncontrolled — (Use additional code to identify manifestation: 362.01-362.07, 365.44, 366.41, 369.00-369.9)
250.51 Diabetes with ophthalmic manifestations, type I [juvenile type], not stated as uncontrolled — (Use additional code to identify manifestation: 362.01-362.07, 365.44, 366.41, 369.00-369.9)
250.52 Diabetes with ophthalmic manifestations, type II or unspecified type, uncontrolled — (Use additional code to identify manifestation: 362.01-362.07, 365.44, 366.41, 369.00-369.9)
250.53 Diabetes with ophthalmic manifestations, type I [juvenile type], uncontrolled — (Use additional code to identify manifestation: 362.01-362.07, 365.44, 366.41, 369.00-369.9)
360.00 Unspecified purulent endophthalmitis ▽
360.01 Acute endophthalmitis
360.02 Panophthalmitis
360.03 Chronic endophthalmitis
360.04 Vitreous abscess
360.13 Parasitic endophthalmitis NOS ▽
360.19 Other endophthalmitis
361.30 Unspecified retinal defect ▽
361.33 Multiple defects of retina without detachment
362.01 Background diabetic retinopathy — (Code first diabetes, 249.5, 250.5) ☒
362.02 Proliferative diabetic retinopathy — (Code first diabetes, 249.5, 250.5) ☒
362.03 Nonproliferative diabetic retinopathy NOS — (Code first diabetes, 249.5, 250.5) ▽ ☒
362.04 Mild nonproliferative diabetic retinopathy — (Code first diabetes, 249.5, 250.5) ☒
362.05 Moderate nonproliferative diabetic retinopathy — (Code first diabetes, 249.5, 250.5) ☒
362.06 Severe nonproliferative diabetic retinopathy — (Code first diabetes, 249.5, 250.5) ☒
362.07 Diabetic macular edema — (Code first diabetes, 249.5, 250.5 Code 362.07 must be used with a code for diabetic retinopathy: 362.01-362.06) ☒
362.20 Retinopathy of prematurity, unspecified ▽
362.22 Retinopathy of prematurity, stage 0
362.23 Retinopathy of prematurity, stage 1
362.24 Retinopathy of prematurity, stage 2
362.25 Retinopathy of prematurity, stage 3
362.26 Retinopathy of prematurity, stage 4
362.27 Retinopathy of prematurity, stage 5
362.54 Macular cyst, hole, or pseudohole of retina

362.56 Macular puckering of retina
362.83 Retinal edema
363.32 Other macular chorioretinal scars
365.44 Glaucoma associated with systemic syndromes — (Code first associated disease: 237.70-237.79, 759.6) ☒
365.83 Aqueous misdirection
366.41 Diabetic cataract — (Code first diabetes: 249.5, 250.5) ☒
369.00 Blindness of both eyes, impairment level not further specified ▽
369.01 Better eye: total vision impairment; lesser eye: total vision impairment
369.02 Better eye: near-total vision impairment; lesser eye: not further specified ▽
369.03 Better eye: near-total vision impairment; lesser eye: total vision impairment
369.04 Better eye: near-total vision impairment; lesser eye: near-total vision impairment
369.05 Better eye: profound vision impairment; lesser eye: not further specified ▽
369.06 Better eye: profound vision impairment; lesser eye: total vision impairment
369.07 Better eye: profound vision impairment; lesser eye: near-total vision impairment
369.08 Better eye: profound vision impairment; lesser eye: profound vision impairment
369.10 Profound, moderate or severe vision impairment, not further specified ▽
369.11 Better eye: severe vision impairment; lesser eye: blind, not further specified ▽
369.12 Better eye: severe vision impairment; lesser eye: total vision impairment
369.13 Better eye: severe vision impairment; lesser eye: near-total vision impairment
369.14 Better eye: severe vision impairment; lesser eye: profound vision impairment
369.15 Better eye: moderate vision impairment; lesser eye: blind, not further specified ▽
369.16 Better eye: moderate vision impairment; lesser eye: total vision impairment
369.17 Better eye: moderate vision impairment; lesser eye: near-total vision impairment
369.18 Better eye: moderate vision impairment; lesser eye: profound vision impairment
369.20 Vision impairment, both eyes, impairment level not further specified ▽
369.21 Better eye: severe vision impairment; lesser eye; impairment not further specified ▽
369.22 Better eye: severe vision impairment; lesser eye: severe vision impairment
369.23 Better eye: moderate vision impairment; lesser eye: impairment not further specified ▽
369.24 Better eye: moderate vision impairment; lesser eye: severe vision impairment
369.25 Better eye: moderate vision impairment; lesser eye: moderate vision impairment
369.3 Unqualified visual loss, both eyes
369.4 Legal blindness, as defined in USA
369.60 Impairment level not further specified ▽
369.61 One eye: total vision impairment; other eye: not specified ▽
369.62 One eye: total vision impairment; other eye: near-normal vision
369.64 One eye: near-total vision impairment; other eye: vision not specified ▽
369.65 One eye: near-total vision impairment; other eye: near-normal vision
369.66 One eye: near-total vision impairment; other eye: normal vision
369.67 One eye: profound vision impairment; other eye: vision not specified ▽
369.68 One eye: profound vision impairment; other eye: near-normal vision
369.69 One eye: profound vision impairment; other eye: normal vision
369.70 Low vision, one eye, not otherwise specified ▽
369.71 One eye: severe vision impairment; other eye: vision not specified ▽
369.72 One eye: severe vision impairment; other eye: near-normal vision
369.73 One eye: severe vision impairment; other eye: normal vision
369.74 One eye: moderate vision impairment; other eye: vision not specified ▽
369.75 One eye: moderate vision impairment; other eye: near-normal vision
369.76 One eye: moderate vision impairment; other eye: normal vision
369.8 Unqualified visual loss, one eye
369.9 Unspecified visual loss ▽
379.22 Crystalline deposits in vitreous
379.23 Vitreous hemorrhage
379.24 Other vitreous opacities
379.25 Vitreous membranes and strands
379.26 Vitreous prolapse
743.51 Vitreous anomaly, congenital
997.99 Other complications affecting other specified body systems, NEC — (Use additional code to identify complications)

ICD-9-CM Procedural

14.74 Other mechanical vitrectomy
14.9 Other operations on retina, choroid, and posterior chamber

HCPCS Level II Supplies & Services

A4305 Disposable drug delivery system, flow rate of 50 ml or greater per hour

67101

67101 Repair of retinal detachment, 1 or more sessions; cryotherapy or diathermy, with or without drainage of subretinal fluid

ICD-9-CM Diagnostic

361.00 Retinal detachment with retinal defect, unspecified ▽
361.01 Recent retinal detachment, partial, with single defect
361.02 Recent retinal detachment, partial, with multiple defects
361.03 Recent retinal detachment, partial, with giant tear
361.04 Recent retinal detachment, partial, with retinal dialysis
361.05 Recent retinal detachment, total or subtotal
361.06 Old retinal detachment, partial
361.07 Old retinal detachment, total or subtotal
361.2 Serous retinal detachment
361.30 Unspecified retinal defect ▽
361.81 Traction detachment of retina
361.89 Other forms of retinal detachment
361.9 Unspecified retinal detachment ▽
362.42 Serous detachment of retinal pigment epithelium
362.43 Hemorrhagic detachment of retinal pigment epithelium

ICD-9-CM Procedural

14.51 Repair of retinal detachment with diathermy
14.52 Repair of retinal detachment with cryotherapy

HCPCS Level II Supplies & Services

A4305 Disposable drug delivery system, flow rate of 50 ml or greater per hour

67105

67105 Repair of retinal detachment, 1 or more sessions; photocoagulation, with or without drainage of subretinal fluid

ICD-9-CM Diagnostic

361.00 Retinal detachment with retinal defect, unspecified ▽
361.01 Recent retinal detachment, partial, with single defect
361.02 Recent retinal detachment, partial, with multiple defects
361.03 Recent retinal detachment, partial, with giant tear
361.04 Recent retinal detachment, partial, with retinal dialysis
361.05 Recent retinal detachment, total or subtotal
361.06 Old retinal detachment, partial
361.07 Old retinal detachment, total or subtotal
361.2 Serous retinal detachment
361.81 Traction detachment of retina
361.89 Other forms of retinal detachment
361.9 Unspecified retinal detachment ▽
362.42 Serous detachment of retinal pigment epithelium
362.43 Hemorrhagic detachment of retinal pigment epithelium

ICD-9-CM Procedural

14.35 Repair of retinal tear by photocoagulation of unspecified type
14.53 Repair of retinal detachment with xenon arc photocoagulation
14.54 Repair of retinal detachment with laser photocoagulation

HCPCS Level II Supplies & Services

A4305 Disposable drug delivery system, flow rate of 50 ml or greater per hour

67107

67107 Repair of retinal detachment; scleral buckling (such as lamellar scleral dissection, imbrication or encircling procedure), with or without implant, with or without cryotherapy, photocoagulation, and drainage of subretinal fluid

ICD-9-CM Diagnostic

361.00 Retinal detachment with retinal defect, unspecified ▽
361.01 Recent retinal detachment, partial, with single defect
361.02 Recent retinal detachment, partial, with multiple defects
361.03 Recent retinal detachment, partial, with giant tear
361.04 Recent retinal detachment, partial, with retinal dialysis
361.05 Recent retinal detachment, total or subtotal
361.06 Old retinal detachment, partial
361.07 Old retinal detachment, total or subtotal
361.2 Serous retinal detachment
361.81 Traction detachment of retina
361.89 Other forms of retinal detachment
361.9 Unspecified retinal detachment ▽
362.42 Serous detachment of retinal pigment epithelium
362.43 Hemorrhagic detachment of retinal pigment epithelium

ICD-9-CM Procedural

14.41 Scleral buckling with implant
14.49 Other scleral buckling

HCPCS Level II Supplies & Services

A4305 Disposable drug delivery system, flow rate of 50 ml or greater per hour

67108

67108 Repair of retinal detachment; with vitrectomy, any method, with or without air or gas tamponade, focal endolaser photocoagulation, cryotherapy, drainage of subretinal fluid, scleral buckling, and/or removal of lens by same technique

ICD-9-CM Diagnostic

361.00 Retinal detachment with retinal defect, unspecified ▽
361.01 Recent retinal detachment, partial, with single defect
361.02 Recent retinal detachment, partial, with multiple defects
361.03 Recent retinal detachment, partial, with giant tear
361.04 Recent retinal detachment, partial, with retinal dialysis
361.05 Recent retinal detachment, total or subtotal
361.06 Old retinal detachment, partial
361.07 Old retinal detachment, total or subtotal
361.2 Serous retinal detachment
361.81 Traction detachment of retina
361.89 Other forms of retinal detachment
361.9 Unspecified retinal detachment ▽
362.42 Serous detachment of retinal pigment epithelium
362.43 Hemorrhagic detachment of retinal pigment epithelium
379.23 Vitreous hemorrhage

ICD-9-CM Procedural

13.90 Operation on lens, not elsewhere classified
14.49 Other scleral buckling
14.51 Repair of retinal detachment with diathermy
14.52 Repair of retinal detachment with cryotherapy
14.53 Repair of retinal detachment with xenon arc photocoagulation
14.54 Repair of retinal detachment with laser photocoagulation
14.71 Removal of vitreous, anterior approach
14.72 Other removal of vitreous
14.73 Mechanical vitrectomy by anterior approach
14.74 Other mechanical vitrectomy

HCPCS Level II Supplies & Services

A4305 Disposable drug delivery system, flow rate of 50 ml or greater per hour

67110-67112

67110 Repair of retinal detachment; by injection of air or other gas (eg, pneumatic retinopexy)
67112 by scleral buckling or vitrectomy, on patient having previous ipsilateral retinal detachment repair(s) using scleral buckling or vitrectomy techniques

ICD-9-CM Diagnostic

361.00 Retinal detachment with retinal defect, unspecified ▽
361.01 Recent retinal detachment, partial, with single defect
361.02 Recent retinal detachment, partial, with multiple defects
361.03 Recent retinal detachment, partial, with giant tear
361.04 Recent retinal detachment, partial, with retinal dialysis
361.05 Recent retinal detachment, total or subtotal
361.06 Old retinal detachment, partial
361.07 Old retinal detachment, total or subtotal
361.2 Serous retinal detachment
361.81 Traction detachment of retina
361.89 Other forms of retinal detachment
361.9 Unspecified retinal detachment ▽
362.42 Serous detachment of retinal pigment epithelium
362.43 Hemorrhagic detachment of retinal pigment epithelium
362.56 Macular puckering of retina

ICD-9-CM Procedural

14.49 Other scleral buckling
14.59 Other repair of retinal detachment
14.71 Removal of vitreous, anterior approach
14.72 Other removal of vitreous
14.73 Mechanical vitrectomy by anterior approach
14.74 Other mechanical vitrectomy
14.75 Injection of vitreous substitute
14.9 Other operations on retina, choroid, and posterior chamber

HCPCS Level II Supplies & Services

A4305 Disposable drug delivery system, flow rate of 50 ml or greater per hour

67113

67113 Repair of complex retinal detachment (eg, proliferative vitreoretinopathy, stage C-1 or greater, diabetic traction retinal detachment, retinopathy of prematurity, retinal tear of greater than 90 degrees), with vitrectomy and membrane peeling, may include air, gas, or silicone oil tamponade, cryotherapy, endolaser photocoagulation, drainage of subretinal fluid, scleral buckling, and/or removal of lens

ICD-9-CM Diagnostic

190.0 Malignant neoplasm of eyeball, except conjunctiva, cornea, retina, and choroid
190.1 Malignant neoplasm of orbit
190.2 Malignant neoplasm of lacrimal gland
190.3 Malignant neoplasm of conjunctiva
190.4 Malignant neoplasm of cornea
190.6 Malignant neoplasm of choroid
190.7 Malignant neoplasm of lacrimal duct
190.8 Malignant neoplasm of other specified sites of eye
190.9 Malignant neoplasm of eye, part unspecified ▽
224.0 Benign neoplasm of eyeball, except conjunctiva, cornea, retina, and choroid
224.1 Benign neoplasm of orbit
224.2 Benign neoplasm of lacrimal gland
224.3 Benign neoplasm of conjunctiva

224.4 Benign neoplasm of cornea
224.6 Benign neoplasm of choroid
224.7 Benign neoplasm of lacrimal duct
224.8 Benign neoplasm of other specified parts of eye
224.9 Benign neoplasm of eye, part unspecified ▽
239.81 Neoplasms of unspecified nature, retina and choroid
249.50 Secondary diabetes mellitus with ophthalmic manifestations, not stated as uncontrolled, or unspecified — (Use additional code to identify manifestation: 362.01-362.07, 365.44, 366.41, 369.00-369.9) (Use additional code to identify any associated insulin use: V58.67)
249.51 Secondary diabetes mellitus with ophthalmic manifestations, uncontrolled — (Use additional code to identify manifestation: 362.01-362.07, 365.44, 366.41, 369.00-369.9) (Use additional code to identify any associated insulin use: V58.67)
250.50 Diabetes with ophthalmic manifestations, type II or unspecified type, not stated as uncontrolled — (Use additional code to identify manifestation: 362.01-362.07, 365.44, 366.41, 369.00-369.9)
250.51 Diabetes with ophthalmic manifestations, type I [juvenile type], not stated as uncontrolled — (Use additional code to identify manifestation: 362.01-362.07, 365.44, 366.41, 369.00-369.9)
250.52 Diabetes with ophthalmic manifestations, type II or unspecified type, uncontrolled — (Use additional code to identify manifestation: 362.01-362.07, 365.44, 366.41, 369.00-369.9)
250.53 Diabetes with ophthalmic manifestations, type I [juvenile type], uncontrolled — (Use additional code to identify manifestation: 362.01-362.07, 365.44, 366.41, 369.00-369.9)
361.00 Retinal detachment with retinal defect, unspecified ▽
361.01 Recent retinal detachment, partial, with single defect
361.02 Recent retinal detachment, partial, with multiple defects
361.03 Recent retinal detachment, partial, with giant tear
361.04 Recent retinal detachment, partial, with retinal dialysis
361.05 Recent retinal detachment, total or subtotal
361.06 Old retinal detachment, partial
361.07 Old retinal detachment, total or subtotal
361.2 Serous retinal detachment
361.31 Round hole of retina without detachment
361.32 Horseshoe tear of retina without detachment
361.33 Multiple defects of retina without detachment
361.81 Traction detachment of retina
361.89 Other forms of retinal detachment
361.9 Unspecified retinal detachment ▽
362.01 Background diabetic retinopathy — (Code first diabetes, 249.5, 250.5) ☒
362.02 Proliferative diabetic retinopathy — (Code first diabetes, 249.5, 250.5) ☒
362.03 Nonproliferative diabetic retinopathy NOS — (Code first diabetes, 249.5, 250.5) ▽ ☒
362.04 Mild nonproliferative diabetic retinopathy — (Code first diabetes, 249.5, 250.5) ☒
362.05 Moderate nonproliferative diabetic retinopathy — (Code first diabetes, 249.5, 250.5) ☒
362.06 Severe nonproliferative diabetic retinopathy — (Code first diabetes, 249.5, 250.5) ☒
362.07 Diabetic macular edema — (Code first diabetes, 249.5, 250.5 Code 362.07 must be used with a code for diabetic retinopathy: 362.01-362.06) ☒
362.20 Retinopathy of prematurity, unspecified ▽
362.21 Retrolental fibroplasia
362.22 Retinopathy of prematurity, stage 0
362.23 Retinopathy of prematurity, stage 1
362.24 Retinopathy of prematurity, stage 2
362.25 Retinopathy of prematurity, stage 3
362.26 Retinopathy of prematurity, stage 4
362.27 Retinopathy of prematurity, stage 5
362.42 Serous detachment of retinal pigment epithelium
362.43 Hemorrhagic detachment of retinal pigment epithelium
362.56 Macular puckering of retina
362.61 Paving stone degeneration of peripheral retina
362.66 Secondary vitreoretinal degenerations peripheral retina
362.73 Vitreoretinal dystrophies
996.59 Mechanical complication due to other implant and internal device, not elsewhere classified
996.69 Infection and inflammatory reaction due to other internal prosthetic device, implant, and graft — (Use additional code to identify specified infections)
996.79 Other complications due to other internal prosthetic device, implant, and graft — (Use additional code to identify complication: 338.18-338.19, 338.28-338.29)
V45.69 Other states following surgery of eye and adnexa

ICD-9-CM Procedural

14.49 Other scleral buckling
14.52 Repair of retinal detachment with cryotherapy
14.54 Repair of retinal detachment with laser photocoagulation
14.59 Other repair of retinal detachment
14.6 Removal of surgically implanted material from posterior segment of eye
14.71 Removal of vitreous, anterior approach
14.72 Other removal of vitreous
14.73 Mechanical vitrectomy by anterior approach
14.74 Other mechanical vitrectomy
14.75 Injection of vitreous substitute
14.9 Other operations on retina, choroid, and posterior chamber

HCPCS Level II Supplies & Services

A4305 Disposable drug delivery system, flow rate of 50 ml or greater per hour

67115

67115 Release of encircling material (posterior segment)

ICD-9-CM Diagnostic

362.56 Macular puckering of retina
379.27 Vitreomacular adhesion
996.59 Mechanical complication due to other implant and internal device, not elsewhere classified
996.69 Infection and inflammatory reaction due to other internal prosthetic device, implant, and graft — (Use additional code to identify specified infections)
996.79 Other complications due to other internal prosthetic device, implant, and graft — (Use additional code to identify complication: 338.18-338.19, 338.28-338.29)
V45.69 Other states following surgery of eye and adnexa

ICD-9-CM Procedural

14.6 Removal of surgically implanted material from posterior segment of eye

HCPCS Level II Supplies & Services

A4305 Disposable drug delivery system, flow rate of 50 ml or greater per hour

67120

67120 Removal of implanted material, posterior segment; extraocular

ICD-9-CM Diagnostic

361.00 Retinal detachment with retinal defect, unspecified ▽
361.01 Recent retinal detachment, partial, with single defect
361.02 Recent retinal detachment, partial, with multiple defects
361.03 Recent retinal detachment, partial, with giant tear
361.04 Recent retinal detachment, partial, with retinal dialysis
361.05 Recent retinal detachment, total or subtotal
361.06 Old retinal detachment, partial
361.07 Old retinal detachment, total or subtotal
361.89 Other forms of retinal detachment
362.56 Macular puckering of retina
368.2 Diplopia

378.60 Unspecified mechanical strabismus ▽
729.90 Disorders of soft tissue, unspecified ▽
729.91 Post-traumatic seroma
729.92 Nontraumatic hematoma of soft tissue
729.99 Other disorders of soft tissue
996.59 Mechanical complication due to other implant and internal device, not elsewhere classified
996.69 Infection and inflammatory reaction due to other internal prosthetic device, implant, and graft — (Use additional code to identify specified infections)
998.30 Disruption of wound, unspecified ▽
998.31 Disruption of internal operation (surgical) wound
998.33 Disruption of traumatic injury wound repair
998.51 Infected postoperative seroma — (Use additional code to identify organism)
998.59 Other postoperative infection — (Use additional code to identify infection)
V43.1 Lens replaced by other means
V45.61 Cataract extraction status — (Use additional code for associated artificial lens status: V43.1)
V45.69 Other states following surgery of eye and adnexa

ICD-9-CM Procedural

14.6 Removal of surgically implanted material from posterior segment of eye

HCPCS Level II Supplies & Services

A4305 Disposable drug delivery system, flow rate of 50 ml or greater per hour

67121

67121 Removal of implanted material, posterior segment; intraocular

ICD-9-CM Diagnostic

379.31 Aphakia
729.90 Disorders of soft tissue, unspecified ▽
729.91 Post-traumatic seroma
729.92 Nontraumatic hematoma of soft tissue
729.99 Other disorders of soft tissue
996.53 Mechanical complication due to ocular lens prosthesis
996.59 Mechanical complication due to other implant and internal device, not elsewhere classified
996.69 Infection and inflammatory reaction due to other internal prosthetic device, implant, and graft — (Use additional code to identify specified infections)
996.79 Other complications due to other internal prosthetic device, implant, and graft — (Use additional code to identify complication: 338.18-338.19, 338.28-338.29)
998.30 Disruption of wound, unspecified ▽
998.31 Disruption of internal operation (surgical) wound
998.33 Disruption of traumatic injury wound repair
998.51 Infected postoperative seroma — (Use additional code to identify organism)
998.59 Other postoperative infection — (Use additional code to identify infection)
V43.1 Lens replaced by other means
V45.61 Cataract extraction status — (Use additional code for associated artificial lens status: V43.1)
V45.69 Other states following surgery of eye and adnexa

ICD-9-CM Procedural

14.6 Removal of surgically implanted material from posterior segment of eye

HCPCS Level II Supplies & Services

A4305 Disposable drug delivery system, flow rate of 50 ml or greater per hour

67141

67141 Prophylaxis of retinal detachment (eg, retinal break, lattice degeneration) without drainage, 1 or more sessions; cryotherapy, diathermy

ICD-9-CM Diagnostic

361.06 Old retinal detachment, partial
361.07 Old retinal detachment, total or subtotal
361.30 Unspecified retinal defect ▽
361.31 Round hole of retina without detachment
361.32 Horseshoe tear of retina without detachment
361.33 Multiple defects of retina without detachment
362.60 Unspecified peripheral retinal degeneration ▽
362.61 Paving stone degeneration of peripheral retina
362.62 Microcystoid degeneration of peripheral retina
362.63 Lattice degeneration of peripheral retina
362.64 Senile reticular degeneration of peripheral retina

ICD-9-CM Procedural

14.31 Repair of retinal tear by diathermy
14.32 Repair of retinal tear by cryotherapy
14.51 Repair of retinal detachment with diathermy
14.52 Repair of retinal detachment with cryotherapy

HCPCS Level II Supplies & Services

A4305 Disposable drug delivery system, flow rate of 50 ml or greater per hour

67145

67145 Prophylaxis of retinal detachment (eg, retinal break, lattice degeneration) without drainage, 1 or more sessions; photocoagulation (laser or xenon arc)

ICD-9-CM Diagnostic

249.50 Secondary diabetes mellitus with ophthalmic manifestations, not stated as uncontrolled, or unspecified — (Use additional code to identify manifestation: 362.01-362.07, 365.44, 366.41, 369.00-369.9) (Use additional code to identify any associated insulin use: V58.67)
249.51 Secondary diabetes mellitus with ophthalmic manifestations, uncontrolled — (Use additional code to identify manifestation: 362.01-362.07, 365.44, 366.41, 369.00-369.9) (Use additional code to identify any associated insulin use: V58.67)
250.50 Diabetes with ophthalmic manifestations, type II or unspecified type, not stated as uncontrolled — (Use additional code to identify manifestation: 362.01-362.07, 365.44, 366.41, 369.00-369.9)
250.51 Diabetes with ophthalmic manifestations, type I [juvenile type], not stated as uncontrolled — (Use additional code to identify manifestation: 362.01-362.07, 365.44, 366.41, 369.00-369.9)
250.52 Diabetes with ophthalmic manifestations, type II or unspecified type, uncontrolled — (Use additional code to identify manifestation: 362.01-362.07, 365.44, 366.41, 369.00-369.9)
250.53 Diabetes with ophthalmic manifestations, type I [juvenile type], uncontrolled — (Use additional code to identify manifestation: 362.01-362.07, 365.44, 366.41, 369.00-369.9)
361.00 Retinal detachment with retinal defect, unspecified ▽
361.01 Recent retinal detachment, partial, with single defect
361.06 Old retinal detachment, partial
361.07 Old retinal detachment, total or subtotal
361.30 Unspecified retinal defect ▽
361.31 Round hole of retina without detachment
361.32 Horseshoe tear of retina without detachment
361.33 Multiple defects of retina without detachment
362.60 Unspecified peripheral retinal degeneration ▽
362.61 Paving stone degeneration of peripheral retina
362.62 Microcystoid degeneration of peripheral retina
362.63 Lattice degeneration of peripheral retina
362.64 Senile reticular degeneration of peripheral retina

ICD-9-CM Procedural

14.33 Repair of retinal tear by xenon arc photocoagulation
14.34 Repair of retinal tear by laser photocoagulation
14.53 Repair of retinal detachment with xenon arc photocoagulation

14.54 Repair of retinal detachment with laser photocoagulation

HCPCS Level II Supplies & Services

A4305 Disposable drug delivery system, flow rate of 50 ml or greater per hour

67208

67208 Destruction of localized lesion of retina (eg, macular edema, tumors), 1 or more sessions; cryotherapy, diathermy

ICD-9-CM Diagnostic

190.5 Malignant neoplasm of retina
190.6 Malignant neoplasm of choroid
198.4 Secondary malignant neoplasm of other parts of nervous system
224.5 Benign neoplasm of retina
224.6 Benign neoplasm of choroid
228.03 Hemangioma of retina
234.0 Carcinoma in situ of eye
238.8 Neoplasm of uncertain behavior of other specified sites
239.81 Neoplasms of unspecified nature, retina and choroid
239.89 Neoplasms of unspecified nature, other specified sites
249.50 Secondary diabetes mellitus with ophthalmic manifestations, not stated as uncontrolled, or unspecified — (Use additional code to identify manifestation: 362.01-362.07, 365.44, 366.41, 369.00-369.9) (Use additional code to identify any associated insulin use: V58.67)
249.51 Secondary diabetes mellitus with ophthalmic manifestations, uncontrolled — (Use additional code to identify manifestation: 362.01-362.07, 365.44, 366.41, 369.00-369.9) (Use additional code to identify any associated insulin use: V58.67)
250.50 Diabetes with ophthalmic manifestations, type II or unspecified type, not stated as uncontrolled — (Use additional code to identify manifestation: 362.01-362.07, 365.44, 366.41, 369.00-369.9)
250.51 Diabetes with ophthalmic manifestations, type I [juvenile type], not stated as uncontrolled — (Use additional code to identify manifestation: 362.01-362.07, 365.44, 366.41, 369.00-369.9)
250.52 Diabetes with ophthalmic manifestations, type II or unspecified type, uncontrolled — (Use additional code to identify manifestation: 362.01-362.07, 365.44, 366.41, 369.00-369.9)
250.53 Diabetes with ophthalmic manifestations, type I [juvenile type], uncontrolled — (Use additional code to identify manifestation: 362.01-362.07, 365.44, 366.41, 369.00-369.9)
362.01 Background diabetic retinopathy — (Code first diabetes, 249.5, 250.5) ☒
362.03 Nonproliferative diabetic retinopathy NOS — (Code first diabetes, 249.5, 250.5) ▽ ☒
362.04 Mild nonproliferative diabetic retinopathy — (Code first diabetes, 249.5, 250.5) ☒
362.05 Moderate nonproliferative diabetic retinopathy — (Code first diabetes, 249.5, 250.5) ☒
362.06 Severe nonproliferative diabetic retinopathy — (Code first diabetes, 249.5, 250.5) ☒
362.07 Diabetic macular edema — (Code first diabetes, 249.5, 250.5 Code 362.07 must be used with a code for diabetic retinopathy: 362.01-362.06) ☒
362.12 Exudative retinopathy
362.16 Retinal neovascularization NOS ▽
362.17 Other intraretinal microvascular abnormalities
362.20 Retinopathy of prematurity, unspecified ▽
362.22 Retinopathy of prematurity, stage 0
362.23 Retinopathy of prematurity, stage 1
362.24 Retinopathy of prematurity, stage 2
362.25 Retinopathy of prematurity, stage 3
362.26 Retinopathy of prematurity, stage 4
362.27 Retinopathy of prematurity, stage 5
362.31 Central artery occlusion of retina
362.35 Central vein occlusion of retina
362.41 Central serous retinopathy
362.42 Serous detachment of retinal pigment epithelium
362.43 Hemorrhagic detachment of retinal pigment epithelium
362.50 Macular degeneration (senile) of retina, unspecified ▽
362.51 Nonexudative senile macular degeneration of retina
362.52 Exudative senile macular degeneration of retina
362.53 Cystoid macular degeneration of retina
362.54 Macular cyst, hole, or pseudohole of retina
362.83 Retinal edema

ICD-9-CM Procedural

14.21 Destruction of chorioretinal lesion by diathermy
14.22 Destruction of chorioretinal lesion by cryotherapy

HCPCS Level II Supplies & Services

A4305 Disposable drug delivery system, flow rate of 50 ml or greater per hour

67210

67210 Destruction of localized lesion of retina (eg, macular edema, tumors), 1 or more sessions; photocoagulation

ICD-9-CM Diagnostic

190.5 Malignant neoplasm of retina
190.6 Malignant neoplasm of choroid
190.9 Malignant neoplasm of eye, part unspecified ▽
224.5 Benign neoplasm of retina
224.6 Benign neoplasm of choroid
228.03 Hemangioma of retina
234.0 Carcinoma in situ of eye
238.8 Neoplasm of uncertain behavior of other specified sites
239.81 Neoplasms of unspecified nature, retina and choroid
239.89 Neoplasms of unspecified nature, other specified sites
249.50 Secondary diabetes mellitus with ophthalmic manifestations, not stated as uncontrolled, or unspecified — (Use additional code to identify manifestation: 362.01-362.07, 365.44, 366.41, 369.00-369.9) (Use additional code to identify any associated insulin use: V58.67)
249.51 Secondary diabetes mellitus with ophthalmic manifestations, uncontrolled — (Use additional code to identify manifestation: 362.01-362.07, 365.44, 366.41, 369.00-369.9) (Use additional code to identify any associated insulin use: V58.67)
250.50 Diabetes with ophthalmic manifestations, type II or unspecified type, not stated as uncontrolled — (Use additional code to identify manifestation: 362.01-362.07, 365.44, 366.41, 369.00-369.9)
250.51 Diabetes with ophthalmic manifestations, type I [juvenile type], not stated as uncontrolled — (Use additional code to identify manifestation: 362.01-362.07, 365.44, 366.41, 369.00-369.9)
250.52 Diabetes with ophthalmic manifestations, type II or unspecified type, uncontrolled — (Use additional code to identify manifestation: 362.01-362.07, 365.44, 366.41, 369.00-369.9)
250.53 Diabetes with ophthalmic manifestations, type I [juvenile type], uncontrolled — (Use additional code to identify manifestation: 362.01-362.07, 365.44, 366.41, 369.00-369.9)
362.01 Background diabetic retinopathy — (Code first diabetes, 249.5, 250.5) ☒
362.02 Proliferative diabetic retinopathy — (Code first diabetes, 249.5, 250.5) ☒
362.03 Nonproliferative diabetic retinopathy NOS — (Code first diabetes, 249.5, 250.5) ▽ ☒
362.04 Mild nonproliferative diabetic retinopathy — (Code first diabetes, 249.5, 250.5) ☒
362.05 Moderate nonproliferative diabetic retinopathy — (Code first diabetes, 249.5, 250.5) ☒
362.06 Severe nonproliferative diabetic retinopathy — (Code first diabetes, 249.5, 250.5) ☒
362.07 Diabetic macular edema — (Code first diabetes, 249.5, 250.5 Code 362.07 must be used with a code for diabetic retinopathy: 362.01-362.06) ☒
362.12 Exudative retinopathy
362.16 Retinal neovascularization NOS ▽

362.17	Other intraretinal microvascular abnormalities
362.20	Retinopathy of prematurity, unspecified ▽
362.22	Retinopathy of prematurity, stage 0
362.23	Retinopathy of prematurity, stage 1
362.24	Retinopathy of prematurity, stage 2
362.25	Retinopathy of prematurity, stage 3
362.26	Retinopathy of prematurity, stage 4
362.27	Retinopathy of prematurity, stage 5
362.31	Central artery occlusion of retina
362.35	Central vein occlusion of retina
362.36	Venous tributary (branch) occlusion of retina
362.37	Venous engorgement of retina
362.41	Central serous retinopathy
362.42	Serous detachment of retinal pigment epithelium
362.43	Hemorrhagic detachment of retinal pigment epithelium
362.50	Macular degeneration (senile) of retina, unspecified ▽
362.51	Nonexudative senile macular degeneration of retina
362.52	Exudative senile macular degeneration of retina
362.53	Cystoid macular degeneration of retina
362.54	Macular cyst, hole, or pseudohole of retina
362.82	Retinal exudates and deposits
362.83	Retinal edema
363.40	Unspecified choroidal degeneration ▽

ICD-9-CM Procedural

14.23	Destruction of chorioretinal lesion by xenon arc photocoagulation
14.24	Destruction of chorioretinal lesion by laser photocoagulation

HCPCS Level II Supplies & Services

A4305	Disposable drug delivery system, flow rate of 50 ml or greater per hour

67218

67218 Destruction of localized lesion of retina (eg, macular edema, tumors), 1 or more sessions; radiation by implantation of source (includes removal of source)

ICD-9-CM Diagnostic

190.5	Malignant neoplasm of retina
190.6	Malignant neoplasm of choroid
190.9	Malignant neoplasm of eye, part unspecified ▽
198.4	Secondary malignant neoplasm of other parts of nervous system
224.5	Benign neoplasm of retina
224.6	Benign neoplasm of choroid
228.03	Hemangioma of retina
234.0	Carcinoma in situ of eye
238.8	Neoplasm of uncertain behavior of other specified sites
239.81	Neoplasms of unspecified nature, retina and choroid
239.89	Neoplasms of unspecified nature, other specified sites
362.16	Retinal neovascularization NOS ▽
362.17	Other intraretinal microvascular abnormalities
362.50	Macular degeneration (senile) of retina, unspecified ▽
362.51	Nonexudative senile macular degeneration of retina
362.52	Exudative senile macular degeneration of retina
362.53	Cystoid macular degeneration of retina
362.54	Macular cyst, hole, or pseudohole of retina
362.83	Retinal edema

ICD-9-CM Procedural

14.26	Destruction of chorioretinal lesion by radiation therapy
14.27	Destruction of chorioretinal lesion by implantation of radiation source

HCPCS Level II Supplies & Services

A4305	Disposable drug delivery system, flow rate of 50 ml or greater per hour

67220

67220 Destruction of localized lesion of choroid (eg, choroidal neovascularization); photocoagulation (eg, laser), 1 or more sessions

ICD-9-CM Diagnostic

190.6	Malignant neoplasm of choroid
198.4	Secondary malignant neoplasm of other parts of nervous system
224.6	Benign neoplasm of choroid
228.09	Hemangioma of other sites
234.0	Carcinoma in situ of eye
238.8	Neoplasm of uncertain behavior of other specified sites
239.81	Neoplasms of unspecified nature, retina and choroid
239.89	Neoplasms of unspecified nature, other specified sites
362.02	Proliferative diabetic retinopathy — (Code first diabetes, 249.5, 250.5) ⊠
362.16	Retinal neovascularization NOS ▽
362.20	Retinopathy of prematurity, unspecified ▽
362.22	Retinopathy of prematurity, stage 0
362.23	Retinopathy of prematurity, stage 1
362.24	Retinopathy of prematurity, stage 2
362.25	Retinopathy of prematurity, stage 3
362.26	Retinopathy of prematurity, stage 4
362.52	Exudative senile macular degeneration of retina
363.30	Unspecified chorioretinal scar ▽
363.31	Solar retinopathy
363.32	Other macular chorioretinal scars
363.33	Other chorioretinal scars of posterior pole
363.34	Peripheral chorioretinal scars
363.35	Disseminated chorioretinal scars
363.40	Unspecified choroidal degeneration ▽

ICD-9-CM Procedural

14.23	Destruction of chorioretinal lesion by xenon arc photocoagulation
14.24	Destruction of chorioretinal lesion by laser photocoagulation

HCPCS Level II Supplies & Services

A4305	Disposable drug delivery system, flow rate of 50 ml or greater per hour

67221-67225

67221 Destruction of localized lesion of choroid (eg, choroidal neovascularization); photodynamic therapy (includes intravenous infusion)

67225 photodynamic therapy, second eye, at single session (List separately in addition to code for primary eye treatment)

ICD-9-CM Diagnostic

190.6	Malignant neoplasm of choroid
198.4	Secondary malignant neoplasm of other parts of nervous system
224.6	Benign neoplasm of choroid
228.09	Hemangioma of other sites
234.0	Carcinoma in situ of eye
238.8	Neoplasm of uncertain behavior of other specified sites
239.81	Neoplasms of unspecified nature, retina and choroid
239.89	Neoplasms of unspecified nature, other specified sites
362.02	Proliferative diabetic retinopathy — (Code first diabetes, 249.5, 250.5) ⊠
362.16	Retinal neovascularization NOS ▽
362.20	Retinopathy of prematurity, unspecified ▽
362.22	Retinopathy of prematurity, stage 0
362.23	Retinopathy of prematurity, stage 1
362.24	Retinopathy of prematurity, stage 2
362.25	Retinopathy of prematurity, stage 3
362.26	Retinopathy of prematurity, stage 4
362.27	Retinopathy of prematurity, stage 5

362.52 Exudative senile macular degeneration of retina
363.30 Unspecified chorioretinal scar
363.31 Solar retinopathy
363.32 Other macular chorioretinal scars
363.33 Other chorioretinal scars of posterior pole
363.34 Peripheral chorioretinal scars
363.35 Disseminated chorioretinal scars
363.40 Unspecified choroidal degeneration

ICD-9-CM Procedural

14.29 Other destruction of chorioretinal lesion

HCPCS Level II Supplies & Services

A4305 Disposable drug delivery system, flow rate of 50 ml or greater per hour

67227-67229

67227 Destruction of extensive or progressive retinopathy (eg, diabetic retinopathy), 1 or more sessions, cryotherapy, diathermy
67228 Treatment of extensive or progressive retinopathy, 1 or more sessions; (eg, diabetic retinopathy), photocoagulation
67229 preterm infant (less than 37 weeks gestation at birth), performed from birth up to 1 year of age (eg, retinopathy of prematurity), photocoagulation or cryotherapy

ICD-9-CM Diagnostic

249.50 Secondary diabetes mellitus with ophthalmic manifestations, not stated as uncontrolled, or unspecified — (Use additional code to identify manifestation: 362.01-362.07, 365.44, 366.41, 369.00-369.9) (Use additional code to identify any associated insulin use: V58.67)
249.51 Secondary diabetes mellitus with ophthalmic manifestations, uncontrolled — (Use additional code to identify manifestation: 362.01-362.07, 365.44, 366.41, 369.00-369.9) (Use additional code to identify any associated insulin use: V58.67)
250.50 Diabetes with ophthalmic manifestations, type II or unspecified type, not stated as uncontrolled — (Use additional code to identify manifestation: 362.01-362.07, 365.44, 366.41, 369.00-369.9)
250.51 Diabetes with ophthalmic manifestations, type I [juvenile type], not stated as uncontrolled — (Use additional code to identify manifestation: 362.01-362.07, 365.44, 366.41, 369.00-369.9)
250.52 Diabetes with ophthalmic manifestations, type II or unspecified type, uncontrolled — (Use additional code to identify manifestation: 362.01-362.07, 365.44, 366.41, 369.00-369.9)
250.53 Diabetes with ophthalmic manifestations, type I [juvenile type], uncontrolled — (Use additional code to identify manifestation: 362.01-362.07, 365.44, 366.41, 369.00-369.9)
361.10 Unspecified retinoschisis
361.11 Flat retinoschisis
361.12 Bullous retinoschisis
362.01 Background diabetic retinopathy — (Code first diabetes, 249.5, 250.5)
362.02 Proliferative diabetic retinopathy — (Code first diabetes, 249.5, 250.5)
362.03 Nonproliferative diabetic retinopathy NOS — (Code first diabetes, 249.5, 250.5)
362.04 Mild nonproliferative diabetic retinopathy — (Code first diabetes, 249.5, 250.5)
362.05 Moderate nonproliferative diabetic retinopathy — (Code first diabetes, 249.5, 250.5)
362.06 Severe nonproliferative diabetic retinopathy — (Code first diabetes, 249.5, 250.5)
362.07 Diabetic macular edema — (Code first diabetes, 249.5, 250.5 Code 362.07 must be used with a code for diabetic retinopathy: 362.01-362.06)
362.12 Exudative retinopathy
362.18 Retinal vasculitis
362.20 Retinopathy of prematurity, unspecified
362.21 Retrolental fibroplasia
362.22 Retinopathy of prematurity, stage 0
362.23 Retinopathy of prematurity, stage 1
362.24 Retinopathy of prematurity, stage 2
362.25 Retinopathy of prematurity, stage 3
362.26 Retinopathy of prematurity, stage 4
362.27 Retinopathy of prematurity, stage 5
362.29 Other nondiabetic proliferative retinopathy
362.35 Central vein occlusion of retina
362.36 Venous tributary (branch) occlusion of retina
362.83 Retinal edema
362.84 Retinal ischemia
365.44 Glaucoma associated with systemic syndromes — (Code first associated disease: 237.70-237.79, 759.6)
365.83 Aqueous misdirection
366.41 Diabetic cataract — (Code first diabetes: 249.5, 250.5)
369.00 Blindness of both eyes, impairment level not further specified
369.01 Better eye: total vision impairment; lesser eye: total vision impairment
369.02 Better eye: near-total vision impairment; lesser eye: not further specified
369.03 Better eye: near-total vision impairment; lesser eye: total vision impairment
369.04 Better eye: near-total vision impairment; lesser eye: near-total vision impairment
369.05 Better eye: profound vision impairment; lesser eye: not further specified
369.06 Better eye: profound vision impairment; lesser eye: total vision impairment
369.07 Better eye: profound vision impairment; lesser eye: near-total vision impairment
369.08 Better eye: profound vision impairment; lesser eye: profound vision impairment
369.10 Profound, moderate or severe vision impairment, not further specified
369.11 Better eye: severe vision impairment; lesser eye: blind, not further specified
369.12 Better eye: severe vision impairment; lesser eye: total vision impairment
369.13 Better eye: severe vision impairment; lesser eye: near-total vision impairment
369.14 Better eye: severe vision impairment; lesser eye: profound vision impairment
369.15 Better eye: moderate vision impairment; lesser eye: blind, not further specified
369.16 Better eye: moderate vision impairment; lesser eye: total vision impairment
369.17 Better eye: moderate vision impairment; lesser eye: near-total vision impairment
369.18 Better eye: moderate vision impairment; lesser eye: profound vision impairment
369.20 Vision impairment, both eyes, impairment level not further specified
369.21 Better eye: severe vision impairment; lesser eye; impairment not further specified
369.22 Better eye: severe vision impairment; lesser eye: severe vision impairment
369.23 Better eye: moderate vision impairment; lesser eye: impairment not further specified
369.24 Better eye: moderate vision impairment; lesser eye: severe vision impairment
369.25 Better eye: moderate vision impairment; lesser eye: moderate vision impairment
369.3 Unqualified visual loss, both eyes
369.4 Legal blindness, as defined in USA
369.60 Impairment level not further specified
369.61 One eye: total vision impairment; other eye: not specified
369.62 One eye: total vision impairment; other eye: near-normal vision
369.64 One eye: near-total vision impairment; other eye: vision not specified
369.65 One eye: near-total vision impairment; other eye: near-normal vision
369.66 One eye: near-total vision impairment; other eye: normal vision
369.67 One eye: profound vision impairment; other eye: vision not specified
369.68 One eye: profound vision impairment; other eye: near-normal vision
369.69 One eye: profound vision impairment; other eye: normal vision
369.70 Low vision, one eye, not otherwise specified
369.71 One eye: severe vision impairment; other eye: vision not specified
369.72 One eye: severe vision impairment; other eye: near-normal vision
369.73 One eye: severe vision impairment; other eye: normal vision
369.74 One eye: moderate vision impairment; other eye: vision not specified
369.75 One eye: moderate vision impairment; other eye: near-normal vision
369.76 One eye: moderate vision impairment; other eye: normal vision
369.8 Unqualified visual loss, one eye

ICD-9-CM Procedural

14.21 Destruction of chorioretinal lesion by diathermy

14.22 Destruction of chorioretinal lesion by cryotherapy
14.23 Destruction of chorioretinal lesion by xenon arc photocoagulation
14.24 Destruction of chorioretinal lesion by laser photocoagulation
14.25 Destruction of chorioretinal lesion by photocoagulation of unspecified type

HCPCS Level II Supplies & Services

A4305 Disposable drug delivery system, flow rate of 50 ml or greater per hour

67250-67255

67250 Scleral reinforcement (separate procedure); without graft
67255 with graft

ICD-9-CM Diagnostic

360.21 Progressive high (degenerative) myopia
871.0 Ocular laceration without prolapse of intraocular tissue
871.1 Ocular laceration with prolapse or exposure of intraocular tissue
918.9 Other and unspecified superficial injuries of eye ▽
921.3 Contusion of eyeball

ICD-9-CM Procedural

12.87 Scleral reinforcement with graft
12.88 Other scleral reinforcement

HCPCS Level II Supplies & Services

A4305 Disposable drug delivery system, flow rate of 50 ml or greater per hour

Ocular Adnexa

67311-67312

67311 Strabismus surgery, recession or resection procedure; 1 horizontal muscle
67312 2 horizontal muscles

ICD-9-CM Diagnostic

368.2 Diplopia
378.00 Unspecified esotropia ▽
378.01 Monocular esotropia
378.02 Monocular esotropia with A pattern
378.03 Monocular esotropia with V pattern
378.05 Alternating esotropia
378.07 Alternating esotropia with V pattern
378.11 Monocular exotropia
378.12 Monocular exotropia with A pattern
378.13 Monocular exotropia with V pattern
378.14 Monocular exotropia with other noncomitancies
378.15 Alternating exotropia
378.16 Alternating exotropia with A pattern
378.17 Alternating exotropia with V pattern
378.18 Alternating exotropia with other noncomitancies
378.21 Intermittent esotropia, monocular
378.22 Intermittent esotropia, alternating
378.23 Intermittent exotropia, monocular
378.24 Intermittent exotropia, alternating
378.35 Accommodative component in esotropia
378.51 Paralytic strabismus, third or oculomotor nerve palsy, partial
378.54 Paralytic strabismus, sixth or abducens nerve palsy
378.73 Strabismus in other neuromuscular disorders
781.93 Ocular torticollis

ICD-9-CM Procedural

15.11 Recession of one extraocular muscle
15.12 Advancement of one extraocular muscle
15.13 Resection of one extraocular muscle
15.19 Other operations on one extraocular muscle involving temporary detachment from globe
15.3 Operations on two or more extraocular muscles involving temporary detachment from globe, one or both eyes

HCPCS Level II Supplies & Services

A4305 Disposable drug delivery system, flow rate of 50 ml or greater per hour

67314-67316

67314 Strabismus surgery, recession or resection procedure; 1 vertical muscle (excluding superior oblique)
67316 2 or more vertical muscles (excluding superior oblique)

ICD-9-CM Diagnostic

368.2 Diplopia
378.07 Alternating esotropia with V pattern
378.11 Monocular exotropia
378.12 Monocular exotropia with A pattern
378.13 Monocular exotropia with V pattern
378.14 Monocular exotropia with other noncomitancies
378.15 Alternating exotropia
378.16 Alternating exotropia with A pattern
378.17 Alternating exotropia with V pattern
378.18 Alternating exotropia with other noncomitancies
378.21 Intermittent esotropia, monocular
378.22 Intermittent esotropia, alternating
378.23 Intermittent exotropia, monocular
378.24 Intermittent exotropia, alternating
378.31 Hypertropia
378.32 Hypotropia
378.45 Alternating hyperphoria
378.51 Paralytic strabismus, third or oculomotor nerve palsy, partial
378.53 Paralytic strabismus, fourth or trochlear nerve palsy
378.54 Paralytic strabismus, sixth or abducens nerve palsy
378.55 Paralytic strabismus, external ophthalmoplegia
378.61 Mechanical strabismus from Brown's (tendon) sheath syndrome
378.87 Other dissociated deviation of eye movements
378.9 Unspecified disorder of eye movements ▽
781.93 Ocular torticollis
802.6 Orbital floor (blow-out), closed fracture
802.7 Orbital floor (blow-out), open fracture

ICD-9-CM Procedural

15.11 Recession of one extraocular muscle
15.12 Advancement of one extraocular muscle
15.13 Resection of one extraocular muscle
15.19 Other operations on one extraocular muscle involving temporary detachment from globe
15.3 Operations on two or more extraocular muscles involving temporary detachment from globe, one or both eyes

HCPCS Level II Supplies & Services

A4305 Disposable drug delivery system, flow rate of 50 ml or greater per hour

67318

67318 Strabismus surgery, any procedure, superior oblique muscle

ICD-9-CM Diagnostic

368.2 Diplopia
378.16 Alternating exotropia with A pattern
378.31 Hypertropia
378.33 Cyclotropia

378.51 Paralytic strabismus, third or oculomotor nerve palsy, partial
378.52 Paralytic strabismus, third or oculomotor nerve palsy, total
378.53 Paralytic strabismus, fourth or trochlear nerve palsy
378.55 Paralytic strabismus, external ophthalmoplegia
378.61 Mechanical strabismus from Brown's (tendon) sheath syndrome
378.71 Duane's syndrome
378.81 Palsy of conjugate gaze
378.9 Unspecified disorder of eye movements ▽
781.93 Ocular torticollis

ICD-9-CM Procedural

15.11 Recession of one extraocular muscle
15.12 Advancement of one extraocular muscle
15.13 Resection of one extraocular muscle

HCPCS Level II Supplies & Services

A4305 Disposable drug delivery system, flow rate of 50 ml or greater per hour

67320

67320 Transposition procedure (eg, for paretic extraocular muscle), any extraocular muscle (specify) (List separately in addition to code for primary procedure)

ICD-9-CM Diagnostic

This is an add-on code. Refer to the corresponding primary procedure code for ICD-9-CM diagnosis code links.

ICD-9-CM Procedural

15.5 Transposition of extraocular muscles

67331

67331 Strabismus surgery on patient with previous eye surgery or injury that did not involve the extraocular muscles (List separately in addition to code for primary procedure)

ICD-9-CM Diagnostic

This is an add-on code. Refer to the corresponding primary procedure code for ICD-9-CM diagnosis code links.

ICD-9-CM Procedural

15.11 Recession of one extraocular muscle
15.12 Advancement of one extraocular muscle
15.13 Resection of one extraocular muscle
15.19 Other operations on one extraocular muscle involving temporary detachment from globe
15.29 Other operations on one extraocular muscle
15.3 Operations on two or more extraocular muscles involving temporary detachment from globe, one or both eyes
15.5 Transposition of extraocular muscles
15.6 Revision of extraocular muscle surgery
15.9 Other operations on extraocular muscles and tendons

67332

67332 Strabismus surgery on patient with scarring of extraocular muscles (eg, prior ocular injury, strabismus or retinal detachment surgery) or restrictive myopathy (eg, dysthyroid ophthalmopathy) (List separately in addition to code for primary procedure)

ICD-9-CM Diagnostic

This is an add-on code. Refer to the corresponding primary procedure code for ICD-9-CM diagnosis code links.

ICD-9-CM Procedural

15.11 Recession of one extraocular muscle
15.12 Advancement of one extraocular muscle
15.13 Resection of one extraocular muscle
15.19 Other operations on one extraocular muscle involving temporary detachment from globe
15.3 Operations on two or more extraocular muscles involving temporary detachment from globe, one or both eyes
15.6 Revision of extraocular muscle surgery
15.9 Other operations on extraocular muscles and tendons

67334

67334 Strabismus surgery by posterior fixation suture technique, with or without muscle recession (List separately in addition to code for primary procedure)

ICD-9-CM Diagnostic

This is an add-on code. Refer to the corresponding primary procedure code for ICD-9-CM diagnosis code links.

ICD-9-CM Procedural

15.11 Recession of one extraocular muscle
15.13 Resection of one extraocular muscle
15.9 Other operations on extraocular muscles and tendons

67335

67335 Placement of adjustable suture(s) during strabismus surgery, including postoperative adjustment(s) of suture(s) (List separately in addition to code for specific strabismus surgery)

ICD-9-CM Diagnostic

This is an add-on code. Refer to the corresponding primary procedure code for ICD-9-CM diagnosis code links.

ICD-9-CM Procedural

15.29 Other operations on one extraocular muscle
15.4 Other operations on two or more extraocular muscles, one or both eyes
15.9 Other operations on extraocular muscles and tendons

67340

67340 Strabismus surgery involving exploration and/or repair of detached extraocular muscle(s) (List separately in addition to code for primary procedure)

ICD-9-CM Diagnostic

This is an add-on code. Refer to the corresponding primary procedure code for ICD-9-CM diagnosis code links.

ICD-9-CM Procedural

15.6 Revision of extraocular muscle surgery
15.7 Repair of injury of extraocular muscle

67343

67343 Release of extensive scar tissue without detaching extraocular muscle (separate procedure)

ICD-9-CM Diagnostic

373.8 Other inflammations of eyelids
378.01 Monocular esotropia
378.10 Unspecified exotropia ▽
378.21 Intermittent esotropia, monocular
378.60 Unspecified mechanical strabismus ▽
378.62 Mechanical strabismus from other musculofascial disorders
378.63 Mechanical strabismus from limited duction associated with other conditions
379.91 Pain in or around eye
379.92 Swelling or mass of eye
728.89 Other disorder of muscle, ligament, and fascia — (Use additional E code to identify drug, if drug-induced)
906.3 Late effect of contusion
921.2 Contusion of orbital tissues

ICD-9-CM Procedural

15.29 Other operations on one extraocular muscle

HCPCS Level II Supplies & Services

A4305 Disposable drug delivery system, flow rate of 50 ml or greater per hour

67345

67345 Chemodenervation of extraocular muscle

ICD-9-CM Diagnostic

378.00 Unspecified esotropia ▽
378.01 Monocular esotropia
378.02 Monocular esotropia with A pattern
378.03 Monocular esotropia with V pattern
378.04 Monocular esotropia with other noncomitancies
378.05 Alternating esotropia
378.06 Alternating esotropia with A pattern
378.07 Alternating esotropia with V pattern
378.08 Alternating esotropia with other noncomitancies
378.10 Unspecified exotropia ▽
378.11 Monocular exotropia
378.12 Monocular exotropia with A pattern
378.13 Monocular exotropia with V pattern
378.14 Monocular exotropia with other noncomitancies
378.15 Alternating exotropia
378.16 Alternating exotropia with A pattern
378.17 Alternating exotropia with V pattern
378.18 Alternating exotropia with other noncomitancies
378.54 Paralytic strabismus, sixth or abducens nerve palsy

ICD-9-CM Procedural

15.29 Other operations on one extraocular muscle

HCPCS Level II Supplies & Services

A4305 Disposable drug delivery system, flow rate of 50 ml or greater per hour

67346

67346 Biopsy of extraocular muscle

ICD-9-CM Diagnostic

190.1 Malignant neoplasm of orbit
190.8 Malignant neoplasm of other specified sites of eye
198.4 Secondary malignant neoplasm of other parts of nervous system
224.1 Benign neoplasm of orbit
234.0 Carcinoma in situ of eye
238.8 Neoplasm of uncertain behavior of other specified sites
239.89 Neoplasms of unspecified nature, other specified sites

ICD-9-CM Procedural

15.01 Biopsy of extraocular muscle or tendon

67400-67405

67400 Orbitotomy without bone flap (frontal or transconjunctival approach); for exploration, with or without biopsy
67405 with drainage only

ICD-9-CM Diagnostic

190.1 Malignant neoplasm of orbit
198.4 Secondary malignant neoplasm of other parts of nervous system
200.11 Lymphosarcoma of lymph nodes of head, face, and neck
224.0 Benign neoplasm of eyeball, except conjunctiva, cornea, retina, and choroid
239.89 Neoplasms of unspecified nature, other specified sites
362.35 Central vein occlusion of retina
368.11 Sudden visual loss
368.8 Other specified visual disturbances
373.9 Unspecified inflammation of eyelid ▽
375.03 Chronic enlargement of lacrimal gland
376.01 Orbital cellulitis
376.32 Orbital hemorrhage
377.39 Other optic neuritis
377.41 Ischemic optic neuropathy
379.91 Pain in or around eye
379.92 Swelling or mass of eye
379.93 Redness or discharge of eye

ICD-9-CM Procedural

16.09 Other orbitotomy
16.23 Biopsy of eyeball and orbit
76.11 Biopsy of facial bone

67412-67413

67412 Orbitotomy without bone flap (frontal or transconjunctival approach); with removal of lesion
67413 with removal of foreign body

ICD-9-CM Diagnostic

190.1 Malignant neoplasm of orbit
213.0 Benign neoplasm of bones of skull and face
216.3 Benign neoplasm of skin of other and unspecified parts of face ▽
224.1 Benign neoplasm of orbit
228.01 Hemangioma of skin and subcutaneous tissue
228.09 Hemangioma of other sites
237.70 Neurofibromatosis, unspecified ▽
237.71 Neurofibromatosis, Type 1 (von Recklinghausen's disease)
237.72 Neurofibromatosis, Type 2 (acoustic neurofibromatosis)
237.73 Schwannomatosis
237.79 Other neurofibromatosis
238.8 Neoplasm of uncertain behavior of other specified sites
239.2 Neoplasms of unspecified nature of bone, soft tissue, and skin
239.89 Neoplasms of unspecified nature, other specified sites
375.12 Other lacrimal cysts and cystic degeneration
376.01 Orbital cellulitis
376.6 Retained (old) foreign body following penetrating wound of orbit — (Use additional code to identify foreign body (V90.01-V90.9))
376.81 Orbital cysts
379.92 Swelling or mass of eye
802.8 Other facial bones, closed fracture
870.4 Penetrating wound of orbit with foreign body
930.8 Foreign body in other and combined sites on external eye
930.9 Foreign body in unspecified site on external eye ▽

ICD-9-CM Procedural

16.09 Other orbitotomy
16.1 Removal of penetrating foreign body from eye, not otherwise specified

67414

67414 Orbitotomy without bone flap (frontal or transconjunctival approach); with removal of bone for decompression

ICD-9-CM Diagnostic

224.1 Benign neoplasm of orbit
242.00 Toxic diffuse goiter without mention of thyrotoxic crisis or storm
246.9 Unspecified disorder of thyroid ▽
368.8 Other specified visual disturbances
374.41 Eyelid retraction or lag

376.21 Thyrotoxic exophthalmos — (Code first underlying thyroid disorder: 242.00-242.9) ☒
378.9 Unspecified disorder of eye movements ▽
473.8 Other chronic sinusitis — (Use additional code to identify infectious organism)

ICD-9-CM Procedural

16.09 Other orbitotomy

67415

67415 Fine needle aspiration of orbital contents

ICD-9-CM Diagnostic

190.1 Malignant neoplasm of orbit
198.4 Secondary malignant neoplasm of other parts of nervous system
224.1 Benign neoplasm of orbit
234.0 Carcinoma in situ of eye
238.8 Neoplasm of uncertain behavior of other specified sites
368.8 Other specified visual disturbances
376.01 Orbital cellulitis
376.30 Unspecified exophthalmos ▽
376.33 Orbital edema or congestion
378.9 Unspecified disorder of eye movements ▽

ICD-9-CM Procedural

16.22 Diagnostic aspiration of orbit

67420-67430

67420 Orbitotomy with bone flap or window, lateral approach (eg, Kroenlein); with removal of lesion
67430 with removal of foreign body

ICD-9-CM Diagnostic

190.1 Malignant neoplasm of orbit
213.0 Benign neoplasm of bones of skull and face
216.3 Benign neoplasm of skin of other and unspecified parts of face ▽
224.1 Benign neoplasm of orbit
228.01 Hemangioma of skin and subcutaneous tissue
228.09 Hemangioma of other sites
237.70 Neurofibromatosis, unspecified ▽
237.71 Neurofibromatosis, Type 1 (von Recklinghausen's disease)
237.72 Neurofibromatosis, Type 2 (acoustic neurofibromatosis)
237.73 Schwannomatosis
237.79 Other neurofibromatosis
238.8 Neoplasm of uncertain behavior of other specified sites
239.2 Neoplasms of unspecified nature of bone, soft tissue, and skin
239.89 Neoplasms of unspecified nature, other specified sites
376.41 Hypertelorism of orbit
376.6 Retained (old) foreign body following penetrating wound of orbit — (Use additional code to identify foreign body (V90.01-V90.9))
870.4 Penetrating wound of orbit with foreign body
930.8 Foreign body in other and combined sites on external eye
930.9 Foreign body in unspecified site on external eye ▽

ICD-9-CM Procedural

16.01 Orbitotomy with bone flap
16.1 Removal of penetrating foreign body from eye, not otherwise specified

67440

67440 Orbitotomy with bone flap or window, lateral approach (eg, Kroenlein); with drainage

ICD-9-CM Diagnostic

224.1 Benign neoplasm of orbit
242.00 Toxic diffuse goiter without mention of thyrotoxic crisis or storm
368.8 Other specified visual disturbances
369.9 Unspecified visual loss ▽
376.01 Orbital cellulitis
376.21 Thyrotoxic exophthalmos — (Code first underlying thyroid disorder: 242.00-242.9) ☒
376.31 Constant exophthalmos
376.41 Hypertelorism of orbit
376.52 Enophthalmos due to trauma or surgery
377.39 Other optic neuritis
377.41 Ischemic optic neuropathy
377.49 Other disorder of optic nerve
473.2 Chronic ethmoidal sinusitis — (Use additional code to identify infectious organism)

ICD-9-CM Procedural

16.01 Orbitotomy with bone flap

67445

67445 Orbitotomy with bone flap or window, lateral approach (eg, Kroenlein); with removal of bone for decompression

ICD-9-CM Diagnostic

242.01 Toxic diffuse goiter with mention of thyrotoxic crisis or storm
368.11 Sudden visual loss
369.00 Blindness of both eyes, impairment level not further specified ▽
376.21 Thyrotoxic exophthalmos — (Code first underlying thyroid disorder: 242.00-242.9) ☒
802.6 Orbital floor (blow-out), closed fracture

ICD-9-CM Procedural

16.01 Orbitotomy with bone flap

67450

67450 Orbitotomy with bone flap or window, lateral approach (eg, Kroenlein); for exploration, with or without biopsy

ICD-9-CM Diagnostic

190.1 Malignant neoplasm of orbit
198.4 Secondary malignant neoplasm of other parts of nervous system
224.1 Benign neoplasm of orbit
234.0 Carcinoma in situ of eye
238.8 Neoplasm of uncertain behavior of other specified sites
239.89 Neoplasms of unspecified nature, other specified sites
379.91 Pain in or around eye
379.92 Swelling or mass of eye
379.93 Redness or discharge of eye

ICD-9-CM Procedural

16.01 Orbitotomy with bone flap
16.23 Biopsy of eyeball and orbit
76.11 Biopsy of facial bone

67500-67505

67500 Retrobulbar injection; medication (separate procedure, does not include supply of medication)
67505 alcohol

ICD-9-CM Diagnostic

115.92 Unspecified Histoplasmosis retinitis ▽
135 Sarcoidosis
249.50 Secondary diabetes mellitus with ophthalmic manifestations, not stated as uncontrolled, or unspecified — (Use additional code to identify manifestation: 362.01-362.07,

365.44, 366.41, 369.00-369.9) (Use additional code to identify any associated insulin use: V58.67)

249.51 Secondary diabetes mellitus with ophthalmic manifestations, uncontrolled — (Use additional code to identify manifestation: 362.01-362.07, 365.44, 366.41, 369.00-369.9) (Use additional code to identify any associated insulin use: V58.67)

250.50 Diabetes with ophthalmic manifestations, type II or unspecified type, not stated as uncontrolled — (Use additional code to identify manifestation: 362.01-362.07, 365.44, 366.41, 369.00-369.9)

250.51 Diabetes with ophthalmic manifestations, type I [juvenile type], not stated as uncontrolled — (Use additional code to identify manifestation: 362.01-362.07, 365.44, 366.41, 369.00-369.9)

250.52 Diabetes with ophthalmic manifestations, type II or unspecified type, uncontrolled — (Use additional code to identify manifestation: 362.01-362.07, 365.44, 366.41, 369.00-369.9)

250.53 Diabetes with ophthalmic manifestations, type I [juvenile type], uncontrolled — (Use additional code to identify manifestation: 362.01-362.07, 365.44, 366.41, 369.00-369.9)

360.41 Blind hypotensive eye

360.42 Blind hypertensive eye

361.9 Unspecified retinal detachment ▽

362.01 Background diabetic retinopathy — (Code first diabetes, 249.5, 250.5) ☒

362.03 Nonproliferative diabetic retinopathy NOS — (Code first diabetes, 249.5, 250.5) ▽ ☒

362.04 Mild nonproliferative diabetic retinopathy — (Code first diabetes, 249.5, 250.5) ☒

362.05 Moderate nonproliferative diabetic retinopathy — (Code first diabetes, 249.5, 250.5) ☒

362.06 Severe nonproliferative diabetic retinopathy — (Code first diabetes, 249.5, 250.5) ☒

362.07 Diabetic macular edema — (Code first diabetes, 249.5, 250.5 Code 362.07 must be used with a code for diabetic retinopathy: 362.01-362.06) ☒

362.10 Unspecified background retinopathy ▽

362.16 Retinal neovascularization NOS ▽

362.20 Retinopathy of prematurity, unspecified ▽

362.22 Retinopathy of prematurity, stage 0

362.23 Retinopathy of prematurity, stage 1

362.24 Retinopathy of prematurity, stage 2

362.25 Retinopathy of prematurity, stage 3

362.26 Retinopathy of prematurity, stage 4

362.27 Retinopathy of prematurity, stage 5

362.53 Cystoid macular degeneration of retina

362.57 Drusen (degenerative) of retina

362.83 Retinal edema

363.21 Pars planitis

364.11 Chronic iridocyclitis in diseases classified elsewhere — (Code first underlying disease: 017.3, 135) ☒

364.3 Unspecified iridocyclitis ▽

364.42 Rubeosis iridis

364.82 Plateau iris syndrome

365.11 Primary open-angle glaucoma — (Use additional code to identify glaucoma stage: 365.70-365.74)

365.83 Aqueous misdirection

366.10 Unspecified senile cataract ▽

371.23 Bullous keratopathy

996.80 Complications of transplanted organ, unspecified site — (Use additional code to identify nature of complication: 078.5, 199.2, 238.77, 279.50-279.53) ▽

996.89 Complications of other transplanted organ — (Use additional code to identify nature of complication: 078.5, 199.2, 238.77, 279.50-279.53)

ICD-9-CM Procedural

16.91 Retrobulbar injection of therapeutic agent

HCPCS Level II Supplies & Services

A4305 Disposable drug delivery system, flow rate of 50 ml or greater per hour

J0178 Injection, aflibercept, 1 mg

J7315 Mitomycin, opthalmic, 0.2 mg

67515

67515 Injection of medication or other substance into Tenon's capsule

ICD-9-CM Diagnostic

115.02 Histoplasma capsulatum retinitis

115.92 Unspecified Histoplasmosis retinitis ▽

361.89 Other forms of retinal detachment

362.36 Venous tributary (branch) occlusion of retina

362.52 Exudative senile macular degeneration of retina

362.53 Cystoid macular degeneration of retina

362.83 Retinal edema

363.21 Pars planitis

364.01 Primary iridocyclitis

364.02 Recurrent iridocyclitis

364.10 Unspecified chronic iridocyclitis ▽

364.3 Unspecified iridocyclitis ▽

366.16 Nuclear sclerosis

373.12 Hordeolum internum

379.91 Pain in or around eye

ICD-9-CM Procedural

16.99 Other operations on eyeball

67550-67560

67550 Orbital implant (implant outside muscle cone); insertion

67560 removal or revision

ICD-9-CM Diagnostic

190.0 Malignant neoplasm of eyeball, except conjunctiva, cornea, retina, and choroid

198.4 Secondary malignant neoplasm of other parts of nervous system

376.40 Unspecified deformity of orbit ▽

376.50 Enophthalmos, unspecified as to cause ▽

871.7 Unspecified ocular penetration ▽

996.59 Mechanical complication due to other implant and internal device, not elsewhere classified

996.69 Infection and inflammatory reaction due to other internal prosthetic device, implant, and graft — (Use additional code to identify specified infections)

996.79 Other complications due to other internal prosthetic device, implant, and graft — (Use additional code to identify complication: 338.18-338.19, 338.28-338.29)

V10.84 Personal history of malignant neoplasm of eye

V43.0 Eye globe replaced by other means

V52.2 Fitting and adjustment of artificial eye

ICD-9-CM Procedural

16.02 Orbitotomy with insertion of orbital implant

16.69 Other secondary procedures after removal of eyeball

16.72 Removal of orbital implant

97.31 Removal of eye prosthesis

67570

67570 Optic nerve decompression (eg, incision or fenestration of optic nerve sheath)

ICD-9-CM Diagnostic

348.2 Benign intracranial hypertension

362.35 Central vein occlusion of retina

365.83 Aqueous misdirection

365.9 Unspecified glaucoma ▼

377.01 Papilledema associated with increased intracranial pressure

377.39 Other optic neuritis

377.41 Ischemic optic neuropathy

950.0 Optic nerve injury

ICD-9-CM Procedural

04.42 Other cranial nerve decompression

67700

67700 Blepharotomy, drainage of abscess, eyelid

ICD-9-CM Diagnostic

373.11 Hordeolum externum

373.12 Hordeolum internum

373.13 Abscess of eyelid

373.9 Unspecified inflammation of eyelid ▼

374.84 Cysts of eyelids

374.9 Unspecified disorder of eyelid ▼

376.01 Orbital cellulitis

780.62 Postprocedural fever

ICD-9-CM Procedural

08.01 Incision of lid margin

08.09 Other incision of eyelid

67710

67710 Severing of tarsorrhaphy

ICD-9-CM Diagnostic

351.9 Unspecified facial nerve disorder ▼

370.21 Punctate keratitis

370.22 Macular keratitis

370.35 Neurotrophic keratoconjunctivitis

371.70 Unspecified corneal deformity ▼

907.1 Late effect of injury to cranial nerve

951.4 Injury to facial nerve

V58.32 Encounter for removal of sutures

V58.49 Other specified aftercare following surgery — (This code should be used in conjunction with other aftercare codes to fully identify the reason for the aftercare encounter)

ICD-9-CM Procedural

08.02 Severing of blepharorrhaphy

HCPCS Level II Supplies & Services

A4305 Disposable drug delivery system, flow rate of 50 ml or greater per hour

67715

67715 Canthotomy (separate procedure)

ICD-9-CM Diagnostic

374.46 Blepharophimosis

ICD-9-CM Procedural

08.51 Canthotomy

HCPCS Level II Supplies & Services

A4305 Disposable drug delivery system, flow rate of 50 ml or greater per hour

67810

67810 Incisional biopsy of eyelid skin including lid margin

ICD-9-CM Diagnostic

171.0 Malignant neoplasm of connective and other soft tissue of head, face, and neck

172.1 Malignant melanoma of skin of eyelid, including canthus

173.10 Unspecified malignant neoplasm of eyelid, including canthus ▼

173.11 Basal cell carcinoma of eyelid, including canthus

173.12 Squamous cell carcinoma of eyelid, including canthus

173.19 Other specified malignant neoplasm of eyelid, including canthus

198.2 Secondary malignant neoplasm of skin

198.89 Secondary malignant neoplasm of other specified sites

215.0 Other benign neoplasm of connective and other soft tissue of head, face, and neck

216.1 Benign neoplasm of eyelid, including canthus

228.00 Hemangioma of unspecified site ▼

228.01 Hemangioma of skin and subcutaneous tissue

232.1 Carcinoma in situ of eyelid, including canthus

238.1 Neoplasm of uncertain behavior of connective and other soft tissue

238.2 Neoplasm of uncertain behavior of skin

239.2 Neoplasms of unspecified nature of bone, soft tissue, and skin

239.9 Neoplasm of unspecified nature, site unspecified ▼

272.0 Pure hypercholesterolemia — (Use additional code to identify any associated intellectual disabilities)

272.1 Pure hyperglyceridemia — (Use additional code to identify any associated intellectual disabilities)

272.2 Mixed hyperlipidemia — (Use additional code to identify any associated intellectual disabilities)

272.3 Hyperchylomicronemia — (Use additional code to identify any associated intellectual disabilities)

272.4 Other and unspecified hyperlipidemia — (Use additional code to identify any associated intellectual disabilities) ▼

272.5 Lipoprotein deficiencies — (Use additional code to identify any associated intellectual disabilities)

272.6 Lipodystrophy — (Use additional code to identify any associated intellectual disabilities) (Use additional E code to identify cause, if iatrogenic)

272.7 Lipidoses — (Use additional code to identify any associated intellectual disabilities)

272.9 Unspecified disorder of lipoid metabolism — (Use additional code to identify any associated intellectual disabilities) ▼

373.2 Chalazion

373.9 Unspecified inflammation of eyelid ▼

374.51 Xanthelasma of eyelid — (Code first underlying condition: 272.0-272.9) ☒

374.84 Cysts of eyelids

379.92 Swelling or mass of eye

696.1 Other psoriasis

701.9 Unspecified hypertrophic and atrophic condition of skin ▼

ICD-9-CM Procedural

08.11 Biopsy of eyelid

67800-67808

67800 Excision of chalazion; single

67801 multiple, same lid

67805 multiple, different lids

67808 under general anesthesia and/or requiring hospitalization, single or multiple

ICD-9-CM Diagnostic

373.2 Chalazion

ICD-9-CM Procedural

08.21 Excision of chalazion

HCPCS Level II Supplies & Services

A4305 Disposable drug delivery system, flow rate of 50 ml or greater per hour

67820-67825

67820 Correction of trichiasis; epilation, by forceps only
67825 epilation by other than forceps (eg, by electrosurgery, cryotherapy, laser surgery)

ICD-9-CM Diagnostic

374.00 Unspecified entropion
374.01 Senile entropion
374.04 Cicatricial entropion
374.05 Trichiasis of eyelid without entropion
374.54 Hypertrichosis of eyelid
374.89 Other disorders of eyelid
379.91 Pain in or around eye
743.63 Other specified congenital anomaly of eyelid
918.1 Superficial injury of cornea

ICD-9-CM Procedural

08.59 Other adjustment of lid position
08.91 Electrosurgical epilation of eyelid
08.92 Cryosurgical epilation of eyelid
08.93 Other epilation of eyelid

HCPCS Level II Supplies & Services

A4305 Disposable drug delivery system, flow rate of 50 ml or greater per hour

67830-67835

67830 Correction of trichiasis; incision of lid margin
67835 incision of lid margin, with free mucous membrane graft

ICD-9-CM Diagnostic

374.01 Senile entropion
374.04 Cicatricial entropion
374.05 Trichiasis of eyelid without entropion
374.54 Hypertrichosis of eyelid
374.89 Other disorders of eyelid
379.91 Pain in or around eye
743.63 Other specified congenital anomaly of eyelid
918.1 Superficial injury of cornea

ICD-9-CM Procedural

08.59 Other adjustment of lid position
08.93 Other epilation of eyelid

HCPCS Level II Supplies & Services

A4305 Disposable drug delivery system, flow rate of 50 ml or greater per hour

67840

67840 Excision of lesion of eyelid (except chalazion) without closure or with simple direct closure

ICD-9-CM Diagnostic

172.1 Malignant melanoma of skin of eyelid, including canthus
173.10 Unspecified malignant neoplasm of eyelid, including canthus
173.11 Basal cell carcinoma of eyelid, including canthus
173.12 Squamous cell carcinoma of eyelid, including canthus
173.19 Other specified malignant neoplasm of eyelid, including canthus
214.0 Lipoma of skin and subcutaneous tissue of face
215.0 Other benign neoplasm of connective and other soft tissue of head, face, and neck
216.1 Benign neoplasm of eyelid, including canthus
228.01 Hemangioma of skin and subcutaneous tissue
232.1 Carcinoma in situ of eyelid, including canthus
238.1 Neoplasm of uncertain behavior of connective and other soft tissue
238.2 Neoplasm of uncertain behavior of skin
239.2 Neoplasms of unspecified nature of bone, soft tissue, and skin
372.51 Pinguecula
372.52 Pseudopterygium
372.54 Conjunctival concretions
372.56 Conjunctival deposits
372.61 Granuloma of conjunctiva
372.62 Localized adhesions and strands of conjunctiva
373.11 Hordeolum externum
373.12 Hordeolum internum
373.9 Unspecified inflammation of eyelid
374.51 Xanthelasma of eyelid — (Code first underlying condition: 272.0-272.9)
374.84 Cysts of eyelids
374.89 Other disorders of eyelid
702.0 Actinic keratosis
702.11 Inflamed seborrheic keratosis
702.19 Other seborrheic keratosis
706.2 Sebaceous cyst

ICD-9-CM Procedural

08.20 Removal of lesion of eyelid, not otherwise specified

HCPCS Level II Supplies & Services

A4305 Disposable drug delivery system, flow rate of 50 ml or greater per hour

67850

67850 Destruction of lesion of lid margin (up to 1 cm)

ICD-9-CM Diagnostic

173.10 Unspecified malignant neoplasm of eyelid, including canthus
173.11 Basal cell carcinoma of eyelid, including canthus
173.12 Squamous cell carcinoma of eyelid, including canthus
173.19 Other specified malignant neoplasm of eyelid, including canthus
216.1 Benign neoplasm of eyelid, including canthus
232.1 Carcinoma in situ of eyelid, including canthus
238.2 Neoplasm of uncertain behavior of skin
239.2 Neoplasms of unspecified nature of bone, soft tissue, and skin
373.2 Chalazion
373.9 Unspecified inflammation of eyelid
374.05 Trichiasis of eyelid without entropion
374.51 Xanthelasma of eyelid — (Code first underlying condition: 272.0-272.9)
374.84 Cysts of eyelids
379.92 Swelling or mass of eye
701.1 Acquired keratoderma
701.9 Unspecified hypertrophic and atrophic condition of skin
706.2 Sebaceous cyst

ICD-9-CM Procedural

08.22 Excision of other minor lesion of eyelid

HCPCS Level II Supplies & Services

A4305 Disposable drug delivery system, flow rate of 50 ml or greater per hour

67875

67875 Temporary closure of eyelids by suture (eg, Frost suture)

ICD-9-CM Diagnostic

173.10 Unspecified malignant neoplasm of eyelid, including canthus
173.11 Basal cell carcinoma of eyelid, including canthus
173.12 Squamous cell carcinoma of eyelid, including canthus
173.19 Other specified malignant neoplasm of eyelid, including canthus
370.04 Hypopyon ulcer
370.06 Perforated corneal ulcer
370.20 Unspecified superficial keratitis

370.34 Exposure keratoconjunctivitis
370.9 Unspecified keratitis
371.40 Unspecified corneal degeneration
372.73 Conjunctival edema
374.05 Trichiasis of eyelid without entropion
374.10 Unspecified ectropion
374.14 Cicatricial ectropion
374.23 Cicatricial lagophthalmos
374.41 Eyelid retraction or lag
378.55 Paralytic strabismus, external ophthalmoplegia

ICD-9-CM Procedural

08.99 Other operations on eyelids

67880-67882

67880 Construction of intermarginal adhesions, median tarsorrhaphy, or canthorrhaphy;
67882 with transposition of tarsal plate

ICD-9-CM Diagnostic

351.0 Bell's palsy
351.9 Unspecified facial nerve disorder
370.01 Marginal corneal ulcer
370.06 Perforated corneal ulcer
370.20 Unspecified superficial keratitis
370.33 Keratoconjunctivitis sicca, not specified as Sjogren's
370.34 Exposure keratoconjunctivitis
370.35 Neurotrophic keratoconjunctivitis
370.40 Unspecified keratoconjunctivitis
371.03 Central opacity of cornea
371.40 Unspecified corneal degeneration
371.42 Recurrent erosion of cornea
374.11 Senile ectropion
374.14 Cicatricial ectropion
374.21 Paralytic lagophthalmos
374.22 Mechanical lagophthalmos
374.34 Blepharochalasis
374.41 Eyelid retraction or lag
378.55 Paralytic strabismus, external ophthalmoplegia
906.5 Late effect of burn of eye, face, head, and neck
918.1 Superficial injury of cornea
940.9 Unspecified burn of eye and adnexa

ICD-9-CM Procedural

08.52 Blepharorrhaphy
08.69 Other reconstruction of eyelid with flaps or grafts

67900

67900 Repair of brow ptosis (supraciliary, mid-forehead or coronal approach)

ICD-9-CM Diagnostic

351.9 Unspecified facial nerve disorder
374.21 Paralytic lagophthalmos
374.30 Unspecified ptosis of eyelid
374.31 Paralytic ptosis
374.32 Myogenic ptosis
374.33 Mechanical ptosis
374.34 Blepharochalasis
374.50 Unspecified degenerative disorder of eyelid
376.30 Unspecified exophthalmos
709.2 Scar condition and fibrosis of skin
709.3 Degenerative skin disorder
743.61 Congenital ptosis of eyelid
743.62 Congenital deformity of eyelid
743.63 Other specified congenital anomaly of eyelid
998.9 Unspecified complication of procedure, not elsewhere classified

ICD-9-CM Procedural

08.36 Repair of blepharoptosis by other techniques
08.59 Other adjustment of lid position

HCPCS Level II Supplies & Services

A4305 Disposable drug delivery system, flow rate of 50 ml or greater per hour

67901

67901 Repair of blepharoptosis; frontalis muscle technique with suture or other material (eg, banked fascia)

ICD-9-CM Diagnostic

368.44 Other localized visual field defect
374.30 Unspecified ptosis of eyelid
374.31 Paralytic ptosis
374.32 Myogenic ptosis
374.33 Mechanical ptosis
374.34 Blepharochalasis
374.46 Blepharophimosis
378.72 Progressive external ophthalmoplegia
701.8 Other specified hypertrophic and atrophic condition of skin
743.61 Congenital ptosis of eyelid
743.62 Congenital deformity of eyelid
743.63 Other specified congenital anomaly of eyelid
743.69 Other congenital anomalies of eyelids, lacrimal system, and orbit

ICD-9-CM Procedural

08.31 Repair of blepharoptosis by frontalis muscle technique with suture

HCPCS Level II Supplies & Services

A4305 Disposable drug delivery system, flow rate of 50 ml or greater per hour

67902

67902 Repair of blepharoptosis; frontalis muscle technique with autologous fascial sling (includes obtaining fascia)

ICD-9-CM Diagnostic

368.44 Other localized visual field defect
374.30 Unspecified ptosis of eyelid
374.31 Paralytic ptosis
374.32 Myogenic ptosis
374.33 Mechanical ptosis
374.34 Blepharochalasis
374.46 Blepharophimosis
378.55 Paralytic strabismus, external ophthalmoplegia
743.61 Congenital ptosis of eyelid
743.62 Congenital deformity of eyelid
743.63 Other specified congenital anomaly of eyelid

ICD-9-CM Procedural

08.32 Repair of blepharoptosis by frontalis muscle technique with fascial sling

67903

67903 Repair of blepharoptosis; (tarso) levator resection or advancement, internal approach

ICD-9-CM Diagnostic

374.30 Unspecified ptosis of eyelid
374.31 Paralytic ptosis

374.32 Myogenic ptosis
374.33 Mechanical ptosis
374.34 Blepharochalasis
743.61 Congenital ptosis of eyelid
743.62 Congenital deformity of eyelid
743.63 Other specified congenital anomaly of eyelid
951.0 Injury to oculomotor nerve

ICD-9-CM Procedural

08.33 Repair of blepharoptosis by resection or advancement of levator muscle or aponeurosis
08.34 Repair of blepharoptosis by other levator muscle techniques
08.35 Repair of blepharoptosis by tarsal technique

67904

67904 Repair of blepharoptosis; (tarso) levator resection or advancement, external approach

ICD-9-CM Diagnostic

351.0 Bell's palsy
368.44 Other localized visual field defect
374.30 Unspecified ptosis of eyelid ▽
374.31 Paralytic ptosis
374.32 Myogenic ptosis
374.33 Mechanical ptosis
374.34 Blepharochalasis
374.46 Blepharophimosis
374.50 Unspecified degenerative disorder of eyelid ▽
374.87 Dermatochalasis
743.61 Congenital ptosis of eyelid
743.62 Congenital deformity of eyelid
743.63 Other specified congenital anomaly of eyelid

ICD-9-CM Procedural

08.33 Repair of blepharoptosis by resection or advancement of levator muscle or aponeurosis
08.34 Repair of blepharoptosis by other levator muscle techniques
08.35 Repair of blepharoptosis by tarsal technique

67906

67906 Repair of blepharoptosis; superior rectus technique with fascial sling (includes obtaining fascia)

ICD-9-CM Diagnostic

368.44 Other localized visual field defect
374.30 Unspecified ptosis of eyelid ▽
374.31 Paralytic ptosis
374.32 Myogenic ptosis
374.33 Mechanical ptosis
374.34 Blepharochalasis
374.46 Blepharophimosis
701.8 Other specified hypertrophic and atrophic condition of skin
743.61 Congenital ptosis of eyelid
743.62 Congenital deformity of eyelid
743.63 Other specified congenital anomaly of eyelid

ICD-9-CM Procedural

08.36 Repair of blepharoptosis by other techniques

67908

67908 Repair of blepharoptosis; conjunctivo-tarso-Muller's muscle-levator resection (eg, Fasanella-Servat type)

ICD-9-CM Diagnostic

368.44 Other localized visual field defect
374.30 Unspecified ptosis of eyelid ▽
374.31 Paralytic ptosis
374.32 Myogenic ptosis
374.33 Mechanical ptosis
374.34 Blepharochalasis
374.46 Blepharophimosis
743.61 Congenital ptosis of eyelid
743.62 Congenital deformity of eyelid
743.63 Other specified congenital anomaly of eyelid

ICD-9-CM Procedural

08.33 Repair of blepharoptosis by resection or advancement of levator muscle or aponeurosis
08.35 Repair of blepharoptosis by tarsal technique

67909

67909 Reduction of overcorrection of ptosis

ICD-9-CM Diagnostic

374.04 Cicatricial entropion
374.30 Unspecified ptosis of eyelid ▽
374.31 Paralytic ptosis
374.32 Myogenic ptosis
374.33 Mechanical ptosis
374.34 Blepharochalasis
374.41 Eyelid retraction or lag
743.61 Congenital ptosis of eyelid
V45.69 Other states following surgery of eye and adnexa

ICD-9-CM Procedural

08.37 Reduction of overcorrection of ptosis

HCPCS Level II Supplies & Services

A4305 Disposable drug delivery system, flow rate of 50 ml or greater per hour

67911

67911 Correction of lid retraction

ICD-9-CM Diagnostic

333.81 Blepharospasm — (Use additional E code to identify drug, if drug-induced)
351.0 Bell's palsy
370.34 Exposure keratoconjunctivitis
374.04 Cicatricial entropion
374.20 Unspecified lagophthalmos ▽
374.21 Paralytic lagophthalmos
374.22 Mechanical lagophthalmos
374.23 Cicatricial lagophthalmos
374.41 Eyelid retraction or lag
374.89 Other disorders of eyelid
376.21 Thyrotoxic exophthalmos — (Code first underlying thyroid disorder: 242.00-242.9) ☒
743.62 Congenital deformity of eyelid
906.5 Late effect of burn of eye, face, head, and neck

ICD-9-CM Procedural

08.38 Correction of lid retraction
08.59 Other adjustment of lid position

67912

67912 Correction of lagophthalmos, with implantation of upper eyelid lid load (eg, gold weight)

ICD-9-CM Diagnostic

374.20 Unspecified lagophthalmos ▽

374.21 Paralytic lagophthalmos
374.22 Mechanical lagophthalmos
374.23 Cicatricial lagophthalmos

ICD-9-CM Procedural

08.59 Other adjustment of lid position

67914

67914 Repair of ectropion; suture

ICD-9-CM Diagnostic

374.10 Unspecified ectropion
374.11 Senile ectropion
374.12 Mechanical ectropion
374.13 Spastic ectropion
374.14 Cicatricial ectropion
375.51 Eversion of lacrimal punctum

ICD-9-CM Procedural

08.42 Repair of entropion or ectropion by suture technique

HCPCS Level II Supplies & Services

A4305 Disposable drug delivery system, flow rate of 50 ml or greater per hour

67915

67915 Repair of ectropion; thermocauterization

ICD-9-CM Diagnostic

374.10 Unspecified ectropion
374.11 Senile ectropion
374.12 Mechanical ectropion
374.13 Spastic ectropion
374.14 Cicatricial ectropion
374.21 Paralytic lagophthalmos
375.51 Eversion of lacrimal punctum

ICD-9-CM Procedural

08.41 Repair of entropion or ectropion by thermocauterization

HCPCS Level II Supplies & Services

A4305 Disposable drug delivery system, flow rate of 50 ml or greater per hour

67916

67916 Repair of ectropion; excision tarsal wedge

ICD-9-CM Diagnostic

374.10 Unspecified ectropion
374.11 Senile ectropion
374.12 Mechanical ectropion
374.13 Spastic ectropion
374.14 Cicatricial ectropion
374.21 Paralytic lagophthalmos
374.30 Unspecified ptosis of eyelid
374.34 Blepharochalasis
375.51 Eversion of lacrimal punctum
728.4 Laxity of ligament

ICD-9-CM Procedural

08.43 Repair of entropion or ectropion with wedge resection

HCPCS Level II Supplies & Services

A4305 Disposable drug delivery system, flow rate of 50 ml or greater per hour

67917

67917 Repair of ectropion; extensive (eg, tarsal strip operations)

ICD-9-CM Diagnostic

333.81 Blepharospasm — (Use additional E code to identify drug, if drug-induced)
370.34 Exposure keratoconjunctivitis
374.11 Senile ectropion
374.12 Mechanical ectropion
374.13 Spastic ectropion
374.14 Cicatricial ectropion
374.21 Paralytic lagophthalmos
374.32 Myogenic ptosis
374.34 Blepharochalasis
374.41 Eyelid retraction or lag
374.50 Unspecified degenerative disorder of eyelid
374.9 Unspecified disorder of eyelid
375.52 Stenosis of lacrimal punctum
376.41 Hypertelorism of orbit
743.62 Congenital deformity of eyelid

ICD-9-CM Procedural

08.44 Repair of entropion or ectropion with lid reconstruction
08.49 Other repair of entropion or ectropion

67921-67924

67921 Repair of entropion; suture
67922 thermocauterization
67923 excision tarsal wedge
67924 extensive (eg, tarsal strip or capsulopalpebral fascia repairs operation)

ICD-9-CM Diagnostic

374.01 Senile entropion
374.02 Mechanical entropion
374.03 Spastic entropion
374.04 Cicatricial entropion
374.34 Blepharochalasis
374.89 Other disorders of eyelid

ICD-9-CM Procedural

08.41 Repair of entropion or ectropion by thermocauterization
08.42 Repair of entropion or ectropion by suture technique
08.43 Repair of entropion or ectropion with wedge resection
08.44 Repair of entropion or ectropion with lid reconstruction
08.49 Other repair of entropion or ectropion

HCPCS Level II Supplies & Services

A4305 Disposable drug delivery system, flow rate of 50 ml or greater per hour

67930-67935

67930 Suture of recent wound, eyelid, involving lid margin, tarsus, and/or palpebral conjunctiva direct closure; partial thickness
67935 full thickness

ICD-9-CM Diagnostic

870.0 Laceration of skin of eyelid and periocular area
870.1 Laceration of eyelid, full-thickness, not involving lacrimal passages
870.2 Laceration of eyelid involving lacrimal passages
870.8 Other specified open wound of ocular adnexa

ICD-9-CM Procedural

08.71 Reconstruction of eyelid involving lid margin, partial-thickness
08.82 Repair of laceration involving lid margin, partial-thickness
08.84 Repair of laceration of eyelid involving lid margin, full-thickness

08.99 Other operations on eyelids

HCPCS Level II Supplies & Services

A4305 Disposable drug delivery system, flow rate of 50 ml or greater per hour

67938

67938 Removal of embedded foreign body, eyelid

ICD-9-CM Diagnostic

374.86 Retained foreign body of eyelid — (Use additional code to identify foreign body (V90.01-V90.9))
379.91 Pain in or around eye
870.0 Laceration of skin of eyelid and periocular area
870.1 Laceration of eyelid, full-thickness, not involving lacrimal passages
918.1 Superficial injury of cornea
930.1 Foreign body in conjunctival sac
930.2 Foreign body in lacrimal punctum
930.8 Foreign body in other and combined sites on external eye
930.9 Foreign body in unspecified site on external eye ▽
998.4 Foreign body accidentally left during procedure, not elsewhere classified

ICD-9-CM Procedural

08.01 Incision of lid margin
08.09 Other incision of eyelid

HCPCS Level II Supplies & Services

A4305 Disposable drug delivery system, flow rate of 50 ml or greater per hour

67950

67950 Canthoplasty (reconstruction of canthus)

ICD-9-CM Diagnostic

173.10 Unspecified malignant neoplasm of eyelid, including canthus ▽
173.11 Basal cell carcinoma of eyelid, including canthus
173.12 Squamous cell carcinoma of eyelid, including canthus
173.19 Other specified malignant neoplasm of eyelid, including canthus
216.1 Benign neoplasm of eyelid, including canthus
232.1 Carcinoma in situ of eyelid, including canthus
238.2 Neoplasm of uncertain behavior of skin
239.2 Neoplasms of unspecified nature of bone, soft tissue, and skin
333.81 Blepharospasm — (Use additional E code to identify drug, if drug-induced)
374.10 Unspecified ectropion ▽
374.11 Senile ectropion
374.14 Cicatricial ectropion
374.20 Unspecified lagophthalmos ▽
374.22 Mechanical lagophthalmos
374.41 Eyelid retraction or lag
374.46 Blepharophimosis
376.36 Lateral displacement of globe of eye
376.41 Hypertelorism of orbit
376.50 Enophthalmos, unspecified as to cause ▽
376.51 Enophthalmos due to atrophy of orbital tissue
376.52 Enophthalmos due to trauma or surgery
743.62 Congenital deformity of eyelid
802.6 Orbital floor (blow-out), closed fracture
870.0 Laceration of skin of eyelid and periocular area
870.1 Laceration of eyelid, full-thickness, not involving lacrimal passages
870.2 Laceration of eyelid involving lacrimal passages
870.8 Other specified open wound of ocular adnexa
906.0 Late effect of open wound of head, neck, and trunk
906.5 Late effect of burn of eye, face, head, and neck
940.0 Chemical burn of eyelids and periocular area
940.1 Other burns of eyelids and periocular area
V10.82 Personal history of malignant melanoma of skin
V10.83 Personal history of other malignant neoplasm of skin
V10.84 Personal history of malignant neoplasm of eye

ICD-9-CM Procedural

08.59 Other adjustment of lid position

HCPCS Level II Supplies & Services

A4305 Disposable drug delivery system, flow rate of 50 ml or greater per hour

67961-67966

67961 Excision and repair of eyelid, involving lid margin, tarsus, conjunctiva, canthus, or full thickness, may include preparation for skin graft or pedicle flap with adjacent tissue transfer or rearrangement; up to 1/4 of lid margin
67966 over 1/4 of lid margin

ICD-9-CM Diagnostic

171.0 Malignant neoplasm of connective and other soft tissue of head, face, and neck
172.1 Malignant melanoma of skin of eyelid, including canthus
173.10 Unspecified malignant neoplasm of eyelid, including canthus ▽
173.11 Basal cell carcinoma of eyelid, including canthus
173.12 Squamous cell carcinoma of eyelid, including canthus
173.19 Other specified malignant neoplasm of eyelid, including canthus
198.2 Secondary malignant neoplasm of skin
198.89 Secondary malignant neoplasm of other specified sites
214.0 Lipoma of skin and subcutaneous tissue of face
215.0 Other benign neoplasm of connective and other soft tissue of head, face, and neck
216.1 Benign neoplasm of eyelid, including canthus
232.1 Carcinoma in situ of eyelid, including canthus
238.1 Neoplasm of uncertain behavior of connective and other soft tissue
238.2 Neoplasm of uncertain behavior of skin
239.2 Neoplasms of unspecified nature of bone, soft tissue, and skin
372.64 Scarring of conjunctiva
373.9 Unspecified inflammation of eyelid ▽
374.05 Trichiasis of eyelid without entropion
374.11 Senile ectropion
374.12 Mechanical ectropion
374.13 Spastic ectropion
374.14 Cicatricial ectropion
374.21 Paralytic lagophthalmos
709.2 Scar condition and fibrosis of skin
728.4 Laxity of ligament
743.62 Congenital deformity of eyelid
870.0 Laceration of skin of eyelid and periocular area
940.0 Chemical burn of eyelids and periocular area
940.1 Other burns of eyelids and periocular area

ICD-9-CM Procedural

08.61 Reconstruction of eyelid with skin flap or graft
08.73 Reconstruction of eyelid involving lid margin, full-thickness
08.74 Other reconstruction of eyelid, full-thickness

HCPCS Level II Supplies & Services

A4305 Disposable drug delivery system, flow rate of 50 ml or greater per hour

67971-67974

67971 Reconstruction of eyelid, full thickness by transfer of tarsoconjunctival flap from opposing eyelid; up to 2/3 of eyelid, 1 stage or first stage

67973 total eyelid, lower, 1 stage or first stage

67974 total eyelid, upper, 1 stage or first stage

ICD-9-CM Diagnostic

171.0 Malignant neoplasm of connective and other soft tissue of head, face, and neck
172.1 Malignant melanoma of skin of eyelid, including canthus
173.10 Unspecified malignant neoplasm of eyelid, including canthus ▽
173.11 Basal cell carcinoma of eyelid, including canthus
173.12 Squamous cell carcinoma of eyelid, including canthus
173.19 Other specified malignant neoplasm of eyelid, including canthus
198.2 Secondary malignant neoplasm of skin
198.89 Secondary malignant neoplasm of other specified sites
214.0 Lipoma of skin and subcutaneous tissue of face
215.0 Other benign neoplasm of connective and other soft tissue of head, face, and neck
216.1 Benign neoplasm of eyelid, including canthus
232.1 Carcinoma in situ of eyelid, including canthus
238.1 Neoplasm of uncertain behavior of connective and other soft tissue
238.2 Neoplasm of uncertain behavior of skin
239.2 Neoplasms of unspecified nature of bone, soft tissue, and skin
372.64 Scarring of conjunctiva
373.9 Unspecified inflammation of eyelid ▽
374.05 Trichiasis of eyelid without entropion
374.10 Unspecified ectropion ▽
374.11 Senile ectropion
374.12 Mechanical ectropion
374.13 Spastic ectropion
374.14 Cicatricial ectropion
374.21 Paralytic lagophthalmos
374.9 Unspecified disorder of eyelid ▽
709.2 Scar condition and fibrosis of skin
728.4 Laxity of ligament
743.62 Congenital deformity of eyelid
940.0 Chemical burn of eyelids and periocular area
940.1 Other burns of eyelids and periocular area
V10.82 Personal history of malignant melanoma of skin
V10.83 Personal history of other malignant neoplasm of skin
V10.84 Personal history of malignant neoplasm of eye

ICD-9-CM Procedural

08.64 Reconstruction of eyelid with tarsoconjunctival flap
08.74 Other reconstruction of eyelid, full-thickness

67975

67975 Reconstruction of eyelid, full thickness by transfer of tarsoconjunctival flap from opposing eyelid; second stage

ICD-9-CM Diagnostic

171.0 Malignant neoplasm of connective and other soft tissue of head, face, and neck
172.1 Malignant melanoma of skin of eyelid, including canthus
173.10 Unspecified malignant neoplasm of eyelid, including canthus ▽
173.11 Basal cell carcinoma of eyelid, including canthus
173.12 Squamous cell carcinoma of eyelid, including canthus
173.19 Other specified malignant neoplasm of eyelid, including canthus
198.2 Secondary malignant neoplasm of skin
198.89 Secondary malignant neoplasm of other specified sites
214.0 Lipoma of skin and subcutaneous tissue of face
215.0 Other benign neoplasm of connective and other soft tissue of head, face, and neck
216.1 Benign neoplasm of eyelid, including canthus
232.1 Carcinoma in situ of eyelid, including canthus
238.1 Neoplasm of uncertain behavior of connective and other soft tissue
238.2 Neoplasm of uncertain behavior of skin
239.2 Neoplasms of unspecified nature of bone, soft tissue, and skin
372.64 Scarring of conjunctiva
373.9 Unspecified inflammation of eyelid ▽
374.05 Trichiasis of eyelid without entropion
374.10 Unspecified ectropion ▽
374.11 Senile ectropion
374.12 Mechanical ectropion
374.13 Spastic ectropion
374.14 Cicatricial ectropion
374.21 Paralytic lagophthalmos
374.9 Unspecified disorder of eyelid ▽
709.2 Scar condition and fibrosis of skin
728.4 Laxity of ligament
743.62 Congenital deformity of eyelid
940.0 Chemical burn of eyelids and periocular area
940.1 Other burns of eyelids and periocular area
V10.82 Personal history of malignant melanoma of skin
V10.83 Personal history of other malignant neoplasm of skin
V10.84 Personal history of malignant neoplasm of eye

ICD-9-CM Procedural

08.64 Reconstruction of eyelid with tarsoconjunctival flap
08.74 Other reconstruction of eyelid, full-thickness
08.85 Other repair of laceration of eyelid, full-thickness

Conjunctiva

68020

68020 Incision of conjunctiva, drainage of cyst

ICD-9-CM Diagnostic

372.54 Conjunctival concretions
372.75 Conjunctival cysts
373.11 Hordeolum externum
373.13 Abscess of eyelid
373.2 Chalazion
374.84 Cysts of eyelids
706.2 Sebaceous cyst
871.0 Ocular laceration without prolapse of intraocular tissue

ICD-9-CM Procedural

10.1 Other incision of conjunctiva

68040

68040 Expression of conjunctival follicles (eg, for trachoma)

ICD-9-CM Diagnostic

076.0 Initial stage trachoma
076.1 Active stage trachoma
076.9 Unspecified trachoma ▽
139.1 Late effects of trachoma — (Note: This category is to be used to indicate conditions classifiable to categories 001-009, 020-041, 046-136 as the cause of late effects, which are themselves classified elsewhere. The "late effects" include conditions specified as such, as sequelae of diseases classifiable to the above categories if there is evidence that the disease itself is no longer present.)
372.02 Acute follicular conjunctivitis
372.55 Conjunctival pigmentations

372.61	Granuloma of conjunctiva
372.64	Scarring of conjunctiva
373.6	Parasitic infestation of eyelid — (Code first underlying disease: 085.0-085.9, 125.2, 125.3, 132.0) ☒

ICD-9-CM Procedural

10.1	Other incision of conjunctiva

68100

68100	Biopsy of conjunctiva

ICD-9-CM Diagnostic

173.10	Unspecified malignant neoplasm of eyelid, including canthus ▽
173.11	Basal cell carcinoma of eyelid, including canthus
173.12	Squamous cell carcinoma of eyelid, including canthus
173.19	Other specified malignant neoplasm of eyelid, including canthus
190.3	Malignant neoplasm of conjunctiva
198.4	Secondary malignant neoplasm of other parts of nervous system
216.1	Benign neoplasm of eyelid, including canthus
224.3	Benign neoplasm of conjunctiva
234.0	Carcinoma in situ of eye
238.8	Neoplasm of uncertain behavior of other specified sites
239.89	Neoplasms of unspecified nature, other specified sites
370.33	Keratoconjunctivitis sicca, not specified as Sjogren's
372.51	Pinguecula
372.75	Conjunctival cysts
372.9	Unspecified disorder of conjunctiva ▽
694.61	Benign mucous membrane pemphigoid with ocular involvement

ICD-9-CM Procedural

10.21	Biopsy of conjunctiva

68110-68115

68110	Excision of lesion, conjunctiva; up to 1 cm
68115	over 1 cm

ICD-9-CM Diagnostic

190.3	Malignant neoplasm of conjunctiva
198.4	Secondary malignant neoplasm of other parts of nervous system
224.3	Benign neoplasm of conjunctiva
234.0	Carcinoma in situ of eye
238.8	Neoplasm of uncertain behavior of other specified sites
239.89	Neoplasms of unspecified nature, other specified sites
372.03	Other mucopurulent conjunctivitis
372.15	Parasitic conjunctivitis — (Code first underlying disease: 085.5, 125.0-125.9) ☒
372.34	Pingueculitis
372.40	Unspecified pterygium ▽
372.45	Recurrent pterygium
372.51	Pinguecula
372.61	Granuloma of conjunctiva
372.71	Hyperemia of conjunctiva
372.74	Vascular abnormalities of conjunctiva
372.75	Conjunctival cysts
372.81	Conjunctivochalasis
372.89	Other disorders of conjunctiva
372.9	Unspecified disorder of conjunctiva ▽
694.61	Benign mucous membrane pemphigoid with ocular involvement

ICD-9-CM Procedural

10.31	Excision of lesion or tissue of conjunctiva

68130

68130	Excision of lesion, conjunctiva; with adjacent sclera

ICD-9-CM Diagnostic

190.0	Malignant neoplasm of eyeball, except conjunctiva, cornea, retina, and choroid
190.3	Malignant neoplasm of conjunctiva
198.4	Secondary malignant neoplasm of other parts of nervous system
224.0	Benign neoplasm of eyeball, except conjunctiva, cornea, retina, and choroid
224.3	Benign neoplasm of conjunctiva
234.0	Carcinoma in situ of eye
238.8	Neoplasm of uncertain behavior of other specified sites
239.89	Neoplasms of unspecified nature, other specified sites
369.9	Unspecified visual loss ▽
370.32	Limbar and corneal involvement in vernal conjunctivitis — (Use additional code for vernal conjunctivitis: 372.13)
372.45	Recurrent pterygium
372.51	Pinguecula
372.61	Granuloma of conjunctiva
372.71	Hyperemia of conjunctiva
372.74	Vascular abnormalities of conjunctiva
372.75	Conjunctival cysts
372.9	Unspecified disorder of conjunctiva ▽
694.61	Benign mucous membrane pemphigoid with ocular involvement

ICD-9-CM Procedural

10.31	Excision of lesion or tissue of conjunctiva
12.84	Excision or destruction of lesion of sclera

68135

68135	Destruction of lesion, conjunctiva

ICD-9-CM Diagnostic

190.3	Malignant neoplasm of conjunctiva
198.4	Secondary malignant neoplasm of other parts of nervous system
224.3	Benign neoplasm of conjunctiva
234.0	Carcinoma in situ of eye
238.8	Neoplasm of uncertain behavior of other specified sites
239.89	Neoplasms of unspecified nature, other specified sites
372.61	Granuloma of conjunctiva
372.62	Localized adhesions and strands of conjunctiva
372.64	Scarring of conjunctiva
372.71	Hyperemia of conjunctiva
372.74	Vascular abnormalities of conjunctiva
372.75	Conjunctival cysts
694.61	Benign mucous membrane pemphigoid with ocular involvement

ICD-9-CM Procedural

10.32	Destruction of lesion of conjunctiva

68200

68200	Subconjunctival injection

ICD-9-CM Diagnostic

190.3	Malignant neoplasm of conjunctiva
224.3	Benign neoplasm of conjunctiva
234.0	Carcinoma in situ of eye
238.8	Neoplasm of uncertain behavior of other specified sites
239.89	Neoplasms of unspecified nature, other specified sites
360.41	Blind hypotensive eye
360.42	Blind hypertensive eye
364.3	Unspecified iridocyclitis ▽

370.34 Exposure keratoconjunctivitis
372.10 Unspecified chronic conjunctivitis
372.61 Granuloma of conjunctiva
372.71 Hyperemia of conjunctiva
372.74 Vascular abnormalities of conjunctiva
372.75 Conjunctival cysts
372.81 Conjunctivochalasis
372.89 Other disorders of conjunctiva
379.00 Unspecified scleritis
379.60 Inflammation (infection) of postprocedural bleb, unspecified
379.61 Inflammation (infection) of postprocedural bleb, stage 1
379.62 Inflammation (infection) of postprocedural bleb, stage 2
379.63 Inflammation (infection) of postprocedural bleb, stage 3
694.61 Benign mucous membrane pemphigoid with ocular involvement

ICD-9-CM Procedural

10.91 Subconjunctival injection

68320-68325

68320 Conjunctivoplasty; with conjunctival graft or extensive rearrangement
68325 with buccal mucous membrane graft (includes obtaining graft)

ICD-9-CM Diagnostic

139.1 Late effects of trachoma — (Note: This category is to be used to indicate conditions classifiable to categories 001-009, 020-041, 046-136 as the cause of late effects, which are themselves classified elsewhere. The "late effects" include conditions specified as such, as sequelae of diseases classifiable to the above categories if there is evidence that the disease itself is no longer present.)
190.3 Malignant neoplasm of conjunctiva
198.4 Secondary malignant neoplasm of other parts of nervous system
224.3 Benign neoplasm of conjunctiva
234.0 Carcinoma in situ of eye
238.8 Neoplasm of uncertain behavior of other specified sites
239.89 Neoplasms of unspecified nature, other specified sites
360.32 Ocular fistula causing hypotony
360.89 Other disorders of globe
372.40 Unspecified pterygium
372.61 Granuloma of conjunctiva
372.62 Localized adhesions and strands of conjunctiva
372.63 Symblepharon
372.64 Scarring of conjunctiva
372.75 Conjunctival cysts
374.04 Cicatricial entropion
374.05 Trichiasis of eyelid without entropion
374.11 Senile ectropion
374.14 Cicatricial ectropion
376.9 Unspecified disorder of orbit
379.11 Scleral ectasia
743.62 Congenital deformity of eyelid
743.69 Other congenital anomalies of eyelids, lacrimal system, and orbit
870.1 Laceration of eyelid, full-thickness, not involving lacrimal passages
871.0 Ocular laceration without prolapse of intraocular tissue
871.1 Ocular laceration with prolapse or exposure of intraocular tissue
871.4 Unspecified laceration of eye
940.2 Alkaline chemical burn of cornea and conjunctival sac
940.3 Acid chemical burn of cornea and conjunctival sac
940.4 Other burn of cornea and conjunctival sac
996.59 Mechanical complication due to other implant and internal device, not elsewhere classified
V10.84 Personal history of malignant neoplasm of eye

ICD-9-CM Procedural

10.42 Reconstruction of conjunctival cul-de-sac with free graft
10.44 Other free graft to conjunctiva
10.49 Other conjunctivoplasty

68326-68328

68326 Conjunctivoplasty, reconstruction cul-de-sac; with conjunctival graft or extensive rearrangement
68328 with buccal mucous membrane graft (includes obtaining graft)

ICD-9-CM Diagnostic

190.3 Malignant neoplasm of conjunctiva
198.4 Secondary malignant neoplasm of other parts of nervous system
224.3 Benign neoplasm of conjunctiva
234.0 Carcinoma in situ of eye
238.8 Neoplasm of uncertain behavior of other specified sites
239.89 Neoplasms of unspecified nature, other specified sites
360.32 Ocular fistula causing hypotony
360.89 Other disorders of globe
372.61 Granuloma of conjunctiva
372.64 Scarring of conjunctiva
372.75 Conjunctival cysts
374.04 Cicatricial entropion
374.05 Trichiasis of eyelid without entropion
374.11 Senile ectropion
374.14 Cicatricial ectropion
376.9 Unspecified disorder of orbit
743.62 Congenital deformity of eyelid
743.69 Other congenital anomalies of eyelids, lacrimal system, and orbit
870.1 Laceration of eyelid, full-thickness, not involving lacrimal passages
871.0 Ocular laceration without prolapse of intraocular tissue
871.1 Ocular laceration with prolapse or exposure of intraocular tissue
871.4 Unspecified laceration of eye
940.2 Alkaline chemical burn of cornea and conjunctival sac
940.3 Acid chemical burn of cornea and conjunctival sac
940.4 Other burn of cornea and conjunctival sac
996.59 Mechanical complication due to other implant and internal device, not elsewhere classified
V10.84 Personal history of malignant neoplasm of eye

ICD-9-CM Procedural

10.42 Reconstruction of conjunctival cul-de-sac with free graft
10.43 Other reconstruction of conjunctival cul-de-sac

68330-68340

68330 Repair of symblepharon; conjunctivoplasty, without graft
68335 with free graft conjunctiva or buccal mucous membrane (includes obtaining graft)
68340 division of symblepharon, with or without insertion of conformer or contact lens

ICD-9-CM Diagnostic

372.63 Symblepharon

ICD-9-CM Procedural

10.41 Repair of symblepharon with free graft
10.49 Other conjunctivoplasty
10.5 Lysis of adhesions of conjunctiva and eyelid

68360

68360 Conjunctival flap; bridge or partial (separate procedure)

ICD-9-CM Diagnostic

139.1 Late effects of trachoma — (Note: This category is to be used to indicate conditions classifiable to categories 001-009, 020-041, 046-136 as the cause of late effects, which are themselves classified elsewhere. The "late effects" include conditions specified as such, as sequelae of diseases classifiable to the above categories if there is evidence that the disease itself is no longer present.)
190.3 Malignant neoplasm of conjunctiva
198.4 Secondary malignant neoplasm of other parts of nervous system
224.3 Benign neoplasm of conjunctiva
234.0 Carcinoma in situ of eye
238.8 Neoplasm of uncertain behavior of other specified sites
239.89 Neoplasms of unspecified nature, other specified sites
351.0 Bell's palsy
360.32 Ocular fistula causing hypotony
370.06 Perforated corneal ulcer
371.23 Bullous keratopathy
372.40 Unspecified pterygium ▽
372.45 Recurrent pterygium
372.61 Granuloma of conjunctiva
372.62 Localized adhesions and strands of conjunctiva
372.64 Scarring of conjunctiva
372.75 Conjunctival cysts
374.20 Unspecified lagophthalmos ▽
743.69 Other congenital anomalies of eyelids, lacrimal system, and orbit
870.1 Laceration of eyelid, full-thickness, not involving lacrimal passages
871.0 Ocular laceration without prolapse of intraocular tissue
871.4 Unspecified laceration of eye ▽
998.30 Disruption of wound, unspecified ▽
998.32 Disruption of external operation (surgical) wound
998.33 Disruption of traumatic injury wound repair
V10.84 Personal history of malignant neoplasm of eye

ICD-9-CM Procedural

10.49 Other conjunctivoplasty
11.53 Repair of corneal laceration or wound with conjunctival flap

68362

68362 Conjunctival flap; total (such as Gunderson thin flap or purse string flap)

ICD-9-CM Diagnostic

139.1 Late effects of trachoma — (Note: This category is to be used to indicate conditions classifiable to categories 001-009, 020-041, 046-136 as the cause of late effects, which are themselves classified elsewhere. The "late effects" include conditions specified as such, as sequelae of diseases classifiable to the above categories if there is evidence that the disease itself is no longer present.)
190.3 Malignant neoplasm of conjunctiva
198.4 Secondary malignant neoplasm of other parts of nervous system
224.3 Benign neoplasm of conjunctiva
234.0 Carcinoma in situ of eye
238.8 Neoplasm of uncertain behavior of other specified sites
239.89 Neoplasms of unspecified nature, other specified sites
351.0 Bell's palsy
360.32 Ocular fistula causing hypotony
370.06 Perforated corneal ulcer
371.23 Bullous keratopathy
371.82 Corneal disorder due to contact lens
372.45 Recurrent pterygium
372.61 Granuloma of conjunctiva
372.62 Localized adhesions and strands of conjunctiva
372.64 Scarring of conjunctiva
372.75 Conjunctival cysts
374.20 Unspecified lagophthalmos ▽
743.69 Other congenital anomalies of eyelids, lacrimal system, and orbit
870.1 Laceration of eyelid, full-thickness, not involving lacrimal passages
871.0 Ocular laceration without prolapse of intraocular tissue
871.4 Unspecified laceration of eye ▽
996.67 Infection and inflammatory reaction due to other internal orthopedic device, implant, and graft — (Use additional code to identify specified infections)
998.30 Disruption of wound, unspecified ▽
998.32 Disruption of external operation (surgical) wound
998.33 Disruption of traumatic injury wound repair
V10.84 Personal history of malignant neoplasm of eye

ICD-9-CM Procedural

10.49 Other conjunctivoplasty
11.53 Repair of corneal laceration or wound with conjunctival flap

68371

68371 Harvesting conjunctival allograft, living donor

ICD-9-CM Diagnostic

V59.8 Donor of other specified organ or tissue

ICD-9-CM Procedural

10.99 Other operations on conjunctiva

68400

68400 Incision, drainage of lacrimal gland

ICD-9-CM Diagnostic

375.00 Unspecified dacryoadenitis ▽
375.01 Acute dacryoadenitis
375.02 Chronic dacryoadenitis
375.03 Chronic enlargement of lacrimal gland
375.31 Acute canaliculitis, lacrimal
375.32 Acute dacryocystitis
375.33 Phlegmonous dacryocystitis
375.55 Obstruction of nasolacrimal duct, neonatal
743.64 Specified congenital anomaly of lacrimal gland
743.65 Specified congenital anomaly of lacrimal passages

ICD-9-CM Procedural

09.0 Incision of lacrimal gland

68420

68420 Incision, drainage of lacrimal sac (dacryocystotomy or dacryocystostomy)

ICD-9-CM Diagnostic

216.1 Benign neoplasm of eyelid, including canthus
375.01 Acute dacryoadenitis
375.02 Chronic dacryoadenitis
375.03 Chronic enlargement of lacrimal gland
375.30 Unspecified dacryocystitis ▽
375.31 Acute canaliculitis, lacrimal
375.32 Acute dacryocystitis
375.33 Phlegmonous dacryocystitis
375.54 Stenosis of lacrimal sac
375.55 Obstruction of nasolacrimal duct, neonatal
375.56 Stenosis of nasolacrimal duct, acquired
375.57 Dacryolith

376.01 Orbital cellulitis
743.64 Specified congenital anomaly of lacrimal gland
743.65 Specified congenital anomaly of lacrimal passages

ICD-9-CM Procedural

09.53 Incision of lacrimal sac

68440

68440 Snip incision of lacrimal punctum

ICD-9-CM Diagnostic

375.15 Unspecified tear film insufficiency
375.20 Epiphora, unspecified as to cause
375.31 Acute canaliculitis, lacrimal
375.41 Chronic canaliculitis
375.42 Chronic dacryocystitis
375.52 Stenosis of lacrimal punctum
375.56 Stenosis of nasolacrimal duct, acquired
375.9 Unspecified disorder of lacrimal system

ICD-9-CM Procedural

09.51 Incision of lacrimal punctum

68500-68505

68500 Excision of lacrimal gland (dacryoadenectomy), except for tumor; total
68505 partial

ICD-9-CM Diagnostic

375.03 Chronic enlargement of lacrimal gland
375.12 Other lacrimal cysts and cystic degeneration
375.13 Primary lacrimal atrophy
375.14 Secondary lacrimal atrophy
375.20 Epiphora, unspecified as to cause
375.21 Epiphora due to excess lacrimation

ICD-9-CM Procedural

09.20 Excision of lacrimal gland, not otherwise specified
09.21 Excision of lesion of lacrimal gland
09.22 Other partial dacryoadenectomy
09.23 Total dacryoadenectomy

68510

68510 Biopsy of lacrimal gland

ICD-9-CM Diagnostic

190.2 Malignant neoplasm of lacrimal gland
224.2 Benign neoplasm of lacrimal gland
234.0 Carcinoma in situ of eye
238.8 Neoplasm of uncertain behavior of other specified sites
239.89 Neoplasms of unspecified nature, other specified sites

ICD-9-CM Procedural

09.11 Biopsy of lacrimal gland

68520

68520 Excision of lacrimal sac (dacryocystectomy)

ICD-9-CM Diagnostic

190.7 Malignant neoplasm of lacrimal duct
224.7 Benign neoplasm of lacrimal duct
234.0 Carcinoma in situ of eye
238.8 Neoplasm of uncertain behavior of other specified sites
239.89 Neoplasms of unspecified nature, other specified sites
375.30 Unspecified dacryocystitis
375.53 Stenosis of lacrimal canaliculi
375.54 Stenosis of lacrimal sac

ICD-9-CM Procedural

09.6 Excision of lacrimal sac and passage

68525

68525 Biopsy of lacrimal sac

ICD-9-CM Diagnostic

190.7 Malignant neoplasm of lacrimal duct
224.7 Benign neoplasm of lacrimal duct
234.0 Carcinoma in situ of eye
238.8 Neoplasm of uncertain behavior of other specified sites
239.89 Neoplasms of unspecified nature, other specified sites
375.30 Unspecified dacryocystitis

ICD-9-CM Procedural

09.12 Biopsy of lacrimal sac

68530

68530 Removal of foreign body or dacryolith, lacrimal passages

ICD-9-CM Diagnostic

375.57 Dacryolith
930.2 Foreign body in lacrimal punctum
930.8 Foreign body in other and combined sites on external eye

ICD-9-CM Procedural

09.99 Other operations on lacrimal system

HCPCS Level II Supplies & Services

A4305 Disposable drug delivery system, flow rate of 50 ml or greater per hour

68540-68550

68540 Excision of lacrimal gland tumor; frontal approach
68550 involving osteotomy

ICD-9-CM Diagnostic

190.2 Malignant neoplasm of lacrimal gland
224.2 Benign neoplasm of lacrimal gland
234.0 Carcinoma in situ of eye
238.8 Neoplasm of uncertain behavior of other specified sites
239.89 Neoplasms of unspecified nature, other specified sites

ICD-9-CM Procedural

09.21 Excision of lesion of lacrimal gland
09.23 Total dacryoadenectomy
76.69 Other facial bone repair

HCPCS Level II Supplies & Services

A4305 Disposable drug delivery system, flow rate of 50 ml or greater per hour

68700

68700 Plastic repair of canaliculi

ICD-9-CM Diagnostic

173.10 Unspecified malignant neoplasm of eyelid, including canthus
173.11 Basal cell carcinoma of eyelid, including canthus
173.12 Squamous cell carcinoma of eyelid, including canthus
173.19 Other specified malignant neoplasm of eyelid, including canthus
190.7 Malignant neoplasm of lacrimal duct
224.7 Benign neoplasm of lacrimal duct

234.0 Carcinoma in situ of eye
238.8 Neoplasm of uncertain behavior of other specified sites
239.89 Neoplasms of unspecified nature, other specified sites
370.33 Keratoconjunctivitis sicca, not specified as Sjogren's
374.10 Unspecified ectropion
374.11 Senile ectropion
375.15 Unspecified tear film insufficiency
375.20 Epiphora, unspecified as to cause
375.21 Epiphora due to excess lacrimation
375.22 Epiphora due to insufficient drainage
375.30 Unspecified dacryocystitis
375.31 Acute canaliculitis, lacrimal
375.32 Acute dacryocystitis
375.33 Phlegmonous dacryocystitis
375.42 Chronic dacryocystitis
375.52 Stenosis of lacrimal punctum
375.53 Stenosis of lacrimal canaliculi
375.54 Stenosis of lacrimal sac
375.55 Obstruction of nasolacrimal duct, neonatal
375.56 Stenosis of nasolacrimal duct, acquired
375.61 Lacrimal fistula
743.65 Specified congenital anomaly of lacrimal passages
870.1 Laceration of eyelid, full-thickness, not involving lacrimal passages
870.2 Laceration of eyelid involving lacrimal passages
870.8 Other specified open wound of ocular adnexa

ICD-9-CM Procedural

09.73 Repair of canaliculus

HCPCS Level II Supplies & Services

A4305 Disposable drug delivery system, flow rate of 50 ml or greater per hour

68705

68705 Correction of everted punctum, cautery

ICD-9-CM Diagnostic

375.51 Eversion of lacrimal punctum

ICD-9-CM Procedural

09.71 Correction of everted punctum

68720

68720 Dacryocystorhinostomy (fistulization of lacrimal sac to nasal cavity)

ICD-9-CM Diagnostic

375.20 Epiphora, unspecified as to cause
375.22 Epiphora due to insufficient drainage
375.31 Acute canaliculitis, lacrimal
375.32 Acute dacryocystitis
375.33 Phlegmonous dacryocystitis
375.42 Chronic dacryocystitis
375.43 Lacrimal mucocele
375.53 Stenosis of lacrimal canaliculi
375.54 Stenosis of lacrimal sac
375.55 Obstruction of nasolacrimal duct, neonatal
375.56 Stenosis of nasolacrimal duct, acquired
743.65 Specified congenital anomaly of lacrimal passages

ICD-9-CM Procedural

09.81 Dacryocystorhinostomy (DCR)

68745-68750

68745 Conjunctivorhinostomy (fistulization of conjunctiva to nasal cavity); without tube
68750 with insertion of tube or stent

ICD-9-CM Diagnostic

375.20 Epiphora, unspecified as to cause
375.22 Epiphora due to insufficient drainage
375.30 Unspecified dacryocystitis
375.31 Acute canaliculitis, lacrimal
375.32 Acute dacryocystitis
375.33 Phlegmonous dacryocystitis
375.42 Chronic dacryocystitis
375.43 Lacrimal mucocele
375.53 Stenosis of lacrimal canaliculi
375.54 Stenosis of lacrimal sac
375.55 Obstruction of nasolacrimal duct, neonatal
375.56 Stenosis of nasolacrimal duct, acquired
743.65 Specified congenital anomaly of lacrimal passages

ICD-9-CM Procedural

09.82 Conjunctivocystorhinostomy
09.83 Conjunctivorhinostomy with insertion of tube or stent

68760

68760 Closure of the lacrimal punctum; by thermocauterization, ligation, or laser surgery

ICD-9-CM Diagnostic

370.20 Unspecified superficial keratitis
370.21 Punctate keratitis
370.23 Filamentary keratitis
370.33 Keratoconjunctivitis sicca, not specified as Sjogren's
370.34 Exposure keratoconjunctivitis
370.8 Other forms of keratitis — (Code first underlying condition: 118, 136.21)
371.42 Recurrent erosion of cornea
371.51 Juvenile epithelial corneal dystrophy
371.52 Other anterior corneal dystrophies
371.53 Granular corneal dystrophy
371.54 Lattice corneal dystrophy
371.55 Macular corneal dystrophy
371.56 Other stromal corneal dystrophies
371.57 Endothelial corneal dystrophy
371.58 Other posterior corneal dystrophies
374.41 Eyelid retraction or lag
375.00 Unspecified dacryoadenitis
375.15 Unspecified tear film insufficiency
710.2 Sicca syndrome

ICD-9-CM Procedural

09.72 Other repair of punctum
09.91 Obliteration of lacrimal punctum

68761

68761 Closure of the lacrimal punctum; by plug, each

ICD-9-CM Diagnostic

370.21 Punctate keratitis
370.23 Filamentary keratitis
370.33 Keratoconjunctivitis sicca, not specified as Sjogren's
370.34 Exposure keratoconjunctivitis
370.8 Other forms of keratitis — (Code first underlying condition: 118, 136.21)
370.9 Unspecified keratitis

371.42 Recurrent erosion of cornea
373.31 Eczematous dermatitis of eyelid
374.41 Eyelid retraction or lag
375.15 Unspecified tear film insufficiency
710.2 Sicca syndrome

ICD-9-CM Procedural

09.91 Obliteration of lacrimal punctum

HCPCS Level II Supplies & Services

A4262 Temporary, absorbable lacrimal duct implant, each
A4263 Permanent, long-term, nondissolvable lacrimal duct implant, each

68770

68770 Closure of lacrimal fistula (separate procedure)

ICD-9-CM Diagnostic

375.61 Lacrimal fistula

ICD-9-CM Procedural

09.99 Other operations on lacrimal system

HCPCS Level II Supplies & Services

A4305 Disposable drug delivery system, flow rate of 50 ml or greater per hour

68801

68801 Dilation of lacrimal punctum, with or without irrigation

ICD-9-CM Diagnostic

375.20 Epiphora, unspecified as to cause
375.22 Epiphora due to insufficient drainage
375.31 Acute canaliculitis, lacrimal
375.32 Acute dacryocystitis
375.33 Phlegmonous dacryocystitis
375.42 Chronic dacryocystitis
375.43 Lacrimal mucocele
375.52 Stenosis of lacrimal punctum
375.53 Stenosis of lacrimal canaliculi
375.54 Stenosis of lacrimal sac
375.55 Obstruction of nasolacrimal duct, neonatal
375.56 Stenosis of nasolacrimal duct, acquired
375.57 Dacryolith
375.61 Lacrimal fistula
375.69 Other change of lacrimal passages
375.81 Granuloma of lacrimal passages
375.89 Other disorder of lacrimal system
743.65 Specified congenital anomaly of lacrimal passages

ICD-9-CM Procedural

09.41 Probing of lacrimal punctum

HCPCS Level II Supplies & Services

A4305 Disposable drug delivery system, flow rate of 50 ml or greater per hour

68810-68816

68810 Probing of nasolacrimal duct, with or without irrigation;
68811 requiring general anesthesia
68815 with insertion of tube or stent
68816 with transluminal balloon catheter dilation

ICD-9-CM Diagnostic

370.33 Keratoconjunctivitis sicca, not specified as Sjogren's
375.22 Epiphora due to insufficient drainage
375.31 Acute canaliculitis, lacrimal
375.32 Acute dacryocystitis
375.33 Phlegmonous dacryocystitis
375.42 Chronic dacryocystitis
375.43 Lacrimal mucocele
375.52 Stenosis of lacrimal punctum
375.54 Stenosis of lacrimal sac
375.55 Obstruction of nasolacrimal duct, neonatal
375.56 Stenosis of nasolacrimal duct, acquired
375.57 Dacryolith
375.61 Lacrimal fistula
375.69 Other change of lacrimal passages
375.81 Granuloma of lacrimal passages
375.89 Other disorder of lacrimal system
743.65 Specified congenital anomaly of lacrimal passages
771.6 Neonatal conjunctivitis and dacryocystitis — (Use additional code(s) to further specify condition)

ICD-9-CM Procedural

09.43 Probing of nasolacrimal duct
09.44 Intubation of nasolacrimal duct

HCPCS Level II Supplies & Services

A4262 Temporary, absorbable lacrimal duct implant, each

68840

68840 Probing of lacrimal canaliculi, with or without irrigation

ICD-9-CM Diagnostic

375.21 Epiphora due to excess lacrimation
375.22 Epiphora due to insufficient drainage
375.30 Unspecified dacryocystitis
375.32 Acute dacryocystitis
375.42 Chronic dacryocystitis
375.51 Eversion of lacrimal punctum
375.52 Stenosis of lacrimal punctum
375.53 Stenosis of lacrimal canaliculi
375.55 Obstruction of nasolacrimal duct, neonatal
375.56 Stenosis of nasolacrimal duct, acquired

ICD-9-CM Procedural

09.42 Probing of lacrimal canaliculi

HCPCS Level II Supplies & Services

A4305 Disposable drug delivery system, flow rate of 50 ml or greater per hour

68850

68850 Injection of contrast medium for dacryocystography

ICD-9-CM Diagnostic

190.7 Malignant neoplasm of lacrimal duct
224.7 Benign neoplasm of lacrimal duct
375.54 Stenosis of lacrimal sac
375.56 Stenosis of nasolacrimal duct, acquired
375.57 Dacryolith
375.9 Unspecified disorder of lacrimal system
743.65 Specified congenital anomaly of lacrimal passages
930.2 Foreign body in lacrimal punctum

ICD-9-CM Procedural

09.19 Other diagnostic procedures on lacrimal system
87.05 Contrast dacryocystogram

Auditory System

External Ear

69000-69005

69000 Drainage external ear, abscess or hematoma; simple
69005 complicated

ICD-9-CM Diagnostic

380.10 Unspecified infective otitis externa
380.11 Acute infection of pinna
380.31 Hematoma of auricle or pinna
680.0 Carbuncle and furuncle of face
706.2 Sebaceous cyst
729.92 Nontraumatic hematoma of soft tissue
738.7 Cauliflower ear
872.11 Open wound of auricle, complicated
920 Contusion of face, scalp, and neck except eye(s)
998.30 Disruption of wound, unspecified
998.51 Infected postoperative seroma — (Use additional code to identify organism)
998.59 Other postoperative infection — (Use additional code to identify infection)

ICD-9-CM Procedural

18.09 Other incision of external ear

HCPCS Level II Supplies & Services

A4305 Disposable drug delivery system, flow rate of 50 ml or greater per hour

69020

69020 Drainage external auditory canal, abscess

ICD-9-CM Diagnostic

380.10 Unspecified infective otitis externa
380.16 Other chronic infective otitis externa
380.21 Cholesteatoma of external ear
380.22 Other acute otitis externa
380.23 Other chronic otitis externa
680.0 Carbuncle and furuncle of face
780.62 Postprocedural fever
872.12 Open wound of auditory canal, complicated

ICD-9-CM Procedural

18.02 Incision of external auditory canal

HCPCS Level II Supplies & Services

A4305 Disposable drug delivery system, flow rate of 50 ml or greater per hour

69090

69090 Ear piercing

ICD-9-CM Diagnostic

V50.3 Ear piercing

ICD-9-CM Procedural

18.01 Piercing of ear lobe

69100

69100 Biopsy external ear

ICD-9-CM Diagnostic

171.0 Malignant neoplasm of connective and other soft tissue of head, face, and neck
172.2 Malignant melanoma of skin of ear and external auditory canal
173.20 Unspecified malignant neoplasm of skin of ear and external auditory canal
173.21 Basal cell carcinoma of skin of ear and external auditory canal
173.22 Squamous cell carcinoma of skin of ear and external auditory canal
173.29 Other specified malignant neoplasm of skin of ear and external auditory canal
198.2 Secondary malignant neoplasm of skin
198.89 Secondary malignant neoplasm of other specified sites
215.0 Other benign neoplasm of connective and other soft tissue of head, face, and neck
216.2 Benign neoplasm of ear and external auditory canal
232.2 Carcinoma in situ of skin of ear and external auditory canal
238.1 Neoplasm of uncertain behavior of connective and other soft tissue
238.2 Neoplasm of uncertain behavior of skin
239.2 Neoplasms of unspecified nature of bone, soft tissue, and skin
380.01 Acute perichondritis of pinna
701.5 Other abnormal granulation tissue
702.0 Actinic keratosis

ICD-9-CM Procedural

18.12 Biopsy of external ear

HCPCS Level II Supplies & Services

A4305 Disposable drug delivery system, flow rate of 50 ml or greater per hour

69105

69105 Biopsy external auditory canal

ICD-9-CM Diagnostic

171.0 Malignant neoplasm of connective and other soft tissue of head, face, and neck
172.2 Malignant melanoma of skin of ear and external auditory canal
173.20 Unspecified malignant neoplasm of skin of ear and external auditory canal
173.21 Basal cell carcinoma of skin of ear and external auditory canal
173.22 Squamous cell carcinoma of skin of ear and external auditory canal
173.29 Other specified malignant neoplasm of skin of ear and external auditory canal
198.2 Secondary malignant neoplasm of skin
198.89 Secondary malignant neoplasm of other specified sites
215.0 Other benign neoplasm of connective and other soft tissue of head, face, and neck
216.2 Benign neoplasm of ear and external auditory canal
232.2 Carcinoma in situ of skin of ear and external auditory canal
238.1 Neoplasm of uncertain behavior of connective and other soft tissue
238.2 Neoplasm of uncertain behavior of skin
239.2 Neoplasms of unspecified nature of bone, soft tissue, and skin
380.21 Cholesteatoma of external ear
380.23 Other chronic otitis externa
701.5 Other abnormal granulation tissue
709.4 Foreign body granuloma of skin and subcutaneous tissue — (Use additional code to identify foreign body (V90.01-V90.9))

ICD-9-CM Procedural

18.12 Biopsy of external ear

HCPCS Level II Supplies & Services

A4305 Disposable drug delivery system, flow rate of 50 ml or greater per hour

69110-69120

69110 Excision external ear; partial, simple repair
69120 complete amputation

ICD-9-CM Diagnostic

171.0 Malignant neoplasm of connective and other soft tissue of head, face, and neck
172.2 Malignant melanoma of skin of ear and external auditory canal
173.20 Unspecified malignant neoplasm of skin of ear and external auditory canal
173.21 Basal cell carcinoma of skin of ear and external auditory canal
173.22 Squamous cell carcinoma of skin of ear and external auditory canal
173.29 Other specified malignant neoplasm of skin of ear and external auditory canal
198.2 Secondary malignant neoplasm of skin
198.89 Secondary malignant neoplasm of other specified sites
215.0 Other benign neoplasm of connective and other soft tissue of head, face, and neck
216.2 Benign neoplasm of ear and external auditory canal
232.2 Carcinoma in situ of skin of ear and external auditory canal
238.1 Neoplasm of uncertain behavior of connective and other soft tissue
238.2 Neoplasm of uncertain behavior of skin
239.2 Neoplasms of unspecified nature of bone, soft tissue, and skin
380.21 Cholesteatoma of external ear
709.4 Foreign body granuloma of skin and subcutaneous tissue — (Use additional code to identify foreign body (V90.01-V90.9))
738.7 Cauliflower ear
872.01 Open wound of auricle, without mention of complication
925.1 Crushing injury of face and scalp — (Use additional code to identify any associated injuries, such as: 800-829, 850.0-854.1, 860.0-869.1)
959.01 Head injury, unspecified
959.09 Injury of face and neck, other and unspecified

ICD-9-CM Procedural

18.29 Excision or destruction of other lesion of external ear
18.39 Other excision of external ear

HCPCS Level II Supplies & Services

A4305 Disposable drug delivery system, flow rate of 50 ml or greater per hour

69140

69140 Excision exostosis(es), external auditory canal

ICD-9-CM Diagnostic

380.81 Exostosis of external ear canal

ICD-9-CM Procedural

18.29 Excision or destruction of other lesion of external ear

HCPCS Level II Supplies & Services

A4305 Disposable drug delivery system, flow rate of 50 ml or greater per hour

69145

69145 Excision soft tissue lesion, external auditory canal

ICD-9-CM Diagnostic

171.0 Malignant neoplasm of connective and other soft tissue of head, face, and neck
172.2 Malignant melanoma of skin of ear and external auditory canal
173.20 Unspecified malignant neoplasm of skin of ear and external auditory canal
173.21 Basal cell carcinoma of skin of ear and external auditory canal
173.22 Squamous cell carcinoma of skin of ear and external auditory canal
173.29 Other specified malignant neoplasm of skin of ear and external auditory canal
198.2 Secondary malignant neoplasm of skin
198.89 Secondary malignant neoplasm of other specified sites
214.9 Lipoma of unspecified site
215.0 Other benign neoplasm of connective and other soft tissue of head, face, and neck
216.2 Benign neoplasm of ear and external auditory canal
232.2 Carcinoma in situ of skin of ear and external auditory canal
238.1 Neoplasm of uncertain behavior of connective and other soft tissue
238.2 Neoplasm of uncertain behavior of skin
239.2 Neoplasms of unspecified nature of bone, soft tissue, and skin
380.21 Cholesteatoma of external ear
380.23 Other chronic otitis externa
680.0 Carbuncle and furuncle of face
701.5 Other abnormal granulation tissue
706.2 Sebaceous cyst

ICD-9-CM Procedural

18.29 Excision or destruction of other lesion of external ear

HCPCS Level II Supplies & Services

A4305 Disposable drug delivery system, flow rate of 50 ml or greater per hour

69150-69155

69150 Radical excision external auditory canal lesion; without neck dissection
69155 with neck dissection

ICD-9-CM Diagnostic

171.0 Malignant neoplasm of connective and other soft tissue of head, face, and neck
172.2 Malignant melanoma of skin of ear and external auditory canal
173.20 Unspecified malignant neoplasm of skin of ear and external auditory canal
173.21 Basal cell carcinoma of skin of ear and external auditory canal
173.22 Squamous cell carcinoma of skin of ear and external auditory canal
173.29 Other specified malignant neoplasm of skin of ear and external auditory canal
198.2 Secondary malignant neoplasm of skin
198.89 Secondary malignant neoplasm of other specified sites
216.2 Benign neoplasm of ear and external auditory canal
232.2 Carcinoma in situ of skin of ear and external auditory canal
238.2 Neoplasm of uncertain behavior of skin
239.2 Neoplasms of unspecified nature of bone, soft tissue, and skin
380.14 Malignant otitis externa

ICD-9-CM Procedural

18.31 Radical excision of lesion of external ear
40.40 Radical neck dissection, not otherwise specified

69200-69205

69200 Removal foreign body from external auditory canal; without general anesthesia
69205 with general anesthesia

ICD-9-CM Diagnostic

931 Foreign body in ear

ICD-9-CM Procedural

18.9 Other operations on external ear
98.11 Removal of intraluminal foreign body from ear without incision

HCPCS Level II Supplies & Services

A4305 Disposable drug delivery system, flow rate of 50 ml or greater per hour

69210

69210 Removal impacted cerumen requiring instrumentation, unilateral

ICD-9-CM Diagnostic

380.4 Impacted cerumen

ICD-9-CM Procedural

96.52 Irrigation of ear

HCPCS Level II Supplies & Services

G0268 Removal of impacted cerumen (one or both ears) by physician on same date of service as audiologic function testing

69220-69222

69220 Debridement, mastoidectomy cavity, simple (eg, routine cleaning)
69222 Debridement, mastoidectomy cavity, complex (eg, with anesthesia or more than routine cleaning)

ICD-9-CM Diagnostic

382.9 Unspecified otitis media ▽
383.00 Acute mastoiditis without complications
383.1 Chronic mastoiditis
383.30 Unspecified postmastoidectomy complication ▽
383.32 Recurrent cholesteatoma of postmastoidectomy cavity
383.33 Granulations of postmastoidectomy cavity
383.89 Other disorder of mastoid
385.30 Unspecified cholesteatoma ▽
385.31 Cholesteatoma of attic
385.33 Cholesteatoma of middle ear and mastoid
388.60 Unspecified otorrhea ▽

ICD-9-CM Procedural

86.28 Nonexcisional debridement of wound, infection, or burn

HCPCS Level II Supplies & Services

A4305 Disposable drug delivery system, flow rate of 50 ml or greater per hour

69300

69300 Otoplasty, protruding ear, with or without size reduction

ICD-9-CM Diagnostic

380.32 Acquired deformities of auricle or pinna
744.22 Macrotia
744.29 Other congenital anomaly of ear
V50.1 Other plastic surgery for unacceptable cosmetic appearance

ICD-9-CM Procedural

18.5 Surgical correction of prominent ear

HCPCS Level II Supplies & Services

A4305 Disposable drug delivery system, flow rate of 50 ml or greater per hour

69310

69310 Reconstruction of external auditory canal (meatoplasty) (eg, for stenosis due to injury, infection) (separate procedure)

ICD-9-CM Diagnostic

380.23 Other chronic otitis externa
380.50 Acquired stenosis of external ear canal unspecified as to cause ▽
380.51 Acquired stenosis of external ear canal secondary to trauma
380.52 Acquired stenosis of external ear canal secondary to surgery
380.53 Acquired stenosis of external ear canal secondary to inflammation

ICD-9-CM Procedural

18.6 Reconstruction of external auditory canal

69320

69320 Reconstruction external auditory canal for congenital atresia, single stage

ICD-9-CM Diagnostic

744.02 Other congenital anomaly of external ear causing impairment of hearing

ICD-9-CM Procedural

18.6 Reconstruction of external auditory canal

Middle Ear

69400-69401

69400 Eustachian tube inflation, transnasal; with catheterization
69401 without catheterization

ICD-9-CM Diagnostic

381.10 Simple or unspecified chronic serous otitis media ▽
381.20 Simple or unspecified chronic mucoid otitis media ▽
381.29 Other chronic mucoid otitis media
381.3 Other and unspecified chronic nonsuppurative otitis media ▽
381.50 Unspecified Eustachian salpingitis ▽
381.51 Acute Eustachian salpingitis
381.52 Chronic Eustachian salpingitis
381.60 Unspecified obstruction of Eustachian tube ▽
381.61 Osseous obstruction of Eustachian tube
381.62 Intrinsic cartilagenous obstruction of Eustachian tube
381.63 Extrinsic cartilagenous obstruction of Eustachian tube
381.81 Dysfunction of Eustachian tube

ICD-9-CM Procedural

20.8 Operations on Eustachian tube

HCPCS Level II Supplies & Services

A4305 Disposable drug delivery system, flow rate of 50 ml or greater per hour

69405

69405 Eustachian tube catheterization, transtympanic

ICD-9-CM Diagnostic

381.10 Simple or unspecified chronic serous otitis media ▽
381.20 Simple or unspecified chronic mucoid otitis media ▽
381.29 Other chronic mucoid otitis media
381.3 Other and unspecified chronic nonsuppurative otitis media ▽
381.50 Unspecified Eustachian salpingitis ▽
381.51 Acute Eustachian salpingitis
381.52 Chronic Eustachian salpingitis
381.60 Unspecified obstruction of Eustachian tube ▽
381.61 Osseous obstruction of Eustachian tube
381.62 Intrinsic cartilagenous obstruction of Eustachian tube
381.63 Extrinsic cartilagenous obstruction of Eustachian tube
381.81 Dysfunction of Eustachian tube

ICD-9-CM Procedural

20.8 Operations on Eustachian tube

HCPCS Level II Supplies & Services

A4305 Disposable drug delivery system, flow rate of 50 ml or greater per hour

69420-69421

69420 Myringotomy including aspiration and/or eustachian tube inflation
69421 Myringotomy including aspiration and/or eustachian tube inflation requiring general anesthesia

ICD-9-CM Diagnostic

381.01 Acute serous otitis media
381.02 Acute mucoid otitis media
381.03 Acute sanguinous otitis media
381.04 Acute allergic serous otitis media
381.05 Acute allergic mucoid otitis media
381.06 Acute allergic sanguinous otitis media
381.10 Simple or unspecified chronic serous otitis media ▽

381.19 Other chronic serous otitis media
381.20 Simple or unspecified chronic mucoid otitis media ▽
381.29 Other chronic mucoid otitis media
381.3 Other and unspecified chronic nonsuppurative otitis media ▽
381.4 Nonsuppurative otitis media, not specified as acute or chronic ▽
381.81 Dysfunction of Eustachian tube
381.89 Other disorders of Eustachian tube
382.00 Acute suppurative otitis media without spontaneous rupture of eardrum
382.3 Unspecified chronic suppurative otitis media ▽
383.00 Acute mastoiditis without complications
383.01 Subperiosteal abscess of mastoid
383.02 Acute mastoiditis with other complications
385.89 Other disorders of middle ear and mastoid
389.03 Conductive hearing loss, middle ear
389.05 Conductive hearing loss, unilateral
389.06 Conductive hearing loss, bilateral

ICD-9-CM Procedural

20.09 Other myringotomy
20.8 Operations on Eustachian tube

HCPCS Level II Supplies & Services

A4305 Disposable drug delivery system, flow rate of 50 ml or greater per hour

69424

69424 Ventilating tube removal requiring general anesthesia

ICD-9-CM Diagnostic

381.10 Simple or unspecified chronic serous otitis media ▽
381.20 Simple or unspecified chronic mucoid otitis media ▽
381.29 Other chronic mucoid otitis media
381.3 Other and unspecified chronic nonsuppurative otitis media ▽
381.4 Nonsuppurative otitis media, not specified as acute or chronic ▽
381.81 Dysfunction of Eustachian tube
382.00 Acute suppurative otitis media without spontaneous rupture of eardrum
382.1 Chronic tubotympanic suppurative otitis media
382.2 Chronic atticoantral suppurative otitis media
996.59 Mechanical complication due to other implant and internal device, not elsewhere classified
996.69 Infection and inflammatory reaction due to other internal prosthetic device, implant, and graft — (Use additional code to identify specified infections)
996.79 Other complications due to other internal prosthetic device, implant, and graft — (Use additional code to identify complication: 338.18-338.19, 338.28-338.29)
V53.09 Fitting and adjustment of other devices related to nervous system and special senses

ICD-9-CM Procedural

20.1 Removal of tympanostomy tube

HCPCS Level II Supplies & Services

A4305 Disposable drug delivery system, flow rate of 50 ml or greater per hour

69433-69436

69433 Tympanostomy (requiring insertion of ventilating tube), local or topical anesthesia
69436 Tympanostomy (requiring insertion of ventilating tube), general anesthesia

ICD-9-CM Diagnostic

381.00 Unspecified acute nonsuppurative otitis media ▽
381.01 Acute serous otitis media
381.10 Simple or unspecified chronic serous otitis media ▽
381.19 Other chronic serous otitis media
381.20 Simple or unspecified chronic mucoid otitis media ▽
381.29 Other chronic mucoid otitis media
381.3 Other and unspecified chronic nonsuppurative otitis media ▽
381.4 Nonsuppurative otitis media, not specified as acute or chronic ▽
381.7 Patulous Eustachian tube
381.81 Dysfunction of Eustachian tube
382.00 Acute suppurative otitis media without spontaneous rupture of eardrum
382.1 Chronic tubotympanic suppurative otitis media
382.3 Unspecified chronic suppurative otitis media ▽
384.81 Atrophic flaccid tympanic membrane
389.02 Conductive hearing loss, tympanic membrane
996.59 Mechanical complication due to other implant and internal device, not elsewhere classified
996.69 Infection and inflammatory reaction due to other internal prosthetic device, implant, and graft — (Use additional code to identify specified infections)
996.79 Other complications due to other internal prosthetic device, implant, and graft — (Use additional code to identify complication: 338.18-338.19, 338.28-338.29)

ICD-9-CM Procedural

20.01 Myringotomy with insertion of tube

HCPCS Level II Supplies & Services

A4305 Disposable drug delivery system, flow rate of 50 ml or greater per hour

69440

69440 Middle ear exploration through postauricular or ear canal incision

ICD-9-CM Diagnostic

384.21 Central perforation of tympanic membrane
384.22 Attic perforation of tympanic membrane
384.23 Other marginal perforation of tympanic membrane
384.24 Multiple perforations of tympanic membrane
384.25 Total perforation of tympanic membrane
384.81 Atrophic flaccid tympanic membrane
384.82 Atrophic nonflaccid tympanic membrane
385.01 Tympanosclerosis involving tympanic membrane only
385.02 Tympanosclerosis involving tympanic membrane and ear ossicles
385.03 Tympanosclerosis involving tympanic membrane, ear ossicles, and middle ear
385.09 Tympanosclerosis involving other combination of structures
385.10 Adhesive middle ear disease, unspecified as to involvement ▽
385.19 Other middle ear adhesions and combinations
385.23 Discontinuity or dislocation of ear ossicles
385.32 Cholesteatoma of middle ear
385.83 Retained foreign body of middle ear — (Use additional code to identify foreign body (V90.01-V90.9))
385.89 Other disorders of middle ear and mastoid
386.41 Round window fistula
386.42 Oval window fistula
386.48 Labyrinthine fistula of combined sites
389.03 Conductive hearing loss, middle ear
389.05 Conductive hearing loss, unilateral
389.06 Conductive hearing loss, bilateral
389.13 Neural hearing loss, unilateral
389.17 Sensory hearing loss, unilateral
389.20 Mixed hearing loss, unspecified ▽
389.21 Mixed hearing loss, unilateral
389.22 Mixed hearing loss, bilateral
872.61 Open wound of ear drum, without mention of complication
872.62 Open wound of ossicles, without mention of complication
872.71 Open wound of ear drum, complicated

ICD-9-CM Procedural

20.09 Other myringotomy

20.39 Other diagnostic procedures on middle and inner ear

69450

69450 Tympanolysis, transcanal

ICD-9-CM Diagnostic

385.10 Adhesive middle ear disease, unspecified as to involvement ▽
385.11 Adhesions of drum head to incus
385.12 Adhesions of drum head to stapes
385.13 Adhesions of drum head to promontorium
385.19 Other middle ear adhesions and combinations
389.03 Conductive hearing loss, middle ear
389.05 Conductive hearing loss, unilateral
389.06 Conductive hearing loss, bilateral
389.08 Conductive hearing loss of combined types
389.13 Neural hearing loss, unilateral
389.17 Sensory hearing loss, unilateral
389.20 Mixed hearing loss, unspecified ▽
389.21 Mixed hearing loss, unilateral
389.22 Mixed hearing loss, bilateral

ICD-9-CM Procedural

20.23 Incision of middle ear

HCPCS Level II Supplies & Services

A4305 Disposable drug delivery system, flow rate of 50 ml or greater per hour

69501

69501 Transmastoid antrotomy (simple mastoidectomy)

ICD-9-CM Diagnostic

383.00 Acute mastoiditis without complications
383.01 Subperiosteal abscess of mastoid
383.02 Acute mastoiditis with other complications
383.1 Chronic mastoiditis
383.9 Unspecified mastoiditis ▽
385.30 Unspecified cholesteatoma ▽

ICD-9-CM Procedural

20.41 Simple mastoidectomy

69502

69502 Mastoidectomy; complete

ICD-9-CM Diagnostic

383.00 Acute mastoiditis without complications
383.01 Subperiosteal abscess of mastoid
383.02 Acute mastoiditis with other complications
383.1 Chronic mastoiditis
383.21 Acute petrositis
383.22 Chronic petrositis
383.9 Unspecified mastoiditis ▽
385.30 Unspecified cholesteatoma ▽
385.33 Cholesteatoma of middle ear and mastoid
385.35 Diffuse cholesteatosis of middle ear and mastoid

ICD-9-CM Procedural

20.49 Other mastoidectomy

69505

69505 Mastoidectomy; modified radical

ICD-9-CM Diagnostic

383.1 Chronic mastoiditis
383.20 Unspecified petrositis ▽
383.21 Acute petrositis
383.22 Chronic petrositis
383.89 Other disorder of mastoid
385.30 Unspecified cholesteatoma ▽
385.31 Cholesteatoma of attic
385.33 Cholesteatoma of middle ear and mastoid
385.35 Diffuse cholesteatosis of middle ear and mastoid

ICD-9-CM Procedural

20.49 Other mastoidectomy

69511

69511 Mastoidectomy; radical

ICD-9-CM Diagnostic

160.1 Malignant neoplasm of auditory tube, middle ear, and mastoid air cells
197.3 Secondary malignant neoplasm of other respiratory organs
231.8 Carcinoma in situ of other specified parts of respiratory system
235.9 Neoplasm of uncertain behavior of other and unspecified respiratory organs ▽
237.3 Neoplasm of uncertain behavior of paraganglia
239.1 Neoplasm of unspecified nature of respiratory system
383.1 Chronic mastoiditis
383.20 Unspecified petrositis ▽
383.21 Acute petrositis
383.22 Chronic petrositis
383.89 Other disorder of mastoid
385.30 Unspecified cholesteatoma ▽
385.31 Cholesteatoma of attic
385.33 Cholesteatoma of middle ear and mastoid
385.35 Diffuse cholesteatosis of middle ear and mastoid

ICD-9-CM Procedural

20.42 Radical mastoidectomy

69530

69530 Petrous apicectomy including radical mastoidectomy

ICD-9-CM Diagnostic

383.20 Unspecified petrositis ▽
383.21 Acute petrositis
383.22 Chronic petrositis
385.21 Impaired mobility of malleus
385.30 Unspecified cholesteatoma ▽
385.33 Cholesteatoma of middle ear and mastoid
385.35 Diffuse cholesteatosis of middle ear and mastoid
744.29 Other congenital anomaly of ear

ICD-9-CM Procedural

20.22 Incision of petrous pyramid air cells
20.42 Radical mastoidectomy
20.59 Other excision of middle ear

69535

69535 Resection temporal bone, external approach

ICD-9-CM Diagnostic

160.1 Malignant neoplasm of auditory tube, middle ear, and mastoid air cells
170.0 Malignant neoplasm of bones of skull and face, except mandible
171.0 Malignant neoplasm of connective and other soft tissue of head, face, and neck
172.2 Malignant melanoma of skin of ear and external auditory canal
197.3 Secondary malignant neoplasm of other respiratory organs
198.5 Secondary malignant neoplasm of bone and bone marrow
235.9 Neoplasm of uncertain behavior of other and unspecified respiratory organs

ICD-9-CM Procedural

20.59 Other excision of middle ear

69540

69540 Excision aural polyp

ICD-9-CM Diagnostic

385.30 Unspecified cholesteatoma
385.31 Cholesteatoma of attic
385.32 Cholesteatoma of middle ear
385.33 Cholesteatoma of middle ear and mastoid

ICD-9-CM Procedural

20.51 Excision of lesion of middle ear

HCPCS Level II Supplies & Services

A4305 Disposable drug delivery system, flow rate of 50 ml or greater per hour

69550

69550 Excision aural glomus tumor; transcanal

ICD-9-CM Diagnostic

194.6 Malignant neoplasm of aortic body and other paraganglia
212.0 Benign neoplasm of nasal cavities, middle ear, and accessory sinuses
216.2 Benign neoplasm of ear and external auditory canal
237.3 Neoplasm of uncertain behavior of paraganglia

ICD-9-CM Procedural

20.51 Excision of lesion of middle ear

HCPCS Level II Supplies & Services

A4305 Disposable drug delivery system, flow rate of 50 ml or greater per hour

69552

69552 Excision aural glomus tumor; transmastoid

ICD-9-CM Diagnostic

194.6 Malignant neoplasm of aortic body and other paraganglia
212.0 Benign neoplasm of nasal cavities, middle ear, and accessory sinuses
216.2 Benign neoplasm of ear and external auditory canal
237.3 Neoplasm of uncertain behavior of paraganglia

ICD-9-CM Procedural

20.51 Excision of lesion of middle ear

69554

69554 Excision aural glomus tumor; extended (extratemporal)

ICD-9-CM Diagnostic

194.6 Malignant neoplasm of aortic body and other paraganglia
212.0 Benign neoplasm of nasal cavities, middle ear, and accessory sinuses
216.2 Benign neoplasm of ear and external auditory canal
237.3 Neoplasm of uncertain behavior of paraganglia

ICD-9-CM Procedural

20.51 Excision of lesion of middle ear

69601

69601 Revision mastoidectomy; resulting in complete mastoidectomy

ICD-9-CM Diagnostic

383.01 Subperiosteal abscess of mastoid
383.02 Acute mastoiditis with other complications
383.1 Chronic mastoiditis
383.21 Acute petrositis
383.22 Chronic petrositis
383.30 Unspecified postmastoidectomy complication
383.31 Mucosal cyst of postmastoidectomy cavity
383.32 Recurrent cholesteatoma of postmastoidectomy cavity
383.33 Granulations of postmastoidectomy cavity
383.81 Postauricular fistula
383.9 Unspecified mastoiditis
385.30 Unspecified cholesteatoma
385.33 Cholesteatoma of middle ear and mastoid

ICD-9-CM Procedural

20.49 Other mastoidectomy
20.92 Revision of mastoidectomy

69602

69602 Revision mastoidectomy; resulting in modified radical mastoidectomy

ICD-9-CM Diagnostic

383.01 Subperiosteal abscess of mastoid
383.02 Acute mastoiditis with other complications
383.1 Chronic mastoiditis
383.21 Acute petrositis
383.22 Chronic petrositis
383.30 Unspecified postmastoidectomy complication
383.32 Recurrent cholesteatoma of postmastoidectomy cavity
383.33 Granulations of postmastoidectomy cavity
385.24 Partial loss or necrosis of ear ossicles
385.30 Unspecified cholesteatoma
385.31 Cholesteatoma of attic
385.33 Cholesteatoma of middle ear and mastoid
385.35 Diffuse cholesteatosis of middle ear and mastoid

ICD-9-CM Procedural

20.49 Other mastoidectomy
20.92 Revision of mastoidectomy

69603

69603 Revision mastoidectomy; resulting in radical mastoidectomy

ICD-9-CM Diagnostic

381.3 Other and unspecified chronic nonsuppurative otitis media
383.01 Subperiosteal abscess of mastoid
383.02 Acute mastoiditis with other complications
383.1 Chronic mastoiditis
383.20 Unspecified petrositis
383.21 Acute petrositis
383.22 Chronic petrositis
383.30 Unspecified postmastoidectomy complication
383.32 Recurrent cholesteatoma of postmastoidectomy cavity
383.81 Postauricular fistula

385.30 Unspecified cholesteatoma ▽
385.31 Cholesteatoma of attic
385.33 Cholesteatoma of middle ear and mastoid
385.35 Diffuse cholesteatosis of middle ear and mastoid

ICD-9-CM Procedural

20.42 Radical mastoidectomy
20.92 Revision of mastoidectomy

69604

69604 Revision mastoidectomy; resulting in tympanoplasty

ICD-9-CM Diagnostic

381.10 Simple or unspecified chronic serous otitis media ▽
381.3 Other and unspecified chronic nonsuppurative otitis media ▽
382.1 Chronic tubotympanic suppurative otitis media
382.2 Chronic atticoantral suppurative otitis media
382.3 Unspecified chronic suppurative otitis media ▽
383.02 Acute mastoiditis with other complications
383.1 Chronic mastoiditis
383.30 Unspecified postmastoidectomy complication ▽
383.32 Recurrent cholesteatoma of postmastoidectomy cavity
383.33 Granulations of postmastoidectomy cavity
384.21 Central perforation of tympanic membrane
384.24 Multiple perforations of tympanic membrane
385.31 Cholesteatoma of attic

ICD-9-CM Procedural

19.4 Myringoplasty
19.6 Revision of tympanoplasty
20.49 Other mastoidectomy
20.92 Revision of mastoidectomy

69605

69605 Revision mastoidectomy; with apicectomy

ICD-9-CM Diagnostic

383.1 Chronic mastoiditis
383.21 Acute petrositis
383.22 Chronic petrositis
383.32 Recurrent cholesteatoma of postmastoidectomy cavity
385.30 Unspecified cholesteatoma ▽
385.33 Cholesteatoma of middle ear and mastoid
385.35 Diffuse cholesteatosis of middle ear and mastoid

ICD-9-CM Procedural

20.49 Other mastoidectomy
20.59 Other excision of middle ear
20.92 Revision of mastoidectomy

69610-69620

69610 Tympanic membrane repair, with or without site preparation of perforation for closure, with or without patch
69620 Myringoplasty (surgery confined to drumhead and donor area)

ICD-9-CM Diagnostic

381.02 Acute mucoid otitis media
382.1 Chronic tubotympanic suppurative otitis media
382.2 Chronic atticoantral suppurative otitis media
382.3 Unspecified chronic suppurative otitis media ▽
384.20 Unspecified perforation of tympanic membrane ▽
384.21 Central perforation of tympanic membrane
384.22 Attic perforation of tympanic membrane
384.23 Other marginal perforation of tympanic membrane
384.24 Multiple perforations of tympanic membrane
384.25 Total perforation of tympanic membrane
389.02 Conductive hearing loss, tympanic membrane
872.61 Open wound of ear drum, without mention of complication
872.71 Open wound of ear drum, complicated
996.59 Mechanical complication due to other implant and internal device, not elsewhere classified
996.79 Other complications due to other internal prosthetic device, implant, and graft — (Use additional code to identify complication: 338.18-338.19, 338.28-338.29)

ICD-9-CM Procedural

19.4 Myringoplasty
19.52 Type II tympanoplasty

HCPCS Level II Supplies & Services

A4305 Disposable drug delivery system, flow rate of 50 ml or greater per hour

69631

69631 Tympanoplasty without mastoidectomy (including canalplasty, atticotomy and/or middle ear surgery), initial or revision; without ossicular chain reconstruction

ICD-9-CM Diagnostic

381.03 Acute sanguinous otitis media
381.10 Simple or unspecified chronic serous otitis media ▽
381.3 Other and unspecified chronic nonsuppurative otitis media ▽
381.4 Nonsuppurative otitis media, not specified as acute or chronic ▽
382.00 Acute suppurative otitis media without spontaneous rupture of eardrum
382.1 Chronic tubotympanic suppurative otitis media
382.2 Chronic atticoantral suppurative otitis media
382.3 Unspecified chronic suppurative otitis media ▽
384.20 Unspecified perforation of tympanic membrane ▽
384.21 Central perforation of tympanic membrane
384.22 Attic perforation of tympanic membrane
384.23 Other marginal perforation of tympanic membrane
384.24 Multiple perforations of tympanic membrane
384.25 Total perforation of tympanic membrane
384.81 Atrophic flaccid tympanic membrane
385.32 Cholesteatoma of middle ear
389.02 Conductive hearing loss, tympanic membrane

ICD-9-CM Procedural

19.52 Type II tympanoplasty

69632

69632 Tympanoplasty without mastoidectomy (including canalplasty, atticotomy and/or middle ear surgery), initial or revision; with ossicular chain reconstruction (eg, postfenestration)

ICD-9-CM Diagnostic

382.00 Acute suppurative otitis media without spontaneous rupture of eardrum
382.01 Acute suppurative otitis media with spontaneous rupture of eardrum
382.3 Unspecified chronic suppurative otitis media ▽
384.20 Unspecified perforation of tympanic membrane ▽
384.25 Total perforation of tympanic membrane
384.81 Atrophic flaccid tympanic membrane
385.02 Tympanosclerosis involving tympanic membrane and ear ossicles
385.21 Impaired mobility of malleus
385.22 Impaired mobility of other ear ossicles
385.23 Discontinuity or dislocation of ear ossicles
385.24 Partial loss or necrosis of ear ossicles

385.31 Cholesteatoma of attic
385.32 Cholesteatoma of middle ear
385.33 Cholesteatoma of middle ear and mastoid
389.02 Conductive hearing loss, tympanic membrane
389.03 Conductive hearing loss, middle ear
389.05 Conductive hearing loss, unilateral
389.06 Conductive hearing loss, bilateral
744.02 Other congenital anomaly of external ear causing impairment of hearing
801.00 Closed fracture of base of skull without mention of intracranial injury, unspecified state of consciousness ▽

ICD-9-CM Procedural

18.6 Reconstruction of external auditory canal
19.3 Other operations on ossicular chain
19.53 Type III tympanoplasty
19.54 Type IV tympanoplasty

69633

69633 Tympanoplasty without mastoidectomy (including canalplasty, atticotomy and/or middle ear surgery), initial or revision; with ossicular chain reconstruction and synthetic prosthesis (eg, partial ossicular replacement prosthesis [PORP], total ossicular replacement prosthesis [TORP])

ICD-9-CM Diagnostic

382.00 Acute suppurative otitis media without spontaneous rupture of eardrum
382.01 Acute suppurative otitis media with spontaneous rupture of eardrum
382.3 Unspecified chronic suppurative otitis media ▽
384.20 Unspecified perforation of tympanic membrane ▽
384.25 Total perforation of tympanic membrane
384.81 Atrophic flaccid tympanic membrane
385.02 Tympanosclerosis involving tympanic membrane and ear ossicles
385.03 Tympanosclerosis involving tympanic membrane, ear ossicles, and middle ear
385.09 Tympanosclerosis involving other combination of structures
385.21 Impaired mobility of malleus
385.22 Impaired mobility of other ear ossicles
385.23 Discontinuity or dislocation of ear ossicles
385.24 Partial loss or necrosis of ear ossicles
385.31 Cholesteatoma of attic
385.32 Cholesteatoma of middle ear
385.33 Cholesteatoma of middle ear and mastoid
389.00 Unspecified conductive hearing loss ▽
389.02 Conductive hearing loss, tympanic membrane
389.03 Conductive hearing loss, middle ear
744.02 Other congenital anomaly of external ear causing impairment of hearing
744.04 Congenital anomalies of ear ossicles
801.00 Closed fracture of base of skull without mention of intracranial injury, unspecified state of consciousness ▽

ICD-9-CM Procedural

19.3 Other operations on ossicular chain
19.53 Type III tympanoplasty
19.54 Type IV tympanoplasty

69635

69635 Tympanoplasty with antrotomy or mastoidotomy (including canalplasty, atticotomy, middle ear surgery, and/or tympanic membrane repair); without ossicular chain reconstruction

ICD-9-CM Diagnostic

382.01 Acute suppurative otitis media with spontaneous rupture of eardrum
382.1 Chronic tubotympanic suppurative otitis media
382.2 Chronic atticoantral suppurative otitis media
382.3 Unspecified chronic suppurative otitis media ▽
383.1 Chronic mastoiditis
384.20 Unspecified perforation of tympanic membrane ▽
384.21 Central perforation of tympanic membrane
384.22 Attic perforation of tympanic membrane
384.23 Other marginal perforation of tympanic membrane
384.24 Multiple perforations of tympanic membrane
384.25 Total perforation of tympanic membrane
384.81 Atrophic flaccid tympanic membrane
385.32 Cholesteatoma of middle ear
385.33 Cholesteatoma of middle ear and mastoid
389.02 Conductive hearing loss, tympanic membrane
389.03 Conductive hearing loss, middle ear
389.05 Conductive hearing loss, unilateral
389.06 Conductive hearing loss, bilateral
389.20 Mixed hearing loss, unspecified ▽
389.21 Mixed hearing loss, unilateral
389.22 Mixed hearing loss, bilateral
744.02 Other congenital anomaly of external ear causing impairment of hearing
801.00 Closed fracture of base of skull without mention of intracranial injury, unspecified state of consciousness ▽

ICD-9-CM Procedural

19.52 Type II tympanoplasty

69636

69636 Tympanoplasty with antrotomy or mastoidotomy (including canalplasty, atticotomy, middle ear surgery, and/or tympanic membrane repair); with ossicular chain reconstruction

ICD-9-CM Diagnostic

382.01 Acute suppurative otitis media with spontaneous rupture of eardrum
382.1 Chronic tubotympanic suppurative otitis media
382.2 Chronic atticoantral suppurative otitis media
382.3 Unspecified chronic suppurative otitis media ▽
384.20 Unspecified perforation of tympanic membrane ▽
384.21 Central perforation of tympanic membrane
384.22 Attic perforation of tympanic membrane
384.23 Other marginal perforation of tympanic membrane
384.24 Multiple perforations of tympanic membrane
384.25 Total perforation of tympanic membrane
384.81 Atrophic flaccid tympanic membrane
385.02 Tympanosclerosis involving tympanic membrane and ear ossicles
385.21 Impaired mobility of malleus
385.22 Impaired mobility of other ear ossicles
385.23 Discontinuity or dislocation of ear ossicles
385.24 Partial loss or necrosis of ear ossicles
389.02 Conductive hearing loss, tympanic membrane
389.03 Conductive hearing loss, middle ear
389.05 Conductive hearing loss, unilateral
389.06 Conductive hearing loss, bilateral
389.08 Conductive hearing loss of combined types
389.13 Neural hearing loss, unilateral
389.17 Sensory hearing loss, unilateral
389.20 Mixed hearing loss, unspecified ▽
389.21 Mixed hearing loss, unilateral
389.22 Mixed hearing loss, bilateral
744.02 Other congenital anomaly of external ear causing impairment of hearing
801.00 Closed fracture of base of skull without mention of intracranial injury, unspecified state of consciousness ▽

ICD-9-CM Procedural

19.3 Other operations on ossicular chain
19.52 Type II tympanoplasty
19.53 Type III tympanoplasty
19.54 Type IV tympanoplasty

69637

69637 Tympanoplasty with antrotomy or mastoidotomy (including canalplasty, atticotomy, middle ear surgery, and/or tympanic membrane repair); with ossicular chain reconstruction and synthetic prosthesis (eg, partial ossicular replacement prosthesis [PORP], total ossicular replacement prosthesis [TORP])

ICD-9-CM Diagnostic

382.01 Acute suppurative otitis media with spontaneous rupture of eardrum
382.1 Chronic tubotympanic suppurative otitis media
382.2 Chronic atticoantral suppurative otitis media
384.20 Unspecified perforation of tympanic membrane
384.21 Central perforation of tympanic membrane
384.22 Attic perforation of tympanic membrane
384.23 Other marginal perforation of tympanic membrane
384.24 Multiple perforations of tympanic membrane
384.25 Total perforation of tympanic membrane
384.81 Atrophic flaccid tympanic membrane
385.02 Tympanosclerosis involving tympanic membrane and ear ossicles
385.21 Impaired mobility of malleus
385.22 Impaired mobility of other ear ossicles
385.23 Discontinuity or dislocation of ear ossicles
385.24 Partial loss or necrosis of ear ossicles
389.02 Conductive hearing loss, tympanic membrane
389.03 Conductive hearing loss, middle ear
389.05 Conductive hearing loss, unilateral
389.06 Conductive hearing loss, bilateral
389.08 Conductive hearing loss of combined types
389.13 Neural hearing loss, unilateral
389.17 Sensory hearing loss, unilateral
389.20 Mixed hearing loss, unspecified
389.21 Mixed hearing loss, unilateral
389.22 Mixed hearing loss, bilateral
744.02 Other congenital anomaly of external ear causing impairment of hearing
801.00 Closed fracture of base of skull without mention of intracranial injury, unspecified state of consciousness

ICD-9-CM Procedural

19.52 Type II tympanoplasty
19.53 Type III tympanoplasty
19.54 Type IV tympanoplasty

69641

69641 Tympanoplasty with mastoidectomy (including canalplasty, middle ear surgery, tympanic membrane repair); without ossicular chain reconstruction

ICD-9-CM Diagnostic

382.1 Chronic tubotympanic suppurative otitis media
382.2 Chronic atticoantral suppurative otitis media
382.3 Unspecified chronic suppurative otitis media
383.1 Chronic mastoiditis
384.21 Central perforation of tympanic membrane
384.22 Attic perforation of tympanic membrane
384.23 Other marginal perforation of tympanic membrane
385.32 Cholesteatoma of middle ear
385.33 Cholesteatoma of middle ear and mastoid
387.0 Otosclerosis involving oval window, nonobliterative
387.1 Otosclerosis involving oval window, obliterative
387.2 Cochlear otosclerosis
387.8 Other otosclerosis
389.02 Conductive hearing loss, tympanic membrane
389.03 Conductive hearing loss, middle ear
389.05 Conductive hearing loss, unilateral
389.06 Conductive hearing loss, bilateral

ICD-9-CM Procedural

19.52 Type II tympanoplasty

69642

69642 Tympanoplasty with mastoidectomy (including canalplasty, middle ear surgery, tympanic membrane repair); with ossicular chain reconstruction

ICD-9-CM Diagnostic

381.19 Other chronic serous otitis media
381.29 Other chronic mucoid otitis media
382.01 Acute suppurative otitis media with spontaneous rupture of eardrum
382.3 Unspecified chronic suppurative otitis media
384.20 Unspecified perforation of tympanic membrane
384.25 Total perforation of tympanic membrane
384.81 Atrophic flaccid tympanic membrane
385.02 Tympanosclerosis involving tympanic membrane and ear ossicles
385.21 Impaired mobility of malleus
385.22 Impaired mobility of other ear ossicles
385.23 Discontinuity or dislocation of ear ossicles
385.24 Partial loss or necrosis of ear ossicles
385.32 Cholesteatoma of middle ear
389.02 Conductive hearing loss, tympanic membrane
389.03 Conductive hearing loss, middle ear
389.05 Conductive hearing loss, unilateral
389.06 Conductive hearing loss, bilateral
389.08 Conductive hearing loss of combined types
389.13 Neural hearing loss, unilateral
389.17 Sensory hearing loss, unilateral
389.20 Mixed hearing loss, unspecified
389.21 Mixed hearing loss, unilateral
389.22 Mixed hearing loss, bilateral

ICD-9-CM Procedural

19.3 Other operations on ossicular chain
19.53 Type III tympanoplasty
19.54 Type IV tympanoplasty

69643

69643 Tympanoplasty with mastoidectomy (including canalplasty, middle ear surgery, tympanic membrane repair); with intact or reconstructed wall, without ossicular chain reconstruction

ICD-9-CM Diagnostic

382.1 Chronic tubotympanic suppurative otitis media
382.2 Chronic atticoantral suppurative otitis media
382.3 Unspecified chronic suppurative otitis media
383.1 Chronic mastoiditis
384.21 Central perforation of tympanic membrane
384.22 Attic perforation of tympanic membrane
384.23 Other marginal perforation of tympanic membrane
384.25 Total perforation of tympanic membrane
385.32 Cholesteatoma of middle ear

385.33	Cholesteatoma of middle ear and mastoid
387.0	Otosclerosis involving oval window, nonobliterative
387.1	Otosclerosis involving oval window, obliterative
387.2	Cochlear otosclerosis
387.8	Other otosclerosis
389.02	Conductive hearing loss, tympanic membrane
389.03	Conductive hearing loss, middle ear
389.05	Conductive hearing loss, unilateral
389.06	Conductive hearing loss, bilateral

ICD-9-CM Procedural

18.6	Reconstruction of external auditory canal
19.52	Type II tympanoplasty
20.41	Simple mastoidectomy
20.49	Other mastoidectomy

69644

69644 Tympanoplasty with mastoidectomy (including canalplasty, middle ear surgery, tympanic membrane repair); with intact or reconstructed canal wall, with ossicular chain reconstruction

ICD-9-CM Diagnostic

382.01	Acute suppurative otitis media with spontaneous rupture of eardrum
382.1	Chronic tubotympanic suppurative otitis media
382.2	Chronic atticoantral suppurative otitis media
383.1	Chronic mastoiditis
384.22	Attic perforation of tympanic membrane
384.25	Total perforation of tympanic membrane
384.81	Atrophic flaccid tympanic membrane
385.02	Tympanosclerosis involving tympanic membrane and ear ossicles
385.03	Tympanosclerosis involving tympanic membrane, ear ossicles, and middle ear
385.21	Impaired mobility of malleus
385.22	Impaired mobility of other ear ossicles
385.23	Discontinuity or dislocation of ear ossicles
385.24	Partial loss or necrosis of ear ossicles
385.32	Cholesteatoma of middle ear
385.33	Cholesteatoma of middle ear and mastoid
389.02	Conductive hearing loss, tympanic membrane
389.03	Conductive hearing loss, middle ear
389.05	Conductive hearing loss, unilateral
389.06	Conductive hearing loss, bilateral

ICD-9-CM Procedural

19.3	Other operations on ossicular chain
19.53	Type III tympanoplasty
19.54	Type IV tympanoplasty

69645

69645 Tympanoplasty with mastoidectomy (including canalplasty, middle ear surgery, tympanic membrane repair); radical or complete, without ossicular chain reconstruction

ICD-9-CM Diagnostic

382.1	Chronic tubotympanic suppurative otitis media
382.2	Chronic atticoantral suppurative otitis media
382.3	Unspecified chronic suppurative otitis media ▽
383.1	Chronic mastoiditis
384.22	Attic perforation of tympanic membrane
385.32	Cholesteatoma of middle ear
385.33	Cholesteatoma of middle ear and mastoid

ICD-9-CM Procedural

19.52	Type II tympanoplasty

69646

69646 Tympanoplasty with mastoidectomy (including canalplasty, middle ear surgery, tympanic membrane repair); radical or complete, with ossicular chain reconstruction

ICD-9-CM Diagnostic

382.01	Acute suppurative otitis media with spontaneous rupture of eardrum
382.1	Chronic tubotympanic suppurative otitis media
382.2	Chronic atticoantral suppurative otitis media
384.22	Attic perforation of tympanic membrane
384.25	Total perforation of tympanic membrane
384.81	Atrophic flaccid tympanic membrane
385.02	Tympanosclerosis involving tympanic membrane and ear ossicles
385.21	Impaired mobility of malleus
385.22	Impaired mobility of other ear ossicles
385.23	Discontinuity or dislocation of ear ossicles
385.24	Partial loss or necrosis of ear ossicles
385.32	Cholesteatoma of middle ear
389.02	Conductive hearing loss, tympanic membrane
389.03	Conductive hearing loss, middle ear
389.05	Conductive hearing loss, unilateral
389.06	Conductive hearing loss, bilateral
389.08	Conductive hearing loss of combined types
389.13	Neural hearing loss, unilateral
389.17	Sensory hearing loss, unilateral
389.20	Mixed hearing loss, unspecified ▽
389.21	Mixed hearing loss, unilateral
389.22	Mixed hearing loss, bilateral

ICD-9-CM Procedural

19.3	Other operations on ossicular chain
19.53	Type III tympanoplasty
19.54	Type IV tympanoplasty

69650

69650 Stapes mobilization

ICD-9-CM Diagnostic

387.0	Otosclerosis involving oval window, nonobliterative
387.8	Other otosclerosis
387.9	Unspecified otosclerosis ▽
389.00	Unspecified conductive hearing loss ▽
389.05	Conductive hearing loss, unilateral
389.06	Conductive hearing loss, bilateral
389.08	Conductive hearing loss of combined types

ICD-9-CM Procedural

19.0	Stapes mobilization

69660-69661

69660 Stapedectomy or stapedotomy with reestablishment of ossicular continuity, with or without use of foreign material;

69661 with footplate drill out

ICD-9-CM Diagnostic

385.03	Tympanosclerosis involving tympanic membrane, ear ossicles, and middle ear
385.09	Tympanosclerosis involving other combination of structures
385.10	Adhesive middle ear disease, unspecified as to involvement ▽
385.12	Adhesions of drum head to stapes

385.19 Other middle ear adhesions and combinations
385.22 Impaired mobility of other ear ossicles
385.23 Discontinuity or dislocation of ear ossicles
385.24 Partial loss or necrosis of ear ossicles
387.0 Otosclerosis involving oval window, nonobliterative
387.1 Otosclerosis involving oval window, obliterative
387.8 Other otosclerosis
387.9 Unspecified otosclerosis ▽
389.00 Unspecified conductive hearing loss ▽
389.02 Conductive hearing loss, tympanic membrane
389.03 Conductive hearing loss, middle ear
389.05 Conductive hearing loss, unilateral
389.06 Conductive hearing loss, bilateral
389.08 Conductive hearing loss of combined types
389.10 Unspecified sensorineural hearing loss ▽
389.13 Neural hearing loss, unilateral
389.17 Sensory hearing loss, unilateral
389.18 Sensorineural hearing loss, bilateral
389.9 Unspecified hearing loss ▽
744.04 Congenital anomalies of ear ossicles
744.09 Other congenital anomalies of ear causing impairment of hearing

ICD-9-CM Procedural

19.11 Stapedectomy with incus replacement
19.19 Other stapedectomy

69662

69662 Revision of stapedectomy or stapedotomy

ICD-9-CM Diagnostic

385.03 Tympanosclerosis involving tympanic membrane, ear ossicles, and middle ear
385.09 Tympanosclerosis involving other combination of structures
385.10 Adhesive middle ear disease, unspecified as to involvement ▽
385.12 Adhesions of drum head to stapes
385.19 Other middle ear adhesions and combinations
385.22 Impaired mobility of other ear ossicles
385.23 Discontinuity or dislocation of ear ossicles
385.24 Partial loss or necrosis of ear ossicles
387.0 Otosclerosis involving oval window, nonobliterative
387.8 Other otosclerosis
389.05 Conductive hearing loss, unilateral
389.06 Conductive hearing loss, bilateral
389.08 Conductive hearing loss of combined types
389.13 Neural hearing loss, unilateral
389.17 Sensory hearing loss, unilateral
389.18 Sensorineural hearing loss, bilateral
744.04 Congenital anomalies of ear ossicles
744.09 Other congenital anomalies of ear causing impairment of hearing
996.70 Other complications due to unspecified device, implant, and graft — (Use additional code to identify complication: 338.18-338.19, 338.28-338.29) ▽
996.79 Other complications due to other internal prosthetic device, implant, and graft — (Use additional code to identify complication: 338.18-338.19, 338.28-338.29)

ICD-9-CM Procedural

19.19 Other stapedectomy
19.21 Revision of stapedectomy with incus replacement
19.29 Other revision of stapedectomy

69666

69666 Repair oval window fistula

ICD-9-CM Diagnostic

385.30 Unspecified cholesteatoma ▽
386.10 Unspecified peripheral vertigo ▽
386.42 Oval window fistula
386.48 Labyrinthine fistula of combined sites
388.61 Cerebrospinal fluid otorrhea
389.17 Sensory hearing loss, unilateral
389.18 Sensorineural hearing loss, bilateral

ICD-9-CM Procedural

20.93 Repair of oval and round windows

69667

69667 Repair round window fistula

ICD-9-CM Diagnostic

386.10 Unspecified peripheral vertigo ▽
386.41 Round window fistula
386.48 Labyrinthine fistula of combined sites
388.61 Cerebrospinal fluid otorrhea
389.17 Sensory hearing loss, unilateral
389.18 Sensorineural hearing loss, bilateral

ICD-9-CM Procedural

20.93 Repair of oval and round windows

69670

69670 Mastoid obliteration (separate procedure)

ICD-9-CM Diagnostic

382.9 Unspecified otitis media ▽
383.1 Chronic mastoiditis
383.30 Unspecified postmastoidectomy complication ▽
383.31 Mucosal cyst of postmastoidectomy cavity
383.32 Recurrent cholesteatoma of postmastoidectomy cavity
385.30 Unspecified cholesteatoma ▽
385.33 Cholesteatoma of middle ear and mastoid
388.61 Cerebrospinal fluid otorrhea

ICD-9-CM Procedural

19.9 Other repair of middle ear

69676

69676 Tympanic neurectomy

ICD-9-CM Diagnostic

352.1 Glossopharyngeal neuralgia
388.5 Disorders of acoustic nerve
388.71 Otogenic pain
527.7 Disturbance of salivary secretion

ICD-9-CM Procedural

20.91 Tympanosympathectomy

69700

69700 Closure postauricular fistula, mastoid (separate procedure)

ICD-9-CM Diagnostic

383.81 Postauricular fistula

ICD-9-CM Procedural

19.9 Other repair of middle ear

69710

69710 Implantation or replacement of electromagnetic bone conduction hearing device in temporal bone

ICD-9-CM Diagnostic

388.12 Noise-induced hearing loss
389.00 Unspecified conductive hearing loss
389.01 Conductive hearing loss, external ear
389.02 Conductive hearing loss, tympanic membrane
389.03 Conductive hearing loss, middle ear
389.04 Conductive hearing loss, inner ear
389.05 Conductive hearing loss, unilateral
389.06 Conductive hearing loss, bilateral
389.08 Conductive hearing loss of combined types
744.02 Other congenital anomaly of external ear causing impairment of hearing
996.60 Infection and inflammatory reaction due to unspecified device, implant, and graft — (Use additional code to identify specified infections)
996.79 Other complications due to other internal prosthetic device, implant, and graft — (Use additional code to identify complication: 338.18-338.19, 338.28-338.29)

ICD-9-CM Procedural

20.95 Implantation of electromagnetic hearing device

69711

69711 Removal or repair of electromagnetic bone conduction hearing device in temporal bone

ICD-9-CM Diagnostic

388.12 Noise-induced hearing loss
389.00 Unspecified conductive hearing loss
389.01 Conductive hearing loss, external ear
389.02 Conductive hearing loss, tympanic membrane
389.03 Conductive hearing loss, middle ear
389.04 Conductive hearing loss, inner ear
389.05 Conductive hearing loss, unilateral
389.06 Conductive hearing loss, bilateral
389.08 Conductive hearing loss of combined types
389.8 Other specified forms of hearing loss
744.02 Other congenital anomaly of external ear causing impairment of hearing
996.69 Infection and inflammatory reaction due to other internal prosthetic device, implant, and graft — (Use additional code to identify specified infections)
996.79 Other complications due to other internal prosthetic device, implant, and graft — (Use additional code to identify complication: 338.18-338.19, 338.28-338.29)
V53.09 Fitting and adjustment of other devices related to nervous system and special senses

ICD-9-CM Procedural

20.99 Other operations on middle and inner ear

69714-69715

69714 Implantation, osseointegrated implant, temporal bone, with percutaneous attachment to external speech processor/cochlear stimulator; without mastoidectomy
69715 with mastoidectomy

ICD-9-CM Diagnostic

389.05 Conductive hearing loss, unilateral
389.06 Conductive hearing loss, bilateral
389.10 Unspecified sensorineural hearing loss
389.11 Sensory hearing loss, bilateral
389.12 Neural hearing loss, bilateral
389.13 Neural hearing loss, unilateral
389.17 Sensory hearing loss, unilateral
389.20 Mixed hearing loss, unspecified
389.21 Mixed hearing loss, unilateral
389.22 Mixed hearing loss, bilateral
389.7 Deaf, nonspeaking, not elsewhere classifiable
389.8 Other specified forms of hearing loss
389.9 Unspecified hearing loss

ICD-9-CM Procedural

20.98 Implantation or replacement of cochlear prosthetic device, multiple channel

HCPCS Level II Supplies & Services

L8690 Auditory osseointegrated device, includes all internal and external components
L8691 Auditory osseointegrated device, external sound processor, replacement
L8692 Auditory osseointegrated device, external sound processor, used without osseointegration, body worn, includes headband or other means of external attachment

69717-69718

69717 Replacement (including removal of existing device), osseointegrated implant, temporal bone, with percutaneous attachment to external speech processor/cochlear stimulator; without mastoidectomy
69718 with mastoidectomy

ICD-9-CM Diagnostic

389.05 Conductive hearing loss, unilateral
389.06 Conductive hearing loss, bilateral
389.10 Unspecified sensorineural hearing loss
389.11 Sensory hearing loss, bilateral
389.12 Neural hearing loss, bilateral
389.13 Neural hearing loss, unilateral
389.17 Sensory hearing loss, unilateral
389.20 Mixed hearing loss, unspecified
389.21 Mixed hearing loss, unilateral
389.22 Mixed hearing loss, bilateral
389.7 Deaf, nonspeaking, not elsewhere classifiable
389.8 Other specified forms of hearing loss
389.9 Unspecified hearing loss
996.59 Mechanical complication due to other implant and internal device, not elsewhere classified
996.69 Infection and inflammatory reaction due to other internal prosthetic device, implant, and graft — (Use additional code to identify specified infections)
996.79 Other complications due to other internal prosthetic device, implant, and graft — (Use additional code to identify complication: 338.18-338.19, 338.28-338.29)
V53.09 Fitting and adjustment of other devices related to nervous system and special senses

ICD-9-CM Procedural

20.98 Implantation or replacement of cochlear prosthetic device, multiple channel

HCPCS Level II Supplies & Services

L8690 Auditory osseointegrated device, includes all internal and external components
L8691 Auditory osseointegrated device, external sound processor, replacement
L8692 Auditory osseointegrated device, external sound processor, used without osseointegration, body worn, includes headband or other means of external attachment

69720-69725

69720 Decompression facial nerve, intratemporal; lateral to geniculate ganglion
69725 including medial to geniculate ganglion

ICD-9-CM Diagnostic

351.0 Bell's palsy
351.8 Other facial nerve disorders
351.9 Unspecified facial nerve disorder

383.1 Chronic mastoiditis
385.33 Cholesteatoma of middle ear and mastoid
386.33 Suppurative labyrinthitis
801.00 Closed fracture of base of skull without mention of intracranial injury, unspecified state of consciousness
801.01 Closed fracture of base of skull without mention of intracranial injury, no loss of consciousness
801.02 Closed fracture of base of skull without mention of intracranial injury, brief (less than one hour) loss of consciousness
801.03 Closed fracture of base of skull without mention of intracranial injury, moderate (1-24 hours) loss of consciousness
801.04 Closed fracture of base of skull without mention of intracranial injury, prolonged (more than 24 hours) loss of consciousness and return to pre-existing conscious level
801.05 Closed fracture of base of skull without mention of intracranial injury, prolonged (more than 24 hours) loss of consciousness, without return to pre-existing conscious level
801.06 Closed fracture of base of skull without mention of intracranial injury, loss of consciousness of unspecified duration
801.09 Closed fracture of base of skull without mention of intracranial injury, unspecified concussion
801.50 Open fracture of base of skull without mention of intracranial injury, unspecified state of consciousness
854.00 Intracranial injury of other and unspecified nature, without mention of open intracranial wound, unspecified state of consciousness
854.10 Intracranial injury of other and unspecified nature, with open intracranial wound, unspecified state of consciousness
951.4 Injury to facial nerve

ICD-9-CM Procedural

04.42 Other cranial nerve decompression

69740-69745

69740 Suture facial nerve, intratemporal, with or without graft or decompression; lateral to geniculate ganglion
69745 including medial to geniculate ganglion

ICD-9-CM Diagnostic

225.1 Benign neoplasm of cranial nerves
351.0 Bell's palsy
351.8 Other facial nerve disorders
351.9 Unspecified facial nerve disorder
383.30 Unspecified postmastoidectomy complication
386.33 Suppurative labyrinthitis
801.00 Closed fracture of base of skull without mention of intracranial injury, unspecified state of consciousness
801.01 Closed fracture of base of skull without mention of intracranial injury, no loss of consciousness
801.02 Closed fracture of base of skull without mention of intracranial injury, brief (less than one hour) loss of consciousness
801.03 Closed fracture of base of skull without mention of intracranial injury, moderate (1-24 hours) loss of consciousness
801.04 Closed fracture of base of skull without mention of intracranial injury, prolonged (more than 24 hours) loss of consciousness and return to pre-existing conscious level
801.05 Closed fracture of base of skull without mention of intracranial injury, prolonged (more than 24 hours) loss of consciousness, without return to pre-existing conscious level
801.06 Closed fracture of base of skull without mention of intracranial injury, loss of consciousness of unspecified duration
801.09 Closed fracture of base of skull without mention of intracranial injury, unspecified concussion
801.50 Open fracture of base of skull without mention of intracranial injury, unspecified state of consciousness
854.00 Intracranial injury of other and unspecified nature, without mention of open intracranial wound, unspecified state of consciousness
854.10 Intracranial injury of other and unspecified nature, with open intracranial wound, unspecified state of consciousness
951.4 Injury to facial nerve
998.2 Accidental puncture or laceration during procedure

ICD-9-CM Procedural

04.3 Suture of cranial and peripheral nerves

69801

69801 Labyrinthotomy, with perfusion of vestibuloactive drug(s); transcanal

ICD-9-CM Diagnostic

370.52 Diffuse interstitial keratitis
386.00 Meniere's disease, unspecified
386.01 Active Meniere's disease, cochleovestibular
386.02 Active Meniere's disease, cochlear
386.03 Active Meniere's disease, vestibular
386.04 Inactive Meniere's disease
386.30 Unspecified labyrinthitis
386.32 Circumscribed labyrinthitis
386.33 Suppurative labyrinthitis
386.34 Toxic labyrinthitis
386.35 Viral labyrinthitis
388.11 Acoustic trauma (explosive) to ear
388.2 Unspecified sudden hearing loss
389.10 Unspecified sensorineural hearing loss
389.12 Neural hearing loss, bilateral
389.13 Neural hearing loss, unilateral
389.14 Central hearing loss
389.15 Sensorineural hearing loss, unilateral
389.16 Sensorineural hearing loss, asymmetrical
389.17 Sensory hearing loss, unilateral
389.18 Sensorineural hearing loss, bilateral
993.0 Barotrauma, otitic

ICD-9-CM Procedural

20.72 Injection into inner ear
20.79 Other incision, excision, and destruction of inner ear
99.29 Injection or infusion of other therapeutic or prophylactic substance

HCPCS Level II Supplies & Services

S2225 Myringotomy, laser-assisted

Inner Ear

69805-69806

69805 Endolymphatic sac operation; without shunt
69806 with shunt

ICD-9-CM Diagnostic

322.9 Unspecified meningitis
386.01 Active Meniere's disease, cochleovestibular
386.03 Active Meniere's disease, vestibular
386.10 Unspecified peripheral vertigo
386.19 Other and unspecified peripheral vertigo
386.50 Unspecified labyrinthine dysfunction
386.58 Other forms and combinations of labyrinthine dysfunction
386.8 Other disorders of labyrinth
386.9 Unspecified vertiginous syndromes and labyrinthine disorders

ICD-9-CM Procedural

20.71 Endolymphatic shunt
20.79 Other incision, excision, and destruction of inner ear

69820

69820 Fenestration semicircular canal

ICD-9-CM Diagnostic

387.0 Otosclerosis involving oval window, nonobliterative
387.1 Otosclerosis involving oval window, obliterative
387.8 Other otosclerosis
387.9 Unspecified otosclerosis ▽
389.00 Unspecified conductive hearing loss ▽
389.05 Conductive hearing loss, unilateral
389.06 Conductive hearing loss, bilateral
389.08 Conductive hearing loss of combined types
389.12 Neural hearing loss, bilateral
389.13 Neural hearing loss, unilateral
389.17 Sensory hearing loss, unilateral
389.20 Mixed hearing loss, unspecified ▽
389.21 Mixed hearing loss, unilateral
389.22 Mixed hearing loss, bilateral
744.02 Other congenital anomaly of external ear causing impairment of hearing

ICD-9-CM Procedural

20.61 Fenestration of inner ear (initial)

69840

69840 Revision fenestration operation

ICD-9-CM Diagnostic

387.0 Otosclerosis involving oval window, nonobliterative
387.1 Otosclerosis involving oval window, obliterative
387.2 Cochlear otosclerosis
387.8 Other otosclerosis
389.05 Conductive hearing loss, unilateral
389.06 Conductive hearing loss, bilateral
389.08 Conductive hearing loss of combined types
389.11 Sensory hearing loss, bilateral
389.12 Neural hearing loss, bilateral
389.13 Neural hearing loss, unilateral
389.17 Sensory hearing loss, unilateral
389.20 Mixed hearing loss, unspecified ▽
389.21 Mixed hearing loss, unilateral
389.22 Mixed hearing loss, bilateral
389.8 Other specified forms of hearing loss

ICD-9-CM Procedural

20.62 Revision of fenestration of inner ear

69905

69905 Labyrinthectomy; transcanal

ICD-9-CM Diagnostic

322.9 Unspecified meningitis ▽
386.01 Active Meniere's disease, cochleovestibular
386.03 Active Meniere's disease, vestibular
386.10 Unspecified peripheral vertigo ▽
386.19 Other and unspecified peripheral vertigo
386.50 Unspecified labyrinthine dysfunction ▽
386.51 Hyperactive labyrinth, unilateral
386.58 Other forms and combinations of labyrinthine dysfunction
386.8 Other disorders of labyrinth
386.9 Unspecified vertiginous syndromes and labyrinthine disorders ▽

ICD-9-CM Procedural

20.79 Other incision, excision, and destruction of inner ear

69910

69910 Labyrinthectomy; with mastoidectomy

ICD-9-CM Diagnostic

383.02 Acute mastoiditis with other complications
383.32 Recurrent cholesteatoma of postmastoidectomy cavity
385.35 Diffuse cholesteatosis of middle ear and mastoid
386.01 Active Meniere's disease, cochleovestibular
386.02 Active Meniere's disease, cochlear
386.03 Active Meniere's disease, vestibular
386.10 Unspecified peripheral vertigo ▽
386.12 Vestibular neuronitis
386.19 Other and unspecified peripheral vertigo
386.2 Vertigo of central origin
386.33 Suppurative labyrinthitis
386.48 Labyrinthine fistula of combined sites
386.50 Unspecified labyrinthine dysfunction ▽
386.9 Unspecified vertiginous syndromes and labyrinthine disorders ▽

ICD-9-CM Procedural

20.41 Simple mastoidectomy
20.79 Other incision, excision, and destruction of inner ear

69915

69915 Vestibular nerve section, translabyrinthine approach

ICD-9-CM Diagnostic

383.02 Acute mastoiditis with other complications
383.32 Recurrent cholesteatoma of postmastoidectomy cavity
385.35 Diffuse cholesteatosis of middle ear and mastoid
386.01 Active Meniere's disease, cochleovestibular
386.02 Active Meniere's disease, cochlear
386.03 Active Meniere's disease, vestibular
386.10 Unspecified peripheral vertigo ▽
386.12 Vestibular neuronitis
386.19 Other and unspecified peripheral vertigo
386.2 Vertigo of central origin
386.48 Labyrinthine fistula of combined sites
386.50 Unspecified labyrinthine dysfunction ▽
386.8 Other disorders of labyrinth
386.9 Unspecified vertiginous syndromes and labyrinthine disorders ▽

ICD-9-CM Procedural

04.01 Excision of acoustic neuroma
04.03 Division or crushing of other cranial and peripheral nerves

69930

69930 Cochlear device implantation, with or without mastoidectomy

ICD-9-CM Diagnostic

385.9 Unspecified disorder of middle ear and mastoid ▽
386.02 Active Meniere's disease, cochlear
389.05 Conductive hearing loss, unilateral
389.06 Conductive hearing loss, bilateral
389.08 Conductive hearing loss of combined types

389.10 Unspecified sensorineural hearing loss ▽
389.11 Sensory hearing loss, bilateral
389.13 Neural hearing loss, unilateral
389.15 Sensorineural hearing loss, unilateral
389.16 Sensorineural hearing loss, asymmetrical
389.17 Sensory hearing loss, unilateral
389.18 Sensorineural hearing loss, bilateral
389.20 Mixed hearing loss, unspecified ▽
389.21 Mixed hearing loss, unilateral
389.22 Mixed hearing loss, bilateral
389.7 Deaf, nonspeaking, not elsewhere classifiable
389.9 Unspecified hearing loss ▽

ICD-9-CM Procedural
20.96 Implantation or replacement of cochlear prosthetic device, not otherwise specified
20.97 Implantation or replacement of cochlear prosthetic device, single channel
20.98 Implantation or replacement of cochlear prosthetic device, multiple channel

HCPCS Level II Supplies & Services
L8614 Cochlear device, includes all internal and external components
L8627 Cochlear implant, external speech processor, component, replacement
L8628 Cochlear implant, external controller component, replacement
L8629 Transmitting coil and cable, integrated, for use with cochlear implant device, replacement

Temporal Bone, Middle Fossa Approach

69950
69950 Vestibular nerve section, transcranial approach

ICD-9-CM Diagnostic
322.9 Unspecified meningitis ▽
386.01 Active Meniere's disease, cochleovestibular
386.03 Active Meniere's disease, vestibular
386.10 Unspecified peripheral vertigo ▽
386.12 Vestibular neuronitis
386.19 Other and unspecified peripheral vertigo
386.50 Unspecified labyrinthine dysfunction ▽
386.8 Other disorders of labyrinth
386.9 Unspecified vertiginous syndromes and labyrinthine disorders ▽

ICD-9-CM Procedural
04.01 Excision of acoustic neuroma
04.03 Division or crushing of other cranial and peripheral nerves

69955
69955 Total facial nerve decompression and/or repair (may include graft)

ICD-9-CM Diagnostic
237.3 Neoplasm of uncertain behavior of paraganglia
351.0 Bell's palsy
351.1 Geniculate ganglionitis
351.8 Other facial nerve disorders
351.9 Unspecified facial nerve disorder ▽
385.33 Cholesteatoma of middle ear and mastoid
801.00 Closed fracture of base of skull without mention of intracranial injury, unspecified state of consciousness ▽
801.50 Open fracture of base of skull without mention of intracranial injury, unspecified state of consciousness ▽
951.4 Injury to facial nerve

ICD-9-CM Procedural
04.42 Other cranial nerve decompression

69960
69960 Decompression internal auditory canal

ICD-9-CM Diagnostic
225.1 Benign neoplasm of cranial nerves
225.2 Benign neoplasm of cerebral meninges
381.52 Chronic Eustachian salpingitis
381.61 Osseous obstruction of Eustachian tube
381.62 Intrinsic cartilagenous obstruction of Eustachian tube
381.63 Extrinsic cartilagenous obstruction of Eustachian tube
385.03 Tympanosclerosis involving tympanic membrane, ear ossicles, and middle ear
385.32 Cholesteatoma of middle ear
385.82 Cholesterin granuloma of middle ear
385.83 Retained foreign body of middle ear — (Use additional code to identify foreign body (V90.01-V90.9))
801.00 Closed fracture of base of skull without mention of intracranial injury, unspecified state of consciousness ▽

ICD-9-CM Procedural
04.42 Other cranial nerve decompression

69970
69970 Removal of tumor, temporal bone

ICD-9-CM Diagnostic
170.0 Malignant neoplasm of bones of skull and face, except mandible
213.0 Benign neoplasm of bones of skull and face
238.0 Neoplasm of uncertain behavior of bone and articular cartilage
239.2 Neoplasms of unspecified nature of bone, soft tissue, and skin

ICD-9-CM Procedural
01.6 Excision of lesion of skull

Operating Microscope

69990

69990 Microsurgical techniques, requiring use of operating microscope (List separately in addition to code for primary procedure)

ICD-9-CM Diagnostic

This is an add-on code. Refer to the corresponding primary procedure code for ICD-9-CM diagnosis code links.

ICD-9-CM Procedural

The ICD-9-CM procedural code(s) would be the same as the actual procedure performed because these are in-addition-to codes.

Appendix A

Add-On Codes

0054T Computer-assisted musculoskeletal surgical navigational orthopedic procedure, with image-guidance based on fluoroscopic images (List separately in addition to code for primary procedure)

0055T Computer-assisted musculoskeletal surgical navigational orthopedic procedure, with image-guidance based on CT/MRI images (List separately in addition to code for primary procedure)

0076T Transcatheter placement of extracranial vertebral or intrathoracic carotid artery stent(s), including radiologic supervision and interpretation, percutaneous; each additional vessel (List separately in addition to code for primary procedure)

0092T Total disc arthroplasty (artificial disc), anterior approach, including discectomy with end plate preparation (includes osteophytectomy for nerve root or spinal cord decompression and microdissection), each additional interspace, cervical (List separately in addition to code for primary procedure)

0095T Removal of total disc arthroplasty (artificial disc), anterior approach, each additional interspace, cervical (List separately in addition to code for primary procedure)

0098T Revision including replacement of total disc arthroplasty (artificial disc), anterior approach, each additional interspace, cervical (List separately in addition to code for primary procedure)

0159T Computer-aided detection, including computer algorithm analysis of MRI image data for lesion detection/characterization, pharmacokinetic analysis, with further physician review for interpretation, breast MRI (List separately in addition to code for primary procedure)

0163T Total disc arthroplasty (artificial disc), anterior approach, including discectomy to prepare interspace (other than for decompression), each additional interspace, lumbar (List separately in addition to code for primary procedure)

0164T Removal of total disc arthroplasty, (artificial disc), anterior approach, each additional interspace, lumbar (List separately in addition to code for primary procedure)

0165T Revision including replacement of total disc arthroplasty (artificial disc), anterior approach, each additional interspace, lumbar (List separately in addition to code for primary procedure)

0172T Insertion of posterior spinous process distraction device (including necessary removal of bone or ligament for insertion and imaging guidance), lumbar; each additional level (List separately in addition to code for primary procedure)

0174T Computer-aided detection (CAD) (computer algorithm analysis of digital image data for lesion detection) with further physician review for interpretation and report, with or without digitization of film radiographic images, chest radiograph(s), performed concurrent with primary interpretation (List separately in addition to code for primary procedure)

0189T Remote real-time interactive video-conferenced critical care, evaluation and management of the critically ill or critically injured patient; each additional 30 minutes (List separately in addition to code for primary service)

0190T Placement of intraocular radiation source applicator (List separately in addition to primary procedure)

0196T Arthrodesis, pre-sacral interbody technique, disc space preparation, discectomy, without instrumentation, with image guidance, includes bone graft when performed; L4-L5 interspace (List separately in addition to code for primary procedure)

0205T Intravascular catheter-based coronary vessel or graft spectroscopy (eg, infrared) during diagnostic evaluation and/or therapeutic intervention including imaging supervision, interpretation, and report, each vessel (List separately in addition to code for primary procedure)

0214T Injection(s), diagnostic or therapeutic agent, paravertebral facet (zygapophyseal) joint (or nerves innervating that joint) with ultrasound guidance, cervical or thoracic; second level (List separately in addition to code for primary procedure)

0215T Injection(s), diagnostic or therapeutic agent, paravertebral facet (zygapophyseal) joint (or nerves innervating that joint) with ultrasound guidance, cervical or thoracic; third and any additional level(s) (List separately in addition to code for primary procedure)

0217T Injection(s), diagnostic or therapeutic agent, paravertebral facet (zygapophyseal) joint (or nerves innervating that joint) with ultrasound guidance, lumbar or sacral; second level (List separately in addition to code for primary procedure)

0218T Injection(s), diagnostic or therapeutic agent, paravertebral facet (zygapophyseal) joint (or nerves innervating that joint) with ultrasound guidance, lumbar or sacral; third and any additional level(s) (List separately in addition to code for primary procedure)

0222T Placement of a posterior intrafacet implant(s), unilateral or bilateral, including imaging and placement of bone graft(s) or synthetic device(s), single level; each additional vertebral segment (List separately in addition to code for primary procedure)

0229T Injection(s), anesthetic agent and/or steroid, transforaminal epidural, with ultrasound guidance, cervical or thoracic; each additional level (List separately in addition to code for primary procedure)

0231T Injection(s), anesthetic agent and/or steroid, transforaminal epidural, with ultrasound guidance, lumbar or sacral; each additional level (List separately in addition to code for primary procedure)

0241T Esophageal motility (manometric study of the esophagus and/or gastroesophageal junction) study with interpretation and report; with stimulation or perfusion during high resolution esophageal pressure topography study (eg, stimulant, acid or alkali perfusion) (List separately in addition to code for primary procedure)

0289T Corneal incisions in the donor cornea created using a laser, in preparation for penetrating or lamellar keratoplasty (List separately in addition to code for primary procedure)

0290T Corneal incisions in the recipient cornea created using a laser, in preparation for penetrating or lamellar keratoplasty (List separately in addition to code for primary procedure)

0291T Intravascular optical coherence tomography (coronary native vessel or graft) during diagnostic evaluation and/or therapeutic intervention, including imaging supervision, interpretation, and report; initial vessel (List separately in addition to primary procedure)

0292T Intravascular optical coherence tomography (coronary native vessel or graft) during diagnostic evaluation and/or therapeutic intervention, including imaging supervision, interpretation, and report; each additional vessel (List separately in addition to primary procedure)

0294T Insertion of left atrial hemodynamic monitor; pressure sensor lead at time of insertion of pacing cardioverter-defibrillator pulse generator including radiological supervision and interpretation and associated injection procedures, when performed (List separately in addition to code for primary procedure)

0300T Extracorporeal shock wave for integumentary wound healing, high energy, including topical application and dressing care; each additional wound (List separately in addition to code for primary procedure)

0309T Arthrodesis, pre-sacral interbody technique, including disc space preparation, discectomy, with posterior instrumentation, with image guidance, includes bone graft, when performed, lumbar, L4-L5 interspace (List separately in addition to code for primary procedure)

01953 Anesthesia for second- and third-degree burn excision or debridement with or without skin grafting, any site, for total body surface area (TBSA) treated during anesthesia and surgery; each additional 9% total body surface area or part thereof (List separately in addition to code for primary procedure)

01968 Anesthesia for cesarean delivery following neuraxial labor analgesia/anesthesia (List separately in addition to code for primary procedure performed)

01969 Anesthesia for cesarean hysterectomy following neuraxial labor analgesia/anesthesia (List separately in addition to code for primary procedure performed)

11001 Debridement of extensive eczematous or infected skin; each additional 10% of the body surface, or part thereof (List separately in addition to code for primary procedure)

11008 Removal of prosthetic material or mesh, abdominal wall for infection (eg, for chronic or recurrent mesh infection or necrotizing soft tissue infection) (List separately in addition to code for primary procedure)

11045 Debridement, subcutaneous tissue (includes epidermis and dermis, if performed); each additional 20 sq cm, or part thereof (List separately in addition to code for primary procedure)

11046 Debridement, muscle and/or fascia (includes epidermis, dermis, and subcutaneous tissue, if performed); each additional 20 sq cm, or part thereof (List separately in addition to code for primary procedure)

11047 Debridement, bone (includes epidermis, dermis, subcutaneous tissue, muscle and/or fascia, if performed); each additional 20 sq cm, or part thereof (List separately in addition to code for primary procedure)

11101 Biopsy of skin, subcutaneous tissue and/or mucous membrane (including simple closure), unless otherwise listed; each separate/additional lesion (List separately in addition to code for primary procedure)

11201 Removal of skin tags, multiple fibrocutaneous tags, any area; each additional 10 lesions, or part thereof (List separately in addition to code for primary procedure)

11732 Avulsion of nail plate, partial or complete, simple; each additional nail plate (List separately in addition to code for primary procedure)

11922 Tattooing, intradermal introduction of insoluble opaque pigments to correct color defects of skin, including micropigmentation; each additional 20.0 sq cm, or part thereof (List separately in addition to code for primary procedure)

13102 Repair, complex, trunk; each additional 5 cm or less (List separately in addition to code for primary procedure)

13122 Repair, complex, scalp, arms, and/or legs; each additional 5 cm or less (List separately in addition to code for primary procedure)

13133 Repair, complex, forehead, cheeks, chin, mouth, neck, axillae, genitalia, hands and/or feet; each additional 5 cm or less (List separately in addition to code for primary procedure)

13153 Repair, complex, eyelids, nose, ears and/or lips; each additional 5 cm or less (List separately in addition to code for primary procedure)

14302 Adjacent tissue transfer or rearrangement, any area; each additional 30.0 sq cm, or part thereof (List separately in addition to code for primary procedure)

15003 Surgical preparation or creation of recipient site by excision of open wounds, burn eschar, or scar (including subcutaneous tissues), or incisional release of scar contracture, trunk, arms, legs; each additional 100 sq cm, or part thereof, or each additional 1% of body area of infants and children (List separately in addition to code for primary procedure)

15005 Surgical preparation or creation of recipient site by excision of open wounds, burn eschar, or scar (including subcutaneous tissues), or incisional release of scar contracture, face, scalp, eyelids, mouth, neck, ears, orbits, genitalia, hands, feet and/or multiple digits; each additional 100 sq cm, or part thereof, or each additional 1% of body area of infants and children (List separately in addition to code for primary procedure)

15101 Split-thickness autograft, trunk, arms, legs; each additional 100 sq cm, or each additional 1% of body area of infants and children, or part thereof (List separately in addition to code for primary procedure)

15111 Epidermal autograft, trunk, arms, legs; each additional 100 sq cm, or each additional 1% of body area of infants and children, or part thereof (List separately in addition to code for primary procedure)

15116 Epidermal autograft, face, scalp, eyelids, mouth, neck, ears, orbits, genitalia, hands, feet, and/or multiple digits; each additional 100 sq cm, or each additional 1% of body area of infants and children, or part thereof (List separately in addition to code for primary procedure)

15121 Split-thickness autograft, face, scalp, eyelids, mouth, neck, ears, orbits, genitalia, hands, feet, and/or multiple digits; each additional 100 sq cm, or each additional 1% of body area of infants and children, or part thereof (List separately in addition to code for primary procedure)

15131 Dermal autograft, trunk, arms, legs; each additional 100 sq cm, or each additional 1% of body area of infants and children, or part thereof (List separately in addition to code for primary procedure)

15136 Dermal autograft, face, scalp, eyelids, mouth, neck, ears, orbits, genitalia, hands, feet, and/or multiple digits; each additional 100 sq cm, or each additional 1% of body area of infants and children, or part thereof (List separately in addition to code for primary procedure)

15151 Tissue cultured skin autograft, trunk, arms, legs; additional 1 sq cm to 75 sq cm (List separately in addition to code for primary procedure)

15152 Tissue cultured skin autograft, trunk, arms, legs; each additional 100 sq cm, or each additional 1% of body area of infants and children, or part thereof (List separately in addition to code for primary procedure)

15156 Tissue cultured skin autograft, face, scalp, eyelids, mouth, neck, ears, orbits, genitalia, hands, feet, and/or multiple digits; additional 1 sq cm to 75 sq cm (List separately in addition to code for primary procedure)

15157 Tissue cultured skin autograft, face, scalp, eyelids, mouth, neck, ears, orbits, genitalia, hands, feet, and/or multiple digits; each additional 100 sq cm, or each additional 1% of body area of infants and children, or part thereof (List separately in addition to code for primary procedure)

15201 Full thickness graft, free, including direct closure of donor site, trunk; each additional 20 sq cm, or part thereof (List separately in addition to code for primary procedure)

15221 Full thickness graft, free, including direct closure of donor site, scalp, arms, and/or legs; each additional 20 sq cm, or part thereof (List separately in addition to code for primary procedure)

15241 Full thickness graft, free, including direct closure of donor site, forehead, cheeks, chin, mouth, neck, axillae, genitalia, hands, and/or feet; each additional 20 sq cm, or part thereof (List separately in addition to code for primary procedure)

15261 Full thickness graft, free, including direct closure of donor site, nose, ears, eyelids, and/or lips; each additional 20 sq cm, or part thereof (List separately in addition to code for primary procedure)

15272 Application of skin substitute graft to trunk, arms, legs, total wound surface area up to 100 sq cm; each additional 25 sq cm wound surface area, or part thereof (List separately in addition to code for primary procedure)

15274 Application of skin substitute graft to trunk, arms, legs, total wound surface area greater than or equal to 100 sq cm; each additional 100 sq cm wound surface area, or part thereof, or each additional 1% of body area of infants and children, or part thereof (List separately in addition to code for primary procedure)

15276 Application of skin substitute graft to face, scalp, eyelids, mouth, neck, ears, orbits, genitalia, hands, feet, and/or multiple digits, total wound surface area up to 100 sq cm; each additional 25 sq cm wound surface area, or part thereof (List separately in addition to code for primary procedure)

15278 Application of skin substitute graft to face, scalp, eyelids, mouth, neck, ears, orbits, genitalia, hands, feet, and/or multiple digits, total wound surface area greater than or equal to 100 sq cm; each additional 100 sq cm wound surface area, or part thereof, or each additional 1% of body area of infants and children, or part thereof (List separately in addition to code for primary procedure)

15777 Implantation of biologic implant (eg, acellular dermal matrix) for soft tissue reinforcement (eg, breast, trunk) (List separately in addition to code for primary procedure)

15787 Abrasion; each additional 4 lesions or less (List separately in addition to code for primary procedure)

15847 Excision, excessive skin and subcutaneous tissue (includes lipectomy), abdomen (eg, abdominoplasty) (includes umbilical transposition and fascial plication) (List separately in addition to code for primary procedure)

16036 Escharotomy; each additional incision (List separately in addition to code for primary procedure)

17003 Destruction (eg, laser surgery, electrosurgery, cryosurgery, chemosurgery, surgical curettement), premalignant lesions (eg, actinic keratoses); second through 14 lesions, each (List separately in addition to code for first lesion)

17312 Mohs micrographic technique, including removal of all gross tumor, surgical excision of tissue specimens, mapping, color coding of specimens, microscopic examination of specimens by the surgeon, and histopathologic preparation including routine stain(s) (eg, hematoxylin and eosin, toluidine blue), head, neck, hands, feet, genitalia, or any location with surgery directly involving muscle, cartilage, bone, tendon, major nerves, or vessels; each additional stage after the first stage, up to 5 tissue blocks (List separately in addition to code for primary procedure)

17314 Mohs micrographic technique, including removal of all gross tumor, surgical excision of tissue specimens, mapping, color coding of specimens, microscopic examination of specimens by the surgeon, and histopathologic preparation including routine stain(s) (eg, hematoxylin and eosin, toluidine blue), of the trunk, arms, or legs; each additional stage after the first stage, up to 5 tissue blocks (List separately in addition to code for primary procedure)

17315 Mohs micrographic technique, including removal of all gross tumor, surgical excision of tissue specimens, mapping, color coding of specimens, microscopic examination of specimens by the surgeon, and histopathologic preparation including routine stain(s) (eg, hematoxylin and eosin, toluidine blue), each additional block after the first 5 tissue blocks, any stage (List separately in addition to code for primary procedure)

19001 Puncture aspiration of cyst of breast; each additional cyst (List separately in addition to code for primary procedure)
19082 Biopsy, breast, with placement of breast localization device(s) (eg, clip, metallic pellet), when performed, and imaging of the biopsy specimen, when performed, percutaneous; each additional lesion, including stereotactic guidance (List separately in addition to code for primary procedure)
19084 Biopsy, breast, with placement of breast localization device(s) (eg, clip, metallic pellet), when performed, and imaging of the biopsy specimen, when performed, percutaneous; each additional lesion, including ultrasound guidance (List separately in addition to code for primary procedure)
19086 Biopsy, breast, with placement of breast localization device(s) (eg, clip, metallic pellet), when performed, and imaging of the biopsy specimen, when performed, percutaneous; each additional lesion, including magnetic resonance guidance (List separately in addition to code for primary procedure)
19126 Excision of breast lesion identified by preoperative placement of radiological marker, open; each additional lesion separately identified by a preoperative radiological marker (List separately in addition to code for primary procedure)
19282 Placement of breast localization device(s) (eg, clip, metallic pellet, wire/needle, radioactive seeds), percutaneous; each additional lesion, including mammographic guidance (List separately in addition to code for primary procedure)
19284 Placement of breast localization device(s) (eg, clip, metallic pellet, wire/needle, radioactive seeds), percutaneous; each additional lesion, including stereotactic guidance (List separately in addition to code for primary procedure)
19286 Placement of breast localization device(s) (eg, clip, metallic pellet, wire/needle, radioactive seeds), percutaneous; each additional lesion, including ultrasound guidance (List separately in addition to code for primary procedure)
19288 Placement of breast localization device(s) (eg clip, metallic pellet, wire/needle, radioactive seeds), percutaneous; each additional lesion, including magnetic resonance guidance (List separately in addition to code for primary procedure)
19297 Placement of radiotherapy afterloading expandable catheter (single or multichannel) into the breast for interstitial radioelement application following partial mastectomy, includes imaging guidance; concurrent with partial mastectomy (List separately in addition to code for primary procedure)
20930 Allograft, morselized, or placement of osteopromotive material, for spine surgery only (List separately in addition to code for primary procedure)
20931 Allograft, structural, for spine surgery only (List separately in addition to code for primary procedure)
20936 Autograft for spine surgery only (includes harvesting the graft); local (eg, ribs, spinous process, or laminar fragments) obtained from same incision (List separately in addition to code for primary procedure)
20937 Autograft for spine surgery only (includes harvesting the graft); morselized (through separate skin or fascial incision) (List separately in addition to code for primary procedure)
20938 Autograft for spine surgery only (includes harvesting the graft); structural, bicortical or tricortical (through separate skin or fascial incision) (List separately in addition to code for primary procedure)
20985 Computer-assisted surgical navigational procedure for musculoskeletal procedures, image-less (List separately in addition to code for primary procedure)
22103 Partial excision of posterior vertebral component (eg, spinous process, lamina or facet) for intrinsic bony lesion, single vertebral segment; each additional segment (List separately in addition to code for primary procedure)
22116 Partial excision of vertebral body, for intrinsic bony lesion, without decompression of spinal cord or nerve root(s), single vertebral segment; each additional vertebral segment (List separately in addition to code for primary procedure)
22208 Osteotomy of spine, posterior or posterolateral approach, 3 columns, 1 vertebral segment (eg, pedicle/vertebral body subtraction); each additional vertebral segment (List separately in addition to code for primary procedure)
22216 Osteotomy of spine, posterior or posterolateral approach, 1 vertebral segment; each additional vertebral segment (List separately in addition to primary procedure)
22226 Osteotomy of spine, including discectomy, anterior approach, single vertebral segment; each additional vertebral segment (List separately in addition to code for primary procedure)
22328 Open treatment and/or reduction of vertebral fracture(s) and/or dislocation(s), posterior approach, 1 fractured vertebra or dislocated segment; each additional fractured vertebra or dislocated segment (List separately in addition to code for primary procedure)
22522 Percutaneous vertebroplasty (bone biopsy included when performed), 1 vertebral body, unilateral or bilateral injection; each additional thoracic or lumbar vertebral body (List separately in addition to code for primary procedure)
22525 Percutaneous vertebral augmentation, including cavity creation (fracture reduction and bone biopsy included when performed) using mechanical device, 1 vertebral body, unilateral or bilateral cannulation (eg, kyphoplasty); each additional thoracic or lumbar vertebral body (List separately in addition to code for primary procedure)
22527 Percutaneous intradiscal electrothermal annuloplasty, unilateral or bilateral including fluoroscopic guidance; 1 or more additional levels (List separately in addition to code for primary procedure)
22534 Arthrodesis, lateral extracavitary technique, including minimal discectomy to prepare interspace (other than for decompression); thoracic or lumbar, each additional vertebral segment (List separately in addition to code for primary procedure)
22552 Arthrodesis, anterior interbody, including disc space preparation, discectomy, osteophytectomy and decompression of spinal cord and/or nerve roots; cervical below C2, each additional interspace (List separately in addition to code for separate procedure)
22585 Arthrodesis, anterior interbody technique, including minimal discectomy to prepare interspace (other than for decompression); each additional interspace (List separately in addition to code for primary procedure)
22614 Arthrodesis, posterior or posterolateral technique, single level; each additional vertebral segment (List separately in addition to code for primary procedure)
22632 Arthrodesis, posterior interbody technique, including laminectomy and/or discectomy to prepare interspace (other than for decompression), single interspace; each additional interspace (List separately in addition to code for primary procedure)
22634 Arthrodesis, combined posterior or posterolateral technique with posterior interbody technique including laminectomy and/or discectomy sufficient to prepare interspace (other than for decompression), single interspace and segment; each additional interspace and segment (List separately in addition to code for primary procedure)
22840 Posterior non-segmental instrumentation (eg, Harrington rod technique, pedicle fixation across 1 interspace, atlantoaxial transarticular screw fixation, sublaminar wiring at C1, facet screw fixation) (List separately in addition to code for primary procedure)
22841 Internal spinal fixation by wiring of spinous processes (List separately in addition to code for primary procedure)
22842 Posterior segmental instrumentation (eg, pedicle fixation, dual rods with multiple hooks and sublaminar wires); 3 to 6 vertebral segments (List separately in addition to code for primary procedure)
22843 Posterior segmental instrumentation (eg, pedicle fixation, dual rods with multiple hooks and sublaminar wires); 7 to 12 vertebral segments (List separately in addition to code for primary procedure)
22844 Posterior segmental instrumentation (eg, pedicle fixation, dual rods with multiple hooks and sublaminar wires); 13 or more vertebral segments (List separately in addition to code for primary procedure)
22845 Anterior instrumentation; 2 to 3 vertebral segments (List separately in addition to code for primary procedure)
22846 Anterior instrumentation; 4 to 7 vertebral segments (List separately in addition to code for primary procedure)
22847 Anterior instrumentation; 8 or more vertebral segments (List separately in addition to code for primary procedure)
22848 Pelvic fixation (attachment of caudal end of instrumentation to pelvic bony structures) other than sacrum (List separately in addition to code for primary procedure)

22851 Application of intervertebral biomechanical device(s) (eg, synthetic cage(s), methylmethacrylate) to vertebral defect or interspace (List separately in addition to code for primary procedure)

26125 Fasciectomy, partial palmar with release of single digit including proximal interphalangeal joint, with or without Z-plasty, other local tissue rearrangement, or skin grafting (includes obtaining graft); each additional digit (List separately in addition to code for primary procedure)

26861 Arthrodesis, interphalangeal joint, with or without internal fixation; each additional interphalangeal joint (List separately in addition to code for primary procedure)

26863 Arthrodesis, interphalangeal joint, with or without internal fixation; with autograft (includes obtaining graft), each additional joint (List separately in addition to code for primary procedure)

27358 Excision or curettage of bone cyst or benign tumor of femur; with internal fixation (List in addition to code for primary procedure)

27692 Transfer or transplant of single tendon (with muscle redirection or rerouting); each additional tendon (List separately in addition to code for primary procedure)

29826 Arthroscopy, shoulder, surgical; decompression of subacromial space with partial acromioplasty, with coracoacromial ligament (ie, arch) release, when performed (List separately in addition to code for primary procedure)

31620 Endobronchial ultrasound (EBUS) during bronchoscopic diagnostic or therapeutic intervention(s) (List separately in addition to code for primary procedure[s])

31627 Bronchoscopy, rigid or flexible, including fluoroscopic guidance, when performed; with computer-assisted, image-guided navigation (List separately in addition to code for primary procedure[s])

31632 Bronchoscopy, rigid or flexible, including fluoroscopic guidance, when performed; with transbronchial lung biopsy(s), each additional lobe (List separately in addition to code for primary procedure)

31633 Bronchoscopy, rigid or flexible, including fluoroscopic guidance, when performed; with transbronchial needle aspiration biopsy(s), each additional lobe (List separately in addition to code for primary procedure)

31637 Bronchoscopy, rigid or flexible, including fluoroscopic guidance, when performed; each additional major bronchus stented (List separately in addition to code for primary procedure)

31649 Bronchoscopy, rigid or flexible, including fluoroscopic guidance, when performed; with removal of bronchial valve(s), each additional lobe (List separately in addition to code for primary procedure)

31651 Bronchoscopy, rigid or flexible, including fluoroscopic guidance, when performed; with balloon occlusion, when performed, assessment of air leak, airway sizing, and insertion of bronchial valve(s), each additional lobe (List separately in addition to code for primary procedure[s])

32501 Resection and repair of portion of bronchus (bronchoplasty) when performed at time of lobectomy or segmentectomy (List separately in addition to code for primary procedure)

32506 Thoracotomy; with therapeutic wedge resection (eg, mass or nodule), each additional resection, ipsilateral (List separately in addition to code for primary procedure)

32507 Thoracotomy; with diagnostic wedge resection followed by anatomic lung resection (List separately in addition to code for primary procedure)

32667 Thoracoscopy, surgical; with therapeutic wedge resection (eg, mass or nodule), each additional resection, ipsilateral (List separately in addition to code for primary procedure)

32668 Thoracoscopy, surgical; with diagnostic wedge resection followed by anatomic lung resection (List separately in addition to code for primary procedure)

32674 Thoracoscopy, surgical; with mediastinal and regional lymphadenectomy (List separately in addition to code for primary procedure)

33141 Transmyocardial laser revascularization, by thoracotomy; performed at the time of other open cardiac procedure(s) (List separately in addition to code for primary procedure)

33225 Insertion of pacing electrode, cardiac venous system, for left ventricular pacing, at time of insertion of pacing cardioverter-defibrillator or pacemaker pulse generator (eg, for upgrade to dual chamber system) (List separately in addition to code for primary procedure)

33257 Operative tissue ablation and reconstruction of atria, performed at the time of other cardiac procedure(s), limited (eg, modified maze procedure) (List separately in addition to code for primary procedure)

33258 Operative tissue ablation and reconstruction of atria, performed at the time of other cardiac procedure(s), extensive (eg, maze procedure), without cardiopulmonary bypass (List separately in addition to code for primary procedure)

33259 Operative tissue ablation and reconstruction of atria, performed at the time of other cardiac procedure(s), extensive (eg, maze procedure), with cardiopulmonary bypass (List separately in addition to code for primary procedure)

33367 Transcatheter aortic valve replacement (TAVR/TAVI) with prosthetic valve; cardiopulmonary bypass support with percutaneous peripheral arterial and venous cannulation (eg, femoral vessels) (List separately in addition to code for primary procedure)

33368 Transcatheter aortic valve replacement (TAVR/TAVI) with prosthetic valve; cardiopulmonary bypass support with open peripheral arterial and venous cannulation (eg, femoral, iliac, axillary vessels) (List separately in addition to code for primary procedure)

33369 Transcatheter aortic valve replacement (TAVR/TAVI) with prosthetic valve; cardiopulmonary bypass support with central arterial and venous cannulation (eg, aorta, right atrium, pulmonary artery) (List separately in addition to code for primary procedure)

33508 Endoscopy, surgical, including video-assisted harvest of vein(s) for coronary artery bypass procedure (List separately in addition to code for primary procedure)

33517 Coronary artery bypass, using venous graft(s) and arterial graft(s); single vein graft (List separately in addition to code for primary procedure)

33518 Coronary artery bypass, using venous graft(s) and arterial graft(s); 2 venous grafts (List separately in addition to code for primary procedure)

33519 Coronary artery bypass, using venous graft(s) and arterial graft(s); 3 venous grafts (List separately in addition to code for primary procedure)

33521 Coronary artery bypass, using venous graft(s) and arterial graft(s); 4 venous grafts (List separately in addition to code for primary procedure)

33522 Coronary artery bypass, using venous graft(s) and arterial graft(s); 5 venous grafts (List separately in addition to code for primary procedure)

33523 Coronary artery bypass, using venous graft(s) and arterial graft(s); 6 or more venous grafts (List separately in addition to code for primary procedure)

33530 Reoperation, coronary artery bypass procedure or valve procedure, more than 1 month after original operation (List separately in addition to code for primary procedure)

33572 Coronary endarterectomy, open, any method, of left anterior descending, circumflex, or right coronary artery performed in conjunction with coronary artery bypass graft procedure, each vessel (List separately in addition to primary procedure)

33768 Anastomosis, cavopulmonary, second superior vena cava (List separately in addition to primary procedure)

33884 Placement of proximal extension prosthesis for endovascular repair of descending thoracic aorta (eg, aneurysm, pseudoaneurysm, dissection, penetrating ulcer, intramural hematoma, or traumatic disruption); each additional proximal extension (List separately in addition to code for primary procedure)

33924 Ligation and takedown of a systemic-to-pulmonary artery shunt, performed in conjunction with a congenital heart procedure (List separately in addition to code for primary procedure)

34806 Transcatheter placement of wireless physiologic sensor in aneurysmal sac during endovascular repair, including radiological supervision and interpretation, instrument calibration, and collection of pressure data (List separately in addition to code for primary procedure)

34808 Endovascular placement of iliac artery occlusion device (List separately in addition to code for primary procedure)

34813 Placement of femoral-femoral prosthetic graft during endovascular aortic aneurysm repair (List separately in addition to code for primary procedure)

34826 Placement of proximal or distal extension prosthesis for endovascular repair of infrarenal abdominal aortic or iliac aneurysm, false aneurysm, or dissection; each additional vessel (List separately in addition to code for primary procedure)

35306 Thromboendarterectomy, including patch graft, if performed; each additional tibial or peroneal artery (List separately in addition to code for primary procedure)

35390 Reoperation, carotid, thromboendarterectomy, more than 1 month after original operation (List separately in addition to code for primary procedure)

35400 Angioscopy (non-coronary vessels or grafts) during therapeutic intervention (List separately in addition to code for primary procedure)

35500 Harvest of upper extremity vein, 1 segment, for lower extremity or coronary artery bypass procedure (List separately in addition to code for primary procedure)

35572 Harvest of femoropopliteal vein, 1 segment, for vascular reconstruction procedure (eg, aortic, vena caval, coronary, peripheral artery) (List separately in addition to code for primary procedure)

35600 Harvest of upper extremity artery, 1 segment, for coronary artery bypass procedure (List separately in addition to code for primary procedure)

35681 Bypass graft; composite, prosthetic and vein (List separately in addition to code for primary procedure)

35682 Bypass graft; autogenous composite, 2 segments of veins from 2 locations (List separately in addition to code for primary procedure)

35683 Bypass graft; autogenous composite, 3 or more segments of vein from 2 or more locations (List separately in addition to code for primary procedure)

35685 Placement of vein patch or cuff at distal anastomosis of bypass graft, synthetic conduit (List separately in addition to code for primary procedure)

35686 Creation of distal arteriovenous fistula during lower extremity bypass surgery (non-hemodialysis) (List separately in addition to code for primary procedure)

35697 Reimplantation, visceral artery to infrarenal aortic prosthesis, each artery (List separately in addition to code for primary procedure)

35700 Reoperation, femoral-popliteal or femoral (popliteal)-anterior tibial, posterior tibial, peroneal artery, or other distal vessels, more than 1 month after original operation (List separately in addition to code for primary procedure)

36148 Introduction of needle and/or catheter, arteriovenous shunt created for dialysis (graft/fistula); additional access for therapeutic intervention (List separately in addition to code for primary procedure)

36218 Selective catheter placement, arterial system; additional second order, third order, and beyond, thoracic or brachiocephalic branch, within a vascular family (List in addition to code for initial second or third order vessel as appropriate)

36227 Selective catheter placement, external carotid artery, unilateral, with angiography of the ipsilateral external carotid circulation and all associated radiological supervision and interpretation (List separately in addition to code for primary procedure)

36228 Selective catheter placement, each intracranial branch of the internal carotid or vertebral arteries, unilateral, with angiography of the selected vessel circulation and all associated radiological supervision and interpretation (eg, middle cerebral artery, posterior inferior cerebellar artery) (List separately in addition to code for primary procedure)

36248 Selective catheter placement, arterial system; additional second order, third order, and beyond, abdominal, pelvic, or lower extremity artery branch, within a vascular family (List in addition to code for initial second or third order vessel as appropriate)

36476 Endovenous ablation therapy of incompetent vein, extremity, inclusive of all imaging guidance and monitoring, percutaneous, radiofrequency; second and subsequent veins treated in a single extremity, each through separate access sites (List separately in addition to code for primary procedure)

36479 Endovenous ablation therapy of incompetent vein, extremity, inclusive of all imaging guidance and monitoring, percutaneous, laser; second and subsequent veins treated in a single extremity, each through separate access sites (List separately in addition to code for primary procedure)

37185 Primary percutaneous transluminal mechanical thrombectomy, noncoronary, arterial or arterial bypass graft, including fluoroscopic guidance and intraprocedural pharmacological thrombolytic injection(s); second and all subsequent vessel(s) within the same vascular family (List separately in addition to code for primary mechanical thrombectomy procedure)

37186 Secondary percutaneous transluminal thrombectomy (eg, nonprimary mechanical, snare basket, suction technique), noncoronary, arterial or arterial bypass graft, including fluoroscopic guidance and intraprocedural pharmacological thrombolytic injections, provided in conjunction with another percutaneous intervention other than primary mechanical thrombectomy (List separately in addition to code for primary procedure)

37222 Revascularization, endovascular, open or percutaneous, iliac artery, each additional ipsilateral iliac vessel; with transluminal angioplasty (List separately in addition to code for primary procedure)

37223 Revascularization, endovascular, open or percutaneous, iliac artery, each additional ipsilateral iliac vessel; with transluminal stent placement(s), includes angioplasty within the same vessel, when performed (List separately in addition to code for primary procedure)

37232 Revascularization, endovascular, open or percutaneous, tibial/peroneal artery, unilateral, each additional vessel; with transluminal angioplasty (List separately in addition to code for primary procedure)

37233 Revascularization, endovascular, open or percutaneous, tibial/peroneal artery, unilateral, each additional vessel; with atherectomy, includes angioplasty within the same vessel, when performed (List separately in addition to code for primary procedure)

37234 Revascularization, endovascular, open or percutaneous, tibial/peroneal artery, unilateral, each additional vessel; with transluminal stent placement(s), includes angioplasty within the same vessel, when performed (List separately in addition to code for primary procedure)

37235 Revascularization, endovascular, open or percutaneous, tibial/peroneal artery, unilateral, each additional vessel; with transluminal stent placement(s) and atherectomy, includes angioplasty within the same vessel, when performed (List separately in addition to code for primary procedure)

37237 Transcatheter placement of an intravascular stent(s) (except lower extremity, cervical carotid, extracranial vertebral or intrathoracic carotid, intracranial, or coronary), open or percutaneous, including radiological supervision and interpretation and including all angioplasty within the same vessel, when performed; each additional artery (List separately in addition to code for primary procedure)

37239 Transcatheter placement of an intravascular stent(s), open or percutaneous, including radiological supervision and interpretation and including angioplasty within the same vessel, when performed; each additional vein (List separately in addition to code for primary procedure)

37250 Intravascular ultrasound (non-coronary vessel) during diagnostic evaluation and/or therapeutic intervention; initial vessel (List separately in addition to code for primary procedure)

37251 Intravascular ultrasound (non-coronary vessel) during diagnostic evaluation and/or therapeutic intervention; each additional vessel (List separately in addition to code for primary procedure)

38102 Splenectomy; total, en bloc for extensive disease, in conjunction with other procedure (List in addition to code for primary procedure)

38746 Thoracic lymphadenectomy by thoracotomy, mediastinal and regional lymphadenectomy (List separately in addition to code for primary procedure)

38747 Abdominal lymphadenectomy, regional, including celiac, gastric, portal, peripancreatic, with or without para-aortic and vena caval nodes (List separately in addition to code for primary procedure)

38900 Intraoperative identification (eg, mapping) of sentinel lymph node(s) includes injection of non-radioactive dye, when performed (List separately in addition to code for primary procedure)

43273 Endoscopic cannulation of papilla with direct visualization of common bile duct(s) and/or pancreatic duct(s) (List separately in addition to code(s) for primary procedure)

43283 Laparoscopy, surgical, esophageal lengthening procedure (eg, Collis gastroplasty or wedge gastroplasty) (List separately in addition to code for primary procedure)

43338 Esophageal lengthening procedure (eg, Collis gastroplasty or wedge gastroplasty) (List separately in addition to code for primary procedure)

43635 Vagotomy when performed with partial distal gastrectomy (List separately in addition to code[s] for primary procedure)

44015 Tube or needle catheter jejunostomy for enteral alimentation, intraoperative, any method (List separately in addition to primary procedure)

44121 Enterectomy, resection of small intestine; each additional resection and anastomosis (List separately in addition to code for primary procedure)

44128 Enterectomy, resection of small intestine for congenital atresia, single resection and anastomosis of proximal segment of intestine; each additional resection and anastomosis (List separately in addition to code for primary procedure)

44139 Mobilization (take-down) of splenic flexure performed in conjunction with partial colectomy (List separately in addition to primary procedure)

44203 Laparoscopy, surgical; each additional small intestine resection and anastomosis (List separately in addition to code for primary procedure)

44213 Laparoscopy, surgical, mobilization (take-down) of splenic flexure performed in conjunction with partial colectomy (List separately in addition to primary procedure)
44701 Intraoperative colonic lavage (List separately in addition to code for primary procedure)
44955 Appendectomy; when done for indicated purpose at time of other major procedure (not as separate procedure) (List separately in addition to code for primary procedure)
47001 Biopsy of liver, needle; when done for indicated purpose at time of other major procedure (List separately in addition to code for primary procedure)
47550 Biliary endoscopy, intraoperative (choledochoscopy) (List separately in addition to code for primary procedure)
48400 Injection procedure for intraoperative pancreatography (List separately in addition to code for primary procedure)
49326 Laparoscopy, surgical; with omentopexy (omental tacking procedure) (List separately in addition to code for primary procedure)
49327 Laparoscopy, surgical; with placement of interstitial device(s) for radiation therapy guidance (eg, fiducial markers, dosimeter), intra-abdominal, intrapelvic, and/or retroperitoneum, including imaging guidance, if performed, single or multiple (List separately in addition to code for primary procedure)
49412 Placement of interstitial device(s) for radiation therapy guidance (eg, fiducial markers, dosimeter), open, intra-abdominal, intrapelvic, and/or retroperitoneum, including image guidance, if performed, single or multiple (List separately in addition to code for primary procedure)
49435 Insertion of subcutaneous extension to intraperitoneal cannula or catheter with remote chest exit site (List separately in addition to code for primary procedure)
49568 Implantation of mesh or other prosthesis for open incisional or ventral hernia repair or mesh for closure of debridement for necrotizing soft tissue infection (List separately in addition to code for the incisional or ventral hernia repair)
49905 Omental flap, intra-abdominal (List separately in addition to code for primary procedure)
51797 Voiding pressure studies, intra-abdominal (ie, rectal, gastric, intraperitoneal) (List separately in addition to code for primary procedure)
56606 Biopsy of vulva or perineum (separate procedure); each separate additional lesion (List separately in addition to code for primary procedure)
57267 Insertion of mesh or other prosthesis for repair of pelvic floor defect, each site (anterior, posterior compartment), vaginal approach (List separately in addition to code for primary procedure)
58110 Endometrial sampling (biopsy) performed in conjunction with colposcopy (List separately in addition to code for primary procedure)
58611 Ligation or transection of fallopian tube(s) when done at the time of cesarean delivery or intra-abdominal surgery (not a separate procedure) (List separately in addition to code for primary procedure)
59525 Subtotal or total hysterectomy after cesarean delivery (List separately in addition to code for primary procedure)
60512 Parathyroid autotransplantation (List separately in addition to code for primary procedure)
61316 Incision and subcutaneous placement of cranial bone graft (List separately in addition to code for primary procedure)
61517 Implantation of brain intracavitary chemotherapy agent (List separately in addition to code for primary procedure)
61609 Transection or ligation, carotid artery in cavernous sinus; without repair (List separately in addition to code for primary procedure)
61610 Transection or ligation, carotid artery in cavernous sinus; with repair by anastomosis or graft (List separately in addition to code for primary procedure)
61611 Transection or ligation, carotid artery in petrous canal; without repair (List separately in addition to code for primary procedure)
61612 Transection or ligation, carotid artery in petrous canal; with repair by anastomosis or graft (List separately in addition to code for primary procedure)
61641 Balloon dilatation of intracranial vasospasm, percutaneous; each additional vessel in same vascular family (List separately in addition to code for primary procedure)
61642 Balloon dilatation of intracranial vasospasm, percutaneous; each additional vessel in different vascular family (List separately in addition to code for primary procedure)
61781 Stereotactic computer-assisted (navigational) procedure; cranial, intradural (List separately in addition to code for primary procedure)
61782 Stereotactic computer-assisted (navigational) procedure; cranial, extradural (List separately in addition to code for primary procedure)
61783 Stereotactic computer-assisted (navigational) procedure; spinal (List separately in addition to code for primary procedure)
61797 Stereotactic radiosurgery (particle beam, gamma ray, or linear accelerator); each additional cranial lesion, simple (List separately in addition to code for primary procedure)
61799 Stereotactic radiosurgery (particle beam, gamma ray, or linear accelerator); each additional cranial lesion, complex (List separately in addition to code for primary procedure)
61800 Application of stereotactic headframe for stereotactic radiosurgery (List separately in addition to code for primary procedure)
61864 Twist drill, burr hole, craniotomy, or craniectomy with stereotactic implantation of neurostimulator electrode array in subcortical site (eg, thalamus, globus pallidus, subthalamic nucleus, periventricular, periaqueductal gray), without use of intraoperative microelectrode recording; each additional array (List separately in addition to primary procedure)
61868 Twist drill, burr hole, craniotomy, or craniectomy with stereotactic implantation of neurostimulator electrode array in subcortical site (eg, thalamus, globus pallidus, subthalamic nucleus, periventricular, periaqueductal gray), with use of intraoperative microelectrode recording; each additional array (List separately in addition to primary procedure)
62148 Incision and retrieval of subcutaneous cranial bone graft for cranioplasty (List separately in addition to code for primary procedure)
62160 Neuroendoscopy, intracranial, for placement or replacement of ventricular catheter and attachment to shunt system or external drainage (List separately in addition to code for primary procedure)
63035 Laminotomy (hemilaminectomy), with decompression of nerve root(s), including partial facetectomy, foraminotomy and/or excision of herniated intervertebral disc; each additional interspace, cervical or lumbar (List separately in addition to code for primary procedure)
63043 Laminotomy (hemilaminectomy), with decompression of nerve root(s), including partial facetectomy, foraminotomy and/or excision of herniated intervertebral disc, reexploration, single interspace; each additional cervical interspace (List separately in addition to code for primary procedure)
63044 Laminotomy (hemilaminectomy), with decompression of nerve root(s), including partial facetectomy, foraminotomy and/or excision of herniated intervertebral disc, reexploration, single interspace; each additional lumbar interspace (List separately in addition to code for primary procedure)
63048 Laminectomy, facetectomy and foraminotomy (unilateral or bilateral with decompression of spinal cord, cauda equina and/or nerve root[s], [eg, spinal or lateral recess stenosis]), single vertebral segment; each additional segment, cervical, thoracic, or lumbar (List separately in addition to code for primary procedure)
63057 Transpedicular approach with decompression of spinal cord, equina and/or nerve root(s) (eg, herniated intervertebral disc), single segment; each additional segment, thoracic or lumbar (List separately in addition to code for primary procedure)
63066 Costovertebral approach with decompression of spinal cord or nerve root(s) (eg, herniated intervertebral disc), thoracic; each additional segment (List separately in addition to code for primary procedure)
63076 Discectomy, anterior, with decompression of spinal cord and/or nerve root(s), including osteophytectomy; cervical, each additional interspace (List separately in addition to code for primary procedure)
63078 Discectomy, anterior, with decompression of spinal cord and/or nerve root(s), including osteophytectomy; thoracic, each additional interspace (List separately in addition to code for primary procedure)
63082 Vertebral corpectomy (vertebral body resection), partial or complete, anterior approach with decompression of spinal cord and/or nerve root(s); cervical, each additional segment (List separately in addition to code for primary procedure)
63086 Vertebral corpectomy (vertebral body resection), partial or complete, transthoracic approach with decompression of spinal cord and/or nerve root(s); thoracic, each additional segment (List separately in addition to code for primary procedure)
63088 Vertebral corpectomy (vertebral body resection), partial or complete, combined thoracolumbar approach with decompression of spinal cord,

cauda equina or nerve root(s), lower thoracic or lumbar; each additional segment (List separately in addition to code for primary procedure)
63091 Vertebral corpectomy (vertebral body resection), partial or complete, transperitoneal or retroperitoneal approach with decompression of spinal cord, cauda equina or nerve root(s), lower thoracic, lumbar, or sacral; each additional segment (List separately in addition to code for primary procedure)
63103 Vertebral corpectomy (vertebral body resection), partial or complete, lateral extracavitary approach with decompression of spinal cord and/or nerve root(s) (eg, for tumor or retropulsed bone fragments); thoracic or lumbar, each additional segment (List separately in addition to code for primary procedure)
63295 Osteoplastic reconstruction of dorsal spinal elements, following primary intraspinal procedure (List separately in addition to code for primary procedure)
63308 Vertebral corpectomy (vertebral body resection), partial or complete, for excision of intraspinal lesion, single segment; each additional segment (List separately in addition to codes for single segment)
63621 Stereotactic radiosurgery (particle beam, gamma ray, or linear accelerator); each additional spinal lesion (List separately in addition to code for primary procedure)
64480 Injection(s), anesthetic agent and/or steroid, transforaminal epidural, with imaging guidance (fluoroscopy or CT); cervical or thoracic, each additional level (List separately in addition to code for primary procedure)
64484 Injection(s), anesthetic agent and/or steroid, transforaminal epidural, with imaging guidance (fluoroscopy or CT); lumbar or sacral, each additional level (List separately in addition to code for primary procedure)
64491 Injection(s), diagnostic or therapeutic agent, paravertebral facet (zygapophyseal) joint (or nerves innervating that joint) with image guidance (fluoroscopy or CT), cervical or thoracic; second level (List separately in addition to code for primary procedure)
64492 Injection(s), diagnostic or therapeutic agent, paravertebral facet (zygapophyseal) joint (or nerves innervating that joint) with image guidance (fluoroscopy or CT), cervical or thoracic; third and any additional level(s) (List separately in addition to code for primary procedure)
64494 Injection(s), diagnostic or therapeutic agent, paravertebral facet (zygapophyseal) joint (or nerves innervating that joint) with image guidance (fluoroscopy or CT), lumbar or sacral; second level (List separately in addition to code for primary procedure)
64495 Injection(s), diagnostic or therapeutic agent, paravertebral facet (zygapophyseal) joint (or nerves innervating that joint) with image guidance (fluoroscopy or CT), lumbar or sacral; third and any additional level(s) (List separately in addition to code for primary procedure)
64634 Destruction by neurolytic agent, paravertebral facet joint nerve(s), with imaging guidance (fluoroscopy or CT); cervical or thoracic, each additional facet joint (List separately in addition to code for primary procedure)
64636 Destruction by neurolytic agent, paravertebral facet joint nerve(s), with imaging guidance (fluoroscopy or CT); lumbar or sacral, each additional facet joint (List separately in addition to code for primary procedure)
64643 Chemodenervation of one extremity; each additional extremity, 1-4 muscle(s) (List separately in addition to code for primary procedure)
64645 Chemodenervation of one extremity; each additional extremity, 5 or more muscle(s) (List separately in addition to code for primary procedure)
64727 Internal neurolysis, requiring use of operating microscope (List separately in addition to code for neuroplasty) (Neuroplasty includes external neurolysis)
64778 Excision of neuroma; digital nerve, each additional digit (List separately in addition to code for primary procedure)
64783 Excision of neuroma; hand or foot, each additional nerve, except same digit (List separately in addition to code for primary procedure)
64787 Implantation of nerve end into bone or muscle (List separately in addition to neuroma excision)
64832 Suture of digital nerve, hand or foot; each additional digital nerve (List separately in addition to code for primary procedure)
64837 Suture of each additional nerve, hand or foot (List separately in addition to code for primary procedure)
64859 Suture of each additional major peripheral nerve (List separately in addition to code for primary procedure)
64872 Suture of nerve; requiring secondary or delayed suture (List separately in addition to code for primary neurorrhaphy)
64874 Suture of nerve; requiring extensive mobilization, or transposition of nerve (List separately in addition to code for nerve suture)
64876 Suture of nerve; requiring shortening of bone of extremity (List separately in addition to code for nerve suture)
64901 Nerve graft, each additional nerve; single strand (List separately in addition to code for primary procedure)
64902 Nerve graft, each additional nerve; multiple strands (cable) (List separately in addition to code for primary procedure)
65757 Backbench preparation of corneal endothelial allograft prior to transplantation (List separately in addition to code for primary procedure)
66990 Use of ophthalmic endoscope (List separately in addition to code for primary procedure)
67225 Destruction of localized lesion of choroid (eg, choroidal neovascularization); photodynamic therapy, second eye, at single session (List separately in addition to code for primary eye treatment)
67320 Transposition procedure (eg, for paretic extraocular muscle), any extraocular muscle (specify) (List separately in addition to code for primary procedure)
67331 Strabismus surgery on patient with previous eye surgery or injury that did not involve the extraocular muscles (List separately in addition to code for primary procedure)
67332 Strabismus surgery on patient with scarring of extraocular muscles (eg, prior ocular injury, strabismus or retinal detachment surgery) or restrictive myopathy (eg, dysthyroid ophthalmopathy) (List separately in addition to code for primary procedure)
67334 Strabismus surgery by posterior fixation suture technique, with or without muscle recession (List separately in addition to code for primary procedure)
67335 Placement of adjustable suture(s) during strabismus surgery, including postoperative adjustment(s) of suture(s) (List separately in addition to code for specific strabismus surgery)
67340 Strabismus surgery involving exploration and/or repair of detached extraocular muscle(s) (List separately in addition to code for primary procedure)
69990 Microsurgical techniques, requiring use of operating microscope (List separately in addition to code for primary procedure)
74301 Cholangiography and/or pancreatography; additional set intraoperative, radiological supervision and interpretation (List separately in addition to code for primary procedure)
75565 Cardiac magnetic resonance imaging for velocity flow mapping (List separately in addition to code for primary procedure)
75774 Angiography, selective, each additional vessel studied after basic examination, radiological supervision and interpretation (List separately in addition to code for primary procedure)
75946 Intravascular ultrasound (non-coronary vessel), radiological supervision and interpretation; each additional non-coronary vessel (List separately in addition to code for primary procedure)
75964 Transluminal balloon angioplasty, each additional peripheral artery other than renal, or other visceral artery, iliac or lower extremity, radiological supervision and interpretation (List separately in addition to code for primary procedure)
75968 Transluminal balloon angioplasty, each additional visceral artery, radiological supervision and interpretation (List separately in addition to code for primary procedure)
76125 Cineradiography/videoradiography to complement routine examination (List separately in addition to code for primary procedure)
76802 Ultrasound, pregnant uterus, real time with image documentation, fetal and maternal evaluation, first trimester (< 14 weeks 0 days), transabdominal approach; each additional gestation (List separately in addition to code for primary procedure)
76810 Ultrasound, pregnant uterus, real time with image documentation, fetal and maternal evaluation, after first trimester (> or = 14 weeks 0 days), transabdominal approach; each additional gestation (List separately in addition to code for primary procedure)
76812 Ultrasound, pregnant uterus, real time with image documentation, fetal and maternal evaluation plus detailed fetal anatomic examination, transabdominal approach; each additional gestation (List separately in addition to code for primary procedure)
76814 Ultrasound, pregnant uterus, real time with image documentation, first trimester fetal nuchal translucency measurement, transabdominal or transvaginal approach; each additional gestation (List separately in addition to code for primary procedure)
76937 Ultrasound guidance for vascular access requiring ultrasound evaluation of potential access sites, documentation of selected vessel patency, concurrent

realtime ultrasound visualization of vascular needle entry, with permanent recording and reporting (List separately in addition to code for primary procedure)

77001 Fluoroscopic guidance for central venous access device placement, replacement (catheter only or complete), or removal (includes fluoroscopic guidance for vascular access and catheter manipulation, any necessary contrast injections through access site or catheter with related venography radiologic supervision and interpretation, and radiographic documentation of final catheter position) (List separately in addition to code for primary procedure)

77051 Computer-aided detection (computer algorithm analysis of digital image data for lesion detection) with further review for interpretation, with or without digitization of film radiographic images; diagnostic mammography (List separately in addition to code for primary procedure)

77052 Computer-aided detection (computer algorithm analysis of digital image data for lesion detection) with further review for interpretation, with or without digitization of film radiographic images; screening mammography (List separately in addition to code for primary procedure)

77293 Respiratory motion management simulation (List separately in addition to code for primary procedure)

78020 Thyroid carcinoma metastases uptake (List separately in addition to code for primary procedure)

78496 Cardiac blood pool imaging, gated equilibrium, single study, at rest, with right ventricular ejection fraction by first pass technique (List separately in addition to code for primary procedure)

78730 Urinary bladder residual study (List separately in addition to code for primary procedure)

81266 Comparative analysis using Short Tandem Repeat (STR) markers; each additional specimen (eg, additional cord blood donor, additional fetal samples from different cultures, or additional zygosity in multiple birth pregnancies) (List separately in addition to code for primary procedure)

82952 Glucose; tolerance test, each additional beyond 3 specimens (List separately in addition to code for primary procedure)

86826 Human leukocyte antigen (HLA) crossmatch, non-cytotoxic (eg, using flow cytometry); each additional serum sample or sample dilution (List separately in addition to primary procedure)

87187 Susceptibility studies, antimicrobial agent; microdilution or agar dilution, minimum lethal concentration (MLC), each plate (List separately in addition to code for primary procedure)

87503 Infectious agent detection by nucleic acid (DNA or RNA); influenza virus, for multiple types or sub-types, multiplex reverse transcription and amplified probe technique, each additional influenza virus type or sub-type beyond 2 (List separately in addition to code for primary procedure)

87904 Infectious agent phenotype analysis by nucleic acid (DNA or RNA) with drug resistance tissue culture analysis, HIV 1; each additional drug tested (List separately in addition to code for primary procedure)

88155 Cytopathology, slides, cervical or vaginal, definitive hormonal evaluation (eg, maturation index, karyopyknotic index, estrogenic index) (List separately in addition to code[s] for other technical and interpretation services)

88177 Cytopathology, evaluation of fine needle aspirate; immediate cytohistologic study to determine adequacy for diagnosis, each separate additional evaluation episode, same site (List separately in addition to code for primary procedure)

88185 Flow cytometry, cell surface, cytoplasmic, or nuclear marker, technical component only; each additional marker (List separately in addition to code for first marker)

88311 Decalcification procedure (List separately in addition to code for surgical pathology examination)

88314 Special stain including interpretation and report; histochemical stain on frozen tissue block (List separately in addition to code for primary procedure)

88332 Pathology consultation during surgery; each additional tissue block with frozen section(s) (List separately in addition to code for primary procedure)

88334 Pathology consultation during surgery; cytologic examination (eg, touch prep, squash prep), each additional site (List separately in addition to code for primary procedure)

88343 Immunohistochemistry or immunocytochemistry, each separately identifiable antibody per block, cytologic preparation, or hematologic smear; each additional separately identifiable antibody per slide (List separately in addition to code for primary procedure)

88388 Macroscopic examination, dissection, and preparation of tissue for non-microscopic analytical studies (eg, nucleic acid-based molecular studies); in conjunction with a touch imprint, intraoperative consultation, or frozen section, each tissue preparation (eg, a single lymph node) (List separately in addition to code for primary procedure)

90461 Immunization administration through 18 years of age via any route of administration, with counseling by physician or other qualified health care professional; each additional vaccine or toxoid component administered (List separately in addition to code for primary procedure)

90472 Immunization administration (includes percutaneous, intradermal, subcutaneous, or intramuscular injections); each additional vaccine (single or combination vaccine/toxoid) (List separately in addition to code for primary procedure)

90474 Immunization administration by intranasal or oral route; each additional vaccine (single or combination vaccine/toxoid) (List separately in addition to code for primary procedure)

90785 Interactive complexity (List separately in addition to the code for primary procedure)

90833 Psychotherapy, 30 minutes with patient and/or family member when performed with an evaluation and management service (List separately in addition to the code for primary procedure)

90836 Psychotherapy, 45 minutes with patient and/or family member when performed with an evaluation and management service (List separately in addition to the code for primary procedure)

90838 Psychotherapy, 60 minutes with patient and/or family member when performed with an evaluation and management service (List separately in addition to the code for primary procedure)

90840 Psychotherapy for crisis; each additional 30 minutes (List separately in addition to code for primary service)

90863 Pharmacologic management, including prescription and review of medication, when performed with psychotherapy services (List separately in addition to the code for primary procedure)

91013 Esophageal motility (manometric study of the esophagus and/or gastroesophageal junction) study with interpretation and report; with stimulation or perfusion (eg, stimulant, acid or alkali perfusion) (List separately in addition to code for primary procedure)

92547 Use of vertical electrodes (List separately in addition to code for primary procedure)

92608 Evaluation for prescription for speech-generating augmentative and alternative communication device, face-to-face with the patient; each additional 30 minutes (List separately in addition to code for primary procedure)

92618 Evaluation for prescription of non-speech-generating augmentative and alternative communication device, face-to-face with the patient; each additional 30 minutes (List separately in addition to code for primary procedure)

92621 Evaluation of central auditory function, with report; each additional 15 minutes (List separately in addition to code for primary procedure)

92627 Evaluation of auditory rehabilitation status; each additional 15 minutes (List separately in addition to code for primary procedure)

92921 Percutaneous transluminal coronary angioplasty; each additional branch of a major coronary artery (List separately in addition to code for primary procedure)

92925 Percutaneous transluminal coronary atherectomy, with coronary angioplasty when performed; each additional branch of a major coronary artery (List separately in addition to code for primary procedure)

92929 Percutaneous transcatheter placement of intracoronary stent(s), with coronary angioplasty when performed; each additional branch of a major coronary artery (List separately in addition to code for primary procedure)

92934 Percutaneous transluminal coronary atherectomy, with intracoronary stent, with coronary angioplasty when performed; each additional branch of a major coronary artery (List separately in addition to code for primary procedure)

92938 Percutaneous transluminal revascularization of or through coronary artery bypass graft (internal mammary, free arterial, venous), any combination of intracoronary stent, atherectomy and angioplasty, including distal protection when performed; each additional branch subtended by the bypass graft (List separately in addition to code for primary procedure)

92944 Percutaneous transluminal revascularization of chronic total occlusion, coronary artery, coronary artery branch, or coronary artery bypass graft, any combination of intracoronary stent, atherectomy and angioplasty; each additional coronary artery, coronary artery branch, or bypass graft (List separately in addition to code for primary procedure)

92973 Percutaneous transluminal coronary thrombectomy mechanical (List separately in addition to code for primary procedure)

92974 Transcatheter placement of radiation delivery device for subsequent coronary intravascular brachytherapy (List separately in addition to code for primary procedure)

92978 Intravascular ultrasound (coronary vessel or graft) during diagnostic evaluation and/or therapeutic intervention including imaging supervision, interpretation and report; initial vessel (List separately in addition to code for primary procedure)

92979 Intravascular ultrasound (coronary vessel or graft) during diagnostic evaluation and/or therapeutic intervention including imaging supervision, interpretation and report; each additional vessel (List separately in addition to code for primary procedure)

92998 Percutaneous transluminal pulmonary artery balloon angioplasty; each additional vessel (List separately in addition to code for primary procedure)

93320 Doppler echocardiography, pulsed wave and/or continuous wave with spectral display (List separately in addition to codes for echocardiographic imaging); complete

93321 Doppler echocardiography, pulsed wave and/or continuous wave with spectral display (List separately in addition to codes for echocardiographic imaging); follow-up or limited study (List separately in addition to codes for echocardiographic imaging)

93325 Doppler echocardiography color flow velocity mapping (List separately in addition to codes for echocardiography)

93352 Use of echocardiographic contrast agent during stress echocardiography (List separately in addition to code for primary procedure)

93462 Left heart catheterization by transseptal puncture through intact septum or by transapical puncture (List separately in addition to code for primary procedure)

93463 Pharmacologic agent administration (eg, inhaled nitric oxide, intravenous infusion of nitroprusside, dobutamine, milrinone, or other agent) including assessing hemodynamic measurements before, during, after and repeat pharmacologic agent administration, when performed (List separately in addition to code for primary procedure)

93464 Physiologic exercise study (eg, bicycle or arm ergometry) including assessing hemodynamic measurements before and after (List separately in addition to code for primary procedure)

93563 Injection procedure during cardiac catheterization including imaging supervision, interpretation, and report; for selective coronary angiography during congenital heart catheterization (List separately in addition to code for primary procedure)

93564 Injection procedure during cardiac catheterization including imaging supervision, interpretation, and report; for selective opacification of aortocoronary venous or arterial bypass graft(s) (eg, aortocoronary saphenous vein, free radial artery, or free mammary artery graft) to 1 or more coronary arteries and in situ arterial conduits (eg, internal mammary), whether native or used for bypass to 1 or more coronary arteries during congenital heart catheterization, when performed (List separately in addition to code for primary procedure)

93565 Injection procedure during cardiac catheterization including imaging supervision, interpretation, and report; for selective left ventricular or left atrial angiography (List separately in addition to code for primary procedure)

93566 Injection procedure during cardiac catheterization including imaging supervision, interpretation, and report; for selective right ventricular or right atrial angiography (List separately in addition to code for primary procedure)

93567 Injection procedure during cardiac catheterization including imaging supervision, interpretation, and report; for supravalvular aortography (List separately in addition to code for primary procedure)

93568 Injection procedure during cardiac catheterization including imaging supervision, interpretation, and report; for pulmonary angiography (List separately in addition to code for primary procedure)

93571 Intravascular Doppler velocity and/or pressure derived coronary flow reserve measurement (coronary vessel or graft) during coronary angiography including pharmacologically induced stress; initial vessel (List separately in addition to code for primary procedure)

93572 Intravascular Doppler velocity and/or pressure derived coronary flow reserve measurement (coronary vessel or graft) during coronary angiography including pharmacologically induced stress; each additional vessel (List separately in addition to code for primary procedure)

93609 Intraventricular and/or intra-atrial mapping of tachycardia site(s) with catheter manipulation to record from multiple sites to identify origin of tachycardia (List separately in addition to code for primary procedure)

93613 Intracardiac electrophysiologic 3-dimensional mapping (List separately in addition to code for primary procedure)

93621 Comprehensive electrophysiologic evaluation including insertion and repositioning of multiple electrode catheters with induction or attempted induction of arrhythmia; with left atrial pacing and recording from coronary sinus or left atrium (List separately in addition to code for primary procedure)

93622 Comprehensive electrophysiologic evaluation including insertion and repositioning of multiple electrode catheters with induction or attempted induction of arrhythmia; with left ventricular pacing and recording (List separately in addition to code for primary procedure)

93623 Programmed stimulation and pacing after intravenous drug infusion (List separately in addition to code for primary procedure)

93655 Intracardiac catheter ablation of a discrete mechanism of arrhythmia which is distinct from the primary ablated mechanism, including repeat diagnostic maneuvers, to treat a spontaneous or induced arrhythmia (List separately in addition to code for primary procedure)

93657 Additional linear or focal intracardiac catheter ablation of the left or right atrium for treatment of atrial fibrillation remaining after completion of pulmonary vein isolation (List separately in addition to code for primary procedure)

93662 Intracardiac echocardiography during therapeutic/diagnostic intervention, including imaging supervision and interpretation (List separately in addition to code for primary procedure)

94645 Continuous inhalation treatment with aerosol medication for acute airway obstruction; each additional hour (List separately in addition to code for primary procedure)

94729 Diffusing capacity (eg, carbon monoxide, membrane) (List separately in addition to code for primary procedure)

94781 Car seat/bed testing for airway integrity, neonate, with continual nursing observation and continuous recording of pulse oximetry, heart rate and respiratory rate, with interpretation and report; each additional full 30 minutes (List separately in addition to code for primary procedure)

95079 Ingestion challenge test (sequential and incremental ingestion of test items, eg, food, drug or other substance); each additional 60 minutes of testing (List separately in addition to code for primary procedure)

95873 Electrical stimulation for guidance in conjunction with chemodenervation (List separately in addition to code for primary procedure)

95874 Needle electromyography for guidance in conjunction with chemodenervation (List separately in addition to code for primary procedure)

95885 Needle electromyography, each extremity, with related paraspinal areas, when performed, done with nerve conduction, amplitude and latency/velocity study; limited (List separately in addition to code for primary procedure)

95886 Needle electromyography, each extremity, with related paraspinal areas, when performed, done with nerve conduction, amplitude and latency/velocity study; complete, 5 or more muscles studied, innervated by 3 or more nerves or 4 or more spinal levels (List separately in addition to code for primary procedure)

95887 Needle electromyography, non-extremity (cranial nerve supplied or axial) muscle(s) done with nerve conduction, amplitude and latency/velocity study (List separately in addition to code for primary procedure)

95940 Continuous intraoperative neurophysiology monitoring in the operating room, one on one monitoring requiring personal attendance, each 15 minutes (List separately in addition to code for primary procedure)

95941 Continuous intraoperative neurophysiology monitoring, from outside the operating room (remote or nearby) or for monitoring of more than one case while in the operating room, per hour (List separately in addition to code for primary procedure)

95962 Functional cortical and subcortical mapping by stimulation and/or recording of electrodes on brain surface, or of depth electrodes, to provoke seizures or identify vital brain structures; each additional hour of attendance by a physician or other qualified health care professional (List separately in addition to code for primary procedure)

95967 Magnetoencephalography (MEG), recording and analysis; for evoked magnetic fields, each additional modality (eg, sensory, motor, language, or visual cortex localization) (List separately in addition to code for primary procedure)

95973 Electronic analysis of implanted neurostimulator pulse generator system (eg, rate, pulse amplitude, pulse duration, configuration of wave form, battery status, electrode selectability, output modulation, cycling, impedance and patient compliance measurements); complex spinal cord, or peripheral (ie, peripheral nerve, sacral nerve, neuromuscular) (except cranial nerve) neurostimulator pulse generator/transmitter, with intraoperative or subsequent programming, each additional 30 minutes after first hour (List separately in addition to code for primary procedure)

95975 Electronic analysis of implanted neurostimulator pulse generator system (eg, rate, pulse amplitude, pulse duration, configuration of wave form, battery status, electrode selectability, output modulation, cycling, impedance and patient compliance measurements); complex cranial nerve neurostimulator pulse generator/transmitter, with intraoperative or subsequent programming, each additional 30 minutes after first hour (List separately in addition to code for primary procedure)

95979 Electronic analysis of implanted neurostimulator pulse generator system (eg, rate, pulse amplitude and duration, battery status, electrode selectability and polarity, impedance and patient compliance measurements), complex deep brain neurostimulator pulse generator/ transmitter, with initial or subsequent programming; each additional 30 minutes after first hour (List separately in addition to code for primary procedure)

96361 Intravenous infusion, hydration; each additional hour (List separately in addition to code for primary procedure)

96366 Intravenous infusion, for therapy, prophylaxis, or diagnosis (specify substance or drug); each additional hour (List separately in addition to code for primary procedure)

96367 Intravenous infusion, for therapy, prophylaxis, or diagnosis (specify substance or drug); additional sequential infusion of a new drug/substance, up to 1 hour (List separately in addition to code for primary procedure)

96368 Intravenous infusion, for therapy, prophylaxis, or diagnosis (specify substance or drug); concurrent infusion (List separately in addition to code for primary procedure)

96370 Subcutaneous infusion for therapy or prophylaxis (specify substance or drug); each additional hour (List separately in addition to code for primary procedure)

96371 Subcutaneous infusion for therapy or prophylaxis (specify substance or drug); additional pump set-up with establishment of new subcutaneous infusion site(s) (List separately in addition to code for primary procedure)

96375 Therapeutic, prophylactic, or diagnostic injection (specify substance or drug); each additional sequential intravenous push of a new substance/drug (List separately in addition to code for primary procedure)

96376 Therapeutic, prophylactic, or diagnostic injection (specify substance or drug); each additional sequential intravenous push of the same substance/ drug provided in a facility (List separately in addition to code for primary procedure)

96411 Chemotherapy administration; intravenous, push technique, each additional substance/drug (List separately in addition to code for primary procedure)

96415 Chemotherapy administration, intravenous infusion technique; each additional hour (List separately in addition to code for primary procedure)

96417 Chemotherapy administration, intravenous infusion technique; each additional sequential infusion (different substance/drug), up to 1 hour (List separately in addition to code for primary procedure)

96423 Chemotherapy administration, intra-arterial; infusion technique, each additional hour (List separately in addition to code for primary procedure)

96570 Photodynamic therapy by endoscopic application of light to ablate abnormal tissue via activation of photosensitive drug(s); first 30 minutes (List separately in addition to code for endoscopy or bronchoscopy procedures of lung and gastrointestinal tract)

96571 Photodynamic therapy by endoscopic application of light to ablate abnormal tissue via activation of photosensitive drug(s); each additional 15 minutes (List separately in addition to code for endoscopy or bronchoscopy procedures of lung and gastrointestinal tract)

97546 Work hardening/conditioning; each additional hour (List separately in addition to code for primary procedure)

97598 Debridement (eg, high pressure waterjet with/without suction, sharp selective debridement with scissors, scalpel and forceps), open wound, (eg, fibrin, devitalized epidermis and/or dermis, exudate, debris, biofilm), including topical application(s), wound assessment, use of a whirlpool, when performed and instruction(s) for ongoing care, per session, total wound(s) surface area; each additional 20 sq cm, or part thereof (List separately in addition to code for primary procedure)

97811 Acupuncture, 1 or more needles; without electrical stimulation, each additional 15 minutes of personal one-on-one contact with the patient, with re-insertion of needle(s) (List separately in addition to code for primary procedure)

97814 Acupuncture, 1 or more needles; with electrical stimulation, each additional 15 minutes of personal one-on-one contact with the patient, with re-insertion of needle(s) (List separately in addition to code for primary procedure)

99100 Anesthesia for patient of extreme age, younger than 1 year and older than 70 (List separately in addition to code for primary anesthesia procedure)

99116 Anesthesia complicated by utilization of total body hypothermia (List separately in addition to code for primary anesthesia procedure)

99135 Anesthesia complicated by utilization of controlled hypotension (List separately in addition to code for primary anesthesia procedure)

99140 Anesthesia complicated by emergency conditions (specify) (List separately in addition to code for primary anesthesia procedure)

99145 Moderate sedation services (other than those services described by codes 00100-01999) provided by the same physician or other qualified health care professional performing the diagnostic or therapeutic service that the sedation supports, requiring the presence of an independent trained observer to assist in the monitoring of the patient's level of consciousness and physiological status; each additional 15 minutes intra-service time (List separately in addition to code for primary service)

99150 Moderate sedation services (other than those services described by codes 00100-01999), provided by a physician or other qualified health care professional other than the health care professional performing the diagnostic or therapeutic service that the sedation supports; each additional 15 minutes intra-service time (List separately in addition to code for primary service)

99292 Critical care, evaluation and management of the critically ill or critically injured patient; each additional 30 minutes (List separately in addition to code for primary service)

99354 Prolonged service in the office or other outpatient setting requiring direct patient contact beyond the usual service; first hour (List separately in addition to code for office or other outpatient Evaluation and Management service)

99355 Prolonged service in the office or other outpatient setting requiring direct patient contact beyond the usual service; each additional 30 minutes (List separately in addition to code for prolonged service)

99356 Prolonged service in the inpatient or observation setting, requiring unit/ floor time beyond the usual service; first hour (List separately in addition to code for inpatient Evaluation and Management service)

99357 Prolonged service in the inpatient or observation setting, requiring unit/ floor time beyond the usual service; each additional 30 minutes (List separately in addition to code for prolonged service)

99359 Prolonged evaluation and management service before and/or after direct patient care; each additional 30 minutes (List separately in addition to code for prolonged service)

99467 Critical care face-to-face services, during an interfacility transport of critically ill or critically injured pediatric patient, 24 months of age or younger; each additional 30 minutes (List separately in addition to code for primary service)

99481 Total body systemic hypothermia in a critically ill neonate per day (List separately in addition to code for primary procedure)

99482 Selective head hypothermia in a critically ill neonate per day (List separately in addition to code for primary procedure)

99486 Supervision by a control physician of interfacility transport care of the critically ill or critically injured pediatric patient, 24 months of age or younger, includes two-way communication with transport team before transport, at the referring facility and during the transport, including data interpretation and report; each additional 30 minutes (List separately in addition to code for primary procedure)

99489 Complex chronic care coordination services; each additional 30 minutes of clinical staff time directed by a physician or other qualified health care professional, per calendar month (List separately in addition to code for primary procedure)

99602 Home infusion/specialty drug administration, per visit (up to 2 hours); each additional hour (List separately in addition to code for primary procedure)

99607 Medication therapy management service(s) provided by a pharmacist, individual, face-to-face with patient, with assessment and intervention if provided; each additional 15 minutes (List separately in addition to code for primary service)

Appendix B

Unlisted Codes

01999 Unlisted anesthesia procedure(s)
15999 Unlisted procedure, excision pressure ulcer
17999 Unlisted procedure, skin, mucous membrane and subcutaneous tissue
19499 Unlisted procedure, breast
20999 Unlisted procedure, musculoskeletal system, general
21089 Unlisted maxillofacial prosthetic procedure
21299 Unlisted craniofacial and maxillofacial procedure
21499 Unlisted musculoskeletal procedure, head
21899 Unlisted procedure, neck or thorax
22899 Unlisted procedure, spine
22999 Unlisted procedure, abdomen, musculoskeletal system
23929 Unlisted procedure, shoulder
24999 Unlisted procedure, humerus or elbow
25999 Unlisted procedure, forearm or wrist
26989 Unlisted procedure, hands or fingers
27299 Unlisted procedure, pelvis or hip joint
27599 Unlisted procedure, femur or knee
27899 Unlisted procedure, leg or ankle
28899 Unlisted procedure, foot or toes
29799 Unlisted procedure, casting or strapping
29999 Unlisted procedure, arthroscopy
30999 Unlisted procedure, nose
31299 Unlisted procedure, accessory sinuses
31599 Unlisted procedure, larynx
31899 Unlisted procedure, trachea, bronchi
32999 Unlisted procedure, lungs and pleura
33999 Unlisted procedure, cardiac surgery
36299 Unlisted procedure, vascular injection
37501 Unlisted vascular endoscopy procedure
37799 Unlisted procedure, vascular surgery
38129 Unlisted laparoscopy procedure, spleen
38589 Unlisted laparoscopy procedure, lymphatic system
38999 Unlisted procedure, hemic or lymphatic system
39499 Unlisted procedure, mediastinum
39599 Unlisted procedure, diaphragm
40799 Unlisted procedure, lips
40899 Unlisted procedure, vestibule of mouth
41599 Unlisted procedure, tongue, floor of mouth
41899 Unlisted procedure, dentoalveolar structures
42299 Unlisted procedure, palate, uvula
42699 Unlisted procedure, salivary glands or ducts
42999 Unlisted procedure, pharynx, adenoids, or tonsils
43289 Unlisted laparoscopy procedure, esophagus
43499 Unlisted procedure, esophagus
43659 Unlisted laparoscopy procedure, stomach
43999 Unlisted procedure, stomach
44238 Unlisted laparoscopy procedure, intestine (except rectum)
44799 Unlisted procedure, intestine
44899 Unlisted procedure, Meckel's diverticulum and the mesentery
44979 Unlisted laparoscopy procedure, appendix
45499 Unlisted laparoscopy procedure, rectum
45999 Unlisted procedure, rectum
46999 Unlisted procedure, anus
47379 Unlisted laparoscopic procedure, liver
47399 Unlisted procedure, liver
47579 Unlisted laparoscopy procedure, biliary tract
47999 Unlisted procedure, biliary tract
48999 Unlisted procedure, pancreas
49329 Unlisted laparoscopy procedure, abdomen, peritoneum and omentum
49659 Unlisted laparoscopy procedure, hernioplasty, herniorrhaphy, herniotomy
49999 Unlisted procedure, abdomen, peritoneum and omentum
50549 Unlisted laparoscopy procedure, renal
50949 Unlisted laparoscopy procedure, ureter
51999 Unlisted laparoscopy procedure, bladder
53899 Unlisted procedure, urinary system
54699 Unlisted laparoscopy procedure, testis
55559 Unlisted laparoscopy procedure, spermatic cord
55899 Unlisted procedure, male genital system
58578 Unlisted laparoscopy procedure, uterus
58579 Unlisted hysteroscopy procedure, uterus
58679 Unlisted laparoscopy procedure, oviduct, ovary
58999 Unlisted procedure, female genital system (nonobstetrical)
59897 Unlisted fetal invasive procedure, including ultrasound guidance, when performed
59898 Unlisted laparoscopy procedure, maternity care and delivery
59899 Unlisted procedure, maternity care and delivery
60659 Unlisted laparoscopy procedure, endocrine system
60699 Unlisted procedure, endocrine system
64999 Unlisted procedure, nervous system
66999 Unlisted procedure, anterior segment of eye
67299 Unlisted procedure, posterior segment
67399 Unlisted procedure, ocular muscle
67599 Unlisted procedure, orbit
67999 Unlisted procedure, eyelids
68399 Unlisted procedure, conjunctiva
68899 Unlisted procedure, lacrimal system
69399 Unlisted procedure, external ear
69799 Unlisted procedure, middle ear
69949 Unlisted procedure, inner ear
69979 Unlisted procedure, temporal bone, middle fossa approach
76496 Unlisted fluoroscopic procedure (eg, diagnostic, interventional)
76497 Unlisted computed tomography procedure (eg, diagnostic, interventional)
76498 Unlisted magnetic resonance procedure (eg, diagnostic, interventional)
76499 Unlisted diagnostic radiographic procedure
76999 Unlisted ultrasound procedure (eg, diagnostic, interventional)
77299 Unlisted procedure, therapeutic radiology clinical treatment planning
77399 Unlisted procedure, medical radiation physics, dosimetry and treatment devices, and special services
77499 Unlisted procedure, therapeutic radiology treatment management
77799 Unlisted procedure, clinical brachytherapy
78099 Unlisted endocrine procedure, diagnostic nuclear medicine
78199 Unlisted hematopoietic, reticuloendothelial and lymphatic procedure, diagnostic nuclear medicine
78299 Unlisted gastrointestinal procedure, diagnostic nuclear medicine
78399 Unlisted musculoskeletal procedure, diagnostic nuclear medicine
78499 Unlisted cardiovascular procedure, diagnostic nuclear medicine
78599 Unlisted respiratory procedure, diagnostic nuclear medicine
78699 Unlisted nervous system procedure, diagnostic nuclear medicine
78799 Unlisted genitourinary procedure, diagnostic nuclear medicine
78999 Unlisted miscellaneous procedure, diagnostic nuclear medicine
79999 Radiopharmaceutical therapy, unlisted procedure
80299 Quantitation of drug, not elsewhere specified

81099 Unlisted urinalysis procedure
81479 Unlisted molecular pathology procedure
84999 Unlisted chemistry procedure
85999 Unlisted hematology and coagulation procedure
86849 Unlisted immunology procedure
86999 Unlisted transfusion medicine procedure
87999 Unlisted microbiology procedure
88099 Unlisted necropsy (autopsy) procedure
88199 Unlisted cytopathology procedure
88299 Unlisted cytogenetic study
88399 Unlisted surgical pathology procedure
88749 Unlisted in vivo (eg, transcutaneous) laboratory service
89240 Unlisted miscellaneous pathology test
89398 Unlisted reproductive medicine laboratory procedure
90399 Unlisted immune globulin
90749 Unlisted vaccine/toxoid
90899 Unlisted psychiatric service or procedure
90999 Unlisted dialysis procedure, inpatient or outpatient
91299 Unlisted diagnostic gastroenterology procedure
92499 Unlisted ophthalmological service or procedure
92700 Unlisted otorhinolaryngological service or procedure
93799 Unlisted cardiovascular service or procedure
93998 Unlisted noninvasive vascular diagnostic study
94799 Unlisted pulmonary service or procedure
95199 Unlisted allergy/clinical immunologic service or procedure
95999 Unlisted neurological or neuromuscular diagnostic procedure
96379 Unlisted therapeutic, prophylactic, or diagnostic intravenous or intra-arterial injection or infusion
96549 Unlisted chemotherapy procedure
96999 Unlisted special dermatological service or procedure
97039 Unlisted modality (specify type and time if constant attendance)
97139 Unlisted therapeutic procedure (specify)
97799 Unlisted physical medicine/rehabilitation service or procedure
99199 Unlisted special service, procedure or report
99429 Unlisted preventive medicine service
99499 Unlisted evaluation and management service
99600 Unlisted home visit service or procedure

Appendix C

CPT® Modifiers

A modifier is a two-position alpha or numeric code appended to a CPT code to clarify the services being billed. Modifiers provide a means by which a service can be altered without changing the procedure code. They add more information, such as the anatomical site, to the code. In addition, they help to eliminate the appearance of duplicate billing and unbundling. Modifiers are used to increase accuracy in reimbursement, coding consistency, editing, and to capture payment data.

22 **Increased Procedural Services:** When the work required to provide a service is substantially greater than typically required, it may be identified by adding modifier 22 to the usual procedure code. Documentation must support the substantial additional work and the reason for the additional work (ie, increased intensity, time, technical difficulty of procedure, severity of patient's condition, physical and mental effort required). **Note:** This modifier should not be appended to an E/M service.

23 **Unusual Anesthesia:** Occasionally, a procedure, which usually requires either no anesthesia or local anesthesia, because of unusual circumstances must be done under general anesthesia. This circumstance may be reported by adding modifier 23 to the procedure code of the basic service.

24 **Unrelated Evaluation and Management Service by the Same Physician or Other Qualified Health Care Professional During a Postoperative Period:** The physician or other qualified health care professional may need to indicate that an evaluation and management service was performed during a postoperative period for a reason(s) unrelated to the original procedure. This circumstance may be reported by adding modifier 24 to the appropriate level of E/M service.

25 **Significant, Separately Identifiable Evaluation and Management Service by the Same Physician or Other Qualified Health Care Professional on the Same Day of the Procedure or Other Service:** It may be necessary to indicate that on the day a procedure or service identified by a CPT code was performed, the patient's condition required a significant, separately identifiable E/M service above and beyond the other service provided or beyond the usual preoperative and postoperative care associated with the procedure that was performed. A significant, separately identifiable E/M service is defined or substantiated by documentation that satisfies the relevant criteria for the respective E/M service to be reported (see Evaluation and Management Services Guidelines for instructions on determining level of E/M service). The E/M service may be prompted by the symptom or condition for which the procedure and/or service was provided. As such, different diagnoses are not required for reporting of the E/M services on the same date. This circumstance may be reported by adding modifier 25 to the appropriate level of E/M service.
Note: This modifier is not used to report an E/M service that resulted in a decision to perform surgery. See modifier 57. For significant, separately identifiable non-E/M services, see modifier 59.

26 **Professional Component:** Certain procedures are a combination of a physician or other qualified health care professional component and a technical component. When the physician or other qualified health care professional component is reported separately, the service may be identified by adding modifier 26 to the usual procedure number.

32 **Mandated Services:** Services related to *mandated* consultation and/or related services (eg, third-party payer, governmental, legislative or regulatory requirement) may be identified by adding modifier 32 to the basic procedure.

33 **Preventive Services:** When the primary purpose of the service is the delivery of an evidence-based service in accordance with a U.S. Preventive Services Task Force A or B rating in effect and other preventive services identified in preventive services mandates (legislative or regulatory), the service may be identified by adding 33 to the procedure. For separately reported services specifically identified as preventive, the modifier should not be used.

47 **Anesthesia by Surgeon:** Regional or general anesthesia provided by the surgeon may be reported by adding modifier 47 to the basic service. (This does not include local anesthesia.) **Note:** Modifier 47 would not be used as a modifier for the anesthesia procedures 00100-01999.

50 **Bilateral Procedure:** Unless otherwise identified in the listings, bilateral procedures that are performed at the same session should be identified by adding modifier 50 to the appropriate 5-digit code.

51 **Multiple Procedures:** When multiple procedures, other than E/M services, Physical Medicine and Rehabilitation services or provision of supplies (eg, vaccines), are performed at the same session by the same individual, the primary procedure or service may be reported as listed. The additional procedure(s) or service(s) may be identified by appending modifier 51 to the additional procedure or service code(s). **Note:** This modifier should not be appended to designated "add-on" codes (see Appendix D).

52 **Reduced Services:** Under certain circumstances a service or procedure is partially reduced or eliminated at the discretion of the physician or other qualified health care professional. Under these circumstances the service provided can be identified by its usual procedure number and the addition of modifier 52, signifying that the service is reduced. This provides a means of reporting reduced services without disturbing the identification of the basic service. **Note:** For hospital outpatient reporting of a previously scheduled procedure/service that is partially reduced or cancelled as a result of extenuating circumstances or those that threaten the well-being of the patient prior to or after administration of anesthesia, see modifiers 73 and 74 (see modifiers approved for ASC hospital outpatient use).

53 **Discontinued Procedure:** Under certain circumstances, the physician or other qualified health care professional may elect to terminate a surgical or diagnostic procedure. Due to extenuating circumstances or those that threaten the well being of the patient, it may be necessary to indicate that a surgical or diagnostic procedure was started but discontinued. This circumstance may be reported by adding modifier 53 to the

code reported by the physician for the discontinued procedure. **Note:** This modifier is not used to report the elective cancellation of a procedure prior to the patient's anesthesia induction and/or surgical preparation in the operating suite. For outpatient hospital/ambulatory surgery center (ASC) reporting of a previously scheduled procedure/service that is partially reduced or cancelled as a result of extenuating circumstances or those that threaten the well being of the patient prior to or after administration of anesthesia, see modifiers 73 and 74 (see modifiers approved for ASC hospital outpatient use).

54 **Surgical Care Only:** When 1 physician or other qualified health care professional performs a surgical procedure and another provides preoperative and/or postoperative management, surgical services may be identified by adding modifier 54 to the usual procedure number.

55 **Postoperative Management Only:** When 1 physician or other qualified health care professional performed the postoperative management and another performed the surgical procedure, the postoperative component may be identified by adding modifier 55 to the usual procedure number.

56 **Preoperative Management Only:** When 1 physician or other qualified health care professional performed the preoperative care and evaluation and another performed the surgical procedure, the preoperative component may be identified by adding modifier 56 to the usual procedure number.

57 **Decision for Surgery:** An evaluation and management service that resulted in the initial decision to perform the surgery may be identified by adding modifier 57 to the appropriate level of E/M service.

58 **Staged or Related Procedure or Service by the Same Physician or Other Qualified Health Care Professional During the Postoperative Period:** It may be necessary to indicate that the performance of a procedure or service during the postoperative period was: (a) planned or anticipated (staged); (b) more extensive than the original procedure; or (c) for therapy following a surgical procedure. This circumstance may be reported by adding modifier 58 to the staged or related procedure. **Note:** For treatment of a problem that requires a return to the operating or procedure room (eg, unanticipated clinical condition), see modifier 78.

59 **Distinct Procedural Service:** Under certain circumstances, it may be necessary to indicate that a procedure or service was distinct or independent from other non-E/M services performed on the same day. Modifier 59 is used to identify procedures or services, other than E/M services, that are not normally reported together but are appropriate under the circumstances. Documentation must support a different session, different procedure or surgery, different site or organ system, separate incision or excision, separate lesion, or separate injury (or area of injury in extensive injuries) not ordinarily encountered or performed on the same day by the same individual. However, when another already established modifier is appropriate it should be used rather than modifier 59. Only if no more descriptive modifier is available and the use of modifier 59 best explains the circumstances should modifier 59 be used. **Note:** Modifier 59 should not be appended to an E/M service. To report a separate and distinct E/M service with a non-E/M service performed on the same date, see modifier 25.

62 **Two Surgeons:** When 2 surgeons work together as primary surgeons performing distinct part(s) of a procedure, each surgeon should report his/her distinct operative work by adding modifier 62 to the procedure code and any associated add-on code(s) for that procedure as long as both surgeons continue to work together as primary surgeons. Each surgeon should report the cosurgery once using the same procedure code. If additional procedure(s) (including add-on procedure[s]) are performed during the same surgical session, separate code(s) may also be reported with modifier 62 added. **Note:** If a cosurgeon acts as an assistant in the performance of additional procedure(s), other than those reported with the modifier 62, during the same surgical session, those services may be reported using separate procedure code(s) with modifier 80 or modifier 82 added, as appropriate.

63 **Procedure Performed on Infants less than 4 kg:** Procedures performed on neonates and infants up to a present body weight of 4 kg may involve significantly increased complexity and physician or other qualified health care professional work commonly associated with these patients. This circumstance may be reported by adding modifier 63 to the procedure number. **Note:** Unless otherwise designated, this modifier may only be appended to procedures/services listed in the 20005-69990 code series. Modifier 63 should not be appended to any CPT codes listed in the **Evaluation and Management Services, Anesthesia, Radiology, Pathology/ Laboratory, or Medicine** sections.

66 **Surgical Team:** Under some circumstances, highly complex procedures (requiring the concomitant services of several physicians or other qualified health care professionals, often of different specialties, plus other highly skilled, specially trained personnel, various types of complex equipment) are carried out under the "surgical team" concept. Such circumstances may be identified by each participating individual with the addition of modifier 66 to the basic procedure number used for reporting services.

76 **Repeat Procedure or Service by Same Physician or Other Qualified Health Care Professional:** It may be necessary to indicate that a procedure or service was repeated by the same physician or other qualified health care professional subsequent to the original procedure or service. This circumstance may be reported by adding modifier 76 to the repeated procedure or service. **Note:** This modifier should not be appended to an E/M service.

77 **Repeat Procedure by Another Physician or Other Qualified Health Care Professional:** It may be necessary to indicate that a basic procedure or service was repeated by another physician or other qualified health care professional subsequent to the original procedure or service. This circumstance may be reported by adding modifier 77 to the repeated procedure or service. **Note:** This modifier should not be appended to an E/M service.

78 **Unplanned Return to the Operating/Procedure Room by the Same Physician or Other Qualified Health Care Professional Following Initial Procedure for a Related Procedure During the Postoperative Period:** It may be necessary to indicate that another procedure was performed during the postoperative period of the initial procedure (unplanned procedure following initial procedure). When this procedure is related to the first, and requires the use of an operating/procedure room, it may be reported by adding modifier 78 to the related procedure. (For repeat procedures, see modifier 76.)

79 **Unrelated Procedure or Service by the Same Physician or Other Qualified Health Care Professional During the Postoperative Period:** The individual may need to indicate that the performance of a procedure or service during the postoperative period was unrelated to the original procedure. This circumstance may be reported by using modifier 79. (For repeat procedures on the same day, see modifier 76.)

80 **Assistant Surgeon:** Surgical assistant services may be identified by adding modifier 80 to the usual procedure number(s).

81 **Minimum Assistant Surgeon:** Minimum surgical assistant services are identified by adding modifier 81 to the usual procedure number.

82 **Assistant Surgeon (when qualified resident surgeon not available):** The unavailability of a qualified resident surgeon is a prerequisite for use of modifier 82 appended to the usual procedure code number(s).

90 **Reference (Outside) Laboratory:** When laboratory procedures are performed by a party other than the treating or reporting physician or other qualified health care professional, the procedure may be identified by adding modifier 90 to the usual procedure number.

91 **Repeat Clinical Diagnostic Laboratory Test:** In the course of treatment of the patient, it may be necessary to repeat the same laboratory test on the same day to obtain subsequent (multiple) test results. Under these circumstances, the laboratory test performed can be identified by its usual procedure number and the addition of modifier 91. **Note:** This modifier may not be used when tests are rerun to confirm initial results; due to testing problems with specimens or equipment; or for any other reason when a normal, one-time, reportable result is all that is required. This modifier may not be used when another code(s) describes a series of test results (eg, glucose tolerance tests, evocative/suppression testing). This modifier may only be used for a laboratory test(s) performed more than once on the same day on the same patient.

92 **Alternative Laboratory Platform Testing** When laboratory testing is being performed using a kit or transportable instrument that wholly or in part consists of a single use, disposable analytical chamber, the service may be identified by adding modifier 92 to the usual laboratory procedure code (HIV testing 86701-86703, and 87389). The test does not require permanent dedicated space, hence by its design may be hand carried or transported to the vicinity of the patient for immediate testing at that site, although location of the testing is not in itself determinative of the use of this modifier.

99 **Multiple Modifiers:** Under certain circumstances 2 or more modifiers may be necessary to completely delineate a service. In such situations, modifier 99 should be added to the basic procedure and other applicable modifiers may be listed as part of the description of the service.

Anesthesia Physical Status Modifiers

All anesthesia services are reported by use of the five-digit anesthesia procedure code with the appropriate physical status modifier appended.

Under certain circumstances, when other modifier(s) are appropriate, they should be reported in addition to the physical status modifier.

P1 A normal healthy patient

P2 A patient with mild systemic disease

P3 A patient with severe systemic disease

P4 A patient with severe systemic disease that is a constant threat to life

P5 A moribund patient who is not expected to survive without the operation

P6 A declared brain-dead patient whose organs are being removed for donor purposes

Modifiers Approved for Ambulatory Surgery Center (ASC) Hospital Outpatient Use

CPT Level I Modifiers

25 **Significant, Separately Identifiable Evaluation and Management Service by the Same Physician or Other Qualified Health Care Professional on the Same Day of the Procedure or Other Service:** It may be necessary to indicate that on the day a procedure or service identified by a CPT code was performed, the patient's condition required a significant, separately identifiable E/M service above and beyond the other service provided or beyond the usual preoperative and postoperative care associated with the procedure that was performed. A significant, separately identifiable E/M service is defined or substantiated by documentation that satisfies the relevant criteria for the respective E/M service to be reported (see **Evaluation and Management Services Guidelines** for instructions on determining level of E/M service). The E/M service may be prompted by the symptom or condition for which the procedure and/or service was provided. As such, different diagnoses are not required for reporting of the E/M services on the same date. This circumstance may be reported by adding modifier 25 to the appropriate level of E/M service. **Note:** This modifier is not used to report an E/M service that resulted in a decision to perform surgery. See modifier 57. For significant, separately identifiable non-E/M services, see modifier 59.

27 **Multiple Outpatient Hospital E/M Encounters on the Same Date:** For hospital outpatient reporting purposes, utilization of hospital resources related to separate and distinct E/M encounters performed in multiple outpatient hospital settings on the same date may be reported by adding modifier 27 to each appropriate level outpatient and/or emergency department E/M code(s). This modifier provides a means of reporting circumstances involving evaluation and management services provided by a physician(s) in more than one (multiple) outpatient hospital setting(s) (eg, hospital emergency department, clinic). **Note:** This modifier is not to be used for physician reporting of multiple E/M services performed by the same physician on the same date. For physician reporting of all outpatient evaluation and management services provided by the same physician on the same date and performed in multiple outpatient settings (eg, hospital emergency department, clinic), see **Evaluation and Management, Emergency Department, or Preventive Medicine Services** codes.

50 **Bilateral Procedure:** Unless otherwise identified in the listings, bilateral procedures that are performed at the same

session should be identified by adding modifier 50 to the appropriate 5-digit code.

52 **Reduced Services:** Under certain circumstances a service or procedure is partially reduced or eliminated at the discretion of the physician or other qualified health care professional. Under these circumstances the service provided can be identified by its usual procedure number and the addition of modifier 52, signifying that the service is reduced. This provides a means of reporting reduced services without disturbing the identification of the basic service. **Note:** For hospital outpatient reporting of a previously scheduled procedure/service that is partially reduced or cancelled as a result of extenuating circumstances or those that threaten the well-being of the patient prior to or after administration of anesthesia, see modifiers 73 and 74 (see modifiers approved for ASC hospital outpatient use).

58 **Staged or Related Procedure or Service by the Same Physician or Other Qualified Health Care Professional During the Postoperative Period:** It may be necessary to indicate that the performance of a procedure or service during the postoperative period was: (a) planned or anticipated (staged); (b) more extensive than the original procedure; or (c) for therapy following a surgical procedure. This circumstance may be reported by adding modifier 58 to the staged or related procedure. **Note:** For treatment of a problem that requires a return to the operating or procedure room (eg, unanticipated clinical condition), see modifier 78.

59 **Distinct Procedural Service:** Under certain circumstances, it may be necessary to indicate that a procedure or service was distinct or independent from other non-E/M services performed on the same day. Modifier 59 is used to identify procedures or services, other than E/M services, that are not normally reported together but are appropriate under the circumstances. Documentation must support a different session, different procedure or surgery, different site or organ system, separate incision or excision, separate lesion, or separate injury (or area of injury in extensive injuries) not ordinarily encountered or performed on the same day by the same individual. However, when another already established modifier is appropriate it should be used rather than modifier 59. Only if no more descriptive modifier is available and the use of modifier 59 best explains the circumstances should modifier 59 be used. **Note:** Modifier 59 should not be appended to an E/M service. To report a separate and distinct E/M service with a non-E/M service performed on the same date, see modifier 25.

73 **Discontinued Out-Patient Hospital/Ambulatory Surgery Center (ASC) Procedure Prior to the Administration of Anesthesia:** Due to extenuating circumstances or those that threaten the well being of the patient, the physician may cancel a surgical or diagnostic procedure subsequent to the patient's surgical preparation (including sedation when provided, and being taken to the room where the procedure is to be performed), but prior to the administration of anesthesia (local, regional block(s), or general). Under these circumstances, the intended service that is prepared for but cancelled can be reported by its usual procedure number and the addition of modifier 73. **Note:** The elective cancellation of a service prior to the administration of anesthesia and/or surgical preparation of the patient should not be reported. For physician reporting of a discontinued procedure, see modifier 53.

74 **Discontinued Out-Patient Hospital/Ambulatory Surgery Center (ASC) Procedure After Administration of Anesthesia:** Due to extenuating circumstances or those that threaten the well being of the patient, the physician may terminate a surgical or diagnostic procedure after the administration of anesthesia (local, regional block(s), general) or after the procedure was started (incision made, intubation started, scope inserted, etc.). Under these circumstances, the procedure started but terminated can be reported by its usual procedure number and the addition of modifier 74. **Note:** The elective cancellation of a service prior to the administration of anesthesia and/or surgical preparation of the patient should not be reported. For physician reporting of a discontinued procedure, see modifier 53.

76 **Repeat Procedure or Service by Same Physician or Other Qualified Health Care Professional:** It may be necessary to indicate that a procedure or service was repeated by the same physician or other qualified health care professional subsequent to the original procedure or service. This circumstance may be reported by adding modifier 76 to the repeated procedure or service. **Note:** This modifier should not be appended to an E/M service.

77 **Repeat Procedure by Another Physician or Other Qualified Health Care Professional:** It may be necessary to indicate that a basic procedure or service was repeated by another physician or other qualified health care professional subsequent to the original procedure or service. This circumstance may be reported by adding modifier 77 to the repeated procedure or service. **Note:** This modifier should not be appended to an E/M service.

78 **Unplanned Return to the Operating/Procedure Room by the Same Physician or Other Qualified Health Care Professional Following Initial Procedure for a Related Procedure During the Postoperative Period:** It may be necessary to indicate that another procedure was performed during the postoperative period of the initial procedure (unplanned procedure following initial procedure). When this procedure is related to the first, and requires the use of an operating/procedure room, it may be reported by adding modifier 78 to the related procedure. (For repeat procedures, see modifier 76.)

79 **Unrelated Procedure or Service by the Same Physician During the Postoperative Period:** The individual may need to indicate that the performance of a procedure or service during the postoperative period was unrelated to the original procedure. This circumstance may be reported by using modifier 79. (For repeat procedures on the same day, see modifier 76.)

91 **Repeat Clinical Diagnostic Laboratory Test:** In the course of treatment of the patient, it may be necessary to repeat the same laboratory test on the same day to obtain subsequent (multiple) test results. Under these circumstances, the laboratory test performed can be identified by its usual procedure number and the addition of modifier 91. **Note:** This modifier may not be used when tests are rerun to confirm initial results; due to testing problems with specimens or equipment; or for any other reason when a normal, one-time, reportable result is all that is required. This modifier may not be used when another code(s) describe a series of test results (eg, glucose tolerance tests, evocative/suppression testing). This modifier may only be used for a laboratory test(s) performed more than once on the same day on the same patient.

Level II (HCPCS/National) Modifiers

Anatomical Modifiers

E1 Upper left, eyelid

E2 Lower left, eyelid

E3 Upper right, eyelid

E4 Lower right, eyelid

F1 Left hand, second digit

F2 Left hand, third digit

F3 Left hand, fourth digit

F4 Left hand, fifth digit

F5 Right hand, thumb

F6 Right hand, second digit

F7 Right hand, third digit

F8 Right hand, fourth digit

F9 Right hand, fifth digit

FA Left hand, thumb

LT Left side (used to identify procedures performed on the left side of the body)

RT Right side (used to identify procedures performed on the right side of the body)

T1 Left foot, second digit

T2 Left foot, third digit

T3 Left foot, fourth digit

T4 Left foot, fifth digit

T5 Right foot, great toe

T6 Right foot, second digit

T7 Right foot, third digit

T8 Right foot, fourth digit

T9 Right foot, fifth digit

TA Left foot, great toe

Anesthesia Modifiers

AA Anesthesia services performed personally by anesthesiologist

AD Medical supervision by a physician: more than four concurrent anesthesia procedures

G8 Monitored anesthesia care (MAC) for deep complex, complicated, or markedly invasive surgical procedure

G9 Monitored anesthesia care for patient who has history of severe cardiopulmonary condition

QK Medical direction of two, three, or four concurrent anesthesia procedures involving qualified individuals

QS Monitored anesthesia care service

QX CRNA service: with medical direction by a physician

QY Medical direction of one certified registered nurse anesthetist (CRNA) by an anesthesiologist

QZ CRNA service: without medical direction by a physician

Coronary Artery Modifiers

LC Left circumflex coronary artery

LD Left anterior descending coronary artery

LM Left main coronary artery

RC Right coronary artery

RI Ramus intermedius coronary artery

Ophthalmology Modifiers

AP Determination of refractive state was not performed in the course of diagnostic ophthalmological examination

LS FDA-monitored intraocular lens implant

PL Progressive addition lenses

VP Aphakic patient

Other Modifiers

AE Registered dietician

AF Specialty physician

AG Primary physician

AH Clinical psychologist

AI Principal physician of record

AJ Clinical social worker

AK Nonparticipating physician

AM Physician, team member service

AQ Physician providing a service in an unlisted health professional shortage area (HPSA)

AR Physician provider services in a physician scarcity area

AS Physician assistant, nurse practitioner, or clinical nurse specialist services for assistant at surgery

AT Acute treatment (this modifier should be used when reporting service 98940, 98941, 98942)

AY Item or service furnished to an ESRD patient that is not for the treatment of ESRD

CA Procedure payable only in the inpatient setting when performed emergently on an outpatient who expires prior to admission

CB Service ordered by a renal dialysis facility (RDF) physician as part of the ESRD beneficiary's dialysis benefit, is not part of the composite rate, and is separately reimbursable

CC Procedure code change (use 'CC' when the procedure code submitted was changed either for administrative reasons or because an incorrect code was filed)

CG Policy criteria applied

CR Catastrophe/disaster related

CS Item or service related, in whole or in part, to an illness, injury, or condition that was caused by or exacerbated by the effects, direct or indirect, of the 2010 oil spill in the gulf of Mexico, including but not limited to subsequent clean up activities

EP Service provided as part of Medicaid early periodic screening diagnosis and treatment (EPSDT) program

ET Emergency services

EY No physician or other licensed health care provider order for this item or service

FB Item provided without cost to provider, supplier or practitioner, or full credit received for replaced device (examples, but not limited to covered under warranty, replaced due to defect, free samples)

FC Partial credit received for replacement device

FP Service provided as part of family planning program

G7 Pregnancy resulted from rape or incest or pregnancy certified by physician as life threatening

GA Waiver of liability statement issued as required by payer policy, individual case

GB Claim being resubmitted for payment because it is no longer covered under a global payment demonstration

GC This service has been performed in part by a resident under the direction of a teaching physician

GD Units of service exceeds medically unlikely edit value and represents reasonable and necessary services

GE This service has been performed by a resident without the presence of a teaching physician under the primary care exception

GF Non-physician (e.g. nurse practitioner (NP), certified registered nurse anesthetist (CRNA), certified registered nurse (CRN), clinical nurse specialist (CNS), physician assistant (PA)) services in a critical access hospital

GG Performance and payment of a screening mammogram and diagnostic mammogram on the same patient, same day

GH Diagnostic mammogram converted from screening mammogram on same day

GJ Opt out physician or practitioner emergency or urgent service

GK Reasonable and necessary item/service associated with GA or GZ modifier

GN Service delivered under an outpatient speech-language pathology plan of care

GO Service delivered an outpatient occupational therapy plan of care

GP Service delivered under an outpatient physical therapy plan of care

GQ Via asynchronous telecommunications system

GR This service was performed in whole or in part by a resident in a department of veterans affairs medical center or clinic, supervised in accordance with VA policy

GT Via interactive audio and video telecommunication systems

GU Waiver of liability statement issued as required by payer policy, routine notice

GV Attending physician not employed or paid under arrangement by the patient's hospice provider

GW Service not related to the hospice patient's terminal condition

GX Notice of liability issued, voluntary under payer policy

GY Item or service statutorily excluded, does not meet the definition of any Medicare benefit or for non-Medicare insurers, is not a contract benefit

GZ Item or service expected to be denied as not reasonable and necessary

H9 Court-ordered

HA Child/adolescent program

HB Adult program, nongeriatric

HC Adult program, geriatric

HD Pregnant/parenting women's program

HE Mental health program

HF Substance abuse program

HG Opioid addiction treatment program

HH Integrated mental health/substance abuse program

HI Integrated mental health and mental retardation/developmental disabilities program

HJ Employee assistance program

HK Specialized mental health programs for high-risk populations

HL Intern

HM Less than bachelor degree level

HN Bachelors degree level

HO Masters degree level

HP Doctoral level

HQ Group setting

HR Family/couple with client present

HS Family/couple without client present

HT Multi-disciplinary team

HU Funded by child welfare agency

HV Funded state addictions agency

HW Funded by state mental health agency

HX Funded by county/local agency

HY Funded by juvenile justice agency

HZ Funded by criminal justice agency

KB Beneficiary requested upgrade for ABN, more than four modifiers identified on claim

KX Requirements specified in the medical policy have been met

KZ New coverage not implemented by managed care

LR Laboratory round trip

M2 Medicare secondary payer (MSP)

PA Surgical or other invasive procedure on wrong body part

PB Surgical or other invasive procedure on wrong patient

PC Wrong surgery or other invasive procedure on patient

PD Diagnostic or related nondiagnostic item or service provided in a wholly owned or operated entity to a patient who is admitted as an inpatient within 3 days

PI Positron emission tomography (PET) or PET/computed tomography (CT) to inform the initial treatment strategy of tumors that are biopsy proven or strongly suspected of being cancerous based on other diagnostic testing, once per cancer diagnosis

PS Positron emission tomography (PET) or PET/computed tomography (CT) to inform the subsequent treatment strategy of cancerous tumor when the beneficiary's treating physician determines that the PET study is needed to inform subsequent anti-tumor strategy

PT Colorectal cancer screening test; converted to diagnostic test or other procedure

Q0 Investigational clinical service provided in a clinical research study that is in an approved clinical research study

Q1 Routine clinical service provided in a clinical research study that is in an approved clinical research study

Q2 HCFA/ORD demonstration project procedure/service

Q3 Live kidney donor surgery and related services

Q4 Service for ordering/referring physician qualifies as a service exemption

Q5 Service furnished by a substitute physician under a reciprocal billing arrangement

Q6 Service furnished by a locum tenens physician

Q7 One Class A finding

Q8 Two Class B findings

Q9 One Class B and two Class C findings

QC Single channel monitoring

QD Recording and storage in solid state memory by a digital recorder

QJ Services/items provided to a prisoner or patient in state or local custody, however the state or local government, as applicable, meets the requirements in 42 CRF 411.4 (B)

QP Documentation is on file showing that the laboratory test(s) was ordered individually or ordered as a CPT-recognized panel other than automated profile codes

QT Recording and storage on tape by an analog tape recorder

QW CLIA waived test

RE Furnished in full compliance with FDA-mandated risk evaluation and mitigation strategy (REMS)

SA Nurse practitioner rendering service in collaboration with a physician

SB Nurse Midwife

SC Medically necessary service or supply

SD Services provided by registered nurse with specialized, highly technical home infusion training

SE State and/or federally funded programs/services

SF Second opinion ordered by a professional review organization (PRO) per section 9401, P.L.99-272 (100% reimbursement - no Medicare deductible or coinsurance)

SG Ambulatory surgical center (ASC) facility service

SH Second concurrently administered infusion therapy

SJ Third or more concurrently administered infusion therapy

SK Member of high risk population (use only with codes for immunization)

SL State supplied vaccine

SM Second surgical opinion

SN Third surgical opinion

SQ Item ordered by home health

SS Home infusion services provided in the infusion suite of the IV therapy provider

ST Related to trauma or injury

SU Procedure performed in physician's office (to denote use of facility and equipment)

SW Services provided by a certified diabetic educator

SY Persons who are in close contact with member of high-risk population (use only with codes for immunization)

TC Technical component. Under certain circumstances, a charge may be made for the technical component alone. Under those circumstances the technical component charge is identified by adding modifier 'TC' to the usual procedure number. Technical component charges are institutional charges and not billed separately by physicians. However, portable x-ray suppliers only bill for technical component and should utilize modifier TC. The charge data from portable x-ray suppliers will then be used to build customary and prevailing profiles.

TD RN

TE LPN/LVN

TF Intermediate level of care

TG Complex/high level of care

TH Obstetrical treatment/services, prenatal or postpartum

TJ Program group, child and/or adolescent

TK Extra patient or passenger, nonambulance

TL Early intervention/individualized family service plan (IFSP)

TM Individualized education program (IEP)

TN Rural/outside providers' customary service area

TR School-based individualized education program (IEP) services provided outside the public school district responsible for the student

TS Follow-up service

TT Individualized service provided to more than one patient in same setting

TU Special payment rate, overtime

TV Special payment rates, holidays/weekends

U1 Medicaid level of care 1, as defined by each state

U2 Medicaid level of care 2, as defined by each state

U3 Medicaid level of care 3, as defined by each state

U4 Medicaid level of care 4, as defined by each state

U5 Medicaid level of care 5, as defined by each state

U6 Medicaid level of care 6, as defined by each state

U7 Medicaid level of care 7, as defined by each state

U8 Medicaid level of care 8, as defined by each state

U9 Medicaid level of care 9, as defined by each state

UA Medicaid level of care 10, as defined by each state

UB Medicaid level of care 11, as defined by each state

UC Medicaid level of care 12, as defined by each state

UD Medicaid level of care 13, as defined by each state

UF Services provided in the morning

UG Services provided in the afternoon

UH Services provided in the evening

UJ Services provided at night

UK Services provided on behalf of the client to someone other than the client (collateral relationship)

UN Two patients served

UP Three patients served

UQ Four patients served

UR Five patients served

US Six or more patients served

V5 Vascular catheter (alone or with any other vascular access)

V6 Arteriovenous graft (or other vascular access not including a vascular catheter)

V7 Arteriovenous fistula only (in use with 2 needles)

Category II Modifiers

1P Performance measure exclusion modifier due to medical reasons

Includes:

- Not indicated (absence of organ/limb, already received/performed, other)
- Contraindicated (patient allergic history, potential adverse drug interaction, other)
- Other medical reasons

2P Performance measure exclusion modifier due to patient reasons

Includes:

- Patient declined
- Economic, social, or religious reasons
- Other patient reasons

3P Performance measure exclusion modifier due to system reasons

Includes:

- Resources to perform the services not available (eg, equipment, supplies)
- Insurance coverage or payer-related limitations
- Other reasons attributable to health care delivery system

8P Performance measure reporting modifier - action not performed, reason not otherwise specified

Dental Modifiers

AZ Physician providing a service in a dental health professional shortage area for the purpose of an electronic health record incentive payment

DA Oral health assessment by a licensed health professional other than a dentist

ET Emergency services (dental procedures performed in emergency situations should show the modifier ET)

ESRD Modifiers

AY Item or service furnished to an ESRD patient that is not for the treatment of ESRD

CD AMCC test has been ordered by an ESRD facility or MCP physician that is a part of the composite rate and is not separately billable

CE AMCC test has been ordered by an ESRD facility or MCP physician that is a composite rate test but is beyond the normal frequency covered under the rate and is separately reimbursable based on medically necessary

CF AMCC test has been ordered by an ESRD facility or MCP physician that is not part of the composite rate and is separately billable

G6 ESRD patient for whom less than six dialysis sessions have been provided in a month

GS Dosage of EPO or darbepoietin alfa has been reduced and maintained in response to hematocrit or hemoglobin level

Q3 Live kidney donor surgery and related services